XXIX International Cong of Psychology

Berlin, Germany, July 20–25, 2008

Abstracts

ICP 2008

published under the auspices of the
International Union of Psychological Science (IUPsyS)

Psychology Press
Taylor & Francis Group

Contents

The abstracts of the XXIX International Congress of Psychology have been typeset from files kindly supplied by CPO HANSER SERVICE GmbH on behalf of the organizing committee. The text of individual presentations is as originally submitted by the authors of the contributions. The arrangement of the presentations in this print volume is in accordance with the planned Congress program at the time the files were passed for publication. Any alterations made between this point in time and the actual date of the Congress will not be reflected in this volume.

Table of Contents

Tuesday 22nd July 2008

Wednesday 23rd July 2008

Thursday 24th July 2008

Friday 25th July 2008

CONGRESS ORGANIZATION

Organizers

German Federation of Psychological Associations, under the auspices of the International Union of Psychological Science (IUPsyS)
The German Federation of Psychological Associations are:
German Psychological Society (DGPs – Deutsche Gesellschaft für Psychologie)
Association of German Professional Psychologists (BDP – Berufsverband deutscher Psychologinnen und Psychologen)

President

Peter A. Frensch

Vice-President

Carola Brücher-Albers

Executive Committee

Chair: Peter A. Frensch
Carola Brücher-Albers
Marcus Hasselhorn
Arthur M. Jacobs
Heinz-Jürgen Rothe

Ralf Schwarzer
Rainer K. Silbereisen
IUPsyS Liaison: Michel Denis
Secretary General: Barbara Schauenburg

Organizing Committee

Chair: Heinz-Jürgen Rothe
Robert Gaschler
Matthias Jerusalem
Helmut Jungermann
Ulf Kieschke
Dietrich Manzey

Michael Niedeggen
Herbert Scheithauer
Peter Walschburger
Hartmut Wandke
Jochen Ziegelmann
Ex Officio: Peter A. Frensch, President

Scientific Committee

Chair: Arthur M. Jacobs
Jens B. Asendorpf
Jürgen Baumert
Niels Birbaumer
Anke Ehlers
Michael Eid
Michael Frese
Joachim Funke
Gerd Gigerenzer
Peter M. Gollwitzer
Kurt Hahlweg
Christoph Klauer
Rainer H. Kluwe

Ulman Lindenberger
Gerd Lüer
Stefan Petri
Frank Rösler
Wolfgang Schneider
Lael Schooler
Sabine Sonnentag
Ursula M. Staudinger
Elsbeth Stern
Hannelore Weber
Hans Westmeyer
Ex Officio: Peter A. Frensch, President

International Advisory Committee

Chair: Rainer K. Silbereisen
Conny H. Antoni
Merry Bullock
Avshalom Caspi
Erik De Corte
Nancy Eisenberg
Rocio Fernandez-Ballesteros
James D. Georgas
Esther R. Greenglass
Buxin Han
Jutta Heckhausen
Michael Knowles
Howard Leventhal
Gerold Mikula
Walter Mischel

Elizabeth Nair
Lars-Göran Nilsson
Arne Öhman
Meinrad Perrez
José M. Prieto
Marc Richelle
Sir Michael Rutter
Juan Jose Sanchez-Sosa
Christiane Spiel
Ingrid Schoon
Wolfgang Stroebe
Richard E. Tremblay
Endel Tulving
Alexander von Eye
Kan Zhang

Honorary Committee

Chair: Paul B. Baltes †
Albert Bandura
Gian Vittorio Caprara
Fergus I. M. Craik
Raymond Fowler
Carl-Friedrich Graumann †
Lothar J. Hellfritsch
Mavis Hetherington
Qicheng Jing
Daniel Kahneman
Walter Kintsch
Jacques Lautrey
David Magnusson
Kurt Pawlik

Lea Pulkkinen
Gavriel Salomon
Wolfgang Schönpflug
Martin E. P. Seligman
Charles D. Spielberger
Robert J. Sternberg
Jan Strelau
Richard F. Thompson
Tuomo Tikkanen
Bernhard Wilpert †
Géry d'Ydewalle
Robert Zajonc
Houcan Zhang

Monday 21st July 2008

PA-001: The laws of learning are always in effect: Implications for all psychologists

Peter A. Frensch (Chair)

(IUPsyS Presidential Address)
Overmier, J. Bruce IUPsyS, University of Minnesota, Minneapolis, USA
Learning phenomena permeate all aspects of psychology and indeed our human lives. Substantial understanding of the principles of learning has come from studies with animals. Findings from animals have indeed influenced practices from schools to therapy. Yet the scientific study of the psychology of learning—and especially that with animals—is virtually disappearing from our universities and certainly from training programs in applied psychology. This would be understandable if we had already learned all we can or if new findings were not relevant to current education or therapy practices. But this is not true as will be illustrated.

IA-001: Psychology and behaviour analysis: The nature of the controversy

Hans Westmeyer (Chair)

Ardila, Ruben Dept. of Psychology, National Univ. of Colombia, Bogota, Colombia
Behavior analysis has traditionally been one of the main areas and main approaches to psychology. It gave origin to a science (the experimental analysis of behavior), to a philosophy (behaviorism), and to a technology (applied behavior analysis). However in the last decades cognitivism as emerged as one of the dominant paradigms in contemporary psychology. The mutual relatioships between behavior analysis and mainstream contemporary psychology will be explored. The controversies concerning fundamental issues will be analyzed. The relevance of behavior analysis for psychology will be pointed out, and also the need for behavior analysis to integrate a number of basic findings from psychology.

IA-002: The cultural construction of self and emotion: Implications for well-being

Wolfgang Schönpflug (Chair)

Misra, Girishwar Dept. of Psychology, University of Delhi, New Delhi, India
Well-being is reciprocally linked with the experiences of self and emotions. Being informed by the cultural meanings and practices selves not only selectively encourage, sustain or constrain the emotional engagements but are also shaped by them. The Indian discourse bridges the gap between emotion and reason and allows emotions to be creatively deployed for movement towards self-realization and ensuring well-being. The self-notions work as intrinsic sources of emotion and direct the course of appraisals of our linkages with environment and generate additional emotional resources. Also, emotional engagement transforms the experience of selfhood in significant ways which furthers people's well-being.

IA-003: A psycho-institutional approach to culture

Kan Zhang (Chair)

Yamagishi, Toshio Japan
Through a series of studies I present in this paper, I demonstrate that some culture-specific behaviors can be better analyzed in terms of default strategies, rather than as simple reflections of preferences. According to this psycho-institutional approach, cultural differences in behavior are viewed as differences in the default adaptive strategies which individuals come to rely on in unspecified situations. An institution, the term which I borrow from comparative institutional economics, refers to a self-sustaining system of shared beliefs, behaviors, and incentives among individuals. Individuals' behaviors collectively create an incentive structure for them and thus provide an equilibrium state.

IA-004: Developing and disseminating effective psychological treatments for anxiety disorders: A cognitive science approach

Thomas Fydrich (Chair)

Clark, David London, United Kingdom
Anxiety disorders are common and disabling. A cognitive science approach to developing effective psychological treatments is outlined. The approach identifies factors that prevent patients' excessively negative appraisals of danger from self-correcting and targets these factors in specialized cognitive therapy programmes. Illustrations of maintaining factors and the way they can be reversed in therapy are presented. A review of controlled trials and the substantial effect sizes that can currently be expected with cognitive therapy leads to a discussion of two challenges. First, how can the treatments be made more effective and efficient? Second, how can they be effectively disseminated?

IA-005: Paternalistic leadership in Chinese context: A full-cycle approach

Joachim Funke (Chair)

Cheng, Bor-Shiuan Taipei, Taiwan
Paternalistic leadership (PL) is an indigenous leadership style prevalent in Chinese organizations. Based on extensive review on case studies and literature of Chinese leadership, PL was defined as a style that combines strong and clear authority with concern, considerateness and element of moral leadership. Since then, a series of multiple approached empirical studies had been conducted to investigate the effects of benevolent, authoritarian and moral leadership for testing PL in a variety of organizational settings of Great China. In this paper, I integrate the research issues, methodology, and findings of PL studies, and offer suggestions for future researches.

IA-007: The co-evolution of event memory and knowledge

Arthur Jacobs (Chair)

Shiffrin, Richard Psychological & Brain Sciences, Indiana University, Bloomington, USA
I present a Bayesian-based theory of the co-evolution of episodic memory and knowledge, and the retrieval of both. Each event produces an episodic memory and also adds information to a developing knowledge trace. Events are coded with the developing knowledge traces. The model is applied to a study involving the learning of initially unknown Chinese characters trained over two weeks to different degrees in a visual search task. We test with: episodic recognition, pseudo-lexical decision, and forced-choice perceptual identification, observing frequency-of-study effects that change direction across these tasks. We show how the model predicts the complete pattern of results.

IA-009: Remembering unfamiliar faces

Buxin Han (Chair)

Bruce, Vicki Humanities & Social Science, University of Edinburgh, Edinburgh, United Kingdom
Our initial encounters with people leave us with visual memories of faces that are fragile and difficult to recollect. In most situations this matters little. If we continue the acquaintance, the visual representation of the person's face will become consolidated into something more robust. I'll describe how representations may shift over time as faces become familiar. But for the eyewitness to a crime, remembering an otherwise unfamiliar face may be critical to the investigation and later apprehension of a suspect. I will describe recent research aimed at understanding and improving systems to help eyewitnesses build images of the faces they have seen.

IA-010: Psychosocial needs assessment of orphans and non-orphans in Uganda: A case study in Masaka District

Juan Jose Sanchez Sosa (Chair)

Baguma, Peter Inst. of Psychology, Makerere University, Kampala, Uganda
Uganda has around 2 million who could be experiencing a lot of psychosocial problems. The study used 203 orphans, 196 non-orphans, 390 caregivers, 75 teachers, 13 key informants. Both qualitative and quantitative analytic procedures were used. Findings focused on prevalence and seriousness of psychosocial problems (negative emotion, stigma, depression and behavioural problems).. Significant differences were found between orphans and non-orphans. Furthermore, significant predictors of psychosocial well being among the children were found. Qualitative results confirmed the existence of physical, sexual, emotional abuse and behavioural problems among orphans compared to non-orphans. The development of psychosocial interventions and OVC policy was recommended.

IA-011: Developmental science: An africentric perspective

Nsamenang, Bame *Resource Centre, Human Development, Bamenda, Cameroon*
This paper anchors on biological embedding and interactive contextualism to profile Africa's holistic worldview and "cultural braid" (Nsamenang, 2002) from a triple heritage (Mazrui, 1986). It presents an African developmental trajectory and articulates its ethnotheories and praxes as "novel theoretical caveats and fresh methodological" insights (Nsamenang, 2007). It notes how lack of culturally informed scholars in "original" indigenous research constrains Africa's input into developmental science. It visualizes progress in "bridging" the "worlds" in Africa's hybridism from an ideological positioning that Africans "have already successfully practised childrearing within the framework" of their rich cultures and timeless traditions (Callaghan, 1998).

IA-012: Conceptual and methodological issues in longitudinal studies of job performance

Dietrich Manzey (Chair)

Chan, David *Singapore, Singapore*
Despite advances in the research on modeling of job performance, studies have almost exclusively focused on either the dimensionality of performance or performance as a dynamic criteria but not both. This presentation will examine performance in terms of both its dimensionality and its dynamics of change over time. The presentation will show that recent advances in latent variable methods could provide a unified conceptual and methodological framework for describing and explaining the different aspects of performance dimensionality and change over time that may occur in longitudinal processes. Implications for future research in the study of job performance will be discussed.

IA-013: Contributions of cross-cultural perspectives to industrial and organizational psychology: Advancements in theory, research and applications

Aycan, Zeynep *Istanbul, Turkey*
Globalization of work activities requires that we understand the role of culture in managing human resources and organizational phenomena. The purpose of the presentation is to provide a critical review of the cross-cultural IO research focusing on the advancements in theory and methodology (e.g., level of theory, assumptions of linearity and unilateral effect of culture on organizations, conceptualization of culture, level of measurement and cross-level data analysis). Examples will be drawn from cross-cultural research on human resource management and leadership. The utility of research in managing cross-cultural interactions in contexts such as, multicultural teams, international joint ventures, and expatriation process will be discussed.

IA-015: Cooperation of complementary learning systems in memory

Arthur Jacobs (Chair)

McClelland, James L. *Mind, Brain and Computation, Stanford University, Stanford, USA*
In this talk I will review the connectionist approach to knowledge representation, learning, and memory. This approach has broad relevance for understanding successes, failures, and distortions in human memory as well as a wide range of developmental phenomena viewed as arising as consequences of a gradual, connection-based learning system. Within that framework I will describe a complementary learning systems theory that addresses a dilemma facing connection-based learning and memory systems and show how the theory is compatible with a wide range of experimental findings spanning cognitive, behavioral, and systems neuroscience. I will then discuss how within the theory the complementary learning systems work together in experiments addressing learning and memory for meaningful materials in normals and amnesics.

IA-016: The topological approach to perceptual organization: Where visual processing begins

Ulman Lindenberger (Chair)

Chen, Lin *Institute of Biophysics, Chinese Academy of Sciences, Beijing, People's Republic of China*
Most traditional models of vision are "local-first": detecting local features first and then integrating them to build objects. In contrast, we have developed a "global-first" topological approach, claiming that topological invariants are extracted at the very beginning of visual processing. To illustrate its applicability, the topological approach is applied to a formal definition of perceptual objects, which is tied to invariance over topological transformation. Behavioral and brain imaging results recently obtained in our lab consistently support the topological definition, demonstrating that the extraction of topological properties serves as the starting point of the formation of an object representation.

IA-020: Time and memory: Combining behavioural, neuroimaging, and neuropsychological approaches

Rainer Kluwe (Chair)

Pouthas, Viviane *LENA-UPR 640, CNRS, Paris, France*
Perception and estimation of time are strongly related to memory processes. But, these memory processes differ depending on the range of durations to be evaluated for an adaptive behavior. First, based on behavioral studies in patients with temporal lobe lesions, the presentation will be devoted to the processing of durations from tens of seconds to several minutes which mainly involved long-term memory. Second, based on MEG-EEG studies, the role of working memory in the perception of hundreds of milliseconds to several seconds will be examined. Finally, the issue of specific memory processes for timing will be addressed.

IA-021: On a psychology of passion

Vallerand, Robert J. *Montréal, Canada*
Passion. For centuries, philosophers and writers have aspired to understand its sources, its ramifications, and its role in our lives. Recently, Vallerand and his colleagues (2003) have proposed a new conceptualization of passion. Passion is defined as a strong inclination or desire for a self-defining activity that we love, value, and spend a considerable amount of time on. Two types of passion are proposed: a harmonious and an obsessive passion. Obsessive passion is involved when people feel that they can't help themselves and have to surrender to their desire to engage in the passionate activity. It is as if the activity controlled the person. Obsessive passion results from a controlled internalization (Deci & Ryan, 2000) of the activity in the person's identity. On the other hand, harmonious passion refers to a strong inclination for the activity that nevertheless remains under the person's control. The person can choose when to and when not to engage in the activity, thus preventing conflict from arising between activity engagement in the passionate activity and other life activities. Harmonious passion results from an autonomous internalization of the activity in identity. In this address, I review research that reveals that harmonious passion is typically associated with adaptive outcomes while obsessive passion is related to less adaptive and at times maladaptive outcomes. These findings have been obtained with respect to a number of affective, cognitive, mental and physical health, relationships, and performance variables with diverse populations. I also address the role of personality and social variables in the development of passion. Finally, some directions for future research are proposed.

IS-001: Analogy-making

Boicho Kokinov *(chair)*
This symposium will explore the role analogy-making plays in human cognition. It will discuss the foundations of analogy - what are the very basic mechanisms underlying analogy-making and how they develop. Experimental work with infants and children will be presented as well as with adults. The influence of analogy-making on perception, category learning, memory, and scientific text understanding will also be explored and computational models will be presented. The symposium will bring together researchers to discuss the core role of analogy and its mechanisms as well as its developmental fate.

The foundations of analogy? Cross-modal sensory mappings in children

Goswami, Usha *Dept. of Education, University of Cambridge, Cambridge, United Kingdom* **Cheah, Victoria** *Dept. of Education, University of Cambridge, Cambridge, United Kingdom* **Soltesz, Fruzsina** *Dept. of Education, University of Cambridge, Cambridge, United Kingdom*
There is growing interest in the idea that shared neural processing mechanisms might explain similarities in the cognitive processing of apparently disparate domains. Here, we explore this hypothesis with respect to the development of analogizing. While cognitive analogies appear to rely on extracting relational similarities between apparently unrelated domains of knowledge, the developmental roots of relational mapping may lie in the operation of our sensory systems. We explore how children aged 3 – 5 years map between pitch, magnitude, size, loudness and luminance. Systematic sensory connections may shape linguistic and conceptual development within a relational mapping framework.

Intermodal mapping of dynamic displays

Pauen, Sabina *Inst. für Psychologie, Universität Heidelberg, Heidelberg, Germany* **Jeschonek, Susanna** *Inst. für Psychologie, Universität Heidelberg, Heidelberg, Germany*
Relational mapping as a core cognitive capacity for analogical reasoning has been found within and between sensory modalities in adults and children (Goswami, 1992, Marks et al., 1987; Mondloch & Maurer, 2004; Wagner et al., 1981). In the present study we are interested in cross-modal correspondences of dynamic changes (e.g. pitch and movement) and explore whether relational mapping is fundamental or learned through linguistic and cultural influence. We tested three infant-age-groups and preschool-children in an auditory-visual matching task containing dynamic displays (i.e. ascending tone/ upward movement; descending tone/ downward movement). The data of all age-groups will be presented and discussed.

The Role of Analogical Reasoning in Category Learning

Bianchi, Cesare Dept. of Computer Science, University College Dublin, Dublin, Ireland *Costello, Fintan* Dept. of Computer Science, University College Dublin, Dublin, Ireland

This research explores if and how Analogical Reasoning is used to learn new concepts, specifically categories, in previously unknown domains. We used sets of colored geometric shapes, which form four different categories: two based on the presence of a distinctive element, two on the numeric relation between the numbers of similar elements. The test has been administered to students, and we analyzed the time taken to learn the different categories and the errors produced. The discovery of a category of one kind considerably helps learning in the other category, but it doesn't help the other kind. We observed that showing two similar objects at the same time, even both completely unknown, helps to find a common or analogical structure.

Using analogy to foster conceptual restructuring

Vosniadou, Stella Philosophy History of Science, University of Athens, Athens, Greece *Skopeliti, Irini* Philosophy and His. of Science, University of Athens, Athens, Greece *Gerakakis, Svetlana-Lito* Philosophy and His. of Science, University of Athens, Athens, Greece

We investigated how an analogy from a different but highly familiar domain can help children restructure their explanations of the day/night cycle. Seventy-three 3rd and 5th grade children participated in the study. The children read expository texts that presented them with the scientific explanation of the day/night cycle with or without the use of an analogy. The results showed that the analogy text helped children change from an initial explanation of the day/night cycle (based on the movement of the sun) to a scientific explanation of the day/night cycle (based on the earth's axis rotation) more than the no-analogy text.

Analogy influences perception and memory

Kokinov, Boicho Dept. of Cognitive Science, New Bulgarian University, Sofia, Bulgaria *Hristova, Penka* Dept. of Cognitive Science, New Bulgarian University, Sofia, Bulgaria *Petkov, Georgi* Dept. of Cognitive Science, New Bulgarian University, Sofia, Bulgaria *Bliznashki, Svetoslav* Dept. of Cognitive Science, New Bulgarian University, Sofia, Bulgaria *Kosev, Svetlin* Dept. of Cognitive Science, New Bulgarian University, Sofia, Bulgaria *Feldman, Veselina* Dept. of Cognitive Science, New Bulgarian University, Sofia, Bulgaria

Experimental work will be presented that demonstrates how analogy-making influences various cognitive processes, including perception and memory. It will be argued for an interactive and emergent approach to human cognition that is based on parallel processing without a central control mechanism; an approach that does not impose boundaries to the so called cognitive processes, but rather integrates them on a common bases. The experimental data demonstrate that the use of specific analogies may change the way we perceive the environment and force us to represent it, may change the way we memorize the events and produce memory distortions and illusory memories.

IS-002: International perspectives on child and adolescent psychopathology: Issues of cross-informant agreement

Leslie Rescorla (chair)

This symposium will examine issues of cross-informant agreement. The first talk will provide a historical overview. The second talk will present findings regarding cross-informant agreement ob-tained in a 20-year longitudinal study of a large Dutch general population sample. The third talk will report behavior genetic findings on cross-informant agreement in a large longitudinal sample of Dutch twins. The fourth talk will compare findings on parent-adolescent agreement obtained for general population samples in 20 different societies. The fifth talk will report agreement between mothers and fathers and adolescents in a German sample over four years. The sixth talk will examine cross-informant agreement from constructivist and epistemological perspectives.

A historical perspective on issues of cross-informant agreement

Achenbach, Thomas Dept. of Psychiatry, University of Vermont, Burlington, VT, USA

Methods have long existed for assessing problems via data from parents, teachers, children, clinicians, and observers. However, until the 1980s, the typical levels of agreement between informants received little attention. Meta-analyses revealed modest agreement that was affected by multiple variables. Since then, use of multi-informant data has become more systematic. Modest agreement on adult psychopathology also requires attention. Variations among data sources must be dealt with to advance assessment and understanding of psychopathology.

Cross-informant agreement: Longitudinal findings over 20 years

Verhulst, Frank Child and Adolesc. Psychiatry, Erasmus Medisch Center, Rotterdam, Netherlands *van der Ende, Jan*

Adolescent self-reports of problems on the Youth-Self-Report (YSR) and parent reports of problems on the Child Behavior Checklist (CBCL) were obtained for 939 adolescents aged 11-17 years from the general population in 1997. Twenty years later we collected information on emotional/behavioral problems, psychiatric diagnoses, and social functioning. Findings on the continuity of self-reported emotional and behavioral problems across a twenty-year follow-up period will be presented. The implications of results on how different levels of agreement between parent and adolescent self-report predicted later functioning will be discussed.

Behavior genetic analysis of cross-informant agreement in Dutch twins

Bartels, Meike Dept. of Biological Psychology, Free University Amsterdam, Amsterdam, Netherlands

Behavior genetic analyses were conducted with longitudinal multiple rater data on internalizing and externalizing problems in a large sample of Dutch twins. Stability in Internalizing and Externalizing scores was mainly accounted for by genetic factors. Rater bias accounted for 10% to 15% of variance overall in rater disagreement. The effect of rater bias in stability appeared to be stronger for INT than for EXT. In interpreting longitudinal data, it should be realized that part of the stability is caused by stability in "rater bias" rather than stability in the "real" behavior of the child, with this effect be larger for INT than for EXT.

Multicultural perspectives on cross-informant agreement: Parent-adolescent agreement in 20 societies

Rescorla, Leslie Dept. of Psychology, Bryn Mawr College, Bryn Mawr, PA, USA *Ginsburg, Sofia*

Adolescent self-reports of problems were obtained with the Youth-Self-Report (YSR) and parent reports of problems were obtained with the Child Behavior Checklist (CBCL) for 22,358 dyads from 20 societies. Correlations between parent and adolescent Total Problems scores ranged widely across societies but were >.40 in half the societies. YSR scores were higher than CBCL scores in all 20 societies. Results indicate considerable variation across societies in level of parent-adolescent agree-ment but a consistent trend across societies for adolescents to report more problems than their parents report about them.

Changes in cross-informant agreement over time: Converging or divergent perspectives of parents and adolescents and links to family functioning

Seiffge-Krenke, Inge Inst. Entwicklungspsychologie, Universität Mainz, Mainz, Germany

Adolescent self-reports on the Youth-Self-Report (YSR) and mothers and fathers reports on the Child Behavior Checklist (CBCL) were obtained over four years in 228 families. Change in symptomatology was linked with changes in parent-child-relationships (FES) over time. Overall, parent-adolescent agreement was low (mean r =.36) and fairly stable over time. Agreement was higher in families with a warmer and more cohesive family climate, and mother-adolescent agreement was higher than father-adolescent agreement. Results indicate considerable variation with respect to respondent and time and illustrate the impact of family functioning on perceived symptomatology of the offspring.

A constructivist perspective on cross-informant agreement: Epistemological aspects

Westmeyer, Hans Inst. für Psychologie, Freie Universität Berlin, Berlin, Germany

Any rating of something by a rater can be conceived of as a personal construction with the following logical structure: x (the rater) constructs y (the entity to be rated) as z (the result of the rating) at t (the time at which the rating takes place). The same rater x may rate the same entity y at different times with different (or the same) results, and the same entity y may be rated by different raters at the same or different times with different (or the same) results. In the last case, the concept of cross-informant agreement becomes relevant. This talk will answer the epistemological question: What does a certain degree of cross-informant agreement express?

IS-003: Language and brain

Pierluigi Zoccolotti, Martin Fischer (chair)

The relationship between language processing and brain functioning is of key importance to a wide field of psychologists and researchers from allied disciplines. Over the past four years a European Research & Training Network on "Language and Brain" (http://www.hull.ac.uk/RTN-LAB/) has examined healthy and impaired language processing, using a range of neuroscientific techniques. This symposium provides an up-to-date survey of our findings.

Analyzing reading processes with MEG

Ellis, Andy Dept. of Psychology, University of York, Heslington, York, United Kingdom *Barca, Laura* ISTC, CNR, Rome, Italy *Urooj, Uzma* Dept. of Psychology, University of York, Heslington, York, United Kingdom *Cornelissen, Piers* Dept. of Psychology, University of York, Heslington, York, United Kingdom *Simpson, Michael* York Neuroimaging Centre, University of York, Heslington, York, United Kingdom

Studies using functional MRI and PET have taught us a lot about the regions of the brain involved in reading. They can tell us relatively little, however, about the time course of reading processes, while those techniques that deliver precise timing information (e.g., ERPs) have poor spatial localization. Magnetoencephalography (MEG) can identify the brain areas involved in a task with reasonable accuracy and can provide very precise timing information. We will illustrate the insights to be gained from MEG with reference to visual word recognition, word learning, hemisphere specialisation, and the similarities between object and word recognition.

Hemispheric processing of poetry

Pobric, Gorana School of Psychology, University of Manchester, Manchester, United Kingdom Lavidor, Michal Brain Research Center, Bar Ilan University, Ramat-Gan, Israel

Previous research suggests that the right hemisphere (RH) may contribute uniquely to the processing of metaphoric language. Transcranial Magnetic Stimulation (TMS) of the right posterior superior temporal sulcus (rPSTS) disrupted processing of novel but not conventional metaphors, while TMS over the left inferior frontal gyrus (IFG) selectively impaired processing of conventional but not novel metaphors. This is the first demonstration of TMS-induced impairment in processing novel metaphoric expressions, and as such confirms the specialization of the RH in the activation of a broader range of related meanings than the LH, including novel, nonsalient meanings.

Interactions between language and motor processes in the brain

Nazir, Tatjana CNRS, Inst. des Sciences Cognitives, Lyon, France

Recently, the notion that cortical or subcortical motor areas maybe crucial to human language has become increasingly popular. In my talk I will present a series of findings from our group that show instant effects of language processes on overt motor behavior and effects of motor processes on language behavior, using ERPs, fine grained analysis of movement and using analyses of language processing in patients with motor deficits. These results will be discussed in the context of Hebbian correlation learning and the human "mirror neuron system".

Lexical reading in Italian typically developing readers and developmental dyslexics

Paizi, Despina ISTC-CNR, Rome, Italy Burani, Cristina ISTC, CNR, Rome, Italy Zoccolotti, Pierluigi Rome, Italy

Readers of transparent orthographies have been theorised to rely on the grapheme-to-phoneme conversion rules in reading acquisition. Lexical effects: lexicality, word frequency, word morphology have been reported for Italian typically developing readers. However, Italian developmental dyslexics' reading is characterised by a striking length effect without specific nonword reading deficit and relatively preserved accuracy implying mainly non-lexical reading. The issue is whether lexical reading is available to Italian developmental dyslexics similarly to typically developing readers. A series of experiments provides evidence towards lexical reading for the dyslexics as well as typically developing readers contrary to previous assumptions for prevalently nonlexical reading.

IS-004: Computational models of episodic memory (Part I)

Stephan Lewandowsky (chair)

This symposium brings together speakers from across a broad range of topics in memory research to present a leading-edge snapshot of current progress in all aspects of computational modeling of memory. Rather than being dedicated to a specific area of memory research, this symposium seeks to survey the breadth of the discipline. Contributors will include researchers with an interest in short-term and working memory on the one hand, and recognition and recall in long-term memory on the other, as well as researchers who believe both short-term and long-term phenomena are best considered together within a unified framework.

On the locus of response suppression in free recall

Davelaar, Eddy USA

In free recall, the sequential output of memoranda gives rise to specific retrieval time distributions. Until now computational theories of free recall memory have not been constrained by these data. In the literature on serial recall, however, models use a retrieval mechanism called competitive queuing that allows parallel activated candidates to be output in sequence. I will show that using this mechanism in models of free recall does not capture the data on retrieval time, and that changing the mechanism to suppression of previous responses at the level of memory selection (instead of at the level of memory activation) does.

Active memory of serial order

Botvinick, Matthew Inst. of Neuroscience, Princeton University, Princeton, NJ, USA

Working memory is widely agreed to depend on active maintenance, that is, sustained neural activation that can preserve information over short delays. One important question is how such a mechanism might support memory not only for individual events, but also for their order of occurrence. Neuroscientific evidence suggests that working memory for serial order relies upon neurons that code conjunctively for item and order information. I'll review a set of computational modeling studies exploring how such a representational regime might explain detailed patterns of serial recall performance, and describe a set of behavioral studies testing predictions of the computational framework.

Time-based models of memory

Brown, Gordon Dept. of Psychology, University of Warwick, Coventry, United Kingdom Morin, Caroline Dept. of Psychology, University of Warwick, Coventry, United Kingdom

Time-based models of memory differ in a number of important ways. Models that represent the locations of items as point sources in time appear to fail on data that require consideration of the temporal extension of items. We describe a new relative-time based model that builds on the positive features of existing temporal models but can yet accommodate data that prove problematic for previous models. We also report the results of a number of experiments designed to test the predictions of the new model.

Temporal effects in serial memory

Hartley, Tom Dept of Psychology, University of York, York, United Kingdom Hursltone, Mark Dept of Psychology, University of York, York, United Kingdom Hitch, Graham Inst. of Psychology, University of York, York, United Kingdom

Irregular timing of items can exert both beneficial and detrimental effects on serial recall performance relative to regular timing. Where items form groups (e.g., Ryan, 1969, QJEP), performance varies with the group sizes. New data are consistent with the idea that auditory grouping effects result from a bottom-up mechanism. A model of serial memory in which a population of oscillators is entrained to the timing of stimuli neatly accounts for these effects, and addresses recent empirical evidence that has been considered incompatible with such models. We suggest that such oscillator models may have been rejected prematurely.

Modeling memory performance in older adults: Assessing the contribution of differences in representation

Neath, Ian Dept. of Psychology, Memorial Univ. of Newfounland, St. John's, Canada Surprenant, Aimée Psychology Dept., Memorial Univ. of Newfoundland, St John's, Canada

We explore whether perceptual deficits in older adults can lead to less discriminable memory representations than those of younger adults and thence to reduced memory performance. In Phase I, similarity ratings were obtained for both auditory and visual stimuli, and the data were analyzed using multidimensional scaling. In Phase II, the same subjects completed a standard immediate serial recall task. The MDS coordinates were used as input to a local distinctiveness model of memory called SIMPLE. The model accounted for the observed age-related differences in memory solely on the basis of differences in the representation.

The role of experience in event memory and knowledge retrieval

Shiffrin, Richard Psychological & Brain Sciences, Indiana University, Bloomington, USA Nelson, Angela __, Indiana University, Bloomington, USA

Participants are trained for two weeks searching displays for initially unknown Chinese characters, different characters occurring different numbers of times. Then participants are tested on episodic recognition, perceptual identification, and pseudolexical decision. High frequency characters do worse in episodic recognition but better in the other tasks. We present a model to explain the storage and retrieval of episodic memories and knowledge, a model that predicts these frequency effects.

IS-005: Lifelong learning: From definition to intervention

Christiane Spiel (chair)

Lifelong learning is proclaimed by the European Commission as a topic of central relevance. But so far a satisfying definition cannot be found neither from the perspective of policy nor within the sciences. Especially Educational and Bildung-Psychology have to deal with LLL as various traditional fields of these domains are decisive for LLL. The symposium presents four papers focusing on a theoretical approach on LLL (Schober et al.) and on interventions promoting core aspects of LLL as motivation (Salmela-Aro) and self-regulated learning (Schmidt & Schmitz, Dresel). The discussion (Sternberg) crystallizes central findings and recommends enhancements and further steps.

Lifelong Learning (LLL) as an educational goal: Theoretical specification and promotion

Schober, Barbara Inst. für Psychologie, Universität Wien, Wien, Austria Finsterwald, Monika University Vienna, Austria Wagner, Petra University Vienna, Austria Aysner, Michael University Vienna, Austria Lüftenegger, Marko University Vienna, Austria Spiel, Christiane University Vienna, Austria

The paper presents a theoretical approach to LLL based on the idea that persistent motivation to learn and the skills to realize this motivation are essential. Following these theoretical specifications a three semester training program for teachers (TALK) to enhance LLL was developed. TALK intends changes in teachers and pupils competencies and alterations in the learning culture of the schools. 40 secondary school teachers participated each with one class, involving 780 schoolchildren. The control group consists of 55 teachers and 1700 pupils. The summative evaluation using questionnaires, training diaries, interviews, and focus groups shows successful promotion of LLL competencies.

Towards work life intervention: Promoting engagement in lifelong learning

Salmela-Aro, Katariina Dept. of Psychology, University of Jyväskylä, Jyväskylä, Finland Vuori, Jukka Institute of Occupational Heal, Finland

Promoting engagement towards Lifelong learning among adolescents during the transition from comprehensive school to education tracks was one of the aims of "Towards work life intervention". A week-long randomized group intervention program was carried out during last year of the comprehensive education among 1035 adolescents (mean age = 15, 520 girls, 515 boys) who were randomized in control (n = 513) or intervention (n = 522) group. The results showed that intervention increased internal motivation towards education and engagement towards goals related to further education. The results are discussed in the context of promoting Lifelong learning.

Training to improve young scientists' self-regulation competencies: promoting lifelong learning
Schmidt, Michaela Inst. für Pädag. Psychologie, Techn. Universität Darmstadt, Darmstadt, Germany Schmitz, Bernhard Technische Universität, Darmstadt, Germany
The aim of the study was the training of young scientists' self-regulation competencies based on a process model of self-regulation. Forty-eight young scientists between the ages of 24 and 39 (41.8% female) participated. Self-regulation was assessed by a diary, which participants filled out over a period of ten weeks. The thus obtained process data were analysed with trend analyses as well as interrupted time-series analyses. The trend analyses show significant effects for variables of all three phases of self-regulation. The interrupted time-series analyses confirmed largely the expected training effects. Results indicate that the training is appropriate to improve self-regulation behavior.

Self-regulated learning with digital media as an important facet of life-long learning
Dresel, Markus Inst. für Pädag. Psychologie, Universität Ulm, Ulm, Germany
A study is presented, with which self-regulated learning with digital media was addressed under the perspective of lifelong learning. A main purpose was to test the effectiveness of a newly designed scaffold. Participants were 70 undergraduates, who worked with "Wikipedia" and were randomly assigned to a treatment or a control group. As measuring instruments, questionnaires and the thinking-aloud-technique were used. Results revealed noticeable deficits in the self-regulation of learning and a substantial training effect. It could be concluded that there is a need to scaffold self-regulated learning with digital media and that the present approach is effective in doing so.

IS-006: Approaches to studying family across cultures

James Georgas (chair)
This symposium presents four issues in the study of the family in cross-cultural psychology. 1) Families and rearing practices of mothers and infants in its cultural context, 2) Family change across cultures, that is, the degree and types of changes in families as a result of the processes of economic development, in particular, transitions from the extended types of family systems to the nuclear family, and one-parent family. 3) Acculturation of immigrant families to the context of receiving societies, and 4) Some methodological issues in studying families in different cultural contexts.

Family relationships as expressed in children's drawings: A cross cultural analysis
Keller, Heidi Inst. für Psychologie, Universität Osnabrück, Osnabrück, Germany
Mainly two family models are discussed in the literature: the model of independence and the model of interdependence This presentation focuses on 4 to 6 years old children' s representations of their family in three different cultural environments: Cameroonian Nso, Indian Hindu and Northern German children. The study analyzes children drawings of their families assessed in kindergartens.

Composition of families, size of the drawings as well as relative position of the family members to each other will be analyzed. In an exploratory analysis, indicators symbolizing equality and hierarchy of relationships will be evaluated.

Persistent traditions and compelling modernity: Dynamics of survival of contemporary Indian families
Kapoor, Shraddha Dept. of Human Development, University of Delhi, New Delhi, India
This presentation focuses on recent research and theory about Asian Indian families. One of the most pertinent questions today concerns the future of the traditional family against the modernising forces of economic progress and social change. This does not place any doubt on the ideology of 'Familism' in India. Most often, the family continues to be the most important affiliation in any person's life. Evidence will also be presented demonstrating the dynamic adaptability of individuals and families through what we call 'elective interdependence', that individuals actively choose when to distance and when to approach another person for desired ends.

Persistent traditions and compelling modernity: Dynamics of survival of contemporary Indian families
Chaudhary, Nandita Dept. of Human Development, University of Delhi, New Delhi, India
A pertinent question facing the traditional Indian family is its survival against modernising forces. Based on research evidence and scholarly discourse, we will present arguments questioning the myth of the harmonious joint family as well as the dynamic adaptability of contemporary Indian families. The pre-eminence of the joint family in traditional Indian society has recently come under question in sociology and gender studies. Evidence will also be presented demonstrating the dynamic adaptability of individuals and families through what we call 'elective interdependence', that individuals actively choose when to distance and when to approach another person for desired ends.

Studying families in a Brazilian network
Seidl de Moura, Maria Lucia Dept. of Psychology, State Univ. of Rio de Janeiro, Rio de Janeiro, Brazil Donato Oliva, Angela Dept. of Psychology, State Univ. of Rio de Janeiro, Rio de Janeiro, Brazil
Families differ on beliefs and child rearing practices as a dynamic result of interconnections between cultural systems and bioecological variables. This study compares mothers from city (UM) and rural areas (RM) of the State of Rio de Janeiro, Brazil on: types of families, sociodemographic variables, mothers' beliefs and related practices. In both groups there was a predominance of nuclear families, with cases of extended families. They differ on all the variables considered and have diverse patterns of social support. Results will be discussed in terms of previous studies on Brazilian mothers and the characteristics and cultural models of these families.

Studying families in a Brazilian network
Donato Oliva, Angela Inst. of Psychology, State Univ. of Rio de Janeiro, Rio de Janeiro, Brazil
Families differ on beliefs and child rearing practices as a dynamic result of interconnections between cultural systems and bioecological variables. This study compares mothers from city (UM) and rural areas (RM) of the State of Rio de Janeiro, Brazil on: types of families, sociodemographic variables, mothers' beliefs and related practices. In both groups there was a predominance of nuclear families, with cases of extended families. They differ on all the variables considered and have diverse patterns of social support. Results will be discussed in terms of previous studies on Brazilian

mothers and the characteristics and cultural models of these families.

Chinese American families in the United States: From everywhere, forever here
Gielen, Uwe Dept. of Psychology, St. Francis College, Brooklyn Heights, USA Lei, Ting Dept. of Social Sciences-N620, BMCC, City Univ. of New York, New York, USA
We report the results of a study of Chinese-origin families in New York Chinatown as seen through the eyes of their adolescent members. Based on interviews with 150 adolescents aged 14-24 years we conclude that many immigrant families face great hardships and make many sacrifices while adopting to their new surroundings. Nevertheless, the structural integrity of most of these families did not seem to be compromised in the face of very difficult circumstances.

Methodological issues and some traps in studying families in different cultures
Georgas, James Dept. of Psychology, University of Athens, Athens, Greece
The two methodological approaches in studies of family in cross-cultural psychology are the cultural or indigenous idiographic, and the cross-cultural comparative and quantitative. Some methodological issues are: the assumption of modernization theory that family changes in countries of the majority world will follow those of Western societies; the traps of demographic measures of family types without studying family networks and the assumption of the independence of cultures (Galton's problem); the identification of psychological universals as well as differences across cultures, the necessity of studying the links between family variables, psychological variables and ecological and sociopolitical variables of cultures.

IS-007: Testing and assessment in emerging and developing countries I: The current state

Marise Born, Fanny M. Cheung (chair)
Testing and assessment of people is a growing activity in emerging and developing countries. This part of the symposium describes the current state of affairs in this area by demonstrating how several major complexities are addressed at present in Singapore, Nigeria and South Africa. Among these difficulties are the education of experts in testing, language issues in multilingual contexts, diverse test taker approaches in questionnaire responding, and non-equivalence issues of measures.

Testing for equivalence of the self description questionnaire I across Australian and Nigerian adolescents
Byrne, Barbara M. Dept. of Psychology, University of Ottawa, Ottawa, Canada
The intent of this study was twofold: (a) to test for equivalence of the Physical Self-concept (SC; Ability, Appearance) and Social SC (Peers, Parents) subscales of the Self Description Questionnaire I (SDQ-I; Marsh, 1992) across Australian (N=497) and Nigerian (N=439) adolescents, and (b) presented with findings of nonequivalence, to identify the possible determinants of this result. Based on analysis of covariance structures within the framework of a confirmatory factor analytic model, findings revealed evidence of both measurement and structural nonequivalence despite similarly specified and well-fitting factor structures for both cultural groups. Results underscore previous caveats regarding preconceived assumptions of instrument equivalence.

Self concepts and response styles in personality testing across cultures

Born, Marise *Inst. of Psychology, Erasmus University Rotterdam, Rotterdam, Netherlands* **Kevenaar, Mitchel** *Optimale Coaching, Korput & Treffers, Oosterhout, Netherlands* **Myburgh, Wim** *Human Capital Assessment, Psymetrics, Cape Town, South Africa*

This study intended to bring together the literature on socially desirable responding (Paulhus, 2002) and on the self-enhancement motive (Heine, 2005; Sedikides et al., 2005) to account for differences in self report personality questionnaire responding across cultural groups. Illustrated with 15FQ+- findings from two South African applicant samples (African language group, N=190; English language group, N=162), possible determinants of different response patterns were sought in cultural self-guide differences, with different weights given to ideal and ought selves (Higgins, 1987).

Psychological testing in Singapore

Leong, Frederick T.L. *Dept. of Psychology, Michigan State University, East Lansing, USA*

Even though psychology has only recently being introduced into Singapore, it appears that psychological testing and assessment has indeed taken hold in this small Island republic. This paper will provide an overview to the status of psychological testing in this country by reviewing (a) the coverage of testing and assessment in the curriculum within the three major academic centers of psychology (i.e., National University of Singapore, Nanyang Technological University, and Singapore Management University), (b) the patterns of test use among practicing psychologists, and (c) the development of a career testing system by psychologists at the National Institute of Education.

Facing the challenge of the language of assessment and test adaptation

Foxcroft, Cheryl D. *Summerstrand Campus, Nelson Mandela Metrop. Uni., Port Elizabeth, South Africa* **de Bruin, Deon** *Department of HRM, University of Johannesburg, Johannesburg, South Africa*

This paper will focus on issues pertaining to the language of assessment when tests are used with diverse cultural groups. Two main themes are addressed. First, whether it is good practice to administer tests in a common (e.g., English) or the dominant language in a multilingual context is explored. Second, issues and good practices related to adapting and translating tests in a multilingual context are highlighted. Reference is made to international good practice guidelines and examples of research and test adaptation studies related to the language issues in assessment in the field of educational, cognitive and personality assessment.

IS-008: Tolerance for ambiguity, creativity, and personality

Katya Stoycheva *(chair)*

Ambiguity tolerance describes individual behaviour in ambiguous situations where one has to act with lack of clarity or lack of information. We shall discuss individual differences in tolerance – intolerance of ambiguity, their measurement, and their relation to creativity and personality. First we will examine the role tolerance for ambiguity plays in creative performance and creative motivation. Then we will consider the relation of ambiguity tolerance to other personality characteristics that describe individual perceptions of and reactions to ambiguity and uncertainty. Correlational data, factor analytical studies and cross cultural comparisons will specify the cognitive, affective and motivational processes in ambiguity tolerance.

The new and the best: Ambiguity tolerance and creativity motivation

Stoycheva, Katya *Inst. of Psychology, Bulgarian Academy of Sciences, Sofia, Bulgaria*

Tolerance for ambiguity correlated positively with creative motivation but was not related to need for achievement across samples of 106 high school students (14 – 19 years) and 135 university students (19 – 34 years). Tolerance for ambiguity and creative motivation related however differently to author's measure of attitudes towards ambiguity tolerant – ambiguity intolerant behaviours. Participants filled in also Bulgarian adaptations of Torrance's Creative Motivation Scale, Norton's Measure of Ambiguity Tolerance, and a Bulgarian scale for measuring need for achievement. Creative motivation items that differentiated individuals with high and low tolerance for ambiguity and high and low need for achievements were identified.

Relationship between tolerance for ambiguity and creative performances

Zenasni, Franck *Inst. of Psychology, University Rene Descartes, Boulogne Billancourt, France*

This study examines the relationship between creativity and tolerance of ambiguity. Participants were parents and their adolescent children. Three measures of creativity were used: a divergent thinking task, a story-writing task and a self-evaluation of creative attitudes and behavior. Participants completed two self-report measures of tolerance of ambiguity: the short version of the "Measurement of Ambiguity Tolerance" (Norton, 1975; Zenasni & Lubart, 2001) and the "Behaviour Scale of Tolerance/Intolerance for Ambiguity" (Stoycheva, 1998, 2003). Tolerance of ambiguity was significantly and positively related to creativity. Creativity of parents was related to their adolescents' creativity. However, parents' tolerance of ambiguity was not related to adolescents' tolerance of ambiguity or creativity.

The dimensions of the complexity tolerance: A synopsis of personality constructs

Radant, Matthias *Inst. für Bildung, Universität Halle-Wittenberg, Halle, Germany* **Dalbert, Claudia** *Educational Psychology, Universität Halle-Wittenberg, Halle, Germany*

The construct complexity tolerance was developed as a super ordinate concept of overlapping constructs like ambiguity tolerance, uncertainty tolerance, need for cognitive closure, and personal need for structure. In a series of three factor analytical studies with a total of N = 690 persons, three factors of complexity tolerance could be identified: the appraisal of complex situations in terms of threat, challenge, or necessity. This threefold factor structure was replicated in 9 studies with N = 943 persons altogether. Construct validity was shown in two studies with N = 440 students, where the dimensions explained different kinds of learning preferences.

Relation of ambiguity tolerance to cognitive and affective needs: A cross cultural content analysis

Stoycheva, Katya *Inst. of Psychology, Bulgarian Academy of Sciences, Sofia, Bulgaria* **Lubart, Todd** *Inst. of Psychology, University Rene Descartes, Boulogne Billancourt, France* **Zenasni, Franck** *Inst. of Psychology, University Rene Descartes, Boulogne Billancourt, France* **Popova, Kalina** *Inst. of Psychology, Bulgarian Academy of Sciences, Sofia, Bulgaria*

Ten Bulgarian and ten French doctoral students in psychology rated each of the 188 items of need for closure, need for structure, need for cognition, need to evaluate, need for precision, intolerance of uncertainty, and need for affect scales. Experts were provided with a written definition of tolerance – intolerance of ambiguity and indicated whether and to what extent these items related to ambiguity

tolerance construct. The strength of items' relation to ambiguity tolerance (weak, moderate, or strong) was compared across expert groups and across scales. Cases of cross-cultural disagreement in judgements and lack of consensus among experts were examined.

IS-009: Transformation and women in the work place: A psychological perspective from Africa

Ann Watts *(chair)*

The third Millennium Development Goal aims to promote gender equality and empower women. However, in Africa women continue to face constraints due to patriarchy, gender discrimination, low levels of education, as well as the burden of family care and poverty. Those in both formal and informal employment confront disparities in development opportunities, and are often under-represented and under-valued. Many also have to contend with sexual harassment. This symposium addresses the psychological issues and challenges facing African woman in formal and informal employment, as well as the transformations that are occurring in the workplace.

The balancing act

Seedat, Fatima *Organisational Psychology, Psych. Society South Africa, Houghton, South Africa*

Women are faced with the challenge of balancing two responsibilities that are crucial to the further development of the country. These are fostering the optimal development of the family and children in particular and contributing to the expansion of the workforce and economy. In South Africa, some women spend a minimum of eight hours in service of the latter and immeasurable time focused on optimal family development. This presentation sketches the promises and challenges of combining these roles within South Africa as an emerging economy.

Exploring the psychosocial factors underlying the uptake of legal provisions against sexual harassment in the workplace

Nyanungo, Kwadzanai *Zimbabwean Psychological Ass., Harare, Zimbabwe*

Research studies have indicated that sexual harassment deserves more attention than current labour practice in Zimbabwe. However, despite legal provision for victims to take this up in the courts of law, under-reporting is the order of the day. This paper reviews research findings, analyses case studies of related court cases and presents victim perspectives. Recommendations are proffered on psychological interventions to support legal provisions within the Zimbabwean cultural context of both the formal and informal employment.

Reforms in Nigeria and the development of women

Mivanyi, Yuwanna Jenny *Education Technical, City University Kaduna, Kaduna, Nigeria*

Reforms could comprise a metamorphosis given the dynamic nature of society. "Reforms could also be necessitated by failures in the extent of operational goals or targets" (Nworgu: 2007). In Nigeria, both types of reforms occur in order to improve the overall quality of life of Nigerians. For women, reforms aim to expand access and achieve equity in the workplace. Colonial reform Acts, were refined into vision 2010, and are subsumed by the Millennium Development Goals. This presentation addresses the nature and extent of the transformation taking place amongst Nigerian working women within the framework of the eight Millennium Development Goals.

The psychological consequences of unemployment and informal work in Namibian women

Kober, Gudrun P.E.A.C.E., Bachbrecht, Namibia
Some research has pointed to the dire psychological consequences of unemployment. Seemingly women are buffered from these consequences because they perceive themselves as doing meaningful work in the family context. However the psychological benefits of having work to do can be overshadowed by poverty and having too much responsibility. This paper will address the following questions in respect of some unemployed Namibian women. What do these women regard as being their work? How do they distinguish between employment and work? To what extent do they derive similar psychological benefits from their work as the formally employed do? How does unemployment affect these women?

IS-010: Psychology and cultural diversity

Thomas Trang (chair)
The first paper discusses psychological issues related to Australian indigenous people and efforts of psychologists in improving their mental health. The second paper reports on two studies that investigated the efficacy of a coping skills program with adolescents in Italy and Australia. The third paper reports on developmental differences about tolerance to human diversity in Australian and American adolescents. The fourth paper reports on a research into the use of a projective personality test for children in the Australian and the Greek cultures. The fifth paper discusses psychological issues related to migrants who made the journey during old age.

Indeginous issues in a multicultural society

Gordon, Amanda Society, Australian Psychological, Melbourne, VIC, Australia
For most city dwelling Australians, the less than 1% of the population that in the early years of the 21st century identifies itself as aboriginal, has been virtually invisible. Decades of disadvantage have created devastating consequences for communities, including significant inequities in life expectancy, morbidity, drug and alcohol abuse, child sexual abuse, domestic violence, youth suicide and high rates of imprisonment. Recent Government interventions in remote aboriginal communities, aimed at promoting mental health, reduce child abuse, domestic violence, etc. and the Australian Psychological Society's support of members working in this area are discussed, plus need for indigenous mental health workforce, strategies for achieving this, based on international best practice.

Improving coping strategies of rural adolescents in Australia and Italy

Frydenberg, Erica Faculty of Education, University of Melbourne, Melbourne, Australia Eacott, Chelsea Faculty of Education, University of Melbourne, Melbourne, Australia Ferrari, Lea Faculty of Psychology, University of Padova, Padova, Italy Nota, Laura Faculty of Psychology, University of Padova, Padova, Italy Soresi, Salvatore Faculty of Psychology, University of Padova, Padova, Italy
This paper reports on two studies that investigated the efficacy of a coping skills program, The Best of Coping. Whilst both focused on at risk rural students, the first reports on a sample of rural Italian adolescents at risk for juvenile psycho-emotional-social problems and the second a sample of adolescents from rural Victoria, Australia at risk for depression. Italian adolescents utilised problem-focused strategies, particularly focus on the positive, post-program and showed increases in self-efficacy concerning decision-making abilities. The Australian adolescents showed overall decreases in use of non-productive coping strategies post-program with greatest reductions seen in use of self-blame.

Cross-cultural examination of adolescents' conceptualization of tolerance to human diversity in Australia and the USA

Witenberg, Rivka Dept. of Psychology, Australian Catholic University, Fitzroy, Australia
This research focused on examining developmental differences about tolerance to human diversity cross-culturally. This presentation will report on the kinds of judgments and justifications in support of tolerance (and intolerance) to human diversity by younger and older adolescents in Australian and the USA. Age and gender related differences have emerged both in previously and in the current research. Similarity and differences have also been noted. For example, fairness is used in both countries to support a tolerance stance while appeal to freedom of speech is more often acceptable to young Australians than young Americans who argue that persuading others is unacceptable.

The Fairy Tale test: A comparison across cultures

Xenos, Sophia Dept. of Psychology, RMIT University, Melbourne, Australia Coulacoglou, Carina Dept. of Psychology, RMIT University, Melbourne, Australia Manikas, Vicky Dept. of Psychology, RMIT University, Melbourne, Australia
The Fairy Tale Test (FTT) (Coulacoglou, 2003) is a projective personality test for children, allowing both quantitative and qualitative interpretation of responses. The current study aimed to provide a cross-cultural comparison of the FTT between a sample of Greek and Australian primary school children. Factor analysis and non-parametric tests revealed that while the number of factors in both samples was similar, the individual variables loading onto each factor varied between the samples. This was mainly due to differences in levels of anxiety, depression and self-esteem that were noted between the two countries. Cultural factors were then explored as possible reasons for these differences.

The mental health of older migrants

Trang, Thomas Melbourne, Australia
This paper reports on research findings about psychological issues related to older people who made the migration journey during their old age. For various political and family reasons, these elderly people had to leave their homeland to settle in an alien society and a prospect of dying in a foreign country. Findings indicate issues include dependency, social difficulties, communication, family relationships, incongruity of expectation about filial duties from children, financial matters, self-esteem and mental health problems. Therefore, more attention should be paid to the psychological factors affecting the settlement of older migrants and more accessible psychological services are needed.

IS-011: Cognitive neuroscience of attention and visual short-term memory

Pierre Jolicoeur (chair)
Although the storage capacity of visual short-term memory (VSTM) is limited to about three objects, passage of visual information through this system appears critical for conscious awareness and cognitive control from visual input. We review research using a variety of methods including psychophysics, electrophysiology (EEG) and the event-related potential method (ERPs), magnetoen-cephalography (MEG), wavelet analysis, and fMRI, that reveal the nature of the representations in VSTM and their role in cognition. We will examine various aspects of encoding, retention, and retrieval in VSTM using behavioural and neuroimaging methods.

Short-term memory capacity as an index of attentional control: A neurally-based individual differences approach

Vogel, Edward Dept. of Psychology, University of Oregon, Eugene, OR, USA
The capacity of visual working memory is well known to be highly limited, but it is also known to vary considerably across individuals. Individual differences in memory capacity appear to be a stable trait of the observer and are often positively correlated with many high-level aptitude measures such as fluid intelligence and reasoning. In this presentation, I will describe recent work from my laboratory in which we examine the relationship between an individual's visual working memory capacity and their ability to control the focus of selective attention. In particular, we use a new event-related potential technique that allows us to measure the active representations of objects within the focus of attention across different task conditions and is highly sensitive to individual differences in memory capacity. In general, we have found that low memory capacity individuals are substantially poorer than high capacity individuals across several tasks in which they must exert attentional control over what information is stored in memory. These results suggest a tight relationship between the constructs of memory capacity and the control of attention.

The neural substrates of visual short-term memory

Marois, Rene Dept. of Psychology, Vanderbilt University, Nashville, TN, USA
Visual short-term memory (VSTM) is thought to be essential for efficient cognition and coherent interaction with the visual world. Yet, despite its fundamental role in cognition, VSTM is severely capacity-limited. This capacity limit is not only apparent in the amount of information that can be held in VSTM, but also in the rate of encoding information in VSTM. In this talk, I will describe experiments comparing and contrasting the neural basis of encoding and maintaining information in VSTM with standard and time-resolved fMRI studies. I will also present studies describing the interdependence of attention and VSTM during encoding and maintenance of information in VSTM.

Is visual working memory capacity for facial identities modulated by emotional face processing?

Sessa, Paola DPSS, University of Padova, Padova, Italy Luria, Roy DPSS, University of Padova, Padova, Italy Gotler, Alex Dep. of Behavioral Sciences, Ben-Gurion University, Negev, Israel Jolicoeur, Pierre Department of Psychology, Université de Montréal, Montreal, Italy Dell'Acqua, Roberto DPSS, University of Padova, Padova, Italy
The goal of this investigation was to discover whether visual working memory (VWM) load for faces is modulated by facial expression using event-related potentials (ERPs). Each trial consisted of memory and test arrays, each including two or four faces with neutral or fearful expressions. A central arrow cued participants to encode the face(s) displayed on just one side of the memory array. The SPCN component of the ERP time-locked to the memory array was used as an index of VWM load. The results suggested that processing fearful faces taxes VWM resources to a greater extent relative to neutral faces.

Electromagnetic explorations of the temporal dynamics of visual short-term memory
Jolicoeur, Pierre Dept. of Psychology, University of Montreal, Montréal, Canada Grimault, Stephan Dept. of Psychology, University of Montreal, Montréal, Canada Robitaille, Nicolas Dept. of Psychology, University of Montreal, Montréal, Canada Lina, Jean-Marc génie électrique, École de Technologie Supérieur, Montréal, Canada
Observers encoded simple visual stimuli from the left or right visual field and remembered them for about two seconds while we recorded brain activity using magnetoencephalography (MEG), electroencephalography (EEG), or functional magnetic resonance imaging (fMRI). Converging resutls from these various, non-invasive, brain imaging methods reveal the functional and neuronal basis of visual short-term memory (VSTM) in the human brain. In this talk we focus on the relationship between increases in induced alpha-band oscillatory power, observed in MEG recordings as VSTM load increased, and other indices of brain activity specifically related to VSTM.

IS-012: Democracy, responsibility and civic participation: A challenge of 21st century

Jana Plichtová (chair)
Democracy is mistakenly understood only in terms of democratic institutions and regular elections. However, healthy democracy requires the steady attention, time, and commitment of large numbers of citizens. Its quality depends upon a literate, knowledgeable citizenry strongly committed to protect and enhance ideas of liberty and equality (equality for themselves as well as for others). Without broad, sustaining participation of citizens, democracy begins to wither and becomes a preserve of a small, selected number of groups and organizations. Even citizens of well-established democracies often take advantage of rights while ignoring responsibilities. In what extent is the young generation in Slovakia and Czech Republic aware of their rights and responsibilities? How they feel about their interdependency? How strong is their belief that, in the end, an open debate will lead to greater truth and wiser public actions than if speech and dissent are stifled? In what extent are they prepared to recognize freedom of conscience/religion of different religious groups? All these questions directed the empirical research which results will be reported in this symposium.

Cross border mobility: Identification(s) and participation: An empirical study of identity construction strategies and civic participation in young Slovaks commuting between Bratislava region and Vienna
Petrjánošová, Magda Dept. of Psychology, Comenius University, Bratislava, Slovak Republic Lášticová, Barbara Dep.of Soc.andBiol.Communicati, Slovak Academy of Sciences, Bratislava, Slovak Republic
European integration supposedly changes perceptions of national/ethnic in/outgroups. A qualitative research project in Slovak-Austrian border region (2004-2007) used semi-structured interviews, focus groups and mental maps to investigate in/outgroups perceptions and civic participation motivations in 60 Slovak commuters (aged 18-32) working or studying in Vienna. It was found that the changing political situation influences possibility for action, but the commuters are not willing to enlarge the space for participation in social, public and political life to both sides of the border. The results are discussed in the framework of social identity perspective (Abrams, Hogg, 2004) and discursive psychology (Potter, Wetherell, 1987).

Dialogue and diversity in public participation
Jeleník, Andrej Dept. of Psychology, Comenius University, Bratislava, Slovak Republic
Many theorists have long extolled the virtues of public deliberation as a crucial component of a responsive and responsible democracy. However many recent authors argue that deliberative procedures and forms of public talk ignore conflicts, emotions, diversity, differences in power and status. Dialogical communication seems to provide a vehicle how to embrace the above mentioned differences. This approach emphasizes relationship building among participants. The presented contribution analyzes current theories on dialogue and confronts it with empirical findings. The potential contribution of Bakhtin's dialogic perspective is explored.

Quality of deliberation and personal responsibility
Plichtová, Jana Dept. of Psychology, Comenius University, Bratislava, Slovak Republic Hapalová, Miroslava Department of Psychology, Comenius University, Bratislava, Slovak Republic
Idea of deliberative democracy is based on implicit assumption that people placed in the "ideal speech conditions" are able to participate in rational discussion. Presented contribution addresses the question to what extent do young people from posttotalitarian countries feel entitled to resolve social problems and which deliberative competences they manifest. Data consist of the discussions in small groups resolving a set of social dilemmas (realized in Slovakia in the period 1996 – 2007). The content analysis is focused on the distinction between hierarchical and egalitarian responsibility. The results are discussed in the context of the potential of civic society in Slovakia.

The debate on novel biotechnologies in Germany: Public deliberation and individual autonomy
Ferretti, Maria-Paola ZERP, Universität Bremen, Bremen, Germany Moulin-Doos, Clair ZERP, University of Bremen, Bremen, Germany
In Germany, local and federal governments often use deliberative models to address controversial societal issues. This paper presents some empirical materials illustrating how some controversies surrounding genetically modified products have been dealt with. Our hypothesis is that court cases are increasingly relevant in the political process and are not limited to establishing winners and losers, but have a spill over effect on public debates, increase public awareness and ultimately have a powerful effect in shaping policies. We defend that the judicial moment should be considered as an integral part of the discursive process that helps generate answers to controversial questions.

Types of responsibility in adolescence
Tyrlik, Mojmir Inst. of Psychology, Masaryk University, Brno, Czech Republic
The sample of 112 students of a training high school evaluate their level of responsibility in various categories of situations. It was found out that there are three groups of life situations towards which adolescents take responsibility in different degree. Full responsibility is attributed to themselves in spending free time, dressing up, choosing a friend and a partner, shared responsibility with their parents for performance in school and preparation for one's profession and full responsibility is attributed to their parents for financial provisioning and housing. Findings are interpreted in relation to the responsibility towards other people, especially peers.

IS-013: Lifespan cognition and neuromodelation: Empirical and computational approaches

Shu-Chen Li, Ulman Lindenberger (chair)
Neuromodulation affects the dynamics of neural representation and information transfer within and between cortical regions. Among various neurotransmitters, the dopaminergic systems play crucial roles in modulating interactions between the prefrontal, midbrain, and striatal regions and consequently influence working memory and episodic memory, as well as reward-based learning and decision making. The maturation and senescence of the dopaminergic systems thus have direct implications for lifespan changes in these neurocognitive functions. Researchers of child development, cognitive aging, and cognitive neuroscience are now combining behavioral, neuroimaging, pharmacological, genetic, and computational approaches to studying the relations between dopamine and lifespan cognitive development.

Dopamine and child cognitive development: The differential impact of DAT1 on reading and inhibitory functions in children with ADHD symptoms
Cornish, Kim Educational Psychology, McGill University, Montreal, Canada
Attention deficit hyperactivity (ADHA) disorder and reading disability frequently co-occur in the child population, indicating possible shared genetic aetiology. We investigated the involvement of the dopamine transporter (DAT1) gene polymorphism in mediating reading disability and poor response inhibition in a population sample of children aged 6 - 11 years in the U.K. We found an independent association between the homozygous DAT1 10/10 repeat genotype and reading disability that was not accounted for by the severity of ADHD symptoms. This is the first finding to suggest that DAT1 polymorphism may influence a common neural mechanism underlying reading acquisition and ADHD symptoms.

Dopaminergic modulation of cognitive function in healthy adolescents
Luciana, Monica Dept. of Psychology, University of Minnesota, Minneapolis, USA
Pharmacological probes suggest that dopamine modulates high-level cognition in adults; this methodology is controversial in developmental research. We have assessed dopamine's modulation of cognition in adolescents using a molecular genetic approach focusing on the gene that regulates Catechol O-Methyltransferase (COMT), an enzyme that catabolizes prefrontal dopamine. Adults homozygous for the MET allele show optimal performance on prefrontal tasks. We find a distinctly different optimal-for-cognition genotype in adolescents, consistent with the idea that adolescents have high functional levels of dopamine relative to other developmental groups. Findings will be discussed in relation to adolescents' vulnerabilities to risk taking behavior.

Dopamine and cognitive aging: New evidence and emerging ideas
Bäckman, Lars Aging Research Center, Karolinska Institute, Stockholm, Sweden
Evidence from animal research, patient studies, pharmacological intervention, genetics, and molecular imaging converges in suggesting that dopamine (DA) systems are implicated in various cognitive functions. Several studies suggest that age-related losses of PET-derived pre- and post-synaptic indicators of striatal DA functions account for a substantial proportion of adult life-span decrements in cognition. Several new evidence on the aging-DA-cognition link will be discussed.

These include: (a) regional specificity within the striatal complex; (b) the connection between DA and intraindividual variability; (c) DA release during executive performance; (d) pharmacological simulation of DA losses in aging; and (e) DA and cognitive plasticity.

Dopaminergic neuromodulation in cognitive aging: Influences of COMT genotype and pharmacological intervention

Heekeren, Hauke Neurocognition of Decision, Max-Planck-Institut, Berlin, Germany *Li, Shu-Chen* Center for Lifespan Psychology, MPI Human Dev, Berlin, Germany *Nagel, Irene* Center for Lifespan Psychology, MPI Human Dev, Berlin, Germany *Preuschhof, Claudia* BNIC, BNIC and MPI Human Dev, Berlin, Germany *Villringer, Arno* Cognitive Neurology, MPI Human Cog and Brain Sci, Berlin, Germany *Baeckman, Lars* Aging Research Center, Karolinska Institute, Stockholm, Sweden

Aging, COMT gene polymorphism, and pharmacological intervention are known to influence dopaminergic neuromodulation. We studied the relationship of these factors and their effects on neuromodulation of cognitive performance and brain activation. We investigated whether lower dopamine (DA) levels associated with aging and COMT polymorphism act additively or interactively in yielding more diffuse fMRI activation patterns that underlie cognitive deficits. Furthermore, we determined whether certain age-COMT allele combinations (i.e., older low-DA val-val carrier) respond positively to D-amphetamine (i.e., more efficient neural activation and improved cognition), whereas others (i.e., younger high-DA met-met carrier) respond negatively, reflecting an inverted U-shaped DA-cognition relationship.

Interactive dynamics of corticostriatal circuits in reinforcementlearning and decision making

Frank, Michael Neurocomputation and Cognition, University of Arizona, Tucson, USA

The basal ganglia and frontal cortex interact intimately to facilitate adaptive action plans while suppressing those that are less adaptive. The dynamics of this circuitry in reinforcement learning and decision-making have been explored via a series of computational models. The models point to 4 distinct neurobiological mechanisms associated with (a) action selection; (b) reinforcement learning from actions most/least likely to yield a positive outcome; (c) dynamic modulation of decision thresholds; and (d) maintenance of decision outcomes in working memory. Novel predictions from these models and associated experimental findings from studies with patient populations, pharmacological manipulation, and genetics will be presented.

Monitoring and learning from feedback in young and elderly healthy persons

Ullsperger, Markus Inst. für Kognitive Neurologie, Max-Planck-Institut, Köln, Germany

Performance monitoring is essential for optimization of action outcomes. Research consistently implicates the rostral cingulate zone in monitoring for unfavorable action outcomes and signaling the need for adjustments. Current theories suggest that phasic dopaminergic signals coding unexpected positive or negative outcomes play a major role in this function. The dopaminergic system declines during aging. I will present a neuroimaging and computational modeling study making use of a polymorphism of a gene (DRD2) that affects gene of the dopamine D2 receptor and an aging study using EEG on the role of dopamine and age effects on probabilistic, feedback based learning.

IS-014: Motivation, recall and information processing

Bo Sanitioso (chair)

The symposium concerns the influence of motivation on recall and information processing. The first three presentations focus on research showing the influence of (self-related) motivation on the semantic content and subjective experience of autobiographical memory recall (Sanitioso), the use of ease of remembering past behaviors as a basis for self-perception (Echterhoff), and processing of general information not directly related to the self (Augustinova). Next, research on the role of internal states in "if-then" plan implemented in goal striving is presented (Achtziger). Finally, Dunning presents data suggesting motivated reasoning can occur below awareness, related to inhibition and to visual stimuli preferences.

Motivated self and recall of autobiographical memories

Sanitioso, Bo Dept. of Psychology, Université Paris Descartes, Paris, France

In several studies, we showed the influence of the motivation to see oneself positively on recall of autobiographical memories. First, motivation influences the semantic content of recall via selective accessibility: When led to believe that a trait is desirable, people remember more of their past behaviors that are consistent (vs. inconsistent) with the trait. Second, motivation influences the subjective experience of remembering relevant past behaviors which, in turn, mediates self-inferences. Remembering past behaviors consistent with a desired trait is experienced as 'easier' than that of inconsistent behaviors. This leads to the inference that they are indeed characterized by the trait.

Memory cues in motivated self-perception: When do people use ease of recall?

Echterhoff, Gerald Inst. für Psychologie, Universität Bielefeld, Bielefeld, Germany

The paper examines the influence of directional motivation on the use of ease-of-recall in self-judgments. In Experiment 1, participants were led to believe that introversion leads to success (introversion desirable) vs. failure (introversion undesirable) and recalled few vs. many introverted behaviors. Participants in the introversion-desirable/ few-behaviors and the introversion-undesirable/ many-behaviors condition relied on ease-of-recall in their self-judgments. In contrast, ease was unrelated to self-judgments in the other two conditions. Experiment 2 showed that motivation effects differed for self versus another person. Apparently, people flexibly use memory cues in their self-perception depending on fit with their directional motivation.

The influence of desired self on the use of base rates

Augustinova, Maria Dept. of Psychology, Université Blaise Pascal, Clermont Ferrand, France

The aim of this presentation is to argue that the influence of the motivated self goes beyond self-related information processing. To this end, I will present research showing that the motivation to achieve a desired characteristic (or to avoid an undesired one) corresponding to an intuitive versus rational cognitive style can lead not only to ensuing self-perceptions but also guides people's probabilistic inferences in the classic lawyers-engineers problem (Kahneman & Tversky, 1974) These findings will be discussed in light of research on the role of the motivated self on general information processing as well as research on motivated reasoning.

Self-control of negative inner states: Goal shielding by means of implementation intentions

Achtziger, Anja Inst. für Psychologi, Universität Konstanz, Konstanz, Germany *Michalski, Norbert* Inst. für Psychologie, Universität Konstanz, Konstanz, Germany *Gollwitzer, Peter M.* Dept. of Psychology, New York University, New York, NY, USA

Forming implementation intentions or "if-then plans" promotes the attainment of different types of goals. So far, research on implementation intentions has focused on delegating action control to the environment by specifying external cues (i.e., situations) in the if-component of an implementation intention. The present study, however, investigated whether people can use implementation intentions to protect goal striving by specifying detrimental inner states in the if-component (e.g., performance anxiety). It was observed that during a competition tennis players who formed implementation intentions performed better than control and goal intention participants by ignoring negative inner states of irritation and performance anxiety.

Motivated reasoning below awareness

Dunning, David Dept. of Psychology, Cornell University, Ithaca, USA *Balcetis, Emily* Dept. of Psychology, Cornell University, Ithaca, USA *Carter, Travis* Dept. of Psychology, Cornell University, Ithaca, USA

In this talk we present data suggesting that the impact of motivated reasoning can occur below awareness, before the product of any motivated distortion reaches the theater of consciousness. We review evidence that people inhibit threatening material appearing at a nonconscious level—thus slowing how quickly they can recognize words related to personal threats. In addition, we show that the visual system can be influenced preconsciously to preferentially present to awareness stimuli that people want to see rather than those they do not.

IS-015: Cognitive functions of the frontal lobe

Susan Iversen (chair)

In vivo neurophysiology and lesion studies in non-human primates, together with brain imaging studies continue to refine our understanding of the functions of cytoarchitecturally defined areas of prefrontal cortex (PFC). The symposium will emphasise the role of PFC in motor and cognitive functions that result in the transformation of the external world into appropriate sequential patterns of mental functions and overt behaviour. Disordered PFC function and the consequent disruption of communication with other brain areas is implicated in schizophrenia, a neuropsychiatric disease that has a strong genetic component.

The frontal granular cortex and behaviour: 40 years on

Iversen, Susan Experimental Psychology, University of Oxford, Oxford, United Kingdom

The structure and function of the prefrontal cortex (PFC) was reviewed in the seminal 1964 symposium "The frontal granular cortex and behaviour". At that time, attempts to find a unitary theory of frontal lobe function dominated the field. But already it was becoming clear that different cytoarchitecturally defined areas of PFC had different afferrent and efferent connections and that lesions to these different areas in animals and Man resulted in dissociable behavioural deficits. In the ensuing decades, with new techniques, including neurophysiology, neurochemistry and fMRI, significant advances have been made in defining the functions of different sectors of PFC.

Functional organization of the primate prefrontal cortex for mnemonic processing

Petrides, Michael Cognitive Neuroscience Unit, McGill University, Montreal, Canada

Evidence will be presented from studies of the effects of lesions to the human and nonhuman primate prefrontal cortex demonstrating that the mid-portion of the dorsolateral prefrontal region (i.e. area 46) is involved in the monitoring of information in working memory. Consistent with these findings, functional neuroimaging work on normal human subjects has shown specific increases of activity in the mid-dorsolateral prefrontal cortex in relation to the tracking of events in working memory. By contrast, the mid-ventrolateral prefrontal region (areas 45 and 47/12) is selectively involved in the active controlled retrieval of information both from working and long-term memory.

Motor and cognitive functions of the ventral premotor cortex

Craighero, Laila Human Physiology Section, University of Ferrara, Ferrara, Italy

Data show that ventral premotor cortex in both humans and monkeys has motor and cognitive functions. In particular, it is part of a series of parietofrontal circuits, working in parallel, involved in space coding. The coordinate frame in which space is coded depends on the motor requirements of the effectors that a given circuit controls. Given this strict link between space coding and action programming, selective attention, the capability of selecting a particular stimulus in space, results from an internal representation of the required response. Experimental evidence indicating that attention is the final outcome of the processing performed in the sensorimotor circuits is presented.

Genetic modulation of pre-frontal cortex function in humans

Meyer-Lindenberg, Andreas ZI für Seelische Gesundheit, Mannheim, Germany

Prefrontal cortex function and interactions between PFC and other brain regions play a key role in normal cognition and neuropsychiatric disorders. Since many of these disorders have a strong genetic component, multimodal neuroimaging can be used to identify neural systems related to variation in susceptibility genes, an approach called "imaging genetics". We review recent convergent evidence that genetic risk for schizophrenia is mediated by an impact on prefrontal signal to noise properties and functional connectivity of PFC with midbrain and neostriatium. Conversely, genetic risk for affective disorders is linked to disturbed interactions between medial PFC and cingulate with regions of the extended limbic system.

IS-016: Neuropsychology and neurodegenerative processes

Jose Barroso (chair)

Considering MCI as an intermediate state between normal aging and dementia and thus being crucial its early diagnosis and treatment, together with the lack of stated biological markers, makes Neuropsychology essential in the neurodegenerative aging field. This symposium presents MCI research status through 5 complementary perspectives: First, we show updated results about MCI prevalence, outcome and subtypes. It is also suggested a more precise operationalization of the diagnostic criteria in order to reduce variability among studies. In addition, the importance of the functional autonomy of MCI patients is highlighted and finally, neuroanatomical correlates and neuroimaging research data are discussed.

Restriction in complex activities of daily living in MCI

Peres, Karine ISPED, Université Victor Segalen, Bordeaux, France Dartigues, Jean-Fraçois Inserm U593, Univerty Victor Segalem, Bordeaux, France Barberger-Gateau, Pascale Inserm U593, Université Victor Segalen, Bordeaux, France

Objectives: 1) To study the natural history of restriction in IADL 10 years before dementia and 2) to assess the impact of IADL-restriction on the progression to dementia and on MCI reversibility. Methods: Results from the PAQUID cohort, a French population-based study on cerebral and functional aging, with 15 years of follow-up. Results/conclusion: The future cases of dementia already performed worse in IADLs 10 years before the diagnosis of dementia, especially in managing finances. In addition, inclusion of IADLs in the criteria of MCI appears to significantly improve the prediction of dementia and the stability of this status over time.

MCI and neuroimaging

Bartres Faz, David Psiqu. y Psicobiology, Universidad de Barcelona, Barcelona, Spain Bosch, Beatriz Department of Neuroscience, Hospital Clinic de Barcelona, Barcelona, Spain Rami, Lorena Department of Neuroscience, Hospital Clinic de Barcelona, Barcelona, Spain Junque, Carme Psiqu. y Psicobiology, Universidad de Barcelona, Barcelona, Spain Molinuevo, Jose Luis Department of Neuroscience, Hospital Clinic de Barcelona, Barcelona, Spain

Objectives: To study brain activity in amnestic Mild Cognitive Impairment (a-MCI) during the performance of cognitive tasks that are not clinically affected. Methods: Twelve healthy elders, 12 subjects with a-MCI and 12 mild Alzheimer's disease cases were recruited. Two functional magnetic resonance imaging acquisitions were obtained for each subject while performing a linguistic and a visuoperceptive task. Results: Amnestic MCI patients showed increased brain activity compared to both groups in visual and linguistic associative areas. Conclusions: Present results reflect possible incipient compensatory mechanisms in a-MCI and suggest that fMRI may be sensitive in identifying subclinical cognitive dysfunctions in these patients.

Prodromal Alzheimeer disease: Neuropsychological characterization

Rami, Lorena Dept. of Neurology, Hospital Clinic of Barcelona, Barcelona, Spain Gómez-Anson, Beatriz Dept. of Neurorradiology, Hospital de Sant Pau, Barcelona, Spain Monte, Gemma Fundacio Clinic, Hospital Clinic de Barclona, Barcelona, Spain Sánchez-Valle, Raquel Dept. of Neuroscience, Hospital Clinic of Barcelona, Barcelona, Spain Bosch, Beatriz Dept. of Neuroscience, Hospital Clinic of Barcelona, Barcelona, Spain Molinuevo, Jose Luis Dept. of Neuroscience, Hospital Clinic of Barcelona, Barcelona, Spain

As memory impairment is usually the earliest feature of Alzheimers disease (AD), amnesic subjects have become a great focus of interest. It seems then desirable to find an homogeneous group of amnesic patients with a high AD conversion rate to be considered as a prodromal stage for AD. By means of prospectively follow-up a group of amnesic patients at risk for Alzheimer disease (AD), we characterised a group of patients whose were intermediate between amnesic mild cognitive impairment (aMCI) and probable AD: prodromal AD (Prd-AD), with distinct neuropsychological features and a higher conversion to AD than aMCI.

Mild cognitive impairment: Prevalence and long-term course of four clinical subtypes

Luck, Tobias Inst. für Psychiatrie, Universität Leipzig, Leipzig, Germany Busse, Anja Department for Psychiatry, University of Leipzig, Leipzig, Germany Guehne, Uta Department for Psychiatry, University of Leipzig, Leipzig, Germany Hensel, Anke Department for Psychiatry, University of Leipzig, Leipzig, Germany Angermeyer, Matthias C. Department for Psychiatry, University of Leipzig, Leipzig, Germany Riedel-Heller, Steffi G. Department for Psychiatry, University of Leipzig, Leipzig, Germany

OBJECTIVE: To examine the prevalence, course, and outcome of mild cognitive impairment (MCI) with four clinical subtypes. METHODS: Community sample of 980 dementia-free individuals (LEILA 75+). Diagnosis of MCI according to original (Petersen et al., 2001) and slightly modified criteria (both with cut-off of 1.0/1.5 SD). RESULTS: The "MCI modified, 1.0 SD" criteria have the highest relative predictive power for the development of dementia. Alzheimer disease was the most common type of dementia at follow-up in all but one subtype. CONCLUSIONS: We can only partially agree that each MCI subtype is associated with an increased risk for a particular type of dementia.

Operationalizing MCI memory impairment criteria

Correia, Rut Dept. de Psicobiología, Universidad de La Laguna, La Laguna, Spain Barroso, Jose Dept. de Psicobiología, Universidad de La Laguna, La Laguna, Spain Nieto, Antonieta Dept. de Psicobiología, Universidad de La Laguna, La Laguna, Spain Ferreira, Daniel Dept. de Psicobiología, Universidad de La Laguna, La Laguna, Spain Sabucedo, María Dept. de Psicobiología, Univ. Santiago de Compostela, Santiago de Compostela, Spain

Our aim was precisely operationalize MCI memory impairment criterion and explore the subsequent effects in MCI prevalence and subtypes classification. 105 healthy old adults were assessed with an extensive neuropsychological protocol with a wide range of memory tasks included. Two different memory impairment criteria based on the existence of different neuroanatomical memory systems were applied in order to classify groups according to their cognitive profile. Results show how subject distribution into the different MCI subtypes varies when applying consolidation vs. acquisition-retrieval memory affection criteria. Our results pinpoint the relevance of accurately define the characteristic memory impairment of every MCI subtype.

IS-017: Joint action: The cognitive mechanisms underlying human coordination

Harold Bekkering (chair)

More and more, we realize that a true understanding of human cognition requires the study of human behaviour beyond isolation. Rather, the social context of everyday life is crucial for shaping for instance language, perception and goal-directed actions. Likely, large parts of our cognitive processes, or as you prefer the correlated brain activities, are modulated by the social environment we are living in. Today's symposium describes new insights from behavioural experiments as well as from studies using neuroimaging techniques (ERP / fMRI). Finally, theoretical implications of these findings are discussed as well as their implementation in social acting autonomous agents.

Joint action and the human brain

Newman-Norlund, Roger NICI, Radboud University Nijmegen, Nijmegen, Netherlands

The study of the human brain is undergoing a general paradigm shift in which cognitive neuroscientists are, with increasing frequency, examining the brain bases of social behaviors. A key question in the emerging field of joint action is how the brain behaves during cooperative social interactions. Evidence from single-cell and neuroimaging experiments is converging on an explanation in which the human mirror neuron system (MNS) plays a fundamental role. In this presentation, recent fMRI experiments implicating specific components of the human MNS in shared cooperative activities tasks will be discussed.

Joint action and the human brain

Erlhagen, Wolfram Dipt. do Mathematics, Universidade do Minho, Guimaraes, Portugal
Many of our social activities during daily life rely on our ability to predict outcomes of others' actions. This allows us to select an adequate complementary behaviour, thereby establishing a joint goal. In my talk I will present a Dynamic Neural Field model for joint action that is strongly inspired by experimental findings about the underlying neuro-cognitive processes. The model implements the idea that motor simulation plays a critical role in goal inference. In addition, it highlights the importance of a flexible mapping between action observation and action execution to cope with constantly changing joint-action situations.

Joint action and the human brain

Bicho, Estela Dipt. do Industrial Elect., Universidade do Minho, Guimarães, Portugal
One of the major challenges for today's robotics is the development of autonomous agents that are able to engage in joint action tasks with humans. I my talk I will present and validate our approach towards socially intelligent robots using as an example a joint construction task. The control architecture is based on the dynamic field model which has been developed to explain important aspects of human perception and action in social context. In particular, I will show that the capacity to predict goals and anticipate actions of the human partner is essential for a fluent team behaviour.

Joint action and the human brain

Knoblich, Günther Dept. of Psychology, Birmingham University, Birmingham, United Kingdom
Successful joint action often requires accurate temporal coordination between co-actors. How is this coordination achieved? There are three candidate mechanisms. First, people have a tendency to spontaneously synchronize their body movements. This basic process could ensure that co-actors share the same general rhythm. Second, mechanisms residing in the motor system provide temporally accurate predictions of the sensory consequences of one's own actions. Such mechanisms could embody others' actions as context and then be used to predict the combined consequences of a jointly performed action. Third, co-actors may strategically coordinate the timing of crucial events resulting from their individual actions.

Joint action and the human brain

Sebanz, Natalie School of Psychology, University of Birmingham, Birmingham, United Kingdom
For many years, cognitive psychologists and cognitive neuroscientists have assumed that we can understand how humans perceive their environment, plan their actions, and encode information by studying these processes in single-person studies, where the interaction between researcher and participant is kept to a minimum. I will give a brief overview of recent two-person studies, suggesting that the social context in which we act modulates how we perceive objects, plan actions, and encode information. This research demonstrates that studying how individuals act together can shed new light on the workings of individual minds.

IS-018: Brain oscillatory correlates of cognitive processes

Wolfgang Klimesch (chair)
The aim of the symposium is to present new findings about the functional meaning of brain oscillations for cognitive processes and memory in particular. Contributions will focus on the role of theta oscillations and cross-frequency coupling for working memory, on the role of alpha for accessing stored information, on the functional meaning of theta and beta frequencies for episodic retrieval, on the role of gamma for mnemonic functions, and of the role of spindle oscillations for memory consolidation.

Oscillatory events in light non-REM sleep

Schabus, Manuel Physiologische Psychologie, Universität Salzburg, Salzburg, Austria Hödlmoser, Kerstin Physiological Psychology, University of Salzburg, Salzburg, Austria Klimesch, Wolfgang Salzburg, Austria Dang-Vu, Thanh Cyclotron Research Centre, University of Liege (Belgium), Liege, Belgium Maquet, Pierre Cyclotron Research Centre, University of Liege (Belgium), Liege, Belgium
Oscillatory events in the 12-15Hz range are prevailing during light human non-REM sleep. These so-called "sleep spindles" drew our attention in the last couple of years. Specifically we addressed their involvement in memory consolidation during sleep. Besides this we recently succeeded in characterizing the cerebral correlates of spindles using simultaneous electroencephalography and functional magnetic resonance imaging (EEG/fMRI) during sleep. Last but not least we tried to artificially enhance sleep spindle activity by using sensorimotor (SMR) conditioning over a 2-week daytime training period. We will review these fascinating results and discuss possible implications.

The neural signature of multi-item working memory

Axmacher, Nikolai Inst. für Epileptologie, Universität Bonn, Bonn, Germany Elger, Christian Inst. für Epileptologie, Universität Bonn, Bonn, Germany Fell, Juergen Inst. für Epileptologie, Universität Bonn, Bonn, Germany
Recent data suggest that the medial temporal lobe (MTL) may play a role for working memory (WM), but the underlying neural mechanisms have remained unknown. Using intracranial EEG (iEEG) in epilepsy patients and functional MRI in control subjects, we found evidence for sustained activity in the MTL during multi-item WM. Phase-synchronization between the inferior temporal cortex and the MTL increased with load, but smaller regions showed correlated BOLD responses with the MTL. Cross-frequency coupling of gamma power to theta phase was more prominent with increasing load, consistent with a computer model where individual items are represented by wavelet cycles.

Gamma oscillations and mnemonic functioning

Gruber, Thomas Inst. für Psychologie I, Universität Leipzig, Leipzig, Germany
It was suggested that the activation of a memory trace is achieved by cortically distributed neural assemblies coordinated by synchronous firing in the Gamma Band range (oscillations >20Hz). Using electroencephalography (EEG) this hypothesis was tested during various implicit and explicit memory tasks. Spectral decompositions of EEG signals revealed that that induced Gamma Band Responses (iGBRs) at approximately 250ms after stimulus are a sensitive marker of encoding- and retrieval-related processes. The results provide support for the view that plasticity within cortical 'gamma networks' is an import mechanism supporting mnemonic functioning.

How retrieval affects the dynamic properties of a memory trace

Hanslmayr, Simon Experimentelle Psychologie, Universität Regensburg, Regensburg, Germany Bäuml, Karl-Heinz Experimentelle Psychologie, Universität Regensburg, Regensburg, Germany
Several behavioral studies have shown that selective retrieval of an episodic memory trace can alter memories for nonretrieved related materials. During selective retrieval related memories are assumed to interfere and to be inhibited to reduce interference. In order to unravel the neural mechanisms mediating interference and inhibition in episodic memory, two EEG experiments were carried out. The results suggest that interference is mainly related to the theta frequency band. In contrast, inhibition was found to be mainly reflected by activity in the beta frequency band. These findings indicate that interference and inhibition in episodic memory are mediated by two different neural correlates.

Brain oscillatory substrates of human short-term memory capacity

Sauseng, Paul Dept. Psychology, University of Salzburg, Salzburg, Austria Klimesch, Wolfgang Dept. Psychology, University of Salzburg, Salzburg, Austria Gerloff, Christian Dept. Neurology, UKE - University of Hamburg, Hamburg, Germany Birbaumer, Niels Inst. Med. Psychol., University of Tuebingen, Tuebingen, Germany Hummel, Friedhelm Dept. Neurology, UKE - University of Hamburg, Hamburg, Germany
Human visual short-term memory (STM) capacity is limited to about three or four items that can be transiently held in memory. Evidence is presented showing that phase-synchronization between slow electroencephalographic (EEG) brain activity at theta frequency (around 5 Hz) and fast oscillatory activity at gamma frequency (beyond 30 Hz) predicts individual memory capacity and represents an actual information storage mechanism. Brain activity at around 10 Hz (alpha activity) also correlates with memory capacity but only at brain sites processing irrelevant information. Therefore, alpha seems rather to be associated with the selection of stored information.

IS-019: Pathways of risk and protection among street youth in India, Indonesia, the Philippines, and South Africa

Suman Verma, Neo Morojele (chair)
This symposium reports findings from a special project on at-risk youth sponsored by CASBS, Stanford. Guided by comparative theoretical framework of risk/ protection, this study examines across countries the extent to which specific domains determine risk and opportunity pathways for street children in metros. The four presenters report on life experiences of street kids in their countries and their strategies of coping with adversities. The focus is on lifestyles that put children's health at risk as also the enabling processes and socio-cultural forms of resilience used effectively to support the child's mental health and well being. The discussant will highlight the emerging themes across cultures with implications for theory and practice.

Examining the lives of children working and living on the streets in India: Associated risk and protective factors

Sharma, Deepali Child Development, Governm. Home Science College, Chandigarh, India
The study examined the domains of risk and protection among street children (N = 120) from a metro city in India, New Delhi. Results, analysed using structural equation modelling, are presented for those children living entirely on the streets.

Findings indicated that the children who spent their entire time on the streets were at a great risk of exhibiting risky outcomes such as stealing and excessive drug usage. However, protection in terms of peer support and resilience was revealed and these acted as the moderators. Implications related to a greater coordination between research institutes and NGOs are discussed.

Comparisons between predictors of anti-social and pro-social behaviors among street children in South Africa

Morojele, Neo Medical Research Council, Alcohol and Drug Abuse Res., Pretoria, South Africa
The study compares predictors of anti-social (violence and drug use) and pro-social behaviors (pro-social outcomes and sense of belonging) among 71 street children in Pretoria. Independent variables included individual, peer, parental and school factors. Both individual (e.g. self-esteem, spirituality) and peer (e.g. risk, support) factors were more strongly associated with anti-social behaviors than with pro-social behaviors. A few parental factors (parental contact, monitoring and cohesion) were associated with both anti-social and pro-social behaviors. School variables (e.g. atmosphere) were associated with both anti-social and pro-social behaviors. Street children programs need to increase the accessibility of supportive school, peer and family environments.

Concomitants of risk and protection among Filipino street youth

Sta. Maria, Madelene Dept. of Psychology, De La Salle University, Manilla, Philippines
The study explored the contribution of family, shelter, peers and school factors to Filipino street youth's risk and positive outcomes. It also examined the influence of individual attributes. Results indicate that the street youth's self-esteem and shelter monitoring significantly predict the sense of community belongingness, while problem solving is significantly predicted by self-esteem, family resilience, and parental monitoring. A strong predictor for risk outcomes is the youth's involvement in risk activities with their peers. The central role of peer activities in contexts of risk and the role of family factors in contexts of protection are further examined and discussed.

IS-020: Self-control and intelligence: What is their relationship?

Jeremy Gray (chair)
Self-control and intelligence are important constructs in health and education, and have rich research traditions. Empirically, self-control and intelligence are often positively related, yet surprisingly little is understood about their relationship. Understanding the extent to which they are similar and the reasons for such similarity will require close attention to definitions, methods, and moderating influences. This symposium brings together experts with diverse perspectives and approaches, including brain imaging, psychometrics, impulsivity, delay of gratification, child development, school-based research, decision making, and social psychology. Understanding how and why individuals and situations vary can potentially foster ways to increase self-control in all people.

Individual differences in self-control: Relation to intelligence

Shamosh, Noah Dept. of Psychology, Yale University, New Haven, USA
Self-control is critical for achieving many goals. Understanding why some individuals exercise more self-control than others can foster the development of ways to increase self-control. More intelligent

individuals tend to prefer larger, later rewards to smaller, sooner ones. Through a meta-analysis of 24 studies, I will demonstrate that this relation is statistically reliable and small to moderate in magnitude (r = -.23). I will also discuss potential mechanistic reasons for this association. Specifically, anterior prefrontal cortex function may mediate the relation between g and delay discounting because it supports integration of diverse, complex information.

Self-control as a multi-dimensional construct: Results from a meta-analysis

Duckworth, Angela Lee Inst. of Psychology, University of Pennsylvania, Philadelphia, PA, USA
My view is that self-controlled behavior as it is observed in the real world (i.e., not under strictly controlled laboratory conditions) is the joint consequence of multiple, separate and interacting processes. This would explain why the intercorrelations among measures of self-control are positive but variable in magnitude – and typically disappointingly low. Different measures tap different aspects (or processes) of self-control. Processes that bear on self-controlled behavior include but are not limited to sensation seeking, motor inhibition, future time orientation, and delay of gratification.

Delay of gratification: Underlying mechanisms and implications for the life course

Mischel, Walter Dept. of Psychology, Columbia University, New York, NY, USA
Affect trumps reason—but not always. What are the mechanisms that can enable individuals to have the "willpower" to stick to their goals in the face of the temptations and situational pressures that easily undermine them? I will discuss findings that begin to demystify willpower, based on experiments and longitudinal studies, on 1. Cognitive-affective and attention control mechanisms that enable goal-directed delay of gratification in the young child; 2. long-term developmental outcomes and protective effects predicted by delay ability assessed in early childhood in diagnostic laboratory situations. Results are conceptualized within a CAPS framework, focusing on the interaction of "hot" and "cool" representations.

IQ / cognitive reflection, risk taking and the role of task instructions

Frederick, Shane Sloan School of Management, MIT, Cambridge, MA, USA
The cognitive reflection test (Frederick, 2005) is a set of three problems designed to suggest a simple intuitive solution which is incorrect. Participants are not only overconfident in their performance, but their estimates of the items difficulty and inversely correlated with performance. Poor performance is due in part to the perceived validity of the initial incorrect heuristic response. I will discuss work conducted with Bob Spunt using the cognitive reflection test in relation to intelligence and impulsivity, including behavioral data, fMRI, and stereotype threat.

IS-021: Why people care about justice (and why they somtimes don't)

Claudia Dalbert (chair)
This symposium brings together scholars highlighting unconscious and controlled processes in justice motivation. Jost investigates why people sometimes tolerate injustices and reveals the unconscious process of system justification. Skitka demonstrates the role of moral convictions for justice motivation. Emler shows that delinquency is better explained as a consequence of social exclusion from justice as of moral reasoning. Dalbert explains justice motivation by two types of justice

motives, one operating on an unconscious and one on a more conscious level. The symposium contributions will be discussed by Montada.

System justification: How do we know it's motivated?

Jost, John Dept. of Psychology, New York University, New York, USA
System justification theory addresses a fundamental question for social science: "Why do people tolerate injustice rather than doing everything they can to change the status quo?" This presentation will highlight survey and experimental evidence indicating that people are motivated to defend and justify the social system, but not necessarily at a conscious level of awareness. Our research shows that system justification: (a) is linked to self-deception and ideological motives, (b) is exacerbated in response to system threat, (c) leads to selective, biased information processing in favor of system-serving information, and (d) exhibits a number of other properties of goal pursuit.

Delinquency as a response to exclusion from justice

Emler, Nicholas Dept. of Psychology, University of Surrey, Guildford, United Kingdom
Objective: To compare the roles of insight into justice, as reflected in moral reasoning level, and confidence in justice processes, as reflected in attitudes to the formal system of authority, in adolescent delinquency Methods: 789 12-15 year olds completed a self-report delinquency measure, and measures of moral reasoning level and attitudes to institutional authority Results: Attitudes reflecting confidence in the formal system guaranteeing justice (r=.47), but not sophistication of moral reasoning (r=.04), predicted self-reported delinquency. Conclusions: Lack of confidence in the official system of delivering justice rather than lack of understanding of justice principles underlies adolescent involvement in delinquency.

On the differentiation of an implicit and a self-attributed justice motive

Dalbert, Claudia Inst. für Pädagogik, Universität Halle-Wittenberg, Halle, Germany
Based on justice motive theory (Dalbert, 2001), this presentation will highlight the hypotheses that justice-related reactions are driven by two processes that differ in their degree of automaticity and that these different processes can be explained by two types of justice motives: the implicit justice motive working on an unconscious level and a self-attributed justice motive, which depicts the justice-related dimension of the motivational self-concept. The self-attributed justice motive better explains controlled reactions, particularly self-presentations. The implicit justice motive better explains more intuitive justice-driven reactions as for example the assimilation of injustices or rule-breaking behavior. Empirical evidence from several studies will be presented.

IS-022: The impact of internet testing on people and society

Iain Coyne (chair)
Recently, Internet testing has seen rapid technological and scientific advances. Although, these advances have positives for the practice of testing, they have also raised a number of challenges for the testing community. This symposium will consider the positives and challenges of Internet testing as it impacts on test-takers and the wider society. We will examine the impact of Internet testing within Occupational and Educational assessment; consider issues around cheating and maximising security of high stakes testing; discuss good practice issues within Internet testing; highlight issues with internet-based self-assessment systems and consider the impact of Internet testing in a developing country

Good practice issues within internet testing

Coyne, Iain Inst. of Work and Health, University of Nottingham, Nottingham, United Kingdom
The International Test Commission's (ITC) recent Guidelines on Computer-based and Internet-delivered testing were focused on: producing a set of internationally developed and recognised guidelines that highlight good practice in computer-based (CBT) and Internet-delivered testing; and raising awareness among all stakeholders in the testing process of what constitutes good practice. This paper will highlight these good practice issues from a test developer, test publisher and test user perspective. Further, the paper will consider the test-taker perspective and examine what a test-taker should expect from an Internet testing session and what is expected of them when taking an Internet test.

Where is occupational testing going? Some indications for the future

Bartram, Dave Research Dept., SHL Group Ltd., Thames Ditton, United Kingdom
Recent developments in harnessing technology to make the remote administration of tests more secure and controllable open the way for a host of new developments in assessment online. These have implications for how assessment may become integrated into other procedures, such as into everyday working for performance management or into training. This paper will consider some possible future scenarios and their implications for standards and good practice In particular it will consider how such developments might impact on the need for revisions to the ITC Guidelines

Self-assessments for prospective students: A new way to increase person-environment fit of college students in Germany by means of internet based tests

Hornke, Lutz F. Inst. für Psychologie, RWTH Universität Aachen, Aachen, Germany Putz, Daniel Inst. für Psychologie, RWTH Aachen, Aachen, Germany
In recent years, several German universities have started to provide computer-based counseling services (SelfAssessment) over the internet. These services attempt to provide prospective students with insights of their fit with an academic program. Some critical issues have been identified in the development of SelfAssessment programs (e.g. consider good practice guidelines and provide valid and helpful recommendations) and this paper illustrates and discusses ways to deal with such critical issues. The paper highlights the use of a new web-based test environment as an example which contains tools for computer-adaptive-testing (CAT) and for computer-based feedback.

Computer-based and internet-delivered testing in South Africa: History and good practice challenges

Foxcroft, Cheryl D. Summerstrand Campus, Nelson Mandela Metrop. Uni., Port Elizabeth, South Africa
The history of CBT and IDT in South Africa will be sketched to highlight the challenges faced when introducing IDT in an emerging country as well as in a country where there is statutory control of the use of psychological tests. This paper will consider implications for standards and good practices when statutory regulations are out of kilter with trends and good practices in the field (e.g. ITC Guidelines). This paper will conclude with reflection on the role of higher education training programmes to retard or stimulate the advancement of CBT and IDT in a country.

Providing secure high-stakes tests over the internet: Practical solutions

Foster, David Kryterion, Inc., Phoenix, USA
This session will present and demonstrate practical and available solutions to providing high-stakes testing over the Internet. New methods of online proctoring, new test and item designs, more test administration options, and tighter security measures are examples of improvements that can make secure high-stakes tests delivered over the Internet a reality. Research on the effectiveness of these new methods and technologies will be presented.

IS-024: Children and adolescents' social competence in cultural context

Xinyin Chen (chair)
Social competence is generally defined as the ability to attain personal or group success in social situations. Cultural norms and values affect the exhibition, meaning, and development of social competence including specific socioemotional functioning and the quality and function of social relationships. The culturally guided social interaction processes such as evaluations and responses may serve as an important mediator of cultural influence on social competence. In this symposium, we will present research on children and adolescents' socioemotional functioning and relationships in different cultures and discuss issues involved in the research from different perspectives.

Cultural aspects of the development of regulatory behaviour: Maternal reactions to children's frustration in Germany and India

Heikamp, Tobias Inst. für Psychologie, Universität Konstanz, Konstanz, Germany Mishra, Ramesh C. Department of Psychology, Banaras Hindu University, Varanasi, India von Suchodoletz, Antje Department of Psychology, University of Konstanz, Konstanz, Germany Trommsdorff, Gisela Inst. für Psychologie, Universität Konstanz, Konstanz, Germany
The study aims to analyze cultural similarities and differences in mothers' and their preschool children's reactions in a disappointment paradigm. Children's emotional reactions, strategies of emotion regulation (emotion focus, distraction), and maternal parenting behaviour were observed in German and in Indian dyads. The results showed significant cultural differences in the mothers' reactions to negative emotions of their children, cultural and gender differences in children's emotional reactions after frustration, and some culture-specific associations among maternal and children's regulatory strategies. The results are discussed with respect to cultural conditions in the development of social competence.

Religious involvement and the social competence of Indonesian Muslim adolescents: A longitudinal study

French, Doran Dept. of Psychology, Illinois Wesleyan University, Bloomington, USA Eisenberg, Nancy Dept. of Psychology, Arizona State University, Tempe, AZ, USA Vaughan, Julie Dept. of Psychology, Arizona State University, Tempe, AZ, USA Purwono, Urip Dept. of Psychology, Padjadjaran University, Bandung, Indonesia Suryanti, Telie A. Suryanti Dept. of Psychology, Padjadjaran University, Bandung, Indonesia
This reports a two year longitudinal study assessing the relation between religious involvement and multiple indices of competence in 13 year old Indonesian Muslim adolescents. Spirituality and religiosity and multiple aspects of social competence and adjustment were assessed using multiple measures and data sources. SEM analyses revealed relations between a religious involvement latent variable and peer status, academic achievement, prosocial behavior, antisocial/problem behavior,

and self-esteem. These results suggest that religious involvement may be integrally related to competence among youth who live in homogeneously religious cultures in which religious values and practices permeate daily life.

Adolescent deviant behaviors across cultures

Dishion, Thomas Child and Family Center, University of Oregon, Eugene, USA
This study compares videotaped interaction dynamics of 680 adolescent friendships, coded with both an affect code and a topic code. The sample consists of 40% European American and 38% African American. The quality of friendship, the interaction dynamics and the levels of deviancy training were compared for the two groups. Second, the predictive validities of the two groups were compared for the observed deviancy training in adolescent friendships to young adult problem behavior such as arrest, self reported antisocial behavior and drug use. Results were interpreted from an ecological systems theory that emphasizes the role of peer reinforcement in adolescence.

Emotional competence in Nepalese and US Children

Cole, Pamela Dept. of Psychology, Penn State University, University Park, USA
This presentation describes a series of studies, comparing two Nepali ethnic groups. Tamang and Brahman cultures differ in terms of 1) children's beliefs about revealing emotion, 2) caregiver socialization of children's emotions, and 3) elders' conceptions of child competence. Tamang actively discourage anger, fostering a child's sense of shame. By first grade, Tamang children do not endorse feeling angry in anger-eliciting situations. Brahmans ignore shame but not anger, modeling emotional constraint. By first grade, Brahman school children endorse feeling angry but assert that anger must not be revealed. Findings are discussed in terms of factors that create different cultural priorities.

Shyness-sensitivity and social, school and psychological adjustment in urban and rural Chinese children

Chen, Xinyin Dept. of Psychology, Unversity of Western Ontario, London, Canada Wang, Li Dept. of Psychology, University of Western Ontario, Beijing, People's Republic of China Wang, Zhengyan Dept. of Psychology, Capital Normal Univeristy, Beijing, People's Republic of China
Shyness-sensitivity may play an important role in social and psychological adjustment in childhood and adolescence. However, the significance of shyness for adjustment may be moderated by social and cultural contexts. The purpose of the present study was to examine how shyness was associated with peer relationships, school achievement and psychological well-being in urban and rural Chinese children. Data on social functioning and adjustment were collected from various sources. The results indicated that shyness was associated with peer rejection, school problems and depression in urban children, but with peer acceptance and school achievement in rural children.

IS-026: Applying the science of psychology to intergroup conflict: Promising results from intractable and prolonged areas of conflict. A USNC symposium

Diane Halpern (chair)
How can we reduce intergroup conflict? The participants in this symposium discuss commonalities and differences across research projects conducted in different places around the world and analyze what worked and did not work in reducing protracted intergroup conflict. The members of this

international panel applied the best of psychological science to the worst of human problems. Panelists have worked to reduce violence and bring about peace in multiple regions around the world including the Israeli-Arab conflict in the Middle East, Catholic-Protestant conflict in Northern Ireland, Christian-Muslim conflict in Indonesia, and Turkish-Armenian conflict in Western Asia and Europe. They are using principles of the psychology of peace in troubled regions where some of the residents have only known war. We can all learn from their failures, celebrate their successes, and build on the hard work of waging peace.

Contact and conflict in Northern Ireland: From long war to long peace

Cairns, Ed Dept. of Psychology, University of Ulster, Coleraine, United Kingdom *Hewstone, Miles* Dept. of Psychology, University of Oxford, Oxford, United Kingdom

Despite the recent positive headlines associated with Northern Ireland, for many people the day-to-day reality is that they live in a segregated (i.e., largely Catholic or largely Protestant) world. This is important because while segregation remains a part of life in Northern Ireland, the seeds of violent conflict, while dormant, lie just beneath the surface. In an attempt to improve the implantation of community relations policy, we have embarked on the first scientific study of intergroup contact in Northern Ireland. In particular we are exploring when cross-community contact works and why it works and how it impacts on intergroup attitudes and in particular on intergroup trust and intergroup forgiveness.

Being socialized in a conflict: Acquisition and development of the image of the enemy in the Israeli-Arab conflict

Teichman, Yona Dept. of Psychology, Tel Aviv University, Tel Aviv, Israel *Bar-Tal, Daniel, Teichmann, Meir*

Recent years have seen an increasing theoretical and empirical interest in the acquisition and development of inter-group representations and attitudes in children. Based on years of research regarding the acquisition and development of intergroup representations and attitudes in the context of the Israeli-Arab conflict, we propose an integrative developmental contextual theory (IDCT) and present part of our findings. Referring to development, we account both for cognitive and personality development. On the cognitive level we acknowledge developmental changes in cognitive abilities and in social perspective. On the personal level, we refer to changes in self- and social identities and related changes in personal needs and motivations (i.e., self-enhancement motivation). The context is accredited as providing conditions which accelerate or delay the development of the representations of social groups and the level of positivity/negativity towards them. In a nut shell, referring to a developmental trajectory for children in a no-conflict multiethnic situation that extends beyond school age, the developmental prediction that stems from IDCT suggests a non-linear pattern of the expression of intergroup stereotypes and attitudes. A pattern in which peaks of negativity toward the out-group are evident in two age groups: preschoolers and adolescents. Conflict, interferes with the developmental course defusing age differences and delaying the moderation toward the out-group to late adolescence. From the empirical perspective, we focus on the issue of assessment (implicit/explicit, and structure/content of intergroup representations), and trace the acquisition and development of children's national identity, their social representations, and attitudes toward the in-and out group in the age range of 2 - 17.

Efficacy of a school-based program to deal with psychosocial distress related to war in low-income countries

Wietse, Tol A. HealthNet, Netherlands

A conflict between Christian and Muslim religious groups has plagued the central region of the island of Sulawesi in Indonesia. Although the causes of the conflict are myriad (colonial historical processes, the power vacuum left after Soeharto, and current political-economic processes have all contributed to the persistence of conflict), religious tension has been one of the main features. The main aim of the study to be described was to examine the efficacy of a school-based psychosocial program to deal with the impact of the conflict on school-aged children. A qualitative study was conducted, aimed at (a) examining the wider public health setting in which the program was implemented, including the cultural "compatibility" of setting and program (b) local perspectives on impact of conflict and available healing methods, and (c) preparation of the RCT, consisting of construction of a local tool for measuring daily functioning, and translation of outcome instruments. Subsequently an experimental design (Randomized Controlled Trial, with waitlist control group) was used to examine the efficacy of a 15-session highly structured school-based psychosocial intervention for children aged 8 to 12. Outcome instruments used were (a) standardized symptom checklists (PTSD, depression, anxiety, aggression), (b) resiliency-focused instruments (coping, social support, family cohesion, hope), (c) socio-metric instrumentation, (d) grades/ absenteeism and (e) a locally constructed daily functioning instrument. At the time of writing, the qualitative results were being examined and the RCT was about to be implemented. Preliminary analyses of the qualitative data show the impact of the conflict on all ecological levels of the child system, and specifically the existence of religious distrust on the peer-level. The outcome instruments were adapted to take into account this religious tension, by the inclusion of socio-metric measurements at the peer-group level.

Psycho-political knots of Turkish-Armenian conflict

Paker, Murat Dept. of Psychology, Istanbul Bilgi University, Istanbul, Turkey

In the heat of the WWI, in 1915, Ottoman Government decided to forcibly remove almost all of its Armenian citizens with the "justification" of self-defense and caused hundreds of thousands Armenians' death. As a result, Armenian population in Ottoman/Turkish State sharply dropped from 10% in the pre-1915 period to 0.1% today. WWI was experienced as a total catastrophe by the Ottoman Armenians, but it was, at the same time, the last dramatic phase of a century-long decline for the Ottoman State, which was barely survived from total disintegration/occupation by the Allied Forces through the emergence of the modern Republic of Turkey in 1923. Since then, Turkey has denied addressing Armenians' suffering caused by the wrongdoings of the Ottoman Government, and Armenians have persistently sought recognition of their trauma. The conflict has recently been locked around the word of "genocide." Fortunately, there have also been some serious recent attempts for dialogue among scholars from both sides. Resolution of this conflict still seems to be far away, but the groundwork for such a resolution appears to have started. This presentation aims to discuss the asymmetric psycho-political difficulties both sides carry along the way of resolution. While 1915 represents a constantly recalled, identity-forming, event that is fixated upon, and hatred-generating negative experience for Armenians, it is a small chain of century-long disastrous, and thus, dissociated, events for the Turkish State and the majority of the society in Turkey. When reminded of what was done to the Armenians in 1915, the typical

Turkish responses include denial, ignorance, rage, or feeling humiliated. Interestingly enough, both sides, for the most part, tend to perceive the other side as extremely homogenous and enemy-like. Also, as a result of the trauma vortex, both sides tend to confuse past and present states of themselves and the other. Identification schemas of both sides are rather illusory. Turkish-Armenian conflict has been suffering from a lack of real relational space. In the absence of this space, intergenerationally transmitted positions of victim/perpetrator cannot be agreed upon by both sides that tend to perceive themselves victims of history in tangential contexts. The presentation ends with some practical suggestions to advance the dialogue/resolution process.

PRIME's two narratives' shared history project: Palestinian and Israeli teachers and pupils learning each other's narrative

Bar-On, Dan Ben Gurion University, Beer-Sheva, Israel *Adwan, Sami*

This paper describes a process of twenty-five workshops (2001-2006) in which seven Palestinian and seven Jewish-Israeli teachers developed a joint textbook, with the help of two historians and the co-directors of PRIME (Peace Research Institute in the Middle East) who also co-authors this paper. The joint schoolbook includes two narratives (an Israeli and a Palestinian) of nine important historical periods in their mutual conflict, covering the period of 1900-2000. The project developed as a kind of an "island of sanity" under fire: working under severe violent conditions of asymmetry of power relations of occupation of the Palestinians and suicide bombings against Israelis. The teachers taught experts of the two narratives in their classrooms and summarized some of their pupils' reactions, as well as their own, before developing additional narratives. Some of the pupils' negative initial reactions helped the teachers express their own negative feelings, but this did not lead them to forgo their commitment to continue their joint work on writing a book that contained the two narratives. The process, described chronologically, helped the teachers realize that they must develop narratives more inclusive and sensitive to each other, more interdependent though still separate as there is currently no chance for a bridging narrative between the two sides.

IS-027: Can happiness change: Implications for theory and policy

Richard E. Lucas (chair)

Subjective well-being reflects a person's subjective sense that his or her life is going well. An important goal–both at an individual and societal level–is to identify the factors that can improve well-being. However, a considerable amount of research shows that personality and other stable factors play a strong role in a person's happiness, and this has led to questions about whether change is possible. The participants will present evidence regarding stability and change in well-being. They will also discuss the implications that this evidence has for theories of well-being and the policies that might foster positive changes.

Health and happiness: The Role of health conditions in subjective well-being

Lucas, Richard E. Dept. of Psychology, Michigan State University, East Lansing, USA

Objectives: Previous research has suggested that people adapt quickly to severe health problems. The goal of the current analyses was to analyze existing datasets to determine how strongly health status and subjective well-being are related. Methods: Various archival datasets were examined, and both cross-sectional and prospective longitudinal analyses were conducted. Results: Cross-sectional and longitudinal analyses showed that health conditions (and changes in health conditions) are associated with subjective well-being, and that effect sizes are often medium to large in size. Conclusions: Health conditions appear to play a strong role in people's subjective well-being.

Greater happiness for a greater number: Is that possible?

Veenhoven, Ruut Faculty of Social Sciences, Erasmus University Rotterdam, Rotterdam, Netherlands
Several psychological theories of happiness imply that great happiness is not possible in a country and neither greater happiness. Yet empirical research on happiness has shown that ga high degree happiness is the rule in most developed nations and that average happiness has risen considerably in most nations over the last 30 years. There are good reasons to believe that we live now longer and happier than ever before in human history. This begs the question why theory diverged so much from reality. Some answers to that question are explored.

Subjective well-being: How do genes and environment contribute to stability and change?

Roysamb, Espen University of Oslo, Oslo, Norway
Vittersø, Joar Psychology, University of Tromsø, Trømsø, Norway
Objectives: First, to review recent findings on genetic and environmental effects on subjective well-being (SWB). Second, to present new results pertaining to stability and change in SWB. Methods: Questionnaire data from the Norwegian Mother and Child Cohort Study (N=75000) and the Twin Panel (N=8000) were analyzed with structural equation modeling. Results: Heritability estimates for SWB range from .20 to .50. Stability in SWB appears to be primarily genetic, whereas change is primarily environmentally caused. Specific life events and conditions influencing SWB change are identified. Conclusion: Happiness can and do change. Effects vary from short to long term.

Intraindividual and interindividual variation in life satisfaction following multiple life events

Luhmann, Maike Freie Universität Berlin, Berlin, Germany Eid, Michael Erziehungsw. & Psychologie, Freie Universität Berlin, Berlin, Germany
Major life events trigger short-term as well as long-term changes in life satisfaction. In a longitudinal study, we investigated whether this reaction varies intraindividually when a specific event occurs multiple times. Using multilevel modeling, we analyzed three life-events: unemployment, marriage, and divorce. Data were obtained from the Socioeconomic Panel (GSOEP), a large-scale representative German panel study. Results show that reaction becomes worse for repeated unemployment (sensitization), it is quite diverse for repeated divorces, and it stays the same for repeated marriages. Demographic, person-related, and event-related variables were tested as moderator variables in order to account for interindividual differences.

Parents' reaction and adaptation to the birth of a child

Dyrdal, Gunvor Marie Dept. of Psychology, University of Oslo, Oslo, Norway Lucas, Richard Dept. of Psychology, Michigan State University, East Lansing, USA
The present study explored how having a child affects life satisfaction among first-time parents participating in the German Socio-Economic Panel study (GSOEP) between 1984 and 2005. Multilevel modeling indicated that life satisfaction increases pre-pregnancy to a peak just after birth and declines shortly thereafter, returning to the initial level within three years postpartum. Older parents

experienced a greater increase in life satisfaction following childbirth. In this study, participants are recruited prior to pregnancy, enabling an examination of baseline and adaptation effects in life-satisfaction following the major life-event of a first child.

Similar changes in spouses subjective well-being

Schimmack, Ulrich Dept. of Psychology, University of Toronto, Toronto, Canada
Longitudinal studies have demonstrated that happiness changes over time. This presentation introduces dyadic latent panel analysis (DLPA) as a new method to examine the contribution of environmental factors to these changes. DLPA examines whether two members of a dyad change in the same direction. The method is applied to married couples in the German Socio-Economic Panel. The results provide strong evidence that environmental factors influence happiness. At the same time, DLPA shows that spouses are also highly similar in the stable dispositions that produce stability in happiness over a period of 22 years. The possibility of assortative mating is discussed.

IS-029: Emotion and the brain

Alfons Hamm (chair)
In this symposium Peter Lang, University of Florida will first present dense-array EEG, brain imaging (fMRI) and psychophysiological measures to elucidate the defense cascade emotional responding. Then David Sanders; University of Geneva will demonstrate that amygdala is central in processing self- relevant information during processing of affective stimuli. Afterwards Margaret Bradley, University of Florida will show that virtual reinforcers (anticipated pain or reward) are potent stimuli in affective learning. Finally, Herta Flor, Central Institute of Mental Health, Mannheim, will demonstrate that genetic variations of the glucocorticoid receptor predict acquistion and extinction of fear learning.

Emotion and motivation: Brain and reflex activation in perception and anticipation

Lang, Peter Dept. of Psychology, University of Florida, Gainesville, USA
The initial response to threat is somatically inhibitory and has a strong vagal component. The functional significance is to facilitate attention. The sympathetic reactions increase if danger is perceived to be more imminent. Furthermore, near the predator's strike zone, the organism is mobilized, increasingly primed for action. This change from attention to action is similarly evoked by appetitive/pleasant stimuli. The presentation will describe human research based on this animal model, using dense-array EEG, brain imaging (fMRI) and psychophysiological measures, and is intended to elucidate patterns of brain activation and reflex physiology in emotional perception and anticipation of punishment or reward.

Testing psychological theories of emotion by investigating the human amygdala

Sander, David NCCR Affective Scien, University of Geneva, Geneva, Switzerland
Patient data and brain imaging studies clearly demonstrate that the amygdala is not a fear-module but rather contributes to the processing of a much wider range of negative and positive affective stimuli suggesting that the amygdala might code the intensity of affective stimulation. However, equally intense stimuli differentially activate the dorsal amygdala contradicting the above view. Converging evidence rather supports the view that the computational profile of the human amygdala meets the core appraisal concept of relevance detection, a view which integrates established

findings on the amygdala and suggests that it may be central in processing self- relevant information.

Defensive learning and the brain: Virtual reinforcers

Bradley, Margaret Dept. of Psychology, CSEA, Gainesville, USA
In humans, learning proceeds quickly under conditions when the reinforcer is only virtual rather than actual. Anticipation of receiving a painful shock elicits a host of defensive reactions in the absence of any specific experience with the painful stimulus itself. Data are presented outlining the nature of defensive learning with virtual reinforcers in somatic, autonomic, reflex and neural (ERP, fMRI) systems. Importantly, individual differences in the fear of pain modulate aversive reactions to threatening shock. Taken together, the mere threat of shock elicits significant defensive reactivity, suggesting that, in humans, virtual reinforcers are a potent stimulus in affective learning.

Brain activation during fear conditioning depends on genetic variations related to functioning of the hypothalamic-pituitary-adrenal axis

Flor, Herta Inst. für Psychologie, ZI für Seeelische Gesundheit, Mannheim, Germany
Posttraumatic stress disorder has been associated with enhanced fear conditioning and dysfunction of the HPA axis. Three glucorticoid-receptor related polymorphisms will be examined testing the hypothesis that the acquisition and/or extinction of conditioned fear id modulated by the risk alleles of the three polymorphisms. Brain imaging data demonstrate that fear acquisition indexed by an increased BOLD signal in the amygdala is positively related to the risk alleles, while during extinction the same alleles showed a negative correlation with prefrontal activation. Cortisol levels as well as early childhood trauma and current stress were also related to fear acquisition and extinction.

Anticipation and exposure to threat

Hamm, Alfons Inst. für Psychologie, Universität Greifswald, Greifswald, Germany
A series of studies will be presented in which patients with specific phobias and panic disorder either anticipate and/or are exposed to their fear specific situations. It will be demonstrated that protective reflexes are potentiated during anticipation and exposure to threat while appetitive stimulation is associated with inhibition of this reflex. Activation of the human amygdala on the other hand is increased both during pleasant and threat related stimulation. Activation of the anterior insular cortex seems to be specific for defensive response mobilization during anxiety disorders.

IS-030: Sleep disturbances in old age: A challenge for psychology

Inger Hilde Nordhus (chair)
The prevalence of insomnia is above 30 % among those 65 years and older. A study on the effect of insomnia on work disability in the second half of life is presented as well as a study on the efficacy of cognitive behavioural therapy (CBT) compared to medical treatment for insomnia in older adults. These are followed by a study examining the efficacy of group CBT on depression, anxiety and sleep disturbances in patients with chronic obstructive pulmonary disease is presented. The fourth study presented has a focus on civilian survivors of war-time bombing and sleep disturbances.

Does age influence the effect of insomnia on work disability?

Overland, Simon Hemil Senteret, University of Bergen, Bergen, Norway
Accumulating evidence suggests that insomnia is a more independent health problem than previously

thought. Insomnia has been demonstrated as an independent predictor of later awards of disability pension and due to high prevalence, insomnia might have a stronger effect on disability pension awards than depression. This presentation will comprise results from several studies, a particular focus will be given to the impact of age upon the association between insomnia and work disability and implications of this interaction will be discussed.

CBT versus pharmacological treatment of insomnia in older adults

Sivertsen, Børge Dep. of Clin. Psychology, University of Bergen, Bergen, Norway Omvik, Siri Dept. of Clinical Psychology, University of Bergen, Bergen, Norway Pallesen, Ståle Dep. of Psychosocial Science, University of Bergen, Bergen, Norway Bjorvatn, Bjørn Dep. of Public Health and Pri, University of Bergen, Bergen, Norway Havik, Odd E Dept. of Clinical Psychology, University of Bergen, Bergen, Norway Kvale, Gerd Dept. of Clinical Psychology, University of Bergen, Bergen, Norway Nielsen, Geir Høstmark Dept. of Clinical Psychology, University of Bergen, Bergen, Norway Nordhus, Inger Hilde Dept. of Clinical Psychology, University of Bergen, Bergen, Norway

Complaints of insomnia are very common, especially in older adults. Previous research has suggested beneficial outcomes of both psychological and pharmacological treatments, but blinded placebo-controlled trials comparing the effects of these treatments are lacking. We compared the short- and long-term effects of CBT and zopiclone in a randomized controlled trial in 46 patients (60 yrs+). CBT resulted in improved short- and long-term outcomes compared with zopiclone on most outcome measures, while zopiclone did not differ from placebo. These results suggest that interventions based on CBT are superior to zopiclone treatment both in short- and long-term management of insomnia in older adults.

Group cognitive behavioural therapy for anxiety, depression and sleep disturbances in patients with chronic respiratory illness

Hynninen, Minna J. Faculty of Psychology, University of Bergen, Bergen, Norway Bjerke, Nina Faculty of Psychology, University of Bergen, Bergen, Norway Pallesen, Ståle Faculty of Psychology, University of Bergen, Bergen, Norway Bakke, Per Department of Thoracic Medicin, University of Bergen, Bergen, Norway Nordhus, Inger Hilde Faculty of Psychology, University of Bergen, Bergen, Norway

The efficacy of group cognitive behavioural therapy (CBT) on anxiety, depression and sleep disturbances was examined in a randomized controlled trial of 51 outpatients with chronic obstructive pulmonary disease (COPD). Seven weeks of CBT was compared with telephone contact. Mixed models were used to characterize change over time across the groups. CBT resulted in a rapid improvement in symptoms of anxiety and depression, and the improvement was maintained at the six-month follow-up. Changes in sleep were minimal. Findings support the implementation of CBT-based interventions for anxiety and depression in COPD patients. Improvement in sleep may require more comprehensive, multidisciplinary interventions.

Civilian survivors of war-time bombing and sleep disturbances in old age

Winje, Dagfinn Faculty of Psychology, University of Bergen, Bergen, Norway

In 1944 allied air forces bombed a primary school in Bergen, Norway. Do the survivors experience psychological distress different from Norwegian and German elderly who also were children during WWII? Symptom Checklist-90-R (SCL-90-R), Impact of Event Scale-R (IES-R) and Pittsburgh Sleep Quality Index (PSQI) were used to assess current symptoms of general psychological distress, post-

traumatic stress, and sleep problems, respectively, in the Norwegian sample. Results (SCL-90-R) indicate that the symptoms of the Bergen sample were significantly different (Effect size, Hedges' g) from the symptoms of elderly good-sleepers, and similar to symptom levels of elderly insomniacs and elderly German child victims of WWII.

IS-031: Advances in the study of personality systems: The self, agency, and personality coherence

Daniel Cervone (chair)

This symposium presents advances in theory and research on a central question of personality psychology: how multiple personality systems interrelate and jointly contribute to the distinctive, enduring patterns of experience and action that distinguish individuals from one another. Speakers address the interactions among cognitive and affective personality systems; the development of personality in social context; the nature of self, personal agency, and processes of meaning construction; and the psychological systems that underlie cross-situational coherence in personality functioning. In total, the presentations address an essential challenge for psychological science: understanding the complex, idiosyncratic individual as a psychological whole.

Social-cognitive systems and personality coherence: The KAPA model of personality architecture

Cervone, Daniel Dept. of Psychology, University of Illinois, Chicago, USA

The KAPA model of personality architecture seeks to advance social-cognitive perspectives on personality in two respects: (1) by specifying a theoretically-grounded model of social-cognitive and affective personality structures and processes, or a model of personality architecture, and (2) by applying that model to the question of cross-situational coherence in psychological response, which is examined through idiographic methodologies. The talk will present data from both correlational and experimental studies that verify a core feature of the model, namely, the hypothesis that situational- and self-knowledge contributes to patterns of cross-situational coherence in self-appraisals that are idiosyncratic yet predictable.

Self-efficacy beliefs across domains of functioning and their relation to traits and values

Caprara, Gian Vittorio Dept. of Psychology, Univers. of Rome 'La Sapienza', Rome, Italy Cugini, Claudia Dept. of Psychology, Univers. of Rome 'La Sapienza', Rome, Italy Gerbino, Maria Grazia Dept. of Psychology, Univers. of Rome 'La Sapienza', Rome, Italy Paciello, Marinella Dept. of Psychology, Univers. of Rome 'La Sapienza', Rome, Italy Tramontano, Carlo Dept. of Psychology, Univers. of Rome 'La Sapienza', Rome, Italy

Previous studies have attested to the merits of a conceptual model positing emotional and interpersonal efficacy beliefs as major determinants of psychological functioning. Recent findings attest to the concerted action of traits, values and self efficacy beliefs in accounting for a large portion of variability in prosocial behavior. Whereas traits, values and self efficacy beliefs attest to the merits of different research traditions in Personality and Social Psychology, the time is now to make convergent efforts to achieve a more comprehensive view of individuals' complexity.

The dialogical self: Between exchange and dominance

Oles, Piotr Dept. of Personality, Catholic University Lublin, Lublin, Poland Hermans, Hubert J. M. Dept. of Psychology, Radboud University, Berg en Dal, Netherlands

The processes of globalization and localization, as globalization's counterforce, require a dialogical conceptualization in which the self is considered as a 'society of mind'. Two factors are described as crucial to understanding the processes of globalization and localization on the individual level: (a) the increasing density and heterogeneity of voices and countervoices; and (b) the role of social power and domination. Some empirical studies are presented that suggest that different positions or voices as parts of the individual self present different narratives, showing the existence of opposite valuations of one and the same person or situation.

Volition and self-development: The dynamics of Ppersonality systems interactions

Kuhl, Julius Inst. für Psychologie, Universität Osnabrück, Osnabrück, Germany Quirin, Markus Inst. für Psychologie, Universität Osnabrück, Osnabrück, Germany

Data from several studies will be provided supporting the hypothesis that experiential access to integrated self-referential knowledge promotes efficient self- and affect regulation. We also demonstrate that experiential self-access but not conscious self-reflection predicts affect-regulatory processes. The results will be discussed with respect to the role of experiential self-access in self-congruent goal pursuit and the maintenance of well-being and health. We use Personality Systems Interactions Theory to discuss the dynamic mechanisms of personality that presumably underlie the affect-regulatory functions facilitating self-access.

IS-032: Lesbian, gay and bisexual health

Clinton Anderson (chair)

Lesbian, gay, and bisexual people are the objects of sexual prejudice. The experience of being targeted for sexual prejudice contributes to minority stress, that is, the extra stress to which individuals are exposed as a result of belonging to stigmatized social groups. The purpose of the symposium is to bring together experts on health within lesbian, gay, and bisexual populations from around the world in an effort to bridge gaps between different theoretical perspectives, cultural perspectives and research traditions and to expand understanding of the relationship between sexual prejudice, sexual minority stress, and health.

Homophobia and discrimination along the life cycle: A psychological perspective

Ardila, Ruben Dept. of Psychology, National Univ. of Colombia, Bogota, Colombia

Homophobia takes different forms in different cultures and at different ages. Children are discriminated if they show behaviors that are not considered gender-correct. It is "appropriate" for boys to play with cars and for girls to pay with dolls. In adulthood, homophobia is addressed towards the people who do not follow the culturally-valued precepts, at work, marriage, etc. Along the life cycle homophobia and discrimination toward minority sexual orientation varies. At old age, sexual discrimination occurs very subtly. Internalized homophobia and self-discrimination influence health and prevention. Giving appropriate health care to different age groups in the LGBT community is pointed out. Key words: homophobia, life cycle, health

Internalized homophobia
Steffens, Melanie Inst. für Psychologie, Universität Jena, Jena, Germany

Most lesbians and gay men grew up in a homophobic society with negative attitudes toward them. According to theory, they should internalize homonegativity, i.e. a spontaneous negative evaluation of lesbians/gay men. After coming-out, they would need to overcome this homonegativity. Recent developments in social cognition enable to measure that kind of automatic cognition. We tested whether automatic homonegativity can be measured by using a version of the Implicit Association Test (IAT) and two Go/No-go Association Tasks (GNATs). As correlation patterns indicate, our measures appear valid for assessing automatic homonegativity. Interestingly, automatic homonegativity appeared low on average in community samples.

Sexual behavior and health of gay men: A psychosocial evolution
Haldeman, Douglas Seattle, WA, USA

Health concerns particular to gay men have historically been linked to sexual behavior and social relationships. Over the past 35 years, sexual practices and eroto-typical values among gay men have evolved in a parallel trajectory to significant events and cultural changes. This presentation will trace historical developments and current trends, as well as the research literature, in sociosexual relating among gay men and the attendant impact on health issues.

Lesbians and breast cancer: Qualitative approaches
Wilkinson, Sue Dept. of Social Sciences, Loughborough University, Loughborough, Leicesters., United Kingdom Fish, Julie Dept. of Social Work, De Montfort Univ. The Gateway, Leitcester, United Kingdom

Lesbians' risk of breast cancer is a contested issue in lesbian health psychology. Particular risk factors for the disease, said to be more prevalent among lesbians, are believed to increase lesbians' susceptibility. Qualitative data collected in the UK Lesbians and Healthcare Survey and in seven focus group discussions is discussed. Five recurrent themes in relation to breast cancer risk perceptions are presented, namely: (i) no children; (ii) drinking alcohol; (iii) being overweight; (iv) reduced participation in breast screening and (v) risk perceptions in relation to heterosexual women. Health psychologists are concerned to make lesbians' health visible without reinscribing pathology.

IS-033: Integrating approaches from education, usability and cognitive science for efficient e-learning deployment: The experience of the WELKOM Leonardo project

Maurice Grinberg (chair)

The main objective of the WELKOM project was to develop and test a tool which will help European companies to integrate, rapidly and at minimal cost, new technologies and new organizational modes enabling them to increase their competitiveness by sustaining, developing, and creating competencies within the company. To meet this goal, an integrated methodology for deployment of Computer Assisted Training (CAT) systems has been developed, applied, and tested. The methodology is based on the integration of various methods used in the field of instructional design, knowledge assessment, and usability research and psychology. The methods were selected to help reducing deployment time, maximize learning and fit maximally the needs and profile of the trainees leading to better

educational achievements and decreased training time. In this symposium, we want to present the results focused on the design and deployment of e-learning systems and the psychology methods used. Moreover, we want to present research, related to adaptive e-learning systems and methods of their design based on the content and the way of delivering it to the learners. The presentations should give the basis of a discussion of the role of methods coming from psychology and cognitive science in the implementation and use of e-learning platforms.

Usability testing during the whole deployment cycle for e-learning systems
Hristova, Evgenia Psychology and Cognitive Scien, New Bulgarian University, Sofia, Bulgaria

The purpose of the usability testing is to make the system easy to use, easy to learn, used without errors, and used with satisfaction. Usability is very important for e-learning systems because achieving educational goals essentially depends on the usability of the system. Five different usability methods are being used in the WELKOM project: learning styles evaluation, heuristic evaluation, user testing, eye-tracking recordings and questionnaires measuring users' satisfaction. Here we present the experience gained from applying usability methods during different phases of e-learning systems' design, development and usage.

Developing and evaluating a prototype of an adaptive tutoring system for English grammar learning
Kremser, Mark Germany Albert, Dietrich Inst. für Psychologie, Universität Graz, Graz, Austria

The aim of our R&D activities was to develop a prototype of an adaptive system for personalized assessment and teaching of English Grammar. This system is based on sound psychological theoretical and empirical findings. The theoretical basis is the Competence-based Knowledge Space Theory. A set of competencies consists of 28 grammar skills which have been ordered due to psycho-linguistic results in the field of learning English as a 2nd language. Empirical basis has been the results of two preliminary investigations by Kremser and Simon. More than 30 paper pencil tasks of the fill in the gap type (competing sentences) have been structured using task analysis methods. The empirical validation of the structures has been mainly successful. The resulting knowledge space has been refined for the current investigation and was again empirically validated - in this case with a computer-based test. In the second step, adaptivity has been added to the system and analyzed by systematic computer simulations. In a third step we developed the prototype of the adaptive tutoring system by adding instructional material and extending the functionality of the system. The resulting prototype was evaluated with a usability test consisting of a guided walk-through and a questionnaire. Although the user interface needs to be improved, participants highly appreciated the systems' functionality regarding the personalization based on psychological grounds.

Game-based learning: Development of a general methodology for creating serious games
Linek, Stephanie Department of Psychology, University of Graz, Graz, Austria Schwarz, Daniel Kickmeier-Rust, Michael Albert, Dietrich Inst. für Psychologie, Universität Graz, Graz, Austria

Game-based learning rests upon the idea of using the enjoyment and motivation within video games in the educational context. Hence, the design of educational games has to address optimizing enjoyment as well as optimizing learning. Within the EC-project ELEKTRA a methodology about the conceptual design of digital learning games was developed. Thereby state-of-the-art psycho-pedago-

gical approaches (e.g., Competence-based Knowledge Space Theory) were combined with insights from media-psychology (e.g., on parasocial-interaction) as well as with best-practice game-design. This interdisciplinary approach was enriched by enclosed empirical evaluation and research studies to answer open questions and achieve further improvements.

IS-034: Metacognition, affect and self-regulation

Anastasia Efklides (chair)

This symposium aims at showing that metacognition, in the form of metacognitive experiences and metacognitive knowledge, is interacting with affect such as interest and anxiety state, as well as with self-concept, motivation, and attitudes as students deal with learning tasks and self-regulate their learning. The interrelations of metacognition, affect, and self-regulation are studied at the online level representing the joint effects of task and situational features and general person characteristics as well. Self-regulation is seen as the outcome of the interaction of two regulatory loops, namely the cognitive and the affective, which are involved in both successful and unsuccessful self-regulation.

Emotions in comprehension monitoring and regulation
Vauras, Marja Faculty of Education, University of Turku, Turku, Finland Kinnunen, Riitta Dept. of Teacher Education, University of Turku, Turku, Finland Salonen, Pekka Dept. of Teacher Education, University of Turku, Turku, Finland

Monitoring of reading comprehension involves metacognition, i.e., evaluating and regulating the level of comprehension. Monitoring was investigated in relation to emotions involved in metacognitive experiences alerting comprehension failures. Participants were ten-year-old 4rth grade students with (n = 30) and without (n = 30) reading comprehension problems. Comprehension Monitoring Tasks include short texts, with or without intended comprehension obstacles, and Prompted Interviews aim to clarify students' comprehension processes and feelings in reading. Tobii Eye Tracker 1750 and Noldus Observer XT were used to track students' reading patterns (e.g., indicative changes in fixation paths, gaze durations, rereading) and emotional expressions in synchrony.

Learning through online information searching: The effects of epistemic metacognition, interest in surfing the web and interest in the topic
Mason, Lucia Dept. DPSS, University of Padova, Padova, Italy Boldrin, Angela Dept. DPSS, University of Padova, Padova, Italy Ariasi, Nicola Dept. DPSS, University of Padova, Padova, Italy

The World Wide Web, with its immense body of information, is one of the most used learning tools, even by young students. To effectively access, identify, and use internet-based material evaluating critically the veracity of online information is required. This paper focuses on 8th graders' epistemic metacognition, i.e., reflections about the source, justification, and nature of knowledge, spontaneously expressed during Web surfing to learn more on a scientifically controversial topic, the extinction of dinosaurs. Results showed that better learners were those who spontaneously activated more epistemic evaluations, had higher interest in online information searching and higher interest in the topic.

Interest: A significant thread binding cognition and affect in the regulation of learning
Ainley, Mary Dept. of Psychology, University of Melbourne, Melbourne, Australia

Self-regulated learning involves complex processes that focus students' affective, cognitive and metacognitive resources. This paper examines the role of interest conceptualized as individual interest and as an on-task affective state, in the network of self-regulatory processes. An online methodology was used to access aspects of young adolescent students' on-task behaviour. The learning task required students to access and use information resources to answer a question on a topical social issue. Analyses indicated significant positive relationships between interest measures and students' on-task efficacy, strategy and control processes. These findings highlight the role of motivational processes such as interest in self-regulated learning.

Students' strategic behavior and its relations to performance and to academic self-concept
Dermitzaki, Irini Dept. of Special Education, University of Thessaly, Volos, Greece Leondari, Angeliki Dept. of Preschool Education, University of Thessaly, Volos, Greece
The aim of the study was to investigate the relations between students' strategic behavior, performance and academic self-concept in mathematics. First and second grade students' cognitive, meta-cognitive, and motivational behaviors were individually recorded by two observers during a mathematical problem-solving situation. The students' self-concept was also individually examined. Data analyses showed that students' performance in the given tasks was closely associated to the use of cognitive and meta-cognitive strategic behaviors, whereas academic self-concept in mathematics was related to strategic behaviors employed to maintain and regulate motivation towards the task at hand.

Is mastery goal orientation associated with state anxiety? The role of attitudes
Efklides, Anastasia Faculty of Psychology, Thessaloniki University, Thessaloniki, Greece Dina, Fotini School of Psychology, Aristotle University, Thessaloniki, Greece
Achievement goal orientations theory associates mastery goal orientation with positive affect and interest, whereas performance goal orientation with anxiety. Attitudes reflect one's affective state towards an object/domain and complement one's goal orientations. The present study tested the joint effect of students' goal orientations and attitudes towards mathematics on anxiety state reported after solving mathematical problems. Participants were 870 students of 7th and 9th grade of both genders. Hierarchical regression analyses showed that, contrary to predictions, mastery goal orientation rather than performance-approach or performance-avoidance goal orientation was positively associated with state anxiety when attitude towards mathematics was entered in the model.

IS-035: RAN (Rapid Automatized Naming) and reading: Current research trends

Prakash Padakannaya (chair)
Rapid Automatized Naming (RAN) is a major topic in current researches on reading acquisition and dyslexia. RAN seems to be a good measure of reading efficiency measures such as comprehension and fluency. The nature of RAN, its relationship with phonological awareness, the validity of RAN as an independent component of reading, its relationship with the general speed of processing, multiple RAN measures and their relative contributions to reading at different levels, neurological correlates of RAN, RAN and transparency of orthography, etc are the central issues of discussion in contemporary researches. The papers will present the state of the art scenario.

Speed of processing, rapid naming, and reading in adult compensated dyslexics
Georgiou, George Department of Ed. Psychology, University of Alberta, Edmonton, Canada Parrila, Rauno Department of Ed. Psychology, University of Alberta, Edmonton, Canada
Several studies have found that dyslexics experience speed of processing (SOP) deficits across a variety of tasks and that SOP may, in turn, underlie the relationship between rapid naming speed and reading. The purpose of the present study was to examine different aspects of SOP (simple-complex, visual-auditory, verbal-nonverbal) and determine whether high-functioning adult dyslexics are reliably different from normally reading adults, and which, if any, of the SOP problems are reliably associated with reading accuracy and fluency. Data are currently analyzed.

Specific reading disorder and specific spelling disorder
Landerl, Karin Inst. für Psychologie, Universität Tübingen, Tübingen, Germany
Empirical data will be presented which indicate that deficits in reading and deficits in spelling may have different cognitive foundations. While children with specific spelling disorder (but age-adequate reading development) display deficits in phonological awareness (PA), but no deficit in rapid automatized naming (RAN), children with specific reading disorder (but age-adequate spelling development) display both, a RAN deficit and a PA deficit. Longitudinal data suggest that the PA-deficit may be a consequence rather than a cause of the reading problem, whereas RAN-deficits are a strong predictor of deficits in reading fluency.

Is fluency an independent component of reading?
Joshi, R. Malatesha Dept. of Literacy Education, Texas University, College Station, USA Binks, Emily College of Education, Texas A & M University, College Station, USA
The National Reading Panel (NRP, 2000) considers 'fluency' one of the five basic components of reading. However, the importance of fluency in effortless reading is not without controversy. Perhaps, the importance of fluency may depend on the orthographic depth of a language; fluency may be part of decoding in deeper orthographies while it may be a separate component in shallow orthographies. Fluency may also be influenced by how it was assessed. In this report, we present some results about the role of fluency in different orthographies and discuss the diagnostic and educational implications.

The relationship between phonological awareness, phonological memory, Rapid Automatized Naming (RAN) and reading in monolingual and bilingual English children
Stainthorp, Rhona Inst. of Education, University of Reading, Reading, United Kingdom Powell, Daisy Psychology, University of Roehampton, Roehampton, United Kingdom Stuart, Morag Institute of Education, University of London, London, United Kingdom Quinlan, Philip DEpartment of Psychology, University of York, York, United Kingdom Garwood, Holly Birkbeck College, University of London, London, United Kingdom
There is debate as to whether the relationship between RAN and reading results from RAN indexing phonological processing, general processing speed, or processes independent of phonology. To address this, tests of > reading, phonological awareness (PA), phonological memory (PM) and RAN were administered to 1008 7- to 9- year-old UK children (897 monolingual; 111 bilingual). There were no differences between the two groups on phonological tasks and reading but the bilingual children were significantly faster on RAN tasks. Structural equation modelling was used to investi-

gate the contribution that PA, PM and RAN make to reading in the two different language groups.

Relationship between Rapid Automatized Naming (RAN), reading comprehension and fluency in English and Kanada alphasyllabary
Padakannaya, Prakash Dept. of Psychology, University of Mysore, Mysore, India G, Sunanda Dept. of Psychology, University of Mysore, Mysore, India Ramanath, Soumya Dept. of Psychology, University of Mysore, Mysore, India
A group of 47 Kannada- English biliterate children were administered a battery of RAN measures, reading comprehension, and fluency in English and Kannada separately. The relationships between the variables were analyzed within and across languages. The results showed that RAN measures were good predictors of reading comprehension in Kannada but not in English. None of the RAN measures seemed to be good at predicting reading comprehension and fluency across languages. The results were discussed in terms of the task analysis of different RAN measures and orthographic features of Kannada and English.

IS-036: Organizational psychology in Ukraine: Main trends and developments

Liudmyla Karamushka (chair)
The symposium is supposed to consider the main trends in and development of organizational psychology in Ukraine being the area of knowledge that has been rapidly developing during the last ten years. The six symposium presentations are grouped so that 1) to consider positive and negative aspects of changes in Ukrainian organizations; 2) to analyze distinctive characteristics of project leaders' work as well as factors that improve team members' competitiveness; 3) to reveal causes of and preventive measures for professional stress in managers; 4) to consider psychological conditions of effective specialists' training (economists, psychologists, etc.). Besides, the symposium participants will know the experience of Ukrainian and German psychologists in joint solving of important problems of organizational psychology in Ukraine.

Positive and negative aspects of change processes in Ukrainian organizations
Karamushka, Liudmyla Organizational Psychology, Institute of Psychology, Kyiv, Ukraine
Objective: To find out ppositive and negative aspects of change making in Ukrainian organizations Methods: The research was done on a sample of 528 school teachers using a questionnaire designed by the presenter. Results: 1. 58.0% of teachers positively assessed organizational changes which included innovative educational technologies, new training courses, participation in international projects, etc. Among the negative aspects of organizational change named by 42.0% of the respondents were untimeliness, ineffectiveness, inadequate orientation toward personnel, etc. 2. 77.0% of the respondents needed psychological support in change making in the form of trainings and individual counseling. Conclusion: A special Change Management Training designed by the presenter has been successfully applied in a number of educational organizations.

Psychological profile of project leaders in business organizations
Berdnikova, Elena Organizational Psychology, Institut of Psychology, Kiev, Ukraine
Objective: To build a profile of project leaders in business organizations. Method: The investigation was performed on 120 project team members using a specially designed questionnaire. Results: 1. 75% of the respondents differentiated project and

standard works in terms, resources, hierarchy, and motivation system. 2. The negative project team leader was unable to set definite tasks, a poor communicator, bad team-roles distributor, and poor motivator oriented toward the process rather than people. 3. The importance of project team leaders' attributes was as follows: personal characteristics – 40%, managerial competencies – 50%, technical skills – 10%. Conclusions: Project leaders should focus their attention on definite areas in order to provide for successful project results.

Organization employees' competitiveness: A team performance improving or aggravating factor?

Fil, Alena Lab. of Organiz. Psychology, Institut of Psychology, Kiev, Ukraine

Objective. Finding out teamwork-critical characteristics of educational organization employees' competitiveness. Methods: R.Blake-J.Mouton Inventory, GET TEST, and SPSS. The sample included 148 educational organization employees. Results. 1) Teamwork orientation statistically significantly (r<0.05) correlated with creativity. 2) Teamwork orientation positively correlated with the ability to take reasonable risks. 3) Teamwork orientation negatively correlated with the achievement need. 4) Teamwork orientation negatively correlated with independence need. Conclusion. To be good teamworkers educational organization employees' have to develop key characteristics of their competitiveness.

Training of organizational psychologists to team building: German-Ukrainian experience

Schmidt-Brasse, Ute Unternehmensberatung, PSYCON - Psychologische, Wildeshausen, Germany

Objective: Analysis of applicability of German team building training methods when training Ukrainian organisational psychologists. Method: Investigation during training graduate and post-graduate students end of 2005 (and during a repeat (with different subject) in 2008). Results (to be supplemented): Slightly modified contents, structure, basic training forms and techniques, as well as students' progress monitoring methods used in team building training in Germany proved quite effective in Ukraine, too. Conclusion (until now): After minor adaptation, German team building training methods can be successfully used in training organizational psychologists in Ukraine.

What causes professional stress in education managers?

Bondarchuk, Olena Dept. of Psychology, Central Inst. after Pedagog., Kiev, Ukraine Karamushka, Liudmyla Organizational Psychology, Institute of Psychology, Kyiv, Ukraine Pankovets, Vitaliy Organizational Psychology, Institut of Psychology, Kiev, Ukraine

0bjectives: finding out causes of professional stress in education managers. Method: The investigation was done on 302 education managers using K.J. Vaiman Level of Professional Stress; Ladanov-Uzarayeva Stressogenic Factors In Managers' Work; and SPSS. Results: 1. 70.2% of the respondents had professional stress. 2. Levels of professional stress statistically significantly correlated (p<0.001; p<0.01) with the psychological overload; tense relationship with the superiors; problems at work; and the respondents' conflictogenity. 3. Level of professional stress statistically significantly correlated (p<0.05) with the respondents' position. Conclusion: The obtained findings show presence of highly developed professional stress in education managers which requires their special anti-stress training.

Development of competitiveness in economics students as a prerequisite of their future efficient work in organizations

Tereshchenko, Kira Dept. of Psychology, Industrial College, Kiev, Ukraine Fil, Alena Lab. of Organiz. Psychology, Institut of Psychology, Kiev, Ukraine

Objective. Finding out levels of development of psychological characteristics of competitiveness in students of economics Method. The investigation was done on 135 college students using V.Petrenko Preparedness for business, V.Shmelyova Inclination to take risks, O.Potyomkina Work-money attitude, and Need of self-development. Results. 1. 22.7% of the respondents had a high level of preparedness for business activity and 26.7% were heavily inclined to take risks. 2. Money orientation dominates over work orientation (32.0% and 21.3% respondents correspondingly). 3. A strong need of self-development was found in 34.7% respondents. Conclusion: Development of the leading characteristics of competitiveness in economics students is a precondition of their future efficient work.

IS-037: Computational models of episodic memory (Part II)

Stephan Lewandowsky (chair)

Memory processes

Dunn, John Dept. of Psychology, University of Adelaide, Adelaide, Australia

The relation between recognition and free recall is complex. While many factors have correlated effects on both forms of memory, other factors have selective or even opposite effects. State-trace analysis is a general method for determining the number and organisation of intervening psychological variables that mediate the effect of two or more independent variables on one or more dependent variables. Applied to recognition and recall, the effects of different variables can be interpreted in terms of relatively simple causal models that resolve the nature and number of underlying memory processes. Preliminary data are reported and implications for theory discussed.

A global memory model of intentional forgetting

Malmberg, Ken Dept. of Psychology, Iowa State University, Ames, USA Malmberg, Kenneth Dept. of Psychology, University of South Florida, Tampa, FL, USA

Forgetting is often unintentional and, hence, it is also unwelcome. Other times forgetting is intentional and may serve to enhance memory for important events or decrease the impact of negative events. Such forgetting is often referred to as the repression, suppression, or inhibition of memory. This presentation describes a new model intentional forgetting. It provides a coherent, quantitative explanation of a variety of directed forgetting phenomena from both free recall and recognition memory procedures, including changes accuracy, serial position effects, condition recall probabilities, and order of output effects that occur as the result of one's intention to forget.

How to say no in short-term recognition: Single- and dual-process models

Oberauer, Klaus Dept. Experimental Psychology, University of Bristol, Bristol, United Kingdom

Single-process models of recognition assume that recognition decisions are based on a single familiarity value, reflecting the match between a probe and all active memory items. Dual-process models assume that familiarity is accompanied by recollection, a process akin to recall. I will apply both types of models to short-term recognition tasks in which probes must be compared to only a subset of the memorized list. The models make differentiable predictions for the serial position curves of three types of probes (positive, new, and probes matching an item in the irrelevant subset). The results of 3 experiments favor a dual-process model.

How a dual-process model of recognition accounts for spurious recollection

Reder, Lynne Dept. of Psychology, Carnegie-Mellon University, Pittsburgh, USA

SAC is a dual-process, computational model of memory that accounts for many results including rapid feeling-of-knowing and spurious feeling-of-knowing, remember and know judgments, contextual fan effects on recognition and priming, interference in cued recall for normal and aging memory and amnesia, and various mirror effects. SAC's account of feeling of knowing also explains spurious recollection. Spurious "remember" responses can occur when features encoded with a foil were also encoded with a studied item. We conducted a series of experiments that allowed us to model spurious recollection without assuming a distribution of unspecified features, using only features that we manipulated.

A unified framework for immediate serial recall, Hebb effects, and the learning of phonological word-forms

Page, Mike Dept. of Psychology, University of Hertfordshire, Hertfordshire, United Kingdom Norris, Dennis Cognition & Brain Sci. Uni, MRC, Cambridge, United Kingdom

There is a substantial body data indicating that phonological working memory is intimately related to the acquisition of phonological word-forms. We propose a unified model that demonstrates how the ordered short-term store that is central to our primacy model of immediate serial recall, interacts with long-term memory, thereby accounting for key features of this relationship. The model is applied to the long-term learning of sequences, as seen in both the Hebb repetition effect and the learning of phonological word-forms. Its application is naturally extended to encompass the recognition of sequences and, hence, of words from continuous speech.

How relative are positional represantions in serial recall?

Farrell, Simon Experimental Psychology, University of Bristol, Bristol, United Kingdom Lewandowsky, Stephan School of Psychology, Univer. of Western Australia, Crawley, Australia

The evidence from serial recall of temporally grouped lists suggests that items are associated with some external positional or timing signal, and that this signal is used to hierarchically organize sequences of items. One particular model of these positional representations, the Start-End Model (Henson, 1998), holds that all items in a group are anchored both to the start and the end of that group: a relative representation. Using a competitive comparison of computational models, we show that the existing evidence, focussing on confusions of terminal group items between groups of different sizes, does not mandate a model in which all items are anchored to the end of a group (i.e, a continuous end marker), but is instead more consistent with a simpler alternative model in which terminal items are discretely tagged as end items (a discrete end marker). We then present some new data using lists grouped in a 4-4 fashion, which allows inspection of confusions of internal items within and between groups. These more discriminating data, and model fits, suggest that a continuous end marker does sometimes play a role in representing order in short-term memory. (Henson, R. N. A. (1998). Short-term memory for serial order: The Start-End Model. Cognitive Psychology, 36, 73-137.)

IS-038: Developmental dyslexia

Heinz Wimmer (chair)
The symposium brings together neurocognitive research on dyslexia from alphabetic scripts and from the Chinese logographic scipt. The first paper deals with the manifestation of dyslexia (e.g., in eye movements) and with associated cognitive impairments. The following papers examine brain dysfunctions with different methods including EEG and functional and structural MRI. The final paper considers potential application of imaging studies for the diagnosis of different types of dyslexia and for prediction of response to remediation.

Behavioral manifestations and cognitive dysfunctions

Wimmer, Heinz NW Fakultät, Universität Salzburg, Salzburg, Austria
From cross-linguistic findings we conclude that the common manifestation of dyslexia in alphabetic orthographies with different levels of regularity is an abnormal increase of word reading time with number of letters. This differs from English-based research which finds misreadings of novel words as main deficit. Second, studies will be presented which find the dyslexic reading speed problem to be associated with slow processing of letter and digit strings but only when name retrieval and not when only visual processing is required. This pattern suggests that brain regions connecting visual with verbal processes are dysfunctional in developmental dyslexia.

Impaired visual tuning for print in dyslexic children learning to read

Maurer, Urs Switzerland Brandeis, Daniel Child and Adolescent Psychiatr, University of Zurich, Zurich, Switzerland
Tuning for print is reduced in dyslexic adults within 200ms of word presentation, as indicated by a reduced N1 specialization in the visual word form area (VWFA). Using electroencephalography-based event-related imaging, we investigated whether impaired N1 tuning for print develops when dyslexic children learn to read. In control children N1 tuning developed strongly with learning to read in occipito-temporal VWFA regions. In dyslexic children visual tuning for print progressed more slowly and was strongly reduced in 2nd grade. The results suggest that delayed initial visual tuning for print critically contributes to the development of dyslexia and to early reading fluency.

Dyslexia: A dysfunction of the visual word form area?

Kronbichler, Martin Psychologie, Universität Salzburg, Salzburg, Austria
We will present data showing profound functional and structural abnormalities of a left occipitotemporal region, roughly corresponding to the Visual Word Form Area, in German dyslexic readers. These dyslexic readers suffered mainly from slow, dysfluent reading. Dyslexic readers not only showed less occipitotemporal activation during word processing, but also failed to exhibit any effect of orthographic familiarity on occipitotemporal activation. Furthermore, dyslexic readers exhibited less occipitotemporal gray matter. As damage to the left occipitotemporal cortex results slow letter-by-letter reading in previously skilled readers, these results suggest a close link between developmental dyslexia and acquired alexia.

Brain dysfunctions and compensatory mechanisms

Hoeft, Fumiko Medicine, CIBSR, Stanford University School of, Stanford, CA, USA
In this talk, we provide evidence that children with developmental dyslexia show reduced activation and gray matter in the posterior brain systems (parieto-temporal and occipito-temporal regions) when compared to age-matched controls and to controls matched for their reading abilities. On the other hand, older (10-16 years of age) but not younger (8-10 years of age) dyslexic individuals show compensatory activation in the inferior frontal region, suggesting that this region is important in the acquisition of compensatory skills. We support this hypothesis by showing that greater inferior frontal activation in adolescents with dyslexia predicts more improvement in reading skills.

Abnormal cortical activation and atypical brain structure in Chinese developmental dyslexia

Tan, Li Hai People's Republic of China Jin, Zhen MRI Lab, Beijing 306 Hospital, Beijing, People's Republic of China Perfetti, Charles LRDC, University of Pittsburgh, Pittsburgh, USA Siok, Wai Ting Dept of Linguistics, University of Hong Kong, Hong Kong, People's Republic of China
In several fMRI experiments with Chinese readers, we found that the neural basis of reading and reading disorders is constrained by language. The left middle frontal region was revealed to play a crucial role in successful Chinese reading. Furthermore, we demonstrated writing system dependent patterns of regional gray matter reduction in dyslexic individuals. Compared with normal controls, children with impaired reading in Chinese exhibited reduced gray matter volume in the left middle frontal gyrus. In contrast, left posterior temporoparietal areas showing structural and functional anomalies in alphabetic language dyslexics showed neither functional nor anatomical differences between Chinese dyslexics and controls.

Neuroimaging studies of dyslexia: Potential applications

Price, Cathy United Kingdom
Will structural or functional neuro-imaging ever be useful for those with developmental and acquired dyslexia? In my talk, I will discuss some recent results that show the variety of structural and functional brain abnormalities associated with different trajectories of reading disability. I will then present hypotheses to suggest that if we could provide neuronal markers for different types of dyslexia, then we should be able to use brain imaging data to predict the functional outcomes of individuals. Ultimately, this may allow us to provide tailor made therapies that facilitate the most efficient course of learning or re-learning.

IS-039: Advances in the research of obsessive-compulsive disorders

Aurora Gavino (chair)
The aim of this symposium is to present recent advances in the research of Obsessive-Compulsive Disorder. Drs. Freeston and Kelly will consider the implications for treatment of the natural interruptions of the obsession-compulsion chain. Dr. Reynolds will explore the validity of cognitive models of obsessive-compulsive behaviours in young people. Drs. Ruiz, Godoy and Gavino will present a descriptive study of obsessive-compulsive behaviours in Spanish children and adolescents from the general population. Dr. Tolin will review research suggesting that behavioural therapies can be enhanced by the use of medications that facilitate neuroplasticity.

Obsessive-compulsive behaviors in children and adolescents in Spain: A descriptive study

Ruiz, Victor M. Dept. of Psychology, University of Malaga, Málaga, Spain Godoy, Antonio Dept. of Psychology, University of Malaga, Málaga, Spain Gavino, Aurora Dept. of Psychology, University of Malaga, Málaga, Spain
This work presents a descriptive study of obsessive compulsive behaviour in childhood. Participants were 1725 Spanish students from fourteen public schools. Spanish versions of the Cognitive Intrusions Questionnaire and of the Childrens Yale-Brown Obsessive Compulsive Scale were applied. The differential frequency of the obsessions and compulsions in the childhood were studied, as well as the associations between the more frequent obsessions and compulsions. The form of the obsessions and the strategies used to manage such obsessions are described. Factors affecting frequency and length of obsessions, as well as effectiveness of the strategies to control intrusions are depicted.

Obsessive-compulsive behaviors in children and adolescents in Spain: A descriptive study

Gavino, Aurora Dept. of Psychology, University of Malaga, Málaga, Spain Ruiz, Victor Manuel Dept. of Psychology, University of Malaga, Málaga, Spain Godoy, Antonio Dept. of Psychology, University of Malaga, Malaga, Spain
This work presents a descriptive study of obsessive compulsive behaviour in childhood. Participants were 1725 Spanish students from fourteen public schools. Spanish versions of the Cognitive Intrusions Questionnaire and of the Childrens Yale-Brown Obsessive Compulsive Scale were applied. The differential frequency of the obsessions and compulsions in the childhood were studied, as well as the associations between the more frequent obsessions and compulsions. The form of the obsessions and the strategies used to manage such obsessions are described. Factors affecting frequency and length of obsessions, as well as effectiveness of the strategies to control intrusions are depicted.

Cognitive models of obsessive compulsive disorder and young people

Reynolds, Shirley Dept. of Medicine, University of East Anglia, Norwich, United Kingdom
Although cognitive models of OCD have been influential with adults their applicability to children and young people requires evaluation. Two experimental studies with children are presented. Study 1 tests the effect of inflated responsibility (Salkovskis, 1985) on OCD related behaviours and affect in children (9 to 12 years). Based on Ladouceur et al., (1995), children sorted sweets into those with and without nuts. They were randomly allocated to 3 levels of perceived responsibility (low, medium, high). Study 2 tested Rachman's Thought-Action Fusion OCD model with children. The results will be discussed in relation their theoretical and clinical implications.

Rules about rules about compulsions in OCD

Freeston, Mark Neurology and Neurobiology, Newcastle University, Newcastle-upon-Tyne, United Kingdom Kelly, Angela Neurology and Neurobiology, Newcastle University, Newcastle-upon-Tyne, United Kingdom
People with OCD can typically describe detailed and rigid rules about how and when rituals must be performed. However, the majority can also report examples of occasions when they can resist, delay, interrupt or otherwise not obey these rules. This study systematically describes 21 people with OCD who were interviewed about 1) their rules about compulsive behaviour, 2) when they do not follow their own rules, and 3) the existence of modifying rules. The results suggest that the phenomenon exists, offers explanations of why this may be so, and considers the therapeutic implications.

Enhancing the efficacy of behavior therapy for OCD with D-cycloserine

Tolin, David F. Anxiety Disorders Center, Hartford Hospital, Hartford, USA

Behavior therapy incorporating exposure and response prevention is the most well-documented treatment for OCD. However, many patients do not respond to this treatment and there is clear room for improvement. Research from animal laboratories suggests that d-cycloserine (DCS), a partial agonist at the N-methyl-D-aspartate gluta-matergic receptor, enhances the extinction of conditioned fear. Meta-analytic results will be discussed, indicating that DCS is most effective when provided a limited number of times, with administration immediately before or after exposure. The growing body of DCS research suggests that behavioral therapies can be enhanced by the use of medications that facilitate neuroplasticity.

Obsessive-compulsive behaviors in children and adolescents in Spain: A descriptive study

Godoy, Antonio Dept. of Psychology, University of Malaga, Malaga, Spain Ruiz, Victor M. Dept. of Psychology, University of Malaga, Malaga, Spain Gavino, Aurora Dept. of Psychology, University of Malaga, Malaga, Spain

This work presents a descriptive study of obsessive compulsive behaviour in childhood. Participants were 1725 Spanish students from fourteen public schools. Spanish versions of the Cognitive Intrusions Questionnaire and of the Childrens Yale-Brown Obsessive Compulsive Scale were applied. The differential frequency of the obsessions and compulsions in the childhood were studied, as well as the associations between the more frequent obsessions and compulsions. The form of the obsessions and the strategies used to manage such obsessions are described. Factors affecting frequency and length of obsessions, as well as effectiveness of the strategies to control intrusions are depicted.

IS-040: Process models for microgenetic concious-perception phenomena

Talis Bachmann (chair)

The symposium is focused on time-course functions of visual perception within the first two hundred milliseconds after a stimulus object has been presented. Microgenesis of contour, form/shape, and surface qualities, insofar as these attributes reach visual awareness, is analysed in terms of possible models that describe it. Pertinent neural mechanisms and computational strategies are dealt with and interrelations between unconscious sensory processing, conscious perception and attention are outlined. The approaches of this symposium are multidisciplinary, covering psychophysics, computational modeling, and electrophysiology of brain processes. However, invariably, the presented data and theory are constrained by the experimental facts.

The "superficial" nature of visual consciousness: Proposal and implications

Breitmeyer, Bruno Dept. of Psychology, University of Houston, Houston, USA

The perception of visual objects depends on the conscious registration of several attributes. At early nonconscious levels of processing the contours and of surface properties are processed separately, with the contour properties processed several tens of milliseconds prior to the surface properties. However, at conscious levels of processing they are perceived simultaneously. Conscious registration of the shape of visual objects occurs only when the surface qualia are filled in between the already established yet nonconsciously processed contours.

The registration of surface properties remains the sine qua non of conscious vision.

Modeling both spatial and temporal aspects of visual microgenesis

Herzog, Michael H. BMI, EPFL, Lausanne, Switzerland Hermens, Frouke Francis, Gregory

Objectives: To jointly model both spatial and temporal properties of visual perception. Methods: Computer simulations of two neural network models of which one was previously been used to explain aspects of depth from disparity and the other one mimicking simple visual processing. Results: Both models explain the shine-through masking effect in which a stimulus is or is not rendered invisible depending on subtle spatiotemporal variations. Both models address different aspects. Conclusions: Theories of visual perception must consider both spatial and temporal aspects of visual perception jointly.

Time-frequency functions of EEG responses: Are there signatures of the microgenesis of visual perceptual awareness

Aru, Jaan Inst. für Psychologie, Humboldt-Universität zu Berlin, Berlin, Germany Bachmann, Talis Institute of Law and ECBHS, University of Tartu, Tallinn, Estonia

Visual backward masking was used in order to find spatiotemporal conditions that are suitable for producing variable correct target perception rate with invariant values of independent variables. Time-frequency broad-band EEG recordings in response to masked and masking stimuli were analysed. Bioelectrical signatures associated with correct and incorrect perception and high versus low subjective confidence in response to masked target presentation were shown to yield different temporal dynamics. The results are interpreted in the context of best-known masking theories and hypothetical functions of various gamma-band oscillatory neural processes.

The microgenesis of non-retinotopic form perception

Öğmen, Haluk Electrical and Computer Eng., University of Houston, Houston, TX, USA

Retinotopic organization and retinotopically localized receptive fields have been two fundamental pillars upon which most theoretical accounts of visual form perception are built. However, perceptual data demonstrate that a retinotopic image is neither necessary nor sufficient for the perception of form. We present a theory for the microgenesis of non-retinotopic form perception and test the predictions of the theory by using perceptual distortions that occur in anorthoscopic viewing. In particular, we show that differences in perceived velocities associated with different parts of the anorthoscopic percept can explain the perceived compression of the form along the direction of motion.

Contributions of attention to the microgenesis of conscious perception

Scharlau, Ingrid Inst. für Kogn. Psychologie, Universität Paderborn, Paderborn, Germany

Attention plays a pivotal role in conscious perception. The contribution of attention to features of the conscious percept or its build-up is currently assessed by quite a variety of experimental paradigms such as the attentional blink, masked priming, peripheral cueing, or attention-related misperceptions such as prior entry or illusory line-motion. So far, however, there are few connections, but some discrepancies among these paradigms. In my talk, I will try to join different experimental paradigms together and elucidate the different ways in which attention contributes to temporal aspects of perception.

Henny Bos, Nanette Gartrell (chair)

The acceptance of same-sex marriage, lesbian parenthood, and homosexuality varies from country to country. In this symposium, we present findings from studies on children in planned lesbian families in Canada, Italy, the Netherlands, South Africa, and the United States. The presentations focus on the children's experiences with and responses to stigmatization. The influence of the larger cultural institutions on everyday activities, family life and the children's well-being will also be addressed. The presenters come from different scientific disciplines (psychology, family studies, social political studies, psychiatry), and the presentations differ in methodology (qualitative, quantitative, and narrative studies).

The experiences of children growing up in same-gendered families in South Africa

Lubbe, Carien Dept. Educational Psychology, University of Pretoria, Pretoria, South Africa

Since the new constitution in South Africa, there appears to be an increasing openness/visibility of same-gender families. The purpose of this paper is to describe the experiences of children growing up in same-gendered families. Findings are based on personal narratives of 8 children. Children exhibit varying levels of comfort, with having two mothers, which is linked to disclosure of their family structure. The children are thoughtful about social responses to their family constellation, and show a need for openness in their relationships with others. They also receive substantial social support from various sources, such as parents, friends, classmates and siblings.

The school experiences of adolescents raised by lesbian mothers in Canada

Vyncke, Johanna D. Dépt. de Psychologie, Univers. du Québec à Montréal, Montréal, Canada

We examined the prevalence and impact of homophobic victimization and perception of homophobia in the school setting in a Canadian sample of adolescents raised by lesbian mothers. Sixty-four adolescents of lesbian mothers (aged 12 to 18) were recruited in 8 Canadian provinces and administered questionnaires on homophobic victimization and perceived homophobia, levels of disclosure about their family and well-being. Thirty-three cent of teens reported some victimization. Disclosure to more peers was associated with an increased risk of victimization. Victimization and perceived homophobia were negatively associated with teens' well-being. Province of residence was also associated with victimization. Implications will be discussed.

Children of lesbians and gays in Italy: The myth of stigmatization

Danna, Daniela Department of Social and Polit, University of Milan, Milano, Italy

Focus of this study is stigmatization of lesbian and gay families within their social environment. In-depth interviews have been conducted with a convenience sample of 22 women and 3 men living in Northern and Central Italy, both in rural and urban environments. On the whole, these families experienced little discrimination from extended family members, friends, peers, or health services personnel. Having children motivates the lesbian and gay parents to participate in the local community. These findings counter the political statements often heard in the Italian media that children of gays and lesbians would be severely disadvantaged because of stigmatization.

The USA national lesbian family study: How 10-year-old children cope with Homophobia

Gartrell, Nanette Dept. of Psychology, University of California, San Francisco, USA

This longitudinal study, initiated in 1986, has been following 78 planned lesbian families in which the children were conceived by donor insemination. When the children were ten years old, they were comparable to children raised in heterosexual families in social and psychological development; the children of unknown donors were indistinguishable from those with known donors in adjustment. More than half of the children were completely out to their peers, and nearly half had experienced homophobia. In this presentation, the children describe their responses to homophobic encounters: they demonstrate a sophisticated understanding of diversity and tolerance.

Stigmatization, psychological adjustment, and the role of protective factors among children in planned lesbian families

Bos, Henny Faculty of Social and Behavior, University of Amsterdam, Amsterdam, Netherlands

The aim of this study was to assess the extent to which children in planned lesbian families in the Netherlands experiencing stigmatization, and the role of protective factors on their psychological adjustment. Data were collected by questionnaires filled out by children themselves (N=63). Results suggest that stigma is related to psychological adjustment. Results also indicate that having frequent contact with other children with lesbian mothers did protect against the negative influence of stigmatization on self-esteem. Our findings support the idea that children in planned lesbian families benefit from the experience of meeting other children in similar family constellations.

S-002: International perspectives on professional training for clinical child and adolescent psychologists

Barry Anton (chair)

Competency based training, licensing challenges, and specialty credentialing in traditional and emerging areas of child and adolescent clinical psychology concern professionals worldwide. The purpose of this symposium is to compare international approaches to training the next generation of child and adolescent clinical psychologists. Psychologists from four countries will compare training requirements, sequencing, pedagogical approaches, licensing demands, and specialty credentialing issues that affect the professional development of child and adolescent clinical psychologists. Emerging issues such as evidence based treatment, psychopharmacology training, multicultural awareness, and access to treatment will be discussed.

Challenges to licensing and credentialing in clinical child and adolescent psychology in the United States

Anton, Barry Dept. of Psychology, University of Puget Sound, Tacoma, USA

This presentation will address challenges to licensing and credentialing for the professional preparation of delivery of clinical services by professionals in the specialty of clinical child and adolescent psychology in the United States. Children are seriously underserved in the United States and the scientific knowledge base is evolving. However, there are significant barriers to practice that include licensing challenges and specialty credentialing for early career psychologists. This presentation will analyze the mental health needs of children and adolescents as well as the present state of licensing and credentialing. Implications for international professionals will be discussed.

Emerging opportunities in child and adolescent mental health in the United States: Psychopharmacology

Brown, Ronald College of Health Professions, Temple University, Philadelphia, USA

This presentation will provide the latest updates on pediatric psychopharmacology for childhood mental health disorders including the most recent research on the safety and efficacy of many of the commonly used medications. In particular, information will be provided on the use of multimodal therapies including the combination of psychotropic medication and psychotherapy for the management of both the internalizing and externalizing mental health disorders in children and adolescents.

Cultural competencies for complex systems (family, school and community): Perspectives on training clinical child psychologists in Aotearoa New Zealand

Evans, Ian Dept. of Psychology, Te Kura Hinengaro Tangata, Palmerston North, New Zealand

Training clinical child psychologists in a bi-cultural country necessitates close attention to the importance of developing cultural competencies. Māori perspectives on children's mental health needs tend to be holistic and to emphasize the role of the extended family. To accommodate the expectations, values and hegemony of both the indigenous and the numerically dominant European populations requires service providers to acknowledge a broad interpretation of evidence-based clinical practice as well as a focus on the systemic influences of home, school, and community, for the benefit of all children.

Clinical psychology training in Ireland: Integrating evidence with clinical practice development

O'Reilly, Gary Dept. of Psychology, University College Dublin, Dublin, Ireland

An over-view of clinical psychology training in Ireland will be presented - emphasising the role of integrating knowledge of theory and research in child clinical practice. In addition the blending of conducting clinically relevant research as a core part of clinical training will be illustrated.

Scientist-practitioner training in clinical child/pediatric psychology in the United States

Roberts, Michael Dept. of Psychology, University of Kansas, Lawrence, USA

This paper will discuss professional preparation for delivery of evidence-based services by scientist-practitioner professionals in the specialty of clinical child and pediatric psychology in the United States. Children are seriously underserved and the scientific knowledge base is developing to meet the needs affecting training. We will analyze mental health needs of children and families as well as the present state of training and education. Advances in the scientific literature and rising needs for qualified professionals in the United States require attention to sequences of predoctoral, internship and postdoctoral training. Implications for international professionalism will be discussed.

Professional training for child and adolescent psychologists in Mexico

Sanchez Sosa, Juan Jose Dept. of Psychology, UNAM Nat. Auton. University, Mexico City, Mexico

Although Clinical Psychology in Mexico is a well defined and established field, training of clinical psychologists to work in the specific area of children and adolescents still receives input from a variety of professionals. As in other Latin American countries, this especialized clinical work is benefiting from the promotion of research-based practice. Educating all the way from politicians to the public in general on these and other issues is therefore a current priority of Mexican psychologists.

Scientist-practitioner training in clinical child/pediatric psychology in the United States

Jackson, Yo Dept. of Psychology, University of Kansas, Lawrence, USA

This paper will discuss professional preparation for delivery of evidence-based services by scientist-practitioner professionals in the specialty of clinical child and pediatric psychology in the United States. Children are seriously underserved and the scientific knowledge base is developing to meet the needs affecting training. We will analyze mental health needs of children and families as well as the present state of training and education. Advances in the scientific literature and rising needs for qualified professionals in the United States require attention to sequences of predoctoral, internship and postdoctoral training. Implications for international professionalism will be discussed.

Cultural competencies for complex systems (family, school and community): Perspectives on training clinical child psychologists in Aotearoa New Zealand

Fitzgerald, John Dept. of Clinical Psychology, The Psychology Centre, Hamilton, New Zealand

Training clinical child psychologists in a bi-cultural country necessitates close attention to the importance of developing cultural competencies. Māori perspectives on children's mental health needs tend to be holistic and to emphasise the role of the extended family. To accommodate the expectations, values and hegemony of both the indigenous and the numerically dominant European populations requires service providers to acknowledge a broad interpretation of evidence-based clinical practice as well as a focus on the systemic influences of home, school, and community, for the benefit of all children.

Cultural competencies for complex systems (family, school and community): Perspectives on training clinical child psychologists in Aotearoa New Zealand

Harvey, Shane Dept. of Psychology, Te Kura Hinengaro Tangata, Palmerston North, New Zealand

Training clinical child psychologists in a bi-cultural country necessitates close attention to the importance of developing cultural competencies. Māori perspectives on children's mental health needs tend to be holistic and to emphasise the role of the extended family. To accommodate the expectations, values and hegemony of both the indigenous and the numerically dominant European populations requires service providers to acknowledge a broad interpretation of evidence-based clinical practice as well as a focus on the systemic influences of home, school, and community, for the benefit of all children.

Cultural competencies for complex systems (family, school and community): Perspectives on training clinical child psychologists in Aotearoa New Zealand

Herbert, Averil Dept. of Psychology, Te Kura Hinengaro Tangata, Palmerston North, New Zealand

Training clinical child psychologists in a bi-cultural country necessitates close attention to the importance of developing cultural competencies. Māori perspectives on children's mental health needs tend to be holistic and to emphasise the role of the extended family. To accommodate the expectations, values and hegemony of both the indigenous and the numerically dominant European populations requires service providers to acknowledge a broad interpretation of evidence-based clinical practice as well as a focus on the systemic influences of home, school, and community, for the benefit of all children.

S-003: Why psychology moves towards the qualitative: Epistemological foundations

Günter Mey, Jaan Valsiner *(chair)*
All over the world it is possible to see the re-emergence of various versions of qualitative methods that offer psychologists in theory and practice new ways of making sense of complex phenomena. This symposium will bring together an internationally representative panel to discuss the epistemological foundations and possible future trajectories of such new developments. It will be demonstrated that all quantitative techniques in psychology are used for qualitatively set hypotheses, and that at the epistemological side of psychology the quantitative traditions become a special case of qualitative general methodology of psychological science.

Rethinking psychological concepts from an epistemology grounded in first philosophy
Roth, Wolff-Michael *Applied Cognitive Science, University of Victoria, Victoria, BC, Canada*
Historically, psychology has taken its concepts from everyday common language. Scientists generally attempt to get a grip on a concept by operationalizing it. However, many fail to question the categorical origins of their concept, and therefore merely reify common sense. A truly scientific psychology, however, constructs concepts that are plausible on evolutionary and cultural-historical grounds, showing how the very concept has (could have) emerged in human history. Using a case study of "responsibility," I show how the concept can be grounded in experiences that precede human-like consciousness; and I show how in everyday conversations, we see the concept at work.

Who shall survive? Psychology that replaces quantification with qualitative mathematics
Valsiner, Jaan *Dept. of Psychology, Clark University, Worcester, USA* **Rudolph, Lee** *Dept. of Mathematics, Clark University, Worcester, USA*
It is well known that contemporary mathematics is primarily qualitative in its nature. Yet psychology continues to use quantification as the standard of scientific nature of its inquiries. Adequacy of that stand is proven unrealistic both by historians of statistics (Theodore Porter) and of science (Lorraine Daston). Contemporary mathematics offers psychologists more options than the use of real numbers—in fact one of us (Rudolph) has demonstrated that real numbers are not adequate fit for most psychological phenomena. We will demonstrate how qualitative psychology can benefit from contemporary qualitative mathematics to model Christian von Ehrenfels' notion of hierarchically growing gestalts.

The importance of conceptual clarity for a thoroughly scientific and reflexive psychology
Sullivan, Gavin Brent *Berlin, Germany*
In debates about psychology, arguing that language has a "constructive" role has led to confusion about the relationship between psychological theories, objectivity, reality and materiality. Moreover, even when reflexivity has been recognized as important to psychology, it has encouraged qualitative research frameworks and practices which have not integrated the discipline. Using an example of qualitative research about theoretical psychology, I explore some of the barriers to emphasizing language and meaning in psychology which could be improved by adopting a framework that envisions conceptual clarification and theoretical work as central to a thoroughly reflexive and scientific psychology.

The researcher as a source of knowledge in qualitative methodology
Mey, Günter *Zentrum für Digitale Systeme, Freie Universität Berlin, Berlin, Germany*
Starting from an empirical example—a single case study in the field of "narrative developmental psychology"—it is demonstrated, in which way a researcher makes sense of the data by referring to theoretical reflections (sensitizing concepts) and biographical and professional experiences within a grounded theory methodology framework, combined with an ethno-psychoanalytical approach as introduced by Devereux. During this process, there is a special attention to the role of the researcher and to the way, knowledge in qualitative research is co-constructed within the epistemological triad of subject, object, and research topic.

Concept analysis as a tool to enhance our practices in qualitative psychology
Cisneros, Cesar *Dept. de Sociología, Universidad Autónoma Metropoli, Mexico City, Mexico*
The role of language on making sense of qualitative data from any approach has been emphasized to build some reflections about the ontological features of our knowledge. Subjectivity and objectivity are still an important dimensions of our current epistemological debates. Based on some examples from teaching qualitative methods in Social Psychology and doing research in the field of collective memories, I explore some theoretical and methodological aspects of how language is shaping our analytical frameworks. Some methods of concept analysis are shown and applied to basic ideas of Psychology to describe theoretical implications of getting clarity, significance and meaning.

A move which can benefit from the past: Re-readings of Vygotsky, Luria, Leontiev
Kölbl, Carlos *Inst. für Pädagog. Psychologie, Universität Hannover, Hannover, Germany*
As far as the epistemological foundations of qualitative methodologies are concerned, in particular in a genuinely psychological perspective, socio-cultural psychology provides important insights. Re-readings of selected writings of the "founding-fathers" of socio-cultural psychology will show this. First special interest will be paid to Vygotsky's "Thinking and Speech" which contains the basic material of any psychological hermeneutics worth its name. Afterwards Luria's expeditions to Central Asia will serve as an example for an empirical study based on these premises. Finally Leontiev's studies on memory and personality will be discussed as to their potential contribution to a move towards the qualitative.

S-004: Motives: Measures, mechanisms, management (Part I)

Hugo M. Kehr, Stefan Engeser *(chair)*
This symposium integrates research on implicit and explicit motives and goals; motive measurement; mechanisms underlying motive arousal and motivation; and volitional and self-regulatory goal management. Session 1 begins with cardiovascular reactivity, a measure of motivational intensity (Gendolla, Richter & Silvia), and computer-based measures of implicit motives (Spangler). Next, the implicit power motive and the necessity of taming its dark side is examined (Winter). Implicit and explicit motives are then differentiated in the compensatory model of motivation and volition (Kehr), which is used to predict flow experience (Schattke & Kehr), leading to an attempt to solve the "paradox of work" (Engeser).

Motivational intensity reflected by cardiovascular reactivity: The role of self-focused attention
Gendolla, Guido *Inst. für Psychologie, Universität Genf, Genf, Switzerland* **Richter, Michael** *Inst. für Psychologie, Universität Genf, Geneva, Switzerland* **Silvia, Paul J.**
Psychophysiological research suggests that the cardiovascular system sensitively responds to the level of experienced task demand. This holds valid for physical and cognitive challenges. As a further test of the cardiovascular system's motivational significance, two experiments tested the role of self-focused attention in this process. Integrating principles of self-awareness theory and motivational intensity theory predicted that focusing attention to the self induces a state of self-evaluation justifying the mobilization of high effort. However, up to the level of justified resources, actual effort intensity should proportionally respond to the level of task demand. Reactivity of systolic blood pressure supported these predictions.

Computer measurement of motives
Spangler, Don *School of Management, Binghamton University, Binghampton, NY, USA*
Traditionally, the measurement of implicit or non-conscious motives has required the manual content analysis of stories written in response to pictures, or the manual analysis of running text. Learning and utilizing these procedures has proven to be tedious and time-consuming, and reliability has been a problem. In this paper I describe the development and validation of a computer program to measure implicit motives. The program analyses materials about and by American CEOs, namely speeches, written materials, interviews, transcripts of meetings, and articles appearing in the business press.

Empirical foundation of the compensatory model of motivation and volition
Kehr, Hugo M. *Inst. für Psychologie, Technische Universität München, München, Germany*
This paper gives an overview of the compensatory model of motivation and volition (Kehr, 2004). The compensatory model synthesizes some previously unrelated lines of research to allow an integrated view on structural and functional aspects of motivation. Structural components of the model are implicit motives, explicit motives, and perceived abilities. Its functional processes are volitional regulation (compensating for inadequate motivation) and problem solving (compensating for inadequate perceived abilities). To provide empirical support for some of the basic propositions derived from the model, I intend to review several studies which were primarily conducted as longitudinal field studies in the management domain.

Does motive-task congruency lead to flow experience?
Schattke, Kaspar *Inst. für Psychologie, Techn. Universität München, München, Germany* **Kehr, Hugo M.** *Inst. für Psychologie, Technische Universität München, München, Germany*
The compensatory model of work motivation and volition (Kehr, 2004) states that flow experience results when the task at hand thematically matches the person's currently aroused implicit motives and when the provided skills and abilities are sufficient. To test this proposition, we assessed participants' implicit achievement motive and their flow experience during a labyrinth task. The experimental condition involved a time limit to arouse the achievement motive. The control condition involved no time limit. In line with assumptions, arousal of task-congruent motives enhanced participants' flow experience. This finding challenges Csikszentmihalyi's (1975) traditional balance-of-skill-and-challenge approach to flow experience.

Flow and happiness at work and leisure
Engeser, Stefan Inst. für Psychologie, Technische Universität München, München, Germany
Flow and happiness/satisfaction of one hundred employees were measured using the Experience Sampling Method (N = 4508 measurements). Flow was highest during work times, but still high during active leisure activity (e.g. sport, communication). Happiness/satisfaction was markedly higher during active leisure activities than during work times. This result might explain individuals prefer leisure activity compared to work, even though flow is highest at work. Additional analysis showed that the affiliation motive foster flow in leisure activities, but the achievement motive failed to explain flow and happiness at work.

S-005: Advances in self-presentation research

Karl-Heinz Renner (chair)
This symposium highlights the significance of self-presentation in various areas of psychology. From the perspective of personality and individual differences, studies on the behavioral genetics of self-monitoring (Wolf et al.), the self-presentation of Adolf Hitler (Laux et al.) and the impact of self-presentation styles on coping with social stress (Renner) are provided. Hewitt and colleagues indicate the importance of perfectionistic self-presentation in clinical settings that involve seeking and establishing a therapeutic alliance. Marcus offers a self-presentation perspective of "faking" in personnel psychology. Blickle and colleagues report on the moderating role of social skills that include managing impressions for performance evaluations.

Individual differences in self-monitoring: A behavioral genetic approach
Wolf, Heike Fachrichtung Psychologie, Universität des Saarlandes, Saarbrücken, Germany Spinath, Frank M. Fachrichtung Psychologie, Universität des Saarlandes, Saarbrücken, Germany Riemann, Rainer Fachrichtung Psychologie, Universität Bielefeld, Bielefeld, Germany Angleitner, Alois Fachrichtung Psychologie, Universität Bielefeld, Bielefeld, Germany Borkenau, Peter Fachrichtung Psychologie, Universität Halle, Halle, Germany
The present study focuses on the relationship between the dimensions of the five-factor model of personality and self-monitoring and its etiology. As part of the German Observational Study of Adult Twins self-reports of personality and self-monitoring were collected for 300 mono- and dizygotic twin pairs. Behavioral genetic analyses showed substantial heritabilities. Moreover, the relationship between personality and self-monitoring was partly mediated by genetic influences. Our findings support the importance of differentiating among the components of self-monitoring. Furthermore, self-monitoring showed unique variance independent of five-factor constructs rendering it a valuable concept for the study of behavior in social interactions.

A self-presentational view of Adolf Hitler
Gessner, Anja Inst. Personal. Psychologie, Universität Bamberg, Bamberg, Germany Laux, Lothar Fakultät für Humanwissenschaft, Universität Bamberg, Bamberg, Germany
Based on a dramaturgical approach, Adolf Hitler and his public performances are analyzed in terms of self-presentation. First, the strategies of staging Hitler used to create the impression of a charismatic leader are explored. Second, a content analysis of diaries written by contemporary witnesses of the Third Reich illustrates how the average citizen and close followers (e.g. Goebbels) experienced Hitler's self-presentation. The results show how Hitler's followers got involved into a charismatic relation-

ship towards him and which factors perpetuated this relationship (e.g. the enhancement of self-esteem) – finally leading to an excessive ruinous commitment to Hitler.

The impact of self-presentation styles on coping with social stress
Renner, Karl-Heinz Inst. für Psychologie, Fern Universität in Hagen, Hagen, Germany Laux, Lothar Fakultät Humanwissenschaften, Universität Bamberg, Bamberg, Germany
Our contribution aims at linking self-presentation and coping both conceptually and empirically. In doing so, we compare the predictive validity of the acquisitive, the protective and the histrionic self-presentation style concerning different coping forms that were assessed in a questionnaire study (N = 571) with a scripted scenario (imagining the moment before an oral exam), in a laboratory study (N = 42) involving a public speaking task and in a diary study (N = 68). Regression analyses show that the three self-presentation styles predict different coping forms. The need for a joint consideration of self-presentation and coping is discussed.

Perfectionistic self-presentation and treatment-related issues
Hewitt, Paul L. Psychology, University of British Columbia, Vancouver, Canada Flett, Gordon Dept. of Psychology, University of British Columbia, Vancouver, BC, Canada
Hewitt and Flett (2002) described perfectionism as involving traits and self-presentational strategies and suggested that whereas perfectionism traits have direct links with psychopathology, perfectionistic self presentation (PSP), is linked indirectly by affecting help-seeking and the development of therapeutic alliances. Two studies assessed these relationships. The first, using community samples, found that PSP facets are associated with behaviors inimical to seeking help for psychological difficulties. The second, using psychiatric patients, found that PSP was associated with more distress, negative appraisals of the therapist, and affective and physiological reactivity during an interview. Perfectionistic self-presentation is discussed as an important predictor of problems affecting treatment.

"Faking" from the applicant's perspective: A theory of self-presentation in personnel selection settings
Marcus, Bernd Inst. für Psychologie (I/O), Fern Universität Hagen, Hagen, Germany
Self-presentation in personnel selection settings is mostly discussed as "faking" from the organization's perspective. Unlike this predominant approach, I offer a process theory, which (a) aims to understand applicant behavior from the actor's point of view, (b) does not assume that self-presentation is illegitimate, (c) broadens the scope of the discussion beyond personality testing and interviews, and (d) predicts effects on criterion-related validity that range from negative, to neutral, to positive. Specifically, four distinct motivational and skills sets of applicants attempting to adapt their projected self-images to situational demands of attracting prospective employers are linked and used to derive predictions.

Self-presentation by political skill and job performance
Blickle, Gerhard Bonn, Germany Solga, Jutta Inst. für Psychologie, Universität Bonn, Bonn, Germany Zettler, Ingo Inst. für Psychologie, Universität Aschen, Aachen, Germany
Based on the socioanalytic perspective of job performance it is tested with 326 target employees and 507 performance raters whether motives to get along and to get ahead produce greater performance when interactively combined with social

effectiveness. Specifically, we investigated whether interactions of the Five-Factor Model constructs of agreeableness and conscientiousness with political skill predict job performance. Our results supported our hypothesis for the agreeableness-political skill interaction. Additionally, after correcting for the unreliability and restricted range of conscientiousness, we found that its interaction with political skill also significantly predicted job performance, although not precisely as hypothesized.

S-006: Comparison of curriculum in professional psychology programs in five countries: Similarities and differences in training psychologists

Sherri McCarthy (chair)
This symposia will provide descriptions of how psychologists are trained in five countries on four continents: Brazil, Malaysia, Mexico, Russia and the U.S. Similarities and differences in curriculum and educational strategies will be highlighted, and implications for the internationalization of the training of professional psychologists will be discussed.

Psychology education in Mexico
Padilla, Alfredo Dept. of Psychology, Unidad Universitaria, Ciudad Guadalupe Victoria, Mexico Tellez-Lopez, Arnoldo Dept. of Psychology, Universidad Autonoma, Monterrey, Nuevo Leon, Mexico
Psychology Specialist programs (5 or 4 years) are designed to allow students to pursue both educational and professional goals. Psychology degree programs include many required psychology courses covering basic, applied and methodological topics. Undergraduate psychology degree programs are mostly general in nature, but specialization is possible. Areas of specialization currently available include: social, political, industrial/organizational, management, forensic, neuropsychology; geriatric; familiar; deviation and developmental retardation, developmental, educational, counseling, social work and sports psychology. The tendency of the programs in psychology is to promote the social and professional pertinence through curriculum based on models of professional competence.

Psychology education in Brazil
Hutz, Claudio Dept. of Psychology, UFRGS, Porto Alegre, Brazil McCarthy, Sherri Dept. of Psychology, Northern Arizona University, Yuma, USA
A 5-year undergraduate curriculum prepares psychologists in Brazil. Additional specialty coursework, and preparation for university teaching and research, is provided in Master's and Doctoral-level programs. Courses generally included at Brazilian universities, typical assignments and teaching methods, and components of both student and institutional evaluation are described.

Psychology education in Malaysia
Jaafar, Jas McCarthy, Sherri Dept. of Psychology, Northern Arizona University, Yuma, USA
This presentation will briefly describe the classes offered and the psychology degree curriculums available at the University of Malaya. This will then be compared to other programs available in Malaysia and discussed in terms of how similar psychology education in Malaysia to other regions within Asia, partcularly Indonesia, India and the Middle East.

Psychology education in the U.S.

McCarthy, Sherri Dept. of Psychology, Northern Arizona University, Yuma, USA

Psychology education in the U.S. has typically followed a different model for preparing professional psychologists than in most of the rest of the world. A four-year undergraduate degree does not prepare professional psychologists, but rather provides general education in a variety of disciplines and prepares students for careers in areas other than psychology. An additional 2 to 4 years at the Master's level may prepare frofessional counselors, while PhD-level training prepares professional psychologists. This presentation will present an overview of the programs, training methodologies and courses typically offered at each level at institutions of higher education within the U.S.

Psychology education in Russia

Karandashev, Victor Dept. of Psychology, Grand Valley State University, Allendale, USA

Psychology Specialist programs (5 years) are designed to allow students to pursue both educational and professional goals. Psychology degree programs include many required psychology courses covering basic, applied and methodological topics. Undergraduate psychology degree programs are mostly general in nature, but specialization is possible. Areas of specialization currently available include: personality, social, political, industrial/ organizational, management, forensic, psychophysiology, deviation and developmental retardation, developmental, educational, counseling, social work and sports psychology. Psychology courses usually account for about two thirds of program curricula for psychology degrees at the undergraduate level. Another third consists of general education courses typical for all undergraduate education.

S-007: Behavioral and brain plasticity in aging

Martin Lövdén, Florian Schmiedek (chair)

Manifestations and mechanisms of plasticity, an organism's capacity for reactive change, is at the heart of several classic matters in the neurosciences and the behavioral sciences, and stretches out across the levels of analysis covered by these domains. The objective of this symposium is to convey the current knowledge about neural and behavioral plasticity in cognitive aging. Specifically, all speakers address the question whether cognitive training has significant beneficial effects on cognitive performance, brain function, and brain structure in old age and discuss the role that mechanisms and manifestations of plasticity may play in behavioral and brain aging.

Training-induced cognitive plasticity in old age

Schmiedek, Florian Center for Lifespan Psychology, Max-Plnack-Institut, Berlin, Germany Lövdén, Martin Center for Lifespan Psychology, Max-Planck-Institut, Berlin, Germany Lindenberger, Ulman Zentrum für Lebenserwartung, Max-Planck-Institut, Berlin, Germany

In the COGITO study, about 100 younger and 100 older adults practiced a computerized battery of twelve content-heterogeneous (numerical, verbal, figural-spatial) perceptual speed, episodic, and working memory tasks over 100 daily one-hour sessions. This intensive and broad intervention led to marked improvements on practiced tasks for younger and older adults, as well as small- to medium-sized effects on several tasks from the same ability domains that were included only in pre- and posttest. Whether the observed effects on unpracticed tasks are due to transfer is currently investigated with a pre-/posttest-only control group.

Structual brain plasticity induced by cogniitve training in old age

Lövdén, Martin Center for Lifespan Psychology, Max-Planck-Institut, Berlin, Germany Schmiedek, Florian Center for Lifespan Psychology, Max-Planck-Institut, Berlin, Germany Lindenberger, Ulman Zentrum für Lebenserwartung, Max-Planck-Institut, Berlin, Germany

Does extensive training of multiple cognitive tasks over 100 occasions in younger and older adulthood result in changes in structure and function of the brain? We report findings from fMRI, MRI, and DTI measurements pre and post extensive cognitive training. Results show functional and structural brain changes that are attenuated in old age.

Behavioral and brain plasticity of executive functions in aging

Dahlin, Erika Integrative Medical Biology, Umeå University, Umeå, Sweden Nyberg, Lars Dept. of Psychology, Umeå University, Umea, Sweden Stigsdotter Neely, Anna Dept. of Psychology, Umeå University, Umea, Sweden Bäckman, Lars Aging Research Center, Karolinska Institute, Stockholm, Sweden

Process-specific training can improve performance on untrained tasks, but the magnitude of gain is variable and sometimes there is no transfer at all. Here we demonstrate transfer to a 3-back task after five weeks of updating training in younger but not older adults. For younger, the behavioral transfer effect was based on a joint training-related activity increase in a striatal region that was recruited pre-training. For older, striatal activation increases were only seen in the criterion task. These findings indicate that generalization of training can occur if the criterion and transfer tasks involve specific overlapping processing components and brain regions.

Behavioral and brain plasticity of working memory in aging

Brehmer, Yvonne Aging Research Center, Karolinska Institute, Stockholm, Sweden Westerberg, Helena Aging Research Center, Karolinska Institute, Stockholm, Sweden Söderman, David Aging Research Center, Karolinska Institute, Stockholm, Sweden Bäckman, Lars Aging Research Center, Karolinska Institute, Stockholm, Sweden

Working memory (WM) is essential for many higher-order cognitive functions and declines in old age. To investigate whether older adults' WM can be improved, we examined 23 older adults (M = 63.7) and 24 younger adults (M = 26.3) in a five-week adaptive computerized WM training study, including psychometric offline testing to assess generalizability of training gains. Furthermore, we measured individuals' brain activity before and after training with functional magnetic resonance imaging (fMRI). Preliminary results indicate that (a) individuals improve their WM performance through training, (b) training benefits can partially be generalized, and (c) age- and training-related changes in brain activity include frontal and parietal regions.

S-008: Psychological factors in cardiac diseases

Amy Ai (chair)

By consensus, psychological factors play a significant role in the prognosis and treatment of cardiac diseases. This interdisciplinary symposium explores not only mental health pathology but positive psychological factors as well. International teams have investigated: 1. attribution, post-traumatic stress and growth following heart attack; 2. spiritual coping and struggle in relation to spiritual transformation in heart failure; 3. association between race and quality of life in heart failure; 4. prediction of secular spirituality for medical outcomes of

coronary bypass surgery; 5. efficacy of psychosocial interventions for smoking cessation in cardiac patients; and 6 therapy of psychological issues in cardiac diseases.

Posttraumatic stress and growth after heart attack

Vázquez, Carmelo Dept. of Psychopathology, Universidad Complutense, Madrid, Spain Castilla, Cristina Dept. of Psychology, Universidad Complutense, Madrid, Spain Karlmayer, Carlos Cardiology, Getafe University Hospital, Getafe (Madrid), Spain Diez-Abad, Paloma School of Psychology, Universidad Complutense, Madrid, Spain

This study investigates the possible course and development of perceived posttraumatic growth (PTG) after suffering a heart attack. Consecutive hospitalized patients where assessed within the first 72 hours after the attack. As part of a longitudinal design, different measures of health habits, general psychopathology, positive and negative emotions and cognitions, trauma-related symptoms, were related to participants' intention to change their lifes as assessed by the Posttraumatic Growth Inventory (PGTI). Our results showed that, in baseline, positive emotions are significantly higher than negative ones and that PGTI scores are significantly correlated with positive emotions but not with negative ones.

Spiritual struggle and transformation in patients with heart failure

Park, Crystal Dept. of Psychology, University of Connecticut, Storrs, USA

Objectives: This study examined the extent to which spiritual coping and spiritual struggle determined spiritual and psychological adjustment to living with congestive heart failure (CHF), a progressive and life-limiting illness. Methods: CHF patients were assessed at two time periods six months apart. Results: Regression analyses indicated that spiritual coping was related to increased daily spiritual experiences of the divine and increased sense of meaning in life, while spiritual struggle predicted declines in meaning in life. Spiritual struggle (negatively) and spiritual coping (positively) were consistently related to depression. Conclusions: Spiritual coping is an adaptive way to deal with CHF, while spiritual struggle reflects difficulties in adjustment.

Race and quality of life in patients with advanced heart failure

Hopp, Faith Dept. of Social Work, Wayne State University, Ann Arbor, USA Vaitkevicius, Peter Cardiology, John D. Dingell VAMC, Detroit, MI, USA Zalenski, Robert Medicine, John D. Dingell VAMC, Detroit, USA Stemmer, Karen Cardiology, VA Ann Arbor Healthcare System, Ann Arbor, USA Hinshaw, Daniel Palliative Care, VA Ann Arbor Healthcare System, Ann Arbor, USA Lowery, Julie Health Services Research, VA Ann Arbor Healthcare System, Ann Arbor, USA Ai, Amy Dept. of Health Sciences, University of Washington, Seattle, USA

Objective: To examine racial differences in quality of life among United States veterans with advanced heart failure (n=86). Methods: The McGill Questionnaire was used to assess quality of life. Separate multiple regression analyses were used to examine the relationships between race and quality of life domains. Results: African Americans (n=31) had higher scores than non-Hispanic Whites (n=53) in overall quality of life (b−0.74, SE−0.29, p < 0.05) and existential scales (b=1.12, SE=0.39, p <.01). Conclusions: Results suggest the need to recognize and support positive approaches to care among ethnically diverse heart failure patients.

Reverence and coronary bypass surgery

Ai, Amy School of Social Work, University of Washington, Seattle, USA Bolling, Steven F. Dept. of Cardiac Surgery, University of Michigan, Ann Arbor, MI, USA Tice, Terrence N. School of Education, University of Michigan, Denver, CO 80210, USA
Objectives: This prospective study examined the multifaceted effect of faith factors on medical outcomes following coronary bypass surgery. Methods: Face-to-face interviews were conducted with 177 patients before heart surgery. Medical variables were retrieved from the hospital's Society of Thoracic Surgeons' Database. Results: Multivariate analyses showed that Respect for life (sense of reverence) predicted fewer postoperative complications (PC) and shorter hospital length of stay (LOS), before PC is introduced into the equation. Prayer was also associated with reduced PC. Neither religious attendance nor spiritual experiences affected outcomes. Conclusions: PC may mediate influences of deep respect for life and prayer on LOS.

Assessment of and intervention with cardiac patients

Bengel, Jürgen Inst. für Psychologie, Universität Freiburg, Freiburg, Germany Barth, Juergen Social and Preventive Medicine, University of Bern, Bern, Switzerland Critchley, Julia Health and Society, Newcastle University, Newcastle Upon Tyne, United Kingdom
Objective: To assess the efficacy of psychosocial smoking cessation interventions in patients with coronary heart disease. Methods: Databases were searched and 16 trials were found. Results: There was a positive effect of interventions on abstinence after 6 to 12 months, but substantial heterogeneity between trials. More intense interventions showed increased quit rates. Conclusion: Smoking cessation interventions should be provided for a minimum of one month.

S-009: Advances in complex structural equation modeling

Karin Schermelleh-Engel, Andreas Klein (chair)
Topics discussed in this symposium encompass complex multitrait-multimethod and nonlinear structural equation modeling. Crayen et al. investigate the performance of multitrait-multimethod-multioccasion models based on CTC(M-1) methodology. Nussbeck et al. combine MTMM and multi-level models for the analysis of non-ordered categorical data. Schermelleh-Engel and Werner discuss problems of model fit and compare test procedures for detecting nonlinear effects. Dimitruk et al. analyze the performance of LMS and QML with varying nonlinear effects and sample sizes. Kelava et al. compare a new Bayesian approach with alternative contemporary approaches under varying predictor multicollinearity.

Performance of structural equation models for multitrait-multimethod-multioccasion data: A Monte Carlo investigation

Crayen, Claudia Berlin, Germany Geiser, Christian Methoden und Evaluation, Freie Universität Berlin, Berlin, Germany Eid, Michael Methoden und Evaluation, Freie Universität Berlin, Berlin, Germany
This Monte Carlo study investigated the performance of structural equation models for multitrait-multimethod-multioccasion data. An extension of the CT-C(M-1) model (Eid et al., 2003) for multiple latent states served as the base. The following conditions were varied: number of indicators per trait-method-occasion unit (2, 3, 4), number of traits (1 vs. 3), number of methods (2 vs. 3), number of occasions of measurement (2 vs. 3), degree of method specificity and temporal stability, and N. The models perform well if the number of indicators and N are sufficiently large. For complex models, the chi-square statistic should be interpreted with caution.

A multilevel Multitrait-Multimethod model for multiple non-ordered categorical data

Nussbeck, Fridtjof W. EZW und Psychologie, Freie Universität Berlin, Berlin, Germany Eid, Michael Department of Psychology, Free University of Berlin, Berlin, Germany
The Mutlitrait-Multimethod (MTMM) matrix has become the most often applied technique to analyze the convergent and discriminant validity of psychological scales. Multilevel (ML) models are most appropriate to analyze nested method structures. In this concribution, we combine the two approaches defining an ML-MTMM model for the analysis of non-ordered categorical data. We present and illustrate the model using a data set from educational measurement. We show how the structure of statistically interchangeable methods can be correctly represented in the model constraints relying on psychometric theory. We explicitly show how convergent and discriminant validity can be inspected in this approach.

How to test nonlinear effects in structural equation modeling: A comparison of alternatives

Schermelleh-Engel, Karin Inst. für Psychologie, Universität Frankfurt, Frankfurt, Germany Werner, Christina Psychology, Goethe University, Frankfurt am Main, Germany
As long as assumptions are fulfilled, testing for linear effects in structural equation modeling is possible by using either chi-square model difference tests or parameters' standard errors. Nonlinear models inevitably violate normality assumptions, so standard errors may be misleading. Nonnormality problems may be further aggravated by predictor multicollinearity. A simulation study compared the appropriateness of standard errors with chi-square difference tests for the detection of nonlinear effects using covariance structure analyses and heteroskedastic methods. Results showed influences of both multicollinearity and model complexity on test results. Implications for empirical analyses of nonlinear models will be discussed.

A comparison of LMS and QML for the analysis of complex nonlinear structural equation models with several nonlinear effects

Dimitruk, Polina Inst. für Psychologie, Universität Frankfurt, Frankfurt, Germany Schermelleh-Engel, Karin Inst. für Psychologie, Universität Frankfurt, Frankfurt, Germany Moosbrugger, Helfried Inst. für Psychologie, Universität Frankfurt, Frankfurt, Germany
Methods developed especially for the analysis of complex latent nonlinear models are LMS and QML. In contrast to LMS, QML has been developed as an efficient, computationally feasible, and more robust estimation technique for complex nonlinear structural equation models with several nonlinear effects. As both methods have not been tested for such complex models yet, an extensive simulation study was carried out in which the number of nonlinear effects and sample size were systematically varied. The results show that - contrary to our expectations - only small differences between QML and LMS exist.

A comparison of a new Bayesian approach for analyzing structural equation models with interaction and quadratic effects with alternative contemporary approaches

Kelava, Augustin Inst. für Psychologie, Universität Frankfurt, Frankfurt, Germany Moosbrugger, Helfried Institute of Psychology, Goethe University, Frankfurt am Main, Germany Schermelleh-Engel, Karin Institute of Psychology, Goethe University, Frankfurt am Main, Germany
Several estimation approaches for analyzing structural equation models with interaction and quadratic effects have been developed within the last 10 years, but most of them have been not examined in the context of multicollinearity. By means of a simulation study we compare the performance of Lee, Song and Tang's Bayesian approach (2007) with Klein and Moosbrugger's LMS (2000), Klein and Muthén's QML (2007), and Marsh, Wen, and & Hau's unconstrained approach (2004) under varying multicollinearity using small, medium and large sample sizes. Results will be presented with respect to the advantages and limitations of the methods.

S-010: On the theoretical status of the habit construct: Latest empirical vidence

Christian Klöckner (chair)
Whereas habit theorists take the finding that habit a strong predictors of behaviour a support for introducing habits into action models (alternatively operationalized as a behavioural script, a heuristic or a neurologically based association of situational cues and behavioural patterns) other authors question the theoretical validity of the construct and attribute the findings to structural stability of other constructs like e.g. intentions, norms or perceived behavioural control. Aim of this symposium is to foster the theoretical discussion about habits as a construct in action models and underline the discussion by latest findings on possible cognitive mechanisms behind effects of habituation.

Are habits just an artificial measure of situational and/or cognitive stability?

Bamberg, Sebastian Inst. für Politikwissenschaft, Universität Gießen, Gießen, Germany
The presentation report results from two studies evaluating the effectiveness of marketing campaigns conducted shortly after a residential relocation. The results indicate that the context change itself triggers a substantive decrease of car use and respective increase of PT use. The treatment significantly amplifies this behavioural change. Further analyses indicate that the voluntary reduction of car ownership and accessibility after the move are central mechanisms mediating the impact of the context change on travel behaviour. The treatment effect is mediated by its positive effect on PT system knowledge and its negative impact on the perceived comfort of car use at the new place of residence.

Routines and decision making

Betsch, Tilmann Sozial- und Organisationswiss., Universität Erfurt, Erfurt, Germany
Adult decision makers possess a huge repertoire of routines and habits, i.e., they have learned behaviors that promoted their goals in repeated choice situations. Cognitive decision research neglected routines over decades. This paper gives an overview of recent research on the influence of routines, habits and prior behavior on decision making. Empirical evidence indicates that routines systematically influence behavior generation, information search, appraisal, choice and the implementation of a chosen behavior in human decision makers. Granting the evidence, a broad theoretical framework is being put forward which views learning of routines as an integral part of decision making.

Habit formation as generalization of script-based choice

Fujii, Satoshi Transportat. Social Psychology, Tokio Institute of Technology, Tokyo, Japan Garling, Tommy Department of Psychology, Goteborg University, Goteborg, Sweden

Habitual behavior is regarded as script-based choice in that it is automatically triggered by limited situational cues. The strength of habit is assumed as ease of retrieval of the script from memory, which in turn depends on generality of the script. It is also assumed that generality would increase after repetition of the behavior in a stable situation, because simplicity of situational cues, that determines generality of the script, increase after repeated choices. Thus, it is argued and shown that habit formation can be regarded as generalization of script-based choice that is led by repeated choices.

Habits and information seeking in changed life situations: Insights from qualitative research

Harms, Sylvia AG Nachhaltige Mobilität, Helmholtz-Z. Umweltforschung, Leipzig, Germany

23 households who had recently relocated have been interviewed in non-standardised qualitative interviews following the grounded theory approach (Glaser & Strauss, 1967). Questions referred to the influence of residential relocations on daily travel mode choice and to information seeking activities about different transport alternatives at the new living place. We could show that the longer the time span between the relocation and our interview the more spontaneous and consistent the answers on travel mode choice were and the less information was searched. The results hint on habit weakening processes around the time of relocation and a continuous re-fixation afterwards.

Habit formation as a result of past behaviour and socialization? Findings from two field studies

Klöckner, Christian Risk Psychology, NTNU, Psykologisk Institutt, Trondheim, Norway

Study 1 (N=430) analysed car choice, car habits, norms and perceived behavioural control in a cross-lagged panel design three times within nine months. Habits showed a substantial temporal stability and relevant cross-lagged effects only of previous car choice on later car habits. Study 2 (N=389) analysed the impact of retrospectively reported travel mode socialization in the context of an action model. In a structural equation model the influence of socialization is mediated by perceived behavioural control, norms, and habit. Habits are directly influenced by "the feeling of autonomy while driving a car (19 years of age)" and "the feeling of vulnerability while walking (9 years of age)".

Habits: Associations between contexts and responses

Wood, Wendy Dept. of Psychology, Duke University, Durham, USA Neal, David Dept. of Psychology, Duke University, Durham, NC, USA

We will present a series of studies demonstrating that habit performance does not depend on a supporting goal. In our view, habits are learned dispositions to repeat past responses. Habits form as people learn patterns of covariation between responses and features of performance contexts (e.g., locations, prior actions) that are then encoded in procedural memory. In this way, habits can be triggered directly by the contexts in which they typically occur. In support of this analysis, our experimental and correlational studies demonstrate that habits are cued regardless of people's behavioral intentions.

S-011: Normative cultural conceptions of life and their influence on autobiographical remembering

Tilmann Habermas (chair)

This symposium brings together two phenomena and research areas. One regards cultural norms for the timing of transitional life events and cultural concepts of biography, specifically life scripts as the set of most salient events in a normal life. The other regards the individual selection of events for inclusion in life narratives. The symposium raises the questions whether individual autobiographical remembering is influenced by cultural norms, whether this influence develops as the norms are acquired, and whether cultural differences in the life as lived and as remembered can be explained by reference to normative cultural conceptions of life.

Acculturational or developmental changes? Expectations about the timing of transitions into adulthood among adolescent immigrants and their native German counterparts

Titzmann, Peter F. Inst. für Psychologie, Universität Jena, Jena, Germany Schmitt-Rodermund, Eva Inst. für Psychologie, Universität Jena, Jena, Germany Silbereisen, Rainer K. Inst. Entwicklungspsychologie, Universität Jena, Jena, Germany

Young ethnic German immigrants come to Germany with expectations to reach autonomy in typical transitions to adulthood later compared with local German adolescents, but gradually adopt the expectations of their local age-mates. The current study compared ethnic German immigrants with local German youth concerning developmental timetables using four annual waves of assessment. A significant change towards earlier timetables was found, but only for immigrant adolescents who had lived in Germany for two years on average and who were at least pre-pubertal at the time of immigration. Effects speak for acculturational and developmental processes as mechanisms for change in autonomy expectations.

The life script across cultures and its relation to the distribution of positive and negative memories across life

Tekcan, Ali Dept. of Psychology, Bogaziçi University, Istanbul, Turkey Tartar, Elif Eda Dept. of Psychology, Bogaziçi University, Istanbul, Turkey

The aims of the present work were to test a) the generality of Berntsen and Rubin's (2002) life-script concept across cultures, genders, and ages, b) the axiom that the dominance of positive events is a prerequisite for the bump obtained during adolescence and young adulthood in life-scripts, and c) the fit of the distribution of word-cued positive and negative autobiographical memories to that predicted by the life-script. The events and age-expectations for these events were consistent across cultures, genders and ages. Distribution of positive and negative word-cued autobiographical memories showed a poor fit to expectations based on the life-script account.

The normative and personal life: Individual and cultural differences in personal life stories and cultural life scripts

Berntsen, Dorthe Psykologisk Institut, University of Århus, Århus, Denmark Rubin, David C. Psychological and Brain Scienc, Duke University, Durham, USA

Life scripts are culturally shared expectations about the order and timing of life events in a prototypical life course. A life story is about the unique life of an individual. We examine the relation between the two notions as mediated by cultural and individual factors. American and Danish undergraduates generated life story and life script events. The life scripts of the two cultures showed only few differences. Measures of depression and PTSD consistently affected the life story but had little effects on the life script. The results underscore the stability of the life script despite variability of the life story.

The development of life story coherence from late middle childhood to adolescence and the acquisition of cultural life scripts

Bohn, Annette Psykologisk Institut, University of Århus, Århus, Denmark

We investigated the relationship between the acquisition of cultural life scripts and the degree of coherence in children's and adolescents' life stories. Participants were 120 Danish children aged 9 to 15 years. Single autobiographical event stories, life stories, and cultural life scripts were collected. Single event stories and life stories were longer and more coherent in older participants. When controlling for age, single event story coherence and life story coherence did not correlate significantly. Life script normativity increased across childhood and adolescence. A significant relationship between the normativity of life scripts and the coherence of life stories, but not the coherence of single event stories, was found.

The development of biographical knowledge from late childhood to late adulthood and its influence life narratives

Habermas, Tilmann Inst. für Psychologie, Universität Frankfurt, Frankfurt, Germany Negele, Alexa Institut für Psychologie, Universität Frankfurt, Frankfurt a.M., Germany Diel, Verena Institut für Psychologie, Universität Frankfurt, Frankfurt a.M., Germany

The theory of the cultural concept of biography posits that in adolescence a set of cultural norms for how to tell a life are acquired and that these norms influence the selection of events for inclusion in a life story. These hypotheses were tested with 140 participants of both genders aged 12, 16, 20, 24, 40, and 60, about 40 of whom were also tested longitudinally across 4 years. They answered two tests of biographical knowledge regarding age norms and biographical salience of life events and recounted life narratives. Results are expected to confirm those of an earlier, smaller study.

S-012: Fostering teaching of psychology: The European perspective

Jörg Zumbach (chair)

In this symposium, six contributions examine how teaching and learning in Psychology education can be fostered. In empirical as well as conceptual approaches the design and outcomes of traditional and technology-enhanced learning are analysed. Starting from a top-down analysis of the Bologna Agreement, over curriculum design up to cultural and target group specific issues, results of all contributions show that fostering teaching of psychology is an important and often neglected aspect of academic profession. The international European perspective contributes here to explain and identify cultural diversity as well as homogeneity and how to improve instructional design in international psychology education.

How to increase students' learning and interest in large university classes: An experimental investigation

Spinath, Birgit Inst. für Psychologie, Universität Heidelberg, Heidelberg, Germany

The present field study employed an experimental approach to investigating which learning arrangements foster students objective and subjective learning and interest in large university classes. In an introductory class to Educational Psychology, N = 451 students were randomly assigned to one out of four conditions, ranging from mandatory presence to optional presence but weekly written short statements. As expected, students who were free to attend the class but had to submit written statements each weak, had better objective learning outcomes compared to all other groups. This effect was mediated by the amount of time invested to class contents.

Teaching psychology in Europe: A network for quality enhancement

Trapp, Annie Dept. of Psychology, University of York, York, United Kingdom

In accord with the Bologna Agreement, universities are moving towards a common framework for degree programmes, for example, EuroPsy, the European certificate in Psychology. The time is therefore right to consider standards of quality in teaching psychology in Europe. This presentation will draw on examples from the Higher Education Academy Psychology Network that have had a positive impact on the teaching and learning of psychology in the UK and how these could be developed within the newly-formed European network to support psychology learning and teaching.

Podcasting a psychology undergraduate audio magazine: An evaluation

Reddy, Peter Dept. of Psychology, Aston University, Birmingham, United Kingdom *Senior, Carl* Dept. of Psychology, Aston University, Birmingham, United Kingdom *Wood, Jon* Dept. of Psychology, Aston University, Birmingham, United Kingdom

The study presented here uses podcasting technology to make available a regular audio magazine (a non-broadcast radio programme) for Aston University psychology students to enhance communication and participation, particularly with new students and with students preparing for and on placement. The programme is created by a placement student employed for the purpose and involves students and staff in interviews, discussion and features. Data from the first year of the audio magazine will be reported including impact on sense of engagement and participation in an academic community, ease of transition to university and to placement employment.

A vertical model for promoting excellence in the teaching of psychology

Bernstein, Douglas Dept. of Psychology, University of South Florida, Bonita Springs, USA

The theme of this contribution is that, because the undergraduates of today will be the graduate students and faculty of tomorrow, the quality of any department's teaching programs will, in the long run, be enhanced if every department were to apply teaching improvement programs at all levels of the organization, including faculty, graduate students, and undergraduates. Examples are provided based on my efforts to develop this vertical teaching model in the psychology department of a major university in the UK.

Competencies, employability, reflective learning, scholarship and personal development: Issues in psychology undergraduate learning and teaching

Rochelle, Kim Dept. of Psychology, Aston University, Birmingham, United Kingdom *Reddy, Peter* Dept. of Psychology, Aston University, Birmingham, United Kingdom *Moores, Elisabeth* Dept. of Psychology, Aston University, Birmingham, United Kingdom

Psychology graduates need awareness of their competencies. Psychology specific competencies are identified by the BPS (2006) and APA (2002) and the Bologna Process. Reflection on these is important for personal development and scholarship. However students may focus solely on academic grades. To overcome this a University Certificate in Personal and Professional Development has been created for students preparing for and taking internships. Students work on reflective learning, self awareness, competency development and employability over three years, before, during and after the internship. Data from the first year at Aston University will be reported.

Tutoring behavior and learners' expertise in problem-based learning

Zumbach, Jörg Bildungswissenschaften, Universität Salzburg, Salzburg, Austria

This contribution addresses issues of tutoring behavior and the level of students' expertise within a Blended Learning Problem-Based-Learning-scenario. In a 2x2-designed experiment, we analyzed the influence of tutor characteristics (tutors with expertise vs. tutors without expertise within the learning domain) on learners with different levels of prior knowledge (beginners vs. advanced learners within the learning domain). While our prior studies on novice learners revealed advantages of expert tutors on learners' knowledge acquisition, the research presented here reveals some benefits of non-expert tutoring in problem-solving groups with advanced learners.

S-013: Psychological approaches to the study of schizophrenia

Ulrich Ettinger (chair)

The aim of this symposium is to discuss the role of psychology in schizophrenia research. Neuropsychological and oculomotor tasks are used to characterise brain dysfunction and cognitive deficits and have been applied in genetic and functional neuroimaging designs (Calkins, Reuter, Ramsey). Recent evidence of impairment in social behaviour (Tse) and research employing pharmacological and psychometric models of schizophrenia (Mason) will be presented. The neural mechanisms of cognitive behavioural therapy in psychosis will be discussed (Kuipers). Overall, the symposium brings together psychologists studying different levels of function in schizophrenia, ranging from genetics through brain function and cognitive/social processes to psychological therapy.

Saccadic eye movements indicate a disorder of volitional action in schizophrenia

Reuter, Benedikt Institut für Psychologie, Humboldt-Universität zu Berlin, Berlin, Germany *Kathmann, Norbert* Inst. für Psychologie, Humboldt-Universität zu Berlin, Berlin, Germany *Franke, Cosima* Institut für Psychologie, Humboldt-Universität zu Berlin, Berlin, Germany

Neuropsychological deficits are an important component of current explanatory models of schizophrenia. Saccadic eye movement address relatively few neuropsychological functions and are particularly useful to identify specific dysfunctions. We conducted a series of studies to test the hypothesis of a deficit in the volitional initiation of saccades. Schizophrenia patients and healthy control subjects performed various experimental tasks that dissociated volitional saccade initiation from other functions such as response inhibition or the shifting of spatial attention. The results support the notion that a disorder of volitional action is a core deficit in schizophrenia.

Schizotypal traits and psychotic states: Acute effects of cannabis and ketamine

Mason, Oliver Clinical Health Psychology, University College London, London, United Kingdom

Drug models of psychosis can usefully be investigated by studying the acute and chronic effects of psychoactive substances in the context of schizotypy. Both ketamine and cannabis have contemporary relevance to the underlying pharmacology of psychotic symptoms as well as the neurocognitive mechanisms by which individuals hypothetically prone to psychosis experience psychosis-like states. We report on a new measure of psychotomimetic experiences when under the influence of drugs (Psychotomimetic States Inventory) in the context of several drug studies. Cannabis was associated with greater increases in positive symptom-like experiences in highly schizotypal individuals, whereas ketamine additionally led to greater cognitive disorganisation.

Neurocognitive impairments as candidate endophenotypes of schizophrenia

Calkins, Monica School of Medicine, University of Pennsylvania, Philadelphia, USA *Gur, Ruben* School of Medicine, University of Pennsylvania, Philadelphia, USA *Richard, Jan* School of Medicine, University of Pennsylvania, Philadelphia, USA *Hughett, Paul* School of Medicine, University of Pennsylvania, Philadelphia, USA *Gur, Raquel* School of Medicine, University of Pennsylvania, Philadelphia, USA

Neurocognitive impairments in schizophrenia are well-replicated and regarded as candidate endophenotypes that may facilitate understanding of schizophrenia genetics and pathophysiology. Several neurocognitive domains meet key endophenotype criteria, including association with illness, trait-like features, and impairment in biological relatives. Three multi-site studies have investigated University of Pennsylvania Computerized Neurocognitive Battery performance in schizophrenia families, including the Multiplex-Multigenerational Investigation (MGI;n=377), Consortium on the Genetics of Schizophrenia (COGS;n=541), and Project Among African-Americans to Explore Risk for Schizophrenia (PAARTNERS;n=1515). Despite differences in ascertainment strategies, heritability estimates are generally similar and significant (ranges: accuracy=0.11-0.66; speed=0.09-0.53). Results support particular neurocognitive abilities as candidate endophenotypes of schizophrenia.

Understanding psychopathology: Contributions of functional MRI research

Ramsey, Nick University Medical Centre, University of Utrecht, Utrecht, Netherlands

Thirty years of neuroimaging research has changed how we think about psychopathology. We have learned how to use functional neuroimaging techniques to test hypotheses about psychopathology, but progress has been slow. One reason is that this research field is so young that we hardly know how the normal brain functions in terms of brain activation. Moreover, analysis techniques advance so rapidly that it is difficult to comprehend the meaning of results of patient studies. I will present some directions of fMRI research that I believe are likely to yield significant contributions to our understanding of the mechanisms of psychopathological disorders.

CBT for psychosis: Potential mechanisms of action

Kuipers, Elizabeth Dept. of Psychology, Institute of Psychiatry, London, United Kingdom *Kumari, Veena* Department of Psychology, Institute of Psychiatry, London, United Kingdom

In psychosis, cognitive behaviour therapy (CBT) addresses positive, behavioural, and emotional symptoms while taking into account the person's individual difficulties. More recently, it has been suggested that therapeutic effects are achieved primarily by targeting negative appraisals and emotional processes associated with symptoms (Garety 2007). Our recent findings support this mechanism and show that effective CBT in schizophrenia targets brain circuits implicated in emotion-cognition regulation; symptom reduction with CBT for psychosis is accompanied by functional changes in brain regions known to be involved in attaching appropriate emotional meaning to events and stimuli and making rational decisions within social and emotional domains.

S-014: Research on mindfulness and mindfulness-based applications

Stefan Schmidt (chair)
The construct of mindfulness has it origins in the ancient Buddhist tradition and attracted recently attention in western psychology. Mindfulness stands for a technique where a person is non-judgmentally and continuously paying attention to the present moment. This acceptance based approach leads to capacities such as improved emotion regulation and meta-cognitive awareness. Interventions based on this concept were success-fully applied in many fields e.g. stress reduction, depression relapse prevention, or psychological treatment for cancer patients. The symposium summarizes research results on the psychological understanding of the construct itself in neurophy-siologic and psychometric studies and demonstrates its applicability in selected areas.

Assessment of mindfulness: A construct and its components

Ströhle, Gunnar Methodenlehre - Evaluationsf., University of Jena, Jena, Germany Heidenreich, Thomas Social Work, Health & Nurs, University of Applied Sciences, Esslingen, Germany Michalak, Johannes Clinical Psychology & Ther, Ruhr-University Bochum, Bochum, Germany Nachtigall, Christof Methodenlehre - Evaluationsf., University of Jena, Jena, Germany
In recent years, research on mindfulness as a psychological construct has received increased interest. The presentation highlights findings from two large German speaking samples (general population, students). To examine the nature of mindfulness, three questionnaires (MAAS, KIMS, FMI-SF) were compared with regard to dimension-ality, reliability and validity. Factor analytic proce-dures showed, that the instruments vary in factor structure and therefore emphasis different aspects of mindfulness. Second, correlational analysis revealed, that apparently equal facets are measured in a slightly distinct way. In general, although all measures assess mindfulness, differences occur in the operationalisation of the construct and its facets.

Effects of mindfulness based stress reduction (MBSR) on the EEG power spectrum, coherence and laterality

Naranjo, Jose Raul Inst. für Umweltmedizin, Universitätsklinik Freiburg, Freiburg, Germany Schmidt, Stefan Inst. für Umweltmedizin, Universitätsklinik Freiburg, Freiburg, Germany
Neuroimaging has deepened our understanding of meditation-related brain processes. As clinical research on mindfulness meditation has proven the efficacy of mindfulness interventions, a quest for the neural mechanisms associated with these benefits is justified. It has been reported EEG changes during mindfulness meditation in the delta, theta, alpha and beta bands. Nevertheless, the gamma band and cortico-cortical coherence during mindfulness meditation has not been investigated so far. Our aim is to investigate with high-resolution EEG (64 channels) both issues in a sample of long-term mindfulness meditators as well as novices undergoing the MBSR health program. Here we report some results.

Effects of Mindfulness-Based Coping with University Life (MBCUL): A pilot study

Lynch, Siobhan School of Social Sciences, University of Northampton, Northampton, United Kingdom Gander, Marie-Louise School of Social Sciences, University of Northampton, Northampton, United Kingdom Walach, Harald School of Social Sciences,

University of Northampton, Northampton, United Kingdom
We explored the feasibility of a mindfulness based program for students. We assessed whether it increased mindfulness, its impact on mental health and the stress system. In a first study, 11 students attended MBCUL and 8 formed a wait-list control group. There was a significant change in mind-fulness, mood, perceived stress, individual symp-toms in the treated but not in the control group. A trend towards lower overall cortisol levels was observed. MBCUL appears to be a useful pro-gramme for students. We will have conducted a further evaluation employing a randomized study on approximately 30 more participants and present further data.

Mindfulness-based stress reduction program as an intervention in patients suffering from fibromyalgia: Results from a three-armed randomized clinical study

Schmidt, Stefan Inst. für Umweltmedizin, Universitätsklinik Freiburg, Freiburg, Germany Grossman, Paul Dep of Psychosomatic & Int, University of Basel Hospital, Basel, Switzerland Jena, Susanne Inst. für Umweltmedizin, Universitätsklinik Freiburg, Freiburg, Germany Schwarzer, Barbara Inst. für Umweltmedizin, Universitätsklinik Freiburg, Freiburg, Germany Naumann, Johannes Inst. für Umweltmedizin, Universitätsklinik Freiburg, Freiburg, Germany Walach, Harald School of Social Sciences, University of Northampton, Northampton, United Kingdom
Mindfulness-based stress reduction (MBSR), an eight-week group program, has been shown to produce health benefits in a number of studies of chronic pain disorders including fibromyalgia. The effectiveness of MBSR on fibromyalgia patients was investigated in a three-arm randomized con-trolled trial. 168 female patients were randomized either to wait list or active control or MBSR. Patients in the MBSR arm significantly improved 8 weeks after the end of the treatment in all outcome variables (generic quality of life, fibromyalgia related complaints, depression, mindfulness, sleep quality, anxiety, pain perception and physical complaints). The other groups showed only weak non-significant improvements.

Mindfulness training for cancer patients: The effectiveness and mechanisms of change of mindfulness based cognitive therapy

Foley, Elizabeth NSW Cancer Institute, Macquarie University, Sydney, Australia Baillie, Andrew Psychology, Macquarie University, Sydney, Australia
This study evaluated the effectiveness of Mind-fulness Based Cognitive Therapy for cancer pa-tients. Over 200 participants with mixed cancer diagnoses (across site and stages) were randomly allocated to either the immediate or delayed treatment conditions. Treatment involved partici-pation in eight weekly sessions of two hours duration, daily meditation and attendance at a full day silent meditation session during the course. Results indicated significant improvements in mind-fulness, depression, anxiety, distress, pain and quality of life for MBCT participants. The path-ways through which therapeutic change occurred were investigated and these findings will be discussed.

S-015: Justice and deserving

Claudia Dalbert, Manfred Schmitt (chair)
Five studies investigated the relationship between justice experiences and its antecedness. Study 1 demonstrates long-term effects of relationship satisfaction on perceived justice and vice versa. Study 2 shows that just-world-belief was positively associated with justification of inequality. In addi-tion, Study 3 reveals that the association between

just-world-belief and justification of inequality is moderated by collective self-efficacy. Study 4 finds that situational and personal uncertainty explains fairness effects. Study 5 introduces an indirect way to assess an implicit justice motive.

Division of family work between the sexes: Perceived justice and relationship satisfaction

Mikula, Gerold Inst. für Psychologie, Universität Graz, Graz, Austria Bodi, Otto Inst. für Psychologie, Universität Graz, Graz, Austria Riederer, Bernhard Inst. für Psychologie, Universität Graz, Graz, Austria
The study analyzes cross-sectional and longitudinal links between the perceived justice of the division of family work and women's relationship satisfaction. The data come from a two-wave panel study with convenience samples of women from dual earner couples with children (N= 389). Cross-lagged panel analyses reveal significant long-term effects of perceived justice on relationship satisfaction and effects of relationship satisfaction on perceived justice. But the signs of the links differ depending on the changes that occurred in the sizes of women's and men's shares in the family work over the 3-years interval between the two surveys.

Belief in a just world, self-efficacy and justification of inequality

Beierlein, Constanze Inst. für Psychologie, Universität Frankfurt, Frankfurt, Germany Preiser, Siegfried Inst. für Psychologie, Universität Frankfurt, Frankfurt, Germany Wermuth, Sonja Inst. für Psychologie, Universität Frankfurt, Frankfurt, Germany Manning, Mark Department of Psychology, Univ. of Massachusetts Amherst, Amherst, MA, USA
A meta-analysis comprising seven heterogeneous samples (N ~ 1000) demonstrated consistently that a strong belief in a just world was accompanied by the justification of inequality and by low social participation. Contrary to expectations, self efficacy did not moderate these relationships. However, while the belief in the possibility of social justice was positively related to the belief in a just world, in multiple regression the belief in the possibility of social justice emerged as a protective factor decreasing the tendency to justify inequality. A further protective factor was the degree of perceived collective efficacy of a social reference group.

Does the belief in a just world always lead to justification of inequality? Moderating role of collective efficacy analyzed using structural equation modeling

Werner, Christina Inst. für Psychologie, Universität Frankfurt, Frankfurt, Germany Beierlein, Constanze Institut für Psychologie, Universität Frankfurt, Frankfurt, Germany Preiser, Siegfried Institut für Psychologie, Universität Frankfurt, Frankfurt, Germany Wermuth, Sonja Institut für Psychologie, Universität Frankfurt, Frankfurt, Germany
Collective efficacy and the belief in a just world may influence both societal participation and justifica-tion of inequality. An assumed moderating effect of collective efficacy on the relationship between the belief in a just world and both outcomes had previously not been established empirically. In a sample of 150 students, nonlinear structural equa-tion modelling has now demonstrated the inter-active effect: if collective efficacy is low, a high belief in a just world increases justification of inequality. If collective efficacy is high, justification of inequality does not increase (buffer effect). Whether this effect also generalizes to behaviour is open to question.

Emotional uncertainty and coping as moderators of fairness effects

Streicher, Bernhard Inst. für Sozialpsychologie, Universität Salzburg, Anger, Germany
In fairness theory different specific moderators of fairness effects are discussed. However, the uncer-

tainty-management-model provides a more general explanation, predicting that people are more sensitive to fairness when dealing with uncertainty in life. Accordingly, people should show stronger fairness effects in uncertain situations (state). Considering person-situation-interactions, it is assumed that personal uncertainty (trait) and ability (coping) should moderate fairness effects as well. In three studies simple slope analyses revealed, that both personal uncertainty and coping moderate fairness effects beyond situational uncertainty. Results are discussed regarding the explanation of former inconsistent outcomes, modifications of the uncertainty-management-model and research implications.

The implicit justice motive measure

*Umlauft, Soeren Inst. für Pädag. Psychologie, Universität Halle-Wittenberg, Halle, Germany **Dalbert, Claudia** Department of Educational Psyc, University of Halle, Halle, Germany*

Based on justice motive theory (Dalbert, 2001) which differentiates an implicit and a self-attributed justice motive, we developed a new measure for the implicit motive. The idea was inspired by the motive superiority measure (Eichstaedt & Scheffer, 2005) and the measure aims to assess chronic pre-activation of justice-related content in memory by word recognition. We present a series of 5 studies to test structure, reliability and validity of the new measure and discuss chances and weaknesses of the measure and the approach.

S-016: Race in a transforming South Africa

Gillian Finchilescu (chair)

The socio-political transformation of South Africa began with the first democratically elected government in 1994. The process has had tangible results in some arenas, but in others the legacy of apartheid still has a stranglehold. Race and race relations represent one of the most contested of these terrains. The symposium will consider how race and racism still manifest in intergroup relations, and in the subjectivities of individuals as they confront these changes. In addition, some papers will reflect on the role of 'race' as a methodological and theoretical concept in the project of transformation.

Is 'race' still a utile variable in South African mental health research?

Duncan, Norman Dept. of Psychology, University of Witwatersrand, Johannesburg, South Africa

Population-level disparities in physical and mental health have been well documented. In South Africa, these patterns have emphasised the utility of 'race' as an important determinant of differential health between apartheid-defined population groups. While 'race' has certainly impacted significantly on patterns of health disparities in South Africa, its uncritical use may have undermined the explanatory contributions of other variables. As part of an ongoing examination of the health disparities between South Africa's social groups, this paper aims to assess the utility of 'race' as a variable in research on determinants of mental health in post-apartheid South Africa.

Is 'race' still a utile variable in South African mental health research?

Bowman, Brett Dept. of Psychology, University of Witwatersrand, Johannesburg, South Africa

Population-level disparities in physical and mental health have been well documented. In South Africa, these patterns have emphasised the utility of 'race' as an important determinant of differential health between apartheid-defined population groups. While 'race' has certainly impacted significantly on patterns of health disparities in South Africa, its

uncritical use may have undermined the explanatory contributions of other variables. As part of an ongoing examination of the health disparities between South Africa's social groups, this paper aims to assess the utility of 'race' as a variable in research on determinants of mental health in post-apartheid South Africa.

Polemics and problematics of race in the context of transformation: Conditions of possibility for deracialisation in South Africa

*Swart, Tanya Dept. of Psychology, University of Witwatersrand, Johannesburg, South Africa **Stevens, Garth** Dept. of Psychology, University of Witwatersrand, Johannesburg, South Africa*

This paper is a theoretical overview and review of research and theorising into race and racism, and highlights its import in the context of South Africa. However, it also looks at newer areas of research and their importance, but then also illustrates the potential circularity of studies into racism and how they often do not take us forward to a point of deracialisation. Finally, the paper concludes with what we think possible key trajectories are in this area that may move us forward, given the contextual constraints of deracialisation.

African motherhood: A blessing or a damning? Developmental psychology's role in implicating mothers in children's development

*Canham, Hugo Dept. of Psychology, University of Witwatersrand, Johannesburg, South Africa **Kiguwa, Peace** Dept. of Psychology, University of Witwatersrand, Johannesburg, South Africa*

The benign and serene picture of mother and child adorns the covers of most developmental psychology texts. This paper argues that this positioning of mother and child is consistent with broader ideologies that implicitly entrench gendered inequalities by locating women within the confines of their childbearing capacity. A focus group of young black parents was conducted to elucidate their lived experiences and perceptions of the bearer of guilt for parenting 'gone wrong' in the parenting roles and expectations parents. We examine if these African discourses are consistent with the findings that see motherhood as deliberately constructed to implicate woman child development to the exclusion of fathers.

African motherhood: A blessing or a damning? Developmental psychology's role in implicating mothers in children's development

*Kiguwa, Peace Dept. of Psychology, University of Witwatersrand, Johannesburg, South Africa **Canham, Hugo** Dept. of Psychology, University of Witwatersrand, Johannesburg, South Africa*

The benign and serene picture of mother and child adorns the covers of most developmental psychology texts. This paper argues that this positioning of mother and child is consistent with broader ideologies that implicitly entrench gendered inequalities by locating women within the confines of their childbearing capacity. A focus group of young black parents was conducted to elucidate their lived experiences and perceptions of the bearer of guilt for parenting 'gone wrong' in the parenting roles and expectations parents. We examine if these African discourses are consistent with the findings that see motherhood as deliberately constructed to implicate woman child development to the exclusion of fathers.

An individual as a critical aspect in transformation projects: Do transforming institutions transform individuals?

Kometsi, Kgamadi Dept. of Psychology, University of Witwatersrand, Johannesburg, South Africa

Transforming societies rely on structural and macro socio-political changes in their pursuit of transformation imperatives. Though essential, these

changes miss out on attending to more subjective experiences of change, and resistances hereof. This presentation explores individual responses in a context of rapid political change. It utilizes psycho-analytic theories to theorize anxieties engendered in historically racist contexts at the advent of change. It poses the question 'where does racism recede to when faced with negative sanctions in a transforming context?'. This presentation proposes that individuals as constituents of society are both 'products' and 'producers' of racism, and it proffers that there is value in expending efforts targeting subjective changes to complement macro socio-political processes to advance transformation imperatives. It uses extracts from a research project that examines interracial subjective experiences.

Schooling, race and masculinity: Personal experiences of young black boys in Alexandra Township

Langa, Malose Dept. of Psychology, University of Witwatersrand, Johannesburg, South Africa

The current study looks at the shifting nature of young masculinities in post-apartheid South Africa. Semi-structured interviews were conducted with young black boys to explore how they negotiate multiple voices of masculinity in a multi-racial school. In their narratives, these boys speak about 'racialised' masculinities in school. The paper discusses how both white and black boys compete to assert and legitimize their masculinities in the school context. Black boys also speak about the difficulties in legitimizing their masculinities. They feel excluded and marginalized in a predominantly white multiracial school. Many of these difficulties are linked to issues of schooling and race.

Race, prejudice and meta-stereotypes: Their role in the persistence of self-segregation

Finchilescu, Gillian Dept. of Psychology, University of Witwatersrand, Johannesburg, South Africa

The radical changes of the past 13 years have transformed the socio-political landscape of South Africa. However these changes have not generally altered interracial relations. In this paper, I will make the argument that rejection sensitivity is one of the more powerful factors that prevent the transformation of race interactions. Drawing on a number of studies conducted by myself and colleagues, I will demonstrate that the belief that the other group thinks negatively of one's own group, contributes to the persistence of racial segregation in a variety of ways.

S-017: Health cognitions and health behaviors

Benjamin Schüz, Mark Conner (chair)

Health Psychology explores health cognitions, health behaviours and their interrelations. This symposium brings together leading contributors working on the relationships between health cognitions and health-related behaviours. In particular, the symposium will contain presentations on the effects of personality variables on health behaviour regulation (Conner), stage theories of health behaviour (DeVet), interplay between illness perceptions and health behaviour (French), impact of self-affirmation on health cognitions and beahviour (Harris), the role of self-efficacy in changing health behaviours (Rodgers), and the role of volitional factors in health behaviour change (Schüz). These individual contributions provide an integrated overview on health cognitions and health behaviours.

Conscientiousness as a moderator of the intention-health behavior relationships

Conner, Mark *Dept. of Psychology, University of Leeds, Leeds, United Kingdom*
Two studies explored the impact of conscientiousness on the relationship between intentions and health behaviors. In Study 1 University students (n = 146) completed measures of conscientiousness and components of the Theory of Planned Behavior (TPB) for exercise. Conscientiousness significantly moderated the intention-behavior relationship for exercise in an unusual context. In Study 2 12-13 year old schoolchildren (n = 539) completed similar measures in relation to smoking and three years later smoking behaviour measures. Conscientiousness moderated the intention-smoking behaviour relationship for both self-reported and objectively assessed smoking behavior. The findings indicate a role for conscientiousness in understanding intention-behavior relationships.

The role of self-efficacy in changing health behaviours: An example from exercise

Rodgers, Wendy *Faculty of PER, University of Alberta, Edmonton, Canada* **Murray, Terra** *Faculty of Physical Education, University of Alberta, Edmonton, Canada* **Scime, Giulia** *Faculty of Physical Education, University of Alberta, Edmonton, Canada* **Bell, Gordon** *Faculty of Physical Education, University of Alberta, Edmonton, Canada* **Courneya, Kerry** *Faculty of Physical Education, University of Alberta, Edmonton, Canada* **Harber, Vicki** *Faculty of Physical Education, University of Alberta, Edmonton, Canada*
Objective: To examine how self-efficacy changes with behaviour change. Method: Expectancies for exercise SE were assessed in two studies of adults (n=117 & 122) before, during and after completing 4 to 6 months of exercise. Participants were assigned to a walking or fitness centre group. Results: Repeated measures MANOVA revealed significant three-way interactions for SE in both studies. SE for walking declined in the walking, but not in the fitness centre group. SE for fitness centre increased in the fitness centre and declined in the walking group. Conclusion: unrealized expectancies may negatively influence motivation.

A test of the transtheoretical model of behavior change

de Vet, Emely *Dept. of Health Sciences, Vrije Universiteit, Amsterdam, Netherlands*
Purpose: to examine the validity of the widely applied Transtheoretical model (TTM) for fruit intake Methods: A longitudinal study examined stability and transitions between TTM stages. An experimental study compared the effects of web-based tailored stage-matched and stage-mismatched feedback on fruit intake. Results: Stage transitions inconsistent with the TTM occurred. Decisional balance, self-efficacy, and processes of change predicted stage transitions, but predictors were not stage-specific. The experimental test failed to show superiority of stage-matched tailored feedback. Conclusion: Although TTM might still have value in describing health behavior, the TTM might not be valid for explaining and changing fruit intake.

Impact of self-monitoring of blood glucose on illness perceptions and behaviour: Results of a randomised controlled trial

French, David *ARCHLI, Faculty of Health, Coventry University, Coventry, United Kingdom* **Wade, Alisha** *Johns Hopkins Univ Schl Med, Johns Hopkins Univ Schl Med, Baltimore, USA* **Neil, Andrew** *Public Health and Primary Care, University of Oxford, Oxford, United Kingdom* **Kinmonth, Ann Louise** *Institute of Public Health, University of Cambridge, Cambridge, United Kingdom* **Farmer, Andrew** *Public Health and Primary Care, University of Oxford, Oxford, United Kingdom*

Objectives Does self-monitoring of blood glucose (SMBG) lead to changes in illness perceptions and self-care behaviours in people with type 2 diabetes? Methods An open, parallel group trial. Patients (n=453) were randomised to usual care, less-intensive self-monitoring and more-intensive self-monitoring. Beliefs about diabetes and SMBG, and self-reports of self-care behaviours (diet, exercise, medication adherence), were assessed at baseline and 12 months. Results Beliefs about Consequences decreased in the control group and increased in the two self-monitoring groups (p=0.004). Neither Control beliefs nor self-reports of behaviour differed between groups Conclusions These results raise doubts over whether illness perceptions cause patient behaviour.

The impact of self-affirming on health cognition and behaviour

Harris, Peter *Dept. of Psychology, University of Sheffield, Sheffield, United Kingdom*
Results of several of our recent studies show that self-affirming (by reflecting upon one's cherished strengths or values) results in less biased processing of health-risk messages, producing potentially beneficial changes in health-related cognitions, including behavioural intentions. Health topics have included breast cancer risks from alcohol, the benefits of eating fruit and vegetables, and graphic warnings on cigarette packs. I will describe these studies, discuss the theoretical underpinnings of this approach, and consider the theoretical and applied implications of our findings.

Volitional factors in health behaviour regulation

Schüz, Benjamin *DZA, Berlin, Germany* **Renner, Britta** *Institute of Psychology, University of Konstanz, Konstanz, Germany* **Mallach, Natalie** *Psychological Methods, Freie Universität Berlin, Berlin, Germany* **Wiedemann, Amelie** *Health Psychology, Freie Universität Berlin, Berlin, Germany*
If-then planning has proven an effective intervention for health behaviour change. Planning interventions have stronger effects in individuals with strong intentions than in those without. This matched/mismatched effect should also affect retention. Research on tailoring interventions suggests that mismatched interventions have detrimental effects on participants' retention. In a RCT over three months, 194 individuals were randomised to planning and control conditions. Significant effects of the intention*intervention interaction on behaviour (η^2=.11) and attrition (OR=2.63) were found. This indicates that planning is effective for behaviour change in individuals with strong intentions, but can contribute to de-motivate non-intending individuals into refusing to participate.

S-018: Health literacy: Why medicine needs psychology

Wolfgang Gaissmaier, Gerd Gigerenzer (chair)
Physicians often think of psychology as useful for emotionally disturbed patients but not for themselves. In contrast, we believe that psychology is vital for medicine if it aims at the ideals of informed patients and shared decision-making. Yet those ideals require health literacy – the ability to properly understand medical evidence. The symposium demonstrates the need for improved health literacy and illustrates how this can be reached. In particular, misunderstandings of risks and benefits of medical treatments can often not be found in patients' and physicians' minds, but rather in the representation of information and in the structure of health institutions.

Psychology and medicine: Helping doctors to understand screening tests

Gigerenzer, Gerd *Max-Planck-Institut, Berlin, Germany*
Most doctors do not understand the outcomes of medical tests (Gigerenzer, 2002; Hoffrage et al., 2000). In cancer screening, this can cause patients unnecessary anxiety. I asked 160 gynecologists to estimate the probability of breast cancer given a positive screening mammogram. Although approximately only 1 out of 10 women who test positive actually has cancer, the majority's answer was 9 in 10. Estimates also showed large variability, over-estimation, and lower than chance-level performance. After a short lesson in using natural frequencies rather than conditional probabilities, these problems largely disappeared. This shows that proper representations can help physicians understand screening tests.

Health literacy in Germany

Gaissmaier, Wolfgang *Max-Planck-Institut, Berlin, Germany* **Silberhorn, Birgit** *ABC, Max-Planck-Institute, Berlin, Germany* **Galesic, Mirta** *ABC, Max-Planck-Institute, Berlin, Germany* **Gigerenzer, Gerd** *Max-Planck-Institut, Berlin, Germany*
Health literacy – the ability to properly understand medical evidence – is an important prerequisite to make informed medical decisions. To get an idea on the status of health literacy in Germany we first investigated the evaluation of a specific early detection method, mammography screening. We assessed how well women who are interested in screening are informed about risks and benefits, which is important as a nationwide program for screening has just started in Germany. Furthermore, we applied the medical data interpretation test (Schwartz, Woloshin, & Welch, 2005) on a broader sample to assess the more general understanding of health information.

Consistency versus accuracy of beliefs: Economists surveyed about PSA

Berg, Nathan *EPPS, University of Texas, Dallas, TX, USA* **Biele, Guido** *Neurocognition, Max-Planck-Institute, Berlin, Germany* **Gigerenzer, Gerd** *ABC, Max-Planck-Institute, Berlin, USA*
We surveyed 133 attendees at the 2006 meeting of the American Economic Association (AEA) about their beliefs and behavior regarding the Prostate Specific Antigen (PSA) test for prostate cancer. Both accuracy of beliefs and their logical consistency (i.e., the relation between the sensitivity of the test and the posterior probability of cancer given a positive PSA) was measured. Contrary to the hypothesis that individuals can be ordered along a uni-dimensional spectrum of rationality, our data reveal negative or no correlation between consistency and accuracy of beliefs. Social influences are much stronger predictors of PSA decisions than beliefs and logical consistency.

The delusive evidence of survival rates

Wegwarth, Odette *Max-Planck-Institut, Berlin, Germany* **Gaissmaier, Wolfgang** *ABC, Max-Planck-Institut, Berlin, Germany*
Survival rates are regarded as necessary information for planning health-care related responses to cancer burdens. This information should elucidate benefits of screening attendance or advantages of receiving one course of treatment over another. However, rather often survival rates underlying studies have not accounted for either the effect of competing causes of mortality or the artifacts of earlier diagnosis. Given the high-scale impact of this information on medical decisions, fifty German physicians are tested for their understanding of differently presented survival rates drawn from several cancer-related journals. Final results will highlight common misunderstandings.

Do analogies help elderly people understand medical information?

Galesic, Mirta *ABC, Max-Planck-Institut, Berlin, Germany* **Birnbaum, Michael** *Dept. of Psychology, California State University, Fullerton, USA* **Barton, Adrien** *Adaptive Behavior & Cognit, Max-Planck-Institut, Berlin, Germany* **Wegwarth, Odette** *Max-Planck-Institut, Berlin, Germany* **Gaissmaier, Wolfgang** *Max-Planck-Institut, Berlin, Germany* **Gigerenzer, Gerd** *Max-Planck-Institut, Berlin, Germany*

To make informed decisions about their health, people need to understand information about medical risks. However, many people have difficulties with understanding numerically presented probabilities and large numbers. We tested whether analogies can improve communication of medical information to elderly people with lower numeracy skills. Recall of information about mortality of different diseases, and consequences of risky behaviors, was much improved when large numbers were accompanied by real-life analogies, and when consequences were presented in tangible rather than abstract terms. The recall was improved without changes in perceived seriousness of risks and credibility of information.

How health insurance systems affect health literacy: A representative study comparing mine European countries

Mata, Jutta *Faculdade de Motricidade Human, Universidade Técnica de Lisboa, Cruz Quebrada, Portugal* **Gigerenzer, Gerd** *Adaptive Behavior & Cognit, MPI for Human Development, Berlin, Germany* **Frank, Ronald** *Bereich Studien, GfK, Nürnberg, Germany*

Does the structure of the national health system influence how much people know about interpreting screening results? We assessed health literacy of a representative sample of 10,228 Europeans from nine countries. The majority of participants largely overestimated the benefit of mammography screening and regular PSA testing. In countries exceeding 20% private contributions to total health insurance costs more men gave an accurate estimate of PSA screening benefits, suggesting some association between health literacy and self-responsibility within a health insurance system. However, women across insurance systems were equally poor at estimating advantages of mammography screening. Implications for policy-making will be discussed.

S-019: Working memory in children with special educational needs

Claudia Maehler, Gerhard Büttner (chair)

The key question underlying the different studies of this symposium is: Are there specific working memory deficits, located in different subsystems, that are associated with specific learning or intellectual disabilities? Working memory is analysed in children with specific mathematical difficulties (Passolunghi), in dyslexic subgroups (Mähler & Schuchardt), in children with intellectual disabilities (Van der Molen et al.) and Down syndrome (Lafranchi et al.). Additionally the structure of working memory in children with learning disabilities is compared to typically developing children (Roick et al.), and a comprehensive review of results in the field is provided (Alloway).

Working memory failure in children with specific arithmetic learning difficulties

Passolunghi, Maria Chiara *Educational Psychology, Universtiy of Trieste, Trieste, Italy*

Several studies have examined the relationship between working memory (WM) and arithmetic achievement, but results are still ambiguous. To examine this relationship, we compared the performance of third and fifth-graders with arithmetic difficulties (AD) and controls of the same age, grade, and intelligence on a battery of working memory tasks, differentiating between different aspects of WM. Children with AD scored significantly lower on active WM tasks requiring manipulation of the to-be-recalled information, but not in passive WM tasks, requiring the recall of information in the same format in which it had been presented, nor in tasks involving word processing.

Working memory differences in dyslectic subgroups

Maehler, Claudia *Georg-Elias-Müller-Institut, Universität Göttingen, Göttingen, Germany* **Schuchardt, Kirsten** *Educational Psychology, Georg-Elias-Müller-Institut, Goettingen, Germany*

Phonological working memory deficits in children with dyslexia have been proved in studies within the multicomponential model provided by Baddeley (1986). However there is an ongoing discussion about the specific problems of children with either reading or writing problems. In our study we administered an extensive test battery for the assessment of phonological, visual-spatial, and central-executive working memory to children with either reading (N = 21) or writing (N = 14) or both difficulties (N = 30) and an unimpaired control group (N = 30). Results reveal a specific deficit of the phonological store in children with reading disabilities.

The structure of working memory in normally achieving and learning disabled children

Roick, Thorsten *Inst. für Bildungssychologie, Freie Universität Berlin, Berlin, Germany* **Schuchardt, Kirsten** *Educational Psychology, Georg-August-University Göttin, Göttingen, Germany* **Mähler, Claudia** *Educational Psychology, Georg-August-University, Göttingen, Germany* **Hasselhorn, Marcus** *Education and Development, DIPF, Frankfurt am Main, Germany*

In his multicomponential model Baddeley provided a broad an influential account of working memory. It is however still largely untested, whether the postulated structure of the working-memory, proven with normally achieving children, is valid also for learning disabled children. 245 children were administered an extensive test battery for the assessment of phonological, visual-spatial, and central-executive working memory. About half of the children fulfilled ICD 10 criteria of a learning disability. Dimensional as well as structural statistical analyses confirmed the view, that the assumption of a tri-partite working memory structure is appropriate for both groups. Therefore, the model can be used for assessing working memory in learning disabled children.

Training working memory in children with below intellectual functioning: Is it effective and does it generalize?

Van der Molen, Mariet *Educational Psychology, University of Utrecht, Utrecht, Netherlands* **Van Luit, Hans** *Department of Education, University of Utrecht, Utrecht, Netherlands* **Van der Molen, Maurits** *Psychology, University of Amsterdam, Amsterdam, Netherlands* **Klugkist, Irene** *Methods and Statistics, University of Utrecht, Utrecht, Netherlands* **Jongmans, Marian** *Educational Psychology, University of Utrecht, Utrecht, Netherlands*

Children with mild intellectual disabilities (MID) suffer from working memory (WM) problems. Ninety-eight 15-year-old children with MID were randomly assigned to a WM training or a control group in order to study if WM performance could be improved. A battery of WM and scholastic tests were administered before and twice after the training (incl. 2 months follow-up). Regression analyses revealed significant effects on some outcome measures (visual WM, arithmetic and story recall; p's .01). The results indicate that children with MID can benefit from training, including generalizability to scholastic activities. Implementing such training within the curriculum should be considered.

Working memory in Down syndrome: Is there a central executive deficit?

Lanfranchi, Silvia *Educational Psychology, University of Padua, Padua, Italy* **Baddeley, Alan** *Psychology, University of York, York, United Kingdom* **Gathercole, Susan** *Psychology, University of York, York, United Kingdom* **Vianello, Renzo** *Educational Psychology, University of Padua, Padua, Italy*

Objectives This study is aimed at analyzing the nature of possible deficits in the central executive component of working memory in Down syndrome. Methods Forty-five individuals with Down syndrome and forty-five typically developing children matched on vocabulary scores completed three verbal and three visuo-spatial working memory tasks that systematically varied central executive involvement, and two further tasks involving different modalities of storage and processing. Results Individuals with Down syndrome performed worse in all verbal task, in visuo-spatial task 3 and in both the mixed double tasks. Conclusions The data indicate that in these individuals with Down syndrome, both the phonological loop and central executive components of working memory were impaired.

Working memory profiles and the link to learning in atypical groups

Alloway, Tracy *Educational Psychology, University of Durham, Durham, United Kingdom*

Working memory refers to the capacity to store and manipulate information for brief periods of time and is closely associated with learning. The aim of this paper is to understand the extent to which deficits in subcomponents of working memory may differentiate different groups of atypical children: those with dyslexia, Specific Language Impairment (SLI), Developmental Coordination Disorder (DCD), Attention Deficit and Hyperactive Disorder (ADHD), and Autistic Spectrum Disorder (ASD). Findings confirming differential memory profiles on the basis of developmental disorders are reported and the implications of these findings are discussed in light of support for learning.

S-020: Causal judgments under uncertainty (Part I)

Manfred Thüring, York Hagmayer (chair)

Causal judgments are of crucial importance for the human understanding of the world. Usually, such judgments are based on available information and are derived from causal knowledge. One key features of this process is that it is performed under uncertainty, i.e., neither explanations nor predictions are totally reliable. In our symposium, a number of theoretical approaches as well as experimental findings are presented that are closely related to this aspect. They address issues of causal knowledge, causal learning, and causal judgments under uncertainty in various application domains, such as clinical reasoning, complex control tasks, legal disputes and decision making.

How people cope with uncertainty and complexity in diagnostic reasoning tasks

Baumann, Martin *Institut für Psychologie, Technische Universität Chemnit, Chemnitz, Germany* **Bocklisch, Franziska** *Inst. für Psychologie, Techn. Universität Chemnitz, Chemnitz, Germany* **Jahn, Georg** *Institut für Psychologie, Technische Universität Chemnit, Chemnitz, Germany* **Mehlhorn, Katja** *Institut für Psychologie, Technische Universität Chemnit, Chemnitz, Germany* **Krems, Josef F.** *Institut für Psychologie, Technische Universität Chemnit, Chemnitz, Germany*

Explaining observations seems to involve the construction of a situation model representing the current best explanation. Observations ambiguously or probabilistically linked to alternative causal explanations increase task complexity because of the amount of information normatively to be represented in the situation model. We report results from experiments testing to what extent reasoners overlook the range of possible explanations and consequences of graded uncertainty by examining the final diagnostic decisions and the situation model content during the reasoning process. The results indicate that task complexity is reduced by implicit comprehension processes that lead to diagnostic decisions comparable to normative model predictions.

Knowing why and guessing when: Does causality warp subjective experience of time?

Buehner, Marc School of Psychology, Cardiff University, Cardiff, United Kingdom
Having and maintaining a sense of how much time has passed between one event and another is of fundamental importance to adaptive cognition. Recent demonstrations of "intentional binding" (Haggard et al., 2002) suggest that people experience a subjective shortening of time between actions and their consequences relative to unrelated events. I will present data that suggests that intentional binding is a special form of 'causal binding' (Eagleman & Holcombe, 2002). Following a reverse interpretation of Hume's principles of causality, I will demonstrate that experienced causality warps our perception of time in line with our expectations of natural timeframes.

The effects of information reliability and cost on the integration of causal information from different sources

Garcia-Retamero, Rocío Psicología Experimental y Fisi, Universidad de Granada, Granada, Spain *Catena, Andrés* Psicología Experimental, Universidad de Granada, Granada, Spain *Maldonado, Antonio* Psicología Experimental, Universidad de Granada, Granada, Spain *Muller, Stephanie* Psicología Experimental, Universidad de Granada, Granada, Spain *Perales, José C.* Psicología Experimental, Universidad de Granada, Granada, Spain
We often base our causal inferences on information that is not reliable and has to be searched in the environment. In our experiments, we manipulated the reliability of the source of information. Participants in the experiments actively search for cause-effect covariation information provided by different sources, and estimated to what extent the potential causal agent generates the effect. Our results showed that the search process was guided by the reliability of the source of information, and that decision-making and causal beliefs updating are based on different information. Participants did not integrate the searched information to make causal judgments.

Causal models in repeated decision making

Hagmayer, York Inst. für Psychologie, Universität Göttingen, Göttingen, Germany *Meder, Björn* Institut für Psychologie, Universität Göttingen, Göttingen, Germany
Most decisions we take in everyday life are repeated decisions. Likelihood × value theories – the currently dominant theoretical framework – assume that probabilities and values of outcomes are learnt and represented. In contrast, causal model theories assume that not only the instrumentality of different actions is learnt, but also the structure of the underlying causal system. Only causal model representations allow for reliable transfer to novel options and modifications of the causal system without further learning. In a series of experiments we found that at least some participants inferred

causal structure and successfully applied this knowledge in later transfer tasks.

The role of temporal factors in causal learning

Krynski, Tevye Brain and Cognitive Science, Massachusetts Inst. of Techn., Oakland, USA *Tenenbaum, Joshua* Brain and Cognitive Sciences, MIT, Cambridge, USA
When one stimulus quickly and reliably follows another, intuition often tells us a causal process is at work. Drawing on Bayesian inferential frameworks, we seek to explain causal learning from very small samples of temporal events as rational statistical inference over a representation of causality that includes a temporal delay between cause and effect. Four experiments show that, as predicted by our model, people learn causal relationships faster when the temporal delay between the putative cause and effect is less variable, and people's tendency to learn better from short delays is an artifact short delays being inherently less variable.

Mind reading aliens: Inferring causal structure from covariational data

Mayrhofer, Ralf Institut für Psychologie, Universität Göttingen, Göttingen, Germany *Waldmann, Michael* Institut für Psychologie, Universität Göttingen, Göttingen, Germany
Although human and nonhuman animals can undoubtedly learn causal model representations, there has been a debate about whether they can infer causal structure from covariation data alone in the absence of other cues (e.g.,temporal order). Using the mind-reading alien paradigm introduced by Steyvers et al. (2003), we found impressive learning performance over a wide range of parameterizations for some causal structures but also systematic failures for others. Our experiments show that people's learning capacities can be explained by pattern-based, heuristic strategies which often lead to the same conclusion as normative inferences based on causal Bayes nets.

S-021: Current psychodrama, sociometry and role-playing in therapy, organizational development, counseling and research

Christian Stadler (chair)
The Symposium shows different aspects of Psychodrama-Research. On the one hand, there are contributions concerning treatment of specific groups of patients as for example psychiatric patients, patients with sexual dysfunctions, psychosomatic disorders and traumatized people. On the other hand there are two meta-analysises on treatment effects of pychodramatic therapy and on the current status of sociometry in todays psychology. A lecture of basic research based upon the "Revised Spontaneity Assessment Inventory" is given.

Psychodrama with psychiatric patients

Bender, Wolfram Klinikum München-Ost, Isar-Amper-Kliniken, Haar, Germany
Demonstrating short examples it will be explained how the psychotherapy method psychodrama can be modified so that it takes into consideration the deficits, resources and needs of psychiatric patients.

Psychodrama in sexual therapy

Kayir, Arsaluys Dept. of Medicin. Psychiatry, Istanbul University, Istanbul, Turkey
The common form of treating sexual dysfunction is couple therapy. In our psychiatric department we treat sexual problems with group psychotherapy, especially with psychodrama. These groups are formed as women's and men's groups. Vaginismus,

rare in western cultures is the most common reason of application to sexual dysfunction treatment units of psychiatry in Turkey. Psychodrama is efficient in group-therapy sessions where social, cultural, religious and traditional issues are worked through besides individual history. Examples from different groups will be given.

Studies on treatment effects of psychodrama psychotherapy

Wieser, Michael Inst. für Klin. Psychologie, Alpen-Adria Universität, Klagenfurt, Austria
This study is concerned with a quantitative systematic overview i.e., a meta-analysis of studies on the effectiveness of psychodrama psychotherapy. The aim is to explore the kind of statistical evidence which researchers have provided for the effectiveness of psychodrama psychotherapy. The analysis shows that there are a few problems with the research design in those studies, which may cast doubts upon the quality of the outcome. A consensus on the kind of measurement instruments to evaluate the effectiveness of psychodrama psychotherapy would be very helpful to evaluate studies.

On the current status of sociometry in psychology: A review of methods and fields of applications

Spörrle, Matthias Dept. for Psychology, Ludwig-Maximilians University, München, Germany
A review of published sociometric techniques and their respective fields of application within psychology and related disciplines is provided. The techniques predominantly focus on the assessment of social status, support and rejection from the social network, and the social skills of the evaluated person. Although developmental and educational settings are the most eminent fields of published applications, sociometric works can also be found in other areas (e.g. organizational and clinical research). Similarities and specifics of sociometric procedures with regard to other forms of network analysis as graph theory and internet network research are outlined.

On the use of psychodrama and art therapy in the treatment of long-lasting psychosomatic conditions

Teszáry, Judith Psychosomatic - Psychotherapy, Karolinska Hospital, Stockholm, Sweden
Psychosomatic patients have often difficulties to think and talk about their emotions, especially in relation to their symptoms, because adequate symbols are lacking. Art and psychodramatic psychotherapy are effective in creating clear emotional states, to provide symbols for experiences of emotional significance and to help the patient integrate repressed memories of early, often preverbal traumatisation. Methods: Psychotherapy with 24 patients with long-lasting psychosomatic conditions. 1. Description of the courses 2. Questionnaires- General Heath, anxiety-depression, psychosomatic symptoms 3. Blood samples Results: decreased anxiety-depression level, increased metabolic activity, one-forth increasing working capacity.

Trauma-treatment with psychodrama

Stadler, Christian Psychologische Praxis, Dachau, Germany
The phase of psychic consolidation plays a decisive role in therapy of traumatized people. The author illustrates proved psychodrama-techniques, which are indicated in the therapeutic work with traumatized people; a spezial emphasis lies on two techniques of consolidation in Psychodrama: the establishment of a Safe Place and the help of an Inner Consultant. A review on current psychodrama-literature concerning the topic is presented. Christian Stadler

Who's afraid of psychodrama research: Empirical studies into spontaneity

Kipper, David A. Dept. of Psychology T1250, Roosevelt University, Chicago, IL., USA

Whereas clinical practice has repeatedly affirmed the therapeutic power of psychodrama based role playing interventions, quantitative research demonstrating these claims was scarce, almost non-existent The reasons for the lack of empirical research are many. Some are rooted in the theory underlying classical psychodrama, and some have been attributed to gross short-sightedness. Psychodrama research may be divided into two broad categories: Outcome research and basic research. The second category concerns the study and validation of the theoretical propositions that serve at the foundation of psychodrama. The lecture will summarize empirical studies with a new Revised Spontaneity Assessment Inventory (SAI-R)and their implication regarding the nature and meaning of 'spontaneity.

S-022: Clinical geropsychology: Prediction, assessment, and treatment of late-life disorders

Simon Forstmeier, Susanne Zank (chair)

This symposium focuses attention on how the contributions of clinical psychology address the problems faced by people in old age. The presentations cover affective and anxiety disorders, insomnia, cognitive impairment, and dementia. Some important research and practical questions are touched: What are predictors of emotional and cognitive disorders in old age? How can the early detection of dementia be improved? Which interventions have been shown to be effective in the treatment of late-life psychiatric disorders? Speakers from six different countries discuss their results that promise to be stimulating for both researchers and practicing clinicians.

Psychotherapy in old people's homes: Conception and evaluation

Laireiter, Anton-Rupert Inst. für Psychologie, Universität Salzburg, Salzburg, Austria Lenzenweger, Ralph Department of Psychology, University of Salzburg, Salzburg, Austria Krammer, Ernestine Department of Psychology, University of Salzburg, Salzburg, Austria Baumann, Urs Department of Psychology, University of Salzburg, Salzburg, Austria Messer, Randolf Seniorenheime, Magistrat Salzburg, Salzburg, Austria

Objectives: Due to general prolongation of life old people need psychotherapy more often. Methods: Cognitive-behavioral therapies of 100 seniors living in residency homes, mean-age 87, suffering from depression, anxiety and adjustment disorders, were evaluated retrospectively in an effectiveness study using data from patients, therapists and nurses. Changes in medication were evaluated by analyzing nursing documentations. Results: Therapies were effective, primarily from the therapists' and nurses' point of view. In addition a significant reduction in antidepressant, analgetic and tranquilizer-medication was found. Conclusions: Psychotherapy can be offered effectively to very old people, however progressive sickness and suffering from dementia limits its outcomes.

Treatment of chronic insomnia with cognitive behavioral therapy vs zopiclone

Sivertsen, Børge Dep. of Clin. Psychology, University of Bergen, Bergen, Norway Omvik, Siri Dept. of Clinical Psychology, University of Bergen, Bergen, Norway Pallesen, Ståle Dep of Psychosocial Science, University of Bergen, Bergen, Norway Bjorvatn, Bjørn Dep Pub Health and Pr H Care, University of Bergen, Bergen, Norway Nordhus, Inger Hilde Bergen, Norway

Complaints of insomnia are very common, especially in older adults. Previous research has suggested beneficial outcomes of both psychological and pharmacological treatments, but blinded placebo-controlled trials comparing the effects of these treatments are lacking. We compared the short- and long-term effects of CBT and zopiclone in a randomized controlled trial in 46 patients (60 yrs+). CBT resulted in improved short- and long-term outcomes compared with zopiclone on most outcome measures, while zopiclone did not differ from placebo. These results suggest that interventions based on CBT are superior to zopiclone treatment both in short- and long-term management of insomnia in older adults.

Motivational reserve: Lifetime motivational abilities contribute to cognitive and emotional health in old age

Forstmeier, Simon Inst. für Psychologie, Universität Zürich, Zürich, Switzerland Maercker, Andreas Inst. für Psychopathologie, Universität Zürich, Zürich, Switzerland

We investigated the influence of lifetime motivational and cognitive abilities on cognitive status and wellbeing in old age. 147 non-demented participants (60-94 years) completed wellbeing questionnaires and cognitive tests. A new procedure was used to estimate lifetime motivational and cognitive abilities on the basis of the occupational history using the Occupational Information Network (O*NET) which provides detailed information on worker characteristics. O*NET-based motivational abilities were associated with cognitive status and wellbeing, even when age, sex, education, and verbal intelligence were controlled. Findings suggest that motivational reserve acts as a protective factor against the manifestation of cognitive impairment and emotional problems.

The diagnosis of early dementia is improved by using computerized validated systems

Bandelow, Stephan Department of Human Sciences, Loughborough University, Leicestershire, United Kingdom

Data from 204 participants from OPTIMA, diagnosed post-mortem using the CERAD histopathological criteria, were used to assess the validity of computerized NINCDS/ADRDA (McKhann, 1984) criteria for AD and the DSM-IV (APA, 1994) clinical criteria for DAT. Three sets of computerized criteria for VaD (NINCDS-AIREN, ADDTC, VCI) were also compared against post-mortem confirmed VaD. Use of the computerized system significantly increased the specificity of the NINCDS/ADRDA diagnoses to 81%, with 'moderate' inter-rater reliability. The ADDTC and VCI criteria for Vascular Dementia (VaD) had good specificity (88%) and sensitivity (75%) for the experienced rater. The DSM-IV and NINCDS-AIREN criteria for VaD showed poor validity and inter-rater reliability.

Results from the longitudinal dementia caregiver stress study

Zank, Susanne Inst. für Psychologie, Universität Siegen, Siegen, Germany Schacke, Claudia Department of Psychology, University of Siegen, Siegen, Germany

The study assessed objective and subjective burden of Dementia caregivers over three years within a stress theoretical framework. Initially, 888 caregivers participated in the study. These subjects completed the Berlin Inventory of Caregivers' Burden at five measurement points. The inventory consists of 20 subscales with 88 items. Complete longitudinal data were gathered from 226 participants. Results show that the intensity of burden varies considerably in different dimensions and changes over time. The loss of a beloved person seems to be the greatest burden for all caregivers. The study proves positive intervention effects of day care facilities and social services.

Caregiver characteristics influence patient behaviour: Findings from the Maastricht study of behaviour in dementia

de Vugt, Marjolein Psychiatry and Neuropsychology, Maastricht University, Maastricht, Netherlands Verhey, Frans Psychiatry and Neuropsychology, Maastricht University, Maastricht, Netherlands

Objectives: The MAASBED study used a prospective design to examine the relationship between caregiver functioning and patient behaviour. Methods: Hundred-nineteen dementia patients and their informal caregivers were followed up for 2 years. Neuropsychiatric symptoms were measured with the NeuroPsychiatric Inventory (NPI). Questionnaires and (semi) structured interviews were used to assess caregiver functioning. Results: Results show that high levels of expressed emotion in caregivers and a non-adapting care strategy were related to higher levels of patient hyperactivity at baseline and 6 months follow up. Conclusions: Results suggest that caregiver functioning is important in predicting patient behaviour. Differentiated interventions should be developed and evaluated.

S-023: Mapping the phenomenal space in somatosensory and tactile perception: concepts, methodology, and application

Jörg Trojan (chair)

This symposium presents an integrated approach to multi-dimensional, multi-modal maps of subjective perception (cf., www.somaps.eu). The mathematical concept of maps offers a framework for measuring spatial and temporal properties of stimuli and objects presented to the body surface. However, the perception of one own's body and its interaction with the outside world not only incorporates sensory, but also affective and evaluative aspects. The mapping approach has the advantage that it can also be applied to the analysis of these more abstract multi-dimensional spaces. The presentations will highlight the conceptual background and report empirical results.

Measuring phenomenal space: The unifying concept of maps

Trojan, Jörg Otto-Selz-Institut, Universität Mannheim, Mannheim, Germany Hölzl, Rupert Otto Selz Institute, University of Mannheim, Mannheim, Germany

Objectives: Maps enable us to depict and analyse stimulation patterns and related brain activations in terms of their spatio-temporal properties. However, likewise approaches to perceived patterns in phenomenal space ('perceptual maps') have been rarely applied to date. Methods: We derived somatotopic maps of perceived stimulus positions on the body surface (e.g., Trojan et al., Brain Research 2006). Results: The map parameters showed specific modulations in response to experimental manipulations (somatosensory illusions, skin irritation) as well as remarkable inter-individual differences. Conclusions: Perceptual maps provide genuinely psychological measures of perceptual processes, complementary to neurophysiological techniques.

Mapping intensity and affect: Multi-dimensional scaling of pain stimuli

Kleinböhl, Dieter Otto-Selz-Institut, Universität Mannheim, Mannheim, Germany von Fournier, Anna Otto Selz Institute, University of Mannheim, Mannheim, Germany

Perception of clinical and experimental pain involves sensory and affective perceptual dimensions including specific qualities and percepts, like sensitization, depending on the type of pain and/ or the specific neuronal process involved. Multi-dimensional Scaling is an exploratory method to analyze distance measures of perceptual judgments to gain insight in the underlying dimensionality of a perceptual space. The application of this technique in perceptual mapping is demonstrated for thermal heat-pain perception, characterized by several psychophysical methods in healthy subjects and pain patients. In this model, pain perception is characterized by a low dimensional space including static vs. dynamic sensitivity and cognitive-evaluative factors.

Multi-modal somatosensation: The thermal grill illusion revisited

Petrini, Laura Health Science & Tech., Aalborg University, Aalborg, Denmark *Li, Xi* SMI, Aalborg Univeristy, Aalborg, Denmark *Arendt-Nielsen, Lars* SMI, Aalborg Univeristy, Aalborg, Denmark

The study investigates thermal grill illusions in healthy volunteers. Participants placed the palm of their right hand on 6 spatially interlaced bars at 38°C (innocuous warm) and 26°C (innocuous cold). Results: a) differences in the location of the pain illusion palm vs. fingers (p<.001), b) higher temperature discrimination on the fingers; c) blurred pain-like sensation only on the palm. The thermal grill produced sensations of "paradoxical pain" accordingly with previous investigations (Craig & Bushnell, Science 1994). However, this sensation differs in intensity and quality different areas of the hand. Psychological contributions at the perceptual level are discussed.

Mathematical models of perception and its relationship to neuronal activity

Buitenweg, Jan Reinoud Biomedical Signals and Systems, University of Twente, Enschede, Netherlands *Meijer, Hil G.E. Gembris, Daniel*

Objectives: Altered perceptual bodymaps or sensation qualities due to spatiotemporal or multimodal stimuli might involve common neuronal circuit behaviour. Therefore, we explore the feasibility of neurophysiologically informed modeling for linking physical stimuli to the perceptual space. Methods: A neurocomputational approach is applied, featuring coupled activity units for representation of discretized bodymaps. Results: The developed modeling platform covers multimodal spatiotemporal interactions. Simulations focus on benchmark experimental datasets, including perceptual and neurophysiological measures. Conclusions: Altered body perception is associated with several pathological states, e.g. phantom limb pain. The proposed modeling could provide markers for monitoring these changes and gain insights for therapy.

S-024: Analyzing pay system effects on employee attitudes, behavior and organizational effectiveness

Conny Herbert Antoni, Matti Vartiainen (chair)

Although compensation is regarded as the most costly human resource intervention, pay systems have not been in the focus of research of European work and organizational psychology. This symposium integrates different European research, which analyzed basic conditions, such as work design, and underlying mechanisms, such as perceptions of organizational justice and psychological contract breach, of pay and reward systems effects on employee attitudes, behaviour and well-being as well as on company outcomes in different businesses settings. Conclusions are drawn for pay system design and implementation as part of strategic HR management.

Use and development of total reward systems in a sample of companies during ten years

Vartiainen, Matti Laboratory of Work Psychology, Helsinki University Technology, Espoo, Finland

Total Reward Systems consist of both monetary and non-monetary reward elements. The purpose of this study was to explore, how the use and composition of Total Reward System have developed in different working life sectors. The hypothesis was that as the complexity of environments grows, increases also the variety of rewards. The data was collected by interviewing from one to three persons in over 130 Finnish companies and public organizations. The interviews were analyzed by using a model of a total reward system. The elements in use were counted, and development over years in different sectors and differences between them were evaluated. The preliminary results show that both the variety and use of different reward elements have grown.

Outcomes and perspectives of pay system research in work and organizational psychology

Antoni, Conny Herbert Arbeits- und Org.-Psychologie, Universität Trier, Trier, Germany

In this paper studies on pay systems and particularly pay for performance systems are reviewed. It is shown that existing research is dominated by cross-sectional studies analyzing pay for performance outcomes allowing no causal inferences. Few studies are analyzing mediating mechanisms to explain how pay systems work or the conditions under which pay systems work to explain the inconsistent findings. Perspectives for analyzing the effects of differential pay systems are discussed, focusing on the mediating role of organizational justice and psychological contract fulfillment, as well as on the moderating role of work design, leadership and implementation strategies.

Interaction effects of work design and pay for performance on employee attitudes and organizational outcomes

Berger, Ansgar Arbeits- und Org.-Psychologie, Universität Trier, Trier, Germany *Antoni, Conny Herbert* Work & Organizat. Psycholo, University of Trier, Trier, Germany

This study tests the assumption, that pay for performance systems, which are not aligned with work design cause stress and impair employee wellbeing as well as company performance. We reanalyzed representative survey data provided by the European Foundation for the Improvement of Living and Working Conditions covering 21 703 respondents in 15 and 5786 managers in establishments of ten European countries. We found support for significant interaction effects between pay systems based on team and company performance and work design characterized by delegating tasks with high variety and autonomy to self-regulating teams on reported stress and company outcomes.

Implementing pay for performance systems: Requirements for leadership

Maier, Christine Arbeits- und Org.-Psychologie, Universität Trier, Trier, Germany *Antoni, Conny Herbert* Arbeits- und Org.-Psychologie, Universität Trier, Trier, Germany

In this study the effects of leadership on pay and job satisfaction and affective organizational commitment were analyzed. It is proposed that the effects of transactional and transformational leadership are differentially mediated by transactional and relational psychological contract fulfillment. 351 employees of four organizations implementing pay for performance systems participated in this study. Results show that both transactional and transformational leadership could significantly explain the variance of pay and job satisfaction and organizational commitment, stressing their importance for pay system changes and outcomes. However, only the indirect effects of transformational leadership via relational contract fulfillment were confirmed.

Use and development of total reward systems in a sample of companies during ten years

Vartiainen, Matti Laboratory of Work Psychology, Helsinki University Technology, Espoo, Finland

Total Reward Systems consist of both monetary and non-monetary reward elements. The purpose of this study was to explore, how the use and composition of Total Reward System have developed in different working life sectors. The hypothesis was that as the complexity of environments grows, increases also the variety of rewards. The data was collected by interviewing from one to three persons in over 130 Finnish companies and public organizations. The interviews were analyzed by using a model of a total reward system. The elements in use were counted, and development over years in different sectors and differences between them were evaluated. The preliminary results show that both the variety and use of different reward elements have grown.

Analyzing reward system effects on employee well-being and organizational effectiveness in elderly care organizations

Hulkko-Nyman, Kiisa Work & Organiz. Psychology, Helsinki Technol. University, Helsinki, Finland *Hakonen, Anu* Work&Organizational Psycho, Helsinki University Technology, TKK, Finland *Sweins, Christina* Work&Organizational Psycho, Helsinki University Technology, TKK, Finland

Our aim is to explore the relationship between pay, pay perceptions (e.g. distributive justice), and well-being (job engagement and stress) as well as perceived organizational effectiveness over time. Previous research on pay attitudes is frequently trying to predict other attitudes. We used questionnaire data from five elderly care organizations. The data was analyzed by using hierarchical multiple regression analysis. Our results indicate that pay perceptions rather than actual pay are associated with both reported well-being and perceived organizational effectiveness. Managing reward systems in a fair way may not only help achieving organizational goals but also promote well-being.

Perceived political behavior in performance appraisal process and its effects on pay satisfaction

Karppinen, Virpi Bit Research Center, Helsinki Technol. University, Helsinki, Finland

The objective of this paper is to find out to what extent political behavior exists in performance appraisal process and whether it is related to pay satisfaction. The data was gathered from one Finnish government agency by questionnaires. The respondents' perceptions of political behavior are described as frequencies and means. Moreover, the relations between research variables were tested with correlations and regression analysis. The results indicate that the respondents have experienced quite a lot of political behavior during their performance appraisals. Furthermore, the results suggest that the higher the perceptions of political behavior are, the lower is the level of overall pay satisfaction.

S-025: Shared leadership in different work contexts: Does it improve team performance?

Julia Hoch, Barbara Künzle Haake (chair)

In this symposium, the issue of shared leadership is addressed. In shared leadership influence is not centred on a formally appointed team leader, but distributed among the team members (Pearce & Conger, 2003). Künzle and colleagues examine the relative effectiveness of shared leadership in Swiss anaesthesia teams. Hoch and colleagues investigate motive dispositions as antecedents of shared leadership in a longitudinal study. Gurtner and colleagues analyse shared leadership in medical emergency teams, whereas Wolf and Nebel examine the impact of organizational structure on shared leadership effectiveness. Finally, Manheim and colleagues review findings from a broad literature review on shared leadership.

The most effective leadership is shared: An empirical analysis of the impact of shared leadership on team effectiveness in Swiss anaesthesia teams

Künzle Haake, Barbara Organisation-Arbeit-Techn., ETH Zürich, Zürich, Switzerland Zala-Mezö, Enikö Organisation-Arbeit-Techn., ETH Zürich, Zürich, Switzerland Kolbe, Michaela Organisation-Arbeit-Techn., ETH Zürich, Zürich, Switzerland Grote, Gudela Organisation-Arbeit-Techn., ETH Zürich, Zürich, Switzerland Wacker, Johannes Institute for Anaesthesia, University Hospital Zurich, Zurich, Switzerland

In order to ensure adequate patient care, anaesthesia teams need to coordinate effectively. Leadership represents one important coordination mechanism. Observations in a simulated anaesthesia setting are used to analyze and compare leadership behaviour of high and low performing teams. We hypothesized that teams are more effective if leadership is shared amongst team members. Results showed that effective leadership is centralized on the team leader in high work load situations, whereas it is shared in phases of lower work load. We will present findings on shared and centralized leadership in anaesthesia teams and discuss their relevance for leadership training.

Achievement or Power?: The impact of individual motive dispositions on the effectiveness of shared and vertical leadership in German product development teams

Hoch, Julia Inst. für Psychologie, Technische Universität Dresden, Dresden, Germany

The goal of the present studies was to analyze individual motive dispositions as impact factors of effective leadership. Study 1 aimed to validate shared and vertical leadership (Pearce & Sims, 2002) in German student product development teams. Study 2 examined the impact of achievement and power motive on the effectiveness of shared and vertical leadership in a three-wave longitudinal study. Results show that superior achievement motive predict shared and vertical leadership. Team member achievement and power motives predict shared but not vertical leadership. This study improves our understanding of motive dispositions and their impact on shared and vertical leadership.

The impact of shared leadership on diagnostic processes in medical emergency driven teams

Gurtner, Andrea Wirtschaft und Verwaltung, Uni. für Angew. Wissenschaften, Bern, Switzerland Tschan, Franziska IPTO, University of Neuchâtel, Neuchâtel, Switzerland Semmer, Norbert K. AOP, University of Bern, Bern, Switzerland Marsch, Stephan C.U. MIPS, University Hospital of Basel, Basel, Switzerland

We analyze leadership communication in diagnostic and therapeutic processes in medical emergency driven teams confronted with a patient with ambiguous and aggravating symptoms. In the diagnostic process ambiguity should be reduced and the correct diagnosis found under high time pressure. Therapy however – given the correct diagnosis – is unambiguous and should be applied immediately. Correct and fast diagnosis and therapy will safe the patient's life. We examine the role of shared leadership (Pearce, 2004) in different phases of the diagnostic and therapeutic process. We discuss the relevance of our findings for leadership in situations with high time pressure, but high or low ambiguity.

The impact of organizational structure on shared and hierachical leadership effectiveness

Wolf, Sandra Arbeits- und Org.-Psychology, Technische Universität Dresden, Dresden, Germany Nebel, Claudia Inst. für Arbeitspsychologie, Technische Universität Dresden, Dresden, Germany

The study investigated whether leadership affects people's health and work satisfaction more strongly in organizations with shared leadership structures compared to organizations with hierarchical organized leadership structures. Preliminary findings on structural equation modelling in a sample of 364 employees reveal that leadership is perceived more intense and affects people's health and well-being in a more positive way, if leadership is hierarchically organized. Results therefore indicate a stronger effect of leadership on employees' psychosocial health and well-being if it's performed by one person. Consequences for organizational structures and assignment of leading roles are discussed.

Shared leadership: A literature review

Manheim, Nele Faculteit Economie en Bedrijfs, University of Groningen, Groningen, Netherlands van der Vegt, Gerben Faculteit Economie en Bedrijfs, University of Groningen, Groningen, Netherlands Janssen, Onne Faculteit Economie en Bedrijfs, University of Groningen, Groningen, Netherlands

Shared leadership is an upcoming concept that goes beyond the role of the formal leader in influencing team members towards the attainment of team-goals. Unfortunately, the literature on shared leadership is in a state of disarray as conceptualizations and operationalizations provided by different researchers vary considerably. We therefore conducted a review of published studies on shared leadership to identify conceptual and methodological inconsistencies. Our analysis shows inconsistencies with regard to the content of shared leadership, with regard to the attribute level of shared leadership (team versus individual), and with regard to the role of the formal leader in shared leadership.

S-026: LIFE: A dynamic interplay between neurobiological predisposition and environmental influences

Karen Bartling, Irene E. Nagel (chair)

There are two opposing views on human ontogeny: One states that neurobiological predisposition plays the major role whereas the other regards cultural and experiential influences as more important. However, accumulating evidence suggests that human ontogeny is better understood as a dynamic reciprocal process between biology and culture. This symposium will provide examples how to explore these interactive processes at various levels (i.e., cultural, behavioural, cognitive, neuronal, and genetic). The six contributions cover the entire lifespan, starting with a study on infants investigating early social interaction and ending with one on old age examining cognitive performance and brain functioning.

Infants' sensitivity to interpersonal timing and its modulation by maternal affect attunement

Bartling, Karen Lifespan Psychologie, Max-Planck-Institut, Berlin, Germany Kopp, Franziska Lifespan Psychology, Max Planck Institute for Human, Berlin, Germany Lindenberger, Ulman Zentrum für Lebenserwartung, Max-Planck-Institut, Berlin, Germany

Early mother-infant interactions are mainly non-verbal, and their success appears to depend on interpersonal timing (e.g., synchronicity, turn-taking). This study examines the development of infants' sensitivity to interpersonal timing and its modulation by individual differences in maternal affect attunement. In a continuous interaction paradigm, mothers and five- or seven-month old

infants were interacting with each other through video screens. Precision of interpersonal timing was manipulated by time-shifting mothers' video sequences. Infants of highly affect-attuned mothers were expected to detect differences between shifts in synchronous and asynchronous interactions earlier in ontogeny than infants of mothers with low affect attunement.

Achievement inequalities as students get older: The case of Hamburg schools

Caro, Daniel Abt. Empir. Bildungsforschung, Humboldt-Universität zu Berlin, Berlin, Germany

This study explores whether the academic achievement gap related to SES changes as students get older and, if so, how it changes. It is based on the Hamburg School Achievement Census 1996 to 2000 (LAU 5, 7 and 9; N ⨉ 14,000) and focuses on the academic achievement in reading and math of students aged 10-14. A set of regression techniques are applied to address this research question. Findings suggest that the gap between low and high SES students narrows with age. Key educational system characteristics to this finding are discussed.

The regulation of distance and closeness in long distance relationships

Jimenez, Fanny V. Inst. für Psychologie, Humboldt-Universität zu Berlin, Berlin, Germany

Results from a study aiming at describing inter-individual and between-dyad differences in distance regulation ability in partnerships by using tools such as 1) organization and decision structures, 2) communication structures, 3) relationship aims and investment, and 4) conflicts are presented. A focus is set on the relation between both personality traits and attachment styles, as relationship traits, and the respective application of regulation tools. The cross sectional online study included a follow up after six months, taking the interdependence of the partners into account at all times.

Genetic liabilities for adolescent problem behavior correlate and

Harden, Kathryn Dept. of Psychology, University of Virginia, Charlottesville, USA Hill, Jennifer E. Dept. of Psychology, University of Virginia, Charlottesville, VA, USA Turkheimer, Eric Dept. of Psychology, University of Virginia, Charlottesville, VA, USA Emery, Robert E. Dept. of Psychology, University of Virginia, Charlottesville, VA, USA

Various intra-familial and extra-familial social experiences are thought to influence adolescent problem behavior; at the same time, adolescents have increased latitude to influence their social environments. In this study, we investigate the extent to which genetic liabilities for adolescent problem behavior correlate with and interact with social experiences, specifically, conflict with parents, affiliation with deviant peers, and involvement in religious communities. Data is drawn from a nationally representative sample of American adolescents and their biological relatives. Results suggest that genetically liable adolescents are more exposed to adverse social environments, and they are more vulnerable to these adverse environments.

Health-related goal pursuit in young and middle adulthood

Reuter, Tabea Gesundheits-Psychologie, Freie Universität Berlin, Berlin, Germany Ziegelmann, Jochen P. Gesundheits-Psychologie, Freie Universität Berlin, Berlin, Germany Wiedemann, Amelie U. Gesundheits-Psychologie, Freie Universität Berlin, Berlin, Germany Lippke, Sonia Gesundheits-Psychologie, Freie Universität Berlin, Berlin, Germany Schüz, Benjamin Lifelong Learning and Institut, Jacobs University Bremen, Bremen, Germany

Health behavior change is a self-regulatory process that consists of goal setting and goal pursuit. The effectiveness of planning for behavior change is assumed to increase with age. The present study is part of a theory-based, longitudinal intervention study (follow-ups 1, 4, and 6 months after baseline) on multiple health behaviors. Planning was found to mediate the intention-behavior relation in older but not in younger adults. As hypothesized, effectiveness of planning strategies increase with age. This demonstrates the need for age-group specific interventions.

Task difficulty affects adult age differences in functional brain activation during a working memory task

Nagel, Irene E. *Lifespan Psychology, Max-Planck-Institut, Berlin, Germany* **Preuschhof, Claudia** *Lifespan Psychology, Max Planck Institute for Human, Berlin, Germany* **Li, Shu-Chen** *Lifespan Psychology, Max Planck Institute for Human, Berlin, Germany* **Lindenberger, Ulman** *Lifespan Psychology, Max Planck Institute for Human, Berlin, Germany* **Heekeren, Hauke R.** *Lifespan Psychology, MPI for Human Development, BNI, Berlin, Germany*
Senescent changes in working memory (WM) functioning were examined by investigating how adult age differences in the involvement of pre-frontal circuitry depend on WM load. In an fMRI study, 16 young (20-30) and 16 older (60-70) healthy adults performed an n-back task. Results from a mixed-effects fMRI group analysis showed that older adults activate additional regions in PFC even when performance levels are equal. Load-related increments in the BOLD response were greater among older adults than in young adults. Results will be discussed in terms of dedifferentiation and compensation views of age-associated changes WM-related activation patterns.

S-027: Current views on scene perception

Ben Tatler, Melissa Vo (chair)
High quality vision is restricted to a small region at the centre of gaze. Thus we must move our eyes to gather information from our surroundings. Understanding the mechanisms that underlie fixation selection is therefore fundamental to understanding visual behaviour. What drives fixation selection remains controversial. In this symposium we present a range of current views and approaches to understanding how we sample the world around us, from accounts suggesting that where we look is determined mainly by the visual characteristics of the scene to those suggesting that where we look is determined mainly by our internal goals and agendas.

Bottom up and top-down guidance of visual attention in natural environments

Itti, Laurent Dept. of Neuroscience, Univ. of Southern California, Los Angeles, CA, USA
The natural world affords a complexity which makes its comprehension highly complex. To cope with this complexity, biological systems have evolved attentional strategies which rapidly focus processing resources on the most important and relevant aspects of the incoming sensory data. Here I describe several exciting new research directions that study the joint stimulus-driven (or bottom-up) and goal-driven (or top-down) influences on attentional allocation. I describe a new computational model which processes video inputs and predicts where observers look under different task conditions. I discuss results of testing this model against human eye movement recordings over several hours of video stimuli.

A probabilistic account of feature-based attention

Vincent, Ben Dept. of Psychology, University of Dundee, Dundee, United Kingdom
How do we direct our eyes around the world? I propose that we might do so by fixating the location most likely to contain a 'target' based upon visual feature information. This was calculated using Bayes equation, allowing predicted visual search performance to be derived and compared to human data. Multiple forms of probabilistic representation were explored; some resulted in better fits to human performance, thus providing insight into our internal representations. This work forms a key component of the emerging probabilistic account of visual attention in its entirety.

Visual attention in natural scenes: A probabilistic perspective

Tatler, Ben Dept. of Psychology, University of Dundee, Dundee, United Kingdom Vincent, Ben Dept. of Psychology, University of Dundee, Dundee, United Kingdom
A probabilistic approach to visual attention is emerging. We highlight how simple, intuitive probabilistic principles can be applied to many attentional phenomena. We base this around the notion that visual attention directs the eyes to the location most likely to contain a 'target' given available cues. Some covert attention effects can be understood as by-products of prior expectation over space. Furthermore, inference in a changing world provides insights into aspects of learning and memory. The probabilistic approach is parsimonious and has strong explanatory power. Further empirical work will evaluate the utility of this approach for understanding visual attention phenomena.

Extraction of 3-D information in scenes

Castelhano, Monica Dept. of Psychology, Queen's University, Kingston, Canada Pollatsek, Alexander Dept. of Psychology, University of Massachusetts, Amherst, MA, USA
Does the visual system construct a usable 3-D representation of a scene after a single view? In the present study, we examine this question by investigating the priming of spatial layout across depth rotations of the same scene. Participants had to indicate which dot (right vs. left) was closer to them in space (Sanocki & Epstein, 1997). Large differences in rotation from prime to probe resulted in little or no improved performance. However, some spatial information was retained for small rotations in depth; suggesting some limited 3D information of a scene's spatial layout can be extracted from a single view.

A glimpse is not a glimpse: Differential processing of Frashed scene previews leads to differential target search benefits

Vo, Melissa Neuro-Kognitive Psychologie, Universität München, München, Germany Schneider, Werner Neuro-Cognitive Psychology, Universität München, München, Germany
The present study investigated the effects of inter-individual differences in rapid scene processing on subsequent eye movements during target search using 3D-rendered images of natural scenes. Participants were shown three different 250 ms previews of the search scene: identical, background, and objects preview. We found that while the objects preview did not result in search benefits, the benefit of identical and background previews greatly depended on the reported ability of the participants to distinguish between previews. The results imply inter-individual differences in establishing initial scene representations, which modulate eye movement control and target search benefits in real-world scenes.

Knowing where to look: The relationships of gaze and action

Land, Michael School of Life Sciences, University of Sussex, Brighton, United Kingdom
For most of the evolutionary history of the human brain, before writing and computer screens, the principal task of vision was to direct action. This involves four cooperating systems: the gaze control, visual and the motor systems, all coordinated by a schema system that selects which acts to perform. In this talk I will give examples from everyday activities such as food preparation, driving and ball sports to illustrate the way these systems work together, and I will speculate about their neural bases.

S-028: Applying time perspective to understand and solve social issues

Nicolas Fieulaine, Taciano L. Milfont (chair)
Time perspective has been a central psychological construct, and recent research has applied this construct to understand and solve relevant social problems. The aim of this symposium is to present an overview of research relating time perspective and social issues, such as social exclusion, antisocial behaviour, socio-cultural contexts, corporate culture or environmental problems. The presentations of this symposium thus highlight the importance of time perspective in psychological research dealing with social issues

Time perspective and social exclusion: Back to Lewin's practical theory of psychological field

Fieulaine, Nicolas Dept. of Social Psychology, University of Lyon, Bron Cedex, France
In his seminal work concerning time perspective (TP), Kurt Lewin underlined the importance of taking into account the temporal dimension of psychological field when analyzing lived experiences of social exclusion [Lewin, K. (1942). Time Perspective and Morale. In G. Watson (Ed.), Civilian Morale. Boston, Houghton Mifflin]. Since, numerous works made appear the central role of psychological time in the impact of unemployment and exclusion on subjective well-being. Based on results from various quantitative field researches performed in France (N=457), this presentation will discuss the stake TP may represent in the context of growing social insecurity in Europe, and its contribution to elaborate evidence-based interventions

Sustainable behavior and time perspective: Present, past and future orientation and their relationships with water conservation behavior

Corral Verdugo, Victor Division de Ciencias Sociales, Universidad de Sorona, Mexico, Mexico Pinheiro, Jose Department of Psychology, U.F.R.N., Natal, R.N., Brazil
300 individuals at a Mexican city responded to Zimbardo's Time Perspective Inventory (ZTPI), and self-reported how frequently they engaged in water conservation practices. Results were processed within two structural equation models, which showed that present orientation negatively affected water conservation. Water conservation did not correlate with past orientation. Yet, that pro-environmental behavior significantly and positively was influenced by Future Orientation. Women reported a higher involvement in water conservation practices, whereas adult individuals (> 18 years old) and those with higher schooling levels presented a higher Future Orientation. Proposals considering these results are discussed aimed at developing sustainable attitudes and behaviors.

Future orientation, cognitive development and antisocial behavior

Frias-Armenta, Martha Law, University of Sonora, Hermosillo, Mexico

The aim of this study was to investigate the interrelations between antisocial behavior, future orientation, impulsivity and risk seeking among college students at a Latin American University; 300 students participated. They responded temporal perspective, impulsivity, risk seeking, and antisocial behavior scales. Results showed that future orientation, impulsivity and risk seeking constituted a second-order factor indicating a deficit in cognitive development, in which future orientation negatively loads on the second-order factor. In turn the deficit in cognitive development had a positive effect on antisocial behavior. These results reinforce the idea that lack in future orientation is a correlate of antisocial behavior.

Turkish adolescents and college students time perspectives

Kislali Erginbilgic, Altinay Dept. of Public Administration, Yeditepe University, Istanbul, Turkey *Artar, Muge* EDUCATIONAL PSYCHOLOGY, Ankara University, Ankara, Turkey

This study aims at comparing a Turkish adolescent group's (N: 750) time perspective with previously measured college students' time perspectives (N: 2750). An individual's time perspective is influenced by one's home culture, dominant religious orientation, socio-economical status, and also the economical/political instability, personal or societal traumatic events etc. The majority of the Turkish population is muslim, and has been living in a very traumatic environment (war in Irak, long lasting in home terrorism, 2001 economical crisis, and 1999 earthquake etc.). Therefore comparisons between different age, gender, socioeconomical etc. groups will be discussed in light of the country's specific conditions.

Organizational time perspective and corporate culture

Nestik, Timofey Social and Economic Psychology, Russian Academy of Sciences, Moscow, Russia

This study investigates the notion and structure of organizational time perspective, the interrelations between attitudes toward organizational past, present and future and characteristics of organizational culture. The exploratory study of 12 organizations (N=429) and among MBA students (N=131) showed that dimensions of organizational time perspective are significantly correlated with organizational trust, strength of corporate culture and its typological characteristics. The dimensions of attitude toward time in social groups and organizations are discussed. Implications for future research of time perspective in social groups are explored.

Time perspective and environmental issues

Milfont, Taciano L. School of Psychology, Victoria Univ. of Wellington, Wellington, New Zealand

There is increasing evidence that human behaviour has been producing unprecedented environmental problems. Several studies have related time perspective orientations to environmental issues. Research has found, for example, that future orientation is related to environmental attitudes and ecological behaviours. In this paper, I first present a brief overview of time perspective research, and then present a review of the use of the time perspective measures, such as the Zimbardo Time Perspective Inventory (ZTPI), in environmental issues research. I illustrate this with data from my ongoing programme of research as well as from other published data. Implications for research on time perspective and environmental psychology are discussed and presented.

S-029: Face processing: Current fields of interest

Claus-Christian Carbon, Janek Lobmaier (chair)

An overview of different recent fields of interests are given. Starting with talks on processing faces in general and emotions and expressions in particular, applied fields such as prosopagnosia and computer simulation of face processing skills are portrayed.

What is the cognitive basis of impairments in congenital prosopagnosia?

Carbon, Claus-Christian Inst. für Psychologie, Universität Wien, Wien, Austria

Prosopagnosia (PA), sometimes termed as "face blindness", is a disorder concerning the recognition of familiar faces. Face research discriminates between an acquired (aPA) and a congenital form of prosopagnosia (cPA). Here, we focused on the underlying processes that are impaired in cPA, which enables to identify processes which are suspected to be the essential ones for processing faces on an expert level. Configural/holistic processing seems to be a key processing mode with respect to general face processing and what we call 'face expertise'.

Emotional expression modulates perceived gaze direction

Lobmaier, Janek School of Psychology, University of St. Andrews, St. Andrews, United Kingdom *Perrett, David I.* School of Psychology, University of St. Andrews, St. Andrews, United Kingdom

Various factors influence the interpretation of gaze perception. Here we show that gaze perception is influenced by the emotional expression of a face. In a forced choice yes-no task participants judged whether a presented face was looking at them or not. Eight faces were used as stimuli, each expressing four different emotional expressions (angry, fearful, happy, and neutral) in different viewing angles. The data revealed that happy faces are relatively more likely to be judged as looking at an observer than angry, fearful or neutral faces. These findings are discussed on the background of the self-referential positivity bias.

The role of global and local information in face processing

Schwaninger, Adrian Inst. für Psychologie, Universität Zürich, Zürich, Switzerland

In this study, face recognition across viewpoint was investigated. In Experiment 1, we found systematic effects of viewpoint; recognition performance increased as the angle between the learned view and the tested view decreased. This finding is consistent with face processing models based on 2D-view interpolation. Experiments 2 and 3 were the same as Experiment 1 expect for the fact that in the testing phase, the faces were presented scrambled or blurred. The results demonstrated that human observers are capable of recognizing faces across different viewpoints on the sole basis of isolated featural information and of isolated configural information.

Identity verification from photographs in travel documents: The role of expertise, race and inversion

Chiller-Glaus, Sarah Inst. für Psychologie, Universität Zürich, Zürich, Switzerland *Schwaninger, Adrian* Inst. für Psychologie, Universität Zürich, Zürich, Switzerland *Hofer, Franziska* Inst. für Psychologie, Universität Zürich, Zürich, Switzerland

At border control, security personnel should identify passengers by means of their passport photograph. The human ability for identification from photographs, however, is limited. In three experiments, we investigated identity verification performance of novices, passport inspectors, and police officers of a specialist investigating task force. Caucasian and Asian photographs were used as stimuli, presentation occurred upright and inverted. The results showed that performance was highly error-prone. Security personnel did not perform better than novices. Results on the other-race effect were ambiguous. Performance was reduced by inversion. Our findings put into question the human ability to reliably verify identity from photographs.

Characteristic dynamic information for facial expression recognition

Cunningham, Douglas WSI / GRIS, Universität Tübingen, Tübingen, Germany

Perhaps one of the most flexible and least understood communication channels is the face. Most experiments on facial communication has focused on at most six "universal" expressions, ignoring the conversational or cognitive expressions. Moreover, they generally used only static stimuli. Human faces, however, are rarely static, demonstrating instead an impressive range and breadth of spatiotemporal characteristics. This talk will briefly describe several experiments that demonstrate conclusively not only that dynamic facial expressions are recognized more easily and accurately than static expressions, but that dynamic expressions are processing an a manner that, at least in part, fundamentally different than static expressions.

Adaptation effects: Where do they lead us to?

Ditye, Thomas Fakultät für Psychologie, Universität Wien, Wien, Austria

Adaptation to configurally distorted faces of famous persons was investigated, with emphasis on the duration of observed adaptation-effects as well as their level of generalization. Due to the adaptation processes participants' evaluation of the faces' veridical version was biased towards the perceived distortion. This effect generalized to other pictures of the same celebri-ties and even transferred to completely new pictures of other famous persons. Further, the effect was still observed one week after the adaptation, yet to a weaker extent. These findings provide valuable insight in how faces are represented in memory and how these representa-tions are organized.

Event-related potentials of face recognition: Geometric distortions and the N250r brain response to stimulus repetitions

Bindemann, Markus Dept. of Psychology, University of Glasgow, Glasgow, United Kingdom *Burton, Mike* Psychology, University of Glasgow, Glasgow, United Kingdom *Leuthold, Hartmut* Psychology, University of Glasgow, Glasgow, United Kingdom *Schweinberger, Stefan* Psychology, Friedrich-Schiller-Universität, Jena, Germany

The N250r ERP has been related to activation of image-independent representations of familiar faces during recognition. However, N250r also shows some image-specificity, with smaller activation across repetitions of two different images of the same face than across the same image, suggesting a component coding visual overlap. This study investigated whether N250r is equally attenuated when stretched faces prime unstretched images of the same face. The results show that N250r is equivalent for same-image priming and priming from stretched onto unstretched faces. This demonstrates that N250r does not simply reflect superficial visual overlap but is related to face recognition.

S-030: Same-sex marriage and legalized relationships: An international perspective

Esther Rothblum (chair)

At a time when heterosexual marriage rates are declining, many countries and localities are advocating for the rights of lesbians and gay men to enter legalized relationships, including marriage. This symposium will present social science research on same-sex couples in legalized relationships (marriages or registered domestic partnerships) in India, France, Scandinavia, Spain, and Iceland. Most of the research on same-sex couples has focused on legal issues, so this will be one of the first international overviews of how same-sex partnership and marriage legislation affects demographic and relationship factors.

Same-sex marriage and legalized relationships in the United States: I do, or do I?

Rothblum, Esther Dept. of Women's Studies, San Diego State University, San Diego, USA
This talk will focus on two research projects. The first compared same-sex couples who had civil unions in Vermont during the first year of any same-sex legislation in the U.S., same-sex couples in their friendship circles who had not had civil unions, and heterosexual married siblings. All three groups were surveyed again three years later to look at changes in relationship satisfaction and relationship termination. The second project compared couples who had civil unions in Vermont, domestic partnerships in California, or same-sex marriage in Massachusetts, to examine the symbolism of marriage for same-sex couples.

Between law and symbol: The meanings of the French "Civil Solidarity Pact"

Rault, Wilfried Démographiques, Inst. National d'Etudes, Paris Cedex 20, France
The French civil solidarity pact applies to both same-sex and different-sex couples. It is supposed to recognize gay and lesbian couples, but it is also a new intermediary status between marriage and concubinage for the heterosexual couples. Because of these two aims, the civil solidarity pact has ambivalent status. As an alternative or a substitute to marriage, a confirmed cohabitation or marriage "for a try," the civil solidarity pact is particularly emblematic of the contemporary transformations of homosexuality.

The demographics of same-sex marriages in the Nordic countries

Andersson, Gunnar Dept. of Sociology, Stockholm University, Stockholm, Sweden Noack, Turid Statistics Norway, Oslo, Norway
In all Nordic countries, same-sex couples today have the legal right to registered partnership, a civil status that in practice does not deviate much from the concept of marriage. As these countries already have some experience of same-sex families, we are here able to provide an accurate insight into the demographic dynamics of such unions: We provide an investigation into the demographics of same-sex marriages, i.e., registered partnerships, in Denmark, Norway and Sweden. We give an overview of the demographic characteristics of the spouses of these partnerships, and study patterns in divorce risks.

¡Viva las novias! Queers getting married in Spain

Pichardo Galan, Josi Ignacio Dept. de Antropologma Social, Univers. Autsnoma de Madrid, Madrid, Spain
A couple of years after same-sex marriage was recognized in Spain is time to look at how lesbian and gay people are using this institution: who is getting married or not, the reasons for doing it and the difficulties in their processes of getting married, the rituals that are taking place, the influence this legal change is having both on queer people lifes and on the perception of sexual diversity in society and public policies.

Going public: Negotiations of public and private life among 'married' same-sex couples in Iceland

Einarsdottir, Anna Fac. of Arts and Human Science, London South Bank University, London, United Kingdom
This paper focuses on the complex negotiations of visibility that the women in my study encountered in their married life. While their relationship had moved from an exclusively private unit to a public establishment, in line with what the campaigners for same sex marriage had envisaged, I argue that the boundaries between public and private are highly sensitive and transitioning between them can be problematic.

S-031: Self-regulated learning with multimedia

Maria Opfermann, Joachim Wirth (chair)
Multimedia learning requires sophisticated self-regulatory abilities when a high amount of learner control is provided. Research, however, has shown that learners often do not show self-regulation behavior spontaneously when confronted with a learning situation but that they rather need some kind of support. Research presented in the symposium investigates learners' pre-requisites of self-regulated learning as well as ways of supporting self-regulated learning with multimedia. As pre-requisites, knowledge of learning strategies and strategy application as well as epistemological beliefs are investigated. Research on ways of support covers internalizing/externalizing of interfaces, implementing pedagogical agents, and metacognitive modeling/representational prompting.

The interaction between hypotheses formulation and experimental design in self-regulated scientific discovery learning

Wirth, Joachim Dept. of educational research, Ruhr-University Bochum, Bochum, Germany Gössling, Jill Instructional Psychology, Duisburg-Essen University, Essen, Germany Thillmann, Hubertina Instructional Psychology, Duisburg-Essen University, Essen, Germany Marschner, Jessica Instructional Psychology, Duisburg-Essen University, Essen, Germany Leutner, Detlev Instructional Psychology, Duisburg-Essen University, Essen, Germany
Klahr and Dunbar (1988) describe self-regulated scientific discovery learning as a search in two spaces, hypotheses space and experiment space. According to their model the interaction between these spaces is crucial for learning. However, to our knowledge this specific interaction has never been investigated empirically. In our study 255 15-year-old students learned self-regulated in a computer-simulated science lab. Results show that students who conducted well-designed experiments related to their hypotheses learned more than students who conducted well-designed experiments, only. Prior knowledge predicted this hypotheses-experiment space interaction substantially. In sum, results support Klahr and Dunbar's model of self-regulated scientific discovery learning.

Learning with hypermedia: Impact of epistemological beliefs on metacognitive processes

Porsch, Torsten Psychologisches Institut III, Universität Münster, Münster, Germany Pieschl, Stephanie Psychological Faculty III, University of Muenster, Muenster, Germany Stahl, Elmar Media Didactics, University of Education, Freiburg, Germany Bromme, Rainer Psychological Faculty III, University of Muenster, Muenster, Germany
Successful learning with hypermedia learning environments requires skills of metacognitive monitoring and controlling. The purpose of this study is to consider experimentally the impact of epistemological beliefs -i.e. beliefs about the nature of knowledge and knowing- on learners' metacogni-

tive adaptation to task complexity. After exposure to an epistemological sensitization 35 students were monitored during a series of learning tasks based on the COPES-model (Winne & Hadwin, 1998). Results show the learner's ability to discriminate and calibrate across learning tasks and that more "sophisticated" epistemological beliefs are associated witch better learning strategies. The results are consistent with a study focussing on students planning.

Supporting self-regulated learning in hypermedia environments

Opfermann, Maria KMRC - Hypermedia, Inst. für Wissensmedien, Tuebingen, Germany Gerjets, Peter Hypermedia, IWM-KMRC, Tuebingen, Germany Scheiter, Katharina Applied Cognitive Psychology, Eberhard Karls University, Tuebingen, Germany
Our studies investigated whether hypermedia learning can be enhanced by providing learners with instructional support that aims at fostering self-regulatory and metacognitive learning behavior. We worked with highschool students and an environment on probability theory and a 2*2 design varying representational prompting and metacognitive modeling. We found that for participants who already possess sophisticated metacognitive abilities, such support is highly detrimental because it might interfere with strategies they have successfully used so far. Participants with low abilities, however, might benefit from such support only if they are aware of how to use it, for instance by means of prior training.

Internalizing vs. externalizing interface elements: How to induce engagement, planning and learning

van Nimwegen, Christof C.U.O., KU Leuven, Leuven, Belgium van Oostendorp, Herre Cognition and Communication, University of Utrecht, Utrecht, Netherlands
Some assume that problem-solving improves when users are assisted by externalized task-related information on the interface. However, we propose the possibility that strategically omitting information (users must internalize information) instigates more metacognitive activity (planning, strategy), better performance and better survival of interruptions. We connect our assumptions to Cognitive Load Theory and investigate how interfaces can provoke high Germane Cognitive Load, contributing to mindful processing. In experiments (constraint-satisfaction scheduling tasks) we varied the amount of external regulation (which task-information users have to infer themselves). A less regulated interface resulted in better performance and transfer, better task-knowledge, and better survival of interruptions.

Using pedagogical agents to support self-regulated learning

Domagk, Steffi Inst. für Bildung, Universität Erfurt, Erfurt, Germany Niegemann, Helmut M. Faculty of Education, University of Erfurt, Erfurt, Germany
Pedagogical agents (PA) are animated characters that guide through multimedia learning environments. They are supposed to facilitate the learners' motivation and their learning outcomes. To examine whether they meet these expectancies, the conducted study consisted of three experimental groups (likable, neutral, dislikable PA) and one control group (no PA). 292 university students learned about visual perception. The application of any pedagogical agent yielded no general motivating or learning facilitating effect. It is rather necessary to take the PA's characteristics into account. The likable-PA-group outperformed all other groups on far transfer tasks. Its application was beneficial for learners without prior knowledge.

S-032: Extending principles of couple interactions to specific populations

Nina Heinrichs (chair)
Previous research affirms that various couple-based interventions produce statistically and clinically significant effects in reducing couples' risk for subsequent relationship problems (Markman & Halford, 2005) as well as reducing current relationship distress (Snyder, Castellani, & Whisman, 2006). Additional studies have extended these findings in indicating the effectiveness of couple-based interventions for a broad range of coexisting emotional, behavioral, or physical health problems in one or both partners. The five papers comprising this symposium will outline five examples on recent empirical and theoretical developments regarding the extension of well-established principles of couple interactions and couple-based interventions to specific populations.

Body image and sexual functioning among women with early stage breast cancer: The impact of a couple-based intervention program

Baucom, Donald H. Dept. of Psychology, University of North Carolina, Chapel Hill, USA Dye, Shiahna Dept. of Psychology, University of North Carolina, Chapel Hill, NC, USA Porter, Laura S. Psychiatry Dept, Duke University Medical Center, Durham, NC, USA Kirby, Jennifer S. Dept. of Psychology, University of North Carolina, Chapel Hill, NC, USA Gremore, Tina M. Dept. of Psychology, University of North Carolina, Chapel Hill, NC, USA Pukay-Martin, Nicole Dept. of Psychology, University of North Carolina, Chapel Hill, NC, USA Keefe, Francis J. Dept. of Psychiatry, Duke University Medical Center, Durham, NC, USA
This paper presents findings exploring body image and sexual functioning for women with breast cancer in the US. First, using pretreatment data, the following issues are examined: the degree to which body image and sexuality are impacted by (a) type of surgery, (b) chemotherapy, (c) women's age, and (d) overall individual and relationship well-being. Second, results showing improvements in body image and sexuality will be presented from a treatment outcome study in which women and their partners are taught how to support each other through the trauma of breast cancer, using strategies from cognitive-behavioral couple therapy.

Fear of progression in partners of women with breast cancer

Zimmermann, Tanja Inst. für Psychologie, Universität Braunschweig, Braunschweig, Germany Heinrichs, Nina Inst. für Psychologie, Universität Bielefeld, Bielefeld, Germany Huber, Birgit Psychosomatik, Universität München, München, Germany Herschbach, Peter Psychosomatik, Universität München, München, Germany
A primary anxiety complaint in cancer patients is the fear of recurrence of the disease. Cancer poses a real threat not only to the patient but also to the partner. Therefore, we assessed fear of progression (FoP) in both. We expected FoP as one of the main reasons for distress in couples and a dyadic interdependence. Partners were expected to have lower mean FoP. Women with Low-FoP-Partners should be less anxious than those with High-FoP-Partners. A high relationship quality – as a protector against anxiety – is expected to be associated with lower FoP. The presentation will report results of 70 couples.

Treating affair couples: An integrative approach to resolving trauma and promoting forgiveness

Snyder, Douglas K. Dept. of Psychology, Texas A & M, College Station, USA Baucom, Donald Dept. of Psychology, University of North Carolina, Chapel Hill,
USA Gordon, Kristina Dept. of Psychology, University of Tennessee, Knoxville, USA
This presentation will describe theoretical and empirical bases to an integrative approach to treating couples following an extramarital affair. This approach draws on theoretical and empirical literature regarding traumatic response as well as interpersonal forgiveness. It incorporates empirically-supported interventions from both cognitive-behavioral and insight-oriented approaches to treating couple distress. This integrative intervention helps couples struggling to recover from an affair to: (1) cope with the initial impact of an affair, (2) develop a shared understanding of factors contributing to the affair, and (3) reach and implement an informed decision about how to move on – either together or separately.

PREP inside and out: Marriage education as an intervention for prisoner reintegration

Markman, Howard Dept. of Psychology, University of Denver, Denver, CO, USA Einhorn, Lindsey Dept. of Psychology, University of Denver, Denver, CO, USA Stanley, Scott Dept. of Psychology, University of Denver, Denver, CO, USA
In the U.S. over 600,000 inmates leave prisons every year, yet within two years, 59% will be rearrested, 39% convicted, and 19% will return to prison. Lower recidivism is predicted by going home to a stable relationship, yet there are few relationship oriented programs being implemented in prisons. We report the results of the Prevention and Relationship Enhancement Program (PREP) adapted for prison populations, on a relationship functioning. Subjects were 254 ethnically and economically diverse inmates in 17 Oklahoma prisons. Significant differences from pre to post were observed on measures of communication, satisfaction, commitment and positive connections. Implications for social policy regarding relationship education in prisons are discussed.

Promoting a positive transition to parenthood: The effect of couple care for parents on the couple relationship and parenting

Halford, Kim Dept. of Psychology, Griffith University, Brisbane, Australia Petch, Jemima School of Psychology, Griffith University, Brisbane, Queensland, Australia Creedy, Debra Health Group Executive, Griffith University, Gold Coast, Queensland, Australia Gamble, Jennifer School of Nursing, Griffith University, Brisbane, Queensland, Australia
Approximately 50% of couples report a moderate to severe decline in relationship satisfaction across the transition to parenthood, which is associated with increased couple conflict, individual psychological distress, and negative parent-child relationships outcomes. is a flexible delivery We report on two randomized controlled trials of 'Couple CARE for Parents' (CCP) with n = 71 pregnant couples, and n = 256 couples. CCP prevented a decline in female relationship satisfaction, reduced parenting stress and observed couple communication negativity relative to the control. Couple relationship education for new parents is an important opportunity to enhance family relationships.

S-033: Words and feelings: Emotions across languages and cultures

Johnny Fontaine, Klaus R. Scherer (chair)
Emotions are often defined and analyzed on the basis of emotion terms in natural languages. This symposium takes a new look at the relationship between emotion words and feelings and the issue of universality vs. cultural specificity, addressing questions such as: Do differences in semantic meaning index cultural variations in values and social structures underlying emotion elicitation?
Are feeling qualia related to the connotations of emotion words? Do words allow the inference of other emotion components? The contributions will reflect on the underlying theoretical issues, present new methods for their empirical study, and report recent data.

The power of emotion words: Cultural definitions of feelings and task masters of emotion theories

Scherer, Klaus R. CISA, Universität Genf, Genf, Switzerland
One of the most powerful determinants of both everyday emotional experience and scientific emotion theorizing and research is the vocabulary of emotion terms. Based on a componential model of emotion, this contribution argues that the feeling component of emotion is strongly affected by the verbal labels chosen to designate ad communicate the respective experience. Often, the semantic field of a term, and its connotations, will add surplus meaning witch subtly changes the conscious experience. Emotion theories have been led by the vocabulary to assume unwarrantedly rigid categories. To elucidate these issues, a crosslanguage semantic profile comparison is suggested.

The GRID approach: An empirical approach to identify the meaning of emotion words across cultural groups

Fontaine, Johnny Dept. of Personnel Managemant, Ghent University, Gent, Belgium Scherer, Klaus R. Dept. of Psychology, University of Geneva, Geneva, Switzerland Roesch, Etienne B. Dept. of Psychology, University of Geneva, Geneva, Switzerland Chen, Yuh-Ling Department of Psychology, National Chung Cheng Universit, Min-Hsiung Chia-Yi, Taiwan
A new approach for empirically identifying the meaning of emotion words within and across cultural groups will be presented. The approach is embedded in the componential emotion framework. It consists of a GRID of 24 emotion terms and 144 emotion features that represent six emotion components, namely the appraisal, the subjective experience, the expression, the psychophysiological, the action tendency, and the regulation component. Data from four language groups and five countries will be presented (Belgium, Switzerland, United Kingdom, USA, and China). In each of the five countries, four basic meaning dimensions emerge, namely evaluation/pleasantness, power/dominance, activation/arousal, and unpredictability.

Where do emotional dialects come from? A comparison of the understanding of emotion terms between Gabon and Quebec

Hess, Ursula Dept. of Psychology, UQAM, Montreal, Canada Thibault, Pascal Dept. of Psychology, Univ. of Quebec at Montreal, Montreal, Canada Lévesque, Manon Dept. of Psychology, Omar Bongo University, Libreville, Gabon Hillary, Elfenbein Haas Schoof of Business, Univ.of California, Berkeley, Berkeley, USA
Recently, Elfenbein et al. (2007) presented evidence for cultural dialects in the expression of certain emotions by Gabonese and Quebecois individuals. The present research aims to test the hypothesis that cultural dialects in expression are due to subtle differences in the meaning of the emotion term. For this 280 each participants from Gabon and Quebec completed the GRID for a total of 10 emotion terms: anger, contempt, disgust, embarrassment, fear, happiness, sadness, serenity, shame and surprise. The similarities and differences between the two cultures in the connotations associated with these terms will be discussed and related to emotional dialects theory.

Exploring words, tastes and feelings in Chinese: The natural semantic

Ye, Zhengdao Coll. Arts and Social Science, Australian National University, Canberra, ACT, Australia

The study of emotions often relies on unpacking the meanings of words describing emotions. This paper demonstrates how the Natural Semantic Metalanguage, a fully-fledged linguistic theory of semantics, can help elucidate those meanings systematically from a culture-internal perspective; deepen our understanding of the relationship between words and feelings; and contribute to the study of universal and culture-specific aspects of human emotions. Empirical case studies will draw on those Chinese taste-describing words that are routinely used to describe feelings and emotions, with a view to analysing their meanings, exploring the relationship between words, tastes and feelings, and identifying cultural scripts informing Chinese attitude towards emotions.

S-034: Decision-making and problem solving in complex scenarios

Joachim Funke, Oswald Huber (chair)

The contributions to the symposium investigate complex scenarios from a problem solving and decision making perspective. For both approaches, the construction of a mental representation of the scenario and the utilization of information is a central topic. From the decision making perspective, complex scenarios are risky decision situations quite different from the common gambling tasks. Decision makers often search for risk defusing operators (a risk decreasing action anticipated by the decision maker to be performed in addition to an available alternative). The papers deal with the construction and quality of the mental representation and with risk defusing.

Risk defusing behaviour: The impact of justification pressure

Bär, Arlette S. Inst. für Psychologie, Universität Fribourg, Fribourg, Switzerland *Huber, Odilo W.* Department of Psychology, University of Fribourg, Fribourg, Switzerland

Under justification pressure decision makers know in advance that they have to justify their decision afterwards. Two hypotheses were investigated: (1) search for risk defusing operators (RDOs) is enhanced under justification pressure, and (2) RDOs are a central element in the justification texts. In Experiment 1, 60 subjects decided in a medical scenario in conditions with and without justification pressure. In Experiment 2 (80 subjects), success of RDO search was varied. Both hypotheses were confirmed in these experiments. In Experiment 2, subjects mentioned in the justification texts also the non-availability of RDOs as argument for not chosing a specific alternative.

Risk-defusing operators for decision making in complex scenarios are scenario-specific

Funke, Joachim Inst. für Psychologie, Universität Heidelberg, Heidelberg, Germany

According to the concept of active risk-defusing behavior, decision makers in risky situations look for additional actions that reduce risk and allow them to favor the more risky alternative. Our study demonstrates that risk-defusing behavior depends on the type of risk (normal, medium, catastrophic or global) as well as on the domain (health, economy, or ecology). Using the interview techniques of active information search and thinking-aloud, 120 interviews about decision-making processes within 12 scenarios were conducted. It shows that active search for different risk-defusing operators depends on type of risk, but even more on the domain of the scenario.

Risky decisions: Mental representation and decision process

Huber, Oswald Inst. für Psychologie, Universität Fribourg, Fribourg, Switzerland

A process model of risky decision making is presented that models – in contrast to predominant decision theories – decisions with successful search for risk defusing operators (RDOs) as well as processes with unsuccessful search or no search at all. The model comprises two types of processes: 1) Procedures for evaluation and preferential selection; 2) procedures relevant for the construction and elaboration of a mental causal model of the alternatives. The model entails testable assumptions about when an RDO is searched for actively and when a detected RDO is accepted. Results concerning different aspects of the model are reported and discussed.

Managing complex personal risks: Cognitive appraisal and emotion in payment protection insurance decisions

Ranyard, Rob Department of Psychology, University of Bolton, Bolton, United Kingdom *McHugh, Sandie* Department of Psychology, University of Bolton, Bolton, United Kingdom

Consumers can defuse the complex financial risks of credit default by taking payment protection insurance (PPI). The bounded rationality of PPI decisions and the role of emotion were investigated in two questionnaire-based experiments. High street bank customers' PPI decisions were significantly influenced by long-term cost information but were insensitive to the level of PPI cover (loglinear analysis). Also, path modelling showed that anticipated worry reduction and current worry both predicted PPI decisions significantly, as did aspects of rational appraisal such as perceived cost. The findings contribute to decision process theory and to understanding how best to facilitate informed decision making.

The quality of information utilization: A central construct to model complex problem solving processes

Rollett, Wolfram IFS, Universität Dortmund, Dortmund, Germany

The aim of the present project was to develop and evaluate a theory-based model of the problem solving process (PSP) when investigating and steering a complex dynamic system, using the DYNAMIS scenario Biology-Lab and a sample of 109 students. Assessment indicators were correctness of task model, quality of strategy use, the newly developed indicator "quality of information utilization" based on discriminating between "generated" and "utilized" system information and subjects' system knowledge. 77% (adj. R^2) of the variance of the acquired system knowledge could be explained. A structural equation model of the investigated PSP showed a very good fit (Chi2=119.3, df=102).

Risk management in complex decision making: A field study

Wearing, Alex J. Department of Psychology, Melbourne University, Melbourne, Australia *Omodei, Mary M.* Department of Psychology, La Trobe University, Bundoora, Australia *McLennan, Jim* Department of Psychology, La Trobe University, Bundoora, Australia *Elliott, Glenn* Department of Psychology, La Trobe University, Bundoora, Australia

Using a specially designed human factors interview protocol, fire fighters in leadership roles during wildfire suppression operations were interviewed as soon as possible after the finish of their shift. Content analyses were carried out on the coded transcripts of these interviews and a number of risk management processes identified. Some implications of the findings both for the study of complex decision making, and the training of emergency

service personnel who have command responsibility are suggested.

S-035: Causal judgments under uncertainty (Part II)

York Hagmayer, Manfred Thüring (chair)

Causal judgments are of crucial importance for the human understanding of the world. Usually, such judgments are based on available information and are derived from causal knowledge. One key feature of this process is that it is performed under uncertainty, i.e., neither explanations nor predictions are totally reliable. In our symposium, a number of theoretical approaches as well as experimental findings are presented that are closely related to this aspect. They address issues of causal knowledge, causal learning, and causal judgments under uncertainty in various application domains, such as clinical reasoning, complex control tasks, legal disputes and decision making.

Modeling causal inferences and uncertainty in ACT-R

Drewitz, Uwe Institut für Psychologie, TU Berlin, Berlin, Germany

Causal Models represent the structure of causal knowledge for a specific domain. We propose to implement rules of such models as a particular chunk type of the declarative knowledge-base in ACT-R. This cognitive architecture provides excellent mechanisms to account for causal inferences, such as explanations and predictions, and for structural changes in a causal model during learning. While ACT-R is well suited to predict the propositional content of causal inferences, no process has been defined yet to account for the subjective probabilities of these inferences. We propose a way for modeling such a process within the ACT-R framework.

Causal diversity effects in clinical psychologists' diagnostic reasoning

de Kwaadsteniet, Leontien Inst. of Psychology, Radboud Universiteit, Nijmegen, Netherlands *Kim, Nancy S.* Department of Psychology, Northeastern University, Boston, USA

When clinical psychologists learn about causal theories for mental disorders, how does this information affect their diagnostic reasoning? We presented causal information from scientific theories for psychological disorders to clinical psychologists. We found that psychologists showed a causal diversity effect, perceiving clients with symptoms far apart in the causal structure as more likely to have a disorder than clients with causally proximal symptoms. Psychologists also rated causally diverse symptoms as more informative than causally proximal symptoms. In no-cause control tasks they showed no such preferences. Implications for clinical reasoning and follow-up directions are discussed.

Binding causal actions to their effects

Lagnado, David Dept. of Psychology, University College London, London, United Kingdom *Haggard, Patrick* Department of Psychology, University College London, London, United Kingdom *Moore, James* Department of Psychology, University College London, London, United Kingdom

Previous research has demonstrated a shift in the perceived time of actions towards their effects (Haggard et al., 2002). Furthermore, both predictive and inferential processes contribute to this shift (Moore & Haggard, 2007). The learning and performance of goal-directed action is, in part, determined by the contingency between action and effect. This study investigates whether the conscious experience of action (as indexed by its perceived time) is sensitive to contingency relations. It was shown that both predictive and inferential contributions to the shift in the perceived time of action were dependent on the contingency relations between action and effect.

Undoing causal knowledge
Osman, Magda Dept. of Psychology, University of Surrey, Guilford, United Kingdom
Previous research on complex problem solving has provided an impoverished understanding of the factors that affect the transference of causal knowledge in complex dynamic environments. The present study was designed to address this by using a control task paradigm. The two most pivotal findings of the study were that along with demonstrations of successful transfer of causal knowledge across analogous dynamic control tasks, an atypical negative transfer effect was revealed in which causal knowledge in the transfer task was impaired relative to the original. The findings are discussed in terms of the relationship between monitoring and control processes.

Transitivity heuristics in causal reasoning
von Sydow, Momme Inst. für Psychologie, Universität Göttingen, Göttingen, Germany Meder, Björn Institut für Psychologie, Universität Göttingen, Göttingen, Germany Waldmann, Michael R. Institut für Psychologie, Universität Göttingen, Göttingen, Germany
Deterministic conditional relations are transitive (A→B, B→C, => A→C). However, probabilistic conditional relations need not to be transitive. In two experiments we provide participants with data that support both probabilistic causal relations, A~>B, and then B~>C (in a developmental context). However, the observed data was designed in a way that there is nonetheless no positive correlation between A and C, or even a negative one. The experiments show that participants judge the overall correlation differently if they got information about the intermediate steps, even if contradicting bottom-up data is available to them.

S-036: The long-term effects of couple education and therapy

Andrew Christensen (chair)
Considerable evidence indicates that interventions to prevent and ameliorate couple problems lead to immediate improvements in relationship skills and satisfaction. However, the long-term effects of these interventions are not clearly established. This symposium includes five research papers and a discussant that examine the long-term effects of couple interventions: three papers report 4, 10 and 11 year follow-up data on relationship education programs, one reports 2 and 5 year follow-up data on couple therapy, and one reports 6-month and 1-year follow-up data on treatment for couples coping with cancer. Collectively the papers demonstrate sustained benefits from couple interventions.

The long-term effects of premarital intervention
Markman, Howard Dept. of Psychology, University of Denver, Denver, CO, USA Rhoades, Galena Dept. of Psychology, University of Denver, Denver, CO, USA Whitton, Sarah Dept. of Psychology, University of Denver, Denver, CO, USA Stanley, Scott Dept. of Psychology, University of Denver, Denver, CO, USA
There is a growing interest at National levels in delivering relationship education programs to couples in order to prevent relationship distress and divorce and strengthen marriages, yet very few long-term evaluations of these programs. We present 10 year follow-up data on the long-term effects of the Prevention and Relationship Enhancement Program (PREP) in a sample of 253 couples who received the intervention premaritally and were followed at yearly intervals. We present a new model of relationship health (communication/ conflict management, positive connections, com-

mitment, satisfaction, stability) and outcome data on each dimension as couples are entering the highest risk period for divorce and distress. Implications for wide spread dissemination of research-based couples interventions are discussed.

The 11-year long-term effects of the EPL-relationship enhancement program
Hahlweg, Kurt Inst. für Psychologie, Universität Braunschweig, Braunschweig, Germany
The literature on the long-term outcome of cognitive-behavioral psychoeducational prevention programs for couples is very limited. In 1994-95, N = 81 couples took part in a randomized controlled study investigating the efficacy of the EPL II: Ein Partnerschaftliches Lernprogram für verheiratete Paare (A Learning Program for Married Couples). In 2005-2006 a 11-year follow-up telephone interview study was conducted with a response rate of 93%. In the EPL-group, the divorce rate was 27,5%, in the non-EPL-group 52,6%. The results will be discussed with regard to refining the intervention strategies.

The 4-year effects of couple care: A flexible delivery couple relationship education program
Halford, Kim Dept. of Psychology, Griffith University, Brisbane, Australia
Flexible delivery relationship education involves self-directed learning that couples can undertake at home, which is intended to make education easier for couples to access than having to attend face-to-face sessions. Couple CARE is a flexible delivery relationship education program that produces similar short term benefits for couple relationships as traditional face-to-face programs. The current paper reports on a 4-year follow-up of the relationship satisfaction and stability of 65 couples who completed Couple CARE, and the predictors of the trajectory of relationship satisfaction across that 4-year period.

Two and five-year follow-up results from a randomized clinical trial of couple therapy
Christensen, Andrew Dept. of Psychology, University of California, Los Angeles, CA, USA Atkins, David Dept. of Psychology, Fuller Graduate School, Pasadena, CA, USA
One hundred thirty-four married couples participated in a randomized clinical trial comparing two forms of behavioral couple therapy. Measurements of relationship functioning were conducted approximately every six months during treatment and during a five year follow-up period. Relationship satisfaction improved during treatment but showed a "hockey-stick" pattern of change during follow-up, falling abruptly at treatment termination but then improving for the first 2 years of follow-up. Approximately 2/3 of couples showed clinically significant levels of improvement at the 2 year follow-up. Data from the 5 year follow-up have just been collected and will be reported at the conference.

Long-term effects of a couple-based intervention for couples coping with cancer
Heinrichs, Nina Inst. für Psychologie, Universität Bielefeld, Bielefeld, Germany Zimmermann, Tanja Inst. für Psychologie, Universität Braunschweig, Braunschweig, Germany Huber, Birgit Institut für psychosomatische, Technische Universität München, München, Germany Herschbach, Peter Inst. für Psychologie, TU München, München, Germany
The cancer diagnosis is a stressful life-event that poses formidable and enduring challenges, not only to the woman but also to their partner. A conjoint process of mutual support has been suggested to be an effective coping strategy. This project aims for gathering data on the potential benefits of a brief psychological intervention to assist couples to cope with cancer. The preliminary treatment outcome

results for about 70 couples assessed for individual and dyadic functioning at pre-, post-, 6- and 12-month-follow-up of a RCT comparing a couple-based intervention to an educational package delivered in a couples context will be presented.

S-037: Enhancing time perspective research: The use of the Zimbardo time perspective inventory across cultures

Nicolas Fieulaine, Taciano L. Milfont (chair)
Time perspective (TP) has been a central psychological construct. Although several scales have been developed to measure TP, the Zimbardo Time Perspective Inventory (ZTPI) seems to overcome most of the limitations of other measures by utilizing multi-item scales and by taking a multidimensional approach to TP (measuring five time frames: Past-Negative, Past-Positive, Present-Fatalistic, Present-Hedonistic, and Future). The aim of this symposium is to present new findings from research using ZTPI across different cultural contexts and several research aims. Therefore, presentations capture the variety and innovative nature of current research using the ZTPI and the importance of TP in psychological research

Zimbardo time perspective inventory: Its Brazilian-Portuguese version and its use in environmental issues research
Milfont, Taciano L. School of Psychology, Victoria Univ. of Wellington, Wellington, New Zealand
The Zimbardo Time Perspective Inventory (ZTPI) has already been translated into several languages and used in different countries. This paper first presents an overview of the ZTPI and then examines the construct and discriminant validity of the Brazilian-Portuguese version of the ZTPI. Overall, the findings support the validity and reliability of the Brazilian-Portuguese version of the ZTPI: The ZTPI five-factor structure (Past-Negative, Past-Positive, Present-Fatalistic, Present-Hedonistic, and Future) provided acceptable fit to the data, and the pattern of relationships between the five time perspective dimensions with other variables were in line with previous studies.

Adjusting the structure of the Zimbardo time perspective inventory scales using Russian data
Mitina, Olga Dept. of Psychology, Moscow State University, Moscow, Russia Blinnikova, Svetlana Psychology, Moscow State University, Moscow, Russia
Data collection using ZTPI and other relevant questionnaires was conducted in Russia (304 ss). According these data ZTPI the traditional structure proposed by Zimbardo was compared with ours. In our interpretation ZTPI includes eight factors. Three of them characterize relations with the past: not realized (loosed) possibilities, the positive emotional past, the positive cognitive past. The present is expressed by two Zimbardo's factors: gedonistic and fatalistic present. The future factor has divided into three factors: orientation on hardworking moral way of life, planning, punctuality. Factors correlate with each other in different degrees. To compare the two models SEM was used

Time perspective profiles from the Zimbardo time perspective inventory
Diaz Morales, Juan Francisco Dept. de Personalidad, Universidad Complutense Madrid, Madrid, Spain
The Zimbardo Time Perspective Inventory (ZTPI) is a multidimensional measure of time orientation that includes positive and negative evaluation of past and present, as well as future evaluation. Examining profiles of how individuals score across more than one time perspective may add depth to understanding psychological time. This communi-

cation analyses the time perspective profiles of 1,067 adults who completed a Spanish version of the ZTPI. Profiles were created using Boyd and Zimbardo's (2005) guidelines, with Future, Present-Hedonistic and Present-Fatalistic dimensions. Prevalence of each time perspective profile and its relationships with participant's demographic characteristics (e.g., sex, age, educational level) are analyzed and discussed.

Zimbardo time perspective inventory : A comparison across cultures
Sircova, Anna Psychology and Education, Moscow City University, Moscow, Russia Mitina, Olga Psychology Department, Moscow State University, Moscow, Russia
The Zimbardo Time Perspective Inventory has been already translated and adapted into many languages. Most of the ZTPI versions show the same five factor structure, but with some amendments in the inventory scales. Focus of the present study was to compare ZTPI results obtained in three countries: Russia, France and Spain. We used method of structured equation modeling to compare the structural models and the measured models (relations between the scales) of time perspective situation in each of these countries. Discussion of these differences pays attention on mentality factors (religion, social situation etc.). Correlations with other scales will include as factors of explanation of differences.

Time perspective issues in the French context: Its social roots and psychological correlates in socially deprived situations
Fieulaine, Nicolas Dept. of Social Psychology, University of Lyon, Bron Cedex, France
From its validation, Zimbardo Time Perspective Inventory enhanced this field of research in French social psychology. After a brief presentation of its French version, we will present original results from a field study in French free care centers (N=182; Mean Age= 39.6), suggesting a mediating effect of time perspective (TP) in the link between social deprivation and psychological distress (anxiety and depression), and its moderating role in the efficiency of coping strategies people used when facing those deprived situations. Discussion will focused on theoretical and practical implications of this intervention of TP in the psychological impact of deprived situations

S-038: Psychological knowledge as commodity: Value added - or lost?

Martin Dege (chair)
Psychology worldwide is facing the transformation of its knowledge base into commodities which are characterized by their assigned economic value—to standardized methods, mandatory data analysis packages, uses of fMRI technologies, extra training courses for pay, etc. In many ways the acts of publication of research results have become commodities (through evaluation of publication sources by their "impact factor"). This commoditization process is about to transform psychological research into profits-oriented business. The objective of this symposium is to analyze the ways in which the commoditization is embedded in the context of educating psychologists in different countries.

Commodity as curse and as condition: A contextual perspective
van Belzen, Jacob A. Dept. of Psychology, University of Amsterdam, Amsterdam, Netherlands
Commoditization is a process that needs a balanced evaluation: it provides conditions for existence and growth, but can also turn into curse, when distracting from the search for fundamental (including non-applicable) insight, when inhibiting dealing with fundamental issues and especially

when taking influence on 1. conceptualizations, 2. types of research and 3. choice of populations and samples. Making comparisons with the international situation, the paper will discuss the ways in which the development of psychology of religion in the Netherlands has been depending on and influenced by its multiple contexts and 'markets'.

A culture-inclusive psychology: Who needs it?
Kölbl, Carlos Inst. für Pädagog. Psychologie, Universität Hannover, Hannover, Germany
A culture-inclusive psychology has in any case normative underpinnings and helps to serve – intentionally or not – different practical and political purposes. This is true for those different enterprises known as cross-cultural, cultural, indigenous and intercultural psychology. Past and present examples will be discussed. Particular attention will be paid to psychological work on intercultural competence. At which point is intercultural competence turned into a commodity? For whom? With which consequences? Are there alternatives? Finally arguments will be presented in favour of a sensitive and differentiated use of all kinds of culture-inclusive psychological knowledge.

Reflexivity and the ability to criticize
Dege, Carmen Inst. für Psychologie, Freie Universität Berlin, Berlin, Germany
The ongoing transformation of the educational system is embedded in a broader change that is strongly related to the diffusion of the discourse of efficiency into different formerly protected areas. Using and introducing the method of de-construction, a focus will be placed on the examination of the very processes that lead to an understanding of knowledge as a commodity. As our analysis shows, the only way to challenge these highly problematic settings is to implement practices that show the inconsistencies of this discourse to transform the hierarchies and make possible other ways of performing and styling education and knowledge.

The school evaluation as a negotiation space: An intriguing picture of "School-family meetings"
Marsico, Giuseppina Dept. of Education Sciences, University of Salerno, Fiselano, Italy
This study documents what happened in a series of "critical" events, during which parents of pre-adolescent children took part, for the umpteenth time, in the "ceremony" of school report cards delivery. This time the rituality was integrated by the presence of a researcher recording the meeting and interviewing twenty-two families to understand their point of view on education and on school evaluation. Results outline school-family meetings as a negotiation space. The child's success or failure in many cases ends up representing the "stakes" in a confrontation between the family's and the school's differing educational views.

The commoditization of yoga
Toise, Stefanie C. Dept. of Psychology, Clark University, Worcester, USA
We studied student's preferences for commoditized learning. Participants chose between commoditized or non-commoditized contexts in which to learn, and were asked to explain their preferences in a choice based survey and short answer format. To elucidate inter- and intra-subject variability, questionnaires focused on learning biochemistry or yoga, which we hypothesized participants would conceive differently. The data from these survey results, and students' explanations for their choices, permit the study of contrasts in their responses.

S-039: New tool for analysis and visualization of teams and populations: Sociomapping

Radvan Bahbouh (chair)
Sociomapping is new data visualization and analytical method that exploits human subconscious cognitive subsystems for easier data exploration by creating landscape-like graphs. It enables to visualize, explore and analyze the structure and dynamics of a system and to present it in a way, which is easy to understand, especially for the public and non-scientific audience. Symposium will introduce this new approach, addressing basic principles of creating and interpreting Sociomaps and the research of the cognitive aspects of Sociomapping. Several applications will be presented from the fields of human resources, psychometrics and organizational psychology.

Title to be announced
Osusky, Michal Analytical Dept., QED Group, Prague, Czech Republic Bahbouh, Radvan analytical, QED GROUP, Prague, Czech Republic
Sociomapping is a new data visualization and analytical method that exploits human subconscious cognitive subsystems for easier data exploration by creating landscape-like graphs. It enables to visualize the structure and dynamics of a system and to present it in a way, which is easy to understand, especially for the public and non-scientific audience. Basic principles of creating and interpreting Sociomaps will be explained. Several case studies from different areas of psychology will be presented to enable fellow scientists to imagine application in their field. This presentation is an introduction to symposium and to following presentations addressing Sociomapping applications.

Title to be announced
Srb, Tomas Analytical Dept., QED Group, Prague, Czech Republic Bahbouh, Radvan analytical, QED GROUP, Prague, Czech Republic
Working with teams as well as other social systems we are facing specific problems that mainly result from difficulty in analyzing and understanding complex relations among team members. An analytical tool Sociomapping enables to analyze and visualize in a comprehensive way different characteristics of team and their combinations (communication, team atmosphere, knowledge sharing). In organizational applications, Sociomapping is used for discovering latent structures and relations inside teams (or departments) and monitoring system dynamics and change. In team coaching context it helps teams to understand mutual relations and monitor development in different areas.

Title to be announced
Rozehnalova, Eva Analytical Dept., QED Group, Prague, Czech Republic Bahbouh, Radvan analytical, QED GROUP, Prague, Czech Republic
In order to introduce Sociomapping as teamwork diagnostic method, several research projects have been done. This paper will briefly introduce some of them. Also, it will focus on inter-rater reliability of interpretation of Sociomaps depicting teamwork. Volunteers were trained in working with Sociomaps and in their interpretation. Then they interpreted several sociomaps and those interpretations were compared. Cohens Kappa, Kendalls W and Interclass Correlation Coefficient were used. Purpose of this study was to find if the interpretation of Sociomaps is independent of interpreting person.

Title to be announced
Hoschl, Cyril Analytical Dept., QED Group, Prague, Czech Republic *Bahbouh, Radvan* analytical, QED GROUP, Prague, Czech Republic
Sociomapping analysis is a new method of visualization of relationships among team members in user-friendly manner. It helps to understand the team structure better and also it enables to display dynamics of team changes. Animation of dynamic Sociomaps shows differences between two teams as well as changes in team behavior. It helps to answer questions such as: What happens when someone leaves the team or someone new comes in? What is the future progress of team changes? Application of dynamic Sociomaps will be presented and also practical use of new software designed for team analysis will be demonstrated.

Title to be announced
Srb, Tomas Analytical Dept., QED Group, Prague, Czech Republic *Bahbouh, Radvan* analytical, QED GROUP, Prague, Czech Republic
If you imagine a profile of a team based on measuring personality, abilities or performance it is usually a graph with sum of individual profiles difficult to analyze or an average profile that is in fact saying nothing about the team. An analytical tool based on Sociomapping – Team Profile Analyzer (TPA) enables to visualize team profiles as a Sociomap - graphical representation of the data resembling a landscape where each team member is represented by a peak having its specific position and a height what can represent various parameters. Thus it is quite easy even for non-statisticians identify significant subgroups (mountains) within a team, analyze and compare them.

Title to be announced
Bahbouh, Radvan QED Group, Prague, Czech Republic
Sociomapping is new data visualization and analytical method that exploits human subconscious cognitive subsystems for easier data exploration by creating landscape-like graphs. It enables to visualize, explore and analyze the structure and dynamics of a system and to present it in a way, which is easy to understand, especially for the public and non-scientific audience. Symposium will introduce this new approach, addressing basic principles of creating and interpreting Sociomaps and the research of the cognitive aspects of Sociomapping. Several applications will be presented from the fields of human resources, psychometrics and organizational psychology.

S-040: Psychological contracts, commitment and identification in organizations

Sabine Räder, Joerg Felfe (chair)
In this symposium, we aim to elucidate the relation between the concepts: psychological contract, identification and commitment. Common roots can be found in social exchange theories, but have not been elaborated. The concepts have been introduced into research models separately. Apart from comparing and integrating identification and commitment, communalities have neither been discussed nor analysed. We explore, in how far the concepts capture similar aspects of the employment relationship and apply comparable assumptions. The presentations will either investigate employment relationships based on one concept or interrelate concepts. The integration of the concepts will be further elaborated in discussion.

Psychological contract and affective organizational commitment: Mediating effects of justice beliefs
Antoni, Conny Herbert Arbeits- und Org.-Psychologie, Universität Trier, Trier, Germany *Bauer-Emmel, Claudia* Work&Organizational Psycho, University of Trier, Trier, Germany
This study tests a mediation model that transactional and relational contract violations have a differential impact on affective organizational commitment, via distributive and procedural justice evaluations as mediating variables. 118 employees in three shops of three different retail companies participated in this study. The results confirm the proposed differential mediation model. Structural equation analysis supports the assumed paths between transactional contract perceptions and distributive justice beliefs and between relational contract perceptions and procedural justice beliefs, both leading to affective commitment. The results show that the suggested integration of organizational justice and psychological contract research seems promising.

A Swedish study on temps: Insecure psychological contract, but willing to stay
Bernhard-Oettel, Claudia Dept. of Psychology, Stockholm University, Stockholm, Sweden *Isaksson, Kerstin* Department of Social Science, Mälardalen University, Västerås, Sweden
Traditional employment theories suggest that job insecurity associates negatively with organizational commitment, and enhances turnover intentions. This study investigates the relevance of this framework in temporary employment, for which job insecurity is a defining element. Analyses of questionnaire data (N = 716) revealed that 1) permanent workers reported lower levels of job insecurity than temporary employees; 2) permanent employees indicated higher organizational commitment than temporaries, but 3) temporary workers reported lower turnover intentions than permanents. The contradiction of low commitment and high intentions to stay may indicate restricted options of exit and is discussed in the framework of psychological contract.

Employment biographies as predictors for psychological contract formation
Rigotti, Thomas Inst. für Psychologie II, Universität Leipzig, Leipzig, Germany
This study aimed to test the role of employment biographies for the formation of psychological contracts. Using a multi facet measure of the psychological contract, study participants (83 trainees) were asked about their expectations regarding their future employment relationship. All participants had been unemployed before starting the trainee program in a paper production plant. The duration of unemployment, time spent in fixed-term, as well as permanent employment contracts showed to be related to the perceived psychological contracts. Furthermore, it could be shown, that for participants with longer periods of being unemployed the relation between perceived employers' obligations and commitment was weaker.

A multilevel model of portfolio workers psychological contracts: Differences in identification and loyalty
Räder, Sabine Dept. of Psychology, University of Oslo, Oslo, Norway *Wittekind, Anette* Organization Work and Technolo, ETH Zurich, Zurich, Switzerland *Inauen, Alice* Institute of Social and Preven, University of Zurich, Zurich, Switzerland
In this study, identification and loyalty were considered as dimensions of the psychological contract. We hypothesised that psychological contracts of portfolio workers (e.g. people working in two or more employment relationships) differ according to employment contracts and individual characteristics (e.g. reasons for portfolio working). Data was collected for two important employment relationships of 149 portfolio workers. Data was analysed by means of multilevel analysis, thus differentiating between employment relationships. Focusing on the dimension of identification, differences pertained to the duration of the contract, the perceived employer contributions, and for the dimension of loyalty to portfolio worker contributions and managerial responsibility.

S-041: Research on Mexican adolescents of different cultural contexts

Alma Vallejo Casarín (chair)
The objective of the symposium is to provide an overview of research conducted with adolescents in different contexts on topics of great importance at this stage of development. Studies are presented in Mexico City, the states of Chiapas and Veracruz and indigenous groups. It reflects on the importance of developing joint research projects to identify similarities and differences between the different cultural groups of this country and the needs for support and counseling from each cultural context.

Depressive symptomatology of Mexican adolescents from urban and totonaca indigenous group
Vallejo Casarín, Alma Dept. of Psychology, Universidad Veracruzana, Poza Rica Veracruz, Mexico *Vázquez, América Mechor, Jasiel Barcia, Roberto Juárez, Luis Enrique Maya, Nayaeli Mazadiego, Teresa Osorno, Rafael*
The purpose of this study is to measure depressive symptomatology through CES-D adapted to Mexican adolescents in adolescents from different cultural backgrounds: one from urban area and another from rural areas of totonaca indigenous group. Method.: 515 totonaca and 496 urban adolescents of both sexes answered de the CES-D adapted to Mexican adolescents. Results: girls from urban and rural areas had higher depressive symptomatology than boys, there were no significant differences in total scores when same sex and cultural background were compared. Analysis of each of the 20 item of CESD revealed significant differences between girls and boys of different cultural background.

Sensation seeking and alcohol drinking in Mexican adolescents
Palacios, Jorge Dept. of Psychology, UNAM, Mexico City, Mexico
The objective of this research was analyzed the influence of sensation seeking in alcohol use in a sample of Mexican youths. The sample studied was formed by 1000 teenagers between 14 and 22 years old, 485 males and 515 females, students of public high schools in Mexico City. New scale measuring sensation seeking was used. The youths completed a survey which assessed alcohol consumption. The results indicated differences between male and female in alcohol use. Regression analyses showed that sensation seeking explaining alcohol drinking. The dimension that accounted part of variance (13%) is the pleasure seeking; this dimension was associated with disinhibition factor. The discussion emphasizes the importance of sensations seeking.

Temperament and parental psychological control as predictors of externalizing problems in Mexican adolescents
Betancourt, Diana Dept. of Psychology, UNAM, Poza Rica Veracruz, Mexico *Andrade, Patricia* Dept. of Psychology, UNAM, México, Mexico
The purpose of this research was determining the effect of temperament and parental psychological

control on the externalizing problems in 587 adolescents, from 11 to 16 years old. In order to measure temperament, a scale was developed it consisted in six dimensions: adaptability, negative reactivity, persistence to the task, inhibition, negative emotionality and level of activity. The Scale of Maternal and Paternal was also used, and for measuring the externalizing problems the adapted version of the Youth Self Report. The temperament and psychological control explained 40% of the externalizing problems.

Students' moral personality, civic knowledge and attitudes in Mexican secondary schools

García Cabrero, Benilde Dept. of Psychology, UNAM, Mexico City, Mexico Haro Solis, Israel Dept. of Psychology, UNAM, Mexico City, Mexico Alvarado Tapia, Ingrid Estrella Dept. of Psychology, UNAM, Mexico City, Mexico

A total of 311 students from public (lay) and private schools (lay & religious) were evaluated using four instruments: DIT (Defining Issues Test (Rest, 1979), Interpersonal Reactivity Index (IRI, Davis, 1980), Pro-social Reasoning Objective Measure (PROM- R, Eisenberg, Carlo & Knight, 1992), and Civic Knowledge and Attitudes' Questionnaire (Torney-Purta, Lehmann, Oswald & Schulz, 2001). Data show differences among males and females and high levels of moral reasoning and empathy. Observations in classroom reveal that this is promoted through the prevalence of norms of interaction set forth by the teacher, as well as by opportunities to discuss topics in which moral reasoning and empathy are involved.

Subjective well-being and attempted suicide in Tuxtla Gutiérrez, Chiapas adolescents

Cañas, Jose Luis Dept. of Psychology, Universidad de Artes y Ciencia, Tuxtla, Mexico Ochoa, Aym Emanuelle Dept. of Psychology, Universidad de Ciencias y Arte, Tuxtla, Mexico Andrade, Patricia Dept. of Psychology, UNAM, México, Mexico Betancourt, Diana Dept. of Psychology, UNAM, México, Mexico

The purpose of this study was determining differences in subjective well-being in adolescents who have and have not attempted suicide. Participants included 1,000 adolescents, from 12 to 19 years old. The subjective well-being dimension Inventory from Protective Factors and Risk was applied on them, as well as 4 indicators of suicide attempt. The 15.4% of adolescents reported have attempted suicide. For purposes of comparison the sample of adolescents and attempts of suicide were matched by age and sex. The results showed adolescents that have attempted suicide had a lower subjective well-being than those who have not.

Coping strategies of Mexican adolescents from urban and totonaca indigenous group measured by CRI-Y

Vallejo Casarín, Alma Dept. of Psychology, Universidad Veracruzana, Poza Rica Veracruz, Mexico Juárez, Luis Enrique Vega, Erika Rivera, Nelly Aquino, Gabriela Quiroz, Laura Mazadiego, Teresa Osorno, Rafael

The purpose of this study is to compare coping strategies in two samples from different cultural backgrounds: one from urban area and another from totonaca indigenous group. Method.: 564 totonaca and 574 urban adolescents of both sexes answered the CRI-Y adapted to Mexican adolescents. Results: Urban adolescents had higher scores than totonaca adolescents in 5 subscales, girls from urban and rural areas scored higher in the 8 strategies compared to their males counterparts. It is necessary to study which coping strategies are used by totonaca indigenous adolescents to face problems.

S-042: Components of arithmetic skills: Their diagnosis, prediction and use in remedial education

Wolfgang Schoppek, Dietmar Grube (chair)

The symposium focuses on the development of arithmetic skills and concepts during childhood with an emphasis on children with special needs. Following issues are addressed: What early risk factors for a delayed development can be identified? How can the current stage of development be diagnosed? How can this information be used for designing interventions? Specifically, how can knowledge about the hierarchical organization of skills be used for the design of individualized computer-assisted instruction? How does individualization affect emotions during practice? Contributions range from longitudinal studies, to psychometric analyses based on item response theory, naturalistic intervention experiments, and detailed single-case analyses.

Mathematical precursors assessed in kindergarten: Can they predict dyscalculia in primary school?

Seitz-Stein, Katja Inst. für Entw.-Psychologie, Kath. Universität Eichstätt, Eichstätt, Germany Seybel-Kroeber, Martina Inst. für Entw.-Psychologie, Kath. Universität Eichstätt, Eichstätt, Germany Zoelch, Christof Inst. für Entw.-Psychologie, Kath. Universität Eichstätt, Eichstätt, Germany Schumann-Hengsteler, Ruth Inst. für Entw.-Psychologie, Kath. Universität Eichstätt, Eichstätt, Germany

The aim of our longitudinal study was to assess mathematical precursors in kindergarten children, especially focussing on indicators that help to identify children being potentially at risk of having dyscalculia. 145 kindergarten children were tested on early numerical and arithmetic competencies as well as working memory capacity. Parents and kindergarten teachers were asked about their children's general arithmetic abilities. Secondly the children were tested in first grade on their general cognitive skills. Teachers were asked to judge arithmetic competencies and risk of having future arithmetic problems. Results indicate correlations between early numerical competencies and teacher estimation in first grade.

What accounts for understanding the place-value system of multi-digit numbers in primary school children?

Krinzinger, Helga Inst. für Neuropsychologie, RWTH Aachen, Aachen, Germany

In previous studies we could show that during early primary school years boys understand the Arabic place-value system of multi-digit numbers earlier than girls. In the literature, several factors have been suggested to account for sex differences in the numerical domain. Employing a longitudinal design and structural equation modelling in n=140 primary school children, we found general visual spatial abilities to have the highest impact on the acquisition of the Arabic base-10 system as well as a much smaller contribution by an emotional factor. Yet, sex itself was still an important influence. Educational implications of this study will be discussed.

Qualitative levels as basis for an arithmetic achievement test for children

Fritz, Annemarie Inst. für Psychologie, Universität Essen, Essen, Germany Ricken, Gabi Fakultät IV, Universität Hamburg, Hamburg, Germany Balzer, Lars Regionalinstitut Zollikofen, EHB Eidgenössisches Hochschuli, Zollikofen, Switzerland

The purposes of our investigations are to gain further knowledge about early arithmetic achievement and to find indicators for risk in the development of arithmetic concepts. Based on

theories of Fuson and Resnick we constructed a developmental model with five qualitative stages and a set of items associated to each stage. This model was tested with data from children aged between 4;6 and 6;5 years with an IQ ranging from 70 to 130. In Rasch analyses we focused on the quality of strategies used in correctly solved items. Results and consequences for test-construction will be discussed.

Making practice efficient: Enhancing arithmetic skills by moderate amounts of computer-assisted individualized practice

Schoppek, Wolfgang Inst. für Psychologie, Universität Bayreuth, Bayreuth, Germany Tulis, Maria Inst. für Psychologie, Universität Bayreuth, Bayreuth, Germany

Practice is one important element of mathematics instruction. Since there are other important elements, practice needs to be efficient. For being efficient, practice needs to be individualized. In our adaptive training software "MMM", individual adaptation is based on a hierarchy of arithmetic skills, which was derived from cognitive task analyses. We tested MMM in an experiment with N=273 third graders. Participants practiced once a week during regular math classes for seven weeks. This moderate amount of individualized practice resulted in better posttest performance (d=0.59) compared with controls. Follow-up measures still showed significant differences. Low and high achieving students benefited alike.

Students' emotions and coping with failure in computer-based learning environments in mathematics

Tulis, Maria Inst. für Psychologie, Universität Bayreuth, Bayreuth, Germany Schoppek, Wolfgang Inst. für Psychologie, Universität Bayreuth, Bayreuth, Germany

Students single out mathematics as the one subject about which they have strong negative feelings. However, there is a lack of empirical insight relating to academic emotions and their impact on learning and achievement - especially in individualized computer-based learning environments. In addition to an inquiry of 5th grade students' process-related emotions while working with a practice-software (N = 119), single cases of high- and low-performance students (concerning emotions linked to error rate) were analysed. Results show a wide range of emotions (not only primarily negative affect) of both high- and low-achieving students, but well depending on mistakes and failure.

S-043: Perspectives in motivational intensity: Psychophysiological processes

Guido Gendolla (chair)

This symposium brings together researchers from three countries whose experiments focus on physiological mechanisms that are involved in the process of resource mobilization during task performance. The contributions stem from laboratories investigating individual, social, and clinical aspects of resource mobilization. Specifically, we report fatigue effects on cardiovascular reactivity, first conclusive evidence that reward elicits beta-adrenergic sympathetic arousal, limitations of this effect in depressed individuals, psychophysiological effects of emotions' motivational function, and the impact of overcommitment on norepinephrine secretion. The reported findings will be integrated and discussed in the broader conceptual framework of motivational intensity theory.

Difficulty and incentive effects on beta-adrenergic response

Richter, Michael Inst. für Psychologie, Universität Genf, Geneva, Switzerland

Empirical research on Wright's integration (Wright, 1996) of motivational intensity theory and Obrist's active coping approach did not yet examined the basic hypothesis that cardiovascular effects of task difficulty and success importance result from cardiac beta-adrenergic impact. Two experiments supported this basic prediction by demonstrating in a 1x4 (task difficulty: low vs. moderate vs. high vs. impossible; N=64) and a 1x3 (reward: low vs. moderate vs. high; N=31) between-persons design that task difficulty determines pre-ejection period—an indicator of beta-adrenergic discharge—as long as task success is possible and that reward determines beta-adrenergic reactivity under conditions of unclear difficulty.

Dysphoria and reward insensivity: Performance incentives do not lead to increased cardiovascular response

Brinkmann, Kerstin Inst. für Psychologie, Universität Genf, Geneva, Switzerland

Dysphoria is characterized by diminished approach motivation and reduced sensitivity to rewards. We tested this with regard to effort mobilization in terms of cardiovascular reactivity. Dysphoric and nondysphoric undergraduates performed a mental task without clear performance standard. We expected effort mobilization to vary with success importance. Results confirmed that nondysphoric participants showed higher reactivity of systolic blood pressure and pre-ejection period in the reward than in the no-reward condition. By contrast, dysphoric participants' reactivity of systolic blood pressure and pre-ejection period did not increase with reward. Our results confirm dysphoric individuals' reduced motivation to expend mental effort for obtaining incentives.

The motivational significance of emotions: Gleanings from psychophysiology

Stemmler, Gerhard Inst. für Psychologie, Universität Marburg, Marburg, Germany

Basic emotions have a strong motivational component which allows organisms to pursue the respective emotion goal. But is the physiology of broad motivational behavior tendencies, that is, approach and withdrawal, distinguishable from the physiology of emotions? In a study with N = 118 male soccer players a sample of 24 somatovisceral variables was registered while participants either imagined anger-approach, anger-withdrawal, fear-approach, or fear-withdrawal soccer scenes. MANOVA showed significant main, but no interaction, effects of Emotion and Motivational Direction. These results support the author's proposal that emotion systems have a bipolar motivational organization.

Higher overcommitment to work is associated with lower norepinephrine secretion before and after acute psychosocial stress in men

Wirtz, Petra H. Inst. für Klin. Psychologie, Universität Zürich, Zürich, Switzerland Siegrist, Johannes Medical Psychology, University of Duesseldorf, Duesseldorf, Germany Emini, Luljeta Clinical Psychology, University of Zürich, Zürich, Switzerland Ehlert, Ulrike Clinical Psychology, University of Zurich, Zürich, Switzerland

We investigated whether overcommitment to work is associated with altered stress hormone levels in response to acute psychosocial stress. In 58 men, we assessed overcommitment and measured norepinephrine and cortisol before and after stress and several times up to 60 min thereafter. Higher overcommitment was associated with lower norepinephrine and cortisol levels before and after stress (p's<0.02) as well as with lower norepinephr-

ine stress reactivity (p=0.02). Higher overcommitment independently explained 13% of the total norepinephrine stress response (beta=-0.46,p<0.01,R2change=0.13). Our findings suggest blunted increases in norepinephrine following stress with increasing overcommitment potentially mirroring blunted stress reactivity of the sympathetic nervous system.

S-045: Environmental psychology's approaches to induce behavioral change

Hans-Joachim Mosler, Ellen Matthies (chair)

An important field of research in Environmental Psychology is on the topic of theoretical informed intervention planning in the domain of pro-environmental behavior. To understand the mode of action of the interventions the underlying psychological principles need to be determined for which well proved theories of psychology have to be used. In this symposium different approaches for deriving interventions will be presented. The symposium will include not only intervention studies, but also studies focusing on action models indicating starting points for interventions, or broader approaches to behavioral change (e.g. social marketing).

Meta-analytical methods for the synthesis of environmental psychological research results

Bamberg, Sebastian Inst. für Politikwissenschaft, Universität Gießen, Gießen, Germany

One can ask whether structural models like TPB or NAM provide an adequate theoretical framework of understanding the process underlying people's change in pro-environmental behaviour. Stage models like the Transtheoretical Model provide a theoretical alternative by conceptualizing behavioral change as a process of passing through a sequence of qualitatively different decision stages. The presentation discusses methodological as well as theoretical problems associated with the application of stage models in the domain of pro-environmental behaviour. Also reported are results from an ongoing research project using a revised stage model as basis for the development of an innovative marketing campain.

Feedback and public commitment to improve the environmental quality of farmlands

Lokhorst, Anne Marike Dept. of Social Psychology, Leiden University, Leiden, Netherlands Staats, Henk Social Psychology, Leiden University, Leiden, Netherlands van Dijk, Jerry Social Psychology, Leiden University, Leiden, Netherlands de Snoo, Geert Social Psychology, Leiden University, Leiden, Netherlands

Farmers have several possibilities to improve the environmental quality of their land by engaging in nature management practices. The Dutch government tries to encourage these practices by subsidizing nature management. However, research has shown that rewards may cause a decline of intrinsic motivation. The goal of this study is therefore to develop and test an intervention that increases this motivation. Based on previous research we developed an intervention package that contains feedback and public commitment. We expect farmers that have received both treatments to show the greatest improvement in their nature management. Data is being collected at the moment.

Planning Interventions on a theoretical basis: Applying a new integrative influence model of pro-environmental behaviour

Matthies, Ellen Inst. für Psychologie, Ruhr-Universität Bochum, Bochum, Germany Hansmeier, Nadine Fakultät für Psychologie, Ruhr-University Bochum, Bochum, Germany

Although psychologists have investigated a great variety of intervention strategies, we still lack a theoretical framework which could be used to inform an optimal selection and combination of strategies. In the paper at hand, an integrated influence model of pro-environmental behaviour is introduced and used for the development of a tailored intervention to reduce energy consumption. Prior to the intervention, motives and cognitive variables concerning energy use were recorded in a randomly chosen sub-sample of the target group (N = 323). Intervention impact was evaluated on the basis of consumption values, behavioural indicators and self-report (N = 966). Implications for further intervention planning are discussed.

Developing dissemination and intervention strategies for a technical innovation

Mosler, Hans-Joachim EAWAG, Universität Zürich, Zürich, Switzerland Tobias, Robert Siam, Eawag, Dübendorf, Switzerland Würzebesser, Christian Siam, Eawag, Dübendorf, Switzerland

In this project we investigate the psychological factors which determine whether households in Vietnam adopt or don't adopt arsenic eliminating sand filter technique. Based on the Protection-Motivation-Theory and the Theory of Planned Behavior a questionnaire was developed containing questions about the decision to construct a sand filter, maintaining it and about the communication behavior concerning the filters. A survey was conducted with 320 households having and not having a sand filter. Several factors were worked out which dispose people to build and maintain a sand filter and to talk about sand filter building issues. From these factors and their coactions different dissemination and intervention strategies were derived.

Providing feedback as a means to empower householders to save electricity: A social cognitive approach

Thogersen, John Aarhus School of Business, University of Aarhus, Aarhus, Denmark Grønhøj, Alice Aarhus School of Business, University of Aarhus, Aarhus, Denmark

Private electricity consumption could be substantially reduced (5 - 25%) without the loss of comfort by using best practice technology and care. Based on Bandura's (2001) social cognitive theory, this paper outlines a conceptual framework for understanding householders' energy saving effort. Detailed feedback about electricity consumption is proposed as a means to change the environment to be more facilitating and empower householders to be more effective in their striving towards this goal. The framework is tested on a survey of Danish householders prior to the onset of feedback intervention. Preliminary results are presented and prerequisites for an effective intervention discussed.

S-046: Reading as the eyes and the brain see it: Evidence from eye-movement and ERP research

Reinhold Kliegl (chair)

Reading research has long relied on eye movements to unravel basic perceptual, oculomotor, and lexical processes. The present symposium reports new experimental evidence in this respect. Moreover, the joint measurement of eye movements and ERP will greatly contribute to our understanding of the complex cognitive skill of reading.

Frequency and predictability effects on event-related potentials and eye-movements

Dambacher, Michael Inst. für Psychologie, Freie Universität Berlin, Berlin, Germany Goellner, Kristin Inst. für Psychologie, University of Potsdam, Potsdam, Germany Nuthmann, Antje Psychology,

University of Edinburgh, Edinburgh, United Kingdom *Jacobs, Arthur* Inst. für Psychologie, Freie Universität Berlin, Berlin, Germany *Kliegl, Reinhold* Psychology, University of Potsdam, Potsdam, Germany

It is debatable whether frequency as bottom-up and contextual predictability as top-down variables affect distinct or common processes during word recognition. In 144 sentences, frequency and predictability were experimentally manipulated in target words; sentence frames were kept constant. Event-related potentials (ERPs) were recorded in two experiments with sentences presented word by word using standard (700 ms) and quasi-normal SOAs (280 ms). Eye movements were collected during normal reading in a third experiment. Interactions between frequency and predictability revealed joint and early effects on word recognition. Furthermore, SOA influenced effect latencies in ERPs. Relations between ERPs and eye movements are discussed.

Simultaneous recording of eye movements and ERPs indicates early access to word meaning in natural, left-to-right reading

Dimigen, Olaf Inst. für Psychologie, Humboldt-Universität zu Berlin, Berlin, Germany *Sommer, Werner* Inst. für Psychologie, Humboldt-Universität zu Berlin, Berlin, Germany *Dambacher, Michael* Inst. für Psychologie, Free University of Berlin, Berlin, Germany *Kliegl, Reinhold* Psychology, University of Potsdam, Potsdam, Germany

Electrophysiological correlates of reading have traditionally been studied with RSVP presentation in the strict absence of eye movements (EM). To investigate the timing of word recognition in natural reading, we simultaneously recorded EM and EEG of 30 participants during self-paced, left-to-right sentence reading. Word predictability and frequency of target words was manipulated, allowing direct comparisons between effects in fixation-locked brain activity and EM behavior. Predictability was found to modulate the ERP 140 ms after fixation onset (N400 onset), suggesting an early access to word meaning in natural reading. ERP effects were compared to two parallel datasets using traditional RSVP presentation.

On the interplay between spatial information, word recognition and the use of context during reading

Juhasz, Barbara Dept. of Psychology, Wesleyan University, Middletown, USA *Cheng, Melanie* Dept. of Psychology, Wesleyan University, Middletown, CT, USA

Interword spaces demarcate saccade targets and provide information about word meaning. Juhasz, Inhoff, and Rayner (2005) investigated spatial information in compound word recognition. The present study follows-up on this research by manipulating the sentence context surrounding a potential compound word. In one context, the meaning of the compound word was implied (During Christmas there is a desire of goodwill...). In another context, the meaning of the two separate words was implied (Grandpa left a good will behind...). Spatial layout was also manipulated. Results indicated a complex relationship between spatial layout and context. Implications for models of reading will be discussed.

Children's reading of disappearing text

Blythe, Hazel Dept. of Psychology, University of Southampton, Southampton, USA *Joseph, Holly* Psychology Department, Durham University, Durham, United Kingdom *White, Sarah* School of Psychology, University of Leicester, Southampton, United Kingdom *Liversedge, Simon* School of Psychology, University of Southampton, Southampton, United Kingdom

We monitored participants' eye movements as they processed sentences that literally disappeared as they read. Adults, children aged 7 to 9 years, and children aged 10 to 11 years read four sets of sentences, one which was normally presented and three in which each word disappeared at varying intervals after fixation onset. Sentences contained a target word that was manipulated for frequency. We found no evidence of a developmental change in the speed of visual information uptake during. Rather, the data suggest that the age-related differences are strategic, allowing the reader to progress through the sentences without making refixations.

Eye movement control in reading Chinese script: The Beijing sentence corpus

Yan, Ming Dept. of Psychology, Beijing Normal University, Beijing, People's Republic of China *Richter, Eike* Psychology, University of Potsdam, Potsdam, Germany *Shu, Hua* Dept. of Psychology, Beijing Normal University, Beijing, People's Republic of China *Kliegl, Reinhold* Psychology, University of Potsdam, Potsdam, Germany

Thirty native Chinese readers were instructed to read 150 sentences while their eye movements were monitored. Although Chinese is written without orthographical word boundaries (i.e., spaces), the results strongly suggest word-based eye-movement control. Readers exhibit a stronger tendency to fixate at the word center in single-fixation cases and at the word beginning in first of multiple fixation cases. The fixed length saccade reading strategy which is a character-based targeting model is also discussed. We conclude that it is the word instead of the character that serves as the saccade target. We propose a two-stage hypothesis about language-independent reading.

Binocular fixations: What happens when each eye looks at a different word?

Kreiner, Hamutal School of Informatics, University of Edinburgh, Edinburgh, United Kingdom *Shillcock, Richard* Informatics, University of Edinburgh, Edinburgh, United Kingdom

Recent studies show that the eyes often don't fixate on the same location during reading. We investigated this phenomenon using binocular recordings of eye-movements from a large English corpus of newspaper articles. While most binocular fixations fall within the same word, in many cases words are fixated by one eye and skipped by the other, and in others the two eyes fixate adjacent but different words. We investigated how visuo-motor (launch-site, word length) and linguistic factors (frequency, predictability, lexical categorization) modulate such dissociative fixations and skips. The implications of these findings for parallel vs. serial models of processing are discussed.

S-047: Mathematical cognition: Development, representation, cerebral mechanisms and individual differences

Isabell Wartenburger, Elke van der Meer (chair)

Learning and mastery of maths are important for in everyday life activities. However, the scientific investigation of the learning and mastery of maths is only a relatively recent enterprise. Due to the rich complexity of maths, it is an ambitious topic for interdisciplinary research to address, and an essential one for any efforts in designing and evaluating educationally effective school settings. With this interdisciplinary symposium we intend to discuss recent questions regarding the nature of mathematical cognition, learning effects in mathematical cognition, its modulation by individual differences, its cerebral correlates, and its development over the life span.

Numerical estimation abilities in primary school children: A comparison of low, normal and high achievers in the mathematical domain

Heine, Angela Inst. für Psychologie, Freie Universität Berlin, Berlin, Germany *Hartfeld, Karolina* Allg. u. Neurokog. Psychologie, Freie Universität Berlin, Berlin, Germany

One crucial constituent skill in mathematical performance is estimation, i.e. the ability to approximate numerical quantities without the execution of exact procedures. We investigated the estimation abilities of matched groups of primary school children, i.e. low, normal and high achievers in the mathematical domain by means of electro-encephalographic measures. The results show that depending on achievement group, children exhibit different patterns of EEG activity with respect to both event-related potentials, and activity in the time-frequency domain when they are confronted with non-symbolic estimation tasks. These findings are interpreted in terms children's differential use of approximate processing strategies.

The development of symbolic and non-symbolic numerical magnitude representation: Evidence from behavioural and brain-imaging studies

Ansari, Daniel Dept. of Psychology, University of Western Ontario, London, Canada

Numerical magnitude can be externally represented using both symbolic and non-symbolic stimuli. I will present data from both behavioral and brain-imaging studies which explore how the processing and representation of symbolic and non-symbolic stimuli develops over time and how developmental changes in numerical magnitude processing are related to children's development of mathematical skills. Our data suggest that symbolic, but not non-symbolic, number processing is associated with individual differences in mathematical skills in the early school years. A developmental perspective is useful in understanding how representations of numerical magnitude emerge and how these are mapped onto cultural, symbolic representations of number.

Brain network for arithmetic as evaluated with functional Magnetic Resonance Imaging (fMRI) and Granger Causality Mapping (GCM)

Krueger, Frank Dept. of Cognit. Neuroscience, NIH-NINDS, Bethesda, USA *Heinecke, Armin* Brain Innovation, Brain Innovation, Maastrict, Netherlands *Landgraf, Seffen* Psychologie, Humboldt Universität, Berlin, Germany *van der Meer, Elke* Inst. für Psychologie, Humboldt-Universität zu Berlin, Berlin, Germany

Recent studies in developmental neuropsychology and human neuroimaging indicate that the human ability for arithmetic has a tangible network of parieto-frontal brain regions. However, the neural connectivity between those regions is still unknown. We combined event-related fMRI and GCM analysis in healthy individuals who performed mental multiplications varying in task difficulty. The results revealed specific directions of information flow between the inferior frontal gyrus, angular gyrus, and horizontal segment of the intraparietal sulcus depending on the number of cognitive operands performed during task solution. The GCM approach provides a useful tool to explore functional connectivity underlying arithmetic functioning.

The relation between mathematical competence and brain activation: Evidence from fMRI studies on mental calculation

Grabner, Roland H. Inst. Verhaltenswissenschaften, ETH Zürich, Zürch, Switzerland *Neubauer, Aljoscha C.* Inst. für Psychologie, Universität Graz, Graz, Austria

Starting from well-established findings of a relation between brain activation and individual differences in general and specific cognitive abilities, two fMRI studies on the role of mathematical competence are presented. The first study compared adult students of lower vs. higher mathematical competence during mental calculation and revealed stronger reliance on task-related parietal brain areas in the more competent individuals. In the second study it was investigated how the individual competence level predicts the change of parietal brain activation following a five-day training of arithmetic problems. These studies provide further insights into neurophysiological changes accompanying the successful acquisition of mathematical knowledge.

Neurophysiological correlates of cognition with a special focus on mathematical cognition
Staudt, Beate Inst. für Psychologie, Universität Graz, Graz, Austria Fink, Andreas Inst. für Psychologie, Universität Graz, Graz, Austria Neubauer, Aljoscha C. Inst. für Psychologie, Universität Graz, Graz, Austria
We focus on research dealing with the exploration of biological correlates of individual differences in mental abilities. Specifically, we review evidence on the relationship between cognitive ability and brain activation patterns in response to the performance of tasks employing different cognitive demands (reasoning, working memory, creative cognition, visuo-spatial abilities, arithmetic). Most of the studies found evidence that brighter individuals display a more efficient brain function when performing cognitive tasks. We also deal with studies showing that cognitive processes can be trained and that training effects are also apparent at the level of the brain. Implications for mathematical cognition will be discussed.

Short-term vs. long-term learning in mathematical cognition: Cerebral correlates, domain impacts and sources of individual differences
Foth, Manja Inst. für Psychologie, Humboldt-Universität zu Berlin, Berlin, Germany Preusse, Franziska Berlin Neuroimaging Center, Charite Berlin, Berlin, Germany van der Meer, Elke Inst. für Psychologie, Humboldt-Universität zu Berlin, Berlin, Germany Wartenburger, Isabell Inst. für Linguistiks, Universität Potsdam, Potsdam, Germany
Mathematics is a complex topic comprising different domains. We report on processing analogies and arithmetics in two groups of adolescents differing in mathematical abilities. Brain activation was monitored via fMRI while resource consumption was measured via pupillometry. Adolescents with superior mathematical abilities outperformed normal controls. However, their pupillary responses were higher compared to normal controls. FMRI-data confirm the positive activation-performance relation. When solving tasks a reduction of brain activation over time was seen, suggesting a more efficient processing through learning. These results stress a cognitive efficiency mechanism that mediates interindividual and intraindividual learning-induced performance differences (cf., Jung & Haier, 2006).

S-048: Gender and health

Monika Sieverding, Claus Vögele (chair)
Although gender is increasingly perceived as a key determinant of health and illness, systematic studies investigating differences in health behaviours are rare. For example, cardiovascular disease has long been seen as a "male" disease, resulting in women being underrepresented in cardiovascular research. In contrast, there are few studies investigating factors affecting men's health protective behaviours. While investigations of adult populations are important for secondary prevention and intervention, results on health behaviour differences in children allow for the improvement of primary prevention. This symposium brings together studies

of gender differences in health behaviours and its determinants across the life span.

Gender issues in secondary prevention of coronary heart disease
Weidner, Gerdi Institute, Preventive Medicine Research, Sausalito, USA Campo, Rebecca Institute, Preventive Medicine Research, Sausalito, USA Ornish, Dean Institute, Preventive Medicine Research, Sausalito, USA
Psychosocial stress is more strongly related to myocardial infarction in women than in men (INTERHEART Study). We examined the relationship of psychosocial stress to lifestyle behaviours (diet, exercise, stress management) and coronary risk factors (obesity, blood pressure, exercise capacity) in 415 women and 782 men in the Multisite Cardiac Lifestyle Intervention Program over 3 months. Both sexes improved in all outcomes. Reductions in psychosocial stress were related to improvements in lifestyle behaviours and coronary risk factors only in women (p<.05). Considering that psychosocial stress presents a major barrier to cardiac rehabilitation of women, increased attention to this variable seems warranted.

The role of social norms in predicting men's cancer screening intentions and behaviour
Sieverding, Monika Inst. für Psychologie, Universität Heidelberg, Heidelberg, Germany Matterne, Uwe Psychological Institute, University of Heidelberg, Heidelberg, Germany Ciccarello, Liborio Psychological Institute, University of Heidelberg, Heidelberg, Germany
We applied the Theory of Planned Behaviour (TPB), extended by descriptive norms, to cancer screening (CS) intentions and uptake in men. A cross-sectional study with 2500 men assessed intention, behaviour was measured in a sub-sample of 1000 men one year later. CS-intention was mainly predicted by psychological variables, whereas the contribution of socio-demographic variables (age, education, income) was marginal. Descriptive norms explained variance over and above the classic TPB-variables and interacted significantly with subjective norms. Significant predictors of CS uptake were intentions and subjective norms. Our results show a strong influence of social norms on men's CS behaviour.

Gender differences in health complaints: The role of society and cultural background
Brähler, Elmar Inst. für Medizin. Psychologie, Universität Leipzig, Leipzig, Germany
Women have consistently reported more body complaints than men. On the basis of three larger representative studies of the West German population (18 to 60 years) we found a strong decrease of sex differences from 1975 to 1994 and 2001. Differences between East and West have exceeded the sex differences. In 2001 East German males have complained of more body symptoms than West German women. Thus, data on sex differences need to be discussed against the background of the epoch and the culture, in which they were collected. Data may not be simply collapsed across different countries and epochs.

Heavy episodic drinking in young adults: Psychological variables mediate sex differences in alcohol consumption
Zimmermann, Friederike Inst. für Psychologie, Universität Heidelberg, Heidelberg, Germany Sieverding, Monika Psychological Institute, University of Heidelberg, Heidelberg, Germany
We investigated sex differences in alcohol consumption and any mediating effects of psychological variables. Three hundred participants completed questionnaires based on the Theory of Planned Behaviour and the Prototype/Willingness Model.

Behavioural data were obtained in telephone interviews after a drinking occasion. Alcohol consumption was higher for men. However, after inclusion of psychological variables this sex difference was no longer significant. Among the most important significant partial mediators of the sex-alcohol-relationship were intention, willingness, attitudes, norms and prototype perceptions. If sex differences in psychological variables decrease in line with changing traditional gender roles, women's alcohol consumption is expected to increase.

Age and gender differences in children's health perceptions and health behaviours
Chater, Angel Division of Psychology, University of Bedfordshire, Luton, United Kingdom Vögele, Claus Human and Life Sciences, Roehampton University, London, United Kingdom Worrell, Marcia Human and Life Sciences, Roehampton University, London, United Kingdom
We investigated age and gender differences in children's cognitions, past behaviour and intentions towards health behaviours. Self-report data was collected from 528 children (259 boys) within UK school year groups 7 (11-12 years) and 10 (14-15 years). Boys held higher generalised self-efficacy beliefs than girls. Perceived importance of healthy eating increased with age for girls, but decreased for boys. Girls held higher intentions to maintain a healthy diet, while boys showed a greater intention to exercise and avoid smoking cigarettes. The results suggest that cognitions towards health protective behaviours decrease with age and that this course is mediated by gender.

Physician-diagnosed obesity in German 6 to 14-year-olds: Prevalence and comorbidity for internal disorders, external disorders and sleep disorders with regard to gender
Kohlmann, Carl-Walter Inst. für Psychologie, Pädagogische Hochschule, Schwäbisch Gmünd, Germany Eschenbeck, Heike Institut für Humanwissenschaft, Pädagogische Hochschule, Schwäbisch Gmünd, Germany Dudey, Stefan Hauptverwaltung, Gmünder ErsatzKasse GEK, Schwäbisch Gmünd, Germany Gross, Cornelia Institut für Humanwissenschaft, Pädagogische Hochschule, Schwäbisch Gmünd, Germany Meier, Stefanie Institut für Humanwissenschaft, Pädagogische Hochschule, Schwäbisch Gmünd, Germany Schürholz, Thomas Hauptverwaltung, Gmünder ErsatzKasse GEK, Schwäbisch Gmünd, Germany
We investigated the prevalence of obesity and co-morbid disorders (ICD-10 classifications) in a population-based sample of children (N = 156.948). Prevalence of obesity was 3.8 %. The prevalence of external disorders, internal disorders, sleep disorders, and stay in hospital was higher in children with obesity compared to normal-weight children. For internal disorders the increased odds ratios were higher in obese girls compared to obese boys. For internal disorders the increased odds ratio was higher in 12-14 year olds compared to younger children with obesity. Implications for gender-sensitive obesity interventions will be discussed.

S-049: Psychiatry meets psychology: Joint perspectives

Frank Schneider, Winfried Rief (chair)
Psychiatry and Psychology are both scientific disciplines which investigate human behaviour and its disturbances and thus share a wide area of research topics and methodological approaches. Still, Psychiatry and Psychology feature their own focuses and methodological approaches. The question how these disciplines can inspire each other is of high relevance for future research efforts especially considering the large scientific intersec-

tion. This symposium is intended to characterize the different viewpoints of these disciplines and to point out a joint perspective for future research. Six different aspects of the joint research agenda and the strength of the different approaches in the fields of interest for Psychiatry and Psychology are presented.

Neuropsychology

Kryspin-Exner, Ilse Inst. für Psychologie, Universität Wien, Wien, Austria

Neuropsychology is associated with various interests within the field of Psychiatry that range from diagnostic issues, cognitive training to the evaluation of therapeutic interventions. Furthermore, neurobehavioural probes offer the possibility of using situations that are analogous to real-life as measures during neuroimaging procedures. In contrast to traditional neuropsychology concentrating on impairments resulting from brain injury, neuropsychology within psychiatry is based on a different interpretative model: The brain-behaviour relationship is discussed as a "final common pathway". Similar dysfunctions appear independently of organic impairment because of the interaction of brain regions responsible for higher cortical functioning; such as decision-making, problem-solving and anticipation.

Current situation of psychotherapy within the health care system

Berger, Mathias Dept. of Psychiatry, University Hospital Freiburg, Freiburg, Germany *Voderholzer, Ulrich*

Data from epidemiological surveys and from health insurance companies indicate an increase of psychiatric disorders within our society. This development implicates an increased demand of psychotherapy which is an integral part of treatment for the majority of psychiatric disorders and the primary form of treatment for many of them. Despite the progress of psychotherapy research showing evidence of efficacy for a variety of disorders, several major issues/problems remain: 1. There is still a large and often confusing variety of many different forms of psychotherapy which are mainly based on "psychotherapy schools" and theories rather than on scientific evidence. 2. A major problem is the implementation of evidence based psychotherapies. 3. In many countries the blueprints of training are more oriented on psychotherapy schools and less on disorders. 4. In some countries, for example in Germany, there is an adequate funding of psychotherapy, but not of primary care of patients with severe mental disorders requiring complex treatments including pharmacotherapy.

Rehabilitation

Rössler, Wulf Psychiatrie und Psychologie, Universität Zürich, Zürich, Switzerland

The goal of psychiatric rehabilitation is to help disabled individuals to establish the emotional, social and intellectual skills needed to live, learn and work in the community with the least amount of professional support. The overall philosophy of psychiatric rehabilitation comprises two intervention strategies: The first strategy is individual-centred and aims at developing the patient's skill to interact with a stressful environment. The second strategy as an ecological approach is directed towards developing environmental resources to reduce potential stressors. Most disabled persons need a combination of both approaches.

Neuroimaging research

Schneider, Frank Psychiatrie und Psychologie, RWTH Universität Aachen, Aachen, Germany

Cognitive and emotional impairments are symptoms in almost every psychiatric disease. As emotions are important human functions in the context of social interactions, these disturbances account for severe impairments of the quality of life. Neuroimaging is a well-established method of studying the neurobiological basis of these disturbed processes. To fully understand the psychiatric disturbances seen in the clinical practice it will be indispensable to establish psychological models of "normal" behaviour, namely emotion and cognition. The understanding of the results of neuroimaging studies will depend on the establishment of widely accepted models of normal brain functions and their neurobiology.

S-050: Psychological reactions to threat

Andreas Kastenmüller (chair)

Different kinds of threat that are in the current discussion (unemployment, war, terrorism, social exclusion, trauma) are considered. In this manner, we discuss societal (e.g. utilization of group-membership, parenting) and personal (e.g. mental health, posttraumatic growth) reactions to these threats.

Trauma recall and posttraumatic growth: In impact of spiritual support

Kastenmüller, Andreas Inst. für Sozialpsychologie, Universität München, München, Germany

Previous research has shown that the recall of a traumatic event (vs. control group) leads to posttraumatic growth, especially to increased life-meaningfulness. By using a standardised posttraumatic growth scale we found evidence within two studies that trauma-recall can additionally increase spiritual growth (Study 1 and 2). Study 2 indicated that this spiritual growth could even increase marginally when people have a high belief (induced by a faked scientific article) that a spiritual power can give support in traumatic situations (e.g. healing severe diseases).

The impact of social exclusion on religiousness

Aydin, Niluefer Inst. für Sozialpsychologie, Universität München, München, Germany

Research has investigated several coping strategies in social exclusion situations, but the role of religiousness in dealing with ostracism has not been studied so far. We postulated that devotion to religion serves as a coping source after social exclusion by showing increased religiousness. Two studies assessed turning to religion as dependent variable. ANOVA analysis revealed that participants, migrated and non-migrated Turks in study 1, German students in study 2, who felt excluded, showed significant higher levels of intrinsic and extrinsic religiousness than participants in the control conditions. Conclusion: Religion serves as coping source in dealing with rejection

Assessing the Connection of Soul (COS) with a transcendental world: A test beyond the belief in literal immortality

Ai, Amy School of Social Work, University of Washington, Seattle, USA

Despite the mounting evidence on Terror Management Theory (TMT), relatively little research has investigated literal immortality (LI), denying physical death as the finality of the life. This paper presents a scale to assess dimensions of belief in the connection of soul (COS), based on different worldviews in the world's dominant cultural traditions. Methods: Principal axis factoring analyses were performed on experimental data. Results: We found a three-factor solution, corresponding to three COS dimensions: secular, God-centered, and cosmic-spiritual views. Other analyses offered initial construct validity and internal consistency. Conclusion: The COS is a reasonable measure for studying LI phenomenon.

The impact of terror salience on authoritarian parenting: First evidence

Fischer, Peter School of Psychology, University of Exeter, Exeter, United Kingdom

Terrorist threat is a form of collective threat and affects a variety of intra- and inter-personal psychological responses, including punishment intentions and authoritarianism. The present research investigates whether terrorist threat fosters authoritarian parenting. A pilot study revealed that watching terrorism-related pictures led to a less negative attitude towards corporal punishment than neutral pictures (Study 1). Two further studies currently test whether a similar effect can be found for established measures of authoritarian parenting style (Study 2) and real parenting behavior in a playing sequence (Study 3).

The value of "We" when "I" fail: Group-based control restoration as reaction to the threat of unemployment

Jonas, Eva Inst. für Sozialpsychologie, Universität Salzburg, Salzburg, Austria *Fritsche, Immo* Social Psychology, Psychology, Jena, Germany

Unemployment threatens people's sense of individual control. As groups may have control restorative value for individuals we hypothesized that people utilize group membership to restore their sense of control. We report two experiments showing that being reminded of the possibility of uncontrollable vs. controllable long-term unemployment increased ingroup bias in the intergroup context of East and West Germans. Furthermore, a field study showed that people suffering from unemployment felt the less powerless the more they identified with other Germans. The findings are discussed in the light of a group-based control restoration account of intergroup behavior.

Enough is enough in the face of threat: Minimal and maximal goal orientations mediate the effect of perceived individual threat on exclusion of norm-breakers

Fritsche, Immo Jena, Germany

I tested the hypothesis that increased negative reactions towards deviants under conditions of individual threat (e.g., Greenberg, Solomon & Pyszczynski, 1997) are mediated by a generalized orientation to set absolute (= minimal) vs. graded (= maximal) goals (e.g., Fritsche, Kessler, Mummendey & Neumann, in press). In support for this assumption, experimentally induced individual threat (vs. reduced threat) increased preference for minimal over maximal goals in Study 1. In Study 2 perceived life threat increased social exclusion inclinations towards deviants. This effect was fully mediated by minimal goal preference. The interplay of individual and collective processes in threat effects is discussed.

S-051: The Leadership Journey: Integration, development, derailment and exit

Judith Blanton (chair)

This symposium will describe various aspects of the leadership journey. The first presentation by Ms. Czegledi-Brown will provide an overview of the key states, challenges and approaches for development of leaders throughout the career journey. Dr. Blanton will summarize research and best practices dealing with how leaders enter and are integrated into an organization. Dr. Li will describe research on assessing cultural intelligence in international executives. Dr. Mobley will focus on issues of potential derailment and Dr. Irving will discuss issues in exiting an organization. Dr. Vandaveer will lead a discussion of implications for developing leaders in organizations.

The leadership journey: Framework and dimensions of success
Czegledi-Brown, Reka RHR International, London, United Kingdom
Reka Czegledi-Brown will present a framework which aims to look at the complex and contextual aspects of the leadership phenomenon. We aim to answer what makes leaders successful throughout their journey. We believe that congruent leadership performance emerges from core values that shape the leadership character and behaviour that will turn the capacity of others toward the achievement of goals. Therefore, the framework focuses on a small number of core leadership attributes, such as values, personal characteristics, behaviors and competences that appear in the formation, performance and sustainability of the leadership journey. Role of executive coaching and other development interventions will be connected to the challenges and attributes.

Executive integration: The first ninety days
Blanton, Judith RHR International, Los Angeles, USA
The presentation summarizes 4 years of research on the integration of executives into a new role. Many executives fail in their initial months on the job but increasing numbers of organizations are initiating activities to enhance integration. Success factors include acceptance, credibility and observable impact. Three major dimensions impacting success were identified: role, relationship and culture. The presentation describes pitfalls as well as effective strategies to address potential derailers during the first three months on the job. In addition to suggesting effective behaviors for the individual, we will describe strategies that organizations have used successfully in their integration efforts.

Developing cultural intelligence in international executives
Li, Lily Business School, China Europe International, Shanghai, People's Republic of China
Lily Li will present a theoretical framework to examine the antecedents of cultural intelligence which reflects the capability of international executives to deal effectively with people from different cultural backgrounds. A diverse set of individual difference constructs including personality, international experience and learning will be discussed. Empirical findings around the importance of these constructs in predicting the level of cultural intelligence will be presented. Finally, important implication of these findings for international executive selection and development will be recommended.

Derailment of executives in international assignments
Mobley, William Mobley Group Pacific, Shanghai, People's Republic of China
Drawing on the relevant research literature and his extensive executive coaching experience, Dr. Mobley will lead an interactive discussion of the causes and consequences of executive derailment in international settings. He will use 5-8 actual mini-cases to focus the discussion; then will seek to draw generalizations from the discussion and relevant literature; and will present an I-O-P conceptual model of the international executive derailment process.. He will suggest a number of steps individuals, coaches and organizations can take to minimize international derailment.

The leadership journey: Transition and exit
Czegledi-Brown, Reka RHR International, London, United Kingdom Irving, Robert RHR International, London, United Kingdom
How individuals join and develop in organisations attracts more attention in the research literature than exits. Dr Rob Irving will talk about the cognitive, emotional and interpersonal components

in transition and exit for senior executives including the legacy issues in transition for senior people, both from a business and person perspective. He will assess how the issues can impact organisational performance (positively and negatively) and the ways in which they can best be managed and monitored from both the individual and organisational perspective. His talk would draw on RHR's research on executive transition including the personality characteristics or behavioral constructs that support or derail this process.

S-052: Recent findings from fatherhood research

Andreas Eickhorst, Heinz Walter (chair)
The father's role in the family, his impact on children's development and his subjective experiences are recent topics in developmental psychology, although until now there is only little systematic research on fathers. Our symposium will present an overview of the current situation in fatherhood research, followed by empirical findings from Costa Rica, Mexico, Argentina, Austria and Germany. Topics are the paternal self concept, the transition to fatherhood, the newborn's impact on the father's emotional setup and the relation between fatherhood experience and children's social competencies. Longitudinal and cross sectional data, surveys, questionnaires, behavioural observations and semi-structures interviews are the methods presented in the symposium.

The father: What is that? Theoretical considerations on fatherhood
Walter, Heinz Inst. für Pädag. Psychologie, Universität Konstanz, Konstanz, Germany
There is no prototypical father. He might have existed in traditional cultures (fathers there were forced to a specific way of living their fatherhood by couvade and other rituals). In modern societies, it seems unrealistic and inhuman to expect men being the one "new", "comitted", "omnipresent" father. Living fatherhood depends on many factors, often not possible to be controled by men themselves. It would be constructive, if social scientists, female partners and professionals in different psychosocial fields would invite fathers to exchange ideas with them, how to live "good enough" fatherhood. Suggestions for different ways of exchange and some hypotheses, which outputs are expected, will be presented and discussed.

Changes in paternal attitudes over a period of 15 years after child's birth
Werneck, Harald Fakultät für Psychologie, Universität Wien, Wien, Austria Rollett, Brigitte Fakultät für Psychologie, Universität Wien, Wien, Austria
The study presented in this paper is part of the longitudinal research project "Family Development in the Course of Life (FIL)", during which 175 Austrian families were investigated six times, from pregnancy up to 15 years afterwards. A lot of instruments were used, e.g. the Parental Role Questionnaire, or the Questionnaire of the Quality of Partnership. Based on the hypothesis that paternal attitudes become more traditional over time, changes in the paternal role concept are analyzed. Using a typological approach, according to which fathers are classified into clusters, different pattern of changes in attitudes can be found.

Experiences of fatherhood, father behaviour and children's social competencies
Eickhorst, Andreas Inst. für Familientherapie, Universitätsklinik Heidelberg, Heidelberg, Germany
This presentation deals with relations between fatherhood experience, father behavior and children's social behaviour. The sample consists of about 600 German fathers with children in the first or second year of elementary school. The methods

are the Alabama Parenting Questionnaire (APQ; German version; Reichle, 2003), the Verhaltensbogen für Vorschulkinder (VBV; questionnaire about children's behaviour; Reichle, 2003) and the Konstanzer Vaeterinstrument (KOVI; Wenger-Schittenhelm & Walter, 2002). This instrument operationalizes the fathers' personal experience with 71 items on eight scales like global paternal competence, relationship to the child or enrichment caused by the father role. The results show positive partial correlations between all three variables.

Fatherhood in Latin America: How does the father express the impact that the birth of his baby produces on him?
Oiberman, Alicia Dept. of Psychology, University of Buenos Aires, Buenos Aires, Argentina
The aim of this article is to assess the emotional impact that the birth of the newborn baby produces on the father. In order to accomplish this, a paternal observation scale (POS) was elaborated. The POS was applied to 60 fathers of babies, during the first 72 hours after birth, in a public hospital in Buenos Aires, Argentina. The observations took place in the rooms where mothers and babies are interned together.

Conceptions of parenting, similarities and differences between Mexican and Costa Rican fathers
Frey, Britta Inst. für Familientherapie, Universitätsklinik Heidelberg, Heidelberg, Germany
Parenting and self-construals are strongly influenced by cultural models. Urban educated families from Central American societies are assumed to follow an autonomous-related self-model. Nevertheless, differences between these cultural communities can be expected. So far, only few studies focus on Latino fathers. Therefore, cultural models of parenting of 20 Costa Rican and 17 Mexican fathers are investigated. Data was analyzed quantitatively and qualitatively focusing on the expression of autonomy and relatedness. First results indicate that fathers from both samples value relatedness to similar degrees, but have different views on autonomy. Further data analysis need to substantiate or modify the first results.

S-053: Women over 50: Psychological perspectives

Varda Muhlbauer (chair)
The shift in cultural representations and life experiences of women at midlife is the product of a substantial transformation in the sociocultural construction of collective gendered-age identity, which has given rise to a blurring and diversification of both age and gender roles. The new gendered-age representations of women over 50 have generated positive meanings and more liberal behavior codes. The present cohort of women over 50 has benefited from the accomplishments achieved by the political movements of the 1960s and 1970s, and they are now rewriting their collective identity in new and empowering ways, some of which we will discuss.

Title to be announced
Chrisler, Joan Dept. of Psychology, Connecticut College, New London, USA
The word "aging" typically brings to mind changes in the body - both superficial (e.g., gray hair, wrinkles) and organic (e.g., chronic illness, infirmity). The speaker will examine the available research on body image issues of women over 50, taking a broad view of embodiment. Much of the available data is not specific to this age group, and how well or poorly midlife women seem to adjust to age-related changes may depend on how the data are acquired (e.g., quantitative vs. qualitative

studies). Suggestions for future research will be given and implications for practice considered.

Title to be announced

Rose, Suzanna Dept. of Psychology, Florida Intern. University, Miami, USA

Women enjoy a renewed experience of friendship after age 50. Changes in the dynamics of women's friendship at midlife and how they are affected by experience, lifestage, personality, race, and sexual orientation will be explored. Directions for future research also will be presented.

Title to be announced

Marván, Maria Luisa Medicine School, Univ Nal Autónoma de México, Mexico City, Mexico

Objective: To explore womens beliefs about mens view on hysterectomy and the actual mens view. Method: Seventy-four women without hysterectomy and 70 men (ages 40-49) answered a Likert scale with positive and negative concepts describing a hysterectomized woman, and three open-ended questions about the issue. Results: Women supposed that men had more negative beliefs than they actually did (p<.0001). The idea that a hysterectomized woman would be "rejected" was the most prominent discrepancy, which was corroborated by the qualitative data. Conclusion: These womens beliefs may cause some patients to delay considering hysterectomy until they are left with no alternative.

Title to be announced

Fimbel Di Giovanni, Joan Tucson, USA

Women artists of the 20th century experienced gender role conflicts between their personal and professional lives. Many struggled throughout adulthood to establish themselves as artists (e. g. Kollwitz, O'Keeffe); others began their artistic expression after age 50 (e. g. Grandma Moses). Midlife artists continue to work due to their postmenopausal zest (Mead) and their generativity (Erikson). Their self-world was defined though their work. The speaker will talk about some biographical aspects of the selected artists and show how some of their works are autotelic illustrations of their defense of self, self-preservation, and self-realization (Csikszentmihalyi).

Title to be announced

Trujillo, Paulina Psychology, Universidad de las Américas-P, Mexico City, Mexico

Objective: To explore womens beliefs about mens view on hysterectomy and the actual mens view. Method: Seventy-four women without hysterectomy and 70 men (ages 40-49) answered a Likert scale with positive and negative concepts describing a hysterectomized woman, and three open-ended questions about the issue. Results: Women supposed that men had more negative beliefs than they actually did (p<.0001). The idea that a hysterectomized woman would be "rejected" was the most prominent discrepancy, which was corroborated by the qualitative data. Conclusion: These womens beliefs may cause some patients to delay considering hysterectomy until they are left with no alternative.

S-054: Predictors of prenatal and postnatal maternal attachment: Implication for lowering at risk-birth outcomes

Anver Siddiqui, Janis B. Feldman (chair)

The purpose of this syposium is to present the prenatal and postnatal significant factors to enhance a mother's relationship to her infant. Predictive factors include maternal prenatal attachment; the mother's childhood history; her attitude, personality, and mood; infant temperament and

partner relationships. While the finding underscore the importance of multiple indicators influencing the mother's relationship to her infant, maternal prenatal attachment emerged as the strongest factor predicting maternal postnatal relationship. The knowledge serves as an important diagnostic tool to identify women who are at-risk for suboptimal attachment to their infant.

Mothers' temperament and its effect on prenatal attachment and postpartum depressed mood

Bielawska-Batorowicz, Eleonora Inst. of Psychology, University of Lodz, Lodz, Poland *Grosicka, Karolina* Inst. of Psychology, University of Lodz, Lodz, Poland

Objective: To test whether (1) mothers' temperament affect prenatal attachment and postnatal depression (2) strong prenatal attachment prevent depressed mood postpartum. Method: 81 primiparas were recruited randomly from pregnant patient of a district hospital. Prenatal Attachment Inventory by Muller and Temperament Questionnaire by Strelau were administered in the third trimester of pregnancy and Edinburgh Postnatal Depression Scale by Cox et al. in the first postpartum week. Results: Higher reactivity was linked to less strong attachment, while higher perseverativity and lower activity to stronger depression. Prenatal attachment had no effect on depression. Conclusion: Temperament can predict postpartum mood and prenatal attachment.

Stability of maternal interpretation of infant facial expression during pre- and postnatal period

Garcia, Danilo Dept. of Psychology, Karlstad University, Karlstad, Sweden *Osmont, Karine* Dept. of Clinical Sciences, Umea University, Umea, Sweden

The study explores maternal ability to perceive and interpret infants' emotional expression during prenatal and postnatal period. 149 pregnant women at their third trimester were recruited for the study. The IFEEL-picture, a projective test is used in pre- and postnatal period. In addition PAI (Prenatal Attachment Inventory) is used to measure prenatal attachment. Results revealed mothers interpreted infant emotion overwhelmingly in positive terms in both periods. However some parity differences were revealed. Moreover the category interest is used more often by medium attached women in both period whereas low attached used the category content more often in both periods.

Prenatal attachment, feeding intention and early cessation of breast feeding

Juergens, Amelie Service de Pedopsychiatrie, Hospital Necker-Enfants Malade, Paris, France *Bauquier, B* Service de Pedopsychiatrie, Hospital Necker-Enfants Malade, Paris, France *Levy-Rueff, M* Service de Pedopsychiatrie, Hospital Necker-Enfants Malade, Paris, France *Golse, B* Service de Pedopsychiatrie, Hospital Necker-Enfants Malade, Paris, France *Goffinet, F* Service de Pedopsychiatrie, Hospital Necker-Enfants Malade, Paris, France

The purpose of this symposium is to present the prenatal and postnatal significant factors found to enhance a mother's relationship to her infant. Predictive factors include maternal prenatal attachment; the mother's childhood history; her attitude, personality, and mood; infant emotions and temperament; and partner relationships. While the findings underscore the importance of multiple indicators influencing the mother's relationship to her infant, maternal prenatal attachment emerged as the strongest factor predicting maternal postnatal attachment. This knowledge serves as an important diagnostic tool to identify women who are at-risk for suboptimal attachment to their infants.

Predictors of mother-infant relationship during early postnatal period

Siddiqui, Anver Dept. of Psychology, School of Social Sciences, Växjö, Sweden

This study examined the predictors of early mother-infant relationships. One hundred pregnant women and their infants at 12- weeks participated in the study. The expectant women completed two self-administered questionnaire: one regarding prenatal attachment and one addressing childhood memories of parenting. At about 12 weeks postpartum mothers completed three additional self administered questionnaire on personality assessments, partner relationship, and maternal perception of infant temperament. Mothers and their infants were observed and videotaped during an en face interaction The results revealed that prenatal attachment and maternal personality were the two most important predictors of the early mother-infant relationship.

The effect of support expectation on prenatal attachment: An evidence-based approach for intervention in an adolescent population

Feldman, Janis B. Dept. of Social Work, University of Texas, Edinburg, TX, USA

This study was designed to determine the variables predicting prenatal attachment in order to assess and intervene to decrease birth risks. Previous related studies demonstrated conflicting findings due to using different theories and methodologies. To ensure consistency, this study infused Bowlby's attachment theory, Levitt's support expectations model, and prenatal relationship research studies. The survey sampled 129 predominately Latina and African American pregnant adolescents attending public school. Measurements included the Prenatal Attachment Inventory (PAI) (Muller). Regression analysis revealed that expectation of support was a significant predictor with pregnancy planning and less stress adding importantly to explain over 33% of variance.

S-055: Motives: Measures, mechanisms, management (Part II)

Hugo M. Kehr (chair)

This symposium integrates research on implicit and explicit motives and goals; motive measurement; mechanisms underlying motive arousal and motivation; and volitional and self-regulatory goal management. Session 2 highlights different levels of self-regulatory mechanisms, starting with unconscious thought as a means to enhance motive/goal congruency (Langens) and with enhancing realization chances of one's fantasies by contrasting them with knowledge about true obstacles (Oettingen). Next, implementation intentions in motivational and volitional mindsets (Gollwitzer) and flexible goal reprioritization (Shah, Leander, Hall & Bodmann) are examined as means of goal management. Lastly, motivation problems in age diverse teams are explored (Shemla, Wegge & Schmidt).

Does unconscious thought increase congruence between implicit motives and goal pursuit?

Langens, Thomas Inst. für Psychologie, Universität Wuppertal, Wuppertal, Germany

Research by Dijksterhuis and colleagues has shown that unconscious thought can increase the quality of decisions and post-choice satisfaction and, more generally, that unconscious thought has the capacity to integrate complex information and affective preferences. The present research investigated whether unconscious thought aligns goal pursuit to implicit motives. Participants decided between two alternative goals – one agentic and one communal – either on the spot, or after 5 minutes of conscious deliberation, or after 5 minutes of distraction. Results are discussed with reference to the distinction between implicit and explicit motives.

Making your fantasies come true: Mechanisms and origins of mental contrasting

Oettingen, Gabriele Inst. für Psychologie, Universität Hamburg, Hamburg, Germany

Mentally contrasting fantasies about a desired future with obstacles of present reality fosters feasibility-guided goal setting (Oettingen, 2000), while only fantasizing about the future or only reflecting present reality leads to goals that fail to respect feasibility. I present research testing scope, mechanisms, and applied implications of mental contrasting effects. Finally, I will discuss context and socialization influences on the self-generation of mental contrasting. The results have important implications for the initiation and maintenance of behavior change.

The interplay of motivation and volition: The case of implementation intentions

Gollwitzer, Peter M. Dept. of Psychology, New York University, New York, NY, USA

Implementation intentions spell out how one wants to strive for a goal and thus enhance the rate of goal attainment (Gollwitzer & Sheeran, 2006). However, motivation to reach the goal needs to be high, no matter whether motivation is assessed (Study 1) or induced (Study 2). Moreover, individuals need to be in a volitional rather than motivational mindset. When asked to reflect on the motivational reasons for reaching the goal, implementation intention effects were no longer observed for both academic (Study 3) and health goals (Study 4). Implications for developing motivational/volitional interventions geared at behavior change are discussed.

Regulatory rotation: The shuffling and shedding of strivings in goal management

Shah, James Dept. of Psychology, Duke University, Durham, NC, USA Leander, Pontus Dept. of Psychology, Duke University, Durham, NC, USA Hall, Deborah L. Dept. of Psychology, Duke University, Durham, NC, USA Bodmann, Shawn Dept. of Psychology, Univ. of Wisconsin-Madison, Madison, WI, USA

An important, although perhaps under-examined, component of effective self-regulation, then, is the manner in which we "juggle" our various pursuits and resolve goal conflict in order to best ensure the successful attainment of as many goals as possible. Our talk will detail recent research examining the various mechanisms involved in such goal management, focusing in particular on the manner in which we rotate amongst our various pursuits and the continual updating of their relative priority. This ongoing research will also be discussed in terms of its implications for the development of a model of goal management.

Motivational problems in workgroups as a function of age and tenure diversity

Shemla, Meir Inst. für Psychology, Technische Universität Dresden, Dresden, Germany Wegge, Jürgen Department of Psychology, Technical University of Dresde, Dresden, Germany Schmidt, Klaus Helmut Department of Psychology, Technical University Dresden, Dresden, Germany

Recent studies reveal that motives of younger and older employees differ substantially. Therefore, we investigated how age diversity in teams is related to motivational problems (e.g., conflict) in 155 groups (N=722) operating in tax-offices. As expected, conflict had negative effects (e.g., low innovation, health problems). Moreover, we found that tenure diversity moderated the relationship between age diversity and conflict. Specifically, as age diversity increased, groups with low tenure diversity showed an increase whereas groups with high tenure diversity showed a decrease in motivational problems. Thus, tenure diversity is an important variable for the management of age-related motivational problems in teams.

S-056: Situating psychology of science

Neelam Kumar (chair)

The symposium aims to bring together psychological studies of science. Science has been subject of study for philosophers, historians and sociologists. Though psychologists have studied science and made important contributions, science has not been the focus of mainstream psychologists. The symposium will address scientists as subjects for psychologists. It will discuss the history, future and the status of Psychology of Science as a sub-discipline. The symposium will also try to explore the place and relationship of Psychology with other disciplines studying science.

The epidemiology of the infinitesimals: A case study in the cognitive history of mathematics

Heintz, Christophe social science, Institut Jean Nicod - EHESS, Paris, France

The 'number sense' is a cognitive ability that performs basic reasoning with quantities. This ability is shown to be cross-cultural and shared with non-human animals. I investigate the role of the number sense in the evolution of mathematics. I first specify how the number sense gets involved in mathematical reasoning: the cognitive ability differentially enriches the cognitive effects that mathematical notions can have. Then I show how these psychological processes have had a role in the history of mathematics: they made the concept of 'evanescent quantities' more appealing, to 18th century French mathematician, than the concept of infinitesimals.

Causal inference and counterfactual reasoning in scientists and children

Gopnik, Alison Dept. of Psychology, University of California at Be, Berkeley, USA

In the "theory theory" I've argued that scientific reasoning and cognitive development share the same basic learning mechanisms. Recently we have been using the causal graphic models or "Bayes Net" foramlism to characterize these mechanisms, and have shown experimentally that very young children use these mechanisms. I'll suggest that the evolutionary advantage of causal knowledge is that it allows counterfactual and hypothetical thought - both in childhood and in science. In turn this allows humans to not only react to their environments but to create new environments.

Scientific reasoning is not necessarily plagued by confirmation bias

Koslowski, Barbara Human Development, Cornell University, Ithaca, USA

Confirmation bias is said to cause several types of flawed reasoning. We presented college students with possible explanations for events, along with information possibly relevant to assessing the explanations. We found: (a) a motivation to confirm results in more accurate judgments about the relevance of information than does a motivation to disconfirm; (b) people place greater emphasis on information that distinguishes between two explanations than on information compatible with both; (c) when evaluating an explanation, people generate and consider the presence of alternative explanations. Thus, we found people have many skills said, in the confirmation bias literature, that they lack.

Trading zones and interactional expertise as a framework for studying technoscientific collaborations

Gorman, Michael E. Science and Technology, University of Virginia, Charlottesville, USA

Science and technology are becoming increasingly interdisciplinary activities. But how can this cooperation occur, given the problems in disciplinary communication caused by incommensurable perspectives and practices? Peter Galison's answer is trading zones - an anthropological concept. Another way is interactional expertise, ability of an expert to communicate effectively with practitioners of another discipline without doing research in that community. Trading zones can be mediated either by inter-language, or interactional expertise, or a combination. This presentation will propose methods by which trading zones and interactional expertise can be empirically observed, using a combination of protocol analysis, interviews and surveys.

Scientist's semantic meaning of the concept of "Tacit Knowledge"

Liberman, Sofia Posgrado. Facultad de Psicolog, Universidad Nacional Autóma de, Mexico City, Mexico Galan, Carlos The Scott Sutherland School, The Robert Gordon University, Aberdeen, United Kingdom

To become a fully-fledged scientist it is not enough to accomplish all explicit curricular tasks required by institutional, academic system. Failure to follow implicit rules and implicit knowledge could cause career failure. Such knowledge is acquired slowly through exposure to, and interiorized in the practice of, subject of study. However, there is neither an operational definition of the concept nor a clear division between tacit and explicit knowledge. We describe meaning of this concept amongst 150 scientists at National University of México using Natural Semantic Networks technique. Results show that scientists' experience and disciplinary knowledge are key definers 'tacit knowledge'.

The making of physical scientists and social scientists: The importance of being thing- or people-oriented

Feist, Gregory Dept. of Psychology, San José State University, California, CA, USA Larson, Adam

Previous work in psychology of science has shown that interest and talent for science is a function of many psychological factors, some of which are cognitive skills and distinct forms of intelligence (Feist, 2006). We predicted that high ability in mechanical reasoning along with high Asperger's quotient (thing-orientation) relates to interest in physical sciences, and high social and emotional intelligence (people-orientation) relates to interest in social sciences. 150 undergraduates, were given online and pen-and-paper tests measuring physical and social intelligence and interest in science. Results supported predictions. Psychological factors are important in shaping scientific interests.

S-057: Human-machine interaction (Part I): Automation and complex systems

Jürgen Sauer, Kai-Christoph Hamborg (chair)

The symposium is concerned with various aspects of work design in highly complex technical systems such as industrial process control. The research papers focus on two elements of work design: training and automation design. With regard to training, the empirical work examined the effectiveness of various training methods under different operational conditions (e.g., unanticipated fault states). The studies on automation are concerned with the advantages of different task allocation methods under changing operational conditions. The work also covers the effects of stressors on operator performance and proposes a quantitative model to determine the degree of automation in a system.

Enhancing knowledge acquisition about complex technical systems by visualising causal system structures

Klostermann, Anne Mensch-Maschine-Systeme, Technische Universität Berlin, Berlin, Germany
Our study investigates two training strategies, both aiming at the promotion of causal knowledge acquisition about complex systems. A text-based training strategy is compared to an augmented training strategy applying the visualisation of causal relations between system components. The experiment is based on a 2x2 factorial design with the factors training type (picture vs. text) and time of system interaction (prior vs. subsequent to knowledge assessment). Forty-eight participants are trained in understanding and manually controlling the simulation of a process control system. Results indicate a strong influence of training type on knowledge acquisition and performance in system interaction.

The effectiveness of emphasis shift training, situation awareness training and drill and practice for system control and fault finding performance in process control

Burkolter, Dina Organisationspsychologie, Universität St. Gallen, St. Gallen, Switzerland Kluge, Annette Organisationspsychologie, Universität St. Gallen, St. Gallen, Switzerland
As our previous studies showed the two main tasks of process control, system control and fault finding, are not correlated. Therefore, they have to be trained in separate entities to support both skills. An emphasis shift training (EST) and an EST combined with situation awareness training (EST/SA) were compared to a drill and practice training. A four-hour training session with a simulated process control environment was held, followed by two test sessions after longer periods of non-use (N = 54). EST and EST/SA trainings supported process control performance best, notably system control performance.

Types of function allocation in complex process control scenarios

Nickel, Peter Dept. de Psychologie, Université de Fribourg, Fribourg, Switzerland Sauer, Jürgen Dept. of Psychology, University of Fribourg, Fribourg, Switzerland
In complex human-machine systems the operator continually adapts to changes in the dynamic process under control and takes action to prevent process disturbances. Although operator performance is assumed to be affected by the type of function allocation in human-machine systems, its effects in process control environments remain largely unclear. In a simulator experiment trained student operators performed process control scenarios under two types of static allocation. Results for performance and psychophysiological parameters and subjective ratings demonstrate differences in static types and suggesting advantages of dynamic allocation. Consequences for subsequent studies on explicit and implicit dynamic function allocation will be discussed.

The influence of time pressure and time on task on orderliness of control

Röttger, Stefan Psychologie und Ergonomie, Techn. Universität Berlin, Berlin, Germany Manzey, Dietrich Inst. of Psychol. and Ergonom., Techn. Universität Berlin, Berlin, Germany
The Contextual Control Model (COCOM, Hollnagel, 1993), describes orderliness as degree of purposefulness, advance planning, and regularity of human operators' control behaviour which constitutes a continuum from random trial-and-error actions to strategically chosen control actions. COCOM predicts that orderliness will decrease with time pressure, resulting in decreased control performance. Familiarity with task and situation is predicted to increase orderliness and performance. These predictions were tested in a controlled experiment using an information theory-based measure of regularity of operator behaviour as an indicator of orderliness (Röttger, Klostermann & Manzey, 2007). Results are in line with COCOM's predictions.

Automation: Levels, types, or amount?

Di Nocera, Francesco Dept. of Psychology, University of Rome, Rome, Italy
The classic approach to the concept of Level Of Automation (LOA) is qualitative in nature: it simply describes the trading of system control between humans and computers. For example, the 10-point scale proposed in Sheridan's seminal work only describes the degree of human (or machine) involvement in system control. Further elaboration of this rationale extended the LOA concept to a four stage information-processing model, thus providing a framework to better design automated systems. Albeit this qualitative approaches are useful for function allocation in the design phase, a more formal model is necessary for experimentation. Here we define LOA in terms of the amount of information traded by humans and machines.

S-211: The Psychology of Sehnsucht (life longings): Connections with related psychological fields

Dana Kotter-Grühn, Susanne Scheibe (chair)
The objective of the symposium is to discuss perspectives of a psychology of "Sehnsucht" (life longings) as well as possible relationships to adjacent research areas. Following a somewhat unusual format, a target presentation will outline a lifespan conceptualization of "Sehnsucht" recently introduced by Paul Baltes and colleagues and first empirical evidence obtained in this framework. Responding to this thesis, and possibly extending on it, a series of commentaries given by representatives of different neighboring fields, including goal theory, lifespan theory, self-regulation, and depression/rumination will explore the extent to which the concept of "Sehnsucht" can be approached by or integrated into these psychological perspectives.

A goal-theory view of Sehnsucht/Longing

Klinger, Eric Division of Social Science, University of Minnesota, Morris, USA
Sehnsucht/Longing can be viewed as preoccupation with a goal the pursuit of which is currently suspended or goal-attainment is still remote and the individual retains some degree of commitment to attaining it. Current-concerns theory of goal pursuit predicts specific forms of emotional and cognitive responses to cues related to this goal, in interaction with the individual's degree of expectancy of goal-attainment.

Evolutionary reasons for problems from Sehnsucht (life longings)

Nesse, Randolph M. Inst. for Social Research, University of Michigan, Ann Arbor, USA
Sehnsucht is joy about past events and future hopes, but it also reflects desires that can never be satisfied. Individual's identities are centered on commitments to pursue some goals and give up others. Sometimes the process goes well, but often individuals long for what they cannot have, the exact situation for which selection has shaped depression. This apparent poor design exists, in part, because the mechanisms that mediate such decisions evolved from those that regulate the behavior of one-celled organisms. However, it is also because selection shapes emotions not for the welfare of individuals but for the benefit of their genes.

A lifespan view on Sehnsucht (life longings)

Staudinger, Ursula M. Zentr. für Lebenslanges Lernen, Jacobs Universität, Bremen, Germany
In the discussion I will compare papers against the theoretical background of lifespan psychology. The role of Sehnsucht in processes of developmental regulation will e.g. be an important aspect.

"If I wrote a novel ...": Sehnsucht for a different I and self-regulatory processes

Greve, Werner Inst. für Psychologie, Universität Hildesheim, Hildesheim, Germany
The main purpose of this discussion will be twofold. First, possible connections of a psychology of Sehnsucht with the psychology of self and identity will be examined (e.g., possible selves, ideal self). Second, I will discuss whether (experienced) feelings of Sehnsucht can be viewed as motivating aspects, that is as causal factors of self-regulation, or rather as emotional states, that is as mere outcomes of disappointing life constellations. As a possible solution, Sehnsucht (as well as related states) might be viewed as indicating ongoing internal adaptive processes.

FP-001: Self-concept, self-determination, and motivation to learn

I Stream: The effects of educational streaming system on self-concept and motivation: A qualitative study with Singaporean secondary school students

Manzano, Anne Adelaine CRPP, Nat'l Institute of Education, Singapore, Singapore McInerney, Dennis M. CRPP, Nat'l Institute of Education, Singapore, Singapore Liem, Arief D. CRPP, Nat'l Institute of Education, Singapore, Singapore Lee, Jie Qi CRPP, Nat'l Institute of Education, Singapore, Singapore Ortiga, Yasmin Y. CRPP, Nat'l Institute of Education, Singapore, Singapore
This study builds on research that emphasizes the importance of a positive self-concept to achievement. Interviews were conducted with 98 Singaporean secondary school students from Express and Normal streams to assess how streaming affects the students' academic self-concept (general, Math and/or English) and achievement motivation. Questions examining self-concept include, "what makes you say you're 'good' at this subject?" Separate focused group discussions with 26 teachers and 18 parents showed how streaming has gained mixed reviews from adults relevant to the students' lives. The findings were assessed in conjunction with the role that streaming plays in Singapore's socio-cultural and economic context.

Big-fish-little-pond-effect: Total long-term negative effects of school-average ability on diverse educational outcomes over 8 adolescent/early adult years

Marsh, Herbert Dept. of Educational Studies, Oxford University, Oxford, United Kingdom
Consistent with theory and previous research, school-average ability had negative effects on school grades, educational and occupational aspirations, long-term educational attainment, and academic self-concept (big-fish-little-pond effect; BFLPE). Longitudinal analyses using complex structural equation modeling were based on nationally representative US data (2,213 students, 89 schools, 5 occasions over eight adolescent/early adult years). Long-term total (direct plus indirect) effects of school-average ability were much more negative than direct effects typically emphasized

and were partially mediated by academic self-concept. Using innovative methodology to extend the substantive implications of the BFLPE and self-concept theory demonstrates the importance of substantive-methodological synergies.

Development and validation of a questionnaire to assess academic learning motivation through measuring regulation styles among Indonesian university students

Soegijardjo, Witriani Faculty of Psychology, University of Padjadjaran, Bandung, Indonesia Sudradjat, Wismaningsih Faculty of Psychology, University of Padjadjaran, Bandung, Indonesia Wiyono, Sudarmo Faculty of Psychology, University of Padjadjaran, Bandung, Indonesia

Failure to complete studies on time was related to lack of motivation for academic learning. Based on Self-Determination Theory (Deci&Ryan, 2000), a questionnaire was constructed to measure motivation ranging from amotivation (non self-determined behavior) to intrinsic motivation (self-determined). Items were constructed and tested on two tryouts (N1=432, N2=392). Content validity was obtained through examination of a panel of experts. Construct validity, reliability ($\alpha > 0.7$), and item analysis were computed resulting in 94 items measuring six Regulation Styles. The questionnaire is valid to detect strengths and weaknesses in learning motivation which can be used for interventions to overcome related problems.

Revisiting the internal/external frame of reference model: Bringing in general cognitive ability and general academic self-concept

Brunner, Martin EMACS Research Unit, University of Luxembourg, Walferdange, Luxembourg Lüdtke, Oliver Educational Research, Max Planck Institute for Human, Berlin, Germany Trautwein, Ulrich Educational Research, Max Planck Institute for Human, Berlin, Germany

The internal/external frame of reference model (I/E model) is a highly influential model of academic self-concept formation. Investigations of the I/E model do not typically incorporate general cognitive ability or general academic self-concept. By applying structural equation modeling the present paper investigates the relation between domain-specific and domain-general abilities and self-concepts within an extended I/E model framework, using representative data from 25,301 ninth-grade students. The extended I/E model permitted meaningful relations to be drawn between general cognitive ability and general academic self-concept, as well as between the domain-specific elements of the model. Implications for academic self-concept formation will be discussed.

Self-determination in Chinese college students' academic learning and social competence

Chen, Xuelian School of Psychology, Huazhong Normal University, Wuhan, People's Republic of China Zhou, Zongkui School of Psychology, Huazhong Normal University, Wuhan, People's Republic of China Zhang, Zhao School of Automation, Wuhan University of Technology, Wuhan, People's Republic of China Song, Shujuan School of Psychology, Huazhong Normal University, Wuhan, People's Republic of China Liu, Huashan School of Psychology, Huazhong Normal University, Wuhan, People's Republic of China

Self-determination is considered to be the most autonomous form of motivation that should predict optimal study and social functioning, even among Chinese students. 300 Chinese students from three different universities participated in this investigation. A structural equation model was applied to test the relations between domain-specific self-determination, academic achievement (including grade point average, GPA) and social competence (e.g., friendships). The results indicated that self-determination could positively predict Chinese students' domain-specific functions (academic and social competence); there were significant gender differences on scores of domain-specific self-determination, GPA and social competence.

Promoting self-determined learning in school

Bieg, Sonja Inst. für Pädagog. Psychologie, Pädag. Hochschule Ludwigsburg, Ludwigsburg, Germany Mittag, Waldemar Educational Psychology, Pädagogische Hochschule, Ludwigsburg, Germany

According to Self-determination theory (Ryan & Deci, 2000), we assume that intrinsic motivation and the process of internalization can be fostered in school. Thus the purpose of the study was to examine the effectiveness of self-determined lessons with autonomy support as a predictor of motivational regulation and academic achievement. In a treatment-control-group design data from about 800 students were collected by questionnaires. Data analyses revealed the effectiveness on perceived autonomy support and academic achievement. However, the effect on intrinsic motivation varied for different school types. In sum, the results support the effectiveness of autonomy support on self-determined learning.

Developing professional identity: Different uses of narrative diary in higher education

Galuppo, Laura Organizational Psychology, Università Cattolica di Milano, Milano, Italy Gilardi, Silvia Labour and Welfare Studies, Università Statale di Milano, Milano, Italy Bruno, Andreina Organizational Psychology, Università Cattolica di Milano, Milano, Italy

The narrative diary is an useful tool to evaluate the development of professional competencies in future psychologists. The paper aims to explore different learning outcomes produced by using narrative diaries in academic training. 40 individual diaries and 40 group diaries, written by students attending two different courses with the same "learning from experience" approach, are analysed through qualitative content analysis. The results show that a different use of narrative diary allows different outcomes in terms of student's reflection on their professional project: while individual diary focuses on students' autoreflexivity, group diary puts the attention on "intersubjective" dialogues and negotiation processes.

FP-002: Social aspects of cognition

Measuring social cognitive process with computer-based cognitive diagnosis theory

Gao, Pengyun Dept. of Psychology, Beijing Normal University, Beijing, People's Republic of China

In this study, based on the newly developed psychometrical method—— cognitive diagnosis theory, the authors devises an ingenious computer program which can divide the critical thinking procedure into several distinctive stages, and diagnose individual logic fallacy instantly. As a CBT (computer based test), it will give in time response for every subject, which is much more efficiently than traditional paper-based questionnaire. Reliability and validity are tested with a sample of 225 high school students. The α-coefficient are 0.85 and the convergent validity with CCTST(The California Critical Thinking Skills Test) were 0.86, and with WGCTA(Watson-Glaser Critical Thinking Appraisal) were 0.76.

Are two heads better than one? Quality of individual and group decision-making in a survivor task

Yan, Greg Dept. of Psychology, Beijing Normal University, Beijing, People's Republic of China Lin, Xuanhui Dept. of Psychology, Beijing Normal University, Beijing, People's Republic of China

The island survivor exercise, similar to the classical NASA moon problem, was used to examine the probability of group performance superior to individual and the best individual. The Quality of decision is defined as the differences from the results given by experts. The less is the better. 560 students (140 4-person groups) from two universities were asked to make decisions individually and collectively, respectively. It was found that 73% group decisions are better than individuals and 66% worse than best member. The probability for group superior to the best member is .20.

Emotional intelligence and persuasiveness

Menges, Jochen Inst. für Leadership + HRM, Universität St. Gallen, St. Gallen, Switzerland Fiedler, Klaus Institute of Psychology, University of Heidelberg, Heidelberg, Germany Spataro, Sandra Johnson Graduate School, Cornell University, Ithaca, NY, USA Salovey, Peter Department of Psychology, Yale University, New Haven, CT, USA

Are speakers with high emotional intelligence (EI) more persuasive than those with low EI? A study with 20 participants provided evidence for the differential role of subscales, or branches of EI. While branch 1 (emotional perception and expression) and branch 2 (emotional facilitation of thought) were not systematically associated with persuasiveness, branch 3 (emotional understanding) and branch 4 (emotional management) showed a significant positive correlation to persuasiveness. Strategic emotional intelligence (combined score of branch 3 and 4) was a significant predictor of persuasiveness and remained significant even when controlling for the Big Five personality traits and nonverbal expressiveness.

The wisdom of ignorant crowds: Collective recognition and forecast combination

Herzog, Stefan Inst. für Psychologie, Universität Basel, Basel, Switzerland Hertwig, Ralph Dep. of Psychology, University of Basel, Basel, Switzerland

Collective recognition can be a successful predictor of real-world phenomena by exploiting the systematic ignorance of laypeople. Collective recognition rates (proportion of people recognizing an object) predicted, for example, political elections, tennis matches and football games. By merging a cognitive model of recognition (ACT-R) with statistical models of forecast combination, we identified conditions that lead to good predictive performance of collective recognition. Formal and empirical analyses show that when using a diverse group of people with noncongruent ignorance, the recognition judgments of merely a few people will already suffice to tap into the wisdom of ignorant crowds.

An exploratory study about the role of epistemological beliefs on learners' solo and duo thinking about an ill-defined issue

Angeli, Charoula Dept. of Education, University of Cyprus, Nicosia, Cyprus Valanides, Nicos Dept. of Education, University of Cyprus, Nicosia, Cyprus

The study explores the relationship between epistemological beliefs and reasoning when thinking about an ill-defined problem in solo and duo problem-solving contexts. The results show that social problem-solving triggers more cognitive and emotional activity than solo thinking. Also, the results showed that different aspects of epistemological beliefs get activated in solo thinking than in group thinking. One finding that we find intriguing is the role of emotions in group thinking but not individual thinking, and the relationship between emotions and some aspects of epistemological beliefs in the duo problem-solving context only.

Simon revisited: Rationality, social representations and organizational identity

Koumakhov, Rouslan People and Organizations, Reims Management School, Reims, France

The paper focuses on some important neglected elements of Simon's paradigm, in particular, on issues related to social representations in organizations. It discusses how the bounded rationality assumptions explicitly lead to outline the interpretative abilities of individuals. Main methodological implications are the following. First, by articulating cognitive and interpretative perspectives on behaviour, Simon predated research programs conducted in terms of social roles and organizational identity. Second, by proposing a theory implying strong connections between various disciplines, Simon anticipated nowadays multidisciplinary approaches (e.g. research on decision-making involving important socio-psychological and philosophical aspects), which associate cognition, coordination and social representations

---

FP-003: Social cognition I

Evidence for the adaptive value of pseudocontingencies

Freytag, Peter Inst. für Psychologie, Universität Heidelberg, Heidelberg, Germany *Fiedler, Klaus* Psychology, University of Heidelberg, Heidelberg, Germany

We present analytical and empirical evidence for the adaptive value of an alternative pathway to contingency assessment in terms of pseudocontingencies (PCs). PCs arise when contingencies are inferred from baserate information. In the analytical part, we relate the need for efficient contingency detection to the observation that skewed baserates restrict the range of possible values of a contingency. Using computer simulations, the empirical part shows that the PC strategy can extract the sign of contingencies as accurately as strategies relying on cell frequency information. Importantly, PCs may be superior to these rather demanding strategies when bivariate information becomes scarce.

The power of pictures: Vertical picture angles and power perceptions

Giessner, Steffen Erasmus University Rotterdam, Rotterdam, Netherlands *Ryan, Michelle* School of Psychology, University of Exeter, Exter, United Kingdom *Schubert, Thomas* Department of Social Psychology, VU University, Amsterdam, Netherlands

The empirical evidence for the commonly accepted principle that vertical camera angles cause the target person to appear more powerful (from below) or less powerful (from above) is mixed. We argue from a social embodiment perspective that vertical camera angle and power judgments are only interrelated if power is cognitively activated. Studies 1a-1d show that media pictures make use of vertical camera angle to present power. Studies 2a-b show that vertical camera angle influences power judgments in a salient power context. Study 3 shows that vertical camera angle only influences power judgments when a power-mindset is activated.

Social facilitation: The facilitation of cognitive processes by mere presence of others

Herfordt, Julia Inst. für Sozialpsychologie, Universität Freiburg, Freiburg, Germany *Klauer, Karl Christoph* Department of Psychology, Social Psychology, Freiburg, Germany *Voss, Andreas* Department of Psychology, Social Psychology, Freiburg, Germany

In Study 1, Zajonc's social facilitation hypothesis was tested with an antisaccade task. Social facilitation could be shown as an acceleration of the prosaccade (dominant reaction), whereas the antisaccade (unfamiliar task) was not affected. These results supports Zajonc's (1965) approach. For Study 2 the Eriksen flanker task was used followed by an unannounced recognition task for the flankers. Participants remember fewer flankers when they were observed than participants working alone. These results might be interpreted as a narrowing of attention focus supporting an alternative account suggested by Baron (1986).

When does communication affect communicators' memory? The role of encoding differences in audience-tuning effects

Kopietz, René Psychological Department, University of Bielefeld, Bielefeld, Germany *Echterhoff, Gerald* Psychological Department, University of Bielefeld, Bielefeld, Germany *Higgins, E. Tory* Department of Psychology, Columbia University, New York, USA

Communicators' memories for original target information (OTI) often reflect the biased view of their audience-tuned message, producing an audience-congruent memory bias. So far, communicators almost exclusively knew the audience's attitude before reading the OTI. We investigated if such biased encoding is necessary for audience-tuning effects, and if encoding differences account for differences in effect size. In two experiments, the memory bias occurred despite unbiased encoding. Furthermore, it depended on whether audience tuning was motivated by a shared-reality goal (versus a compliance goal). Consistent with shared-reality theory (Hardin & Higgins, 1996), the communication-goal effect was partially mediated by epistemic trust.

You don't know what I know: The effect of information sources on the empathy process

Shi, Songqu Psychology, Peking University, Beijing, People's Republic of China *Wang, Lei* Psychology, Peking University, Beijing, People's Republic of China

This article argued that two different imputations in opposite directions may occur at the starting point of the empathy process and that whether the information of imputation comes from external or internal source will determine which one really happens. We tested our hypothesis by experiments both in the cognitive and emotional area. We manipulated the source of information and instructed participants to guess what choices would be made by other people without that information. The results showed that the difference of information source affected the way how participants used the information to infer what other people would know and act.

Social representations: Their main contrasts defining their roles and meanings

Lopez Alonso, Alfredo Oscar Psycholy, CONICET - University Salvador, Buenos Aires, Argentina

Objectives: To analyze social representations from their inferential bases and structures as cognitive processes. Methods: Alternative methods of grouping subjects, such as cluster-analysis or Venn-diagrams on inferential structures are briefly revised and explained. Results: It's shown how different significant effects and features emerge and may be used to better describe and understand social representations in their complexity, multiple roles and variations, such typicality/atypicality, coherence/incoherence, divergence/convergence, information and communication contexts, etc.. Conclusions: This cognitive-inferential approach to social representations has proved to discover new facets and systematic effects contrasting their implied literal meanings against their inferential meanings in information and communication statements.

FP-004: Statistical and mathematical methods and models

An empirical comparison of Cronbach's alpha with ordinal reliability coefficients alpha and theta

Gadermann, Anne Educat. & Couns. Psychology, University of British Columbia, Vancouver, Canada *Guhn, Martin* Dept. Educational Psychology, University of British Columbia, Vancouver, Canada *Zumbo, Bruno D.* Educat. & Couns. Psycholog, University of British Columbia, Vancouver, Canada

Cronbach's alpha assumes continuous data. Likert type response formats, however, commonly provide ordinal data. Accordingly, Zumbo, Gadermann, and Zeisser (2007) introduced ordinal reliability coefficients, alpha and theta, using the polychoric correlation matrix (rather than the Pearson). The present study compares the ordinal coefficients to Cronbach's alpha, using Early Development Instrument (EDI; Offord & Janus, 1999) data from 43,644 kindergarten children. The ordinal coefficients consistently estimate EDI subscale reliabilities higher than Cronbach's alpha (.83—.97 versus .43—.95), with differences depending on the number of response options. The findings coincide with previous simulation research, confirming the usefulness of these ordinal reliability coefficients.

Adjusting for confounding covariates in multilevel designs

Nagengast, Benjamin Institut für Psychologie, FSU Jena, Jena, Germany *Steyer, Rolf* Institut für Psychologie, FSU Jena, Jena, Germany

An extension of the theory of individual and average causal effects for non-randomized multilevel designs, e.g. non-randomized group-designs or multisite-trials, is presented. The core assumptions of this extension are outlined and sufficient conditions for causal inference in multilevel designs are discussed. New adjustment methods developed within this framework are presented. These methods correct the influence of confounding covariates on individual- and group-level when there are interactions between treatment and covariates. A simulation study shows that regression based adjustment methods perform adequate under a variety of conditions when heteroscedastic level-1-errors and stochastic covariates are accounted for. Recommendations for applications are given.

Testing mediation by moderation: Some conceptual suggestions

Jacoby, Johann AG3, Inst. f. Wissensmedien, Tübingen, Germany

While Baron and Kenny's (1986) distinction between mediator and moderator variables provides invaluable conceptual clarification, reception of this distinction has lead to blurred distinctions between theoretical conception on one hand, and research designs and statistical tools on the other. It will be demonstrated that theoretical mediation hypotheses can be reformulated as moderation hypotheses in design and are in principle amenable to tests based on designs commonly used for moderation tests (i.e., statistical interaction terms). Criteria for when a mediation may well be tested as a moderation and strategies to recover conceptual mediation behind empirical moderation hypotheses will be proposed.

Relation analysis: A proper way for testing hypotheses logically

Maderthaner, Rainer Basic Psychological Reseach, Faculty of Psychology, Vienna, Austria

Objectives: Demonstration of the inadequacy of correlational association methods and the recommendation of Relation Analysis. The correlation coefficient is principally used by many complex statistical methods (e.g. factor analysis, regression analysis, structural equation modelling), even though its weaknesses always have been obvious. Method: The program version RELOG enables multivariable, multifunctional, and causal hypotheses testing as well as the simulation of propositional data structures. Results: Computer simulations will be presented to illustrate that correlational association measures are unable to deal with the complexity of psychological theories. Conclusion: Hypotheses should be formulated and tested statistically with regard to mathematical logic.

FP-005: Social values, family, and culture

Emotional and social maturation: Intervening factors in achieving different kinds of love

Tabae Emami, Shirin Psychology, Isfahan Univercity, Isfahan, Islamic Republic of Iran Tabaeian, Sayedeh Razieh Psychology, Isfahan Univercity, Isfahan, Islamic Republic of Iran

Objectives: The purpose of the present study was to examine the role of emotional and social maturation in achieving different kinds of love. Methods: One hundred students at University of Isfahan were evaluated based on the Passionate Love scale (PLS), Compassionate Love scale (CLS), Emotional Maturity scale (ELS), and Roao's social Maturity Scale (PLS). Results: The results of Regression analysis suggest a significant relationship between achieving emotional and social maturity and the kind of love among the students (p<05). Conclusions: Emotional and social maturity among students seem to be involved in achieving different kinds of love.

Social value orientation among different Chinese cohorts

Huangfu, Gang School of management, Beihang University, Beijing, People's Republic of China Zhu, Liqi Institute of Psychology,, Chinese Academy of Sciences, Beijing, People's Republic of China

China was traditionally a very socio-morally-oriented society. With rapid social and economic reform, does the development of a market economy affect people's social value orientation? This study investigated whether a cohort effect existed. Six hundred seventy-two participants from different age groups (elderly, middle-aged and young) in China were recruited. They were shown a revised Decomposed Game based on Van Lange (1996). Results showed that, though the majority of Chinese subjects were pro-social, the proportion of pro-social choices decreased and the proportion of individualistic choices increased from the elderly to the young.

"I or we": Family socialization values in a national probability sample in Taiwan

Kao, Shu-Fang Dept. of Applied Psychology, Hsuan Chuang University, Hsinchu, Taiwan Lu, Luo Dept. of Business Administrati, National Taiwan University, Taipei, Taiwan

The aim of this research was to explore antecedents and consequences of family socialization values emphasizing independence or interdependence, using a Taiwanese national probability sample. Analysis of variance revealed that those who were male, older, and less educated emphasized greater interdependence values. In contrast, those who were younger, with higher social status and urban residents emphasized greater independence values. Multiple regression analysis further revealed that valuing interdependence was related to preferring a greater number of offspring, a higher endorsement on filial piety, greater marital and life satisfaction. Finally, in this national sample, endorsement on independence and interdependence values was equivalent.

The influence of parental child-rearing practices on Spanish adolescent values

Martínez, Isabel Psychology, UCLM, Cuenca, Spain Navarro, Raul Psychology, UCLM, Cuenca, Spain

In this work we investigate in a sample of Spanish adolescents (12 to 14 year-old) the influence of parenting in the priority given to Schwartz's self-transcendence and conservation values. To asses parenting styles we classified adolescents' families into 1 of 4 groups (Authoritative, Authoritarian, Indulgent, and Neglectful) based on adolescents' answers to the ESPA29 Parental Socialization Scale. Adolescents then answered to the 27 items of the Schwartz Value Inventory measuring self-transcendence and conservation values. The Multivariate analysis of variance reveals that adolescents from authoritative and indulgent households assign higher priority to those values than adolescents from authoritarian and neglectful homes.

Value inculcation across generations: Different patterns, similar aims!

Sharma, Divya Human Development and Family, University of Baroda, Vadodara, India Mohite, Prerana Human Devp. & Family Studi, M.S. University of Baroda, Baroda, India

Study examines parents' perceptions regarding the transmission of values and strategies used by them to develop values in children of 9-12 years of age, belonging to urban middle class families of Udaipur City, India. Interviews were carried out and data was analyzed from the perspectives of gender and family type. Parents focused on inculcating religious values and generating interest of children in their culture. The strategies like giving instructions, explanation and providing guidance were most commonly used across generations. Sharing adequate time with children and being a good role model are the upcoming dimensions to bridge the gap between the generations.

Do social values guide behavior by synergistic or by compensatory person x situation interactions?

Strack, Michaela G.E.-Müller Inst. für Psychol., Universität Göttingen, Göttingen, Germany Schmitt, Manfred Fachbereich Psychologie, University of Koblenz-Landau, Landau, Germany

Psychology treats values as personality variables, social sciences as cultural, contextual or situational forces. Work on interactionism (Schmitt, Eid & Maes 2003; Schmitt & Sabbagh 2004) predicts a synergistic interaction of functionally equivalent person and situation factors. However, < it is necessary to find methods of representing person and environment in common terms > (Lewin 1936). But we are endued with an universal content structure of values (Schwartz 1992ff)! Considering that value preferences sensitize a person to situational clues for value-fulfillment, we predict the synergistic interaction type. Our contribution discusses relevant value-fit research, problems imposed by the bipolarity of value dimensions, and designs for the person x situation interaction test.

FP-006: Social psychology

Recovering fractal spaces via parameterization of cyclic invariants: Niche construction through niche operations-

Caraiani, Claudiu Bucharest, Romania Cicei, Cristiana Catalina Psychology, Faculty of Psychology, Bucharest, Romania

The goal of our paper is to study the possible existence of simplex structures, isomorphic to feedback cycles, in social psychological phenomena. The objects that undergo our study are known as sociological niches. We introduce some ideas on how to recover and study these simplex structures through studying local interactions rules in certain lattices. We analyze classes of symmetries and synchronization of chaotic phenomena through

the consideration of the correlation between cyclic invariants. We conjecture that these simplex structures are universal spaces under certain restrictive conditions.

Media and fear of crime: The implicit relationship

Chadee, Derek Psychological Research Centre, University of the West Indies, St. Augustine, Trinidad and Tobago

A review of available international evidence indicates that crime features regularly in the media. New data shows that this is also true for Trinidad. Elsewhere, it has been shown that newspaper crime news concentrates heavily on infrequently occurring crimes involving sex and/or violence. Data from a representative sample of Trinidadian respondents (n=705) undertaken in 2000 indicate no relationship between media consumption and fear of crime. Data show a weak relationship. This data is complemented by two content analysis of newspapers, (1) undertaken utilize the three daily newspapers in Trinidad for the period May to August 2001, (2) undertaken for the period January 2003 to January 2004. Findings are discussed from a social psychological perspective on fear of crime.

Quality of life among students abstaining, experimenting and habitualy using drugs

Hedzelek, Mateusz Dept. of Social Psychology, Faculty of Psychology, Warsaw, Poland Wnukiewicz, P. Silakowski, K. Wnuk, M.

The research concerns a comparison of a conglomerate of quality of life, sense of life and sense of coherence factors between university students abstaining, experimenting and habitualy using drugs. Following factors have been measured: desire to live, passion for life, feeling of happiness, global contentment of life concerning the past, present and future, particular satisfaction rates of contentment of different life areas. Ninety participants were evaluated. The comparison has been done between three groups of thirty participants. The research indicated that there were significant differences in quality of life, sense of life and sense of coherence measures beteween these three groups.

Surveying the role of emotional intelligent in mental health of students

Nikpour, Gholam Ali Dept. of Psychology, Medical Clinic of Dr. Mosavi, Babol, Islamic Republic of Iran Azadfallah, Hossein Dept. of Psychology, University of Allameh Tabatab, Tehran, Islamic Republic of Iran Taghypour, Hassan Dept. of Psychology, Sampad, Babol (Amirkola), Islamic Republic of Iran Homayouni, Alireza Dept. of Psychology, Islamic Azad University of Ban, Babol (Amirkola), Islamic Republic of Iran Mosavi Amiri, Seyed Jalal Dept. of Psychology, Dr. Mosavi Clinic, Babol (Amirkola), Islamic Republic of Iran

The study is to clarify role of emotional intelligent in mental health of students.73 students were randomly selected and Shutt Emotional Intelligent Inventory(SEII) and General Health Questionnaire (GHQ) administered on them. Data analyzed with Pearson correlation formula. Results showed negative and significant correlation between components of emotional intelligent especially in regulation and expression of emotions and components of mental illness in GHQ specially in social dysfunction. It indicates that applying of plans in the field of increasing emotional intelligent in students can help them to manage the bad problems and event and as a results reduce mental illness.

Which concepts of self can predict implicit self-esteem of Japanese adolescents?

Shiomura, Kimihiro Iwate Prefectural University, Iwate, Japan

The two contrastive targets (Self and Other) were focused and measured by GNAT which is one of derivative types of IAT (Implicit Association Test).

The analyses were performed whether some types of cultural-self concepts and explicit self-esteem can be predictive of the implicit self-esteem. Seventy-six Japanese university students participated in both GNAT and explicit self-rating questionnaires on cultural-self and self-esteem. The results indicate that implicit self-esteem was predicted only by Relational-Interdependent Self-Construal Scale (Cross et al., 2000) among some cultural-self concepts. It must be important to note that the other cultural-self scales could not predict implicit self-esteem of Japanese adolescents.

Declarations and reaction latencies as complementary indicators in the attitudes research

Samarcew, Alicja Faculty of Psychology, Warsaw University, Warszawa, Poland Stec, Magdalena Inst. for Social Studies, Warsaw University, Warszawa, Poland Giersz, Paulina Faculty of Psychology, Warsaw University, Warszawa, Poland

Implicit measures of attitudes rely either on reaction latencies or declarations. Our data suggests that it may not be enough. In our studies participants concentrated on positive vs. negative statements. Subsequently, the subliminal affective priming paradigm was applied. We hypothesized that neutral stimuli will be judged more positively when primed with faces expressing positive emotions or representing the own race. The hypothesis was confirmed in participants who concentrated on positive statements. Declarations of participants concentrated on negative statements did not differ. This might suggest that negative affect impedes the implicit processing. Yet, reaction latencies differed in all experimental conditions.

FP-007: Social support and chronic disease

Back to school after cancer: How children, parents and teachers perceive support from the school environment

Jutras, Sylvie Dept. de Psychologie, Université du Québec, Montréal, Canada Lauriault, Christiane Psychologie, Université du Québec à Montréa, Montréal, Canada Tougas, Anne-Marie Psychologie, Université du Québec à Montréa, Montréal, Canada Labonté, Nathalie Éducation, Université de Sherbrooke, Sherbrooke, Canada

Objective: To determine how the perceived support from the school environment contributed to successful reintegration into the school setting, and this, from the point of view of 22 children with cancer, 21 parents, and 10 teachers. Method: Individual interviews were conducted on the types, sources of support, and perceived benefits of school support. Content analysis of open-ended questions revealed the salience of emotional and cognitive support provided by teachers and peers. Children, parents and teachers associate in a distinct way the forms and sources of support, thus demonstrating their specific patterns of contribution to psychosocial adjustment and school performance.

Disabled persons' mental health and self-esteem in relation to perceived parental support

Vlachou, Anastasia Special Education, University of Thessaly, Volos, Greece Kleftaras, George Dept. of Special Education, University of Thessaly, Volos, Greece

The present research aimed at investigating: a) disabled person's perceptions of the received parental support, b) the impact of this support on both mental health and self-esteem and c) the differential impact of mothers' and fathers' support on their psychological well-being. 101 disabled persons completed three questionnaires: Goldberg's-General-Health, Rosenberg's-Self-Esteem and Family-Support. The results indicate that parental support is of a great importance for the

psychological well-being of disabled persons. What was not expected is the differential impact of mothers and fathers' support. Mothers' support is mostly related to general perception of mental health, while fathers' support to anxiety.

Family involvement in psychosocial interventions for adults with chronic physical diseases: A Cochrane review

Hartmann, Mechthild Abt. Psychosomatik, Universitätsklinik Heidelberg, Heidelberg, Germany Bäzner, Eva Psychosomatic and General Inte, University Hospital, Heidelberg, Germany Herzog, Wolfgang Psychosomatic and General Inte, Univerity Hospital, Heidelberg, Germany

Objective: Families have a powerful influence on health equal to traditional medical risk factors. Consequently interventions were developed in recent years to involve family or spouse in the treatment of chronic diseases. This systematic review will examine the effects of family or spouse interventions in adults with chronic physical diseases. Methods: The review is performed according Cochrane guidelines. Main outcome criteria are psychological, physical and social functioning of the patient. Results: 89 studies met inclusion criteria. Data extraction is still in progress. Conclusions: This systematic review will provide evidence for the question "Can family involvement be beneficial in the treatment of physical diseases?"

Social support in general and chronic patients

Sacramento Zanini, Daniela Dept. de Psicologia, Universidade Catolica de Goias, Goiânia, Brazil Verolla, Adriana Dept. de Psicologia, Universidade Catolica de Goias, Goiânia, Brazil

Many studies have pointed associations between social support and health (ex. Matsukura, Marturano & Oishi, 2002). However, though this theme has received been largely studied (Cobb, 1976; Griep; et al, 2005; Ribeiro, 1999) there isn't one measure valid for different cultures and contexts. The objective of this study is to compare a measure in Social Support in general population and chronic patients. 129 university students were accessed. The Social Support Questionnaire (Sherbourne & Stewart, 1991) was used. The results point to good adequation of the scale in both population and are discussed based in the literature in the area.

FP-008: Personality assessment I

Within- and between-person variability: The benefits of different perspectives on personality

Beckmann, Nadin Accelerated Learning Labratory, University of New South Wales, UNSW, Australia Minbashian, Amirali Australian School of Business, University of New South Wales, Sydney, Randwick, Australia Wood, Robert E. Australian School of Business, University of New South Wales, Sydney, Randwick, Australia

We compare a within-person conceptualization of personality with the traditional trait approach. Employing event sampling methodologies, 73 managers were assessed multiple times daily, over several weeks in work- and laboratory-settings. Within- and between-person variation in personality indicators was analysed using hierarchical linear modelling. Findings indicate that analyzing personality as a dynamic within-person phenomenon reveals relationships not captured by the trait approach. E.g., while Conscientiousness and Neuroticism were negatively correlated at the between-person level, this relationship was reversed at the within-person level. Results are discussed in terms of person- and situation-factors. Implications for contemporary models of personality are considered.

Predictive validity of a student selection procedure on the basis of experiment-based behavioural tests

Litzenberger, Margarete Psychological Assessment, University of Vienna, Vienna, Austria Haiden, Daniela Psychological Assessment, University of Vienna, Vienna, Austria Haslgrübler, Karin Psychological Assessment, University of Vienna, Vienna, Austria

The purpose is the introduction of an evaluation of a proficiency assessment procedure conducted at the University of Applied Science. The sequential qualifying procedure generally comprises two methods: three initial assessment centre tasks and a set of experiment-based behavioural tests. The evaluation focuses on determining if potentially qualified applicants fall victim to premature elimination and the question of the predictive validity according to external criteria (specialized knowledge-test, grades). A total of 194 candidates were analyzed. The results show, that the sequential procedure is adequate and does not discriminate any candidates. Furthermore the predictive validity can be considered as satisfactory.

Predicting expatriate job performance: Using the normative NEO-PI-R or the ipsative OPQ32i?

Kusch, Rene Immanuel Inst. für Sozialwissenschaften, Helmut-Schmidt-Universität, Hamburg, Germany Deller, Jürgen Business Psychology, Leuphana University, Lüneburg, Germany Albrecht, Anne-Grit Business Psychology, Leuphana University, Lüneburg, Germany

Although the application of ipsative personality measures for inter-individual comparisons is still controversial research comparing the criterion validity of ipsative and normative instruments is rare. In a field study 145 German speaking expatriates were assessed with the normative NEO-PI-R, the ipsative OPQ32i and a 17 item measure of job performance (self report and other ratings). Controlling for several demographic variables multiple regressions, incremental validities over and above each instrument and cross validations were calculated. Results with respect to the differences in how valuable both instruments are for predicting expatriate job performance are presented and discussed.

Do personality traits influence the effect in personality-IATs twice?

Fleischhauer, Monika Inst. für Psychologie, Techn. Universität Dresden, Dresden, Germany Enge, Soeren Department of Psychology, TU Dresden, Dresden, Germany Dreisbach, Gesine Department of Psychology, TU Dresden, Dresden, Germany Strobel, Alexander Institute of Psychology, J. W. Goethe University, Frankfurt am Main, Germany Strobel, Anja Department of Psychology, TU Dresden, Dresden, Germany

The Implicit Association Test (IAT) provides a RT-based instrument to assess personality traits. There is evidence that personality inherently influences the performance on RT-measures (speed, RT-variability). In a task-switching-paradigm (N=156) we observed extraversion, openness, need for cognition and positive emotionality to be negatively and neuroticism to be positively correlated with different RT-measures. These results raised the question whether IAT-effects might also be influenced by traits independent of the personality construct to be measured. We present a study that aimed to investigate this influence. Conclusions for the development of an IAT to assess the trait need for cognition will be drawn.

Optimal trait level and self-enhancement bias

Borkenau, Peter Halle, Germany Zaltauskas, Katrin Psychology, Martin-Luther University, Halle, Germany

Although one extreme is more desirable than the opposite extreme on most trait dimensions, neither extreme constitutes the most favorable level of the trait. This is important for research on self-enhancement bias. Using a round-robin design, 76 groups of 4 persons indicated optimal levels for, and described themselves and each other on, 30 trait dimensions. Participants tended to assign trait levels equal to the optimal level to themselves, but trait levels beyond the optimal level to their peers. Trait levels perceived as optimal predicted self-reported trait levels. A new measure of self-enhancement bias, unrelated to actual trait levels, is suggested.

Cross-cultural differences in socially desirable responding: A framework for theory and practice
Odendaal, Aletta Human Resource Management, University of Johannesburg, Johannesburg, South Africa de Bruin, Gideon Human Resource Management, University of Johannesburg, Johannesburg, South Africa
Objective We examine whether recent findings in respect of social desirability (SD) in high stakes occupational assessment replicate in a multicultural African context. Method We employed IRT and moderated multiple regression to examine SD across cultural groups. Results The construct of SD appears universal, but it manifests differently across cultures. The relations of SD with substantive personality traits differ across cultures. Discussion American and European findings partially replicate in the African context. The meaning of existing SD scales may differ across cultures. We present a framework for understanding SD across cultures and for developing unbiased measures of SD.

FP-009: Social issues: Children and youth I

A comparison of social skills of partially hearing impaired students in integrated versus nonintegrated schools
Beh-Pajooh, Ahmad Special Education, Faculty of Psychology and, Tehran, Islamic Republic of Iran
The present study was conducted to compare social skills of male students with partially hearing impairment (PHI) in integrated versus nonintegrated schools in Tehran, IRAN. In this ex post facto research, 60 PHI students participated and two different kinds of educational settings were considered as an independent variable and social skills of PHI students was regarded as a dependent variable. To measure social skills of PHI students, Social Skills Rating System developed and adapted. Results revealed that mean score of PHI students in integrated setting was higher than their peers in nonintegrated settings. This difference, however, was not statistically significant.

Fiscal consciousness in the young
Alarcon-Garcia, Gloria Economia y Empresa, Universidad de Murcia, Espinardo (Murcia), Spain Penaranda, Maria Psicologia Basica y Metodologi, Universidad de Murcia, Espinardo, Spain Quiñones Vidal, Elena psicologia basica y metodologi, universidad de murcia, Espinardo (Murcia), Spain
The concept of fiscal consciousness is related to other concepts, such as fiscal ethics or fiscal moral. But, have all these concepts the same meaning in those population segments, in which as taxpayers, the youth is supposed to be supportive and optimistic, to have primacy of ethical feelings and fairness are predominant over compulsory tax paying. In our research we have focused on the study of fiscal consciousness in the young Spaniards, including the taxpayers' moral and ethics as well.

The occupational values and orientations of recent graduates: A comparative European study
Woodley, Alan IET, Open University, Milton Keynes, United Kingdom Hick, Rod Westminster Business School, Westminster University, London, United Kingdom Braun, Edith Schul und Unterrichtsforschung, FU Berlin, Berlin, Germany
This paper will examine the value that recent higher education graduates place on a range of job characteristics such as job security, high earnings, and social status. Drawing on a 36,000-strong graduate survey, conducted as part of an EU-Commission funded project, it will examine the different values held by graduates in eleven European nations and consider possible implications for the Bologna Agreement. Early results indicate significant differences in such valued characteristics and explanations will be sought in terms of differences between the various higher education systems, national social and economic contexts and demographic variables.

The study of relationship between religious attitude and optimism in college students
Sharyati, Maryam Psychology, University of Isfahan, Birjand, Islamic Republic of Iran Ghamarani, Amir Psychology, University of Isfahan, Isfahan, Islamic Republic of Iran
Objectives: the purpose of this study was study the relationship between religious attitude and optimism in college students. Method: we recruited 100 students (50 male & 50 female) with randomize sampling and survey with two instruments (religious attitude scale & self – report scale of optimism). Result: result indicated that: 1- females religious attitude was stronger than male, 2- total optimism was stronger in the male, 3- optimism was correlated with religious attitude, 4-high level religious attitude was the best predictor of the optimism.

The relationship between family process and quality of life in Shiraz high school students
Rahimi, Mehdi Shiraz, Islamic Republic of Iran Samani, Syamack Educational Psychology, Shiraz University, shiraz, Islamic Republic of Iran
The aim of study was examining the prediction of quality of life dimensions, included Physical health, psychological health, social relationships and perception of life environment by family processes. The sample of the study included 435 boys and girls students selected by cluster random sampling from different high schools of Shiraz. Brief version of World Health Organization Quality Of Life (WHO-QOL) scale and samani's family processes scale were administered. Cronbach alpha coefficient and internal consistency showed acceptable reliability and validity of the instruments. Results of multiple regression revealed that family communication and family cohesion were positive and significant predictors of quality of life.

Study of the effect of family patterns style on shyness in high school students of Shiraz
Zarnaghash, Maryam Dep. of Educational Psycholog, Shiraz University, Shiraz, Islamic Republic of Iran Samani, Siamak Dep. of Educational Psycholog, Shiraz University, Shiraz, Islamic Republic of Iran
The aim of this study was examining the effect of different family parenting styles on shyness. The sample includes 200 high school students (85 girls and 115 boys) with a mean age 16 and SD 0.98 from Shiraz city. Revised version of cheek Shyness Questionnaire and Schaefen Family Patterns Style Questionnaire were used. Results showed that students in family with authoritarian and neglectful patterning style in comparison with students in family with authoritative and permissive patterning style have higher score in Shyness scale. Also the results revealed that the authoritarian parenting style is too powerful factor to predict shyness.

FP-010: Conditioning I

Base-rate neglect based on base-rates in experience based contingency learning
Kutzner, Florian Abt. Sozialpsychologie, Universität Heidelberg, Heidelberg, Germany Freytag, Peter Abtl. Sozialpsychologie, Universität Heidelberg, Heidelberg, Germany Fiedler, Klaus Abtl. Sozialpsychologie, Universität Heidelberg, Heidelberg, Germany Vogel, Tobias Abtl. Sozialpsychologie, Universität Heidelberg, Heidelberg, Germany
Predicting criterion events based on probabilistic predictor events, humans often lend excessive weight to predictor event information and insufficient weight to criterion event base-rates. In three studies with 119 student subjects, we used a matching-to-sample paradigm (Goodie & Fantino, 1996) to demonstrate that similarity between predictor and criterion in terms of base-rates skewed in the same direction produces a contingency illusion interpretable as base-rate neglect. In line with the pseudocontingency illusion (Fiedler & Freytag, 2004), analyses of variance indicate that predictions are biased toward the more (less) frequently reinforced response option following the more (less) frequently presented sample cue.

Neural basis of reinforcement-guided decision-making: Insights from reinforcement learning theory
Park, So-Young Q. Psychiatrie - Psychotherapie, Charité (CCM), Berlin, Germany Kahnt, Thorsten Dep. Psychiatry/Psychotherapy, Charité (CCM), Berlin, Germany Beck, Anne Dep. Psychiatry/Psychotherapy, Charité (CCM), Berlin, Germany Cohen, Mike X. Department of Epileptology, University of Bonn, Bonn, Germany Heinz, Andreas Dep. Psychiatry/Psychotherapy, Charité (CCM), Berlin, Germany Wrase, Jana Dep. Psychiatry/Psychotherapy, Charité (CCM), Berlin, Germany
Successful decision making requires at least two basic processes: The ability to learn which decisions lead to rewards (reinforcement learning), and the ability to flexibly adapt behavior to modified circumstances (dynamic decision adjustment). To investigate both processes in one task, we used model-based functional magnetic resonance imaging (fMRI) and a probabilistic reversal learning task with 19 healthy subjects. A computational reinforcement learning model was able to predict both subjects' learning behavior and dynamic decision adjustment. On neural level, the model was able to reveal new findings of neural activity in such complex tasks predicting reinforcement learning and dynamic decision adjustment.

Pattern vs. visual cue learning in rats
Cole, Mark Dept. of Psychology, Huron University College, London, Canada Clipperton, Amy Psychology, University of Guelph, Guelph, Canada Peck, Margaux Psychology, Huron University College (UWO), London, Canada Quirt, Julie Psychology, Huron University College (UWO), London, Canada
Rats searched for food atop 4 of 16 towers set in a 4 X 4 matrix. Baited towers, visually distinctive, or not, were always in a 2 X 2 pattern, during training. Removal of visual cues did not lead to performance worse than that by rats that never had visual cues. In Experiment 2, on probe trials, rats chose a visually marked tower outside the pattern over an unmarked tower completing the pattern. In Experiment 3, performance declined more when visual cues, rather than pattern cues, became unreliable. Pattern learning occurs but appears weaker than learning based on visual cues.

FP-011: Psychotherapy - Research and treatment methods I

Changes in attachment characteristics and depression following inpatient psychotherapy

Kirchmann, Helmut Friedrich-Schiller-University, Psychosocial Medicine, Jena, Germany Strauss, Bernhard Friedrich-Schiller-University, Psychosocial Medicine, Jena, Germany

In a control group design (200 controls; 150 consecutively recruited inpatients out of five psychotherapeutic hospitals) changes in attachment characteristics (attachment security, anxiety, and avoidance) and depression were analyzed related to pre-, post- and follow-up measures. Results indicated significant pre-post-changes in depression (decrease) and attachment security (improvement) following psychotherapy. Moreover changes appeared remarkably stable with regard to follow-up. Preliminary analyses revealed significant prediction of pre-post-changes in depression by pretreatment attachment security as well as post-follow-up-stability in depression by pre-post-changes in attachment security.

Nonverbal synchrony in psychotherapy: Coordinated movement, the therapeutic relationship and outcome

Ramseyer, Fabian Inst. für Psychotherapie, Univ. Psychiatrischer Service, Bern, Switzerland Tschacher, Wolfgang Dpt. of Psychotherapy, Univ. Psychiatric Services, Bern, Switzerland

Objectives. Nonverbal coordination in dyadic psychotherapies was quantified with a video-based algorithm allowing us to explore behavioral synchrony between patient and therapist. Methods. We analyzed movement patterns of (N=125) randomly selected sessions. Motion energy analysis (MEA) was carried out by an automated examination of video sequences. Behavioral synchrony was measured as the simultaneous or time lagged correlations between movements of interacting persons. Results. Higher levels of synchrony corresponded to a higher quality of the therapeutic bond and better outcome at the end of treatment. Conclusions. Our analysis showed that coordinative nonverbal behavior is a crucial variable for the therapeutic alliance.

Quality monitoring in ambulatory psychotherapy: A cluster-randomized trial

Voelkle, Manuel Psychology II, University of Mannheim, Mannheim, Germany Steffanowski, Andrés Psychology II, University of Mannheim, Mannheim, Germany Kriz, David Psychology II, University of Mannheim, Mannheim, Germany Wittmann, Werner W. Psychology II, University of Mannheim, Mannheim, Germany

Design and first results of a large-scale evaluation study in ambulatory psychotherapy will be presented. About 400 therapists have been randomly assigned to an intervention or control group. While the latter treated their clients as usual, the former received additional psychometric information on the status and progress of their patients (N =1500). In addition, the standard procedure of calling an expert opinion has been suspended in the intervention group. Since the randomization took place at the level of the therapists, appropriate statistical techniques are required to account for the clustered structure of the data. It will be demonstrated how to analyze such data and first results will be presented.

FP-012: Psychophysics

Consciousness science as Fechner's "Inner Psychophysics"

Faw, Bill Dept. of Psychology, Brewton Parker College, Mount Vernon, USA

Gustav Fechner (1860) called his techniques "outer psychophysics": deriving bridge laws between physics and psyche, but, for then, ignoring mediating physiology. Fechner anticipated a later "inner psychophysics" to develop bridge laws betweenphysics and physiology (developed in psychophysiology) – and between physiology and psyche (developed in biopsychology). The new field of Consciousness Science uses all the techniques of outer and inner psychophysics to understand very specific parts of the "psyche" – differentiating among conscious, pre-conscious, subliminal, and non-conscious: perceptual, mental, emotional, and motor functioning – precisely the science that fulfills Fechner's projection for an "inner psychophysics"!

Magnitude estimation is eccentricity invariant: Enhanced adult discriminability in a foveal-peripheral sequential magnitude discrimination task

Madon, Stewart Dept. of Psychology, Lakehead University, Thunder Bay, Canada Vanderleest, Lisa Psychology, Lakehead University, Thunder Bay, Canada Wesner, Michael Psychology, CBTC-Lakehead University, Thunder Bay, Canada

Using a sequentially-presented magnitude discrimination task we determined if elements presented in the foveal or peripheral visual fields produce discriminability differences. Subjects (N=24) were presented with 20-30 dots contained within concentric center (9° dia)-surround (9° inner - 18° outer dia) fields. Surprisingly, we found high magnitude discriminability in our adult population (3% differences were detected better than chance), and these high sensitivities were found in both the center and surround regions. The only difference between eccentricities was reaction time at sub-threshold levels, with longer latencies observed in peripheral field responses [t(23)=2.258, p<0.05]. Potential for clinical depression markers will be discussed.

Assessing the role of spatial-frequency content on slant-from-texture

Rosas, Pedro Santiago, Chile Wichmann, Felix Modelling of Cognition, TUB and BCCN Berlin, Berlin, Germany

We report two psychophysical experiments assessing the influence of the spectral content of our stimuli on slant-from-texture discrimination. First, our masking experiment suggests that a narrow band of spatial frequencies is sufficient for the task. Second, an adaptation experiment suggests a similar spatial frequency band to be necessary for the task. The location and width of the critical band varies with texture type. We interpret these results as suggesting that a local frequency analysis is critical for slant-from-texture perception similar to the notion of a "channel" suggested as a front-end to spatial vision.

FP-013: Neural bases of cognition I

Response-time corrected averaging of event-related potentials

Gibbons, Henning Psychological Assessment, University of Göttingen, Göttingen, Germany Stahl, Jutta Psychological Assessment, University of Göttingen, Göttingen, Germany

In cognitive tasks, one can assume substantial latency variability of late components in the event-related potential (ERP). Hence, in traditional stimulus-locked ERP averages smearing of components like P300 and N400 will make them appear less distinctive. We therefore introduce a novel response-time (RT) corrected ERP averaging procedure: Prior to the averaging procedure, single-trial ERP waveforms are warped in time to match mean RT. We demonstrate for a set of priming data that certain RT-corrected averaging procedures outperform both, the traditional stimulus- and response-locked averages, regarding the ability to detect priming effects on amplitude of a late ERP component, i.e., P500.

Neurocognitive evidence of defective magnocellular visual processing in configurational apperceptive prosopagnosia

Bliem, Harald Rudolf Inst. für Psychologie, Universität Innsbruck, Innsbruck, Austria

Detailed investigations of a new case of configurational apperceptive prosopagnosia due to right ventral occipito-temporal lesions are reported. Detection and recognition experiments with two-color face pictures at isoluminance and at varying luminance contrasts revealed a selective inability to perceive a human face indicating intact local detail processing but impaired configurational processing. Further recognition experiments varying spatial frequency contents of faces and chairs showed face-specific impairment of global gestalt-like form perception. All experiments reveal a lesion-induced defect of the magnocellular visual subsystem in high level configurational face processing which is partly embodied in the fusiform face area.

Distinct neural mechanisms for repetition effects of visual objects

Guo, Chunyan Education Science College, Capital Normal University, Beijing, People's Republic of China Jiang, Yang Behavioral Science Department, University of Kentucky, Lexington, USA

Repetition of visually common objects was examined in relation to prior intentional learning and memory status using a delayed match-to-sample task. Two temporally separate event-related potential (ERP) components indexed repetition.The early repetition effect (200–550 ms) evoked more ERP responses for repeated visual objects. In contrast, the late repetition effect (after 550 ms) evoked reduced ERP activation for repeated items, and was not affected by prior learning.Meanwhile, the early and anterior repetition effect, in temporal pole and frontal cortices, is modulated by explicit memory mechanisms.

FP-014: Mental representation

How does the mind represent numbers?: A simple neural network model

Brockhaus, Friederike Techn. Universität Chemnitz, Chemnitz, Germany Sedlmeier, Peter Inst. für Psychologie, Techn. Universität Chemnitz, Chemnitz, Germany

Concerning the representation of numbers in the mind, Verguts et al. (2005) proposed a neural-network model that overcomes some shortcomings of prior approaches. Nonetheless, also their model uses several ad hoc assumptions and is restricted to numbers up to 15. We simplified their model, extended the number range, and examined whether the model still reproduced established empirical effects. It turned out that not all assumptions are needed to mimic basic judgments about numbers. Our model reproduced also, for the first time, the "compatibility effect", another well-known result, that consistently appears in the comparison of two-digit numbers.

Object representations in long-term memory as feature sets derived from affordances

Eren, Selda Cognitive Science, Middle East Technical Univ., Ankara, Turkey

This study tests whether object representations in LTM consist of features encoding affordances. Participants were familiarized with fifteen slides where an 'active' object hits a 'passive object'. Each object had four features (border, color, shape, pattern). In five slides, the active object had a 'pushing' affordance. During recognition, sixteen objects (same/novel), with two, one or zero affordance-relevant features were shown. A two-way ANOVA revealed that novel objects with affordance-relevant features were recognized as familiar, as frequently as truly identical stimuli. Thus, objects are preferentially recognized in terms of their affordance-relevant features, disregarding other defining features.

FP-015: Media effects: The psychological, social, and cultural impact of mass media I

5-Dimensional media culture virtuality model
Naydonova, Lyubov A. Psychol. of Mass Communication, ISPP, Kyiv, Ukraine
Mass media are an important part of the modern culture, significance of which is being increased during societies' transition to digital era. Media have potential to create virtual worlds in recipients' minds. They become the part of everyday life as post-virtual reality and play the same role as the natural and the social reality. Virtuality investigation is the way to understand the diversity of media culture. We suggest 5 dimensions of virtuality: contextual weaving, realistic simulation, interactivity, reflexivity, resource ability. 5DV-questionnaire is proposed. All-Ukrainian representative survey (n=2250) data show differences of media culture of the different age cohorts.

The impact of information validity and need for affect on the persuasion through fiction
Maleckar, Barbara Bildung und Psychologie, Universität Linz, Linz, Austria Appel, Markus Education and Psychology, University of Linz, Linz, Austria
Recent persuasion research has demonstrated strong effects of narratives on beliefs irrespective of the source label and need for cognition. In the present project, we linked models of narrative persuasion with research on the false-information effect. A narrative introduced as a lie story was assumed to be less persuasive than conventional source labels (fact, fiction), rather to evoke a contrast effect. We further predicted that the trait need for affect moderates the advance-information/ label effect. In an experiment with 18-40 year-old British on-line panelists, a mediated moderation model of emotional persuasion was supported, including text-, label-, and recipient factors (state/ trait).

Effects of television and video games on psychophysiological variables in adolescent boys
Maass, Asja Inst. für Psychologie, Universität Bielefeld, Bielefeld, Germany Poggenpohl, Henrike Psychology, University of Bielefeld, Bielefeld, Germany Lohaus, Arnold Psychology, University of Bielefeld, Bielefeld, Germany
The use of electronic media is one of the main recreational activities of adolescents. This study investigates changes in physiological and psychological indicators of stress associated with watching television and playing video games. Besides the type of media two genres (violent vs. non-violent) were compared. Differential changes in physiological factors (heart rate, cortisol, alpha-amylase) and subjective experiences were expected between the treatment groups. Participants were N=100 boys aged 12 to 14. The expected differences in psychophysiological reactions were supported by analyses of variance. The results underline the role of certain types of media and genres for the emergence of stress.

FP-016: Acquisition of language I

Error analysis of english word recognition and students' reflections on a balanced reading instruction program
Leou, Yea-Mei General Education, Tainan Institute of Nursing, Tainan, Taiwan Huang, Shiu-Hsung Education Department, National University of Tainan, Tainan City, Taiwan Fang, Chin-Ya Center for Teacher Education, National Kaohsiung Normal Univ, Tainan City, Taiwan
The purposes of this study are to explore the students' error analysis of word recognition before and after the intervention of a balanced reading program which combines phonics with whole language, and to explore the students' reflections on this program. The participants in the experimental group and the controlled group were 61 fourth graders in Taiwan. A standard assessment named English Word Recognition is used before and after the intervention. The questionnaire of reading is used to explore the students' reactions to the program. Besides the results of error analysis and students' reflections, some suggestions are provided.

Interrelation between supporting language acquisition and the development of language and cognitive abilities in preschool children
Gasteiger-Klicpera, Barbara Inst. für Bildungspsychologie, Pädag. Hochschule Weingarten, Weingarten, Germany Patzelt, Doreen Educational Psychology, University of Education, Weingarten, Germany Knapp, Werner Educational Psychology, University of Education, Weingarten, Germany Kucharz, Diemut Educational Psychology, University of Education, Weingarten, Germany Vomhof, Beate Educational Psychology, University of Education, Weingarten, Germany
A program of the Landesstiftung Baden-Württemberg to support language acquisition for children with German as first or second language was evaluated. 864 children participating in intervention groups were tested with SSV (Grimm, 2003) and CPM (Bulheller/Häcker, 2002) as well as 294 children as a control group. Language related and cognitive skills were assessed at the beginning and end of the period of support. First results showed a developmental improvement in all of the children. Despite these, differences in achievement were shown between the two groups of children in the examined developmental domains. Consequences of the results for supporting language acquisition of children are therefore assumed.

Experts' evaluation of the effectiveness and feasibility of interventions aiming to improve cognitive-academic language proficiency of multilingual migrant pupils
Rösselet, Stephan IVP / ZFE, PH Bern, Bern, Switzerland Müller, Romano IVP/ZFE, PH Bern, Bern, Switzerland
By means of a two-round Delphi-expert-questionnaire a panel of 176 language-education and migration experts (CH, D, A) rated the effectiveness and feasibility of 174 interventions aiming at the improvement of cognitive-academic language (educational language) proficiency and school success of migrant pupils. The rating resulted in a high consensus both between individual experts and groups of experts respectively. Two groups of interventions proved to be most important in the judgement of the experts: (1) educational interventions, e.g. individualisation, cooperative learning and literacy-education; (2) institutional interventions, e.g. implementation of integrative measures, sustaining both first and second language and reforming the selection procedures.

FP-017: Burnout and social support I

Effectiveness of coaching, quality circles, and supervision for the reduction of job related burdens in police personnel
Kleiber, Dieter Edu.Sciences & Psychology, Freie Universität Berlin, Berlin, Germany Chwallek, Katharina Edu.Sciences & Psychology, Freie Universität Berlin, Berlin, Germany Burkhard, Gusy Edu.Sciences & Psychology, Freie Universität Berlin, Berlin, Germany Auckenthaler, Anna Edu.Sciences & Psychology, Freie Universität Berlin, Berlin, Germany
In a pre-post-test control-group-design, three types of interventions (coaching, health related quality circles, and supervision) were provided for police officers working in particularly burdening fields at a state office of criminal investigation in Berlin. The interventions' differential effectiveness was investigated using qualitative group interviews and standardised questionnaires. Compared to control-group participants, participants from the intervention groups reported reduced emotional exhaustion, more positive subjective perceptions of working conditions, and stronger feelings of connectedness to the workplace as well as of social support from superiors.

Occupational mental health among nurses in Argentina: The moderating effects of absence, job satisfaction and social support
Tourigny, Louise Management Dept., C-5052, Univ. of Wisconsin-Whitewater, Whitewater, USA Baba, Vishwanath Management, McMaster University, McMaster, Canada Monserrat, Silvia Inés Facultad de Cs. Económicas, Universidad Nacional del Centr, Campus universitario Tandil, Argentina Mayoral, Luisa Facultad de Cs. Económicas, Universidad Nacional del Centr, Campus universitario Tandil, Argentina Lituchy, Terri Management, Concordia University, Montreal, Canada
This study focuses on the impact of role overload on stress and depression. The restorative effect of absence is assessed in conjunction with job satisfaction and social support. Data were collected from 304 nurses in Argentina. Hierarchical moderated multiple regressions with 3-way interaction terms were used for data analysis. Findings indicate that role overload demonstrates significant main effects on stress and depression. Job satisfaction is particularly relevant in the context of high absence in buffering the effect of role overload on depression. Social support moderates of the impact of role overload on job stress in the context of high absence.

A structural model of professional burnout in high school and collegue professors
Arias Galicia, Fernando Dept. of Psychology, Morelos University, Cuernavaca, Mexico
The purpose of this study is to test a structural model with antecedent and consequent variables associated with burnout in Mexican teachers. The burnout is meant as a response to prolonged emotional and interpersonal chronic stressors at work, with three dimensions: exhaustion, depersonalization and inefficiency. The sample consisted in 227 high school and college teachers. Statistical analysis was performed using a model of structural equations. Results show social support and relationships with peers as predictive variables of burnout and health and job satisfaction as consequent variables, upon analysis of adequate adjustment indexes. Suggestions for further research are offered.

FP-018: Psychological disorders I

Defocused mode of attention: Further evidences from perceptual eccentricity and memory
Fazilat Pour, Masoud Psychology, Cardiff University, Cardiff, United Kingdom von Hecker, Ulrich Psychology, Cardiff University, Cardiff, United Kingdom
Changes in attentional processes have been proposed to play a functional role in depressed mood. Drawing on the defocused mode of attention hypothesis, we examined perceptual eccentricity (Studies 1a & 1b), and memory for irrelevant aspects of stimuli (study2). Overall, the results indicate that depressed participants maintained attention for stimuli in spite of differences in eccentricity and valence. Additionally, they showed greater sensitivity to periphery stimuli as compared to focal

stimuli. Furthermore, relative to nondepressed individuals, depressives demonstrated more accurate memory for irrelevant stimuli. The pattern of results is in line with recent theorizing on the functional value of attentional changes in depressed mood.

Peritraumatic experiences of abusive behaviours

Hawkes, Amy School of Psychology, University of Tasmania, Hobart, Australia

This study investigated the peri-traumatic psychological and psychophysiological responses to four types of abusive experiences: sexual; physical; psychological and sexual harassment. This was done through imagery scripts, which depict exactly the participants abusive experience, allowing for accurate recording of the physiological response during the trauma. Information from abusive experiences were put into staged imagery scripts and delivered to participants. Physiological and psychological measures were recorded for each of the scripts. It was hypothesised that sexual and physical abuse groups would show greater distress to traumatic abuse scripts, particularly at the incident stage. The results supported hypotheses and showed that abusive exprinces that contain a sexual element produced higher ratings of personal violation.

Long-term course of post-traumatic stress disorder: A meta-analysis

Morina, Nexhmedin Department of Psychology, Friedrich-Schiller-University, Jena, Germany Franke, Lydia Department of Psychology, Friedrich-Schiller-University, Jena, Germany Mitte, Kristin Department of Psychology, Friedrich-Schiller-University, Jena, Germany Stangier, Ulrich Department of Psychology, Friedrich-Schiller-University, Jena, Germany Priebe, Stefan Social & Community Psychia, Queen Mary, Univers. of London, London, United Kingdom

Research indicates that post-traumatic stress disorder (PTSD) is one of the most common mental disorders. However, little is known about its longitudinal course. The goal of the current meta-analysis was a quantitative integration of all previous results on the long-term course of PTSD. Data sources were comprehensive computerized literature search (PubMed, PsycInfo, Pilots, and Psyndex), hand searches, and contact with authors. All observational studies on the course of PTSD following any kind of traumatic stress with a follow-up of at least 10 months were included. The studies are currently being analysed and the results will be presented at the conference.

Autobiographical memory bias and posttraumatic stress disorder

Silvestre, César Mem-Martins, Portugal Cláudio, Victor Psicologia, ISPA, Lisboa, Portugal

Research has shown that biases in autobiographical memory have a deep impact in Posttraumatic Stress Disorder (PTSD). In this study, two groups were compared - individuals with PTSD (n=12) and individuals without psychopathological evidence (n=13) – using the Autobiographical Memory Task, Impact Event Scale, Beck Depression Inventory and State-Trait Anxiety Inventory. The results demonstrated that individuals with PTSD evidenced a significant level of categorical and negative recall of autobiographical memories. We suggest these biases have an important role in the origin and maintenance of this disorder and are related with intrusive and avoidance symptoms of PTSD.

FP-019: Contemporary and advanced approaches to well-being at work I

Multimethod validation of a screening instrument for job related affective well-being

Uhmann, Stefan Klinische Psychologie, TU Dresden, Dresden, Germany Wendsche, Johannes Arbeits- und Organisationspsy., TU Dresden, Dresden, Germany Tomaschek, Anne Arbeits- und Organisationspsy., TU Dresden, Dresden, Germany Richter, Peter Arbeits- und Organisationspsy., TU Dresden, Dresden, Germany

Research has mainly focused on non-specific affective states at the work place: stress and satisfaction. Based on a two-dimensional model of affect (valence, activation) we tested the validity of a one-click, semantic-free screening instrument assessing job-related affective states. As proposed, the "affective grid" corresponds to the Positive and Negative Affect Schedule (Study 1). Furthermore, its sensitivity was examined by applying it before and after oral examinations (Study 2). Studies 3 and 4 showed associations to performance, perceived job strain and cardiovascular reactivity in virtual and assembly-line work.

A first examination of the structure of the Utrecht Work Engagement Scale in an italian sample

Lo Presti, Alessandro Dipt. Scienze dell'E., Università di Bologna, Bologna, Italy Pace, Francesco Dipartimento di Psicologia, Università di Palermo, Palermo, Italy Nonnis, Marcello Dipartimento di Psicologia, Università di Cagliari, Cagliari, Italy Sprini, Giovanni Dipartimento di Psicologia, Università di Palermo, Palermo, Italy

Work Engagement is defined by Schaufeli and colleagues as a positive, fulfilling work-related state of mind that is characterized by Vigor, Dedication and Absorption. A questionnaire (UWES) was developed in different versions and languages, to be used in organizational contexts. We tried to confirm the factorial structure of the scale (either about the 9 and 17 items' versions) using responses from an overall sample of 1080 Italian workers. Results confirmed the good structure of the UWES, consistent to Schaufeli's findings. Concluding, the UWES can be used as a good measure of work engagement in Italian organizational contexts as well.

Stress Audit Scale for organizational performance

Bommareddy, Udayakumar Reddy Rural Development, National Institute of, Hyderabad, India

Stress audit is an organizational approach to stress risk assessment that identifies the locations, extent, causes and effects of stress within the organization. OBJECTIVES: To construct a Stress Audit Scale (SAS) and examine the Model validity. METHODS: Procedurally, SAS was constructed and sharpened through pilot study. Stress Audit was also conducted for Rural Development Organizations on a sample of 322 employees drawn from four corners of India. Analysis includes Factor Analysis, Multiple Regression and Bivariate Correlation. RESULTS: "F" value found significant statistically, SAS developed has proved valid. CONCLUSIONS: As such SAS can be used for other organizations effectively.

FP-020: Consequences of occupational stress I

Is the relation between work characteristics and depression biased by self-reports about work characteristics?

Rau, Renate Inst. für Psychologie, Universität Marburg, Marburg, Germany Hoffmann, Katja Psychology, Philipps-University Marburg, Marburg, Germany Morling, Katja Psychology, Philipps-University Marburg, Marburg, Germany

The relation between work characteristics and depression were measured in 320 men and women employed in the health sector, civil service and banks. Depression was measured with a symptom severity index of depression,and by a standard clinical interview according to DSM-IV criteria. Since depression itself may bias reporting of work characteristics, job demands and job control were assessed twice: by job analysis experts, and by self-reports. Results show that both expert rated and self-reported job demand but not job control were significantly associated with a symptom severity of depression. Results indicate that the difference in work characteristics were associated with depression and can not be better explained by distorted response behaviour due to the depression.

Causal directions in the relationship between organizational justice and employee depressive symptoms

Lang, Jessica Aachen, Germany Bliese, Paul D. Medical Research Unit-Europe, U.S. Army, Heidelberg, Germany Lang, Jonas W.B. Institut für Psychologie, RWTH Aachen University, Aachen, Germany Adler, Amy B. Medical Research Unit-Europe, U.S. Army, Heidelberg, Germany

The goal of our study was to investigate the role of each causal direction between organizational justice and employee depressive symptoms using a full cross-lagged panel design. Participants (N=134 military reservists) were surveyed 3 and 6 months after activation for a non-combat deployment. Structural equation modeling revealed that both organizational justice influenced depressive symptoms (-.19, p<.05) and vice versa (-.35, p<.01). Supplementary analyses showed that the justice effect on depressive symptoms was only considerable for procedural justice. The findings suggest that addressing depressive symptoms is a fruitful alternative to improve justice in organizations.

From abusive supervision to subordinates' emotional exhaustion: The mediating effects of subordinates' justice perception and emotional labor

Wu, Tsung-Yu Dept. of Psychology, Soochow University, Taipei, Taiwan

In the current study, I explore the mediating process from abusive supervision to subordinates' emotional exhaustion. I also investigate the moderating effect of supervisory power on the relationship between abusive supervision and its consequences. I collect 223 valid questionnaires from full-time employees in Taiwan. Using hierarchical regression, the results show that abusive supervision predicts emotional exhaustion through subordinates' justice perception and emotional labor. In addition, supervisory power moderates the relationship between abusive supervision and emotional labor such that the relationship is stronger when individuals perceive more supervisory power. The results contribute to the literature of both negative leadership and emotion.

FP-021: Ethic behavior and trust I

Implementing meeting results: The impact of trust and transactivity in IT-teams

Henschel, Angela Inst. für Psychologie, Tech. Universität Braunschweig, Braunschweig, Germany Kauffeld, Simone Institut für Psychologie, TU Braunschweig/Germany, Braunschweig, Germany
To enable implementation of solutions found in a meeting, a certain team climate is required: team members should feel that they can trust each other. We expect a mediating effect of transactivity in this context. Team members who trust each other should engage in a more vivid exchange of knowledge. In consequence, any measures discussed in a team meeting should be implemented more efficiently. This assumption was tested in a study with 46 IT employees (15 teams). The results showed a positive influence of trust on the implementation of meeting results. Moreover, transactivity within the IT teams mediated this influence.

Antecedents of initial trust formation: A quasi-experimental analysis

Xie, Xiaoyun School of Management, Zhejiang University, Hangzhou, People's Republic of China Ye, Qing School of Management, Zhejiang University, Hangzhou, People's Republic of China
Many studies stated that people exhibited high-level trust even at their first interaction, which were paradoxical to that trust developing over time. 176 subjects were employed to attend a quasi-experiment, which aimed to develop antecedents of Initial trust through a policy-capturing design. We administrated a mixed factorial design to assess the effects of trust propensity and (a) trustor-trustee gender match, (b) extraversion-introversion match of trustor-trustee on initial trust. Results showed that all antecedents have significant main effect and interacted with each-other on initial trust. The present study increased our understanding on organizational trust and contributed to team-based personnel selection (NSFC70602015/ NPFC2005038627).

Moral leadership, organizational justice, and employee engagement

Hassan, Arif Business Administration, IIUM, Kuala Lumpur, Malaysia
Moral leadership involves leader's ethical conduct and the capacity to inspire others to promote ethical culture within the organization. It is expected that such leaders will practice organizational justice which will, in turn, contribute to employees' engagement. Organizational justice is a multi dimensional construct consisting of distributive, procedural, interactional, and informational justice facets. Employees' engagement is measured in terms of cognitive, emotional and physical involvement with the organization. The paper is based on a study conducted in Islamic banks in Malaysia which provided a suitable context for this study. In general, results were in the hypothesized direction.

FP-022: Caregiving and external aids for older adults

Apathy and facial expressions in demented nursing home residents

Lüken, Ulrike Inst. für Klin. Psychologie, Technische Universität Dresden, Dresden, Germany Seidl, Ulrich Section Geriatric Psychiatry, University of Heidelberg, Heidelberg, Germany Kruse, Andreas Institute of Gerontoloy, University of Heidelberg, Heidelberg, Germany Schröder, Johannes Section Geriatric Psychiatry, University of Heidelberg, Heidelberg, Germany
Objectives. In dementia, non-verbal communication becomes increasingly important in caregiver-patient interactions. We aimed to investigate influences of cognitive and neuropsychiatric symptoms on facial expressions. Methods. Facial expressions, cognitive and neuropsychiatric symptoms were assessed in 58 nursing home residents with varying degrees of dementia. Results. Even after controlling for cognitive deficits, apathy correlated substantially with facial expressions (Pearson's partial correlations: r=-0.24 to r=-0.54). Apathy mediated the relationship between cognitive status and facial expressions. Conclusion. Results highlight the impact of apathy on facial expressions in dementia. Reductions of facial expressiveness may contribute to a disregard of patients' needs in everyday life.

Dementia caregiving as a risk for morbidity and mortality within the Longitudinal Dementia Caregiver Stress Study (LEANDER-Study)

Opterbeck, Ilga Fachbereich 2, Universität Siegen, Siegen, Germany Schacke, Claudia Fachbereich 2, Universität Siegen, Siegen, Germany Zank, Susanne Fachbereich 2, Universität Siegen, Siegen, Germany
The study examines the impact of caregiver burden in Dementia on the risk for (caregivers) morbidity and mortality. In addition Dementia caregivers' state of health after the death of the patient is investigated. Data was used from the 888 subjects, who completed the Berlin Inventory of Caregivers' Burden during the LEANDER-study. The measurement allows to assess the strain of caregiving in a multidimensional way as the inventory consists of 20 subscales with 88 items. Using regression analysis, those dimensions of the caregiving burden were identified, that predicted caregivers' poor health most significantly.

Design of small touch screen interfaces for older users: The impact of screen size, task difficulty and task complexity

Oehl, Michael Universität Lüneburg, Lüneburg, Germany
A broad user group increasingly uses mobil touch screen devices in business and private areas. The limited screen space in small screen devices imposes considerable usability challenges: objects displayed on the small screens should be big enough to be hit successfully, but also small enough to house several objects on the screen. This is addressed in the present experimental study. Users' age (younger vs older adults), screen size, task difficulty (Fitts' Law) and complexity of pointing task (single vs serial) were examined. Results allow ergonomic guidelines for an optimized design of touch-based screen devices in terms of an inclusive design.

FP-023: 'Social Media': Social processes and social interaction in mass media I

The significance of others in TV reception: The reference-group model

Trepte, Sabine Inst. für Medienpsychologie, Medienschule Hamburg, Hamburg, Germany Dohle, Marco Kommunikationswissenschaft, University of Duesseldorf, Düsseldorf, Germany Hartmann, Tilo Dep. of Communication Science, Vrije Universiteit - Amsterdam, Amsterdam, Netherlands
Two groups of persons are relevant for users of entertaining TV content: protagonists of the TV show on the one hand and other audience members watching the same show on the other hand. A series of studies investigated the importance of these groups leading to the development of the reference-group model. Accordingly, in case of analytic reception, users engage in social comparison processes (Social Identity Theory, Tajfel, 1989) with protagonists and the anonymous co-audience, striving for positive distinction. In case of involved reception, however, a comparison of similarity or dissimilarity to the protagonists takes places ("similarity breeds attraction", Byrne, 1971).

Getting no answer? An experimental study on unavailability in SMS communication

Arlt, Dorothee Media Design/Media Psychologie, Technische Universität Ilmenau, Ilmenau, Germany
The presented study analysed how people deal with the problem of unavailability in SMS communication. A sample of N = 499 students took part in an experiment. They had to complete an online questionnaire presented in three versions, thereby realising different stimulus materials. The 3x2-design enabled to look for main effects of unavailability and sex. The results showed that the duration of unavailability and the sex of the subjects had different effects on human behaviour. Main effects of duration of unavailability on the subjects' emotions could be shown. Moreover, personal and motivational factor proved to be influential on emotional reactions.

FP-024: Self concept and identity

Dialogicality and other dimensions of human nature

Oles, Piotr Dept. of Personality, Catholic University Lublin, Lublin, Poland
The purpose of this paper is to propose dialogicality as dimension of human nature. Dialogicality is defined as an ability to communicate and conduct internal dialogical activity: to conduct monologues and internal dialogues and to change point of view. Other features of human nature are discussed: self-awareness and self-reflection, intentional activity and self-regulation, adaptation and flexibility, using of language and meaning giving, permanent learning and creativity, imagination and self-transcendence. This notion of human nature, and others proposed on the ground of psychodynamic approach, social cognitive theory, sociobiology, Five Factors Theory of personality, humanistic psychology, and narrative approach are compared.

Abused girls and adolescents gender identity

Obando Salazar, Olga Lucia Área de Cognicion, Instituto de Psicologia, Cali, Colombia
This presentation deals with the question of how to construct free gender identity within diversity (Foucault, Butler 1990, Lauretis 1990-1994), when girls and adolescents have been subject to the oppressing experience of abuse in different situations and ways. The content evolves around the analysis of an intervention experience with the "Luna Roja" project, which aims at putting the disempowered victim in a position where she can develop the appropriate strategies to overcome the physical and psychological effects of gender-based abuse. Methods: Study exploring, Participant actions research as methodologies of investigation and intervention emancipators. Participants: 60 adolescents. Discourse analyses

Whoami? Self-definition based on genetic phylogenies

Morf, Martin Dept. of Psychology, University of Windsor, Windsor, Canada
An examination of the gap between the geneticist's haplogroups and the human populations of interest to psychologists and the public. DNA analysis providers offering to link clients to contemporary and ancestral populations assume that this gap has been bridged. The focus here is on overlap between haplogroups and human populations, and between haplogroups based on Y chromosome DNA and on mitochondrial DNA. The conclusion reached is that these overlaps are sufficiently large to make efforts like those of the National Geographic Genographic Project interesting new tools for understanding the nature of self and identity, both of individuals and as constructs.

A study on the correlation of college students' self-confidence and internal-external control tendency

Che, Liping College of Management, USST, Shanghai, People's Republic of China

The paper explored the correlation between college students' self-confidence and internal-external control tendency by sampling 270 college students as subjects, based on college students' self-confidence questionnaire and the Adult Nowicki-Strickland Internal-External Control Scale (ANSIE). By means of canonical analysis, linear regression, and path analysis, it found that there were significant negative correlation between dimensions of self-confidence and internal-external control tendency in different degrees; academic self-confidence, social self-confidence and overall self-confidence had significant predictive function to internal-external control; there were obvious differences between students in different groups of internal-external control scores on the dimensions of self-confidence.

Critical thinking, identity styles, and commitment: A study among middle adolescents

Hejazi Moughari, Elaheh Educational Psychology, University of Tehran, Tehran, Islamic Republic of Iran

Based on a social-cognitive framework, the relations between critical thinking, identity styles and commitment were investigated. 380 Tehrani (190 male -190 female) eleventh grade students were selected randomly. Two questionnaires were administrated: California critical thinking disposition inventory (CCTDI), identity styles inventory (Berzonsky, 1992).Confirmatory factor analysis and Hierarchal regression were used for analyzing the data. The results showed that critical thinking was able to predict significantly, 28% variance of informational identity, 11%variance of normative identity and 22% of commitment but was not able to predict diffuse-avoidant identity. The gender difference in critical thinking and diffuse-avoidant identity were significant (p<0.5).Due to the results, thinking styles are able to influence the process of self-relevant information.

Mindfulness as a self-concept integrating factor

Jankowski, Tomasz Inst. of Psychology, Catholic University Lublin, Lublin, Poland

Mindfulness is a kind of receptive, non-jugdemental awareness of current experience. Some authors suggest that mindfulness has experience integrating function. To see if mindfulness is important factor explaining integrating processes in self-concept, 144 students reported disposition to be mindful in every day life as well as several aspects of self-concept structure. Based on correlation matrix exploratory model was proposed. Path analysis revealed indirect impact of mindfulness on self-differentiation, impact of mindfulness on self-discrepancy mediated by self-esteem and impact of mindfulness on self-clarity mediated by rumination.

FP-025: Social issues: Religion

Religiousness as a predictor of personality traits, locus of control and ways of coping

Akdeniz, Ceren Dept. of Psychology, Middle East Technical Univers., Ankara, Turkey

The following study aimed to look at whether religiousness predicts a specific type of personality trait, locus of control and coping mechanism. It is hypothesized that high religiousness will be correlated with high agreeableness, internal locus of control and emotional coping. Related inventories are applied to 350 university students from 7 different regions of Turkey. This study will reveal important results in terms of large scale religiousness profile of Turkish university students and relationship between religiousness and stated psychological terms. The statistical analyses of the study have not been completed yet.

Investigation of religious orientation and mental health in senile people

Mosavi Amiry, Seyed Jalal Medical Clinic, Babol, Islamic Republic of Iran Homayouni, Alireza Dept. Psychology, Medical Clinic, Babol, Islamic Republic of Iran Nikpour, Gholam Ali Dept.Psychology, Medical Clinic, Babol, Islamic Republic of Iran Emadi Haieri, Marzieh Dept.Nutrition, Medical Clinic of Dr Mosavi, Babol, Islamic Republic of Iran

The study aims to investigate the role of religious orientation and mental health in senile people. Hypothesis: People with internal religious orientation have more mental health.70 senile people were randomly selected and Alport's religious orientation scale and General Health Questionnaire(GHQ) were administered on them.Data wereanalyzed with Chi Square. Results showed negative and significant correlation between internal religious orientation and mental illness and positive significant correlation between external religious orientation and mental illness.Being religious Specially internal religious can reduce bad effects of bad events in life and causes person feels satisfaction and self-confidence and as a results mental illnesses have the least effects specially in senile period .

Relationship between attachment to god and reliance on god

Ghobary Bonab, Bagher Faculty of Psychology & Educ., University of Tehran, Tehran, Islamic Republic of Iran Yousefi-Namini, Avazeh Sadat Faculty of Psychology & Ed, University of Tehran, Tehran, Islamic Republic of Iran

This study investigates relationship between "attachment styles to God" and "Reliance on God". 500 college students were selected by means of multistage cluster sampling. Attachment to God Inventory (Rowatt, and Kirkpatrick, 2002) and Collaborative Coping Strategies in Challenging Life Events (Ghobary et al., 2003) were used. Multiple correlation indicated positive significant correlations between dimensions of reliance on God and secure attachment style. Also, negative significant correlation were observed between dimensions of reliance on God and anxious or avoidant styles. Males showed more avoidant attachment styles whereas females were higher in all dimensions of reliance on God and surrender to God.

The development and the psychometric investigation of the Muslim Religious Orientation Scale (MROS)

Harlak, Hacer Dept. of Psychology, Adnan Menderes University, Aydin, Turkey Eskin, Mehmet PSYCHIATRY, ADNAN MENDERES UNIVERSITY, AYDIN, Turkey Demirkiran, Fatma SCHOOL OF HEALTH, ADNAN MENDERES UNIVERSITY, AYDIN, Turkey

Religion plays an important part in the lives of many people. Religious orientation is a concept that defines the motivational styles of how people believe in religion. The literature delineates three religious orientations as extrinsic, intrinsic and quest. Scales were developed to measure these three religious orientations for Christian populations. There are no equivalent measures for people who believe in Islam. Therefore, we have undertaken a series of studies for developing a religious orientation scale for Muslims. As a conceptual framework we used the extrinsic, intrinsic and quest dimensions in this endeavour. We have conducted three studies to assess the psychometric properties of the Muslim Religious Orientation Scale (MROS).

Cross-confessional research of religious worldviews

Petrenko, Victor Faculty of Psychology, Moscow State University, Moscow, Russia Ulanovsky, Alexey Faculty of Psychology, Moscow State University, Moscow, Russia

The aim of our study was to compare different religious worldviews using psychosemantic approach and methodology (Petrenko, 1982, 1997, 2005; Petrenko & Mitina, 1997). The approach is close to methodology of G.Kelly. Semantic space was constructed using evaluations of canonical texts' fragments, that were given by adepts of several religions (Christian, Islam, Buddhism, Hinduism) and ideologies (fascism, communism). Several axes of semantic space were developed using factor analysis. Each religion got its coordinates in the semantic space. Projection of Russian population's positions on semantic space allowed to sort out social and religious attitudes.

From religious commitment to spiritual practices?: Religious change in the Netherlands

Popp-Baier, Ulrike Art, Religion and Culture, University of Amsterdam, Amsterdam, Netherlands

Different scholars in psychology of religion have noticed a growing trend toward uncoupling religion (declining) and spirituality (emerging) in modern Europe. Relying on survey data published by the Dutch Social and Cultural Planning Office in 2006 and on additional in-depth interviews with people of different religious affiliations and religious interests, religious changes in the Netherlands are discussed. The so-called spiritual revolution claim (Helaas, Woodhead et al. 2005) cannot be sustained by the results of these studies. The concept of controlled religiosity is introduced in order to understand contemporary trends in personal religion in the Netherlands.

FP-026: Social issues: Unemployment

The relationship among job search self-efficacy, job search behaviors and outcomes of Chinese seniors

Chang, Xue-Liang School of Psychology, Beijing Normal University, Beijing, People's Republic of China

The current study surveyed a sample of 384 university graduates to test the relationship among job search self-efficacy, job search behaviors (job search intensity and job search effort) and outcomes (job interviews, job offers and the satisfaction with the job which participants had signed up). The results demonstrated that job search intensity and effort predict the amount of job interviews; job interviews and job search self-efficacy predict the amount of job offers; job search self-efficacy and job search effort predict the satisfaction with the job which participants had signed up. The implications of these results for job search research and practice are also discussed.

Health behaviors and health risk behaviors among job-seekers

Freyer-Adam, Jennis IES, Universität Greifswald, Greifswald, Germany Coder, Beate IES, University of Greifswald, Greifswald, Germany Pockrandt, Christine IES, University of Greifswald, Greifswald, Germany Lau, Katharina IES, University of Greifswald, Greifswald, Germany John, Ulrich IES, University of Greifswald, Greifswald, Germany

Objective: To investigate the distribution of health behaviors (physical activity, fruit and vegetable intake) and health risk behaviors (smoking, unhealthy alcohol use, illicit drug use) among job-seekers. Method: Over a period of two weeks, all job-seekers of one job-agency (n=2251) were asked to be screened. Results: The sample (n=1672, M=34 years) reported less health behaviors and increased risky behaviors compared to the general population and nationwide guidelines. Long term unemployed persons had increased risks of smoking and drug use compared to short term unemployed persons. Conclusions: The high rates of risky behaviors indicate the demand for intervention programs for job-seekers.

Effects generated for the unemployment in the social and psychic spheres

Garcia Rodriguez, Rosalba Robotica Recreativa A.C., Henderson, USA Lopez Garcia, Rosa Esther Director, Robotica Recreativa A.C., Henderson TX, USA

The presented research is developed on studies of case of unemployed people from the automotive industry in Mexico; the answer generated by the corporation regularly is based in economical conditions, but once the individuals are dismissed, the psychic or social rupture caused and the anguish that live themselves, are diluted or they are ignored facing the necessity to react to the economic necessities. Support in studies of case of individuals dismissed and the narrative and analysis of their histories of life, the founded results invite to rethink the unemployment based on its own actors and turn the sight to the person.

The effects of different counselling methods on job search behaviour

Schmeink, Claudia Franziska Inst. für Psychologie, Techn. Universität Darmstadt, Darmstadt, Germany Rüttinger, Bruno Institut für Psychologie, TU Darmstadt, Darmstadt, Germany

Metaanalysis found individual career counselling generally to be the most effective and efficient treatment, while self-administered treatment is the most cost-effective. This study compares the effects of different types of counselling on 55 long-term unemployed. Initially, all subjects attended a workshop to clarify their current situation and to develop personal goals and action plans. To support their subsequent goal striving actions the three counselling treatments – individual, peer-group,and self-administered –were applied. Multivariate analysis of longitudinal data confirmed the predominance of individual counselling on job search behaviour, followed by peer-counselling. Self-administered counselling was found to be inadequate in supporting long-term unemployed.

Predictors of psychological distress and satisfaction with life in a sample of Portuguese unemployed adults

Sousa-Ribeiro, Marta Lisbon, Portugal Coimbra, Joaquim Luís Ct. Career Guid. Lifelong Lear, Fac. of Psychology and Educati, Porto, Portugal

In the light of the Jahoda's Latent Deprivation Model, this study investigated the contribution of the deprivation of the latent and manifest benefits of employment (time structure, collective purpose, activity, social contact, status, financial resources) in predicting psychological distress (anxiety, loss of confidence, discouragement) and satisfaction with life in a sample of 218 unemployed adults (mean age = 49.1 years). Four hierarchical multiple regression analyses were conducted, showing that deprivation of the latent and manifest benefits accounted for the variance in the dependent variables though not all to the same extent. Study limitations and its implications for practice are discussed

Predicting the interindividual difference of the intraindividual changes in job seeking behavior of the unemployed: A latent growth model approach

Zhou, Fan School of Management, Zhejiang University, Hangzhou, People's Republic of China Leung, Kwok Department of Management, City University of Hong Kong, Hong Kong, People's Republic of China

Previous studies have not investigated intraindividual change of job seeking behaviors of the unemployed. In this study, through the use of latent growth modeling approach, we checked the intraindividual changes in job seeking behavior of the unemployed. Data were collected from 632

unemployed individuals on four waves with a interval of three months. The results indicated several predictors for the interindividual difference in intraindividual change. The relationships were discussed.

FP-027: Smoking and alcohol abuse

Application of self-determination theory to smoking reduction: Role of relationally-autonomous motivation

Yeung, Nelson Chun Yiu Dept. of Psychology, Chinese Univer. of Hong Kong, Hong Kong, China, People's Republic of : Hong Kong SAR Mak, Winnie Wing Sze Psychology, Chinese University of HK, Hong Kong, China, People's Republic of : Macao SAR Teng, Yue Dept. of Psychology, Chinese Univ. of Hong Kong, Hong Kong, China, People's Republic of : Hong Kong SAR

Viewing that smoking is the greatest cause of preventable deaths, exploring factors facilitating smoking reduction is thus important for community health. This study applies the Self-Determination Theory (SDT) to smoking reduction with several theoretical extensions, including the incorporation of family-oriented concerns of smoking reduction into the SDT model. Throughout the 1-month follow-up study, self-reported measures and biochemical validations of smoking status were administered among a hundred of Hong Kong smokers who intended to reduce smoking. Findings from this study showed added value both in theoretical and practical perspectives, offering grounds for future smoking cessation campaigns and clinical services.

The new smoking ban policy in Hong Kong: relationship between attitudes toward the policy and social cognitive determinants of smoking

Tang, Jessica Janice I-WHO, University of Nottingham, Nottingham, United Kingdom Mo, Phoenix Kit Han I-WHO, University of Nottingham, Nottingham, United Kingdom

A new smoking policy, which required the majority of indoor public places to ban smoking, was implemented in 2007. This study applied the Theory of Planned Behavior to investigate factors associate with attitudes toward the policy and intention to smoke among 172 Hong Kong residents. Structural Equation Modeling showed that attitudes toward smoking and perceived behavioral control predicted intention to smoke. Attitudes toward the policy mediated the relationship between attitudes toward smoking and intention to smoke. Knowledge about the policy had no significant effect. To promote smoke-free, the government should focus on both attitudes toward the policy and smoking.

Can smoking attentional bias be changed? An examination of attentional retraining in smokers, smokers attempting to quit and non-smokers

Cane, James Edward Department of Psychology, University of Kent, Canterbury, United Kingdom

Research has shown that greater smoking attentional bias (AB) increases the chance of relapse during a quit attempt. The present research examines whether smoking AB can be manipulated and whether manipulations affect smoking behaviour. 38 smokers, 30 smokers attempting to quit, and 37 non-smokers received Attentional Retraining either towards smoking stimuli (towards condition), away from smoking stimuli (avoid condition), or equally to smoking and neutral stimuli (unbiased condition). Smokers showed reduced AB in the avoid and towards conditions. Effects also generalised to a new task in the towards condition, indicating the short-term effectiveness of Attentional Retraining in reducing AB.

Underage drinking: For adults!

Carius, Roland Centre de Prévention (CePT), Luxembourg, Luxembourg Michaelis, Théràse -, Centre de Prévention (CePT), Luxembourg, Luxembourg

In 2007, the CePT launched a long-term campaign in order to sensitize the adult population of Luxembourg to have a responsible and health-conscious handling of alcoholic drinks when youngsters are involved. This project combines structural and educational measures: (a) a broad-based media campaign, (b) the nationwide diffusion of information material, customized for various target groups, (c) the implementation of pilot projects in several municipalities. An intermediate evaluation indicates that the conveyed positive image, combined with factual information, enhances the commitment of the involved adults.

Family disharmony and sexual disadaptation of patience with alcohol dependence and program of cognitive psychotherapy and psychoprevention

Tolmacheva, Svetlana Sexological Service, Mental Health Research Institu, Tomsk, Russia Abolonin, Alaexey Addictive State Department, Mental Health Research Institu, Tomsk, Russia Dremov, Georgy Sexological Service, Mental Health Research Institu, Tomsk, Russia

Our investigation has shown a low level of sexual knowledge in patients with alcohol dependence. Most patients (87,6%) are not familiar with bases of psychohygiene of family life. This circumstance is a consequence of low sexual culture of the nearest during his/her puberty. Such level of sexual culture does not allow conducting with patients the psychotherapeutic work directed immediately at correction of sexual marital disharmonies. In this situation psychotherapist-sexologist is forced to begin his/her activity from informational-educative work with the patient. Creation of some informational basis of sexual culture allows further proceeding to other kinds and methods of psychotherapy.

FP-028: Social and economic transition

Exploring the expectations and experiences of new generation learners

Adams, Byron Human Resource Management, University of Johannesburg, Johannesburg, South Africa Uys, J.S. Human Resource Management, University iof Johannesburg, Johannesburg, South Africa

This study compares actual academic experience of the new generation learner with their expectations, in a South African context. We posed undergraduate students with open ended questionnaires and repertory-grid interviews. It explored the possible questions and expectations learners have compared to previous generations. The data were qualitatively analyzed. Results presented evidence regarding presentation methods in contact sessions and lecturing styles. It could also be inferred that learners have a shorter term focus, engaging more in the "here and now", relative to previous generations. This indicates possible characteristics of new learners entering tertiary education.

Envisioning the future in at risk youth in the South African context

Ahmed, Rashid Dept. of Psychology, University of the Western Cape, Cape Town, South Africa Mosavel, Maghboeba Cntr Rdcing Health Disparities, Case Western Reserve Univ, Cleveland, USA Simon, Chris Bio-Ethics, Case Western Reserve Univ, Cleveland, USA Van Stade, Debbie Dept of Social Welfare, Local Government Western Cape, Cape Town, South Africa

Objectives The present study sought to explore the future orientation of youth in high-risk communities. Method A grounded theory design was utilised to explore the perceptions of high school students from a low-income community in Cape Town. Fourteen focus group discussions were held and the data was analysed by using thematic analysis. Results The magnitude of the risk factors in the community powerfully shaped youths perceptions of their community and future. A sense of altruism, a strong need to transform social conditions and embeddedness in their community were the dominant themes. Conclusion These cross-cultural differences in future orientation and resilience merit further investigation.

Idols from an intergroup perspective

Dumont, Kitty Dept. of Psychology, University of Fort Hare, East London, South Africa Lupke, Lyn Psychology, University of Fort Hare, East London, South Africa Malgas, Lucky Psychology, University of Fort Hare, East London, South Africa
The study of children's and adolescents' idols has an over 100-year tradition. The meta-analysis of Teigen (2000) showed that idols which are commonly understood as role models, changed over the last century which is attributed to changes in the social context. The present paper argues that Social Identity Theory and related research offers an appropriate framework to conceptualize changes in the social context by assuming a functional relationship between idols and identity management strategies. The assumed functional relationship was established in a survey which investigated idols of Black and White South Africans before and after 1994.

Marginalized model citizens: Civic engagement patterns of undocumented immigrant youth in the United States

Perez, William Los Angeles, CA, USA Ramos, Karina Education, Claremont Graduate University, Claremont, CA, USA Coronado, Heidi Education, Claremont Graduate University, Claremont, CA, USA Cortes, Richard Education, Claremont Graduate University, Claremont, CA, USA
An estimated 12 million undocumented immigrants live in the United States and about 65,000 graduate from American high schools annually. This study examines the civic engagement patterns of undocumented immigrant adolescents. Over 108 students were recruited using snowball sampling methodology to participate in the study. They completed an online survey and participated in a one-hour interview. Results indicate that high achieving undocumented youth exhibit high levels of civic engagement. The present study suggests that existing laws that maintain these youth marginalized need to be revised so that communities and society at large can benefit from the potential of these students.

The strategies for coping with the migrational stress of migrants

Roznowski, Bohdan Inst.. of Psychology, Catholic University Lublin, Lublin, Poland
On the basis of the literature (the Hugo's migrational stress model, the ways of cognitive stress combating by Lazarus and Folkman) we can put forward a hypothesis, that the migrants experience stress in different ways. They use different strategies for coping with migrational stress. Qualitative research consisting of ten deep surveys conducted on the Polish citizens in Italy illustrates how migrants cope with the stress when being abroad. Secondary appraisal of the situation (Lazarus), whose aim is to reduce the stress factor-migrational employment, is worth special attention. These mechanisms are specifically strong in the case of people who have not succeeded. The latter strategies refer to the support quest and different ways of combating stress.

Social changes and life quality of the Romanian adolescents

Sassu, Raluca Dept. of Psychology, University, Sibiu, Romania
This pilot – study aims to identify the fundamental aspects of teenagers' lives in Romania, and to determine how relationships affect different life aspects. Those aspects contribute considerable to the future's adult personality; this study investigates the following domains: family, friends, school, education, self-development, social values, and career. This study aims to emphasize how the latest economical and social changes and the integration in the E.U. influence the new generations. The methodology contains an opinion questionnaire - SAR-20, STAI X1, STAI X2, Beck Depression Inventory. The questionnaire will be used to identify the researched aspects and to measure the changes.

FP-029: The role of home and family in development

A comparison of family structure perception and ideal between parents and their young children

Mazaheri, Mohammad A. Family Research Institute, Shahid Beheshti University, Tehran, Islamic Republic of Iran Haidari, Mahmood Family Research Institute, Shahid Beheshti University, Tehran, Islamic Republic of Iran Sadeghi, Mansoureh S. Family Research Institute, Shahid Beheshti University, Tehran, Islamic Republic of Iran
The present study is aimed to compare family structure's perception and ideal between parents and their young adult children. 367 families (n =1128). members of families participating in the project completed Family Adaptability and Cohesion Evaluation Scale (third version, FACES-III, Olson et al., 1985) separately. The results of the present study indicate that there's not a significant generation gap in the field of family structure and function. Moreover, comparing the results is indicative of significant differences between perceived and ideal conditions of youth as well as perceived and ideal conditions of parents.

The long-term negative effects of parental conditional regard on students' intrinsic motivation and self worth

Kuttner, Simon Dept. of Psychology, University of Otago, Dunedin, New Zealand Murachver, Tamar Psychology, University of Otago, Dunedin, New Zealand
This study examined students' perception of parental conditional regard (PCR) and its relation to intrinsic motivation and self-evaluation. 120 New Zealand students (M = 21 years) completed 4 creativity tasks and the Intrinsic Motivation Inventory. Subsequently, participants completed a PCR measure, the Impostor Phenomenon Scale, and the Self Handicapping Scale. Pearson correlations indicated that students higher in PCR displayed higher levels of compulsion to perform creativity tasks and showed increased levels of impostor feelings. Higher levels of compulsion mediated this relationship. The results highlight the long-term negative effects of controlled parenting on students' self-worth and intrinsic motivation.

Applicability of subjective well-being model in Korean children

Lee, Jeong-Mi BK21 Group of Multicultural, Sungkyunkwan University, Seoul, Republic of Korea Lee, Yang-Hee Child Psychology & Educati, Sungkyunkwan University, Seoul, Republic of Korea
The purpose of this study was to examine the applicability of a structural equation model for Korean children's subjective well-being, which was developed in the previous study. 1,481 elementary school children (781 boys and 700 girls) participated in this study. The structural model, which consisted

of perceived parental conflict, maternal behavior, social support, and children's subjective well-being, was analyzed across gender and grade. The results are discussed in terms of the relative influences of the latent variables on children's subjective well-being. The findings identify the importance of social support as a mediator that can be a target of intervention program.

Home environment and personal values on adolescents of single parent families: An impact study In Goa

Pinheiro, Michelle Abbe Faria P.G Dept of Psycho, St. Xavier's College, Mapusa, Goa, India Antoa, Nisha Abbe Faria P.G Dept of Psychol, St. Xavier's College,, Mapusa, Goa, India
This research was formulated with the purpose to understand if an adolescent's home environment plays an important role in developing his/her Personal Values. The research used the Home Environment Inventory Scale by Dr. Karuna Shankar Misra and the Personal Value Questionnaire by Dr. (Mrs.) G.P. Sherry and (Late) Prof. R.P. Verma on adolescents (N=160) between the age group of 10 -22 years in the state of Goa. The adolescents were of two groups, namely those who lost a parent and those whose parent worked abroad. Analysis of the findings suggests a significant difference in adolescents who had lost one parent and whose one parent worked abroad in terms of home environment.

Intimacy in romantic relationships during young adulthood: The role of the mother-daughter relationship

Coetzer, Elizabeth Psychology, University of Fort Hare, East London, South Africa Nicholas, Lionel Psychology, University of Fort Hare, East London, South Africa
This paper addresses the role of the mother-daughter relationship on the daughter's development of the capacity for intimacy with a romantic partner. Adolescents and young adults often become preoccupied with romantic feelings and experiment sexually. Young adulthood is therefore a critical time to study the development of sexual and non-sexual behaviour and how the mother-daughter relationship impacts on the daughter's capacity for romantic intimacy with a romantic partner. This study will report whether separateness in mother-daughter relationships is related to sexual and non-sexual intimacy in romantic relationships, and whether mother-daughter interactions significantly explains romantic intimacy in young women while taking into account other individual variables.

Direct and indirect effects of parenting on adolescents' psychosocial adaptation: The role of self disclosure and perceived parental knowledge among Turkish adolescents

Kindap, Yeliz Dept. of Psychology, Hacettepe University, Ankara, Turkey Sayil, Melike Dept. of Psychology, Hacettepe University, Ankara, Turkey
It was previously demonstrated that dimensions of parenting were related with adolescents' problem behaviors via perceived parental knowledge and self-disclosure (Soenens et al., 2006). These relations were examined in a different culture. Adolescents (352 boys and 428 girls) from 7th to 10th grade responded to the Adolescent Family Process-Parental Closeness, Behavioral and Psychological Control, Deviant Friends and Loneliness Scales. Structural equation modeling analyses revealed similar relations confirming the proposed model. However direct relations were found between parental control (behavioral and psychological) and adolescent's adaptation (loneliness and deviant friends). Also parental knowledge positively related with deviant friends in Turkish sample.

FP-030: Team performance

Creativity in teams across cultures

Bechtoldt, Myriam Work & Organizational Psychol., Universiteit van Amsterdam, Amsterdam, Netherlands de Dreu, Carsten Work & Organizational Psyc, Universiteit van Amsterdam, Amsterdam, Netherlands Nijstad, Bernard Work & Organizational Psyc, Universiteit van Amsterdam, Amsterdam, Netherlands Choi, Hoon-Seok Dept. of Psychology, Sungkyunkwan University, Seoul, Republic of Korea

Under what conditions do teams working on creative problem solving tasks make optimal use of their group members' potential? The Motivated Information Processing Model in Groups (De Dreu, Nijstad, & Van Knippenberg, 2007) suggests that affecting team members' epistemic and social motivation is decisive. We tested this assumption in three experimental studies with three-person groups from the Netherlands and Korea engaging in a brainstorming task. Results confirmed the model's predictions. However, whereas ideas of the Dutch teams became more original under high epistemic and pro-social motivation, those of the Korean teams became more feasible. The impact of culture is discussed.

Simultaneous emotional arousal in teams leads to better performance

de Boer, Robert Industrial Design Engineering, Delft University of Technology, Zeist, Netherlands

This paper discusses the role of group emotions in the creation of a shared or team mental model. We propose that the shared mental model improves if the group process leads to simultaneous emotional arousal in individual team members. We have measured emotional arousal through heart beat measurements while conducting a management case. Using different teams, we found that simultaneous arousal of the subjects is correlated to better team performance. We propose a framework to explain these findings, that combines cognitive aspects with the emotional characteristics of the group process. These results are relevant to a better understanding of team processes.

Social responsibility as trigger of motivation gains in groups: The representer effect

Hertel, Guido Psychology III, University of Muenster, Münster, Germany

The effort persons exert during teamwork is usually explained based on individualistic utility models, neglecting collectivistic motives such as responsibility for others. This study compares effects of individualistic competition motives (coactor being present or absent) with collectivistic social responsibility motives (working as a representative of a group or not) in a 2 x 2 experimental design with 64 participants performing a physical task. The results of a MANOVA revealed that both individualistic and collectivistic motives significantly increased participants' performance and subjective motivation compared to individuals working alone. However, social responsibility led to much stronger gains than social competition.

The role of intragroup respect in task performance in and for (in)groups

Renger, Daniela Dept. of Social Psychology, CAU Kiel, Kiel, Germany Simon, Bernd Dep. of Social Psychology, University of Kiel, Kiel, Germany

Previous research on intragroup respect demonstrated that respectful as opposed to disrespectful treatment increases collective identification and intended group-serving behaviour. The present research extends prior work by considering two different dimensions of respect (equality-based and performance-based respect) as independent variables as well as actual task performance in and for the ingroup as an additional dependent variable. A series of laboratory experiments was conducted which replicate the traditional effects of respect, but also demonstrate the role of respect in actual task performance. Implications for research on task performance in small groups are discussed.

Does competence feedback improve group performance in quantitative judgment tasks?

Schultze, Thomas Wirtsch.- u. Sozialpsychologie, GEMI für Psychologie, Göttingen, Germany Klocke, Katharina Wirtschafts- und Sozialpsy., GEMI für Psychologie, Göttingen, Germany Mojzisch, Andreas Wirtschafts- und Sozialpsy., GEMI für Psychologie, Göttingen, Germany Schulz-Hardt, Stefan Wirtschafts- und Sozialpsy., GEMI für Psychologie, Göttingen, Germany

Group judgments have tremendous impact on our daily lives. In the present study, we investigated whether providing group members with feedback about each other's expertise improves group performance in quantitative judgement tasks. Participants first worked on ten tasks individually and, thereafter, solved another twenty in three-person groups. Members of feedback groups were informed about each other's mean absolute percent error during the ten individual trials. Control groups received no feedback. Regression analysis showed that, after correcting for the group members' initial competence, feedback significantly increased group performance. This effect was stronger for groups consisting of members with low initial competence.

PROMOD (PROcedural MODeration): Theoretical background and empirical results on an innovative group facilitation technique

Witte, Erich H. Psychology, Institute of Social Psychology, Hamburg, Germany

Derived from theoretical postulates on how to moderate groups, we developed a facilitation technique which structures group interaction from the beginning to the end. The technique begins with the exhaustion of individual knowledge and continues by integrating it into group knowledge. These steps lead to a final group decision process (Witte, 2007). This technique has been used with different tasks: technology assessment, highly complex and dynamical problems, structured problems, escalated commitment, and ethical committees. With continuing effort to customize this technique for diverse group tasks, PROMOD has proved its superiority over unguided processes in naturally interacting groups.

FP-031: Team work

Impact of interpersonal competence, goal setting, and team building competencies' on personal effectiveness and job satisfaction

Srivastava, Kailash B.L. Humanities and Social Sciences, Indian Institute of Technology, Kharagpur, India Misra, Sunil Humanities & Social Sciences, I.I.T. Kharagpur, Kharagpur, India Tewari, H.R. Humanities & Social Scienc, I.I.T. Kharagpur, Kharagpur, India

This study examines the relationship of certain managerial competencies like goal setting, team building and interpersonal competence with job satisfaction and personal effectiveness and differences in perception across hierarchy, and the moderating effect of leadership style. Data were collected from 307 executives from banking sector using survey questionnaire and analyzed using correlation and multiple-regression analysis techniques. The results showed that managerial competencies had significantly predicted job satisfaction and personal effectiveness and leadership style moderated this relationship, and employees' perception differed across hierarchy for leadership and personal effectiveness. It had implications for management that employee should make use of these competencies and transformational leadership style to improve effectiveness.

New institutional approaches to foster inter- and transdisciplinary collaboration

Clases, Christoph School for Applied Psychology, UAS Northwestern Switzerland, Olten, Switzerland Ulbrich, Sebastian School for Applied Psychology, UAS Northwestern Switzerland, Olten, Switzerland Bäuerle, Florian School for Applied Psychology, UAS Northwestern Switzerland, Olten, Switzerland

The call for inter- and transdisciplinary collaboration as a means to cope with the complexity of real-world problems has become more and more popular in recent decades. However, academia including its implicit and explicit reward systems for career building still is dominantly organized around disciplines. The paper will discuss two case studies – one in a Swiss institute for advanced studies, the other in a Swiss university of applied sciences – that describe new types of institutional arrangements to foster inter- and transdisciplinary collaboration. The presentation of results will focus on the relation between organizational incentives and the emergence of interdisciplinary projects.

Virtualness, cohesiveness, extra-role performance and team climate in Indian software development teams

Ganesh, M.P. Humanities & Social Sciences, Indian Institute of Technology, Mumbai, India Gupta, Meenakshi Humanities & Social Scienc, Indian Institute of Technology, Mumbai, India

The paper studies the effect of group cohesiveness on team climate and extra-role performance of team members and the moderating effect of virtualness in this relationship. The sample consists of 192 team members from 33 software development teams. The following scales were used for measurement: Virtualness Index (developed for this study), Team Climate Inventory (Anderson & West, 1994), Group Cohesiveness Index (Seashore, 1954) and Organizational Citizenship Behaviour (OCB; Podsakoff & MacKenzie, 1989). Results showed that group cohesiveness significantly influences all OCB and team climate dimensions. Virtualness moderates the relationship between cohesiveness and some dimensions of OCB and team climate.

Task and relationship conflicts: Are they inseparable twins?

Kearney, Eric Bremen, Germany Schäffner, Mélanie Human Resources, Technical University Berlin, Berlin, Germany Diether, Gebert Human Resources, Technical University Berlin, Berlin, Germany

Based on De Dreu and Weingart's (2003) meta analysis, this study analyses moderator variables in the relationship of task and relationship conflicts. In an empirical study with 88 new products and services development teams, an expected highly significant positive correlation between the two described conflict types was found. We therefore introduce two possible moderators in this relationship: team identity and a sfinancial win win situation. Simple Slope analysis though showed that the undesired relationship between task and relationship conflict can only be reduced under the condition of a high team identification. Furthermore, the moderation effect of team identification varies dependent on the intensity of the existing task conflict. We discuss the theoretical and practical implications of these findings.

Knowledge exchange: Fostering performance of new services development teams through the combination of team meetings and cross functional communication

Gebert, Diether Berlin, Germany Schäffner, Màlanie Human Resources, Technical University Berlin, Berlin, Germany Kearney, Eric Human Resources, Jacobs University Bremen, Berlin, Germany

Knowledge exchange between all members of a team and between team members of different functional backgrounds each entail chances and risks concerning team performance. This study with 55 service development teams shows that neither of the mentioned knowledge exchange strategies on its own is positively related to team performance. Simple slope analyses though demonstrated that the combination of both, knowledge exchange in team meetings and cross functional communication within teams, fosters team performance: Cross functional communication was positively related to team performance only, if there existed a high frequency of team meetings. Conversely, team meetings were positively related to team performance only, if cross functional communication often took place.

Individual communicative styles of international space station astronauts
Yusupova, Anna Psychology, Moscow State University, Moscow, Russia **Gusev, Alexei** *Psychology, Moscow State University, Moscow, Russia* **Gushin, Vadim** *O-004, Inst. for Biomedical Problems, Moscow, Russia*
The objective of the study are the individual communicative styles of International Space Station (ISS) crewmembers. The content analysis of crew-ground communication in the course of four ISS missions was designed to detect the presence of three communicative functions (informative, regulatory and affective), defined in ten categories. After detection and description of communicative styles, we compared our results with a POMS questionnaire completed by the crews during space flights and with weekly ground control expert commission decisions. We found significant correlations between our data and the compared methods data and confirmed our communicative styles results.

FP-032: The development of cognition and metacognition across the lifespan

Developmental differences in performance and metacognitive accuracy in different cognitive domains from adolescence to middle adulthood
Bakracevic Vukman, Karin Dep. of Pedagogy & Psychology, Faculty of Arts, Maribor, Slovenia **Demetriou, Andreas** *Dep. of psychology, University of Cyprus, Nicosia, Cyprus*
This study was designed to provide evidence about the development of three types of thinking and metacognitive evaluations from adolescence to middle age. The study involved participants from four age groups: 13-15, 23-25, 33-35 and 43-45-year-olds. These participants solved tasks addressed to spatial, verbal and social reasoning, evaluated their own performance and difficulty of the tasks. To specify possible differences in metacognitive accuracy, the metacognitive accuracy index was created. No significant developmental differences were found in spatial and verbal domain. Social reasoning improved systematically until the age of 45. The accuracy of metacognitive evaluations also increased with age.

Lifespan age differences in monitoring and selecting task difficulty
Schäfer, Sabine Lifespan Psychology, MPI for Human Development, Berlin, Germany **Riediger, Michaela** *Lifespan Psychology, MPI for Human Development, Berlin, Germany* **Li, Shu-Chen** *Lifespan Psychology, MPI for Human Development, Berlin, Germany* **Lindenberger, Ulman** *Lifespan Psychology, MPI for Human Development, Berlin, Germany*
We predict that young adults are more accurate in judging their capacities in a given task than children and older adults. Furthermore, when given the chance to choose the difficulty of a given task, we expect older adults to underestimate their ability, and children and teenagers to overestimate their ability. Participants played a modified version of the BINGO game, in which task difficulty was determined by the number of cards played simultaneously. As expected, young adults were most accurate in choosing a suitable task-difficulty level, and children were least accurate. All age groups showed a tendency to overestimate their capacity.

Adolescents' mental health and images of self and parents
Ybrandt, Helene Dept. of Psychology, Umeå University, Umeå, Sweden
The relation between self-concept and the mental health problems; aggression, delinquency, somatic problems and anxiety/depression was studied in a sample of 199 adolescents (13 - 17 years). Regression analyses showed for girls a strong relation between self-blame and parental blame and low self-affirm/self-love and mental health problems. For boys self-neglect and too little self-autonomy predicted both externalized and internalized problems and compared to girls parental behaviour showed a stronger relation to mental health problems. A multidimensional gender specific perspective of the relation between self-concept and adolescent mental health problems is necessary.

Development of children's meta-cognition and effects on problem solving
Hao, Jiajia Department of Psychology, Institute, Beijing, People's Republic of China **Chen, Yinghe** *Department of Psychology, Develpmental Psychology, Beijing, People's Republic of China*
This study was conducted to explore the development of meta-cognition of children selected from 2-6 grades (N=169) and effects on problem solving. Three Matching Puzzle Tasks with different complexity were shown by computers, and the process and time of problem solving were recorded. MANOVA was used and the results revealed: (1) children's meta-cognition increased rapidly from grade four; (2) children with high meta-cognition regulated strategy better than the others as task complexity changing; (3) in complex task, the more time was spent on planning, the less time problem solving took, while in simple task by no means so.

Mission cognition: specially designed video games for the development of higher cognitive functions
Haddad Zubel, Rosita Psychology, University of fribourg, Fribourg, Switzerland
MissionCognition is a set of video games that encourages children's own control over their changing strategies for higher-level thinking. The games target strategies across spatial cognition, intuitive physics, number, and combinatorial thought, and have been tested on a population of 700 children between 7 and 12 years of age, yielding developmental trajectories for each cognitive domain across the entire age span. We discuss the implications of our findings as a tool for large-scale macro-developmental research and fine-tuned micro-developmental studies, both cross-sectional or longitudinal, as well as for educational practice aimed at typically developing children and those presenting developmental disorders.

Meta-analysis of sex differences in Piaget's water-level tasks: Summarizing 50 years of research
Pavlovic, Stefanie Inst. für Psychologie, Universität Wien, Wien, Austria **Voracek, Martin** *School of Psychology, University of Vienna, Wien, Austria* **Formann, Anton** *School of Psychology, University of Vienna, Wien, Austria*
Performance on Piaget's water-level tasks (WLT), originally devised for investigating children's development of the concept of horizontality invariance, shows a sex effect (boys outperform girls) and persistence of errors into adulthood. We report on the results of an extensive, topical meta-analysis on sex differences in WLT performance (140 samples, >20,000 individuals) that overcomes clear limitations of existing reviews on this theme (which are outdated, incomplete, or no formal meta-analyses). Sex differences in WLT performance are of medium size (d=0.6, one-third larger than previously believed), are commensurate for children, adolescents, and adults, and have not diminished over the past decades.

FP-033: Teacher competence, teacher beliefs and concepts of knowledge

Does students' immigration status matter? Teachers' diagnostic accuracy in the evaluation of students' mathematical achievement
Hachfeld, Axinja Erziehungswiss.&Bildungssystem, Max Planck Institut, Berlin, Germany **Grabbe, Yvonne** *Erziehungswiss.&Bildungssy, Max Planck Institut, Berlin, Germany* **McElvany, Nele** *Educational Research, Max Planck Institute, Berlin, Germany* **Kunter, Mareike** *Educational Research, Max Planck Institute, Berlin, Germany*
Accuracy in diagnostic judgment is a precondition for providing students with appropriate support. The poor performance of immigrant students in international assessment studies has been linked to teachers' difficulties in evaluating their (domain-specific) achievement. The present study used data from N = 305 secondary mathematics teachers to compare teacher ability to correctly diagnose the achievement of German and non-German students. Teachers were asked to indicate whether their students would answer specific mathematical problems from an achievement test correctly. Results reveal that teachers tended to overestimate the achievement of non-German students. Consequences of these findings will be discussed.

Pre-service teachers' epistemological beliefs and conceptions about teaching and learning: A Hong Kong study
Wong, Angel K.Y. of Education, Hong Kong Institute, Tai Po, China, People's Republic of : Hong Kong SAR **Chan, Kwok Wai** *EPCL, HK Institute of Education, Tai Po, China, People's Republic of : Macao SAR* **Lai, Po Yin** *EPCL, HK Institute of Education, Tai Po, China, People's Republic of : Macao SAR* **Cheung, Ho Yin** *EPCL, HK Institute of Education, Tai Po, China, People's Republic of : Macao SAR*
A survey was conducted with 604 pre-service teacher education students in Hong Kong to examine their epistemological beliefs, conceptions about teaching and learning, and the relationships between these beliefs and conceptions. For epistemological beliefs, the students tended to conceive knowledge as tentative, attained by effort rather than given by authority or limited by ability. They endorsed the constructivist conception more than the traditional conception about teaching and learning. Structural equation modeling and path analysis showed that epistemological beliefs predict students' conceptions about teaching and learning. Helping teachers understand their epistemological beliefs would subsequently facilitate them to adopt appropriate instructional approach.

Intuition in the teacher's activity
Gilmanov, Sergey Pedagogics and Psychology, Yugorskiy State University, Khanty-Mansiysk, Russia
Objectives Our purpose was to reveal the functions of intuition in teacher's activity, its psychological basis. Methods Supervision, interviewing, written interrogation by teachers (n = 270) was carried out. We have allocated four kinds of the decisions of teachers: impulsive (purely affective reaction); stereotyped (based on found decisions); logic (mediated by reasoning); intuitive (unrealized, direct, fast). The functions of intuitive decisions were defined by cluster analysis. Results There are 6 functions of intuition: compensatory, regulatory,

orientation, integrating, forecasting, optimization. Conclusions The professional pedagogical intuition is formed as dynamic cognitive-emotional model of the pedagogical actuality (DCEM).

What can we reliably know? Teacher's concepts of knowlegde at the beginning and at the end of teacher training and after several years of teaching experience

Fiechter, Ursula IVP, Pädagogische Hochschule Bern, Bern, Switzerland **Weinmann-Lutz, Birgit** Fachbereich Psychologie, Universität Trier, Trier, Germany **Meili, Barbara** IVP, Pädagogische Hochschule Bern, Bern, Switzerland **Trösch, Larissa** IVP, Pädagogische Hochschule Bern, Bern, Switzerland

Assuming that personal epistemology influences the quality of teaching, the goal of this study was to characterize and compare the personal epistemologies of teaching students at the beginning and the end of their training and experienced teachers. We expected differences along the advancement in training and professional experience as well as with the diversity of educational and occupational experiences in the life-course. 300 reflective judgement questionnaires were collected and 24 dilemma interviews were undertaken. Multivariate analyses of variance and content analyses were performed. Additionally important curricular documents were analysed to provide information about the intended impact of the training.

Pedagogical knowledge as an aspect of teacher competence: Conceptualization and test construction

Dubberke, Thamar Inst. für Bildungsforschung, Max-Planck-Institut, Berlin, Germany **Kunter, Mareike** Educational Research, Max Planck Institute, Berlin, Germany **McElvany, Nele** Educational Research, Max Planck Institute, Berlin, Germany

Teachers need to draw on a rich knowledge base in order to create powerful learning situations. Besides subject-related knowledge, this knowledge base covers generic aspects of instruction. We present a comprehensive conceptualization of teachers' general pedagogical knowledge (PK) and the development of a test—a battery of multiple-choice and short-answer items and videotaped vignettes—designed to tap different aspects of PK. Seventy-one teachers completed the items and rated their relevance for teaching and their content generality. Teachers' ratings were very positive and reliable subscales were established to tap PK as one significant aspect of teacher competence.

FP-034: Stressful life events

Emotions, social support and recovery in crime victims

Abbiati, Milena Faculté de Droit, Universite de Geneve, Geneve, Switzerland **Languin, Noelle** Faculté de droit, UNIVERSITE DE GENEVE, Geneve, Switzerland **Rauschenbach, Mina** Faculté de droit, UNIVERSITE DE GENEVE, Geneve, Switzerland

This study aims at exploring crime victims' emotional reactions about their aggression and the impact of lay support and criminal justice system experience. 60 crime victims were asked, using a semi-structured individual questionnaire, to recall the overall emotional intensity of the traumatic event just after the assault and currently and to report lay support and criminal justice experience. Correspondence factorial analyses indicate that criminal justice experience have a detrimental impact on victims' psychological adjustment and coping of actual everyday life, whereas positive lay support and absent criminal justice experience appear to help recovery. These results suggest that more efforts are needed to offer more adequate legal and social interventions to support crime victims and to prevent eventual secondary victimization.

Psyschosocial impact of terrorism-induced migration on the Kashmiri women

Vinayak, Seema Dept. of Psychology, Panjab University, Chandigarh, India

Study aimed to understand the psychosocial impact of terrorism-induced migration on the Hindu women from the Kashmir region of India. 70 such women victims and the same number of women from terrorism-free parts of India, in the age range of 20-50 years, were randomly selected. Death Anxiety, Stress, Depression and Coping Scales were administered. Statistical analysis revealed the women in younger age group showed more depression,less stress and anxiety than women in the higher age group of terrorism-affected sample. Against terrorism-free population, the Kashmiri women migrants were higher on depression and death anxiety. Coping strategies used were also analysed.

Stress and extreme poverty in Peruvian women

Arévalo Prieto, María Victoria Dept. of Psychology, Pontifical Catholic University, Lima 32, Peru

The study focused on understanding the stress reaction of poor women under extreme poverty. The study propose a relational model which comprised the stressload generated by the accumulation of the negative impact of continuous exposure to difficulties, the coping styles, personal assets (attribution styles and sense of coherence) and, social resources, namely perceived relief Participants were 80 adults women that live in an extreme poverty area in Lima. The results were presented in a descriptive form and the chronic stress reaction regression model was tested. The study results showed that in extreme poverty three variables were significant in explaining chronic stress reaction, i.e., stressload, Sense of Coherence and Perceived Emotional Relief due to Social Support.

Stress and resilience in paramedics

Baenninger-Huber, Eva Psychology, University of Innsbruck, Innsbruck, Austria **Juen, Barbara** Psychology, University of Innsbruck, Innsbruck, Austria

The present study focuses on the subjective experience of stress and coping strategies of different high risk professions. Participants were 31 train drivers, 31 mountain rescuers, 26 paramedics and 10 undertakers (n=98). Based on their narratives of traumatic events experienced during their work, the specific stressors, subjective experience and symptoms during and after the event, cognitive evaluations and coping strategies were analysed. The results show how specific stressors are linked to specific coping strategies in each of the groups. The results allow the differentiation between more general as well as specific needs of the various professions with regard to psychosocial support after traumatic experiences.

Occupational hazards and coping mechanisms of sex workers in south-western Nigeria

Popoola, Bayode Educational Found & Counseling, Obafemi Awolowo University, Ile Ife, Nigeria

The study investigated occupational hazards and coping mechanisms of sex workers in Nigeria. A questionnaire was administered on 112 female sex workers from Southwestern Nigeria to collect information on occupational hazards and coping mechanisms. Findings revealed that 63% of sex workers joined the profession for socio-economic reasons. Reported occupational hazards included poor health (65%), risk of STD's (78%), police harassment (91%) and loss of social prestige (62%). Major coping mechanisms included bribing law officials (83%), enduring public ridicule (87%) and spiritual help (68%). The paper stressed the need for economic empowerment of women to reduce their involvement in sex work

Psychosocial support services for HIV/AIDS orphans in Zimbabwe

Mutepfa, Magen Counselling Dept., Zimbabwe Open University, Harare, Zimbabwe **Mpofu, Elias** Counselor Education and Reha., The Penn State University, University Park, USA

Objective. The study examined the nature and accessibility of psychosocial support services for HIV/AIDS orphan children in two districts of Harare, Zimbabwe. Method. A total of 105 pupils (mean age= 13.1 years), six schoolheads and three community agency directors took part in this study. Pupils reported on the types of support that they received. Caregivers reported on the different types of support provided to orphans. Results. Orphans received support mainly in the form of school fees whereas medical care and psychological and emotional was minimal. Conclusion: Gaps in psychosocial supports for orphans lowered their quality of life.

FP-035: Child and adolescent psychopathology I

Neuroticism and its relationship with depressive symptoms and explanatory style in children

Ludlow, Tracy Dept. of Psychology, Griffith University, Gold Coast, Australia **Conlon, Elizabeth** School of Psychology, Griffith University, Gold Coast, Australia

An association between depression, neuroticism and explanatory style is reported in research. These associations were measured in two studies with children (mean age = 10.9). Positive associations were found between depressive symptoms, neuroticism and explanatory style measured with the Children's Attributional Style Questionnaire, which has poor reliability. When explanatory style was measured reliably with a causal interview no significant association was found between explanations for negative events and neuroticism, but was found between depressive symptoms and the same explanations for negative events. Differences in explanations of negative events following retrospective or immediate failures and the influence of neuroticism are discussed.

Parenting styles in families of adolescents with and without emotional/behavioral disorders in Iran

Goodarzi, Alimohammad Education, University of Social welfare ., Tehran, Islamic Republic of Iran **Alizadeh, Hamid** Psychology & Education, University of Allameh Tabataba, Tehran, Islamic Republic of Iran **Galavi, Najmeh** Psychology, Islmic Azad university, Birjand, Islamic Republic of Iran

Objective: This study examines parenting styles in families of adolescents with and without emotional/ behavioral disorders (EBD) in Iran. Method: 10 high schools were selected in Zabol, and 180 14-18 year old students were diagnosed utilizing CBCL. Parenting styles (PS) were evaluated by Robinson et al., (2001). Results: Analysis of data with utilization of Pearson correlation and Chi-square revealed that there exists a negative relationship between authoritative styles and EBDs. The findings show a significant correlation between authoritarianism and EBDs. The parents apply similar PS in the groups. Conclusion: This study helps to get a better understanding on the etiology and clinical intervention for adolescents with EBDs. Keywords: Parenting Styles, Adolescents, Emotional/Behavioral Disorders

Appearance-related social pressure as a risk-factor in the development of body dissatisfaction and disordered eating

Helfert, Susanne Inst. für Psychologie, Universität Potsdam, Potsdam, Germany **Warschburger, Petra** Inst. für Psychologie, Universität Potsdam, Potsdam, Germany

Social influences are crucial for the development of body dissatisfaction and eating disorders. Since most studies are limited to one aspect, research is needed that investigates the influence of several sources (e.g. parents, peers) and several kinds (e.g. comments, norms) of social pressure. We will therefore present the results of a 10-month longitudinal study. 340 high-school students aged 12-16 completed a questionnaire including measures regarding different kinds and aspects of social pressure and eating pathology. Results support the crucial role of appearance-related social pressure for the development of body dissatisfaction and eating disturbance. Different mechanisms will be discussed.

Fetal head growth mediates associations of maternal folate in early pregnancy with behavioural problems in childhood

Schlotz, Wolff School of Psychology, University of Southampton, Southampton, United Kingdom Jones, Alexander MRC Epidemiology Resource Cent, University of Southampton, Southampton, United Kingdom Gale, Catharine R. MRC Epidemiology Resource Cent, University of Southampton, Southampton, United Kingdom Godfrey, Keith M. MRC Epidemiology Resource Cent, University of Southampton, Southampton, United Kingdom Robinson, Sian M. MRC Epidemiology Resource Cent, University of Southampton, Southampton, United Kingdom Phillips, David I.W. MRC Epidemiology Resource Cent, University of Southampton, Southampton, United Kingdom

Objective: To examine for a neurodevelopmental mechanism in the association of maternal folate levels during pregnancy with the child's behavioural adaptation later in life. Methods: In a prospective birth cohort (N=100), we tested if fetal growth mediated associations of maternal folate (physiological folate levels; total folate intake) during early pregnancy with behavioural problems of their children at 7-9 years of age. Results: Lower maternal folate in early pregnancy was associated with higher levels of hyperactivity and peer problems in their children; these associations were partially mediated by fetal head growth. Conclusions: These results suggest a neurodevelopmental mechanism for long-lasting folate effects.

FP-036: Psychotherapy - Research and treatment methods II

Interventions with Aboriginal street youth in Western Canada: A narrative exploration of experiences with counseling

Brunanski, Dana Counselling Psychology, University of British Columbia, Vancouver, Canada

Indigenous youth are at high risk of street-involvement in many nations, including Canada. The scant research suggests that despite experiencing problems that could be benefited by counseling, most Canadian Aboriginal street youth do not access counseling. The present study aimed to explore youths' experiences and opinions of counseling using qualitative narrative methods. Interviews with youth focused on their experiences with counseling in the context of their lives on the street, as did a focus group with street youth counsellors. Youths' narratives of counseling will be presented to illustrate themes in counseling with Aboriginal street youth and implications for counseling practice.

The effect of psychological and educational family-centered early intervention on parents mental health of children's with Down syndrome

Faramarzi, Salar Dept. of Education, University of Isfahan, Isfahan, Islamic Republic of Iran Afrooz, Gholamalli psychology, university of tehran, tehran, Islamic Republic of Iran Malekpour, Mokhtar

educational science, university of isfahan, isfahan, Islamic Republic of Iran

The purpose of this study is to examine the effect of family-centered early psychological and educational interventions on parents' mental health of isfahanian children's with Down Syndrome. An experimental and a pretest-posttest control group design method was applied. parents of 36 children with Down Syndrome were chosen as sample size of the study. General Health Questionnaire was used to evaluate the mothers' mental health. The analyses of covariance revealed that, the difference between the performance of the control group and the experimental group in the mental health test was statistically significant, and family-centered early psychological and educational interventions have positive effect on parents' mental health state.

Presenting Pa.B.I.c.: Psychological-anamnestic bereavement interview for caregivers

Guarino, Angela Dipt. di Psicologia 1, Università La Sapienza, Roma, Italy Serantoni, Grazia Fondazione Lefebvre D'Ovidio, Fondazione Lefebvre D'Ovidio, Roma, Italy Benini, Franca Fondazione Lefebvre D'Ovidio, Fondazione Lefebvre D'Ovidio, Roma, Italy Cornaglia Ferraris, Paolo Fondazione Lefebvre D'Ovidio, Fondazione Lefebvre D'Ovidio, Roma, Italy

"Psychological-Anamnestic Bereavement Interview for caregivers" (Pa.B.I.c.) is a structured guide for psychologists/psychotherapists, useful for conducting a clinical interview with bereaved parents. This interview collects information about the life, the family and the experiences – during the disease of the child and after his death for incurable disease – of bereaved parents. This clinical guide is divided in three sections: first section collects anagraphic information about the caregiver and his/her family; second section collects anamnestic information about the dead child, his incurable disease and the quality of received care; third section investigates the psycho-emotional sphere of caregiver and possible received psychological support.

Improving psychotherapy services for LGBT clients: Perspectives of clients, therapists and administrators

Israel, Tania Gevirtz Grad. School of Educ., UC Santa Barbara, Santa Barbara, USA Sulzner, Joselyne CCSP, UCSB, Santa Barbara, USA Walther, William CCSP, UCSB, Santa Barbara, USA Gorcheva, Raia CCSP, UCSB, Santa Barbara, USA

The aim of this study was to develop recommendations for improving psychotherapy services for lesbian, gay, bisexual, and transgender (LGBT) therapy clients. The researchers conducted interviews with 42 LGBT therapy clients, 12 therapists, and nine mental health service administrators in the United States. The interviews explored a wide range of variables related to helpful and unhelpful experiences of LGBT therapy clients. The interview data were analyzed using content and case study analyses. This presentation will describe recommendations made by participants, as well as those ascertained by the researchers through analyses of the helpful and unhelpful experiences that the participants described.

FP-037: Clinical neuropsychology I

Genes influence emotional memory: A deletion variant of the alpha(2B)-adrenoceptor is related to enhanced intrusion symptoms in posttraumatic stress disorder

Kolassa, Iris-Tatjana Inst. für Psychologie, Universität Konstanz, Konstanz, Germany Ertl, Verena Onyut, P. Lamaro Neuner, Frank Psychology, University of Konstanz, Konstanz, Germany Elbert, Thomas Psychology, University of Konstanz, Konstanz, Germany Papassotiropoulos, Andreas de Quervain, J.-F.

Emotional events are recalled better than neutral events, because of enhanced noradrenergic transmission within the brain during emotionally arousing situations. Intrusions constitute a pathological form of emotional memory in posttraumatic stress disorder (PTSD). We investigated whether a deletion variant of the gene encoding the alpha(2b)-adrenergic receptor influences intrusion symptoms in PTSD. Among 202 survivors of the Rwandan genocide, deletion carriers showed higher intrusion symptoms per traumatic event type than noncarriers, independent of PTSD. While under normal circumstances a deletion-variant-related enhancement of emotional memory might be adaptive.

Electrophysiological parameters of individual psychological pecularities

Lebedev, Artur Psychophysiology, SU-HSE, Moscow, Russia

In our earlier experiences it was established, that only two EEG parameters permit to predict quantitatively many psychological pecularities. Later we have found that individual psychological portraits constituted by known MMPI scales may be computed without any questions, if we use individual EEG parameters of a subject. The accuracy of these diagnosis were verified in blind cheek experiments. The multiple linear regression equations were used with this purpose. At last it was found that intellectual possibilities of persons, their moral characteristics, sport's achievements, leaders qualities and even individual anthropological parameters may be predicted using individual EEG parameters. In our experiments mentioned above were participated about thousand subjects at all.

FP-038: Preschool, primary schools and transitions between schools

Positive Transition: Promoting sucess and school adjustment in elementary school transition

Coelho, Vitor Costa de Caparica, Portugal Sousa, Vanda Projecto Atitude Positiva, Académico de Torres Vedras, Torres Vedras, Portugal

This study analyzes the impact of a program designed to facilitate school transition from elementary to middle school. In Portugal this transition is considered an ecological transition (Rudolph, Lambert, Clark e Kurlakowski, 2001) that takes place from 4th to 5th grade. The sample was composed by 424 students who took part in a 21 weekly sessions in two consecutive school years. Results show decreases in levels of school absenteeism, retention, as well as lower levels stress associated with transition when compared to control groups and students from previous years. These results underline the importance of proper programming for school transitions.

Study impact of preschool on social development and educational progress of male students in the elementary stage in Tehran

Aliakbari, Mahnaz Dept. of Psychology, Payame Noor University, Tehran, Islamic Republic of Iran Aliakbari Dehkordi, Mahnaz PSYCHOLOGY, PAYAME NOOR UNIVERSITY, TEHRAN, Islamic Republic of Iran

In the present study, impact of preschool on social development and educational progress of male students in the elementary stage in Tehran is investigated. In this study, 3 main hypotheses and 14 minor ones are addressed: There are differences in terms of educational progress between students who participated in preschool and those who did not. There are differences in terms of social development between students participated in preschool and those who did not. There are certain relations between social development and educational progress of school students. To study hypotheses provided, a sample consisted of 150 students was taken through cluster sampling. And, to measure social development, Vineland questionnaire was used. According to the results: All three hypotheses were confirmed.

FP-039: Culture and human development I

The psychological measurement of honesty in Russia

Bormotov, Alexander Faculty of Psychology, South Ural State University, Chelyabinsk, Russia
Recent time, the common level of the social honesty is reducing steady, but number of dishonest persons is permanently rising. The scientific researches on this problem are significant because of social importance of these phenomenons and lack of differential knowledges about. The pearson's questionnaires are most popular used in evaluation of integrity. Bit it's also necessary to take into consideration cultural, historical and national peculiarities of russian people for mesurement of honesty as a person's trait. That's why we can't use diagnostic tools of any different origins but russian. And creation of such psychological tool was our aim to get.

Role of attachment in the perception of general ethnic discrimination and stress

Narchal, Renu School of Psychology, University of Western Sydney, Penrith South, Australia
This study examined the relationship between attachment styles, perceived general ethnic discrimination and perceived stress in a university student sample. Two hundred seventy seven participants indicated their attachment styles, perceived general ethnic discrimination over a period of one year, their entire lifetime and stress levels emanating from perceived general ethnic discrimination. Fearful, preoccupied attachment styles were found to be positively related to perceived ethnic discrimination and perceived stress. Attachment styles were not found to mediate relationship between perceived ethnic discrimination and perceived stress. Findings are discussed in the context of attachment and discrimination frameworks.

Exploring Filipino mothers' concept of hope

Tolentino, Laramie Counseling & Educational Psych, De La Salle University,Manila, Manila, Philippines
Concurrent theories of hope (Snyder, 1994, 2002)) define it as having two dimensions related to agency and pathways. The study seeks to reconceptualize hope in the Philippine context through the identification of cultural mediators. Twenty-five Filipino mothers from rural and urban communities were interviewed regarding their personal experience and understanding of hope. The gathered responses were evaluated to determine its alignment with the existing hope theory. Likewise, emerging themes were drawn from the interview responses through content analysis. Results indicate the need to define additional dimensions of hope in the Philippine context. Potential implications for research are discussed.

Involuntary remembering as a function of activity: A hypothesis of the historical evolution of mental functions

Yasnitsky, Anton CTL/HDAP, OISE/UT, Toronto, Canada Mazhirina, Evgeniya Department of Psychology, Kharkiv National University, Kharkiv, Ukraine Falenchuk, Olesya Education Commons, OISE/UT, Toronto, Canada Ivanova, Elena F. Department of Psychology, Kharkiv National University, Kharkiv, Ukraine
The objective of this study was to investigate historical evolution of involuntary remembering as a function of activity. To that end, we replicated a classical study done in the Soviet Union in the mid-1930s (Zinchenko, 1939) so that 1) original experimental methodology was thoroughly replicated; 2)

experimental sample with similar demographic characteristics was used, and 3) similar analytic techniques were utilized. The results of this study indicate that although developmental trends (by age groups) in involuntary remembering undergo insignificant historical change, the absolute capacity of memorization in most age groups changed dramatically over the period of the last 70 years.

FP-040: Cross-cultural comparisons I

A cross-cultural investigation about content of plays in preschool classes

Güler, Tülin Preschool Education, Hacettepe University, Ankara, Turkey Kargi, Eda Preschool Education, Hacettepe University, Ankara, Turkey
The aim of this study is to analyze the content of free time plays that three to five year-old children play during their free playing time. Research carried out with 100 children from Turkey, Germany and United States. This study is based on content analysis model. The researchers observed and recorded the plays of each group during school day. All records were coded on Saracho (1996) play observation check-list. Types of plays children's preferred in their free time plays were categorized accordance Piaget's and Smilansky's play classification. It was found out that play behaviors had been differentiated in intercultural level.

Cross-cultural identity issues in a comparison between Romanian and German female students

Joja, Oltea Clinical Psychology, Institute for Endocrinology, Bucharest, Romania von Wietersheim, Joern Psychosomatic Medicine, University of Ulm, Ulm, Germany
The study attempts to explore cross-cultural differences concerning social ideal, gender stereotypes and self-image. We compared 114 Romanian to 110 German female students using a grid-questionnaire for social roles. For Germans, the social ideal consisted of fewer masculine gender stereotype traits than for Romanians. Both groups showed a social ideal differing largely from the feminine stereotype. There were many discrepancies in the Romanian group between the social ideal and the self-images. In the German group, there were no differences between the social ideal and the self-images in the dimensions career expectancies, supporting others and sliminess. The results are discussed for their significance as vulnerability factors for the development of eating disorders in young women.

Essentialism, naturalism, entitativity and the expression of stereotypes

Pereira, Marcos Dept. of Psychology, Universidade Federal da Bahia, Salvador, Brazil Alvaro, José Luis Social Psychology, Univ. Complutense de Madrid, Madrid, Spain
The main purpose of this study is to evaluate the impact of essentialistic beliefs on the expression of social stereotypes. Studies about automatism in stereotyping processes suggest that categories such as age, gender and race are automatically applied, but are there any cultural differences in beliefs about naturalistic categories (gender, race and age) and entitativity categories (ethnic origins, religion beliefs, political affiliation, economic and social background)? The results obtained in this cross-cultural research show a similar pattern in essentialistic beliefs in Brazilian and Spaniard participants, although some differences were detected. The implications of these findings are discussed and its implications for stereotyping are evaluated.

FP-041: Space, shape, and motion I

Treading a slippery slope: Perception of the slopes of hills

Bridgeman, Bruce Dept. of Psychology, University of California, Santa Cruz, USA Hoover, Merrit psychology, University of California, SC, Santa Cruz, USA
Since some cortical neurons respond only to objects within arm's reach, we compared verbal and motor estimates of slopes in near and far space. Verbal estimates greatly overestimated slopes; overestimates increased logarithmically with distance. Proprioceptive estimates were more accurate at all ranges. When observers traverse a hill before judging it, they continue to overestimate slopes just as much as non-walkers, despite experiencing more accurate slope perception at near distance on every part of the slope; appearance trumps experience. We conclude that geometric layout of the world interacts with effort required for locomotion, but more strongly for verbal than for motor measures.

The dynamic prediction effect of saccade directions in re-mapping visual space

Chou, Yu-Ju Clinical and Counseling Psy., Nat. Dong Hwa University, Shoufeng, Taiwan
This study aims to examine saccade-contingent spatial mislocalization and how the mechanism of visual-motor coordination keeps space constancy during eye-saccades. The presentation will base on behavioural data to show how horizontal and vertical saccade directions may affect the accuracy of spatial localization? and the dynamic prediction effect of saccade directions in re-mapping visual space prior to the execution of a saccadic eye movement.

Effects of surface lightness on the perceived height of rooms

Oberfeld, Daniel Inst. Experimen. Psychologie, Universität Mainz, Mainz, Germany Hecht, Heiko Experimental Psychology, Johannes Gutenberg-Universität, Mainz, Germany
Although it is commonly held that ceilings that are lighter than the walls appear higher, while those that are darker appear lower, these effects have never been studied psychophysically. In two experiments conducted in a virtual reality setting, observers judged the height of rooms varying in physical height and surface color. Experiment 1 showed a significant effect of ceiling lightness. The rooms appeared higher with the lightest rather than with a medium light ceiling. Unexpectedly, there was a pronounced effect of wall lightness at the darkest ceiling color. Experiment 2 demonstrated that floor lightness has no significant effect on perceived height.

FP-042: Acquisition of language II

Handwriting and learning to recognize Chinese characters

Shiu, Ling-Po Dept. Educational Psychology, Chinese Univ. of Hong Kong, Shatin, China, People's Republic of : Hong Kong SAR Cheng, Pui-wan Educational Psychology, Chinese Univ. of Hong Kong, Shatin, China, People's Republic of : Macao SAR
Previous research has showed that Chinese children's writing-related skills predict their reading achievement. In the present study, 345 Chinese grade 2 children learned to recognize some Chinese characters by one of three methods – (1) writing the characters twice in the normal stroke order, (2) in the reverse stroke order, or (3) looking at the characters. Results show that the first group of children was more able than the other two groups to recognize the characters in a recognition test, while the latter two groups did not differ significantly. The implications for children learning to read Chinese will be discussed.

The impact of drama-based literacy preparation program on the 5-6 year olds' phonological awareness skills

Karaman, Gökçe Primary Education, Ankara University, Ankara, Turkey

This experimental study examines the impact of drama based literacy preparation program on the 5-6 year olds' phonological awareness skills. The study group is composed of 43 children in courses at Ankara University Kindergarten. One 5 year old group formed the control group whereas the other one with 10 week program treatment was the experiment group. The data collection tool of this study as both a pre and post test is 'Test of Phonological Awareness' developed by Torgesen and Bryant in 1994. The study will then discuss the differences between the groups of phonological awareness skills.

Evaluation of a phonological awareness program in kindergarten

Pocinho, Margarida Dept. of Psychology, University of Madeira, Funchal, Portugal *Correia, Armando* Psychology, Department of Education, Funchal, Portugal

Objectives: Testing the effectiveness of a phonological awareness program in 418 children aged 5-6 years old. Methods:The pre-test of the children's phonological awareness was done through an Portuguese adaptation of the Prueba de Segmentación Lingüística (PSL). The attained results led to the establishment of two homogeneous groups, (experimental, n=127; control, n=120).A phonological training was applied to the experimental group. Scores assessed with the PSL indicate a growth of the phonological awareness levels after the post-test. Results: Tests indicate significant differences in the experimental group (t=4,69; p<.001). Conclusions: Results sustain that training Programs intervention such as this one can improve pre-readers children metalinguistic competences.

FP-043: Burnout and social support II

Work design and psychological work reactions: The mediating effect of psychological strain and the moderating effect of social support

Panatik, Siti Aisyah Hamilton East, New Zealand

The aims of the present study were twofold: First, I examined the moderating influence of social support on the relationship between job design (job demands and job control) and psychological strain, job satisfaction and turnover intentions. Second, in providing a more comprehensive link between job design and job satisfaction and turnover intentions, I examined psychological strain as a mediator of that relationship. Participants were 443 technical workers at Telecom Malaysia. Social support was found to moderate the job design-psychological work reactions. Moreover, psychological strain significantly mediated the relationship job design-job satisfaction and turnover intentions. Implications of this study are discussed from theoretical and applied perspectives

Psychosocial factors associated to mental health outcomes among human service professionals in México City

Juárez García, Arturo Graduate School of Psychology, Morelos University, Cuernavaca, Mexico

Human Service Organizations (HSO) are characterized by psychosocial and emotional demands on workers. This research was aimed to identify factors associated to mental health outcomes in HSO professionals in Mexico. A cross-sectional study was carried out to test the association between Psychological Demands, Job Control, Job Insecurity, Social Support, Self Efficacy and Emotional Control with different Mental Health Outcomes (MHO) in HSO workers (nurses, physicians,

psychologist, social & educational workers, etc.) (N=197). Multivariate Analyses showed that most psychosocial factors were associated significantly to MHO even though job insecurity was an outstanding variable which is a growing problem in Latin-American countries.

Workplace health management (WHM) as a key concept for "classic" safety and "progressive" health issues

Lueken, Kai Prevention, Unfallkasse Rheinland-Pfalz, Andernach, Germany *Stoewesandt, Antje* Prevention, Unfallkasse Rheinland-Pfalz, Andernach, Germany *Simon, Wenke* Prevention, Unfallkasse Rheinland-Pfalz, Andernach, Germany

Classic safety at work and industrial psychology approaches often deal with strategies based on workplace enhancement considerations. Modern concepts like workplace-health-promotion often place emphasis on lifestyle enhancement strategies. Workplace-health-management combines all these approaches if certain units are established in the target organisation. Step-by-step these units carry over relevant safety and health issues from initial supervision teams founded in the course of WHM-projects. The results of a large study (n ⪲ 11.000) are introduced to show in which way a workplace health management is established in the public sector which integrates all facets of modern and traditional occupational safety and health.

FP-044: Personality and mental health I

Preliminary analysis of the MMPI results of migrant and non migrant Mexicans

Garcia, Camilo Dept. de Psicología, Universidad Veracruzana, Veracruz, Mexico *Rivera-V., Natanael* Psicología, Universidad Veracruzana, Xalapa, Veracruz, Mexico *Medina, Esteban* Psicología, Universidad Veracruzana, Xalapa, Veracruz, Mexico *Clairgue, Erika* Psicología, Universidad Veracruzana, Xalapa, Veracruz, Mexico *Jaimes, Esteban* Psicología, Universidad Veracruzana, Xalapa, Veracruz, Mexico *Herrera, Rodolofo* Psicología, Universidad Veracruzana, Xalapa, Veracruz, Mexico

We compared the profiles of migrant and non migrant populations of Mexico in order to assess the differences, if any, of the impact of migratory experiences. A 2X2 factorial design was carried out. The first was sex and the second migrant experience. The MMPI was applied to 50 young participants. ANOVA showed statistical differences for migrant factor on the paranoia and Schizophrenia. Even when the application wasnt carried out for strict clinically valid interpretations, the results seem to show the effect of a migrant experience over the psychological one. It's consistent with previous studies that report perceptual alterations:depression and anxiety.

A taxometric analysis of health anxiety

Ferguson, Eamonn Dept. of Psychology, University of Notingham, Nottingham, United Kingdom

There is a long standing debate concerning whether health anxiety is dimensional or categorical. The answer to this debate has important implications for theory, research and clinical practice. To date no studies have directly address this question using taxometric procedures. This study provides a taxometric analysis in a healthy (receiving no current medical treatment) community sample of 501 adults. Results from three taxometric procedures (MAMBAC, MAXEIGEN and L-Mode factor analysis) indicated that health anxiety is dimensional rather than categorical. This implies a multiple causal model and that clinical practice requires a shift to using empirically derived multiple diagnostic categories

Rigidity in the dispositional model of fixed forms of behavior

Zalevskiy, Genrikh Faculty of Psychology, Tomsk State University, Tomsk, Russia

Purpose and hypothesis: To what degree may be explanatory the dispositional model of fixed forms of behavior, which supposes that mental rigidity is presented in the structure of personality. Methodes: The original Tomsk questionnaire of rigidity, based on the system structure-level conception. In the study took part over 2000 normal and mentally diseased subjects. Results and conclusions: Hypothesis is corroborated, role of rigidity increased from the norm to psychic pathology, correlation to age is not linear, gender peculiarities are in the different substructures of personality, trait and state rigidity are differentiated, "local and total rigid personality" can be defined.

FP-045: Contemporary and advanced approaches to well-being at work II

Resources, requirements, and stressors at the workplace in retail: The research project RASA

Iwanowa, Anna Institut für Psychologie, Innsbruck, Austria *Lampert, Bettina* Institute of Psychology, University of Innsbruck, Innsbruck, Austria *Unterrainer, Christine* Institute of Psychology, University of Innsbruck, Innsbruck, Austria

The retail sector is known for a big number of employees, competitive conditions, and an increasing demand on flexible working hours. Up to now, in this field working-conditions and their impacts on employees' health have been rarely taken into account by research. Against this background, two condition-related instruments of analysis, namely objective observational interviews and self-report surveys, were especially developed for the retail and applied in the research project RASA (funded by the OeNB Österreichische Nationalbank). With respect to the measurements validity relations between working-conditions (resources, requirements, and stressors), and job satisfaction, health-indicators, and work-life-balance are reported (n = 520).

Occupational stress in managers: Specification of stress syndromes in top and middle management positions

Kachina, Anastasia Psychology, Moscow State University, Moscow, Russia

The purpose of the study was to investigate the influence of job position and work content on the manifestation of occupational stress among managers. A Managerial Stress Survey (Leonova, 2001) method was used to collect data from 131 (46 top and 85 middle management level) managers. The results show that the development of stress syndromes depends on the level and content of job position in managerial' work. Gender and age indirectly influence the level of occupational stress. Dynamics in stress syndromes demonstrates the cumulative character in the enhancement of negative stress effects when individuals' stress level increases.

Relationship of job dimensions and stress among personnel of Saipa Car Company

Oreyzi, Hamid Reza Pschology, Isfahan University, Isfahan, Islamic Republic of Iran *Golparvar, Mohsen* Psychology, University of Khorasgan, Isfahan, Islamic Republic of Iran *Nouri, Aboulghasem* Psychology, University of Isfahan, Isfahan, Islamic Republic of Iran *Moradi, Babak* Psychology, Car of company, Isfahan, Islamic Republic of Iran

Three hundred jobs were classified according to Position Analysis Questionnaire via interview with personnel of Saipa car company. Job stress instrument was administered and relationships between Job stress and job dimensions were significant (P<

0.05). Findings indicated that certain aspect of job introduce stress. Implication for evaluation were discussed.

FP-046: Consequences of occupational stress II

Work-related stress and depression susceptibility of employees in the financial services industry

Wang, Xiao Lu Chinese Academy of Sciences, Institute of Psychology, Beijing, People's Republic of China Shi, Kan Chinese Academy of Sciences, Management School, Beijing, People's Republic of China Tsang, Hector Wing Hong the HK Polytechnic University, D. of Rehabilitation Sciences, Hong Kong, China, People's Republic of : Hong Kong SAR Fong, Mandy Wing Man the HK Polytechnic University, D. of Rehabilitation Sciences, Hong Kong, China, People's Republic of : Hong Kong SAR

Depression cases have been reported among workers in the financial services sector, one of the most stressful occupations. The study aimed to identify depression susceptibility and stressors which may act as etiological factors among workers in this sector and their influences on workers' well being and productivity. Twenty semi-structured interviews among workers randomly recruited from a list of licensed stockbrokers in Hong Kong were conducted, audio-taped and transcribed. Content analysis shows depressive symptoms prevailed among our respondents. Employees suffered a range of work stressors which were mostly uncontrollable and unavoidable. Negative impacts on non-work life areas, e.g., work-family conflict, and damages to their attention, decision and judgment abilities were revealed.

Top managers and anxiety: An explorative qualitative study

Harding, Gabi Inst. für Psychologie LG AO, Fern-Universität Hagen, Hagen, Germany

Research on anxiety in leaders is scarce. This is even more astonishing since fear or anxiety are part of almost every typology of basic emotions (e.g. Ekman, 1984). Why should such fundamental emotions be experienced by each individual except for leaders – especially against the background of a task including risky decisions (Hirschhorn, 2000)? This explorative study investigates the work-related anxieties of top managers. Qualitative, in-depth, semi-structured interviews were carried out with top managers of profit organisations. Research questions were whether the leaders experienced anxiety and how they dealt with it, whether anxieties were induced by the task or the organisation.

Learned helplessness among the subordinates of abusive supervisors

Rashid, Tabassum Psychology, Effat College, Jeddah, Saudi Arabia

The present study was aimed to explore the relationship between subordinate's perception of abusive supervision and learned helplessness among a sample of 255 employees and their supervisors in a multinational company. It was surmised that abusive supervision might adversely affect the motivation of subordinates and thereby generate the learned helplessness. As predicted learned helplessness was greater among the subordinates of abusive supervisors. The results are discussed in the light of previous researches carried out to study the implications of abusive supervision for organizations and employees, and vis-à-vis learned helplessness.

FP-047: Ethic behavior and trust II

Antecedents and consequences of unethical behavior: Does economic development make a difference?

Tang, Thomas Li-Ping Management and Marketing, Middle Tennessee St University, Murfreesboro, USA Tang, Theresa Application Development, Affinion Group, Franklin, Tennessee, USA Arias Galicia, Fernando Graduate School of Psychology, Morelos University, Cuernavaca, Mor, Mexico Charles-Pauvers, Brigitte French Chinese Management Cent, University of Nantes, Nantes, France Garber, Ilya Economic Sociology, Saratov State Socio-Economic U, Saratov, Russia Garcia de la Torre, Consuelo Marketing Administration, Technological Institute of Mon, Monterrey, Mexico Nnedum, Anthony Department of Psychology, Nnamdi Azikiwe University, ANAMBRA, Nigeria Sutarso, Toto Information Technology Divisio, Middle Tennessee St University, Murfreesboro, USA Vlerick, Peter Personnel Management, Ghent University, Ghent, Belgium

Using survey data from managers of 29 geopolitical entities (7 geopolitical entities in the high GDP group, 12 in the median GDP group, and 10 in the low GDP group) across six continents around the world (N = 6,081), we found that high corporate ethical values and low love of money were related to high ethical behavior that was related to low job stress and high life satisfaction. Our results varied across the three GDP groups. The median GDP group had the lowest corporate ethical values, the highest unethical behavior, the highest percentage of bad apples, the highest job stress, and the strongest relationship between love of money and unethical behavior.

The role of trust and organizational support in transactive memory development and job satisfaction

Brauner, Elisabeth Dept. of Psychology, Brooklyn College, CUNY, Brooklyn, USA Robertson, Rommel Department of Psychology, Brooklyn College, CUNY, Brooklyn, NY, USA

Transactive memory enables members to coordinate their work by referring to each other, assigning areas of expertise, and delegating subtasks to competent colleagues. Transactive memory thus allows more complex tasks to be accomplished. However, building transactive memory systems requires resources and has social-dynamic implications. We assessed transactive memory in a department of a public organization (N=40) using the Q-Tracks questionnaire and standardized scales for measurement of trust, support, and job satisfaction. Multivariate analyses show that transactive memory is affected by trust and cognitive interdependence, but not by organizational support. Barriers to knowledge sharing impede both transactive memory and job satisfaction.

Moral development of future Ukrainian managers by training

Vynoslavska, Olena Psychology and Pedagogics, Kyiv Polytechnic Institute, Kyiv, Ukraine

Objectives. To create training on ethical grounds of professional culture for future managers. Methods. Theoretical analyzes, modeling, training. Results. Psychological model of managerial culture is formed by decision-making and distribution of responsibilities; human resources management; establishment of conditions for productive working activity; communication and interpersonal relations with subordinates and top managers as system-forming component. The core of model is spiritual basis of managerial ethics, which includes ethical attitudes, ethical behavior, ethical relations in professional communications, and openness to ethical norms in international cooperation. Con-

clusion. Moral development of future managers is possible by their raining in spiritual basis of professional ethics.

FP-048: Cognitive development in childhood I

What do young infants learn from observing goal-directed actions: Means, ends, or both?

Elsner, Birgit Inst. für Entw.- Psychologie, Universität Potsdam, Golm, Germany

A looking-time study investigated how infants (N=72; 7, 9, 11 months) perceive the components of goal-directed actions. Infants were habituated to a novel action, and then, either the movement or the outcome was changed. Eleven-month-olds dishabituated to both changes, indicating that they had encoded both components. Not all infants in the younger age groups fully processed the habituation information. Of those who did, the 9-month-olds encoded both action components, whereas the 7-month-olds focused mainly on the movement. In sum, the perception of goal-directed actions changes during the first year of life, affecting how infants may understand other persons' actions.

Modulation of attention by emotional faces in 7-month-old infants

Peltola, Mikko Dept. of Psychology, University of Tampere, University of Tampere, Finland Leppänen, Jukka M. Psychology, University of Tampere, University of Tampere, Finland Hietanen, Jari K. Psychology, University of Tampere, University of Tampere, Finland

7-month-old infants show an attentional bias to fearful faces, as indicated by looking time and event-related potential (ERP) measures. In three studies, we investigated whether these effects are specific to 7-month-olds and, specifically, whether the disengagement component of visual attention is sensitive to modulation by emotional faces in infants. The results indicate that in 7-month-olds, but not 5-month-olds, fearful faces produce longer looking times and a larger mid-latency negativity in ERPs as compared to happy faces. Furthermore, such capture of attention by emotionally significant stimuli is also expressed in the modulation of the latency and frequency of attentional disengagement.

A comparative study on cognitive development of time between children with ADHD and normal children

Fang, Ge Institute of Psychology CAS, Beijing, People's Republic of China Yang, Lili Developmental Psychology, Institute of Psychology CAS, Beijing, People's Republic of China Zhu, Xiuhua Developmental Psychology, Institute of Psychology CAS, Beijing, People's Republic of China Fang, Fuxi Institute of Psychology CAS, Beijing, People's Republic of China Zhao, Jia Developmental Psychology, Institute of Psychology CAS, Beijing, People's Republic of China

Prior Studies demonstrated that there is a sluggish growth of cognition of time in children with ADHD. What are explicit index in this field for diagnosing them? We addressed this question by conducting three tasks (estimating time duration, recognizing the time of clock-face and retelling stories with time threads) to examine and compare the performances between them and normal children. The results revealed that all of performances of children with ADHD were lower than those of normal children, specially at age of 7 - 9. Therefore, the variables of age and tasks should be concerned for diagnosing children with ADHD.

Facilitating socio-cognitive development of primary school children through creative drama
Sharma, Charru Dept. of Child Development, University of Delhi, New Delhi, India Misra, Girishwar Dept. of Psychology, University of Delhi, New Delhi, India
The role of creative drama (CD) in fostering social and cognitive development among children in a Government school in Delhi was investigated. Following a longitudinal strategy the children participated in a CD intervention programme for a period of two and half years. Working as facilitator the researcher used participant observation and examined changes in creative ability and academic performance across five time points. CD emerged to be a powerful intervention to promote cognitive and social interactive skills in primary school children. It may revolutionize pedagogical practices by making school learning experiential and joyful for children and fosters their holistic development.

FP-049: Psychological disorders II

Sleep disorders in patients with Schizophrenia: A review
Bosch, Margaretha Support & Psychose, ggnet Groenlo, Groenlo, Netherlands van den Noort, Maurits biological and medical psychol, university of bergen norway, bergen, Norway
Objectives Sleep disorders are underestimated in patients with schizophrenia, because other symptoms attract more attention. Methods An extensive review on the available literature on sleep in patients with schizophrenia was conducted. Results Patients complain of persistent insomnia, report nightmares and increased sleep disturbances preceding an acute episode of the illness. During acute phases, sleep is deeply disturbed: global insomnia and periods of reversal of the sleep-wake cycle are observed. Specific increases in sleeping problems were found in elderly patients. Conclusion Although specific patterns were found, more research in this group of patients is needed.

Emotional changes and paranoia: An experience sampling study
Thewissen, Viviane Dept. of Psychology, Open University Netherlands, Heerlen, Netherlands Bentall, Richard Psychology, Bangor University, Gwynedd (Bangor, Wales), United Kingdom à Campo, Joost Social Cognition, Mondriaan Zorggroep, Heerlen, Netherlands van Lierop, Thom Social Cognition, Mondriaan Zorggroep, Heerlen, Netherlands van Os, Jim Psychiatry & Neuropsycholo, Maastricht University, Maastricht, Netherlands Myin-Germeys, Inez Psychiatry & Neuropsycholo, Maastricht University, Maastricht, Netherlands
Objectives: To investigate the role of negative emotional processes (depression, anxiety and anger) in the development of paranoid symptoms. Methods: The Experience Sampling Method (a structured self-assessment diary technique) was used to examine paranoia and emotional processes in the daily life of 79 patients with a clinical diagnosis of psychotic disorder. Multilevel linear regression analyses were performed to temporal associations between paranoia and emotional processes. Results: Paranoid beliefs not only generate, but independently also arise from increases in negative emotional experiences. Conclusions: Paranoia may be emotion-driven, rather than serving an immediate defensive function against negative emotions.

Screening attitudes towards schizophrenia
Yüksel, Muazzez Merve Dept. of Psychology, Middle East Techn. University, Ankara, Turkey Karanci, Nuray PSYCHOLOGY, MIDDLE EAST TECHNICAL UNIVERSI, ANKARA, Turkey
Backround: This study aimed to develop a scale to examine the attitudes of lay individuals towards schizophrenia. Method: Participants [n:268] who were university students completed a 63-item questionnaire rated on a five points scale. The items included beliefs about aetiology, treatment of schizophrenia and preferred social distance to schizophrenic patients. Results: Five factors were extracted and labeled as "general negative attitude", "rejection and social distance", "introversion and instability", "general positive attitude" and "negative prognosis". Cronbach Alpha coefficients were satisfactory. The total variance explained was 37.88 % by the five factors. The scores from the five factors differed according to gender and familiarity with schizophrenia.

FP-050: Identity and self-development in adulthood

Coping with social change: The role of self-efficacy and control-beliefs
Grümer, Sebastian Inst. Entwicklungspsychologie, Universität Jena, Jena, Germany Silbereisen, Rainer K. Inst. Entwicklungspsychologie, Universität Jena, Jena, Germany Heckhausen, Jutta Dept. of Psychology, UC Irvine, Irvine, USA
Macro-level phenomena of social change like globalization manifest themselves in new demands at work or in family life. Based on control and coping theories, the study investigated, first, whether perceived demands of social change were related to coping-strategies and subjective well-being, and second, whether self-efficacy and control beliefs moderated this coping process. We found that well-being was negatively related to work and family-related demands, and positively related go coping-strategies (primarily active-coping). Additionally, self-efficacy and control beliefs indeed moderated the relationship between demands and coping-strategies. Overall, the results emphasize the interplay between social change, coping, and control beliefs in individuals' well-being.

Positive relationships and self-worth in lifespan development
Becker, Martina Educational Sciences, Vienna University, Vienna, Austria
In the development of personality it is of particular importance to experience self-worth. Starting from a first qualitative research where 20 people were interviewed about experiencing self-worth in biographical retrospection, a questionnaire was developed to collect biographical experiences of self-worth in different spheres and relationships. The reliabilities of the single scales lie between .77 and .94 Cronbachs Alpha. In a further investigation 149 students were asked with this questionnaire and quantitative coherences were calculated between the reported experiences and measures for mental well being and satisfaction with life. The results show the outstanding importance of the experience of appreciating, empathical and relationships in the course of biography.

The training of creativity as a means of students' self-actualization development
Bykova, Anastasia Ulan-Ude, Russia
The core of the research is the idea of interrelation between the level of creativity and parameters of self-actualization in different social groups of students. Creativity is viewed as an integral part of personal growth and self-actualization. The aim of the research is to reveal the role of creativity training in the development of students' self-actualization. Training seems to be the most effective way of creativity intensification. The results of the research prove the hypothesis of interrelations between creativity and personality's self-actualization. They testify the training's importance in the development of personality's self-actualization.

Living on the edge: A scale of risk behaviors for young adults
Banozic, Adrijana Dept. of Psychology, Faculty of Philosophy, Požega, Croatia Udovicic, Martina Department of psychology, Faculty of philosophy, Zagreb, Zagreb, Croatia Vojnic Tunic, Ana Department of psychology, Faculty of philosophy, Zagreb, Zagreb, Croatia Prot, Sara Department of psychology, Faculty of philosophy, Zagreb, Zagreb, Croatia Stamenkovic, Barbara Department of psychology, Faculty of philosophy, Zagreb, Zagreb, Croatia Plosnic, Fani Department of psychology, Faculty of philosophy, Zagreb, Zagreb, Croatia
The goal of this study was to test a newly constructed 20-item scale of risky behaviors for young adults. Participants were 250 men and women from 18 to 35 years of age. The scale proved to be heterogeneous (the average inter-item correlation was r = 0.13), measuring a wide range of risky activities. The results of this preliminary sample show that the most common risky behaviors were regular use of alcohol (61%) and daily smoking (22%). Significant sex differences were found - men were slightly more prone to engage in risky behaviors than women (t = 4.41, p < 0.05).

Attitudinal responses to lifestyle changes and their consequences
Maass, Vera Living Skills Institute, Inc., Indianapolis, USA
Change is the only constant element today. How do people react to changes that uproot or alter significant parts of their lives? At transition points from one lifestyle to anopther individuals are challenged to focus on losses or on options and opportunities. Sometimes their awareness of alternatives is limited or they may refuse to decide. Researchers seek explanations from a variety of theories, such as personality constructs or decision-making theories. A structured process to apply at transition points, exploring options that takes into account aspects, such as likely consequences, cognitive/emotional appeal, necessary actions, and probable obstacles will be presented.

FP-051: Health and psychological adjustment in aging

Network structures, perceived support exchange and life appraisal: A comparison of home dwelling elderly and nursing home residents
Michels, Tom INSIDE, University of Luxembourg, Walferdange, Luxembourg Albert, Isabelle INSIDE, University of Luxembourg, Walferdange, Luxembourg Ferring, Dieter INSIDE, University of Luxembourg, Walferdange, Luxembourg Donven, Nathalie INSIDE, University of Luxembourg, Walferdange, Luxembourg
The present study addressed the differential impact that quantitative and qualitative indicators of social support may have on indicators of psychological adjustment in the elderly. The study sample comprised 120 elderly persons; of these 50 percent were home dwelling and 50 percent were living in a nursing home respectively. The study followed two objectives: First, to investigate the relative impact of quantitative network characteristics and subjective exchanges of emotional and instrumental support on indicators of life appraisal; second, to compare network characteristics and support exchange patterns of independently living elderly and nursing home residents.

Behavioural independence and psychological well-being in very old age: Can housing make a difference?
Oswald, Frank Psycholog. Alternsforschung, Universität Heidelberg, Heidelberg, Germany Wahl, Hans-Werner Dept. Psych. Ageing Research, University of Heidelberg, Heidelberg, Germany Schilling, Oliver Dept. Psych. Ageing Research,

University of Heidelberg, Heidelberg, Germany
Fänge, Agneta Dept. of Health Sciences, Lund
University, Lund, Sweden **Iwarsson, Susanne** Dept. of
Health Sciences, Lund University, Lund, Germany
One challenge of very old age is how to maintain
functional capacity and well-being in given contexts. In this study we want to identify subgroups of
elders representing profiles across domains of
perceived housing, and to explain outcomes of
behavioural independence and psychological well-
being. Data were drawn from the ENABLE-AGE
Survey including 1,918 very old people aged 75 to
89 years, living alone at home in Sweden, Germany,
England, Hungary and Latvia. Latent class analyses conducted on the perceived housing indicators
revealed evidence for heterogeneity in terms of
subgroups of participants representing different
patterns of perceived housing across national
samples.

Socioeconomic determinants of self-rated health among older Malaysians: Non-comparative and age-comparative models

Rosnah, Ismail Psychology and Social Work,
University Malaysia Sabah, Kota Kinabalu, Malaysia
Tengku-Aizan, Hamid INSTITUTE OF
GERONTOLOGY, UNIVERSITI PUTRA MALAYSIA,
KUALA LUMPUR, Malaysia **Low, Wah Yun**
PSYCHOLOGICAL MEDICINE, UNIVERSITI MALAYA,
KUALA LUMPUR, Malaysia
The study was to determine the effect of selected
socioeconomic variables on self-rated health (SRH)
of older persons. Total respondents is 2,980. Mean
age is 70 years old (M=70.43, SD=7.23), males
(50.5%), Malays (56.9%), married (56.2%) and
primary education (44.6%), median income is
USD106 a month. The independent variables
accounted for 7.4% of variance in noncomparative
SRH (F=35.33, df=6, p=0.000), with greatest effect
is age, education, ethnicity, marital status and
monthly income. Results indicated differences in
the two measures of SRH, as the age-comparative
single item naturally has weaker correlation with
age. The study investigated the direct impact of
socioeconomic factors on SRH and compared two
separate models.

Elders on long term care existential and psychological concerns: A qualitative study

Rivera, Luz Dept. of Clinical Psychology, Carlos Albizu
University, Gurabo, Puerto Rico **Altieri, Gladys**
Clinical Psychology, Carlos Albizu University, Gurabo,
Puerto Rico
The aim of the present study was to look beyond
elder's placement on long term care, and to find out
their perception of concepts related to a healthy
aging and self actualization. Semi-structured interviews were conducted with a sample of fifty elders
ages 65 and over. Interview themes included;
perceived dignity, autonomy and independence.
The interviews were transcribed verbatim and the
resulting data was analyzed using the Interpretative
Phenomenological Analysis. Shared existential
themes were identified which captured the essence
of the participants views of their life as elders and
life satisfaction.

Predicting physical activity in older people: Social-cognitive determinants and health related dispositions

Lucidi, Fabio Department of Psychology, Sapienza.
University of Rome, Rome, Italy **Grano, Caterina** Dept.
of Psychology, University 'La Sapienza', Rome, Italy
Zelli, Arnaldo Educ. Sciences for PA & Sp, Univ, of
Sport & Movem Sci, Rome, Italy **Violani, Cristiano**
Department of Psychology, Sapienza. University of
Rome, Rome, Italy
Constructs defined in the theories of planned
behavior (TPB), self-efficacy and health-related
dispositions, were considered in two studies pre-
dicting physical activity in older adults. The first

study considered 1095 active older exercisers
(Mage=69; 917 were females). The second one
considered 317 sedentary older people (Mage=74.81
+ 6.08; 159 were females). SEM analyses were used.
In the exerciser sample, perceived behavioral
control (PBC) and self-efficacy were the strongest
predictors of intention. Intention moderately predicts behavior. In the sedentary sample, attitudes
and PBC strongly influenced intentions. The effects
of health related dispositions on the intention to
attend physical activity sessions were mostly
mediated by TPB variables.

FP-052: Social psychological responses to terrorism and state violence

A report about the psychological consequences of the war on terrorism

Kimmel, Paul Saybrook Grad Schl/Res. Center, Los
Angeles, USA
This presentation will trace the history of a Task
Force (TF) set up in 2003 by the American
Psychological Association (APA) to assess American efforts to prevent terrorism. It will discuss key
findings and recommendations of the TF and their
implications for organized psychology and governmental policies. Questions will be raised about the
APA's rejection of the TF Report and subsequent
events within the Association. A book based on the
TF findings will be discussed, featuring ethical
issues faced by peace psychologists in doing policy
work. The presenter was the Chair of the TF and
co-editor of the book.

The Jena terrorism study: Behind terrorism attitudes

Orlamünder, Nicole Jena, Germany
This paper presents the results of a qualitative
analysis from a selection of halfstandardized interviews of the three wave longitudinal Jena Terrorism
Study. Against the background of the Terror-
Management-Theory (Pyszcynski, Greenberg, Solomon, 1997) the social motivation hidden behind
the general attitudes towards terrorism as well as
behind the causal explanations were questioned.
Special attention was therby on the mortality
salience effects – the construction of the cultural
worldview and the from-following acceptance of
terrorism and/or anti-terrorism actions. Additionally these statements were compared to interviews
which are not characterised by a reflection on such
a meta-level. Keywords: The Jena-Terrorism-Study,
Qualitative Research, Terrorism, Terror-Manage-
ment, Social Motivation

Psychological aspects in research of terrorism

Zinchenko, Yury Faculty of Psychology, Moscow
State University, Moscow, Russia
Terrorism as a quickly growing phenomenon of last
years became one of the important threat of
security in contemporary society. There are certain
potentials in basic and applied psychology that
should be used in security enforcement and terrorism prevention: (1) formation of adequate conceptions about terrorism; (2) analysis of
transformational processes leading radical groups
to extremist organizations; (3) classification and
differentiation of conflict situations, provoked by
terrorism; (4) ways and principles of effective
negotiations; (5) minimization consequences of
terrorist acts and decreasing suffering of victims
and their relations; (6) special trainings for professionals, participating in antiterrorist actions.

Attitudes to peace and a state's rights to violence: A South African survey

Akhurst, Jacqueline Human and Life Sciences, York
St. John University, York, United Kingdom **Leach,
Mark** Psychology, University of Southern Mississ,
Hattiesburg, USA **Dass-Brailsford, Priscilla**
Counseling and Psychology, Lesley University,
Cambridge, MA, USA
Given South Africa's turbulent and violent political
history, over 300 adult South Africans were polled
via an internet questionnaire regarding their attitudes toward human rights issues and state rights to
violence. Quantitative analysis and thematic coding
were used to analyze the cognitive processes related
to expressed attitudes. Variables considered included age, sex, educational level, ethnic identity
and current domicile. Thematic differences highlighted the spread of opinions and illustrate the
complexity of post-apartheid attitudes regarding
governmental rights and responsibilities. Human
rights discussion in relation to South African
history, current governmental influences, and global context will be provided.

Listening to the experiences of military service personnel

Hector, Mark New Market, TN, USA **Herrera,
Catherine** Psychology, University of Tennessee,
Knoxville TN, USA **Whitesell, Allison** Psychology,
University of Tennessee, Knoxville TN, USA
An undergraduate university course is described in
which students learn how to listen to and under-
stand the experiences of military service personnel.
The listening methods taught are based on phe-
nomenological research interviewing strategies
which are described in "The Phenomenology of
Everyday Life" by Pollio et al. (1997) and "Listen-
ing to Patients: A Phenomenological Approach to
Nursing Research and Practice" by Thomas et al.
(2002). Topics covered in the course include:
Phenomenological Interviewing, Hermeneutics, Ex-
istentialism, Military Training, Military Life and
Culture, Military Experience in War Zones, Posttraumatic Stress Syndrome, Cultures of Peoples in
War Zones and Ethics of Phenomenological Interviewing.

FP-053: Research in fields of environmentally relevant behavior

Verbal interaction in brand-communication: Social and psychological aspect

Brovkina, Julia Dept. Sociology and HR, State
University of Management, Moscow, Russia
The purpose of the said research is the following.
First, it has to reveal social and psychological
mechanisms of the social subjects verbal interaction
in the brand communication. Second, it has to
study the said mechanisms influence upon how the
brand is perceived in various social groups. The
research methods used are: an experiment and an
interview. As a result of the study, there have been
revealed the social and psychological mechanisms
of the cognitive (explicit and implicit) argumentation. The said mechanisms influence in the following social groups have been considered: branding
products consumers; loyal consumers; the brand
creators; the trade mark right holders; competitors;
associations sharing the brand ideology and occasional communicators etc.

Psychological determinants of the importance of energy consumption within car purchase

Peters, Anja D-UWIS, IED, NSSI, ETH Zürich, Zürich,
Switzerland
The purchase of energy-efficient new cars is a
decisive factor towards reducing CO_2 emissions
from road transport. Traditional models forecasting car choice rarely include psychological variables. A first study pointed out the importance of
including these when evaluating effective measures

to promote consumers' shift to more energy-efficient vehicles. In order to provide the basis for the selection of variables to be included, two studies utilizing surveys conducted in Switzerland aimed to identify the relevant psychological variables determining the importance of energy consumption for car buyers within car choice. An outlook will be given how to proceed with these results.

Segmenting owners of clean cars: Effects of values, beliefs, norms and habits on consumers eco-friendly behavior

Nordlund, Annika *Dep of Psychology, Umeå University, Umeå, Sweden* **Marell, Agneta** *Umeå School of Business, Umeå University, Umeå, Sweden* **Jansson, Johan** *Umeå School of Business, Umeå University, Umeå, Sweden*

This study aims to investigate a group of individuals who have chosen to change to a clean car. Although the amount of clean cars are increasing, only a fraction of the car fleet can today be defined as environmentally friendly. It is therefore important to study these early adopters in order to gain more knowledge about them. The study will present results from a survey conducted in Sweden 2006, and focus on the possibility of segmenting owners of clean cars from owners of traditional cars based on the factors included in the Values-Beliefs-Norm Theory and on the strenght of car habits.

Motivation component of fund-raising activities of environmental NGOs

Karamushka, Victor *Fundamental Studies, CIPGES, Kyiv, Ukraine*

The investigation was aimed at the analysis of motivation of Ukrainian environmental NGOs participating in grants' programs supported by foreign donors. Methodology included content-analysis of the project proposals (over 350) and targeted interviews of the participants. Features of motivation are analysed and discussed in details. It was revealed that motivation of the fund-raising activity has multifunctional structure, and receiving funds as such is not less important task for environmental NGOs than getting funds for environmental initiatives. Moreover, grant recipients mostly do not consider the donors' motivation. Analysis of the obtained data resulted in conclusion that striving to improve environment if not the only objective of the activities of environmental NGOs within the international cooperation programs.

FP-054: Psychology of disaster

Gender attitudes and approaches in disaster risk reduction

Mukhopadhyay, Durgadas *Education, Sparta Inst. of Social Studies, Pin, India*

Disaster affects man and women differently. Gender relations and attitude pre-condition people's ability to anticipate, prepare for, survive, cope with, and recover from disasters. Women affected by Gujarat earthquake and Orissa super cyclone were interviewed and data collected through participant observation. 150 women from these areas were interviewed in detail The vulnerability of women is much greater because of their subordinate position in the family arising out of patriarchy and traditionally embedded cultural values. Conclusion: Gender mainstreaming in disaster reduction refers to fostering awareness about gender equity and equality and to help reduce the impact of disasters.

Attachment and social trauma of young survivors of Gujarat earthquake and riots

Kumar, Manasi *Dept. of Clinical Healthpsych., University College London, London, United Kingdom*

The proposed paper is an attempt to look into attachment trauma of children affected by both 2001-02 earthquake-and-riots in Gujarat. The prime focus of ongoing research is to differentiate the trauma of earthquake-affected-children from those children who were affected by riots or social violence. To address this question, at first, recent disaster psychology literature is evaluated to illuminate prominent mental health implications for young survivors of extreme trauma and disasters. Secondly, the paper how child and adolescent mental health post disaster concerns are relatively underdeveloped and underreported areas in world wide disaster literature. Thirdly, the paper raises methodological and theoretical debates associated with working with children in disasters in developing countries.

Resilience promotion in disaster area of Peru

Alcalde, Aurea *Lima, Peru* **Alcalde Alcalde, Maria Julia** *Education, Colegio Huerta Santa Ana, Seville, Spain*

On August 15th 2007 an earthquake in Peru destroyed 80% of buildings killing half a million people. Devastation affected thousands of people's houses, work and life projects. The aim of this project was to prevent permanent trauma from instaling in participants and to strengthen survivors in overcoming their critical condition so they could go on with their lives in search of development and well-being. Promotion of the development of individual and group resilient resources was worked through workshops. Participants were community leaders (professionals of health, education and social workers). Promotors resilience factors were identified through a psychological assessment, and workshop effectiveness was also assessed in order to improve its future quality.

Global assessment and comparison of children's reactions after an earthquake disaster

Bulut, Sefa *Counseling Psychology, Abant Ýzzet Baysal Üniversity, Bolu, Turkey*

This study aimed at examining the disaster survivor children's global psycho-social reactions with a multidimensional assessment scale. Children in the high impact and low impact groups were compared to investigate their differential diagnosis, educational, emotional problems and behavioral disorders after the earthquake. Eleven months after the 1999 Turkish earthquake, 200 elementary school children were screened with a Behavior Assessment Systems for Children and compared via Analysis of Variance. The results revealed that these two groups differed in anxiety and social stress sub-scales. It seems that after such a huge catastrophe, children can develop not only PTSD, but also other emotional and behavioral problems.

Strategic process, entrepreneurial orientation, human capital and success of accommodation business's entrepreneurs in 2004 Tsunami disaster area, Thailand

Pavakanun, Ubolwanna *Prakorn, Thailand* **Ekamonpun, P.** *Psychology, Thammasart university, Bangkok, Thailand* **Gorsanan, S.** *Bangkrai, P.*

This research is to study the attributions, the patterns relations, and to find the prediction equation of entrepreneurial success by strategic process, entrepreneurial orientation, human capital of 156 entrepreneurs in accommodation business in 2004 Tsunami disaster area; to whom considering successful in the business and exist now. The individual structured interview and questionnaires are the tools of data collection. Success results correlated with all type in strategy process. Strategy process are found significant correlation with human capital. Success also showed the correlation to some aspects of entrepreneurial orientation. Critical point planning, opportunistic strategy, and Innovativeness can predict the entrepreneurial success.

FP-055: Persuasion and communication I

The pretrial effects of narrative and argumentative writing style of press articles

Lepastourel, Nadia *Psychologie Sociale - Bat I, Université Rennes 2, Rennes, France* **Testé, Benoît** *Psychologie sociale - Bat I, Université Rennes 2, Rennes, France*

This work extends the researches on pretrial publicity (Studebaker & Penrod, 1997) which mainly focus on prejudicial informations to the defendant. The effects of syntactic characteristics of media communication are investigated : narrative and argumentative (moderate vs affirmative). An experimental study was conducted. 248 participants read a press article on a judicial inquiry, either in a narrative (vs not narrative) or in a moderate (vs affirmative) syntactic style. Results indicate that narrative and affirmative style are both prejudicial to the defendant. Implications for journalists and legal actors are discussed considering particularly the story model effects (Pennington & Hastie, 1992).

The persuasiveness of ambiguous information: If they advertise it, it must be good

Wänke, Michaela *Inst. für Psychologie, Universität Basel, Basel, Switzerland* **Reutner, Leonie** *Institut für Psychologie, Universität Basel, Basel, Switzerland* **Friese, Malte** *Institut für Psychologie, Universität Basel, Basel, Switzerland*

Based on Grice's cooperative principle in communication we argue that even meaningless or ambiguous information may work as a persuasive argument as long as it is perceived in in the context of a persuasion attempt. According to a contribution to a conversation should be relevant to the purpose of the ongoing conversation. Thus, information that is presented with the goal to persuade will likely be interpreted as potentially persuasive. Five experiments within the context of advertising support this hypothesis. The effects are more pronounced for consumers high in Need for Cognition suggesting that the inference is due to effortful processing.

Reactance and defense-motivated information processing

Ziegler, Rene *Inst. für Psychologie, Universität Tübingen, Tübingen, Germany* **Santorinakis, Johannes** *Psychologisches Institut, Universitaet Tuebingen, Tuebingen, Germany*

Perceived threat to attitudinal freedom may cause reactance, a state of motivational arousal that leads to attempts at restoring freedom. Few research has studied the mediating cognitive processes. We postulate that reactance triggers defense-motivated systematic processing, i.e., the cognitively effortful defense of an attitudinal position contrary to the one being advocated. Results of an experiment in which participants read a recommendation of a tourist agent support our predictions. Evaluations of the agent, the recommended journey, and thought valence were less affected by argument strength under high (vs. low) threat. Nonetheless, thought valence correlated with evaluations irrespective of threat level.

The Influence of electronic-word-of-mouth on purchase intention and attribution of post-purchase regret

Li, Tsz Wai Gloria *Department of Psychology, Chinese University of HK, Hong Kong, China, People's Republic of : Hong Kong SAR*

Electronic-word-of-mouth (eWOM) refers to word-of-mouth happened in the electronic platform. This paper presents a conceptual model of eWOM exploring relationships among interpersonal forces, sender's and receiver's characteristics, and purchase intention. This study employed a 2 by 2 between-subject factorial design: expertise and homophily. One hundred twenty undergraduates were recruited. The present research showed an interaction effect between expertise and homophily level on (a) perceived sender's expertise and (b) perceived purchase intention. Additionally, causal attribution of product failure was also examined. Results show that main effects for (a) internality; (b) stability; (c) uncontrollability; and (d) an interaction effect of three.

FP-056: Person perception & impression formation I

Job applications, voting behavior and university recruitment: Evidence for a multidimensional attractiveness-gender bias in selection contexts

Agthe, Maria Inst. für Psychologie, Universität München, München, Germany *Spörrle, Matthias* Department of Psychology, Ludwig-Maximilians-University, Munich, Germany *Dörfler, Rebecca* Department of Psychology, Ludwig-Maximilians-University, Munich, Germany *Försterling, Friedrich* Department of Psychology, Ludwig-Maximilians-University, Munich, Germany

Four studies (N > 4000) using different selection contexts (job application, elections, application for a course of study, application for scholarships) revealed an overall consistent multidimensional interaction pattern of respondent's sex with candidate's sex and candidate's physical attractiveness, indicating a general preference of attractive opposite-sex targets, while favoring less good-looking candidates with regard to same-sex individuals. Studies include paper-based paradigms and simulated videotaped interviews, between-subjects and within-subject designs, as well as rating and ranking procedures. Results' consistency with hypotheses derived from evolutionary psychology is delineated. The findings shed new light on previously documented gender and attractiveness biases.

The (dis)order of impression formation: Order information in person memory

Costa, Rui S. Lisboa, Portugal *Garcia-Marques, Leonel* Social Psychology, FPCE-UL, Lisboa, Portugal *Sherman, Jeff* Psychology Department, UC, Davis, Lisboa, Portugal

Person memory models describe impressions as dense networks of inter-behavioral associations, these networks facilitate item memory but hinder memory for item order. However, the implications for order memory remain untested. Four experiments were conducted to address this gap, contrasting impression formation (IF) with memorization (M) processing goals and using order information measures along with item information measures. The information described single and multiple targets. Results show that order and item information are better recalled under IF conditions. These new findings suggest that IF preserves order information and shed new light on the way we represent information about people.

Women's attractiveness depends more on their age than men's: New evidence for a double standard of aging

Felser, Georg Wirtschaftspsychologie, Hochschule Harz, Wernigerode, Germany *Bendel, Martina* Wirtschaftspsychologie, Hochschule Harz, Wernigerode, Germany *Völler, Dominic* Wirtschaftspsychologie, Hochschule Harz, Wernigerode, Germany *Wegner, Anja* Wirtschaftspsychologie, Hochschule Harz, Wernigerode, Germany

In research on the dependence of a person's physical attractive on her or his age results are often confounded with numerous variables (i.e. appearance of a certain individual, historical time in which the target is presented...). Our research

controls for these variables by using the same photograph of a person digitally changed into different stages of physical development. Portraits of ten different persons were presented on a computer screen to N = 383 participants who judged the targets' physical attractiveness. Results indicate that in the course of aging physical attractiveness remains much more stable for men than for women.

Doing better when knowing less: The influence of feedback and reasoning on the validity of person perception

Fetchenhauer, Detlef and Social Psychology, Dept. Economic, Cologne, Germany *Pradel, Julia* Economic and Social Psychology, University of Cologne, Koeln, Germany

In three studies we investigated the influence of intuition and deliberation on the validity of person perception. Stimulus-persons on short videotapes had to be estimated according to their prosociality or their personality strength. The validity of estimates were the best, when they were made intuitively. Validity declined, when judges were asked to deliberately reason about the cues that they used or when during a "training period" judges were given feedback on the stimulus-persons' actual values on the target variable. We will discuss the relevance of our findings for the ongoing discussion of intuitive versus deliberate reasoning and decision-making.

What is beautiful leads good? Attractiveness, masculinity, femininity and ascribed leadership skills

Hoffmann, Mareike Wirtsch.- u. Sozialpsychologie, Universität zu Köln, Köln, Germany *Pradel, Julia* Economic and Social Psychology, University of Cologne, Cologne, Germany *Fetchenhauer, Detlef* Economic and Social Psychology, University of Cologne, Cologne, Germany

The present study examines the ascription of leadership skills toward unknown strangers and the cues that are factored into such judgements. Therefore N=264 judges saw 20second silent videotapes of 80 target persons and judged them on different dimensions. As a result, significant correlations between perceived personality strength (i.e., leadership skills) and intelligence, attractiveness, extraversion, femininity and masculinity were found. Whereas generally male and female target persons were ascribed an equal level of personality strength, women achieved higher ratings when they were perceived as more feminine, whereas men achieved higher ratings when they were perceived as more masculine.

FP-057: Job attitudes

Relationships between organizational processes and job attitudes in the personnel of a steel factory in Ahvaz, Iran

Shokrkon, Hossein Dept. of Psychology, Shahid Chamran University, Ahvaz, Islamic Republic of Iran

This research was conducted to test hypotheses concerning the relationships between Likert's organizational processes and job attitudes. The sample consisted of 478 Ss, selected randomly. Four questionnaires were used to measure the research variables. Correlation and regression analyses were employed to analyze the data. The findings indicated that 60 of the 80 simple correlation coefficients were significant, with a range from 0.10 to 0.28. The results of the regression analyses showed that the significant multiple correlation coefficients between the predictors and the criteria had a range from 0.130 to 0.301. Implications of the findings were discussed for the improvement of productivity and quality of work life. Key words; organizational characteristics, job attitudes

How income plays a crucial role on the personnel's attitudes toward different aspects of their organization

Samavatyan, Hossein Psychology, Isfahan University, Isfahan, Islamic Republic of Iran *Nouri, Aboulghasem* Psychology, Isfahan University, Isfahan, Islamic Republic of Iran *Oreyzi, Hamid Reza* Psychology, Isfahan University, Isfahan, Islamic Republic of Iran *Sanati, Javad* Occupational HSE, Polyacril of Iran Corporation, Isfahan, Islamic Republic of Iran *Mojib, Mahmoud* CEO, Polyacryl of Iran Corporation, Isfahan, Islamic Republic of Iran

Income, as an important factor which can affect numerous organizational variables, was investigated in the present study. 409 participants were selected randomly from the list of personnel of a large industrial company and their attitudes toward several aspects in their organization were measured after categorizing them on the basis of their salary. ANOVA indicated significant differences among the personnel with different levels of income on job satisfaction, attachment, perceived justice, and motivation (p<0.01). The findings may have several implications indicating how any change in salary could result in changes in the personnel attitudes on organizational aspects.

Leadership culture as a predictor of quality of working life: A hierarchical linear model approach

Ulferts, Heike Inst. für Wirtsch.-Psychologie, Universität Wien, Wien, Austria *Korunka, Christian* Economic Psychology, University of Vienna, Vienna, Austria *Scharitzer, Dieter* Marketing Management, University of Business, Vienna, Austria

Employee commitment, job satisfaction and stress are three facets of quality of working life (QWL). Leadership culture may have a considerable effect on QWL. A multilevel model, postulating different effects of leadership culture on the three facets of QWL on individual and work unit levels was developed and tested. 6020 employees of a corporate group of companies working in 51 clearly defined work units participated in a survey study. The model was tested by use of hierarchical linear modelling (HLM) procedures. The model could be confirmed. Leadership culture significantly influences QWL with different effect sizes of the two hierarchical levels on the three QWL facets.

A study on the relations among the teachers' competency, self-efficiency, performance and job satisfactory

Xu, Jianping School of Psychology, Beijing Normal University, Beijing, People's Republic of China

This study discussed the relations of teacher's competency, self-efficiency, performance and job satisfactory. It investigated 500 teachers in primary and secondary schools by teacher's competency questionnaire, self-efficiency questionnaire and job satisfactory questionnaire. After analyzed these data with SEM and HLM, the conclusions were that the teacher's competency and self-efficiency can forecast the teachers' teaching performance well, the teachers in different level of competency and self-efficiency performed differently in job satisfactory, while the teachers in either gender performance almost the same.

Relationship of approaches of job-design (mechanistic and motivational approaches) with job attitudes in four industrial companies

Oreyzi, Hamid Reza Pschology, Isfahan University, Isfahan, Islamic Republic of Iran *Zareyi Shmsabadi, Fahime* Psychology, University of Isfahan, Isfahan, Islamic Republic of Iran *Askaripour, Nastaran* Psychology, University of Isfahan, Isfahan, Islamic Republic of Iran

The aim of the current research is to provide empirical evidence that job-design based on Mechanistic approach correlate negatively with job satisfaction, job involvement and job commitment (critical variables). Participants were 125 subjects with correspondence job. Each job was seen by one trainee observer. The instrument was Multi-method Job Design Questionnaire (MJDQ). The method of cononical corrolation has used for data analysis. Findings showed that Mechanistic approach correlates negatively with critical variable. Mechanistic approach negatively effect on job attitudes of personnel and Motivational approach has the significant impact on produce positive job attitudes of personnel.

FP-058: Inhibitory processing

Topological properties in preview search: Inhibition of feature-based in prioritizing selection
Hao, Fang Institute of Psychology, Renmin University of China, Beijing, People's Republic of China Fu, Xiaolan Chinese Academy of Sciences, Institute of Psychology, Beijing, People's Republic of China Yu, Guoliang Renmin University of China, Institute of Psychology, Beijing, People's Republic of China
This study is concerned with the role of topological properties in preview search. All participants completed three conditions: half-element, all-element and preview conditions, each of which contained two types of stimuli, the same topological properties and the different topological properties. The results showed: (1) topological properties exerted a significant influence on the preview benefits, (2) topological properties had different impacts on three search conditions, which indicated that the inhibition of feature-based was not necessary in prioritizing selection in preview search.

Inhibition of color-based in prioritizing selection
Yu, Guoliang Inst. of Psychology, Renmin University, Beijing, People's Republic of China Hao, Fang Institute of Psychology, Renmin University of China, Beijing, People's Republic of China Fu, Xiaolan Institute of Psychology, Chinese Academy of Sciences, Beijing, People's Republic of China
This study is concerned with how color influenced on prioritizing selection in preview search. All participants completed three preview conditions, each of which contained targets of different colors. The results showed: (1) RTs of the targets with same color with new objects were slower than the targets with same color with old objects; (2) RTs of the targets with new color did not have difference with the targets with the same color with old objects. The inhibition of feature-based in prioritizing selection in preview search was discussed.

Proactive inhibitory control on simple reaction time: Event-related fMRI study
Jaffard, Magali INRETS, Salon-de-Provence, France Longcamp, Marieke LAPMA, Université de Toulouse, Toulouse, France Velay, Jean-Luc INCM, CNRS, Salon de provence, France Benraïss, Abdelrhani LPMC, Université de Poitiers, Poitiers, France Anton, Jean-Luc centre d'IRMf de Marseille, CNRS, Marseille, France Roth, Muriel centre d'IRMf de Marseille, CNRS, Marseille, France Nazarian, Bruno centre d'IRMf de Marseille, CNRS, Marseille, France Boulinguez, Philippe LPMC, Université de Poitiers, Poitiers, France
Questions about attention are usually addressed by cueing tasks. Most current interpretations suggest that a warning signal (WS) provokes an "alerting" effect resulting in faster processing of both sensory and motor events. However it also triggers undesired motor activations and proactive response inhibition is needed to prevent false alarms (Jaffard et al., 2007; Boulinguez et al., 2008). ER-fMRI reveals that the medial prefrontal cortex and the inferior parietal cortex mediate such inhibition. We claim that a strong executive control biasing RT is involved in simple visual detection tasks. It consists in switching from tonic inhibition to automatic processing.

Backward inhibition effect on the attentional blink
Sdoia, Stefano Dept. of Psychology, University of Rome, Rome, Italy Ferlazzo, Fabio Psychology, U.Rome, Rome, Italy
Task switching is supported by the inhibition of the abandoned task (backward inhibition) as shown by slower reaction times on alternating than on non-alternating runs (CBA vs ABA). We recently found a stimulus-related component of task inhibition, occurring before response selection. Here we investigated whether a backward inhibition mechanism can account for the Attentional Blink effect by asking our participants to report three targets, embedded in a RSVP task and presented in ABA and CBA sequences. Results are interpreted in terms of a general inhibition mechanism that ensures the successful switching between tasks also at very early processing stages.

Inhibition of return found in dynamic search
Wang, Zhiguo Institute of Psychology, Beijing, People's Republic of China Zhang, Kan Chinese Academy of Sciences, Institute of Psychology, Beijing, People's Republic of China
Klein (1988) suggested that inhibition of return (IOR) might operate to facilitate inefficient searches. The present study investigated IOR in dynamic search by combining the dynamic search task with a probe detection task. Participants were asked to search for a target among distractors while the display items traded places every 200 ms. Sixty ms after the search response, a luminance-detection probe was presented either at a location previously occupied by a distractor (on-probe) or at an empty location (off-probe). IOR effects were observed in dynamic search, suggesting that IOR was not the foraging facilitator in serial search.

FP-059: Neuropsychology I

Restoration of vision after optic nerve lesions by electrical brain synchronization
Sabel, Bernhard Inst. für Medizin. Psychologie, Universität Magdeburg, Magdeburg, Germany Fedorov, Anton B. Neurosurgery, State Neurosurgical Institute, Saint-Petersburg, Russia Chibisova, A.N. Neurosurgery, State Neurosurgical Institute, Saint-Petersburg, Russia Jobke, Sandra Inst Medical Psychology, University of Magdeburg, Magdeburg, Germany Gall, Carolin Inst Medical Psychology, University of Magdeburg, Magdeburg, Germany
Objectives: Patients suffering impaired vision following brain damage experience serious limitations in daily living. We now electrically stimulated residual vision to activate neuronal functioning of surviving neurons. Methods: 446 patients with optic nerve lesions caused by trauma, inflammation, tumor or vascular malfunction received non-invasive electrical stimulation (< 1mA) for 10 days using electrodes attached to the skin near the eyeball. Results: Visual field enlargements of 1.9-2.3% (p<0.001) were observed in 34.6% of the patients and visual acuity significantly improved also. Conclusions: Electrical stimulation can improve some of the lost visual function, possibly inducing neuroplasticity through neuronal synchronization of residual networks.

Cortical inhibition in adult attention-deficit/hyperactivity disorder patients measured by transcranial magnetic stimulation
Richter, Melany M. Department of Psychiatry, Laboratory of Psychophysiology, Würzburg, Germany Ehlis, Ann-Christine Department of Psychiatry, Laboratory of Psychophysiology, Würzburg, Germany Dresler, Thomas Department of Psychiatry, Laboratory of Psychophysiology, Würzburg, Germany Fallgatter, Andreas J. Department of Psychiatry, Laboratory of Psychophysiology, Würzburg, Germany
Cortical excitability measured by transcranial magnetic stimulation (TMS) reflects inhibitory and facilitatory brain functions. Inhibitory deficits associated with attention-deficit/hyperactivity disorder (ADHD) have been found in children (Moll et al. 2000). We investigated adult ADHD patients (N=10): Inhibition was measured using double-pulse TMS (inter-pulse intervals (IPI): 2ms, 3ms) and compared (t-tests) to ten healthy controls. Reduced inhibition (IPI 2ms: p=.007) in ADHD was found along with larger variability (both IPIs: F>4.67; p<.016). Inhibitory deficits seem to be related to ADHD regardless of age. Inhibitory variability in adult ADHD will be discussed introducing new data of 20 patients where inhibition was correlated with the symptom focus.

FP-060: Childhood and adolescence in the presence of socioeconomic disadvantage or physical disorder

Development of playing activity in children aged 1 to 3 years reared in institutions
Kostadinova, Krasimira Child&School Health Protection, Nation.Center PublicHealthProt, Sofia, Bulgaria
Purpose: to establish the specific characteristics of playing activity of children reared in different social conditions. Two groups were compared: 34 children from kindergartens aged 1 to 3 and experimental group of 83 children from institutions. Methods: Developmental scale, Vineland Social Maturity Scale, scale about assessment of play. Results: established significant lower level of playing development of children from institutions; a correlative relationship between children's developmental level of playing activity and level of mental and social development. The reasons of these evidences are discussed. The development of play in early childhood can be improved by stimulating of mental and social development.

Improving computer literacy and initiating positive development by peer tutoring in Germany and Siberia: The pc4youth program
Grob, Alexander Inst. für Psychologie, Universität Basel, Basel, Switzerland Vogelwiesche, Uta University of Dortmund, Institut of Gerontology, Dortmund, Germany
In two cultural contexts, pc4youth — a three-level prevention program — was adopted in order to create turning point experiences of socially disadvantaged adolescents. Herein, adolescents acquire computer literacy in an extra scholar program while they are tutees. If they succeed they can become a tutor, and later a consultant. At each level, they can widen their ICT competency. While the adolescents stay in the program, their commitment increases and they take more social and personal responsibility. These principles advance positive development. In Germany and in Siberia, 520 tutees, 129 tutors, and 14 consultants participated in the program. Participants substantially increased in ICT competency and positive development. The principles of empowerment of adolescents at risk are discussed.

Emotional disturbances and family organization in eating disorders
Rommel, Delphine Psychologie URECA, Université Lille 3, Villeneuve d'Ascq Cedex, France Nandrino, Jean-Louis Psychologie URECA, Université Lille 3, Villeneuve d'Ascq Cedex, France Victor, Laetitia Psychologie URECA, Université Lille 3, Villeneuve d'Ascq Cedex, France Antoine, Pascal Psychologie URECA, Université Lille 3, Villeneuve d'Ascq Cedex, France Delecourt, Francois endocrinologie diabétologie, GHICL Saint Philibert, Lomme Cedex, France Dodin, Vincent Psychiatrie Adulte, GHICL Saint Vincent, Lille Cedex, France

Objectives: To explore the relation between emotional disturbances and the family organization in eating disorders. Methods: Patients suffering from anorexia nervosa or bulimia and controls answered questionnaires about alexithymia (TAS-20), emotion regulation (ERQ), emotional awareness (LEAS), family cohesion and adaptability (FACES-III) and parental bonds (PBI). Results: Patients are alexithymic and more suppressive. Although they do not present a deficit of emotional awareness, we observe a positive correlation between low level of emotional awareness and overprotection in the family. Conclusion: We discuss the idea of an emotional deficit as a characteristic of the family interaction rather than the patient's sole concern.

FP-061: Psychopharmacology I

The stimulant-like properties of dietary caffeine are non-existent after controlling for physical dependence and withdrawal reversal

James, Jack Psychology, National University of Ireland, Galway, Ireland **Keane, Michael** Psychology, National University of Ireland, Galway, Ireland
Although it is widely believed that caffeine can enhance human performance and mood, and that it has stimulant-like electrophysiological effects (EEG), most of the findings said to confirm such beliefs are ambiguous. The central question is whether superior performance, improved mood, and EEG effects after caffeine represent net effects, or whether differences between caffeine and control conditions are due to reversal of adverse withdrawal effects. We present findings from several experiments, in which we controlled for confounding due to physical dependence and withdrawal reversal, showing that caffeine has essentially no reliable stimulant-like properties on performance, mood, or EEG.

Effect of DNA methylation in hippocampus and prefrontal cortex on acquisition and expression of cocaine-induced place preference in C57 mice

Han, Jin Key Lab of Mental Health, Institute of Psychology, CAS, Beijing, People's Republic of China **Li, Yonghui** Key Lab of Mental Health, Institute of Psychology, CAS, Beijing, People's Republic of China **Wang, Dongmei** Key Lab of Mental Health, Institute of Psychology, CAS, Beijing, People's Republic of China **Sui, Nan** Key Lab of Mental Health, Institute of Psychology, CAS, Beijing, People's Republic of China
To examine the effect of DNA methylation in addiction, we injected DNA methyltransferases inhibitor, 5-aza-deoxycytidine (5-AZA) into hippocampus CA1 and prelimbic cortex (PrL) in the acquisition and expression of cocaine-induced place preference in C57 mice. The shift values (preference of test minus pretest) of each group were analyzed by using one-way analyses of variance. Results show that intra-CA1 not intra- PrL injections of 5-AZA impaired the acquisition, and intro-PrL not intra-CA1 reduced the expression of cocaine-induced place preference. In conclusion, DNA methylation in different brain regions exerts different roles in the specific period of drug-related learning and memory.

Different effects of imipramine and fluoxetine on anhedonia and anxiety-related behavior induced by chronic mild stress in adolescent rats

Wang, Weiwen Key Lab of Mental Health, Institute of Psychology, CAS, Beijing, People's Republic of China **Xie, Xi** Key lab of mental health, institute of psychology, CAS, beijing, People's Republic of China **Lin, Wenjuan** Key lab of mental health, institute of psychology, CAS, beijing, People's Republic of China **Sun, Meng** Key lab of mental health, institute of psychology, CAS, beijing, People's Republic of China **Wang, Donglin** Key lab of mental health, institute of psychology, CAS, beijing, People's Republic of China

Qi, Xiaoli Key lab of mental health, institute of psychology, CAS, beijing, People's Republic of China
The purpose of the research was to examine whether depressed adolescents respond differently to antidepressant imipramine and fluoxetine treatment. Chronic mild stress (CMS)-induced behavior alterations and the effects of drug treatments were investigated in rats aged 32-53 days. The data showed that fluoxetine but not imipramine reversed the decrease of sucrose preference intake, index of anhedonia. Anxiety-related behaviors induced by the stress were restored by both drugs in elevated plus maze test. No differences in open field were observed between groups. These results suggest that imipramine and fluoxetine exert different effects on anhedonia induced by CMS in adolescent rats.

Effects of the basolateral amygdala inactivation on defensive responses of morphine abstinence rats in elevated T-maze

Li, Jie KLMH, Institute of Psychology, Beijing, People's Republic of China **Li, Yonghui** KLMH, Institute of Psychology; Chine, Beijing, People's Republic of China **Sui, Nan** KLMH, Institute of Psychology;Chines, Beijing, People's Republic of China
The authors investigated inhibition avoidance (IA) and escape responses of rats in morphine abstinence and the role of basolateral amygdala (BLA) in these responses. Thirty days after morphine (10mg/kg, 3 days) administration, rats were submitted to elevated T-maze task after intra-BLA injections of muscimol. Data were analyzed by using two-way analyses of variance. Morphine abstinence shortened latencies of IA, which was reversed by BLA inactivation that impaired IA in naive rats. There might be bidirectional regulation over IA related to detection of threatening stimuli in BLA. BLA dysfunction appears to be related to change of IA by prolonged morphine abstinence.

FP-062: Ethnic and race issues I

Ethnopsychological peculiarities of self-actualization and its development

Buzhgeyeva, Elena Buryat State University, Ulan-Ude, Russia
The following research is devoted to the study of Buryat and Russian students' self-actualization ethnopsychological peculiarities. The interrelations between parameters of self-actualization and peculiarities of ethnic identity are revealed. So, higher characteristics of self-actualization correspond to the positive ethnic identity and its less expressed demonstrations. And, on the contrary, low characteristics of self-actualization correspond to vividly expressed demonstrations of hyper-identity. Ethnopsychological training is one of the conditions of self-actualization development. The results of the carried out experiment testify to the smoothing of negative ethnic stereotypes. It leads, in its turn, to the increase of students' self-actualization level.

Impact of sociodemographic variables and stressful life events on the mental health of Ecuadorian immigrants in Spain

Gonzalez Castro, Jose Luis Ciencias de la Educación, Universidad de Burgos, Burgos, Spain **Ubillos, Silvia** Ciencias de la Educación, Universidad de Burgos, Burgos, Spain **Lopez, Cristina** Ciencias de la Educación, Universidad de Burgos, Burgos, Spain
The impact of social and economic variables, and stressful life events on mental health of a group of immigrants from Ecuador in Spain will be analyzed. Participants evaluated their current mental health using the GHQ-12 scale. Their perception of life in Spain was mainly positive. The GHQ results were explained by certain life events, whereas sociodemographic or economic factors did not significantly affect this rating. Perceived discrimination, social contact and social support, either from fellow

Ecuadorians or native population, did not have an effect on mental health. Results will be interpreted within immigration policies in Spain.

The acculturation process in a mine in South Africa

Jackson, Leon Industrial Psychology, NWU - Potchefstroom Campus, Potchefstroom, South Africa
The main contempory acculturation frameworks are to a large extend empirically based. According to these frameworks, the acculturation process involves group-level and individual-level variables. These frameworks depict cross-cultural transitions as potentially stressful life events that elicit coping resources to deal with them. The aims of this research were to determine the nature of the acculturation context in a mine in South Africa and to determine the impact of acculturation context variables on health and perceived work success. Results indicated that situational as well as individual factors could be used to predict work-related outcomes in the acculturation process.

Germans in Ukraine: Depression as indicator of ethnofunctional disadaptation

Kayger, Valeriy Psychology, Odessa Mechnikov University, Odessa, Ukraine
In paper results of ethnopsychological research of depressions at Germans-citizens of Ukraine are considered. In frameworks ethno-functional approach the concept 'the ethnocaused depression' is entered. It is shown, that one of the reasons of occurrence of the ethnocaused depressions is the conflict between disharmonious image of ethnic self-identification and its high importance for respondents. It is underlined, that the ethnocaused depressions are widespread among a considerable part most socially active age group, and it requires the help of the ethnopsychologist-psychotherapist.

FP-063: Risk and decision making I

Simple strategies in decisions from experience

Hau, Robin Inst. für Psychologie, Universität Basel, Basel, Switzerland **Pleskac, Timothy J.** Department of Psychology, Michigan State University, East Lansing, USA **Hertwig, Ralph** Department of Psychology, University of Basel, Basel, Switzerland
In real-life decisions, more often than not, people base their choices on experience with similar situations. In studies of decisions from experience, participants are therefore allowed to gather experience with their options prior to making their choice. This experience substitutes the summary information that is given to respondents in decisions from description. We investigate the gap between the two modes of decision making by analyzing what cognitive strategies people employ in both situations. We find that remarkably simple strategies that embody risk-neutral or even risk-seeking behaviour are best able to account for decisions from experience.

Representation format and contextual factors in simple probability judgments

Navarrete, Gorka Psicologia Cognitiva, Universidad de La Laguna, La Laguna, Spain **Santamaría, Carlos** Psicologia Cognitiva, Universidad de La Laguna, La Laguna, Spain **Fernandez-Berrocal, Pablo** Psicologia Basica, Universidad de Malaga, Malaga, Spain
In the debate over the favored status of frequencies for probability calculus, some confusion might have arisen from subtle contextual factors. We tested representation format (frequencies vs. probabilities) together with two different contextual factors (Instructions-Response Matching and Explicit vs. Implicit Complementary Category). Only one of these contextual factors (Instructions-Response Matching) became a relevant variable to account for the participants' accuracy in their probability judgements. Our experiment involved simple-prob-

ability judgements about series of events. Results conflict with frequentist approaches pointing contextual factors as more important than representation formats and hence, arguing against the evolutionary basis of frequency format advantages.

Keeping in mind what you cannot have: Memory advantages for excluded options in choice situation
Ritter, Johannes O. Inst. für Psychologie, Universität Zürich, Zürich, Switzerland *Freund, Alexandra M.* Inst. für Psychologie, Universität Zürich, Zürich, Switzerland
We propose an information-processing model that hypothesizes that losing a formerly available option affects the choice process and the evaluation of the remaining options. Specifically, we posit that the excluded option accentuates specific attributes of the remaining alternatives by serving as a standard of comparison in the revaluation process. Two studies using an incidental memory paradigm with different stimulus material tested and confirmed the first step of this model, namely that exclusion of an option leads to higher accessibility of its features. Results will be discussed regarding different models of the choice process.

FP-064: Risk assessment in young offenders I

Idiographical assessment of risk of reoffence: Is there some incremental predictive validity relative to established standardized measures?
Dahle, Klaus-Peter Institute Forensic Psychiatry, Charité, Berlin, Germany *Schneider, Vera* Institute Forensic Psychiatry, Charité, Berlin, Germany *Ziethen, Franziska* Institute Forensic Psychiatry, Charité, Berlin, Germany
Objective: Purpose of the study was the question, whether a well-guided idiographic approach enhances the reliability of criminal risk assessments relative to standardized measures. Methods: Two samples of male prisoners (unselected offenders, N=307; violent offenders, N=230) were assessed using standardized measures (LSI-R, HCR-20, PCL-R) and a structured idiographic assessment procedure. Results: The standardized measures achieved predictive validity similar to international findings. However, the idiographic assessment improved the validity of predictions significantly and mitigated some weaknesses of the nomothetic measures. Conclusions: A thorough and well-guided idiographic approach in addition to standardized measures can improve the results of risk assessments.

Psychopathy and violent crime: Case study in Estabelecimento Prisional de Paços de Ferreira
Filipe Saraiva, Carlos Augusto Faculdade de Ciências Humanas, Universidade Fernando Pessoa, Matosinhos, Portugal *Soares Martins, José* Faculdade de Ciências Humanas, Universidade Fernando Pessoa, maia, Portugal
The individual diagnosed with psychopathy as been associated with the notion of human predator, with unique characteristics, in specific literature like lack of emotions, feelings and violent crime. Our investigation had the goal to obtain specific data of the genesis of the psychopathy that could enlight us the risk factors for the psychopathic personality. Our subject is a convicted inmate. The conclusions were similar to the specific literature existent. The presence of maltreatment, unstructured parental education, existence of perceived and acceptable violence, all this aspects support the theoretical aspects of psychopathy and its association with criminal activity. Keywords: Psychopathy, inmate, violent crime, PCL-R, case study.

FP-065: Social-cognitive mechanisms I

Discontinuity patterns and stage transitions in relation to the uptake of a kidney screening tool: An application of the Precaution Adoption Process Model (PAPM)
van Empelen, Pepijn Dept. of Health Psychology, Leiden University, Leiden, Netherlands *van Grieken, Amy* Health Psychology, Leiden University, Leiden, Netherlands
Objectives. It was examined whether (1) stages and (2) stage transitions could be predicted. Methods. In a prospective survey among 321 adult Dutch people stages, knowledge, risk perception, subjective norm, pros, cons, precaution effectiveness and action planning were assessed. ANOVA with polynomial contrasts was used. Results The PAPM stages were collapsed into 3 groups (unaware, undecided, action). Linear trends were found for most predictors. Discontinuity patterns were found for pros, cons and action planning. Stage transition could not be predicted. Conclusion Partial support was found for health-behavior stages. Of importance, action planning differentiates actors from non-actors. Change mechanisms remain unclear.

Relationship of protect motivation theory and condom use among female sex workers in China
Ran, Zhao and Economy, Central University of Finance, Beijing, People's Republic of China *Fang, Xiaoyi* psychology department, Beijing Normal University, Beijing, People's Republic of China *Li, Xiaoming* medical school, Wayne State University, Detroit, USA
This study examines association between PMT and condom use with clients among 452 Female Sex Workers in Guangxi, China. Consistent condom use level of FSWs was lower in China. Three factors of PMT can predict HIV risk behavior of FSWs with clients. Condom use self-efficacy (γ=0.11) was positively associated with condom use frequency and condom use intention. External reward (γ=-0.24) and internal reward (γ=-0.15) was negatively associated with condom use frequency. This finding suggested that HIV prevention programs targeted the FSWs should take into consideration affecting factors of Psychosociology, and tailor to characteristics of high risk groups.

Health related risk factors of excessive internet use among adolescents
Meixner, Sabine Inst. für Pädag. Psychologie, Humboldt-Universität zu Berlin, Berlin, Germany *Jerusalem, Matthias* Humboldt-Universität zu Berlin, Berlin, Germany
Objectives: The study was done to validate an internet addiction scale (IAS) and to identify risk and protective factors of addictive internet use in adolescence. Methods: N=5000 German pupils filled in a questionnaire containing the 20-Item IAS and further measures to assess protective and risk factors. Results: Results indicate that online assessment of internet addiction may lead to higher prevalence rates than offline assessment. In multivariate analyses self-efficacy turned out to be a strong protective factor. Positive outcome expectations, distress, unfavorable coping and social anxiety are potential risk factors. Conclusions: Consequences and implications for school based prevention are discussed.

FP-066: Special needs and strengths of particular learner groups: ADHD, at-risk-learners, and gifted students I

Behavioral parent training for children with ADHD: A meta-analytic study
Lee, Pei-Chin Occupational Therapy, Chung Shan Medical University, Taichung, Taiwan *Niew, Wern-Ing* Special Education, National Kaohsiung Normal Univ, Kaohsiung, Taiwan *Yang, Hao-Jan* Public Health, Chung Shan Medical University, Taichung, Taiwan *Huang, Shu-Chi* Psychiatry, Chung Shan Medical University, Taichung, Taiwan
Behavioral parent training has been one of the popular forms of intervention for children with Attention deficit hyperactivity disorder (ADHD) and many studies have been published to examine its effectiveness since 1980s. This study was intended to differentiate the effects of behavioral parent training, and behavioral parent training combined with other forms of intervention through a meta-analytic review. Thirty-nine studies met the criteria and were included in this meta-analysis. This meta-analysis will further examine how study design, child's characteristics, parental factors, and methods of assessment moderate the training effects. Implication for clinical practice and future research will be discussed.

Self beliefs, school context and Attention Deficit Hyperactivity Disorder (ADHD): Perception from Brazilian teenagers and young adults
Loos, Helga Dept. Educational Psychology, Federal University of Paraná, Curitiba, Brazil *Rangel Junior, Edison* Educational Psychology, Federal University of Paraná, Curitiba, Brazil
This study is aimed at investigating how school influences the psychosocial development among ADHD diagnosed students. 21 teenagers and young adults (age: M=23,5; 15 male, 6 female) were interviewed about their perceptions concerning the role of formal academic contexts on their self-beliefs. Negative feelings were frequently reported, mainly involving memories of incomprehension, negative judgment, and inadequate treatment from teachers at school. Low self-concepts and self-esteems were detected, and most participants considered themselves unable to cope with academic difficulties. By not having appropriate resources to deal with ADHD students, school seems to heavily contribute to a poor development of their self-beliefs.

FP-067: Stereotypes and categorization I

How subtyping shapes perception: Predictable exceptions to the rule reduce attention to stereotype-associated dimensions
Deutsch, Roland Lehrstuhl für Psychologie II, Universität Würzburg, Würzburg, Germany *Fazio, Russell* Psychology, Ohio State University, Columbus, OH, USA
Two experiments examined the relation between stereotype disconfirmation and attentional processes. Using an instrumental learning-paradigm, we simulated stereotype acquisition and the subsequent subtyping of disconfirming exemplars. While replicating established markers of subtyping, the present research demonstrates a hitherto neglected cognitive consequence of subtyping: Predictable stereotype disconfirmation increased attention to features that facilitated discriminating between confirming and disconfirming exemplars, and reduced attention to features associated with the original stereotype. These effects were not observed when stereotype disconfirmation was not easily predictable and, hence, subtyping proved difficult. The discussion focuses on implications for research on subtyping and stereotype change.

Discriminated groups' belief validation and change: The role of heterogeneity and consensus information

Lopes, Diniz Social and Organ. Psychology, ISCTE, Lisbon, Portugal *Vala, Jorge* Social Psychology, ICS - UL, Lisbon, Portugal *Silva, Pedro* Social and Organ. Psychology, ISPA, Lisbon, Portugal

There is little empirical evidence regarding the effects of informational or normative influence on validation of beliefs and attitudes towards discriminated groups. Two experiments showed that participants (N = 136) holding negative attitudes towards Blacks changed to more positive evaluations after receiving consensual feedback from a reference group supporting a positive attitude towards Blacks. More interestingly, these studies show that heterogeneous reference groups holding positive evaluations of Black immigrants exert a greater pressure reducing prejudice in participants holding negative evaluations than homogeneous groups. These results are analysed at the light of informational and normative influence accounts of belief change.

Open your mind: Reduction of cognitive ingroup projection by priming complex superordinate categories

Waldzus, Sven ISCTE, Lisboa, Portugal *Rosa, Miriam* CIS, ISCTE, Lisboa, Portugal *Meireles, Claudia* CIS, ISCTE, Lisboa, Portugal *O'Sullivan, Clodagh* Department of Psychology, Univerity of Fort Hare, East London, South Africa *Dumont, Kitty* Department of Psychology, University of Fort Hare, East London, South Africa

Ingroup projection is the tendency to generalize ingroup characteristics to superordinate categories. Two experiments with Portuguese and South-African participants tested whether a) ingroup projection is partly a result of cognitive bias and thus can be reduced by inducing a more tolerant mindset leading to a complex representation of superordinate categories and b) whether this effect is opposite for low prototypic groups. Tolerant mindset was induced by priming the simultaneous use of many vs. few orthogonal dimensions in information processing. Results show that mindset priming reduced ingroup projection for high prototypical groups but had no effect for low prototypical groups.

Don't just look – listen! Influence of auditory cues on social categorization

Rakic, Tamara Psychology, University of Jena, Jena, Germany *Steffens, Melanie* Psychology, University of Jena, Jena, Germany *Mummendey, Amélie* Psychology, University of Jena, Jena, Germany

This project investigated (a) whether "non salient" visual cues (e.g., typical Italian vs. German look) can activate categorization; (b) if it is possible to extend the phenomenon using auditory cues (accents); and (c) in case of cross categories based on these two dimensions (visual and auditory cues) which one is stronger in activating the category. Using Taylor et al.'s (1978) "Who Said What" paradigm in a series of studies we tested these assumptions. Results showed that not only look (visual cue) but also the accent (auditory cue) of a person plays an important role in how that person is categorized.

FP-068: Stress and mental health I

Individual and group stress reactions

Sedrakyan, Sedrak Psychology, Urartu University, Yerevan, Armenia

In modern scientific literature there are existing approximately 60 definitions of "stress" conception. It must be noticed, that in stressiology stress reactios are usually discussed at individual level. Simultaneously, it is obvious that both the perception of stressors and stress reactions of a group

(large or small) as a whole have their specifications and differ from individual ones. Surely, stress classification to individual and group types is relative as any individual stress influences on the microenvironment where the individual acts and visa versa. The recent research done by us in stress area proved that the mechanisms of withstanding stress actively function in collective, especially in families. The higher collective value orientation the easier it is to withstand stress.

Creating an interprofessional culture in mental health services

Vingilis, Evelyn Population & Community Health, The University of Western Onta, London, Canada *Forchuk, Cheryl* School of Nursing, The University of Western Onta, London, Canada *Orchard, Carole* Faculty of Health Sciences, The University of Western Onta, London, Canada

Objectives: To facilitate and evaluate an interprofessional (IP) mental health care educational intervention. Methods: Through workshops, online modules and practice site settings, students have the opportunity to learn and practice new skills. Participatory Action Research was used, informed by IP research and theory. Mixed methods, multimeasures (focus groups, validated instruments, feedback forms) evaluation is being conducted with students, faculty, practitioners and clients. Results: Early results found participants expressed desire to learn more about team processes (i.e. leadership, conflict resolution, care coordination, etc) and the issues they may encounter in practice. Final results on realization of learning objectives will be presented.

Internal picture of actual state of person in the total score of his health state

Zalevskiy, Genrikh Faculty of Psychology, Tomsk State University, Tomsk, Russia *Kuzmina, Yulia* Faculty of Psychology, Tomsk State University, Tomsk, Russia

Purpose and hypothesis: To study the productivity of conception "internal picture of actual state" supposed its bigger potentiality in estimating of pre-pathological states and groups of risk in comparative with the concepts "internal picture of health" (IPH) and "internal picture of illness" (IPI). Methods and material: Original questionnaire of subjective estimate of actual state (IPAS), tests of IPI and IPH. 200 subjects from "group of risk" took part – smoking and pregnant women. Results and conclusions: For health psychology, oriented on communication with "between health and illness groups" and prevention of health disorders, more productive is "actual state orientation" the concept of IPAS and not "illness" and "health orientation".

Study of terrible and emotional films influence on "sIgA"

Hakim Javadi, Mansour Dept. of Psychology, Guilan University, Rasht, Islamic Republic of Iran

we investigate the influence of terrible and emotional films on "IgA" .the findings on the relation between stress and "sIgA" indicated that the rate of "sIgA" become desynchronize under chronic stress and the rate of "sIgA" increase under acute stress. In a repeated measure procedure the impact of stress on "sIgA" was controlled with covariance analysis. The results suggest that After showing the films for each group the increase of "sIgA" in experimental group was very higher than baseline and was significantly different from control group. This research showed that the terrible films have critical impact on immune system and increase the rate of "sIgA".

FP-069: Substance abuse / epidemiology, course and intervention I

A longitudinal test of the acquired preparedness model for alcohol use in an adolescent community sample: Results of the Greifswalder family study

Stopsack, Malte Klinische Psychologie, Universität Heidelberg, Heidelberg, Germany *Ulrich, Ines* Clinical Psychology, University of Heidelberg, Heidelberg, Germany *Barnow, Sven* Clinical Psychology, University of Heidelberg, Heidelberg, Germany

Aim of the Study was to test the Acquired Preparedness Model (APM) for alcohol use longitudinally which indicates that the relationship between impulsiveness and alcohol use is mediated by alcohol expectancies. Method: 381 adolescents (aged 11 – 18 years and five years later) from a community sample in Pomerania were analyzed using Structural Equitation Modeling. They were questioned regarding impulsiveness, alcohol expectancies and different measures for alcohol problems. Results: The APM was confirmed solely for male adolescents and some alcohol measures (e. g. binge drinking). Conclusions: The results are discussed with respect to applications and additions of the model.

Drug addiction: A study on subjective well-being as a function of socioeconomic status and place of residence

Khan, Mozibul Huq Azad Dept. of Psychology, Rajshahi University, Rajshahi, Bangladesh

The study was designed to investigate the subjective well-being (SWB) of drug addicts and non-addicts as a function of socioeconomic status and place of residence in the context of Bangladesh. SWB Questionnaire of Nagpal and Sell (1985) was administered on 348 addicts following the criteria of addiction suggested by DSM-IV. The scale was also administered on 348 non-addicts employing matched pair technique. The results showed that drug addicts had significantly poorer SWB than the non-addicts and also found no significant effects of socioeconomic status and place of residence on SWB of the addicts.

Preventing substance abuse among the secondary school adolescents in Nigeria through self control

Fayombo, Grace Adebisi School of Education, University of West Indies, Bridgetown, Barbados

Objectives: This experimental study investigated the effectiveness of self-control in preventing substance abuse among the Secondary School Adolescents in Nigeria. Methods: 302 adolescents were purposefully selected from 10 secondary schools in Ogun State, Nigeria, 152 in experimental group, 150 in control group. Adolescents' Self Control Rating Scale (ADSCRS) was used to collect the data, which was analysed using Analysis of Covariance (ANCOVA). Results: Self control is effective in preventing substance abuse, effect of gender in the prevention of substance abuse is not significant, and the interaction effect of the treatment and gender on the dependent measure is significant. Conclusion Substance abuse can be prevented through self control when promptly addressed.

Brief motivational interventions for sexual risk reduction in alcohol detoxification

Brems, Christiane Behav Health Research & Svcs, University of Alaska Anchorage, Anchorage, Alaska, USA *Johnson, Mark E.* Behav Health Research & Sv, University of Alaska Anchorage, Anchorage, Alaska, USA *Dewane, Sarah L.* Behav Health Research & Sv, University of Alaska Anchorage, Anchorage, Alaska, USA *Eldridge, Gloria D.* Behav Health Research & Sv,

University of Alaska Anchorage, Anchorage, Alaska, USA

Objectives: An NIH-funded sexual risk reduction clinical trial in alcohol detox tested feasibility, safety, and motivations about sexual risk of three intervention: 1) standard-care control; 2) brief motivational intervention (BMI); and 3) BMI with biological feedback. Method: Through random stratification, three groups of 25 participants were assessed, received intervention, and were followed up. Results: BMI, regardless of biological feedback, enhanced motivation for change. Risk behavior did not change statistically significantly; additional analyses and context suggested negative biological feedback resulted in slightly increased level of sexual activity. Conclusions: The study demonstrated that BMI is feasible in short-term detoxification with positive outcomes.

FP-070: Assessment and prediction of the attainment of domain-specific and cross-curricular competencies I

Assessing the attainment of educational standards: Gains in measurement efficiency by multidimensional adaptive testing
Frey, Andreas PISA 2006, IPN Kiel, Kiel, Germany Seitz, Nicki-Nils Educational Sciences, IPN, Kiel, Germany
Simulation studies showed that adaptive tests based on multidimensional Item-Response-Models (MAT) are more efficient than unidimensional adaptive tests (CAT) or fixed-item-tests (FIT). The objective of the present simulation is to examine gains in efficiency if MAT is used within a scenario typical for the assessment of educational standards. Data generation was based on population parameters empirically obtained from a study assessing the attainment of German educational standards in mathematics (N=9577). Using MAT, 20% fewer items are needed compared to CAT, 60% compared to FIT, measurement precision held constant. Thus, the number of presented items can be substantially reduced by MAT.

Psychometric assessment of interpersonal skills: Their inclusion in the selection processes of medical and health science courses
Nixon, Judy Australian Council of Ed Res, Camberwell, Australia Bryce, Jennifer Assessment and Reporting, Australian Council of Ed Res, Camberwell, Australia
'Understanding People' is a component of the Undergraduate Medicine and Health Sciences Admission Test (UMAT), constructed by the Australian Council for Educational Research, for the UMAT consortium of universities. This component is designed to be an objective measure of candidates' ability to understand and reason about people. We provide a rationale for testing 'interpersonal understanding' as a cognitive ability rather than a personality trait. We address the issues that arise from inferring interpersonal ability from multiple-choice items, which are analysed using a combination of classical test theory and factor analysis, on an annual testing cohort of approximately 14,000 students.

Application of many-facet Rasch model in rater training for subjective items
Li, Zhongquan School of Psychology, BNU, Beijing, People's Republic of China
Rating of subjective items may be influenced by many factors, such as knowledge, ability and individual preference of raters. In the present study, many-facet Rasch model was applied in rater training for a national examination. 60 raters were randomly divided into two groups, to complete rating on a subjective item during pre-training and post-training sessions. The only difference between

the two groups was whether they receive individual feedbacks on rater error which was identified by many-facet Rasch model during the interval. Results indicated that this kind of rater training was effective in reducing rater's effects and improving rater reliability.

FP-071: Assessment and job performance I

What do assessment centers really measure?: Complex problem-solving behaviour as a contribution to the construct validity of Assessment Centers
Schültz, Benjamin Human Resource Consulting, Atrain GmbH, Bamberg, Germany König, Anja Human Resource Consulting, atrain GmbH, Bamberg, Germany Hübner, Oliver Human Resource Consulting, atrain GmbH, Bamberg, Germany Stempfle, Joachim Human Resource Consulting, atrain GmbH, Bamberg, Germany
By moving away from the traditional approach of attempting to improve the construct validity of Assessment Centers by enhancing design characteristics, our study identifies complex problem-solving behavior (CPS) as a predictor of AC ratings. For N=49 students, we found a significant correlation (r=.5) between CPS communicative behavior, as assessed through a multi-level coding system and an overall AC rating. Subsets of CPS abilities yielded differential validity: a task-oriented set of CPS categories, for example, predicted a task-oriented factor of AC ratings, but did not predict a team-oriented factor. Implications for utilizing CPS in ACs are discussed in our study.

The impact of technology on changing practice in psychological assessment
Bartram, Dave Research Dept., SHL Group Ltd., Thames Ditton, United Kingdom
The presentation will outline the way in which the Internet has produced a major change in the way assessment is carried out in work and organizational settings. Not only has the volume of test use increased dramatically but also the way in which tests are used has changed. Unproctored or unsupervised modes of assessment has been the biggest growth area and the most controversial, raising issues of test security, increased possibilities of cheating and candidate authentication. However, technology, both in IT and in psychometrics has developed to meet these challenges.

The exploring the Chinese managers' ability to execute
Fang, Liluo Inst. of Psychology, Chinese Academy of Sciences, Beijing, People's Republic of China Ling, Li DEPARTMENT OF PSYCHOLOGY, PEKING UNIVERSITY, Beijing, People's Republic of China Wang, Yao The Aushou Biosystem Company, The Aushou Biosystem Company, BURLINGTON, MA, USA
The results shown that (1)The five dimensions of Chinese managers' ability to execute are ability to digest, to plan, to conduct, to coach and to innovate.(2)The organizational factors which restrict execution were regulations being incomplete, processes being unscientific, organizational climate being undesirable, organizational structure being inappropriate. (3)All restriction factors at organizational level had negative effects on the managers' ability to conduct and had significant negative effects on division performances.(4) The managers' self-efficacy acted as a mediator between the managers' execution competence and his/her management effectiveness; the leader's participation moderated the relation between the manager's execution competence and he/her management effectiveness.

FP-072: Memory processes I

Directed forgetting of rats' memory for event duration
Santi, Angelo Psychology, Wilfrid Laurier University, Waterloo, Canada McMillan, Neil Psychology, Wilfrid Laurier University, Waterloo, Canada Van Rooyen, Patrick Psychology, Wilfrid Laurier University, Waterloo, Canada
Rats were trained to discriminate 2-s versus 8-s of magazine light illumination by responding to either a stationary lever or a moving lever. During training, comparison response alternatives were always presented following a brief remember (R) cue, but never presented following a brief forget (F) cue. During testing, accuracy was significantly poorer on F-cued trials than on R-cued trials. Additional testing involved increasing the duration of the R- and F-cues, manipulating cue location in the retention interval, and successively presenting both cues. The implication of the results for active control of event duration memory by rats will be discussed.

Framing effects in children's intentional forgetting
Aslan, Alp Inst. für Psychologie, Universität Regensburg, Regensburg, Germany Bäuml, Karl-Heinz Department of Psychology, Regensburg University, Regensburg, Germany
We examined framing effects in children's directed forgetting - the ability to intentionally forget out-of-date information when cued to do so. Children and adults were provided with two different versions of the forget cue, telling them that a to-be-forgotten list was just for practice (practice condition) or telling them that it was presented by mistake ("whoops" condition). Fourth graders and adults showed efficient directed forgetting regardless of framing. In contrast, first graders showed efficient forgetting in the "whoops" condition but not in the practice condition. The results challenge the view that young children are unable to intentionally forget out-of-date information.

Retrieval induced forgetting and transfer appropriate processing
Wilbert, Jürgen Inst. für Humanwissenschaften, Universität zu Köln, Köln, Germany Gerdes, Heike Faculty of Human sciences, University of Cologne, Cologne, Germany
We tested the hypothesis that retrieval induced forgetting (RIF) refers to the attended information during the initial practise phase. Therefore, we conducted four experiments, in which we used a clarification procedure as a memory test. We manipulated whether a cue was displayed during the practise and the clarification task. The results show a significant RIF-effect when cues were present or absent during both tasks, but no effect when only one task had cues. Accordingly, RIF can be explained by the constitution of context specific cues during practise phase and transfer appropriate processing during the recall task.

FP-073: Categorization and conditional reasoning I

Algorithmic distances versus geometrical distances in categorization processes
Mathy, Fabien Auxon-Dessous, France
This presentation reports a series of experimental studies aiming to assess the compressibility of information in categorization processes. Our results show that 1) The patterns of response times are function of the decompression times produced by algorithmic models 2) When investigating the learning times by manipulating the training samples, rule-based presentations substantially facilitate learning over similarity-based orders 3) The effect of mutual information on repeated learning of

categories suggests that subjects use some relational information between variables. This series of results show that models based on algorithmic distances better explain categorization processes than models based on geometrical distances.

Sustain and heterogeneous category representation

Yang, Lee-Xieng Cognitive Institute, National Cheng-Kung University, Tainan, Taiwan *Wang, Chung-Yu* Institute of Cognitive Science, National Cheng-Kung University, Tainan, Taiwan

The exemplar models in categorization, such as ALCOVE, holds a stance that exemplars are homogeneously represented in the psychological space, as the same dimensional weights are used for all items while computing similarity. However, the past two studies (Aha & Goldstone, 1990; Yang & Lewandowsky, 2004) challenged this stance. This study shows SUSTAIN can account for the data from these two studies, because its winner-takes-all algorithm and its cluster forming mechanism can reserve the uniqueness of local items. In addition, the superiority of SUSTAIN over ATRIUM in this study suggests that the heterogeneity of categorization can have a single-system explanation.

Poster Session Monday Morning 09:00

Is theory of mind; associated with reading skills among high-functioning children with autism spectrum conditions?

Åsberg, Jakob Dept. of Psychology, Göteborg University, Göteborg, Sweden *Dahlgren, Sven Olof* Autismforum, Stockholm habilitation service, Stockholm, Sweden *Dahlgren Sandberg, Annika* Department of Psychology, Göteborg University, Göteborg, Sweden

Measures of 1st and 2nd-order false belief understanding (FB), word decoding and reading comprehension were administered to 37 higher-functioning children with autism spectrum conditions. Children who failed 1st-order FB had significantly lower word decoding and reading comprehension relative to passers. The differences on the comprehension measures remained significant after controlling for chronological and verbal mental age, but the word decoding measure did not. When the same analyses were made for 2nd-order FB, null results were obtained for all reading measures. Findings are discussed in relation to the connections between oral and written language and different levels of theory of mind.

The extent of gathering information on academic programs among Iranian university candidates

Abdi, Beheshteh Social sciences, National Organization for Educ, Tehran, Islamic Republic of Iran

This study examines the extent of gathering information on the academic program selection among Iranian university candidates. A questionnaire was designed which had adequate psychometric properties in pilot study.The final sample consisted of 1737 (949 women and 788 men). Using a factor analysis test, revealed two factors(media/books and advising). Also based on a Mean Confidence Interval Estimation, the extent of gathering information on academic programs was low (48 percents) while there is a gap (of 52 percent). Findings showed the higher mean of gathering information through media-books among girls and humanities applicants.These findings address the importance of providing information gathering opportunities for university applicants.

An investigation of the effect of organizational entrepreneurship teaching on entrepreneurial inclination of university's employees

Adibrad, Nastaran Dept. of Counseling Psychology, Shahid Beheshti University, Tehran, Islamic Republic of Iran *Adsibrad, Mojtaba* Counseling Psychology, Abbas Abad- Sarafraz, Tehran, Islamic Republic of Iran

Method: At first, 40 individuals were chosen voluntarily of university employees. they were devided randomly into 2 groups of 20 people (experimental and control groups) all participates respond to organization entrepreneurial inclination test as a pre-test and post test.The organizational entrepreneurship teaching was done just for the experimental group by a 10 sessions workshop. Results: Resultes showed the significant differents between pre- test and post- test in experiment group in significant level of P< 0/001 in problem solving, self efficancy and significant differents in level of 0/01, between post- test of experimental group and control group in problem solving, self efficancy and perservernece.

Predicting clinical depression in adolescents by self - reports

Aebi, Marcel Kinder- und Jugendpsychiatrie, Universität Zürich, Zürich, Switzerland *Winkler Metzke, Christa* Child and Adoles. Psychiatry, University of Zurich, Zurich, Switzerland *Steinhausen, Hans-Christoph* Child and Adoles. Psychiatry, University of Zurich, Zurich, Switzerland

Objectives: The diagnostic accuracy of the DSM – oriented depression scale of the Youth Self Report (YSR) and the Centre of Epidemiological Studies – Depression Scale (CES-D) in the prediction of clinical depression in adolescent clinical and community samples. Methods: Subjects with clinically evaluated ICD -10 diagnoses were compared with a non-referred community sample and a clinical sample referred for other psychiatric disorders. The areas under the curve (AUC) based on ROC analyses of the two scales were compared. Results: Both scales showed high diagnostic accuracy in the prediction of depression in community subjects but only moderate accuracy in clinical subjects. Conclusion: The two scales are very effective screening instruments in the field but not in clinical samples.

The development of facial expressions of emotion in indian culture

Agrawal, Priyanka Indian Institute of Technology, Humanities and Social Sciences, New Delhi, India *Bhaya Nair, Rukmini* Humanities and Social Sciences, Indian Institute of Tech-Delhi, New Delhi, India *Narsimhan, Bhuvana* Language Acquisition Group, MPI- NL, Nijmegen, Netherlands *Chaudhary, Nandita* Child Dev, Lady irwin College, University of Delhi, New Delhi, India *Keller, Heidi* Psychology, University of Osnabrück, Osnabrück, India

The development of emotions in the offspring of any species, especially humans, is one of the most important and complex processes necessary to ensure their survival. Although other nonverbal expressions of emotion such as body movements provide valuable clues, facial expressions in human infants are arguably the most crucial component in tracking emotional responses. Tracing the developmental path of facial expressions is thus the aim of this longitudinal research study which explores mother-child interactions from infancy to pre-school in Indian culture via video-taped datasets recorded as part of multiple projects spanning Indian universities (IITD, JNU, DU), Osnabrück University and MPI-Netherlands.

Relationships between gender, gender role orientation and work-family and family-work conflicts

Aguilar-Luzon, Maria del Carmen Psychology, University of Jaen, Jaen, Spain *Calvo-Salguero, Antonia* Social Psychology, University of Granada, Granada, Spain *Salinas, José Maria* Social Psychology, University of Granada, Granada, Spain *Martin Tamayo, Ignacio* Social Psychology, University of Granada, Granada, Spain

In this study the relationships that exist between gender, gender role orientation and work-family and family-work conflicts were examined. A sample of 267 workers (128 men and 139 women) was taken from three different work posts within a Spanish public organisation. Pearson correlation analyses and regression analyses were carried out. The results showed that gender and gender role orientation were related. Men are more masculine than women, and women are more feminine than men. While gender did not predict any of the two types of conflict, feminine gender role orientation did predict work-family conflict.

Gender differences in masculinity and femininity with regard to the active paternity atage

Aguilar-Luzon, Maria del Carmen Psychology, University of Jaen, Jaen, Spain *Calvo-Salguero, Antonia* Social Psychology, University of Granada, Granada, Spain *García-Martínez, J. Miguel A.* Social Psychology, University of Granada, Granada, Spain *Monteoliva Sánchez, Adelaida* Social Psychology, University of Granada, Granada, Spain *Carrasco González, Ana María* Psychology, University of Huelva, Huelva, Spain

The objective was to ascertain whether there are differences between genders and within each gender in gender role orientation depending on whether a person is going through active paternity or not. A sample of 240 workers (115 men and 125 women). We carried out difference in averages analyses and the results indicated that there were differences between genders in masculinity and femininity both when the two genders had children and when they had no children. Women are more feminine than men and men are more masculine than women. On the other hand, there were no differences between women with children and women without children in gender role orientation. However, men with children were more masculine than men without children.

The effect of group training organizational behavior on organizational climate, organizational commitment and job satisfaction in Isfahan municipality personnel

Ahmadi, Elaheh Tehran, Islamic Republic of Iran *Nouri, Abolghasem* Psychology, Isfahan university, Isfahan, Islamic Republic of Iran *Samavtyan, Hossein* Psychology, Isfahan university, Isfahan, Islamic Republic of Iran

The purpose of this study was to investigate the effect of group training on organizational climate, organizational commitment and job satisfaction in Isfahan Municipality personnel. Data of 60 personnel in Isfahan Municipality was obtained by three inventories in the pre- and post- stages of the training workshop. ANOVA and MANOVA confirmed the main hypothesis, meaning that training is effective on the propsed variables. It may be concluded that organizational climate can be promoted by applying the relevant training and it increases organizational commitment and job satisfaction.

Social referencing in chimpanzees: Responses to the fear presentation by humans

Akagi, Kazushige Faculty of Education, Mie University, Tsu, Japan *Hayashi, Misato* Primate Research Institute, Kyoto University, Inuyama, Japan

Matsuzawa, Tetsuro *Primate Research Institute, Kyoto University, Inuyama, Japan*
The purpose of the present research was to investigate the ability of social referencing in chimpanzees (Pan troglodytes). Six chimpanzees participated in the present experiment. The chimpanzees were tested in a situation that the experimenter opened a box and showed fear toward something in it. As a result, all of the chimpanzees looked at the experimenter and the box alternatively within 15 seconds. Moreover they behaved with caution toward the box. These findings demonstrated the ability of social referencing was robust in chimpanzees. The results were discussed from the view point of the social referencing in comparison to human infants.

Linguistic and conceptual equivalence of Conners' revised rating scales in a Sudanese sample

Al-Awad, Ahmed *Psychology, University of Gezira, Medani, Sudan*
Sudanese parents and teachers completed behaviour rating scales on a stratified sample of 100 children. These instruments were based on Conners parent and teacher revised questionnaires. Following a reliable translation into Sudanese Arabic the test-retest reliability of the items and the internal consistency of the original Conners' scales were explored. Both instruments displayed good reliability and the original Conners scales had satisfactory internal consistency. As far as linguistic and conceptual equivalence with previous studies in different cultures was concerned it appeared that the Sudanese raters' views of problems mirrored their western counterparts.

The interaction between sibling's cognitive development and parent-child relationships

Alekseeva, Olga *Psychological Institute, Moscow, Russia*
The aim of the study: to analyze parental influences on sibling's cognitive development. Subjects 70 nonstep families with two children. Methods: 1. Russian versions of WAIS and WISC; 2. Child-parent interaction questionnaire (Markovskaya, 1998). Results: Higher score in scale of Mother Control was related with lower VIQ estimations of older sibling (-.25) and lower VIQ, PIQ, IQ estimations of younger sibling (-.46; -.38; -.45). Higher PIQ estimation of older sibling was related with lower score of Mother Cooperation (-.22) and higher score in scale of Father Cooperation (.23). Father Cooperation was related with IQ of younger sibling (.27).

The identification of nine groups of gender types of employed gouples and comparing their emotional intelligence

Aliakbari, Mahnaz *Dept. of Psychology, Payame Noor University, Tehran, Islamic Republic of Iran*
The purpose of this study was to identify gender types among Ahvaz employed women and their husbands. Other purpose of the study was comparing of nine groups of gender types of employed couples with respect to emotional intelligence. The sample of this study consisted of 724 employed women and their husbands (total 1448) that were selected randomly. The instruments used in this study were:Sex- Role Inventory (Bem,1981)& Emotional Intelligence Inventory (Petrides & Furnham, 2000). The result of this study showed: There is a significant difference between the frequencies of androgen, feminine and masculinity gender in employed women and their husbands. Also There is significant difference between nine groups of emotional intelligence.

Impressions on facial appearance and their influence on HR selection process

Alves Lino de Souza, Altay *Evolutionary Psychol, Sao Paulo University, Sao Paulo, Brazil*
To analyze the influence of first impressions based on facial appearance on hiring decision, 141 consultants of 20 Brazilian companies evaluated a resumé associated to the photograph of a bearded or a clean shaved candidate for a Corporative job (Financial Director) and for a Free-lancer job (Web Designer). GLM model showed significant positive effect of beard on the evaluation for a Free-Lancer Job (p<.05) and a negative effect for a Corporative Job (p<.05). Our findings suggest that beard was associated with unconventionality and that a clean shaved face was associated with the establishment, influencing hiring decisions in spite of resumé.

Primary School children's drawings of Europe: A study on Italian children

Amann Gainotti, Merete *Scienze dell'Educazione, Università degli Studi Roma, Roma, Italy* **Pallini, Susanna** *Scienze dell'Educazione, Università di Roma, Roma, Italy* **Scalesse, Antonella** *Dip di Scienze dell'Educazione, Università degli Studi RomaTre, Roma, Italy*
The study is part of a wider research (Amann Gainotti, 2006 ; Amann Gainotti, Pallini, 2006,2007) that aimed at gaining knowledge about European children's spontaneous ideas and representations of Europe before being taught about Europe in schools. 150 Italian children from first to fifth grade of primary school were asked, after a short interview, to make a drawing of Europe. Results show that children's graphic representations of Europe follow precise developmental patterns, that outline their very first spatial and geographical notions and give an idea about how "cognitive maps" of a complex entity as Europe are constructed during childhood.

M. Montessori and Jean Piaget 's writings on peace education

Amann Gainotti, Merete *Scienze dell'Educazione, Università degli Studi Roma, Roma, Italy*
Maria Montessori (Italy, 1870-1952) and Jean Piaget (Switzerland, 1896-1980) are outstanding and world famous figures in the fields of education and of developmental psychology. The purpose of our study was to conduct a historical and comparative analysis of the converging interests of Montessori and Piaget for peace education, which they expressed in two international meetings (1932,1934) and in a number of written works. Special attention will be paid to the very different political and social backgrounds in which their interest for peace education was fostered.

Development of preventive intention scale for sexually transmitted diseases on Japanese university students

Amazaki, Mitsuhiro *Graduate School, J.F. Oberlin University, Tokyo, Japan* **Shimizu, Yasuo** *College of Health and Welfare, J.F. Oberlin University, Tokyo, Japan* **Mogi, Toshihiko** *College of Health and Welfare, J.F. Oberlin University, Tokyo, Japan* **Mori, Kazuyo** *College of Health and Welfare, J.F. Oberlin University, Tokyo, Japan*
The purpose of this study was to develop the Preventive Intention Scale for Sexually Transmitted Diseases (STD) on Japanese university students. The subjects of 335 Japanese university students (male=177, female=158, mean age=20.20) were asked to answer the questionnaire that was composed of 7 items which were derived from the Sexual Risks Scale (DeHart. et al., 1997). All the items of this questionnaire were translated from English into Japanese. Exploratory factor analysis identified a one-factor solution with 5 items. The results of reliability analysis and confirmatory

factor analysis supported the reliability and structural validity of this Scale.

Understanding early leaving in adult learners literacy program

Amenyah, Efua Irene N. *PSP/PSED, Université Catholique Louvain, Louvain La Neuve, Belgium*
This research investigates reasons why adult learners do not complete their training sessions. Motivational framework was drawn on achievement goals and related behaviors. Participants were 96 adult women from 7 literacy centres. Structural survey has assessed features as work environment, utility value and achievement goals. Results indicated that 96% do not complete planned sessions. 64% sustained that they completed sessions. Results also showed that learners are able to use acquired skills at work, at home and in social life. We concluded that learners linked competence beliefs and utility value and are more focused only on acquired skills that will help them achieve important goals.

Biomembrane correlates of personality: New strategy of psychobiological assesment to people of risk-professions

Aminev, Evarist *RGUFC, Moscow, Russia* **Aminev, Gesiod** *Applied Psychobiology Lab, Hi-tech Psychology Central Ins, Moscow, Russia* **Minnibaev, Marsel** *Pathophysiology, Kazan State Medical University, Kazan, Russia* **Gunter, Nina** *Therapy, Clinical hospital N 6 FMBA RF, Moscow, Russia* **Wang, Qing** *Administration Management, UIBE, Beijing, People's Republic of China* **Truskalov, Vadim** *Military Psychobiology Lab, Hi-tech Psychology Central Ins, Moscow, Russia* **Safronova, Helena** *Penitentiary Psychology, Ufa legal Institute MVD RF, Moscow, Russia*
People of risk-professions have no fear before the God, but before a captivity. Affects cause personal-cognitive disturbances (F.R.Brush, J.B.Overmier). Project-aim: psychobiological rehabilitation-system developing. Methods. Data of 450 volunteers resumes, diagnoses (ICD-10/F45.30-32), testing (R.Kettell, J.Streljau, K.Maslach), EEG, EVP, operative-memory stress-stability were used. Individual mitochondrion, K+, Ca++, H+-channels inhibition sensitivity were measured according Hoorweg-Weiss (electroskin thresholds, stimulus 5, 10 msec). Results. NeuroSolution professional reliability forecast and efficiency of psychobiological rehabilitation was shown (Bell's zones acupuncture, bioprotectors in comparison with auto-training, double blind method, t=2.91, P<0.01). The conclusion. Psychobiology assessment - a strategic direction of personal rehabilitation.

Youth and addiction: Treatment of co-morbid disorders

Andorfer, Ute *Frauenabteilung, Anton Proksch Institut, Wien, Austria* **Feselmayer, Senta** *Frauenabteilung, Anton Proksch Institut, Wien, Austria* **Scheibenbogen, Oliver** *Frauenabteilung, Anton Proksch Institut, Wien, Austria* **Beiglböck, Wolfgang** *Frauenabteilung, Anton Proksch Institut, Wien, Austria*
Young female addicts have different and more co-morbid disorders than older patients. First empirical data from our qualitative study supports a more differentiated therapeutic approach. Besides clinical pictures, anxiety disorders and trauma-related disorders it is above all eating disorders, emotional instable personality disorders and "multi-impulsive personalities" in which multiple self-destructive behaviour reflects a personality that has lost control. Neglect and non-treatment of these co-morbidities massively increases the probability of relapses and prevents full recovery. At the Anton Proksch Institute a treatment programme specifically developed for young female addicts addresses all relevant co-morbidities. Therapeutic work fo-

cues inter alia on the development of a "self-care" attitude.

Can web-based feedback facilitation enhance the effect of feedback on performance?

Anseel, Frederik Personnel Management, Ghent University, Ghent, Belgium Lievens, Filip Personnel Management, Ghent University, Ghent, Belgium Schollaert, Eveline Dept. de Psychologie, Universiteit Gent, Gent, Belgium

An unanswered question is whether web-based feedback facilitation can enhance the effects of feedback on performance. Drawing from research on dual-process models, we test a web-based feedback facilitation technique aimed at deeper elaboration of the feedback message. Results (N = 640) show that performance improvement on an in-basket exercise was stronger in a group receiving web-based feedback facilitation as compared to a group wherein only a feedback report was provided. The effect of feedback facilitation on performance was partially mediated by feedback responses. These findings suggest a practical and cost-effective strategy for enhancing feedback interventions in a web-based context.

The relation between acculturation orientations preferred by both immigrants and host society and immigrants' school success

António, João Dept. of Psychology, ISCTE, Lisboa, Portugal Monteiro, Maria Benedicta Psychology, ISCTE, Lisboa, Portugal

The impact of acculturation orientations on immigrant adolescents' school success is the main issue of this study. It was hypothesised that is not only the immigrants' orientations but also their perception of majority group preferences that contribute to best predict school success. 140 students of African immigrant background answered a questionnaire during regular school classes. Acculturation orientation was accessed by 2x2 combinations of items measuring adoption of host culture and maintaining of immigrant heritage independently. Main results showed that perceiving majority group as defending the adoption of host culture by immigrants was the best predictor of participants' school success.

Becoming parents of a premature baby: Parental adjustment facing a preterm birth - a 3 year follow-up

Araujo-Pedrosa, Anabela UNIP - Psychology, Maternidade Daniel d Matos HUC, Coimbra, Portugal Canavarro, Maria Cristina UNIP - Psychology, FPCEUC/Maternidade D. de Matos, Coimbra, Portugal Moura-Ramos, Mariana UNIP - Psychology, Departamento MMFGRH - HUC, Coimbra, Portugal

Objectives With this paper we aim to compare parents of premature infants in terms of parental and marital adjustment along a 3-year follow up. Design and methods Subjects are 96 parents of premature infants needing NICU care, assessed at 4 moments. Data was obtained using different assessment instruments. Results Differences were found in the adjustment of mothers and fathers and in their marital satisfaction. Conclusions Preterm birth may cause exceptional demands to the family, with consequences that remain overtime. Further studies are needed to clarify risk and protective factors that may interact in these processes of adjustment.

Locus of distractor rejection in rapid serial visual presentation

Ariga, Atsunori RCAST, University of Tokyo, Tokyo, Japan Watanabe, Katsumi RCAST, University of Tokyo, Tokyo, Japan

Presenting a target-like distractor in a rapid serial visual presentation task deteriorates the detection performance of the following target. Interestingly, when observers have prior knowledge about the identity of the distractor, the cost of the distractor processing, presumably a rejecting process, emerges belatedly. In this study, using several types of cues (e.g., auditory cues) that indicated the distractor's identity, we investigated at which level of representation the distractor is rejected. The results suggest that the visual system uses a local representation involving a perceptual pattern, not an abstract representation, in rejecting the distractor.

High school students' motive of achievement and assertiveness

Arnaudova, Violeta Psychology, Faculty of Philosophy, Skopje, The former Yugoslav Republic of Macedonia

This paper presents and illustrates an approach on the relation between motive of achievement and assertiveness of high school students with different gender. Achievement Motive Test and Assertiveness Test were distributed to 90 high school students (47 female and 43 male). The results show significant correlation between general motive of achievement and assertiveness (r=-.27, p<.01). It was found significant difference between male and female students regarding emotional inhibition (t=2.82; p<.05). Shown results are expected concerning the factors of socialization that support assertiveness at male students, and motive of achievement is stimulated at both gender in today's conditions of life.

Positive illusion in romantic relationship and its correlation with relationship satisfaction, quality and stability

Arnaudova, Sofija Social work and Social policy, Faculty of Philosophy, Skopje, The former Yugoslav Republic of Macedonia Ivan, Trajkov Social work and Social policy, Faculty of Philosophy, Skopje, The former Yugoslav Republic of Macedonia Denkova, Frosina Social work and Social policy, Faculty of Philosophy, Skopje, The former Yugoslav Republic of Macedonia

The study has been conducted in order to explore the existence of positive illusion in romantic relationships and to research the nature of its correlation with the indicators of relationship achievement: relationship satisfaction, relationship quality assessment and relationship stability appraisal. The participants were 418 Macedonian couples living together for a year. As hypothesized, positive illusion in partner evaluation was found. It was manifested through overestimating partner's qualities on Mate Value Inventory (MVI-7) in comparison to his own estimates on the same Inventory. Furthermore, the positive correlation between the degree of positive illusion and the tree relationships achievement indicators was measured.

Development of temporally extended emotions understanding: From the perspectives of the interaction with a person and the emotional attribution

Aso, Ryota Kyushu University, Fukuoka, Japan Maruno, Shun'ichi Faculty of Human-Environment, Kyushu University, Fukuoka, Japan

This study investigated whether development of temporally extended emotions understanding differs depending on (1) working with a person or alone and (2) what type of causes of emotional attribution children have. Participants ages 3 to 5 watched four videos where a character with negative experience confronts the objects related to his/her past experience. After that, they inferred present emotion of the character and explained the inference they made. The results suggested that in development of temporally extended emotions understanding, there is a stage to understand past emotions through re-experiencing them in a present situation and through working with a person.

Development of preparatory attention

Auclair, Laurent LPNCog - CNRS, Université Paris Descartes, Boulogne-Billancourt Cedex, France

Preparatory attention was evaluated in 6- to 14-year-old children and in young adults, using a detection task developed by LaBerge, Auclair and Siéroff (2000, Consciousness and Cognition, 9, 396-434). A visual target was presented 2 seconds after a warning signal, and was sometimes preceded by a distracter, whose probability was varied across blocks in order to modulate the attentional preparation. Six- to eight-year-old children were most sensitive to frequent distracters, showing a difficulty to prepare to the target. Also, the use of instructions reinforcing attention showed that preparation was weaker in 12- to 14-year-old children than in young adults.

An evaluation of the career centers' services in Turkish universities

Büyükgöze Kavas, Aysenur Dept. Educational Sciences, Middle East Technical Univ., Ankara, Turkey

The purpose of this descriptive study is to evaluate the provided services of the career centers in Turkish universities. There are 115 (85 state and 30 private) universities in Turkey; however, most of them do not have a career center. The data gathered from career center websites. Results of the study indicated that preparing cv, providing information for job interviews and opportunities, job placements, and conducting several other organizations to introduce some companies to students are most offered services by university career centers. Findings of the study will be, discussed concerning the implications for career centers.

Indigenization of psychology in Sudan: The case of doctorate thesis in psychology

Babikir, Muna Dept. of Psychology, Unversity of Blue Nile, Damazine, Sudan

This study examines trends and degree of Indigenization of Psychology in Sudan. The sample of the study (N=50 PhD theses) and the indigenization scale developed by Adair, et al (1993) was used. It showed that Khartoum is the preferred place for data collection (46%), the percentage of education Psychology (46%), students sample (48%), male supervisors (98%) female researchers (72%). The level of cultural sensitivity in local concepts (0%), high documentation of validity (80%) and reliability (80%) test. Concepts of indigenization are not mention in (88%) of the studies. There was a lack of cross–cultural discussion in (66%) of the studies.

Young children's comprehension of deception in folk stories and their manipulation of deceptive acts in games

Babu, Nandita Psychology, University of Delhi, Delhi, India

Children's understanding of deception in folk stories and it's comparison with their manipulation of deceptive acts in games is reported in two different studies done on children in India. The research was conducted on a group of 3- to- 5 year old children in the first study and on a group of 3-to -11 year old children in the second study. They were administered a number of folk stories involving deceptive scenario and games requiring manipulation of deceptive acts. Comprehension of deceptive scenario was easier than the manipulation of deceptive acts. Findings were interpreted in terms of socialization practices in Indian families.

Can 2x2 Factors of achievement goal orientation be found empirically: A German adaptation of the achievement goal orientation questionnaire

Bachmann, Gerhard Inst. für Psychologie, Universität Frankfurt, Frankfurt, Germany Werner, Christina Institute of Psychology, JW Goethe-University, Frankfurt, Germany

Elliot & McGregor's (2001) Achievement Goal Questionnaire is based on a 2x2 framework of achievement goal orientation, constituted by competence evaluation (mastery vs. performance) and valence (approach vs. avoidance). This instrument was translated to German and answered by 322 students (mean age: 23; 98 male). A confirmatory factor analysis revealed problems with two items, but excluding these from analysis, the hypothesized 4-factor model shows acceptable fit. The previously controversial mastery-avoidance dimension could be established without problems, while surprisingly items of the well established performance-avoidance component turned out to be problematic. Interpretations for this unexpected result will be discussed.

What factors modulate attitudes towards homosexuality in a small Canadian University located in a semi-rural setting?

Bacon, Benoit A. *Dept. of Psychology, Bishop's University, Sherbrooke, Canada* **Bellhouse-King, Mathew** *Psychology, Bishop's University, Sherbrooke, Canada* **Stout, Dale** *Psychology, Bishop's University, Sherbrooke, Canada* **Standing, Lionel G.** *Psychology, Bishop's University, Sherbrooke, Canada*
Attitudes towards homosexuality have been well assessed in large, urban centers but not in smaller, more rural settings. Two scales measuring attitudes towards homosexuality were administered to 263 students in a small-town Canadian University (Bishop's). Scores were correlated to a number of sociological variables. Males were more homophobic than females and gender differences were greater in attitudes towards gay men than towards lesbians. Age, religiosity and conservative political affiliation were positively correlated to homophobia. Business and science students were more homophobic than education or humanities students. Overall, attitudes and trends were surprisingly similar to those obtained in large, urban centers.

Negative effect of organizational changes on employees' well-being and its psychological correction

Barabanshchikova, Valentina *Psychology, Moscow State University, Moscow, Russia* **Kazakova, Yulia** *Psychology, Moscow State University, Moscow, Russia*
The aim of the study was to develop an intervention program for reducing negative effects of organizational changes on employees' well-being in small business. Data from a small Russian company (25 employees) were analyzed. Measures of employees' well-being and organizational status were collected at 3 occasions over 1,5 year. The intervention program was started after the second measurement occasion. Before the intervention the level of employees' stress had risen due to the organizational changes. After the intervention significant improvements in employees' psychological well-being were observed. We conclude that the proposed intervention program can effectively correct consequences of faulty organizational decisions.

The relationship between marital adjustment and relationship standards

Barazandeh, Hoda *Mashhad, Islamic Republic of Iran* **Sahebi, Ali** *Family therapy, sydney university, Mashhad, Islamic Republic of Iran* **Aminyazdi, Amir** *psychology, Ferdowsy university, Mashhad, Islamic Republic of Iran*
we studied the relationship between marital adjustment and relationship standards. 50 female high school teachers and their husbands in Mashhad district completed (ISRS) and (DAS) scales. The correlation between the relationship-focused standards in three major dimentions of marital functioning (boundaries, power, and investment), and marital adjustment was significant. satisfaction from meeting relationship standards was signifi-

cantly related to marital adjustment. The relationship standards predicted 25% of marital adjustment. The results of the stepwise regression technique showed that the expressive investment was the only standard that significantly predicted marital adjustment. Differrences between spouse's standards also were related to marital adjustment.

Chronic physical complaints of adolescents in Germany: A population-based cross-sectional survey

Barkmann, Claus *Abt. Kinder-Psychosomatik, UKE Hamburg-Eppendorf, Hamburg, Germany* **Brähler, Elmar** *Medical Psychology, University of Leipzig, Leipzig, Germany* **Schulte-Markwort, Michael** *Child Psychosomatics, University Hospital Hamburg, Hamburg, Germany*
Compared to mental health problems, the type and distribution of chronic physical complaints in adolescence have to-date been examined in only few empirical studies. Data were gathered by means of a questionnaire including the Giessen Physical Complaints Inventory based upon a population-based sample of N=1027 11-18 year olds. The overall distress caused by the ailments across all complexes remained relatively constant with increasing age for boys and intensified with puberty for girls. The clinical significance of these findings lies above all in the provision of a representative benchmark for the assessment in specific populations.

Patterns of categorization on the life-death line

Barrera, Kirareset *Posgrado en Psicología, UNAM, México City, Mexico* **León, Rigoberto** *Posgrado en Psicología, UNAM, Cuidad de México, Mexico* **Palafox, Germán** *Posgrado en Psicología, UNAM, Cuidad de México, Mexico* **Eraña, Angeles** *IIF, UNAM, Cuidad de México, Mexico*
The objective of this study is determine if children's concepts of "life" and "death" are coherent and if they are restricted to the biological domain, we presented children (N= 89) with ages from 4 to 13, first with a classification task in which they had to separate living things from non living things. A second classification task in which they had to determine whether those thing could die or not. The analyses of conditional probabilities showed that children's conceptions about "life" and "death" were related. A log-linear analyze demonstrated that these conceptions were related with the age.

Selection of applicants for apprenticeship positions in Public Administration: Construction and validation of a test to measure concentration

Bartholdt, Luise *Chemnitz, Germany* **Schütz, Astrid** *Personality Psychology, University of Chemnitz, Chemnitz, Germany*
We present a paper-and-pencil concentration test that assesses processing speed and accuracy of performance. Subjects are asked to mark two types of targets (ei with two dots and ie with one dot) without being distracted by non-targets (with different numbers of dots). Psychometric properties of the measure were tested in samples of applicants for apprenticeship positions, pupils, students and the unemployed. The reliability for separately timed halves is sufficient. The instrument shows convergent and discriminant validity and is moderately related to school grades. Norms based on more than 350 applicants from middle schools and high schools are reported.

Parenting and socio-personal development in contexts of social vulnerability

Bartau Rojas, Isabel *M.I.D.E., Facultad F.I.C.E., Universidad del País Vasco, San Sebastian, Spain* **de la Caba, Angeles** *M.I.D.E., Facultad F.I.C.E., Universidad del País Vasco, San Sebastian, Spain*
The aim is to assess an educational program for improving the socio-personal development of min-

ors living in situations of social vulnerability, and the parenting skills of their parents. The sample group comprised both fathers, mothers and children. 10 families participated in the first phase and 6 participated in the second phase. A pretest-posttest design was used, assessing the process using questionnaires and diaries. Improvements were found in the emotional and cooperation skills of the children, as well as in parents' ability to respond to their children's needs. The educational intervention helps develop values such as 'learn to care for' in contexts of social vulnerability.

Mothers of aggressive children: insights on how to prevent transgressor behavior in the future

Basaglia, Aline *Instituto de Psicologia, Universidade de São Paulo, Sao Paulo, Brazil* **Souza, Maria Abigail** *Instituto de Psicologia, Universidade de São Paulo, Sao Paulo, Brazil*
Objectives: To investigate psychic functioning of mothers of aggressive boys on educational environment and, therefore, formulate preventive strategies for transgressor behaviors in the future. Methods: 30 mothers were assisted on psychodiagnostic process, submitted to two interviews (one about the son and the other about herself), and to the Rorschach test. Results: The mothers showed a fragile control of emotions, difficult to establish interpersonal contact, insecurity feelings, and depressive distress. Conclusion: These characteristics might produce negative effects (i) on maternal function performance as well as (ii) on proportionate a stable and protective environment to theirs sons.

The aggressor identity vs target effect on representation of the terrorism

Battistelli, Piergiorgio *Dipt. di Psicologia, Università di Bologna, Bologna, Italy* **Palareti, Laura** *Psicologia, Università di Bologna, Bologna, Italy* **Passini, Stefano** *Psicologia, Università di Bologna, Bologna, Italy*
Everyday mass media reports about war against terrorism, terrorist acts and preventive war but what characterize an action as terrorism? There is disagreement on a common definition of terrorism. The aim of this research is to study the influence of different variables on the interpretation of some violent actions as war or terrorism acts. Results on 325 university students sample confirm that the basic criterion for the evaluation is the distinction between military or civilian targets (target effect) but also that some subjects use also as criterion the ethnic-cultural identity of the aggressor (actor effect).

Protective and risk factors of being bully and victim in a Turkish adolescent sample

Bayraktar, Fatih *Dept. of Psychology, Ankara University, Ankara, Turkey* **Say, Melike** *Psychology, Hacettepe University, Ankara, Turkey* **Kumru, Asiye** *Psychology, Abant Izzet Baysal University, Ankara, Turkey*
Adolescents' individual, peer and parental risk factors of being bully/ victim were investigated. Adolescents (262 girls, 168 boys) from 9th-10th grade high school students were participated in the study. Individual and school related variables, peer relations, and perceived parental control were entered respectively in sequential logistic regression analyses. Results indicated that protective factors were school belonging and peer attachment for victimization; parental behavioral control and negative peer relationships for bullying. On the other hand, anger was risk factor for both bully-victims. As a conclusion, while behavioral control seems to be a protective factor, psychological control is not a risk factor.

Contexts to deny: When people produce negations

Beltran, David *Psicología Cognitiva, Universidad de La Laguna, Tenerife, Spain* **Orenes, Isabel** *PSICOLOGÍA COGNITIVA, UNIVERSIDAD DE LA LAGUNA, TENERIFE, Spain* **Santamaria, Carlos** *PSICOLOGÍA COGNITIVA, UNIVERSIDAD DE LA LAGUNA, TENERIFE, Spain*

Comprehension studies suggest that negation is more plausible in some contexts than others. We present two experiments to examine if the production of negation depends also on the context. The participants read stories where a sentence is false, and were asked to produce a sentence that could be true. In the first experiment they produced more negations from multiple than bipolar adjectives. In the second experiment the context was logically dichotomized by adding disjunctions. In this case, implausibility improved negation. Consequently, when there is a clear alternative, negation is seldom spontaneously produced even if it denies a presupposition.

Rhetorical figures in persuasion

Berardi, Rocco *Linguistics, University of Bari, Bari, Italy* **Defilippis, Domenico** *Dipartimento di Scienze Umane, University of Foggia, Foggia, Italy* **di Iasio, Domenico** *Dipartimento di Scienze Umane, University of Foggia, Foggia, Italy* **Sinatra, Maria** *Department of Psychology, University of Bari, Bari, Italy*

Starting from the concept of πιτανουργα and through crowd psychology our research aims at focusing the crucial historical moments pointing to the establishment of the actual models of persuasion. In this way, we could contextualize better a category of consciousness which is free from the various prejudices accumulated in the time. In this context, psychology, philosophy, literature as well as linguistics play a very important role, especially when they are considered in their interconnection. On this matter we show some concrete examples gained from different textual typology (for ex.: press, media, therapeutic language).

Influence of time pressure on the inspection performance in nuclear power plants

Bertovic, Marija *BAM, Berlin, Germany*

Human factor is in non-destructive testing an unsolved problem. In order to investigate human factors occurring during in-service inspections in nuclear power plants a human factor model had been built. Parts of this model will be tested in an ongoing project. 10 inspectors will perform manual ultrasonic inspection of 25 artificially produced flaws on a mock-up version of a reactor pressure vessel under three different levels of time pressure. Stress coping strategies, mental workload of the task, stress reaction and organizational factors as well as their influence on the inspection performance under different levels of time pressure will be tested.

Logic thinking and formation of leading mental functions of primary school children

Bespanskaya, Ekaterina *General and Clinical Psycholog, Belarusian State University, Minsk, Belarus*

Methodological base of this research is the function-stage model of ontogenetic development (Y.N. Karandashev, 1981). In this model a child mental development is considered as a development of system of mental functions. Purpose of research: the empirical analysis of correlation of leading mental functions and logic thinking in primary school age. 120 primary school children took part in research. We used the diagnostic techniques, which were constructed and approved by ourselves. Statistical method of data processing: the correlation analysis. The result of the research: development of leading mental functions is interconnected with development of thinking of primary school children.

Prevalence and chronicity of dating violence among a sample of South African university students

Bhana, Kerlanie *Dept. of Psychology, University of Fort Hare, East London, South Africa* **Nicholas, Lionel** *Psychology, University of Fort Hare, East London, South Africa*

This study used the Conflict Tactics Scale 2 to investigate the prevalence of dating violence at a South African university. This study provides data on rates of perpetration of physical assault, physical injury, sexual coercion and psychological aggression. The purpose of the current study was to identify the presence of any differences in the experiences of dating violence relative to gender.

Fear of heights and fear of victimization: Are they evolved subtypes of fear?

Binser, Martin Josef *Inst. für Psychologie, Universität München, München, Germany*

The present experiment gathered empirical evidence for at least two evolved subtypes of fear. In a reflex modulation study (N = 33) evidence was found that fear of heights and fear of victimization prepare different defense reflexes. The study examined how height and aggressor situations presented with immersive virtual environment technology modulate the startle response. In the aggressor situation fingers moved towards a flexion, which corresponds to the defense reaction of the startle response. However, in the height situation fingers moved towards an extension, which matches the reaction of the parachute reflex and other reflexes that aim to avoid injury by falling.

Interdisciplinary work and linkage to the Academy of Science - Development of the Institute of Psychology at Humboldt-University, Berlin

Blauwitz, Julia *Berlin, Germany*

The development of the Institute of Psychology at Humboldt-University, Berlin is summarized with special emphasis on links to the Academy of Science in Berlin. The former directors of the institute, Carl Stumpf, Kurt Gottschaldt, and Friedhart Klix, were members of the academy. Furthermore, the Academy of Science sent Wolfgang Köhler to Tenerife where he conducted the famous studies on intelligence in primates. In 1969 the Central Institute of Cybernetic and Information Processes was founded, starting a long tradition of interdisciplinary collaboration amongst the researchers at the Institute of Psychology and the Academy of Science.

The Butler Project: First results of usability validation of a cognitive and emotional tele-assistance system for elderly

Botella, Cristina *Dept. of Psychology, Universitat Jaume I, Castellón, Spain* **Castilla, Diana** *Psychology, Universitat Jaume I, Castellón, Spain* **Lozano, Jose Antonio** *Diseño Grafico Ingenieria, Univ. Politecnica Valencia, Valencia, Spain* **Alcañiz, Mariano** *Diseño Grafico ingenieria, Univ. Politecnica Valencia, Valencia, Spain* **Breton, Juana** *Psychology, Universitat Jaume I, Castellón, Spain* **Baños, Rosa** *Psychology, Universitatd de Valencial, Valencia, Spain* **García Palacios, Azucena** *Psychology, Universitat Jaume I, Castellón, Spain* **Quero, Soledad** *Psychology, Universitat Jaume I, Castellón, Spain*

The Butler Project offers a cognitive and emotional tele-assistance system for elderly people that allow carrying out early diagnosis, intervention, and monitoring of the physical, cognitive, and emotional state of elderly with the aim of improving their quality of life and preventing their social isolation. For this purpose it uses several tools based on telecommunication (e-mail, chat and videoconference) and virtual reality techniques (e.g., to induce positive emotional states). This work describes the first results on usability valida-

tion of the system in a sample selected from users without previous experience in the use of computers and users with some experience.

Burnout: A vulnerability factor for PTSD

Boudoukha, Abdel Halim *UFR de Psychologie, Université de Nantes, NANTES cedex 3, France*

The research aimed to study the effect of the burnout as a possible vulnerability factor for PTSD among French correctional professionals (CO's). 350 CO's participated in this study and filled in questionnaires of burnout, PTSD and questions about aggressions (with gun, physical, verbal or none). We have created a measure called "burnout level" according to a high, a moderate or a low burnout level. Results show that PTSD levels of CO's physically or by guns aggressed are significantly higher than those verbally or non aggressed but only when the "burnout level" is high. This suggests that burnout acts like a vulnerability factor for PTSD in "potentializing" the traumatic effect of an aggression.

Effects of community-social- and spouse-support on women's work-family-conflict in privatized vs. non-privatized Israeli kibutz

Braunstein-Bercovitz, Hedva *Tel-Aviv, Israel*

Differential effects of community social support (CSS) and spouse support (SS) on work-family-conflict (WFC) were examined in privatized (PV) and non-privatized (NPV) Israeli kibbutzim. Sixty women from dual-career families, 30 PV and 30 NPV, completed the Career-Family-Conflict and the Spouse-Support questionnaires. Stepwise regression (controlling for relevant variables) indicated that CSS ($p<0.03$) and SS ($p<0.007$) were significantly predictors of WFC. However, work-interfere-family (WIF) was predicted only by CSS ($p<0.02$), and family-interfere-work (FIW) only by SS ($p<0.001$), for both time and pressure. The relationships between WFC/WIF/FIW and CSS/SS are discussed.

The reform of Italian university and effects on teaching practices: A research with Psychology graduates at the Catholic University of Milan

Bruno, Andreina *Psychology Department, Università Cattolica, Milano, Italy* **Kaneklin, Cesare** *Psychology Department, Università Cattolica, Milano, Italy*

The study aims to monitor the changes introduced by the didactics reform in university (law decree n. 509 of 11/3/1999) on teaching setting and practices and on learning outcomes. The object is the Psychology degree course at the Catholic University in Milan. Methods: qualitative research using semi-structured interviews with 24 Psychology graduates matriculated in 2001. The results indicate that changes are in these areas: professionalism; the connection between the university and the labour world; the methodology of learning from experience. Finally, this study evidences the importance of learning setting and devices in order to support the reform of Italian university.

The role of self-discrepancy in eating disordered women's body image

Brytek-Matera, Anna *Dept. of Psychology, University of Silesia, Katowice, Poland*

Objective: Evaluation of domains of the self in women suffering from eating disorder. Methods: The Figure Rating Scale (Stunkard et al., 1983) was administered to 26 women with anorexia nervosa and 35 women with bulimia nervosa. Results: Anorexics present slimmer ideal-self ($p<0,001$) and ought-self ($p<0,01$) than bulimics. The results revealed significant differences between anorexics' and bulimics' actual-self and ideal-self (AN and BN), between ideal-self and ought-self (AN and BN) and between actual-self and ought-self (BN). Conclusion: The results suggest that eating disordered patients have an unrealistic ideal of their body image and demand as to how they should look.

Subjective body experience and attitude toward one's body in patients with eating disorder

Brytek-Matera, Anna Dept. of Psychology, University of Silesia, Katowice, Poland

Objective: Examining the relationship between body attitude and dissatisfaction with physical appearance among undergraduate females. Methods: Participants were 61 eating disordered patients. The measures include The Body Attitude Test (Probst et al., 1995) and the Body Image Avoidance Questionnaire (Rosen et al., 1991). Results: Significant relationships were seen between negative appreciation of body size and social outings, avoidance of tight-fitting clothes and eating restraint. Lack of familiarity with one's own body correlated with avoidance of tight-fitting clothes and social outings. General body dissatisfaction was dependent on the social outings, the avoidance of tight-fitting clothes and eating less. Conclusion: Negative self-evaluation with negative body image plays an important role in the eating disorder.

Lifetime prevalence and impact of stalking: Epidemiological data from Eastern Austria

Burger, Christoph School of Psychology, University of Vienna, Vienna, Austria Schild, Anne School of Psychology, University of Vienna, Vienna, Austria Stieger, Stefan Core Unit f. Medical Education, Medical University of Vienna, Vienna, Austria

Community-based studies of stalking in European countries are scarce. Our survey consisted of a stalking questionnaire and the WHO-5 well-being scale. We were able to replicate the data on the lifetime and point prevalence of stalking in a German speaking community reported by Dressing, Kuehner and Gass (2005). Almost 11% (n=43, 37 women, 6 men) of a total of 401 participants from Eastern Austria could be identified as stalking victims. Affected persons scored significantly lower on the WHO-5 well-being scale. We were unable to find any significant difference in stalking and well-being between participants in rural and urban areas.

To go or not to go: Chimpanzees' understanding of a human's goals

Buttelmann, David Inst. für Entw.-psychologie, Max-Planck-Institut EVAN, Leipzig, Germany Carpenter, Malinda Dept. of Develop. & Comp., Max Planck Institute EVAN, Leipzig, Germany Call, Josep Dept. of Develop. & Comp., Max Planck Institute EVAN, Leipzig, Germany Tomasello, Michael Dept. of Develop. & Comp., Max Planck Institute EVAN, Leipzig, Germany

In previous studies of great apes' understanding of others' goals, apes could have used subtle behavioral cues to pass. We ruled out such cues by making the experimenter's behavior identical in experimental and control test phases; the only difference was the context prior to test. Chimpanzees learned that when a human stood up she would feed them at another location, but when a novel, unexpected event happened, they changed their expectation - presumably based on their understanding that this event led to a new goal (Fisher's test: T+=46.0, N=10, p=.032). This suggests that apes are able to read others' goals.

Foraging in the Radial-Arm Maze: Anticipatory responses to predictable food

Cabrera, Felipe CEIC, University of Guadalajara, Guadalajara, Mexico

Operant procedures simulating foraging behavior had been widely used in experimental scenarios. In this experiment the objective was to analyze the foraging strategies of rats in an environment where multiple patches were available in the Radial-Arm Maze, where the prey values in patches were arranged according to an eight concurrent Fixed-Interval schedule of reinforcement. The results showed the pattern of choices among patches according to the systematic changes in the global prey density and the pattern of search and food procurement within the different patches. It is discussed the implications for the models in foraging behavior and spatial memory.

Causal reasoning in great apes: The tubes task

Cacchione, Trix Psychologie, Universität Zürich, Zürich, Switzerland

We investigated if great apes (as other species) show a gravity bias when tested with the tubes task or if they appreciate the causal function of the tube. Apes were confronted with four versions of the task: A transparent, an "acoustic", a "silent" and a painted two-dimensional (non-causal) "tube". Results indicate that apes do neither have a reliable gravity bias, nor understand the causal function of the tube. Even though there was evidence that they could integrate tube related causal information, they depended mainly on non-causal inferences when searching for an invisibly displaced object.

How do infertile couples following IVF-treatment consider their frozen embryos?

Cailleau, Françoise CP-122, Université Libre de Bruxelles, Bruxelles, Belgium Mottrie, Cindy CP-122, Université Libre de Bruxelles, Bruxelles, Belgium

Cryopreservation of embryos is a common practice of assisted reproduction techniques. It allows to replace only a small number of embryos at a time and to freeze surplus embryos for future use. Published literature suggest that infertile couples consider their embryos as potential children. A descriptive statistical analysis of 200 Informed Consents and clinical interviews of infertile couples following IVF-treatment confirm the hypothesis of an attachment to their frozen embryos.

EG and topography frequency in alcohol dependence offenders

Calzada, Ana Neurophysiology, Legal Medicine Institute, Havana, Cuba

Deficiency information processing capacity of CNS contribute to increase the likelihood of criminal act in alcohol dependence offenders The resting electroencephalogram was recorded in 12 alcohol dependence offenders, evaluated for forensic psychiatric and compared with 9 offenders without psychiatrics disorders. The features at visual inspection of the Electroencephalogram and the use of frequency domain quantitative analysis techniques are described. A high incidence of electroencephalographic abnormalities was found in the alcohol dependence offenders. Electrogenesis alterations attenuated alpha rhythm and global delta-theta slow activity and excess of beta activity in posterior regions. The quantitative analysis confirmed the results of EEG visual analysis.

Quality and quantitative EEG abnormalities in offenders with Antisocial Personality Disorder

Calzada, Ana Neurophysiology, Legal Medicine Institute, Havana, Cuba Alvarez, Alfredo Neurophysiology, Cuban Neuroscience Center, Havana, Cuba

This investigation contributes to electrophysiological characterization of the offenders. Resting electroencephalogram was studied in a group of offenders evaluated at Psychiatric Department at the Legal Medicine Institute in Cuba (18 with ASPD and 10 without psychiatric diagnosis). Characteristics of the EEG visual inspection and quantitative analysis techniques are described. Both groups were compared to Cuban normative database. High incidences of electroencephalographic abnormalities were found. The most frequent: electrogenesis alterations, attenuated alpha rhythm and theta and delta activities increase in the frontal lobe. The quantitative analysis theta and delta frequencies were increased and alpha activity was decreased in both groups.

Primary documents sources of history of psychology: Constitution of the archives of documents from the selection and professional Orientation Service (1949-1994)

Campos, Regina Célia Faculdade de Educação, Univ. Estado de Minas Gerais, Belo Horizonte, Brazil Bellico, Anna Edith Faculdade de Educação, Univ. Estado de Minas Gerais, Belo Horizonte-MG, Brazil

The research intends to communicate to the scientific community the new documentary sources on History of Psychology in Brazil, originated of the Service of Orientation and Professional Selection-SOSP(1949-1994): psychological findings and tests of selection for the ingression in agencies and schools. The documentary research formed a Data Base: (1)Adolescents: 326 archives with 12.307 tests; (2)Adults: 690 archives with 41.953 tests; (3)Children: 212 archives with 9.282 tests. Moreover, 8.219 psychological findings to orientation, individually applied. The debate on the contributions of psychological evaluation in History of Psychology is in opened, is an invitation for the interlocution between the fields to know.

Parental characteristics and practices and children early disruptive behaviours

Carbonneau, Rene Paediatrics, University of Montreal, Montreal, Canada Liu, Xuecheng GRIP, University of Montreal, Montreal, Canada Boivin, Michel Psychology, Laval University, Montreal, Canada Tremblay, Richard Paediatrics, University of Montreal, Montreal, Canada

The aim of this study was to investigate the association between parental characteristics and parental practices and the trajectories of Disruptive Behaviours (DBs) during early childhood. Method: Trajectories of DBs were assessed based on annual mother interviews from 17 to 60 months for a Canadian population-representative birth cohort (N=2057). Results: Frequency of DBs increased from 17 to 41 months and then tended to decline. Parental characteristics and parental practices were both associated with chronic trajectories of DBs. Conclusion: Early childhood is a critical period to prevent later DBs during school years that leads to psychosocial maladjustment during adolescence and adulthood.

Attachment to peers and depressive symptomatology: A study in preadolescents

Carmen, Senra Rivera Clinical Psychology, University Santiago Compostela, Santiago de Compostela, Spain Seoane, Gloria Methodology, University Santiago Compostela, Santiago de Compostela, Spain Vilas, Vanessa Clinical Psychology, University Santiago Compostela, Santiago de Compostela, Spain

This study analyzed the influence of peer attachment pattern in depressive symptoms in a sample of Spanish preadolescents. Participants were 656 children, 334 boys (Mage = 13.36; SD =0.55) and 322 girls (Mage = 13.29; SD =.47). All of them filled the peer attachment subscale of the Inventory of Parent and Peer Attachment (Armsden & Greenberg, 1987) and the Children Depression Inventory (Kovacks, 1992). The results indicated significant main effects for attachment and sex in depression symptoms, but not the interaction between depression variable and sex. The findings support the hypothesis that the vulnerability to depression differs in function of peer attachment pattern, independently of gender.

Gender, guilt and parenting styles: A comparison between employed and non-employed mothers

Carrasco, Maria Jose Dept. de Psicologia, Universidad Pontificia Comilla, Madrid, Spain *Martinez, Pilar* Psicologia, Universidad Pontificia Comilla, Madrid, Spain *Aza, Gonzalo* Psicologia, Universidad Pontificia Comilla, Madrid, Spain *Blanco, Angeles* Metodos de Investigacion y Dia, Universidad Complutense de Mad, Madrid, Spain *Espinar, Isabel* Psicologia, Universidad Pontificia Comilla, Madrid, Spain

The aim of this poster is to present the results of an ongoing research project with a sample of employed and non-employed Spanish mothers with children at a very demanding age (between 3 and 6 years). The selected variables are parental stress, feelings of guilt about childrearing, parenting styles, maternal role ideology, and child psychological development. Three main objectives of this research should be highlighted: a) to examine the differences in guilt feelings and intensive mothering ideology b) to test the relationship between guilt and permissive parenting styles and c) to evaluate differences in socioemotional development between children.

Beyond a single pattern of mixed emotional experience: Sequential, prevalent, inverse, and genuine simultaneous

Carrera, Pilar Psicologia Social y Metodologi, Universidad Autonoma de Madrid, Madrid, Spain *Oceja, Luis* Psicologia Social y Metodologi, Universidad Autonoma de Madrid, Madrid, Spain

We designed an Analogical Emotional Scale to measure mixed emotions (Carrera & Oceja, 2006). This scale permits the analysis of how two opposite emotions (e.g., happiness and sadness) evolve from the beginning to the end of the experience, allowing discrimination between simultaneous and three patterns of sequential mixed emotional experiences. Distinguishing between these patterns is important, since it sheds light on the theoretical controversy between the bipolar and bivariate models of emotions and the AES opens up an interesting field of research on the factors that may cause one pattern or another and, more importantly, the potential consequences on behaviors.

History of early-modern psychological healing in Brazil and Portugal

Carvalho da Silva, Paulo José Graduate Program, PUC- SP, São Paulo, Brazil

Consoling those who are in pain has a long history. We focus on some early-modern Portuguese-language writings on consolation, gathered in historical archives. A comparative analysis suggests diverse authors developed guides to relieving emotional distress such as sorrow, grief and despair. Their main goal was to bring comfort and to advise about the expression of emotions. We discuss how the study of this ancient form of psychological healing enhances our understanding of the history of psychological treatments.

Spoken and written dream communication: Differences and methodological aspects

Casagrande, Maria Dipartimento di Psicologia, Roma, Italy *Cortini, Paolo* Dipartimento di Psicologia, "sapienza" Università, Roma, Italy

Based on structural differences between spoken and written language, the purpose of this paper was to investigate whether spoken and written communication imply a different representation in reporting an experienced dream. Three hundred subjects tape recording their own dreams and putting them down in writing. The reports were analyzed by a psycholinguistic system. Results indicated that the report modality is able to affect the dream experience representation, conditioning the figurative (re)translation carried out by the tester: written forms show a loss of hallucinatory information and a non-complete correspondence also of the bizarreness features with respect to the spoken texts.

Psychology at the Gregorian University in Rome

Ceglie, Flavio Pathological Anatomy, University of Bari (Italy), Bari, Italy *Monacis, Lucia* Department of Psychology, University of Bari (Italy), Bari, Italy

The Pontifical Gregorian University in Rome merits attention because of its role in the psychological training of the international Catholic clergy. The aim of our research is concerned with the reconstruction of the various courses in experimental psychology, starting from the teaching held by Joseph Fröbes. His appointment was a step of special significance because it was a formal recognition of psychology as separate and independent from philosophy in circles which traditionally regarded psychology as an integral part of philosophy. Moreover, our attention focuses on up-to-day forgotten psychologists as J. Lindworsky, A. Willwoll, P. Siwek, A. Godin, and F. Gaetani.

On university students' self-confidence personality and its development

Che, Liping College of Management, USST, Shanghai, People's Republic of China

Nowadays we paid more attention to creative education and all-around development of students, we should attach great importance to self-confidence personality development of the talented person. This paper provided some suggestions for the university students' self-confidence personality development and the college educational reformation by two models. One is to start special training curriculum for self-confidence education; The other is to make the self-confidence personality education melt into the existed education. The university education would benefit from following aspects: promoting self-confidence consciousness; strengthening achievement motivation educating; increasing success experience of students; giving timely feedback and affirmation appraisals; carrying on moderate frustration education.

The Cross-Country Comparison of the Related Sequence Model in science achievement, science attitude, and learning participation: Taking seven Asia counties for example

Chen, Shin-Feng Education, National Pingtung University, Taiwan, Taiwan

This study was based on the structural equation modeling built by TIMSS 2003 survey, including the Taiwan fourth graders' family resource, school learning atmosphere, scientific attitude and science achievement. This Taiwan structural equation modeling was used to compare with the Japan, Singapore, Hong-Kong, Australia, New Zealand, and Philippines. All the results fitted the hypotheses in this study. Most of the potential factors showed positive and direct effects.

Gender-differentiated biases of perceived facial emotions in anxious and dysphoric individuals

Chen, Sue-Huei Dept. of Psychology, National Taiwan University, Taipei, Taiwan *Tseng, Huai-Hsuan* Psychiatry, NationalTaiwanUniversity Hosp., Taipei, Taiwan *Huang, Yu-Lien* Psychology, National Taiwan University, Taipei, Taiwan

Research evidences and clinical observations suggest that depressed individuals tend to negatively perceive other's emotions. This study aimed to explore if gender as well as interpersonal sensitivity and depression together play any roles in negatively biased perception of facial emotions. We first developed a series of photos with various facial expressions and then designed computerized presentation for individual assessment. Preliminary findings suggest that interpersonal anxiety and depression may bias perception of various facial emotions differently for males and females. Future research concerning culture-relevant and gender-specific biases of facial emotion perception and plausible clinical applications are accordingly discussed.

Possessing absence: An exploratory study of a hijra's life

Cherian, Diana Dept. Clinical Psychology, Fortis Flt. Lt. Rajan Dhall H, New Delhi, India *Nagpal, Ashok* Psychology, Arts faculty, Delhi University, New Delhi, India

"Hijras"- this institutionalized third gender has been ignored by psychological research, resulting in erroneous analogies drawn between them and transsexuals in Western nations. This study investigates the subjective meanings of lives as narrated by a hijra. A case study format has been adopted and thematic analysis utilized to interpret qualitative data obtained from the semi structured interview. Numerous themes emerged including individualized gender construction, perceptions of a sexual relationship, and conception of self concept. The central theme was the incapacity to possess one relationship in totality. The absence of a figure that can be possessed emotionally, sexually and mentally surfaced as the essence of their existence.

Eye-tracking investigation of cognitive flexibility in preschoolers

Chevalier, Nicolas LPC (UMR 6146), University of Provence, Marseille, France *Blaye, Agnès* LPC (UMR 6146), University of Provence, Marseille (cedex 3), France

Cognitive flexibility contributes to executive functioning and is assessed in preschoolers with tasks such as the Advanced Dimensional Change Card Sort (DCCS; Zelazo, 2006) which requires switching between picture-matching rules by shape and colour. This study assessed what information preschoolers consider while switching or maintaining matching rules. Five- to 6-year-old children's eye movements were collected on versions of the Advanced DCCS that differed in interference level (integrated vs. dissociated dimensions on the stimuli). Comparison of eye fixation patterns – a novel methodology in this field of research – offered new insight in the processes underlying cognitive flexibility in preschoolers.

Stimulus-location based analysis of visual fields by combining an eye tracker with the campimetric assessment

Cieslik, Silvana Institut of Medical Psychology, Otto-von-Guericke University, Magdeburg, Germany *Günther, Tobias* Institut of Medical Psychology, Otto-von-Guericke University, Magdeburg, Germany *Müller, Iris* Institut of Medical Psychology, Otto-von-Guericke University, Magdeburg, Germany *Sabel, Bernhard A.* Institut of Medical Psychology, Otto-von-Guericke University, Magdeburg, Germany

Eye movements are an important natural behavior to explore visual scenes. Especially in hemianopic subjects who suffered from brain damage, eye movements are used to compensate for visual field loss. To measure the visual field independent of eye movements, we present an interface between a campimetric diagnostic system and an infrared-based eye tracker (50 Hz, long term error <1°) which allows to measure eye movements explicitly for each presented stimulus. By using this newly designed interface, we are able to analyze fixation instability in computer-based assessments of visual field defect. For validation of this new interface, data of visual field diagnostics of hemianopic and healthy subjects are used.

Effectiveness of culturally adapted violence prevention with children from Latin America: A multi-country report

Clinton, Amanda Dept. of Psychology, Universidad de Puerto Rico, Rincon, Puerto Rico *Amesty, Elvia* Director, Fundación Senderos, Maracaibo, Venezuela

This study evaluated a culturally adapted violence prevention program for very young children from three countries: Guatemala, El Salvador, and

Venezuela. In each country, 100 children received a school-based intervention program during the academic year; 100 controls received no treatment. ANOVA completed on data from individual child interviews, parent questionnaires, and teacher questionnaires indicated a statistically significant decrease (p<.005) in aggressive behavior and a statistically significant increase in pro-social behavior (p<.001); controls demonstrated an increase in aggression and no change in social skills. Conclusions address the importance of universal violence prevention within a cultural context beginning at very young ages.

The relationships between clinical and personality features in a non-clinical sample
Combaluzier, Serge Dépt. de Psychologie, Université de Rouen, Mont-Saint-Aignan, France
The aim of this communication is to explore the relationships between clinical and personality features in a sample of 153 students. The data collected by using SCL 90r and PDQ4 has been computed on statistical software (SPSS) and let us produce a model of interactions between global severity index and clinical and personality features that has been validated by structural modelling equation software (Amos.5 ®).

Television and the Family Context
Conde, Elena Psicología Evolutiva, University of La Laguna, La Laguna, Spain León, Nieves Psicología Evolutiva, University of La Laguna, La Laguna, Spain Torres, Esteban Psicología Evolutiva, University of La Laguna, La Laguna, Spain
This work analyses familiar habits of television viewing on a sample of 527 families with children who responded to the questionnaire on consumption habits, family audiovisual context, attitudes toward the contents of television and media administration. The results show what variables are related to the high consumption of television in children. Finally, we will be giving some strategies to reduce the level of television viewing among children and how to mediate in the children's experience in front of television.

The parents working in Europe migration's effects on the behavior of Romanian children
Constantinescu, Maria Sociology and Social Work, University of Pitesti, Pitesti, Romania Constantinescu, Cornel Sociology and Social Work, University of Pitesti Romania, Pitesti, Romania
The study marks out the consequences of living away parents on the children's personality. We analyzed a lot 250 of pupils using direct observation, the interviews technique, questionnaires and the study of school documents. The results show that the children' separation from their parents determines different behaviors depending on the child's age and the person (institution) that takes care of the child. The children who live with grandparents have good school performances. On the emotional plan they are more troubled. Those who are in Care Institutions have almost the same performances. On the emotional plan, they present negative emotional states.

Is gambling satisfactory?
Contini, Paolo Dept. of Psychology, University of Bari, Bari, Italy
The present research aims at analysing the kind of correlation between gambling and Bingo players' well-being and pleasureness. The empirical investigation involved 2200 Italian subjects ranging in age from 28 to 57, and it was divided into four phases. Participants rated: 1. their agreement on a 5-Likert scale, 2. the amount of money, 3. their frequency of gambling; 4. the level of their introversion/extroversion. Findings, analysed by Manova, showed that: 1. the level of well-being/pleasureness was in inverse relation to the amount of money; 2. there was a

direct relation between well-being/pleasureness and their capacity for relationships.

A measure of response inhibition with single trial resolution
Contreras Ros, David Experimental Psychology, Universidad de Granada, Granada, Spain Gómez Cuerva, Julia Psychology, Bangor University, Bangor, United Kingdom Catena, Andrés Experimental Psychology, Universidad de Granada, Granada, Spain
This study aimed to find a reliable electroencephalographic (EEG) measure of response inhibition with single trial resolution. Sixteen volunteers performed, in a single experimental session, three tasks assumed to require motor inhibition (Eriksen, stop-signal, go/no-go) while EEG activity (62 channels) was recorded. Using intrasubject independent component analysis (ICA) we identified a mediofrontal component in 11 of the participants that was more active in inhibitory (no-go, incompatible, and stop) trials than in non-inhibitory trials, and had a timing consistent with an inhibitory function. Since ICA does not involve averaging across trials, these results show ICA can provide an index of response inhibition with single-trial resolution.

Evolutionary trade-off: Inter and intersexual differences in propensity to casual sex and alcohol comsumption on different age Brazilian samples
Correa Varella, Marco Antonio Psicologia Experimental - IP, Universidade de Sao Paulo, Sao Paulo, Brazil Ferreira, José Henrique Psicologia Experimental - IP, Universidade de São Paulo, São Paulo, Brazil Bussab, Vera Silvia Psicologia Experimental - IP, Universidade de São Paulo, São Paulo, Brazil
We test if the same trade-off between mating and parental domains explains inter and intrasexual variations in sociosexuality and alcohol consumption (doses in parties). 221 undergraduates (21 years) and 81 adults (38 years) answered the Sociosexual Orientation Inventory (Simpson & Gangestad, 1991). Risk taking was associated with lower parental investment. As predicted, in both age groups: men were more unrestricted and consume more alcohol doses (ANOVA); and women (both ages) and men (undergraduate) more unrestricted consume more alcohol doses (r-Pearson). Trade-offs Allocation Theory of Relevant Effort supplies a unified explanation for sex differences and individual variations in each sex.

The dietary intake of people with pre-diabetes: A comparison between two self-report measures
Crafti, Naomi Faculty of LSS, Swinburne University, Hawthorn, Australia Hackworth, Naomi Psychology, Swinburne University, Hawthorn, Australia Moore, Sue Psychology, Swinburne University, Hawthorn, Australia
In diabetes prevention and treatment, as in other areas of lifestyle management, an accurate assessment of dietary intake is essential. This study evaluated a sample of data collected from 500 pre-diabetic participants in a lifestyle intervention and compares eating patterns assessed using the Food Choices Questionnaire (FCQ), a 16 item measure of eating patterns based on the Dietary Guidelines for Australian Adults (NHMRC, 2003) and a Three – Day Food Diary. The contribution of fibre, fat and other nutrients to overall energy intake was assessed and compared to nutritional recommendations. Correlations between food intake determined by the food-diary and the FCQ were also calculated. The results have implications for the use of dietary assessment instruments in nutritional interventions.

The developmental of children's perceptions of oral health and disease
Croker, Steve Dept. of Psychology, University of Derby, Derby, United Kingdom Buchanan, Heather IWHO, University of Nottingham, Nottingham, United Kingdom
Objectives: This study aimed to explore age-related differences in children's perceptions of oral health and disease. Methods: 71 children aged 4-11 were interviewed in schools. Questions were based on knowledge of behaviours that contribute to oral health. The data were coded used content analysis. Results: Even very young children demonstrated a basic understanding of behaviours that contribute to oral health. However, older children were more likely to mention that drinks (p<0.005) and oral care (p<0.001) affect the health of teeth. Conclusions: Children's knowledge of oral health develops over time. This has implications for oral health promotion to different age groups.

Masculinity: An overview
Cronan, Kerry Richard Counselling Centre Ltd., Professional Consulting and, Eagle Farm, Australia
Gender awareness and research has become a topic of increasing interest, particularly in Western psychology. The greatest interest would appear to come from the Anglo-Celtic based professional psychological interest in the psychotherapeutic perspective. The subject of masculinity is slowly becoming mainstream in academic institutions, but has captured a wide interest in academic journals as an undoubted preliminary to becoming more widespread at the tertiary studies level. This presentation will trace the history of the development of the psychological study of masculinity, evaluate the progress and integration of these studies, and project future opportunities for the development of this burgeoning topic.

Oh psychologist, where art thou?
Cronan, Kerry Richard Counselling Centre Ltd., Professional Consulting and, Eagle Farm, Australia
The development of the profession of psychology in its short history has been slow in comparison to other professions. It is now often forgotten that psychology grew out of the long-standing study of philosophy. In some instances, e.g. the recent studies of the psychology of wisdom, there has been a return to and acknowledgment of this philosophical background. This presentation will trace the historical progress of the profession of psychology from its origins in philosophy and also evaluate the barriers in the pathway of its development thus far, and promote future opportunities for integrated advancement.

"Girls just wanna have fun?" Impact of students gender on status and growth in their emotional development during language instruction
Cronjäger, Hanna Konstanz, Germany
Aim of this study is to investigate students emotional development in foreign language instruction e.g. whether emotional status and growth can be regarded as dependent of students gender. To investigate this question, N = 779 sixth graders were asked four times over their first year of learning French as foreign language to indicate their experienced emotions (anxiety, anger, boredom and joy), as well as other relevant predictors of emotions in a survey study. Analysis of multilevel hierarchical modelling yielded over all significant effects for students gender with regard to status and growth for all but anxiety.

In-group favoritism in leadership evaluations: A gender perspective
Cuadrado, Isabel Dept. de Psicologia Social, Open University Madrid, Madrid, Spain Molero, Fernando PSICOLOGÍA SOCIAL Y DE LAS ORG, OPEN UNIVERSITY (MADRID, SPAIN, MADRID, Spain Garcia

Ael, Cristina PSICOLOGÍA SOCIAL Y DE LAS ORG, OPEN UNIVERSITY (MADRID, SPAIN, MADRID, Spain
The aim of this study is to analyze gender differences in leadership style and work-related traits. 613 participants evaluated to their respective managers using the MLQ-5X and a 27-adjective list. Analysis of variance showed an interaction effect between the sex of the leader and the sex of the subordinate: women and men show in-group favoritism in their evaluations. On the other hand, both men and women think that efficacy-related traits are more applicable to male than to female managers, and women applies stereotypically feminine characteristics to describe their leaders. These results are interpreted according to psychosocial literature about gender.

The effectiveness of psychological health-protection exercise for alleviating students' learning fatigue

Cui, Lizhong Department of Psychology, Anhui Normal University, Wuhu, People's Republic of China
Objectives: Test the effectiveness of Psychological Health-protection Exercise which combined Progressive Muscular Rlaxation with Chinese tai chi chuan and Indian yoga for alleviating students' learning fatigue in their spare time. Methods: In school situations, experimental group do the exercise everyday for a month while the control group act as usual, and do one decoding test per week for each group. Analyze the difference of decoding score between them by T-test. Results: The experimental group was significantly superior to the control group. Conclusions: The exercise is generally suitable for 6-24 years-old male and female students and should be popularized for large-scale.

Down syndrome parents worries about their children: Iranian family pattern

Dadkhah, Asghar Dept. of Clinical Psychology, University of Welfare & Rehab., Tehran, Islamic Republic of Iran Pourmohammadi Roudsari, Moloud Dept. of Clinical Psychology, University of Welfare & Re, Tehran, Islamic Republic of Iran Hemmati, Sahel Dept. of Clinical Psychology, University of Welfare & Re, Tehran, Islamic Republic of Iran
To find out how children with down syndromes get on with life is one main source of worry. Some children's physical or mental disabilities mean that extra provision will always have to be made for them. Totally 61 persons with Down syndrome out of 127 available populations ages between 3 to 18 years were selected. In four stages by questionnaire and interview of families and specialists the problem was find out and categorized. The major worries of families were: at birth have physical problems, their health, poor explanation condition by professionals, and not a structural program and organizations for referral.

Consciousness changing the photoelectric conversion principle by slow mass wave

Dayong, Cao Sciences, Beijing Natural Providence, Beijing, People's Republic of China
The experiment results show that human consciousness can change Voc and Isc of solar cell at isolation air. This is the first record of consciousness signal through an experiment in the world. (2002,Oct,22) Consciousness can control the slow mass wave of the brain signal to act on photoelectric system. The system magnifies it. Consciousness' behavior and it's evolves is aggressively and self-determined, and it is in a spiritual level, which has the psychological defense mechanism; The brain signal and it's evolves is a receiving process which results in stimulation, it's in physiological terms, which has the psychological offense mechanism.

Mood and effort mobilization: Context rules!

de Burgo, Joana Dept. of Psychology, University of Geneva, Geneva, Switzerland
Based on the Mood-Behavior-Model and the mood-as-input approach, two experiments tested moods' informational impact and manipulated demand appraisals on effort-related cardiovascular response. 79 students were randomly assigned to a 2 (Mood) x 3 (Effort Rule) x 2 (Time) design, including habituation, mood manipulations, and a mental task. Data analysis revealed the expected interaction: systolic blood pressure reactivity was stronger in a positive mood in the enjoy-rule condition, whereas in a negative mood more effort was mobilized in the no-instructions and enough-rule conditions. Therefore, mood effects on effort mobilization were moderated by the judgment for which mood was used as information.

Concepts of mental health and barriers to help services from the perspective of children and parents: Recent results from the AMHC-(Access to Mental Health Care in Children)-Study

de Oliveira Käppler, Christoph Special Education, Univ. of Education Ludwigsburg, Reutlingen, Germany Goncalves, Marta Child & Adolescent Psychia, Univ. of Zurich, Zurich, Switzerland Gianella, Daria Child & Adolescent Psyicha, Univ. of Zurich, Zurich, Switzerland Zehnder, Sabine Child & Adolescent Psychia, Univ. of Zurich, Zurich, Switzerland Peng, Aristide Child & Adolescent Psychia, Univ. of Zurich, Zurich, Switzerland Mohler-Kuo, Meichun Social and Preventive Medicine, Univ. of Zurich, Zurich, Switzerland
The AMHC-(Access to Mental Health Care in Children)-Study conducted initionally in Switzerland and now extended internationally (to Italy and Brazil) aims at a better understanding of concepts and needs in mental health and of existing barriers to prevention and intervention from the perspective of children and their families. Results show similarities and many differences in concepts of mental health and illness as well as on help seeking strategies between generations and different clinical/ risk groups. Also cultural differences were found. A better knowledge of those concepts of mental health/illness and help-seeking strategies is needed to bridge the need-service gaps for children, adolescents and their families.

A microgenetic study of the development of indirect addition as an alternative strategy for doing two-digit subtraction

de Smedt, Bert Dept. of Educational Sciences, Katholieke Universiteit Leuven, Leuven, Belgium Stassens, Nick Educational Sciences, Katholieke Universiteit Leuven, Leuven, Belgium Torbeyns, Joke Educational Sciences, Katholieke Universiteit Leuven, Leuven, Belgium Ghesquière, Pol Educational Sciences, Katholieke Universiteit Leuven, Leuven, Belgium Verschaffel, Lieven Educational Sciences, Katholieke Universiteit Leuven, Leuven, Belgium
This microgenetic study investigated the development of indirect addition (IA) as an alternative strategy for doing two-digit subtraction in two IA-favouring instructional conditions. Thirty-five third-graders who did not master IA participated in a strong (n=20) or weak (n=15) IA-favouring condition. Over a period of six weeks, children participated in nine individual sessions: four training sessions, three test sessions, one transfer session, and one retention session. The results revealed that throughout the study IA was used only rarely, even by children who got explicit instruction and practice in IA during the training sessions. But when used, IA was executed remarkably efficiently.

Academic achievement and personality in prosocial students of secondary education

Delgado Domenech, Beatriz Dept. of Health Psychology, M. Hernandez Univ. of Elche, Elche, Spain Ingles Saura, Candido Jose Health Psychology, Miguel Hernández University, Elche, Spain Torregrosa Diez, Maria Soledad Health Psychology, Miguel Hernández University, Elche, Spain Garcia Fernandez, Jose Manuel Education, University of Alicante, San Vicente del Raspeig, Spain
Objective. To analyze the Eysenck's personality variables, and the predictive value of these variables on the academic achievement in Spanish prosocial students of secondary education. Method. Teenage Inventory of Social Skills (TISS) and Eysenck Personality Questionnaire (EPQ) were administered to 978 participants. Descriptive analyses, means differences and logistic regression were used. Results. Prosocial students showed significantly higher scores in neuroticism and extraversion and significantly lower scores in psychoticism than non prosocial students. Psychoticism turned out as a risk factor for academic success. Conclusions. Psychoticism was a negative and significant predictor of academic achievement in prosocial adolescents.

Academic achievement and personality in antisocial Spanish adolescents

Delgado Domenech, Beatriz Dept. of Health Psychology, M. Hernandez Univ. of Elche, Elche, Spain Torregrosa Diez, Maria Soledad Health Psychology, Miguel Hernandez University of, Elche, Spain Ingles Saura, Candido Jose Health Psychology, Miguel Hernandez University of, Elche, Spain Garcia Fernandez, Jose Manuel Education, University of Alicante, San Vicente del Raspeig, Spain
Objective. To analyze Eysencks personality traits and its predictive value on academic achievement in antisocial secondary education students. Method. Antisocial Behavior subscale of the Teenage Inventory of Social Skills (TISS) and Eysenck Personality Questionnaire (EPQ) were used. Data were analysed through mean differences and logistic regression. Results. Antisocial students showed significant lower scores in Neuroticism, Extraversion and Psychoticism than their non-antisocial peers. Logistic regression states that Psychoticism is as a risk factor for antisocial students academic performance. Conclusions. Antisocial students differed from their non-antisocial peers in personality traits. Psychoticism was found as a negative predictor of antisocial students school success.

Academic achievement and personality in social anxious students

Delgado Domenech, Beatriz Dept. of Health Psychology, M. Hernandez Univ. of Elche, Elche, Spain Ingles Saura, Candido Jose Health Psychology, Miguel Hernández University, Elche, Spain Torregrosa Diez, Maria Soledad Health Psychology, Miguel Hernández University, Elche, Spain Garcia Fernandez, Jose Manuel Education, University of Alicante, San Vicente del Raspeig, Spain
Objective. To analyze the Eysenck's personality variables, and the predictive value of these variables on the academic achievement in Spanish students of secondary education with social anxiety. Method. Social Phobia and Anxiety Inventory (SPAI) and Eysenck Personality Questionnaire (EPQ) were administered to 978 participants. Descriptive analyses, means differences and logistic regression were used. Results. Adolescents with social anxiety showed significantly higher scores in neuroticism and lower scores in extraversion than students without social anxiety. Psychoticism appeared as a risk factor for academic achievement. Conclusions. Psychoticism was a negative predictor of the school success in adolescents with social anxiety.

Psychopathology in a sample of Greek Cypriot students

Demetriou, Andreas *Psychology, University of Cyprus, Larnaca, Cyprus* **Kapsou, Margarita** *Psychology, University of Cyprus, Nicosia, Cyprus* **Georgia, Panayiotou** *Psychology, University of Cyprus, Nicosia, Cyprus*

The Child Behavior Checklist was administered in a sample of 121 Greek Cypriot Students (63 boys, 58 girls; M age=11.73) and their mothers. The mother's and children's reports indicated good overall agreement. Overall, boys tended to report psychopathology within the clinical range more than girls. Mothers were significantly more likely to report clinical scores on any of the subscales for boys. Chi square tests in the children's reports identified a statistically significant gender difference only for the oppositional-defiant problems scale. Interestingly, mothers were much more likely to report anxiety and emotional problems within the clinical level for boys.

The correlations between playing computer games involving violence and displays of aggression by the players

Denglerova, Denisa *Department of Social Pedagogy, Masaryk University, Brno, Czech Republic*

The paper addresses phenomenon of playing computer games. Respondents were divided into three groups (occasional-players, regular-players and computer-game-addict) according to time spent on playing. The results show the correlation between intensive playing of violent computer games and higher scores in Caprara Tolerance-toward-Violence Scale. Important is the high correlation between the respondent's own appraisal of aggression in games and total score in Caprara scales (especially Dissipation-Rumination Scale. The results show, that objective measurement of violent scenes (their number, intensity and life-likeness) doesn't sufficiently explain how they affect player's personality. Next research should aim to semantic methods and individual diagnostic detecting how the person construes the violent scenes presented in computer games.

Brazilian fathers participation during pregnancy and childbirth

Dessen, Maria Auxiliadora *Developmental and Educational, Institute of Psychology, Brasilia, Brazil* **Oliveira, Maira Ribeiro** *Developmental and Educational, Institute of Psychology, Brasilia, Brazil*

Recent literature has shown that father's contribution to the familys welfare during the period of gestation and immediately after children are born is important, especially considering mothers. This study aims to report fathers' participation during this period, according to 45 pregnant women and 42 women with babies from the working class. Data was collected by the administration of a family social demographic questionnaire and a semi-structured interview. The results show that fathers engage in few domestic tasks, and have only specific obligations to children. However, the majority of mothers reported that they are satisfied with the fathers' engagement in family life.

Brazilian grandparents' influence on family life during the birth of their grandchildren

Dessen, Maria Auxiliadora *Developmental and Educational, Institute of Psychology, Brasilia, Brazil* **Oliveira, Maira Ribeiro** *Institute of Psychology, University of Brasilia-UnB, Brasilia, Brazil*

Grandparents play a very supportive role to their children and their new family, especially during transitions due to the birth of a baby. This study aims to describe the grandparents' participation during this period, according to 45 pregnant women and 42 women with babies from the working class. A family social demographic questionnaire was administered and a semi-structured interview was carried out with the mothers. Most of them reported that grandparents, particularly grand-mothers, use counselling as the main strategy to transmit values and beliefs to the family, especially in relation to the grandchildren's education and the couple's relationship.

Do infants differentiate the unwilling state from the unable state?

Destrebecqz, Arnaud *Cognitive Science Unit, Universite Libre Bruxelles, Bruxelles, Belgium* **Legrain, Laure** *S.R.S.C., Université Libre de Bruxelles, Bruxelles, Belgium* **Cleeremans, Axel** *S.R.S.C., Université Libre de Bruxelles, Bruxelles, Belgium*

Three years ago, Behne, Carpenter, Call and Tomasello (2005) showed that infants react differently when the experimenter refuses to give them a toy or when she can not give it. In this replication, we used a mechanical display in order to make the experimenter's inability to give the toy more explicit and to control for eye contact between the infant and the experimenter. Even though we did not observe the same patterns of results, we observe, as in the original study, several differences in infant's behavior depending on the experimenter's intention. As we extent and replicate Behne et al's results, we also conclude that infants attribute intentional states from 9 months up.

Medicine and the clinic psychology

Diandomba, Andre *Dept. of Psychiatry, Service Medical Armee du Salut, Brazzaville, Congo, Democratic Republic of the*

Medicine and the clinic psychology or the psychology of health is an approach of the models and theories psychological concerning health and the disease and articulation with the related fields. The psychologist, doctor must acquire knowledge on the aspects cognitive, emotional, behavioral, biological and social which exert an influence on health. To know at the same time of the ideal models (biomedical, psychosomatic, bio-psycho-social), of the methods of intervention and the fields of application of the psychology of health. Psychological health thus approaches: - beliefs and representations of health and the disease; - the factors of the environment which affect physical health, psychic and social of the individuals; - individual factors of vulnerability and protection to the disease; - mediators of the relations between individual and environmental antecedents and criteria of health (including the well-being and the quality of life). the psychological good being acts on physical and psychicologic health human. Psychological health rests primarily on three pillars: the society, work and the person.

Measuring need to evaluate: A Spanish exploration

Diaz, Dario *Dept. of Social Psychology, Universidad Autonoma de Madrid, Madrid, Spain* **Briñol, Pablo** *Social Psychology, Universidad Autonoma de Madrid, Madrid, Spain* **Horcajo, Javier** *Social Psychology, Universidad Autonoma de Madrid, Madrid, Spain* **Gandarillas, Beatriz** *Dept. of Social Psychology, Universidad Autonoma de Madrid, Madrid, Spain*

Introduction and Objetives. Individual differences in need to evaluate can be reliably assessed with the Need to Evaluate (NE) Scale (Jarvis & Petty, 1996). The main purpose of the present work was to adapt the NE scale to Spanish, and to assess its reliability, factorial validity, and psychometric properties. Results and Conclusions. The first study revealed that the Spanish version of the NE scale had a good internal consistency. Factorial analyses suggested a bifactorial solution (Need to Evaluate – Preference for Neutrality). The second study confirmed that the scale also showed good properties in terms of convergent and discriminatory validity.

Age of acquisition and proficiency on L2 syntactic processing

Diaz, Begoña *GRNC, Parc Científic UB, Esplugues, Spain* **Sebastián Gallés, Núria** *GRNC, Parc Científic UB, Esplugues, Spain* **Erdozia, Kepa** *Unité INSERM 562, Serv. Hosp. Frédéric Joliot, Paris, France* **L. Mueller, Jutta** *Neuropsychology, Max Planck Institute, Leipzig, Germany* **Laka, Itziar** *Philology&General Linguist, University oftheBasque Country, Bilbao, Spain*

Electrophysiological studies have shown that high proficient late L2 learners show native-like patterns of event related potentials (ERP) when processing an L2. In the present study two typologically very different languages have been chosen to explore syntactic processing: Basque and Spanish. Early and Late Basque learners (L1 Spanish) performed a grammatical judgment task with Basque sentences. Different types of syntactic violations (either existing or non-existing in the participants' L1) were used. The results show distinct ERP patterns as a function of language proficiency, even for the group of late learners.

Morningness-Eveningness, seasonality and somatic symptoms: Gender differences in adolescents

Diaz Morales, Juan Francisco *Dept. de Personalidad, Universidad Complutense Madrid, Madrid, Spain* **Delago Prieto, Pedro** *Dpto. Individual Differences, Universidad Complutense Madrid, Madrid, Spain* **Escribano Barreno, Cristina** *Dpto. Individual Differences, Universidad Complutense Madrid, Madrid, Spain*

Most of studies on mood seasonality have been realized among adults and there are few available data on children and adolescents. Relationship between morningness-eveningness, seasonality and somatic symptoms were evaluated among boys and girls adolescents aged 12 to 16 years. Spanish versions of Morningness-Eveningness Scale for Children (MESC), Seasonal Pattern Assessment Questionnaire (SPAQ), and Symptom Checklist-90-R (SCL-90-R) were administered to 408 adolescents (224 girls and 184 boys). The results indicated that seasonal sensitivity (Global Seasonality Score, GSS) was higher in girls. Morningness-eveningness was negatively related to Seasonality in women, but not in men. Girls self-reported greater somatic symptoms than boys.

Evolution of attitudes and knowledge in the field of human research ethics, in medical students, Bogota, Colombia

Diaz-Amado, Eduardo *Instituto de Bioetica, Universidad Javeriana, Bogota, D. C., Colombia* **Escobar, Hugo** *Dept. of Psychology, Universidad Javeriana, Bogotá, Colombia*

Nowadays ethical aspects are central in medical research investigation. In Colombia, in general, medical students are still taught on research ethics in a very informal way. This study was carried out during 2007 in a private medical school in Bogota and analyzed the evolution of attitudes and knowledge of medical students in the field of Human Research Ethics. A complex scale of attitudes, an inquiry about ethical knowledge and two focus groups were used. Attitudes seem to be progressing relatively and there are discordances with respect to the ethical knowledge acquired throughout the medical training.

Depression and feelings of loneliness in a sample of Greek primary school children

Didaskalou, Eleni *Special Education, University of Thessaly, Volos, Greece* **Kleftaras, George** *Dept. of Special Education, University of Thessaly, Volos, Greece*

The present study explores the relationship between childhood depression and loneliness. 323 pupils from fifth to sixth grades completed the Greek versions of: a) the Children's Depression Invetory (CDI) and b) the Louvain Loneliness Scale for Children and Adolescents. High scores in CDI are associated with high scores in Loneliness Scale. Some significant discrepancies are observed between boys and girls on interpersonal problems (CDI subscale), suggesting that boys experience more interpersonal problems than girls. Furthermore, children's scores in parent subscale (loneliness) are strongly associated with scores in CDI. Additionally, children's relationship with their mother affects significantly their feelings of loneliness.

Peculiarities of the hemispheric interactions in gifted children with different cognitive orientation

Dikaya, Ludmila Dept. of Psychologie, Southern Federal University, Rostov-on-Don, Russia Ermakov, Pavel Psychology, Southern Federal University, Rostov-On-Don, Russia

The aim of the research is to compare the peculiarities of the cerebral hemispheric interactions in the gifted pupils with cognitive orientation to natural and to social sciences. With the help of gaploscopical method which is based on the binocular competition the activity of hemispheres and interhemispheric relations of each intellectually gifted pupil had been measured from the 8-th to the 11-th grades. The results: there is a direct correlation between increase of the right hemispheric activity in thinking and the development of orientation to natural sciences; among the gifted pupils with orientation to social sciences those who belong to the combined type of cerebral organization have the highest level of general abilities.

The specificity of formulating questions and answers in deaf and hearing Children

Dimic, Nadezda Faculty of Special Education, University of Belgrade, Belgrade, Serbia Isakovic, Ljubica Faculty of Special Education, University of Belgrade, Belgrade, Serbia, Kovacevic, Tamara Deaf and Hard of Hearing Child, School Radivoj Popovic, Belgrade,

The aim of this study was to examine the success achieved by deaf and hearing children - grades three to eight, nine to fifteen years of age, when answering questions, as well as posing questions for the given answers. Instrument was The Language Corpus for the evaluation of lexical-style related characteristics (Dimic, Isakovic). Sample was consisting of 94 deaf and 60 hearing children. A quantitative and qualitative analysis of the obtained results. Deaf children of all grades obtained better results in answering questions then in asking them, while hearing children had shown the same rate of success in both tasks.

Psychometric properties of the TCI-R in a Serbia and Montenegro

Djuric Jocic, Dragana Inst. for Psychiatry, Clinical Centre of Serbia, Belgrade, Serbia Pavlicic, Nevenka Inst. for Psychiatry, Clinical Centre of Montenegro, Podgorica, Montenegro

The research set out to check the factor structure of seven factor model in our population, to compare our and USA population according to the main dimensions of temperament and character and to check if TCI-R is a valid and reliable test for clinical/ research use in our environment. 500 subjects were investigated with TCI-R questionnaire (Cloninger, 2000) The proposed factorial structure of 4 temperament and 3 character dimensions was partialy confirmed. TCI-R was found to be a reliable and valid test for use in our environment, but certain modification or elimination of some cultural sensitive items should be carried out.

Self-concept and social anxiety in stuttering children

Domsch, Holger Inst. für Psychologie, Universität Bielefeld, Bielefeld, Germany Drechsler, Marion Department of Psychology, Marburg University, Marburg, Germany Peglow, Sabine Department of Psychology, Bielefeld University, Bielefeld, Germany Lohaus, Arnold Department of Psychology, Bielefeld University, Bielefeld, Germany

Although stuttering is a common disorder during childhood studies about this issue are relatively rare. The present study examines the self-concept and social anxiety in a group of stutterers. A sample of 51 stuttering children and a control group were examined. No differences were found between the two groups with respect to the self-concept. Nonetheless, a more severe symptomatic of stuttering was negatively correlated with the self-concept. Furthermore, stuttering children showed significantly more social anxiety in comparison to the control group. The results have practical implications for the diagnosis and therapy of stuttering children.

Developmental trends in the relation between verbal and visuospatial working memory

Dong, Jimei Dept. Educational Psychology, Institute of Education, Hong Kong, China, People's Republic of : Hong Kong SAR

A latent-variable study examined whether verbal and visuospatial working memory capacity measures reflect a domain-general construct or there is a developmental trend in the relationship between them by testing 228 participants ranged form grade 2 to 5 in an elementary school. Confirmatory factor analysis and structural equation models indicated that 8 years is the turning point of the developmental trend in the two kinds of working memory. Before 8 years, they reflected a domain-general construct, while became distinct and separate beyond 8 years. The findings supported a developmental trend relation view of the two kinds of working memory capacities.

Clinical and counseling psychology: The psychological profile of the hemodialized patients

Drobot, Loredana D.P.P.D., Resita, Romania

Our paper tries to focus on the hemodialized patients. The research paper objective is to identify the evaluative rational and irrational cognitions having a general character. The research' instruments used are: USAQ (Unconditional Self Acceptance Questionnaire), GABS (General Attitude and Beliefs Scale), PAD (Profile of the Affective Distress), SCID I and SCID II. The sample consists of 27 subjects. The research hypothesis: if there are identified the cognitions, dysfunctional emotions, the qualitative level of the hemodialized patient, then there is possible to identify the adequate therapeutic interventions. The research findings will be used as items in the professional forming of the medical personnel.

What evaluation depends on: Interactions of explicit and implicit emotions in the conditions of stimulating right or left hemisphere

Dyderska, Anna Dept. of Psychology, Warsaw University, Warsaw, Poland Kobylinska, Dorota Psychology, Warsaw University, Warsaw, Poland

A study is presented, in which goal was to verify the impact of suboptimal priming by using an affective stimulus on conscious judgements about neutral stimulus. Also the possibility of modifying this influence through distraction and self-control personality predispositions was considered. Sixty two participants were engaged in an experiment using affective priming paradigm. Before the procedure of affective priming manipulation concerning positive or cognitive distraction was proceeded (or no distraction in control group). After the procedures

participants filled in Mood Regulation Scales. As predicted, the results confirmed the contrast effect and interaction of positive distraction and priming valence. Results showed that people with higher ability to control mood were more prone to be influenced by implicit affective stimuli.

Families of agricultural and urban zone: Characteristics and conceptions of adolescents

Ebner Melchiori, Ligia Dept. of Psychology, São Paulo State University, Bauru, Brazil Faco, Vanessa Psicologia, São Paulo State University, Bauru-SP, Brazil Dessen, Maria Psicologia Escolar e do Desenv, Brasília University, Bauru-SP, Brazil

The study investigated conceptions about the family, by reports of 48 adolescents of areas agricultural and urban in Brazil, by a questionnaire and an interview. The mean of the concept and the characterization of the familiar structure for these adolescents, shows that the mother is primordial figure in the social net of support, followed of the father who get others social functions, not only the traditional financial sustentation. Conflicts in the familiar net are more related by adolescents in the urban zone, although, for both groups, the conceptions on family had been based on the emotional and affective support.

Relationship between body mass index, obesity and total body fat with depression in 15 to 49 years old females

Eftekhari, Mohammad Hassan Nutrition, Shiraz University, Shiraz, Islamic Republic of Iran Ahmadi, Mehdi Nutrition, Shiraz University, Shiraz, Islamic Republic of Iran Firoozabadi, Ali Psychology, Shiraz University, Shiraz, Islamic Republic of Iran Soveid, Mahmood Endocrinology, Shiraz University, Shiraz, Islamic Republic of Iran

Background: Depression are associated with serious metabolic complications. Objective: To investigate the rate, the intensity and different types of obesity in depressed female patients. Methods: A total 90 subjects(depressed,obese&control) were selected. Anthropometric indices were measured. Total body fat &body mass index were calculated. Results: Compression of mean of BMI, WHR, TBF between the depressed & control groups showed a significant difference. There was not a significant relationship between the intensity of depression with the intensity & type of obesity. Conclusion: Obesity & the type of android obesity in depressed patients are of higher intensity in comparison to obese patients.

A smile is just a smile: But only for men. Gender differences in response to faces scales

Elfering, Achim Department of Psychology, University of Bern, Bern, Switzerland Grebner, Simone Department of Psychology, University of Michigan, Mount Pleasant, USA

Objectives: This study tested measurement equivalence of the faces scale that is often used to assess emotions, attitudes and well-being. Methods: Multilevel analysis of 10584 two-alternative-two-forced-choice judgments (sad versus happy) of 11 faces from 72 participants. Results: Women judged a "neutral face" more often sad than happy and significantly more often sad than men. Moreover, women showed a contrast effect: within predominantly smiling faces a mild smile was judged to be sad, while within predominantly griming faces a mild grim was judged to be happy. Conclusions: There are considerable gender differences in meaning of faces within faces scales.

Biases in pigeons' choices with computer-generated, multi-item visual arrays: relative numerosity as a potential cue in foraging decisions

Emmerton, Jacky Dept. of Psychological Science, Purdue University, West Lafayette, USA

This study tested whether pigeons might use relative numerosity as a foraging cue by operantly rewarding one group for choosing an array containing more items, and another for choosing an array containing fewer. The hypothesis was that the first group should perform better than the second. When array quantities differed in acquisition, birds trained to choose more items performed better. ANOVAs on test data still yielded this performance advantage when arrays were equated in area and luminance, but asymmetries in the salience of local features also affected performance. Relative numerosity differences may be one cue that influences pigeons' foraging decisions.

Pursuing a career in a technological field: Barriers and motivating factors

Endepohls-Ulpe, Martina Inst. für Psychologie, Universität Koblenz, Koblenz, Germany **Ebach, Judith** Fachhochschule Koblenz, Ada Lovelace Projekt, Remagen, Germany **von Zabern, Janine** Universität Koblenz, Institut für Psychologie, Koblenz, Germany

The presented study is part of a European research project (UPDATE) that aims at improving science and technology teaching in Europe, especially for girls. A questionnaire based on theories of gender role development, research on gender related vocational choices and effects of mentorship/role models, was administered to a German sample of 100 students, 50 from courses of study of different technology fields, 50 from courses of study for primary school teachers. The results are discussed in terms of differences concerning tradition in family, experiences in the educational system as well as self-image, image of science/ engineering and career expectations.

The creative unconscious: The contribution of Georg Groddeck

Faneco Maniakas, Georgina Psychology, UniversidadeFederaldeSãoCarlos, São Carlos, Brazil

In Groddeck the supposition by which the body and its organs are symbolic and the body "speaks" through the disease, opposes to the characterization of the somatic illness like an assymbolic expression of discharges in a body reduced to the pure materiality. The Groddeck's unconscious Es – symbolic matrix from where emanates all psychosomatic existence -, in its essence, it isn't psychical nor somatic. Based on textual analysis we intend to show the importance of Groddeck's thought and his influence on Freud's last ideas, to point of Freud taking into account, in 1938, an integration between somatic and psychical processes.

Biogenesis of death drive

Faneco Maniakas, Georgina Psychology, UniversidadeFederaldeSãoCarlos, São Carlos, Brazil

Although Freud hasn't mentioned the russian embriologist Elie Metchnikoff in Jenseits des Lustprinzips (1920), through textual analysis we found a remarkable similarity between the freudian project and Etudes sur la nature humaine (1903), essay where Metchnikoff postulated a death instinct counterpositioned to a life instinct. Freud heard about Metchnikoff in Sabina Spielrein's presentation to Vienna's psychoanalytic circle in 1911. We intend to show that as well as Spielrein, Metchnikoff also can have inspired Freud to conceive the death drive like a basic biological phenomenon.

Effect mechanism of family functioning on adolescent's emotional problem

Fang, Xiaoyi Inst. of Developm. Psychology, Beijing Normal University, Beijing, People's Republic of China **Xu, Jie** Institute of Developmental Psy, Beijing Normal University, Beijing, People's Republic of China **Zhang, Jintao** Institute of Developmental Psy, Beijing Normal University, Beijing, People's Republic of China

To explore the relationship between family functioning process and outcome on adolescents' emotional problems, 422 Chinese adolescents from

one ordinary school and one key school were selected to file the Olson's Family Adaptability and Cohesion Evaluation Scale, Skinner's Family Assessment Measure, Radloff's Depression Scale, Zung's Self—Rating Anxiety Scale. Correlation analysis, Hierarchical Regression, Structural Equation Modeling analysis were done, the results showed: All dimensions of family functioning process were significant correlated with the dimensions of family functioning outcome; the predict power of Family functioning process on adolescent's emotional problems were much higher that that of family functioning outcome; Family functioning outcome predicted not only directly, but also indirectly adolescents' emotional problems via family functioning outcome.

Relationship between leadership style of managers and conflict management methods

Fathi-Ashtiani, Ali Behavioral Sciences Research C, Baqiyatallah University of Med, Tehran, Islamic Republic of Iran **Zarnooshe-Frahani, Mohammad-Taqi** Behavioral Sciences Research C, Baqiyatallah University of Med, Tehran, Islamic Republic of Iran **Taofiqi, Shahram** Strategic Research Center, Baqiyatallah University of Med, Tehran, Islamic Republic of Iran

The study investigates the relationship between leadership styles of managers and conflict management methods. 48 high and middle level managers of a general hospital were selected. We used leadership style and conflict management inventories. Statistical analysis has Chi-Square and ANOVA. Results indicated 62.5% of managers had tendency to favoritism while 20.8% were conscientious, 16.7% were socially independent. From the point of conflict management methods, 4.2% had tendency to anti-conflict approach, 50% had tendency to problem solving, and 45.8% had tendency to applying control. There was a significant relationship between age and managing methods same as between history of management and Managing methods.

Empirical research on Managers Meta-competence Model and Its relationship with performance

Feng, Ming Chongqing, People's Republic of China **Yin, Mingxin** Chongqing University, Economic and Business Admin, Chongqing, People's Republic of China **Guo, Yali** Chongqing University, Economic and Business Admin, Chongqing, People's Republic of China **Chen, Wan** Chongqing University, Economic and Business Admin, Chongqing, People's Republic of China

We use behavioral event interview to develop the meta-competence and performance questionnaires, and revise them. From 585 large samples analysis we conclude that meta-competence contains ideation, learning and applying ability, self-development ability, and have characteristics of cross-industry and transferability of managerial levels. The results show that it is necessary for top manager to possess strong ideation, for middle-level manager learning and applying ability, and for grass roots self-development ability. The further research suggests that adaptive performance can promote task and contextual performance, ideation can enhance contextual and adaptive performance, learning and applying ability is good for promoting one's whole performance.

Prevalence of dominating and jealous tactics in adolescent and young adult dating relationships

Fernández González, Liria Psic. Biológica y de la Salud, Universidad Autónoma de Madrid, Madrid, Spain **Muñoz-Rivas, Marina Julia** PSIC. BIOLÓGICA Y DE LA SALUD, UNIVERSIDAD AUTÓNOMA DE MADRID, Madrid, Spain **Gámez-Guadix, Manuel** PSIC. BIOLÓGICA Y DE LA SALUD, UNIVERSIDAD AUTÓNOMA DE MADRID, Madrid, Spain **González**

Lozano, Pilar PERS., EVAL. Y PSIC. CLÍNICA, UNIV. COMPLUTENSE DE MADRID, Madrid, Spain

Objective: To assess the prevalence of dominating and jealous tactics in dating relationships. Method: The participants were 4,097 Spanish adolescents and young adults of both genders, between ages of 16 and 26 years. Results: Overall, 45.5% and 70.7% of the men, and 55.7% and 80.1% of the women, reported perpetrating some form of dominant tactic and jealous behaviour, respectively. Trend analysis for age groups showed that jealousy decreases with age for both genders, but dominance dropped exclusively for males. Conclusions: Dominant and jealous tactics are very frequent in this section of the population, especially for women. Prevention efforts appear necessary.

Development of children's graphic representations achieved from tactile or visual exploration of bidimensional shapes

Fernandes, Viviane Dept. of Psychology, Université de Bourgogne-LEAD, Dijon, France **Vinter, Annie** Psychology, Université de Bourgogne-LEAD, Dijon, France

This research aims at studying the mental images that children aged 4 to 10 years elaborate, from a visual or haptic exploration of bidimensional geometric shapes. The children were asked to explore visually or haptically different shapes, and to draw them. The drawings were made from memory or under a copy condition. As expected, the results revealed interesting performance in the tactile condition. However, it was below the one observed in the visual condition for shape production, but not for size production. Drawings from memory were not systematically less good than drawings from copy.

P.-J.-G. Cabanis' thought in the history of ideas

Ferrandes, Carmela Letterature mediterranee, University of Bari, Bari, Italy

P.-J.-G. Cabanis, maître à penser of the "Idéologues", established the principal elements of a "whole" education of the future ideal citizen on the basis of the medical knowledge of his time. The current paper is divided into two parts. The first one traces the elements concurring to the definition of individuals' physical and social well-being through education and sharpening of their potentialities in sight of realizing a happy State. The second part examines the influence of Cabanis' thought on the literary production of his contemporaries and pupils (Staël, Constant, Stendhal), as well as on the Freudian interpretation of language.

Television and aggression: A test of a mediated model

Ferreira, Joaquim Faculdade de Psicologia, Universidade de Coimbra, Coimbra, Portugal **Matos, Armanda** Faculdade de Psicologia e Ciên, Universidade de Coimbra, Coimbra, Portugal **Haase, Richard** Division of Counseling Psychol, University at Albany, Albany, USA

We conducted a study to test the hypothesis that identification with violent TV heroes, enjoyment of TV violence, and perceived reality in TV violence would mediate the relationship between TV violence and aggression. The sample consisted of 722 students from the 4th, 6th and 8th grades and self-report measures were used. A multivariate structural equation model on latent variables was adopted. The results showed that the relationship between TV violence and physical aggression is mediated by enjoyment of TV violence and identification with violent TV heroes. We found no evidence of a mediated relationship between TV violence and verbal aggression.

Social representations of boredom in french primary school

Ferriere, Severine Bron, France

This study explores the social representations of boredom, in a school context. It is a neglected topic in psychology, contrary to the concept of motivation. We can distinguish motivation in success and demotivation in failure. Yet, boredom is an ambivalent process recalling in success vs failure at school. We hypothesis that teacher's social representations vary according to the pupil's school position. 258 primary school teachers were questionned on their expectations on bored students. Two variables are studied : failure vs success at school and boy vs girl. The categorical and prototypical analysis was used to reveal differences of social representations.

Career priority patterns among managerial women in Turkish banks: Benefits of putting career first?

Fiksenbaum, Lisa Dept. of Psychology, York University, Toronto, Canada *Burke, Ronald J.* Schulich, York University, TORONTO, ON, Canada *Koyuncu, Mustafa* School of Tourism, Erciyes University, Nevsahar, Turkey

This research examined antecedents and consequences of different career priority patterns among 215 managerial women working in large Turkish banks. Two career priority patterns advanced by Schwartz (1992) were considered: Career-primary (CP) and Career-family (CF). Using anonymously completed questionnaires, data revealed that CP and CF women were similar on personal demographic and work situation characteristics (age, marital status, job and organizational tenure). CP women were more satisfied with their jobs and careers, were more engaged with their work and reported higher levels of psychological well-being. These findings were consistent with an earlier study carried out in Turkey but somewhat different from those obtained earlier in Canada suggesting possible country and culture differences.

Distinctive features of development of the need of further improvement in organization employees

Fil, Alena Lab. of Organiz. Psychology, Institut of Psychology, Kiev, Ukraine *Karamushka, Liudmyla* Organizational Psychology, Institute of Psychology, Kyiv, Ukraine *Kozubai, Nataliya* Organisational Psychology, Institut of Psychology, Kyiv, Ukraine

Objective. To find out distinctive features of development of the need of further improvement in organization employees. Methods: The investigation was done on a sample of 148 educational organization employees using GET TEST and SPSS. Results. 1. Most respondents (66.9%) had the need of further improvement at low level. The high level was found in 10.5% of the respondents. 2. Different categories of employees had different levels of development of the need in question: a) high level was found in 20.0% of methodists of district (city) departments of education; 11.5% school principals, and 2.4% school psychologists. Conclusion. The findings call for educators' development of the need of further improvement using a special training course.

Usability of priming effect for research of unconscious content of motivational structure of the personality

Filippova, Margarita Psychology, Saint-Petersburg University, Sain-Petersburg, Russia

The aim of the research is verification of the idea of possibility of calling and registration uncontrolled manifestation of the personality (by the example of motivation) with application of "priming" methodology. For adaptation of that experimental paradigm for new research tasks we registered time of reaction on neutral stimuli with previously sub-liminally exposed control words (time of exposure 30 ms with mask). Control words are related to different needs by classification of Murray. Results are interpreted as perceptive defense and vigilance and demonstrate effectiveness of subliminal exposition of testing stimuli for examination the structure of unconscious or covert motives.

Obsessive compulsive symptoms in Asperger's disorder and high functioning autism

Fischer, Christian Psychology Department, University of Hamburg, Hamburg, Germany *Probst, Paul* Psychology Department, University of Hamburg, Hamburg, Germany

Although rituals, stereotypies and special interests are a core feature of autistic disorders, substantial data related to those obsessive-compulsive phenomena are lacking. Recent research results indicate that autistic individuals frequently suffer from distressing obsessions and compulsions according to DSM- IV criteria of Obsessive- compulsive disorder. Although OCD and autism overlap in symptoms, comorbidity, neurobiology and genetics, autism- related obsessive- compulsive phenomena have to be differentiated carefully from OCD-symptoms. Further research will have to determine if obsessive- compulsive symptoms in autistic disorders are to be diagnosed as symptoms of a distinct condition which is comorbid OCD.

Self-concept of male and female conduct-disordered adolescents

Fischer, Pascal S. Oberried, Germany *Güntert, Marion* Psychology, Freiburg Univ. of Education, Freiburg, Germany *Schleider, Karin* Psychology, Freiburg Univ. of Education, Freiburg, Germany

Several studies point out, that the self-concept can be understood as one possible factor within the multifactorial model of aetiology for emergence and maintenance of mental and behavioural disorders. Purpose of this study is the comparison of the self-concept of adolescents with and without conduct-disorders (ICD-10) in specific consideration of gender- and age-specific aspects. For this the self-concept of 450 adolescents between 11 and 17 years was collected, by using the Inventory of Self-Concept (Georgi & Beckmann, 2004). The first results exhibit significant differences between disordered and controll group. Furthermore specific influences of gender and developmental issues can be found. The results are discussed regarding implications for prevention and intervention.

Relative time, choice delay and delay of reinforcement in conditional discrimination

Flores, Carlos CEIC, Universidad de Guadalajara, Guadalajara, Jalisco, Mexico *Mateos, Rebeca* CEIC, Universidad de Guadalajara, Guadalajara, Jalisco, Mexico

Rats were trained on a conditional discrimination procedure. In Experiment 1 the intertrial interval (ITI) was increased for a group, while for another group was constant, concurrently the retention interval was increased. The effects of retention interval were smaller with longer ITIs. In Experiment 2 the delay of reinforcement was increased. In both groups the accuracy was constant. The occurrence of relative time effects in Experiment 1, but not in Experiment 2, suggest that different types of delay intervals depend upon different psychological processes.

Creating ourselves: Ethnic arts participation and adaptation in New Zealand

Fox, Stephen Psychology, Victoria University, Wellington, New Zealand

This research investigates arts participation by ethnic minority individuals in New Zealand, focusing on its effects adaptation outcomes. It was found that arts were perceived to be an important part of identity creation and maintenance. Arts were also perceived to reduce intergenerational conflict, improve relations with other ethnic groups, provide coping resources, and generally improve self-esteem and efficacy. These results suggest significant effects of ethnic arts participation on acculturative outcomes and well-being. Subsequently, a survey to test mechanisms of this process and resulting level of well-being was developed. Its validation and initial results of the overall survey shall be discussed.

Conflict resolution and dominance in 4-year-old Portuguese preschool children

Fragoso, Sara Lisboa, Portugal *Carreiras, Joana* UIPCDE, ISPA, Lisboa, Portugal *dos Santos, António José* UIPCDE, ISPA, Lisboa, Portugal

Preschoolers, like non-human primates, develop conflict resolution strategies, such as reconciliation, in order to minimize the costs of resource competition. Our objective is assessing the relation between reconciliation and dominance in 25 4-year-old preschool children, using an ethological approach. Data on reconciliation were collected by means of PC-MC method (de Waal & Yoshihara, 1983). David's Score (Gammell et al., 2003) was used to quantify dominance relationships. Dominants showed higher levels of reconciliation. They used prosocial and coercive strategies. Dyadic analysis revealed that the smaller the status difference between opponents, the greater their conciliatory tendency, maybe as a result of attraction to adjacent rank.

Differential predictors to explain persistence and academic achievement of first-year university students

Frenay, Mariane Dept of Educational Psychology, University of Louvain UCL, Louvain-la-Neuve, Belgium *Neuville, Sandrine* Dept of Educational Psychology, University of Louvain UCL, Louvain-la-Neuve, Belgium *Noel, Bernadette* Center for University Teaching, FUCAM, Mons, Belgium *Wertz, Vincent* Faculty of Engineering, University of Louvain UCL, Louvain-la-Neuve, Belgium *Schmitz, Julia* Faculty of psychology and educ, University of Louvain UCL, Louvain-la-Neuve, Belgium *Boudrenghien, Gentiane* Faculty of Psychology and Educ, University of Louvain UCL, Louvain-la-Neuve, Belgium

The aim of this study is to understand the process leading students, who are entering for the first time into higher education, to an academic and social integration, and how it may affect them to persist and succeed. We hypothesize – from 2 theoretical frameworks (Tinto; Eccles) - that predictors are different for persistence and success. 2637 first-year university students were surveyed. Multiple regression analyses were performed. Results suggest differential predictors of persistence and achievement: certainty of study choice, expectancy and value perceptions predict best persistence while school past, mother' education, expectancy, academic engagement and intention to persist predict performance.

How college students build anticipatory confidence to succeed in their future careers: The impact of experiences gained trough college activities

Fujimura, Makoto Faculty of Economics, Kyushu University, Fukuoka, Japan *Furukawa, Hisataka* Department of Human Sciences, Kyushu University, Fukuoka-city, Japan

The purpose of this study is to identify the sources of confidence college students feel about succeeding in future careers. Two types of confidence are proposed: "experience-based confidence," which describes confidence college students gain during college, and "anticipatory confidence," which represents confidence college students feel about succeeding in jobs in the future. "Experience based confidence" gained from academic achievement and interpersonal relationships during college demonstrated positive effects on "anticipatory confidence" about job-related tasks and relationships in the future. Results suggest that confidence college students feel about future careers is derived from experiences in participating in various activities during college.

Discipline styles used by Spanish parents: a preliminary study

Gámez Guadix, Manuel Universidad Autonoma de Madrid, Madrid, Spain Almendros, Carmen Department of Psychology, Autonomous University Madrid, Madrid, Spain Carrobles, José Antonio Department of Psychology, Autonomous University Madrid, Madrid, Spain

Objective: To describe Spanish parents' use of corrective discipline styles as reported by university students. Method: The sample was composed of 290 participants that retrospectively reported on the disciplinary acts that they received at age ten. Results: Explain/Teach was the most frequent discipline technique used by both mothers and fathers through the referent period (92% and 84%, respectively), followed by Penalty Tasks and Restorative Behavior (74% of mothers and 68% of fathers) and Reward (73% of mothers and 67% of fathers). Conclusions: This study provides useful preliminary information on the discipline used by Spanish parents and opens up the possibility of making transcultural comparisons.

Can societal language amendments change gender representation? The case of Norwegian

Gabriel, Ute Dept. of Psychology, NTNU, Trondheim, Norway Gygax, Pascal Psychology, University of Fribourg, Fribourg, Switzerland Sarrasin, Oriane Psychology, University of Fribourg, Fribourg, Switzerland

The influence of stereotypical information and the grammatical masculine on the representation of gender in Norwegian was investigated by applying a sentence evaluation paradigm. Participants had to decide whether a second sentence containing explicit information about the gender of one of more of the characters (e.g. ...one of the women...) was a sensible continuation of a first sentence introducing a role name (e.g. The spies ...). Participants' representations were biased by the stereotypicality of the role names when reading female (e.g. nurses) and male (e.g. pilots) stereotyped role names, but male biased when reading neutral role names. Thus, the Norwegian language policy has only partly been successful.

The quality of the training ecperience: Predictor variables of satisfaction and career exploration

Gamboa, Vitor Dept. de Psicologia, Universidade do Algarve, Faro, Portugal Paixão, Maria Paula Psicologia e de C. Educação, Universidade de Coimbra, Coimbra, Portugal Jesus, Saul Psicologia, Universidade do Algarve, Faro, Portugal

The quality of the apprenticeship can have differentiated impacts on the students' lives and on their vocational development. Brooks et al. (1995), talk about the value of work experience as the most realistic way of vocational exploration. However, the efficiency of work experiences is extremely variable (Ainley, P., 1990; Smith & Harris, 2000). The present study (N=310) seeks to highlight which qualities of the apprenticeship are predictors of satisfaction and career exploration in a group of students. Multiple linear regressions (Stepwise) revealed that the learning opportunities and the social support of the supervisor are the significant predictor variables.

The effects of work experiences on values of the high school students

Gamboa, Vitor Dept. de Psicologia, Universidade do Algarve, Faro, Portugal Gomes, Rubina Psicologia, Universidade do Algarve, Faro, Portugal Vieira, Luís Psicologia, Universidade do Algarve, Faro, Portugal

This study examined the effects of the work experiences on career development, specifically on values of 119 students from a High School. Were analysed the work experiences (duration of the experience, weekly hours, wages and whether the experience was coincidence with the period of classes), the quality of work contexts, as well the values of students. When compared the students in function of the presence or not of work experiences, we verified significant statistically differences in favour of the not workers. Significant differences were not verified in the dimensions of the quality in function of the work contexts.

Gender differences during adolescence in factors of the socio-emotional development

Garaigordobil, Maite Dept. of Clinical Psychology, University Basque Country, San Sebastián, Spain Maganto, Carmen Clinical Psychology, University Basque Country, San Sebastián, Spain Pérez, José Ignacio Clinical Psychology, University Basque Country, San Sebastián, Spain

The study objective was to analyze the existence of gender differences in socio-emotional development. The sample consists of 285 adolescents aged 15 to 16. The study uses a descriptive methodology. The ANOVAs confirm that women had significantly higher scores in: violence rejection and prosocial cognitions, empathy, perception of classmates, ability to resolve conflicts positively, knowledge of constructive strategies to face violent behaviour, anger internal control, and positive social behaviours. However, men had significantly higher scores in: violence acceptance cognitions, aggressive style of dealing with conflicts, knowledge of aggressive strategies to face violent behaviour, anger internal expression, and negative social behaviours. The ANOVA results did not reveal gender differences in self-concept.

Risk-sensitivity in humans and rats: Comparatives results

García Leal, Óscar CEIC, Universidad de Guadalajara, Guadalajara, Mexico Díaz Lemus, Carlos Augusto CEIC, Universidad de Guadalajara, Guadalajara, Mexico Saldivar Olivares, Gamaliel CEIC, Universidad de Guadalajara, Guadalajara, Mexico Galindo Oceguera, Alma Karina CEIC, Universidad de Guadalajara, Guadalajara, Mexico Olivo Salinas, Carmen Paola Guadalupe CEIC, Universidad de Guadalajara, Guadalajara, Mexico Ramírez de la Torre, Elizabeth CEIC, Universidad de Guadalajara, Guadalajara, Mexico

Two different experimental tests were developed to check risk-sensitivity in humans and rats. The main results are compared, to argue about some of the factors or variables that determine the preference between two different alternatives of response, one of them with a certain outcome, and the other with an uncertain result, in spite of the differences between species.

Program of education of skills for the prevention of the violence in the pair in the educational context

García-Baamonde Sánchez, Maria Elena Psicología y Antropología, Universidad de Extremadura, Badajoz, Spain Blázquez Alonso, Macarena Psicología y Antropología, Universidad de Extremadura, Badajoz, Spain Moreno Manso, Juan Manuel Psicología y Antropología, Universidad de Extremadura, Badajoz, Spain Rabazo Méndez, María José Psicología y Antropología, Universidad de Extremadura, Badajoz, Spain

Let's sense beforehand a workshop directed to anticipating the violence of genre in the educational context. Its directed for pupils of ages included between 12 and 17 years. The program tries to clarify concepts in relation to the violence of genre (types, reasons, consequences ...); to orientate the young men in order that "they" "denounce" those situations that might end in mistreatment; to analyze the influence of communication brings over of the sexist stereotypes, which are given in the mass media; and to arouse the pupils of the gravity of the problem, since they are our present and future society.

Gender differences in school anxiety: Study with a sample of Spanish middle and high school students

García-Fernández, José Manuel Developmental and Educational, University of Alicante, Alicante, Spain Ingles, Cándido J. Developmental and Educational, University of Miguel Hernandez, Elche, Spain Martínez-Monteagudo, Carmen Developmental and Educational, University of Miguel Hernandez, Elche, Spain Redondo, Jesús Developmental and Educational, University of Miguel Hernandez, Elche, Spain

Objetive: The purpose of this study was to analyze gender differences in school anxiety. Method: The Questionnaire of School Anxiety (CAE; Garcia-Fernandez e Ingles, 2006) was administered to 1,409 adolescents (47.9% males) from 12 to 18 years. Results and conclusion: Significant gender differences were founded. Girls reported significant higher levels of anxiety than boys in the three response systems (cognitive, physiological, and motor), and in the four school situations (anxiety faced with school failure and punishment, anxiety faced with aggression, anxiety faced with social evaluation, and anxiety faced with school evaluation). In general, these differences had a moderate effect size.

Attitudes towards deaf people in adolescence

García-Fernández, José Manuel Developmental and Educational, University of Alicante, Alicante, Spain Guillen-Gosalvez, Carmen Developmental and Educational, University of Alicante, Alicante, Spain Valero-Rodriguez, Jose Evolutive Psychology and Didac, University of Alicante, Alicante, Spain Gomis-Selva, Nieves Evolutive Psychology and Didac, University of Alicante, Alicante, Spain

Objective: This piece of work assesses the different attitudes towards deaf people among secondary school students according to their age and sex. Method: In order to achieve our aim we recruited a sample of 471 secondary school students who were assessed by means of EAPDA –Attitudes Towards Deaf People Scale- (Guillén y García-Fernández, 2007). Results and conclusion: The results reveal that the girls show better attitudes in every factor of the scale. According to the age, the most positive attitudes are developed at the beginning and end of the dolescence period.

Sociometric variables and attitudes towards deaf people

García-Fernández, José Manuel Developmental and Educational, University of Alicante, Alicante, Spain Guillen-Gosalbez, Carmen Developmental and Educational, University of Alicante, Alicante, Spain Pérez-Sanchez, Antonio M. Developmental and Educational, University of Alicante, Alicante, Spain Inglés-Saura, Candido J. Developmental and Educational, University of Miguel Hernández, Elche, Spain

Objective: This piece of work establishes the different attitudes towards the deaf people among subjects according to their high or low sociometric status, high or low punctuation in popularity and high or low punctuation in unfriendliness or rejection. Method: In order to achieve our aim, we recruited a sample of 471 students, who belonged to six different secondary schools, and who were assessed by means of a sociogram and the EAPDA–Attitudes Towards Deaf People Scale-(Guillén y García-Fernández, 2007). Results and conclusion: The results reveal that those subjects who have a high status or/and are popular or/and are not rejected show better attitudes.

Resiliency, well being, and future life planning in the lives of school and non school going street/working children in India

Garg, Seerat Roshan Bhawan, Punjab, India

The present study examined the lives of street/working children in India in relation to their schooling status. The sample (N = 100; M= 13.6 years, SD= 3.88) was from three groups: non-school going (n=50), children enrolled with formal education system (n=35), and children with non-formal education (n=15). ANOVA results for resiliency, well-being, and ability to plan for future demonstrated the scores on these variables to be the highest for children with formal education system followed by children with non-formal education system, and then non-school going children. Results highlight the importance of schooling as an important predictor of adjustment among children.

Self-regulatory strength lessens rumination and increases self-confidence

Geisler, Fay C.M. Inst. für Psychologie, Universität Greifswald, Greifswald, Germany Kubiak, Thomas Institut für Psychologie, Ernst-Moritz-Arndt-Universität, Greifswald, Germany Weber, Hannelore Institut für Psychologie, Ernst-Moritz-Arndt-Universität, Greifswald, Germany

We hypothesized, that self-regulatory strength operationalized through self-reports and tonic heart rate variability (tHRV) lessens rumination and increases affective self-confidence. Psychology students were randomly assigned to a treatment failure feedback or a control success feedback condition. The experience and mechanisms of rumination were assessed. Afterwards participants took the test again they had received feedback for. Only after failure feedback self-regulatory strength correlated significantly with rumination and affective self-confidence. Tonic HRV outperformed self-reports, insofar as it is was not only associated with the experience of rumination, but also with its underlying mechanisms. Furthermore, only tonic HRV was associated with affective self-confidence.

Psychosocial profiles of bullies, victims and bully-victims

Georgiou, Stelios Dept. of Psychology, University of Cyprus, Nicosia, Cyprus

The aim of this study was to develop a theory driven model describing personal and familial parameters of peer violence at school and to test its ability to fit empirical data. The participants were 377 twelve-year-old Greek Cypriot children and their mothers. It was found that bully-victims were more temperamental, more different than the typical student and more socially isolated (p<.05). Also, the same group members tended to use external attributions for explaining the causes of peer violence. Maternal monitoring was negatively related to child participation in peer violence, while maternal depressiveness was positively related to such experiences.

Social competence, emotional intelligence and its relations with academic achievement in a group of students of compulsory education

Gilar, Raquel Dept. Developmental Psychology, University of Alicante, Alicante, Spain Sanchez, Barbara Dept. Developmental Psychology, University of Alicante, Alicante, Spain Cantero, Pilar Dept. Developmental Psychology, University of Alicante, Alicante, Spain Gonzalez, Carlota Dept.

Developmental Psychology, University of Alicante, Alicante, Spain

In this work we analyse the existing relations between emotional intelligence and social competence, as well as the relations between these variables and academic achievement. The participants were 200 students of Compulsory Education and the instruments used were: the BarOn EQ-i:YV (S), the LSSP (Spence, 1980), and the MESSY (Matson et al., 1983). The results of multiple correlation and regression analysis show that the variables that contribute most significantly to explain the Social Inadequance are the Interpersonal Factor and Stress management (EQ-i). In addition, variables which contribute to explain the academic achievement are Interpersonal Factor, Stress Management and Adaptability (EQ-i). Finally, the results show the importance of the development of these socioemotional competences in Compulsory Education.

A model of unprotected sexual activity among gay-identified men

Gillis, Joseph Roy Dept. Counselling Psychology, University of Toronto, Toronto, Canada Schulter, Daniel P. Adult Ed. & Counselling Ps, University of Toronto, Toronto, Canada

Detailed semi-structured interviews were carried out for a sample of 16 gay, bisexual or queer identified men in Toronto, Ontario, Canada that focused on the meanings attributed by participants to incidences of "bare-backing" or unprotected receptive anal intercourse. Findings indicated that "treatment optimism", "safer-sex fatigue", monogamy, substance use, low self-esteem, and feelings of poor self-efficacy all factored into the participants' decisions regarding bare-backing. These factors were intertwined in complex ways, each combination a different possible route to bare-backing. A model is presented to conceptualize these pathways, and to guide future HIV prevention intervention efforts with this population.

Experiences of hospitalization among children under Bon Marrow Transplantation: A qualitative study

Godarzi, Zahra Pediatric Nursing Department, School of Nursing and Midwifer, Tehran, Islamic Republic of Iran

Introduction: Hospitalization considered as a challenging experience especially in children. The aim of this qualitative study was to describe the feelings of children hospitalization experiences during their BMT. Data were gathered by collecting the children written memories in the Shariati Hospital of Medical Sciences of Tehran University. Methodology: In this qualitative study 10 stories were analyzed using latent content analysis. Finding: Three main themes were emerged included: fear of cancer disease, worry about the potential pain of the procedure and finally the importance of nurses and physician communication and their sympathy. Conclusions: The findings of this study confirmed the importance of psychological support and consultation of nurses and physicians. Key words: Cancer, Qualitative, Child experiences, BMT, Nursing.

Problems in treating Prolonged Incestual Violence (PIV): Research clinical, and ethical issues: The impact on treatment outcomes of nondisclosure vs self-disclosure

Goldberg, Greta Psychelp, Sydney, Australia

Case studies presented within the linked conceptual and research frameworks of systemic and developmental/attachment theories. Fear, silence and shame perpetuate complex betrayal and disrupted bonding even with the " non-offending" parent whose silence may reflect dissociated denial of their own childhood abuse. Within prolonged therapy the client's failure to disclose PIV poses ethical/

social /legal challenges about perpetuating silence. Parallels are drawn between the dissociated denial which keeps certain mothers from seeing what is going on, and the therapist/client barriers and double dissociations which can inhibit client's disclosure to a therapist with unresolved history of abuse.

A cultural understanding of risky behavior engagement amongst Chinese adolescents

Goldfinger, Marc Dept. of Psychology, McGill University, Montreal, Canada Auerbach, Randy P. Psychology, McGill University, Montreal, Canada Abela, John R.Z. Psychology, McGill University, Montreal, Canada

The goal of the current study is to examine whether materialism moderates the relationship between stress and engagement in risky behaviors in Chinese youth. At time 1, 411 adolescents from Yue Yang, Hunan, China (ages 14-19) completed measures assessing engagement in risky behaviors and the occurrence of negative events. Follow up assessments occurred once a month for six months. In line with our hypotheses, results of hierarchical linear modeling analyses indicated that adolescents who exhibited high levels of materialism were more likely than individuals possessing lower levels of materialism to report increased engagement in risky behaviors following negative life events.

The evaluation of teachers on multiple intelligences in preschool and primary

Gomis Selva, Nieves Educatıvonal Psychology, University of Alicante, Alicante, Spain Valero Rodriguez, Jose Evolutive Psychology and Didac, University of Alicante, Alicante, Spain Castejón Costejón, Juan Luís Educatıvonal Psychology, University of Alicante, Alicante, Spain Pérez Sánchez, Antonio Miguel Educatıvonal Psychology, University of Alicante, Alicante, Spain García Fernández, Jose Manuel Educatıvonal Psychology, University of Alicante, Alicante, Spain

Researching made by experts confirm the existence of multiple intelligences in children of school age, but there is a little showing what perception that teachers have on the abilities of their students. Aim: Evaluation of MI of students by teachers. Participants: 8 teachers (tutors and specialists) and 144 pupils. Instruments: SPECTRUM inventories for teachers. Factorial Analysis with SPSS. The results indicate that teachers do not identify different capacities related MI in their students. Teachers identify a general intelligence, musical intelligence, kinesthetic-bodily and some aspects of interpersonal intelligence. Conclusion: These results are fundamental and complementary to develop a dynamic assessment of the students and encourage reflection on the type of methodology and activities that teachers propose in the classroom.

Job strain, negative sensitivity and health in Venezuelan professionals

Goncalves Oliveira, Lila Behavioral Cience and Technol., Universidad Simón Bolívar, Caracas, Venezuela Felman, Lya Behavioral Cience and Tecnolo, Universidad Simón Bolívar, Caracas, Venezuela Guarino, Leticia Behavioral Cience and Tecnolo, Universidad Simón Bolívar, Caracas, Venezuela

Objective: to determine the relationship between job strain (Demand-Control Model), negative egocentric sensitivity and health in venezuelan professionals. Method: Using a non-experimental cross-sectional design, correlation coefficients were performed on data from 441 professionals from Caracas, Venezuela. Results: negative egocentric sensitivity was positively related to job demands, anxiety, depression, reports of illness, symptoms and indixes of morbidity, and inversely related to job control, job support, self-esteem and well-being. Conclusion: Findings support the expected relations among personality, psychosocial variables and health in a group of working people. Key words: job strain, negative egocentric sensitivity, health

Sexual aggression in dating relationships of Spanish students during high school and university

González Lozano, Pilar *Pers., Eval. y Psic. Clínica, Univ. Complutense de Madrid, Pozuelo de Alarcón (madrid), Spain* **Sebastián Herranz, Julia** *Psic. Biológica y de la Salud, Universidad Autónoma de Madrid, Madrid, Spain* **Muñoz-Rivas, Marina Julia** *Psic. Clínica y de la Salud, Universidad Autónoma de Madrid, Madrid, Spain* **Fernández González, Liria** *Psic. Biológica y de la Salud, Universidad Autónoma de Madrid, Madrid, Spain*

Objective: To assess the prevalence and forms of sexual aggression in Spanish dating couples. Method: The participants were 4,052 adolescents and young adults of both genders, between ages of 16 and 26 years. Results: About 34% of males and 14% of females reported that they are engaged in some form of sexual aggression, being verbal pressure the most prevalent. Analysis of the age group differences showed that, overall, sexual coercion increases with age. Conclusions: Sexual aggression in dating relationships is more common and serious than it is thought. Moreover, results provide useful introductory information to design prevention and intervention programs.

Examining early adaptation difficulties among 3-year-old children with difficulties in attention and hyperactivity: The role of biological risk-factors, family stressors and parenting practices

Gosar, David *Department of Neurology, University Children's Hospital, Ljubljana, Slovenia* **Holnthaner, Rok** *Child & Adolescent Psychia, Mental Health Service, Maribor, Slovenia*

The systematic psychological survey of 3-year-olds authored by Peter Praper is a screening survey, which allows early detection of children at risk in their cognitive, social or emotional development. Using data from a representative sample of 3210 Slovenian 3-year-olds included in the survey we investigated the adaptation difficulties of children for whom parents reported hyperactivity and/or difficulties in attention. This group of children was 8-times more likely to score beyond the cut-off point for severe adaptation difficulties. In addition, difficulties during pregnancy and brain impairment were more common. Parents also reported more interpersonal difficulties and less optimal parenting practices.

Effects of exposure to mass media on human drawings of four-year olds

Goshiki, Toru *Fuculty of Education, Shizuoka University, Shizuoka, Japan* **Koyasu, Masuo** *Fuculty of Pedagogy, Kyoto University, Kyoto, Japan*

This study examined the effects of exposure to mass media on the drawings of 885 four-year-old children (465 boys and 420 girls) living in Kawasaki City, Japan. Children were asked to draw a male and a female figure. Their parents assessed the degrees to which the children were exposed to television, video, and video games in their daily lives. The results suggest that girls can draw better human figures than boys, and that longer video viewing time in four- and three-year-olds produced a lower score, but that longer television viewing time in three-year-olds produced a better score in their drawings.

The family in the contemporary society: Shared tasks?

Goulao, Maria de Fatima *Universidade Aberta - CEMRI, Lisboa, Portugal*

Family is the first subjects' agent of socialization, providing experiences and examples that can come to perpetuate or to change representations, atti-

tudes and behaviours. We intended to know the opinion of a group of teenagers, on aspects that link with the division of tasks between both couple's members relatively the children's education. The sample is composed of 172 teenagers of both sexes and the average age is 15. A questionnaire with 2 parts was used. The results appear, in agreement with this group of youths, for a shared commitment in assuming the linked tasks to the children's education.

Conditioned place preference induced by forced running in rats

Grant, Virginia *Dept. of Psychology, Memorial Univ. of Newfoundland, St. John's, Canada* **Tobin, Stephanie** *Psychology, Concordia University, Montreal, Canada* **Rice, Patricia** *Psychology, Memorial U of Newfoundland, St. John's, Canada*

Rats running voluntarily in wheels develop a conditioned place preference (CPP) for a place experienced after running. Thus the after-effects of voluntary running appear rewarding. Two similar experiments determined if forced running also produces CPP. Male Sprague-Dawley rats were forced to run in a motorized wheel and then confined in a novel place. After six such pairings, the rats were allowed free access to that place and another equally familiar place. Compared to controls, rats spent more time in the place paired with running (p<.05). The after-effects of forced exercise, like voluntary exercise, produce CPP and thus are rewarding.

Is ethnic identity in children worth measuring?: The development of an ethnic identity scale for majority and minority group children

Griffiths, Judith *School of Psychology, Griffith University, Queensland, Australia*

The current study was conducted to redress the absence of a measure of ethnic identity in ethnic majority and minority children. Following a consultation process, an initial scale was constructed. The responses of 279 ethnic majority and minority children to this initial scale were subjected to factor analysis. This analysis revealed three factors (ethnic pride, ethnic comparison, and involvement in ethnic activities) characterising ethnic identity in children. Reliability analysis supported the reliability of these scales. The results of confirmatory factor analysis from an additional 475 ethnic majority and minority children provided support for the utility of the original factor structure.

Body-experience in breast cancer patients: A study with the repertory grid technique

Grimm, Anne *Klinik für Psychosomatik, Charité Berlin, Berlin, Germany* **Voigt, Barbara** *Med. Klinik m.S. Psychosomatik, Charité, Berlin, Germany* **Klapp, Burghard F.** *Med. Klinik m.S. Psychosomatik, Charité, Berlin, Germany* **Rauchfuß, Martina** *Med. Klinik m.S. Psychosomatik, Charité, Berlin, Germany*

Objectives: Breast cancer has an effect on the body-experience of the affected women. The repertory grid technique as a diagnostic instrument can be used to ascertain the central dimensions on the basis of which breast cancer patients structure their body experience. Methods: 58 women with breast cancer were questioned by the repertory grid technique. Results: The subjective connotations of representations of individual body parts will be presented. We found dissociation tendencies of representations of breast, genital and skin. Conclusion: The repertory grid technique can make specific body-experience profiles accessible to therapeutic treatment. A questionnaire based on subjective self-descriptions is planned.

Psychometric instruments for measuring and preventing the risk of complicated grief in bereaved parents

Guarino, Angela *Dipt. di Psicologia 1, Università La Sapienza, Roma, Italy* **Serantoni, Grazia** *Fondazione Lefebvre D'Ovidio, Fondazione Lefebvre D'Ovidio, Roma, Italy*

The aim of this clinical research is the application of a specific battery of psychometric instruments (tested on a group of more than 10 parents) for measuring and preventing the risk of complicated grief in bereaved parents; the psychological constructs investigated and correlated are: psychological reactions to grief and risk factors – with "Hogan Grief Reaction Checklist (Hogan et al., 2001)" and "Inventory of Complicated Grief (Prigerson et al., 1995)" – and the cognitive traits of changes in life outlook and time perspective with "Changes in Outlook Questionnaire (Joseph et al., 2005)" and "Zimbardo Time Perspective Inventory (Zimbardo & Boyd, 1999)".

God, fairies and Superman: Children concepts about non-human agents

Guerrero, Silvia *Psychology, University of Castilla-Mancha, Cuenca, Spain* **Jiménez, Laura** *Developmental Psychology, Univ. Complutense of Madrid, Madrid, Spain* **Callejas, Carolina** *Developmental Psychology, Universidad Autónoma, Madrid, Spain* **Dopico, Cristina** *Developmental Psychology, Univ. Complutense of Mad, Madrid, Spain*

Previous studies have shown that the early comprehension of human-agents follows three stages: Teleological-agency, mentalistic-agency and representational-agency. However, much less is known about the non-human agent. Seventy-two Spanish children from three age-groups (5-6, 7-8, 9-10) faced a false belief task about the mental state of different kinds of agents: Human agents (p.e., a friend), animal agents (p.e., a dog) and non-human agents (Superman, a fairy, and God). Preliminary results show that older children make some distinctions between the non-agent concepts, specifically between God and the other two kinds of non-agents. However, these differences were not found among younger children.

The attitudes, beliefs, and emotions about mathematics of primary education students of the University of Extremadura

Guerrero Barona, Eloisa *Psicología y Antropología, Universidad de Extremadura, Badajoz, Spain* **Caballero, Ana** *Didáctica CC.Experimentales, Universidad de Extremadura, Badajoz, Spain* **Blanco, Lorenzo** *Didáctica CC.Experimentales, Universidad de Extremadura, Badajoz, Spain* **Brigido Mero, Maria**

We studied the affective domain (attitudes, beliefs, and emotions) of primary education students at the University of Extremadura (Spain) with respect to mathematics teaching, given the importance of these aspects in pupils' attainments and acceptance or rejection of this discipline. The sample consisted of four years of primary education undergraduates who were given a questionnaire of 48 items scored from 1 ("strongly disagree") to 4 ("strongly agree"). A descriptive and inferential analysis revealed hopeful results as long as there was improvement in the affective factors of these students.

The effect of a verbal pretraining on the post-contact descriptions on a matching-to-sample task

Guerrero Radillo, Alejandra Paola *CEIC, Universidad de Guadalajara, Guadalajara, Mexico* **Ortiz, Gerardo** *CEIC, Universidad de Guadalajara, Guadalajara, Mexico* **Herrán Galaviz, Antonio** *Facultad de Psicologia, Universidad de Guadalajara, Guadalajara, Mexico*

Instructions are often defined as descriptions of contingencies presented to the individual prior to contact with them, while rules are defined as descriptions elaborated after such contact, being abstractions of verbal elements relevant to the task. The identification of these elements can be affected if there is a verbal repertoire to designate them or not. In the present study we observed the effects of a verbal pretraining on the post-contact descriptions of college students. The results show a differential effect on the type of post-contact description due to feedback frequency and the precision of the received instructions.

The effect of housing group size and gender on emotional behavior indexes in rats

Gulatowska, Judyta Dept. of Psychology, University of Warsaw, Warsaw, Poland

The purpose of present study was to find out, whether the size of the housing group affects emotionality in rats of different sexes. Sprague-Dawley rats were housed in small, medium, large groups. After two months open field and elevated plus maze tests were done. Standard indexes of emotionality were measured and ultrasonic vocalization (22 kHz frequency) were recorded. Two-factor analysis of variance was used to asses differences. It was found that males vocalized more during both anxiety tests. There was statistical significant effect of the group size on defecations and freezing.

Some neglected ethical impulses for psychology in the past and their actuality for the future

Guski-Leinwand, Susanne Bad Honnef, Germany

In the history of psychology some remarkable ethical impulses were published and should be remembered and discussed in their meaning in the past and for the future. Ethic will be discussed in fields of responsibilities of psychology. Various psychological theories - like "Ganzheitspsychologie" and "differentielle Völkerpsychologie" - are presented in their basic statements as well as ethical-scientifical claims.

Bioethical aspects of medico-genetic assistance in psychiatry

Gutkevich, Elena Laboratory, Mental Health Research Institu, Tomsk, Russia

Principles of global bioethics in psychiatry are personal autonomy, justice, non-malfalcence and beneficence, verity, confidentiality and informed consent. Investigations of genetic bases of mental disorders show their multi-factorial nature. However, results of genetic analysis of mental disorders indicate only alteration of degree of risk for carrier of revealed mutations. Genetic counseling regarding family planning or abortion should be conducted with account for system of values of the patient, it is necessary to help patients in independent optimal decision making giving them sufficient medical and psychiatric information.

Technical precision of measurement in computerized psychological assessment on windows platforms

Häusler, Joachim Psychological Assessment, SCHUHFRIED GmbH, Mödling, Austria *Sommer, Markus* Psychological Assessment, SCHUHFRIED GmbH, Mödling, Austria *Chroust, Stefan* Psychological Assessment, SCHUHFRIED GmbH, Mödling, Austria

Reaction time based measures are used to assess a variety of elementary cognitive functions. Typically the inter-individual variance is small in the sense that the central 50 percent of a norm population range within less than 100ms. Thus systematic errors of measurement may seriously affect the validity of diagnostic judgments. Using an "artificial respondent" several computerized tests of attention have been evaluated on a wide range of computer configurations with respect to their technical precision of measurement. The results

range up to biases greater than 20 percentile ranks. Self-calibration devices are presented as a means of quality control and assurance.

Positive evidence for Eysenck's arousal hypothesis: Combining electroencephalogram and magnetic resonance imaging methods

Hagemann, Dirk Institute of Psychology, University of Heidelberg, Heidelberg, Germany *Hewig, Johannes* Department of Psychology, University of Jena, Jena, Germany *Walter, Christof* Department of Radiology, Brüderkrankenhaus Trier, Trier, Germany *Naumann, Ewald* Department of Psychology, University of Trier, Trier, Germany

Eysenck's arousal hypothesis was tested in several studies that used the electroencephalogram (EEG) to index cortical arousal, but empirical findings are inconsistent. The aim of the present study was to test this hypothesis with EEG measures of arousal while controlling for a static nuisance variable, i.e. individual differences in skull thickness. Resting EEG was acquired on three occasions of measurement, skull thickness was quantified with anatomical magnetic resonance imaging (MRI), and extraversion was assessed by questionnaire. There was a positive association between alpha activity and extraversion, which was not affected by skull thickness. This finding is consistent with the hypothesis.

The effect of positive adolescent choices training (a cognative-behavioral program) on violence prevention in adolescents of Tehran

Hajati, Fereshteh Sadat Faculty of Psychology, Al_Zahra University, Tehran, Islamic Republic of Iran

The objective of this study is to investigate the effect of cognitive-behavioral, positive adolescent choices training (PACT) program on violence reduction and prevention in adolescents of Tehran. For this purpose the Adolescents' Aggression Inventory(AAI)& Anger Control Inventory (ACI) were developed and administered to 200 adolescents. A sample of 48 students, who had obtained the highest scores on (AAI), and the lowest scores on (ACI), were selected and divided randomly into two groups of experimental and control. The experimental group received the intervention program in 12 sessions.Then the two inventories were administered again to the experimental and control groups as post-test. The hypotheses were verified by ANOVA, and were confirmed.

Single mother families, stepfather families, and intact families: Children's psychosocial adjustment & mothers' experience of parenthood

Hakvoort, Esther Educational Sciences, University of Amsterdam, Amsterdam, Netherlands *Bos, Henny* Educational Sciences, University of Amsterdam, Amsterdam, Netherlands *van Balen, Frank* Educational Sciences, University of Amsterdam, Amsterdam, Netherlands *Hermanns, Jo* Educational Sciences, University of Amsterdam, Amsterdam, Netherlands

Assuming that family composition influences family processes, children and mothers in single-mother-families (n=51), stepfather-families (n=30), and intact-families (n=67) were studied. In a representative sample, children (8-12 years) were interviewed and mothers filled in a questionnaire. A 3 (family type) x 2 (gender) MANOVA was carried out. Boys in single-parent-families showed more conduct problems than girls, while the opposite was found in stepfather-families. For mothers, single mothers reported less competence, more stress, and more parental justification compared to mothers in other family types. These results support the assumption that the presence of a second parent positively influences mothers' experience of parenthood.

Theory of mind acquisition and use in deaf college students

Hao, Jian Dept. of Psychology, Peking University, Beijing, People's Republic of China *Su, Yanjie* Department of Psychology, Peking University, Beijing, People's Republic of China

The present study aimed to investigate whether theory of mind delay in deaf children from hearing families is a permanent deficit. Participants were 45 deaf students from hearing families (20 prelingual signers, 15 prelingual bilinguals and 10 postlingual bilinguals), 8 deaf students from deaf families and 32 hearing students. The results indicated that most deaf groups produced less mentalisitc terms and the prelingual groups did poorly in theory of mind story understanding. However, all the participants seemed to ignore others' mind in the communication game. It was suggested that prelingual deaf adults from hearing families might still have mentalizing difficulties.

Does work experience make a difference in the expression of gender role behavior?

Harring, Kathleen Dept. of Psychology, Muhlenberg College, Allentown, USA *Edelman, Laura* Psychology, Muhlenberg College, Allentown, USA

We investigated whether sexist attitudes influence workplace behavior and if work experience affects gender role behavior. College undergraduates (N=137) and alumni (N=77) completed the Ambivalent Sexism Inventory (Glick & Fiske, 1996) to assess their level of sexism. Participants rated the extent to which they engaged in various workplace behaviors or traits. A factor analysis was used to group the behaviors and traits into four categories: negative agentic, positive agentic, negative communal, positive communal. Results indicated that the alumni were less sexist, more agentic, and overall rated themselves higher on positive than negative traits than did the college students.

Internal motivation in academic performance

Hart, Alex Psychology, Clark University, Worcester, MA, USA *McGovern, Arthur* Psychology, Nichols College, Dudley, MA, USA

The present study sought to find if linguistic differences found in samples of students' expressive writing were associated with differences in academic performance. US students (n=38) were assigned to write on either the emotional issues of transitioning to college life, or a mental simulation exercise about attaining academic goals. Students' writings were analyzed using LIWC (Pennebaker and Frances, 1996) showing 72 different linguistic dimensions. There were no significant differences between the groups. However across both groups those students who wrote more about money had a higher semester GPA (r= .399 p= .016). We discuss whether internal motivation has become reduced in a globalized system of pressure for success.

The novelty of the laboratory

Hart, Alex Psychology, Clark University, Worcester, MA, USA

There is an ever increasing novelty within the psychological laboratory, settings are increasingly artificial and thus if the goal of psychology is to examine the mental processes and behavior of man within natural settings, psychology must adapt procedures to meet such an end. The informed consent form often makes participants uncomfortable, rather than assuring them of their rights, its intended purpose. Questioned also is the notion of applied \\ field psychology- what is observed is not necessarily natural as for observer effects. However, minimizing these effects and working toward a more person centered psychology will be discussed, in so far as one can reduce extraneous variables such as informed consent, ill familiarity and only then truly examine the concept desired.

Undergraduate conceptions of the institutional review board

Hart, Alex Psychology, Clark University, Worcester, MA, USA

To challenge undergraduate students in a capstone psychology course to reexamine notions in psychology that are generally accepted without second thought was the focus of this study. Students were challenged to rethink everyday activities within their laboratories and studies. Students felt the relative absurdity of the IRB, in that their mission had changed from ethical protections to legal and fiscal protections within Universities. Students challenged that data belongs to the participant and the participant should be acknowledged if he so desires, not be automatically anonymous. These results should raise questions about the relatively accepted principles of psychology within our race to consistently publish and not perish in an increasingly productive but decreasingly novel field.

The effects of perinatal hypothyroidism on the attentional ability in rats

Hasegawa, Masashi Sapporo, Japan Kida, Ikuhiro Dental Medicine, Hokkaido University, Sapporo, Japan Wada, Hiromi Psychology, Hokkaido University, Sapporo, Japan

Thyroid hormone is essential for proper development of the CNS; disruption of this hormone causes cognitive dysfunctions. We examined effects of perinatal hypothyroidism on attentional abilities, using vigilance tasks and magnetic resonance imaging (MRI). Pregnant dams were treated with Methimazole by adding it to the drinking water from gestational day 15 to postnatal day 21. In the vigilance task, hypothyroid rats displayed significantly lower rates of correct responses. The MRI studies did not detect significant differences in hippocampus/brain proportions between normal and hypothyroid rats. These results suggest that hypothyroidism impairs to shift attention but does not affect the hippocampal sizes.

Infants appreciate cooperativeness in imperative communication

Hauser, Gerlind Developmental Psychology, Max Planck Institute EVA, Leipzig, Germany Behne, Tanya School of Psychology, University of Manchester, Manchester, United Kingdom Moll, Henrike Developmental Psychology, Max Planck Institute EVA, Leipzig, Germany Carpenter, Malinda Developmental Psychology, Max Planck Institute EVA, Leipzig, Germany Tomasello, Michael Developmental Psychology, Max Planck Institute EVA, Leipzig, Germany

Human communication rests on a basic assumption of partner cooperativeness. For imperatives, it is unknown whether infants appreciate this assumption of cooperativeness or manipulate their partner on an instrumental basis. In our first study an adult ambiguously requested an object from an infant. To disambiguate the request the infant had to assume that the adult was acting cooperatively and rationally. In the second study we manipulated the reaction of an adult to infants' requests, by either understanding or misunderstanding and giving the right or the wrong object first (modelled after a study by Shwe and Markmann, 1996). Results indicate that infants just beginning to acquire language already understand the cooperative logic of imperative communication.

The role of movement in the action-sentence compatibility effect

Hauser, Christiane Inst. für Psychologie, Max-Planck-Institut, Leipzig, Germany Massen, Cristina Psychology, Max Planck Institute CBS, Leipzig, Germany Rieger, Martina Psychology, Max Planck Institute CBS, Leipzig, Germany Glenberg, Arthur Psychology, University of Wisconsin, Madison, WI,

USA Prinz, Wolfgang Psychology, Max Planck Institute CBS, Leipzig, Germany

In line with research on embodied language, the action-sentence compatibility effect (ACE) shows that sensibility judgements for sentences are faster when the direction of the described action matches the direction of the movement required to make the response. We investigated whether the ACE results from compatibility between sentence direction and movement direction or direction of the movement effect and whether movement amplitude influences the size of the ACE. Movements were dissociated from their effects by presenting transformed action effects on a screen. The ACE turned out to be predominantly movement-related and its size was independent of the movement amplitude.

Analyzing the cognitive, emotional, and motor development of hyperactive children with the Intelligence and Developmental Scales (IDS)

Heckmann, Carmen P. Inst. für Psychologie, Universität Freiburg, Freiburg, Germany Hansen, Miriam Cognition, Emotion & Commu, Albert-Ludwigs-Universität Fre, Freiburg, Germany Spada, Hans Inst. für Psychologie, Universität Freiburg, Freiburg, Germany

The Intelligence and Developmental Scales (IDS; Grob, Meyer & Hagmann) were recently constructed for children between 5 and 11 years and are currently standardized for Switzerland, Germany, and Austria. The sixteen subscales provide a comprehensive developmental profile including cognitive, emotional, motivational, and motor abilities. We tested 30 hyperactive children between 8 and 11 years and compared their achievement to the data of 30 children (matched in age) from the German standard population. The results implicate differences in attention related development but also in some new subscales as the socio-emotional development. Implications for using IDS in clinical diagnostics will be discussed.

The structure of Holland's RIASEC types in Serbia and Croatia

Hedrih, Vladimir Psychology, Faculty of Philosophy, Nis, Serbia Sverko, Iva Psychology, Institute of Social Sciences, Zagreb, Croatia

The goal of this study was to examine the level of fit of four models of Holland's RIASEC vocational interest structure on samples of high school students from Serbia and Croatia. Holland's Self-directed Search was administered to 362 high school students from Serbia and 384 from Croatia. Levels of fit of Holland's hexagonal, Gati's hierarchical, Rounds-Tracey's and Liu-Rounds' models were examined using the randomization test of hypothetical orders and Myors' test. High level of fit was obtained for the hexagonal model in both countries, while the fit of other models was not uniformly high.

Performance of the bootstrap Rasch model test in the presence of crossing item characteristic curves: Complex answers to a simple question

Heene, Moritz Inst. für Pädog. Psychologie, Universität München, München, Germany Ziegler, Matthias Psychological Methodology, Psychological Institute, Muenchen, Germany Bühner, Markus Psychological Methodology, Psychological Institute, Muenchen, Germany

The Rasch model (Rasch, 1960) has been widely applied to test data because of its properties of unidimensionality and specific objectivity (Rasch, 1977). The extent to which these properties are met depends on the data-model fit. Results of this simulation study pinpoint the weaknesses of the bootstrap model test (Davier, 1997) with respect to detection rates of model violations in the form of intersecting item characteristic curves. The results revealed low detection rates and complex effects between the distributional type of item slope and

item difficulty. The drawbacks of global versus local model fit testing are discussed.

Developmental changes in affective decision-making: The effects of age and sex in 3 and 4-year old children

Heilman, Renata Dept. of Psychology, Babes-Bolyai University, Cluj-Napoca, Romania Miu, Andrei Psychology, Babes-Bolyai University, Cluj-Napoca, Romania Benga, Oana Psychology, Babes-Bolyai University, Cluj-Napoca, Romania

The present study used Children's Gambling Task (CGT) to investigate age and sex differences in affective decision-making in 3-year old and 4-year old children. Our main findings were that 4-year old children displayed better performance than 3-year olds, and boys outperformed girls in CGT. Also, there was a significant correlation between the level of declarative and metacognitive knowledge and behavioral performance in 4-year old, but not 3-year old children, and in boys, but not girls. These results indicate that the development of CGT performance undergoes a critical period between 3 and 4 years, being faster in boys than girls.

Implicit association test and children's concept of alcohol

Heim-Dreger, Uwe Inst. für Psychologie, Pädagogische Hochschule, Schwäbisch Gmünd, Germany Eschenbeck, Heike Psychology, University of Education, Schwäbisch Gmünd, Germany Kohlmann, Carl-Walter Psychology, University of Education, Schwäbisch Gmünd, Germany

The implicit association test (IAT, Greenwald et al., 1998) has been adapted to measure primary school children's concept of alcohol (N = 67, age: 8 to 10 years). Target categories were children vs. adults and alcoholic vs. soft drinks. Questionnaires measured explicit attitudes concerning drinking alcohol and taste of alcohol. Correlations were found for IAT-alcohol (high scores indicating associations between adults and alcohol) with positive attitudes towards drinking alcohol (r = .37, p < .01), "alcohol tastes good" (r = .39, p < .05), and "I would try it again" (r = .41, p < .05). Diagnostic implications will be discussed.

A subtle measure of prejudice: Development and validation of a German version of the Racial Argument Scale

Heitland, Kirsten Bielefeld, Germany Bohner, Gerd Social Psychology, University of Bielefeld, Bielefeld, Germany

On the Racial Argument Scale (RAS), respondents rate how well arguments support conclusions that are positive or negative toward Blacks (Saucier & Miller, 2003, PSPB). These ratings provide a subtle measure of racial prejudice. A German version of the RAS was adapted to Turks as the target group and validated with a diverse sample of adults (N = 194). High correlations of the RAS with related measures of prejudice, right-wing authoritarianism, and social dominance orientation, and a null correlation with a social desirability scale provide evidence for convergent and discriminant validity. Potential applications for the German RAS will be discussed.

Effects of gender and ethnicity on gender beliefs, identity styles, and social well-being

Hejazi Moughari, Elaheh Educational Psychology, University of Tehran, Tehran, Islamic Republic of Iran

In order to identify the effects of gender and ethnicity on gender beliefs, identity styles, and social well-being,830(430 Fars-400 Kurds)tenth grade students were chosen randomly from Tehran and Sanandaje.They completed 3 questionnaires: identity styles inventory(ISI,Berzonsky,1992),social well-being scale(SWS,Keyes,1998), and gender beliefs scale(Hejazi,Zohrevand,2004). A 2(gender) ×2(ethnic) analysis of variance (ANOVA) was used to analyze identity styles, gender beliefs, and social well being scores. The results indicated that; the gender and ethnicity differences in identity styles, commitment and social well being were significant ($p<.05$).The effects of gender and ethnicity on gender stereotype beliefs were significant ($p<0.05$).

German speaking psychology in Prague

Heller, Daniel Dept. of Cognitive Psychology, Institute of Psychology, Prague, Czech Republic

Since dividing Charles university to German and Czech universities in 1882, there were two universities in Prague, the Czech one (until 1939 and again since 1945) and the German one (until 1945). Many persons important for the history of psychology were teaching there: Christian von Ehrenfels, Josef Eisenmeier, Ewald Hering, Johannes Lindworsky, Ernst Mach, Anton Marty, Carl Stumpf, Emil Utitz and others. Max Wertheimer was born and studied in Prague. The author focuses on this historical heritage and its contribution to the European, as well as world psychology.

Assessing infant behaviour: Acceptance and accuracy of electronic diaries

Hemmi, Mirja Helen Universität Basel, Basel, Switzerland Müller, Silvana Universität Basel, sesam, Basel, Switzerland Schneider, Silvia Universität Basel, Fakultät für Psychologie, Basel, Switzerland

To date, no studies have collected important infant behaviour by electronic diaries. However, electronic diaries seem to obtain more accurate data than a paper-pencil version. Moreover, the usability of electronic diaries might lead to greater acceptance and to a reduced probability of retrospection errors. Method: 120 German—Speaking women are asked to fill out an electronic and written diary about important behaviour of their 6-month-old child. The two diaries will be compared to examine their accuracy. Additionally, questionnaires will be used to assess the acceptance of both diaries. First results of the study and their implications will be presented and discussed.

The role of goal focus for success in dieting

Hennecke, Marie Inst. für Psychologie, Universität Zürich, Zürich, Switzerland Freund, Alexandra M. Inst. für Psychologie, Universität Zürich, Zürich, Switzerland

Focusing on the process (food preparation, eating behavior) vs. the outcome (weight, figure) of the goal to loose weight might influence the success of dieting. A total of $N = 135$ young, middle-aged and older women are taking part in a diet program that manipulates goal focus using a diary method focusing participants either on the outcome or the process. Success of dieting is assessed longitudinally over 3 months in terms of weight loss and maintenance of diet. The impact of goal-focus on success in dieting and possible age-related differences will be reported.

Parents and children in custody disputes

Heubeck, Bernd School of Psychology, Australian National University, Canberra, Australia Connor, Sue School of Psychology, Australian National University, Canberra, Australia

Divorce can generate considerable conflict which often lingers for years. A small minority of parents (in Australia $< 6\%$) will pursue their disagreements to such an extent that they finally require a judge to make a custody decision for their child/ren. Custody disputes represent a particular conflict constellation. Family conflict is generally known to adversely affect parents and children. However, the literature on how parents and children respond to the particular demands of custody disputes is limited. This study is based on a series of 100 families referred for custody evaluations by the court and considers the patterns of their relation-

ships as well as indicators of mental health within a triadic framework.

Body consciousness moderates the effect of message framing on intentions to use sunscreen

Hevey, David Dept. of Psychology, Trinity College Dublin, Dublin, Ireland Pertl, Maria School of Radiation Therapy, Trinity College Dublin, Dublin, Ireland Thomas, Kevin School of Psychology, Trinity College Dublin, Dublin, Ireland Maher, Laura School of Radiation Therapy, Trinity College Dublin, Dublin, Ireland Craig, Agnella School of Radiation Therapy, Trinity College Dublin, Dublin, Ireland Ni Chuinneagain, Siobhan School of Radiation Therapy, Trinity College Dublin, Dublin, Ireland

Objectives: to examine moderating effects of body consciousness on the relationship between responses to gain or loss-framed health messages describing appearance or health benefits and subsequent intentions to use sunscreen. Methods: Questionnaire data from a sample of 590 young adults were analysed using factorial ANOVA. Results: A statistically significant interaction between message frame and body consciousness was found, such that gain-framed health or appearance messages had the strongest effect on sunscreen use intentions for those high in body consciousness compared to those low in body consciousness. Conclusion: Message framing effects on precautionary sun behaviour intentions are moderated by body consciousness.

Community force: Ethnic networks for social inclusion

Hinding, Barbara TU Dortmund, Dortmund, Germany Borowczak, Anja Organisationspsychologie, TU Dortmund, Dortmund, Germany Kastner, Michael Organisationspsychologie, TU Dortmund, Dortmund, Germany

Migrants and ethnic minorities often develop an active community life in their host countries. These ethnic communities hold an enormous self-help potential. For example, inhabitants of a socially deprived residential district often build a community and develop social strategies and organisational forms to support and help each other to protect their interests. Regarding this, ethnic groups threatened by social exclusion were examined by means of qualitative social network analysis. Case studies show the significance of individual networks as well as ethnic self-organizations for the individual mastering of social exclusion in the context of different cultures.

Effects of interior color on emotion in full-scale modeling

Hirschmüller, Anna Katharina CDSS, University of Mannheim, Mannheim, Germany Irtel, Hans Faculty of Social Sciences, University of Mannheim, Mannheim, Germany Schlegel, Markus I. international Trendscouting, HAWK Hildesheim, Hildesheim, Germany

The influence of interior room color attributes on emotional response was systematically explored by using full-scale room modeling. 25 complex interior-models were designed each of them representing a distinct color intensity (lightness & chroma) and hue category. The emotional responses of 91 participants to the room-models were investigated using Self-Assessment Manikin scales. Results show that dominant hue has a significant influence on emotional responses and indicate furthermore the combined influence of lightness and chroma as well as an interaction between hue and intensity attributes.

Sense of coherence and illness experience

Horike, Hiroko Dept. of Psychology, Tohoku-Gakuin University, Sendai, Japan

The concept of "sense of coherence (SOC)" is notable to investigate the illness experience in health

psychology. Horike (2004, ICP) extracted the three components of SOC from the illness narrative of Japanese breast cancer patients. In this study, adult female patients with breast cancer and children with chronic illness were asked to answer our Japanese version of SOC scales for adults (Antonovsky, 1987) or for children (Margalit, 2005version; personal letter). The participants were also asked to write or talk about their illness experience. The narrative categories on the illness experience were related with the SOC sub-scores respectively.

Argumentation and knowledge inquiry

Horng, Ruey-Yun Dept. Industrial Engineering, National Chiao Tung University, Hsinchu, Taiwan Lin, Tzu-Jung Educational Psychology, University of Illinois, Champaign, IL, USA

Objectives: The effect of argumentation practice on knowledge inquiry was examined. Methods: Ninety-five participants were assigned to the argumentation or non-argumentation training condition to argue for two claims proposed in two science texts. They were then asked to recall the original texts and argue from their own position. Results: Argumentation training increased the number of new concepts, new propositions and evidences explored by participants when they encountered claims regarding some states of knowledge. The cost of argumentation on memory intrusion was minimal. Conclusions: Self-argumentation is useful as a means to expand one's knowledge inquiry attempts.

The gender differences in the pattern of major and college selection and the mental health

Hsu, Chong-Shiann Dept. of Clinical Psychology, Chang Jung Christian Uni., Tainan, Taiwan

This study investigates the reasons for major decision and college selection and the impact of the preceding reasons on the mental health. There are 47,465 samples from the Taiwan Higher Education Data System. The t-test and the structural equation modeling are used. It is found that before going to college, the female freshmen make major and college selection on the basis of school quality, career plan, academic interest, suggestions from significant others, and placement prediction more than the male ones. The freshmen who decide a major on the basis of their own needs perform great mental health.

Gendered Guanxi: How women managers in information technology field in China network

Huang, Jiehua School of Business, Lappeenranta University, Lappeenranta, Finland Aaltio, Iiris School of Business and Economi, Jyväskylä University, Jyväskylä, Finland

This empirical study is on the characteristics of guanxi (personal ties) bases of women managers in information technology (IT) in Mainland China, especially on what comprise them and how they affect women managers' career and life. Using questionnaire, in-depth interview, statistic and interpretive analysis, we found, (1) guanxi bases of these IT women are limited, (2) a significant effect of female-to-male dyads, which are mainly within power- and work-related guanxi, (3) female-to-female dyads are mostly related to 'socialize' guanxi. Our study indicates that women IT managers have two constructions of networks (work- and life-related), which are illustrative of a gendering process. Implications for human resource management are discussed.

Work environment, work-nonwork interface, and quality of life offreelance teleworkers

Huang, Qinghai Personnel Decisions Internatio, Shanghai, People's Republic of China Johansson, Gunn Department of Psychology, Stockholm University, Stockholm, Sweden

This study was to examine freelance teleworkers' work environment, work-nonwork interface, and quality of life. The results showed men reported better physical work environment and health level than women, especially than home-based working women. Too high a work centrality was significantly related to high work demand, more work-to-nonwork conflict, low nonwork satisfaction and health. Those who chose freelance work for the reason of autonomy and freedom reported better psychosocial work environment, which was especially seen in women. It was found that work environment, work-nonwork interface, and quality of life were significantly related, and work-nonwork interface was a significant mediator.

The relationships between Taiwanese family boundary and adolescent school adjustment: A multilevel approach

Huang, Tsung-Chain Guidance and Counseling, National Changhua University, Changhua City, Taiwan

This article extended the scope of previous research to employ family as an unit of analysis to characterize members' interactions Subjects were from a metropolitan area in Taiwan, each of four members in 362 families, including father, mother, two adolescent children. The results showed that the variances of adolescent school adjustment were significantly predicated by the family-level, dyadic-level and individual-level of family boundary. Surprisingly, clear family boundary did not show better adjustment as predicted. However, for adolescent, those who perceived higher level of dominance and higher level of alliance have the best adjustment outcome. The influential cultural-specific effects such as "person in relations", filial piety, as well as clinical applications were discussed.

A temporal perspective of psychological ownership and employee extra-role behavior

Hui, Chun Management Dept., Chinese Univers. of Hong Kong, Shatin, China, People's Republic of : Hong Kong SAR Lee, Cynthia College of Business Admin, Northeastern University, Boston, USA Liu, Jun Business School, Remin University of China, Beijin, China, People's Republic of China

We attempt to conceptualize employer-employee relationship in terms of employee's psychological ownership of their job and examine the role of psychological ownership in employee's extra-role contribution. We adopt a temporal perspective in understanding how to enhance psychological ownership. We suggest that involving employees in the future of the organization is critical to the development of psychological ownership. We also suggest that there must be consistency between the employee's own temporal orientation and the organization's temporal orientation in order that employee's involvement in the future of the organization may have the strongest effect on psychological ownership and subsequently, employee extra-role contribution.

Self-actualization in Japan: A history of discourse on self in consumer society

Igarashi, Yasuhiro Aesthetics and Health Sciences, Yamano College of Aesthetics, Tokyo, Japan

The conception of self-actualization was introduced into Japan in 1960s with translation of Abraham Maslow's work. His theory of motivation was widely accepted and soon incorporated into psychology textbook. Along with Erik Erikson's theory of ego-identity, it became popular by 1980s. Self-actualization had liberating impetus for people looking for their unique ways of lives in society where traditional collective culture and Confucian ethics curtailed individual freedom. With changes in society in recent years, discourses concerning self-actualization are also changing. The way they serve as technology of subjectivity in contemporary

Japanese society and their implications will be discussed.

Science education of the brain and mind for junior high school students: The experiential cognition and development of e-learning program

Ikeda, Masami Ochanomizu University, Tokyo, Japan Tanaka, Miho International Communication, Gunma Prefectural Women's Univ, Gunma, Japan Ishiguchi, Akira Graduate School, Ochanomizu University, Tokyo, Japan

This research is a new investigation that incorporates the "visual phenomena" treated in psychology into science education for junior high school students. Specifically, using the visual phenomenon of "visual illusions" as materials, we (i) developed a "visual illusion experiment tool"; (ii) conducted classes using the experiment tool; and (iii) measures the effects of the classes. The results of this study showed that through the process of measuring their own visual reactions, the students gained an increased interest in humans and science, and at the same time developed a greater understanding of the workings of the brain and the mind.

Family relationship in the rural areas of Bangladesh: A comparative study on Muslim and Santal community

Islam, A.K.M. Shafiul Dept. of Sociology, Rajshahi University, Rajshahi, Bangladesh

This study will provide a detail perspective of family relationship pattern between Muslim and Santal communities, and explore the family relationship norms, marriage relationship and developing bond. This study also compares the sexual behaviour, marriage relationship pattern and marriage role relationship among these communities. Family relationship pattern depends on various influencing factors in Bangladeshi culture. It will try to depict factors which influence the relationship pattern among the Muslim and Santal communities in rural Bangladesh. It's based on a significant sample of Muslim and Santal families collected through survey and participant-observation methods from selected study areas in Bangladesh.

Effect of employees' self-esteem and the discrepancy between self-appraisal and reflected self-appraisal on relationships with superordinates

Isobe, Chikae Graduate of I.A.S, Hiroshima University, Higashihiroshima, Japan Li, Xuemei Graduate of I.A.S, Hiroshima University, Higashihiroshima, Japan Ura, Mitsuhiro Graduate of I.A.S, Hiroshima University, Higashihiroshima, Japan

Effect of employees' self-esteem and the discrepancy between self-appraisal and reflected self-appraisal from a superordinate on the relationship with superordinates was investigated. It was predicted that employees with high self-esteem would feel close to their superordinates, if they perceived that superordinates estimated their job competence higher than themselves, whereas this would not be true for low self-esteem employees. The hypothesis was examined in a study with 148 participants using 2 (self-esteem: High vs. Low) x 3 (appraisal discrepancy: overestimate, equal, under estimate) ANOVAs. Results supported the hypotheses. It is suggested that appraisal discrepancy and self-esteem were related to organizational relationships.

The relationships among motivational beliefs, self-regulated learning strategies and four language skills

Ito, Takamichi Faculty of Education, Aichi University of Education, Kariya, Japan

This study examined the relationships among motivational beliefs, self-regulated learning strategies, and four language skills in Japanese junior and senior high school students. Students (N = 511)

completed self-report questionnaires. The three motivational beliefs were self-efficacy, anxiety for learning and intrinsic motivation, and the four language skills were speaking, listening, reading, and writing. Self-regulated learning strategies were investigated by two aspects: cognitive and self-motivational strategies. The relations among motivational beliefs, strategies, and the four skills were examined by analysis of covariance structures. Findings are discussed with regard to their implication for both self-regulated learning theory and instruction.

Developmental study on conservation of probability

Itoh, Tomoko Graduate School of Education, Waseda University, Nagareyama, Japan

This study investigated development of probability conservation essential to quantification of probability. The experiment examined whether children's judgment on the likelihood of drawing a winning lot was influenced by irrelevant factors. 22 kindergarteners, 26 second graders and 35 fifth graders were presented with two bags which contained both one winning and two losing chips but were different in chip size, and asked from which bag he/she was more likely to draw a winning chip. 18%, 35% and 74%, respectively, answered correctly (χ^2=19.397, df=2, p<.001). This shows the concept of probability conservation is not an early acquisition but is progressively constructed.

Personal features of children with educational problems

Ivashchenko, Nina Moscow, Russia Ivashchenko, Fedor Chemistry, MSU, Moscow, Russia Gruzdeva, Svetlana Family Club, Open Education Found, Moscow, Russia Shehovtsev, Igor Psychology, HSE, Moscow, Russia

EEG of children with educational problems in age of 7 - 12 were recorded and estimated using prof. Lebedev method. Individual profiles in MMPI scales were obtained. An evident sign of presence in elements of zero (0SI) and second (2DD) scales. All subjects have no signs of high values of third (HY) and sixth (PA) scales. We assumed that the obtained data should be helpful in future approach to training.

Girls and mathematical education: Results of a longitudinal study

Jüling, Inge Schulpsychologische Beratung, Landesverwaltungsamt, Magdeburg, Germany Lehmann, Wolfgang Institut für Psychologie, Universität Magdeburg, Magdeburg, Germany

A ten-year longitudinal study investigated the development of girls in a school setting dominated by males. Different approaches try to explain gender differences. Methods were tests and questionnaires. 75 students with equal cognitive preconditions were selected for a school with mathematical-scientific profile. Girls achieve better school marks but in mathematics, informatics and physics there are no gender differences. The girls' self-estimation of cognitive and motivational characteristics is lower. Only in the girls' subgroup marks in mathematics explains a part of school and examination anxiety. The girls' inappropriate emotional state impacts their vocational orientation more than high mathematical and scientific abilities.

Neuroticism in everyday life: A general population momentary assessment study

Jacobs, Nele Dept. of Psychology, Open University Netherlands, Heerlen, Netherlands Wichers, Marieke Psychiatry and Neuropsychology, Maastricht University, Maastricht, Netherlands Derom, Catherine Center for Human Genetics, Catholic University Leuven, Leuven, Belgium van Os, Jim Psychiatry and

Neuropsychology, Maastri cht University, Maastricht, Netherlands

Neuroticism has consistently been linked with increased risk for psychopathology, but it is still unclear how this concept can be translated into everyday life psychological processes. Using the experiencing sampling method in a large female twin sample, cross-twin cross-trait multilevel regression analyses revealed that neuroticism in one twin was associated with increased momentary levels of negative affect, increased instability in negative affect as well as with increased reactivity to minor daily life stressors in the co-twin. These findings clearly show that neuroticism represents a familial vulnerability to different forms of negative affect in daily life.

Factors associated with psychological responses after a grandparent's death

Janowski, Konrad Milano, Italy Niedbal, Kornelia Dep. of Clinical Psychology, Catholic University of Lublin, Lublin, Poland

The objective of this study was to verify if repeatable patterns of psychological responses to a grandparent's death exist and, if so, what factors are associated with them. High school and graduate students was surveyed retrospectively with a questionnaire asking about various aspects of their relationships with their grandparents, including responses to a grandparent's death if this had occurred within their lifetime. Several different patterns of psychological responses to a grandparent's death emerged, ranging from indifference to severe grieving. They were most closely related to the quality of the relationship between the grandparent and grandchild, to the grandchild's age at the moment of the grandparent's death and to the parental response to the death.

Worrying and performance on attention tasks: Gender differences

Janowski, Konrad Milano, Italy Gradus, Ilona Dep. of Clinical Psychology, Catholic University of Lublin, Lublin, Poland Niedbal, Kornelia Dep. of Clinical Psychology, Catholic University of Lublin, Lublin, Poland Kaczmarek, Lukasz Dep. of Clinical Psychology, Catholic University of Lublin, Lublin, Poland Kossowska, Magdalena Dep. of Clinical Psychology, Catholic University of Lublin, Lublin, Poland Steuden, Stanislawa Dep. of Clinical Psychology, Catholic University of Lublin, Lublin, Poland

The objective of this study was to assess gender differences in the relationships between the worrying tendency and performance on tasks measuring attention functions. Fifty female and fifty male graduate students took part in the study. They completed the Penn State Worry Questionnaire and were examined by means of three attention tasks. Higher worrying was found to be statistically significantly related to better performance on these tasks in female participants, whereas no associations between worrying tendencies and attentional functions were observed in male participants. These results suggest that gender differences may exist in the impact of worrying tendencies on performance on tasks involving attention.

Differences between revenge and retaliation

Janson, Michal Dept. of Social Sciences, Catholic University of Lublin, Lublin, Poland

In psychological literature two terms: revenge and retaliation, are similar and seem equal. However purpose of two studies was to reveal important differences. Laboratory experiment (N=72) tested (MANOVA) whether intensity of response is an effect of: frustration level, trait of vengefulness or number of possibilities to response. Results show important differences between revenge and retaliation. Experimental data suggest differences in the aggressive mechanism: retaliation seems to be the

example of impulsive aggression, revenge is rather instrumental. Questionnaire survey (N=210) provide with the arguments for differentiation of these two psychological categories on dimensions: strength, openness, time and social acceptability.

Comparative evaluation of adaptability in families with handicapped member

Javadian, Reza Khomeinishahr Branch, Islamic Azad University, Esfahan, Islamic Republic of Iran Akbari, Leila social work, Islamic Azad University, Esfahan, Islamic Republic of Iran Yarahmadi, Arezoo social work, Islamic Azad University, Esfahan, Islamic Republic of Iran

The purpose of this was to see the Family adaptability and cohesion in families with handicapped member(s) and to determine whether the adaptability differ normal families. For, 150 subjects (100 handicapped and 50 normal people) from Esfahan city were randomly chosen. The data was conducted by Family adaptability and cohesion Evaluation scale (FACES-III) and was analyzed by T-test and ANOVA. The Results indicated that Family adaptability, cohesion and communion in families with handicapped member(s) were higher than normal families. Also, there was significant relationship between family cohesion and the number of family members.

The effect of demographic factors on elderly people's general health

Javadian, Reza Khomeinishahr Branch, Islamic Azad University, Esfahan, Islamic Republic of Iran Behzadmanesh, Maryam social work, Esfahan Welfare Organization, Esfahan, Islamic Republic of Iran Hajjian, Gholamreza social work, Islamic Azad University, Esfahan, Islamic Republic of Iran

The purpose of this study was to see the elderly people's general health and to determine whether the demographic indices affect on general health. For, 200 elderly persons from Esfahan were randomly chosen. The data was conducted by GHQ-28 questionnaire and was analyzed by T-test, ANOVA and multiple regressions. The Results indicated that 29.4% of elderly persons were unhealthy. They reported severe depression (4.9%), somatic symptoms (38.2%), social dysfunction (70.6%), and anxiety (20.6%).The Results of multiple regressions analysis showed, 31.5% of general health variance was predicted by demographic factors (p<0.0005) and the affect of age, sex, and children's educations was significant.

Life styles and study methods scale for the university students

Jesus, Saul Psychology, University of Algarve, Faro, Portugal Martins, Alda Psychology, University of Algarve, Faro, Portugal

The Life Styles and Study Methods Scale was made to know the learning styles and the organizational skills related to the life styles of the university students. This instrument intends to be easy to understand and with fast application. This scale presents two different sub-scales related with the concepts of life style and study methods: personal organizational skills sub-scale and study methods sub-scale. In this research (n=151), the scale presented a good internal consistence as a global scale ($\alpha = 0,853$). The two sub-scales have also presented good levels of reliability: $\alpha=0,779$ for the personal organizational skills sub-scale; and $\alpha=0,789$ for the study methods sub-scale.

The developmental characters of emotion regulation strategy of children

Jiang, Yuan Sport Psychology, Beijing Sport University, Beijing, People's Republic of China Fang, Ping Psychology, Capital Normal University, Beijing, People's Republic of China Chen, Manqi Psychology, Capital Normal University, Beijing, People's Republic

of China Li, Yang Psychology, Capital Normal University, Beijing, People's Republic of China

In this study, 792 students from grade five in the primary school and grade two in the junior and senior school participate in the questionnaire investigation. The study investigates the developmental characters of emotion regulation strategy of children. The results of the study indicate: Tendency of the use of different emotion regulation strategies shows certain characteristics in terms of grade, gender and learning level. Senior students and higher learning level students prefer to use cognitive reappraisal strategy. Males use expression suppression strategy more frequently than females.

Feminine identity in teenagers with abuse experience who entered to government protection programs in Colombia

Jiménez Flórez, Mauricio Hernán Instituto de Psicologia, Universidad Del Valle, Cali, Colombia

This abstract presents the following research: "Feminine identity in teenagers with abuse experience who entered to Government protection programs in Colombia". It was a qualitative study. Its main objective is to diagnose the consequences of physical and psychological abuse in an early age. Based on Participative Action Research method, we found that abuse experiences build a "victim identity". However, those same experiences arouse a wish to build an "autonomy-based identity".

Differences on collective identity and ethnic pride and differentiation between whites and half-castes in Chile

Jimenez, Amaia Social Psychology, University of Basque Country, San Sebastián, Spain Martxueta, Aitor Social Psychology, University of Basque Country, San Sebastián, Spain Basabe, N. Páez, Darío Social Psychology, University of Basque Country, San Sebastián, Spain

According to Chile's 2002 census, Chile is composed of 72% of Half-castes, 22% of Whites and 4.6% of Indigenous population. The objective of this study is to examine the differences on collective identification and self-esteem between those who identify themselves as Half-castes and Whites. Design: a survey of a sample of 270 students of Degree in Psychology from 4 Chilean regions. Results: There were no significant differences on ethnic pride and belonging neither in identification with Chile. However, Whites reported more ethnic differentiation and identification with Europeans whereas Half-Castes reported more identification with Indigenous populations and Latin-Americans.

The influence of time management disposition training on mental health and academic performance in junior middle school students

Jin, Junwei Department of Psychology, Institute of Psychology, Jinhua, China, People's Republic of China Xie, Xuehui Department of Psychology, Institute of Psychology, Jinhua, China, People's Republic of China Li, weijian Department of Psychology, Institute of Psychology, Jinhua, China, People's Republic of China

Purpose: Investigate the influence of time management disposition training on mental health and academic performance. Method: Experiment method. Conclusion: 1.The junior middle school students' time management disposition can be improved by training. 2. The training has some effect on the improvement of junior middle school students' mental health. 3. The effect of time management disposition training on the academic performance is not significant. 4. In the effect of time management disposition training, there is gender effect. The effect of time management disposition training to the male students is not significant. But to the female students, it is significant.

Dynamic predicative model of cognitive load in a dual task environment

Jinbo, Li Psychology of Science, Zhejiang University, Hangzhou, People's Republic of China Baihua, Xu Psychology, Zhejiang University, Hangzhou, People's Republic of China Wuheng, Zuo Psychology, Zhejiang University, Hangzhou, People's Republic of China

A dual task experiment is designed to obtain the subjective evaluation, performance measurement and eye movement indexes concerning the cognitive load during different phases of operation. A model is built via Elman artificial neural network to analyze and predict the cognitive load dynamically, the result of which informs the approach of Elman neural network prediction of the cognitive load is credited with the top accuracy. This provides initial evidence for the potential use of generalized dynamic predicative models in multitask cognitive load assessment.

Health and cultural beliefs unique to the Caribbean University student

Johnson, Lockie Behavioral Science, AUC School of Medicine, Cupecoy, Sint Maarten, Netherlands Antilles

The purpose of this study was to collect information on health and personal beliefs of the Caribbean student. Little data exists on unique culturally held beliefs about the nature of self and others and personally held attitudes about health care in the Caribbean. The students enrolled in the University of St. Martin filled in questionnaires, responding to detailed scales and questions. Results indicate that the Caribbean student holds many personal and health care beliefs that are not prevalent in Western Medicine. Culturally competent care of the Caribbean patient will be enhanced through understanding of this unique set of beliefs.

The influence of intelligence on early mortality is explained by household income: National longitudinal study of youth

Jokela, Markus Dept. of Psychology, University of Helsinki, Helsinki, Finland Kivimäki, Mika Department of Epidemiology, University College London, London, United Kingdom Elovainio, Marko Department of Psychology, University of Helsinki, Helsinki, Finland

Objective: To examine whether the inverse association between IQ and mortality risk is explained by socioeconomic achievement over the life course. Methods: The participants were 11914 women and men participating in the National Longitudinal Study of Youth (aged 16–23 years at baseline and 30–47 at the end of follow-up). Income and educational achievement were assessed as time-varying covariates. Results: High IQ predicted decreased mortality risk (standardized relative risk=.77, $p<.001$). This association disappeared when household income was controlled for (RR=.95, $p>.05$). Conclusions: The inverse association between IQ and mortality risk may be due to income differences associated with IQ.

Health-related quality of life in thyroid diseases: Relative validity of two generic instruments

König, Dorothea Inst. für Klin. Psychologie, Universität Wien, Wien, Austria Jagsch, Reinhold Inst. für Psychologie, Universität Wien, Wien, Austria Kryspin-Exner, Ilse Inst. für Psychologie, Universität Wien, Wien, Austria Koriska, Karl Department of Nuclear Medicine, Kaiserin Elisabeth Hospital, Vienna, Austria

Objectives: To evaluate the relative validity of two generic instruments measuring health-related quality of life (HRQL) in thyroid patients. Methods: The HRQL questionnaires Short-Form-36 Health Survey (SF-36) and Nottingham Health Profile (NHP) were administered to 241 patients with various thyroid diseases. For calculations of the generic instruments' relative validity HRQL was compared across different levels of subjective health-ratings. Results: Analyses of relative validity identified SF-36 and NHP as appropriate and complementary measures of HRQL in patients with different thyroid diseases. Conclusions: For the subjective evaluation of HRQL in thyroid disorders the combination of the questionnaires SF-36 and NHP proved suitable.

Relationships between mindfulness and perfectionism with mental health

Kabirnezhad, Sanaz Tabriz, Islamic Republic of Iran Mahmoud Alilou, Majid psychology, colleges, Tabriz, Islamic Republic of Iran

At the present research, the relationships between Mindfulness and Perfectionism with Mental Health have been studied. To this aim, 150 students from Tabriz university took part in the research and, these students completed General Health Questionnaire (GHQ), subscale Perfectionism of Dysfunctional Attitude Scale (DAS) and Mindful Attention Awareness Scale (MAAS). correlation coefficient between Mindfulness and Perfectionism with Mental Health was found – 0.30 and 0.44 respectively. also there was no significant difference in Mental Health between women and men. In sum, the results of the present research showed that there is significant relationship between Mindfulness and Perfectionism with Mental Health. In therapy fields and prevention we can use this relationship. Keyword : Mindfulness, Perfectionism, Mental Health

Effectiveness of parental education in language performance of children with hearing impairment

Kako Jouibari, Aliasghar Tehran, Islamic Republic of Iran

In this study two groups of parents and their hearing impaired children were selected.The participants were 26 children,1.5 to 4 years, with moderate,severe and profound hearing lose who lived in Tehran. They didn't have any additional disability.Two groups of 13 parents and their children were matched. First group,the experimental group of parents, they learned skills to live with their hearing impaired children. another group didn't educate. The children had the same program of language training. results showed that language performance in experimental group of children was increased in compare to another group, in aspect of speech and speech reading ;not hearing.

Long-term influences of past bullied experience on mental health in late adolescence

Kameda, Hideko Dept. of Social Welfare, Seitoku University, Koshigaya, Japan

The purpose of this study is to examine the long-term influences of bullied experience on current mental health of college students. A total of 1039 Japanese college students completed two kinds of questionnaires on their bullied experience when they were children and their current mental health. The major finding was as follows: college students bullied for a long time have mental health problem. The result was discussed in terms of developmental theories on human relationship and person perception.

Factor analysis of Brief COPE in a sample of Greek Cypriot adults

Kapsou, Margarita Dept. of Psychology, University of Cyprus, Nicosia, Cyprus Demetriou, Andreas Psychology, University of Cyprus, Nicosia, Cyprus Panayiotou, Georgia Psychology, University of Cyprus, Nicosia, Cyprus Kokkinos, Constantinos Educations, Democretus University Thrace, Alexandroupolis, Greece

The brief COPE test consists of 28 items which examine the way individuals deal with stress. Greek Cypriot adults (N=1132; 633 women; 499 men; Age Range: 16 to 66) completed the Greek version of the questionnaire. Exploratory factor analyses yielded 3 main factors and 5 others that contained one scale (cronbach alphas>.60). These factors seemed to correspond well with the original 14 factors of the Brief-COPE (Carver, 1997), although some of them tended to cluster together. The Bref-COPE can to be a sufficiently sensitive measure of coping style in Greek Cypriot adults, but further study is needed.

Considerations regarding the use of screening tools in the identification of children with Attention Deficit Hyperactivity Disorder (ADHD)

Karaba, Rania Psychological Center, Athens, Greece Zournatzis, Vaggelis Psychological Center "ARSI, Psychological Center, Athens, Greece Kakouros, Efthimios Psychological Center "ARSI, Psychological Center, Athens, Greece Christodoulea, Stilianna Psychological Center "ARSI, Psychological Center, Athens, Greece

The study investigates the reliability of two screening tools for AD/HD. Parents of 170 children diagnosed with AD/HD completed the "AD/HD Rating Scale IV" and the "CBCL". Almost 30% of children diagnosed with AD/HD were reported to fall in the abnormal range of the CBCL and almost half of them in the abnormal range of the AD/HD Rating Scale. The correlation of the two screening tools was r=.704 (p=0.01). Although AD/HD is one of the most well-studied disorders with several assessment strategies being used, the field is challenged to further improve the identification process based on behavior rating scales, in order to lead to an accurate diagnosis of AD/HD.

Spontaneous activity of mice in various structures of space: From an open field to complex mazes

Kato, Katsunori Inst. of Psychology, University of Tsukuba, Tsukuba, Japan Betsuyaku, Toru College of Human Sciences, University of Tsukuba, Tsukuba, Japan Hanazato, Toshihiro Institute of Art and Design, University of Tsukuba, Tsukuba, Japan

Animals change their activities depending on the structure of a space. Mice and rats, specifically, show anxiety-related behaviors in an open space. In a six-day study, mice preferred complex mazes to an open field. However, a single wall added to the open field greatly reduced this preference. In addition, mice indicated preferences for different types of mazes. During the testing period, changes in locomotor activities were affected by the patterns of spatial structures. Complex mazes generally inhibited habituation except when they were connected with an open field. The role of spatial cognition is discussed.

Emotion understanding of children with ADHD and its relation to social problems

Kats-Gold, Inna Psychology, Ben-Gurion University, Rehovot, Israel

Objectives. The EU (emotion understanding) of boys at risk of ADHD (Attention Deficit Hyperactivity Disorder), and its associations with their SS (social skills) was investigated. Methods. Based on Conners' questionnaire scores 152 boys (grades 4 - 6) were assigned to an At-risk (n=66) or to a comparison (n = 86) group. Group differences in EU were evaluated and the role of EU in SS was investigated using SEM (structural equation modeling). Results. Children with ADHD had lower EU scores and SEM revealed a significant relation between EU and SS in the At-risk group. Conclusions. At-risk boys' less mature EU may be partly responsible for their poor social functioning.

Infant typical-color knowledge for natural objects modifies chromaticity selections in recognition task

Kawabata, Miho Dept. of Psychology, Sapporo International Univ., Sapporo, Japan Sasaki, Mikuko Psychology, Hokkaido University, Sapporo, Japan Kasai, Yuriko Psychology, Hokkaido University, Sapporo, Japan Fujii, Tetsunoshin Psychology,

Hokkaido University, Sapporo, Japan **Kawabata, Yasuhiro** Psychology, Hokkaido University, Sapporo, Japan

The present study explored the typical color knowledge of natural objects for 3-6 years-old infants. The experiment was divided in two parts. In Session 1, memory task for the color of eight natural object drawings presented in a display was performed. The drawings were familiar for them. In Session 2, ten-minutes later, participants imagined the color of session1 stimuli and performed the color recognition task. Pointing for the drawings in a 3*5 matrix was performed and each of the 15 drawings was assigned one of 15 different colors. Selected colors were close to the typical chromaticities for natural objects.

Kine-Cluster-System evaluates the effects of antianxiety drugs and repetition experience on open-field behaviors of rats

Kawasaki, Katsuyoshi Dept. of Psychology, Hoshi University, Tokyo, Japan **Takahashi, Aki** Mouse Genomics Resource Labora, National Institute of Genetics, Mishima, Japan **Koyama, Takamasa** Psychology, Japan Wimen's University, Kawasaki, Japan **Yoshikawa, Yasuhiro** Biomedical science, The University of Tokyo, Tokyo, Japan **Kuroda, Yoichiro** Science, Tokyo Univeresity of Science, Tokyo, Japan

The aims of present study were to clarify changes in behaviors by antianxiety drugs and repetition experience, and to verify the availability of Kine-Cluster-system (KCS) developed for easy and objective analysis of Open-field behaviors. Twenty-one F344 rats were divided into three groups: diazepam-0.5mg/kg, diazepam-1.0mg/kg and saline. The assigned drug was administered to each subject 10 min. before it was introduced in the Open-field. Open-field behaviors were VTRed for 9 min. and analyzed by KCS. This Open-field-test was conducted again one month later. Both characteristic changes by the diazepam injection and repetition experience were found. This result proved the availability of KCS.

Couples' communication style and marital attribution in Japan

Kawashima, Akiko Ochanomizu University, Tokyo, Japan **Sugawara, Masumi** Depertment of Psychology, Ochanomizu University, Bunkyo, Tokyo, Japan **Sakai, Atsushi** Division of School Education, University of Yamanashi, Yamanashi, Japan

The research was conducted in order to examine the relationship between marital attribution and communication style using Japanese samples. We hypothesized that preceding marital communication would predict the way of appreciating the negative events happening in their marital relationship. Sixty-four Japanese couples have participated in the dyadic communication tasks using the procedure of Social Support Interaction Coding System, developed by Bradbury and Pasch (1994). They have also completed the Relationship Attribution Measure, developed by Fincham and Bradbury (1992). The result suggested the link between preceding communication patterns and later attribution patterns for both husbands and wives.

A nation-wide computer-based school monitoring program

Keller, Ulrich FLSHASE/EMACS, University of Luxembourg, Walferdange, Luxembourg **Martin, Romain** FLSHASE/EMACS, University of Luxembourg, Walferdange, Luxembourg **Reichert, Monique** FLSHASE/EMACS, University of Luxembourg, Walferdange, Luxembourg **Brunner, Martin** FLSHASE/EMACS, University of Luxembourg, Walferdange, Luxembourg **Busana, Gilbert** FLSHASE/EMACS, University of Luxembourg, Walferdange, Luxembourg

Around the world, school systems are being re-organized, moving away from input-orientation

(e.g. fixed curricula) to output-orientation: more autonomy for schools, which are held accountable for their results. This necessitates the development of efficient assessment and reporting tools. We will demonstrate a flexible, open source system for large-scale assessment of students' competencies (TAO) in the context of the Luxembourgian school monitoring program. It enables web-based testing of thousands of students and generation of detailed reports for school administrators in a largely automated fashion. Our practical experience and the system's future development will also be discussed.

The effect of critical thinking instruction on students' hypothesis creation (Science creation mechanism in universities)

Khalkhali, Ali Dept. of Educational Sciences, Islamic Azad University, Tonekabon, Islamic Republic of Iran **Sadooghi, Mitra** Dept. of Educational Sciences, Islamic Azad University, Tonekabon, Islamic Republic of Iran

"Hypothesis Creation" plays significant role in the process of science production. The research was exploring to this hypothesis that instruction of critical thinking effects on students' Hypothesis Creation as a mechanism to create science by critically thinking relations between teacher, content and student in universities. The methodology is of an experimental design according to the Solomon four-group design. The participations include 60 students, (30 =15+15 experimental and 30=15+15control group). The Two Way Analysis of Variance, T-test, Tuki and the one-way ANOVA were used to analyze the data. The findings show that critical thinking instruction will increase students' Hypothesis Creation.

A study on the gender differences between intimacy dimensions of married college students

Khamseh, Akram Women Research Center, Alzahra University, Tehran, Islamic Republic of Iran **Hossienian, Siemien** Psychology Faculty, Alzahra University, Tehran, Islamic Republic of Iran

Intimacy has been conceptualized as a very important pattern of behavior with a strong aspect of emotion and social relationships. The aim of this study is comparison of gender differences in intimacy dimensions between married college students. One hundred married college students were randomly selected from Tehran universities. Three questionnaires were used: 1.Marital Intimacy Needs Questionnaire, 2.Marital Intimacy Questionnaire, 3.General demographic questionnaire. Results show that there are significant gender differences in the total score of the intimacy (t=2.56,df=98, p<0.01),.But there are not significant gender differences in social, esthetic, spiritual- thought dimensions of intimacy. Results have been discussed according to the different patterns of socialization and a multidimensional model of intimacy.

Mothers expressed emotion towards children with and without autism: Study in Iran

Khodabakhshi Koolaee, Anahita Counseling Psychology, Allamhe Tabatabaee University, Tehran, Islamic Republic of Iran

Introduction: The Expressed Emotion (EE) concept (Leff & Vaugn, 1985), measures of attitudes and behavioral patterns of relatives toward patients (Widemann et al, 2002). Objectives: To propose of this study, is to identify factors with maternal expressed emotion (EE) towards their child with Autistic Disorder. Design and Method: A total of 35 mothers who had a child with Autism and at least one child without Autism between 3-11 years participated in this study. Mothers completed Family Questioner (Widemann et al, 2002) and also for assess the Autistic Disorder using the criteria of DSM-IV-R (APA, 2000). Results:

Mothers with High EE towards the child with Autism and with Hostility. Key words: Expressed Emotion, Autism, Iran.

Pleasant activities as reinforcers and indicators of quality of life: Their impact on depression in the elderly

Kleftaras, George Dept. of Special Education, University of Thessaly, Volos, Greece

This reduced engagement in pleasant activities and consequently the reduced positive reinforcement that they receive appears to be responsible for depressive symptoms in the elderly. The present study aimed at: a) confirming the relationship between pleasant activities' level and later life depression in Greece and b) determining which pleasant activities are mood-related. 100 community living elderly persons completed the Pichot-Questionnaire-of-Depressive-Symptoms and the Pleasant-Activities-Questionnaire. The results confirm the relationship between pleasant activities and depression and clearly demonstrate that only certain types of pleasant activities are mood related and should be seriously considered in treating depressive symptomatology in old age.

Feelings of loneliness and family coherence in children

Kleftaras, George Dept. of Special Education, University of Thessaly, Volos, Greece **Didaskalou, Eleni** Special Education, University of Thessaly, Volos, Greece

Family coherence seems to be associated with the quality and kinds of support children receive and the feelings of loneliness that may experience. A sample of 323 primary school Greek children responded to the Louvain Loneliness Scale for Children and Adolescents and to the Family Coherence Scale. The results support the hypotheses of this study and as it was expected, they indicate significant relationships between family coherence and feelings of loneliness in children. Of special interest is the differential impact of particular dominant patterns of family interaction and ways of support on specific types of loneliness that children experience.

Memory for serial order in bilingual speakers

Klingebiel, Kathrin Dept. of Psychology, University of Sussex, Brighton, United Kingdom **Majerus, Steve** Cognitive Science, University of Liàge, Liàge, Belgium **Weekes, Brendan** Psychology, University of Sussex, Brighton, United Kingdom

Our aim was to investigate the memory for serial order in bilingual language processing. We compared memory for serial order and memory for lexical items using behavioural and EEG methods. Our hypothesis was that memory for serial order would activate specific brain regions. We used an EGI (128 channel) net and recorded activity on trials involving memory for word sequences and memory for the items themselves. Bilingual language proficiency was assessed using a battery of tests. We identified independent ERP components associated with serial order and item memory. Memory of serial order is an important predictor of language processing.

Readiness to bereavement: The change of men's prospect before the death of their wife

Kobayashi, Shinichi kyouto-shi, Japan

For near century, bereavement theorists have assumed that recovery from loss requires a period of grief work. And some researcher revealed anticipatory grief plays important role. Generally, many men believe to die earlier than their wife. Namely, they doesn't think to live alone after the death of spouse. This study investigated the readiness to bereavement of men. 8 widower(-age:61-84,widowed period:1year-11year) were interviewed about their prospect for the future before the consciousness of bereavement and anticipatory grief. 3 fundamental categories (changed prospect, obscure prospect, error prospect)were found and process of anticipatory grief of widower will be indicated.

Are optimists better in emotional self-control

Kobylinska, Dorota *Faculty of Psychology, University of Warsaw, Warsaw, Poland* **Demicka, Dorota** *Faculty of Psycholog, University of Warsaw, Warsaw, Poland*
Our research program refers to positive psychology. We concentrate on the relation between positive emotions and effective emotional self-control. The aim of the study was to check wheather (1) positive emotions as dispositions will positively correlate with emotional self-control, (2) inducing negative emotional state will influence ability of emotional self-control, (3) there is relationship of positive emotions as dispostions and the influence of induced negative emotional state on emotional self-control. The results confirm the hypotheses and show that people in negative emotional state are less able to effectively control themselves than those in neutral state. Moreover people who generaly feel more positive emotions were more imune to negative emotions and more effective in controlling themselves.

The psychometric properties of the Greek Questionnaire on Teacher Interaction (G-QTI)

Kokkinos, Constantinos *Dept. of Primary Education, Democritus University of Thrac, Alexandroupolis, Greece* **Charalambous, Kyriakos** *Elementary Education, Democritus University, Komotini, Greece* **Davazoglou, Aggeliki** *Primary Education, Democritus University of Thrac, Alexandroupolis, Greece*
The psychometric properties of the Greek translation of the Questionnaire on Teacher Interaction (G – QTI) were investigated in a sample of 273 Cyprus public elementary school 10 – 12 years old students. In general, while the data did not seem to support the construct validity of the 48-item scale, when Confirmatory Factor Analyses were used, a psychometrically reliable and valid 27-item instrument emerged, significantly confirming its a priori structure, with the exemption of the Uncertain dimension. The interscale correlations confirmed the circumplex nature of the scale. The findings suggest that the G – QTI should be applied cautiously with Greek-Cypriot samples.

The "blind spot" in personnel selection: The role of unconscious factors in job interviews

Kolominski, Stephan *Psychologie, Fernuniversität Hagen, Hagen, Germany*
In personnel selection unconscious factors are rarely investigated. The theoretical part of this work relates different psychological approaches (e.g. organizational-, social-, neuro- and cognitive-psychological issues) to unconscious decisions in the job interview. Human-Resource-Managers (N=26) were asked in semi-structured interviews about hard and soft factors (e.g. work qualification and stereotypes) underlying their decisions based on selection interviews. The results of this study give hints to the impact of unconscious factors in job interviews and in personnel selection.

Development of the "Mannheim Stress Test"

Kolotylova, Tatyana *Psychosomatische Medizin, ZI für Seelische Gesundheit, Mannheim, Germany* **Koschke, Mandy** *Psychiatry and Psychotherapy, University Jena, Jena, Germany* **Bär, Karl-Jürgen** *Psychiatry and Psychotherapy, University Jena, Jena, Germany* **Bohus, Martin** *Psychosomatic Medicine, Central Inst.of Mental Health, Mannheim, Germany* **Schmahl, Christian** *Psychosomatic Medicine, Central Ins. of Mental Health, Mannheim, Germany*
The aim of this study was to develop an economical stress paradigm for the investigation of stress reactions in a laboratory setting. 10 healthy females

were included. The "Mannheim Stress Test "(MST) consisted of mental stress, noise and emotional pictures and showed significant increases in heart rate and subjective stress levels. Furthermore, we tested the MST on 32 healthy females to evaluate the physiological response to MST stimulation. Significant changes in heart rate variability, barore-flex sensitivity and cardiac output were found. We conclude that the MST is an economical method to investigate stress reactions in a laboratory setting.

The effects of adrenergic system on level of anxiety in rat

Komaki, Alireza *Dept. of Physiology, Hamadan University, Hamadan, Islamic Republic of Iran* **Shahidi, Siamak** *Department of Physiology, Hamadan University of Medical, Hamadan,, Islamic Republic of Iran* **Alaei, Hojatollah** *Department of Physiology, Isfahan University of Medical, Isfahan,, Islamic Republic of Iran* **Malakouti, S. Mansour** *Department of Physiology, Hamadan University of Medical, Hamadan,, Islamic Republic of Iran* **Lashgari, Reza** *Neuroscience Research Center, Shaheed Beheshti University, Tehran, Islamic Republic of Iran* **Noorbakhsh, S. Mohammad** *Neuroscience Research Center, Shaheed Beheshti University, Tehran, Islamic Republic of Iran* **Haghparast, Abbas** *Neuroscience Research Center, Shaheed Beheshti University, Tehran, Islamic Republic of Iran* **Heshmatian, Behnam** *Department of Physiology, Hamadan University of Medical, Hamadan,, Islamic Republic of Iran*
Anxiety is a psychological and physiological complex response, which is manifested by tachycardia, increase in blood pressure and respiratory rate. In this investigation we studied the effect of adrenergic system on the anxiety, using Vogel's test. The effect of drugs on increasing the number of conflict responses in rat is corresponding to an anxiolytic action in human. Our result showed that Propranolol, a β antagonist and Clonidine a $\alpha 2$ agonist, increased conflict responses. In contrast, Atenolol, a $\beta 1$ antagonist and Yohimbine, a $\alpha 2$ antagonist, produce anxiogenic effect. These results provide further support to the involvement of adrenergic system in anxiety.

Task switching and attentional selection in young children

Konde, Zoltan *Dep. of General Psychology, University of Debrecen, Debrecen, Hungary* **Inántsy-Pap, Judit** *Dep. of Pedagogical Psychology, University of Debrecen, Debrecen, Hungary*
Executive control is supposed to be necessary for efficient and appropriate adaptive behavior and to be manifestation of numerous correlative processes including planning, selection of action, switching of task settings, memory updating. Several aspects of executive functioning develop in the preschool years, but they are hard to investigate during that period as a source of methodological difficulties. It was aimed to investigate the developmental aspects of executive functioning and to develop computerized, touchscreen versions of well-known executive tests. We present preliminary results of our experiments with groups of children aged 61 and 108 months using stroop like and task switching tasks.

Psychometric properties of Polish adaptation of the Postpartum Depression Screening Scale

Kossakowska-Petrycka, Karolina *Institute of Psychol, University of Lodz, Lodz, Poland*
Objectives: The aim of the study was to adapt and validate a Polish version of the Postpartum Depression Screening Scale (PDSS). Methods: A multiple translation model was used to achieve semantic equivalence with translation the PDSS to polish-language version. 384 women were examined. Results: The analysis of the psychometric properties of Polish version of PDSS shown that the reliability and validity were slightly lower, but within the acceptable range Conclusions: PDSS

can be used as a good measure for screening for postpartum depression.

Investigating sexual strategies in a social community website

Krause, Martin *Inst. für Psychologie, Universität München, München, Germany* **Spörrle, Matthias** *Dept. for Psychology, Ludwig-Maximilians University, München, Germany*
In this exploratory study we tried to corroborate existing findings of Sexual Strategies Theory (SST, Buss & Schmitt, 1993) by using data collected from an online community. A random sample of 460 German user profiles was drawn from "MySpace", a social networking website. Sexual interests reported by the users were analyzed separately for men and women: "Dating" served as indicator of short-term and interest in "Serious Relationship" as an indicator of long-term sexual strategy. Consistent with SST, a higher percentage of male than female users were interested in dating. However men were also more interested in serious relationships, indicating that online partner search itself might be a short-term sexual strategy.

Fair enough: Comparing and evaluating different approaches of test score adjustment in statewide assessments

Kuhl, Poldi *Berlin, Germany* **Pant, Hans Anand** *Institute for School Quality, Freie Universitaet Berlin, Berlin, Germany* **Wendt, Wolfgang** *Institute for School Quality, Freie Universitaet Berlin, Berlin, Germany*
Being confronted with disparate student populations teachers and principals - particularly in socially disadvantaged urban neighborhoods - call for adjusted performance feedback systems that take into account schools' varying socio-economic and ethnic compositions. Using statewide assessment data of grade-2 students in Berlin; Germany in 2005 (N= 1955), in successive multilevel models we compared and evaluated extant approaches relying on data from parents, teachers, schools, and socio-spatial statistics. The approaches are discussed with respect to their utility for providing schools with adjusted performance feedback in terms of adjustment power and data accessibility.

A study of self concept, adjustment and academic achievement of adolescents in relation to socio-demographic variables

Kumar, Parmod *Dept. of Education, Kurukshetra University, Kurukshetra, India*
A comparative study on 100 adolescents of Secondary schools having different socio-economic and demographic backgrounds was conducted to see effect of these backgrounds on their self concept, adjustment and academic achievements using Adjustment Inventory(Mittal), Self-concept (Saraswat), matriculation marks taken into account for Academic achievement. Pearson's product moment correlation, Means, S.D, t-ratio used. Findings indicated males adolescents had better self-concept, health adjustment but low academic achievement as compared to female counterparts. Adolescents of deprived sections, low economic status were more adjusted and had better self-concept but low academic achievement. Study has implications for government, school authorities, teachers, social and community leaders.

The mental health of adolescents in Rural South Australia: Perspectives of human service providers

Kurtin, Marijeta *Dept. of General Practice, University of Adelaide, Adelaide, Australia* **Barton, Christopher** *General Practice, The University of Adelaide, Adelaide, Australia* **Edwards, Jane** *Commerce, University of South Australia, Adelaide, Australia* **Winefield, Tony** *Psychology, University of South Australia, Adelaide, Australia*

Objectives To investigate the views human service providers hold regarding the mental health of adolescents in rural South Australia and to determine if services are perceived as appropriate to cope with the volume of mental health needs. Methods Four focus groups and fourteen interviews were conducted with 38 service providers working across four regions. Results Thematic analysis identified 90 themes, subsequently categorised into five key areas: Community/Society Factors, Occupational Factors, Service Delivery/Utilisation, Youth Issues and Indigenous Culture. Conclusions Service providers identified significant mental health issues in rural adolescents. Deficits in service provision and service utilisation need to be addressed further.

Biological factors and psychosocial stress as contributors to coronary artery disease among veterans with traumatic blindness

Kushnir, Talma Dept. of Health Sciences, Ben-Gurion University, Beer-Sheva, Israel Defrin, Ruth Physiotherapy, Tel Aviv University, Tel Aviv, Israel Levy, David Heruti, Rafi Ehrenfeld, Mally Orbach, Yaffa Bor, Ariela Ohri, Avi Drory, Jacob

Objectives: There is a very high prevalence of coronary artery disease (CAD) among veterans with traumatic blindness (TBL) unexplained by well-known risk factors. We studied the contribution of oxidative stress, homocystein, CRP, folic acid, B12, stress, PTSD and social support. Method: Questionnaires and blood samples were collected from 21 veterans with TBL and CAD (TBLC); 25 veterans with TBL without CAD ; 16 healthy siblings of TBLC. Results: Compared with the control group, TBLC exhibited significantly higher levels of CRP, homocystein and stress; and lower social support. Conclusions: CAD among veterans with traumatic blindness is associated with high levels of CRP, stress, post-traumatic symptoms and low social support.

Performance evaluation with within-individual comparisons: A prospect theory approach

Kwong, Jessica Y.Y. Marketing Dept., Chinese Univ. of Hong Kong, Hong Kong, China, People's Republic of : Hong Kong SAR Wong, Kin Fai Ellick Management of Organizations, HKUniv of Science & Techno, Hong Kong, China, People's Republic of : Macao SAR

This research examines performance evaluation with within-subject comparisons. Study 1 found that performance evaluation of a person was polarized by changing the frame of reference for a performance attribute. Study 2 found that the performance of an individual between two time points appeared more divergent when the performance information was presented in small numbers than when it was presented in large numbers. These findings are consistent with the reference dependence and diminishing sensitivity assumptions of prospect theory, suggesting that this theory is a useful theoretical framework to help increase understanding of performance evaluation beyond between-individual comparisons.

The Negative Bias: Related to current mood or to persisting depressive symptoms?

Lüttke, Stefan Inst. für Psychologie, Universität Potsdam, Potsdam, Germany Werheid, Katja Department of Psychology, Humboldt University at Berlin, Berlin, Germany Heuser, Isabella Clinic for Psychiatry, Charité University Medicine, Berlin, Germany Kathmann, Norbert Department of Psychology, Humboldt University at Berlin, Berlin, Germany

The 'Negative Bias', a tendency towards negative evaluation of emotional stimuli, is a common phenomenon in Major depression. However, it is unclear whether the negative bias is rather related to actual mood or to more persisting signs of depression, or personality traits. In the present

study, a stratified sample of 50 healthy participants evaluated standardized facial portraits with neutral, positive, or negative emotional expression according to valence and arousal. Additionally, they performed scales for state- and trait-like depression and a personality inventory. The results show that biased emotional judgments are rather related to persistent depressive symptoms than to current mood.

Impact of the speed of visual and auditory stimuli on the perceptive and comprehensive aspects of communication in children with autism

Lainé, France Centre Psyclé, Aix-en-Provence, France Tardif, Carole psychology, centre psyclé, aix en provence, France Gepner, Bruno CNRS UMR 6057, laboratoire parole et langage, aix en provence, France

Processing of facial/body gestures and speech is impaired in subjects with autism, partly due to their excessive speed in the everyday life. Slowing down facial, body and verbal stimuli may help autistic subjects to process them. Nineteen children with autism, and 3 matched control groups are compared on their ability to recognize facial expressions and words, understand and execute verbal instructions, and imitate facial/body gestures. Stimuli are displayed on a computer, at three different speeds. Results show that autistics subjects, especially those having the more severe symptomatology or the lower mental age, perform better at low speeds presentations. These findings may open new perspectives for reeducation.

Foreign language acquisition by using precision eaching method

Larcan, Rosalba Scienze dell'Educazione, University of Messina, Messina, Italy Oliva, Patrizia Scienze dell'Educazione, University of Messina, Messina, Italy Cuzzocrea, Francesca Scienze dell'Educazione, University of Messina, Messina, Italy

The purpose of study was to explore the potential of Precision Teaching software (PT) for improving English as foreign language. Three groups of students were compared; two experimental groups have used PT by using computer with or without review the errors. The control group followed a traditional textbook-based approach. The students who used PT showed a better learning than students who did not use it. The same students had increased scores in memory, attention and concentration tasks. The results imply that the PT has great potential for improving learning' accuracy and fluency, with positive influence on some cognitive abilities.

Pecularities of constructive thinking of 8-9 years old children

Latysh, Natalia Creativity psychology, Institute of Psychology, Kyiv, Ukraine

The peculiarities of constructive thinking displaying in process of decision of creative tasks are the research object. The individual experiment and developing training has based on our research. The regular decision of creative tasks directed on formation of abilities to search analogues, antipodes, to combine structures and functions, to find original variants of the task decision assists the development of constructive thinking, though the designing will be more successful, when the pupil imagines more detailed and more precisely, and the design is consisted of such parts, as these parts are connected.

Transfer effect and emotional context: Evidence for memory domains

Laukka, Seppo J. Unit of Psychology, University of Oulu, Oulu, Finland Sozinov, Alexei A. Russian Academy of Sciences, Institute of Psychology, Moscow, Russia Tuominen, Tuulikki Unit of Psychology/LearnLab, University of Oulu, Oulu, Finland Nopanen, Markku Unit of Psychology/

LearnLab, University of Oulu, Oulu, Finland Alexandrov, Yuri I. Russian Academy of Sciences, Institute of Psychology, Moscow, Russia

Studying the relation of transfer effect to emotions, we have recently found the negative transfer effect only in the negative emotional situation, when the break between the two visual discrimination tasks was five minutes. In this study our aim was to explore whether the relation between emotions and transfer is evident after a 72-hour break. The positive transfer effect was found only in the negative emotional situation. Persistence of emotion-dependent transfer effect for at least three days is consistent with our standpoint that outwardly similar behavior in the negative and positive emotional contexts is provided by systems belonging to different memory domains.

Leadership in market-oriented contexts

Laumann, Maja Advanced Research Studies, Flensburg School for, Flensburg, Germany Rybnikova, Irma Human Resource Management, Technische Universität Dresden, Ascheberg-Herbern, Germany

If firms introduce market elements to gain more flexibility, it does not fundamentally change leadership patterns: both superiors and subordinates obviously stick to conventional leadership instruments and behaviours and reproduce hierarchy-oriented leadership processes. This is revealed by qualitative studies on leadership in market-oriented organisational contexts such as virtual co-operation of firms and interim management, whereby 88 qualitative interviews with managers and subordinates were conducted. The researchers disprove normative statements which suggest an increase of self-leadership in such contexts and give valuable input to the theoretical discussion on how the 'move-to-the-market' is affecting leadership relations within organisations.

Psychological determinants of industrial enterprise managers' responsibility

Lazorko, Olha Dept. of Psychology, Volyn University, Lutsk, Ukraine

Background. Problem of the psychological determinants of industrial enterprise managers' responsibility is an urgent issue. The aim of this research lies in the elucidation of the above-mentioned determinants. Methods. 16 PF Questionnaire, Locus of control scale, Professional Motivation Test, Word Association Test. Results. The main objective psychological determinants (age, gender, work experience, manager's status) and subjective psychological determinants (individual characteristics, professional motivation and qualities, locus of control) of managers' responsibility and the degree of their influence on formation of the personality feature development are outlined. Conclusions. The technology of the managers' responsibility correction depends on the studied psychological determinants.

Professional motivation and organizational commitment

Lebedeva, Nataliya Donbass technical university, Kiev, Ukraine Dmitriy, Samoilenko Psychology, Donbass technical university, Kiev, Ukraine

Objective. To test a hypothesis that realization of employees' professional motives affects their organizational commitment. Method. J.Meyer & N.Allen Organizational commitment, V.Dominyak Motives realization. The sample included 354 employees from different organizations. Results. 1) Organizational commitment (OC) significantly correlated with 11 professional motives; 2) reduction in the sense of stability and safety negatively correlated with the desire to quit (r=-0.368, r=0.05); 3) OC most correlated with the motives of professional self-realization (r=0.572, r=0.001) and professional development (r=0.491, r=0.001) and career growth (r=0.567, r=0.001). Conclusion. The investigation confirmed the hypothesis and its findings can be used in developing employees' organizational commitment.

Peer pressure in adolescence

Lebedina-Manzoni, Marija *Dept. of Behavioral Disorders, University of Zagreb, Zagreb, Croatia* **Lotar, Martina** *Dpt. of Behavioral Disororders, University of Zagreb, ERF, Zagreb, Croatia*

The aim of this research is the construction of the Adolescents' Peer Pressure Scale. Scale will include specific questions about peer pressure in terms of adolescents' behaviour and thoughts. Four focus groups with adolescents (conducted in two elementary and two high schools in Zagreb) will serve as an empirical background for defining peer pressure domains. First scale draft will be applied on sample of adolescents who are 12 to 17 years of age. Sample size will depend on number of items. Final version of scale will be determined according to the results of factor analysis, inter-item correlations and item-total correlations.

The development of narrowing the window of attention: Relationship with the reading level

Leclercq, Virginie *Centre Henri Piéron, Boulogne Billancourt, France*

Endogenous narrowing of attention was investigated in 7- and 9-year-old children, and in young adults. Participants detected a target in a horizontal display of 5 characters. Targets were preceded by cues of different sizes. Small cues indicated the exact target location; middle-size cues indicated the visual field in which the target appeared; the size of large cues was identical to the whole display. Results showed that the ability to narrow the window of attention increased with age. Moreover, in 7-year-olds, this ability differed with the reading level of children.

Couple relations scales between non-violent and violent couples

Lee, Sang-Bok *Pastoral Counseling Graduate, Kangnam University, Yongin, Republic of Korea*

Objective: To study mediating factors on marital violence on South Korea.Methods: 572 Korean wives in Kyunggi-Do, South Korea (Mean Age=45, SD=5.7), Non-violent couples (n=272), Lightly violent couples (Group 1: n=252), Violent couples (Group 2, n=48). There would be significant correlations among marital violence, role conflict, family cohesion, marriage satisfaction, and depression. Results: Multiple Regression Analysis of Wife Abuse Inventory Factors by Groups (1 & 2) – Husband's character (p<0.005); role conflict (p<0.01); conflict in-law (p<0.05). The correlation Matrix – Significant in violence and conflict (r=.56, violence and depression (r=.38), violence and family cohesion (r=.29), and violence and marriage satisfaction (r=.45).

The longitudinal relationship between conduct problems and depression of Korean adolescents

Lee, Suk-Hi *Dept. of Psychology, Chungbuk National University, Cheongju, Republic of Korea* **Hwang, Soon-Taeg** *Department of Psychology, Chungbuk National University, Cheongju, Republic of Korea*

This study aims to examine the longitudinal relationship between Conduct Problems(CP) and depression of adolescents from Korea participated in the present study. Data were collected from 2556 Middle school students through the Korean Youth Panel survey (KYPS), and carried out 3 year follow-up study. The feature of three groups (CP, depression, and comorbid group) were compared on CP, depression, anxiety, stress, life satisfaction items. Results showed that in comorbid group, stress is the highest and anxiety and life satisfaction is the lowest level among 3 groups, whereas in CP group, stress is the lowest and anxiety and life

satisfaction is the highest level, and in depression group, all variable is middle level.

What do you tell your students what school is for and how does it affect their motivation? A study in the Singaporean context

Lee, Jie Qi *CRPP, NIE, Singapore, Singapore* **McInerney, Dennis** *CRPP, Nat'l Institute of Education, Singapore, Singapore* **Liem, Arief D.** *CRPP, Nat'l Institute of Education, Singapore, Singapore* **Ortiga, Yasmin** *CRPP, Nat'l Institute of Education, Singapore, Singapore*

Is it healthy to emphasize future economic benefits as the incentives for academic achievement? This study examines the relationship between perceived utility value of education and achievement motivation. Achievement motivation is important in shaping learning processes and academic achievement. The Inventory of School Motivation (McInerney & Ali, 2006) was administered to 5,000 Singaporean secondary school students. Students' motivational goals were correlated with their perceived utility value of education. Questions to be addressed are: How do students perceive the utility value of education? How does it affect their achievement motivation? This study discusses possible interventions in motivating students in Singapore context.

What is emotion dysregulation related to?

Leroy, Tanguy *UFR de Psychologie, University of Lille 3, Villeneuve D'asque Cedex, France* **Christophe, Veronique** *UFR de Psychologie, University of Lille 3, VILLENEUVE D'ASCQ CEDEX, France* **Nandrino, Jean-Louis** *UFR de Psychologie, University of Lille 3, VILLENEUVE D'ASCQ CEDEX, France*

Objectives: This study aims to assess links between emotion dysregulation and other constructs such as alexithymia, anxiety, impulsivity and behavioural activation and inhibition. Methods: 83 students completed a questionnaire composed of the DERS (emotion dysregulation), BVAQ (alexithymia), STAI-Y-B (trait anxiety), BIS-10 (impulsivity) and BIS/BAS scales (behavioural activation and inhibition). Results: The emotion dysregulation score was highly positively correlated to the anxiety and behavioural inhibition scores. Conclusions: Emotion dysregulation seems to be related to a hypersensitivity to punishment that we assume to be of social nature. It is neither related to alexithymia nor impulsivity.

Social competence of adolescents having schizophrenia

Levikova, Ekaterina *Dept. of Psychology, Moscow State University, Moscow, Russia* **Pechnikova, Leonora** *Psychology, Moscow State University, Moscow, Russia*

The research is based on comparison of social adaptation levels of adolescents (ages 13-16) having schizophrenia and those with no psychiatric disorders. Two clinical groups (15 males, 15 females) were assessed against the control group (62 adolescents) using Gilford-Salliven's and Goldstein's tests. Norms for adolescents were derived "from scratch" based on assessment results and existing norms for adults. Among the key findings are: deficit of emotional language and inability to differentiate own personality from social environment (for both clinical groups), and negligible gender differences in social competence at given age.

Is there a role for psychology on neurosciences?

Lhullier, Cristina *Porto Alegre, Brazil* **Furstenau de Oliveira, Lucas** *Biology, ISE/CESUCA, Porto Alegre, Brazil*

For the past several years, neurosciences have been providing data and explanations for phenomena traditionally investigated by the psychological science. This trend is only becoming more present

and psychological theories are being set aside. Our objective is to provide guidelines on how psychology may collaborate with neuroscientific investigation. A review on current literature allow us to conclude that neuroscience and psychology can both benefit from each other, specifically with the latter providing problems to be investigated by the former. This way, our understanding on the psychobiological basis of human behavior may advance in more directed and comprehensive manner.

An experimental research on children's concepts of bullying and their coping styles

Li, Xinyu *Department of Psychology, Zhejiang Normal University, Jinhua, People's Republic of China* **Li, Weijian** *Department of Psychology, Zhejiang Normal University, Jinhua, People's Republic of China*

[Aim]To investigate children's concepts of bullying and their coping styles. [Subjects] 54 children whose ages were from 4 to 6. [Methods]Picture-test was used. There were two different situations–one was bullying and another was playing. After observing the two different situations, the subjects were asked three different questions about their concepts of bullying and their coping styles. [Results]There were significant difference between 4 years old children and 6 years old children on their concepts of bullying. More 4 years old children have confusion on these two different situations. It maybe means 4 years old children's theory of metal still not to be mature.

A designing of rating scale of number sense of sixth grader in China

Li, Yanxia *Shangdong Normal, JINAN, China, People's Republic of : Macao SAR* **Jiwei, Si** *psychology department, Shangdong Normal, JINAN, China, People's Republic of : Macao SAR*

The purpose of this study was to design a "Rating Scale of Number Sense of Sixth Grader". we discussed the term meaning of number sense and element composition, and designed "The Sixth Grade Number Sense Rating Scale" according to Chinese Machmetial Curriculum Criterion. Then, we chosed 530 students of sixth grade from two public schools in Jinan of Shandong province using random sampling and carried out test. The data collected were put in SPSS14.0 and analysed. the results of this study are as follows: The Scale has very good reliability and validity. The reliability consists both of the coefficient of internal consistency and the test-retest reliability. The validity includes the specialist validity, content validity and construct validity.

The relationship between feedback types and emotional responses

Li, Yang *Dept. of Psychology, Capital Normal University, Beijing, People's Republic of China* **Fang, Ping** *Psychology, Capital Normal University, Beijing, People's Republic of China* **Chen, Manqi** *Psychology, Capital Normal University, Beijing, People's Republic of China* **Jiang, Yuan** *Sport Psychology, Beijing Sport University, Beijing, People's Republic of China*

This study explored the relationship between feedback types and emotions. 99 High-middle-school students with different levels of self-regulated learning competence (SRLC) participated in the experiment. The results showed that: feedbacks influenced those students' emotional physiological arousing, affective priming and subjective feeling experience differently. The respiration frequency of people received negative feedback was faster than those ones who received positive and neural feedback significantly; people received non-feedback thought more fake-words as positive ones, and their judgment-times was longer than the others' significantly. And the level of SRLC can adjust the students' feelings to feedbacks.

The survey and analysis of mental stress and coping manner of Chinese college students

Liao, Xiangrong School of of Administration, University of Changsha, Changsha, People's Republic of China Long, Xiaodong School of Administration, University, Changsha, People's Republic of China

A mental stress and coping manner survey was conducted by a youngsters life event scale and coping manner questionnaire for chinese college students, the results show that mental stress differences among groups are not obvious, but coping manner differences are significant; average mental health level is higher for groups using coping manner of problem-solving and ask-for-help and lower for self-blame and fantasy. methods such as correct identification of mental stress, ripe coping manner etc. were recommende to and adopted by the students, the survey made six months later proves that the methods can make chinese colloge students overcome their mental crises during their college years.

The prevalent of child sexual abuse and its association with risky behaviours among rural adolescent in Hunan province, China

Lin, Danhua School of of Psychology, Beijing Normal University, Beijing, People's Republic of China Fan, Xinghua School of of Psychology, Beijing Normal University, Beijing, People's Republic of China Li, Xiaoming Pediatric Prevention Research, Wayne State University, Detroit, USA Fang, Xiaoyi School of of Psychology, Beijing Normal University, Beijing, People's Republic of China

The study aimed to find out the prevalent of child sexual abuse(CSA) and its relationship with risky behaviors. A sample of 707 rural adolescents in Hunan province, China was recruited. Chi-square analysis and logistic regression were employed to find out the association of CSA with risky behaviors. Results showed 18% of rural adolescent reported ever experienced CSA, with more girls experiencing CSA than boys (20.4% vs. 13.9%). Adolescent experienced CSA were more likely to report smoking, alcohol use, suicide attempt and suicide intention after controlling for demographic variables. More attention should be paid in this population regarding CSA.

Psychological tests used in Romania during the last 50 years

Lita, Stefan Centre for Psychosociology, Ministry of Interior, Bucharest, Romania Mihalcea, Andreea Department of Psychology, Titu Maiorescu University, Bucharest, Romania Ana Maria, Marhan Department of Psychology, Romanian Academy, Bucharest, Romania

The aim of the study is to present the most frequently used tests in Romania. A content analysis was performed on the papers published in Journal of Psychology edited by Romanian Academy during the communism period (1960-1989) and the post-communism period (1990-2007). The preliminary results revealed that (a) 39% of the papers published during before 1989 were based on test's results, while only 25% of the papers used test's results after this year (b) the most used abilities tests were those build by Raven and Torrance and the most used personalities inventories were those build by Eysenck, Cattell and Gough.

Application of generalizability theory in estimating the inter-rater reliability of emotional assessment

Liu, Ye Institute of Psychology, Chinese Academy of Sciences, Beijing, People's Republic of China Wei, Ling Department of Psychology, Fujian Medical University, Fuzhou, People's Republic of China Fu, Xiaolan Institute of Psychology, Chinese Academy of Sciences, Beijing, People's Republic of China

As affective computing research springs up in computer science and psychology, the assessment methods of emotion expressed by dynamic video get much more attention. The present study applied Generalizability Theory to estimate the inter-rater reliability of emotional assessment. Four raters assessed emotional states of 80 video segments by Chinese version of the abbreviated Pleasure-Arousal-Dominance (PAD) emotion scales. The G coefficients of the PAD dimensions were .95, .74, and .55, and the indexes of dependability were .93, .73, and .52, respectively. The results showed increasing the number of raters had a large effect on the G coefficient and index of dependability.

Effect of play therapy group counseling on life adjustment of shy children

Liu, Xuanwen Children's culture Institute, Zhejiang Normal University, Jinhua, People's Republic of China Xu, Er Education College, Zhejiang Normal University, Jinhua, People's Republic of China

The study is to discuss the effect of play therapy group counseling on life adjustment of shy children. 20 shy children in fourth and fifth grade were investigated, who joined a play therapy group counseling for 60 minutes a time, twice a week, 12 times in total. Experiment-control group method was designed in the study. Statistic analysis showed that play therapy group counseling had an immediate effect in posttest, but not in following test. All the members in experimental group had gained some progress. In the process, such play characteristics as special issues, relationship with the leader, topic, verbal expression and nonverbal expression made a change.

Campus violence in Chinese high school

Liu, Xuanwen Children's culture Institute, Zhejiang Normal University, Jinhua, People's Republic of China Wang, Qi Education College, Zhejiang Normal University, Jinhua, People's Republic of China

This paper, based on related literature review, attempted to find out the distribution and causes of campus violence in Zhejiang Province, China by questionnaire. 1256 students from different kinds of high school were investigated. The result showed that high school mostly embodied the intensity of campus violence. Boys' tendency of violence is superior to that of girls'. Higher grades students are more offensive. Poor students' possibility of violence is superior to that of excellent students'. Family environment effects campus violence. Finally, strategies avoiding campus violence had been put forward.

The relationships of personality, social support, and the preference for using internet services in Chinese adolescent

Liu, Mingxin Institute of Psychology, Chinese Academy of Sciences, Beijing, People's Republic of China Lei, Li Institute of Psychology, Chinese Academy of Sciences, Beijing, People's Republic of China Hu, Weiping Institute of Psychology, Chinese Academy of Sciences, Beijing, People's Republic of China Shi, Jiannong Institute of Psychology, Chinese Academy of Sciences, Beijing, People's Republic of China

This study explores the relationships of personality, social support, and the preference for using internet services by surveying a sample of 339 adolescents. The result shows that (1) adolescents' preference for using the internet services includes four factors: social, information, recreational and trade service. Only front three factors are involved in this study;(2)different components of personality have direct on different internet services use, and also have indirect influence through social support;(3) the use of social support have significant negative effects on the use of three services provided by internet.

The mentoring program in the university as a measure of quality in the learning students's process: A proposal for action at the University of Alicante

Lledo Carreres, Asuncion Psicologia Evolutiva, Universidad de Alicante, Alicante, Spain Alvarez Teruel, Jose Daniel Psicologia Evolutia, Universidad de Alicante, Alicante, Spain Grau Company, Salvador Psicología Evolutiva, Universidad de Alicante, Alicante, Spain Gonzalez, Carlota Psicologia Evolutiva y Didacti, Universidad de Alicante, Alicante, Spain Roig Vila, Rosable Didacticas Específicas., Universidad de Alicante, Alicante, Spain Lorenzo Lledó, Gonzalo Psicologia evolutiva y didácti, Universidad de Alicante, Alicante, Spain Tortosa Ybañez, Maria Teresa Developmental Psychology, University of Alicante, Alicante, Spain

The subject of our research is to analyze the situation of action tutorial program at the University of Alicante, after the launch of the project in line with the framework of the European Higher Education Area, seeks action tutorial program towards university student as a measure of support and assessment in this college career advice. The methodology used is within the so-called investigation-action, and the data about the subjects have been analyzed in a qualitative method. And the conclusions findings reflect the demand and the necessity to the action in the tutorial of the new students' entrants at the University of Alicante.

Hereditarism and environmentalism in the formation of character according to Giuseppe Sergi

Lombardo, Giovanni Pietro Clinical Psychology, University, Rome, Italy Bartolucci, Chiara CDept. of linical Psychology, University of Rome, Terni, Italy

The present work aims at reconstructing, within the sphere of evolutionism, the contribution given by Giuseppe Sergi (1841 - 1936) to the specification of heredity and environmental influence on the psycho-physical formation of the individual. The anthropologist Sergi, a pioneer of Italian psychology, proposed a dynamic theory according to which the character was formed by a modular stratification of the hereditary ("fundamental") elements with the acquired ("adventitious") ones (Sergi, 1893). In fact, the author believed that the characteristics acquired by the subject throughout his life could mould his genetic patrimony and be transmitted hereditarily. This conception led Sergi to make use of psycho-pedagogical science in order to favor an optimal development of the character (Sergi, 1890).

Evaluation of content descriptions on conceptual behavior

Lopez Islas, Mario Zapopan, Mexico Rodríguez Pérez, Maria Elena CEIC, Universidad de Guadalajara, Guadalajara, Mexico

Matching-to-sample tasks have been used to study conceptual behavior. Previous research have shown that conceptual behavior is faster acquired when participants describe own behavior. However, there is not a clear correlation between performance and content descriptions in terms of level of abstraction (describing physical properties vs. non-apparent properties). In this study, participants were trained with a matching-to-sample task promoting descriptions with different level of abstraction through differential feedback. Data is discussed in terms of how descriptions affected learning.

Development of speech synthesizer for the blind capabilities in slavic language

Losik, George Lab. Identification System, Institute Information Problem, Minsk, Belarus Parhomenko, Darria Lab of Eginiring Psychology, BSURI, Minsk, Belarus Nekhaev, Evgenij Lab of Engineering Psychology, BSURI, Minsk, Belarus

We currently train Blind people to use speech synthesizer in Belarus. It is difficult for Blind to perceive the speech from PC. This aspect has relating to engineering psychology. Unlike well-known JAWS-system for Blind we designed an intellectual program "Search Echo" which has internal speech comments in on human acts and computer answers. It reflects the computer's dynamics, but not the monitor's static. We have developed training programs on a keyboard, on reading, writing. Results: We have found 3 psychological phenomena: concerning space images, speech synthesizers is more human-like, a perfect command of the oral form.

Current mood state and affective startle modulation

Mörsen, Chantal Patricia Medizinische Psychologie, Johannes Gutenberg-Universität, Mainz, Germany *Wölfling, Klaus* Medizinische Psychologie, Johannes Gutenberg-Universität, Mainz, Germany *Grüsser, Sabine Miriam* Medizinische Psychologie, Johannes Gutenberg-Universität, Mainz, Germany

The aim of the present study was to determine the influence of the current mood state on startle modulation. Forty-five healthy volunteers viewed affective stimuli while eye blink responses, subjective emotional ratings and current mood state were assessed. Compared to subjects in a positive mood those in a more negative mood showed significantly reduced startle amplitudes after viewing the negative and neutral stimuli. The results of the present study show that changes in startle responses are not only related to the current state of psychopathology but also to the general affective state of the participants during the assessments.

The characters of development

Ma, Chuan Dept. of Psychology, East China Normal University, Shanghai, People's Republic of China

With the invalidation of Reductionism and the development of complexity theory, the perspective and the methodology ought to be transformed in the research of developmental psychology. The individual exchange the information with interpersonal and circumstance, so it's a open and self-organization process. The dynamics of development is depended on the interactive with the interpersonal and circumstance so it's un-reversible. The attractors which comes from the chaos theory and be used in the dynamic system theory makes the process is unbalance and nonlinear.

The investigation in relationtion between identity status and loving styles to other sex freind in high school at Tehran city

Mahmoodi, Maliheh Shahid Beheshti S University, Isfahan, Islamic Republic of Iran *Noranipor, Rahmatollah* beheshti, Shahid Beheshti S University, tehran, Islamic Republic of Iran *Salehe Sedghpoor, Bahram* beheshti, Shahid Beheshti S University, tehran, Islamic Republic of Iran

Abstract: This study has been done on 200 subjects who have been selected through available sampling to investigate the relationship between identity status and loving style to the other sex friend. The statistical method used was correlation and the questionnaire was Sternberg's love scale and Eom – EIS2. To analyse the data used the independent sample T- test, chi square, multiple analyses of regression, V crammer, Anova and HSD. The result showed that gender has direct effect on the achieved identity and no effect on diffusion and loving style. Diffusion has a reverse relationship with intimacy, commitment and loving style and a direct relationship with passion. Capability is in direct relationship with intimacy, commitment and loving style.

The mental health service needs of children and adolescents in the South East of Ireland

Martin, Maeve Dept. of Psychology, Health Service Executive, Co Tipperary, Ireland *Carr, Alan* Psychology, University College Dublin, Dublin, Ireland

The aim of this study was to establish the prevalence of psychological disorders in the south east of Ireland and to make recommendations for service delivery.A 2-stage design method was adopted. In Stage 1, 3,191 children age between 2 and 18 years, were screened using the Child Behaviour Checklist or youth Self report form, this represented over 70% of the total population of under 18 year olds.In Stage 2, cases that screened positive and a random sample of those that screened negative for mental health problems were interviewed with the Diagnostic Interview Schedule for Children 1V. Results. Estimated prevalence rate for at least one Psychological disorder was 19%. Recommendations for service development are presented.

A study of subjective well-being and health of Spanish nurses of healthcare organizations

Martinez, Fermin Health Psychology. Edf. Altami, University Miguel Hernandez, Elche, Spain *Orgiles, Mireia* Health Psychology. Edf. Altami, University Miguel Hernandez, Elche, Spain *Solanes, Ángel* Health Psychology. Edf. Altami, University Miguel Hernandez, Elche, Spain *Benavides, Gemma* Health Psychology. Edf. Altami, University Miguel Hernandez, Elche, Spain *Pastor, Yolanda* Health Psychology. Edf. Altami, University Miguel Hernandez, Elche, Spain

The objective of this study is to examine whether subjective well-being self-reported (happiness) is associated with mental and physical health in nurses working in healthcare organizations. It also explores the relationship between these variables and the burnout. Participants are 287 nurses from Spanish healthcare organizations, who responded individually to the assessment tests. The results show that the more happiness, better physical and mental health. Besides, the participants with higher scores in work stress and burnout had more symptoms of mental and physical diseases (anxiety, depression, flu, etc.). The clinical implications of these findings are discussed.

Bullying: Aggression and emotions

Martins, Maria José D. Ciências da Educação, Escola Sup. de Educação Port., Portalegre, Portugal

The objective of this study is to understand the relations between the conditions of being an aggressor, a victim, and a victim/aggressor with emotions and the role of emotions in this kind of behaviour, both in school settings and leisure in adolescence. We use a self-report to assess aggression and victimization and the emotional skills and competence questionnaire developed by Taksic (2000) to assess emotions, specifically competence to manage and regulate emotions, to express and label emotion, and to perceive and understand emotion. Results emphasize the role of emotions in aggression and prevention programs of bullying should include emotional learning.

Envy, resentment, indignation and sense of injustice

Matarazzo, Olimpia Dept. of Psychology, Second University of Naples, Caserta, Italy

Rowls's (1971) assumption about the distinction between envy and resentment or indignation based on subjective vs. objective injustice was tested. 160 students (50% male, 50% female), aged 19-26 (M=21.16; s.d=1.42), participated in this experiment. In the 2 x 2 design the type of injustice and the auto- vs. other-attribution of elicited emotions were manipulated. Objective and subjective injustice perception acted as manipulation check. Data were analyzed through ANOVAs and multivariate standard regressions. Results showed no effects of independent and mediational variables on resentment and indignation, while envy augmented in function of objective injustice and of other-attribution. Rowls's assumption was disconfirmed.

Central processing of emotional faces in eating disorders

Matthias, Ellen Inst. für Psychologie, Universität München, München, Germany *Pollatos, Olga* Psychology, LMU, Munich, Germany

The classification of emotional faces is known to be impaired in eating disorders. To date, it is unclear whether this deficit is reflected in indices of central processing. Visual evoked potentials to emotional faces were assessed in anorexic and bulimic females and matched controls. Anorexic females showed no modulation of emotional face processing and displayed significantly decreased VEPs in response to unpleasant emotional faces, while bulimic patients showed enhanced VEPs in the P300 time range as compared to healthy controls. These marked differences might contribute to difficulties in the correct recognition of facially expressed emotions and deficits in social functioning.

Posttraumatic stress disorder in women experiencing partner violence in El Salvador and Spain

Matud, Pilar Personality, Assessment, La Laguna University, La Laguna, Spain *Bermúdez, Paz* Psychology, Granada University, Granada, Spain

Objective: To analyze Posttraumatic Stress Disorder in women from two different countries (El Salvador and Spain) who experienced partner violence. Methods: Cross-sectional study of a sample of 252 women experiencing partner abuse; 126 of them were living in El Salvador and the rest in Spain. Measures: Severity of Symptoms of Posttraumatic Stress Disorders Scale; Physical and Psychological Abuse Scale; Domestic Violence Interview. Statistical analysis: Multivariate Analysis of Variance, correlations, and Chi-squared tests. Results. 55.6% of the Salvadoran and 56.3% of the Spanish women suffered from Posttraumatic Stress Disorder. In both samples posttraumatic stress symptoms correlated with intensity of partner abuse.

Parenting the disruptive child: From cope to hope: Parental satisfaction and treatment outcomes in the evaluation of successive parenting and children's social skills groups in a clinical setting

Maunula, Stephen Child and Adol. Mental Health, Calgary Health Region - RRDTC, Calgary, Canada *Murdoch, Douglas* Child & Adol. Mental Healt, Calgary Health Region - RRDTC, Calgary, Canada *Barsky, Valerie Wendt, Mila*

Evaluation of the Parents & Children Series (PCS) and Community Parent Education (COPE) programs led to a new combined parent management training/social skills program (PMT/SS). Objective: Improve PMT/SS through Continuous Quality Improvement (CQI) and Program Evaluation (PE). Methods: 100 families of children with disruptive behaviour problems seen through a children's hospital clinic. Measures included behaviour and social skill checklists, parent satisfaction & efficacy scales and Goal Attainment Scales (GAS). Results: Improvements demonstrated on satisfaction, efficacy, behaviour and GAS. Conclusions: Program evaluation led to an improved, effective program package of parenting and child groups.

Longitudinal predictors of English vocabulary knowledge among Hong Kong Chinese-speaking children

McBride-Chang, Catherine *Psychology, Chinese U. of Hong Kong, Hong Kong, China, People's Republic of : Hong Kong SAR*

We examined longitudinal predictors of English receptive vocabulary knowledge among 127 Hong Kong Chinese-speaking children (56 males, 71 females) followed over six years. Parental reports of comprehension of English words at age 2, nonword repetition at ages 3 and 4, and syllable and phoneme awareness at ages 4 and 5 were uniquely associated with subsequent English vocabulary knowledge; age and gender were not. Overall, 29% of the variance in year 6 English vocabulary knowledge could be predicted from these early phonological and language-related variables. Among the strongest correlates of English vocabulary skill were nonword repetition and phoneme onset awareness.

Comparision of visual motor coordination ability, attention, intelligence, learning disorders and behavioral disorders in immature and normal children

Mehri Nejad, Seyyed Abolghasem *Dept. of Psychology, Alzahra University, Tehran, Islamic Republic of Iran*

the purpose of this research was to compare the visual motor coordination ability, attention, intelligence, Learning disorders and behavioral disorders in premature and normal children. Research sample comprised 250 premature student and 250 normal students. the subjects completed tests of Bender Gestalt, Tools Piron, Wechsler (Wisc-R form), Micheal Bust and Ratter (teacher form). the results showed that premature children are lower than normal children are lower than normal children in intelligence quotient, attention and visual motor coordination ability, and Prevalence of learning disorders and behavioral disorders in premature children is more than that of in normal children.

In job interviews, the behaviour of an interviewer affects the reaction of the job candidate

Meier-Faust, Thomas *München, Germany* **Strack, Micha** *Wirtschafts- und Sozialpsych., G.-E.-Müller Inst. f. Psych., Göttingen, Germany* **Revenstorf, Dirk** *Psychologisches Institut, Universität Tübingen, Tübingen, Germany*

Interviews should assess, not simply produce words! 36 structured interviews were videoed and divided into 5 phases: introduction, three main interview phases of equal length, and feedback. Two trained assessors rated the behaviour of the candidate within each phase using 6, and the behaviour of the interviewer using 8 categories (RIVDI, Meier-Faust et al., 2007). Analysis (canonical correlation, cross-lag path) demonstrates the reciprocal interaction between interviewer and candidate. The more distanced and controlling the interviewer was, the less cooperative the candidate. The study shows that communication processes in structured interviews have a significant impact on candidate behaviour and thus on the assessment of their suitability.

Cognitive load and rating accuracy during the observation of an assessment center group discussion

Melchers, Klaus G. *Inst. für Psychologie, Universität Zürich, Zürich, Switzerland* **Meyer, Marion** *Psychologisches Institut, Universität Zürich, Zürich, Switzerland* **Kleinmann, Martin** *Psychologisches Institut, Universität Zürich, Zürich, Switzerland*

It has been suggested that the large cognitive demands during the observation of assessment center participants impair assessors' rating accuracy. An aspect that is especially relevant in this regard is the number of candidates assessors have to observe at the same time in group discussions. In the present experiment assessors had to observe only one candidate or all six candidates at the same time. Participants (N = 71) were shown three videotaped group discussions and had to evaluate candidates on three dimensions. Participants experienced significantly higher cognitive load and showed significantly lower levels of rating accuracy in the latter condition.

Social images of genetic counselling

Mendes, Álvaro *Ciências da Saúde, Universidade de Aveiro, Aveiro, Portugal* **Patrão, Marta** *Ciências da Saúde, Universidade de Aveiro, Aveiro, Portugal* **Guerra, Sara** *Ciências da Saúde, Universidade de Aveiro, Aveiro, Portugal* **Sousa, Liliana** *Ciências da Saúde, Universidade de Aveiro, Aveiro, Portugal*

This study aims at identifying images associated to genetic counselling. A semi-structured interview was administered to two focus-groups (16 participants): i) involved in genetic counselling; ii) never involved in genetic counselling. Main findings suggest that: i) all participants show a vague knowledge about genetic counselling which is related to family inherited; ii) those involved in genetic counselling reveal benefits in terms of health prevention and anxiety reducing; iii) participants associate genetic counselling to some culpability connected to descendents mutation transmission. These findings indicate topics that should be included in future psycho-educational programmes.

Negative affect in focal epilepsy: The role of quality of life perception

Meneses, Rute F. *FCHS, Universidade Fernando Pessoa, Porto, Portugal* **Ribeiro, José P.** *FPCE, Universidade do Porto, Porto, Portugal*

Objective: To identify the best Quality of Life (QoL) predictors of Negative Affect (NA) in Focal Epilepsy (FE). 75 Portuguese outpatients with FE were assessed (40 female; M=37.59 years, SD=12.32, 16-70) with the SF-36 and the HADS. Pearson correlations were used. Correlations (p<.0001) were found between NA and all 8 SF-36 scores. Mental Health, Physical Functioning, General Health, and Social Functioning were the best predictors (R2a=.747). Physical and psychological dimensions should be considered when assessing/intervening in the NA of FE.

Triviality of social research findings, information processing and social cognition: State of the art and methodological applications for the communication of research results

Menold, Natalja *GESIS-ZUMA, Mannheim, Germany*

A problem for the communication of psychological research findings is their apparent triviality and irrelevance from the point of view of a non scientistic audience. To foster the acceptance of social science findings methodological approaches for their effective communication are necessary. The starting point is a model of information processing on the part of the audience. This process can be inhibited through biased and heuristic social cognition: priming and construct-salience, confirmation bias, hindsight bias and false consensus effect. The methodological applications are presented and discussed, e.g. prediction of results (against the hindsight bias) or perspective taking (against the false consensus effect).

Assessing user experience through retrospective time estimation

Meyer, Herbert A. *artop, Humboldt-University Berlin, Berlin, Germany* **Hildebrandt, Michael** *Industrial Psychology Division, OECD Halden Reactor Project, Halden, Norway*

User experience (UX) is often assessed directly through questionnaires. We propose an indirect measure of UX using a time estimation paradigm. The approach is based on an empirically confirmed assumption concerning subjective estimates of the duration of actions: Episodes filled with engaging activity are overrated in retrospective duration judgments, and vice versa. The approach was validated in two experimental studies using a simulated website. Engagement was manipulated by systematically varying the system response time (SRT), while the number of stimuli in the session was held constant. As expected, SRT was correlated with retrospective duration judgment. Applications and limitations are discussed.

The relationship between employment relationship and flexible workforce occupational fatigue, job insecurity

Miao, Qing *Scholl of Public Admin., Zhejiang University, Hangzhou, People's Republic of China* **Yao, Xian-Guo** *Department of Psychology, School of Public Admin., Zhejiang Hangzhou, People's Republic of China*

This research focus on the influence of employment relationship(ER) on the flexible worker's occupational fatigue(OF) and job insecurity(JI), and predicting the moderating role of industrial union(IU). The nation-wide survey(n=1451) was measured by the scale of ER(Tusi,2005), OF(Beurskens,2000), and JI(Ashford,1989). The analysis of variance indicated the quasi-spot-contract ER led to the highest level of OF and JI, the mutual-investment ER caused to the lowest level of OF and JI, while the other two having no difference. If the flexible workers being members of IU, their OF and JI would decrease, especially for the categories of quasi-spot-contract ER and underinvestment ER.

Psychometric studies on coping responses inventory (cri-a) Argentinian adaptation

Mikulic, Isabel Maria *Faculty of Psychology, University of Buenos Aires, Buenos Aires, Argentina* **Crespi, Melina Claudia** *Faculty of Psychology - UBA, CONICET, Buenos Aires, Argentina*

Present study shows results obtained analyzing psychometric properties of Coping Responses Inventory (CRI-A, Moos, 1993) adapted version (Mikulic, 1998) developed to assess approach and avoidance coping It was administered to a sample of 805 participants residing in Buenos Aires, ages between 20 and 50 years old. Alpha found shows high internal consistency (.84). Construct validity was examined and factorial analysis identified two main components in correspondence with Moos theoretical approach. There is a difference in only one scale that loaded on the opposite factor. These findings highlight the importance of reevaluating how coping is conceptualized and measured when adapting instruments

The study of faculty members' attitude towards distance learning as a strategy in development of this type of education

Mirzaie, Sharareh *Tehran, Islamic Republic of Iran*

The present research tries to investigate the attitudes of Faculty members who adopt traditional, distance or both educational systems towards distance learning. The ex post facto method was used in this study and population of the survey included faculty members of Basic Sciences and Technology Universities of Tehran. The instrument was used a questionnaire containing some questions about Faculty beliefs towards electronical learning. The method of analysis was used MANOVA. In conclusion, it appears that skill development is a fundamental factor for proffesors to adopt distance learning. On the other hand, those who didn't have enough familiarity with distance learning issue, were more reluctant to apply it.

Follower emotional responses to leader communications

Mitchelson, Jacqueline *Psychology, Auburn University, Auburn, USA* **Dickson, Marcus** *Psychology, Wayne State University, Detroit, USA*

This study tests regulatory focus predictions regarding followers' emotional responses to leader messages. Specifically, when leader message is promotion-focused, emphasizing advancement (Higgins, 1999), followers experience higher excitement at high goal attainment and higher depression at low goal attainment. When leader message is prevention-focused, emphasizing protection, followers experience higher relaxation at high goal attainment and higher distress at low goal attainment. A 2 (leader message) x 2 (goal attainment) between-subjects experimental design was conducted with 278 followers. Support for hypotheses were found only amongst followers most involved in the message topic and only using a circumplex model and not emotional frequency model of emotions.

Correlations between temperament measured J. Strelau FCB-TI and demographic characteristics sex and age

Mitina, Olga *Dept. of Psychology, Moscow State University, Moscow, Russia*

The results show that six scales are not homogeneous: it was possible to extract different numbers of subscales within each scale. This is important because subscales correlate differently with sex and age. At the same time combining all items in one scale is expedient from the standpoint of system effect maintenance (when the whole is not the simple sum of it's components). Thus, the analysis of parameters on each of temperamental scales should be done at two levels: separate subscales and integrating them scales. Alternative models were testing using structural equation modeling and discussed from theoretical and statistical points of view.

Multimode independent component analysis and relaxing independence assumption

Miyamoto, Yusuke *Dept. of Human Sciences, Osaka University, Suita, Japan*

In classic Independent Component Analysis (ICA), mutual independence between components is assumed and most of ICA algorithms search for a solution that achieves this assumption as much as possible. However, in most cases, the independence assumption is too strong to hold practically. Then, several methods relaxing the independence assumption has been proposed. The basic idea of these methods is to find components with "independent clusters" using external information. This study attempts to show that the idea could be extended to Independent Component Analysis model for multimode (typically 3-mode) data.

Imitation of model tool use in children and adults

Mizuguchi, Takashi *Early Childhood Education, Iwaki Junior College, Iwaki, Japan* **Deguchi, Toshisada** *Educational Science, Tokyo Gakugei University, Koganei, Japan*

This study investigated the imitation of tool use by children and adults, and the comparison of their errors. 32 preschoolers and 32 college students participated. The action model we used consisted of five variable aspects that were a series of tool use movements. Results indicated that the pattern of error was similar in children and adults, but children omitted some variable aspects from the action model. The findings suggest that children and adults engage in goal-directed imitation with a similar mechanism. Moreover, the limit of memory span was related to the omission of the action model.

A prelude on moral prism in education: case study: teachers' moral prism

Moghimi, Mohammad *Qom, Islamic Republic of Iran* **Khanifar, Hossein** *Education and psychology, University of Tehran, Qom, Islamic Republic of Iran* **Bayan Memar, Ahmad** *Education and psychology, University of Qom, Qom, Islamic Republic of Iran*

Pedagogy has an important role in learners' socialization along with their families and completing their roles. Fundamentally, because that pedagogy system faces with a raw material called human, it plays a vital role. Meanwhile, moral prism with its long history (religious, civilization, and training) is retainable in educational systems of countries. In this article, we try to address various items of teachers' and educational leaders' moral prism and introduce some models. Research methodology is content analysis and elite method is applied. Moral prism is considered in religion, philosophy, morality and educational management. By considering psychological and philosophical origins, we have reviewed different opinions.

Estimation of multiple intelligences in Kordofan State

Mohammednour, Obeidallah *Dept. of Psychology, University of Kordofan, Elobied, Sudan*

this study investigates the estimation of multiple intelligences (MI) in Kordofan State, Sudan. a constructed measure of nine multiple intelligences was applied to a group of 562 pupils in primary education (11-15 years), both males (50%) and female (50%) from urban (64%) and rural areas(36%). the study showed that there was a significant difference in most aspects of MI between male and female participants, favoring the later. furthermore, it showed that there was a significant difference in the estimated MI between rural and urban areas favoring the later. finally, many suggestions and recommendations were reached.

Emotional competence of children and adolescents

Monigl, Eszter *Inst. für Psychologie, Pädagogische Hochschule, Schwäbisch Gmünd, Germany* **Behr, Michael** *Psychology, University of Education, Schwäbisch Gmünd, Germany*

Research conveys that emotional competence has a major influence on children's personal development. Therefore measures of emotional competence are pivotal in many evaluations of learning and developmental processes. A multi-dimensional measure examining children's and adolescents' emotional competence (EKO-KJ) was developed on a paper-pencil base and for use with children from the age of 10. The EKO-KJ covers three essential subjects of emotional competence: personal emotions, other people's emotions and knowledge about emotions. All sub-constructs are measured both on subjective and objective scales. Data from an evaluation study with students from age 10 to 18 will be demonstrated.

Media role in a crisis psychological intervention

Monov, Hristo *Sofia University, Sofia, Bulgaria*

The purpose of the report is to present the role of the media in a crisis psychological intervention. The used methods are "case studies" and "content analysis".The cases that are analysed are a drown of 12 bulgarian children in an accident in Republic of Monte Negro and a drown of 8 people after a flood. The conclusion is that media have very important role in the model of crisis psychological intervention in natural disasters,accidents,crashes and terroristic acts.

Post traumatic stress disorder and psychological functioning in spinal cord injured patients

Moodley, Nancy *Behavioural Medicine, University of KwaZulu-Natal, Durban, South Africa* **Pillay, Basil** *Dept. Behavioural Medicine, University of KwaZulu-Natal, Durban, South Africa*

Objectives: To investigate psychological functioning in patients with spinal cord injury (SCI). Method: Participants at spinal units were assessed over a year. A semi-structured interview and questionnaires (Impact of Event, Posttraumatic Diagnostic, General Health, Beck Depression, Symptom Checklist and Hospital Anxiety and Depression) were administered. Group differences were explored using ANOVA, $\chi 2$ and post hoc tests. Results: High levels of Depression & PTSD impacted on overall level of functioning and general satisfaction with life. Females were at a greater risk. High road traffic accidents and crime were contributing factors to SCI and PTSD. Conclusion: The discussion emphasises multicultural issues prevalent.

A study of effectiveness of structural family therapy approach in treatment of 6-12 years old children with separation anxiety disorder

Mousavi, Rogayyeh *Tehran, Islamic Republic of Iran* **Moradi, Alireza** *Psychology, Tarbiat Moallem University, Tehran, Islamic Republic of Iran* **Mahdavi Harsini, Esmaeil** *Counseling Psychology, University of Masachoset, Tehran, Islamic Republic of Iran*

The main aim of the present research is to investigate the effects of the structural family therapy approach on the treatment of children with separation anxiety disorder. 40 families with at least one child who suffer from the SAD participated in this study. All families were randomly divided in two main groups including experimental and control groups. A battery of the instruments include Separation Anxiety Scales (Spence; 1998), Enrich Satisfaction Test (Enrich, 1999), and Family Performance Inventory (Mousavi; 2005) were used. The experimental group was received 10 sessions of the family intervention program, while control group were on the waiting list. The results indicated that the family structural intervention was significantly treated the separation anxiety disorder (p<0.001).

Gestural reference in mother and babies over the second and the third years

Muñetón Ayala, Mercedes Amparo *Dept. Developm. Psychology, University of La Laguna, La Laguna, Spain*

Gestural reference mediated by pointing was examined during daily routines. Eight mothers and their 1- and 2-year-old babies were observed during one year every three months. Episodes of pointing were selected to examine whether they are produced alone or accompanied by a verbal utterance/vocalization, the referent target and whether it is visible, occluded or absent. Results indicated that pointing gestures were produced very frequently by both, followed a significant positive trend with age and were accompanied with verbal utterances/vocalizations. Referent target for both is mainly external and visible/occluded and becomes more absent with age indicating a displacement of reference.

Verbal deictics in Spanish children between 12-36 months of age: A longitudinally study

Muñetón Ayala, Mercedes Amparo *Dept. Developm. Psychology, University of La Laguna, La Laguna, Spain*

This study examined longitudinally during one year, the rate of deictic production in four Spanish 1-and 2-years-old children in interactive situations with their mothers at home. First, we observed the order of deictic emergence. Second we analyzed its production changes taking into account their semantic dimensions (spatial, personal, temporal);

their grammar categories (pronouns, adjectives, adverbs), and their morphological features (gender, number, distance). The results indicated that the deictic words help to anchor the speaker's and the addresses' discourse to the deictic center (I, here, now, this). Also the spatial domain seemed to be relevant for the development of personal deictics.

Illicit drug use, alcohol use and perpetation of dating violence among Spanish adolescents

Muñoz-Rivas, Marina Julia Psic. Biológica y de la Salud, Universidad Autónoma de Madrid, Madrid, Spain Gámez-Guadix, Manuel Psic. Biológica y de la Salud, Universidad Autónoma de Madrid, Madrid, Spain Fernández González, Liria Psic. Biológica y de la Salud, Universidad Autónoma de Madrid, Madrid, Spain González Lozano, Pilar Pers., Eval. y Psic. Clínica, Univ. Complutense de Madrid, Madrid, Spain Objective: The goal of study was to analyze the association between Spanish adolescents' alcohol and illicit drug use and perpetration of violence against a dating partner. Method: The sample was composed of 1887 students between 15 and 19 years old. K-means cluster analysis yielded three groups of alcohol and illicit drug users: low, intermediate and high substance use clusters. Results: Members of the high alcohol and drug use cluster were significantly more likely than participants in low substance use cluster to report perpetrating verbal, physical or sexual violence against a dating partner. Conclusions: Findings suggest that substance use is a relevant risk factor for perpetration of dating violence.

Design of a research experiment for the training in motivationals competencies through educational innovation in personality and social psychology subjects

Muela, José Antonio Personality Psychology, Universidad de Jaén, Jaén, Spain Lopez Zafra, Esther Dept. of Social Psychology, Universidad de Jaén, Jaén, Spain García León, Ana María Personaligy Psychology, Universidad de Jaén, Jaén, Spain Augusto, José María Social Psychology, Universidad de Jaén, Jaén, Spain The implementation of the European Credit Transfer System (ECTS), in Spain is a challenge that needs to develop new activities favoring the development of competencies. Our activity within Social and Personality Psychology wanted to develop cognitive and values competencies, by means of a participation in an empirical research. 57 students of the first course of Psychology participated in this study (13 male and 44 female) representative of the gender distribution in class. Pre- and post- assessment of the experience show that students enhanced their level of commitment and performance, although the impact over the performance was to be discussed.

Developmental change and diversity of children's beliefs about the origin of personal, intellectual and physical traits

Mukai, Takahisa Graduate School of Human Env., Kyushu University, Fukuoka, Japan Maruno, Shunichi Faculty of human-environment s, Kyushu university, Fukuoka(city) East-Ward, Jordan We investigated developmental change and diversity of children's beliefs about the effects of 'nature and nurture' on personal/intellectual/physical traits. 87 first to third graders participated were asked to evaluate the degree of likelihood about the four possible causal models (nature and/or nurture, or others) concerning the origin of traits. The results indicated that with age, children think that the origin of personal/intellectual traits is nurture, and that of physical traits is nature. However, the majority of children showed plural conflicting beliefs (causal models) on each trait, which insinuates the plural beliefs as a possible preparatory state for the belief change.

Burden of care: Measuring the impact of pediatric psychiatric, emotional and behavioral disorders on caregivers

Murdoch, Douglas Dept. of Clinical Psychology, University of Calgary, Calgary, Canada Rahman, Abdul CAMHP-Specialized Services, Calgary Health Region, Calgary, Alberta, Canada Barsky, Valerie CAMHP-Specialized Services, Calgary Health Region, Calgary, Alberta, Canada Maunula, Stephen CAMHP-Specialized Services, Calgary Health Region, Calgary, Alberta, Canada Wosnock, Natasha CAMHP-Specialized Services, Calgary Health Region, Calgary, Alberta, Canada Cawthorpe, David Faculty of Medicine, University of Calgary, Calgary, Alberta, Canada The emotional, financial and social impact on caregivers of pediatric psychiatric, emotional and behavioral disorders has been poorly documented. Objective: Determine the utility of the Burden Assessment Scale (BAS) with this population. Methods: 300 parents seeking services with the Calgary Health Region were interviewed using the BAS. Results: The BAS was clear, acceptable and comprehensive for >80% of participants. Burden was associated with the degree of impairment. Factor analysis revealed four factors compared to the two factors found with adults. Conclusions: the BAS had a utility with this population and would be a valuable addition to standard information gathered.

Progress in gesture-speech synchrony and early lexical uses in children 9- to 12-months-olds

Murillo, Eva Psicología Basica, Universidad Autonoma de Madrid, Madrid, Spain Belinchón, Mercedes Psicología Básica, Universidad Autónoma de Madrid, Madrid, Spain Objectives: To study how gestures and vocalizations "codevelop" in normally developing children from 9 to 12 months, and to test whether among the crucial skills for the acquisition of first words is the ability to use these two systems in an integrated way. Method: Ten children were longitudinally recorded in a semi-structured play situation with an adult. Observational codes and the Program "Praat" were used in analyses. Results: Differences in topography, function and frequency were found when gestures and vocalizations are used separately vs. jointly across this period. Conclusions: Changes toward a gesture-speech synchrony are paralleled by early lexical development, and could be viewed as a prerequisite for it.

Relationship of narrative and theory of mind in children with high function autism

Nagasaki, Tsutomu Disability Sciences, University of Tsukuba, Narashino, Japan Maruyama, Daiki school, Kotoni Elementary School, Sapporo, Japan Nagasaki, Yuko resource room, Dai-Ni Junior High School, Narashino, Japan Relationship of performance level of personal narrative and five tasks of theory of mind(TOM) was observed in seven children with high function autism of elementary school. As a result, in the aspect of content of narratives, the children with autism who didn't pass the tasks of TOM rarely referred to mental states of self and others. In the aspect of narrative structure, the children with autism who didn't pass the tasks of TOM narrated events enumerated, not sequenced. These results shows the closely relationship between narrative and theory of mind in children with high function autism.

The effect of Emotional Intelligence Training (EIT) on aggressiveness in male students

Naghdi, Hadi Divandareh, Islamic Republic of Iran The aim this research was to show effectiveness of emotional intelligence training on the aggression of male students. this research was experimental type; therefore They randomly selected two groups. The experimental group participated in teaching cycle of emotional intelligence at eight teaching workshops. The results of covariance analysis show that emotional intelligence training decreased the amount of aggression in students. Emotional intelligence training decreased physical aggression, verbal aggression and anger in students, but emotional intelligence training didn't decrease the amount of students' hostility. Conclusion: we can say that emotional intelligence training was effective in decrease of aggression in male students.

Why do people smoke cigarettes? Different reasons for different people

Nahari, Galit Criminology, Bar-Ilan University, Ramat-Gan, Israel For better understanding of cigarettes smoking behavior, the current study was focused on testing an integrative model which combines personality and motivational factors of smokers, within the framework of Eysenck's smoking model. 121 smokers filled up a motivational questionnaire which was developed in a pilot study, as well as a set of personality questionnaires (EPQ-R-S, I7, BIS-11, SSS-V) and smoking habitual questionnaire. A differentiation in smoking motivation by personality traits has emerged: smokers have different motives to begin smoking and to continue smoking as a function of their personality traits. Giving a reference to variance between smokers may contribute for developing smoking preventing or treatment programs.

Does sugar turn life into sweet or bitter? The psychological influences of sucrose intake on the change of emotional stress

Naito, Mayumi Dept. of Economics, Takasaki City University, Takasaki, Japan The aim of this study was to examine whether sugar intake in everyday life affects our emotional stress in positively or negatively. People often hold two opposite images of sugar. One image is that sweetness gives us relief, which implies that sugar intake decreases emotional stress. Another is that sugar gets associated with health problem (e.g., obesity), which implies that its intake increases emotional stress via making health apprehension high. These potential influences were investigated in two-wave panel study for 433 people in their teens to fifties. Analysis of covariance structure supported both positive and negative influences of sugar intake.

Effects of endogenous opioids on the passive avoidance learning and memory of female rats during estrus cycle

Najafi, Atieh Physiology, Hamadan University of Medical, Hamedan, Islamic Republic of Iran Shahidi, Siamak Physiology, Hamadan University of Medical, Hamedan, Islamic Republic of Iran Farhadinasab, Abdollah Psychiatrics, Hamadan University of Medical, Hamedan, Islamic Republic of Iran Komaki, Alireza Physiology, Hamadan University of Medical, Hamedan, Islamic Republic of Iran The purpose of this study was to define the physiological functions of endogenous opioids on passive avoidance learning and memory during estrous cycle in rat. The pro-estrus and estrus female rats were trained in the passive avoidance task. The rats received naloxone (an opioid receptors anatagonist) or saline before or after training or before retrieval test. Administration of naloxone before training had no effect on trials to acquisition in the estrus and pro-estrus rats. Naloxone facilitates consolidation and retrieval of memory in the estrus phase. Thus, endogenous opioids impair consolidation and retention of passive avoidance during estrus but not pro-estrus.

Is an inference rule Modus Ponens really an early acquisition?

Nakagaki, Akira Graduate School of Education, Waseda University, Tokyo, Japan

Modus Ponens, the most fundamental inference rule in conditional reasoning, is generally believed to develop at latest at 6 years old. Our experiment examined the validity of this belief. Each participant (23 first, 21 third, and 21 fifth graders) was presented with two boxes and the conditional statement: 'if there is A in a box, then there is also B in it' and was asked whether he/she could or could not determine if B was in it. In spite of insufficient information, 96%, 76%, 71%, respectively, answered affirmatively. This result cast serious doubt on the early acquisition of Modus Ponens.

Maternal exposure to BPA feminized social behavior of cynomolgus male infants (Macaca fascicularis)

Nakagami, Akiko Dept. of Psychology, Japan Women's University, Kawasaki, Japan Kawasaki, Katsuyoshi Psychology, Hoshi University, Tkyo, Japan Kuroda, Yoichiro Neuroscience, Tokyo Metropolitan Institute, Tokyo, Japan Negishi, Takayuki Chemistry and Biological Scien, Aoyama gakuin University, Sagamihara, Japan Yoshikawa, Yasuhiro Biomedical science, Tokyo University, Tokyo, Japan Koyama, Takamasa Psychology, Japan Women's University, Kawasaki City, Japan

It has been recently discussed that low does exposure to the endocrine disrupting chemical in critical point of fetal period affects permanently development of its own offspring. In the present study, we administrated to BPA in amount of 10 μg/kg/day via subcutaneously implanted pumps experimentally controlled cynomolgus monkeys in order to examine adverse effect of perinatal exposure to and we observed social behaviors between infant and its mother during lactation period. Perinatal exposure to BPA significantly altered BPA-exposed male infant behaviors toward female infant's ones. These results suggest that behavioral sexual differentiation in male monkeys should be a target of BPA, which would be useful to understand risk of BPA-exposure in human.

Taste aversion learning based on physical exercise in rats

Nakajima, Sadahiko Psychology, Kwansei Gakuin University, Nishinomiya, Japan

Physical exercise such as running in an activity wheel or swimming in a water pool works as an effective unconditioned stimulus (US) to establish conditioned taste aversion in rats. This paper gives a brief review of the experiments conduced in my laboratory in the last 9 years and presents our currently ongoing studies. The topics include demonstrations of exercise-based taste aversion learning, surveys on some basic parameters such as the length of exercise and the taste-exercise interval, and investigations regarding (1) effect of US pre- or post-exposures, (2) degraded contingency effect, and (3) overshadowing effect on exercise-based taste aversion learning.

Effects of attention on early and late syntactic processes in 3 to 4 years old children

Nikolaizig, Franziska Max-Planck-Institut, Leipzig, Germany Friederici, Angela D. Neuropsychology, MPI CBS, Leipzig, Germany

In a recent study (Hahne, & Friederici, 1999) it was shown that the two-pass syntactic parsing process is reflected by an early left anterior negativity and a late positivity with only the latter being influenced by attentional factors. As we were interested in how attention might influence a sentence processing system which is still under development we tested 3 to 4 year-olds in a passive listening task containing different proportions (20% vs. 80%) of syntactically

correct and incorrect sentences, respectively. We found an ELAN and no P600 for both conditions, thus showing a different pattern compared to the adult data.

The matrix of the unconsciousness

Nikolova, Vyara Phylosophy, South-West University, Sofia, Bulgaria

The aim of this study is to fulfill two tasks: first to define a principle which determines a system of terms for discovering the human nature. For this purpose, the Psychoanalysis is a central paradigm because it is explanatory principle applicable in a broader scope of phenomena – social, psychological, cultural, religious and historical. Second, to describe an invariant principle in the human nature as a general motivating factor of human behavior, wishes and ideas. These are considered as fundamental strives for significance which derives from biological principle of surviving.

Developmental outcomes in children with very-low-birth-weight

Noi, Mika Faculty of Health and Welfare, Seinan Jo Gakuin University, Kitakyushu, Japan

Since the mid-1980's, along with progress in neonatal medicine, there has been a marked increase in the survival rate of very-low-birth-weight (VLBW) and extremely-low-birth-weight (ELBW) infants. Several studies have showed that the development of VLBW children without major complications catches up with the development of children born at term. However, the developmental status may be affected and vary, as the technology in neonatal medicine proceeded. In this study, 438 children with VLBW were classified into 3 cohorts (children who were born in 1986-1990, 1991-1995, and 1996-2000). Total IQ, verbal IQ, and performance IQ were compared among these 3 groups.

A comparison of printed-page versus web-based data obtained from older adult study participants

O'Rourke, Norm Dept. of Gerontology, Simon Fraser University, Vancouver, Canada Chou, Ben Centre on Aging, University of Victoria, Victoria, Canada

Use of the Internet for participant recruitment and data collection has become increasingly prevalent in social science research. Despite this, negative perceptions persist about the reliability of web-based data. Results of the current study, however, suggest that few demographic or personality differences distinguish older adults who provide responses via the Internet as reported by self-report and collateral informants. Furthermore, the reliability of responses does not appear to differ between methods. Most notable, invariance analyses suggest that patterns of response are largely indistinguishable between the two. These findings suggest that social science researchers can embrace the Internet with greater confidence as a cost effective and reliable means of participant recruitment and data collection.

Science discourse in the digital age

Odonoghue, Raphael Foreign Language, National Institute of Fitness, Kanoya, Kagoshima, Japan

Arbitrariness of meaning of language is more visible in electronic communication. Communicating electronically, from one discourse domain to another, one language to another, and between cultures is prone to misunderstanding. 'Technology-inspired informality of expression that didn't exist before' (Ross, 2006) creates problems when used in science discourse. On-line journals, submissions, proposal applications, topic alerts and computer based research groups are now shaping science discourse. The linguistic and discourse features and strategies used in this shaping, and how these are embedded in native language communication styles is surveyed quantitatively

and qualitatively for a sample of on-line and manuscript-based science discourse.

The role of executive function in Japanese children's prediction and explanation of other person's false action

Ogawa, Ayako Osaka, Japan

Recent studies on the child's developing theory of mind (ToM) have identified that the development of executive function (EF) as a factor which contributes to children's understanding of false belief. But cross-cultural studies what the relationship between ToM and EF was showed inconsistent results in Asia and Western countries. The present study examined what aspect of EF is related to understanding of false belief in Japanese children. 3- to 5-year-olds were given prediction and explanation false belief tasks, a receptive vocabulary test, and executive function tasks. The results showed that the working memory was significantly related to ToM.

Discrimination threshold of inclination angle against vertical is 10 degree in Goldfish

Ohi, Shuzo Faculty of Education, Gifu University, Gifu, Japan

It is known that goldfish can discriminate between vertical and horizontal lines. But it has not been clarified how much degree of inclination angle the goldfish requires to discriminate between 2 types of inclined lines. We measured the threshold of inclination angle against vertical line by means of descending a difference of angle between vertical and oblique lines. There are two rotating directions to make oblique line approach to vertical: clockwise series and counter-clockwise. At 10 degree of inclination from vertical in both series, it was shown that fifty percent of subjects could discriminate successfully and the other half not.

A support system of students' error by probabilistic modeling

Ohmori, Takuya Managm. & Information Science, Tama University, Tokyo, Japan

A new student support system which is based on Bayesian network model is proposed. In this system, students' error on arithmetic are assumed to be based on Buggy model. To diagnose the type of error, we also assume the network structure on test items, which contains testlet. We show the simulation study of applying to the real data, and comparison to IRT model.

Effects of attachment on evaluation of emotions

Okumura, Yayoi Human-Enviroment Studies, Kyushu-University/Japan, Fukuoka, Japan

This study focused on how peoples evaluate their own emotions (evaluation of emotions). I hypothesize that attachment style have effects on the evaluation of emotions (sadness and anger). 149 university students completed questionnaire. Main results of multiple regression analysis shows that preoccupied style had positive effect on negative evaluations of emotions ("negative self-conscious emotions about emotions" and "emotions as burden"), negative effect on positive evaluation of emotions ("necessity of emotions"). Therefore, these results suggested that attachment style have effects on evaluation of emotions that is supposed to be associated with function of emotions.

Peer-group norms regarding abusive behavior: The case of Japanese junior high school students

Onishi, Ayako Omura Miyahigashi Mansion, Nagoya, Japan Yoshida, Toshikazu Omura Miyahigashi Mansion 2D, Nagoya University, Nagoya, Japan

The purpose of this study was to examine the relationships between class enjoyment, exclusivity in peer-group, trust and peer-group norms regarding abusive behavior. Participants were 355 junior high school students who responded to a questionnaire survey. The results indicated that: (1) exclusivity of the peer-group has a direct effect on norms for preventing abusive behavior. (2) class enjoyment has a direct effect on norms for despising abusive behavior. The importance of classroom management to keep classes enjoyable, and maintaining trust between classmates was discussed.

The role of the ventral premotor cortex in sequencing linguistic information

Opitz, Bertram Psychology, Saarland University, Saarbrücken, Germany Kotz, Sonja A. Cognitive and Brain Science, Max Planck Institute for Human, Leipzig, Germany

Recent fMRI evidence demonstrated a differential involvement of the inferior frontal gyrus (IFG) and the ventral premotor cortex (PMv) in syntactic processing. Our main goal is to specify the precise role of PMv in processing sequential structures and whether these processes are a necessary prerequisite for successful language acquisition. We tested patients with PMv lesions in an artificial grammar (AG) learning task. Compared to matched controls patients exhibited impaired acquisition of the AG. This impairment was more pronounced for local (referring to adjacent elements within an AG string) as for long-distance dependencies, indicating a PMv involvement in processing local sequential information.

Acceptability and usability of technical solutions in old age

Oppenauer, Claudia Inst. für Klin. Psychologie, Universiätsklinik Wien, Wien, Austria Prazak-Aram, Barbara Biomedical Engineering, Austrian Research Center GmbH, Wiener Neustadt, Austria Hochgatterer, Andreas Biomedical Engineering, Austrian Research Center GmbH, Wiener Neustadt, Austria Kryspin-Exner, Ilse Inst. für Psychologie, Universität Wien, Wien, Austria

Motivational and emotional factors highly influence acceptability and usability of technical devices in old age. Within the project Safety Assistant For the Elderly (S.A.F.E.) a information and emergency system has been developed which registers every movement and activity in the assisted senior citizen apartments and forwards acoustic signals to the residents and the care staff. The aim of this study is to evaluate the project from a psychological point of view. Participants of the project will be interviewed with psychological questionnaires, and changes in psychological variables will be assessed. Preliminary results of this evaluation will be presented and ethical aspects discussed.

Give me your tired, your poor, your huddled masses: Mortality salience, physicality and immigration

Osborne, Randall Dept. of Psychology, Texas State University, San Marcos, USA Mazzetti, Francesco Psychology, Texas State University-San Mar, San Marcos, USA

Problem Mortality Salience was hypothesized to lead participants to view immigrants described with physical jobs more negatively than immigrants described with nonphysical jobs. Methods Participants were randomly assigned to non-mortality salience (NMS) or MS groups and rated the effect immigrants with physical and nonphysical jobs would have on American society. Results Results revealed lower means for non-physical job descriptions after MS induction, greater difference between the MS and NMS groups for physical job descriptions and an interaction between job type and MS. Conclusions MS led to lower ratings of immigrants. Perspectives on immigration appear shaped by mortality salience and physicality of immigrant groups.

Post-transgressional repair intention: Its relationship with consequence severity, trait favorability and responsibility attribution

Pak, S. Tess Dept. of Psychology, University of Hong Kong, Hong Kong, People's Republic of China Chao, An An Psychology, The University of Hong Kong, Hong Koong, China, People's Republic of : Macao SAR Hui, C. Harry Psychology, The University of Hong Kong, Hong Koong, China, People's Republic of : Macao SAR

Research indicates that offence severity predicts and moderates forgiveness behavior. Our study of real life transgression events reported by 91 individuals replicates and extends past research to show: (a) consequence severity hinders both offenders' and victims' intention to repair relationship; (b) offender's perceived trait favorability promotes the victim's intention to repair relationship; (c) the association between consequence severity and victim's repair intention varies with the offender's trait favorability. In line with studies conducted in collectivist cultures, responsibility attribution has relatively negligible effect on repair intention. Equality of predictors' strength on repair intention between offenders and victims is also discussed.

Women as victims of violence: Analyses of the effectof prevention campaings in young people's attitudes

Palacios, Maria Soledad Dept. of Psychology, University of Huelva, Huelva, Spain Morales Marente, Elena Department of Pscyhology, University of Huelva, Huelva, Spain Pérez Flores, Miguel Consejería de Educación, I.E.S. José Caballero, Huelva, Spain Abrio, Inmaculada Department of Pscyhology, University of Huelva, Huelva, Spain

The aim of this study is to analyse the effect of the campaigns that Spanish Government carry out for the prevention of violence against women. These campaigns are focused on the complicity of people who keep silent when are witness of this violence. We try to demonstrate that it is not enough. Recent studies have showed that people blame the victims. With an experimental design we compare 2 prevent campaigns focused in both topics (complicity vs blame victim). The main dependent variable was attitude toward gender violence. Participants are 68 students from the University of Huelva (Spain). Results showed significant differences of the two types of campaigns for attitudes toward gender violence.

Ambivalent sexism in young people: Prediction of attitudes toward violence in the couple

Palacios, Maria Soledad Dept. of Psychology, University of Huelva, Huelva, Spain Pérez-Flores, Miguel Consejería de Educación, IES José Caballero, Huelva, Spain Morales Marente, Elena Department of Pscyhology, University of Huelva, Huelva, Spain Torrico, Esperanza Department of Pscyhology, University of Huelva, Huelva, Spain

The aim of this study is to analyse the relationship between ambivalent sexist ideology and attitudes toward physical and psychological violence against women. Specifically, we would like to know if any of the two components of ambivalent sexism predicts attitudes toward one of the types of violence. Participants were 193 young students ofthe University of Huelva (Spain), 79.3% women. We administrated the next scales: Ambivalent Sexism Inventory (Spanish version, Expósito, Moya & Glick, 1998); and a questionnaire on attitudes toward physical and psychological violence created for this study. We made correlational and lineal regression analysis, and found gender differences in attitude toward violence against women, and in the prediction of these attitudes by ambivalent sexism

Conversational awareness and false belief tasks: A training study with children of a low socioeconomic level

Panciera, Sara UNICSUL, São Paulo, Brazil Maluf, Maria Regina Psychological developmental, Universidade Catolica de SP, São Paulo, Brazil Deleau, Michel CRPCC, Universite Rennes2, Rennes, France

This study uses a training procedure to investigate precedence relationships between language and the performance in false-belief-tasks. Twenty-eight children of a low socioeconomic level took part in the experiment, between ages 3.10 and 5.3; these children formed an experimental and a control group. The training was in the pragmatic aspect of language (conversational awareness). The Wellman and Liu scale of theory-of-mind (2004) was applied to the pretest and post-test. Results showed that children belonging to the experimental group had a significantly better performance in the theory-of-mind tasks in the post-test (p<0,0001), as compared to children belonging to the control group.

Comprehensibility of warning symbols

Paridon, Hiltraut und Gesundheit, BGAG Institut für Arbeit, Dresden, Germany Hupke, Marlen research and education, BGAG Institute Work and Health, Dresden, Germany Ottersbach, Hans-Jürgen BGIA, DGUV, Sankt Augustin, Germany

A warning symbol and a prohibitory sign were developed for personal safety equipment against falls and crashes. Before using the symbols their comprehensibility was to be investigated. Different drafts were designed and rated by experts regarding compatibility, standardization, familiarity, and understandability. On the basis of the experts ratings the best drafts were selected and user had to evaluate the drafts. The ratings show that none of the drafts is sufficient comprehensible. On the basis of the results the drafts are revised at present.

Effects of social stress on state-dependent learning: A comparison of lab and real life settings

Peper, Martin Inst. für Neuropsychologie, Universität Marburg, Marburg, Germany Braner, Mike Biological Psychology, University of Freiburg, Freiburg, Germany Löffler, Simone Biological Psychology, University of Freiburg, Freiburg, Germany

Social stress is typically induced by free speech situations. Here, we compared the effects of an artificial lab situation ("Trier Social Stress Test", TSST) and a realistic seminar setting with respect to physiological activation and subsequent state-dependent learning (N=48). Ambulatory assessment (Freiburg Monitoring System) was used to register emotional activation and for presenting word lists. Although subjective stress ratings were similar, nonmetabolic heart rate accelerations were stronger in the lab (TSST). In real life, social stress was more ambivalent and influenced by additional factors. State-dependent learning could not be demonstrated but a trend for the effect was found in women.

Parental rearing styles and adjustment patterns in Portuguese school-aged children

Pereira, Ana Isabel IPC - FPCE -UC, Coimbra, Portugal Canavarro, Maria Cristina FPCE, FPCE -UC, Coimbra, Portugal Mendonça, Denisa ICBAS, ICBAS, Porto, Portugal

The purpose of this study is to identify family correlates of four groups of children: externalizing, internalizing, mixed-problems and well functioning. The sample consisted of 519 children. Parental rearing styles were measured through the administration of EMBU-C. Adjustment was measured through CBCL and TRF. Multinomial logistic regression analysis indicate that: a) children with higher parental control are significantly more likely to be internalizers than well functioning, b) children with lower emotional support from parents are significantly more likely to be externalizers than well functioning, c) children reporting higher parental rejection are significantly more likely to be categorized as mixed problems than well functioning.

Representations of 'being dead': Cognitive and cultural constraints

Pereira, Vera Lisbon, Portugal *Sá-Saraiva, Rodrigo* Psychology, University of Lisbon, Lisbon, Portugal *Faisca, Luis Miguel*

We studied how the representations of being dead are determined by cognitive constraints and explicit beliefs about the afterlife. We interviewed young adults for information about the implicit and explicit representations of being dead and the degree in which experience is perceived as body dependent. The results point to a general tendency to imagine the state of being dead as a continuation of the conscious self, even if the belief in the afterlife is denied. The parts of the self that 'continue' tend to be perceived as less body dependent. The explicit cultural beliefs about the afterlife interact with this general tendency.

Reflections about relationships in later life: The old people and their families

Perez-Marin, Marian Faculdad de Psicologia, Universidad Catolica Valencia, Valencia, Spain *Molero-Zafra, Milagros* FACULTAD DE PSICOLOGIA, UNIVERSIDAD DE VALENCIA-UVEG, VALENCIA, Spain *Barreto-Martin, Pilar* FACULTAD DE PSICOLOGIA, UNIVERSIDAD DE VALENCIA-UVEG, VALENCIA, Spain

The main aim of this paper is to analyze the circumstances that can bring the best quality of life possible for old people and their relatives at the end of their lives. The framework of this idea is humanitarian, ethical and professional. From this point of view, we present some reflections on the results and conclusions from the scientific literature on this topic. Thereby, it is important to consider the old person's resources and capacities, his/her family conditions and the support both receive from the different informal and governmental organizations.

How do organizational values and individual differences determine patterns of sensemaking?

Perry, Anthony School of Psychology, Northcentral University, Prescott Valley, USA

Sensemaking within the military organization has gained much attention. Studies examining sensemaking have been descriptive or theoretical, with few empirical studies. This study explored correlates of sensemaking, and examined individual differences including aggression, organizational culture, cultural preferences, and their relationships to sensemaking and how information is prioritized during sensemaking within battle scenarios. One hundred participants in the Corps of Cadets were presented with one battle scenario and asked what they would do and why. Results showed a number of siginficant relationships between indiviudal differences and sensemaking and that the concept of using scenario to capture the sensemaking process was viable.

Features of emotional and body experience Oof the children with the Burn Trauma

Pervichko, Elena Psychology, Moscow State University, Moscow, Russia

There were serveyed 100 children with a burn trauma (subjects) and 50 healthy chil-dren. Results: qualitative and quantitative distinctions in the organization of body experi-ence of the subjects revealed (the volume of the subjective vocabulary of the bodyness is wider; the category structure of body experience 40% of cases is diffused); the signs of distor-tion of «the Image of the physical self» are

expressed with clear distinction; negative attitude of subjects to the body and body experience; max-imum degree of sharp affective reactions at the moment of trauma reception and directly after; depressive and ipokhondric emotions start to prevail eventually.

Not estimated discovery of Mashhour Madjid: On the relationship between subjective time, space and velocity

Pestov, Alexey Internet Community, SGTP, Moscow, Russia

The equation relating subjective velocity to sub-jective space and time was derived theoretically and verified empirically; it describes subjective velocity as being directly proportional to subjective space raised to a power, and indirectly proportional to subjective time raised to another power, or stated equivalently, subjective velocity is a power function of the ratio of subjective space to subjective time. It was indicated that perception of velocity, like perception of space, is immediate in nature, thus being basically independent of physical time and space magnitudes which are large enough to be experienced within the 'psychological present'. STOCKHOLM UNIV. PSYCHOL. LABS. 1963.

The association of respiratory symptoms with depressive mood is distinct from the association with anxiety

Petersen, Sibylle Inst. für Psychologie, Universität Hamburg, Hamburg, Germany *Ritz, Thomas* Psychology, Southern Methodist University, Dallas, USA

Research on interactions between respiration and psychopathology has mainly focused on anxiety disorders. Less is known about respiration in depressed mood. 197 individuals rated 25 respira-tory sensation descriptors regarding their frequency of experience and completed the Hospital Anxiety and Depression Scale. Depressive mood remained a significant predictor of reported dyspnea after controlling for demographic and health-related variables and anxiety, but only for sensations of obstruction and arrest of breathing, and not for other qualities of dyspnea, such as effortful breath-ing. Respiratory symptoms are thus significantly associated with depressive mood over and above any association with anxious mood.

Risk factors and protectors of suicide behavior in secondary school students

Pinto Loria, Maria de Lourdes Facultad de Medicina, UNIV. AUTONOMA DE YUCATAN, MERIDA, YUCATAN, Mexico *Flores Galaz, Mirta Margarita* Facultad de Medicina, UNIV. AUTONOMA DE YUCATAN, MERIDA, YUCATAN, Mexico *Serrano Pereira, Mario Gerardo* Facultad de Medicina, UNIV. AUTONOMA DE YUCATAN, MERIDA, YUCATAN, Mexico

The OMS (2006) reported suicide as the 13th cause of death between the ages of 15 and 34. Mexico is among 10 Latin American countries with higher rates. The objective is to determine the risk factors and protectors of suicide behavior among second-ary school students in the state of Yucatan; divided by sex and ecosystem. Tests were applied which explore the protector factors and suicide risk. The analysis of association and differences are presented by variable criteria. The results revealed that the suicide behavior can be prevented by strengthening the protector factors with the focus on Abilities for Life.

The contribution of changes in diet, exercise and stress management to changes in cardiovascular risk factors in patients at risk for heart disease

Pischke, Claudia Research Institute, Preventive Medicine, Sausalito, USA *Weidner, Gerdi* Institute, Preventive Medicine Research, Sausalito, USA

Ornish, Dean Research Institute, Preventive Medicine, Sausalito, USA

We examined associations of dietary fat intake, exercise, and stress management with cardiovascu-lar risk factors (CRF) in 1041 patients (69 % female) with $\geq$ 3 CRF or diabetes over 3 months. All patients were enrolled in the Multisite Cardiac Lifestyle Intervention Program. All 3 health beha-viors were independently related to CRF (reduced fat intake: weight, hemoglobin A1c, mental health, depression; increased exercise: weight, physical health, depression; increased stress management: perceived stress). Exercise interacted with fat intake, predicting reduced LDL-cholesterol, and with stress management, predicting reductions in perceived stress. Patients with elevated CRF benefit from improving all 3 health behaviors.

Comparative impact of being the bearer of a chronic illness on quality of life (QOL), health locus of control (HLOC) and perceived social support (PSS) at Glaucoma and Osteoarthritis patients

Popa-Velea, Ovidiu Dept. od Medical Psychology, University of Medicine, Bucharest, Romania *Peciu-Florianu, Iulia* Faculty of Medicine, Univ.of Medicine, Bucharest, Romania *Coclitu, Catalina* Faculty of Medicine, Univ.of Medicine, Bucharest, Romania *Dobrota, Rucsandra* Faculty of Medicine, Univ.of Medicine, Bucharest, Romania *Cernat, Bogdan* Faculty of Medicine, Univ.of Medicine, Bucharest, Romania

This study examined QoL, LOC, HLOC and PSS in patients with glaucoma and osteoarthritis. Two groups of 30 patients each were tested for these parameters, using SF-36, Rotter, Walston and Duke Questionnaires. Independent t-tests and ANOVA analysis were run to evaluate the sig-nificance of differences. Both groups had low SF-36 scores, with no significant differences regarding LOC and HLOC. External HLOC was significantly more prevalent in both groups (2,39 and 2,85, respectively), reflecting a pessimistic attitude versus disease. PSS was significantly higher in glaucoma patients (41,71 vs. 35,10; p < 0,05). These results can lead to more focused psychological interven-tions.

The effect of picture exchange communication system on behavioral problems of children with Autism spectrum Disorders

Pouretemad, Hamid Psychology, Shahid Beheshti University, Tehran, Islamic Republic of Iran *Mamaghaniah, Maryam* Psychology, Shahid Beheshti University, Tehran, Islamic Republic of Iran *Ahamadi, Fatamah* PECS, Center for the Treatment of Au, Tehran, Islamic Republic of Iran *Khoshabi, Katayoun* Psychiatry, University of Social Welfare a, Tehran, Islamic Republic of Iran

The current research is examining the effect of Picture Exchange Communication System (PECS) on behavioral problems of 4 Iranian Children suffering from Autism Spectrum Disorders (ASD). Four non-verbal children (age 4-7 years) with ASD were recruited from the Center for Treatment of Autistic Disorders - Tehran. They were received PECS training for duration of four months, three sessions per week. The results indicate that all children showed significant decrease on behavioral problems, associated with enhanced non-verbal communication skills.

Coping strategies in parents of children with pervasive developmental disorders

Pouretemad, Hamid Psychology, Shahid Beheshti University, Tehran, Islamic Republic of Iran *Jalali-Moghadam, Nilofar* Psychology, Shahid Beheshti University, Tehran, Islamic Republic of Iran *Saleh-Sedghpour, Bahram* Psychology, Shahid Beheshti University, Tehran, Islamic Republic of Iran *Khoshabi,*

Katayoun Psychiatry, University of Social Welfare a, Tehran, Islamic Republic of Iran
Objectives: This study was aimed to explore coping strategies used by parents of children with Pervasive Developmental Disorders (PDD) as compared with a control group. Methods: the Coping Responses Inventory (Billings & Moos,1981), was individually completed by 43 pairs of parents with PDD child recruited from The Center for the Treatment of Autistic Disorders - Tehran; and a sex, age and education matched control group. Results: PDD parents predominantly used somatic control based coping strategies. Conclusion: Less effective coping strategies was shown in parents of children with PDD.

The agressive behaviour questionnaire (QCA): Two validation studies

Raimundo, Raquel FPCE-UL/ FCT, Costa de Caparica, Portugal Marques Pinto, Alexandra Psychology, FPCE-UL, Lisboa, Portugal
The QCA is a 6-item, hetero-report scale designed to evaluate students and teachers perceptions about students aggressive behaviours. 443 students from the 5th to the 9th grades, participated in the first study; 157 children, from the 4th grade, in the second. The studies demonstrated the QCA to have strong internal consistency and adequate test-retest reliability. It also showed factorial, empirical and discriminant validity. The factor analysis suggested the existence of a single factor, explaining more than 75% of variance. The QCA proved to be sensitive, as an outcome measure, to the implementation of social and emotional learning programs.

Male groups at risk for violence-related mortality in South African cities

Ratele, Kopano Inst. of Social & Health Scie., University of South Africa, Lenasia, South Africa Laher, Hawabibi Inst. of Social & Health S, University of South Africa, Lenasia, South Africa Seedat, Mohamed Inst. of Social & Health S, University of South Africa, Lenasia, South Africa
The study aims to identify 'at-risk' male groups for violence-related fatalities (2001-2005) across four South African cities where the National Injury Mortality Surveillance System (NIMSS) has full coverage. Using NIMSS, data on males across the cities were analysed for age, elevated blood alcohol levels, race, day and time of day. Descriptive, correspondence, and cluster statistical analysis were performed. Preliminary analysis suggests that black males aged 20-29 with elevated blood-alcohol levels, are at highest risk for violence-related death over weekends. The paper attempts to explain the results with help of masculinity theory.

Mental health, risk and resilience in German children and adolescents. Results from the BELLA study within the German Health Interview and Examination Survey for Children and Adolescents (KiGGS)

Ravens-Sieberer, Ulrike School of Public Health, Universität Bielefeld, Bielefeld, Germany Wille, Nora School of Public Health, University of Bielefeld, Bielefeld, Germany Erhart, Michael School of Public Health, University of Bielefeld, Bielefeld, Germany Study Group, BELLA School of Public Health, University of Bielefeld, Bielefeld, Germany
To examine mental health, risk and resilience in a national representative sample of 2,863 families with children aged 7-17. Mental health problems were assessed with standardised screening measures via telephone and mail-survey. 21.9% of the children showed mental health problems (anxiety 10.0%, conduct problems 7.6%, depression 5.4%). Adverse family climate and low socioeconomic status stand out as risk factors. Positive individual, family and social resources coincide with less mental health problems. Far of the children with mental health problems are receiving treatment.

Identifying high risk groups therefore requires the assessment of available resources in addition to the usual risk factors. These resources should be strengthened in prevention and interventions.

"Who is Susie's mother?": Preschooler's understanding of identity statements

Rendl, Bibiane Department of Psychology, University of Salzburg, Salzburg, Austria Perner, Josef Department of Psychology, University of Salzburg, Salzburg, Austria
We investigated children's ability understanding identity statements, for example, that Susie's mother is the teacher. Performance of 59 3- and 4-year-old children on an identity-question ("Who is Susie's mother?") in relation to a control-question ("Who is Susie's mother searching for?") was analyzed. The identity-story (including the identity-question) deals with Susie's mother who is the teacher and the control-story (including the control-question) is about Susie's mother who is searching for the teacher. Results revealed that 3-year-olds did better on the control-question than on the identity-question, whereas 4-year-olds showed no significant difference. Children's performance improved significantly with age only on the identity-question.

The development of magnitude representations: A cross-sectional comparison

Reynvoet, Bert Department of Psychology, University of Leuven, Leuven, Belgium Depestel, Isabel Department of Psychology, University of Leuven, Leuven, Belgium De Smedt, Bert Dep.of Educational Sciences, University of Leuven, Leuven, Belgium
Magnitude representations (MRs) were traditionally examined using comparison tasks, where reaction times increase when numbers are closer to each other (distance effect). Based on this, MRs proved to become more exact with age. However, since this distance effect emerges in a variety of comparison tasks using different stimuli, it might reflect a general phenomenon rather than exposing underlying MRs. Therefore, the present experiment used a better indicator of MRs in children and adults: the quantity priming effect (i.e. faster latencies on targets preceded by numerically close primes). Gradually, a more precise MR was observed, consistent with claims in numerical cognition.

Nurses imagens of old age

Ribeiro, Antonio Pedro Secção Autonoma de Ciências, Universidade de Aveiro, Aveiro, Portugal Figueiredo, Daniela Secção Autonoma de Ciências, Universidade de Aveiro, Aveiro, Portugal Vicente, Henrique Secção Autonoma de Ciências, Universidade de Aveiro, Aveiro, Portugal Sousa, Liliana Secção Autonoma de Ciências, Universidade de Aveiro, Aveiro, Portugal
Ageing is an inevitable process and a social construction (image). The main objective of this exploratory study is to characterize the images of old age and aging in nurses. The scale ImAges (Sousa, Galante & Cerqueira, 2002) was administered to 60 nurses (30 females). Main findings suggest that images are multidimentional, moderate and incongruent involving "maturity, activity and affection" as well as "cognitive and relational incompetence". The promotion of realistic images towards aging constitutes an important strategy in the promotion of the status of the elderly within an ageist society.

Effective anger management at work: Individual and contextual factors

Rivera, Cristina Genàve, Switzerland Wranik, Tanja Affective sciences, University of Geneva, Genàve, Switzerland
Cristina Rivera & Tanja Wranik Poster Effectively dealing with anger in the workplace means regulat-

ing ones own anger as well as managing the anger of others. We compared how individual differences (gender, personality, emotional competence, culture) influence regulation strategies and regulation effectiveness for three types of anger experiences: anger at another person, anger at the self, and another person's anger. We found that the three anger experiences differ in intensity, length, appraisal, and behaviors. Moreover, individual differences influence anger regulation strategies, and anger management effectiveness is dependent on individual factors, type of anger, and context. We will discuss the uses and functions of anger at work.

The development of the conception of pollution: A cross-age study

Rodriguez, Manuel Developmental Psychology, Universidad Autonoma of Madrid, Madrid, Spain Kohen, Raquel Developmental Psychology, UNED, Madrid, Spain Delval, Juan Developmental Psychology, UNED, Madrid, Spain
Eighty Spanish children and adolescents were interviewed using the clinical-critical method to study their representations about pollution and global warming. We expect, more than a change in the concepts they use, an evolution in the kind of relationships they can make with those concepts. The qualitative analysis showed that the youngest participants have representations based on visible features whose impacts are local and direct. This representations change into a chemical-molecular conception of pollution with global and progressives impacts. Knowing deeply the development in the kind of relationships they establish about pollution might be very useful to improve the environmental education.

The psychophysiology of disgust

Rohrmann, Sonja Inst. für Psychologie, Universität Frankfurt, Frankfurt, Germany Hopp, Henrik Psychology, University of Frankfurt/ Main, Frankfurt am Main, Germany Hodapp, Volker Psychology, University of Frankfurt/ Main, Frankfurt am Main, Germany
The peripher-physiological correlates of disgust are insufficiently known. Therefore two film clips representing the main domains of disgust (disease related and food intake related disgust) were shown to 100 volunteers in randomly order. Electrodermal, blood pressure and hemodynamic responses were compared with baseline levels via t-tests for repeated measures. Both disgust stimuli led to pronounced psychophysiological responses representing sympathical as well as parasympathical activation of the vegetative nervous system (coactivation). Disgust responses seem to be complex emotionspecific interplay of vagal, alpha-adrenergic and beta-adrenergic reactions which function requires further research.

Psychometric properties of the health and anxiety inventory in a non-clinical Spanish sample

Romero Sanchiz, Pablo Salud Mental, Hospital de Jaén, Jaén, Spain Godoy Avila, Antonio Personalidad, evaluación y tra, Universidad de Málaga, Málaga, Spain Gavino Lázaro, Aurora Personalidad, evaluación y tra, Universidad de Málaga, Málaga, Spain Nogueira Arjona, Raquel Personalidad, evaluación y tra, Universidad de Málaga, Málaga, Spain
The Health Anxiety Inventory (HAI, Salkovskis, Rimes, Warwick & Clark, 2002) is a self-rated scale that is used for measure health anxiety in people who suffers physical illness or different levels of health concerns. The aim of this work is to validate this measure in a Spanish sample of University students with or without physical or mental illness. The results indicate that the HAI is a reliable measure in this sample and that it has a good

convergent and discriminant validity with different measures of anxiety and depression.

Evaluation of the quality of life in Iranian women with fibromyalgia

Roshan, Rasol *Department of Psychology, Shahed University, Tehran, Islamic Republic of Iran* **Shariat Panahi, Shamsa** *Department of Psychology, shahed university, Tehran, Islamic Republic of Iran* **Tavoli, Azadeh** *Department of Psychology, shahed university, Tehran, Islamic Republic of Iran* **Ghafori, Zeinab** *Department of Psychology, shahed university, Tehran, Islamic Republic of Iran*

OBJECTIVE: To compare quality of life among Iranian females with Fibromyalgia and healthy group. METHODS: A sample of women with Fibromyalgia attending to rheumatology unit of Mostafa Khomeini hospital were submitted to (SF36). t-test was used for comparisons. RESULTS: 80 women with FM and 74 healthy women who were comparable in demographic features, were studied. FM group showed a lower degree of role physical functioning(P=0.001), physical functioning(P=0.001), general health(P<0.001), vitality (P=0.001) and role emotional functioning(P=0.042) and higher level of bodily pain(P=0.004) than healthy group. CONCLUSION: the study has demonstrated that Iranian women with Fibromyalgia are affected in many dimensions of their QOL.

The acquisition of phonotactic rules: Evidence from a combined event-related brain potentials and near-infrared spectroscopy study

Rossi, Sonja *Berlin Neuroimaging Center, Berlin, Germany* **Juergenson, Ina** *Neurology, Berlin Neuroimaging Center, Berlin, Germany* **Hanulikova, Adriana** *Linguistics, Humboldt University Berlin, Berlin, Germany* **Obrig, Hellmuth** *Neurology, Berlin Neuroimaging Center, Berlin, Germany* **Wartenburger, Isabell** *Inst. für Linguistiks, Universität Potsdam, Potsdam, Germany*

Phonotactics describes the language-specific combinatory rules of phonemes in different syllabic positions. In the present study we compared phonotactically legal to illegal pseudowords. The rationale was to investigate both ERPs between legal and illegal phonotactics and lateralization effects of cortical oxygenation changes simultaneously measured by near-infrared spectroscopy. In adults we found a stronger N400 and a stronger left-hemispheric lateralization for legal pseudowords. As little is known about the neurocognitive development of phonotactic knowledge during infancy, we are presently conducting the same study in infants below sixth month of age. Preliminary results indicate sensitivity towards language-specific phonotactics at that age.

Visuo-spatial working memory in face processing from preschool to adulthood

Rossmeisl, Uwe *Gunzenhausen, Germany* **Zoelch, Christof** *Developmental Psychology, Cath. University of Eichstätt-, Gunzenhausen, Germany* **Seitz-Stein, Katja** *Developmental Psychology, Cath. University of Eichstätt-, Gunzenhausen, Germany*

The present study aims to explore the role of visuo-spatial working memory (Logie & Pearson, 1997; Baddeley, 1990) in face processing from preschool to adulthood. 100 six-, eight-, and ten-year-olds and adults participated in a face recognition task where either featural or relational information was manipulated. The retention interval was filled with visual or spatial interference. Baseline measures indicate that all age groups perform above chance without interference tasks and that performance increases with age. No age x information type (featural, relational) interaction was observed. Interference tasks influenced face recognition of the age groups differentially. Results are discussed within the working memory model.

Validation of a German version of the state self-esteem scale

Rudolph, Almut *Inst. für Psychologie, Techn. Universität Chemnitz, Chemnitz, Germany* **Schütz, Astrid** *Department of Psychology, Technical University Chemnitz, Chemnitz, Germany* **Schröder-Abé, Michela** *Inst. für Psychologie, Techn. Universität Chemnitz, Chemnitz, Germany*

Self-esteem is often used as dependent, independent or moderator variable. To assess temporary changes in self-esteem, measures of state self-esteem have been developed. In three studies, psychometric properties of a German-language version of the State Self-Esteem Scale (SSES; Heatherton & Polivy, 1991) were evaluated. The results confirmed the factor structure (performance, social, appearance), reliability, and construct validity of the scale (Study 1). Additionally, sensitivity of the SSES to experimental manipulation (social feedback; Study 2) and naturally occurring events (test grade performance; Study 3) was analysed. The potential in detecting SE changes with the SSES in experimental and natural settings is discussed.

An approach to an emotional regulation model: The case of fear

Sánchez Aragón, Rozzana *Dept. of Social Psychology, UNAM, México City, Mexico*

Among the contributions in Emotional Regulation subject, there is a lack of studies in Latin American contexts. Due to this, the present research –based on several previous studies (Gross & Thompson, 2007) - looked for propose a theoretical model to be empirically tested in the situation of the emotion of fear. This study integrate variables as regulatory resources (emotional perception, expression, understanding and self-monitoring), strategies used during the coping with emotional events and self-efficacy as precursors of well-being. Findings show the importance of each variable in the way Mexican males and females feel with themselves and in their personal relationships.

Comparative study in number transcoding from verbal to digital form in French, German and Syrian first-grader children

Saad, Lana *LEAD, Université de Bourgogne, Dijon, France* **Lecas, Jean-François** *Psychology, université de Bourgogne, LEAD, Dijon, France* **Barrouillet, Pierre** *Psychology, université de Genàve, Genàve, Switzerland*

Our study aims at evaluating the impact of linguistic structure as well as the influence of the direction of writing, on the acquisition of number transcoding rules. We investigate number transcoding from verbal to digital code in French, German, and Syrian first-grader children. The results reveal an influence of both the linguistic structure and the direction of writing on the acquisition of number transcoding rules. These findings are discussed within the theoretical framework provided ADAPT (A Developmental Asemantic Procedural Transcoding) model recently proposed by Barrouillet et al. 2004 for transcoding numbers from verbal to Arabic form.

The role of inner speech in task-set selection: An examination using a random task-cuing procedure

Saeki, Erina *Tokyo, Japan* **Saito, Satoru** *Education, Kyoto University, Kyoto, Japan*

The role of inner speech in action control was examined in a task-switching paradigm using a random task-cuing procedure. In Experiment 1, the task cues informed the participants as to whether they should repeat or switch a task. In Experiment 2, each task cue specified the current task directly. Mixing costs in Experiment 1, not in Experiment 2, were greater under articulatory suppression than under tapping. The results suggest that inner speech

is useful for selecting the current task set with reference to the previous trial information.

S-R correspondence in a simple response task: The effect of switching hands

Saenger, Jessica *Experimental Psychology, Heinrich-Heine-Universität, Duesseldorf, Germany* **Hoffmann, Sven** *an der Uni Dortmund (IfADo), Institut f. Arbeitsphysiologie, Dortmund, Germany* **Grosjean, Marc** *an der Uni Dortmund (IfADo), Institut f. Arbeitsphysiologie, Dortmund, Germany* **Wascher, Edmund** *an der Uni Dortmund (IfADo), Institut f. Arbeitsphysiologie, Dortmund, Germany*

In choice response tasks, a stimulus (S) is generally responded to faster when the required response (R) shares spatial features with the stimulus than when it does not. This S-R correspondence effect (a.k.a. Simon effect) has also been observed in simple response tasks when representations of alternative response locations are somehow activated by the experimental context. In the present study, participants responded to laterally presented stimuli first with their left/right hand and then with their right/left hand. In line with the response-discrimination account of spatial compatibility effects, a S-R correspondence effect was observed only after participants switched their responding hand.

Marital conflict causes : Based on family process and content model

Samani, Siamak *Dept. Educational Psychology, Shiraz University, Shiraz, Islamic Republic of Iran*

The aim of this research was to determine the important factors of marital conflict between spouses. The sample of this study includes 200 men and 200 women. To determine the important factors for marital conflict a likert scale was used. This scale includes 5 demographic items and 19 questions about the important factors of conflicts. The results of this study revealed that the first five important factors of marital conflict are personality trait, love and interest, communication skills, commitment, and family background. The findings of this research showed that there are two general factors for marital conflict: family processes and family contents.

Cognitive development of deaf children interacting with hearing mothers

Sanchez Barba, Mayra *gaciones en Comportamiento, Centro de Estudios e Investi-, Zapopan, Mexico* **Quintana, Carmen** *Environmental Sicences, University of Guadalajara, Guadalajara, Mexico* **Salcedo, Jorge** *Psychology, ITESO, Guadalajara, Mexico*

It is accepted that deaf children of hearing mothers experience more cognitive difficulties compared to other children (Galenson, 1979). In order to test this hypothesis, we compared one hearing mother and her deaf child with other two dyads. They were observed using a multidimensional observational system focusing on the specific teaching behaviours of the mother and their direct effects on the cognitive achievements of the child. Results confirm the initial hypothesis, deaf child of hearing mother showing less cognitive achievements. We discuss in terms of the implications of this results to improve intervention programs with this kind of dyads.

A deconstruction of the psychology

Santos, Élison *Clinical, Élison Santos, Varginha, MG, Brazil*

The objective is to develop a new line of thought about the conception of Man in the beginning of the 21st century, by raising a discussion about the concepts that have driven the Psychology in the last century, analyzing the possibilities and changes of society and confronting the ideas of the essence of Man. The methodology consists on a dialogue between two schools: Psychoanalisys, Sigmund Freud and the Logotherapy, Viktor Frankl. Points of these two schools will help us to cover a holistic vision of man for the Psychology in a new conception of understanding.

Psychological disorders among salvadorean women victims of domestic violence

Santos, Pablo Granada University, Granada, Spain Gutiérrez, Olga Developmental Psychology, Granada University, Granada, Spain Lenarduzzi, Eveling Psychosocial assistance cente, Supreme Court of Justice, Sonsonate, El Salvador Castro, Ángel Developmental Psychology, Granada University, Granada, Spain

OBJECTIVE. The aim of this study was to know the psychological disorders of salvadorean women who suffered domestic violence. METHOD. A group of 50 women who had been, or were currently being, victims of domestic violence was compared to a group of 51 womed who did not suffer abuse. RESULTS. Results show a higher frequency of psychological abuse, followed by both psychological and physical abuse. Also, women who suffered abuse show problems in adaptation to everyday life, more depressive and postraumatic stress symptoms, and have less self-steem. CONCLUSIONS. Implications of this study for clinical practice and future research in this field are commented.

She has a long neck and he has big ears: How grammatical gender affects the concepts of animals

Schalk, Lennart Inst. Verhaltenswissenschaften, ETH Zürich, Zürich, Switzerland Saalbach, Henrik Inst. of Behavioral Sciences, ETH Zurich, Zurich, Switzerland Imai, Mutsumi Dep. of Environm. Information, Keio University, Endoh, Japan

In languages with a grammatical gender (e.g., German) the assignment of grammatical gender to an animal name is mostly independent of the referent's biological sex. Children's understanding of this independency was examined by comparing German and Japanese (no grammatical gender) preschoolers' patterns of deductive inference about sex-specific biological properties. German preschoolers' inferences were strongly predicted by the grammatical gender of the animal, whereas Japanese preschoolers' inferences were predicted by the animal's typicality, as measured by adult ratings and children's deductive inferences of non-sex specific biological properties. Our findings suggest that grammatical gender affects the conceptual representation of animals.

Politics and voters appeal of boot camps vs. psychologically based early childhood intervention for the prevention of antisocial behavior

Schlauch-Rigby, Gisela Service, Psychological Counseling, Yakima, USA

The literature review shows that US style boot camps are ineffective in the reduction of recidivism of antisocial behavior. It is argued that increased criminal activity could result since boot camps are not based on psychotherapeutic programs. In contrast, intervention during early childhood becomes prevention, when it is based on psychological principles. The model presented incorporates teacher training in stages of child development, the use of positive behavioral interventions instead of suspensions, thus reducing learning deficits, frustration, anger, school drop outs and antisocial behavior. School based mental health counseling for children and families is available.

The general model for negative priming

Schrobsdorff, Hecke BCCN Göttingen, Göttingen, Germany Ihrke, Matthias BCCN Goettingen, Uni Goettingen, Goettingen, Germany Behrendt, Jörg BCCN Goettingen, Uni Goettingen, Goettingen, Germany Herrmann, J. Michael BCCN Goettingen, Uni Goettingen, Goettingen, Germany Hasselhorn, Marcus BCCN Goettingen, Uni Goettingen, Goettingen, Germany

Various theoretical accounts have been developed to explain the negative priming effect. However, the very complex pattern of empirical results does not clearly favor one theory over the others. In order to reveal which of the theories can account for what part of the pattern, a straightforward computational implementation of negative priming theories is desirable. We therefore developed a general model for stimulus-based action selection which attempts to incorporate all mechanisms relevant to selective attention giving a concretion of negative priming theories. Reaction time differences in various priming conditions emerge by an interplay of all model components.

Asymmetry of body and brain as determinants of believing in paranormal phenomena

Schulter, Günter Department of Psychology, University Graz, Graz, Austria Papousek, Ilona Department of Psychology, University Graz, Graz, Austria

The significance of several laterality measures of the body and brain for explaining belief in paranormal phenomena was investigated. Direction and degree of several trait aspects of functional hemisphere asymmetry were quantitatively assessed in a large sample (n=68 men and n=68 women). Additionally, measures of finger length were taken to calculate directed body asymmetry scores and indicators of fluctuating asymmetry. Results indicated that a stronger belief in paranormal phenomena was associated with fluctuating asymmetry of finger length, and that this aspect of body asymmetry was related to greater intraindividual variability in the degree of 'atypical' lateralization of brain functions.

Person-situation interaction in adaptive emotional functioning

Schutte, Nicola Dept. of Psychology, University of New England, Armidale, Australia Malouff, John Dept. of Psychology, University of New England, Armidale, NSW, Australia Price, Ian Dept. of Psychology, University of New England, Armidale, NSW, Australia Walter, Samantha Dept. of Psychology, University of New England, Armidale, NSW, Australia Burke, Greg Dept. of Psychology, University of New England, Armidale, NSW, Australia Wilkinson, Catherine Dept. of Psychology, University of New England, Armidale, NSW, Australia

Objectives: A person-situation model explored the effect of emotional affordances of situations. Methods and Results: Participants rated their emotional functioning as more extensive in situations classified as high in emotional affordance. Participants who scored higher on the individual difference characteristic of emotional intelligence were more interested in entering high emotional affordance situations than and participants who scored higher on emotional intelligence were rated by others as being more successful in high emotional affordance situations than individuals lower in emotional intelligence. Conclusions: These results provide preliminary evidence that interactions between emotional intelligence and situations may influence emotional functioning.

Depressive mood and cardiovascular responses to stress: A matter of context

Schwerdtfeger, Andreas Inst. für Psychologie, Universität Mainz, Mainz, Germany

Depressive mood has been associated with attenuated parasympathetic activation, thus, increasing risk for cardiovascular diseases. Two studies will be presented that examined cardiovascular responses to different stressors in healthy volunteers with varying depression scores. Results varied as a function of social context. Within a social-evaluative context, depression and heart rate variability were negatively associated, thus, confirming other findings. However, depression was associated with attenuated systolic blood pressure responses and attenuated lf/hf ratio to social-evaluative self-threatening stressors, possibly documenting motivational deficit. The results suggest that social context and stressor type moderate cardiovascular stress responses in individuals with varying depression scores.

Right of life and health

Semke, Valentin Borderline States Department, Mental Health Research Institu, Tomsk, Russia

We suppose to pay attention to the most relevant social sections of penitentiary medicine including declaring the right of faithful life and dignity for persons convicted to deprivation of liberty with account for demands and possibilities of the modern society, ethics of life and moral problems of interpersonal relations under penitentiary conditions, psychological and psychopathological aspects of forced loneliness and limitation of personality freedom, finely, discussion of vitally important bases of preventive and rehabilitative interventions directed at heightening of convicts' quality of life. Pointed out by us "main" questions are without doubt of social-political and moral significance.

Multimethod design as a way to add breadth and depth to research analyses

Setiawan, Jenny Lukito Universitas Ciputra, Surabaya, Indonesia

Qualitative and quantitative approaches provide a different type of contribution in the effort of search for knowledge. This paper aims to discuss the use of multimethod design to achieve deep and rich research analyses. By exemplifying a study investigating students' attitudes to counselling, the paper explores the contribution of each approach to understanding the research issues. The study used questionnaire as the data collection method in the quantitative approach, and individual interview as well as Focus Group Discussion in the qualitative end. Results showed that multimethod design generated complementary findings which add the breadth and depth to the analyses.

Relationship model in cross-cultural thinking aloud usability testing

Shi, Qingxin Dept. of Informatics, Copenhagen Business School, Frederiksberg, Denmark

Culture plays an important role in the global market today. This paper aims at investigating culture's impact on thinking aloud usability testing from a theoretical perspective. First, two kinds of relationships in thinking aloud usability testing are introduced, and then we discuss culture and culture theories, such as Nisbett's culture theory and Hong's dynamic constructivist approach to culture. Based on the discussion and previous researches, we extract the potential factors which may influence cross-culture usability testing and then propose a relationship model. Finally, we discuss how the two thinking aloud approaches may be used in cross-culture usability testing.

The problems of classification in psychology

Shilko, Roman Faculty of Psychology, Moscow State University, Moscow, Russia

Classification is one of the basic level that underlies construction of theory. There are some key principles in philosophy and methodology of science on what is classification and how to construct it. Unfortunately, the principles are not fully explicit while constructing classification in psychology. Classification in psychology applies to different objects: phenomena, methods, and processes. There are classifications which differentiate kinds of objects and types of objects. Some classifications are used in basic research whereas others are used in applied psychology. The latter are concerned with practical issues and often should be more related to general conceptual points of theory.

The construct validity of the Santa Barbara Sense of direction scale in the Greek population

Shimi, Andria *Dept. Experimental Psychology, University of Oxford, Oxford, United Kingdom* **Avraamides, Marios** *Dept. of Psychology, University of Cyprus, Nicosia, Cyprus*

Objectives: The psychometric properties of the Santa Barbara Sense of Direction Scale (SBSOD) were examined in a Greek sample. Methods: A Greek translation of the SBSOD was administered to 97 university students. An exploratory factor analysis was carried out to extract factors and establish the validity and reliability of the questionnaire. Results: In contrast to the one dimensional factor structure of the original questionnaire, our analyses revealed two distinct factors with high reliability: quality of mental map and understanding spatial information from symbolic media. Conclusion: Cultural reasons are discussed in order to account for the difference in results.

When task pleasantness helps negative mood: Evidence from cardiovascular and facial EMG reactivity

Silvestrini, Nicolas *Dept. of Psychology, University of Geneva, Geneva, Switzerland* **Gendolla, Guido** *Psychology, University of Geneva, Geneva, Switzerland*

This study investigated whether task pleasantness could eliminate the motivational deficit of people in negative moods facing difficult tasks. Students were assigned in a 2 (Mood) x 2 (Task valence) x 2 (Task difficulty) x 2 (Time: Mood inductions vs. Task) mixed model design. We assessed cardiovascular and facial EMG reactivity. Results confirmed that, for the pleasant task, systolic blood pressure reactivity in the negative mood/difficult condition was stronger than in other conditions, indicating the elimination of the motivational deficit. Facial EMG reactivity supported efficient mood manipulations. Findings demonstrate the effect of context's valence on resource mobilization in negative moods.

Hardiness differently predicted in men and women in the Czech sample

Solcova, Iva *Dept. of Health Psychology, Institute of Psychology, Prague 1, Czech Republic*

A sample of 162 healthy adults completed a survey concerning personality characteristics. Physiological and biochemical measures were taken. The physiological cardiovascular risk, and psychological cardiovascular risk were calculated. The sum gave the total cardiovascular risk. The psychological cardiovascular risk was gender dependent (more risk in men). The physiological cardiovascular risk differed according to age. The odds ratio of 1.56 was calculated for subjects older than 35 years, i.e., already from the middle age the psychological cardiovascular risk means heightened probability of physiological cardiovascular risk. Hardiness was differently determined in men and women, the buffering effect being better expressed in men.

Evolutionary determinants of feelings of joy of the helper in an altruistic context

Spörrle, Matthias *Dept. for Psychology, Ludwig-Maximilians University, München, Germany* **Wolf, Sebastian** *Psychology, LMU München, München, Germany*

Based on evolutionary psychology assumptions we investigated the influence of success, reciprocity, and biological kinship on feelings of joy of the helping person in a life or death situation. Correspondingly manipulated scenarios were presented to a German student sample (N = 240) in an experimental between subjects design. Results indicated significant main effects for success and

relatedness and a marginal significant effect for reciprocity. Moreover, we found significant interactions indicating that success resulted in increased levels of joy especially in situations of high relatedness and increased probability of future reciprocity. Results underscore the role of joy as a stimulation of evolutionary functional activity.

Level of automation: Effects on train drivers' vigilance

Spring, Peter *School of Safety Science, University of New South Wales, Sydney, Australia* **Baysari, Melissa T. Caponecchia, Carlo D. McIntosh, Andrew S.**

The effect of train driving automation on certain Human Factor (HF) issues and their impact on driver performance was investigated. Undergraduate students were trained to drive a computer simulated passenger train on an intercity route. Driver vigilance and other performance measures were recorded while manipulating two IVs: (1) level of automation and (2) failure detection event type. A vigilance decrement was predicted to occur over extended driving periods and be more severe at higher levels of train automation, when the failure to be detected was of low salience or when the event was a failure of the automation itself.

Work-family conflict and coping in Germany and Sweden

Staar, Henning *Work and Org. Psychology, University of Hamburg, Hamburg, Germany* **Busch, Christine** *Inst. für Psychologie, Universität Hamburg, Hamburg, Germany* **Aborg, Carl** *Dept. of Behavioural Science, University Örebro, Hamburg, Germany*

The intercultural study examines differences in the value dimension masculinity, in the level of work-family conflict and in coping strategies with German and Swedish workers. Results indicate that the Germans (n=98) reported more masculine attitudes and, especially German women, experienced more conflict between the two life domains. The Swedish sample (n=105) used more collective coping strategies and Swedish men were more likely to use emotion-focused strategies than their male German counterparts.

Parental attributions and the risk of physical punishment: How do situational ambiguity and personality of the parents interact?

Steinmetz, Martina *Inst. für Psychologie I, Universität Würzburg, Würzburg, Germany*

In research referring to "hostile attribution bias" a link between attributions of hostile intent to another person and aggressiveness to this person is supposed, especially in ambiguous situations. In an experimental study n = 153 parents read different written scenarios depicting problematic behaviors of children and judged the probability of physical punishment for the child. Situational ambiguity with respect to the responsibility of the child for his behavior was varied (three conditions: child clearly not responsible, child clearly responsible, responsibility ambiguous). Results about the relations of parental attributional styles, attributions and punishment judgments in the three different conditions are reported.

"The mote in thy brother's eye": Does recognizing faces of a different ethnicity rely on the telling detail?

Stenberg, Georg *Bunkeflostrand, Sweden* **Holmberg, Ulf** *Psychology, Kristianstad University, Bunkeflostrand, Sweden* **Sjögren, Erika** *Psychology, Kristianstad University, Bunkeflostrand, Sweden*

Recognition of faces belonging to other ethnicities is generally poorer than recognition of one's own. This study tested the proposition that same-race faces enjoy the advantage of holistic, configurational processing, whereas other-race faces rely on detail perception. Experiment 1 confirmed the own-race effect in groups of Chinese and Swedish

students. Experiment 2 replicated it in a group of Swedish students recognizing African and European faces, and further documented that distinctiveness interacted with ethnicity, such that distinctiveness was essential for recognition of other-races. Experiment 3, using spatially high-pass and low-pass filtered images, found an advantage for high frequencies in other-race faces only.

Relationship between anxiety and quality of life among cardiac patients undergoing the home rehabilitation

Stepnowska, Monika *Cardiac Rehabilitation, National Inst. of Cardiology, Warsaw, Poland* **Leszczynska, Kinga** *Cardiac Rehabilitation, Institute of Cardiology, Warsaw, Poland* **Kowalska, Monika** *Personality Psychology, UKSW, Warsaw, Poland* **Tylka, Jan** *Cardiac Rehabilitation, Institute of Cardiology, Warsaw, Poland* **Baranowski, Rafal** *Cardiac Rehabilitation, Institute of Cardiology, Warsaw, Poland* **Piotrowicz, Ryszard** *Cardiac Rehabilitation, National Institute of Cardiolo, Warsaw, Poland*

OBJECTIVE OF WORK: Determination of a relation between the level of escalation of anxiety and the quality of life in cardiac patients undergoing the home based rehabilitation, after 4 and 8 weeks. MATERIAL: study included 40 patients (post MI or/and CABG, aged 39-81; x=65) taking part in the multi-centre program of the telemedical home based rehabilitation METHODS: The following research methods were used in this work: STAI and SF-36 RESULTS: The change in the physical dimension of the quality of life after the first 4 weeks of rehabilitation was related to the change in anxiety symptoms– correlation coefficient - r=0,33

I want (my) children to sleep in a safe place: Experimental analysis of human sleeping site preferences from an evolutionary point of view

Stich, Jennifer *München, Germany* **Spörrle, Matthias** *Dept. for Psychology, Ludwig-Maximilians University, München, Germany*

Based on evolutionary assumptions of habitat selection and parental investment the hypotheses are tested that adults choose sleeping sites (1) in which children have safer bed positions than the adults themselves and (2) in which own children have safer bed positions than unrelated children. Both hypotheses could be confirmed in a questionnaire study (N = 220) with experimentally manipulated floor plans in a 3 (number of children: no vs. one vs. two) x 2 (kinship: own vs. unrelated child) factorial between-subjects design.

Ethnical identity and social adaptation in the different culture spheres for different ethnical groups

Strode, Diana *Dept. of Psychology, Higher School of Psychology, Riga, Latvia* **Plotka, Irina** *psychology, Higher School of Psychology, Riga, Latvia* **Bluminau, Nina** *psychology, Higher School of Psychology, Riga, Latvia*

Authors examines: ethnic identity and person's social adaptation in a foreign state and culture. Methodics: 1) "Test of ethnic identity typology" G.Soldatova and S.Rizhova; 2) "Questionnaire, the person's adaptation in a new cultural environment" L.Yankovska. Participants: 480 persons. The study is based on different correlations: 6 types of adaptation and 6 types of ethnic identity indices, focusing on Latvians, residing in Russia and Russians in Latvia. Investigation shows that Russians in Latvia and Latvians in Russia are mainly positive-minded towards the surrounding cultural identities. Both groups have high indicators of interactivity, and it demonstrates that both groups are engaged in new social sphere.

Testing the reverse self-inference hypothesis: The case of anger

Studtmann, Markus Inst. für Psychologie, Universität Greifswald, Greifswald, Germany *Weber, Hannelore* Institute for Psychology, University of Greifswald, Greifswald, Germany *Reisenzein, Rainer* Institute for Psychology, University of Greifswald, Greifswald, Germany

According to the reverse self-inference hypothesis, people use their subjective experiences to infer the presence and intensity of their behavioral reactions to emotion-eliciting events. In the present study, we tested this hypothesis for anger. Anger was induced through unfair treatment in an allocation game. 66 participants were angered in either a social or a solitary situation. In both conditions, they significantly overestimated the intensity of their facial expression of anger compared to observer-ratings. Supporting the reverse self-inference hypothesis, regression analyses found that beliefs about facial expressions could be predicted by feelings of anger but not actual facial expressions.

Discrepancy between autonomeous reaction and conscious psychic perception following acute mental stress after the disaster of 9-11 in New York

Stueck, Marcus Institute of Psychology, University of Leipzig, Leipzig, Germany *Witruk, Evelin* Institute of Psychology, University of Leipzig, Leipzig, Germany *Braun, Jan-Matthias* Clinical Immunololology, University of Leipzig, Leipzig, Germany *Sack, Ulrich* Clinical Immunology, University of Leipzig, Leipzig, Germany

Three hours before the last of four measurements belonging to an interventional study 11 probands from Germany were confronted by radio/TV with the terrorist attacks at the 9-11-2001 in the USA. Psychological, immunological and endocrinological parameters were determined. Compared to the first three measurements psychometric data showed no negative influence concerning the psychological condition. However, immuno-endocrinological monitoring revealed typical stress relevant and significant changes. It seems as if coping techniques play an important role here which may be explained with denying the existence of a potential existential threat. This is the first study about acute reactions after the 9-11.

Language development in profoundly deaf children

Suarez, Maria Developmental Psychology, University of La Laguna, La Laguna, Spain *Rodríguez, Carmen* DIDACTIC RESEARCH IN EDUCATION, UNIVERSITY OF LA LAGUNA, LA LAGUNA. TENERIFE, Spain *Leal, Elena* DIDACTIC RESEARCH IN EDUCATION, UNIVERSITY OF LA LAGUNA, LA LAGUNA. TENERIFE, Spain

The aim of this study was to evaluate the language development of deaf children with and without cochlear implants (CI). The participants were 20 deaf children: 5 of them received a CI prior to 2 years of age; another 5 children were implanted at an older age; and 10 deaf children weren't implanted. Children's language development was assessed using the Illinois Test of Psycholinguistic Abilities (ITPA; Kirk, McCarthy & Kirk, 1996) and the Peabody Picture Vocabulary Test (TVIP; Dunn, 1986). The discussion will be focused on the gap between language age and chronological age in the different groups of participants.

Expanded and upright postures reduce depressive mood

Sugamura, Genji Tokyo, Japan *Takase, Hiroki* Center of Excellence, Tokyo Denki University, Hiki, Saitama, Japan *Haruki, Yutaka* Human Sciences, Waseda University, Tokorozawa, Saitama, Japan *Koshikawa, Fusako* Psychology, Waseda University, Shinjuku, Tokyo, Japan

The present study examined how expressive postures affect current depressive mood. Sixteen healthy volunteers were asked to induce a depressive mood by listening to sad music and recalling prior depressive events, and then to adopt slumped, upright, and expanded postures respectively. Postures were indirectly manipulated by changing the height of the desk and chair. The order was counterbalanced across participants. The results showed that "humble," "weak," "subordinate," and "inferior" moods experimentally induced were maintained longer when participants adopted a slumped posture. It is suggested that upright and expanded postures have a function to diminish current depression.

Development of problem behaviours among Japanese children: A behavioural genetic approach

Sugawara, Masumi Dept. of Psychology, Ochanomizu University, Tokyo, Japan *Sakai, Atsushi* Division of School Education, University of Yamanashi, Kofu, Japan *Tanaka, Mami* Department of Psychology, Ochanomizu University, Tokyo, Japan *Matsuura, Motoko* Department of Psychology, Ochanomizu University, Tokyo, Japan

The purpose of this study is to investigate contributions both genetic and environmental factors to development of children's problem behaviors considering the role of children's personality. For a prospective study of problem behaviors in Japanese twins, a total of 2,147 twin pairs (age 0 ~age15, monozygotic twins: n=892 pairs, 41.5%; dizygotic twins: n=1,160 pairs, 54.0%; unidentified: 95 pairs, 4.4%) and their parents participated in a questionnaire survey. In this study, problem behaviors were assessed using Child Behavior Checklist 4-18 version and 2-3 version, and personality was assessed by Temperament & Character Inventory Junior version and Preschool version.

Asperger Spectrum Quotient (ASQ) and electroencephalographic topograph-analyses

Sugawara, Masakazu Dept. of Psychology, Iwate University, Morioka, Japan *Mikami, Hiroki* Psychology, Iwate University, Morioka, Japan *Suzuki, Kohichi* Psychology, Iwate University, Morioka, Japan

Objectives:Our understanding of Asperger adolescence is full of unknowns and speculation. The present report investigated (i) the correlation of Asperger Spectrum Quotient (ASQ) and social skill in normal adolescence, (ii) the electroencephalographic (EEG) topograph-analyses with ASQ. Methods:ASQ subjecs were 193 normal students. EEG stpectrum potentials recorded monopolarly from 16 placements over frontal, central, parietal, temporal, and occipital scalp-locations with the international 10-20 system in 40 subjects. The statistical significance of psychological and neurophysiological differences was evaluated by ANOVA. Results & Conclusions:The high ASQ subjects showed significantly the decreased social-skill coefficients and beta 2 power spectra at frontal, central, and parietal.

Can the internet replace postal surveys?

Sullman, Mark Dept. of Psychology, University of Hertfordshire, Hatfield, United Kingdom

Objective: To investigate whether the internet produces data which was more or less representative than that collected using a postal survey and whether these two methods produced similar results. Method: This research compared data collected on driving anger using the internet with that collected by post using a random sample of 3000 voters. Results: The results found that the internet sample had a demographic profile which was more similar to the population of drivers, and that there were also many more similarities than differences in the relationships found between the DAX and the demographic variables measured.

Conclusions: The results of this research confirm that the internet is a viable and efficient alternative for conducting surveys.

Does general situation awareness exist?

Sun, Xianghong Institute of Psychology, Beijing, People's Republic of China *Zhang, Kan* Engineering Psychology Lab, Institute of Psychology, CAS, Beijing, People's Republic of China

Ensley divided Situation Awareness (SA) into three stages: awareness to information in environment, recognition and judgment to the current situation, and prediction to future status of a system. In each stage, a specific situation and task is necessary for people to deal with. Therefore SA has always been studied to a specific professional group, especially for the measurement of SA. The way to measure pilots' SA is different from the way to measure car drivers' SA. 20 firefighters and 20 taxi drivers were asked to take several SA tests. Results showed that there were some common components existed among different SA tests, which implied that each person could have general SA and domain specific SA.

Psychological factors of adult patients with sustained atopic dermatitis

Takaki, Hiroko Waseda University, Tokyo, Japan *Sano, Ayako* Graduate,School of Letters,Art, Waseda University, Tokyo, Japan *Ishii, Yasutomo* Faculty of Letters,Arts and Sc, Waseda University, Tokyo, Japan

Adult patients with atopic dermatitis(AD) have been increasing because of stress society and steroid bashing which is characteristic in Japan. The purpose of this study was to find psychological factors of AD patients with different courses. Japanese adult people (N=460) were surveyed using the Center for Epidemiologic studies Depression(CES-D), Sense of Coherence(SOC) and others. They were classified into four groups, healthy persons, patients with sustained AD, patients with recrudescent AD and persons who had been AD patients childhood. Results showed that patients with sustained AD had higher score than the other groups in CES-D.

The effects of regulatory focus and self-construal on affective experiences in daily life

Takehashi, Hiroki Environmental studies, Nagoya university, Nagoya, Japan *Karasawa, Kaori* Humanities and Sociology, The university of Tokyo, Tokyo, Japan

This study examined the effects of regulatory focus and self-construal on subjective experiences of affects. One-hundred and ten participants were asked to indicate their affective experiences in daily life, and answered on the regulatory focus scale and the self-construal scale. The results found that the promotion focus and independent self-construal were correlated with positive affects and energetic arousal whereas the prevention focus and interdependent self-construal were correlated with negative affects and tense arousal. However, regression analyses revealed that affects were directly determined by only regulatory foci, not by self-construals. The discussion considered the relationship between self-construal and regulatory focus.

Gaze-following but not perspective-taking in golden monkeys (Rhinopithecus roxellana)

Tan, Jingzhi Dept. of Psychology, Peking University, Beijing, People's Republic of China *Su, Yanjie* Department of Psychology, Peking University, Beijing, People's Republic of China

Three experiments were conducted to evaluate how golden monkeys, Rhinopithecus roxellana, understand seeing. In experiment 1, three subjects revealed capability to co-orient a human experimenter's gaze direction. However, in experiment 2, three subjects failed to exploit various experimenter-given cues including gazing, pointing and tapping to locate hidden food. The third experiment showed that subjects were not able to discriminate competitors who can see them from who cannot in a multiple-trail stealing task. These findings suggest that gaze-following has evolved in golden monkey, but whether this ability reflects perspective-taking remains unclear. Finally, the appropriateness of using a competitive paradigm was discussed.

Is the love of money the root of evil? Machiavellianism as a mediator and college major and gender as moderators

Tang, Thomas Li-Ping Management and Marketing, Middle Tennessee St University, Murfreesboro, USA Chen, Yuh-Jia Management and Marketing, Middle Tennessee St University, Murfreesboro, USA

We investigate the efficacy of ethics intervention and test a model that the love of money is directly or indirectly related to evil across major and gender. Business ethics intervention had a significant impact on business students' conceptions of evil and propensity to engage in theft behavior. Psychology students without intervention did not have these changes. We identified a significant path (the Love of Money –> Machiavellianism –> Evil) for the whole sample; for business students, but not for psychology students; for male students, but not for female students; and for male business students, but not for female business students.

Measurement invariance of internet-administrated imagery tests: A comparison between anonymous and undergraduate participants

Tang, Yun Psychology, The Ohio State University, Columbus, USA Zhang, Houcan Psychology, Beijing Normal University, Beijing, People's Republic of China

The present study investigated the measurement invariance for the internet-based testing compared with traditional methods. A computer-based mental rotation test was developed and the Individual Differences Questionnaire (IDQ, Paivio, 1971) was adapted for internet-administration. Participants included 206 anonymous individuals randomly collected via internet and 113 undergraduate students. ANOVA and SEM were used to detect measurement invariance. Results indicated that the two samples behaved and scored similarly on mental rotation test. For IDQ, the metric invariance and scalar invariance were verified. These findings suggested a measurement invariance of the two imagery tests and may guarantee their use in internet-based studies.

Are they all the same? The influence of subcategorization on the perception of group variability in a Polish and German sample

Tauber, Joanna Psychology, University of Hamburg, Hamburg, Germany Petersen, Sibylle Psychology, University of Hamburg, Hamburg, Germany Orth, Bernhard Psychology, University of Hamburg, Hamburg, Germany

Perception of group-variability has been shown to influence the application of stereotypes in social judgement. We explored the influence of subcategorization on perceived variability of national groups. 121 Polish and 120 German participants were assigned to four conditions. They were asked to create subgroups of (1)none of the groups, (2)the ingroup, (3)the outgroup, or (4)both, before answering questions on group variability in general and regarding negative and positive stereotypical traits. Only within the German subsample subgrouping led to the perception of higher general group-variability. Regarding stereotypic traits, the influence of subcategorization depended on trait-valence and group membership.

Hemodynamic response to stimuli with varying temporal complexity in healthy neonates

Telkemeyer, Silke Inst. für Neurologie, Charité Universitätsmedizin, Berlin, Germany Obrig, Hellmuth Department of Neurology, Charité University Medicine, Berlin, Germany Steinbrink, Jens Department of Neurology, Charité University Medicine, Berlin, Germany Rossi, Sonja Department of Neurology, Charité University Medicine, Berlin, Germany Wartenburger, Isabell Department of Neurology, Charité University Medicine, Berlin, Germany

The ability to decode different temporal features of the auditory stream is mandatory during language acquisition. Despite its relevance little is know about the underlying pathways and the development of interhemispheric specialization for processing auditory information from birth on. In this study we presented fast (< 25 ms) and slowly (> 160 ms) modulated acoustic stimuli to 24 neonates while recording Near-Infrared-Spectroscopy. Our results reveal a stronger activation for fast compared to slowly modulated stimuli in left auditory areas while slowly modulated stimuli show a stronger right hemispheric activation. These data suggest an asymmetric sampling of temporal features in neonates.

Determinants of the attitudes of Ukrainians and Russians in Ukraine to ethnic and social-economic issues

Tereshchenko, Kira Dept. of Psychology, Industrial College, Kiev, Ukraine

Objectives. To find out how the Ukrainians' and Russians' attitudes toward ethnic and social-economic issues are influenced by micro-level factors (education, age and gender). Methods. The investigation was done on a sample of 832 respondents using an INTAS designed questionnaire and SPSS. Results. Young Ukrainians and Russians had a stronger republican identity (p<0.05) and more positive opinions of their personal economic status and the general economic situation in Ukraine (p<0.05) than seniors. Conclusions. Age is the strongest determinant of the Ukrainians' and Russians' attitudes toward ethnic and social-economic issues whereas education and gender are less influential factors.

Academic causal attribution in antisocial Spanish adolescents

Torregrosa Diez, Maria Soledad Health Psychology, Miguel Hernandez University of, Elche, Spain Ingles Saura, Candido Jose Health Psychology, Miguel Hernandez University of, Elche, Spain Delgado Domenech, Beatriz Dept. of Health Psychology, M. Hernandez Univ. of Elche, Elche, Spain Garcia Fernandez, Jose Manuel Education, University of Alicante, San Vicente del Raspeig, Spain

Objective. To assess the academic causal attribution pattern of antisocial Spanish adolescents. Method. Antisocial Behavior subscale of the Teenage Inventory of Social Skills (TISS), and Sydney Attribution Scale (SAS) were administered to a sample of 2,022 secondary education students. Mean differences were used to analyse the data. Results. Antisocial students attributed their failure in a higher extent to ability and effort and in a fewer to external causes than their non-antisocial counterparts. Furthermore, antisocial students attributed success to effort and external causes in a fewer extent than their non-antisocial peers. Conclusions. Antisocial students tend to attribute failure to intrinsic causes.

Effects of the acute restraint stress on recovery and extinction of a spatial learning task in rats

Torres Berrio, Angelica Bogota, National University of Colombi, Bogota, Colombia Munera, Alejandro Bogota, National University of Colombi, Bogota, Colombia Lamprea, Marisol Bogota, National University of Colombi, Bogota, Colombia

Acute stress has been reported to impair spatial memory recovery, but this effect has not been evaluated on an extinction process yet. In other to test the acute stress effect on recovery and extinction, forty one Wistar rats were trained in a Barnes Maze task and given either zero, one or four hours of acute restraint stress before the recovery and extinction of the task. Results show that animals stressed had a better performance in recovery but differences on extinction were not found. These results suggest the effect of the acute stress would depend on intensity of the stress applied.

Effects of perpetrator status and punishment on feelings of revenge

Torvik, Fartein Ask RBUP, INM, DMF, NTNU, Trondheim, Norway

A survey experiment (n=200) among Norwegian students examined the effects of perpetrator social status and formal punishment on assumed revenge behaviour. Results revealed that after violence, perpetrator punishment reduced revenge behaviour. More revenge was also directed towards high status offenders if not punished. The respondents' willingness to impose formal punish was low, and feelings of revenge were low when respondents imagined being victim of a crime themselves versus a socially close person. This suggests a low degree of vengefulness, and that people find it more important to impose justice on high status persons when responsibility is assigned.

Franz Anton Mesmer: The first psychotherapist of the modern age?

Traetta, Luigi Dipartimento di Scienze Umane, University of Foggia, Foggia, Italy

On the basis of traditional historiographic trends that recognize the origin of dynamic psychology in the Mesmerian model, the current essay deals with the reconstruction of the scientific path of Mesmer by analysing those works which marked the shift from "animal gravity" to "animal magnetism". The aim is to show how the thesis of the derivation of dynamic psychology from the Mesmerian theory produces a reductio of the animal magnetism doctrine to curative aspects: what emerges is a new theoretical Mesmerian system, a sort of "tree of knowledge" on which the curative approach represents only one of many branches.

The phenomenon of second brooding in Black-headed gull (Larus ridibundus). The attempt of explanation in terms of numerical competence

Trojan, Maciej Dept. of Psychology, Warsaw University, Warsaw, Poland Reinholz-Trojan, Anna Psychology, Warsaw University, Warsaw, Poland Gulatowska, Judyta Psychology, Warsaw University, Warsaw, Poland Dzierzak, Ewa Psychology, Warsaw University, Warsaw, Poland

We studied broodig behaviour in a Black-headed gull colony. The observation area was divided into fields, marked with poles, forming the network 135 squares. 110 nests, fulfilling the conditions necessary for further experimental manipulation, were selected and marked. In the case of 55 nests containing three eggs, one egg was taken and moved to one of 55 other nests, where only two legs were laid during the similar period. Second brooding was observed in 34.5% of the nests from which an egg had been removed. Not even a single case of egg loss was observed in any of these nests. However, egg loss was observed in 18.9% of the nests to which an egg was added.

Do dogs have the theory of mind?

Trojan, Maciej Dept. of Psychology, Warsaw University, Warsaw, Poland Reinholz-Trojan, Anna Psychology, Warsaw University, Warsaw, Poland

In first part of project dogs decided which container with award to choose on the basis of pointing by the experimenter. The effectiveness of good choices was about 90%. In the second part of the experiment the experimentator showed the container and when he was leaving, the other experimentator was putting the containers back into the previous position in the presences of the dog. Afterwards the first experimentator was coming back and pointing the old position the container again. The effectiveness of good choices dropped drastically (40%). In the third part of fthe experiment not a location of containers was being exchanged but an award was being moved. In this less abstract situation the effectiveness of choices was about 80%.

The 100 most eminent psychologists of the 20th century on the internet: Do internet page counts provide latent indicators of scientific eminence?

Tumasjan, Andranik Inst. für Psychologie, Universität München, München, Germany *Männich, Matthias* Fakultät Math./Nat., Technische Universität Dresden, Dresden, Germany *Spörrle, Matthias* Dept. for Psychology, Ludwig-Maximilians University, München, Germany

Recently, Haggbloom et al. (2002) established a rank-ordered list of the 100 most eminent psychologists of the 20th century meticulously measured by several quantitative and qualitative indicators. We aimed at replicating this listing by simply using page counts obtained from three major internet search engines using different search queries and five points of measurements. The resulting highly reliable indicators of internet frequency were consistently positively associated with the existing ranking and this correlation reached significance when the field of research was included in the query. We conclude that frequency data obtained by this method can be considered a simple and valid indicator of scientific impact and discuss additional applications of this method.

Children's comprehension of Chinese narratives with full versus reduced anaphoric coherence: A behavior and computational exploration

Tzeng, Yuhtsuen Center for Teacher Education, National Chung Cheng Universit, Min-Hsiung, Chia-Yi, Taiwan

Both anaphoric and causal coherence are essential for comprehension but they generally co-occur in natural discourse. Taking advantages of Chinese, grammatical texts with causal yet no/low anaphoric coherence between sentences were created to dissect their relative contribution for comprehension. 4th grade readers' comprehension was degraded by low anaphoric coherence texts whereas 6th graders showed the opposite with 5th graders remained unaffected. When students were asked to revise texts, 5th and 6th readers added more referents for the low-anaphor versions but no difference for the 4th graders. Simulations based on a computational model shed lights on the possible cognitive processes involved.

A longitudinal narrative study of psychological acculturation of immigrants in Finland

Varjonen, Sirkku Dept. of Social Psychology, University of Helsinki, Helsinki, Finland

The purpose of my study is to examine and understand acculturation in the context of individual lives by using longitudinal life story data of 25 immigrants living in Finland. I focus on the changes in the ways the participants narrate their acculturation experiences and negotiate their identities in the continuum of their stories. The narrative-discursive analysis of the data shows that contrary to what acculturation theories might suggest, the narrated acculturation processes and identities are often constructed in reference to social categories other than ethnic or national groups. These categories

could be considered as alternative points of reference in acculturation research.

Personal control variables and body image dissatisfaction

Vivas, Eleonora Behavioral Science and Techn., Simon Bolivar University, Caracas, Venezuela *Guzmán, Rosana* Behavioral Science and Technol, Simon Bolivar University, Caracas, Venezuela *Lugli, Zoraide* Behavioral Science and Technol, Simon Bolivar University, Caracas, Venezuela

Objective: Determine the predictive level of self-regulation, self-efficacy and weight locus of control on body image dissatisfaction in obese people. Method: Using a non-experimental cross-sectional design, a multiple regression analysis was performed on data from 243 obese patients in Caracas, Venezuela. Results: Self-efficacy, chance and powerful others beliefs in weight control predict dissatisfaction with body image. Conclusion: The importance of considering personal control variables as influencing factors on satisfaction with body image in obesity treatment are suggested.

Psychosocial determinants of health care use by obese adults: Findings from KORA, Germany

von Lengerke, Thomas Med. Psychologie (OE 5430), Medizin. Hochschule Hannover, Hannover, Germany *John, Jürgen* Institute of Health Economics, Helmholtz Center Munich, Oberschleißheim-Neuherberg, Germany

Findings from the "Cooperative Health Research in the Region of Augsburg (KORA)"-platform on determinants of health care use by obese adults are presented. Specifically, it is scrutinized whether outpatient care use is driven "only" by co-morbidity or body experience and health-related beliefs. Data from the S4-1999/2001-Survey (N=4261, response: 67%) show excess use of general practitioners by obese adults (OR=1.7, p<.05), which is associated with co-morbidity. In contrast, obesity-attributable excess use of physical therapy and especially alternative practitioners (OR=2.3, p<.05) is associated with body weight dissatisfaction. In conclusion, results indicate lacks of primary prevention and narrative-based medicine in obesity care.

Posterior versus anterior EEG theta activity: A correlate of personality traits related to incentive motivation

Wacker, Jan Inst. für Psychologie, Universität Marburg, Marburg, Germany *Chavanon, Mira-Lynn* Department of Psychology, Philipps-Universitaet Marburg, Marburg, Germany *Stemmler, Gerhard* Department of Psychology, Philipps-Universitaet Marburg, Marburg, Germany

We have recently reported that agentic extraversion (i.e., a trait hypothesized to be based on dopaminergically modulated individual differences in incentive motivation) is related to more posterior (versus anterior) EEG theta activity (4-8 Hz) under resting conditions. Measuring the resting EEG in 106 healthy males we have now not only replicated this association in a larger sample, but also demonstrated that it is specific to the theta and sub-theta range (< 8 Hz) and that it generalizes to a different trait (sensitivity of Gray's behavioral approach system) likewise hypothesized to be related to incentive motivation and brain dopamine.

Object permanence in Sichuan Golden Monkey (Rhinopithecus roxellana)

Wan, Meiting Dept. of Psychology, Peking University, Beijing, People's Republic of China *Su, Yanjie* Department of Psychology, Peking University, Beijing, People's Republic of China

Sichuan golden monkey is endemic to China and this study aimed to assess the level of object permanence of them. The effective subjects were 2

captive adult males and received 9 tests of object permanence, of which included visible displacement and invisible displacements tasks. The performances of subject 1's were all higher than chance level and showed Stage 6b object permanence capabilities. However, subject 2 only reached Stage 6a because of his insufficient attention during tests. The result suggests that this species can represent the existence and movements of unperceived objects, and find out the hidden objects using incomplete information.

Online game and aggressive behavior of college students

Wang, Chih-Chien Information Management, National Taipei University, Taipei Countyt, Taiwan

Playing online games now become a popular entertainment activity for college students. However, many online games contain violent materials which make the players continually involve in bloodiness scenarios. People are concern the negative effect of online game on individuals' aggressive behavior, although there is no consensus on this issue. This study conducted a questionnaire survey for 246 college students. According to the empirical results, players of fighting role-playing game have higher level of physical aggression, anger and hostility than non-players. However, players of casual online game, such as playing card and online sport, have lower level of hostility than non-players.

Free labeling of emotion in children at ages 3 to 6 years: The different developmental trend under two label task conditions

Wang, Zhenhong The Department of Psychology, Shaanxi Normal University, Xi'an, People's Republic of China *Tian, Bo* The Department of Psychology, Shaanxi Normal University, Xi'an, People's Republic of China *Cui, Xuerong* The Department of Psychology, Shaanxi Normal University, Xi'an, People's Republic of China

Object: This study explored the different age trend under two free labeling conditions in children. Method: 130 children at ages 3, 4, 5, and 6 years were assessed on their ability to freely label facial expressions and emotional situations. Result: labeling emotional situations were better than labeling of facial expressions. Accuracy of free labeling of emotion increased rapidly at ages 3 to 5 years. For free labeling of facial expressions, it reached to a plateau after 5 years, for free label of emotional situations, it continuously increased after 5 years. Conclusion: there's the different age trend in two label tasks.

Do we make more mistakes in memory while using a foreign language? The side effect of foreign language on recognition memory

Wen, Wen Dept. of Psychology, University of Tokyo, Tokyo, Japan *Takano, Yohtaro* Psychology, University of Tokyo, Tokyo, Japan

This study examined the effects of foreign language processing on false recognition by Japanese-English bilinguals. They studied those words that were related or unrelated to a common theme, and then recognized them by identifying the line drawings that had the same meanings as those words among distracters that were related or unrelated to that theme. A linguistic task in Japanese or English was performed simultaneously with the recognition task. The foreign language task increased the false recognition of the related distracters and decreased the correct recognition of the related targets when the number of the related distracters was large enough.

The development of a cognitive-behavior group intervention program to reduce the hostility level of coronary heart disease patients and its effect on blood coagulation function

Weng, Chia-Ying Dept. of Psychology, Chung-Cheng University, Chiayi, Taiwan Lin, Chin-Lon Cardiology/ Internal Medicine, The Tzu Chi General Hospital, Chia-Yi, Taiwan Lin, Tin-Kwang Cardiology/Internal Medicine, The Tzu Chi General Hospital, Chia-Yi, Taiwan Hua, Chen-Tung Psychology, Chung-Cheng University, Chia-Yi, Taiwan Chou, Ying-Yu Psychology, Chung-Cheng University, Chia-Yi, Taiwan

The purpose of this study is to develop an intervention program to reduce the hostility levels of coronary heart disease (CHD) patients and to examine its effects. Eleven male CHD patients (mean age = 63.27) participated in weekly two-hour sessions and did homework for two months.The results indicate that the hostility level decreased t=2.45, p= .028, and participants' prothrombin time and activated partial thromboplastin time increased (t=-2.91, p= .020 and t=-3.53, p= .008) after the intervention. The results suggest that psychological intervention may reduce the risk of disease recurrence for CHD patients.

Doing science: What does it mean? The disciplinary matrices of psychology, physics, biology and sociology

Witte, Erich H. Psychology, Institute of Social Psychology, Hamburg, Germany Stauch, Jakob Social Psychology, Universirty of Hamburg, Hamburg, Germany Junger, Lisa Social Psychology, Universirty of Hamburg, Hamburg, Germany Strohmeier, Charlotte Eva Inst. für Sozialpsychologie, Universiät Hamburg, Hamburg, Germany

Differences of "disciplinary matrices" (cp. Kuhn, 1974) of psychology, physics, biology and sociology are investigated. Research methods and focus of these disciplines and prototypical groups of projects of the disciplines (derived from cluster analysis) are compared with ANOVA. The disciplinary matrix of psychology can be characterized by "testing a theory quantitatively". It is more similar to the life science of biology than to sociology, which is best characterized by working qualitatively and not doing correlational studys.

Cruelty to animals among Chinese children referred to psychiatric service

Wong, Siu Yi Ann Dept. of Psychology, Chinese Univ. of Hong Kong, Hong Kong, People's Republic of China Luk, Siu Iun, Ernest Psychiatry, The Chinese University of HK, hong kong, China, People's Republic of : Macao SAR Lai, Yee Ching Kelly Psychiatry, The Chinese University of HK, hong kong, China, People's Republic of : Macao SAR

Objectives: To examine pattern of cruelty to animals among children referred to psychiatric service in Hong Kong Methods: Parents of 658 children were asked to complete Children's Attitudes and Behaviors towards Animals Questionnaire (CABTA) and Strengths and Difficulties Questionnaire. Results: 7.2% of children were rated to have harmed animals while 12.5% have been rough with animals. Children who had harmed animal engaged in more frequent, intentional, secretive, solitary and pleasurable harming than those who were rough to animals. Conclusions: Cruelty to animals exists among HK children. 19.7% of children in psychiatric service have either been rough towards or harmed animals.

Impact of visualization type and individual factorson human reliability with monitoring systems

Wuheng, Zuo Dept. of Psychology, Zhejiang University, Hangzhou, People's Republic of China Baihua, Xu Psychology, Zhejiang University, Hangzhou, People's Republic of China Jinbo, Li Psychology of Science, Zhejiang University, Hangzhou, People's Republic of China

We explore and test ways of conveying information to the user that can achieve more reliability in their interaction with monitoring systems. Tasks were tested using two types of graphical visualization interface in which experienced and inexperienced human operators had to perform tasks of an easy, moderate, and difficult nature in the experiment. Results revealed that the two types of graphical visualization significantly reduced response errors, particularly with inexperienced users performing difficult tasks. Our results imply that some graphic information visualization displays for monitoring systems can increase the probability of successful implementation and enhance the reliability of human operators.

Usability test of voice-operated cellular phone services

Wuheng, Zuo Dept. of Psychology, Zhejiang University, Hangzhou, People's Republic of China Baihua, Xu Psychology, Zhejiang University, Hangzhou, People's Republic of China Jinbo, Li Psychology of Science, Zhejiang University, Hangzhou, People's Republic of China

A usability assessment was conducted on a voice-operated cellular phone by determining the effectiveness, efficiency, and user satisfaction of service. Two different versions of a mock mobile shopping guide service using a hierarchically structured menu system were evaluated in a mobile setting. One numbered menu style service, and another service which contained terms derived from underlying real-world referents, were implemented. User performance and attitudes to the services were recorded. Results showed that significantly more participants prefer to the metaphor-based service. Research findings suggest that proper interface metaphor could significantly enhance the system's usability.

Syntactic and reading-related cognitive skills in Chinese children

Xiaoyun, Xiao Psychology, The University of Hong Kong, Hongkong, China, People's Republic of : Hong Kong SAR Connie Suk-Han, Ho Psychology, The University of Hong Kong, Hongkong, China, People's Republic of : Macao SAR

The present study was conducted to examine the contributions of syntactic and reading-related cognitive skills to reading comprehension in Chinese children. Different measures of syntactic skills, linguistic skills (Chinese word reading ability, semantic, and oral language skills) and cognitive skills (working memory and visual sequencing memory) were administered to 188 Chinese children. It was found the unique contributions of Chinese word reading ability, semantics, oral language abilities, and syntactic skills to reading comprehension, but not of working memory and visual sequencing memory. The results suggest that linguistic skills especially syntactic skills have direct contributions to reading comprehension, whereas memory skills involve a more general underlying process, rather than specific to reading comprehension.

Enhanced learning-memory associated with BDNF upregulation in hippocampus and striatum in rats

Xu, Bo College of Physical Education, East China Normal University, Shanghai, People's Republic of China

To explore a relationship between excise and learning-memory and the mechanism underlined, 36 male adult rats were randomly assigned into control and experiment group (N=18). For experiment group, an 8-week no-load swimming session (1 hour x 6 times/week) was performed. Learning-memory was screened by MWM test and BDNF expression was analyzed by a RT-PCR.In contrast to control, swimming not only enhanced performance on water maze, but significantly increased BDNF expression in hippocampus and striatum by 38% (P?0.01) and 14 % (P?0.05) respectively. The results indicate an association of improved learning-memory by the swimming paradigm with BDNF expression.

Spatial distribution of Zenk-positive neurons for song perception in the brain of budgerigars

Yamazaki, Suteo Psychology, Gifu University, Gifu, Japan Satoh, Ryohei Physiology, Kitasato University Sch. Med., Sagamihara, Japan Eda-Fujiwara, Hiroko Chemical & Biological Scie, Japan Women's University, Tokyo, Japan Miyamoto, Takenori Chemical & Biological Scie, Japan Women's University, Tokyo, Japan

Budgerigars develop elaborate songs used in social interactions. The neural activities for the song stimuli elicit activity-dependent genes, such as ZENK. We investigated the gene product Zenk in the NCM (caudomedial nidopallium) and the CMM (caudomedial mesopallium) of the telencephalic auditory areas in female budgerigars exposed to male songs. Little is known about the spatial distribution of subdivisions in these nuclei for the conspecific song complexity. We got a sign of increased clustering of neurons induced by the complex songs compared with simple ones, suggesting that the song- complexity-dependent neuronal arrangement might exist in these areas.

Several ways on interpreting dreams in ancient China

Yan, Liang-Shi Faculty of Education Science, Hunan Normal University, Changsha, People's Republic of China Wang, Ya-qian Faculty of Education Science, Hunan Normal University, Changsha, People's Republic of China

Cultural psychology concerning dreams in ancient China is unique. In ancient China, dream embodies not only individual's desire but also collective's or society's. Furthermore, dream was considered as a communication between the ghosts & gods world and the real world in ancient China, of which is different from Freud's consciousness and unconsciousness. Therefore, our ancestors have created some ways of Chinese style to interpret dreams, such as interpreting dreams by symbol, divining by interpreting dreams with Chinese characters, interpreting dreams by orientation, interpreting dreams by dual persons confirming together with divination reference, positive interpreting on nightmares, etc..

Research on counseling skill analysis based on chinese ancient great five elements philosophy

Yang, Wensheng Psychological Counseling, Shanghai Jiao Tong University, Shanghai, People's Republic of China Wang, Zhongming

Chinese ancient great-five-elements philosophy was introduced to counseling research. Skills were classified into looking, listening, asking, bian (identifying) and dao(influencing) and corresponded with fire, water, gold, earth and wood. Fixed relationships existed: dao (wood) was facilitated by listening (water) and restrained by asking (gold); looking (fire) was facilitated by dao (wood) and restrained by listening (water); bian (earth) was facilitated by looking (fire) and restrained by dao (wood); asking (gold) was facilitated by bian (earth) and restrained by looking (fire);listening (water) was facilitated by asking (gold) and restrained by bian. Then, skills formed a dynamic system.

Consideration on the shift of sentence processing strategies

Yong, Zhai Graduate School of Humanities, Kyushu University, Fukuoka, Japan Sakamoto, Tsutomu Faculty of Humanities, Kyushu University, Fukuoka, Japan

Objectives: The present study addresses the gradual shift of general strategy to linguistic strategy. Methods: Sixty Chinese children (from grades 1 to 5) participated in this experiment. After reading the sentence, participants are instructed to answer questions by YES/NO key. Results: The Classification Trees Analysis revealed that the participants were divided into three groups. Conclusions: The strategy has gradually shifted through three stages. In the earlier stages of language acquisition, a general-purpose strategy is dominant. After one acquires linguistic knowledge, a specific language strategy becomes dominant.

The effect of biofeedback treatment under stress situation on test anxiety

Yuan, Xiaojiao Psychology, Beijing Normal University, Beijing, People's Republic of China Zhang, Yubin Psychology, Beijing Normal University, Beijing, People's Republic of China Zhuo, Ran Psychology, Beijing Normal University, Beijing, People's Republic of China Su, Wenliang Psychology, Beijing Normal University, Beijing, People's Republic of China Fang, Xiaoyi Psychology, Beijing Normal University, Beijing, People's Republic of China

Objective: To study the effect of biofeedback treatment on test anxiety under different situations. Method:Try on the freshman; divide them into three groups; train group A with biofeedback under stress situation, group B under non-stress situation, and the control group did ont receive the intervention. Result: The intervention of biofeedback in Blood Volume Pulse(BVP), Peripheral Temperature(PT) and Skin Conductance(SC) is effective, especially the PT; The intervention of biofeedback under the stress situation can help one master and transfer the skill of relaxation better, as well as perform better in other stress situations.

A proposed model of safety climate: Contributing factors and consequences

Yucebilgic, Harika Dept. of Human Resources, Man Türkiye A.S., Ankara, Turkey Sümer, H. Canan Psychology, METU, Ankara, Turkey

The aim of the present study was to propose a model on safety climate by investigating the relationship between safety climate perceptions of employees and their safety-related behaviors in the workplace, along with the effects of risk taking/sensation seeking tendencies on this relationship. A hundred and eighty-five blue-collar employees working in a manufacturing firm in Turkey participated in the study. The outcome variables included compliance with safety rules and percentage of safety equipments used. Employees who had more positive perceptions of safety climate were found to report more compliance with the rules. Also, protective equipment usage was more for employees who scored less on sensation seeking.

Relationship between loneliness and self, Reported health among university students

Zardeckaite-Matulaitiene, Kristina Dept. of General Psychology, Vytautas Magnus University, Kaunas, Lithuania Stankute, Edita General Psychology, Vytautas Magnus University, Kaunas, Lithuania

The aim of the study was to disclose relationship between loneliness and self-reported health. A group of 177 students from various universities in Kaunas, Lithuania were evaluated using The Loneliness Scale by De Jong Gierveld & Kamphuis and 9 questions about physical and mental health. As a result, it was found that men students reported greater loneliness than women. No significant difference in loneliness between first–year and later–year students was discovered. A significant relation between loneliness and self-reported health was found. The analysis showed that more lonely students reported poorer physical and mental health than those who were less lonely.

Proposition of a new theory of aphasia: A cognitive model

Zellal, Nacira Algiers University, Director of Laboratory, Algiers, Algeria

The main challenge in neuropsycholinguistic field was, since 1915, the creation of theoretical models. In this proposal, we'll synthetize our 30 year reflexion. We started our researches in neuropsychology in 1977 (Paris VI, Faculty of Medicine). We have worked in description, then classification (N. Z., Glossa, n° 23,1991), then interpretation (N. Z., IALP, Septembre 1998), then rehabilitation (N. Z., I.A.L.P, Cairo, 1995) of aphasic deficits. We have used a program - the first Algerian neuropsychological battery plurilingual tasks : the "MTA"2002, financed in the frame of a French-Algerian agreement project. Starting from our neurolinguistic typology and cognitive interpretation of aphasic impairments, we'll present a cognitive theoretical model of aphasia based upon temporo-spatial structuration concepts.

Adolescents' cognition of projectile motion: Differences and characteristics

Zhao, Jun-yan Institute of Psychology, Chinese Academy of Sciences, Beijing, People's Republic of China

To explore the dissociation between conceptual knowledge and action knowledge in adolescents, a projectile motion experiment was conducted. The participants were 160 middle school students. In the action task, participants were asked to swing ball A of a bifilar pendulum to some height then release it to collide with ball B. Ball B was then projected to hit a target. In the judgment task, participants judged the angles through which ball A was swung. Unlike what has been found in previous studies with adults, dissociation between the two knowledge systems still exists among adolescents. This suggests that the two knowledge systems follow different developmental trajectories. The effects of formal physics education are discussed.

Poster Session Monday Afternoon 14:00

The relationships between mother's rearing types and aggression in children and adolescents

Ángel Carrasco, Miguel Personality Dept., UNED, Madrid, Spain del Barrio, Victoria Personality Dept., UNED, Madrid, Spain Rodriguez, Miguel Personality Dept., UNED, Madrid, Spain Holgado, Pablo Personality Dept., UNED, Madrid, Spain

The present study explores how aggression in children is related to different rearing subtypes of mothers. The sample consisted of 524 children (45,2% girls and 54,8 boys) ranging from 7 to 14 years old (means 11.11; Standar Desviation 1.56). Children completed the Childs Report Behavior Parenting Inventory (Shaefer, 1965) and The Physical and Verbal aggression Questionnaire (Caprara et al., 1993). Cluster analysis identified three distinct groups of mothers: hostile mothers, balaced mothers and affective mothers. Mothers profiles differed significantly on physical and verbal aggression in children. Membership in hostile mother cluster (high control and high hostility and low affect) was related with higher scores in physical and verbal aggression. From a bidirectional perspective aggression.

Automatic thoughts and locus of control as factors for academic success

Ackovska-Leskovska, Elena Faculty of Philosophy, Skopje University, Skopje, The former Yugoslav Republic of Macedonia

Many studies have shown that students with high basic abilities, good working habits and learning skills could fail because of some internal mediating cognitive processes. The aim of this study is to investigate influence of different types of automatic

thoughts (positive and negative) and locus of control (internal and external) on students' academic success. Student Automatic Thoughts Questionnaire and Scale for Locus of Control were distributed to 161 university students. The results indicate that students with negative automatic thoughts and external locus of control are more successful. Findings don't confirm the contribution of positive automatic thoughts in achieving academic success.

Incidental probability learning test

Aczel, Balazs Experimental Psychology, University of Cambridge, Cambridge, United Kingdom Brown, Jamie Experimental Psychology, University of Cambridge, Cambridge, United Kingdom Cserep, Csongor Experimental Psychology, Implicit Laboratory Assn., Budapest, Hungary

Objectives: To construct a novel incidental learning paradigm, in which knowledge is acquired about the probabilistic location of non-sequential stimuli. Methods: A Serial Reaction Time design was constructed in which stimuli were random-ordered and the colour of the screen frame probabilistically predicted the location of the stimuli. Reaction times (RT) on the more and less probable locations were compared using a 2x5 repeated-measures ANOVA. Results: RTs were longer on the less probable locations than on the more probable ones (p<.05), reflecting learning about the probabilistic associations. Subjects were unaware of the probabilistic contingencies. Conclusions: The novel paradigm is capable of producing and assessing incidental probability learning.

Mental health of the patients seeking cosmetic rhinoplasty

Afkham Ebrahimi, Azizeh Dept. of Clinical Psychology, IUMS, Tehran, Islamic Republic of Iran Afkhamebrahimi, Shirin Dept. of Foreign Languages, Tehran University, Tehran, Islamic Republic of Iran Mousavi, Fatolah Dept. of ENT, IUMS, Tehran, Islamic Republic of Iran Akbari Barcheloi, Zahra Dept. of Medicine, IUMS, Tehran, Islamic Republic of Iran Afkham Ebrahimi, Azadeh Student affairs, Australian Embassy in Tehran, Tehran, Islamic Republic of Iran

Background: Cosmetic surgery is now carried out increasingly in an attempt to solve the psychological and social problems of people who are discontent with a particular facet of their appearance. Method: A total of 69 patients who were seeking cosmetic rhinoplasty were selected and completed SCL-90-R, a 90 item self-report symptom inventory which measures 9 primary symptom dimensions. Results The statistical findings showed high levels of somatization, obsessive-compulsive, interpersonal sensitivity and anxiety symptoms in both gender. Women reported more interpersonal sensitivity and anxiety than men. Conclusion: Our results points to linkages between negative body image and certain impairments of psychosocial functioning.

Gender differences in the degree of environmental concern

Aguilar-Luzon, Maria del Carmen Psychology, University of Jaen, Jaen, Spain Calvo-Salguero, Antonia Social Psychology, University of Granada, Granada, Spain Salinas, José María Social Psychology, University of Granada, Granada, Spain Berrios Martos, M. Pilar Psychology, University of Jaén, Jaén, Spain López-Zafra, Esther Psychology, University of Jaén, Jaén, Spain Augusto Landa, José María Psychology, University of Jaén, Jaén, Spain

Traditionally, studies carried out of attitudes towards the environment have suggested that women, in comparison with men, show a higher degree of awareness regarding environmental subjects or issues. However, given the socio-cultural changes which have come about in the last decades, one would expect these differences to have been reduced, at least among the younger generations. In order to verify this, for this study a sample of 523 young people were selected (309 women and 214 men) who responded to the New Environmental Paradigm (NEP) Scale. Contrary to expectations, the results indicated the existence of differences in gender, and that it was women who showed a higher degree of environmental concern.

The relationship between environmental concern and the consumption of ecological products

Aguilar-Luzon, Maria del Carmen Psychology, University of Jaen, Jaen, Spain Calvo-Salguero, Antonia Social Psychology and Methodol, University of Granada, Granada, Spain García-Martínez, J. Miguel A. Social Psychology, University of Granada, Granada, Spain Monteoliva-Sánchez, Adelaida Social Psychology, University of Granada, Granada, Spain Sánchez Santa-Bárbara, Emilio Social Psychology, University of Granada, Jaén, Spain

The objective was to ascertain whether the degree of concern for the environment is related to a greater tendency towards the consumption of ecological products. 154 housewives responded to the New Ecological Paradigm Scale and to a Likert-type scale regarding the frequency of consumption of ecological products. Having carried out correlation analyses and a difference in averages test between the groups of high and low environmental concern, the results indicate a positive and significant correlation between the degree of environmental awareness and the level of consumption of ecological products. Thus, the housewives showing a high level of environmental concern obtained a significantly higher average in the level of consumption than those of low environmental concern.

Clinical significance of WISC- 111 for the gifted children

Ahmed, Khalil Psychology, Adrak, Khatoum, Sudan

This study aimed at examining the clinical significance of WISC- 111 for the gifted children in Sudan. The sample comprised (293) pupils at gifted schools. The researcher employed WISC- III, for Childers (9-12 year). The results revealed that: average of gifted children in Sudan, mean for verbal (110.85), performance (117.80) Total (117.63). No significant statistical differences were found on intelligence level between males and females, and also there were significant differences on subtests performance related to gender, and there was significant correlation between parent's education, verbal intelligence, and general intelligence

Difficulty of stimulus discrimination and reaction times for negative emotional pictures

Akamine, Aki Nagoya, Japan Kida, Mitsuro
Department of Psychology, Aichi Gakuin University, Nisshin, Japan

Reaction times (RTs) for negative and neutral people stimuli were assessed using a Stop/NoStop task. In the task, participants were instructed to react ("NoStop") to every stimulus (including people) that was not a "Stop" stimulus. Three task conditions were defined by a combination of NoStop people and Stop stimuli (simple geometric shapes, cars, and animals). More the stimulus discrimination became difficult, more the RTs increased. Moreover, RTs were longer for the negative compared to neutral stimuli except for the easy condition. Results suggest that negative emotions have little effect on performance when stimulus discrimination is completed quickly.

Psycho-somatic factors of the health of the elderly athletes

Al-Obadi, Inessa MCPSO, Moscow Sport Committee, Moscow, Russia Sagitova, Venera sport medicine, RSUPES, Moscow, Russia

Compared the group of the masters of the sport of elderly age, who continue to be occupied by sport with the group of the masters of sport, who ended

occupations, 114 veterans of sport and 100 - not occupying by the sport 40-70 years. Health, psycho physiologic status, psychological characteristics were investigated using clinical, laboratory, instrumental, and test indices. We found that physical activity, employment by the dear matter, good friendly relations - important factors of a good health at the elderly age. The curtailment of occupations by sport reliably adversely affects the health of elderly professional athletes.

Sensitivity to vowel categories in bilingual infants

Albareda, Barbara PCB & Dept. Psicologia BÀsica, GRNC, Esplugues (Barcelona), Spain Pons, Ferran PCB & Dept. Psicologia BÀ, GRNC, Esplugues (Barcelona), Spain Sebastián-Gallés, Núria PCB & Dept. Psicologia BÀ, GRNC, Esplugues (Barcelona), Spain

Certain studies have shown that at 8 months of age, infants raised in bilingual environments fail to discriminate some native contrasts (Bosch & Sebastián-Gallés, 2003). The present study aims at further exploring this issue. To this end, the anticipatory eye movement methodology (McMurray & Aslin, 2004) was adapted. Infants from monolingual (Catalan and Spanish) and bilingual (Catalan-Spanish) families were tested on a Catalan-specific vowel contrast. Results evidence that Catalan monolinguals and Catalan-Spanish bilinguals were able to anticipate the reinforcer. Thus, the lack of discrimination previously reported for 8-month-old bilinguals disappears when tested with a technique sensitive enough.

Indigenization of psychology in the Sudan

Altayp, Anas Spychology, Alniliyen, Khartoum, Sudan

This study examines the degree of indigenization of psychology in the Sudan with respect to the content analysis of master theses (N = 60) that were awarded 1990 – 2002. It showed that percentage of educational psychology (45%), descriptive method (76.6%), the sample was small in number (76.6%), old references (82%), majority of researchers were females (63.3) while majority of supervisors were males (92.6%). The level of cultural sensitivity in local concepts was (0%), local references (9%), and local issues (11.6). Indigenization and similar concepts not mention in 79% of the studies and there is alack of cross-cultural discussion in 95% of the studies.

Influence of perceptual and emotional cues on risky driving

Alvarez, Vanessa Experimental Psychology, Faculty of Psychology, Granada, Spain di Stasi, Leandro Luigi Experimental Psychology, Faculty of Psychology, GRANADA, Spain Serrano, Jesús Experimental Psychology, Faculty of Psychology, GRANADA, Spain Canas, José Juan Experimental Psychology, Faculty of Psychology, GRANADA, Spain Maldonado, Antonio Psicologia Experimental, Universidad de Granada, Granada, Spain Cándido, Antonio Experimental Psychology, Faculty of Psychology, GRANADA, Spain Catena, Andrés Experimental Psychology, Faculty of Psychology, GRANADA, Spain

This research is part of a larger project "Risk behaviour: cognitive, emotional and neuropsychological basis" supported by Honda Motor. In this paper, we will present experiments that investigate the role of perceptual and emotional cues during a static riding simulation. Our results indicate that risky decisions were affected by the time when the cues were presented and by whether these cues induced specific emotions. The final goal of this series of experiments is building a model of risk behaviour to predict decisions under uncertainty, and to design programs for evaluating, preventing and controlling risk behaviour.

Is it possible to combine discourse analysis and survey methods? A theoretical account

Anderssen, Norman Dep. of Psychosocial Science, University of Bergen, Bergen, Norway

Objective: Identify key concerns in combining discourse analysis and survey methods. Theory: Discourse analysis means studying language in use, often with specific interest in power. Survey methods imply questionnaires putting strong restrictions on communication between informant and researcher. To combine the methods one needs to phrase questionnaire items in non-essentialist terms (e.g. in attitudes-surveys on lgbt), and one needs to realize that survey responses must be understood as acts of meaning within the specific forms of language in use that surveys constitute. Conclusions: A discouse analytical framework may fruitfully incorporate survey methods.

Psychological support for patients with diabetes mellitus in clinical practice

Ando, Shinichiro Okayama Citizens Hospital, Okayama, Japan Ando, Mikayo Dep. Clinical Psychology, Okayama University, Okayama city, Japan

Methods of psychological support for patients with diabetes were explored in experience of clinical practice. Involvement of a clinical psychologist in a diabetic education program with group work and individual counseling improved quality of life of patients. Presenting data of studies on the impact of reducing HbA1c, blood pressure, LDL-cholesterol and triglyceride increased patient motivation. For depressive patients psychological assessment, antidepressant including SSRI, SNRI and psychotherapy by a clinical psychologist were useful to improve depression and diabetic control. Self-monitoring of body weight, blood pressure and blood glucose were helpful for most of patients to enhance confidence of self-management.

Binge eating assessment in Spanish population

Andrés, Ana Methodology Behavioral Science, University of Barcelona, Barcelona, Spain Saldaña, Carmina Department of Personality, University of Barcelona, Barcelona, Spain Lecube, Albert Obesity Unit, Hospital Vall d'Hebrón, Barcelona, Spain Gómez, Juana Methodology Behavioral Science, University of Barcelona, Barcelona, Spain

Objectives. The aim of this study is to present the preliminary results of the Questionaire on Eating and Weight Patterns-Revised (QWEP-R; Spitzer, Yanovski and Marcus, 1994) adaptation to Spanish population. Methods. The scale was applied to an experimental group of overweight and obese people (n = 100) and to a control group of general population (n = 50). Results. The analyses carried out provide psychometric properties regarding the discrimination indexes of the items and test reliability (Cronbach's alpha). Conclusions. This study presents the psychometric properties of the first questionnaire aimed to assess binge eating in Spanish population.

Personality in caregivers of the aged

Aparicio, Marta Diferencial y Trabajo, Universidad Complutense, Madrid, Spain Sánchez-López, M⍨ Pilar Diferencial y Trabajo, Universidad Complutense, Madrid, Spain Díaz Morales, Juan Francisco Diferencial y Trabajo, Universidad Complutense, Madrid, Spain Fernández Martínez, M⍨ Teresa Psicología, Residencia Villaverde-Alzheime, Madrid, Spain Castellanos Vidal, Beatriz Psicología, Residencia Villaverde-Alzheime, Madrid, Spain Tena Fontaneda, Angela Diferencial y Trabajo, Universidad Complutense, Madrid, Spain

Objectives: To analyse the relationships between personality and physical health in the case of formal and informal caregivers. Methods: Those taking part are 100 formal and informal caregivers who work or have members of their family in old peoples' homes. The instruments used were the MIPS (and a medical evaluation to analyse physical health. Several MANOVAS were performed to analyse differences between the various health variables. Results: The caregivers with the lowest rates of personal adaptability characteristics in the MIPS will be those obtaining the worst values in physical health. Conclusions: Personality impinges on health problems that people suffer, in such a way that people who are most involved with others have the worst health.

Disease attitude and self-concept of haemophiliac adolescents (HA) in connection with parental attitude

Aralova, Marina Rostov-on-Don, Russia Aslanyan, Karapet Hematology, Regional Children's Hospital, Rostov-Don, Russia Goncharova, Ludmila Hematology, Regional Children's Hospital, Rostov-Don, Russia Shaydarova, Nataliya 12 department, Bureau medical-social examinat, Rostov-Don, Russia
HA's disease attitude and self-concept in connection with parental attitude were studied. Hypothesis: parental attitude determines HA's self-concept and disease attitude. Main and control groups of 42 adolescents aged 12-16 and their mothers were inquired. Methods: self-concept and parental influence questionnaires (S. Pantileev, A. Vargi - respectively), "unfinished sentences" (V. Mikhal), SPSS 13,0. Results: Main HA's disease attitude types – anosognosiac and neurasthenic. Mothers' attitude (factor analysis) is ambivalent – types: "little loser"; symbiosis; authoritative hypersocialisation; cooperation; aversion – it significantly determines HA's reflected self-concept (33% of variance) without influencing HA's disease attitude. The results help understand the process of adolescents' self-actualization .

Professors' job satisfaction in Mexico

Arias Galicia, Fernando Dept. of Psychology, Morelos University, Cuernavaca, Mexico Camacho-Cristiá, Carmen Business Administration School, Universidad Veracruzana, Coatzacoalcos, Mexico
Traditionally human behavior has been analyzed in private sectors firms. Less attention has been directed towards people working in other type of organizations for instance educational institutions. Even less frequent is research regarding this matter in underdeveloped countries. For this reason we surveyed 349 Mexican college professors. The main interest was to ascertain the relative weight of Compromise with the profession, Satisfaction with Supervision, Satisfaction with Peers and Organizational Support on Job Satisfaction. After a regression analysis Satisfaction with Supervisor emerged as the variable with the highest beta. Theoretical implications as well as suggestions for further research are posited.

Intelligence assessment and their impact in the formulation of educational policies in Colombia

Arias Patino, Erika Servicio de Atención Psicológi, Nation. University of Colombia, Bogota, Colombia
It is analyzed the impact that presents the intelligence assessment by objective tests, in the formulation of educational public policies, especially in the identification of children with educational special needs. it is carried out an analysis of public policies from the conceptual frame proposed by Shonkoff (2000), by means of documental analysis and interviews. Conclusions: In Colombia the educational policies assume as referent a unidimensional intelligence theory, proposing their evaluation through standardized instruments as the scales Weschler, with the purpose of assuring the justness and equality, standing out incongruities between the psychological knowledge and their appropriation for the political actors.

Construction of inventories assessing metacognitive ability

Asamura, Akihiko Hokkai-Gakuen University, Sapporo, Japan Yoshino, Iwao Dept. of Educ. Psychology, Hokkaido Univ. of Education, Sapporo, Japan Kaketa, Koichi Dept. of Educ. Psychology, Hokkaido Univ. of Education, Asahikawa, Japan Miyazaki, Takuya Dept. of Educ. Psychology, Hokkaido Univ. of Education, Asahikawa, Japan
The purpose of this research is to construct new inventories assessing metacognitive ability and to compare the inventories with another constructed by a previous research (Schraw & Dennison, 1994). 464 participants rated 40 items and 87 of them also rated the Schraw-and-Dennison inventory. Factor analysis suggested that two inventories could be constructed to measure knowledge about cognition and regulation of cognition respectively. High correlation between our inventories and the Schraw-and-Dennison inventory suggested validity of our inventories. Since our inventories represent various concrete situations, assessing metacognitive ability with our inventories may be more accurate than assessing with the Schraw-and-Dennison inventory.

The relationship of job characteristics with job dimensions of managers in two industrial companies

Askari Pour, Nastaran Psychology, University of Isfahan, Isfahan, Islamic Republic of Iran Oreyzi, Hamid reza psychology, university of Isfahan, Isfahan, Islamic Republic of Iran
The purpose of this study was to examine the relationship between job characteristics and job dimensions of manager. The participants were 100 managers of two companies. To measure job characteristics has been used the Job Characteristics Inventory and job dimensions measured by Professional and Managerial Position Questionnaire.100 manager participated in this study. Method of data analysis was multiple regressions. Findings indicated that job characteristics have significant relationship with job dimensions ((p<0.005). The research findings may have important implications for fitness between managers and their jobs and decision makings including managers' career planning and implementation.

Relationship of managers' role breadth with aptitude in three industrial companies

Askari Pour, Nastaran Psychology, University of Isfahan, Isfahan, Islamic Republic of Iran Oreayzi, Hamid Reza psychology, university of Isfahan, Isfahan, Islamic Republic of Iran
The purpose of this study was investigating any kind of relationship between the managers' role breadth and aptitude as well as predicting the possible critical variable of managers' role breadth. 86 male and female managers participated and the managers' role breadth was measured by applying the Professional and Managerial Position Questionnaire. Managers also completed the General Aptitude Test Battery. Using the Multiple regression method, the findings indicated meaningful relationships among role breadth and managers' cognitive abilities (p<0.001). The research findings may have important implications for managers' decision makings including career planning and implementation, appraisal performance and job evaluation.

Relationship of approaches of job-design with job satisfaction, job involvement and job commitment in four industrial companies

Askari Pour, Nastaran Psychology, University of Isfahan, Isfahan, Islamic Republic of Iran
The purpose of this study was investigating relationships among approaches of job-design(Motivational,Biological and Motor-perception approaches) with job attitudes. participants were 125

subjects with correspondence job. Each job was seen by one trainee observer. The instrument was Multi-method Job Design Questionnaire (MJDQ) and job attitude was evaluated by Job Descriptive Index, Job Involvement Inventory and Organizational Commitment Inventory. Using the cononical corrolation method, the findings indicated positively significant relationships between motivational approachjob-design and job attitudes. Implications of the findings are important in implementing positive job attitudes towards jobs in the personnel industrial organization.

Effects of computerized adaptive testing and feedback on test-taking motivation and achievement

Asseburg, Regine der Naturwissenschaften, Leibniz-Institut für Pädagogik, Kiel, Germany Frey, Andreas Educational Science, IPN, Kiel, Germany
While the psychometric and statistical aspects of computerized adaptive testing have been intensely investigated during the last decades, the psychological correlatives of adaptive testing are not yet thoroughly understood. Given the conflicting research results and divergent opinions concerning the effects of adaptive testing on test-taking motivation, the present study analyses the effect of adaptive testing and feedback on test-taking motivation and achievement. First results from an online-experiment (N = 500) are presented and discussed with respect to an application of computerized adaptive testing that is optimal regarding test-taking motivation and achievement.

Introducing a model for decision making process in organizations

Atashpour, Hamid Psychology, Azad University, Isfahan, Islamic Republic of Iran Salahshouri, Nasrin Psychology, Azad University, Isfahan, Islamic Republic of Iran Samsam Shariat, Mohamad Reza Psychology, Azad University, Isfahan, Islamic Republic of Iran Samavatyan, Hossein Psychology, Isfahan University, Isfahan, Islamic Republic of Iran
Decision making, one of the main duties of managers, can be considered as an indication of the degree of success in organizations. In this study, 90 managers and supervisors in a large organization were consulted and after analyzing their performance, a practical model for determining successful and unsuccessful organizations was proposed. The model can be also used as a strategy for identifying the kind of problems, analyzing them, and showing how they can be solved. It shows how the situations can be categorized and what steps should be taken to solve them.

Atypical workers and prefiguration of the future: The role of self-efficacy and contextual variables

Avallone, Francesco Department of Psychology, La Sapienza, Roma, Italy Petitta, Laura Department of Psychology, University La Sapienza, Roma, Italy Pepe, Silvia Department of Psychology, University La Sapienza, Roma, Italy
Atypical workers (N=1043) were administered a questionnaire measuring self-efficacy, values, needs, perceptions of the organizational constituencies, job burnout, psycho-somatic disturbances, and prefiguration of the worker's future. Results from SEM showed that prefiguration of the worker's future was mainly explained by perceptions of organizational reward, self-efficacy in job search, need for protection, and cynicism. Furthermore, cynicism was mainly explained by values, self-efficacy in work fulfilment, perceptions of negative behaviours. Practical implications for developing atypical workers' job search strategies is discussed.

The effectiveness of mindfulness training on the degree on dysfunctional attitudes and automatic thinks in the students of Isfahan University

Azargoon, Hassan *Psychology, Isfahan University, Isfahan, Islamic Republic of Iran* **Kajbaf, Mohammad Bagher** *psychology, isfahan university, isfahan, Islamic Republic of Iran*

In this research the effectiveness of mindfulness training on depression and rumination of students was examined. Therefore a sample of 36 depressed (12 men and 24 women) were randomly selected and assigned to training and control groups. All patients completed Dysfunctional attitudes and Automatic Thinks Questionnaires pre and post of the training. The training groups received 8 weekly two hours sessions of mindfulness training. The control group did not receive any training. The results of analysis of covariance. Showed a significant reduction in depression and rumination of the training group as compared to the control group (p<.01).The qualitative observation showed that this method could also be effective in increasing concentration. Keywords: Mindfulness, Rumination, Depression

Possible cognitive processes involved in the creation of the concept of four-dimensional spacetime

Babb, Richard *Rehabilitation Medicine, Harlem Hospitality Centre, New Rochelle, USA* **Jirik-Babb, Pauline** *Psychology, Iona College&Montefiore Me, New Rochelle, New York, USA*

Cognitive processes underlying psychology of science are involved in geometric concepts and awareness of space and time. Originally, the belief was that geometries of mathematics and the world are identical, resulting in Newton producing a physical theory in which time and space are separate and absolute. In contrast, Einstein, using intuition and symmetry concepts, related electrodynamic theory and speed of light-constancy to the formulation of space and time as not being absolute. This prompted Minkowski to create the concept of time and space being merged into a single, four-dimensional, spacetime geometry, leading to the General Relativity Theory.

Emotions in elite sports

Baenninger-Huber, Eva *Psychology, University of Innsbruck, Innsbruck, Austria* **Juen, Barbara** *Psychology, University of Innsbruck, Innsbruck, Austria*

Engaging in elite sports means the experience of strong emotions such as joy, anger, fear or disappointment. In the study presented here, narrative interviews with 20 former top athletes have been conducted. Starting from a model of the elicitation, phenomenology and regulation of emotion they were asked about their most important positive and negative emotions experienced during their carrier. The data analysis shows that the capacity for an effective regulation of negative emotions is crucial for success. Furthermore, successful athletes have to be able to maintain a balance between their fears and risk taking. Positive thinking and basic beliefs of fairness in sports on the other side are additional requirements for high-performance.

Evaluating the role of cognitive and motivational strategies in the student academic achievement and psychologic problem reduction

Baezzat, Fereshteh *Dept. of Psychology, Shahid Beheshti University, Tehran, Islamic Republic of Iran* **Sadinam, Mohsen** *psychology, Shahid Beheshti University, Tehran, Islamic Republic of Iran* **Milani, Farideh** *Dept. of Psychology, Shahid Beheshti University, Tehran, Islamic Republic of Iran* **Sadinam, Nasim** *Dept. of Psychology, Shahid Beheshti University, Tehran, Islamic Republic of Iran*

Abdmanafi, Vahid *Dept. of Psychology, Shahid Beheshti University, Tehran, Islamic Republic of Iran*
The present study concerned with the effects of cognitive and motivational self regulation techniques training on academic improvement and the possible reduction of psychological problems in Iranian students. 272 students at Shahid Beheshti University in Tehran were randomly divided into two experimental groups, given eight weeks training on self regulation techniques and two control groups given no training at all. Evaluation of subjects academic improvements was done by comparing their mean grades in two academic terms. A questionnaire measuring subjects' academic problems, Cattells Anxiety Scale and MSLQ were also administered. Results showed those given training, reported fewer problems than those not given training.

Effects of neuropsychological treatment on the reading efficiency of Iranian students with developmental dyslexia

Baezzat, Fereshteh *Dept. of Psychology, Shahid Beheshti University, Tehran, Islamic Republic of Iran* **Sadinam, Mohsen** *psychology, Shahid Beheshti University, Tehran, Islamic Republic of Iran*
This research investigates the effects of neuropsychological treatment on reading efficiency of students suffering from developmental dyslexia.165 students suspected of dyslexia were selected from elementary schools through cluster sampling, of which after diagnostic tests sixty students were selected. The evaluated sample was then randomly divided into four categories based on Bakker's classification. After pretests, the L-type and the P-type experimental groups received neuropsychological treatments (HSS) through 20 sessions. Control groups received no treatments. Subsequently post-tests with follow-up tests were made. Results showed neuropsychological interventions, increases reading accuracy and comprehension of the L-type and reading speed and comprehension of p-type dyslexic students.

"Locomotion-space" representation of visually impaired persons: Impact of personality, environmental factors and new technologies on the urban space management

Baltenneck, Nicolas *Institut de Psychologie, Université Lyon 2, Bron Cedex, France* **Portalier, Serge** *Institut de Psychologie, Université Lyon 2, Bron Cedex, France*
This thesis study space representation and management for blind persons. How the blinds construct, structure and tame their environment? Kitchin (1994) reminds us the existing interdependence between behavior and environment. Thus, what impact personality profiles can have on the urban space management? First, we will try to define a "displacement style" concept. These "displacement styles" rest on interaction between type of aid used (long canes etc.) in one hand, personality profile in the other hand, and type of visual impairment. We used a questionnaire with 135 blind subjects. It's based on 2 traits of EPQ (Eysenck, 1975) and SSS (Zuchermann, 1983). We also introduce originals items about risk-taking. We are currently working on data processing, achieved April 2008.

Communication, participation and community: The use of internet among Portuguese adolescents

Barros Duarte, Carla *Faculty of Social and Human, University Fernando Pessoa, Porto, Portugal* **Cardoso, Paulo** *Faculty of Social and Human, University Fernando Pessoa, Porto, Portugal* **Sacau, Ana** *Faculty of Social and Human, University Fernando Pessoa, Porto, Portugal*
Framed in the area of Media Psychology, this study analyses the habits and preferences of Portuguese Teenagers when they use Internet. Specifically, the

study aims to know how much time is spent on Internet and which are the most visited web sites. Using a qualitative/quantitative approach, a questionnaire was administrated to a sample of 250 Portuguese teenagers. Results revealed that young internet user's preferences involve interpersonal communication, group participation and a sense of community that go beyond geographic boundaries.

Procedural learning in obsessive-compulsive disorder compared to anxiety disorder

Bauer, Anja *Klinik Roseneck, Prien, Germany* **Geissner, Edgar** *Psychosomatic, Klinik Roseneck, Prien, Germany* **Endraß, Tanja** *Clinical Psychology, Humboldt University Berlin, Berlin, Germany* **Kathmann, Norbert** *Clinical Psychology, Humboldt University Berlin, Berlin, Germany*
Neuropsychological research associates obsessive-compulsive disorder (OCD) with disturbed fronto-striatal brain systems. This dysfunction is assumed to affect procedural learning. We adopted the serial reaction time task to test this prediction. Single and dual task versions were used to control the role of explicit strategies, and anxiety disorder patients were included as a clinical control group. OCD patients showed robust deficits confirming prior studies. These deficits were independent of concurrent working memory load. Performance of anxiety patients was reduced under single task but not under dual task demands. In conclusion, procedural learning is impaired in OCD supporting the fronto-striatal dysfunction model. Anxiety patients show a different deficit profile.

The study of the validity and reliability of the Trait Meta-Mood Scale (TMMS) among students

Bayani, Ali Asghar *Dept. of Psychology, Islamic Azad University, Azadshahr, Islamic Republic of Iran* **Kocheki, Ashour Mohamad** *Dept. of Psychology, Islamic Azad University, Azadshahr, Islamic Republic of Iran*
Since Salovey and Mayer's (1990) conceptualization of emotional intelligence (EI), the construct has generated wide spread interest and attention. Several different models of EI now exist, and a number of assessment measures have been developed. The main objective in this study was to examine the reliability and validity of TMMS on a sample of Iranian students. The reliability of TMMS was tested through three methods of Cronbach's alpha, test –retest.. The validity TMMS of was evaluated through construct validity. In general, The Persian Version of TMMS Scale showed to have fairly acceptable level of reliability and validity.

Validation and norming the Computerized Adpative Test of Anxiety ('A-CAT')

Becker, Janine *Clinic of Psychosomatics, Charite Univeritätsmedizin, Berlin, Germany* **Fliege, Herbert** *Clinic of Psychosomatics, Charite Univeritätsmedizin, Berlin, Germany* **Kocalevent, Rüya-Daniela** *Clinic of Psychosomatics, Charite Univeritätsmedizin, Berlin, Germany* **Bjorner, Jakob** *Science Team, QualityMetric Inc, Waltham, MA, USA* **Rose, Matthias** *Science Team, Quality Metric Inc, Waltham, MA, USA* **Walter, Otto** *Methods and statistics, Univeritty of Munster, Münster, Germany* **Klapp, Burghard** *Clinic of Psychosomatics, Charite Univeritätsmedizin, Berlin, Germany*
Previous validation studies of a Computerized Adaptive Test to measure anxiety (A-CAT) in psychosomatic patients showed the tool to be brief, reliable, and valid. This study was conducted to validate and norm the CAT in a population sample. N=300 healthy subjects were asked to complete the CAT, an acceptance survey and two subscales of the Perceived Health Questionnaire. Descriptive and correlational statistics were calculated. Cut-off scores to differentiate between healthy subjects and

patients with high anxiety levels were developed. The study demonstrated the A-CAT to be a brief, well accepted, precise, and valid tool for the general population.

Contingency Awareness in operant conditioning of pain perception

Becker, Susanne Otto-Selz-Institut, Universität Mannheim, Mannheim, Germany Kleinböhl, Dieter Otto-Selz-Institute, University of Mannheim, Mannheim, Germany Hölzl, Rupert Otto-Selz-Institute, University of Mannheim, Mannheim, Germany

Recent research showed that, perceived pain intensity can be altered by operant conditioning. However, it is still being discussed whether contingency awareness is needed by underlying learning mechanisms. To modulate pain sensitivity by operant learning an experimental psychophysical method was used. Within this paradigm contingency awareness was measured by an implicit and an explicit method. Both measurements indicated that contingency awareness was not needed to produce gross changes in pain sensitivity by operant learning. These results support the significant role of unaware operant learning mechanisms and thereby might explain the increasing hypersensitivity in pain becoming chronic without a person's knowledge.

Cognitive flexibility, selective attention and semantic verbal fluency in three schizophrenic dimensions: Psychotic, negative and disorganisation (P.A.N.S.S)

Bejaoui, Moez Dept. de Psychologie, PsyCLE, Aix-en-Provence, France Bonnet, Agnàs psuchology, PsyCLE, Aix En Provence, France Pedinielli, Jean-Louis psuchology, PsyCLE, Aix En Provence, France

The aim of this study was to explore specific pattern of cognitive dysfunctions related to three schizophrenic dimensions: disorganisation, negative and psychotic resulting from principal component analyse applied to P.A.N.S.S's items. We assessed executive functions/dysfunctions in 42 schizophrenics (APA, 1994). Results : component analyse identify homogenous schizophrenic dimensions. Disorganisation dimension was associated with low performances in selective attention (Stroop test), Negative dimension were associated to low performances in cognitive flexibility (Wisconsin Card Sorting Test) and in semantic verbal fluency. However, no significant correlation was found between psychotic dimension and cognitive dysfunctions. On the whole, our study contributes to the comprehension of specific patterns of cognitive disorders in the schizophrenic dimensions. Results are detailed and discussed.

The positive impact of irrational beliefs? A mutual connection with justice sensitivity

Bekk, Magdalena Department of Psychology, Ludwig-Maximilians University, München, Germany Baumert, Anna Psychology, Universität Koblenz-Landau, Landau, Germany Spörrle, Matthias Psychology, Ludwig-Maximilians-Universität, München, Germany

Rational-Emotive-Behavior Therapy (REBT, Ellis, 1962, 1994) postulates that irrational thinking implies demanding thoughts about punishing people for their evil activities. Hence, irrational thinking should be associated with increased individual sensitivity concerning unfair social events. Results of our study (N = 108) confirm this hypothesized correlation between Irrationality and Justice Sensitivity. Notably, the strongest correlation was found between low frustration tolerance, a subdimension of irrationality, and justice sensitivity from the perspective of a victim. This indicates that easily frustrated individuals are particularly prone to suffer when being treated unfairly and are, therefore, eminently susceptive to justice sensitivity.

Individual/organizational tactics' influence on the outcomes of the newcomers' organizational socialization process

Bellò, Benedetta Elmas (CA), Italy Mattana, Veronica Dept. of Psychology, University of Verona, San Vito, Italy

A longitudinal research is carried out through a questionnaire on a sample of 148 newcomers (54% male; average age: 35) employees of a public administration. The aim was to understand which individual/organizational tactics influence the 6 outcomes (Chao et al., 1994) of the organizational socialization process which enables newcomers to acquire values, behaviors and knowledge of the organization to which they belong (Van Maneen & Schein, 1979). The results show that individual tactics influence all of the outcomes but only History, Goal & Value and People are influenced by organizational tactics. Limitations and research's future perspectives will be discussed.

Lived experience of patients hospitalized in a palliatives care unit: A phenomenological analysis

Bellouti, Rym Faïrouz Lille, France

The study aims to apprehend, by a phenomenological approach and an inductive method, lived experience of six adults receiving palliative care. Non-directive integrally tape-recorded interviews and phenomenological observation served to collect data. Discourses were qualitatively analyzed and results were articulated with clinico-theoretical data. The study reveals three main common dimensions : The need for belonging to a community, the search for experience's sense and a temporo-spatial dimension. It also shows the importance of subjectivity to understand lived experience and that common dimensions are related to individual problematics and to life's perception. Moreover, the study reveals ethical difficulties in the clinical research on dying persons and discusses about the social taboo of death.

Psychosocial determinants of the dimensions of depression in adolescence

Benavides, Gemma Psicología de la Salud, University Miguel Hernández, Elche, Spain Pastor, Yolanda Psicología de la Salud, University Miguel Hernández, Elche (Alicante), Spain Martinez, Fermin Psicología de la Salud, University Miguel Hernández, Elche (Alicante), Spain

The aim of this paper was to analyse the influence of different psychosocial variables in the levels of depression of a sample of 648 Spanish adolescents (M age=13.4, SD=1.7, Range=11-16 years). A validated Spanish version of the "Dimensions of Depression Profile for Children and Adolescents" (Harter, 1987; Benavides, Pastor, et al., 2004) was used for this purpose. The hierarchical multiple regression analyses showed that the less physical appearance, self-steem, behaviour adequacy, academic competence, social adjustment and social support adolescents perceived, the higher depression was in its different dimensions (depressive mood, sense of fault, lack of energy and interest, and suicidal thinking-out).

Depression in adolescence: Gender and grade differences

Benavides, Gemma Psicología de la Salud, University Miguel Hernández, Elche, Spain Martinez, Fermin Psicología de la Salud, University Miguel Hernández, Elche (Alicante), Spain

The purpose of this paper was to examine, in a sample of 648 adolescents, differences on the "Dimensions of Depression Profile" (Harter, 1987) by gender (52% boys, 48% girls) and grade (three academic levels, M age=13.4). Results showed a significant interaction gender by grade. In boys, depressive mood and suicidal thinking-out increased by grade, whilst sense of fault was lower

in the middle grade. In girls, sense of fault increased by grade, being depressive mood and suicidal thinking-out higher in the middle grade. It could be concluded that during adolescence depressive symptoms seem to appear earlier in girls than in boys.

Architects' and non-architects' perception of exposed concrete as a building material

Benz, Irmela Dept. of Psychology, Otto-von-Guericke-University, Magdeburg, Germany Rambow, Riklef Architecture, BTU Cottbus, Cottbus, Germany

Two studies were carried out to determine differences in the perspectives of experts and laypeople in architecture. Exposed concrete was chosen as the object of perception, because there is a multitude of anecdotal evidence showing the controversial connotations of this material, but systematic research is lacking. In the first study N = 96 laypersons were interviewed in front of two prominent built examples of exposed concrete architecture. In the second study differences were confirmed by a systematic comparison of architects (N = 65) and non-architects (N = 75) by means of a semantic differential technique and additional open questions.

The role of entitativity in the perception of neighbourhoods in urban areas

Bernardo, Fátima Psychology Department, UNiversity of Évora, Évora, Portugal

It is hypothesized that perceptions of entitativity (i.e. seeing social targets as possessing unity and coherence) can be a useful concept to understand perception of the neighbourhoods in urban areas. A group of 189 participants rated a sample of 20 neighbourhoods in Lisbon accordingly to 5 properties of groups, 14 physical properties of the area (e.g., size, age, degree of functionality) and perceived entitativity. Correlacional analyses were used to determine the group and physical properties most strongly related to entitativity. Clustering and factor analyses identified 3 main dimensions in neighbourhoods perception and allows to distinguish 5 clusters of neighbourhoods in terms of its properties, notably the entitativity perception.

A factorial exploratory analysis of Minnesota multiphasic personality inventory adolescents (MMPI-A)

Berrío, Angela Dept. of Psychology, Nation. University of Colombia, Bogotá, Colombia Arias Patino, Erika Servicio de Atención Psicológi, Nation. University of Colombia, Bogota, Colombia

It explores the operation of the MMPI-A in a sample of Colombian adolescents without antecedents of psychiatric illness (N= 72), executing a factorial analysis for main components with the clinical, supplementary and content scales, by means of the statistical program SPAD-4. Results: Three factors explain 71,51% of the total variance, (Psychopathology 45,19%; Control 17,61%; Social Competence 8,71%). Conclusion: The MMPI-A, it is similar in their characteristics to the original version for adults, discriminating against between normal and Psychopathology personality, and identifying a common factor respect to the social competition. The "control of impulses", arises as an analytic new factor.

The role of person-organization fit in the newcomer socialization processes: A latent growth modeling approach

Bian, Ran School of Psychology, Beijing Normal University, Beijing, People's Republic of China Lin, Xuanhui School of Psychology, Beijing Normal University, Beijing, People's Republic of China Che, Hongsheng School of Psychology, Beijing Normal University, Beijing, People's Republic of China

Using a 2nd-order factor latent growth modeling approach to data collected from a sample of 92 newcomers in 6 organizations, this 3-wave long-itudinal study examined the pattern of change in person-organization (P-O) fit over time, and its relationships with socialization tactics and socialization outcomes. Results indicated P-O fit changed linearly across time, and these intraindividual changes had significant interindividual differences. A significant association was found between socialization tactics and change trajectories of P-O fit, and also the change trajectories of P-O fit and socialization outcomes. These results supported the mediating role of P-O fit change in the process of socialization.

Metropolitan characteristics and environment related human needs

Bieniok, Majken *Kognitive Psychologie, HU - Institut für Psychologie, Berlin, Germany* **Beyer, Reinhard** *Kognitive Psychologie, HU - Institut für Psychologie, Berlin, Germany* **van der Meer, Elke** *Kognitive Psychologie, HU - Institut für Psychologie, Berlin, Germany*

Permanently changing life conditions due to globalisation processes and population changes evoke the demand of new urban development concepts especially for metropolises. The aim of the current investigation was to identify environment related human needs and relevant characteristics of a metropolis, their emotional valence and their interrelation. Different methods like interview-techniques, q-sort and pupillometry were used and statistically analysed. A significant correlation between a higher relevance and positive evaluation of metropolitan characteristics and the capacity to fulfill environment related human needs could be found. The results can provide advice for urban development concepts based on the needs of metropolitan inhabitants.

Factors influencing applicant attraction to job openings

Bilgiç, Reyhan *Dept. of Psychology, Middle East Tech. University, Ankara, Turkey* **Acarlar, Gizem** *Psychology, Middle East Tech. University, ANKARA, Turkey*

The main purpose of the present study was to explore the effects of characteristics of information given in a job advertisement (amount and specificity of the information) on the potential applicants' willingness to apply to the job opening with the mediating roles of credibility of and satisfaction from the information, and attraction to the organization. One hundred and fifty four METU students from Electrical and Electronics Department were used to examine the hypotheses of the study. The students were randomly assigned to the three different versions of job advertisement. The results supported most of the main hypotheses and the proposed model except for the mediating effect of satisfaction.

Neural correlates of aversive conditioning

Blümel, Isabelle *Psychiatrie und Psychotherapie, Universitätskrankenhaus Aachen, Aachen, Germany* **Kellermann, Thilo** *Psychiatry and Psychotherapy, UK Aachen, Aachen, Germany* **Schüppen, André** *IZKF Biomat, UK Aachen, Aachen, Germany* **Jansen, Andreas** *Psychiatry and Psychotherapy, UK Aachen, Aachen, Germany* **Kircher, Tilo** *Psychiatry and Psychotherapy, UK Aachen, Aachen, Germany*

Neutral visual stimuli have been associated with a white noise as unconditioned stimuli in an aversive classical conditioning paradigm. Subjects performed the usual three experimental phases of learning. First preliminary results indicate greater activation in the contrast between CS+ and CS- in regions known to be involved in emotional processing. Subjective ratings give also evidence for behavioral conditioning. The paradigm will be used in a multicenter study with patients with panic disorder. We expect significant faster conditioning

and slower extinction in panic patients compared to healthy subjects and a hyper reaction of the amygdala.

Psychological determinants of addiction to the internet

Blachnio, Agata *Psycho. Emotion and Motivation, Catholic University of Lublin, Lublin, Poland* **Przepiorka, Aneta** *JP II, Catholic University of Lublin, Lublin, Poland*

The aim of this study was to define psychological determinants of addiction to the Internet. There were 353 subjects who were interviewed through various measurements. The following methods have been applied: Rotter's Locus of Control Scale, Satisfaction of life (Diener, Emmons, Larsen i Griffin, 2004), Scale of Addiction to Internet (Young, 1996). The results showed that the subjects who gained more points on the addiction scale had a higher level of neurotism and extraversism. Additionally, people who declared that they used the computer more often than they used the Internet displayed an even higher level of addiction to Internet.

Freud's China connections

Blowers, Geoffrey *Dept. of Psychology, University of Hong Kong, Hong Kong, China, People's Republic of : Hong Kong SAR*

This paper explores the work of three Chinese scholars, Zhang Shenfu (1893-1986, Zhang Zhizhao (1881-1973) and Dai Bingyeung (1899-1996) who made significant contributions to the importation and impact of Freudian ideas into China during the Republican period (1912-1949), and considers their contributions and significance for the emergence and development of a psychoanalytic psychotherapeutic culture in China today.

Selection of applicants for apprenticeship positions in Public Administration: Construction and validation of a method to capture the ability to reason

Boessneck, Andre *Oelsnitz, Germany* **Schütz, Astrid** *Sachsen, TU Chemnitz, Chemnitz, Germany*

To predict the success of apprenticeship, an instrument to capture logical thinking has been developed. The method consists of verbal, numerical and figurate analogical tasks of the type: A relates to B like C to D. Psychometric properties of the measure were tested among others on two samples of pupils (class eight to ten) and one group of students. The method is sufficiently reliable, meets the strict criteria of the Rasch-model, shows convergent and discriminant validity, and correlates moderately with school grades and teacher judgements. With a time for completion of approximately 20 minutes, it is a very economical selection instrument.

Workplace deviant behaviors: The role of organizational climate and sanctions

Bollmann, Grégoire *Dept. of Management - HEC, Université de Lausanne, Lausanne, Switzerland* **Krings, Franciska** *Department of Management - HEC, Université de Lausanne, Lausanne, Switzerland* **Facchin, Stéphanie** *Department of Psychology, University of Pittsburgh, Pittsburgh, USA* **Simon, Aude** *Psychologie du Travail, Université de Neuchâtel, Neuchâtel, Switzerland*

This study examined if organizational factors intended to manage deviant behaviors at work – sanction probability in case of rule violation, rules climate (a dimension of ethical climate) – actually reduce their occurrence. Questionnaire data were gathered from 84 employees, coming from various companies. Hierarchical regression analyses revealed that sanction probability was negatively related to work organizational deviance as defined by Robinson & Bennett (1995). Further, rules climate interacted with sanction probability sug-

gesting that organizational climate may effectively reduce deviant behaviors, especially when the probability of being sanctioned is low.

Messurement of professional self-understanding at practising psychologists

Bondarenko, Alexander *Dept. of Psychology, Kiev National University, Kiev, Ukraine* **Kucherovskaya, Nataliya** *Psychology, Kiev National University, Kiev, Ukraine*

This research was aimed at extracting the most general categories for assessment of professional self-understanding at practising psychologists. The referent sample of the subjects were 25 of the most qualified Russian Psychologists, working in the field of Counselling and Therapy for more than 20 years. Factor and cluster analysis were used to single out the principal dimensions which might be the basic poles of a Semantic Differential (SD). The constructed SD comprised the following scales: subjectivity - objectivity; quick results - postponed results; ideology oriented- technique oriented; presupposed involvement- presupposed noninvolvement; innovatory- traditionalistic; presupposed development - presupposed homeostasis.

Disordered eating and body dissatisfaction in aesthetic sports: A study of adolescent high-performance athletes

Bonekamp, Eva *Inst. für Psychologie, Universität Potsdam, Potsdam, Germany*

Eating disorders are more prevalent in aesthetic sports such as figure skating, rhythmical gymnastics and ballet compared to normal population. It is hypothesized, that the focus on body weight and appearance in aesthetic sports sets the athlete at greater risk. The current study investigates a sample of 60 high-performance aesthetic athletes aged 12-18 years regarding risk and protective factors known from the aetiology of eating disorders. Additionally possible sports-related risk-factors like pressure by trainer or the belief to increase performance by loosing weight are examined. Specific mechanisms for the group of aesthetic athletes will be discussed.

On the validity of specific cognitive abilities for predicting training success in Germany: A multi-level meta-analysis

Borgmann, Lars *Inst. für Psychologie, Unversität Münster, Münster, Germany* **Hülsheger, Ute R.** *Work and Organizational Psycho, Unversity of Maastricht, Maastricht, Germany* **Maier, Günther W.** *Department of Psychology, Unversity of Bielefeld, Bielefeld, Germany*

A meta-analysis on the validity of specific cognitive abilities (verbal, numerical, perceptual, spatial-mechanical and reasoning) for the prediction of training success in Germany is presented. The database consisted of K=67 independent samples (N=9,513) providing 722 correlation coefficients. The meta-analysis was conducted using a multi-level approach in order to account for dependencies between validity estimates. Corrected validities of specific cognitive abilities varied considerably, ranging from $\rho=.288$ for spatial-mechanical ability to $\rho=.369$ for numerical ability. Results indicate that validities vary according to the g-loading of the respective cognitive ability, a finding which is discussed with regard to Carroll's Three-Stratum Theory.

Gender differences on the Mental Rotation Test: No item specificity

Bors, Douglas A. *Dept. of Psychology, University of Toronto, Toronto, Canada*

It has been argued (Voyer & Hou, 2006) that item types defined in terms of various target or distractor properties (structurally different, mirror image, presence of significant occlusion) were related to the magnitude of the gender differences found on the Mental Rotation Test (MRT; Vandenberg & Kuse, 1978). Diverse analyses of MRT data collected on a large sample of university students failed to support this hypothesis. In terms of factor structure, it is argued that the MRT is best conceptualized as a consistent set of non-independent items, all contributing to the gender effect.

The development of sport interest factors in female adolescents

Bosnar, Ksenija *Faculty of Kinesiology, University of Zagreb, Zagreb, Croatia* **Prot, Franjo** *Faculty of Kinesiology, University of Zagreb, Zagreb, Croatia*

Simple analyses of sport popularity among females show similar results in different age groups. The aim of this study is to compare latent structures of sport preferences in four samples of 5th to 8th grade elementary school girls. The total sample of 1001 girls was given the list of 52 sports to be evaluated on five-point scale. Hierarchical factor analyses were done on separate grade samples. At third level, two-factor solution was obtained in all samples. First dimensions were defined as general interest in sport factors. Differences in other factor solutions suggest complex sport preference development pattern in female adolescents.

Brain, mind and thinking: Three different entities?

Botia Sanabria, Maria Lucero *National Office of Research, Antonio Nariño University, Bogotá, Colombia* **Orozco Pulido, Luis Humberto** *National Office of Research, Antonio Nariño University, Bogotá, Colombia*

To formulate an explicative problem solving theory we need to found a useful and enough theoretical background but we failed; based on critical analysis this study shows limits and advantages of eight theoretical models: four that look for explain the brain-mind relation (as neuropsychology, evolutionarism) and four about the mind-thinking relationship (as mental models, computing, constructivism). Facing the conceptual fragilities of them we propose a theoretical model that looks for explain the brain-mind-thinking problem as virtual, systemic, complex, constructivist, reflexive, auto-organized, developing related entities, taking care of not to be eclectic at all.

Teenagers and magazines: Which social representations do they share?

Boyer, Isabelle *Paris, France* **Cormier, Béatrice** *IUT TC, UCP, Cergy Saint Christophe, France*

The aim of this study is to analyse which beliefs are present in the French press for teenagers, and on the other hand, are these conceptions or some of them shared by the teenagers themselves? the contents and the structure of the summary and the covers of 6 magazines were analysed and also 150 students filled in questionnaires. First results show that the social representations in the magazines are very conventional, for example adolescence is a period of doubt and change. The analysis of the questionnaire demonstrates that teenagers have a large number of those beliefs in common but not all of them. (preliminary results).

URMEL-ICE, controlled randomized school-based obesity prevention in Ulm, Germany: Which and how many elements of the intervention were implemented by teachers?

Brandstetter, Susanne *Sport- ud Rehamedizin, Universtitätsklinikum Ulm, Ulm, Germany* **Wartha, Olivia** *Universtitätsklinikum Ulm, ZNL, Ulm, Germany* **Steinacker, Jürgen** *Universtitätsklinikum Ulm, Sport- & Rehamedizin, Ulm, Germany* **Berg, Swantje** *Universtitätsklinikum Ulm, Kinder- und Jugendmedizin, Ulm, Germany* **Galm, Christoph** *Universtitätsklinikum Ulm, Kinder- und Jugendmedizin, Ulm, Germany* **Klenk, Jochen** *UniverstitätUlm, Institut für Epidemiologie, Ulm,*

Germany **Peter, Richard** *Universität Ulm, Institut für Epidemiologie, Ulm, Germany* **Prokopchuk, Dmytro** *Universitätsklinikum Ulm, Sport- & Rehamedizin, Ulm, Germany* **Steiner, Ronald** *Universitätsklinikum Ulm, Sport- & Rehamedizin, Ulm, Germany* **Wabitsch, Martin** *Universitätsklinikum Ulm, Kinder- und Jugendmedizin, Ulm, Germany*

Aim is to describe how well teachers fulfilled intervention-guidelines for obesity prevention over one school year. 32 second grade teachers rated frequencies they used a healthy lifestyle promoting units (~60 min) and activity sessions (5 min) and their satisfaction. Mean use was 23.1 (1st, 3rd quartile: 20.5, 29.0) of 29-yearly required units (significant decrease over time) and 3.8 (1st, 3rd quartile: 2.0, 5.0) of 10-weekly required activity sessions. Over all, teachers had been satisfied with the teaching materials. The discrepancy between the satisfaction with the materials and their use reveals problems have to be considered in further studies.

Innovative business culture implementation in small and medium-sized enterprises (SME)

Bremser, Indra *A.U.G.E.-Institut, Hochschule Niederrhein, Krefeld, Germany* **Packebusch, Lutz** *A.U.G.E.-Institut, Hochschule Niederrhein, Krefeld, Germany* **Herzog, Barbara** *IAP, Hochschule Niederrhein, Krefeld, Germany*

During the course of this German/Dutch project a coaching strategy to implement an innovative business culture in SME was developed, introduced and pre- and post tested for SME (n=30). The concept "innovation" is generally used in terms of the development of new products. Our study states that structural and social innovations as well as innovation of processes have much greater impact on the innovative team climate and, hence, on the overall success of the enterprise. It is also to be tested that the different cultural (German/Dutch) background has a significant influence on the success of the coaching. Final results based on qualitative and quantitative data will be available in spring 2008.

The incremental validity of irrationality for the prediction of life satisfaction

Breugst, Nicola *Inst. für Ökonomie, Universität Duisburg-Essen, Essen, Germany* **Spörrle, Matthias** *Department Psychology, Ludwig-Maximilians-University, München, Germany* **Welpe, Isabell** *Munich School of Management, Ludwig-Maximilians-University, München, Germany*

A central tenet of Rational Emotive Behavior Therapy (REBT) is that irrational cognitions are associated with maladaptive emotions which in turn should reduce individual life satisfaction. Previous research has already provided some preliminary evidence of this connection between irrationality and life satisfaction. By administering established self-assessment measures of the involved constructs to a student sample (N = 343) in a multiple regression approach we tried to guard this relation against the influence of potential covariates. Results confirmed that irrationality still provided incremental predictive validity when simultaneously including sex, age, social desirability, the big five, and emotional intelligence.

How many psychologies do we need?

Brinkmann, Svend *Department of Psychology, University of Aarhus, Aarhus C, Denmark*

Psychology has always been a science with two sides: Aristotle distinguished the natural scientific explanation of anger as "boiling of the blood" from the rhetorical explanation of anger as a response to unfairness. Dilthey's distinction between Erklären and Verstehen captures this. From this follows a taxonomy of three positions: Erklären-monism (all psychology should seek causal laws), Verstehen-monism (all psychology should be hermeneutic), and Verstehen-Erklären dualism arguing for

"peaceful coexistence in psychology" (Charles Taylor) or even the creation of a hybrid psychology (Rom Harré). I defend the latter dualistic position, but argue that the Verstehen-side necessarily enjoys primacy in psychological explanations.

High abilities, gifted, moral and ethics / HSME

Bulkool Mettrau, Marsyl *Rio de Janeiro, Brazil* **Simão Linhares Barreto, Márcia** *Mestrado in Psicology, UNIVERSO, Niterói - RJ, Brazil* **Rangel, Mary** *Mestrado in Education, UFF, Niterói - RJ, Brazil*

This study aims to evaluate instruments of measurement of maturity on moral judging in use in Brazil. Having tested 20 students, from both sexes, from the eighth grade, in the average 12 to 14 years old with the SROM. We have used pre-test and post-test, an attitude questionnaire concerning the students that were recognized as academic talents, constituted of 10 items. Having calculated the average of the pretest (=1,51). Other subjects have increased their average (zero to 1,42). The relation between the grades of participation in the discussions and the scores was significant ($x2 = 7,68$; $p<0,01$).. The differences found among the samples can be due to the cultural diversity among Brazilians.

Effective cognitive work and individual response to external factors of activity

Burov, Oleksandr *Kiev, Ukraine* **Burova, Kateryna** *Student, Kyiv Municipal Pedagogic Un-ty, Kiev, Ukraine* **Filatova, Iryna** *Psychophysiology, RIMM, Irpin, Ukraine*

Objectives. Securing high accuracy of operator's work reliability depending on psychological type and cognitive style. Methods. Computer system for psychophysiological research. Tests performance, measurement of physiological parameters. Data analysis based on regression models. Results. Values of psychophysiological parameters of cognitive activity depend on character of tasks and infradian rhythms. Pace and reliability of activity is determined by parameters of physiological security and solar activity (R = 0.95, $p<0.01$). Prognosis models reliability increases (R=0.97). Conclusions. Significance is to demonstrate ways to achieve a high accuracy of human performance prediction.

Psychology of money: Values and symbolization in postmodern consumers behaviour

Bustreo, Massimo *Istituto di Consumi, IULM University, Feltre, Italy*

This research highlights the socio-psychological symbolizations of money as an absolute aim in post-modern consumerist society. Here money is studied as the expression and the instrument of mutual dependence between consumers. Through a deep analysis of a specific form of literature, the research underlines the psychoanalytic aspects of money as a «real abstraction» and as an instrument for both possessing goods and emotions: a powerful symbol of unlimited power. A new history of money reality stands out from this multi-disciplinary research: a psychosocial approach to study peoples' attitudes and motivations, whether from an individual standpoint or whether considering group dynamics.

Avatar, shops and Linden dollars in Second Life: New consumers between reality and virtuality

Bustreo, Massimo *Istituto di Consumi, IULM University, Feltre, Italy* **Missaglia, Anna** *Consumi, comportamento e comun, IULM University, Milano MI, Italy* **Jabes, Davide** *Consumi, comportamento e comun, IULM University, Milano MI, Italy*

Internet 2.0 is a revolution also for market and consumers. Communication, interpersonal relationships, interactive strategy, and the symbolic dimension of private and public life are changing, following, anticipating or placing side by side the new media influences (Kiesler, 1997; Suler, 2000).

The aim of this study – according to a psycho-sociological method – is to explore the representation of consumers Self between real and virtual life. The present research explore the importance of origins, basic structure, functions, development of Second Life. In particular, the limit between real and virtual opportunity is considered as the new space for cyberconsumers identity and behaviour.

Occasional excessive use of alcohol an emotional ambivalence

Caballero, Amparo Social Psychology, Universidad Autonoma de Madrid, Madrid, Spain Carrera, Pilar Social Psychology, Universidad Autonoma de Madrid, Madrid, Spain Muñoz, Dolores Social Psychology, Universidad Autonoma de Madrid, Madrid, Spain

We have studied the differential and complementary role in the prediction of the intention to repeat a risk behaviour in the immediate future played by the TPB variables, and the emotions felt when the participants recall and describe a previous experience of that risk behaviour. We have chosen the behaviour of occasional (not habitual) excessive drinking are characterized by evoking attitudinal ambivalence and by eliciting mixed emotions, joy and sadness. The results show, firstly, that the emotional ambivalence is not equivalent to the attitudinal ambivalence. They may have a differential and complementary consideration. Secondly, that this emotional information is relevant for predicting the intention to repeat the risk behaviour in the near future, enhancing the prediction of the TPB model.

The Health Scale for Chinese Drug Abuser (HSDA):Development, reliability, and validity

Cai, Taisheng Central South University, Psychological Center, People's Republic of China Junhui, Guo Central South Univercity, psychological center, People's Republic of China

Objective: this study was to initially develop a drug abuser comprehensive multidimensional assessment scale for assessing the overall level of health of Chinese drug abuser and examine the reliability and validity of this scale. Methods:The health data got from the measurement of 949 cases were used to evaluate the scale. Results: scale was composed of 120 items. Except for validity scale, it included 11 factors: Each factor of test-retest reliability was well, such as Cronbach'sα, was from 0.615 to 0.879 Conclusion:initially a new scale was developed, and thought confirmatory factor analyses studies showed the structure of the scale was reasonable.

Life satisfaction among immigrant and native adolescents in Spain

Calderón López, Sonsoles Psicología Evolutiva, Universidad Complutense, Madrid, Spain

Satisfaction with life, as the global evaluation of a persons quality of life based on personal criteria (Shin & Johnson, 1987), will be examined among immigrant Latino adolescents in relation to acculturation process (length of residence in the country, identification with Spanish culture, perceived discrimination) and social support variables (peer acceptance, support from parents and teachers). Results will be compared with the perspective of native adolescents from same age and school contexts. Implications for intervention programs to improve psychological adaptation among young immigrants will be discussed.

Sensitivity to pain, auto-regulation, coping and personality in healthy adult women

Calero, M. Dolores Faculty of Psychology, Granada University, Granada, Spain Lopez Perez, Angel Faculty of Psychology, Granada University, Granada, Spain

Objectives: to investigate the relation between sensitivity to pain, subjective intensity of pain and

certain psychological variables. Method: the sample consisted of 74 women without pain symptoms. Experimental pain was induced by the Dolorimeter®. Subjective intensity of pain was evaluated using a Visual Analog Scale. Psychological characteristics studied were self-government, stress-coping, sensitivity to anxiety and personality. Results: we found a positive relation between sensitivity to pain and subjective intensity of pain. ANOVA showed differences between groups in same of these variables. Conclusions: we could identify psychological factors related to perception of pain to consider in the psychological treatment of pain.

Anxiety and the fear of death in health professionals

Campelos, Cristina Faculdade de Ciencias Humanas, Universidade Fernando Pessoa, Maia, Portugal Soares Martins, José faculdade de ciencias humanas, universidade fernando pessoa, maia, Portugal

This study has like objectives to understand if the nurses that more frequent and directly live together with the death feel more anxiety and fear face to the same one and which demographic variables and perspectives of the death could be associated to it. The results show up that do not exist significant differences in the death anxiety levels in the two groups (Institut of Oncology and other institutions). Relatively to the perspectives of the death the conclusion was that there are significant differences between the several groups and that these are correlated positively with the anxiety face to the death.

Academic performance in college: Study of the effects of interaction person-context with Portuguese students

Candeias, Adelinda Dept. of Psychology, University of Evora, Évora, Portugal Martins, Alexandre Dept. of Sociology, IPP, Portalegre, Portugal Guerra, Cristina CIEP, University of Evora, Évora, Portugal Pires, Heldemerina Dept. of Psychology, University of Evora, Évora, Portugal Saragoça, José Dept. of Sociology, University of Evora, Évora, Portugal

In this paper we present the study of how student's perceptions about self, tasks and interaction with others interact with its performance. Such purpose was sustained in the model of experience in development from Sternberg et al., (2000) and ecological model from Bronfenbrenner (1993). For this purpose we developed a Multidimensional Questionnaire that involves: Self-Perception of Tacit Knowledge, Family Support, Socio-Cultural and Economic Levels, Impact of Transition. We applied the questionnaire to the high and low academic performance courses (N=200). We present the psychometric characteristics regarding the sensitivity, reliability and internal and external validity that point out for a strong tool.

Relations between family and/or school disconnection, gender, and adolescents' health

Cartierre, Nathalie Dept. of Psychology, University of Lille 3, Lille, France Demerval, René Psychology, University of Lille 3, Lille, France Coulon, Nathalie Psychology, University of Lille 3, Lille, France Nandrino, Jean-Louis Psychology, University of Lille 3, Lille, France

Objectives. This study aims at investigating the relations between contextual disconnection (poor quality of transaction person-context), gender, and adolescents' health. Method. 1006 eighth grade students were classified in No disconnected, Family disconnected, School disconnected, or Double disconnected group. We considered three dimensions of the Duke Health Profile: self-esteem, anxiety, depression. Results. Disconnected participants show lower health scores than no disconnected ones. Double disconnected participants show lower scores than simple disconnected parti-

cipants (to one context). Results are different according to gender and contexts. Conclusion. Inspired by the bioecological model, this study shows the interest to consider the adolescents' health in context.

Hemispheric transfer in alexithymic subjects

Casagrande, Maria Dipartimento di Psicologia, Roma, Italy Maccari, Lisa Dipartimento di Psicologia, "Sapienza" Università, Roma, Italy Mereu, Stefania Dipartimento di Psicologia, "Sapienza" Università, Roma, Italy

The emotion-feeling dissociation, which characterizes alexithymic subjects, has been ascribed to an impairment in callosal transfer of information. However, the results are not always unambiguous and they are often found using low sensitive interhemispheric transfer measures. We proposed to evaluate this hypothesis using a Poffemberger paradigm on half alexithymic and half non-alexithymic subjects. Results showed shorter RT in the uncrossed as respect to crossed conditions and an impairment, specific for the transfer from the right hemisphere to the left, only in the non alexithymic subjects, suggesting a specific disadvantage for the emotional hemisphere.

Specific contribution of cognitive-motivational variables to the academic achievement's prediction

Castejon, Juan-Luis Inst. for Developm. Psychology, University of Alicante, Alicante, Spain Cantero, Pilar Developmental Psychology, University of Alicante, Alicante, Spain Miñano, Pablo Developmental Psychology, University of Alicante, Alicante, Spain

This study contrast a causal sequence of cognitive-motivational variables that predict the academic performance: General Intelligence, Causal Attributions, Academic Self-concept, Goals and Learning Strategies. We carry out correlation and multiple regression analysis ("stepwise" and "hierarchical" procedures), taking as a criterion the marks in Maths and Language, as well as the Global Marks. Data are obtained from a 168 student sample, who are studying the first year of Secondary Obligatory Education in Alicante (Spain). The results show a satisfactory support to the model. Academic self-concept, attributions, goals and strategies own an additional contribution in the prediction of the academic performance.

Learning social attitudes: Children's sensitivity to the nonverbal behaviors of adult models during interracial interactions

Castelli, Luigi DPSS, University of Padova, Padova, Italy

The origin of early interracial attitudes is to a large extent still unclear. In two studies, we tested the possibility that White preschool-aged children are particularly sensitive to the nonverbal behaviours performed by White adults during interracial interactions. Children were exposed to a video displaying a White-Black interaction, and the nonverbal behaviours of the White adult were manipulated (e.g., closeness vs. distance). Results confirmed the hypothesis revealing that participants perceived the meaning of subtle nonverbal behaviours and shaped their attitudes toward Black targets accordingly. These findings demonstrate that early interracial attitudes may be influenced by subtle adults' behaviours.

Sexual behaviour in adolescents immigrants: HIV risk analysis

Castro, Ángel University of Granada, Granada, Spain Bermúdez, María Paz Psychology, University of Granada, Granada, Spain Buela Casal, Gualberto Psychology, University of Granada, Granada, Spain

OBJECTIVE. To study the population of immigrant adolescents in Spain, due to they could be infected with HIV and/or they could be taking sexual risk behaviours. METHOD. 218 adolescents (109 natives and 109 immigrants) who are living in Spain, respond to the questionnaire, which evaluates HIV risk behaviours. RESULTS. Immigrant adolescents carry out more HIV risk behaviours than natives, such as not use of condom, drugs abuse, etc.. CONCLUSIONS. Due to differences between natives and immigrants, counseling and information programs aimed at immigrant population are proposed.

Study of social apprehension in primary care and its relationship with the frequency of medical visits and psychosocial distress

Cebrià, Jordi Psychology, Blanquerna Faculty, Barcelona, Spain Palma, Carol Psychology, Blanquerna Faculty, Barcelona, Spain Ferrer, Marta Psychology, Blanquerna Faculty, Barcelona, Spain Ger, Sandra Psychology, Blanquerna Faculty, Barcelona, Spain Domenech, Marga Psychology, Blanquerna Faculty, Barcelona, Spain Segarra Gutiérrez, Gerard Ramon Llull University, Blanquerna Faculty Psychology, Barcelona, Spain Segura, Jordi Psychology, Blanquerna Faculty, Barcelona, Spain

Objectives: To compare the differences in social apprehension between Primary Care patients with high and low level of frequentation and its relationship with psychosocial distress. Methods: 594 patients (stratified random sample) were interviewed and tested with Symptom Check List, and Social Apprehension Scale. Student test analysis and Pearson correlations were used. Results: There are ssignificant differences were observed between the groups(p=0.015). We observed a relationship between social apprehension, obsessive and paranoid thoughts(p=0.000; p=0.000) and anxious-depressive symptoms(p=0.000). Conclusions: We observed a relation between high levels of social apprehension and frequentation in Primary Care. These findings show its relationship with psychosocial distress.

Sexual behavior among Brazilians adolescents: Does religiosity matter?

Cerqueira Santos, Elder Instituto de Psicologia, UFRGS, Porto Alegre, Brazil Raffaelli, Marcela Developmental Psychology, University of Nebraska, Lincoln, USA Wilcox, Brian Developmental Psychology, University of Nebraska, Lincoln, USA Koller, Silvia Instituto de Psicologia, UFRGS, Porto Alegre, Brazil

Objectives: Investigate associations between religiosity and sexuality among impoverished Brazilian youth. Methods: 4078 youth ages 14-24 (M = 16.14; 53.5% females) completed self-report questionnaires at schools and non-governmental organizations. Results: 47% of respondents had initiated sexual activity (M age sexual debut = 14.24). Analyses revealed that highly religious youth were significantly less likely to be sexually active but (after their sexual debut) significantly more likely to engage in sexual risk-taking. Girls scored significantly higher than boys on religiosity and sexual risk-taking. Conclusions: Religiosity is associated with delays in sexual debut, but may increase sexual risk-taking after initiation of sex. Potential reasons are discussed.

Colours' perception in the advertisement of the beverages: A consumer perspective

Cesniene, Ilona Department of Psychology, Mykolas Romeris University, Vilnius, Lithuania Kuzinas, Arvydas Department of Psychology, Mykolas Romeris University, Vilnius, Lithuania

Results of previous research show that visual elements are very important for an effective advertising. However, consumer's perception of colour in advertisements is ambiguous. The purpose of this study was to explore what properties are attributed to different colours and which colours are best suited for advertising of beverages. A

detailed questionnaire was completed by undergraduate students. Respondents were asked to give their views on how they perceive various colours and how they understand handling of colours. The results revealed that different colours are strongly associated with different properties of beverages. Suggestions for future research and practical recommendations are provided.

What happens when students' majors mismatch with career interests? Mediating effects of life satisfaction towards academic burnout and engagement in China

Cham, Heining Dept. of Psychology, Peking University, Beijing, People's Republic of China Jin, Jing Department of Psychology, Peking University, Beijing, People's Republic of China Gan, Yiqun Department of Psychology, Peking University, Beijing, People's Republic of China Zhou, Le Department of Psychology, Peking University, Beijing, People's Republic of China Li, Yanjie Department of Psychology, Peking University, Beijing, People's Republic of China

Objectives Mismatch between career interests and majors was common among Chinese college students. An inventory assessing the belief of students' mismatch in their career interests and their current majors was developed and its relationship with academic burnout, engagement and satisfaction was investigated. Results (1) The new inventory had good reliability and validity. (2) Structural equations modeling showed that life satisfaction acted as mediators between the mismatch and academic burnout and engagement. Conclusions The mismatch phenomenon may impede their attitudes and behaviors towards study. Counseling and educational reforms are called in order to alter the current situation in China.

Role of women in teaching of children

Chaturvedi, Niharika Dept. of Humanities, SRK PG College Firozabad, Firozabad, India

This paper is about the contribution of women to the moral health and uprightness of African society. It begins with a discussion of the role of women as moral teachers in African families and underscores the centrality of women in the moral upbringing of children. As part of their traditional care-giving roles, African women have been in a unique and strategic position not only to produce and sustain life but also to instill socio-religious values and moral standards in the family and society.

Environmental perception and public participation in infrastructural development projects in developing countries

Chauhan, Pawan New Delhi, India Rana, Neeti Dept. of Applied Psychology, EMPI Business School, New Delhi, India

The present paper highlights the environmental perception & public participation in Environmental impact assessment (EIA) process adopted in India. It has been demonstrated that substantive, early investments in public participation can benefit the project proponent, the public and the final plan. An effective public participation program does not happen by accident; it must be carefully planned. A proactive effort will lead to a more effective process and outcome than a reactive, minimalist approach to public involvement. We draw upon the results of the case studies to provide suggestions for improving public participation programs in infrastructural development projects in developing countries.

Generalizability models applied to analyzing reliability of multidimensional questionnaire on medical students' attitudes towards family medicine

Chen, Xiaojuan Educational Psychology, CUHK, Shatin, N.T., China, People's Republic of : Hong Kong SAR Hau, Kit-Tai Educational Psychology, CUHK, Shatin, N.T., China, People's Republic of : Macao SAR

In estimating reliabilities of psychological instruments or questionnaires, generalizability theory (GT) extends classical test theory (CTT) and has its unique contributions. In this study, the similarities and differences between CTT and GT were examined and displayed through an empirical investigation. In the one-facet $p \times i$ UGT design, it can be shown that the generalizability coefficient is equal to the Cronbach's alpha if the questionnaire length in the D- and G-study are the same. However, UGT provides more information than those in CTT. Importantly, MGT provides further information and has obvious advantages in the reliability analyses of multidimensional questionnaires.

Developing test tools to analyze and diagnose Mathematical creativity in junior high students in Taiwan

Chen, Lee-Chou Eduation and Counseling, NTNU, Taipei, Taiwan

The main purpose of this study was to develop test tools to analyze mathematical creativity of elementary students. The findings indicate that?(1) test battery was good in reliability and validity in analyzin mathematical creativity of elementary students; (2) this battery is comprised of novelty, insight, automaticity, analogical thinking and meta-cognitive ability; (3) high meta-cognition students and field-independents scored higher than low meta-cognition students and field-dependents; and (4) mathematical achievement was closely related to mathematical creativity, due to common components in mathematical problem-solving such as meta-cognitive ability, automaticity, novelty and analogical reasoning.

Exploring trend in male body nudity in a men's fashion magazine and male body image in Taiwan

Chen, Sue-Huei Dept. of Psychology, National Taiwan University, Taipei, Taiwan Lu, Hsueh Chao Psychology, National Taiwan University, Taipei, Taiwan Pan, Yuan-Chien Psychology, National Taiwan University, Taipei, Taiwan

Objectives: Male body image has been obtaining more public and research attention to its role in men's psychosocial functions. Such trends could be reflected in men's fashion magazines. Methods: We developed a rating system of six-degree body nudity and applied to evaluate the male figures of the fashion section in a leading men's magazine from 1998 to 2005. Results: A significant correlation between the year of publication and the degree of nudity was found. Conclusions: Exposure to male body in print media is rising up over recent years and may increase its influence in men's attitudes toward their body image.

The effects of B to C website characteristics on female shopping behaviors

Chen, Hsin-Hung Business Administration, NTUST, Taipei, Taiwan Pin, Luarn Business Administration Dep., NTUST, Taipei, Taiwan Chen, I-Jen Business Administration Dep., NTUST, Taipei, Taiwan Kao, Yi-Ting Business Administration Dep., NTUST, Taipei, Taiwan

This article examines what woman perceptions about the website and their responses. The study includes 401 female respondents have experience with on-line shopping. The results showed that woman has different perceptions about the website, and these impact their shopping behaviors and emotional states. The Useful Information dimension has negative impact on woman behaviors. This means all business to consumer website must pay more attention with it. The other two dimensions (Rich Design, Superior Product Quality) are important in the formation of positive emotional states (trust, pleasure, arousal), then impact purchase intention, intended loyalty, satisfaction, and time spent on the site.

Providing psychiatric care to a small and remote Island population

Cheney, Alan Dept. of Behavioral Science, Saba Univ. School of Medicine, Saba Island, Netherlands Antilles
An island of only 13 sq km and 1400 population, the Dutch Caribbean island of Saba is a microcosm of mental health problems found in larger populations as almost all DSM/ICD disorders are represented there. Until recently, however, there has been only one physician and no psychologists serving the island. In this seminar, the two American psychologists now practicing on the island, two Dutch physicians, and a native Caribbean nurse will discuss the challenges and creative solutions being employed to provide psychiatric care to the tiny and remote island population.

The visual mediaculture of a personality

Cherepovska, Natalia psy of mass commun, ISPP, Kyiv, Ukraine
The purpose of experiment was studying of a visual component of the mediaculture of a personality. The sampling composed of 95 persons of 14-15 years old. The questionnaire included questions directed on revealing the criticality of thinking of the teenagers concerning a visual aspect of mass-media. The results of questioning: 26 % pay attention to quality of polygraph images, 58 % - to picture quality of telecasts; 57 % - watch over operator's methods of the filming camera; 78 % - note the technology of using of a beautiful object for the purpose of a manipulation of consciousness.

The relationship between Interparental conflict and adolescents' affective well-being: Mediation of cognitive appraisals and moderation of peer status

Chi, Liping Preschool Education Department, China Women's University, Beijing, People's Republic of China Xin, Ziqiang School of Psychology, Beijing Normal University, Beijing, People's Republic of China
This study examined the mediation effect of cognitive appraisals and the moderation role of peer status in the association of interparental conflict and adolescents' affective well-being based on an investigation of 549 Chinese adolescents from 7th to 12th grades. The results of structure equation modeling showed that: cognitive appraisals totally mediated the association between marital conflict and adolescents' affective well-being; peer status moderated the effect of marital conflict on adolescents' positive affect, but not for negative affect; and the relationship between marital conflict and positive affect showed different patterns for adolescents in different social status.

A factor analysis of the Mini-Mental State Examination in Taiwanese schizophrenic patients

Chiang, Shih-Kuang Dept. of Clinical Psychology, Yu Li Veterans Hospital, Yuli Town, Taiwan Shiah, Yung-Jong General Education Center, Chienkuo Technology University, Changhua, Taiwan Tam, Wai-Cheong Carl Psychology, ChungYuan Christian University, Chung Li, Taiwan Wu, Ming-Hsun International Business, Chienkuo Technology University, Changhua, Taiwan
The Mini-Mental State Examination (MMSE) is a widely used method for assessing cognitive mental status both in clinical practice and in research. Because of its brevity, it has been frequently used to assess cognitive deficits in schizophrenic patients. Therefore, it is surprising that till now only one paper to study factor analysis of MMSE in schizophrenic patients.The goal of this study is to elucidate what neuropsychological domains were measured by the Chinese version of Mini Mental State Examination in Taiwanese schizophrenia. The data has being analyzed. The result and clinical implications of this study will be reported.

Using community studies to improve pupils' environmental perception and cognition

Chilala, Michael Research and Test Development, Examinations Council of Zambia, Lusaka, Zambia
As part of the Outcome Based Curriculum of 2003, the Ministry of Education in Zambia introduced a new learning area, Community Studies. The community studies aims at enabling learners appreciate the immediate social/economic environment and positively participate in the community development process. This presentation explains how the community studies learning area has been used to improve the way pupils perceive the local environment, identify local community resources and explore the environment to positively participate in the social economic activities in their immediate communities.

Predictors of Competitive State Anxiety among Filipino university athletes

Ching, Victoria Graduate School, University of Santo Tomas, Quezon City, Philippines Mordeno, Imelu Psychology Department, University of San Carlos, cebu city, Philippines Untalan, John Hermes graduate school, University of Santo Tomas, metro manila, Philippines
This study explores demographic profile, sports motivation, and athletic coping skills as predictors of competitive state anxiety among Filipino university athletes. A sample of 192 university athletes in two types of sports—basketball and table tennis—participated in this study answered the Sports Motivation Scale (SMS), Athletic Coping Skills Inventory (ACSI-28) and the Competitive State Anxiety Inventory (CSAI-2). Descriptive, t-test of independent means, correlation, and multiple regression analysis are used to establish the significant predictors of CSA among athletes. Implication of the study is discussed. (85 words) Keywords: competitive state anxiety, sports motivation, athletic coping skills, basketball, table tennis.

Evaluation of the design of the packages of Japanese canned coffee beverages using "change blindness" paradigm

Choi, Jeong-Seo Dept. of Design Psychology, Chiba University, Chiba, Japan So, Moon-Jae Chiba University, Chiba, Japan Koyama, Shinichi Koyama Design Psychology Unit, Chiba University, Chiba, Japan Hibino, Haruo Design Psychology Unit, Chiba University, Chiba, Japan
Packages of Japanese canned coffee beverages contain design elements such as brand names and logos to catch consumers' attention. We investigated how much attention each element in the package design would attract consumers by using "change blindness (O'Regan et al. 1999)" paradigm. In the experiment, we presented pictures of canned coffee beverages in the change blindness paradigm and recorded how quickly the subjects could detect changes. The results showed that the subjects detected changes more quickly in the graphical elements than in characters. We concluded that the graphical elements are more salient than characters in Japanese canned coffee beverages.

The Influence of personal characteristics, behavior specific-cognitions and psychological factors on exercise commitment of Thai adult populations in the Northeast

Choosakul, Chairat Health and Sport Science, Mahasarakham University, Mahasarakham, Thailand Taweesuk, Duangkrai Health and Sport Science, Mahasarakham University, Mahasarakham, Thailand Piyasuwan, Suttinee Health and Sport Science, Mahasarakham University, Mahasarakham, Thailand
The author explored the factors of exercise commitment among adult populations at the Northeast of Thailand. A sample of 962 randomly selected with the greater than 20 years olds and completed a survey that included questions about personal informations, and behavior-specific cognitions and psychological factors. Multiple regression analysis suggested that five factors of behavior-specific cognitions and psychological (perceived benefits, perceived barrier, intrinsic motivation, task and ego goal orientations) had significant effect on exercise commitment with 39 percent accounted of variance. These results could be assisted health care providers or educators to establish methods for promoting exercise adherence and commitment behavior.

The support of the existence of preferred landing position in the recognition of Chinese words with high frequency

Chou, Yu-Ju Clinical and Counseling Psy., Nat. Dong Hwa University, Shoufeng, Taiwan Sio, Lok-Teng Clinical and Counseling Psy., No. 1, Sec. 2, Da Hsueh Rd., S, Shoufeng, Hualien, Taiwan
From the perspective of the split fovea model, words are initially divided between the hemispheres when they are fixated.To test the information contour in Chinese words, the present study examined the effect of five positions inter- and intra- Chinese two-character words. (i.e. ??). Equal numbers of nonwords were matched in numbers and made by switching the orders of two characters. (i.e. ??,??). The result showed that the fixation points in the LVF elicit quicker lexical decisions and higher accuracy in word recognition, compared with those in the RVF, and thus support the existence of preferred landing position and Left Visual Field Advantage in the recognition of Chinese words.

Use of symbolic methods to explore the cognitive processes used by people to evaluate a sailing boat

Cian, Luca Dep. of Political Sciences, University of Trieste, Trieste, Italy Cervai, Sara dep. of political sciences, University of Trieste, Trieste, Italy
The aim was to study which cognitive processes are used by people to evaluate (and after purchase) a sailing boat; indeed, people seem to not choose it in a logical way. To test this, we have used, on a sample of 25 potential costumers, Photosort (a projective technique) and Q-sort to elicit the emotional and symbolic attributes. Though the data collected we created a questionnaire which included a self-correspondence test. The result shows that people, to evaluate the boat, is leaded by specific symbols (especially linked with the inside of the boat). So, not-direct methods seem preferable in this field.

Translation and cross-cultural adaptation of assessment instrument for working alliance in child psychotherapy

Ciucurel, Manuela Mihaela Psychology, University of Pitesti, Pitesti, Romania Vasile, Alina Psychology, University of Pitesti, Pitesti, Romania Ionescu, Claudia Maria Psychology, University of Pitesti, Pitesti, Romania Stan, Andreea Psychology, University of Pitesti, Pitesti, Romania Nita, Daniela Psychology, University of Pitesti, Pitesti, Romania
Objectives. The purpose of this study was to adapt an assessment instrument for working alliance in

child psychotherapy on Romanian population. Methods. We started from the Working Alliance Inventory (Horvath & Greenberg, 1989) and we achieved four steps: translation, back-translation, pre-test, statistical analyses (for identifying controversial items and establishing reliability, validity and new norms). Results. The results indicate that our assessment instrument presents a good level of reliability and validity (internal consistency of the subscale: 0.77-0.87). Conclusions. The comparison of the translated inventory with reported data on the original instrument suggests that some differences appeared in the response style.

Genders differences in sexual risk behavior to HIV/AIDS

Claudio, Victor Clinical Dept., ISPA, Lisbon, Portugal Sousa, Paula Clinical, ISPA, Lisbon, Portugal
In this study we compare between genders the attitudes and beliefs, in a cognitive perspective, relation with HIV/ AIDS risk behavior in a population with ages between 15 and 30 years old, in fives Portuguese regions. We tested near 4000 subjects from both sex. We used three questionnaires, with open and closed questions and also with free associations questions. The results indicate some particular beliefs and attitudes related with differences by genders, with implications in the risk behavior. We also present, agree with the results, different HIV/AIDS primary preventive programs.

Conflict behaviour in innovation processes

Clausing, Anne Inst. für Psychologie, Humboldt-Universität zu Berlin, Berlin, Germany Schulze, Anna Dorothea Institute of Psychology, Humboldt University of Berlin, Berlin, Germany
The genesis of new ideas, technologies or products in scientific innovation processes is often characterized by controversies and conflicts. Constructive behaviour in conflicts appears to enhance ongoing innovation processes. Problem-centred interviews (N=45) with scientists from applied and basic research institutes within the field of genetic engineering were conducted and analyzed with quantitative-content analysis techniques. A set of different conflict issues is found to be relevant in innovation processes. Conflict styles depend on the hierarchical positions of the parties and the issue involved. Opponents are primarily described as displaying dominant conflict behaviour while self-descriptions reflect more variation – mainly integrating or obliging styles.

Understanding of the emotions felt by the protagonist of a story: Impact on the meaning of the story

Clavel, Céline UFR SPSE, Université Paris X Nanterre, Nanterre, France Cuisinier, Frédérique UFR SPSE, Université Paris X Nanterre, Nanterre, France
Understanding a story requires specific knowledge about emotions. However the understanding of emotions develops progressively and personal differences can be observed (Pons & Harris, 2005). We can investigate the characteristics of the pupils who correctly determine the protagonist's emotions. 256 children (5th grade) have read three stories whose emotional valence varied (positive vs. negative vs. ambiguous). At the end of each reading, they had to answer questions on the text. Preliminary precautions had been taken (checking the French and reading levels of pupils and of the difficulty of the texts). The children who correctly identified the characters' emotional experience have a better understanding of the negative and ambiguous stories. Their assessment of the valence of the story is much better.

Standardised measuring of informal/non-formal learning in a disadvantaged job-seeking population

Clifford, Ian Research Dept., Ballymun Job Centre, Dublin, Ireland Powell, Lorna Research, Ballymun Job Centre, Dublin, Ireland Whelan, Nuala Research, Ballymun Job Centre, Dublin, Ireland
An Online tool has been developed to quantify informal and non-formal learning in disadvantaged job seekers. Highlighting the learning people acquire in their own community serves to increase self-esteem, self-efficacy and help them choose a pathway to education, training or employment. A task analysis was carried out on time use in order to find out what activities the target population were spending time on and learning from. This EU supported study was informed by social learning theory, experiential learning, emotional intelligence, key competences and rooted in positive, community & diversity psychology. Analyses of cross-country informal learning will be presented.

Passageless comprehension of the Nelson-Denny Reading Test: Well above chance for university students

Coleman, Chris 335 Milledge Hall, UGA RCLD, Athens, GA, USA Gregg, Noel 339 Milledge Hall, UGA RCLD, Athens, GA, USA Lindstrom, Jennifer 354 Milledge Hall, UGA RCLD, Athens, GA, USA Lindstrom, Will 352 Milledge Hall, UGA RCLD, Athens, GA, USA
We examined the validity of the comprehension section of the Nelson-Denny Reading Test (NDRT) by asking university students (n=115) to answer the comprehension questions without reading the passages. Overall accuracy rates were well above chance, and the students were particularly successful with inferential questions. These results raise validity concerns about the widely-used instrument, which may measure verbal abilities (e.g., background knowledge and reasoning) more than the intended construct (reading comprehension).

The Narcissistic Personality Inventory: Psychometric characteristics in a Turkish sample

Coskan, Canan Psychology, METU, Ankara, Turkey Gencoz, Tulin Psychology, METU, Ankara, Turkey
This research is aimed to examine psychometric characteristics of Narcissistic Personality Inventory (Raskin, & Hall, 1979; Raskin, & Terry, 1988) in a Turkish sample. For this aim, after the translation and back-translation processes, data were collected from 500 university students from Turkey. As for the reliability analyses, internal consistency, split-half reliability and test-retest reliability coefficients will be examined. Principle Components Factor Analysis will be used to test for the construct validity, and several related questionnaires will be used to assess for the criterion validity. It is expected that Narcissistic Personality Inventory will reveal satisfactory reliability and validity coefficients in a Turkish sample, indicating cross-cultural utility of the scale.

Causal attributions to academic failure, personal conceptions of intelligence, academic failure, perception of feedback messages from parents and teachers

Couceiro Figueira, Ana Paula IPC, Faculty of Psychology, University of Coimbra, Coimbra, Portugal Lobo, Rita
It becomes pertinent to study features capable of influencing academic achievement. It was our goal to study the existing relationships among causal attributions, personal conceptions of intelligence and the perceptions of the feedback messages given by parents and teachers in situations of academic failure. The participants were 520 students from 5th to 9th grade. One might conclude that there is similarity among the students who ascribe their failures to external, stable and incontrollable causes and those who have static conceptions of intelli-

gence, among those who have indiscriminate conceptions of intelligence, ascribe their failure to ability and receive person-oriented feedback and among those who ascribe failure to effort and receive strategy-oriented feedback

The role of self-efficacy, past habit and action plans in children's fruit intake

Craciun, Catrinel Health Psychology, Freie Universitat Berlin, Berlin, Germany Baban, Adriana Health Psychology, Babes Bolyai University, Cluj, Romania
The study aimed to explore children's motivation to eat a fruit snack in school and test the effectiveness of a volitional intervention based on forming action plans. Data were gathered from a sample (N=233) of 10-year old children. Intention, self-efficacy, previous habit and fruit intake were measured using an adapted version of the Pro Children Questionnaire (Sandvik et al., 2005). Motivated children who formed action plans ate more fruit snacks in school than those from the control group, both two weeks and three months after the intervention showing the importance of using volitional interventions to promote healthy eating in children.

Identity, commitment, infidelity: An organizational study

Crescentini, Alberto Scienze dell'Educazione, Alta Scuola Pedagogica, Locarno, Switzerland Galardi, Annalisa Scienze Politiche, Università Cattolica del S. C., Milano, Italy
This study wants to examine the relationship between personal identity, commitment and potential infidelity in an organizational context. A questionnaire adapted from a previous study was given to four organizations of northern Italy. The most important results are: confirmation of the literature's findings about the role of working identity in the personal identity and about nested identities, prevalence of moral commitment, aspiration to greater career opportunities and to self development, dominant infidelity for economic reasons. Management can play on workers' search for personal opportunities to increase affective commitment and to reduce the economically based infidelity.

Obtaining recommendations for vocational training from vocational interests: An automated algorithm using the inventory of vocational interests of the German Federal Employment Agency (BA-BII)

Crost, Nicolas Psychologischer Service, Bundesagentur für Arbeit, Nürnberg, Germany
The process of obtaining explicit recommendations regarding vocational training from vocational interests is not very well investigated. Therefore a transparent algorithm generating such recommendations was to be developed. 437 professions were rated on 27 different vocational interests measured by the Inventory of Vocational Interests of the German Federal Employment Agency (BA-BII) regarding whether they satisfy them. Recommendations resulting from different algorithms using different processes and weighting of the participants' responses were compared and validated using data from 2831 persons who filled out the BA-BII and specified their desired vocational training. The final algorithm is presented and its properties are discussed.

Conflict management strategies and gender: A qualitative analysis

Cunha, Pedro Faculty of Human and Social Sc, University Fernando Pessoa, Porto, Portugal Correia Jesuino, Jorge ISCTE, Technical University of Lisbon, Lisboa, Portugal
In line with current trends within conflict and gender theories, our research aims to analyse the relationship between gender and negotiation orien-

tation in conflict management situations. Using the critical incidents method we made a content analysis of the data provided by nine skilled Portuguese negotiators (5 female and 4 male) related with the detailed techniques used by them in mediating conflict management in family and labour contexts. The findings suggest that concessions appear as particularly relevant for the conflict management outcomes. Gender might have a significant moderating role in family and in working fields and, more specificaly, when choosing a conflict management strategy, women look more to relational aspects than men.

Can mental images be rotated and examined?

Dósa, Zoltán Dept. of Human Sciences, Sapientia University, Târgu Mures, Romania Séra, László Dept. of Psychology, Kodolányi University College, Székesfehérvár, Hungary Révész, György Inst. of Psychology, University of Pécs, Pécs, Hungary

There are investigations that failed to confirm the transformation of the mental images of ambiguous pictures. Other experiments however, gained evidence that mental images can be transformed and rotated, although not in the case of all subjects. In the present study we examined the role of the practise of mental turning in the transformation of ambiguous images that presuppose the rotation of the reference frame. The experimental tasks involved the practise of turning of two- and three-dimensional objects, as well as mental synthesis tasks. Our findings reveal the transfer effect of practise in the interpretation of ambiguous images.

Children's preference of television programs

D'Alessio, Maria Clinical Psychology, Faculty of Psychology 1, Rome, Italy Laghi, Fiorenzo Clinical Psychology, Faculty of Psychology 1, Rome, Italy Baiocco, Roberto Faculty of Psychology 1, Universita di Roma, Rome, Italy Raffone, Antonino Clinical Psychology, Faculty of Psychology 1, Rome, Italy

Objectives: Recently, it has been shown that many consumer behaviours follow a "long tail" distribution, with a remarkable presence of non-shared choices. We investigate preference of television programs in 4 to 8 years old children. Method: The sample was composed of 1500 children. We obtained data using interview concerning preferred Tv program. Results: There is a considerable dispersion of preferences below 5% threshold of sharing. The preference distribution in our sample follows a long-tail Zipf distribution. Conclusion: The findings revealed that the transition from Gaussian to long-tail profiles of consume-affecting preference are expressed in developmental age.

A multidimensional view of temperament: Correlation between parental reports and observational methodology

D'Ocon, Ana Department of Psychology, University of Valencia, Valencia, Spain Simó Teufel, Sandra Dept. of Psychology, University of Valencia, Valencia, Spain Banacloche, Diana Department of Psychology, University of Valencia, Valencia, Spain

This study is focused on the measurement of infant temperament and analyzes the correspondence between two different assessment techniques: on one side temperamental data obtained by parental reports and, on the other side, observational assessment made by a trained observer on several rating scales on infant temperament dimensions. Subjects in the study were 40 assessed at 6 months. Parents fill out the Infant Behavior Questionnaire (IBQ-R; Gartstein and Rothbart, 2003) and children were observed during a structured episode through the Revised Behavioral Rating Scales on Infant Temperament (DOcon and Simó, 2007). This instrument evaluates ten infant temperament dimensions: irritability, sadness, pleasure; social orientation, cooperativeness, activity; attention, reactivity, soothability and stability.

A dynamic view of temperament: Interdependence of temperament and interactional dimensions

D'Ocon, Ana Department of Psychology, University of Valencia, Valencia, Spain Simó Teufel, Sandra Dept. of Psychology, University of Valencia, Valencia, Spain Trenado, Rosa Department of Psychology, University of Valencia, Valencia, Spain

The aim of the study is to clarify the bidirectional influence of temperamental dimensions and interactional experience. Subjects in the study were 40 children assessed at 6 months. Parents filled out the Infant Behavior Questionnaire (IBQ-R; Rothbart, 1981) and children and their parents were observed during a five minute semistructured play situation through the "Early mother-child interaction coding system" (CITMI-R; Trenado y Cerezo, 2004). The IBQ include following dimensions: Activity Level, Smiling and Laughter, Fear, Distress to Limitations, Duration of Orienting, and Soothability, Vocal Reactivity, Positive Anticipation (Approach), Falling Reactivity, Attentional Shifting, High and Low Intensity Pleasure, Perceptual Sensitivity, Fear, Social Fear, and Sadness.

A study of factor structure of 3, 9 and 14-item per-construct Persian versions of Ryff's scales of psychological well-being in male and female university students

DaneshvarPour, Zohreh Dept. of Psychology, Teacher Training University, Tehran, Islamic Republic of Iran Shokri, Omid psychology, Teacher Training University, Tehran, Islamic Republic of Iran Dastjerdi, Reza psychology, Teacher Training University, Tehran, Islamic Republic of Iran

The aim of the research was to examine the factor structure of 3, 9 and 14-item versions of SPWB encompasses 6 domains self-acceptance, positive relations with others, autonomy, environmental mastery, purpose in life & personal growth. Three competing models for each of 3, 9 and 14-item versions were evaluated using CFA.CFA revealed while the multidimensional SPWB model in the 3, 9 and 14-item versions had an acceptable fit to the data; the hierarchical SPWB model demonstrated a superior fit. The unidimensional SPWB was shown to be an unacceptable measurement model in this sample in the 3, 9 and 14-item versions.

Relation between personality characteristics and electroencephalografic feature in athletes

Danoiu, Suzana Patophysiology, University of Medicine and Pha, Craiova, Romania Danoiu, Mircea Physiology, University of Craiova, Craiova, Romania Zavaleanu, Mihaela Kinesiology, University of Craiova, Craiova, Romania Rosulescu, Eugenia Kinesiology, University of Craiova, Craiova, Romania Davitoiu, Aurelian Psychology, Cartest Laboratory, Tg-Jiu, Romania Badea, Petrica Biostatistics, University of Medicine and Pha, Craiova, Romania

Purpose: To assess the relationship between personality and bioelectric activity of the brain in athletes. Methods: Electroencephalographic (EEG) band was recorded on a EEG machine according to international standards. For the psychological testing we used The R.B. Cattell 16. P.F. Questionary. Subjects: Sample I: 32 athletes (average age 22.37 years SD 2.12). Sample II: 28 nonsportsfellows (average age 19 years SD 2.01). Setting: Romania. Results: Personality characteristics of the athletes were significantly correlated with the higher energetical index (based on Pearson's correlation). Conclusions: Application of the results could aid in the development of better selection and orientation in sports.

Exposure to an evolutionary psychology theory affects moral judgments

Dar-Nimrod, Ilan Psychology, University of British Columbia, Vancouver, Canada Heine, Steven Psychology, University of British Columbia, Vancouver, Canada

The crux of evolutionary psychology (EP) has been heavily criticized on scientific grounds as well as moral-political grounds. Many critics of EP suggested that it contributes to undesirable inequality and sexism in society. Following this commonplace critique, in two studies we examined whether EP arguments affect evaluations of deviant sexual behaviors. Participants were exposed to arguments representing an EP perspective, a social constructionist (SC) perspective or a control prime. Analyses on covariance indicated that participants who were exposed to EP arguments evaluated sexual deviant behaviors more leniently than participants who were exposed to SC arguments. Further analyses and implications are discussed.

The parenting style impact to resiliency and identity status on the late adolescence

Dariyo, Agoes Psychology Faculty, Tarumanagara University, Jakarta, Indonesia

The purpose of this study was to examine the differences of parenting style impact to the resiliency and identity status on the late adolescence. This study used analysis of variance (ANOVA), with SPSS as a tool of analysis. Total 500 research data were collected. Findings that there were the differences of parenting style impact to the resiliency and identity status on the late adolescence. The authoritative parenting style has the significant influence on the resiliency and identity achievement status (than permissive or authoritarian style) on the late adolescence.

Processing non-adjacent dependencies

Destrebecqz, Arnaud Cognitive Science Unit, Universite Libre Bruxelles, Bruxelles, Belgium

Theories of Grammar Learning propose different putative mechanisms: rule abstraction, similarity with stored instances, or sensitivity to statistical properties of the input. These models, however, cannot account for how sensitivity to nonadjacent dependencies is modulated by the variability of the intervening material. Gomez (2002) showed that learning nonadjacent dependencies improves when the embedded material is highly variable. We report on simulation studies that demonstrate that this effect can be accounted for by a Simple Recurrent Network trained to predict the the successor to each element of input sequences. We conclude that statistical learning might be more powerful than previously anticipated.

Clustering e-learning strategies

Diaz, David Universidad Autonoma de Madrid, Madrid, Spain Shih, Pei-Chun Psychology, Universidad Autonoma de Madrid, Madrid, Spain Martinez Molina, Agustin Psychology, Universidad Autonoma de Madrid, Madrid, Spain Muñoz, Dolores Psychology, Universidad Autonoma de Madrid, Madrid, Spain

Using Web sites allows us to design new e-learning environments. We analyze in this study the relations between different e-learning strategies, and two achievement indices: task performance and knowledge acquisition. 189 students participated in Web-based activity. The data were grouped by web navigation variables. A hierarchical cluster and a discriminant function were employed to describe, classify and predict Web navigation patterns. Achievement indices were compared between different navigation groups. We identify Exploratory and Task Oriented behaviors in the activity. Differences between strategies were observed in knowledge acquisition only (t=2.594 p=.012). Exploratory strategy shows better knowledge acquisition than Task Oriented strategies.

Early electrophysiological evaluation of central auditory pathway in patients with alcoholism

Diaz Martinez, Carina Clinical Neurophysiology, General Hospital, Guantanamo, Cuba *Cespedes Fernandez, Pedro Luis* Clinical Neurophysiology, General Hospital, Guantanamo, Cuba *Annia, Diaz Martinez* Internal Medicine Department, General Hospital, Guantanamo, Cuba

Objectives: Explore objectively the neurotoxic effects of alcohol over Nervous System (NS) at the first stages of alcoholism. Methods: 50 patients in the first week after diagnosis were evaluated using Brain Auditory Evoked Potential (BAEP). Latencies were analyzed and compared with those obtained in 50 controls. Descriptive statistic and ANOVA test were used. Results: 48% of cases showed a significant latency prolongation. Conclusions: Toxic effects of alcohol affect significantly the activity of central auditory via. BAEP are useful to reveal dysfunctions when clinical signs are difficult to identify.

Perceived injustice and perceived humiliation similarly influence observer judgments in a conflict situation

Dimdins, Girts Dept. of Psychology, University of Latvia, Riga, Latvia

The study explored the influence of perceived injustice and humiliation on observers' judgments about a conflict. The participants read an essay about one side rejecting a Palestinian-Israeli peace plan. The side and its arguments were manipulated between participants. When either injustice or humiliation was used as basis for rejecting the plan, the participants evaluated the sides' arguments as more legitimate and increased their support for the sides' position. The results were independent of which side was rejecting the plan, and of participants' sympathies in the conflict. The results complement previous findings that collective humiliation is closely related to perceived injustice.

View from preschools in Turkey

Dincer, Caglayan Preschool, Ankara University, Ankara, Turkey *Ergul, Aysegul* Preschool, Ankara University, Ankara, Turkey

History of preschool education in Turkey goes back to 1915. There were 80 preschools, 136 teachers and 5.880 children in 1923, the number of schools, teachers and children increased and reached 20.675 classrooms, 24.775 teachers and 640.849 children in 2007. This article puts forth the numerical differences related to preschool education and documents the changes which have occured over the past 80 years. With a sample from Ankara, this article explains variety of today's preschools, characteristics, quantity, aims and principles. Physical conditions of these preschools will be compared with the ideal conditions and the acquired data will be visually presented.

Psychometric properties of Lithuanian version of the Intelligence Structure Test 2000-R

Dragunevicius, Kestutis General Psychology, Vilnius University, Vilnius, Lithuania *Gintiliene, Grazina* General Psychology, Vilnius University, Vilnius, Lithuania *Bagdziuniene, Dalia* Organizational Psychology, Vilnius University, Vilnius, Lithuania *Zukauskaite, Irena* Organizational Psychology, Vilnius University, Vilnius, Lithuania

Objective of this study was to investigate the reliability and construct validity of Lithuanian version of I-S-T 2000 R (Amthauer et al., 2001). The sample of 1120 Lithuanians aged from 16 to 73 was tested with basic and additional modules of I-S-T 2000 R. Data of item analysis and internal consistency showed the high reliability of the scales. Confirmatory factor analysis supported the original factor structure model. Since differences in scores were found between Lithuanian and German samples, Lithuanian norms were established. Current data showed IST-2000-R as reliable and valid instrument for assessment of reasoning abilities of Lithuanian population.

Development and validation of entrepreneurial competence in Chinese private enterprises

Du, Hong Center for HRM & SM, School of Management ZJU, Hangzhou, People's Republic of China *Xie, Xiaoyun* Center for HRM & SM, ZJU, School of Management ZJU, Hangzhou, People's Republic of China

With reference of the theoretical model, a content analysis was conducted firstly to identify Entrepreneurial competence (EC) elements based on interviewing with 28 successful business owners. After building a conceptual model of EC, 248 entrepreneurs from various private companies had completed a validating questionnaire. The results showed that EC model was comprised of fundamental competences (FC, such as conceptual, commitment, learning, emotional) and dynamic competences (DC, such as organizing, strategic, opportunity, GUANXI); Each of these dimensions showed promising effect on venture performance, but the DC had exhibited higher-level predictability of the venture's growth than FC at start-up stage.

Adaptation and validation of the positive affect and negative affect schedule to Chile

Dufey, Michele Escuela de Psicologia, Universidad Diego Portales, Santiago de Chile, Chile *Fernandez, Ana Maria* Laboratori de Neurociencia C, Universidad Diego Portales, Santiago, Chile

The Positive Affect and Negative Affect Schedule (PANAS; Watson, Clark & Tellegen, 1988) is a brief affective measure widely used internationally. The study sought to evaluate the psychometric properties of the PANAS in its general and present versions, with a sample of 434 undergraduate students. The results are comparable to its original versions, with both scales showing a high reliability (test retest, and internal consistency), as well as an appropriate bi-factorial structure that sustains its validity. Additionally, intercorrelations of the scales with other constructs theoretically related were confirmed, supporting the use of the adapted version of the PANAS in Chile.

Detection of malingering in prepared and unprepared experimental simulators

Eberl, Axel Neurologische Klinik, Lüdenscheid, Germany *Heusler, Marcella* Klinikum Lüdenscheid, Neurologische Klinik, Lüdenscheid, Germany *Schimrigk, Sebastian* Klinikum Lüdenscheid, Neurologische Klinik, Lüdenscheid, Germany

The purpose of this study was to verify the quality of neuropsychological tests and a special simulation-test to detect simulation. Eighty subjects has been examined with different neuropsychological tests and a computerized simulation-test. The countrol and patient group became the instruction to perform all tests as best they can. Both experimental groups got the instruction to perform the test-battery like someone who want to feign a memory disorder. The data-analyis shows that neither the unprepared nor the prepared simulators could mislead the results of the used special simulation-test in contrast to the other neuropsychological tests.

Fast visual stimulus system using LED

Eda, Hideo Photonics Innovations, Hamamatsu, Japan *Kiyohara, Kosuke* GPI, GPI, Hamamatsu, Japan *Eura, Shigeru* Systems Division, Hamamatsu Photonics K.K., Hamamatsu, Japan

Vision research is one of the main themes in brain science. If in charge of a vision stimulus, the liquid crystal display by PC control is used in many cases. However, unlike a cathode-ray tube screen, the display of a high speed is impossible and the liquid crystal display cannot perform exact time control of stimulus presentation. We developed the stimulus equipment using LED light source. This can have the accuracy of a micro second and can choose free arrangement and a free color by selection of LED. This system can also control by the external transistor-transistor logic.

Computer-assisted quality of life assessment in the daily clinical routine of a neurooncological outpatient unit

Erharter, Astrid Biologische Psychiatrie, Universitätsklinik Innsbruck, Innsbruck, Austria *Schauer-Maurer, Gabriele* Biologische Psychiatrie, Universitätsklinik für Psychia, Innsbruck, Austria *Stockhammer, Günther* Neurologie, Universitätsklinik Innsbruck, Innsbruck, Austria *Muigg, Armin* Neurologie, Universitätsklinik Innsbruck, Innsbruck, Austria *Giesinger, Johannes* Biologische Psychiatrie, Universitätsklinik für Psychia, Innsbruck, Austria *Rumpold, Gerhard* Medizinische Psychologie, Universitätsklinik Innsbruck, Innsbruck, Austria *Sperner-Unterweger, Barbara* Biologische Psychiatrie, Universitätsklinik für Psychia, Innsbruck, Austria *Holzner, Bernhard* Biologische Psychiatrie, Universitätsklinik für Psychia, Innsbruck, Austria

Purpose Aim of this project was to implement a software tool for computerized collecting, processing and real-time presenting longitudinal quality of life data at the neurooncological outpatient unit of Medical University Innsbruck. Methods QOL was evaluated with EORTC QLQ-C30/+BN20. For computerized assessment in patients with primary brain tumors a specially designed software tool called Computer-based Health Evaluation System was used. Results Within two years QOL was assessed in 107 patients (48.6% female, age: 47.86+/-12.57 years) at 565 time-points. Conclusion QOL-assessment in the daily clinical routine is feasible and an effective approach for improving neurooncological practice and individualization of medical treatment.

Wisdom and values in older adults

Etezadi, Sarah Psychology - CRDH, Concordia Univerity, Montreal, Canada *Burr, Andrew* Psychology - CRDH, Concordia Univerity, Montreal, Canada *Pushkar, Dolores* Psychology - CRDH, Concordia Univerity, Montreal, Canada

This research investigated the relation between wisdom and values in recently retired individuals. 320 participants (mean age 59) completed a series of questionnaires including the Three-Dimensional Wisdom Scale (Ardelt, 2003), the Portrait Values Questionnaire (Schwartz et al., 2001) and the Everyday Activities Questionnaire (Pushkar et al., 1997). Hierarchical regression analyses revealed that the values of benevolence and universalism predicted wisdom. An interaction between values and value-congruent activity levels also predicted wisdom. Results support the theoretical link between wisdom and an orientation toward the common good, and are further discussed in terms of the connection between wisdom-related knowledge and wise behaviour.

Development and validation of an assessment procedure to identify therapy related interpersonal behaviour of postgraduate student therapists (TRIB)

Eversmann, Julia Inst. für Klin. Psychologie, Universität Osnabrück, Osnabrück, Germany *Schoettke, Henning* Clinical Psychology, Institute of Psychology, Osnabrueck, Germany *Wiedl, Karl Heinz* Clinical Psychology, Institute of Psychology, Osnabrueck, Germany

Aim: Besides technical competence, establishing and maintaining a positive therapeutic relationship represents a therapeutic skill, influencing treatment outcome. The aim was to develop a short rating instrument to identify "pretraining interpersonal competence" of student therapists, which might be related to training and treatment success. Methods: 82 student therapists were judged by 3 clinical experts using a pool of 9 items related to group dynamic behaviours and rank ordered according to their global therapeutic aptitude. Results: PCA suggested one factor explaining 77, 5 % of variance (Cronbach's Alpha α = 0.96). Correlations with training and treatment success have been partially confirmed.

The moderating effect of self-appraised life stress on mood clarity-vital satisfaction relationship

Extremera, Natalio Social Psychology, University of Málaga, Malaga, Spain *Durán, Auxiliadora* Social Psychology, University of Málaga, MALAGA, Spain *Rey, Lourdes* Personality Psychology, University of Málaga, MALAGA, Spain

This study examined the relations between mood clarity, self-appraised life stress and vital satisfaction in a sample of 369 university students. Our hypothesis posits that the positive relationship between mood Clarity and vital satisfaction is moderated by the levels of self-appraised life stress. According to our hypothesis, our results indicated that the link between mood clarity and vital satisfaction was significantly higher for less stressed students. These results provide preliminary support for an interactive prediction model of vital satisfaction involving mood clarity and self-appraised life stress.

Titles' validity and effects on users' mental model

Eyrolle, Hélàne MDR Université Toulouse Mirail, CLLE-LTC UMR CNRS 5263, Toulouse, France *Cauchard, Fabrice* MDR Université Toulouse Mirail, CLLE-LTC UMR CNRS 5263, Toulouse, France

The question of the titles' validity in representing the content of the text is examined in relation with research in cognitive psychology. An exploratory study was carried out with real-life technical documents. Linguistic analyse of the content of the Subject item at their beginning were developed. They led us to consider them as titles. The results showed that the titles were not, in the majority, valid to represent the documents contents and that users globally did not detect this lack of validity. The study led to several proposal for documents design and to new research questions in the area of linguistic-cognitive psychology.

The four factor personality test based on 4 elements

Fajmonova, Dana Qed Group a.s., Prague, Czech Republic *Bahbouh, Radvan* Psychology, Qed Group a.s., Prague, Czech Republic

The four factor personality test based on 4 Elements and its psychometric properties will be introduced. One of the biggest advantages of this test is that people are able to understand the four factors very quickly and use as psychological tool, since it is based on our rich experience with elements in everyday life. We verified this assumption by testing correlation between the real results of the test and the estimation of the factors by tested people. It shows that even after short introduction of this personality model, people are able to make good estimations of their profiles based on intuitive understanding.

Personnel selection process research based on multi-level fit perception assessment

Fan, Wei Academy of Personnel Science, Ministry of Personnel PRC, Beijing, People's Republic of China

Traditional personnel selection focused on individual competency based on person-job fit. But, traditional personnel selection technique can't satisfy the organizational need now. Therefore, researches and practitioners emphasis the impor-

tance of person-organization fit more and more in personnel selection. That means emphasizing on recruiters' multi-dimension fit perceived in personnel selection. In our research, New ASD(attraction-selection-development) perspective suggest a implicit multi-level fit perceived assessment model. Through experimental and field study, we tracked more than 1195 subjects and confirmed the multi-level fit perceived model finally. A Multi-level fit assessment model included value congruence, personality congruence, need-supplies fit and demands-abilities fit can influent person development in different career stages.

The role of dynamic testing in assessing cognition competence of children

Fang, Ping Dept. of Psychology, Capital Normal University, Beijing, People's Republic of China *Cai, Hong* Psychology, Capital Normal University, Beijing, People's Republic of China *Chen, Manqi* Psychology, Capital Normal University, Beijing, People's Republic of China *Li, Yang* Psychology, Capital Normal University, Beijing, People's Republic of China

Dynamic testing can supply hints to the individuals; therefore, we proposed it can assess cognitive potential. This study evaluated 76 normal intelligence children's cognition competences by dynamic and static testing, who were aged 8-11 years. The results showed that: those Low-score and High-score children identified by static testing had no significant difference in dynamic testing, and no significant difference between genders was found. Moreover, dynamic testing improved the validity of exploration to children's potentials. It's concluded that the combination of using dynamic and static testing can reflect the panorama of children's developments of intelligence.

The role of dynamic testing in diagnosing reading disabilities

Fang, Ping Dept. of Psychology, Capital Normal University, Beijing, People's Republic of China *Qi, Li* Psychology, Capital Normal University, Beijing, People's Republic of China *Jiang, Yuan* Psychology, Beijing Sport University, Beijing, People's Republic of China *Li, Yang* Psychology, Capital Normal University, Beijing, People's Republic of China

Dynamic testing supplies opportunities to show what individuals are capable of doing for its guided instruction during the testing process. Therefore, we proposed dynamic testing can diagnose reading disabilities more effectively. 36 children aged 9-10 years participated in this study; half of them were reading disabilities and the others were normal students identified by static test. Experimental results suggested that: the gain-scores of reading disable students weren't significantly different from those scores of normal ones in dynamic testing, however, their gain-scores improvements varied with individual differences. It's concluded dynamic testing can classify reading disabilities children identified by static test further.

Autotelic need for touch, affective response, and persuasion: The moderating role of country-of-origin image

Fang, Wenchang Business Administration, National Taipei University, Sansia Township, Taiwan *Hsu, Ya Hui* Business Administration, National Taipei University, Sansia Township, Taiwan *Hidaka, Yoshino* Business Administration, National Taipei University, Sansia Township, Taiwan

Prior research assumes that the opportunity to touch products increases affective response and persuasion, but it neglects the moderating role of country-of-origin image (COI). This study fills the research gap, using an analytical sample comprising a total of 360 housewives. Using analysis of variance (ANOVA), experimental findings suggest that (1) touch, autotelic NFT, and COI have significantly positive effects on affective response

and persuasion; (2) the positive effect of touch on persuasion significantly influenced is associated with a high level of COI, even if the touch produces negative sensory feedback.

Electronic word-of-mouth and purchase intentions: The mediating role of conformity tendency

Fang, Wenchang Business Administration, National Taipei University, Sansia Township, Taiwan *Hsu, Ya Hui* Business Administration, National Taipei University, Sansia Township, Taiwan *Sung, Kunlin* Business Administration, National Taipei University, Sansia Township, Taiwan

Previous research rarely examines the relationship between electronic word-of-mouth (eWOM) and purchase intentions. Moreover, most studies neglect the mediating effect of conformity tendency in the relationship between eWOM and purchase intentions. The results of this study are based on empirical data from 356 participants, and are generated by the regression analysis method. Results show that eWOM actually improves purchase intentions through conformity tendency. In addition, the notion of conformity tendency holds implications for the theory and practice of psychology.

Desensitization to media violence

Fanti, Kostas Dept. of Psychology, University of Cyprus, Aradippou, Cyprus

The study investigated whether desensitization can occur during a short period of time. 96 college students (50% female) watched 9 violent movie scenes and reported whether they enjoyed the violent scenes or were sympathetic toward the victim. Multiple group mixture modeling was incorporated to investigate how aggressive and non-aggressive individuals responded to the different violent scenes across time. The findings suggested that with repeated exposure to media violence both aggressive and non-aggressive viewers reported less sympathy toward the victims of violence and more enjoyment of media violence. These findings are important because reduce inhibitions toward violence might result in increased aggressive behavior.

The structural validity of the coping strategies questionnaire for teachers

Faraci, Palmira Department of Psychology, University of Palermo, Palermo, Italy *Sprini, Giovanni* Department of Psychology, University of Palermo, Palermo, Italy *Miragliotta, Antonino* Department of Psychology, University of Palermo, Palermo, Italy

The present study is aimed to validate the factor structure that best represents a new instrument addressed to assess teachers' coping strategies. Participants were 260 high school teachers. Self-report 24-item questionnaires were administered during the class break by trained examiners. The hypothesized four factor structure (Problem-oriented coping, Emotion-oriented coping, Seeking Support and Avoidance) was examined using confirmatory factor-analytic techniques. According to the fit indexes, the 4-factor model seems to be an adequate explanation of the data, suggesting that the questionnaire is comprised of four unidimensional subscales. These findings provide evidence for the construct validity of the scale.

Is there a self-concept change after participation in outdoor education programs? An evaluation study

Fengler, Janne Education and Counselling, Universität Düsseldorf, Düsseldorf, Germany *Schwarzer, Christine* Adult Education and Counseling, Heinrich-Heine-University, Duesseldorf, Germany

The objective of the study is to empirically investigate the impact of outdoor education programs on participants' self-concept. In this quantitative longitudinal three-wave study (pre-post-post) 917 adolescents were tested with the Frankfurter Selbstkonzeptskalen (FSKN; Deusinger, 1986 - Frankfurt Self-Concept Scales). Highly significant immediate and sustainable effects can be stated for the whole sample. The comparison between different subsamples gives remarkable insights into the relationships between self-concept change and both person-variables and situation-variables in regard to greatest progress and greatest need for support. The study provides important impulses to target-group-selection and -support and also to learning-objective specific conceptualisation of outdoor education programs.

Psychometric properties of the interpersonal reactivity index in a sample of Chilean university students

Fernandez, Ana Maria Escuela de Psicología, Universidad de Santiago, Santiago, Chile **Dufey, Michele** Laboratorio de Neurociencias C, Universidad Diego Portales, Santiago, Chile

The Interpersonal Reactivity Index (Davis, 1980) measures cognitive and affective components of empathy: Fantasy, Perspective-Taking, Empathic-Concern, and Personal-Distress. In order to adapt it to the Chilean context of university research, a backward translation procedure was used. After piloting and adjusting the items, the scale was applied to a total of 436 students. The results showed an appropriate reliability which is comparable to its original version in English. Sex differences in empathy sustained its validity in Chile, as well as the intercorrelations of the subscales, and the confirmation of predicted relationships with measures of self-esteem, anxiety, and social avoidance.

Service users' views of the benefits of and barriers to mental health research participation

Finn, Erica Dublin, Ireland **McNulty, Muireann** Psychology Department, Cluain Mhuire Service, Dublin, Ireland **Carr, Alan** Psychology Department, University College Dublin, Dublin, Ireland **O'Callaghan, Eadbhard** Psychiatry Department, Cluain Mhuire Service, Dublin, Ireland

The aim of the present study was to investigate the perceived benefits of mental health research, and the barriers to participation, from the perspective of the service user. Participants were 105 service users recruited from a psychiatric service's outpatient clinic. A newly developed Benefits and Barriers Questionnaire (BBQ) was administered. The BBQ demonstrated good reliability and discriminant validity. Benefits included helping others and reducing stigma, while lack of confidentiality and feedback were perceived as barriers. Results are discussed in terms of tailoring research to maximise benefit to both service user and researcher, and reducing barriers to increase participation.

Feasibility and validity of a computer-adaptive test for the assessment of depression

Fliege, Herbert Abt. Psychosomatik, Charité Berlin, Berlin, Germany **Becker, Janine** Psychosomatik, Charité, Berlin, Germany **Walter, Otto** Psychologisches Institut, Universität Münster, Münster, Germany **Rose, Matthias** Psychosomatik, Charité, Berlin, Germany **Klapp, Burghard** Psychosomatik, Charité, Berlin, Germany

A computerized adaptive test (CAT) to assess depression, based on Item Response Theory, was evaluated in clinical application. The CAT, supplied by a bank of 64 items, was administered to 423 patients (78 with depression). Patients' acceptance was assessed. Items are adaptively administered until a reliability of 0.90 is attained. Conventional depression questionnaires and standardized diagnostic interviews (CIDI) were included. The CAT was time-saving, well accepted and reliable after an

average administration of 6 items. Correlations with depression questionnaires ranged between r=0.68 and 0.77. The CAT distinguished well between diagnostic groups. It proved an efficient, well feasible and reliable tool.

Mental health service users: Empowerment through training-EMILIA project

Flores Martinez, Paz Dept. of Psychiatry, Hospital Centre Forum, Barcelona, Spain **Masferrer, Carmen** Psychology, Hospital Forum, Barcelona, Spain **Izquierdo, Roser** Psychology, Hospital Forum, Barcelona, Spain **Palomer, Eduard** Psychology, Hospital Forum, Barcelona, Spain **Ní Laocha, Eithne** Research, Hospital Forum, Barcelona, Spain

Objectives • Training programs based on Lifelong learning(LLL) to empower users, facilitate social inclusion, creation and promotion of access to normalized work. Method: • Training programmes focus on users personal strengths and experience in the mental health services using LLL method. • Target group: bi-polar, schizophrenia, unemployed, users' families, staff. • Five blocks; Personal Development Profile, Recovery/Integration, EMILIA workplace EMILIA jobs Training clinical staff Results • 6 months training completed • 12 users • 4 users incorporated into mental health institution as co-teachers in training programme. Conclusions: • Through LLL training programme users are more empowered

Can blogs tell me who you are? Personality impression based on blogs in Japan

Fuji, Kei University of Tsukuba, Tsubaka, Japan **Yoshida, Fujio** Institute of psychology, University of Tsukuba, Tsukuba, Japan

This research examined the accuracy of personality impressions based on blogs, a growing medium for self-expression. Based on the Vasire & Gosling (2004), self-ratings of blog-authors (n=38) about themselves were compared with ratings of readers (n=38) about author's personality as well as those of author's friends (n=38) on the Big Five dimensions. Although there were high correlations between authors and friends, no significant correlations was found between authors and readers, contrary to Vasire & Gosling (2004). These findings suggest that, in Japan, personality impressions based on blogs are inaccurate and there are cultural particularities of self-expression on Internet.

Relationship between problems and frustrations of students in Japan, Sweden, Denmark and Finland

Fujii, Yoshihisa Iwate Prefectural University, Morioka, Japan

The International Version of Problem Diagnostic Scale and the International Version of Frustration Scale were developed for investigating the relationship between problems of students and their frustrations. Participants were 1827 students(fourth to ninth grades) in Japan,Sweden,Denmark and Finland.The results of multiple regression analysis?there was a close relationship between problems related to Relationships with friends and the demand for security:between problems related to Self-complex and problems related to Relationships with parents and the demand for belonging:and between problems related to Relations with teachers and the demand for approval.

How does the belief in a just world influence attitudes regarding people accused of crimes?

Fukakusa, Mari Dept. of Behavior Science, Hiroshima University, Hiroshima, Japan **Ura, Mitsuhiro** Behavior Science, Hiroshima University, Higashi-Hiroshima, Japan

Effect of just world beliefs (JWB) and trust in institutions (TII) on the attitude that people are presumed innocent until proven guilty was investigated in this study. Participants read a newspaper

article on a target person who was released from custody for lack of evidence and then completed an attitude scale regarding the target person. Results indicated that participants with high JWB and low TII scored lower on positive attitudes compared to those with high JWB and high TII. This finding suggests that people with no TII, but desire to maintain JWB are more likely to punish the target person.

The Wide Eyes of Dyslexics: Indication of increased Mental Effort in Dyslexic Reading

Gagl, Benjamin Psychology, University of Salzburg, Salzburg, Austria **Hawelka, Stefan** Psychology, University of Salzburg, salzburg, Austria **Wimmer, Heinz** Psychology, University of Salzburg, salzburg, Austria

In addition to standard eye movement measures (number and duration of fixations), we measured the pupil size (SR Research Eyelink 1000) of dyslexic readers and and age matched controls (N = 18/18) during reading of the 144 sentences of the Potsdam sentence corpus. Main findings were that the dyslexic readers exhibited much more fixations and that their pupil size was markedly increased after about 200 ms of sentence presentation. For both groups, difficult sentences tended to lead to larger pupil size. The increased pupil size of dyslexic readers is taken to reflect the higher mental effort during reading.

Social competences, positive mental health and community projects

Galinha, Sonia ESE, IPS, Povoa Santa Iria, Portugal **Ferreira, Christina** ESE, IPS, Santarem, Portugal **Quintal, Octavia** ESE, IPS, Santarem, Portugal **Carmo, Ines** ESE, IPS, santarem, Portugal **Vieira, Carolina** ESE, IPS, santarem, Portugal

The purpose of this study is present projects train community in order to implement a personal and social competence health promotion programme. The projects advocate positive menthal health and prevent personal and social malajustment. Participants: 5-16, adult, aging. During the process of adapting, implementing and evaluation, suggestions were recorded. After intervention plan, authors show results and conclusions about.

Functional disability and rehabilitation outcome in neglect patients with and without hemianopia

Gall, Carolin Inst. für Medizin. Psychologie, Universität Magdeburg, Magdeburg, Germany **Hoffmann, Maria** Humboldt-Universität zu Berlin, Institute of Psychology, Berlin, Germany **Michalik, Romualda** Humboldt-Universität zu Berlin, Institute of Psychology, Berlin, Germany **Kaufmann, Christian** Humboldt-Universität zu Berlin, Institute of Psychology, Berlin, Germany **Kasten, Erich** University of Lübeck, Institute of Medical Psychology, Lübeck, Germany **Fydrich, Thomas** Humboldt-Universität zu Berlin, Institute of Psychology, Berlin, Germany **Sabel, Bernhard A.** University of Magdeburg, Institute of Medical Psycholog, Magdeburg, Germany

Two approaches to reduce chronic neglect (lesions older than 6 months) were evaluated in a multiple-baselines-cross-over design. 20 neglect patients with associated visual field defects in 15 cases underwent both treatments for 30-60 minutes daily on a personal computer at home over a period of six months. While one strategy aimed at improving visual exploration the other prevented eye movements and covert attention to stimuli moving to the left was trained. After both treatments detections in perimetry and visual exploration significantly improved. Treatment specific effects were observed in single cases. Improvements transferred to reading speed and vision-related quality of life.

Internet self-efficacy and career Information search on the internet

Gamboa, Vitor Dept. de Psicologia, Universidade do Algarve, Faro, Portugal Inácio, Patricia Psicologia, Universidade do Algarve, Faro, Portugal
The main goal of this investigation is to analyse self-efficacy, on schooling and professional information search on Internet, in students of the 7th, 9th and 12th grade. In this study, we took a sample of 187 students (M=15,01; SD=2,142) from both genders, in which 33,2% are from the 7th grade, 34,2% from the 9th grade and 32,6% from the 12th grade. Multiple regressions analyses (stepwise method) indicate that high levels of Internet self-efficacy on career information search predict a wider exploratory activity. Moreover, the level of self-efficacy increases along with the level of scholarship.

Reactions to the professional injustices according to the level of belief in a just world of Argentinean salaried employees and unemployed persons

Gangloff, Bernard Ciencias Sociais Aplicadas, Univ. Federal da Paraiba, Joao Pessoa, Brazil
The feelings of injustice can conduce to various reactions, some resulting in passivity, others in protest. We wanted to study here if the level of belief in a just world, among salaried employees on the one hand, and among unemplyed persons on the other hand, had an influence on these reactions. Thus we presented, in a questionnaire, different cases of professional injustices to Argentinean workers, differentiated according to their statute (salaried employees versus out of work) and their level of belief in a just world, and we asked them to indicate the reactions that they would adopt. Our results, and their discussion, will be about the different types of reactions induced by our independent variable.

Timing models and second order conditioning preparations

García Leal, Óscar CEIC, Universidad de Guadalajara, Guadalajara, Mexico Díaz Lemus, Carlos Augusto CEIC, Universidad de Guadalajara, Guadalajara, Mexico Alfaro Hernández, Luís CEIC, Universidad de Guadalajara, Guadalajara, Mexico
According to associative models, in a second order conditioning preparation an association forms between CS2 and CS1, so the activation may be conducted to the US via de primary association. Timing models assumes that what is learned is not the association between two events, but the temporal interval between two signed events. So, the organism learns to estimate the interval form CS2 to the US, and it is assumes that this interval is the sum of the interval between CS2 and CS1 and the interval between CS1 and the US. The present work is about this hypothesis.

Effects of continuous and partial reinforcement over the acquisition of a specific criterion of response in rats

García Leal, Óscar CEIC, Universidad de Guadalajara, Guadalajara, Mexico Saldívar Olivares, Gamaliel CEIC, Universidad de Guadalajara, Guadalajara, Mexico Díaz Lemus, Carlos Augusto CEIC, Universidad de Guadalajara, Guadalajara, Mexico Alfaro Hernández, Luís CEIC, Universidad de Guadalajara, Guadalajara, Mexico
Two groups of rats were exposed to a different program of reinforcement: continuous vs partial reinforcement. The rate of responses was not considered as a measure of learning. The rats should wait for twenty seconds after a signal to response and get the reinforcer. If the rats response before twenty second the timekeeper was reinitialized. One group got the reinforcer every time the criterion of response was satisfied; the other got the reinforcer with a probability equal to 0.5. Data

about the acquisition and extinction of the response criterion are presented. Likewise, the distributions of the responses are discussed.

Self-inventory of attitudes and skills of moral and spiritual intelligence

Garcia Fernandez, Carmen Irma Dept. of Clinical Psychology, CCIF, Inc., Guaynabo, Puerto Rico Altieri, Gladys Psy.D. Program, Carlos Albizu University, Guaynabo, Puerto Rico Quintero, N. Ph.D. Program, Carlos Albizu University, San Juan, Puerto Rico
Based on Gardner's conception of Multiple Intelligence, this paper presents the validation and normalization of the Self-Inventory of Attitudes and Skills of Moral and Spiritual Intelligence based on its high congruency with the Ethics of Reverence for Life of Albert Schweitzer. This tool has two subscales, Moral (Alpha Crombach .96) and Spiritual (Alpha Crombach .97); sample consisted of 152 men and women of 21 years plus, chosen by availability. Z / T scores were obtained for each scale. Higher ethic's acceptance, higher score for each scale with significant relationship between sex, age and volunteer work and participant score.

The influence of a valence focus on evaluative conditioning

Gast, Anne Inst. für Psychologie, Universität Jena, Jena, Germany
Examined the role of an evaluative task focus on Evaluative conditioning (EC, transfer of valence of a positive or negative stimulus (US) onto a neutral stimulus (CS) after paired presentation). In two experiments conditioning trials were combined with two equally demanding secondary tasks (Likeability judgment versus judgment on a non-evaluative dimension). As an ANOVA shows, the EC-effect is diminished through the non-evaluative task. This supports the impact of an evaluative focus. Further results indicate that CS-US-associations are established under both tasks. The non-evaluative task, however, suppresses the valence of the US temporarily. If valence is reinstated, so is the EC-effect.

Significant improvement of early reading competencies through differentiated classroom tuition

Gasteiger-Klicpera, Barbara Inst. für Bildungspsychologie, Pädag. Hochschule Weingarten, Weingarten, Germany Fischer, Ute Educational Psychology, University of Education, Weingarten, Germany
163 children were tested with a diagnostic instrument, enabling a differentiation of ability in specific reading strategies (phonological recoding and lexical reading) after 10 weeks of lessons. 100 children participated in a 10 hour support course during their normal German lessons, whilst 63 control children continued to attend their usual lessons. The children in the support groups practiced reading according to a differentiated teaching concept linked to their reading abilities. The results of pre-, post and follow up tests at the end of the school year are reported. The intervention group showed a significantly greater improvement in reading skills.

The dependability of the defensive functioning scale of diagnostic and statistical manual of mental disorders (DSM-IV)

Ghamari Givi, Hossein Dept. of Psychology, University of Mohaghegh Ardebi, Ardebil, Islamic Republic of Iran
The aim of this research is to evaluate the dependability of the defensive functioning scale proposed by D.S.M-IV. One sample including 280 subjects with generalized anxiety disorder(GAD)and major depressive disorder(MDD) and normal persons were selected and asked to complete the defensive functioning and Folkman and Lazarus coping ways questionnires. Analysis of

varianc suggests that there is only significant difference in high adaptive level and level of defensive dysregulation among three groups. The results indicate that the defensive levels can discriminate normal population from clinical one but cannot discriminate clinical syndromes absolutely from each other.

Relationship between intrinsic-extrinsic religious orientation and mental health

Ghobary Bonab, Bagher Faculty of Psychology & Educ., University of Tehran, Tehran, Islamic Republic of Iran Kalantari, Mitra Educational Psychology, University of Tehran, Tehran, Islamic Republic of Iran
This study investigates relationship between internal-external religious orientations with college students' mental health status. Religious Attitude Scale (Khodayarifard et al., 1999) and General Health Questionnaire (Goldberg, 1972) were administered on 500 randomly selected college students. Independent "t" test revealed that college students with intrinsic religious orientation showed less depressive symptoms in compare to students with extrinsic religious orientation (t = 2.11, P < 0.03). In other dimensions of GHQ, significant differences were not found between internal and external religious orientation. Moreover, results indicated that students with higher scores on Religious Attitude Scale were psychologically healthier than other students.

The effect of violent and non-violent computer games on cortisol in adolescent boys

Ghorbani, Saeed Physical Education, Ali Abad Azad Univeristy, Ali Abad Katul, Islamic Republic of Iran Tartibian, Bakhtiar physical education, Urmia University, Urmia, Islamic Republic of Iran
Computer games have become a popular pastime among children and adolescents. Current study includes a report of the effect of these games on secretion of the stress hormone cortisol in adolescent boys. Participants were 50 adolescent boys with age range 17-19. Four saliva samples were taken, that is, before practice (T1), in 15th min of beginning of the playing (T2), immediately after the end of the playing (T3), and 20 minutes after the end of the experiment (T4). The results of MANOVA showed that violent game increases cortisol significantly during playing and its level remain constant in the immediately after playing, but non-violent computer game don't increase cortisol level in participants (P<0/05).

Instrumental leadership: Validity and reliability of a new scale

Gleich, Heike Osnabrück, Germany Rowold, Jens Psychologisches Institut II, Westfaelische Wilhelms-Univers, Muenster, Germany
The full range leadership theory (FRLT) describes transformational, transactional, and non-leadership styles. There exists considerable evidence for the factorial and criterion-oriented validity of this theory. Instrumental leadership adds additional variance in outcome criteria of leadership, over and above leadership constructs of the FRLT (Antonakis & House). The present study explores psychometric properties of a German version of this scale. Three independent studies (N = 840) investigated the factorial and criterion-oriented validity as well as reliability of this scale. Several outcome criteria yield a fuller picture of the effects of instrumental leadership. The results confirmed adequate psychometric properties of this construct.

The role of family in creating desired nutritional habits of children and youth

Glowacka-Rebala, Alicja Dept. of Health Science, University of Science, Poznan, Poland Mojs, Ewa Dept. of Health Sci., Poznan, University of Science, Poznan, Poland Jakubek, Ewa Dept. of Health Sci., Poznan, University of Science, Poznan, Poland

The obesity of children and youth comprises a large problem of modern world. This occurrence is determined by many of factors. To find out main reasons of this problem the research engaged 100 children in preschool-age of 5 years old and 100 children in age of 13-14 years old. Besides children there were in research also engaged parents and protectors of those children. The results of all tests were statistically elaborated and they are one of the elements of complex researches of this topic which are directed on factors of creating wrong, dangerous health habits in family – especially nutritional habits and indicating desired changes.

A study with children on family in animal drawing test (Familie in Tiere Test) by Brem Græser

Goktas, Goksu Clinical Psychology, Ankara University, Ankara, Turkey Erden, Gulsen CLINICAL PSYCHOLOGY, ANKARA UNIVERCITY, ANKARA, Turkey

The aim of this research is to determine, the patterns of family relations, the gender roles,and the perceptions of the kids about their families and how these perceptions reflect to "Family in Animal Drawing Test" According to the aim,a test called "Family in Animal" by Brem Græser was translated to Turkish and applied to 300 kids attending to pre-school and first grades of two primary schools. The data were examined in total numbers and as percentages.The result of the analysis points that some animals were drawn more than the others and this attributes that the animals have similar features. The results were discussed under the theories and studies related to the literature.

Suicide attempts during adolescence: An identity quest?

Goldsztein, Sasha Psychologie du Developpement, Universite Libre de Bruxelles, Bruxelles, Belgium Vercruysse, Nathalie Psychologie Clinique, Universite Libre de Bruxelles, Bruxelles, Belgium Duret, Isabelle Psychologie du Developpement, Universite Libre de Bruxelles, Bruxelles, Belgium

The objective of this clinical study is to explore the ways in which adolescents who attempted suicide imagine their family bonds and picture themselves in their genealogical trees. Imaginary and free genograms, and a semi-directed interview, were administered to18 adolescents hospitalized after several suicide attempts. Results show that suicidal attempts during adolescence should be understood in the context of interactive transgenerational family processes. Specifically, they indicate that suicidal attempts during adolescence could, in some cases, be understood as growth-producing or resilient behaviors, and not necessarily explained as a deliberate will to die but rather by a true wish to exist.

Interference between cues needs a causal frame

González Martín, Estrella Málaga, Spain Luque, David Departamento Psicología Básica, Universidad de Málaga, Málaga, Spain Cobos, Pedro L. Departamento Psicología Básica, Universidad de Málaga, Málaga, Spain López, Francisco J. Departamento Psicología Básica, Universidad de Málaga, Málaga, Spain

We examined whether interference-between-cues (IbC) could be caused by associative mechanisms, and be independent of causal reasoning processes. This was achieved by testing participants in two conditions: 1) a causal-scenario condition, in which a diagnostic causal scenario was provided through instructions to make sense of the relationships programmed between cues and outcomes; 2) and a non-causal-scenario condition, in which no causal scenario was provided through instructions. IbC was only found in the causal-scenario condition. This result is consistent with causal reasoning models of causal learning and raises important difficulties for associative explanations of IbC.

Social dominance, values and sexism in a sample of Venezuelan students

Gonzalez Castro, Jose Luis Ciencias de la Educación, Universidad de Burgos, Burgos, Spain Oliveros, María Alejandra Psicologia, Universidad Nacional Abierta, San Cristobal, Venezuela

With a sample of Venezuelan students (n=300) we will test the relationships between values (measured using Schwartz's PVQ scale), Social Dominance Orientation (Pratto et al) and a series of measures of neosexism (Tougas et al) and ambivalent sexism (Glick & Fiske). Results show adequate psychometric values for the scales. As expected, those who stress more conservative values tend to endorse more ambivalent sexism, whilst those who propose more universalistic values tend to be less sexist. Social Dominance Orientation also is an important variable in explaining neosexism results. Gender differences will also be presented.

Values and preference for ethical products

Grankvist, Gunne Dept. of Social and Behavioral, University West, Trollhattan, Sweden

Objectives Investigate associations between importance attached to values and preference for ethical (fair trade labelled) alternatives. Method Data was collected by questionnaires. A total of 99 Swedish high school students participated on a voluntary basis. Mean age was 17.9 (S.D. = 0.64). Importance attached to values was measured by the List of Values scale. Associations between values and preference were calculated by use of Spearman rank-order correlation coefficient. Results Rate values "Warm relationships with others" or "Self-fulfillment" as more important was statistically significantly associated with being more positive towards ethical (fair-trade labelled) alternatives. Correlations were 0.26 and 0.24 respectively.

Factors of perfectionism in adolescent football players

Greblo, Zrinka Faculty of Kinesiology, University of Zagreb, Zagreb, Croatia Bosnar, Ksenija Faculty of Kinesiology, University of Zagreb, Zagreb, Croatia Sporis, Goran Faculty of Kinesiology, University of Zagreb, Zagreb, Croatia

With aim to verify two-factor model of perfectionism in athlete population, the sample of 167 junior players of first Croatian football league clubs were given 40-items Positive and negative perfectionism scale by Lauri Korajlija (2004). Two component analyses were done on the matrix of item correlations. First analysis was done with fixed number of two factors. The results indicated that factors are corresponding to those obtained in school surrounding, but are not identical. Second hierarchical factor analysis showed two factors at the third level more complexly defined than those theoretically proposed, which can be explained by specific sport context.

Antonovsky's sense of coherence theory and mental disorder

Griffiths, Chris Mental Health, Middlesex University, Coventry, United Kingdom

This poster presents Antonovsky's sense of coherence theory in relation to mental disorder and mental health recovery. The reader will be given a description of relevant aspects of the EU's EMILIA project. The poster will show how sense of coherence theory has relevance in understanding the existence, development, treatment of and coping with mental disorder. The results of this research endorse care and treatment for those with mental disorder that is based on salutogenic principles. They also point to the application of this theory in areas such as early intervention and recovery.

Semiotic analysis of Bradesco Seguros publicity campaign "We take good care of everything you care for"

Grubits, Sonia Dept. of Psychology, Dom Bosco Catholic University, Campo Grande, Brazil Paula Pessôa, Luis Alexandre Grubits de Dept. of Psychology, PUCRJ, Campo Grande, Brazil Pessoa, Diana Luz Dept. of Psychology, USP, Campo Grande, Brazil

This work contributes for a better understanding of the engenderment of the consumption ideology on the individuals and the society, using as the starting point the analysis of marketing discourse and its potential effects on the consumer's behavior.In the light of the French approach to discursive-semiotics, an attempt was made to point out the senses derived from the publicity campaigns and to reveal their role on the designers' manipulative strategies on the consumers.The results showed that sense effects produced by the campaigns are coherent to the advertisers' objectives, with eminence on the support of the brands emotional attributes.

Pregnancy in adolescence: Repercussions and the partner's expectations

Grubits Freire, Heloisa Bruna Dept. of Psychology, Dom Bosco Catholic University, Campo Grande, Brazil Silva, Melissa Cristina Dept. of Psychology, Dom Bosco Catholic University, Campo Grande, Brazil Cabral, Zuleide Dept. Gynecology and Obstetric, Univ.Federal do Mato-Grosso, Campo Grande, Brazil

Goal: To know the psychological-social-cultural expectations and repercussions of the pregnant girls' partner attended at the prenatal clinic specialized on the attendance of adolescents. Methodology: 35 half-structured interviews were made with adolescents' partners during their pre-natal consults. Conclusions: The paternity in this group has not occasioned the suspension of the studies, nor the acceleration of the ingression in the work market. The data points as well the lack of dialogue and sexual guidance between parents and children, knowledge and inadequate use of contraception methods and that the partner's pregnancy is well received by the couple and relatives.

Reacting to perceived prejudice: The moderating role of the actor's social beliefs and prior contact

Guan, Yanjun Psychology, Chinese University Hong Kong, Hong Kong, China, People's Republic of : Hong Kong SAR Bond, Michael Psychology, Chinese University Hong Kong, Hong Kong, China, People's Republic of : Macao SAR Zhang, Zhiyong Psychology, Peking University, Beijing, People's Republic of China Deng, Hong Psychology, Peking University, Beijing, People's Republic of China

This study examined the moderating effects of personal contact and social beliefs on the relation between inter-group outcomes. Results showed that for Mainland Chinese who have had prior contact experience with the Hong Kong Chinese, the relation between reflected prejudice and the intention to interact was stronger than for those without such experience. For those Mainland Chinese without experience of contact with Hong Kong Chinese, the relation between these inter-group outcomes was moderated by their "Spiritual Transcendence" beliefs. These results were discussed in terms of the function of worldview and the uncertainty reduction effects of contact with out-group members.

The professional development of Sardinian psychologists: Analysis of present trends

Guicciardi, Marco Ordine Psicologi Sardegna, Cagliari, Italy Garau, Tullio Ordine Psicologi Sardegna, Ordine Psicologi Sardegna, Cagliari, Italy Mura, Federico CDLS Psicologia, CDLS Psicologia, Cagliari, Italy Murranca, Antonella Ordine Psicologi Sardegna, Ordine Psicologi Sardegna, Cagliari, Italy

Soriga, Antonello *Ordine Psicologi Sardegna, Ordine Psicologi Sardegna, Cagliari, Italy*
To explain the improvement of the vocations in psychology and analyze the areas of professional development in Italy, several researches are conducted in regional contexts, for example, in Liguria and Emilia Romagna, Lombardy and Lazio. The present research examines in Sardinia the educational path, skills and professional status of chartered psychologist. Through a multiple correspondence analysis we have evaluated the different professional fields in which the psychological competencies in Sardinia are developing. Obtained results can give useful information for professional and educational guidance of young graduates in psychology and potential students, in order to make conscious career choices.

The imaginary audience, personal fable and pathological internet use of Chinese adolescents
Guo, Fei *Inst. of Developm. Psychology, Institute of Psychology, CAS, Beijing, People's Republic of China* **Lei, Li** *Social Psychology, Institute of Psychology,Renmin, Beijing, People's Republic of China*
This research examined the relations between the imaginary audience, personal fable, preference of the Internet social service and pathological Internet use (PIU) among Chinese adolescents. Results from 689 adolescents indicate that (1) the preference of the Internet social service has a direct positive effect on PIU; (2) the imaginary audience significantly influence PIU; (3) the imaginary audience has a indirect positive effect on PIU through the preference of the internet social service; (4) both the omnipotence and the invulnerability of personal fable have indirect influences on PIU through the preference of the internet social service.

Reading and spelling patterns in bilingual dyslexic children
Gupta, Ashum *Psychology, University of Delhi, Delhi, India*
The present study aims to analyze the reading and spelling patterns of bilingual dyslexic readers in Hindi and in English. The participants were 30 right- handed dyslexic readers. Word reading and spelling tasks in Hindi and English were devised. The findings indicated that in case of word reading, the dyslexic readers were more accurate in Hindi than in English. Hindi reading accuracy was significantly greater than Hindi spelling accuracy while there was no significant difference between English word reading and word spelling accuracy. In both the languages, reading and spelling errors produced were predominantly nonword than word errors.

Relationship between metacognition, anxiety and depression among mothers of deaf and normal children
Hakim Javadi, Mansour *Dept. of Psychology, Guilan University, Rasht, Islamic Republic of Iran*
purpose of this study was investigate the relationship among metacognition, anxiety and depression in mothers of deaf and normal children.50 deaf children mothers and 50 normal ones selected in a random method.MCQ-30 and (TAI) and BECK inventory were administered. there were significant differences between two groups of mothers in anxiety and depression with control of age. Depression of mother of deaf children were very higher than mothers of normal ones. in metacognition means of two groups were analogous. Anxiety variable had meaningful relationship with depression and metacognition. results showed that metacognition had meaningful relationship with depression in two groups but was not meaningful with anxiety in mothers of deaf children.

The efficacy of assertiveness training amount of social phobia and assertiveness in people with visual impairment (low vision, blindness)
Hakim Javadi, Mansour *Dept. of Psychology, Guilan University, Rasht, Islamic Republic of Iran*
we investigate on affectivess of assertiveness training on assertiveness and social phobia in people with visual impairment. analysis of variance showed that the rate of social phobia decreased in all groups (but significantly more in training group)after training course. while the rate of assertiveness skill increased in all three groups and this rate of increasing was not different from control groups. the results showed that by considering social phobia variable, the assertiveness workshop was more effective than text but about assertiveness skill the effects of two ways were the same. Considering the outcomes, assertiveness training program was affective on decreasing the rate of social phobia in people with visual impairment.

Is opinion about energy efficiency linked to values?
Hammer, Beatrice *ICAME, EDF-R&D, Clamart Cedex, France* **Wach, Monique** *DYRESO, CMH, Clamart cedex, France*
Using the results of an international survey conducted in 2007 in six countries (France, Germany, Great Britain, Sweden, Italy, Czech Republic) on national samples (1000 in each country) including questions about energy efficiency and values, we propose to check whether a link can be drawn between opinion towards energy efficiency and the importance one gives to values (Schwartz's PVQ plus two additional values). To analyse this link, we use regression and correspondence analysis. We find that being in favour of energy efficiency goes together with giving a higher importance to Universalism, and a lower importance to Hedonism.

Remembering advertisements leads to forgetting other advertisements
Hanita, Kenji *Dept. of Social Sciences, Hitotsubashi University, Tokyo, Japan* **Murata, Koji** *Social Sciences, Hitotsubashi University, Kunitachi, Tokyo, Japan*
Previous research has demonstrated that the act of retrieving can prompt the inhibition of related items in memory. We examined this phenomenon, retrieval-induced forgetting, on perception of product advertisements. Participants learned printed advertisements for several categories, and then practiced retrieving a subset of advertisements. After some delay, participants were asked to recall as many advertisements as possible. In general, results showed a significant pattern of retrieval-induced forgetting. Also, it was shown that some participants' attributes could moderate this effect. Implications to research on forgetting and possible influence on consuming behavior of these findings were discussed.

Taboos and value conflicts: Styles of cognitive processing in moral decision making
Hanselmann, Martin *Inst. für Psychologie, Universität Zürich, Zürich, Switzerland* **Tanner, Carmen** *Psychologisches Institut, Universitaet Zuerich, Zuerich, Switzerland*
Sacred values (SV) refer to the phenomenon that people often hold certain values or attributes as absolute. Based on findings that SV can facilitate decision making, we analyzed the underlying style of information processing. Utilizing several decision tasks, we examined the effect of SV on information processing (e.g., assessed by sensitivity to argument strength) and decision difficulty. Tasks promoted heuristic processing and were perceived as easy when they involved one single SV. However, when tasks involved conflicting SV, they promoted systematic processing and high decision difficulty.

In conclusion, information processing in moral decision making strongly depends on situational factors.

Life events, online games and pathological internet use of Chinese early adolescents
Hao, Chuanhui *Beijing, People's Republic of China* **Lei, Li** *Institute of Psychology, Beijing, People's Republic of China*
The physical and psychological development of adolescents makes them suffer much special stress which may correlate with their internet use behavior. This study explored the relationship of life events, online games and pathological internet use(PIU) in Chinese adolescents. With questionnaires, 316 early adolescents participated in the research and the results indicated that subjective and objective stress of life events can predict PIU directly and positively. Moreover, online games could predict PIU positively. Finally, online games partially mediated the relationship of objective stress and PIU in Chinese adolescents.

Loneliness, self-regulation and pathological internet use of Chinese early adolescents
Hao, Chuanhui *Beijing, People's Republic of China* **Lei, Li** *Institute of Psychology, Beijing, People's Republic of China*
With the rapid development of internet in China, as a two edged sword, it's leading to some problems, one of which is Pathological Internet Use(PIU) among adolescents. According to CNNIC(China Internet Network Information Center), there has been about 162 million internet users in China until July 2007, and the percentage of adolescent internet users under 18 years old is 17.7%, about 28.7 million. This study examined the effects of loneliness and self-regulation on PIU in Chinese early adolescents. The results indicated that self-regulation could directly, negatively predict PIU. Loneliness could predict PIU through self-regulation indirectly.

Studies of the influence of parents and teachers' interaction on students' psychological health and learning qualities
Hao, Ruoping *Dept. of Education, Taiyuan Teachers College, Taiyuan, People's Republic of China*
We invite 1,581 people (712 parents, 347 teachers, and 522 students) to take part in this experiment. The result is: the parents' three-dimensional interactions (cognition, emotion and strategy) of the experimental class are much better than that of the ordinary class; the psychological health, learning qualities and every other factor of the experimental class are higher than the ordinary class; and the relationships between teachers and students, parents and children and ways of teaching and training of the experimental class are better. Key words: parents and teachers' interaction; psychological health; learning qualities; training

Exploring the nature of attitudes towards career mothers: A look at the Canadian academic work environment
Harriman, Rebecca *Dept. of Psychology, University of Saskatchewan, Saskatoon, Canada*
Qualitative accounts suggest that career mothers often perceive negative attitudes and subtle forms of discrimination at work; what is not known is the nature or content of these attitudes. The research conducted addressed this issue through the development of a scale designed to measure contemporary attitudes toward career mothers. Items for the Career Mothers Inventory (CMI) were generated and subsequently distributed via an Internet questionnaire. Two Prairie province universities (faculty) were sampled. Respondents (N=287) indicated their endorsement of negative attitudes toward career mothers. The items were then

analysed and reduced via factor analysis. Results and future directions are discussed.

A study of the psychological traits on being injured athletes

Hashimoto, Taiko Clinical Psychology, Obirin University, Machida-shi, Japan

Researcher investigated psychological traits of injuerd athletes useing Baume test, SCTand Attachment scale. The group which was a presence of being injured in sports showed emotionally unstable and had dificult in having good relations with their parents and coach.It is important psychological support systems for athletes in order to prevent from being injury.

Stimulus generalization in evaluative conditioning

Hayashi, Mikiya Fuculty of Human Sciences, Matsuyama Shinonome College, Matsuyama, Ehime, Japan

An experiment was conducted to examine the effect of the stimulus generalization in evaluative conditioning. In the acquisition phase, country names were repeatedly paired with positive or negative adjectives. In the test phase, pictures of national flags corresponded to country names used in the previous phase were presented as prime stimuli for SOA 300 emotional priming procedure. Participants were required to make evaluative judgements for positive and negative Japanese logographs presented immediately after prime stimuli. Response latencies for logographs were measured. The analysis for latencies revealed significant emotional priming effect. Results showed that semantic generalizaion phenomenon occurred in evaluative conditioning.

The double-deficit hypothesis in Spanish children with Dyslexia

Hernandez Valle, Isabel Developmental & Educational, Faculty of Psychology, La Laguna, Spain Jimenez Gonzalez, Juan E. Developmental and Educational, Faculty of Psychology, La Laguna, Santa Cruz Tenerife, Spain Rodriguez, Cristina Developmental and Educational, Faculty of Psychology, La Laguna, Santa Cruz Tenerife, Spain Guzman Rosquete, Remedios Didactic Educ. Investigation, Faculty of Education, La Laguna, Santa Cruz Tenerife, Spain Diaz Megolla, Alicia Developmental and Educational, Faculty of Psychology, La Laguna, Santa Cruz Tenerife, Spain

The objective of this study was to explore the Double Deficit Hypothesis of developmental dyslexia in a sample of Spanish children between the ages of 7 and 12 years. Four groups were formed based on their performance in phonemic awareness and naming speed, and compared on measures of lexical access, fluency, orthographic abilities and reading comprehension. The results are partially consistent with the predictions of the Double Deficit Hypothesis. It is concluded that, in Spanish, naming speed is more important than phonological processing for some aspects of reading as fluency, orthographic skills or reading comprehension.

Listening to music affects performance and psychophysiological changes in sport

Horikawa, Masami Dept. of Psychology, Kwansei Gakuin University, Nishinomiya, Japan Yagi, Akihiro psychology, Kwansei Gakuin University, Nishinomiya, Japan Ukita, Jun psychology, Kwansei Gakuin University, Nishinomiya, Japan

Many athletes and sports teams adopt listening to music for a performance gain and maintenance when they feel pressure. It is thought that a feeling is guided by listening to music and lets psychophysiological changes occur, and affects performance. In this study, we examine whether listening to music affects performance and psychophysiological changes. Therefore we operate pressure by instruc-

tion and use the number of the lacrosse goal success, State-Trait Anxiety Inventory rating, Multiple Mood Scale rating and the number of heartbeat.

Inequity enhancing rejection of unfair offers: Comparison of the ultimatum, impunity, and private impunity games

Horita, Yutaka Graduate School of Letters, Hokkaido University, Sapporo, Japan Yamagishi, Toshio Graduate School of Letters, Hokkaido University, Sapporo, Hokkaido, Japan

Previous ultimatum game (UG) studies have revealed that recipients reject unfair allocation to reduce inequality. To investigate another reason, we compared rejection rates between the UG, the impunity game (IG) and the private impunity game (PIG). In the IG and PIG, rejection enhances inequality. Moreover, in the PIG, partners don't know that recipients have the option to reject. Rejection rates in the IG and PIG were about half of the UG, suggesting that maintaining self-image plays an important role in the UG. In this presentation, we will show the results of second experiment in which the procedure was changed.

The finitude belief scale: Exploration of general beliefs about how human is limited

Huen, Jenny M.Y. Dept. of Psychology, Chinese Univer. of Hong Kong, Hong Kong, China, People's Republic of : Hong Kong SAR Mak, Winnie W. S. Department of Psychology, Chinese Univeristy of HongKong, New Territories, China, People's Republic of : Macao SAR

The present study explored a new psychological construct known as human finitude (the awareness of how human is limited in different aspects of human functioning). Finitude Belief Scale (FBS) was developed by polling open-ended responses on human limitations from the general public through qualitative content analysis. Subsequent validation of the FBS in another sample reported adequate reliability and validity. Factor analyzes revealed these finitude beliefs to fit into a five-factor structure. Implication of finitude beliefs will be discussed in terms of a new potential model of individual differences in social cognition, through a nomological network with other related individual-difference constructs.

Intergroup contact: The case of Cyprus

Husnu, Senel Dept. of Psychology, Eastern Mediterranean Univ., Magosa, Cyprus Mertan, Biran Psychology, Eastern Mediterranean Universi, Magosa, Cyprus Rustemli, Ahmet Psychology, Eastern Mediterranean Universi, Magosa, Cyprus

The aim of the current study was to determine the effects of intergroup contact by measuring the outgroup attitudes of Turkish Cypriots toward Greek Cypriots in the Cyprus context. A questionnaire of positive and negative adjectives was administered to two different samples of Turkish Cypriots throughout two periods of sociopolitical change on the island. Results showed that the opportunity for contact with the partial opening of the borders between North and South Cyprus, led to a significant decline in positive attitudes; accompanied by an increase in negative attitudes. The implications for intergroup contact and relations within a contextual framework are further discussed.

How we perceive people's excuses

Ida, Masashi Dept. of Human Science, Tokiwa University, Mito, Japan

How do people explain their conduct that could be criticized by others? Cluster analysis was applied to classify types of such "excuses." Participants in the study were 90 university students who were asked to evaluate using the SD method impressions on 18 published examples of excuses or explanations.

They could be classified into three clusters–"denying intentionality," "evading responsibility" and "justification." The categories achieved through the method of quantitative psychology are similar to those suggested by Semin and Manstead (The Accountability of Conduct, Academic Press, 1983)

A review of Japanese psychological studies on Japanese comics: The first step to materialize 'manga-psychology'

Ieshima, Akihiko Graduate School of Education, Kyoto University, Kyoto, Japan

The aim of this paper was twofold: first, I reviewed relevant research on typical Japanese comics (so-called "manga") in recent psychological studies in Japan; then I explored the impact of manga on development. The presentation will include a review of relevant literature, which makes it clear that it is necessary to study the impact of reading manga from a viewpoint of psychology. I will introduce research undertaken in this study. Twenty university students who grew up with manga participated in a semi-structured interview and talked about their experiences regarding manga.

Tip-of-the-tongue states and aging: Does vocabulary have any effect?

Ijuin, Mutsuo of Gerontology, Tokyo Metropol Institute, Tokyo, Japan Kondo, Tadahisa Communication Science Labs., NTT Corporation, Kanagawa, Japan Shimanouchi, Aki Psychology, Meiji Gakuin University, Tokyo, Japan Sato, Shinichi Psychology, Meiji Gakuin University, Tokyo, Japan

The tip-of-the-tongue (TOT) states were compared in younger and older adults. An experiment was conducted in two age groups, twenty-five young adults (18-20 years old) and twenty-eight old adults (65-84 years old), controlled for group differences in WAIS-III vocabulary scores. The participants were requested to name 320 pictured objects or motions with high or low frequency names to elicit TOTs. The results revealed that the age-related increase in TOTs was not because of increased vocabulary but because of the general breakdowns in the word retrieval systems of older adults. Two theoretical views: decrement view and incremental-knowledge view are discussed.

Attiudes toward food, and the role of food in the life in Japanese women

Imada, Sumio Dept. of Psychology, Hiroshima Shudo University, Hiroshima, Japan Hasegawa, Tomoko Department of Human Sciences, Taisho University, Tokyo, Japan Masuda, Hisashi Psychology, Hiroshima Shudo University, Hiroshima, Japan Takagaki, Atsuo Marketing Headquaters, House foods Corporation, TOKYO, Japan Sakamoto, Takashi Marketing Headquaters, House foods Corporation, TOKYO, Japan Koyama, Hiroki Marketing Headquaters, House foods Corporation, TOKYO, Japan Pribyl, Charles Communication & Culture St, Otsuma Women's University, Tokyo, Japan

In the past few decades, there has been a wide-reaching diffusion of fast food as well as industrially processed foods in Japan. In line with this diffusion, perceptions and attitudes about food among Japanese consumers have also changed. We conducted an initial online survey of 2233 Japanese women to examine these changes in detail. Based on the initial results, four hundred of the initial respondents were selected for a second detailed survey. Results are discussed from generational, marital, global and definitional points of view.

The prevalence of reading disability among primary school children in Japan: A school-based screening study using a questionnaire for teachers

Ishizaka, Ikuyo Special Education, Fukuoka Univ. of Education, Munakatashi, Japan Watanabe, Toru Special Education, Miyagi University of Education, Sendaishi Aobaku, Japan Hosokawa, Toru Graduate School of Education, Tohoku Uniersity, Sendaishi Aobaku, Japan Tatsuta, Nozomi Graduate School of Education, Tohoku Uniersity, Sendaishi Aobaku, Japan China, Aoko Graduate School of Education, Tohoku University, Sendaishi Aobaku, Japan Suzuki, Keita Graduate School of Education, Tohoku University, Sendaishi Aobaku, Japan Chua, Yi-Lynn Stephanie Graduate School of Education, Tohoku University, Sendaishi Aobaku, Japan

The purpose of this study was to estimate the prevalence rate of reading disability (RD) among primary school children in Japan. The target population consisted of first to sixth grades children in Sendai city. A stratified sampling selected 22 schools of different size. All children were assessed by their classroom teachers using a screening questionnaire. Although 185 (2.2%) of 8510 children were identified as RD or probable RD, only 61 (0.7%) children were satisfied the critical features of RD. The estimated prevalence rate in this study was so small as compared with previous studies reported in other countries.

Attitude, awareness and knowledge towards safety among school children in Malaysia

Ismail, Rozmi School of Psychology, Universiti Kebangsaan Malaysia, Bangi Selangor, Malaysia

This study is aimed to investigate the level of knowledge and attitude towards road safety among school children. The questionnaires used containing several aspects of safety There were 2220 school children (aged between 7-12 years old) involved in this study. Results revealed that generally school children have medium level of knowledge and atitude towards road safety. Demograpical factors such as age, parents income and school location found to be related to their kowledge and attitudes towards roa safety. Student from urban area were significantly more kwnowledgble then pupils of rural area. Whereas children age 9-12 years were significantly higher knowledge than children age 7-8 years.

Developing of "A View in Mind" Scale (VMS)

Ito, Yoshimi Dept. of Psychology, Nagoya University, Nagoya, Japan Kurino, Rieko Psycholpgy, Nagoya University, Nagoya, Japan Obata, Atsumi Psycholpgy, Nagoya University, Nagoya, Japan Takahashi, Michiko Psycholpgy, Nagoya University, Nagoya, Japan Kim, Kyoung Mi Psycholpgy, Nagoya University, Nagoya, Japan Koike, Harumi Psycholpgy, Nagoya University, Nagoya, Japan Araki, Chiharu Psycholpgy, Nagoya University, Nagoya, Japan Tresno, Fiona Psycholpgy, Nagoya University, Nagoya, Japan

The purpose of this study was to develop "A View in Mind" Scale(VMS). One hundred and fifty participants drew a picture of their mental state twice. The VMS was composed of selected words that other participants described freely about their impressions of the pictures. A separate group evaluated the pictures with the VMS. Result of factor analysis revealed 3 factors: neeling(α=.96), matureness(α=.80) and dynamics(α=.77). T-test revealed a significant difference between the first score and the second one(p<.05). In conclusion, drawing their "view in mind" could bring about internal positive changes.

Image focusing (TIF) and Mind View focusing (MVF) as self-help focusing

Ito, Yoshimi Dept. of Psychology, Nagoya University, Nagoya, Japan

Tsubo image focusing(TIF) and Mind View focusing(MVF) in Japan are very unique and effective as self-help focusing. These two kinds of focusing,their characters and their merits are introduced and clarified. Tsubo(Japanese container) image focusing is the method of floating worrisome matters, and putting one matter in one tsubo by dividing them. Then, a focuser enters into an imaginary healing tsubo and is cured in it. TIF can be used as both mini focusing and full focusing. Mind View focusing(MVF) is the felt sense drawing method,feeling one's felt sense and drawing it as the scenary and/or the weather.This is performed twice continuously to produce an experiencing step of inner change process clearly.

Affect of media exposure upon adolescent self-esteem

Jansson-Boyd, Cathrine Psychology, Anglia Ruskin University, Cambridge, United Kingdom Bloomfield, Susan Psychology, London Metropolitan University, London, United Kingdom

This study set out to explore whether there is a relationship between media exposure and self-esteem in UK adolescents. Hundred and nine participants aged 13-14 provided information on their levels of use of TV, the Internet, magazines, and movies. They also completed a Rosenberg self-esteem scale (Rosenberg, 1989), providing measures of global as well as positive and negative self-esteem (Owens, 1994). A significant positive correlation between boys Internet use and their global self-esteem was found (r =.283, n=52, p<0.05, two-tailed) and between Internet use and positive self-esteem (r = .428, n =52, p<0.05, two-tailed). Results indicate that the Internet can aid self-esteem in adolescent boys.

Do materialists feel less good about themselves and have fewer friends?

Jansson-Boyd, Cathrine Psychology, Anglia Ruskin University, Cambridge, United Kingdom Spiers, Rupert Psychology, London Metropolitan University, London, United Kingdom

Hundred and seventy three participants in the UK took part in a study that investigated to what extent social support affect the relationship between materialism and subjective well being (SWB). New sets of scales that measure social support, SWB and materialism were developed. The results showed that there were significant negative correlations between materialism and SWB, and between materialism and social support. A multiple regression also found that when controlling for social support the influence of materialism upon SWB was reduced in strength. Demonstrating that materialists tend to feel less good about themselves but the decrease in SWB is also affected by the lack of social support.

Contrasting the immediate desensitizing effects in two ways of exposing to violent video games

Jiang, Guang-Rong School of Psychology, Huazhong Normal University, Wuhan, People's Republic of China Guo, Xiao-Li School of Psychology, Huazhong Normal University, Wuhan, People's Republic of China

Objectives: to compare the effects of desensitization caused by contacting violent video game in two conditions, active playing and passive viewing games. Method: 44 male graduate-subjects included. Two independent variables were the degree of violence and the way of exposure to violent game. The change of skin conductance and heart rate were adopted as the index of emotional desensitization. Result and Conclusion: exposing to violent video games caused desensitization; the different violence exposures made no difference on desensitization; the active playing subjects had more positive feelings and cognitions about the game compared to the passive subjects.

The relationship between emotion regulation strategy and physiological response of children

Jiang, Yuan Sport Psychology, Beijing Sport University, Beijing, People's Republic of China Fang, Ping Psychology, Capital Normal University, Beijing, People's Republic of China Li, Yang Psychology, Capital Normal University, Beijing, People's Republic of China Chen, Manqi Psychology, Capital Normal University, Beijing, People's Republic of China

In this study, 336 students from grade five in the primary school and grade two in the junior and senior school participate in the experiment. The study analyses the relationship between emotion regulation strategy and physiological response. The results of the study indicate: The changes of subjects with sadness, cognitive reappraisal strategy's physiological response is less than expression suppression strategy's; while those of subjects with pleasure, two strategies have the same efficiency. The physiological responses of female students, primary school pupils, or lower learning level students are stronger than the others.

The predicting effect of achievement motivation and gender for risk attitude

Jie, Li Psychology Department, Peking University, Beijing, People's Republic of China Dingguo, Gao Psychology Department, Sun Yat-sen University, Guanzhou, People's Republic of China Xiaofei, Xie Psychology Department, Peking University, Beijing, People's Republic of China Yin, Zheng Psychology Department, Zhongshan University, Guangzhou, People's Republic of China

For exploring the relationship between achievement motivation and risk propensity, Certainty Equivalents (CEs) of six risk prospects were generated to represent the risk attitude. 110 students completed a series of choice tasks in the experiment. No significant difference of risk attitude was found between subjects with high achievement motivation and those with low. But subjects with different propensity to avoid failure showed significant discrepancy of risk attitude in gains domain. The study suggested that the motive to avoid failure is a more sensitive factor to predict risk attitude than the motive to approach success in gains domain. Moreover, women were more risk-seeking in loss domain under high and middle probabilities.

Representation of four-dimensional spacetime as separate spatial and temporal mental images

Jirik-Babb, Pauline Psychology, Iona College&Montefiore MedCtr, New Rochelle, USA Babb, Richard Rehabilitation Medicine, Harlem Hosp. Ctr.- Columbia U., New Rochelle, New York, USA

Information from events in the spacetime world is carried to the retinae and visual cortex, where left and right representations are processed to form three-dimensional spatial images, while psychological time, which is not detected by a sensory system, derives from holding sequences of events cognitively. Spatial awareness is separately produced by ventral and dorsal pathways projecting from the visual cortex to the superior temporal gyrus, and awareness of subjective time is created by cognitively processing sequentially organized event-information by the medial temporal and prefrontal cortical areas. Thus, actual spacetime is analyzed into mental spatial awareness and time awareness.

Intercorrelations between professional adaptation of students and university image forming

Jivaev, Nickolay Psychology, Yaroslavl State University, Yaroslavl, Russia

Purpose – to reveal intercorrelations between university image forming and adaptation of students to professional work. Due to the subjects are students of all courses to find out the characters and dynamics of intercorrelations. Professional adaptation, professional motivation level, professional identity, emotional and cognitive sphere and other indicators of adaptation were diagnosed. University image and it's departments were diagnosed according to present models of organization image. The influence of university image on professional adaptation of the students was revealed. The process of professional adaptation of the students influencing on the universities image forming on different stages of learning was determined.

No evidence for abstraction with extended exposure in artificial grammar learning

Johansson, Tobias Dept. of Psychology, Lund University, Lund, Sweden

Some theories of implicit learning hold that exposure to regularities gives rise to abstract knowledge that is independent from the surface features of the exposure material. In three experiments, participants were tested on an artificial grammar learning task, contrasting long and short exposure to regularities. The results showed that long exposure did not give rise to increasingly abstract knowledge compared to short exposure. Instead, long exposure was associated with increased knowledge tied to the surface features of the regularities. The results are consistent with a variety of computational models and provide no evidence for automatic abstraction in artificial grammar learning.

Error processing while switching between addition and multiplication

Jost, Kerstin Inst. für Psychologie, Universität Marburg, Marburg, Germany Hahn, Tim Psychiatrie und Psychotherapie, Universitätsklinikum Würzburg, Würzburg, Germany Rösler, Frank Psychology, Philipps-Universität Marburg, Marburg, Germany

We measured event-related brain potentials while 15 participants verified single-digit addition and multiplication problems presented intermixed. Interfering incorrect solutions were either correct for the other operation (e.g., 4*3=7), or a multiple of one of the operands (e.g., 4*3=15). Both types of incorrect solutions were more often accepted as correct than non-interfering incorrect solutions (e.g., 4*3=5 or 17). However, "between operation" errors should demand better adaptation when switching between operations is required. Consistent with this hypothesis, error processing differed as indicated by the "error-related negativity" (ERN): the ERN amplitude was larger for between-operation than for within-operation errors.

Psychology in postmodern settings: Theoretical and practical challenges

Jovanovic, Gordana Dept. of Psychology, University of Belgrade, Belgrade, Serbia

The aim is to examine theoretical and practical challenges psychology is facing in postmoderrn settings. Having in mind that psychology is a fundamentally modern undertaking (its social genesis encompasses the epochal framework of modernity with its fundamental structures - an autonomous individual, social order understood as an aggregation of free individuals, nature subjected to progressive control) and taking into account postmodern questioning of basic modernist assumptions (autonomous rational individual, universalistic claims, belief in progress) it should be examined what kind of implications these changes have for psychological theorizing and practice. Can psychology abandon the individual as it once abandoned the soul?

Biography, personality and behavior: An empirical study on the validity and utility of two online questionnaires as pre-selection instruments for leadership positions

König, Anja HR Consulting, atrain GmbH, Bamberg, Germany Stempfle, Joachim atrain GmbH, Bamberg, Germany Schültz, Benjamin atrain GmbH, atrain GmbH, Bamberg, Germany Hübner, Oliver atrain GmbH, atrain GmbH, Bamberg, Germany

This study investigates to what extent an online biographical questionnaire, an online personality questionnaire and grade point average (GPR) are suitable criteria for pre-selecting applicants for leadership positions, utilizinhg a sample of university graduates (N=109). Significant correlations emerged between the biographical questionnaire and the results of an Assessment Center (r=0.45) and the personality questionnaire and the AC result (r=0.41). GPR was uncorrelated to the AC result. Utilizing the two questionnaires as an entry filter leads to a considerable increase in the number of suitable candidates in the subsequent Assessment Center. Thus, utilizing online questionnaires for pre-selection allows for realizing considerable savings.

State-dependent learned valuation determines food choice

Könnecke, Katja Inst. für Psychologie, Universität zu Kiel, Kiel, Germany Wiesner, Christian Dirk Department of Psychology, Christian-Albrechts-University, Kiel, Germany Ferstl, Roman Department of Psychology, Christian-Albrechts-University, Kiel, Germany

Previous animal studies [e.g. Pompilio et al., 2006] have shown that food preferences reflect the energetic state subjects were in when experiencing novel foods for the first time. Under deprivation food gains a higher reward value and is therefore preferred later on. In the present experiment we used a counterbalanced within-subjects design. Sixteen healthy subjects repeatedly consumed two novel drinks in either a deprived or presatiated state. After a learning phase a forced-choice preference decision confirmed state-dependent valuation. Moreover, the preference appeared to be independent from the energetic state at the time of choice and the subjectively rated valence.

The role of categorisation for implicit sequence learning

Kühnel, Anja Berlin, Germany Gaschler, Robert Allgemeine Psychologie, Humboldt Universität zu Berlin, berlin, Germany Frensch, Peter A. Allgemeine Psychologie, Humboldt Universität zu Berlin, berlin, Germany

Implicit learning in the serial reaction times task is a stable phenomenon over a variety of stimulus-response-formats. Participants implicitly learn an inherent sequence which is, unbeknownst to the subjects, build in the task. In virtually all studies a categorisation or choice between responses is necessary to solve the task. The present study observes if implicit learning takes place when these processes are spared. In four experiments the amount of categorisation necessary to conduct the serial reaction times task was manipulated in terms of the stimulus-response-format and a Go/NoGo manipulation. The results demonstrate the importance of categorisation for implicit sequence learning.

Georgian adolescents' ethnic attitudes, beliefs and personal values

Kacharava, Tea General Psychology, Institute of Psychology, Tbilisi, Georgia

Georgian adolescents' ethnic attitudes, beliefs and personal values Tea Kacharava Institute of Psychology, Tbilisi, Georgia Objectives To reveal ethnic stereotypes toward various nations; "Ours" and "Others" in the context of "important" nations; Attitudes and beliefs toward countries future and present; Methods "Repertory Grid" method; Incomplete sentences; Free-response scenarios; Sociometry (quantitative method for measuring social relationships); Participants 50 adolescents of 15-16 years old from public school in Tbilisi; Type of statistical analysis Content analysis; SPSS (average evaluations, frequency); Results In most cases religious similarity factor determines members in "our" group; Positive image of Europeans comparing with Americans or Russians exposed by Georgian participants can be examined as a striving toward the EU.

Gender differences in beliefs about driving skills for male and female drivers

Kamenov, Zeljka Department of Psychology, University of Zagreb, Zagreb, Croatia Pleic, Neda Department of Psychology, University of Zagreb, Zagreb, Croatia

The aim of this study was to examine the existence of gender differences in beliefs about male and female driving skills: perceptual motor skills and safety concerns. Participants were 443 graduate students, average age of 33. Contrary to our expectations, overall results on the driver skill inventory showed women to be better drivers. There was an evident difference between the sexes: female participants consider women to be better drivers, and male participants consider men to be better drivers. Men are perceived to be better in perceptual motor skills, while women are perceived to be better in safety concerns.

Psychological need-satisfaction moderates the impact of physical activity on subjective well-being

Kanning, Martina Sport and Exercise Science, Universität Stuttgart, Stuttgart, Germany

A person can regulate his subjective well-being (SWB) by setting and pursuing personal valued goals because the achievement of this goals influence psyhological need-satisfaction (PNS) and SWB (self-concordance model). This longitudinal study analyses whether the impact of physical activity (PA) depends on the amount a person experiences PNS while being physically active. For 16 selected participants, daily self-monitoring of SWB and PNS while being physically active or inactive respectively were assessed for ten weeks and modeled using time series methods. The experience of PNS moderates the impact of PA on SWB. Therefore, the impact of PA is not consistently.

Dynamics of the parameters of functional states while playing and working on a computer

Kapitsa, Maria Psychology, Moscow State University, Moscow, Russia Blinnikova, Irina Psychology, Moscow State University, Moscow, Russia Rudina, Natalia Psychology, Moscow State Linguistic Univer, Moscow, Russia

Dynamics of functional states in different computerized activities was investigated. 44 subjects either played an Internet game "Warcraft", or accomplished text editing task (average time - 84.7 min). Subjects were interrupted four times for evaluation of their states. ANOVA revealed opposite tendencies in the dynamics of the level of Anxiety and Activity. These parameters radically increased while playing and permanently decreased while working. Mood did not change while working and became worse closer to the end of the game. It was also demonstrated a mobilizing effect of computerized activity. Obtained results can be explained in terms of general resources distribution.

Effects of variable information in perception and recognition for indoor scenes

Kasai, Yuriko Dept. of Psychology, Hokkaido University, Sapporo, Japan

Visual scenes we see in daily life involve a lot of variable information such as illumination, figural information of objects, and so on. How this type of information represent accurately in memory? In this research, we measured change sensitivity of some variable information in indoor scenes; a field of view, brightness and chromatic purity of flood-light illumination, and object color. In experiments, subjects retained a standard scene representation for a few seconds or several minutes, and compared with variations of the study image. The stimuli were made by CG software, and they presented on large sized screen.

Google's sense of semantics

Kaser, Armin Psychology, University of Innsbruck, Innsbruck, Austria Kolar, Gerald Psychology, University of Innsbruck, Innsbruck, Austria Sachse, Pierre Psychology, University of Innsbruck, Innsbruck, Austria

Studies concerning searching engines (e.g. Griffiths et al., 2007) have investigated how far algorithms like "PageRank" and the knowledge representation in the semantic memory resemble. Our study shows that searching engines may facilitate elements of a semantic system. 2,500 terms of a natural data record were matched pairwise in 270,000 queries with hits in searching engines as well as web catalogs by the program "Semantic Collector" (© Kaser, 2008). It was found that semantically resembling terms of the natural data scored more hits than terms in farther semantic distance. Consequences: 1) Statement which support form (searching engine vs. web catalog) may be preferred for which content-related context. 2) Support of human information processing.

Consumer skepticism toward advertising: A scale validation study

Katzer, Juliane Flensburg, Germany Bohner, Gerd Sozialpsychologie, Universität Bielefeld, Bielefeld, Germany

Skepticism toward advertising is an individual-difference variable related to consumer information processing. We present a German adaptation of the SKEP scale, a 9-item scale measuring skepticism toward advertising (Obermiller & Spangenberg, 1998). A translation by Florack and Ineichen (2006) was revised to reduce item difficulty, and 2 items were added. Male students (N = 181) completed this German SKEP scale and other questionnaires. Exclusion of 4 items resulted in a unidimensional and reliable 7-item scale (Cronbach's α = .75). Negative correlations with Personal Need for Structure and ratings of advertiser honesty support the construct validity of the German SKEP scale.

The task of imitating meaningless upper-limb movements for detecting early-stage Alzheimer's disease

Kawano, Naoko Dept. of Geriatrics, Nagoya University, Nagoya, Japan Saito, Hirofumi Information Science, Nagoya University, Nagoya, Japan Umegaki, Hiroyuki Department of Geriatrics, Nagoya University, Nagoya, Japan Suzuki, Yusuke Department of Geriatrics, Nagoya University, Nagoya, Japan

To detect mild cognitive impairment (MCI) caused by Alzheimer's disease (AD), we investigated the error rates in a task involving imitating meaningless upper-limb movements (IM-) in three groups: AD, MCI, and controls. IM- was carried out in combination with tasks involving pantomiming and imitating meaningful movements and a neuropsychological battery including the Mini-Mental State Examination (MMSE). Of the groups, AD had the highest error rates on the IM- and the controls had the lowest. The correlation between the MMSE scores and error rate in the IM- was significant. These results suggest that the IM- is practicable for screening early-stage AD.

Video phone use in intimate relationship under mobile communication

Kawaura, Yasuyuki Tokyo Keizai University, Tokyo, Japan Miura, Asako Social Psychology, Kobe Gakuin University, Kobe, Japan Niida, Sumaru Research and Development, KDDI R&D Laboratories, Saitama, Japan

The development of mobile technology enable us to do anytime anywhere video communication as well as photo communication. Conventional video communication (i.e., fixed videophone) has been unpopular among people. However mobile video phone make us to be colorcasters. This study intended to investigate the qualitative description of communication accompanied with some live pictures by mobile video phone. Field experiments were conducted on intimate terms (i.e., parent and child, lovers, and close friends) for a week. We discussed that the participants felt empathy towards their experiences each other by synchronous pictures.

The effects of mental training program for mental health and competitive performance of Kyudo (Japanese archery) athletes

Kemuriyama, Chihiro Graduate School, J. F. Oberlin University, Tokyo, Japan Shimizu, Yasuo College of Health and Welfare, J. F. Oberlin university, Tokyo, Japan Mogi, Toshihiko College of Health and Welfare, J. F. Oberlin university, Tokyo, Japan

The purpose of this study was to investigate the influence of mental training program to enhance competitive performance of Kyudo. The subjects were 15 Japanese university Kyudo athletes (male=4, female=11, mean age=19.80) who participated in the mental training program that is based on relaxation training. The subjects were asked to answer a questionnaire composed of State-Trait Anxiety Inventory in Japanese (Hidano et al., 2000) and Mental Health Pattern (Hashimoto et al., 2000). A hierarchical multiple regression analysis showed that the state anxiety and the physical stress were negatively correlated directly or indirectly with the rate of hitting the mark.

Dissonance in how we make decisions and how we want to make decisions

Kerimi, Neda Dept. of Psychology, Stockholm University, Stockholm, Sweden

Thirty-five university students indicated their indecisiveness, how they made important decisions, and how they wished they made decisions, in a validated 65 item questionnaire. T-tests showed that participants identified as dependent, avoidant, and spontaneous, desired to have less characteristics associated with those styles. Even though one might expect these individuals to be more indecisive, regression analysis showed no such significant relationship. It remains to be seen why these individuals do not actively work towards changing their decision making style, though they are aware of and unhappy about it and also why are they not indecisive as previous research suggests.

Meaning of the money, and its relationship with individualism collectivism: A research on Kyrgyzian and Turkish college students

Keser, Askin IIBF, Kocaeli University, Izmit-Kocaeli, Turkey Özbek, Ferhat Türk Dünyası İş, İktisat ve Girişimci, İstanbul, Turkey

Money is most important thing our life. We always dream to have it and we are afraid to lose money. In this article we are trying to explain meaning of the money, and its relationship with individualism & collectivism. In this purpose, we use well known three money scales (money importance scale, money ethic scale and money belief and behavior scale), and individualism & collectivism scales. A cross-sectional questionnaire survey among college students in the two Kyrgyzstan and Turkey. We use the regression models. Dependent variables of our models are importance of money, money ethic and money belief and behaviors, and independent variables are individualism & collectivism. We use reliability, factor analyzes, correlations and regression analyze.

Physical psychology and ethics

Khanifar, Hossein Qom, Islamic Republic of Iran Bayan Memar, Ahmad Education and psychology, University of Qom, Qom, Islamic Republic of Iran Moghimi, Mohammad Management and pgychology, University of Tehran, Qom, Islamic Republic of Iran

Islam frankly emphasizes the body health and physical training. In this survey, besides physical education and physical psychology during the history and different religions, we discuss these things: fairness, justice, chivalrousness, heroic and bodily and spiritual and mental considerations, and even physical ethics among the children, teenagers and women. This survey mentions the effects of physical exercises between the middle- and old-aged; because they can improve their mentality. Nowadays, the motto "Being old in fine fettle" is spread all around the world from the physical, mental and ethical points of view. So, in this survey we are going to introduce the psychological theories and ethical instructions which are related to physical education.

Locus of control and parenting style in runaway girls

Khorramabadi, Razieh Family Research, Shahid Beheshti, Tehran, Islamic Republic of Iran Talebian Sharif, Jafar Psychology, Ferdosi university, Mashhad, Islamic Republic of Iran Abarashi, Zohre Family Research, shahid Beheshti, Tehran, Islamic Republic of Iran

Locus of Control and Parenting Style in Runaway Girls The purpose of this study was investigate the locus of control and parenting style of runway girls. The sample included 50 runaway girls. Information collected with I-E scale (Rotter, 1966) and perceived parenting style (Asgari and Akbarnejad, 1999).The result showed that their locus of control was external and the most perceived parenting style was authoritarian. There were significant positive relation between authoritarian parenting style and external locus of control and authoritative parenting style and internal locus of control(p<0.05). There were significant negative correlation between external locus of control and democratic parenting style (p<0.05).

Problem solving and parenting style in runaway girls

Khorramabadi, Razieh Family Research, Shahid Beheshti, Tehran, Islamic Republic of Iran Talebian Sharif, Jafar Psychology, Ferdosi University, Mashhad, Islamic Republic of Iran Safavi Shamlu, Malihe Psychology, Ferdosi University, Mashhad, Islamic Republic of Iran

Problem Solving and Parenting Style in Runaway Girls The goal of this study was investigate the problem solving and parenting style of runway girls. The sample included 50 runaway girls. Information collected with problem solving test (Kacidy& Lung, 1996) and perceived parenting style(Asgari,1999).The result showed that the most perceived parenting style was authoritarian. They used of problem solving control less than other factors. There were significant positive relation between problem solving helplessness and authoritarian parenting style, problem solving creativity, problem solving confidence and democratic parenting style(p<0.05). There were significant negative relation between problem solving helplessness and democratic parenting and problem solving creativity and authoritarian parenting (p<0.05).

The effects of the deception as a result of varying contents concerning the possibility of occurrence on ratings of truthfulness and forgiveness

Kikuchi, Fumitoshi Dept. of Psychology, Tohoku University, Sendai, Japan Sato, Taku Psychology, Tohoku university, Sendai, Japan Abe, Tsuneyuki Psychology, Tohoku university, Sendai, Japan Nihei, Yoshiaki Psychology, Tohoku university, Sendai, Japan

In this study, we examined whether deception as a result of varying contents concerning the possibility of occurrence influences ratings of truthfulness and forgiveness. One hundred and eighty-three college students were required to read scenarios wherein an acquaintance provided deceptive reasons for arriving late for an appointment. Then, they rated the degrees of truthfulness, forgiveness, and negative emotion for each reason. The results revealed that deception with commonplace events resulted in high ratings of truthfulness and low ratings of forgiveness, and vice versa. Furthermore, this study suggested that the forgiveness ratings originated from the raters' suppression of their negative emotion.

A comprehensive action determination model of conservationism: Empirical support for a holistic approach

Klöckner, Christian Risk Psychology, NTNU, Psykologisk Institutt, Trondheim, Norway Blöbaum, Anke AG Umwelt- und Kognitionsps., Ruhr-Universität Bochum, Bochum, Germany

This poster displays and empirically tests a first sketch of a Comprehensive Action Determination Model (CADM) of conservationist behaviour that combines intentional, normative, situational, and habitual influences on environmental friendly behaviour. The model is tested with structural equation modelling on a sample of 389 students of the German University of Duisburg-Essen in the domain of travel mode choice. The results show a strong support for the proposed integrated model, variables from all four possible influence sources significantly determine car choice behaviour of students. Situational influences account for approximately half of explained variation, intentional, normative, and habitual influences share the other half. The explained variation of actual car choice behaviour is with R2=.68 very high.

Functional magnetic resonance neuroimaging of fear conditioning by using aversive pictures as unconditioned stimuli

Klucken, Tim B.I.O.N., Gießen, Germany Stark, Rudolf B.I.O.N., B.I.O.N., Gießen, Germany Tabbert, Katharina B.I.O.N., B.I.O.N., Gießen, Germany Hermann, Andrea B.I.O.N., B.I.O.N., Gießen, Germany Vaitl, Dieter B.I.O.N., B.I.O.N., Gießen, Germany

The aim of the study was to explore whether unpleasant pictures can be used as unconditioned stimuli (US) in a Pavlovian conditioning experiment. Using functional magnetic resonance imaging, subjects were presented with a geometric shape (CS+) followed by aversive pictures, whilst another visual stimulus (CS-) was paired with neutral pictures. In addition, skin conductance responses (SCR) and valence ratings were assessed. We found differential valence ratings and increased SCR to the CS+ in relation to the CS-. Furthermore, enhanced activity was found in fear-relevant brain areas (e.g. amygdala). Our results indicate that the picture-picture paradigm is a worthwhile procedure in human conditioning experiments.

Marijuana use initiation and mental health of adolescents

Kocon, Katarzyna Psychology&Mental HealthPromot, InstituteOfPsychiatry&Neurolog, Warsaw, Poland Okulicz-Kozaryn, Katarzyna Psychology&Mental HealthPr, InstituteOfPsychiatry&Neur, Warsaw, Poland

Objective: To analyze the relationship between age of cannabis initiation and adolescent mental health. Method: Students from randomly selected Warsaw middle-schools participated in the follow-up survey (N=664). Comparisons were made between cannabis abstainers (78%), those who initiated at age 13 (4%) and 15 (18%). Results: Abstainers have better mental health than adolescents who use cannabis. Age of initiation does not influence mental health. Only boys who indicated at 13 have significantly lower self-esteem than boys from other two groups. Conclusions: Mental health problems related to early initiation of cannabis use reveal later in life.

Effects of the color environments on the human cognitive function

Kodama, Takayuki Res. Inst. of Brain Diseases, Kurume University, Kurume, Japan Morita, Kiichiro Res Ins of Brain diseases, Kurume University, Asahi-Machi Kurume-Shi, Japan

Objective: To perform a detailed examination of regions with nervous activities specifically reacting to the emotional effects of the color environments, we analyzed the P300 component of ERPs by LORETA. Methods: Twenty healthy subjects were recruited. We examined the effects of color environments of red, green, and black (darkness) on the cognitive function using the P300 component of ERPs to visual oddball paradigms and LORETA. The P300 segment was determined by the microstate segmentation method using the P300 component in tasks presence or absence. Results: Nervous activities of the red color environment in the limbic system and prefrontal cortex were significantly higher in task presence than absence. Conclusions: These results suggested that the color environments enhance cognitive function.

The connection between flow experience and performance in tennis

Koehn, Stefan Dept. of Health Innovation, Central Queensland University, Rockhampton, Australia

The purpose of this single-case study was to examine the link between flow and performance during tennis matches. Junior ranking-list players with several years of competition experience completed a short form of the flow state scale during each break of the match. Performance was measured through a combined score of direct winners and unforced errors. Results showed similarities between flow state and performance; a higher level of flow coincided with more winners. The conclusion can be drawn that there are similar patterns between flow state and match performance, but it is not clear whether this relationship is one-directional or reciprocal.

Anxiety as predictor of flow state in tennis competition

Koehn, Stefan Dept. of Health Innovation, Central Queensland University, Rockhampton, Australia

The purpose of this study was to examine the relationship between anxiety and flow state. Junior tennis players completed the Competitive State Anxiety Inventory-2 and the Flow State Scale-2 following a competition match. Stepwise multiple regression analyses showed that confidence was the only significant predictor of global flow (β=.72, p<.001) and of all flow dimensions, except time transformation, with beta values ranging between .52 and .66. In conclusion, the results indicated that confidence is a stronger predictor of flow state than cognitive and somatic anxiety. This provides more

evidence that confidence is one of the main personality variables underlying flow.

Mindfulness: A personality variable underlying flow

Koehn, Stefan Dept. of Health Innovation, Central Queensland University, Rockhampton, Australia

The purpose of this study was to examine the relationship between mindfulness and flow state. Junior tennis players completed the Kentucky Inventory of Mindfulness Skills and the Flow State Scale-2 following a competition match. Results showed significant and meaningful (r>.30) correlations between mindfulness and global flow (r=.43, p<.01) and for flow dimensions of challenge-skills balance (.44), action-awareness merging (.36), clear goals (.43), unambiguous feedback (.35), sense of control (.31), and autotelic experience (.34). In conclusion, mindfulness is a potentially important personality variable underlying flow state. Future studies should further investigate the link between mindfulness, using a sport-specific measure, and flow.

The development of confidence and performance during a tennis match

Koehn, Stefan Dept. of Health Innovation, Central Queensland University, Rockhampton, Australia

The purpose of this study was to examine the development of confidence and performance during a tennis match. In this single-case study, two ranking-list players assessed their confidence level during each break of the match. Differences in players' confidence are evaluated through visual inspection at break-time scores (0:1, 1:2, 3:2). Results showed that a change in performance, as reflected by the score, generally lead to a change in confidence, but the level of confidence was not indicative for upcoming performance. This leads to the conclusion that the relationship between performance and confidence might be one-directional, but not necessarily reciprocal.

The relationship between anticipation and performance during a two-set tennis match

Koehn, Stefan Dept. of Health Innovation, Central Queensland University, Rockhampton, Australia

The purpose of this study was to examine differences in players' anticipation for winning and losing performance in a tennis match. In this single-case study, two ranking-list players assessed their levels of anticipation during each break. Differences in anticipation were evaluated through visual inspection at scores of 0:1, 1:2, 3:2, and so on. Results showed that the winner maintained a constantly high level of anticipation throughout the match, whereas the loser's anticipation dropped substantially towards the end of each set. In conclusion, anticipation appears to be a crucial variable for the performance outcome. More research on anticipation is necessary.

Associations between pre-competition confidence and flow state

Koehn, Stefan Dept. of Health Innovation, Central Queensland University, Rockhampton, Australia

The purpose of this study was to examine the link between pre-competition confidence and flow state during a tennis match. Junior tennis players (N=59) completed the State Sport Confidence Inventory before and the Flow State Scale-2 after a competition match. Results showed significant and meaningful (r>.30) correlations between confidence and global flow (r=.38, p<.01) and for flow dimensions of challenge-skills balance (.36), action-awareness merging (.40), unambiguous feedback (.32), concentration on the task at hand (.32), loss of self-consciousness (.32), and autotelic experience (.38). In conclusion, the level of pre-competitive confidence might an important factor influencing flow state.

Cognitive anxiety: Side effects of an imagery intervention to increase flow state in tennis competition

Koehn, Stefan Dept. of Health Innovation, Central Queensland University, Rockhampton, Australia Morris, Tony School of HMRP, Victoria University, Melbourne, Australia Watt, Anthony P. School of Education, Victoria University, Melbourne, Australia
Csikszentmihalyi (1999) proposed anxiety as the antithesis of flow, whereas confidence facilitates flow. In an imagery intervention, Koehn, Morris, and Watt (2007) aimed at increasing flow state and confidence in tennis competition. In this paper, we examine side effects of the intervention on cognitive anxiety. The results of this single-case study showed that beside the increase of flow and confidence, cognitive anxiety decreased from baseline to post-intervention phase. In conclusion, the results indicated that the increase in flow state and confidence indirectly affected cognitive anxiety, which was not part of the intervention.

Personality traits influencing flow state

Koehn, Stefan Dept. of Health Innovation, Central Queensland University, Rockhampton, Australia Morris, Tony School of HMRP, Victoria University, Melbourne, Australia Watt, Anthony P. School of Education, Victoria University, Melbourne, Australia
The purpose of this study was to examine personality traits, including confidence, absorption, action control, and imagery use, as antecedents of flow state in tennis competition. Participants were junior tennis players with several years of training and competition experience. Stepwise multiple regression results showed that action control (β=.39, p<.001) and confidence (β=.21, p<.01) significantly predicted flow, accounting for 19.89% of the variance. In conclusion, a combination of personality traits appears to underlie flow. For future interventions, imagery could be used as an intervention technique taking into account action control and confidence as critical personality variables to enhance flow state.

Comparing of competitive trial and state anxiety degree in team and individual fields sportsmen

Kohandel, Mahdi Physical Education, Azad Universitu Karaj Branch, Karaj, Islamic Republic of Iran Kasbparsat, Mehdi physical education, azad universitu karaj branch, Karaj, Islamic Republic of Iran Zarei, Fereshteh physical education, azad universitu karaj branch, Karaj, Islamic Republic of Iran
The purpose of this study was comparing of competitive trait anxiety and competitive state anxiety degree between sportsmen selected team and individual sport fields that participated in university competition. We selected 90 athletes in team sports and 62 athletes in individual sports randomly. To find of anxiety degree in subjects used of Martinez the competitive state and trial anxiety inventory. The results shown that trial anxiety in team sport fields athletes(15.93)was more than individual fields athletes(15.51).the degree of physical anxiety was 18.97,19.56 respectively in individual and team athletes. Self confidence in team athletes was more than individual athletes.

Internal activeness as a sense of wisdom - From the transcendental point of view of Heidegger

Kojima, Yasuji Business Information, Hokkai-Gakuen University, Sapporo, Japan
Modern Westerners are gradually being troubled by the suspicion that an external activeness may have been only a controversial concept. Post-modern thoughts, introduced by Nietzsche, Freud, and Heidegger, who argued that the spirit of human should be out of control by itself, commonly denied the existence of unconditional external activeness. Another type of activeness needs contradictorily an absolute passiveness since the gravy is something like a blessing or a godsend, which one can not actively get it by oneself but rather only can passively accept it by one's own will.

Individual differences of declarative memory from infancy to childhood

Kolling, Thorsten Inst. für Psychologie, Universität Frankfurt, Frankfurt, Germany Goertz, Claudia Psychology, Psychology, Frankfurt / Main, Germany Frahsek, Stefanie Psychology, Psychology, Frankfurt / Main, Germany Knopf, Monika Psychology, Psychology, Frankfurt / Main, Germany
Deferred imitations assess declarative memory in infants. Experimental studies demonstrated that with increasing age, infants learn faster, and retain more target actions over longer retention intervals. Furthermore, individual stability correlations are moderate throughout the second year. However, multivariate approaches focusing on inter-individual differences of deferred imitation are largely missing. The present four-wave (12-, 18-, 24- and 36-month-old infants), multivariate, longitudinal study analyzed deferred imitation in line with cognitive, motor, emotional, social, language and self-development. A person-centered approach demonstrated inter-individual differences in intra-individual change. Multivariate analyses revealed differences between developmental groups. Results are discussed against the background of contemporary developmental theories.

Influence of Byelorussian stage of creativity of Vygotskogo on development of psychology in Russia, Byelorussia

Kolominsky, Yakov Psychology, Belarus State Pedagogical Univ, Minsk, Belarus Kandibovich, Lev Psychology, Belarus State Pedagogical Univ, Minsk, Belarus Komkova, Elena Psychology, Belarus State Pedagogical Univ, Minsk, Belarus
Vygotskogo's heritage have come into the theory of development of psychology in the world. His activities during work in Belarus in Gomel (1917-1926) had huge value for his further creativity (works «Psychology of art», «Pedagogical psychology»). In this period many theoretical ideas was generated by Vygotsky. As is known, Vygotsky has died in Moscow in the age of 37 years. Representation of historical importance of Gomel period for all activity of the great psychologist is an overall objective, actual for training and education not only hundreds, but also thousand young psychologists in Byelorussia, Russia and other countries.

The asymmetric relationship between facial identity and facial expression: The influence of facial expression

Komatsu, Sahoko Human-Environment Studies, Kyushu University, Fukuoka, Japan
We examined the relationship between facial identity and facial expression by using a selection task. Participants were asked to find the matching individual/expression from amongst four alternatives. There were two types of tasks: one was to select from four alternatives, all of the same expression or identity (base task), and the other from four alternatives of varying expressions and identities (filter task). Reaction times (RTs) for expression selection were independent of identity variation, but RTs for identity selection were influenced by variation of expression. The results suggested an asymmetric relationship between identity and expression.

The irony from mobile: Impact of multi task on egocentrism over celluar phone message

Komori, Megumi Tokyo, Japan Murata, Koji Naka, 2-1, Tokyo, Japan
This study examined the automaticity of egocentric bias in perspective taking in a mobile-based e-mail communication. Recent research(Krueger, Epley, Parker, & Ng, 2005) demonstrated that we tend to assume similarity in interpretation of ironic messages in e-mail communication. We tested this bias in Japan, using mobile celluar phone as a communication means. We also manipulated cognitive busyness of the mail sender for the purpose of investigating the nature of this bias. It was hypothesized and partly confirmed that egocentric bias in sender would be heightened if he/she suffers from multi task.

Impact of differing grades of anthropomorphism and embodiment on Theory of Mind (ToM). An fMRI study

Krach, Sören Psychiatrie & Psychotherapie, Universitätsklinikum Aachen, Aachen, Germany Hegel, Frank Social Robotics, Bielefeld University, bielefeld, Germany Wrede, Britta Social Robotics, Bielefeld University, bielefeld, Germany Buschkämper, Stefan Psychology, Bielefeld University, bielefeld, Germany Sagerer, Gerhard Social Robotics, Bielefeld University, bielefeld, Germany Kircher, Tilo Psychiatrie & Psychotherap, Universitätsklinikum Aachen, Aachen, Germany
Inferring intentions of others is referred to Theory-of-Mind. Neural correlates of Theory-of-Mind have been investigated by means of the Prisoners' Dilemma in combination with fMRI. It remains unclear what exactly manifests the neural correlates of Theory-of-Mind. We present fMRI-data of subjects playing the PD against four opponents, stepwise increasing in anthropomorphism & embodiment: computer, functional robot, anthropomorphic robot and human. All partners elicited Theory-of-Mind associated activity. However, human-human interaction evoked strongest Theory-of-Mind activity. It is the first study to apply fMRI-methods on human-robot interaction on a higher cognitive level such as ToM.

Subarachnoid haemorrhage and quality of life: One year follow-up

Kramska, Lenka Dept. of Neurosurgery, Regional Hospital Liberec, Liberec, Czech Republic Preiss, Marek Psychiatry, Psychiatric Center of Prague, Praha, Czech Republic Koblihova, Jana Psychology, Ustredni vojenska nemocnice, Prague, Czech Republic Dusankova, Erika Psychology, FFUK Prague, Liberec, Czech Republic Netuka, David Neurosurgery, Ustredni vojenska nemocnice, Prague, Czech Republic Bernardova, Lenka Neurosurgery, Ustredni vojenska nemocnice, Prague, Czech Republic Benes, Vladimir Neurosurgery, Ustredni vojenska nemocnice, Prague, Czech Republic
55 patients one year after neurosurgery for SAH were assessed with semi-structured interview focused on health, social and psychological sequelae of SAH. 22% of the group visited a doctor for some kind of psychological problems but none was hospitalized due to such problems. Average sick leave period after neurosurgery was 5,3 months (SD=3,6 months). We found 8 persons still on sick leave (15% of the group), which lasted 12 months and was not closed yet, in the one-year-after examination. 47% of the group was active, either studying or working. 30% of the group was in some form of disability pension.

The relationship between an attachment style and emotional intelligence among adolescents

Kricman, Katija Strukovna Skola Eugen Kumiàiæ, Rovinj, Croatia
The aim of this study was to examine the relationship between four types of an attachment style in adolescence and corresponding emotional intelligence which was measured by two questionnaires: emotional competence and regulation of negative emotions. Attachment style was explored with family figures. Results are gathered on 194 high school students of both sexes. Findings suggest that anxious dimension of attachment is correlated with less efficient regulation of negative emotions and avoidance dimension is correlated with weaker

emotional competence. It seems that securely attached adolescents are more emotional competent than adolescents with avoidant attachment style at the particular dimension of self regulation of emotion and regulation of emotion in others. The results are discussed within a context of attachment theory.

A health psychology perspective on therapy of sexual delinquency

Krischke, Norbert Inst. für Psychologie, Uversität Oldenburg, Oldenburg, Germany Tomczyk, Joanna Health Psychology, Carl von Ossietzky University, Oldenburg, Germany

The objective of this pilot study is to identify different states of risk perception of sexual deviant persons according to Health Action Process Approach Model of Schwarzer (2001). Next to data of the standardised Multiphasic Sex Inventory, half structured interviews were conducted with seven inpatients of forensic psychiatry. Results indicate that the determinants of the HAPA-Model are qualified for the clarification of the insight into the illness and the insight into the therapy of sexual deviant persons. Key words: health behaviour model, risk perception, sexual delinquency

The impact of value on self-regulation

Krohn, Jeanette Inst. für Psychologie, Universität Greifwald, Greifswald, Germany Friedrich, Sandra Psychologie, Ernst-Moritz-Arndt Universität, Greifswald, Germany Hilbrich, Anja Psychologie, Ernst-Moritz-Arndt Universität, Greifswald, Germany Hüning, Christin Psychologie, Ernst-Moritz-Arndt Universität, Greifswald, Germany Schmidt, Luise Psychologie, Ernst-Moritz-Arndt Universität, Greifswald, Germany Schneider, Silvia Psychologie, Ernst-Moritz-Arndt Universität, Greifswald, Germany

Contrary to expectancy-value theories we hypothesized, that value is a more important predictor for self-regulation than expectancy. 300 students were randomly assigned to one cell in a 2 (high vs. low value) x 2 (high vs. low expectancy) design. Anticipated commitment and effort were assessed as well as the perceived value and expectancy for each scenario. A twoway ANOVA indicated that value has a positive significant impact on commitment and effort with notably stronger effects than in case of expectancy. Correlation analyses supported this. Hence, value may play a much more important roll than expectancy, necessitating further refinements of theory.

Trust in E-commerce

Kumbruck, Christel Institute for Ergonomics, University of Kassel, Kassel, Germany

The dfg-sponsored TrustCaps(ules) project aims at identifying and implementing technological solutions for the psychological, jurisprudential and technological conditions that enable users to trustfully participate in E-commerce. The resulting trustworthy environment was tested November 2007 in a simulation study. Like in a qualitative experiment, consumers and suppliers were observed for two days while conducting sales processes as instructed to determine whether a secure environment generates system trust and the supporting icons and communication possibilities induce personal trust. An increase in trust was found for technically experienced users but not for technically inexperienced ones. Further research on sensitization and training is required.

Gender differences in first-grade mathematics strategy use: Is there reason for concern?

Kurz-Milcke, Elke Inst. für Mathematik, Pädag. Universität Ludwigsburg, Stuttgart, Germany Pawelec, Bärbel Psychology, University of Education, Ludwigsburg, Germany

Research indicates that gender differences in mathematics strategy use occur as early as elementary school. In a study with first graders (N=161, 82 girls) randomly selected from their classrooms (n=33) we have been studying strategy use in early arithmetic. Children were interviewed and video-taped twice in individual sessions (first and second grade). A coding scheme was developed (see Carr & Jessup 1997; Fennema et al. 1998). An advantage for boys in using knowledge-based strategies (d=0.55) was determined, whereas effect sizes for mental calculation and overt strategies (fingers and counters) were small. There seems to be reason for concern.

Soccer World Championship 2006: Explaining changes in Germans' national identification

Kutscher, Jörn Faculty of Education, Bundeswehr University Munich, Munich, Germany Maes, Jürgen Inst. für Bildung, Universität der Bundeswehr, München, Germany Pahl, Holger Faculty of Education, Bundeswehr University Munich, Munich, Germany

During the soccer world championship 2006, German as well as foreign observers stated a change in German mentality: Germans seemed to develop a more relaxed way to deal with their national identity and national symbols. During this time, we conducted a longitudinal online-study including 10 measure points (t1 and t2 before, t3 to t9 during, t10 after the championship). Data confirm the above-mentioned observations: We found an increase in a positive national identification with Germany (and an increase in extraversion). Using longitudinal path analyses, this increase could be causally linked to emotions and attributions concerning the performances of the German soccer team.

Outcome evelution of behavior therapy in an outpatient university psychotherapy unit

Löcker, Kristin Klinische Psychologie and Psyc, Universität Göttingen, Göttingen, Germany Ruhl, Uwe Georg-Elias-Müller-Institut, Universität Göttingen, Göttingen, Germany Kröner-Herwig, Birgit Georg-Elias-Müller-Institut, Universität Göttingen, Göttingen, Germany

Objectives: In this study the therapeutic outcome of the Outpatient University Psychotherapy Unit of the University of Goettingen is evaluated. The effectiveness of the treatment is affirmed which thus assures the requirements of quality management. Considering high dropout rates, predictors for therapy completion are analysed. Methods: The design of the study is naturalistic and the outcome classifies as phase-IV evidence with 6-months follow-up. Results: Robust effects are attained in all scales. The variables age and maximum vocational education qualify as predictors for therapy dropout.

Identity status and time perspective in adolescence

Laghi, Fiorenzo Faculty of Psychology 1, Univers. of Rome 'La Sapienza', Rome, Italy Baiocco, Roberto Faculty of Psychology 1, Universita di Roma, Rome, Italy d'Alessio, Maria Clinical Psychology, Faculty of Psychology 1, Rome, Italy Gurrieri, Grazia Clinical Psychology, Faculty of Psychology 1, Rome, Italy Mazza, Marco Clinical Psychology, Faculty of Psychology 1, Rome, Italy

Objectives: The study aims to examine the relationship between Marcia's ego identity status and Time Perspective in adolescence. Method: A survey was conducted in a sample of 2,000 italian adolescents. We obtained data using questionnaires concerning ego identity status, self-esteem, time perspective, and family characteristics. Data were analyzed using bivariate and multivariate analyses. Results: The survey revealed that more advanced statuses (achievement and moratorium) and the less advanced statuses (diffusion and foreclosure) differ in terms of time perspective dimensions. Conclu-sion:The findings of this study emphasize the importance of considering the time perspective in future research on identity formation.

Correlates of identity statuses among adolescents in Hong Kong

Lam, Rebecca Dept. of Education Studies, Hong Kong Baptist University, Hong Kong, China, People's Republic of : Hong Kong SAR Tam, Vicky Education Studies, Hong Kong Baptist Univeristy, Hong Kong, China, People's Republic of : Macao SAR

The study investigates identity statuses of adolescents in Hong Kong and examines psychological and contextual correlates of identity development. Data were collected using questionnaires from 1445 Secondary Two to Four Chinese students. Results in general support the prediction of identity theory. Specifically, identity achievement was linked to positive school-related performance and psychosocial outcomes, while identity diffusion was associated with negative outcomes. In addition, boys exhibited higher levels of identity foreclosure and achievement than girls did, and identity foreclosure tended to decrease with grade level. Overall, findings provide in-depth understanding on identity development in a Chinese cultural context.

Profiling optimal performance: A case study of peak performance in foreign exchange dealing and boxing environments

Lane, Andy Dept. of Sport Psychology, University of Wolverhampton, Walsall, United Kingdom Lane, Richard Business Consultancy, OptimizeFX,, Broxbourne, United Kingdom Lane, Helen Sport Psychology, Winning Lane, Lichfield, United Kingdom

This case study aims to explore emotional intelligence and emotional states associated with optimal performance in two high-performance environments. An experienced foreign exchange dealer whom also competed as an amateur boxer completed mood measures and offered qualitative in relation to optimal performance states related to each environment. Results indicated comparative emotional profiles between optimal performance, although optimal boxing performance was linked with high calmness and happiness. Tension was motivational when coupled with positive emotions, and de-motivational when experienced with depression (Lane & Terry, 2000). Findings indicate the potential transferability of emotional control training between sport and occupational environments.

Psychology of eating and food control: A case study

Lane, Andy Dept. of Sport Psychology, University of Wolverhampton, Walsall, United Kingdom Lane, Helen Sport Psychology, Winning Lane, Lichfield, United Kingdom

Evidence indicates that many athletes develop dysfunctional attitude to diet. The present case study investigates intervention work designed to enhance attitudes to eating in an experienced athlete. The Test of Exercisers Eating Scale (TEES) was completed before and after a cognitive-behavioural intervention programme designed to enhance self-confidence to exert self-control around food and to challenge using eating as a mood-regulation strategy. Questionnaire and interview data revealed that the client reduced using eating as a food regulation strategy, coupled with changing beliefs that exercise legitimised excessive eating. Findings indicate that the TEES provides useful data when monitoring interventions.

Emotional intelligence, mood states and optimal and dysfunctional performance

Lane, Andy Dept. of Sport Psychology, University of Wolverhampton, Walsall, United Kingdom Lane, Helen Sport Psychology, Winning Lane, Lichfield, United Kingdom

This study investigated the mediating effect of emotional intelligence on mood states associated with optimal and dysfunctional performance. Forty-nine athletes completed a modified Brunel Mood Scale (Lane et al., 2007) to assess optimal and dysfunctional mood states and the Emotional intelligence scale (Schutte et al., 1998). MANOVA results indicated that emotional intelligence was associated with optimal mood states (Wilks lamba = .27. P < .01, Eta2 = .23), with low emotional intelligence being associated with anger, tension and depression coupled with low happiness. Future research should investigate the efficacy of emotional intelligence interventions on mood states associated with performance.

What is the meaning of life? An analysis of university students' writing about life

Lang, Ya-Chin *Counseling Center, Da-Yeh University, Changhwa, Taiwan*
This is a qualitative study of analyzing a group of university students' writing about life. The researcher asked her students firstly to finish a sentence,' Life is as....', and to state their explanation. The whole process took about 10 minutes. The purpose of this study is to understand if students hold positive or passive attitude toward their lives. Through their writings and later discussion, it is hoped that students may cherish their lives more. Further, researcher may sort out some high risky students and try to help them.

Anorexic young women and their mothers: Psychodynamic approach of a contemporary clinic

Lange, Elaine *Dept. of Psychology, Universidade São Francisco, Ribeirão Pires- SP, Brazil*
This study investigated the intrapsychic dynamic from pacients diagnosed as restrictive anorexic, clinically analysed according to psychoanalytical approach. A semi-structured interview and Family Drawing with Histories were conducted in three anorexic patients and their mothers. The results showed a supremacy of primitive defenses, an excessive attempt to control the offensive impulses, that could be mistaken for obsessive-compulsive disorder, became evident in the anorexic patients. The relationship between both has proved to be excessively fragile and ambivalent. Feelings of envy from daughters towards mothers and lack of continence from mothers to daughters were observed, representing the poor reciprocal relationship between both.

Online games, self-regulation and pathological internet use of Chinese early adolescents

Lei, Li *Institute of Psychology, Beijing, People's Republic of China* **Hao, Chuanhui** *Capital Normal Uni., Dept. of Psychology, Beijing, People's Republic of China*
The rapid development of internet in China has lead to some problems, one of which is Pathological Internet Use(PIU). According to CNNIC(China Internet Network Information Center), there has been about 162 million internet users in China until July 2007, and the percentage of adolescent internet users under 18 years old is 17.7%, about 28.7 million. This study examined the effects of online games and self-regulation on PIU in Chinese adolescents. The results indicated that online games can predict PIU directly and positively. Moreover, self-regulation could predict PIU negatively. Finally, self-regulation partially mediated the relationship of online games and PIU.

Early adolescents' life events, instant messaging and pathological internet use

Lei, Li *Institute of Psychology, Beijing, People's Republic of China* **Ma, Liyan** *Capital Normal Uni., Dept. of Psychology, Beijing, People's Republic of China*

A survey from China Internet Network Information Center in 2007 demonstrated that adolescent internet users reached to 28.67 million, the impact of internet on Chinese teenagers has been one of foci in public and research. In order to explore the relation among life events, Instant Messaging (IM) and Pathological Internet Use (PIU) for early adolescents, 215 students were surveyed. The results indicated that subjective stress caused by life events could positively predict PIU; IM could predict PIU positively; objective stress have a positive effect on PIU, and at the same time it could indirectly predict PIU through IM.

Social fear as a peculiar phenomenon of adolescence

Lemeshchuk, Viktoriya *Institute of Psychology, Kyiv, Ukraine*
Fear is a complex notion. It can be observed as an emotion, a psychological state and a highest human feeling. In the development of a personality it has two main periods of occurence: childhood and adolescence. However the quality of fear differs a lot. As main activities of the ages concerned vary, it suggests the difference in the shape and image of fear while the object or threat remains the same. In adolescence fear aquires a new trait — social. The new penomemenon the age introduces is «Social Fear». It reaveals the danger as it involves all the precesses and spheres of developing personality.

Cross-cultural study of the affordances of children's urban environments in Russia and Switzerland

Leonova, Tamara *Department of Psychology, University of Fribourg, Fribourg, Switzerland* **Baumeler, Marie-Paule** *Department of Psychology, University of Fribourg, Fribourg, Switzerland* **Shmeleva, Irina** *Department of Psychology, University of St-Petersbourg, St Petersbourg, Russia*
The goal of current study is to explore the perception of physical affordances of urban environment by Swiss and Russian children. Affordances are defined as functional properties of environment that open opportunities for action. The study was based on individual interviews with 8-9 year-old children in Russia (n = 68) and in Switzerland (n = 65). The ANOVAs performed on the scores of different categories of affordances found no significant differences between the countries, age and gender in affordance availability, in level of affordances (perceived, used, and shaped) and the distribution of affordances within the categories of the taxonomy.

The classification and discriminate of social adjustment

Li, Xiaowei *Psychology, Developmental Psychology, BeiJing, People's Republic of China* **Zou, Hong** *Psychology, Developmental Psychology, BeiJing, People's Republic of China*
We selected 718 students from Beijing and Xi'an, used K-means cluster and discriminant analysis, and studied the categories of adolescent's social adjustment. The result showed: According to four internal indicators of social adjustment (self-esteem, interpersonal competence, loneliness, and problem behavior), the adolescent could be classified into three kinds: harmonious adjustment (45.0%), low interpersonal relationship-low emotional adjustment (30.5%), and low self-esteem more problem behaviors (24.5%). We also established the discriminant function of adolescent social adjustment and will provide a primary diagnose for educational and mental problem diagnoses.

Adolescents' multimedia recreation of internet, self-regulation and coping style

Li, Dongmei *Psychology, Capital Normal University, Beijing, People's Republic of China*
Multimedia Recreation (such as MP3, Flash) has been one of the most popular, frequently used service of the Internet. This study investigated 306 adolescents from 7 to 11 grade to explore the relationship of multimedia recreation of internet, self-regulation and coping style with Structure equation Model. The results showed that, firstly ?there was no significant effect between gender on multimedia recreation of internet, and so was grade on it. Secondly, self-regulation had significant negative effect on it. Thirdly, the asking for help coping style had significant positive direct and indirect effect through self-regulation on multimedia amusement of internet. At last, the avoiding coping style had significant positive direct effect on it.

Paired associated learning by Chinese children with dyslexia

Li, Hong *School of Psychology, Beijing Normal University, Beijing, People's Republic of China* **Shu, Hua** *School of Psychology, Beijing Normal University, Beijing, People's Republic of China*
Two experiments examined whether 82 Chinese children, with and without dyslexia, differed in establishment, long-term retention, and utilization of rules in paired associate learning tasks. Children were asked to learn visual-verbal and visual-visual associates in Experiment 1. Experiment 2 required children to learn visual-verbal association with systematic and arbitrary correspondences. Result indicated that two reader groups did not differ in the visual-visual learning task and long-term retention tests. But the normal readers learned more efficiently overall in visual-verbal learning tasks, and the major differences between groups occurred on the task involving symbol-sound correspondence rules.

The effect of mental loading on meta-memory monitoring

Li, Jian *School of Psychology, Beijing Normal University, Beijing, People's Republic of China* **Zhang, Houcan** *school of psychology, Beijing Normal University, Beijing, People's Republic of China*
Studies showed that metacognitive monitoring accuracy was affected by difficulty, familiarity, knowledge etc. The present research investigated the effect of mental loading on 45 graduate students' meta-memory monitoring at the character recalling task. By calculating the absolute accuracy, relative accuracy and monitoring bias as indexes, both prospective monitoring and retrospective monitoring were assessed. Results showed that the accuracy declined as mental loading aggravated. However, when the mental loading aggravated gradually, the monitoring bias changed from "No bias" to "Over confidence", then to "No bias", and finally to "Under confidence", along the path similar an " inversed U" curve.

The problematic history of New Media

Liano, Enrico *Sem. di Storia della Scienza, University of Bari, Bari, Italy*
According to a current approach to new media, if the old media could have been used in an individual way creating a personal relationship man/machine, the new ones by translating information into action encourage their collective use and reduce the subjective identity. This paper analyses Finholt's, Johansen's, and Turoff's viewpoints, according to which we can no longer proceed developing technologies with our eyes closed to their effects on our psychological habits. Indeed, new media reflect back on their activities producing voices that render events and processes symbolic so that they

become knowable according to their one-sided way of thinking.

International assessment of learning in scientific literacy between Germany and Taiwanese on PISA 2006

Lin, Hsiao-Fang Inst. of Teaching Art, Ming-Dao University, Chang-Hua, Taiwan

Recently, students' learning has become a more important subject worldwide. PISA was built by OECD under the plan of Programme for International Student Assessment. It is based on a dynamic model of lifelong learning in which new knowledge and skills are necessary for successful adaptation throughout life. PISA2006 will be released on 04 December 2007 focusing on scientific literacy. The participants mainly are 15-year-old students. To verify the theoretical model fitness, researcher used SEM as an analyzing tool. The implication of the findings may promote students' lifelong learning capability and benefit Germany and Taiwanese youngsters, parents, teachers, and principals.

Early sexual intercourse among adolescents and parenting processes

Lin, Siu-Fung Dept. Applied Social Studies, City University of Hong Kong, Kowloon, China, People's Republic of : Hong Kong SAR Poon, Emily C.L. Applied Social Studies, City University of Hong Kong, Kowloon, China, People's Republic of : Macao SAR

Adolescent are becoming sexually active. Despite the lifelong and irreversible harm caused by early sexual intercourse, the age of onset of sexual intercourse is decreasing. Parenting processes and age of adolescents' first sexual intercourse has not been investigated although the importance of family factors is known. 300 secondary Chinese students were recruited to investigate Chinese concepts of behavioral control- "jiao xun" (training) and "guan" (to love and to govern); four dyadic relationships and their relationships with the onset of early sexual intercourse. It is important that concepts to be evaluated in an indigenous context and from adolescents' perspective.

The development and use of Romanian system for reviewing and certification of psychological tests

Lita, Stefan Centre for Psychosociology, Ministry of Interior, Bucharest, Romania Stan, Aurel Department of Psychology, A.I. Cuza University, Iaşi, Romania Sava, Florin Department of Psychology, Babeş Bolyai University, Cluj, Romania

The paper describes the strategy used in Romanian for assessing the quality of psychological tests. In 2004, the practice of the psychology was regulates by the law 213 and presently, the Methodology Commission represents the institution which certifies tests in Romania. The paper has two main objectives: (a) to present the Romanian rating system for test quality (an adaptation of COTAN System) and the results obtained in the last 2 years, and (b) to show which are the most frequently used tests in Romania, based on a three criteria: a content analysis of the papers published, a survey of psychologists' opinion and the list with the tests certified by the Commission.

Emotional variation exhibited by medical students, Chinese and Russians

Liu, Huiying Dept. of Psychology, Moscow State University, Moscow, Russia

418 Chinese students and 180 Russians students (212 males & 206 females aged 12 to 16) are tested for 16 types of basic emotions during lessons. The date is categorized according to age, sex and nationality. Scatter diagram analysis reveal that there is a correlation exists between boys & girls between the ages of 12 to 14.Differences begin at the age of 15 and are clearly evident by the age of 16. Boys aged 12 to 16 exhibit constant emotions,

while girls' emotions change from the age of 15.This conclusion results from an analysis of both Chinese & Russian students. Key word: emotional variation, medical students

Stereotype and affect toward science in Chinese secondary school students

Liu, Mingxin Institute of Psychology, Chinese Academy of Sciences, Beijing, People's Republic of China Hu, Weiping Institute of Psychology, Chinese Academy of Sciences, Beijing, People's Republic of China Shi, Jiannong Institute of Psychology, Chinese Academy of Sciences, Beijing, People's Republic of China

Current study explored gender-science stereotype and science affect in a sample of Chinese secondary school students. The results showed (a) science-gender stereotype is more and more apparent as students' progress in the specialization of science subjects. girls appeared to start earlier in stereotypical thinking compared to boys, though their difference is not statistically significant; (b) the implicit science-unpleasant/ humanities-pleasant association is more and more apparent as the specialization of science subjects' progresses. in self-report, girls prefer humanities to science, while boys prefer science to humanities; (c) that the Science-gender stereotype is correlated closely with implicit affective experience may lead to development of more effective strategies for decreasing students' gender stereotyped thinking.

Inhibitory control of children with mathematics learning disabilities

Liu, Ming Dept of Special Education, East China Normal University, Shanghai, People's Republic of China

In order to investigate the developmental relationship between ability of inhibitory control and mathematics learning disabilities, 60 elementary school children with only mathematics learning disabilities (MLD) or with mathematics and reading disabilities (MRD) were recruited and their abilities of inhibiting dominant responses were assessed by Stroop tasks and color match reversal tasks. The results show that children with MLD only have comparable abilities of learning new tasks to normal children, however, they have significantly worse performance in tasks of inhibiting dominant responses; whereas children with MRD score lower on both new-task learning and inhibiting dominant responses than normal children.

Qualitative analysis of marriage and romantic love perceived by never-married PhD female students in a Chinese culture

Liu, Ling Dept. of Psychology, Liaoning Normal Universtiy, Dalian, People's Republic of China

The purpose of the study was to explore the marriage and romantic love perceived by never-married PhD female students in a Chinese culture. Five women were interviewed. The results revealed a positive attitude toward and evaluation of these women's single life option. Most of the source of stress was coming from parents. Most participants thought that the reason of single was high academic qualifications. They wanted equality in love and marriage. Most participants paid special attention to protecting marital fidelity and thought that it was immoral to have sex before marriage and extramarital love.

Emotional separation in parent-adolescent relationship: The role of adolescent personal characteristics

Lo Cricchio, Maria Grazia Dept. of Psychology, Università di Palermo, Palermo, Italy Ingoglia, Sonia Department of Psychology, Università di Palermo, Palermo, Italy Lo Coco, Alida Department of Psychology, Università di Palermo, Palermo, Italy

Liga, Francesca Department of Psychology, Università di Palermo, Palermo, Italy

The study was aimed at analyzing the role played by adolescents' disposition to empathic responsiveness, self-orientations, and self-other differentiation on emotional separation from parents. The oderator role of gender was examined. Participants were 331 Italian adolescents. They were administered a series of self-report measures. Hierarchical regression analysis assessed the predictive value of adolescents' personal characteristics on emotional separation, after controlling for other aspects of their relationship. For boys, it was positively predicted by connected self and self-other differentiation, and negatively by empathic concern and separate self. For girls, it was positively predicted by self-other differentiation and negatively by perspective taking.

Investigation and cause analysis of mental health for impoverished undergraduates in China

Long, Xiaodong Dept. of Psychology, Changsha Uni.of Science&Techn, Changsha, People's Republic of China

Abstract: In present China the mental health of impoverished undergraduates tends to deteriorate. The demonstrative result of this investigation shows that there is a marked difference between the impoverished undergraduates and other students in psychological anxiety, depression, human relationship sensitivity and inferiority complex, resulting in a higher proportion of study failure and problematic behavior. It is put forward that universities should, on the basis of education, pay close attention to the mental health of the impoverished undergraduates by providing financial aid and creating harmonious campus culture, by encouraging work-study program and building the awareness of self-esteem, and by integrating active mental health education and pertinent psychological consultation. The mental health of the impoverished undergraduates shall thus be improved.

Athlete's styles of behavior under conditions of risk

Lozhkin, Georgiy Psychology, Institute of Psychology, Kiev, Ukraine Predko, Stanislav Psychology, Institute of Psychology, Kiev, Ukraine

Style of behavior in exercising sport is a holistic formation, including conscious and unconscious mechanisms of activity and passive adaptation. Object. Definition of styles of behavior under conditions of risk. Methods: observation, interviews, questionnaires of G.Shubert and Elers. Results. Style of behavior depends on individual features and environment. Determining factors: readiness to risk; motivation in reaching goal. Behavioral types distinguished: "adventures", "careful", "creative". Characteristics of behavior under conditions of risk could be underlain in athlete's psychological potential.

Adolescent's identity, attachment to parents and family environment

Lubenko, Jelena Dept. of Psychology, University of Latvia, Riga, Latvia Sebre, Sandra Psychology, University of Latvia, Riga, Latvia

This study examined associations between family environment, attachment to parents and adolescent identity achievement status. A sample of 114 pupils of secondary schools in Latvia, 17 – 19 years of age, completed questionnaires regarding identity status, parent and peer attachment and family environment. The results show that achieved identity status ratings are associated with various aspects of family environment and relationships with parents. The achieved identity status of adolescent females is predicted by family cohesion, less family conflict and family achievement orientation. The achieved identity status of adolescent males is predicted by family achievement orientation, family intellectual-cultural orientation and family control.

The effect of music and light upon indoor cycling
Lufi, Dubi Kibbutz Yifat, Yifat, Israel
The present research assessed the effect of music and light on the physical performance and the subjective feelings of participants in indoor cycling (spinning). The participant performed four sessions of different conditions of music and light. The results showed that the energy level, sense of pleasure, and feelings of satisfaction were significantly higher when there was a music during the training. Light did not have any effect on any of the subjective measures. Light and music did not have any effect upon physiological measures: exertion of energy (measured by heart rate) and energy expenditure (measured in calories).

Obesity and life satisfaction: A path analysis
Lugli, Zoraide Behavioral Science & Technol., Simón Bolívar University, Caracas, Venezuela Guzmán, Rosana Behavioral Science and Technol, Simón Bolívar University, Caracas, Venezuela
Objective: Determine the relationship between obesity, body image dissatisfaction, teasing perception and attitude towards physical appearance and the influence of these variables on life satisfaction. Method: Using a non-experimental, cross-sectional design, a path analysis was performed on data from 328 obese patients in Caracas, Venezuela. Results: Obesity doesn't predict life satisfaction. This was predicted by teasing perception and body image dissatisfaction. Attitude towards physical appearance has an indirect effect on life satisfaction. Conclusion: What makes obese people dissatisfied is an interiorized aesthetic ideal which is unreachable. This is expressed by emotional susceptibility to teasing and dissatisfaction with body image.

Integration of action effects in mental task representations
Lukas, Sarah Kognitive Psychologie, RWTH Aachen, Aachen, Germany Philipp, Andrea M. Cognitive Psychology, RWTH Aachen, Aachen, Germany Koch, Iring Cognitive Psychology, RWTH Aachen, Aachen, Germany
The aim of our study was to examine how processes that take place after the response affect mental task representations. We used a task-switching paradigm in which the response triggered irrelevant but predictable task-specific action effects. Subjects experienced these task-response-effect combinations in several learning blocks. In a subsequent transfer block, the predictable action effects changed into random effects. This change led to higher reaction times and switch costs. We assume that anticipated action effects are integrated in task representations and influence the implementation and execution of tasks.

The impact of hands-on experience: Are gender differences important?
Madill, Helen Health Promotion Studies, University of Alberta, Edmonton, Canada York, Mandy Educational Psychology, University of Alberta, Edmonton, Canada Kujat-Choy, Sonya Health Promotion Studies, University of Alberta, Edmonton, Canada Campbell, Rachel Sociology, University of Alberta, Edmonton, Canada
To determine the impact of hands-on experience on undergraduates' educational, career decision-making, and commitment students participating in summer research experiences were surveyed (n=200, 42% return rate) and interviewed (n=10) in 2007. Results indicated that hands-on experiences were key to persistence. Women were more likely to cite the importance of social support and supportive environments than men. Graduate students played critical roles in students' decision-making. Five themes emerged (aspirations, pivotal

experiences, strategies and skills, resources, and career decision-making) using an empirically derived framework of career commitment (Madill, Campbell et al 2007).

Structural analysis of brand equity based on the cognition of consumers: From the survey of foundation-cream brands
Maeda, Hiromitsu Kansai University, Osaka, Japan Takagi, Osamu Faculty of Sociology, Kansai University, Yamatecho 3chome, Suita City, Japan
The purpose of this study is to verify the brand equity model (Maeda, 2004). In this study, brand equity is defined, from the cognitive aspects of consumers, as "a set of brand values perceived by consumers based on past brand-marketing conducted by a corporation". 381 female participants were responded to the questionnaire of foundation-cream brand. The main findings were as follows: Brand equity consists of primary values (qualitative values) and secondary values (incremental values beyond product quality). Second, the value consumers attribute to a corporation affects brand equity. Third, Brand equity causes "consumer-brand relationships". Finally, these "relationships" influence secondary value.

Local and global process of stimuli in autism using face
Malkoç, Gokhan Psychology, Dogus University, Istanbul, Turkey
The aim of the study was how people with autism configure faces. We collected data from autistic and normal children. In a lighted room participants were presented with 24 stimuli constructed by three dots configuring a face. Stimuli were provided in upright or inverted and symmetric or asymetric, which are determined by the relative distances and positions among dots making either face or no face. The error rate was measured. The results showed that autistics showed a significant error when the face stimuli were presented inverted fashion, suggesting that they focused on local feature in face processing.

Skin cancer prevention for adolescents: Theory-based determinants for behavioral interventions
Mallach, Natalie Methods and Evaluation, Freie Universität Berlin, Berlin, Germany Eid, Michael Methods and Evaluation, Freie Universitaet Berlin, Berlin, Germany
Skin cancer incidence rates have increased rapidly over the past 30 years. Particularly adolescents form an at-risk group. A systematic literature review was conducted in order to identify determinants explaining sun protection behavior and deliberate sun exposure, the main risk factor for skin cancer. On the basis of these determinants intervention blocks were specified and put into an integrative theoretical framework. Randomized controlled trials (RCT) are indispensable for testing the effectiveness of such interventions. Multilevel modeling and latent class analysis are valuable methods for analyzing such data. Preliminary results from an ongoing RCT on skin cancer prevention will be presented.

Women and science: Girls-only schools improve women's attitude to science
Manassero Mas, Maria-Antonia Dept. of Psychology, Univ. of the Balearic Islands, Palma de Mallorca, Spain Vázquez-Alonso, Angel Ed.Sciences & Psych.Educat, U of the Balearic Islands, Palma de Mallorca, Spain
Science and technology display a male bias: boys exhibit better science related attitudes than girls, which causes a smaller election of science and technology careers among women. This communication compares hundred of attitudes variables between 16-year old women educated in one girls-only school and coeducated boys and girls. A

discriminant analysis of attitudinal variables shows that the girls-only group achieve more positive attitudes than do the coeducated girls, and even than boys. This result fuels the debate on the advantages and disadvantages of the single-sex education to improve girls attitudes to gender-biased science and technology.

Gender and power at the workpace - two studies about women's and men's leadership in Polish organization
Mandal, Eugenia Inst. of Psychology, University of Katowice, Katowice, Poland
Abstract The aim of the abstract is the presentation of the problems of power in an organization at the workplace from the perspective of gender. Data are presented concerning the access to economic resources (among other things: remunerations, pensions, promotion, information) and the problem of women's and men's leadership in an organization. Two studies are discussed: (1) investigation into women's male subordinates' opinions concerning leadership in an organization, (2) investigation into personality characteristics (femininity-masculinity, locus of control, social competences, professional burnout) of women and men differing from each other in the extent of their power in the same professional organization –superiors and subordinates. Key words power, leadership, gender, femininity, masculinity, social competences, professional burnout

Aggressive trends in adolescents with criminal behavior
Mandel, Anna Addictive States Department, Mental Health Research nstitu, Tomsk, Russia
Problematic adolescents represent risk group regarding development of behavioral and emotional problems. We have conducted investigation into aggressive and hostile trends in minor offenders - 117 male adolescents (mean age $17,1 \pm 0,9$ years) under conditions of a penitentiary institution. Analysis of data of Bass-Darkey test has revealed high values of index of suspiciousness, physical aggression, irritability, indirect aggression (destruction of inanimate objects). High values of index "verbal aggression" (expressing negative feelings through scream, squeal, imprecations, threatening) in adolescents – offenders exceed permitted level $7,73 \pm 2,01$ (norm 3-7). Adolescents are inclined to hostile reactions using all forms of aggressiveness but verbal aggression dominates.

Personality traits and pregnancy related worries
Marin Morales, Dolores Servicio de Obstetricia, Hospital de Fuenlabrada, Fuenlabrada (Madrid), Spain Carmona Monge, Francisco Javier Ciencias de la Salud II, Universidad Rey Juan Carlos, Alcorcón (Madrid), Spain Peñacoba Puente, Cecilia Psicología, Universidad Rey Juan Carlos, Alcorcón (Madrid), Spain Carretero Abellán, Isabel Psicología, Universidad Rey Juan Carlos, Alcorcón (Madrid), Spain Moreno Moure, Amparo Servicio de Obstetricia, Hospital de Fuenlabrada, Fuenlabrada (Madrid), Spain
Objective The aim of the present study is to identify any possible relation between pregnant women personality and specific pregnancy worries Methodology Sample: 99 pregnant women from Fuenlabrada Hospital. Measurement instruments: Cambridge Worries Scale and NEO-FFI. All questionnaires were cumplimented during the first trimester of pregnancy. Results Significant correlations were found between neuroticism and consciousness and most of the items in the Cambridge Worries Scales. Scores in the remaining personality traits didn't correlate with these worries. Conclusions High scores in neuroticism and consciousness could influence the development of specific pregnancy worries. Women could take advantage of

specific psychological attention during pregnancy according to their personality profile.

The strategy of self-handicapping: Self-handicapping effects in different future goals conditions

Marumoto, Nao Dept. of Social Psychology, Kansai University, Osaka, Japan Takagi, Osamu social psychology, Kansai University, Osaka (Suita), Japan
This study examines characteristics of strategies of self-handicapping (SH) process. 365 college students answered to two questionnaires. They attempt to measure the extent of aroused affective effects on two kinds of tasks: Task 1 has high-level self-involvement and low rate of success and Task 2 with opposite condition. The result of Task 1 shows that 'avoidance from difficulty' was related negatively with self-claimed strategy. In Task 2 'fear of failure' was negatively related with self-claimed strategy, and 'acceptance of failure' was positively correlated with acquired strategy. The results seem to imply that the task conditions may influence the SH processes.

Deficits of cognitive, emotional and social functioning in children with a cerebellar lesion

Maryniak, Agnieszka Warsaw, Poland
Purpose: analysis of emotional and social functioning in children with a cerebellar lesion. Participants: 66 children (aged 6-18) who underwent surgery for cerebellar astrocytoma pilocyticum. Methods: parents questionnaire addressing children's linguistic functioning, emotion regulation and social behaviour; neuropsychological tests according to the child's age and abilities. Results: intellectual function of most children (86%) was found to be normal; however, disturbances of initiative and performance (77%), problems in affect regulation (65%), and communication disorders (46%) were observed. Children with cerebellar lesion often suffer setbacks and helplessness in social relationships and are incapable of normal functioning in the social environment.

Illness and health recovery: Experiences of patients with supraventricular arrhythmia treated with ablation

Maryniak, Agnieszka Warsaw, Poland Walczak, Franciszek Cardiac Rhythm Disturbances, Institute of Cardiology, Warsaw, Poland Orczykowski, Michal Cardiac Rhythm Disturbances, Institute of Cardiology, Warsaw, Poland Bodalski, Robert Cardiac Rhythm Disturbances, Institute of Cardiology, Warsaw, Poland Szumowski, Lukasz Cardiac Rhythm Disturbances, Institute of Cardiology, Warsaw, Poland Urbanek, Piotr Cardiac Rhythm Disturbances, Institute of Cardiology, Warsaw, Poland
Purpose: psychological study of patients with supraventricular arrhythmias successfully treated with ablation. Participants: 133 patients, aged 15–77; disease duration: 6 months to 40 years. Methods: semi-structured interview, questionnaire of symptoms, SF-36 (before ablation and 6–12 months after). Results: before ablation patients reported permanent anxiety and life disorganization due to unpredictable arrhythmia paroxysms. Ablation improved their emotional functioning and quality of life (SF-36: 51;9/78,6; p=0,00001). However, during first weeks after ablation patients still monitored their heart beats, feeling "phantom arrhythmias". The study reveals that patients recovering from a long-term illness experience the difficult "adaptation to health" process.

Worker's education and social inclusion in Brazil

Matos Coelho, Maria Inês Mestrado em Educaçåo, UEMG, Belo Horizonte, Brazil
The purpose of this article is to analyze the public politics of the Brazilian government toward Professional Education since 2003. Recognizing that complex formulation we develop the analysis of

the historical construction of the politics discourses that have founded the integrated professional education into the basic education. This reform has been based on the Gramsci's conception of unitary school. Finally, we discuss this reforms possibilities and challenges on the methodology applied to the formation of the professionals or workers in the social context of inequality and exclusion that characterized brazilian society.

Picture superiority in conceptual implicit memory tests

McBride, Dawn Dept. of Psychology, Illinois State University, Normal, USA Braithwaite, Jeremy Psychology, Illinois State University, Normal, USA
The present study examined picture superiority in conceptual implicit memory tests. In two laboratory experiments, university students completed category production tasks for studied words and pictures with levels of processing study tasks. In both experiments, item-specific processing was emphasized to test the distinctiveness view of picture superiority effects. Percentage of target responses data were analyzed with Analysis of Variance, which indicated significantly greater target completions for words than pictures with both semantic and graphemic study tasks in the implicit tests. Results are not consistent with the distinctiveness view of picture superiority effects.

Social anxiety and progesterone: Maladaptive responses to social rejection

Mcclure, Christopher Dept. of Psychology, Florida State University, Tallahassee, USA
This current research aims to show that people with high social anxiety tend to exhibit maladaptive responses when they are socially rejected, and that these responses are related to deficits in the neuroendocrinological substrate progesterone. The setting is a small room, laboratory setting; the participants are undergraduate students; the study is a 2x2 design (male/female, control/rejection groups). The results will show that people with high social anxiety will display negative responses (e.g. withdrawing socially) when socially rejected, mediated by reductions in progesterone.

Family relationships in childhood, pubertal timing and reproductive strategies of adolescents

Meckelmann, Viola Entwicklungspsychologie, Institut für Psychologie, Potsdam, Germany Pfeifer, Caroline Entwicklungspsych., Institut für Psychologie, Potsdam, OT Golm, Germany Rauh, Hellgard Entwicklungspsych., Institut für Psychologie, Potsdam, OT Golm, Germany
Empirical evidence of the evolutionary theory of socialization of Belsky, Steinberg and Draper (1991) was investigated in a longitudinal sample of 26 adolescents who were born during German unification, and their mothers. Consistent with theory, pubertal timing of the girls (but not of the boys) was predicted by the quality of parental relations in childhood, and pubertal timing of the girls (but also not of the boys) was a significant predictor for the age of first intercourse. Furthermore indications of a context-sensitive hereditary transmission of pubertal timing of girls were found in this sample.

Interpersonal cognitions, psychological adjustment and rehabilitation after a cardiac event

Medved, Maria Dept. of Psychology, University of Manitoba, Winnipeg, Canada
This study explored whether self-silencing, that is, believing that self-inhibition is needed to maintain intimate relationships was predictive of post-cardiac psychological adjustment and rehabilitation activities. Adults (110) enrolled in a cardiac treatment program completed questionnaires to assess psy-

chological adjustment, self-care and self-silencing. Regression analyses indicated that a high endorsement of such beliefs was predictive of anxiety, anger-in and depressive symptoms. Females who endorsed high levels of self-silencing were less likely to participate in rehabilitation activities; this relationship was not present for males. These findings suggest that a gender-differentiated stance might be helpful in promoting rehabilitation adherence.

Gender differences in vocational development

Merino Tejedor, Enrique Dept. of Psychology, University of Valladolid, Segovia, Spain
The aim of this study was to analyse the results obtained in the application of a program for vocational development. Two dependent variables were considered, career self-efficacy and vocational maturity, comparing the differences between men and women. The sample used in this investigation consisted of 179 students of Secondary Education. In order to assess career self-efficacy it was used the Vocational Self-Efficacy Scale; meanwhile the Vocational Maturity Questionnaire was used to assess vocational maturity. There were no significant differences between men and women in the experimental group. However, significant differences appeared in the control group, where women scored higher than men in three variables.

First-year university student adjustment: Factor structure and profiles in different faculties

Miezitis, Solveiga Dept. of Psychology, University of Latvia, Riga, Latvia Voitkane, Sarmite Psychology, University of Latvia, Riga, Latvia Rascevska, Malgozata Dept. of Psychology, University of Latvia, Riga, Latvia
The purpose of this study was to survey student needs at the beginning of the first year of studies. A Questionnaire of University Adjustment was administered in 2006 to first-year students (N=1863; 539 males and 1324 females; age 18-22) in 13 faculties at the University of Latvia. Data analysis yielded 3 second-order factors. 1) Social involvement; 2) Self-regulated learning 3) Stress symptoms. Significant differences were found between faculties relating to difficulties in social relationships, clarity of study goals, and gaps in study skills. Implications for remedial interventions were discussed.. Keywords: psychosocial risk factors; first-year student adjustment; initial university study support

Gender differences in leadership styles of Russian students

Mikosha, Valeriya Moscow State University, Moscow, Russia Skatova, Anna Psychology, Moscow State University, Moscow, Russia
Previous research demonstrated gender differences in behavioral strategies of leaders in the work settings (Eagly, 2001). Our goal was to examine if male and female student-leaders use different behavioral styles in achieving their goals during group discussions, and, if yes, what personality factors can explain those differences. 79 students filled in abilities' test, personality questionnaires and participated in small-group discussions. Two leaders were chosen from every group. The results revealed no significant differences in general abilities and personality traits between male and female leaders. However, we found significant differences in the range of behavioral styles between male and female students-leaders.

Contribution of cognitive-motivational variables in the explanation of the academic achievement from a expectation-value model

Minano Perez, Pablo Dept. of Developm. Psychology, University of Alicante, Alicante, Spain Castejón, Juan-Luis Developmental Psychology, University of Alicante (Spain), Alicante, Spain Cantero, Pilar

Developmental Psychology, University of Alicante (Spain), Alicante, Spain

This study analyze the predictive capacity of cognitive-motivational variables about the students' academic achievement, taking as a reference the expectation-value model proposed by Wigfield and Eccles (2002), in Language and Mathematical areas. As a predictive variables are included: General Intelligence/Aptitudes, Causal Attributions, Academic Self-Concept, Goals, Feelings, Expectations and Task's Subjective Value. The correlation and multiple regression analyses (hierarchical method) are carried out about the information obtained from a 168 student sample, who are studying Secondary Obligatory Education in Alicante (Spain). The results show a satisfactory adjustment of the model, especially in Language area. These results are discussed in terms of their theoretical and practical implications for the improvement of the teaching-learning process.

Safety perception among patients of Spanish hospitals

Mira, Jose Joaquin Health Psychology, Universidad Miguel Hernandez, Elche, Spain Rodríguez-Marín, Jesús HEALTH PSYCHOLOGY, UNIVERSIDAD MIGUEL HERNANDEZ, ELCHE, Spain Pérez-Jover, Virtudes HEALTH PSYCHOLOGY, UNIVERSIDAD MIGUEL HERNANDEZ, ELCHE, Spain Ortiz, Lidia HEALTH PSYCHOLOGY, UNIVERSIDAD MIGUEL HERNANDEZ, ELCHE, Spain Vitaller, Julian HEALTH PSYCHOLOGY, UNIVERSIDAD MIGUEL HERNANDEZ, ELCHE, Spain Ziadi, Medhi HEALTH PSYCHOLOGY, UNIVERSIDAD MIGUEL HERNANDEZ, ELCHE, Spain

Objective: To describe the clinical safety perception. Methods: 227 patients replayed a postal survey after discharge. Results: 25 (11%) believed that they had a high chance of suffering a medical mistake. 33 (14,5%) patients suffered an AE. No significant differences were isolated in the safety perception between male and female (p=0,963). The worry for suffering an AE was similar between the age groups considered (p=0,602). Conclusions: One of four patients believe that they have a high chance of suffering a medical mistake. The frequency of AE was associated to the clinical safety perception.

An attempt at stress management using self-relaxation

Mizota, Katsuhiko Faculty of Rehabilitation, Nishikyusyu University, Saga, Japan Murata, Shin Faculty of Health Science, Himeji Dokkyo University, Himeji, Japan

A self-relaxation technique was performed by students of a physiotherapy department as a stress-coping measure during stressful clinical training, and its effectiveness was evaluated. During the last 15 minutes of a 90-minute class, the author taught a self-relaxation technique to 56 students. The effects were evaluated by using a questionnaire incorporating a stress symptom scale, and a short version of the Profile of Mood States, and shoulder and low back pain (visual analogue scale), which was performed at the beginning and end of the class. The same questionnaire was given to 44 control students. In the self-relaxation group, the stress symptom scale decreased significantly, suggesting that self-relaxation is effective as a measure for stress management.

Parents' attitudes towards girl-child education: A study of rafi local government area of Niger State, Nigeria

Mohammad, Rahila L. Social Development, Kaduna Polytechnic, Kaduna, Nigeria Kato, Rosemary Social Develpment, Kaduna Polytechnic, Kaduna, Nigeria Kontagora, Hafsatu L. Social Development, Kaduna Polytechnic, Kaduna, Nigeria

In November 2004, the Federal Government of Nigeria, DFID and UNICEF, initiated the Girls' Education Project (GEP) to eliminate gender gaps in education in northern Nigeria. Parents' negative attitude towards girls' education constitutes one major obstacle to education in that region. The purpose of this paper is to assess GEP's impact on parents' attitudes towards girls' education by comparing GEP and non-GEP communities in Niger State, Nigeria. Instruments of study will be guided questions in questionnaire format and Focus Group Discussions. Recommendations will then be made to stakeholders and advocacy made for initiatives that influence positive attitudes towards girls' education.

A study of the relationship between emotional intelligence and human resources management, group effective leadership and employment progress

Mokhtaripour, Marzieh Education, University of Isfahan, Isfahan, Islamic Republic of Iran

Nowadays adaptive changes are one of the main requirements of the effective permanence and competition. Permanence and growth in new environments needs special characteristics that generally challenge manager's abilities. One of the most important abilities that can help leaders and managers to answer these changes is emotional intelligence. Managers who have emotional intelligence are effective leaders that acquire their goals with maximum productivity and staff satisfaction and commitment. In this article will be stated emotional intelligence and its application in staff selection, development of employment abilities, education and improvement of human resources management.

First step for a behavioural analysis of the therapeutic relationship: Development of therapist's verbal behaviour coding system and study of its reliability

Montaño, Montserrat Faculty of Psychology, Autonoma University of Madrid, Madrid, Spain Calero, Ana Faculty of Psychology, Autonoma University of Madrid, Madrid, Spain Ruiz, Elena Faculty of Psychology, Autonoma University of Madrid, Madrid, Spain Frojan, Maria Xesus Faculty of Psychology, Autonoma University of Madrid, Madrid, Spain

OBJECTIVE: The goal of this work is to present the process of development of a therapist's verbal behaviour coding system. METHOD: This procedure was carried out through observational analysis of the recordings of 50 clinical sesions from 11 cases treated by 5 cognitive-behavioural therapists. Categories, based on Catania's behavioural taxonomy, were coded and registered using The Observer XT software. RESULTS: The new coding system consists of 8 categories and presents acceptable values of intra and interobservers agreement. CONCLUSIONS: The future development of this new research is expected to produce a more complete understanding of the learning mechanisms underlying psychotherapeutic change.

Students' emotional appraisal mechanisms to academic events and their relation to attitude toward their professors

Morales, Guadalupe Dept. of Psychology, UANL, Monterrey, Mexico Lopez, Ernesto Dept. of Psychology, UANL, Monterrey, Mexico Hedlefs, Isolde Dept. of Psychology, UANL, Monterrey, Mexico

68 Bachelor's students were required to perform two experimental tasks. Both were based on the affective priming paradigm. Pairs of facial stimuli (professor and unfamiliar faces) and words (academic and non academic) were presented at automatic conscious and unconscious level with an SOA of 300 ms and one ISI of 50 ms. The goal was to determine emotional appraisals toward professors and the impact of this appraisals on the emotional evaluation of academic events. Results showed that only few students had an effect related to professors' emotional facial information, but these students have a strong influence over the emotional perception of their classmates for the teacher. Educational Implications are discussed at the end of the paper.

Which factors do affect transfer of training to the work place?

Moreno Andres, Maria Victoria Pedagogia Sistemàtica i Social, Universitat Autònoma Barcelona, Bellaterra (Cerdanyola V.), Spain

Nowadays, training effectiveness is one of the areas of Human Resources Development which are cause of worry of professionals. Not all the competences learnt in training are finally transferred to the workplace so the sources invested in training do not result effective. Furthermore, there are a lot of factors which inhibit workers from incorporating new competences in their performance. The aim of the research carried out was to detect which factors could affect the process of transfer of training. The work field consisted in thirteen interviews to experts. The main result showed that identification of workers needs before training was one of the most relevant factors for transfer.

The effect of data characteristics on mean estimation

Morris, Bradley Psychology, Grand Valley State University, Allendale, USA Masnick, Amy Psychology, Hofstra University, Hempstead, USA Natschke, Christa Psychology, Grand Valley State University, Allendale, USA Spenner, Adrianne Psychology, Grand Valley State University, Allendale, USA Hammond, Stephanie Psychology, Grand Valley State University, Allendale, USA Kearney, Deardra Psychology, Grand Valley State University, Allendale, USA

Humans represent number as analog magnitudes with error variance. However, it is unclear how representational format influences approximate mathematical operations such as mean estimation. Twenty participants estimated the mean of 80 data sets; number of observations (2-6) and coefficient of variation (10% or 20% of the mean) varied. Ten participants calculated means as rapidly as possible, ignoring accuracy; ten participants calculated means as accurately as possible, ignoring time. Although reaction times were significantly longer in the accurate condition, accuracy did not differ between conditions. Across conditions reaction times increased with the number of observations, and with larger relative variance.

Psychological causes of employees' resistance to change in organizations

Mozhvilo, Ilena Organizational Psychology, Institut of Psychology, Kiev, Ukraine

Objective. Finding out psychological causes of resistance to change in organizations. Method. The research was done on mid-level managers in a private building company in Dnipropetrovsk region using L.Karamushka Resistance to change questionnaire and SPSS. Results. The leading causes of employees' resistance to change were found to be (most important first): fear of salary decrease and unemployment, incomprehension of new activities, unawareness of rewards brought about by new activities, anxiety due to uncertainty, and ignorance of new work principles. Conclusion. The findings call for a development of a special joint employees' and managers' training course in overcoming resistance to organizational change.

Mixed emotional messages to prevent the occasional excessive drinking behavior

Muñoz, Dolores Social Psycology, Universidad Autónoma, Madrid, Spain Carrera, Pilar Social Psychology, Universidad Autónoma, Madrid, Spain Caballero, Amparo Social Psycology, Universidad Autónoma, Madrid, Spain

The risk behaviour is, in general, difficult to predict. The fact is that attitude does not predict real behaviour. In this work we induce emotions presenting to the students, in laboratory situation, two types of emotional messages, negative versus mixed, with the aim of studying their differential effect on the probability estimated by participants of repeating the behaviour of occasional excessive drinking in the near future. The results show that the two types of emotional messages had a differential effect. These results suggest that mixed emotional messages could be more effective in campaigns for the prevention of this risk behavior.

Computer competence and gender: Differences in test-performance and attribution under stereotype threat

Mueller, Stephanie Experimental Psychology, Institut of Psychology, Granada, Spain Koch, Sabine Department of Psychology, University of Heidelberg, Heidelberg, Germany Sieverding, Monika Department of Psychology, University of Heidelberg, Heidelberg, Germany

The study investigated the influence of Stereotype Threat (ST) on performance in a computer-test and attribution patterns after failure. Participants were assigned to conditions according to the ST-paradigm (positive, negative, neutral), followed by a learning test at the computer and a final task, providing an experience of failure (faulty memory stick). Overall, no gender-differences emerged in the computer-test. Women showed better results in the negative than in the neutral condition, potentially suggesting a reactance effect. Gender- and threat-specific attribution patterns emerged in the negative threat condition: women attributed failure rather internally (own inability), men externally (faulty technique).

Success factors in Human resource consulting

Mueller, Andrea Winterthur, Switzerland

In research and practise a new understanding of human resource management's role arises (Kesler & Law, 1997; Oertig, 2006). The presented results are preliminary results of the first phase of a research project, which purpose is to validate procedures, criterions of quality and impact on human resource consulting. In a first step a document analysis is realized. N=12 case documentations of consulting in eight notable Suisse companies was coded by a grid model allowing differentiated in best and worst consultations. The results will be flow in university courses and in the development of a prototype for HR-consulting.

Comparison of competence assessment by self and supervisory ratings vs. performance tests on technically skilled personnel

Muellerbuchhof, Ralf Math.-Nat., Psychologie, Tech. Universität Dresden, Dresden, Germany

Validity and economic considerations make it difficult to decide between different methods of competence assessment. However, an exhaustive operationalization of the competence construct is commonly used. Hence the overlap of rating and performance data had to be estimated in triplicate. Self-concept of competence, supervisory ratings, and tests of vocational performance of low and high experienced technically skilled personnel were measured in a new canonical approach (N=138). Results showed weak bivariate correlations but medium to high explained variance in Cohen's set correlation. Implications are both a confirmation of meta-analytical findings and a recommendation of multi-methodical use of different sources of competence assessment.

Man-environment bond: A community based study

Mukherjee, Jhuma Psychology, Ashutosh College, Kolkata, India

Environment is a broad concept encompassing the whole range of diverse surrounding in which man perceive, experience and react to events and change. Current study examined how perception of community dwellers was affected by their identity bond. Data were collected from urban community dwellers (N=200) through perceived values of dwelling environment inventory and perceived family environment inventory. Statistical analysis revealed that favourable environmental perception of urban dwellers was affected by their sweet past memories, ideas, pleasant values and good interpersonal relationship with family members due to attractive physical environmental features, modern infrastructural facility and planned and scientific environment.

Cognitive performance in patients with MDD: Profile, dynamics and factors

Navratilova, Petra Dept. of Psychiatry, The Faculty Hospital Brno, Brno, Czech Republic Kucerova, Hana Department of Psychiatry, The Faculty Hospital Brno, Brno, Czech Republic Ustohal, Libor Department Of Psychiatry, Faculty Hospital Brno, Brno, Czech Republic

Objectives: This study investigated profile and dynamics of cognitive performance in patients with MDD. We tried to find, whether predicted factors (depressive symptomatology, response to treatment, current emotional state, personality characteristics) are related to cognitive performance. Methods: 25 in-patients with MDD (ICD-10) were assessed by comprehensive neuropsychological test battery at the beginning and at the end of acute treatment. Assessment of predicted factors was made simultaneously. Results and Conclusion: Cognitive performance was partly improved after acute treatment and was related to depressive symptomatology and response to treatment. This work was supported by the Ministry of Education Czech Republic (Project MSM0021622404).

Personality development in strong environments

Ness, James Gruppe Wehr Psychologie, Streitkräfteamt, Bonn, Germany

One process of domestication is canalizing behavior through the imposition of strong stable environments. If an institution is a strong environment, then individuals' tendencies should canalize toward an ideal. The USMA class of 2006 were given the NEOPIR their freshman and junior years. Randomly selected faculty, staff, and seniors responded to the NEOPIR with the ideal Cadet in mind. Freshmen NEOPIR scores didn't differ from those of the general population and didn't predict attrition. NEOPIR profiles changed reliably from freshmen to junior year toward the ideal. Strong environments canalize behavior but interviews suggest that "havens" are needed to manage strain.

Psychology in health education

Neu, Eva Dept. Physiology, Inst. Umweltmedizin/ICSD e.V., Muenchen, Germany Schulz, Guntram Dept. Physiology, Inst. Umweltmedizin/ICSD e.V., Muenchen, Germany Schumitz, Angela Dept. Physiology, Inst. Umweltmedizin/ICSD e.V., Muenchen, Germany Schratz, Michael Dept. Physiology, Inst. Umweltmedizin/ICSD e.V., Muenchen, Germany Michailov, Michael Ch. Dept. Physiology, Inst. Umweltmedizin/ICSD e.V., Muenchen, Germany

Psychology is fundamental discipline in anthropological-sciences considering human spheres (consciousness, cognitive, emotional, etc.). The future needs founding of integral anthropology for total health of all spheres via scientific evaluation and application of occidental (Buddhism-Brahmanism-Christianism-Confucianism-Mohammedanism-Mosaism) psychological, philosophical, theological, medical, pedagogical approaches and their integration in holistic-multidimensional health-education (health-teacher) and psychotherapy in context of psychosomatics (Th.v.Uexküll) and somatopsychics (Y.Ikemi). This could support UNO-Agenda-21 for global better education, health economy, ecology incl. foundation of international university (B.Russel)/experimental schools (I.Kant) [Congr.-Books: Int.-Congr.-Philos.-279-280/2007/FISP-Istanbul; Int.-Congr.-Psychol.-1028.62/3028.96/2004/Beijing; J.-Psychosom.-Res.-58/6:S85-6/2005].

Two perspectives on the modular mind

Ni, Yujing Dept. Educational Psychology, Chinese Univ. of Hong Kong, Hong Kong, China, People's Republic of : Hong Kong SAR

The purpose of this paper is to clarify the concept "modular mind" as theorized by Chomsky and Fodor. The focus of the discussion is on four questions that relate to the divergence occurring in current research in the field of cognitive science. The first question deals with defining what is meant by "the priori," followed by the question of whether "the priori" plays a central part in cognitive processing. The next question examines domain-specific aspects of "the priori," and the final question asks to what extent is "the priori" developmentally constant.

The influence of academic self-efficacy and work values on career awareness of elementary school, junior high school and high school students

Niimi, Naoko Graduate School of Education, Hiroshima University, Hiroshima, Japan Maeda, Kenichi Graduate School of Education, Hiroshima University, Higashi-Hiroshima, Japan

The influence of academic self-efficacy and work values such as interpersonal orientation and status orientation on career awareness of elementary school, junior high school, and high school students was investigated. Participants (196 elementary, 427 junior high, and 453 high school students) completed the Academic Self-Efficacy scale, Work Values scale, and Career Awareness scale. Canonical correlation analyses indicated that academic self-efficacy and interpersonal orientation were positively related to four areas of career awareness in each educational stage. Furthermore, the relationship between academic self-efficacy and career awareness became lower as the educational stage increased.

Effects of the health education program with gaming simulation for college students

Nishigaki, Etsuyo Dept. of Psychology, Wakayama Medical University, Wakayama, Japan

Objectives: This study examined the health education program involving the gaming simulation was more effective in participants' cognitive and behavioral changes than the program without gaming. Methods: One hundred and eighteen college students participated in the program. Only the experiment group experienced the game. All participants practiced two everyday healthy habits they chose for two weeks. Results: The results showed that the experiment group attained higher achievement in the healthy habits, and their scores of health locus of control were significantly different from those of the control group. Conclusions: The gaming simulation was effective to promote college students' healthier habits.

The relationship between students' attitude towards entrepreneurship, value, personality and achievement motivation: A case study in Malaysia

Nordin, Nor Akmar FPPSM, University Technology Malaysia, Skudai, Malaysia **Panatik, Siti Alsyah** FPPSM, UNIVERSITY TECHNOLOGY MALAYSIA, SKUDAI, Malaysia **Abdul Wahab, Shah Rollah** FPPSM, UNIVERSITY TECHNOLOGY MALAYSIA, SKUDAI, Malaysia

This paper is designed to study the relationship between students' attitude towards entrepreneurship, value, personality and achievement motivation. The differences of students' attitude towards entrepreneurship are also assessed from University Technology of Malaysia. A Likert Scale instrument that consisted of five parts was used to measure students' attitude, value, personality, achievement motivation and demographic factors. The correlation analyses indicated that the relationship between students' attitude, value, personality and achievement motivation was significant. While, only faculty factor showed the significant differences of students' attitude towards entrepreneurship. Results were discussed on the light of others' findings and results.

Cognitive aging and decision quality in consumer choice

Nunes, Ludmila Almada, Portugal **Mata, Rui** Psychology, University of Lisbon, Lisbon, Portugal

The impact of limited information search and use of simpler strategies due to aging was evaluated by simulating the decision process of elderly consumers with computational models of decision strategies and measuring the quality of the decision outcomes using objective criteria such as expert and consumer product ratings from a popular website. Our results suggest that there is on average little value lost when using a noncompensatory strategy, which leads to better than chance performance. Thus, the study supports the notion that old adults' limited information search and use of simpler decision strategies may not lead to poorer decision quality.

Explaining academic achievement: The roles of procrastination and executive functioning

Nutter-Upham, Katherine Dept. of Psychology, City University of New York, Brooklyn, USA

Procrastination, or the tendency to defer tasks, is commonly observed in educational settings. Aspects of executive functioning, known to be associated with academic achievement (Spinella & Miley, 2003), may be related to the tendency to procrastinate. Research, however, has yet to investigate the interrelation of executive functioning, procrastination, and academic achievement. One hundred undergraduates completed the Procrastination Scale (Lay, 1986) and Behavior Rating Inventory of Executive Functioning (Roth et al., 2004). Structural equation modeling suggested that the relationship between executive functioning and academic performance (measured by GPA) was moderated by procrastination. Implications for pedagogical practice and intervention will be discussed.

Continuing initiatives for Nigerian psychology in the present century

Nwachuku, Viktor Faculty fo Education, Abia State University, Uturu, Umuahia, Nigeria

The practice of psychology in Nigeria dates to over forty years. However, its application to scientific, technological and social problems is yet to make appreciable impact. Given this reality some initiatives are proposed that could be undertaken to bring about real progress. fFirst, rather than function as distinct entities, professional bodies in psychology need to band themselves together so that they can make cohesive statements regarding the interface between the discipline and modern development process. In thi way, practitioners will begin to decipher ways in which psychological knowledge can address the several problems that are sources of concern for Nigeria.

Factors predicting career iIndecision for Japanese liberal arts, education, and business majors

Obana, Maki Counseling and Psychological S, University of California-Berke, Bribane, USA

The purpose of this study was to examine Japanese college students' career indecision (CI): whether career decision-making self-efficacy (CDMSE), career maturity (CM), and anxiety were predictive of CI. Additionally, it was hypothesized that college major (liberal arts/education versus business) would moderate the predictor-criterion relations. Participants included 252 liberal arts/education students and 211 business students. Results from multiple regression indicated that CI was related to CDMSE, CM, and anxiety. The study concluded that CDMSE was a stronger predictor of CI for liberal arts/education students than business students. CM was significant only for liberal arts/education majors. Anxiety was significant for both majors.

Phenomenological study about students' cognition of campus environment

Ohta, Hirohiko Dept. of Human Sciences, Kansai University, Kobe, Japan

This study examines how students subjectively recognize their campus with using phenomenological methodology. The participants were 9 male and 7 female students of a university. They were inquired by means of in-depth interviews. After qualitative analysis, seven main categories of cognitive aspects were extracted; Relationships with university, Recognition about teachers, Environmental changes, Relationships with others, Characteristics of himself/herself, Evaluation of campus environment, and Comparison with other universities. The present results indicate that students' cognition is constructed through synthesis of physical, social, and cultural aspects of campus environment. Students' viewpoints should be reconsidered for better planning of campus construction.

Strategic model for learning from reading at the college tutoring

Ortega Andrade, Norma Angélica Area académica de psicología, UAEH, Pachuca Hidalgo, Mexico **García Cruz, Rubén** Area académica de psicología, UAEH, Pachuca Hidalgo, Mexico **Romero Ramírez, Mucio Alejandro** Area académica de psicología, UAEH, Pachuca Hidalgo, Mexico

Reading is one of the most important mechanism for the transmission of knowledge (Gonzalez, 2004), at the top level, however, the college student has not developed the need for reading as a means of learning; Well then, the present work research aimed at implementing a strategic model to learn from reading through mentoring. Based on a design multivariate 2x2, it was found that students changed their procurement processes, organization, development, implementation and information retrieval read, after the intervention with the model.

Students psychoeducational diagnosis II: Self-regulation and academic performance

Osés Bargas, Rosa Maria Dept. of Psychology, Universidad Autónoma d Yucatán, Mérida, Mexico **Mezquita Hoyos, Yanko** Psychology, Universidad Autónoma d Yucatán, Mérida Yucatán, Mexico **Aguayo Chan, Jorge** Psychology, Universidad Autónoma d Yucatán, Mérida Yucatán, Mexico **de Lille Quintal, José** Psychology, Universidad Autónoma d Yucatán, Mérida Yucatán, Mexico

It was identified the correlation of the self-regulation with the academic performance of a group of students. With this purpose, we validated psycho-metrically the modification of a self-regulation questionaire of 20 reactives with 206 undergraduate students of psychology. Subsequently it was correlated the scores of 56 of these participants with their academic performance and it was found a significative correlation between the component of organization with the mathematics module: moment product coefficient of pearson = .28, p < .05. The results were discussed accordingly to the participants token and accordingly to the convergence between learning and self-regulation strategies.

Sex differences in heart rates, anxiety and estimated time under paired cooperative task situations

Osato, Eiko International Communication, Fukuoka Internat. University, Fukuoka, Japan

This study examined sex differences in the effects of three conditions, verbal condition that may talk each other, nonverbal condition that may not talk each other during performing a task, and instruction only for a way of the task, on heart rates, STAI scores, and estimated duration of the task performance in a cooperative task situation to do in a pair of the same sex. Subjects were 62 Japanese students, 38 men and 24 women, aged from 20 to 22. Instructions were conveyed by VTR. As results, there were sex differences on heart rates and state anxiety scores.

Self-esteem as the buffer in relation between occupational stress and health in medical profession

Ostrowski, Tadeusz Marian Inst. of Applied Psychology, Jagiellonian University, Kraków, Poland

The aim of research was to discover psychological factors that may reduce a pathogenetic influence of occupational stress on health in medical profession. House's model of relation between occupational stress and health provided theoretical underpinnings for this research. Methods: Group of 121 physicians has been examined. Interview and psychological questionnaires were used. Results: Physicians' self-esteem plays a crucial role in coping with occupational stress. The social support has salutogenetic role in relation between stress and health because it improves self-esteem and it diminishes perceived stress of work. Conclusion: The stress management training for physicians should be focused on self-esteem.

Using learning diaries to evaluate training effects on students' self-regulated learning

Otto, Barbara Inst. für Pädag. Psychologie, Universität Frankfurt, Frankfurt, Germany **Perels, Franziska** Educational Psychology, Institute of Psychology, Darmstadt, Germany

This study aimed on the development and evaluation of a training to enhance students' self-regulated learning. The training bases on a process model of self-regulation, which differentiates three phases. Altogether, 105 4th graders of German elementary school participated within the intervention study. During this time the students filled out a learning diary. These process data were analyzed with trend analyses as well as interrupted time-series analyses. For almost all variables, significant trends were found. The interrupted time-series analyses confirmed partly the expected effects. By these results the conclusion can be drawn that students' self-regulatory competences can be enhanced by training.

Academic achievement in university students through motivation, quality of life and lifestyles

Pacheco, Andreia Dept. of Psychology, University of the Algarve, Faro, Portugal **Jesus, Saul** Psychology, University of the Algarve, Faro, Portugal **Martins, Alda** Psychology, University of the Algarve, Faro, Portugal

The present research aim is to understand the relations between the variables lifestyles, motivation, quality of life and academic achievement in university students. The 684 students, from the University of the Algarve, answered four on-line questionnaires. The results suggest that, on one hand, socio-demographical variables have influence on motivation, quality of life and lifestyles, and, on the other hand, these variables influence academic achievement. Therefore, it seems important, to improve academic results, to intervene both on motivational and health aspects.

The influence of self-efficacy and social support on life-satisfaction and academic achievement: Longitudinal analysis of the transition from elementary to high school

Park, Young-Shin Dept. of Education, Inha University, Incheon, Republic of Korea Choi, Jung-Sook Education, Inha University, Inchon, Republic of Korea Kim, Uichol Business administration, Inha University, Inchon, Republic of Korea

This study examines longitudinally the influence of self-efficacy and social support on life-satisfaction and academic achievement starting at Grade 6 through Grade 11 and Grade 12. A total of 961 elementary school children completed a questionnaire when they were Grade 6. First, social support received from parents has a direct and positive influence on students' self-efficacy, which in turn increases their academic achievement. Second, self-efficacy has a direct and positive influence life-satisfaction. Third, although social support received from friends had no impact at the elementary school level, at the high school level, it has a direct and positive influence on their life-satisfaction.

How psychology is given its importance in the Early Childhood Teacher Education Program adopted in METU

Parlak Rakap, Asiye Elementary Education, METU, Ankara, Turkey

The purpose of the current study is to investigate whether psychology is taken into consideration in the Early Childhood Teacher Education Program adopted in METU. For this purpose, syllabuses of thirty eight courses were examined. Thirty four of those courses were must courses and four of them were electives opened at elementary department. To determine, the number of times the word "psychology" appears in the course objectives were listed. The data were coded by manifest content. It is found that the word "psychology" used in the syllabuses 13 times. This result is quite questionable.

Health promotion with a bounce: Conveying well-being and lifestyle

Paulos, Carlos Centre de prévention - CePT, Luxembourg, Luxembourg Biver, Cynthia CePT, Centre de prévention, Luxembourg, Luxembourg Carius, Roland CePT, Centre de prévention, Luxembourg, Luxembourg Duscherer, Katia CePT, Centre de prévention, Luxembourg, Luxembourg Godart, Astrid CePT, Centre de prévention, Luxembourg, Luxembourg Herz, Anne-Carole CePT, Centre de prévention, Luxembourg, Luxembourg Michaelis, Théràse CePT, Centre de prévention, Luxembourg, Luxembourg

For decades, addiction prevention projects focused on information and dissuasion campaigns. Recently, the framework of prevention shifted towards the promotion of well-being and life skills development. In order to reach a broad audience, the CePT designed the project "Trampolin – Sprongkraaft am Alldag" (i.e. Trampoline – the daily vitality), an interactive exhibition that toured for two years through Luxembourg. In this context the attendees were encouraged to reflect on their own habits and personal well-being. After a brief description of our

methodology, the relationship between well-being, lifestyle and addiction prevention will be discussed.

Artificial grammar learning in primary school children with and without developmental dyslexia

Pavlidou, Elpis Edinburgh, United Kingdom Kelly, Louise PPLS, University of Edinburgh, Edinburgh, United Kingdom Williams, Joanne The Moray School of Education, The University of Edinburgh, Edinburgh, United Kingdom

We explore implicit learning in children (9-12yrs) with and without developmental dyslexia using a modified Artificial Grammar Learning Task, which consists of a learning phase (Perfect Free Recall) and a testing phase (classification judgments). Preliminary results show that dyslexic children require more trials to achieve PFR for items of higher complexity compared to non-dyslexic, but perform in a similar way during the testing phase (repeated measures ANOVA (Group x Grammaticality x Chunk strength) revealed only a main effect of Grammaticality). The theoretical and practical implications on the notion of implicit learning (and the resulting knowledge) in childhood are discussed.

Functional MRI investigation of neural networks in implicit sequence learning in schizophrenic patients

Pedersen, Anya Abt. Psychiatrie, Universitätsklinik Münster, Münster, Germany Bauer, Jochen Psychiatry, University of Muenster, Münster, Germany Kugel, Harald Clinical Radiology, University of Muenster, Münster, Germany Arolt, Volker Psychiatry, University of Muenster, Münster, Germany Ohrmann, Patricia Psychiatry, University of Muenster, Münster, Germany

Introduction: We examined neural correlates associated with implicit learning in schizophrenia patients compared to controls. Methods: Nineteen schizophrenia patients and 21 healthy controls were studied with 3 Tesla functional MRI while performing a serial reaction-time task (SRT). Brain activation in sequential blocks and random blocks was contrasted. Results: Impaired implicit learning was associated with decreased activation of the striatum (both groups) and of the hippocampus and middle occipital cortex (schizophrenia patients). Simple motor performance was not related to striatal activation. Discussion: These present results support the engagement of a fronto-striatal network during implicit sequence learning in schizophrenia patients and controls.

The effects of efficiency of human resources management on the performance of accounting firms in Northeastern region

Peemanee, Jindarat Management Dept., Mahasarakham University, Mahasarakham, Thailand Pratoom, Karun Management, Mahasarakham University, Mahasarakham, Thailand Srisurach, Sirintip Management, Mahasarakham University, Mahasarakham, Thailand

This research for study investigate the effects of efficiency of human resources management (HRM) on the performance of accounting firms. Samples were 170 entrepreneurs of accounting firms and responded by 139 entrepreneurs. Analysed of data by F-test (ANOVA and MANOVA), multiple correlation analysis, and MRA. The findings revealed that entrepreneurs of accounting firms had opinions about efficiency of HRM both wholly and singly at high level. In conclusion, efficiency of HRM positively affected the performance of accounting firms.

Predicting academic success in college courses: General intelligence, personality traits and emotional intelligence

Perez, Nelida Psicologia Evolutiva, Universidad de Alicante, Alicante, Spain

Intelligence and personality have played central roles in the investigation of determinants of human performance. Recently, the construct of emotional intelligence (EI) has emerged as an additional explanatory concept. However, associations between academic performance and EI are inconsistent. In this study, the capacity of emotional intelligence to predict academic achievement was examined in a sample of 608 undergraduate university students, using grades as criterion. The predictive validity of emotional intelligence was compared with general intelligence, g, and the Big Five dimensions of personality. Hierarchical regression analysis revealed the incremental validity of EI beyond personality and over and above general intelligence.

Health-promoting lifestyle profile of psychologist university students in Mexico

Perez Fortis, Adriana Tlaxcala, Mexico Ulla Díez, Sara CC. Educación y Humanidades, Universidad de Castilla La Man, Cuenca, Spain Franco Franco, Soledad Facultad de Psicología, Universidad Autónoma de Puebla, Puebla, Mexico

Objective: To examine health behaviors in university students. Method: A cross-sectional study was conducted, using a convenience sample (n=307) from the Autonomous University of Puebla, México. Instruments used were the HPLP II (Walker & Hill-Polerecky, 1996), and a questionnaire to assess demographic and health information. Results: Only 34.2% of the students had a health-promoting lifestyle. The scores on some dimensions of the HPLP-II differed significantly ($P < 0.05$) by gender, age, marital status, economic situation and parental educational status. Conclusions: University students have unhealthy habits which are influenced by their socio-demographical characteristics. These results provide information for health promoting interventions.

Odor from industrial sources: Defining and predicting resident's annoyance

Pierrette, Marjorie UFR SPSE, Université Paris x, Nanterre cedex, France

Studies about olfactive annoyance highlight interindividual differences despite similar odor concentrations (Miedema, Walpot et Steunenberg, 2000). The main purpose of our research is to identify individual and contextual factors which could predict the olfactive annoyance felt by residents living near waste processing of animal origin. 187 residents answered a questionnaire. The results show four predictive factors which are percieved olfactive sensitivity, estimated pollution level of the industrial site, unpredictability and intensity of odors. To go futher we could compare the annoyance produced by another industrial source with a more positive image.

"Air pollution is bad to my health": Children's knowledge of the role of environment in health and illness

Piko, Bettina Dept. of Behavioral Sciences, Universtity of Szeged, Szeged, Hungary Pluhar, Zsuzsanna Dept. of Behavioral Sciences, Universtity of Szeged, Szeged, Hungary Kovacs, Szilvia Dept. of Neurosis, Children's Hospital of Buda, Budapest, Hungary Uzzoli, Annamaria Dept. of Regional Geography, Eötvös Loránd University, Budapest, Hungary

Objectives: The study reported here describes 9-11-year-olds' lay beliefs and knowledge about harmful environmental effects and environment-borne disease. Methods: Data were collected among children aged 9-11 (N = 448) in Hungary. The 'draw-and-write' technique was used in the data collection.

Results: Most respondents clearly described the man-made environmental risks (e.g., noise, air pollution). Among the environment-borne diseases, most of the children mentioned infectious diseases which were followed by allergy. A great number of them did not mention a specific disease but trivial symptoms. Conclusions: Children are aware of the environmental health hazards and they are both environment and health conscious at this age.

The cognitive functions and psychopharmacology
Pluzhnikov, Iliya Psychology, Moscow State University, Moscow, Russia
There was a research of the affect of different psychopharmacological drugs on the cognitive functions (perception, memory, attention and thinking) of people with different psychiatry disorders (schizophrenia, affective pathology and addictions). All of the drugs could be divided in two groups: drugs, which improve cognitive functions and drugs which worsen their operation. The best way to reveal this affect is to use either the modern psychometric method or the syndromes analysis method, developed by the Russian school of A.R. Luria and B.V. Zeygarnik. In the further research these methods should be used all together.

Diversity management in organizations: Context specific effects of culturally diverse workforces
Podsiadlowski, Astrid Wien, Austria
Besides increasing cultural diversity in organizations the effects of diversity management measures on individual and organizational outcomes have rarely been studied. Based on an integrative research model this paper is going to present results of organizational surveys conducted in different national contexts. Employers in New Zealand, Indonesia and Singapore answered open and closed questions on the demographic composition of their organization and their experience in managing a culturally diverse workforce. Results stretch the importance of cultural distance and employers attitudes for employing minority group members and implementing diversity management measures. This research provides implications for successful diversity management in organizations.

Neuroendocrine responses to academic stressors
Preuß, Diana Inst. für Psychologie, Ruhr-Universität Bochum, Bochum, Germany *Schoofs, Daniela* Psychology, Ruhr-Universität Bochum, Bochum, Germany *Wolf, Oliver T.* Psychology, Ruhr-Universität Bochum, Bochum, Germany
Objectives: To compare the neuroendocrine response to different academic stressors. Methods: Salivary cortisol was assessed before and after an oral presentation (without grades) and before and after a written exam (with grades). Results: Compared to a control day cortisol levels were markedly elevated before the oral presentation and continued to rise during it. In contrast cortisol levels were only moderately increased before the written exam and decreased during the course of it. Conclusions: Social evaluative threat associated with an oral presentation has a stronger influence on the cortisol stress response than the academic pressure associated with a written exam.

Latent structure of sport interests of female and male adolescents controlled for general attitude toward sports, achievement in sport and level of activity
Prot, Franjo Faculty of Kinesiology, University of Zagreb, Zagreb, Croatia
The structure of sport interests of 942 female and 988 male adolescents have been studied. Achievement in sports, general attitude scale toward sports, level of sport activity and questionnaire consisting of the list of 52 available sports (to evaluate their interest in each of them) have been measured.

Latent structure of sport preferences controlled for general attitude toward sports, achievement in sport and level of activity was established by component analysis. Congruences of three corresponding orthoblique factors are 0.951 (outdoor and adventurous activities), 0.892 (marital art and male dominant) and 0.692 (bipolar factors of aesthetic sports and indoors sport games).

School dropout and self-esteem at the early elementary school
Rambaud, Angelique Psychologie (EA 3259), Universite de Nantes, Nantes Cedex 3, France *Rambaud, Angélique* Psychologie (EA 3259), Université de Nantes, Nantes Cedex 3, France *FLORIN, Agnès* Psychologie (EA 3259), Université de Nantes, Nantes Cedex 3, France
The purpose of this research is to study the relation between repeating at the early elementary school, self-esteem and reading abilities of 178 pupils of grade one and two. Among 87 pupils of grade one, 10 repeated grade one and among 91 pupils of grade two, 13 repeated grade one. Self-esteem was measured by a french adaptation of Harter's Self perception Profile (1982) and reading abilities were evaluated using the Identification of Written Words Test (Khomsi, 1997). Results indicate that pupils who repeated grade one reported a significantly lower level of self-esteem and reading abilities than pupils in grade two who had never repeated.

Evaluation of a learning organization questionnaire: Adaptation, validity and reliability
Ramirez L., Jorge J. Ciencia y Tecnología Comportam, Universidad Simón Bolívar, Caracas, Venezuela *Mayorca, Romulo* Ciencia y Tecnología Comportam, Universidad Simón Bolívar, Caracas, Venezuela
The present work evaluated the adaptation of Dimensions of the Learning Organization Questionnaire (DLOQ) to the Venezuelan context (Watkins and Marsick, 1997). In the English version, the instrument has seven dimensions of the organizational learning in the organizations that learn: continuous learning, dialogue and inquiry, team learning, embedded system, system connection, empowerment and provide leadership. The sample was conformed by 250 worker-students of MBA. The instrument was translated to Spanish and adapted to the local context, a factorial analysis showing that the items are integrated in only six dimensions. The internal consistency was 0.80, and for the dimensions it was between 0,71 and 0,86.

Semantic priming between verbal and pictorial codes in visual modality
Rebernjak, Blaž Department of Psychology, Faculty of Philosophy, Zagreb, Croatia
Assuming that concepts can be activated by both pictures and words, and that the activation can spread to neighboring concepts, we demonstrated experimentally the effect of semantic priming between verbal and pictorial codes of visual modality. The reduction of reaction time was evident when words and pictures were preceded by semantically related pictures and words, respectively. The next step is to reduce the overall reaction time to avoid conscious contamination by adopting a lexical decision paradigm and applying it to pictorial stimuli.

Reading motivation: Decline in adolescence and relations to sex, reading behavior and literacy
Retelsdorf, Jan Inst. für Psychologie, Universität zu Kiel, Kiel, Germany *Möller, Jens* Department of Psychology, Christian-Albrechts-University, Kiel, Germany
The assumption of a "reading crisis" (i.e. decrease of reading motivation) at transition from childhood to adolescence is widespread. However, only little empirical support from longitudinal studies exists.

Latent change analyses with 1508 German secondary school students (5th to 8th grade) support this assumption for "reading enjoyment" and "reading for interest". Thereby, the decrease of "reading enjoyment" was lower for girls than for boys, while there were no sex differences concerning "reading for interest". Moreover, "reading enjoyment" turned out as a significant predictor of reading behavior and literacy, while "reading for interest" only predicted reading behavior.

Neural activation shifts during implicit sequence learning in old age: An fMRI study
Rieckmann, Anna Aging Research Center, Karolinska Institute, Stockholm, Sweden *Fischer, Håkan* Aging Research Center, Karolinska Institute, Stockholm, Sweden *Bäckman, Lars* Aging Research Center, Karolinska Institute, Stockholm, Sweden
Older adults often demonstrate relatively well preserved implicit learning (IL) despite volumetric and neurochemical losses in key brain areas (i.e., the striatum). This study explores possible compensatory brain mechanisms during IL in aging. Younger and older adults performed a serial reaction time task during fMRI acquisition. Both age groups evidenced similar IL and recruited a similar striatal-cortical network. However, in a direct comparison, older adults showed more activation in cortical areas, whereas younger adults showed more activation in striatal regions. Results are interpreted in terms of compensatory neural shifts that may contribute to successful IL in old age.

Negative life events and styles of coping, in relation to hopelessness depression: Analysis in females in comparison with males
Rodriguez Naranjo, Carmen Personality Dept., University of Malaga, Malaga, Spain *Cano Gonzalez, Antonio* Basic Department, Malaga University, Malaga, Spain *Romero Ballaltas, Macarena* Personality Dept., Malaga University, Malaga, Spain
This study explores how negative life events and coping styles are related to hopelessness depression in adolescents. A sample of 488 students aged 12 to 18 completed the Life Experiences Survey, the Coping Across Situations Questionnaire and the Hopelessness Depression Symptoms Questionnaire. As expected, the regression analyses revealed that negative life events predicted hopelessness depression in both boys and girls. However, less active, more internal and more withdrawal coping styles predicted depression in girls and not in boys. Negative life events in girls interacted with less active and more internal coping styles to predict depression. These findings convey important implications regarding the focus of intervention for hopelessness depression in adolescents.

Productivity measurement and enhancement system among knowledge-intensive services
Roth, Colin Colin Roth OE, Koblenz, Germany
We report the first application of ProMES among knowledge-intensive high-tech services. Performance data was collected over a period of 24 months on a workgroup in an international market research company. The project turned out to be effective in the first feedback condition (d=1.7) and even more effective in the second, internally moderated feedback condition (d=2.8). In addition, team climate was assessed: After the implementation of ProMES, substantial changes occurred on all measured dimensions. Throughout the project, however, only task relevant aspects of cohesion evolved. We conclude with the discussion of issues when conducting ProMES with organizations tackling knowledge intensive service tasks.

Evolution of place attachment and place identity

Ruiz, Cristina Dept. de Psicología Cognitiva, Universidad de la Laguna, La Laguna, Spain Vidal, Tomeu Psicología Social, Universidad de Barcelona, Barcelona, Spain Valera, Sergi Psicología Social, Universidad de Barcelon, La Laguna, Spain Tabernero, Carmen Psicología, Universidad de Córdoba, Córdoba, Spain Hidalgo, M. Carmen Psicología Social, Universidad de Málaga, Málaga, Spain

Place attachment feelings could turn into feelings of pride for the place of residence, providing personal and social identity. From this perspective, this would be a proof that attachment precedes to identity. To verify this evolution, attachment and identity to the neighbourhood were measured in 936 students of Barcelona and La Laguna. A factorial design of repeated measurements revealed that for subjects with less time living in the neighbourhood, attachment is significantly superior to the identity, whereas for participants with more time in the neighbourhood, these differences disappear, in such way that identity is significantly superior to attachment.

Assessment of imagination use in inner conflict resolution with thematic apperception test

Ryzhov, Andrey Neuro- and Clinical Psychology, Moscow State University, Moscow, Russia

The ability to use invented stories (reflected in Thematic Apperception Test performance) as means of conflict resolution (as opposed to defensive use of imagination) was studied. The importance of story structure is stressed. It is conceived as a series of representations of conflict, with special attention to compromising ones, called mediators after Claude Levi-Strauss's work. For each TAT table various models of conflict resolution (prototales) are described. It is argued that subject's story should be assessed within the frame of corresponding model, because they differ in the way the transformations of conflict are used and the strategy of conflict resolution.

Developmental ability of reversibility perception of the ambiguous figures

Séra, László Dept. of Psychology, Kodolányi University College, Székesfehérvár, Hungary Révész, György Inst. of Psychology, University of Pécs, Pécs, Hungary Dósa, Zoltán Dept. of Human Sciences, Sapientia University, Târgu Mures, Romania

Ambiguous figures trigger two incompatible perceptions. Two experiments were done with children between the ages of 3.5 and 9 years. In the first experiment we assessed the proportion of the spontaneous reversal of images, the relationship between the reversal of the informed condition ambiguous figures, and the results of theory of mind tests, and those of tests assessing interpretation differences (False Belief, Droodle task). In the second experiment we aimed to explore the relationship of reversals and executive functions in the case of both monolingual and bilingual children. Selective attention, inhibition, attentional switch and mental imagery abilities connected to the central executive function contribute to the complex perception-based process of reversal.

Relationship between fiction games and mind theory

Saiz Manzanares, Maria Consuelo Education Sciences, Universidad de Burgos, Burgos, Spain Ortego, Jesus EDUCATION SCIENCES, BURGOS UNIVERSITY, BURGOS, Spain

Mind theory is a reflection of a mental subsystem which may construct and manipulate certain mental representations (meta-representations) which are a product of a certain type of cognitive operation (Fodor, 1983). Fiction games would be a deliberate distortion of reality and would require both primary (real representations of the world) and secondary representations (meta-representations). In this study we will analyze the relationship between the indices regarding the pre-requisites of mental theory and those of symbolic game within a sample of 12 – 24 month old children.

Effects of a psychological self-regulation system on the promotion of well-being alongside productivity in workers and top performance in athletes

Sakairi, Yosuke Health and Sports Sciences, University of Tsukuba, Tsukuba, Japan Nakatsuka, Kentaro Health and Sports Sciences, University of Tsukuba, Tsukuba-shi, Japan Kizuka, Tomohiro Health and Sports Sciences, University of Tsukuba, Tsukuba-shi, Japan Soya, Hideaki Health and Sports Sciences, University of Tsukuba, Tsukuba-shi, Japan

This research developed a system to self-regulate the psychological condition of both workers and athletes so as to ensure a suitable state for displaying one's capacity. The system consisted of a self-monitoring process in which the vitality and stability scores of psychological state were self-rated through a cellular phone version of the Two-Dimensional Mood Scale (Sakairi & Soya, 2003), and a self-control process in which the individual's condition was adjusted via relaxation or activation techniques. The results showed that the system was effective for decreasing anxiety and depression levels while increasing work efficiency and sports performance.

What changed about writing activities through repeated writing practice?

Sakihama, Hideyuki Teacher Training Course, Nagoya University of Arts, Nisshin, Japan

This study examined changes of writers' attitude toward writing activities through repeated writing practice.40 college freshmen participated in this study and they were asked to write a text about psychology for high school students within 600 characters (about 250 words in English) every week, based on the content they learned in psychology class during 6 months. They were asked to answer the questionnaire about "attitude toward writing (Verninger et al, 1996)"at the beginning and at the end. Results showed that they did not emphasize so much on "revising" and "planning" activities at the end.

A psychosocial model for breast cancer protective behaviour

Saldivar, Alicia Depto. de Sociología, Universidad Autonoma Metropoli, Col. Vicentina, Mexico

In México, breast cancer is one of the most important causes of death in productive age women. The most effective way to detect a breast tumour is the self examination of breasts; unfortunately, a minor number of women practice this self-exploration once a month. This study was carried out with 500 urban Mexican women to whom where applied the Scale of related factors with breast cancer for Mexican women. Results show that only a minor number of participants examine their breasts once a month, but the recognize the risk factors easily. Model fits adequately to explain women's protective behaviour.

Gender and health: The gender perspective in health made operative by masculinity/femininity measurement

Sanchez Lopez, Pilar Dept. Psicología Diferencial, Univers. Complutense de Madrid, Madrid, Spain Díaz Morales, Juan Francisco Psicología Diferencial, Universidad Complutense de Mad, Madrid, Spain Aparicio García, Marta Psicología Diferencial, Universidad Complutense de Mad, Madrid, Spain

Objective: To introduce the gender variable (evaluated by means of Masculinity/Femininity) and test how it relates to objective measurements of health 250 Participants Instruments: CM/CFNI (Mahalik et al., 2005, 2006) and standardised health measurements Statistical Analysis: Odds Ratio and Stepwise Logistic Regression Results: Masculinity (more than just the fact of being a man) and femininity (more than just the fact of being a woman) are related to indexes of health. Conclusions: To apply the gender perspective to health it is not sufficient to evaluate sex, rather it is necessary to evaluate gender for a better understanding of indexes of health.

A therapeutic form of body exercise for over 50-year-old women

Sarje, Aino Sport sciences, University of Jyväskylä, Helsinki 20, Finland

The weakening of capability of moving may begin already at the age of 50, so that it is impossible to make use of generally available exercise services. At that age, women may also have a negative body-image which may cause inhibitions concerning the exercise environment. My "gentle exercise" program consists of imagination, relaxation and stretching exercises in a gentle group. I tested it on women aged 55-75 years and asked about their physical, psychological and social experiences. I studied the action-oriented and intrapsychic copings of the participants. Their attitudes to their corporeality became more positive. They enjoyed of belonging into the group and reported the increase of positive moods and better stress management in everyday life.

Self-regulation and inhibition in children with comorbid Attention Deficit Hyperactivity Disorder (ADHD): An evaluation of executive functions

Sarkis, Stephanie Sarkis Family Psychiatry, Gainesville, USA

Study examined the relationship between executive function and comorbid diagnoses in ADHD children. We assessed 106 children using the TOL (test of executive function), and the K-SADS-PL (diagnostic interview). All children met the diagnosis of ADHD. Most children had comorbid anxiety disorders, mood disorders, or Oppositional Defiant Disorder. Age was found to be predictive in all three measures of executive function as assessed by the TOL. Gender was predictive of total initiation time and total rule violations. Comorbid disorders were found to not have significance on executive function. The study concluded that comorbid disorders may not affect executive function.

Gender difference in psychological impact of disasters among survivors in India in last three decades

Satapathy, Sujata PPCCI, NIDM, New Delhi, India

India is a theatre of multiple disasters. A retrospective study of disaster related reports, research, & documentation revealed a pattern of gender differentiation at all levels of disaster process: exposure to risk, risk perception, preparedness, response, physical impact, psychological impact, recovery and reconstruction. Findings revealed that psychological distress was significantly more among females in earthquakes, tsunami, and cyclone, while slow onset disasters like drought and floods affected the males the most. Although gender difference in research on fire related disasters was not systematically addressed, females reported higher distress in few incidents. In few disasters, the distressed women when involved in community disaster psychosocial recovery and rehabilitation programme, the distress level was lowered.

Socialization and learning in a professional sport team

Scatolini, Ezio Bologna, Italy Liuni, Alessandra Psychology, University, Firenze, Italy

Abstract: (Objectives) This exploratory qualitative research is aimed to investigate how socialization tactics affect the learning of successful values and behaviours in a professional football young team. (Methods) Assuming socialization as part of organizational culture, some organization's key-people were interviewed using the narration method through self-stories. (Results) The data analysis indicated the presence of some recurrent tactics in the socialization process related to attitudes outcomes and sport performances. (Conclusions) Results suggest that the investigation of socialization practices allows to interiorize messages, social rules and culture of the new organization.

Cognitive processes speeded by implicitly learned visual context: An event-related brain potential study

Schankin, Andrea Inst. für Psychologie, Universität München, München, Germany Schuboe, Anna Inst. für Psychologie, Universität München, München, Germany

Searching for a task-relevant object (or target) among task-irrelevant objects (distractors) is faster when the arrangement of distractors (or context) is repeated (contextual cueing). To investigate which cognitive processes are speeded, event-related brain potentials were measured while 16 participants performed a visual search task in either new or repeated displays. The shift of attention to the target (reflected by differences in N2pc amplitude) and response selection processes (indicated by differences in P3 amplitude and LRP onset) were affected by display repetition. Probably, an implicitly known context not only predicts the target position but also reduces the response selection threshold.

Ordinal position information in implicit learning

Schuck, Nicolas Inst. für Psychologie, Humboldt-Universität zu Berlin, Berlin, Germany Gaschler, Robert Psychology, Humboldt University Berlin, Berlin, Germany

Against the background of results of a) the verbal learning tradition with humans and b) reinforced sequential learning with animals, it becomes interesting to explore if ordinal position information is acquired in human implicit sequence learning. In a visual search task participants acquired implicitly knowledge about two sequences of unique target locations. Afterwards one learned target location appeared in a new sequence together with other previously unused target locations at either the right or wrong ordinal position. Results suggest that implicit learning in humans can result in ordinal position knowledge.

Individual difference in face memory and eye fixation patterns during face learning

Sekiguchi, Takahiro Dept. Educational Psychology, Tokyo Gakugei University, Tokyo, Japan

Examined relationship between individual difference in face memory and eye fixation patterns on faces. Participants watched short movies of 20 faces and were divided into good and poor memory groups based on recognition memory for them. Both groups made longer fixations on the internal region of faces (eyes, nose, and mouth) than the external region during learning. The fixation time to the internal region was longer in the good than the poor memory group. This finding suggests that fixations on the internal region facilitate face memory, and eye fixation patterns are related to the individual difference in face memory.

Intelligence, creativity and outstanding academic achievements of gifted students

Sekowski, Andrzej Dept. of Psychology, Catholic University of Lublin, Lublin, Poland

The hypotheses assume that outstanding academic achievements are mainly connected with analytical intelligence. The higher the level of education and the stricter the criteria for outstanding achieve-

ments, the greater the significance of creative abilities. The tests used in the study include Raven's Progressive Matrices Scale, APIS Test of Intelligence, Urban and Jellen's Test for Creative Thinking-Drawing Production and Schutte Emotional Intelligence Test. Statistical analyses include analysis of variance, canonical analysis and regression analysis. The significance of individual dimensions depends on the level of achievements and on whether they are achievements in humanities, math or art.

PTG and behavioral indices consistency among the survivors of myocardial infarction patients

Senol-Durak, Emre Dept. of Psychology, Abant Izzet Baysal University, Bolu, Turkey

Posttraumatic Growth (PTG) has seen an "illusory" concept due to overestimation problems of positive parts of events following traumatic experiences. Consistency between PTG scores and other behavioral measures related to changes in life conditions may demonstrate whether PTG is really experienced. In the present study, the validity of the self report of PTG was assessed with the group of myocardial infarction patients (MIP) (N= 151). The MIP paid more attention to dietary, doing sports, not gaining weight, not smoking cigarette, and not drinking alcohol, after the crises than before the crises. Findings are discussed within the scope of current literature

A comparative study of psychological problems of children suffering from cancer, epilepsy and asthma

Shah, Ashiq Ali Psychology, Kwantlen University College, Surrey, Canada Othman, Azizah Psychology, Int. Islamic University, Kuala Lumpur, Malaysia

The study examined psychological problems of chronically ill Malaysian children. The sample consisted of 63 parents of children suffering from cancer, epilepsy and asthma. Child behavior checklist was used. The data were collected Kuala Lumpur General Hospital. The data were analyzed for differences between cancer, epilepsy and asthma children using one-way ANOVA. Result showed that children suffering from cancer, epilepsy and asthma differed in the degree of their psychological problems. The results demonstrated that children suffering from cancer had more internalizing problems as compared to the children suffering from epilepsy and asthma. Further, they indicated that epileptic children showed more thought, attention and social problems as compared to cancer and asthmatic children.

Personality hardiness distinguishes elite-level sport performers

Sheard, Michael Faculty of Health, York St. John University, York, United Kingdom

Objectives: Hardiness has three components: Commitment to full involvement in life, belief in personal control over events, and enjoyment of challenge and opportunity. Evidence from a variety of work environments, but little in sport, suggests that hardiness buffers stress, which facilitates optimal functioning. This study examined the potential of hardiness in distinguishing elite-level athletes. Methods: Volunteers (N = 1786), drawn from 38 sport classifications and competing at one of four representative levels, completed the Personal Views Survey III-R. MANCOVA revealed that International competitors scored significantly highest (p < .001) in all hardiness attitudes. Conclusion: A psychological profile that includes high hardiness appears to distinguish elite-level competitors.

Personality correlates and analytical ability among senior bank executives

Shejwal, Bhaskar Dept. of Psychology, University of Pune, Pune, India

The study investigated the relationship between personality factors measured by NEO Five Factor

Inventory by Costa & McCrae and Myers Briggs Type Indicator and their relation with analytical ability. Sixty senior bank officers answered NEO-FFI, MBTI, and Advanced Progressive Matrices Test. The analytical ability was positively correlated to openness and the MBTI dimensions of Perception and Intuition. Conscientiousness was negatively correlated to Intuition, whereas Openness correlated positively with Intuition and Feeling. Agreeableness correlated positively with Feeling. Extraversion showed positive correlation with Perception. Implications for HRM are discussed.

Application of the transtheoretical model to healthy eating in Japanese college students: Preliminary findings

Shiba, Eri Hiroshima, Japan

This study investigates psychological factors related to cooking to examine the relationship between stages of change (Transtheoretical Model) for healthy eating and self-efficacy variables. Japanese college students (n=268) completed questionnaires, considering stages of change, self-efficacy, and frequency of cooking. The frequency of cooking was higher for students in preparation stage compared with contemplation stage. Self-efficacy in cooking was also greater for students in preparation compared to contemplation. These results suggest that cooking may be essential for healthy eating. Therefore how to get accustomed to cooking should be discussed for future intervention programs that attempt to promote healthy eating in students.

Accreditation process and quality assurance of education in the professional school of clinical psychology in Japan

Shibui, Susumu Institutional Research Office, Kagoshima University, Kagoshima, Japan Ida, Masaaki University Evaluation, NIAD-UE, Kodaira-shi, Tokyo, Japan

We report the accreditation system of the professional school of clinical psychology in Japan. Training courses of the professional schools and graduate schools of clinical psychologists are certificated by the Japanese certification board for clinical psychologist. Moreover, all the kinds of professional schools are required to be accredited by accreditation organization or perform self-evaluation in the light of general guidelines established by accreditation organization every five years. We investigated the case example of quality assurance of education under these situations and examined the adequate application of the general guidelines for self-evaluation consulting the accreditation guidelines proposed by American Psychological Association.

Deciding the means of suicide

Shigemori, Masayoshi Safety Psychology Lab., Railway Technical Resarch Inst, Tokyo, Japan Murakoshi, Akiko Ergonomics LAB, Railway Technical Resarch Inst, Tokyo, Japan

To account for the selective process of suicide means, in a group setting, we asked 88 female undergraduates (average age of 18.23) to answer the suicide means sequentially corresponding to what comes to mind (ill-considered test), and to rank the means if they adopt them and reasons they adopt and avoid them (well-considered test). The results showed that the order of means in the ill-considered test corresponded better to that of real means adopted by suicidal people than that of means in the well-considered test. We concluded that people tend to decide suicide means which come to their mind first.

Psychodynamics of well-being

Shukla, Aradhana *psychology, K.U. Campus, Almora India, Almora, India*

In this paper author has raised some querries which are generally asked by a person while dealing with the psychodynamics of well being. They are as follows. 1.What is well being? 2.What is the coverage of well being? 3.What is structure and process of well being? 4.What are the essentials of well being ? 5.What are the qualityies of a person having higher sense of well being?. 6.What are the changing systems of society and modern system views regarding the construct of well being ? 7.What are the discrepancies and similarties in eastern and western thoughts of well being ?

How health educators and their audience perceive influence of attitude, subjective norms and behavioural control on health behaviours

Simeone, Arnaud *ISPEF, Université Lyon 2, Lyon, France* **Al Atrach, Julie** *ISPEF, Université LYON 2, LYON, France*

Objective: The research investigates how health educators and their audience take into account different factors which could influence health behaviours. It is based on the Functional Theory of Cognition and the Theory of Planned Behaviour. Design and Methods: 20 health educators and 20 college students were to judge acceptance for a young woman of a contraceptive method. This method is described in a series of scenario, elaborated using an orthogonal factorial design. The factors used are Attitudes, Subjective Norms, and Behavioural control (3 x 3 x 3). Results: Attitude factor is perceived more important than Subjective norms or Behavioural control factors. The model of integration of these factors is formalized.

Emotional labor and work engagement on nurses in Bali and Kupang, Indonesia

Sinambela, F. Christian *Dept. of Psychology, University of Surabaya, Surabaya, Indonesia*

Nurse was one of three professions that susceptible to feel decreasing of work engagement. The indicators are low levels of energy and mental resilience, lack of a sense of significance, enthusiasm, inspiration, pride and challenge while working. This paper had an aim to test the relationship between emotional labor and work engagement on nurses. Result indicated that there was positive correlation between surface acting and work engagement (r = 0,416 ; p = 0,001) and there was no significance positive correlation between deep acting and work engagement (r = 216, p = 0,058). The implications of these findings for health-care worker are discussed.

Triple world, triple realm model of life: A chaotic system for understanding psychology

Snyder, Roslyn *Falcon, Australia*

The triple world, triple realm model of life (3x3) is a paradigm shift, which synthesises scientific research and theory from multiple disciplines to provide a real world workable model. The 3x3 model is actually a chaotic system (a mathematical model in picture form) and like other chaotic systems, appears simple and is fractal in nature, yet any psychological theory or research finding will be found within the model. The 3x3 is a step-by-step stage-by-stage mind development model, a model of mental dysfunction, a model for individual/organizational/social behaviour. An overview will be presented.

Development and validation of a questionnaire to assess academic learning motivation through measuring regulation styles among Indonesian university students

Soegijardjo, Witriani *Faculty of Psychology, University of Padjadjaran, Bandung, Indonesia* **Sudradjat, Wismaningsih** *Faculty of Psychology, University of Padjadjaran, Bandung, Indonesia* **Wiyono, Sudarmo** *Faculty of Psychology, University of Padjadjaran, Bandung, Indonesia*

Failure to complete studies on time was related to lack of motivation for academic learning. Based on Self-Determination Theory (Deci&Ryan, 2000), a questionnaire was constructed to measure motivation ranging from amotivation (non self-determined behavior) to intrinsic motivation (self-determined). Items were constructed and tested on two tryouts (N1=432, N2=392). Content validity was obtained through examination of a panel of experts. Construct validity, reliability (α>0.7), and item analysis were computed resulting in 94 items measuring six Regulation Styles. The questionnaire is valid to detect strengths and weaknesses in learning motivation which can be used for interventions to overcome related problems.

Metatheoretical integration model proposal to explain psychological problems as well as positive psychology

Sosa Correa, Manuel *Psicología, Universidad Autónoma de Yucatá, Mérida Yucatán, Mexico* **Peniche Aranda, Cyntia Cristina** *Psicología, Universidad Autónoma de Yucatá, Mérida Yucatán, Mexico*

This work, is a "Metatheoretical Integration" model according to Fiexas& Miró (1993) which purpose is to describe, explain, predict and intervene in psychology problems. A clinical case is analyzed with this model, explaining the problem and posing the intervention with models 1) Psychodynamics referencing conscience levels; 2) Humanists referencing the I separation; 3) Cognitive like the Bandura's Selfsystem and 4) Cognitive Behavior Therapy related to Activator Stimuli, Thought, Emotion and Behavior according to Ellis & Beck regarding complexity dimensions of Csikszentmihalyi.

Relationship between perfectionism and goal orientations in sport context

Sporis, Goran *Faculty of Kinesiology, University of Zagreb, Zagreb, Croatia* **Greblo, Zrinka** *Faculty of Kinesiology, University of Zagreb, Zagreb, Croatia*

The aim of the study was to examine the relationship between perfectionism and goal orientations on the sample of junior players of first Croatian football league clubs (N = 272). Athletes completed Croatian versions of Positive and Negative Perfectionism Scale (Lauri Korajlija, 2004) and Task and Ego Orientation in Sport Questionnaire (Barić and Horga, 2007). As expected, negative perfectionism was positively associated with ego orientation while positive perfectionism was positively correlated with both goal orientations. Results are discussed in the context of Skinnerian concepts of positive and negative reinforcement and Hamachek's (1978) conceptualization of adaptive and maladaptive perfectionism.

Managing knowledge for intellectual capital growth: The role of culture, communication, trust and involvement

Srivastava, Kailash B.L. *Humanities and Social Sciences, Indian Institute of Technology, Kharagpur, India*

This paper examined the role of organizational culture, communication, trust, and employee involvement in predicting a firm's Knowledge Management (KM) processes, and Intellectual Capital. Data were collected from 345 respondents across hierarchy using structured interview schedule from Indian software R&D firms. The findings indicated that all these variables significantly predicted KM processes and intellectual capital. It was concluded that Knowledge acquisition enhanced firm's human capital; dissemination resulted in an increased knowledge base and responsiveness in growth of customer capital. It has implications for management that effective KM can help firms to achieve competitive advantage by developing its Intellectual Capital.

Positive self-presentation in personnel selection: Which behaviors are common, which are appropriate?

Stadelmann, Eveline H. *Psychologisches Institut, Universität Zürich, Zürich, Switzerland* **Jansen, Anne** *Psychologisches Institut, Universität Zürich, Zürich, Switzerland* **König, Cornelius J.** *Psychologisches Institut, Universität Zürich, Zürich, Switzerland* **Kleinmann, Martin** *Psychologisches Institut, Universität Zürich, Zürich, Switzerland*

Objectives: This study examines to what extent applicants use strategies for positive self-presentation (i.e. impression management (IM) vs. faking) and how these strategies are evaluated by HR professionals. Methods: 416 applicants took part in an online survey that used the randomized-response technique. 53 HR professionals rated the appropriateness of the applicant behaviors. Results: Applicants reported more IM behavior than faking. HR professionals rated IM behavior more appropriate than faking. Applicants used only strategies that corresponded to HR professionals rated appropriateness. Conclusion: IM strategies of positive self-presentation seem to be both prevalent and advisable as they are expected by HR professionals.

A set of new scales measuring self and collective efficacy beliefs in sport

Steca, Patrizia *Psychology, University of Milan, Milan, Italy* **Militello, Jessica** *Psychology, University of Milan, Milan, Italy* **Greco, Andrea** *Psychology, University of Milan, Milan, Italy* **Andena, Sara** *Psychology, University of Milan, Milan, Italy* **Castellini, Francesca** *Psychology, University of Milan, Milan, Italy* **Monzani, Dario** *Psychology, University of Milan, Milan, Italy* **Caprara, Gian Vitttorio** *Psychology, University of Rome, Rome, Italy*

Aim of the study is to present six new scales aimed to measure self- and collective efficacy beliefs in three sports: basket, soccer, and athletics. A large group of basket and soccer players, and athletes filled in the new scales measuring seven dimensions of personal efficacy and four dimensions of collective efficacy; questionnaires measuring motivational orientation and team cohesion were also administered. Results demonstrated the good psychometric properties of the scales as well as significant differences due to sex and seniority. Furthermore, athletes' self-efficacy beliefs positively correlated with achievement motivation, whereas their collective efficacy beliefs were associated with team cohesion.

Selection of applicants for apprenticeship positions in public administration: Development and validation of a work motivation test

Stein, Susanne *Burgstädt, Germany* **Schütz, Astrid** *Department of Psychology, University of Technology, Chemnitz, Germany*

The development and validation of a 10-item self-description questionnaire to assess work motivation are described. Psychometric properties of the measure were tested in a sample of 111 applicants for apprenticeship positions (administration, printing, and library services) from middle schools and high schools (ages 15-26). Internal consistency was .75 and item-total correlations ranged from .36 to .53. The data provide evidence for convergent and discriminant validity. The measure correlated above

.5 with school grades and .3 with interview evaluations. It seems useful in human resource management and can be used to screen applicants for apprenticeship positions.

Long-term impact of repeated strong Hypothalamus pituitary adrenal axis activations on basal Glucocorticoid sensitivity

Strahler, Jana Inst. für Psychologie, Technische Universität Dresden, Dresden, Germany *Berndt, Christiane* Psychology, TU Dresden, Dresden, Germany *Kirschbaum, Clemens* Psychology, TU Dresden, Dresden, Germany *Rohleder, Nicolas* Psychology, University of British Columbia, Vancouver, B.C., Canada

To investigate the long-term impact of repeated strong hypothalamus-pituitary-adrenal-axis activations on basal glucocorticoid (GC) sensitivity, 17 ballroom dancers were recruited and compared to 17 age and sex-matched controls. GC sensitivity was assessed by in-vitro inhibition of lipopolysaccharide-stimulated production of interleukin-6 by different concentrations of dexamethasone in whole blood. We found no main effect of group or gender but a significant interaction effect of both. In ballroom dancers men show a higher basal GC sensitivity than male controls, whereas women hardly differ from female controls. These different patterns may be due to dysregulations of stress hormones, probably reflecting allostatic load factors especially affecting male ballroom dancers.

Development of the multidimensional scale of irrational beliefs

Strobel, Maria Inst. für Psychologie, Universität München, München, Germany *Bekk, Magdalena* Psychology, LMU München, München, Germany *Fischer, Josef* Psychology, LMU München, München, Germany *Spörrle, Matthias* Dept. for Psychology, Ludwig-Maximilians University, München, Germany *Försterling, Friedrich* Psychology, LMU München, München, Germany

The Multidimensional Scale of Irrational Beliefs (MSIB) is a brief and theoretically founded measure of irrational thinking as conceptualized by Albert Ellis in his most recent works on Rational Emotive Behavior Therapy (e.g. Ellis, 2003). With a total of 18 items, it captures demandingness, negative self-evaluation, and low frustration tolerance as the three core aspects of irrationality. Unlike previous irrationality instruments, it is a highly reliable, purely cognitive measure and avoids measuring aspects which are consequences or correlates of irrational thinking (e.g. emotions). Three studies (n = 757) are reported that repeatedly indicate high internal consistency of all subscales (Cronbach's alpha: .85-.90), factorial validity, and convergent validity with earlier measures.

Analysing dynamical process-systems in psychology by means of cointegration methodology

Stroe-Kunold, Esther Heidelberg, Germany *Brosig, Burkhard* University Clinic Giessen, Clinic f. Psychosomatic Medici, Giessen, Germany

Time series analysis as a method of process research has been introduced to psychology in order to evaluate psychotherapy. Various psychological processes are unstable (i.e., non-stationary) as well as mutually interconnected, thus forming a dynamic system. The approach of cointegration methodology allows treating non-stationary (i.e., integrated) time series as a multivariate system if their linear combination is stationary. Nevertheless, these methods are almost unfamiliar to psychologists. The presentation aims at demonstrating in which way cointegration methodology offers flexible techniques for analysing human dynamics. An empirical example of clinical psychology demonstrates the performance of these methods in a typical research situation.

Vocal recognition in golden monkeys (Rhinopithecus roxellana)

Su, Yanjie Dept. of Psychology, Peking University, Beijing, People's Republic of China

This study aimed to investigate the vocal (calls) recognition in golden monkeys (Rhinopithecus roxellana) of Shanghai Wild Animal Park and Beijing Wild Life Park. The results of playback experiments showed that 5 adult females responded significantly stronger to the contact calls of Alfa-male than those of other males, and 4 mothers responded significantly stronger to the spoiled calls of their own infants. These data indicated that golden monkeys were able to distinguish the calls uttered by different individuals and suggested that there was individual identity information in golden monkey's vocal communication.

Survey of living conditions of employees who were absent due to mental health disorders

Sugimoto, Yoko Dept. of Mental Diseases, Matsushita Health Care Center, Moriguthi, Japan *Takahara, Ryuji* Department of Social Psycholog, International Economy & Wo, Osaka, Japan *Shinohara, Hiroko* Depertment of Mental Diseases, Matsushita Health Care Center, Moriguthi, Japan

Employees with mental health problems were surveyed to define the relation between life patterns during the leave of absence and adjustment to work after returning. Probit analysis was used to analyze the influencing factor. A negative influence on mental status after reinstatement was observed among employees who suffered early morning awakening during their leave and those who spent their time using a computer during their leave. Also employee's contact with their manager during their leave hindered a smooth return to work while contact with medical staff promoted it. Guidelines for employees on leave of absence are needed.

Effect of the 'participatory communication game' on environmental education

Sugiura, Junkichi Aichi University of Education, Aichi, Japan

'Participatory communication game' for problem solving was developed based on "persuasion game" (Sugiura, 2003), and is used in environmental education. In this game, players are assigned one of two roles, i.e., those who persuade or are persuaded. They constantly exchange interactions regarding the implementation of environmental behavior. The educational effects of the game were as follows: The participants of the game would become to understand the idea of environmental protection by accounting for the merits and demerits of environmental behavior. The possible elaboration of knowledge through mutual understanding of participants was discussed.

The eye movement research of the influence of music on cognition

Sui, Xue Education School, Liaoning Normal University, Dalian, People's Republic of China

The study mainly investigated the difference between musical and nonmusical background. The results are that comparing to nonmusical condition, musical condition disturbed cognition efficiency. There is more influence on hard question than on easy question. Music resulted in using much more time to accomplish cognition task, process speed become slower. Music changes the model of eye movement. There are more fixations, lower fixation frequency, longer duration time of fixation points, and shorter saccadic distance. The results suggested that music change the model of eye movement during cognition process, and result in debasing cognition accuracy.

An exploration for Frankl's psychology of religion

Sui, Guangyuan Zhejiang Normal University, Jinhua, People's Republic of China

Viktor Frankl is the founder of "The Third Vienna's Psychoanalysis School ". His thoughts of psychology of religion have not been received enough attention, and even people have divarication on the property of his thoughts of psychology of religion. This study pointed out that Frankl's psychology of religion had three characteristics: emphasizing that religion was to search for Ultimate Meaning; emphasizing that the relationship between man and God was unconscious; emphasizing spiritual dimension man subsisted on. The paper proposed the basis of his thoughts was psychology, and evaluated his contributions and limits.

Cognitive and executive functions in schizophrenia: Does it matter to quality of patients life?

Sumcovová, Petra Psychiatry, Faculty Hospital, Plzeò, Czech Republic

Schizophrenia has been found to be associated with dysfunction in cognitive and executive processes. Focus of the study is to find out to what degree are those impairments responsible for lower quality of life of schizophrenic patients. In the study cognitive and executive performance was measured by standardized neuropsychological methods. The outcome of frontal lobe tests was correlated to outcome of cognitive tests commonly used by clinical psychologists to assess cognitive impairment in schizophrenics. Executive functions appear to be of higher importance in preserving the high life quality of those patients than cognitive performance.

Loneliness in middle childhood and its relation to multi-level peer experience

Sun, Xiaojun Psychology, Hua Zhong Normal University, Wuhan, People's Republic of China *Zhou, Zongkui* Psychology, Hua Zhong Normal University, Wuhan, People's Republic of China *Zhao, Dongmei* Psychology, Hua Zhong Normal University, Wuhan, People's Republic of China *Cohen, Robert* Psychology, University of Memphis, Memphis, USA *Hsueh, Yeh* College of Education, University of Memphis, Memphis, USA

Relations between children's social behavior, peer relationship, self-perceived social competence and loneliness have been an important topic in child developmental psychology. 430 Chinese children in an elementary school from grade three to five participated in this investigation.A hypothesized structural equation model was applied to test the relations between multi-level peer experience(e.g., peer relationship, friendship quality) and loneliness. The results indicated that social behavior had impact on loneliness through the multiple mediating effects of peer relationship and self-perceived social competence,self-perceived social competence was the most powerful predictor of loneliness.

The time factor and effective learning

Sun, Hechuan RIEEA, Shenyang Normal University, Shenyang, People's Republic of China *Feng, Cailing* School of Educational Sciences, Shenyang Normal University, Shenyang, Liaoning, People's Republic of China *Guo, Lili* RIEEA, Shenyang Normal University, Shenyang, Liaoning, People's Republic of China *Ge, Hui* RIEEA, Shenyang Normal University, Shenyang, Liaoning, People's Republic of China *Wang, Ting* RIEEA, Shenyang Normal University, Shenyang, Liaoning, People's Republic of China *Hao, Yan* RIEEA, Shenyang Normal University, Shenyang, Liaoning, People's Republic of China

[Abstract] This study explored the relationship between time and effective learning. It investigated 16 senior secondary schools (SSS) located in different school districts in Shenyang, China. Over

1400 SSS students completed the surveys which identified the time factors that positively or negatively influenced student learning, and which ranked their relative importance. Factor analysis was used to analyze the data. The important findings include: the students' learning outcome performance at three different types of SSS in Shenyang, and the relationship between the time factor (e.g. time spent at schools, time focused on tasks in the classroom, time spent on doing homework per day, go-to-bed-time, get-up-time, etc.) and effective learning. [Key words] time, effective learning, relationship

Structural equation model of the causal relations between consumption values and basic life values in Chinese urban adolescents

Sun, Qi Chaoyang, Institute of Psychology, Beijing, People's Republic of China Zheng, Gang Institute of Psychology, the Chinese Academy of Scienc, Beijing, People's Republic of China

Since adolescents are a large group of future consumers in China, the purpose of this study was to investigate the consumption values in urban adolescents and to demonstrate how basic life values should determine consumption values. The possible influences of the factors of gender and age were also analyzed. A total of 5875 Chinese middle school students participated in the questionnaire survey. Results showed that Chinese adolescents inclined to keep frugality, and their consumption values could be influenced by gender and grade. The structural equation model analyses demonstrated the causal relations between the basic values of individualism/collectivism and consumption.

Gender differences in the role of linguistic style on impression formation

Suppes, Alexandra Dept. of Psychology, Columbia University, New York, USA Krauss, Robert M. Psychology department, Columbia University, New York City, USA Bolger, Niall Psychology department, Columbia University, New York City, USA

How does a talker's linguistic style affect an argument's evaluation? Undergraduates recorded arguments on high- and low-involvement topics. An argument's Type-Token Ratio (the proportion of unique words), an index of lexical diversity, was positively related to listener's evaluations of it. This relationship was strongest for low involvement topics and for female talkers. For women speaking on low involvement topics, the effect was three times greater compared to men speaking on high involvement topics. These effects were independent of the listener's gender. The findings indicate that the effects of linguistic style on evaluation depend on the talker's gender and topic involvement.

Dietary life of Japanese college students: The relationship among dietary habits, mental health and eating disorder

Takano, Yuji Dept. of Psychology, Senshu University, Kawasaki, Japan Takano, Haruka Psychology, Child-Family Support Center, Chiyoda-ku, Tokyo, Japan Nouchi, Rui Psychology, Chuo University, Hachioji-shi, Tokyo, Japan Kojima, Akiko Psychology, Meijigakuin University, Minato-ku, Tokyo, Japan Sato, Shinichi Psychology, Meijigakuin University, Minato-Ku, Tokyo, Japan

A scale was constructed to investigate the dietary habits of Japanese college students. Cluster analysis revealed four typical dietary patterns: "dietary mood oriented", "dietary regulation oriented", "deprecating diet", and "deprecating dietary regulation". In terms of mental health, the dietary regulation oriented pattern was the healthiest, and the deprecating diet pattern was the unhealthiest. In terms of eating disorders, the deprecating dietary regulation pattern was the riskiest, and the dietary mood oriented pattern was the safest. These results suggest that eating a regulated diet in accordance

with the dietary mood lead to a healthy dietary life for Japanese college students.

Wundt and stumpf collections in Japan

Takasuna, Miki Dept. of Clinical Psychology, Tokyo International University, Tokyo, Japan Mizoguchi, Hazime Dept. of Social Welfare, Rissho University, Kumagaya, Japan

In 1922, Tanenari Chiba (1884-1974), a psychologist at Tohoku Imperial University, represented his university in purchasing Wilhelm Wundt's personal collection of books, journals, and reprints for the university library. Around 1923, Kanae Sakuma (1888-1970), a psychologist at Kyushu Imperial University, likewise purchased Carl Stumpf's privately owned collection for his university's main library. Why these Japanese psychologists took extraordinary measures to obtain these collections is the subject of this article and is discussed first in terms of Japan's burgeoning field of psychology in the 1920s and each university's subsequent desire to distinguish themselves from less progressive academic institutions.

Different forgetting rates of implicit and explicit knowledge in a serial reaction time task

Tamayo, Ricardo Inst. für Psychologie, Humboldt-Universität zu Berlin, Berlin, Germany Frensch, Peter A. Inst. für Psychologie, Humboldt-Universität zu Berlin, Berlin, Germany

We tested the forgetting rates of implicit and explicit knowledge in a SRT task. Implicit and explicit tests were carried out after two retention intervals. The results showed that explicit knowledge decays rapidly toward asymptote as predicted by a power function whereas implicit knowledge showed initial retention and later forgetting. A simulation with a single-system model only fits the empirical data when the error term for the explicit measure is allowed to fluctuate at different times of assessment. We interpret these findings as incompatible with the assumption that error terms simply reflect different sensitivities of implicit and explicit tests.

IT professionals as potential applicants: Do fancy job titles in recruitment advertisements make a difference?

Templer, Klaus J. Nanyang Business School, Nanyang Technological U., Singapore, Singapore

Companies create new prestigious sounding job titles and 'uptitle' jobs with higher-level titles. Research has not theoretically explained nor proven the effects of fancy job titles. Drawing from marketing research (instrumental-symbolic framework; adaptations of self-theories) and from expectancy theory, I hypothesized that fancy job titles would lead to positive reactions in potential applicants. In an experimental study, 187 male IT professionals in Singapore evaluated a recruitment advertisement with either a fancy or traditional job title. ANOVA results showed that IT professionals exposed to the fancy job title had higher expectations of job prestige (p<.01) and higher intentions to apply (p<.05).

Gender difference in emotional intelligence

Tolegenova, Aliya Dept. of Psychology, Kazakh National University, Almaty, Kazakhstan Matthews, Gerald psychology, University of Cincinnati, USA, Cincinnati, USA Jakupov, Satybaldy M. psychology, Kazakh National University, Almaty, Kazakhstan Kustubayeva, Almira psychology, Kazakh National University, Almaty, Kazakhstan

Objective: To test for gender differences in Emotional Intelligence (EI) in a Kazakh sample. Subjects and Method: 140(70 male and 70 female, age M=19.38 y.o., SD=2.05) students of the Kazakh National University were volunteers. EI was measured by the Russian version of Trait Meta-Mood Scale that will be used for EEG

research in emotion regulation. Results: Bonferroni-corrected t-tests revealed gender differences in the Attention to Emotion subscale significantly at the 0.05 level. No significant differences in the Clarity and Repair subscales between female and male groups were found. Conclusion: Females are more inclined to pay attention for their emotions than males.

Effect of socio economic status on academic achievement and emotional competencies among Indian adolescents

Tomar, Sapna House # 4&5, Lane 6, , Dehradun, India Joshi, Renuka PG Department of Psychology, DAV (PG) College, Dehradun, India

The study involved 200 adolescents (equal number of both sexes) to evaluate the influence of socio-economic status (SES) on Achievement Motivation (AM) and Emotional Competence(EC) using standardized Indian tools. Low SES subjects revealed lower levels of AM as against high level SES subjects. High and low subjects differed significantly (gender levels as well) on total AM and its dimension (academic motivation, academic challenges, meaningfulness of task, attitude towards teacher, interpersonal relations, relevance of college personal relations) and EC and its dimension (depth of feeling, expression, control of emotions, ability to cope with problem emotions, encouragement of positive emotions).

The effects of sex-role attitudes and gender types on the process model of work-family conflicts in dual-career couples

Tomida, Makiko Psychology, Nagoya University, Nagoya, Japan Kato, Yoko Psychology, Sugiyama Jogakuen University, Aichi-Ken, Japan Kanai, Atsuko Psychology, Nagoya University, Nagoya, Japan

The purpose of this study is to examine the comprehensive process model of work-family conflict. As the precedent factors in WFC, we examined gender types and sex-role attitudes. First, in psychological androgyny, which is characterized by high masculinity and high femininity, both job and family involvement were higher, and higher frequency coping behavior of WFC occurred than the other gender types. Second, egalitarian sex-role attitudes of females showed coping behavior at a higher frequency, and had a higher degree of mental health than females with traditional sex-role attitudes. Gender types and sex-role attitudes are important as precedent factors in the process of WFC.

Effects of varying reinforcement availability using temporally defined schedules

Torres, Carlos CEIC, Universidad de Guadalajara, Guadalajara, Mexico Vargas-Calleros, Karla CEIC, Universidad de Guadalajara, Guadalajara, Mexico Rosales-Barrera, Erick CEIC, Universidad de Guadalajara, Guadalajara, Mexico

Twelve rats, experimentally naïve at the start of the study, were used to evaluate the effects of varying the temporal availability of water delivery in a temporally defined schedule. The rats were assigned to a three different groups. The study consisted in three experimental phases in which the probability of reinforcement was 1.0, 0.5 and 0.1. Each experimental phase was divided into four blocks with different discriminative time proportion or $\bar{T}$ values (1.0, 0.5, 0.3 and 0.1). The results will be discussed by contrasting functional differences between response frequencies and temporal distribution of response.

Analyzing temporal contiguity with a sensory preconditioning task

Torres Berrio, Angelica Bogota, National University of Colombi, Bogota, Colombia de la Casa Rivas, Gonzalo Experimental Psychology, University of Seville, Seville, Spain

Two sensory preconditioning experiments with rats were conducted to check the Temporal Coding Hypothesis (Savastano & Miller, 1998). In the first experiment, the animals received simultaneous, forward or backward pairings between a tone and a light in the sensory preconditioning phase. Subsequently, one of the stimuli (either the tone or the light, counterbalanced) was simultaneously presented with the US (food pellets). At testing, we registered the conditioned response to the preconditioned stimulus. In the second experiment, the temporal relationship was reversed (simultaneous presentation of the tone and the light at preconditioning stage and simultaneous vs. Forward vs. backward pairings at conditioning). Keywords: Temporal Coding Hypothesis, contiguity, sensory preconditioning.

Clinical characteristics of ADHD in Thai children

Trangkasombat, Umaporn Dept. of Psychiatry, Chulalongkorn University, Bangkok, Thailand
Objectives: To study clinical characteristics of ADHD. Method: A retrospective chart review was conducted on 202 ADHD cases. Results: Most cases were in the 6-12 years age group. The most frequent chief complaints were school problems. Almost one-fourth came for problems not directly related to ADHD, the most frequent of which were aggressive and oppositional behaviors. Comorbidity was found in 53.5% with oppositional defiant disorder, anxiety disorder and depressive disorders as the three most common diagnoses. Behavioral management was successful in 38%. In 62% psychostimulants were needed. Conclusion: Clinicians should be aware of varied presentations of ADHD. Proper treatment of comorbidity is imperative in the care of ADHD children.

Methods for the analysis of urban environments and wayfinding

Troffa, Renato Cagliari, Italy Nenci, Anna Maria Psychology, LUMSA University, Rome, Italy
An ad-hoc software was developed to allow a navigation task in a real urban environment, with the aim to test two assumptions of Space Syntax Theory (the influence of angular incidence and visibility on route's choice, Hillier 2006). Participants were divided according to their knowledge of the neighbourhood (high/low). They had to choose their route taking a given number of choices (straight/curve). The visibility level of each junction was manipulated, and a spatial ability test completed the toolset. Data were analysed through correlational and log-linear analyses. Results showed a significant influence of angular incidence and visibility manipulation on wayfinding.

Coronary hearth disease patients treated by stent: Illness perception and self-efficacy relationship

Trovato, Guglielmo Internal Medicine & Health Psy, University of Catania, Catania, Italy Pace, Patrizia Internal Medicine & Health, University of Catania, Catania, Italy Catalano, Daniela Internal Medicine, University of Catania, Catania, Italy Martines, Giuseppe Fabio Internal Medicine & Health, University of Catania, Catania, Italy
Objectives: Illness perception and self-efficacy assessment in coronary heart disease patients. Method: Eighty patients with angina, treated with percutaneous coronary procedure and stent completed IPQ-r and General Self-Efficacy Questionnaire. Results: Men perceived greater personal control and reported more symptoms than women. Older patients have an higher personal illness control score. GSE has linear positive correlation with identity and treatment control and a linear inverse correlation with emotional representation. Conclusions: Patients can take advantage and can be supported for a better illness coping by modifying and restructuring their personal illness models

and enhancing life skills, self-efficacy and perceived control.

The influence of opportunities of role taking and guided reflections on moral judgment competence of students in institutions of higher education

Trups-Kalne, Ingrida Rezekne, Latvia
The aim of the quasi experimental study is to discover the influence of factors of learning environment (opportunities of role taking and guided reflections) on students' moral judgment competence in institutions of higher education. The sample consists of 144 pedagogical, law and medical students. Methods: Moral Judgment Test (MJT, Lind, 2000) and the ORIGIN/u Questionnaire (Lind&Schillinger-Agati, 2005). Results of analysis of variance show the students who have opportunities of role taking produce higher level of moral judgment competence. The effect of opportunities of guided reflections is not statistically significant. Key words: moral competence, role taking, guided reflection

School aged children symptoms of examination stress measured by the Greek adjustment of the Test concerning Abilities for Study and Examination (T.A.ST.E.)

Tsakalis, Panayiotis Dept. of Psychology, University of Crete, Rethymno, Greece
Purpose of this study is to scrutinise the symptoms of examination stress (psychosomatic symptoms, study avoidance, negative self-evaluations of competence, studies-graduation evaluation, and study dedication) of approximately 450 school aged Greek children who responded to the T.A.ST.E. (Kalantzi-Azizi & Karademas, 1997). Mean comparisons of the five factors in relation to sociocultural/demographic characteristics, as well as comparisons among the factors, are thoroughly conducted. The reliability analysis of all the items is high (a=.874). Children's ability of study isn't significantly correlated to sociocultural/demographic characteristics. In contrast, symptoms/factors of examination stress present statistically significant inter-correlations, affecting children's physical performance and psychological resiliency/health.

Ratings of depression syndrome among university athletes

Tsuji, Kosaku Graduate school of sports, University of Tsukuba, Tsukuba, Japan
The purpose of this study was to examine depression syndrome ratings among university athletes. Depression syndrome was measured via the Zung Self-Rating Depression Scale (SDS), and athletes who scored more than 50 on the SDS were categorized as having depression syndrome. This group comprised 19.7% (41/208) of the total sample, which was about twice as high as the percentage for university students. The results showed that depression syndrome ratings of low-status athletes were significantly higher than those of high-status athletes. These findings suggest a need to address mental health, and especially depression syndrome, in university athletes.

The development of the concept of death among Japanese kindergarteners

Tsujimoto, Tai Dept. of Human Science, Osaka University, Suita, Japan
This study aimed to investigate development of the concept of death among Japanese kindergarteners and to examine the relationship between death concept development and their parents' attitudes toward death. 200 children of 3-6 years were interviewed individually about the death concept, and the interview consisted of three components: finality, irreversibility and universality. Their responses were scored by reference to a scoring

manual from Smilansky(1987). Additionally, their parents were administered a questionnaire about attitudes toward death, religious beliefs, and belief in the afterlife. The findings suggested that death concept development differed among age groups and was related to their parents' attitudes toward death.

An eye-tracking analysis of context effects in multi-attribute, multi-alternative decision making: Examining the attraction effect and the compromise effect

Tsuzuki, Takashi Dept. of Psychology, Rikkyo University, Niiza, Japan Shirai, Toshiyuki Graduate School of Psychology, Rikkyo University, Niiza, Japan Ohta, Akira Graduate School of Psychology, Rikkyo University, Niiza, Japan Matsui, Hiroshi Graduate School of Sociology, Rikkyo University, Tokyo, Japan Honma, Motoyasu Psychology, Rikkyo University, Niiza, Japan
Two major findings regarding context-dependent choice, the attraction effect and the compromise effect, warrant specific attention, since they constitute violations of rational choice axioms. We used an eye movement recorder to examine the underlying cognitive process of these context effects in multi-attribute decision making. Seventeen undergraduates participated in an experiment where they were presented with twelve hypothetical purchase problems comprising three alternatives described along two attributes. Significant effects resulted from the manipulation of the third alternative for choice proportions, fixation duration, and frequency of saccade. These results support our stochastic comparison-grouping model of the multi-attribute decision making processes.

Self-concept, subject value and coping with failure in the math classroom: Influences on students' emotions

Tulis, Maria Inst. für Psychologie, Universität Bayreuth, Bayreuth, Germany Riemenschneider, Ingo Instit. of Product.Engineering, University of Technology Graz, Graz, Austria
Academic emotions (except test anxiety) have been neglected in psychological and educational research for a long time. Thus more research effort is needed to investigate determinants for their formation. 5th grade (N=685) students' emotions and other relevant variables (mathematical self-concept, achievement, subject value and dealing with failure in the classroom-setting) were analysed using partial least squares (PLS) and structural equations modelling (SEM). Results indicate that "error culture in the math classroom" (where errors are seen as learning opportunities instead of indicators of failure) is a strong predictor for students' emotions. Furthermore individual antecedents such as self-concept and subject value are important.

Chance for young heart - Education program

Tylka, Jan Cardiac Rehabilitaton, Institute of Cardiology, Warsaw, Poland Naruszewicz, Marek Cardiac Rehabilitaton, IMedical Academy of Warsaw, Warsaw, Poland Kozowska-Wojciecho, Magorzata Cardiac Rehabilitaton, Medical Academy of Warsaw, Warsaw, Poland
Model and results of own elaboration cardiac prevention program Chance for Young Heart. This project is accomplishment through school-teachers in 100 elementary and grammar schools. Innovatory activity of our program was specific preparation of teachers as healthy trainers. The main educational issues were grouped in six lessons, "Mysteries of Your Heart", "What is Loving for Your Heart, and What is Intolerably", "I Think No, and I Speak No!", "Can You Help All Family Hearts?", "What to Eat? – Cardiac Irresolution.", "How to Prevent to Hypertension?." Over 11 600 participants were included the educational program, which results are very promising.

Duration to prepare against natural disasters: Fail to plan or plan to fail

Unagami, Tomoaki Graduate School of Education, Nagoya University, Nagoya, Japan Motoyoshi, Tadahiro Graduate School of Education, Nagoya University, Nagoya, Japan Takai, Jiro Graduate School of Education, Nagoya University, Nagoya, Japan Yoshida, Toshikazu Graduate School of Education, Nagoya University, Nagoya, Japan

The authors examined the tendency of procrastinating disaster prevention plans. Despite the fact that failure to accomplish one's disaster prevention plans may result in a catastrophe, not much had been revealed about procrastination of disaster prevention acts. The authors conducted an experiment which asked undergraduates to estimate the time they had to spend to accomplish certain disaster prevention tasks. The discrepancy between the time claimed by the participants and the actual time they had spent to accomplish the tasks were measured. Procrastination was explained from the risk perception, and social consideration perspectives. Implications for effective risk communication were also discussed.

Personality characteristics (self-concept) perceived between parents and permanent couple: A correlation

Valdez, José Luis CIENCIAS DE LA CONDUCTA, UAEM, Toluca, Mexico González Arratia L.F., Norma Ivonne CIENCIAS DE LA CONDUCTA, UAEM, Toluca, Mexico Laura Mireya, Sánchez CIENCIAS DE LA CONDUCTA, UAEM, Toluca, Mexico

Some authors affirm that couple's election is principally based by finding similar characteristics between couple and parents. In this way, women would look for a man who's similar to her father, meanwhile men could be oriented to choose for a girl like their mother. Results shows that man obtained a 76% of their answers referred to their mother and couple, while women only obtained a 46%. So, it's possible to say that men perceive a higher relation between their mother and their couple, in comparison with female.

The impact of primary school transition on the development of mathematical achievement

van Ophuysen, Stefanie Inst. für Schulentwicklung, Universität Dortmund, Dortmund, Germany

How does the transition from primary to secondary school affect pupils' learning development in the highly selective German school system? About 1000 German students filled in achievement tests in mathematics at up to three measurement times in grade four (primary school), five and six (secondary school). To quantify individual developmental trajectories and its predictors, longitudinal data were analysed with HLM. Next to sex and migration background, school type revealed to be of high relevance for test scores at grade four, growth in time and the impact of transition itself. Results are discussed within the context of school type-specific developmental milieus.

Gender identity: An integrated approach

Vasconcellos, Doris Dept. of Psychology, University of Paris 5, Paris, France

Research on love shows that young men and women differ significantly in their expectations concerning intimate relationships. Although evolutionary theory sounds quite relevant to explain these facts, human sexuality differs from animal sexuality because, in humans, the correlation between reproduction and sexuality masks their separate meanings. We have to consider other approaches like social gender role theory that takes into consideration the relativity of cultures, implicitly acknowledging the plasticity of human beings during their early development. From this perspective, we can introduce the interactional construction of sexuality linking developmental

and psychodynamic theories, explained by neuroscience research.

Personality culture from gender viewpoint

Verzhybok, Halina Psychology, Minsk Linguistic University, Minsk, Belarus

Changes, taking place in our social world, cause certain transformations of traditional psychological roles, appearing of numerous viewpoints on gender problem. Cultural characteristics help appear certain systems of drives for acquisition of masculine or feminine patterns of behavior. Culture parameters and characteristics are subject to environmental and individual modifications. The problems of intercultural dialogue nowadays should be solved on the basis of understanding masculine and feminine behavior in different cultural groups as society humanization is closely linked to changes in gender ideology and culture. It will help broaden the informational range of a person's ties with other people, find individual peculiarity and diversity.

Determination of physical self-concept characteristics within different sport disciplines

Viciana, Jesus Physical Education and Sport, University of Grenade, Granada, Spain Cocca, Armando Physical Education and Sport, University of Grenade, Granada, Spain Salinas, Francisco Physical Education and Sport, University of Grenade, Granada, Spain Lozano, Luis Physical Education and Sport, University of Grenade, Granada, Spain Martínez, Juan Carlos Physical Education and Sport, University of Grenade, Granada, Spain

As self-concept determines personality, and since activity and sport environment also determine individual character, we centred our study on the typical characteristics that different sport disciplines formed in athletes with the aim of using them in future experimental situations. We studied the physical component of self-concept through the Physical Self Description Questionnaire (Marsh et al.,1994), applied to 104 subjects (average age 21 years) in eight sports (swimming, soccer, volleyball, handball, rugby, judo, sport gymnastics and basketball). The results of the ANOVA analysis showed significant differences in eight of the 11 dimensions among the studied sport disciplines.

Comparison of sportpersonship orientation among sport disciplines

Viciana, Jesus Physical Education and Sport, University of Grenade, Granada, Spain Cocca, Armando Physical Education and Sport, University of Grenade, Granada, Spain Salinas, Francisco Physical Education and Sport, University of Grenade, Granada, Spain

Differences between sport disciplines respect to sportsmanship orientation were evaluated. We selected 59 subjects who had practiced soccer, handball, swimming, basketball or rugby for at least 2 years. Multidimensional Sportspersonship Orientation Scale was used. We applied a posthoc Anova with Bonferroni and Tamhane tests for multiple comparisons. Results were high for all disciplines and categories. Significant differences were found in 'Commitment' between soccer and swimming compared to rugby; 'Opponents' between handball and soccer compared to swimming; 'Negative Approach' between swimming and soccer compared to rugby; 'Rules and Officials' between swimming and rugby. No differences were found in 'Social Conventions'.

Effect of feedback quality on motor learning in alpine skiing

Viciana, Jesus Physical Education and Sport, University of Grenade, Granada, Spain Martínez, Juan Carlos Physical Education and Sport, University of Grenade, Granada, Spain Román, Blanca Physical Education and Sport, University of Grenade, Granada, Spain Gómez, Pablo J. Physical Education and Sport,

University of Grenade, Granada, Spain Lozano, Luis Physical Education and Sport, University of Grenade, Granada, Spain

We studied the feedback quality given by ski teachers (n=24) and its effect on student motor learning (n=142). We used a mixed design (repeated measures with 10 trials each and unifactorial groups). We provided the teachers with immediate visual feedback at the conclusion of the skiing class (histograms in laptop), comparing to it to a pre-established model. ARIMA analysis detected a reduction in variability of measures and convergence toward to this model in experimental group (EG). Convergence toward the model resulted in pupils' improved learning, generating differences between the control group and EG (P=0.001).

Comparison between sports and psychological information given by coaches during competition

Viciana, Jesus Physical Education and Sport, University of Grenade, Granada, Spain Cocca, Armando Physical Education and Sport, University of Grenade, Granada, Spain Salinas, Francisco Physical Education and Sport, University of Grenade, Granada, Spain Lozano, Luis Physical Education and Sport, University of Grenade, Granada, Spain

We studied the amount of sports information compared to psychological information given by football coaches to their players during competition. Instructions of 10 coaches (age 25-44) in 10 matches to 15-17 year-old players were analysed, using a multidimensional category system created by Viciana and Sanchez (2002). Results showed that 42.62% of information given was technical-tactical, 30.7% related to motivation and 4.92% directed to attention, calmness, responsibility and incitement to aggressiveness. This emphasizes the importance of psychological information during competition, helping to categorize coaches as having positive or negative attitudes to education.

Individuals with disabilities and their relations with parents: Self-esteem and psychological well-being

Vlachou, Anastasia Special Education, University of Thessaly, Volos, Greece Kleftaras, George Dept. of Special Education, University of Thessaly, Volos, Greece

The current study investigates: a) disabled individuals quality of relationships with their parents, b) its impact on both their mental health and self-esteem, and c) the differential impact of the relationship with parents on self-esteem and psychological well-being. 101 adults with different impairments participated in this study and were administered: the Goldberg-General-Health-Questionnaire, the Rosenberg-Self-Esteem-Questionnaire and a questionnaire concerning their relationships with their parents. The relationship with parents was significantly correlated with disabled people's self-esteems as well as with certain dimensions of their psychological well-being. Interestingly, only the relationship with fathers was related to the psychological health of disabled individuals.

Study on modeling the characteristics of distance learners

Wang, Ying Distance Education Institution, China Central Radio & TV Uni., Beijing, People's Republic of China

The higher distance education all over the world develops rapidly, so is that in China with expanding development scale. In order to clarify the actual needs and realities of adult distance learners for teaching, it is necessary to explore and study the characteristics of distance learners. This paper defined some relevant key concepts of distance learners, introduced a theoretical framework called Bernice Neugarten theory, and explored the topic from demographical, support, motivational and strategic perspectives. Based on above researches and questionnaire to survey 207 distance learners, a tentative model on studying the characteristics of distance learners has been set up.

Rater goals, performance level and rating patterns: An experimental examination

Wang, Xiaoye Management of Organizations, Univ. of Science & Technology, Hong Kong, China, People's Republic of : Hong Kong SAR

Departing from the traditional psychometric and cognitive perspective of performance rating, this experimental study examined rater's rating from goal-based perspective. 154 subjects watched a 20-min video about six team members' performance, and gave ratings based on their rating goals. ANOVA results showed raters pursuing a harmony goal will increase mean ratings more for low performer than high performers, raters pursuing a motivation goal will increase rating means both for high and low performers. Raters pursuing a harmony goal and motivation goal will decrease overall discriminability among all team members, but not local discriminability within high or low performers.

Effects of communication training

Weisweiler, Silke Inst. für Psychologie, Universität München, München, Germany Hammerl, Marianne Sozialpsychologie, Universität Regensburg, Regensburg, Germany

The purpose of the present study was to examine the effects of communication training in a university setting. A sample of 87 students from different fields participated in a one-day-training focusing on interaction in conflict situations. Different parts of communication behaviour were measured with questionnaires (IPS, Schaarschmidt & Fischer, 1999; SPCC, McCroskey & McCroskey, 1988 and ROCI, Rahim, 1983) before and three month after training. Results reveal a significant effect for self-rated assertiveness. Applications for evaluation designs in field of soft skill trainings are discussed.

The influence of health concepts on health promoting leadership

Wilde, Barbara Inst. für Psychologie, Universität Freiburg, Freiburg, Germany Hinrichs, Stephan Institute of Psychology, University of Freiburg, Freiburg, Germany Bahamondes Pavez, Carolina Institute of Psychology, University of Freiburg, Freiburg, Germany Schüpbach, Heinz Institute of Psychology, University of Freiburg, Freiburg, Germany

Leaders have different options to influence their employees' health: a considerate leadership style, the design of healthy working conditions and the support of workplace health promotion, summarized as health promoting leadership. This study examined whether leaders' health concepts are associated with health promoting leadership. Leaders were asked in a questionnaire about the perceived influences on employees' health and their health promoting leadership behaviour. As expected, the perceived influence in terms of leadership as well as working-conditions and workplace health promotion on employees' health was associated with health promoting leadership behaviour. Implications for companies and further research will be discussed.

The impact of achievement motivation on the development of job skills: First results from the longitudinal study "LEARN" at Heilbronn University

Wilpers, Susanne Inst. für Psychologie, Universität Heilbronn, Heilbronn, Germany

The effect of self rated self-efficacy as well as achievement motivation on subsequent career achievement is well known. But how are different job skills affected by personality variables and how is procrastination tendency involved in this development? These central questions are the main focus of the longitudinal study "LEARN", which takes place since 2006 at Heilbronn University. 200 subjects repeatedly answer questions regarding skills such as team orientation, learning behavior, personal goals, and contentiousness. First results confirm the relationship between achievement motivation and self-efficacy but also show a longitudinal impact of these variables on specific skills such as goal orientation.

The role of symmetry and repetition in material when learning implicitly an artificial grammar

Witt, Arnaud Université de Bourgogne-LEAD, Dijon, France Vinter, Annie Psychology, Université de bourgogne-LEAD, Dijon, France

This experiment aims at showing that in an implicit learning episode, subjects become sensitive to salient features of the material (symmetry, repetition), sometimes to the detriment of non specific chunks. Children aged 5 to 8 years were confronted with a grammar made of colours, in a game involving flags' production. They were divided into three groups: control group (random items), symmetry group and repetition group. Whatever the age, child learnt specifically the grammatical symmetries in the symmetry group, while they learnt also the repetition structure, independently of grammaticality, in the repetition group.

Will positive performance feedback improve or deteriorate subsequent performance? Evidence from professional jockeys

Wong, Kin Fai Ellick Management of Organizations, HKUST, Hong Kong, China, People's Republic of : Hong Kong SAR Kwong, Jessica Y.Y. Marketing, CUHK, Hong Kong, China, People's Republic of : Macao SAR

There have been debates on the effects of positive feedback on performance. We attempt to solve this debate by drawing upon Dweck's (1989) implicit theories of ability, proposing that the effect of positive feedback on good performers, who believe that they can change their ability through increasing efforts, is qualitatively different from the effect of positive feedback on poor performers, who believe that their ability is unchangeable. Consistent with this notion, performance data from professional jockeys showed that poor jockeys performed significantly worse than their baseline performance after winning, whereas good jockeys performed slightly better than baseline after winning.

Analysis of risk communication channels and emotional significance

Xie, Xiaofei Dept. of Psychology, Peking University, Beijing, People's Republic of China Li, Jie Psychology, Peking University, Beijing, People's Republic of China

Participants were presented with real-life materials on environmental risks to explore the effects of type of risks, image information, of inputs from different sensory channels, through two communication media and of emotions on risk perception. Study 1 showed that man-made risks produced more perceived risk than natural risks, that image information increased perceived risk, but there was no difference elicited by inputs through different sensory channels, Simulation of risk-related information transmission of real-world TV news and webpage was adopted in study 2, found a result consistent with that derived from study 1, with emotions playing a mediating role as well.

Application of the theory of planned behavior to exercise participation among Chinese undergraduates

Xiong, Mingsheng School of Psychology, Huanzhong Normal University, Wuhan, People's Republic of China

The purpose of this study was to examine the predictive utility of The Theory of Planned Behavior for explaining exercise intention and behavior among Chinese undergraduates. Participant were 187 undergraduates (146 boys, 41 girls) aged 20-25 who completed anonymous questionnaires of their attitude, subjective norms, perceived behavioral control (PBC), intentions and exercise behavior. Hierarchical regression analyses indicated that attitude and subjective norm and PBC explained 71% of the variance in intention; intention and PBC explained 29% of the variance in exercise behavior. Particularly, subjective norm is a significant predictor of intention.

The simulation experiment study on construct validity of assessment center

Xu, Jianping School of Psychology, Beijing Normal University, Beijing, People's Republic of China Wang, Haixia Faculty of Education, Shaanxi Normal University, Xi'an, People's Republic of China

This article simulated the exercises of employing excellent mathematics teacher for some middle school, and confirmed construct validity and the influences of different rating methods to assessment center. The results indicated: 1.assessment center had well convergent validity and exercise effect is higher than dimension effect, 2. assessors estimated the assessees' ability by the person characteristic model. The finding of this study showed that assessment center had well convergent validity, but its discriminant validity was low and assessors estimate the assessees' ability by the person characteristic model.

Sandplay therapy's process and effect for a 11 year old girl with selective mutism

Xu, Jie Institute of Developmental Psy, BeiJing Normal University, Beijing, People's Republic of China Zhang, Risheng Institute of Developmental Psy, BeiJing Normal University, beijing, People's Republic of China Zhang, Wen Institute of Developmental Psy, BeiJing Normal University, beijing, People's Republic of China Chen, Shunsen Applied Psychology, Zhangzhou Normal University, Fujian?Zhangzhou, People's Republic of China

Objective: To explore effective psychotherapy for Selective Mutism and enlarge the clinical application of sandplay therapy. Method: An 11 year old girl diagnosed, using criteria from the DSM-IV, with Selective Mutism was given 18 individual sandplay and 4 family sandplay sessions. Result: The quality of the girl's sandtrays changed from monotony to abundance, from static to dynamic. The case had positive long-term changes in mutism behavior, as evinced by school adaptation, and the parent-child relationship. These changes symbolized the strengthening of her ego. Conclusion: The girl showed dramatic improvement through sandplay therapy. The sandplay therapy was effective in Selective Mutism.

Rawls's principles of justice: From a thought experiment to an empirical study

Xu, Huanu Educational Psychology, The Chinese U of Hong Kong, Hong Kong, China, People's Republic of : Hong Kong SAR Wong, Wan-chi Educational Psychology, The Chinese U of Hong Kong, Hong Kong, China, People's Republic of : Macao SAR

Under the "veil of ignorance", will people derive Rawls's principles of justice like the case in his thought experiment? Twenty Chinese undergraduates, with five in a group, were asked to conduct a discussion concerning the arrangement of social life and the distribution of resources in the approximation of Rawls's "original position". After lengthy discussions, unanimous agreement was reached in two groups. Major principles, endorsed collectively or individually, were characterized by a concern of the worst-off members on one hand, and by the affirmation of distributive justice according to merits and/or status on the other. These diverged much from the principles of Rawls's theory of justice. The validity and implications of this study will be discussed.

The effects of watchng athletes' playing videos on their psychological and performance aspects

Yamazaki, Masayuki Human Environment Studies, Kyushu University, Kasuga, Japan Sugiyama, Yoshio Human Environment Studies, Kyushu University, Kasuga City, Fukuoka Prefectur, Japan

The purpose of this study was to examine the effects of videos based on self-modeling theory on athletes' psychological and performance aspects. Participants were 40 college badminton players. They were randomly assigned to the experimental group and the control group. The experimental group watched own playing videos. Both groups completed psychological questionnaire and successful shot rates as performance evaluation were calculated. In analyses, Group (2) × Times (2) in repeated measure of ANOVA were performed. The results indicated that the experimental group improved psychological and performance aspects more than the control group.

Effects of reference point in trust decisions

Yan, Jin School of management, Zhejiang University, Hangzhou, People's Republic of China Chen, Kangli School of management, Zhejiang University, Hangzhou, People's Republic of China Pan, Huizhen Jiaxing Branch, Zhejiang Mobile Telecom, Jiaxing, People's Republic of China

The effects of reference point in trust decisions have been studied by simulation in this research. 97 subjects participated in the study. The results showed that the reference point have significant effects on trustor' decision. The trustor thinks more about the reciprocal ratio more than the overall return. When the reference point changed, the judgment of the trustor will also transfer.

A servey of mental status of Taiwan students in a certain medical college in Beijing

Yang, Fengchi Dept. of Humanities, Capital Meidical University, Beijing, People's Republic of China

objective To investigate the psychological features, including coping style, Loneliness, Interaction anxiousness and self-Esteem, of the college students from Taiwan,and to provide the foundation of psychological education. Methods A totle of 30 college students from Taiwan and 49 continental students were enrolled in the survey by the way of clustering sample, and then compared by Simplified coping style scale, UCLA Loneliness scale, Interaction Anxiousness Scale and The self-Esteem Scale. Results There was significance defferences between continental and Taiwan students in loneliness and self-Esteem. Conclusion As a result, developing the self-esteem and overcome lonliness have important influence for the mental status of Taiwan students.

Middle school students' personal epistemology: Theoretical construct and development of a personal epistemology inventory

Yang, Xiaoyang Dept. of Psychology, Sun Yat-sen University, Guangzhou, People's Republic of China Shen, Jiliang School of Psychology, Beijing Normal University, Beijing, People's Republic of China

In this study, it was supposed that the middle school students' personal epistemology is the conceptions that the students have about knowledge and knowing. 459 students in grades 7, 8, and 10 completed the inventory about personal episte-mology. The results showed that: (1) after data analysis and item adjustment, the inventory has significant item differential validity, construct validity and internal consistency reliability; (2) the theoretical construct of personal epistemology which proposed by us was confirmed through confirmatory factor analysis; (3) the findings of the present study were consistent with existent outcomes. Key Words Personal epistemology; Middle school student; theoretical dimensions

The influence of field independence-field dependence cognitive style on set effect among middle school students

Yao, Jingjing Psychology, Zhejiang Normal University, Jinhua, People's Republic of China

Using Embedded Figure Test and Luchins' set experiment, cognitive styles and set effects among middle school students were investigated. And the relationship between cognitive style and set effect was also studied. Results: female students' field independence was significantly higher than male students but there was no significant difference in cognitive styles among different grades. Male students had more set effects than female students, and the effects increased in accordance with grades. Junior middle school students had no significant differences in set effects among different cognitive styles. High School Students with field-dependence style presented significant more set effects than field-independence students.

Determinants of children's waste reduction behavior

Yorifuji, Kayo IEWRI, Osaka, Germany Ando, Kaori Human Life and Environment, Nara Women's University, Nara, Japan Ohnuma, Susumu School of Letters, Hokkaido University, Sapporo, Japan Sugiura, Junkichi Faculty of Education, Aichi University of Education, Kariya, Japan Usui, Junko Human Life and Environment, Nara Women's University, Nara, Japan

We explored the determinants of children's waste reduction behavior. We distributed questionnaires at elementary school in Japan for the children of 9 and 10 years old and one of their parents. We analyzed the 348 pairs of data which was matched between children and parents. The result showed that communication with parents had a significant influence on children's awareness of consequences (AC) and subjective norm (SN). AC had strong influence on personal norm, which was related to the waste reduction behavior. SN didn't have significant influence on personal norm, but it was directly related to the behavior.

The effect of teacher's teaching behaviors on Chinese junior high school student's English learning motivation and achievement

Zeng, Xihua Educational Psychology, The Chinese University of HK, Hong Kong, China, People's Republic of : Hong Kong SAR Wang, Yun Beijing Normal University, Beijing Normal University, Beijing, People's Republic of China

The effect of Teachers' teaching behaviors on students' learning motivation and achievement in EFL (English as foreign language) contexts was tested with English test scores and questionnaire responses of 662 Chinese Junior high school students. Students had higher intrinsic regulation, English learning self-efficacy and English achievement when English teachers provided more autonomy support. However, students' had higher external regulation when teachers gave more control, and had higher intrinsic regulation but lower scores when teachers were more involved in their studies. Students' regulation and self efficacy partially mediated the effect of teacher's teaching behaviors on students' English achievement.

The influence of metaphor and plan of development introductions on the evaluation of student essays

Zengaro, Franco Murfreesboro, USA Zengaro, Sally Educational Psychology, University of Alabama, Murfreesboro, USA Iran-Nejad, Asghar Educational Psychology, University of Alabama, Tuscaloosa, USA

Objectives: This research examined the influence of the type of introduction on the evaluation of student essays. Methods: A plan of development introduction and a metaphor introduction were written for two student essays. Eighty-eight university students evaluated the essays. One-way ANOVA tests were conducted on the data. Results: The essays with metaphor introductions received higher grades and were considered the best. Conclusions: These results follow Iran-Nejad (1987) on the causes of affect and liking; presenting a "clue" leads to greater interest than presenting all the information first and then elaborating.

Chinese rural migrant workers' social attitude personality and poverty attribution

Zhang, Jianxin Chinese Academy of Sciences, Institute of Psychology, Beijing, People's Republic of China

To explore poverty attributions of Chinese rural migrant workers. the study developed Chinese Poverty Attribution Questionnaire (CPAQ), and used Just World Belief Scale(JWBS), HAR, DIS and ANT subscales of CPAI-2 among 398 participants. CPAQ has five factors of Overburden-Fate, System-Unjustness, Education-Skills, Individual-Family, and Region-Environment. The rura workers endorsed less in JWBS, and scored lower in HAR and ANT, but higher in DIS subscales. DIS predicted positively Overburden-Fate and Region-Environment poverty attribution. JWBS predicted negatively System-Unjustness and Education-Skills attribution. It seems that Chinese rural worker still tend to criticize themselves but society and system for their poverty.

A survey on stress level of the employees in nuclear power plants in China

Zhang, Meiyan Dept. of Psychology, Jinan University of Shandong, Jinan, People's Republic of China Tong, Yuehua Dept. of Psychology, Jinan University of Shandong, Jinan, People's Republic of China

The present study was to investigate the stress level in employees working in nuclear power plants in China. 262 employees completed the Stress Scale. The results showed that psychological stress of employees in nuclear power plants was significantly higher than that of employees in other plants. In three age groups such as the group under age 30, the group between age 30 and 40, and the group above age 40, employees above age 40 reported higher stress level than those under age 30, with the group between age 30 and 40 the least. Implications for stress management program are discussed.

Other-regarding preference in 3.5- to 5-year-old children

Zhang, Zhen Department of Psychology, Peking University, Beijing, People's Republic of China Su, Yanjie Department of Psychology, Peking University, Beijing, People's Republic of China

The existence of concern for the welfare of others was investigated in 120 (3.5- to 5-year-old) children, using two-alternative choice task adapted from Silk et al. (2005) in chimpanzees. Results showed that only girls chose the option benefiting both sides more often when another person was present than when they were alone. For boys, however, the variance of the frequency choosing altruistic option was heterogeneous between conditions, which implied individual difference on other-regarding preference in boys. These findings suggest that there is positive other-regarding preference in girls but the preference is heterogeneous in boys in this age period.

New issues of implicit learning and its influence on research of expertise

Zhang, Yingping Children's Culture Institute, Zhejiang Normal University, Jinhua, People's Republic of China *Liu, Xuanwen* Children's Culture Institute, Zhejiang Normal University, Jinhua, People's Republic of China

The paper discussed new issues of implicit learning and its influence on research of Expertise. New progress on implicit learning was gained in many areas, such as on abstraction characteristic, representation mechanism, the relationship between implicit learning and explicit learning, and the applied area of implicit learning. The new issues of implicit learning indicated that the difference of the expert and novice possibly laid its root in difference of representation of abstract knowledge. The studies of implicit learning provide a brand-new research field for research of expertise in its interior mechanism and its expertise acquired approach.

The relationship between theory of mind and executive function: Evidence from children with ASD or ADHD

Zhou, Shijie Second Xiangya Hospital, Central South University, Changsha, People's Republic of China

Objective: To investigate the relationship between theory of mind and executive function. Methods: 20 children with autism spectrum disorders (ASD), 26 children with Attention Deficit Hyperactivity Disorder (ADHD), and 30 normal control subjects were compared on two batteries of ToM tasks and EF tasks. The data was analyzed with Kruskal-Wallis H test, Chi-square test, correlation analysis and covariance analysis. Results: After nonverbal IQ was partialled out, ToM composite score was significantly related to EF scores in ADHD group; while in autism group, ToM composite score was only significantly related to WCST scores. Conclusion: ToM has relationship with EF, but the relationship varies with the groups and components.

Theory of mind in children with autism spectrum disorders

Zhou, Shijie Second Xiangya Hospital, Central South University, Changsha, People's Republic of China *Yang, Juan* The Second Xiangya Hospital, Central South University, Changsha, People's Republic of China

Objective: To investigate the theory of mind(ToM) of children with autism spectrum disorders, and to examine the theory of mind deficit hypothesis. Methods: 17 autistic children and 30 normal children were tested by the appearance-reality task, the unexpected-location task and the unexpected-content task. Results: Correlation analysis showed that there was a significant correlation between "location false-belief" and "content false-belief" for autistic children, and significant correlations between each other ToM tasks for normal children. Children with autism spectrum disorders get significantly lower scores in all ToM tasks than the normal group. Conclusions: Autistic children had a great deficit in ToM.

The relationship between the character and the sport strategy of the elite golf athletes in China

Zhu, Da Peng Health Science Department, Wuhan Institute of P.E., WuHan, People's Republic of China

In order to examined the relationship between the character and the strategy of training and competition among the excellent golf athletes, this study tested 14 golf athletes' character, strategy of training and competition of the national golf team(male=8,female=6,average age=21). The results suggested that there is a significant relationship between the athletes' character and the strategy of training and competition($p<.05$); also the strategy of training has a significant relationship with the competition strategy($p<.05$). Significant gender differences were found in some dimensions of the training strategy and competition strategy.

Convergent, discriminant, and predictive validity of a measure of implicit motives based on word recognition latencies

Zinn, Frank Aviation and Space Psychology, German Aerospace Center, Hamburg, Germany *Oubaid, Viktor* Aviation and Space Psychology, German Aerospace Center, Hamburg, Germany *Köhler, Antje* Social Psychology, Helmut-Schmidt-University, Hamburg, Germany *Eichstaedt, Jan* Industrial and Organiz. Psy., Helmut-Schmidt-University, Hamburg, Germany

A measurement approach is introduced for assessing the implicit affiliation, achievement, and power motive, based on visual word recognition (Eichstaedt, Scheffer, Köhler & Driemeyer, submitted). Motive-relevant target words are tachistoscopically presented and masked in repetition until recognized. Words related to the individual's motives are recognized quicker than unrelated words. Results of two independent studies demonstrate convergent validity with TAT-measured implicit motives and discriminant validity with self-attributed motives. Two further studies among trainees and pilot candidates provide evidence for predictive validity regarding assessment center results, academic achievement and career success. The new measure's internal consistency is evidenced to be sufficient.

Career types and a specialist's motivation

Zolotova, Natalia Dept. of Human Resources, GE, Chisinau, Moldova

Hypothesis: Horizontal and Vertical careers - are the different ways for a specialist to develop. It is chosen by specialists with different types of personal qualities and motivation. Based on factorial analysis marks from tests where created personality models of a specialist with a horizontal and vertical career. Such models are characterized by mutual and differing traits. There for, the presence in the power industry of specialists with a vertical outer based and horizontal, intrapreneurs, inner based career: harmonizes the professional environment, allows to take into consideration personal qualities of a young specialist, makes the process of developing a specialists motivation more purposeful. This increases the working efficacy of specialists.

Tuesday 22nd July 2008

BL-001: Executive attention: Its origins, development, and functions

Peter A. Frensch (Chair)

(Paul-B.-Baltes Lecture)
Posner, Michael Dept. of Psychology, University of Oregon, Eugene, USA
Various functions of attention are mediated by separate brain networks. One of these, the executive attention network, is important for self-regulation. We have traced the origin of this network to infancy and its development in childhood. Although common to all, its efficiency differs among individuals, partly due to genetic variation. We discuss several alleles of dopamine and serotonin genes that are related to network function. One of these variations appears to behave differently in children depending upon the quality of parenting. The implications of this finding for the development and evolution of the human brain will be discussed.

IA-008: The cultural psychology of globalization

Sik-Hung Ng (Chair)

Chiu, Chi Yue Psychology, University of Illinois, Champaign, USA *Cheng, Shirley* Psychology, University of Illinois at Urba, Urbana-Champaign, USA
In this paper, we discuss how individuals may respond to the cultural implications of globalization. We begin with a discussion of the possible cultural impacts of globalization and the basic cognitive and motivational principles that mediate some cultural processes. Based on these principles, we describe the hot (emotional, identity-driven, exclusionary) and cool (thoughtful, goal-oriented, integrative) responses to the cultural impacts of globalization. We argue that simultaneous activation of two cultural representations increases the likelihood of both cool and hot responses. We also argue that the need for firm answers and existential anxiety increase (decrease) the likelihood of hot (cool) responses.

IA-022: How to detect lies with statistics

Helmut Jungermann (Chair)

Bar-Hillel, Maya Jerusalem, Israel
"How to lie with statistics" is the title of a famous book. Can statisics be used for the purpose of detecting lies, too? I will present a number of historical cases, from my own research and that of others. where statistical tools were used to detect scientific fraud or misbehavior. I will discuss the possibilities and obstacles for developing a standard toolkit for screening suspect data, and/or for uncovering "secret" data.

IA-023: Passions: What emotions really are

Frijda, Nico Dept. of Psychology, University of Amsterdam, Amsterdam, Netherlands
The presentation will sketch an effort towards an integrative theory of "emotions". It will start from the several prominent features of behavior and experience. Seeking to account for those features leads to considering the central characteristic of emotions to be passionate: that is, to represent states of motivation, including having reached the end of striving and the loss of striving. Those motive states (called states of action readiness) concern readiness to establish or change subject-object relationships, functioning to enhance adaptation but also to produce exaptation. Most emotions are elicited by events with the intervention of information processes (called "appraisal") that engage the individual's interests (called "concerns"). Passions exemplify major aspects of human and animal mental architecture.

IA-024: Environmental stressors: The context of South Asia

Marc Richelle (Chair)

Pandey, Janak Behav. and Cognitive Sciences, University of Allahabad, Allahabad, India
The presentation will be based on the findings of a series of studies using multiple methodologies related to environmental and economic stressors in a variety of contexts (rural, urban, large size gatherings, and deprived slums) in the South Asia. Stressors interact and influence physical-mental health and overall well being. The lowest strata of the society, particularly the slum dwellers, have to continuously cope with both economic and environmental stressors. These stressors are partly source of migration, from rural to urban centers. A number of socio-cultural variables would be discussed to explain findings such as greater tolerance to crowding by women than men.

IA-026: Parent-child relationship, academic achievement and quality of life: The role of self-regulation, social support, and efficacy beliefs in Korea

Michael Knowles (Chair)

Park, Young-Shin Dept. of Education, Inha University, Incheon, Republic of Korea
The author examines factors that influence academic achievement and quality of life in Korea by focusing on parent-child relationship, social support and efficacy beliefs. In international studies (PISA, TIMSS, 2003), Korean students are top performers in academic achievement. Cross-sectional and longitudinal studies indicate that their success can be traced to cultural, relational and psychological factors (e.g., emphasis on education and effort, parental devotion and sacrifice, feeling of indebtedness, respect and trust of parents, and high efficacy beliefs). The pattern of results found in Korea challenge Western theories that emphasize individualistic values, but support the social cognitive theory advanced by Albert Bandura.

IA-027: The best-worst method for the study of preferences: Theory and applications

Christiane Spiel (Chair)

Marley, Anthony A.J. Dept. of Psychology, University of Victoria, Victoria, Canada
Over the past decade, a choice design in which a person is asked to select both the best and the worst option in a set of available options has been gaining favor over designs where a person, say, selects the best option; ranks the options; or rates the options. I present various models for such best-worst choices that are closely related to Luce's choice model and demonstrate that simple data analyses ("scoring" rules) "work" for those models. I illustrate the approach with an application in medicine. As time allows, I mention applications in voting theory and relevant open mathematical problems,

IA-030: Intrinsic multiperspectivity: On the architectural foundations of a distinctive mental capacity

Erik de Corte (Chair)

Mausfeld, Rainer Kiel, Germany
It is a characteristic feature of our mental make-up that the same perceptual input situation can simultaneously elicit conflicting mental perspectives. This ability, to which I refer as intrinsic multiperspectivity, pervades our perceptual and cognitive domains. Striking examples are the dual character of pictures in picture perception, pretence play, or the ability to employ metaphors and allegories. I will argue that corresponding achievements (i) share important structural properties and (ii) are brought forth by a specific type of modular functional architecture in which the same sensory input can be exploited by different types or systems of conceptual forms.

IA-031: Solving the puzzles of hypnosis

Kurt Hahlweg (Chair)

McConkey, Kevin Newcastle, Australia
Although researchers have strived to solve the puzzles of hypnosis from the vantage point of science, its essential nature continues to elude. I survey the domain of hypnosis, and argue for a new way of hypnosis research to progress the field. I explore why hypnosis research has evolved in the way it has, and why it has asked particular questions about hypnosis. I illustrate this with examples of experimental and applied research into or using hypnosis. I suggest questions to ask and methods to use in the next generation of theoretical and empirical work on hypnosis.

IA-032: Personal values and socially significant behavior

Ingrid Schoon (Chair)

Schwartz, Shalom Dept. of Psychology, Hebrew University of Jerusalem, Jerusalem, Israel
Do the basic values we proclaim influence behavior, or are they mere lip-service to justify our behavior? I will discuss the nature and functions of personal values and then derive a set of ten basic value categories that include the values recognized across cultures. Values form an integrated structure of conflicts and compatibilities that clarifies why it often appears that values do not relate to behavior. I will present methods to measure values that have been used around the world. I will then discuss how values influence behavior and provide examples of the value bases of numerous socially significant actions.

IA-034: Bayesian approach can be descriptive for cognition and learning

Buxin Han (Chair)

Shigemasu, Kazuo Tokyo, Japan
Bayesian approach has been believed to be normative and not appropriate for descriptive purposes. One of its justifications has been that the Bayesian approach never fits the typical responses for a number of probability-related problems (e.g., the Three Prisoners Problem) that are often considered paradoxical. But contrary to the "common sense" of cognitive psychologists, the Bayesian orthodox axiom system does not contradict real data. We argue that through deep understanding of the Bayesian axioms, the direct application of the basic principles proves to be consistent with the real data for paradoxical problems.

IUPsyS-001: Social change and psychosocial development in adolescence and adulthood

Rainer K. Silbereisen (chair)
The political changes in the 1990s, and the challenges that followed due to globalization and demographic shifts, produce uncertainty and individual demands that reflect a mismatch between the established behavioral repertoire and new requirements. Individuals react by various ways of coping dependent on opportunity structures and their change. The studies presented include the effect of social change on the cultural appreciation of shy behaviors in China, on the restoration of traditional family behaviors in Vietnam, transition pathways and career trajectories in the UK, and the role of post-transformation challenges on well-being in Germany. All studies share a comparative format by utilizing systematic comparisons between cohorts and regions, and also utilize longitudinal assessments.

Social change in Vietnam and its implications for youth

Jayakody, Rukmalie Population Research Inst., Pennsylvania State University, University Park, USA
Dramatic changes have characterized Vietnam during the past few decades, including prolonged periods of war, socialist collectivization, and a recent transition to a market economy. Although the economic consequences of renovation policies are well documented, the impact on families has received far less research attention. Understanding the impact of these changes on adolescents and young adults is vital given that 32% of Vietnam's population is under 15 and a little over half the population is under 25. The majority of our analyses use data from the Vietnam Surveys of Family Change and the Survey and Assessment of Vietnamese Youth.

Social change and transitions into adult roles: Mapping transition pathways and career trajectories

Schoon, Ingrid Inst. of Education, University of London, London, United Kingdom
Objective: To map changing transition pathways among men and women born in 1958 and 1970 Method: Drawing on longitudinal data from two British Birth cohorts, employment and family histories of over 20,000 individuals are charted, providing empirical evidence of transition experiences among the 'baby boom' versus the 'baby bust' generation Result: Findings suggest increasing destandardisation of transitions in the later born cohort, although there are no dramatic changes. Transitions have become more polarized, and women's careers are far more diverse than men's Conclusion: Diversity and differentiation in transi-

tion experiences challenge normative views of life course patterns

Adolescent traits as predictors of success in the emerging market societies in post-Soviet countries

Titma, Mikk Dept. of Psychology, Stanford University, Stanford, USA
We present findings from the longitudinal surveys "Paths of a Generation" begun in 1983 in 15 regions of the USSR and later in 8 post-Soviet countries. We estimated various multivariate models to examine the impacts of human agency on socio-economic behaviors and success in 1991, 1997, and 2004. Most surprising result is the consistent effects of traits in adolescence and early adulthood on outcomes when the same individuals are in their thirties or early forties. We conclude that longitudinal studies provide a unique opportunity to investigate the persistent impacts of individual traits in rapidly changing societies.

Effects of individuals' coping with demands of social change: A German study

Silbereisen, Rainer K. Inst. Entwicklungspsychologie, Universität Jena, Jena, Germany **Pinquart, Martin** Fachbereich Psychologie, Universität Marburg, Marburg, Germany
The study analyzes whether perceived demands due to social change, problem-focused coping and distancing from demands, would be related to depressive symptoms in 1,975 German adolescents and adults. A higher number of perceived demands in the areas of work and family life were associated with higher levels of depressive symptoms. Higher levels of problem-focused coping and lower levels of distancing were related to less depressive symptoms. Problem-focused coping buffered the effect of family-related demands but not of work-related demands on depressive symptoms. Finally, distancing buffered the effects of family-related demands but amplified the effects of work-related demands on depression.

Children's social functioning and adjustment in changing Chinese society

Chen, Xinyin Dept. of Psychology, Unversity of Western Ontario, London, Canada
In a program of research on social change and child development in China, we examined children's social functioning, peer relationships and adjustment in different circumstances. A series of differences were found among urban, rural, and rural-to-urban migrant children in social behaviors and relationship patterns. For example, shyness-inhibition was associated with social, school and emotional problems in urban children. However, similar to the results in the early 1990s in China, shyness was associated with social and psychological well-being in rural and rural-to-urban migrant children, although shy rural children started to experience the pressure due to the rapid change in the society.

Class, stratification and personality under conditions of apparent social stability and of radical social change: A multi-nation comparison

Kohn, Melvin L. Dept. of Sociology, Johns Hopkins University, Baltimore, USA
My collaborators and I have carried out rigorously comparative studies of social structure and personality in the United States, Japan, Poland when socialist, Poland (again) in transition to capitalism, Ukraine (longitudinally, during radical social change), and - currently - China, during "privatization." We have found overwhelming similarities in the interrelationships of class and stratification with job conditions and personality in all these countries, during times of apparent social stability and of radical social change. We have also found one poignant difference between socialist Poland and

the capitalist countries, which disappeared as Poland and Ukraine became capitalist and is nowhere to be found in transitional China.

IUPsyS-002: How diagrams promote thought

Barbara Tversky (chair)
Diagrams are an ancient external device designed to augment human cognition. They reflect, represent and convey thought, and do so by selecting and augmenting critical information. Among other things, they serve memory, communication, inference, and creativity. Five speakers will describe diverse ways that diagrams augment and reflect thought across several domains and populations.

Diagrams are visual analogies

Gattis, Meredith School of Psychology, Cardiff University, Wales, United Kingdom
Diagrams, graphs, and other figures are visual analogies drawing on the same cognitive processes as analogical reasoning in non-visual domains. Like other analogies, creating and interpreting diagrams relies on a structure-based mapping of relations between a source and a target. In this talk, I will present studies of learning and reasoning with graphs, Chinese characters, and other abstract spatial representations. The results of these studies demonstrate that similarity of relational structures influences the interpretation of diagrams and other spatial representations.

Handling spatial models in astronomy: With gestures and diagrams

Ramadas, Jayashree Homi Bhabha Centre for Science, Tata Institute of Fundamental, Mumbai, India
Handling spatial models in astronomy - with gestures and diagrams Jayashree Ramadas and Shamin Padalkar HBCSE, TIFR, Mumbai, India Understanding of the sun-earth-moon system requires visuospatial reasoning including mental rotation, perspective-taking and distance scales much beyond our experiences. In our classroom design study with Indian middle school students we develop a pedagogy for the sun-earth system. We focus on these students' attempts to work with large distance scales within a classroom environment that encourages use of models, experiences, gestures and diagrams. Gestures mediate between the concrete physical model and the diagrams: first in arriving at diagrammatic representations and then in relating the inferences from the diagrams back to the real situation.

IUPsyS-003: Challenges in diagnostic classification: The IUPsyS-WHO collaboration on mental and behavioural disorders for ICD

Pierre L.-J. Ritchie (chair)
The major international diagnostic classification system is that promulgated by the World Health Organization, the current version of which is commonly known as ICD-10. IUPsyS strategic priorities include maintenance of Official Relations with WHO generally and the revision of the International Classification of Diseases (ICD) project in particular. This work occurs within the framework of the Official Relations established between IUPsyS and WHO in 2002. Psychology's primary focus is the Revision Process for the ICD chapter on Mental Disorders and Substance Abuse. This symposium addresses the broad goals for ICD-11 as well as psychology's particular perspective and contributions.

Beyond psychiatry and psychiatrists: Making ICD-11 useful to all mental health care providers
Saxena, Shekhar Evidence and Research, World Health Organization, Geneva, Switzerland
Diagnosis and classification of mental and behavioral disorders has traditionally been considered an exclusive preserve of psychiatry and psychiatrists. However, less than 10% of all persons having such a disorder are treated by psychiatrists. WHO is revising ICD-10 and has decided that the revision will be done in close collaboration and consultation with all stakeholders including researchers, public health experts, non-governmental organizations and consumer and family groups. The scope of these collaborations and consultations will be international and multi-professional/multidisciplinary, including all providers of mental health care. WHO has established a mechanism to achieve these objectives as a part of the revision process.

Public health implications of substance use diagnosis
Tucker, Jalie Dept. of Health Behavior, Univ. Alabama at Birmingham, Birmingham, USA
Historical and contemporary issues in clinical diagnosis of substance use disorders are considered from a population-based public health perspective. The utility of different diagnostic approaches is discussed in relation to the behavioral epidemiology of substance use and misuse over the life-span, measurable dimensions of substance use and related harm that can support diagnosis and outcomes assessment, and prevention strategies that variously identify high-risk individuals for targeted protective interventions or attempt to control determinants of population incidence. Development of diagnostic schemes can be informed by public health, but differences in clinical and public health goals and applications make integration challenging.

New Zealand psychologists' use and perceptions of mental disorders classification systems
Lutchman, Raksha Psychology Psychiatrics, Waikato District Health Board, Hamilton, New Zealand
This presentation focuses on a study of registered New Zealand psychologists regarding their use and perceptions of diagnostic classification systems for mental disorders, including ICD-10 and DSM-IV. Psychologists feel that these systems do not reflect psychological explanations of clients' presentation, and question the biomedical approach as a basis for mental health classification. They would prefer a system that is less complex, considers cultural identity, is flexible with regard to individual differences, and more clearly informs and guides treatment. The results of this study will be compared with those of similar studies of psychiatrists and other groups of mental health professionals.

Psychology's participation in ICD-11: A call to action
Reed, Geoffrey IUPsyS, Madrid, Spain
Historically, the fit between psychology and the psychiatric model of diagnostic classification has been an uneasy one. One obstacle to the more widespread use of psychological treatments has been the dominance of a health services model based on acute medical treatment of infectious disease. Mental health problems are "medicalized" by conceptualizing them as discrete disease entities, with overly specific criteria creating the illusion of specific and curative medical treatments for each. Psychology has an unprecedented opportunity to participate in the revision of the ICD-11 Mental and Behavioural Disorders classifications, which has critical implications for both psychology and public health.

IUPsyS-004: Resiliency and capacity building: Four years post-tsunami

Elizabeth Nair (chair)
Psychologists in four Asian countries began a collaborative journey after the 2004 Indian Ocean tsunami. They met in May 2005 in Singapore to share their professional experiences and plans for psychosocial and community resiliency support in their respective countries: Indonesia, Thailand, India and Sri Lanka. In this Berlin symposium, they will present their action research status review and current challenges.

Meusigo Bangket: Challenges of the post tsunami social intervention in Indonesia
Ismail, Rahmat Himpunan Psikologi Indonesia, HIMPSI, Jakarta, Indonesia Marieta, Josephine Himpunan Psikologi Indonesia, HIMPSI, Jakarta, Indonesia Nurdadi, Surastuti Himpunan Psikologi Indonesia, HIMPSI, Jakarta, Indonesia Dewanti, Retno Himpunan Psikologi Indonesia, HIMPSI, Jakarta, Indonesia
The Meusigo Bangket programme is a series of planned change activities initiated by the Indonesian Psychological Association with the main objective of supporting the resilience and self sufficiency of the people of Durueng area, Aceh, following on from the devastation wreaked by the 2004 tsunami. The programme relied heavily on the participation of the local village people. Villagers learned to transform problems found in the area into solutions with planned action, beginning with two groups of women and youth followed by a program for the men. Outcome measures have been positive. Confirming sustainability and marking HIMPSI's exit will follow.

Disaster preparedness of Indian psychologists: The post-tsunami scenario
Manickam, L. Sam S. Dept. of Clinical Psychology, JSS Medical College Hospital, Mysore, India Undurti, Vindhya Dept. of Psychology, CESS, Hyderabad, India
Following the 2004 Indian Ocean tsunami, national level Training of Trainers program was conducted in 2005 and 2006 at two different geographical locations in India. 52 psychologists were trained. In turn, they trained 165 Masters level psychologists, 50 lay volunteers and 7 psychiatrists. The training of trainers program on psychosocial support is the only one of its kind in the history of the national psychology associations in India. It evolved out of the capacity building initiatives of IUPsyS and IAAP. Monitoring strategies at the national level need to be strengthened to evaluate the longer term impact of the program.

Impact of 2004 Asian tsunami disaster on Thai youth and their families
Sirivunnabood, Puntip Faculty of Psychology, Chulalongkorn University, Bangkok, Thailand Tuicomepee, Arunya Faculty of Psychology, Chulalongkorn University, Bangkok, Thailand L. Romano, John Faculty of Psychology, University of Minnesota, Minnesota, USA
Helping youth and their families cope with and adjust to a massive seems to be critical. Although a variety of disaster studies have been in place in the affected provinces, little is known about how the youth and their families navigate through this devastating experience. In addition, most of the studies on affected youth and families come from either cross-sectional or traditional longitudinal studies with time lags that often exceed one year. Therefore, our study is to collect data by interviewing about the daily lives of the 200 impacted children and families in Phang Nga provice, Thailand. Ways to minimize effectively future psycho-

social, behavioral and educational problems of the affected youth and their families are discussed.

Action research four years post Asian tsunami: Quo vadis?
Nair, Elizabeth Dept. of Psychology, Work & Health Psychologists, Singapore, Singapore
The Indian Ocean tsunami provided a unique opportunity for collaboration amongst the four Asian countries most severely affected by the devastation. Each country shared some commonalities, while maintaining vast differences in religious adherence and cultural practices. Psychologists involved in psychosocial rebuilding in their respective countries have shared their experiences over the last four years. This final paper in this symposium will examine the merit of continuing this process as a longitudinal action research program, to understand the evolution of different intervention programs in the four countries, and the relative impact achieved.

IUPsyS-005: Ecological psychophysics: From laboratory experiments to complex real world

Sonoko Kuwano, Jürgen Hellbrück (chair)
Many psychophysical studies have been conducted and important laws between physical quantities of the stimuli and sensation were found from the results of the basic psychophysical studies. It is now sought to apply the basic findings to our real life situations. Ecological validity should be taken into considerations when the problems in real life situations are treated. Real life situations are complex and many factors are involved. Though it is not easy to approach this topic, its importance has been recognized and the studies are increasing. This symposium would provide a good opportunity to promote the research into ecological psychophysics through discussions from various viewpoints.

Psychophysical and psychophysiological measurements of visual functions in laboratories and in everyday life
Yagi, Akihiro Dept. of Psychology, Kwansei Gakuin University, Nishinomiya, Japan
In rigorous psychophysical and psychophysiological experiments on visual functions, a subject has to stop eyes at a stimulus on a display for long time. The eye fixation related potential (EFRP) that is obtained with averaging EEGs at offset of saccades. EFRP is a measurable Event Related Brain Potential in eye movement situations. We compared data of EFPR with those in psychophysical studies. EFRP varies with characteristics of visual stimuli and attention like psychophysical study. EFRP enables to assess visual functions temporally and in real-time. We show studies of EFRP in laboratories, virtual reality or simulating situations, and practical fields.

Estimating the mass of real objects in collision by means of videos
Guski, Rainer Inst. für Psychologie, Ruhr-Universität Bochum, Bochum, Germany
Two experiments used videos of two metal cylinders on tracks, colliding in the middle of the screen. In the first experiment, the collision was filmed and presented audio-visually from two different viewing positions. Subjects estimated the mass of each cylinder. Results: the percentage of correct mass relations differed between positions, and the average estimation of each mass depended on the physical mass of the other object. – In the second experiment, videos from the vertical position were used in three conditions: audio-visual (AV), visual (V), and auditory (A). The visual condition showed the poorest results. Considerable inter-individual variance was observed in the A condition.

Mitigation psychophysics and soundscape quality

Berglund, Birgitta Dept. of Psychology, Stockholm University, Stockholm, Sweden Nilsson, Mats E. Dept. of Psychology, Stockholm University, Stockholm, Sweden

New psychophysical knowledge on soundscapes was obtained by developing the laboratory experiment and the listening walk. Sound level mitigation of noise by propagation and barriers overpredicts the perceptual effects on the soundscape because of counteracting relative low-frequency increase. Soundscape quality is best measured by four bipolar quantities (pleasant-unpleasant, exciting-boring, eventful-uneventful, chaotic-tranquil) and improved by combining nature and human-activity sounds. Ecological settings affect our interpretation of soundscape quality, thus, higher sound levels are accepted outdoors than indoors (<50 vs. 30-40 dBA). Below these soundscape levels it would still be possible to introduce positive sounds from nature in urban soundscape design.

Environmental design and psychology: Human response to thermal, visual and acoustic environment

Matsubara, Naoki Faculty of Human Environmen., Kyoto Prefectural University, Kyoto, Japan

Psychological study is useful in the design of interior and architectural space. It seems that designers in the wide sense are doing their work using the psychological effect of the physical environmental stimuli based on their personal experience. We have been conducted several multimodal experiments, which was suggested from these traditional wisdom We have shown that the discomfort caused by the hot environment might be lesson by some of the visual and auditory stimuli, e.g. visual stimuli such as cool color, river and environmental sounds. Facilitatory effects of the environmental sound on hue-heat phenomena was also shown.

IUPsyS-006: Presenting the public face of psychology

Merry Bullock, Jose Maria Prieto (chair)

An important function of scientific professional societies is to inform the public about the goals, content and applications of research and applications. This symposium explores how psychological societies educate the public through media use and outreach. Presenters from four psychological associations describe a range of initiatives to educate and engage the public.

National Psychology Week and other media opportunities

Gordon, Amanda Society, Australian Psychological, Melbourne, VIC, Australia

A deliberate goal of the Australian Psychological Society is presenting the public face of psychology in a positive light. We prepare media releases when psychological evidence can contribute to the public debate, and use the media and website to promote our messages. The presentation will discuss the development of the annual National Psychology Week, with over 400 national events in 2007. Members are assisted by media consultants in presenting their research to the public and APS releases results of research on an issue of national concern. The flow-on effect throughout the year of this initiative will be discussed.

Creating online and multimedia culture in a national or international association of psychology: Proactive minds

Prieto, Jose Maria Faculty of Psychology, Complutense University, Madrid, Spain

This presentation traces the history of communication by Scientific Societies from early communications to a 21st Century model based on the Internet and Cyberculture. It outlines new media standards, including Blogs and Youtube and the challenges of introducing an interactive and multimedia culture in psychological association and divisions. New expertise is needed to develop corporate discourse and multimedia and interactive communication formats among members of an organization. Although Psychology graduates are Internet users, few keep a proactive mind in devising new psychological developments based on web and digital standards or innovations. Suggestions for new approaches and outcomes are offered.

Presenting the public face of psychology: Strategies and opportunities

Farberman, Rhea Public Communications, American Psychological Ass., Washington, USA

One primary mission of the American Psychological Association is educating the public about the value of psychological research and interventions. This presentation will focus on APA's primary tools for communicating with the general public including news media relations and the APA website - APR.org. APA's news media relations effort is an extensive program including publicity for research, response to breaking news, preparing APA members for news interviews and a media referral service. The presentation will discuss what reporters are interested in vis-à-vis psychology, how psychologists can be most helpful to them in their reporting process, and use of the internet.

On-line readings in testing and assessment

Born, Marise Inst. of Psychology, Erasmus University Rotterdam, Rotterdam, Netherlands Foxcroft, Cheryl D. Summerstrand Campus, Nelson Mandela Metrop. Uni., Port Elizabeth, South Africa

The International Test Commission supports the scientifically and ethically sound development and use of psychodiagnostic tools across the world for the public good. This presentation will discuss ORTA, a project to foster the teaching and practice of testing and assessment, especially in developing countries, through on-line readings on broad topics from psychometric principles and cross-cultural testing to specific domains. Issues include encouraging the international community of scholars to contribute, and providing readable texts for people whose 1st language is not English. The current state of the project, findings from a readability study, and general challenges will be presented.

IUPsyS-008: Behavioral medicine: Promoting viable collaboration among professionals from diverse disciplines

Juan Jose Sanchez Sosa (chair)

Epidemiology points toward an increase in chronic diseases worldwide and a permanence of infectious diseases in developing regions, in addition to a complex HIV/AIDS map. Although human behavior is seen as key ingredient of the health-disease continuum, once individuals enter healthcare systems, their recovery depends mainly on effective coordination among professionals, acting on the basis of scientific findings. Recent experiences worldwide point in this direction but professional interaction between psychologists, physicians and other professionals does not always achieve the articulated interface required by the patients' care. The symposium analyzes experiences by top experts and presents options for improvement.

The psychologist as health care team development expert: Experiences in the United States, Europe and Asia

Garcia-Shelton, Lindamaria Dept. of Family Medicine, Univ. of Southern California, Los Angeles, USA

Providing health care is complex because of the many needs people present and the social/economic constraints presented by the national health care system of the country. Some medical practices around the world have expanded beyond physicians and nurses to include psychologists, nutritionists, clinical pharmacists, and other health professionals. Introducing people from a variety of health professions to a practice does not automatically lead to good team functioning. This presentation will focus on the ways one psychologist went about responding to explicit requests to assist several primary care practices and systems in three different countries improve the care they provide.

Improving the clinical care delivered by physicians: The opportunities of multiprofessional teamwork in patients with chronic diseases

Wollersheim, Hub Medical Center, Radboud University, Netherlands

Care delivery has shifted from the individual doctor-patient relationship into multiprofessional team work. Various types of physicians, nurses and allied health care workers, who often work in different departments or organisations participate, leading to more in-depth subspecializations. Aging of the population and higher cure rates of diseases formerly showing high death rates (like AIDS and cancer) lead to higher numbers of chronic patients. These developments require new ways of health care delivery, and multidisciplinary care coordination. We will discuss the pinciples and effects of new healthcare programmes and instruments and methods needed to measure various aspects of these programmes.

The contest over professional jurisdiction: Physicians and psychologists in an ambiguous institutional setting

Mizrachi, Nissim Tel Aviv University, Tel Aviv, Israel

Psychologists often collaborate with physicians in many institutional settings such as hospital wards, nursing homes, mental institutions and other frameworks. Drawing on fieldwork in a hospital for children with severe disabilities that functions as a boarding school. We examine the relationships between psychologists, physicians and other staff over professional jurisdiction. Special attention is drawn to the contest over space and visibility, exclusivity of knowledge and daily decision making. The analysis touches upon broader theoretical issues and some practical implications regarding the ongoing collaboration of physicians and psychologists in institutional environments.

Professional collaboration between psychologists and other health professionals in healthcare settings in Latin America

Sanchez Sosa, Juan Jose Dept. of Psychology, UNAM Nat. Auton. University, Mexico City, Mexico

Although Clinical Psychology in Mexico is a well defined and established field, training of clinical psychologists to work in the specific area of children and adolescents still receives input from a variety of professionals. As in other Latin American countries, this especialized clinical work is benefitting from the promotion of research-based practice. Educating all the way from politicians to the public in general on these and other issues is therefore a current priority of Mexican psychologists.

IS-023: Psychology in Middle East: Present and future challenges

Adnan Farah (chair)
This symposium will discuss the current problems and future challenges confronting psychology in the Middle East such as the training, qualifications, and practice of psychologists, as well as the challenges in advocacy, organizing, and policy-making. The symposium will focus on the implications of social justice and political violence for psychologists, and the need for indigenous psychology, which can enrich the development of a true global understanding. Finally, the symposium will examine the contexts that have affected the development of modern psychology in the Arab world and its relation to international traditions. The symposium includes distinguished participants from different counties such as Jordan, Lebanon, Sudan, Turkey and Yemen.

Training and qualifications of psychologists at Arab Regional Countries
Kassim Khan, Hassan Dept. of Psychology, University of Aden, Aden, Yemen
Training qualification of Psychologists in MENA Arab Countries is a corner stone in the development of the discipline as a science and profession and also to meet needs and challenges facing these countries. In recent year an overwhelming growing concern is witnessed in almost all Arab counties to review and assess Psychology University Curriculums for updating the discipline and meeting societal needs. The objectives of the presentation is to assess the present situation of Training of Psychologists in these countries pointing out achievements and also barriers and problems, recommending proposals to overcome it.

Social Justice: Implications for counseling psychologists
Ayyash-Abdo, Huda Social Sciences Department, Lebanese American University, Chouran Beirut, Lebanon
Social Justice: Implications for counseling psychologists Over the past few years, parts of the Middle East have witnessed phenomenal growth as well as violence. These changes have altered the socio-political map. Many social justice issues that impact the day-to-day life of people have been considered as less important given the threat political violence. What are the implications of social justice and political violence on counseling psychologists? This presentation offers a personal account of the situation with implications to counseling psychology education programs.

Present and future challenges for psychology in Turkey
Degirmencioglu, Serdar M. Istanbul, Turkey
In the last 20 years, universities in Turkey have undergone major transformations. New regulations led to pressures and incentives to publish more and obtain external funding. The 1999 earthquakes shook the ivory tower approach many psychologists were accustomed to. The country, too, was shaken by a military government, oppression and ongoing human rights abuses, as well as economic crises and increasing poverty. Psychologists are now faced with a free-market system, a volatile socio-political climate, increasing violence and a young population. The challenges in training, practice, advocacy and organizing, and policy-making are enormous. The paper concludes with a set of recommendations.

Indigenization of psychology in the Arab world
Khaleefa, Omar Dept. of Psychology, University of Khartoum, Khartoum, Sudan
The study investigated indigenization of psychology in the Arab world. Content analysis method was used for analyzing 50 refereed studies both empirical (n=35), and theoretical (n=15), published in 18 journals, local (n=15) and international (n=3). The study showed that Arab research is characterized by a single paradigm, which is descriptive in contrast to worldwide research and the process of indigenizing is slow. However, research published by Arab psychologists in international journals was more sensitive than research published in regional ones. The study suggested the need for indigenous psychology which can enrich the development of a true global understanding.

Historical, sociological and empirically grounded perspectives on the development of intellectual movements in psychology in the Arab world
Zebian, Samar Dept. of Psychology, Lebanese American University, Beirut, Lebanon
Danziger (2006) advocates a polycentric history of Psychology which examines the relations between sites that produce and consume psychological knowledge and the socio-political contexts that shape knowledge production and transfer. I attempt to contribute to a polycentric approach by examining the contexts and conditions that have affected the development of modern psychology in the Arab world and its relation to various local traditions and to Western psychology. Using content analyses of published work and interviews with prominent professionals, as well as sociological perspectives, this paper offers a perspective on the history and future direction of psychology in the Arab world?

IS-025: Improving learning and memory through differential outcomes procedures

Luis Jose Fuentes (chair)
Trapold and Overmier (1969; vide 1972) theorized conditional discrimination learning could be improved when unique reward outcomes for each choice condition are arranged. Each separately later confirmed this empirically in rats and dogs, respectively; it is termed the "differential outcomes effect" (DOE). Researchers have since extended these findings in both animals and humans with and without learning or memory deficits. Evidence suggests that DOE is a powerful tool to improve learning and memory that can be dissociated from traditional non-differential outcomes procedures in terms of behaviour, neurochemistry, and anatomy. This symposium will present recent findings assessing that contention

The neuroanatomical substrates of the differential outcomes effect
Savage, Lisa Dept. of Psychology, State University of New York, Binghamton, USA
The Differential Outcomes Procedure (DOP) has been shown to reduce or eliminate the learning and memory impairments associated with amnesia and dementia. This powerful effect has led to the question of how such a simple manipulation exerts such dramatic influence on learning and memory. Our data with animals demonstrate that not only are different cognitive strategies, but different brain regions are used when subjects are trained with the DOP relative to the Nondifferential Outcomes procedure (NOP). These data support the theory that different brain structures are evoked as a function of the type of associative structure used by the organism.

Dissociable neural systems underlie conditional discriminations with and without differential outcomes
Easton, Alexander Dept. of Psychology, University of Durham, Durham, United Kingdom
Differential reward outcome (DRO) is applied to a conditional discrimination learning task in monkeys and humans. DRO does not increase the rate of learning, but the mechanisms of learning are different, with DRO allowing the transfer of information about newly learnt stimuli to older information. In addition, the DRO task is not reliant on interactions of the frontal cortex and inferior temporal cortex, whilst conditional discrimination not using DRO is reliant on these interactions. We discuss the possibility that DRO allows for efficient categorisation of stimuli.

Differential outcomes and retention interval influence spontaneous retrieval in children
Romero, Mucio Dept. de Psicología, UAEH, Hidalgo, Mexico García, Rubén Dept. de Psicología, UAEH, Hidalgo, Mexico Martínez, Juan Patricio Dept. de Psicología, UAEH, Hidalgo, Mexico Chávez, Berenice Dept. de Psicología, UAEH, Hidalgo, Mexico
The aim of the experiments reported here was to explore the effect of the retention interval and the presence of differential outcomes procedure (DOP) on retrieval of the information using a successive reversal discrimination paradigm in a matching-to-sample task across an acquisition phase, a reversal phase, and, a final test of reversal with children. Results demonstrated an interaction of retention interval and DOP. These results suggest that the presence of the DOP generates conditioned expectancies about the stimulus reinforcer that can be a contextual-like cue that interacts with retention interval to modulate delayed retrieval of information.

Training with differential outcomes is effective in children with developmental dyslexia
Vivas, Ana Dept. of Psychology, City College, Thessaloniki, Greece
Discriminative learning of symbolic relations can be enhanced when specific outcomes follow responses to each relation to be learned. Furthermore, this procedure has been demonstrated to be effective in special populations with cognitive deficits. In the present study we investigated if the use of the differential outcomes procedure would improve performance of a group of children and adolescence with developmental dyslexia in a symbolic conditional discrimination task. The results suggest that the differential outcome procedure may be effective in improving discriminative learning in developmental dyslexia, and as an intervention of dyslexia-related deficits such as phoneme or word discrimination.

Enhancing short-term memory in adults through differential outcomes
Estévez, Angeles F. Neurociencia y CC SS, Universidad de Almería, Almería, Spain Plaza, Victoria Neurociencia y CC SS, Universidad de Almería, Almería, Spain Martínez, Lourdes Neurociencia y CC SS, Universidad de Almería, Almería, Spain Fuentes, Luis Psicología Básica y Metodología, Universidad de Murcia, Murcia, Spain
It has been widely demonstrated that the differential outcomes procedure (DOP) facilitates both learning of conditional relationships and memory for the conditional stimuli in delayed matching-to-sample tasks in animal subjects. Regarding conditional discriminations in humans, the DOP also produces an increase in speed of acquisition and/or final accuracy. In the present study, we aimed to test whether this procedure improves the execution of a short-term memory task in healthy adults. Participants showed a significantly better delayed face recognition when DO were arranged. This

finding suggests that the DOP can be a technique to facilitate short-term memory performance in humans.

Human fMRI evidence for the neural correlates of the differential outcomes effect

Mok, Leh-Woon National Institute Education, Nanyang Tech. University, Singapur, Singapore

In conditional discrimination choice tasks, one learns to make a choice conditionally based on the presenting discriminative/cue stimulus. Prior research has shown that when each type of correct choice is followed by a cue-unique trial outcome (differential outcomes procedure), learning is faster and more accurate than when a single, common outcome is delivered for all types of correct choice. This learning effect has been termed the differential outcomes effect (DOE). Results are discussed here for brain regions that are active in mediating the DOE, while healthy young adults performed delayed conditional discrimination under event-related functional magnetic resonance imaging (fMRI).

IS-041: Object perception: New views

Marlene Behrmann, Mary A. Peterson (chair)

The theme of this symposium concerns the processes whereby visual input becomes organized and coherent. The visual world consciously perceived is very different from the raw retinal mosaic of intensities and colors. Hence, some internal processes of organization must be responsible for producing a coherent percept. Exactly what these processes are remains poorly understood despite the roughly 100 years since the Gestalt psychologists first articulated the principles of perceptual organization. Here, we highlight new and converging research emanating from behavioral, developmental, neurophysiological and neuropsychological approaches in an effort to enhance our understanding of the processes mediating perceptual organization.

Perceptual organization: Acquisition and breakdown

Behrmann, Marlene Dept. of Psychology, Carnegie Mellon University, Pittsburgh, USA

Efficient face recognition is thought to depend on the ability to derive global structure from visual input. Here, we explore the relationship between perceptual organization and face recognition in three different populations: (a) in typical individuals across the course of development; (b) in individuals who fail to apprehend a multi-element stimulus as a whole following acquired brain damage (integrative visual agnosia); and (c) in individuals with autism in whom perceptual organization and face processing is atypical. In all cases, there was a clear and robust association between the failure to derive a global whole and the ability to process faces.

Reconceptualizing figure-ground perception

Peterson, Mary A. Dept. of Psychology, University of Arizona, Tucson, USA

The processes producing shape perception are not yet understood. A fundamental assumption has been that figure-ground segregation is early stage in the process, but this assumption is mistaken. I will review behavioral and neurophysiological evidence indicating that figure-ground perception results from competition between two candidate shapes that might be seen and that suppression is an integral part of this process. This evidence suggests that figure-ground perception lies on a continuum of processes explained by the biased competition model of attention.

Processing local signals into global patterns

Sasaki, Yuka Athinoula A Martinos Center, Harvard Medical School, Charlestown, MA, USA

Perceptual organization or grouping is one of the central issues in vision research. Recent reports in the neuroimaging literature suggest that perceptual organization is mediated by distributed visual areas that range from the primary visual cortex to higher visual areas, depending on the availability of grouping cues. Further studies that include deliberate controls for confounding factors such as attentional artifacts and radial orientation bias, are needed to clarify how spatiotemporal information in visual areas is integrated to give rise to perceptual organization.

What goes with what? Development of perceptual organization in infancy

Quinn, Paul C. Dept. of Psychology, University of Delaware, Newark, DE, USA

A program of research will be reviewed that has been investigating the origins and development of perceptual organization during infancy. The data suggest that infant perception of visual pattern information is guided by adherence to organizational principles (including continuity, common region, proximity, similarity, and connectedness) that become functional over different time courses of development, are governed by different developmental determinants, and that not all principles are readily deployed in the manner proposed by Gestalt psychologists. In addition, there is evidence that the principles are soft-wired and subject to interference, and that they yield perceptual units of an abstract nature.

Perceptual organization and visual attention

Kimchi, Rutie Dept. of Psychology, University of Haifa, Haifa, USA

Can perceptual organization affect the automatic deployment of attention? Participants were presented with an element display. On some trials a subset of the elements grouped into an object. The object was task irrelevant and unpredictive of the target. No abrupt onset or any other unique transient was associated with the object. Target identification or discrimination was better when the target appeared in the object than in a different location than the object. Similar results emerged even when the target appeared after the display offset. These findings demonstrate that a perceptual object can capture attention by its mere objecthood.

Extremal edges and gradient cuts: New cues to depth and figure-ground perception

Palmer, Stephen E. Dept. of Psychology, University of California, Berkeley, USA Ghose, Tandra Dept. of Cognitive Science, University of California, Merced, CA, USA

Extremal edges (EEs) and gradient cuts (GCs) are powerful cues to depth and figure-ground organization that arise from shading and texture gradients, where convex surfaces partly occlude themselves (EEs) or are partly occluded by other surfaces (GCs). Ecological constraints imply that EEs should be seen as closer/figural, and we show that they are: EEs readily dominate all figure-ground cues we have studied. GCs are generally seen as farther/ground to a degree that depends on the relation between the shared edge and the gradient's equiluminance contours. Together EEs and GCs strongly determine the perception of relative depth and figure-ground assignment.

IS-042: Terrorism and peace

Noraini N. Noor (chair)

This symposium presents an overview of current psychological research in terrorism, considers the relationship between Islam and terrorism, and how basic memory process interact with certain media

reports. The second part of the symposium considers the contribution of psychology to diplomacy, peace and the mitigation of terrorism, by examining the case of Northern Ireland, and of humanitarian relief work in conflict areas.

An overview of the psychological literature on peace and terrorism

Blumberg, Herbert Dept. of Psychology, Goldsmiths University, London, United Kingdom

Psychological research on terrorism shows an upward trend starting prior to September 2001 and now reaching approximately 500 publications per year. Classification schemes and some main findings are summarized in the present paper.<'"BR>Approximately 16% of the publications are general works and overviews, 51% deal with terrorism and terrorists themselves, 16% concern victims of terrorism. The remaining 10% are interdisciplinary or elucidate special topics. There is an ongoing need to integrate findings and to build a comprehensive, contextualized picture of the (diverse) aetiology of terrorism, of how it can be constructively minimized, and of how best to serve its actual and potential victims.

Islam and terrorism

Noor, Noraini N. Dept. of Psychology, Intern. Islamic University, Kuala Lumpur, Malaysia

The words "Islam" and "terrorists" are being used synonymously in contemporary public discourse. Why are Muslims perceived as terrorists, a menace to civilization and universal values of democracy? To respond, a) we introduce Islam and its principles regarding relations between Muslims and non-Muslims, b) we consider the historical and political contexts of the Muslim/non-Muslim relation to see why and how the connection between Islam/Muslims and terrorism is made, c) we provide social psychological explanations to understand this interpretation of Muslims as terrorists, and d) we offer some guidelines for peaceful co-existence between Muslims and non-Muslims.

Misinformation and the 'war on terror': When memory turns fiction into fact

Lewandowsky, Stephan School of Psychology, Univer. of Western Australia, Crawley, Australia Stritzke, Werner Oberauer, Klaus Psychology, University of Bristol, Bristol, United Kingdom Morales, Michael Psychology, SUNY Plattsburgh, Plattsburgh, NY, USA

We describe how basic human memory processes can interact with certain types of media reports to (a) create false memories for events related to the 'War on Terror' in a substantial proportion of people, and (b) create resistance to changing of beliefs that were initially formed on the basis of misinformation, even if that information was subsequently corrected or retracted. We review research that identifies suspicion and skepticism as crucial psychological variables that can enable people to respond to corrections or retractions. We present and validate a new scale to measure skepticism and show that it predicts people's beliefs about the reasons for the invasion of Iraq in 2003.

Contributions of psychologists to diplomacy, peace and the mitigation of terrorism

Christie, Daniel Dept. of Psychology, Ohio State University, Marion, USA

The worldwide contributions of psychologists to domestic policies that promote human well being and international policies that support war preparation and operations have been amply documented. The current presentation identifies and documents ways in which psychologists around the world have promoted peace and diplomacy, in some cases by directly influencing the thinking and actions of political elites. Roles for psychologists in civil society movements around the world that seek to address the roots of terrorism and promote peacebuilding will also be identified.

From war leaders to peace leaders: The Northern Ireland experience

Cairns, Ed Dept. of Psychology, University of Ulster, Coleraine, United Kingdom

This paper will review the roles, both positive and negative, that paramilitary leaders have played in the peace process in Northern Ireland. Using a Social Identity based approach evidence will be examined that reveals how former terrorists have through their leadership roles either helped to promote or discourage intergroup contact in Northern Ireland. Finally, implications for contact theory as a way of promoting peace in divided societies recovering form political violence will be discussed.

Peace psychology and humanitarian relief work in conflict areas: Challenges and potential

Abdul Majid, Hariyati Dept. of Psychology, Intern. Islamic University, Kuala Lumpur, Malaysia

This paper discusses the role and contributions of, as well as the challenges faced by peace psychology, as a discipline, in humanitarian relief efforts in disaster afflicted and conflict areas. Although still in its infancy, peace psychology is making gradual but significant impact in the delivery and sustainability of humanitarian relief efforts to afflicted survivors of disasters and conflicts. Based on advancements in research on mental health, socio-cultural and geo-political nature of conflicts, the needs of humanitarian relief agencies, and the author's personal experiences in relief work, several strategies and recommendations are provided to make peace psychology further relevant to the field of humanitarian relief efforts.

IS-043: Clinical reasoning

Antonio Godoy (chair)

The aim of this symposium is to present recent advances in the research of clinical reasoning. Dr. Ahn will present the cognitive implications of changing the current system of classification of personality disorders from discrete categories to dimensional traits. Drs. Lopez and Cobos will discuss the role of causal knowledge in diagnostic reasoning. Dr. Garb will propose changing clinical-decision-making from causal reasoning to probabilistic reasoning. Dr. Witteman will review research about the role of training and experience in clinical reasoning. Dr Haynes will discuss the presentations by the previous authors from the perspective of the training of clinicians.

Cognitive processes involved in diagnostic inferences

Lopez, Francisco Psicologia Basica, University of Malaga, Malaga, Spain Cobos Cano, Pedro Luis Dept. of Psychology, University of Malaga, Malaga, Spain Flores, Amanda Dept. of Psychology, University of Malaga, Malaga, Spain

Diagnostic inference is central to causal induction processes. Understanding how diagnostic inferences are made would be benefited if greater attention was paid to the specific cognitive processes that produce them. In this sense, our research has shown that different types of cognitive processes may mediate inference making: (a) intuitive processes based on the computation of statistical covariations; (b) complex processes relying on the use of causal knowledge concerning the nature of causal relationships. In our view, different kinds of causal knowledge may be involved in diagnostic inferences, and delimiting their specific influences would greatly benefit the field.

Cognitive implications of eliminating categories in personality disorders

Ahn, Woo-Kyong Dept. of Psychology, Yale University, New Haven, USA

One prominent proposal for the DSM-V is to eliminate categories of personality disorders and to use traits, based on the Five-Factor Model. Existing cognitive theories of concepts and expertise predict that eliminating categories and imposing trait-based reasoning on clinicians would disrupt communicability of, memory for, and inferences about patients. However, dimensional systems might have great clinical utility if clinicians feel that the current taxonomy is incomplete or invalid. In this talk, I will present results from a recent study testing clinical utilities of Five-Factor models, and discuss the implications in terms of cognitive theories of concepts.

Causal versus probabilistic reasoning in clinical judgment

Garb, Howard USA Air Force, San Antonio, TX, USA

Research from clinical psychology and social psychology indicates that case formulation is the most difficult task facing mental health professionals. Simply put, it is more difficult to explain than to describe. Not only is it difficult to make valid causal judgments, but when clinicians make diagnoses and predictions, they often rely on causal formulations. Yet, if their causal formulations are invalid, this can undermine the validity of their diagnoses and predictions. Data will be presented on efforts to modernize decision making processes in the United States Air Force.

Diagnostic decision making

Witteman, Cilia Radboud University, Nijmegen, Netherlands

My research focuses on the diagnostic decision maker. The diagnostician's experience seems to be an important determinant of decision outcomes. I will discuss differences in client representations and in reasoning with these representations, from more rational to more intuitive, over the diagnostician's practice years. And I will discuss the 'intermediate effect', i.e. a temporal dip in performance by diagnosticians who are more advanced than novices but who are not yet fully experienced. I will address the question which representation and which style of clinical reasoning underlies this intermediate effect, and the development of competence in clinical diagnostic reasoning in general.

IS-044: Coherent mental activity in perception and semantic cognition

James L. McClelland (chair)

The symposium will consider how different parts of the brain work together when we think and perceive. The viewpoint underlying the symposium is the notion that brain areas do not function as discrete modules that work independently. Instead, thinking and perception involve dynamic functional systems distributed across multiple brain regions. The activities of participating neurons are mutually interdependent, allowing a synergistic combination of different types of influence to affect processing in each participating area. The symposium will begin with a historical and theoretical overview by the organizer and conclude with a brief panel discussion among the participants.

Neural synchrony and selective attention

Desimone, Robert McGovern Institute, MIT, Boston, USA

Top-down attentional selection appears to involve an increase in high-frequency (gamma) synchronization of neurons carrying critical information about the location or features of the behaviorally relevant stimulus. Increases in gamma synchrony are found during both spatial attention and featural

attention engaged during visual search, and the presence of synchrony predicts faster responses in visual tasks. Recent evidence suggests that the frontal eye fields in prefrontal cortex may be an important source of synchronizing activity in visual cortex, during tasks of spatially directed attention.

Cortical integration of information in perception and attention

Haynes, John-Dylan Bernstein Zentrum, Universitätsmedizin Berlin, Berlin, Germany

The degree to which cortical integration of information is required for conscious perception and attention is still a matter of debate. Here we provide evidence for the important role of cortical connectivity during tasks involving spatial attention and visual perception. Selective spatial attention led to increased connectivity within the representations of individual stimuli in the visual system, both within and between brain areas. In visual masking, the connectivity between remote regions in early and high-level visual cortex was significantly increased when stimuli were more visible. This suggests that both attention and awareness require intact large-scale connectivity within the visual system.

The proactive brain: Top-down predictions in cognition

Bar, Moshe Martinos Center - Radiology, Harvard Medical School, Charlestown, USA

Object recognition is traditionally viewed as a hierarchical, bottom-up neural process. This view has been challenged recently by theoretical models and by findings indicating that top-down processes are involved in facilitating recognition. We propose that such top-down facilitation is triggered by coarse information projected early and rapidly to the prefrontal cortex. I will describe behavioral, neuroimaging and computational studies aimed at testing this proposal. Our findings provide strong support by showing that fast magnocellular projections linking early visual and inferotemporal object recognition regions with the prefrontal (orbitofrontal) cortex facilitate object recognition by enabling the generation of early predictions.

Bringing it all together: The critical role of anterior temporal lobes in semantic memory

Lambon Ralph, Matthew Neuroscience and Aphasia Unit, University of Manchester, Manchester, United Kingdom

Semantic cognition requires a number of interactive, neurocognitive elements including amodal semantic representations. These representations license appropriate generalisations and inferences made on the basis of semantic rather than superficial similarities. Classical neurological models and many contemporary neuroscience theories suggest that conceptualisation represents the conjoint action of multiple, modality-specific brain regions. Data from multiple convergent methods (neuropsychological studies, fMRI, rTMS, MR tractography, computational modelling) indicates that in addition to these regions, the bilateral anterior temporal lobes provide a critical structure which not only binds together information into amodal concepts but provides the foundation for appropriate semantic generalisations and inferences.

IS-045: Transformation of intimacy in the context of citizenship, culture and participation

Gabriel Bianchi (chair)

Symposium presents results of empirical studies diging into particular aspects of intimacy and its transformation. Exploration of needs and conflicts in the public space related to alternative sexualities, national/ethnic minorities, people with chronic disease and/or physical handicap. Identity issues of clients in the sex business, concerning mainly transformation of their social network, intimate partnerships, subjective meanings of sexuality, sex and intimacy. Transformation of discourses and practices in the field of sexual education, their relatedness to power and political influences during the period of a "redemocratization" of the post-totalitarian country. Ethnic identity of immigrants and its implications to their civic participation.

Identity transformation of clients in sex business

Popper, Miroslav *Social and Biol. Communication, Slovak Academy of Sciences, Bratislava, Slovak Republic*

Objectives: A posteriori aim of the study of sex business (conducted by national teams in Hungary, Poland, Slovakia and Slovenia) was to find out how intimacy is perceived by the clients of prostitutes. Methods: Thematic analysis of the semi-structured interviews (approximately 20 in each country) was used. Results: Clients' transformation of the relationships with their closest social network and of the meanings of sexuality was revealed. Conclusion: The same clients view intimacy in different perspectives, based on their assessment of various types of (steady and paid) sexual partners as well as on how clients are assessed by their social network.

Transformation of discourses and practices in sexual education

Luksik, Ivan *Faculty of Education, Comenius University, Bratislava, Slovak Republic* **Markova, Dagmar** *Faculty of Social Science, Constantine the Philosopher U, Nitra, Slovak Republic*

The study solves the question: when an ideological discourse of sexual education becomes more powerful in society than expert arguments, existing law and curriculum framework. A discursive analysis concentrates on a public discourses, discourses from the round tables of experts and evaluation of teachers experience from sexual education.

Ethnic identity and civic participation of migrants in Slovakia

Szeghyova, Petra *Social and Biol. Communication, Slovak Academy of Sciences, Bratislava, Slovak Republic*

The qualitative study aims to explore the relation between ethnic identity and its implications to civic participation of immigrants in Slovakia. The emphasis is put on the influence of social phenomenons, such as discrimination, to the ethnic identity and its transformation after migrats relocation to the destination country. As a method, the thematic content analysis of semi structured interviews and focus group discussions with immigrants was used (N= 20). Migrants perception of the domestic population and relevant institutions attitudes towards immigrants plays a crucial role in the transformation of ethnic identity, determining the overall migrants integration into society and civic participation.

Conflicts of intimate needs in the public space

Bianchi, Gabriel *Social and Biol. Communication, Slovak Academy of Sciences, Bratislava, Slovak Republic*

Objectives: The study is aimed at identification of intimate needs, particularly needs of people belonging to specific groups (chronically ill/handicapped, foreigners/migrants, gays/lesbians), and conflicts (explicit and implicit) occuring during the process of their satisfaction in the public space. Methods: In-depth semi structured individual interviews (20) analyzed with thematic and discursive analysis. Results: Results will be analysed on the background of the major discourses on intimacy and its transformation in the society. Conclusion: The expected conclusions will focus on possibilities for conflict prevention in the public arena.

IS-046: Inhibitory tags that guide orienting

Raymond Klein (chair)

Using uninformative peripheral cues and the model task pioneered by Posner for exploring covert orienting, Posner & Cohen (1984) discovered that the well-known, immediate benefits at a cued location (attributed to attentional capture by the cue) were followed by costs. These costs came to be labeled and understood as "inhibition of return" (IOR): an inhibition of orienting toward previously inspected objects and locations that could therefore serve as a foraging facilitator. Using behavioral and neuroscientific data from free choice, visual search, and cuing tasks, symposium presenters will inform the audience about the behavioral presentation and neural underpinnings of IOR.

Inhibitory tags that guide orienting

Klein, Raymond *Dept. of Psychology, Dalhousie University, Halifax, Canada*

Orienting refers to the overt or covert selection of an input pathway. When orienting is produced by an attention-grabbing uninformative peripheral event, the initial facilitation of performance produced by capture of attention is followed by an inhibitory aftereffect (IOR) that discourages subsequent orienting to the original location or object. Using such a cuing paradigm, much has been learned about the nature of IOR, notably that it has those properties necessary for it to function as a foraging facilitator. The discovery of inhibition of re-orienting during and after episodes of search confirms the proposal that inhibitory tags guide orienting.

Neurophysiological correlates of covert and overt orienting

Munoz, Doug *Centre Neuroscience Studies, Queen's University, Kingston, Canada*

Salient events in the visual world have consequences on future actions. An abrupt visual onset can capture attention overtly via an express saccade or covertly without an eye movement. Many of the behavioural consequences of reflexive overt and covert orienting arise from direct mapping of visual signals onto motor systems that need not implicate higher brain structures or strategies. We use an oculomotor cueing task to investigate bottom-up and top-down components of overt and covert orienting and we monitor neuronal activity in the superior colliculus (SC), where top-down inputs can interact directly with bottom-up signals to alter behaviour.

IOR and orienting of attention: Is attentional disengagement necessary?

Lupiáñez, Juan *Dept. de Psicología Experim., Universidad de Granada, Granada, Spain* **Chica, Ana B.** *Dept. de Psicología Experim., Universidad de Granada, Granada, Spain* **Funes, María Jesús** *Dept. de Psicología Experim., Universidad de Granada, Granada, Spain*

Appearance of new objects captures attention so that stimuli are better and/or faster processed at its location. However, facilitation is later followed by a negative effect called Inhibition of Return, widely assumed the result of the inhibitory tag created at the cued location/object once attention is disengaged from it. We present behavioural and electrophysiological data showing that IOR, as measured by reduced P1, reduced accuracy, and increased RT, can be observed independently of whether or not attention is disengaged from the cued location. The mechanism underlying IOR might alternatively be related to the detection cost associated to previously cued locations/objects.

The effects of visual signals on spatial decision making

Danziger, Shai *School of Management, Ben Gurion University, Beer Sheva, Israel*

We examined the effect of irrelevant visual transients on deciding where to look for a hidden object. In 4 experiments participants also performed a conventional 'inhibition of return' localisation task. There was a bias to select the cued location in the spatial decision task. IOR was observed only when the localisation task preceded the spatial decision task in experiments in which the two tasked were blocked and was not observed in experiments in which they were randomly interleaved. These findings demonstrate that spatial decisions engage a different 'foraging mode' than those engaged when searching for visual transients.

An early inhibitory mechanism in visual search

Takeda, Yuji *Institute for Human Science, National Institute of Advanced, Higashi, Japan* **Sogo, Hiroyuki** *Department of Psychology, Ehime University, Matsuyama, Japan*

Objectives: Inhibition of return (IOR) arises several hundred milliseconds after the attentional shift. It was argued that this delay would be too long to inhibit several recently examined distractors in visual search. I examined the possibility that an early inhibitory mechanism other than IOR works in preventing reexaminations of these distractors. Method: Saccade trajectories during serial visual search were measured. Results: The saccade trajectories curved away from previous fixations. This inhibition arose immediately after the gaze shift and lasted 600ms. Conclusion: The inhibitory mechanism generating curved saccades possibly work in conjunction with IOR in preventing reexaminations in visual search.

Memory mechanisms make search efficient during static and dynamic search

Boot, Walter *Dept. of Psychology, University of Illinois, Champaign, USA* **McCarley, Jason** *Dept. of Psychology, University of Illinois, Champaign, USA* **Peterson, Matthew** *Dept. of Psychology, George Mason University, Fairfax, USA* **Kramer, Arthur** *Dept. of Psychology, University of Illinois, Champaign, USA*

Search is made more efficient by mechanisms that reduce refixations. However, the capacity of search memory appears to be influenced by several factors, both internal and external. Memory is improved when participants try to intentionally avoid re-inspecting items. When saccade planning is prevented, memory capacity drops substantially. A hybrid visual search / multiple object tracking paradigm suggests that although oculomotor search memory is decreased when item location is no longer constant, memory is still evident and surprisingly robust. Together, these findings demonstrate that several mechanisms make search efficient, including visio-spatial memory, inhibition-of-return, saccade planning, and multiple-object tracking.

IS-047: Correlates and co-determinants of health across the life-span

Sun-Kyo Kwon (chair)

At the interface of physical health and psychology, this symposium has been organized to elucidate the nature of objective and subjective health indices further. In the first part, Mrozek et al., and Wurm & Tesch-Römer, present empirical evidence about health in association with personality and life events. Kwon describes some structural properties of subjective health. A more comprehensive model is introduced by Spivak et al. Chung et al. offer an alternative methodological approach for investigating health. Finally, from an interventionist perspective, Rogers expounds on existentialist underpinnings in health-preventive interdisciplinary practice, while Lee presents an on-going program for adaptive health behavior.

Effects of neuroticism and widowhood on mortality

Mroczek, Daniel K. Dept. of Psychology, Purdue University, West Lafayette, USA Turiano, Nick Karakurt, Gunnur Spiro, Avron

Previously, we demonstrated that men with greater increases in neuroticism had a higher mortality risks. Death of one's spouse is also associated with earlier mortality. We hypothesized that men who increased in neuroticism with age and experienced widowhood would be at greater risk of mortality than men who experienced either. Those who had decreasing neuroticism and did not experience the death of their spouse lived the longest, whereas those with one/both risk factors had a higher mortality risk. These findings may be explained by the effect of negative emotions on physiological processes, which can lead to cardiovascular and neural damage.

Physical and subjective health in middle adulthood: Causes and effects of early vs. normal retirement

Wurm, Susanne Altersfragen, Deutsches Zentrum für, Berlin, Germany Tesch-Römer, Clemens Deutsches Zentrum Gerontologie, Berlin, Germany

In the past, early retirement was common practice to adjust to a tight job market. Compared to normal retirement, early retirement is considered more as an "off-time event" (Neugarten, 1996). Based on longitudinal data of a sub-sample of the German Aging Survey (N = 776, aged 45-64), we compared the importance of physical and subjective health for individuals who retired early or normally. Results revealed that poor physical health only increases the risk of early retirement. Moreover, early (but not normal) retirement is accompanied by a worsening of subjective health, which suggests that early retirement is perceived as a strain.

Does age make a difference for predicting nutrition behavior of South Koreans?

Spivak, Youlia Jacobs University, Internal Research Officer, Bremen, Germany Renner, Britta Inst. für Psychologie, Universität Konstanz, Konstanz, Germany Schwarzer, Ralf

Social cognition models of health behavior are commonly understood as being universal, implying that they are applicable to groups that vary in age or cultural background. Cultural uniqueness and characteristics of life span development, however, necessitate the study of differential effects. The Health Action Process Approach (HAPA) was examined in younger and older adults from South-Korea (N = 697) who participated in a longitudinal health screening study. The HAPA model had a good fit within both samples. However, structural differences among groups were found, e.g., regarding risk perception. The results suggest a different motivation for the adoption of nutrition behavior as a function of age.

Differential effects of individualized feedback on selected conditions: The role of subjective health

Kwon, Sun-Kyo Inst. of Mental Health, Hanyang University, Seoul, Republic of Korea

Social cognition models of health behavior are commonly understood as being universal, implying that they are applicable to groups that vary in age or cultural background. Cultural uniqueness and characteristics of life span development, however, necessitate the study of differential effects. The Health Action Process Approach (HAPA) was examined in younger and older adults from South-Korea (N = 697) who participated in a longitudinal health screening study. The HAPA model had a good fit within both samples.

However, structural differences among groups were found, e.g., regarding risk perception. The results suggest a different motivation for the adoption of nutrition behavior as a function of age.

A framework of user customized healthcare management using a neural network approach

Jung, Insung Industrial Engineering, Ajou University, Suwon, Republic of Korea Park, Peom Park, Rae-Woong Wang, Gin-Nam

The objective of this paper is to describe the design of a user-customized healthcare management system using a neural network approach. Current and near future users' general health information related to the metabolism and the like are base data. This framework consists of a vital sign acquiring device, a database, a clinical decision support system learning device and a computer-aided prediction system. The engine generates patterns of user health conditions and a suitable food and fitness list of recommendations. We expect that this algorithm can be utilized to manage prevention of sudden death and metabolic syndromes in a homecare environment.

Interdisciplinary approaches to methodologies in prevention

Rogers, Sherome Dept. of Psychology, Mokpo Maritime University, Mokpo City, Republic of Korea

We endeavor to identify an ever-reappearing trend of many disciplines that indicate the need for interdisciplinarity in prevention. We pinpoint its sources in various disciplines, particularly in health psychology. The fields of study are discussed which consciously and willfully made attempts to become interdisciplinary in their approach, and also attempt to identify their progress and outcomes. The advantages and disadvantages of such an interdisciplinary approach will be highlighted and discussed from an existential perspective of psychology.

A coaching approach for the promotion of adaptive health behaviors

Lee, Hwayun Johns Hopkins HealthCare LLC, Johns Hopkins University, Baltimore, USA

This study examines the correlates of activation levels for healthy behavior changes among employees at John Hopkins. All eligible employees will receive a new health promotion program working with a health coach. For four months, the health coach will collaborate with the employees to encourage and sustain a healthy lifestyle. Health risk assessment, patient activation measure (PAM) and SF-12 data will be collected at baseline. PAM will be conducted monthly, and after 6 and 12 months together with the SF-12. It is hypothesized that employees at a higher activation level will have increased compliance in adopting or maintaining healthy behaviors.

IS-048: Visual expertise

Narayanan Srinivasan, Cees van Leeuwen (chair)

'Visual expertise' is used to cover a variety of remarkable abilities that involve the visual system, often emerging through extensive practice. Typical examples are reading, figural creativity, the astonishing diagnostic skills found in echoscopy experts, or the skills of highly trained surgeons. Past research has treated the visual system and our cognitive and motor abilities as separate. Under the banner of visual expertise, we will discuss: 1) the ways in which different aspects of visual information interact, 2) the way the visual, cognitive and motor systems interact with each other and 3) the way these interactions are modified by expertise.

Contrasting congruency in letters and shapes: Domain-specific perceptual integration strategies

van Leeuwen, Cees Laboratory for Perceptual Dyn., Riken Brain Science Institute, Saitama, Japan Lachmann, Thomas Inst. Sozialwissenschaften, Universität Kaiserslautern, Kaiserslautern, Germany Plomp, Gijs Laboratory for Perceptual Dyn., Riken Brain Science Institute, Saitama, Japan

We review our results showing task-specific contrasts between congruence effects in letters and shapes. This effect dissociation was understood as based on a learned differentiation between letters and shapes, in which global symmetry information is suppressed in an early stage of visual processing. Results so far were based on reaction times. We present new evidence from neuro-imaging using MEG. The differentiation was observed in normal adults, and develops differently in normal reading children and children with developmental dyslexia. We discuss the implication of these finding for theories about how children learn to read.

Visual processing strategies in developmental dyslexics

Lachmann, Thomas Inst. Sozialwissenschaften, Universität Kaiserslautern, Kaiserslautern, Germany van Leeuwen, Cees Laboratory for Perceptual Dyn., Riken Brain Science Institute, Saitama, Japan

In some studies dyslexics reached normal scores in visual processing tasks and the conductors concluded that visual processing deficits are not involved in the syndrome. These tasks, however, may have been insensitive to anomalous visual information processing strategies used to compensate for an underlying deficit. We present results showing that differences in processing speed between dyslexics and controls depend on task and material. Furthermore we present an experiment in which dyslexics performed even faster than controls. We will show that an anomalous processing strategy leads to this seemingly paradoxical result for the particular task.

Practice effects on EEG phase synchrony during attentional blink

Nakatani, Chie Lab. for Perceptual Dynamics, Riken Brain Science Institute, Saitama, Japan Baijal, Shruti Centre for Behavioural and Cog, University of Allahabad, Allahabad, India van Leeuwen, Cees Laboratory for Perceptual Dyn., Riken Brain Science Institute, Saitama, Japan

Whereas a single target presented in a sequence of non-target items is detected easily, even when each item is presented less than 100 ms, when the number of targets is increased to two, the second target report becomes more difficult. When the lag from the first target (T1) is 200-500 ms and followed by a distracter, the second target (T2) is often missed (i.e., attentional blink). The attentional blink attenuates with practice. We report the results of a study using cross-lag EEG phase synchronization measures to examine the practice effect on attentional blink

Effect of color on motion-defined form detection in camouflage

Srinivasan, Narayanan CBCS, University of Allahabad, Allahabad, India Srivastava, Priyanka CBCS, University of Allahabad, Allahabad, India Kant, Vivek CBCS, University of Allahabad, Allahabad, India

We investigated the effect of color on word identification with a display consisting of broken stationary black lines arranged randomly embedded with a word (made up of broken lines) not visible when stationary. The word stimulus moved horizontally left and right till it was identified. We had found that identification was faster with red compared to green background. In addition, identification was faster with words defined by green lines compared to red lines. The results indicate interactions between motion and color for form perception and support models of figure-ground organization based on activities of the two visual pathways.

Motor performance impacts Fitts' law effect in action-perception
Chandrasekharan, Sanjay Faculty of Kinesiology, University of Calgary, Calgary, Canada Binsted, Gordon Health and Social Development, University of British Columbia, Kelowna, Canada Welsh, Timothy Faculty of Kinesiology, University of Calgary, Calgary, Canada
Recent work has demonstrated that perceptual judgment of the speed-accuracy trade-off in biological motion follows Fitts' Law. We investigated whether this effect is based on implicit enaction of the perceived task. Participants first judged whether a series of hand movements shown on screen were possible or impossible. They then executed the same hand movements, and the movements on screen were judged once again. The analysis of perception judgments pre and post action-execution indicates that motor performance has a significant impact on action perception. This suggests that the Fitts' Law effect in action perception is based on implicit enaction.

IS-049: Early syntactic acquisition and its impact on word learning

Anne Christophe (chair)
Learning new words is hard work, especially so for young children who do not yet possess a large vocabulary. Lila Gleitman and her collaborators have convincingly shown that some syntactic knowledge would help children to acquire the meaning of words, and especially verbs (the syntactic bootstrapping hypothesis). In this symposium, we will present and discuss experimental work with infants between 1 and 3 years, that investigate what kind of syntactic knowledge they possess, how they might have acquired it (before they knew many words), and how they use it to constrain their acquisition of new words.

Verb learning and the early development of sentence comprehension
Fisher, Cynthia Dept. of Psychology, University of Illinois, Champaign, USA Gertner, Yael Beckman Institute, University of Illinois, Urbana, IL, USA Scott, Rose Dept. of Psychology, University of Illinois, Champaign, IL, USA Yuan, Sylvia Dept. of Psychology, University of Illinois, Champaign, IL, USA
Children use syntax to interpret verbs. Our account of early syntactic bootstrapping has two main premises: First, children attempt to interpret each noun in a sentence as a semantic argument of a predicate term. This simple bias toward the one-to-one mapping of nouns onto participant-roles leads young children to assign appropriately different meanings to transitive and intransitive verbs. Second, children represent language experience in an abstract mental vocabulary that permits rapid generalization to new verbs. Thus, language-specific grammatical learning, such as detecting the significance of English word order, transfers rapidly to novel verbs, permitting progressively finer constraint on verb learning.

Little words, big impact: Early grammatical access to function words
Kedar, Yarden Dept. of Psychology, Ben-Gurion University, Be'er-Sheva, Israel
Infants of 12-, 18- and 24 months tested in a preferential-looking task oriented faster to target following grammatical sentences using the determiner 'the' (e.g., can you see the book?) rather than ungrammatical conditions in which 'the' was substituted with another English function word or with an unfamiliar word, or omitted. Around the 1-year marker, infants begin incorporating syntactic

information regarding function words in sentence processing. This early grammatical access enables the syntactic categorization of words and facilitates reference determination, suggesting that both lexical categories as well as functional categories are developing in tandem during this critical period in language acquisition.

Syntactic categorization of new words: Distributional and morphological cues to form class
Höhle, Barbara Inst. für Linguistiks, Universität Potsdam, Potsdam, Germany Wang, Hao Psychology, University Southern California, Los Angeles, USA Mintz, Toben Psychology, University Southern California, Los Angeles, USA
One aspect of establishing lexical representations for new words is their assignment to a syntactic category. Recent research has shown that English 12-month-olds use distributional information in form of frequent frames to categorize verbs (Mintz, 2002). Based on an analysis of German child directed speech we will argue that the concept of frequent frames is not simply transferable to a language with a more flexible word order and a richer inflectional system. Instead, the inflectional endings typical for German verb forms provide another cue that infants may use for categorization. Results of experiments testing this hypothesis will be presented.

The syntactic skeleton: Partial syntactic structure through function words and prosody
Christophe, Anne Dept. Etudes Cognitives, CNRS, Paris, France Millotte, Séverine Psychology, Université de Genàve, Geneva, Switzerland Alves Limissuri, Rita Dept. Etudes Cognitives, CNRS, Paris, France Margules, Sylvie Dept. Etudes Cognitives, CNRS, Paris, France
Many recent results show that infants, before 18 months of age, are sensitive to the function words of their native language as well as to its prosody. We propose that infants are able to exploit these two sources of information to build a partial syntactic structure, the syntactic skeleton (Christophe et al. in press, Language & Speech). Using a word detection task, we observed that 18-month-old French infants, just like adults, are able to predict the syntactic category of incoming words. Such information may help infants to constrain their acquisition of word meanings (e.g. noun = object, verb = action).

Processing of functional morphemes and early lexical acquisition
Shi, Rushen Dept. de Psychologie, Univers. du Québec à Montréal, Montréal, Canada Cyr, Marilyn Dept. of Psychology, Université du Québec, Montreal, QBC, Canada
In previous work we showed that infants begin to recognize function words from continuous speech and represent specific functors during the second half of the first year of life, with highly frequent functors being perceived already at six months of age. In this talk we will present the evidence that infants use frequent function words and bound functional morphemes to segment content words before one year of age. We will also present data showing that functional elements play an important role in infants' subsequent word learning and language comprehension after one year of age.

IS-050: Organizational behavior and culture

Shahrnaz Mortazavi (chair)
Organizatonal behaviors will be discussed from the following perspectives: The validity of individualism and collectivism as cultural constructs measured on national, organizatonal and individual levels.The second presentation is related to self-

presentation and personal values in the employment interview. The third paper discusses Intercultural Issues in Multinational corporations based in Iran. The last two presentations are related to "work stress and alcohol use across cultures" and "collectivsm and undesirable physical work conditions related to absenteeism in an Iranian industrial organizaiton".

Individualism/collectivism measured on national, organizational and individual levels
Mortazavi, Shahrnaz Education and Psychology, University of Shahid Beheshti, Tehran, Islamic Republic of Iran
Organizations are embedded within their national cultures. It is suggested that values used to describe cultural level phenomena are also meaningful at the organizational and individual levels (Robert & Wasti, 2002). In this research, a) Indices measuring individualism/collectivism were used to compare 476 subjects from three national cultures (America, Ukraine and Iran). b) The same measures were applied on organizational level to compare family and work settings in Iran, and c) The data was used to study the relationships of work-family-conflict and individualism/collectivism at individual levels. Differences were not significant at national level, but functionally meaningful at organizational and individual levels.

Self-presentation and personal values in the employment interview: A comparison between Afro-American and Euro-American student
Sandal, Gro Mjeldheim Dept. Psychological Sciences, University of Bergen, Bergen, Norway
Empirical evidence shows that job applicants engage in impression management behaviour in the job interview, and that such strategies influence hiring recommendations. The study examines whether ethnic groups differ in expectancies regarding favourable self-presentation, and relationships with Schwartz' Personal Value Questionnaire. A factor analysis of the Culture Impression Management Scale yielded six factors, labelled Competence, Compliance, Independence, Flawlessness, Modesty, and Collegiality. Euro-American students (N=156) favour the Competence strategy more and the Modesty strategy less than the Afro-American students (N=89). Associations of personal values with self-presentation strategies differ across ethnic groups. Insights are useful for training both interviewers and job applicants.

Intercultural issues and challenges in multinational corporations based in Iran
Namazie, Pari Atiehroshan, Tehran, Islamic Republic of Iran Namazi, Pari Atiehroshan, Tehran, Islamic Republic of Iran
This paper addresses intercultural issues and challenges multinational corporations face when their expatriates work with Iranian local staff. National culture factors from Hofstede and Hall have been used to show cultural differences. The paper examines literature and uses qualitative research on 12 semi structured and in-depth interviews with Iranian and expatriate staff in 8 corporations. Findings have been content analyzed. Conclusions suggest tools to deal with the other culture and how MNCs need be locally responsive as well as globally consistent in intercultural and work practice considerations.

Work stress and alcohol use across cultures
Mohr, Cynthia Dept. of Psychology, Portland State University, Portland, USA Wang, Mo Dept. of Psychology, Portland State University, Portland, USA Wendt, Staci Dept. of Psychology, Portland State University, Portland, USA Liu, Songqi Dept. of Psychology, Portland State University, Portland, USA
Employee alcohol consumption can undermine productivity and safety (Frone, 1999; 2004). In this

research we examine work stress-related alcohol consumption in Japan, China, and the U.S. Among the questions we consider: Are there cultural differences in workplace alcohol climate and work stress-drinking relationship? Are there cultural differences in the social contexts in which people drink after a stressful day at work? Workers from each culture participated in a daily process study. Daily reports were gathered via telephone (China), Internet (Japan), and programmable handheld computer (U.S.) for periods of 28-30 days. The utility and flexibility of daily process methodology was demonstrated.

Cultural collectivism and undesirable physical work conditions related to absenteeism

Mansour, Mahmoud Dept. of Psychology, University of Tehran, Tehran, Islamic Republic of Iran **Mortazavi, Shahrnaz** *Dept. of Psychology, University of Shahid B eheshti, Tehran, Islamic Republic of Iran*

Our sample consisted of 296 employees, who had high absenteeism records. The criteria variable was the amount of absenteeism. Predictive variables were: a) Cultural collectivism, b) undesirable physical work conditions, c) attitudes such as job satisfaction, organizational commitment, organizational culture etc., c) work-family-conflict, d) demographic variables and e) feeling distressed. Linear regression analysis showed that collectivistic values of work environment was positively related to attitudes (job satisfaction, organizational commitment etc.) and negatively related to work-family-conflict. Absenteeism could be predicted by feeling distressed, which could be predicted by family-to-work conflict, undesirable physical work conditions and low education.

IS-051: International Test Commission Guidelines and methodology for adapting educational and psychological tests

Ronald Hambleton (chair)

Interest has been growing for years in the topic of translating and adapting educational and psychological tests from one language and culture to others. Today, many of the popular intelligence and personality tests are translated and adapted into 50 or more languages; achievement tests such as those used in the large scale international assessments are translated and adapted into more than 30 languages and cultures; and in the United States, as one approach for handling cultural diversity and accommodations, many states are making their state assessments available to students in more than one language. Progress too has been made in the methodology for translating and adapting tests. The purposes of this symposium are to introduce (1) the widely-respected second edition of the International Test Commission (ITC) Test Adaptation Guidelines, (2) validated steps for adapting tests, and (3) examples of good test adaptation practices. The 17 guidelines were presented for the first time at the ITC Conference in Brussels in 2006 and at this symposium, the latest revision of the guidelines will be presented. Each of the participants will discuss aspects of the guidelines and their relevance for test adaptation practices in cross-cultural assessments. Four of the five participants, and the chairperson were part of the ITC committee with the responsibility of producing the second edition of the guidelines. Single abstracts are not being prepared. All of the participants will speak to the second edition of the ITC Test Adaptation Guidelines.

IS-052: Sensory-motor foundations of cognition and language

Michael Masson, Daniel Bub (chair)

Behavioral and neurophysiological evidence will be presented that indicates that mental representations of manual and other sensory-motor actions influence the orientation of visual attention to objects in the environment and contribute to fluent identification and evaluation of those objects. This evidence also shows that action representations are evoked during skilled comprehension of language. These results illustrate some of the ways in which cognitive skills depend on interactions between the human body and the environment, and they reveal some crucial constraints regarding embodied cognition and mental simulation.

Modulation of visual attention by hand actions

Masson, Michael Dept. of Psychology, University of Victoria, Victoria, Canada

Evidence suggests that handled objects attract attention. Furthermore, these objects may show alignment effects in that reaction times are shorter when the response hand is aligned with the object's handle. Alignment effects do not always occur, however, and our work shows that they are strongly tied to the nature of the response that subjects make. In particular, key-press responses to an object attribute like color show no handle alignment effects, but the very same judgment produces robust effects when the response requires reaching and grasping. These constraints imply interesting interactions between visual attention and the motor system.

The roles of neuroanatomy and experience in shaping visuomotor representation

Handy, Todd Dept. of Psychology, University of British Columbia, Vancouver, Canada

When viewing a graspable object, the human motor system has the ability to automatically activate the motor programs associated with that object's use. In a set of fMRI experiments, we have elucidated at three key factors mediating the nature of these visuomotor representations: The spatial location of the object relative to the observer, the observer's prior motor experience with the object, and whether or not the object's spatial location is actively attended. Taken together, these data suggest that visuomotor representations are not monolithic in nature. Rather, they appear to dynamically vary depending on present circumstances and past experience.

Conceptual representations embodied in perception and action

Kiefer, Markus Inst. für Psychiatrie, Universität Ulm, Ulm, Germany

Classical models assume that conceptual knowledge is represented in an amodal format distinct from the sensory and motor systems. More recent models, however, propose that concepts are embodied in the sense that interactions with objects form their conceptual memory traces in distributed sensory or action-related modality-specific brain areas. In neurophysiological experiments, we show that conceptual tasks activate brain areas involved in the processing of visual, acoustic and action-related conceptual information. Activity emerges early within the first 200 ms of stimulus processing rendering imagery unlikely. Our results therefore strengthen the notion of modality-specific conceptual representations grounded in perception and action.

Athletic expertise enhances language comprehension

Beilock, Sian Dept. of Psychology, University of Chicago, Chicago, USA

Do we understand action-related language differently depending on whether such actions are part of our skill repertoire? We examined how novice and expert ice-hockey players and experienced hockey fans (with viewing, but no playing experience) comprehend everyday and hockey-specific action scenarios they read about. Results demonstrate that hockey expertise not only differentiates performers on the ice rink, but also impacts the comprehension of hockey-action language - even when there is no intention to act. Neuroimaging and behavioral data points to the differential recruitment of motor-related brain regions in experts, novices, and fans while reading about ice-hockey, but not everyday, actions.

Evocation of action representations by words and sentences

Bub, Daniel Dept. of Psychology, University of Victoria, Victoria, Canada

Manipulable objects are inherently ambiguous with respect to the actions they afford. We distinguish between functional action representations (F) having to do with actions carried out when using an object, and volumetric action representations (V) that are applied when lifting or moving an object. Theoretical considerations imply that evocation of these representations should depend on context. We describe a novel method for measuring the evocation of F and V action representations to manipulable objects. We report a series of experiments showing how linguistic context modulates the time course of the activation of these representations.

IS-053: Psychology of sustainable development and environmental sustainability

Mirilia Bonnes, Giuseppe Carrus (chair)

The symposium will introduce the sustainable development concept and its implications for psychological research, for the promotion of environmental sustainability and pro-environmental human behavior. Major theoretical perspectives and related empirical problems characterizing this domain of environmental psychology will be presented and discussed. Different psychological approaches, relevant for environmental sustainability, bridging the individual and collective levels of psychological processes will be presented, ranging from more intra-disciplinary topics (change of environmentally relevant attitudes/behaviors, normative influence in environmental behavior, dispositional factors driving sustainable lifestyles), to more inter-disciplinary and policy-oriented approaches to person-environment relationship (psychological restoration in nature, cooperation in environmental social dilemmas).

The hidden power and real difficulties on changing environmental attitudes

Kaiser, Florian Human-Tech. Interct., University of Technology, Eindhoven, Netherlands

Attitude change is greatly underestimated as a means for behavior change. This is because "behavioral spillover effects" require behaviors to be interdependent. Objectives: To date, there is no evidence for the existence of behavioral spillover. Methods: With a pre-post design, we compared 196 persons in four conditions. Results: After the intervention, only the group that received personalized energy advice revealed significantly augmented environmental attitudes. Conclusions: Successful attitude change is demanding as it involves individualizing messages. Eventually, it pays off, when behavioral spillover, the hidden power of attitude change, occurs. However, recognizing spillover requires a novel way of thinking about attitudes.

Normative concerns and environmental behavior

Steg, Linda Dept. of Psychology, University of Groningen, Groningen, Netherlands

Pro-environmental behaviour is often associated with high behavioural costs. For example, it is less convenient to travel by bus, and ecological products are often more expensive. In such cases, pro-environmental behaviour mainly results from biospheric values and normative concerns. I will discuss results of a series of studies aimed to examine which factors strengthen normative concerns, among which biospheric values, awareness of environmental consequences of behaviour, and ascription of responsibility for these consequences. Moreover, I will indicate under which circumstances normative concerns will most strongly affect behaviour.

Psychological dimensions of pro-sustainability orientation

Corral Verdugo, Victor Division de Ciencias Sociales, Universidad de Sorona, Mexico, Mexico

Environmental psychology is committed to searching psychological and contextual factors inciting sustainable lifestyles. Pro-Sustainability Orientation (PSO) is a set of dispositional variables presumably leading individuals to the goal of environmental protection, both at the social and biophysical levels. According to a number of studies, PSO is characterized for future orientation tendencies, affinity towards bio and socio diversity, pro-environmental competency, the perception of environmental norms, tendencies towards equity, feelings of indignation due to environmental deterioration, and a group of sustainable lifestyles including altruistic, frugal and pro-environmental behaviors. Models of PSO developed and tested by our research group are presented and discussed.

The psychology of sustainability: Contributions from the study of restorative environments

Hartig, Terry Inst. Housing and Urban Res., Uppsala University, Gävle, Sweden

The study of restorative environments aids the pursuit of sustainability in two general ways: it provides insights on how to enhance environmental livability and on how to reduce human environmental impacts. In this presentation, I will overview empirical studies that exemplify these contributions. Some of the studies concern a planning dilemma: How can development realize the ecological benefits of compact cities while avoiding the psychosocial costs of dense urban structure? Other studies concern the challenge of motivating people to behave ecologically. All of the studies speak to the importance of restorative experiences in natural environments for people in urbanized societies.

A general model of social dilemmas

Gifford, Robert Dept. of Psychology, University of Victoria, Victoria, Canada

The symposium will introduce the sustainable development concept and its implications for psychological research, for the promotion of environmental sustainability and pro-environmental human behavior. Major theoretical perspectives and related empirical problems characterizing this domain of environmental psychology will be presented and discussed. Different psychological approaches, relevant for environmental sustainability, bridging the individual and collective levels of psychological processes will be presented, ranging from more intra-disciplinary topics (change of environmentally relevant attitudes/behaviors, normative influence in environmental behavior, dispositional factors driving sustainable lifestyles), to more inter-disciplinary and policy-oriented approaches to person-environment relationship (psy-

chological restoration in nature, cooperation in environmental social dilemmas).

IS-054: Personnel psychology and vocational psychology: Competing paradigms or twins separated at birth?

Frederick T.L. Leong (chair)

Despite having a central focus on work and workers, these two subfields of Personnel Psychology and Vocational Psychology have tended to traverse parallel but non-intersecting pathways. Each subfield has its own associations, handbooks, journals, and graduate programs. The goal of the symposium is to have industrial-organizational psychologists and vocational psychologists present their ideas on these two related fields and why there have not been more cross-fertilization and interactions. In addressing this question, the presenters will also provide some ideas on whether synergistic interactions are possible and desirable and what mechanisms may support such interactions.

What differences make a difference: An organizational psychologist's perspective on vocational psychology

Ryan, Ann Marie Dept. of Psychology, Michigan State University, East Lansing, USA

This presentation will provide background on how the identities of professions are formed and changed, and how the process of identity development of professions relates to the fields of personnel psychology and career counseling. The ways in which the fields differ in terms of research paradigms, methodological foci, topics addressed, and general aims will be covered. Key differences in identity between the two arenas will form the basis for a discussion of neglected opportunities for synergy.

Personnel psychology and vocational psychology: A family reunion for siblings separated since adolescence

Savickas, Mark Dept. of Behavioral Sciences, NEOUCOM, Rootstown, USA

First half of the presentation will provide a précis of the origins and early development of the application of the person-environment paradigm to problems of vocational guidance, personnel selection, and military classification. Pioneers in applied psychology worked synergistically on all three problems, and traversed fluid boundaries between academia, industry, and the military. Only after applied psychology was firmly established did vocational psychology split from personnel psychology. The second half of the presentation will describe the difficulties vocational psychologist now face and why they need assistance from their colleagues in personnel psychology.

The IO psychologist's handshake with the counselor

Born, Marise Inst. of Psychology, Erasmus University Rotterdam, Rotterdam, Netherlands

For individual employees, well-being and satisfaction are desirable outcomes. Yet, happiness at work is only weakly related to performance outcomes (Judge et al., 2001).To improve worker productivity, personnel psychologists therefore prefer to base personnel screening and training on g and job knowledge. Using improved study designs, satisfaction and well-being however demonstrate having links to performance (Wegge et al., 2007). Will these findings convince personnel psychologists of the importance of affective influences? Will they then start adding dispositional affect to the list of predictors in personnel selection? This contribution discusses risks and opportunities when the counselor and the personnel psychologist meet.

Personnel and vocational psychology: A lewinian analysis of centripetal and centrifugal forces

Leong, Frederick T.L. Dept. of Psychology, Michigan State University, East Lansing, USA

Using a Lewinian force-field analysis, this paper discusses the cultural environment underlying the two separate subfields of personnel and vocational psychology. The centripetal forces (center-seeking) that maintains the integrity of each of these subfields and gives each its unique identity and boundary conditions will be delineated. In addition, the centrifugal forces (center-fleeing) exerted on each subfield will also be discussed (e.g., psychology's resurrected interest in personality, the increasing importance of cultural factors in understanding human behavior). Finally, it is proposed that the degree of divergence or convergence of these two subfields will depend on the balance of these opposing forces.

IS-055: The role of psychology for human and social development: From research to policy

Susan Pick (chair)

The science and the practice of Psychology has a series of tools, both theoretical and methodological which have been used to enhance the wellbeing of individuals and communities' both in developed and developing countries. Representatives from a wide spectrum of countries come together to analyze different perspectives on this very central topic. They do so from both a purely psychological as well as from an interdisciplinary perspective; both basic and applied views will be integrated. The presentations address the role which Psychology has had, and can have in different areas of human and social development policy.

Comprehensive community development programs: Targeting mulitiple behaviors

Givaudan, Martha IMIFAP, Mexico City, Mexico *Pick, Susan* President, IMIFAP, Mexico City, Mexico *Leenen, Iwin* Evaluation, IMIFAP, Mexico City, Mexico *Martínez, Rocio* Evaluation, IMIFAP, Mexico City, Mexico *Barriga, Marco* Training and Community Develo, IMIFAP, Mexico City, Mexico *Bernal, Miriam* Training and Community Develo, IMIFAP, Mexico City, Mexico

There has been a long standing debate regarding the possibility of targetting multiple behaviors in interventions vs targetting individual ones. This paper refers to the process and results of a comprehensive health education development program. It has reached over 250,000 rural and indigenous women and their offspring in Central Mexico. For all the targeted behaviors a common base of life skills and opportuniites for reduction of psychological barriers together with specific knowledge has been built. The program has been carried out with a multi behavior, multipopulation and multistrategy perspective. Longitudinal data are analyzed comparing control and experimental groups as well as the efect of the program related with the level of participation of different target groups in the comunities.

Agency and wellbeing: The role of psychology in making Sen's capabilities approach operative

Pick, Susan Dept. of Psychology, National University of Mexico, Mexico City, Mexico

One of the most widely acclaimed perspectives in development in the last decade is Amartya Sen's capability approach. It departs from the philosophical position that economic wellbeing is an instrument rather than an end for development. It is enhancing peoples capabilities i.e. alternatives for realizing their potential, which should be the man target of development. It is in this way that people's freedoms are strengthened and being reached. Psychological theory and methods have a central role to play in such an approach given that it relies strongly on human development as the bases for development in general. The Framework for Enabling Agentic Empowerment (FENAE) has evolved from field work with marginalized urban, rural and indigenous communities in 14 countries.

Applying psychological knowledge elsewhere: The factor "culture"
Poortinga, Ype Dept. of Psychology, Tilburg University, Tilburg, Netherlands
The application of psychological tools and techniques in other populations as where they were developed repeatedly is widely criticised as cultural imposition, but at the same time steadily increasing. After mentioning the rationale for transfer I will propose tentative standards for responsible professional practices focussing on (i) consultation of intended clients and other stakeholders, (ii) the role and position of psychologists as experts, and (iii) empirical justification.

Efforts to modify health-related behaviors have been dominated by health education perspectives
Vinck, Jan Inst. for Behavioural Science, Hasselt University, Diepenbeek, Belgium Lengerke, Thomas Von Medical Psychology Unit, Hannover Medical School, Hannover, Germany
Efforts to modify health-related behaviors have been dominated by health education perspectives. Recently, more ecological views have evolved stating that health-related behavior is also regulated by habitual processes and, especially in terms of behavioral prevalences, environments (meta-/ macro-contingencies). Obesogenic environments are a well-known case in point. Thus, while it is evident that health psychologists (nor the populations concerned) do not have direct control over environmental variables, they have to organize collaboration with economic, political, and media actors who impact environments. This is a role health psychologists are neither trained nor prepared for, and will have to learn to take up professionally

Antecendents and effects of political participation: A behavioral epidemiological review
von Lengerke, Thomas Med. Psychologie (OE 5430), Medizin. Hochschule Hannover, Hannover, Germany Vinck, Jan Institute for Behavioural Scie, Hasselt University, Diepenbeek, Belgium
Political participation and participation in formal social activities more generally are key links between micro and macro levels of social systems. Simultaneously, they have received mixed appraisals as to their health promoting effects and capacities, in particular regarding individual health. This paper reviews studies both on the antecedents and health effects of participation. Regarding the former, policy-related (e.g., social climate) and individual-level (educational resources, social responsibility) variables predict political participation. Regarding effects on health, in line with social psychological theories both from sociology and psychology, strong control beliefs are central preconditions for participation to be promotive of individual health.

Conducting research with children and adolescents in street settings in Brazil
Koller, Silvia Helena Dept. de Psicologia, Univers. Fed. do Rio Grande, Porto Alegre, Brazil Neiva-Silva, Lucas Dept. de Psicologia, Univers. Fed. do Rio Grande, Porto Alegre, Brazil Morais, Normanda Dept. de Psicologia, Univers. Fed. do Rio Grande, Porto Alegre, Brazil Paludo, Simone Dept. de Psicologia, Fundação Univ. de Rio Grande, Rio Grande, Brazil
At the Center for Psychological Studies on Street Children (CEP-RUA) at the Federal University of

Rio Grande do Sul, Brazil, researchers conduct empirical research and applied projects to improve the quality of life of at-risk populations. One focal population is "street youth" – children and adolescents who spend much of their time in settings characterized by physical need, lack of adult supervision, drug use, and psychological neglect. This presentation will describe ethical and methodological challenges encountered when working with street youth and present examples of how they have been overcome during the Center's 15 years of existence.

IS-056: Prevention and treatment of behaviour problems in children and adolescents

Manfred Döpfner (chair)
In this symposium we will focus externalizing behaviour problems, which encompass a heterogeneous group of overlapping behaviour poroblems and disorders, especially Attention Deficit-/ Hyperactivity Disorders (ADHD), Oppositional Defiant Disorders (ODD) and Conduct Disorders (CD). These disorders are common, stable and hard to treat especially as a chronic condition. Psychosocial interventions have been proven to be effective in these disorders. Parent focused treatment approache seem to be more important than patient focused interventions. The high prevalence rates and the chonicity of disruptive disorders require the development of preventive interventions which may help to reduce behavior problems at a very early stage of development of the disorder. In this symposium current research findings on unversal and indicated prevention als well as self-help interventions and the long-term outcome of treatment will be provided.

The 3-year efficacy of a parent-training in the universal prevention of child behavior problems
Kahlweg, Kurt Dep. of Clinical Psychology, TU Braunschweig, Braunschweig, Germany Heinrichs, Nina Inst. für Psychologie, Universität Bielefeld, Bielefeld, Germany Kuschel, Annett Rehabilitationswissenschaften, Humboldt Universität Berlin, Berlin, Germany Naumann, Sebastian Bertram, Heike
The long-term efficacy of the Triple P parent group training as a universal prevention strategy was investigated from the perspective of mothers. Based on their respective preschool, families were either randomly assigned to a prevention program (parent training) or a control group. The long-term efficacy was analysed with a multimethod and multimodal assessment in 212 two-parent families. At the long-term follow-up's 1, 2 and 3 years later, most of the significant post-treatment changes were maintained. Mothers reported an improvement in parenting and a reduction in child behavior problems. Mothers' psychological distress was significantly reduced and their relationship satisfaction improved.

Prevention Program of Externalizing Problem Behavior (PEP): Efficacy and effectiveness in 3 studies
Hautmann, Christopher Psychiatrie und Psychotherapie, University of Cologne, Köln, Germany Plück, Julia Meyer, Ilka Döpfner, Manfred Psychiatrie und Psychotherapie, Universität Köln, Köln, Germany
The Prevention Program for Externalizing Problem Behavior (PEP) addresses parents and kindergarten teachers of children (3 to 10 years) with symptoms of Attention-Deficit/Hyperactivity Disorder (ADHD) and Oppositional Defiant Disorder (ODD). PEP has been evaluated in three different studies. The first study was planned as a randomized controlled efficacy study with high experimental control and internal validity. The two other studies tested the program components under "real-

world conditions" (effectiveness study). All three studies demonstrate that PEP is effective in reducing externalizing behavior problems of the child and improving parenting behavior. The results of the three studies are compared with each other.

The effects of self-help interventions for parents of children with disruptive behavior problems
Döpfner, Manfred Psychiatrie und Psychotherapie, Universität Köln, Köln, Germany Kierfeld, Frauke
Parent trainings either in a group or an individual format has proven to be effective for children with disruptive behaviour problems. However, these kinds of interventions are time consuming and expensive. A self-help program for parents of children with disruptive behaviour problems may be helpful to cover a broader range of children and families and may also reduce the treatment costs. Two studies were conducted to assess the feasibility and the efficacy / effectiveness of a self-help-program for parents of children with disruptive behaviour problems. The studies demonstrated the efficacy of that approach with moderate to large intervention effects.

Long-term outcome of psychosocial and multimodal interventions for children with ADHD
Wolff Metternich, Tanja Psychiatrie und Psychotherapie, University of Cologne, Köln, Germany Döpfner, Manfred Psychiatrie und Psychotherapie, Universität Köln, Köln, Germany
Attention Deficit-/ Hyperactivity Disorder (ADHD) is a serious and chronic condition in children and adolescents. Studies on long-term effects are rare and contradictive. In this presentation the results of a study on the long-term outcome of ADHD children treated with an adaptive and individually tailored multimodal intervention will be presented. The original sample consisted of 75 school-children aged 6-10 years with a diagnosis of ADHD/HKD. After an initial psychoeducation an adaptive and individually tailored therapy including medication and psychosocial interventions was delivered. In an 8year follow-up most of the ADHD children had a good prognosis.

IS-057: Lessons learned: Cross-cultural perspectives on education and development

Kevin Miller (chair)
Cross-cultural comparisons show dramatic differences in beliefs about education and development and in the enactment of these beliefs in schooling and child-rearing. This symposium looks at how details of children's experience – with orthographies, graphical representations, and classroom discourse – serve as mediators of cognitive development and educational achievement. Papers describe (1) differentiation of graphic genres in preschool, (2) relations among phonological, semantic, and orthographic information in learning to read Chinese; (3) how orthographic structure affects literacy; (4) opportunities to learn mathematics in Chinese and American classrooms; (5) cultural scripts in teaching in China and the US.

The roles of phonological, semantic and orthographic information for reading development in Chinese
Chen, Shiou-Yuan Early Childhood Education, Taipei Municipal University, Taipei, Taiwan
Previous studies showed the importance of phonological awareness in learning alphabetic languages, and the importance of morphological awareness in learning Chinese. This study examined the roles of phonological, semantic, and orthographic information in learning Chinese multiple-character words. The results had two major findings. First, both phonological and orthographic information influ-

enced children's semantic judgments. Second, for experienced young readers, the impact of phonological information alone on semantic judgments was limited. In sum, the results showed that young readers' comprehension of multiple-character words were influenced by the phonological and orthographic factors, and the impact of these "unrelated" factors gradually decreased.

Grown-ups won't tell you this: A few observations on how children learn to read
Feng, Gary Psychology and Neuroscience, Duke University, Durham, USA
Some important conceptual and perceptual learning in reading acquisition occurs without explicit instructionn. Here I will present 3 examples. First, pre-reading English-speaking children approach written words as individual symbols, and fail to understand the symbol system nature of writing. Second, Chinese preschoolers who know only a few characters spent much time scanning texts even though most of the words do not make sense to them. Last, we never teach children how to move their eyes and yet they learn to adapt to the script they read. Implications to learning to read in different languages will be discussed.

Opportunities to learn in Chinese and American math classes: what and how
Perry, Michelle Educational Psychology, University of Illinois, Champaign, IL, USA Schleppenbach, Meg McConney, Marc Sims, Linda
Do Chinese students have different opportunities to learn than U.S. students? And, if so, is this a function of what the students bring to the classroom or how the teachers structure the learning environment? From analyses of 1st- and 5th-grade mathematics lessons from both countries, we found that students seem remarkably similar (e.g., produce the same number of mathematical errors), but teachers' responses to students and their structuring of the lessons are quite different in China than in the United States. We conclude that Chinese students have opportunities to engage in more complex mathematical work than U.S. students and teachers provide differential opportunities to learn.

IS-058: Drug addiction: Behavioral and neurobiological advances

Klaus A. Miczek (Chair)
Latest developments in the neurobiology of addiction: Beyond dopamine and the accumbens
Zernig, Gerald Exp. Psychiatrie, Med. Universität Innsbruck, Innsbruck, Austria Crespo, Jose A. Stöckl, Petra Zorn, Katja Fritz, Michael Saria, Alois
While of incalculable value for the advancement of the drug abuse research field, the dopamine theory of reward, with the nucleus accumbens as its prime brain region, has to be considerably modified. A number of brain regions and neurotransmitters other than dopamine have been shown to at least modulate drug-seeking behavior, e.g., glutamatergic inputs into the AcbC and AcbSh from the medial prefrontal cortex (PrL, IL; P.W.Kalivas and coworkers) or nicotinic and muscarinic acetylcholine receptors in the AcbC (C.R.Schuster, G.Mark, E.Acquas and G.diChiara and coworkers as well as our own work). It has also been shown that in chronic, habit-like drug taking behavior, the center of activity shifts away from the Acb to the dorsal striatum (CPu; B.J.Everitt, T.W.Robbins and coworkers).

Psychobiological features associated with cocaine addiction-like behavior in rats
Deroche-Gamonet, Véronique Physiopath. de l'Addiction, INSERM NeuroCentre U862, Bourdeaux, France
We used an addiction model recently developed that takes into account the hallmarks of drug addiction, i.e. compulsivity, inter-individual vulner-

ability, and its temporal dimension. This model provides evidence for both rats that develop an addiction-like behavior and rats that do not, despite an equal exposure to cocaine. We investigated behavioral and neurobiological characteristics associated with cocaine addiction. Behaviorally, we demonstrated that addiction-like behavior is specifically preceded by the occurrence of a burst-like pattern of intake and an increased cocaine-induced craving. Using complementary approaches that range from system neuroscience to gene profiling techniques, cocaine addiction was shown to be associated with alterations in the meso-accumbens dopaminergic and prefrontal-accumbens glutamatergic transmissions.

Neurobiological processes in alcoholism
Spanagel, Rainer Dept. of Psychopharmacology, ZI Mannheim, Mannheim, Germany
This presentation adheres to a systems biology perspective such that the interaction of alcohol with primary and secondary targets within the brain is described in relationship to the behavioural consequences. As a result of the interaction of alcohol with these targets, alterations in gene expression and synaptic plasticity take place that lead to long-lasting alteration in neuronal network activity. As a subsequent consequence, alcohol-seeking responses ensue that can finally lead via complex environmental interactions to an addictive behaviour.

Social stress, cocaine binges and role of BDNF
Miczek, Klaus A. Neuroscience and Psychiatry, Tufts University, Medford, USA
Ostensibly aversive stress experiences can intensify cocaine taking. Intermittent episodes of social defeat stress increase the motivation for cocaine and the cumulative intake during cocaine binges, whereas continuous subordination stress blunts rewards such as cocaine. Changes in brain derived nerve growth factor correlate with the sensitizing vs. attenuating effects of stress. Feedback from the prefrontal cortex to the ventral tegmentum and to the raphe via glutamate appears critical for these divergent stress effects on intensely rewarding cocaine taking, possibly pointing to a mechanism for compulsion.

IS-059: False belief attribution: Cultural and methodological issues

Maria-Regina Maluf (chair)
The six papers in this symposium focus on young children developmental changes in acquisition of an explicit theory of mind. Data collected in different cultural settings are discussed. Deficits in the ability to attribute mental states to others are related to language and communication problems. Issues raised by research results in different languages and cultures are presented and their implications for linguistic and educational practices are considered.

Promoting the development of theory of mind in young children
Maluf, Maria-Regina Developmental Psychology, PUC/SP, Sao Paulo, Brazil Panciera, Sara-Del-Prete Developmental Psychology, UNICSUL, Sao Paulo, Brazil
Many children under 5 years in developing countries are exposed to risk factors which prevent from attaining their developmental potential. This study aims to verify the effects of language training on theory of mind development. False belief tasks were applied as pre and post tests to 56 children aged 3 to 5. Results showed that differences previously found between children from two sociocultural contexts were reduced. We concluded that conversational situations which include mental verbs use and incite

perspective changes can be viewed as strategies to prevent or ameliorate the loss of developmental potential in children from underprivileged families.

A cultural-historical approach to childrens talk about psychological states: Four case studies
Rodríguez Arocho, Wanda Dept. of Psychology, University of Puerto Rico, San Juan, Puerto Rico Martinez, Frances Dept. of Psychology, Universidad de Puerto Rico, San Juan, Puerto Rico
Current research suggests that autism involves deficits in the acquisition of a theory of mind. Accordingly, these children seem to be specifically impaired in their ability to attribute mental states to themselves or others. These deficits have been related to language and communication problems. Our study focused on the early development and use of mental states terms in preschoolers. We present and discuss the results of four case studies with children aged 4-6 in which spontaneous talk and talk during the realization of instructional tasks was collected and analyzed. We focused on utterances referring to desires, perception, cognition and emotions. A cultural-historical framework is used to analyze data.

Language as a window into theory of mind
Hollanda Souza, Debora Developmental Psychology, Federal University São Carlos, São Carlos, Brazil
In recent years, a substantial body of research has been conducted on the links between theory of mind and language. Many researchers have argued that an important prerequisite to false belief attribution is an understanding of the meaning of mental state terms. Results from three different studies conducted on childrens developing understanding of think and know will be discussed. The first two were aimed at exploring possible differences between U.S. English-speaking and Brazilian Portuguese-speaking children in their understanding of these two terms. The third one was aimed at investigating the emergence of these two terms in Brazilian childrens vocabulary.

Childrens mistrust: Attention to false statements or false beliefs?
Koenig, Melissa Inst. of Child Development, University of Minnesota, Minnesota, USA
Children rely extensively on other people to learn about the world. From early on, children's reliance on testimony is tempered by selective trust in particular informants. New data from studies of children's evaluation of reliable and unreliable informants will be presented. Although the relation between children's selective trust and false belief understanding remains unclear, I will argue that selective trust is likely to involve the mentalistic appraisal of speakers rather than surface generalizations of their behavior. One issue raised by this research is the extent to which false statements are treated as markers of unreliability by different languages and cultures.

Test of emotion comprehension: A Portuguese-language adaptation
Dias, Maria-da-Graça Dept. of Psychology, UFPe, Recife, Brazil
Objective: The goal of this study was to translate, perform the necessary adaptations and evaluate the applicability in Brazilian Portuguese of the Test Emotion Comprehension, developed by Pons, Harris and Rosnay. Method: The Portuguese version, complying with internationally accepted criteria for transcultural adaptation of instruments, was administered to 87 children who differed regarding their sociodemographic variables, age and gender. Results: Subjects of this sample demonstrated good acceptance and understanding. Conclusions: The utilization with individuals of different sociodemographic strata enabled the necessary adaptations to the Brazilian sociocultural

reality. The adaptation of the instrument to Brazil should continue with larger samples.

IS-060: Infants' and very young children's affinity for animals

Judy DeLoache (chair)
DeLoache, Judy Charlottesville, USA **Bloom Pickard, Megan**
Recent work on infants' and toddlers' preference for animate over inanimate stimuli will be discussed. Visual attention studies with infants reveal that they look longer at animals moving through a landscape than at moving inanimate objects. Another set of studies establish that toddlers are highly interested in animals, with one of the major aspects of their behavior being greater emotional response to animals over other stimuli. These results will be discussed in the general context of the existence of a special affinity on the part of human infants and very young children for other animals.

IS-061: The personalization of politics

Gian Vittorio Caprara (chair)
The symposium is the occasion to bring together a number of scientist that in recent years have focused their investigation on the intersection and interactions between personality and politics. In reality, the individual characteristics of leaders and voters have assumed greater importance in political discourse, as political choices increasingly depend on voters' distinctive patter of habits, attitudes and values, and perception of politicians. The aim of the symposium is to debate major contributions attesting to the impact of leaders' and voters' personality to political choices and its implications for global democracy.

Basic values, core political values and political preference
Schwartz, Shalom Dept. of Psychology, Hebrew University of Jerusalem, Jerusalem, Israel **Vecchione, Michele** Dept. of Psychology, Universita di Roma La Sapienza, Rome, Italy
We examine relations to voting of basic personal values and core political values. Italian adults responded before (n=1699) and after (n=1030) their 2006 national election. Basic values explained 19% of the variance in voting and completely mediated effects of age, gender, education, and income. Core political values fully mediated the impact of basic values and explained 58% of the variance in voting. Basic values explained substantial variance in each of the political values (24% to 53%). The dimensions that organize basic values (self-enhancement vs. self-transcendence and openness vs. conservation) appear to structure and gave coherence to people's systems of political values.

The political consequences of perceived threat and felt insecurity
Huddy, Leonie Dept. of Political Science, Stony Brook University, Stony Brook, NY, USA **Feldman, Stanley** Dept. of Political Science, Stony Brook University, Stony Brook, NY, USA **Weber, Christopher** Dept. of Political Science, Stony Brook University, Stony Brook, NY, USA
Data from the National Threat and Terrorism Survey (N=1549) is used to explore the impact of a need for security and threat on Americans' support for security policies. Among the minority of Americans who felt insecure, perceived terrorist threat increased support for domestic and international security policy. Threat had no effect on support for domestic security policies among the majority who felt secure after the 911 attacks, however. Our findings underscore the diverse ways in which individuals react politically to a common external threat. Our approach draws from both attachment and terror management theory.

"Elective affinities": On the psychological bases of left-right differences

Jost, John Dept. of Psychology, New York University, New York, USA
Theoretical and empirical relationships between psychological variables and political orientation will be discussed. Converging lines of research that link basic personality, cognitive, motivational, and neurophysiological processes to ideological differences between left and right will be summarized. Also situational factors that are capable of inducing "liberal" and "conservative" shifts in political attitudes will be discussed. Findings suggest that, contrary to received wisdom in recent decades, ideology is a meaningful force in people's lives and that it may be rooted in fundamental psychological antinomies, including preferences for stability vs. change, order vs. complexity, familiarity vs. novelty, conformity vs. creativity, loyalty vs. rebellion.

Impact of personality traits and values on level of political involvement in women and on facing glass-ceiling hurdles

Francescato, Donata Dept. of Psychology, Univers. of Rome 'La Sapienza', Rome, Italy **Mebane, Minou** Dept. of Psychology, Univers. of Rome 'La Sapienza', Rome, Italy **Sorace, Roberta** Dept. of Psychology, Univers. of Rome 'La Sapienza', Rome, Italy
Personality of women with different levels of political engagement has been investigated: 109 members of the Italian Parliament, 255 elected to regional and local offices, 101 activists in extremist groups, 155 activists of moderate parties and 1369 voters were administered self-report questionnaires measuring traits, values and coping skills. Both traits and values differ in the five groups, with local and national politicians scoring higher in energy, agreeableness and emotional stability and lower in hedonism than extremists, activists and voters. Traits and values were also related to coping with glass-ceiling obstacles.

Selecting politicians: Individual differences as predictors of electoral performance among UK parliamentary candidates

Silvester, Jo Dept. of Psychology, City University London, London, United Kingdom
There is growing interest in the possibility that individual differences are associated with effective political leadership. Validation of a multi-trait multi-method assessment process for the Conservative Party was achieved by comparing candidate scores at assessment with their performance during the 2005 General Election. Critical thinking skills (and to a lesser extent communication skills) predicted the percentage swing and percentage of votes achieved by candidates. Subsequent work designing a selection process for the Liberal Democrat Party raises issues about the need to differentiate between assessing political candidates on political values as well as behavioural performance criteria.

IS-062: Intersensory interaction

Roberta Klatzky (chair)
The last decade has seen an exciting surge of psychological research on interactions among sensory modalities. This symposium invites an international group of speakers to describe current intersensory research from multiple perspectives. Topics include how inputs from the senses are combined in relation to statistically optimal integration, how attention is distributed between and across modalities, and how sensory systems interact in acquiring information about objects. Neurophysiological research will be described that addresses how the physiological properties of individual multisensory neurons and neural networks contribute to intersensory interaction. Applications re-

lated to interactions across the senses will also be of interest.

Cortex and midbrain conspire to synthesize information from different senses in order to mediate adaptive behavior

Stein, Barry Multisensory Research Group, Wake Forest School of Medicine, Winston-Salem, NC, USA
Some neurons synthesize information from different senses, thereby markedly enhancing their sensitivity to external events and facilitating overt behavior. This capacity is neither innate nor pre-specified, nor is it present in every neuron receiving cross-modal inputs. Rather, a specific circuit is crafted based on extensive postnatal experience to adapt the processes to the environment in which they will be used. The specifics of the circuit; the principles that normally govern it; the early life experiences that give rise to these principles; and the utility of the process for adapting behaviors to the demands of the environment will be discussed.

Multisensory perception during locomotion

Ernst, Marc Multisensory Perception and ct, MPI for Biological Cybernetics, Tuebingen, Germany **Souman, Jan** Multisensory Perception &, MPI for Biological Cybernetics, Tuebingen, Germany **Frissen, Ilja** Multisensory Perception and ct, MPI for Biological Cybernetics, Tuebingen, Germany
A multitude of sensory signals and perceptual processes are involved in the control of human walking. In return, also the human walking behaviour has a profound effect on the way we perceive the world. To investigate the interaction between multisensory perception and locomotion we constructed different locomotion environments containing a treadmill and some visualization. We focus here on the perception of visual motion and the interaction with walking speed. In several studies we found that motion perception is increased for high visual speeds and decreased for low visual speeds. The results will be discussed in terms of multisensory integration.

The effect of non-informative, cross-modal information on haptic spatial perception

Newell, Fiona Dept. of Psychology, Trinity College Dublin, Dublin, Ireland **Finucane, Ciara** Psychology, Trinity College Dublin, Dublin, Ireland **Pasquallotto, Achille** Psychology, Trinity College Dublin, Dublin, Ireland **Chan, Jason** Psychology, Trinity College Dublin, Dublin, Ireland
We investigated the effects of noninformative vision and audition on haptic memory for layouts of objects. Participants first learnt a scene of objects and were tested on their recognition of that scene through touch only. We found better haptic performance during the non-informative visual condition than when participants were blindfolded. Furthermore, visuo-spatial information was necessary to enhance haptic memory performance. In contrast to vision, non-informative audition was not associated with an improvement in haptic performance. Our findings suggest that spatial cognition is multisensory and the relative precision of spatial information in other modalities determines cross-modal spatial performance.

Neural correlates of multisensory integration

Vroomen, Jean Dept. of Psychology, Tilburg University, Tilburg, Netherlands
Purpose: Electrophysiological (ERP) studies have found that auditory neural activity (the N1-component) induced by speech is suppressed when speech is accompanied by concordant lip movements. We examined whether this effect occurs with audiovisual non-speech events. Results: The auditory-evoked N1 was suppressed by the video of natural actions like handclapping. This effect was not influenced by whether the auditory and visual information were congruent or incongruent. N1-

suppression was absent, though, when the video did not contain anticipatory motion. Conclusion: Auditory N1-suppresion is not speech-specific, but crucially depends on whether vision predicts when a sound will occur.

IS-063: Cultural variations in childrearing values and practices

Peeter Tulviste (chair)
Parental views regarding children and childrearing have received considerable attention in developmental psychology because of their importance in understanding and explaining the variation in people's parenting behaviors. The main aim of the symposium is to address the nature and extent of cultural differences in general socialization values as well as in more specific childrearing beliefs (e.g. parents' causal attributions concerning their children's academic achievement and normative beliefs about aggression). The questions of how cultural models of development are reflected in childrearing values and to what extent socialization values change over time along with the societal changes will also be addressed.

Cultural variations in childrearing values and practices
Tulviste, Peeter Dept. of Psychology, University of Tartu, Tartu, Estonia
Parental views regarding children and childrearing have received considerable attention in developmental psychology because of their importance in understanding and explaining the variation in people's parenting behaviors. The main aim of the symposium is to address the nature and extent of cultural differences in general socialization values as well as in more specific childrearing beliefs (e.g. parents' causal attributions concerning their children's academic achievement and normative beliefs about aggression). The questions of how cultural models of development are reflected in childrearing values and to what extent socialization values change over time along with the societal changes will also be addressed.

Continuity of mothers socialization goals across cultures
Keller, Heidi Inst. für Psychologie, Universität Osnabrück, Osnabrück, Germany Schröder, Lisa Inst. für Psychologie, Universität Osnabrück, Osnabrück, Germany
Socialization goals define scripts for child rearing practices. Cultural differences refer especially to the emphasis put on autonomy and relatedness. This study reports mothers socialization goals assessed when their children were three months and three years. Four cultural environments were selected which can be assumed to differ with respect to the emphasis put on autonomy and relatedness, urban middle class families in Berlin, Germany, rural subsistence based families from Gujarat, India, and urban middle class families of Delhi, India and San Jose, Costa Rica. The discussion refers to socialization as a long term project is adapted to contextual variation.

How do parents explain their children's success and failure at school? Parental causal attributions of primary school children
Natale, Katja Dept. of Psychology, University of Jyväskylä, Jyväskylä, Finland
In the JEPS-Study 207 children and their parents were followed up from kindergarten to 2nd grade. The LGM results showed that especially highly educated parents attributed their children's success increasingly to ability and decreasingly to teaching. Further, when parents thought their children succeeded because of ability, children's subsequent performance increased.

Parenting practices, beliefs concerning children's aggression and evaluations of primary school children's behaviour
Tropp, Kristiina Dept. of Education, University of Tartu, Tartu, Estonia
Estonian and Finnish parents' parenting practices, approval of aggression, and reports about their children's problematic and prosocial behaviour were studied. Sample: 230 Estonian, 150 Finnish 7- to 8-year old children, their parents and teachers. A child's behaviour was assessed by teachers and parents with the same original questionnaire. A modified version of the NOBAGS (Huesmann & Guerra, 1997) was used for studying beliefs, and items from the APQ (Shelton et al., 1996) for studying parenting practices. Differences in preferred parenting practices and the approval of aggression emerged between Estonian and Finnish parents. Parenting profiles were associated to behaviour ratings.

Socialization values and cultural change: A comparative study of Estonia and Sweden
Tulviste, Tiia Dept. of Psychology, University of Tartu, Tartu, Estonia
The present study addressed socialization values of mothers of adolescents in Estonia – a country in transition – to those in Sweden. One hundred sixty four ethnic Estonians, 95 Russian immigrants in Estonia, and 149 Swedish mothers living in Sweden filled in the Child-Rearing Goals Questionnaire. The study found mothers to be similar in emphasizing characteristics related to benevolence and self-direction the most. In comparison with the Swedish mothers, mothers residing in Estonia stressed simultaneously the conformity values (being polite, respecting elders, etc.), attached a greater significance to being smart and hard-working, while not valuing self-confidence as highly as the Swedes.

The mutual influence of social class and their own children on Brazilian parents' child-rearing values
Tudge, Jonathan Dept. of Human Development, University of North Carolina, Greensboro, USA Lopes, Rita Inst. of Psychology, U. F. Rio Grande do Sul, Porto Alegre, Brazil Piccinini, Cesar Institute of Psychology, U. F. Rio Grande do Sul, Porto Alegre, RS, Brazil Sperb, Tania Inst. of Psychology, U. F. Rio Grande do Sul, Porto Alegre, RS, Brazil
Data were gathered on 45 Brazilian parents' child-rearing values when their children were 3, 36, and 72 months. Middle-class parents were more likely to value autonomy and less likely to value conformity at each age than were their working-class counterparts. However, when their children were 36 months the parents from both classes were significantly less likely to value autonomy and valued conformity more than at other times. Our data suggest that the parents' relatively abstract values while their children were babies were influenced by their developing children but that thereafter a process of mutual adaptation between parents and children occurred.

IS-064: Motivational structure: Theory, measurement, applications

Iva Stuchlikova (chair)
The motivational structure refers to the individual's pattern of goal-striving.The symposium will introduce the concept of motivational structure, its theoretical roots, development and validation of the measurement tools and its applications in addictive disorders treatment. The identification of adaptive or maladaptive motivational patterns will be discussed and interventions for changing motivational structure will be presented.

Motivational structure and its relations to some personality variables
Stuchlikova, Iva Dept. of Psychology, University of South Bohemia, Ceské Budejovice, Czech Republic Man, Frantisek Dept. of Psychology, University of South Bohemia, Ceské Budejovice, Czech Republic
There is a consistency in a way people choose their goals and strive for them. This pattern was labeled motivational structure and could be operationalized via idiotetic tools evaluating the person's current concerns. The indices of motivational structure are relatively stable and can be seen as habitual variables. Their relations to some potential relevant personality variables (social desirability, trait anxiety, level of autonomy, Big five personal factors) were investigated. The results show that the relation of personality factors and motivational structure are moderated by social desirability and level of autonomy.

Volitional and emotional correlates of the motivational structure questionnaire
Baumann, Nicola Inst. für Psychologie, Universität Trier, Trier, Germany
The Motivational Structure Questionnaire (MSQ) showed theoretically consistent relationships with self-report measures of self-regulation (state versus action orientation), depression and anxiety. In addition, MSQ indices captured motivational differences between wishes, duties, and intentions. Furthermore, MSQ indices predicted actual goal enactment. Consistent relationships were also found for implicit, non-reactive measures of self-infiltration (i.e., false self-attribution of externally controlled goals or activities) and alienation (i.e., difficulties to perceive and enact emotional preferences). The experimental data suggest that specific motivational structures are associated with volitional inhibition and/or self-inhibition. In sum, findings contribute to the validity of the MSQ.

Motivational restructuring
Cox, W. Miles Dept. of Psychology, Bangor University, Bangor, United Kingdom Klinger, Eric Dept. of Psychology, University of Minnesota Morris, Morris, USA Fadardi, Javad S. Dept. of Psychology, Ferdowsi University of Mashhad, Mashhad, Islamic Republic of Iran
Sufferers of addictive disorders and many other kinds of psychological disturbance show maladaptive patterns of motivation, which significantly cause or contribute to the disorder. The following will be included in this presentation: (a) an assessment instrument (the Personal Aspirations and Concerns Inventory) that identifies maladaptive motivational patterns, and (b) interventions for changing those patterns. The latter include Systematic Motivational Counseling (an individual therapy), Zielaktivierung und Zielklärung [Goal Activation and Clarification] and the Life Enrichment and Advancement Programme (group interventions), and a computerized intervention (for self-help). Results obtained with the assessments and interventions will also be presented.

The big two: Getting deeper into motivational structure and attentional bias
Fadardi, Javad S. Dept. of Psychology, Ferdowsi University of Mashhad, Mashhad, Islamic Republic of Iran Cox, W. Miles Dept. of Psychology, Bangor University, Bangor, United Kingdom
We will present the results of our recent study that investigated the relationships among motivational structure (adaptive vs. maladaptive), attentional bias for alcohol-related stimuli, and alcohol consumption. The results of our study (a) supported previous evidence on the importance of both maladaptive motivation and alcohol-attentional bias in predicting drinking behaviour and (b) suggested the independence of motivational structure and alcohol-attentional bias in predicting the

amount of alcohol consumption. The importance and application of the results for both assessment and intervention will be discussed.

Individual and combined effects of information-enhancement and goal-setting on improving motivational structure

Shamloo, Zohreh Dept. of Psychology, Ferdowsi University of Mashhad, Mashhad, Islamic Republic of Iran Shamloo, Zohreh S. Dept. of Psychology, Ferdowsi University of Mashad, Mashad, Islamic Republic of Iran Cox, W. Miles Dept. of Psychology, Bangor University, Bangor, United Kingdom

Motivational structure affects people's success or failure at goal pursuits and their mood regulation (e.g., by using chemicals). We will present results showing that manipulations (enhancement-information; goal-setting) that increase sense of control and intrinsic motivation also improve individuals' motivational structure. There were four experimental conditions: No-Intervention; Goal-Setting; Information-Enhancement; both Goal-Setting and Information-Enhancement. Task-specific versions of the Personal Concerns Inventory (PCI), Shapiro Control Inventory, and Intrinsic Motivation Inventory were administered. On post-test PCI adaptive motivation, the groups were ordered as follows: Combination > Information- Enhancement > Goal-Setting > No-Intervention. The improvement was maintained at a 45-day follow-up.

IS-065: Diverse methodological challenges in cross-cultural research

Barbara M. Byrne (chair)

Psychological research that focuses on cross-cultural comparisons has increased considerably during the last decade. Of particular import is its popularity within mainstream psychology. Thus, cross-cultural research can no longer be considered the sole domain of experts trained in this area. Paralleling this growth has been an equally notable expansion of advances in quantitative psychology related to measurement, statistics, and research design. These advances bear importantly on studies of cultural differences. The intent of this symposium is twofold: (a) to heighten awareness to methodological complexities associated with cross-cultural research, and (b) to elucidate how these methodological advances can address cross-cultural comparisons.

Comparing people from different cultural backgrounds

Bartram, Dave Research Dept., SHL Group Ltd., Thames Ditton, United Kingdom

Within the context of organisations seeking to make comparisons between people coming from different national or cultural backgrounds on the basis of their personality scores, the issue of criteria for aggregation of samples across cultures is discussed. This raises the questions of: What is meant by 'culture'? How can it be operationalized? Some key issues are identified including evidence supporting construct and structural equivalence of scales across samples; the impact of DIF on scale scores; the need to control the demographics of different samples; and the need to avoid general biases associated with instrument formats and modes of administration.

Challenges of globalization vs. indigenous measures

Cheung, Fanny M. Dept. of Psychology, Chinese Univ. of Hong Kong, Hong Kong, China, People's Republic of : Hong Kong SAR

With globalization, there is increasing use of personality assessment across cultures. Imported

tests are often used in countries where few local instruments are available. I will address the basic problems of test translation and adaptation in personality assessment, bilingual equivalence, and implications on test interpretation when using imported tests. While well adapted imported tests allow cross-cultural comparison on universal constructs, the problem of gaps in culturally relevant dimensions remains. I will illustrate good practices in test translation and in development of indigenous measures with examples from the Chinese MMPI-2 and the Cross-Cultural (Chinese) Personality Assessment Inventory (CPAI).

Threats to cultural validity in clinical assessment

Leong, Frederick T.L. Dept. of Psychology, Michigan State University, East Lansing, USA

Borrowing from Campbell and Stanley's (1966) concept of threats to validity, the lack of cultural validity in clinical diagnosis and assessment can be also conceptualized to be due largely to a failure to recognize or a tendency to minimize cultural factors among researchers and clinicians. Illustrated with the case of Asian Americans, the following factors may serve as the sources of threats to cultural validity in clinical assessment: (a) pathoplasticity of psychological disorders, (b) cultural factors influencing symptom expression, (c) therapist bias in clinical judgment, (d) language capability of the client, and (e) inappropriate use of diagnostic and personality tests.

Cognitive biases in cross-cultural research

van de Vijver, Fons Dept. of Psychology, Tilburg University, Tilburg, Netherlands

Cross-cultural psychologists show five cognitive biases which impede progress in the field: (1) a lack of balance between uncritical acceptance and rejection of observed cross-cultural score differences; (2) a Euro-American dominance in the methods used, the theoretical orientations adopted, and the topics chosen to study; (3) methodological preconceptions (e.g., insufficient concern for equivalence of instruments); (4) a paradigmatic organization of cross-cultural research; (5) a lack of attention for measurement of the cultural context of the study.

Ethical issues related to cross-cultural research

Oakland, Thomas Dept. Educational Psychology, University of Florida, Gainesville, USA

Psychological research, including that conducted cross-culturally, is subject to both legal and ethical standards in those countries in which research is conducted. Ethics codes may help define acceptable procedural and methodological issues associated with research. Procedural issues include confidentiality, protection from harm, informed consent, plagiarism, and publication credit. Methodological issues include and are not limited to competence in conducting cross cultural research. The purpose of this presentation is to summarize information on ethical issues associated with conducting cross-cultural research.

IS-066: Bicultural self and social change

Sik-Hung Ng (chair)

The confluence of cultures resulting from cultural contact has accelerated in recent decades under the influence of globalisation and the spread of information technology. Individuals with bicultural (or multicultural) knowledge are on the rise in numbers and social influence, many of whom have also developed bicultural selves beyond the mere acquisition of knowledge about other cultures. This symposium reports theoretical and applied studies of biculturals, their self-concepts and issues of psychological integration, language and behavioural decisions.

Social identities, bicultural selves and perceived social change

Ng, Sik-Hung Dept. Applied Social Studies, City University of Hong Kong, Hong Kong, China, People's Republic of : Hong Kong SAR Kim, Jung-Sik Fairhaven College of Interdisc, Western Washington University, Bellingham, Vatican City State

Since its reunification with China in 1997, Hong Kong SAR has experienced various significant changes. This paper summarises studies to show, first, that people who perceived the changes to be fast preferred single identities ("I am a Chinese", or "I am a Hongkonger") over dual identities (e.g., "I am a Chinese but also a Hongkonger"). This correlation was mediated by perceived social uncertainty as predicted. Second, social identities correlated positively with biculturality. Biculturals who were strong in both Chinese and Western selves, when compared to others who were strong in only one self or none, embraced multiple identities more strongly.

Indigenous identity, language and social change: Some considerations from Bolivia and Canada

Sachdev, Itesh Oriental and African Studies, University of London, London, United Kingdom

In the Americas, indigenous peoples, who are effectively bicultural, are referred to by a variety of group labels, though few studies have explored their self-categorisations. In this paper the relationship between self-categorisation and language was explored amongst 198 members of 3 indigenous communities in Bolivia and Canada. Survey data, on self-categorisations, bilingual behaviour and attitudes, revealed systematic associations. Specifically, whereas colonially imposed categorisations were associated with the status quo, self-determined categorisations were seen as the harbingers for social change. Overall, the survival of indigenous peoples depends on self-determined categorizations in their appropriate socio-structural and temporal contexts.

Biculturals, conformity motives and decision making

Briley, Donnel Marketing Dept., University of Sydney, Sydney, Australia

Prior research suggests that biculturals shift the values they espouse depending on cues such as language. The paper examines whether the effects of language extend to a potentially less malleable domain, behavioural decisions. Studies of Hong Kong biculturals found that language manipulation (Cantonese vs. English) increases tendencies to choose compromise options in a product decision task, endorse associated decision guidelines, defer decision making in problems where it can be postponed, and endorse decision guidelines that advocate caution rather than decisive action. A motivational explanation of these effects was confirmed.

The individual- and social-oriented chinese bicultural self: Testing the theory

Lu, Luo Dept. of Business Administrati, National Taiwan University, Taipei, Taiwan

A Chinese bicultural self theory (individual- and social-orientation) was proposed and tested in a series of five studies. The social-orientation is rooted in traditional Chinese conceptualization of the self, while the individual-orientation is rooted in the Western culture but brought in through social change. A total of 977 students in Taiwan were tested. The individual self aspect was related to individualism, independence, individualistic motivation, and subjective well-being, whereas the social self aspect was related to collectivism, interdependence, social motivation, holistic thinking, interpersonal harmony and a communal orientation. The bicultural self model was thus generally supported.

IS-067: Development of psychological and biological resources in children at risk

Maria Cristina Richaud (chair)
In this symposium problems concerning children at risk by poverty and by cultural changes due to emigration, will be presented. Characteristics of biological and psychological resources of children at poverty will be shown. At the same time, the effects of intervention strategies and temperament or innate self control over reinforcement of attachment, executive functions and social skills will be analyzed. With respect to children that have emigrated to a different country of that of origin, differential impact of child-rearing styles, depending on the culture of origin, over prosocial and aggressive behaviour will be studied.

How to reinforce psychological resources in children at risk by poverty

Richaud, Maria Cristina Buenos Aires, Argentina
Theoretical support for an intervention proposal to reinforce psychological resources in children at poverty is developed. Results referring to the effects of a curriculum integrated program are presented. The sample was made up of 100 children, both sexes, from a state school, randomly selected from schools under poverty level. The control group – 'not at risk'– was formed by children attending a middle class school. The results obtained through a before and after design with control group support the premise that reinforcing the child's resources lowers menace perception and ensures more successful coping and that discontinuity in the intervention produce a resources weakening.

Hostility, neglect and permissiveness in parent-child relation: Influence in behavioural development

Mestre, Vicenta Psicologia Basica, Universidad de Valencia, Valencia, Spain Samper, Paula Psicologia Basica, Universidad de Valencia, Valencia, Spain Tur, Ana Psicologia Basica, Universidad de Valencia, Valencia, Spain Latorre, Angel Psicologia Basica, Universidad de Valencia, Valencia, Spain Cortés, Maite Psicologia Basica, Universidad de Valencia, Valencia, Spain
Hostility, neglect and permissiveness within the family have a negative effect on the child's psychological and behavioural development. This paper aims to confirm the impact of this family climate on children in populations from different cultures. 2788 subjects with a mean age of 12.15 years filled the Child's Report of Parent Behaviour (Schaefer, 1965; Samper, Cortés, Mestre, Nácher and Tur, 2006), the Prosocial Behaviour Scale, the Physical and Verbal Aggression Scale (Caprara and Pastorelli, 1993; Del Barrio, Moreno and López, 2001) and the Inventory of Empathy for Children and Adolescents (Bryant, 1982). The findings show a differential impact of child-rearing styles depending on gender, age and culture of origin.

Parental disciplining practices, sympathy and prosocial behaviors among Mexican American and European American families

Carlo, Gustavo Dept. of Psychology, University of Nebraska, Lincoln, NE, USA Knight, George Dept. of Psychology, Arizona State University, Tempe, AZ, USA
Parental inductions are associated with positive morality and punitiveness is associated with negative morality. However, these relations might vary across ethnic groups and social behaviors and sympathy might mediate these relations. Participants were 322 adolescents (212 Mexican Americans; M age = 10.9 years; 50% girls). Students completed measures of disciplining practices, sympathy, and prosocial behaviors. Correlations

showed that inductions were related positively to sympathy, dire, emotional, anonymous, and compliant but not significantly related to altruism or public helping. Punitiveness was related negatively to sympathy and altruism, and positively to public helping. Discussion will focus on prosocial development among US Latinos.

Personality role in resilience promotion in children at risk by poverty

Lemos, Viviana CIIPME, CONICET, Buenos Aires, Argentina
As part of a research and intervention project which attempts to foster affective, cognitive, and linguistic resources in at-risk children due to extreme poverty backgrounds, this study assess the role of child personality and its modulatory role in the strengthening of some of these resources, as related to the resilience construct. One hundred children —who attend one of the 1,000 most socially vulnerable schools in Argentina— took part in the study. Results —consistent with the theory on the subject— show that personality traits may function as positive (e.g. extraversion and a more controlled temperament) or negative catalysts (e.g. neuroticism) of the intervention, allowing for interventions adjusted to the dispositional profile of children.

Development of psychosocial resources of vulnerable children in Brazil

Koller, Silvia Helena Dept. de Psicologia, Univers. Fed. do Rio Grande, Porto Alegre, Brazil Dell'Aglio, Débora Dept. de Psicologia, Univers. Fed. do Rio Grande, Porto Alegre, Brazil Poletto, Michele Dept. de Psicologia, Univers. Fed. do Rio Grande, Porto Alegre, Brazil Siqueira, Aline Dept. de Psicologia, Univers. Fed. do Rio Grande, Porto Alegre, Brazil Lieberknecht Wathier, Josiane Dept. de Psicologia, Univers. Fed. do Rio Grande, Porto Alegre, Brazil
This study investigated risk and protective factors of 297 impoverished 7-16 year old children, both sexes, comparing those living at home (G1, n= 142) to sheltered (G2, n= 155). Sheltered children informed higher scores on stressing life events inventories, and negative emotions, and depression scales (p <0,001). No group and sex differences were found on life satisfaction, positive emotions, and social networks (p >0,05), but negative emotions (girls scored higher; p<0,05). In spite of the poverty and adversities, some resilience processes were identified on the higher scores of protective factors.

IS-068: Psychosocial risk analysis and prevention at work

Jose M. Peiro (chair)
The world of work is experiencing important transformations in a global economy and in a complex and multi-cultural, connected, and technological society. Demographic and value changes in these multicultural societies are also inducing changes in organizations. These changes are raising emergent risks at work of a psychosocial nature. They also posit new challenges and opportunities for work and organizational psychology. The aim of this symposium is to present theoretical models and empirical evidence which support relevant contributions Work and Organizational Psychology is making to improve work places and organizations in order to promote safe and healthy people in healthy organizations.

Emergent psychosocial risk conditions in current work places: Evaluation and prevention strategies

Korunka, Christian Fakultät für Psychologie, Universität Wien, Wien, Austria
Changes in the society and the organizations in Western countries result in continuously changing working conditions of employees. The aging work

force, increasing customer demands, a comeback of Taylorism, new form of work contracts and an increasing permeability of the work-life interface are only few examples of the wide range of "new" psycho-social risks. Theoretically and empirically well-developed frameworks exist in Industrial and Organizational psychology to describe and evaluate these changes from a perspective of human work design. It is argued that these frameworks should be used to evaluate the abovementioned new risk conditions. Examples of these evaluations will be given.

Psychosocial risks at work and their prevention in Finland

Lindström,, Kari Psychology, Finnish Institute of Occupat., Helsinki, Finland
Psychosocial risks at work can be monitored at national level using survey methods. At the organizational level, common approaches constitute surveys on work climate and task-level methods based on the observation of risks at work. Results gained through these methods may be used for improvements in organizational development, job redesign, and change management. National level interventions comprise policy making and national action programmes. A holistic approach combining these actions has been formed based on the healthy organization model, a multilevel intervention approach. The results of these interventions are evaluated from the perspective of future challenges, learning, expected results, and context.

Stress prevention and management in the workplace: Concepts, findings and desiderata

Semmer, Norbert Inst. für Psychologie, Universität Bern, Bern, Switzerland
For many, changing work characteristics seems a "natural priority" for stress prevention. Nevertheless, person-related interventions are dominant, and their effectiveness has been shown. Changing work characteristics has yielded mixed results, due partly to the complexity of the social systems involved, and to implementation problems. Common features of successful include a thorough analysis, a participative approach, and management support. Improvements cannot be expected in all parameters, and may be restricted to certain subgroups of participants. Methodological improvement should focus not only on design issues but also on careful, quantifiable documentation of the project. Person-focused and organization-focused approaches should be combined.

Beliefs, accident analysis, risk perception and prevention

Kouabenan, Rémi Psychology, UFR SHS, University of Grenoble 2, Grenoble Cedex 9, France
Psychological studies carried out on accidents have demonstrated the value of taking into account the systems of values and beliefs of subjects non-initiated in safety matters, in the understanding of risk-taking and the explanation of accidents (Kouabenan, 1998; Cadet & Kouabenan, 2005; Helmreich & Merritt, 2001). This perspective is particularly crucial in this era of globalization where organisation become more and more large, and when workers from different backgrounds are relocating, and increasingly complex technology is being used. In this paper, we would examine the way laypeople, perceive risks and explain accidents and the possible influence of their systems of values and beliefs on the efficiency of safety measures and campaigns.

Cross-cultural perspectives on coping with work-family conflict

Tetrick, Lois Dept. of Psychology, George Mason University, Washington, DC, USA Gonzalez-Morales, M. Gloria Dept. of Psychology, George Mason University, Fairfax, VA, USA

Considerable research has been conducted examining the conflict that can arise from the demands of both work and family. Work and organizational psychology, primarily based on research in the USA, has characterized work-family conflict as arising from time-based, strain-based, and behavior-based conflicts and it has been demonstrated that work-family conflict can have negative consequences for employees and their families. However, little work has been done to understand how individuals cope with work-family conflict and whether coping mechanisms extend across cultures. We will report the results of a cross-cultural approach (United States and Spain) to examine work-family conflict and coping mechanisms.

Psychosocial risk prevention: An approach from positive psychology
Peiro, Jose M. Dept. of Social Psychology, University of Valencia, Valencia, Spain Rodriguerz, Isabel Dept. of Social Psychology, University of Valencia, Valencia, Spain
Psychosocial risk analysis and prevention may largely benefit from the long tradition and the contributions made by research on stress in general and more specifically on work stress. However, research on stress has mainly focused on distress phenomena and its negative consequences. Recently, Nelson and Simmons (2003) have defined eu-stress as "a positive psychological response to a stressor, as indicated by the presence of positive psychological states" (p.104). Thus, new questions arise in stress research and its analysis certainly will contribute to improve the present psychological armamentarium for risk assessment and prevention. In the present paper we will analyze this issues and we will provide some empirical evidence on them.

IS-069: Negotiation theory and negotiation practice: Bridging the divide

Peter Carnevale, Kwok Leung (chair)
We address the divide between theory and practice of negotiation in Australia, China, Spain, Turkey, The Netherlands and elsewhere. Important aspects of the theory-practice divide include issues of trust (Olekalns and Smith), fundamental conceptions of negotiation affected by culture (Zhang and Liu), the context of integrative agreements (Ismet & Beriker), the challenges of co-mediation (Martinez-Pecino, Munduate, Medina & Euwema), and how negotiators deal with complex constituencies who send mixed signals (Steinel & De Dreu). This will be followed by some distinctly pithy, insightful discussant comments that tie it all together by Leung and Carnevale.

The moves you make: Sense-making in negotiation
Olekalns, Mara Melbourne Business School, University of Melbourne, Carlton, Australia
Negotiators receive a steady stream of information from their opponents. Because this information provides important clues about the other party's goals and motives, negotiators use it to update their own strategic approach. Over the last decade, we have investigated how what negotiators say (or don't say) shapes both their relational and substantive outcomes. Three themes emerge from our research. First, unexpected events are pivotal to outcomes. Second, trustworthiness shapes decisions to deceive the other party. Finally, many of the relationships we identify between strategic behavior and outcomes are context-dependent.

Differences in negotiation mentality between Chinese and American
Zhang, Zhixue Guang Hua School of Management, Peking University, Beijing, People's Republic of China
There are more and more business negotiations occurring between American—the largest developed country, and China—the largest developing country. It has been widely reported that business negotiations between the two large economic entities often ended with misunderstanding and impasses. The barriers to the business negotiations between the two countries arise from the fundamental differences in the mentality between Chinese and American negotiators. To examine the differences, we asked part-time MBA students from both China and America to answer a semi-structured questionnaire and a survey. Both qualitative and quantitative data show significant differences between Chinese and American in the conception of negotiation.

Integrative bargaining strategies in the Turkish finance sector: Theory, practice and context of integrative agreements
Beriker, Nimet Arts and Social Sciences, Sabanci University, Istanbul, Turkey
In this study we investigate real-life business negotiations conducted in the Turkish financial sector in order to achieve a fine tuned picture of real-life integrative agreements. For this purpose, we collected 6 narrated negotiation cases, and analyzed the outcomes of negotiations on the basis of distributive and integrative divide, and looked at the nature of the integrative outcomes by using Pruitt's classification of integrative agreements. In addition, we investigated the relationship among negotiation processes, bargaining styles, and the outcomes of negotiations. The findings showed that, almost in all cases negotiations ended with integrative agreements, and showed more complicated patterns than what has been described in Pruitt's categories.

Mediating in teams: Opportunities and challenges
Munduate, Lourdes Dept. of Social Psychology, University of Sevilla, Sevilla, Spain
Mediating in teams or co-mediation may present different characteristics and challenges compared to mediations conducted by a single individual. In contrast to negotiating teams, where there is ample literature that allows giving advices to negotiators, practitioners in mediation may feel the need for scientific research that traces bridges between theory and practice and let them know how to face specific demands for mediation teams. We present an observational study of real mediation cases, analyzing how different mediation teams faced different challenges and situations and the outcomes they achieved.

When constituencies have opposing factions
Steinel, Wolfgang Social and Organiz. Psychology, Leiden University, Leiden, Netherlands
We examined how people negotiate on behalf of a constituency in which opposing factions send different signals. Experiment 1 showed that representatives follow the majority of their constituents, yet competitive (but not cooperative) minorities could challenge the majority's influence. Experiment 2 replicated this finding across different decision rule conditions. Competitive minorities were influential, no matter whether the group would decide unanimously or with majority vote. Experiment 3 showed that competitive members had more influence than cooperative members, even when factions were equally large. We conclude that the influence of a minority faction in intergroup negotiation depends on the specific content of the faction's message, and its strategic implications.

IS-070: Couple and family dynamics in the mirror of experience and behaviour sampling method

Meinrad Perrez (chair)
The main purpose of the symposium is to give a representative insight into the current psychological research on couple and family dynamics on the base of ambulatory assessment methods. Different variants of behavior sampling and of multi-method approaches will illustrate new possibilities to study couple and family processes under daily life conditions with repeated measures from both parents and children, and from couples. Methodological strengths and limits of this research approach outside the confinements of laboratories and questionnaires will be discussed.

Emotional lives of mothers, fathers and young children: Are they connected?
Rönkä, Anna Family Research Center, University of Jyväskylä, Jyväskylä, Finland Malinen, Kaisa Family Research Center, University of Jyväskylä, Jyväskylä, Finland Lämsä, Tiina Family Research Institute, University of Jyväskylä, Jyväskylä, Finland Tolvanen, Asko Family Research Institute, University of Jyväskylä, Jyväskylä, Finland
The objective of this study was to analyze if parents' and young children's daily moods are related. Data on 107 families was collected during a one-week period in November 2006 using different kinds of diaries. Parents answered ten structured questions about their mood and interactions three times a day by mobile diary, sending text messages. More detailed information about daily events and interactions was gathered by means of paper-and pencil diaries. A child diary gathering data on children's mood and interactions were filled in by parents and day care personnel. Multi-level modeling was used to analyze the data gathered from three family members.

A new approach to the study of couple and family dynamics: Zeroing in on a week in the life of a family
Repetti, Rena Dept. of Psychology, University of California, Los Angeles, USA
Data from the Alfred P. Sloan Center for the Everyday Lives of Families at UCLA will illustrate a novel approach to studying the dynamics of family life. The study uses a variety of repeated measures data that were collected from both parents and children: diary measures of mood and stressors (taken at scheduled points during the day), samples of cortisol (taken at the same points each day), and daily video tapes of family interaction. The integration of self-reports with biological samples and naturalistic observations of family life presents both opportunities and challenges for family and couple researchers.

Self-esteem and the coregulation of emotions in married couples' daily life
Schoebi, Dominik Dept. of Psychology, University of California, Los Angeles, USA Perrez, Meinrad Dept. of Psychology, University of Fribourg, Fribourg, Switzerland
The study investigates interpersonal coregulation of affect in marital relationships, and how self-esteem affects these processes. In two studies, 655 dual-earner couples participated in an electronic diary procedure. Both partners reported on their affect, their expectancies and their perceptions of the partner's affect, several times per day over the course of a week. The results suggest that men's low self-esteem shapes how affective experience are transmitted between spouses. Moreover, low self-esteem moderated within-person patterns of associations between expectancies about the partner's

affect and reports of marital distress at night. These patterns predicted change in relationship satisfaction across 3 years.

Emotional transmission in couples under stress

Bolger, Niall Dept. of Psychology, Columbia University, New York, USA **Lida, Masumi** Dept. of Psychology, Kent State University, Kent, USA **Stadler, Gertraud** Dept. of Psychology, Columbia University, New York, USA **Paprocki, Christine** Dept. of Psychology, Columbia University, New York, USA **Shrout, Patrick** Dept. of Psychology, New York University, New York, USA

Close relationships are defined as those where one partner's psychological states and behaviors have the capacity to influence those of the other. We investigated this process of emotional transmission in couples under stress. Participants were 216 couples where one partner was preparing to take a legal certification test typically experienced as highly stressful. They provided daily diary reports of emotional states for 44 days surrounding the event. Examinees' angry mood was related to partners' angry mood on the same day. However, emotional transmission diminished as the examination approached and rebounded afterwards. Couples differed considerably in the strength of transmission.

Mood synchronization in family-members' daily lives

Cook, William L. Centre for Psychiatry Research, Portland, USA **Wilhelm, Peter** Department of Psychology, University Fribourg, Fribourg, Switzerland

Reciprocity of negativity is one of the most ubiquitous findings in the family dynamics literature. Reciprocity can produce positive correlations in dyad members' moods, but other factors such as trait-based similarity can too. If processes of reciprocity explain mood similarity, family-members' moods should be higher synchronized when they are together than when apart. To test this hypothesis we analyzed time-series diary data of 96 families with adolescent children. Family members' moods were more similar when they were together than when apart. This difference was partially explained by conflict (reciprocity of negativity).

The design and psychometrics of ambulatory assessment

Pawlik, Kurt Inst. für Psychologie I, Universität Hamburg, Hamburg, Germany

Ambulatory assessment (AA) methods are devised to study human behavior outside the confinements of laboratory or other experimenter-designed conditions of observation. Different from classical "stationary" interindividual difference assessment, AA also captures intraindividual sources of variation (with respect to states, settings etc.). AA enables a researcher to draw upon these sources of variation (and their correlation and interaction!) so as to meet chosen criteria of ecological representativeness. Principal study designs of AA will be presented and discussed with respect to strengths and weaknesses. This will be followed by a taxonomy of psychometric standards and illustrative sample results from the presented papers.

IS-071: Learning in context: Constructing knowledge through sociocultural mediated activity

Néstor Roselli (chair)

This symposium aims to present the most recent developments in theory and research on learning from a sociocultural framework. Many concepts developed inside this approach have already been incorporated to the background of educational discourse. Meanwhile, in recent times new topics have arisen: the computer supported collaborative learning, the sociocultural view of the executive functions, the semiotic function of the teaching strategies, the distribution cognition systems, the communities of practice, the creative and motivational support of learning, and the new kind of subjectivity emerging in a high technological world. The symposium is particularly focused on these recent topics.

Teaching strategies as instruments of semiotic mediation

Roselli, Néstor Faculdad de Education, CONICET / UNER, Rosario, Argentina

Teaching strategies are not only the way to learn culture; they are cultural instruments by themselves. In this way, they have a semiotic effect on learning and the mental construction of knowledge. This presentation focuses on the cognitive and affective effects of three teaching modalities: classical-expositive, participative-guided and peer-collaborative. These effects concern the linguistic formulation of knowledge, the permanence in memory, the transfer to concrete situations, the links to other concepts and fields, and the motivation and attitude disposition of learners. Results are discussed from the sociocultural approach, regarding specially the different models of teacher-student interaction involved in each strategy.

The subjective processes and their significance in learning: Unfolding consequences from an historical-cultural approach in psychology

González Rey, Fernando Luis Centro de Ciencias da Vida, PUC-Campinas, Brasilia, Brazil

This presentation focuses on one interpretation about Vygotskys work which has not been common among Vygotskys followers in Western Psychology: the consequences of the emotional-cognitive and emotional symbolical unities of psyche for the analysis of psychological processes. Fantasy, emotion, feelings and personality received a prior attention from Vygotsky. Starting from an historical-cultural view of subjectivity, this presentation discusses how learning is affected by those symbolical – emotional consequences of child's social life, which in some cases "paralyzed" their socialization into the school and also his cognitive capacities, which are inseparable of the subjective configured student's personalities resulting from their social histories

Cognitive education: Sociocultural mediated activity for learning problems remediation

Rodríguez Arocho, Wanda Dept. of Psychology, University of Puerto Rico, San Juan, Puerto Rico

In their seminal works on the historical, cultural and social foundations of cognitive development Lev S. Vygotsky and Alexander R. Luria emphasized the role of mediation in learning. In spite of the fact that remedial education and cognitive rehabilitation was a main area of concern for both of them, this aspect of the sociocultural framework has not received the attention it deserves until very recently. In this presentation we discuss the basic principles of rehabilitation and remediation from a sociocultural perspective and examine their application in an intervention designed to address learning difficulties, specifically reading problems, in elementary school children.

Collaborating in virtual learning environments: Conversation vs. product elaboration tasks

Mauri, Teresa Psicología Evolutiva, Universidad de Barcelona, Barcelona, Spain **Onrubia, Javier** Psicología Evolutiva, Universidad de Barcelona, Barcelona, Spain

The aim of our paper is to study collaboration processes in two different instructional activities in a text-based asynchronous environment with university students. Two activities on the same content have been registered: a conversation forum and a collaborative writing task. Results show differences between the two activities related with how students manage the task, how common knowledge is established and how students assist each other both in management and knowledge construction processes. These results are discussed from a sociocultural view of learning in virtual environments

Looking at education reform projects from a socioconstructivist approach to knowledge

Bravo Vick, Milagros Graduate Studies in Education, University of Puerto Rico, San Juan, Puerto Rico **Moreno, Mary Annette** Graduate Studies in Education, University of Puerto Rico, San Juan, Puerto Rico

The Puerto Rico Collaborative for Excellence in Teacher Preparation, and the Puerto Rico Math and Science Partnership (Josefina Arce, PI; NSF-sponsored) have as its ultimate goal improvement of student science and mathematics learning. The first tackles transforming teacher preparation programs and the second teacher professional development and school culture. Both involve scientists, mathematicians and educators working in communities of learning and practice that integrate basic principles of the sociocultural framework and related research-based approaches on how people learn. We present its major processes and results and analyze them from a socioconstructivist perspective addressing some original central concepts and recent developments.

The influence of different cultural settings in the modes of discourse and ways of thinking

Cubero Pérez, Mercedes Psicología Experimental, Universidad de Sevilla, Sevilla, Spain

We started from a theoretical perspective in which the activity settings are related to the use of different discourse genres and different ways of thinking. From this perspective, an empirical study was conducted. Individuals from two different levels of education, three different generations, and from the two sides of the border area between Tamaulipas-Texas participated in the study. They solved a task of concept formation in which they had to answers formal and informal questions about the concept of border area. Similarities and differences between the participants were interpreted in terms of the hypothesis of the heterogeneity of verbal thinking.

IS-072: Achievement motivation and achievement attribution among Asian students: Insights from qualitative data

Allan B.I. Bernardo (chair)

Most theories of achievement motivation and achievement attribution have been developed from research involving learners in Western educational systems. Asian psychologists have investigated how these theories apply to learners in Asian educational contexts. This symposium features papers that use qualitative data to determine how meanings, processes, and factors influencing achievement motivation and attribution in Asian students may be similar to or different from Western students. The papers shall highlight how meanings, processes, and factors need to be understood with reference to the students' particular cultural meanings and practices, and how theories could take into account the cultural dimensions of achievement.

Academic achievement and the role of the self and relationship

Muramoto, Yukiko International Graduated School, Yokohama National University, Yokohama, Japan

In an open-ended questionnaire, Japanese undergraduates were asked to recall their positive and negative life events and make attributions. Most participants mentioned their academic success and failure and made self-effacing attributions for them. At the same time, they expected that others who are significantly related to them would make internal attributions for their success more than for their failure. Especially they tended to believe that others would emphasize their effort as the most important cause of the success. The quantitative analysis in our subsequent research further examined the meaning of effort among Japanese and the role of the self and relationship in achievement attribution.

How do future goals affect academic motivation and learning? A qualitative study with Singaporean secondary school students

McInerney, Dennis OER, Nation. Institute of Education, Singapore, Singapore Liem, Arief Darmanegara National Inst. of Education, Nanyang Technological Univers., Singapore, Singapore

This study examines how secondary school students' future goals are related to their academic motivation and learning at school. A hundred Singaporean students were randomly selected for an interview that probed their future goals, perceived utility value of schooling, immediate achievement goals, and learning. This qualitative information was analysed to search for cultural themes related to the abovementioned psychosocial components and their dynamic interactions in affecting student motivation. Parents' and teachers' views about their roles in students' future goals and motivation were also investigated. The findings are discussed in relation to the sociocultural and educational contexts of Singapore.

Cultural models of achievement of Singaporean Malay and Chinese students

Chang, Weining C. Division of Psychology, Nanyang Technological Univers., Singapore, Singapore

The present project aims at identifying (1) the meaning of achievement, its related (2) achievement goal conceptualization and (3) their relationships to parental philosophies concerning their desired outcomes for their children. It is proposed that a cultural model of achievement motivation can be identified through parents' goals and expectations of the child. These goals and expectations will in turn guide parents' interaction with the child. Through these interactions a cultural model is developed. Children might internalize these cultural models as their own internal working model of achievement

Motivation and amotivation: Conceptions of Filipino students

Bernardo, Allan B.I. Counseling and Edu. Psychology, De La Salle University, Manila, Philippines Salanga, Maria Guadalupe C. Counseling and Edu. Psychology, De La Salle University, Manila, Philippines Aguas, Karla Marie C. Counseling and Edu. Psychology, De La Salle University, Manila, Philippines

Many psychological theories of motivation have defined the important categories of students' purposes for learning (motivation) and their reasons for not being motivated in their studies (amotivation). Do these categories adequately describe the dimensions of Filipino students' motivation and amotivation? Using a questionnaire with open-ended questions, we asked 713 Filipino students to describe what motivates them to achieve in school and what factors cause them not to be motivated. The core ideas in the responses were categorized. The results reveal some categories that converge with those in existing theories, and some new ones, including some that describe personal instrumental motivations.

(Tentative) European American and Taiwanese mothers' conversations with their children about school learning

Li, Jin Dept. of Education, Brown University, Providence, USA Fung, Heidi Institute of Ethnology, Academia Sinica, Taipei, Taiwan Liang, Chi-Han Institute of Ethnology, Academia Sinica, Taipei, Taiwan Resch, Jennifer Education Department, Brown University, Providence, RI, USA Luo, Lily Education Department, Brown University, Providence, RI, USA Lou, Lucy Education Department, Brown University, Providence, RI, USA

Children develop learning beliefs under the influence of parental socialization. One important form of socialization is daily talking between parents and children about learning. We examined how European American (EA) and Taiwanese mothers addressed learning with their children. We recorded 167 mother-child conversations about an incidence of the child's good learning attitude/behavior. Analysis of conversational styles revealed that EA mothers guided for self-discovery of past achievement whereby Children were led to recount and to feel positive about themselves. Taiwanese mothers guided for self-betterment from past achievement. Children were steered to construct the strategies that they could use in the future.

IS-073: Child rights in South Asia: Psychosocial aspects

Murshida Ferdous Binte Habib (chair)

A large majority of the children, all over the world, are not properly treated according to the CRC. Therefore, the researcher attempted to know the situation of child rights practice in some developing countries of South Asia. It was found that the nature, causes, and magnitude of exploitation varies in different forms in different countries but it causes serious damages to psychosocial development of the children. However, some children are getting better treatment where Zakah system is being practiced than those who do not have the advantage. Finally some recommendations are made to uplift child rights situation in these countries.

Child rights and mentally retarded children in Bangladesh

Sultana, Sabina Dept. of Psychology, University of Rajshahi, Rajshahi, Bangladesh

With the dissemination of knowledge about mental retardation people are becoming conscious about the preventive measures about it. The researcher found that the span of life of retarded people, special school, social acceptance etc. have increased significantly during last few years. But most of the people are not yet aware of rights of mentally retarded as children. Therefore, these children are being deprived from their basic rights and are facing lot of sufferings. They do not get any social welfare benefit even. Finally some suggestions were recommended to make the situation of child rights better for mentally retarded children.

Child rights and child labour in Bangladesh

Habib, Murshida Ferdous Binte Dept. of Psychology, University of Rajshahi, Rajshahi, Bangladesh

Children of this sub- continent have to work hard to earn, even their own bread, though there are many laws related to child labour. In this study attempts have been taken to explore the child labour situation in Bangladesh from child right perspectives. It was found, in most of the cases, that the employers without being aware of child rights have treated the children engaged as labourers cordially. The employers in rural areas are more caring to their child labourers compared to their urban counterparts. Lack of education and awareness has been identified as important reasons in violating child rights.

Child rights and girls of Bangladesh

Habib, Farzana Quobab Binte Business Administration, University of Kebangsaang, Bangi, Malaysia Quoquab binte Habib, Farzana Business & Management, University of Kebangsaang, Bangi, Malaysia

Protection of consumer rights is a new dimension in some of the countries of South Asia. Children are considered a significant market to the business world. But their rights as a consumer is not practiced or protected properly. In this study child rights have been investigated from consumer rights perspective. The situation is better in Malaysia, Thailand, and Singapore than that of in Indian sub continent. In Bangladesh people are hardly aware of their consumer rights let alone child rights as consumers. Finally some recommendations have been made for the development of consumer rights protection in these countries.

Child rights and education in Bangladesh

Haq, Enamul Dept. of Psychology, University of Rajshahi, Rajshahi, Bangladesh

Having proper education is a basic right of children. It is also included in MDGs. The scenario is somewhat promising in Bangladesh in this sector. Not only the government but also some NGOs have come forward with the mission of providing education. Therefore, underprivileged children are also getting the opportunity to have education along with the children of solvent families. But they are having non- formal education. The study found that the number of girls taking education is higher than that of the boys. The percentage of children having education is increasing but the figure is neither significant nor satisfactory.

Rights of the children as consumers

Saha, Nitai Dept. of Psychology, Rajshahi College, Rajshahi, Bangladesh

Girls are more vulnerable to be abused physically and psychologically as compared to boys in South Asia. Although the articles in CRC and other laws are equally applicable to girls as it is for boys they are not properly treated. This study tried to reveal condition of girls in Bangladesh from child right perspectives. The maltreatment from the family and others hinders their mental development and causes various problems. In recent years few measures have been taken to make the situation better which added little contribution. Some other suggestions have been made in this study to make the situation better.

IS-074: Authenticity in the communication of emotion

Pierre Gosselin (chair)

Although we often regulate our emotional expressions, authenticity is a key factor in successful social transactions, not only in the context of intimate relationships but also in the context of political and artistic performances. In this symposium, contributors will discuss the continuity between genuine, regulated and simulated expressions, identify the parameters that are central to perceived authenticity within a public performance, and report new data on the cultural aspects of smile authenticity. Finally, developmental evidence pertaining to the perception of smiles and to the understanding of real and apparent emotions will be presented.

The presentation of emotion in everyday life

Scherer, Klaus R. CISA, Universität Genf, Genf, Switzerland

Calling dichotomous distinctions between "real-life, authentic" and "acted, stereotypical" displays into question, a Goffmanian analysis of emotion expression is suggested. Just as Goffman argued that we continuously "present" our idealized self as actors on the interactional stage, we suggest that, with the rare exception of sudden, spontaneous "affect bursts", we almost always monitor and regulate our emotional expressions (and the emotions themselves) in line with strategic intentions and normative constraints. In consequence, there are no sharp boundaries between authentic, regulated, and acted emotions but rather a continuum. Implications for research are discussed on the basis of recent data.

Performing authentic emotions on the political and operatic stages: Multimodal analyses of synchrony

Mortillaro, Marcello Dept. of Psychology, University of Geneva, Geneva, Switzerland Goudbeek, Martijn Dept. of Psychology, University of Geneva, Geneva, Switzerland Dael, Nele Dept. of Psychology, University of Geneva, Geneva, Switzerland Mehu, Marc Dept. of Psychology, University of Geneva, Geneva, Switzerland

Authenticity is a key-factor for successful communication in many performance domains. In this contribution we propose that synchronous activation of multiple modalities lies at the heart of perceived authenticity of a public performance. Two different instances are presented. First, political discourse is considered through the example of the last French presidential debate. Second, stage performance is investigated through the comparison of different opera singers. Analyses of voice, face and body movements are used to explain the perceived authenticity of performers. The discussion of the multimodal approach to authenticity and synchronization will be central to our contribution.

Cultural aspects of smile authenticity

Thibault, Pascal Dept. of Psychology, UQAM, Montreal, Canada

Duchenne smiles are postulated to be markers of authentic enjoyment, but it is still unknown whether this is the case universally. In this study, Gabonese, Chinese and French-Canadians rated the intensity of smiles differing in intensity and Duchenne marker presence. Participants from these cultures posed authentic and non-authentic smiles, which were FACS coded and judged by decoders from the same groups. Absence of Duchenne markers increased perceived inauthenticity, but only for French-Canadian smiles decoded by French-Canadians. The posed smiles varied in intensity and presence/absence of the Duchenne marker. The Duchenne marker does not seem to function as such in some non-Western contexts.

Children's perception of enjoyment smiles

Gosselin, Pierre Dept. od Psychology, University of Ottawa, Ottawa, Canada Perron, Mélanie Department of Psychology, LaurentianUniversity, Sudbury, Canada

Children's knowledge of the distinction between enjoyment and nonenjoyment smiles was investigated by presenting participants with short video excerpts of smiles. Enjoyment smiles differed from non-enjoyment smiles by greater symmetry and by appearance changes produced in the eye region by the orbicularis oculi action. The results indicate that 6- and 7-year-old children have the perceptual abilities to detect these differences and are able to interpret them with above chance level accuracy. Sensitivity was higher for the symmetry of the smiles than for the appearance changes produced in the eye region and improved in later childhood.

Children's understanding of real and apparent emotions

Perron, Mélanie Dept. of Psychology, Laurentian University, Sudbury, Canada Gosselin, Pierre Dept. of Psychology, University of Ottawa, Ottawa, Canada

We investigated children's understanding of real and apparent emotions between the ages of 5 and 10 years. Participants were read stories designed to elicit display rules and asked to predict the facial expressions the protagonists would make to hide their emotions. Five- and 6-year-olds were found to have an implicit understanding of the difference between real and apparent emotions. However, they had more difficulty understanding the simultaneity of real and apparent emotions and were less likely to think that apparent emotions might mislead an observer.

IS-075: Self-regulation and health: Perspectives from social and personality psychology

Bärbel Knäuper, Christine Stich (chair)

This symposium presents current theory and research on self-regulation of health cognitions and behaviors. The discussion will highlight current conceptual and methodological challenges in this field and explore directions for future research.

Cortisol, negative affect, sleep, and health

Wrosch, Carsten Dept. of Psychology, Concordia University, Montreal, Canada

This longitudinal study examined whether health effects of cortisol level would emerge particularly among older adults who experience high levels of negative affect or exhibit poor sleep. High cortisol was associated with increases in physical symptoms among older adults who experienced high levels of negative affect and poor sleep. By contrast, cortisol level did not predict changes in physical symptoms among older adults who experienced either low negative affect or efficient sleep. This suggests that cortisol secretion are particularly likely to contribute to older adults' physical symptoms if they co-occur in the context of other emotional and behavioral problems.

Health behavior and successful aging: Interplay of mental resources and self-regulation

Ziegelmann, Jochen Inst. für Psychologie, Freie Universität Berlin, Berlin, Germany Lippke, Sonia Health Psychology, Freie Universität Berlin, Berlin, Germany

Objectives: To model motivational and volitional processes of health behavior change in individuals with differing degrees of mental resources. Methods: 368 individuals in rehabilitation completed questionnaires assessing the amount of physical activities performed pre-rehabilitation and 36 months thereafter as well as motivational and volitional variables. Mental resources were assessed with the mental component score of the SF12. Results: Analyses revealed different motivational and volitional patterns in individuals with differing degrees of mental resources. Conclusions: The motivational and volitional processes seem to depend on mental resources. This demonstrates the need for specific interventions tailored to those resources.

Smoking-specific compensatory health beliefs and smoking behaviour in adolescents

Radtke, Theda Inst. für Psychologie, Universität Zürich, Zürich, Switzerland Scholz, Urte Inst. für Psychologie, Universität Zürich, Zürich, Switzerland Keller, Roger Inst. für Psychologie, Universität Zürich, Zürich, Switzerland Hornung, Rainer Inst. für Psychologie, Universität Zürich, Zürich, Switzerland

Objective: Compensatory Health Beliefs (CHBs) are beliefs that negative consequences of an unhealthy behaviour can be compensated for by engaging in a different healthy behaviour. Method: A newly developed questionnaire for smoking-specific CHBs in adolescents was tested for its validity and reliability as well as its predictive value for smoking behaviour in a sample of 187 adolescents aged 14-19 years. Results: We found first evidence for the reliability and validity of the smoking-specific CHB scale. Moreover, the construct proved useful in predicting adolescent smoking behaviour. Conclusions: CHBs provide one possible explanation why adolescents fail to change their smoking behaviour.

Prototype-distancing and the theory of planned behavior: Prediction of quitting in women and men

Dohnke, Birte Center for Gender in Medicine, Charite Berlin, Berlin, Germany Weiß-Gerlach, Edith Department of Anaesthesiology, Charite Berlin, Berlin, Germany Spies, Claudia D. Department of Anaesthesiology, Charite Berlin, Berlin, Germany

To integrate prototype perception, gender, and theory of planned behaviour (TPB). Distancing from the typically male smoker should support quitting beyond TPB variables. A cross-sectional and a longitudinal study were conducted with 298 and 183 smokers, respectively. Prototype perception was assessed by desirable masculine traits and similarity to the self-concept. High masculinity and high dissimilarity contributed to the prediction of quitting intentions over and above TPB variables in women. Study 2 confirmed this finding regarding quitting intentions and attempts at 4-weeks follow-up. Health promotion targeting women should facilitate distancing from the male smoker in addition to strengthen evidence-based social-cognitive factors.

Trying to restrain: Unsuccessful weight regulation is related to paying more attention to food

Stich, Christine Dept. of Psychology, McGill University, Montreal, Canada Knäuper, Bärbel Dept. of Psychology, McGill University, Montreal, Canada Leigh Lyons, Chrystal Dubé, Laurette Faculty of Management, McGill University, Montreal, Canada

Inhibitory control (IC) is defined as the ability to inhibit on-going or pre-potent actions. We propose the idea of food-specific IC and investigated its relationship to self-reported weight fluctuation (WF) as indicator of the ability to regulate weight using a newly developed food-specific stop-signal-task. If food-specific IC exists then individuals with lower food-specific IC should report higher WF. As expected results show that individuals with higher WF paid significantly more attention to food pictures and had shorter stop-signal-delays than individuals with low WF. Moreover, high WF individuals more often failed to inhibit responses to food than to non-food pictures.

IS-076: Eye movements in reading: Experiments, models, and corpus analyses

Reinhold Kliegl (chair)

Current research on eye movements in reading is based on experiments manipulating specific words in sentences, on analyses of eye movements including all fixations during reading of sentences or paragraphs, and on computational models of eye-movement control. Presentations of new results relating to these three lines of research are presented in this symposium.

The role of computational models and experimental data in understanding eye movements during reading

Rayner, Keith Dept. of Psychology, University of California, San Diego, CA, USA

Some influential computational models of eye movement control during reading have recently been proposed. I will review these different models focusing primarily on the E-Z Reader and SWIFT models. Some recent research findings will be presented to illustrate the value of these models. I will also discuss the role that these models play in furthering our knowledge base about the control of eye movements in reading, as well as the role of experimental and corpus based data in this domain. My primary argument will be that the models and data need to go hand in hand in furthering our understanding.

Raednig wrods with jmulbed ltetres

Liversedge, Simon *Dept. of Psychology, University of Southampton, Southhampton, United Kingdom*
I will report data from three eye movement experiments that investigated how people process text with jmulbed ltetres (letter transpositions). We manipulated externality, distance and position of transposition, and whether transpositions were of consonants, vowels, or both. Also, in one experiment parafoveal preview of transposed text was available and in another it was not. We obtained a number of key results, however, the primary finding was that external word beginning transpositions were maximally disruptive (regardless of the availability of preview). The results as a whole will be considered in relation to letter position encoding in word recognition during reading.

Reading and ocular dominances

Shillcock, Richard *Dept. of Informatics, University of Edinburgh, Edinburgh, United Kingdom* **Roberts, Matthew** *Dept. of Informatics, University of Edinburgh, Edinburgh, United Kingdom*
Reading is more effective with two eyes than with one. This fact begs the question of the interaction of the two eyes. How does the brain coordinate the reading-related eye-movements of the two eyes, and what are the implications of the fact that the two eyes frequently do not fixate conjointly on the text? We present new data and theory to show the varied and task-dependent nature of ocular dominances, the importance of reading direction and the fact that the brain evolved to cope with the unitary perception of scenes in depth.

Limited parallel word processing during reading

Radach, Ralph *Dept. of Psychology, Florida State University, Tallahassee, USA* **Inhoff, Albrecht** *Psychology, State University of New York, Binghamton, USA* **Glover, Lisa** *Dept. of Psychology, Florida State University, Tallahassee, FL, USA*
Models of continuous reading differ on two dimensions, the extent to which reading behavior is controlled by visuomotor vs. cognitive forces and whether word processing proceeds in a strictly serial or a more parallel fashion. We present evidence from paradigms probing the spatial and temporal extent of concurrent word processing. Eye movement contingent image manipulations were used to completely or temporarily restrict availability of information on a parafoveal word n+1 or n+2 while fixating on n. Results indicate that while there is temporal overlap in the processing of consecutive words, the spatial extent of this parallel processing appears quite limited.

Broadening the scope of eye-movement research in reading: Oral reading and proof reading

Laubrock, Jochen *Inst. für Psychologie, Universität Potsdam, Potsdam, Germany* **Bohn, Christiane** *Psychology, Universität Potsdam, Potsdam, Germany*
Most eye-movement research in reading deals with silent, comprehension-motivated reading. We extent the scope and impose constraints on reading models by presenting empirical results on how the eye movement system adapts to different task demands. First, we provide data on a different output system and show how the eye-voice span available from oral reading protocols is modulated by textual variables. Second, we simulate reading with an external pacemaker (someone reading something to you) by asking listeners to read along a recorded voice with electronically varied speed.

Third, we analyze eye movements of proof-readers, who place relatively little emphasis on comprehension.

Reading strategies and their implementation in the SWIFT model of eye-movement control

Kliegl, Reinhold *Inst. für Psychology, Universität Potsdam, Potsdam, Germany*
Differences in reading strategies (by instruction and by individual habits or dispositions) have been the hallmark of early eye-movement research but were largely limited to global characteristics (e.g., skipping and regression rate, fixation durations). Linear mixed-effect models allow the simultaneous assessment of effects of text characteristics and both instruction effects and individual differences in reading strategy. We illustrate this procedure with analyses of a large corpus of reading eye movements. In addition, we present how individual differences in reading strategies are implemented in SWIFT, a computational model of eye-movement control, and how they promote the further development of this model.

IS-077: Restoration and restorative environments

Terry Hartig *(chair)*
With its concern for excessive demands on adaptive resources, stress research has long proved helpful for mapping relations between environment and health. In recent years, researchers and practitioners have also come to value a complementary body of work that is primarily concerned with restoration of depleted adaptive resources. By directing attention to variations in restoration processes and the environments where they occur, that body of work provides another perspective on problems in adaptation. The presentations in this symposium address some of the concerns of the restoration perspective, in particular the arrangements in everyday life that support versus thwart support restoration.

The restoration perspective: Another view of human adaptation

Hartig, Terry *Inst. Housing and Urban Res., Uppsala University, Gävle, Sweden*
This presentation sets the stage for the symposium by contrasting the restoration perspective with two other, better known perspectives on human adaptation, namely, the stress perspective and the coping perspective. The three perspectives are contrasted in terms of their theoretical and practical premises, and interrelations among them are noted.

A longitudinal study on the benefits of recovery experiences on job performance

Binnewies, Carmen *Work &Organizational Psych., University of Konstanz, Konstanz, Germany* **Sonnentag, Sabine** *Inst. für Psychologie, Universität Konstanz, Konstanz, Germany* **Mojza, Eva** *Inst. für Psychologie, Universität Konstanz, Konstanz, Germany*
Recovery experiences during leisure time, such as psychological detachment from work, mastery experiences, and relaxation benefit employee health. We assumed that recovery experiences also foster job performance, because employees can increase resources during recovery that benefit job performance. Results from a longitudinal study over six months with a sample of 358 employees showed that mastery experiences were positively related to personal initiative, and relaxation was positively related to creativity. Psychological detachment was associated with perceiving work as less effortful. Unexpectedly, psychological detachment was negatively related to creativity, personal initiative and OCB. Recovery experiences were unrelated to task performance.

Urban slums in South Asia: Residents' prospects for psychological restoration

Pandey, Janak *Behav. and Cognitive Sciences, University of Allahabad, Allahabad, India*
The South Asian countries share harsh socio-economic and environmental realities like high population density, poverty, illiteracy, and inequalities in living conditions, as well as cultural characteristics like collectivism and hierarchical social order. Massive rural to urban migration has caused serious problems particularly in the cities, where many people live in crowded slums. Together with environmental problems and cultural characteristics, South Asians probably share psychological characterestics. This paper examines the perceptions and coping of slum dwellers in some South Asian capital cities, including issues related to where they find possibilities for psychological restoration in a difficult everyday environment.

On-site evaluation of restorative environments: The effect of actual place experience upon the perceived restorativeness of natural and built historical environments

Carrus, Giuseppe *Cultural and Education Studies, University of Rome, Rome, Italy* **Scopelliti, Massimiliano** *Inst. Cognitive Sciences Tech., National Research Council, Rome, Italy* **Bonaiuto, Marino** *Dept. Social and Devel. Psych., Sapienza University of Rome, Rome, Italy* **Romoli, Elisa** *Dept. of Education, University of Roma Tre, Rome, Italy*
Research on restorative environments consistently has shown positive outcomes of nature experience. However, assuming that actual environmental experience plays a key role in whether restoration can occur, it was predicted that actual immersion in either natural or built/historical settings would moderate the perceived restorativeness of different types of environments: individuals immersed in natural settings were expected to be more sensitive to restorative qualities of nature, while individuals immersed in built/historical environments were expected to be more sensitive to restorative qualities of artistic/historical buildings. A study (N = 153) tested and supported these hypotheses. Theoretical and practical implications are discussed.

Restoration in nature as a promoter of conservation

Kaiser, Florian *Human-Tech. Interct., University of Technology, Eindhoven, Netherlands*
Do personal benefits from experiences in natural environments, such as psychological restoration, underlie people's concern about the environment and, ultimately, motivate people to act for environmental conservation? Employing self-reports from 468 students, we examined the relationships between use of natural environments for restoration, environmental concern, and conservation behavior. Based on hierarchical regression analyses, we found the use of nature for restoration to promote environmental concern. Concern, in turn, predicted conservation behavior; however, the degree of mediation varied with the type of environmental concern measure used. Apparently, psychological restoration in nature motivates people to engage more in environmental conservation.

IS-078: Pathways to health and healing in diverse cultures

Elias Mpofu *(chair)*
Constructions of health within cultural communities influence the processes for its sustenance, restoration and promotion. We explore resources for well-being in five ecological settings: rural South Africa, Botswana, post-civil war Liberia and Rwanda, workplace environments in Australia and Canada. Optimism explained the subjective well-being in rural South Africans. Religiosity in Botswana teenagers protected their health. Resi-

lience transitioned survivors of civil war in Liberia from survivors to helpers. Post-trauma appraisal by survivors of Australian and Canadian industrial accidents influenced their recovery and work capacity. Pathways through which health and healing are filtered or otherwise appropriated influence subjective well-being.

Does religiosity predict health outcomes in Botswana teenagers?

Mpofu, Elias Counselor Education and Reha., The Penn State University, University Park, USA
Muchado, Jabulani Educational Foundations, University of Botswana, Gaborone, Botswana
Moswela, Bernard Educational Foundations, University of Botswana, Gaborone, Botswana Jensen, Kipton Theology and Religious Studies, Univeristy of Botswana, Gaborone, Botswana Tlhabiwe, Pinkie Educational Foundations, Univeristy of Botswana, Gaborone, Botswana

Objective. We investigated religiosity as a health protective in Batswana teenagers from STIs and alcohol abuse. Method. Two hundred and fifteen teenagers completed the Botswana Youth Health Survey (BYHS), which included measures of religiosity/spirituality, STIs and alcohol abuse risk. Logistic regression modeling was used to predict health risk from STIs and alcohol abuse with religiosity. Results. Religiosity was a valid construct with Batswana teenagers. High religiosity scores predicted lower risk for STIs and alcohol abuse in Batswana teenagers. Conclusion. Religiosity influences STIs and alcohol abuse risk in Batswana teenagers and should be considered in prevention programming.

Prevention of post-concussional syndrome in north american workers: The importance of early intervention on vocational outcome

LeBlanc, Jeanne Private Practice, Vancouver, Canada
Objectives: Examination of the effectiveness of early education and interdisciplinary intervention to prevent Post-Concussional Syndrome in workers after a concussion during employment. Method: Two approaches to intervention (generalized (N=26) versus individual (N=23)) were utilized, in an outpatient clinic in Vancouver, British Columbia. Return to work status was compared, (Fisher's Exact Test). Results: The individualized approach resulted in significantly more returning to work or having a planned return to work than the general treatment (87% versus 58%, respectively, p = .024). Conclusion: Early individualized and educational approach, reinforcing abilities rather than deficits, is an effective approach for most individuals post-concussion.

Psychological predictors of work capacity: Improving pathways to health for injured workers

Matthews, Lynda Faculty of Health Sciences, University of Sydney, Lidcombe, Australia Harris, Lynne Faculty of Health Sciences, University of Sydney, Sydney, NSW, Australia Cumming, Steven Faculty of Health Sciences, University of Sydney, Sydney, NSW, Australia
Objectives: This study examined trauma-related appraisals and posttraumatic responses of injured workers to determine their usefulness in predicting work capacity. Methods: Demographics, physical function, psychological health, and perceptions of work capacity were documented in 69 survivors approximately 8-months post-accident. Multiple regression identified predictors of work capacity. Results: Occupation, physical function and PTSD severity were associated with work capacity. While PTSD severity and trauma-related appraisals were correlated, appraisals were significant predictors of work capacity independent of PTSD severity. Conclusions: Targeting trauma-related appraisals may improve work capacity, particularly if inter-

ventions that challenge appraisals are introduced early in rehabilitation before they become well-rehearsed and habitual.

Perceived health needs of elderly South Africans in a rural area

Sodi, Tholene Dept. of Psychology, University of Venda, Thohoyandou, South Africa
Objectives: The aim of the study was to explore the perceived health needs of a group of elderly South Africans drawn from a rural community. Method: Semi-structured interviews were conducted with 20 elderly people to gain insight regarding their perceived health needs. Results: Whilst ageing for some of the elderly people is associated with physical ill health, loneliness and poverty, there were also indications to suggest that this period may be psychologically meaningful if understood within a particular cultural context. Conclusion: Culturally appropriate intervention strategies need to be put in place to address the health needs of elderly people.

Transcending trauma and relentless hope: Peer support counselors, indicators of Posttraumatic Growth (PTG) and what they carry

Vogel, Gwen Int. Center of Disast. Psych., Salus World, Boulder, USA
Objective: An analysis of the impact of vocation on psycho-social counselors with trauma histories. Method: Appreciative Inquiry (AI) technique was used with 22 counselors in post-war Liberia. Particular emphasis was placed on indicators of vicarious trauma, resiliency and post traumatic growth (PTG). Results: A dimensional analysis of narrative interviews with Liberian counselors' uncovered: 1) two dimensions of recovery that prevented recurring symptoms of PTSD and, 2) three mechanisms of resiliency that created personalized order and control. Conclusion: Established mechanisms and experiences of PTG resulted in significantly more reports of work satisfaction, indicating a successful journey from victim to survivor to provider.

Urgent mental health needs in Rwanda: Culturally sensitive training interventions

Lopez Levers, Lisa Counseling Psychology, Duquesne University, Pittsburgh, USA
Objectives: Rwanda has experienced the tragic consequences of genocide (1994). While the Rwandan government has done much to restore the country's infrastructures and civil society services, the lingering psychosocial effects of the genocide remain relatively unaddressed. An invited consultation assessed how need for intervention could be translated into effective strategic planning. Methods: Consultative activities involved a situational analysis, interviews and focus groups with relevant actors, and other relevant data collection. Results: Consultation outcomes supported the need for culturally appropriate community-based trauma recovery counseling. Conclusions: Results pointed to the need for building capacity to deliver services through appropriate training endeavors.

Counselling needs of adolescents and youth living with HIV/AIDS in the Eastern Cape Province, South Africa

Mayekiso, Tokozile Faculty of Arts, Nelson Mandela Met. University, Port Elizabeth, South Africa
Objectives: Assessment of the counselling needs of adolescents and youth living with HIV/AIDS. Methods: Data was collected from a sample of 30 participants using semi-structured interviews. Results: Acceptance of diagnosis and condom usage and deaths were some of the areas that were reported by the majority of the participants. Adolescents and youth were mainly concerned about issues relating to death. In terms of the main concern of family members of adolescents and

youth, all three groups were of the perception that family members would be concerned about the prospect of premature death of their loved one. Conclusion: Counsellors need to provide the adolescents and youth the space to express their fears and to accept the HIV positive status.

IS-102: International perspectives on the new draft of the Universal Declaration of Ethical Principles for Psychologists

Janel Gauthier (chair)
Since 2002, an international group is working under the auspices of IUPsyS, IAAP, and IACCP to develop a universal declaration of ethical principles for psychologists. A draft declaration was released for consultation in 2005. The purpose of the symposium is to discuss the newly revised version of the Draft Universal Declaration, its overall significance and implications for individual psychologists and psychology organizations, and how best to use it for the international advancement of ethics in psychology. The symposium includes distinguished participants from Africa, Asia, Europe, the Middle East, North America, and South America. Carola Brücher-Albers (Germany) will act as Discussant.

African considerations for a universal declaration of ethical principles for psychologists

Watts, Ann Medical Center, Entabeni Hospital, Durban, South Africa
The relevance of the newly revised draft of the Universal Declaration of Ethical Principles for Psychologists for South African psychology will be addressed within the context of its historical complicity in supporting apartheid and its human rights abuses. The appropriateness of definitions, concepts and language contained in the Declaration, as well as its significance for South Africa's multi-cultural psychological context will be discussed within the framework of South Africa's post-democracy Constitution, Bill of Rights, and pertinent legislation. The Declaration's relevance for Africa and the majority world will also be considered in terms of the challenges facing psychology in these regions

The universal declaration of ethical principles for psychologists: Guidelines for a plan of action

Farah, Adnan Jordan Psychological Society, Irbid, Jordan
The proposed Universal Declaration of Ethical Principles for Psychologists consists of a set of basic ethical principles from which specific applications can be drawn. It reflects what is expected from psychologists at the personal, professional, and global level. The reality of globalization requires that we learn to embrace diversity and plurality while fostering an innate sense of unity and harmony. As psychologists, we must seek to equip ourselves with the tools that will enable us to comprehend our fellow human beings more profoundly and to conduct ourselves in an appropriate and universally acceptable manner, regardless of particular ideology, race or religion.

South American perspectives on ethical principles for psychologists

Ferrero, Andrea Dept. of Human Sciences, National University, San Luis, Argentina
Most Southamerican psychology ethics codes include ethical principles that provide a moral framework for professional practice. Sometimes, those principles transcend national borders and lead to regional agreements such as the Ethical Principles Framework for Professional Practice of Psychology in the Mercosur and Associated Countries, endorsed by six countries. Endorsing common

ethical principles in Southamerica has strengthened commitment for ethical behaviour in the psychology community and helped some countries to develop their own ethics code. We believe that the proposed Universal Declaration of Ethical Principles could have similar positive effects and guide psychologists worldwide toward highest professional and scientific ethical ideals.

Asian perspective on the proposed universal declaration of ethical principles

Nair, Elizabeth Dept. of Psychology, Work & Health Psychologists, Singapore, Singapore

This paper will review the extent to which practice and research in Asian psychology can be in alignment with a Universal Declaration of Ethical Principles. Cultural nuances, ethnic beliefs, and social norms for acceptable behaviour are disparate across Asian countries. The paper will review the language, terminology, and interpretations that may pose difficulties for acceptance and adherence in the Asian context. The Declaration has the potential to move world psychology towards acknowledging a shared perspective on ethical principles for the profession across national boundaries. Effective procedures for translating these Principles to Codes of Ethics in Asian countries will be discussed.

The cultural dimensions of a universal declaration of ethical principles for psychologists: A European perspective

Lindsay, Geoff University of Warwick, Coventry, United Kingdom

For the Declaration to have universal applicability, ethical principles must either be uncontentiously universal or 'located' and made relevant within a cultural context. My position is the latter. This requires specific attention to the cultural dimensions when producing the Declaration. The European Federation of Psychologists Associations' Meta-code of Ethics provides a template for EFPA national associations when developing their codes. The lessons learned from this process have relevance to the present initiative and will be presented as part of the process for making the Universal Declaration optimally useful.

Viewing the universal through the lens of the local: The universal declaration and the APA ethics code

Behnke, Stephen Ethics Office, American Psychological Ass., Washington, USA

This presentation will discuss the final revised draft of the Universal Declaration of Ethical Principles for Psychologists as it relates to the Ethical Principles of Psychologist and Code of Conduct (2002) of the American Psychological Association. The presentation will explore the "universality" of the final revised draft, and will discuss the relationship between such universality and the cultural underpinnings of a national ethics code which is, by definition, written for a specific group of psychologists at a particular moment in time. The presentation will examine the implications of the Revised Draft for psychologists under the American Psychological Association ethics code.

S-058: The integration of scientific knowledge: Ontological knowledge and consciousness

Larissa A. Tsvetkova (chair)

Ontopsychological method as contribution to the integration of the psychological knowledge with the other sciences will be explained. The process of development of many sciences and their practical applications is directly connected to theoretical and applied psychology. The result given is the change of social role and the importance of psychology. In

particualr, the problem of knowledge and consciousness and its psycho-social implications will be highlighted. Applications and results in Russia, Brazil and Europe will be discussed.

Ontopsychology in the strategic guidance to develop the faculty of psychology, State University of St. Petersburg, Russia

Tsvetkova, Larissa A. St. Petersburg University, St. Petersburg, Russia

Current education for graduate and post graduate studies at Faculty of Psychology of St. Petersburg State University is characterised by integration of humanistic and applied sciences. Strategic objective is to study human person in all his/her different aspects above all leader psychology. By leader it is meant a person who chooses to have the leading role for his/her life and works to improve social environment. Faculty mission is to become a center of integration of scientific research activity to contribute to solve psychology task in social, political and economic field. Interdisciplinary educational projects and interdisciplinary scientific research are carrying out.

Ontological knowledge and consciousnss

Meneghetti, Antonio Dept. of Ontopsychology, A.I.O., NGO in UN Cons. Status, Rome, Italy

Aim of the work is to give contribution to one of the topic of psychology: the critical problem of knowledge. The three basic levels of elementary perception: esteroceptive, proprioceptive and egoceptive have been analysed, in particular the extinction mechanisms as a result of a conditioning generalization. Total phenomenological understanding and epochà (Husserl) can produce a cmplete personal change in favour of the whole existential development. Optimal egoceptivity would be a decisional and operative compensation in correspondent reflection to the total organismic. Interdisciplinary research at St. Petersburg University, psychology faculty, ontopsychology chair has been carried out.

The further reaches of the psychology of being: Ontopsychology

Grishina, Natalia V . Dept. of Ontopsychology, St. Petersburg University, St. Petersburg, Russia

In his essay Towards a psychology of being, Maslow declared that Humanistic Psychology, the third force was a groundwork for a fourth force. He concluded that Sutich already had defined all this in a word: Ontopsychology, but the scientist, who could have indicated this process, was still missing. We find ourselves to realize this fourth force, announced by the most advanced international psychology, founded by Meneghetti and formalised in 2004 at the chair of ontopsychology, faculty of psychology, Saint Petersburg State University. Our contribution to realize an epistemic psychology as interdisciplinary to all other sciences will be highlighted.

Responsibility and creative evolution: Prospectic synthesis of instruments and application

Lacerda e Silva, Wesley ABO - F.O.I.L., Brazil, Sao Paulo, Brazil

The object of ontopsychology is the psychological experience; it individuates the causes that constitute this experience and the elements that cansolve it. It has indvidual and world positive vision: human being as a responsible protagonist, can base on virtuality which can attain personal growth. Diagnosis and intervention instruments as intercultural approach will be described. Analysis of the application in Russia, Brazil, Europe and China will be discussed. Results highlights importance of training approach based on identificaiton, isolation and application of positive inner part (in-itslef) for creative evolution independently from age, sex, nationality.

The concept of authentication: Methodological aspects and psycho-social implications

Dmitrieva, Victoria Dept. of Ontopsychology, St. Petersburg University, St. Petersburg, Russia

Ego problem is not an easy question to solve, above all for the frequency of a fictitious Ego, that is a consciousness based on strong interpretative styles of reality. This is to be found in most of the persons, including many teachers, researchers and politicians. Object of the paper is to describe the function of the authentication counseling and its application. Through case-histories the author will explain the training method to: a)identify the semantic field; b)isolate the verbalization of her/his in-itself; c)apply the optimal or specified choice/action; d)results: consciousness can reflect reality overcoming stereotypes.

Ethical principles and political decision-making across international boundaries

Argenta, Roberto Economics and Politics, Brazilian Ass. Ontopsychology, Sau Paulo, Brazil

Ethics is the ethical person. We can define the ethical choice as what best safeguards the individuality within the whole. Politics, in its essence, is the art of centering the different situations and to solve them in progress, at benefit within the whole. Ideologies must not be saved as such, they must be verified and followed only if they are functional to social conviviality. Thus, it is a problem of psychological matter. Training application in Brazil Europe and Russia will be described.

S-059: Emotion: Development and functions in adulthood and old age

Michaela Riediger, Ute Kunzmann (chair)

Recent life-span theories suggest that emotional competencies remain stable or even improve during the second half of life. Empirical evidence for age differences as well as the functions of emotions during adulthood and old age is, however, sparse. This symposium brings together an international group of researchers who investigate emotional aging from different perspectives and by employing various methodologies. Presentations deal with age differences in emotional reactivity and emotion regulation, motivational aspects of the emotion system, and the interplay of cognition and emotion during adulthood and old age. Methodologies include experience sampling, measurement bursts, experimental and long-term longitudinal designs.

Age-related differences in emotion regulation effectiveness

Blanchard-Fields, Fredda Psychology, Georgia Institute of Technolog, Atlanta, USA

In a dual task paradigm, older adults who were instructed to regulate their emotions performed better on a working memory task than those who were instructed to maximize negative emotions. Young adults who were instructed to regulate their emotions performed more poorly on the working memory task than those who were not instructed to do so. Older adults' emotion regulation may not require as many cognitive resources. In a second study instructing young adults to use strategies typically used by older adults resulted in better mood outcomes than for young adults' spontaneous use of strategies in a No Instructions condition.

Couplings of daily events and cognitive performance: Is daily affect a mediator in younger and older adulthood?

Brose, Annette für Bildungsforschung, Max-Planck-Istitut, Berlin, Germany *Schmiedek, Florian* Psychology, Humboldt University Berlin, Berlin, Germany *Lindenberger, Ulman* Zentrum für Lebenserwartung, Max-Planck-Institut, Berlin, Germany

Exposure to events affects cognitive performance. In the present study, 200 younger and older adults were tested at 100 occasions. Central interest is whether on a daily basis, affective correlates (positive, negative affect) of minor and major events are coupled with working memory performance, e.g., because of suboptimal arousal. Older as compared to younger adults are described to be more motivated to regulate emotions, therefore might direct attention to emotions instead towards cognitive tasks. Contrariwise, performance might be unaffected by affective fluctuations if emotion regulation takes place habitually. Results are discussed with regard to emotional development and declining cognitive abilities.

Age differences in emotional reactivity: Cognitive status makes a difference

Kunzmann, Ute Inst. für Psychologie I, Universität Leipzig, Leipzig, Germany Richter, David Inst. für Psychologie I, Universität Leipzig, Leipzig, Germany
Recent evidence has suggested that older people react with greater sadness and anxiety to fundamental age-related losses than younger adults. This increase may be restricted to older adults with relatively low cognitive resources - arguably because down-regulating negative emotional reactions may pose particular difficulties to them. This prediction was supported in a study with 240 adults (age range 20 to 70), who watched films about existential age-related losses and reported their emotional reactions after each film. The evidence suggests that a simultaneous consideration of cognitive and emotional functioning will lead to a more comprehensive understanding of the aging mind.

Me against myself: Motivational conflicts and emotional development in adulthood

Riediger, Michaela Zentrum Lifespan Psychologie, Max-Planck-Institut, Berlin, Germany
We report two studies on adult changes in the prevalence and emotional consequences of everyday motivational conflict experiences. Data were obtained using diary and experience-sampling methodologies. Both studies showed that emotional well-being increased, while motivational conflict prevalence decreased with age, and that motivational conflicts were associated with impaired emotional well-being. Mediational analyses revealed that the age-related decrease in motivational conflicts accounted for age-related improvements in emotional well-being. These findings were robust to controlling for age differences in everyday activities. This suggests that motivational conflicts are among the factors underlying the positive development of emotional well-being into young old age.

Do age-related preferences in visual attention facilitate affect regulation?

Isaacowitz, Derek Dept. of Psychology, Brandeis University, Waltham, USA
Older adults report high levels of emotional control and fairly positive mood profiles. Recent evidence has suggested that older adults show preferences in visual attention toward positive and away from negative stimuli; it has been assumed that these preferences facilitate successful mood regulation, but no study to date has tested this directly. The current study induced young and older adults into various mood states, then assessed real-time changes in mood along with eye tracking of attentional preferences. While preferences were activated most when a negative mood needed to be regulated, whether the preferences actually improved mood was less clear.

The dynamics of later life cognitive-emotional development

Labouvie-Vief, Gisela Socio-Emotional Development, University of Geneva, Geneva, Switzerland
This paper discusses the function of emotions in later life development and presents supporting data. It proposes that suggest that changes in cognitive function and homeostatic regulation stimulate feelings of awareness of vulnerability. Whether individuals can integrate those towards growth and expansion or develop a sense of protective self-constriction depends on already available coping resources. I discuss four completed and ongoing studies that demonstrate these divergent patterns in the context of attachment styles and their relation to emotion regulation in the context of emotional Stroop performance, dyadic discussion, and 12 year longitudinal patterns of change in emotion regulation strategies.

S-060: Decision-making in experimental games: influence of context, development, and culture

Michaela Gummerum, Monika Keller (chair)
This symposium explores sharing in two tasks from experimental economics across development and in different cultures. In Dictator Game a proposer is requested to share a sum of money with an anonymous receiver, who can only accept. In Ultimatum Game the receiver can reject and then nobody gets anything. We are interested in children's individual and group behavior in these games, its relation to toher psychological variables, and group negotiations about sharing. Behaviour and psychological correlates were studied in pre-school- and elementary-school children, adolescents and adults in different cultures (European / Asian). The results support the assumption of a simple fairness heuristic across the life-span and reveal processes how this norm is negotiated.

Prosocial sharing and social competence in preschool children

Gummerum, Michaela School of Psychology, University of Plymouth, Plymouth, United Kingdom
This study investigates the relationship between prosocial sharing in the dictator game and social competence in a longitudinal sample of Canadian preschool children. Participants either got training in a social competence program or not (control sample). They were interviewed individually on a number of questionnaires measuring their social-emotional development, and their social behavior was rated by the day-care teachers. Prosocial sharing was examined with the dictator game. The longer children participated in the social competence program, the more they shared in dictator game. Sharing was predicted by children's empathy, but not by their understanding of basic emotions.

Decisions and group discussions in dictator game

Keller, Monika für Bildungsforschung, Max-Planck-Institut, Berlin, Germany Gummerum, Michaela School of Psychology, University of Plymouth, Plymouth, Devon, United Kingdom Takezawa, Masanori Dep.of Social&Economic Psy, MPI Human Development, Tilburg, Netherlands Canz, Thomas
The study interconnects behavioural game theory and moral development. Sharing behaviour in dictator game is analyzed in five different age groups from childhood to adulthood, comparing individual decisions and group negotiations for a common decision. Quantitative results reveal equal split as the dominant offer in all age groups, however adults are least generous compared to all other groups. Arguments in discussion were coded according to different categories. Results reveal that negative evaluation of others' arguments had the most salient effect for lower offers while fairness arguments correlated positively with higher offers.

Implications of these results are discussed from the perspective of behavioural economics and moral development theory.

Formal analysis of children's group discourse on fairness: Application of mathematical group decision making models in developmental data

Takezawa, Masanori Psychology and Society, Tilburg University, Tilburg, Netherlands
A quantitative method to analyze moral group discourse is presented. Instead of analyzing the details of individual dialogues, mathematical functional forms best describing the relationships between individual opinions measured before the group discussion and the group agreement is estimated using the models of group decision making processes developed in social psychology. By analyzing the data reported by the other presenters in this session, I demonstrate that such highly abstract models allow us to quantify which opinion (e.g., selfish or altruistic arguments) is socially amplified or vanished in the course of group discussion and nicely complement qualitative discourse analysis.

Children's prosocial behaviors and moral emotions

Malti, Tina Hall-Mercer Laboratory, Harvard University, Belmont, MA, USA
Objectives: The study's aim was to investigate the concurrent and longitudinal relations between children's prosocial behavior with sympathy and moral emotion expectancies. Methods Participants were 175 six-year-old children. Prosocial behaviors and sympathy were assessed by different observational measures and self- and other-ratings. Emotion expectancies were assessed by a moral interview. Results Children's prosocial behaviors were concurrently and longitudinally predicted by moral emotions, but the relations depended on type of measure, informant, and gender. Conclusions The findings support early links between children's prosocial behaviors and moral emotions and are discussed in regard to early precursors of the moral self.

How Chinese children play economic games

Zhu, Liqi Institute of Psychology, Chinese Academy of Sciences, Beijing, People's Republic of China Keller, Monika Max Planck Institute for Human, Max Planck Institute for Human, Berlin, Germany
This study compares group decision-making behavior of German and Chinese participants. As in the study presented by Keller et al., children of 3rd, 6th, 8th grade and college freshman made an offer individually and then negotiated a decision (video-taped) as a group in both Dictator and Ultimatum Game. Quantitative results reveal effects of culture (Chinese participants give significantly more) and gender (females in both cultures are more generous) in Dictator but less salient differences in Ultimatum Game. Furthermore, a comparison of the qualitative analysis of arguments according to a coding scheme developed for the German data will be presented.

S-061: Integrating western comparative psychological science and indigenous environmental science

Ethel Tobach, Regina Kressley (chair)
Development of new sciences addressing planetary health and ecology of all species has made it necessary for comparative psychology to examine its theory and practice. Comparative psychologists working with species in all parts of the world need to learn the indigenous enviromental science of the relation of people, animals, and ecology that has served people in the countries in which comparative

psychologists work. An integration of the two knowledge sets, Western scientific comparative psychology and indigenous enviromental practices will be discussed by two comparative psychologists of industrialized nations, Colombia (Ruben Ardila) and Japan (Miki Takasuna) and two indigenous scholars who hve been working in environmental science (Diogenes Ampam Wejin [Peru] and Jacinta Mimigari [Papua New Guinea]).

On animals, humans and culture: Comparative psychology in Iberoamerica

Ardila, Ruben Dept. of Psychology, National Univ. of Colombia, Bogota, Colombia
The native cultures of the Americas were integrated with nature and the ecological systems in which they lived. The behavior of animals was very relevant for those original cultures. At the present time comparative psychology has developed as a scientific discipline in many countries of the world, including Latin America and Spain, and their findings could contribute to sustainable development. The equilibrium between nature and culture is a goal to which the science of animal behavior could greatly contribute. Key words: comparative psychology, native cultures, Latin America, Spain.

Development of comparative psychology in Japan: An Asian point of view

Takasuna, Miki Dept. of Clinical Psychology, Tokyo International University, Tokyo, Japan
The field of comparative psychology that exists in Japan today has different aspects from Western precursors in terms of its development. First, with a background of Buddhism, which influenced the general view of wildlife, Japanese did not delineate a rigid boundary between humans and animals. It was in 1887 that Darwinism was officially accepted and with relative ease. Further, I will discuss post-World War II influences on comparative psychology in Japan and the inception of primate research. For example, during the 1950s, neobehaviorism became prevalent, and in 1967, the Primate Research Institute at Kyoto University was established.

Ancient Awajun practices in the use of natural resources

Ampam Wejin, Diogenes Peru Conservation Group, Lima, Peru
The heads of the clans worked for the community, based on honesty and transparency; they guided the community to develop the same mentality; thus community loyalty was gained. The community guided all to continue collective policies: "All for one and one for all." Our ancestors taught their descendants how to treat all resources, e.g., plants and animals. By having knowledge of animals, such ants and frogs, they learned how to deal with their resources. The ant builds a community. The frog selects its food and conserves what it does not eat for the next day. Today the indigenous communities are vulnerable because they do not control necessary resources; they need to integrate new technology with ancient indigenous skills.

The culture that was born of the sea and then turned its back to it

Abugattas, Daniel Center for Environmental Sust., Universidad Peruana Cayetano, Lima, Peru
Lack of information about behavioural and psychological relationships that Lima maintains with its marine and coastal environment (ecosystems) is a barrier to natural resource conservation and sustainability. In addition, the lack of statistically reliable and valid instruments to assess these is critical. A psychometric instrument (a = 0.839) to assess expectations of the future, attitudes, and behaviours towards marine conservation was developed through a pilot assessment of the instrument with local people. With the new and tested

psychometric instrument, scientists had information to guide public awareness campaigns by knowing the current perceptions, attitudes and behaviours towards marine conservation in Lima. Objectives for conservation were linked with behavioural modification programs and recommendations resulted to direct conservation efforts in populated marine areas.

The people of Managalas Plateau and traditional/cultural methods of environmental conservation

Mimigari, Jacinta NGO-Non Govern. Organization, Partners with Melanesians, Port Moresby, Papua New Guinea
Partners with Melanesians (PWM) is an environmental NGO that works with indigenous rural people of Papua New Guinea to protect the natural environment, biological diversity, sustainable livelihoods and cultural heritage in high value conservation areas. The people of Managalas have a special relationship with the plants and animals in the forest. They know their environment; the type of ecosystems and the relationship among each, and have always lived in harmony with their surroundings. However, the Managalas communities lack knowledge about the consequences of industrialized development for traditional practices that impact their environment and livelihood. Solving this problem calls for integrating recent and traditional practices in protecting the environment so that all can live in harmony with the environment.

S-062: Real-world psychology: Lessons learned from applying ambulatory assessment

Ulrich W. Ebner-Priemer (chair)
Symposium speakers have been gathered to demonstrate innovative applications of ambulatory assessment for capturing behavior, physiology, thoughts and feelings during everyday life. Kubiak will report on symptom perception and blood glucose feedback in diabetes; Conner will present associations of the serotonin transporter gene with daily stress reactivity; Mehl tracked moment-to-moment ambient sounds to study participants' social lives; Peter Wilhelm assessed how well spouses know their partners' feelings; Frank Wilhelm examined daily-life experience and symptoms related to anxiety; and Ebner-Priemer investigated emotional instability patterns in personality disorders. Together, presentations support the significance of a psychological science oriented towards real-world behavior.

Ambulatory assessment at the interface of psychology and genetics: An illustration with the serotonin transporter gene

Conner, Tamlin S. Dept. of Psychology, University of Otago, Dunedin, New Zealand
Ambulatory assessment techniques are potentially powerful tools at the interface of psychology and genetics. In this talk, I will present research combining ambulatory assessments with genotyping from saliva samples. Participants (N = 345) were genotyped for variation in the serotonin transporter gene. They also reported their feelings daily over the Internet for 30 days. Participants with the risky genetic variant reported greater anxiety, particularly on high stressor days, compared to low genetic risk individuals. No genetic differences were found with traditional questionnaires. Findings suggest that ambulatory assessments may be more sensitive than traditional approaches for detecting some genetic vulnerabilities.

Exploring symptom perception in diabetes mellitus: Putting ambulatory assessment techniques to clinical use

Kubiak, Thomas Inst. für Psychologie, Universität Greifswald, Greifswald, Germany Kulzer, Bernhard Research Institute, Diabetes Center Mergentheim, Mergentheim, Germany Hermanns, Norbert Research Institute, Diabetes Center Mergentheim, Mergentheim, Germany
In a set of studies, we investigated the use of hand-held computer (HHC) based ambulatory assessment methods for assessing symptom perception in diabetes mellitus patients. Combined signal- event sampling schemes were employed. In two studies (N=20, N=87), our findings demonstrated the added diagnostic value of our approach as compared to relying solely on questionnaires. Furthermore, in Study 3 (N= 59), where we extended the HHC procedure with a blood glucose / symptom feedback function, we were able to observe beneficial effects with regards to improving symptom perception pointing towards novel, relevant uses of HHC assessment in clinical care.

Anxiety in everyday life

Wilhelm, Frank H. Institute for Psychology, University of Basel, Basel, Switzerland Pfaltz, Monique C. Institute for Psychology, University of Basel, Basel, Switzerland Michael, Tanja Institute for Psychology, University of Basel, Basel, Switzerland Margraf, Jürgen Institute for Psychology, University of Basel, Basel, Switzerland
Anxiety is a fundamental emotion that evolved to guide behavior under conditions of threat. Although modern life is characterized by few threats to life anxiety is exceedingly common. Surprisingly little is known about the architecture of anxiety in modern life. Using state-of-the-art methods of ambulatory assessment we investigated a wide range of experiential, physiological and contextual variables during daily life in healthy individuals and patients with anxiety disorders. Results indicate that anxiety episodes in healthy individuals are typically brief and mild, while anxiety patients experience extended periods of moderate to intense anxiety and are rarely free of bodily symptoms.

Assessing affective instability in an emotionally unstable personality disorder

Ebner-Priemer, Ulrich W. Inst. für Psychosomatiks, ZI für Seelische Gesundheit, Mannheim, Germany
The study of psychopathology has witnessed rapid advancements in laboratory research; however, traditional methods are often unable to provide information about psychopathology outside of these settings. Affective instability is an essential criterion for borderline personality disorder (BPD), but empirical studies are spares and conflicting. Using electronic diaries, we assessed repeatedly affective states of 50 patients with BPD and 50 healthy controls during a 24-hour period of everyday life. In contrast to previous studies, heightened affect instability was exhibited in BPD and self-injuries and skills were identified as emotion regulation strategies. Results suggest the promise of electronic diaries for clinical research.

Empathic inference and assumed similarity in couples' daily lives

Wilhelm, Peter Department of Psychology, University Fribourg, Fribourg, Switzerland Perrez, Meinrad Department of Psychology, University of Fribourg, Fribourg, Switzerland
So far research on empathic inference has been limited to short laboratory interactions. Therefore, we investigated how well spouses know how their partners are feeling during their daily lives. We conducted two computer assisted diary studies with 95 and 77 couples. Spouses recorded their own feelings and their partners' feelings six times each

day during an ordinary week. Results based on multilevel analyses allow the following Conclusions: In daily life spouses' judgments of their partners' feelings rely substantially on their own feelings (assumed similarity). However, their inference is quite accurate, even when assumed similarity is controlled.

Eavesdropping on personality: A naturalistic observation approach to studying individual differences in daily life

Mehl, Matthias R. *Dept. of Psychology, University of Arizona, Tucson, USA*

This talk provides an overview of a novel ambulatory assessment method called the Electronically Activated Recorder (EAR). The EAR is a portable audio recorder that periodically samples ambient sounds from participants' momentary environments. In tracking moment-to-moment ambient sounds, it yields an acoustic log of a person's day as it naturally unfolds. As a naturalistic observation method, it provides an observer's account of daily life and is optimized for the assessment of audible aspects of participants' social lives. The talk will address conceptual and methodological issues around the method, highlight recent empirical findings, and discuss the method's potentials for personality research.

S-063: Molecular genetics of individual differences

Marcus Ising, Burkhard Brocke (chair)

The increasing availability of high-throughput genotyping methods provided a major boost for the research on individual differences. We want to summarize recent findings regarding molecular genetics of personality traits and coping strategies, stress response and emotional reactions. Further, we will discuss methodological aspects of genetic and environmental sources of variance for mental and somatic functions. We will argue that the molecular genetic findings of individual differences are important sources to learn about the somatic mechanisms underlying individual differences. Since these differences can translate into disease vulnerability, these findings contribute also to our understanding of pathomechanisms in related disorders.

Molecular genetics in win cohorts

Busjahn, Andreas *HealthTwiSt GmbH, Berlin, Germany*

Andreas Busjahn, HealthTwiSt GmbH, Berlin, Germany Classical twin studies estimate genetic variance (heritability) by comparing trait resemblance between monozygotic (MZ) and dizygotic (DZ) twins. Using the same logic, linkage analysis in DZ is estimating the genetic variance explained by a measured gene locus by comparing pairs identical by descent 0, 1 and 2. Association analysis in twin pairs results in stratification-free quantitative estimates. Trait correlation can be dissected into genetic and environmental correlation, resulting in genetic factors with enhanced power for gene discovery. These methods will be discussed in the context of studies on psychological and cardiovascular traits from the Berlin twin register.

Genetic variation of serotonin function and negative emotionality

Strobel, Alexander *Allgemeine Psychologie II, Universität Frankfurt, Frankfurt, Germany* **Armbruster, Diana** *Differentielle Psychologie, Technische Universität Dresden, Dresden, Germany* **Lesch, Klaus-Peter** *Psychobiologie, Universität Würzburg, Würzburg, Germany* **Brocke, Burkhard** *Differentielle Psychologie, Technische Universität Dresden, Dresden, Germany*

To further elucidate the role of genetic variation of serotonin (5-HT) function in the modulation of Negative Emotionality (NE), healthy volunteers

were genotyped for functional polymorphisms in the genes encoding the 5-HT1A receptor (5-HT1A), the 5-HT-synthesizing enzyme tryptophan hydroxylase 2 (TPH2), and the 5-HT transporter (5-HTTLPR) in three studies (N≥284). We observed associations of different measures of NE with 5 HT1A and TPH2 polymorphisms, but found no association with 5-HTTLPR. In another study (N=66), however, 5-HTTLPR was associated with the acoustic startle response, an endophenotype of NE. These findings highlight the significance of 5-HT in modulation of individual differences in NE.

Polymorphisms in the angiotensin-converting enzyme gene region are associated with coping styles in healthy adults and depressed patients

Heck, Angela *Molekulare Psychologie, Max-Planck-Institut, München, Germany* **Lieb, Roselind** *Epidemiology and Health Psycho, University of Basel, Basel, Switzerland* **Pfister, Hildegard** *Molekulare Psychologie, Max-Planck-Institut, München, Germany* **Lucae, Susanne** *Molekulare Psychologie, Max-Planck-Institut, München, Germany* **Erhardt, Angelika** *Molekulare Psychologie, Max-Planck-Institut, München, Germany* **Himmerich, Hubertus** *Psychiatry and Psychotherapy, University hospital Aachen, Aachen, Germany* **Horstmann, Sonja** *Molekulare Psychologie, Max-Planck-Institut, München, Germany* **Kloiber, Stefan** *Molekulare Psychologie, Max-Planck-Institut, München, Germany* **Ripke, Stephan** *Molekulare Psychologie, Max-Planck-Institut, München, Germany* **Holsboer, Florian** *Molekulare Psychologie, Max-Planck-Institut, München, Germany* **Ising, Marcus** *Molekulare Psychologie, Max-Planck-Institut, München, Germany*

Objectives: Coping styles are affected in stress-related disorders and angiotensin-converting enzyme (ACE) gene influences the vulnerability for these disorders. We investigated whether ACE polymorphisms are associated with coping styles. Methods Using a candidate gene approach we investigated 15 single nucleotide polymorphisms (SNPs) and quantitative coping phenotypes with data from the Munich Antidepressant Response Signature project, including 541 mentally healthy controls and 195 depressed inpatients. Results In healthy controls, SNP rs8066276 and rs4305 were associated with coping factors Distraction and Devaluation/Defense, respectively. This effects could be partly replicated in patients. Conclusions These results suggest that ACE is involved in the development of positive coping strategies.

Interaction effect of D4 Dopamine Receptor Gene (DRD4) and Serotonin Transporter Promoter Polymorphism (5-HTTLPR) on the stress induced cortisol response

Armbruster, Diana *Inst. für Psychologie II, Technische Universität Dresden, Dresden, Germany* **Müller, Anett** *Institute of Psychology I, University of Technology, Dresden, Germany* **Moser, Dirk** *Department of Neuro-Behavioral, University of Trier, Trier, Germany* **Brocke, Burkhard** *Differentielle Pers.-Psychol., Technische Universität Dresden, Dresden, Germany* **Kirschbaum, Clemens** *Institute of Psychology I, University of Technology, Dresden, Germany*

Serotonin and dopamine have been linked to stress responsivity in animals. Here, we investigated the impact of genetic variation of serotonin (5-HTTLPR) and dopamine function (DRD4) on the cortisol stress response in 84 adults. Saliva cortisol was measured during and after the Trier Social Stress Test. Carriers of the DRD4 7R allele were found to exhibit lower cortisol responses. Additionally, a DRD4 by 5-HTTLPR interaction emerged: 5-HTTLPR LA/LA homozygotes showed smaller cortisol responses, if they possessed at least one copy of the DRD4 7R allele. The results point to independent and joint effects of these polymorphisms on stress responsivity.

Glucocorticoid and mineralocorticoid receptor gene variants are associated with ACTH, cortisol and cardiovascular responses to psychosocial stress

Wüst, Stefan *Inst. für Psychobiologie, Universität Trier, Trier, Germany* **Kumsta, Robert** *Inst. für Psychobiologie, Universität Trier, Trier, Germany* **DeRijk, Roel H.** *Center for Drug Research, Leiden University, Leiden, Netherlands* **Entringer, Sonja** *Inst. für Psychobiologie, Universität Trier, Trier, Germany* **van Rossum, Elisabeth F. C.** *Internal Medicine, Erasmus MC, Rotterdam, Netherlands* **de Kloet, E. Ron** *Center for Drug Research, Leiden University, Leiden, Netherlands* **Hellhammer, Dirk H.** *Inst. für Psychobiologie, Universität Trier, Trier, Germany* **Koper, Jan W.** *Center for Drug Research, Leiden University, Leiden, Netherlands*

Objectives: A chronic hypothalamus-pituitary-adrenal axis (HPAA) dysregulation is associated with several stress-related pathologies. Methods: We investigated if polymorphisms of corticosteroid receptor (MR and GR) genes modulate HPAA activity. Results: In males, MR180V carriers showed enhanced cortisol and cardiovascular responses to psychosocial stress. In a sample of males and females four GR gene polymorphisms were assessed (ER22/23EK, N363S, BclI, 9beta). We found significant associations between GR genotype and HPA axis stress responses and with ACTH levels after dexamethasone administration. Furthermore, sex by genotype interactions were observed. Conclusions: Our data suggest a sex specific impact of corticosteroid receptor polymorphisms on endocrine stress responses.

Molecular genetics of individual differences: What can we learn for related disorders?

Ising, Marcus *Molekulare Psychologie, Max-Planck-Institut, München, Germany* **Silja, Adena** *RG Genetics of Depression, MPI of Psychiatry, Munich, Germany* **Lucae, Susanne** *RG Genetics of Depression, MPI of Psychiatry, Munich, Germany* **Siebertz, Anna** *RG Molecular Psychology, MPI of Psychiatry, Munich, Germany* **Depping, Anna-Mareike** *RG Molecular Psychology, MPI of Psychiatry, Munich, Germany* **Modell, Sieglinde** *Director Neuroscience, Bristol.Myers Squibb, Munich, Germany* **Müller-Myhsok, Bertram** *Statistical Genetic, MPI of Psychiatry, Munich, Germany* **Holsboer, Florian** *Director, MPI of Psychiatry, Munich, Germany*

Patterns of personality traits, altered stress response, and stress response regulation are discussed as vulnerability markers for affective disorders. Genetic factors contribute to individual differences observed in these variables. We investigated personality traits, stress response, and stress response regulation in healthy subjects with elevated risk for depression and in subjects from the general population. We observed genetic associations that could be replicated in patients suffering from depression. We conclude that the molecular genetic investigation of disease related individual differences in healthy subjects is an important source to learn about genetic factors contributing to the risk for related disorders.

S-064: Social competence in childhood and adolescence: Issues in assessment and development

Karl-Heinz Arnold (chair)

The development of social competence is one of the major outcomes of both the socialization within the private sector of societal life (family, peers) and the education received in schools and other educational institutions. To determine the personal growth in this competence is a matter of several areas of psychological research. The symposium brings together actual research results on the assessment of social competence that contribute to the multi-trait and multi-informant nature of the construct and that allow for its contextual analyses in terms of group composition factors.

Multisource assessment of children's and adolescents' social competence: Issues in validity, consistency and concomitants
Junttila, Niina Centre for Learning Research, University of Turku, Turku, Finland *Vauras, Marja* Centre for Learning Research, University of Turku, Turku, Finland
The paper discusses concomitants of children's and adolescents social competence, based on multi-source assessment. First, we present the validity and consistency indices of the scale and correlations between the evaluators (self, peer, teacher, parent) and between the social competence factors (co-operating skills, empathy, impulsivity, disruptiveness). Second, we present structural equation models of 10, - 13-, and 17-years old students' (n=985, n=191, n=419, respectively) social competence related to aspects of school achievement, socio-emotional well-being (self-esteem, loneliness, social anxiety, burn-out, depression) and parenting. The context-related effects and developmental significance of social competence to children's and adolescents socio-emotional well-being will be discussed.

Perception of children's social competence in Greece: Self-reports from students, teachers and parents
Metallidou, Panayiota School of Psychology, University of Thessaloniki, Thessaloniki, Greece *Efklides, Anastasia* School of Psychology, University of Thessaloniki, Thessaloniki, Greece *Gonida, Eleftheria* School of Psychology, University of Thessaloniki, Thessaloniki, Greece *Vauras, Marja* Dpt. of Teacher Education, University of Turku, Turku, Finland *Junttila, Niina* Dpt. of teacher Education, University of Turku, Turku, Finland *Dina, Fotini* School of Psychology, University of Thessaloniki, Thessaloniki, Greece *Dousi, Ioulia* School of Psychology, University of Thessaloniki, Thessaloniki, Greece
This study examined the construct validity of the Multisource Assessment of Social Competence Scale (MASCS) produced in Finland on a Greek sample of 4th graders. Participants were 161 students, 122 parents and 7 teachers. Principal component analysis supported a two-factor solution representing the two main theoretical dimensions of MASCS, namely, prosocial and antisocial behavior, instead of the four-factor solution confirmed in the Finnish sample (cooperating skills, empathy, impulsivity, and disruptiveness). The two factors were found in all three sources of data, namely students, parents, and teachers. The results provide evidence for cultural and/or educational differences between the two countries.

Assessing the self-concept of social competence of primary school students
Lindner-Müller, Carola Inst. Bildungswissenschaften, Universität Hildesheim, Hildesheim, Germany *Chudaske, Jana* Institute of Education, Universität Hildesheim, Hildesheim, Germany *Hentschel, Martin* Institute of Education, Universität Hildesheim, Hildesheim, Germany *Arnold, Karl-Heinz* Institute of Education, Universität Hildesheim, Hildesheim, Germany
Interacting in classrooms and receiving feedback on social behavior, students get some impression of their respective ability. According to the model of Shavelson, this information contributes to the development of the self-concept of social competence (SCSocComp) that was assessed by giving about thousand students questions in the Harter-format to reduce social desirability. Language proficiency was tested by HSET. SDQ-ratings (self and teacher report form) and sociometric indices functioned as validation criteria. Indices of internal

consistency as well as a structural equation model investigating convergent validity and a possible moderator effect of language proficiency will be presented.

Social competence in multi-ethnic elementary schools: Looking beyond friendship measures
Fortuin, Janna Education and Child Studies, Leiden University, Leiden, Netherlands *Vedder, Paul* Dept. of Education, University of Leiden, Leiden, Netherlands
An important aspect of social competence is having meaningful relations with peers. In contrast to the research on friendship, relatively few studies have described social interaction networks of children. We studied both friendship and social interaction networks within elementary school classes, while focusing on the role that ethnic identity and ethnic background play in the network processes. We expected ethnic identity and ethnic background to influence the networks. This was confirmed in half of the classes in our current sample. Issues with regard to integration in the classroom will be discussed during the presentation.

Telling a richer story about relations between child factors and social competence in 'Kindergarten' and the transition to school period
de Rosnay, Marc School of Psychology, University of Sidney, Sidney, NSW, Australia *Lecce, Serena* Department of Psychology, University of Pavia, Pavia, Italy *Fink, Elian* School of Psychology (A18), University of Sydney, Sydney, NSW, Australia *Fritz, Kristina* School of Psychology (A18), University of Sydney, Sydney, NSW, Australia
There is a considerable literature linking young children's socio-cognitive understanding (SCU) with their social competence in a (pre)school setting. Relatively little is known, however, about the influence of children's empathic arousal (EA) on their peer interactions; and the interplay between SCU and EA has evaded investigation in the context of children's social competence. We present data from three ongoing studies that investigate (1) the relation between children's SCU and their EA to distress, and (2) the influence of these factors on children's social competence. Preliminary findings indicate that higher SCU moderates the expression of EA in socially adaptive ways

Social-information-processing as risk and protective factor for antisocial behavior problems in pre- and elementary school children
Beelmann, Andreas Inst. für Psychologie, Universität Jena, Jena, Germany *Lösel, Friedrich* Institute of Criminology, University of Cambridge, Cambridge, United Kingdom *Stemmler, Mark* Department of Psychology, University of Bielefeld, Bielefeld, Germany *Jaursch, Stefanie* Instiute of Psychology, Univers. of Erlangen-Nuremberg, Erlangen, Germany
The paper presents five-year-longitudinal data from the Erlangen-Nuremberg Prevention and Intervention Study. 600 preschooles were assessed according to their social-information-processing competence and its influence on social development in early and late elementary school years based on parents and teacher behavioral ratings. Results showed that social-cognitive skills increased markedly within the preschool years showing that this period is essential for developing social-cognitive skills. In addition, longitudinal analysis identified social-information-processing as important risk and protective factor for antisocial behavior problems in children. These results are discussed in the light of previous research and the designing of intervention measures for this age group.

Markus Quirin, Julius Kuhl (chair)
Motivation and self-regulation are indispensable for the enactment of goal-directed behavior. This symposium brings together different lines of current research dealing with the engagement of the left and right brain in motivation and self-regulation. Findings will be presented on hemisphere asymmetries in approach-withdrawal motivation (Harmon-Jones), power vs. affiliation motivation (Kuhl), attention and self-regulation (Foerster), and implicit vs. explicit representations of approach-withdrawal emotions (Quirin). Not least, animal models of asymmetry in approach-withdrawal motivation will be presented (Vallortigara). Implications for psychological models of motivation and self-regulation will be discussed.

Asymmetrical frontal cortical activity and approach-withdrawal motivation regulation
Harmon-Jones, Eddie Department of Psychology, Texas A&M University, College Station, USA
Much research has suggested that the left and right frontal cortices are asymmetrically involved in approach and withdrawal motivational processes. Conceptual models guiding this research have assumed that approach vs. withdrawal motivation is implemented in the left vs. right prefrontal cortex (PFC), respectively. I will review research suggesting, however, that it is the dynamic interplay of the left and right PFC that is important for approach-withdrawal motivation. Specifically, during approach motivational states, the left PFC is activated and the right PFC is deactivated, whereas during withdrawal motivational states, the right PFC is activated and the left PFC is deactivated.

Levels of personality functioning and approach versus avoidance systems: Opposing hemispheric asymmetries for power and affiliation motivation
Kuhl, Julius Inst. für Psychologie, Universität Osnabrück, Osnabrück, Germany
In a dot-probe paradigm drawing on visual half-field presentations, we tested and confirmed the hypothesis that power motivation activates the left hemisphere being typically associated with approach motivation, and that affiliation motivation activates the right hemisphere being typically associated with avoidance motivation. In addition, performance in a remote associate task being associated with a right hemispheric advantage can be facilitated or impaired depending on affiliation- vs. power-related priming, respectively. The findings are discussed with respect to a recent model of levels of personality functioning that suggests an evolutionary advantage of the relationships found (Kuhl & Koole, 2007).

On the relation between scope of attention and regulatory focus: Mediation by brain hemisphere activation
Förster, Jens Dept. of Psychology, Universiteit Amsterdam, Amsterdam, Netherlands
Our research shows that a promotion, relative to prevention, focus expands attentional scope on both the perceptual and conceptual levels. These effects were mediated by right hemisphere activation. Notably, our results suggest that it is the sheer self-regulatory focus on desired versus undesired end-states, as opposed to the elicitation of elated versus tense arousal, that drives these effects of motivational state on relative hemispheric activation and attentional scope. We will present theory and recent results using both diverse measures of scope of attention and diverse inductions of

regulatory foci. Implications for neurobiological, emotion and motivation theories will be discussed.

The IPANAT: An implicit measure for the assessment of state and trait variation in approach-avoidance motivation

Quirin, Markus Inst. für Psychologie, Universität Osnabrück, Osnabrück, Germany

Self-reports of motivational and affective processes may be criticized for their validity. This is because many of these processes are not consciously accessible. Even if they are, individuals can easily bias them, intentionally or unintentionally. A novel measure, the IPANAT, will be introduced for the assessment of implicit positive-approach vs. negative-avoidance representations. Data supporting reliability and validity will be presented. Particularly, a study will be reported where implicit but not explicit representations of avoidance motivation predicted right prefrontal activation in resting electroencephalography. Implications for the use of implicit measures in brain research on motivation will be discussed.

Cerebral asymmetry in emotional/motivational behaviour in non-human species

Vallortigara, Giorgio Center for Brain/Mind Sciences, University of Trento, Trieste, Italy

Evidence collected in different taxonomic groups suggests a general pattern of cerebral lateralization among vertebrates, with the right hemisphere specialized to attend to novelty and execute rapid responses, and the left hemisphere specialised to categorize stimuli and control considered responses. Some of these lateralized functions are manifested as side biases that would be disadvantageous for survival, as in the case of enhanced reactivity to predators approaching on the animal's left side, which leaves prey more vulnerable to predators on their right side. Evidence is discussed of how these disadvantages may be counterbalanced by computational and social-ecological advantages.

S-066: International perspectives on invasion, reconciliation, peace, and security

Sherri McCarthy (chair)

The proposed symposium would include papers from contributors to an international study of citizens' views on governmental aggression and peace. Participants in all the represented countries completed a mixed-methods (qualitative & quantitative) survey in which they responded to items such as "Children have the right to grow up in a world of peace." There were generally more than 100 respondents per country. In general support for peace was high but respondents varied across countries in perspectives concerning the rights of governments to invade other countries, the possibility of peace, the nature of reconciliation, and the meaning of security.

Perspectives on invasion: The United States, Portugal and Germany

Barbosa, Mariana Dept. of Psychology, Universidade do Minho, Braga, Portugal Machado, Carla Psychology, Universidade do Minho, Braga, Portugal Matos, Raquel Psychology, Universidade Católica do Porto, Porto, Portugal Zaveri, Tanvi International Relations, Boston University, Boston, USA Leembruggen-Kallberg, Elisabeth Azusa Theological College, Free University, Nieuwegein, Netherlands

Participants from three countries (100 participants per country) with different histories of involvement in armed conflict—i.e., Portugal, the USA, and Germany-provided quantitative and qualitative responses to the PAIRTAS item: "Sometimes one country has the right to invade another country". An overall analysis of qualitative responses in the sample as a whole showed that "self-defense" and "humanitarian causes" appeared as major justifications in favor of war, whereas the search for non-violent solutions and a concern with ulterior motives (e.g., power, oil) appeared as major arguments against invasion.

Perspectives on reconciliation in England, Australia, Canada, India and the United States

Castanheira, Helena Dept. of Psychology, Boston University, Boston, USA Borrelli, Scott Psychology, University of Maryland, Europe, Malaga, Spain Puri, Ellora Political Science, University of Jammu, Jammu and Kashmir, India West, Doe Psychology, Boston University, Boston, USA

Publications on reconciliation have been more theoretical than empirical and few studies have addressed lay people's understandings of reconciliation. Open-ended definitions of reconciliation from 50 Canadian, 50 Australian, 50 English, 50 Indian, and 100 American participants were coded into two major categories– process and end-state–and several subcategories. Chi squares revealed statistically significant differences among countries in definitional categories. For example, as compared with other nationalities, Australians gave significantly more responses defining reconciliation as a process of forgiveness, while English participants gave significantly more responses defining it as an end state of peace and end of conflict.

Eastern perspectives on reconciliation: Israel and Lebanon

de Sivilya, Helena Psychology, Emek Yezreel College, Kibbutz Merhavia, Israel Yassour-Borochowitz, Dalit Psychology, Emek Yezreel College, Kibbutz Merhavia, Israel Youssef, Rouba Psychology, Boston University, Boston, USA Tastle, William School of Business, Ithaca College, Ithaca, USA Yalcinkaya, Alev Psychology, Yeditepe University, Istanbul, Turkey Turan, Feryal Psychology, Ankara Univerisy, Ankara, Turkey

The Jewish-Palestinian conflict, and conflicts in Turkey, continuing for over 100 years, have clearly visible repercussions in Middle Eastern and Eurasian attitudes towards reconciliation. Quantitative and qualitative responses from over 300 Israeli citizens (Jewish and non-Jewish), Lebanese citizens (Christian and Muslim), and Turkish citizens were analyzed. An apology as a mechanism for reconciliation received moderate support at best. The minority of the respondents who endorsed apology view it as a first step for reconciliation, albeit insufficient condition. The presentation will provide the statistical data as well as elaborate on central themes that have emerged from the qualitative data.

European perspectives on reconciliation and peace: Serbia, Portugal and Sweden

Petrovich, Nebojsa Dept. of Psychology, Belgrade University, Belgrade, Serbia Salmberg, Mathilde Counseling & Psychiatric S, Georgetown University, Washington DC, USA Zaveri, Tanvi International Relations, Boston University, Boston, USA Machado, Carla Psychology, University of Minho, Braga, Portugal Matos, Raquel Psychology, Catholic University of Porto, Porto, Portugal

Swedish, Serbian, and Portuguese participants' responses on seven-point PAIRTAS scales addressing children's right to peace, everyone's right to peace, and the achievability of world peace were analyzed and compared. Results have shown almost complete agreement with the rights in all three subsamples, but also a discrepancy between that desired state and possibility of its realization. Special attention in the presentation will be given to the qualitative responses – participants' explanations of their degree of agreement. There are several categories of obtained reasons ("it's a basic human right", "human nature is selfish", etc) which appear in all subsamples but in different percents.

Latin American perspectives on peace: Nicaragua and Peru

Clinton, Amanda Dept. of Psychology, Universidad de Puerto Rico, Rincon, Puerto Rico DeSouza, Eros Psychology, Illinois State University, Normal, USA Stevens, Michael Psychology, Illinois State University, Normal, USA

The current study, which forms part of a larger international project, addresses Nicaraguan and Peruvian citizens' opinions of peace. A sample of 200 citizens, 100 from each country, voluntarily completed the seven-point PAIRTAS Peace Scale regarding the right to and the possibility of peace. Distinctions and commonalities between countries were coded. Analyses of data indicated a pattern of themes describing peace as the absence of war, terror, and torture, in lieu of which personal and social prosperity and harmony exist. Latin American data suggest that, having lived through war, its absence is the definition of peace.

Perspectives on security in Russians, Russian Americans and European Americans

McCarthy, Sherri Dept. of Psychology, Northern Arizona University, Yuma, USA Medveda, Anna International Relations, St. Petersburg University, St. Petersburg, Russia Castanheira, Helena Psychology, Boston University, Boston, USA Tochilnikova, Elina Psychology, Boston University, Boston, USA Trosky, Abram International Relations, Boston University, Boston, USA Corgan, Michael International Relations, Boston University, Boston, USA Malley-Morrison, Kathleen Psychology, Boston University, Boston, USA

Perspectives on security in Russians, Russian Americans, and European Americans To assess Russian American and European American perspectives on security, quantitative and qualitative responses to two PAIRTAS items were analyzed: "It is important to support the government in time of war" and "National security is essential for individual and family security." T tests revealed that European Americans scored marginally significantly higher than Russian Americans on the importance of supporting the government in wartime, and provided more arguments in support of the statement that national security is essential to personal/family security. Further analyses including a Russian sample will be presented.

S-067: Inference from recognition: Uncovering the mind's adaptive heuristics

Julian Marewski (chair)

The recognition heuristic is a simple strategy that can yield highly accurate inferences about uncertain events in the world. Inferences are based solely on recognition—even when other information is known. It is not surprising that it has stirred a large amount of research. This symposium gives an overview of current debates concerning the conditions under which people use it, demonstrates how this heuristic can be used to forecast the outcomes of Wimbledon tennis matches and political elections, presents new findings concerning people's use of it, and examines the accuracy and use of a related recognition-based heuristic, the fluency heuristic.

Inference from ignorance: An adaptive mental tool?

Pachur, Thorsten Cognitive and Decision Science, Universität Basel, Basel, Switzerland

The recognition heuristic is a prime example of how, by exploiting systematic structures in the environment, a simple inference rule can lead to effective decision making. The heuristic requires only little information and ignores probabilistic cues beyond recognition. In this talk I will present empirical evidence concerning two key predictions of the recognition heuristic: (a) that in their decisions people use recognition adaptively, that is, contingent on characteristics of the decision task, and (b) that people use recognition noncompensatorily (i.e., that contradicting information is ignored). Moreover, I discuss the boundary conditions of the heuristic in light of these findings.

Predicting Wimbledon with mere player name recognition

Scheibehenne, Benjamin Center for Adaptive Behavior, Max-Planck-Institut, Berlin, Germany *Bröder, Arndt* Allgemeine Psychologie, Universität Bonn, Bonn, Germany

The outcome of actual Wimbledon tennis matches was predicted by mere player name recognition. Amateur tennis players and laypeople indicated players' names they recognized and predicted match outcomes. Predictions based on recognition rankings aggregated over all participants correctly predicted 70% of all matches. These recognition predictions were equal to or better than predictions based on official ATP rankings and the seedings of Wimbledon experts while online betting odds led to more accurate forecasts. When applicable, individual amateurs and laypeople made accurate predictions by relying on individual name recognition. The study shows that simple heuristics can lead to highly accurate forecasts.

Ignorance-based election forecasts

Gaissmaier, Wolfgang Max-Planck-Institut, Berlin, Germany *Marewski, Julian* Zentrum Adaptives Verhalten, Max-Planck-Institut, Berlin, Germany

'Bad press is better than no press', many a politician might believe, reflecting the idea that being highly recognized is important to be successful in democratic elections. Studying a wide range of elections, ranging from the federal to the national level, we investigated the relation between recognition and electoral success more systematically. We found that people can and do rely on mere recognition of parties and candidates to successfully predict election outcomes. People intuitively seem to put a high weight on recognition, as it often even outweighs highly predictive conflicting information such as party affiliation.

Identification and success of using or not-using the recognition heuristic

Pohl, Rüdiger F. Inst. Verhaltenspsychologie, Universität Mannheim, Mannheim, Germany *Hilbig, Benjamin E.* Center for Doctoral Studies, University of Mannheim, Mannheim, Germany

The recognition heuristic is hypothesized to be a frugal inference strategy assuming that inferences are based on recognition alone. We propose an index to identify true users of the heuristic contrasting them to decision makers who incorporate further knowledge beyond recognition. The properties and applicability of the proposed index are investigated in the re-analyses of four published experiments and corroborated by a new study designed to remedy shortcomings of the reanalyzed experiments. Applying the proposed index we found that more knowledgeable participants made use of additional information beyond recognition and thereby achieved the highest proportion of correct inferences.

Recognition revisited: The influence of valence, conflicting cues, and non-size/dominance settings

Vitouch, Oliver Inst. für Allgem. Psychologie, Universität Klagenfurt, Klagenfurt, Austria *Zdrahal-Urbanek, Julia* Dept. of Psychology, Universität Wien, Wien, Austria

In the last years, the recognition heuristic has been identified to be a domain-general guide for decision-making under uncertainty; fulfilling both the requirements of existence (behavioral experiments) and reliability (additional simulations). This paper

gives a condensed overview of three independent experiments, demonstrating that the use of recognition information (1) is often intrinsically linked to valence information, (2) can lead to a subtly graded trade-off when conflicting cues are presented, and (3) is not limited to size/dominance settings. Results show that while the definition of the recognition heuristic needs qualifying in some respects, its scope can even be extended in others.

The fluency heuristic: A highly specialized tartle heuristic?

Marewski, Julian Zentrum Adaptives Verhalten, Max-Planck-Institut, Berlin, Germany *Schooler, Lael* Center for Adaptive Behavior a, Max Planck Institute for Human, Berlin, Germany

The fluency heuristic is a simple strategy. It bases inferences on the speed with which information is retrieved from memory. Other strategies base such inferences on explicit knowledge. The mechanisms for strategy selection between the fluency heuristic and these knowledge-based strategies are unknown. In computer simulations and experiments, we show how human memory limits the situations in which the fluency heuristic competes with knowledge-based strategies for strategy selection: In contrast to the recognition heuristic which is often used instead of available knowledge, the fluency heuristic is most likely relied on when a person is unable to recall knowledge.

S-068: Advice and trust in decision making

Matt Twyman (chair)

When a person wants to make a judgment or decision, they may attempt to improve the quality of their decision by taking advice. Such advice may take a range of forms, including recommendations for action, numerical quantities, or graphical representations of data. The question of how such information may be integrated, weighted, trusted, or otherwise assessed before influencing one's judgment is the focus of a growing area of research. The symposium will cover some of the key applications of this research, from financial forecasts and consumer recommendations to risk communication, change detection paradigms, and studies of consensus.

On the appeal of vague financial forecasts

Budescu, David Dept. of Psychology, University of Illinois, Champaign, USA *Du, Ning* Accountancy, De Paul University, Chicago, USA

Management earnings forecasts are an important source of information for investment decisions. We examined earnings forecasts made by corporate managers. We observed a clear preference, and documented higher hit rates, for range forecasts. Our analysis indicates that managers' decisions about the format of the forecasts are driven by their perception of the imprecision of the situation. We also investigated investors' perception of forecasts. Respondents were more confident when they received range forecasts, and expected them to be more accurate, informative and credible. These results support the hypothesis that investors prefer imprecise information if it matches the perceived underlying vagueness.

Compatibility effects in the aggregation of consumer recommendations

Maciejovsky, Boris Sloan School of Management, MIT, Boston, USA *Budescu, David* Department of Psychology, University of Illinois, Champaign, USA

Many websites provide consumers with product information by displaying verbal reviews and numerical ratings, assuming that consumers can aggregate the information across both presentation modes. Research on compatibility effects between stimulus and response formats, however, suggests

that preference consistency is higher (lower) in cases of compatible (non-compatible) formats, implying that information aggregation across the two modes is inefficient. The results of three experiments confirm this conjecture. Information aggregation and preference reversals were systematically affected by the compatibility of the stimulus and response format, especially for high variance products. Decision makers were not aware of this effect.

Determinants of trust in advice: Studies of the effectiveness of risk communication

Harvey, Nigel Dept. of Psychology, University College London, London, United Kingdom *Twyman, Matt* Department of Psychology, University College London, London, United Kingdom *Harries, Clare* Department of Psychology, University College London, London, United Kingdom

Siegrist et al (Risk Analysis, 2003) proposed a two-route model of risk communication in which communicative effectiveness depends on trust in the advisor's motives and trust in the advisor's competence. The model has received support from questionnaire studies. We tested it behaviorally in advice-taking experiments. Participants estimated risk levels associated with various types of hazard (transport, occupational, leisure, drug-taking) on the basis of advice from a government agency and a consumer organization. Greater reliance on an advisor provided a behavioral measure of trust. Results broadly support the two-route model but some of its details are brought into question.

How much do people use advisors' previous accuracy when weighting advice from multiple sources?

Reimers, Stian Dept. of Psychology, University College London, London, United Kingdom *Harvey, Nigel* Psychology, University College London, London, United Kingdom *Harries, Clare* Psychology, University College London, London, United Kingdom

When people receive quantitative advice from multiple sources, they often have access to information about advisors' accuracy on previous occasions, particularly when people receive advice from the same advisors on many occasions. Regression-based models show that people weight good advisors more strongly than poor advisors. However, we have demonstrated this may be a statistical artifact from using aggregation strategies such as taking the trimmed mean. We investigate this by varying the information a participant has available about an advisor's previous predictions. Results show that people use different weighting strategies when they have track-record information, suggesting they do use such information.

Using time series information to detect change

Twyman, Matt Psychology, University College London, London, United Kingdom *Harvey, Nigel* Psychology, University College London, London, United Kingdom *Lagnado, David* Psychology, University College London, London, United Kingdom

Matyas & Greenwood (1990) showed that sequential dependence in a non-trended data series, as used in certain graphical forms of advice, impairs detection of a change in level. In noisy series, it may be harder to detect changes in trended data, because salience of the change is reduced. An experiment investigated effects of sequential dependence type and trended data on ability to detect change. Type of sequential dependence, data trends and judgment frequency are influences on the efficacy of change detection in time series, but the pattern of effects is more complicated than that described by Matyas & Greenwood (1990).

Illusory consensus of opinion and belief updating

Yaniv, Ilan Psychology, Hebrew University of Jerusalem, Jerusalem, Israel *Choshen-Hillel, Shoham* Psychology, Hebrew University of Jerusalem, Jerusalem, Israel *Milyavsky, Maxim* Psychology, Hebrew University of Jerusalem, Jerusalem, Israel

In making advice-based decisions, an important cue that guides people's confidence is consensus of opinion. Illusory consensus occurs when opinions are obtained from interdependent sources. We tested people's accuracy and confidence in tasks that required them to revise their initial judgment on the basis of advice. The advisory opinions were either independent or interdependent (a function of the participant's initial judgment). Decision makers underestimated the detrimental effect of interdependence and, thus, yielded to illusory consensus. Specifically, they exhibited a confidence-accuracy reversal such that they were systematically more confident in their less accurate judgments. Implications for individual- and group-decision are drawn.

S-069: Individual differences in face processing

Grit Herzmann (chair)

Face processing is one of the most important human abilities. There are enormous differences in face processing between people, ranging from prosopagnosia, where learning and recognizing new faces are highly impaired, to astonishing cases of memory for faces over many years. In the symposium we will try to answer the following questions: In what way and to which extent do people differ in their abilities to process faces? How can individual differences be measured? Differences between people with prosopagnosia and healthy participants, between policemen and students, between women and men, and individual differences within the general population will be discussed.

Developmental prosopagnosia and fractionating the face processing system

Garrido, Lúcia Inst. Cognitive Neuroscience, University College London, London, United Kingdom

Developmental prosopagnosia (DP) is a condition in which individuals experience severe face recognition difficulties. They do not report any history of brain damage or visual impairments that could have caused those difficulties. Despite their impairments in face recognition tasks, DPs' performance on other visual tasks is highly variable. Thus, the study of DPs provides a great method to fractionate the face and visual recognition system. Recent evidence from DPs supports a dissociation of face and object processing. We will also present evidence suggesting the separation of mechanisms within face processing, such as facial identity, facial emotion and facial gender.

Variability in accuracy and confidence in face matching

McNeill, Allan Dept. of Psychology, Glasgow Caledonian University, Glasgow, United Kingdom

Megreya & Burton (2006) demonstrated wide-ranging variability (50% to 95% accuracy) in a simple face-matching task. Here we investigate further what might drive this variability by comparing accuracy and confidence levels for policemen and students in a range of tasks: upright/inverted face matching, Matching Familiar Figures Task, and matching from CCTV. Accuracy was found to be generally equivalent for both groups. However, confidence levels differed in the face-matching tasks. Here policemen were more confident than students for upright faces, but not for inverted faces. The implications of these findings will be discussed from both applied and theoretical perspectives.

Sex differences in face recognition: The role of attention

Herlitz, Agneta Dept. of Neurobiology, Karolinska Institutet, Stockholm, Sweden *Rehnman, Jenny* Aging Research Center, Karolinska Institutet, Stockholm, Sweden *Lovén, Johanna* Department of Psychology, Stockholm University, Stockholm, Sweden

Women are generally better than men at recognizing faces and are especially efficient at recognizing female faces. Here, the reasons behind women's superior face recognition ability and own-sex bias will be discussed. By manipulating participants' perception of gender, and by hindering participants to use their full attention when encoding faces, we have investigated how attention and social categorization affect men's and women's ability to remember female and male faces. Our preliminary results suggest that women show an own-sex bias because they allocate more attention to female than to male faces, resulting in higher memory performance for female faces.

I thought I was prosopagnosic, but it turns out I am just below average: Individual differences in face recognition

Righi, Giulia Dept. of Cognitive Psychology, Brown University, Providence, USA *Tarr, Michael* Dept. of Cognitive Psychology, Brown University, Providence, RI, USA

Face recognition abilities are considered homogenous among normal subjects; similarly differences in individual neural responses are not given much diagnostic weight. Our approach combines fMRI with: i) behavioral tasks sufficiently sensitive to capture individual differences in face recognition; ii) "standard" measures of face processing, e.g., the inversion and composite effects. Preliminary data suggest that face recognition performance is normally distributed across the "normal" population, and that individuals differ significantly from one another on measures of face processing. These behavioral data serve as covariates with fMRI data, providing a theoretically meaningful method for predicting the variability of neural responses to faces.

Measuring face processing: Structure and correlates of behavioral data

Kunina, Olga Inst. für Qualitätsentwicklung, Humboldt-Universität zu Berlin, Berlin, Germany *Wilhelm, Oliver* Inst. für Qualitätsentwicklung, Humboldt-Universität zu Berlin, Berlin, Germany *Herzmann, Grit* Inst. für Psychologie, Humboldt-Universität zu Berlin, Berlin, Germany *Sommer, Werner* Inst. für Psychologie, Humboldt-Universität zu Berlin, Berlin, Germany

The structure and correlates of individual differences in face processing were investigated with broad task collections. In Study 1 (N=151) a measurement model for face processing postulating latent factors for Face memory, Face perception, and Speed of face processing was established. In Study 2 (N=209) a modified battery of face processing tasks and indicators for fluid intelligence, general memory, object recognition, and clerical speed tasks were used to replicate and extend the model. The results clearly support the idea that the battery for face processing captures unique abilities reflecting the speed and accuracy of face memory and face perception.

Individual differences in face processing: Psychophysiological indicators

Herzmann, Grit Inst. für Psychologie, Humboldt-Universität zu Berlin, Berlin, Germany *Kunina, Olga* IQB, Humboldt-Universität zu Berlin, Berlin, Germany *Wilhelm, Oliver* IQB, Humboldt-Universität zu Berlin, Berlin, Germany *Sommer, Werner* Inst. für Psychologie, Humboldt-Universität zu Berlin, Berlin, Germany

Event-related potentials are associated with distinguishable aspects of face processing and might serve as indicators of individual differences in face processing abilities. In an extensive study (N = 86) we investigated the extent to which such individual differences can be captured with the N170, difference due to memory, early and late repetition effects, and the old/new effect. Latent factors for the behavioral measures of face processing correlated moderately with the repetition effects, the old/new effect, and the N170 latency. Thus, individuals with faster structural encoding and higher activation during recognition showed better face recognition performance.

S-070: Real-time monitoring of nonlinear processes in psychotherapy - A new approach to evidence-based practice

Christoph Wölk, Günter Schiepek (chair)

In this symposium different ways of real time monitoring (RTM) in psychotherapy are presented. Some of them use paper-pencil-tests, others hand held PCs or mobile phones (SMS) as input devices. All systems generate a broad data basis for high differentiated analyzing techniques, all monitoring nonlinear dynamics of psychotherapeutic processes. Empirical data applying these two-level-techniques lead to an evidenced based practice in psychotherapy.

Identifying nonlinear phase transitions and critical instabilities by means of real-time monitoring: A method for evidence-based treatment control and the timing of fMRI-measures during psychotherapy processes

Schiepek, Günter Inst. für Psychology, Universität München, München, Germany *Tominschek, Igor* Inst. für Psychology, Universität München, München, Germany *Hauke, Walter* Inst. für Psychology, Universität München, München, Germany *Karch, Susanne* Inst. für Psychology, Universität München, München, Germany *Pogarell, Oliver* Inst. für Psychology, Universität München, München, Germany *Zaudig, Michael* Inst. für Psychology, Universität München, München, Germany

An internet-based system is used to visualize and analyse patient's self-ratings during psychological treatment processes. The data input is done by internet terminals or PDA, using different process and outcome questionnaires. Daily ratings result in valid and equidistant time series data. The time series are analyzed by means of nonlinear measures (dynamic complexity, recurrence plots, complexity resonance diagrams, dynamic synchronization analysis), all being sensitive to dynamic nonstationarity. The method helps for the control of treatment processes, and for the timing of repeated fMRI measures applied to identify the neural correlates mental phase transitions during the psychotherapy process.

SMS monitoring of subjective state in subjects suffering from obsessive compulsive disorder, trichotillomania and healthy controls

Wölk, Christoph Inst. für Psychology, Universität Osnabrück, Osnabrück, Germany *Onken, Rieke* Inst. für Psychology, Universität Osnabrück, Osnabrück, Germany *Brandt, Nadja* Inst. für Psychology, Universität Osnabrück, Osnabrück, Germany *Seebeck, Andreas* Inst. für Psychology, Universität Osnabrück, Osnabrück, Germany

In a quasi-experiment three groups of subjects (n=20 each): obsessive compulsive disorder (OCD), trichotillomania and controls rated their subjective state via SMS (mobile phone) over 4 weeks 3 times per day. The hypothesis was, that this ambulatory assessment led to a normalisation in the emotionality of the two clinical groups. Results: The mean values of the subjective state (i.e. mood, activities, physical and mental fitness) remained different from the controls, but the variability of the ratings sent per day systematically declined after four weeks of monitoring. This is interpreted as a normalization of the subjective state of both clinical groups.

Real-time monitoring of OCD inpatient treatment

Aigner, Martin Inst. für Psychiatrie, Medizin. Universität Wien, Wien, Australia Unger, Annemarie Inst. für Psychiatrie, Medizin. Universität Wien, Wien, Australia Demal, Ulrike Inst. für Psychiatrie, Medizin. Universität Wien, Wien, Australia Lenz, Gerhard Inst. für Psychiatrie, Medizin. Universität Wien, Wien, Australia

Traditionally effects of psychotherapy have been measured at the beginning and at the end of therapy. A new method of measuring the effects of psychotherapy takes the dynamic nature of psychotherapy into account and allows us to grasp phases of critical instability in order to gain a better understanding of how psychotherapy works. Daily evaluations in the course of an eight-week intensive behavioural therapy were made. The evaluations were administrated in an on-line computer program called "synergetic navigation system." The therapy process can be displayed with SNS and can be interpreted before the background of the theory of self organisation.

Synergetic generic principles about nonlinear processes in psychotherapy enable better understanding of therapeutic factors

Mozina, Miran Faculty for Social Work, University of Ljubljana, Ljubljana, Slovenia Kobal Mozina, Leonida Faculty for Social Work, University of Ljubljana, Ljubljana, Slovenia

According to Lambert's meta analysis of therapeutic factors the correlation between psychotherapeutic techniques and outcome is relatively small (around 5 %). Much more important are client's life or extratherapeutic (40%), common (35%) and therapist's factors (20%), which are neglected in the classical Randomized Clinical Trial design. We need a new frame of understanding and of doing practice and research in psychotherapy. Synergetics is one of possible new frames. The knowledge about generic principles derived from synergetics enables better understanding and research of the therapeutic factors and that self-organized non-linear processes of the therapeutic action are organized, symplified and based.

Emotional learning in patients with borderline-personality disorders

Remmel, Andreas Waldviertel, Psychosomatisches Zentrum, Eggenburg, Austria Richarz, Britta Psychosomatische Medizin, Waldviertel-Zentr. für Psycho., Eggenburg, Austria Walter, Thomas Psychosomatische Medizin, Waldviertel-Zentr. für Psycho., Eggenburg, Austria Cynthia Mioczka-Distler, Cynthia Psychosomatische Medizin, Waldviertel-Zentr. für Psycho., Eggenburg, Austria Woeber, Verena Psychosomatische Medizin, Waldviertel-Zentr. für Psycho., Eggenburg, Austria Schütt, Astrid Psychosomatische Medizin, Waldviertel-Zentr. für Psycho., Eggenburg, Austria

Psychotherapy is a learning process, whereas a system has to be open, secure, mildly stressed, and well balanced between fluidity and stability. Patients with BPD show the opposite: their mental states rapidly changing, being stressed with high inner tension, feeling unsecure and avoiding emotions. Treatment of BPD is highly effective, when emotional learning is continuously being enabled within psychotherapy. We present data of 25 patients, showing highly effective emotional learning during a 12 week-specialized inpatient treatment. These empirical data have great an impact on integrating different methods in building up emo-

tional learning and an evidence based treatment for BPD.

S-071: Genes and cognition: Lesson from the study of genetic disorders with mental deficiency

Pierre Roubertoux (chair)
There is a longstanding debate on the genetic bases of intelligence. The results from wide genome scan with IQ indicate several linkages but no gene has been identified. The study of genetic disorders with cognitive deficits provide an alternative approach to decipher the genes involved in cognition. Molecular and clinical analyses with persons with extra chromosomal region, deletion, or allelic mutated forms have permitted to identify genes associated with cognition. Animal models have provided information on the neurobiological and molecular pathways from gene to cognition. The aim is to present a comprehensive view of the results in the field.

Genes involved in cognitive disorders of trisomy 21 (down syndrome)

Roubertoux, Pierre Dept. of Medical Genetics, INSERM, Marseille, France
The first cause of mental deficiency is Trisomy21 (TRS21) or Down syndrome that results from an extra copy of chromosome 21 (HSA21). HSA21 has been sequenced and the question is to decipher which of the 285 genes carried by HSA21 are linked with the cognitive profile of TRS21. The gene-phenotype correlation has taken advantage of the similarities between HSA21 and mouse chromosomes 16, 10 and 17. One region including 7 genes and limited by Cbr1 and Cldn14 and two genes (Dscr3 and Dyrk1a) are responsible of most of brain and cognitive impairment seen in TRS21.

Atypical lateralities in persons with genetic disorders and mental deficiency

Carlier, Michàle Dept. de Psychologie, Aix Marseille Université, Marseille, France
It has been shown that mental disability is linked to atypical laterality (with more non-right handedness or more mixed-handedness in mentally deficient populations) but it is not clear if this atypical laterality is the consequence of mental impairment or a specific feature of the syndrome itself. To address with question it is necessary to compare persons with different genetic disorders and mental deficiency. Recent published data on persons with Trisomy 21 and Williams Beuren syndrome suggest that atypical laterality could be due to gene dosage effect rather developmental disability

Genes and cerebellar disorders associated with cognitive deficits

Goldowitz, Dan Dept. of Psychology, University of Tennessee, Memphis, USA
The cerebellum is emerging from its role as a computational machine toward a new role as the conductor of a symphony orchestra. We have been using genetic mutations that perturb cerebellar development in very specific ways to dissect the contributions that this strucure plays in motor and cognitive learning. Our results suggest that there are components of cerebellar function, as modeled in the mouse, that are critical to higher function.

Cognitive-behavioral profiles of children with subtelomeric deletions

Fisch, Gene Dept. of Psychology, NYU Bluestone Clinic. Research, New York, New York, USA Carey, John Dept Pediatrics, University of Utah Medical Ctr, Salt Lake City, USA Simensen, Richard Dept Genetics, Greenwood Genetics Center, greenwood, sc, USA Battaglia, Agatino Dept. of Neurology, University of

Pisa, Pisa, Italy Youngblom, Janey Dept. of Biology, CSU Stanislaus, turlock, CA, USA
Cognitive-behavioral features of children with subtelomeric deletions have not been systematically assessed. We examined 27 children with either del2q37, del8p23, del11q25, or 4p-, using a neuropsychological battery to evaluate cognitive ability, adaptive behavior, emotionality, attentiveness/hyperactivity, and autistic-like features. We found an unusually high proportion of our sample (8/27 or 30%) could be diagnosed as autistic-like. In addition, each disorder was associated with a different cognitive-behavioral profile. Children with del11q25 had significantly higher cognitive abilities, while those with del4p16 were significantly lower. Adaptive behavior was significantly higher among children with 11q25. Cognitive-behavioral profiles also differed among the groups.

Gene-gene interactions modulate adult cognitive development

Chicherio, Christian Zentrum Lifespan Psychology, Max-Plank-Institut, Berlin, Germany Li, Shu-Chen Center for Lifespan Psychology, MPI for Human Development, Berlin, Germany Heekeren, Hauke R. Berlin Neuroimaging Center, Charité Université Medicine, Berlin, Germany Nagel, Irene E. Center for Lifespan Psychology, MPI for Human Development, Berlin, Germany von Oertzen, Timo Center for Lifespan Psychology, MPI for Human Development, Berlin, Germany Sander, Thomas Molecular Medicine, Max-Delbrück-Center, Berlin, Germany Villringer, Arno Bäckman, Lars Aging Research Center, Karolinska Institute, Stockholm, Sweden Lindenberger, Ulman Zentrum für Lebenserwartung, Max-Planck-Institut, Berlin, Germany
Gene-behavior association studies allow investigating how genetic polymorphisms affect individual differences in cognitive lifespan development. In a large-scale study, we tested whether relations among adult age, dopamine, and cognition are modulated by genetic variations. As predicted, we found: (a) that age differences in executive functions are modulated by a common val/met polymorphism affecting the Catechol-O-Methyltransferase(-COMT) enzyme degrading dopamine in prefrontal cortex; (b) that COMT effects on cognition interact with another common val/met polymorphism affecting the brain-derived neurotrophic factor(BDNF), which is associated with mediotemporal lobe associative memory processes. Results underscore the importance of gene-gene interactions for understanding adult cognitive development.

S-072: Behavioral finance

Ekkehard Stephan (chair)
Tax compliance, risk preference, and laypeople's understanding of the economy are topics of this symposium. Kirchler and Wahl et al. show how purely economic models of tax compliance may be improved substantially by psychological explanations. Mölders & Witte look at the perceived fairness of Germany's tax law. Bittner & Neumann study predictors of risk taking by managers, specifically implicit vs. explicit measures of risk attitude. Epper et al. argue that hyperbolic discounting of future payoffs may be explained by nonlinearly probability weighting. Haferkamp and Christandl et al. analyze differences between experts' and laypeople's understanding of economic processes and measures.

Why paying taxes? A review of tax compliance decisions

Kirchler, Erich Inst. Wirtschaftspsychologie, Universität Wien, Wien, Austria
Surveys, laboratory experiments and analyses of aggregate data revealed ambiguous evidence with regard to the standard tax behavior model. This

presentation reviews various studies and concludes that compliance decisions can only partly be explained by the rational choice approach. Depending on the climate in a society, compliance bases on two factors. In a climate of distrust, high power of authorities is needed to enforce tax compliance and increasing fines and audit probabilities may be an effective tax policy. In a climate where taxpayers trust the authorities of social psychological factors gain importance. In this case, fines and audits can corrupt tax morale.

Influence of participation and tax money use on cooperation

Wahl, Ingrid Ökonomie und Psychologie, Universität Wien, Wien, Austria *Muehlbacher, Stephan* Ökonomie und Psychologie, Universität Wien, Wien, Austria *Kirchler, Erich* Ökonomie und Psychologie, Universität Wien, Wien, Austria

Is tax compliance, i.e., cooperation with the state, influenced by participation opportunities and the uses of tax money? In a public good experiment (101 triads, N=303) we manipulated whether participation was possible or not, and whether the collected money would be returned to group members or donated to charities. ANOVAs showed that participation significantly increased cooperation for own profit, but only when the group voted for a risky option. Over time, cooperation decreased significantly more when group members profited themselves. Results suggest that group information – gained from voting and interaction with other citizens – plays a role in tax compliance.

Germany's income tax law: How justice is implemented by the parliament

Mölders, Christina Inst. für Sozialpsychologie, Universität Hamburg, Hamburg, Germany *Witte, Erich H.* Inst. für Sozialpsychologie, Universität Hamburg, Hamburg, Germany

People's compliance to pay taxes is assumed to rise as their perceived taxation fairness increases. Criticism on Germany's income tax law generally focuses on the countless exceptions made. We examined whether these exceptions serve the higher purpose of implementing justice and whether people consider them to be fair. Basing our research on the German parliament's tax justifications, we show that justice does not play the outstanding role expected when exceptions are introduced. However, taxpayers rate most of the exceptions to be more or less just, although no structured pattern of their judgement can be detected. A report on what taxpayers consider to be a just tax rate will conclude this talk.

Implicit attitudes towards risk taking in decision making processes of managers

Bittner, Jenny Inst. für Psychologie, Universität Kassel, Kassel, Germany *Becker, Johannes* Inst. für Psychologie, Universität Kassel, Kassel, Germany *Neumann, Tanja* Inst. für Psychologie, Universität Kassel, Kassel, Germany

Indirect methods allow for the measurement of unconscious attitudes, while direct methods are used to measure reflective attitudes. Decision making processes are assumed to involve both implicit and explicit attitudes towards risk taking. This study examined managers in middle-level management positions to see whether implicit and explicit attitudes towards risk are useful predictors of realistic decisions. An Implicit Association Test (IAT) was constructed to measure implicit risk taking and compared to an explicit risk questionnaire in it's influence on management decisions. The IAT turned out to be the better predictor for highly risky decisions. It can be concluded that implicit attitudes towards risk strongly influence managers' decision making.

Financial decision making: The relationship between time preferences and risk

Epper, Thomas Technology and Economics, Swiss Federal Institute of, Zürich, Switzerland *Schubert, Renate* Technology and Economics, Swiss Federal Institute of, Zürich, Switzerland *Fehr, Helga* Technology and Economics, Swiss Federal Institute of, Zürich, Switzerland *Bruhin, Adrain* Technology and Economics, Swiss Federal Institute of, Zürich, Switzerland

Financial decisions vary in two dimensions: riskiness and time delay of payoffs. New theoretical models, drawing on the idea that future payoffs are inherently uncertain, show that the frequently observed pattern of hyperbolic discounting is compatible with a constant rate of time preference. Specifically, hyperbolic discounting may be the effect of nonlinear probability weighting, another commonly observed regularity of average behavior. Consequently, people who tend to weight objectively given probabilities of risky outcomes nonlinearly, should also be prone to hyperbolic discounting. Based on a laboratory experiment with real monetary incentives, we demonstrate that, in support of the theoretical prediction, individual sensitivity to changes in probability and declining discount rates are strongly correlated.

Views on the economy: Do economic laypeople judge different from economic experts?

Haferkamp, Alexandra Ökonomie und Soz.-Psychologie, Universität zu Köln, Köln, Germany *Fetchenhauer, Detlef* Dep. of econ. & social psy, University of Cologne, Cologne, Germany *Christandl, Fabian* Ökonomie und Soz.-Psychologie, Universität Köln, Köln, Germany

It was measured how economic laypeople (N=1141 German citizens) and economic experts (N=80 professors of economics) judge on various political reform measures. Our results reveal substantial differences between these two groups. Experts judge a measure favourable if it serves certain macroeconomic goals (e.g., if it lowers unemployment or creates economic growth). To the contrary, laypeople mainly focus on the question, whether a certain measure appears to be fair and just. We will show that in these judgments laypeople are influenced by a number of cognitive and moralistic biases (e.g., fixed pie bias, status quo bias, do no harm heuristic).

The pitfalls of living in a linear world: How laymen and experts underestimate the effect of economic growth

Christandl, Fabian Ökonomie und Soz.-Psychologie, Universität Köln, Köln, Germany *Fetchenhauer, Detlef* Ökonomie und Soz.-Psychologie, Universität Köln, Köln, Germany

In a series of four experiments it was examined, how economic laymen and experts estimate long-term effects of economic growth, what influences the accuracy of their estimations, and which procedures they use. Participants were either economic laypeople or experts. The growth rates, incentives, and settings were varied. One study used the "thinking-aloud method". It was found that very different procedures were used, and that most participants clearly underestimated the normative values. Experts provided slightly better estimations. It is concluded that many people lack the understanding of the dynamics behind exponential effects. Further implications of these findings are discussed.

S-073: Psychosocial resources and health in later adulthood: Findings from population based longitudinal studies

Clemens Tesch-Römer, Susanne Wurm (chair)

Health and its development is a key topic in psychology. Although there is an average decline in health over the life span and especially in old age, there are large variations in the health status between individuals of the same age. Hence, the role of personal and social resources for health changes in adulthood is worth exploring. In particular, the relation between psychosocial resources and health behaviour seems to be crucial. In the current symposium, findings from population based longitudinal studies from Europe and the United States will be presented.

The health-promoting effect of a positive view on aging: Longitudinal findings from the German ageing survey

Wurm, Susanne Altersfragen, Deutsches Zentrum für, Berlin, Germany

Recent studies have shown that individuals' view on aging can affect (premature) mortality in later life. This raises the question of which views on aging are beneficial for physical and subjec-tive health. We examined this question with the longitudinal data of the German Aging Survey (N = 1,286, aged 40-85) using SEM analyses. Individuals who viewed their aging as ongoing development maintained better health over a six-year period than those with a less positive view. Moreover, viewing aging as ongoing development was beneficial up to old age and even re-mained beneficial in the wake of a health-related critical life event.

Psychosocial resources and health in adulthood: Findings from the Health and Retirement Study (HRS)

Smith, Jacqui Inst. for Social Research, University of Michigan, Ann Arbor, USA *Antonucci, Toni* Inst. for Social Research, University of Michigan, Ann Arbor MI, USA *Clarke, Philippa* Inst. for Social Research, University of Michigan, Ann Arbor MI, USA *Weir, David* Inst. for Social Research, University of Michigan, Ann Arbor MI, USA

Theory suggests that personality, self-related beliefs, and social relationships have unique and shared associations with health and well-being in the second-half of life. Empirical investigations of such proposals are rare in nationally representative samples. In 2006, a module of psychosocial measures was added to the Health and Retirement Study (HRS). This addition complements ex-tensive longitudinal data about trajectories of disability, health, and economic well-being in co-horts born in and prior to 1953. Multivariate analyzes indicated that, beyond socioeconomic and demographic factors, specific profiles of psychosocial resources contributed to the classification of subgroups with different levels of multimorbidity and subjective well-being.

Effects of age on the associations between personality traits and depression in later life

Steunenberg, Bas Dept. of Clinical Psychologie, Vrije Universiteit Amsterdam, Amsterdam, Netherlands *Kerkhof, A.J.F.M.* Dept of Clinical Psychology, Vrije University Amsterdam, Amsterdam, Netherlands *Beekman, A.T.F.* Dept of Clinical Psychology, Vrije University Amsterdam, Amsterdam, Netherlands *Deeg, Dorly* Dept of Clinical Psychology, Vrije University Amsterdam, Amsterdam, Netherlands

Several models about the relationship between personality and depression have been proposed. We investigated whether personality traits in later life still have a direct or a moderator effect on the level of depressive symptoms. We hypothesized that these effects were affected by aging it-self or by age-related deteriorations. Analyses were performed on the community-based sample of elderly aged between 55-85 years of the Longitudinal Aging Study Amsterdam (LASA), followed during the last 15 years. Results and Conclusions: Personality stays, even in old age, an important prognostic factor for depression.

Pathways into chronic disease: Findings from the interdisciplinary longitudinal study of adult development (ILSE)

Jopp, Daniela Institute of Gerontology, Heidelberg University, Heidelberg, Germany Schmitt, Marina Marina, Schmitt Institute of Psychology, Heidelberg University, Heidelberg, Germany

The development of chronic diseases represents an important research topic. The present study investigated the impact of psychosocial resources on disease development in middle and old age. Based on 600 participants of the Interdisciplinary Longitudinal Study of Adult Development (ILSE) who were investigated at three measurement occasions (T1-T3: 12 years), we explored the role of resources (e.g., sociodemographic and cognitive characteristics, social network, personality, and control beliefs) with respect to the occurrence of major groups of chronic diseases (e.g., cardiovascular illness, sensory-motor limitations, and metabolic diseases). Differential predictive patterns were found which are discussed in the framework of resource theory.

Social inequality, psychological resources and health in adulthood: Findings from the German ageing survey

Herbrich, Ina für Gerontologie, Deutsches Zentrum, Berlin, Germany Tesch-Römer, Clemens Deutsches Zentrum Gerontologie, Berlin, Germany

Consistently, it has been shown that lower socioeconomic status (SES) is related to worse health. It has been proposed that psychosocial factors function as mediators or moderators within this relationship. Models have been developed incorporating these factors into a larger framework and it has been suggested that the mechanisms underlying the SES-health association might be age-specific. Data from the German Ageing Survey (Nbaseline_1996 = 4,838, 40-85 years) will be used to investigate psychosocial and other mediating factors within the SES-health relationship as well as their differential impact in the second half of life.

S-074: Psychology and globalization: Past, present and future

Adrian Brock (chair)

The term, 'globalization' is rarely out of news. It can have many meanings but it is sometimes used to denote the expansion of psychology around the world, often to places with cultures that are very different from the Euro-American culture in which it arose. This process began in the nineteenth century but technological innovations since World War II have served to accelerate it. In this symposium, psychologists from six different countries will discuss various aspects of the relationship between psychology and globalization. They include some of the most prominent figures in history of psychology, theoretical psychology and international psychology.

Impact of globalization on U.S. psychology

Stevens, Michael Dept. fo Psychology, Illinois State University, Normal, USA

Although psychology is international in origin, the discipline as situated in the U.S. grew increasingly isolated and parochial during the latter half of the 20th century. The dynamics of globalization have recently challenged the ethnocentrism and hegemony of U.S. psychology. This paper will highlight noteworthy worldwide trends in psychology and more closely examine emerging conceptual models, research methods, applied practices, and ethical guidelines that are compelling a re-evaluation of the strengths and limitations of U.S. psychology. The paper concludes by posing questions about the future identity of U.S. psychology, including the training of U.S. psychologists.

Psychology in cultural contact zones: Indigenous psychologies in India and the Phillipines

Pickren, Wade Dept. of Psychology, Ryerson University, Toronto, Canada

A decade ago, Dutch psychologist Hubert Hermans wrote about the polyvalence of cultural transmissions at the confluence of contrasting cultures, intimating that culture is to be understood as dynamic, fluid, and permeable. Hermans labeled these points of confluence, cultural contact zones. Using this construct as a point of departure, this paper examines post-WWII developments of psychology in India and the Philippines and explores the implications of cultural contact zones for the future of psychology.

Collaboration between psychologists and traditional healers: The South African case

Brock, Adrian School of Psychology, University College Dublin, Dublin, Ireland Louw, Johann Dep. of Psychology, University of Cape Town, Rondebosch, South Africa

Health services are beyond the reach of many citizens of developing countries, either due to the inability of governments to fund them or the inability of individuals to pay, but many of these countries have an untapped resource in traditional healers. South African writers have been arguing for collaboration between psychologists and traditional healers for over thirty years. These views have long had the support of the World Health Organisation. In spite of this, we were unable to find any examples of genuine collaboration. The reasons for this situation and the prospects for the future will be outlined and discussed.

Psychology goes 'GLOCAL': Psychology's adventure in Turkey as a case in point

Gulerce, Aydan Dept. of Psychology, Bogazici University, Istanbul, Turkey

This presentation departs from a picture of psychology's 'development' in Turkey that is caught up between the direct influence of international relations and global sociopolitical dynamics and the enduring historical, religious and cultural discourses. Against the common modernist developmental view of this 'arrest' as deviance (from Western norms), or the lack of a truly indigenous psychology as something to be realized, it seeks some insights in divergent historical accounts, not only for alternative theories and practices to the hegemonistic psychology, but also for possible revisions of its metatheoretical core in the hands of self-reflexive psychologists.

The lasting past of academic colonialism

Staeuble, Irmingard Inst. für Psychologie, Freie Universität Berlin, Berlin, Germany

Academic colonialism was not only an integral part of colonial domination; it outlasted the achievement of political autonomy. What Euro-American academics celebrate as 'internationalisation' of social science means for academics in Asia, Latin America and Africa that they are faced with a Eurocentric order of disciplines in which the definition of problem areas, methods of research and standards of excellence remain defined by the West. This phenomenon will be analysed in terms of the imbalanced power structure of international academic knowledge production, with a focus on intellectual relations of dependency in Third World psychology and social science.

S-075: Workplace bullying: Antecedents, consequences and interventions (Part I)

Uwe Rose (chair)

Workplace bullying, often labeled by other names like psychological aggression, harassment and

mobbing targets a wide range of behaviour at the workplace. Therefore the starting point for the symposium comments on construct validity of workplace bullying. Inferences one can legitimately make from the current operationalizations will be focus of the longitudinal study presented first. This is followed by presentation of empirical studies targeting aetiological aspects of bullying like working conditions or conflict style. The final presentations will concentrate on interventions and organizational measures against bullying in institutions.

On construct validation of bullying at work: Personal and organisational preconditions

Eisermann, Jens Industr. und Socialpsychologie, Freie Universität Berlin, Berlin, Germany

Assumptions on antecedences of bullying at work are deduced from a causal model in terms of exposures, demands and strains at work. Two organizations of civil services in Germany are examined regarding personal and organisational features in a cross lagged panel design. We test assumptions of how patterns of personal and organisational variables correlate with subsequent bullying by means of stressors and how features serve as protective resources. There are different patterns with respect to two different indicators of bullying: self-designation and LIPT31. This should be considered in prevention of bullying and aftercare for persons affected by bullying.

Towards a job characteristics approach to explain workplace bullying

Notelaers, Guy Dept. of Psychology, Katholieke Universiteit Leuven, Leuven, Belgium

It is the intent of this paper to investigate a range of task-related antecedents of bullying. In this respect, we use Warr's (1987; 1994) framework of environmental features to formulate hypotheses on the relationship between task-related antecedents and workplace bullying. This framework invites testing relationships between task-related antecedents and workplace bullying simultaneously, which in addition allows to investigate the relative importance of various task-related antecedents while taking into account a number of socio-demographic variables. A particular strength of this study compared with earlier studies relates to the large and very heterogeneous sample as well as to the use of well-established, valid and reliable measurement instruments.

From conflict escalation to workplace bullying: A dual concern theory oriented analysis

Baillien, Elfie Dept. of Psychology, Katholieke Universiteit Leuven, Leuven, Belgium Notelaers, Guy Dept. of Psychology, Katholieke Universiteit Leuven, Leuven, Belgium de Witte, Hans Department of Psychology, Katholieke Universiteit Leuven, Leuven, Belgium

We investigated the moderating effect of specific conflict management styles based on the Dual Concern Theory (Pruit & Rubin, 1986; Thomas, 1992; Van de Vliert, 1997). We assumed a stronger relationship between conflicts and bullying when 'forcing' and 'avoiding' are dominant. The relationship between conflicts and bullying will be weaker when 'problem solving' and 'accomodating' are dominant. Hypotheses were investigated within 20 Flemish organizations (N = 5062). Results show a significant contribution from the interactions 'conflict frequency – forcing', 'conflict frequency - problem solving', and 'conflict frequency – accomodating'. In these cases, hypotheses were confirmed.

How do working conditions affect bullying

Roscher, Susanne Arbeits-, und Org.-Psychologie, Universität Hamburg, Hamburg, Germany

The present study investigates the assumption that poor working conditions serve as a risk factor for bullying. 848 employees in three German hospitals answered a survey questionnaire. Several analyses compared employees evaluations of their work environment in departments with high and low levels of bullying. In order to obtain objective results, this study included the rating scores of bullied and non-bullied employees in the same work settings. Results showed significant departmental differences in the working conditions which remained, even when the bullied employees were removed from the statistical analysis. The results indicate that working conditions affect the occurrence of bullying.

Occupational mobility and bullying
de Costanzo, Elisabetta Arbeit-, und Org.-Psychologie, Freie Universität Berlin, Berlin, Germany
This study targets different personal resources and organisational characteristics related to bullying at workplaces with frequent foreign assignement. Mental health is included as a correlate of exposition to antisocial behaviour. A questionnaire was submitted to employees of an administration in Italy and abroad. Changes of social relationships abroad increase the risk of being affected by bullying.

Anti-bullying policies in Finnish municipalities: Contents and recommended procedures
Salin, Denise Dept. of Management, Swedish School of Economics, Helsinki, Finland
The aim of this study was to examine the contents of written anti-bullying policies. In line with recommendations provided by researchers (e.g. Richards & Daley, 2003) the documents typically included a definition of bullying, statements about the unacceptability of bullying and advice to targets. In contrast, there was a lack of advice to alleged perpetrators, little information on investigation procedures and contact persons were seldom named. Identical sentences were used in many of the documents, indicating that the process might be driven by imitation rather than by individual organisational needs, which may have a negative effect on effectiveness.

S-076: Emotions and emotional representations

Christian Kaernbach, Sylvia D. Kreibig (chair)
Emotions have been explained by a number of different theoretical approaches. Two divergent underlying conceptualizations can be identified therein: On the one hand, the search for discrete emotional response patterns within the basic emotions camp, based on the conception of emotions as evolutionary adaptations to prototypical ecological situations; on the other hand, the aim for reducing the complexity of emotional manifestations by identifying a limited number of abstract dimensions of emotions, primarily derived from the study of subjective feelings. The present symposium compares these views, presents recent research, and explores to which extent these approaches may inspire each other.

Emotional experience: Are dimensions helpful?
Kaernbach, Christian Inst. für Psychologie, Universität zu Kiel, Kiel, Germany
Since Wundt (1896) it has been popular to describe emotional experience according to a certain number of dimensions, which often include valence and arousal. This talk argues that dimensional models of emotional experience may not help in understanding the underlying mechanisms. A comparison is drawn against dimensions of gustatory experience. Data are presented concerning the dimensional representation of gustatory experience, and the latter is confronted with what is known on the basic tastes. While this comparison is inspiring fruitful search for the next stage of gustatory

processing, too little is known on basic emotions to profit from a similar comparison.

Pleasant and unpleasant music: fMRI and peripheral physiological studies
Koelsch, Stefan Dept. of Psychology, University of Sussex, Falmer, United Kingdom
This paper will present studies on emotional processes during listening to pleasant and unpleasant music, with musical stimuli evoking similar "arousal". fMRI data show that stimuli with positive emotional valence elicit activity in a dorsal aspect of the amygdala (which is functionally and anatomically connected to the ventral striatum and the orbitofrontal cortex), whereas stimuli with negative valence elicit activity in the central amygdala (which is connected with the hippocampal formation, the parahippocampal gyrus, and the temporal pole). Peripheral physiological data show that the valence of music modulates heart rate, breathing rate, and heart rate variability.

Goosebumps and electrodermal activity as indicators of emotional arousal
Benedek, Mathias Inst. für Psychologie, Universität zu Kiel, Kiel, Germany Kaernbach, Christian Inst. für Psychologie, Universität zu Kiel, Kiel, Germany
While electrodermal activity (EDA) is known as a sensitive indicator of general arousal, the phenomenon of goosebumps is believed to accompany the strong experience of a specific emotional quality. The development of an optical recording system allows for the objective and continuous assessment of goosebump intensity. In the present study goosebump intensity, EDA and subjective feedback were recorded while participants listened to a selection of emotionally moving audio tracks. The correspondence pattern of goosebumps and EDA corroborates the notion that goosebumps may assess an emotional quality that can not be fully explained on the more basic level of general arousal.

A discrete or dimensional affective landscape? Evidence for emotion discreteness from a multiple-response-levels analysis of film-induced fear and sadness
Kreibig, Sylvia D. Inst. für Psychologie, Universität Genf, Geneva, Switzerland Wilhelm, Frank H. University of Basel, University of Basel, Basel, Switzerland Roth, Walton T. Department of Psychiatry, Stanford University, Stanford, USA Gross, James J. Department of Psychology, Stanford University, Stanford, USA
The affective space model predicts emotional response differentiation along the dimensions of valence and arousal. The present study examined two negatively valenced emotional states, fear and sadness, matched on both dimensions. According to the tested model, the investigated emotions would be expected to affect emotional responding similarly. To test this hypothesis, 34 subjects viewed two sets of 10-min film clips inducing fear, sadness, and a neutral emotional state. Emotion was assessed on four response levels: feelings, expressions, physiology, and behavior. Results indicate differential responding for fear and sadness across response levels. We discuss implications of findings for models of emotion.

Arousal modulates affective evaluation
Weinreich, André Inst. für Psychologie, Humboldt-Universität zu Berlin, Berlin, Germany
Studies that examined the effects of stimulus valence and arousal on direct and indirect measures of evaluative processing suggest that stimulus arousal plays an important role in human affective evaluation. The experiments presented here extend the knowledge on valence-arousal interaction by manipulating the prime stimulus arousal in a conceptual replication of the affective priming paradigm according to Murphy & Zajonc (1993).

Findings show that the arousal level modulates the prime stimulus' affective impact on evaluative judgment of the target. These results are discussed in the light of predictions of recent theoretical assumptions about the influence of arousal on information processing.

Distance effects in differential conditioning and choice reaction tasks
Angstmann, Steffen Inst. für Psychologie, Universität zu Kiel, Kiel, Germany
We compare differential conditioning to choice-reaction tasks. Participants were exposed to a series of tones varying in pitch. One of the tones was the critical one. Participants were to respond to this tone by pressing a special key (choice reaction) or the critical tone was followed by a mild electric shock (differential conditioning). We measured reaction time and electrodermal activity for the non-critical stimuli as a function of the pitch distance to the critical stimulus. The distance effect shows a similar pattern for both paradigms. These results are discussed in the scope of the low-road / high-road model of LeDoux.

S-077: How relationships influence health: From large scale epidemiology to daily process research to interventions

Gertraud Stadler (chair)
Relationships play an important role in health status and behavior. Five presentations offer new insights into the behavioral processes that mediate this role. The first presents data from a large epidemiological study of how social isolation influences health behavior in men. The second looks at social interactions and health behavior in cardiovascular patients. The next two focus on social interactions and health in everyday life in healthy adults and diabetes patients. The fifth reports results of a couple intervention on behavior change in prostatectomy patients. The discussant is an expert in psychometrics and biostatistics and has extensive experience in health research.

Family support and risk factors of coronary heart disease in middle-aged men
Julkunen, Juhani Dept. of Psychology, University of Helsinki, Helsinki, Finland Igna, Cornel Dept. of Psychology, University of Helsinki, Helsinki, Finland Vanhanen, Hannu Finnish Heart Association, The Finnish Heart Association, Helsinki, Finland
We aimed to explore the relationship of family support and marital status to risk factors of coronary heart disease (CHD). A sample of middle-aged men (N=1005) participated. A self-report questionnaire was used to assess the atmosphere among family members. Strong family support was associated with being physically active, infrequent alcohol use, and non-smoking. Living alone was related to physical inactivity, heavy drinking, and smoking. For men some key indicators of CHD risk are associated with living alone, or if men are married, with low family support. The direction of causality remains unclear. Men living alone deserve special attention in preventive trials.

Two facets of social interactions: Social support and social undermining in health behavior change
Dohnke, Birte Center for Gender in Medicine, Charite Berlin, Berlin, Germany Nowossadeck, Enno Rehabilitation Sciences, Charite Berlin, Berlin, Germany Plonait, Sabine Rehabilitation Sciences, Charite Berlin, Berlin, Germany Müller-Fahrnow, Werner Rehabilitation Sciences, Charite Berlin, Berlin, Germany
We aimed to examine the sex-specific importance of social support and social undermining regarding

exercise using the health action process approach (HAPA). A cross-sectional and a longitudinal study were conducted in which 108 and 300 cardiac patients participated, respectively. Patients assessed received social support and social undermining from partners and friends. The results indicate that social undermining is more predictive of exercise over and above HAPA variables, particularly in women. Study 2 provides predictions of exercise at 6-month follow-up. The role of both social influences will be discussed under consideration of stage of change, source, and sex.

Intimacy and psychosomatic symptoms in daily life

Stadler, Gertraud Dept. of Psychology, Columbia University, New York, USA Bolger, Niall Dept. of Psychology, Columbia University, New York, USA Paprocki, Christine Dept. of Psychology, Columbia University, New York, USA Iida, Masumi Dept. of Psychology, Kent State University, Kent, OH, USA
People who are happy in their intimate relationships show better health than people who are unhappy. How does this effect come about on a day-to-day level? Both partners in 294 couples completed daily diaries over a 30-day period during which one partner prepared for a stressful examination. To the extent that examinees felt emotionally and physically closer to their partner on a given day, they had lower psychosomatic symptoms. This result held over and above the effects of state anxiety, trait emotional stability and prior day's symptoms. These results confirm the role of daily intimate relationships in health symptoms.

Determinants of support provision from spouses of type 2 diabetic patients

Iida, Masumi Dept. of Psychology, Kent State University, Kent, USA Stephens, Mary Ann Parris Dept. of Psychology, Kent State University, Kent, OH, USA Franks, Melissa M. Karmanos Cancer Institute, Wayne State University, Detroit, MI, USA Rook, Karen S. Dept. of Psychology, University of California, Irvine, CA, USA Salem, James, K. Endocrinology, Kent State University, Kent, OH, USA
In intimate relationships, coping with serious chronic illness, like Type 2 diabetes, can be a relationship stressor. This paper examines support for patients' dietary choices provided by caregivers (N = 85) using 24-day electronic diaries. We hypothesized that daily patient factors (e.g., symptom severity), caregiver factors (e.g., spouses' stress levels), and relationship factors (e.g., interaction quality) each contribute to support provision. We found that recipients' symptom severity, spouses' positive mood, and positive relationship interaction were important predictors of support provision. Implications for future research and theoretical models of dyadic coping are discussed.

Dyadic planning as an interactive self-regulatory strategy in health behavior change: A study with prostatectomy patients and their spouses

Burkert, Silke Inst. für Medizin. Psychologie, Charité Berlin, Berlin, Germany Knoll, Nina Medical Psychology, Charité Universitätsmedizin, Berlin, Germany Gralla, Oliver Urology, University Hospital, Cologne, Germany
Along with other social-cognitive variables, planning with a partner (dyadic planning) was investigated as a predictor of the implementation of pelvic floor exercise. Data of 110 prostatectomy patients and their spouses were assessed at three times up to 6 months postsurgery. Couples were randomly assigned to dyadic versus individual planning groups. Variables assessed included pelvic-floor exercise, planning, action control, and social support. Positive effects of dyadic planning on patients' pelvic-floor exercise were mediated by action control and support. Including a partner in the

planning process should enhance self-regulation and health behavior change.

S-078: Modern concepts in basic research on obsessive-compulsive disorder (OCD)

Norbert Kathmann (chair)
OCD is a disabling disorder with unclear etiology and pathogenesis. However, research has revealed promising models and hypotheses. This symposium exemplifies modern approaches in basic research on OCD. Animal models map brain regions involved in OCD-like mechanisms (Joel). Family studies support the role of genetic factors but also show the need for subtyping OCD (Wagner). Brain imaging studies look at the role of fronto-striatal and limbic brain regions (Kaufmann). Cognitive-behavioral mechanisms like the paradoxical effect of checking on certainty try to explain symptom maintenance (van den Hout). Analysis of memory performance suggests that confidence rather than memory per se is disturbed in OCD (Moritz). Finally, action monitoring appears to be another prominent locus of cognitive dysfunction (Endrass).

What can we learn from animal models of obsessive-compulsive disorder?

Joel, Daphna Dept. of Psychology, Tel Aviv University, Tel Aviv, Israel
Objectives: To use animal models of obsessive-compulsive disorder (OCD) to promote understanding of neural mechanisms, etiology and therapy of OCD. Methods: Several animal models were used to map brain regions whose high frequency stimulation exerts an anti-compulsive effect; test the autoimmune hypothesis of OCD; test the role of ovarian hormones in OCD. Results: Stimulating subthalamic nucleus and nucleus accumbens exerted an anti-compulsive effect. Immunizing rats with a Streptococcal extract tended to induce compulsive behaviors. Estradiol exerted an anti-compulsive effect. Conclusions: Results are in agreement with data from OCD patients and provide the basis for new therapeutic approaches.

Familiarity and genetics of OCD

Wagner, Michael Inst. für Psychiatryie, Universität Bonn, Bonn, Germany Grabe, Hans Dept. Psychiatry, Univ Greifswald, Stralsund, Germany Pukrop, Ralf Dept. Psychiatry, Univ. Köln, Köln, Germany Rampacher, Friederike Dept. Psychiatry, Univ. Bonn, Bonn, Germany Ruhrmann, Stephan Dept. Psychiatry, Univ. Köln, Köln, Germany Falkai, Peter Dept. Psychiatry, Univ Göttingen, Göttingen, Germany Maier, Wolfgang Dept. Psychiatry, Univ. Bonn, Bonn, Germany
Obsessive-compulsive disorder is a clinically heterogenous disease of unknown etiology. The risk for OCD is increased about fourfold in first degree relatives of OCD cases. Molecular genetic findings are inconsistent, results from the first whole genome association analysis (> 1000 cases vs. NIMH controls, 1 MB Affymetrix) are expected for 2008. We will review family and recent genetic findings in OCD, and highlight current attempts to parse the clinical heterogeneity into psychological subtypes or dimensions in order to better identify genetic and environmental factors contributing to the development of OCD.

Functional brain imaging of fronto-striatal and limbic brain areas in OCD

Kaufmann, Christian Dept. of Psychology, Humboldt-Universität, Berlin, Germany Simon, Daniela Inst. für Klin. Psychologie, Humboldt-Universität zu Berlin, Berlin, Germany Kathmann, Norbert Dept. of Psychology, Humboldt-Universität, Berlin, Germany
Neuroanatomic models of OCD emphasize an imbalance of excitatory and inhibitory pathways

within the cortico-basal ganglia-thalamo-cortical circuits. The disease is likely to be associated with dysfunctions of thalamic, striatal, and orbitofrontal regions resulting in deficient inhibitory effects. These brain regions are also involved in reward processing which may be altered in OCD. This is in line with clinical impressions that patients are more sensitive to punishment and negative feelings. We present brain imaging data supporting the notion that anticipated reward and loss-avoidance is cortically mediated. OCD patients were relatively more sensitive to losses and less sensitive to rewards. However, there is no general activation abnormality in the reward circuitry.

Paradoxical effects of compulsive perseveration

van den Hout, Marcel Dept. of Psychology, Utrecht University, Utrecht, Netherlands
Obsessive compulsive patients distrust their memory for checked events and they repeat the checking in order to increase memory confidence. Repeated checking however has paradoxical effects: it decreases memory vividness, detail and confidence. The observations were made in a series of experiments in our lab and succesful replications were reported from Canada, the USA and Austrralia. This suggests that compulsive perseveration is a counter productive manouevre that serves to maintain and increase uncertainty. The main findings will be presented, theoretical explanations will be suggested and applications to other forms of obsessive uncertainty (e.g. uncertainty about perception) will be discussed.

Memory and metamemory performance in Obsessive-Compulsive Disorder (OCD): Time to forget the forgetfulness hypothesis of OCD?

Moritz, Steffen Inst. für Psychiatrie, Universität Hamburg, Hamburg, Germany Jelinek, Lena Dept Psychiatry, Universität Hamburg, Hamburg, Germany
The memory deficit hypothesis of obsessive-compulsive disorder (OCD) suggests that some OCD symptoms may be accounted for by deficits in memory accuracy or confidence. The present study aimed to provide a fair test of its various formulations: (1) memory dysfunction in OCD is ubiquitous (2) memory dysfunction is seen for non-verbal but not verbal material and (3) memory dysfunction affects confidence rather than accuracy. 43 OCD patients and 46 healthy controls were tested on the Picture Word Memory Test, which provides several parameters for nonverbal and verbal memory accuracy and confidence. Replicating earlier work, samples displayed similar performance. None of the different formulations of the memory deficit hypothesis was supported.

What is wrong with action monitoring in patients with obsessive-compulsive disorder (OCD)?

Endrass, Tanja Inst. für Psychologie, Humboldt-Universität zu Berlin, Berlin, Germany Kathmann, Norbert Inst. für Psychologie, Humboldt-Universität zu Berlin, Berlin, Germany
Patients with OCD repeat actions due to uncertainty about their correctness. We aimed at specifying cognitive mechanisms and neural underpinnings of these symptoms. Event-related brain potentials (ERPs) were used to assess action monitoring processes after errors and correct responses in OCD patients and control subjects. Significance of errors was manipulated by monetary consequences. Response-locked ERP-amplitudes to correct as well as to erroneous responses were larger in patients. Amplitudes increased during risky actions in controls but not in patients. The source of this action monoring-related brain potential is probably located in the anterior cingulate cortex. OCD patients show inflexible and overactive action monitoring. This may be caused by chronically hyperactive fronto-striatal loops in the forebrain.

S-079: Wellbeing and coping in couple relationships: A longitudinal approach

Katrin Spiegler, Dorothea E. Dette-Hagenmeyer
(chair)
Throughout the family life cycle, couples need to efficiently cope with a variety of stressors to maintain high well-being. This symposium provides a forum for five longitudinal studies that focus on inter- and intrapersonal processes in couples' relationships. Specifically, the studies examine the role of emotions in the process of coping, the mediating role of marital and non-marital stress for interpersonal well-being, actor and partner effects of coping on marital quality, work and family variables affecting individual well-being on an individual and dyadic level, and parents' specific coping strategies during marital conflicts with children's social and school adjustment.

Coping with restrictions in the family life cycle and relationships with marital satisfaction

Burkhardt, Martina Stuttgart, Germany Reichle, Barbara Pädagogische Psychologie, Päd. Hochschule Ludwigsburg, Ludwigsburg, Germany
Relationships between attributions, emotions, coping and marital satisfaction were investigated longitudinally. Four waves were conducted with initially n=190 parents of three months-olds and n=105 at the last assessment 13 years later. Participants completed questionnaires assessing their marital satisfaction, attributions, emotions (anger, resentment, hopelessness, and sadness), and coping with restrictions experienced in the course of their family life cycle. Structural equation modeling showed the critical role of emotions in coping with experienced restrictions for the prediction of marital satisfaction.

Daily stressful experiences, marital processes and the development of personal and interpersonal well-being

Schoebi, Dominik Dept. of Psychology, University of California, Los Angeles, USA Perrez, Meinrad Dept. of Psychology, University of Fribourg, Fribourg, Switzerland Bradbury, Thomas N. Dept. of Psychology, University of California, Los Angeles, CA, USA
The study investigates longitudinal effects of daily marital and non-marital stress on personal and interpersonal well-being, and the moderating role of marital processes. In two studies, more than 300 dual-earner couples participated in electronic diary procedures. On the basis of diary and longitudinal questionnaire data (two years later), the results showed that relationship external stress spilled over into marital interactions and specific patterns of marital interactions predicted longitudinal increase in depressive symptomatology. Moreover, in a sample of 172 couples, we examined the relevance of marital interactions for longitudinal course of depressive symptomatology over the first 12 years of marriage.

Strategies in coping with daily hassles and their contribution to marital

Dette-Hagenmeyer, Dorothea E. Inst. für Pädagog. Psychologie, Pädag. Hochschule Ludwigsburg, Ludwigsburg, Germany Reichle, Barbara Educational Psychology, University of Education, Ludwigsburg, Germany
Successful coping has often been shown to heighten well-being, especially in couples' relationships. We tested the longitudinal effects of coping with daily hassles on marital quality using structural equation modelling on dyadic longitudinal data from 215 heterosexual German couples. As expected, positive coping was followed by an increase in marital quality, and dysfunctional coping was followed by a

reduction in marital quality. Moreover, in addition to strong actor effects we found strong support for equally important partner effects on marital quality. Results are discussed with respect to the existing literature.

Wellbeing and partnership quality in working couples: A diary study

Spiegler, Katrin Inst. für Entw.-Psychologie, Universität Erfurt, Erfurt, Germany Kracke, Bärbel Inst. für Entw.-Psychologie, Universität Erfurt, Erfurt, Germany
A longitudinal approach was applied to investigate influences on individual wellbeing. The aim was to show that wellbeing is also influenced by variables on a dyadic level. Answers to daily experiences in the work and family domain have been collected from 71 working couples over 14 consecutive days. Results of hierarchical multivariate level modelling demonstrate that on an individual level satisfaction with home life and partnership quality are associated with higher wellbeing whereas work related variables are not. On the dyadic level being moderately satisfied with the division of housework and childcare is related to less wellbeing.

Transmission of marital conflict on the social adaptation of elementary school children

Franiek, Sabine Pädagogische Psychologie, Päd. Hochschule Ludwigsburg, Ludwigsburg, Germany Reichle, Barbara Inst. für Bildungspsychologie, Pädag. Hochschule Ludwigsburg, Ludwigsburg, Germany
Differential relations of marital quality and parents' specific coping strategies during marital conflicts with children's social and school adjustment were investigated longitudinally over six months. A sample of 151 couples with elementary school children completed the Hahlweg (1996) Partnership Questionnaire, a newly developed instrument assessing coping with conjugal conflict, and a short version of the child behavior checklist. For 53 children, teachers assessed children's school adaptation and achievement. Structural equation modeling showed direct and indirect effects of marital conflict.

S-080: Cognitive and socio-emotional changes in four year olds: Are they manifestations of a common underlying process?

Norbert Bischof (chair)
Toward the end of the fourth year several seemingly unrelated competences emerge, among them level-II perspective taking (theory of mind), the use of a temporal buffer to anticipate non-actual motivational states (mental time travel), the consolidation of gender constancy, and a differentiation of children's affective attitude toward their parents. The symposium deals with experiments demonstrating age-independent correlations between the features named and examines the hypothesis that these correlations are due to a special mechanism enabling the subject to reflect upon frames of reference. Moreover, new methodologies in the investigation of emotional consequences of cognitive development shall be discussed.

Frame-of-reference awareness as a key to the developmental changes occuring around age four

Bischof, Norbert Bernried, Germany
"Frame of reference" is a construct introduced by Gestalt theorists to account for the essentially relative character of apparently absolute phenomena. While mostly inconspicuous, its functioning can under certain conditions be reflected upon. This capacity for frame-of-reference awareness is assumed to be specifically human and owing to a mechanism that is responsible for the synchronous

development of several seemingly unrelated cognitive and emotional competences around age four, among them a theory of mind. It will be argued that the adaptive funcion of this mechanism is not primarily "common-sense mentalism" but a new and more efficient motivational priority management strategy.

Gender constancy and time comprehension in early childhood

Zmyj, Norbert Inst. für Psychologie, Max-Planck-Institut, Leipzig, Germany
Gender constancy requires the concept of an identical Self extending from the past into the future. Therefore, the development of gender constancy and of time comprehension should coincide. This hypothesis was tested with 53 children aged 3 to 5 years. In the gender constancy task, participants watched a video showing the cross-dressing of a boy and a girl and were asked about their beliefs regarding the permanency of the protagonists' apparent sex changes. Time comprehension was tested by comparing hour-glasses of different duration. Both competences correlated age independently (rSpearman$=.48$, $p<.001$).

The re-organization of familiar attachment structure in three to five year olds, as tested with a projective doll-play technique

Groh, Eva-Maria Inst. für Psychologie, Universität München, München, Germany Schubert, Johanna Inst. für Psychologie, Universität München, München, Germany
Following a Lewinian suggestion, we hypothesized that frames of reference control not only perceptual, but also affective issues, particularly children's experience of their family "atmosphere". With frame-of-reference awareness developing, children should realize that parental perspectives diverge, which may cause transient uneasiness. To test this hypothesis we invited 104 children (aged 3 to 5) to play with dolls in a three-dimensional landscape offering ample opportunities to express social relations through interactive and spatial behavior. A computer-based evaluation of the play styles, validated by parental interviews, clearly confirmed our expectation. The findings offer an alternative to Freud's allegation of an "Oedipal" crisis.

Quantifying quality: How to teach the computer to interpret and evaluate a projective test

Kappler, Gregor Inst. für Psychologie, Universität München, München, Germany
"Qualitative" categorizations based on the clinical evaluation of children's play are notoriously non-objective. In order to ensure that all subjects in the experiment reported by Groh & Schubert were evaluated equally, without sacrificing the subtlety of intuition, this intuition was transformed into a computer program. First, the concrete play events were protocolled in a syntactically simplified formal language. Next, this protocol was evaluated by an expert system calculating semantic fingerprints for every play. Finally, a neural network detected patterns within these fingerprints, thus assigning the children to psychologically meaningful play style categories. The methodology of this procedure will be discussed.

Perspective taking, mental time travel, gender constancy and child-parent-relationship in four year olds: How they connect

Bischof-Köhler, Doris Inst. für Psychologie, Universität München, München, Germany
Three studies with 183 children (aged 3 to 5) yielded highly significant correlations around .6 (age-independently, .4) between the onset of theory of mind (false belief, perspective taking), time comprehension, the ability to delay gratification, planning for the future, gender constancy, and socio-emotional uneasiness indicating an alienation of the

other-sexed parent. Contrary to the present emphasis on the domain-specific modularity of cognitive capabilities the remarkable correspondence, both onto- and phylogenetical, of these features suggests re-considering the existence of domain-general mechanisms. The nature and possible evolutionary function of such mechanisms will be discussed.

S-081: New directions in cross-cultural psychology

Astrid Podsiadlowski (chair)
Cross-cultural psychology seeks to address a possible ethnocentric bias when psychological concepts are investigated within one (mostly Western) culture and transferred to other cultural groups. This symposium will highlight psychological concepts that have rarely been the object of research in cross-cultural psychology including ethnic groups that have often slipped the focus of attention. This symposium shall contribute to our understanding of culture and its impact on individual's attitudes and preferences by introducing six relatively new constructs from a cross-cultural perspective covering a wide range of topics. Future directions in cross-cultural research and its implications will be discussed.

The functions of music across cultures

Boer, Diana School of Psychology, VUW, Wellington, New Zealand Fischer, Ronald School of Psychology, VUW, Wellington, New Zealand
Music has many psychological functions: It can affect individuals emotionally (Juslin & Sloboda, 2001), cognitively (Levitin, 2006), socially (Rentfrow & Gosling, 2003), and their self-identity (Hargreaves & North, 1999). In this presentation we will propose a holistic model of functions of music listening. Based on a qualitative study (N=222 from 29 countries) the model was conceptualized and a scale measuring functions of music was constructed. The scale measuring functions of music listening was validated across multiple cultural samples. Cross-cultural universalities of music as well as differences in its functions and implications for future research will be discussed.

Cross-cultural perspectives on environmental attitudes

Milfont, Taciano L. School of Psychology, Victoria Univ. of Wellington, Wellington, New Zealand Hawcroft, Lucy J. Department of Psychology, University of Auckland, Auckland, New Zealand
There has been an increase in cross-cultural studies of environmental attitudes (EA) over the last 10 years. These studies have generally taken either an individual-level or cultural-level approach. Individual-level studies focus on cross-cultural variations in the relationship between individuals' levels of EA and other individual-level variables. Cultural-level studies focus on cross-cultural variations in the relationship between nations' levels of EA and other cultural-level variables. This paper presents a critical review of these studies. The review shows that there is considerable variation in the causes and correlates of EA across cultures. Implications for further cross-cultural research on EA are discussed.

Moral values in different cultures

Vauclair, Melanie School of Psychology, Victoria Univ. of Wellington, Wellington, New Zealand
Morality and values are conceptually linked through their mutual concern with obligation and ideals. Thus, values may provide ideals influencing people's belief about what they regard as right or wrong. We assessed moral values by measuring the extent of feeling guilty if a value is violated. We hypothesize that respondents from collectivistic cultures feel guiltier after violating 'conformity' and 'tradition' values as they represent an 'ethic of

community'. We assume that these self-restraining values are also related to a less permissive attitude regarding issues of personal and sexual morality. This is tested with samples from New Zealand, Brazil, and Germany.

The meaning and dynamics of intergroup forgiveness in Western and Asian contexts

Hanke, Katja School of Psychology, VUW, Wellington, New Zealand Liu, James H. School of Psychology, VUW, Wellington, New Zealand
Forgiveness could function as a facilitator of reconciliation and sustainable peace in post conflict societies (Roe, 2007). The present study employed a culture-sensitive model of intergroup forgiveness consisting of representational (e.g. perception of conflict), psychological (e.g. attributions) and process-oriented factors (e.g. seeking vs. rejecting the need of forgiveness). Participants of third generation after World War 2 (East-Asian vs. Western European countries) will be compared in terms of their propensity to forgive the victimizing nation. Furthermore, we will compare the perceived costs and benefits of forgiveness from both sides (victim vs. victimizer). First results, implications and future directions will be discussed.

Critical thinking about critical thinking: How does it relate to culture?

Lun, Vivian School of Psychology, Victoria University, Wellington, New Zealand
The cultivation of critical thinking ability is considered one of the essential aspects of university education. However, previous research on international education noted some potential challenges involved in teaching critical thinking to students of diverse cultural backgrounds, such as that critical thinking being "Western based" concept or that Asian cultures endorse less critical thinking in education. In this presentation, cross-cultural research involving comparison between Asian and Western cultures will be reviewed. Moreover, the proposition of analytic versus holistic thinking in the cross-cultural psychology literature will be discussed in relation to its implication on the relationship between critical thinking and culture.

Collectives in collectivism: Relational and group collectivism of four ethnic groups in the New Zealand context

Podsiadlowski, Astrid Wien, Austria
Brewer and Chen (1997) argue for a conceptual confusion about the meaning of in-groups as a target of collectivism and postulate a need to distinguish between relational and group collectivism when measuring this dimension of cultural variation on an individual level. This paper presents findings from two studies with Maori, New Zealand European, Pacific Island and Chinese participants. If we distinguish between the items according to their content analysis of the scales used, their conceptual model is supported. Additional variance is explained and results show the predicted effects adding to the body of available international and intra-national multiethnic data.

S-082: Participative organizational culture, ethical climate and democratic enterprise structures

Wolfgang G. Weber (chair)
The frame concepts organizational culture, ethical work climate, and organizational democracy represent practice-oriented examples of interdisciplinary work research. Partially, they emerged through organizational psychologists' references to cultural studies, ethics, and political science. Between these concepts interrelations exist, e.g. interventions to improve organizational ethical climate or to promote democratic decision-making in workgroups

interact with basic beliefs and traditional value orientations of managers and employees. Referring to organizational culture, climate, and democracy current analysis instruments, intervention concepts, and empirical findings relating to outcome variables (e.g. innovation activities, social responsibility, role conflicts, socio-moral atmosphere) will be presented. Furthermore, theoretical problems will be considered.

Ethical aspects of organizational culture, climate and procedural justice reconsidered

Weber, Wolfgang G. Inst. für Psychologie, Universität Innsbruck, Innsbruck, Austria Pircher-Verdorfer, Armin Institute of Psychology, University of Innsbruck, Innsbruck, Austria
This theoretical-methodological contribution (conceptual review excerpts) compares research on ethical aspects of organizational climate, culture, or procedural/interactional justice is referring to - foundation within psychological theories (e.g. moral development, social exchange) - foundation within moral philosophy (justice or discourse ethics, human rights, economistic utilitarianism) - theoretical problems (reification of socially constructed economic 'laws' and organizational norms; neglect of conflicting interests; anthropomorphizing) - methodological problems (discrepancy: constructs vs. superficial operationalizations) Combining approaches inherent to considered concepts of organizational culture, climate, and justice that can contribute to solve such problems, research proposals will be presented (e.g. stronger reference to interdisciplinary basic theories).

A look on ethical programs and innovation climate in German companies

Eigenstetter, Monika Inst. für Psychologie, Universität Jena, Jena, Germany Löhr, Albert Lehrstuhl für Sozialwissenscha, IHI Zittau, Zittau, Germany
It is not clear how ethical programs (e.g. ethical codes) are effectively implemented in German companies yet. Nor is it known how these programs correlate with ethical work climate (EWC, Victor & Cullen 1988), affect innovation climate or attitudes and behavior of employees. In a pilot study 132 of 600 personal managers participated. Ethical codes show no correlations with attitudes or behavior but with subscales of EWC. As predicted, they correlate with Commitment, OCB and counterproductive work behavior. EWC subscales "team spirit" and "social responsibility" are related to innovation climate, confirming studies that innovation corresponds with participative organizational culture.

Sociomoral atmosphere and democratic value orientations in enterprises with different levels of structurally anchored participation

Unterrainer, Christine Inst. für Psychologie, Universität Innsbruck, Innsbruck, Austria Höge, Thomas Institute of Psychology, University of Innsbruck, Innsbruck, Austria Weber, Wolfgang G. Institute of Psychology, University of Innsbruck, Innsbruck, Austria
This study examines effects of structurally anchored organizational democracy on perceived sociomoral atmosphere and on employees' prosocial, democratic behavioral orientations. Data result from the ODEM research project. Within this project, 30 small and medium sized enterprises from Austria, North Italy, Germany, and Liechtenstein (542 participants) were surveyed with questionnaires, interviews and document analyses. Based on organizational criteria, eight types of enterprises were derived and pooled into three groups of organizational democracy (no democracy – medium democracy – high democracy). Multivariate group analyses show significant differences between those groups in parts of their prosocial and democratic behavioral orientations and in sociomoral atmosphere.

Culture of participation and its effects on employees

*Horsmann, Claes S. Arbeits-, Organis.-Psychologie, Universität Rostock, Rostock, Germany **Martins, Erko** Organiz.& Business Psychol, University of Rostock, Rostock, Germany **Pundt, Alexander** Organiz.& Business Psychol, University of Rostock, Rostock, Germany **Nerdinger, Friedemann** Organiz.& Business Psychol, University of Rostock, Rostock, Germany*

This contribution describes the empirical development of the "Organisational Culture of Participation" (OCP) concept, which is useful for studying systems of employee participation holistically. Based on qualitative research in eight companies, three types of OCP were identified, which may be distinguished by the actors dominating the participation systems: (1) leader-promoted, (2) employee-promoted and (3) institution-promoted OCP. Results from two quantitative studies indicate that work attitudes and innovative behaviour of employees differ between types. Implications for future research and corporate practice will be discussed.

Works councils in organizational innovations: Role conflicts and potential strategies of resolution

*Stracke, Stefan Arbeits,- und Org.-Psychologie, Universität Rostock, Rostock, Germany **Nerdinger, Friedemann W.** Arbeits,-Organis.-Psychologie, Universität Rostock, Rostock, Germany*

The objective of a qualitative study in 14 companies was to analyse the involvement of works councils in processes of change: What are the particular preconditions to strengthen the competitiveness of companies and to take into account the interests of the employees at the same time? The analysis shows that works councils have to adopt different roles resulting from requirements/expectations of the company/management, the workforce and the members of the works council itself which are in part contrary. The quality and significance of role conflicts of works councils will be discussed, and strategies to solve them will be presented.

S-083: Breaking the habits: Individual characteristics, team climate, leadership and organizational system as antecedents of workplace innovation

Diana Krause (chair)
Despite the voluminous body of research on organizational innovation, the understanding of innovations in organizations still remains underdeveloped. The objective of this symposium is therefore to address gaps in the current literature by presenting new insights and findings on the antecedents and consequences of innovations using different approaches at the individual, team, and organizational level. The results of a meta-analysis conducted in the Netherlands and several single studies conducted in Canada, Germany, Switzerland, and the U.S. suggest that self-efficacy, motivation to change, facets of leadership, and team climate are the most powerful predictors of innovative behaviors.

Conflicts in scientific and economic innovation processes

Scholl, Wolfgang Organiz. and Social Psychology, Humboldt University Berlin, Berlin, Germany
In a study on innovation processes in the fields of Nano and Gene Technology it was hypothesized that collaborative conflict management would have positive consequences on knowledge growth, action capability, and effectiveness whereas a contending style would have the opposite consequences. It was also explored whether there are differences in this respect between scientific institutes and private

firms. N = 300 active researchers and developers answered our questionnaire. The main hypotheses were supported. No major differences between science and economy were found. Top researchers also used more often problem solving. Implication of these results will be discussed.

Individual characteristics of the innovator and leadership as stimuli for innovative behaviors at work

Krause, Diana Dept. of Social Science, University of Western Ontario, London, Canada
To further understand innovative behaviors at work, two survey studies were conducted in Canadian organizations of different sizes and sectors. Results of Study 1 (N = 286 managers) explored the individual characteristics of the innovator and found that self-efficacy and intrinsic motivation to innovate are more important for innovative behaviors (e.g., idea generation/testing and implementation) than other individual characteristics. With respect to leadership as stimuli, Study 2 (N = 340 managers) confirmed, as hypothesized, main effects of delegative-participative leadership and consultative-advisory leadership on the implementation of innovations.

What drives innovative behavior in organizations?: A meta-analysis at the micro- and meso-organizational level of analysis

*Hülsheger, Ute Regina Dept. of Psychology, University Maastricht, Maastricht, Netherlands **Anderson, Neil** 2Universiteit van Amsterdam Bu, Amsterdam, Netherlands **Salgado, Jesus** Uni. Santiago de Compostella,, Santiago de Compostella, Spain*
One of the most frustrating features of the voluminous body of research into the antecedents of innovation is that effect sizes are varying in direction and magnitude, making it difficult to get a clear picture of the differential impact of predictor variables. The aim of the present study was therefore to summarize existing research quantitatively and to compare the influence of predictors at the individual- and team-level of analysis. The meta-analysis included 200 studies and revealed that individual variables like personal initiative and self-efficacy and team variables like team climate and transformational leadership are the most powerful predictors of innovative work behavior.

Leadership and organizational system influences on employees' inspiration and organizations' performance

*James, Keith Industrial and Organizational, Portland State University, Portland, USA **Lahti, Ken** PreVisor, Inc., Portland, USA*
The impact of transformational leadership on performance at the individual, group, and organizational level has recently been the center of major lines of work on leadership and organizational strategy. However, no model has been proposed or tested of how leadership comes together with organizational system operations to influence employees' vision, inspiration and, through it, organizational outcomes. We developed an integrative leadership and system model. Results of two quantitative studies (N = 1,662; N = 70) indicate that model factors are significantly related to levels of inspiration; and that levels of inspiration are significantly related to expert-rated and objective organizational performance.

Organizational learning climate to learn from errors, transformational leadership and workplace innovation

*Kluge, Annette Organisationspsychologie, Universität St. Gallen, St. Gallen, Switzerland **Schilling, Jan** RWTH Aachen, Inst. für Psychol, Aachen, Germany*
Organizational learning from errors at work should be systematically fostered to support workplace

innovation. In parallel, it is widely accepted that transformational leadership supports employees' strive for innovation, excellence and continuous learning. Given that, we investigated the relationship between charismatic goal orientation, passive-avoidant leadership, management-by-exception, and components important for organizational learning from errors (namely error-related leadership behaviors, support of other team members, task characteristics, organizational values) in three studies conducted in Swiss manufacturing organizations. Among other things, results of a stepwise regression analysis supported the dominant impact of charismatic goal orientation on all four learning components.

S-084: Recent perspectives on the development and treatment of Posttraumatic Stress Disorder (PTSD)

Birgit Kleim (chair)
Recent research has increased our understanding of factors involved in the development and maintenance of PTSD, and has started to explore mechanisms of change in PTSD treatment. Much of this research focuses on individual differences in information processing, the resulting difficulties, and on how these can be approached in treatment. The presentations in this symposium focus on factors involved in the emergence of PTSD and on those involved in its successful treatment. Recent findings of studies using various methods in a range of different trauma populations (journalists, road traffic accident, assault and torture survivors) will be described.

Witnessing trauma in the newsroom: Everyday exposure to violent film scenes and posttraumatic intrusions in TV journalists

*Weidmann, Anke Psychotherapie u. Somatopsych., Humboldt-Universität zu Berlin, Berlin, Germany **Papsdorf, Jenny** Psychotherapie u. Somatopsych., Humboldt-Universität zu Berlin, Berlin, Germany*
Journalists working in TV newsrooms frequently watch film scenes depicting traumatic events. It is unclear whether they subsequently experience intrusive memories and psychological distress. We conducted an online survey with 81 German newsjournalists regularly working with those images. Sixty percent reported recurring intrusions and rated them as moderately to severely distressing. Intrusion characteristics were similar to those of clinical cases. Furthermore, the extent of intrusive re-experiencing and avoidance was significantly predicted by self-reported distress with regard to film exposure. Thus, newsroom workers can be considered as a potential risk group for secondary traumatic stress.

Trauma memory characteristics in PTSD: Testing the disorganisation hypothesis

*Ehring, Thomas Dept. of Clinical Psychology, University of Amsterdam, Amsterdam, Netherlands **Weidmann, Anke** Dept. of Psychology, Humboldt University, Berlin, Germany **Gerger, Heike** Dept. of Psychology, University of Bielefeld, Bielefeld, Germany **Ehlers, Anke** Inst. of Psychiatry, University of London, London, United Kingdom*
Objectives: The study aimed to test the hypothesis that trauma memory disorganization is involved in the development of PTSD. Method: Different indices of trauma memory disorganization were assessed in two samples of road traffic accident (RTA) survivors (total N = 248). Results: There was some indication showing that the trauma memory is more disorganized in PTSD patients than controls and that this is especially true for 'hotspots' in the trauma memory. However, results differed greatly according to the measures used. Conclusions: Despite preliminary supporting evi-

dence, the results suggest that important modifications of the disorganization hypothesis are necessary.

Social cognition in PTSD: Two studies on empathy and social exclusion

Nietlisbach, Gabriela Int. für Psychopathologie, Universität Zürich, Zürich, Switzerland Maercker, Andreas Inst. für Psychopathologie, Universität Zürich, Zürich, Switzerland

Objectives: Trauma survivors with PTSD often show significant psychosocial impairments. In two studies, we (1) assessed differences in social perception and empathy, and (2) experimentally investigated social exclusion with a ball tossing game to test social exclusion as a possible maintenance factor for PTSD. Methods: A sample of trauma survivors with PTSD (N=16) and healthy controls completed various empathy tests (1) and participated in the experiment (2). Results: Individuals with PTSD showed less empathy in questionnaire measures and in objective empathy tests. Conclusions: Our results support the assumption of lower empathy in individuals with PTSD following the experience of trauma.

Cognitive mediation during cognitive therapy for PTSD

Kleim, Birgit Dept. of Psychiatrie, King's College London, London, United Kingdom Grey, Nick Center for Anxiety Disorders, Institute of Psychiatry, London, United Kingdom Hackman, Ann Psychiatry, Oxford University, Oxford, United Kingdom Wild, Jennifer Psychology, Institute of Psychiatry, London, United Kingdom Ehlers, Anke Inst. of Psychiatry, University of London, London, United Kingdom

Objectives: Cognitive Therapy for PTSD (CT, Ehlers & Clark, 2000) has been shown to be effective, but there is yet little empirical evidence on the hypothesized mechanisms of change. We tested the hypothesis that change in appraisals characteristic for PTSD mediate symptom reduction with treatment, and that appraisal change precedes symptom change. Methods: We analysed weekly measures from CT sessions. Results: Preliminary analyses suggested that change in cognitive appraisals from initial assessment to mid-treatment mediate symptom reduction with CT from by the end of treatment. Conclusion: Symptom reduction in cognitive PTSD therapy can be explained by cognitive change during therapy.

Efficacy and feasibility of CBT biofeedback in traumatised migrants

Knaevelsrud, Christine Research, Center for Torture Victims, Berlin, Germany Karl, Anke School of Psychology, University of Southampton, Southampton, United Kingdom Denke, Claudia Charite Virchow-Clinic, Department of Anaesthesiology, Berlin, Germany Müller, Julia Department of Psychiatry, University Hospital Zürich, Zürich, Switzerland

Background: Somatoform pain disorder (SPD) and PTSD are frequently seen in migrants. We examined the efficacy and feasibility of a short-term CBT-biofeedback (BF) approach focusing on trauma-related pain. Method: We treated 11 migrants suffering from SPD and PTSD with BF. Before and after treatment and at 3 months follow-up psychiatric status, pain related conditions and psychotherapy toleration was assessed. Results: We found significantly increased cognitive and behavioral pain-related coping and significant reduction of heart rate reactivity to stressful and painful diagnostic conditions after treatment and at follow-up. Conclusion: Findings are in support of BF intervention for management of trauma-related pain.

Annekathrin Schacht (chair)

Emotional stimuli tend to involuntarily draw attentional resources and elicit preferential and sustained processing, possibly caused by their high intrinsic relevance. This symposium focuses on the processing of emotional aspects of written or spoken language and its neurophysiological substrates. Results will be presented from intracranial recordings during emotional prosody encoding and from different reading paradigms using event-related potentials, ranging from single words to complex sentences. Further, different effects of positive and negative emotional valence on memory performance are investigated. In a final section the presented data will be summarized and integrated by a discussant.

The synchronized brain in emotional prosody decoding

Grandjean, Didier Dept. of Psychology, University of Geneva, Geneva, Switzerland

How are emotionally salient events perceived and represented by our central nervous system? How do neuronal assemblies interact to allow humans to have appropriate adaptive responses to cope with unexpected situations? Local field potentials (LFPs) obtained by intracranial recordings in humans can be studied using recent methods in order to better understand distributed neural networks involved in emotional prosody decoding. The quantification of neuronal synchrony of LFPs now allows us to measure how the neuronal activities of distant brain regions interact dynamically during the perception of emotionally relevant events. Evidences of amygdala and orbito-frontal neuronal coupling will be discussed.

Detecting and remembering emotional words

Kensinger, Elizabeth Dept. of Psychology, Boston College, Chestnut Hill, USA

Emotional words are detected and remembered more often than nonemotional words. However, the valence of the words (whether pleasant or unpleasant) influences the processes that support these enhancements. Negative words seem to capture attention, resulting in poorer memory for words presented in proximity to those negative words. Detection of positive words, by contrast, results in no detrimental effects on memory for surrounding words. In fact, detection of positive arousing words seems to broaden attention, making people more likely to notice and remember other words presented in close temporal proximity to the positive words.

Emotional connotation in spontaneous word processing

Kissler, Johanna Inst. für Psychologie, Universität Konstanz, Konstanz, Germany

When people read sequences of words varying in emotional connotation, event-related potentials (ERPs) to the pleasantly and unpleasantly arousing words differ from ERPs to the neutral ones. Distinct effects are found at functionally different stages in the processing stream: An early posterior negativity is reliably enhanced during reading of emotionally arousing words, possibly reflecting facilitation of lexical access. Second, the late positive potential (LPP) is also enlarged to emotionally significant words, but it displays a more variable pattern, often with an advantage for pleasant contents. The emotional modulation of the LPP during reading is paralleled by subsequent incidental memory performance.

Contributions of emotional valence and arousal to visual word processing in sentences: Central and peripheral psychophysiological indicators

Bayer, Mareike Inst. für Psychologie, Humboldt-Universität zu Berlin, Berlin, Germany Schacht, Annekathrin Department of Psychology, Humboldt-University at Berlin, Berlin, Germany Sommer, Werner Department of Psychology, Humboldt-University at Berlin, Berlin, Germany

Dimensional models describe emotions as a function of valence and arousal. In event-related potentials (ERPs), both pictorial and verbal emotional stimuli elicit effects in the Late Positive Complex (LPC), but so far it remains unclear, to what extent these effects are attributable to emotional valence or arousal. In the present study, subjects performed a semantic decision task on sentences with neutral, syntactically correct initial sentence parts, and negative and neutral verbs at the final position. Irrespective of valence, pure arousal affected early stages of word processing but not the LPC, an effect that seems to be unreported as yet.

Emotion in word and face processing: Early and late cortical responses

Schacht, Annekathrin Inst. für Psychologie, Humboldt-Universität zu Berlin, Berlin, Germany Sommer, Werner Department of Psychology, Humboldt-University at Berlin, Berlin, Germany

For the first time we directly compared emotion effects in word and face processing on event-related brain potentials (ERPs). Participants performed lexical decisions on emotionally positive, negative, and neutral verbs, and decisions on the integrity of happy, angry, and neutral faces. Two emotion effects were found in both domains: Enhancements of a Late Positive Complex were seen at comparable latencies but with different scalp distribution, indicating contributions of domain-specific brain systems. Still earlier emotion effects, apparently arising in domain-general brain systems occurred much faster for faces than words corroborating more rapid access to emotional meaning in faces.

Ilan Meyer, Theo Sandfort (chair)

Minority stress theory suggests that lesbians, gay men, and bisexuals (LGB) are exposed to more stress related to stigma, prejudice, and discrimination than their heterosexual counterparts and that this stress leads to more health problems among LGBs. However, little research has examined minority stress cross-culturally. Yet, only in cross-cultural comparisons can the unique aspects of the social environment stand out. Our symposium addresses this gap in research by bringing together researchers who study cultures that vary in the level of acceptance of homosexuality and legal protections afforded LGBs. We critically assess cross-cultural differences and commonalities in minority stress and health.

Cultural and structural determinants of acceptance of homosexuality: A cross national comparison

Sandfort, Theo Psychiatry, Columbia University, New York, USA

Although worldwide acceptance of homosexuality is increasing, there are substantial differences in the acceptance of homosexuality between countries. Based on the World Values Survey and additional data sources, we compared over 40 countries. Acceptance of homosexuality could be predicted by the extent to which countries have values favoring self-expression versus group survival and secular versus traditional values. These value patterns have been shown to be strongly informed by economic development. Countries in which tolerance had increased over recent decades showed less uncertainty avoidance. These findings challenge our thinking about how to further acceptance of homosexuality in less fortunate situations.

Minority stress and quality of life in Flemish gays, lesbians and bisexuals
Vincke, John Dept. of Sociology, Voorzitter Vakgroep Sociologie, Gent, Belgium *von Lengerke, Thomas* Med. Psychologie (OE 5430), Medizin. Hochschule Hannover, Hannover, Germany
Objectives: To investigate the impact of internalised homophobia, stigma consciousness and being discriminated at work as indicators of minority stress. Methods: On line survey of 2921 respondents. Male (66.5%). Age distribution : < 26yrs 42%, 27-45 yrs 43.7%, > 45% 14.3%. 70% finished higher education (university 29.2%; non university 39.9%). We used analysis of variance and multiple regression analysis. Results: Internalised homophobia (beta – 0.191; 0.307), stigma consciousness (beta -0.208; 0.309) and experience of discrimination (beta -0.172;0.228) lead to a perception of bad physical health and depression. Conclusions: Internal and external stressors related to minority status result in lower experienced levels of quality of life.

Relationship problems, sexual violence and health care needs: A comparison between Dutch lesbian, gay, bisexual and heterosexual individuals
Kuyper, Lisette Research Department, Rutgers Nisso Groep, Utrecht, Netherlands
Objective Assuming that sexual minority stress leads to sexual health problems, we examined whether LGBs (lesbians, gays and bisexuals) have more relational stress, experiences with sexual violence, and health care needs than heterosexuals. Method Data from a population survey (n = 4285) on sexual health in the Netherlands is used to test the differences between LGBs and heterosexual persons. Results LGBs had more frequently experienced sexual violence, reported more relational stress, and had a higher need for health care than heterosexuals. Conclusion Probably due to minority stress, Dutch sexual minorities have more sexual health problems than their heterosexual counterparts.

The unbearable comfort of privacy: Experiences of transparent closet in Slovenia
Kuhar, Roman Faculty of Arts - Sociology, University of Ljubljana, Ljubljana, Slovenia
The paper is based on the research on everyday life of gays and lesbians in Slovenia (N=443) which showed that for gays and lesbians public space often functions as a panopticon, where the threat of violence, even if manifested only in the form of subtle regulating processes (meaningful looks, stares or whistles), contributes to self-control and mimicry. Similarly when an individual comes out in the family, the information is often noted but pushed aside, establishing a transparent (or family) closet with implicit expectations that "this subject" should not be discussed. In both cases a form of "privatization" of homosexuality takes place contributing to stress situations, discussed in the paper.

Factors affecting vulnerability to depression among South African gay men and lesbians
Nel, Juan Centre for Applied Psychology, University of South Africa, Pretoria, South Africa *Polders, Louise* Psychology, University of South Africa, Pretoria, South Africa
Risk factors consistently cited in the literature on depression among gay men and lesbian women were examined in this Masters study to determine their ability to predict vulnerability to depression. Data was collected from 385 participants who self-

identified as lesbian or gay in metropolitan Gauteng, South Africa, using a purposive quota sampling technique to ensure representation across age, gender, race and socio-economic status lines. Multiple regression analysis indicated that lowered self-esteem and more frequent experiences of hate speech were the only significant predictors of vulnerability to depression. The regression model accounted for 21.7% of the variance in vulnerability to depression scores.

Social stress and mental health outcomes in lesbians, gay men and bisexuals: Divergences and commonalities in cross-cultural perspectives
Meyer, Ilan Mailman School of Publ. Health, Columbia University, New York, USA
Results from Project Stride, a study of minority stress regarding sexual orientation, race/ethnicity and gender in 524 NYC lesbian, gay men, and bisexuals (LGB). Hypotheses: disadvantaged social position is related to excess exposure to social stress and increase in rates of mental disorders. The evidence is mixed, supporting social stress prediction sometimes (e.g., regarding social stress exposure among blacks and Latinos) but contradicting it in other instances (e.g., regarding rates of disorders of black and Latino LGBs). I will discuss the implication of this and other research presented in the symposium to minority stress theory.

S-087: Towards an interdisciplinary understanding of aesthetic emotions

Winfried Menninghaus, Klaus R. Scherer (chair)
The symposium is aimed at reviewing and redirecting recent research on the distinctive features of art-related emotions. While current research on the topic receives only marginal attention within the fields of psychology, philosophy,and the neurocognitive sciences, and moreover lacks interdisciplinary cooperation, the symposium will bring together psychologists with scholars from philosophical aesthetics, rhetoric, and literary studies. Papers will focus on the crucial – and mostly unresolved – question of how to demarcate "real" emotions, "represented" emotions, and, most importantly, the specific kind of "aesthetic emotions" elicited by the artistic representation itself.

Psychology and the art: Perception, cognition and fluency?
Leder, Helmut Inst. für Psychologie, Universität Wien, Wien, Austria *Jacobs, Arthur* Bildung und Psychologie, Freie Universität Berlin, Berlin, Germany
A recently proposed psychological model aims at specifying the cognitive and emotional processes involved in processing of art (Leder, et al., 2004). Concerning aesthetic emotions the model claims that changes of affect and emotion can occur at any processing stage eventually resulting in strong positive aesthetic emotions. We discuss how the possible emotions elicited by the processing of artworks are in accordance with psychological approaches of affect and emotion. Moreover, we present results from experimental studies in which effects of fluency in aesthetic appreciation were investigated, and give an outlook on paradigms that might contribute to solve the open questions.

Cold narrators: Modern fiction and the power of unspoken emotion
von Koppenfels, Martin Fak. für Ling. und Literaturw., Universität Bielefeld, Bielefeld, Germany
Modern fiction is rich in instances of indirect emotional communication. The wide-spread phenomenon of "cold" narrative yielding strong emotional effects in the reader can be considered on various levels: first, historically, in its relation to a dominant emotional discourse; second, from a

functional, and thirdly, from an aesthetic point of view. The paradox of "non-verbal" emotional transactions taking place in the exclusively verbal medium of literary narrative raises questions concerning the nature of textual emotions: How are they negotiated between text, reader and society? Can we call them "fictional" in the same way we speak about fictional plots or characters?

Prolegomena to a theory of aesthetic 'feelings' in the wake of Aristotle and Kant
Menninghaus, Winfried Comparative Literature, Freie Universität Berlin, Berlin, Germany
Starting with Aristotle's account of the pleasure taken in the tragic mimesis of uxoricide or parricide –, apparently paradoxical features have haunted theories of aesthetic emotion. The paper will argue that most accounts of these theories fail to systematically maintain two key distinctions: first, the basic differences between real emotions and their artful simulation, and, secondly, Aristotle's and Kant's indications that aesthetic pleasure must primarily be accounted for in purely dimensional terms, with interplays of represented discrete emotions serving to promote such pleasure. Implications for notions of "catharsis", "affect conversion", and other functional hypotheses will be discussed.

Aesthetic vs. utilitarian emotions in listening to music
Scherer, Klaus R. CISA, Universität Genf, Genf, Switzerland
Research on emotional reactions to music has been limited by an excessive reliance on basic emotion models. While some program music may iconically represent fear or anger, these basic emotions will rarely be elicited as they are "utilitarian" in the sense of serving situationally appropriate adjustment functions. It is suggested that psychological research on affective reactions to music should focus on subtler forms of emotion and specifically the "aesthetic" emotions which are generally neglected by established emotion theories (largely due to hypocognition and the lack of readily available verbal labels). The theoretical analysis is illustrated with research examples.

On the relationship between curiosity and affect in Euripides' Bacchae
Schlesier, Renate Inst. für Religionsstudien, Freie Universität Berlin, Berlin, Germany
In approaching the relationship between curiosity and affect in ancient Greek tragedy, one encounters an immediate problem: there are no synonyms for the terms curiosity and affect in ancient Greek language, at least before the emergence of philosophical theories of emotion. On the other hand, curiosity as a phenomenon is clearly exhibited in some Greek tragedies, as an intellectual and emotional behavior which leads to serious consequences. This issue will be addressed in the contribution.

S-088: Media as a go-between nature and nurture

Frank Schwab, Dagmar Unz (chair)
Since the 1980ies evolutionary thinking is more and more of note in psychology, not only focussing on cognitive processes, but also broaching the issues of art, aesthetics, media, literature and entertainment. Sherry (2004) criticized traditional "media effects"-theories for their nature blindness and described them as "learning-only approaches" thus asking for an integration of biological, neurological and genetic aspects in media research. The panel addresses the question to what extend the media can be analyzed as a go between nature and nurture. The contributions refer to traditional and

new media, to processes of media selection and reception, and to media effects.

The neurophysiology perspective in media psychology

Weber, Rene Dept. of Communication, University of California, Santa Barbara, CA, USA **Sherry, John** Communication, Michigan State University, East Lansing, USA

In this presentation, we argue for an updating of the ontology and epistemology of our field to better reflect current advances in scientific thought. To this end, we advance an approach to media and communication science that embraces a neurophysiological perspective and includes a move toward 'why' explanations based on probabilistic relationships, dynamic systems theory, evolutionary explanations, an emphasis on emergence, and openness to exploratory and descriptive research. We describe such a perspective for those not familiar with this approach, enumerate key distinctions, provide an introduction to the methodologies used, and give examples of current work in this vein.

Digit Ratio (2D:4D) and theatre movie selection and preferences

Schwab, Frank Medien und Organ.-Psychologie, Universität des Saarlandes, Saarbrücken, Germany **Unz, Dagmar C.** media & organ. psychology, Saarland University, Saarbruecken, Germany

The presentation addresses the question to what extend the darwinian architecture of human nature - especially sex and hormonal aspects - influences media selection and preferences. Two studies use digit ratio (2d:4d) as a marker of prenatal concentrations of sex hormones. A field studie (N = 116), examines the influence of digit ratio on movie selection. A survey (N = 200), uses sex, digit ratio and sex roles as predictors for genre preferences. Congruent with evolutionary explanations, the results show an influence of sex and hormonal aspects, thus arguing against "learning only" approaches in media psychology.

Reception of frightening movies

Suckfüll, Monika Universität der Künste, Berlin, Germany

The reception of fear arousing movies is a popular form of entertainment even though fear is a negative emotion in every day life. To systematize the complex processes of reception I differentiate three analytic levels: a phylogenetic, an ontogenetic and a situational level. Evolved psychological mechanisms can help to explain the reception of frightening movies in several ways. My main hypothesis is that inhibiting the expenditure of energy on costly behavioural responses in a situation, in which the existence of threats is ambiguous, has an adaptive function. First results of an empirical study testing parts of the model are reported.

Differences in experience of 2 D and 3 D movies

Tan, Ed Dept. of Communication, University Amsterdam, Amsterdam, Netherlands **Visch, Valentijn** Psychology, University of Geneva, Geneva, Switzerland

Differences in experience of 2 D and 3 D movies An experiment is reported in which immersiveness of the projection of a movie is varied. Categorisation, emotion and aesthetic impression were the dependent variables. The results show that with increasing immersion, self-reported experience of the movie tends to unify, with various components becoming indistinguishable. They may illustrate the determination of experiencing paradigm scenarios by nature vs. nurture. The most "realistic" viewing condition may offer the best opportunity for developing adaptive functions like hunting and escaping (Steen & Owens, 2001). In the most immersive condition, the movie triggers interest

and an explorative response, while aesthetic judgments loose their analytic character. Alternative explanations are discussed in the paper.

Social reactions to virtual agents: Evolutionary foundations

Krämer, Nicole Inst. für Sozialpsychologie, Universität Duisburg-Essen, Duisburg, Germany

Embodied conversational agents are expected to facilitate future human-computer-interaction since they draw on human communication mechanisms. This, however, does not only lead to increased usability but also to unwarranted social reactions on the part of the human user. Several explanations for these reactions have been proposed that range from misunderstandings and superficial demand characteristics of the experimental situation to the argument that users are social animals that cannot help but mindlessly react socially to social cues. Drawing on evolutionary theory, a review on recent research (including three own studies) will be given that provides empirical evidence for the latter thesis.

S-089: New research concepts of modeling and measuring change in clinical psychology and psychotherapy

Wolfgang Lutz (chair)

Recently several approaches have been developed to improve the empirical bases of psychotherapy. It seems not enough, that a treatment approach has shown to be efficient, the question about the effectiveness under routine conditions as well as how change happens are getting important. Several topics about the appropriate research methods, design and measurement issues will be discussed in that panel. Alan Kazdin is presenting about the mediators and mechanisms of change. Jutta Joormann investigates cognitive and psychobiological indicators of change, Werner Wittmann will present on cost-effectiveness, Franz Caspar on the responsiveness of therapists, Ferdinand Keller on growth mixture modeling and Wolfgang Lutz on new methods to predict change under routine care conditions.

Mediators and mechanisms of psychotherapy: Changes are needed in the focus and design of psychotherapy research

Kazdin, Alan E. Dept. of Psychology, Yale University, New Haven, USA

Remarkable advances have been made in clinical research. Nevertheless, after decades of research, we cannot provide evidence-based explanations for how or why even our most well-studied interventions produce change, that is, the mechanism(s) through which treatments operate. This presentation will convey why the study mechanisms is critical, the requirements for demonstrating mechanisms rather than correlates of change, and promising lines of basic and treatment research. Two areas will be illustrated that are often considered to explain why therapy produces change (e.g., therapeutic alliance, changes in cognitions). Changes needed in conceptualizing mechanisms of change, the types of studies completed, and design and data evaluation methods will be highlighted.

The impact of cognitive-behavioral interventions on cognition, stress reactivity and emotion regulation in social anxiety disorder

Joormann, Jutta Dept. of Psychology, University of Miami, Coral Gables, FL, USA **LeMoult, Joelle** Dept. of Psychology, University of Miami, Coral Gables, FL, USA **Tran, Tanya B.** Dept. of Psychology, University of Miami, Coral Gables, FL, USA **D'Avanzato, Catherine** Dept. of Psychology, University of Miami, Coral Gables, FL, USA

Recent models emphasize the importance of integrating research on psychological and biological factors of emotional disorders. Although previous studies have investigated the role of individual differences in psychophysiological and neuroendocrine responses to stressors in depression and anxiety disorders, few studies have used these measures to investigate the impact of psychological treatments. In this project, we assessed HPA-axis reactivity and psychophysiological responses to a stress task in combination with measures of interpretive biases to evaluate the efficacy of a cognitive-behavioral group treatment for social anxiety disorder. Pre-post measures of stress reactivity and emotion regulation were compared to more established self-report and observational outcome measures. Our findings support the usefulness of an integrative psychobiological assessment of treatment outcome.

Growth mixture models

Keller, Ferdinand Kinder- und Jugendpsychiatrie, Universität Ulm, Ulm, Germany

Objective: An early prediction of individual treatment courses may allow early decisions for adequate interventions. Methods: Growth mixture modelling (GMM) assumes that there is not only one growth curve with persons having individual differences in level but subgroups who exhibit different trajectories. Results: The method will be illustrated with longitudinal data sets, e.g. the Treatment of Adolescent Depression Study (request for data is in progress), with special emphasis on the question of how early it is possible to classify patients into "problematic" classes. Conclusion: GMM is a promising approach to identify and predict clusters of change.

Reliability of measuring change via in-session ratings

Caspar, Franz Dept. für Psychologie, Universität Bern, Bern, Switzerland

Some patients don't fit standardized treatments for reasons of comorbidity or context variables. In such cases, therapist responsiveness to the individual situation is needed. Some authors (e.g. Beutler) hold that maximizing treatment effects beyond the possibilities of standardized treatment includes in general a certain extent of therapist responsiveness. Therapist responsiveness is, although clinically desired, a methodological problem. It spoils, for example, direct correlations between process variables and outcome. If different patients need different degrees of therapist directivity, a misleading zero correlation between directivity and outcome may result. Several possibilities of dealing with responsiveness will be described and discussed.

Cost-effectiveness

Wittmann, Werner W. Inst. für Psychologie, Universität Mannheim, Mannheim, Germany

Change in health related outcome measures is very well documented by research and meta-analysis. What is less known are the specific causal mechanisms, how cost-effective different interventions are, and what the cost-benefit effects are, given outcome measures with monetary impact. The idea of how to compute an effect size (ES) measured at the break-even point is presented. This concept can be applied a-priori to any intervention study and tells how much change must be produced to balance the costs. Once the real ES is known, the return on investment (ROI) can be estimated as the quotient of the real ES by the break-even one. Examples are shown to demonstrate the monetary benefits.

New trends in patient-focused psychotherapy research

Lutz, Wolfgang Inst. für Psychologie, Universität Trier, Trier, Germany

Background: All clinical services require decision making i.e., modifications based on diagnostic configurations and on an ongoing assessment of progress. Objective: Using concepts from avalanche research, this paper presents a strategy to disaggregate datasets into homogeneous subgroups to get optimal individual profiles to track patients in psychotherapy. Methods: The paper is based on data of approximately 1000 patients in outpatient psychotherapy treated with different treatment modalities in three federal states of Germany by 349 therapists. Results: A feedback system about the course of treatment was developed to support clinical decisions. Conclusions: Implications of this prediction and feedback model for supporting treatment decisions as well as possibilities of sharing specific clinical knowledge to improve clinical services are discussed.

S-090: Interplay of physical and psychological factors and their impact on health issues

Tanja Zimmermann (chair)
This symposium illustrates the interplay of psychological and physical factors and their impact on health issues regarding pregnancy, cancer and couples, and burn injury. First the demand of psychological counselling in obstetric inpatients treated to prevent preterm birth was examined. Second changes of quality of life in breast cancer patients were demonstrated. Third the impact of body image in breast cancer patients on psychological functioning and relationship issues will be demonstrated. Fourth, in reducing marital stress emotional and physical reactions of couples during a dyadic coping task will be examined. Finally psychosocial variables in providing valuable information for physical and mental health and quality of life after severes burninjuries will be discussed.

Psychological liaison counseling in obstetric inpatients treated to prevent preterm delivery
Ditzen, Beate Inst. für Psychologie, Universität Zürich, Zürich, Switzerland Hunkeler, Carol Inst. für Psychologie, Universität Zürich, Zürich, Switzerland Zimmermann, Roland Forschungsabt. Geburtshilfe, Universitätsspital Zürich, Zürich, Switzerland Ehlert, Ulrike Inst. für Psychologie, Universität Zürich, Zürich, Switzerland
Demand of psychological counseling (PC) in obstetric inpatients treated to prevent preterm birth was determined. We characterized standard interventions and treatment success in those women receiving PC. We analyzed medical records and psychological treatment protocols of 326 obstetric inpatients receiving PC between 2002 and 2007. If available, duration of pregnancy, birth weight and APGAR scores were analyzed as variables indicating treatment success. Medical data were unrelated to demand/ receipt of PC. Treatment rationale and methods of PC focused on emotion regulation and reduction of anxiety. Data on treatment success are currently analyzed and will be presented at the conference.

Quality of life of breast cancer patients at follow-up and the impact of demographic, oncological and psychological factors
Härtl, Kristin Psychosomatische Abteilung, Universitätsfrauenklinik, München, Germany Müller, Marianne Psychosomatische Abteilung, Universitätsfrauenklinik LMU, München, Germany Sommer, Harald Ludwig-Maximilians-Universität, Universitätsfrauenklinik, München, Germany Reinecker, Hans LS Klinische Psychologie, Universität Bamberg, Bamberg, Germany Friese, Klaus Ludwig-Maximilians-Universität, Universitätsfrauenklinik, München, Germany
We examined changes of quality of life (QoL) in breast cancer patients at follow-up and the impact of demographic, oncological and psychological factors. 236 women with primary diagnosis of

breast cancer completed the questionnaires after surgical treatment, 6 and 12 months postoperative. QLQ-C30 questionnaire, HADS, Life orientation questionnaire and nonparametric tests were used. QoL scores improved over time, but impairments in terms of anxiety, body image and sexual functioning were still observed. Younger patients were more likely to be distressed. Operation modality, tumor prognostic factors, living situation, being married seemed to play a minor role, whereas optimism is strongly linked with QoL. The importance of subjective versus objective predictors of QoL in women with breast cancer is discussed.

Am I still beautiful? Body-image in women with breast cancer
Zimmermann, Tanja Inst. für Psychologie, Universität Braunschweig, Braunschweig, Germany Heinrichs, Nina Inst. für Psychologie, Universität Bielefeld, Bielefeld, Germany Huber, Birgit Psychosomatik, Universität München, München, Germany Herschbach, Peter Psychosomatik, Universität München, München, Germany
Women with breast cancer have to address medical and psychological issues. These issues converge in the area of body image which appears to be related to their overall well-being, and their partners' attitudes towards their bodies influence the women's own views of their bodies. We evaluate whether body image is impacted by surgery and chemotherapy. Is a mastectomy more difficult for younger women because of the premium placed on physical beauty for younger women in society? We also report the degree to which women's body image is related to their overall psychological well-being and relationship quality and how they think their male partners perceive their body.

Psychological and physiological reactions of couples
Schaer, Marcel Inst. for Family Research, University of Fribourg, Fribourg, Switzerland
Previous studies revealed that couples' heath is associated with their coping with stress. To improve dyadic coping, the way how couples deal with stressors together, Bodenmann (2004) developed the 3-phase-method. This method trains couples how to address emotion-centred communication skills and how to mutually support each other (exchange of dyadic coping). The aim of this study is to examine physical and emotional reactions during the 3-phase-method to detected specific reactions of both partners during the intervention. Results reveal higher emotional and physiological reactions, and more empathic reactions in women compared to men. Further implications of the study are discussed.

Predictors of quality of life after severe burn injury
Renneberg, Babette Berlin, Germany Ripper, Sabine Brandverletzten Zentrum, BG Unfallklinik, Ludwigshafen, Germany Seehausen, Annika Brandverletzten Zentrum, Unfallkrankenhaus Berlin, Berlin, Germany
Objectives: To investigate the predictors for ability to work and quality of life one year after a severe burn injury. Methods: Socio-demographic, medical and psychological variables were assessed during inpatient treatment for the burn injury, at 6-months und 1 year follow-up. Data from 103 patients were available for all three assessments. Results: Severity of burns and depressive coping during acute care predicted ability to work one year later. Furthermore, quality of life was mainly predicted by psychosocial factors assessed during the hospital stay. Conclusions: Psychosocial variables provide valuable information for physical and mental health and quality of life after severe burn injuries.

S-091: Values, community, engagement and burnout: International perspectives

Michael Leiter (chair)
Research in Europe (Spain, Switzerland, Italy) and Canada considers models of job burnout in terms of organizational characteristics. An integrative theme for the session is the concept of person/organization fit. The presentations consider the implications of findings for positive constructs, specifically work engagement. SEM analyses identify common themes across the international samples. The session emphasizes the congruence of personal and organizational values as a major determinant of worklife quality. Presentations also examine distinct models for managers in contrast to point of care providers. The sessions consider the implications of the findings for interventions to enhance the quality of worklife.

The role of value congruence in the burnout process
Maslach, Christina Dept. of Psychology, University of California, San Francisco, USA
Italian health care providers (N=2688) completed surveys of burnout and perceptions of worklife. Structural equation modeling (SEM) confirmed a central role for value congruence for all three aspects of job burnout (exhaustion, cynicism, and inefficacy). The analysis confirmed a mediating role for exhaustion in the relationship of workplace qualities with cynicism and with inefficacy. The results are discussed in the context of a comprehensive model of job burnout. The presentation discusses implications for value-based interventions, as well as the importance of clear professional values for providers and a well articulated and implemented organizational vision.

Distinct predictors of burnout for health care managers and point of care providers
Leiter, Michael COR&D, Acadia University, Wolfville, Canada
Managers (N=219) and point of care providers (N=2337) from Italian hospitals complete surveys of burnout and areas of worklife during a health care regionalization process. Managers reported more positive evaluations on all measures. The relationships among the measures differed significantly between the two groups. A series of SEMs confirmed that for point of care providers, value congruence and fairness played a more important role in predicting exhaustion and cynicism. Further, negative social environment among workgroups were associated with a much greater vulnerability for burnout. The presentation considers implications for management training and leadership among hospital personnel.

Personal and organizational paths to burnout: Implications for interventions
Greenglass, Esther Dept. of Psychology, York University, North York, Canada
Burnout is defined in terms of emotional exhaustion, depersonalization and lack of personal accomplishment. Emotional exhaustion is most responsive to stressors. The role of efficacy beliefs in burnout is not clear. Lack of personal accomplishment does not have a strong relationship with depersonalization or emotional exhaustion. Rather than one path, there may be two paths to burnout, a cognitive one associated with the individual is manifested in lack of personal accomplishment and an emotional path reflected in a sense of overload resulting in emotional exhaustion and lack of organizational support. Depression may be a mediator between the paths. These observations have implications for interventions to alleviate the

deleterious effects of burnout at both the organizational and personal levels.

Worklife predictors of burnout in Spanish doctors and nurses

Gascón, Santiago Medicina Legal, Universidad de Zaragoza, Zaragoza, Spain *Martínez Jarreta, Begoña* Medicina Legal, Universidad de Zaragoza, Zaragoza, Spain

Hospital-based nurses (N=832) and doctors (N=603) in Spain completed a survey of job burnout, areas of worklife, and management issues. Analysis of the results provided support for a mediation model of burnout that depicted employees' energy, involvement, and efficacy as intermediary experiences between their experience of worklife and their evaluation of organizational change. The study confirmed a structured pattern of relationships among the areas of worklife. It supported a central role for first-line supervisors in employees' experience of worklife. Of the areas of worklife, workload received the most diverse ratings, with significant differences noted between men and women and between doctors and nurses. Female doctors evaluated supervision significantly more negatively than did other participant groups.

Work empowerment, engagement and burnout

Laschinger, Heather School of Nursing, University of Western Ontario, London, Canada *Wong, Carol* School of Nursing, Univ. of Western Ontario, London, Canada *Finegan, Joan* PSUCHOLOGY, Univ. of Western Ontario, London, Canada

We tested a model derived from Kanter's work empowerment theory linking staff nurse empowerment to their perceived fit with 6 areas of worklife and work engagement/ burnout in a cross-sectional survey of 322 randomly selected staff nurses in Ontario hospitals. Fifty-three per cent reported severe levels of burnout. Overall empowerment had an indirect effect on emotional exhaustion through nurses' perceived fit in 6 areas of worklife. The final model fit statistics revealed a good fit (χ^2 = 32.4, df = 13, GFI = 0.97, IFI = 0.97, CFI = 0.97, RMSEA= .07). These findings have implications in the current nursing shortage.

Job engagement and burnout: Opposite poles or correlates?

Schulze, Beate Universität Zürich, Zürich, Switzerland Objectives: Occupational psychology is currently experiencing a positive turn. Interventions are being re-framed to aim at building engagement rather than preventing burnout. Job engagement is defined as the opposite pole of burnout. In contrast, high job commitment is among the risk factors for burnout. Methods: Data were collected as part of an online survey among service professionals (n= 400). Results: Analysis is ongoing. It explores the role of engagement in preventing and/or contributing to burnout, and the mediating factors at play. Conclusion: Understanding the benefits and risks of engagement is essential to promoting occupational health and sustainable performance.

S-092: Spatial cognition: New approaches to assessing and explaining individual differences in spatial cognition (Part I)

Judith Glück, Claudia Quaiser-Pohl (chair)
Current research on individual differences in spatial cognition shows two new developments: First, new technologies are increasingly being used for ecologically valid assessment. Second, predictors of spatial performance are conceptualized in a dynamic way, including interactions of biological and environmental predictors. This symposium brings together researchers using a variety of assessment methods, including real-life tasks, virtual-reality

tasks, and tasks using moving stimuli. Performance predictors include age, gender, experience, strategies, executive functioning, and hormonal status. The goal of the symposium is to gain a deeper understanding of how predictor variables relate to one another and to different aspects of spatial performance.

Spatial tests and spatial activity: How do they contribute to spatial orientation in familiar macro environments?

Popp, Michael Luft- und Raumfahrtt, Universität der Bundeswehr, Neubiberg, Germany *Neidhardt, Eva* Inst. für Psychologie, Universität Frankfurt, Frankfurt, Germany

From many studies we know that preschool children are able to point to locations they cannot see, as for example to the starting point of the path they have just walked. Are spatial tests and spatial orientation in macro environments based on common abilities? Spatial tests show small but consistent effects on spatial orientation performance. Studies postulate correlations between macro orientation experience and spatial test performance. The contributions of spatial abilities and of spatial experience to spatial orientation measures are discussed.

Map understanding: Developmental marker in childhood, marker for neurological impairment in adulthood?

Peter, Michael Anton-Proksch-Institut, Wien, Austria *Glück, Judith* Entwicklungspsychologie, Alpen-Adria-Universität, Klagenfurt, Austria *Beiglböck, Wolfgang* Anton-Proksch-Institute, Anton-Proksch-Institute, Vienna, Austria

A new test of map understanding was constructed based on developmental models of spatial ability and representational understanding. In a sample of 3- to 9-year-old children, performance patterns confirmed the construction rules, and results showed correlations to measures of general cognitive development. The test may also be a useful screening of executive functioning in adults. First results of an MRI study of alcohol-addicted patients with organic psychosyndrome, compared to a healthy reference population, are presented.

Components of variance in neural networks of spatial cognition

Jordan, Kirsten Inst. für Medizin. Psychologie, Universität Göttingen, Göttingen, Germany *Wüstenberg, Torsten* Inst. für Medizin. Psychologie, Universität Göttingen, Göttingen, Germany
Environmental and biological factors change the performance and behavior in complex spatial cognition tasks. We were interested in the common neural networks of spatial cognition and the impact of those factors on the neural networks. We conducted various fMRI-studies examining different influencing factors in spatial cognition like sex differences, experience, training, strategies and sexual hormones. The parietal cortex and the motor/premotor areas constitute the invariant part of this network mainly manipulated by biological factors. The whole network of spatial cognition involves brain regions in the frontal, temporal, parietal and occipital lobe mainly manipulated by environmental factors.

Virtual teacups, cubes and head-mounted displays: The development of a dynamic spatial test in augmented reality

Strauß, Sabine Inst. für Psychologie, Universität Klagenfurt, Klagenfurt, Austria *Strasser, Irene* Inst. für Psychologie, Universität Klagenfurt, Klagenfurt, Austria *Csisinko, Mathis* IMS, Vienna University of Technolog, Vienna, Austria *Kaufmann, Hannes* IMS, Vienna University of Technolog, Vienna, Austria *Glück, Judith* Inst. für Psychologie, Universität Klagenfurt, Klagenfurt, Austria

In a cooperation of psychologists and software engineers, we are developing a new spatial test: Using augmented reality, items can be presented in actual 3D. Items consist of cube figures to be mentally rotated and assembled. In a first study, 40 items, constructed according to pre-defined rules, were evaluated (N=240), and verbal strategy reports were collected. Results confirm the validity of the construction rules. In addition, gender differences and strategy descriptions were related to item characteristics and performance level. Based on these findings, we are currently developing an adaptive training in order to eventually assess status and learning potential.

Sex-specific solution strategies in spatial tasks

Schönfeld, Robby Inst. für Psychologie, Universität Halle-Wittenberg, Halle, Germany *Leplow, Bernd* Inst. für Psychologie, Universität Halle-Wittenberg, Halle, Germany

We utilized two spatial navigational tasks using desktop virtual environments. Place learning abilities which require the construction of a cognitive map were assessed with a computerized Morris water task. Spatial updating abilities by means of path integration were assed using a compass pointing task. Age differences with younger subjects outperforming the elderly were always seen in both navigation tasks throughout many of our studies whereas sex differences only occurred in place learning. Further investigations have shown that spatial solution strategies interact with gender in that older subjects used more non-spatial strategies and more females than males behaved like the elderly.

Individual and sex differences in solution strategies when facing dynamic spatial tasks

Rubio, Victor Dept. de Psicología, Universidad Autónoma de Madrid, Madrid, Spain *Contreras, María José* Dept. Psicología Básica, UNED, Madrid, Spain *Santacreu, Jose* Departamento de Psicología, Universidad Autónoma de Madrid, Madrid, Spain
Individual and sex differences in performance quality and speed as well as in the response patterns employed emerge when individuals perform spatial tasks. Nevertheless, neither educational differences nor performance factors have fully explained this effect. The aim of this research is to identify the different response patterns used by individuals when performing a dynamic spatial task such as the Spatial Orientation Dynamic Test (SODT-R). We analyze the relationships between strategy/ response effectiveness and the frequencies with which men and women use these strategies. Future applications would provide an effective method for training in order to improve spatial performance.

S-093: Innovations in organizations

Eva Bamberg, Liudmyla Karamushka (chair)
Summary Within the symposium, innovations within different organizations are discussed. We focus especially on those factors that are a risk or a help for innovation and change. In a first step a study is presented that deals with the topics which are associated with the term innovation. In a second step studies on the role of the customer in the innovation process are outlined. In a third step we present studies that deal with factors that influence innovations in organizations. On the background of these studies innovation-related interventions can be evaluated.

What do people in organizations have in mind when they talk about innovation?

Martins, Erko Inst. Organisationspsychologie, Universität Rostock, Rostock, Germany *Pundt, Alexander* Organizational Psychology, University of Rostock, Rostock, Germany *Horsmann, Claes S.*

Organizational Psychology, University of Rostock, Rostock, Germany Nerdinger, Friedemann W. Organizational Psychology, University of Rostock, Rostock, Germany

Company stakeholders seem to value innovation, regardless of their particular interests. However, it is completely unclear what these stakeholders think of when using the term 'innovation'. To address this question, we conducted 40 semi-standardized interviews with leaders, works councillors, and HR managers from eight different companies. We asked company representatives for the topics they associate with the term 'innovation' and what they refer to as 'innovative'. Results indicate that innovation is often associated with new product development or the improvement of procedures or technologies. Besides that, creating value for the customer seems to be an important topic associated with innovation.

Innovativeness and customer orientation of firms: Friends or foes?

Kindermann, Andrea Hamburg, Germany

Taking a systems theory perspective neither innovation nor customer orientation come easily to an organization that is built on continuity and a certain amount of conformity. Psychologically one might expect difficulties to combine necessary motivational traits. Also role conflicts could arise. A quantitative study in nine small enterprises showed, that – while there are no negative correlations between indicators for innovativeness and customer orientation – one need to pay more attention to the fact that innovativeness and customer orientation ask for similar, usually scarce resources. The resulting conflicts must be solved on the organizational level. They cannot be delegated to the employees.

Facilitating innovation and change in organizations

Bamberg, Eva Inst. für Psychologie, Universität Hamburg, Hamburg, Germany Dettmers, Jan Department of Psychology, University of Hamburg, Hamburg, Germany Marggraf-Micheel, Claudia Department of Psychology, University of Hamburg, Hamburg, Germany Stremming, Saskia Department of Psychology, University of Hamburg, Hamburg, Germany

With members of trade organizations a training programm was conducted; the aim of the training was to enhance the inclusion of customers in the innovation process. Between the sessions of the training, the participants had to conduct meetings with the staff. Results of the evaluation study show that the training was useful for the participants. The training had slight effects on factors that influence innovations but it had no effects on the number of innovations that took place in the organization.

Building innovation management teams in organizations

Karamushka, Liudmyla Organizational Psychology, Institute of Psychology, Kyiv, Ukraine Fil, Alena Lab. of Organiz. Psychology, Institut of Psychology, Kiev, Ukraine

Objectives: To find out distinctive features of innovation management teams in educational organizations. Methods: The investigation was done on 236 educators using Karamushka & Fil questionnaire. Results: 1. Occurrence of innovation management teams in organizations was low (29.15%). 2. Employees' teamwork motives correlated with age: a) those younger 30 were most position- (r<0.05) and prestige-oriented (r<0.01); b) those aged 31-40 were most oriented toward maintaining the organization's competitiveness (r<0.01); c) those aged 55-60 were most adaptation-oriented (r<0.01). 3. Females were more position (r<0.05) and innovation-oriented (r<0.001) than men. Conclusion: The findings can

be helpful in creating innovation management teams.

Factors that hamper innovative processes in educational organizations

Ivkin, Vladimir M. Lab of Org. Psychology, Institute of Psychology, Kyiv, Ukraine Karamushka, Lyudmila Lab of Org. Psychology, Institute of Psychology, Kyiv, Ukraine

Objectives: To find out factors that hamper innovative process in educational organizations Methods: The investigation was done on 358 school principals and teachers in 2007 using a specially designed questionnaire and statistics. Results: 1. Factors which reduce effectiveness of innovations were grouped as follows: a) inadequate consideration of employees' interests; b) employees' poor understanding of innovation contents and aims; c) organizational and material factors; d) inadequate care about employees' psychological health. 2. Organization-centered motives prevail over the employee-centered motives (p<0.001; p<0.01) Conclusion: To make innovations effective education managers should take into account employees' interest and engage them in innovation process.

Organizational openness: Risk or success factor for innovations?

Hagenah, Meike Dept. of Org. Psychology, Humboldt University of Berlin, Berlin, Germany Scholl, Wolfgang Dept. of Org. Psychology, Humboldt University of Berlin, Berlin, Germany

The willingness to engage in an open dialog is said to be critical to promote innovations (e.g. Hauschildt, 2004; 2007). 30 interviews with researchers and developers showed that the necessity of openness is recognized, but that it stands in conflict with the fear of losing competitive advantage. In a follow-up study (N=224) we explored how openness is taking shape in science and economy. Additionally, we used data from patent and publication indices to test the hypothesized positive relation between openness and several indicators for innovation success. Results indicate a positive relationship between openness and general as well as personal success.

S-094: Self-regulatory strength and ego depletion: A decade later

Alex Bertrams (chair)

In 1998, for the first time the strength model of self-control was empirically confirmed and the term ego depletion was established for a state of reduced self-control power. Since then, a number of studies based on or related to the strength model have been carried out. The symposium addresses new research directions and newest findings regarding self-regulatory strength: Underlying physiological processes (Matt Gailliot), differentiation from other processes (Brandon Schmeichel), extension to decision making and risk behavior (Alexander Unger), and several possibilities to build regulatory strength (Megan Oaten, Alex Bertrams & Oliver Dickhäuser).

Ego depletion and cognitive load: What's the difference?

Schmeichel, Brandon J. Department of Psychology, Texas A&M University, College Station, USA

Both cognitive load and ego depletion undermine self-control. Do they operate via the same mechanism? The current experiment indicates they do not. Sixty-six women either did or did not perform a self-control task prior to a test of pain tolerance. Participants who performed the self-control task persisted less on the pain test. Participants also did or did not carry a cognitive load during the pain test. Participants persisted longer on the pain test under cognitive load. Hence cognitive load and ego depletion had independent and opposite effects on

pain tolerance, demonstrating that load and depletion operate via distinct mechanisms.

Influence of ego-depletion on risk-behavior

Unger, Alexander Inst. für Angw. Wissenschaften, Universität Ludwigshafen, Ludwigshafen, Germany

Ego-depletion theory postulates a cognitive resource, necessary for self-regulation, including decision-making. In study 1 we analyzed the influence of ego-depletion in an investment scenario. Two alternative hypotheses were considered: 1.) A general decrease in risk-behavior independent of risk-proclivity. 2.) Depleted persons rely more on their risk-proclivity. In study 2-3, the subjects had to edit a time-measurement, to test if depleted subjects are more risk-averse, if the risk-behavior was established without requirement of demanding cognitive processes. We consider a mediation of subjective time-perception-change (Vohs & Schmeichel, 2003) and test alternative hypotheses about the effectiveness of time-perception-change.

Increasing self-control capacity by regular complex thinking

Bertrams, Alex Nürnberg, Germany

Success in self-control and complex thinking (e.g., logical reasoning, reading comprehension) depends on a resource comparable to the strength of a muscle. This regulatory strength can be boosted by regular self-control effort. In several studies, we examined whether frequent complex thinking also increases self-control capacity. As predicted, need for cognition (that is associated with regular complex thinking) was positively related to self-control capacity. This relation was robust across different samples (undergraduate students, high-school students). In addition to this cross-sectional support, the presentation will also address the question of causality between complex thinking and self-control capacity using longitudinal data.

S-095: Prosocial behaviors in adolescence across cultures

Asiye Kumru, Maria Rosario de Guzman (chair)

Prosocial behavior is valued in all cultural communities and for that reason is a central part of socialization process. Cultural values and socialization practices might promote/accent moral motives deemed particularly substantial to specific cultures. This symposium will bring together five research teams from the UK, USA and Turkey who use a cultural approach to study prosocial development. The presentations discuss the continuity/discontinuity issues and parental ethnotheories regarding prosocial behavior, a range of factors that promote different forms of prosocial behaviors, and provide an integrated model of maternal peer management and adolescent prosocial behavior with self-disclosure as intervening variable in adolescence.

Continuities and discontinuities in prosocial behaviour, disruptive behaviour and intellectual ability from early childhood to adolescence

Hay, Dale F. Dept. of Psychology, Cardiff University, Cardiff, United Kingdom Pawlby, Susan Perinatal Psychiatry, Institute of Psychiatry, London, United Kingdom

The aim of the paper is to examine prosocial behaviour from childhood to adolescence. The children of 171 mothers recruited in pregnancy were assessed for prosocial and disruptive behaviour, and IQ, at 4, 11 and 16 years of age. Individual differences in prosocial behaviour were stable from 11 to 16, and negatively related to disruptive behaviour at both time points. Cooperation at 4 predicted low rates of disruptive behaviour in adolescence, and higher IQ at 16, even when controlling for early cognitive ability. Early co-operativeness may foster more general opportunities for learning

Beliefs about children's prosocial behaviors and the parenting practices that promote them: A study of Mexican- and European-American mothers' ethnotheories

de Guzman, Maria Rosario Dept. of Psychology, University of Nebraska, Lincoln, USA

The current study examines parental ethnotheories regarding children's prosocial behaviors and the parenting practices that promote them. A total of 60 mothers of young adolescents participated in one of six focus groups in the United States. Three groups were composed of Mexico-born, Spanish-speaking Mexican-Americans; two groups of US-born, English-speaking Mexican-Americans; and one of European-Americans. In addition to group discussions, participants free-listed their responses on paper. Materials were coded using a Grounded-Theory approach, and results indicate both similarities and differences in themes across groups. Patterns reflect shared and unique expectations and socio-cultural contexts, and highlight the interplay between parenting and culture.

Prosocial behaviors: The ifferential roles of individual, interpersonal and parental variables in Turkish early and middle adolescents

Kumru, Asiye Dept. of Psychology, Abant Izzet Baysal University, Bolu, Turkey

This study explores the differential roles of empathy, self-perception of behavioral conduct, friendship quality dimensions, parental ideologies, behavioral/psychological control, and attachment. Participants were 555 adolescents and their parents in Turkey. Results indicated that empathy, support of friendship, parent's positive ideology and behavioral control predicted proactive prosocial behavior; Self-perception of behavioral conduct (negatively), companionship and conflict dimension of friendship, parent's negative ideology and psychological control predicted proactive prosocial behavior; Parent attachment predicted positively both types of prosocial behaviors. Finally, for girls support and negative ideology and for boys conflict, attachment and psychological control were more important predictors of prosocial behaviors.

The relations between parenting practices and prosocial behaviors in Mexican American early adolescents

Carlo, Gustavo Dept. of Psychology, University of Nebraska, Lincoln, NE, USA

Scholars are interested in identifying parenting practices that are predictive of social behaviors. Based on prior theory and research (Eisenberg, 1986; Staub, 1979), social rewards, experiental learning, moral conversations, and discursive communicative practices were expected to be positively related to prosocial behaviors. Material rewards were expected to be weakly or negatively associated with prosocial behaviors. Participants were 322 adolescents (212 Mexican Americans; M age = 10.9 years; 50% girls). Students completed a measure of parenting practices and of prosocial tendencies. Correlational analyses showed general support for the hypotheses. The findings suggest the need to examine different forms of prosocial behaviors.

S-096: The developmental significance of peer groups

Beate Schwarz (chair)

Peer groups are important developmental contexts of children and adolescents for the acquisition of specific skills, attitudes and behaviors and for their well-being. The objective of the six studies in the symposium is to investigate which specific characteristics of peer groups affect the development of school-aged children and adolescents. With respect to the outcome variables a major focus is on social integration, problematic behavior, engagement and motivation in the school setting. The perspective is

extended to peer group effects on school-to-work transitions and well-being. Gender differences and other sources of influence such as families and teachers are considered.

With a little help from their friends: Within-clique interpersonal harmony as a predictor of children's dominance position in the peer group

Olthof, Tjeert Faculty of Psychology and Educ, VU University Amsterdam, Amsterdam, Netherlands Lam, Anna Developmental Psychology, VU University Amsterdam, Amsterdam, Netherlands Aleva, Liesbeth Developmental Psychology, Utrecht University, Utrecht, Netherlands Goossens, Frits A. Dpt of Special Education, VU University Amsterdam, Amsterdam, Netherlands Van der Meulen, Matty Developmental Psychology, Groningen University, Groningen, Netherlands Vermande, Marjolijn Psychosocial Development, Utrecht University, Utrecht, Netherlands

Hawley (1999) argued that children who use both coercive and pro-social strategies to influence other children are most likely to obtain dominance within their peer group. We hypothesized that dominance would also depend on the quality of children's interpersonal relationships within their clique, i.e., the group of peers they hang out with. Children's (N = 1008) strategy use, dominance (perceived popularity and resource control) and clique membership, were measured using peer nominations. Within-clique interpersonal harmony was measured using 'liking'-ratings that children gave each other. Membership of a harmonious clique actually was related to dominance, even when controlling for strategy use.

What makes a popular woman? Social dominance strategies and social integration in early adolescence

Ittel, Angela Fakultät für Pädagogik, Bundeswehr Universität München, Neubiberg, Germany

Girls and boys use a variety of strategies to obtain and maintain their social status within the peer group. Girls are assumed to exhibit more pro-social behaviours while boys are assumed to use more coercive strategies. In this study we used a peer rated measure of social integration and strategies to obtain once social status within the class context. Well integrated boys and girls used more pro-social strategies. Well integrated girls used more relational aggressive strategies while less well integrated girls used more aggressive and manipulative strategies. Discussion will consider the genderspecific meanings of social integration within the peer network.

Peer group influences on sixth graders' school motivation and achievement

Kindermann, Thomas Dept. of Psychology, Portland State University, Portland, USA

Peer effects on academic motivation were examined in the entire cohort of 366 sixth graders in a small town. Peer groups were assessed using Socio-Cognitive Mapping; as an indicator of motivation, classroom engagement was measured using teacher reports (87% participation rate). Peer groups were moderately homogeneous in terms of engagement. Despite member turnover across the school year, groups maintained their motivational composition. Engagement levels of students' groups in fall predicted changes in students' motivation over time. The magnitude of effects was small, but evidence for peer influences persisted when effects of peer selection and teacher and parent involvement were controlled.

Peer group influences on fifth graders' reading motivation

von Salisch, Maria Inst. für Psychologie, Universität Lüneburg, Lüneburg, Germany Philipp, Maik Dept. of Education, Leuphana University Lueneburg, Lueneburg, Germany Gölitz, Dietmar Dept. of

Education, Leuphana University Lueneburg, Lueneburg, Germany

Although family and school factors affecting children's reading motivation are known, little is known about the influence of their peer group's attitude towards reading. Therefore N = 501 fifth graders attending three different tracks of German schools filled in questionnaires about family reading climate, school motivation, reading motivation and behavior and answered questions on a newly constructed questionnaire about their peer group's attitude towards reading (alpha = .80). Hierarchical regressions suggest that their peer group's attitude towards reading predicted fifth graders' reading motivation above and beyond gender, school track (ability level), familiy reading climate, and school motivation, especially among girls.

Peer support in the preparation of the school-to-work transition

Kracke, Bärbel Inst. für Entw.-Psychologie, Universität Erfurt, Erfurt, Germany

The transition from school to work is a major challenge for adolescents. To prepare this transition they have to collect a lot of new information in situations which they might not have experienced before (e.g., job centers, internships). The present study addresses the role of peers for adolescents information seeking regarding occupations in 240 15 year-old adolescents. Results show that girls more often talk about occupational issues with their friends than boys. For both genders holds that the perception of ones friends as being supportive in exploration situations correlates positively with more general occupation related information seeking behaviors.

Associations between antisocial friends, friendship quality and adolescents' adjustment

Schwarz, Beate Inst. für Psychologie, Universität Basel, Basel, Switzerland Walper, Sabine Dept. of Education, University of Munich, Munich, Germany

The study investigated the effects of contact with antisocial friends, quality of the relationship with the best same-sex friend and their interaction on adolescents' internalizing and externalizing behavior. Self-report data of N = 314 adolescents from Germany (51% girls; 66% from separated, 34% from intact families) with a mean age of 15.50 years (SD=1.68) were analyzed across a 1-year period. Regression analyses revealed only effects of antisocial friends but not of friendship quality on change in adjustment. Interaction effects showed that the negative effects of antisocial friends were pronounced when the relationship with the best friend was of high quality.

S-097: Gender and career prospects: Charting women's paths through the labyrinth

Sabine Sczesny, Alice H. Eagly (chair)

To achieve career success, women navigate a labyrinth of impediments. Among these impediments are stereotypes dictating that women lack the qualities needed for success. Occasional failures damage the self-esteem of women more than men. Motherhood ideology encourages women to accept a disproportionate share of domestic responsibility. In the workplace, women have work that is either unchallenging or impossibly difficult and risky. Nevertheless, women's careers have become more successful. Also, cultural shifts have eroded the perceived incongruity between the characteristics of women and those of leaders. Nevertheless, there is no room for complacency about the challenges that women continue to face.

Effects of gender schemata on women's math and science career choices

Cherney, Isabelle D. Dept. of Psychology, Creighton University, Omaha, USA

The gender disparity in the fields of science, technology, engineering, and mathematics (STEM fields) has received renewed attention. The purpose of this study was to explore how gender schemata can explain some important aspects of this female underrepresentation. A survey was administered to 921 adolescents and young adults. The findings showed that, besides several gender-based differences in personality and motivation, women also had more inaccurate representations of what science is and their prior experiences suggest that patterns of socialization which shape the male gender role are more conducive to success in the academic and professional culture in the physical sciences.

Failure-as-an-asset

Stahlberg, Dagmar Inst. für Sozialpsychologie, Universität Mannheim, Mannheim, Germany

In two studies it is shown that only members of high-status groups (i.e., men and students of business administration) but not members of low-status groups (i.e., women and students of teaching profession) react with an increase in state self-esteem after their own alleged poor performance in a fictitious intelligence test. This Failure-as-an-Asset (FA-) effect is only observed when the high-status ingroup (i.e., men) is outperformed by a low-status outgroup (i.e., women). In this case, a poor performance indicates high ingroup prototypicality. Our experimental data support this idea that high ingroup identification of high-status group members mediates the reported FA effect.

Viewing women's career progression through the lens of motherhood ideology

Dikkers, Josje S.E. Management and Organisation, Vrije Universiteit Amsterdam, Amsterdam, Netherlands *van Engen, Marloes* Human Resource Studies, University of Tilburg, Tilburg, Netherlands *Vinkenburg, Claartje* Management and Organisation, Vrije Universiteit Amsterdam, Amsterdam, Netherlands

Differential career progression of women and men in organisations may be explained by motherhood ideology: social norms about what it means to be a mother and appropriate behaviours for mothers. This ideology ranges from traditional (maternal sacrifice) to contemporary (shared childcare). Motherhood ideology influences career patterns and outcomes of women and men through the (implicit) expectations and decisions of supervisors and human resources staff. We studied the relationship between motherhood ideology of supervisors and HR staff, the utilization of family-friendly arrangements, and subjective and objective career outcomes of women and men. Data were collected in a variety of Dutch organisations.

Think-manager-think-male? Perceptions of managers, men and women in the past, present and future

Bosak, Janine Inst. für Psychologie, Universität Bern, Bern, Germany *Sczesny, Sabine* Psychology, University of Bern, Bern, Switzerland *Diekman, Amanda* Psychology, Miami University, Oxford OH, USA

The image of a successful manager is more congruent with the stereotype of men than with the stereotype of women. A decrease in this perceived incongruity between the female gender role and leadership roles might follow from a change in these roles. To investigate the dynamics of managerial sex-role stereotyping, management students of both sexes judged a target group (men/women/executives) in a specified year (1950/present/2050) with regard to gender-stereotypic leadership

traits. Altogether, our findings concerning stereotypes about managers, men, and women of the past, present, and future indicate a less traditional projection of leadership as times moves on.

Through the labyrinth: How women encounter and overcome impediments to their career success

Eagly, Alice H. Dept. of Psychology, Northwestern University, Evanston, USA

Women's career success and labor force participation have been steadily increasing in Western nations. Nevertheless, women's careers still lag behind men's careers. This talk frames the obstacles that women face as a labyrinth of complexities and impediments. This metaphor captures the situation of contemporary women in Western nations far better than the familiar glass ceiling metaphor. This labyrinth theme incorporates the analyses featured in the five talks that preceded this integrative presentation. Also described is a new meta-analysis that shows the partial erosion over time of one of the impediments that women face: The "think manager—think male" phenomenon.

S-098: Towards defining counselling psychology in the global context

Richard Young (chair)

Counselling psychology is a recognized field of scientific inquiry and professional practice in many countries. In other countries, similar practices and domains of inquiry are known by other names. As a discipline and field of practice, it is influenced by and/or influences developments in psychology, cultural differences, and the emerging global context. This symposium highlights the challenge of defining counselling psychology by examining its development of in three countries, China, France, and Greece, and proposing two different conceptual frameworks that can be used to identify commonalities across national borders and between cultures.

Current directions and future directions for counselling psychology in Greece

Malikiosi-Loizos, Maria Early Childhood Education, University of Athens, Athens, Greece

The current status and future directions for counselling psychology in Greece will be presented. The presentation will focus on topics such as the identity of counselling psychology in Greece, its strengths and weaknesses, opportunities for development, objectives and strategies for its advancement. It will be based on SWOT analysis. Its strengths include the rapid growth of professional and research activity. Weaknesses include the small recognition counselling psychology has compared to clinical psychology and the lack of a clear professional identity. Opportunities concentrate around the possibility to start graduate programs in counselling psychology and to incorporate counselling psychology services in education and many employment organizations.

How to develop counselling psychology in France?

Guichard, Jean INETOP, CNAM, Paris, France

This presentation, based on a review of various reports, surveys, etc., aims at giving an overview of the French situation regarding counseling and at pondering diverse means to improve it. The situation appears paradoxical: the number of counselors is high and still increasing. But, these counselors work in different domain and they don't think of themselves as belonging to a same family. This is probably due tot the fact that their training (when any) is heterogeneous. A clear identification of "counseling psychology" as an academic subject along with the creation of professional and

scientific associations could be ways to improve the current situation.

Counselling and clinical psychology: The differentiated dilemma in training and practice in China

Hou, Zhi-Jin Dept. of Psychology, Beijing Normal University, Beijing, People's Republic of China

Counseling psychology and clinical psychology belong to two different but related disciplines in western countries. In US, they are in two separated professional divisions in APA. However, in other countries like China, either counseling or clinical psychology is still in its starting stage. The combination of counseling and clinical psychology in training and practice is very popular in the author's observation. In this paper, the author with report the results from the survey of the perception of counseling and clinical psychology with students in psychology department in order to see how they view these two related discipline.

Social justice: A model for international counselling psychology

Sinacore, Ada Educ. and Counselling Psychol., McGill University, Montreal, Canada

Counselling psychology with its focus on diversity and social justice offers research and knowledge that is salient in an international context. Social justice models require an analysis of the distribution of resources within society and how that distribution results in the advantaging and disadvantaging of different groups of people. While these models have focused predominately within societies, they are easily expanded to provide an analysis of the distribution of resources between societies. The goal of this paper is to discuss the theoretical foundations of social justice models and their application to the development of an international definition of counselling psychology.

The contribution of action theory to defining counselling psychology in the global context

Young, Richard Counselling Psychology, University of British Columbia, Vancouver, Canada *Valach, Ladislav* Klinik Schossli, Universtat Zurich, Oetwil a.S., Switzerland

Objectives: To describe how action theory can contribute to defining counseling psychology in the global context. Methods: A range of challenges facing counseling psychology are described, including cultural and national differences, the tension between theory and practice, and the prevalence of global psychological issues. These problems are analyzed from an action theory perspective, in which the centrality of goal-directed, joint action is highlighted. Results: Counseling psychology can be understood as culturally related discourse grounded conceptually in action theory and methodologically in the action-project method. Conclusions: Action theory provides a suitable means to uncover implicit approaches to defining counseling psychology.

S-099: Psychology and torture - Prohibition, prevention and reparations

Nora Sveaass (chair)

The symposium will focus on different aspects of psychological practice and psychology. The ethical challenges will be discussed, especially in times of crises, conflict and threat of terror. Torture is gendered, and a number of serious violations related to gender are now considered acts of torture. This will be addressed. Ways of assessment and documentation of signs and consequences of torture will be presented, together with outlines of psychological rehabilitation and social integration in the aftermath of torture. Psychologists and their work with reparations after serious human rights violations is an important issue, and it will discussed with a focus on health and mental health aspects of reparation.

Psychological values and ethics in a context of threats to international human rights law
Sveaass, Nora Ref Health and Forc Migration, NKVTS, Oslo, Norway
Psychological knowledge has been misused in the context of torture for years. It is a challenge for psychologists to work against all forms of torture. In the wake of the "war against terror", psychologists' participation in interrogation of terror suspects has been debated. Reports from human rights organisations and from political and military sources indicate that psychological methods are systematically used in interrogation in ways that may amount to torture. The relationship between interrogation, CIDT and torture will be explored, as well as role and position of psychologists, and our codes of ethics in relation to this problem.

Gender-based torture and psychology
Patel, Nimisha Medical Foundation, University of East London, London, United Kingdom
The use of torture, against both men and women, in 'peacetime', in war and in the 'war on terror' is considered specifically in relation to gender. Sexual torture of women, a tool of terror and oppression, is understood within the context of the historical devaluation, marginalization and discrimination of women, violence against women, the feminization of the 'other', the degradation and positioning of women as passive victims without agency. Against the backdrop of developments in international human rights law, this paper critiques psychological approaches to theorizing and working with rape and other forms of sexual torture, from a human rights perspective.

Torture survivors and rights - tortured asylum seekers in Europe: The truth and its (professional) consequences
Bittenbinder, Elise Germ Ass. Psy-centres Refugees, BAFF, Berlin, Germany
Health professionals working with victims of torture often produce reports for the asylum process. But professional trauma discourse is ambivalent on determining truth in this context. Whereas the perspectives of trauma victims are generally seen as possessing a special truth, this assumption does not apply to torture victims seeking asylum in Europe. Clinical knowledge about trauma is used to justify decision-making and political processes. However, asylum remains primarily a political and social question—and not a question of diagnostics or treatment methods. At the same time medical or psychological reports may influence the debate. Here professionals face a dilemma.

Challenges on documentation of torture for asylum applications
Ozkalipci, Onder Program Unit, IRCT, Copenhagen, Denmark
Wide range of different practices in asylum applications exists in Europe such as medical and psychological examinations from having no value on or being influential on asylum decisions. Research examples of medical documentation practice of torture allegations during asylum applications from different EU countries, similarities between EU countries and non democratic regimes on documenting torture and different training project initiatives for using Istanbul Protocol standards on asylum application and researches will be discussed.

Detention, asylum and social integration
Schlar Ozkalipci, Caroline Dept. of Psychology, Impact Positif, Geneve, Switzerland
Long time imprisonment has to be considered while analyzing social integration of the asylum seeker. While proceeding psychological documentation long imprisonment in history should receive special interest. Geneva is one of the important cities of Switzerland with huge number of asylum seekers and internationals. Despite the international responsibilities of Swiss government, human tragedies cant be prevented. Long time imprisonment, asylum and social integration will be analyzed with their connection with each other. Possible approaches for strengthening social well being of asylum seekers will be discussed with special stress on long time imprisonment and social integration.

S-100: How do values affect behavior? Let me count the ways

Lilach Sagiv (chair)
In this symposium we aim to show the multiple and complex paths through which values affect behavior. Six studies, presenting data from six countries, combine to exemplify some of these processes. Values impact behavior directly (Levontin), especially when rendered accessible (Sagiv & Grant). Values also affect behavior through more complex mechanisms: The relationships of values to behavior are sometimes moderated by personal attributes (Caprara et al). Values also interact with other personal attributes (Vauclair) and with contextual characteristics (Roccas & Amit) to affect behavior. Finally, individuals are ambivalent toward targets with conflicting values (Gebauer et al).

Values and resistance to change
Levontin, Liat School of business administrat, The Hebrew University, Jerusalem, Israel
This study examined the relations between personal values (Schwartz,1992) and resistance to change (RTC, Oreg, 2003). Studying 131 students, we hypothesized and found that RTC correlated positively with stimulation and self direction values, that reflect openness to new ideas and experiences ($r= -.40, -.21$, respectively; $p<.05$) and negatively with tradition, conformity and security values, that reflect a preference for maintaining the status quo ($r= .29, .17, .34$, respectively; $p<.05$). When entered to a regression, values explained 21% of the variance in RTC ($F(5,125)=6.72$; $p<.001$). Also as expected, values correlated most strongly with the routine-seeking aspect of RTC.

From pro-social values to pro-social behavior
Sagiv, Lilach School of Business Administr., Hebrew University, Jerusalem, Israel
Benevolence values reflect concern and care for the welfare of others and were found to correlate with pro-social behavior. In the current research we present a 30-minute intervention designed to enhance the importance of benevolence values. In Study 1 (US, N=37), participants in the "benevolence" condition attributed higher importance to benevolence values than participants in the control condition (t=2.15; p<.01). Study2 (Israel, N=56) replicated this finding and examined the behavioral consequences of the intervention: Following the "benevolence" intervention, 47% of participants agreed to volunteer in a pro-social organization compared to 24% only in the control group (x=4.68, p<.01).

Prosocial agency: Values and self-efficacy beliefs as determinants of prosocial behavior
Caprara, Gian Vittorio Dept. of Psychology, Univers. of Rome 'La Sapienza', Rome, Italy
A variety of personal determinants may contribute to individual's tendency to behave prosocially. The present study extend previous findings attesting to the contribution of values and self efficacy beliefs to prosocial behavior. Italian adults filled out self-report questionnaires aimed at evaluating values, affective and social self-regulatory efficacy beliefs; also two relatives and two friends evaluated the target subject's prosocial behavior. Findings corroborate the posited conceptual model in which self-reported values and self-efficacy beliefs in the domain of affect regulation and social relations, operate in concert to promote prosocial behavior as resulting from both self evaluation and others' evaluation.

Linking moral values to self-control: The moral personality as a moderator
Vauclair, Melanie School of Psychology, Victoria Univ. of Wellington, Wellington, New Zealand
Our study examines the relationship between moral values and self-control as moderated by moral chronicity. The latter is defined as the chronic accessibility of moral schemata indicating moral personality. Self-control refers to the ability to override immediate impulses to conform to socially desirable standards instead of pursuing selfish goals. We hypothesized that the preference for moral values relates to self-control but only for moral chronics. This was confirmed for 'conformity' values in a sample of 166 New Zealand students. Moral chronics also showed higher levels of self-control than moral non-chronics. Implications for linking moral values to moral action are discussed.

The role of personal and group values in explaining identification with groups
Roccas, Sonia Education and Psychology, Open University of Israel, Raanana, Israel Amit, Adi Jerusalem, Israel
We tested the hypothesis that the relationship of personal values to identification with a group depends on the values emphasized by that group. Study 1 included three samples (US, Switzerland & Israel). Participants reported their personal values and their identification with four prototypical groups that differ in their values. Findings indicate that identification depends on the congruency between personal and group values. In Study 2 Israeli participants reported their values and their perception of the values emphasized by real-life groups. Findings indicate that perception of group values moderates the relationships between personal values and identification.

Value structure and ambivalence
Maio, Gregory R. School of Psychology, Cardiff University, Wales, United Kingdom Gebauer, Jochen School of Psychology, Cardiff University, Cardiff, United Kingdom
Three laboratory experiments, using psychology students as participants, tested whether people are more ambivalent towards target persons who simultaneously endorse structurally incongruent values (e.g., helpful and successful) than towards target persons who endorse structurally congruent values (e.g., helpful and forgiving). Regression analyses revealed that structural incongruence predicted ambivalence, even after controlling for incongruence due to valence of the values. Mediation analyses revealed that conscious perception of structural incongruence mediated this effect. This research is the first that identified a source of ambivalence other than valence incongruence of the attributes of an attitude object.

S-101: Psychology of mental health: An Asian perspective on affectivity, stages of change and coping

Ai-Girl Tan (chair)
The symposium of "psychology of mental health" is proposed as well-being, health, affectivity, coping

and help seeking have attracted attention of professional and lay Asian communities. Specifically this is true in both Singapore and Malaysia societies. The roles of mental health professionals such as psychologists have recently been enhanced and revived. Five papers are presented in this symposium; each examines the reliabilities and validity of measures (e.g., affectivity, coping, stages of change and decisional making) used in different clinical and social contexts, and/or the relations between the measures. The studies in their small ways contribute to the understanding of mental health behavior of Asians living in fast-pace, modernized, and relatively affluent societies.

Psychology of mental health: An Asian perspective on affectivity, stages of change and coping

Tan, Ai-Girl Psychological Studies, Nanyang Techn. University, Singapore, Singapore Tan, Sooyin Psychological Studies, 1 Nanyang Walk, Singapore, Singapore Chou, Chih-Chin Dept of Psychology, University of Arizona, USA, USA

A total of 120 rehabilitation patients rated theri affectivity and meaning of life. The reliabilities of the measures were high, more than .7. Exploratory and confirmatory factor analyses were employed to establish validity of the measures. Positive correlations were observed between Positive Affect, Subjective Happiness, Satisfaction with Life and the Presence of Meaning of Life (.37 and .46, p <.01), and between Negative Affect and the Presence of Meaning of Life (MoL_P) (.-.31, p <.01).

Exploring stages of change of two Asian samples

Chou, Chih-Chin Dept. of Psychology, University of Arizona, USA Tan, Ai-Girl Psychological Studies, Nanyang Techn. University, Singapore, Singapore Tan, Sooyin Nanyang Technological Uni, Psychological Studies, Singapore, Singapore Ting, Steven Independent Researchers, Simei Centre, Singapore, Singapore Too, Martha Independent Researcher, Simei Centre, Singapore, Singapore

TThe Stages of Chang e (SoC) Questionnaire was administered to 120 mental health patients and 595 high school students in Singapore. Using the principal component analysis, varimax or oblimin rotation, factor structures of SoC of the two groups were compared. For both groups, Cronbach's Alphas of the stages of change were high, ranged between .72 and .80. Cluster analysis showed that mental health patients can be grouped into four clusters: Pre-contemplation, contemplation, action and maintenance, but only three for the high school student group. Discussion on the suitability of the use of SoC with reference to contextual specificity is highlighted.

Coping behavior of HIV/AIDS patients

Teoh, Chloe Psychological Studies, Nanyang Techn. University, Singapore, Singapore Tan, Sooyin Psychological Studies, 1 Nanyang Walk, Singapore, Singapore Tan, Ai-Girl Psychological Studies, Nanyang Techn. University, Singapore, Singapore

A total of 595 students in Singapore participated in a study on making a decision (pro and con) to change their gaming behavior. Two measures were adopted: Decisional balance scale (DBS, pro and con) and Task-Specific Efficacy Scale (TSES, symptom management, help-seeking, family and school). Their factor structures were examined using the principal component, oblimin/varimax orientation. All scales were with high Cronbach's Alpha reliabilities. DBS_con correlated with one sub-scale of TSES (symptom management, .18, p<.01), but DBS_pro with all sub-scales of TSES (.11-.16, p<.01). Discussion on the suitability of the use of DBS with reference to the context of gaming behavior is highlighted.

Positive affect and coping

Chin-Chin, Chia Psychological Studies, Nanyang Techn. University, Singapore, Singapore Tan, Ai-Girl Psychological Studies, Nanyang Tech. University, Singapore, Singapore

Based on Lazarus and Folkman's (1984) coping theory and Fredrickson's (1998) theory of positive emotions, a study was conducted to explore the relation between coping strategies and affect. 123 year two and 182 year three Singapore student nurses completed the Ways of Coping scale and PANAS experienced for clinical or academic stressors. Results showed adaptive strategies were correlated positively with positive affect (p<.01); less adaptive strategies with negative affect (p<.05, p<.01). Positive reappraisal and social support predicted positive affect (p<.001). Student nurses in clinical stress used more problem-focused strategies and likely benefited more from the upward spiral of positive emotions.

S-102: Spatial cognition: Individual and gender differences in mental rotation (Part II)

Claudia Quaiser-Pohl, Judith Glück (chair)
The study of individual differences in mental-rotation ability, especially of gender differences in mental-rotation test performance has a long tradition in psychological research. There are still many open questions, however, with regard to the factors influencing their emergence and their course of development. The papers of the symposium, on the one hand, deal with different factors responsible for performance differences in the Mental Rotation Test (e.g. the response format). On the other hand, papers are presented that analyze the origins of individual differences in mental rotation in childhood more properly from a developmental perspective.

Sex differences in mental rotation: Now you see them, now you don't

Peters, Michael Dept. of Psychology, University of Guelph, Guelph, ON, Canada
Sex differences in mental rotation are reliably observed when cube stimuli of the Shepard and Metzler type are presented in the Vandenberg & Kuse mental rotation (MR) paradigm. In contrast, when the same stimuli are presented pair-wise, sex differences in performance are either not observed or quite small. This observation prompts an interpretation of the cause of sex differences in MR that places less emphasis on differences in spatial ability and more emphasis on sex differences in approaching mental rotation tasks.

The solution strategy as an indicator of the developmental stage of mental-rotation ability of pre-school children

Quaiser-Pohl, Claudia Inst. für Pädag. Psychologie, Universität Siegen, Siegen, Germany Rohe, Anna Department of Psychology, University of Siegen, Siegen, Germany
The development of mental-rotation ability has been studied with the Picture Rotation Test with N=565 pre-school children (aged 4;0 to 6;11). By qualitative and quantitative analyses (Latent-Class-Analysis) six solution strategies were identified which were further classified in appropriate, semi-appropriate and non-appropriate strategies. The relationship between performance level, age, and strategy usage proved the strategy to be an indicator of the developmental stage of mental rotation. In addition, the results of a training study are reported showing that the solution strategy and thus the development of mental rotation in pre-school children can be influenced successfully by different forms of training.

Gender differences in the mental rotation test: An effect of response format?

Glück, Judith Inst. für Psychologie, Universität Klagenfurt, Klagenfurt, Austria Fabrizii, Claudia Dept. of Psychology, University of Vienna, Vienna, Austria
Gender differences in the Mental Rotation Test (MRT) are larger than gender differences in response time-based measures of mental rotation. One possible reason is the response format of the MRT, where two responses are chosen from four alternatives. This format may induce extensive cross-checking in individuals with low spatial self-confidence. In a study with 288 students, an MRT version was used where 0 to four alternatives could be correct. Gender differences were significantly smaller than in the original MRT, but only when the standard time limit was used. Thus, subtle factors such as item presentation can affect gender differences markedly.

Do 9 years-old already show the well-known (male superiority) gender effect in a classical mental rotation test?

Vorstius, Corinna Inst. für Exp. Psychologie, Universität Düsseldorf, Düsseldorf, Germany Jansen-Osmann, Petra Institute of Exp. Psychology, Heinrich-Heine-University, Duesseldorf, Germany Heil, Martin Institute of Exp. Psychology, Heinrich-Heine-University, Duesseldorf, Germany
This study focused on the age, at which the well-known gender effect – favoring males – in mental rotation performance develops. Two groups of children with a mean age of 9.3 and 10.3 years and adults answered the classical mental rotations test (MRT, Peters et al., 1995). 10.3 years old children and adults showed the expected large gender effects (Johnson & Meade, 1987), whereas the 9.3 years old children did not, although effect sizes indicate a small to medium effect. Possible reasons for these differences will be introduced and a consecutive planned study will be presented.

Lateralized brain activation during mental rotation is not ontogenetic, but determined by familiarity

Lange, Leonie F. Inst. für Exp. Psychologie, Universität Düsseldorf, Düsseldorf, Germany Heil, Martin Institute of Experimental Psyc, Heinrich-Heine-University, Duesseldorf, Germany Jansen-Osmann, Petra Institute of Experimental Psyc, Heinrich-Heine-University, Duesseldorf, Germany
Recent publications suggest that there is a developmental-based change of lateralization of brain activity during mental rotation from left to bilateral. One explanation might be the amount of familiarity with the stimuli material, i.e. adults might be more familiar with letters than children. To test this, ERPs of 3 agegroups (7-8, 11-12 and adults) were measured during mental rotation with animal drawings. Children's left lateralization observed with characters was not replicated. Instead, a left lateralization for adults was found. Probably, adults are not as familiar with the drawings as children. This might have caused the left laterality.

S-103: Social power and political skill in politics and organizations

Gerhard Blickle (chair)
The analysis of power in politics and organizations is a promising field of applied psychological research. The symposium will deal with the effective and ineffective social power strategies, facework in political discourse, perception of politics in organizations, political skill (interpersonal influence, social astuteness, networking ability, impression management), and the consequences on social conflict and the implementation of innovation in organizations. Data from field studies in organizations, discourse analyses, and theoretical contributions will be presented. Political skill is seen as a

resource to constructively use social power, i.e., create trust, neutralize stress, deal constructively with conflicts, and implement successfully organizational change.

A critical incident approach to the analysis of power/ interaction in political confrontation
Raven, Bertram Los Angeles, USA
The critical incident technique is applied to effectiveness of social power strategies. Using as our tools the Bases of Power and the Power/Interaction Model, we examined intensively three such critical incidents: one successful–Hitler's influence on Austrian Prime Minister Kurt von Schuschnigg; one ultimately successful–Winston Churchill's attempts to influence President Franklin Roosevelt during World War II; one questionably successful–Harry Truman's attempts to restrain General MacArthur from dangerous aggressive action in the Korean War. These analyses not only help to clarify the power/interaction process, but provide support for the theory with indications for modifications, extension, and further development.

Face and facework in political discourse
Bull, Peter Dept. of Psychology, University of York, York, United Kingdom
The focus of this paper is on the extent to which political discourse can be understood in terms of the concepts of "face" and "facework". A series of analyses of British politicians have been conducted by the author in three distinctive genres: political speeches, televised political interviews, and parliamentary question time. Overall, it will be argued that face and facework are central preoccupations of politicians and central to an understanding of political discourse. It will be further argued that the results of these analyses are highly relevant to our understanding of political language in organizations.

Internal politics in the academia: Theoretical and empirical analysis of its relationship with social capital and job performance
Vigoda-Gadot, Eran School of Political Science, University of Haifa, Haifa, Israel Talmud, Ilan Dept. of Sociology, University of Haifa, Haifa, Israel Peled, Aviv Department of Sociology, University of Haifa, Haifa, Israel
The prime goal of this study was to examine perceptions of organizational politics (POPS) as viewed from the scholarly chair of faculty staff in a public university. POPS and individuals' social capital (i.e., trust, social support and reciprocity, and social tradeoffs) are hypothesizes to be related with job performance (i.e., job satisfaction, organizational commitment, stress and strain, and burnout). We surveyed 142 junior and senior faculty members of a large public Israeli university and tested three competing models of direct and indirect relationships. Major results, based on Structural Equation Modeling (SEM) analysis indicate that the direct model is superior to any other alternative.

Antecendents and consequences of political skill: A longitudinal investigation over two years with newly hired employees
Blickle, Gerhard Bonn, Germany Ferris, Gerald Department of Management, University of Florida, Talahasse, USA
Political skill has been demonstrated to predict important work outcomes, to facilitate the effectiveness of influence tactics, and to neutralize the dysfunctional effects of stressors on strain reactions.The present study reports on longitudinal data gathered from newly hired employees over the course of two years testing hypotheses regarding the dispositional and developmental experience antecedents, career-related consequences, and mediation of these antecedents and outcomes by political skill. Implications of these results, strengths and

limitations, and directions for future research are discussed.

The impact of wielded power on idea generation and implementation of innovations
Krause, Diana Dept. of Social Science, University of Western Ontario, London, Canada
The purpose of this presentation is to propose a framework that explains the effects of wielded power on idea generation and the implementation of process innovations (e.g., introduction of a new project management approach, performance appraisal system). Two studies have been conducted to provide preliminary evidence for the validity of the model. Confirmatory factor analyses in study 1 did not support the distinction between 11 bases of power as proposed by Raven et al. (1998). Study 2 supported the higher functionality of soft power bases compared to harsh power bases for both, idea generation as well as implementation.

Conflicts and political skill in organizations
Solga, Marc Inst. für Psychologie, Universität Bonn, Bonn, Germany
In their meta-analysis, De Dreu and Weingart (2003) showed intragroup conflict to be negatively correlated with group member's subjective well-being as well as with team performance. Among others, Jehn and Bendersky (2003) called for research on variables moderating the afore mentioned relationships. Linking research on intragroup conflict and political skill – two fields of research with little connection to date – this presentation approaches the role of political skill as a neutralizer, or even ameliorator, of intragoup conflict's detrimental effects on well-being and team performance.

S-104: Do infants have a theory of mind?

Beate Sodian, Diane Poulin-Dubois (chair)
Recent research has addressed infants' ability to attribute knowledge, including false beliefs, to other people. This symposium presents new and converging findings, based on visual attention and interactive research paradigms, suggesting that infants become increasingly competent in taking others' knowledge and beliefs into account when making sense of their behavior. The papers address lean and rich interpretations of these findings, asking whether infants' competencies are based on mental state attribution and therefore truly indicate that they possess an early form of folk psychology.

Understanding of knowledge/ignorance in one-year-olds
Carpenter, Malinda Evolutionary Anthropology, Max-Planck-Institut, Leipzig, Germany
We demonstrate in a series of studies that 1-year-old infants use their understanding of knowledge/ ignorance to make sense of others' behavior and to communicate appropriately. For example, 12-month-olds point differently for knowledgeable and ignorant adults. Fourteen-month-olds know not just which objects are known to adults but also what particular experiences adults have had with the objects – but only if infants have shared some of those experiences with the adults. Finally, in progress studies suggest that 14-month-olds imitate differently based on the competence of the demonstrator and that young children may demonstrate understanding of false belief in a helping paradigm.

Who knows best? Infants selectively attribute knowledge to others
Poulin-Dubois, Diane Dept. of Psychology, Concordia University, Montreal, Canada Chow, Virgina Dept. of Psychology, Concordia University, Montreal, Canada

This study examined whether 16-month-olds use the past reliability of a person's looking behavior in their attribution of true beliefs. Infants were administered a Search Task in which they observed an experimenter show excitement while looking inside a box that contained either a toy (Reliable Looker) or was empty (Unreliable Looker). Infants were then administered a True Belief Task in which the experimenter searched for the toy in a location that was congruent or incongruent with her belief about its location. Results indicated that only infants in the Reliable Looker condition looked longer at the incongruent display.

Early understanding of false belief: Rule-based or mentalistic?
Traeuble, Birgit Inst. für Psychologie, Universität Heidelberg, Heidelberg, Germany Marinovic, Vesna Inst. für Psychologie, Universität Heidelberg, Heidelberg, Germany Pauen, Sabina Inst. für Psychologie, Universität Heidelberg, Heidelberg, Germany
The idea that even young infants might appeal to others' mental states (Onishi & Baillargeon, 2005) is challenged by authors who propose that infants' responses in nonverbal false belief tasks might be based on an behavioural rule that "actors look for an object where they last saw it" (Ruffman & Perner, 2005). The behavioural-rule argument is tested by using a balance-beam apparatus that allows the actor to manipulate the location of an object without watching it. This allows a decoupling of the seeing-searching relation in false belief tasks. The data of 50 15-month-olds will be presented and discussed.

False belief understanding in 18-month-olds' anticipatory looking behavior: An eye-tracking study
Neumann, Annina Inst. für Psychologie, Universität München, München, Germany Thoermer, Claudia Inst. für Psychologie, Universität München, München, Germany Sodian, Beate Inst. für Psychologie, Universität München, München, Germany
The ability to predict people's actions based on their beliefs is a critical feature of a Theory of Mind. While recent looking-time studies claim false-belief understanding in infants as young as 15.5 months, belief-based action prediction has not yet been shown below the age of 24 months. In the present study we applied eye-tracking to analyse 18-month-olds' performance in a non-verbal false-belief paradigm. We found evidence for correct anticipation of the protagonist's action. Further, we provide evidence that infants did not use simple rule-based strategies, such as "agents search for an object where they last saw it".

Infants' understanding of false beliefs about the location, identity and properties of objects
Scott, Rose M. Dept. of Psychology, University of Illinois, Champaign, USA Baillargeon, Renee Dept. of Psychology, University of Illinois, Champaign, IL, USA
Recent work suggests that infants in the second year of life can attribute to others false beliefs about objects' location. Do these findings truly represent an understanding of false belief? If so, this understanding should not be limited to objects' location: infants should also be able to reason about other types of false beliefs, just as older children do. Here we present experiments demonstrating that by 18.5 months, infants can attribute false beliefs about objects' identity and internal properties. Together with previous results, these findings suggest that by the second year infants already possess a robust understanding of false belief.

S-105: Portrait of contemporary adolescence: An attempt to explore and explain young people's value, attitudes, behaviours and coping in everyday life

Siu-Fung Lin (chair)

Adolescents today live in a technologically advanced society and are facing stressors new to the earlier generations. This is an attempt to explore a new portrait of contemporary young people. A range of behaviours was chosen for discussion on their decision makings and attitudes on choices of idol worship, sexual behaviours, internet and video game use; suicide attempt and on stress coping. Attributes including personality, self-efficacy and parenting style towards these decisions will be explored. The effect of dispositional optimism on daily hassles and young people's mental health appears to be a stress-buffering strategy.

Optimism moderates the impact of hassles on mental health in Hong Kong Chinese undergraduates

Lai, Julian Dept. of Psychology, City University of Hong Kong, Hong Kong, China, People's Republic of : Hong Kong SAR

The moderating effect of dispositional optimism on the link between daily hassles and mental health was investigated in a group of 234 Chinese undergraduates in Hong Kong. Optimism was measured by a Chinese version of the revised Life Orientation Test (Lai et al., 2005), which had been shown to be represented by a single factor using confirmatory factor analysis in a separate sample of 750 Hong Kong Chinese (RMSEA = 0.038, NNFI = 0.924, and CFI = 0.955). Results of multiple regression analyses showed that more optimistic participants fared better than their less optimistic peers under stress.

S-106: Emotion regulation and mindfulness

Matthias Berking (chair)

The concepts of "emotion regulation" and "mindfulness" have gotten increasingly popular in recent years among practitioners and researchers in the field of clinical psychology. This development has taken place in spite of the fact there are still comparatively few studies that a) try to clarify the nature of these concepts, b) investigate their importance for mental health and treatment outcome and c) evaluate different interventions designed to improve emotion regulation or enhance mindfulness. Thus, the goal of this panel is to address these questions and present studies that help to understand how useful these concepts can be for improving outcome in psychotherapy.

Lower levels of mindfulness in currently and formerly depressed patients

Heidenreich, Thomas Inst. für Psychologie, Fachhochschule Esslingen, Esslingen, Germany Steil, Regina Psychosomatic Medicine, CI of Mental Health, Mannheim, Germany Michalak, Johannes Department of Psychology, University Bochum, Bochum, Germany Pommersheim, Karin Department of Psychology, University of Frankfurt, Frankfurt, Germany Baum, Corinna Department of Psychology, University of Frankfurt, Frankfurt, Germany Bohus, Martin Psychosomatic Medicine, CI of Mental Health, Mannheim, Germany

Objectives: To examine whether patients suffering from major depressive disorder (MDD) show lower levels of mindfulness compared to healthy controls. Methods: SCID-diagnosed currently depressed patients, formerly depressed patients and healthy community controls were compared using the Mindful Attention Awareness Scale (MAAS). Results: Both currently and formerly depressed patients show significantly lower levels of mindfulness than healthy controls. Additional analyses revealed moderate to high correlations of mindfulness with depressive symptoms. Conclusions: Lower levels of mindfulness can not only be detected in currently depressed patients but also in formerly depressed patients. Mindfulness might be an important target for increasing emotion regulation in depression.

Does mindfulness change the way people walk?

Michalak, Johannes Inst. für Klin. Psychologie, Ruhr-Universität Bochum, Bochum, Germany Troje, Nikolaus Psychology, Qeens's University Kingston, Kingston, Ontario, Canada Schulte, Dietmar Psychology, Ruhr-Universität Bochum, Bochum, Germany Heidenreich, Thomas Psychology, Hochschule Esslingen, Esslingen, Germany

Objectives: (1) Do dynamic gait patterns of currently and formerly depressed patients differ from never depressed people (2) Does mindfulness-based cognitive therapy (MBCT) normalize gait patterns of formerly depressed patients? Methods: Gait patterns of 30 formerly depressed patients participating in MBCT, 14 currently depressive inpatients and 30 never depressed participants were analyzed by fourier-based descriptions and computation of linear classifiers. Results: Gait patterns of currently depressed patients and formerly depressed patients differ form never depressed people. MBCT has some normalizing effect on the way patients walk. Conclusions: Mindfulness might change proprioceptive-bodily feedback important in the generation of depressive states.

The role of emotion suppression in vulnerability to depression: Results of two experimental studies

Ehring, Thomas Dept. of Clinical Psychology, University of Amsterdam, Amsterdam, Netherlands Bösterling, Andrea Dept. of Psychology, Universit of Bielefeld, Bielefeld, Germany Schnülle, Jewgenija Dept. of Psychology, University of Bielefeld, Bielefeld, Germany Fischer, Silke Dept. of Psychology, University of Bielefeld, Bielefeld, Germany Tuschen-Caffier, Brunna Dept. of Psychology, University of Freiburg, Freiburg, Germany

Objectives: Depression vulnerability has been suggested to be related to emotion suppression and a lack of emotion acceptance. Our studies aimed to test this hypothesis experimentally. Method: Recovered depressed and never depressed individuals were randomly assigned to the induction of emotion suppression or a functional emotion regulation strategy (study 1: reappraisal; study 2: acceptance) before undergoing a negative mood induction. Results: Recovered depressed individuals showed emotion suppression as their dominant response to the mood induction and benefited less from functional strategies than controls. Conclusions: The studies provide preliminary experimental evidence for a role of dysfunctional emotion regulation in depression-vulnerable individuals.

Emotion suppression in borderline personality disorder: An experience sampling study

Chapman, Alexander Dept. of Psychology, Simon Fraser University, Burnaby, BC, Canada Rosenthal, M. Zachary Cognitive Behavioral Research, Duke University, Durham, NC, USA Leung, Debbie Department of Psychology, University of Washington, Seattle, WA, USA

Objective: Examine the effects of emotion suppression in the natural environment among individuals with borderline personality (BPD) features. Methods: Participants who were high (n = 30) and low (n = 39) in BPD features observed or suppressed their emotions and monitored their emotions, impulsive urges, and behaviours over four days. Results: High-BPD participants reported greater negative emotions and stronger urges to engage in impulsive behaviours. For low-BPD participants, suppression led to higher negative emotions. Among high-BPD participants, suppression led to higher positive emotions and lower urges. Conclusion: Findings indicate negative effects of emotion suppression for low-BPD but not high-BPD participants.

Can we enhance the effectiveness of today's psychological interventions by adding an intensive emotion regulation skills training?

Berking, Matthias Dept. of Psychology, University of Washington, Washington, USA Reichardt, Alexander Psychology, University of Bern, Bern 9, Switzerland Pejic, Tanja Psychology, University of Giessen, Gießen, Germany Dippel, Alexandra Psychology, Vogelsberg Clinic, Grebenhain OT, Germany Franz, Caspar Psychology, University of Bern, Bern 9, USA

Objectives: Deficits in general emotion regulation skills have been shown to be important for the development and maintenance of mental disorders. Thus, adding an intensive training of these skills to empirically validated treatments should further enhance treatment outcome. Methods: 289 patients suffering from diverse mental disorders were randomly assigned to (inpatient) cognitive behavioral therapy (CBT) or to CBT plus an intensive training of emotion regulation. Results: Patients in the skills training condition showed greater improvements with regard to affect, emotion regulation skills, and depression. Conclusions: Adding an intensive emotion regulation skills training to empirically validated treatments can enhance treatment outcome.

S-107: Adaptive goal adjustment and well-being

Christel Salewski, Manja Vollmann (chair)

Adaptive goal adjustment in life situations that endanger goal attainment has been recognized as an important aspect of self-regulation. The aim of the symposium is to gather current research focussing on two aspects of goal adjustment, namely goal disengagement and goal reengagement. The importance of goal disengagement and reengagement with regard to psychological and physical well-being is examined in different life domains. The studies include subjects undergoing life transitions, participants in an occupational rehabilitation program, and patients with chronic/life-threatening illnesses. Both facets of adaptive goal adjustment contribute differentially to well-being, together with other variables such as optimism and illness representations.

Goal adjustment and well-being: Does the attainability of goals matter?

Salewski, Christel Rehabilitation Studien, FH Magdeburg-Stendal, Stendal, Germany Vollmann, Manja Psychological Assessment, Universität Konstanz, Konstanz, Germany

Objectives: The study aims at analyzing the relationship between adaptive goal adjustment and well-being in persons facing and not facing unattainable life goals. Method: In two studies with 111 participants in an occupational rehabilitation program and 200 students, dispositional optimism, goal adjustment and three health-related outcomes were assessed. Results: In both groups, goal reengagement explains significant amounts of variance of well-being. Additionally, goal disengagement was import for persons undergoing an occupational rehabilitation program. Conclusion: Depending on actual experiences with unattainable goals, the two components of goal adjustment are differentially predictive of well-being in the two groups.

Does goal adjustment moderate the relationship between optimism and well-being?
Vollmann, Manja Psychological Assessment, Universität Konstanz, Konstanz, Germany Salewski, Christel Psychology of Rehabilitation, University of Applied Sciences, Stendal, Germany
Objectives: The aim of the present research was to examine whether the relation between optimism and health-related outcomes are mediated by adaptive goal adjustment (i.e., disengagement and reengagement). Method: In two studies with 111 participants in an occupational rehabilitation program and 200 students, dispositional optimism, goal adjustment and three health-related outcomes were assessed. Results: In both samples, the relationship between optimism and health-related outcomes was partially mediated by goal-reengagement. Conclusion: The effect of optimism on health outcomes seems to be influenced, at least to some extent, by the ability of optimists to set new goals.

Goal adjustment profiles and well-being trajectories during a life-span transition
Haase, Claudia CADS, Universität Jena, Jena, Germany Silbereisen, Rainer K. Inst. Entwicklungspsychologie, Universität Jena, Jena, Germany
Objectives: This longitudinal study examined well-being trajectories of young adults with different profiles of goal adjustment (i.e., disengagement and reengagement) during a life-span transition. Combining disengagement with reengagement was expected to be most adaptive. Method: We followed 523 university graduates in a 4-wave longitudinal study until one year after graduation. Data was analyzed using latent growth curve modeling. Results: Well-being trajectories were most favorable for individuals with high goal disengagement and high goal reengagement. Selective goal disengagement was associated with unfavorable trajectories. Implications: Adaptive goal adjustment requires both disengagement and reengagement, particularly during life-span transitions. Selective goal disengagement is maladaptive.

Goal disengagement and goal reengagement among multiple sclerosis patients: Relationship to wellbeing and illness representation
Neter, Efrat Dept. Behavioral Sciences, Ruppin Academic Center, Emeq Hefer, Israel Litvak, Anat Dept. of Behavioral Science, Tel-Aviv Jaffa College, Tel-Aviv, Israel Miller, Ariel Department of Neurology, Carmel Medical Center, Haifa, Israel
Objectives: The study examines whether goal adjustment is related to well-being, illness representation and disease characteristics in a clinical population of multiple sclerosis (MS) patients. Methods: 101 MS patients participated. Questionnaire tapped goal adjustment, anxiety, depression, purpose in life, illness intrusion, illness perception and background variables. Results: Significant results emerged only on depression, where an interaction between goal disengagement and re-engagement was uncovered. Participants high on disengagement and low on re-engagement were more affected by depression. Unexpectedly, the least depressed are those low on both disengagement and re-engagement. Implications: Differences between healthy individuals vs. patients' populations are discussed.

Goal adjustment and well-being in cancer patients: The role of prognosis
Fleer, Joke Graduate School for Health, UMC Groningen, Groningen, Netherlands Ranchor, Adelita V. Graduate School for Health Res, UMCG, RB Groningen, Netherlands
Objectives. Assess how goal adjustment and intrusive thoughts relate in cancer patients with different prognoses. Measurements. Goal Disengagement (GD)/Goal Reengagement (GR) Scale;

Intrusion Scale of the Impact of Event Scale. Results. In patients with an unfavorable prognosis more intrusive thoughts related to lower levels of GR; in patients with an uncertain prognosis they related to lower levels of GD. No significant relations were found in patients with a favorable prognosis. Implications. Different adjustment strategies might be beneficial for cancer patients with different prognoses. Findings will be interpreted using theoretical frameworks of Martin and Tesser (1996) and Wrosch et al. (2003).

S-108: Psychology in the Arab world

Uwe Gielen, Ramadan A. Ahmed (chair)
This symposium reviews the state of selcted areas of psychology in the Arab world. Ramadan Ahmed and Uwe Gielen present a general overview of psychology in Arab countries, Maan A. Bari Saleh discusses clinical psychology in Yemen, Jasem Al-Khawajah analyzes the applications of cognitive therapy in Kuwait, Ahmed Megreya presents an overview of cognitive psychology, Uwe Gielen introduces a proposal to establish an institute of Arab psychology, and Juris Draguns presents an integrative discussion of these papers from an international and regional perspective.

The state of psychology in the Arab world
Ahmed, Ramadan A. Dept. of Psychology, Kuwait University, Kaifan, Kuwait Gielen, Uwe Dept. of Psychology, St. Francis College, Brooklyn Heights, USA
We critically review the state of psychology in the Arab world by tracing its history, describing prevailing research interests, comparing its situation to the situation in other developing countries, tracing some of the existing Arab psychology associations, describing psychology's pedagogic situation, outlining available professional and publishing opportunities, noting psychology's generally weak public image, and mentioning some recent efforts to connect psychology more closely to Islam. We conclude that Arab psychologists need to achieve a number of specified goals before their discipline can be said to constitute an intellectually convincing and socially effective force for professional education and training, and for positive social change.

Clinical psychology and counseling in Yemen
Saleh, Maan A. Bari Dept. of Behavioral Sciences, Aden University, Aden, Yemen
In Yemen, general and clinical psychology took root in the 1970s. This paper highlights psychology's history in Yemen, including the developmental origins of clinical psychology and its implementation as an applied science in hospitals, private clinics, and accredited university programs. Related issues in the field are discussed: legislation, assessment, therapeutic teams, and capacity building. Two established Yemeni counseling services are highlighted: the Hotline for Psychological Aid and the Aden School Counseling Program. Both programs offer services from a community orientation in order to support abused women and children. Finally, the role of Yemeni clinical psychologists at the national, regional and international levels is discussed.

Using cognitive therapy in Kuwait
Al-Khawaja, Jasem A.M. Dept. of Psychology, Kuwait University, Kaifan, Kuwait
In the 1950's, psychoanalytic theory and therapy constituted the only approaches to the treatment of psychological disorders in the Arab countries. Subsequently, a number of Arab psychologists began to examine alternative theories in psychology, finding that there are different treatment methods for psychological disorders. In this paper,

cognitive psychotherapy will be presented as one treatment method for psychological disorders in Kuwait with the help of five case studies. It is suggested that many concepts in cognitive therapy are supported by Islamic ideas especially when adapted to culturally specific behaviors. This is the reason why many cases treated by this method progress successfully.

Cognitive psychology in the Arab countries
Megreya, Ahmed M. Dept. of Psychology, Menoufia University, Menoufia, Egypt
This paper focuses on the history of cognitive psychology in Arab countries: its beginnings, development, and present status. The paper also discusses the main research areas in Arab cognitive psychology which show that some topics in cognitive psychology, such as cognitive styles, have received extensive attention by Arab psychologists while other topics have received little or no attention. Suggestions for improving the status of cognitive psychology in Arab countries will be discussed.

Proposal to establish institute of Arab psychology
Gielen, Uwe Dept. of Psychology, St. Francis College, Brooklyn Heights, USA
Although psychology in the Arab countries has steadily developed, it has nevertheless fallen behind in relation to some other economically, politically, and culturally emerging regions of the world. In order to strengthen the presence of psychology in the Arab world, it is proposed that an Institute of Arab psychology be established. The institute could organize conferences, workshops, and courses in psychology and overlapping areas of endeavor, serve as a model for establishing a research culture, support interdisciplinary cooperation in the context of joint research projects, train researchers and practitioners of psychology, and periodically publish a survey of Arab psychology.

S-109: The social psychology of avatars and agents: Real life effects of virtual communication

Sabine Trepte, Nicole Krämer (chair)
Avatars and agents have become the major forms of media access to virtual environments. Avatars are virtual representations of people, e.g. in computer games. Players can create their avatars according to their needs and the requirements of the game. Agents are human-like embodiments designed to assist the users in virtual communication. Via an avatar or agent a player can elicit all kinds of social interaction. Thus, communication between user and avatar or agent evolves to a new form and it has potential effects on user identity as well as on the experience of virtual communication.

The effects of social avatars and emotional valence on facial muscle movements in an immersive virtual environment
Eric, Vanman Dept. of Psychology, University of Queensland, Brisbane, Australia Philipp, Michael Department of Psychology, University of Queensland, Brisbane, Australia
This research explored the effectiveness of measuring facial muscles that are elicited in virtual environments containing avatars. In two studies, participants viewed positive and negative pictures in a virtually rendered environment. Depending on condition, they were either seated in the virtual lab alone or with two human avatars. The two studies differed in the extent to which the avatars were made salient. Surface electrodes recorded brow and cheek electromyography throughout the experimental sessions. Analyses revealed responses to the pictures consistent with previous studies in real-

world settings. Moreover, these affective responses were augmented in the presence of the avatars.

The impact of nonverbal signs transmitted by avatars on collaborative performance

Allmendinger, Katrin Industrial Engineering, Fraunhofer-Institut, Stuttgart, Germany Guadagno, Rosanna Psychology, University of Alabama, Tuscaloosa, USA Blascovich, Jim Psychology, University of California, Santa Barbara, USA Beall, Andrew Psychology, University of California, Santa Barbara, USA

In our experiment, dyads were asked to play a modified game of dominos in an immersive collaborative virtual environment. The availability of rendered head movements and the presence of a virtual pointer were varied. The results show that when participants were able to augment their discussion via the use of a virtual pointer, their performance was higher than in the condition without pointer. Head movement information did not impact the number of correct responses suggesting that it was a too broad source of direction information in this context. The study shows that not merely adding channels helps optimizing virtual collaboration.

Keep smiling: An embodied agents impact on users evaluation and smiling behavior

Sommer, Nicole Sozialpsychologie, Universität Duisburg-Essen, Duisburg, Germany Krämer, Nicole Inst. für Sozialpsychologie, Universität Duisburg-Essen, Duisburg, Germany Kopp, Stefan Artificial Intelligence group, University Bielefeld, Bielefeld, Germany Becker, Christian Artificial Intelligence, University Bielefeld, Bielefeld, Germany

Recent studies demonstrate that people show social reactions when interacting with virtual agents. Although they would consciously evaluate this behavior as inappropriate, they e.g. behave in a socially desirable way, show increased cooperation or apply human-like communication forms. Within the present study we analyzed whether humans reciprocate an agents smile. In a between subjects design, 104 participants conducted a ten-minute small talk conversation with an agent that either did not smile, engaged in casual smiles or displayed frequent smiles. Results show that people did not only evaluate the smiling agent more favorably but that they themselves smiled more frequently.

Competition or coping: The effects of task structure and satisfaction with life on the choice of avatar features

Trepte, Sabine Inst. für Medienpsychologie, Medienschule Hamburg, Hamburg, Germany Reinecke, Leonard Media Psychology, Hamburg Media School, Hamburg, Germany Behr, Katharina-Maria Media Psychology, Hamburg Media School, Hamburg, Germany

In a 2(competitive game vs. non-competitive game) x 2(high vs. low satisfaction with life) quasi-experiment the effects of task structure and satisfaction with life on the choice of Avatar features were investigated. 483 participants read descriptions of 6 computer games and designed an Avatar for each game by choosing from a set of personality characteristics. Participants designed their Avatars according to game requirements in case of the competitive games and in line with their own personality in case of the non-competitive contexts. Participants with low satisfaction with life show a tendency to compensate for own deficits by creating idealized Avatars.

Avatar creations and individual goals: An empirical investigation of avatar designs and user motivation in second life

Misoch, Sabina Soziologisches Seminar, Universität Luzern, Luzern, Switzerland

One of the most important questions regarding user representation using avatars is to analyse why users represent themselves in a special manner and to determine the conscious aims underlying these representations. Previous studies have shown a tendency towards representations using human avatars that correspond to (stereotype) images of maleness and femininity – and thus the ideal of beauty prevalent in our culture. To identify a correlation between the proxy designs employed and the individual goals underlying these avatar creations, the data analysis from a current study (visual data analysis; qualitative interviews) about self-representation in Second Life will be presented.

S-110: Interplay between epistemological beliefs and different media during learning processes

Elmar Stahl, Dorothe Kienhues (chair)

There exists growing empirical evidence that learners' epistemological beliefs, i.e. their beliefs about the nature of knowledge and knowing, are important predictors for learning processes and outcomes. Also, learners' beliefs depend on their experiences within learning scenarios. Media like textbooks, instructional films, or the Internet are essential components for learning. Therefore it is reasonable to assume that learners' epistemological beliefs should affect and should be affected by different kinds of media. Nevertheless little research exists about this interplay. This symposium aims to present current studies giving evidence that epistemological beliefs are highly related to the use of media

Epistemological thinking of sixth graders during online learning

Barzilai, Sarit Snunit Center, Hebrew University of Jerusalem, Jerusalem, Israel Zohar, Anat School of Education, Hebrew University of Jerusalem, Jerusalem, Israel

The Internet fundamentally changes the ways in which information is accessed and organized, thus requiring a better understanding of how students gather, evaluate, and integrate information online. The purpose of this study is to characterize the epistemological thinking of students as they learn online. The study uses an epistemological understanding questionnaire (Kuhn et. al, 2000) and thinking aloud during two open-ended online tasks, followed by retrospective interviews (Hofer, 2004). Participants are 42 Israeli sixth graders. Preliminary results show that epistemological thinking plays a key role in online learning processes. The study analyzes the interplay between epistemological metacognition and strategic performance.

The interplay between students' scientific epistemological beliefs and science learning in internet-enhanced environments

Tsai, Chin-Chung Graduate School, National Taiwan University, Taipei, Taiwan

Numerous educational psychologists highlight the importance of epistemological beliefs, but little research has addressed the role of epistemological beliefs in student learning in Internet environments. By gathering research data from some high school students in Taiwan, this study found that students with more sophisticated constructivist-oriented scientific epistemological beliefs (SEBs) tended to benefit more from online science learning environments. Moreover, students with more constructivist SEBs tended to express not only more higher-level conceptions of science learning, but also those of

Internet-based learning; they perceived learning science or Internet-based learning as "understanding" and "seeing in a new way," rather than "memorization."

Epistemological analyses of educational materials: Elementary school books and curricula in English, science and mathematics

Haerle, Florian Educational Psychology, University of Nevada, Las Vegas, USA Bendixen, Lisa Educational Psychology, University of Nevada, Las Vegas, USA

The aim of this presentation is to demonstrate how epistemic messages of school books and curricula can influence the epistemic climate of elementary classrooms; how knowledge is portrayed by teachers and experienced by students in classrooms. We argue that epistemic messages of educational materials can influence (1) the beliefs of students about knowledge and knowing and (2) the beliefs of teachers about knowledge, teaching, and assessment. Our claims stem from research in US and German elementary classrooms (4th & 6th Grade). The study encompassed a variety of methods, such as document analysis, interviews with teachers and students, and classroom observations.

Impact of epistemological sensitization and context on source preferences

Porsch, Torsten Psychologisches Institut III, Universität Münster, Münster, Germany

The critical evaluation of sources of information is an important element of critical thinking, which has become all the more important since the Internet has become an important source of information on many topics. This study examines the impact of epistemological beliefs and search context on source evaluation. After an epistemological sensitization high school students rated several sources (e.g. Internet, books, and teachers) in the context of a homework task and in the context of a personal problem. Results show that the impact of epistemological beliefs on source preference is moderated by the context of information search.

Effects of different kinds of representational formats on epistemological judgements

Stahl, Elmar Medieninstiut, Pädagog. Hochschule Freiburg, Freiburg, Germany

Learners with little prior knowledge in a discipline can refer to the reliability of the source to judge the certainty and validity of information. This study examines whether the representational format also effects epistemological judgements so much, that information presented in more concrete representations like film is seen as more certain and valid than information presented in more abstract representations like texts. Students received the same content presented as a film, a text-picture-combination, a text or a short abstract and made epistemological judgements. Results are discussed in relation to the interplay between epistemological beliefs, media and information processing.

FP-074: Heuristics and frequency estimation

Children's understanding of cognitions and emotions: A longitudinal study on the links between theory of mind and metacognition

Lecce, Serena Dept. of Psychology, University of Pavia, Pavia, Italy Zocchi, Silvia Psychology, University of Pavia, Pavia, Italy Palladino, Paola Psychology, University of Pavia, Pavia, Italy Pagnin, Adriano Psychology, University of Pavia, Pavia, Italy

This longitudinal study aims at exploring the links between children's metacognition and their ToM, comparing beliefs vs. emotions and controlling for vocabulary. 71 children (Time1: mean age 120.7, SD=6.5; Time2: mean age 131.59, SD=5.9) were tested for vocabulary, ToM and metacognition. Correlational analyses showed a positive association between children's understanding of cognition and their metacognition at both times also controlling for vocabulary. Furthermore, children's understanding of cognition significantly predicted their later metacognition over and above language and metacognition at T1 (F (4,66) = 10.99; p < .01). Overall, our results extend the literature on children's knowledge about the mind.

Probability communication with verbal expressions: The role of directionality

Honda, Hidehito Human System Science, Tokyo Institute of Technology, Tokyo, Japan *Yamagishi, Kimihiko* Human System Science, Tokyo Institute of Technology, Tokyo, Japan

People often communicate probability information with verbal phrases (we call verbal probabilities, VPs). Literature has shown that VPs have a feature called "directionality." We explored the role of the directionality in communication of probability information. We hypothesized that, in the communication of uncertainty with VPs, a speaker would choose the directionality on the basis of his/her reference point for a situation. Results from two experiments suggested that reference points influenced speaker's choice of the directionality of VPs in communicating probability, and that listeners made accurate inferences about speaker's reference point on the basis of the directionality being used.

Conjunction 'Fallacies' with natural frequency formats and ratings: Bayesian logic

von Sydow, Momme Inst. für Psychologie, Universität Göttingen, Göttingen, Germany

Bayesian logic (BL) is proposed as a rational model explaining conjunction fallacies (CFs). The probability judgment P(Girls from the Linda school become bank tellers) < P(Girls from the Linda school become bank tellers who are feminist) involves a CF. P(A&B) can never be larger than P(A). BL calculates the posterior probability that a frequency pattern is generated by 'probability tables', corresponding to (probabilistic) logical connectors. BL takes distributions into account and predicts CFs under particular conditions. In two studies we used contingency tables and a rating format – nonetheless, we obtained CFs and double CFs as predicted by BL.

Simplicity of simple heuristics: The role of the central executive

Gula, Bartosz Inst. für Pychologie, Universität Klagenfurt, Klagenfurt, Austria *Vitouch, Oliver* Department of Psychology, Klagenfurt University, Klagenfurt, Austria

In the simple heuristics approach (Gigerenzer et al., 1999) decision models describing probabilistic inferences from memory have been promoted. Adding to previous work by Bröder & Schiffer (2006) the empirical validity of these models was addressed in two studies. First, the think aloud technique was used to assess the kind and number of cues participants spontaneously use. The results support the notion of one-reason and recognition-based decision making. Second, the impact of the central executive (tapped by a tone monitoring task) on strategy selection was assessed in a dual task paradigm. The results suggest that participants switch to simpler strategies under cognitive load conditions.

The influence of criterion knowledge on the recognition heuristic

Hilbig, Benjamin E. Universität Mannheim, Mannheim, Germany *Pohl, Rüdiger F.* Lehrstuhl für Psychologie III, University of Mannheim, Mannheim, Germany *Bröder, Arndt* Allgemeine Psychologie 2, University of Bonn, Bonn, Germany

The recognition heuristic (RH) assumes that people make inferences based on recognition in a non-compensatory fashion. This assumption has been

questioned by several studies. However, some of these findings have been refuted by the argument that they could stem from conclusive criterion knowledge which renders a heuristic decision obsolete. In an experiment with 81 participants making inferential choices between pairs of cities we show that one specific type of criterion knowledge indeed influences participants' non-use of the RH. However, we also replicate findings which clearly contradict the RH while strictly controlling for such criterion knowledge.

An analysis to information search processes of female mate choice

Liu, Yongfang Dept. of Psychology, East China Normal University, Shanghai, People's Republic of China *Su, Lina* Department of Psychology, East China Normal University, Shanghai, People's Republic of China

A experiment was conducted to examine the information search processes of female mate choice using information board technique.The subjects were 68 unmarried women.Results show that:(1) the numbers of male candidates affect time of decision-making, depth of information processing and pattern of information search;(2) Subjects prefer to search information based on alterrnatives instead of cues;(3) The degree of the subject's satisfaction for search results did not improve due to increase of the number of male candidates and decision time;(4) personality, health state and responsibility of male candidates are the 3 key factors in the female mate choice.The conclusation of the research is that female mate choice is a bounded rational search process.

FP-075: Stereotypes, prejudice and discrimination

Stereotypes of physically and speech disabled persons as detected with partially structured attitude measures

Stern, Steven Johnstown Campus, University of Pittsburgh, Johnstown, USA *Mullennix, John* Johnstown Campus, Psych, University of Pittsburgh, Johnstown, PA, USA *Flaherty, Mary* Johnstown Campus, Psych, University of Pittsburgh, Johnstown, PA, USA *Grounds, Benjamin* Johnstown Campus, Psych, University of Pittsburgh, Johnstown, PA, USA *Hutchison, Erica* Johnstown Campus, Psych, University of Pittsburgh, Johnstown, PA, USA *Steinhauser, Elizabeth* Psychology, Florida Institute of Technolog, Melbourne, FL, USA

Partially Structured Attitude Measures (PSAM, Vargas, et al., 2004) are measures of implicit attitudes in which ambiguous statements are interpreted differently by participants depending upon existing attitudes. In a series of studies we sought to refine the method, use the method to examine stereotypes of the speaking and physically disabled, and to validate by comparison to other measures. We found evidence that participants stereotyped speech disabled and physically disabled persons as asexual, unappealing, dependent, entitled, isolated, and unemployable. Further, we found evidence that type of disability affected stereotyping, and that stereotypes were most evident for people with both disabilities.

Imagine being an outgrouper: The impact of perspective taking on intergroup helping intentions

Bilewicz, Michal Psychology, Warsaw University, Warsaw, Poland

People are more willing to help those who belong to their own group than to the outgroup. Research on perspective-taking has shown that many forms of ingroup favoritism disappear when people take perspective of the outgroup. The current research explores the possibility of increasing the level of intergroup helping by a perspective-taking manip-

ulation. Experiments performed in Poland demonstrated that Polish participants who were made to imagine that they became members of an outgroup (perspective-taking manipulation) were more willing to help outgroup members. The moderating role of perceived power is discussed in the context of the perspective-taking theory.

Stereotypes and identity: Romanians and European Union citizens

Glaveanu, Vlad-Petre Faculty of Psychology, University of Bucharest, Bucharest, Romania

The study focuses on the stereotype representations persons from Bucharest have regarding Romanians and European Union citizens as well as the degree in which they embrace the European citizenship after January 2007. The research included a sample of 466 persons from Bucharest and followed a methodology inspired by the social representations prototypical-categorical technique. The results are discussed considering previous research as well as social psychology theories: social identity, system justification and social creativity. The main conclusion, with great practical relevance, is that respondents put an obvious psychological distance between the two groups revealed by the dissimilarity in associated attributes.

"The Germans will never forgive the Jews for Auschwitz": Does group-based guilt predict positive intergroup attitudes?

Imhoff, Roland Inst. für Sotialpsychologie, Universität Bonn, Bonn, Germany *Erb, Hans-Peter* Social Psychology, Helmut-Schmidt University, Hamburg, Germany

Collective guilt, an aversive emotional reaction on ingroup atrocities, is commonly associated with positive phenomena such as the motivation to make amends. However, sociologically oriented authors have postulated the opposite. Theories of secondary anti-Semitism assume that feelings of guilt lead to more outgroup aggression toward the (historical) victims. 4 studies (total N = 432) were conducted to test whether guilt is a better predictor for positive intergroup attitudes than regret and responsibility. Regret predicted less negative views of the victim group, whereas guilt had no such relation. The results question the positive effects implied in the literature on collective guilt.

Generalised attitude of young adults towards Moslems

Kerimova, Izumrud Moscow, Russia

This research presents findings from an empirical investigation of the stereotypes that people hold towards Moslem. Purpose: investigation of the differences in perception of the general image of typical Moslem and typical local Moslem. Methods: associative test, attitude analysis method, 60 participants (Moscow students, 20-25). Results: stereotypes of typical Moslem and typical local Moslem differ according to the criteria of generalization and vector of relation. The image of typical Moslem is positive and has a single meaning (high level of generalization) though the stereotype of the typical local Moslem is negative and has various meanings (low level of generalization).

FP-076: Stress and coping

Gender and negative affectivity effects on stressor appraisal and coping selection: A test of the differential vulnerability hypothesis

Bradley, Graham Dept. of Psychology, Griffith University, Gold Coast, Australia *Eaton, Rebecca* Psychology, Griffith University, Gold Coast, Australia

To investigate the role of gender and negative affectivity in stressor appraisal and coping selection, exposure to stressors was controlled by requiring the 216 participants to rate the stressfulness of identical hypothetical scenarios. As predicted, females rated the scenarios as more stressful than males, and perceptions of stressfulness increased with negative affectivity. In terms of coping selection, females endorsed emotion-focused strategies more than males, even when perceived stressfulness was controlled. NA predicted selection of both emotion- and avoidance-focused coping, although only the latter remained significant controlling for stressor appraisals. Implications for the prediction and management of stress are discussed.

Social support in cyberspace and appraisal of coping with cancer

Seckin, Gul *Sociology and Anthropology, University of Maryland, Baltimore, USA*

Objective: This presentation will provide a discussion of a research that examined the associations between cancer patients' appraisal of coping with their illness and receipt of social support in cyberspace through participation internet cancer support groups. Methods: An internet survey was conducted with 350 cancer patients. Bivariate and multiple regression analyses were performed to examine the data. Results: A significant associations were found between illness appraisal, psychological well being and receipt of online support. Discussion: Results suggested that social support, even if it is in cyberspace, plays an important role in illness appraisal and psychological well-being.

Emotional disclosure buffers the negative effect of motive-incongruence on health

Schüler, Julia *Department of Psychology, University of Zurich, Zurich, Switzerland* **Job, Veronika** *Inst. für Psychologie, Universität Zürich, Zürich, Switzerland* **Fröhlich, Stefanie** *Department of Psychology, University of Osnabrück, Osnabrück, Germany* **Brandstätter, Veronika** *Department of Psychology, University of Zurich, Zurich, Switzerland*

In two cross sectional studies the beneficial effect of emotional disclosure on health was examined with respect to motive-incongruence as a hidden stressor. It was assumed that emotional disclosure would help individuals with incongruence between their implicit and explicit affiliation motive to buffer the negative effects of this incongruence. Both studies confirmed the hypothesis. In Study 1 (N = 93) participants with a motive incongruence used less medication when they practiced emotional disclosure. Study 2 (N = 51) revealed the same result pattern for somatization. The role of emotional disclosure for the resolution of intrapersonal conflict is discussed.

Stressors, coping strategies and stress level among adolescents in West Java Indonesia

Mansoer, Winarini *Psychology, University of Indonesia, Depok, Indonesia* **Mansoer, Wilman Dahlan** *Psychology, University of Indonesia, Depok, Indonesia* **Herwina, Mila** *Psychology, University of Indonesia, Depok, Indonesia*

Aim of this study was to examine stressors, coping strategies and stress levels among adolescents. The results showed that the greatest stressor among the whole participants and middle adolescents was problems in parent-child relationship, while the greatest stressor among early adolescents was relationships with peers. Among the whole participants and early adolescents, active coping, avoidance coping, emotion-focused coping, acceptance coping, and religious-focused coping strategies had significant contribution on stress level. Among middle adolescents active coping and religious-focused coping strategies had the negative contribution on stress level. Avoidance coping, emotion-focused coping, and acceptance coping strategies had positive contribution on stress level.

Adult attachment and ways of coping with stress

Khoshnevis, Elaheh *Dept. for Psychology, Islamic Azad University, Tehran, Islamic Republic of Iran*

This study examined how adult individuals cope with stress as a function of their attachment style (God attachment, parental and adult attachment). Data were gathered from 195 adult individuals (university student from Tehran University) included measures of attachment to God, attachment to adults, ways of coping and whom the respondent would turn to in times of stress. Adults' God, parental and adult attachment security was positively related to positive ways of coping and negatively related to negative ways of coping such as escape-avoidance. Attachment insecurity was positively related to negative ways of coping.

Disaster psychosocial support; Mental health services in SAARC countries: A synthesis

Satapathy, Sujata *PPCCI, NIDM, New Delhi, India* **Bhadra, Subhasis** *Disaster Mental Health, American Red Cross, New Delhi, India*

Commonalities and differences in approaches and practices in disaster psychosocial and mental health; nature of services - curative, preventive or promotive; post-disasters service delivery; trained manpower; service providers; institutional funding mechanisms for project/program implementation; and major constraints were critically analyzed. Findings highlighted the prevalence of project based ad-hoc approach in service provisions; absence of proper institutional mechanism with mandatory guidelines; grossly inadequate trained manpower; weak community based referral system; inadequate psychological need assessment; and ad-hoc funding sources. Nevertheless, a strong trend has also emerged to integrate this into disaster policy, planning, relief and rehabilitation services; seek regional cooperation in capacity building; and to build a community-based disaster psychological service delivery system.

FP-077: Speech and reading comprehension

The effect of a learning strategies programme on the cognitive process of comprehension

Bilimória, Helena *IEP, Universidade do Minho, S. Mamede de Infesta, Portugal* **Almeida, Leandro** *Inst. de Educação e Psicologia, Universidade do Minho, Braga, Portugal*

The intent of this investigation is to illustrate the effects of a learning strategies programme – SABER – on the comprehension process. Within an experimental design, with two assessment moments: pre, post-test, and two groups: experimental and control, we applied the AME scale (Vasconcelos & Almeida, 2000) to both groups (60 7th grade students) at both assessment moments; SABER was applied between the assessment moments on the experimental group. A repeated measures analysis indicates positive effects of SABER on comprehension: F(1, 58) = 12, 184; p=0,001). The program was validated to train comprehension skills.

Development of reading skills in second language learning and teaching

Bojovic, Milevica *Cacak, Serbia*

Institution: Faculty of Agronomy, Cacak Reading as a language skill is an aspect of language performance and achieving competence in second language learning. Reading comprehension is an objective of reading process, product of reading a particular text. Complexity of reading process in second language learning is presented by describing and analyzing models and types of reading, reading techniques, strategies and activities aiming at improving reading skills in usual second language situations or in reading for academic purposes. Adopting a range of reading styles in a second language necessary for successful interaction with

authentic texts implies more efficient second language reader and learner.

Evaluating the effects of age and noise on spoken word identification using eye-tracking

Pichora-Fuller, M. Kathy *Dept. of Psychology, University of Toronto, Mississauga, Canada* **Ben-David, Boaz** *Dept. of Psychology, University of Toronto, Mississauga, Canada* **Chambers, Craig** *Psychology, University of Toronto, Mississauga, Canada* **Daneman, Meredith** *Psychology, University of Toronto, Mississauga, Canada* **Reingold, Eyal** *Psychology, University of Toronto, Mississauga, Canada* **Schneider, Bruce A.** *Psychology, University of Toronto, Mississauga, Canada*

Most speech tests measure accuracy of word identification without revealing how the listener processes incoming speech as the word unfolds. Eye-tracking provides an on-line measure of speech processing. Here, eye movements were recorded as older and younger adults followed spoken instructions, presented in quiet or noise, that referred to displayed pictures. We measured the extent to which listeners momentarily considered (fixated on) the target picture (e.g., candle) relative to a phonologically similar alternative sharing onset (candy) or rhyme (e.g., sandal). Both groups identified targets highly accurately, but older adults considered alternatives to a greater extent, especially onset alternatives in noise.

Methodology of system-and-activity approach to reading researches within INLOKKS teaching technology as the basis for the projects of A. A. Leontiev International Reading Institute

Usacheva, Irina *Leadership, Leontiev International Reading, Moscow, Russia*

One of the main activities of the International Reading Institute is the development of the programs based on INLOKKS technology (informational, logical, rhetorical and communicative culture of the specialist.) The following projects will be discussed at the Congress: - system-and-activity approach to understanding of reading; - speech and thinking development of students; - system of teacher training at the International Reading Institute, and others.

The role of orthography and phonology in reading Chinese sentence

Ren, Guiqin *Institute of Psychology, Beijing, People's Republic of China* **Han, Yuchang** *psychology, Liaoning normal university, Dalian, People's Republic of China* **Yang, Yufang** *Institute of Psychology, Institute of Psychology, Beijing, People's Republic of China*

Objectives: to explore the role of orthographical and phonological codes in Chinese lexical access in sentence context. Methods: two eye tracking experiments were conducted and Chinese single character words were selected as the targets. Results: In the high-constraint sentence context, the first fixations made on both the homophonic and graphically similar targets were higher than on the congruent targets. In the low-constraint sentence context, the gaze durations and total fixations made on the homophone targets were lower than on the controls Conclusions: The role of orthography and phonology of Chinese words in lexical access depends on the prior sentential context.

FP-078: Pain

Psychological risk factors for recurrent pediatric headache

Morris, Lisette *Klinische Psychologie, GEM-Institut für Psychologie, Göttingen, Germany* **Gaßmann, Jennifer** *Klinische Psychologie, GEM-Institut für Psychologie, Göttingen, Germany* **Heinrich, Marion** *Klinische Psychologie, GEM-Institut für Psychologie, Göttingen, Germany* **Kröner-Herwig, Birgit** *Klinische*

Psychologie, GEM-Institut für Psychologie, Göttingen, Germany

Psychological risk factors for the development of recurrent pediatric headache were investigated in a longitudinal study. Postal questionnaires assessing these factors and headache frequency were sent to 8800 families with a child aged 7 to 14 (year 1). Twelve months later all responding families were questioned again (year 2). Using logistic regression analyses the following variables (assessed year 1) were identified as predictors for the development of weekly headache (year 2): gender, anxiety/depression, outward expression of anger, aggressive coping strategies and aggressive behavior. Implications for treatment and prevention will be discussed.

Families in pain: 6-months prevalence of headache, back pain and abdominal pain within families for parent and child

Steur, Hester Klin. Psych. u. Psychotherapie, GEM-Institut für Psychologie, Göttingen, Germany Morris, Lisette Klin. Psych. u. Psychotherapie, GEM-Institut für Psychologie, Göttingen, Germany Gaßmann, Jennifer Klin. Psych. u. Psychotherapie, GEM-Institut für Psychologie, Göttingen, Germany Heinrich, Marion Klin. Psych. u. Psychotherapie, GEM-Institut für Psychologie, Göttingen, Germany Kröner-Herwig, Birgit Klin. Psych. u. Psychotherapie, GEM-Institut für Psychologie, Göttingen, Germany

The aim of this study is to assess the prevalence of headache, back pain and abdominal pain within families. Questionnaires were sent to a randomly drawn regional sample of 8800 households with a child aged seven to fourteen. Descriptive statistics showed that in 84.4% of the families, at least one member has had headaches. This corresponds to 98.6% and 92.6% for back and abdominal pain, respectively. The prevalence of multiple pains is highest for the mother. Associations between the parent's pain and that of the child are significant for all locations. The highest association is found between mother and child.

Identification, measurement and efficacy of different modalities of headache treatment

Tanwir, Shahida 210-B, Lahore, Pakistan Najam, Najma Applied Psychology and Psychol, Punjab University, Lahore, Pakistan

Objectives: To compare the efficacy of various modalities of headache treatment. Method: Headaches sufferers (N=37: ages 15-55) diagnosed with Migraine /Tension Headaches were recruited from hospitals, underwent diagnostic clinical examination. Those who met criteria (Ad hoc Committee For The Classification of Headaches (1962)) were referred to the clinical psychologist assessment and treatment. Pre and post assessments using Interview, MPQ, Faces test, Rating scales, medication index and subjective report of pain were carried out. All participants underwent six weeks of intervention in their respective groups. Conclusion: Significant differences were found among treatment groups indicating implications for headache interventions.

Psychopathologies in migraine and tension headaches sufferers

Tanwir, Shahida 210-B, Lahore, Pakistan Najam, Najma Applied Psychology and Psychol, Punjab University, Lahore, Pakistan

Objectives: The present research investigated the underlying psychopathologies leading to headaches. Methods: 100 participants, 15-55 years diagnosed with Migraine/ Tension Headaches were recruited from hospitals. Only those fulfilling the criteria (Ad hoc Committee for the Classification of the headaches (1962) were referred to the Clinical Psychologist for psychological assessment. CCEI was used to measure underlying psychopathology. Rating scales and other pain assessment were also adminis-

tered Results: Significantly higher levels of depressive psychopathology., free floating anxiety, hysteria and somatic scales were found in headache patients. These findings shed light to help headache patients and the clinicians to achieve effective management of headaches.

Chronic pain: Study of structure and determinants of cognitive and emotional illness representations

Marchetti, Elise GRC University of Nancy 2, Nancy Cedex, France Batt, Martine Lorraine, GRC University of Nancy 2, Nancy, France Trognon, Alain Lorraine, GRC University of Nancy 2, Nancy, France

Objective: Study cognitive and emotional representations of the chronic pain patients about their pain and the influence of demographic and medical data. Methods: 215 subjects completed questionnaires about demographic, professional, social, pain data and the revised Illness Perceptions Questionnaire. Correlations, mean comparisons and multiple regressions were performed. Results: Gender, pain severity, pain localisation, work status, relationship with healthinsurance influence representations about pain. The more the participants have a non coherent pain perception, the more severe they assess the pain consequences on their life, the more they have negative emotions. To conclude, clinical outcome of these data will be discussed.

Rehabilitation after amputation: Psychotherapeutic intervention module in Indian scenario

Srivastava, Kalpana Dept. of Psychiatry, Armed Forces Medical College, Pune, India Saldanha, Daniel Department of Psychiatry, Armed Forces Medical College, Pune, India Ryali, V.S.S.R. Department of Psychiatry, Armed Forces Medical College, Pune, India Goyal, Sunil Department of Psychiatry, Armed Forces Medical College, Pune, India

Objectives: To propose an effective psychotherapeutic intervention module (PIM) for rehabilitation of amputees in Indian setting. Methods: Limb amputees were randomly assigned to PIM (n=90) and treatment-as-usual (TAU) groups (n=83). PIM group was given six therapy sessions focusing on Reassurance, Ventilation, Acceptance of self, Therapeutic milieu & Reintegration. All subjects were evaluated on Carroll-Rating-Scale-for-Depression (CRSD), State-Trait-Anxiety-Inventory (STAI), Amputees-Body-Image-Scale (ABIS), and Impact-of-Event-Scale (IES) before & after two months of therapy. Results: PIM group showed significant reduction in scores on CRSD, STAI, ABIS and IES whereas TAU group showed reduction only on ABIS. Conclusion: Proposed module was highly efficacious in alleviating distress.

FP-079: Memory and cognition

The function of positive and negative memories

Rasmussen, Anne Scharling Dept. of Psychology, University of Aarhus, Aarhus, Denmark Berntsen, Dorthe Psychology, University of aarhus, Aarhus, Denmark

The paper examines directive, social and self-functions of autobiographical memory as a function of the emotional valence of the remembered events. We expected positive memories to be rated higher on social and self-function than negative memories, and negative memories to be rated higher on directive function. 136 undergraduates (115 females, average age 25.7 years) participated as part of a psychology course. The analysis was paired-sampled t-tests. The hypotheses were supported, although there was only a statistical trend for the results concerning self-function. Positive memories serve important social and self-functions. Negative memories direct thought and behaviour and prevent future mistakes.

The effect of state anxiety on processing efficiency and performance effectiveness on reading span test

Moradi, Alireza Dept. of Psycohlogy, Tarbiyat Moallem University, Tehran, Islamic Republic of Iran Cheraghi, Fereshteh Psycohlogy, Tarbiyat Moallem University, Tehran, Islamic Republic of Iran

The main aim of this study is to investigate the effect of state anxiety on processing efficiency and performance effectiveness on working memory task. 35 high anxious and 28 low anxious university students participated in this study. Measurement of task accuracy was taken as an indicator of performance effectiveness. Time taken to complete task and mental effort were taken as measurements of performance efficiency. The results indicated significant differences between two groups on task accuracy, rating of mental effort and rating of time for Reading Span task. These findings are in line with Eysenck and Calvo's processing efficiency theory.

Rumination is associated with increased reliving in negative autobiographical memories

Kirkegaard Thomsen, Dorthe Department of Psychology, University of Aarhus, Aarhus, Denmark

Rumination has been related to poorer recall of specific memories and may be expected to be associated with less emotional reliving of memories. This was investigated in three studies, where students completed rumination-questionnaires, recalled positive and negative memories and rated memories on emotional reliving. In studies 1 and 3, correlations showed that higher degree of rumination was related to increased reliving in negative memories (rs(76 and 125)=0.20 and 0.21, ps<0.10 and 0.05). The higher emotional reliving suggests that ruminators have not emotionally processed their negative memories and indicate that rumination may not always hinder recall of specific memories

Effect of glucose ingestion on recognition memory for emotionally arousing stimuli

Sunram-Lea, Sandra Psychology, Lancaster University, Lancaster, United Kingdom Brandt, Karen Psychology, University of Keele, Keele, United Kingdom

Previous data suggest that glucose administration facilitates recognition memory that is accompanied by recollection of contextual details and episodic richness. Research on emotion and memory has shown the presence of an emotional enhancement effect such that emotional stimuli are more memorable than their more neutral counterparts. This paper discusses whether the recognition memory facilitation effect associated with glucose would emerge for emotional material that already benefits from a memory advantage. The results suggest that the additive effect of glucose ingestion and a rise in glucose levels due to the emotional nature of the stimuli shifts the previously observed dose-response curve.

Investigating cognitive mechanisms underlying the modality effect in multimedia learning

Fürstenberg, Anne Inst. für Psychologie, Universität des Saarlandes, Saarbrücken, Germany Rummer, Ralf Psychology, Saarland University, SB, Saarbruecken, Germany Schweppe, Judith Psychology, Saarland University, SB, Saarbruecken, Germany

When learning with text and pictures, why does auditory text presentation lead to better learning outcome than visual text presentation? For theoretical reasons, we doubt that this is due to written text and pictures causing an overload in visual working memory. Two experiments tested alternative explanations in line with current working memory research. The results suggest that it is rather aspects of sensory processing (e.g. eye movements) than a matter of working memory capacity that yield the auditory advantage. We infer that this advantage is highly restricted with regard to the materials features and to the succession of text-picture presentation.

Reference frames in spatial navigation: Human brain dynamics is influenced by path complexity

Müller, Markus Inst. für Psychologie, Universität München, München, Germany Gramann, Klaus SCCN, UC San Diego, San Diego, USA

Two experiments analyzed brain dynamics accompanying path integration based on distinct reference frames. Participants, preferentially using an allocentric or an egocentric reference frame, traversed virtual tunnels of varying path complexity. Tunnels contained either one turn, two turns into the same, or two turns into opposite directions. At the end of a passage participants indicated their momentary position relative to the starting point (point to origin). ICA was used to identify spectral perturbation patterns underlying distinct reference frames. The results demonstrate an influence of path complexity on spectral activity in distinct brain areas dependent on the reference frame used.

FP-080: Work-family-interface: Balance, conflict, facilitation

A new framework model for research on work-family conflict

Haun, Sascha Inst. for Psychologie, Mainz University, Mainz, Germany Dormann, Christian Institute of Psychology, Johannes Gutenberg-University, Mainz, Germany

A review of the literature on work-family conflict (WFC) reveals that the concept is rooted in organizational stress theory. However, most common conceptualizations and measures have several shortcomings that have already been identified and criticized in other areas of organizational stress research. We will discuss common flaws like conceptual overlap, item overlap and the lack of objective measurement, which may spuriously inflate correlations among WFC, its antecedents and its consequences. We base our claims on empirical evidence and propose a new framework model for future research on WFC.

Associations of work-life-balance with objective and subjective work characteristics and health

Morling, Katja Work&Organizational Psychology, Philipps University Marburg, Marburg, Germany Roesler, Ulrike Work&Organizational Psycho, Philipps University Marburg, Marburg, Germany Hoffmann, Katja Work&Organizational Psycho, Philipps University Marburg, Marburg, Germany Rau, Renate Work&Organizational Psycho, Philipps University Marburg, Marburg, Germany

The study investigated how work-life-balance (WLB) influences the association between objectively and subjectively measured work characteristics and health outcomes (e.g. blood pressure, vital exhaustion). Hierarchical regression analyses in a sample of 360 employees from 3 industry sectors (health and financial services, public administration) confirmed the importance of WLB. WLB was significantly associated with health outcomes above and beyond work characteristics as assessed by the Job-Demand-Control-Model and the Effort-Reward-Imbalance-Concept. Additional variance explained by WLB ranged between 2.4% for systolic blood pressure and 25.4% for vital exhaustion. Mediator analyses indicated that work-life-balance mediates the relation between job demands and health.

The work-family facilitation among Thai nursing staff

Tengpongthorn, Chatsaran Guildford, United Kingdom McDowall, Almuth Psychology, University of Surrey, Guildford, United Kingdom

Thai female nurses are assumed to experience Work-family conflict, because they are responsible for both family matters and the elderly support, while they are expected to maintain the long-term relationship with their organizations. So how to balance loyalty to and the demands of the family on the one side and the loyalty to and demands of the organization on the other side was investigated. Twenty-six nurses in 3 university hospitals were interviewed. By using Template Analysis, the preliminary result show that notions in line with a collectivist culture appear to facilitate the interface of work and families; where work is also experienced as a 'family'.

Modelling multiple causes of work-family balance: Application of a formative measurement approach

Ellwart, Thomas Schule für Angew. Psychologie, Uni. für Angew. Wissenschaft, Olten, Switzerland Konradt, Udo Institute of Psychology, University of Kiel, Kiel, Germany Hoch, Julia Institute of Psychology, Uniiversity of Technology, Dresden, Germany

Previous reflective measures of work-family balance (WFB) focus on outcome-related variables such as conflict or satisfaction. This study introduces a formative measurement approach that emphasizes on distinct and relevant causes of imbalanced life domains. The formative WFB scale was evaluated in two samples of 698 and 2210 participants. Formative indicators assessed work, family, and time demands. Partial Least Squares analyses indicated that the formative scale has convergent and content validity and predicts reflective WFB, as well as satisfaction. Formative indicator weights also provide information about the specific impact of each cause. Conclusively, formative scales provide an innovative and complementary alternative for research.

A longitudinal test of the job demands-resources model in Australian university staff

Boyd, Carolyn Psychology, University of South Australia, Adelaide, Australia Winefield, Anthony Psychology, University of South Australia, ADELAIDE, Australia Bakker, Arnold Institute of Psychology, Erasmus University Rotterdam, Rotterdam, Netherlands

A longitudinal test of the Job Demands-Resources Model (Demerouti et al., 2001) was conducted in a sample of Australian academic staff (n = 796). Using structural equation modelling, job demands (work pressure, work-home conflict) and job resources (autonomy, fairness, trust in supervisors) at Time 1 (2000) were used to predict psychological strain and organizational commitment at Time 2 (2003). As expected, Time 1 demands and resources predicted Time 2 strain and commitment, respectively. However, Time 1 commitment also predicted Time 2 resources, suggesting that strong organizational identification may exert a lasting effect on staff perceptions of working conditions.

Work-family conflict and employees' well-being: The moderating effects of job characteristics

Karimi, Leila Research and Development, Helen Macpherson Institute, Melbourne, Australia

This study aimed at examining the effects of work-family conflict on the perceived wellbeing of employees, after controlling for job-characteristics. The participants of the study consisted of Iranian employees from a variety of organizations. The effects of three dimensions of the job-strain model and six forms of work-family conflict (WFC) on affective wellbeing were assessed. The results of

canonical correlation and hierarchical multiple regression analysis revealed that strain-based WIF along with the job characteristic variables (i.e. supervisory support, job-demands, and job control) make a significant contribution to the prediction of an employee's affective wellbeing, particularly their job satisfaction. Implications and recommendations are made regarding future research and interventions in the workplace.

FP-081: Memory processes II

Motivation for weight loss affects recall from autobiographical memory in dieters

Johannessen, Kim Berg Dept. of Psychology, University of Aarhus, Aarhus, Denmark Berntsen, Dorthe Psychology, University of Aarhus, Aarhus, Denmark

Two studies examined the connection between motivation and autobiographical memories. We expected memories recalled in response to dieting-related cue words to be more central to the person's identity and life story and to contain more body and weight related elements for dieters than for non-dieters. We expected no differences on memories recalled in response to neutral cue words. Study 1: 29 normal/overweight dieters and 48 non-dieters participated. Study 2: 18 obese dieters and 19 non-dieters participated. We conducted repeated measures tests. The hypotheses were supported, which support the concept of current concerns and the theory of the working self.

Evidence for the memorizing effort heuristic: Fluency effects on judgments of learning and study times

Undorf, Monika Inst. für Psychologie III, Universität Mannheim, Mannheim, Germany Cüpper, Lutz Chair of Psychology III, University of Mannheim, Mannheim, Germany

Koriat, Ma'ayan, and Nussinson (2006) proposed the memorizing effort heuristic to account for the negative correlation of judgments of learning (JOLs) and study times typically observed in self-paced learning. Although several empirical findings are compatible with this heuristic, there is a lack of direct evidence for it. We report two experiments in which memorizing effort was reduced by experimental manipulations that are known to enhance processing fluency, i.e., visual clarity (experiment 1) and priming (experiment 2). As predicted by the memorizing effort heuristic, elevated processing fluency resulted both in a decrease in study time and in an increase in JOLs.

Adaptive memory updating in the musical realm

Strauß, Sabine Inst. für Psychologie, Universität Klagenfurt, Klagenfurt, Austria Vitouch, Oliver Department of Psychology, University of Klagenfurt, Klagenfurt, Austria

The perception of extremely accelerated versions of familiar pieces of music affects judgments about the original musical tempo. Similar effects have recently been shown for pitch shifts. We here focus on the stability of this "musical adaptation effect" (MAE) over time. In four experiments, we tested influences of different music material and different presentation conditions on the persistency of MAE in the time and pitch domain. Results show strong correspondence to other modalities, and point to MAE being a facet of a domain-general long-term memory mechanism for context-dependent template updating.

Influence of self-centred spatial information on episodic memory

Gomez, Alice UMR 5105, LPNC-CNRS, Grenoble, France Rousset, Stéphane Cognitive Psychology, LPNC, CNRS UMR 5105, Grenoble, France

From episodic memory models (Burgess, 2002; Nadel & Moscovitch, 1998), we investigated which spatio-contextual information (self-referenced / allocentrically-referenced) is crucial to episodic memory. We designed tasks maximizing one or the other type of spatial information during a word study-phase. Participants' episodic memory was assessed using recall and recognition tests associated to a Remember-Know-Guess procedure. Results show that more items are recalled and recognized after a learning maximizing self-referenced spatial components. Crucially, these results dissociate over phenomenological aspects: this advantage is observed only for remember responses. Findings point toward a causal link between observer-centred information and phenomenological aspects of episodic memory.

Objects can be conditioned, places need to be configured

Lange-Küttner, Christiane Dept. of Psychology, London Metropolitan University, London, United Kingdom

In three studies (N = 131), object and place memory in three spatial arrays was tested in 6- to 9-year-old children and adults using a reaction time/accuracy paradigm. In both children and adults, object memory was always better than place memory in the early stages of the experiment, but place memory subsequently selectively improved. More explicitly structured spatial arrays improved recognition performance, but this occurred independently of the gradual spatial learning. With constantly novel memory sets, the performance gap between object and place memory was closed, but with constantly repeated sets, object memory was more strongly reinforced than place memory.

Does the advantage of familiar real-person sources remain after a one-week delay in 3-, 4- and 5-year olds source monitoring performance?

Kraus, Uta Inst. für Psychologie, Universität zu Kiel, Kiel, Germany Pruesch, Angelika Inst. für Psychologie, Universität zu Kiel, Kiel, Germany Koehnken, Guenter Inst. für Psychologie, Universität zu Kiel, Kiel, Germany

The effect of familiarity was examined for different real-person sources. Thirty-six children (M=42, M=52, M=68) were presented 4 sticker book pages. On each page, two person-sources (child-adult/child-child) per source term (reality-monitoring familiar; realty-monitoring unfamiliar; external source monitoring; external; internal source monitoring) chose two wildlife-stickers, pasted them into the book and described what each animal was doing. Source recall was examined after a one-week delay. Results (t-tests) showed the advantage of familiarity in the familiar reality monitoring term in all children after the delay. In contrast, the advantage of familiarity was not found in external source monitoring in each age group.

Cognitive control in working memory: Event-related brain potentials (ERPs) dissociate between different processes of attentional allocation

Berti, Stefan Inst. für Psychologie, Universität Mainz, Mainz, Germany

Attentional allocation is an important function of cognitive control. These processes are tapped by event-related brain potentials (ERPs), especially the P3a and a late frontal negativity. In three experiments these ERP components were obtained in different paradigms, i.e. re-orientation after a distracting event, task switching, and object switching. Importanlty, both components were correlated with reaction time costs. These results suggest that the P3a and the late negativity reflect different processes of attentional allocation: an initial preparation for the switch – presumably by decoupling of the task-set – and a subsequent switch of the

focus of attention to relevant information in working memory.

Memory load effects on the executive control: An event-related potential study

Wang, Xiang Medical Psychological Center, Second Xiangya Hospital, Changsha, People's Republic of China Yao, Shuqiao Medical Psychological Center, Second Xiangya Hospital,CSU, Changsha, Hunan, People's Republic of China

Objective: To examine the working memory (WM) load effects on the event-related potentials (ERPs) in a parametric executive control task. Method: ERPs were recorded during 20 healthy volunteers performed an n-back task with three levels (0/1/2-back). Results: P3 peak amplitude decreased progressively as WM load increased. The difference wave N450 was consistently identified by subtracting the lower load task from higher load task. Conclusions: The progressively decreased P3 reflected the effectively distributing and switching attention. The N450 on prefrontal and parietal areas may reflect the updating and coding in executive control process and the short-term storage process, respectively and simultaneously.

Two executive sub-functions: Set shifting and inhibition impacting Chinese phonemic and semantic fluencies?

Lu, Aitao Dept. of Psychology, Chinese Univers. of Hong Kong, Hong Kong, China, People's Republic of : Hong Kong SAR Zhang, Jijia Mo, Lei Zhang, Xuexin

Motivated by the recent demonstration that set shifting played an important role in two verbal fluencies using a dual-task paradigm (Rende et al., 2002), the present study focused on both set shifting and inhibition in two Chinese verbal fluencies. We examined whether the findings based on English language could be extended to Chinese, and whether the role of inhibition was substantially reliable. Results from dual-task paradigm showed that there was no interaction between task type (namely, single task vs. dual task) and fluency type, suggesting that two Chinese fluencies shared the same mechanism with respect to set shifting and inhibition.

The relationship between executive functions and problem solving among primary school children

Wang, Jing Inst. of Developm. Psychology, Beijing Normal University, Beijing, People's Republic of China Chen, Yinghe Beijing Normal University, BNU, Developmental Psychology, DPI, Beijing, People's Republic of China

This study was conducted to explore the relationship between executive functions and problem solving, especially in ToL task.121 7~11 years old children were tested both executive functions (including Go/no-go task, working memory task and switching task) and ToL tasks (two problem parameters: subgoaling and suboptimal alternative) by computers. Moving solutions of ToL problems were analyzed and repeated-measures MNOVA were used. The results revealed that working memory was the basic function in problem solving, while inhibition influenced the performance when the structure of problem needed to inhibit some reactions, such as suboptimal alternative, whereas cognitive flexibility had no significant effect on it.

Developmental relations between working memory and early literacy among young children aged 3 to 8 years

Hoskyn, Maureen Educational Psychology, Simon Fraser University, North Vancouver, Canada

In this study, developmental relations between working memory and early literacy is investigated in a longitudinal study of 170 children aged 3 to 8 years. Multilevel modeling procedures were used to document developmental trajectories in working

memory capacity and the factors that mediate this growth including inhibitory control and processing speed. Results show that a working memory executive develops earlier in childhood than past theories would predict and that growth in a general working memory system rather than absolute size of working memory capacity best predicts performance on measures of early reading and writing.

The influencing factors of Chinese and English reading span: A latent variable analysis of three hypotheses

Yang, Qiwei Education Science Department, Zunyi Normal University, Zunyi, People's Republic of China Zhang, Fuchang Life Science Department, Northwest University, Xi'an, People's Republic of China

This study had two major goals: to test three hypotheses concerning the nature of individual difference tapped by working memory span tasks, and to find out the influencing factors of English and Chinese reading span. We used 10 tasks to test 159 seniors of English and Chinese major. The General resource tapped by English and Chinese reading span, digital working memory span and n-back task had significant path coefficients for these manifest variables except for n-back task. The latent variable analysis challenged controlled attention view. The task-switching hypothesis was not supported by the fact that Chinese reading span was not influenced by the changing of sentence length. All data could be explained by resource-sharing model.

Processing segmental and prosodic information during Cantonese word production

Wong, Andus Wing-Kuen Dept. of Psychology, The Chinese University, Hong Kong, China, People's Republic of : Hong Kong SAR

Three picture-word interference experiments were conducted to investigate how sub-syllabic, syllabic, and prosodic information is processed in Cantonese word production. Facilitatory effects in naming latencies, relative to a control condition, were obtained when the targets and the distractors shared a) the same rhyme and the same tone (Experiment 2), b) the same syllable (Experiment 3), or c) the same syllable and the same tone (Experiment 3). The priming effect in the syllable + tone-related condition was found significantly larger than that in the syllable-related condition. These results indicate that the facilitatory effects generated by different phonological components are not additive.

Feedback consistency effect in visual and auditory word recognition

Petrova, Ana Psychologie, Université Paris Descartes, Boulogne-Billancourt Cedex, France Ferrand, Ludovic Psychology, University Blaise Pascal, Clermont-Ferrand, France Ziegler, Johannes Psychology, University Aix-Marseille, Marseille Cedex 1, France

Two experiments investigated the role of feedback consistency (i.e. sound-spelling consistency) in the visual and auditory lexical decision tasks in adults. Experiment 1, done in French, showed strong feedback consistency effects in the auditory modality but no such effects in the visual modality (consistency was manipulated at the onset and the rime). In Experiment 2, exactly the same pattern of results was found in English. Our results thus clearly show that sound-spelling consistency affects spoken but not visual word recognition. We further show that previous reports of feedback consistency in the visual modality can be explained without assuming feedback mechanisms.

Conscious and unconscious processing of emotional words

Van den Noort, Maurits Biological and Medical Psych., University of Bergen, Bergen, Norway *Bosch, Peggy* NICI, Radboud University Nijmegen, Nijmegen, Netherlands *Van Kralingen, Rosalinde* Foodstep, Foodstep B.V., Wageningen, Netherlands

Objectives: The processing of emotional words was tested. Methods Thirty-five, right handed males participated in the study. A divided visual field technique with different presentation times (10ms, 120ms, 1000ms) was used. Results At the conscious level, in contrast to the unconscious level, emotional words that were presented in the right visual field were processed significantly faster and better than words that were presented in the left visual field. Conclusion At the unconscious level, no strong support for either the valence- or the right hemisphere theory is found. At the conscious level, however, normal language processing is the most dominant process.

Lexical representations do not contain open bigrams

Kinoshita, Sachiko MACCS, Macquarie University, Sydney, Australia *Norris, Dennis* CBU, MRC, Cambridge, United Kingdom

A letter string generated by transposing letters within a word (e.g., jugde from judge) is perceived as being more similar to the word than a string generated by replacing letters in the corresponding positions (e.g., junpe). "Open bigram" accounts explain this transposed-letter (TL) similarity effect by proposing that lexical representations are coded in terms of bigrams. We present data using the masked priming procedure that suggests that, if there are open bigrams, they are not part of lexical representations. We suggest that TL similarity effects are better interpreted in terms of uncertainty associated with individual letter positions during perceptual sampling.

Hemispheric asymmetry profiles during beginning reading: Effects of reading level and word type

Porta, Maria Elsa Psicologia Evolutiva, INCIHUSA-CRICYT-CONICET, Mendoza, Argentina *Kraft, Rosemarie* HUMAN & COMMUNITY DEVELOPM, UNIVERSITY OF CALIFORNIA, Davis, USA *Harper, Lawrence* HUMAN & COMMUNITY DEVELOPM, UNIVERSITY OF CALIFORNIA, Davis, USA

We evaluated how right- and the left-temporal lobe activation of first (1stLR), second (2ndLR), and third (3rdLR) level readers (n=60; Age=6-to-9 years) varied with reading level, word characteristics, and cognitive abilities by using electroencephalogram measurements while the children read high-frequency/high-imageability, high-frequency/low-imageability, and nonsense words. The ANOVA showed significant interaction effects: 1stLR had greater right-hemispheric activation than 3rdLR, who had greater left-hemispheric activation; for nonsense words, 1stLR had lower left-hemisphere activation than that of 2ndLR and 3rdLR. The EEG measure of hemispheric asymmetry indicated a developmental effect on lateralized activity in the temporal lobes of beginning readers during word recognition.

Learning to read in Chinese in Hong Kong: The linguistic demands of learning Chinese characters in the grade-one classroom

Cheng, Pui-Wan Dept. Educational Psychology, Chinese Univers. of Hong Kong, Hong Kong, China, People's Republic of : Hong Kong SAR *Luk, Sau-Ha* Educational Psychology, Chinese U. of Hong Kong, Hong Kong, China, People's Republic of : Macao SAR

This study examines the linguistic properties of a pool of Chinese characters most frequently used in Hong Kong grade-one textbooks for semantic and morphological features, phonetic regularity and consistency, and orthographic structure and complexity. It concludes that while written Chinese has certain systematic features that can be explicitly taught to young children, the regularity and transparency of these features are less evident in the initial learning stage, thus making the first steps of learning Chinese particularly difficult for struggling readers. Implications for differentiated instruction are discussed.

Deliberate self harm and attachment to parents and peers

Covic, Tanya School of Psychology, University of Western Sydney, Penrith South, NSW, Australia *Hallab, Lisa Frances* School of Psychology, University of Western Sydney, Penrith South, NSW, Australia

Objectives: The aim of the study was to examine the relationship between deliberate self harm (DSH) and attachment to parents and peers. Methods: Participants were 114 first-year university students (mean age = 18.9 years). They completed an online survey consisting of measures of deliberate self harm, parents and peers attachment, self esteem and mood. Results: The DSH group reported poorer attachments, more depression, anxiety and stress compared to the non-DSH group. Within the DSH group it was also found that attachment to peers was significantly stronger than to parents. Conclusions: The findings of this study highlight the need to consider DSH within a developmental framework.

The cognitive predictors of obsessive compulsive disorder

Davoudi, Iran Psychology, Chamran University, Ahvaz, Islamic Republic of Iran

The present study examined cognitive variables as the predictors of Obsessive Compulsive Disorder. The sample consisted of 103 with OCD and 103 nonclinical Iranian subjects. The instruments used in this study were: Obsessive Belief Questionnaire-44 (Obsessive-Compulsive Cognition Working Group, 2005), Interpretation of Intrusion Inventory (OCCWG, 2005), White Bear Suppression Inventory (Wegner and Zanakos, 1994), Thought Control Questionnaire (Wells and Davis, 1994) and Thought Control Ability Questionnaire (Luciano, Algarabel, Tomas & Martinez, 2005). Stepwise discriminate analysis identified that thought suppression, perfectionism / certainty, and two thought control strategies (distractibility and punishment) contributed most to the discrimination of groups.

Axis I comorbidity and psychopathological correlates in patients with autodestructive syndromes

Fliege, Herbert Abt. Psychosomatik, Charité Berlin, Berlin, Germany *Grimm, Anne* Psychosomatik, Charité, Berlin, Germany *Lee, Jeong-Ran* Psychosomatik, Charité, Berlin, Germany *Klapp, Burghard* Psychosomatik, Charité, Berlin, Germany

Factitious disorder and (non-suicidal) deliberate self-harm may be seen as subtypes within the autodestructive behaviour spectrum, basically differing in concealment. We investigated axis I diagnoses and psychopathological correlates in factitious disorder and self-harm patients. 194 psychosomatic patients were assessed using the WHO Composite International Diagnostic Interview (CIDI) and self-rated questionnaires. 37 patients with self-destructive behaviour were matched with 37 patients without self-destruction. Overt self-harmers were more frequently diagnosed with anxiety, depression, substance dependence, or eating disorders than factitious disorder patients (n=19) or those without self-destructive behaviour, and they reported more stress. When psychopathologically assessed factitious disorder patients present themselves inconspicuous.

Self-mutilation: Processes associated with self-injury in borderline and non-borderline patients

Haines, Janet School of Psychology, University of Tasmania, Hobart, Australia *Bowe, Erin* School of Psychology, University of Tasmania, Hobart, Australia

Although understood as a diagnostic criterion for Borderline Personality Disorder, little information exists about the similarities or differences in the processes associated with self-mutilation in people with and without Borderline Personality Disorder. A guided imagery methodology was used to examine psychophysiological and psychological processes associated with self-mutilation in people with and without BPD. Results indicated few differences with a strong tension reduction mechanism being identified in both groups. Results indicated that, irrespective of trigger or intention, the processes of self-mutilation are fundamentally similar with or without borderline personality disturbance.

Effect of shame and guilt on coping by meaning making

Chan, Raymond Applied Social Studies, City University of Hong Kong, Kowloon Tong, China, People's Republic of : Hong Kong SAR

Shame and guilt have been the focus in coping studies, but not many on their relations with meaning making. This study is to explore the gap. Structured questionnaires were completed by 193 university students. Results showed that with high intensified grief reaction, people in guilt were ready to make meaning out of their loss experience among low self-esteem group (beta=0.291, p=0.036) but opposite effect in shame (beta=-0.272, p=0.050). It concludes that low self-esteem and intensified emotional experience at time of loss facilitate coping that guilt favors but shame hinders cognitive processing. Working through guilt can be constructive in meaning making.

The effectiveness of family systems acute psychiatry

Crameri, Aureliano Angewandte Psychologie, ZHAW, Zürich, Switzerland

The effectiveness of family systems therapeutic interventions in the treatment of psychiatric inpatients is investigated. The entire multiprofessional teams of six psychiatric wards in Germany were trained during altogether 150 hours to perform family systems interventions in practice routine. 187 inpatients treated with the new interventions were matched 1:1 on propensity score with controls treated before the team training in the same wards. Outcome measures included BSI and BPRS. No significant outcome improvement could be determined after the team training and implementation of the additional interventions. The short training duration has been presumed as a reason for the missing effect.

Impact of patients' subjective experience on the effectiveness of psychotherapy in schizophrenia

Schmidt, Friederike Charite Berlin, CBF, Berlin, Germany *Körtner, Katrin* Psychiatry and Psychotherapy, Charite Berlin, CBF, Berlin, Germany *Auckenthaler, Anna* Klinische Psychologie, Freie Universität, Berlin, Berlin, Germany *Dettling, Michael* Psychiatry and Psychotherapy, Charite Berlin, CBF, Berlin, Germany

Patients' subjective experience and attitudes supposedly are critical for the effectiveness of therapeutic interventions. This hypothesis is tested in a prospective randomized controlled psychotherapeutic-psychoeducative study with follow-ups of in- and outpatients with schizophrenia. Special attention is paid to the extensive assessment of self-esteem, quality of life, satisfaction with treatment and illness-concepts and to the establishment of the psychometric quality of key instruments. Multigroup structural equation modelling will be used to test relations between classic outcome criteria and subjective variables for data from the first two years. Consequences for further improvement and differential indication of psychotherapeutic interventions in schizophrenia are drawn.

Chronic Fatigue Syndrome - Psychodynamic and psychotherapeutic aspects: A case study

von Buelow, Gabriele Dt. Akademie für Psychoanalyse, Berlin, Germany

The case study is about a 40 years old male patient 'being too tired to be depressive. Etiological background are neurotic guilt feelings concerning the death of his brother as well as a severe early attachment- and developmental trauma. His ability to contact was fundamentally disturbed: contact to himself, his feelings and needs (alexithymia), to people and things.

FP-086: Conflicts and cooperation in organizations

Organizational identification and intergroup conflict handling strategies

Joensson, Thomas Department of Psychology, University of Aarhus, Aarhus C, Denmark Jeppesen, Hans Jeppe Department of Psychology, University of Aarhus, Aarhus C, Denmark

Objectives: To investigate whether organizational identification is positively associated with approach strategies in intergroup conflicts and negatively associated with avoidance and yielding strategies. Methods: A cross-sectional field study at a hospital department was conducted using questionnaires distributed to medical secretaries, physicians and nurses (166 = 75,8% replied). Regression analyses were applied. Results: Organizational identification statistically predicted approach strategies (Beta=.34, Adj.R2=.11) but not avoidance nor yielding strategies. Conclusions: The results may imply that strategies enhancing organizational identification can be applied to stimulate employees' engagement in interdisciplinary conflict solutions. The results are especially valuable for organizations based on cooperation between groups.

The antecedents of constructive controversy: Beyond cooperative goal

Wang, Zhen Institute of Psychology, Chinese Academy of Sciences, Beijing, People's Republic of China Tjosvold, Dean Department of Management, Lingnan University, Hong Kong, China, People's Republic of : Hong Kong SAR Shi, Kan Institute of Psychology, Chinese Academy of Sciences, Beijing, People's Republic of China

Constructive controversy is proved to be one important team process variable and cooperative goal is evidenced to be one antecedent of constructive controversy. The purpose of this study was to explore the impact of deep-level diversity (agreeableness) on constructive controversy. Hypotheses were tested by doing a survey in 60 customer service teams. Hierarchical regression analysis revealed that besides the effect of cooperative goal, team members' agreeableness diversity had a supplementary effect on constructive controversy, and it would be more likely to result in constructive controversy when team agreeableness level is higher than when it is low.

Which motivational types experience more work alienation?: A study among academicians

Erben, Gül Selyn Business Administration, Maltepe University, Istanbul, Turkey Guneser, Ayse Begum —, —, ISTANBUL, Turkey

One way to bring about alienation is going too far away from what one essentially is and wants to be, that is: being too far away from ones basic motives. The purpose of the study was to find out which motivational types predict work alienation better. 170 academicians participated to the study and filled out the questionnaire. Results were analyzed by using regression analyses. Findings showed that specific motivational types of individuals explain work alienation more than other types. Sociability seekers experience less work alienation whereas authenticity seekers experience more work alienation.

The floor between us: A context-specific model of contact between workgroups

Koschate, Miriam Social and Organizational, Universität Koblenz-Landau, Landau, Germany van Dick, Rolf Social Psychology, Goethe Universität, Frankfurt/Main, Germany

Based on the social identity approach and intergroup contact theory, we propose a context-specific model of contact between workgroups. Depending on the contact context (informal vs. work-related), different categorization levels become salient, leading either to interpersonal or intergroup outcomes, respectively. Different categorization levels as well as changes in affect and knowledge about the outgroup are proposed as mediating processes. Initial evidence is provided by a study with 283 employees of a German mail-order company and a three-wave longitudinal study of student project groups. Implications for future research and the management of intergroup relations between workgroups are discussed.

FP-087: Mental health and counseling I

Spirit possession: Professional perceptions and lay experiences

Shubha, Ranganathan Humanities & Social Sciences, Indian Institute of Technology, Mumbai, India Bhattacharya, Tanmay Humanities & Social Scienc, Indian Institute of Technology, Mumbai, India Parthasarathy, D. Humanities & Social Scienc, Indian Institute of Technology, Mumbai, India Gupta, Meenakshi Humanities & Social Scienc, Indian Institute of Technology, Mumbai, India

In this paper, the experience and understanding of possession by supplicants and healers at a temple is compared with the perceptions of possession held by mental health professionals. The study was conducted in a temple reputed for healing spirit-related problems in the state of Maharashtra in India. Methods included participant and non-participant observations and interviews with nine individuals undergoing possession, their families, and two healers. Five mental health professionals working outside the temple were also interviewed. The study found considerable differences between professional and lay perceptions of possession. These results have been analysed and discussed in the paper.

Social capital, human autonomy and health: A cross-cultural analysis

Chirkov, Valery Dept. of Psychology, University of Saskatchewan, Saskatoon, Canada Lebedeva, Nadezhda Psychology, Moscow School of Economics, Moscow, Russia Molodtsova, Inna Psychology, University of Saskatchewan, Saskatoon, Canada Tatarko, Alexander Psychology, Moscow School of Economics, Moscow, Russia

In this presentation we will discuss the role human agency and autonomy play in people's functioning in domains of health and organizational innovations. Conceptual distinction of autonomy vs. agency will be elaborated. The role of social conditions, such as social capital and horizontal relations in promoting human autonomy will be examined. The results of several cross-cultural studies of health behavior and attitudes of young people from Canada and Russia will be reported and discussed. In conclusion, the role of human agency in modern plural worlds will be highlighted.

Perception of depression among Pakistani adults in early adulthood: Need for culturally relevant mental health intervention

Khan, Bushra Inst. of Psychology, University of Karachi, Karachi, Pakistan Talat Hussain, Rakhshinda

Objective: To explore the perception of depression, in understanding, recognition, manifestations, risk factors and treatment, among adults in early adulthood. Method: An interview based survey was conducted on a sample of 100 males and females, aged 20-23.Data was analyzed qualitatively and quantitatively. Results: Depression was perceived as a disorder, with cognitive manifestations and was recognized through facial expression and general behavior. Oversensitivity and economic instability were important risk factors. Majority reported self treatment through various strategies, only few favoured treatment by specialists. Slight gender differences were also found. Conclusion: Need for indigenous mental health intervention in early adulthood was highlighted.

Enlisting Asian American churches in the fight to reduce stigma and increase access to mental health treatment

Yamada, Ann Marie Los Angeles, USA Dinh, Tam Social Work, Univ of Southern California, Los Angeles, USA Lee, Kyeung-Hae Social Work, Univ. of Southern California, Los Angeles, USA Song, Lucian Social Work, Univ of Southern California, Los Angeles, USA Nguyen, Diana Social Work, Univ of Southern California, Los Angeles, USA Lee, Vincy Social Work, Univ of Southern California, Los Angeles, USA

This presentation aims to explore the role of Asian-American Christian churches in providing mental health care for persons with stigmatized forms of severe mental illness. Data were collected with semi-structured in-depth interviews with 15 well-respected (Chinese, Korean, Vietnamese) pastors in California. Using a grounded theory approach, three themes emerged: Pastors are not trained to provide church-based mental health services; stigma is a barrier to use of mental health services; culturally appropriate, Christian-based mental health services are lacking in the local communities. Solutions to encourage and support Asian-American churches in addressing the mental health needs of their congregations will be presented.

FP-088: Media effects: The psychological, social, and cultural impact of mass media II

Representations of mental health in the Polish press

Jacennik, Barbara Dept. of Psychology, Uvers. of Finance and Managmt., Warsaw, Poland Anna, Ulanowicz Psychology, U. of Finance and Management, Warsaw, Poland

Representations in the press can influence the formation of attitudes and beliefs about mental illness. The methodology of Commers, Visser, de Leeuw (2000) was adapted in a study of representations of mental health in the Polish press. The objective was to verify their consistency with the health promotion guidelines. A total of 680 articles from two national newspapers were subjected to content analysis. The mental health representations only partly followed the health promotion guidelines, and in some aspects were overly medicalized. The issue of mental health was not attributed high significance in the analyzed data.

Impact of youth oriented television programs on Pakistani youth

Naz, Sajida Behavioral Sciences, Fatima Jinnah Women University, Rawalpindi, Pakistan **Muzammil, Hina** Behavioral Sciences, Fatima Jinnah Women University, Rawalpindi, Pakistan

The present study investigated the impact of youth oriented television programs of Pakistani television channels. The data was collected by a self-devised questionnaire (r, 0.8). Data was collected from 100 youngsters (50 males and 50 females) falling in the age limit of 15 to 24 years, from different colleges and university of Rawalpindi and Islamabad. The findings showed that a strong negative impact has been seen and youth was not satisfied with the programs showing on Pakistani channels. According to their responses these programs must be according to Pakistani cultural and social setup in order to compete with the world standers.

Game over: Back in reality? Results of a questionnaire for transfer processes between the virtual and real world

Luthman, Stefanie Inst. für Psychologie, Universität zu Kiel, Kiel, Germany

The presentation will show results of a questionnaire investigating effects of video gaming. Based on the model of transfer processes by Fritz (1997) a questionnaire containing various cognitive, affective, and behavioral effects of gaming was developed. Factor analyses of the data of gamers (N = 597; mean age 19.60 years, SD = 6.40) revealed five factors showing high reliability (Cronbach's αs from .71 to .79). These are "game reflection", "mental and behavioral transfers", "general excitation", "obsessive gaming", and "moral framing". Regression analyses show that variables such as time spent with gaming, game preferences, and personality traits can predict these transfers.

Internet addiction: Debating the diagnosis

Czincz, Jennifer Dept. of Psychology, University of Ottawa, Ottawa, Canada

A question that is receiving significant attention in both research and practice is whether it is possible to develop a diagnosable addiction to the Internet. The current status of research in this area will be reviewed, with a focus on proposed diagnostic criteria, assessment measures, and suggested treatment recommendations. Groups that have been demonstrated as being at higher risk of developing problematic internet use will be reviewed based on demographic criteria, personality characteristics, and psychopathology. Gaps in the existing literature will be identified and implications for how to address problematic internet use from both an individual and societal perspective will be discussed.

FP-089: Lesbian, gay, bisexual and transgender concerns

Body image, masculinity, homonegativity and eating disorders in a sample of Latino gay men

Toro Alfonso, Jose Dept. of Psychology, University of Puerto Rico, San Juan, Puerto Rico **Borrero-Bracero, Nestor** Psychology, University of Puerto Rico, San Juan, Puerto Rico **Nieves, Karen** Psychology, University of Puerto Rico, San Juan, Puerto Rico

Objectives: To explore the body image of a sample of young Latino gay men and their eating beliefs. Explore possible relations between culture, body image, eating disorders, and sexual orientation. Methods: An exploratory survey of 100 young Latino gay men in Puerto Rico was developed exploring these issues. Results: 12% of the participants reported eating disorders symptoms. One fourth reported high levels of body dissatisfaction while 20% showed medium to high levels of homonegativity. Discussion: Masculinity image endorsed by society and high levels of homonegativity could represent difficulties which make these

young Latino males to demonstrate complex ideas about their body and their eating habits.

A deeper insight in a Greek homophobia study: What affects homophobic reports, and why?

Chiotis, Georgios Dept. of Psychology, City University, London, United Kingdom

The aim of this paper was to investigate in a deeper mode the results produced from the distribution of the Wright, Adams, & Bernat Homophobia Scale (1999) to 700 college students in Greece. A combination of quantitative detailed statistical analyses and qualitative interviews is presented to shed light and highlight the overt and covert homophobic beliefs and behaviours, suggesting a variety of factors observed as strengthening homophobic attitudes, and presenting a possible matrix of variables that might affect the study of homophobia as a general research area. This possibly enriches our understanding of the processes involved in understanding homophobia.

Rocking the cradle: Gay parenting

Curl, Layton Psychology - Campus Box 54, Meto State College of Denver, Denver, USA **Watson, Mary Ann** Psychology - Campus Box 54, Meto State College of Denver, Denver, USA

In this study a licensed clinical and social psychologist reviewed the current literature, laws, and family options available for gay and lesbian couples in the United States. Five gay and lesbian families along with their children were chosen for interview. An educational video was produced from the interviews coving the topic of gay parenting by adoption, insemination, and co-parenting. The authors review the current literature and illustrate the change in parenting trends among gay and lesbian couples. The research suggests that gay and lesbian couples serve as capable and loving parents, while facing prejudice, discrimination, and challenging legal obstacles.

FP-090: Learning and emotion: School climate, attitudes towards learning, well-being

Academic performances and psycho social well being in the university environment

Negovan, Valeria Dept. of Psychology, University of Bucharest, Bucharest, Romania

The purpose of the study is to examine the dynamics of the relationship between students' academic performances and psycho-social well being, related to factors such as need of achievement and self-evaluation bias. Participants in the study were 600 university students, in the 1st year and the 3rd year of faculty (a public and a private one). This is a diagnostic study, 10 self report scales were used, inferential statistics tested our hypotheses (multiple regression especially). As the main results we report some clear patterns of presumed relationship. As conclusions some implications for educative practices in the university environment are highlighted.

Children with general learning difficulties: Feelings of loneliness and depressive symptomatology

Didaskalou, Eleni Special Education, University of Thessaly, Volos, Greece **Kleftaras, George** Dept. of Special Education, University of Thessaly, Volos, Greece

The aims of the present research are: a) to estimate the proportion of primary school children with general learning difficulties presenting loneliness and depressive symptomatology and b) to explore the relationship between feelings of loneliness and depressive symptoms. 100 pupils with general learning difficulties, aged 10 to 12 years, completed the Greek versions of the Children's Depression

Inventory and the Louvain Loneliness Scale for Children and Adolescents. A considerable percentage of students with general learning difficulties reach high scores of self-reported feelings of loneliness and depressive symptoms. Additionally, significant correlations were identified between level of depression and loneliness.

Socio-emotional school climate in relation to adjustment among sighted and visually impaired students

Yadav, Rajender Singh Dept. of Eduction, Kurukshetra University, Kurukshetra, India

The study was conducted on 32 visually impaired and 32 sighted students selected on purposive basis from two residential special schools and two general schools using Sinha and Bhargava Socio-Emotional School Climate Inventory and Asthanas Adjustment Inventory. Mean, SD, Standard Error of difference were used. Visually impaired had more favourable perception of their Socio-Emotional school climate and also showed better adjustment to school climate as compared to sighted students. There was significantly positive correlation between perceived SE school climate and the adjustment level of students. The study has implications for the administrators, teachers of residential special schools and general schools.

Relationship of perceived school climate and school adjustment for middle schoolers

Yu, Yibing Yingdong Building, Room 255, Beijing Normal University, Beijing, People's Republic of China **Minggui, Ge** College of Psychology, Anhui Normal University, Wuhu, People's Republic of China

The author investigates the relationship between five dimensions of perceived school climate (teacher-student relationships, order and discipline, students interpersonal relationships, academic pressure and multiple development) and school adjustment for middle school students. The result shows:(1)specific relations have been found between different dimensions of perceived school climate and school adjustment ;(2)gender effect between perceived school climate and adjustment exists, especially in teacher-student relationships, academic pressure and adjustment.(3)the influences of perceived school climate on school adjustment is by direct or indirect method, in which school attitude play mediator effect for some relations.

FP-091: Job choice

Can work values and career orientations predict the final choice of workplace?

Kefalidou, Despina-Maria Athens, Greece

Objectives: This study examines the work values and career orientations of the sample and whether they can predict the choice of workplace, also taking into account demographical data. Method The sample consisted of 235 professionals from the region of Attica, Greece, selected through simple random sampling. The psychometric tools used were a translation of the Career Orientations Inventory (Schein, 1990) and Work Values Test (Kantas et al., 2001). The statistical analysis performed was factor and regression analysis. Results Work values predict the career orientations which, in turn, predict the choice of workplace. Conclusions This study provides useful advice about HR management and career orientation counselling.

Are ability-related demands at the workplace still the same after 30 years?

Sander, Nicolas Dst. 19-622, Bundesagentur für Arbeit, Nürnberg, Germany

The German Federal Employment Agency utilizes occupation-specific norms in the field of non-academic professions based on measures of intelligence to facilitate appropriate job choices. Given the rapid changes at workplaces, verifying the validity of these norms is permanently indicated. To circumvent repeated conduction of extensive norming studies, an index was developed based inter alia on the current ratio of school types previously visited by freshmen of individual apprenticeships. Since this index predicts almost perfectly measures of occupational aptitude from 30 years ago, it can be concluded that although operational characteristics at the workplace underwent dramatic changes ability-related demands remain largely stable.

Using institutional theory to explain the (non-) use of personnel selection procedures

König, Cornelius J. Universität Zürich, Zürich, Switzerland Berchtold, Matthias Institute of Psychology, University of Zurich, Zürich, Switzerland Klehe, Ute-Christine Arbeids-Organisatiepsychologie, Universiteit van Amsterdam, Amsterdam, Netherlands Kleinmann, Martin Institute of Psychology, University of Zurich, Zürich, Switzerland
Objectives: The scientist-practitioner gap is especially large in the personnel selection field. We used institutional theory to explain the (non-)use of selection procedures. Methods: 521 HR professionals filled out an online survey on selection procedures used in their organizations. Multilevel logistic regression was used to analyze the data. Results: The highest odd ratios belonged to the factors applicant reactions, costs, and diffusion. Lower (but significant) odds ratios belonged to the factors predictive validity, selection as a recruitment tool, and legality. Conclusions: In line with institutional theory, the decision whether to use selection procedures is based on several factors.

Institutional pressures affecting the adoption of personnel selection procedures among German HR-managers

Klehe, Ute-Christine Arbeids-Organisatiepsychologie, Universiteit van Amsterdam, Amsterdam, Netherlands König, Cornelius Arbeids&Organisationspsych, Universität Zürich, Zürich, Switzerland Kleinmann, Martin Arbeids&Organisationspsych, Universität Zürich, Zürich, Switzerland
This study tests Klehe's (2004) theoretical model on why practitioners use certain personnel-selection procedures. In an online-questionnaire, 274 German HR-managers reported their use of different selection procedures and evaluated procedures on diverse dimensions. Multilevel-analyses confirmed that practitioners used procedures of high perceived costs-effectiveness (moderated by financial resources and being a stock-corporation), applicant-acceptance (moderated by applicant-numbers and selection-ratio), dissemination among other HR-practitioners, and manager-control in hiring decisions. The procedures' perceived validity only predicted usage in the case of high applicant-numbers and low selection-ratio, and perceived legal defensibility did not influence decisions. This confirms that multiple factors beyond validity and legality matter.

FP-092: Business in the digital age: E-commerce, advertisement and digital marketing I

The effect of virtual spokes-character type upon on-line advertisements

Fang, Wenchang Business Administration, National Taipei University, Sansia Township, Taiwan Hsu, Ya Hui Business Administration, National Taipei University, Yonghe City, Taipei County, Taiwan Lyu, Yi-Lan Business Administration, National Taipei University, Sansia Township, Taiwan
To fill the research gap regarding spokes-characters, this study examines the rarely discussed influence of lip-syncing in on-line advertisements.

This study tests different types of virtual characters effects on advertisement effectiveness, including attention, credibility, and attitude. The main experiment includes eight conditions, in which each character has a different gender (male vs female), facial appearance (human-like vs cartoon-like characters), and lip-syncing (adult vs child), presenting a sentimental animated on-line advertisement. Using analysis of variance (ANOVA), this study reveals that human-like/male characters with adult lip-syncing and cartoon-like/female with child lip-syncing presented in the on-line advertisements cause more positive advertisement effectiveness.

Measuring congruity between self-concept and brand image: Testing moderators of predictive value of different methods

Stachoń-Wójcik, Maria Chémoelski, Poland Gorbaniuk, Oleg Katedra Psychologii Eksperymen, Katolicki Uniwersytet Lubelski, Lublin, Poland
The aim of the research was answering the question whether there are any significant differences in predicting attitude towards the brand on the basis of measuring congruity between self-concept and brand image using an indirect and direct method. The moderators of predictive accuracy were: brand exposure (public vs private), brand symbolism (symbolic vs non-symbolic) and type of self-concept (individual vs social, real vs ideal). The research involved 232 women. Result: the direct measurement of self-congruity is the most accurate indicator in predicting attitude towards the brand and intention to purchase the brand (the biggest in individual self-concept).

The research of online shopper decision-making's influencing factors

Chen, Hui Economic & Management School, Beijing University, Beijing, People's Republic of China
The objective was to find out the web sites factors and individual factors that influence the buying decision-making of online shopper. 190 online shoppers as subjects, we required them to browse two web stores which sell similar goods 15 minutes respectively, let them buy one goods on one of given sites, then filled in a few questionnaires, we used path analysis to verify the hypothesis. The results showed that ease of use of web sites, product information, entertainment, and trust remarkably influence online shoppers' satisfaction, which turns out it significantly influence on buying intention and buying behavior.

FP-093: Child and adolescent psychopathology II

Mental health issues among Aboriginal street-involved youth in Western Canada

Brunanski, Dana Counselling Psychology, University of British Columbia, Vancouver, Canada Bingham, Brittany N/A, McCreary Centre Society, Vancouver, Canada Smith, Annie N/A, McCreary Centre Society, Vancouver, Canada Saewyc, Elizabeth School of Nursing, University of British Columbia, Vancouver, Canada
This study explored health issues of younger Aboriginal street-involved youth (<19 years) from nine communities of a Western Canadian province. A participatory research population-based survey (N = 762) found disproportionate Aboriginal representation (54%) vs. census data (~9%). Despite high levels of risk exposures, Aboriginal youth reported connectedness to family and school, and hope for the future. Mental health problems, including suicidality, self-harm, and problem substance use were common, yet few youth accessed mental health services. Analysis within community discussions emphasized societal factors, including the legacy of colonization, cultural dislocation, diversity of Aboriginal cultures, and the importance of culturally-relevant interventions.

Effectiveness of cognitive behaviour group therapy on shyness among adolescents in Iran

D'Souza, Lancy Maharaja's College, University of Mysore, Mysore, India
Effectiveness of Cognitive Behaviour Group Therapy in reducing shyness was verified among 56 Iranian adolescents (28 experimental and 28 control). Shyness Assessment Test (SAT) developed by D'Souza (2006) was employed to measure levels of shyness in 3 domains: Cognitive/affective, Physiological and Action oriented. In the intervention program, after the introduction the researcher explained the CBT theory and evaluated the problems regarding CBT, identified Negative Automatic Thoughts (NAT) and trained the subjects to cope with NAT. At the end of CBGT, again, SAT was applied and data collected on 3 dimensions of shyness. Results revealed that CBGT is highly effective in reducing the shyness of adolescents in all the 3 domains.

Three-eight year outcome of a clinical sample of depressed adolescents

Dudley, Amanda CDPP, Monash University, Melbourne, Australia Tonge, Bruce CDPP, Monash University, Melbourne, VICTORIA, Australia Gordon, Michael CAMHS, Southern Health, Melbourne, VICTORIA, Australia King, Neville Faculty of Education, Monash University, Melbourne, VICTORIA, Australia Ford, Sarah CDPP, Monash University, Melbourne, VICTORIA, Australia Melvin, Glenn CDPP, Monash University, Melbourne, VICTORIA, Australia Klimkeit, Ester CDPP, Monash University, Melbourne, VICTORIA, Australia
Depression is a significant health problem and is associated with a range of negative sequelae including impaired social and academic adjustment, sensitisation to recurrent episodes of depression, self-harming behaviour and an increased risk of suicide. This longitudinal study involves the assessment of a clinical sample of depressed adolescents 3 – 8 years after acute treatment. Assessment comprises a semi-structured diagnostic interview and self-report measures of depression, general functioning, and family functioning/parent-child interactions. This paper presents the outcomes of young adults who experienced depression and findings will assist with the identification of risk factors for relapse and may contribute to treatment guidelines.

A longitudinal study of subthreshold depression in Chinese mainland adolescents

Yao, Shuqiao Medical Psychological Research, The Second Xiangya Hospital, Changsha, People's Republic of China Zhang, Chenchen The Second Xiangya Hospital, Medical Psychological Research, Changsha, Hunan, People's Republic of China Ling, Yu The Second Xiangya Hospital, Medical Psychological Research, Changsha, Hunan, People's Republic of China Zhu, Xiongzhao The Second Xiangya Hospital, Medical Psychological Research, Changsha, Hunan, People's Republic of China Abela, John R. Z. McGill University,, Department of Psychology,, Montreal (QC), Canada
Very few studies have been reported about the subthreshold depression (SD) in mainland of China, and some features of SD, especially the relationship with major depression (MD), are still unclear. We use both K-SADS interviews and self-report questionnaires assessing a variety of psycho-social factors including depressive symptoms and other symptoms, negative events, cognitive factors, interpersonal protective factor, personality, culture-related factors to a sample of high school students in China, once every six months, for 18 months. The prevalence of SD among Chinese adolescents is reported, possible relationship between SD and MD is analyzed, and the related biopsychosocial model of SD is discussed in this paper.

FP-094: Cognitive information processing and learning I

Improving the effects of strategy instruction on reading comprehension in elementary school children

Ennemoser, Marco Inst. für Psychologie, Universität Gießen, Gießen, Germany *Diehl, Meike* Department of Psychology, University of Gießen, Gießen, Germany

Two studies were conducted to optimize the effects of strategy instruction on reading comprehension in young elementary school children. Study 1 provided evidence that supplementing a basic rehearsal strategy to conventional strategy instruction leads to additional gains in reading comprehension (n = 254). The rationale for this strategy is that it takes into account the limited decoding abilities and consequential working memory load of young readers. Study 2 investigated if benefits can be further improved by the instructional approach of reciprocal teaching (n = 72). Results were only partially supportive and to some extent even contrary to our hypotheses.

The assessment of executive control functions in children: Implications for learning

Musso, Mariel Social and Behavioral Sciences, Leiden University / CONICET, Leiden, Netherlands

This research focuses on the assessment of indicators of appropriate emergence of inhibition in the activation of inhibitory responses. Processes were studied with measures for latencies, corrections, and other responses. Interventions over executive control mechanisms were designed for and adapted to situations of school instruction/learning. It was hypothesised that children improve their performance in executive control mechanisms after intervention. Results showed significant improvement of Executive Control after interventions, and that the novel assessment methods designed were efficient and reliable for application in school environments. Findings have concrete application in the development of better school-centred intervention programmes improving learning outcomes.

The influence of abacus training on intelligence and speed

Khaleefa, Omar Dept. of Psychology, University of Khartoum, Khartoum, Sudan

To examine the possible influence of abacus training on the intelligence and speed for children (7-11 years) both males (51%) and females (49%) IO and speed before and after training was assessed for the controled group (N=1144) and experimental group (N=1348). The study showed a statistically significant difference between the controled group and the experimental one on both intelligence and speed on 0,001 level.

FP-095: Cognitive and affective development in childhood and adolescence I

Analysing children's colloquial pain stories

Ostkirchen, Gabriele Gerda Inst. für Klin. Neurologie, Universität Duisburg-Essen, Essen, Germany

This project analyses colloquial pain stories of children and reports empirical findings. The 'Pediatric Pain Inventory' asks the children to describe the pain and to specify probable causes, coping strategies and attachment relationships. The utterances were categorised (CAT_SYS_PED_PAIN) exhaustively. Children generate in total 3088 utterances (mean 10,3): H=654/21,2%; AP=998/32,3%; INJ=603/19,5; BIC=833/27,0%. Relative frequencies within different pain situations vary from 21,4%-28,6%. High interrater reliablities are provided. Children talk about their pain with interest but without exaggeration. This study is a

contribution to acquire empirical knowledge that could provide the basis of a new way of looking at this issue.

Adaptation of Danva 2 in Romania

Rosan, Adrian Special Education Department, BBU Cluj Napoca, Cluj Napoca, Romania

The objective is the relationship between the capacity of recognising facial expressions, empathy and the adaptation in Romania of a range of tools: the Diagnostic Analysis of Nonverbal Accuracy with the two subtests: Danva 2- Test of Facial Expressions of Adults (Danva - AF) and Danva 2 – Test of Facial Expressions of Children (Danva - CF) with role in the screening of the risk of violent behaviour in puberty. Participants: 500 teenagers, age between 14-16. Anova Test for interpretation statistical data. The results will be used as support in applying a soft program for preventing violent behavior in puberty.

The curse of knowledge in children's false belief tasks

Li, Xiaodong Dept. of Psychology, Shenzhen University, Shenzhen, People's Republic of China *Xu, Jian* psychology, Shenzhen University, shenzhen, People's Republic of China *Liu, Ping* psychology, Shenzhen University, shenzhen, People's Republic of China *Zhou, Shuangzhu* psychology, Shenzhen University, shenzhen, People's Republic of China

The study was aimed to examine whether there was a cures of knowledge in False belief tasks. Three tasks were designed: unexpected transfer, unexpected content and auditory task. Each task includes four contexts: child-knowledgeable while puppet-ignorant, child-ignorant and puppet-ignorant, child-ignorant while puppet-knowledgeable, child-knowledgeable and puppet -knowledgeable. Subjects were 60 children aged 3-5. The results showed that there was a significant difference between child-knowledgeable and child-ignorant when puppet didn't know the truth and children obviously overestimate others' knowledge when they themselves know the truth; however, there was no significant difference between the two contexts when the puppet know the truth. These results demonstrate the curse of knowledge does exist.

FP-096: Educational assessment I

The interaction between cognitive learning styles and lingual background of the high school learners

Beygi, Ali Reza Psychology, Arak Azad University, Arak, Islamic Republic of Iran *Maghsudi, Mojtaba* English, Arak Bahoonar T.T.C., Arak, Islamic Republic of Iran

The present project was going to study the relationship between cognitive learning styles and bilingualism; therefore, a group of male and female high school students (n =236) with English or Kannada as medium in the city of Mysore, India comprised the sample of the present study. Appling T-test and one-way ANOVA, indicated: Independent subjects scored higher than dependent ones in English Achievement Test, subjects with English scored higher than subjects with Kannada Medium of instruction in Learning Style Test and finally it was indicated that there is NO significant interaction between students' linguality and gender in their cognitive Style scores.

The development and application of the wisdom assessment for college students

Cheng, Ying-Chen Measurement and Statistics, National University of Tainan, Tainan, Taiwan *Huang, Hsiu-Shuang* Measurement and Statistics, National University of Tainan, Tainan, Taiwan

The purpose of this study was to develop the evaluation in the wisdom of the undergraduate

students. The wisdom assessment consisted of three facets, a total of 8 items. Those subjects were 464 undergraduate students in Taiwan. The wisdom assessment performance was divided into five levels. The performance of the subjects was in the third level. In accordance with the IRT, each of the dimensions of difficult questions was between .038 - .761, the internal consistency reliability was .776, reliability was .875, and with a good construct validity.

Relationship between study habits, educational ability and study problems among secondary school students in Rawalpindi, Pakistan

Hussain Kanwal, Rabia Behavioral Sciences, Fatima Jinnah Women University, Rawalpindi, Pakistan

The present study investigated relationship between study habits, study problems, educational abilities among secondary school students in schools of Rawalpindi. The Educational Ability Test (ETS), Study Habits and Attitude Questionnaire, Mooney Problem Checklist were administered to 200 students, matched on gender, age, and grades. Findings indicated significant high correlation between scores of Study Habits and Attitude Questionnaire. However, Problem Checklist was negatively correlated with Study Habits and Attitude Questionnaire. The problems concerned with teachers were more significant in boys as compared to girls on problem checklist. These findings are helpful in strategic curriculum planning for secondary school students.

Mapping values and achievement goals using smallest space analysis

Liem, Arief Darmanegara Cent. for Res. in Pedagogy, Nat. Inst of Education, S'pore, Singapore, Singapore

Boekaerts et al. (2006) propose that Schwartz's (2006) circular model of values should guide our innovative approach to studying achievement and non-achievement goals that students bring to the classroom. Using a multidimensional scaling application called smallest space analysis, the present study aims to map out students' values and achievement goals on a two-dimensional projection. Two measures, the Portrait Values Questionnaire (Schwartz et al., 2001) and the Inventory of School Motivation (McInerney & Ali, 2006), were administered to 5000 Singaporean secondary school students. The result will address a question, "Is students' pursuit of multiple goals underpinned by their basic values?"

FP-097: Environmental perception and cognition I

Conceptions about environment and environmental education: From theory to practice

Stoltz, Tania Thery and Fundaments of Educat, Federal University of Paraná, Curitiba, Brazil *Carneiro, Sônia* Thery and Practice of Educatio, Federal University of Paraná, Curitiba, Brazil *Vestena, Carla* Education, UNESP, Guarapuava, Brazil *Nogueira, Valdir* Education, Centro Universitário de Jaragu, Curitiba, Brazil *Pieczarka, Thiciane* Education, Federal University of Paraná, Curitiba, Brazil *Sotero Costa, Roberta Rafaela* Education, Federal University of Paraná, Curitiba, Brazil

This study aims to analyze the conceptions about environment and Environmental Education of Geography teachers of the States of Parana and Santa Catarina in Brazil. Thirty teachers working at primary and secondary schools were interviewed. It was verified that even though the teachers have a major in Geography, which has as object of study the relation society and nature, among them predominate a fragmented and naturalistic conception of environment. In terms of the conception about Environmental Education it is predominantly a practice without thoughtfulness, not presenting in a significant way the development of environmental values and attitudes. As a conclusion there is a need for restructuring the courses of educators' formation in relation to the environmental issue in Education.

Space appropriation as an academic achievement factor: A study on a population of University Institute of Technology students in France

Rioux, Liliane EA3984 département psychologie, Université de Paris X-Nanterre, Nanterre Cedex, France

The principal aim of our research is to study the relation between space appropriation and the IUT students'academic achievement. 167 students in region Centre (France) answered a questionnaire meant to assess some socio-demographic (age, culture, types of housing), individual (professional project, relational network), and psychosocial (academic satisfaction and motivation, space appropriation) variables. The results show that the IUT space appropriation is dependent, in a large part, with the academic achievement. Moreover a step-wise regression analysis showed that five variables, i.e. age, environmental stimulation, having an open professional project, environmental discomfort and degree in amotivation are predictors of IUT students'academic achievement.

FP-098: Work motivation and engagement

A content valid measure of organizational engagement: Its relationships with job satisfaction, empowerment, affective commitment and turnover intentions

Albrecht, Simon Psychology and Psychiatry, Monash University, Caulfield East, Australia

The research aimed to validate a face valid measure of organizational engagement. Factor analysis and regression analyses were conducted on data drawn from 280 full-time employees working across a range of roles and industry sectors. The measure demonstrated acceptable reliability and could be reliably distinguished from an existing measure of engagement (the UWES) and from job satisfaction (JS), empowerment, affective commitment (AC), and turnover intentions (ITO). It explained significant additional variance in AC and ITO beyond JS and empowerment. The new measure will provide academics and practitioners with a useful and reliable way to measure engagement.

The effect of learning goals on performance: A simulation and 5 questions for future research

Seijts, Gerard Richard Ivey School of Bus., University of Western Ontario, London, Canada

Recent studies have shown that, on tasks that require the acquisition of knowledge and skill, a learning goal rather than a performance goal should be set in order to facilitate performance. The results of the experiment show that a specific, high learning goal leads to higher performance on a complex 90 minute business simulation than a specific, low learning goal. Other correlates of complex task performance included self-efficacy, goal commitment, and dispositional goal orientation. The results of the experiment and other goal-setting studies lead to five questions that will help in moving research on learning goals forward.

What are people looking for? Personality traits and importance of work motivation factors

Bipp, Tanja Human Performance Management, Technical University Eindhoven, Eindhoven, Netherlands

Based on two different work motivation theories, the relationships between personality traits (Big Five, CSE: core self-evaluation) and the importance of various job aspects was investigated. In Study I (N=118), graduates with high scores on Openness

to experience and Agreeableness placed emphasis on Herzberg's motivation factors, whereas no relations were found for hygiene factors. In Study II (N=117 employees), the Big Five accounted for 30% of the variance in importance of the motivating potential of a job (Job Characteristics Model) and CSE showed incremental validity. Results are discussed regarding person-job fit and the practical utility of the CSE construct.

Biopsychosocial correlates of work motivation

Liesienė, Justina Dept. of Psychology, Vytautas Magnus University, Kaunas, Lithuania Endriulaitien, Auks General Psychology, Vytautas Magnus University, Kaunas, Lithuania Bukšnyt, Loreta Theoretical Psychology, Vytautas Magnus University, Kaunas, Lithuania

The objective of this study was to find the most important biological, psychological and social factors related to work motivation. 310 Lithuanian employees were examined. The questionnaire constructed according to the instructions of Vroom Expectancy Theory was used to assess work motivation. Personality traits were assessed by Big Five Inventory. Correlations, comparison of averages and Path analysis was used to analyze the data. Results showed that extraversion, conscientiousness, openness to experience, better health and leading position are related to work motivation. Structural equation modeling showed that work motivation through subjective work effectiveness could be best predicted by extraversion and conscientiousness.

Designing and testing a model of important precedents and outcomes of work motivation of national Iranian south oil company employees in Ahvaz region, Iran

Arshadi, Nasrin Dept. of Psychology, Shahid Chamran University, Ahvaz, Islamic Republic of Iran Shokrkon, Hossein Psychology, Shahid Chamran University, Ahvaz, Islamic Republic of Iran Shehni Yailagh, Manije Psychology, Shahid Chamran University, Ahvaz, Islamic Republic of Iran

The purpose was to test a proposed model of antecedents and consequences of work motivation in Iran. A model of work motivation was developed, depicting motivational traits, Islamic work ethic ... as determinants of work motivation and considered job attitudes, job performance ... as outcomes. To assess the fitness, SEM was employed, using the maximum likelihood methods of AMOS-7. Taken together, the model showed good fit. Better fit and more meaningful results were obtained by developing an optimal model. The results indicated that the model can identify specific leverage points that can affect work motivation and therefore, important organizational outcomes.

The relation between socio-relational self-efficacy and work engagement in an Italian sample of social workers

Pace, Francesco Dept. of Psychology, University of Palermo, Palermo, Italy Mistretta, Rosalia University of Palermo, Palermo, Italy Salvo, Francesca Psychology, University of Palermo, Palermo, Italy Rigano, Rosalia Psychology, University of Palermo, Palermo, Italy Gallina, Carmela Psychology, University of Palermo, Palermo, Italy Foddai, Elena Discipl. Chir. ed Oncologiche, University of Palermo, Palermo, Italy Guadagna, Paola Psychology, University of Palermo, Palermo, Italy Di Maggio, Maria Gemma Psychology, University of Palermo, Palermo, Italy

This study examined how much in social workers the confidence about perceived socio-relational competencies is related to work engagement. We used a questionnaire delevoped to assess the socio-relational self-efficacy (according to the Bandura's theory), and the UWES (Schaufeli & Bakker, 2003), a measure of work engagement, defined as a

positive, fulfilling work-related state of mind. Subjects were interviewed in therapeutic communities (for drug addicts, for abused women etc.) or family communities. It was found that some aspects of relational competence (like to feel able to understand others' feelings) are strongly related to work engagement.

FP-099: Understanding aggression

Is the Implicit Association Test a valid tool for measuring aggressiveness?

Bluemke, Matthias Inst. für Psychologie, Universität Heidelberg, Heidelberg, Germany Zumbach, Jörg Bildungswissenschaften, Universität Salzburg, Salzburg, Austria

The Implicit Association Test (IAT) is a flexible categorization task that can be adapted to measure cognitions related to aggressiveness and, possibly, impulsive aggressive behaviour. We tested if IATs are suitable for experimental and diagnostic purposes. The current presentation draws on a review of three studies, including one quasi-experimental online-study and two experimental lab studies, in which we applied different variants of IATs in order to establish a connection to (a) consequences of violent computer gaming, (b) explicitly-reported aggression, and (c) behavioural indicators. Our findings show that not all aggressiveness-IATs are created equal.

Culture of honour and gender identity: The impact of sex, age and educational level on the predisposition to violence

Lopez Zafra, Esther Dept. of Social Psychology, Universidad de Jaén, Jaén, Spain Rodríguez Espartal, Noelia Social Psychology, Universidad de Jaén, Jaén, Spain Jiménez, María Isabel Social Psychology, Universidad de Jaén, Jaén, Spain

Culture of Honour is reaching a height at the present time as a variable that may explain or affect the violence against women. Culture of the honour justify and use violence as a form to defend honour and to dominate the relationship. This problem is present in our society. In our study 406 individuals fill out a questionnaire that measures culture of honour, gender identity and socio-demographic variables. Our results show a relationship between this concept and socio-demographic variables as age, sex and level of studies. Moreover, we find that a masculine-agency gender identity is significantly related to a higher importance given to culture of honour.

A social-cognitive look at the catharsis hypothesis: How goal-fulfillment reduces aggression

Denzler, Markus Dept. of Social Psychology, University of Amsterdam, Amsterdam, Netherlands

A model predicting cathartic-like effects is suggested: It is assumed that the goal to aggress increases accessibility of aggression-related constructs. This heightened accessibility looses its functionality after goal-fulfillment and is hence inhibited. This model is applied to two different aspects of the catharsis-hypothesis: Experiment 1/2 demonstrate that accessibility of aggression-related constructs is increased before and inhibited after goal-fulfillment; aggressive behavior is also reduced upon goal-fulfillment. Experiment 3/4 show that playing a violent computer-game with the goal to aggress inhibits the accessibility of aggression-related constructs when the goal is fulfilled. The relationship to previous catharsis research and practical implications are discussed.

Peer aggression and coping

Méndez, Claudia Personality, Assessment, University of Barcelona, Barcelona, Spain Forns, Maria PETRA, University of Barcelona, Barcelona, Spain

Peer aggression is a significant problem among adolescents. This study aims to analyze peer aggression, adolescents coping strategies and how they influence adaptive functioning. Participants were 400 adolescents aged 11-16 years from Barcelona Secondary Schools. Data were obtained from three self-report measures: a peer aggression and bullying questionnaire (instrument created ad-hoc for this investigation), Adolescent-Coping Orientation for Problem Experiences (Patterson,J. M., McCubbin, H), and Behavior Assessment System for Children Self-Report (Reynolds, C. R. & Kamphaus, R. W.). The results suggest that successful adaptation is related to the type of coping strategies used.

An attempt of a social psychological analysis on the contemporary concepts of aggression

Zografova, Yolanda Institute of Psychology - BAS, Sofia, Bulgaria

Based on the comparative analysis of contemporary models of aggressive behavior - personological and information-processing - an approach to the construction of concepts of aggressiveness are presented. The proposed approach includes the achievements of the discussed models as well as new aspects in the perspective of definition of aggression's different subject levels – individual and social-group. Empirical evidence is presented to illustrate the impact of different factors like personal aggressiveness, social and cultural environment, situational context of the interpersonal relationships and factors such as some frustrating, social, economical and psychological changes in Bulgaria on the person's/groups' aggressive dispositions and behaviour. In conclusion the necessity of elaboration of new treatment of the different aggressiveness' subject levels is discussed.

Teenage population's reactions to a terrorist attack

Valero Valero, Maria Oficina de Cooperación, Universitat Jaume I, Castellón de la Plana, Spain García Renedo, Mónica Oficina de Cooperación, Universitat Jaume I, Castellón de la Plana, Spain Gil Beltrán, José Manuel Oficina de Cooperación, Universitat Jaume I, Castellón de la Plana, Spain

Our aim is to examine the reactions and perceptions to a terrorist attack of secondary school students geographically distant from the scene of the incident. The sample is made up of 87 subjects aged between 12 and 16, whose average age is 13.8 (s.d.=1.309). The data analysis was carried out with the statistical analysis software SPSS 14.0. The results reveal how adolescents show a wide range of reactions and cognitions regardless of their age. These results can be useful to design strategies that allow parents and teachers to have enough knowledge to meet the psychosocial needs that they may manifest after a crisis situation.

FP-100: Understanding semantics

Comprehension of metaphorical statements

Repeko, Alexander Collegium Europaeum, Poznan University, Gniezno, Poland

Comprehension of different types of statements including metaphorical ones was checked under different conditions. Participants were asked to evaluate truthfulness of statements under explicit requirements to consider them either as formal expression or to use their imaginary. It was found that metaphors was treated in a different way then true or false statements and that requirement to use imagery alter the time to judge the truthfulness of a statement.

Affect primacy in embodied word processing

Domingos, Ana Psychology, ISPA, Lisbon, Portugal Garcia-Marques, Teresa Psychology, ISPA, Lisboa, Portugal Niedenthal, Paula Psychology, Université Blaise Pascal, Clermont-Ferrand Cedex, France

Together affective-primacy and embodiment approaches predict that our face muscle activity reacts to valenced information. In our studies participants perform affective/non-affective judgments while facial muscles activity was manipulated. In lexical decisions frowning participants revealed facilitation for positive compared to positive negative and nonwords. Bite and blocking manipulations impaired positive word recognition. In study 2, negative words, elicited greater amount of disliking judgments in blocking and biting conditions, than in frowning mimicry. Positive words, elicit less liking in the biting condition. As expected mimicry impacts valenced-word processing however, our pattern of results did not revealed the expected congruency effect.

Cognitive and emotional dimensions of narrative engagement

Bilandzic, Helena Medien und Kommunikation, Universität Erfurt, Erfurt, Germany Busselle, Rick Murrow School of Communication, Washington State University, Pullman, USA

This study validates a scale describing cognitive and emotional engagement with filmic narratives. Items derived from a model of narrative engagement were tested on a developmental sample of 443 US-American students who watched a television show. Four dimensions were found in factor analysis: Narrative Understanding, Attentional Focus, Emotion and Being There. The subscales were replicated in two test samples of 60 German students with two shows. Secondary task reaction times were taken in this study at intense and less intense moments. Reaction times were slower in suspenseful, but faster in emotional scenes. Implications for the relationship between resource allocation and narrative engagement are discussed.

Describing sense-making processes

Nystrom, Monica Medical Management Centre, Karolinska Institutet, Stockholm, Sweden

The purpose of the study was to test methods for investigating sense-making processes. Three researchers analyzed transcribed interviews and summarized them. A method for following the process was used, resulting in segments of text and process comments. Quantitative and qualitative analyses examined meta-cognitions and the discourse of interpretation. Results showed sense-making as a mixture of bottom-up and top-down cognitive processing. Variation concerned type and amount of information reacted on in relation to previous knowledge. Text influence, strong in the beginning, weakened during the process. Potential sources for variation in cognitive processing were suggested. The proposed measurement design was found useful.

Influence of inhibition of return on semantic processing: Evidence from a semantic stroop task

Zhang, Yang Dept. of Psychology, Northeast Normal University, Changchun, People's Republic of China Ming, Zhang psycology, NortheastNormal university, Changchun, People's Republic of China Linyun, Wang psycology, NortheastNormal university, Changchun, Germany

Objective: The goal of the present study is to determine whether IOR can modulate semantic process by combination the semantic Stroop and IOR procedure. Methods: Seventeen undergraduate students with a mean age of 22.75 ± 2.38 years old were recruited as participants Results and Conclusions: The results showed that the semantic stroop effect was eliminated when the stimuli presented in cued locations. Therefore, in consistent with atten-

tional hypothesis of IOR, IOR appears to arise from inhibition of attention rather than disconnecting perceptual representations with their motor representations.

How semantic knowledge affects object recognition: Electrophysiological evidence for early perceptual modulations

Abdel Rahman, Rasha Inst. für Psychologie, Humboldt-Universität zu Berlin, Berlin, Germany

Expertise in object recognition is based on extensive perceptual experience and in-depth semantic knowledge. In contrast to well-attested effects of perceptual experience, little is known about the influence of in-depth knowledge recognizing objects. A series of experiments with event-related brain potentials (ERPs) demonstrates that the amount knowledge acquired about objects modulates visual ERP components already 120 milliseconds after object presentation and causes gradual variations of activity within a later time window associated with meaning access. Thus, in-depth knowledge not only affects involuntary semantic memory access but also penetrates early visual processes that are traditionally held to be immune to such influences.

FP-101: Transformational leadership

Transformational leadership and employee well-being: An examination of the mediating role of self-efficacy and trust in the leader

Liu, Jiayan Institute of Psychology, Beijing, People's Republic of China Siu, Oi-ling Department of Politics & S, Lingnan University, Hong Kong, China, People's Republic of : Macao SAR Shi, Kan N/A, Institute of Psychology, Beijing, People's Republic of China

Based on survey data collected from 745 employees from the People's Republic of China (Hong Kong, n = 448; Beijing, n = 297), regression results revealed that transformational leadership was positively related to employees' self-efficacy, trust in the leader, and job satisfaction, and negatively related to perceived work stress and stress symptoms. Employees' self-efficacy and trust in the leader partially mediated the influence of transformational leadership on job satisfaction, and fully mediated the influence of transformational leadership on perceived work stress and stress symptoms. Implications of these findings for practice and research are discussed.

Psychological capital as a mediator between transformational leadership and employees' work-related outcomes

Zhong, Lifeng School of Business, Renmin University, Beijing, People's Republic of China Li, Mei School of Business, Renmin University of China\\, Beijing, People's Republic of China

Building on previous research, this study proposed that transformational leadership would boost followers' task performance and organizational citizenship behavior by enhancing their psychological capital. Using a sample of 167 supervisor-subordinate dyads from China, a two-step process of analysis with LISREL 8.50 was employed to test the hypotheses. The results indicated that both transformational leadership and psychological capital were positively related to employees' task performance and organizational citizenship behavior, and employees' psychological capital mediated the relationship between transformational leadership behavior and employees' job performance and organizational citizenship behavior. Limitations and practical applications were offered. Keywords: transformational leadership, psychological capital, job performance, organizational citizenship behavior

Are personnel trainers leaders?

Silva Peralta, Yamila Social Psychology, Universidad de Barcelona, Barcelona, Spain

This is an exploratory and qualitative study which purpose is to know about Personnel Trainers' Leadership. It was oriented to the discovery of deductive categories in the experiences of non-success of the trainers and the exploration of regularities among the categories. Taking into account the theoretical model of Bass and Avolio (2004) a content analysis of 41 trainer's critical incidents was performed. The results showed transformational and transactional styles combined in most of the critical incidents. The incidents were linked to the self-criticism as a trainer and the irregularities during the training process. Theoretical and practical contributions are presented.

Transformational leadership and innovation implementation: The mediating role of commitment to change and moderating function of climate for initiative

Michaelis, Björn I&O Psychologie, Universität Heidelberg, Heidelberg, Germany Stegmaier, Ralf I&O Psychology, University Heidelberg, Heidelberg, Germany Sonntag, Karlheinz I&O Psychology, University Heidelberg, Heidelberg, Germany

This questionnaire-based study investigates the relationship between six transformational leader behaviors and subordinates' innovation implementation behaviors. Findings from 198 employees working in the R&D section in a multinational automotive company indicate that transformational leadership is consistently related to implementation behaviors, given controls for numerous individual differences in subordinates' personality, satisfaction, and job demography. As assumed, this relationship is shown to be mediated by subordinates' affective commitment to change. Further, climate for initiative moderates the relation between transformational leadership and subordinates' innovation implementation behaviors. Implications for practice and future research are discussed.

The relationship between the Big Five personality traits and transformational and transactional leadership styles

Sattari, Fatemeh Tehran, Islamic Republic of Iran Shokrkon, Hossein psychology, Shahid Chamran University, Ahvaz, Islamic Republic of Iran

This research studies simple and multiple correlations between the personality traits and the leadership styles of the managers in an organization in IRAN. The hypothesis was that the big five Neo P-IR factors are positively correlated to the transformational and transactional leadership styles. 118 managers completed the Neo P-IR and Multifactor Leadership questionnaires. Data were analyzed using Correlation and Multiple Regression. Extraversion, Neuroticism, Conscientiousness, and Openness and their sub-factors had significant correlation with transformational leadership. Extraversion and Conscientiousness and their sub-factors had significant correlation with transactional leadership. Indications of findings have been discussed for the improvement of the two leadership styles.

Followers self-regulation and preferences for transformational versus transactional leadership: A conjoint-analytical approach

Galais, Nathalie Organ.- und Sozialpsychologie, Universität Erlangen-Nürnberg, Nürnberg, Germany Halbig, Michael Organizational and Social Psy., University Erlangen-Nürnberg, Nürnberg, Germany

The study (N = 481) focuses on the effects of followers' goal-orientation and regulatory focus on preferences for transformational versus transactional leadership. We applied a conjoint-analytical approach that was realized through an online study and enables to interactively assess preferences on

the basis of multiple comparisons. Results indicate that individual self-regulation do not predict a general preference for transformational/transactional leadership but preferences for specific motivational facets of transformational leadership. Whereas learning oriented individuals and those with high promotion-focus prefer leaders who offer visions and challenge followers, those with high performance-orientation prefer leaders who act as role-models. Prevention-focus had no effects.

FP-102: The learning environment: Student-teacher relationship, teacher effectiveness, learning opportunities

Identification of effectiveness factors in English (EFL) teachers and the study of the relationships between these factors and students'attitudes with students' outcomes

Takrimi, Azimeh Teaching English, Teacher Training School, Ahvaz-Kooye, Islamic Republic of Iran Khojaset Mehr, Reza counselling, sahahid chamran university, Ahvaz,KooyeOstadane Daneshghe, Islamic Republic of Iran

This study was designed to identify the English teachers' effectiveness factors and to investigate the relationships between these factors and students'attitudes with their outcomes.215 teachers participated, selected according to multi-stage sampling. Instruments were a 50-item questionnaire on effectiveness factors,Aiken's attitude scale,and students' final scores.Factor analysis revealed four factors as Instructional strategies,Comunication skills,Personality characteristics,and Knowlege.Results also show a simple and multiple correlation between these factors and students'attitudes with students'outcomes.This study has implications for language teachers,teacher training centers,and principals.

Children's adaptive and maladaptive motivational patterns and teacher-child relationships

Patrick, Helen Educational Studies, Purdue University, West Lafayette, USA Mantzicopoulos, Panayota Educational Studies, Purdue University, West Lafayette, USA Samarapungavan, Ala Educational Studies, Purdue University, West Lafayette, USA French, Brian Educational Studies, Purdue University, West Lafayette, USA

We identified different motivational profiles of 110 kindergarteners, and examined whether demographic, achievement, and teacher-child factors were associated with these patterns. Using cluster analysis we identified three profiles involving children's perceived competence in, liking, and ease of science. The largest group expressed high motivation. A smaller group expressed low competence but high liking, and another reported low liking with moderate competence. The profiles did not differ by demographics or achievement. The low competence/ high liking group perceived less teacher support than did children with high motivation. Discourse analysis of teacher-child interactions during science lessons showed interaction differences by motivational profile.

Learning environments and schooling engagement in secondary qualifying education

Frenay, Mariane Dept of Educational Psychology, University of Louvain UCL, Louvain-la-Neuve, Belgium Archambault, Isabelle Dept of Psychoeducation, University of Montreal, Montreal, Canada Paul, Cecile Dept of Educational Psychology, University of Louvain UCL, Louvain-la-Neuve, Belgium Dayez, Jean-Baptiste Dept of Educational Psychology, University of Louvain UCL, Louvain-la-Neuve, Belgium Galand, Benoît Dept of Educational Psychology, University of Louvain UCL, Louvain-la-Neuve, Belgium

This study investigates effects of learning environments on students' engagement and achievement. We hypothesize differential effects of specific teaching practices on value perception and on academic achievement. Promoting instrumentality would increase utility value while supporting learning will raise attainment value and academic achievement. 2207 vocational and technical secondary students (grade 9 & 11) were surveyed twice during school year. Controlling for demographics and prior motivation, utility value was predicted by teaching promoting instrumentality, but, surprisingly, no change in R^2 was found for attainment value while academic achievement was best predicted by teaching supporting learning. Theoretical and practical implications are discussed.

Learning opportunities and math achievement of third grade Mexican children

Contreras, Carolina Pruebas y Medición, INEE, México City, Mexico

The main purpose of this study was to determine whether achievement scores differ significantly across different levels of learning opportunities. A two phase, stratified SRS, PPS national representative sample of 55312 students was used. Children were evaluated on math using a standardised test of 80 items with a .79 reliability. Learning opportunities were assessed through four items answered by children and scaled with the Rasch model. Three groups were created according to Rasch scores on learning opportunites. Achievement means were compared using PISAs macros for complex samples. Significant differences were found among the three groups.

Critical analysis of ideas on the learning readiness of children

Quibuyen, Liezl Elementary Department, College of the Holy Spirit, Tarlac City, Philippines

This study investigated the indicators of learning readiness of thinkers as applied in the classroom of a private school. Three questions were generated: What learning ideas are common among the thinkers? ; What are the common indicators of learning readiness assumed by the thinkers? ; what principles of learning readiness are applied in the classroom? Results proves that the principles of readiness exemplified by the thinkers are present in the observable skills of the pupils.There is commonality in the learning ideas of the thinkers and the indicators of readiness. Analysis of data suggests that teachers need to foster an environment that strengthens the creative capacities and interest of children.

The study of factors affecting educational degradation in learning English among non-English major students

Rahbar, Mohammad Dept. of Foreign Language, Quchan Azad University, Quchan, Islamic Republic of Iran

The present research considers six hypotheses that might affect students, degradation in learning English. The research instrument was a 36 item questionnaire with the following sub-scales: 1.very low effect, 2.low effect, 3.moderate effect, 4.high effect, and 5.very high effect. To analyze the gathered data, SPSS software was used. The results showed that factors such as family financial problems, lack of educational facilities and inexperienced teachers did not have such a great effect on students' degradation in learning English, but factors such as improper educational planning, lacks of motivation, and social environment problems were of most important factors.

FP-103: Motivation and goal orientation

Why positive expectations do not always work?

Moà, Angelica Dept. of General Psychology, University of Padova, Padova, Italy

Previous research has shown that the way you think of your abilities affects your performance in a related domain. The present study explores an additional explanation/factor i.e. time pressure. Three experiments were run with high school students (mixed-gender, all-males, all-females) who were required to complete a mental rotation test and told that men generally perform better than women for either genetic reasons or a stereotype or time pressure. Results showed an increase in performance in the time pressure condition for males and a decrease in the genetic reasons condition in the mixed group. Discussion focuses on the underlying motivational mechanisms.

A study of motivation on the peasant distance learners in urbanization

Zhang, Yan Research, 6/F TCL Building OPEN, Beijing, People's Republic of China *Song, Yu* research, 6/F TCL Building OPEN, Beijing, People's Republic of China

To examine Self-Determined Learning Intervention Model (SDLIM), we investigate 87 peasant distance learners from Beijing, Ningbo, Guangzhou, where the teaching reform project of MOE of China "To establish and demonstrate the Digitalized Learning Port and Lifelong Learning Society" is undertaken. This study adopts types of motivation based Self-determination to measure the intrinsic motivation, extrinsic motivation and amotivation level of peasant distance learner. By analyzing with their different characteristics in urbanization, it shows that because of their different occupations, their motivation levels vary considerably, SDLIM is also more complex.

Goal orientation and motivation to lead: A self-organization theory perspective

Zhang, Kai School of Business, Renmin University of China, Beijing, People's Republic of China *Jiao, Changquan* Faculty of Business Administra, Lakehead University, Thunder Bay, Canada *Li, Binyu* Department of Human Resource, Beijing Institute of Economic, Beijing, People's Republic of China *Tan, Shuang* School of Business, Renmin University of China, Beijing, People's Republic of China

The conceptualization of goal orientation in past studies has focused on individual achievement goals. Based on self-organization theory, this study broadens goal orientation conceptualization to include teamwork goal orientation and investigates the relationship between employee goal orientation and motivation to lead (MTL). Factor analyses, correlation analyses, and hierarchical regression analyses were employed to test the hypotheses. The results show that teamwork goal orientation can be distinguished from other three goal orientations. We also found that teamwork goal orientation significantly predicts benefit-related MTL, and learning goal orientation significantly predicts power-related and social-normative MTL. Implications for future research and practices are discussed.

Achievement goals, learning strategies and academic achievement among Peruvian highschool students

Matos, Lennia Dept. of Psychology, University of Lima, Lima, Peru *Lens, Willy* Psychology, University of Leuven, Leuven, Belgium *Vansteenkiste, Maarten* Psychology, University of Gent, Gent, Belgium

Achievement goal theory was used to study the role of motivation in the academic context of a Peruvian sample of highschool students (N = 1505). The purpose of this cross-sectional study was to examine the relationship between students' achievement goals, their use of learning strategies and academic achievement. Multiple Regressions identified, as predicted, positive effects of mastery goals (i.e. more use of learning strategies, higher academic achievement), and negative effects of performance-avoidance goals (i.e. lower academic achievement). Mixed results were found for pursuing performance-approach goals. The present findings support the external validity of achievement goal theory in a sample of students from a culture that is understudied in the motivational literature.

Could optimal self lead to optimal adjustment? Actions to achieve goals larger then the self and their beneficial effects

Lin, Yicheng Department of Psychology, National Taiwan University, Taipei, Taiwan *Huang, Chinlan* Division of General Education, The National Taiwan University, Taipei, Taiwan

Crokers & Park (2004) proposed that the key to achieve the optimal self-esteem is to consciously choose goals larger than the self. In the current study, three types of actions including actions of hope, actions to show gratitude, and actions to make oneself and one's partner happy were executed three times a week and consecutively for two weeks in a fixed order. Pre and post measures of psychological adjustments, life satisfaction, and emotional experiences were assessed. Both the beneficial effects and moderating mechanisms of taking actions to achieve inclusive goals larger then the self were examined.

Finding Mr. Right: Implicit affiliation motive and affect regulation moderate partner choice

Fröhlich, Stephanie M. Abteilung Bad Rothenfelde, Institut für Rehaforschung, Bad Rothenfelde, Germany *Kuhl, Julius* Dep. of Human Sciences, Universität Osnabrück, Osnabrück, Germany

The implicit affiliation motive is a desire for close relationships. We hypothesize that people with a high implicit affiliation motive look for partners with matching high implicit affiliation motives. Persons with good access to their inner motives should be more successful in finding a suitable partner. We obtained data from 51 couples. Hierarchical regression analyses were conducted. Individuals having a strong implicit affiliation motive and the ability to downregulate negative affect have partners with comparable affiliation motives. Affect regulation plays an important role in finding a partner who is similar to oneself in the strength of the implicit affiliation motive.

FP-104: Motivational and social aspects of sport

Interrelations between anxiety, personality, motivation and performance in 15 years old top-level fencers

Rosnet, Elisabeth Research Department, INSEP, Paris, France *Gillet, Nicolas* Laboratory of Applied Psycholo, University of Reims, REIMS, France

In order to test the interelations between anxiety, personality, motivation and performance, more than 300 15 years old fencers have completed the STAI, the Gordon Personality Inventory and the Echelle de Motivation dans les Sports (EMS). Fencers are from the 20 national best at this age in foil, epee and sabre. Data are collected during several years. Performance is assessed by the national ranking at the time of the psychological measures and also 2 years later. Gender is also taken into account. Results are discussed according to the self-determination theory of motivation.

Relationship maintenance strategies in the coach-athlete relationship

Rhind, Daniel School of Sport and Exercise S, Loughborough University, Loughborough, United Kingdom *Jowett, Sophia* School of Sport and Exercise S, Loughborough University, Loughborough, United Kingdom

Objectives: Although the investigation of relationship maintenance strategies has received considerable attention in romantic/marital and familial relationships, no research has yet investigated the use of such strategies in the coach-athlete relationship. Methods: Twelve one-to-one interviews were conducted with 6 coaches (4 males and 2 females) and 6 athletes (2 males and 4 females), from team and individual sports, regarding their perceptions of the strategies which help maintain coach-athlete relationships. Results: Using content analysis, the following 7 categories emerged: Conflict Management, Openness, Motivational, Positivity, Advice/ Feedback, Support and Social Networks. Conclusions: Similar strategies were identified to those revealed in personal relationship research, however, some sport-specific strategies were also highlighted/ emerged.

The Power Motive Scale - Sports- 4 Stages (PMS-Sports-4S): A sports specific power motive scale according to McClellands four stage model

Krippl, Martin Foren. Psychiatrie u. Psychol., Universität Göttingen, Göttingen, Germany

Objectives: On the basis of McClelland's four stage model of the power motive a sports specific questionnaire of the power motive was developed. Measures 162 sports students (M=22.13; SD= 2.64, men: 86) of the universities of Potsdam and Erlangen in Germany filled out the questionnaire. An explorative factor analysis was conducted in order to also identify not intended factor structures. Results The result is a four-factor structure (Kaiser-Guttman-Kriterium) with a different number of items for each factor/stage. Cronbach's Alphas for all scales are above .70. The alpha for the whole scale is .80. Conclusions The factor structure is satisfying, as well as the internal consistencies of the subscales.

Testing achievement motivation and volition in sport

Wenhold, Franziska Inst. für Sportpsychologie, Universität Potsdam, Potsdam, Germany *Elbe, Anne-Marie* Department of Exercise and Spo, Univerity of Copenhagen, Copenhagen, Denmark *Beckmann, Jürgen* Sportpsychology, Technical University Munich, Munich, Germany *Ehrlenspiel, Felix* Sportpsychology, Technical University Munich, Munich, Germany

Due to a deficit of German sport specific psychological questionnaires the German Federal Institute for Sport Science financially supported the development of four questionnaires measuring motivational and volitional personality aspects, which are main prerequisites for athletic peak performance. Test control criteria analysis showed sufficient results for all four instruments, namely the Achievement Motives Scale-Sport (Elbe& Wenhold, 2005a), the German Sport Orientation Questionnaire (Elbe, 2004), the Action Control Scale-Sport (Beckmann, 2003) and the Volitional Components Questionnaire-Sport (Elbe& Wenhold, 2005) and norms were established. The questionnaires are available as manuals, via an internet portal and are currently being implemented in the sport psychological consultation of elite athletes.

Educational needs of actors involved in soccer youth sectors

Gozzoli, Caterina Dipartimento Psicologia, Universita Cattolica, Milano, Italy *Frascaroli, Daniela* Dipartimento Psicologia, Università Cattolica, Milano,

Italy **D'Angelo, Chiara** *Dipartimento Psicologia, Università Cattolica, Milano, Italy*
This research aims to investigate representations and needs of young players, parents, coaches and chiefs in soccer youth sectors, as well as relations and the quality of the relation between these actors. We will also compare and link these four lifespaces, by investigating and analysing educational needs. 13 soccer clubs were involved (500 players, 300 parents, 50 coaches, 30 chiefs). We conducted group-interviews, ethnographic observations and semi-structured interviews (further data are being collected), then analysed through content-analysis (with Atlas.ti software for qualitative analysis). Different representations, complex relations, crucial issues, efforts and resources emerged; these results are essential to get a deeper understanding of sport as lifespace and to plan educational paths.

Role of sports in student stress coping

Bommareddy, Udayakumar Reddy *Rural Development, National Institute of, Hyderabad, India*
Childhood is the critical time for developing healthy attitudes and adaptive stress coping, which persist into adulthood. OBJECTIVES: To examine the health-related behaviours and sports training of school children. METHODS: Structured interview schedule was prepared and Scientific Survey conducted on 1275 Students as a sample from 162 Schools in India. Analysis includes Descriptive Statistics and Bivariate Correlation. RESULTS: Majority of the sample revealed "Stress" in their day-to-day life and found "Playing Sports" as their Stress Coping but suffered from sports injuries, nervous at play. CONCLUSIONS: Negligence of scientific sports training and sports sciences makes sports an ineffective stress coping

FP-105: Motor learning, decision making and expertise in sport

A longitudinal investigation of expertise-based differences in search and option-generation strategies

Raab, Markus *Köln, Germany* **Johnson, Joseph** *Psychology, Miami University, Oxford, Ohio, USA*
In a 2-year longitudinal study, we investigate changes of athlete's performances strategy (three expertise levels) to generated options and subsequent choices in handball. Search pattern were identified via eye-tracking data to independently verify decision strategies previously inferred from patterns of generated options. A verbal protocol identified the option-generation process for each individual prior to an allocation decision. Although athletes of varying expertise generated the same number of options on average, these options differed in quality between levels of expertise for both their initial and final choices. These results are formalized to elaborate a model presented recently (Raab & Johnson, 2007).

Attribution biases in foul calls: Laboratory and field evidence for the "all players foul small players" heuristic in soccer

van Quaquebeke, Niels *Inst. für Sozialpsychologie, Universität Hamburg, Hamburg, Germany* **Giessner, Steffen R.** *Organization and Personnel Man, RSM Erasmus University, Rotterdam, Netherlands*
There is no video-evidence in soccer. Consequently, for ambiguous misconduct, referees have to rely upon heuristics to infer foul probabilities. We propose that one heuristic relates height to aggressiveness. Study 1 revealed that over all fouls of the last seven European Champions League seasons, the last seven Bundesliga seasons, and the last three World Cups (altogether n1=123,857 fouls), perceived foul perpetrators were on average taller than their victims. Further experimental studies (n2=198, n3=327), in which the height of two soccer players chasing a ball was manipulated, confirmed that

participants were more likely to call a foul on taller players.

The effects of attentional focus strategies on the performance and learning of soccer-dribbling task in children and adolescents

Bahram, Abbas *P.E. and sport sciences, Tarbiat Moalem University, Tehran, Islamic Republic of Iran* **Abdolahi Pour, Reza** *-, Ministry of Education, Arak, I, arak, Islamic Republic of Iran* **Shafizadeh, Mohsen** *P.E. and sport sciences, tarbiat moalem university, tehran, Islamic Republic of Iran*
The aim of this study was to determine the effects of internal versus external focus strategies on the performance and learning in novice children and adolescences. At practice phase, participants, without prior experience were required to dribble a colorful soccer ball. They will be asked to recall part of the foot (internal) or color of the ball (external). Retention and transfer (external evaluation) tests performed without instructions or reminder on day 2. MT and errors data were analyzed. The results showed, at practice phase the internal focus condition had lower errors, but at transfer the external focus group showed faster MT.

Effects of different external attention of focus on the motor learning and error-detection capability: Perception-action approach

Shafizadeh, Mohsen *Physical Education & Sport, Tarbiat Moallem University, Tehran, Islamic Republic of Iran*
The objective of present study was to determine the effect of different sources of external attention of focus on motor skills.30 students were participated voluntarily and were divided according to type of attention. All subjects performed 60 trials of golf putt skill in acquisition and retention phases. ANOVA results have shown that action-perception focus group had better learning than other groups but perception focus group had better error-detection than action focus group. Thus, the external focus instruction that helps the performer to perceive the condition of extrinsic target and planning the action is more useful than other external of focus instructions. These results propose the role of ecological theory on the effects of external focus of attention.

Physical misconceptions in football professionals

Rauch, Jan *Inst. für Psychologie, Universität Zürich, Zürich, Switzerland* **Daum, Moritz M.** *Psychology, Max Planck Institute, Leipzig, Germany* **Wilkening, Friedrich** *Psychology, University of Zürich, Zürich, Switzerland*
The field of intuitive physics in psychology has shown that adults - even experts - often show astonishing misconceptions about physical laws. The present study investigated the performance of football professionals regarding their ability to redirect a cross ball in order to score. In a post-hoc analysis of all 64 games of the 2006 World Cup in Germany, even these football professionals showed a misconception when redirecting balls with the head, but not when redirecting with the foot. A follow-up experimental study with amateur and professional football players examined possible reasons for the misconception.

The psychology of playing at home in Italian Serie A football

Zengaro, Franco *Murfreesboro, USA* **Zengaro, Sally** *Educational Psychology, University of Alabama, Murfreesboro, USA*
Objectives: The purpose of this study was to examine the relationship between aggression and home field advantage for Italian Serie A. Methods: Penalties, yellow cards, and red cards from 2003-2007 were examined. Data were analyzed through chi square, Pearson correlation, and regression. Results: The results indicated a significant advan-

tage for home teams in penalty kicks ($\chi2$ (8) = 168.538; p = .000). There were moderate correlations of yellow cards, red cards, and team classification. Conclusions: Away teams may adopt a defensive strategy leading to more cards and penalties. However, crowd support, player profile, and team reputation may influence referee decisions.

FP-106: Multilingualism I

Relations between working memory, language awareness and multiliteracy of young, Chinese immigrant children in early French immersion programs

Hoskyn, Maureen *Educational Psychology, Simon Fraser University, North Vancouver, Canada*
Chinese-immigrant parents in Canada have the option of enrolling their children in either English or French immersion language programs at school entry. In this study, the relative importance of educational placement (i.e., language experience), working memory and meta-cognitive language awareness on literacy outcomes (i.e., in English, French and Mandarin/Cantonese) of 120 young Chinese immigrant children is investigated. Results of hierarchical regression analyses suggest that working memory mediates, but does not entirely explain the role of meta-cognitive language awareness on literacy outcomes in English and French and these relations exist irrespective of children's educational placement.

Transfer of phonological skills in L2 lexical learning

Xiao, Wen *Dept. of Psychology, CUHK, Hong Kong, China, People's Republic of : Hong Kong SAR* **Cheng, Jeremy Chi-Yeung** *psychology, CUHK, Hong Kong, China, People's Republic of : Macao SAR* **Cheung, Him** *psychology, CUHK, Hong Kong, China, People's Republic of : Macao SAR*
The study shows that Chinese (L1) phonological awareness predicts English (L2) receptive vocabulary over and above English phonological awareness in a group of bilingual 9-year-olds. No such transfer effect however emerges with orthographic awareness. In addition, transfer of phonological skills appears to be restricted to relatively sparse phonological neighbourhoods. Our results are discussed in the light of the lexical restructuring hypothesis as applied to bilingual learning, and the universality of phonological processing across languages adopting different writing systems.

Bilingual reading and vocabulary development in relation to speech perception and metalinguistic awareness

Cheung, Him *Dept. of Psychology, Chinese Univers. of Hong Kong, Hong Kong, China, People's Republic of : Hong Kong SAR* **Chung, Kevin** *Curriculum and Instruction, HongKong Instituteof Education, N.T., Hong Kong SAR, China, People's Republic of : Macao SAR* **Wong, Simpson** *Psychology, Oxford University, Oxford, United Kingdom* **McBride-Chang, Catherine** *Psychology, Chinese University of HongKong, N.T., Hong Kong, China, People's Republic of : Macao SAR* **Penny, Trevor** *Psychology, National University of Singapo, Singapore, Singapore* **Ho, Connie** *Psychology, University of HongKong, Pokfulam, Hong Kong, China, People's Republic of : Macao SAR*
This study examines the intercorrelations among speech perception, metalinguistic awareness, reading, and vocabulary in three age cohorts of Chinese-English bilingual children, aged from 5 to 9 years. Results showed that: (1) speech perception followed slightly different developmental paths in the two languages; (2) metalinguistic awareness was related to reading and vocabulary in the two languages in similar ways; (3) speech perception was more predictive of metalinguistic awareness, reading, and vocabulary in the L1 than L2; (4) L1 speech

perception and metalinguistic awareness uniquely predicted L2 reading but not vocabulary. The findings are discussed in the context of cross-language transfer.

Willingness to communicate and communicative apprehension in the Japanese context

Gladman, Tehmina Miyazaki International College, Kiyotake, Japan *Curl, Layton* Psychology, Metropolitan State College, Denver, USA

This study looks at the differences in levels of willingness to communicate in English and communicative comprehension in a sample of Japanese college students from both a traditionally structured Japanese university as well as from an international college in Japan. Many private colleges have recently opened with the express purpose of teaching an international curriculum in English to predominantly Japanese students. This study will discuss whether these English immersion colleges are significantly increasing Japanese students' willingness to communicate while reducing their intercultural communicative apprehension as compared to students taking a more traditional Japanese curriculum with traditionally designed English classes.

Priming in the mental lexicon between mother tongue and a foreign language in bilinguals and interpreters

Polonyi, Tünde Éva Budapest, Hungary

This research studied lexical retrieval in bilinguals. The specific question was whether in a disambiguating context the processing of an ambiguous word in one language facilitates the access of both of its meanings in the other language of the mental lexicon. Students majoring in English, Hungarian-English bilinguals and interpreters (N=87) took part in the experiment. A cross-modal priming experimental setup was applied. Results showed no clear time-course of lexical access that after multiple access of meanings comes selective access. A factor revealed by our study that is capable of influencing priming effects is word class of prime and target.

FP-107: Learning strategies I

The role of Self-Regulated Learning (SRL) and Self-Efficacy (SE) on mathematics and biology learning (a study carried out in high schools in Indonesia which conducted accelerated program for the gifted)

Kusumawardhani, Dianti Endang School of Education, Flinders University, Jakarta, Indonesia

Indonesian first year students (N=240) from accelerated and regular classes from three different high schools were assigned to either an intervention (teaching sessions fostering students' knowledge of SRL strategies) or a non-intervention condition. The proposition was there is an effect of the intervention on Mathematics and Biology learning that operates through SRL or SE. PLS, AMOS, and HLM programs were used to examine the pattern of relationships and to track change over time. The result showed although the direct effect of intervention on Mathematics and Biology learning on SE dropped after the intervention, an indirect effect operates through SRL, particularly in learning Biology.

Age differences in the metacognitive control of workplace learning

Roßnagel, Christian Jacobs Centre, Jacobs University Bremen, Bremen, Germany *Schulz, Melanie* Jacobs Centre, Jacobs University Bremen, Bremen, Germany

We investigated the effects of low memory self-efficacy (MSE) on work-related learning. 90 workers participated in a computer-based training. They were assigned to a 2(age: < 36yrs vs. >50yrs) x 2 (high vs. low MSE) x 2(reflection prompts vs. no prompts) design. Participants in the prompts group received self-reflection prompts on learning goals and learning strategies. For older learners, prompts enhanced performance in the low MSE group, but not the high MSE group. Unlike low MSE older learners, high MSE older learners did not rate learning as being of negative affective quality. Results show that MSE affects the metacognitive control of learning.

Comparing the study methods of Iranian and American high school students from the perspective of cognitive and metacognitive strategies

Shaghaghi, Farhad Dept. of Psychology, Paiam Noor University, Tehran, Islamic Republic of Iran

Abstract This research is about comparing the study method of Iranian and American high school students from the perspective of cognitive and metacognitive strategies. The tow groups of subjects were selected randomly from Iranian and American high school students within the range of 15 to 18 years old who studied in Tehran (Iran) and New York. For the purpose of comparing the study methods of these subjects, each group of subjects was separately ask to fill out a questionnaire on study methods. The results indicated that Iranian students apply more cognitive strategies, however Iranians use more metacognitive strategies for studying their subject matters.

Competence-based knowledge space theory and self-regulated learning: Mission impossible or happy marriage?

Albert, Dietrich Inst. für Psychologie, Universität Graz, Graz, Austria *Steiner, Christina M.* Department of Psychology, University of Graz, Graz, Austria

Two apparently conflicting research trends in e-learning are picked up. Competence-based Knowledge Space Theory (CbKST) provides a knowledge representation framework which, since its invention by Doignon and Falmagne, has been successfully applied in various e-learning systems (e.g. ALEKS, ELEKTRA) providing automated personalisation to learners' competence. Principles of self-regulated learning (SRL), pioneered by e.g. Zimmerman, argue for increased learner control, thus resulting in giving learners greater responsibility over their e-learning. It is shown that CbKST-based guidance and SRL-based autonomy are noway conflicting but rather complementing each other towards an integrated approach of self-regulated personalised learning, demonstrated by the iClass system.

Computer-assisted analysis of online collaborative learning process

Li, Yanyan Educational Technology, Beijing Normal University, Beijing, People's Republic of China

To explore the students' interaction process during online collaborative learning by adopting the computer assisted approach, the asynchronous discussion transcripts of 18 graduate students taken in course "Introduction of E-learning" were analyzed. Semi-auto content analysis results showed that students' interaction process could be described in terms of cognitive, metacognitive and social activity. Their interaction mainly focused on emotional greeting at the social dimension, and information sharing, questioning, debating, negotiation at the cognitive dimension, but occasionally related to metacognitive dimension. It was concluded that online discussion during learning was still superficial, and learning-related deep discussion seldom occurred.

Self-regulation and feedback in learning from texts

Chen, Qishan Dept. Educational Psychology, Chinese Univers. of Hong Kong, Hong Kong, China, People's Republic of : Hong Kong SAR *Shiu, Ling-Po* Educational Psychology, Chinese University of HongKong, Hong Kong, China, People's Republic of : Macao SAR

How accurately can students monitor and regulate their learning? In this study, 100 college students were asked to re-study some texts they had read and on which they had taken a comprehension test. The texts for re-study were selected by either the students themselves or the computer on the basis of the comprehension test. Our results show that students in the latter condition outperformed those in the former condition in a second comprehension test. However, students in these two conditions did not differ significantly had they generated five keywords at a delay after reading the texts for the first time.

FP-108: Consequences of occupational stress III

Relationship between health and coping in human service workers

Morán, Consuelo Psychology, Sociology and Ph., University of León, León, Spain *Alonso, Nieves* Psychology, Sociology and Ph., University of León, León, Spain

Objective: To explore the exposure to workplace bullying and his repercussion in general health and differences in coping strategies. Design and methods: Human services, 394 workers, 136 men. Diagnosis study. Multivariate Analysis, Pearson correlation, Cluster analysis. Results: 10% of subjects considered targets of bullying. The results indicated differences within targets and no-targets in all of dimension of health. A greater distress appears in target males. Differences in coping strategies appear. Conclusion: Workplace bullying was a strong risk factor for general health loss. This study suggested that targets must used more healthy strategies of coping (positive reinterpretation, acceptance, planning).

Study on the relative factors of workaholism and work engagement

Jiang, Jiang School of Psychology, Beijing Normal University, Beijing, People's Republic of China *Zheng, Fangfang* School of Psychology, Beijing Normal University, Beijing, People's Republic of China *Yu, Shengkai* School of Psychology, Beijing Normal University, Beijing, People's Republic of China

The study examined workaholism and work engagement on work demands, work support and perceived health by related scales. The sample consisted of 436 employees in China securities agencies. Correlation analysis and regression analysis showed workaholism had significant positive correlation with engagement which meant the one who was workaholic scored high on engagement. Workaholism and work engagement both positively related to work demands and support. Workaholism was negatively associated with physical health. In contrast, work engagement had no significant relation with total health. Work support could predict the status of engagement and working excessively could predict poor health.

Workplace bullying in Italy: Some empirical findings

Giorgi, Gabriele Psychology, University of Firenze, Firenze, Italy

This research addresses the prevalence of bullying in Italy. Above 1500 Italian employees compiled the Negative Acts Questionnaire Revised (NAQ-R) across more than 20 organizations. The database of the research came indeed from a work of organizational diagnosis. Results showed that bullying prevalence in Italy is high. Findings also highlighted that bullying is clearly linked to the organizational system, though the nature of the experience varies among companies. Finally a strong relation was found between workplace bullying and organizational climate. Team, leadership, job description and dynamism were the most important predictors of bullying at work.

The occupational stress of public sector employees

Neelakandan, Rathinam Psychology Wing, Annamalai University, Chidambaram, India

The present study aims to find out the level of occupational stress of different cadre of employees working in a public sector organization. A samples of 320 employees selected randomly were studied using Srivasthava and Singh Occupational Stress scale. Statistical measures such as Mean, SD, SEM, t-tests and Analysis of Variance, were used to interpret the obtained data. The results revealed that employees differed in occupational stress on the basis of marital status, education and year of service.

FP-109: Conscious and unconscious processes I

Electrophysiological correlates to changes in state of consciousness during meditation

Hinterberger, Thilo Inst. für Umweltmedizin, Universitätsklinikum Freiburg, Freiburg, Germany

Psychophysiological measurements comparing meditation and non-meditation conditions have been conducted over decades. This study focuses on the detection of state changes during meditation. Therefore, twenty highly experienced meditators have been measured with 64 channels of EEG (Electroencephalogram) and additional peripheral measures during self-paced and guided meditation. After referencing the data to a resting state condition the state changes during meditation could be visualized. Most meaningful correlates were found in the Theta and Gamma range of the EEG which mostly matched the mediators' reports. These results encourage us to develop an online monitoring device for states of consciousness.

The effect of preparation time and foreknowledge on task switching

Huang, Silin School of of Psychology, Inst. of Developm. Psychology, Beijing, People's Republic of China *Lin, Chongde* school of psychology, institute of developmental Psy, beijing, People's Republic of China *Hu, Qingfen* school of psychology, institute of developmental Psy, beijing, People's Republic of China *Luo, Liang* school of psychology, institute of developmental Psy, beijing, People's Republic of China *Chen, Guang* school of psychology, institute of developmental Psy, beijing, People's Republic of China

An explicit task-cuing paradigm was used to explore the effect of preparation time and foreknowledge on task switching. The results as follow: (1) The interaction between the preparation time and the foreknowledge was significant. With prolonging the preparation time, the RT in repetition task and switch-to task reduced significantly. However, the RT in switch-away task didn't reduced. There were not the preparation effects; (2) Compared to the switch-to task, the RT and switch cost in switch-away task were longer; (3) the preparation effect did not depend on the predictability of the preparation time.

The nature of practice-related changes of dual-task control

Strobach, Tilo Inst. für Psychologie, Humboldt-Universität zu Berlin, Berlin, Germany *Frensch, Peter A.* Department of Psychology, Humboldt University Berlin, Berlin, Germany *Schubert, Torsten* Department of Psychology, Ludwig-Maximilians-University, Munich, Germany

Studies on dual-task practice suggest that participants acquire skills of inter-task coordination to control simultaneously processed component tasks. However, the nature of these skills is still a matter

of debate. We assumed that participants acquire skills to accelerate the switch between the bottleneck stages in a dual-task situation and compared the dual-task performance of dual-task and single-task learners after extensive practice. The results showed that dual-task learners speed up the start of the processes after switching between the two component tasks in a dual-task situation. These findings suggest improved bottleneck switching as an important skill resulting from extensive dual-task practice.

Unconscious determinants of free decisions in the human brain

Soon, Chun Siong Attention & Awareness, MPI CBS, Leipzig, Germany *Brass, Marcel* Experimental Psychology, Ghent University, Ghent, Belgium *Heinze, Hans-Jochen* Department of Neurology II, Otto-von-Guericke University, Magdeburg, Germany *Haynes, John-Dylan* BCCN Berlin, Charité – Universitätsmedizin, Berlin, Germany

Are decisions influenced by unconscious brain processes? Here we investigated to which degree the outcome of a free decision could be predicted from fMRI signals at various timepoints before it was made. Participants spontaneously decided between a left or right button press and immediately executed their choice while also reporting when their conscious decision was formed. Using a pattern classifier applied to fMRI signals we were able to predict the outcome of a decision up to 7s before it was made from frontopolar and parietal cortex. This suggests that a sequence of unconscious processing stages precedes a free conscious decision.

FP-110: Neural bases of cognition II

Using ERPs to probe phonological short-term memory deficits in children with SLI

Barry, Johanna Inst. für Neuropsychologie, Max-Planck-Institut, Leipzig, Germany *Hardiman, Mervyn* Experimental Psychology, University of Oxford, Oxford, United Kingdom *Yasin, I.* Experimental Psychology, University of Oxford, Oxford, United Kingdom *Bishop, Dorothy* Experimemtal Psychology, University of Oxford, Oxford, United Kingdom

The event-related potential components called the mismatch negativity (MMN) and late mismatch negativity (LDN) were used to investigate phonological short-term memory deficits in children with Specific Language Impairment (SLI). Stimuli comprised 4-syllable standard and deviant CV-strings. We predicted significantly reduced MMN and LDN responses to consonant changes particularly in the third and fourth syllables due to more rapid fading of the sensory memory trace. This paper reports our findings and the implications for understanding sensory memory deficits in SLI.

Object-specificity in human brain activity without the objects?

Mnatsakanian, Elena HNA Laboratory, Institute of Neurophysiology, Moscow, Russia *Tarkka, Ina Maria* Neurophysiology, Brain Res&Rehab Center Neu, Kuopio, Finland

We studied brain activity elicited by the preparation to compare pairs of consecutive targets superimposed with the ignored stimuli. The tasks were: pattern comparison where targets were abstract patterns, same for all series, and real object comparison where targets in different series were 1) personally familiar faces, 2) unfamiliar faces, 3) animal figures. The target type to compare was defined by the preceding cues - dot patterns, same for all series. The 128-channel event-related potentials elicited by the cue were analyzed in 12 volunteers. The cue-elicited activity showed differences related to the specificity of the objects to be compared later.

The effect of subthalamic deep brain stimulation on processes of response selection in patients with Parkinson's disease: Evidence from a Simon task

Plessow, Franziska Department of Psychology, University of Technology, Dresden, Germany *Volkmann, Jens* Department of Neurology, Christian-Albrechts-University, Kiel, Germany *Schubert, Torsten* Department of Psychology, Humboldt-University, Berlin, Germany

The aim of this study was to investigate the involvement of the basal ganglia (BG) in mechanisms of response selection. Patients with Parkinson's disease and therapeutic deep brain stimulation (DBS) of the subthalamic nucleus performed a Simon task, in which they responded to a relevant stimulus dimension while inhibiting competing response tendencies due to irrelevant stimulus dimensions. DBS was used to systematically switch between physiological (ON) and pathological (OFF) functioning of the BG. Results show a reliable Simon effect in the ON but not in the OFF condition. This suggests that the BG play a role in response selection processes.

Invariant decoding of object categories from human visual cortex

Chen, Yi Attention and Awareness, Max-Planck-Institut, Leipzig, Germany *Haynes, John-Dylan* BCCN Berlin, Charité – Universitätsmedizin, Berlin, Germany

Categorical representations of objects in visual cortex have been intensively investigated using fMRI in humans. However it remains unclear to which degree specific brain regions encode objects invariant of their defining features. We approached the problem using 3D rendering of objects rotating along a randomly changing axis. Multivariate techniques were used to decode objects from fMRI signals. We investigated whether changes of speed, size and colour of objects affected the degree to which they could be decoded. Our results support the notion that object representations in temporal cortex can be decoded independently of their precise spatial representation in retinotopic regions.

FP-111: Psychotherapy - Research and treatment methods IV

A compensation model of online therapy

Akmehmet, Sibel Educational Sciences, Bogazici University, Istanbul, Turkey

Systematic qualitative research on actual experience of online therapists is lacking. This study aimed to demystify the experience of e-therapy practitioners by collecting in-depth interview data from four therapists residing in three different countries. Triangulation was achieved through the interviews, member-checking, and their web sites. A qualitative analysis of each narrative revealed that e-therapists tend to adjust the face-to-face therapy processes rather than totally transforming them. A "compensation model" was supported particularly regarding visual cues. In addition, an "online therapeutic relationship model" focusing on the interaction of compensation and transformation was devised to conceptualize the adjustment process.

Computer supported training based on latent semantic analysis and the expertise of psychotherapists

Caspar, Franz Dept. für Psychologie, Universität Bern, Bern, Switzerland *Wenning, Katrin* Dept. für Psychologie, Universität Freiburg, Freiburg, Germany *Wahl, Sonja* Dept. für Psychologie, Universität Freiburg, Freiburg, Germany *Berger, Thomas* Dept. für Psychologie, Universität Bern, Bern, Switzerland

Research on the development of expertise shows that "deliberate practice" with explicit fast feedback, and the possibility of improving performance is an efficient avenue to expertise (Ericsson). Unfortunately, such possibilities hardly exist naturally in psychotherapy practice and too little in common psychotherapy trainings. This may partly explain why consistently only modest differences are found between novice and experienced psychotherapists. Unfortunately, intensive deliberate practice with human support would be too costly. Therefore, a computer tool based on Landauer et al's "Latent Semantic Analysis", which "understands" freely formulated text and gives feedback has been successfully used in an experimental comparison with traditional feedback

Psychodiagnostic decisions
Sjödahl, Lars Lund, Sweden
To exemplify a category-system over false diagnostic inferences (attributions) a number of case studies will be presented, based on patients' first person accounts and their patient charts. Educational measures to improve clinicians' diagnostic skill are suggested. The following aspects are discussed and empirically illustrated from the case material. Idiographic or nomothetical approach to the diagnostic task: consequences? Validity criteria for diagnostic attributions, coherence or correspondence criteria? Categorial and/or dimensional attribution of the client: consequences? Dispositional versus episodic attribution of the client: consequences? A category system covering 36 categories of false attributions, in terms of contextual explanations is presented.

Effects of university training and practical experience on expertise in clinical psychology
Spada, Hans Inst. für Psychologie, Universität Freiburg, Freiburg, Germany Hauser, Sabine Department of Psychology, University of Freiburg, Freiburg, Germany Rummel, Nikol Department of Psychology, University of Freiburg, Freiburg, Germany Caspar, Franz Department of Psychology, University of Bern, Bern, Switzerland
We examined the effects of university training and growing practical experience on expertise development in clinical psychology, and in particular psychotherapy. 85 persons (novice, intermediate, and advanced students, graduated trainee therapists, and therapists with at least 10 years of practical experience) took part in our study. They completed a test measuring basic and clinical knowledge and worked on case studies. Up to the level of trainee therapists the results were consistent with the positive picture known from expertise development in medicine. However, at the level of experienced therapists several variables decreased. A possible explanation of these results will be presented.

FP-112: Cognitive processes

Railroad illusion in railroad profession
Druzhinin, Georgy IEAP, Moscow, Russia
Visual illusions were studies by interactive version of psychophysical methods. Applying to railroad problems the question whether railroad employees see railroad illusion (Ponzo illusion) was studied in details. Locomotive drivers and railway men see this illusion and work with it every day but never think about it. Locomotive drivers see the cabin equipment in light inverse perspective, see the railway in direct perspective and try to locate the front window as the border between the direct and inverse perspective in the area of neutral perspective. The structure of visual space of railroad personnel will be discussed.

Behavioral intention: Motivation to protect among young drivers faced to human versus automatic road speed control
Kergoat, Marine Dept. de Psychologie EA 3984, University Paris X, Nanterre, France Delhomme, Patricia Psychologie de la conduite, INRETS, Arcueil cedex, France Meyer, Thierry Psychology EA 3984, University Paris X, Nanterre cedex, France
Based on the motivation protection model (Rogers, 1983), the present research is about understanding the way young drivers cognitively process speed control messages while driving on a highway. Young drivers had to imagine themselves in a specific situation where control type (automatic vs. policemen) and situation controllability (control location known vs. unknown) were manipulated. Measures of speed behavioral intention and coping evaluation were collected. Variance and regression analyses were performed. In a controllable situation, only information concerning police control had a deterrent effect. Self-efficacy and motivation as explanatory factors are discussed.

Traffic "Incivilities" in Romania: Attributions and social representation of traffic infrastructure
Holman, Andrei Iasi, Romania Havarneanu, Cornel Psychology, "Al. I. Cuza" Universi, iasi, Romania Dumitru, Marian Psychology, "Al. I. Cuza" Universi, iasi, Romania Havarneanu, Grigore Iasi, Romania
The research is aimed at revealing the connections between the Social Representation of traffic infrastructure in the Romanian population and driving "incivilities", taking into account as a possible mediator the attribution process. Our hypothesis is that drivers justify their "rude" (and even risky) attitudes and behaviors through the bad state of Romanian traffic infrastructure, their attributions being aimed at the carelessness of authorities in this regard. We researched the links between the content and structure of this social representation, on one hand, and the attributions, attitudes and behavioral intentions in various traffic situations, on the other.

Assessing focus of attention during driving with visual secondary tasks: Development of a new experimental design
Gradenegger, Barbara IZVW, Würzburg, Germany Rauch, Nadja Psychologie 3, IZVW, Würzburg, Germany Krüger, Hans-Peter Psychologie 3, IZVW, Würzburg, Germany
In a driving simulation study drivers' gaze behaviour during visual secondary tasks was simulated via occlusion. Change blindness for changes occurring to moving, driving relevant and irrelevant objects was used to measure focus of attention. Relevance for driving was only dependent on speed and headway of surrounding vehicles; all other aspects were kept constant. Results for N=16 subjects show influence of expectation and relevance on focus of attention. Due to unattended situational developments failures with severe consequences for driving safety occurred. Therefore, the new experimental design seems promising for a detailed analysis of attentional strategies in driving with secondary tasks.

FP-113: Cognitive development in childhood II

The development of attentional orienting after non-predictive, predictive or counter-predictive cues
Leclercq, Virginie Centre Henri Piéron, Boulogne Billancourt, France Siéroff, Eric LPNCog, centre Henri Piéron, Boulogne Billancourt, France
Orienting of attention was investigated in 6- to 10-year-olds and in adults, in experiments using non-predictive, predictive or counter-predictive cues and various delays between the cue and the target. With non-predictive cues, IOR was found in all groups, but was delayed in younger children. With predictive cues, the advantage of valid over invalid trials occurred in all participants, showing an ability to endogenously orient the attention even in younger children. However, a weaker ability to inhibit the capture of attention by a counter-predictive cue, leading to a delayed endogenous reorienting of attention, was found in children compared to adults.

Age of beginning formal reading instruction and later literacy: Evidence from longitudinal research
Suggate, Sebastian Dept. of Psychology, University of Otago, Dunedin, New Zealand Schaughency, Elizabeth Psychology, University of Otago, Dunedin, New Zealand Reese, Elaine Psychology, University of Otago, Dunedin, New Zealand
This study compares developing literacy in children attending schools where literacy instruction begins earlier or later. Participants (N = 450) comprised eight cohorts of children (5-12 years) across seven years, attending state (instruction begins at 5) or Rudolf Steiner (instruction begins around 7) schooling. Measures assessed included: home literacy/demographic practices, receptive vocabulary, narrative story retell, phonemic and alphabetic awareness, decoding, and comprehension. Literacy growth and absolute performance were investigated with hierarchical linear analyses, while accounting for participant characteristics. Preliminary results suggest students beginning reading instruction later generally catch up to their earlier-starting peers. Further findings and implications will be presented.

Validation of the early childhood behavior questionnaire in Chinese setting
Tao, Ye Inst. for Psychology, Zhejiang University, Hangzhou, People's Republic of China Xu, Qinmei Inst. for Psychology, Zhejiang University, Hangzhou, People's Republic of China
The Early Childhood Behavior Questionnaire (Putnam, 2006) was translated into Chinese. Parents of 126 children (63 male, 63 female, M = 38.14 months, SD=13.55) were asked to complet the Chinese version. Results showed the internal consistency of the scale and 17 dimensions except attentional shifting ranged from 0.60 to 0.86. A three-factor structure of Effortful Control, Negative Affectivity, and Extraversion was validated. Chinese children were lower in High Intensity Pleasure, Soothability, and Sociability, but higher in Motor Activation, Sadness, Fear, Discomfort, Shyness, Perceptual Sensitivity, and Positive Anticipation than American ones. Both of age and gender differences emerged in several dimensions.

Five-month old babies' manual motor behaviors in interactions with their mothers
Vicente, Carla Rio de Janeiro, Brazil Seidl de Moura, Maria Lucia Social Psychology, State University of Rio de Jan, Rio de Janeiro, Brazil
This study investigated manual motor behaviors of reaching and grasping in five-month old babies during 114 interactional events with their mothers, in order to understand the role of this interactional mediator on joint attention over objects. The participants were 35 urban dyads of the Rio de Janeiro and they were video-recorded in their home. A descriptive analysis was performed considering categories of babies' behaviors and maternal stimulation. The results show that manual behaviors take part in 61.4% of interactions, together with maternal stimulation. Thus, babies' manual behaviors seem to be co-constructed by the dyad in a process of joint attention.

FP-114: Cognitive development I

Not smarter, but wiser: Dialectical reasoning across lifespan
Grossmann, Igor Dept. of Psychology, University of Michigan, Ann Arbor, USA Na, Jinkyung Psychology, University of Michigan, Ann Arbor, USA Varnum, Michael Psychology, University of Michigan, Ann Arbor, USA Kitayama, Shinobu Psychology, University of Michigan, Ann Arbor, USA Nisbett,

Richard Psychology, University of Michigan, Ann Arbor, USA

Are older people wiser? Despite the lay belief, researchers have failed to provide a clear answer to this question. Re-conceptualizing wisdom as a dialectical style of reasoning, we invited a randomly selected community sample of younger (n=63) and older people (n=65) to read stories about social group conflicts and give their prognosis for future events. Participants' responses were coded on five dialecticism dimensions, including recognition of limits of knowledge and compromise. Older participants used dialectical reasoning more often than younger adults. Cognitive ability tests did not predict dialecticism for either younger or older participants.

Institute of Psychology of Russian Academy of Education: Methods of prognosis and design of social situation for children with neurological illnesses

Bulanova, Olga Centre, Diagnostics and Consulting, Moscow, Russia

Prognosis of children's predisposition to illnesses with help of experimental database analysis by means of neural networks and methods of multi-dimensional statistical analysis. We used "Intelligent Problem Solver" in STATISTICA Neural Networks package and received optimal instruments for classification. Neural networks for aim of prognosis and data analysis are effective modelling method allowing to relatively easily reproduce complicated non-linear dependencies. Networks on radial basic elements proved to be the most effective (80% of correct prognoses). In process of investigation we singled out most influential factors for prognosis of neurological illnesses, which ensures effective designing of rehabilitation conditions for development and improvement of a sick child's life standard.

The comparison on the development of visual attention between the hearing impaired population and hearing population

Zhang, Xingli Developmental and Educational, Institute of Psychology,CAS, Beijing, People's Republic of China *Shi, Jiannong* developmental and educational, Institute of Psychology,CAS, Beijing, People's Republic of China *Wang, Kenan* For the Deaf, Beijing No.2 School, Beijing, People's Republic of China

We used the visual search task to investigate the development of visual attention between the hearing impaired and hearing population. The two group participants were matched in age and IQ. The results showed that the visual attention developmental speed of the hearing impaired children was slower than that of the hearing ones. However, their selective skill improved with age. Therefore, in the adulthood, hearing impaired students showed the slight advantage in the selective attention skill over the hearing ones. The present study suggested that visual attention development depended on the integration of multimodal sensory information.

FP-115: Organizational development

The dynamic process of person-environment fit in episodic organizational change: A longitudinal case study in China

Pan, Lushan School of Management, Zhejiang University, Hangzhou, People's Republic of China

While it is recognized that implementing organizational changes impact both employee and organizational health, there is a lack of research that focus on the interactions between the employee and changing environment. This study examines Person-Environment (P-E) fit during the changing period and takes a longitudinal perspective on P-E fit. By examining how P-E fit are imbalanced and rebalanced through specific phases of the changing period, this research also provides insights about the role of employee's adaptation to organizational change as the key driver of shifts in P-E fit rebalancing.

Unconscious conflicts of values as socio-psychological barriers to organizational development

Zakharova, Lyudmila Administration Psychology, NNSU, Nizhny Novgorod, Russia

The presentation identifies the values, determining decision making of Russian managers and their influence on building the market organizational culture. Significant difference in officially accepted and de-facto affecting decision making values is found. 50% of managers agree that market culture values are the most efficient for their enterprise but only 14,5 5 use them in decision making. Unconscious conflict of values is a barrier for developing market relationships. This conflict leads to forming an amorphous organizational culture, reproduction of outdated management styles and block market oriented development.

Logo-OD: The applicability of logotherapy as an Organisation Development (OD) intervention

Burger, Daniel Human Resource Management, University of Johannesburg, Johannesburg, South Africa *Crous, Fredrik* Human Resource Management, University of Johannesburg, Johannesburg, South Africa *Roodt, Gert* Human Resource Management, University of Johannesburg, Auckland Park, Johannesburg, South Africa

This study investigated the applicability of logotherapy as an OD intervention by examining the relationship between the constructs of resistance to–readiness for change and meaning seeking, and determining whether a logotherapy-based intervention – or Logo-OD – would impact on resistance to change. A quasi-experimental design was applied to test the study's hypotheses. Whereas a significant relationship was established between the above-mentioned constructs, no significant effect of Logo-OD on resistance to change was observed. These results largely supported the primary conclusions emanating from the literature review: the role of Logo-OD is one of a positive trigger event for organisational change.

Organization development in an Iranian industrial corporation: The diagnosis phase

Nouri, Aboulghasem Psychology, University of Isfahan, Isfahan, Islamic Republic of Iran *Samavatyan, Hossein* Psychology, University of Isfahan, Isfahan, Islamic Republic of Iran *Oreyzi, Hamid Reza* Psychology, University of Isfahan, Isfahan, Islamic Republic of Iran *Sanati, Javad* Occupational HSE, Polyacryl of Iran Corporation, Isfahan, Islamic Republic of Iran *Mojib, Mahmoud* CEO, Polyacryl of Iran Corporation, Isfahan, Islamic Republic of Iran

Based on the organization development literature, a long-term and multi-phased study was planned in an Iranian industrial corporation. In the first phase, the aim was to achieve the organization diagnosis. Following a comprehensive study of the system, identifying its key components and discussing with key members of the corporation, a questionnaire was developed and finalized after the pilot study. A classified random sample of 425 persons participated. The results indicated some significant degrees of congruence between the corporation and the personnel's goals. Implications for the next phase of a planned intervention as well as the relevant model are proposed.

FP-116: Diversity management

Does age matter in leadership? Age relations between leaders and followers as determinants of leadership effectiveness

Kearney, Eric Bremen, Germany *Voelpel, Sven* JCLL, Jacobs University Bremen, Bremen, Germany

Despite the abundant literature on leadership, there is little knowledge of how leadership effectiveness may depend on age relations between leaders and followers. Given that in today's organizations there are often considerable age differences between leaders and followers (e.g., old leaders and young followers or vice versa), we present a comprehensive model of how leaders can adapt their leadership behaviors not only to the age of their followers, but especially to their own age relations with followers. Moreover, we present the results of two pertinent empirical studies and discuss the theoretical and managerial implications of our findings.

Age as a factor in leadership situations

Muecke, Anja School of Business, University of Applied Sciences, Olten, Switzerland

Demographic change will make it necessary to manage and maximise the performance and potential of a workforce that is growing older. Supervisors play a crucial role in the challenge to keep employees at all ages motivated and effective (Tuomi et al., 1997). However, little is known how "age" is perceived by supervisor in everyday leadership situations. 348 critical leadership situation were worked out using leadership diaries, interviews and workshops with 28 Swiss line managers. Attributional theory (e.g. Mitchell, 1982) and the theory of age effects by Lawrence (1987) were used as theoretical basis. Results will be presented.

Diversity management and social representations of diversity

Cardu, Helene Fondements Pratiques Education, Universite Laval, Quebec, Canada *Costalat-Founeau, Anne-Marie* Psychologie, Université Montpellier III, Montpellier, France

In this presentation, we describe the results of a study taking place in Canada (3 regions: Quebec, Ontario and Western Canada) which aims to analyse social representations of diversities and competencies in diversity management among Canadian managers (N=180). Results were obtained via a multimethodological approach with both content analysis on managers' discourse and factorial and correlational analysis from questionnaires on diversity and competencies managers' representations. Results show the importance of cultural and regional variations on diversity management practices and representations. We highlight the relation between diversity and competencies representations and regional variations are described using the action and identity representation theorethical model (Costalat-Founeau, 2005) Our discussion will focus on international comparizons of diversity management models from Canada and France.

FP-117: Environmental perception and cognition II

Environmental issues in Sudanese press: Psychological view

Ahmed, Asma Psychology, University of Khartoum, Khartoum, Sudan

Abstract The Present study explores the wide range of Psychological significance of the press coverage of issues related to environment in the Sudan. The sample consists of three daily Sudanese national newspapers: Al- Ayyam, AlRai ElAam, and Al Sahafi ad- Dawli during year (2000). Content analysis method was used as a tool for the present study. The study showed that there were differences in environmental issues tackled by the press, variation in forms of presentation concerning environmental issues, the prevailing attitudes regarding environmental issues were divided into negative and positive attitudes. There was a positive relation between the attitudes and both of the correct behavioral patterns and the behavioral trend concerning environmental issues.

Perceptions of genetically modified food and crops

Shengelia, Tamara Milton Keynes, United Kingdom
Developments in agricultural biotechnology, namely, genetically modified (GM) crops and food are of a growing significance and resonance at both national and transnational level, and form part of our daily life. In this context, it is especially important to study research perceptions of these biotechnological innovations. The objective of this study is to explore perceptions of GM crops and food among young people in Georgia. The study employed a qualitative method to address these issues. Specifically a method of written accounts (essays) was used. Study provides insights about the interwoven character of the environmental cognition and perceptions of biotechnological innovations.

Ecological ethics and morality in perception of experts during globalization

Mamonova, Olga Moscow, Russia *Irina, Sosunova* Scientific programs, IIUEPS, Moscow, Russia
The present study examined the phenomenon of ecological ethics and ecological morality in contemporary Russia on its way from totalitarian society to democracy. The main hypothesis of research is that in Russia the ecological morality is latent and is only a part of bigger system of values. Ecological morality is developed in the conditions of social-ecological tension or conflict and can be presented by the relation to environment. In-depth formal interviews were used, 100 experts participated in the research. The findings show that in spite of the serious concern about environment, experts are not ready to sacrifice to economic development.

FP-118: Business in the digital age: E-commerce, advertisement and digital marketing II

Impact of eroticism on product and brand recall in advertising

Stachoń-Wójcik, Maria Chémoelski, Poland
Gorbaniuk, Oleg Psychologia Eksperymentalna, Katolicki Uniwersytet Lubelski, Lublin, Poland
Szymona, Tomasz Psychologia Eksperymentalna, Katolicki Uniwersytet Lubelski, Lublin, Poland
The study of the impact of erotic content on brand recall was conducted in two stages among 200 respondents aged 19-35. The first stage examined the influence eroticism, sex of recipients and situational shame on brand recall. The second stage examined strength of erotic content, sex of actor and sex of recipient. It was concluded that: (1) strong eroticism in ads facilitate brand recall; (2) erotic content causes more mistakes in recognition of the advertised brands in the case of men; (3) ads featuring women facilitate better product and brand recognition; (4) sex of recipients moderates effectiveness of erotic ads.

Readability assessment of advertisements and signs using electronic paper

Hishinuma, Takashi Tokyo, Japan *Masuda, Takuya* Design Science, Chiba University, Chiba, Japan *Takahashi, Shihomi* Design Science, Chiba University, Chiba, Japan *Ohira, Yuko* Design Science, Chiba University, Chiba, Japan *Nakamura, Hiroomi* Design Science, Chiba University, Chiba, Japan *Yoshizawa, Yosuke* Design Science, Chiba University,

Chiba, Japan *Koyama, Shinichi* Design Science, Chiba University, Chiba, Japan *Hibino, Haruo* Design Science, Chiba University, Chiba, Japan
Electronic paper (E-paper) can be useful for advertisements and emergency signs because it is light and energy-saving. In order to develop E-paper, we tested the readability of the smallest-possible Japanese characters (composed of 12 pixels x 12 pixels; each pixel 4 mm x 4 mm) presented on the E-paper at the distance of 4 m from the observer, under different visual conditions (illumination and spacing). Our results showed that the minimal illumination was lower than 0.5 lux and the optimal character and line spacing was 25% and 50% respectively. Based on our results, we proposed layout designs for E-paper.

An exploratory study on the relationship between the goals of internet users and their behavior

Gutschmidt, Anne Computer Science Department, Universität Rostock, Rostock, Germany *Nerdinger, Friedemann W.* Business Administration, University of Rostock, Rostock, Germany *Cap, Clemens H.* Computer Science Department, University of Rostock, Rostock, Germany
An exploratory study was conducted to identify behavioral characteristics suitable for the automatic recognition of an Internet user's current goal. On an on-line newspaper, 20 participants solved tasks corresponding to the predefined goals Fact Finding, Information Gathering and Just Browsing. Their behavior was captured by recording every action in the browser, namely clicks on hyperlinks, the use of browser interface elements like the back button etc. The analysis of variance indicates that all three goals can be distinguished using behavioral characteristics such as the average time a user spends on a page and the number of news categories visited.

FP-119: Child and adolescent psychopathology III

Autism: Is there a spontaneous preference for details and not meaning?

Müller, Christoph Köln, Germany *Nußbeck, Susanne* Department of Human Sciences, University of Cologne, Köln, Germany
It was investigated if children with autism-spectrum-disorders (ASD) differ in their processing-style in terms of spontaneously preferring details instead of meaning. Subjects included 25 high-functioning children with ASD and 25 typically developing children comparable in age, IQ and sex. In two experiments children were asked to match a picture to one of two other pictures either by congruence in details but wrong meaningful relations or vice versa. Children with ASD matched items at a significantly higher rate congruent in details, although it was made sure that all subjects had recognized the meaningful relations. It is concluded that they tend to spontaneously focus on details despite their knowledge of the meaning at hand.

Assessment of attention bias in children with separation anxiety disorder using an eye-movement paradigm

In-Albon, Tina Inst. für Psychologie, Universität Basel, Basel, Switzerland *Kossowsky, Joe* Clinical Child and Adolescent, Institute of Psychology, Basel, Switzerland *Schneider, Silvia* Clinical Child and Adolescent, Institute of Psychology, Basel, Switzerland
Objectives: Procedures such as the dot-probe-paradigm or the emotional Stroop-task capture only a snapshot of attention processes. In contrast, the advantage of an eye-movement paradigm is its assessing of a continuous measure of gaze. Methods: Eye-tracker methodology was used to investigate the attentional bias in children with separation

anxiety disorder in comparison to normal and clinical controls. Results: Preliminary results suggest that the attentional bias can be assessed with this eye-movement paradigm. No hypervigilance pattern was found, however, compared to normal controls, children with SAD showed a late avoidance of threatening pictures. Conclusions: Preliminary results partially support the hypervigilance-avoidance model.

Successful innovations for young people with autism spectrum/disorders (dispositions)

Lawson, Christine Dept. of Psychology, CAMHS, Isle of Man, Southam, United Kingdom
Lawson(2003) described a boy with Asperger syndrome and marked dyspraxia who drew people after forming specific Object Assembly items from the WISC-R(UK) and WAIS-R(UK). Also, he participated in activities which encouraged the fast apprehension of small numerosities associated with dots and schematic facial features. Noticeable improvements were shown concerning human figure drawings and arithmetic/mathematics alongside increasing maturity artistically and socially. Similar performances were demonstrated by individuals with autism spectrum disorders(ASD) receiving similar assessments and interventions presented by Lawson(2004 and 2005b) and by young people whose ASD characteristics were not acknowledged until adolescence discussed by Lawson(2005a) and in the presentation here.

Transgenerational transmission of traumata

Ammon, Maria Psychoanalyse, Deutsche Akademie für, Berlin, Germany
Transgenerational transmission of psychic trauma plays an important role in the etiology of many psychic disorders. First, the development and recognition of this concept in psychoanalysis is reviewed. Second, mechanisms of transgenerational transmission taking place in everyday interactions between parents and children are described. Third, family dynamics built around parental trauma are analyzed. Then an own study is reported, in which the interplay between parental trauma, transmission processes in the family and schizophrenia of a child in later life was investigated (M. Ammon 2002). Finally, recommendations for the psychoanalytic treatment of patients with transgenerational traumata are given.

FP-120: Self and identity in childhood and adolescence

Development of the gender concept in children in age of 3-6 years

Shahni, Razieh Dept. of Psychology, Shahed University, Tehran, Islamic Republic of Iran *Shairi, Mohammad* psychology, shahed university, Tehran, Islamic Republic of Iran
Developmental theorists believe that understanding of children from their environment is according to the level of their development.two hypothesis were designed; the first, children understanding of Gender in variant ages is different, and also development of the gender concept in children is function of their total development.(using comprehension model of Kohlberg's gender development) In this study, children in age of 3-6 years (n=120 in 4 groups) were investigated.Using instrument is Gender concept Interview of slaby, R. G. & Fery, k. s. Not only using descriptive statistics,but also to compare groups in questions according to chi-square test.The results revealed that two designed hypothesis are approved. Key words: Development, Gender, Child.

Research on the features of Mongolian adolescent mental adaptation

Yang, Yisheng Department of psychology, Inner Mongolia Normal Universi, Hohhot, People's Republic of China

Adaptation scale for Adolescent was adopted to investigate 1768 Mongolian students' developmental trend and features of mental adaptation. The results showed that Mongolian adolescent' mental adaptation had significant differences in gender, type of school, family source and grade. (1)Physiological adaptation and social adaptation of boys were significantly higher than girls, interpersonal adjustment was significantly lower ;(2) In addition to the physiological adaptation, all the adaptation of students who were from key secondary school were significantly higher than general school;(3) The adaptation showed gradation that urban> township> rural;(4) With the higher grade, the level of mental adaptation showed undulated upward trend

Psychological correlates of self's differentiation

Clinciu, Aurel Ion Dept. of Psychology, University Transilvania, Brasov, Romania

The survey was developed on 232 high school pupils and students from Brasov, using the instruments: Bowen's Scale of Self's Differentiation, Andreas & Bond's Defense Style Questionnaire, Clinciu's Self Perception and Body Self Perception, Sherer's Self Efficacy, Levenson's Multidimensional Locus of Control, Sperry's Questionnaire of Hemisphere Preference, Eysenck Personality Questionnaire. The defined hypotheses anticipate existence of some connections between level of self's differentiation (Witkin) and structure of defences, self-esteem or feeling of self-efficacy, hemispheric specialization, locus of control. Results confirm significant connections between criterium and studied variables. We finally built a regressive model (R=.67) combining the strongest predictors in an equation.

FP-121: Cognitive and affective development in childhood and adolescence II

The developmental characteristics of children's faux pas detection and understanding in 5-to-8-year-olds

Wang, Yifang Department of Psychology, Capital Normal University, Beijing, People's Republic of China Su, Yanjie Department of Psychology, Peking University, Beijing, People's Republic of China

The operant definition of faux pas detection and understanding is whether individuals can recognize when someone unintentionally says something that would hurt or insult the other. One hundred and twenty 5-to-8-year-olds children's faux pas detection and understanding ability was measured through story-picture presentation in self-other, other-self, and other-other situations. The results showed that 7-to-8-year-olds had the ability to detect and understand faux pas. And the development of faux pas detection and understanding in 6-to-8-year-olds was synchronous in three situations, yet 5-year-olds performed significantly better in the other-self situation than did in the self-other situation.

Children's implicit and explicit knowledge about steady and accelerated speed in motions

Ebersbach, Mirjam Inst. für Psychologie, Universität Halle-Wittenberg, Halle, Germany van Dooren, Wim Educational Sciences, University of Leuven, Leuven, Belgium Verschaffel, Lieven Educational Sciences, University of Leuven, Leuven, Belgium

This study investigated the development of implicit and explicit knowledge about two types of motions. Kindergartners, 2nd, 5th, and 10th graders judged the distances covered by vehicles travelling on a horizontal and an inclined plane, given information

about travel duration. Tasks were presented either as realistic situations, requiring action-based responses (implicit knowledge) or as word problems requiring quantified responses (explicit knowledge). Even a considerable proportion of 10th graders estimated the covered distances on the inclined plane as linearly related to travel duration, particularly in the word problems. The relation between implicit and explicit knowledge will be discussed.

Ostension production by children aged 7 to 24 months old

Dimitrova, Nevena Social and Political Sciences, Institute of Psychology, Lausanne, Switzerland

Signs that the child produces (e.g. ostension) and which underly appropriation-differenciation of object's conventional (culturally determined) use transform thought development (Vygotsky 1934/1997, Moro & Rodrîguez, 2005). Mother-object-child (children from 7 to 24 moths old) interactions are observed longitudinally during play situations. Interactions are coded and sign productions are examined in order to trace out the developmental progression of object's conventional use. Preliminary results show that conventional use appropriation is acquired at 13 months but sign production was not investigated specifically. This study help clarify semiotic development (productions, functions etc.), essential in thought development processes.

FP-122: Educational assessment II

Classificatory stream analysis in the prediction of expected reading readiness: Understanding student performance

Cascallar, Eduardo Katholieke Universiteit Leuven, Brussels, Belgium Musso, Mariel Social and Behavioral Sciences, Leiden University and CONICET, Leiden, Netherlands

This research describes the application of a neural networks approach in the prediction of readiness for reading upon entry to primary education. Machine-learning techniques used offer an iterative methodology that is capable of discovering complex relationships and interactions in the inputs and outcomes. The approach maximized classification accuracy, and was able to model various outcome patterns from the over 700 students studied. Results based on hypotheses of student characteristics using these predictive modeling achieved a total accuracy of 98% in the identification of "students-below-readiness-threshold". The presentation explains the processes and the stream analysis technique utilized, and explores various alternative models.

Theory-making and scale-creating for investigating the value system and status of Iranian high-school; pre-university students' attitude toward globalization

Lotfabadi, Hossein Psychology, Shahid Beheshti University, Tehran, Islamic Republic of Iran Nowroozi, Vahideh Psychology, Globalization Project, Tehran, Islamic Republic of Iran

Brief Abstract Objective: Theory-making & scale creating for assessing value-system Method: Descriptive Results: Value system assessment skills Conclusions: Ten categories of individual values, family values, economic values, political values, social values, artistic values, scientific and theoretical values, religious identity values, national identity values, and worldviews (or globalization) values might be distinguished by conducting this value system assessment scale. Long Abstract The process of "globalization", which appeared after the 2nd Word War in the most industrialized Western countries, is rapidly expanding across the world. This process has shown itself as one of the most challenging issues of the past and..

Measuring text reading comprehension in admitted university students: Validating retrieval contexts

Castañeda Figueiras, Sandra Postgraduate Psychology, National Autonomus University, México City, Mexico González Lomelí, Daniel Graduated Psychology, UNISON, Mexico, Mexico

The factorial structure of two retrieval contexts was tested (recognizing and remembering) of the Castañeda (1996) text comprehension test, in a sample of 187 students beginning five majors. Both subscales possess internal consistency. A confirmatory factorial analysis allowed to build a structural model integrated by two first order latent variables: recognizing and remembering, with statistical and practical goodness of fit ($\chi2=15$, 17 gl., p=.54, IBBAN=.94, IBBANN=.99, IAC=.99, RMSEA=.000). Implications to improve admittance examinations to majors in Mexico are discussed

FP-123: Psychological disorders IV

Risk factors for postpartum depression among low income Brazilian women

Andrade da Silva, Gabriela Experimental Psychol, Universidade de São Paulo, São Paulo, Brazil Matos Viegas, Lia Experimental Psychology, Universidade de São Paulo, São Paulo, Brazil Otta, Emma Experimental Psycholgy, Universidade de São Paulo, São Paulo, Brazil

Risk factors for postpartum depression (PPD) were investigated in a sample of 92 low income Brazilian mothers. Participants answered Edinbourgh Postnatal Depression Scale (EPDS) 2-4 months after delivery. PPD prevalence was 31.5% (cut-point 11/12). A linear regression showed that women with high EPDS scores were more likely to report bad relationship with parents during childhood (b=1.587, p<0.001), and high marital conflict (b=0.364, p=0.014). High social support was negatively correlated with EPDS scores, but it did not enter the final model. There was a high prevalence of PPD in our study associated with perceived relationships with past and present attachment figures.

The role of autobiographical memory in depression

Claudio, Victor Clinical Dept., ISPA, Lisbon, Portugal

In this study we assess the relationship between information processing and the major depression. The approach used, based on a cognitive perspective, relates emotions, depression and its memory characteristics. We used an autobiographical memory task applied to forty-two major depresses subjects, twenty-height panics subjects and fifty-one subjects without psychological disorder. We concluded about the existence of differences in the processing and evocation of information in function of the depression severity, the started and maintained depression are more related with the codification and evocation process, directed by the negative self-schemas, than the negative thoughts.

Rumination and worry in depressive and non-depressive persons: What makes the difference?

Rischer, Angela Tagesklinik, Psychiatrische Univ.-Klinik, Erlangen, Germany Kornhuber, Johannes Tagesklinik, Psychiatrische Univ-Klinik, Erlangen, Germany

Both nonclinical and depressive persons ruminate and worry. What makes the difference? So far, only one study compared rumination and worry in an nonclinical and a clinical sample (Papageorgiou & Wells 1999a,b). Therefore, our aim was to compare repetitive thinking in depressive and nondepressive persons. Patients with Major Depression (n=104) and nondepressive subjects (n=390) were questioned with the Cognitive Intrusion Questionnaire (Watkins et al. 2005). We found a rumination/

worry profile that differed in both groups concerning specific appraisals, emotions and coping strategies. Implications for the treatment of rumination/worry and relapse prevention will be discussed.

Detection of depression in cancer patients

Singer, Susanne Inst. für Sozialmedizin, Universität Leipzig, Leipzig, Germany Klein, Andrea Radiotherapy, Leipzig University, Leipzig, Germany Krauß, Oliver Psychiatrie, Park-Krankenhaus Leipzig, Leipzig, Germany Slesazeck, Heike Social Medicine, Leipzig University, Leipzig, Germany Schwarz, Reinhold Social Medicine, Leipzig University, Leipzig, Germany

Objectives: To determine the ability of two screening methods - a questionnaire versus the view of the oncological team – to detect depression in tumour patients. Methods: 329 tumour patients completed the Hospital Anxiety and Depression Scale (HADS) and a clinical interview. Physicians and nurses assessed the mental health of the patients. Analysis was done using ROC statistics. Results: Physicians indicated 13 (AUC .486), nurses 9 (AUC .564), and the HADS 8 (AUC .802) of the 28 depressed patients as not being depressed. Conclusions: The HADS performed better in detecting depressed cancer patients than physicians and nurses did.

FP-124: Innovation I

Future visions: Time-related characteristics of sustainable innovations and their innovators

Wastian, Monika Inst. für Soziologie, Techn. Universität München, München, Germany

In this qualitative-quantitative study we investigated how innovators in the field of mobility – 67 project managers, strategists and researchers (53 % in the private sector, 47 % in the public sector) – construct future visions for a sustainable mobility and how their constructions correlate with their individual time perspectives (future-oriented and present-hedonistic scales of the Zimbardo Time Perspective Inventory). Innovators focused on short-term visions and were more optimistic for technical than for non-technical visions. Individual time perspectives predicted the innovativeness of the visions, the probability and time to put the visions into practice, and also attributions of responsibility for barriers.

No climate for innovation without commitment

Feinstein, Ingrid Lehrstuhl Psychologie I, Universität Mannheim, Schöneck, Germany Bladowski, Beate Lehrstuhl Psychologie I, Universität Mannheim, Mannheim, Germany Madukanya, Virginia Lehrstuhl Psychologie I, Universität Mannheim, Mannheim, Germany

Commitment and innovation are important determinants for companies' success. However, only few studies address the question, whether a causal relationship between these two exists. It is hypothesized that employees' commitment contributes to a positive climate for innovation. In order to test this hypothesis a longitudinal study was conducted in a pharmaceutical company in the context of an employee opinion survey. The results of the statistical analysis (cross-lagged model) provide evidence for a positive impact of commitment (t1) on innovation climate (t2). This finding emphasizes the importance of commitment as a prerequisite to climate for innovation and innovative behavior.

Values as predictors of leadership, altruism and innovation

Rank, Johannes Management Dept., University of Surrey, Guildford, United Kingdom Vogel, Jana Psychology, University of Giessen, Giessen, Germany

The purpose of this field study was to investigate the role of managers' and employees' values in influencing leadership, altruism and innovation. Based on theories of leadership and models of values, we examined main and moderating effects of four individual-level values (universalism, benevolence, stimulation and self-direction). The sample was composed of 71 supervisor-subordinate dyads working in an electronics company in the Netherlands, Germany and Poland. Multiple hierarchical regression analyses revealed significant positive relationships between the values held by supervisors and subordinate ratings of their leadership behaviors. For example, universalism was associated with consideration, which in turn predicted altruistic subordinate behavior.

The relationship between job satisfaction and innovative performance of Chinese science-technology talents

Jiang, Hong Beijing, People's Republic of China Sun, Jianmin School of Labor and HR, Renmin University of China, Beijing, People's Republic of China Mu, Guibin School of Labor and HR, Renmin University of China, Beijing, People's Republic of China

Innovation ability in Science and Technology is the country's core competency, and the Innovative Performance of Science-Technology Talents (STTs) is the basis of the whole organization and country innovation. Based on the statistical analysis of a sample of 5180 STTs from 30 provinces and seven national institutes of China, this paper analyzed the relationship between job satisfaction and innovative performance of the Science-Technology talents in China. The regression analysis result shows that job satisfaction of STTs leads to the innovative performance. This paper also analyzed the moderator effect of the district between the relationship of job satisfaction and innovative performance.

High performance work system's diversified impact on firm's innovation performance in entrepreneurial firms

Zang, Zhi School of Psychology, Zhejiang University, Hangzhou, People's Republic of China

This study covered several linked field: high performance work system(HPWS) in new ventures, development zones' entrepreneurial policy and status quo, entrepreneurial opportunities exploration and resource allocation, and entrepreneurial performance. We strongly supposed that new venture's HPWS had unique theory frame and particularity in the setting of national-level economic and technical development zone (ETDZ) in China. Author sampled 192 firms and 92 goverment officials in ETDZ. This report concluded with high performance work system's function pattern in high-tech new ventures, and ETDZ's entrepreneurial policy measures' effect on HPWS and new venture's procedural & performance. Job-related HPWS dimensions had a significant positive impact on innovation, opportunity & resources usage.

FP-125: The impact of goals, goal-orientation, and volitional processes on learning I

The effect of student involvement in homework on academic outcomes: A study on Hong Kong primary school students

Tam, Vicky Dept. of Education Studies, Hong Kong Baptist University, Hong Kong, China, People's Republic of : Hong Kong SAR

This research fills a research gap on the effect of homework involvement on academic outcomes by studying Chinese primary school students in Hong Kong. Data were collected from 2361 students studying at Primary One to Primary Six using self-report questionnaires. Results of Multivariate Analysis of Variance showed a significant interaction effect between homework involvement and grade level on academic outcomes. Whereas students at Senior Primary Level benefited from higher homework involvement, negative associations were found between homework involvement and academic outcomes among Junior Primary students. Findings were discussed in terms of the views on homework in the Chinese cultural context.

When it's not a matter of choice: Future goals and the utility value of schooling for students in Singapore's lower streams

Ortiga, Yasmin Patrice CRPP, National Inst. of Education, Singapore, Singapore McInerney, Dennis CRPP, National Institute ofEducation, Singapore, Singapore Liem, Arief CRPP, National Institute ofEducation, Singapore, Singapore Manzano, Ann Adelaine CRPP, National Institute ofEducation, Singapore, Singapore Lee, Jie Qi CRPP, National Institute ofEducation, Singapore, Singapore

For the lowest 25% of Singapore's secondary school cohort, life after graduation leads to only one path: the Institute of Technical Education (ITE). This study investigates how this affects these students' future goals and the role school plays in their lives. Based on interviews with 50 students and focus group discussions with 30 teachers, we discuss how students set future goals not based their own aspirations but what their examination results allow them to do. Using the theory of future time perspective, we also show how this can have negative effects on their motivation to do well in school.

Activation and inhibition of self-regulated learning

Magno, Carlo Counseling and Educational Psy, De La Salle University-Manila, Manila, Philippines

The study investigated the factors that activates and inhibits self-regulated learning (SRL). The factors that activate SRL are action control and self-determination while the inhibition includes anxiety, worry, fear of negative evaluation, and thought suppression (negative affect). A series of questionnaires measuring the constructs mentioned were administered to 1454 participants using a longitudinal design. It was found in the study that action control and self-determination activates SRL and negative affect has a negative effect on SRL. But it was also shown that in a separate model, experiencing negative affect leads to SRL especially if there are high activation factors.

Goal attainment scaling: Practical application in educational psychology research

Woolfson, Richard Educational Psychology Service, Renfrewshire Council, Paisley, United Kingdom

Educational psychologists often evaluate services for children and young people. One of the challenges is to find sufficiently sensitive measurement tools which are responsive to subtle changes in an individual's progress. This presentation discusses the use of Goal Attainment Scaling (GAS), devised by Kiresuk & Sherman (1968), in a three-year evaluation of an intervention which provided support for pupils at risk of school exclusion. The results show that GAS had major impact on both assessing and improving the effectiveness of the intervention. The session will discuss the practicalities of implementing this measurement technique in real-world research.

FP-126: Substance abuse and addiction I

Types of recreational drug users: Exploring a hidden population online

Stetina, Birgit U. Forschung und Ausbildung, Universität Wien, Wien, Austria Jagsch, Reinhold Clinical, Biological and Diffe, University of Vienna, Vienna, Austria Kryspin-Exner, Ilse Clinical, Biological and Diffe, University of Vienna, Vienna, Austria

Objectives: Intention of the study was to reach the hidden population of recreational drug users online and evaluate the possible existence of different types. Methods: An international cross-sectional online-study surveying recreational drug users (N=9268) was carried out. The online obtained data was evaluated by means of statistical inference, descriptive and structure-discovering (cluster analysis) procedures. Results: Three different groups of recreational drug users were identified who differ regarding consumption patterns and demographic variables. Conclusions: Looking at the results it seems that the Internet could not only be a relatively new but also a better tool for this specific area of research.

The failure to anticipate regret and persistence in gambling

Tochkov, Karin Dept. of Psychology, Texas A&M University, Commerce, USA

Cognitive distortions have been identified as a major risk factor in problem gambling (Ladouceur, 2004). The present study focused on the failure to anticipate regret, and tested whether the gap between anticipated and actual regret is different for social (n=42) and problem gamblers (n=40). The results revealed that problem gamblers committed a larger error in predicting regret than social gamblers. Negative mood was found to affect the anticipation error of social but not of problem gamblers. The role of inaccurately anticipated regret as a possible contributor to excessive gambling and its implications for the treatment of pathological gambling are discussed.

A revised screening measure for cannabis misuse: The Cannabis Use Disorders Identification Test

Adamson, Simon Psychological Medicine, University of Otago, Christchurch, New Zealand Sellman, Doug Psychological Medicine, University of Otago, Christchurch, New Zealand Kay-Lambkin, Frances Centre for Brain & Mental, University of Newcastle, Newcastle, Australia Baker, Amanda Centre for Brain&Mental He, University of Newcastle, Newcastle, Australia Lewin, Terry Centre for Brain&Mental He, University of Newcastle, Newcastle, Australia Thornton, Louise Centre for Brain&Mental He, University of Newcastle, Newcastle, Australia Kelly, Brian Centre for Rural Mental Health, University of Newcastle, Orange, Australia

Objectives: To revise the CUDIT (Adamson & Sellman, 2003), originally developed by directly modifying the alcohol-oriented AUDIT. The original published findings of the CUDIT noted that whilst it performed adequately as a screening instrument some items were not optimal. Methods: 134 cannabis-using patients in a CBT clinical trial completed the t-CUDIT, a trial version containing the original items plus ten candidate substitute items at intake, with half completing a one week retest. Results: An improved version of the CUDIT was developed which showed good psychometric properties. Conclusions: The revised CUDIT-R is an effective screening tool for cannabis use disorders.

Dimensions of personality in cannabis users

Afkham Ebrahimi, Azizeh Dept. of Clinical Psychology, IUMS, Tehran, Islamic Republic of Iran Eftekhar, Mehrdad Dept. of Psychiatry, IUMS, Tehran, Islamic Republic of Iran Azimi, Hamed Dept. of Psychiatry, IUMS, Tehran, Islamic Republic of Iran Afkham Ebrahimi, Azadeh Students' affairs, Australian embassy in Tehran, Tehran, Islamic Republic of Iran

Objective: The aim of this study is to examine Eysenck personality dimensions in a number of young cannabis users. Method: 100 regular cannabis users were selected and completed the Eysenck Personality Questionnaire (EPQ) which measures Neuroticism (N), extraversion-Introversion (E-I) and Psychoticism (P) dimensions of Eysenck personality structures. Results. The scores of 51%

of cannabis users were higher than mean in all dimensions of EPQ. Conclusion. This research reinforces our call for a public health information campaign about a drug which may young people still see as being risk-free. Psychiatric morbidity could be prevented by discouraging cannabis use among vulnerable youths.

FP-127: Gender and cultural influences on development

The prevalence of gender atypical behavior in Chinese school-aged children: A preliminary study

Yu, Lu Department of Education, The University of Hong Kong, Hong Kong, China, People's Republic of : Hong Kong SAR Xie, Dong Psychology and Counseling, University of Central Arkansas, Conway, Arkansas, USA

This study investigated the prevalence of gender atypical behaviors on a sample of Chinese school-aged children (6-12 years old) with a newly revised Child Play Behavior and Attitude Questionnaire (CPBAQ). Parents of 486 boys and 417 girls completed CPBAQ and a demographic information sheet. The frequency distribution and developmental trends for each gender-related behavior were analyzed. Results indicated that Chinese boys and girls had different developmental tendencies in their exhibition of gender atypical behaviors. Possible effects of Chinese specific culture and the one-child policy on Chinese children's gender atypical behavior were discussed.

Gender and generation differences on vertical and horizontal individualism-collectivism and religiosity among Turkish people

Tapdemir, Nagihan Ankara, Turkey sakallı-uğurlu, nuray psychology, metu, ankara, Turkey

This study investigated gender and generation differences on vertical and horizontal individualism-collectivism and religiosity. 225 Turkish families participated in the study and completed the measures of vertical and horizontal individualism-collectivism and religiosity. Results indicated a significant main effect on VC, VI, HC, HI. Mothers and fathers scored higher on VC than did their children. Children scored higher on VI than did their mothers. Fathers scored higher on VI than did mothers. Mothers were higher on HC than their children. Children scored higher on HI than did both their mothers and fathers. There was no significant difference between groups on religiosity.

Exploring the acculturation of young new arrivals in Hong Kong via the reconstruction of life space: An application of Lewinian Field Theory

To, Chan Curriculum and Instruction, Chinese Univer. of Hong Kong, Hong Kong, China, People's Republic of : Hong Kong SAR Wong, Wan-chi Curriculum and Instruction, Chinese University of HK, Hong Kong, China, People's Republic of : Macao SAR

This study attempted to integrate Lewin's field theory and Berry's framework of acculturation. 21 subjects participated in two in-depth interviews. The first interview consisted of an acculturation questionnaire and the co-construction of topological diagrams of life space before and after the immigration. In the second interview, acculturation styles identified by these two approaches were presented to the participants for an inter-subjective scrutiny. Results of the questionnaire indicated that all subjects were integrative in acculturation. Nonetheless, four different acculturation styles were identified from the typological diagrams, with "integration" occupying 52.38%. All participants except one held that what revealed via the Lewinian method was closer to the truth and more individualized.

Gender differences and developmental analysis of blatant and subtle prejudice in multicultural schools

Fernandez Castillo, Antonio Develop.-Education. Psychology, University of Granada, Granada, Spain

The objective of this study is to seek dimensions that explain the arisen of social prejudice in childhood and to describe developmental and gender characteristics. The sample was composed of a total of 572 Spanish children aged 9-14. The results reveal, first, the presence of social prejudices in the childhood, as well as interesting differences according to age in the studied sample. The blatant prejudice scores decreased with increasing age, especially from the age of 12. This pattern was not followed in the case of subtle prejudice, which tended to maintain similar levels of intensity among the older children.

Sleuthing for gender differences in reading experience: A study with thriller-type short stories

Schreier, Margrit School of Humanities, Jacobs Univer. Bremen gGmbH, Bremen, Germany Thies, Yvonne School of Humanities, Jacobs Univer. Bremen gGmbH, Bremen, Germany Odag, Oezen School of Humanities, Jacobs Univer. Bremen gGmbH, Bremen, Germany

It is tested whether the reading experience (DV) of men and women varies with text topic (inner world orientation versus action orientation) and sex of main character. Readers' gender and affinity to literature are included as covariates. Four authentic thriller-type short stories were selected so as to represent the variation of the independent textual variables. 99 persons (59 women, 40 men; aged 20 to 66) participated in the study. Analyses of variance show that texts with a female main protagonists result in a more intense reading experience. Contrary to the hypotheses, readers' sex and gender have no effect.

FP-128: Language disorders

Importance of symbols in developing language

Hathazi, Andrea Special Education Department, UBB Cluj Napoca, Cluj Napoca, Romania

In the case of a child with severe impairment or reduced ability of acquiring and developing language abilities, the use of symbols in forming the necessary concepts, representations and structures is very important. The associations of symbols with oral or written language, the repetitions in the routines and activities, the feed-back and the immediate reward that it is given, control, anticipation and negotiation give the child the opportunity to understand meaning and signification of communication and implicit words. Symbols are the key when the natural process of learning language is affected from a certain reason.

Syntax, semantics and memory functioning in school-aged children with language learning impairment

Spanoudis, George Psychology, University of Cyprus, Nicosia, Cyprus Natsopoulos, Demetrios Psychology, University of Cyprus, Nicosia, Cyprus

Two groups of children each of 22, aged 8 to 12, one with language learning impairment and one typically developing matched on age, nonverbal intelligence and varying significantly in verbal ability (receptive and expressive level) were tested on a battery of language (syntax and semantics) and memory (short-term, working and long-term memory) measures. The conventional statistical analysis indicated that the two groups differed significantly in all measures. A logistic regression analysis performed revealed that working and long-term memory functioning was the most robust discriminant markers of classification. The findings are explained in relation to results stemming from the current literature.

Language aquisition of grammatical category: Plural form of nouns in Bulgarian children with dyslexia

Todorova, Ekaterina Cognitive Science & Psychology, New Bulgarian University, Sofia, Bulgaria

The present study focuses on the realization of the morphological language capacity in a grammatical unit – the plural of nouns, with children with dyslexia. For the purposes of the study, a unique experimental instrument was constructed. The data has been processed by using the hi-squire test and ANOVA. The results indicate specific language performance in dyslexic children – over generalization errors, usage of non-existing phonetic rules and no clear distinction between the different forms of plural. These errors reveal not only specific deficit in children with dyslexia, but also the strategies which young children use to acquire this part of grammar.

The pattern of auditory deficit in adult dyslexic readers

Fostick, Leah Ariel University Center, Ariel, Israel Bar-El, Sharona School of Education, Bar-Ilan University, Ranat-Gan, Israel Ben-Artzi, Elisheva Psychology, Kinneret College, Jordan Valley, Israel Babkoff, Harvey Psychology, Ashkelon College, Ashkelon, Israel

Objectives: To identify the pattern of auditory sensory/perceptual deficit in dyslexic readers. Method: Forty-six adult normal readers were compared with 51 adult dyslexic readers on cognitive, linguistic, and auditory psychophysical tasks. Results: Dyslexics showed significant deficits in (1) auditory and visually based linguistic tasks; (2) verbal, but not spatial, short- term and working memory; (3) three auditory temporal discrimination tasks, but no deficit in auditory thresholds or in intensity discrimination. Conclusions: Adult dyslexics with general auditory and visually based linguistic difficulties also present deficit in discrimination based on the auditory temporal, but not on an auditory intensity stimulus dimension.

A cross-linguistic study of reading and spelling in children with severe speech and physical impairment

Larsson, Maria Dept. of Psychology, Göteborg University, Göteborg, Sweden Dahlgren Sandberg, Annika psychology, göteborg university, GÖTEBORG, Sweden Smith, Martine Speech&communication scie, Trinitiy college, Dublin, Ireland

One Swedish- and one English-"speaking" group of 15 children with severe speech and physical impairment were tested on phonological awareness, memory, reading and writing. The aim was to study early reading and writing abilities and possible differences between the two groups that might depend on the structure of the spoken language, and to compare the relationship between phonological awareness and literacy abilities in the groups. The English-speaking children were more proficient in reading and less reliant on rhyming ability and phonological memory, suggesting greater use of the orthographic route to reading than the Swedish children.

FP-129: Entrepreneurship and management

"Guanxi" orientation and entrepreneur's ethical decision-making: Evidence from China

Jin, Yanghua School of Management, Zhejiang Gongshang University, Hangzhou, People's Republic of China Yang, Jian Human Resource Department, Zhejiang Mobile Communication, Hangzhou, People's Republic of China

Using situational judgment test, this study examined the relationship between "guanxi" orientation and entrepreneur's decision-making from a sample of 318 Chinese entrepreneurs. Structural equation modeling results demonstrated that entrepreneur's ethical decision-making involved ethical awareness, judgment, and behavior, "rent-seeking" guanxi affect ethical decision making negatively, but "favor-seeking" guanxi wouldn't. Cluster analysis distinguished entrepreneurs into four types with ethical behavior and "guanxi" orientation, that is, "favor-seeking ethic keepers", "guanxi oriented ethical actors", "neutral ethical actors", "guanxi oriented unethical actors". Organizational profitability of "favor-seeking ethic keepers" and "guanxi oriented ethical actors" were higher than "neutral ethical actors" and "guanxi oriented unethical actors" significantly.

An empirical research on the relationship between entrepreneurial intellectual capital and venture growth in hi-tech enterprises

Zhang, Wei School of Management, Hangzhou Dian Zi University, Hangzhou, People's Republic of China

Abstract?Intellectual capital is an important organizational knowledge asset. The study investigated small and medium technology new firms in china via multi- level behavioral questionnaires?and verified the model of entrepreneurial intellectual capital structured by four dimensions of human capital, structural capital, customer capital and innovation capital. It revealed that entrepreneurial intellectual capital had a prominent positive effect on venture growth of technology new firms, and stated that the entrepreneurial intellectual capital would change dynamically according to different entrepreneurial stage and organizational background. Keywords?Entrepreneurial intellectual capital; Confirmatory factor analysis; Structural model; Venture growth

The Chinese undergraduate students' entrepreneurial cognition and entrepreneurial awareness

Li, Lingji Educational college, Peking University, Beijing, People's Republic of China Hu, ping Public Administration School, Renmin University of China, Beijing, People's Republic of China

This study investigated the Chinese undergraduate students' entrepreneurial cognition and the forming process characteristic of entrepreneurial awareness based on the previous researches about the career choice theory. Respondents were Mainland Chinese undergraduate students (N=105). Results indicated: (1) masculine trait of personality was significantly influencing the forming of entrepreneurial awareness, but the attachment type, gender, age, specialty had no relationship with the entrepreneurial awareness; (2) the developmental and reputational factor in the career value have interactive influence on the forming of entrepreneurial awareness, (3)entrepreneurial cognitive level was not relative with the entrepreneurial awareness. The author discussed the forming process of entrepreneurial awareness from individual, group and cultural factors and raise further issues for future research.

Decision-making processes in family-owned companies: A process-model for succession planning

Eberhardt, Daniela Embrach, Switzerland

Objective of the study was the development of a process-model for succession planning in family-owned companies. The multi-level qualitative research was focused on the decision-making process of entrepreneurs and successors. Based on the results of a pre-study semi-structured interviews with entrepreneurs and successors (N = 22) and an expert panel had been used for content analysis and case comparisons. Decision-making processes in succession planning can be distinguished for

entrepreneurs and successors and be grouped in phases. The phase-specific decision has an impact on the handling of the situation as well as possible scenarios in the area of business administration and law.

The effects of organizational change and entrepreneurship strategies as mediated by organizational learning among Chinese firms

Wang, Zhongming School of Management, Zhejiang University, Hangzhou, People's Republic of China Zang, Zhi School of Management, Zhejiang University, Hangzhou, People's Republic of China Li, Shiyang School of Management, Zhejiang University, Hangzhou, People's Republic of China

Organizational change is crucial for global entrepreneurship among Chinese firms. In a field study supported by NSFC on organizational change, managers in local firms were interviewed and surveyed among two kinds of industries: information technology and automobile component manufacturing. A scale of organizational learning was distributed to test its mediating effects on change and entrepreneurship strategies. The results showed that the dimensions of organizational learning positively mediated the effects of organizational change strategy on performance whereas its influence on entrepreneurship strategies was largely depended upon venturing stages and types of industries. The implications of person-organizaiton fit were highlighted.

FP-130: Effects of environmental and family contexts on developmental outcomes

Negative knowledge: How families learn from their children's mistakes

Oser, Fritz Dept. of Education, University of Fribourg, Fribourg, Switzerland Hattersley, Lisa Education, University, Fribourg, Switzerland

On the basis of video analyses we developed a questionnaire on norm deviations (mistakes) of children/adolescents in families. We conducted a study with 100 families (50 with a child aged 9-11, 50 with a child aged 14-17) testing the questionnaire. The theoretical basis consists in the so-called negative knowledge, which protects a person from making the same mistakes again, gives security in similar situations and marks off opposites like cold and warm, in and out etc. The hypothesis is that families with a culture of mistakes enable a better development of their children than families without.

Examining the physical difficulties experienced by twins in Greece

Markodimitraki, Maria Pre-School Education, University of Crete, Rethymnon, Greece Kypriotaki, Maria Pre-School Education, University of Crete, Rethymnon, Greece

The aim of this developmentally oriented study was to explore the physical difficulties in 50 pairs of non-identical, pre-school twins. The data collection of this study derives from the administration of the questionnaire constructed by Pat Preedy (1994). It was found that the proportion of twin children experiencing difficulties with speech and language development was significantly higher than other physical difficulties experienced by twins of the same age. The implications of these results are discussed in terms of the main idea that some multiples may have special needs, but being a multiple in itself must not be regarded as a handicap.

Relationship between mother distress and fetal growth during pregnancy

Shafizadeh, Mohsen *Physical Education & Sport, Tarbiat Moallem University, Tehran, Islamic Republic of Iran* **Mehdizadeh, Mehrzad** *MEDICAL SCHOOL, TEHRAN UNIVERSITY, TEHRAN, Islamic Republic of Iran*

The aim of present investigation was to study the relationship between mothers' distress and fetal growth.106 pregnant women selected randomly and completed Depression Anxiety Stress Scale before ultrasound measurement of fetus. The results of structural equation model have shown that the overall model has been accepted (X2 = 36.4, d.f= 24, P>.05). In fact, by increasing mothers' stress and anxiety the fetus heart rate was increased and it decreased the height, weight, head circumference and width and femur length of fetus. In conclusion, one of the environmental variables that have negative effect on the fetus growth is mother distress, because it can stimulate the fetal autonomic nervous system through the mediating of heart rate.

The impact of prenatal substance exposure on pediatric psychology

Battaglia, Suzanne *MCSTART, Salinas, USA*

Objectives: To offer evidenced-based early intervention services to improve developmental and neurobehavioral functioning for at risk young children prenatally exposed to alcohol or other drugs. Methods: The MCSTART multidisciplinary team in Salinas, California diagnoses and treats children with deficits resulting from trauma and substance exposure through medical assessment, psychological testing, occupational therapy, and customized psychotherapies focusing on attachment and social-emotional issues. Results: Significant functional improvements in deficit areas of social-emotional, motor skills, and communication occurred in 570 children served in 2005-06. Conclusions: Many substance-exposed children have derived benefit from accurate diagnosis and appropriate treatment modalities targeted to their functional deficits.

Talking to the child: Teaching the child being a tolerant person?

Pakalniskiene, Vilmante *Dept. of Psychology, Mykolas Romeris University, Vilnius, Lithuania*

Objectives: The literature suggests that tolerance towards refers to an attitude of openness. Family could play a big role in teaching tolerance. Drawing on the ideas from the literature, it seems that open atmosphere in the family could be the base for tolerance towards other people. Methods: 300 Lithuanian youths' (15-18 years) data were used. Results: Even though open atmosphere and open communication in the family are related to tolerance towards other people, latent profile analysis suggested some variation in this relation. Conclusions: It seems that there could be several ways how open atmosphere is related to tolerance.

FP-131: Dyslexia and dyscalculia

The behavioural and neurophysiological effects of a computer-based morphological awareness training on the spelling and reading skills of young dyslexics

Weiss, Silvana *Learning and Instruction, ETH Zürich, Zürich, Switzerland* **Grabner, Roland** *Learning and Instruction, ETH Zurich, Zurich, Switzerland* **Kargl, Reinhard** *Reading and Spelling, LRS Graz, Graz, Austria* **Purgstaller, Christian** *Reading and Spelling, LRS Graz, Graz, Austria* **Fink, Andreas** *Differential Psychology, University of Graz, Graz, Austria*

Compared to phonological awareness little is known about the role of morphological awareness in dyslexia. This study examined the effects of a computer-based morphological training in children

with poor spelling and reading abilities. Thirty-five students (grades 3-9) were trained over 2-3 weeks and contrasted with a control group of 59 students. The training improved morphological awareness, spelling and reading skills with older students (grades 5-9) benefiting most. Furthermore, neurophysiological effects of the training were examined in a subsample by means of EEG. The results are interpreted within the framework of a step-model of learning to spell and read.

Dyslexia in different language systems: A comparison of Cantonese, Arabic and German speaking dyslexic children

Witruk, Evelin *Inst. für Psychologie, Universität Leipzig, Leipzig, Germany* **Raziq, Oafa** *Institute of Psychology, Leipzig University, Leipzig, Germany*

Working memory performances in Chinese, Moroccan and Ger-man dyslexic and normally-achieving children were compared and the language dependency of working memory functions was tested. Phonological and visual-spatial loop together with diffe-rent automated Central Executive functions were investigated on the basis of four computerised, adaptive task sets, using non-language materials and accuracy -, reaction time measurement. The study involved 235 Chinese, Moroccan and German dyslexic and non-dyslexic children with an averaged age of 10.26 years. The findings support the assumption of a dyslexia specific deficit in working memory functions, the Chinese superiority in working memory performances and the cultural specific role of anxiety and motivation in dyslexics.

Comparison of neuropsychological aspect of dyslexic and normal children

Faramarzi, Salar *Dept. of Education, University of Isfahan, Isfahan, Islamic Republic of Iran* **Abedi, Ahmad** *education, university of isfahan, isfahan, Islamic Republic of Iran* **Hamidreza, Oreyzi** *education, university of isfahan, isfahan, Islamic Republic of Iran*

The aim of the Current research was to investigate and Compare neuropsychological of dyslexic and normal Third grade Children of Isfahan Schools. To administer The study, 118 Students were selected from Isfahan third grade students Population according to randomized multi- step cluster sampling that were Suspected to be dyslexic. Among them 30 students were selected by diagnostic tests (namely Wexler Children Intelligence tests and dyslexic recognition checklist) and compare with 30 normal children Via ex- post facto design by Nepsy test. Obtained data were analyzed by statistical method of t independent test. Findings indicate that dyslexic children were inferior relative to normal children in attention/ execution functions, language, Sensory motor, Spatial Processing and memory and learning and memory significantly.

Relationship between Attention Deficit Disorder (ADHD) and Dyslexia in assessing basic writing skills

Ignatova, Albena *Cognitive Scince and Psycholog, New Bulgarian University, Sofia, Bulgaria*

Purpose: to evaluate the ability for writing dictation in children with Dyslexia and ADHD. Hypothesis: there is difference between the mistakes the two diagnostic groups demonstrate. Method includes 3 groups- dyslexia, ADHD and controls. Groups consists of 20 boys and 20 girls at age between 9-12 years, diagnosed by the ICD-10 criteria. All computations have done by SPSS (V.15). Results:- No difference between groups according to dictation of letters (p=0.862). For all groups p<0.0001. There are difference between dyslexia and ADHD in dictation words and sentences. There are difference between two experimental groups and controls in dictation.

Basic number processing difficulties and dyscalculia in children with Velo-Cardio-Facial Syndrome (22q11 deletion syndrome)

de Smedt, Bert *Dept. of Educational Sciences, Katholieke Universiteit Leuven, Leuven, Belgium* **Reynvoet, Bert** *Experimental Psychology, Katholieke Universiteit Leuven, Leuven, Belgium* **Swillen, Ann** *Centre for Human Genetics, Katholieke Universiteit Leuven, Leuven, Belgium* **Verschaffel, Lieven** *Educational Sciences, Katholieke Universiteit Leuven, Leuven, Belgium* **Ghesquière, Pol** *Educational Sciences, Katholieke Universiteit Leuven, Leuven, Belgium*

It has been proposed that dyscalculia emerges due to impairments in basic number processing. We examined this hypothesis in Velo-Cardio-Facial Syndrome, a genetic disorder with a high prevalence of dyscalculia. Twenty-five children with VCFS and 25 individually matched controls participated. Children with VCFS showed a consistent pattern of deficits in number comparison, large addition/ subtraction and the use of procedural back-up strategies, indicating an impaired quantity subsystem and intraparietal dysfunction. However, the verbal subsystem (number reading, multiplication and fact retrieval) was preserved. Furthermore, correlational data showed that basic number processing skills directly accounted for single-digit arithmetic performance and strategy use.

FP-132: Death and dying

Effective use of metaphor and stories in grief therapy

Leaver, Vincent *Psychology - Counseling, Walden University, Ft. Myers, USA*

Effective use of metaphor and stories to guide and facilitate individual and group grief therapy is described in the context of hospice bereavement program. Presentation will include basic theory of metaphor therapy, sources of methphors and stories appropriate for grief work, and how these are applied to grief concepts and theories. The issue of baseline and assessment in grief is addressed.

Healing from trauma reactions through indigenous health beliefs: A cultural psychological inquiry among the survivors of Kachchh earthquake

Priya, Kumar Ravi *Humanities and Social Sciences, Indian Institute of Technology, Kanpur, India*

A study of the experience of trauma reactions and healing was conducted using ethnographic method and semi-structured interviews in the aftermath of an earthquake that hit Kachchh, India, in 2001. Constructivist grounded theory was used to analyze the survivors' narratives. Besides depression, 're-experiencing of the traumatic event' was the predominant trauma reaction. Survivors' socio-centric belief in karma (internalized duty towards family, community and nature) facilitated healing from trauma reactions by enabling the survivors realize a new meaning for their lives by motivating them to attain satisfaction or equanimity by working for and taking care of their family and community.

Suicide and suicidal behaviours: Social representation of health care professionals

Rothes, Inês *Faculdade de Psicologia da UP, Porto, Portugal* **Henriques, Margarida** *Centro de Psicologia da UP, Faculdade de Psicologia da UP, Porto, Portugal*

This study intends to determine how Health Professionals explain suicide behaviours and to explore the differences between three different groups: Psychologists, Psychiatrists and other Physicians. The Free Association Technique is the method used for data collection and the Factorial Association Analysis is used to work and interpret the results. The results are consistent with a theoretical perspective based on integrated interpretation, thus indicating a multifactor and complex causality phenomenon. The results based on different groups indicate that this is a modelling variable of differences in representational contents and provide significant clues for the planning of training strategies.

Suicide prevention workshops: Do they influence the number of completed suicides?
Steyn, Renier Graduate School of Business, University of South Africa, Unisa, South Africa
In this study the effect of Suicide Prevention Workshops (SPW's) on completed suicides in an organisational setting was assessed. Pearson product-moment correlations between the number of SPW's and the completed suicides were calculated. Analyzing the observations collected over a 6 year period and at 10 sites revealed a positive correlation between the number of SPW's and completed suicides (r=0.48; p<0.01; N=60). It is concluded that SPW's have no positive effect on suicidal behaviour and that they may indeed have an adverse effect. Suggestions are made regarding the monitoring of SPW's and collection of data for future research.

Religious beliefs and health: A study of Mumukshu's in Kashi
Shankar, Shail Dept. of Psychology, University of Allahabad, Allahabad, India
Mumukshus are individuals who willingly come to Kashi/Varanasi for a natural death with the belief that "Kashyam marnam mukti (Death in Kashi is liberation)". Many of them have major health crisis. The present research explores how religious beliefs of mumukshu help them in living with their health problems. Unstructured interviews were conducted on forty mumukshus from various ashrams/religious institutions, located in Varanasi (India). Relational Content analysis reveals that religious beliefs were associated the peace of mind and sense of freedom from daily hassles of worldly life. Mumukshu were found to have low death anxiety and fear of disease that they have.

FP-133: Cross-cultural differences

Work resources, work/family conflict and their consequences: A Chinese-British cross-cultural comparison
Lu, Luo Dept. of Business Administrati, National Taiwan University, Taipei, Taiwan Chang, Ting-Ting Industrial Management, Lunghwa University, Taoyuan, Taiwan
The aim of this research was to explore relations between work resources, work/family conflict, and work- and non-work related outcomes in a cross-cultural comparative context involving Taiwanese and British employees. For Both Taiwanese and British employees, work resources were negatively related to work/family conflict, but positively related to work satisfaction. Family-to-work conflict (WFC) was negatively related to family satisfaction, which in turn, was positively related to happiness. More importantly, we found that nation moderated the relationship between supervisory support and WFC: supervisory support had a stronger protective effect for Taiwanese than British.

Cross-cultural differences in applicants' faking behaviors
Jansen, Anne Institut für Psychologie, Universität Zürich, Zürich, Switzerland Stadelmann, Eveline H. Institut für Psychologie, Universität Zürich, Zürich, Switzerland Hafsteinsson, Leifur G. School of Business, Reykjavik University Iceland, Reykjavik, Iceland König, Cornelius J. Institut für Psychologie, Universität Zürich, Zürich, Switzerland Kleinmann, Martin Institut für Psychologie, Universität Zürich, Zürich, Switzerland

Objectives: Nearly all what we know about faking is based on US samples. This study examines whether the frequency and magnitude of faking among Swiss and Icelandic applicants parallels that of US applicants. Methods: Data of 416 Swiss and 245 Icelandic graduates who took part in surveys using the randomized-response technique were compared with data from the US. Results: Faking base rates in Switzerland and Iceland were comparable, but lower than those in the US. European applicants only engaged in mild faking behaviors. Serious faking (e.g. fabrication of information) was non-occurring. Conclusion: Differences are possibly due to different cultural values.

Trust-building processes in context for German-Indonesian cooperation
Schwegler, Ulrike Philosophische Fakultät, Universität Chemnitz, Korb, Germany
The aim of the present study is to identify characteristics and conditions of trust building procedures in contexts for German-Indonesian cooperation, specifically in German multinational companies operating in Jakarta, Indonesia. The proposed paper used qualitative research methods, comprising interviews with 25 Indonesian and 25 German managers. The results of the analysis support the assumption that there are differences regarding trust-related "signs and signals" between the samples. In addition, the findings serve to question accepted assumptions on the metric dimension of trust. Given that very little research has investigated the challenges of trust-building processes across cultural boundaries, this present study makes a relevant contribution to the field.

FP-134: Personality and mental health II

Individual differences and the prevalence of psychiatric symptoms in medicine and psychology students
Bore, Miles Psychology, University of Newcastle, Callaghan, Australia Ashley-Brown, Gillian Psychology, University of Newcastle, Callaghan, Australia Gallagher, Emma Psychology, University of Newcastle, Callaghan, Australia Powis, David Psychology, University of Newcastle, Callaghan, Australia
Poor mental health has been associated with low self-control, high neuroticism, low agreeableness, low conscientiousness, and introversion. We administered the Brief Symptom Inventory (BSI: Derogatis & Spencer, 1982) as a measure of mental health to medical school students (n = 270) and psychology students (n = 102). Neuroticism and self-control were significant predictors of poor mental health. Of note, however, is that 24% of 1st Year Psychology students and 31% of the 1st Year Medical students produced BSI global scores greater than the BSI norm for adult psychiatric inpatients. Is this a psychometric artefact or a high-achiever norm?

Existential trauma and the system of values
Mamcarz, Peter Dept. of Health Psychology, Catholic University of Lublin, Lublin, Poland Popielski, Kazimierz Health Psychology, Catholic University of Lublin, Lublin, Poland Suchocka, Lila Health Psychology, Catholic University of Lublin, Lublin, Poland
The aim of this paper is to find a link between existential trauma and the system of values, as well as confirming the psychometric values of the Existential Trauma Questionnaire (KTE). In the research the following group of tests were applied to a random selection of people (n=170): Cattell's Questionnaire, K. Popielski's Scale of Value Preferences, Popielski's Noodynamics Test, Popielski's Noopsychosomatic Symptoms List, and Mamcarz's KTE. Person's correlation factor r was applied, as

well as multiple regression analysis and analysis of variance. The conclusion of this paper gives the research results, corroborating the hypothesis of people who tend to experience trauma being in general functioning essentially different from the ones with low trauma vulnerability.

Visual impairments and anxiety
Balyanin, Konstantin IEAP, Moscow, Russia
Comparative experimental research between groups of graduating students of boarding schools for children with severe visual impairments and groups of students of the same age without vision disabilities showed differences in anxiety level. Higher level of personal anxiety is naturally typical for people with visual impairments, while higher level of reactive anxiety is discovered to be common for respondents without serious visual pathologies. Having known these psychological differences, some aspects of social and professional adaptation for people with visual impairments will be discussed.

FP-135: Psychological theories I

Historiography of psychology: Challenges of postmodernism
Ye, Haosheng Dept. of Psychology, Nanjing Normal University, Nanjing, People's Republic of China
Traditional historiography of psychology (THP), in search for objective truth of history, adopted the correspondence theory of truth, and took the natural science model as its ideal. It regarded the development of psychology as a linear, one-dimensional and accumulative process, in which all the nations and cultures in different historical periods dealt with the same subject of psychology. In striking contrast with THP, postmodern historiography of psychology takes the history of psychology as a social construction. It claims that history of psychology is socially constructed by psychologists. The narratives of history are not representation of historical facts, but the construction of historians. Key Words: historiography; history of psychology; postmodernism; objectivity; subjectivity

Maria Zambrano and hopeness psychology
Penaranda, Maria Psicologia Basica y Metodologi, Universidad de Murcia, Espinardo, Spain Quiñones-Vidal, Elena psicologia basica y metodologi, Universidad de Murcia, Espinardo, Spain
Maria Zambrano (1904-1991) is an outstanding thinker summarizing the dramatic history of the 20th century, Spanish Civil War, liberal and democratic intelligence exile in Europe during the Second World War, democracy crisis by totalitarian regimes. She intended to change not only the way of current occidental thought since the Greeks and transformed the main categories of ethics and policy but also concepts such as person, people, democracy and intellectual commitment, mercy, etc. which she herself lived and used as her own thought.

Environmental psychology and postmodernism
Imamichi, Tomoaki Environmental Psychology, City University of New York, Hoboken, USA
Inspired by Kvale's (1992) Psychology and Postmodernism and the 2006 International Congress of Applied Psychology, this presentation is going to explore the relationship between Environmental Psychology and Postmodernism by examining its diverse roots, orientations, and directions. 2007 marked the 20 year anniversary of the Handbook of Environmental Psychology (Stokols & Altman, 1987) with a section: Environmental Psychology: Prospects for the Future, with provoking chapters by Barker, Wapner, Proshansky and Sommer. It also marked the 20 year anniversary of the Journal of Environmental Psychology special issue on Clark

University, with authors reflecting on the beginnings of environment-behavior research.

Psychological anthropology and philosophical psychology

Michailov, Michael Ch. Inst. für Physiologie, Inst. Umweltmedizin/ICSD e.V., München, Germany *Neu, Eva* Dept. Physiology, Inst. Umweltmedizin/ICSD e.V., Muenchen, Germany *Weber, Germain* Dept. Physiology, Inst. Umweltmedizin/ICSD e.V., Muenchen, Germany

General anthropology (philosophical, pedagogical, medical) considers human from biophysics to theology [J.-Psychosom.-Res. 58/6:S85-6/2005]. Psychology has a central position in general and special anthropology (natural/social): Human interaction with nature/society. This way psychology must be implied obligatory in education of anthropological sciences (theology, philosophy, etc.). Philosophical psychology (Aristoteles, Kant) in context of ethics, epistemology, aesthetics, ought to develop holistic-multidimensional psychological anthropology incl. psychosomatics for better education and health in all countries according to UNO-Agenda-21 in frames of international university (Russel) [Congr.-Books: Int.-Congr.-Philos. 279-280/2003/ FISP-Istanbul; Int.-Congr.-Psychol., 1028.62/ 3028.96/2004/Beijing].

FP-136: Sensory-motor interactions I

The impact of working memory load on the Simon effect

Nattkemper, Dieter Inst. für Psychologie, Humboldt-Universität zu Berlin, Berlin, Germany *Aru, Jaan* Department of Psychology, Humboldt-University Berlin, Berlin, Germany

We studied the impact of working memory (WM) load on the Simon effect by requiring participants to memorize letters while responding to visual objects. In Experiment 1 stimuli and response keys were vertically arranged, and we obtained a Simon effect not being modulated by WM-load. In Experiment 2 where stimuli and response keys were horizontally arranged the Simon effect was modulated by WM-load: it was absent when WM-load was high. The key finding for understanding the differing pattern of results seems to be that the memory items evoked interference in the latter study but not in the first study.

Dissociation between perception and action? Not if reality is an illusion!

Gilster, René Inst. für Physiologie, Universität zu Kiel, Kiel, Germany *Kuhtz-Buschbeck, Johann P.* Institute of Physiology, Christian-Albrechts-University, Kiel, Germany *Ferstl, Roman* Institute of Psychology, Christian-Albrechts-University, Kiel, Germany *Illert, Michael* Institute of Physiology, Christian-Albrechts-University, Kiel, Germany

The two visual systems hypothesis (Milner and Goodale, 1995) has been tested by studies using "visual illusions". By abandoning the distinction between reality and illusion, we argue that dissociations between perception and action cannot be taken as evidence for the hypothesis. We used the Müller-Lyer and Ponzo illusions and show that 1) the same motor response (saccades) dissociates from perception for one illusion but not for the other 2) different motor responses (saccades and grasping) either dissociate or not for the same illusion. Dissociations can be explained by only one system that translates internal concepts to specific motor responses.

Explicit and implicit adjustments of drawing movements to changes in visuo-motor gain

Sülzenbrück, Sandra Inst. für Arbeitsphysiologie, Dortmund, Germany *Heuer, Herbert* Transformierte Bewegungen, Institut f. Arbeitsphysiologie, Dortmund, Germany

Adjustments of movements to changes of the visuo-motor gain can occur implicitly, with participants not being aware of them. We investigated the interplay of explicit information regarding changes of the visuo-motor gain and these implicit adjustments. In the experiment 24 participants had to draw circles of a constant size with a stylus on a writing pad. Movements had to be adjusted due to changes in visuo-motor gain occurring during drawing. Radii of drawn circles were analysed using ANOVAs. Results showed additivity of explicit and implicit adjustments even when these had opposite directions.

A response bias produces conflict-adaptation effects in the Simon task

Wühr, Peter Psychologie und Sportwissen., Universität Erlangen-Nürnberg, Erlangen, Germany

Stimulus-Response congruency effects are often smaller after an incongruent than after a congruent trial. This finding has been attributed to conflict-adaptation mechanisms that are able to gate the processing of relevant and/or irrelevant stimulus information. We investigated conflict-adaptation effects in two- and three-choice Simon tasks, where response conflict arises from noncorresponding stimulus and response locations. Results showed conflict adaptation (i.e. reduced costs from noncorresponding conditions after noncorresponding trials) in two-choice, but not in three-choice tasks. Results suggest that noncorresponding conditions in the Simon task induce a bias to respond incompatibly to stimulus location, which produces the conflict-adaptation effect in this task.

FP-137: Risk and decision making II

Psychological distortions in multiple-criteria decision making

Seri, Raffaello Dipt. di Economia, Università dell'Insubria, Varese, Italy *Bernasconi, Michele* Dipartimento di Economia, Università dell'Insubria, Varese, Italy *Choirat, Christine* Dept of Quantitative Methods, Universidad de Navarra, Pamplona, Spain

We start from recent results about separable representations in magnitude ratio estimation that identify two different distorsions, a sensorial and a cognitive one embodied respectively in two functions called "psychophysical" and "subjective weighting" functions. We investigate theoretically and empirically the presence of biases in a multiple-criteria decision method, the Analytic Hierarchy Process. Using the theory of matrix differentials, we are able to separate the contributions of sensorial and cognitive distorsions and individual unexplained heterogeneity and to evaluate their relative weights. In particular we show that the customary implementation of the method allows for controlling the impact of cognitive biases.

Testing risky choice models

Brandstätter, Eduard Sozial- und Wirtschaftspsych., Universität Linz, Linz, Austria

I present a new method for investigating choice processes, called mind-reading. In a mind-reading experiment participants guess how most people had decided previously. Immediately after their guess (majority chose gamble A or B), participants receive feedback, whether their guess was right or wrong. They make 25 guesses, after each guess they get immediate feedback, and every five guesses they are requested to formulate the majority's choice rule. These choice rules indicate that participants often use simple heuristics, such as the priority heuristic (Brandstätter, Gigerenzer, & Hertwig, 2006). I

compare the results with those obtained from mouse-lab and think-aloud protocols.

Probability meaning of motivation: A theoretical and experimental study of Monty Hall Dilemma

Yu, Daxiang Automation College, Nanchang HangKong University, Jiangxi Nanchang, People's Republic of China *Zhujing, Hu* college of educational science, Jiangxi Normal University, Jiangxi Nanchang, People's Republic of China *Qin, Qiu* college of education science, Jiangxi normal University, Jiangxi Nanchang, People's Republic of China

The study aimed at finding out the main factors that cause Monty Hall dilemma. A mathematical theorem, Probability Lumping Theorem, was presented and proved based on the axiom of probability and the mathematical structure of Monty Hall problem. Compared with the solution based on Bayes's theorem, the Monty Hall problem can be solved easily and intuitively with this theorem. An experiment was designed and performed. Sixty graduate students majored in science and technology volunteered to participate in the experiment. The results obtained demonstrate that failing to distinguish stochastic lumping and non-stochastic lumping of probability is the main factor that causes Monty Hall dilemma.

The cognitive processes underlying quantitative estimations: Comparing recent estimation models

von Helversen, Bettina ABC, Max-Planck-Institut, Berlin, Germany *Rieskamp, Jörg* ABC, MPI for Human Development, Berlin, Germany

Recently, Helversen & Rieskamp (in press, JEP: General) proposed a new heuristic model for quantitative estimation, the mapping model. For the present contribution the mapping model was tested against an exemplar model. In two experiments we investigated, how the task structure influences which model captures participants' estimations best. Our results show that prior cue knowledge is decisive. When knowing the direction of the cue-criterion correlation and the correlations' magnitude, the mapping model was best in describing participants' estimations. When knowledge about the cues was not available and hard to acquire, participants' estimations were better predicted by the exemplar model.

FP-138: Risk perception

Students' competence in systemic thinking related to climate change: Computer-assisted assessment approach based on concept maps

Boll, Thomas EMACS Research Unit, University of Luxembourg, Walferdange, Luxembourg *Faber, Théid* EMACS Research Unit, University of Luxembourg, Walferdange, Luxembourg *Busana, Gilbert* EMACS Research Unit, University of Luxembourg, Walferdange, Luxembourg *Martin, Romain* EMACS Research Unit, University of Luxembourg, Walferdange, Luxembourg *Latour, Thibaud* Centre for IT Innovation, CRP Henri Tudor, Luxembourg-Kirchberg, Luxembourg

Study presents a computer-assisted approach for assessing student's competence in systemic thinking related to climate change. Using a concept map paradigm 800 13th-graders were shown 20 concepts (10 relevant, 10 irrelevant to the issue). Firstly, they had to select up to 10 concepts which they regarded as relevant and arranged them on the screen. Secondly, they had to draw arrows between them indicating causal relationships. Measures of systemic thinking were derived: Ratio of relevant/ irrelevant concepts, ratio of correctly/incorrectly indicated causal relationships, complexity of causal modelling. Reliability and validity data are presented and further applications in assessment and education are outlined.

From natural hazards to disasters: How human decisions exacerbate or mitigate risk

Eiser, Richard Dept. of Psychology, University of Sheffield, Sheffield, United Kingdom

Despite improved monitoring and prediction, worldwide losses from natural disasters continue to increase. Human activity contributes to this increase, through extreme weather events reflecting climate change, degradation of vulnerable ecosystems, and poor decision-making accentuating population risk exposure and vulnerability. Surveys of at-risk communities identify processes including: risk perception and trust in risk communicators; the impact of feedback and motivation on risk beliefs: how longer-term environmental consequences are weighed subjectively against short-term economic gain; (dis)empowerment of vulnerable communities and inequities in risk exposure. A theoretical synthesis of these psychological processes is presented with implications for future policy.

Perception of climate change risks: A multi-agent simulation

Seidl, Roman CESR, Universität Kassel, Kassel, Germany Ernst, Andreas CESR, University of Kassel, Kassel, Germany

Floods and drinking water shortages are likely consequences of future climate change. In order to understand how such risks are perceived, we developed and implemented a psychological process model. It is based on qualitative and quantitative data from interviews and questionnaires, and theoretical aspects of cognition and emotion in risk perception. It forms part of an integrated social science – natural science model that simulates the water cycle, including drinking water, in a large German river basin. We assess the spatial and temporal dynamics of risk perception and its relation to natural impacts and sustainability indicators under different climate scenarios.

Risk perception assessment in Argentina: Research, results and relevance

Mikulic, Isabel Maria Faculty of Psychology, University of Buenos Aires, Buenos Aires, Argentina

This presentation will illustrate why risk is a multifacetted concept and which factors determine how people think about risks and make their judgments about hazards in Argentina. As no measurement tools exist in Argentina, Rohrmanns Hazard Evaluation Questionnaire has been adapted and ecologically validated for a contrast-group design with representative samples of groups with specific societal, professional and cultural orientations.This instrument is based on respondentsview of their principal standpoint in risk situations. Results indicate that risk attitudes are multidimensional and that motivations for accepting risks vary considerably depending on the type of hazard. Potential implications for further research are discussed.

The social-cognitive mechanisms regulating adolescents' use of doping substances

Mallia, Luca Dept. of Psychology, Universita 'La Sapienza', Rome, Italy Lucidi, Fabio of Psychology, Sapienza. Univerity of Rome., Rome, Italy Zelli, Arnaldo Educ Sciences for PA & Spo, Univ. of Sport &Movem. Sci, Rome, Italy Grano, Caterina Psychology, Sapienza. Unviersity of Rome, Rome, Italy Violani, Cristiano Psychology, Sapienza. University of Rome, Rome, Italy

The study assessed the longitudinal effects of social-cognitive mechanisms on the self-reported use of doping substances among Italian high school students. 1,232 students completed questionnaires measuring various psychological factors hypothesized to influence students' intention to use substances. Of these, 762 filled out the same questionnaires three months later and also reported their use of substances. Adolescents' intention to use doping substances increased with stronger attitudes about doping, stronger beliefs that significant others would approve their use, a stronger conviction that doping use can be justified, and a lower capacity to resist situational pressure or personal desires. In turn, stronger intentions and moral disengagement contributed to a greater use of doping substances during the last three months.

Attentional bias and positive changes in breast cancer patients: A cross-sectional survey and an experimental study

Chan, Michelle Wing Chiu Department of Psychology, The University of Hong Kong, Hong Kong SAR, China, People's Republic of : Hong Kong SAR Ho, Samuel Mun Yin Department of Psychology, The University of Hong Kong, Hong Kong SAR, China, People's Republic of : Macao SAR

Objectives. To investigate the relationship between attention to positive and negative information and self-perceived positive changes among women with breast cancer. Methods. Study 1 is a cross-sectional study. 150 eligible patients completed a set of psychological inventories. In Study 2, 60 eligible patients completed three experimental tasks measuring attentional bias (change-detection task, dot-probe task and affective-picture memory task) at the outpatient clinic. Results. Patients' attentional bias might influence the content valence of cancer-related cognitive processing, which in turn might affect self-perceived positive changes. Conclusion. Attentional style and cognitive processing may render as therapeutic leverages in facilitating self-perceived positive changes.

The structure of the generalized health-related self-concept: A structural modelling approach

Wiesmann, Ulrich Inst. für Medizin Psychologie, Universität Greifswald, Greifswald, Germany Niehörster, Gabriele Institute for Medical Psycholo, University of Greifswald, Greifswald, Germany Hannich, Hans-Joachim Institute for Medical Psycholo, University of Greifswald, Greifswald, Germany

Starting out from Markus' dynamic self-concept theory, we explore health-related knowledge structures about the self that are generalized over different health-related areas and over experiences at different points in time. 436 college students (70.5% women) filled out the revised general health-related self-concept (GHSC) scale which assesses five dimensions: health-protective dispositions, health-protective motivation, vulnerability, health-risky habits, and external, avoidant motivation. Using structural equation modelling, we found support for a hierarchical factor structure. The five first-order factors, representing different health resources and deficits, are explained by a single second-order factor of GHSC.

Processes of change assessment in overweight and obese patients

Andrés, Ana Methodology Behavioral Science, University of Barcelona, Barcelona, Spain Saldaña, Carmina Department of Personality, University of Barcelona, Barcelona, Spain Gómez, Juana Methodology Behavioral Science, University of Barcelona, Barcelona, Spain

Objectives. The aim of this study is to validate a processes of change scale, according to the transtheroretical model, to be used with overweight and obese patients. Methods. The above mentioned questionnaire was specifically developed to be used among overweight and obese patients. It was applied to a clinical sample of overweight and obese people (n = 200) and to general sample (n = 200). Results. The psychometric properties of the scale obtained in this study are referred to discrimination indexes, test reliability (Cronbach's alpha) and criterion validity. Conclusions. This study offers the validation of a processes of change questionnaire.

Appropriate strategies for gifted education to enhance affective development

McCarthy, Sherri Dept. of Psychology, Northern Arizona University, Yuma, USA Stutler, Susan Psychology, Northern Arizona Univ.-Yuma, Yuma, USA

Qualitative data was gathered on 9 pre-adolescent (age 11) enrolled in a gifted education program at an elementary school in the Southwestern U.S. Follow-up interviews 10 years later were used to determine educational experiences viewed as most important for affective development. Small-group discussions of books read in common with other gifted girls ("book talks') were perceived as most useful.

Relationship between goal-orientation and motivational self-regulation in the gifted students

Safe, Diba Special Education, Shiraz University, Shiraz, Islamic Republic of Iran Bashash, Laaya Special Education, Shiraz University, Shiraz, Islamic Republic of Iran

This research examines the relationship between goal-orientation and motivational self-regulation strategies (mastery self talk, performance self talk, interest enhancement, environmental control and self-consequent). To this end 334 gifted high school students (172 girls and 162 boys) were participated in this study. Motivational Beliefs Scale about Mathematics (MBSM) and Self-Regulation Scale for Learning Mathematic (SRSLM) were used as measurement instruments. Validity and reliability of these scales were confirmed in the present study. Multiple regression analyses revealed that mastery goal orientation is the strongest predictor of motivational self-regulated strategies in gifted students. Results were interpreted in the light of self regulation models.

Inclusive education in Slovenia

Adlesic, Irena Crnomelj, Slovenia Grah, Jana School counseling, Prymary school, Murska Sobota, Slovenia Mataic Salamun, Mihaela School counseling, Primary school, Beltinci, Slovenia Jerman, Janez

In Slovenia we take care of pupils with special needs. We have focused inclusive teams to help schools with pupils with special needs. Each team includes a psychologist, a teacher, a special pedagogue and social pedagogue or a speach therapist. We did a research in which we wanted to establish the inclusive climate in those schools. We made questionnaires for pupils, teachers and parents about positive and negative experiences with inclusive education. With statistical methods we established areas in which the parents, teachers and pupils (a pupil with special need and his/her schoolmates) have positive or negative opinions respectively. Result help us develop future programmes - for pupils, parents and teachers.

Validity of commonly-used measures of effort when used with adults demonstrating learning disabilities or AD/HD

Lindstrom, Jennifer RCLD, University of Georgia, Athens, USA Lindstrom, William RCLD, University of Georgia, Athens, USA Gregg, Noel RCLD, University of Georgia, Athens, USA Coleman, Chris RCLD, University of Georgia, Athens, USA

This study investigated the construct validity of the Word Memory Test (WMT; Green, 2003), the Test of Memory Malingering (TOMM; Tombaugh, 1996), and the Word Reading Test (WRT; Osmon et al., 2006) for the classification of adults. Four groups (N=20/group) were included: students with LD, LD-simulators, a control group, and an AD/HD clinical comparison group. ANOVAs and post hoc tests were used to determine the discriminatory capacity of each measure. The sensitivity, specificity, positive predictive validity, and negative predictive validity of each measure were determined. Findings question the validity of the WMT and the TOMM as measures of malingering.

FP-141: Cooperation and prosocial behavior in childhood and adolescence

The importance of hermeneutics to developmental process
Jardim, Maria Faculdade de Ciências Humanas, Universidade Fernando Pessoa, Porto, Portugal Oliveira, Jorge Faculdade de Ciências Humanas, Universidade Fernando Pessoa, Porto, Portugal
We shall focus on narratives hermeneutics to prove how this method helps to develop our moral in order to become an ethical human being. Hermeneutics is therefore a tool to go deeper inside our own personalities, ways of seeing the world and inter-acting with it. Interpretation and evaluation turn out to be self interpretation as well as self evaluation and the world we live asks to be re-interpreted by the subject.

Use six-step method to improve children's cooperation
Wang, Lei Shool of Psychology, Central China Norm. University, Wuhan, People's Republic of China Zhou, Zongkui shool of psychology, CentralChina Normal University, Wuhan, People's Republic of China Liu, Jiujun shool of psychology, CentralChina Normal University, Wuhan, People's Republic of China
What factors would influence the children's co-operation? The former researches have found the level of empathy, expression, strategies on clash played important roles. How to integrate those factors to improve children's cooperation? We used a 6-week program named "six-step method on children's clash". Two schools in suburb were involved; one as experimenting group. In each of the two schools we selected children in grade three and grade five. The results demonstrated that children in experimenting school used more effective strategies to resolve clash, while the controlling school students remain unchanged. This method can be applied to improve the children's cooperation. Key words: cooperation, children's clash, intervention, behavior training

Conceptual representation of early adolescents' prosocial behavior
Kou, Yu Inst. of Developm. Psychology, Beijing Normal University, Beijing, People's Republic of China Zhang, Qingpeng Institute of Developmental Psy, Beijing Normal University, Beijing, People's Republic of China
This study focuses on the early adolescents' conceptual representation of prosocial behavior. 609 participants (average age=13.0, SD=1.49) were asked to assess 43 prosocial items those were nominated by early adolescents in focus group interview with the method of centrality rating. The paper exploring the conceptual structure with the method of hierarchical cluster analysis and exploring factor analysis. The results show: the concept of early adolescent's prosocial behavior was represented in a prototype model; their prototype of prosocial behavior was structures of four dimensions- commonweal and rule, personality trait, interpersonal relationship, and altruism; four opti-

mum examples are kin altruism, enhancing friend-ship and helping respectively.

Self-perception, attachment, peer relations and parental peer management as predictors of prosocial behavior sub-types among Turkish female and male adolescents
Bayraktar, Fatih Dept. of Psychology, Ankara University, Ankara, Turkey Kumru, Asiye Psychology, Abant Izzet Baysal Univer, Bolu, Turkey Sayl, Melike Psychology, HacettepeUniversity, Ankara, Turkey
This study investigated how individual, peer and parental variables related to proactive and reactive prosocial behaviors and how they differentiate among male and female adolescents. 1110 adolescents (650 girls, 550 boys) were recruited between 7th-10th grades in Ankara, Turkey. Individual variables, peer relations, perceived parental practices, and parental peer management styles were entered respectively in hierarchical regression analyses. Results revealed that the predictors of proactive and reactive prosocial behaviors differentiated among boys and girls. Finally, psychological control seems to be the indicator of authoritarian parental style functioned in the same way on prosocial behavior sub-types being remarkably different from Western cultures.

FP-142: Memory processes III

Memory and music: Mozart effect or interference?
Czerniawska, Ewa Faculty of Psychology, University of Warsaw, Warsaw, Poland
Four experiments concerning the role of music in memory processes are presented. The first experiment showed that English vocal decreased the recall of earlier memorized English words while instrumental music increased it. The second and third experiment demonstrated that the influence of music accompanying memorization or preceding recall was very weak, although in line with the hypothesized positive influence of Mozart and Abba, and negative of Chinese music. In the last investigation, no significant effects of music preceding or accompanying memorization were found. The results are discussed with reference to the Mozart effect and interference.

Origins of the enactment effect: A recall-based view
Spranger, Tina Inst. für Psychologie, Universität Frankfurt, Frankfurt, Germany Knopf, Monika Institut für Psychologie, Goethe-Universität Frankfurt, Frankfurt am Main, Germany
The basis of the enactment effect is still unclear. We suggest a recall-based view, focussing on differences in the recall process for verbally vs. subject-performed actions. Recall of action phrases was analysed as a function of encoding and age: Younger and older adults were tested in a within-subjects design using direct (experiment 1) as well as in a between-subjects design using delayed free recall (experiment 2). Experiment 3 was a replication of Experiment 1 with 7- and 10-year-olds. Across experiments subject-performed actions were consistently recalled faster than actions encoded verbally. Theoretical implications of these findings are discussed.

A simplified conjoint recognition paradigm for the measurement of verbatim and gist memory
Stahl, Christoph Inst. für Psychologie, Universität Freiburg, Freiburg, Germany Klauer, Christoph Institute for Psychology, University of Freiburg, Freiburg, Germany
The distinction between verbatim and gist memory traces postulated by Fuzzy Trace theory has furthered our understanding of numerous phenomena in various fields, such as false memory research, research on reasoning and decision making, and

cognitive development. To measure verbatim and gist memory empirically, an experimental paradigm and multinomial measurement model has been proposed, but rarely applied. In the present article, a simplified Conjoint Recognition paradigm and multinomial model is introduced and validated as a measurement tool for the separate assessment of verbatim and gist memory processes. A Bayesian metacognitive framework is applied to validate guessing processes. Similarities and differences of the new paradigm and the Source Monitoring paradigm are also highlighted.

FP-143: Agreement and information sharing in groups I

The communication bias toward preference-consistent information in groups: Dependent on decision preference salience and partner communication?
Kerschreiter, Rudolf Inst. für Psychologie, Universität München, München, Germany Seibold, Angelika Psychology Department, Ludwig-Maximilians-University, Munich, Germany Schweizer, Tatjana Psychology Department, Ludwig-Maximilians-University, Munich, Germany Mojzisch, Andreas Institute of Psychology, Georg-August-University, Göttingen, Germany Schulz-Hardt, Stefan Institute of Psychology, Georg-August-University, Göttingen, Germany
This experiment focused on the communication of preference-consistent vs. preference-inconsistent information in groups. Participants worked on a decision-making task and exchanged information in written form with a bogus partner next door. We manipulated the salience of participants' decision preference and the amount of preference-consistent information contained in the handwritten information list participants received from their bogus partner. Results revealed a systematic bias toward preference-consistent communication: Participants mentioned, repeated, and asked for more preference-consistent information than preference-inconsistent information. This bias was slightly larger when decision preference salience was high and when the partner communicated predominantly preference-inconsistent information.

Supporting the collaborative drawing of inferences from distributed information in groups
Meier, Anne Inst. für Psychologie, Universität Freiburg, Freiburg, Germany Spada, Hans Inst. für Psychologie, Universität Freiburg, Freiburg, Germany
Based on research on group decisions in "hidden profiles", the impact of information distribution as well as instructional support on collaborative inferences and solution quality in group problem-solving were investigated. In a first experiment (n=27 dyads), information distribution had a significant impact on the number of inferences drawn, with inferences from unshared, distributed information the most difficult. Instructional support positively affected solution quality. A follow-up experiment investigates the effectiveness of feedback based on an online analysis of inference patterns. Both experiments point towards the importance of individual-level cognitive processes also in group-level problem solving.

Don't tell me which candidate you prefer: The negative impact of learning the other group members' preferences on processing effort and decision quality
Mojzisch, Andreas Inst. für Psychologie, Universität Göttingen, Göttingen, Germany Schulz-Hardt, Stefan University of Goettingen, Institute of Psychology, Goettingen, Germany
Hidden profiles are decision tasks in which the superior alternative is hidden from group members when considering their prediscussion information. We propose a new explanation for the failure of

groups to solve hidden profiles. Accordingly, learning the other members' preferences reduces the effort devoted to processing the information exchanged and, hence, impedes the detection of the correct solution. The results of three experiments show that participants who were not informed about the other members' preferences were more likely to detect the correct solution than those who received bogus information about the others' preferences. This effect was mediated by processing effort.

FP-144: Aging and health I

Motives and determinants of volunteering in older volunteers

Grano, Caterina Dept. of Psychology, University 'La Sapienza', Rome, Italy Lucidi, Fabio Department of Psychology, Sapienza. University of Rome, Rome, Italy Zelli, Arnaldo Educ. Sciences for PA & Sp, Univ. Sport & Movem. Scien, Rome, Italy Violani, Cristiano Department of Psychology, Sapienza. University of Rome, Rome, Italy

Objects: Self-efficacy, and constructs from the theories of planned behavior (TPB) and self-determination theory (SDT) were combined in a study of older adults' volunteering. Motives from SDT were considered antecedents of TPB variables and self-efficacy. Methods: A longitudinal investigation was conducted with 615 older volunteers (Mage=66.32; 312 were males). SEM analyses were used. Results: The analysis yielded a very good model fit (CFI = .96; NNFI = .95; SRMSR= .04; RMSEA=.04). Findings suggest that SDT motives predict TPB variables and self-efficacy. General hypotheses from TPB were confirmed. Conclusions: The integration of SDT and TPB can result in a more complete understanding of volunteer behavior in older volunteers.

Future orientations, age and self construals

Guler-Edwards, Ayca Dept. of Psychology, Middle East. Tech. University, Ankara, Turkey Imamoglu, E. Olcay Psychology, Middle East Tech. University, Ankara, Turkey

The present research investigated the relation between future orientations, age, and self-construals by using Balanced Integration and Differentiation (BID) Model of Imamoglu. Four hundred four adults from different age groups (young, middle-aged, older) participated in the study. ANOVA tests indicated the effect of age on future orientations except for related-individuated respondents, representing the optimal development by the BID Model. Contrary to the other self types (i.e., separated patterning, related patterning, separated individuation), related-individuated respondents had open future perspective, low anxious and high planful attitudes towards future at all ages.

Elderly perception of their quality of life – a Brazilian exploratory study using WHOQOL OLD

Silva, Eleonora Psicologia, Universitas - FEPI, Taubate, Brazil

The purpose of the research was to evaluate how elderly perceive their quality of life. It has been conducted in a countryside region of Brazil, and the instrument used was the WHO scale. The sample was composed by 300 volunteers over 60 years of age. The results showed that most elderly find their lives meaningful and more than half believes they have a good quality of life even having health and financial problems. The most common complains were regarding quality of relationships and poor leisure. It is hoped the research can subsidy future social and psychological interventions with this population.

FP-145: Aggression and violence at school I

Socio-emotional competencies in violent contexts: Evaluation of the multicomponent program Aulas en Paz

Jiménez, Manuela Psychology, Universidad de los Andes, Bogotá, Colombia Chaux, Enrique Psychology, Universidad de los Andes, Bogotá, Colombia

Aulas en Paz is a multicomponent school-based program that promotes the development of socio-emotional competencies among children living in violent neighborhoods. It includes classroom sessions, peer group activities, family workshops, phone calls and home visits. This study seeks to evaluate its effectiveness. Eleven 4th and 5th-grade classrooms (440 students) in three schools in Bogotá, Colombia, were randomly assigned to three conditions: 1) multi-component program; 2) classroom sessions only; 3) control group. Measures of classroom climate, academic achievement and several socio-emotional competencies are being collected in a pre-test post-test quasiexperimental design. Results will be ready by the time of the conference.

Aggressive teacher behavior in Germany and Japan: A cross-cultural study

Baudson (née Klein), Tanja Gabriele Hochbegabtenforschung, Universität Trier, Trier, Germany Stiensmeier-Pelster, Joachim Pädagogische Psychologie, JLU Gießen, Gießen, Germany Fujihara, Takehiro School of Sociology, Kwansei Gakuin Daigaku, Nishinomiya, Hyogo, Japan

"Violence at school" usually targets student aggression. Teachers' aggression against students has been largely ignored in empirical research, despite its serious consequences. Not only the amount, but also the type of aggression is determined by sociocultural norms: With group cohesion, subtlety of aggression increases as well. In addition, Japanese teachers, unlike their German counterparts, focus on managing their classes as much as on conveying knowledge. We expected Japanese teachers to show less and relatively more indirect aggression, which was partly confirmed by a survey of over 1,200 German and Japanese junior high school students. Implications of the results are discussed.

Effects of teacher-student relationships on students' reports of school aggression and victimisation

Lucas Molina, Beatriz Madrid, Spain Martinez Arias, Rosario DEVELOPMENTAL AND EDUCATIONAL, COMPLUTENSE UNIVERSITY OF MADR, MADRID, Spain

The effects of school factors on aggression and victimisation behaviour in primary school children has rarely been investigated. As yet there has been few studies focusing clearly on fundamental aspects of school, such as teacher-student relationships (Yoneyama & Naito, 2003). The present study aims to expand the knowledge in this field. Participants were 2050 children aged 8-13 from 27 primary schools of the Region of Madrid. Multiple regression analysis showed that both student aggression and victimisation were predicted by being victimised by teachers and by perceiving low support from them. These results highlight some important directions for future prevention programs.

FP-146: Aggression and sexual abuse I

Outcome of the treatment program of the Department of Social Welfare and Development (DSWD) for incest victims at Marillac Hills: A qualitative-quantitative analysis of cases

Agcaoili, Suzette SWIDB, Dept. of Social Welfare & Devt, Quezon City, Philippines

Objective: This study analyzed the outcome of treatment program of the Department of Social Welfare and Development to twenty-one minor incest victim-survivors in Marillac Hills, Alabang, Muntinlupa City. Methods: There were 21 father-daughter incestuous cases provided with bio-psychosocial intervention programs, and used the qualitative-quantitative in-depth, multiple case-study analysis, and combination of descriptive-correlational method. Results: The Spearman's correlation is 0.569 or 0.57 at .01 level of significance (2 tailed) of the Total Score of Piers-Harris-2 Self-Concept and the total score of Client Satisfaction Qustionnaire-8, concluded that there's a moderately high significant correlation between the two variables.

Attitudes toward victims of rape: A comparison on different times and places

Jasso-Lara, Martha Julia Special Education Needs, UAPNEE, Chihuahua, Mexico Luna Hernandez, Jesus Rene SPECIAL EDUCATION NEEDS, UAPNEE, CHIHUAHUA, Mexico

Although many laws against sexual violence have been reinforced in recent years, victims of rape are still being stereotyped and discriminated. Pictures of two women, one considered as attractive and other as not attractive, and different scenarios were associated to an attitude scale designed to measure how respondents perceive and react to female victims of rape. Data was gathered originally in 1995 in three cities of the north of Mexico and is compared to 2007 responses to a similar instrument in Ciudad Juarez. Overall, the main effects are with the type of picture shown and the interaction picture-scenario.

Sibling abuse

Carvalho Relva, Ines Telões, Portugal Monteiro Fernandes, Otilia Education and Psychologie, UTAD, Vila Real, Portugal

In this work we have studied the maltreatment amongst siblings, a reality which is not well known in Portugal, but with a wide range of investigation in other countries. The aim of this study is to verify if in the gathered sample any kind of aggression amongst siblings exists. First characterize the various forms of child maltreatment and the risk factors which are implied. We use qualitative and quantitative methods. On quantitative research we use a questionnaire applied to younger who have siblings. We also use an interview. We have found that there are many situations of maltreatment amongst siblings.

FP-147: Theoretical and philosophical psychology I

Cultural bases of psychological theories: A challenge for intergrating world psychology

Mironenko, Irina Dept. of Social Psychology, SPb Univers. Humanities, St. Petersburg, Russia

World psychological science is integrating. The time when psychological empires lived relatively independent one from another is over and a structure of an integrate psychological science is emerging. Russian psychology is facing a challenge to join the international mainstream. Gathering together psychological knowledge demands laying bare differences in implicit cultural bases of psychological theories. Things which are not stated in scientific reasoning but taken for granted must be taken into account to promote mutual understanding between psychological schools. A system of implicit beliefs about human nature underlying Russian psychology is compared to the one underlying Western psychological theories.

The problem of consciousness in psychology, philosophy and religion: Three ways or one?

Bogoslovskiy, Stanislav Dept. of Chemistry, State Technological University, Moscow, Russia

The aim is comparison of approaches in the study of consciousness in psychology, philosophy and religion. "Vanishing subjectivity" paradox; "subjective coloring"; laboratory equipment limitations; social consciousness as a censor of ideas. New opportunities of interdisciplinary approaches in the study of consciousness. The place of ethics in the study.

Psychology in search for new methods and approaches

Smirnov, Sergey Department of Psychology, Moscow State University, Moscow, Russia Kornilova, Tatiana Department of Psychology, Moscow State University, Moscow, Russia

Contemporary discussion on psychology methods has committed two substantive errors. The first one is connected to separating and confronting two psychologies, exploratory (descriptive) and explanatory (causal) ones. The second one is connected to assertion of the so-called unbreakable connection between experimental psychology and positivism. Recognition of ideas of pluralism in psychological literature should mean acceptance of multiple methods instead of rejection of methods already mastered by a professional psychology. Any psychological method predetermines a selection of explanatory principles only with regard to making inferences about a sought after empirically based discovery, but not to content-driven foundations of psychological explanation.

FP-148: Career: Its meaning and development

Has the meaning of "career" shifted?: A vignette study exploring four generations' career-related attitudes

Dries, Nicky AROR, Vrije Universitet Bruxelles, Brussel, Belgium Pepermans, Roland AROR, VUB, Brussel, Belgium de Kerpel, Evelien AROR, VUB, Brussel, Belgium

This study examined whether different generations hold different beliefs about career. Career type, career success evaluation and importance attached to organizational security were scrutinized for each generation. 750 people completed a vignette task (5x2), rating the career success of 32 fictitious people. The majority of participants still had rather "traditional" careers, although younger generations displayed larger discrepancies between career preferences and actual career situation. Overall, satisfaction appeared to be the overriding criterion used to evaluate other people's career success. No significant differences were found between generations.

An exploratory factor analysis of career management in teachers of middle school

Zhang, Shuhua School of Management, Shenyang Normal University, Shenyang, People's Republic of China Sun, Lili School of Management, Shenyang Normal University, Shenyang, People's Republic of China Yi, Weijing School of Management, Shenyang Normal University, Shenyang, People's Republic of China

Abstract Objective: The study aims at developing the Career Management Inventory for teachers of middle school. Method:According to the results of 200 teachers by exploratory factor analysis, the Organizational Career Management (OCM) is

consist of occupational exploration, career plan, morality culture, occupational development, teaching tactic and interrelationship; The individual career management inventory (ICM)is consist of justice in assessment and promotion, occupation development facilitation and learning sustainment. Conclusion:The inventory had good internal consistency and reliability level. Key Words Organizational career management, Individual career management, Exploratory factor analysis

General perceived self-efficacy and locus of control as mediating factors to the perception of career-related barriers

Dragova, Sonya Cognitive Science & Psychology, New Bulgarian University, Sofia, Bulgaria

The study investigates the relationship between general self-efficacy and locus of control and the perception of barriers to career development. Studied categories of barriers are: social, attitudinal and interactional barriers. Research methods include: Inventories of perceived barrier hindrance; General perceived self-efficacy scale of Schwarzer and Jerusalem; Spector's Occupational locus of control method. The sample consists of 879 participants from Bulgaria, Poland and Russia. Results show that participants ascribe average hindrance to career-related barriers. The expected relationship is cofirmed to some extent. It is more salient in the Bulgarian sample and does not exist in the Russian one.

Comparison of general aptitudes and career motives in three levels of jobs in Saipa car company

Oreyzi, Hamid Reza Pschology, Isfahan University, Isfahan, Islamic Republic of Iran Golparvar, Mohsen psychology, Khorasgan University, Iran, Islamic Republic of Iran Amiri, A. tehran, Saipa car company, Iran, Islamic Republic of Iran

Three levels of careers in career ladder development was identified in 80 Jobs (240 position).Aptitudes were identified by administering General Aptitude Test Battery on Owners of these prostitutions. Aptitudes were compared in three levels. Findings indicate that higher level positions need certain aptitudes also, career motives were significantly different. Implications for selection decisions discuss.

FP-149: Depression and loneliness in old age

Development of a screening scale for geriatric depression

Heidenblut, Sonja Fachbereich 2, Universität Siegen, Siegen, Germany Zank, Susanne Fachbereich 2, Universität Siegen, Siegen, Germany Schacke, Claudia Fachbereich 2, Universität Siegen, Germany

Purpose: Purpose is the development of a new depression-scale, that is particularly suitable for the use on geriatric inpatients. Methods: From an empirically proved Item-pool a short scale was constructed considering the discriminatory power of the items as well as the intended form and content of the instrument. The Scale was validated among a sample of N=300 geriatric inpatients, using a structured clinical interview as gold standard criterion for depression. Results: Preliminary findings show promising psychometrical qualities for the new instrument. Reliability and validity as well as the effectiveness of the scale as a screening-instrument will be presented.

Autobiographical memory specificity in older adults with major depression

Latorre Postigo, Jose Miguel Dept. of Psychology, Faculty of Medicine (UCLM), Albacete, Spain Serrano Selva, Juan Pedro Health Psychology, Faculty of Medicine (UCLM), Albacete, Spain Ros Segura, Laura

Health Psychology, Faculty of Medicine (UCLM), Albacete, Spain Aguilar Corcoles, Maria Jose Health Psychology, Faculty of Medicine (UCLM), Albacete, Spain Navarro Bravo, Beatriz Health Psychology, Faculty of Medicine (UCLM), Albacete, Spain

Increased recall of categorical autobiographical memories is a phenomenon present in depressed young adults. The aim of this study was to compare the autobiographical memory performance in older adults with major depression compared to non-depressed older adults, using the Autobiographical Memory Test procedures (Williams & Broadbent, 1986). Thirty-three older adults with major depression and thirty-three non-depressed older adults were asked to generate specific memories in response to a series of positive and negative cue words. Evidence of overgeneral memory (OGM) was found for the depressed group. While OGM effect size in depressed young adult is d = 1.12 (Williams et al., 2007) effect size in older adult sample is d = 0.88.

Therapeutic usefulness life review focused on life events specific positives (ReVISEP) in the treatment of major depression in old age

Serrano Selva, Juan Pedro Psicología, Facultad de Medicina, Albacete, Spain Latorre, Jose Miguel Psicología, Facultad de Medicina, Albacete, Spain Ros, Laura Psicología, Facultad de Medicina, Albacete, Spain Navarro Bravo, Beatriz Psicología, Facultad de Medicina, Albacete, Spain Córcoles, José Psicología, Facultad de Medicina, Albacete, Spain

The technique ReViSEP has shown its effectiveness in improving mood in the elderly with depressive symptoms (Serrano Latorre, Gatz and Montañés, 2004). The aim of this study was to examine the efficacy of ReViSEP in the treatment of TDM in the elderly, in the context of the Primary Care. 16 elderly [15 women, mean age = 76.4 (SD = 8.6). The subjects after four sessions ReViSEP found a statistically significant increase in the specific memory, showed fewer depressive symptoms and improved life satisfaction.

FP-150: Risk assessment in young offenders II

Patterns of elevated PAI validity indices across assessment contexts and presenting psychopathology: Implications for assessment

Yoxall, Jacqueline School of Psychology, Bond University, Robina, Australia Bahr, Mark School of Psychology, Bond University, Robina, Queensland, Australia

Objective: To determine whether elevations of validity indices on the Personality Assessment Inventory (Morey, 1991) vary across assessment contexts and types of clinical presentation. Method: A review of 400 cases presenting across different forensic contexts (worker's compensation claims, victims of crime compensation claims, personal injury compensation claims; and pre-sentence) where the PAI was administered as part of a psycho-legal evaluation. Discriminant function analysis was employed. Results & Conclusions: Base rates for elevation of validity indices on the PAI may vary across assesment context and reported psychopathology. Implications for assessment using the PAI are discussed.

Leaking as a warning sign in cases of school shootings and Severe Targeted School Violence (STSV)

Bondü, Rebecca Erz.wissenschaft u. Psychol, Free University Berlin, Berlin, Germany Dölitzsch, Claudia Erz.wissenschaft u. Psychol, Free University Berlin, Berlin, Germany Scheithauer, Herbert Erz.wissenschaft u. Psychol, Free University Berlin, Berlin, Germany

Several studies have identified warning signs of school shootings and STSV in American samples.

The transferability of these results to German cases has long been questionable. Prior announcements of the offences called "leaking" and other warning signs such as violent fantasies, depressive tendencies or access to weapons may be valuable starting-points for a threat assessment approach. We present data on German single cases based on analyses of files of inquiry within the Berlin Leaking-Project. Comparisons of German and American data reveal both overlaps and specifics in the samples with regard to leaking and other risk factors preceding the offences.

Gambling, risk and vulnerability

Chadee, Derek Psychological Research Centre, University of the West Indies, St. Augustine, Trinidad and Tobago

This paper assesses the relationship between gambling and risk factors of teenagers. Among the risk factors are low neighborhood attachment; community disorganization; transitions and mobility; and perceived availability of the following: drugs, substance use, crime, violence, gangs and delinquency. The main hypothesis of the study is: the greater the perceived risk the more likely teenagers are to participate in gambling and other delinquent behaviour. A sample of 850 secondary school teenagers in the 14 -16 age cohort in a Caribbean country is studied using the survey design. Results are discussed in the context of prevent of occurrence of gambling problem, identifying risk indicators and reduce vulnerability.

The effect of self-awareness intervention programme on children's self-perception and antisocial behaviour

Shulruf, Boaz Faculty of Education, University of Auckland, Auckland, New Zealand

This study measured the effect of an intervention programme aiming at altering at-risk primary students' self-perception and social awareness as an avenue to mainstream citizenship rather than delinquency. The students participated in an intervention programme operated once weekly over four months. Programme activities were focused on raising awareness of antisocial and anti-environmental behaviours and awareness of personal life quality. The evaluation applied a mixed-methods approach using both quantitative and qualitative data. Evidence for improvement in children's self-perception was identified as well as effective methods facilitating such changes. It was concluded that focused self-awareness intervention programmes may positively affect antisocial behaviour

FP-151: Risk and uncertainty

Personality and decision-making in neuropsychological tasks measuring decisions under risk and decisions under ambiguity

Brand, Matthias Inst. Physiolog. Psychologie, Universität Bielefeld, Bielefeld, Germany Altstötter-Gleich, Christine Differential Psychology, University of Koblenz-Landau, Landau, Germany

In this contribution we firstly report a study in which we assessed 58 healthy volunteers (30 males) with two neuropsychological decision-making tasks, the Iowa Gambling Task (IGT) and the Game of Dice Task (GDT) and several specific personality traits. We found strong correlations between performance in the GDT and specific core facets of perfectionism while other personality traits were unrelated to decision-making under risk. IGT performance was unrelated to all personality traits assessed. Thereafter, we compare data of patients with pathological gambling, anorexia and bulimia nervosa, showing that impulsivity and perfectionism are related to decision-making, but not other personality traits.

The role of risk in intertemporal choice

Sun, Yan Chinese Academy of Sciences, Beijing, People's Republic of China Li, Shu Institute of Psychology, Chinese Academy of Sciences, Beijing, People's Republic of China

The purpose of this study is to examine the preference change of intertemporal choice caused by risk. Different versions (i.e., certain vs uncertain) of the questionnaires on time discounting were presented to undergraduate students to evaluate the degree of discounting future. Previous research found that adding a time delay to all the alternatives will decrease the degree of time discounting. Thus, introducing an external uncertainty will also decrease the degree of time discounting if risk and delay were psychologically interchangeable. However, our three experiments indicated adding uncertainty to all the intertemporal alternatives will increase the degree of time discounting.

A fuzzy logic model of successful coping with uncertainty

Eierdanz, Frank Inst. für Psychologie, Universität Kassel, Kassel, Germany Lantermann, Ernst-Dieter Universität Kassel, Institut für Psychologie, Kassel, Germany Gerhold, Lars Freie Universität Berlin, Institut Futur, Berlin, Germany Döring-Seipel, Elke Universität Kassel, Institut für Psychologie, Kassel, Germany

People are facing many uncertainties in modern times, for instance uncertain employments, weaker social systems, terrorism and global change. Some people manage to cope well with individual uncertainties and apply active coping strategies. Other people appraise uncertainty as a threat and stay passive. The paper presents a Fuzzy Logic Model of coping with uncertainty based on psychological stress theories and developed from qualitative interview data. Purpose of the model is (i) to show that Fuzzy Logic offers a method to quantify and systemize qualitative interview data and (ii) to predict successful or non-successful coping with uncertainty.

When people chase risk, and when they don't: Role of regret personality and regret behavior

Lai, Zhigang Institute of Psychology, Chinese Academy of Sciences, Beijing, People's Republic of China Shi, Kan Institute of Psychology, Chinese Academy of Sciences, Beijing, People's Republic of China

This study focused on the temporal dynamics of the relationship between regret personality and risk taking behaviors. We developed a model concerning regret orientation, regret behavior and risk preference to examine how people with different regret orientations make decision under different uncertainties. Survey was conducted among 121 undergraduates. Results showed that, generally, participants with higher regret orientation exhibited higher risk avoidance, but when the regret under the gain frame was induced, participants with higher regret orientation contrarily exhibited higher risk taking behavior. This is a very interesting preference reversal. The same effect was not found under the loss frame.

FP-152: Psychotherapy - Research and treatment methods V

Phenomenological analysis of the use of voice training for Parkinson's patients

Janzen, Henry L. Educational Psychology, University of Alberta, Edmonton, Canada Wiens, Harold Department of Music, University of Alberta, Edmonton, Canada

The purpose of this research study was to examine the effects of the use of voice training as a therapeutic intervention for Parkinson's patients. Two pilot studies with high stress subjects and depressed patients showed positive effects. Ten Parkinson's participants were given 15 voice training sessions. The final session was a performance concert in which all patients sang one of their favorite songs. In-depth interviews were analyzed by qualitative methods. Our results confirmed the therapeutic effect of voice training, including a lessening of motor tremors and an increased feeling of greater satisfaction of life.

Narrativity of decision-making in psychotherapy

Polkinghorne, Donald Dept. of Education, Univ. of Southern California, Pasadena, USA

In psychotherapy, therapists are required to make ongoing decisions in response to changing client actions. The paper explores two modes of deciding how to respond—the paradigmatic and narrative modes. In the paradigmatic mode, decisions are informed by indentifying a client action as an instance of a type. In considering the appropriate response, the therapist selects the type of response determined to be helpful to the type of client action. In the narrative mode, decisions are informed by their contribution to the distinctive story of a particular unfolding client-therapist interaction. Narrative decision-making emphasizes the in-situation meaning of the therapist's response.

Peculiarities of open and closed space perception in the process of motor action regulation

Polyanychko, Olena Physical Education, IAPM, Kyiv, Ukraine

The abstract focuses on the characteristics that are the highlights of perception of the open and closed space involved in the motor action control. Open space perception depends on the atmospheric pressure, on casual lack of landmarks, on phobias. Closed space perception depends on its depth, on compulsory motion restriction, on comprehension of landmarks, on body postures change, and on phobias. The skills acquired in a specific space type are not transferable to a different kind of motor action. Therefore, the means is provided to reach the adequate perception of the reflected space for the purpose of motion control, casual trauma prevention, and elimination of phobias and illusions related to the space perception in motor action regulation.

An integrated, multidimensional method for the treatment of trauma in children and adolescents

Schlauch-Rigby, Gisela Service, Psychological Counseling, Yakima, USA

The effectiveness of an integrated, multidimensional therapeutic method for the treatment of sexual abuse trauma in female subjects, ages 6-16, is demonstrated. Therapy consists of five phases. Key points of intervention are explained and graphed. Developmental stages, one at the beginning of treatment, and one during which the abuse occurred, are assessed. The uncovering of the abuse and abreaction, and the client's awareness of a change from an 'abuse influenced' schema to a more 'normative' schema, results in symptom reduction and increased social-, and psychological functioning. Results, reported by the client, caregiver and therapist, are correlated.

FP-153: Evolutionary issues

Mothers baby, fathers maybe: A multinomial model for the estimation of nonpaternity rates

Wolf, Michael Inst. für Exp. Psychologie, Universität Düsseldorf, Düsseldorf, Germany Musch, Jochen Exp. Psychology, University of Duesseldorf, Duesseldorf, Germany Erdfelder, Edgar Psychology III, University of Mannheim, Mannheim, Germany

Knowing the prevalence of nonpaternity in a population is of considerable interest to evolutionary psychologists; its exact determination is however costly. We present a multinomial model allowing to estimate nonpaternity rates by means of Mendelian inconsistencies using easy-to-collect phenotype data. Our model allows for an asymptotically unbiased and efficient estimate of nonpaternity rates in a population even though the single genetic markers on which the model is based have low efficiency for detecting nonpaternity in individuals. In a reanalysis of data sets from different countries and decades, the proposed model is successfully validated against more expensive methods.

Innovation: Novel behaviours in humans and non-human animals from an evolutionary perspective

Toelch, Ulf Innovation, Univeriteit Utrecht, Utrecht, Netherlands Bruce, Matthew J. Behavioural Biology, Universiteit Utrecht, Utrecht, Netherlands Meeus, Marius T.H. Organisational Sciences, Univeriteit Tilburg, Tilburg, Netherlands Reader, Simon M. Behavioural Biology, Universiteit Utrecht, Utrecht, Netherlands

Innovation, the production of novel behaviour patterns not previously found in a population, is puzzling since innovations are often costly and their benefits hard to assess. We investigated the conditions promoting innovation by testing human participants in a 3D computer game where they could discover several behavioural strategies that lead to differential rewards. Before playing, players saw high-scores that were manipulated according to experimental treatment. We found that more novel strategies were discovered when social aspiration levels increased. We discuss these results in relation to social intelligence hypotheses and in comparison with our findings on innovation in non-human animals.

High cost helping behaviour is driven by benevolence rather than altruism

Ferguson, Eamonn Dept. of Psychology, University of Notingham, Nottingham, United Kingdom Lawrence, Claire Psychology, University of Notingham, Nottingham, United Kingdom Farrell, Kathleen Psychology, University of Notingham, Nottingham, Germany

Is human helping behaviour driven by altruistic or egoistic motives that are dependent on the cost of the behaviour? Theorizing in economics, psychology and biological suggests that benevolence should predict high cost helping and empathy (altruistic motive) low cost helping. These predictions were supported across 3 studies (prospective, cross-sectional and experimental) contrasting altruistic (empathy, societal benefit), egoistic (hedonism) and benevolent (both donor recipient benefit) motivations for high (blood donation) and low cost (fundraising) helping behaviours. The results provide the first integration across these different theoretical perspectives (economic, psychology and biology). Implications for models of human altruism are drawn

FP-154: Educational environment, resilience, and problem behaviors in childhood and youth

Community and Individual aspects of Russian youth resilience

Makhnach, Alexander Inst. of Psychology, Russian Academy of Science, Moscow, Russia Laktionova, Anna Russian Academy os Sciences, Institute of Psychology, Moscow, Russia

The resilience of four groups of adolescents (age of 15-19 years) was investigated. Sample was: high school students, orphans, students with emotional and behavioral difficulties, university students (n=233). The interrelation of individual and community aspects of teens' resilience was investigated: coping stress behaviour, achievements motivation, a locus of control, acceptance/nonacceptance of

self/others, domination/dependence, level of emotional comfort/discomfort (individual aspects). The interrelation of social and individual aspects with resilience of adolescents was found. Among social aspects the most important for resilience of teenagers are a community and peers. The family is secondary on the value. The differences between groups are presented.

Future time perspective, coping and risk behaviours among Latin American adolescents

Chau, Cecilia Psychology, PUCP, Lima, Peru Herrera, Dora Psychology, PUCP, Lima, Peru

The aims: to know the relations of future time perspective (FTP), coping and risk behaviours in adolescents from high schools in Peru. The participants were 419 students (230 males and 189 females), 16 years old average. Instruments: Method of Induction Motivacional (PTF), Time Perspective of Zimbardo, Questionnaire of problems and coping across the situations, PRAI (Version Rr). The study used descriptive and inferencial statistics. Results are compared by variance analysis. Significant differences were found between private and public schools with respect to their future time perspective and hedonistic present. The stressors of male and female students differ significantly (future and parents). The proneness to be a problematic drinker is higher than in other risk areas.

Relations beween behaviour problems at age 8 and adjustment at age 9: The influence of the child-teacher relationship

Rydell, Ann-Margret Dept of Psychology, Uppsala University, Uppsala, Sweden Bohlin, Gunilla Dept of Psychology, Uppsala University, Uppsala, Sweden Diamantopoulou, Sofia Dept. of Psychology, Uppsala University, Uppsala, Sweden Thorell, Lisa Dept of Psychology, Uppsala University, Uppsala, Sweden

We investigated the effects of the teacher relationship on children's adaptation. At 8 years, parents and teachers rated behavior problems of 130 children using the Rutter CBQ and ADHD-criteria. Teachers rated the child-teacher relationship using the Pianta STRS. At age 9 teachers rated behaviour problems and peer relations were assessed in a sociometric procedure. Effects of the teacher relationship were studied in regression analyses. There were independent effects of conflicted teacher relations on later adjustment. Further, there were protective effects of teacher closeness and exacerbating effects of teacher conflicts for children with high problem levels at age 8.

FP-155: The impact of students' family background on learning I

The educational and psychological support of educators to include learners from child-headed homes in urban classrooms

Pillay, Jace Faculty of Education, University of Johannesburg, Johannesburg, South Africa Taggert, Nadia

The purpose of this inquiry was to determine what educational and psychological support educators need to include learners from child-headed homes in their classrooms and schools. A qualitative research design was used to collect data from several stakeholders in different schools in Gauteng. On the basis of the negative experiences of the educators we argue that educators need to be supported within a framework of critical and community educational psychology if they are to be successful in educating learners from child-headed homes. Several recommendations on how this could be accomplished are made.

Parental involvement in schooling: The perceptions and attitude of secondary school teachers in a local government area in Nigeria

Omoteso, Bonke Dept. of Educ. Founds & Couns, Obafemi Awolowo University, Ile-Ife, Nigeria

This study investigated how secondary school teachers in a Local Government Area (LGA) in Nigeria perceived parental involvement in their children's schooling. It also examined their attitude to parental involvement. A sample of 120 teachers was randomly selected from this LGA. An instrument titled "Questionnaire on Parental Involvement" was used to collect data from the teachers. Data were analysed using simple percentages, correlation and t-test. Analyses revealed that large proportion of the teachers perceived parental involvement in their schools as fair and most of the teachers were favourably disposed to parents being involved in their children's academic and other school activities.

Educational and social exclusion: The social context as a school failure setting

Serna, Cristina Psychology, University Castilla-La Mancha, Cuenca, Spain Yubero, Santiago Psychology, University Castilla-La Mancha, Cuenca, Spain Larrañaga, Elisa Psychology, University Castilla-La Mancha, Cuenca, Spain

Previous research has related different socio-cultural factors with the academic performance. This work explores the relation of adolescents' academic motivation and expectations with the laboral, economical and educational situation of their families. 1016 Spanish students from secondary schools (12 to 18 year-old) completed measures to assess this relation. The outcomes have been organised into eight categories according with the level of risk of school failure that has been establish through two objective indicators (number of repetitions and failed subjects) and a perceptive one (personal valuation of achievement). Contingencies and correlational analyses showed different directions depended on diverse socio-cultural factors. The logistic regression confirmed the results obtained at descriptive level.

FP-156: Psychopharmacology II

Adverse effects of midazolam premedication on children's post-operative cognitive function

Millar, Keith Psychological Medicine, Glasgow University, Glasgow, United Kingdom Asbury, John Anaesthesia, Glasgow University, Glasgow, United Kingdom Bowman, Adrian Statistics, Glasgow University, Glasgow, United Kingdom Hosey, Marie Therese Paediatric Dentistry, Glasgow University, Glasgow, United Kingdom Musiello, Toni Psychological Medicine, Glasgow University, Glasgow, United Kingdom Welbury, Richard Paediatric Dentistry, Glasgow University, Glasgow, United Kingdom

Administration of midazolam to children before surgery reduces their anxiety, but it is unknown whether the drug impairs post-operative cognition. We conducted a randomised controlled trial of cognitive function before and after midazolam premedication in 179 children aged 5 to 10 years having day-surgery with general anaesthesia. Reaction time, psychomotor co-ordination and recall were significantly impaired at the time of discharge when compared to placebo. When tested 48 hours later, children who had received midazolam continued to show significantly impaired recall. The results confirm the risk to children's safety and well-being in the days following anaesthesia with midazolam premedication.

Effects of methylphenidate on oculomotor prediction as a function of Dopamine Transporter (DAT1) genotype

Ettinger, Ulrich Institute of Psychiatry, London, United Kingdom Joober, Ridha Douglas Hospital, McGill University, Montreal, Canada Pintsov, Oliver Centre for Neuroimaging Scienc, Institute of Psychiatry, London, United Kingdom de Guzman, Rosherrie Douglas Hospital, McGill University, Montreal, Canada O'Driscoll, Gillian Department of Psychology, McGill University, Montreal, Canada

Methylphenidate, a stimulant drug that blocks reuptake of both dopamine and noradrenaline by inhibiting the dopamine transporter, is known to improve cognitive function. We investigated methylphenidate effects on predictive oculomotor control as a function of dopamine transporter (DAT1) genotype. 29 healthy male volunteers were administered 20mg oral methylphenidate in a repeated-measures, double-blind, placebo-controlled design. Saccades to predictable and non-predictable visual targets were recorded. Methylphenidate improved saccadic amplitude, particularly in 9R-carriers and on non-predictive saccades. Methylphenidate effects on saccadic latency were moderated by order of administration, with participants who received methylphenidate first showing a carry-over effect into the second session.

Cognitive effects of creatine ethyl ester supplementation

Ling, Jonathan Dept. of Psychology, Keele University, Newcastle-under-Lyme, United Kingdom Kritikos, Minos Psychology, Keele University, Newcastle-under-Lyme, United Kingdom Stephens, Richard Psychology, Keele University, Newcastle-under-Lyme, United Kingdom

Objectives: Supplementation with creatine-based substances to enhance athletic performance has become widespread. Until recently, the effects of creatine supplementation on cognitive performance had rarely been examined. Methods: The current study investigated whether creatine ethyl ester supplementation would improve performance in five cognitive tasks in a double-blind, placebo controlled study. Results: Results showed that in three out of five tasks creatine dosing led to a significant improvement over the placebo condition. Conclusions: Creatine supplementation appears to improve some areas of cognitive performance. This improvement is discussed in the context of research examining the influence of brain energy capacity on cognitive performance.

FP-157: Eyewitness identification and credibility

Hugo Münsterberg's (1908) on the witness stand: A pioneering work on the psychology of eyewitness testimony?

Sporer, Siegfried L. Inst. für Psychologie, Universität Gießen, Gießen, Germany

In many textbooks, Hugo Münsterberg's (1908) "On the Witness Stand" is celebrated as the key work that marks the beginnings of psychology and law. Some also note that Münsterberg's book was criticized by legal scholars which may have been the cause why psychology and law was not as successful as it might have been. To assess Münsterberg's influence, I review the origins of (experimental) psychological research at the first decades of the 20th century in Central Europe and compare these developments with those in the United States. Much can be learned from the successes and failures of those times.

Eyewitness identification dilemma: Video portrayal vs. photo array in target-absent line-up

Pateraki, Eleni PSYCHOLOGY, DERRE COLLEGE, ATHENS-Ag.Paraskevi, Greece Nega, Chrisanthi PSYCHOLOGY, DERRE COLLEGE, ATHENS-Ag.Paraskevi, Greece Chiotis, Georgios Dept. of Psychology, City University, London, United Kingdom

The present experiment investigated whether agreement between the modes of presenting a crime and identifying it affects recognition accuracy in target-present lineup. Ninety-six undergraduate students were randomly assigned to one of four conditions: video presentation-video identification, photo sequence presentation-photo identification, video presentation-photo identification and photo sequence presentation-video identification. Results showed better recognition when presentation and identification modes were identical. Additionally, participants identified overall more accurately the perpetrator in the video portrayal mode, with more accurate nonchoosers in the target-absent condition. Findings underline the importance of matching presentation and identification modes and reveal the superiority of video portrayal of suspects over photo presentation in identification.

Eyewitness identification: Cultural differences in susceptibility to weapon focus

Lorenz, Jan L. Pädagogische Psychologie, Tech. Universität Braunschweig, Braunschweig, Germany Yan, Song Cognitive Psychology, Universität Göttingen, Göttingen, Germany

The presentation addresses a study conducted in Germany and China, examining an interaction of two variables influencing eye-witness identifications: 'weapon-focus' and culture. 160 mockwitnesses watched a video-presentation depicting a criminal act with or without gun-use. They described the culprit and identified him in a sequential line-up. Free descriptive measures (ANOVA) and final identification frequencies (Chi^2) support the hypothesis that East-Asians are less impaired by a gun's presence in their ability to describe and identify culprits than 'Westerners'. The results indicate that there are cultural differences in susceptibility to weapon focus. Design issues, theoretical and practical implications will be addressed.

An ERP study of the acquired process about self-referring information

Ding, Xiaopan Psychology,School of Education, Zhejiang Normal University, Jinhua, People's Republic of China Fu, Genyue psychology,shool of education, Zhejiang Normal University, Jinhua, People's Republic of China

Prior ERP studies used to compare the incidentally acquired information with the concealed autobiographical information. The present study aims to explore the process of how to acquire self-referring information. In the mock-spy task, ten subjects were told to pretend spy and investigated every week for three times. They need to respond on true, fictitious, irrelevant, and target items. The EEG was recorded from 128 scalp sites using electrodes mounted in HydroCel GSN cap. The results shows that the differences between the P300 which elicited by the true and factitious self-referring information become smaller after two weeks.

FP-158: Ethnic and race issues II

Relationship of socio-economic status, accomodation type and marital status with mental health well being among Turkish migrant women in the UK

Cakir, Gulfem Dept. of Educational Sciences, Middle East Technical Univers., Ankara, Turkey

The purpose of this study was to analyse the relationship of marital status, accomodation type, employment status, and income level of migrant women living in the UK with their mental health well being. A sample of 232 Turkish migrant women completed the questionnaire including demographic questions and General Health Questionnaire. Factorial ANOVA results suggested that employment status were associated with mental health well being of migrant women. However, marital status, accomodation type, and income level of migrant women had no significant effect on their mental health well being. Implications of these findings are drawn for practice and further research.

Multiculturism and cultural, social and political integration: The case of the immigrant Chinese Community in Bilbao (Basque Country)

Rubio Ardanaz, Eduardo Psicología Social, University of Basque Country, Leioa, Spain Fang, Xiao Director, Chinese Studies Center, Bilbao, Spain Rubio Ardanaz, Juan Antonio Antropología Social, University of Extremadura, Bilbao, Spain

The degree of integration of the Chinese immigrant community was analyzed by considering cultural, social and political parameters, which allowed for a comparision with the local native population. The study was realized in Bilbao, Basque Country, where data was compiled on the Chinese immigrant community by means of ethnographic techniques, either with interviews or by direct observation. All data was analyzed qualitatively. Findings indicate correlated levels of participation with the local community, whether it be high or low, leading to the conclusion that increased participation facilitates integration and a mutually enriching multiculturalism.

Having more humane and responsible citizens by teaching them history

Guerra, Elida Psychology, UAQ, Queretaro, Mexico Guerra, Gabriela Master in Education, Universidad Contemporanea, Queretaro, Mexico Salinas, Rolando Javier Psychology, UAQ, Queretaro, Mexico

This article suggests a didactic approach to promote the development of a more humane and informed citizenship at schools. Our findings show that a new perspective on the way lessons of the Colonization and Independence of Mexico are presented promoted on high school students to make the essential connection between history and the choices they confront in their own lives. It engaged students in an examination of identity, racism and intolerance, as well as the need to be responsible of their own actions since they affect the community as a whole. Students realized that the problem is collective as well as the solutions.

Race encoding within São Paulo undergraduates: A contextual comparison

Nascimento, Leandro São Paulo, Brazil Marui Cosenti, Leonardo Antonio Psicologia Experimental, Instituto de Psicologia, USP, São Paulo, Brazil Macedo Gonçalvez, Diego Departamento de Fisiologia, Centro de Biociencias, UFRN, São Paulo, Brazil Otta, Emma Psicologia Experimental, Instituto de Psicologia, USP, São Paulo, Brazil Yamamoto, Maria Emilia Departamento de Fisiologia, Centro de Biociencias, UFRN, Natal, Brazil

To compare context influences in race encoding, the race variation of Kurzban et al. (2001. Can race be erased?, PNAS, 98, 15387–15392) experiment was applied in São Paulo. 84 undergraduates were exposed to a sequence of sentences, each paired with one of eight speakers' photos, and afterwards asked to attribute the sentences to the speakers' photographs. Participants formed two groups, control and coalition clued. Analyzing the errors effect size, the race encoding difference between the groups was inverted, in comparison to the original experiment: the encoding was higher in coalition clued group. Context was revealed essential for race encoding.

FP-159: Multisensory processing

Effects of spatial compatibility and consistency across simultaneously executed saccades and manual responses

Huestegge, Lynn Inst. für Psychologie, RWTH Aachen, Aachen, Germany Koch, Iring Inst. für Psychologie, RWTH Aachen, Aachen, Germany

In the present study, we search for underlying mechanisms of between-task crosstalk. In a series of experiments, subjects responded to auditory stimuli with manual responses, saccade responses, or both. The spatial compatibility of response locations with the imperative auditory stimulus was systematically varied. Overall, the systematic introduction of response-code conflict between tasks modulated the pattern of dual-task performance. However, the consistency of spatial response codes across tasks could override the adverse effects of S-R incompatibility. We propose response-code confusability as an underlying mechanism of crosstalk, which is modulated by the spatial cross-task consistency of response codes.

Visual, proprioceptive, and inertial cue-weighting in travelled distance perception

Campos, Jennifer Inst. Biologische Kybernetik, Max-Planck-Institut, Tübingen, Germany Butler, John Biological Cybernetics, Max Planck Institute, Tübingen, Germany Mohler, Betty Biological Cybernetics, Max Planck Institute, Tübingen, Germany Bülthoff, Heinrich Biological Cybernetics, Max Planck Institute, Tübingen, Germany

When moving through space, visual, proprioceptive, and inertial information contribute to the perception of distance travelled, yet little is known about how each are weighted when simultaneously available. In this study participants moved through a large, fully tracked space by either walking or being passively driven by a robotic wheelchair (proprioception removed) and were asked to judge the distance travelled. Visually travelled distances (presented via a head-mounted display) were either congruent or incongruent with the proprioceptive/inertial inputs. Responses reflect a higher weighting of body-based cues during walking and a relatively equal weighting of inertial and visual cues during passive movement.

Spatial attention affects the processing of tactile and visual stimuli presented at the tip of a tool: An event-related potential study

Yue, Zhenzhu University of Hamburg, biological psy. and neuropsy., Hamburg, Germany Bischof, Gérard-Nisal University of Hamburg, biological psy. and neuropsy., Hamburg, Germany Zhou, Xiaolin Department of Psychology, University of Peking, Beijing, People's Republic of China Spence, Charles Department of Experimental Psy, University of Oxford, Oxford, United Kingdom Röder, Brigitte University of Hamburg, biological psy. and neuropsy., Hamburg, Germany

An ERP experiment was conducted in order to investigate crossmodal links in spatial attention during tool-use. Vibrations were delivered from the tips of two sticks, held in either a crossed or an uncrossed posture, while visual stimuli were presented along the length of each tool. Participants had to detect tactile deviant stimuli at the end of one stick, while ignoring all other stimuli. Somatosensory and visual ERPs were enhanced to tactile and visual stimuli presented at the tip of the attended tool. These results suggest that tool-use results in a shift of visuospatial attention towards the tip of the tool.

Ignoring complex tactile patterns: Tactile versus visual negative priming

Frings, Christian Inst. Verhaltenspsychologie, Universität des Saarlandes, Saarbrücken, Germany

In a Negative Priming (NP) task, participants selectively respond to targets accompanied by distractors; repeating a distractor as the target usually impairs performance. Here I analyze this phenomenon in the tactile domain (participants identify complex vibro-tactile patterns), and furthermore compare tactile NP with visual NP. Results showed that tactile NP 1) produces larger effect sizes than visual NP and 2) is observed under conditions, in which visual NP is not (constantly absent probe distractors). It is discussed whether tactile and visual NP reflects modality-free selection.

FP-160: Need assessment and treatment of offenders

Moral development of solo juvenile sex offenders

Stams, Geert Jan Education, University of Amsterdam, Amsterdam, Netherlands van Vugt, Eveline Education, University of Amsterdam, Amsterdam, Netherlands

This study compared moral development of solo juvenile male sex offenders (n = 20) and juvenile male non-offenders (n = 76), aged 13 to 19, from lower socioeconomic and educational backgrounds. Moral judgment was assessed with the Sociomoral Reflection Measure – Short Form (SRM-SF), with questions added on sexual offending and the offender's own victim(s). No differences in moral judgment were found. However, lower stages of moral judgment were observed when the offenders' own victim was involved, confirming specific moral deficits in solo juvenile sex offenders. Delay in moral judgment proved to be associated with cognitive distortions.

How juveniles attribute their delinquent behavior: A presentation of preliminary results

Ricijas, Neven Dept. for Behavioral Disorders, Faculty of Educ. and Rehab., Zagreb, Croatia

The main goal of this research is a development of Criminal Attribution Scale for Juvenile Delinquents. The Scale was constructed in a preliminary research with the Weiner attribution theory and Risk / Need perspective of criminal behavior as theoretical background. Research was conducted on a sample of 108 male juvenile delinquents in the city of Zagreb, and included juvenile delinquents within three types of sanctions: (1) probation, (2) open institution facility, (3) closed institution facility. Results will be presented within the context of attribution categories and differences according to the type of sanction and intensity of criminal activity.

Psychological rehabilitation of children in conflict with law

Rath, Pratap Psychology, Utkal University, Bhubaneshwar, India Mohapatra, Kasturi Social Activism, Open Learning Systems, Bhubaneshwar, India

The Maslow's (1954) model emphasized biological needs instead of the right to life with dignity (RLD) as primary. This is unfortunately allowing many abuses to be seen as acceptable if the biological needs are met. In a paradigm shift, emphasizing RLD, 50 children (< 18 years), alleged to have committed offenses were released on bail from Observation Homes. Initially, the attitude of the Home authorities, the children themselves and the parents were negative. Repeated intervention emphasizing the RLD yielded substantial change in attitude. For long-term impact, the children are being given vocational training and support for entrepreneurship.

Characterizing adolescents' deviant group identity

Zhang, Chunmei Dept. of Psychology, Wuhan University, Wuhan, People's Republic of China Zou, Hong Developmental Psychology, Beijing Normal University, Beijing, People's Republic of China

This research aimed to exam whether delinquent group would fulfill important function for delinquent adolescents, namely, deviant group identity, and it contribute to their delinquency and delinquent association. 13 incarcerated youths from Hubei juvenile prison were selected through theory sampling of qualitative research, and by line-by-line coding analyzing, the results showed that there were five important components: group figure categorizing identification, interacting experience and sense of coherent affiliations, group reputation management, group norms, and positive feeling and commitment to group, which could be called the characters of deviant group identity. The characters of juveniles' deviant group identity were discussed.

The "Hits" keep coming: Examining parole practices for violent offenders in New York State

Marquez, Carla Social_Personality Psychology, CUNY Graduate Center, New York, USA Fine, Michelle Social-Personality Psychology, CUNY Graduate Center, New York, USA Boudin, Kathy Not Applicable, Columbia University, New York, USA DeVeaux, Mikail Not Applicable, Muslim Re-entry Initiative, New York, USA Martinez, Migdalia Not Applicable, Not Applicable, New York, USA Pass, Michael G. Not Applicable, John Jay College, New York, USA Waters, William E. Not Applicable, The Osbourne Association Inc., New York, USA White, Sharon Not Applicable, Not Applicable, New York, USA Wilkins, Cheryl Not Applicable, Lehman College, New York, USA Vargas, Felipe Not Applicable, The Doe Fund, Inc., New York, USA

Since 1995, there has been an "unofficial" practice of denying parole to people convicted of violent felonies, based primarily on the nature of the original crime. These "hits" have forced people to serve lengthy prison sentences despite maintaining clean institutional records and undergoing extreme transformations behind prison walls. This study examines these parole procedures. By analyzing narratives of 34 women and men convicted of violent crimes (namely murder), who have stayed out of prison post-release, we are able to operationalize the process and offer evidence of transformation and rehabilitation. Finally, we offer suggestions for revisions to the current parole process.

FP-161: Negative affect

The share of somatization, anxiety, social maladjustment, and depression in predicting addiction potential among theoretical high school male students in Freidan City

Moradi, Azam Psychology, Isfahan University, Isfahan, Islamic Republic of Iran Ghamarani, Amir psychology, isfahan university, isfahan, Islamic Republic of Iran Oreizi, Hamid Reza psychology, isfahan university, isfahan, Islamic Republic of Iran Rezaie, Sedigheh psychology, isfahan university, isfahan, Islamic Republic of Iran

The purpose of this study was determine the share of somatization, anxiety, social maladjustment, and depression in predicting addiction potential among high school male students. The sample consisted of 220 students who were selected randomly from high school male students in Freidan city. addiction potential and psychological characteristics measured by APS and GHQ-28. Results of stepwise regression showed that anxiety and somatization variables are best predictors for addiction potential respectively (for both P=0.00); but adding social maladjustment, and depression to former variables can't increase the predicting power of addiction potential significantly.

Acculturation stress and homesickness of Turkish migrants in Germany

Uslucan, Haci-Halil Inst. für Psychologie, Universität Potsdam, Potsdam, Germany

The psychological well-being of migrants is one of the neglected domains both of clinical psychology and health psychology. This empirical study with 357 Turkish people in Berlin at the age of 13 to 66 specify the psychological burdens of Turkish migrants exemplified at acculturation stress, feelings of homesickness and depression. The results show high psychological strain both by the first working migrant generation and the next generations. Personal resources like high self-esteem and social supporting networks could buffer the pains of homesickness and depression. The results have implications both to clinical-psychological praxis as well as to social policy of immigration.

Individuals with paraplegia from spinal cord injury: Self-esteem and depressive symptoms

Psichouli, Pavlina Occupational theraphy, Techn.ed.inst.of athens, Volos, Greece Kleftaras, George Dept. of Special Education, University of Thessaly, Volos, Greece

The present study aimed at investigating the differences in depressive symptomatology among low, moderate and high self-esteem individuals with spinal cord injuries. 96 paraplegic adults (aged 16 to 71) responded to the Pichot-Questionnaire-of-Depressive-Symptoms and the Rosenberg-Self-Esteem-Scale. Statistically significant differences were found among low, moderate and high self-esteem paraplegic individuals in terms of how depressed they feel. Furthermore depressive symptomatology was not related to the period of time an individual lives with the spinal cord injury. Finally an important protection against depression appeared to be the individual's active participation to social events and happenings. Implications for counselling and rehabilitation are discussed.

Depressive symptoms and all-cause mortality after heart transplantation

Havik, Odd Erik Dept. of Clinical Psychology, University of Bergen, Bergen, Norway Sivertsen, Børge Department of Clinical psychol, University of Bergen, Bergen, Norway

Heart transplantation (HTx) is associated with increased depression. However, the impact of depression on the prognosis for HTx-patients has not been sufficiently established. The aim of the study was to investigate the influence of depression on mortality in 147 HTx-patients. Depressive symptoms assessed by Beck's Depression Inventory at inclusion increased the risk of mortality during a 5 years follow-up period. This remained significant after adjusting for several risk factors. The adjusted relative risk associated with depression was comparable to the adjusted relative risk associated with time since HTx. Conclusion: Depression predicts mortality independent of somatic and lifestyle risk factors.

The effect of systematic desensitization on test anxiety and school performance of girl third grade guidance school students in Behbahan

Mehrabizade Honarmand, Mahnaz Psychology, Shahid Chamran University, Ahvaz, Islamic Republic of Iran Kazemian Moghaddam, Kobra Psychology, Shahid Chamran University, Ahvaz, Islamic Republic of Iran

This research aimed at studying the effect of systematic desensitization method on test anxiety and the performance of girl third grade guidance school students. The participants of the study included 42 students suffering from test anxiety These students were selected using the multi-phase method. The instrument in this study were: Speilberger's Test Anxiety Questionnaire. Besides descriptive statistics such as mean, standard devia-

tion, in order to analysis the data, inferential statistics like MANOVA were also used. The results showed that systematic desensitization method decrease test anxiety and improve educational performance of experimental group in compare with the control group.

The comparative and stady mentalhealth on street women and normal women

Alavi, Tahere Ferdowsy University, Mashhad, Islamic Republic of Iran Gharaie, Vajiheh Psychology, Payamenoor University, Mashhad, Islamic Republic of Iran

Main objective in this research is study and comparative mental health in street women and normal women in Mashhad.A comparative - causative design was use.Sample group was composed of 60 women, who were randomly allocated into two groups. In this study we used GHQ questionnaire (physical symptom, anxiety, depression, social dysfunction). The data analysis was taken place using SPSS version and independent t-test was used.The results revealed that there was a significant difference (α=0/05) between two groups in mental health scores.The average mental health scores in four subtest was significantly high in street women.So mental health street women is lower than normal women.

Working memory and the language system: fMRI evidence for a procedural model of verbal working memory

Fiebach, Christian Dept. of Psychology, University of Heidelberg, Heidelberg, Germany

The functional neuroanatomy of the verbal working memory system is generally described in the context of Baddeley's multi component model of working memory, i.e., as a phonological loop consisting of a passive phonological store and a subvocal articulatory rehearsal system. However, this model fails to account for lexical effects on working memory performance, observed in behavioral studies, and is partly incomptible with neurocognitive models of language. In this talk, I will present a series of studies that explore how different language systems in the brain contribute to verbal working memory. The results support procedural, or active memory, models of working memory.

The neural signature of multi-item working memory

Axmacher, Nikolai Inst. für Epileptologie, Universität Bonn, Bonn, Germany Elger, Christian Department of Epileptology, University of Bonn, Bonn, Germany Fell, Jürgen Department of Epileptology, University of Bonn, Bonn, Germany

Recent data suggest that the medial temporal lobe (MTL) may play a role for working memory (WM), but the underlying neural mechanisms have remained unknown. Using intracranial EEG (iEEG) in epilepsy patients and functional MRI in control subjects, we found evidence for sustained activity in the MTL during multi-item WM. Phase-synchronization between the inferior temporal cortex and the MTL increased with load, but smaller regions showed correlated BOLD responses with the MTL. Cross-frequency coupling of gamma power to theta phase was more prominent with increasing load, consistent with a computer model where individual items are represented by wavelet cycles.

Effects of shape similarity in short-term visual recognition

Mate, Judit Psicologia Bàsica, Universitat Autònoma Barcelona, Barcelona, Spain Baques, Josep Psicologia Bàsica, Universitat Autònoma Barcelona, Cerdanyola del Vallàs, Barcelo, Spain

The aim of this research was to examine the effects of shape similarity in visual working memory using a span recognition task of Chinese characters. Shape similarity among items was manipulated at encoding and retrieval in order to assess in which phase similarity impairs performance in a greater degree. Moreover, half of the participants were required to suppress articulation. Results revealed a significant main effect of suppression and also a significant interaction between phases, showing the greatest effect when items were dissimilar at encoding but similar at retrieval. Visual similarity effects and the role of verbal contribution to recognition of similar and dissimilar items are discussed.

Links between working memory and episodic memory in a virtual environment

Plancher, Gaen Descartes CNRS, University Paris, Boulogne-Billancourt, France Gyselinck, Valerie LPNCog, University ParisDescartes CNRS, Boulogne-Billancourt, France Nicolas, Serge LPNCog, University ParisDescartes CNRS, Boulogne-Billancourt, France

In order to expand our knowledge about the links between working memory and episodic memory, the effect of a verbal memory load was tested on the recall of episodic memory components within an ecological virtual environment. 58 undergraduate psychology students navigated in a virtual town and half of them had concurrently to count the number of two kinds of garbage. Subjects' memory of the elements (factual), their position (spatial) and their sequence (temporal) was tested. Results show that the load of working memory reduces temporal episodic recall, but not factual nor spatial recall. Thus, verbal component of working memory contributes to the construction of temporal episodic traces.

Working memory declined by normal aging: What kind of tasks are the most damaged by this process?

Rodríguez, Raquel Metodología de las CC del Comp, UNED, Madrid, Spain González Marqués, Javier Psicología Básica II, UCM - Facultad de Psicología, Pozuelo de Alarcón (Madrid), Spain

The main decrements on memory performance by aging were in working memory. Our aim was to analyse alterations in different working memory tasks. 71 individuals, between 55 to 75 years old, were evaluated in the following tasks: Digit span, Spatial span, Letters and numbers, Mental control, Stroop test, D2 test, Trail Making Test, a searching task, a switching task, a dual task and a task based on the Daneman and Carpenters task (1980). We found statistical significant differences in a few tasks. Our experiment provides evidence that age is a crucial factor in working memory, especially from 65 years old.

Spatial learning with navigation assistance

Münzer, Stefan Universität des Saarlandes, Saarbrücken, Germany Zimmer, Hubert Department of Psychology, Saarland University, Saarbrücken, Germany Baus, Jörg Computer Science Department, Saarland University, Saarbrücken, Germany

Navigation assistance systems provide support for wayfinding at the cost of spatial learning (Münzer et al., 2006, J. Environm. Psy.). The goal of the study was to support incidental spatial learning. First-time visitors to an university campus took a guided tour. Across a series of experiments, the wayfinding presentation on their navigation assistance varied with respect to modality (verbal, visual), perspective (egocentric, allocentric), alignment (north-aligned, rotated), and completeness of information. While route knowledge was not affected, better survey knowledge was aquired with allocentric spatial information. Thus information presented on assistance systems contribute to incidental orientation learning. In addition, large individual differences were found which were related to visuo-spatial working memory capacity.

FP-163: Memory processes IV

Influence of response-stimulus interval (RSI) on sequence learning

Chambaron, Stephanie SRSC, Universite Libre de Bruxelles, Bruxelles, Belgium Destrebecqz, Arnaud SRSC, Universite Libre de Bruxelles, BRUXELLES, Belgium Ginhac, Dominique LE2I, Universite de Bourgogne, DIJON, France Cleeremans, Axel SRSC, Universite Libre de Bruxelles, BRUXELLES, Belgium
We investigated the role of response-stimulus intervals (RSI) on sequence learning in serial reaction time tasks. We assumed that random RSIs would disturb chunk formation and have detrimental effects on learning. In two experiments, we compared sequence learning using random and constant RSIs. Moreover, the RSI average values could be either short (Expt. 1) or long (Expt. 2). Our results reveal that (1) random RSIs had no impact on SRT performance; (2) recognition of sequence fragments was only observed with constant RSIs. It is therefore argued that sequence temporal organization is mandatory for explicit sequence learning to take place.

The emergence of awareness during learning

Rose, Michael Medizin. Universität Hamburg, Hamburg, Germany
The development of explicit, aware memory during incidental learning offers a new perspective on consciousness. Here, we were able to show that the emergence of awareness during incidental learning is accompanied by an increase of high frequency coupling between distant brain areas as observed with EEG and increased neural activity as indexed by fMRI. More importantly, the increase in neural coupling and FMRI signal increase was observed even before awareness occurred behaviourally. Thus, our data provides direct evidence for the notion of large scale coupling as the basis for conscious awareness and the temporal precedence strongly suggests causality.

Examining the strategy hypothesis: On the functional relation between explicit knowledge and implicit visuomotor adaptation

Hegele, Mathias Bewegungskoordination, Insitut für Arbeitsphysiologie, Dortmund, Germany Heuer, Herbert Movement coordination, Insitut f. Arbeitsphysiologie, Dortmund, Germany
According to the strategy hypothesis, deliberate strategic adjustments based on explicit knowledge of visuomotor regularities should facilitate adaptation to novel visuomotor relations. In the present set of experiments, we examined the characteristics of implicit and explicit adaptive shifts and tried to elucidate the hypothesis' scope of validity. Subjects performed aiming movements to targets of different amplitude and direction while visuomotor relations were manipulated. Results showed different generalization characteristics of implicit and explicit adaptative shifts as well as a more complete adaptation for subjects who accumulated more explicit knowledge. Potential preconditions for the generation of explicit knowledge are discussed.

Context-sensitive adjustments of cognitive control: Conflict-adaptation effects are modulated by processing demands of the ongoing task

Fischer, Rico Inst. für Psychologie, Techn. Universität Dresden, Dresden, Germany Dreisbach, Gesine Department of Psychology, Technische Universität Dresden, Dresden, Germany Goschke, Thomas Department of Psychology, Technische Universität Dresden, Dresden, Germany
Adjustments of cognitive control due to interference from irrelevant stimulus attributes have repeatedly been shown. Here we investigated how these control adjustments are modulated by the processing demands of a primary task. A primary number comparison task was combined with a Simon task. Control adjustments revealed sequential modulations of the Simon effect. In addition, we found sequential modulations of the numerical distance effect and an interaction of both effects. Therefore, not only response conflict due to interference from task irrelevant features but also processing demands of task relevant features determine the level of control adjustment in the subsequent trial.

Autobiographical memory and self of Chinese college students

Wang, Qiaohong rm 619 34A bldg, Peking University, Beijing, People's Republic of China
This study aimed to investigate the characteristics of autobiographical memories of Chinese college students. Participants reported memory events cued by emotion words, together with the emotional valences and strengths. The results indicated that memories related to others were more specific than those related to self. Emotional strengths were lower for the negative memories than those for positive ones, which was possibly a strategic self-defense mechanism. The results suggested that significant others might be important in self-construal for Chinese students therefore such memories were more specific, while the generic retrieval of memories related to self might save the cognitive resources.

Transfer and rule based learning problem solving

Meo, Maria Psychology, University of Rome, Rome, Italy Marucci, Francesco S. Psychology, University of Rome, Rome, Italy
Main goals of this study were: 1) to investigate the high processes related to transfer of learning in problem solving, 2) to evaluate the plausibility of Anderson's Theory of learning, in order to investigate if rule based learning is the preferential way used by child cognitive system during information processing. Problem solving tasks with figural, verbal and numeric stimuli are used to transfer knowledge in different domain. Anderson's theory is evaluated comparing effectiveness of rule-based text versus descriptive text in training sessions of all tasks. Results indicate that people took advantage by rule based training

FP-164: Mental health and counseling II

Counselling in the Greek culture

Malikiosi-Loizos, Maria Early Childhood Education, University of Athens, Athens, Greece Christodoulidi, Fevronia School of Education, University of Manchester, Manchester, United Kingdom
The purpose of the present study was to investigate the helping relationship patterns of Greeks, with the ultimate goal of generating a culture-specific counselling model. A questionnaire designed to cover situations of natural helping and counselling styles was administered to N=265 Greeks, 17 to 55 years old. Multiple correspondence and cluster analyses showed Greeks offering and receiving emotional support from their immediate family, using a more active influencing style of helping, based on advice and directives. The findings suggest various culture-specific factors that illuminate the possible implications for training and the shaping of the counselling profession within the Greek cultural context.

Culture-sensitive and resource oriented peer-groups (CROP-G) as a community based intervention for trauma survivors: A pilot randomized trial with asylum seekers and refugees from Chechnya

Renner, Walter Inst. für Psychologie, Universität Innsbruck, Innsbruck, Austria Peltzer, Karl Social Aspects of HIV/AIDS and, Human Sciences Research Counci, Pretoria, South Africa
Objectives. Testing culturally sensitive peer-counselling. Methods. N=94 Chechens were randomized to 2 peer-counselling (CROP-G), 2 Cognitive Behaviour Therapy (CBT), 2 wait-list control groups, and to an individual short intervention. Measures: Hopkins-Symptom-Checklist (HSCL-25), Harvard-Trauma-Questionnaire (HTQ), Post-traumatic-Growth-Inventory (PGI). (Repeated-measures ANOVA, pre/post/follow-up design). Results. On HSCL-25 and HTQ, CROP-G and CBT groups did not differ significantly from each other, but were significantly superior to the waiting condition (effect sizes around 1.00). Individual short treatment was not effective. Regarding PGI-scores, none of the interventions worked sufficiently. Conclusions. As CROP-G are a promising alternative where psychotherapy is unavailable, larger trials are strongly recommended.

Assessment of sociocultural issues in the delivery of culturally appropriate mental health services

Yamada, Ann Marie Los Angeles, USA
This presentation introduces an interview-based assessment tool to illicit social and cultural issues affecting mental health service delivery. A mixed-method design was used to develop the instrument. Surveys and in-depth narratives (using grounded theory) from 20 diverse patients with severe mental illness attending a mental health rehabilitation program were analyzed. Subtle sociocultural experiences and internalized stigma expressed by patients were classified into six themes and social support and stigma were the most salient issues. Use of our newly developed assessment tool may aid clinicians to examine the relevance of their interventions for the diverse groups they encounter in everyday practice.

Use of non-conventional venues to extend counseling services in a majority world country: An exploratory study in Goa, India

Desouza, Karl St. Xaviers College, Goa, India
Indian society is in transition. They are becoming more westernized. At the same time due to stigma traditional venues and models of counseling have not gained acceptance either at the clinic or hospital. On the other hand spaces where people used to traditionally go to seek psychological help, at the temple or village well is diminishing. The objective of this study was to explore areas in which counseling services could be made accessible to a larger segment of the people, using western and traditional Indian models. For this study interviews and focus group discussion was carried out.

Some representations on health: Observations from a focus group study from India (Bihar)

Verma, Jyoti Psychology, Patna University, Patna, India
The objective was to study the culture specific representations of health. Method comprised of focus group discussions in camera with 35 Bihari, Indians. Results, suggested that in common sense understanding, health referred to being able to perform one's social and professional duties and clinically, health represented mental and physical fitness. The culture specific categories of food as Satwik (balanced, non-vegetarian food), rajsic (rich food which exhilarates body's metabolic rate) and tamsik (toxic, rotten food) had important implications for health. In conclusion, health was a holistic concept referring to a harmonious functioning of

mind and body while Biharis believed in a traditional and modern conceptualization health.

Diversity in Community Mass Syndrome (CMS)
Singh, Anita Puri Dept. of Psychology, Girls P.G. College, Bhopal, India
The Community Mass Syndrome (CMS) was first reported in fifteen century as "Tarantism "in context to normal behavior in Germany and rest of Europe where it was known as St.Vitus's dance. With time some symptoms were added or eliminated, changing its form to religious to political to commercial adding diversity. Since 12th to 13th century in Hajj,the feast of fools etc are the symbol of religious CMS. The carnival tradition, the Mardi Gras still flourishes in Belgium, Italy, France, and West Germany. The Political CMS is observed all over the world. The objective of this study was to explore the evidence based diversity in community mass syndrome.

FP-165: Organizational diagnostics and development

Learning organizations and individuals: Learning organizational anchors
Glaveanu, Vlad-Petre Faculty of Psychology, University of Bucharest, Bucharest, Romania
The main assertion of this theoretical paper is that the path of organizational learning is closely related to the beliefs and expectations adults have regarding learning in organizational settings. These "implicit theories" lead to the formation of psycho-behavioral anchors such as: the Self-Sufficiency Anchor, the External Anchor, the Situational Anchor, the Discovery Anchor, the Maintenance Anchor and the Expansion Anchor. Each is discussed from the point of view of the learning process and its outcomes, at both an individual and organizational level. Identifying these learning anchors is a central task for psychologists involved in personnel selection and adult learning programs.

Methods and tools: A case study of organizational culture diagnosing to a private company in China
Yongrui, Li School of Management, Beijing Normal University, Beijing, People's Republic of China Juan, Qin School of Management, Beijing Normal University, Beijing, People's Republic of China Jidong, Liu School of Management, Beijing Normal University, Beijing, People's Republic of China Yangyingxue, Li School of Management, Beijing Normal University, Beijing, People's Republic of China Zhihong, Xiao School of Management, Beijing Normal University, Beijing, People's Republic of China Changhai, Wang School of Management, Beijing Normal University, Beijing, People's Republic of China
In order to investigate the status quo of a private company in China, and to provide its organizational change with basically theoretical foundations. Structural interview, coding, and questionnaire as the diagnosing methods/tools were used, Results showed that the conclusions by qualitative methods of structural interview, coding and by quantitative of questionnaire reinforced and explained each other, but couldn't be replaced by the other. Both the methods combing qualitative tools with quantitative ones, and the questionnaire self-developed in this study could be used for reference in the field of organizational diagnosing and change.

Practical evaluation of questionnaire results for organizational quality management
Oesterreich, Rainer Computer Science, Technische Universität Berlin, Berlin, Germany
Employee and costumer enquiries often are conducted to compare the quality of organizational

units. At the Technische Universität Berlin, a methodical concept was developed and established to evaluate courses. This concept is generally appropriate for benchmarking organizational units, e.g. departments in a company. The evaluation results in standardized integer values having the following characteristics. Positive/negative integers designate ratings above/below the mean, differences of the integers are directly linked to Cohen's systematic of effect sizes, and the differences' significance is readily identifiable. Strengths and shortcomings within each unit, and changes for the better and for the worse can easily be identified.

Human resources as the basic component of contemporary business context: The experience of an application of the ontopsychological method
Kaluga, Vladimir HR-Management, Counsulting Group FOIL, Moscow, Russia
In most cases the enterprise analysis demonstrates the impossibility to explain the processes in the organization if the psychic dynamics is not taken into account. The knowledge and capacity to exact analysis of the psychic activity permit to manage and create any function necessary to organization. The actuality of the application of ontopsychological knowledge in the field of hr-management is connected with the effectiveness of instruments of Ontopsycology that make possibile the in-depth analysis of a human potential of an enterprise, rapidly reaction to the changes and rationally use of intuition, that is demonstrated by the application of the ontopsychological method in the field of business consulting in Russia.

A measurement of Fuzzy Delphi Theory to personal communication dyad referral reward programs
Liu, Fangyi Business Administration, NTUST, Mituo Township, Taiwan Hung, Yi-Jung Operations and Marketing, Swire Coca-Cala (S&D) Ltd., Mituo Township, Kaohsiung Coun, Taiwan
Word of mouth (WOM) communication dyad, at one time viewed as a psychological and sociological phenomenon to be observed and described, is increasingly considered a cognitive marketing tool to be managed. Because referral reward programs reward existing customers and build the customer base, firms use them to encourage customers to make recommendations to others. In this research, by fuzzy Delphi theory, it provides a basis for identifying what is understood, hence, exploitable of the designs in personal referral reward programs. Overall, this proposed examine the importance weights of WOM motivations, personal referral reward attributes, and management technologies of referral likelihood.

Application of rough sets and neural networks to the study of competency assessment
Yu, Jiayuan Department of Psychology, Nanjing Normal University, Nanjing, People's Republic of China
The objective of this study was to explore whether rough sets(RS) and neural networks(NN) could be applied in the competency assessment. The rating scale which included 21 attributes was used for assessing 195 civil servants' competency. The data was discretized with seven methods and reduced with two ways in RS. The 14 reduced groups of attributes were set up prediction models with NN and ordinal regression respectively. The results showed RS and NN could predict competency more accuracy than ordinal regression.

FP-166: Occupational stress and burnout

Occupational stressors and stress outcomes in Canadian academic staff: Preliminary findings
Catano, Victor Dept. of Psychology, Saint Mary's University, Halifax, Canada Francis, Lori Psychology, Saint Mary's University, Halifax, Canada Haines, Ted Occupational Health, McMaster University, Hamilton, Canada Kirpalani, Haresh Occupational Health, McMaster University, Hamilton, Canada Shannon, Harry Occupational Epidemiology, McMaster University, Hamilton, Canada Stringer, Bernadette Occupational Health, McMaster University, Hamilton, Canada Lozanski, Lorna Occupational Health & Safe, Canadian Association of Univer, Ottawa, Canada
Surveys in UK and Australia universities demonstrate high occupational stress levels. To investigate occupational stressors and stress outcomes at Canadian universities. Randomly selected staff from 56 universities were surveyed via web-based questionnaires. Response rate was 27%. On the General Health Questionnaire (GHQ), 13% of the 1470 respondents reported high distress. 22% reported elevated stress-related symptoms on the Physical Health Questionnaire. In regression analyses, less secure employment status and work-life imbalance strongly predicted job dissatisfaction; work-life imbalance strongly predicted increased GHQ scores. Despite the low response rate, the results are consistent with other research. Strategies to improve stress outcomes are needed.

Prevention of teacher burnout begins in the university: A training for teachers students
Wangler, Jutta Psychosomatische Medizin und P, Universitaetsklinikum Freiburg, Freiburg, Germany Vogelbacher, Angelika Zentrum für Lehrerbildung, Universität Freiburg, Freiburg, Germany Bohnsack, Antje Zentrum für Lehrerbildung, Universitaet Freiburg, Freiburg, Germany Bauer, Joachim Psychosomatische Medizin, Universitätsklinikum Freiburg, Freiburg, Germany
Previous studies from our group showed high rates of mental health problems and burnout in German school teachers. In an attempt to contribute to health prevention, around 400 teacher students in the second year of their studies received the offer to take part in a prevention training program in order to improve behavior, body language, and to optimize the appropriate use of the voice in the classroom. The intervention (84 participants) was accompanied with a survey of the students mental health (GHQ). Our data show i. that teacher students report a remarkable degree of mental stress and ii. highly appreciate the offered program.

Burnout and organizational factors in hospitals affecting nurses
Lu, Jinky Leilanie National Institutes of Health, Manila, Philippines Lu, Yung Chang Human Resource and Mangement, Sophia Mineral Services, Quezon City, Philippines
This is a cross sectional study which looked into the interaction between situational factors, role stressors, hazard exposure and personal factors among. More than half (58.5%) of the respondents have reported being ill from work in the past 12 months, and 59.3% have said that they have missed work because of an illness. After multiple regression analysis, organizational role stress (p= .000), migraine (p= .001), age (p= .018) and illness in the past 12 months (p= .000) were found to be significant predictors of burnout. Significant interactions were also found between self-efficacy and hazard exposure, self-efficacy and organizational role stress. The contribution of the study is seen in advancing new concepts burnout.

Stress in university teachers and possibilities of coping with it

Bulotaitè, Laima General Psychology, Vilnius University, Vilnius, Lithuania Pociute, Birutè General Psychology, Vilnius University, Vilnius, Lithuania Bliumas, Remigijus General Psychology, Vilnius University, Vilnius, Lithuania

Roles, competences and life of university academic staff are changing under the influence of education reform, social and economical changes. The aim of the study was to investigate the relationship between stress factors in university teachers everyday work, job satisfaction, somatic complains and to ascertain teachers' stress-coping strategies. Teachers from different faculties of Vilnius University participated in the study. A specially designed questionnaire, Minnesota Satisfaction Questionnaire and Coping Strategies Questionnaire were used. The results of this research prove the necessity for stress management programs for university teachers in order to decrease the negative consequences of stress.

Burnout in relation to the motivational needs of workers in the business process outsourcing industry

Lohumi, Shama UCOL, CIIS, Mohali, India

Objectives: To identify the relationship between the motivational needs of BPO workers (power, achievement and affiliation) with burnout. Method: Questionnaire survey of 80 BPO workers in India, utilising a range of established psychological inventory tools. Data was analysed with ANOVA. Results: The extent of depersonalisation and personal accomplishment in workers varied according to their different motivational needs, and was also gender sensitive. Conclusion: The motivational needs of prospective BPO workers should be assessed prior to thier appointment to reduce the incidence of burnout.

FP-167: Organizational citizenship behavior: Personal and situational factors

Personal characteristics as predictors of organizational citizenship behavior in Thailand

Smithikrai, Chuchai Dept. of Psychology, Chiang Mai University, Chiang Mai, Thailand

This study aimed to examine whether relationships between personal characteristics and organizational citizenship behavior (OCB) in Thailand are similar to those in western context. The sample consisted of 1,933 persons working in government offices and private companies in Thailand. Survey questionnaires were used to assess OCB, personality traits, and demographics. Hierarchical multiple regression analyses were used to test the hypotheses. Unlike the western findings, the results indicated that extraversion, among personality traits, appeared to play the most significant role in determining OCB and its facets. Furthermore, the results showed that demographic variables exerted small but significant effects in predicting OCB.

Is empowering leadership always welcomed by employees?: That depends on what they think and how they feel

Yang, Jane Dept. of Management, City University of Hong Kong, Hong Kong, China, People's Republic of : Hong Kong SAR Huang, Xu Dept of Management & Marke, Hong Kong Polytechnic Universi, Hong Kong, China, People's Republic of : Macao SAR

We investigate organizational cynicism and trust in supervisor as psychological states leading to organization-directed citizenship behavior (OCBO) and voice behavior, and the moderating role of empowering leadership climate. Data were collected from 267 employees nested within 54 groups from a Fortune-500 company. Hierarchical Linear Modeling results indicate that cynicism is negatively

related to supervisor-rated OCBO, and high levels of empowering leadership climate make this association stronger; trust is positively related to supervisor-rated voice behavior, and high levels of empowering leadership climate make this association weaker. Whether empowering leadership facilitates employees' proactive behavior appears to depend on their attitudes and feelings.

Work environment characteristics and its motivating effect: A preliminary study in knowledge workers

Wu, Zhiming School of Economics & Managmt., Tsinghua University, Beijing, People's Republic of China Wu, Xin School of Economics & Managemt, Beihang University, Beijing, People's Republic of China

The current study explored the motivating effect of work environment characteristics in knowledge workers. Specifically, we empirically investigated the impact of work environment characteristics on psychological empowerment, task performance and organizational citizenship behavior(OCB). 277 knowledge workers and their supervisors in high-tech organizations participated in this study. The results showed that the "achievement and growth" dimension of work environment characteristics was positively related to both psychological empowerment and OCB; the "work meaningfulness" dimension of work environment characteristics was positively related to both psychological empowerment and task performance; the "social support" dimension of work environment characteristics had a positive effect on OCB.

The influence of positive characteristics on organizational citizenship behaviors

Goel, Abhishek Organizational Behavior, IIM Ahmedabad, Ahmedabad, India Vohra, Neharika Organizational Behavior, IIM Ahmedabad, Ahmedabad, India

This study tested the relationship of dispositional optimism, resilience, hope, subjective well-being, and generalized self-efficacy with engagement in organizational citizenship behaviors (OCB). Superior's ratings for an individual's OCB and positive characteristics and individuals' self-report of characteristics were collected for 334 respondents. Regression analysis of data from independent sources showed small but significant positive relationship between hope, resilience, SWB and OCB. Individuals who were low or high on certain characteristics showed negative relationship with engagement in OCB. The relationship between positive characteristics and OCBs of an individual was strong when the superiors' rating was considered for both. Implications for theory, measurement of behaviors, and practice have emerged.

The relationship between organizational citizenship behaviours (OCBs) and counterproductive work behaviours (CWBs) of Malaysian automotive workers

Mehdad, Ali Khorasgan Branch, Islamic Azad University, Esfahan, Islamic Republic of Iran Arifin, Zainal Psychology, University Kebagsaan Malaysia, KL, Malaysia Rozmi, Ismail Psychology, University Kebangsaan Malaysia, KL, Malaysia

The main purpose of this research is the study of the relationship between OCBs and CWBs and related dimensions. Also this research compare the OCBs levels and CWBs scores between women and men workers and Standardize the OCB and CWB measures in Malysia.This research is the first phase of researches which will be conducted in Asian developing countries because of the lack of same research in these countries. This research is a cross-sectional field survey study.The subjects are 300 workers. The results show that there is a negative relationship between OCBs and CWBs. This result is consistent with findings in western countries.

Citizenship performance: Relative importance of personal and situational antecedents

Wesche, Jenny Sarah Dep. of Social Psychology, Ludwig-Maximilians-University, Munich, Germany Muck, Peter M. Work and Organisationational, University of Bielefeld, Bielefeld, Germany

A comparative analysis of antecedents of citizenship performance from different categories (organization, team, leadership, task, personality, and attitudes) was performed based on self-report data of 101 job incumbents. Citizenship performance was assessed by a newly developed German measure based on the three-dimensional hierarchical model originally proposed by Coleman and Borman (2000). The new instrument showed satisfactory reliability. Internal and external construct validity were confirmed. Dominance analysis (Azen & Budescu, 2003) was applied to evaluate the relative importance of the different predictors with regard to variance accounted for. Conscientiousness dominated all other personal and situational antecedents in all possible subsets.

Country image and organizational attractiveness: A marketing perspective

Froese, Fabian Business School, Korea University, Seoul, Republic of Korea Vo, Anne Management, Wollongong University, Wollongong, Australia

In today's globalized world, multinational companies need to attract talent not only in the domestic market but also in overseas markets. This study introduces the country image framework from the marketing literature to the recruitment context in order to examine why foreign companies are (not) attractive to local job seekers exemplified for the case of Japanese companies in Vietnam. Survey results of more than 300 participants confirmed the robustness of our postulated framework. Image of human resource practices, image of Japanese people, and general country image predicted attractiveness of Japanese companies. Detailed explanations and practical implications are provided.

FP-168: Organizational commitment

Organizational climate and job commitment among Nigerian workers

Mogaji, Andrew A. Dept. of Psychology, University of Lagos, Lagos, Nigeria

The study was aimed at examining the relationship between organizational climate variables and job commitment among Nigerian workers. Data were collected from 600 workers randomly selected from three industries in Lagos, Nigeria. The sample included 450 junior workers, 90 supervisors and 60 managers. Analysing data with the Pearson's product-moment correlation shows that all the nine dimensions of organizational climate are positively and significantly related to job commitment at p < .01 respectively. The implication of the results is that the Nigerian organizational climate facilitates job commitment.

Downsizing: The impact of fairness on commitment

Jacobs, Gabriele Personnel and Organisation, Erasmus University, Rotterdam, Netherlands van Dierendonck, Dirk Rotterdam School of Management, Erasmus University, Rotterdam, Netherlands

The experience of a dismissal has a serious impact not only on victims, but also on survivors. We provide a meta-analytic overview of the impact of fairness on organizational commitment for survivors and victims after a downsizing operation. Among 34 samples (including 10534 persons), a positive overall relationship was found for fairness and organizational commitment ($\rho = .39$). Procedural fairness is more strongly related to commitment in the downsizing context than distributive fairness ($\rho = .41$ vs. $\rho = .31$). Furthermore, indications were found that survivors are more sensitive for procedural fairness, whereas victims are more sensitive for distributive fairness.

Antecedents and consequences of service quality in public administrations
Gehring, Frank Inst. für Psychologie, Universität Würzburg, Würzburg, Germany Hertel, Guido Psychology, University of Würzburg, Würzburg, Germany

Public organizations are increasingly perceived as service providers. However, service quality has only marginally been examined in the public sector. As part of an organizational development project in the administration of a large university, administration employees and their in-house clients (scientific and non-scientific staff, university students) participated in an online survey (N=3500). As potential antecedents of service quality, employees' work satisfaction and motivation were measured. As potential consequences, clients' Organizational Citizenship Behavior and affective commitment towards university were taken into account. Using regression and path-analyses, we analyzed whether the relationship of employee and client data is mediated by service quality.

Antecedents of organizational commitment among higher level employees
Suman, Shanti Dept. of Psychology, Banaras Hindu University, Varanasi, India

This study investigated the role of various antecedents of organizational commitment (OC) among employees of higher level. Personal (age, tenure and locus of control) and perceived organizational (job characteristics and organizational structure) characteristics of employees were studied as the antecedents of OC. 140 employees from a Public Sector production organization participated in this study. Multiple linear regression (simultaneous) analysis was carried out in order to estimate the relative impact of various antecedents on employees' OC. Results indicated that perceived job characteristics were the most dominant predictor of OC followed by perceived organizational structure and locus of control. However, the contributions of age and tenure were found to be insignificant.

Escalation of commitment as planned behavior
Soucek, Roman Lehrstuhl für Psychologie, Universität Erlangen-Nürnberg, Nürnberg, Germany Beutner, Susanne Lehrstuhl für Psychologie, Universität Erlangen-Nürnberg, Nürnberg, Germany

Escalation of commitment describes continuing investments into a failing course of action. The present study examined escalating commitment from the perspective of the Theory of Planned Behavior. Ninety-six subjects participated in an interactive computer-based investment scenario with repeated negative feedback. Results show the particular relevance of both the attitude towards further investments and the subjective norm for escalation behavior. Furthermore, the results reveal a change in attitude and subjective norm during an escalation of commitment. In particular, subjects remain committed to a losing course of action, although their attitude and subjective norm towards further investments significantly decline.

The chicken-and-egg problem in the climate-firm performance link
Winkler, Silvan Arbeits- & Organisationspsy., Psychologisches Institut, Zurich, Switzerland Kleinmann, Martin Arbeits- & Organisationsps, Psychologisches Institut, Zurich, Switzerland

The objective of this research project was to determine the causal order of the relation between engagement climate and firm performance (financial performance, customer satisfaction, turnover). Analysis was conducted within one single firm,

allowing the observation of stable, homogenous entities. Data from 35 market areas from a Swiss financial service provider was analyzed for three consecutive years. Lagged analysis was used permitting exploration of priority in likely causal orderings. Analysis revealed statistically significant and stable relationships across various time lags. The reciprocal relationship between employee engagement and financial performance is consistent with previous research on the organizational level of analysis.

Poster Session Tuesday Morning 09:00

How child maltreatment experiences relate to adult sexual offenders' emotional appraisals
Abbiati, Milena Faculté de Droit, Universite de Geneve, Geneve, Switzerland Mezzo, Belinda CHUV, SMPP, Prilly, Switzerland Gravier, Bruno CHUV, SMPP, Prilly, Switzerland

This study aims at exploring the emotional reactions expressed by sexual offenders about their childhood traumatic events and the impact of child abuses experiences. Until now, 54 sexual offenders were assessed, using a semi-structured clinical questionnaire. Correspondence factorial analyses indicate that victimizations in childhood influence further sexual offenders' emotional appraisal of traumatic life events; notably reducing acknowledgement and reinforcing denial of their traumatic experiences. We conclude that maltreatment in childhood is one factor of vulnerability which has to be considered in further sexual delinquency prevention.

The influence of psychosocial stress on the expression of clock genes
Abbruzzese, Elvira A Psychological Institute, University of Zurich, Zürich, Switzerland Birchler, Thomas Clinical Immunology, University Hospital of Zurich, Zürich, Switzerland Fontana, Adriano Clinical Immunology, University Hospital of Zurich, Zürich, Switzerland Ulrike, Ehlert Psychological Institute, University of Zurich, Zürich, Switzerland

The Circadian Clock strongly influences behavioral, biochemical and physiological circadian processes. The neuronal structure of the SCN acts as central pacemaker and synchronizes the expression of clock genes in the peripheral cells by neuronal and/ or hormonal signalling. First data report on the coherence of physiological and/ or physcological disturbances and diseases and the disruption of the circadian clock. Currently we are analyzing gene expression of the clock genes Per1 and Per2 in thirty healthy men before, during and after a psychosocial stress test as well as in a control situation. First data will be presented at the conference.

The effect of academic acceleration, on the socioemotional and the cognitive development of the gifted and talented children
Abrahim, Azza Dept. of Education, Al-Neelin Unversity, Khartoum, Sudan

The study aims to design a scale for measuring the effect of academic acceleration, on the socioemotional and the cognitive development of the gifted and talented children. Either by early admission or by grade skipping, in the Sudan. The subjects in the sample are (60) males 83.3%., Females 16.7%.The researcher used some statistical methods for processing data. Of these were the frequencies, percentage ratios, average standard deviation, T-Test, Pearson's Correlation Coefficient, and Spearman's Correlation Coefficient. (SPSS). The researcher found that, the measurement has showed high indicators of validity and reliability. This makes it a good measurement for the effect of academic acceleration on the socioemotional and cognitive development.

The relationship between long proceedings of divorce for a woman who acted to divorce; her mental health
Adibrad, Nastaran Dept. of Counseling Psychology, Shahid Beheshti University, Tehran, Islamic Republic of Iran Adibrad, Mojtaba Counseling Psychology, Abbas Abad-Sarfraz, Tehran, Islamic Republic of Iran

This search has been done on 60 women who had acted to divorce & they responded to General Health Questioner, some questions about their characteristics & the proceedings of their divorce. The result showed that the 32% of the reasons for women's divorced were physical abuses & 38% were husbands abnormal behaviors. There was a significiant relationship between the length of the divorce proceedings for woman & her depression (P<0.05) & anxiety (P<0.01). The result indicated that there was a relationship between the length of divorce proceedings & mental disorder in women who acted to divorce.

The effect of group cognitive behavioral training on self-esteem and mental health in infertile women
Aghaei Jeshvaghani, Asghar Khorasgan Branch, Islamic Azad University, Isfahan, Islamic Republic of Iran Atashpour, Sayed Hamid Psychology, University Khorasgan-Isfahan, Isfahan, Islamic Republic of Iran Khayatan, Shahin Psychology, University Khorasgan-Isfahan, Isfahan, Islamic Republic of Iran Almasi, Maryam Psychology, University Khorasgan-Isfahan, Isfahan, Islamic Republic of Iran

This study has addressed the effect of group cognitive-behavioral training on self-esteem and mental health in infertile women. The method was quasi-experimental. The statistical population was infertile women in Isfahan. The sample size comprised 15 subjects (treatment group) and 15 subjects (control group) selected randomly The treatment group only received 8 weekly sessions of cognitive-behavioral training. The measurement instrument comprised two questionnaires: Cooper Smith's self-esteem, mental health (GHQ).Results: The mean scores of self-esteem and mental health of the training group was significantly higher than the control group (P<0.0001).

Burnout (Emotional exhaustion) in doctors of two hospitals of the city of Lima: Peru
Aguilar Angeletti, Ana Dept. of Psychology, Cayetano Heredia University, Lima, Peru Gutierrez, Ramiro Psychology, Cayetano Heredia University, Lima, Peru Ojeda, GianCarlo Psychology, Cayetano Heredia University, Lima, Peru

Fifty-four doctors from two hospitals of Lima, Peru were studied in order to identify the relations between the three dimensions of Burnout (Emotional Exhaustion, Depersonalization and Personal Accomplishment), Social-Demographic-Labour Characteristics, and Working Environment. There is a greater presence of emotional exhaustion and depersonalization in men than in women, unmarried, contracted and internal of medicine of the hospitals. The dimension personal accomplishment appears with greater averages in women, married, named doctors and resident doctors. The working environment protects them of the emotional exhaustion, the depersonalization; and; it favours the personal accomplishment.

Relationship of worry and eating behaviors in young women
Ahlawat, Aditi Dept. of Psychology, Delhi University, Noida, India Singh, Jayshree Department of Psychology, MataSundri College for Women,, New Delhi, India

The participants in the study were divided into high and low worry groups on the basis of Student Worry Questionnaire-30(SWQ-30) and correlated with the Eating Attitude Test-26(EAT-26). 13.77 % of the sample showed unhealthy eating and 5% had highly abnormal eating behaviors; 30% indicated high-worry and 70% low worry levels; a significant difference (F = 7.281 at p < 0.01) between the groups on correlations of scores was found which established the relationship between the abnormal eating attitudes and high worry levels in the sample.

Geriatric centres: Emotional indicators older people

Aizpurua Sanz, Alaitz Psychology Faculty, University of Basque Country, San Sebastian, Spain Lizaso, Izarne Psychology, University of Basque Country, San Sebastian, Spain Sanchez de Miguel, Manuel Psychology, University of Basque Country, San Sebastian, Spain

Few studies have investigated systematically emotional situation of older adults living in geriatric centres. This study claims to analyze several emotional indicators of 121 older adults (89 females and 32 males, Mage = 82.21) from a geriatric centre. After examination of cognitive status (MMSE), anxiety (GADS, HAS) and depression (GADS, GDS/15) levels were tested in 56 participants. 21% showed sings of anxiety and 10% signs of depression. These results are consistent with findings of previous studies. Authors emphasize the need of psycho-affective intervention in these cases.

The search for adolescent health-related advice in the cyber space: An examination of online usage by Southern African youths

Akand, Bo GSB, The University, Marine Parade, South Africa Adebo, Will GSB, The University, Marine Parade, South Africa

In Africa, youths go online to look for information on sexuality and health; however, there is scanty of literature about the online usage of children. Following Borzekowski, Fobil and Ashante (2005, we explored and provided latest information, regarding online practice of youths in Maseru, Johannesburg and Tshwane, concerning gathering of internet-based literature on sexuality and health. Half of the population had gone online (50%) Of all these Internet users, 59% had sought online health information, and this percentage cut across in all the cities by gender, age, ethnicity. These youth revealed interest, high motivation, and positive perceptions of online health-related information.

When our memories fail us: Exploring the accuracy and inaccuracy of memory

Alberts, Joyce Dept. of Psychology, University of Canterbury, Christchurch, New Zealand

Objectives: Susceptibility to false memories was examined in relation to the ability to ignore irrelevant information. Specifically, whether children and adults demonstrating less-efficient inhibitory control produce more false memories. Method: Greater percentage of Stroop interference was classified as less-efficient inhibition, whereas lesser Stroop interference was classified as more-efficient inhibition. The intrusion of non-presented lure-words was classified as false memories. Results: Statistical analyses revealed less-efficient inhibitors produced significantly more false memories than more-efficient inhibitors. Conclusion: The results of this study provide evidential support for the hypothesis that inhibitory control plays a crucial role in memory, particularly in false memories.

The study of comparison between hardiness; multiple coping styles in MS (multiple sclerosis) patients Iranian

Aliakbari, Mahnaz Dept. of Psychology, Payame Noor University, Tehran, Islamic Republic of Iran Aliakbari Dehkordi, Mahnaz PSYCHOLOGY, PAYAME NOOR UNIVERSITY, TEHRAN, Islamic Republic of Iran

The main idea of following research is about different type of coping style and its relationship with coping style in multiple sclerosis patients. The number of cases is 102 all staying in Tehran and

supporting by MS society whom selected randomly To measure hardiness, inventory (Maddi& kobasa, 1984)) And coping style inventory with stress (Andler & parker 1990) have been used. Results are shown that the number of those patients who are using coping style in order to cover stress & also those who have a high rate of hardiness, are following problem .focused coping more than other group.

Comparative study of religious attitude's influence on mental health among residents of nursing homes and unresident aged

Aliakbari, Mahnaz Dept. of Psychology, Payame Noor University, Tehran, Islamic Republic of Iran Aliakbari Dehkordi, Mahnaz PSYCHOLOGY, PAYAME NOOR UNIVERSITY, TEHRAN, Islamic Republic of Iran Aghababaei, M. PSYCHOLOGY, PAYAME NOOR UNIVERSITY, TEHRAN, Islamic Republic of Iran

The main purpose of this research is a comparative study of resident aged and unhesitant aged in respect of mental health and the effect of religious attitude on it. In this research, a sample including of 100 persons of resident aged and unhesitant aged selected by the use of random sampling and available sample methods and studied with attention of purposes and assumptions. The measurement tools in this research were included General Health Questionnaire (GHQ = 12) and Religious Orientation Test. The result show there is significant relation between mental heath and religious attitude also there is significant difference between subjects.

Dimensions of school health from the teachers' point of view

Altenstein, Christine Inst. für Medizin. Psychologie, Universität Greifswald, Greifswald, Germany Wiesmann, Ulrich Western-Pomerania, Institute of Medical Psycholog, Greifswald, Germany Möbius, Kati Western-Pomerania, Institute of Medical Psycholog, Greifswald, Germany Hannich, Hans-Joachim Western-Pomerania, Institute of Medical Psycholog, Greifswald, Germany

We wanted to identify health relevant features of the school system from the teachers' point of view. 553 teachers filled out a 112-item questionnaire generated by a focus group. Using PCA, we found a four-component solution which accounted for 37.4% of the total variance. The components were interpreted as Cooperation at the workplace, Professionalization of handling work-related stresses and strains, Support during work-related stresses and strains and Organization of the school business. We conclude that interventions should be interdisciplinary and multidimensional instead of focusing specific needs at the individual teacher level.

Relationship between visuospatial impairment and facial recognition ability in parkinsons disease: Mediator variables

Amayra, Imanol Dept. of Psychology, University of Deusto, Bilbao, Spain Maranon, Daniel Dept. of Psychology, University of Deusto, Bilbao, Spain Martínez, Silvia Psychology, University of Deusto, Bilbao, Spain Uterga, Juan María Neurology, Basurto Hospital, Bilbao, Spain

The aim of the present study was to examine the role of processing speed (PS) and three executive function measures as mediators between visuospatial impairment and facial recognition ability in Parkinsons disease (PD) without dementia following the method described by Baron and Kenny (1986). The Judgment of Line Orientation Test (JLO), Benton Facial Recognition Test (BFRT), Five Point test, Verbal Fluency, Stroop Test and the Trail Making Test were administered to thirty PD patients and thirty matched normal controls. The results confirm the mediating role of PS and

three executive function measures in JLO and BFRT only in PD patients.

Social skill therapy for college student with social adjusment difficulty

Ambarini, Tri Kurniati Psychology, Airlangga University, Surabaya, Indonesia

social adjusment was crucial to gain mental health. people who cant do social adjusment expreience stress and deppression. This effect become more worst for Indonesian college student, which in transition phase from high school to college. the pressure not just from their self but also from environment. this research aim to improve the social skill of the student, so they can do social adjusment, through social skill therapy. these therapy applying using group therapy. the group consist 6 person who having same problem. their felt incapable to do social adjusment.

Emotional priming-of-popout in visual search

Amunts, Liana Psychology, Tel Aviv University, Tel Aviv, Israel Lamy, Dominique Psychology, Tel Aviv University, Tel Aviv, Israel

When searching for an unpredictable singleton along a simple dimension, target feature repetition speeds search, an effect known as Priming-of-Popout (PoP). We present the first report of emotional-PoP (ePoP). This effect occurred for valenced expressions, not for neutral ones. Target emotion repetition did not reduce search slopes, suggesting that ePoP does not affect attentional priority. While the face-in-the-crowd effect (FCE) - search slope reduction for angry relative to neutral faces - was similar with upright and inverted faces, face inversion eliminated ePoP. The contrast between ePoP and FCE challenges the notion that emotional salience cannot be dissociated from physical salience.

Anxiety, depression, somatic symptoms, social dysfunctions and social demographic variables as predictors of physical health in graduate students

Angelucci, Luisa Dept. de Psicología, Universidad Católica Andrés Be, Caracas, Venezuela

OBJECTIVE: Analyze the influence of gender, marital status, age, body mass index, smoking habits, anxiety, depression, somatic symptoms and social dysfunctions on physical health. METHOD: Using a non-experimental, cross-sectional design, a path analysis was performed on data from 631 graduate students in Universidad Católica Andrés Bello, Caracas, Venezuela. RESULTS: Low level of problems in physical health and depression, and moderate levels of anxiety, somatic symptoms and social dysfunctions were found. The gender, anxiety, somatic symptoms and social dysfunctions directly influenced physical health. CONCLUSION: Physical Health is explained through gender and mental health indicators.

Effects of error types on error negativity

Armbrecht, Anne-Simone Differential Psychologie, Universität Göttingen, Göttingen, Germany Gibbons, Henning Differential Psychol, Institute for Psychology, Göttingen, Germany Stahl, Jutta Differential Psychol, Institute for Psychology, Göttingen, Germany

According to response-conflict theory, the magnitude of error negativity (Ne/ERN) is associated with the strength of conflicting response processes. In an electrophysiological study, 30 participants performed a 3-digit flanker task, combined with an adaptive stop-signal paradigm. Due to number of conflicting responses and delayed response activation, Ne/ERN should vary with error types and with delay between digit and stop-signal onsets. Ne/ERN differences were not expected for single-errors (hand or stop errors), but between single- and double-errors (hand and stop errors), and for longer stop-signal delay, as well. The results supported aspects of response-conflict and reinforcement-learning theories of Ne/ERN. supported by DFG Sta 1035/1-1.

Exploring the construct validity and factor structure of the Persian translation of the Sternberg Triarchic Abilities Test (STAT) with Iranian students: Using confirmatory factor analysis

Asgari, Ali Educational Psychology, Tehran University, Tehran, Islamic Republic of Iran *Sadat Musavi, Parastoo* Psychology, Hesabi Research Institute, Tehran, Islamic Republic of Iran *Shahruzi, Razie Shahruzi* Psychology, Hessabi Research Institute, Tehran, Islamic Republic of Iran *Azizi, leila* Psychology, Hessabi Research, Tehran, Islamic Republic of Iran *Faraji, Hamidreza* Psychology, Hessabi Research institute, Tehran, Islamic Republic of Iran

The study aimed to investigate construct validity and factor structure of the Sternberg Triarchic Abilities Test (STAT) in Iranian population. 428 (133 male and 294 female) Iranian junior high students were measured using the STAT's grades 4-5. Using Cronbach's alpha coefficients for the test and Analytical, Practical and Creative subtests were .91, .83, .80 & .71 respectively. CFA results, based on LISREL, confirmed the STAT's construct validity and showed the second-order factor which added three first-order factors (the 9 sections) fit the data better and was aligned with Sternberg theory. The significance differences between the 3 grades of junior high students' means showed STAT's differential validity.

Alignment effects in spatial reasoning about described scenes

Avraamides, Marios Dept. of Psychology, University of Cyprus, Nicosia, Cyprus *Kelly, Jonathan* Psychology, Vanderbilt University, Nashville, USA *Kyranidou, Melina* Psychology, University of Cyprus, Nicosia, Cyprus

Objectives: The study examined the presence of encoding and retrieval alignment effects with reasoning about linguistically-encoded spatial locations. Methods: Participants encoded in memory object locations and then pointed to them from imagined perspectives. Testing occurred either in the same or in an adjacent room. Results: A performance advantage for the imagined perspective aligned with the learning orientation occurred in both testing conditions. An independent advantage for the perspective aligned with the orientation of the participants at test was present but only with same room testing. These findings document the presence of distinct alignment effects due to encoding and retrieval.

Internalizing disorders in dyslexic children

Bétrisey, Carine Department of Psychology, University of Fribourg, Fribourg, Switzerland *Ribeiro, Bruna* Department of Psychology, University of Fribourg, Fribourg, Switzerland *Leonova, Tamara* Department of Psychology, University of Fribourg, Fribourg, Switzerland

The study explores internalizing disorders in French-speaking dyslexic children. The assumption is that dyslexic children show higher depressive and anxiety scores than non-dyslexic. Non dyslexic children were compared to dyslexic children attending traditional school and dyslexic children attending special school. Their depression and anxiety were measured by the CDI and the R-CMAS. Results of the MANOVA did not reveal any difference in symptoms of dyslexics versus non-dyslexic children (Group F (10, 48) = .59 p > .05, Sex p > .05, interaction p > .05). There is no difference between internalizing symptoms in dyslexic and control children.

Stability of rater judgments in holistic and analytic essay-coding in primary school

Böhme, Katrin IQB, Humboldt-Universität zu Berlin, Berlin, Germany *Robitzsch, Alexander* IQB, HU Berlin, Berlin, Germany

The judgment of writing ability is an important aspect in the assessment of productive language skills in primary school. In a nationwide representative German sample of 3rd and 4th graders (N = 5.382) data of narrative, argumentative and informative writing were collected. Trained raters coded the student essays twice with a time-lag of approx. 12 weeks using a combined coding approach including analytic and holistic ratings. Findings of variance decomposition according to Generalizability theory as well as results of IRT-modeling show no systematic shifts over time but effects attributable to individual raters or single variables.

Risk and security perceptions during the FIFA World Cup 2006

Baasch, Stefanie Inst. für Psychologie, Universität Magdeburg, Magdeburg, Germany

The SWC 2006 was labeled as one of the major security challenge in Germany. In the public discussion the main fields of threat were terrorism, hooliganism and right-wing extremism. This contribution represents the results of an empirical study which compares estimations of local experts, the security discourse in the local media and official statements in governmental publications on the basis of a case study in Hamburg. It focuses on similarities and differences in risk perceptions, attitudes towards security measures as well as their legitimating. The study demonstrates the effect of event driven security policies.

Screening for clinical depression in Iranian post-MI patients with the Beck Depression Inventory for Primary Care

Bagherian, Reza Psychiatry, Isfahan Univ. of Med. Sciences, Isfahan, Islamic Republic of Iran

The purpose of this study was to ascertain psychometric properties of BDI-PC in screening for clinical depression in the post MI patients. The BDI-PC and Hospital anxiety and depression scale (HADS) were administered to 176 post MI. Also the structured interview for DSM-IV was used to diagnose clinical depression. Cronbach's alpha of the BDI-PC was 0.88, and the construct validity of BDI-PC was 0.86.8. A BDI-PC cutoff score of 5 and above yielded 91% maximum clinical efficiency with 84% sensitivity and 97% specificity rates, respectively, for identifying patients with and without clinical depression. The BDI-PC proved as an effective case-finding instrument for screening clinical depression among post-MI patients.

The effect of educational games on the IQ of the mentally retarded children

Bahrololoomi, Mohamad Hossein Shiraz, Islamic Republic of Iran

This research is an experimental one and its design is up to the pretest-post test,control group design with utilization of randomization. of 187 educable mentally retarded children seven to fourteen years old and living in Shiraz, 64 people were selected randomly,and according to Veksler's intelligence Test equalized into two matched groups: experimental and control.educational games were done in experimental group tests for 12 weeks. Results: 1.educational games caused,significantly,the IQ improvement of educatable mentally retarded children. 2.the people who made higher score of intelligence in primary test,showed more improved IQ at the end of the experimental course.

Are there effective smoking cessation interventions that help women remain smoke free?

Bahrs, Darlene Stop Smoking Program at SFGH, SF Department of Public Health, San Francisco, USA

Smoking rates for the general population in the USA have declined over the past 20 years, yet have increased for women (USDHHS, 2004). Additionally, there is evidence that women have less success quitting and remaining abstinent for longer periods of time than do men (Fiore, et al., 1989). The paper reviewed the literature on interventions that effectively help women quit smoking.Methods that appear most promising are telephone quit lines, proactive recruitment techniques, antidepressant medication, and comprehensive cessation programs. Research methodological limitations will be addressed. Future studies should give greater attention to relapse prevention efforts and the social and contextual conditions that reinforce smoking behavior.

Neural and cognitive mechanisms of addiction

Baker, Travis Dept. of Psychology, University of Victoria, Victoria, Canada *Holroyd, Clay Stockwell, Tim Barnes, Gordon*

Drawing on recent biologically inspired models of addiction, the specific aim of this project tested the hypothesis that many of the cognitive and behavioral impairments attributed to addiction result from the impact of abnormal reinforcement learning signals carried by the midbrain dopamine system on frontal brain areas involved in cognitive control and decision making. We propose that this disturbance of the dopamine system may result not only from extended drug abuse, but may exist even before the addiction develops in individuals who are at a high risk of becoming addicted. We tested this hypothesis with electrophysiological measures and Addiction Inventory data.

Coping strategies in two samples of Mexican adolescents living in poverty conditions

Barcelata, Blanca Psychology Faculty, National Autonomous University, México City, Mexico

The objective of the study was to assess coping strategies in adolescents with and without emotional problems living in poverty. The participants were 80 male and female adolescents, aged 13 to 17 years old, 40 adolescents attending mental health institute from a psychological services, and 40 high school adolescents from a public school. T Student values (1.245, p. 05) show significant differences. Adolescent with emotional problems use avoidant coping. The adolescent students use active strategies such as social support from pairs and family. The study confirms that avoidant strategies are related to psychological problems, and that active ones work as stress-environmental moderators, which might serve as help to mexican adolescents.

Nonshared environment in Russian adolescent twins

Barsky, Philipp Devlopmental Behavior Genetics, Psychological Institute of RAE, Moscow, Russia *Lobaskova, Marina* Devel. Behavior Genetics, Psychological Institute of RAE, Moscow, Russia *Gindina, Elena* Devlopmental Behavior Genetics, Psychological Institute of RAE, Moscow, Russia *Malykh, Sergey* Developmental Behavior Genetic, Psychological Institute of RAE, Moscow, Russia *Kobanov, Vladimir* Devlopmental Behavior Genetics, Psychological Institute of RAE, Moscow, Russia

There exists well documented evidence of genetic influence on measures of family environment (Plomin & Bergeman, 1991), as well as of importance of nonshared environment in development (Plomin & Daniels, 1987). However, no research of this kind was previously reported for Russian sample. We have collected scores on Russian version of Sibling Inventory of Differential Experience (SIDE: Daniels & Plomin, 1985) from Russian 11-17-years old monozygotic and dizygotic (of same-sex and of different-sex) twin pairs, 225 pairs in overall. Model-fitting was used to investigate genetic, shared environmental and nonshared environmental effects on SIDE factors.

Neural mechanisms underlying the integration of costs and benefits in decision making

Basten, Ulrike Inst. für Psychologie, Universität Heidelberg, Heidelberg, Germany *Biele, Guido* for Human Development, Max Planck Institute, Berlin, Germany *Stippich, Christoph* Neuroradiology, University of Heidelberg, Heidelberg, Germany *Heekeren, Hauke R.* for Human Development, Max Planck Institute, Berlin, Germany *Fiebach, Christian J.* Psychology, Neurology, University of Heidelberg, Heidelberg, Germany

Neural processes underlying cost-benefit integration in decision making were determined by identifying brain regions whose activity covaries with integration difficulty. Twelve subjects were trained to associate stimulus-characteristics with financial consequences and decided in a fMRI study to accept or reject three types of stimuli: pure gain, pure loss, or combinations of gain and loss. Decisions about combined outcomes activated medial and dorsolateral PFC. Decision difficulty modulated response times and brain activation independent of absolute gain- /loss-magnitude and behavioral choice. Easier integrative decisions were associated with increased ventromedial PFC activation, suggesting ventromedial PFC as a neural basis for cost-benefit integration.

The relationship between socio- economic status, physical health and perceived physical health

Bazzazian, Saeideh Human Science, Islamic Azad University, Abhar, Tehran, Islamic Republic of Iran *Rajaei, Yadollah* Human Science, Islamic Azad University, Abhar, Zanjan, Islamic Republic of Iran

This study investigated the relationship between socio-economic status (SES) (income, education, and occupation), physical health and perceived physical health. 150 employees completed physical Health Checklist (PLC) and demographic information form. Data were analyzed using One- Way ANOVA and Chi- Square. According to the results, there were significant relation between indexes of SES, physical health and perceived physical health. Significant differences were found between men and women in perceived physical health but not in physical health. Finding under sure the connection between SES and physical health and can be helpful in planning appropriate policies for promoting public health.

Social representations about inclusion in official documents and their implications on the implementation of inclusive public politics in education

Bellico da Costa, Anna Edith Mestrado em Educação, FAE / UEMG, Belo Horizonte, Brazil

Objectives: to identify the social representations regarding the inclusive public politics; b) to analyze current implications of these representations in implementation of inclusive actions. Methodology: bibliography research about social representations and documental analysis of the legislation on inclusion. Results: 1. multiple social representations about inclusion concept linked with some social exclusion; 2. the inclusion concept in the documents always goes from the passive acceptance of "segregation"; 3. punctual inclusive politics, contingencies for the exclusion; 4. education while "normalization" of the differences as inclusion instrument. Preview analysis of the practical social representations of them can facilitate the execution of inclusive politics.

Relationship between anxiety, depression, perceived exertion and level of physical function in patients undergoing routine rehabilitation after valvular heart replacement

Bertolotti, Giorgio Psychology, Maugeri Foundation, Tradate, Italy

Literature on valvular heart surgery patients contains almost no information on the role played by psychological variables on outcomes of in hospital multidisciplinary rehabilitation programme. Aims:explore relationship between anxiety, depression, perceived exertion and the level of physical function as measured by the 6-minutewalkingtest. SF-36assessed quality of life at 45days after discharge. 95patients were enrolled in a multidisciplinary rehabilitation programme led to significant improvement in metres walked at the 6MWT,RPE scores,STAI-XI and Depression Questionnaire (DQ) scores in both sexes and all age groups. Higher depression at the end of rehabilitation negatively influenced quality of life (SF36-PCS p=.006). Results recommends screening to assess depression in valvular heart surgery patients.

Socio-economic and academic correlates of Anaemia among adolescent girl students at secondary school level in rural India: A study

Berwal, Sandeep Dept. of Distance Education, Kurukshetra University, Kurukshetra, India

Out of thousand adolescent girls tested for Haemoglobin, 746 were found Anaemic. Incidence was significantly higher amongst those having low scholastic achievements, poor economic background, and illiterate mothers. No significant difference between urban and rural subjects was observed. Significant association of Anaemia with socio-economic status, poor school attendance, high drop-out rate, low academic achievement and mother's education indicates the need to develop strategies for intensive community education, better nutrition and diet, and awareness about regular intake of Iron-folic acid supplements during menstruation. The study has its implications for school administrators, health specialists, parents, government and community leaders.

Electroconvulsive Therapy (ECT): Attitudes, knowledge and experience of patients

Besani, Chiara Inst. of Neuroscience, Trinity College, Dublin, Ireland *Hevey, David* School of Psychology, Trinity College, Dublin, Ireland *Mangaoang, Maeve* Research, St. Patrick's Hospital, Dublin, Ireland *Lucey, Jim V.* ECT, St. Patrick's Hospital, Dublin, Ireland

Objectives: to examine the relationships between ECT patients' knowledge of the treatment, attitudes towards ECT, experience of side-effects, and perceived improvement in quality of life (QOL). Methods: Questionnaire data from a sample of 64 patients were analysed using standard multiple regression. Results: Although 87% of the sample experienced side-effects after ECT, almost 80% believed the treatment improved their QOL. Perceived improvement in QOL explained 20% (p<.05) of the variance in attitudes. Conclusion: Perceived improvements in QOL after ECT are associated with positive attitudes towards the treatment. Results are considered in relation to previous literature on attitudes towards ECT.

Psychological benefits of high self-complexity for women with and without children

Besta, Tomasz Dept. of Psychology, School of Social Psychology, Wejherowo, Poland *Barczak, Agata* Dept. of Psychology, School of Social Psychology, Wejherowo, Poland *Bazinska, Róza* Psychology, Warsaw School of Social Psycho, Sopot, Poland

The purpose of the study was to investigate the relationships between Self-Complexity (based on Linville's model) and various psychological variables linked to well-being. We hypothesized that those relationships may be moderated by the type of the group: young mothers (where one social role is salient) and young women without children. Sample consisted of 80 participants (40 mothers). Regression analysis showed Self-Complexity to be significant predictor of perceived increase of one's resources, Depression, Self-Esteem, Self-Reliance, perceived decrease of resources and emotional style of coping with stressful events. Last four results were moderated by the type of the group.

The strengths and difficulties questionnaire in a community sample of children and adolescents in Switzerland

Betrisey, Carine Dept. de Psychologie, Universite de Fribourg, Fribourg, Switzerland *Corpataux, Joanne* Department of Psychology, University of Fribourg, Fribourg, Switzerland *Leonova, Tamara* Department of Psychology, University of Fribourg, Fribourg, Switzerland

Our goal was to validate the French version of the Strengths and Difficulties Questionnaire completed by teachers (N = 574) of children and adolescents aged 6-16. SDQ is a brief measure for screening behavioural and emotional problems in children and adolescents aged 4 - 16. Our data provide evidence for five-factor solution. Internal consistency and interrater reliability of different subscales were found to be satisfactory. The results suggest that teacher-report form of the SDQ is a reliable screening measure for the purpose of identifying behavioural and emotional problems in a community sample of children and adolescents aged 6 - 16.

Non-invasive brain stimulation and psychology: New approaches on cognitive and behavioral investigations

Boggio, Paulo Psychology, Universidade Mackenzie, Sao Paulo, Brazil

Transcranial magnetic stimulation (TMS) and transcranial direct current stimulation (tDCS) are both non-invasive and painless techniques to modulate brain function that can be applied to conscious human being. Using these techniques, it is possible to generate virtual transient lesions in healthy people or modulate the brain activity, increasing or decreasing cortical excitability related to the stimulated areas. In this paper we present a series of studies in which broad aspects of psychology (such as neuropsychological functions (memory and executive functions) and behavior (response to emotional stimuli and food, alcohol and tobacco cue-induced craving)) have been evaluated following or during the application of TMS or tDCS.

The current state of parental alienation syndrome in Spain (PAS)

Bonasa Jimenez, Pilar Centre de Diagnostic Tarragona, Tarragona, Spain *Cartil Ferré, Conxita* FAMILY EXPERT WORKING TEAM, OFF. COLLEGE OF PSYCOLOGIST, Tarragona, Spain *Espada Sánchez, Carme* FAMILY EXPERT WORKING TEAM, OFF. COLLEGE OF PSYCOLOGIST, Tarragona, Spain *Adan Chavarria, Pilar* FAMILY EXPERT WORKING TEAM, OFF. COLLEGE OF PSYCOLOGIST, Tarragona, Spain *Punset Decoppet, Vanessa* FAMILY EXPERT WORKING TEAM, OFF. COLLEGE OF PSYCOLOGIST, Tarragona, Spain *López Carrillo, Andreu* FAMILY EXPERT WORKING TEAM, OFF. COLLEGE OF PSYCOLOGIST, Tarragona, Spain *López Novella, Judit* FAMILY EXPERT WORKING TEAM, OFF. COLLEGE OF PSYCOLOGIST, Tarragona, Spain *Checa Casado, Maria* FAMILY EXPERT WORKING TEAM, OFF. COLLEGE OF PSYCOLOGIST, Tarragona, Spain *Viola Pardina, Elena* FAMILY EXPERT WORKING TEAM, OFF. COLLEGE OF PSYCOLOGIST, Tarragona, Spain *Vázquez Orellana, Nuria* FAMILY EXPERT WORKING TEAM, OFF. COLLEGE OF PSYCOLOGIST, Tarragona, Spain

The target of our investigation is to know the state of PAS in Spain. The methodology to be followed consists in search for information about PAS until December 2007, through articles, associations, courses, bibliographies, opinions, court sentences, etc. Principally through the internet and on-line databases. Latterly a qualitative and quantitative analysis of the information will be carried out to determine its position with respect to the PAS controversy. Even though PAS is known in Spain, it's still a phenomena in process of evolution to consolidation. There's still no agreement between professionals about its existence as a syndrome.

Body and affect words: Valence, cognitive specificity and temporal change among young women

Bone, Meagan E. Dept. of Psychology, University of Ottawa, Ottawa, Canada Davis, Ron Psychology, Lakehead University, Thunder Bay, Canada Gomes, Lezlie Psychology, Lakehead University, Thunder Bay, Canada

This study examines the relationship between extreme attitudes and schematic functioning in the development eating disorders. Over the course of two phases (pre- and post-psychoeducational intervention) participants provided demographic information, valence ratings of stimulus words, and self-report ratings on measures of eating disorder symptomatology, affect, and self-esteem. A significant relationship between scores of eating disorder symptomatology, body mass index, and the valence and extremity ascribed to body-related stimuli was found. Additionally, self-esteem was found to moderate this relationship. Post-treatment assessment revealed that participants reported significant reductions in eating and body image concerns and rated "thin body" stimuli more moderately.

Longitudinal assessment of quality of life, coping and social support in women with breast cancer and their caregivers

Bonnaud-Antignac, Angélique ERSSCA, Faculty of Medicine, Nantes, France Sebille-Rivain, Véronique Biostatistiques, Faculty of Pharmacy, NANTES, France Hardouin, Jean-Benoit Biostatistiques, Faculty of Pharmacy, NANTES, France Hartmann, Anne LAUREPS/CRPCC, Université Rennes 2, RENNES, France

This study was conducted through the Regional Center Against Cancer in Loire-Atlantique (France). It focused on quality of life, coping and social support both in one hundred women treated surgically for breast cancer and their associated caregivers. Target psychological parameters were longitudinally evaluated before surgery, after radiotherapy/chemotherapy treatments, and six months later. Our first hypothesis was that the patient's quality of life is partially predictable by their "research of social support" coping dimension. Our second hypothesis was that a significant correlation exists in terms of coping between these patients and their caregivers, that was effectively confirmed by our results.

Interdisciplinary evaluation of 5th year medical students capabilities to announce cancer diagnosis based on simulated and filmed consultations

Bonnaud-Antignac, Angélique ERSSCA, Faculty of Medicine, Nantes, France Supiot, Stéphane Département de radiothérapie, CRLCC, NANTES, France Campion, Loïc Unité de Biostatistiques, CLCC, NANTES, France

This study was conducted on the Nantes University's Faculty of Medicine (France). It goal was to perform an interdisciplinary evaluation of the pedagogical objectives defined for 5th year's students, i.e. (1) memorize the 6-point protocol for disclosing a cancer diagnosis, (2) use appropriate communication techniques, (3) cope with

difficulties encountered in unsettling situation. This evaluation used dedicated questionnaires, simulated/filmed consultations, and real-time analyses by a physician/psychologist duet. Our hypothesis was that such integrated/interactive course may improve the self-assessed competences in the field of cancer diagnosis disclosure (patient-centred approach), which was demonstrated by our first results collected from 104 students.

Self-esteem as a resource for coping with developmental tasks in emerging adulthood

Born, Aristi Inst. für Psychologie, Universität Magdeburg, Magdeburg, Germany Krause, Daniela Department of Psychology, University of Magdeburg, Magdeburg, Germany

This study explores the significance of developmental tasks for emerging adults in Germany. It focuses on the ambivalent feeling of having reached adulthood (Arnett, 2000) as well as on self-esteem as a multidimensional resource that eases coping with these tasks and increases well-being. Regression and structural analyses based on the questionnaire data of 80 males and 80 females between 17 and 24 years old show e.g. that a stronger or weaker ambivalent feeling of adulthood predicts the various dimensions of self-esteem, the pattern of developmental tasks, and their predictive power for well-being in a differentiated way.

Testing the Caregiver Stress Model with the caregivers of children with Leukemia

Bozo, Özlem Psychology, Middle East Technical Uni., Ankara, Turkey Demirtepe, Dilek Psychology, Middle East Technical Uni., Ankara, Turkey

This study tests Caregiver Stress Model (Pearlin, et al., 1990) in caregivers of children with leukemia. According to model, primary stressors (caregiving tasks, problematic behaviors etc.) and secondary stressors (problems in daily life, interpersonal relationships etc.) impact on the health outcomes; and coping and social support mediate the process. Obtained data will be used to test six mediation models. The expected results are: (1) both primary stressors and secondary stressors will negatively affect outcome variables (depression, anxiety, general physical health), and (2) coping and social support will mediate the relationship between primary and secondary stressors, and the outcome variables.

The effect of dispositional optimism on posttraumatic growth: Testing the moderator role of ways of coping between dispositional optimism and posttraumatic growth in Turkish breast cancer patients

Bozo, Özlem Psychology, Middle East Technical Uni., Ankara, Turkey Büyüka, Canan Psychology, Middle East Technical Uni., Ankara, Turkey Gündo, Elçin Psychology, Middle East Technical Uni., Ankara, Turkey

This study examined the relationship between dispositional optimism and posttraumatic growth (PTG) in postoperative breast cancer patients and the moderator effect of coping strategies on this relationship. Participants were 104 women receiving postoperative chemotherapy/radiotherapy in hospitals. Hierarchical multiple regression analyses indicated that dispositional optimism predicts PTG; although both predicting PTG, compared to problem focused coping, emotion-focused coping has more power in predicting PTG; and the patients being in love are more likely to develop PTG. Nevertheless, coping strategies were not moderating the relationship between dispositional optimism and PTG. Strengths and limitations were discussed.

Ventromedial prefrontal cortex processing during emotional evaluation in late-onset depression: A longitudinal fMRI-study

Brassen, Stefanie Inst. Neurowiss. Systeme, UKE Hamburg-Eppendorf, Hamburg, Germany Kalisch, Raffael Inst. for Systems Neuroscience, UKE, Hamburg, Germany Weber-Fahr, Wolfgang Translational Imaging, ZI, Hamburg, Germany Braus, Dieter F. Psychiatry, HSK Wiesbaden, Wiesbaden, Germany Büchel, Christian Inst. for Systems Neuroscience, UKE, Hamburg, Germany

Objective: Given reported structural changes in aging we wondered whether highly prevalent but understudied late-onset depression (LOD) is accompanied by similar functional alterations in the ventromedial PFC (vmPFC) as observed in younger patients. Method: A homogeneous sample of LOD patients and healthy controls were scanned during emotional evaluation using fMRI. LOD patients were rescanned after 7 months. Results: LOD patients showed an altered pattern of vmPFC functioning which was positively correlated with disease severity and which had normalised at follow-up. Conclusions: These findings indicate vmPFC dysfunction as a biological state marker of geriatric depression.

Influences on the civic engagement of adolescents in Thailand

Braverman, Marc HDFS, Corvallis, USA Sutabutra, Harin Secretariat, Thailand Parliament, Bangkok, Thailand

Objectives: To investigate influences of parenting, school characteristics, media exposure, and traditional Thai cultural variables on adolescents' civic engagement in Thailand. Methods: Stepwise regressions on group-administered data from 1,105 students, 15-18, in Bangkok. Dependent variables: civic knowledge, skills, attitudes, participation. Independent variables: parents' civic attitudes, parenting practices, school characteristics, media exposure, cultural values of respect, group cohesion, wisdom. Results: Thai cultural values predicted components of engagement most strongly. Other independent variables significantly predicted aspects of civic attitudes, participation, engagement. Conclusions: Development of adolescents' civic engagement differs in Thailand compared to Western societies. Cross-national research on youth civic engagement should incorporate cultural characteristics.

The structure of the causal attribution belief network of patients with obesity

Brogan, Amy School of Psychology, Trinity College Dublin, Dublin, Ireland Hevey, David School of Psychology, Trinity College Dublin, Dublin, Ireland

Objectives: To explore the structure of causal attributions in 72 (22 male, 50 female) obese individuals. Methods: Participants completed a questionnaire based on the matrix grid network analysis technique. Inductive Eliminative Analysis and multidimensional scaling were used to produce the network. Results: 70% of participants endorsed the network, which indicated Traumatic events, Family Problems, and Addictive personality were perceived as distal causes of Over-eating and Comfort eating, while More passive behaviours, Less physical activity, Over-eating, and Comfort eating were proximal causes of Obesity. Family history did not contribute. Conclusions: Obese individuals hold a highly consensual and complex representation of obesity.

Reasons for misdiagnosis of bipolar disorder

Bruchmueller, Katrin Klin. Kinder- u. Jugendpschol., Universität Basel, Basel, Switzerland Meyer, Thomas D. School of Neurology, Neurobiol, Newcastle University, Newcastle, United Kingdom

Objectives: Bipolar disorders are often not recognized. It was hypothesized that this occurs because clinicians do not strictly adhere to DSM-IV criteria. Instead, subjective explanations for manic symptoms ("being in love") and the absence of a prototypic symptom ("reduced sleep") may increase the likelihood of misdiagnosis. Methods: A case vignette was sent to 400 psychotherapists. This vignette described a case of bipolar disorder but was varied in respect to the two factors named above. Results and Conclusion: Both subjective explanations and the absence of prototypic symptoms influenced the frequency of misdiagnosis.

Effect of acute exercise on the concentration of testosterone in the salvia and the reaction to fearful faces in high school students

Budde, Henning Department of Movement, Institute of Sportscience, Berlin, Germany Pietrassyk-Kendziorra, Sascha Department of Movement- and Tr, Institute of Sportscience, Berlin, Germany Voelcker-Rehage, Claudia Department of Movement- and Tr, Institute of Sportscience, Berlin, Germany

Several studies show decreased anxiety reactions after an acute aerobic physical stress. Cognitive functions in students are negatively affected by fear (Aronen et al., 2005). The response to threatening stimuli appears to be dependent on the testosterone concentration (Schultheiss & Wirth 2007). In our study we questioned whether a standardized exercise performed in school breaks can lower anxious behaviour (test: dot probe; measuring atten-tional bias; fearful faces vs. neutral) and improve cognitive performance (d2-test, Letter-Digit-Span) compared to control and whether these changes are dependent on the testos-terone levels in the salvia. The study included 25 students of the 9th grade.

A web-based quality control system for assessment processes

Busana, Gilbert EMACS Research Unit, University of Luxembourg, Walferdange, Luxembourg Koenig, Vincent EMACS research unit, University of Luxembourg, Walferdange, Luxembourg Martin, Romain EMACS research unit, University of Luxembourg, Walferdange, Luxembourg Latour, Thibaud Technologies de l'information, CRP Henri Tudor, Luxembourg-Kirchberg, Luxembourg Plichart, Patrick CITI department, CRP Henri Tudor, Luxembourg, Luxembourg Jadoul, Raynald CITI department, CRP Henri Tudor, Luxembourg, Luxembourg

At a time where more and more education systems are heading towards output-oriented systems, the existence and availability of high quality assessment instruments for an ever-growing variety of measurable competencies becomes more and more important. As these assessment instruments will be the most important steering instruments in output-oriented systems, the question of the quality of these instruments but also the question of the quality of the assessment process into which these instruments are embedded has to be risen. The aim of this communication is to present a quality control system for assessment processes integrated into a computer based testing platform (TAO).

Perceptions of vulnerability and preparedness for terrorism and emergencies: A preliminary Australian study

Caponecchia, Carlo School of Safety Science, University of New South Wales, Sydney, Australia

The perception that "it won't happen to me" has been identified as a significant challenge for counter terrorism efforts in Australia. The current study examines perceptions of Sydney residents regarding the likelihood of personally experiencing emergency events (terrorism, natural disasters), compared to the likelihood of others in Sydney, and other parts of Australia, experiencing these events. The degree to which personal perceptions of vulnerability is related to knowledge of local emergency plans and degree of personal preparations was also assessed.

Data will be discussed in terms of the importance of personal risk perception in managing a community's emergency response.

Construct validation of a graduating examination for psychologists

Castañeda Figueiras, Sandra Postgraduate Psychology, National Autonomus University, México City, Mexico

With answers from 456 clinic psychologists, 231 educative and 255 labour psychologists to major graduating examination, construct validity for cognitive demand and cultural background features was established. By means of a confirmatory factorial analysis, the models generated practical fit indexes that back them up: in clinic psychology seven levels of cognitive demands that explained the 89.2% of the variance were validated (IBBAN=.91, IBBANN=.89, CFI=.92 0 and RMSEA=0.08); educational psychology model validated five that explained 87% (IBBAN=.93, IBBANN=.97, IAC=.97 and RMSEA=0.06) and labour model validated five, explaining 99% of the variance (IBBAN=.93, IBBANN=.97, CFI=.97 and RMSEA=0.06). Cultural background indirectly explained scores.

Personality traits moderate the impact of chronic stress on depression-like behaviors and hippocampal neurogenesis

Castro, Jorge Brain and Mind Institute, EPFL, Lausanne, Switzerland Varea, Emilio Histology Department, UMH, San Juan de Alicante, Spain Marquez, Cristina Brain and Mind Institute, EPFL, Lausanne, Switzerland Cordero, Maria Brain and Mind Institute, EPFL, Lausanne, Switzerland Sandi, Carmen Brain and Mind Institute, EPFL, Lausanne, Switzerland

Emerging evidence in humans and rodents has associated the anxiety trait with both resilience and vulnerability to stress-induced depression. We hypothesize that a combination of personality traits might help characterizing predispositions to develop depression-like alterations and changes in hippocampal neurogenesis following chronic stress. Sprague-Dawley rats were behaviorally characterized and three principal traits identified and named: anxiety, exploration and activity. After exposure to chronic stress, depression-like behaviors and hippocampal neurogenesis were evaluated. The results indicate that both the direction and intensity of the impact of stress on behavior are dependent on traits configuration and correspond to different patterns of neurogenesis impairment.

Perceived stress and licit psychoactive substance consumption among employees

Cerclé, Alain Sciences Humaines/Psychologie, Université Haute Bretagne, Rennes, France Pain, Karine Sciences Humaines/Psychologie, Université Haute Bretagne, Rennes cedex, France

Many studies reveal (Cooper, 1991 ; Cerclé, 1998 ; Burck, 2002) undoubted relations between usual stress and licit psychoactive substance uses (alcohol, tobacco, medicine..). However, the direct link between the event stressors and the substance consumption is not clearly demonstrated. But, the transactional stress models or the substance use models (Lazarus, 1993 ; Frone, 1999) both show the mediator role of a cognitive variable : the perceived stress. That's what our study, realised in France, in the hospital field (n = 203 employees), confirms, according to the statistic methods of factorial analysis.

Superficial processing in question-answering activities

Cerdan, Raquel Faculty of Psychology, Catholic University Valencia, Valencia, Spain Gilabert, Ramiro Faculty of Psychology, University of Valencia, Valencia, Spain

Some strategies to answer questions (i.e., copying verbatim information corresponding to the wording of the question) are not always helpful to find the right answer. We designed an experiment manipulating questions and texts so that the wording of half of the questions corresponds to sentences in the text, but these do not have the right answer. 40 secondary school students were measured on comprehension level and then performed a question-answering task. Preliminary data show that in half of the manipulated questions poor level comprehension students copied the information from the wrong locations, without awareness of the correction of their answers.

The assessment of the quality of the learning outcome in vocational courses

Cervai, Sara Dept. of Political Sciences, University of Trieste, Trieste, Italy Fabbro, Barbara Anna Political Sciences, University of Trieste, Trieste, Italy Cian, Luca Political Sciences, University of Trieste, Trieste, Italy

Inside Leonardo da Vinci Action, it has been developed a theoretical model aimed to analyze the learning outcome of HTE courses (Higher Technical Education). It takes in consideration the variety of the stakeholders and the role of the expectations in order to evaluate quality. We used both customer satisfaction both service quality strategies to assess the quality level. Focus groups, semi structured interviews, and questionnaires were used to test different indicators of the learning outcome. Particular attention was given to the influence of the Image of the school. The model was tested inside schools from 5 countries (Italy, Slovenia, Spain, Lithuania and Bulgaria).

Peculiarities of investigative interviews in child sexual abuse cases: Lithuanian perspective

Cesniene, Ilona Department of Psychology, Mykolas Romeris University, Vilnius, Lithuania Grigutyte, Neringa Department of Psychology, Vilnius University, Vilnius, Lithuania

Forensic interviewing of children in an adapted for child's needs interview room started in Lithuania only three years ago. The aim of this study is to explore the experience of investigative interviewing of children alleged in sexual abuse. 50 videotaped interviews were analyzed with regard to verbal and nonverbal behavior of children. The effectiveness of interviews depending on children's willingness to testify, question type and complexity, stage of interview and some other variables as well as implications for further practice are discussed.

Who comes first? Balance and emotional ambivalence

Chang, Yenping Department of Psychology, National Taiwan University, Taipei, Taiwan Lin, Yicheng Department of Psychology, National Taiwan University, Taipei, Taiwan Huang, Chinlan General Education, NTUST, Taipei, Taiwan Cheng, Yi Department of Psychology, National Taiwan University, Taipei, Taiwan Chen, Mengting Inst. of Behavioral Medcine, National Cheng Kung University, Tainan City, Taiwan

What would you like to do if you win a 500-million-dollar lottery prize? In the current study, participants were asked to prioritize their top three choices imagining if they do win the prize. These responses were then classified into 3 categories, including instant pleasure, altruism, and prolonged pleasure. Their attachment tendencies were also measured. Results showed if one chose to take instant pleasure at beginning, he/she would show the highest ambivalent score. However, if one took instant pleasure at last, his/her ambivalence score lowered significantly. The findings supported that orderly balancing the self and "something bigger than the self" reduced emotional ambivalence in life effectively.

Effects of intrinsic and extrinsic cues on judgments of learning

Chen, Gongxiang Dept. of Psychology, University of Jinan, Jinan, People's Republic of China Fu, Xiaolan Division of Cognitive Psycholo, Institute of Psychology, Beijing, People's Republic of China

Four experiments were conducted to examine the effects of the intrinsic cue (relatedness) and the extrinsic cues (presentation order and presentation time) on judgments of learning (JOLs) by using paired-associate learning. These cues were presented in three modes: between-participants, blocked-list, and mixed-list. The results showed that relatedness influenced JOLs no matter how it was presented. The time required to produce judgments was longer for unrelated items than for related items, which suggested that a mnemonic cue, namely ease of processing, might exert influence on JOLs. The effects of extrinsic cues were unstable in the present four experiments.

Prevalence of insomnia of nursing and midwifery students

Cheraghi, Fatemeh Faculty of Nursing, Hamadan University of Medical, Hamadan, Islamic Republic of Iran Shamsaei, Farshid nursing, Hamedan University of medical, Hamedan, Islamic Republic of Iran

Objectives: The aim of this study was to assess the prevalence of sleeping problems in the nursing and midwifery students. Methods: This research is a descriptive study. The participants consist of 321 individual were selected by census sampling. Data were collected by questionnaire. Results: Nearly one-fourth of suffered nursing and midwifery students from insomnia. The percentage was significantly higher among women (28.1%) than among Men (18.1%). Conclusion: Sleep disorders distracted the physical and mental health of student's Emotional stress and anxiety are some factors of sleep disorders, with recognizing these factors, we can operate effective interventions.

Alexithymia and basic hope among prisoners

Chmielewska, Anna Inst. for Social Studies, University of Warsaw, Warsaw, Poland Wawrzyniak, Malgorzata Psychology, SWPS, Warsaw, Poland

The purpose of the research was to determine the level of alexithymia and basic hope among prisoners. Study 1 included male and Study 2 included female inmates. The test subjects have been divided into three groups according to their end of isolation perspectives defined as the beginning, middle or end of the incarceration period. It was found that the level of basic hope is high. The high level of alexithymia in both tests differs depending on the end of isolation perspectives, but the higher level has been found in group, which have been in the middle of the incarceration period.

Assessment style and learning motivation

Cocorada, Elena Psychology, University Transilvania, Brasov, Romania Luca, Marcela Rodica Psychology, University Transilvania, Brasov, Romania

Article presents a bi-dimensional model of the evaluative behaviors with the axis: the degree of Exigency and the Direction of assessment. The evaluation styles are categorized in normative, formative, populist, and conventional. The perceived evaluative styles of five teachers were measured by 385 students in relationship with their learning motivation. The formative and the conventional perceived styles are associated with the perception of the task control; populist perceived style is associated with extrinsic motivation; normative style is associated with intrinsic motivation. There are differences between the perceptions of the students in the same class according to their learning performances.

Factorial structure of the screen for child anxiety related emotional disorders

Cosi, Sandra psicologia, universitat rovira i virgili, Tarragona, Spain Canals, Josepa psicologia, universitat rovira i virgili, Tarragona, Spain Chico, Eliseo psicologia, universitat rovira i virgili, Tarragona, Spain Vigil, Andreu Psicologia, Universitat Rovira i Virgili, Tarragona, Spain

The SCARED is a wide used self-reported instrument to screen anxiety disorders and to diagnose the different types of anxiety disorders, Nevertheless different studies have shown that there is a lack of consensus about their factorial structure. We administered SCARED to a sample of 1490 children and split the sample into two random subsamples used for exploratory (EFA) and confirmatory factor analysys (CFA). EFA on one subsample showed a four factor structure that was confirmed by a restricted CFA on the other subsample The factorial structure of SCARED seem to replicate the four categories of anxiety disorders proposed by DSM-IV.

Undergraduate students' attitudes towards online versus face-to-face counseling

Cui, Lixia Psychology, Beijing Normal University, Beijing, People's Republic of China

[Abstract] Objective: To study undergraduates' attitudes towards online versus face-to-face counseling and accele- rate their changes. Methods: We sent 608 questionnaire packets including four scales to five universities to investia- te the undergraduate Students' attitudes towards online versus face-to-face counseling to examined the influence of gender,grades, experience (ever counseling or never), and personal psychological variables (i.e., stigma, social anxiety,and self-concealment) on these two kinds of attitudes. Results: The stigma, self-consealment and communication apprehension could predict attitude towards face- to-face counseling, but they could not predict attitudes towards online counseling. Conclusion: Online counseling can alleviate risk factors and promote students' asking help behaviors.

Voters' susceptibility to a multidimensional attractiveness-gender bias in electoral politics

Dörfler, Rebecca Neufahrn, Germany Agthe, Maria Department of Psychology, Ludwig-Maximilians-University, Munich, Germany Spörrle, Matthias Department of Psychology, Ludwig-Maximilians-University, Munich, Germany Försterling, Friedrich Department of Psychology, Ludwig-Maximilians-University, Munich, Germany

Since elections are of high societal importance, we tested whether voter and candidate characteristics bias voting decisions. Using a 2 (respondent sex) X 2 (stimulus person sex) X 3 (stimulus person attractiveness: high, average, low) between-subjects design, participants (N = 173) evaluated fictitious candidates on various scales. Consistent with hypotheses derived from evolutionary psychology and previous findings (FPA, 2007), analyses yielded a three-way interaction indicating an overall preference for attractive opposite-sex candidates, while favoring less attractive same-sex targets. Implications for elections are discussed.

Subjective well being on young adult and relatedness to emotional intelligence, optimism and self esteem

Dachlan, Rostiana Dept. of Psychology, Tarumanagara University, Jakarta, Indonesia

This research is aimed to describe subjective well being (SWB) on young adult based on personality characteristics, such as Emotional Intelligence, Self Esteem and Optimism. Data were collected from 160 university students by using questionnaires and to be analyzed based on statistic techniques. The results showed the level of SWB participants is high (mean = 3,096, SD = 0,2644; the range of the scale

is 4). The connection between personality characteristics and SWB is significant { F(3,1.706) = 45,905; p<0,01} and all independent variables accounted 47% to SWB. This research also found the modes of positive affect participants is 'blessing' and the modes of negative affect is 'confusing'.

Effect of social and family factors on committing suicide among university students in Iran

Dadkhah, Asghar Dept. of Clinical Psychology, University of Welfare & Rehab., Tehran, Islamic Republic of Iran Pourmohammadi, Moloud Lolagar hospital, University of Iran Medical sci, Tehran, Islamic Republic of Iran Motamedi, Seyyed Hadi clinical psychology, University of welfare & Re, Tehran, Islamic Republic of Iran

Committing suicide among the young people, especially university students is a great social problem. It is also a matter of concern for mental health specialists. The aim of this study is to investigate the relationship between social and family factors and the idea of committing suicide among university students in Iran. 100 university students (50 male, 50 female) from University of Welfare and Rehabilitation sciences were randomly selected and participated in the study. The samples were taken randomly. So it was found out that the singles were more inclined to commit suicide than the married ones. Divorce, failure in education, and family background also increase it. Among the other increasing factors old age and female sex should be indicated

Prediction of the school performance following from the WISC–III test

Dan, Jiri Dept. of Psychology, Faculty of Art and Letters, Ruzomberok, Slovak Republic

The WISC-III test was localized on the population in the Czech Republic. The sample of the population covered 1455 children at the age of 6;0 to 16;11, 1015 of them were pupils of the elementary schools. In our survey the school performance is represented by the average marks, the mark in maths and the teachers evaluation of loud reading. The multiple stepwise regression analysis method was used. The value and importance of the subtests in WISC-III, Czech Edition as predictors of the school performance varies in the individual years.

The impact of Transactional Analysis (T.A) method on increasing self-knowledge and marital compatibility of incompatible couples

Danesh, Esmat psychology, shahid behashti, Karaj, Islamic Republic of Iran Saliminia, Narguesse psychology, shahid behashti, tehran, Islamic Republic of Iran

The aim of this pseudo-experimental research was to determine the effect of the Transactional Analysis method on increasing marital compatibility of incompatible couples. 14 married couples were chosen among the couples were volunteer, and randomly assigned to experimental and control groups. Spanier's dyadic adjustment scale and the questionnaire of self-knowledge were used as the research tools. The results indicated that: the Transactional Analysis, increased self-knowledge and marital compatibility of the experimental group compared to pretreatment and compared to the control group, and activates behaviors derived from adult ego-state more than behaviors derived from the parent and the child ego-states.

Dissociation major risk factor for the development of secondary traumatization

Daniels, Judith Kinder- und Jugendpsychiatrie, Universitätsklinik Hamburg, Hamburg, Germany

Objectives: The role of dissociative processing in the development of secondary traumatization was investigated. Methods An online-study was conducted with a sample of German-speaking therapists (n=1.124). Secondary traumatization was measured with a German questionnaire (FST, α =.94). Peritraumatic dissociation was evaluated with a set of items derived from scientific literature (PD, α=.79). Results The two instruments correlate with Kendall-Tau-b = .390 (p < .000). The effect size for this correlation is .85. PD predicted FST scores in a hierarchical regression analysis with R2=.29. Conclusions Ideosyncratic peritraumatic processing of client's trauma material predicts secondary traumatization better than work setting, work experience or education. Specialized supervision is advised.

Improving metacognitive monitoring and regulation by means of collaborative tests

de Carvalho Filho, Moises Kirk Kyoto University, Kyoto, Japan

This study investigated the effects of metacognitive skills, test types, and test social conditions on students' test performances and monitoring processes. Undergraduates were categorized according to their metacognitive skills and had their test performances and monitoring processes in two types of tests compared in individual and collaborative test conditions. Results showed that low-metacognitive students' monitoring was improved when tests were taken collaboratively. Consequently, although in individual tests, high-metacognitive students presented higher performance and confidence, those differences disappeared when students took tests collaboratively. The discussion focuses on the results' educational implications and gives specific suggestions on how to improve academic assessment.

The place of the clinical psychology in our time: Singularities in the world of globalization

de Farias, Francisco Ramos Fundamentos da Educ., UNIRIO / PPGMS, Rio de Janeiro, Brazil Tarré de Oliveira, Gilsa F. Depto de Psicologia, UNESA, Rio de Janeiro, Brazil

Objectives: reflections about the uses of transference in the clinic experience nowadays. Methods: rescue freudian's concept of transference: an obstacle in the course of the speech, full of passion, but also full of the presence of the analyst. Results: transference, if used properly, can be an effective tool: allow pacients to reexperience and reenact old singular feelings through the relationship with their therapist. Conclusions transference is a key point that can orientate our practice according its ethical proposal: preserve the singularity of the subject. It's worthwhile to remember Freud's recommendation: individual psychology can't be separated of social psychology.

The aesthetic of suffering and of satisfaction in psychological clinic of contemporaneousness

de Farias, Francisco Ramos Fundamentos da Educ., UNIRIO / PPGMS, Rio de Janeiro, Brazil

Objectives: Starting from in inquiry on the situations of clinic experience in the current times, it points to analyse the changes of the psychological clinic of news symptoms. Method: Suffering and satisfaction are analysed for distinct tracks: in the history of patient and on enjoyment of caption of aesthetic pain as experience pleasant. Results: It was found that the pain is reverted in pleasure and the suffering changes in satisfaction on the life experiences. Conclusions: Sublimation, joy and pain are devices that define the life in contemporary age. The symptoms present a aesthetic based on forgotten of differences.

Psychological peculiarities of political socialization of students

Dembitska, Natalia Dep. of Social Psychology, G.S. Kostyuk Institute, Kyiv, Ukraine

The investigation exposes the political socialization as a process of forming and development of personalities political qualities, which is based on the interiorization of the semantic-symbolic order of the Ukrainian political culture and the next subject-object personality realization in relationships with political authority. These relationships must be based on constructive partner principals. The presupposition about contradictory of student's political representation maintenance in conditions of political system's transformations and the hypothesis about ties between semantical-symbolical characteristics of political representations and peculiarities of psychological involving in the political life of students has been confirmed.

A meta-analysis of neuroimaging studies reporting Amygdala Activation

Derix, Johanna Epilepsie-Zentrum, Universität Freiburg, Freiburg, Germany Wentlandt, Johanna Epilepsy Center, University of Freiburg, Freiburg, Germany Mutschler, Isabella Department of Psychiatry, University of Basel, Basel, Switzerland Eickhoff, Simon C&O Institute, University of Düsseldorf, Düsseldorf, Germany Schulze-Binhage, Andreas Ball, Tonio Epilepsy Center, University of Freiburg, Freiburg, Germany

Amygdala function is in the focus of interest of many neuroimaging studies, in particular in the context of emotion research. We have conducted a coordinate-based meta-analysis of previous neuroimaging studies reporting amygdala activation, determining the probability of reported activation peaks to belong to the amygdala using a probabilistic map (Amunts et al., 2005). We find that 1/3 of reported amygdala peaks are not probabilistically assigned to the amygdala complex, but to neighboring structures, including the hippocampus. Therefore, across studies, previously reported amygdala activation most likely represents a mixture of true amygdala responses and of responses originating from outside the amygdala.

Psychological aspects involved in drug allergy

Diaconescu, Liliana Veronica Dept. of Medical Psychology, University of Medicine, Bucharest, Romania

Objective: Analysis of some of the psychic factors involved in allergic type reactions. Methods: In the study were included 55 patients with drug allergic type reactions and 55 patients with no drug allergy. The subjects underwent the tests: Hospital Anxiety and Depression Scale, Perceived Stress Scale, Life Event Stress Scale. Results: The patients with drug allergy present a higher anxiety score (77%), a higher grade of depression (54%), higher scores at Life Event Stress Scale (with many stressful events in precursory months before the drug allergy) and also elevated scores of perceived stress. Conclusions: Personality traits, such as stress vulnerability, individual reactivity to stress, anxiety, depression and phobia have a certain influence upon the allergic reactions.

Attentional mechanisms in the generation of sympathy

Dickert, Stephan Max Planck Institute, Bonn, Germany Slovic, Paul Psychology, Decision Research, Eugene, USA

The effects of emotions on attention are well documented, but the effects of attention on emotions have only recently been studied (Fenske & Raymond, 2006). We tested whether sympathy depends on the ability to visually attend to victims in need. In a 2x2 repeated-measures design, participants expressed more sympathy for victims shown alone (vs. part of a group) and when sympathy judgements were made online (while attending) vs. from memory. Our results indicate that attentional mechanisms are an ingredient in the generation of sympathy, and have important implications for theoretical and applied research on attention, emotion, and charitable behavior.

Blood Pressure and pain: The everyday suffering in hypotension

Dietel, Anja Biological Psychology, Ludwig Maximilians University, Munich, Germany Duschek, Stefan Biological Psychology, Ludwig Maximilians University, Munich, Germany Schandry, Rainer Biological Psychology, Ludwig Maximilians University, Munich, Germany

Recent studies have shown that hypotension is accompanied by higher sensitivity to experimental pain. This study investigated whether these findings can be confirmed by the everyday experience of pain. Twenty-nine hypotensive and 33 normotensive participants of a study assessing laboratory heat pain sensitivity additionally rated everyday pain experienced over the last 2 months. Hypotensives did not report a higher frequency, but significantly higher mean everyday pain intensity and impairment than normotensives (T-test). Correlation analysis revealed a significant association between laboratory pain sensitivity and everyday pain. Results underline that a condition that is commonly perceived as beneficial may deserve clinical attention.

The effect of the guilty movement polygraph tests on lie detection: A variation of the guilty knowledge test

Ding, Xiaopan Psychology,School of Education, Zhejiang Normal University, Jinhua, People's Republic of China Fu, Genyue psychology,shool of education, Zhejiang Normal University, Jinhua, People's Republic of China Ma, Yan psychology,shool of education, Zhejiang Normal University, Jinhua, People's Republic of China

This study developed a new variation of Guilty Knowledge Test (GKT) - Guilty Movement Test (GMT) which is based on the feature-matching theory and emphasizing the criminal action of the guilt. Thirty-six subjects were randomly assigned to one of the 3 experimental groups – guilty, innocent, and innocent knowledgeable of the crime. Study results indicated that the GMT not only improved the accuracy of judging the innocent knowledgeable group(75%)but remained highly accurate in judging the innocent(91.7%)and guilty (100%) groups as well.

Emotions affected attention performance in adolescents with learning disabilities

Dong, Yan Institute of Psychology, Renmin University of China, Beijing, People's Republic of China Yu, Guoliang Institute of Psychology, Renmin University of China, Beijing, People's Republic of China

Using feedback of performance induced emotions, this study examined emotions affected performance of selective and sustained attention in adolescents with learning disabilities. Experiment 1 examined emotions affect on selective attention using visual search task. Experiment 2 examined emotions affect on sustained attention using CPT-AX task. The results showed that: (a) Subjects had better selective attention performance in positive low-arousal emotions than in negative emotions. (b) Subjects with negative high-arousal emotions had more errors of commission and less inhibit ability than those with other emotions for sustained attention. The positive high-arousal emotions upgraded the β value and consumed more cognitive resources.

The emotion evoking effect of emotional faces in challenging cognitive tasks

Dong, Guangheng Department of Psychology, Liaoning Normal University, Dalian, People's Republic of China Yang, Lizhu Department of Psychology, Liaoning Normal University, Dalian, People's Republic of China Shen, Yue Department of Psychology, Liaoning Normal University, Dalian, People's Republic of China

Event-related potentials were used to study the emotion evoking effect of emotional faces in different conditions. The Participants (13 normal adults) performed two kinds of tasks. In the first task, there were pictures of single face they had to focus on, but don't need to react. The second task, they had to decide whether faces presented in pairs were same or different, and press relative keys immediately. In task one, significant main effect was found for different emotional faces (positive, neutral, negative); but in task two, no significant main effect was found. We gave a deep discussion about the results.

How much suspense is good for the recipe?

Dreisörner, Thomas Pädagogische Psychologie, GEMI für Psychologie, Göttingen, Germany Sickert, Janine Pädagogische Psychologie, GEMI für Psychologie, Göttingen, Germany

We compare two computer based test procedures for the diagnosis of attention deficit hyperactivity disorder (ADHD) in children. Thirty children diagnosed with ADHD and a control group completed the "Testbatterie zur Aufmerksamkeitsprüfung" (TAP, Zimmermann & Fimm, 1993) and the adapted version for children called KI-TAP(2005). In contrast to the TAP the KITAP exhibits a more suspenseful user interface. Our study examines if both test procedures differentiate well between children with and without ADHD. We discuss the criteria a test procedure for diagnosing children with ADHD need to satisfy.

Peer pressure or social support?: An empirical analysis of internet-based self-injury support groups

Eichenberg, Christiane Inst. für Klin. Psychologie, Universität zu Köln, Köln, Germany

Self-injuring (SI) adolescents using online-groups are viewed with concern because of possible detrimental effects on coping. To assess the impact of SI-forums, an online-study was conducted with N=300 adolescents. Focus was to survey subjective impact of these forums, relationships and symptoms. Results mainly showed that among a sample of highly impacted adolescents (using BSI and PTSS-10) constructive motivation and communication are essential in forum-use. Merely among 8%, participation in forums frequently set off SI, 64% exhibited increased motivation to seek professional help. Overall findings demonstrated that users of SI-forums largely experience social support -more than within families, according to self-evaluations.

Emotional reasoning as social information processing in preschool and first grade children

Eivers, Areana Inst. of Psychology, University of Oslo, Oslo, Norway Brendgen, Mara Department of Psychology, University of Quebec, Montreal, Montreal, Canada Borge, Anne Inger Helmen Institute of Psychology, University of Oslo, Oslo, Norway

The present study compared emotional reasoning responses of preschool and first grade children to two hypothetical scenarios depicting emotionally challenging events. It was hypothesised that both children rated as high in prosocial and antisocial behaviour, by parents and teachers, would show significantly different emotional reasoning patterns than other children already in preschool, but more obviously at school-age. 487 Norwegian children, aged 28 to 89 months (M = 65.6, s.d. = 14.1), were interviewed. Parents and teachers rated behaviour. Significant differences in emotional reasoning were found, particularly for antisocial and school-aged children. Links to social information processing theory are discussed.

The effects of internalization of corporate principles and confidence in superiors on employees' job attitudes

Enami, Junko Behavior Seiences, Hiroshima University, Higashihiroshima-City, Japan Ura, Mitsuhiro Behavior Seiences, Hiroshima University, Higashihiroshima-city, Japan Isobe, Chikae Behavior Seiences, Hiroshima University, Higashihiroshima-city, Japan Orimo, Hiroya head office, Human With, Inc., Tokyo, Japan

In order to examine the effects of internalization of corporate principles and confidence in superiors on employees' job attitudes, we conducted an employee satisfaction survey (n=184). Two(high or low internalization of corporate principles) × 2(high or low confidence in superiors) ANCOVAs on employees' job attitudes (covariate was a loyalty to the company) were conducted. Results showed the main effect of confidence in superior and a two-way interaction effects on employees' career perspective were significant. These results suggest that not only internalization of corporate principles but also good relationship with superiors is necessary to clarify employees' career perspectives.

How to present evidence in a criminal trial: Order effects in judicial decision making

Enescu, Raluca Lausanne, Switzerland

Contrary to social impression formation and according to studies using legal evidence, it has been hypothesized that a recency effect would influence the verdict's choice. Six groups among the total amount of swiss criminal judges (N = 1840) have been constituted, each of them receiving a filmed mock trial with one order of evidence stemming from the combination of two discriminating witnesses and one incriminating expert. Results show a recency effect based on a witness whose audience in the last position provoked significantly more acquittals. The defense should be consulted in the choice of evidence order in a criminal trial.

Relations between personal norm and car use in facilitating and inhibiting contexts

Eriksson, Louise Dept. of Psychology, Umeå University, Umeå, Sweden Garvill, Jörgen Department of Psychology, Umeå University, Umeå, Sweden Nordlund, Annika M. Department of Psychology, Umeå University, Umeå, Sweden

Contextual factors may put boundaries on the relation between attitudinal factors and behavior. Since distance is an important contextual factor for travel mode choices, the relation between a personal norm to reduce car use and self-reported car use for individuals living at different distance from various destinations were analyzed in a sample of car users (N = 658). A significant relation between personal norm and car use was generally found for individuals living at an intermediate distance indicating that attitudinal factors and behavior is mainly related when the context is neither too facilitating nor too inhibiting.

Focusing on resources of health: The contribution of the salutogenesis for health promotion and education

Eriksson, Monica Health Promotion Programme, Folkhalsan Research Centre, Helsinki, Finland Lindstrom, Bengt Health Promotion Programme, Folkhalsan Research Centre, Helsinki, Finland

Objective: Provide a comprehensive understanding of the salutogenic concept Sense of Coherence and the relation with health. Methods: A worldwide systematic and analytical research synthesis 1992-2003 based on 458 scientific papers and 13 doctoral theses. Results: The synthesis, the most extensive available to date, shows SOC is strongly related to perceived good health, especially mental health. SOC seems to have a main, moderating or mediating role in the explanation of health.

Further, the SOC reduces stress and predicts good health and quality of life. The salutogenic framework could guide public health, health promotion and education, in a new direction.

Psychological effects of noise in elementary school children

Estrada Rodríguez, Cesáreo Facultad de Psicología, UNAM, México City, Mexico

Objectives. Identify the psychological effects of noise in elementary school children. Methods. The descriptive study was conducted in eight elementary school classrooms in 189 pupils. The evaluation included recording noise in the classrooms and measuring its psychological effects. SEM was used to analyze the data. Results. The impact of noise and physical design from an emotional effect and on reading comprehension was identified, also identifying a direct influence of emotional impact on comprehension, as well as the influence of age on speech intelligibility and the influence of speech intelligibility on pupils' reading comprehension (Chi Sq.=52.32 P=0.00 CFI=0.90 RMSEA=0.11). Conclusions. This initial empirical analysis is consistent with the theoretical premises.

Berlin stays fit: Motivational and volitional strategies for mental and physical exercise of elderly women

Evers, Andrea Inst. für Psychiatrie, Charité CBF, Berlin, Germany Klusmann, Verena Psychiatry, Charité CBF, Berlin, Germany Schwarzer, Ralf Health Psychology, FU Berlin, Berlin, Germany Dimeo, Fernando Sports Medicine, Charité CBF, Berlin, Germany Reischies, Friedel Psychiatry, Charité CBF, Berlin, Germany Heuser, Isabella Psychiatry, Charité CBF, Berlin, Germany

This randomized controlled trial aims at assisting 252 elderly women in performing a demanding new health behaviour, either attending a fitness training or a computer course, for 6 months, 3 times a week. We expect beneficial cognitive effects in those women who attend their courses regularly. To promote motivational and volitional strategies, we conducted a planning (after 1.5 months) and a feedback intervention (after 4 months) to bridge the intention-behaviour gap. Preliminary results (ANOVA; Regression analyses) indicate that these interventions have differential effects on adherence to the behaviour and on psychosocial outcomes.

The relation between time management and subjective well-being in undergraduate students

Fan, Cuiying School of Psychology, Huanzhong Normal University, Wuhan, People's Republic of China Liu, Huashan School of Psychology, Huanzhong Normal University, Wuhan,Hubei, People's Republic of China Zhou, Zongkui School of Psychology, Huanzhong Normal University, Wuhan,Hubei, People's Republic of China Sun, Xiaojun School of Psychology, Huanzhong Normal University, Wuhan,Hubei, People's Republic of China

The objective of the present study is to explore the relation between time management and objective well-being in Chinese undergraduate students. Data were collected from 520 students. Correlation analysis, variance analysis and regression analysis were applied to explore the data. Results suggest that the relation between time management disposition and subjective well-being is significant across the gender and grade level; undergraduate student's time supervision and time effect feelings can positively predict their subjective well-being significantly, time effect feeling can positively predict positive feeling and affective balance significantly, meanwhile, negatively predict negative feeling significantly.

An experimental study on the relationship between interference and affective priming

Fang, Ping Dept. of Psychology, Capital Normal University, Beijing, People's Republic of China Chen, Manqi Psychology, Capital Normal University, Beijing, People's Republic of China Jiang, Yuan Sport Psychology, Beijing Sport University, Beijing, People's Republic of China Li, Yang Psychology, Capital Normal University, Beijing, People's Republic of China

In order to investigate the relationship between interference and affective priming, present study uses cue-target paradigm to arrange supraliminal affective priming and subliminal affective priming under interference and without interference. The research shows that: 1) there are significance supraliminal affective priming and subliminal affective priming under both conditions; 2) interference decreases the effect of supraliminal affective priming but can't moderate the effects of subliminal affective priming. The results suggest that supraliminal and subliminal affective priming are dependent differently on attention, they may belong to different processing systems.

The influence of feedback types on cognition in different post-feedback interval

Fang, Ping Dept. of Psychology, Capital Normal University, Beijing, People's Republic of China Li, Yang Psychology, Capital Normal University, Beijing, People's Republic of China Chen, Manqi Psychology, Capital Normal University, Beijing, People's Republic of China Jiang, Yuan Psychology, Capital Normal University, Beijing, People's Republic of China

This study explored the influence of feedback types on cognitions in different post-feedback interval, which consists of a lab experiments with 99 High-middle-school students in different levels of self-regulated learning competence (SRLC), and a field experiment with 60 additional High-middle-school students. The results showed that: in short post-feedback interval, the feedback types and SRLC had no effects on reaction accuracy, and only positive feedback extended reaction time significantly; while the feedback types and SRLC had interaction on reaction accuracy in long post-feedback interval. It is concluded that SRLC could adjust the process of feedbacks affected cognition in long post-feedback interval.

A research on cognitive generating mechanism of organizational justice: An attributional perspective

Fang, Xuemei Psychology, East China Normal University, Shanghai, People's Republic of China

The current organizational justice literature focuses on relationship between perceived justice and the associated behavioral consequences without really examining the process that leads to the determination of why a certain event is fair or unfair. The present study proposes an attributional process as the cognitive antecedent to perceived justice. The result suggests causal attribution is an important cognitive antecedent of judgment of justice.

Gender differences in non-fatal suicide attempts among psychiatric and medical patients in Pakistan

Farooqi, Yasmin Applied Psychology, University of the Punjab, Lahore, Pakistan

This research investigates gender differences in non-fatal suicide attempts; nature of precipitants and methods used by Pakistani psychiatric and medical patients. The sample was composed of 30 psychiatric and 20 medical patients (25 males and 25 females). A questionnaire and psychiatric / medical records were used. The research findings suggest that female patients have a higher rate of non-fatal suicide attempts with less violent methods as compared to their male counterparts. These results have implications for helping professionals in

screening those at risk for suicide and for gender sensitive treatment and management of suicide cases.

Relationship between identity style, commitment, and friendship

Fartash, Soheila Dept. Educational Psychology, University of Tehran, Tehran, Islamic Republic of Iran Hejazi Mughari, Elahe educational psychology, university of Tehran, Tehran, Islamic Republic of Iran

The purpose of this study is to investigate the relation between identity style and commitment with quality of friendship among the students in third grade of high school. 400 participants from nineteen educational districts were chosen randomly. Three questionnaires were used: Identity style inventory, the quality of friendship, the reciprocity of friendship. The results indicated that informational style is able to predict the variances of three components of friendship quality (intimacy and self-disclosure, loyalty and trust, and reciprocity). Normative style and diffuse/ avoidant style are not able to predict the components of friendship quality. Key words: identity style, commitment, quality of friendship.

Violence experienced by youths involved with drug traffic

Feffermann, Marisa Health Institut of São Paulo, São Paulo, Brazil

Objectives: To present the violence to which these Youths are submitted. Methods: four-year field study carried out among youngsters inserted in drug traffic in the outskirts of São Paulo. Results: The violence which is associated: the drug, "crack" - that causes high dependence degree; the police which acts in a cruel and corruptible way; the drug traffic, with its dispute for the dealing-points and its exemplary punishments; the violence perpetrated by these youngsters - victims and, in many cases, executioners. Conclusions: Fear, bribery, corruption permeate this reality. In fact, they are the mechanisms of crime and power.

Climate for innovation in companies: A multilevel approach on the analysis of antecedents and consequences

Feinstein, Ingrid Lehrstuhl Psychologie I, Universität Mannheim, Schöneck, Germany

Three studies were conducted in several large to middle-sized german companies to analyze various variables predicting or resulting from climate for innovation that theory and empirical studies so far propose. In the literature perspectives are taken exclusively either for the individual, group or organizational level. Here a thoroughly multilevel perspective is taken. The scope was first to verify whether isomorphism can be assumed across levels. In study 2 and 3 antecedents and consequences were to be localized on the level of functioning. Results suggest isomorphism. Differences can be observed with respect to antecedents.

Influence of job-role quality, anger and social support on health in working women

Feldman, Lya Ciencia y Tecnologia del Compo, Simon Bolivar University, Caracas, Venezuela Angelucci, Luisa Ciencia y Tecnologia del Compo, Simon Bolivar University, Caracas, Venezuela

Objective: To analyze how job-role quality, anger and social support influence direct and indirectly on the presence of symptoms report, risk habits of health and cholesterol Method: Using a non-experimental, cross-sectional design, a path analysis was performed in a sample of 402 working women in Caracas, Venezuela. Results: Health risk habits, job support and job rewards were associated with more symptoms. Indirect relationships between Job-role quality were observed and the number of symptoms is mediated by job support. Conclusion: The findings allowed to verify relations in the health

area, emotions and role quality in working women and can be very useful for intervention programs in organizational settings.

Relationship between the sense of loneliness and mental health of college students

Feng, Huiru Dept. of Psychology, Kaifeng University, Kaifeng, People's Republic of China

AIM: To explore the relationship between the sense of loneliness and mental health of college students with different sexes, majors and grades. METHODS: The College Student Loneliness Structure Questionnaire and SCL-90 Symptom Self-Report Scale were used to measure and get data. RESULTS: 330 valid questionnaires were involved in the result analysis. The social loneliness and development loneliness were correlated significantly with mental health, which had strong positively prediction power on nine factors of SCL-90 Symptom Self-Report Scale. CONCLUSION: Those students with higher-level loneliness have lower levels mental health. College should strengthen the education and mental regulation on loneliness.

Emotional responses to visual pictures with controlled facial muscle activation

Ferreira, Ana Dept. of Psychology, ISCTE, Lisboa, Portugal Esteves, Francisco Psychology, ISCTE, Lisboa, Portugal

The aim of the present experiment was to investigate effects of the manipulation of facial muscles on the emotional responses of the participants. Sixty student volunteers were exposed to 21 pictures from the International Affective Picture System, depicting different contents and previously evaluated as positive, negative and neutral. Stimuli were exposed for six seconds and randomly presented. Two manipulations of the Zygomatic muscle (inhibition and activation) were compared to a control condition (without manipulation). In general, a clear differentiation between positive, negative and neutral pictures was obtained on all measures, and zygomatic manipulation was associated with lower emotionality.

Behaviour disorders and the search of identity by an adolescent twin: Study case

Ferreira, Olga Rita Psychiatry and Mental Health, Hospital Nossa Sr.♀ do Rosário, Barreiro, Portugal

The author looks to expand on the subject of the identity construction of a 17 years old adolescent female twin who has started a psychiatric and psychological treatment for behaviour disorders, such as nervous anorexia and suicide attempt. The method used is the Case Study, considering the evolution of counselling sessions over 6 months. The objective is to comprehend the symptoms, considering the effects of being a twin on the development of identity and during the stage of adolescence. The need to differentiate from her twin sister has been observed, resulting in difficulties on this process such as behavioural symptoms.

Presenteeism and positive organizational behavior

Ferreira, Aristides IEP, Minho University, Carvoeira-Mafra, Portugal Fructuoso Martinez, Luís Psicologia, Universidade Lusíada, Lisboa, Portugal Vieira da Cunha, João Faculdade de Economia, Universidade Nova de Lisboa, Lisboa, Portugal Manuel Sousa, Luís DGRH, Hospital Curry Cabral, Lisboa, Portugal

In this study, we evaluate the relation between two dimensions of presenteeism ('completing work' and 'avoided distraction') and one construct associated with positive organizational behavior (hope). The sample consists of 158 workers mainly from research and health-related areas submitted to the Stanford Presenteeism Scale (SPS-6) and the hope scale. Results show that 'avoided distraction' is associated with the low hope cluster workers. On the other hand, high hope cluster workers reveal higher values in 'completing work'. Moreover, psychological causes of presenteeism – anxiety and depression – seem to be associated with low levels in the hope scale.

Affective priming of emotional facial expressions independent of perceptual similarity

Fesche, Arne Berlin, Germany Werheid, Katja Klinische Psychologie, Humboldt-Universität zu Berlin, Berlin, Germany Kovács, Gyula Dept. Cognitive Science, Budapest Univ.Techn.and Econo., Budapest, Hungary Sommer, Werner Biologische Psychologie, Humboldt-Universität zu Berlin, Berlin, Germany

In our study we investigated affective priming, the acceleration of responses following the second of two sequentially presented, affectively congruent faces. Morphed faces were used to disentangle affective and perceptual similarity. Twenty-six participants were presented with either congruent or incongruent pairs of face morphs, having identical physical distance, in an emotion discrimination task. Reactions to affectively congruent pairs were faster and more accurate as compared to incongruent pairs, even if they were of equal perceptual similarity. Our results indicate that congruent pairs are processed more efficiently, and that this processing advantage is due to affective and not perceptual priming.

An initial imprinting of the self-help groups of narcotics anonymous and alcoholics anonymous in Greece

Flora, Katerina Dept. of Psychology, Aristotle University, Thessaloniki, Greece

The purpose of this study is the representation of Alcoholics Anonymous (AA) and Narcotics Anonymous (NA) in Greece. This study is a survey.The sample is 82 members who filled a 55-item questionnaire. We made a quantitative analysis using the Statistical Package for Social Sciences 12 and a qualitative thematic analysis.The findings present demographic features, data concerning substance abuse, group participation, uncovered needs and opinions about professionals. The findings present the profile of the people who approach AA and NA and signify the necessity for recognising their needs and for the linking of the mental health professionals with the groups.

The impact of alcohol and drug intoxication on Canadian perpetrators' memories of violent crimes

Foellmi, Melodie Department of Psychology, University of British Columbia, Vancouver, Canada Griesel, Dorothee Department of Psychology, University of British Columbia, Vancouver, Canada Ternes, Meg Department of Psychology, University of British Columbia, Vancouver, Canada Cooper, Barry Department of Psychology, University of British Columbia, Vancouver, Canada Yuille, John Department of Psychology, University of British Columbia, Vancouver, Canada

Many violent crimes are committed by offenders under the influence, yet field research in this area is scarce. This study examines the impact of drug and alcohol consumption on perpetrators' memories of their own acts of violence. One hundred fifty inmates were asked to recall acts of instrumental and reactive violence. These violent acts will be compared for quantity of details and differences in rate of intoxication at the time. The types of substances will be analyzed in relation to type of violence, as well as quantity of details recalled. Implications for the criminal justice system will be discussed.

The financing of care at mental health: Challenges to public health system from Brazil

Freire, Flávia Helena Rio de Janeiro, Brazil Amarante, Paulo ENSP, FIOCRUZ, Rio de Janeiro, Brazil Porto, Silvia ENSP, FIOCRUZ, Rio de Janeiro, Brazil

Objective: To discuss financing of Brazilian Public Health Care System and analyze its implications to the mode of producing care at substitutive web of mental health care. Method: Theoretical review about substitutive model to mental health care and analyses of normative documents that regulate the financing of Public Health Care System. Results: Financing model has been characterized by procedures focused on disease and diagnosis code. The substitutive clinic requires differentiate and singular modes of inventing lives of persons in mental disorder. Conclusion: Financing system shows inadequate to provide new kind of care required at substitutive web of mental health care.

Existential threat changes motives of pro-environmental behaviour

Fritsche, Immo Jena, Germany

Motives of pro-environmental behaviour are proposed to change under conditions in which people perceive threat to their individual existence. In line with terror management theory mortality salience increased the relative importance of anthropocentric (protecting humans) compared to biocentric (protecting nature) pro-environmental motivation in Study 1. In Study 2 people indicated both more altruistic and more biospheric but less egoistic environmental concern following a death reminder. I will discuss societal and theoretical implications of these findings focussing on the meaning of nature under conditions of threat.

Emotional expressions within the N-back working memory paradigm: Performance in early Parkinsons disease

Fusari, Anna Basic Psychology II, UNED Univ. Nac. Ed.a Distancia, Madrid, Spain García Rodríguez, Beatriz Basic Psychology II, UNED Univ.Nac.Ed.a Distancia, Madrid, Spain Ellring, Heiner Psychology, Julius Maximilian University, Wurzburg, Germany Molina Arjona, José Antonio Neurology, Hospital XII de Octubre, Wurzburg, Germany

Associated with dorsolateral prefrontal cortex impairments, working memory (WM) deficits have been found in patients with Parkinsons disease (PD). The purpose of this study was to assess WM performance in early and unmedicated PD patients with emotional facial expressions stimuli. Participants were 20 de novo unmedicated PD patients and 40 controls. Subjects were tested on an emotional N-back task in one control task (0-back) and three experimental tasks (1-, 2-, 3-back). Results showed an impaired performance of PD patients inversely related to task difficulty. The N-back paradigm with emotional expressions may be a preclinical marker for the detection of PD.

School inspection in Germany: Initial data on the quality of school inspection as an instrument for diagnosing school quality

Gaertner, Holger Inst. für Schulqualität, Freie Universität Berlin, Berlin, Germany

School inspection is a new instrument of quality assurance in Germany. This study examines the reliability and validity of inspection results. The data are based on inspection reports from 218 schools in the years 2005 to 2007. Analyses show that a priori assignments of inspectors' quality ratings to dimensions of quality do not meet classical reliability criteria ($0.18 < \alpha < 0.79$). As a consequence, criterion validity is expected to be low. Moreover, not only unreliable dimensions but almost all composite quality measures failed to show associations with school-level aggregated results from achievement tests. These results suggest

that inspection instruments must be improved considerably.

Productive versus active aging: Differential effects on personal wellbeing and cognitive abilities

García Rodríguez, Beatriz Dept. of Basic Psychology II, UNED, Madrid, Spain Sarabia, Carmen Fusari, Anna Basic Psychology II, UNED, Madrid, Spain Ellring, Heiner Department of Psychology, Universität Würzburg, Würzburg, Germany

We investigate to what extent a professional activity in aging influences cognitive abilities and subjectively reported personal wellbeing. We tested three groups of participants: productive elderly, retired/active elderly and younger controls. Participants wellbeing personal state was assessed by questionnaires and cognitive abilities by executive functions tasks (WCST, n-back task). Our results show mainly two things: 1) productive elderly report a better personal wellbeing then retired/active elderly, similar to the younger control group, 2) cognitive abilities keep stable in productive aging, starting to decay when subjects retire. Moreover, no intergroup differences were found in cognitive abilities performance of productive elderly and younger controls.

Preliminar psychometric data of the questionnaire of school anxiety

García-Fernández, José Manuel Developmental and Educational, University of Alicante, Alicante, Spain Inglés, Cándido J. Developmental and Educational, University of Miguel Hernandez, Elche, Spain Martínez-Monteagudo, Carmen Developmental and Educational, University of Miguel Hernandez, Elche, Spain Redondo, Jesús Developmental and Educational, University of Miguel Hernandez, Elche, Spain

Objective: This study evaluated the reliability and validity of the Questionnaire of School Anxiety (QSA; García-Fernández e Inglés, 2006). Method: The CAE was administered to 1,409 adolescents (47, 9 % males) from 12 to 18 years. Results: The exploratory factor analysis revealed a four-factor structure: Anxiety faced with School Failure and Punishment, Anxiety faced with Aggression, Anxiety faced with Social Evaluation, Anxiety faced with School Evaluation, which accounted for the 74.92% of the total variance. The confirmatory factor analysis revealed a good fit for the four-factor model. The internal consistency was high (.93). Conclusion: The CAE shows promise as a screening instrument for school anxiety.

The influence of causal knowledge and empirical evidence on causal inference and decision making

Garcia Retamero, Rocio Experimental Psychology, Granada, Spain Maldonado, Antonio Psicologia Experimental, Universidad de Granada, Granada, Spain Perales, Jose Cesar Dept. Psicología Experimental, Universidad de Granada, Granada, Spain Mueller, Stephanie Experimental Psychology, Institut of Psychology, Granada, Spain Cándido, Antonio Psicología Experimental, Universidad de Granada, Granada, Spain Catena, Andrés Psicología Experimental, Universidad de Granada, Granada, Spain

The independent and joint effects of prior causal beliefs and observed cause-effect covariation on causal judgment and decision-making were analyzed in several experiments. Prior causal beliefs were the main factor guiding participants' inferences and decisions when no covariation data were available. However, training with valid neutral cues that were not causally linked to the effect abolished the influence of prior causal beliefs. Whereas current theoretical frameworks mainly focused either on causal or covariation knowledge, our research shows that both factors are required to explain the flexibility and complexity of human causal inferences and decisions.

The role of emotional maturity in the development of Irritable Bowel Syndrome (IBS) among adolescents

Garg, Niyati D. H. 217, Niyati Garg, Meerut, India **Sharma, Vandana** Meerut College, Department of Psychology, Meerut, India

In the present study emotional stability, emotional progression, social adjustment, personality integration and independence were selected as indepndent variables and IBS as dependent variable. The sample consist of 200 adolescents (100 IBS and 100 non IBS). Rome II criteria was applied for screening IBS students and Emotional Maturity Scale by Singh and Bhargava to measure variables related to emotional maturity. Multiple regression analysis was employed. Findings reveled that emotional stability and social adjustment were contributing in the development of IBS with beta value (.27 and .20), t-value (3.24 and 2.49) and multiple R (.42) which is significant at .01 level of confidence. Result indicates that IBS group lacks emotional stability and social adjustment.

Study on the influence of the environment sounds on the human creativeness

Gatej, Emil-Razvan Dept. of Psychology, Bucharest University, Bucharest, Romania **Mihai, Madalina-Andreea** Psichology, Bucharest University, Bucharest, Romania

The objective of this study is to reveal the influence of the environment sounds on the human creativeness. The experiment means the testing of the assumption on two lots comprising 40 subjects each. The study shows the effect of natural environment sounds presented as a relaxing method, then the effect of urban and industrial noises and sounds, on the creativeness tested in a specifc way. The obtained results will be examined with the "T Test" procedure for independent samples. These results will show the influence of the environmental conditions on the development of human creative skills.

Future time perspective in health behavior change: Moderation of the intention-behavior relation

Gellert, Paul Berlin, Germany **Ziegelmann, Jochen Philipp** Health Psychology, Freie Universitaet Berlin, Berlin, Germany **Reuter, Tabea** Health Psychology, Freie Universitaet Berlin, Berlin, Germany **Wiedemann, Amelie Ulrike** Health Psychology, Freie Universitaet Berlin, Berlin, Germany **Lippke, Sonia** Health Psychology, Freie Universitaet Berlin, Berlin, Germany

Objectives: Bridging the intention-behavior gap by planning, and assessing future time perspective (FTP) as moderator. Method: 78 workers of a German railway company participated in a health change intervention. Social-cognitive and behavior variables were assessed by questionnaires prior to and 1 month after intervention. Bootstrapping resampling was used for statistical analyses. Results: Planning mediates the intention-behavior relation. Controlling for age, FTP moderates the effect of planning on physical activity, but not the effect of intention on planning. Conclusions: Planning is not related to physical activity in same intensity in all individuals, but depends on the level of future time perspective.

Recognition of speech emotional prosody valence in stimuli of different time structure (aging aspects)

Gelman, Victor ICT, Med. Acad. for Postgrad. Stud., St. Petersburg, Russia **Dmitrieva, Elena** Bioacoustics, Inst. Evol. Physiol. RAS, St-Petersburg, Russia

The impact of ageing on recognition of emotions' valences in speech signals of different durations was examined. Neural mechanisms underlying emotional prosody perception were studied by comparing the reaction time and accuracy of recognition. The ANOVA of the data revealed "emotion's valence", "stimuli duration", "age" and "gender" factors to be highly significant for speech emotions' recognition. The signal temporal structure affected more strongly the valence evaluation in the eldest group (51-65-year-olds). Threshold duration in this group was longer indicating the weakening of human ability to process the speech affective intonation with ageing. The support of RFH grant: 07-06-00821à.

The relation of medical and psychological risk factors to cardiovascular disease

Gholamali Lavassani, Massoud Psychology and Education, University of Tehran, Tehran, Islamic Republic of Iran

Objectives: This study investigated the relation of medical and psychological risk factors to cardiovascular disease in 100 Iranian patients. Methods: Finally the data of 72 men aged 35 to 65 years were considered appropriate for evaluation. Multiple regression analysis examined relationship of coronary artery disease with blood glucose and lipids, cigarette smoking, hypertension, body mass index, heart disease precedent, trait anxiety, stress, anger, hope and type A behavior. Results:The results showed that only heart disease precedent, hypertension, and stress have significant coefficients (P

Epistemological beliefs, motivation, and learning strategies as predictors of medical students' academic success

Giesler, Marianne Inst. für Medizin. Psychologie, Universität Freiburg, Freiburg, Germany **Fabry, Götz** Medical Psychology, Albert-Ludwigs-University, Freiburg, Germany

Objectives: This research analyzes the relationships between epistemological beliefs, motivation, and learning strategies and the extent to which these variables predict academic success of medical students. Methods Two cohorts of medical students (N approx. 300) completed questionnaires assessing the aforementioned learner characteristics at three occasions during their first year of study. Academic success was measured by open-answer- and multiple-choice-questions. Results Use of the learning strategy "critical review" declines during the first year of medical education and strategies such as "effort" and "attention" are most important in predicting academic success. Results of further analyses currently being performed will also be reported.

Optimism and pessimism about the future of the environment: An 18-nation study

Gifford, Robert Dept. of Psychology, University of Victoria, Victoria, Canada **Scannell, Leila** Dept. of Psychology, University of Victoria, Victoria, Canada **Kormos, Christine** Dept. of Psychology, University of Victoria, Victoria, Canada

Perceptions of current, and expectations of future, environmental conditions were investigated at the local, national, and global spatial levels with a sample of 3130 community participants in 18 nations. Current environmental perceptions showed spatial bias ("things are worse over there") in 15 of 18 countries, and future expectations showed temporal bias ("things will get worse") in all countries except one. Assessments of current national conditions were positively associated with an expert ranking of national environmental quality. Aside from the intrinsic value of understanding global trends in environmental assessments, the results have important implications for policy and risk management strategies.

Measuring workplace bullying in Japan

Giorgi, Gabriele Psychology, University of Firenze, Firenze, Italy **Asakura, Takashi** Health Psychology, Tokyo Gakugei Univeristy, Tokyo, Japan **Ando, Mikayo** Counseling Psychology, Okayama University, Okayama, Japan

This research addresses the prevalence of bullying in Japan. The agreed method used in bullying surveys, the operational classification method, has been employed. Furthermore a two step cluster approach was used to analyze the data, which was obtained by using the Negative Acts Questionnaire Revised (NAQ-R) administered to employees in Japan (n > 700.). The results showed that when comparing the traditional operational classification method with the two step cluster analysis there was a high overlap in identifying bullying victims and non victims. Furthermore bullying prevalence in Japan appeared to be quite elevated, higher than other European Countries.

Do children with deficits in basic cognitive functions profit from mixed age primary schools?

Goelitz, Dietmar Inst. für Psychologie, Leuphana Universität Lüneburg, Lüneburg, Germany **Hasselhorn, Marcus** DIPF, Bildung und Entwicklung, Frankfurt am Main, Germany

The study examines if children with deficits in working memory, phonological awareness or counting knowledge profit in academic skills when taught in age mixed schools in grade 1 and 2. Cognitive functions were measured at the beginning of the first grade in age mixed (N= 564) and age homogenous schools (N= 476). Achievement measures were taken during grades 1 to 4. The results indicate interactions between cognitive deficits and mixing: risk children profit from mixed age classes in the language domain, but should be taught in age homogenous classes when having deficits in phonological awareness. Research consequences are discussed.

Confirmatory analysis of a social-cognitive model of sexual risk behaviour: A contribute to the explanation of condom use

Gomes, Alexandra FCHS - Psicologia, University of Algarve, Faro, Portugal **Nunes, Cristina** FCHS - Psicologia, University of Algarve, Faro, Portugal

Contribute to socio-cognitive models that explain sexual risk behaviour by including demographic, intrapersonal, interpersonal and situational variables. 165 questionnaires were applied to university students. Exploratory and confirmatory analyses were made to confirm the applicability of the constructed model. The confirmatory analysis, with intrapersonal, interpersonal and situational variables adjusted on the fit measures. Attitudes had the higher predictive value to explain previous condom use, and the one explaining the intention was the previous behaviour of use. Further studies are necessary to integrate a contextualized and interpersonal vision on the condom use behaviour in order to increase the effectiveness of prevention programs.

The Kuwait University anxiety scale: Psychometric properties under item response theory

Gomez Benito, Juana Metodologia C. Comportamiento, Universitat de Barcelona, Barcelona, Spain **Hidalgo, M. Dolores** Metodologia C. Comportamiento, Universidad de Murcia, Murcia, Spain **Tomás-Sábado, Joaquín** Esc. Univ. Enf. Gimbernat, Univ. Autónoma de Barcelona, Barcelona, Spain

The Kuwait University Anxiety Scale (KUAS) developed by Abdel-Khalek (2000) was analyzed in an item response framework, using both dichotomous and polytomous models. Several models were applied: Graded Response Model (Samejima, 1969), Generalized Partial Credit Model (Muraki,

1992), Partial Credit Model (Masters, 1982), Dichotomous Logistic Model (2-parameters) (Birnbaum, 1968). The results indicated that the items satisfy the assumptions of generalized partial credit model. Moreover, test precision at different points along the latent trait continuum is presented. Finally, are showed item information function in order to examine the contribution of each item on test information function.

Social identity theory: A historical review from the perspectives of social and industrial and organizational psychology

Goncu, Asli Inst. of Psychology, Middle East Technical Univ., Ankara, Turkey

The present study aims to summarize the literature regarding Social Identity Theory (SIT) in the context of social psychology as well as in relation to Industrial and Organizational Psychology. The present research firstly summarizes the development and main assumptions of SIT. In addition, the research regarding SIT, main findings and application fields in the social psychological research are explained. Finally, organizational identification as a research area stimulated by SIT in the Industrial and Organizational Psychology literature is summarized along with the main findings and relevant concepts (i.e. identification with the work-group, identification with the leader).

That's it we're having more insulation! Will householders change behaviours and attitudes after being shown an infrared image of their homes leaking heat?

Goodhew, Julie Dept. of Psychology, University of Plymouth, Plymouth, United Kingdom Auburn, Tim Psychology, University of Plymouth, PLYMOUTH, United Kingdom Pahl, Sabine Psychology, University of Plymouth, PLYMOUTH, United Kingdom

This longitudinal pilot study explored the impact of infrared images (of homes leaking heat) on energy consumption and attitudes. British householders were randomly allocated to three groups: image + carbon footprint, carbon footprint or control. We measured qualitative (interviews) and quantitative data (attitudes, intentions, behaviours, actual energy usage). Participants had high environmental awareness but attitudes did not correlate with carbon emissions. Interview data suggest specific links between information in the image and energy saving behaviours. Follow up measures are currently being analysed. The data will help evaluate and develop the use of infrared images as prompts for energy saving behaviours.

Informational and energetic models of influence of activity results on emotions

Gorbatkow, Aleksander Pedagogic University of Kielce, Kielce, Poland

Influences of activity results on emotions are mediated by "informational" (competence, abilities) and "energetic" ("expenses" necessary for activity performance) factors. Proposed "informational" and "energetic" models of these influences differ from each other by ratio nonmonotonous asymmetrical curves of positive and negative emotions. Considered dependences determine contrast of nonlinear sinusoidal dynamics of emotional balance with growth by functioning results (fall-growth-fall in the first model and growth-fall-growth in the second one) and mutual resemblance of emotional activation curves. Modal zones (corresponding with "ordinary" activities) of two models are characterized by similar bell-shaped curves of positive emotions and contrary linear trends of monotonous curves of another three emotional dimensions.

An investigation of the influence of "informational" and "energetic" activity factors on emotions

Gorbatkow, Aleksander Pedagogic University of Kielce, Kielce, Poland

This study tested "informational" and "energetic" models of influences of activity parameters on emotions (in "modal zones", relevant to "ordinary" activities). The undergraduate students estimated emotions experienced in task-solving process. Informational (skills) and energetic (difficulty-wearisomeness) activity factors were assessed as independent variables. Results revealed that influences of skills and difficulty-wearisomeness on emotions can be described by similar symmetrical single-peaked curves of positive emotions, monotonous curves of negative emotions (accordingly, descending and ascending), asymmetrical single-peaked curves of emotional balance (accordingly, with ascending and descending tendencies) and monotonous curves of emotional activation (accordingly, descending and ascending). These findings supported the hypotheses of the study.

Determinants of school achievement: Hints from a twin study

Gottschling, Juliana Inst. für Psychologie, Universität des Saarlandes, Saarbrücken, Germany Spinath, Frank M. Psychology, Saarland University, Saarbruecken, Germany Spinath, Birgit Inst. für Psychologie, Universität Heidelberg, Heidelberg, Germany Wolf, Heike Psychology, Saarland University, Saarbruecken, Germany

The study presented is part of CoSMoS, a twin study about Cognitive Ability, Self-Reported Motivation, and School Achievement (Spinath & Wolf, 2006), which provides data from more than 400 pairs of monozygotic and dizygotic twin children. As a first step we examined the complex phenotypic interrelations between several individual and familial determinants of school achievement (e.g., motivation and parenting style). To elucidate the sources of individual differences in these variables and to gain a deeper understanding of the sources of their interrelations, we additionally conducted univariate and multivariate genetic analyses. Results and implications for future research are discussed.

Measuring uncertainty in the observation and evaluation process in assessment centres. Possible antecedents of uncertainty and its relationship to rating accuracy

Greco, Riccardo Köln, Germany Maier, Günter W. Abteilung für Psychologie, Universität Bielefeld, Bielefeld, Germany Stumpp, Thorsten Abteilung für Psychologie, Universität Bielefeld, Bielefeld, Germany

The purpose of this study was first to research possible antecedents (expertise of observer, criteria-dimension-fit) of uncertainty occurring throughout the observation and evaluation process in assessment centres and to investigate its relationship to rating accuracy. Therefore observers with different levels of experience (N=56) observed and judged video-taped exercises and rated their uncertainty for each assessed dimension. In a second step rating accuracy was measured and correlated with the established level of uncertainty. Results indicate that uncertainty largely depends on expertise of observer, especially regarding dimensions with a high fit to the criteria. However, a correlation between uncertainty and rating accuracy cannot be confirmed.

Mental health, quality of life and the coping of stress of undergraduate students from Brazil

Grubits Freire, Heloisa Bruna Dept. of Psychology, Dom Bosco Catholic University, Campo Grande, Brazil

A cross-sectional study was carried out in a sample of 466 undergraduate students who were attending their first and last year in 5 major areas of knowledge. To assess their Mental Health (MH), GHQ-60, SF-36 for Quality of Life (QoL), Billings & Moos Coping Scale to measure coping strategies to deal with stressful events were used. The students did better in the physical component of QoL than in the mental one. They predominantly used active strategies to cope with stressful events. There were gender differences as regards MH and QoL performances. The worst MH scores were for males from Human and Social Sciences.

Relationship between the values of organizational culture and human resource management practices from a gender perspective

Grueso, Merlin Patricia CIDI, Univ. Pontificia Bolivariana, Palmira, Colombia Anton, Concha Salamanca, Universidad de Salamanca, Salamanca, Spain

The purpose of this research was to identify the values of the organizational culture which take effect in the implementation of human resources practices regarded as fair from a gender perspective. It used a sample of employees from three organizations in Cali Colombia and was administered through a questionnaire that analyzed five values of the corporate culture and six best human resource practices from gender perspective. The results indicate that the values power distance, masculinity - femininity, uncertainty tolerance, individualism - collectivism and long term – short term orientation, predicting significantly implement good human resources practices from gender perspective although differently.

The relationship between moral characteristics and abilities of gifted persons

Gudzik, Svetlana Psychology Department, BSPU, Minsk, Belarus

One of the important tasks that faces scientists and practical workers with gifted children is how to preserve the high level of abilities through all life cycle of gifted person. In the context of this task the revealing of the connections between the abilities (general and special) and moral characteristics of personality let us to determine the benefits for personal and social activities of gifted person's potential realization. In the paper the results of investigation of moral characteristics and different abilities of gifted children are presented and discussed. Some comparisons are made with the group of ordinary children.

Informal caregivers of elderly people: Social network and life satisfaction

Guerra, Sara Dept. of Health Sciences, University of Aveiro, Aveiro, Portugal Vicente, Henrique Health Sciences, University of Aveiro, Aveiro, Portugal Figueiredo, Daniela Health Sciences, University of Aveiro, Aveiro, Portugal Sousa, Liliana Health Sciences, University of Aveiro, Aveiro, Portugal

This study aims at characterizing informal carers of elderly people's networks and its impact on satisfaction with life. IARSP-R (Analysis Instrument of Social Network) and SWLS (Satisfaction with Life Scale) were administered to 30 carers of elderly dependent people. Main findings suggest that: i) caregivers' tend not to include the elderly person as a member of their network; ii) networks are based on family and neighbours; iii) life satisfaction is positively correlated with the number of friends and relatives in the network. Caregivers' networks need to be strengthening, mainly through making use of the potential of the already existing ties.

Effectiveness of humanistic child and adolescent psychotherapy

Hölldampf, Dagmar Psychology, University of Education, Schwäbisch Gmünd, Germany Theresa, Jakob Psychology, University of Education, Schwäbisch Gmünd, Germany Behr, Michael

Psychology, University of Education, Schwäbisch Gmünd, Germany

Meta analysis about Child- and Adolescent-Psychotherapy show considerable differences. Over the past 50 plus years, humanistic child and adolescent psychotherapy has been the subject of over 100 studies reporting pre-post results. The authors are using meta-analysis methods to statistically combine the results of these studies. The following hypothesis are surveyed: Children and adolescents who participate in humanistic psychotherapies show significant amounts of change over time; in randomized clinical trials against untreated control groups, children who participate in humanistic psychotherapies typically show substantially more change than comparable untreated clients.

Neuroimaging of therapeutic effects in schizophrenia

Habel, Ute Psychiatrie und Psychotherapie, RWTH Aachen, Aachen, Germany Koch, Kathrin Psychiatry and Psychotherapy, University of Jena, Jena, Germany Kellermann, Thilo Psychiatry and Psychotherapy, RWTH Aachen University, Aachen, Germany Reske, Martina Psychiatry and Psychotherapy, RWTH Aachen University, Aachen, Germany Fromann, Nicole Psychiatry and Psychotherapy, University of Düsseldorf, Düsseldorf, Germany Wölwer, Wolfgang Psychiatry and Psychotherapy, University of Düsseldorf, Düsseldorf, Germany Zilles, Karl Neuroscience and Biophysics, Research Center Jülich, Jülich, Germany Shah, N Jon Neuroscience and Biophysics, Research Center Jülich, Jülich, Germany Schneider, Frank Psychiatry and Psychotherapy, RWTH Aachen University, Aachen, Germany

Objectives: Longitudinal neuroimaging studies addressing therapeutic effects on the cerebral dysfunctions underlying emotion and cognitive deficits are lacking. Methods: Repeated fMRI was used during long-term studies testing psychotherapeutic effects of a Training of Affect Recognition and a training of attention as well as pharmacotherapy effects on the neural correlates of these processes. Results: A specific behavioural improvement could be observed in trained patients only. In parallel, an activation increase was observed in occipital, frontal and parietal areas in patients who had undergone training compared to those who had not. Conclusion: Specific training effects are probably reflecting more efficient use of attentional, perceptual or cognitive strategies.

Choosing how many options to choose from: Does it depend on affective priming?

Hafenbrädl, Sebastian HEC, Université de Lausanne, Lausanne, Switzerland White, Chris M. HEC, Université de Lausanne, Lausanne, Switzerland Hoffrage, Ulrich HEC, Université de Lausanne, Lausanne, Switzerland

When making purchase decisions, how many options do people wish to choose from (i.e., what is their desired-set-size, or DSS)? An experiment examined the extent to which DSS depended on: whether participants approached the issue in a computational or affective frame of mind (manipulated via priming), and the number (5 vs. 10) and type of items they could select. Participants also reported their willingness-to-pay (WTP) for the selected items. The results suggest that participants who received computational priming were, as predicted, sensitive to the number of items, whereas those who received affective priming were not, again as predicted.

Mentoring and privacy: The relationship of environmental privacy and personal disclosure

Hager, Mark J. Psychology, Russell Center 6, Menlo College, Atherton, USA

This study examined the interaction of perceived privacy with academic and psychological mentoring

outcomes in a school-based mentoring program in the USA. College students (N=42; 28 female) mentoring elementary and secondary students were surveyed about their perceptions of privacy in different campus settings. Chi square analyses confirmed higher levels of acoustic and visual privacy were significantly related to increased psychosocial mentoring activities while low levels of acoustic and visual privacy were related to increased academic activities (p < .0001 and p < .0005). The interaction of privacy and self-disclosure has significant implications for program design, mentor training and outcomes assessment.

Internet child pornography: The psychology and psychophysiology of viewing child pornography

Haines, Janet School of Psychology, University of Tasmania, Hobart, Australia

The aim of this study was to examine the psychophysiological and psychological processes associated with viewing Internet child pornography. A comparison was made between those with and without a history of child sex offending. In both cases, criminal charges for viewing child pornography were being faced. A guided imagery methodology was used to examine responses to personal experiences. Fundamental differences in the response to viewing child pornography were noted with non-offending being associated with a strong tension reduction process. Results have implications for understanding the motivations for this behaviour and providing explanations for the court.

Does the presence of a weapon shrink the functional field of view?

Hakoda, Yuji Dept. of Psychology, Kyushu University, Fukuoka, Japan Yamakawa, Akio Department of Psychology, Kyushu University, Fukuoka, Japan Nobata, Tomoe Department of Psychology, Kyushu University, Fukuoka, Japan Ninose, Yuri Department of Computer Science, Fukuoka University, Fukuoka, Japan

This research investigated the effect of a weapon on the functional field of view. Two series of affective pictures consisting of negative pictures with and without a weapon were presented to the participants. They were required to identify the letter presented at the fixation point along with the numbers occurring at each corner. Results revealed that the identification of the numbers was significantly low in the case of negative pictures with a weapon as opposed to that of negative pictures without one. This result indicates that the existence of a weapon shrinks the functional field of view.

The investigation of secondary traumatic stress levels observed in emergency service personnel in terms of dissociation level, perceived social support and coping strategies

Haksal, Pinar Ankara, Turkey Dag, Ihsan Psychology Department, Hacettepe University, Ankara, Turkey

In this study, secondary traumatic stress levels of health personnel working at emergency services are examined in terms of dissociation level, perceived social support and coping strategies. Health personnel working at hospital polyclinics were included in the study for comparison purposes. 159 emergency service worker and 153 polyclinic worker received five scales to investigate the relationship between work place and post-traumatic stress symptoms, psychopathology symptoms, dissociation level, perceived social support and coping strategies. Among the analysis, post-traumatic stress symptoms, psychopathology symptoms and dissociation levels of the employers at polyclinics were significantly higher than that of the employers at emergency services.

The psychosocial adaptation for displaced youth (age 16-20) Alsalam area Rabak, White Nile State Sudan

Hamadain, Osman Psychology, University of Blue Nile, Edamzine, Sudan

The aim of this study is to examine the psychosocial adaptation for displaced youth because of wars or others (age 16-20) Alsalam area Rabak, White Nile State Sudan. Hugh.M.Bell questionnaire for adaptation was used for a random sample 200 persons analyzed by SPSS. The outcomes are: 1. There were statistical significant differences in psychosocial adaptation between displaced youth. a. Worked or do not in favor of worked. b. Ethnic groups, in social dimension in favor of Arabs, Southerners, Noba. c. Educated and non educated. d. Age. e. Time spent in displaced area. 2. No differences in the causes of displacement.

Personal-organizational orientation of needs for job application and its effect

Han, Ying Dept. of Psychology, Peking University, Beijing, People's Republic of China Wang, Lei Department of Psychology, Peking University, Beijing, People's Republic of China

This study explored different job application need orientations using a self-developed questionnaire. A total of 285 employees or applicants participated in the survey. Two factors were identified by EFA, named as "personal need orientation" (α=.76) and "organizational need orientation" (α=.72), both significantly correlated to work value, self-efficacy or individualism/collectivism. The hierarchy regression analysis showed that personal-need-orientated individuals have a lower level of job satisfaction and higher level of turnover intention; organizational-need-orientation individuals have a lower level of turnover intention but no significant correlation with job satisfaction. The findings may help organizations reduce turnover rate.

A new strategy for learning highly-similar concepts

Hannon, Brenda Dept. of Psychology, Univ. of Texas at San Antonio, San Antonio, USA

In educational settings, students are often expected to learn pairs of concepts, such as fluid intelligence/ crystallized intelligence. For many students these concepts are difficult to learn because they have similar definitions that are easy to confuse. The challenge of learning these similar, yet often confused concepts is further complicated by the fact that students are often examined about differences between the concepts. This research tests the efficacy of a new strategy—called differential+associative processing–for learning highly similar concepts. The results revealed that differential+associative processing is better than elaboration and that it might even spontaneous transfer to new contexts.

The role of deliberate practice in the acquisition of AOC e-sports expertise

Hao, Ning Dept. of Psychology, East China Normal University, Shanghai, People's Republic of China Wu, Qinglin Department of Psychology, East China Normal University, Shanghai, People's Republic of China

This study explored the role of deliberate practice in the domain of AOC E-sports by analyzing the appraisement of 16 different domain activities made by 97 top experts. Then 271 players of 3 different skill levels were selected as subjects to investigate how the accumulative time spent on deliberate practice activities affects the player's skill level. The study shows that there are 3 kinds of deliberate practice activities in the AOC E-sport s domain and that the time different subjects spent on these activities causes significant differences. We suggest that the time spent on deliberate practice activities can effectively forecast the player's skill level while experience can't be used as a predictor.

The method of the measurement about fear of crime by a projective technique

Harada, Akira Koshien Junior College, Hyogo, Japan Toda, Hidetoshi Graduate School of Humanities, Koshien University, Takarazuka, Hyogo, Japan Kagemura, Yukihiro Graduate School of Humanities, Koshien University, Takarazuka, Hyogo, Japan Sugasawa, Hironari Graduate School of Humanities, Koshien University, Takarazuka, Hyogo, Japan

This study attempted to measure fear and risk perception of crime by a projective method. The experiment of constructing a desirable town for participants to live in was submitted. On the sheet that a virtual town area including their home was printed, the participants arranged the cards that the elements of a town were painted, for example, house, hospital, parking, bank and so on. After the construction was finished, they were asked where they have felt fear and risk perception of crime. The result suggested the relation between a position of home and a location of feeling them.

Self-Regulation as a predictor of delinquent behavior and socially inconsiderate behavior

Harada, Chika Education & Human Development, Nagoya University, Nagoya, Japan Yoshizawa, Hiroyuki Faculty of Education, Gifu Shotoku Gakuen University, Gifu, Japan Yoshida, Toshikazu Education & Human Developm, Nagoya University, Nagoya, Japan

This study focused on the temperament and ability facets of self-regulation, and examined their effect on delinquent and socially inconsiderate behavior. Temperament was assessed by the Behavioral Inhibition System / Behavioral Approach System scales, and the Effortful Control scale, and ability was assessed by the Social Self-Regulation (SSR) scale. Data were collected from 414 high school students, and 227 college students in Japan. Results of structural equation modeling revealed that the direct effect of SSR was stronger than temperament, and different factors of self-regulation influence delinquent behavior versus merely socially inconsiderate behavior. These differences and similarities were discussed.

Context and information reduction

Harsanyi, Geza Institute of Psychology, Humboldt University at Berlin, Berlin, Germany Frensch, Peter A. Institute of Psychology, Humboldt University at Berlin, Berlin, Germany

Individuals learn to optimize performance speed by reducing task-irrelevant information (Haider & Frensch, 1996). The nature of context affecting information reduction was investigated. Participants performed two categories of the same task, for one category information reduction was valid, for the second information reduction was invalid. The categories were indicated by contextual cues, which were either arbitrary for the task (Experiment 1) or were structural components of the task (Experiment 2). Results suggest that the categories were not discriminated on the basis of surface characteristics. Rather the categories were established, and information reduction was learned when structural characteristics affect task-processing.

Interaction of organizational environment and employees personality characteristics as predictor of counterproductive workplace behaviors in employees of an Iranian industrial company

Hashemi Sheykhshabani, Sayedesmaeil Dept. of Psychology, Shahid Chamran University, Ahvaz, Islamic Republic of Iran Shokrkon, Hossein Dept. of Psychology, Shahid Chamran University, Ahvaz, Islamic Republic of Iran Neissi, Abdolkazem Dept. of Psychology, Shahid Chamran University, Ahvaz,

Islamic Republic of Iran Shehni Yeilagh, Manijeh Dept. of Psychology, Shahid Chamran University, Ahvaz, Islamic Republic of Iran Haghighi, Jamal Dept. of Psychology, Shahid Chamran University, Ahvaz, Islamic Republic of Iran

Interaction relationships of important environmental variables and personality characteristics to counterproductive behaviors were investigated. 546 employees randomly selected were surveyed. Moderated regression analyses showed that personality characteristics moderated relationships between environmental variables and counterproductive behaviors. That is, the relationships between environmental variables and counterproductive behaviors were stronger for individuals high in trait anxiety and anger and low in agreeableness and conscientiousness than for individuals low in trait anxiety and anger and high in agreeableness and conscientiousness. Personality characteristics did not moderate the relationships of organizational constraints and counterproductive behaviors. In addition, trait anger and conscientiousness moderated the relationship of distributive justice to counterproductive work behaviors, but trait anxiety did not.

Behavioral outcomes associates with emotional contagion: A study among direct selling agents

Hashim, Junaidah Business Admin., KENMS, Intern. Islamic University, Kuala Lumpur, Malaysia Wok, Saodah DEPT OF COMMUNICATION, KHSIRK, INTERNATIONAL ISLAMIC UNIVERSI, KUALA LUMPUR, Malaysia

This study investigates how members in the group are affected by the happiness of their high achievers, what factors influence the emotional contagion to occur, and what are the effects of emotional contagion on group and organization. A total of 86 respondents participated in this study. It is found that emotional contagion is positively related with personal outcomes, it has an impact on both the group and the team. Emotional contagion is also related to organizational outcomes. The findings of this research expand previous researches by identifying the outcomes of emotional contagion on personal, groups, and organization.

Correlation between JIFP and prefrontal activity: A NIRS study

Hashimoto, Teruo Psychology, Keio Univ., Yokohama, Japan Yoshimitsu, Kaeko Psychology, Keio Univ., Tokyo, Japan Omori, Takahide Psychology, Keio Univ., Tokyo, Japan Kojima, Shozo Psychology, Keio Univ., Tokyo, Japan

JIFP_Japanese version of IFEEL (Infant Facial Expressions of Emotion from Looking at Pictures)_was used to study the reactions of potential caregivers (14 university students) to the varied emotions of infants, as revealed in their interpretations of a set of 30 pictures of 1-year-olds. The prefrontal activity was simultaneously measured by the near infrared spectroscopy which can easily measure neural response. This study was approved by the ethical committee of Keio university. The interpretations was quantified, and it's correlation with prefrontal activity showed emotion-related and/or attachment-related processes. This preliminary study suggests the usefulness of JIFP for screening the aptitude for child rearing is suggested.

Motives of criminal behavior among prison inmate in Khartoum state, Sudan

Hassan, Khalid Psychology, Elneelein, Khartoum, Sudan

This research was conducted on (300) inmates :(216) males, (83) Females to examine the motives of criminal. To fulfill this aim, the researchers administered scale for measuring motives of criminal behavior. The collected data were analyzed statistically by T-test for on sample, Mann Witney test, One Way Analysis (ANOVA) and product

moment correlation. The results showed that: Economic motives were predominantly higher compared to psychological and social motives. No significant statistical differences were found in criminal behavior related to gender. There were significant statistical differences on motives of criminal behavior among inmates attributed to the type of crime, and there was negative correlation between crime motives and education level.

Intelligence testing among students in greater Khartoum

Hassan, Hajshrife Psychology, Wight Nil, Khartoum, Sudan

This study examines intelligence testing among students in greater Khartoum, Sudan. The sample of study (N= 5549) selected randomly from primary, secondary schools and universities. The Standard Progressive Matrices was applied to both males (N=2961) and females (N=2588) and their age is ranged between 9-20 years. The study showed that (a) scores of intelligence increased with the increase of age (b) significant differences in intelligence scores between males and female participants was found in age group 10,11 12, 13 and 18 years and no significant differences in other ones.

Disproportionate allocation of cognitive resources during thought suppression in depressed individuals

Hattori, Yosuke Nagoya University, Nagoya, Japan Karasawa, Minoru Graduate School of Enviroment, Nagoya university, Nagoya, Japan

Depressed individuals often fail to control their unwanted thoughts. In order to reveal psychological mechanisms underling this phenomenon, we compared response latencies among depressed and non-depressed college students under a lexical decision task. Seventy-three participants judged whether a presented letter string was a word or not while thinking or not thinking various concepts. The depressed individuals showed a better performance than the non-depressed, only under the suppression instruction, suggesting that the depressed failed to allocate cognitive resource to the main task in this condition. Implications for the study of cognitive processes taking place among the depressed are discussed.

The ERPs N400 variation by difference of semantic relation between words

Hayashi, Nao Dept. of Psychology, Japan Women's University, Kawasaki, Japan Koyama, Takamasa Psychology, Japan Women's University, Kawasaki, Japan Kawahara, Yuri Psychology, Japan Women's University, Kawasaki, Japan

The effect of difference of semantic connection and relation between words on semantic priming was investigated by a specific word in a series of successively presented words. Ten participants were asked to judged semantic connection and relation under 3 condition of word connections antonym, category and syntactic. Results showed that reaction time was shortest the under the antonym condition and the longest under the same category condition. This phenomenon suggested that priming effect were larger in order of antonym > syntactic > category on RT. Therefore the number of expected items would effect on difference of semantic priming. The N400 results showed that attenuation were not occurred on type of non-related target.

The BDNF Val66Met polymorphism influences olfactory processing

Hedner, Margareta Dept. of Psychology, Stockholm University, Stockholm, Sweden Nilsson, Lars-Göran Psychology, Cognitive Psychology, Stockholm, Sweden Olofsson, Jonas Psychology, Psychology, Umeå, Sweden Hummel, Thomas

Otorhinolaryngology, Otorhinolaryngology, Dresden, Germany **Eriksson, Elias** Pharmacology, Pharmacology, Göteborg, Sweden **Melchoir, Lydia** Pharmacology, Pharmacology, Göteborg, Sweden **Larsson, Maria** Psychology, Psychology, Stockholm, Sweden

This study explored the relationship between allelic variations of the brain-derived neurotrophic factor (BDNF) and olfactory memory in normal subjects (n=827). Participants were derived from the Betula project, a large-scale population-based study focusing on memory and aging. Preliminary data suggest that the BDNF Val66Met polymorphism affects the individual variation in olfactory proficiency, such that met/met carriers were significantly poorer in identifying odors than val/val carriers. The Val66-Met effect did not interact with age, suggesting that the genetic effect is independent of the well-known aging effect on olfactory functioning.

Effectiveness of leadership styles in the non-profit sector: Results from a multi-sample study

Hehn, Verena FB Psychologie, Universität Münster, Münster, Germany **Rowold, Jens** 2: Applied and Work Psychology, WWU Münster, FB Psychologie, Münster, Germany

It seems important to compare and contrast several leadership theories both from a theoretical and empirical perspective. Consequently, the present study contributes to the nomological network of six leadership styles: Transactional, transformational, and ethical leadership, LMX, initiating structure and consideration. Based on data from several samples (i.e., public and private industries, profit and non-profit organizations) from the CoLeS (Context and Leadership Styles) project, evidence for criterion-oriented validity of these leadership styles is presented. Implications for leadership theory and practice are discussed.

Evaluation of the cognitive, behavioral and physiological responses to two versions of the Stroop test

Hernandez, Melba Behavioral Science and Tech., Simon Bolivar University, Caracas, Venezuela

Two Stroop test versions were used to evaluate physiological, behavioral and cognitive responding. Participants: 100 Venezuelan engineering students aged 18-25. Method: participants were exposed to both classically and computer administered Stroop tests. Blood pressure, heart rate, and ratings of test difficulty and state-anxiety were obtained after each test. Results: significant differences were observed in both cardiovascular response and perceived test difficulty relative to the two Stroop versions. Classically administered Stroop tests elicited greater physiological reactivity and higher ratings of test difficulty. No significant correlations between perceived test difficulty and state-anxiety were found; by contrast, a relationship was observed between perceived test difficulty and high physiological reactions.

Relation between temporal perspective and motivation towards the socio-labour integration of minors under judicial measures

Hernandez, Bernardo Psicologia Social, Universidad de La Laguna, La Laguna, Spain **Ruiz, Cristina** Psicologia Social, Universidad de La Laguna, La Laguna, Spain **Martín, Ana** Psicologia Social, Universidad de La Laguna, La Laguna, Spain **Hernández Fernaud, Estefania** Psicologia Social, Universidad de La Laguna, La Laguna, Spain

The study of the social rehabilitation processes of minors under judicial measures has revealed the importance of cognitive and motivationals variables in the efficiency of the intervention programs. This work analyses the relation between the temporal perspective and the motivation to realize behaviours related to the socio-labour integration. The questionnaires were administered individually to

171 minors under judicial measures. It was found positive and significant correlations between orientation to the future, negative past and positive past measures and motivation measures, but hedonistic present and fatalistic present measures did not correlate with those of motivation.

The parent version of the preschool Social Skills Rating Scale (SSRS) – Analysis of factorial structure and psychometric properties with a German sample

Hess, Markus Freie Universität Berlin, Berlin, Germany **Wille, Nora** Gesundheitswissenschaften, Universität Bielefeld, Bielefeld, Germany **Scheithauer, Herbert** Erz.wiss u. Psychologie, Freie Universität Berlin, Berlin, Germany **Kleiber, Dieter** Erz.wiss. und Psychologie, Freie Universität Berlin, Berlin, Germany **Kocalevent, Rüya** Erz.wiss. und Psychologie, Freie Universität Berlin, Berlin, Germany **Ravens-Sieberer, Ulrike** Gesundheitswissenschaften, Universität Bielefeld, Bielefeld, Germany

The Social Skills Rating Scale (SSRS) is a commonly used tool for measuring social skills. However recent studies have questioned the factorial structure of the SSRS (parent version). Therefore the present study tested the factorial structure of the parent version of the preschool SSRS with a German sample of 365 children (mean age 4.5 years) stemming from the BELLA-study. We conducted explorative factor analyses based on an ordinal data level. In addition internal consistencies, item-total, and inter-item correlations were used for scale construction. We will present a revision of the original 4-factor structure of the social skills scale with a reduced item pool.

Effects of leadership styles on branch-level profit

Hessmer, Stefan Inst. für Arbeitspsychologie, Universität Münster, Münster, Germany **Rowold, Jens** Arbeitspsychologie Prof. Hell, Westfälische Wilhelms-Uni, Muenster, Germany

Over the last 50 years, several leadership theories emerged. Empirical research demonstrated the positive relationship between each of these leadership styles and performance. However, empirical research that compares and contrasts the relative effects of these leadership styles on outcome criteria is virtually nonexistent. Thus, the present study compared the simultaneous effect of six leadership styles (initiating structure/consideration, transactional/transformational leadership, LMX, and ethical leadership) on objective performance (i.e., profit). Followers (N = 855) assessed these leadership styles of their respective supervisor (N = 178), who was the head of one branch of an international bank company. Results revealed that LMX, initiating structure and transformational leadership both contributed to branch-level profit, independently from each other.

Learning by note-taking vs. learning by drawing as a follow-up strategy for learning from texts

Hilbert, Tatjana School and Instrut. Psychology, Universität Göttingen, Göttingen, Germany **Nückles, Matthias** School and Instructional Psych, University of Goettingen, GEMI, Göttingen, Germany **Gierk, Benjamin** School and Instructional Psych, University of Goettingen, GEMI, Göttingen, Germany **Zander, Steffi** School and Instructional Psych, University of Goettingen, GEMI, Göttingen, Germany

Learner-generated drawings or notes are successful strategies for learning from texts. In a 2x2-experiment, on the one hand, we varied whether learners were instructed to take notes on six short texts or to draw an illustration of the texts' contents. On the other hand, learners were either allowed to use their notes/illustration for answering the posttest or not. Preliminary results showed that learners were better able to draw conclusions from the learning texts when they were allowed to use their notes/illustrations in the posttest. Also, drawing led to a more

coherent knowledge of the texts contents than note-taking.

Selective attention to visual motion is modulated by emotional distractors

Hindi Attar, Catherine Department of Psychology, University of Leipzig, Leipzig, Germany **Rose, Michael** Dep. of Systems Neuroscience, University Med. Center Hamburg, Hamburg, Germany **Büchel, Christian** University Med. Center Hamburg, University of Leipzig, Hamburg, Germany **Müller, Matthias M.** Department of Psychology, University of Leipzig, Leipzig, Germany

There is an ongoing debate over the extent to which selective attention can prevent the processing of task-irrelevant emotional distractors. In this fMRI study subjects attended a display of moving random dots and were asked to detect short intervals of coherent motions under two levels of task difficulty. Concurrently, neutral and emotional faces were presented in the background which were always task-irrelevant. Within motion-sensitive area MT we observed a significantly steeper decrease in activation with increasing task demands for fearful face distractors compared to neutral. This finding implicate a prioritized processing of unattended threat-related stimuli despite sparse attentional resources.

Different effects of Schubert's and Berlioz's music on emotion and incidental psychophysical responses

Hirooka, Mizuho Psychology, Japan Women's University, Kawasaki, Japan **Kawahara, Yuri** psychology, Japan Women's University, Kawasaki, Japan **Mochizuki, Toshiko** psychology, Japan Women's University, Kawasaki, Japan

To examine effects of music on emotion and incidental psychophysical responses, we recorded blood volume pulse (BVP) and respiration (RESP) while the subject listened to Schubert's and Berlioz's music. After the music presentation, Multiple Mood Scale (MMS) test was done. When the Schubert's music was presented, there were increases in BVP rate and RESP amplitude, and MMS test revealed introverted and affirmative emotion. When Berlioz's music was presented, there were decreases in BVP rate and RESP amplitude, and MMS test revealed extroverted and negative emotion. Thus, Schubert's music appears to be relaxing while Berlioz's music appears to make one nervous.

Which aspects of assessment-tasks matter for student learning?: The role of expectations and conceptions of assessment

Hirschfeld, Gerrit Inst. für Psychologie, Universität Münster, Münster, Germany **von Brachel, Ruth** Psychology, Ruhr University Bochum, Bochum, Germany

This paper investigates how students' expectations of particular assessment-tasks (e.g. 'naming definitions', 'justifying an own opinion') and conceptions of assessment (e.g. 'assessment as feedback', 'ignoring assessment results) influence the quantity and quality of students' learning. 356 students from different German universities completed an online-questionnaire about their expectations, conceptions and use of individual and cooperative learning strategies. In a SEM-model the assessed five expectation-factors and four conception-factors predicted significantly how much time students spent learning and which strategies they used. Implications for a model of self-regulated learning that contains both short-term (expectations) and long-term (conceptions) factors are discussed.

Validity of an implicit association test for assessing the big five personality dimensions

Hirschmüller, Sarah Inst. für Psychologie, Universität Leipzig, Leipzig, Germany Stopfer, Juliane Inst. für Psychologie, Universität Leipzig, Leipzig, Germany Back, Mitja Department of Psychology, University of Leipzig, Leipzig, Germany Schmukle, Stefan Department of Psychology, University of Leipzig, Leipzig, Germany Egloff, Boris Department of Psychology, University of Leipzig, Leipzig, Germany

The Implicit Association Test was adapted to measure the Big Five personality dimensions. We present a behavioral study that aimed at assessing the predictive validity of this Big Five-IAT: Participants were observed and videotaped in a variety of socially relevant situations. Behavioral criteria were derived to represent the five dimensions as well as varying degrees of automaticity and control. Results demonstrate that the IAT shows incremental predictive validity for neuroticism and extraversion but not for the other dimensions. Moreover these findings were not due to general effects of valence. Implications for theory and measurement of implicit self-concepts are discussed.

Measuring mathematics in pre-school age: Rasch model analyses for determining the dimensionality of competences

Hirschmann, Nicole Psychology, Vienna University, Wien, Austria Deimann, Pia Psychology, Vienna University, Wien, Austria Kastner-Koller, Ursula Psychology, Vienna University, Wien, Austria

Based on research concerning numerical abilities of preschool-children, an item pool for the assessment of mathematical abilities of three- to six-year-olds was constructed. Five scales were shown to conform to the assumptions of the Rasch model. They exhibited high reliabilities and good criterion-validities. Only low correlations with achievements in spatial and logical thinking emerged. Age-progress of the children could be represented well with the scales. Due to floor- and ceiling-effects however, none of the scales seemed appropriate for developmental diagnosis. Therefore, a new scale with an age-dependent starting-point was constructed, which also conformed to the assumptions of the Rasch model.

Individualized assessment of quality of life in old age

Holzhausen, Martin Berlin, Germany Martus, Peter Biometry & Clin. Epidemiol, Charité - Universitätsmedizin, Berlin, Germany Tesch-Römer, Clemens Director, Dt. Zentrum für Altersfragen, Berlin, Germany

Many elderly suffer from multiple chronic health-conditions. To avoid floor effects, assessment of quality of life should focus on life-satisfaction instead of function-related variables. A questionnaire was developed that enables participants to individually define domains constituting their quality of life. This individualized approach was chosen due to vast heterogeneity of impairments and resources in old age. Domain-specific ratings of satisfaction and importance are integrated into an overall life-satisfaction score. The questionnaire was successfully pilot-tested and pre-validated in an elderly sample. It allows for comparison of sum-scores as well as for detailed individual trajectories of domain-specific and content changes over time.

Attachment behavior style: Different influence on attribution and emotion

Hu, Ping Public Administration School, Renmin University of China, Beijing, People's Republic of China Guan, Yu Public Administration School, Renmin University of China, Beijing, People's Republic of China

Two studies examined attachment behavior style difference in attribution and emotion. The results indicated that (1)the attachment behavior had clear and significant influences on the social relationship satisfaction; (2)the attachment behavior styles had influences on both attribution and emotion. Regression analysis indicated behavior reactive was explained by two attachment behavior styles, two kinds of reactive emotion and one attribution dimension. These findings are consistent with the idea that adults with different internal working models of attachment are predisposed to think, feel and reactive differently in their relationships.

Relation among trauma, trait coping, and students' suicide attitude after super typhoon Saomai

Huang, Xiaozhong Institute of Psychology, Zhejiang Normal University, Jinhua City, People's Republic of China Li, Weijian Institute of Psychology, Zhejiang Normal University, Jinhua City, Zhejiang province, People's Republic of China

Based on theory of ego psychology model and relational model of stress, the present study was to explore the relation among trauma, trait coping, and students' suicide attitude after super typhoon Saomai. With 650 participants (10-18 years old) around landing places of Saomai, Post-trauma Symptom Reaction Questionnaire, Trait Coping Styles Questionnaire, and Suicide Attitude Questionnaire were used. The results indicated that (a) post-trauma symptom reaction had direct effect on suicide attitude; (b) the cognitive dimension of post-trauma symptom reaction had significant predictive effect on suicide attitude. The results took sides with relational model of stress, coping had the contextual feature. cognitive therapy is recommended to adopt for traumatic students.

Women managers' careers in information technology field: A cross-cultural comparison between China and Finland

Huang, Jiehua School of Business, Lappeenranta University, Lappeenranta, Finland Aaltio, Iiris School of Business and Economi, University of Jyvaskyla, Jyvaskyla, Finland

This study explores women managers' career in information technology (IT) in China and Finland. Used Q-methodology, in-depth interview and interpretive analysis as background methodology, which are based theoretical on a feminist standpoint, cultural sensitive career theory and Individual Difference Theory of Gender and IT, this study links the real experience of women IT managers' career with the concrete historical, political, and economic structures of nation and organization. Results show the career scripts and guanxi (network) bases of women mangers in cross-cultural context, which imply the gendered nature of IT and cultural notions of what is an ideal woman. Implications for HRM are discussed.

Emotions in the process of risky decision making: Spontaneous verbal expressions

Huber, Odilo W. Psychology Department, University of Fribourg, Fribourg, Switzerland Bär, Arlette S. Psychology Department, University of Fribourg, Fribourg, Switzerland

An experiment investigates spontaneous verbal expressions of emotions during information search in quasi-naturalistic risky scenarios. 198 Subjects got a scarce description of the decision situation. Subsequently they asked questions, and got matching answers. Spontaneous verbal statements were recorded and later coded regarding emotional content. As expected, respective emotions were connected with evaluation of positive and negative consequences. Further, process related negative emotions emerged due to risk taking in choice, and positive ones if subjects terminated the process with the choice of an alternative after having successfully searched for possibilities to defuse its risky negative outcome.

General knowledge and need for cognition – Is there a mediating role of behavioral habits?

Huic, Aleksandra Psychology, University of Zagreb, Zagreb, Croatia Urch, Drazen Psychology, University of Zagreb, Zagreb, Croatia Tonkovic, Masa Psychology, University of Zagreb, Zagreb, Croatia Tomisa, Tia Psychology, University of Zagreb, Zagreb, Croatia Ljubotina, Damir University of Zagreb, Zagreb, Croatia Sverko, Dina Psychology, University of Zagreb, Zagreb, Croatia

Personality and behavioral correlates of general knowledge were examined. General knowledge was assessed with an advanced vocabulary test (consisting of words of latin and greek origin). Need for Cognition Scale (Caccioppo and Petty, 1992) was administered, along with questions about behavioral habits in relation to theaters, museums, movies and libraries. We also assessed the respondents exposure to different kinds of media information – TV, radio, Internet, daily news, scientific and entertainment magazines and books. Total of 600 respondents (50% male and 50% female; 49% high school and 51% higher education) participated in the study. Applied and theoretical implications are discussed.

Self-consciousness and different ways of measuring stress

Huic, Aleksandra Psychology, University of Zagreb, Zagreb, Croatia Kamenov, Zeljka Psychology, University of Zagreb, Zagreb, Croatia Jokic-Begic, Natasa Psychology, University of Zagreb, Zagreb, Croatia Lauri Korajlija, Anita Psychology, University of Zagreb, Zagreb, Croatia

Self-consciousness is a tendency of the individual to focus onto him/herself. It consists of two factors – private and public self-consciousness. Research that tried to link self-consciousness with levels of stress is inconclusive. The aim of this study was to examine individual differences in self-consciousness in relation to different ways of stress measurement. Self-consciousness scale was administered together with three instruments measuring levels of stress. 418 individuals, aged 22 to 68, participated in the study. Relations among measured variables are discussed with regard to Trapnell and Campbell's (1999) distinction to two self-consciousness motives-rumination and reflection.

Different perspectives in treating post-traumatic stress disorder patients after mass disasters and terrorist attacks

Icoz, Ferhat Dept. of Psychology, Istanbul Bilgi University, Istanbul, Turkey

This poster is a comparative archival research on treatment methods of victims of mass disaster and terrorism, focusing on different instances from the U.S.A, Israel, Turkey, Finland and Germany. This poster contains three parts, firstly briefly introducing PTSD, secondly introducing different incidents from these countries and symtoms that were revealed after the incident, and lastly compares methods used in different indicents. The aim of this research is to identify different methods and perspectives used in different incidents in different countries, to compare possible problems during treatment and outcomes for patients of these treatment methods.

Environmental competence in destination marathon runners

Imamichi, Tomoaki Environmental Psychology, City University of New York, Hoboken, USA

This project will examine environmental competence (the ability to deal with one's surroundings in an effective and stimulating manner) via destination marathon runners. A semi-structured interview of destination marathon runners will provide insight into environmental competence: how they have dealt with an unfamiliar environment and with the challenge of the marathon. In order to successfully (bodily and experientially) complete a destination marathon, the smooth transition with one's surroundings is essential. Planning and dwelling practices to achieve this smooth transition, and bodily and experiential aspects are examined; concepts of flow and restorative environments are reevaluated.

Preliminar psychometric properties of the Portuguese version of the questionnaire about interpersonal difficulties for adolescents

Ingles, Candido J. *Dept. of Health Psychology, Universidad Miguel Hernandez, Elche, Spain* **Castanheira, Joao** *Health Psychology, Miguel Hernandez University, Elche, Alicante, Spain* **Ribeiro, Filipe** *Health Psychology, Miguel Hernandez University, Elche, Alicante, Spain* **Garcia Fernandez, Jose M.** *Psychology, University of Alicante, Alicante, Spain*

This study evaluated the psychometric properties of the Questionnaire about Interpersonal Difficulties for Adolescents (QIDA) in a sample of Portuguese adolescents. Exploratory and confirmatory factor analyses supported a four-factor structure of the QIDA in the Portuguese sample: Assertiveness, Heterosexual Relationships, Public Speaking, and Family and Friends Relationships. Internal consistency ($\alpha = 0.91$) and test-retest reliability (r = 0.84) were appropriate. The results revealed a clear and predictable pattern of relationships between the QIDA and the Social Anxiety Scale for Adolescents, the School Anxiety Questionnaire and the International Personality Item Pool.

The roll of encoding strategies on face recognition memory

Ito, Yoshie *Institute of HSC, Nihon University, Tokyo, Japan*

This study investigated the influence of facial expressions and encoding strategies on recognition memory. Participants looked some happy and neutral faces they had never seen before, and judged with distinctive feature judgment assumed to be isolated of facial features, or distinctive expression judgment supposed to lead the configural processing of the faces. About thirty minutes later, an unexpected recognition test was carried out. In this retrieval, upright or inverted faces were presented. The results showed changing expressions between encoding and retrieval decreased the recognition performance. Furthermore, the encoding strategies did not influence the memory performance.

Verbal abuse and cognition in the developing mind

Ittyerah, Miriam *CNRS/ MNHN 5145, Musee de l'Homme, Paris, France* **Kochar, Reema** *Psychology, University of Delhi, Delhi, India* **Babu, Nandita** *Psychology, University of Delhi, Delhi, India*

The study investigated the detrimental effects of verbal abuse on children. A Verbal abuse scale was administered to abused and non-abused children of three age- groups (8 years, 11 years, 15 years) and self reported measures of verbal abuse were collected from 180 children. The Cognitive Assessment Schedule was administered. Results indicated that overall boys performed better than the girls and abused children performed poorly than the non-abused children. Developmental changes were found for the attention and coding tasks, whereas gender differences were seen only for the attention tasks. Therefore verbal abuse has consequences that are detrimental to development.

Determinants of public opinion on sentences and their preference for different types of sentences

Iviàiæ, Ines *Institute of Social Sciences, Zagreb, Croatia* **Franc, Renata** *psychology, Institute of Social Sciences, Zagreb, Croatia* **Sakic, Vlado** *psychology, Institute of Social Sciences, Zagreb, Croatia*

The aim of study was to examine the sociodemographic variables, crime attributions and sentencing goals as determinants of opinions on sentences and preference of sentence for burglary. Data (N=1004) were analyzed by discriminant analysis. Depending on the type of dependent variable canonic correlation related to the first significant function ranged from .25 to .36 while classification results showed that in average from 49% to 66.1% of cases were correctly classified. Definition of first function showed to be related to the type of dependent variable, but in each case it was mostly defined by punishment or rehabilitation as sentencing goals.

Unexpected action effects elicit deviance-related brain potentials and cause attentional distraction

Iwanaga, Mio *Hiroshima University, Higashi-Hiroshima, Japan* **Nittono, Hiroshi** *Cognitive Psychophysiology Lab, Hiroshima University, Higashi-Hiroshima, Japan*

To examine how people perceive the effects of their actions, we recorded event-related potentials during a self-paced, random generation task. Sixteen participants randomly pressed one of two buttons once every 1–2 s. Each press triggered either a 1000 or 2000 Hz tone. The button–tone combination was initially fixed, and then became variable. When a press produced a tone that was initially associated with the opposite button (p = .15), N2, P300, and a positive slow wave occurred. Intervals between each press increased after mismatched tones compared with matched ones. Action effects that differ from the expectation cause attentional distraction.

Everyday life heroes (in white): The end of a dream job? Burnout of general practitioners (GP)

Iwanowa, Anna *Institut für Psychologie, Innsbruck, Austria*

This study focuses on the investigation of burnout and mental health by GP. The specific resources, requirements and demands in the job of GP as well as socio-demographic variables were explored by interviews and questionnaires. A total of 2,500 completed questionnaires were returned and evaluated. Job burnout was measured by MBI and general health by the GHQ. A new questionnaire of specific job requirements was developed and used to test the linkage between job characteristics, exhaustion, cynicism and a perception of low personal accomplishment and general health. The mediating role of burnout was tested with Structural equation modelling analysis.

Differences in perceptions of the ward atmosphere among patients and staff in psychiatric inpatient care

Jörgensen, Kjetil Nordbö *Dept. of Psychology, Norwegian Univ. of Sci. & Tech, Trondheim, Norway* **Römma, Vidat** *Dept. of Psychology, Norwegian Univ. of Sci. &, Trondheim, Norway* **Rundmo, Torbjörn** *Dept. of Psychology, Norwegian Univ. of Sci. &, Trondheim, Norway*

Previous research using the Ward Atmosphere Scale (WAS) has shown that patients and staff from the same wards may perceive the treatment environment differently. The aim of the present study was to replicate the finding that patients and staff may respond differently to the WAS, and furthermore to assess the level of agreement between their scores. 65 patients and 60 staff members from four different ward units completed the Ward Atmosphere Scale questionnaire. Significant differences between patients' and staff's scores were found. Staff tended to view the ward environment in a more positive way than patients.

The utility of the personality-interest test in predicting changes in chronic fatigue in adolescents: A two-year longitudinal study

Janowski, Konrad *Milano, Italy* **Luszczak, Krzysztof** *Dep. of Clinical Psychology, Catholic University of Lublin, Lublin, Poland* **Szewczyk, Leszek** *Dep. of Clinical Psychology, Catholic University of lublin, Lublin, Poland*

The objective of this study was to evaluate the potential utility of Personality-Interest Test in predicting changes in chronic fatigue in adolescents. 103 high school students took part in the study and were evaluated by means of the Personality-Interest Test and Cumulative Fatigue Index on their first year at high school and two years later. The initial levels of fatigue were found non-significant in predicting the change in the level of fatigue. Three subscales from the Personality-Interest Test were found to predict the future change in fatigue: prosocial attitudes, linguistic and literary interests and the preference for living and work in the countryside.

The relationship between emotion regulation strategy and memory of children

Jiang, Yuan *Sport Psychology, Beijing Sport University, Beijing, People's Republic of China* **Shen, Deli** *Psychology, Tianjin Normal University, Tianjin, People's Republic of China* **Bai, Xuejun** *Psychology, Tianjin Normal University, Beijing, People's Republic of China*

In this study, 336 students from grade five in the primary school and grade two in the junior and senior school participate in the experiment. The study is about the relationship between emotion regulation strategy and memory. The results of the study indicate: Recognition RT of the subjects who adopt cognitive reappraisal is faster than expression suppression whether word or figure condition. There is no significant difference in recognition RT between word and figure condition when the subjects adopt expression suppression; recognition RT of word condition is faster than the one of figure condition when the subjects adopt cognition reappraisal.

Time as a key factor for a new dynamic model of job satisfaction: Theoretical concept and empirical data

Jiménez, Paul *Inst. für Psychologie, Universität Graz, Graz, Austria*

The aspect of job satisfaction has been seen as a relatively static concept. The estimation of changes which influence job satisfaction has to explained in a new way: A new instrument which makes it possible to relate dynamic changes to job satisfaction and also the latest results in research - from a representative survey in Austria with 1500 persons - are presented. The scale of development-estimations shows a high internal consistency with r>.8. The correlations with external scales show different validity in the expected direction. The scale helps to analyse the work situation and also to implement intervention strategies.

Danger Ideation Reduction Therapy (DIRT): Preliminary findings with three obsessive-compulsive checkers

Jones, Mairwen *Behav. & Community Health, University of Sydney, Sydney, Australia* **Menzies, Ross** *Behavioural & Community Hl, The University of Sydney, Lidcombe Sydney, Australia* **Vaccaro, Lisa** *Behavioural & Community Hl, The University of Sydney, Lidcombe Sydney, Australia*

Objectives: Investigated a new treatment package for Obsessive Compulsive Disorder (OCD) checkers. Methods: Three OCD checkers received eight to 14 individual sessions of Danger Ideation Reduction Therapy (DIRT). Assessment with the Maudsley Obsessional-Compulsive Inventory, Beck Depression Inventory-II and Global Assessment of

Severity was conducted at pre, post and follow-up. Results: DIRT was associated with significant decreases in OCD symptoms across all measures and was maintained over the four-month follow-up period in all three cases. Conclusions: Strong support for the efficacy of DIRT was found. All three cases had a longstanding OCD history (12-30 yrs), yet still responded rapidly to DIRT.

Psychometric properties of two generalized anxiety disorder questionnaires in Mexican residents

Jurado, Samuel Facultad de Psicología, UNAM, México, Mexico Campos, Patrica Psicología Aplicada, INP"RFM", México, D.F., Mexico

Objective: determine reliability and validation of the PSWQ and GAD-Q-IV in residents of México City. Methods: 1504 participants (733 men and 771 women), between 12 and 78 years old (X=26.35, SD=12.38) answered the spanish version of both questionnaires. Cronbachs Alfa for the PSWQ was .76. Concurrent validity between the PSWQ and GAD-Q-IV was Spearman Rho = .53. Conclusions: Both instruments are psychometrically relevant to assess the construct of worry.

Some personal correlates of justice sensitivity

Jurkin, Marina Dept. of Psychology, University of Zadar, Zadar, Croatia Cubela Adoric, Vera Department of Psychology, University of Zadar, Zadar, Croatia

The aim of this study was to investigate how the justice sensitivity from victim, observer and beneficiary perspectives relates to justice beliefs, Machiavellianism, empathy and anomy. A questionnaire package was administered in a group of 178 students at the University of Zadar, Croatia. The relationships with justice variables and empathy were similar for the three perspectives. Machiavellianism correlated negatively with beneficiary and observer sensitivity, whereas the anomy was associated with the victim and observer perspectives. These results provided partial support for previous findings and suggest that future research would benefit from exploring justice sensitivity in different cultures.

Age differences in social emotions recognition

Justo, Mariline Psychology, University of the Algarve, Olhão, Portugal Simão, Cláudia Psychology, University of the Algarve, Olhão, Portugal Martins, Ana Psychology, University of the Algarve, Olhão, Portugal

The main objective of this study was to understand age effect in social emotion (Arrogance, Guilt and Jealousy) recognition. A hundred and one participants were distributed by age groups (children, adolescents and adults). They had to recognize 27 photos representing social emotions. It was asked the dominant emotion in each photo. All participants were screened with cognitive tests. Our results suggest that age has an influence in the recognition of social emotions in study.

Computer-assisted cognitive training as a trauma-unspecific intervention for posttraumatic stress disorder

König, Dorothea Inst. für Klin. Psychologie, Universität Wien, Wien, Austria Lueger-Schuster, Brigitte Clinical and Health Psychology, University of Vienna, Vienna, Austria Kryspin-Exner, Ilse Clinical and Health Psychology, University of Vienna, Vienna, Austria

Objectives: Posttraumatic stress disorder (PTSD) often produces impairments of cognitive functions such as concentration and memory. The aim of the pilot study was to evaluate a computer-assisted cognitive training (CCT) in patients with PTSD. Methods: Using the programme COGPACK ten sessions were arranged focusing on exercises regarding concentration and memory. Results: After the CCT objective and subjective evaluations of the patients' cognitive capacity indicated significant improvements, symptomatology was significantly decreased. Secondary effects such as increasing self-esteem were observed. Conclusions: The evaluation of the CCT provides first indications of the effectiveness of a trauma-unspecific intervention for patients with PTSD.

Investigation of responsibility attitude's validity and reliability

Kabirnezhad, Sanaz Tabriz, Islamic Republic of Iran Mahmood Ali, Majid TABRIZ UNIVERSITY, PSYCHOLOGY, tabriz, Islamic Republic of Iran Sharifi, Mohammad Amin TABRIZ UNIVERSITY, PSYCHOLOGY, tabriz, Islamic Republic of Iran

At the present research, the validity and reliability of Responsibility Attitude Scale (RAS) was studied.The result of this research showed that RAS had acceptable validity coefficient. In this research, correlation between Responsibility Attitude Scale, Maudsley Obsessional and Compulsive Inventory and between Responsibility Attitude Scale, Dysfunctional Attitude Scale were 0.45 and 0/51, respectively, also validity of the RAS was evaluated by exploratory factor analysis. In the second research 76 students from Tabriz took part in order to study reliability of RAS. The test-retest reliability coefficient of the scale in one-week interval, correlation odd and even items and splitting were 0.84, 0.92, and 0.61 respectively. The internal consistency of the RAS was 0.94.

Self-regulation for learning in primary school: Relations to achievement goals and school adaptation

Kambara, Masahiko Educational Psychology, Chiba University, Chiba, Japan Taketsuna, Seiichiro Psychology, Gakushuin University, Tokyo, Japan Ogata, Ryoko Psychology, Gakushuin University, Tokyo, Japan Takizawa, Eri Psychology, Gakushuin University, Tokyo, Japan Saito, Sumiko Psychology, Gakushuin University, Tokyo, Japan Sakai, Fujiko Psychology, Gakushuin University, Tokyo, Japan

The purpose of this study was to investigate the relations of self-regulation to achievement goals and children's school adaptation. In study I, a questionnaire on self-regulation for learning was administered to 131 sixth-grade students. Factor analysis revealed that self-regulation for learning was constructed by three factors: general, concentration and self-reward. In study II, 111 sixth-grade students answered a questionnaire on self-regulation for learning, learning strategies, achievement goals and school adaptation. Path analysis showed the positive effect of mastery-approach goal on general self regulation and also the latter had positive effect on learning behaviors,mastery-avoidance goal showed negative effect on leaning behaviors.

Executive control of attention benefits from positive emotion: ERP evidence

Kanske, Philipp Inst. für Neuropsychologie, Max-Planck-Institut, Leipzig, Germany Kotz, Sonja A. Neuropsychology, Max Planck Inst Cogn Brain Sci, Leipzig, Germany

We previously showed that executive control of attention is more efficient in the presence of emotionally negative words (Kanske & Kotz, 2007). Here we addressed the question whether executive attention also benefits from positive emotion. Emotionally positive words (e.g. kiss, happiness) were presented in a version of the flanker task. The RT conflict effect (incongruent-congruent) was reduced in emotional trials, the conflict N200, indexing conflict processing, was enlarged. These results resemble those for negative words suggesting that executive control of attention is more efficient in both emotionally salient positive and negative situations.

Methods to assess preschool age children reactions to bombing

Kapor Stanulovic, Nila Dept. of Psychology, University of Novi Pazar, Novi Pazar, Serbia Stanulovic, Ada Center for research, University of Novi Pazar, Novi Pazar,

Preschool children's cognitive functioning is limited to operations characteristic for preoperational stage of cognitive development This means that they cognitively function best when given concrete visual tasks. In addition, preschool children have limited capacity to differentiate among various emotional states and often have poorly developed vocabulary to name own feelings. A visual scale that allows a child to express the intensity of own emotional state by pointing out on a visual scale its intensity resolves the above mentioned limitations. Data from a study assessing the amount of fear reactions to the experience of bombing will be presented in which a visual scale to describe the intensity of fear has been used.

The place attachment and the mental representations of a public space in a Turkish big city

Karakus, Pelin Dept. of Social Psychology, Ege University, Izmir, Turkey Göregenli, Melek Social Psychology, Ege University, Izmir, Turkey

The study aims to determine the mental representations and levels of place attachment of a public space (Fair area-Kültürpark) in one of the big cities of Turkey, Izmir. The data has been collected with hand-drawn mental maps, semi-structural interview forms (Francescate & Mebane, 1973; Lynch, 1960; Manzo, 2005) and questionnaires (Lalli, 1992). Interviews, maps and questionnaires were conducted with 279 people (135 women and 144 men). The results show that people who live in Izmir generally evaluate this public space as an important part of their personal, cultural and symbolic history and they think this public space should be conserved and be improved according to upcoming interests and demands.

Supervisor behavior and employees' job neglect: A study of Australian employees

Karimi, Leila Research and Development, Helen Macpherson Institute, Melbourne, Australia

We investigated the extent to which supervisor behavior is associated with employees' job neglect. We also investigated the efficacy of the Kidwell-Robie measure of job neglect in a non-U.S. sample. Australian employees from three organizations reported on their supervisor's behavior, as well as their levels of job neglect. Results from correlation and multiple regression analysis support our hypothesis that both positive and negative supervisor behavior is associated with job neglect. Our findings provide additional evidence for the important effects supervisors can have on employees.

Psychological constitution of effectivization of self-learning

Kasatkina, Olga Psychologie of Education, MSUPE, Moscow, Russia

The goal of this research is to understand the psychological aspect of self-study and find a method that would simplify the process and give more results. The methods used: 1) the theoretical analyses; chosen the "Mind Maps" (T. Buzan)(the "MM"-method); 2) an empirical research (a forming experiment). The data were processed with the help of content analyses and expert evaluation. The students were taught the "MM"-method and used it on the purpose of self-learning. The results of the experiment held prove that using the "MM"-method makes the process of self-learning more productive, which has a positive impact on the level of knowledge of students.

Measurement invariance between a traditional and a web-based application of the German Anxiety Sensitivity Index–3 and its psychometric quality
Kemper, Christoph Psychology, Gutenberg University, Mainz, Germany
Web-based psychometric research using adaptations of paper-and-pencil personality/psychopathology measures is on the rise. Although web-based versions may be reliable and valid, they may not necessarily measure the same constructs as their traditional antecedents. Measurement invariance is rarely tested. Within a confirmatory factor-analytic framework, measurement invariance of a traditional and a web-based version of the Anxiety Sensitivity Index–3 (ASI-3; Taylor, Zvolensky, Cox, Deacon, Heimberg & Ledley et al., 2007) was evaluated and fully confirmed (N=3360). Reliability and validity coefficients are reported. The ASI-3 displayed sound psychometric properties irrespective of its mode of application. Theoretical and practical implications will be discussed.

Obligations and duties: Hong Kong students' conceptions of citizenship responsibilities
Kennedy, Kerry Curriculum & Instruction, The HK Institute of Education, Tai Po, China, People's Republic of : Hong Kong SAR
Citizenship responsibilities have been measured in different ways. Little attention has been paid to how adolescents as future citizens construct these responsibilities. This paper will report on a project concerned with adolescents in Hong Kong and how they understood the responsibilities of 'good citizens'. Drawing on data from the IEA Civic Education Study, all items relating to student conceptions of the 'good citizen' were re-analyzed using exploratory and confirmatory factor analysis. A 3 –factor model was identified showing adequate fit to the data. This model suggested that students identified obligations and duties as the main responsibilities of citizens.

Effect of mental simulation training on educational performance between talented and normal students in Iran
Khalili, Fatemeh Psychology, Shahid Beheshti University, Tehran, Islamic Republic of Iran Minakari, Mahmood Psychology, Shahid Beheshti University, Tehran, Islamic Republic of Iran Pakdaman, Shahla Psychology, Shahid Beheshti University, Tehran, Islamic Republic of Iran
The purpose was to investigate how intelligence could modulate the effect of mental simulation on educational performance. Hypothesies : educational performance improve with mental simulation strategies. Instruments, for educational performance we used EPT(Taylor,1999) and for mental simulation trainning, different strategy. Sampeling .208 talented and normal students were selected, then divided to 4 categories. Results: Educational performance improved with mental simulation training.It could regulate five skills which form educational performance, Based on investigating the effects of IQ, talented students used more outcome simulation and normal student used more process simulation.Outcom simulation is more intresting for tallented student becouse they used process simulation apparently.

Tele-therapy: An approach to provide mental health services to remote and rural areas
Kharkwal, Meena Haucourt Moulaine, France
Mental health services are totally unavailable to rural and remote India. Mental illnesses are still considered as life long handicap and most of the time remain untreated. The objective of the present study was to find out how the patients from remote areas can be benefited by tele-therapy. The area of present study includes a town and surrounding villages of Himalayan region. The data base is

patients records from researcher's private practice. The findings of the study show that it is possible to provide professional mental health services to rural and remote areas through telecommunication and one trained worker in community. The probable misuse of this approach has also been discussed.

Earthquake behavior rules for disable people
Kirakosyan, Hasmik Psychology, Urartu University, Yerevan, Armenia
In Armenia disabled people comprise 4,4% of the population while the people with psychical problems comprise 0,5% of the population. In absolute numbers they are 141368 and 15998 respectively. Therefore our purpose is to develop the earthquake behavior rules and relevant techniques for those people. The problem may be solved as follows: • Study and outline the safety means for people with physical and psychical defects • Develop guidelines for the guardians of those people • Teach the people and their guardians for behavior rules through lectures and workshops. The necessary assistance and safety means are selected and implemented at several special schools.

Increased rumination is associated with poor internalisation of personal strivings
Kirkegaard Thomsen, Dorthe Department of Psychology, University of Aarhus, Aarhus, Denmark Tønnesvang, Jan Department of Psychology, University of Aarhus, Aarhus, Denmark Schnieber, Anette Department of Psychology, University of Aarhus, Aarhus, Denmark Hammershøj Olesen, Martin Department of Psychology, University of Aarhus, Aarhus, Denmark
Individual differences in rumination may be explained by differing degrees of internalization of personal strivings in self-regulation processes. Six-hundred-and-seventy-seven students completed an e-based survey including the Rumination-Reflection Questionnaire, listed five important personal strivings and rated these on four questions measuring internalisation (extrinsic, introjected, identified, intrinsic). Correlations showed that a higher degree of rumination was associated with more extrinsic strivings (r(674)=0.21, p<0.001), more introjected strivings (r(675)=0.30, p<0.001), less identified strivings (r(675)=-0.15, p<0.001) and less intrinsic strivings (r(675)=-0.15, p<0.001). The results suggest that theories of rumination should include self-regulation processes and motivation.

The employability development of business students
Kirovova, Iva Management Dept., Faculty of Economics, Ostrava, Czech Republic
The educational system should enhance graduates' employability. Graduates need to be equipped with the knowledge, skills, and personal qualities required by organizations and the labor market. Objective: To determine how students perceive the effectiveness of their university studies. Hypothesis: Students evaluate what they gain through university studies in accordance with employability characteristics. Setting for the study: Faculty of Economics, Technical University of Ostrava. Methods: questionnaire, focus group. Respondents: N=190, MA students (final year) specializing in management. Results: Significant differences exist between the general employability characteristics now required and those developed through university studies.

Risk and protective factors for juvenile delinquencies in children with pervasive developmental disorders: Findings from life-story research
Kita, Yosuke Graduate School of Education, Tohoku University, Sendai, Japan Tanaka, Mari Graduate school of Education, Tohoku University, Sendai, Japan Kikuchi, Takekatsu Graduate school of Education, Tohoku University, Sendai, Japan

Based on life-stories that reflect their internal worlds, this study explores risk and protective factors for juvenile delinquency in children with pervasive developmental disorders (PDD). Life-story interviews have been continuously conducted with an adolescent boy with PDD who committed an assault. We have identified two risk factors, poor acquisition of social skills and unstable family and school environment, and one protective factor, presence of stable relationships and emotional bonds. These factors demonstrate three actions for comprehensive support for them: to teach social skills, to put in place measures to control a delinquent activity, and to support their internal worlds.

Mood states and processing of stereotype information
Kitamura, Hideya Sociology, Toyo University, Tokyo, Japan Sato, Shigetaka Sociology, Toyo University, Tokyo, Japan
The influence of processing of stereotype information on the recipients' mood states were investigated. Forty-three participants were presented with information which was congruent or incongruent of the stereotype(the university clubs), and their affective responses were measured by self-rating scales and electrodermal activities. The results showed the level of elaborative thinking functioned as a moderate variable. Highs in elaborative thinking kept their attention level throughout the difficult task including incongruent information, while lows in elaborative thinking did not keep their effort and were most pleasant when they read congruent information of stereotypes. The relation of affect with cognitive performance was discussed.

Underactivation of left occipitotemporal cortex in developmental dyslexia: General or specific?
Klackl, Johannes Salzburg, Austria Wimmer, Heinz NW Fakultät, Universität Salzburg, Salzburg, Austria Kronbichler, Martin Psychologie, Universität Salzburg, Salzburg, Austria
The reduced left occipitotemporal (OT) activation characteristic for dyslexic reading may be specific to words or reflect a general dysfunction. 13 dyslexics and 15 controls participated in a functional MRI study. They had to detect the presence of two identical adjacent characters in words and strings of consonants and false fonts. Controls, but not dyslexics, exhibited increasing OT activation from false font strings to consonant strings to words. The group difference was largest for words and smallest, but still reliable, for false fonts. This pattern speaks for a general OT dysfunction which becomes most evident for words.

Measurement equivalence of written C-tests and multiple-choice C-tests
Klemmert, Hella Bundesagentur für Arbeit, Nürnberg, Germany
C-Tests are integrative written tests of general language proficiency based on the concept of reduced redundancy. Multiple-Choice (MC) C-Tests offer economical advantages, but their validity is unclear. Therefore n=1061 customers of the Psychological Service of the German Federal Employment Agency completed an established German C-Test and a computerized MC-Version in randomized order. Confirmatory factor analyses and item response theory analyses revealed separable but highly correlated constructs (r=.95). The MC-Version is not biased with respect to sex, age or german language proficiency. Due to the positive results now an English MC C-Test is under development. Preliminary results will be presented.

Rasch-scalability of a revised German version of the Family Relations Test

Kleylein, Meike Inst. für Psychologie I, Universität Würzburg, Würzburg, Germany Hommers, Wilfried Department of Psychology I, University of Würzburg, Würzburg, Germany

The Family Relations Test is used to compare parents in matters of custody and visitation disputes. Therefore, the psychometric properties of a revised German version of the Family Relations Test were examined using item response theory. The difference scores "Mother minus Father" of the scales "Positive", "Negative", "Dependency", "Sum of positive and negative", and "Emotional balance" were obtained from a sample of 922 children between 3 and 8 years in age. The results showed that the scales "Positive" and "Dependency" were consistent with the Rasch-model after eliminating items. Rasch-scalability of the difference scales was compared with classical approach.

Measurement differences of verbal cognitive ability tests in native speakers vs. second-language speakers

Klinck, Dorothea Psychologischer Dienst, Bundesagentur für Arbeit, Nürnberg, Germany

What do verbal cognitive ability tests measure when applied to second-language speakers in comparison to native speakers? Scores of verbal, numerical and figural ability tests completed by 65000 second-language and 115000 first-language clients of the German Federal Employment Agency were analysed using SEM: Intercorrelations between the different verbal tests are of comparable size in both groups, but in the second-language speakers the verbal ability construct is more clearly separated from the figural and numerical ability construct. Therefore with second-language speakers a verbal overall-score can be computed, but it reflects more language proficiency aspects and should not be aggregated with nonverbal scores.

Development and evaluation of a computerized adaptive test for the measurement of stress perception (Stress-CAT)

Kocalevent, Rüya-Daniela AB Psychosoziale Prävention, Freie Universität Berlin, Berlin, Germany Becker, Janine Psychosomatik, Charité, Berlin, Germany Rose, Matthias QualityMetric Incorporated, QualityMetric Incorporated, Richmond, USA Walter, Otto Psychological Institute IV, Westfaelische Wilhelms-, Münster, Germany Fliege, Herbert Psychosomatik, Charité, Berlin, Germany J.B., Bjorner HealthLab, Qualitymetric, Richmond, Germany Kleiber, Dieter AB Psychosoziale Prävention, Freie Universität Berlin, Berlin, Germany Klapp, Burghard Psychosomatik, Charité, Berlin, Germany

This study aimed to develop and evaluate the first computerized adaptive test for the measurement of stress perception in terms of two dimensions: exposure to stress and stress reaction. 1,092 psychosomatic in- and outpatients were studied. In the first simulation study CAT scores could be estimated with a high measurement precision (SE<0.32) using 7.0 +/- 2.3 stress reaction items and 11.6 +/- 1.7 stress exposure items. Second simulation study reanalyzed real patients data: 5.6 +/- 2.1 for the dimension stress reaction and 10.0 +/- 4.9 for the dimension stress exposure. Cut-off scores to differentiate between healthy and subjects and patients with high stress levels were developed.

Questionnaire modification to increase diagnostic accuracy

Koehn, Stefan Dept. of Health Innovation, Central Queensland University, Rockhampton, Australia Morris, Tony School of HMRP, Victoria University, Melbourne, Australia

Psychological measurements commonly involve either state or trait assessments. The study's purpose was to examine flow state in tennis by employing a measure consisting of intensity and frequency scales to increase diagnostic value. Results on dispositional flow showed a mean of 3.75 (response format 1 to 5; 3=some of the time). Using a bipolar flow-state measure (-5=strongly disagree; +5=strongly agree), in combination with a frequency scale (1=never; 7=always) revealed a range from -10.52 to 30.39 (M=10.92). In conclusion, highly negative scores indicated the absence of positive experiences over time, which assists in detecting participants for interventions to increase flow experiences.

The influence of different trait measures of absorption on the assessment of dispositional flow experiences in sport

Koehn, Stefan Dept. of Health Innovation, Central Queensland University, Rockhampton, Australia Morris, Tony School of HMRP, Victoria University, Melbourne, Australia Watt, Anthony P. School of Education, Victoria University, Melbourne, Australia

The study's purpose was to examine the relationship between dispositional flow (DFS-2) and absorption. Previous results (Koehn, Morris, & Watt, 2005) showed nearly zero correlation (r=.01) between flow and the Tellegen Absorption Scale (TAS), a general trait measure of absorption. Participants (N=320) were physical education students who completed the DFS-2 and a sport-specific absorption questionnaire. The sport absorption measure showed a strong correlation (r=.71) with dispositional flow, supporting the connection between both constructs as proposed by Jackson and Csikszentmihalyi (1999). In conclusion, the results indicated the importance of context specific measures when assessing relationships of personality traits in sport.

The "blind spot" in personnel selection: The role of unconscious factors in job interviews

Kolominski, Stephan Psychologie, Fernuniversität Hagen, Hagen, Germany

In personnel selection unconscious factors are rarely investigated. The theoretical part of this work relates different psychological approaches (e.g. organizational-, social-, neuro- and cognitive-psychological issues) to unconscious decisions in the job interview. Human-Resource-Managers (N=26) were asked in semi-structured interviews about hard and soft factors (e.g. work qualification and stereotypes) underlying their decisions based on selection interviews. The results of this study give hints to the impact of unconscious factors in job interviews and in personnel selection.

Psychiatric disorders and childhood trauma in German prisoners with antisocial personality disorder

Kopp, Daniel Greifswald, Germany Dudeck, Manuela Psychiatrie Stralsund, Ernst-Moritz-Arndt Universität, Greifswald, Germany Spitzer, Carsten Kuwert, Philip Barnow, Sven Orlob, Stefan Lüth, Holger Freyberger, Harald J.

Given the high prevalence of mental disorders and trauma among prisoners reported in recent studies, the comorbidity and childhood trauma experiences in criminals with antisocial personality disorder were investigated. Associations of antisocial personality disorder and early traumatic experiences with the age at first conviction and the duration of prison sentences over lifespan were examined. High rates of comorbid lifetime and current disorders as well as childhood trauma experiences were found. Physical abuse and neglect in childhood and adolescence were positively correlated with duration of prison sentences over lifespan, antisocial personality disorder was negatively correlated with the age at first conviction.

The moderating effect of marital satisfaction on the relationship between type-A personality and the level of blood pressure

Korkmaz, Melike Nuray Dept. of Psychology, Middle East Technical Univers., Ankara, Turkey Bozo, Özlem Psychology, Middle East Technical Uni., Ankara, Turkey Onur, Seda Psychology, Middle East Technical Uni., Ankara, Turkey

The purpose of this study was to investigate the influence of Type A personality and marital satisfaction on hypertension. The sample of the study consisted of 100 participants provided from Ankara by ad hoc sampling (49 men, 51 women). All participants completed Medical History Questionnaire Blood Pressure Battery, Type-A Behaviors Inventory, and Dyadic Adjustment Scale. Moreover, blood pressure levels of participants were measured before and after the administration of questionnaires. Moderated regression analysis was performed to test the hypotheses. The results indicated that Type A personality, marital satisfaction, and their interaction did not significantly predict the level of blood pressure.

Emotional interference in health anxiety and the moderating role of working memory load

Kornadt, Anna Inst. für Psychologie, Universität Mannheim, Mannheim, Germany Schmidt, Erika Psychologisches Institut, Universität Heidelberg, Heidelberg, Germany Witthöft, Michael Clinical Psychology, Central Institute of Mental He, Mannheim, Germany Bailer, Josef Clinical Psychology, Central Institute of Mental He, Mannheim, Germany

Objectives: Though proposed in cognitive-behavioral models of health anxiety (HA), there is no clear evidence of selective attention to threat cues in HA. Therefore we investigated the moderating effect of working memory load (WML) on selective attention in HA. Method: An emotional stroop task (EST) with high and low WML was administered to students high in either HA (N=27) or depression (D; N=28), and controls (CG; N=29). Results: Compared to CG and D, students with HA show a significantly larger EST effect for symptom words only during low WML. Discussion: Implications regarding refinements of cognitive models of HA are presented.

Peculiarities of time identity of Latvian people's

Korniseva, Alona Dept. of Social Psychology, Daugavpils University, Daugavpils, Latvia

Each epoch demands definite social roles and task of a person is to correlate peculiarities of epoch and personal period of his development for successful performance of these roles. Time orientation means adequate usage of social roles which are demand of time. Research on the problem of time demonstrates that there are differences between psychological and social time. The objectives of the research are directed on discovering influence of personal and social factors on peculiarities of time orientation and life strategy. The results of this study confirms the significance of personal and social factors in the individual's time orientation, time attitude and views of past, present and future objects.

The priming effect of negative emotional words on a dichotic listening task

Kouri, Katherine Ilioupolis, Greece

Following the attenuation theory (Treisman, 1960), the present experiment investigated whether negative emotional words, verified by GSR measure, had a priming effect in comparison to neutral words on a dichotic listening task. Forty-eight undergraduates received in the attended channel either a passage or a list of neutral words. The non-attended message for both conditions consisted of a mixture of neutral and emotional words (Affective Norms of English Words) controlled for length and abstractedness. Participants were tested on an implicit (word fragment) memory test having words from the non-attended message mixed with new of relative meaning. Results showed overall superiority of emotional words over neutral, with greater effect on the list condition.

Remembered or forgotten?: The collective remembering the Holocaust and the crimes of the communist systems

Kovacs, Monika Faculty of Psychology, Eotvos Lorand University, Budapest, Hungary
The aim of the study was to examine what kind of differences are there between generations as regards their picture of history? How is the memory of the Holocaust related to the memory of communism? A representative sample of the Hungarian population was surveyed. Most of the people simple do not communicate about the past with members of their family and with friends, however there is a visible difference between different age groups concerning their knowledge level and involvement in discussing the historical past. While on the political level – in public discourse - it seems there is a strong division in facing the past, it does not exist on the personal level.

The interaction between parent-child relationships and siblings' personality traits

Kozlova, Irina Psychological Institute, Moscow, Russia
The aims of the present study were to compare intrapair similarity of siblings in personality traits and to estimate parental influences on personality development. Subjects:70 nonstep families with 2 children. Siblings' age ranged from 12 to 22 years old. Methods: EPI; Sensation Seeking Scale; Parent-child interaction questionnaire. The sibling correlations obtained for sensation seeking scale were significant. Paternal neuroticism was related to older sibling neuroticism. Maternal locus of control correlated with older sibling's locus of control. Influences of father-child relationships on personality traits of both older and younger siblings were less in comparison with maternal influences

Assessing implicit self-esteem with affective priming procedures: Improving reliability by using pictures of participants as primes

Krause, Sascha Inst. für Psychologie, Universität Leipzig, Leipzig, Germany Schmukle, Stefan Inst. für Psychologie, Universität Leipzig, Leipzig, Germany Back, Mitja Inst. für Psychologie, Universität Leipzig, Leipzig, Germany Egloff, Boris Inst. für Psychologie, Universität Leipzig, Leipzig, Germany
Research on implicit self-esteem suggests that affective priming does often not allow for a reliable assessment of interindividual differences. In two studies, we analyzed the reliability of affective priming procedures with an adaptive response-window. In Study 1 (N=76) initials served as primes. Results revealed neither a significant priming effect nor an adequate reliability. In Study 2 (N=85) pictures of participants were used as primes. In contrast to Study 1, we found both a significant priming effect and a moderately high reliability. Implications of these findings for the improvement of affective priming procedures and the assessment of implicit self-esteem are discussed.

Feedback processing and moral decision making in adolescents with behavioral problems: An EEG study

Kreuter, Joerg Kognitive Neuropsychologie, Freie Universitaet Berlin, Berlin, Germany Witt, Lisa Kognitive Neuropsychologie, Freie Universitaet Berlin, Berlin, Germany Tamm, Sascha Kognitive Neuropsychologie, Freie Universitaet Berlin, Berlin, Germany Boesel, Rainer Kognitive Neuropsychologie, Freie Universitaet Berlin, Berlin, Germany

12 male adolescents recruited from youth welfare services (attended because of delinquency, drug abuse, etc.) passed the Iowa Gambling Task (IGT) and a short personality screening based on NEO-PI-R items. All participants obtained remarkable scores for sensation-seeking but showed inconspicuous IGT performance compared to same-aged controls (cf. Witt et al., 2007). In addition these adolescents were requested to imagine moral dilemmas in order to make judgements about proposed action alternatives (cf. Kreuter et al., 2007). EEG data show increased theta power at frontal electrodes when rejecting proposed impersonal alternatives. This can be interpreted as high effort in generating desirable solutions.

Fair School Comparisons – Using previous knowledge as additional covariate for the adjustment of school achievement scores

Kroehne, Ulf Inst. für Methodologie, Universität Jena, Jena, Germany Nagengast, Benjamin Department of methodology, FSU Jena, Jena, Germany
The value of school comparative tasks relies on the fairness of the reference scores for the expected outcome of participating classes. From the theory of individual and average causal effects different adjustment methods for such fair references can be derived. In the "Thüringer Kompetenztests" references are estimated based on a saturated regression model. In our longitudinal approach previous knowledge from recent tests can be used as additional covariates. Pre-knowledge can be included in two different ways: Predicting a) performance or b) class membership of each scholar based on previous knowledge. The effects of different parameterizations are presented with empirical data and in a Monte Carlo Simulations.

An evaluation of a Norwegian vocational rehabilitation program

Krogstadmo, Borghild Dept. of Psychology, Norwegian Univ. of Sci. & Tech, Trondheim, Norway Rundmo, Torbjörn Dept. of Psychology, Norwegian Univ. of Sci. &, Trondheim, Norway
The main focus for this study is to evaluate a vocational rehabilitation program. According to a theory on vocational rehabilitation, health conditions and other factors will influence the rehabilitation process. The result is based on a self completion questionnaire carried out among participant in a vocational rehabilitation program (n = 94). The questionnaire was distributed at three different times. The response rate was 100%. The results showed that only optimism about the future was a significant predictor for the benefit of the vocational rehabilitation program. The oldest participants showed the least degree of optimism about the future during the program.

The impact of ipsative and social standards on affective reactions depends on the goal

Krohn, Jeanette Inst. für Psychologie, Universität Greifwald, Greifswald, Germany Faisst, Scarlett Psychologie, Ernst-Moritz-Arndt Universität, Greifswald, Germany Kücükbalaban, Pinar Psychologie, Ernst-Moritz-Arndt Universität, Greifswald, Germany Sperrhacke, Katrin Psychologie, Ernst-Moritz-Arndt Universität, Greifswald, Germany Schildhauer, Katja Psychologie, Ernst-Moritz-Arndt Universität, Greifswald, Germany Schönpflug, Martin Psychologie, Ernst-Moritz-Arndt Universität, Greifswald, Germany
We investigated, if the emotional consequences of social and ipsative standards during goal attainment depend on the nature of the goal. 278 students were randomly assigned to one cell in a 2 (above vs. below social standard) x 2 (above vs. below ipsative standard) design. They received both, a performance and qualitative goal scenario. Anticipated intensity of affective reactions was assessed. A threeway ANOVA revealed significant toway inter-

actions between the nature of the goal and both standards. Descriptive analyses suggest a stronger impact of social standards for performance goals and a stronger impact of ipsative standards for qualitative goals.

The dimensions of the perception of Polish politicians' personalities

Krulikowska, Anna Experimental Psychol, Catholic University of Lublin, Lublin, Poland Gorbaniuk, Oleg Experimental Psychol, Catholic University of Lublin, Lublin, Poland Baszczyk, Ewa Experimental Psychol, Catholic University of Lublin, Lublin, Poland
The aim of the undertaken research was to set the basic dimensions of personalities, with which the Polish politicians are perceived. The research was conducted in the stream of the trait theory, using the material found in Polish lexical research by Szarota (1995), with the extension of the adjectives specific for politicians. 700 people, aged 18-75, were describing 24 politicians with a scale of 148 adjectives. The analysis of 24 factor structures let us extract some common dimensions of the politicians' perceived personalities: Competence, Extraversion, Agreeableness. The fourth dimension, Honesty, has only been found in 7 of 24 factor structures.

Investigating the structure of attention: How do characteristics of attention and concentration tests influence their relationship?

Krumm, Stefan Inst. für Psychologie, Universität Marburg, Marburg, Germany Schmidt-Atzert, Lothar Department of Psychology, Philipps-University Marburg, Marburg, Germany
Studies examining the structure of concentration and attention seldom considered different test modi as a source of variance. We examined 110 participants and administered concentration and attention tests in five different modi (paper-pencil, self-paced item-blocks, self-paced single items, force-paced item-blocks, force-paced single items). Original versions of different tests correlated only moderately; tests corresponding in terms of modus showed strong correlations. A model was established with two test factors and three modus factors. The latter accounted for 60% of variance. Apparently, the validity of attention and concentration tests strongly depends on specific task characteristics.

Coordination as a crucial component of performances in a sustained attention test: The digit-symbol substitution test

Krumm, Stefan Inst. für Psychologie, Universität Marburg, Marburg, Germany Schmidt-Atzert, Lothar Department of Psychology, Philipps-University Marburg, Marburg, Germany
Different researchers proposed a mechanism responsible for the coordination of single processes. It was also considered as a component of paper-pencil sustained attention (SA) tests. Previous research identified single processes in the Digit-Symbol-Substitution-Test (DSST), which is regarded as a SA test. In study 1 (n=199) we predicted the overall DSST performance with its single processes. Validity results confirmed that the residual reflected the coordination of single processes. Study 2 (n=132) showed that gains over practice in the DSST can also be attributed to the coordination of single processes. This represented the first evidence for a coordination mechanism in SA tests.

The influence of anxiety on memory proccesses and the role of music in mood modification

Kudlik, Agata Faculty of Psychology, University of Warsaw, Warsaw, Poland
The purpose of the study was to investigate the relationship beetwen anxiety and memory and the influence of music on mood. We assumed that high - state anxious would have lower memory results in

general and better remembering of threatening words. The experiment was carried out on adolescents with STAI and different emotional words list. High - state anxious achieved lower general memory results than low - state anxious at a tendency level. Both low and high state anxiety was connected with neutral and positive words preference. Relaxing and threatening music had an influence on mood's dimensions, measured by UMACL.

The predictive ability for pupil's achievement in mathematics

Kuku, Hamdon Dept. of Psychology, University of Kordofan, Elobied, Sudan

The predictive ability for pupil's achievement in mathematics This study examines the predictive ability for pupils' achievement in mathematics by suing three instruments namely, The Standard Progressive Matrices (SPM), Torrance Battery for Creativity (TBC) and Mathematical Intelligence Indicator (MII). The instruments were applied to a group of (210) pupils both males (107) and females (103) selected randomly from Kordofan Basic schools. The results of the study showed a significant positive correlation between both SPM, MII and pupils achievement in mathematics (P<0.05), and significant positive correlation between the fluency and flexibility dimension of the TBC and pupil's achievement in mathematics (P<0.01).

Posttraumatic symptoms were worst among quake victims with injuries following the Chi-chi quake in Taiwan

Kuo, Hsien-Wen Dept. of Public Health, China Medical University, Taichung, Taiwan

Objectives: We investigate the posttraumatic stress disorder (PTSD) and psychological health status among earthquake victims one year after the quake. Method 272 quake victims from temporary housing units were interviewed. PTSD was assessed using the Davidson Trauma Scale, Chinese version. Psychological health status was measured using the Chinese Health Questionnaire. Results Based on linear and logistic regression models, age and injury were the only two factors that significantly affected post-traumatic symptoms and CHQ total scores. Conclusion It is vitally important to continue providing psychological counseling and social support for quake victims, particularly victims who sustained an injury.

Correlation between adolescent illicit drug use and family characteristics in Taiwan

Kuo, Hsien-Hwa Nursing Dept., Tao Yuan General Hospital, Tau-Yuan, Taiwan

Objective: The relationship between adolescent illicit drug use and family characteristics in Taiwan was investigated. Methods 12,327 students were selected using stratified sampling and interviewed using a structured questionnaire which included demographic information, life style behavior, history of illicit drug use and achievement in school. Results 1.6% of prevalence rate with illicit drug use was reported from study adolescents. Multivariate analysis, adjusted for covariates, revealed that the risk of illicit drug use among adolescents correlated significantly with low levels of trust from their parents (OR=3.1). Conclusion It is necessary to create a better level of awareness and understanding of the issues and risk factors regarding adolescent drug use.

Minimization of answer distortion in personality questionnaires: Does the ipsative OPQ32i capture normative variances?

Kusch, Rene Immanuel Inst. für Sozialwissenschaften, Helmut-Schmidt-Universität, Hamburg, Germany
Deller, Jürgen Business Psychology, Leuphana University, Lüneburg, Germany Beauducel, André

Humanities and Social Sciences, Helmut-Schmidt-University, Hamburg, Germany Albrecht, Anne-Grit Business Psychology, Leuphana University, Lüneburg, Germany

Ipsative personality questionnaires can reduce the effects of social desirability. However, the answering-format induces artificial dependencies, which raises questions about its normative interpretability. In a field study 145 German speaking expatriates were assessed with the ipsative OPQ32i (SHL, 1999) and the normative NEO-PI-R (Ostendorf & Angleitner, 2004) in seven countries. A significant set correlation shows that the OPQ32i captures normative variances (R2shrunk= 0.99). According to a multi-trait-multi-method matrix relationships between scales and factors of both instruments are interpretable conceptually. Therefore, ipsative questionnaires seem to be applicable for inter-individual comparisons if some specific conditions are met.

Temperamental determinants of depletion of self: Control resources in the emotional control situation

Kwapis, Krzysztof Dept. of Psychology, Catholic University of Lublin, Lublin, Poland

The aim of the research is answering the question what kind of an increase in energy features of temperament favours an increased depletion of self-control resources and what kind of the increase in these features favours retaining self-control resources in the situation of repression of emotions. The research will investigate the relation between temperament features and depletion of emotional resources. The research is an experiment with participation of students. The regression analysis will be used for the purpose of analyzing of the data. The research is in progress, the results will be presented during the conference.

Culturally-derived protective factors in blacks at risk for suicide

Kyle, Jennifer Dept. of Social Science, BMCC - CUNY, New York, USA

For Black youth age 15-24, suicide is the 3rd leading cause of death. The following study hypothesizes that the rise in the rate of suicide is attributable to the erosion of culturally derived protective factors for Blacks. A battery of self-report instruments were chosen to assess the following variables: suicidality, family, social support and protective factors. Data analysis was performed using logistic regression to investigate relationships between the predictor (independent) variables and to estimate the probability of the outcome variable i.e. suicidal behaviors. Family involvement and spiritual faith are significantly related to, and predictive of lifetime suicidal ideation.

Symbolic variables involved in the use of private-cars

López Sáez, Mercedes Dept. of Social Psychology, UNED, Madrid, Spain Lois, David Social Psychology, UNED, Madrid, Spain

The excessive use of private vehicles has negative consequences in terms of environmental impact, health and social well-being. The traditional approach to these problems has focused almost exclusively on their technical aspects, neglecting the existing psychosocial aspects. The study takes into account, through structural equations methodology, symbolic variables in private-car use, and related to several transportation motives. Sample: 501 participants, from cities varying in population size. Main results displayed the influence of socio-affective and instrumental aspects on the emotion elicited by car use. The effect of emotion displayed a predictive power of 12% of the variance of car use.

The relationship between time management disposition and test anxiety of undergraduates

Lan, Yujuan Psychology, Huazhong normal university, Wuhan, People's Republic of China

Objective:To explore the relationship between time management disposition and test anxiety. Method:302 undergraduates were investigated by adolescence time management disposition inventory(ATMD) and the test anxiety inventory(TAI). Results:(1)The grade differences in time management disposition is significant. (2)The general appraisement of time management disposition, time efficacy and time monitor had significantly negative correlations with test anxiety and its two components. (3)Time efficacy was a direct predictor for test anxiety, while time value and time monitor had indirect effects on test anxiety by time efficacy.Conclusion:The test anxiety of undergraduates related to their time management disposition,especially related to their time efficacy.

Is the correlation between test anxiety and test performance rooted in feelings of low competence in test anxious individuals?

Lang, Jonas W. B. Inst. für Psychologie, RWTH Aachen, Aachen, Germany Lang, Jessica no affiliation, no affiliation, Aachen, Germany

Researchers disagree whether the correlation between test anxiety and test performance is causal or explainable by third variables. A core idea in causal theories is that test anxious individuals perceive themselves to be incompetent. We designed two studies (N=415) with high school students experimentally heightening feelings of competence using a priming intervention. The association between one component of test anxiety – test worry – and test performance diminished in the priming conditions (Study 1: p<.03; Study 2: p<.01) suggesting that the association is rooted in a causal low competence mechanism. Findings for the other component of test anxiety – test emotionality – were mixed.

Impacts of organizational leadership and culture on organizational trust: The moderating role of job cadre

Lawal, Olufemi Psychology, Olabisi Onabanjo University, Ogun State, Nigeria

This study sampled 362 junior and 192 middle cadre employees towards investigating the extent to which their work performance orientations and their ratings of their immediate superior's leadership quality may dictate the amount of cognitive and affective trusts they hold for the superiors. Data analysis via two separate 2X2X2 ANOVA revealed significant main influences of leadership quality and performance orientation on both affective and cognitive trusts. The interaction between leadership quality and employee cadre was significant on affective trust but not on cognitive trust. Mean comparisons and post hoc shed more light on the directions of the significant influences.

What are the core attributes of humanity?

Lee, Sau-Lai Dept. of Psychology, Nanyang Technological Univ., Singapore, Singapore Lau, Ivy Yee-Man Sch of Social Sciences, Singapore Management Universit, Singapore, Singapore

The aim of this research is to study the core attributes of humanity. In Study 1, we asked participants to list characteristics that can define humanity, differentiate human from robot, or differentiate human from animal. In Study 2, we asked the participants to rate a set of entities on their humanity. Some of these entities lacked the important attributes in defining humanity as suggested by the results of Study 1. We found three kinds of attributes are important in defining humanity and individuals rates entities without these attributes as less human.

Attitudes reflecting national identity in Lithuanian young people population

Lekaviciene, Rosita Dept. of Psycology, Kaunas University, Kaunas, Lithuania Antiniene, Dalia Dept. of Psycology, Kaunas University, Kaunas, Lithuania

The aim of the research is to determine the content and peculiarities of national identity among Lithuanian youth. The goals of the research are: to analyze from the phenomenological point of view the structure of their national identity and to determine indicators representing the cultural context of the country. National identity attitudes were investigated employing an original, anonymous close-type questionnaire. The structure of the national identity was established with the help of multistage factorial validation. We discovered that the attitudes rather clearly polarize into the components reflecting modern and traditional attitudes towards nationality. Multidimensional Scaling was used to obtain the model of gradation of national identity expression.

Discrimination of facial emotional expressions during early perceptual processing indexed by the N170 ERP component

Leleu, Arnaud Laboratoire PSY.CO EA1780, Université de Rouen, Mont St. Aignan Cedex, France Drouin, Héloïse Université de Rouen, Laboratoire PSY.CO EA1780, Mont Saint Aignan Cedex, France Charvin, Heidi Université de Rouen, Laboratoire PSY.CO EA1780, Mont Saint Aignan Cedex, France Fiori, Nicole Université Paris V, UPR 640, CNRS, Boulogne-Billancourt, France Bernard, Christian Université de Rouen, Laboratoire PSY.CO EA1780, Mont Saint Aignan Cedex, France Lalonde, Robert Université de Rouen, U614, IFRMP 23, Rouen, France Rebaï, Mohamed Université de Rouen, Laboratoire PSY.CO EA1780, Mont Saint Aignan Cedex, France

Objectives: determine how the valence of emotional expressions could have an effect during early perceptual processing when subjects had to compare two expressions. Methods: 18 subjects performed the discrimination expression task. ANOVAs were used on behavioral and electrophysiological data. Results: Electrophysiological data indicate a valence effect as early as the perceptual encoding stage reflected by the N170. This effect led a reduction of electrophysiological and behavioral responses when a negative expression is primed. Conclusions: There is an effect of emotional valence during early perceptual stage whereas expression is not yet categorized. This effect modulates behavioral responses of subjects.

Self-esteem in French-speaking dyslexic children of special school

Leonova, Tamara Department of Psychology, University of Fribourg, Fribourg, Switzerland Grilo, Gaëlle Department of Psychology, University of Strasbourg, Fribourg, France

Researchers have given little attention to self-perceptions in dyslexic children. To date, the results are inconsistent and external validity of these studies is limited to English-speaking dyslexics. There is no study focused to the self-esteem in pupils with dyslexia in special schools. Our study explored self-esteem in French-speaking dyslexics attending special school in Switzerland. Thirty-five dyslexics children were compared on different subscales of self-esteem (Harter, 1985) to 31 children without dyslexia. Results suggest no significant difference for the perceived social and physical competence ratings, appearance and general self-worth ratings. However, on the cognitive subscale, dyslexics tend to have lower self-esteem than normal children of the same age and sex.

Effectiveness of meditation and music technique as a mechanism of wellness for incarcerated drug addicts

Leuterio, Ray Dept of Psychology, Colegio San Juan de Letran, Calamba City, Philippines

This research studied the effectiveness of Meditation and Music technique as a mechanism of wellness for incarcerated drug addicts. The design is a multiple pretest-posttest randomized control group design. 30 selected drug addicts from the Bureau of Correction were assigned and matched to 2 treatment groups and a control group. Three mixed ANOVAs with Tukey's HSD found that meditation with music significantly improved on measures of anxiety and depression while the meditation group improved significantly on psychological health. The study suggests that meditation and music technique are effective in creating change on the wellness measures among incarcerated drug addicts

Attention resources competition accounting for specific spatial working memory affected by emotional context

Li, Xuebing Key lab of mental health, Psychology of institute,CAS, Beijing, People's Republic of China Ouyang, Zhengzheng School of Psychology, Southwest University, Chongqing, People's Republic of China Luo, Yue-jia State lab Cogn Neurosci learn, Beijing Normal University, Beijing, People's Republic of China

To explore how emotional context selectively modulates dissociating spatial and verbal working memory (WM), event-related potentials were recorded from 16 subjects during WM tasks (n-back) and control tasks (visual search). Parietal P300 of the spatial WM task was impaired in emotional context (both negative and positive) relative to neutral context. This effect was not observed for verbal WM. In control tasks, the P300 of both verbal and spatial tasks were affected by emotional context. The results suggest a specific disruption of spatial WM by emotional context, indicating more attention resources competition between emotional distraction processing and spatial WM.

Social Desirability Response (SDR) in China: Dimension analysis and situation effects

Li, Feng Institute of Psychology,CAS, Beijing, People's Republic of China

The Balanced Inventory of Desirability Response (BIDR) was administered in three studies to explore the dimensions and situation effects of SDR. In the first study, four dimensions were extracted by EFA (N= 683) which indicated the split of enhancement and denial on both self-deception and impression management. Then in the different job analysis situations, only was the scores of enhancement and denial of impression management significantly higher when declaring that the results of job analysis were for salary reform (N=123). But in the third study, there was significant difference on four dimensions between the applicants' scores (N=55) and non-applicants' (N=64).

A comparative study of different types of scales with online survey and paper-and-pencil assessment

Li, Yuhui School of Human Resource, Renmin University, Beijing, People's Republic of China Ma, Lili Psychology, Institute of Psychology, CAS, Beijing, People's Republic of China Ye, Jieyou Psychology, Institute of Psychology, CAS, Beijing, People's Republic of China Zhang, Jianxin Psychology, Institute of Psychology, CAS, Beijing, People's Republic of China

The study aimed to examine the equivalency of two administration methods (paper-and-pencil and Internet) of NEO-FFI, General Attitude Scale (GAS), and Chinese Personality Assessment Inventory (CPAI). A total of 3074 participants in mainland China took part in the study with in-group and between-group design. Analyses with IRT, SEM, and mean differences supported the equivalence of Internet and traditional paper-and-pencil administrations of personality tests (NEO-FFI and CPAI), but differences found in GAS. In conclusion, the application of personality scale on the internet was proved in this study, but for attitude scale, we need to choose prudently.

Screening executive dysfunction in Parkinson's disease with the Frontal Assessment Battery

Lima, Cesar Psychology, Universidade do Porto, Porto, Portugal Meireles, Laura Psychology, Universidade do Porto, Porto, Portugal Fonseca, Rosália Psychology, Universidade do Porto, Porto, Portugal Garrett, Carolina Faculty of Medicine, Universidade do Porto, Porto, Portugal Castro, São Luís Psychology, Universidade do Porto, Porto, Portugal

The Frontal Assessment Battery (FAB; Dubois, Slachevsky, Litvan and Pillon, 2000) is a short tool for the assessment of executive functions. We compared the performance on the FAB test by normal controls (N = 122) and patients with Parkinson's disease (PD; N = 50). Correlations with formal measures of executive functioning were also carried out. We observed that FAB scores are lower in PD as compared to controls and correlate with performances in verbal fluency, Wisconsin Card Sorting Test and Trail Making Test. These results show that the FAB test is a useful tool to identify executive dysfunction in PD.

The health effects of indoor air quality in two workplaces

Lin, Ping-Yi Nottingham, United Kingdom Kuo, Hsien-Wen College of Public Health, Environmental Health, Taichung, Taiwan

Objectives: The purpose of this study is to investigate the health effects related to indoor air quality in two kinds of building. Methods Indoor air pollution, sick building syndrome (SBS) and quality of life (QOL) of employees were measured in two kinds of workplace, hospital center and office in high building. Results QOL scores in workplace were affected by satisfaction toward indoor air quality in office, work stress and perceived indoor pollution score and severity of SBS. Conclusions The health effects related to indoor air pollution are chronic not acute, therefore, follow up is needed in this study.

Factorial structure of the CES-D Scale among Chinese high school students

Ling, Yu Medical Psychological Research, The Second Xiangya Hospital, Changsha, People's Republic of China Wei, Yong Test Development Department, Education Examination Board, Changsha, People's Republic of China

The Chinese version of CES-D was completed by 1044 Chinese high school students residing in urban area and rural area. Confirmatory factor analyses were employed to obtain a final solution. The results of confirmatory factor analyses ($\chi2$/ df = 4.344?GFI=0.934?IFI=0.915?CFI=0.915?NNFI=0.900? RMSEA=0.057) indicated that the original four factors provide a reasonable good fit for Chinese high school students: depressed affect, positive affect, somatic-retardation, interpersonal relationship.

Trait anxiety modulation of neural responses to automatic and elaborated processing of threat-related pictures

Lipka, Judith Biolog. und Klin. Psychologie, Universität Jena, Jena, Germany Miltner, Wolfgang H. R. Jena, Germany Straube, Thomas LS für Biolog. & Klin. Psy, Institut für Psychologie, Jena, Germany

Using fMRI, we investigated effects of trait anxiety on BOLD-signal changes during explicit and implicit emotional processing of threat-related versus neutral pictures. Thirty-eight healthy volunteers participated in this study. Higher levels of trait anxiety proved to be correlated with relative signal increases in the insula during the explicit condition only, whereas moderate levels of anxiety predicted augmented signal intensity of the dorsal ACC during the implicit condition. Thus trait anxiety may interact with attentional focus to determine brain responses to threat-related information. Furthermore, activation in the insula and ACC might represent main mediators of individual differences in the anxious phenotype.

The event-related potentials study of deceptive responses to characters and pictures

Liu, Hongguang *Elementary Education College, Capital Normal University, Bejing, People's Republic of China*
The event-related potentials(ERPs) of 20 healthy subjects were recorded during deceptive responses and truthful responses to the two kinds of stimuli. We come to the following conclusions: 1. Executive control process of deceptive responses includes a series of sub-task, which might consume the limit psychological resources. The amplitude of P300 evoked by deceptive responses is smaller than truthful responses. 2. Pictures can activate more related information than characters, and the speed is faster than the latter. 3. Comparing to characters, the cognitive process of pictures showed picture superiority effect during deceptive responding too.

The junior middle school students' mathematical estimation performance and its relationship with their metacognitive ability

Liu, Xiaozhen *Psychology Department, Shandong Normal University, Jinan, People's Republic of China*
This research aims to explore the middle school students' mathematical estimation performances and its relationship with metacognitive ability by using estimation tasks and the questionnaire of metacognition to test 547 middle school students in Grade seven, eight and nine. The results showed that: the junior middle school students' mathematical estimation ability is generally low; there is a strong positive correlation between estimation performance and metacognitive ability. Among the four factors of metacognition, self-consciousness had positive correlations with measurement estimation, computational estimation; plan had strong correlations with numerical estimation, computational estimation. Self-consciousness had significant predictable effect on the students' estimation performance.

Developing measure of team emotional climate in China

Liu, Xiaoyu *Labor and Human Resources, Renmin University, Beijing, People's Republic of China* *Sun, Jianmin* *Labor and Human Resources, Renmin University, Beijing, People's Republic of China* *Härtel, Charmine E.J.*
A four-factor theory of workgroup emotional climate is derived from a review of the organizational climate and emotion literature, and the procedures used to operationalize this model into a survey measure is described. Data attesting to the underlying factor structure, internal homogeneity, predictive validity and factor replicability across workgroups of the measure are presented. An initial sample of 396 workgroup members provides the data for the exploratory factor analysis of this measure. Responses from 334 workgroup members are subsequently used to apply confirmatory factor analysis techniques. The resulting four-factor, 18-item questionnaire demonstrates robust psychometric properties, with acceptable reliability and validity.

Effects of emotional activation on state-dependent learning in daily life

Loeffler, Simone Nadine *Biolog. und Diff. Psychologie, Institut für Psychologie, Freiburg, Germany* *Braner, Mike* *Biolog. und Diff. Psychologie, Institut für Psychologie, Freiburg, Germany* *Peper, Martin* *Neuropsychologie, Philipps-Universität Marburg, Germany*
The aim of the study was to investigate interactions of emotional state and declarative memory in natural settings to evaluate the validity of laboratory results. We used the Freiburg Monitoring System for recording subjective state and physiological measures to trigger palmtop presentations of to-be memorized word lists (N=70). Analyses of variance showed significant differences for the number and valence of remembered words depending on the valence of the learning situation and on the intensity of physiological activation. The results illuminate the ecological validity of laboratory studies of mood state-dependent learning suggesting a more differentiated view than previous work.

Emotional experience and regulation of action by coping with stress: Functional and conceptual issues

Loos, Helga *Dept. Educational Psychology, Federal University of Paraná, Curitiba, Brazil* *Fernandes, Rosseline* *Educational Psychology, Federal University of Paraná, Curitiba, Brazil*
From a self-regulatory view, our objective is to understand the role of emotional processing when coping with stress, disagreeing with the self-deprecatory roles of emotion in traditional coping research. 51 children (aged 9-14) from a public school in Curitiba/Brazil were asked for a true-life stressful situation. Sadness (42%), followed by anger (31%) and fear (21%), were the most common experienced emotions. Despite this, many children also managed the problem directly and successful. According to a functional perspective, emotion should be analyzed as a 'factor' of coping, because any emotional experience activates reorganization and action programs, towards an adaptive solution.

Deaf children performance in the Universal Nonverbal Intelligence Test

Lopes, Ederaldo *Experimental Psychology Lab., Institute of Psychology, Uberlandia, Brazil* *Lopes, Renata Ferrarez* *Experimental Psychology Lab., Institute of Psychology, Uberlandia, Brazil* *Borges, Claudia* *Experimental Psychology Lab., Institute of Psychology, Uberlandia, Brazil* *Damas Cardoso, Carolina* *Experimental Psychology Lab., Institute of Psychology, Uberlandia, Brazil* *Oliveira, Flávia* *Experimental Psychology Lab., Institute of Psychology, Uberlandia, Brazil* *Almeida, Ana Paula* *Experimental Psychology Lab., Institute of Psychology, Uberlandia, Brazil* *Pacheco, Ana Carolina* *Experimental Psychology Lab., Institute of Psychology, Uberlandia, Brazil*
The goal of this work was to carry out an ipsative analysis of deaf children through the Universal Nonverbal Intelligence Test (UNIT). Fifteen girls and 4 boys from a music school took part in this research. Teh Compuscore data show the only meaningful difference in the frequency of cognitive characteristics was found in the comparison of the items of the secondary scale, Cochran's Q = 11.8, df = 1, p < 0.001. Analyzed as a whole, the ipsative data show that these deaf children present a good cognitive performance when they are evaluated through a nonverbal test.

Psychometric properties of the Universal Nonverbal Intelligence Test: A Brazilian study

Lopes, Ederaldo *Experimental Psychology Lab., Institute of Psychology, Uberlandia, Brazil* *Lopes, Renata Ferrarez* *Experimental Psychology Lab., Institute of Psychology, Uberlandia, Brazil* *Moreira, Ana Paula* *Experimental Psychology Lab., Institute of* *Psychology, Uberlandia, Brazil* *Guimaraes, Claudiane Aparecida* *Experimental Psychology Lab., Institute of Psychology, Uberlandia, Brazil* *Borges, Cláudia* *Experimental Psychology Lab., Institute of Psychology, Uberlandia, Brazil* *Aguiar, Reginaldo* *Experimental Psychology Lab., Institute of Psychology, Uberlandia, Brazil* *Abdo, Fabiana* *Experimental Psychology Lab., Institute of Psychology, Uberlandia, Brazil* *Lemes, Paula* *Experimental Psychology Lab., Institute of Psychology, Uberlandia, Brazil* *Silva, Gabriel* *Experimental Psychology Lab., Institute of Psychology, Uberlandia, Brazil* *Pacheco, Ana Carolina* *Experimental Psychology Lab., Institute of Psychology, Uberlandia, Brazil* *Lopes, Challynne* *Experimental Psychology Lab., Institute of Psychology, Uberlandia, Brazil*
This work aimed to evaluate the validity of construct and the reliability of the standard battery of the Universal Nonverbal Intelligence Test (UNIT) in a sample of 163 students, men and women, in the age within 5-17 years. The data of the full scale in each subtest were submitted to an analysis of principal components (PC) (eigenvalue > 1). The results showed the presence of one component (56.5% of the total variance). The reliability (Spearman-Brown) was .77. These results are promising for the effective use of this test in the Brazilian context.

Exploring male body image in Taiwan: Drive for muscularity and its relationship to self-esteem and quality of life

Lu, Hsueh-Chao *Dept. of Psychology, National Taiwan University, Taipei, Taiwan* *Chen, Sue-Huei* *Psychology, National Taiwan University, Taipei, Taiwan*
Objectives: Recently, there is a rapid rise of research interest in the muscularity dimension of body image among men. Concern for muscularity is suggested to play a central role in men's mental health. Methods: We examined the relationships among drive for muscularity, self-esteem, and quality of life in a sample of 200 male college students in a cross-sectional design. Results: Evaluative component of drive for muscularity was related to poor self-esteem, and behavioral component was related to positive quality of life. Conclusions: Various aspects of concern over masculinity may play different roles in Taiwanese college males' psychological functions.

Assessment style and learning motivation in students

Luca, Marcela Rodica *Psychology, Transilvania University, Brasov, Romania* *Cocorada, Elena* *Psychology, Transilvania University, Brasov, Romania* *Pavalache-Ilie, Mariela* *Psychology, Transilvania University, Brasov, Romania* *Clinciu, Aurel Ion* *Psychology, Transilvania University, Brasov, Romania* *Hilbert, Rozemarie* *Psychology, Transilvania University, Brasov, Romania*
Studies in educational psychology focused on the factors that influence students' motivation for learning. This correlational study investigated the relationship between the evaluative style of the teacher and the students' motivation. The 394 students, age 16.83, in 16 English classes, answered questionnaires on intrinsic/ extrinsic motivation (Amabile, adapted), perceived value of activity, competence and locus of control (Viau) as well as the perceived evaluative style (Cocorada) of five teachers, in four schools. The results indicate differentiated perception of the same evaluative style in connection with intrinsic/ extrinsic motivation, perceived value of activity, perceived competence and internal/ external locus of control.

Neural correlates of dissociative states in patients with borderline personality disorder

Ludäscher, Petra *Psychosomatische Medizin, ZI für Seelische Gesundheit, Mannheim, Germany* **Schmahl, Christian** *Klinik für Psychosomatik, ZI für Seelische Gesundheit, Mannheim, Germany*

Objective: To investigate the neural correlates of dissociation in patients with BPD. Methods: Eighteen patients with BPD were investigated. Two autobiographical scripts, one neutral and one stress-associated script, were presented during fMRI. Three outcomes were assessed during the script presentations: 1. dissociation, 2. pain sensitivity and 3. BOLD signal changes. Results: During the stress-associated script patients showed 1. increased dissociation, 2. lower pain sensitivity and 3. increased activation of the cingulate gyrus as compared to the neutral script. Conclusions: Increased activation of the cingulate gyrus during dissociation in patients with BPD is consistent with previous studies investigating neural correlates of dissociation in patients with post traumatic stress disorder.

The development of young adults' dating relationships: The role of antecedent and personality

Lussier, Yvan *Psychology, University of Quebec, Trois-Rivieres, Canada* **Alain, Michel** *Psychology, University of Quebec, Trois-Rivieres, Canada* **Lemelin, Carmen** *Psychology, University of Quebec, Trois-Rivieres, Canada*

The aim of the present study was to examine antecedent (e.g., child abuses, family violence, parental divorce, sexual orientation) and personality variables related to the development of young adults' dating relationhips. Participants (N = 1070) were aged between 16 to 18 years. Of this total, 557 participants had an intimate relationship. The participants completed sociodemographic, background, personality and close relationship questionnaires. Results showed that violence in family was related to violence in dating relationships. The higher the age of the first sexual relationship, the stronger is the actual sexual satisfaction. Personality variables are significantly associated to couple adjustment.

The neglected dimension of physical environment in counselling: Influence of the consulting room on perceived quality of care

Lyng, James *Dept. of Psychology, Cluain Mhuire Family Centre, Dublin, Ireland* **Guilfoyle, Michael** *Psychology, University of Dublin, Trinity, Dublin, Ireland*

The study investigates whether the physical environment of the consulting room relates to the perceived quality of care in counselling. It was hypothesised that perceived care would be greater where consulting rooms appeared warm and nicely furnished than where rooms appeared cold and poorly furnished. Participants (N=102) rated 28 photographic projections depicting a range of consulting rooms for perceived quality of care. Factor analysis produced factors consistent with the hypothesis and subsequent analysis of variance found factors differed significantly from each other (p < .001). As perceptions of care relate to therapeutic outcome, the consulting room may have clinical relevance.

Smoking cessation in psychiatric patients

Mühlig, Stephan *Inst. Klinische Psychologie, Tech. Universität Chemnitz, Chemnitz, Germany*

Compared with the general population, psychiatric patients have a significant higher prevalence of smoking and nicotine dependence. There is an increasing awareness for the necessarity to develop specific interventions for smoking cessation for these specific subgroups. Conversely, smoking cessation in individuals with past mental disorders is associated with a significantly increased risk of developing exacerbations or relapses of their psychiatric disorder. This presentation systematically reviews the etiological associations as well as the body of evidence regarding to the efficacy of specific smoking cessation approaches for smokers with concomitant mental disorders.

World social memory and oblivion of Greeks and Germans

Madoglou, Anna *Dept. of Psychology, Panteion University, Athens, Greece* **Melista, Anastassia** *Psychology, Panteion University, Athens, Greece* **Liaris-Hochhaus, Sylvia** *Psychology, Panteion University, Athens, Greece*

This research investigates the events which compose world social memory and oblivion. The participants, 243 Greek and German students, were asked to write three events from the world history that they wished to remember and three others that they wished to forget, and, then, to evaluate them according to their positiveness and importance. Correspondence Analysis (SPAD) was applied to data. The content of world memory refers to revolutions, inventions and civilization, whereas oblivion is surrounded by silences. Despite the uniqueness of the world history, Greeks and Germans constructed the memory through the national viewpoint focusing on their particular historical-national identity.

Facial expression - The recognition of basic emotions in alcoholic dependents: Empirical study with Portuguese

Magalhães, Freitas *Facial Emotion Exprssion Lab., Faculty of Health Sciences, Porto, Portugal* **Érico, Castro** *Facial Emotion Expression Lab, Faculty of Health Sciences, Porto, Portugal*

This research presents the effect of alcohol in the in the identification and recognition of the basic emotions (joy, sadness, anger, surprise, disgust, fear and contempt). The sample involved 65 Portuguese (20 women and 45 men) diagnosed with the use of alcohol disorders (DSM-IV-TR, 2000), aged between 25 and 70 years. The results confirm that the alcoholic dependents present difficulties in the identification and characterization of the universal basic emotions with exception of the sadness and anger. The results confirm, still, that the women are more spontaneous in the identification and characterization of the basic emotions than men.

Values, emotional affinity toward nature and proenvironmental behaviour

Maier, Kathrin *Weißenfeld, Germany* **Müller, Markus M.** *Social and Organizational Psyc, Catholic University Eichstaett, Eichstätt, Germany* **Kals, Elisabeth** *Social and Organizational Psyc, Catholic University Eichstaett, Eichstätt, Germany*

Building on value-belief-norm theory (Stern et al., 1999), an extended hierarchical model regarding the role of value structures for proenvironmental behaviour is proposed. First, with critical reference to the purely cognitive approach in VBN-theory, we suggest to integrate emotional affinity toward nature (Kals, Schumacher, & Montada, 1999). Second, it is assumed that the link between general personal values and environmental beliefs is mediated by a person's specifically environmental value orientation. Results from a questionnaire study (N=400) support the mediation model. Including an emotional factor and specific environmental values shows to improve the validity of the VBN model.

Effectiveness of cognitive-behavioral techniques on performance improvement of student with medium dyslexia in Iranian primary school students

Majidi, Abed *Shahid Beheshti University, Tehran, Islamic Republic of Iran* **Baezzat, Fereshteh** *psychology dept., shahid beheshti university, tehran, Islamic Republic of Iran* **Khosh Konesh, Abiolghasem** *shahid beheshti university, psychology dept., tehran, Islamic Republic of Iran*

The aim of this study is to examine the effect of self-instruction technique on reading performance of students with medium dyslexia. So, among the student educating in third and forth grade of arak public primary school, 32 students were selected and they were divided in two groups of experimental and control. Results indicated that self-instruction technique is significant effective in reading performance improvement of student. After 4 months, results from performed pursuit shows that although students marks in experiment group have decreased to some extent, but yet, difference between experiment and control groups are significant. key words:Cognitive-Behavioral techniques;self-instruction;medium dyslexia.

The influence of proactive personality and coping on commitment to STEM majors

Major, Debra *Psychology, Old Dominion University, Norfolk, USA* **Oborn, Kurt** *Psychology, Old Dominion University, Norfolk, USA* **Meert, Shannon** *Psychology, Old Dominion University, Norfolk, USA*

Increasing recruitment and retention in science, technology, engineering, and math (STEM) education and careers is a major focus in the United States as well as an international concern. Using web-based survey data from 296 STEM majors at two universities, results showed that proactive personality is positively associated with commitment to one's STEM major. Additionally, the relationship is fully mediated by students' coping strategies. Proactive personality is positively linked to coping through active planning and is negatively linked to coping through behavioral disengagement. In turn, active planning is positively linked to commitment and behavioral disengagement is negatively linked to commitment.

Genetic and environmental influences on temperament in Russian early adolescents

Malykh, Sergey *Developmental Behavior Genetic, Psychological Institute of RAE, Moscow, Russia* **Lobaskova, Marina** *Developmental Behavior Genetic, Psychological Institute of RAE, Izhevsk, Russia* **Gindina, Elena** *Developmental Behavior Genetic, Psychological Institute of RAE, Moscow, Russia*

The aim of current study was to evaluate the contributions of genotype and environment to individual differences in temperament in adolescence. Early Adolescent Temperament Questionnaire by M.K.Rothbart (Russian adaptation) was administered to 57 pairs of monozygotic, 35 pairs of same-sex dizygotic, and 28 pairs different-sex dizygotic twins. The children were 10-14-years old. Structural equation modeling was used for assessment of contributions of genetic and environmental factors. Results: genetic factors account for 12% of variance for Inhibitory control scale, 19% for Perceptual sensitivity, 19% for Shyness, 35% for Affiliation, 41% for Frustration, 48% for Pleasure Sensitivity, and 53% for Depressive Mood.

Checklist for screening behavioural problems in Greek preschool children

Manolitsis, George *Preschool Education, University of Crete, Rethymno, Greece* **Tafa, Eufimia** *Preschool Education, University of Crete, Rethymno, Greece*

The purpose of this study was the development of a checklist for screening behavioural problems in Greek preschool children and the investigation of the checklist's psychometric properties. Preschool teachers administered the Behaviour Checklist for Preschool Children (BCPC) to 800 children aged 3-6 years old, who attended public kindergarten or day care classrooms in Greece. Four factors revealed from exploratory and confirmatory factor analysis: Disruptive behaviour, Isolation/Immaturity, Anxiety/Insecurity, and Psychosomatic Problems. Inter-rater reliability and internal consistency reliability have been shown to be at a high level. Moreover, results indicated a satisfactory concurrent validity with other similar behaviour scales.

Some new classification methods in attribution hierarchy model

Mao, Meng-Meng Nan Chang, People's Republic of China *Ding, Shu-Liang* Computer Information, Jiang Xi Normal University, Nan Chang, People's Republic of China *Chen, Qing* Computer Information, Jiang Xi Normal University, Nan Chang, People's Republic of China *Zhu, YU-Fang* Computer Information, Jiang Xi Normal University, Nan Chang, People's Republic of China

Leighton et al. (2004) proposed a cognitive diagnostic model named Attribute Hierarchy Method (AHM). There are two classification methods for AHM, named Method A and Method B. However, there are some defects in these two methods. To fill this flaw, several kinds of new classification methods for AHM are proposed. The new methods are based on establishing a series of indices of the similarity between expected response pattern and observed response pattern. The results of simulation indicate that the new methods are better than methods A and B. And with the slips increasing the advantage is especially obvious.

Communication within a post-secondary institution: Analysis and recommendations

Marasigan, John Dept. of Psychology, Kwantlen University College, Surrey, Canada

This exploratory study analyzes the levels of communication within a university-college along ten dimensions of communication. Being the first investigation on the topic in this institution, it explores the reality of what the latter spouses as open communication within the organization. One-hundred-ninety-five employees, including management, faculty, and staff, volunteered to respond to a 10-item survey. Data analysis, both descriptive and multivariate, reveals disparity among the three levels of employment in several dimensions. Overall, open communication is high but its effectiveness is average. Recommendations for improvement from respondents abound.

Who helps victims of natural disasters? An examination of predictors of helping

Marjanovic, Zdravko Psychology, York University, Toronto, Canada *Struthers, C. Ward* Psychology, York University, Toronto, Canada *Greenglass, Esther R.* Psychology, York University, Toronto, Canada

Little is known about why people help natural-disaster victims. The present investigation examines the contributions of demographics (age, gender), social attitudes (prejudice, political orientation), and personality traits (cognitive empathy, affective empathy, social responsibility) in predicting helping. In Study 1, participants read about a bogus, devastating earthquake in South Korea. In Study 2, participants reported retrospectively on their attitudes about Hurricane Katrina. Results of hierarchical regressions showed that, across studies, the predictor variables accounted for significant variance in helping intentions and helping behavior toward natural-disaster victims. The utility of a model that combines demographics, social attitudes, and personality traits is discussed.

Uncertainty and the detection of deception

Marksteiner, Tamara Inst. für Sozialpsychologie, Universität Mannheim, Mannheim, Germany *Reinhard, Marc-Andre* Social Psychology, University of Mannheim, Mannheim, Germany *Müller, Patrick* Social Psychology, University of Utrecht, Mannheim, Germany

Higher uncertainty leads to more systematic processing of information about the quality of social exchange relationships. Therefore we hypothesize that uncertain individuals use more verbal-cues when making credibility judgments. The study followed a 2 (Uncertainty: low vs. high) x 2 (Verbal-cues: deceptive vs. truthful) x 2 (Nonverbal cues: deceptive vs. truthful) factorial design. Lay persons saw a film where nonverbal and verbal-cues has been systematically manipulated. Consistent with the hypothesis verbal-cues only affected the credibility judgment of uncertain individuals (deceptive: M = 4.22 vs. truthful: M = 5.56) but not of certain individuals (M = 4.57 vs. M = 4.37).

The effect of religious orientation, political ideology, fundamentalism, and social dominance orientation on political intolerance

Markum, M Enoch Department of Psychology, University of Indonesia, Depok, Indonesia *Ekaputra, Idhamsyah* Department of Psychology, University of Indonesia, Depok, Indonesia

This paper examined the effects of religious orientation, religious conservative political ideology, religious fundamentalism, and social dominance orientation on political intolerance. Data gathered from 300 subjects with Islamic background. Structural Equation Modeling was employed to test the fit of the proposed model. Results of the study showed that religious conservative political ideology has direct effect on political intolerance. Religious fundamentalism and social dominance orientation mediated the effect of religious orientation, religious political conservative ideology on political intolerance. In testing the moderating effect, it was found that social dominance orientation better served as the moderator of the relation between religious conservative political ideology and political intolerance.

The impact of attachment style on subjective well-being

Marrero, Rosario J. Dept. de Personalidad, Universidad de La Laguna, La Laguna, Spain *Carballeira, Mónica* Personalidad, Ev. y Trat. Psic, Universidad de La Laguna, La Laguna, Spain

The purposes were to analyze the factor structure of the Adult Attachment Scale (Collins y Read, 1990) in Spanish people and to examine the role of attachment in well-being. 500 adult participants completed attachment, self-esteem, social support and subjective well-being measures. Factor analyses revealed five dimensions, only three were according with the authors' model: closeness, depend-dismissing and anxiety-fearful. ANOVA analyses have been conducted to know the well-being level depending on attachment style. Close individuals had more satisfaction with partner and leisure, positive emotion, happiness, self-esteem, life satisfaction, social support; and less negative emotion than depend-dismissing and anxiety-fearful individuals.

Do presentation modes of nature influence the effect on human well-being?: A comparison of laboratory and field results

Martens, Dörte Economics and Social Sciences, Swiss Fed. Research Institute, Birmensdorf, Switzerland *Bauer, Nicole* Economics and Social Sciences, Swiss Fed. Research Inst. WSL, Birmensdorf, Switzerland

Research about the influence of nature onto human well-being is strongly influenced by experiments using visual stimulations representing different environments. We tested if the effect is different depending on the presentation mode. In an experimental setting, we randomly assigned participants (n = 197) to either a natural walk in the laboratory or in the field. The participants assessed well-being in a pre-post-design. Confirming our hypotheses, the results show a significantly stronger positive effect of the field condition on well-being than the laboratory condition. This indicates that field research is needed to analyze the effect of natural environment more specifically.

Assessing multidimensional quality of life: Construct validation of selected World Health Organisation Quality of Life 100 facets

Martinez, Carissa Education and Social Work, University of Sydney, Sydney, Australia *Martin, Andrew* Education and Social Work, University of Sydney, Sydney, Australia *Colmar, Susan* Education and Social Work, University of Sydney, Sydney, Australia

Previous research suggests that quality of life is a multidimensional construct comprised of psychological and physical factors. This study tests the construct validity of a selection of key psychological and physical health facets from the WHOQoL-100, hypothesized to be most relevant to young adults. Based on data from N=705 young adults, this paper reports on the psychometric properties of the facets by assessing descriptive and distribution properties, reliability, factor structure using confirmatory factor analysis and invariance of this structure across gender. The present construct validation findings provide detailed information on the structure underpinning selected facets of the WHOQoL-100 and quality of life more generally – as relevant to young adults.

Career pattern and mental health of women in the child-rearing years

Matsuura, Motoko Ochanomizu University, Tokyo, Japan *Sugawara, Masumi* Graduate School of Human Cultu, Ochanomizu University, Otsuka, Tokyo, Japan *Atushi, Sakai* Divison of School Education, Ochanomizu University, Otsuka, Tokyo, Japan

The purpose of this study is to examine the relationship between career pattern and women's mental health, as mediated by situation of child-rearing and life dissatisfaction. A questionnaire survey was carried out using a mailed questionnaire, and 752 women completed (average age 39.8 years). Women asked to answer questions regarding to their (positive and negative) feeling toward child-rearing, life dissatisfaction, and self-rating depression scale. The major findings are as follows : (1) Career pattern related to husband's income, negative feeling toward child rearing, life dissatisfaction, and depression. (2) Life dissatisfaction and low positive feeling toward child-rearing were correlated with higher depression.

Individual differences in multiple-cue learning: When mathematically proficient students fail to learn nondeterministic environments

Matton, Nadine University of Toulouse, Toulouse, France *Raufaste, Eric* Psychology, University of Toulouse, Toulouse, France *Vautier, Stephane* Psychology, University of Toulouse, Toulouse, France

Objectives: The purpose of the study was to investigate individual differences in the learning of a multilinear correlational relationship between cues and criteria. Methods Two samples of mathematically proficient students (N = 401 and N = 448) performed two experimental tasks. Cluster analyses on rolling achievement indices were computed. Results In either experiment four learning profiles were identified and 12% of each sample failed to learn even the simplest relationship between cues and criteria. Conclusions Correlational tasks can discriminate among mathematical proficient students.

The structure of national currency perception

Mazurek, Joanna Dept. of Psychology, Catholic Univeristy Lublin, Lublin, Poland *Kozak, Agnieszka* Psychology, Catholic Univeristy of Lublin, Lublin, Poland

The purpose of this study is to describe the structure of perception of a national currency and compare it to perception of another currencies recognized as significant to participants. The semantic differentials were used to collect the opinions of 228 participants from Belgium, Poland and the United States of America. Participants evaluated such currencies as: the Dollar and the Euro, Polish participants evaluated also the Polish Zloty. We report an attempt to elucidate some differences between evaluations of examined currencies and perception of a national currency modified by emotional attachment to it.

Choosing between office buildings and converted heritage houses for professional services

McCunn, Lindsay Psychology, Universtiy of Victoria, Victoria, Canada *Gifford, Robert* Psychology, Universtiy of Victoria, VICTORIA, Canada

How do building facades influence consumers' choices? In two studies, two building types (office buildings and converted heritage houses) were shown to student and community participants, who chose between them for various services, and rated them on other dimensions. Participants in both studies reported that they would be more comfortable using office buildings for dental, financial, and medical services. Community participants expected to be more comfortable visiting converted heritage houses for their legal needs. Participants in both studies expected better dental, financial, and medical service in office buildings, but community participants expected higher quality legal service in converted heritage houses.

Gender dissatisfaction among Iranian youth

Mehryar, Amir Hooshang Behavioral Studies, Inst for Research on Planning, Tehran, Islamic Republic of Iran

Objective: To examine degree of satisfaction of youth with their given sex. Methodology: A survey of 15000 men and women aged 15-29 years randomly selected from capital cities of all 30 provinces of Iran. Measure of Gender Dissatisfaction: Expressed wish to have been born male (in the case of girls) or female (in the case of boys). Major Findings: Over two-fifth of girls as compared with only 16% of boys expressed a desire to have been from the other sex. Comparing youth dissatisfied with their gender with the rest of sample revealed significant differences in a number of characteristics.

A study of family alienation among Iranian adolescents

Mehryar, Amir Hooshang Behavioral Studies, Inst for Research on Planning, Tehran, Islamic Republic of Iran

Objective: To explore contemporary Iranian adolescents' perception of and attitude to family environment and determine extent of family alienation (defined in terms of expressed wish to have been born in another family). Methodology: Survey covering a random sample of 5600 boys and girls aged 15-19 years taken from capital cities of all 30 provinces. Main findings: The overwhelming majority of subjects live in intact parental homes and describe their parents' relations as close. Yet, 17% wish they had been born in another family. They differ from the rest of the sample in a number of social, behavioral and attitudinal characteristics.

The effects of event sponsorship on product evaluations: The role of company's corporate social responsibility

Messner, Matthias Social Psychology, University of Mannheim, Mannheim, Germany *Reinhard, Marc-André* Social Psychology, University of Mannheim, Mannheim, Germany

Across two studies, it was predicted and found that products of retailers with negative reputations for social responsibility are evaluted less favorably than those of retailers with positive reputations. Furthermore, students penalized socially irresponsible retailers for sponsoring socially responsible events (Special Olympics) compared to when they simply advertised their products. By contrast, students rewarded socially responsible retailers for supporting the Special Olympics. Sponsoring an event lower in perceived social responsibility (Olympics) led to better product evaluations for both irresponsible and responsible corporations. These effects were found to be mediated by students' global attitudes toward the sponsor.

Spontaneous emotion regulation following affective events: Do we have a choice how to regulate our emotions?

Meyenschein, Kerstin Köln, Germany

People frequently (have to) control their emotions – this is especially important in the work place, where successful emotion regulation is crucial for the success of interpersonal relationships. Evidence suggests that different forms of emotion regulation have different costs for the individual. But what influences the individual's choice of a specific emotion regulation strategy in a given situation? Drawing on Affective Events Theory, the authors use "affective events – vignettes" to examine the relative contributions of the personality, the situation and the personality X situation interactions in the emotion regulation process in an experimental setting. Results and their implications are discussed.

Students psychoeducational diagnosis I: Learning strategies and academic performance

Mezquita-Hoyos, Yanko Psychology, Universidad Autonoma d Yucatan, Merida, Mexico *de Lille-Quintal, Jose* Psychology, Universidad Autonoma d Yucatan, Merida Yucatan, Mexico *Oses-Bargas, Rosa* Psychology, Universidad Autonoma d Yucatan, Merida Yucatan, Mexico *Aguayo-Chan, Jorge* Psychology, Universidad Autonoma d Yucatan, Merida Yucatan, Mexico

It was identified the learning strategies which are correlated to a succesful students'academic performance. With this purpose, we validated psychometrically a questionaire of 50 reactives of learning strategies with 206 udergraduate students in psychology. Subsequently it was correlated the scores of 56 of these participants with their academic performance and it was found a correlation which was significative between the strategy of organization of acitivities and time with the module of mathematics: moment product coefficient of pearson = .27, p < .05. The results were discussed in theoretical terms, psychometrically, as well as by the academmic planning of the students.

Change processes in higher education: Moderating effects of personality variables on the relationship between commitment to change and change support behaviour

Michel, Alexandra Inst. für Organ.-Psychologie, Universität Heidelberg, Heidelberg, Germany *Stegmaier, Ralf* Organizational Psychology, University of Heidelberg, Heidelberg, Germany *Sonntag, Karlheinz* Organizational Psychology, University of Heidelberg, Heidelberg, Germany

In the context of organizational change in higher education, the present study examined the moderating role of personality variables, such as resistance to change, on the relationship between commitment to change and change support behaviour. Predictions were tested using self-reported questionnaire data of 315 members of academic staff at a German university. Results revealed that positive effects of commitment to change on change support behaviour were stronger for employees low on resistance to change than for those with high levels of resistance to change. No significant moderating effects were found for other personality variables under investigation.

Profiling voters in Vojvodina

Mihic, Vladimir Department of Psychology, University of Novi Sad, Novi Sad, Serbia *Mihic, Ivana* Department of Psychology, University of Novi Sad, Novi Sad,

Although Serbia in the last fifteen, or so years, is burdened by the politics much more than needed, only a few of the researches in the past years deal with the question: who is an average voter in Serbia and how does he looks like? The sample of this research consisted of 352 subjects. We used some classic variables, but also an attitude scale about some important political issues in Serbia, as well as BFI for the measurement of personality traits. The results show that differences can be found in almost all of the political attitudes concerning preferences of the political parties, but out of five personality traits measured, only one proved statistically significant (agreeableness).

The phenomenon of immigration: Cultural values and cultural diversity in Europe

Miryam, Rodriguez Dpt. of Social Psychology, Univ. Complutense de Madrid, Madrid, Spain *Inge, Schweiger* Dpt. of Social Psychology, Univ. Complutense de Madrid, Madrid, Spain *José Luis, Álvaro* Dpt. of Social Psychology, Univ. Complutense de Madrid, Madrid, Spain

It is an undeniable issue that the phenomenon of the immigration is lived in Europe with preoccupation and certain pressure because of its consequences. In the present research, we based on the European Social Survey Questionnaire (2002) and the Portrait Values Questionnaire (Schwartz, 1992, 2001) to focus on the relevance of the criteria which determine the acceptance or the immigrant's rejection, their consequences, as well as its relationship with cultural values. Finally, we emphasize the importance of cultural values -like Harmony or Egalitarianism- for any initiative or politics in migratory matter in a European context.

The effects of kinship cue on empathy and helping intentions

Mitani, Nobuhiro Nagoya University, Aichi, Japan

This study investigated whether the detection of kinship cue would affect the elicitation of empathy and help intentions. The existence of kinship cue was manipulated by similarity in high heritability attitudes. Total 155 participants completed the questionnaire consists of target person's attitude, evaluation of attitude similarity, scenario, and the rating of empathy and helping intentions. Regression analyses revealed that similarity significantly predicted empathy and helping intentions. Furthermore, empathy mediated the relationship between similarity and helping intentions. These results imply the possibility that detection of kinship cue elicit empathy, which functions as an emotional kinship cue that leads to helping behavior.

Attachment styles and emotional availability to infants in young adult females

Miyamoto, Kunio Psychology, Tokaigakuin University, Gifu-shi, Japan

The objective was to investigate the relations between attachment styles of female university students and their emotional availability to infants. Attachment styles were assessed by two questionnaires of attachment internal working models and emotional availability was assessed by Japanese edition of IFeel Pictures (facial expressions of infants). Range of used categories was correlated positively and number of popular responses was correlated negatively to secure scores. Anxious individuals showed more popular responses to infant facial expressions. These results suggested that young female adults with secure attachment have the readiness to read emotions and motivations of infants more flexibly.

Creative processes of community revitalization from narrative approach: A case study from Chuetsu earthquake

Miyamoto, Takumi Atsumi Lab., Human Sciences, Osaka University, Suita, Japan *Atsumi, Tomohide* Atsumi Lab., Human Sciences, Osaka University, Suita city, Japan

The 2004 Chuetsu Earthquake destroyed many mountainous villages in Niigata Prefecture, Japan. It accelerated the depopulation and aging of the communities. How can the local residents achieve any creative revitalization? Authors have been conducting a long-term participatory observation in the region. We are concerned with the ways the survivors and the outside supporters collaboratively created new narratives about their community. We found that if the local residents' narratives on their community changed, they could start their community revitalization positively and outside supporters could help it. Finally, we discussed what group dynamics would do for the revitalization as an action research.

Self-immunization in adolescence: Does the functionality of self-stabilizing processes vary with age?

Moessle, Regine Institut für Psychologie, Universität Hildesheim, Hildesheim, Germany *Greve, Werner* Institute of Psychology, University of Hildesheim, Hildesheim, Germany

This research addresses the question whether the buffering effect of self-immunization on the burdening effect of stressful experiences on subjective well-being changes during adolescence. Two pilot questionnaire studies (n1 = 1387; n2 = 122; ages 12-22) are conducted. Study 1 comprises several general measures (including self-immunization, self esteem, stressful life events); study 2 contains more fine-grained measures of self-immunization with respect to six traits, ability, centrality and complexity of these traits, stressful experiences and subjective well-being. The first study indicates that the buffering effect is more pronounced in early adolescence (<16); first analyses of study 2 support this finding.

Atypical lateralization in auditory regions of dyslectic children: Is there a reduced right hemispheric contribution to temporal integration and segmentation?

Mohamed, Wessam Inst. für Klin. Psychologie, Universität Konstanz, Konstanz, Germany *Paul, Isabelle* clinical psychology, university of konstanz, konstanz, Germany *Wienbruch, Christian* clinical psychology, university of konstanz, konstanz, Germany *Elbert, Thomas* clinical psychology, university of konstanz, konstanz, Germany

For speech perception, segmentation of the auditory stream into discrete representations is a prerequisite, producing neural activity with corresponding frequency content. We hypothesize that degraded auditory representations trigger temporal integration deficits in developmental dyslexia. Using magnetoencephalographic source imaging, we mapped focal slow waves in 48 dyslexic and 20 normal readers (aged 8.2 -11.4) during a passive auditory odd-ball paradigm. A repeated measure ANOVA showed hemispheric asymmetry differences in the density of magnetic slow waves in perisylvian regions, whereby dyslexic children

showed less right hemispheric delta activity. Results unprecedentedly suggest impaired right hemispheric contribution to the speech sound segmentation in dyslexia.

First accreditation to specialist in forensic psychology by the psychologist's official college of Cataluña, in Spain

Molina Bartumeus, Asuncion COPC, Barcelona, Spain *Almenara, Jaume* Decano, COPC, Barcelona, Spain *Cartil, Conxita* vicepresidenta sección, COPC, Barcelona, Spain *Farre, Merce* secretary, COPC, Barcelona, Spain *Carmona, Anna* Tesorera, COPC, Barcelona, Spain *Espada, Carme* vocal sección, COPC, Barcelona, Spain *Antolin, Andreu* vocal sección, COPC, Barcelona, Spain *Franquesa, Emilia* vocal sección, COPC, Barcelona, Spain *Arch, Mila* vocal sección jurídica, COPC, Barcelona, Spain

This poster presents the process of accreditation as Specialist in Forensic Psychology which was initiated last autumn (2007) by the psychologist's Official College of Cataluña, in Spain. After the official recognition of the speciality in Clinical Psychology, a wide movement of accreditation is beginning in our country in other psychological specialities that could draw the final plan of the state of the profession as a common line with specialities that demand skills and specific capacities. Here are exposed the conceptual bases of this process for the Forensic Psychology and the criteria that are demanded to accede to the accreditation, which offer us then the suitable training level for an expert in this discipline.

Neuropsychological, psychological and social correlates of antisocial behavior among Peruvian adolescents in conflict with the penal law: A study from Moffitt's taxonomic theory

Morales, Hugo Faculty of Psychology, San Marcos National University, Lima, Peru

The early identification of those individual and social characteristics that discriminate among offender adolescents who maintain their antisocial delinquent behavior along their life span and those who don't, constitutes an important strategy for the design of efficient prevention policies for juvenile delinquency. Using a discriminant analysis, significance Scheffe Test, variance analysis for significant differences between Groups and Levenes variance homogeneity test, it was corroborated if the typology of the antisocial behavior development taxonomy established by Moffitt is replicated in the studied sample. The results suggest that the Moffitt tipology has cross-culture validity and to explain different profiles at risk amog offender adolescents.

Influence of psychopolitical variables in reactions to traumatic and hopeful events

Morales Marente, Elena Dept. of Psychology, University of Huelva, Huelva, Spain *Palacios, María Soledad* Department of Psychology, University of Huelva, Huelva, Spain *Willis, Guillermo* Department of Psychology, University of Huelva, Huelva, Spain *Pérez, Jose María* Department of Psychology, University of Huelva, Huelva, Spain

Researchers have been analysed the influence of psychopolitical variables in stresful and traumatic events as 11S, 2001. We have used them also to explore its influence in a hopeful event. In our research we present two studies (a traumatic event, 11M, 2004 in Madrid –N= 300- and a hopeful one, the cease of fire of ETA, 2006 –N= 198) conducted in Spain. We tested hypothesis related with the influence of individual's values and ideological factors on hopes and fears for the future and other indexes of out-group prejudice. Analysis showed which psycho-political variables predicted fears and hopes.

The HRM perspective on conflict in organizations: The Portuguese case

Moreira, Ricardo Fac. Human and Social Science, University Fernando Pessoa, Porto, Portugal

Contemporary debate concerning organizational conflict, independently the different analitical perpectives, goes beyond the question of its (dys)functionality. In line with current trends about conflict and negotiation theories, Portugal has witnessed an increase of academic research concerning negotiation in organizations, however has not been given great attention to the political perspective of HR Management. Many pathways can be explored regarding the connection between negotiation and Human Resource Department. Crossing statistical and content analysis, our investigation seeks to interpret the views of portuguese human resources managers concerning organizational conflicts and the impact these views exert on organizational efficacy, in an effort to build a close alignment with the HRM role in negotiation.

Personality judgments based on email addresses of mobile phones

Mori, Tsutako Dept. of Human Science, Konan Women's University, Kyoto, Japan *Takahira, Mieko* Research and Development, NIME, Chiba, Japan

This study investigated the accuracy of personality judgments based on email addresses of mobile phones, which are very popular personal media among young people in Japan. The holders' personalities of 121 addresses were rated by two judges with the Big Five scale, and the ratings were compared with the holders' real-self or ideal-self ratings. Judge consensus for personality ratings was significant in all five dimensions. Also, judge ratings were significantly correlated with Extraversion of real-self ratings and with Agreeableness of ideal-self ratings. These findings suggest that email addresses are used as tools for impression management as well as self-expression.

What is the first cause of tendency to addiction? Psychological, environmental or physical

Mosavi Amiry, Seyed Jalal Medical Clinic, Babol, Islamic Republic of Iran *Nikpour, Gholam Ali* Dept. of Psychology, Medical Clinic of Dr. Mosavi, Babol, Islamic Republic of Iran *Homayouni, Alireza* Psychology, Islamic Azad University of Ban, Babol, Islamic Republic of Iran *Emadi Haeri, Marzieh* Addiction studies, Dr Mosavi Medical Clinic, Babol(Amirkola), Islamic Republic of Iran

The aim of the research is to test this question what is the first cause of addiction? Psychological, Environmental or Physical causes.80 addicted people were randomly selected and Abuse Drug Assessment Inventory (ADAI) were administered on them. Chi Square formula was used to analyze the results. Results showed 55 percent of tendency to addiction was psychological. Also more analyzing showed 80 percent of continuing causes of addiction were psychological factors such as fear, anxiety, sorrow. In regard to result we should put more emphasise on psychological prevention and treatment methods so that both tendency to addiction and continuing causes of addiction decrease and control.

Public acceptance of wind turbines in Tokyo

Motosu, Memi Interdisciplinary Information, University of Tokyo, Tokyo, Japan *Arakawa, Chuichi* Interdisciplinary Information, The University of Tokyo, Tokyo, Japan

The purpose of this study is to examine the public's viewpoint regarding wind turbines in the landscape of metropolitan city, Tokyo.The author conducted 30 interviews, showing pictures of different districts in Tokyo. The result indicates that there are different viewpoints depending on the district, considering that the design of the wind turbines should harmonize with the landscape. The study concludes that it is necessary for wind turbines to capture the distinctive features of districts in order to get public acceptance. If the appropriate design is followed, the landscape with wind turbines should be acceptable in the urban area.

Explicit and implicit values of grandmothers and their granddaughters

Mudyñ, Krzysztof Inst. Applied Psychology, Jagiellonian University, Krakow, Poland Pietras, Karolina Management and Social Com., Jagiellonian University, Cracow, Poland

The aim of the study was to examine the correspondence of implicit and explicit values measures and the convergence of grandmothers and their granddaughters values.Schwartz's SVS and Mudyn's RN-02 was administered to 80 grandmothers (aged 64-86) and their 80 grand-daughters (aged 18-30).The results revealed many inter-correlations, especially between religious or-ientation and tradition (r=0,63), benevolence (r=0,36), security (r=0,31), self-direction (r=-0,47) or stimulation (r=-0,35). The similarities between grandmothers and granddaughters appeared in universalism (r=0,51), achievement (r=0,31) and hedonism (r= 0,33). Further research concerning the consequences of grandmothers' stimulation value is recommended.

Exploring new dynamics of job-involvement: An empirical study of life-orientation, gender and occupational stress

Mukherjee, Debjani Bhilai - Chattisgarh, India Singh, Promila Psychology, Pt.Ravishankar ShuklaUniversit, BHILAI (CHATTISGARH), India

Industries facing twin challenges of being viable and competitive in global scenario, exploit man-power resource by facilitating job-involvement. Breaking socio-cultural ethos of the east, women are also joining the industrial sector. In this study 400 (140 females, 260 males) steel industry executive's life-orientation, gender and occupational stress were empirically treated to explore their impact on job-involvement. Results of 2x2 ANOVA show sig-nificant interaction effect of life-orientation and gender on job-involvement F-77.3(P<.001), whereas life-orientation, gender and occupational stress in 2x2x3 ANOVA was not significant F-2.66(P<.05). Results support reconceptualizing the major determinants of job-involvement and refor-mulation of placement policies by H.R.M. depart-ments.

Peace psychology of grassroot reconciliation: Lesson learned from "Baku Bae" peace movement

Muluk, Hamdi Department of Psychology, University of Indonesia, Depok, Indonesia Malik, Ichsan Department of Psychology, Indonesian Peace Building Inst, Depok, Indonesia

This paper explored the community-based reconci-liation process mediated by civil society compo-nents – known as "The Baku Bae Movement" – as an alternative to conflict resolution and reconcilia-tion in current Indonesian political context. This movement applied some principles from peace psychology such as; multitrack diplomacy, inter-active problem solving workshop and other media-tion technique contextualized with indigenous values. This unique conflict resolution strategy consists of five stages ranging from dialog to interactive problem solving workshop, creating peace zone, and economic empowerment. The successful of Baku Bae movement suggest the benefit of bottom-up approach and the role of civil society in strengthening and empowering survivor to make their own reconciliation.

Differential prefrontal EEG activity between sport amateurs and non-sport amateurs during video clip viewing

Muramatsu, Ayako Psychology, Japan Women's University, Kawasaki, Japan Kawahara, Yuli Psychology, Japan Women's University, Kawasaki, Japan Mochizuki, Toshiko Psychology, Japan Women's University, Kawasaki, Japan

To examine whether prefrontal activity differs depending on the amusingness of the video clip, prefrontal EEG activity was compared between Sport amateurs and Non-sport amateurs by show-ing three kinds of video clips; 1) basketball game (group sport), 2) snowboard game (individual sport), 3) non-sport documentary. We measured Beta/Alpha ratio of the prefrontal EEG, and found that the ratio during the basketball video viewing was higher in Sport amateurs than in Non-sport amateurs. This indicates that Sport amateurs are more amused and show more PFC activity by videos of dynamic and social sports than Non-sport amateurs.

Brain areas activated during listening to piano music

Mutschler, Isabella Freiburg, Germany Speck, Oliver Hennig, Jürgen Seifritz, Erich Schulze-Bonhage, Andreas Ball, Tonio Epilepsie-Zentrum, Universität Freiburg, Freiburg, Germany

In this study functional MRI (fMRI) was combined with cyto-architectonically defined probabilistic maps to analyze brain responses in 18 healthy subjects presented with classical piano music and the relation of these brain responses to the personality trait of affect intensity. Significant fMRI responses related to music perception were demonstrated in the auditory cortex, right and left inferior frontal cortex (including Broca's area), supplementary motor area (SMA), cerebellum, and in the amygdala. Correlation of music related responses with affect intensity were found in a network of brain areas previously implicated in emotion recognition (Adolphs et al. 2005), includ-ing primary somatosensory cortex.

Social intelligence of pedophile sex offenders

Nötzold, Janine Inst. für Psychologie, Universität Magdeburg, Magdeburg, Germany Hähnel, Nadine Institut für Psychologie, Universität Magdeburg, Magdeburg, Germany Süß, Heinz-Martin Institut für Psychologie, Universität Magdeburg, Magdeburg, Germany Witzel, Joachim Forensische Psychiatrie, LKH Uchtspringe, Uchtspringe, Germany

The study tested the hypothesis on pedophile sex offenders (N = 25) being deficient in social under-standing and perception when compared to matched controls (N = 26). Research indicates pedophiles having problems to perceive emotions appropriately and to understand social cues in certain context using victim-specific material. Social understanding and perception were measured ac-cording to the performance based Social Intelli-gence Test Battery Magdeburg (Weis, Seidel & Süß, 2007) by new tasks with children as target stimuli. ANCOVAs showed no differences in social under-standing and perception between the groups when speed performance was statistically controlled indicating a revision of former theories.

Relationships between organizational obstacles and innovation organizational climate in the personnel of an industrial organization

Naami, Abdolzhara Psychology, Shahid chamran, Ahvaz, Islamic Republic of Iran

the present study examind the relationship between organizalobstacles as measureed by Karen, Brown and Mitchlell and the climate for innovation measure (scott and Bruce) A sample of employees (N=143), completed quanstionnaires. Results com-firm the hypothesis by indicating that component of organizational obstacle (work information, informa-

tion timeliness, work materials, co-workers job training, avallability of training, guality of training, work enviroment,work schedule, decision author-ity, role demand and priorities) were negatively correlated with climate for innovation.

The relation between behavior of consulting and psychological distress among Japanese junior high school students

Nagai, Satoru Inst. of Psychology, University of Tsukuba, Tsukuba, Japan

The purpose of this study was to investigate the pattern of consulting behavior among junior high-school students. Two thousand, three hundred eighty-three junior high-school students (1245 male and 1138 female) were asked about consulting behavior, severity of concerns and Depression Self-Rating Scale for Children (DSRS). Results indi-cated that, students with more concerns presented higher level of consulting behavior. On the other hand, although high level of consulting behavior was related with low level of "declining activity and pleasure (one of factors of DSRS)", relation between consulting behavior and "depressive mood (one of factors of DSRS)" was very little.

The relationship between intelligence and learning processes

Narváez Rullán, María Dept. of Psychology, Autónoma University of Madrid, Madrid, Spain Lozano, José Héctor Department of Psychology, Autónoma University of Madrid, Madrid, Spain Hernández, José Manuel Department of Psychology, Autónoma University of Madrid, Madrid, Spain Santacreu, José Department of Psychology, Autónoma University of Madrid, Madrid, Spain

The present study attempts to analyze relationships between intelligence and two different types of learning: a) the acquisition of specific discriminative learning; b) the improvement in the accuracy during execution of a dynamic spatial task, which is assumed not to involve any verbal or discriminative ability. 267 participants were assessed through computer-based tasks. A significant relationship was found between discriminative learning and intelligence while intelligence was not related to the improvement shown during the dynamic spatial task. The results support Sternberg's hypothesis (1989) that intelligence is related to the type of learning that involves discriminative or verbal abilities.

Self-regulation in vocabulary learning

Nett, Ulrike Erziehungswissenschaften, Universität Konstanz, Konstanz, Germany Frenzel, Anne Inst. für Psychologie, Universität München, München, Germany

This presentation addresses how self-regulation ability and external constraints regarding the allocation of study time affects performance in vocabulary learning tasks. Participants had to learn Swahili-German translation equivalents and to rank the perceived difficulty of each pair before learning (pre-trial JOLs). Self-regulation ability, operationalized as the relationship between pre-trial JOLs and self-allocated study time, was positively related to performance (Experiment 1). However, total performance was identical when learning times were externally fixed, based on objective pair difficulty (Experiment 2). We speculate about the existence of differentially adequate learning envir-onments for different types of learners.

Status quo of dysfunctional thoughts in Chinese senior elementary school students and middle school students

Ni, Jie Educational Psychology, Hong Kong, China, People's Republic of : Hong Kong SAR Sang, Biao Psychology, East China Normal University, Shanghai, People's Republic of China

The purpose of present studies was to discover the status quo of the dysfunctional thoughts -"sick, false, or unreasonable thoughts that cause the appearance of maladjustment and what's more, the emotion disorders"- in Chinese elementary and middle school students. 851 students completed the dysfunctional thoughts scale developed in previous study. The results showed the status quo of the dysfunctional thoughts in elementary and middle school students was beyond optimistic, "Demanding for best treatment" and "over-perfectionism" were the two most severe problems in Chinese students. Significant gender and age differences were also found. Our findings gave important instructive suggestion to school counseling, mental health education and learning guidance.

Is a happy worker a productive one?

Niklas, Claudia D. Work, Organizational &Business, Psychologisches Institut / Uni, Mainz, Germany Dormann, Christian I/O Psychology, Gutenberg-Universität Mainz, Mainz, Germany

Although this question is discussed since the beginning of organizational psychology, results are still inconsistent. Using multiple state and trait measurements obtained in a two-week diary study (N = 116), job satisfaction, as well as positive and negative affect (PA, NA) were related to extra-role and in-role behavior. Our results showed that PA and NA predicted job satisfaction, which in turn mediated the relationship of PA and extra-role behavior. In-role behavior was only influenced by PA, whereas NA failed to influence any performance component. These results support happy-productive worker thesis and enlarge affective events theory.

Personality characters as a predictor of tendency to addiction

Nikpour, Gholam Ali Dept. of Psychology, Medical Clinic of Dr. Mosavi, Babol, Islamic Republic of Iran Mosavi Amiry, Seyed Jalal Medical Clinic, Babol, Islamic Republic of Iran Homayouni, Alireza Dept. of Psychology, Medical Clinic of Dr. Mosavi, Babol (Amirkola), Islamic Republic of Iran

The aim of this research is to test this question that are there specific personality characters that lead to addiction? Method research is causative-comparative (Ex post facto).153 addicted people and 153 nonaddicted people were randomly selected and Mocioly's Characterlogy Inventory (MCI) administered on them.The inventory assess personality based on eight characters: sanguine, indifferent,-nervous,indolent,indignant,passionate,sentimentee,amorphous.Results showed addicted people are much more indifferent, sanguine and passionate than nonaddicted people. Conclusion: In regard to people with these characters are much more at risk, they should be trained with special plans and be cared so that tendency to addiction in them decrease or control.

Relations among prosocial tendency, guilt and problem actions in Japanese junior high-school students

Ninomiya, Katsumi Dept. of Policy Studies, Aichi Gakuin University, Nisshin, Japan

The present study examined the relations among adolescents' prosocial tendency, guilt, and problem actions. Participants were 1,446 Japanese adolescents (708 males and 738 females) who were seventh graders (age: 12-13 years). They answered a questionnaire concerning prosocial tendency (7 items), guilt (25 items), and problem actions (22 items) on a 4-point scale. Females scored higher in prosocial tendency and guilt than males. The partial correlation coefficient was significantly positive between prosocial tendency and guilt. A positive partial correlation was also found between prosocial tendency and problem actions. However, there was a negative partial correlation between guilt and problem actions.

Longitudinal study of socio-environmental experiences, self-worth and emotional/ behavioral problems among junior high school students

Nishino, Yasuyo Seto, Japan Ujiie, Tatsuo Education, Nagoya University, Nagoya, Japan Ninomiya, Katsumi Education, Aichi-Gakuin University, Chita, Japan Igarashi, Atsushi Education, Fukushima University, Fukushima, Japan Inoue, Hiromitsu Education, Chiba College of Health Scienc, Chiba, Japan Yamamoto, Chika Education, Nagoya-Bunri University, Nagakute, Japan

This study aimed to investigate the role of self-worth as a mediator of relationships between socio-environmental experiences and emotional/ behavioral problems using a sample of 359 junior high school students. They participated in a questionnaire survey three times every four months. Socio-environmental experiences were assessed using self-report questionnaire measures of social support and stressful events. SEM was conducted, and it was revealed that social support had significant effects on emotional problems via indirect effects indicated a mediating role for self-worth. The results of present study reinforced the need for further inquiry into specific processes through which adolescents would become depressed.

Training evaluation: Effectiveness, learning styles and modes of assistance

Nocera, Antonio Psicologia e Antropologia, Università di Verona, Verona, Italy Pasetto, Sara Psicologia e Antropologia, Università di Verona, Verona, Italy Cubico, Serena Psicologia e Antropologia, Università di Verona, Verona, Italy Bellotto, Massimo Psicologia e Antropologia, Università di Verona, Verona, Italy

The aim of the research is to evaluate the influence selected individual variables may have on effectiveness of training; effectiveness of the training actions supposedly depends also on the link between training provided and the learning styles of the participants. The sample is 100 Italian Public Administration employees. The survey instruments are: Kolb Questionnaire on Learning Styles, multiple-choice questionnaires on learning, supported by a time survey on video lesson use. Analysis of the data highlights significant correlations among the progress made by the participants, measured behaviours and learning style.

The influence of reflection and brooding to depressive symptom: Examination from subtypes of rumination

Noguchi, Rieko Teacher Education, Hyogo University of, Joetsu, Japan Fujiu, Hideyuki Science of School Education, Hyogo University of Teacher Ed, kato, Japan

This study examined relation among rumination, coping, stress response and depression symptom, classified rumination into reflection and brooding. Research subjects were 835 undergraduate and graduate students. The results showed that reflection items were classified into controlled coping, brooding items were classified into automatic stress response in Responses to Stress Questionnaire. Moreover, in female, definition of problem scores, including reflection items, were negatively correlated to BDI-II scores. In both male and female, negative thought tendency scores, including brooding items were positively correlated to BDI-II scores.

History as a content of individual autobiographical memory

Nourkova, Veronika Psychology, Moscow State University, Moscow, Russia

With regard to their perspective toward historical event individuals may be labeled Participant, Witness, Contemporary, and Successor. To what extent people employing each of those perspectives are sensitive to historical information? From 240 Russian participants 20% spontaneously included historical events in their life stories. There were 20 different historical events. 40% of historical events mentioned by participants referred to war ("evacuation", "Victory day", "wounding near Moscow"), while 38% - referred to politic ("perestroika", "collapse of USSR", "XX Party Congress"). People included in their life story events which were experienced from Participant or Witness perspective. There was just one case when Contemporary perspective was employed ("9/11").

Second-order retrospective revaluation in human contingency learning

Numata, Keitaro Psychology, Kwansei Gakuin University, Nishinomiya, Japan Shimazaki, Tsuneo Psychology, Kwansei Gakuin University, Nishinomiya, Japan

Two Experiments were conducted to demonstrate the second-order retrospective revaluation with 3 cues, T1, T2, and C, and an outcome, in human contingency learning. Experiment 1 revealed that ratings about the relation between a target cue T2 and an outcome heightened when first two training phases involved CT1+ and T1T2+ trials followed by third phase containing C+ trials, and the ratings lowered by the third phase containing C- trials. In Experiment 2, the order of first two phases in the Experiment 1 was changed, and still the results of Experiment 1 were replicated. These results clearly demonstrated the phenomena of second-order retrospective revaluation.

The authenticity of manager

Nuslauerova, Pavla Dept. of Psychology, Charles University, Chomutov, Czech Republic

The presented poster concerns the issue of authenticity with the focus on the context of the managerial profession. It is a presentation of the author's research. The main aim of the research was the meaning of the concept of authenticity for managers and its better understanding within the context of managers' working activity. The research includes 17 interviews with 16 participants (1 lecturer and 15 managers from various levels) and observation of 13 managers. In conclusion, based on the obtained data, the author refines the definition of authenticity and recommends paying more attention in developing the managers' self-reflection.

Adaptive behavior and skills of young children with autism

Oakland, Thomas Dept. Educational Psychology, University of Florida, Gainesville, USA Woolf, Steve Psychological Services, Beacon Services, Milford, MA, USA

This study identifies the adaptive behaviors and skills of 172 children, ages 2 and 3, who display an Autistic Disorder. Their mean general adaptive behavior is at the 2nd percentile. The rank order of their 10 adaptive skills follows: functional academic (the highest) motor, self-direction, community resources, leisure, home living, health and safety, social communication, and self-care skills.

Political participation of youths who have dropped out of armed conflict and rejoined civil life

Obando Salazar, Olga Lucia Área de Cognicion, Instituto de Psicologia, Cali, Colombia

The main objective is to discover the types of political participation of young men who have dropped out of the armed conflict in Colombia and its incidence in the formulation and implementation of public policy for youth. The research methodology was qualitative and exploratory, through Participant Action Research (PAR) as an research method and intervention for emancipation. 60 subjects participated, among them youths who have dropped out of the conflict, agents from government, from NGOs and from financial organizations. Results include new elements about diversity in the conception of the settings, instances, mechanisms and processes of political participation of the youths.

Red moon: Strengthening of feminine identity in mistreated girls and adolescents

Obando Salazar, Olga Lucia Área de Cognicion, Instituto de Psicologia, Cali, Colombia

Problem: the supposition of the existence of a deficit in the state of development of a feminine identity in girls and adolescents with maltreatment experience. Corpus: results of the investigation and intervention project: "Red Moon: strengthening of feminine identity in mistreated girls and adolescents through artistic, psychological and pedagogic activities" by the light of: the contributions of the Social Psychology. Results: the existence of a feminine subject, that is stereotyped, unreal, cultural, ethnic and socially out of context, when it is comparing with what they say to be and to feel as women. Methods: Study exploring, Participant actions research as methodologies of investigation and intervention emancipators. Participants: 60 adolescents. Discourse analyses.

When does trust in authority and procedural fairness affect social acceptance of public policy?

Ohana, Kyosuke Environmental studies, Nagoya University, Nagoya, Japan Hirose, Yukio Environmental studies, Nagoya University, Nagoya, Japan

Our study explored the effect of trust in authority and procedural fairness on poeple's acceptance of his policy when information about policy content is available or not. When people did not know the content, their acceptance was based on whether the authority was trustworthy or not. People used procedural fairness as alternative cue when neither content nor trust information was available. However, when people knew the content, their acceptance was based on both of content and trust information, but not on procedural fairness. Results suggested that procedural fairness affected acceptance only when neither policy content nor trust was available.

Relationship between communication, commitment, identification, job satisfaction and turnover intentions

Ok, Afife Dept. of Psychology, Atilim University, Ankara, Turkey Bilgic, Reyhan psychology, middle east technical uni., Ankara, Turkey Sumer, Hayriye psychology, middle east technical uni., Ankara, Turkey

The aim of this study was to examine the relationships between organizational communication, organizational commitment, organizational identification, job satisfaction, and turnover intentions. Questionnaires were administered to a sample of 321 white-collar bank employees who are working in different branches of different banks in Ankara. The results revealed that both job satisfaction and organizational identification were significant positive predictors of organizational commitment. Organizational commitment was found as a significant negative predictor of turnover intentions. Significance of indirect effect of job satisfaction and organizational identification on turnover intentions through organizational commitment confirms the mediation of organizational commitment.

Participation in school-based extracurricular activity and adolescent's school adjustment

Okada, Yuji Hino, Japan

The purpose of this study was to investigate the relation between school-based extracurricular activity and adolescent's school adjustment, by focusing on adolescent's morale to the activity. 824 adolescents answered self-report questionnaire, which consisted of participation in the extracurricular activity, morale to the activity and school adjustment. Two-way (gender and participation) ANOVAs revealed that adolescents with high morale to the activity indicated high adjustment score compared with adolescents with low morale and adolescents those who don't participate any activities. It was suggested that, for adolescents with low morale, participation in the extracurricular activity doesn't have positive effect on school adjustment.

Determining the attitude toward characters in television commercials using text data mining: An analysis of Japanese commercials that feature famous actresses

Okano, Masao Information and Communication, Bunkyo University, Chigasaki, Japan Okano, Masami Bunkyo University, Chigasaki, Japan

This research examined the reason for viewers' liking or disliking characters in television commercials. For this purpose, commercials featuring Japanese actresses were shown to 200 college students. After the presentation, the students were asked to provide answers pertaining to the following: their attitude toward the actress in the commercial shown on a 4-point scale and the reasons behind their like or dislike in the form of free answers. The results of textminig of the free answers revealed that the reasons for viewers' liking or disliking the characters matched the brand images of the products the latter endorsed.

Influence of consumers' perception toward online shopping on online shopping behavior

Okano Asakawa, Masami Junior College, Bunkyo University, Chigasaki, Japan Okano, Masao Junior College, Bunkyo University, Chigasaki, Japan

This study examined the factors influencing consumers' perception toward online shopping and developed a causal model that explains how this perception affects their online shopping behavior. We framed a questionnaire survey for 160 college students. Utilizing 13 questions pertaining to consumer perceptions, we conducted a factor analysis that revealed three factors—security, convenience, and navigation. Based on this result, a causal model was developed, and its validity was investigated using covariance structure analysis. It was found that while the "security" factor negatively influences online shopping behavior, the "convenience" factor positively influences it.

"Connectedness with nature scale": Validity and reliability in the Spanish context

Olivos Jara, Pablo Psicología Social, Univers. Complutense de Madrid, Madrid, Spain Aragonés, Juan Ignacio Psicología Social, Univ. Complutense de Madrid, Madrid, Spain Amérigo, María Psicología, Univ. de Castilla la Mancha, Toledo, Spain

The Connectedness with Nature Scale (CNS) has been one of the most interesting measures related with environmental identity. Three studies have been carried out in order to adapt this scale into a Spanish context. Two of them have been developed with university students and the other one with inhabitants of Madrid. The results obtained by mean of Principal Component Analysis and Internal Reliability; suggest just a few changes in the original scale. The correlation analysis of CNS with other measures of connectedness, environmental identity, and Anthropocentric and Biospheric scales, confirms its convergent and discriminant validity, and also its internal consistency.

College and technical college student's self-presentation: Examination of the evaluation to own self-presentation and the other's self-presentation

Ono, Miwa Graduate School of Literature, Chuo University, Tokyo, Japan

The purpose of this study was to examine self-presentation from the following two points; (a) evaluation and (b) self-concept represented by speaker and recognized by others.The investigation methods were self-evaluation test (Rosenberg, 1965), questionnaire and interview. Participants were two handred students. In brief, High Self Esteem person have caught own presentation and other's presentation from same viewpoint. On the other hand, Low Self Esteem person have caught own presentation and other's one from different viewpoint. Based on these findings, it suggested that evaluation of own self-presentation was related to evaluate other's presentation.

Relationship of deficiency in abilities and responsibility of managers with their personality in gas company

Oreyzi, Hamid Reza Pschology, Isfahan University, Isfahan, Islamic Republic of Iran

Managers of Iran Gaz company in two provinces responded a Job analysis structured interview instrument. They identified certain aspects of jobs that make big difference in job performance when managers have deficiencies and have responsibility for thoes dimensions of jobs. significant relationship were found between the results job analysis and personality dimension of managers (P< 0.05) Findings implications for career development of managers were identified.

Relationship of job complexity and managers aptitude in Iran gas company

Oreyzi, Hamid Reza Pschology, Isfahan University, Isfahan, Islamic Republic of Iran

59 managerial position of Iran Gas company were analyzed by applying Professional and Managerial Position Questionnaire. Managers also completed to General Aptitude Test Battery. There were significant relationship between complexity dimension of jobs and five aptitudes(P<0.05). Implications of the Findings are current research is considerable for career development of managers.

Profile analysis of training in Saipa car company

Oreyzi, Hamid Reza Psychology, Isfahan University, Isfahan, Islamic Republic of Iran Nouri, A. psychology, Isfahan university, Iran, Islamic Republic of Iran Amiri, S. psychology, Isfahan university, Iran, Islamic Republic of Iran

Profile analysis is the method that investigate configuration and pattern of data especially in clinical psychology instruments. In the current research pattern of data namely training scores and job analysis were correlated via cattle index. Conclusions indicate there is deficiency in training in Scc.

The effect of orthographic regularity on dyslexic children' spelling

Ortiz, Rosario Developmental Psychology, University of La Laguna, Santa Cruz de Tenerife, Spain

The aim of this work is to study the effect of orthographic regularity on the spelling in children with dyslexia. Normal readers (NRD) and dyslexics (RD) were tested on written spelling tasks. A 2(Group-RD vs. NRD) x 4 (Regularity- regular, irregular, ruled word and pseudoword) multivariate analysis of variance revealed an interaction Group x Regularity. The findings support the hypothesis that Spanish children with RD experience serious difficulties in spelling, and that the orthographic regularity and lexicality have effects on their performance in written spelling.

Motivation on science and mathematics across elementary school to junior high school

Oye, Mayumi Dept. of Bunri, Tokyo Woman's Christian Univ., Tokyo, Japan *Fujie, Yasuhiko* Department of literature, Kansai University, Suita-city, Japan

The purpose of this present study was to investigate development of motivation, academic engagement, and attitude of students toward mathematics and science before and after the transition to junior high school. A survey of students in fifth, sixth graders' and seventh and eighth graders'(N=1818)was conducted for the purpose of developing a questionnaire to assess Japanese students' mathematics motivation. In addition, academic engagement, attitude on mathematics and science were investigated. The result suggested that motivation in mathematics was undermined according to grade, on the other hand, motivation in mathematics was distinguished among sex.

Facing a real Person: An ERP Study

Pönkänen, Laura Tampere, Finland *Hietanen, Jari* Department of Psychology, University of Tampere, Tampere, Finland *Peltola, Mikko* Department of Psychology, University of Tampere, Tampere, Finland *Kauppinen, Pasi* Medical Technology, Ragnar Granit Institute, Tampere, Finland *Haapalainen, Antti* Medical Technology, Ragnar Granit Institute, Tampere, Finland *Leppänen, Jukka* Department of Psychology, University of Tampere, Tampere, Finland

The present event-related potential (ERP) study examined whether the processing of faces is different depending on whether participants (N = 19) are viewing faces live or as pictures. In both conditions, the participants were shown a face of a real person and a face of a dummy. The ANOVA showed that early posterior negativity (EPN) differentiated between the real face and the dummy only in the live condition. The result reflects the fact that a live face is a potentially interacting stimulus. Therefore, a live face is processed differently as compared with an inanimate face at the early processing stages.

May vocational experience affect the pattern of vocational interests?

Pösse, Bianca PFE, Bundesagentur für Arbeit, Nürnberg, Germany *Dorothea, Klinck* PFE, Federal Employment Agency, Nuremberg, Germany

We explored the influence of vocational experience on vocational interests. A sample of 2650 customers of the Psychological Service of the German Federal Employment Agency completed the agency's proprietary interest inventory measuring 27 vocational interests. We compared the vocational interests of 1659 adolescents (making a school-to-work transition) to those of 991 adults (planning a career change). In general, adults obtained higher vocational interest scores. Further analyses of specific interests revealed that adults with an interest-congruent job outperformed adults with interest-incongruent job. Results suggest that career counselling has to take vocational experience into account especially when using an interest inventory.

Parental coherence and transmission of attributional style to the conflicts between parents and adolescent

Padrón, Iván Developmental Psychology, Faculty Psychology, La Laguna, Spain *Rodrigo, Maria Jose* Developmental Psychology, Faculty Psychology, La Laguna, Spain

Causal (locus, stability, controllability) and intentional (hostile, positive) attributions to the conflicts between parents and adolescent were examined. Open-ended responses to six conflicts of the father, mother and adolescent from 270 two-parent families were categorized. Parental coherence of the attributional style was significantly moderate in every dimension especially for the girls no matter

adolescents age. Fathers transmission of attributions to adolescents was more robust and consistent regardless of their sex, whereas mothers transmission was only observed to the girls. Overall, content of the attribution transmitted by parents was more positive for girls than for boys.

Perpetuating the inequality: Tokenism and ideologies that legitimize the system

Palacios, Maria Soledad Dept. of Psychology, University of Huelva, Huelva, Spain *Morales Marente, Elena* Department of Pscyhology, University of Huelva, Huelva, Spain *Vélez, Jonatan* Department of Pscyhology, University of Huelva, Huelva, Spain *Portal, Javier* Department of Pscyhology, University of Huelva, Huelva, Spain

The aim of this study is to check if tokenism context could promote ideologies that justify/legitimize the system and/or the social structure. We compare this context with a control, a discriminatory and a meritocratic context, that we primed by a text about recent scientific results over the access of women to the work place. The design was a factorial intergroup 2 (gender) x 4 (control, tokenism, discriminatory and meritocratic context). The main dependent variable was a questionnaire about ideologies that legitimize the status quo. Participants were 63 students from the University of Huelva. Results showed significant differences between contexts: tokenism is clearly related with justification ideologies. Also were found gender differences.

Exploring factor structure of the CDI_TW in Taiwanese adolescents

Pan, Yuan-Chien Psychology, NTU, Taipei, Taiwan *Chen, Sue-Huei* Psychology, National Taiwan University, Taipei, Taiwan *Wu, Chih-Hsun* Psychology, National Taiwan University, Taipei, Taiwan

The Children's Depression Inventory (CDI) is a widely used tool to measure depressive symptoms of children and adolescents. The present study aimed to explore underlying factor structure of the Taiwan version of the CDI (CDI_TW) with 1446 students aged 13-16 in Taiwan. By using exploratory factor analysis, the results yielded four factors, i.e., self-deprecation, sadness, interpersonal problem, and lack of interest. Being different from the findings of European and American samples, our findings suggest of potential cultural differences on depressive symptom manifestations between Taiwanese and Western children and adolescents. Further verification of such four-factor structure of the CDI_TW is needed.

Adolescence identity status: It's relation to applied creativity and self-esteem in Greek adolescents

Paraskevopoulou, Polyxeni Athens, Greece *Pischos, Charalampos* PSYCHOLOGY, UNIVERSITY OF ATHENS, ATHENS, Greece

J. Marcia's adolescence identity statuses (identity diffusion, identity foreclosure, identity moratorium and identity achievement) are detected in Greek adolescent pupils, by "identity status interview"). Levels of applied creativity and self-esteem are obtained, as well, by Guilford's and Torrance test and by Rosenberg's scale, accordingly. The study examines the relation between each adolescence identity status to levels of creativity and self-esteem.

An exploratory study of some sexual behaviours and psychological adjustment of Indian gay and bisexual youths

Parekh, Suresh Dept. of Psychology, Shri M.M.Ghodasara Mahila Col., Junagadh, India

This research may be viewed as the beginning, with a tiny step, in the totally unexplored field of the study of homosexuality and bisexuality in India. The study was carried out with 136 gay and

bisexual participants in the age range of 16 to 26 years and the mean age of 20.8 years. A 49 items/questions Interview Schedule, covering demographic items and various sexual behaviour items was developed and used. Both similarities and differences have been found on various sexual behaviours. The correlation analysis showed that gay or bisexual identity was highly and positively related to psychological adjustment or ego-strength.

Psychological characteristics of run away youth

Parsian, Monireh Psychology, Teacher Training University, Tehran, Islamic Republic of Iran *Parsian, monireh* psychology, teacher training university, tehran, Islamic Republic of Iran *Moradi, Ali Reza* psychology, teacher training university, tehran, Islamic Republic of Iran *Shahraray, Mehrnaz* psychology, teacher training university, Tehran, Islamic Republic of Iran

The main aim of the current research is to investigate the family risk factors with runaway youth. 107 youth people in two groups including runaway groups and normal control groups participated in this study. Two groups were mached by sex, age, IQ and the number of sisters and brothers.The instruments were used in this study include the Family Functioning Scale,, Raven Intelligence Test. The results showed that there is a significant relationship between family risk facrtors such as cohesion, expressiveness, confilict with parent, active orientation, cultural orientation, religious orientation, organization, external locus of control, family idealization, cancellation, democratic, lassize-faire and authoritarian family style, interweave and runaway youth.

High schizotypy is related to increased response bias and decreased visual sensitivity for detecting faces embedded in noise

Partos, Timea Dept. of Psychology, University of Melbourne, Parkville, Australia *Cropper, Simon* Psychology - Redmond Barry Bdg, The University of Melbourne, Parkville, Australia *Rawlings, David* Psychology - Redmond Barry Bdg, The University of Melbourne, Parkville, Australia

Schizotypy has been linked to hallucination-like visual experiences. We investigated whether response biases (beta) or variations in visual sensitivity (d-prime) were driving this relationship. Schizotypy questionnaires were administered to a non-clinical sample, along with a computerized signal-detection task requiring the discrimination of faces-in-noise from noise-only images. Incorrect expectations regarding the ratio of face to noise images were created for some participants. False-alarm rates shifted towards participants' expectations, regardless of schizotypy. High schizotypy was consistently associated with higher beta and lower d-prime. These results implied that decreased visual sensitivity (along with bias) may influence visual perception in individuals high in schizotypy.

Positive illusions in the mating domain: When thinking good about yourself while feeling bad is a crucial part of your fitness

Pass, Jessica Dept. of Sociology, University of Groningen, Groningen, Netherlands *Lindenberg, Siegwart* Sociology, University of Groningen, Groningen, Netherlands *Park, Justin* Psychology, University of Groningen, Groningen, Netherlands

Positive illusions have been proposed to be adaptive (Haselton & Nettle, 2006). We examined whether maintaining certain positive illusions (e.g., "I am desirable as a mate") may be essential for motivating functional approach behavior when fitness-relevant beliefs are threatened. In two experiments participants received bogus feedback on their mate-value. The results revealed that after mate rejection, participants experienced negative affect and lowered self-esteem. Women's self-esteem was only lowered when the reason for rejection was their physical attractiveness; for men when competence and status were the cause of rejection. However, as expected, positive illusions and functional approach behavior were maintained.

Treatment evaluation of psychosomatic in-patient rehabilitation

Pausch, Jana Clinical Psychology, Technical University Chemnitz, Chemnitz, Germany **Muehlig, Stephan** Clinical Psychology, Technical University Chemnitz, Chemnitz, Germany

The effectiveness of psychosomatic in-patient rehabilitation with a cognitive-behavioral orientation was evaluated (N=229) using patients subjective health rating and objective criteria. In addition predictors of treatment outcome were investigated. Predictor variables were assessed using a battery of standardized clinical instruments. Pre-post differences over the treatment duration showed a positive medium effect size. Multiple regression analysis and discriminant analysis identified predictors associated with a worse treatment outcome: younger age, absent partnership, lower level of education, absent employment, somatoform disorders, larger number of pretreatment, higher degree of comorbidity, application for a pension and period of disability over 25 weeks. Implications are discussed.

Perceptions of European and national identities of Turkish Cypriot students

Pehlivan, Ahmet Turkish Language Teaching, Cyprus International Univers., Nicosia, Cyprus **Pahin, Feride Sulen**

Nowadays, how children perceive the European and national identities is important in North Cyprus. Because political and identical issues are still in discussion in Turkish Cypriot community. The aim of the study is to determine how students construct European and national identities on their mind. The test which was based on Philippou (2005) and Barrett and his colleagues' studies, and a focus group interview were used in this study. Tests were completed by 100 15-year-old Turkish Cypriot students in 5 classes and the group interview were conducted with only groups of four pupils from every class totaling twenty students in all. Data analysis is still in progress.

Repressors are unable to suppress, unless it is threatening: Coping styles influence intentional forgetting

Peters, Jan Hendrik Inst. für Psychologie, Universität Mainz, Mainz, Germany **Hock, Michael** Psychology, University Mainz, Mainz, Germany

Repressors remember less negative information than non-repressors. Using a think/no-think task, we tested whether this is caused by intentional suppression of unwanted memories: Participants (N = 88) learned unrelated word pairs (cues and responses). Subsequently, depending on the presented cue, responses had to be recalled or inhibited. One-third of the cues were not presented during this phase (baseline). Finally, all responses had to be recalled. While most participants could permanently inhibit memory independent of word-valence, repressors showed intentional forgetting only for threatening words. Consequently, intentional forgetting interacts with the valence of the to-be-suppressed material and with an individual's coping style.

The influence of internet on the political activity of Ukrainian youth: The possibilities of positive dynamics

Petrunko, Olga ISPP, Kyiv, Ukraine

According to the sociological researches carried out in Ukraine, the majority of Ukrainian Net segment users are interested in politics, because they visit political sites and discuss political news very active. However an interest to politics in fact does not guarantee that many young people participate in

elections and there is a doubtful evidence of their political activity. The virtual political activity and creativity in the Charts and on the Forums allegedly displace the need in the real actions. The influence of Internet on youths' political activity is significantly limited by the culture imaging, users' stereotypes, intellectual-professional level of hypertext.

Self-monitoring in the structure of personality and the factors of its genesis

Polezhaeva, Ekaterina Dept. of Psychology, Moscow State University, Moscow, Russia

The aim of our study was to analyze the structure of personality traits, including self-monitoring, as well as to understand intra-family similarity of personality traits, especially - the dependence of children's self-monitoring on different personality features of their parents. The sample comprised 540 participants - Moscow and Dubna university students, their siblings and parents. The most remarkable results were the following: 1) significant correlation between self-monitoring and personal features linked with the phenomenon of power, 2) more significant correlations between fathers' and their off-springs' traits, including self-monitoring, than between mothers and their off-springs, 3) self-monitoring as the basic building block feature in the correlation matrix of children and their parents.

Purpose-in-life-test: Reliability, factorial structure and relation to mental health in a Greek sample

Psarra, Evangelia Special Education, University of Thessaly, Volos, Greece **Kleftaras, George** Dept. of Special Education, University of Thessaly, Volos, Greece

The purpose of the present study was a) to adapt the Purpose-in-life-Test (PIL) in Greece, b) to gather empirical evidence on the psychometric properties of the Greek version of the PIL, including reliability and factorial structure and c) to investigate the relationship between meaning-in-life and psychological health. 401 newly recruited men for their navy-national-service completed the Greek versions of the "Purpose-in-life-Test" and the "General-Health-Questionnaire". PIL was found to have a good reliability and factor analysis showed that four factors were abstracted from the scale, namely, "sense-of-fullness", "goal-achievement", "freedom-of-choice" and "death". Finally, PIL factors were significantly correlated to general health dimensions.

Comparison of the actual and theoretical (cube-in-globe) structures of the individual sleep-wake adaptability

Putilov, Arcady Berlin, Germany **Putilov, Dmitriy**

The three-dimensional Cube-in-Globe model was propounded to explain the structure of sleep-wake adaptability. The model distinguishes between two types of dimensionality, underlying and overt. Three axes of Globe represent three independently variable underlying neurobiological parameters, while 12 ribs of Cube inscribed in this Globe represent six bipolar overt dimensions (they are delineated by fixing two underlying parameters in the area of extreme values, and allowing variation of the third parameter). Application of the tetra-circumplex criterion to questionnaire data (n=680) provided empirical evidence of similarity between the actual and theorized structures of the sleep-wake adaptability.

Neurocognitive correlates of public risk

Qin, Jungang Dept. of Psychology, Peking University, Beijing, People's Republic of China **Han, Shihui** Psychology, Peking University, Beijing, People's Republic of China

Although public risk has come to more and more dominate individual and collective consciousness, the cognitive and neural processes involved in

public risk identification remain unknown. We recorded brain activities when observers identified potential risks involved in public events. Relative to safe public events, identification of risky public events resulted in larger amplitudes of P200 and of LPP. fMRI results further localized these neural correlates in the vACC and PCC. Both the P200/LPP amplitudes and the PCC activation magnitudes positively correlated with subjective rating scores of risky events. Our findings support public risk identification is subserved by an early process of threat detection and a late evaluation process based on retrieval of emotional experiences.

Fractal patterns in collective bahaviour. Trends in political psychology

Quezada, Ariel Psicología, Universidad Adolfo Ibáñez, Viña del Mar, Chile

This study talks about the evidence of political behaviour as an emergency of a Complex Adaptive System (CAS). CAS are integrated systems constituted by excitable and interacting individual components that generate self organization and facilitate spontaneous behavioural patterns, different from its origin and not reducible to it. Analyzing monthly trends in Political Identification in Spain and Chile, it could describe patterns of volatility and change in long-term time series. The methodology employed to analyze this time series was Hurst's Exponent, a tool from Fractal Geometry. This methodology allows discover the pattern and forecast future trends of this collective behaviour. The results give support to the operation of feedback mechanism regulating collective behaviour in political psychology.

Quality of work life: Findings from a Portuguese study

Rafael, Manuel Faculty of Psychology, University of Lisbon, Lisbon, Portugal

Attention to human capital within organizations and to Quality of Work Life (QWL) is an essential topic in the agenda of human resource management. This poster describes the development of a Portuguese QWL study with 250 participants. Main results are presented, namely the identification of relative importance of QWL' dimensions (job, career, work relations, personal life and work conditions, e.g.) with the evaluation of the real existence of QWL events, and relationship with other psychological dimensions, namely satisfaction and job stress. Usefulness of findings for promoting QWL within an humanistic tradition are discussed.

The circumplex model of organizational citizenship behavior in a military context

Rafael, Manuel Faculty of Psychology, University of Lisbon, Lisbon, Portugal **Abreu, Rute** Faculty of Psychology, University of Lisbon, Lisbon, Portugal

The circumplex model of Organizational Citizenship Behavior (OCB) was recently proposed by Moon, Dyne & Wroble (2005) and in the authors' words can guide both theoretical and empirical research. This poster presents a study with 461 college students in a military institution that completed a questionnaire intended to evaluate Helping, Innovation, Sportsmanship and Compliance dimensions of OCB. Findings indicated satisfactory levels of reliability of the results. Also support partially the circumplex model with the clearly emergence of Helping, Innovation, and Compliance factors/dimensions. Results are discussed on implications for future research in human resource management.

The role of verbal and non-verbal tests in determining of laterality in schizophrenic and depressive patients

Rahimi Taghanaki, Changiz Clinical Psychology, Shiraz University, Shiraz, Islamic Republic of Iran

We studied the role of verbal and non-verbal tests in determining of laterality in schizophrenic and depressive patients. 36 schizophrenic and 27 depressive patients completed two verbal and non-verbal memory tests including "Worterlerntest" and "pare-Assoziation-Test von abstrakten Figuren". Analyzing the row values using t test showed that, the difference between two groups was only in verbal memory test significant (P<0.05). It seems verbal fluency test, in opposite of non-verbal memory test, can determine laterality in schizophrenic and depressive patients.

Factors associated in the moral development in engineering students: An approach multivariante, Analysis of main components

Ramirez L., Jorge J. Ciencia y Tecnología Comportam, Universidad Simón Bolívar, Caracas, Venezuela

The present work studied the association between demographics factors and academic abilities with the level of moral development in a sample of students of Engineering. The version of the instrument "Defining Issues Test" - DIT- (Rest, 1979) adapted to Venezuelan context by Zerpa and Ramirez (2004) was used. The sample was 281 students. An analysis of main components shows two factors of grouping high and low moral development; first associated with the feminine sex, age between 16 and 17 years, parents with superior formation. The second factor under development, associated with parents and mothers with incomplete high school. Will discuss results.

Life attitude and environmental perception of women in detention

Rana, Neeti Dept. of Applied Psychology, EMPI Business School, New Delhi, India

Herein, an attempt has been made to investigate life attitude and environmental perception of Indian women in detention (N=300). ANOVA by 2x2x2 factorial design with repeated measures and unequal cell entries showed that elderly under-trial women prisoners with no social support had lowest self control, highest perception of crowding, and maximum negative attitude towards life. The young convicts with social support had highest self control, lowest perception of crowding and maximum positive attitude towards life. It is concluded that women in detention have special needs and steps to be taken for preparing them for subsequent release and reintegration into society.

Symbolic battles around a bronze soldier: Estonian version of intergroup disagreement

Raudsepp, Maaris Psychology, Tallinn University, Tallinn, Estonia Wagner, Wolfgang Social and Economic Psychology, Johannes Kepler University, Linz, Austria

The study aims to analyze the development of a intergroup conflict (which culminated in violent events in April 2007), related to interpretation of the consequences of II World War in Estonia. Qualitative content analysis of Estonian and Russian language media texts and accompanying discussions in the internet reveals systems of hetero-referential representations, which form various barriers to intergroup dialogue – institutional and political, on the one hand (manipulation with threatened identities), and socio-psychological – on the other (collective emotions, intercultural incompetency, procedural injustice, disrespect and lack of recognition, intensifying distrust). In conclusion, some possibilities for promoting conflict resolution and conciliation are discussed.

Self-reports and peer-reports of depression and social behaviour: Results of a 4-year longitudinal study in adolescence

Reicher, Hannelore Inst. Bildungswissenschaften, Universität Graz, Graz, Austria

Concurrent and longitudinal relations among self- and peer-reported depression, positive and negative social behaviour, and perceived family functions (scales assessing task-fulfillment, role behavior, communication, emotionality, affective establishment of relations, control, values and norms) were assessed in 32 pupils starting from grade 9 and four years later in grade 13. Self-reported depressive symptoms and positive social behaviour were stable over time. Self- and peer-reports of depression and negative social behaviour are not correlated. Significant increases in some family function scales were found. In general, these results are discussed with regard to interpersonal aspects of emotional problems and developmental tasks in adolescents.

Is there a common construct underlying the need for cognition, perfectionism, industriousness and persistence?

Reyes-Lagunes, Isabel Fac.de Psicología, UNAM, Mexico, Mexico Luis, Garcia Mexico, Mexico Correa-Romero, Fredi E. Psicología, UAM, Mexico, Mexico

In this poster is presented the adaptation and validation of five scales from four different theoretical approximations, the constructs evaluated were Need for cognition, Perfectionism (2 different scales), industriousness and Persistence. The sample was no probabilistic, intentionally conformed by 446 participants (male = 47%; Age mean=23, SD=9) from Mexico City. The scales present Cronbach's Alpha values from 0.78 to 0.91, factor and structural equation modeling analysis were performed, the results shows an underlying theoretical construct to the four constructs referred previously.

Genetic predictors of mood variability in women: An examination of the estrogen receptor, androgen receptor and serotonin transporter genes

Richards, Meghan Dept. of Psychology, Lakehead University, Thunder Bay, Canada Bird, Jessica Psychology, Lakehead University, Thunder Bay, Canada Oinonen, Kirsten Psychology, Lakehead University, Thunder Bay, Canada

We examined whether genetic polymorphisms on the estrogen-receptor (ERα), androgen-receptor (AR), and serotonin transporter (5-HTT) genes affect mood reactivity or mood variability in women. Over the course of three phases, participants engaged in: demographic screening, DNA sample collection, an experimental anxiety induction, and self-report affect ratings. Preliminary results for the mood induction procedure revealed trends suggesting greater overall mood and positive-affect change for the homozygous long group, and a greater amount of negative-affect change for the heterozygous group for the ERα gene. In addition, we observed greater positive-affect change for the 8/10-9/10 allele group of the 5-HTT gene.

'Long term care' vs 'independent living'': Exploring identity concepts

Rivera, Luz Dept. of Clinical Psychology, Carlos Albizu University, Gurabo, Puerto Rico Altieri, Gladys Clinical Psychology, Carlos Albizu University, Gurabo, Puerto Rico

This paper presents a phenomenological analysis of semi-structured interviews with 12 elders; 6 living on long term care facilities and 6 living independently. The motivation behind the study was to identify common themes on the narratives from elders regarding identity, self image, self esteem and self care. Results showed the importance of self actualization development for their perception of

life satisfaction and well being (personal experience of self and their world).

Age differences in workplace learning competency

Roßnagel, Christian Jacobs Centre, Jacobs University Bremen, Bremen, Germany Schulz, Melanie Jacobs Centre, Jacobs University Bremen, Bremen, Germany

In an ageing workforce, the informal workplace learning participation of older workers is increasing. We explored how age affects the learning competency required for informal learning and assessed learning, control and self-regulation strategies in three age groups of workers (18-35, 36-50, and 51-65yrs). Independent of age, unsuccessful learners reported fewer control strategies. This effect was more pronounced for older workers and was linked to higher cognitive load. Negative affect was higher for both successful and unsuccessful older learners and was coupled with declining self-efficacy for unsuccessful learners. Learning competency was only weakly correlated with general cognitive ability. Findings inform the age-differentiated development of workplace learning.

Relation between objective school competence and perceived school competence in gifted and non-gifted 9th grade students

Rodrigues da Costa, Ana Faculdade de Ciências Humanas, Universidade Fernando Pessoa, Porto, Portugal

Objective: To analyse the relation between objective competence and perceived school competence in gifted and non-gifted 9th grade students. Method: A cohort of 171 students (28 gifted and 143 non-gifted), aged between 13 and 18, answered to Raven Progressive Matrix, Verbal and Numeric Thinking Test, Self-Concept and Self-Esteem Scale, and to a Socio-Demographic Questionnaire. Results: Results suggest that perceived school competence is related to objective school competence in 9th grade students. Moreover, data analysis also suggests that this relation is stronger in gifted students. Discussion: These results suggest that gifted students present a more realistic perception concerning their competence.

Perceived school-competence and socio-demographic characteristics: Comparison between gifted and non-gifted 9th grade students

Rodrigues da Costa, Ana Faculdade de Ciências Humanas, Universidade Fernando Pessoa, Porto, Portugal

Objective: To analyse if there are differences concerning perceived school-competence between gifted and non-gifted 9th grade students, considering gender and socio-economic status. Method: A cohort of 171 students (28 gifted and 143 non-gifted), aged between 13 and 18 answered to Verbal and Numeric Thinking Test, Self-Concept and Self-Esteem Scale, and to a Socio-Demographic Questionnaire. Results: Gender and socio-economic status in gifted students revealed not to be relevant to perceived school-competence. However, male and high income non-gifted students report higher perceived competence. Discussion: Socio-demographic characteristics are relevant in the study of non-gifted students' perceived school-competence, but not of gifted students.

Evaluation of visual perception and creativity in the university classroom

Rodriguez, Maria Elena CEIC, Universidad de Guadalajara, Guadalajara, Mexico Orozco, Rosalba CUAAD, Universidad de Guadalajara, Guadalajara, Mexico Maciel, Cristobal CUAAD, Universidad de Guadalajara, Guadalajara, Mexico

In order to evaluate the level of visual perception and creativity of 227 students (113 male and 114 female) of 4 university programs in architecture and design of the University of Guadalajara, two tests were used: (1) Rey complex figure and (2) Torrance Test of Creativity Thinking. Both tests were adapted to the Mexican context by Beristáin. Tests were applied at the beginning and the end of the first semester and at the end of the fourth and eighth semester. Results showed a statistically significant increment after the first semester but not after the fourth and eighth.

Family conflicts, have the same solution depending of children's age?

Rodriguez Ruiz, Beatriz Psicologia Evol. y de la Educ., University of La Laguna, La Laguna, Spain Rodrigo López, Maria Jose Psicologia evol. y de la educ., University of La Laguna, La Laguna, Spain

One of the most significant changes in the Spanish family system has been the sons and daughters stay at home till later ages. In this study we analyze the participation and the use of strategies and goals in the solution of conflicts depending of the age of sons/daughters. This sample is composed of 150 families with son/daughter between 15 and 25 years old. The ANOVA results showed that there are differences in the conflicts participation. Parents use similar strategies and goals, whereas sons and daughters use more negation with age. In sun, it is necessary to promote different family interventions depending of children's age.

French social representation of war and peace

Roland-Levy, Christine Paris, France

Based on recent French history -World War 2, the war with Algeria during the 60s, and on terrorism attacks in 1995, we assume that these events contribute to the building of a "national" discourse. Thus, these events, having shaped today's social representation of peace and war, help us interpret the discourse used in France about peace, terrorism and/or wars. In terms of methodology, association tasks were carried out with three samples, men and women, aged 18-25; 35-60; 65 and above; these age groups were chosen because of their proximity with at least one of the previously mentioned events.

The dark side of mindfulness: Why mindfulness interventions are not beneficial for everyone

Rosing, Kathrin I/O Psychologie, Universität Gießen, Gießen, Germany Baumann, Nicola Dept. I - Psychology, University of Trier, Trier, Germany

This experimental study (N = 57) tested the effects of a mindfulness induction (i.e., mindfully eating a raisin) on the susceptibility to expert recommendations of extrinsic goals. Susceptibility was operationalized as the tendency to misperceive recommended extrinsic goals as self-selected. Results indicated that individuals who have trouble knowing their own preferences (i.e., low access to their self-system) are likely to be invaded by expert recommendations of extrinsic goals after a mindfulness induction. These results show that a mindfulness intervention might be harmful for some people – i.e., with low self-access – and is not as universally beneficial as prior studies suggest.

Using commitment to encourage public transportation use to go to work

Rubens, Lolita Hauts de seine, Université Paris 10 UFR SPSE, Nanterre, France

Our study aims at comparing the effectiveness of commitment and cognitive dissonance in the environmental field. We expect people to choose alternative transportation mode instead of their car to go to work everyday when they are committed. We have two different studies, the first one manipulate the level of commitment and the arguments given to participants. The second one make participants feel dissonant about their behaviour. We expect "committed and hypocrite" participants to give up their car more often than

the control group. The studies are in progress and the results will be presented during the congress.

The role of emotion and issue ownership in explaining pro-environmental behavior in organizations

Russell, Sally UQ Business School, University of Queensland, Brisbane, Australia Ashkanasy, Neal M. Faculty of Business, Economics, The University of Queensland, Brisbane, Australia

Based on the social psychological theory of issue ownership, we present a model of the emotional antecedents of pro-environmental behavior. We argue that more intense emotional reactions to environmental issues result in stronger issue ownership, and therefore increased displays of pro-environmental behavior. The hypotheses underlying this model were supported using a structural equation modeling analysis of questionnaire data from three large Australian organizations (N=325). The findings make a significant contribution to both the environmental psychology and environmental management literatures by offering a greater understanding of how emotional reactions and issue ownership predict proenvironmental behaviors within organizations.

Citizenship and counterproductive behavior in organizations and employees' social identity

Rutkowska, Dorota Faculty of Psychology, Warsaw University, Warsaw, Poland Latawiec, Paulina Faculty of Psychology, Warsaw University, Warsaw, Poland

Employees' social identity may be connected with organizational citizenship and counterproductive behavior (OCB and CPB). There seem to be two most salient reference groups people identify with in work context: a group of co-workers (organizational identification) and a group of the same profession holders (professional identification). In the correlation study among physicians (n=83) it was shown that for employee's whose professional identification is poor strong identification with an organization increases OCB level and reduces CPB level. However, the strength of organizational identification does not modify the level of OCB and CPB in employees who strongly identify with their professional group.

Achievement goals in social interactions: Which goal promotes learning?

Sülz, Christoph Institut für Psychologie, Universität Greifswald, Greifswald, Germany

In the present study (N=99) participants in different goal conditions (mastery, performance-approach, performance-avoidance, and control group) studied a text, together with an alleged partner connected via Ethernet. Periodically they were interrupted to answer a question. After each answer participants received a manipulated feedback from their "partner" (agreement vs. disagreement). Contrary to Darnon and colleagues' findings (2007), participants in the performance-approach goal condition benefited from disagreement and performed better in the subsequent multiple-choice test. But under agreement both performance goals, compared to mastery and control condition, lead to worse learning.

Gender stereotypes about technology: Prototypes about people involved in technology

Sainz, Milagros Internet Interdisciplin. Inst., UOC, Castelldefels, Spain López Sáez, Mercedes Social and Organizational, UNED, Madrid, Spain

A great body of literature evidences the existence of gender stereotypes about technology that exclude women from technological fields (Eccles, Barber and Jozewoficz, 1999; Eccles, 2005). In this study, we have used parametric and non- parametric statistical proofs in order to analyze some of those stereotypes in a sample of 550 adolescents (293 girls and 250 boys, average age=15, s.d=1.73) in Spain.

Our findings proved the existence of gender stereotypes about people involved in technology-related fields concerning their intellectual capacities and lack of social skills. Role models in technology-related works are masculine. We discuss our findings and their practical implications.

Interval timing behavior was affected by circadian rhythm in rats

Sakata, Shogo Dept. of Behavioral Sciences, Hiroshima University, Hiroshima, Japan Hattori, Minoru Behavioral Sciences, Hiroshima University, Higashi-Hiroshima, Japan Hasegawa, Takayuki Behavioral Sciences, Hiroshima University, Higashi-Hiroshima, Japan

Animals have own internal clocks that were called the circadian rhythm and the interval timing mechanism. Six Wistar male rats were trained for five days a week in PI 30-s procedure at the same time of the day over 60 sessions. The 3-s bin of lever press responses on probe trials showed a clear peak point. Response temporal distributions had the peak time of regression curve fitting with the Gaussian distribution. The peak time corresponded to near the 30-s with reinforcement durations. Then a run of three days experiments were done. Temporal distributions showed clearly dependent on the circadian rhythm.

Perceived justice: How different demographic characteristics can predict it in an organization

Samavatyan, Hossein Psychology, Isfahan University, Isfahan, Islamic Republic of Iran Nouri, Aboulghasem Psychology, Isfahan University, Isfahan, Islamic Republic of Iran Oreyzi, Hamid Reza Psychology, Isfahan University, Isfahan, Islamic Republic of Iran Sanati, Javad Occupational HSE, Polyacryl of Iran Corporation, Isfahan, Islamic Republic of Iran

Perceived justice has been investigated among the personnel of a large industrial setting. The randomly selected 420 participants responded to an attitude questionnaire measuring their attitude about different aspects of justice in their organization. Selective demographic characteristics (such as education, income, gender, and employment status) were also measured to find out any possible relationship and effect on the perceived justice. The results revealed some significant correlations as well as differences in perceived justice. Factor analysis was also conducted to indicate the similar factor patterns. The findings showed how some demographic factors can change and form the personnel's perception of justice.

Psychometric properties of negative attitudes toward masturbation inventory on a sample of Salvadorian adolescents

Santos, Pablo Granada University, Granada, Spain Sierra, Juan Carlos Personality, Assessment and Ps, Granada University, Granada, Spain Perla, Felipe Psychology, Orient University, San Miguel, El Salvador

OBJECTIVE. This work shows the first psychometric data of Negative Attitudes Toward Masturbation Inventory (NAMI; Abramson y Mosher, 1975) on Salvadorian adolescents. METHOD. A sample of 610 adolescents filled in the NAMI, together with Sexual Opinion Survey. RESULTS. The three factors which were obtained explained 33.53% of the total variance, corroborating the structure which was proposed by the authors: Personally experienced negative affects associated with masturbation (? =0.84), Positive attitudes toward masturbation (? =0.75), and False beliefs about the harmful nature of masturbation (? =0.64). The total scale achieved an internal consistency of 0.82. Two of the three factors significantly correlate with erotophilia.

Navigational and learning strategies in hypermedia learning environments

Schellhas, Bernd *Inst. für Psychologie, Universität Potsdam, Potsdam, Germany*

Hypermedia learning environments allow learners to move through information networks with self-regulated learning strategies. Forty 10th grade students were asked to gather information on the outbreak of Word War I for a knowledge test. Subsequently, they were confronted with the recorded replay of their hyperspace behavior interviewed regarding their intentions and their proceeding. Learning strategies assessed via this direct analysis proved to be more reliably related to learning outcomes as well as to motivation, test anxiety, and cognitive abilities (questionnaires) than did previously reported learning strategies (questionnaire). Deep/nonlinear vs. surface/linear strategies were differentiated, the first being more effective.

The processing of food cues in binge eating disorder: An fMRI study

Schienle, Anne *Inst. für Klin. Psychologie, Universität Graz, Graz, Austria* **Schäfer, Axel** *Clinical Psychology, University of Graz, Graz, Austria* **Hermann, Andrea** *Clinical Psychology, University of Giessen, Giessen, Germany* **Vaitl, Dieter** *Clinical Psychology, University of Giessen, Giessen, Germany*

We investigated reward sensitivity in patients afflicted with binge eating disorder (BED) via functional magnetic resonance imaging. BED is characterized by recurrent overeating episodes, which are not followed by regular compensatory behaviors. Patients suffering from BED, bulimia nervosa and healthy controls were exposed to pictures depicting food and non-food stimuli. BED patients reported elevated reward sensitivity and showed enhanced activation in the anterior cingulate cortex, the insula and the nucleus accumbens during processing of food cues. Their valence ratings for food pictures were positively correlated with involvement of the nucleus accumbens, the central structure of the brain reward system.

Effects of studying abroad on national identity: A longitudinal field study with German exchange students

Schneider, Henrike Alexandra *Arbeits- und Org.-Psychologie, Tech. Universität Braunschweig, Braunschweig, Germany* **Weitekamp, Katharina** *Differentielle Psychologie, Helmut Schmidt University, Hamburg, Germany* **Deutsch, Werner** *Abteilung f. Entwicklungspsych, TU Braunschweig, Braunschweig, Germany*

Does a stay abroad have an effect on national identity? National identity was measured by an online questionnaire concerning "national feeling" and "political pride", which was completed by 292 German high school students. 203 students (treatment group) left Germany for a stay abroad while the remaining 89 (control group) stayed in Germany. The survey was repeated twice over a period of eight months. Results of MANOVA indicate that "national feeling" does increase in the treatment group during the stay abroad, whereas "political pride" remains constant. This implies that national identity can be modified by intergroup contact.

Training of visual-auditory integration in dyslexia

Schumacher, Bettina *Inst. für Psychologie II, Universität Kaiserslautern, Kaiserslautern, Germany* **Koether, Ralf** *Psychology, University of Bamberg, Bamberg, Germany* **Scheller, Kerstin** *Psychology, University of Bamberg, Bamberg, Germany* **van Leeuwen, Cees** *PDL, Brain Science Institute, Riken, Wako-shi, Japan* **Lachmann, Thomas** *Psychology II, University of Kaiserslautern, Kaiserslautern, Germany*

AudiLex ® is a commercial training program that aims to practice accuracy and speed of visual-auditory integration in children with reading problems in order to enhance their reading skills. Some researchers have found positive effects on reading time after training, others failed. The present study evaluated the effect of long term training on speed / accuracy of visual auditory integration in children with dyslexia compared to controls, the impact on reading speed in both groups and the stability of the effects. The results were compared to those of a regular reading program conducted with different groups, dyslexics and controls.

Improving the prediction of recycling behavior: A cross-cultural comparison of the subjective evaluation of social norms and experienced emotions in Spain and Brazil

Schweiger Gallo, Inge *Psicología Social, U. Complutense de Madrid, Madrid, Spain* **Torres, Ana** *Psychology Department, Catholic University of Goiás, Goiânia, Brazil* **Corraliza, José Antonio** *Psicología Social y Metodologí, U. Autónoma de Madrid, Campus de Cantoblanco, Spain* **Rodriguez Monter, Miryam** *Psicología Social, U. Complutense de Madrid, Pozuelo de Alarcón (madrid), Spain* **Álvaro, José Luis** *Psicología Social, U. Complutense de Madrid, Pozuelo de Alarcón (madrid), Spain*

Starting from the premise that the evaluation of the social norm and experienced emotions should improve the prediction of carrying out recycling behavior, we analyzed which factors underlie the subjective evaluation of the social norm, as well as the emotions associated with recycling behavior. The results revealed that in both Spain and Brazil the most relevant emotions associated with recycling behavior were joy, responsibility and affective evaluation. Both emotions and affective evaluation also accounted for a significant increase of the explained variance. Thus, future research might take into account these variables for increasing our capacity to predict recycling behavior.

The collective unconsciousness in politics

Sedrakyan, Sedrak *Psychology, Urartu University, Yerevan, Armenia* **Sedrakyan, Anahit** *Psychology, Urartu University, Yerevan, Armenia*

Nowadays in the light of socio-economic and political changes psychological factors play an important role. In this sense it is important to reveal the political consciousness. Irrational, unconsciousness, together with political consciousness and self-consciousness plays an important role in politics. The main content of collective unconsciousness (K. Jung) is archetypes, universal a priori behavior schedules, special type over-personal (group and typical) perception types and reaction types of people from definite "collective". Collective unconsciousness becomes very dangerous if it opposes politics. There are existing psychological methods of impact on politics. In modern civilized society its influence has decreased and appears only in extreme situations. Usually in stable socio-political systems the collective unconsciousness is expressed too weak.

Well-being across cultures: An investigation of cultural, individual, and job characteristics impact on employee well-being

Septarini, Berlian Gressy *Faculty of Psychology, Airlangga University, Surabaya, Indonesia* **Smith, Leigh** *School of Psychology, Curtin Univ of Technology, Perth, Australia*

The prediction of cultural, individual and job characteristics on occupational well-being (job satisfaction, anxiety-comfort, and depression-enthusiasm) were investigated in two countries. Hypotheses were tested in 458 university employees of two universities located in Indonesia and Australia using canonical correlation analysis and hierarchical multiple regression. Employee well-being, indicated by the first canonical variates, centred on Depression-Enthusiasm and Extrinsic Jobsat for the Indonesia sample; whereas all well-being variables loaded on the first dimension for Australia. Only job characteristics and some individual factors were found to be predictive, demonstrating that well-being has culture-specific dimensions and is related to a complex array of personality and job factors.

Social projection on environmental concern

Sevillano, Verónica *Dept. of Psychology, Castilla-La Mancha University, Toledo, Spain* **Aragonés, Juan I.** *Social Psychology, Complutense University, Pozuelo de Alarcón (Madrid), Spain*

Do we overestimate or underestimate the prevalence of our own attitudes / behaviors related to the environment? One hundred and ninety one college students filled in a questionnaire concerning pro-environmental behaviors and attitudes, and the estimated percentage of people who hold attitudinal and behavioral items. From standard analysis of the False Consensus Effect (FCE), results suggest that for all items Endorsers' consensus estimates of agreement were higher than non-endorsers' consensus estimates [p values among $p<.001$ to $p<.016$]. From TFCE (Truly False Consensus Effect) analysis, the significant positive correlations between the difference scores (diff) and endorsements (end) indicated the TFCE, meanall $r(diff, end) = 0.32$ ($p<.0001$).

Workplace bullying in the voluntary sector: Is there a need for concern?

Sheik Dawood, Shariffah Rahah *Dept. of Psychology, Internat. Islamic University, Kuala Lumpur, Malaysia*

This study investigates the nature and prevalence of workplace bullying in the voluntary sector. Twenty two interviews and 178 questionnaires, from 29 British voluntary organisations were analysed. Fifteen percent of the respondents were bullied over the last 1 year and 28% in the last 5 years. The prevalence is higher than among the NHS trusts, higher education, and civil service sectors, while almost parallel to the police service and the post/telecommunications—which have high prevalence rates. The independent sample t-test identified overt behaviour and personal harassment as least prevalent, and work-related harassment as most prevalent; hence urging the management to address this issue.

Natural language analysis of written description of impressions of science and language subjects

Shimoda, Hiroko *Dept. of Medicine, Kyoto University, Kyoto, Japan* **Okamoto, Yuji** *Department of medicine, Osaka university, Osaka, Japan* **Fukuyama, Hidenao** *Department of medicine, Kyoto university, Kyoto, Japan* **Matsuyama, Takashi** *Dept Intelligence Science, Kyoto university, Kyoto, Japan* **Takahashi, Ryosuke** *Department of medicine, Kyoto university, Kyoto, Japan*

This research conducted for the purpose of trying to analyze written description of impressions, clarifying the difference of impressions between science and language subjects and discussing structure of sentences and profitability of this method. Subjects are Japanese university students. We analyzed written description of impressions. The results are we clarified the difference of impressions between science and language subjects, expressly quality of words and structure of sentences. We found the profitability of this method of clarifying the difference of science and language subjects.

Loving the school... no problem!: The influence of social skills training in attitudes toward school
Silva, Carla Funchal, Portugal Sousa, Pedro Educação Fisica, Escola B. S. do Porto Moniz, Porto Moniz, Portugal
With this investigation, we pretend to analyze the influence of the participation in a social skills training program in the participant's attitudes toward school, expecting to observe a positive correlation between the two variables. The program is being implemented to approximately 44 students of Porto Moniz Basic and Secondary School, and is being evaluated with a pre/post-test, using the Questionário de Atitudes Face à Escola (Candeias, 1996) and a set of personal and social skills evaluation scales (Jardim & Pereira, 2006). Results and conclusions will only be available in June, because the program implementation will only be completed in May.

Relationships between teachers and parents in the island of Crete
Simopoulou, Agapi Nursery, University of Ioannina, Rethymno, Greece
The aim of the study was to define the interpersonal processes and relationships between teachers and parents. It was carried out the year 2006 with N=169 teachers and 1568 parents in 33 urban, semi-urban and agricultural elementary schools of Crete. For the purpose of this study a common questionnaire consisted of 21 close questions for both groups was designed. It focused on three main topics: Communication, cooperation and perception – attitudes. Results: Communication based on pupils' performance, behavior and home works. Cooperation is restricted in financial support. Attitudes and perception show a significant deviation in basic pedagogical beliefs and a significant congruity in point of the socioeconomic role of school.

Justice violations and reactions: Role of justice cognitions as mediator
Singh, Purnima Humanities and Social Sciences, IIT Delhi, Delhi, India
Violations of justice norms is frequently seen in social situations. The three studies examine respectively the reactions to violations of distributive, procedural and interactional justice. The studies further examine the mediating role of justice cognitions. Respondents were presented with vignettes where some justice violation had occurred and their reactions were examined. Reactions were in terms of justice restoring mechanisms used- retribution, restoration, forgiveness and others. Results showed that justice cognitions play a mediating role. Results are explained in terms of current theory in justice reserach. Implications of the results are discussed.

Realtime fMRI and fNIRS based neurofeedback
Sitaram, Ranganatha Inst. of Med. Psychology, University of Tuebingen, Tuebingen, Germany
Functional Magnetic Resonance Imaging (fMRI) and Functional Near Infrared Spectroscopy (fNIRS) based BCIs are non-invasive techniques to induce localized changes in brain response, using online detection and feedback of the BOLD signal, to study behavioral effects associated with specific brain regions and their connectivity. fNIRS offers portability, affordability and ease of use for bedside monitoring and applications. Despite their potential, fMRI-BCI and fNIRS-BCI are still in infancy and waiting to be further explored. The intention of this talk is to encourage wide-spread usage, by presenting details of the methods and applications of fMRI-BCI and fNIRS-BCI.

Can evil be moral?: Moral representations of good and evil in people with different need for cognitive closure
Skupele, Irina Riga, Latvia
The study looks at such terms as "good" and "evil" from the point of view of different authors in moral psychology, and also there is also practical research done, looking for associations between NFCC level (Kruglanski) and five moral foundations. The research addresses moral representations of a good and evil person, moral systems ascribed to an "extremely good" and "extremely evil" person, as well as diferences in these representations among people with low and high NFCC level and people having different moral foundations. KEY WORDS: Good, Evil, Need for Cognitive Closure, 5 Foundations of intuitive Ethics, Moral Representations.

Fast and frugal or complex and calculating? Modelling police judgments regarding the veracity of suicide notes
Snook, Brent Psychology, Memorial University, St. John's, Canada Mercer, Jamison Psychology, Memorial University, St. John's, Canada
This poster reports the results of a comparison of the ability of two cognitive models to capture police officers' decisions regarding the veracity of suicide notes. Thirty-eight police officers indicated their decisions regarding the authenticity of 30 suicide notes. Participants' decisions are modelled by the matching heuristic and Franklin's Rule. It is argued that the matching heuristic is a more accurate and frugal model of police decisions on this task, and generalizes better to novel data than Franklin's Rule. The implications of the results for the ongoing rationality debate and police decision-making are outlined.

Violence and maltreatment in the family and in the group of peers as juvenile delinquency predictive variables
Soares Martins, Jose Manuel Faculdade de Ciências Humanas, Universidade Fernando Pessoa, Maia, Portugal
This investigation aimed to know whether physical and emotional maltreatment experimented by the subjects through the parents and the group of peers, as well as emotional and physical violence observed in the parents and in the group of peers, can explain the conducts of theft, rules infraction, consumption and drug dealing, vandalism and aggression against people. From this investigation, one can conclude that the several forms of violence and maltreatment, whether in the family or in the group of peers, are predictive of the various types of delinquent behaviours in the young students, as well as the parents' negligence. Key-words: observed emotional violence; observed physical violence;phisical maltreatment; emotional maltreatment;negligence; juvenile delinquency.

The construction of attitudes toward nations: Valence effects of priming with person vs. non-person exemplars
Spanuth, Claudia Sozialpsychologisches Labor, Universität Bielefeld, Bielefeld, Germany Jung, So-Rim Social Psychology Lab, University of Bielefeld, Bielefeld, Germany Siebler, Frank Social Psychology Lab, University of Bielefeld, Bielefeld, Germany Bohner, Gerd Social Psychology Lab, University of Bielefeld, Bielefeld, Germany Echterhoff, Gerald Social Psychology Lab, University of Bielefeld, Bielefeld, Germany
To construct attitudes, people need to retrieve pertinent information. For complex social attitude objects like nations or organizations, different types of information (e.g., person exemplars, non-person exemplars, abstract attributes) can be used. This construction process may be affected by priming. Consistent with our rationale, three experiments

reveal effects of subliminal and supraliminal priming of exemplar types: When participants were primed to construe attitudes toward nations based on person (vs. non-person) exemplars (e.g., faces vs. non-faces) they reported more positive evaluations. Additional evidence suggests that this valence effect is partly due to the person-positivity bias (Sears, 1983).

Pathways to collective protest: Calculation, identification or emotion? A critical analysis of the role of anger in social movement participation
Stürmer, Stefan Inst. für Psychologie, Fern-Universität in Hagen, Hagen, Germany Simon, Bernd Psychology, Christian-Albrechts-University, Kiel, Germany
Two studies examined the role of anger in collective protest. Study 1, a field study in the context of the German students' movement (N = 201), suggested that, when intergroup conflict is intense, anger may provide an independent pathway to protest. Study 2, a laboratory experiment (N = 182), showed, however, that this emotional path is rather "fragile". First, analyses demonstrated that the effect of anger was restricted to the prediction of "cathartic" protest activities. Second, the anger effect was reduced to nonsignificance when participants, before indicating their willingness to participate, encountered an alternative opportunity to reduce their negative tensions. The implications of these findings for "entrepreneurs" of movements are discussed.

Personal and interpersonal determinants of dating violence in adolescence and young adulthood
Stavrinides, Panayiotis Psychology, University of Cyprus, Nicosia, Cyprus
Purpose of this study was to investigate the factors that predict the intensity of dating violence at its three main dimensions: psychological, physical, and sexual violence. The participants were 300 adolescent and young adult women. Hierarchical regression analysis shows that dating violence is significantly predicted by the victim's self-esteem, neuroticism, insecure attachment, and prior engagement in violent relationships. At the interpersonal level, the results show that young women with authoritarian and neglectful parents are more likely to be victims of dating violence.

Competencies of successful entrepreneurs
Steensma, Herman Soc. and Organizat. Psychology, Leiden University, Leiden, Netherlands
Objectives. Determine the core competencies of successful entrepreneurs. Methods. From a list of 46 competencies, entrepreneurs (N=36) had to select the 7 criteria that are most essential. Next, they listed these 7 items in order of importance. Results. Pro-activity, vision, and willingness to take chances were by far the most important criteria, followed by customer-oriented, result-oriented, managementskills, innovative, networking, creativity, charisma, self-efficacy. Entrepreneurs scoring high on essential competencies also scored highest on: sales volume; future perspective; innovation. Discussion. It is possible to assess entrepreneurial quality. Knowledge of the profile of successful entrepreneurs is useful for investment bankers.

Individual differences in working memory capacity: Effects of dopamine-related gene-gene interactions are task-dependent
Stelzel, Christine Inst. für Psychologie, Universität Heidelberg, Heidelberg, Germany Basten, Ulrike Inst. für Psychologie, Universität Heidelberg, Heidelberg, Germany Montag, Christian Inst. für Psychologie, Universität Bonn, Bonn, Germany Reuter, Martin Inst. für Psychologie, Universität Bonn, Bonn, Germany

Fiebach, Christian *Inst. für Psychologie, Universität Heidelberg, Heidelberg, Germany*

Dopamine modulates cognition like working memory (WM) or cognitive control. We tested WM capacity depending on two dopamine-related genetic polymorphisms influencing prefrontal dopamine concentration and D2 receptor density: Catechol-O-methyl-transferase(COMT) val158met and DRD2/ANKK1-Taq-Ia, respectively. COMT effects on WM depended on D2 receptor density and the specific WM subprocess. VAL- participants outperformed VAL+ participants in the manipulation of WM contents when D2 receptor density was high. VAL+ participants with low D2 receptor densities inhibited distracting information more successfully when the working memory task was sufficiently challenging. This reveals the importance of considering gene-gene interactions and different WM subprocesses in genetic association studies.

Sustainable development in office building environments: Contributions of environmental psychology
Stumpf, Michael *Institut für Psychologie, Universität Freiburg, Freiburg, Germany* **Spada, Hans** *Institut für Psychologie, Universität Freiburg, Freiburg, Germany* **Scheuermann, Michael** *Institut für Psychologie, Universität Freiburg, Freiburg, Germany* **Rummel, Nikol** *Institut für Psychologie, Universität Freiburg, Freiburg, Germany* **Steck, Jürgen** *Abteilung Umweltschutz, Universität Freiburg, Freiburg, Germany*

Ongoing climate change and increasing expenses for resources require a sustainable use of energy in office environments. Initiated by the Sustainable University Work Group, the Department of Psychology at the University of Freiburg has developed, implemented and evaluated several types of interventions with the aim to promote knowledge, attitudes, norms and behaviour concerning energy saving. By combining these psychological interventions with technical adjustments (e.g. modifications to the schedule of the central heating system) the department was able to decrease the consumption of energy significantly, i.e. by approx. 25%. Current work focuses on stabililizing the established effects.

Behavior problems and motivation of criminal behavior in adolescence
Stupish, Svetlana *Psycholody, Belarussian University of Law, Minsk, Belarus*

The purpose of this study was to examine the relationship between behavior problems and mechanisms of criminal behavior development. Three sample (N=220) were took part in research: law-obedient adolescents without behavior problems, adolescents with externalizing behavior problems and adolescents committed different kinds of punishable acts, including homicide, rape, violence, burglary and robbery. Methods: "The Subjective Control's Level Scale" (Bajhyn) and projective technique "The Criminal Behavior Motivation" (Stupish). Results showed that behavior problems are strongly related with locus of control and could increased risk of criminal offending. There some correlations between level of subjective control and motivation of criminal behavior.

Letter length and lexicality effects on left occipitotemporal activation in developmental dyslexia
Sturm, Denise *Inst. für Psychologie, Universität Salzburg, Salzburg, Austria* **Kronbichler, Martin** *Psychologie, Universität Salzburg, Salzburg, Austria* **Wimmer, Heinz** *NW Fakultät, Universität Salzburg, Salzburg, Austria*

Objectives: This study examined letter length and lexicality effects in the left occipitotemporal cortex (OTC) in dyslexia. Methods: Brain activity during visual word processing in 17 dyslexic and 18 fluent readers was measured with functional MRI. Re-

sults: Fluent readers showed higher OTC activation for pseudowords than words, and for long compared to short pseudowords, but no length effect for words. Dyslexic readers showed less OTC activation and failed to exhibit any effects of lexicality or length. Conclusions: In dyslexic readers, OTC activity was not affected by reading demands. These results suggest a profound dysfunction of the OTC in developmental dyslexia.

Are different career patterns related to personality traits?
Suchar, Marek *SWPS, Sopot, Poland*

The study explores advantages of using a concept of occupational career in personnel assessment and selection. Biographical data of 400 job applicants were statistically analyzed which allowed to identify 6 different career patterns. At the second stage of the study the sample of 150 was tested with Polish version of NEO FFI and their individual career patterns were diagnosed. The result revealed correlations between career dimensions (changebility, dynamism, verticality) and Five Personality Dimensions. The findings general agree with reports of other authors aditionaly enabling to specify and clarify the nature of relations between personality and occupational career providing us with arguments that the course of individual career can be to some extent predicted by personality characteristics.

The Influence of perceptual self-mother relations, self-image,and reflective self-image from mother on formation and developmental change of cognitive self concept through life
Sugita, Chizuko *Education and Psychology, Bukkyo University, Kyoto, Japan*

This research aims to find out influencalworking factors by people's mothers on the formation and advancement of self-concept throughout life. I realized that People do not take copies of their experience in memory, but in the situation which self awareness activates, they would reconstruct their object in. I like to propose several hypotheses. Hoevere it is impossible because of scarce of space. First of all, people who easily change their perceptual structure about self (including self-image and reflective self-image from mother) as perceptual object were Ss who have self -concept concernig environment-oriented self in childhood, conflict about separation from mother, and devoting themselves to any work. Ss are college students in England.

Self-regulation in informal learning environment: A case study of web-based reading
Sung, Yao-Ting *Edu. Psy., National Taiwan Normal Univ., Taipei, Taiwan* **Chang, Kuo-En** *Dept. Computer and Information, National Taiwan Normal Univers, Taipei, Taiwan*

The purpose of this study was to examine whether different types of formative tests on hypermedia integrated learning environment would influence learners' self-regulated behaviors. The participants were 357 junior high school students in Taipei County. They were randomly assigned to four treatment groups (mastery group, non-mastery group, non-formative-test group, and non-reminding group). All participants read four chapters of a supplementary article and took formative and summative tests in a wed-based environment. According to the recorded reading time, reviewing frequencies, and reviewing time, the experiment results showed that the feedback from the formative did not improve the self-regulated behaviors of students.

Personality in adolescence: Are the Big-Five domains still stable at the second glance?
Szirmak, Zsofia *Inst. für Psychologie, Freie Universität Berlin, Berlin, Germany*

The focus of the present study is the investigation of the adequacy of an adult self-rating Big Five personality measure in adolescence. The FFPI (Five Factor Personality Inventory) was administered to 1100 pupils (M=12,4 years). CFA were conducted on both halves of the total sample in order to investigate the convergence of the adolescent personality structure to the lexically defined adult Big-Five dimensions and to test measurement invariance. Though at a first glance major similarities to the adult Big Five domains are obvious, a closer look reveals some developmentally important differences. The assumption of measurement invariance could not be confirmed.

The impact of significant other's expectancies on self-stereotyping in Japan
Takabayashi, Kumiko *Sociology, Hitotsubashi University, Kunitachi, Japan* **Numazaki, Makoto** *Graduate School of Humanities, Tokyo Metropolitan University, Kunitachi, Japan*

We examined the effects of a significant other's expectancies on self-stereotyping. Female participants responded to whether their mother expected them to be feminine or masculine and rated the scale of egalitarian sex role attitude. About two months later, participants were told to make a picture of their mother (mother-prime condition) or their campus (control condition). After that, they rated themselves on feminine and masculine traits. As a result, participants' ratings on masculine traits were more consistent with their mother's expectancies in mother-prime condition than in control condition. Furthermore, this tendency was apparent among participants who had traditional sex role attitudes.

A study of self-help focusing (SHF):Comparison between "Tsubo image focusing" and "Mind View focusing"
Takasawa, Keiji *Graduate School of Environment, Nagoya University, Nagoya, Japan* **Ito, Yoshimi** *Graduate School of Environment, Nagoya University, Nagoya, Japan* **Tsuda, Hisamitsu** *Graduate School of Environment, Nagoya University, Nagoya, Japan* **Yamazaki, Akira** *Graduate School of Environment, Nagoya University, Nagoya, Japan* **Okada, Atsuhi** *Graduate School of Environment, Nagoya University, Nagoya, Japan* **Mori, Toshinobu** *Graduate School of Environment, Nagoya University, Nagoya, Japan* **Oguro, Daichi** *Graduate School of Environment, Nagoya University, Nagoya, Japan*

111 undergraduates conducted "Tsubo (Japanese container) image focusing" and "Mind View focusing", two kinds of self-help focusing. Participants described what they experienced through focusing. Authors classified their experiences by KJ method and compared "Tsubo image focusing" experiences with "Mind View focusing" ones. In addition, authors assessed the depth of the experience. Main results were as follows. (1) The experience of "Keeping a distance from problems" was reported more frequently in "Tsubo image focusing" experiences than in "Mind View focusing" ones. (2) The experience of "self-examination" was reported more frequently in "Mind View focusing" experiences than in "Tsubo image focusing" ones.

The study of the effects of social climate (milieu) of girls high school on fostering their social skills
Talebzadeh Nobarian, Mohsen *Faculty of Education, University of Shahid Beheshti, Tehran, Islamic Republic of Iran*

Dr.Mohsen,Talebzadeh Ensi,Keramaty The Study Of The Effects Of Social Climate (Milieu) Of Girls High School On Fostering Their Social Skills

Abstract: The major objectives of this study are: 1) Describing school climate (milieu) in two forms (open and closed milieu). 2) The study of the effects of the milieu on fostering students social skills. Therefore the study tested this hypothesis: The milieu of schools has effects on fostering of students social skills (social skills here are: self-assertion, cooperation, empathy and assuming responsibility).Findings, the research shows that :milieu of schools has effects not only on students social skills but also on common variance of above-mentioned social skills.

Deception about the crime leads to memory distortion
Tanaka, Mio Dept. of Psychology, Nihon University, Tokyo, Japan Itukushima, Yukio Psychology, Nihon University, Setagaya-Ku, Tokyo, Japan
Deceptions of eye-witnessed event leads to memory distortion. Previous studies showed three possibilities which affected the memory distortion after deception. These are disturbing memory rehearsal, retrieval induced forgetting, and reality monitoring. This study investigated which factors affect the memory distortion after deception. First, we examined that deceptions of eye-witnessed event disturb to rehearsal original memory. We compared memory recall after deception to memory recall without deception and memory rehearsal. Second, we examined that deceptions of eye-witnessed event reads to memory confusion between deceptive memory and original memory.

For what proselfs eat and travel?
Taniguchi, Ayako Risk Engineering, University of Tsukuba, Tsukuba, Japan Fujii, Satoshi Civil engineering, Tokyo Institute of Technology, Meguro, Tokyo, Japan
To solve or manage real world social dilemmas, knowledge about characteristic of proselfs who tend to defect is important. Proselfs are assumed to prioritize self-interest rather than other's interest. We hypothesize that proselfs try to maximize physical self-interest more strongly, and therefore maximize spiritual self-interest less strongly, than non-proselfs. We collected data from students and faculties in University of Tsukuba, Japan by questionnaire survey (n = 4,900). In this survey, we observed egoistic attitude, attitude toward rapidness and cheapness in travel and attitude toward volume of meal. All of the correlation coefficients between these factors were significantly positive.

How much for your honesty?: The role of values and incentives in determining honest behavior
Tanner, Carmen Inst. für Psychologie, Universität Zürich, Zürich, Switzerland Gibson, Rajna Swiss Banking Institute, University of Zurich, Zürich, Switzerland Wagner, Alexander Swiss Banking Institute, University of Zurich, Zürich, Switzerland Berkowitsch, Nicolas Department of Psychology, University of Zurich, Zürich, Switzerland
Economic theories assume that people are opportunists and behave honestly when it is in their self-interest to be so. Conversely, the approach of sacred/protected values maintains that people feel committed to honesty and keep telling the truth even though they may forgo gains. We examined the influences of values and incentives on honesty, the focus being on behaviors of managers and investors. Experiment 1 revealed that non-opportunistic CEOs were somewhat less sensitive to costs of telling the truth than opportunistic CEOs. In Experiment 2, investors were more likely to invest into CEOs who were perceived to be committed to honesty.

Personality traits and value orientation on the high risk police settings
Tat, Cristina Centre for Psychosociology, Ministry of Interior, Bucharest, Romania Bozai, Violeta Centre for Psychosociology, Ministry of Interior, Bucharest, Romania Turc, Mirela Centre for Psychosociology, Ministry of Interior, Bucharest, Romania
The aim of the study was to identify the value orientation of the personnel carrying on high-stakes settings and the relation between the personality traits and their personal values. The participants were 42 police officers working within a rapid intervention structure. We used California Psychological Inventory "CPI-260" and Rokeach Value Survey. The results show that individual values are more important than the social ones. There are also significant correlations between some values and personality traits. The practical implications are given by the approach of the values as a part of psychological selection and also to the study of the values in organizational context.

Standards of web based course evaluation
Thielsch, Meinald T. Psychologisches Institut 1, Münster, Germany Haaser, Kristof Psychologisches Institut 5, Universität Münster, Münster, Germany
Web-based course evaluation can successfully meet both evaluation and online methodology requirements. Pros and cons are discussed and standards of web based evaluations depicted. Fulfilling these standards is of great importance since the evaluation results may have personal consequences for teachers as well as for the whole organization. Evaluation standards help to raise the acceptance of the survey on the side of evaluated teachers as well as on the side of participating students. Standards are derived from own findings of different studies (N=577), experiences from regular course evaluations (about N=2500 every term) as well as the relevant literature.

The Parental-Representation-Screening-Questionnaire (PRSQ): A new screening questionnaire to assess risks in the parental relationship from the perspectives of children and adolescents
Titze, Karl Kinder- und Jugendpsychiatrie, Universität Zürich, Zurich, Switzerland
The study presents main psychometric properties of the PRSQ. The PRSQ consists of 36 items representing 8 scales (cohesion, identification, autonomy, conflicts, rejection/ neglect, punishment, emotional burden and fears/ overprotection). A school-based sample of 649 participants and a clinic-referred consecutive sample of 194 outpatients aged 10 to 20 years (mean: 14.6), were surveyed. Construct validity was shown by exploratory and confirmatory factor analyses. The internal consistencies of 13 of the 16 PRSQ scales were above .80. All PRSQ scales where significantly correlated with psychopathological symptoms (CBCL, YSR). Furthermore, they showed convergent correlations to the German EMBU (Schumacher et al., 2000).

Self-efficacy, self-regulation, proactive attitude, proactive coping and academic performance of Filipino students
Tolentino, Joanna Guidance Center, La Salle College Antipolo, Antipolo, Philippines
The study explores the relationship between self-efficacy, self-regulation, proactive attitude, proactive coping and academic performance of 187 Filipino college students. Correlational analysis revealed significant positive associations between self-efficacy, self-regulation, proactive attitude, proactive coping subtypes and academic performance. T-test revealed significant gender differences in proactive coping, instrumental support seeking, emotional support seeking and academic performance; year level differences in terms of self-

efficacy, proactive attitude, strategic planning, instrumental support seeking and academic performance. Agentic nature influences one's cognitive, affective, and goal-directed behaviors. Findings of the study can be used as a basis for an intervention program to enhance agentic nature of students.

Factors affecting students' self-educational ability: Learning goal, attribution of success and failure, self-efficacy and implicit theory of intelligence
Toshiaki, Mori Dept. of Education, Hiroshima University, Hiroshima, Japan Masuharu, Shimizu Literature, Kobe Women's University, Kobe, Japan Mihoko, Tominaga Nursing and Nutrition, Siebold University of Nagasaki, Nagasaki, Japan
This study investigated the relationships between students' self-educational ability and their attitude toward learning. A total of 768 students were examined on their self-educational ability in their college age, high school age, and elementary school age by retrospective questionnaires. They were also examined on their learning goal, attribution of success and failure, self-efficacy, and implicit theory of intelligence. The results showed that students with more self-educational ability have higher mastery goal and self-efficacy, and they regard intelligence as changeable. Implications of these results were discussed in relation to recent educational reform in Japan to foster self-educational ability.

Symptom understatement is gender-related in patients with arrhythmia: A suggestion for timely clinical intervention
Trovato, Guglielmo Internal Medicine & Health Psy, University of Catania, Catania, Italy Catalano, Daniela Internal Medicine, University of Catania, Catania, Italy Pace, Patrizia Internal Medicine & Health, University of Catania, Catania, Italy Marttines, Giuseppe Fabio Internal Medicine & Health, University of Catania, Catania, Italy
Objectives: Assessment illness perception, quality of life and anxiety and depression of patients with arrhythmias. Method: Sixty patients with arrhythmia completed the IPQ-r, the SF36 and the HADS. Results: Men perceived greater personal and treatment control and reported a more symptoms than women. Men reported a better perceived quality of life than women. No significant difference in the HADS was observed. Conclusions: Women report less symptoms and have a less focused perspective of their own illness. If disease is inappropriately minimized, serious troubles can derive both on patients' compliance and to the work of diagnostic and rehabilitation teams.

Self-concept instability in everyday classroom learning: Does it predict long-term school performance?
Tsai, Yi-Miau Zentrum für Bildungsforschung, Max-Planck-Institut, Berlin, Germany
Daily classroom learning and frequent competition and evaluation may pose challenge for students to maintain a positive and stable self-concept. The present study focuses on short-term fluctuation in students' academic self-concept and its relation with school achievement. Diary data were collected from 209 adolescents for an average of eight times within a 3-week period. In addition, school achievement was surveyed twice over a period of one school year. Short-term academic self-concept in the three subjects was positively related, pointing to consistent individual difference across academic domains. Moreover, higher self-concept instability predicted lower grades at the end of the school year.

Identity statuses in relation to parenting styles and well being

Tung, Suninder Psychology, Guru Nanak Dev University, Amritsar, India

The study investigated the relationship of Identity Statuses to the Parenting Styles and Well Being in adolescents. 210 adolescents (99 boys and 111 girls) in the age ranging between 17 to 20 yrs comprised the sample. The data was analyzed using Factor analysis. Five factors for each sample were obtained accounting for 68.3% and 66% variance respectively. Results show maternal and paternal concentration to be positively associated with achievement in boys whereas in girls maternal concentration was found to be positively associated with the lower statuses. Well being has not correlated very significantly with Identity statuses. Results have been discussed within the Indian cultural context.

Adolescents and their parents post-comprehensive educational aspirations

Tynkkynen, Lotta Psychology, University of Jyväskylä, Agora, Jyväskylä, Finland Salmela-Aro, Katariina Psychology, University of Jyväskylä, Agora, University of Jyväskylä, Finland

This study explored adolescents and their parents post-comprehensive educational aspirations. We examined whether the educational aspirations of the adolescents and parents would be congruent and what kinds of antecedents and consequences the congruency had in terms of SES, gender, school achievement and post-comprehensive education. The study is longitudinal and includes three measurement points. At the baseline there were 513 participants. Parents were examined at first measurement point. We found that there was more congruency in educational aspirations among those of higher school achievement and among those entering senior secondary school. In addition, associations between gender, SES and congruency were found.

The emotional modulation of the startle and post-auricular reflexes in non-criminal psychopathy

Uzieblo, Katarzyna Dept. of Psychology, University Ghent, Ghent, Belgium Verschuere, Bruno Psychology, University Ghent, Ghent, Belgium de Clercq, Armand Applied Mathematics & Comp, University Ghent, Ghent, Belgium Crombez, Geert Psychology, University Ghent, Ghent, Belgium

To assess which specific affective states may be impaired in psychopathy, we examined the effects of psychopathy on the emotional modulation of startle blink and post-auricular reflexes during six distinct affective events (erotic, thrill, love, threat, victim, and sad) in 72 male undergraduates. It was expected that psychopathic traits would be related to deviant emotional modulation of the reflexes. However, no such relation was found in this study. Only distinct associations between self-report ratings and psychopathy were established. The authors propose tentatively that aberrant startle modulation is mainly characteristic for individuals with emotional-interpersonal traits who also exhibit chronic antisocial behaviour.

Career and education oriented adults' beliefs about life

Uzole, Tatjana Social Psychology, Daugavpils University, Daugavpils, Latvia

The research aims to study the career and education oriented adults' beliefs about life. The responses on question - what is life – will be analyzed using the qualitative content analysis complemented by quantitative analysis of data. 170 Master students of Management participated in the research. The analysis revealed 12 different categories of beliefs about life. The first three ranks were allotted for the life as a period of time (25%), as my reality (14%), and process/reaching aim (13%). The results show

the tendency toward the diffuse beliefs about life as aimless, horizontal, self-regulated, and materialistically oriented limited period of time.

Biases in contingency learning: Are outcome predictions more accurate than causal judgements?

Vadillo, Miguel A. Dept. de Psicología, Universidad de Deusto, Bilbao, Spain Musca, Serban C. Departamento de Psicología, Universidad de Deusto, Bilbao, Spain Blanco, Fernando Departamento de Psicología, Universidad de Deusto, Bilbao, Spain Matute, Helena Departamento de Psicología, Universidad de Deusto, Bilbao, Spain

It is sometimes assumed that predictions involve simpler and more accurate cognitive processes than causal judgements. In our experiment, college students were exposed to a standard contingency learning task in which both outcome predictions and causal judgements were requested. Statistical analyses showed that, contrary to previous studies, a well-documented bias, namely the cue-density bias, was actually stronger in predictions than in causal judgments.

Host acculturation orientation

Verma, Jyoti Psychology, Patna University, Patna, India

The objective was to study the host acculturation orientation of 100 French students of a S. France University. The instrument used was a 9 items Host Acculturation Scale. Observations impressed that the students gave significantly 'more importance' to the idea that the immigrants maintained their heritage culture in their home rather than in general or at work. Furthermore, it was only 'partially important' that the immigrants adopted the French culture in general and at work and 'not important at all' to do so in their homes. Ethnic groups were not perceived as threatening and comparatively speaking, they were more accepted than liked.

Social distance of ethno-communicative relation in Latvia: Psychological analysis

Vidnere, Mara Dept. of Psychology, Daugavpils University, Jurmala, Latvia Igonin, Dmitry Psychology, Latvian University, Riga, Latvia Plotka, Irina Psychology, Daugavpils University, Riga, Latvia

Objective is personality's ethnical self awareness and civic identity. Methods. The empirical methods : - survey of social-psychological indices was developed (by M.Vidnere, D.Igonins); - modified Bogardus social distance scale; Study base. We received of 720 questionnaires. In the result of social distance scale (SDS) treatment, we obtained two factors. The first factor in the total factor interpretation shows that in general we can observe respondents' "orientation towards the West". The second factor that can be called "orientation towards familiar national neighbourhood" shows that the highest significance and social acceptance (favourability) is granted to Polish, Lithuanians, Estonians, Hebrews).

Psychology and interprofessional training and collaboration: Results of a comprehensive program to promote client-centred collaborative teamwork in mental health services

Vingilis, Evelyn Population & Community Health, The University of Western Onta, London, Canada Forchuk, Cheryl School of Nursing, The U of Western Ontario, London, Canada Orchard, Carole Interprofessional Health Educa, The U of Western Ontario, London, Canada Nicholson, Ian Population & Community Hea, London Health Science Centre, London, Canada

Interprofessional (IP) training and collaboration has become an expectation in Canadian health care, with much funding available for training and health care centres to provide IP care. Yet, virtually all newly funded training programs and health care centres do NOT include psychologists. This study,

ending June 2008, provides results of a mixed methods, multi-measures evaluation of the only Health Canada funded comprehensive IP initiative in mental health services and homeless that includes psychology. Given the strong international push for IP, this presentation will provide results on successes and barriers of psychologists and other health care providers in IP training and collaboration.

Beyond egoism, equality and equity: On the role of justice in the ultimatum and dictator game

von Sydow, Momme Inst. für Psychologie, Universität Göttingen, Göttingen, Germany

Game theory often refers to the rationality of self-interested individuals (homo economicus). Ultimatum and Dictator Game have been claimed to rebut this idea, showing that subjects often seek an equal split of some endowment given to them, even as 'dictator'. In two experiments, participants first contributed differently to some common endowment. The splits (and punishments) in the ultimatum and dictator games then corresponded to their contribution, if this contribution took effort (favoring equity over egoism and equality). However, if this was not linked to effort, the splits favored equality. Overall, the results favor a non-consequentialist notion of justice.

Neural correlates of different self-conscious emotions identified by functional magnetic resonance imaging

Wagner, Ullrich Inst. für Fundam. Neurowiss., Universität Genf, Geneva, Switzerland N'Diaye, Karim Inst. für Fundam. Neurowiss., Universität Genf, Geneva, Switzerland Ethofer, Thomas Inst. für Fundam. Neurowiss., Universität Genf, Geneva, Switzerland Vuilleumier, Patrik Inst. für Fundam. Neurowiss., Universität Genf, Geneva, Switzerland

Affective neuroscience has revealed the neural bases of fundamental emotions like fear and disgust, but little is known about the specific neural correlates of more complex "self-conscious" emotions like guilt, shame, and pride. During functional magnetic resonance imaging (fMRI) scanning, subjects reinstated emotional states of personal past situations (previously specified in a questionnaire) that were associated with strong feelings of guilt, shame, and pride. This is the first study that directly compares the neural correlates of guilt, shame and pride. Preliminary results point to distinct patterns of brain activation specifically in prefrontal and temporal areas for these emotions.

The influences of work and family values on Chinese and Taiwanese young urban workers' marriage and childbearing intentions

Wang, Chung-Kwei Dept. of Psychology, Soochow University, Taipei, Taiwan Lo, Kuo-Ying Department of Social Work, Soochow University, Taipei, Taiwan

An indigenous work value scale, which contains both individual and social oriented work end values, was developed and administered to 497 Chinese and Taiwanese young urban workers. Men are less willing than women to accept non-traditional marriage and childbearing practices. Chinese are less likely than Taiwanese to accept these practices. Workers who emphasized more on autonomy and independence work end values and less on family values were more likely to accept these practices. Those who emphasized more on social benefits work end values and more on family value were less likely to accept non traditional marriage and childbearing practices.

Impact of public policy-making procedures on policy accestability

Wang, Er Ping Center for S-E Behaviors, Institute of Psychology, CAS, Beijing, People's Republic of China Li, Da Zhi Graduate School, Cinese Academy of Sciences, Beijing, People's Republic of China

This research hypothesizes that improving procedures policy-making may make policies more acceptable. A pilot study was interviewing ten scholars of vary disciplines. They criticized current public policies as lacking sensitivity to public issues and resolving problems ineffectively. Study 2 tracked the procedure of a public policy. Findings indicated that the hearing of witnesses was not able to delegate the opinions of the public, so the policy failed to resolve the problem. Study 3 designed a quasi-experiment on two Internet website exhibitions of original photo. Results indicated that inviting visitors to express their desires and suggestions on the exhibition rules increased the rules' acceptability.

Experiment on Chinese postgraduates remembering 100 common English sentences by using MMOASAPMI

Wang, Hong-Li School of of Education Science, Guizhou Normal University, Guiyang, People's Republic of China Li, Jinghua School of Education Science, Guizhou Normal University, Guiyang, People's Republic of China Liu, Hong School of of Education Science, Guizhou Normal University, Guiyang, People's Republic of China Luo, Jing School of Education Science, Guizhou Normal University, Guiyang, People's Republic of China

A experiment was conducted in which Chinese postgraduates remembered 100 common English sentences by using the Natural Numeral Imagery Memory (Method by Memorizing Concrete Objects Associated with the Shapes of Arabic Numeral to produce Marvelous Imagination, MMOASAPMI). The result indicates: with the MMOASAPMI materials can be recited on random sequence and only around 2 seconds is needed for each randomly chosen item; the method can effectively remove the interference of proactive and retroactive inhibition, keeping memory for a longer time with less loss; the method turned out to be practical and efficient in common English sentences learning.

Impacts of impression regulating on smoking cessation in Taiwan

Wang, Jui-Hsing China Medical University Hospi, Taichung City, Taiwan Suen, Mein-Woei Chung Shan Medical University, Chung Shan Medical University, Taichung City, Taiwan Ho, M-C Chung Shan Medical University, Chung Shan Medical University, Taichung City, Taiwan

The ways to help smoking cessation is rare based on Social Psychology. This study aims at improving success of smoking cessation by increasing smokers' impression regulations in order to avoid negative impressions formed by smoking. Our survey is to understand negative impressions on female smokers (negative gender stereotypes). An experiment is conducted as a 2(stereotype: threat vs.non-threat) × 2(situation: regulation vs. non-regulation) design. Survey results will be expected to reveal typical negative stereotypes on female smokers. The experiment results also expected to show that, in regulation condition while stereotype activated, female smokers tempt to decrease their smoking-associated motivation and performance.

From terror to tolerance

Williams, Kinga Agnes Psychological Consultancy, MENSANA Intercultural, Goring-on-Thames, United Kingdom

Various cultures create their own world-views by construing reality in particular ways, while rendering alternative world-views threatening. The same is true of the present cultural-political climate, and mindfulness of its workings is imperative. The poster gives an overview of two possibilities of global psychological management of cultural diversity. One route is a negative feedback-loop, resulting in increased other-culture intolerance - the other is pointing forwards, towards greater other-culture

tolerance. The poster maps out the connection among Existential Anxiety, Culture-Distance, Culture-Shock, Constitutive and Regulative Rules, Cognitive Errors, Terror Management Strategies, Culture Learning and Intercultural Dialogue, as well as the relevant theories and hypotheses.

Development of a brief daily hassles scale for use with adolescents

Wright, Michalle School of Psychology, Griffith University, Bundall, Australia Creed, Peter School of Psychology, Griffith University, Bundall, Australia

Day-to-day hassles may be stronger predictors of psychological maladjustment than negative life events. Previous measures of daily hassles are critiqued. An initial focus group was conducted. Items were collapsed and tested on two samples. Items that reflected infrequent daily hassles and gender bias were removed. Principal axis factoring with an Oblimin rotation yielded two robust factors: Family Hassles and Peer Hassles, each containing 5 items. The two-factor structure was confirmed with the second sample using structural equation modelling. The two factors showed high alpha reliabilities. Daily hassles scores were significantly, positively correlated with self-reported anxious and depressive symptoms.

The application of cue-reactivity paradigm in smoking cessation: A biofeedback study

Wu, Yang School of Psychology, Beijing Normal University, Beijing, People's Republic of China Fang, Xiaoyi School of Psychology, Beijing Normal University, Beijing, People's Republic of China Deng, Linyuan School of Psychology, Beijing Normal University, Beijing, People's Republic of China

Cue-reactivity paradigm is widely used by researchers to elicit desires and cravings for tobacco, alcohol and drugs. Evidence has demonstrated its effectiveness through self-report craving, physiological responses and brain imaging. However, studies on the effect of its practical applications in drug cessation are quite limited. This study uses cue-reactivity paradigm by presenting picture stimulus to help sixty light and heavy smokers to control their desires for cigarette smoking through four-session biofeedback training.

Memory bias of emotional words in depression: ERP evidence in negative affective priming

Xiao, Zhongmin Nanchang, People's Republic of China Liu, Mingfan Department of Psychology, Jiangxi Normal university, P.R, Nanchang, People's Republic of China Yao, Shuqiao The Medical Psychological Rese, Second Xiangya Hospital, Centr, Changsha, People's Republic of China Liu, Jianping Department of Psychology, Jiangxi Normal university, Nanchang, People's Republic of China

The study aims to investigate electrophysiological measures of memory bias processes for emotional words using event-related potentials. Data collected from 18 patients with unipolar depression and 18 controls was analyzed in a negative affective priming task (NAP) with degraded target stimuli. Both depressed patients and normal controls showed longer time in response to positive and negative experimental targets. The depressed patients showed larger late positive component (LPC) difference amplitude in response to negative experimental trials than normal controls, however, normal controls showed larger LPC difference amplitude in response to positive experimental trials than depressed patients.

The experimental study of the transmitting relationship from weather to the expectation of stock returns in China

Xu, Shaojun College of Economics, Zhejiang University, Hangzhou, People's Republic of China Jin, Xuejun college of economics, Zhejiang University, Hangzhou, People's Republic of China

This study examined the relationships among weather, mood, personality and the expectation of stock returns, which were evaluated by experiment (N=481) conducted on an internet platform. The results showed that mood can mediate the relationship between weather and the expectation of stock returns, good weather is apt to cause positive mood which will cause optimistic expectation of stock returns. And the extraversion and neuroticism of personality can moderate the relationship between negative mood and the expectation of stock returns. So the result demonstrates the limit of "effective market theory" and shows that investors are not always rational.

AIDS awareness among post graduate students of Kurukshetra University, Kurukshetra (India)

Yadav, Rajender Singh Dept. of Eduction, Kurukshetra University, Kurukshetra, India

100 Postgraduate students of Arts and Science faculties were randomly selected and given AIDS Awareness Test. Percentages and t-test were used. Male students had more awareness than female students regarding the fact that AIDS is a viral disease. Female students had better understanding than male students about the fact that AIDS virus attack immune system. On certain items male and female students did not differ significantly. Science and arts students differed significantly and did not differ on some items. Study has implications for Doctors, Government, Teachers, Social workers and Community Leaders and highlights the need for AIDS Awareness among masses.

The experimental study on the preschool eyewitnesses

Yajing, Liu Psychology Depart., East China Normal University, Shanghai, People's Republic of China Wenxiu, Geng Psychology Depart., East China Normal University, Shanghai, People's Republic of China

The present study conducts three sets of comparative experiments simulating policemen inquiry strategies, doll-aids and picture-aids inquiry strategies to explore different impacts on the accuracy of the Chinese preschool eyewitnesses. As the suggestive and misleading impact?the results suggest that after free-recall?preschoolers should be enquired with open-ended leading questions immediately, and be asked three-choices forced question for crux if the former doesn't work. Judicial application of doll-aids is promising because testimony accuracy is improved distinctly with doll-aids and no additional misleading effects are found. The preschoolers exhibit much better performance after showing them prepared pictures containing open-ended leading information, but misleading effect is also disclosed after exposure to misleading pictures.

Longitudinal development of global self-worth and school adjustments during early adolescence in Japan

Yamamoto, Chika Junior college, Nagoya Bunri University, Nagoya, Japan Ujiie, Tatsuo Departmen of Education, Nagoya University, Nagoya, Japan Ninomiya, Katsumi Department of Policy Studies, Aichi Gakuin University, Nisshin, Japan Igarashi, Atsushi Human Development and Culture, Fukushima University, Fukushima, Japan Inoue, Hiromitsu Health Science, Chiba College of Health Scienc, Chiba, Japan

The purpose of this study was to examine the longitudinal development of global self-worth and school adjustments during early adolescence in Japan, by using latent growth curve models. School adjustments were assessed positive attitudes to club activities, negative attitudes to study, relationships with teachers, and adjustments to class. Participants were 449 junior high school students (197 males and 252 females). Results suggested that there were declines in global self-worth, and initial level of adjustments to class was related to initial level of global self-worth, but changes in School adjustments did not influence changes in global self-worth.

Rule-based learning of older adults in perceptual speed and inductive reasoning

Yang, Lixia Psychology, Ryerson University, Toronto, Canada Reed, Maureen Psychology, Ryerson University, Toronto, Canada Russo, Frank Psychology, Ryerson University, Toronto, Canada Wilkinson, Andrea Psychology, Ryerson University, Toronto, Canada

In this study, we investigated rule-based learning in older adults. Thirty-three older adults (ages 57-82, M = 70.30) were enrolled in an 8-session training program. Equivalent versions of psychometric measures of Perceptual Speed (i.e., Digit Symbol) and Inductive Reasoning (i.e., Letter Series and Number Series) were administered across different sessions. To ensure that learning was rule-based rather than memorization of specific items, same rules were applied but there was no overlap in items between different versions of the same test. The results demonstrated substantial learning effect, suggesting that older adults are able to apply self-learned rules to solve new items.

Detection of malingering: A survey of Australian psychologists' current practices

Yoxall, Jacqueline School of Psychology, Bond University, Robina, Australia Bahr, Mark School of Psychology, Bond University, Robina, Queensland, Australia Barling, Norman PO Box 1405, Private Practice, Broadbeach, Queensland, Australia

Objective: To explore Australian psychologists' beliefs & practices in the detection of malingering & to establish a retrospective estimation of malingering prevalence. Method: One hundred psychologists (in psycho-legal practice) completed a survey adapted from Slick et al. (2003). Statistical analysis included non-parametric tests & discriminant function analysis. Results: Respondents retrospectively estimated a 10% prevalence of malingering in psycho-legal arena, but differed in endorsment of explanatory models. Conclusion: Estimation of malingering prevalence in Australia appears similar to that derived from North American studies. There is indication that exposure to psycho-legal assessments, beliefs about malingering, and use of detection strategies may predict psychologists' retrospective estimation of malingering prevalence.

The role of a local community's discussion forum in creating social capital: Study of a gated community in Warsaw

Zajac, Aleksandra Faculty of Psychology, University of Warsaw, Warsaw, Poland

The widespread use of Computer-Mediated Communication and Internet in communal activities can have fundamental influence on local communities and level of social capital represented by their members. Starting with theoretical frames of social capital, an attempt to describe the role of a local internet forum in creating sense of community and its relations with social capital measures was made. 57 inhabitants of a gated community in Warsaw filled a social capital questionnaire. Results showed that frequent forum users where more active and more trustful than non-users. Moreover their social networks were broader and wider.

Worked example learning about the rules of the four fundamental admixture operations of arithmetic

Zhang, Qi Dept. of Psychology, Liaoning Normal University, Dalin, People's Republic of China Lin, Hongxin Psychology, Liaoning Normal University, Dalin, People's Republic of China

We hypothesized that second Grade pupils could learn the rules of the four fundamental admixture operations of arithmetic and adopted worked examples having operation step annotations or not and representing worked examples alternating, and 48 second Grade pupils were tested in the study. The results showed that the most of participants could learn the rules of the fundamental admixture operations of arithmetic with brackets by worked examples; the operation step annotations had obvious effect on participant's learning about the more difficult rules; the participants needed different quantities of worked examples when learning different difficult operation rules.

Citizens' environmental concern in China: From perspective of environmental psychology

Zheng, Quanquan Psychology, Zhejiang University, Hangzhou, People's Republic of China Pan, Lingyun Psychology, Zhejiang University, Hangzhou, Zhejiang Province, People's Republic of China

This research explored the mental structure of environmental concern from the perspective of psychology. Based on the reviews on domestic and abroad research materials and interviews of citizen, an environmental concern questionnaire was developed with relative high level of reliability and construct validity, and then an investigation was conducted involving a sample of 1066 subjects by this questionnaire to find out the total state of the citizen's environmental concern approximately. At the same time, the relationship of the local identity and environmental concern was analyzed, as well as the future environmental protection behaviors using the Theory of Planned Behavior (TPB).

Sign systems related to user wayfinding behavior in interchanging in under-ground stations

Zheng, Meng Cong Chiba, Japan

The purpose of this study is to understand how signs correspond to various user wayfinding behaviors and serve their needs when interchanging in under-ground stations. Two different distance interchange routes were set up for wayfinding experiments. Conversations with the subjects were coded and categorized based on their wayfinding process. It is found that the subjects followed some fixed patterns for finding a sign, recognizing the direction shown on the sign, determining the direction, moving, and looking for the next sign. The act of confirmation is not done by memory but depends on finding the same sign continuously.

Investigating economy resources and living means of unemployed drug addicts

Zhu, Mianmao of Political Science and Law, Hainan Institute, Haikou, People's Republic of China He, Jiaofei Haikou, Qiongshan Middle School, Hainan, People's Republic of China

Objective: Investigating economy resources and living means of 400 unemployed drug addicts who declared unemployed when they were taken to the hospital. Methods: By talking to addicts, confirming with their mates and inquiring of their relatives. Results: 57% cases had committed various crimes violating the executive regulations and laws. The three tops ranked on the list were: 16% cases concerned with gambling, 15% cases concerned with pornography and 9% cases were thieves respectively. 18% cases included entertainment and commerce. Conclusions: The majority of so-called unemployed addicts might have their illegal means: committing crimes or undertaking inglorious jobs.

Is virtual nature equally restorative as "physical" nature? An experimental comparison study

Ziesenitz, Anne Inst. für Psychologie, Universität Kassel, Kassel, Germany Krömker, Dörthe Psychology, University of Kassel, Kassel, Germany

Nature can help to restore depleted attention resources or reduce stress. We examined if different presentation modes of urban nature are equally restorative. We conducted a combined field/laboratory experiment, using a between-subject design to manipulate presentation modes of a walking-track through an urban park. After performing a stress-inducing task, participants (N=118) were randomly assigned to three presentation modes (in situ, a video recording, a computer-simulation) or a control group. We measured salivary alpha-amylase, affect and attention. First analyses show differences in the in situ and laboratory conditions, which indicate methodological and practical implications for further studies in that field.

Self-regulation procedures as a mean of optimization professional's states during business-trainings

Zlokazova, Tatyana Psychology, Moscow State University, Moscow, Russia

The purpose of the study was to investigate effectiveness of self-regulation techniques in optimizing professional's state during business-training. Subjects: 92 training participants. Optimizing procedures: self-organized rest, progressive relaxation, progressive relaxation with autogenic training elements. Dependent measures: self-estimation scales, physiological indicators, task performance test. Results showed negative changes in participant's state after five hours of intensive education and specific positive effects of each optimizing procedure. We conclude that self-regulation techniques, unlike spontaneous regulation, shows system optimization effect which occurs both on the psychological and the physiological level. Complex self-regulation procedures, including verbal auto-suggestions, allow forming state more adequate to tasks demands.

Poster Session Tuesday Afternoon 14:00

Investigation the relationship between personality and demographic factors with happiness in pharmachological students in Kermanshah Medical Sciences University

Abaspour, Parastoo Dept. of Medical Sciences, Kermanshah University, Kermanshah, Islamic Republic of Iran Solgi, Zahra psychology factualy, Eslamabad payamenor university, kermanshah, Islamic Republic of Iran Karimi, Maryam medical sciences, kermanshah university, kermanshah, Islamic Republic of Iran

This study has examined the relationship between Personality and demographic factors with Happiness. it was hypothesized that it would be significant differences between males and females in their happiness and personality factors. Predicting happiness via personality and demographic factors was one of our aims. On 48 students Personality factors inventory(costa,1985); Oxford Happiness Inventory (argyle,1989) with some demographic questions were applied. The results showed that there is a negative significant relationship between the neuroticism and happiness but there are positive significant relationship between the others personality factors and happiness. about sex, just the relationship between happiness and sex was statistically significant. Furthermore extroversion itself explained %39 of happiness by adding agreeableness and sex it would be%53.

Lexical cohort activation and the dynamic microstructure of speech production

Abdel Rahman, Rasha Inst. für Psychologie, Humboldt-Universität zu Berlin, Berlin, Germany

Semantic interference in speech production has long been viewed as a prime indicator of competition during lexical selection. However, recent conflicting findings - suggesting that these effects are restricted to categorical relations - have put doubt on the lexical competition assumption. A series of behavioural and electrophysiological experiments demonstrates that modulating the extent of lexical cohort activation by meaningful contexts, interference can be observed for associates and even unrelated items. This suggests that lexical selection is competitive, that lexical cohort activation is a major determinant for interference effects, and that the microstructure of speech production is highly flexible and dynamic.

Spouse selection criterias

Abedi, Fariba *Ward of Psychology, Dr. Hamidiye Clinic, Tehran, Islamic Republic of Iran* **Shahraray, Mehrnaz** *faculty of psychology, teacher training university, tehran, Islamic Republic of Iran*
The purpose of this study was of investigating about Spouse Selection Criterias .step 1: we reviewed criterias in other studies on mate selection.step 2: we finded specialist view, prepared an open ended list of criterias and administered to 80 university students Step 3: with results of step 2 we prepared new list of criterias inclusive 50 adjectives and administered to 235 university students. after factor analysis we made a list of Spouse Selection Criterias in 3 factor: 15 adjectives in factor 1, 13 adjectives in factor 2 and 10 in factor 3.

Mental health improves as a function of social support

Acuna, Laura *Psychology, National University of Mexico, Mexico City, Mexico* **Bruner, Carlos A.** *Psychology, National University of Mexico, Mexico City, Mexico*
University students (N=649) responded the Health and Daily Living Form (HDL) and the Social Support Questionnaire (SSQ). Scores on the sections of self-confidence, depression and psychosomatic symptoms of the HDL were analyzed as a function of perceived number of lenders of help in situations of need on the SSQ. Consistent with Social Impact Theory, increases in perceived social support resulted in marginal increases on self-confidence and decreases in depression and psychosomatic symptoms.

Affective picture processing in traumatized victims of war and torture: An MEG study

Adenauer, Hannah *Inst. für Psychologie, Universität Konstanz, Konstanz, Germany* **Catani, Claudia** *Psychology, University of Konstanz, Konstanz, Germany* **Keil, Julian** *Psychology, University of Konstanz, Konstanz, Germany* **Aichinger, Hannah** *Psychology, University of Konstanz, Konstanz, Germany* **Neuner, Frank** *Psychology, University of Konstanz, Konstanz, Germany*
In the present study the influence of traumatic stress on the processing of emotional stimuli was examined using a visual steady state MEG paradigm with flickering pictures of varying affective valence. 28 torture victims with Posttraumatic Stress Disorder (PTSD) and 38 matched subjects without PTSD (subdivided into a traumatized and a non-traumatized group) were compared. A minimum norm estimation (MNE) technique was used for source localization. The enhanced processing of unpleasant arousing stimuli in visual and parietal regions in PTSD patients will be discussed in the framework of present theories about elaboration and memory representation of threatening cues in PTSD. The study was supported by DFG and European Refugee Fund.

The impact of a reminiscence program on the psychological well-being in aged Portuguese people

Afonso, Rosa *Dept. of Psychology, University of Beira Interior, Covilhã, Portugal* **Bueno, Belén** *Psychology, University of Salamanca, Salamanca, Spain*
Throughout the investigation it was tested whether the individuals exposed to the reminiscence sessions would significantly increase their psychological well-being in relation to the subjects who did not

receive this type of intervention. 90 individuals over 65 years-old participated in this study. They were divided into three groups: an experimental group, who was exposed to the reminiscence sessions, a control group and a placebo control group. All the subjects carried out pretest and posttest evaluations answering The Psychological Well-Being Scales. According to the t tests based on the statistic program SPSS 15.0, there were significant statistical increases in the general psychological well-being within the experimental group.

The relationship between shyness and some demographic variables of Sultan Qaboos University students

Al-Damen, Monther *Psychology, Sultan Qaboos University, Al Khod, Oman*
This study will investigate the relationship between shyness and gender, type of college and acheivement of Sultan Qaboos University students. As we know, shyness is an emotion that affects how a person feels and behaves around others. It means feeling uncomfortable, self-conscious, nervous, timid, or ensecure. It can be analayzed into verious components : cognitive, affectional and behavioral. A random sample consisting of 400 male and female students from different colleges at the University will be selected for this purpose. A twenty item shyness questionnaire will be distributed to be answered by the study sample after finding its validity and reliability. A statistical analysis such Means, Standard Deviations, T-tests, Chi-square and Anova will be used in this study.

Characteristics of personality traits and personal behaviour of future ballet dancers

Aleksandrovich, Maria *Department of Psychology, Academia Pomeraniensis, Slupsk, Poland*
Objectives: The purpose was to study the correlation of personality traits of future ballet dancers with forms of their personal behaviour. Methods: NEO-FFI questionnaire (Costa & McCrae, polish adaptation, 1998) and self-reports on Study of Personal Behaviour (Senko, 1998). Sample: 103 ballet dancers (54 girls, 49 boys), 14-19 y.o. Results: There is significant correlation between personality traits "Extraversion", "Neuroticism", "Conscientiousness", "Agreeableness" and different forms of personal behaviour. There is no correlation between personality trait "Openness to experiences" and any form of personal behaviour. Conclusions: Our data enrich the psychological portrait of such a closed professional community as ballet group is.

Psychopathology and quality of life of bariatric surgery candidates

Andrés, Ana *Methodology Behavioral Science, University of Barcelona, Barcelona, Spain* **Lecube, Albert** *Obesity Unit, Hospital Vall d'Hebrón, Barcelona, Spain* **Saldaña, Carmina** *Department of Personality, University of Barcelona, Barcelona, Spain* **Quesada, Marta** *Psychiatry Division, Hospital Vall d'Hebrón, Barcelona, Spain* **Gómez, Juana** *Methodology Behavioral Science, University of Barcelona, Barcelona, Spain*
Objectives. The aim of this study is to assess psychopathology and quality of life of bariatric surgery candidates. Methods. The participants (n=100) of this study were obese patients waiting for the Roux-en-Y gastric bypass surgery. The patients completed some demographical data and the following questionnaires: DASS-21, BSI and IWQOL-Lite. Results. The results obtained in this study describe the profile of these patients regarding anxiety, depression or stress, among other psychopathological factors. Also, it describes the quality of life of these patients before surgery. Conclusions. This study offers a psychological profile of bariatric surgery candidates.

Prisoner's Dilemma Games and the Autism-Spectrum Quotient

Annen, Yasumasa *Department of Human Sciences, Aichi Mizuho College, Toyota, Japan*
The relationship between performances in prisoner's dilemma games (PDG) and the Autism-Spectrum Quotient factors (AQ-f) was investigated with student participants (n=120). Twenty-seven performances in PDG matched by two strategies (21 trials each with Random, and Tit-For-Tat) were analyzed using multiple linear regressions. Results indicated that when a partner used Random, AQ-f governed PDG performances significantly more under the non-rewarded condition when the partner was recognized as human. Conversely, in the case of Tit-For-Tat, AQ-f governed PDG performances significantly more under the rewarded condition. The AQ-f influences are discussed in relation to partner's strategies, recognition of a partner, and reward.

Epistemic beliefs in elementary school children

Anschütz, Andrea *Inst. für Pädagogik, Universität Oldenburg, Oldenburg, Germany* **Wernke, Stephan** *Institut für Pädagogik, Universität Oldenburg, Oldenburg, Germany* **Moschner, Barbara** *Institut für Pädagogik, Universität Oldenburg, Oldenburg, Germany*
Subjects in most of the studies about epistemic beliefs are students, only a few deal with elementary school children. In our study we questioned if it is possible to assess their beliefs by standardized questionnaires. For answering this question we investigated epistemic beliefs of 3rd and 4th graders in different ways. In the first study 145 children answered a questionnaire. In study 2 we interviewed 32 subjects of study 1 about their understanding of the questionnaire items. Results show that children are able to verbalize their thoughts about epistemic beliefs, but they had severe difficulties to understand some of the questionnaire items.

Character strengths and the relationship with well-being for children and students in Japan

Aoki, Tazuko *Graduate School of Education, Hiroshima University, Hiroshima, Japan* **Miyazaki, Hiroshi** *Faculty of Education, Okayama University, Okayama, Japan* **Hashigaya, Yoshimasa** *Faculty of Education, Okayama University, Okayama, Japan* **Yamada, Tsuyoshi**
This study examined the relationships between character strengths and well-beings in Japan. Forth graders, sixth graders and eighth graders participated in this research. We used six character strengths and two kinds of feeling to classify some categories by cluster analysis. We found five categories; courage, wisdoms, justice, respect and positive feeling. We analyzed the relations between each cluster category and well-being scales by multiple regression analysis. We found courage, justice and respect were related with well-being. However wisdom was not related with it. All character categories were related with hope scale. We discussed about the relations between character strengths and well-being.

Self-esteem and social attitudes in intellectual disabled people

Armas Vargas, Enrique *Person., Evaluat. & Psychology, Psychology Faculty, Tenerife, Spain*
This study offers empiric results that show disabled people evaluation of their Self-Esteem and their Support & Comprehension (S&C) attitudes as well as Autonomy & Independence (A&I) perceived in their social environment. Intellectual disabled people (n=50) (Light M. R.), 27 men, 23 women (20-55 years). CAE (Self-Esteem Questionnaire) and CAFA (Social Attitudes Questionnaire) by Armas-Vargas. CAE (55% variance), factors: Valuation of Efficiency/Utility (alpha=.84); He himself (alpha=.73); The Others (alpha=.73); Negative

Comparison with Others (.74). CAFA, (50% variance), factors: A&I (alpha=.87); S&C (.80). The valuation of Utility/Efficiency is positively associated to A&I attitudes (r= .49, p

Superiority of left three-quarter views in face recognition: Right hemisphere advantage hypothesis

Arnold, Gabriel Institut de Psychologie, Boulogne-Billancourt, France Sieroff, Eric Labo Psychologie Cognitive, Institut de Psychologie, Boulogne-Billancourt, France

We evaluated the right hemisphere advantage explanation of the superiority of left three-quarter views (main features in the left visual field) over right three-quarter views, in face recognition. We used a sequential matching task of faces presented in the left (LVF) or right (RVF) visual fields, or in the middle of the visual field. Response times were faster in the middle presentation than in the LVF, and in the LVF than in the RVF. The left three quarter advantage was found only with the middle presentation. These results are in favour of the right hemisphere advantage hypothesis.

Relationships between self-description and dominant structure of word meaning

Arro, Grete Inst. of Psychology, Tallinn University, Tallinn, Estonia

597 men participated in a study on relationships between dominant structure of word meaning, personality characteristics and free-response self-description. The analysis revealed that the individuals who primarily used everyday concepts thinking systematically had fewer self-descriptions. Metatrait was related more with scientific concepts thinking than everyday concepts thinking. Secondly, the result in NEO-PI-R inventory correlated less with the free-response personality descriptions in individuals using primarily everyday concepts thinking. Thus the structure of word meaning can be one factor mediating the personality as for the scientific concept thinkers there are available substantially different mental tools as for everyday concept thinkers.

Goal orientation and initial motivation: An integrated approach

Bachmann, Gerhard Inst. für Psychologie, Universität Frankfurt, Frankfurt, Germany

To explain the role of motivation in learning, goal orientation (Elliot & McGregor, 2001) and the cognitive-motivational-process-model (Vollmeyer & Rheinberg, 1998) were integrated. 41 participants' goal orientation was measured with the Achievement-Goal-Questionnaire and initial motivation with the QCM after introducing the task (Sudokus). Performance was measured as solved numbers. Mastery-approach and challenge correlate (r=.32*), as well as performance-avoidance and fear of failure (r=-.36*). Regressing performance on initial motivation and goal orientation yielded low accounted variance, F(8)=2.5, p=.03, with interest as best predictor. Relating the two explanations to another helped clarifing each explanation and supported the importance of interest.

A unified framework to study motorcyclists' risk awareness

Banet, Aurélie LESCOT, INRETS, Bron, France Bellet, Thierry LESCOT, INRETS, Bron, France Martin, Robert LEACM, Université Lyon2, Lyon, France Bonnard, Arnaud LESCOT, INRETS, Bron, France Goupil, Céline LESCOT, INRETS, Bron, France

Research Objective is to provide a common methodological framework to study motorcyclists' risk awareness at two complementary levels: "Social Attitudes" towards risk, and "Cognitive Abilities" to detect risks of accident while driving. The Methods developed are based on video sequences showing critical driving situations. Participants had

to watch these sequences then appraise and qualify the criticality of the situations through a Likert scale and an Osgood Semantic Differential. Then they completed Attitudes Questionnaires. Twenty-one riders participated in this experiment. The Results obtained enable us to highlight different categories within the motorcyclists' population in terms of risk awareness.

Effect of stimulus eccentricity on the timing of inhibition of return

Bao, Yan Dept. of Psychology, Peking University, Beijing, People's Republic of China Li, Hui Department of Psychology, Peking University, Beijing, People's Republic of China Zhou, Bin Human Science Center, University of Munich, Munich, Germany

Recent evidence shows that inhibition of return (IOR) is much stronger in far peripheral areas relative to the more central visual field. The present study further examined the time course of IOR in the two regions with stimuli presented at either 7 or 21 degree eccentricity. Twenty-five university students performed a detection task, in which a target appeared randomly following a peripheral cue with a varied time interval. Results showed that IOR disappeared approximately 1 second later at 21 degree relative to 7 degree stimulus eccentricity. Possible reasons underlying the eccentricity effect of the timing of IOR were discussed.

Educational needs assessment of nurses work in hospitals of Tehran University of Medical Sciences about life skills

Barough, Nasrin community health, Nursing&Midwifery of Tehran U., Tehran, Islamic Republic of Iran Sharifi, Nahid community health, Nursing&Midwifery of Tehra, Tehran, Islamic Republic of Iran Taghavi Larijani, Taraneh community health, Nursing&Midwifery of Tehra, Tehran, Islamic Republic of Iran

Objectives: Determination educational needs of nurses about (Decision making, problem solving, Stress management, Critical thinking) Material &Method This research is a descriptive analytical study. The sample was randomly219 The instrument was a quantitative questionnaire with 35 items about life skills The data were Analyzed by SPSS software. Results The nurses had high educational needs in Decision making, problem solving, stress management and there was low educational need in critical thinking. Conclusion. It is useful to consider results and to detect abilities, weakness of nurses and do the future programming in a way which have the most effectiveness.

Negotiation habilities

Barros, Manuela Faculty Human and social scien, University Fernando Pessoa, Porto, Portugal

Our investigation defines as general objective to realize a study about negotiation habilities, namely to analyse the relation between a wide set of socio-demographic variables, negotiation efficacy and assertiveness in commercial context. In a portuguese sample of 300 subjects, we analyse the relevance of the relation between negotiation efficacy and assertiveness in commercial management and, for such, we used CEN II (Questionnaire of Negotiation Efficacy) and EHS (Scale of Social Habilities). Data, obtained by statistical analysis in SPSS, show that most of our hipothesis have confirmation. Research implications are discussed more deeply in conection with strategic pertinence of having some negotiation habilities in a commercial context.

The role of auditory sensory memory in explaining differences in nonword repetition ability

Barry, Johanna Inst. für Neuropsychologie, Max-Planck-Institut, Leipzig, Germany Weiss, Benjamin Psychology, Paris Lodron Universitaet, Salzburg, Austria Sabisch, Beate Neuropsychology, Max Planck Institute, Leipzig, Germany Brauer, Jens Neuropsychology, Max Planck Institute, Leipzig, Germany

Deficits in nonword repetition are heritable and may be a risk factor for Specific Language Impairment (SLI). These deficits may derive from a rapid decay of sensory memory. This hypothesis was investigated by measuring frequency discrimination thresholds at different ISIs in two groups of parents (control versus SLI). A greater increase in discrimination threshold (JND) with increasing inter-stimulus interval was not observed in parents of SLI children, and performance on the task was not correlated with phonological working memory measures, suggesting a dissociation between sensory memory and phonological working memory. Our findings have implications for models describing phonological working memory.

Temporal resolution is enhanced by temporal preparation

Bausenhart, Karin Maria Inst. für Psychologie, Universität Tübingen, Tübingen, Germany Rolke, Bettina Psychologisches Institut, Universität Tübingen, Tübingen, Germany Ulrich, Rolf Psychologisches Institut, Universität Tübingen, Tübingen, Germany

In two experiments, we investigated whether temporal preparation influences the temporal resolution of the visual system. Temporal resolution was assessed by a temporal-order judgment (TOJ) task. To manipulate temporal preparation, we varied the time between a warning signal and a subsequent target stimulus (foreperiod). In this foreperiod paradigm, short foreperiods enable better temporal preparation than long foreperiods. The results are clear-cut: Short foreperiods improved TOJ for two spatially adjacent dots (Experiment I) and for two spatially overlapping stimuli (Experiment II). Thus, temporal preparation improves the temporal resolution of the visual system.

Cross-modal correspondences between weight, pressure, brightness and spatial position

Benarzi, Elisheva Dept. of Psychology, Kinneret College, Emek Hayarden, Israel

Objectives: To propose and examine an ecological account for cross-modal correspondences. Method: Participants made similarity judgments of pairs of cross-modal stimuli differing in weight or pressure and in brightness or spatial position, and magnitude estimates of weight or pressure with varying levels of contextual brightness or spatial position. Dimensions were presented at five levels each. Results: Consistent congruence relationships among all pairs of dimensions emerged. Moreover, findings indicated a consistency in the directions of correspondences across dimensions and tasks, providing support for the ecological account for cross-modal correspondences, as they underlie most perceptual dimensions.

The relationship between perfectionism and psychological symptoms among university students

Benk, Asli Altis psychological counseling, Istanbul, Turkey

In this study, following independent variables considered: age, gender, year, the type of number of sibling, birth order, the educational background of their parents, and whether parents live together or not, and whether they are alive or not, parents' occupations, the perceived socio-economical status,perceived mother-father-child relations, perceived parenting style and perceive perfectionism levels from their parents. In order to measure perfectionism, Multi Dimensional Perfectionism Scale (MPS), to measure the level of psychological symptoms, Symptom Check List (SCL-90) and to reach demographic data, Demographic Data Sheet have been used in this study. Findings shows that perfectionism has significant relationship between all psychological symptoms and most of choosen independent variables.

What does cloze measure?: The French validation of a shortened form of standard cloze test
Bennacer, Halim Université d'Orléans, Tours, France
The cloze research has been rather inconclusive with regard to what cloze tests are measuring (Brown, 2002). This study describes the validation of a shortened form of standard cloze test, with a sample of 561 French pupils aged 11 to 17 from junior high schools. It also allows identifying the determinants of cloze achievement. The results show that this tested form has good psychometric properties, and evaluates primarily two factors: grammatical structures and vocabulary acquisition (Exploratory factor analysis). They support the cogency of use of rational cloze.

Interaction involvement of university students of prosocial professions
Bjekic, Dragana Technical Faculty, Cacak, Serbia Zlatic, Lidija Educational Psychology, Faculty of teacher education, Uxice, Zlatkovic, Blagica Educational Psychology, Faculty of teacher education, Vranje, Stojiljkovic, Snezana Department of psychology, Faculty of philosophy, Nis,
Communication skills are important professional/job skills, especially for social interactive professions. The study of interaction involvement compared students of prosocial oriented professions (realized in social interaction process, as teachers of different courses, psychologists, etc.) and nonprosocial oriented professions (engineers, technologists, etc.) by using Interaction involvement scale. The results of the first phase of the research (realized in the Serbian universities): there are not differences between students of two professional groups in the first years of study, but there are differences between the students of the final years of study. University education for prosocial professions improves the interaction involvement.

Influence of patients' characteristics on nursing students' perceptions of cancer situation
Blois, Stephanie Social Psychology Department, University of Provence, Aix-en-Provence, France Dany, Lionel Social Psychology Department, University of Provence, Aix-en-Provence Cedex 1, France Mahieuxe, Magali Oncology Service, Dunkerque Hospital Center, Dunkerque Cedex 1, France Morin, Michel Social Psychology Department, University of Provence, Aix-en-Provence Cedex 1, France
Objectives. This study explored how nursing students integrate informations about cancer patients into gravity and social support needs perception. Methods. 719 nursing students completed a questionnaire including a scenario describing a cancer patient. Each of the 16 scenarios varied according to four informations: patient gender; physical state; psychological state; relatives availability. Results. MANOVA showed that the four main effects were significant but the more important results concerned psychological state and relatives' availability. There are also interaction effects between these four factors. Conclusion. Nursing students' evaluation of patients' situation is influenced by patients' bio-psycho-social characteristics and the way they cope with cancer.

Impulse-control disorders in young adults
Bohne, Antje Psychologisches Institut I, Universität Münster, Münster, Germany Meiners, Sinje Psychologisches Institut I, Universität Münster, Münster, Germany
Objective: Assessment of impulse-control disorders (ICD) with focus on their prevalence and co-occurrence of impulsive symptoms. Method: DSM-IV-based screenings for intermittent explosive disorder, kleptomania, pyromania, pathological gambling, and trichotillomania as well as pathological buying as an ICD not otherwise specified. Results: Work is still in progress. We expect to present data of 400 individuals. By now the database incorporates 160 participants (68.7% female, age: M=21.9 years). Detailed results will be presented on our poster. Conclusion: The results will provide information on the prevalence and co-occurrence of ICDs and impulsive symptoms in young adults.

Academic, social and emotional adjustment among Mandarin/English-speaking students studying in Canada
Both, Lilly Dept. of Psychology, University of New Brunswick, Saint John, Canada Di Tommaso, Enrico Psychology, University of New Brunswick, Saint John, New Brunswick, Canada
Adjusting to university can be a difficult transition for many students. Students from China have added stressors as they cope with this transition in a new culture and a second language. Thirty-five students participated in this study which assessed their adjustment. Students with a secure attachment were less likely to report social and emotional loneliness, and were more likely to feel socially connected and socially assured. Individuals with an insecure attachment were more likely to be worried about school, and were less satisfied with life. Results will be discussed in terms of possible interventions to make this transition easier for international students.

Specificity and universality of the attentional bias in Generalized Anxiety Disorder
Brassard Lapointe, Marie-Laure École de psychologie, Université Laval, Québec, Canada Langlois, Frédéric Département de psychologie, UQTR, Trois-Riviàres, Canada Tremblay, Sébastien École de psychologie, Université Laval, Québec, Canada
Several studies show an attentional bias towards threatening information for Generalized Anxiety Disorder (GAD) patients, though the same bias is also observed with normal individuals. In the present study, we compared the extent to which both groups were biased in processing threatening information within the attentional blink (AB) paradigm. Participants had to identify two targets (threatening or neutral) among distractors. Although, overall identification was poorer for GAD patients, the magnitude of the AB was similar across groups with little impact of threat. Specificity and universality of the attentional bias are discussed in relation to pathology and task parameters.

Interpersonal relations in different types of groups: Mapping social combinations of relational models
Brito, Rodrigo CIS, ISCTE, Lisbon, Portugal Waldzus, Sven CIS, ISCTE, Lisbon, Portugal
This study builds on research with relational models theory and seeks to map models used in interpersonal relations onto types of social groups. We first asked student participants in a questionnaire study to rate acquaintances on items of the four relational models scales, and then to identify types of groups to which each relation belonged. Relations within different types of groups were associated to different relational models. For instance, authority ranking combined with communal sharing in families, but with market pricing in

organisations. We conclude that the cultural definition of groups determines the combinations of relational models used.

Linkages between auditory perception and action: Acoustic affordances
Burton, Joel Psychology, Cardiff University, Cardiff, United Kingdom Macken, Bill Psychology, Cardiff University, Cardiff, United Kingdom Jones, Dylan Psychology, Cardiff University, Cardiff, United Kingdom
The studyinvestigated whether the presence of auditory motion in bimodal displays facilitatated congruent movement towards a visual target. Participants were asked to make a visual left right discrimination task whilst simultaneously being presented with moving auditory stimuli. When the participants response and auditory stimuli were in the same direction participants were faster to responded than when the auditory stimuli was moving in the opposite direction. The results indicate that sounds moving in the same direction did afford participants to move in the direction of the sound.

Measurement equivalence of the interviewing self-efficacy scale across samples from Ghana, Russia, Turkey and Italy
Bye, Hege H. Faculty of Psychology, University of Bergen, Bergen, Norway Sam, David L. Faculty of Psychology, University of Bergen, Bergen, Norway Sandal, Gro Mjeldheim Faculty of Psychology, University of Bergen, Bergen, Norway
Objectives: The objective of this study was to investigate the measurement equivalence of the interviewing self-efficacy scale (I-SE) across samples from four different countries. Methods: University students from Ghana (n=442), Russia, (n=251), Turkey (n=407) and Italy (n=383) completed questionnaires including the I-SE scale. The data were analysed by means of a multigroup confirmatory factor analysis. Results: The analyses support the configural and metric invariance of the scale across the four samples. Conclusions: The invariance of the I-SE scale across the samples suggests that the scale is applicable for research and practice in a cross-cultural setting.

Generalized Anxiety Disorder in older adults: Testing Dugas' conceptual model
Cabrera, Isabel Dept. de Psicologia Biologica, Universidad Autonoma de Madrid, Madrid, Spain Montorio, Ignacio Psicología BIOLOGICA Y DE LA S, UNIVERSIDAD AUTÓNOMA DE MADRID, MADRID, Spain Izal, Maria Psicología BIOLOGICA Y DE LA S, UNIVERSIDAD AUTÓNOMA DE MADRID, MADRID, Spain Marquez Gonzalez, Maria Psicología BIOLOGICA Y DE LA S, UNIVERSIDAD AUTÓNOMA DE MADRID, MADRID, Spain Nuevo, Roberto Psychiatry Service, Hospital de la Princesa, MADRID, Spain
Objective: to test Dugas' conceptual model of Generalized Anxiety Disorder in older adults. Method: 111 community-dwelling older adults completed measures of severity-of-worry (SW), beliefs-about-worry (BAW), negative-problem-orientation (NPO), cognitive-avoidance (CA) and Intolerance-of-Uncertainty (IU). Results: a hierarchical regression analysis with the SW as a dependent variable indicated that IU explained a significant (p=.034) percentage of variance in predicting SW after controlling for gender, age, BAW, NPO and CA (Total adjusted $R2=.401$). ONP and IU were the only significant predictors. Conclusions: these results partially support Dugas' model of GAD in older adults and highlight the role of IU in this disorder.

9.5 months old infants prefer Picasso over Monet

Cacchione, Trix *Psychologie, Universität Zürich, Zürich, Switzerland* **Bertin, Evelyn** *Psychologie, Universität Zürich, Zürich, Switzerland*

We examined infants' visual attention to works of two painters, namely Picasso and Monet. 24 infants were randomly assigned to either a Monet or a Picasso condition. In the Picasso condition, infants were habituated to paintings by Picasso and were then presented with an unfamiliar painting by Picasso and a painting by Monet (and vice versa in the Monet condition). Results suggest that infants discriminate between different paintings and painting styles but that they display a spontaneous preference for paintings by Picasso. We are currently conducting control experiments investigating infants' basis for their Picasso preference.

Using inertial information alone to estimate linear self-displacement with varying durations of constant velocity

Campos, Jennifer *Inst. Biologische Kybernetik, Max-Planck-Institut, Tübingen, Germany* **Reimann, Michael** *Biological Cybernetics, Max Planck Institute, Tübingen, Germany* **Beykirch, Karl** *Biological Cybernetics, Max Planck Institute, Tübingen, Germany* **Butler, John** *Biological Cybernetics, Max Planck Institute, Tübingen, Germany* **Bülthoff, Heinrich** *Biological Cybernetics, Max Planck Institute, Tübingen, Germany*

During self-motion in the absence of vision and proprioception, inertial information can be used to compare different magnitudes of linear self-displacement. However, during periods of constant velocity, no inertial information is available, thus, how perceived displacement is evaluated during different durations of constant velocity is unknown. Here, participants judged which of two inertially experienced distances was longer. Three durations of constant velocity (1, 3, 5s) were included in order to evaluate whether estimates of distance would vary as a function of constant velocity duration. The results are described using a model which accounts for both duration and peak velocity.

Reversal of typical effect of task switching for random switch

Carmona, Encarna *Neurociencia y CC de la Salud, University of Almeria, La Cañada de San Urbano, Spain* **Plaza-Ayllón, Vanesa** *Neurociencia y CC de la Salud, University of Almeria, La Cañada de San Urbano ALME, Spain* **Alvarez, Dolores** *Neurociencia y CC de la Salud, University of Almeria, La Cañada de San Urbano ALME, Spain* **Noguera, Carmen** *Neurociencia y CC de la Salud, University of Almeria, La Cañada de San Urbano ALME, Spain*

In this study we used a task switching paradigm. Shift between tasks was associated with an impairment in people's performance know as switch cost. This cost is characterized for an increment in reaction time (RT) and errors compared to a situation in which no shift is required. The relevant experimental conditions are: predictable task switching (AABBAA...) and random task switching (ABBABA...). In the predictable condition, we found the classic results; an increase in TR for switching block (general cost) and an increase in TR for switch trial in switching block (specific cost). Nevertheless, in situations of random, we obtain the reversal typical effect in specific cost. We conclude that the expectancies are important for the use of control strategies.

Anger, depression and aggression in children: A comorbidity study

Carrasco, Miguel *Personalidad, Universidad UNED, Madrid, Spain* **del Barrio, Victoria** *Personalidad, Universidad UNED, Madrid, Spain* **Gordillo, Rodolfo** *Personalidad, Universidad UNED, Madrid, Spain*

The purpose of this study was to explore the comorbidity between depression and aggression in children and adolescents from Clark and Watsons model. The sample was composed by 721 children and adolescents from public schools (Mean age = 12.6; SD = 1.44; 308 boy). Results shown that: (a) depression, anger and aggression were significant correlated; (b) depressive children and aggressive children shown both higher levels of aggression as well as depression; (c) depression and aggression shared the emotion of anger and refusal a underlying common structure and (d) a three model factors were better adapted to the structure of comorbidity proposal.

Future time perspective and education: Organizational and pedagogical challenges

Carvalho, Renato Gil *Dept. de Psicologia, DRE/UMa, Campanário, Portugal*

The study approached students' future time perspective (FTP), with the goal of characterize it, analyze its behaviour expression and debate which impact it can have in educative interventions. Participants were 9th grade students from a rural school in Madeira, Portugal. There were used both quantitative and qualitative research techniques. Results have shown a consolidation of pupils' FTP during school year, especially when they've experienced specific activities, such as orientation procedures. Results demonstrate as well the association between FTP and academic success, and emphasize some agents' role, namely teachers and school psychology services, in the construction of student's life projects.

The Azorean Schizophrenia high risk study

Carvalho, Célia *Ciências da Educação, Universidade dos Açores, Ponta Delgada - Açores, Portugal* **Nunes Caldeira, Suzana** *Ciências da Educação, Universidade dos Açores, Ponta Delgada - Azores, Portugal* **Medeiros, Helena** *SUNY Upstate Medical Universit, Center for Psychiatric and Mol, Siracuse, USA* **Pato, Carlos** *Center for Psychiatric and Mol, SUNY Upstate Medical Universit, Ponta Delgada - Açores, USA* **Pato, Michelle** *Department of Psychiatry, SUNY Upstate Medical Universit, Ponta Delgada - Açores, Portugal*

The most significant risk for developing schizophrenia is being related to a patient suffering from the same illness. This pattern argues strongly for a genetic component in the transmission of schizophrenia. Early experiences of care and abuse and self perceptions in adult life also seem to be related to the onset of the disease. Recently, we have identified a number of promising genetic linkages in the families we have been studying in the Azores. Now we are studying personal, relational and social variables in the onset of illness in this high-risk population, using inquiry methods.

Automatic and voluntary orienting of attention in visual search: Two independent processes?

Casagrande, Maria *Dipartimento di Psicologia, Roma, Italy* **Marin, Ioana Alexandra** *Dipartimento di Psicologia, Sapienza - University of Rome, Roma, Italy* **Mereu, Stefania** *Dipartimento di Psicologia, Sapienza - University of Rome, Roma, Italy* **Marotta, Andrea** *Dipartimento di Psicologia, Sapienza - University of Rome, Roma, Italy* **Martella, Diana** *Dipartimento di Psicologia, Sapienza - University of Rome, Roma, Italy*

Eighteen subjects performed two visual search tasks, characterized by different cognitive load, which required to identify a vertical segment between other segments, all with the same orientation, and a distractor that could be presented or not. By varying the orientation of both targets and distractors, it was manipulated the salience and the similarity between them, deemed considerable for bottom-up and top-down components respectively. Results showed a salience by similarity interaction, suggesting that, while in high cognitive load conditions endogenous and exogenous components

can act independently, when the task requires mild attentional resources, the two processes give rise to an interaction.

Effects of vigilance decrease on exogeneous and endogeneous visual orienting

Casagrande, Maria *Dipartimento di Psicologia, Roma, Italy* **Martella, Diana** *Dipartimento di Psicologia, Roma, Italy* **Mereu, Stefania** *Dipartimento di Psicologia, "Sapienza" Università, Roma, Italy* **Marotta, Andrea** *Dipartimento di Psicologia, "Sapienza" Università, Roma, Italy* **Bottaro, Giusi** *Dipartimento di Psicologia, "Sapienza" Università, Roma, Italy*

It is an aim of this study to assess whether a decrese of vigilance, obtained by means of a sleep deprivation, affects automatic and voluntary orienting of attention. Visual orienting was induced by both central (endogenous) and peripheral (exogenous) cues. Results show that the decrease of vigilance do not affect peripheral orienting, but induces a selective reduction of the facilitation effects, in the central cueing task. The specific impairment in the ability to intentionally follow the cue, suggests that the reducion of allerting produces a worsening of the voluntary control of attention.

Convergent validity between the dentist's report on dental treatment anxiety and the patient's self-report

Caycedo, Claudia *Psychology, Fundación Universitaria Konrad, Bogotá, Colombia* **Cortes, Omar Fernando** *Psychology, Fundación Universitaria Konrad, Bogotá, Colombia* **Caycedo, Martha Lucia** *Odontología, Colegio Odontológico Colombian, Bogotá, Colombia* **Palencia, Rafael** *Odontología, Colegio Odontologico Colombian, Bogotá, Colombia* **Barahona, German** *Odontología, Colegio Odontologico Colombian, Bogotá, Colombia*

The convergent validity between the dentist's report and the patient's self- report concerning dental treatment anxiety is analyzed. The sample was composed of 132 dentists and 913 patients. A standarized interview was administered to the dentist and both MDAS and SDAI rating scales were administered to the patients. The results, which showed the reports to be highly convergent, were analyzed by using descriptive, corelational statistics, and a model of structural equations which allowed to identify the main behavioral anxiety indicators for the dentist as well as the intervention strategies obtained from them.

Variations of the level of alertness and performance during a prolonged driving simulation task: Effects of rest

Chóliz, Mariano *Psicologia Basica, Universidad de Valencia, Valencia, Spain* **Tejero, Pilar** *Psicología Básica, University of Valencia, Valencia, Spain* **Roca, Javier** *INTRAS, University of Valencia, Valencia, Spain* **Pastor, Gemma** *Psicología Básica, University of Valencia, Valencia, Spain*

Several factors has been linked to the appearance of drowsiness, reduced alertness and passive fatigue during a prolonged monotonous task. We studied the variations of the level of alertness and performance during a prolonged driving simulation task in habitual drivers. Then we compared those results with results obtained in a different group of participants, habitual drivers too, but who were allowed to rest by the middle of the task duration. Results are discussed with respect to the recommendation that drivers should interrupt driving to overcome the fatigue caused by prolonged driving.

The influence of parent-child relationship and self-efficacy on quality of life among university students and their parents

Chang, Woo-Giy Education, Inha University, Inchon, Republic of Korea *Park, Young-Shin* Dept. of Education, Inha University, Incheon, Republic of Korea *Kim, Uichol* Business administration, Inha University, Inchon, Republic of Korea

This study examines the influence of parent-child relationship and self-efficacy on quality of life among university students and their parents. A total 873 participants (a matched sample of 291 university students and their parents) completed a questionnaire. The results indicate students' quality of life is positively influenced by self-efficacy and emotional support received from their parents. Their fathers' quality of life is positively influenced self-efficacy and by emotional support received from their children. Their mothers' quality of life is positively influenced by self-efficacy and emotional support received from their spouse. For university students, relational efficacy was the best predictor of quality of life.

Examining the components of worry-trait

Chang, Ben-Sheng Psychology, Soochow University, Taipei, Taiwan *Chung, Shih-Ming* Psychology, Soochow University, Taipei, Taiwan

Three core components of worry (excessive worry, uncontrollable worry, and intolerance of uncertainty) are defined by many scholars. The purpose of the study is to test the construct validity of worry. Taiwanese college students (248 students) filled out worry, anxiety, and depression questionnaires. Results of the study are as follows: (a) Worry with three core features is supported; (b) Construct validity and reliability of the worry trait scale are supported; (c) The worry trait scale is better than the PSWQ in validity and reliability; (d) The worry-trait scale is more effective than the PSWQ in screening GAD.

Verbal violence towards homosexual individuals: How is it justified in a Greek population?

Chiotis, Georgios Dept. of Psychology, City University, London, United Kingdom

The present study investigated people's justification of violence towards Lesbian and Gay individuals, and its relation to overt and covert homophobia. A story portraying an incident of verbal abuse was created along with a questionnaire measuring attitudes towards these events, complemented with the Wright, Adams, & Bernat Homophobia Scale (1999). The story varied in the sex and the sexual orientation of the victim, creating 10 groups in which 700 students were assigned. Results showed that participants justified more easily verbal violence towards Gay & Lesbian individuals, and this was correlated with their measured homophobia levels.

Remembering, normal aging and executive function

Clarys, David Dept. of Psychology, University of Tours, Tours, France *Bugaïska, Aurélia* Department of Psychology, University of Tours, TOURS, France *Tapia, Géraldine* Department of Psychology, University of Tours, TOURS, France *Baudouin, Alexia* Department of Psychology, University of Tours, TOURS, France

Objectives: In this study we investigated the relations between the executive functions and age-related decline in remembering. Methods: Younger and older adults undertook a word recognition test including the Remember/Know/Guess procedure and were assessed with three specific executive task (updating, shifting and inhibition) and a complex executive task. Results: Older adults exhibited a decline in the number of "R" responses but not in the number of "K" responses. Analyses showed that controlling for updating function strongly

removed the age-related variance in remembering. Conclusions: These findings support the idea of a central role of updating decline in understanding age-related deficit in remembering.

Threats of climate change can increase authoritarian tendencies

Cohrs, Christopher Inst. für Sozialpsychologie, Universität Jena, Jena, Germany *Fritsche, Immo* Dept. of Social Psychology, University of Jena, Jena, Germany *Bauer, Judith* Dept. of Social Psychology, University of Erlangen, Erlangen, Germany

Threats to social order and stability can increase authoritarianism, because authoritarian responses may be perceived as functional to counter specific threats. We tested the further assumption that even an unrelated type of threat can produce such effects. We manipulated (N=44 students) the salience of threats of climate change to Germany and found increased authoritarianism and negativity toward deviant groups. The effect on authoritarianism was mediated by perceived threats of climate change. The results point to previously neglected possible social consequences of climate change. Ongoing research examines the potential moderating role of how threats of climate change are framed.

Mental bipolarity and personnel development practices in organizations

Colautti, Christian Università IULM, Milano, Italy *Monducci, Valentina* Facoltà di Psicologia, Università degli Studi Firenze, Firenze, Italy *Bellotto, Massimo* Facoltà di Lettere e Filosofia, Università degli Studi Verona, Milano, Italy

Drawing from Group-analytic (Napolitani, 1987) and Work&Organization Psychology theories (Bellotto & Trentini, 1988), we hypothesize a new framework and explore, through a storytelling approach, whether managers tend to re-actualize four relational orientations/polarities (conservation, innovation, uniqueness and openness) with their co-workers, corresponding to relational models introjected during early years. With ATLAS.ti 4.2 software, we qualitatively analyzed 30 stories by managers attending managerial seminars and found a prevailing innovation relational orientation. This method could be used to support managers to become aware of their relational styles and to promote co-workers harmonic development through an equilibrium between practices related to different relational polarities.

The role of attention in object and gist perception

Constantinou, Elena Kokkinotrimithia, Cyprus *Koushiou, Maria* Department of Psychology, University of Cyprus, Strovolos, Nicosia, Cyprus *Avraamides, M.N.*

A dual-task experiment was conducted to investigate low and high level of processing under conditions of inattention. Thirty-seven students performed an attentionally demanding central task while responding to a secondary task, that is object categorization (high level) or gist identification (low level) in natural scenes. Central task performance was comparable with participants being unexpectedly more accurate on object than gist categorization (p< .001). A second experiment comparing the secondary task stimuli confirmed our initial results suggesting that saliency of object figures facilitates their recognition and renders gist perception more difficult contradicting previous literature.

Self esteem and affective temperaments in psychiatric nurses

Cordeiro, Raul CESM, Escola Sup. Saude Portalegre, Portalegre, Portugal *Sónia, Galinha* Educ. e Currículo, Esc. Sup. Educação de Santarém, Santarém, Portugal

Analysing Self Esteem and Affective Temperaments of Nurses in Psychiatric and Mental Health Services, have a crucial importance, because this

fact will influence many phenomena's in nursing practice. A total of n=47 nurses, of both sexes, with average age of 38,57 years, working in Mental Health and Psychiatry Departments. In the Questionnaire, were introduced some measures: TEMPS-A Scale (Akiskal, 1998), and Scale of Self Personal Appreciation Scale (Ribeiro, 2006). The results indicate that the population, have a Hyperthymic Temperament. Affective temperament of nurses seems to be a good predictor of leadership capacity in violence situation at psychiatric services.

Development and initial validation of an infant rearing pactices instrument

Cortés-Moreno, Assol DIP Aprendizaje Humano, UNAM FES Iztacala, Tlalnepantla, Mexico *Romero Sánchez, Patricia* DIP Aprendizaje Humano, UNAM FES Iztacala, Tlalnepantla, Edo. Mex, Mexico

Rearing practices moderate undernourishment effects on psychological child development. This study describes development and psychometric data in support of Responsive Practices and Stimulation Questionnaire (CuPRE), a caregiver-report measure of actions oriented to assure the survival and child development. The initial items were derived from interviews to 48 caregivers. Item reduction and reliability were complete with a sample of 242 caregivers. Principal components analysis yielded a five-factor structure (composed of 23 items), accounting for 49.9% of total variance. The CuPRE was found to have good internal consistency (alpha = 0,83). The results suggest the CuPRE can be a useful instrument to value rearing practices.

Demographics, rearing practices and health history: Its relation with nutrition and child development

Cortés-Moreno, Assol DIP Aprendizaje Humano, UNAM FES Iztacala, Tlalnepantla, Mexico *Avilés Torres, Ana Laura* DIP Aprendizaje Humano, UNAM FES Iztacala, Tlalnepantla, Edo. Mex, Mexico

The effects of undernourishment on psychological development varies according psychosocial factors. This study assesses the impact of demographic, organic and rearing variables on nourishment and psychological development in children aged complementary feeding. A sample of 124 child-caregiver dyads from four different socioeconomic and nutritional index communities participed. Anthopometrics and child development were assessed. Demographics, rearing practices, and family health were measured as possible factors. Multiple regression models obtained illustrate a major impact of birth weight on nourishment condition. This factor is followed by demographic and rearing variables, which become more important for psychological child development.

The predictive power of short term goals in academic adjustment

Cretu, Romeo Zeno Dept. of Psychology, University of Bucharest, Bucharest, Romania *Amza, Madalina* Psychology, University of Bucharest, Bucharest, Romania

The present research, undertakes a multi-level analysis of the role that many goals categories, defined as person variable, have in the differential adaptation of students (N=332) at academic requests. The goals were considered repeated measures nested in person and formed the 1st level of our hierarchical analysis. Three personality superfactors – extraversion, conscientiousness and neuroticism – were introduced at the 2nd level of our analysis, with the aim of investigating the between-subject variation. The results of hierarchical analysis show that associative relations are not identical for all the persons. The personality's superfactors succeeded explaining a significant part of the intercepts variation.

The use of bodywork in the psychotherapeutic context

Cronan, Kerry Richard Counselling Centre Ltd., Professional Consulting and, Eagle Farm, Australia
The use of the body in the healing process has a long history in the treatment of human beings. The integration of the body into a recognized psychological therapeutic process is slowly gaining recognition from the work of the Touch Research Institute led by Dr Tiffany Field. There has also been another significant recent study in a prestigious psychological journal, and a new journal has been published devoted to Body, Dance and Movement in Psychotherapy. Arguments concerning the physical and consequential psychological advantages of bodywork will be introduced and testimonials presented.

Effects of instructional precision and frequency feedback on instrumental and verbal performances during training and transfer sessions in adults

Cruz Alaniz, Yuria Posgrado Cs del Comportamiento, Universidad de Guadalajara, Guadalajara, Mexico Ortiz, Gerardo CEIC-CUCBA, Universidad de Guadalajara, Guadalajara, Mexico
In the present study, we explored the effects of a) the precision of the response component of pre-contact descriptions (i.e. instructions) given in training and transfer test and, b) feedback density on instrumental and verbal performances (i.e. rules) of pre-graduated students, in a first order matching-to-sample task. Results show better instrumental and verbal transfer performances in subjects that received specific and pertinent instructions, suggesting interesting implications about teaching-learning processes.

Intergroup prejudice of immigrants and natives in Spain: The influence of ethno cultural origin and its relation with acculturation process

Cuadrado, Isabel Dept. de Psicologia Social, Open University Madrid, Madrid, Spain Navas, Marisol Ciencias Humanas y Sociales, University of Almeria, Almeria, Spain Carmen, Gomez-Berrocal Psicologia Social, University of Granada, Granada, Spain Antonio, Rojas Ciencias Humanas y Sociales, University of Almeria, Almeria, Spain Oscar, Lozano Psychology, University of Huelva, Huelva, Spain
Starting from the Relative Acculturation Extended Model (Navas et al., 2004, 2005), this paper is focused on the relation between prejudice and the acculturation attitudes (Berry et al., 1989) preferred by various groups of immigrants and by the native population. There participate 1389 Spanish persons and 1293 immigrant persons (397 from Maghreb; 343 from Sub-Saharan Africa; 293 from Romania; and 260 from Ecuador), all of them residing in municipalities from Eastern and South Spain. Results show that the natives who prefer "exclusion" or "segregation", present the highest levels of prejudice towards the out-group, while those who prefer "integration" show the lowest levels. This pattern is shared by the studied immigrants groups

Parent training for families with mental retarded children

Cuzzocrea, Francesca Scienze dell'Educazione, University of Messina, Messina, Italy Larcan, Rosalba Scienze dell'Educazione, University of Messina, Messina, Italy Oliva, Patrizia Scienze dell'Educazione, University of Messina, Messina, Italy
The aim of this research was to explore parent-child interaction processes. Particularly, it was experimented a parent training in order to: a) modify wrong parents' believes on mental retardation and behavioral child's problems; b) reduce parental stress and increase parenting skills. 24 couples of parent with mental retarded children were tested. The experimental group was trained with communication and self-regulation strategies, and beha-vioral and educational techniques for child management. The results proved the parent training efficacy. Compare to parents of control group, the experimental one showed significant exchanges in perception of children problems, lower stress level and greater parental competences.

Creative movement performance of Slovak dancers

Daniskova, Klaudia Dept. of Psychology, Catholic University, Ruzomberok, Slovak Republic
Creativity as a personal trait of dancers was mostly measured by figural tests. Researches were not focused on specific creativity domain of dancers. The study identifies factors in creative movement performance of dancers. Torrance Figural Test of Creative Thinking and Test of Creative Movement and Motor Associations were implemented with research sample of 146 subjects. By factor analysis we found out that originality, elaboration, and stimulative freedom participate on creative movement performance. We hypothesized and found that criterions of figural and motor creativity are different. Answers on motor stimuli and movement performance represent particular category of divergent production.

Associations between nutrition and cognitive functioning in older adults

Danthiir, Vanessa CSIRO Human Nutrition, Adelaide, Australia Wilson, Carlene Human Nutrition, CSIRO, Adelaide, Australia Nettelbeck, Ted Psychology, University of Adelaide, Adelaide, Australia Burns, Nick Psychology, University of Adelaide, Adelaide, Australia Wittert, Gary Medicine, University of Adelaide, Adelaide, Australia
Research indicates a possible role for nutrition in the maintenance of cognitive functioning in older age. We are running a parallel double-blind randomised controlled 18-month clinical trial (N=400), supplementing normal community-dwelling older adults (65-90 years) with omega-3 fatty acids. Cognitive functioning is assessed comprehensively; factor scores represent the domains of working memory, fluid intelligence, short-term memory, long-term memory and retrieval, inhibition, processing speed and perceptual speed. These results report the baseline associations between the cognitive domains and various nutrients (e.g., omega-3 fatty acids, B vitamins), reflecting both systemic status and intake estimated from food frequency questionnaires, and health-related bio-markers.

Action monitoring and perfectionism in severe major depression

de Bruijn, Ellen R.A. Nijmegen Institute for Cognit., Radboud University Nijmegen, Nijmegen, Netherlands Schrijvers, Didier CAPRI, University of Antwerp, Wilrijk, Belgium Maas, Yvonne NICI, University of Nijmegen, Nijmegen, Netherlands Hulstijn, Wouter CAPRI, University of Antwerp, Wilrijk, Belgium Sabbe, Bernard CAPRI, University of Antwerp, Wilrijk, Belgium
Given the reported impact of affective distress on the error-related negativity (ERN) and error positivity (Pe) in healthy subjects, this study will explore the effect of perfectionism on action monitoring in severe major depression. Severely depressed patients (n=35) participated in an ERN session and completed the Concern over Mistakes (CM) and Doubt about Actions (DA) subscales of a perfectionism questionnaire. Analyses revealed larger amplitudes for the ERN in high DA patients, and for the Pe in high CM patients relative to low DA and CM participants respectively, indicating that action monitoring in severe depression indeed is influenced by perfectionism traits.

The development of the Workplace Self-Directed Learning Scale

de Bruin, Karina Psychology, University of Johannesburg, Johannesburg, South Africa
Self-directed learning is highly applicable in the rapidly changing world of work. The aim of this research was to develop an instrument to measure self-directed learning in the workplace. Participants were 280 employees from various corporate environments. The initial 22 items that reflected the underlying construct of self-directedness were fitted to the Rasch rating scale model. The final questionnaire contains 14 items which measures a single unidimensional construct. Cronbach's coefficient alpha for the scale was 0.92. The instrument is useful to practitioners in workplace settings as part of their strategies to increase self-directedness in employees.

The relationship between self-directed learning and career adjustment amongst women employees in South Africa

de Bruin, Karina Psychology, University of Johannesburg, Johannesburg, South Africa
The aim of this research was to investigate the relationship between self-directed learning and various factors related to the career adjustment of women. The Workplace Self-Directed Learning Scale and the Career Attitudes and Strategies Inventory were completed by 180 working women. The instruments yielded acceptable Cronbach's coefficient alphas > 0.70. Pearson's product-moment correlation coefficients revealed positive relationships between self-directed learning and work involvement, skills development and dominant style respectively and a negative relationship between self-directed learning and career worries. The results of the study have important implications for the facilitation of the career adjustment and development of women employees.

Visual and auditory ARAS (Advanced Rider Assistance Systems) in road safety decision-making

Di Stasi, Leandro Luigi Experimental Psychology, University of Granada, Granada, Spain Serrano Jiménez, Jesus Inst. Experimental Psychology, Universidad de Granada, Granada, Spain Álvarez, Vanessa Experimental Psychology, University of Granada, Granada, Spain Garcia Retamero, Rocio Experimental Psychology, University of Granada, Granada, Spain Antolí, Adoracion Experimental Psychology, University of Granada, Granada, Spain Catena, Andres Psicologia Experimental, Universidad de Granada, Granada, Spain
This study shows that auditory and visual warnings can either facilitate or slow down the detection of risk in a simulated car-driving scene. The visual warning cued both location and time point of the scene target; auditory warnings indicated only the point in time of the target. The slowest reaction time was observed when both auditory and visual warnings were present, and the scene was risky. This effect was independent of the type of auditory cue: speech message, auditory icon or abstract sound. Our results indicate that simultaneous warnings from different sensory modalities possibly will impair the detection of risk

In-group favouritism in minimal group situations: Does competition change automatic inter-group evaluation?

Dickel, Nina AE05 Social Psychology, University of Bielefeld, Bielefeld, Germany Degner, Juliane Department of Psychology, Saarland University, Saarbrücken, Germany Wentura, Dirk Department of Psychology, Saarland University, Saarbrücken, Germany
Within a minimal group setting, we tested the effect of competitiveness of inter-group context on automatic inter-group evaluations assessed by masked

affective priming. Participants were assigned to minimal groups allegedly according to their performance in a perception test. To manipulate intergroup context, they watched a recording of a computer game played by in- and out-group team members with high vs. low competitiveness. For high competitiveness, we predicted dissociation between possessor- and other-relevant evaluations. The competitiveness manipulation did affect neither explicit nor automatic inter-group evaluation. However, we found explicit and automatic in-group favouritism, only for other-relevant evaluations. Theoretical implications are discussed.

Psychophysiological prerequisites of effectiveness of advertising impact

Dikiy, Igor Dept. of Psychology, Southern Federal University, Rostov-on-Don, Russia

The objective of the research is to study interrelationship between effective advertising impact and individual psychophysiological consumers peculiarities. 32 students took part in the research. Research methods - semantic differential, Torrens's techniques, gaploscopic techniques (Talanov), techniques of functional brain asymmetry (Tsagarelly) and Aminov-Shalven Preference Questionnaire. A degree of advertising effectiveness with predominating emotional impact is interrelated with a low degree of psychic activity and weak tension. The degree of advertising effectiveness with rational effect is interrelated with high activity of the left hemisphere and predominance of creative approach to information processing in consumers of advertising products.

The effect of implicit priming on risk investment

Ding, Xianfeng Department of Psychology, Huazhong Normal University, Wuhan, People's Republic of China Guo, Dongdong Department of Psychology, Huazhong Normal University, Wuhan, People's Republic of China

This study examined the effect of implicit priming on risk investment in a simulated risk investment game. 89 college students were divided into 3 random groups. The first group is called "risk group" which is expected to be induce risky attitude, the second is called "conservative group" which is expected to be induce the conservative attitude. The third is control group. "Unrelated Events Priming" is used to induce different risk attitudes. The results indicated that the effect of implicit priming is significant. The risk behaviors in risk group are more notable than conservative group and control group.

Changes on parental representations

Diniz, Eva Lisboa, Portugal Rocha, Ana Paula Psicologia, ISPA, Lisboa, Portugal

The study aims to identify the impact that the transition from husband/wife to father/ mother role have on parent's representations. Participants were four parents-baby triads who answered the Interview-R (Stern et al., 1989) during the pregnancy (28th -32nd weeks) and eight weeks after the baby's birth. Although data cannot be generalised, the results appeared to be interesting: all parents showed changes on their self-descriptions, on the relationship with their own parents and on the perception they had about the baby. Findings reveal that pregnancy plays an important role on modifying personal's internal representations. Keywords – Parent's representations, pregnancy, parental role changes.

Social / emotional functioning as predictive of Kindergarten readiness and success

Dixon, David Dept. of Psychology, Missouri State University, Springfield, USA

This study contrasted social / emotional vs. conceptual / language / motor development as predictors of kindergarten readiness and success.

Just before and at the start of kindergarten, children were administered the Devereaux Early Childhood Assessment (DECA; social / emotional development) and the DIAL-3 (conceptual / language / motor development) and assessed for K-readiness. Near the end of kindergarten, children were reassessed for K-readiness and evaluated for K-success. Both DECA and DIAL-3 predicted concurrent readiness (R = .715) and later readiness and success (Rs = .574 and .583, respectively). In stepwise analyses, DECA scores ranked above DIAL-3 scores as predictors.

The integrated computerized system in the analysis and prediction of the human behaviour

Dorofte, Ionel Dept. of Education, Technical University of Iasi, Iasi, Romania Dorofte, Tatiana Dept. of Education, Technical University of Iasi, Iasi, Romania

The beginning of the hereby research was the dissatisfaction offered by the classical psychometrical diagnosis for the drivers especially. We have developed methodological and instrumental improvements in three directions: 1. More complex interactive psychometrical tests. A simulator auto oriented to psycho diagnosis was made and experimented. 2. A new methodology for statistic analysis based on the new concept of the «Mobile Static Functions», internationally published with the title of «Statistica Nova» [«Nova Statistics »]. 3. New metrics of human performances based on an informational interpretation of the empirical data curve. Being corroborated in an Integrate Computerized System, we succeed in obtaining a validity coefficient of more than 0.5.

Successful ageing: A psychological approach

Duarte, Mafalda UNIFAI, UNIFAI, Porto, Portugal Paúl, Constança UNIFAI, UNIFAI, Porto, Portugal

Objectives: Check which are the dimensions mentioned by elders as contributes to ageing well. Method: apply the instrument – Perception about Successful Ageing – to 51 elders, from 65 to 75 years old. Results: From the data analysis (SPSS,15.0) it is shown that, at first it is associated to the health state. Later it associates with variables of psychological aspect, as the ability to face the implicit demands of the ageing process itself – associated coping mechanisms; absence of feelings of loneliness and a balanced balance between gains and losses. Conclusion: It assumes a multidimensional perspective, in which the psychological dimension is very important. Key-words: Elders, Successful Ageing; Adaptation Strategies.

The dynamics of changes of executive functions in patients with traumatic brain injuries

Dzierlak, Ewa Dept. of Psychology, University of Warsaw, Warsaw, Poland

The purpose of the study was to observe the dynamics of changes of executive functions in patients with light and mild traumatic frontal lobes injuries. Patients with changes indicated in CT, were presented with a set of neuropsychological methods (i.e. Tower of London, Trail Making Test), three times during two weeks following the brain trauma. Dynamics of change may differ according to individual factors (Leon-Carrion et al.), however in results obtained the general pattern of improvement may be observed (F (1; 12) = 2.5, p<0.05), which gives hope for the future evaluation of methods in neuropsychological rehabilitation.

Evaluation of a psychoeducational boardgame to promote gender equity and children rights

Echeverria, Rebelin Facultad de Psicología, Univ. Autónoma de Yucatán, Mérida, Mexico Castillo León, Teresita Facultad de Psicología, Univ. Autónoma de Yucatán, Mérida YUcatán, Mexico

The aim for this paper is to present the evaluation of a psychoeducational board game designed to promote gender equity and children rights through discussing about integral sexuality and a life free of violence. The board game was designed through a participatory action research methodology with the participation of children, parents and professors of elementary schools in Merida, Yucatan, Mexico. The board game is described as well as the evaluation of the construction process and its application. The results are discussed considering content, structure, language, format and utility.

Increasing traffic safety concerning individual differences

Ehrenpfordt, Ingmar Inst. of Transportation Sy., DLR, Braunschweig, Germany Kullack, Anke IPMB, University of Technology, Braunschweig, Germany Eggert, Frank IPMB, University of Technology, Braunschweig, Germany

Traffic Safety can be increased by refining the typical assistance systems. Route calculation with reference to individual differences will lead to better driving performance on the generated route. This is due to a possible reduction of individual stress and allows choosing stress less infrastructural based situations associated with less stress thereby enhancing the driver's performance. Two new basic route planning characteristics were developed: one to enable a more stress less routing and the other one as a training mode to increase drivers' experience. Stressful situations were identified and known avoidance strategies of elderly people were additionally considered.

Pooling unshared information: An experiment comparing two different type of computer-mediated group discussions with face-to-face group discussion

Eisele, Per School of Managment, Blekinge Inst. of Technology, Ronneby, Sweden

The aim of the study was to examine effects of computer-mediated information on the use of unshared information during group discussion. The participants (N=77) were psychology students (37 men and 40 women with a mean age of 28,4) that were randomised into three different conditions, IT based on writing, IT based on talking and face-to-face interaction. The result indicate that IT based on writing affect the use of unshared information but not IT based on talking, as compared to face-to-face interaction. Discussions of this result are being provided.

A field experiment examining effects of an intervention to increase work group effectivity on role stress (ambiguity and conflict)

Eisele, Per School of Managment, Blekinge Inst. of Technology, Ronneby, Sweden

The aim of the present study was to examine a social psychological intervention effects on attitudes toward role ambiguity and role clarity. The experimental manipulation consisted of two different type of interventions (role relevant and role neutral) compared with a control group. The sample consisted of 4128 participants. Result showed, contrary to the hypotheses, that both role ambiguity and role conflict increased after the intervention. But data collected six months later showed that role stress (ambiguity and conflict) not only decreased but did so significantly below the first measurement.

A two-year tracking study of the language awareness of immigrant mothers' children

Fang, Chin-Ya Center for Teacher Education, National Kaohsiung Normal Univ, Kaohsiung City, Taiwan Leou, Yea-Mei General Education, Tainan Institute of Nursing, Tainan, Taiwan

In Taiwan, the number of foreign spouse's children increases with years. The Study attempts to realize the difference of language awareness ability among these children, and explore whether socioeconomic status would be related to the difference. The study gets the information by tracking for two years with the materials, including phonological awareness test, character awareness test, word awareness test, word recognition test and comprehension test. Besides the results of two-year tracking, some suggestions are provided.

Teenage mothers: Which relationships in comparison with adult mothers?
Faoro-Mottrie, Cindy Clinic psychology, Université Libre de bruxelles, Brussel, Germany *Cailleau, Françoise* Clinic psychology, Université Libre de bruxelles, Brussel, Belgium *De Coster, Lotta* Clinic psychology, Université Libre de bruxelles, Brussel, Germany
According to the literature, we expect that first pregnancy and motherhood for teenage mothers will act as an operator of change in the relationships with their parents ; whereas these relationships would rather take place in a process of continuity for adult mothers. Across eight case studies based on semi-directive discussions and "génogrammes", we will demonstrate that results will be confirmed for most of the teenage mothers and for all of the adult mothers.

Issues, goals and methods to succeed in Educational Psychology: Defies from a globalised world
Ferreira de Almeida, Ana Cristina Fac. Psic. e Ciências da Educ., University of Coimbra, Coimbra, Portugal
Educational Psychology fostered in a changing world invites pointing out major goals, issues and focal methods. Our hypothesis is for succeed, academe and professionally, educational psychology ought to be comprehensive, unified. Reviewing literature and consulting psychologists in educational settings, from pre-school to life span opportunities of education, from classrooms to self-helping groups, we've based the analysis on qualitative research. Defy of inclusion in multiple, unpredictable contexts and of planning or solve influential society problems with impact in health, justice, ...evolve levels of cognitive, emotional and moral skills requiring educational psychologists to excel in projects at the modern global world.

Validity of the Work Efficiency Test
Fischer, Anika Institut of Psychology, University of Magdeburg, Magdeburg, Germany *Seidel, Kristin* Institute of Psychology, University of Magdeburg, Magdeburg, Germany *Süß, Heinz-Martin* Institute of Psychology, University of Magdeburg, Magdeburg, Germany *Kersting, Martin* Institute of Psychology, RWTH Aachen, Aachen, Germany
Efficient working behaviour and routine development are important demands in clerical occupations. The Work Efficiency Test (AET, Seidel & Kersting, in preparation) is assumed to simulate processes of skill acquisition (e.g. Ackerman, 1989) and to predict training performance. 77 bank trainees worked on the computerised AET, tasks of the well established Berlin Intelligence Structure Test (Jäger et al., 1997) and the NEO-FFI questionnaire. Training performance was measured by supervisor-ratings and grades in vocational school. Autoregressive trajectory models and regression analyses indicate routine development during task completion. AET performance is significantly correlated with trainees' grades confirming its importance for aptitude diagnostic.

Auditory temporal judgments
Fostick, Leah Ariel University Center, Ariel, Israel *Ben-Artzi, Elisheva* Psychology, Kinneret College, Jordan Valley, Israel *Babkoff, Harvey* Psychology, Askeolon College, Askelon, Israel
Objectives: To compare young-controls, dyslexics and elderly individuals in judgment of spectral TOJ (temporal order of different frequency tones) at varying inter-stimulus intervals. Methods: 46 young-controls, 51 dyslexics, and 29 elderly subjects were tested on cognitive and psychophysical tasks, including spectral TOJ. Results: The number of high- accuracy vs. low-accuracy responders within groups differed significantly: Young subjects, 50%-50%; dyslexics and elderly, 25%-75%. Hearing thresholds, education, cognitive ability and speech comprehension did not predict TOJ accuracy. Stimulus duration (5-40 msec) predicted the number of high-accuracy responders for all groups. Conclusions: Spectral TOJ is a frequency-modulation paradigm which improves with stimulus duration.

Starters in the gay scene: Sexual behavior of young gay men at the start of their coming-out
Franssens, Dirk Work & Social Psychology, Maastricht University, Maastricht, Netherlands *Hospers, Harm J.* Work & Social Psychology, Maastricht University, Maastricht, Netherlands
Objective: To assess rates of sexual risk behavior of young gay men (YGM) during coming-out. Method: Participants (N=185) within one year of coming-out, completed an online questionnaire on sexual risk behavior, and on the role of internet in partner selection. Results: YGM reported substantial levels of risk behavior with steady and casual partners. Interestingly, the most common sexual partners were "regulars" -, i.e., acquaintances with whom they regularly had sex, but not a steady relationship. Internet was an important source for finding sexual partners. Conclusion: These findings have important implications for safer sex prevention efforts, which will be discussed.

The education of personality and development of skills for life: A relationship recurrent training school student of the media
García, Rubén Area de Psicología, UAEH, San Agustin Tlaxiaca, Mexico *Cáceres Mesa, Maritza* Area de Psicología, UAEH, San Agustin Tlaxiaca, Hgo,Méxi, Mexico *Romero Ramírez, Mucio Alejandro* Area de Psicología, UAEH, San Agustin Tlaxiaca, Hgo,Méxi, Mexico *Ortega Andrade, Norma Angelica* Area de Psicología, UAEH, San Agustin Tlaxiaca, Hgo,Méxi, Mexico *Guzman Saldaña, Rebeca María Elena* Area de Psicología, UAEH, San Agustin Tlaxiaca, Hgo,Méxi, Mexico
This study is based on an intervention program at the Technical Secondary School No. 38 in Pachuca, Mexico, Hidalgo; the main arms were to promote the development of skills between students, for a process of professionalization of teaching, from the treatment of Education of personality in the context of the student's personal growth, and the treatment of resilience as a generating capacity of these psychological constructs; arguments theoretical underpinning model performance of teachers in terms of the changes that educational reform in Mexico requires the school from the demands of contemporary society.

Cortisol reactivity and personality
Garcia de la Banda, Gloria Facultad de Psicologia, Universidad Islas Baleares, Palma de Mallorca, Spain *Meisel, Victoria* Facultad de Psicologia, Universidad Islas Baleares, Palma de Mallorca, Spain *Chellew, Karin* Facultad de Psicologia, Universidad Islas Baleares, Palma de Mallorca, Spain *Riesco, Maria* Laboratorio Analisis Clinicos, Hospital Son Dureta, Palma de Mallorca, Spain *Perez, Gerardo* Laboratorio Analisis Clinicos, Hospital Son Dureta, Palma de Mallorca, Spain *Fornes, Joana* Facultad de Psicologia, Universidad Islas Baleares, Palma de Mallorca, Spain
Introduction: Individual differences in cortisol reactivity may be related to personality. Objectives: 1 To compare baseline versus stressful cortisol secretion. 2 To determine the relationship between cortisol and personality. Methods: Two saliva samples were collected from 55 students during a stressful condition and two in the baseline condition. EPQ-R and NEO-FFI questionnaires were used to evaluate personality. Results: Cortisol increased significantly on stressful condition compared with baseline. Cortisol differences correlated positively with conscientiousness and agreeableness and negatively with psychoticism. Conclusions: These results are consistent with the literature where conscientiousness is considered a good predictor of healthy status and longevity.

Coping responses and resilient behaviors in adolescents attending public high schools in Buenos Aires
Garcia Labandal, Livia Beatriz Faculty of Psychology, University of Buenos Aires, Buenos Aires, Argentina *Mikulic, Isabel María* FACULTY OF PSYCHOLOGY, UNIVERSITY OF BUENOS AIRES, Buenos Aires, Argentina
Present study aims to analyze transition from Primary to High School of Buenos Aires students.500 adolescents, from 13 to 15 years and 68 professors have been administered a battery of five instruments specially adapted: Coping Responses Inventory, Perceived Quality of Life, Life Stressors and Social Resources Inventory and Structured Interviews to Assess Students Strengths and Teachers' Educational Practices. Findings show that teachers are perceived as resilient guides for students transition from primary to high school. Family and school contexts are perceived as sources of resilient behaviors and social support. Coping responses, positive reappraisal and problem solving, contribute to school transition.

Violent work encounters on public transport: A concept to prevent public transport employees from third party violence
Gehrke, Anne Forschung und Beratung, BGAG Dresden, Dresden, Germany *Erb, Rainer* Prävention, BG BAHNEN, Hamburg, Germany
Public transport employees who are in contact with customers, e.g. bus drivers or ticket inspectors, are at an elevated risk of third party violence. As a result a growing demand for specific training programs for the prevention of work-related violence emerges. A specific multiplier training program for the prevention of work-related violence was developed. The multiplier training program is based on a three-dimensional modular concept, comprising the phase prior to a conflict, the conflict phase in itself, as well as the phase after a conflict situation.

fMRI during affective processing in tinnitus patients and normal controls
Georgiewa, Petra Klinik für Psychosomatik, Charité - Universitätsmedizin, Berlin, Germany *Rothemund, Yvonne* Klinik für Psychosomatik, Charité - Universitätsmedizin, Berlin, Germany *Bohner, Georg* Klinik für Neuroradiologie, Charité - Universitätsmedizin, Berlin, Germany *Bauknecht, Christian* Klinik für Neuroradiologie, Charité - Universitätsmedizin, Berlin, Germany *Mazurek, Birgit* Tinnituszentrum, Charité -Universitätsmedizin, Berlin, Germany *Klingebiel, Randolf* Klinik für Neuroradiologie, Charité -Universitätsmedizin, Berlin, Germany *Klapp, Burghard F.* Klinik für Psychosomatik, Charité -Universitätsmedizin, Berlin, Germany
Brain imaging studies suggest that the functional connectivity of various limbic, prefrontal, and temporal brain structures can be understood as the basis for tinnitus. Following the hypothesis of changes in affective processing in tinnitus set of tasks was applied in a fMRI-study. Ten patients with tinnitus and 10 matched healthy controls were scanned during blocks of auditory stimuli of different emotional quality: pleasant sounds of chimes, unpleasant peep tones, neutral words, words with affective valence, off-periods. The comparison of patterns of activation in tinnitus

patients and controls revealed significant differences in limbic regions, prefrontal cortex and temporal brain regions.

The effect of writing on short-term and long-term semantic memory

Georgiou, Georgia Dept. of Psychology, University of Cyprus, Nicosia, Cyprus Avraamides, Marios Dept. of Psychology, University of Cyprus, Nicosia, Cyprus
Objectives: This study examined whether writing about expected learning material leads to superior retention than simply previewing material. Methods: Participants in the experimental group read the main points of a psychology film that would follow and wrote down what they knew about the topic and what they expected to learn from watching the film. Those in the control group simply previewed the main points. Results and Conclusion: The experimental group outperformed the control group on both immediate and delayed memory tests suggesting that writing is an effective method for promoting the encoding and retention of new information in semantic memory.

Effect of velocity on cortical processing of auditory motion

Getzmann, Stephan IfADo, Dortmund, Germany
The study investigated the processing of sound motion, employing a psychophysical motion detection task in combination with high-density electroencephalography. Following stationary acoustic stimulation from a central space position, the onset of motion elicited a specific cortical response that was lateralized to the right hemisphere with both left- and rightward motion. Higher motion velocity was associated with larger and earlier cortical responses and with shorter reaction times to motion onset. The results indicate a close correspondence of brain activity and behavioral performance in auditory motion detection and support the notion of a motion-specific analysis system.

Attributional style and academic performance

Gherasim, Loredana Ruxandra Psychology, Iasi, Romania
The reformulated model of learned helplessness assumes that attributional style has a certain impact on depression and performance through the intermediary effect of expectations about the occurrence of future outcomes. We used 2 short-term longitudinal designs to examine whether attributional style for negative and positive events and expectancies work in combination with perception of control style (Study 1; N=135), academic goals, self-efficacy and motivational orientation (Study 2; N=280) to predict students' grades. Results indicated that attributional style predicts grades, 6 weeks later, in interaction with expectations, specific causal attributions and control perception. These findings support diathesis-stress model of depression.

Elders' mental health in nursing house

Ghoreyshi Rad, Fakhrossadat Tabriz, Islamic Republic of Iran
Until recently, aging psychological disorder has been neglected by mental health experts. As the proportion of people who lives beyond age sixty-five continues to grow, it will become ever more important to learn about the disorders by some older people suffer from and the most effective means of preventing them. The researches have shown in that pre-industrial and also in industrial societies, until mid 20th century, there was nothing as "elders' problems". Up to that time, aged people were never left the society, and there were not so many people in need of care and attention. On the other hand, in past times, elders worked till whenever they could, while now a day they retire at early years. The problems of old age are not identical in all of the societies and their historical periods; they are also different in industrial and non-industrial, developed and non-developed, rural and urban societies. In this bereave, I'm going to show role of nursing home and other extended cares and facilities in Iranian society, as well as the outcome of cultural view point on their lives. The mental health of elders (women and men) in nursing house are compared with each other. The subjects of this research have been 60 elders living in nursing house; and the instrument was the Goldberg health questioner (G.H.Q. 1972). The results reveal such health problems such as depression, physical problems, etc. in correlation with economical status of the elders. Keywords: Aging and culture - mental health -psychological disorders- elders.

Attitudes toward young and older persons: Extended version of the German Aging Semantic Differential

Gluth, Sebastian Human Development, Max Planck Institute, Berlin, Germany Ebner, Natalie C. Department of Psychology, Yale University, New Haven, USA Schmiedek, Florian Human Development, Max Planck Institute, Berlin, Germany
We used an extended version of the German Aging Semantic Differential to assess attitudes toward young and older persons. Multiple-group confirmatory factor analysis replicated the 4-factor solution reported in the literature. Young and older participants described young persons as more personally satisfied and peaceful and as more active and adaptive to change, whereas older individuals were described as more autonomous and self-sufficient. More agreeable, extraverted, and positively tempered participants reported less negative attitudes toward other people. Results support the use of the German Aging Semantic Differential and are discussed in the context of multidimensional assessments of aging stereotypes.

An ethnographic study with college students in and from the classroom

González, Yetzabé Behavioral Science and Techn., Simon Bolívar University, Caracas, Venezuela
Objective: To understand significant aspects experienced by students during their college studies. Method: Based on educational ethnography, it uses the case study and participant observation to build information in Venezuelan students. The information is organized into categories that emerge during the investigation. Results: Time is the key dimension. The trimester term is very demanding and tense, it requires almost exclusive dedication to their studies and alters food and sleep. It is very important to have a good study group. Conclusion: The balance between personal and academic life constitute the key to cope and finish college studies.

Depression, spirituality and quality of life in Mexicans elderly

Gonzalez Celis, Ana Fes Iztalaca Posgrado, Universidad Nacional de Mexico, Estado de Mexico, Mexico Ruiz Carrillo, Edagardo FES IZTACALA POSGRADO, UNIVERSIDAD NACIONAL DE MEXICO, Estado De Mexico, Mexico Trón Álvarez, Rocío FES IZTACALA POSGRADO, UNIVERSIDAD NACIONAL DE MEXICO, Estado De Mexico, Mexico Chávez Becerra, Margarita FES IZTACALA POSGRADO, UNIVERSIDAD NACIONAL DE MEXICO, Estado De Mexico, Mexico
The purpose was to describe the relation of depression, spirituality and Quality of Life (QoL) in 75 Mexicans elderly. They applied the Geriatric Depression Scale (GDS), the WHOQoL-100 (QoL) with six factors (health, psychological, independence, social relations, environment, spirituality). The results exhibited a correlation between GDS and QoL (r =-0.482, p <0.000); and difference in all dimension of QoL between older persons whithout and with low and high level depression (F=19.84, p<0.000; F=29.02, p<0.000; F=19.54, p<0.000; F=6.71, p<0.002; F=9.22, p<0.000; F=0.76, p>0.47) excepted for spirituality. It's concludes that the spirituality may be one coping for well-being of the Mexicans elderly.

Evaluation of educational processes for developing management skills in sports

Gozzoli, Caterina Dipartimento Psicologia, Universita Cattolica, Milano, Italy Gorli, Mara Dipartimento Psicologia, Università Cattolica, Milano, Italy Frascaroli, Daniela Dipartimento Psicologia, Università Cattolica, Milano, Italy D'Angelo, Chiara Dipartimento Psicologia, Università Cattolica, Milano, Italy
This research aims to evaluate processes and outcomes of 5 editions of the II Level Master "Sport and Psychosocial Management: Promoting Cooperation, Mediating Conflict" (a training-research project promoted by the Postgraduate School of Psychology "Gemelli", Catholic University, Milan). Focus is on job skills developed (planning and coping with complex initiatives, managing problems related to the new context's complexity, developing specific relational competences) through this pilot experience in the Italian Academy context. The research analyzes evaluation questionnaires, narrative notes and board diaries of 90 postgraduate students and 8 interviews to the Master trainers. Analysis is conducted through two specific softwares: Atlas.ti and Spss. Data analysis and results are still ongoing and in progress (end of 5th edition: February 2008).

Assessing social indicators in PIRLS 2001

Groeneveld, Imke IQB, Humboldt-Universität zu Berlin, Berlin, Germany
In this study the number of books as an indicator of a students social background was examined using the German subsample of PIRLS 2001. It was analysed whether children of Primary school age already possess the cognitive capacity to estimate the number of existing books at home correctly. This skill was identified by Wößmann (2004) as a social indicator for 15 year olds in PISA 2000. The results of this study show that the number of books in PIRLS 2001 related to the German sampling can be seen as a meaningful indicator of a students social background.

Informal and formal learning of blue-collar workers: A qualitative approach to characterize and contrast operative learning processes

Grund, Axel Inst. für Sozialwissenschaften, Universität Karlsruhe, Karlsruhe, Germany Jöns, Ingela Social science, University of Mannheim, Mannheim, Germany
Though widely used in advanced vocational training, the concept of informal learning is lacking a substantive theoretical and empirical background. An inductive empirical study was conducted to provide further insights. Based on 27 learning episodes from interviews with blue-color workers, informal learning processes were characterized and linked to various psychological constructs. Configural-frequency-analysis indicates that informal rather than formal learning is associated with self-determination and self-efficacy in learning, a prospective, continuous and self-driven learning-cycle, the acquirement of processing-knowledge, a direct impact on business success and fewer problems in learning transfer. Implications for future studies are deduced from a theoretical framework.

Framing the frame: Goodness-of-fit for probe shapes within rectangular frames

Guidi, Stefano Firenze, Italy Palmer, Stephen Psychology, UC Berkeley, Berkeley, USA
We studied the internal structure of rectangular frames using judgments of perceived goodness-of-fit for simple shapes at different positions, orientations, and directions. Perceived fit appears to be driven mainly by the symmetry structure of the frame, with circular probes fitting best in the center,

along symmetry axes, and at positions symmetrical to or frame-aligned with a contextual element, when present. Triangular probes revealed strong orientational and directional effects that also depend on symmetry and alignment. Regression models using these variables account for 70-90% of the variance. Further experiments reveal that perceived fit is systematically related to aesthetic preference.

A study on floating children's school adaptation and Its relationship with teacher interpersonal style

Guo, Li-Yan School of Teacher Education, Shenyang Normal University, Shenyang, People's Republic of China *Wang, Yang* Institute of Teacher Training, Institute of Teacher Training, Yingkou, People's Republic of China

The current study explored school adaptation among floating children from Northeast China and examined the effect of teacher's interpersonal style on children's school adaptation. A total of 899 school students (including 455 floating children and 444 local children) participated in the questionnaire study. Results found that levels of self-acceptance, teacher-student interaction and academic performance were lower for floating children than for local children. Results also showed that teacher's empathy exerted the greatest effect on school adjustment of floating children. Implications for educational improvement of floating children were discussed.

Emotional and typological peculiarities of professional identity among teachers and students of teacher training programmes

Guseva, Svetlana Daugavpils University, Daugavpils, Latvia *Dombrovskis, Valerijs* Dept. Educational Psychology, Daugavpils University, Daugavpils, Latvia *Murasovs, Vadims* University, Daugavpils, Latvia *Ilisko, Dzintra* Pedagogy and Educ. Psychology, Daugavpils University, Daugavpils, Latvia

This research aims to study the interdependence between peculiarities of professional identity of educators, personality typology and professional burn-out problem. The objective of the research is to study the ways the professional burn-out expresses itself among school teachers and students of teacher training programmes, then linking this process to the typological peculiarities of personality. Research methods include D.Keirsey Temperament Sorter II and Professional Burn-out Detection Test. The research points to a significant correlation between personality types and the most common characteristics of emotional burn-out syndrome. The burn-out syndrome begins during the university training, and continues with teacher's employment in schools.

Relationship between spirituality and wellness in university students sample

Gustainiene, Loreta Theoretical Psychology, Vytautas Magnus University, Kaunas, Lithuania *Pranckeviciene, Aiste* General Psychology, Vytautas Magnus University, Kaunas, Lithuania

Objectives. To examine the relationship between students' spirituality and health oriented lifestyle. Methods. 136 first-second year bachelor students of Vytautas Magnus University were assessed using Five Factor Wellness Inventory (Myers, Sweeney, 2005) and Daily Spiritual Experience Scale (Underwood, Teresi, 2002). Results. Spirituality was significantly related to general wellness both in males and females. More spiritual females paid more attention to their physical health issues, were more creative, active, and more resilient to stress. Spirituality was related to stronger gender and cultural identity, and positive self-care for both genders. Conclusion. Spirituality is positively related with health oriented lifestyle of students.

Relationship among aspects of wellness and job satisfaction in Lithuaninan male managers

Gustainiene, Loreta Theoretical Psychology, Vytautas Magnus University, Kaunas, Lithuania *Pranckeviciene, Aiste* General Psychology, Vytautas Magnus University, Kaunas, Lithuania

Objectives. To evaluate the relationship between health-oriented life style (wellness) and job satisfaction among male managers. Methods. 103 male managers from building and engineering companies in Kaunas (Lithuania) were assessed by Five Factor Wellness Inventory (Myers, Sweeney, 2005) and job satisfaction scale generated by the authors of the study. Results. Younger managers scored higher on Wellness scales (except the Essential self). Married managers scored higher on the Essential self scale. Positive correlation was observed among General wellness scale and its components, and job satisfaction. Conclusion. Job satisfaction is positively related to health-oriented life style (wellness).

Effects of alcohol at low doses on driving-related performance and self-evaluation

Haga, Shigeru Department of Psychology, Rikkyo University, Niiza, Japan *Masuda, Takayuki* Department of Psychology, Rikkyo University, Niiza, Saitama, Japan *Pong, Neng-on* Department of Psychology, Rikkyo University, Niiza, Saitama, Japan *Oya, Hana* Department of Psychology, Rikkyo University, Niiza, Saitama, Japan

The effects of alcohol on driving-related performance and self-evaluation were tested at breath alcohol concentration levels of 0.15 mg/liter and 0.30 mg/liter (equivalent to a blood alcohol concentration of 0.03% and 0.06% respectively). Student participants performed various driving-related cognitive and psycho-motor tasks in laboratory experiments. Following a dose of alcohol, they predicted their own task performances and repeated the same tasks. Results showed that alcohol intake, even at very low doses, impairs performance on some tasks. However, there was no clear effect of alcohol on self-evaluation of task-performance ability.

An fMRI study on crossmodal interactions during object processing

Hagemann, Cordula Dept. of Systems Neuroscience, Univ. Medical Center Hamburg, Hamburg, Germany *Klinge, Corinna* Dept. of Systems Neuroscience, Univ. Medical Center Hamburg, Hamburg, Germany *Schneider, Till* Neuro- and Pathophysiologie, Univ. Medical Center Hamburg, Hamburg, Germany *Röder, Brigitte* Biological Psychology, University of Hamburg, Hamburg, Germany *Büchel, Christian* Dept. of Systems Neuroscience, Univ. Medical Center Hamburg, Hamburg, Germany

This study aimed to investigate brain regions involved in the integration of multisensory object information. Familiar objects were presented in an S1-S2 paradigm. The modality of S1 was varied blockwise (visual, haptic, auditory), while S2 was always auditory. Within a trial, S1 and S2 either referred to the same object or to two different objects. Thirty-one participants took part in this event-related fMRI study. We compared BOLD responses in object-incongruent and object-congruent trials. In the crossmodal conditions, the dorsolateral prefrontal cortex (DLPFC) was significantly more activated in object-incongruent than in object-congruent trials. Thus, these data suggest a significant role of the DLPFC in multisensory object recognition.

Consequences of the school entry age policy in Iran: A cross-sectional study of students' academic achievement, creativity and social adjustment

Hameedy, Mansoor Dept. Educational Psychology, Alzahra University, Tehran, Islamic Republic of Iran *Safe, Susan Afrooz, Gholaamali* Educational Psychology, Alzahra University, Tehran, Islamic Republic of Iran *Maghame, Afsaneh* Educational Psychology, Alzahra University, Tehran, Islamic Republic of Iran

The Iranian children can start schooling only if they have reached the age of six during the previous school year. To study the consequences of this regulation, a cross sectional study was undertaken in which the academic achievement, creativity, and social adjustment of two groups of second, fifth, eight, and eleventh graders were compared. Each of the two groups consisted either of students born within the first or the second half of the year. Results show that there were significant differences between the two groups in academic achievement and creativity with the older students being superior across all grades.

Adult playfulness, organizational playfulness climate, teaching innovation behavior, job satisfaction and work performance among teachers in three areas of China

Han, Cheng-Min Suzhou Vocational University, Suzhou, People's Republic of China

There are 1,413 teachers involved to investigate in three areas (Mainland China, Taiwan and Hong Kong). There is no significant difference of adult playfulness among teachers of the three regions. Teachers from Taiwan perceive higher organizational playfulness climate than teachers in Mainland China, who perceive higher organizational playfulness climate than those from Hong Kong. Teachers' innovation behavior is higher in Mainland China than Taiwan or Hong Kong. Teachers' job satisfaction is higher in Taiwan than Mainland China or Hong Kong, but teachers from Mainland China perceive higher work performance than those from Hong Kong. Further discussions are generated. Keywords: playfulness; organizational playfulness climate; creativity; innovation; job satisfaction; work performance

The evaluation of constructing educational accountability system in China local government: The application of Fuzzy Delphi Method

Han, Cheng-Min Suzhou Vocational University, Suzhou, People's Republic of China

Based upon data of literature review and questionnaire, conclusions have been reached as follows: The purpose of educational accountability system is to offer both teachers and the principal opportunities to develop professionalism. Teachers are the main persons who take responsible for educational accountability. Educational accountability system should take responsible for the students. Taking students' and schools' diversity into consideration in evaluation is the most important development criterion of educational accountability system. Teacher training and curriculum development are prior items in the educational report. Professional model is more feasible than other educational accountability models. Keywords: educational accountability system; accountability; Fuzzy Delphi method

Evidence for the malleability of group-based emotions: The role of pride, guilt, and sympathy in social interaction

Harth, Nicole Social Psychology, FSU Jena, International Graduate College, Jena, Germany

This research investigates the particular ways, in which social inequality is experienced. Findings from vignette studies and experimental games will be presented that show how distinct group-based emotions motivated different inter-group behaviour. It was found that a) pride is based on a focus on legitimate in-group advantage, b) guilt is based on a focus on illegitimate advantage, and c) sympathy is based on a focus on the out-group's illegitimate disadvantage. Whereas pride motivated in-group favouritism, sympathy stimulated out-group support. I will also demonstrate the malleability of these emotions and subsequent behavioural change when the out-group's response is taken into account.

The influences of deviation in harmony to the processing of musical context: A study using event related brain potentials (ERP)

Hashimoto, Midori Saijo-Cho, Misonou 5614 C-202, Hiroshima-pre, Japan *Konishi, Kenzo* School of Psychology, Kibi International University, Takahashi, Japan *Nezu, Chikako* Department of Education, Mie University, Tsu, Japan

The aim of this study was to investigate the influence of a preceding musical context to the unexpected chords using physiological index (ERP). Subjects consisted of two groups; one having absolute pitch, the other not having absolute pitch. Chords with unexpected notes elicited two ERP effects which are an early right hemispheric preponderant-anterior negativity (ERAN) and the late negativity (N5).These components were investigated relate with the deviation of chords and the processing of unexpected chords, and compared to two groups(with absolute pitch or without absolute pitch).

The relationship between cosmetic behavior and higher brain function with aging

Hatta, Takeshi Nagoya, Japan *Hatta, Taketoshi* psychology, nagoya, Nagoya, Japan *Iwahara, Akihiko* psychology, nagoya, Nagoya, Japan

The aim of this study was to examine the relationship between cosmetic behavior and higher brain function of middle and aged female people. Participants (N=181) of 39 to 91 yrs old had a cognitive test battery as a part of medical checkup. The used cognitive test consisted of items for the examination of prefrontal brain function. Results showed that the participants habitually having the care cosmetic behavior were higher than the participants habitually did not in several cognitive tests. These results suggest a relationship between sustaining of cosmetic behavior and decline of higher brain function in the aged people.

Objective detection of goosebumps and its course over the body

Hausmann, Barbara Emotion & Motivation, Institut für Psychologie, Kiel, Germany *Kaernbach, Christian* Inst. für Psychologie, Universität zu Kiel, Kiel, Germany

The feeling of goosebumps is often reported to be perceived as a reaction spreading over the body. We objectified these findings in our study. By parallel skin recordings of different body parts we examined differences and synchronicities of the goosebump appearance at a particular time. The objective examination was carried out with two models of our custom-built GooseCam. The results show a variety of time delays between appearances of goosebumps in the upper and lower parts of the body. It would be interesting to see whether the goosebump reaction follows particular patterns, due to definite types of stimuli.

Recognition and transmission process of skill acquirement in the Japanese traditional crafts and modern factories

Hayashibe, Keikichi Dept. of Informatics, Shizuoka University, Hamamatsu, Japan *Amenomiya, Masahiko* Informatics, SHIZUOKA University, Hamamatsu, Japan

Cognitive and transmission process of acquiring skills of craftsmen was investigated in order to effectively inherit the skills in Japanese traditional craft and modern factories to the next generation. In traditional acquirement of crafts in Japan, the original educational system unlike the gradual and systematic method in school is adopted. The transmission of the traditional craft in Japan takes the apprentice system. Long-term period such as some ten years is necessary for apprentices to acquire crafts. The support system based informatics for the effective craft acquirement based on the recognition process is proposed in our study.

The boundary effect and its elimination in Chinese text reading: The event-duration effect

He, Xianyou Department of Psychology, South China Normal University, Guangzhou, People's Republic of China

A Moving window technique was used to explore the effect of temporal segmentation markers on boundary effect in Chinese text reading. Experiment 1 examined whether boundary effect could be observed. Experiment 2 and 3 explored whether temporal segmentation markers could eliminate boundary effect. The results showed that the effect of temporal segmentation markers on boundary effect depended on the temporal relationship between the markers and the event before them, which was referred as event-duration effect. The results were discussed in terms of the possible ways of how the markers eliminated boundary effect.

Visuomotor uncertainty influences the frames of reference supporting motor output

Heath, Matthew Neurobehavioural Laboratory, University of Western Ontario, London, Canada

We report two experiments examining the nature of the visual information supporting motor output. Participants completed grasping and simple reaching movements to targets within pictorial illusions under predictable and unpredictable visual feedback schedules. Maximal grip aperture (Experiment 1) and endpoint accuracy (Experiment 2) for unpredictable – but not predictable - feedback trials were "tricked" by the pictorial illusions. Moreover, analysis of trajectory formation (Experiment 2) indicated that unpredictable feedback schedules engendered a mode of control wherein responses were structured in advance of movement onset. These results suggest that strategic adaptations to visuomotor uncertainty influence the visual information supporting motor output.

Understanding the internet: Psychological word norms as indicators of query-specific internet word frequencies

Heine, Joerg-Henrik Ismaning, Germany *Spörrle, Matthias* Department Psychology, Ludwig-Maximilians-Universität, München, Germany

By using existing psychological word norms obtained by rating procedures we try to predict the frequencies of search hits derived from internet search engines. We used several major search engines and repeated measurement to develop a highly reliable scale of internet word frequency. We presumed that psychological criteria like typicality and valence of nouns predict the frequencies of search-operator-specific frequencies of internet search hits. Regression analysis confirmed this assumption indicating that the verbal content of the internet as interactive mass medium can be predicted by already existing and established psychological characteristics of words.

Comparison of a sustained attention to response and a continuous performance format in a letter-detection task

Helton, William Psychology, Michigan Tech University, Houghton, USA

A sustained attention to response task (SART), unlike a typical continuous performance task (CPT), requires responding to frequent distracters and withholding responses to rare targets. Sixteen participants performed perceptually identical letter detection tasks using either a SART or CPT response format. Perceptual sensitivity (d') was higher and bias (c) was more conservative in the CPT format than in the SART, p < .001. Bias became more conservative over trials in the SART, but stayed relatively constant in the CPT. The SART response format is much more challenging and demonstrates different changes over time than the CPT response format.

General health and loneliness in elders living with their own families in compare to elders who were living in nursing homes in Tehran city

Hemati Alamdarlo, Ghorban Tehran, Islamic Republic of Iran *Dehshiri, Gholam Reza* psychology, psychology, tehran, Islamic Republic of Iran *Shojaee, Setareh* psychology, exceptional children, tehran, Islamic Republic of Iran *Hakimirad, Elham* psychology, exceptional children, tehran, Islamic Republic of Iran

Aim of the study was to compare general health and loneliness between two groups of elders, living with their families or in nursing homes in Tehran city. Two hundred eighteen elderly consisted our sample. GHQ and loneliness questionnaires were administered on them. Results of two way analysis of variance indicated that General health of elders living in nursing homes were significantly lower and their loneliness were significantly more than elders who were living with their families. Based on psycho-cultural situation of elders in Iran, home based environment is the best place of nurturing psychological needs of elderlies in Iran.

Learning music as aesthetical experience

Hernández, Marisela Comportamiento, Universidad Simón Bolívar, Caracas, Venezuela

This research aimed to assess children and young people personal and social changes related to their musical education. Here, we highlight some results concerning the Aesthetical Sense, understood as sensitivities and feelings implied in appreciating artistic forms and their connections to dailylife. We were guided by principles and methods allied to Social Phenomenology, so it is assumed that composers, musicians and audiences, interpret music as long as they feel and communicate sensations and emotions. Data was obtained through qualitative interviews and field notes. The results has been organized in three Core Meanings: Senses in action, Extraordinary Dailylife, Me and Others.

Women and education: An approximation to women empowerment

Hernandez, Julieta Dept. of Educacion, Juarez Autonomous University, Villahermosa, Mexico *García Falconi, Renan* Psychology, Juarez Autonomous University o, Villahermosa, Mexico *Campos, Josefina* Educacion, Juarez Autonomous University o, Villahermosa, Mexico *Garcia Hernandez, Renan Jesus* Psychology, Del Valle University, Villahermosa, Mexico

Education is an essential tool to insure equality of conditions between women and men in decision making positions. This qualitative study was to analyze the level in which the educational background of women influences their becoming leaders, and how education influences their actual leadership situation. A sample of Mexican political women were interviewed, deepening in several axes of analysis. In this paper only the results on education are discussed. It was found that formal education played an important role and that this influence goes both ways, since the occupation of positions of power, make women thrive for higher and further education.

Defense style in Iranian sample

Heydarinasab, Leila Psychology, Shahed University, Tehran, Islamic Republic of Iran Shaeeri, Mohammad reza psychology, Shahed university, Tehran, Islamic Republic of Iran

This study has examined defense style in iranian sample with psychometric properties defens style questionaaire (DSQ -40). 1067 subjects in a non-clinical sample (666 students, age mean : 16.61 SD: 1.13 and 401 college students, age mean:21.3 SD: 3.8, 527 female,540 male) participated in this investigation. results : It was found that students (age mean:16.61) used immature defense styles more than college students. more over famels used neurotic styles more than males, men were found to be immature more than women. This study considers DSQ-40 a valid instrument for evaluating iranian defense styles and shows the crucial role of sex and age in using defense mechanism.

The stress coping model of a case with mild traumatic brain injury in Taiwan

Ho, Hsueh-Lin Psychology (S115), National Taiwan University, Taipei, Taiwan Yang, Chi-Cheng Psychology (S115), National Taiwan University, Taipei, Taiwan Wu, Yin-Chang Psychology (S115), National Taiwan University, Taipei, Taiwan

Traumatic brain injury (TBI) is a significant public health problem in Taiwan. Patients with mild traumatic brain injury (mTBI) often suffered from a variety of neuropsychological and psychosocial difficulties. However, past studies focused on stress coping processes were limited in scope and number. A case study with semi-structured interview was designed to comprehensively describe the stress coping process of a case with mTBI. The results displayed the patient's subjective experiences, included stressors, coping strategies, interactive processes between stress and coping, and related environmental and personal factors. Moreover, appraisal might be an important moderator for mTBI patient's psychosocial adjustment.

Standard perimetry reflects perceptual and premotor deficits in hemispatial neglect

Hoffmann, Maria Inst. für Psychologie, Humboldt-Universität zu Berlin, Berlin, Germany Kaufmann, Christian Humboldt-Universität zu Berlin, Institute of Psychology, Berlin, Germany Fydrich, Thomas Humboldt-Universität zu Berlin, Institute of Psychology, Berlin, Germany Sabel, Bernhard A. University of Magdeburg, Inst. of Medical Psychology, Magdeburg, Germany Gall, Carolin University of Magdeburg, Inst. of Medical Psychology, Magdeburg, Germany

Impairments in detecting targets and initiating motor responses in contralesional space characterise hemispatial neglect which is often associated with hemianopic field defects. A modified line bisection task (Bisiach et al., Neurology, 1990) was assessed to evaluate perceptual and motor-intentional deficits in 30 patients with chronic neglect. Perimetry revealed visual field defects in 76% of the patients. Larger visual field defects were observed in patients with perceptual impairments. Patients with premotor deficits showed prolonged reaction times in perimetry. Thus, perimetry reflects both perceptual impairments as well as impairments in motor initiation although motor responses in contralesional space were not required during perimetry.

Personality constructs and responsibility in gifted and normal students in high school

Homayouni, Alireza Dept. of Psychology, Islamic Azad University, Bandargaz, Islamic Republic of Iran Taghypour, Hassan Dept. of Psychology, University, Babol, Islamic Republic of Iran Begic, Ivana Dept. of Psychology, I University of Croatia Zagreb, Zagreb, Croatia Nikpour, Gholam Ali Dept. of Psychology, Islamic Azad University, Babol, Islamic Republic of

Iran Mosavi Amiri, Seyed Jalal Dept. of Psychology, Medical Clinic, Babol, Islamic Republic of Iran Allahyari, Rajab Ali Dept. of Sociology, Payame Noor University(PNU), Babol, Islamic Republic of Iran

The research investigated the role of personality constructs based on Jungian personality types and responsibility in gifted and normal students. Research question:Is there significant difference between personality constructs and responsibility in gifted and normal students? 92 gifted and 93 normal students were randomly selected from three educational districts and Hogan- Champagne's Personal Style Inventory (PSI) and California Personality Inventory (CPI) were administered on them. Results showed that Gifted are more intuitive, thinking, perceiving and responsible than normal students. In regard to results we can set curriculum plans in educational places that empower and reinforce these constructs to have more responsible, creative and gifted people.

Learning styles as a predictor of achievement motivation and academic performance

Homayouni, Alireza Dept. of Psychology, Islamic Azad University, Bandargaz, Islamic Republic of Iran Mohammadzadeh, Rajab Ali Nikpour, Gholam Ali Dept. of Psychology, Islamic Azad University of Toa, Mahmoudabad, Islamic Republic of Iran Mosavi Amiri, Seyed Jalal Dept. of Addiction Studies, Medical Clinic of Dr. Mosavi, Babol, Islamic Republic of Iran

The research is aimed to investigate the role of learning styles in achievement motivation and academic performance.Rsearch question:Do particular learning styles have more achievement motivation and academic performance.300 students were randomly selected and Kolb's learning styles inventory and Hermans's achievement motivation questionnaire were administered on them.Data were analyzed with ANOVA.Results showed that there is significant differences between means of variables in different learning styles.Converger and assimilator learning styles have high achievement motivation and better in academic performance than other styles.The results can be used in planning for educational goals in order to increasing the characters of this styles in educational settings so that students can have better achievement motivation and better academic performance.

The effects of donepezil on the sleep EEG of healthy older adults: Implications for sleep-related memory consolidation

Hornung, Orla Department of Psychiatry, Charité (CBF), Berlin, Germany Regen, Francesca Department of Psychiatry, Charité (CBF), Berlin, Germany Dorn, Hans Department of Psychiatry, Charité (CBF), Berlin, Germany Anghelescu, Ion Department of Psychiatry, Charité (CBF), Berlin, Germany Kathmann, Norbert Institute of Psychology, Humboldt University Berlin, Berlin, Germany Schredl, Michael ZI Mannheim, ZI Mannheim, Mannheim, Germany Danker-Hopfe, Heidi Department of Psychiatry, Charité (CBF), Berlin, Germany Heuser, Isabella Department of Psychiatry, Charité (CBF), Berlin, Germany

Aging is associated with cholinergic hypofunction and memory decline. Cholinergic activity also plays a crucial role in sleep-dependent memory consolidation. The effects of an acetylcholinesterase-inhibitor on the sleep EEG of healthy older adults were investigated focussing on features, which have been linked to plasticity-related processes, i.e. sigma and delta activity. Forty-two participants (60-77 years) received 5mg of donepezil 30 minutes before bedtime in a placebo-controlled, double-blind design. Donepezil led to an increase in sigma activity during stage 2 NREM-sleep and delta activity during slow-wave-sleep (p<.05). These results suggest that an acetylcholinesterase-inhibitor triggers processes of sleep-dependent memory consolidation in old age.

Psychological distress and well-being: Overlapped or distinct outcomes in the acute aftermath of cancer diagnosis?

Hou, Wai Kai Psychology, The University of Hong Kong, Hong Kong, China, People's Republic of : Hong Kong SAR Law, Chi Ching Clinical Oncology, The Queen Elizabeth Hospital, Hong Kong, China, People's Republic of : Macao SAR

Objective: To test whether psychological distress and well-being are separate outcomes in the acute aftermath of cancer diagnosis. Methods: A consecutive cohort of Chinese colorectal cancer (CRC) patients (N = 234) were recruited and administered measures of optimism (C-LOT-R), hope (AHS), social relationships (ChSRQS), depression (HADS) and positive affect (CAS) immediately and 3-month postdiagnosis. Results: Multinomial logistic regressions identified separate predictors for depression and absence of positive affect 3-month after CRC diagnosis, suggesting the importance of assessing and intervening well-being as well as distress in newly diagnosed cancer patients.

Different patterns between children with and without learning disabilities: The effects of encoding fluency and retrieval fluency on judgments of learning

Hou, Ruihe Psychological Counselling, Renmin University, Beijing, People's Republic of China Yu, Guoliang Institute of Psychology, Renmin University, Beijing, People's Republic of China

Pattern differences between children with and without learning disabilities (LD) in the effects of fluency on Judgments of learning (JOLs) were investigated. JOLs were elicited either immediately after study, short or longer delay. When study time was self-paced, the effects of encoding fluency (EF) on JOLs decreased with delay, whereas those of retrieval fluency (RF) increased. When study time was manipulated, JOLs increased with both EF and RF. These were true only for normal children, children's with LD JOLs mainly based on RF across conditions, which demonstrated normal children utilized flexibly different cues to make JOLs, but not their counterpart.

The neuropsychology of second language (L2) pronunciation talent

Hu, Xiaochen Hertie Institut, Medizin. Universität Tübingen, Tübingen, Germany Reiterer, Susanne Department of Neuroradiology, University of Tübingen, Tübingen, Germany Ackermann, Hermann Clinical Brain Research, Hertie Institute, Tübingen, Germany

The current study aimed at the investigation of the determinants of the L2 pronunciation talent. 75 German students were assessed with respect to their English pronunciation ability, intelligence, working memory, musicality, personality and their English learning histories. A subgroup was assigned to the brain imaging examination. Preliminary analysis of behavioural data revealed a significant positive relationship between L2 pronunciation talent and exposure time in native speaking country, with openness, and with empathy. A multiple regression analysis using backward elimination indicated that, exposure time, neuroticism, conscientiousness and empathy contributed to the talent. Further brain structural and functional analysis is needed to understand the foundation of this unique skill.

Differences in chronic patients cared by different medical settings

Huang, Yun-Hsin Psychology (S115), National Taiwan University, Taipei, Taiwan Cheng, Yih-Ru Psychology (S115), National Taiwan University, Taipei, Taiwan Wu, Chih-Hsun Psychology (S115), National Taiwan University, Taipei, Taiwan Huang, Yang-Wen Psychology (S115), National Taiwan University, Taipei, Taiwan Wu, Yin-Chang Psychology (S115), National Taiwan University, Taipei, Taiwan

Dealing with chronic patient's emotional problems had become an important issue in many primary care settings. The aim of this study is to investigate if there were differences in chronic patients among two local primary care clinics, one in higher (H) and the other in lower (L) SES area, and a family medicine (FM) clinic in large medical center in Taiwan. Negative emotions and disturbed level were evaluated by questionnaires. The results show that patients cared by the L clinic reported less anxiety and felt less disturbed, which might imply that patients with lower SES might accepted the disease better.

Adapting to the disease: Differences in emotional reactions between chronic and non-chronic disease patients in Taiwan

Huang, Yang-Wen Dept. of Psychology (S115), National Taiwan University, Taipei, Taiwan Wu, Chih-Hsun Psychology (S115), National Taiwan University, Taipei, Taiwan Cheng, Yih-Ru Psychology (S115), National Taiwan University, Taipei, Taiwan Huang, Yun-Hsin Psychology (S115), National Taiwan University, Taipei, Taiwan Wu, Yin-Chang Psychology (S115), National Taiwan University, Taipei, Taiwan
The purpose of the current study is to understand the differences in emotional reactions between the patients with chronic disease and the patients with recoverable problems (e.g. stomachache), while they were adapting to the changes in his/her life. Emotional reactions, disturbed level caused by (1) increased daily hassles (e.g. taking pills) and (2) changes in one's functions were measured by inventories. The results show that chronic disease patients reported less negative emotions and lower level of disturbances caused by functional changes. These results suggested that most of the chronic patients might adapt better to the changes caused by the disease.

Measurement equivalence in Norwegian and American hardiness scales

Hystad, Sigurd Psychosocial Science, University of Bergen, Bergen, Norway Eid, Jarle psychosocial science, University of Bergen, Bergen, Norway Brevik, John Ivar Institute of Epidemiology, Norwegian Armed Forces Medical, Sessvollmoen, Norway Johnsen, Bjørn Helge psychosocial science, University of Bergen, Bergen, Norway Laberg, Jon Christian psychosocial science, University of Bergen, Bergen, Norway Bartone, Paul T. psychosocial science, University of Bergen, Bergen, Norway
Objective: To explore measurement invariance in newly revised Norwegian and American Dispositional Resiliency (hardiness) Scales. Methods: Using LISREL 8.8, a baseline model allowing all parameters to be freely estimated for Norwegian (N = 7264) and American (N = 1101) respondents was compared to a constrained model. Results: Based on the changes in goodness-of-fit indexes between the baseline and more restricted model, results provided support for measurement equality in the Norwegian and American scale. Conclusions: Measurement equivalence is pivotal if meaningful comparison between different cultures and countries are to be made. The current result suggests that both Norwegian and American subjects respond to the revised hardiness scale in a similar manner.

The moderating role of group identification in complementary stereotype effects

Ikegami, Tomoko Psychology, Osaka City University, Osaka, Japan
System justification theory contends that people idealize existing social arrangements by relying on complementary stereotypes, which ascribe compensating virtues to the disadvantaged and corresponding vices to the advantaged. This study investigates how ingroup identification moderates this complementary effect. A questionnaire is given to Japanese university students to assess their stereotypical

images of a higher- or lower-status out-group university. Contrary to traditional social identity theory, ingroup identification accentuated this effect by enhancing both perceived competence of a higher-status university and perceived friendliness of a lower-status university. This suggests that a collective system-justification motive overrides group-level interests.

Preparing children for school education: The sustainability perspective

Ilisko, Dzintra Pedagogy and Educ. Psychology, Daugavpils University, Daugavpils, Latvia Guseva, Svetlana Daugavpils University, Daugavpils, Latvia Dombrovskis, Valerijs Dept. Educational Psychology, Daugavpils University, Daugavpils, Latvia
The study presents an analysis of different aspects of development in the process of preparing pre-school children for school education. The objective of this study is justification of child's development in pre-school educational environment that uses sustainability elements, based on a synergetic unity of children's affective and cognitive spheres. The method used in this research is Gutkina's tests that determine children's readiness for school education. The authors conclude that in the pre-school educational environment arranged without sustainability elements the level of child's development regarding their affective-cognitive personality sphere is not as high as in the environment oriented towards sustainability.

Mothers beliefs about restrictions in child dietary

Ingrassia, Massimo Pedagogia e Scienze dell'Ed., Università di Messina, Reggio Calabria, Italy Benedetto, Loredana Dept. of Educational Sciences, Messina University, Reggio Calabria, Italy Rosano, Mariagrazia Pedagogia e Scienze dell'Ed., Università di Messina, Messina, Italy
The study investigates maternal beliefs induce them to select foods that children may eat. Hupkens et al. (1998) found parents with higher instruction levels are more restrictive and their dietary habits are more in line with the recommendations for a healthy child feeding. 147 mothers of elementary school-age children were divided into two groups (low instruction vs. middle-high instruction level). A self-report questionnaire served to measure the maternal motivations of their dietary restrictions. Results show low instructional-level mothers more responsive to excessive food consumption and child refusal. The other group seems to be significantly more attentive to choice "healthy" foods.

The function of the bilingual approach in language development of preschool deaf children

Isakovic, Ljubica Faculty of Special Education, University of Belgrade, Belgrade, Serbia Vujasinovic, Zdravka Deaf and Hard of Hearing Child, School Radivoj Popovic, Belgrade, Serbia Dimic, Nadezda Faculty of Special Education, University of Belgrade, Belgrade, Serbia
The aim of study was to examine the function of the bilingual approach in language development of preschool deaf children. The sample - 14 children. We used the picture dictionary and picture story-book. A qualitative and quantitative analysis was completed. The results show that the use of nonverbal communication is significant for the language development and the personality of deaf children. Children who have a richer sign language also, have a richer lexicon, make better use of sentences and are better at connecting them, and are able to observe the relations between a series of pictures.

The effects of a peer health education program on peer educator's self health behavior modification

Ishikawa, Rie Health Psychology, J. F. Oberlin University, Tokyo, Japan Matsuda, Yoriko Health Psychology, J. F. Oberlin University, Tokyo, Japan Okuta, Noriko Health and Welfare, YMCA college of Human Services, Kanagawa, Japan Kamba, Naoko Health Psychology, J. F. Oberlin University, Tokyo, Japan Shibata, Keiko Health Psychology, J. F. Oberlin University, Tokyo, Japan Kawano, Rika Health Psychology, J. F. Oberlin University, Tokyo, Japan
Objectives: To examine whether peer health educators change their own health behavior or increase motivation for change as a result of their educating peers, observing peers' health behavioral change and being appreciated by peers. Methods: The intervention participants were 25 Japanese undergraduates. The participants were assigned to either Group(1) who received health education or Group(2) who received health education and provided health education to peers with similar health behavioral problems. Results: Group(2) increased perceived importance for healthy behavior and self-efficacy in achieving healthy behavior. Conclusions: Health education for peers with similar problems enhances health educators' motivation for healthy behavior.

Social exclusion and inequality of the rural elderly in Bangladesh

Islam, A.K.M. Shafiul Dept. of Sociology, Rajshahi University, Rajshahi, Bangladesh
This study examines the level of exclusion and inequality of the elderly people in the rural areas of Bangladesh. Bangladesh is agro-based and least developing country. The vast majority of the people of rural areas are related to agriculture and agro-based commerce. The elderly people of rural areas are becoming vulnerable due to socioeconomic marginalization. With increasing age, the rural elderly decline their role and status. Basically, they are excluded from income generating activities, decision-making process, rural politics and other social institutions except religious institution. This study mainly focuses on the socioeconomic deprivation of the rural elderly.

The relationship between pain experience, functional disability and generic health related quality of life in children with juvenile idiopathic arthritis in biological therapy

Jeppesen, Johanne H. Psykologisk Institut, Aarhus Universitet, Aarhus, Denmark Thastum, Mikael Aarhus Universitet, Psykologisk Institut, Aarhus C, Denmark Herlin, Troels Skejby, Aarhus Universiteshospital, Aarhus N, Denmark
This study examined the relationship between health-related quality of life (HRQOL), experience of pain and functional disability in children with juvenile idiopathic arthritis (JIA) in biological therapy. Thirty-seven children aged 5-17 year (M=12.49year, SD=3.45year) with JIA in biological therapy and one of their parents completed measures of pain experience, functional disability and generic HRQOL. Significant correlations were found between children and parents HRQOL-ratings and children's pain experience (children: R= -0.723; parents: R=-0.610, p=0.0001), as well as functional disability (children: R=-0.784, parents: R=-0.680, p=0.0001). HRQOL in children with JIA is highly affected by levels of pain experience and functional disability.

Semantic relatedness among objects promotes the activation of multiple phonological codes during object naming

Jescheniak, Jörg D. Inst. für Psychologie, Universität Leipzig, Leipzig, Germany Görges, Frauke Inst. für Psychologie, Universität Leipzig, Leipzig, Germany Oppermann, Frank Inst. für Psychologie, Universität

Leipzig, Leipzig, Germany **Schriefers, Herbert** NICI, Radbout University Nijmegen, Nijmegen, Netherlands

In two picture-word interference experiments the authors demonstrate that a semantic-categorical relation between a target object and a context object (e.g., target: flute, context object: harp) promotes the phonological activation of the to-be-ignored context object (as indexed by interference from a distractor phonologically related to the context object, e.g., heart). No such activation is observed if the objects are semantically unrelated. This observation further supports the notion that the possibility to establish a coherent representation among multiple objects affects the information flow in the conceptual-lexical system during speech planning (cf., Oppermann et al., in press, JEP:LMC).

Attitudes toward homosexuality and bisexuality in adolescents between 15 and 19 years old, in rural and urban areas of the north of Portugal

*Jesus Ferreira, Ana Ciencias Humanas e Sociais, Universidade Fernando Pessoa, Vila Nova de Gaia, Portugal **Soares Martins, Jose** Ciencias humanas e sociais, Universidade Fernando Pessoa, maia, Portugal*

The purpose of this study was to understand the adolescent's attitudes toward homosexuality and bisexuality, studding differences associated to gender, area of residence (urban or rural), and religion, using the LFHS (Hansen, 1982) translated by the authors. The sample is formed by 265 students, ages 15 to 19, from V.N.Gaia (urban) and Lousada (rural). The results showed that, in general, adolescents have favorable attitudes toward homosexuality and toward bisexuality, and there are significant differences concerning gender (girls' presenting more favorable attitudes). However, we didn't find significant differences concerning to the area of residence and to religion. We found that homosexuality and bisexuality are positive co-related, and that attitudes toward bisexuality tent to be more unfavorable.

Psychological and social recources that increase resilience through adulthood

*Jiménez Abriz, María Guadalupe Psicología Clñinica y la Salud, Universidad Autónoma de Madrid, Madrid, Spain **Izal, Maria** Psicología Clínica y la Salud, Universidad Autónoma deMadrid, Madrid, Spain **Montorio, Ignacio** Psicología Clínica y la Salud, Universidad Autónoma deMadrid, Madrid, Spain*

Resilience is a dynamic process that includes the positive adaptation within contexts of significant adversity (Luthar, Cicchetti and Becker, 2000). The goal research was to find the psychological and social resources that buffer stress and serve as resilience constellation. Additionally mediation - moderation of age and country between resources, stress and life satisfaction was probed. Sample was 325 mexican and spaniers, age 18 to 87. Results shown that self esteem, control perception, optimism, acceptance coping, search emotional support coping and socioeconomical level can predict life satisfaction and protect upon stress impact. Furthermore, age served as mediation and country as moderation variable.

How does the temporal attentional selection work: Under illusion paradigm

Jin, Mingxuan Dept. of Psychology, Chinese Univ. of Hong Kong, Hong Kong, People's Republic of China

In current study, we developed the illusion paradigm to investigate the mechanism of temporal based attentional selection. The illusion picture was used as materials to measure and compare the point of subjective equality under two conditions. The result indicated the basic temporal selection that the temporal gap could diminish the effect of illusion. We further investigated two core hypothesis about the characteristic of this process. Finally, we

proposed to test the neuropsychology base of the temporal attentional selection. The results suggested that temporal selection is a robust phenomenon wherein temporal cues are used for selected attention.

Is fluency an independent component of reading?

*Joshi, R. Malatesha Dept. of Literacy Education, Texas University, College Station, USA **Sha, Tao** Psychology, Beijing University, Beijing, People's Republic of China **Binks, Emily** Education, University of Hull, Scarborough, United Kingdom*

The National Reading Panel (NRP, 2000) considers 'fluency' one of the five basic components of reading. However, the importance of fluency in effortless reading is not without controversy. Perhaps, the importance of fluency may depend on the orthographic depth of a language; fluency may be part of decoding in deeper orthographies while it may be a separate component in shallow orthographies. Fluency may also be influenced by how it was assessed. In this report, we present some results about the role of fluency in different orthographies and discuss the diagnostic and educational implications.

The role of phonological analysis act

Jung, Hyewon Dept. of Literature, Chuo University, Tokyo, Japan

In this research, I examined the role of phonological analysis. Phonological awareness is concerned with the understanding of the linguistic characteristics of each language, and being able to operate the smallest units in words. The ability to segment and isolate phonemes is critical to the development of decoding and spelling skills. The child was required to place small magnets on the table for the number of phonemes. This way a problem is solved in the form of an external act. When an external act is made, something is learned or internalized.

Decoding control signals for visual spatial attention from ventral prefrontal cortex

*Kalberlah, Christian Attention and Awareness, MPI CBS, Leipzig, Germany **Haynes, John-Dylan** BCCN Berlin, Charité - Universitätsmedizin, Berlin, Germany*

Both dorsal and ventral regions of prefrontal cortex are known to be involved in top-down control of visual spatial attention. However, it has remained unclear whether ventral areas encode the spatial distribution of attention rather than unspecific mechanisms related to detecting and reorienting, task difficulty or perceptual load. Using multivariate decoding of fMRI signals (Haynes & Rees 2006), we succeeded in decoding the focus of attention from occipital, parietal, and prefrontal, especially right ventral prefrontal areas where topographic mapping approaches failed to identify an "attention-o-topic" map. Multivariate decoding is thus a powerful tool for revealing topographically organised cortical information.

The role of anxiety, multitasking and task complexity in psychomotor task performance

*Kanwal, Harpreet Dept. of Psychology, Panjab University, Chandigarh, India **Chhabra, Preeti Nagpal***

The present study was carried out on a total sample of 200 female students in the age range of 15 to 19 years. Classification on Anxiety levels finally made 165 students available for further study. Four multitasking conditions and three task complexity levels based data was subjected to a 3*4*3 repeated measures ANOVA. The results pointed at a significant effect of each variable on the psychomotor task performance. An interesting differential impact of the four chosen multitasking conditions was seen.

Psychophysiological control: Getting goosebumps when you feel like it

*Katzur, Björn H. Inst. für Psychologie, Universität zu Kiel, Kiel, Germany **Kaernbach, Christian** Inst. für Psychologie, Universität zu Kiel, Kiel, Germany*

Goosebumps as a reaction to cold or strong emotional experiences are known to most people and are controlled by the autonomic nervous system. Interestingly, however, there are individuals able to induce goosebumps by conscious effort. We investigated 14 participants; six of them being able to induce goosebumps during additional physiological measurements. The occurrence of goosebumps was in some (but not all) cases correlated with changes in skin conductance, heart rate, blood pressure and respiration. Furthermore, results from an internet study are presented in which we investigated how many people have this ability and how their techniques differ.

Higher cognitive control reduces conflicts in visual spatial attention: Electrophysiological correlates

*Kehrer, Stefanie Berlin, Germany **Kraft, Antje** Neurology, Charité, Berlin, Germany **Irlbacher, Kerstin** Neurology, Charité, Berlin, Germany **Koch, Stefan P.** Neurology, Charité, Berlin, Germany **Hagendorf, Herbert** Psychology, Humboldt University, Berlin, Germany **Kathmann, Norbert** Psychology, Humboldt University, Berlin, Germany **Brandt, Stephan A.** Neurology, Charité, Berlin, Germany*

We investigated the role of selection difficulty on conflict processing in the location negative priming (NP) paradigm. We hypothesized that a more difficult target selection leads to stronger attentional top-down control, reducing the effects of arising conflicts. Event-related potentials were recorded in 25 subjects. A significantly delayed reaction time for NP- compared to control-trials was only evident in the easy task. Interestingly the frontocentral N2 was generally enhanced in the difficult task as compared to the easy task. Thus, we conclude that stronger cognitive control is involved in the difficult task, resulting in a reduced behavioral NP conflict.

Social skills in traffic: Connections to driver's age, sex, experience and driver group

*Keskinen, Esko Dept. of Psychology, University of Turku, Turku, Finland **Katila, Ari** Department of Psychology, University of Turku, Turku, Finland **Laapotti, Sirkku** Department of Psychology, University of Turku, Turku, Finland **Hernetkoski, Kati** Department of Psychology, University of Turku, Turku, Finland **Lammi, Antero** Department of Psychology, University of Turku, Turku, Finland*

Social skills are important in traffic but how driver's age, sex, experience and driver group are connected to them? As part of a larger research project a mail survey (n=798) was made for "everyday" drivers, professional drivers, driving instructors and novice drivers. Questions concerned attitudes concerning safety and scales measuring perceived phenomena and own behaviour while driving. Anova (separately male/female) revealed that age (males and females) and driver group (males) were connected to pro- and antisocial behaviour and irritation and driver group (males) also to communication. However experience did not have expected connections to social skills and behaviour in traffic.

Noun and verb generation investigated with fMRI: Testing the sensory-motor hypothesis of semantic representations

*Khader, Patrick Inst. für Psychologie, Universität Marburg, Marburg, Germany **Jost, Kerstin** Psychology, Philipps-Universität Marburg, Marburg, Germany **Mertens, Michelle** Psychology, Philipps-Universität Marburg, Marburg, Germany **Rösler,***

Frank Psychology, Philipps-Universität Marburg, Marburg, Germany

Are semantic representations of nouns and verbs located in visually vs. motor-related brain areas, according to the "sensory-motor hypothesis"? Seventeen participants generated nouns and verbs triggered by a minimal sentence context (e.g., "carpenter cuts...wood" or "carpenter wood...cuts"). Noun generation activated occipital-temporal areas more than verb generation, indicating stronger recruitment of visual representations. In contrast, stronger activation for verbs was not found, as expected, in the motor cortex, but in the left prefrontal cortex, presumably reflecting processing differences that are due to the grammatical status of the two word categories. Therefore, these results are only partially consistent with the sensory-motor hypothesis.

Simbir project for identification of gifted children in Sudan

Khalifa, Gowaher Dept. of Pyshology, Ministry of Science, Khartoum, Sudan

This study investigates the identification and promotion process for gifted children (N=3000) both males (50%) and females (50%) in primary schools(9-11 years) in Sudan. The project is named "Simbir", a famous bird in Sudan a good omen marking the beginning of the planting season. Several tools were used in the identification process including intelligence, creativity, aptitude and imagination scores. Three special schools were established in 2005 for the extremely gifted children and supported financially by the government. Special enrichment curriculum was designed for the gifted children. Highly trained teachers and psychologists were selected for promoting giftedness among children.

Elderly males social benefit through dog walking

Kikuchi, Kazumi Dept. of Gerontology, JF Oberlin Universty, Tokyo, Japan *Osada, Hisao* gerontology, JF Oberlin Universty, Tokyo, Japan

In Japan, the number of pets is larger than the number of children. People treat their pets like family. We conducted case studies of elderly men and their personal networks created by dog walking. To clarify the benefits of dog walking networks, we used a Physiological Distance Map to chart their ego-central networks and compared these networks with other regular activities within the community. We found that the dog walking networks were larger and had a lower density, were multi-generational, of various backgrounds and had a larger number of weak tie.

Implicit change detection: Evidence from event-related brain potential

Kimura, Motohiro Nagoya University, Nagoya, Japan *Katayama, Junichi* Graduate School of Education, Hokkaido University, Sapporo, Japan *Ohira, Hideki* Department of Psychology, Nagoya University, Nagoya, Japan

Objectives: Some "change blindness" studies have provided behavioral evidences of implicit change detection. The present purpose was to identify brain activities associated with implicit change detection using event-related brain potential (ERP). Methods: Two successive visual displays were presented, where color change (66%) and no change trials (33%) were randomly occurred. Participant's task was to report whether or not color changed between the two displays. Results: Compared to no changes, undetected color changes were associated with anterior positive ERP at around 160-180 ms. Conclusions: Implicit change detection is associated with anterior positive ERP, which provides an electrophysiological evidence of implicit change detection.

Which trauma is the worse of them all? The effects of collective identity trauma/racism and discrimination

Kira, Ibrahim Center for Cumulative Trauma, Hamtramck, MI, USA *Templin, Thomas* Health Research, Wayne State Unversity, Detroit, MI, USA *Lewandowski, Linda* Nursing, Wayne State University, Hamtramck, MI, USA *Ramaswamy, Vidya* Center for Peace and conflict, Wayne State University, Detroit, MI, USA *Ozkan, Bulent* Research, Wayne State University, Detroit, MI, USA *Mohanesh, Jamal* Research, Center for Cumulative Trauma, Hamtramck, MI, USA

A new taxonomy of traumas proposes that collective identity trauma/ discrimination (Type III trauma) is the most damaging as it is ongoing. To check this assumption we conducted two studies. The first study utilized a sample of 501 of Iraqi refugees in Michigan. We used measures for cumulative trauma dose and types, PTSD, CTD and poor health. The second study utilized 399 mental health clients using similar measures. Both studies found that collective identity trauma is the most damaging compared to other traumas. Results partially validate the proposed taxonomy of traumas, and give a new challenge to clinicians in the assessment and treatments of traumatized minority populations and to community leaders and policy makers.

How does angry face capture attention?: Evidence from attentional blink paradigm

Kirita, Takahiro Dept. of Psychology, Iwate Prefectural University, Iwate, Japan *Endo, Mitsuo* Psychology, University of the Ryukyus, Nishihara, Okinawa, Japan

Using attentional blink (AB) as a measure, we examined the impact of facial expressions of first targets (T1) on the discrimination of second targets (T2). Experiment1, where T1 and T2 were presented at different locations, demonstrated that when T1 was an angry face, participants quickly shifted their attention to T1 but held it for longer duration, resulting in maximum AB. The results of Experiment2, where shift of attention was not required, showed that happy and angry expressions of T1 yielded the same magnitude of AB, suggesting that it was delayed disengagement from angry faces that caused maximum AB in Experiment1.

From the biography of women entrepreneurs to predictions of success: Innovative approaches to practices of consultation and finance

Kissel, Dorothea European Business School, Oestrich-Winkel, Germany *Chlosta, Simone* chair for entrepreneurship, European Business School, Oestrich-Winkel, Germany *Klandt, Heinz* chair for entrepreneurship, European Business School, Oestrich-Winkel, Germany

German women are still less likely to start a business than men. Evaluations of consultations with female founders reveal that at the pre-start-up stage particular conditions of the interview-situation can exhort a negative impact on the success forecast of an enterprise. The aim of this study is to increase the number of female entrepreneurs by providing a standardised instrument for consultation and success estimation. Qualitative and quantitative methods are employed to capture biographic data, relevant for success prediction. The first wave of data-collection involves expert interviews (half-standardized). The biographic questionnaire to be developed supports a solid risk-estimation by the consultants.

Sources of small group motivation in early adolescence

Klassen, Robert Dept. Educational Psychology, University of Alberta, Edmonton, Canada *Krawchuk, Lindsey* Educational Psychology, University of Alberta, Edmonton, Alberta, Canada *Job, Jenelle*

Educational Psychology, University of Alberta, Edmonton, Alberta, Canada

This study examines early adolescent collective motivation, with particular focus on the sources of collective efficacy in small work groups in school settings. Eleven focus group interviews were conducted with 58 participants in grades six through nine, with discussion centered on the role played by collective efficacy beliefs, the sources of collective efficacy beliefs, and early adolescents' perspectives on the characteristics of effective small groups. The results from the study provide direction for future research in early adolescent small group motivation.

Teachers' occupational well-being and the quality of instruction: The important role of self-regulatory patterns

Klusmann, Uta Educational Research, Max-Planck-Institut, Berlin, Germany *Kunter, Mareike* Educational Research, Max Planck Institute, Berlin, Germany *Luedtke, Oliver* Educational Research, Max Planck Institute, Berlin, Germany *Trautwein, Ulrich* Educational Research, Max Planck Institute, Berlin, Germany

The present article investigates the role of engagement and resilience as two work-related self-regulatory dimensions that predict teachers' occupational well-being and teachers' instructional performance. In Part 1 of the study, data from 1,789 German mathematics teachers were subjected to a latent profile analysis, yielding four self-regulatory types (healthy-ambitious, unambitious, excessively ambitious, and resigned) that differed statistically significantly on emotional exhaustion and job satisfaction. In Part 2, the association between teachers' self-regulatory type and instructional performance was examined in a subsample of 318 teachers. Results showed that teachers' self-regulatory type predicted the quality of instruction and differences in students' motivation.

Berlin stays fit: A 6-month intervention study to improve cognitive fitness

Klusmann, Verena Psychiatrie und Psychotherapie, Charité Universitätsmedizin, Berlin, Germany *Evers, Andrea* Psychiatry & Psychotherapy, Charité Universitätsmedizin, Berlin, Germany *Schwarzer, Ralf* Health Psychology, Freie Universität Berlin, Berlin, Germany *Dimeo, Fernando C.* Sports medicine, Charité Universitätsmedizin, Berlin, Germany *Reischies, Friedel M.* Psychiatry & Psychotherapy, Charité Universitätsmedizin, Berlin, Germany *Heuser, Isabella* Psychiatry & Psychotherapy, Charité Universitätsmedizin, Berlin, Germany

The study examines the differential effects of a physical and a mental 6-month intervention on cognitive performance. Additionally, we presume well-being and motive pattern to be important moderators of cognitive fitness. 252 elderly women were randomly assigned to a physical fitness course, a computer course (three times a week each) and a control group. Measures (pre, inter, post) contain cognitive tests (e.g., executive control, episodic memory, verbal fluency, processing speed) and questionnaires (e.g., well-being, motives). Statistical analyses include ANOVA, MANOVA and regression analysis. Preliminary results indicate that performing a new activity in old age might help to prevent cognitive decline.

A new measure to assess family functioning in young adults

Knestel, Andrea Institute of Psychology, Syracuse, USA

Evidence suggests a relationship between family functioning and mental health. The types of relationships students have with their families of origin, and their perceptions thereof, may be an important predictor of their subsequent psychological functioning. A 20-item measure of family cohesion and enmeshment was developed to assist in the assessment of common young adult problems. Upon administration to 158 freshmen in an introductory psychology course, a factor analysis was conducted. Family cohesion and enmeshment emerged as two separate constructs. This questionnaire can provide clinicians with a snapshot of how family functioning may contribute to common presenting concerns in young adults.

An attitude survey on relations between blood type and personality

Kobayashi, Sayoko Early Childhood Education, Nagasaki Women's Junior Colleg, Nagasaki, Japan
This survey was conducted to clarify an attitude to relations between blood type and personality, by asking questions to 245 woman college students. 1. Their answer shows that they believe in existence of relations at some 60% of probability. All blood types showed the same result. 2. After statistical procedure, 10 significant differences out of 95 types of personality and behavioral idiosyncrasy, depending on blood types, were found. 3. There are significantly more AB type students than others who feel repulsion for blood type judgment. A prevalent negative character image for AB type may affect this result.

A trial to change the social representations of the real community

Kobayashi, Hitoshi Dept. of Human Sciences, Osaka University, Osaka, Japan *Atsumi, Tomohide* Center for the Study of Commu, Osaka University, Osaka, Japan *Hanamura, Chikahiro* Center for the Study of Commun, Osaka University, Osaka, Japan *Honma, Naoki* Center for the Study of Commun, Osaka University, Osaka, Japan
The objective of this research was to reverse the process of forming social representations of a real community –Osaka University. We implemented a project named as DATA HANDAI Project (DHP). The project member was the students and faculty members of the university. They collected data of the university and designed information-cards presenting new aspects of the university. The authors participated in the project as a member and took field notes. Through this practice, we tried to reverse the forming process of the social representations. As a results, the participated members changed their perspectives and remarks before joining the project.

Motor learning in suppressed tracking tasks

Kobori, Satoshi Dept. of Elec. and Information, Ryukoku University, Otsu, Japan *Abe, Yosuke* Dept. of Elec. & Info., Ryukoku University, Otsu, Japan *Nakazono, Shogo* Dept. of Elec. & Info., Ryukoku University, Otsu, Japan
We measured tracking performance in two groups while either the target or the manual cursor was suppressed for a brief period during each trial. We used this manipulation to show that motor learning involves acquiring predictive models of the target motion and also of one's own hand movement. We also found clear positive transfer from learning to predict one's own manual action to learning target motions, and no transfer in the reverse direction. This asymmetric transfer suggests specific predictive neural mechanisms for learning to control one's own action, as opposed to general prediction of external events.

Extending the human life span: Assessing pro- and anti-longevity attitudes

Kogan, Nathan Center for New Constructs, Educational Testing Service, Princeton NJ, USA *Tucker, Jennifer* Psychology, New School for Social Research, New York, NY, USA *Porter, Matthew* Templeton Fellows, The HealthCare Chaplaincy, New York, NY, USA

Successful efforts by biologists to extend the natural life span of lower animals has raised the possibility of extrapolation to humans, which in turn has given rise to bioethical argumentation, pro and con. These arguments were converted into pro- and anti-longevity items yielding a 35-item Life Extension Questionnaire (LEQ). This was administered to a mixed-age sample of 164 respondents. Factor analysis of the LEQ yielded 3 factors labelled Personal Emotional Rejection, Utopian Vision, and Social Economic Burden. Age correlated significantly with Utopian Vision, older individuals more readily endorsing pro-longevity items.

The study of relationships among prosocial behavior and three attitude-components toward person in need in elementary school children

Kohyama, Takaya Graduate School of Education, Hiroshima University, Hiroshima, Japan *Miyasato, Tomoe* Graduate School of Education, Hiroshima University, Higashi-Hiroshima, Japan *Yamada, Yohei* Graduate School of Education, Hiroshima University, Higashi-Hiroshima, Japan *Suzuki, Yumiko* Graduate School of Education, Hiroshima University, Higashi-Hiroshima, Japan *Ishii, Shinji* Graduate School of Education, Hiroshima University, Higashi-Hiroshima, Japan
The purpose of this study was to clarify relationships among prosocial behavior and three attitude-components toward person in need by the questionnaire survey of elementary school children. One hundred and forty-seven 5th and 6th graders participated in this survey. The results showed that most of children had high attitude score on a cognitive component but it was less corresponding to prosocial behavior than affective and behavioral ones. This result indicated that the importance of affective approach to cultivate prosocial behavior of children.

How Japanese first-time parents arrange object-based child-rearing environments during transition to parenthood

Kojima, Yasuo Dept. of Psychology, Chukyo University, Nagoya, Japan
Ten Japanese first-time mothers were asked to record everything that they acquired (purchased, received as a gift, or borrowed) until one year after their infant's birth. Monthly interviews complemented the data. The items could be classified into several categories, including those that were intended to aid the parent, and those that were intended to support the development of cognitive or physical skills and to promote the safety of the infant. Interview data revealed that items were not only useful in close parent-child interaction, but also triggered conflict between them.

Diagnostic of social phobia: Psychometric properties of the SASKO (Social Anxiety - Social Competence Deficit)

Kolbeck, Sabine Hamburg, Germany *Maß, Reinhard Dahme, Bernhard Hand, Iver*
The SASKO is a new self-rating scale for the differential measurement of social anxiety and social deficits, including four subscales which have been developed by factor analysis: two subscales describe aspects of social anxiety (speaking, acting under observation; rejection), two subscales aim at symptoms of social deficits (performance; competence). In the present study, the diagnostic validity of the SASKO was investigated in a sample of N=68 inpatients with social phobia and a comparison group of healthy controls (N=242). The total scale shows good internal consistency (Cronbach's alpha = .96), good convergent validity (.64-.80) and outstanding sensitivity (.93) and specifity (.92).

Spoken word intelligibility of young and old adults with Familiarity-controlled Word lists 2007 (FW07)

Kondo, Tadahisa Communication Science Labs, NTT Corporation, Atsugi, Japan *Ijuin, Mutsuo* Institute of Gerontology, Tokyo Metropolitan, Itabashi-ku, Tokyo, Japan *Amano, Shigeaki* Communication Science Labs, NTT Corporation, Soraku-gun, Kyoto, Japan *Sakamoto, Shuichi* Res. Ins. of Elec. Comm., Tohoku University, Sendai, Miyagi, Japan *Suzuki, Yôiti* Res. Ins. of Elec. Comm., Tohoku University, Sendai, Miyagi, Japan
To assess aging effects on spoken word recognition, 16 young adults (20 - 38 years old) and 24 old adults (69 - 83 years old) participated in a spoken word intelligibility test with the Familiarity-controlled word lists 2007 (FW07). The results revealed the significant effects of word familiarity (WF) and signal to noise ratio (SNR) as well as the significant interaction between WF and SNR. However, the interaction was weaker for old adults than young adults. These results suggests that old adults depend much on word familiarity in spoken word recognition.

Coming out: The role of the internet for meeting potential (sex)partners among young gay men

Koning, Maaike Work and Social Psychology, Maastricht University, Maastricht, Netherlands *Hospers, Harm* Work and Social Psychology, Maastricht University, Maastricht, Netherlands
Objectives: To examine the role of the internet in the coming-out process for meeting potential (sex)partners. Methods: Twenty-nine young gay men, who had their coming-out in the preceding year, are interviewed biannually for a period of three years about the coming-out process. The first two waves were analyzed. Results: Between the two waves a shift occurred from the internet as the primary meeting place for sex(partners) to the public gayscene. Conclusions: The internet plays a large role in the beginning stage of the coming-out process, when it is mainly used as a means of contacting other young gay men.

An examination on coping in interpersonal stress of narcissistic personality

Konishi, Mizuho Dept. of Psychiatry, Shiga Univ. of Medical Science, Otsu, Japan *Yamada, Naoto* Psychiatry, Shiga Univ. of Medical Science, Otsu, Shiga, Japan *Sato, Suguru* Psychology, Doshisha University, Kyoto, Japan
Objectives: The objective of this study was to investigate the coping in interpersonal stress of narcissistic personality and influence on mental health. Methods: Participants; 127 college students. Questionnaire; Narcissistic Personality Inventory-35 (NPI-35; Konishi, Okawa, & Hashimoto, 2006), Interpersonal Stress-Coping Inventory (ISCI), Happiness Scale and Stress Response Scale (includes 7 subscales; e.g. depression, physical fatigue). Results and Conclusion: Multiple regression analyses were conducted to identify the effects from NPI-35 to ISCI and influences on mental health. When the person who had the high NPI-35 goes through the stress, he/she strives for positively improving the relationship. And then, he/she feels depressive mood.

Children's biological theories on the role of inheritance

Kornilaki, Ekaterina Preschool Education, University of Crete, Rethymno, Greece *Kitrou, Paraskevi* Preschool Education, University of Crete, Rethymno, Greece
Children's understanding of the biological basis of parent-offspring relations was examined. The study was not only restricted on children's theories on the role of inheritance of physical characteristics, as most studies did, but also examined its role on a set of psychological traits, skills, preferences and

beliefs. Ninety four children aged 7, 9 and 11 were read stories about babies of biological and adoptive parents and were asked to judge to whom the child would resemble. Most young children attributed all the characteristics to the biological parents, while the eldest children attributed psychological traits, skills, preferences and beliefs to the adoptive parents.

The categorical structure of the perception of painting: A study of landscape

Korotchenko, Evgeniya Inst. of Psychology, Russian Academy of Education, Moscow, Russia Petrenko, Viktor General psychology, Moskow State University, Moskow, Russia

Purpose: psychosemantical research of categorical structure of the perception of painting. Methods: - Multidimensional scaling of landscapes and their verbal descriptions. The respondents had to compare 100 landscapes according to the emotions each landscape evoked. Then they had to compare those verbal descriptions of their moods. Individual matrices of similarity, received after scaling, were factorized. -Miller's classification. The respondents classified 100 landscapes into some groups. The data were converted into a cluster tree. The results indicated qualitative difference between the figurative and verbal languages and gave the grounds for advancing assumptions about the structure and features of "the language of art".

Effectiveness of group creativity for different ways of group organization

Kozlova, Maria Psychology, Moscow State University, Moscow, Russia

The aim of our study was to examine the relation between organization of group activity and creative problems solving effectiveness. For this purpose the scheme of multifactor experiment and the Russian version Torrance Tests of Creative Thinking were used. The sample comprised of 35 groups. If there was a nominal group, then group became effective in fluency, flexibility and originality of ideas. If there was an interactive group, than the group was effective in resistance to premature closure and abstractness of titles. If a common-successive activity was organized in a group, than this group was effective in elaboration of ideas.

Audio-visual simultaneity judgments in rapid serial visual presentation

Kranczioch, Cornelia Southampton, United Kingdom Thorne, Jeremy Institute of Hearing Research, MRC, Southampton, United Kingdom Debener, Stefan Institute of Hearing Research, MRC, Southampton, United Kingdom

We investigated the accuracy of audio-visual simultaneity judgments in a RSVP task. Healthy participants indicated which RSVP stimulus was presented simultaneously with a tone. Data analysis confirmed a bias towards perceiving the visual stimulus that was presented one lag before the tone as being presented simultaneously with the tone. This constellation was perceived as simultaneous in about 20% more trials than the truly simultaneous constellation. This effect is likely related to the higher processing speed in the auditory modality. Further analyses will explore whether this misperception is affected by the length of the RSVP sequence preceding the audio-visual stimulus pair.

Mediating effect of job attribution on role stress and health strain

Krishna, Anshula Psychology, Vasanta College for Women, Varanasi, India

The study examined mediating effect of causal attributions on experience of job stress and its effect on health in a sample of 300 technical employees. Participants' role stress, attributional style and health status were assessed through psychometric tools. The results suggest that attribution to ability,

effort and luck/chance for success/failures in job positively mediate (buffer) the experience of role stress, while attributions to working condition, boss, colleagues, nature of job, and management policies intensify the role stress. It was also noted that attribution to ability, effort, and luck/chance moderate, while attribution to other job factors elevate, the degree of positive relationship between role stress and health strains.

People older age and life contentment

Kulas, Kristina Zaprešiæ, Croatia Carija, Martina Preventive programme MPPI, Udruga Igra, Zaprešiæ, Croatia Niksic, Dubravka Psihologija, Filozofski fakultet, Zagreb, Croatia Galic, Mia Psihologija, Filozofski fakultet, Zagreb, Croatia

The goal was to find how personal assessment of one's health, way of using free time, social support and place of living effects life contentment of the people older age. Two questioner was completed. The first one consisted of questions concerning general data, health, way of using free time, social support. In the second one they estimated their life contentment. Personal assessment of one's health, social support and way of using free time shows to be the best predictors of life contentment. The place of living was significantly associated with subjective health.

Development of driver assistance-systems based on behavioral strategies

Kullack, Anke Inst. für Psychologie, Tech. Universität Braunschweig, Braunschweig, Germany Ehrenpfordt, Ingmar Transportation Systems, German Aerospace Center, Braunschweig, Germany Eggert, Frank Psychology, TU Braunschweig, Braunschweig, Germany

In order to improve lane-keeping-assistance-systems we applied behavioral strategies. Classical lane-keeping-systems can be regarded as cognitive systems because an association between an arbitrary signal and the required reaction has to be established by means of learning processes. Since this association is subjected to interference and decay, the functionality of cognitive systems is in principle suboptimal. These disadvantages can be avoided by eliciting a steering-reflex. This behavioral approach was tested in a simulator-study with 28 participants. First results demonstrate the functionality of the principle. It could be of considerable importance in the prevention of accidents caused by road-departures.

Effects of extended video stimulation on visual cognition in preadolescent children

Kumari, Santha Dept. SMSS, Thapar University, Patiala, India Ahuja, Simerpreet SMSS, Thapar University, Patiala, India

Present study investigated the detrimental effects of video stimulation on visual cognition in preadolescents. School going children, boys and girls(N=1100) of the age range 9-12 years participated. Using a television viewing questionnaire, 300 children were categorized as heavy and light viewers. They were compared on three different cognitive variables :attention span, visual memory, and creative imagination. Light viewers performed significantly better than heavy viewers on all variables studied. Findings are explained in terms of the inhibitory effect of formal features of video on cognitive mechanisms underlying the evolution of rich imagery and processes linked to creative imagination, free play of fantasy etc.

Aging related changes in processing and retention for visual information

Kunimi, Mitsunobu Dept. of Psychology, Jinai University, Fukui, Japan Matsukawa, Junko Psychology, Kanazawa University, Kanazawa, Ishikawa, Japan

Ageing related changes in visual working memory were examined using matrix patterns. Participants, in their 20s to 70s, were investigated using the cross-sectional method, and the N-back task. Zero-back task that requires only retention and 1-back task that requires processing and retention were compared. In the 0-back task, recognition was different between the 20-59 year-olds and the 60-79 year-olds. Conversely, in the 1-back task, significant differences were observed between the 20-29 year-olds and the 40-79 year-olds. These results suggest a relatively rectiline decline in the 0-back task during the 30s and a rapid decline after the 60s.

Prediction of school achievement: A prospective longitudinal study from kindergarten to elementary school

Kuschel, Annett Rehabilitationswissenschaften, Humboldt Universität Berlin, Berlin, Germany Bertram, Heike Department of Psychology, Braunschweig University, Braunschweig, Germany Naumann, Sebastian Department of Psychology, Braunschweig University, Braunschweig, Germany Staender, Dagmar Health Centre, Bildungsinstitut nds.Justiz, Celle, Germany Heinrichs, Nina Department of Psychology, Bielefeld University, Bielefeld, Germany Hahlweg, Kurt Department of Psychology, Braunschweig University, Braunschweig, Germany

This study followed 204 children from kindergarten trough elementary school to assess which characteristics are predictors of school achievement. The various predictor variables were assessed during the preschool years and follow-up and represented different domains (i.e. demographic variables, IQ, phonological awareness, behaviour problems). The criterion measures were assessed from first Grade on with standardized tests in reading, spelling and mathematics on achievements at school. Important predictors are phonological awareness, intelligence and family income in reading, but not in spelling, mathematics. About 30% of the variance was explained by these factors. Implications for prevention and early intervention will be discussed.

Elementary school boys (but not girls) show a negative correlation between creativity and feelings that the teacher encourages them to share their work

Kyle, Stephanie Dept. of Psychology, Bishop's University, Lindsay, Canada Bacon, Benoit Psychology, Bishop's University, Sherbrooke, Canada Stout, Dale Psychology, Bishop's University, Sherbrooke, Canada

The present study originally aimed at producing a valid English translation of the "My Classroom" scale (De Souza Fleith & De Alencar, 2005), and assessing whether its items correlated with creativity scores of grade two, three and four children, as measured with the Williams Exercise in Divergent Thinking (Form A) (Williams, 1986). Creativity scores did not vary significantly across ages, but the evaluations of the climate for creativity became significantly more negative with age. Interestingly, the item "The teacher encourages me to share my work with other students" was negatively correlated with creativity in boys, but not in girls.

Nutrition scholarship education and relation in preference and selection food choices: Application to four behavior programs

López Gamiño, María del Refugio UIICSE, FESI UNAM, Tlalnepantla, Mexico Cortés Moreno, Assol UIICSE, FESI UNAM, Tlalnepantla, Mexico Alarcón Armendariz, Martha Elba UIICSE, FESI UNAM, Tlalnepantla, Mexico

This study assessed a nutritional education strategy and its relation with preferences and food choices. A 116 elementary school children sample particiced. Pretest-postest design with comparison groups was employed. The scholarships were assignment to four behavior programs: not instrumental, situational instrumental, extrasituational and transituational. Body Mass Index was evaluated, also preference and food choices. Results showed scholarships preferered natural food, but selection painted to industrial food. Significant differences in extrasituational and transituational programs sign the preferences and selection food were modificated after intervention in fourth and sixth grade. Results suggest to begin nutritional education starting around nine years.

Testing the relationship between personality and well-being: Contrasting visually and auditory impaired older adults

Langer, Nadine Psychological Ageing Research, Institute of Psychology, Heidelberg, Germany *Wahl, Hans-Werner* Psychological Ageing Research, Institute of Psychology, Heidelberg, Germany *Heyl, Vera* Blindenpädagogik, University of Education, Heidelberg, Germany *Jonas, Jost* Department of Ophtalmology, University of Mannheim, Mannheim, Germany *Rohrschneider, Klaus* Department of Ophtalmology, University of Heidelberg, Heidelberg, Germany

This paper focuses on the interplay between personality and subjective well-being in sensory impaired and unimpaired older adults. Results (based on 151 visually impaired, 100 auditory impaired and 150 unimpaired adults between 75 and 94 years, mean: 83 years): Besides considerable similarities between groups concerning the correlation of extraversion/neuroticism and well-being, for example, only in the visually impaired and in the unimpaired group neuroticism correlates with positive affect (-) and cognitive well-being (+). Extraversion correlates with cognitive well-being (+) only in the impaired groups. There is first evidence that the personality-wellbeing-connection may be questioned when it comes to sensory impairment.

Disrupting face biases in visual attention

Law, Anna Dept. of Psychology, John Moores University, Liverpool, United Kingdom *Langton, Stephen* Psychology, University of Stirling, Stirling, United Kingdom

Objectives: To investigate whether a working memory load disrupts face biases in visual attention. Methods: Undergraduate participants attempted a dot-probe task known to produce bias towards faces (Bindemann, M., Burton, A. M., Langton, S. R. H., Schweinberger, S. R., & Doherty, M. J. (2007). The control of attention to faces. Journal of Vision, 7(10):15, 1-8), both alone and with a digit-rehearsal secondary task. Results: At 100ms delay between cue and target: no modulation of face bias. At 500ms delay: elimination of face bias for participants attempting dual-task condition before single-task. Conclusions: Working memory load can disrupt attentional orienting to faces.

Participatory research in a school setting: A process of acculturation

Leblanc, Raymond Dept. d'Education, Université d'Ottawa, Ottawa, Canada *Ducharme, Daphne* Speech and Language disorders, Université d'Ottawa, Ottawa, Canada

The purpose of the study was to measure the impact of a training program in phonological awareness that was offferd to 64 grade 1 and grade 2 teachers in a francophone school board of the province of Ontario, Canada. We examined the teacher's teaching practices in reading and in their students' reading achievement. An action research and training framework guided the collaborative work between university researchers and teacher participants. Findings suggest that teacher training in phonological awareness did produce better achievement in reading for at-risk students in grade one

and even more significant progress for reading disabled second grade students.

Intrinsic and extrinsic motivation and school-achievement

Lehmann, Wolfgang Inst. für Psychologie, Universität Magdeburg, Magdeburg, Germany *Rombusch, Marita* Insitut für Psychologie, Universität Magdeburg, Magdeburg, Germany *Jüling, Inge* Schulpsychologische Beratung, Landesverwaltungsamt, Magdeburg, Germany

This study investigates connections of motivation and achievement. Basis is the theory of intrinsic and extrinsic motivation. Six-grade-students attending different school types worked on an intelligence test, an English test and motivation questionnaires. In students' self-appraisal extrinsic motivation has a more important meaning than intrinsic motivation but intrinsic motivation shows higher correlations to school marks. Facets of intrinsic motivation are more closely related to test performances than extrinsic motivation. Extrinsic motivation in one subject seems to radiate to the other subject while intrinsic motivation in one subject has only weak or no connections to intrinsic motivation in the other subject.

From national glorification through moral disengagement to appraisals of justice

Leidner, Bernhard Dept. of Psychology, New School for Social Research, New York, USA *Slawuta, Patricia* Psychology, New School for Social Research, New York, USA *Castano, Emanuele* Psychology, New School for Social Research, New York, USA

Proposing an integrated perspective of research on moral disengagement strategies and collective emotions, the process of moral disengagement in the context of reminders of ingroup atrocities is investigated. In our current study, American participants read a newspaper article about fictitious but reality-related prison tortures in Iraq, allegedly committed by U.S. soldiers. By means of path modeling it is shown that the more participants glorified the U.S., the more they minimized the victims' suffering and explicitly infrahumanized them, which, in turn, led to less intensive group-based distress, compared to non-glorifiers. Moral disengagement and distress ultimately predicted retributive and restorative justice.

Predicting driving manoeuvres via eye movements

Lethaus, Firas Inst. Transportation Systems, German Aerospace Center (DLR), Braunschweig, Germany

The aim of this study was to establish whether characteristic eye movement patterns precede particular driving manoeuvres. Drivers' gaze behaviour was measured prior to and during the execution of five different driving manoeuvres performed in real traffic on three different types of road using the DLR research vehicle ViewCar. The eye movement data were analysed using Markov matrices of zero- and first-order. It was found that significantly distinct gaze patterns precede each of the driving manoeuvres analysed. The study indicates that eye movement data might be used as input to advanced driver-assistant systems in order to recognise intended driving manoeuvres.

Some latest advances in cognitive load theory research and it's teaching implications

Li, Yinghui Shandong Normal University, Ji Nan, People's Republic of China *Si, Jiwei* School of Psychology, Shandong Normal University, Ji Nan, People's Republic of China

The classification of cognitive load have been more detailed, acceded to the concept of Germane cognitive load. The mechanism of cognitive load combined with Schema construct theories were discussed. Some new measurement method appeared, such as production system, self-report

psychological effort, EEG technology, rapid assessment test. As to the impacting factors of cognitive load, the level of expertise and multimedia displaying method have been investigated. Results of research on cognitive load theory quickly applied to teaching practice, guided the mode of instruction, teaching programs, and teaching software.

The relationship between metacognitive regulation ability and job performance

Li, Jian School of Psychology, Beijing Normal University, Beijing, People's Republic of China *Zhang, Houcan* school of psychology, Beijing Normal University, Beijing, People's Republic of China

With 260 employees from an IT company as subjects, the relationship between metacognitive regulation ability and job performance was investigated. Their information of position ranks, job performances were collected and metacognitive regulation abilities assessed. Analyzed by the hierarchical linear and logistic regression methods, differences between four career posts were obtained: Middle managers of sales department had higher off-line generalizing level and on-line monitoring level, while those from support department had higher off-line insight level. But for the employees, low level of on-line monitoring led to bad sales credits, whereas low level of off-line global-planning led to more creative activities.

Mental health status of Chinese elders

Li, Juan Inst. of Psychology, Chinese Academy of Sciences, Beijing, People's Republic of China *Wu, Zhenyun* Institute of Psychology, Chinese Academy of Sciences, Beijing, People's Republic of China

Objectives: To evaluate mental health status of Chinese elders. Methods: Mental Health Inventory for Chinese Elders, which included emotion, self-conception, interpersonal relationship, cognition and adaptation components, was administered to 4208 elders above 55 from all over China. Results: The status of Chinese elders' mental health was well $(3.21 \pm 0.39$ with score can range 1-4). The status of mental health declined with aging increasing and educational degree decreasing. The married couple had higher scores of mental health than the divorced and widowed. The level of elders' mental health in various areas was inconsistent with that of economy development of those areas.

Can apology repair the trust?: The role of locus of control in trust-game

Liao, Zongqing Dept. of Psychology, Peking University, Beijing, People's Republic of China *Su, Yanjie* Department of Psychology, Peking University, Beijing, People's Republic of China

The present study examined the influence of apology, LOC (the locus of control) on individual's trust in 44 Chinese college students. A trust-game was designed to measure trust behaviors and beliefs, and LOC score was assessed by Rotter's scale. The results indicated an interaction (F (1, 18) =5.709, p <0.05) between apology and LOC. The internal LOC individuals accepted the apology more easily and showed a positive effect, while the external ones were opposite. It was suggested the relation between trust repair and apology may take a different form when situational cues and individual traits are taken into account.

Semantic interference in delayed picture naming: Evidence from a new set of stimuli and language

Lima, Cesar Psychology, Universidade do Porto, Porto, Portugal *Castro, São Luís* Psychology, Universidade do Porto, Porto, Portugal

Seventy-two Portuguese college students named pictures of common objects with superimposed distractor words in two naming conditions, immediate or delayed, according to the design of Janssen, Schirm, Mahon and Caramazza (in press). A new set of pictures (of high or low frequency) and distractor words (that were either semantic category coordinates of the target pictures or unrelated) was tested. A frequency effect was obtained only in immediate naming, but semantic interference occurred both in immediate and in delayed naming. These results give robustness to the claim that semantic interference in the picture-word interference paradigm arises at a post-lexical level of processing.

How information structure affects semantic integration in question-answer pairs: A semantic illusion phenomenon

Lin, Wang Institude of Psychology, Chinese Academy of Science, Beijing, People's Republic of China *Yang, Yufang* Institude of Psychology, Chinese Academy of Science, Bei Jing, People's Republic of China *Li, Xiaoqing* Institude of Psychology, Chinese Academy of Science, Bei Jing, People's Republic of China *Li, Weijun* Institude of Psychology, Chinese Academy of Science, Bei Jing, People's Republic of China

ERP was used to explore the role of information structure (IS) in the processing of WH question-answer pairs. IS was manipulated by questions such as who bought vegetable to cook today? /which vegetable did mum buy to cook today? Relative to the context, the alternative critical words in the answers (Mum bought eggplant/beef to cook today.) were either focus or non-focus which was semantic appropriate or inappropriate. The results showed that compared to focus, non-focus elicited larger N400. Moreover, on non-focus but not on focus there was a semantic illusion effect. The results suggested that IS can manipulate attentional resources allocation during language comprehension and that subjects could make immediate discourse integration.

Self-supporting of children aged between 6 and 12 years: Theoretical construct and development of questionnaire

Ling, Hui Department of Psychology, Hunan Normal University, Changsha, People's Republic of China *Huang, Xiting* School of psychology, Southwest University, Chongqing, People's Republic of China

Objective: Self-supporting is a Chinese traditional virtue, this study attempts to explore the connotation, structure and theoretical explanations about self-supporting in Chinese children. Methods: In this study we intend to construct the structure of self-supporting behavior of 6-12 years old children from two dimensions: the major fields related to children's self-supporting behavior, and the mental functions of such behaviors. Results: The Self-supporting Questionnaire was constructed according to the hypothesis. Exploratory and Confirmatory factor analysis found that Self-supporting Questionnaire of Children had clear factor structure, high reliability and validity. Conclusions: The multi-layered structure model of two dimensions for children's self-supporting behavior was proposed by this study.

An experimental research on self-schema of children with different self-supporting levels

Ling, Hui Department of Psychology, Hunan Normal University, Changsha, People's Republic of China *Huang, Xiting* School of psychology, Southwest Normal University, Chongqing, People's Republic of China

Objective: To validate whether there exist self-schema of self-supporting and to look into the differences in amount of recall, amount of recognition and reaction time between children with high score of self-supporting and those with low score. Methods: The self-referent encoding task(SRET) was assigned to the two groups. Results: The amount of recognition of self-supporting words by the two groups is larger than that of non-self-supporting words; The reaction time of the high self-supporting group is longer than that of the

other group; there is no significant difference in the amount of correct recognition. Conclusion: Self-supporting is not a dichotomy concept of self.

An experimental research on self-imposed delay of gratification of children with different self-supporting levels

Ling, Hui Department of Psychology, Hunan Normal University, Changsha, People's Republic of China *Huang, Xiting* School of Psychology, Southwest University, Chongqing, People's Republic of China

Objective: To explore the self-imposed delay of gratification of children with different self-supporting levels. Methods: Levels of self-supporting of 272 grade one students were assessed by the Self-supporting Behavior Questionnaire. Then the Self-imposed Delay of Gratification experimental task of Mischel was assigned to the high self-supporting group and the low self-supporting group. Results: The delay time and the delay strategy has significant difference between children with high self-supporting and those with low self-supporting. Conclusion: the development levels of self-supporting of children can be used to predict children's ability of self-imposed delay of gratification.

Belief in a just world and value for Chinese students

Liu, Chang-Jiang School of Management, Shenyang Normal University, Shenyang, People's Republic of China *Guo, Li-Yan* School of Teacher Education, Shenyang Normal University, Shenyang, People's Republic of China

Previous research has showed cultural differences of personal and general beliefs in a just world between eastern and western worlds, and current study examined whether the pattern of relationship between BJW and value in China was different from that in western world. Chinese students whose age varied from 13 to 26 completed measures on BJWs and various values. Results showed that general BJW was significantly predicted by power and universalism values, whereas personal BJW was predicted by achievement and universalism values after controlling the effect of age. Implications for cultural variations in the nature of BJW and value were discussed.

The relationships among mothers' ego development, mother-child communication and adolescents' ego development and autonomy

Liu, Yih-Lan Center for Teacher Education, National Tsing Hua University, Hsinchu, Taiwan

Objective: This study investigated how mothers' ego development affected adolescents' ego development and autonomy by ways of mother-child communication. Methods: subjects were 137 8 th graders and their mothers in Taiwan. They completed questionnaires to measure their ego development, perceived mother-child communication (mothers and adolescents) and autonomy (adolescents only). Results: Regression analyses indicated that mothers' ego development and mother-child's rational communication style significantly and positively predicted adolescents' relating vs. individuating autonomy. Mothers' ego development and mother-child communication did not predict adolescent ego development. Conclusions: Mothers who had higher ego development and used rational communication style tended to facilitate adolescents' autonomy.

The relationship among the perceived classroom structure, science epistemological belief, misconception and academic achievement

Liu, Pei-Yun Education and Human Resource, Hsuan Chuang University, Hsinchu, Taiwan

The purpose of this study was to investigate the relationship among the perceived classroom structure, science epistemological belief, misconception and academic achievement. Three hundred and

thirty-one seven-grade students completed a self-report survey assessing their perceived classroom structure, science epistemological belief and misconception. Results included that (a) constructivist perceived classroom structure exerted significant positive effects on individual science epistemological belief and academic achievement, but exerted negative effects on misconception. (b) individual science epistemological belief was the mediating variable between the perceived classroom structure and misconception. Based on findings, the implications for theory and practice, and for further research, are also discussed.

Gender differences in health in people over 55

Lizaso, Izarne Dept. of Psychology, Univ. of the Basque Country, San Sebastian, Spain *Sansinenea, Francisco* PSYCHOLOGY, UNIVERSITY OF THE BASQUE COUNT, SAN SEBASTIAN, Spain *Aizpurua, Alaitz* PSYCHOLOGY, UNIVERSITY OF THE BASQUE COUNT, SAN SEBASTIAN, Spain *Sanchez de Miguel, Manuel* PSYCHOLOGY, UNIVERSITY OF THE BASQUE COUNT, SAN SEBASTIAN, Spain

This study claims to analyse gender differences in physical, psychological and social health in people over 55 (Mage= 66 years, SD= 6.35). A semi-structured interview was used with 161 adults (80 women and 81 men). Also, the following psycho-social questionnaires were administered: GADS - screening -, GDS/30, HAS, PGC, Inventory of Social Resources and COOP-WONCA. Statistically significant differences were found in several factors: i.e., women display more sings of depressive and a lower degree of social support in comparison to men. This psycho-social questionnaire battery can be useful to know possible gender differences in health of people over 55.

Effects of a relaxation programme in older adults' state of mind

Lizaso, Izarne Dept. of Psychology, Univ. of the Basque Country, San Sebastian, Spain *Sanchez de Miguel, Manuel* PSYCHOLOGY, UNIVERSITY OF THE BASQUE COUNT, SAN SEBASTIAN, Spain *Aizpurua, Alaitz* PSYCHOLOGY, UNIVERSITY OF THE BASQUE COUNT, SAN SEBASTIAN, Spain

In this study the effects of a relaxation programme in state of mind and quality of life in a group of 89 (81 women and 8 men) older adults (Mage = 72; Mrange = 53–86 years) were analysed. Anxiety (GADS; Cautela's Inventory of Tension and Anxiety Indicators) and depression level (GADS; GDS/15) and quality of life (Health-Related Quality of Life COOP-WONCA) were evaluated. Pre-post treatment comparisons indicate statistically significant differences in anxiety (GADS) and depression (GADS and GDS) but not in tension-anxiety nor quality of life. Relaxation programmes may improve older adults' state of mind thus their application is suggested.

Production of a normative speech and role of expression context: Young people's relationship with alcohol

Lo Monaco, Gregory Laboratory of Socialpsychology, University of Provence, Aix-en-Provence, France *Lheureux, Florent* Laboratory of socialpsychology, University of Provence, Aix-en-Provence, France *Chianàse, Laure* Laboratory of socialpsychology, University of Provence, Aix-en-Provence, France *Codaccioni, Colomba* Laboratory of socialpsychology, University of Provence, Aix-en-Provence, France *Halimi-Falkowicz, Severine* Laboratory of socialpsychology, University of Provence, Aix-en-Provence, France

Students, producing verbal associations about alcohol, were confronted either with an agent of health or with a student, and were speaking either for themselves or as the students would do in general. The results show that the individuals, placed in front of an agent of health and directly implied in the beliefs that they express, tend to adopt the speech wished by this agent. However, this manifest adhesion only appears to be circumstantial, insofar as the speech of the individuals is different when they are expressed vis-a-vis a member of its group and in the name of this one.

Ways of overcoming psychological barriers

Lozhkin, Georgiy Psychology, Institute of Psychology, Kiev, Ukraine Volyanyuk, Nataliya Psychology, Central Institute of Post-Grad, Lutsk, Ukraine

Research object: peculiar features of psychological barrier manifestations in educational environment. Methods: self-diagnostics of psychological barriers (Y.Yermolayeva). Results. It was determined that psychological barriers are various forms of "fear syndrome" manifestations having two sides: fear of losing the habitual, and fear of the new, unusual. Conclusions. Ways of overcoming psychological barriers in educational environment imply the activity in two directions: elimination (liquidation or decrease) of a psychological barrier; and psychological barrier neutralization without its actual elimination.

Work health psychology of women workers in work settings

Lu, Jinky Leilanie National Institutes of Health, Manila, Philippines

The study aimed at looking into problems caused by organizational factors to mental health of women workers. This was conducted in an export zone involving 31 industries and an interview with 613 women workers. The results showed that there were several interactions between variables which include the following- the need for new quality for products is associated with the need to upgrade knowledge and skills, fast-pace work is associated with heavy physical load, andpoor health and safety policies. The study proposed for a massive review of the existing regulations for work and its relations to mental and psychological health.

A study on the present status and causes of university students' loneliness

Lu, Yiping Department of Psychology, Beijing Normal University, Beijing, People's Republic of China

This study investigates the present status of university students' loneliness and its causes from four scales, namely, friendship, relation with family members, relation with lovers and relation with larger groups. The results shows:(1) undergraduates' loneliness is at a higher level, especially those introvert ones; meanwhile, loneliness is the most severe on the relation with lovers scale, and the least severe on the relation with family members scale. (2) unfulfilled needs for love, lack of interpersonal trust, deficiency in communication skills and weakened relation with parents are the main causes of undergraduates' loneliness.

Psychosocial and health issues in the workplace

Lu, Yung Chang Quality Control, Sophia Mineral Services, Quezon City, Philippines

The study aimed at looking into the problems caused by organizational factors such as job autonomy, content of job, nature of task, to mental health of women workers. This was conducted in an export zone involving 31 industries and an interview with 613 women workers. Results showed that the overall good physical health of workers is affected by overtime and mental work. Moreover The study suggests that psychosomatic medicine must be considered by occupational doctors to promote occupational health in industries. Policies and counseling that covers psychosomatic medicine must also be formulated for the industrial setting.

The evaluation on the effect of happiness enhancing activities

Luo, Yueh-Chuan National Taiwan Unversity, Taipei, Taiwan

This study aims to evaluate the effect of happiness enhancing activities. The participants were 7th grade students. The experimental groups participated in 4 various intentional activities to obtain hope, gratitude, strengths, and the best job; while the control group simply recalled life experiences. All of the five groups were administered the pre-test before the experimental treatment, the post-test two weeks after the experimental intentional activity, and the delay test one month after. The results showed the experimental groups had higher authentic happiness and lower depression than the control group on both the post-test and the delay test.

An experimental research of the influence of past feeling experience on self-esteem

Lv, Houchao School of Psychology, Chongqing, People's Republic of China Huang, Xiting School of Psychology, School of Psychology, BeiBei District, Chongqing, People's Republic of China

This research is aimed to explore the influence of past feeling experience on self-esteem. Results show that: Individuals with positive feelings tend to be high self-esteem, and negative individuals tend to be low self-esteem. When recalling high-self-esteem words, the subjects with positive feelings is significantly better than negative subjects; when recalling low-self-esteem words, the subjects with positive feelings is significantly worse than negative subjects. Within subjects of positive feelings, the recalled number of high-self-esteem words is higher than that of low-self-esteem words; and within negative subjects, the recalled number between high-self-esteem words and low-self-esteem words has no significant difference.

Negated directives in the context communicative competence

Maciuszek, Jozef Inst. of Applied Psychology, Jagiellonian University, Krakow, Poland

The presentation shows the research into effects of negations usage in directives. Three experiments tested effects of 'pay attention to' and 'don't pay attention to' commands on focusing attention. The indicator of attention focusing was the level of recollection of details of comic read before. In following experiments this indicator was time needed to name the stimulus words' colors and the level of these words' recollection after the previous task. The results show the paradox of negated commands which cause similarly great attention focus on the key objects as direct commands and far greater focus than in the control conditions.

Motivation strategy as factor devolepment person of the school children

Malkin, Valery Centre Psychology, Ural University, Ekaterinburg, Russia Rogaleva, Liudmila centre psychology, Ural university, Ekaterinburg, Russia

Physical culture lessons are considered not only to be a means of physical development of students, but a matter of their personal development that are able to develop their possibilities. The solution of this problem is possible under the circumstance if the students aware themselves as the subject of the activity. Motivative technology of the decision of this task consisted of 4 steps: 1.formation positive emotions to Physical culture lessons. 2.formation motivation of achievement of the group and individual aims. 3.formation motivation to creative activity. 4.formation motivation for self-realisation and self-development

Heterosexual men as targets of gay men's coming out: Exploring experiences in friendship

Manalastas, Eric Julian Dept. of Psychology, University of the Philippines, Quezon City, Philippines

If sexual identity is truly socially constructed, then research on coming out of the closet needs to include perspectives not just of gay individuals, but also of the recipients ("targets") of coming out. Using in-depth interviews, I explored the lived experiences of N = 12 young heterosexual men who have male friends come out to them as gay. Coming out was experienced in diverse, usually indirect ways, involving mixed affect, identity support, stereotype-based perceptions, and occasional homoerotic tension. Interviewees' normative suggestions for gay men coming out and for their heterosexual male friends were also analyzed.

An overview of relationship between marital adjustment and relational beliefs of employed and married women in Shahid Beheshti University, Iran

Mansour, Ladan Counseling (psychology), University of Shahid Beheshti, Tehran, Islamic Republic of Iran Abdlo-Mohammadi, Kobra counseling (psychology), University of Shahid Beheshti, tehran, Islamic Republic of Iran Etemad, Samar counseling (psychology), University of Shahid Beheshti, tehran, Islamic Republic of Iran

To study the relationship between marital adjustment and relational beliefs in employed and married women, 100 married women employee randomly were selected from Shahid Beheshti University, Iran. We used Relations belief indicator (RBI) and dyadic adjustment scale (DAS) as research tools, one way variance and variable regression assessments for analyzing data. The results indicate that there is a meaningful difference between the relational beliefs of couples (mindset expectation, undermining opposition, sexual perfectionisms, disinterested in changeability of partner) and marital adjustment (partner satisfaction and agreement) at different educational levels of assessments. The outcome of this research can be applied for cognitive education between employed couples and their corrections in some ineffective beliefs. Key Words: relational beliefs, marital adjustment, women employee.

Student's perception regarding the degree of aggressivity concerning types of school behavior

Marian, Claudia Baia Mare, Romania Tofane, Vasile foundation, Il quadrifoglio foundation, baia mare, Romania

The research is focused on the perception of 595 students on the degree of aggressivity of 18 types of school behavior. Concerning aggressive level, Likert's scale attached to each investigated behavior indicates that all types of behavior are perceived relatively undifferentiated by school age children. However, ANOVA two-ways underlines the presence of some perception patterns depending on age and gender. In agreement with social cognition theory, multiple regression show that perception is both cause and effect for the frecquence of some aggressive type of aggression but this causalities do not cover more than 20% from variance.

Predicting cognitive functioning among centenarians

Martin, Peter Dept. of Gerontology, Iowa State University, Ames, USA Cho, Jinmyoung Gerontology, Iowa State University, Ames, USA MacDonald, Maurice Gerontology, Iowa State University, Ames, USA Margrett, Jennifer Gerontology, Iowa State University, Ames, USA Poon, Leonard Gerontology Institute, University of Georgia, Ames, USA

Objectives: The purpose of this study was to assess a resource and adaptation model predicting cognitive function among centenarians. Methods: Two hundred and eighty five centenarians and their proxies participated in this study. Multiple regression analyses were used to test predictors of general cognitive functioning (MMSE). Results: All hypotheses received support. The strongest associations with cognitive functioning were obtained for residence, functional health and openness to experience. Centenarians residing in their own homes, in good functional health and those relatively high in openness had higher MMSE scores. Conclusions: Health, individual and social resources are important predictors of general cognitive functioning.

Physical health as a predictor of quality of life and self-esteem: A proposed model and implications for education- and health-related policy and practice

Martinez, Carissa Education and Social Work, University of Sydney, Sydney, Australia Martin, Andrew Education and Social Work, University of Sydney, Sydney, Australia Colmar, Susan Education and Social Work, University of Sydney, Sydney, Australia

This paper proposes and tests a model of the predictive relations between physical health and the outcome factors quality of life and self-esteem. Unlike much of the recent quality of life literature that focuses on in-patient or clinical populations, this study involves a general population of young people, with a view to understanding perceived physical health and quality of life in the general population. Based on a sample of N=705 young adults (341 male, 364 female), structural equation modelling showed significant relationships amongst hypothesised variable sets. The significance of this study manifests in the important outcome factors that can be predicted by physical health and the implications the findings have for education- and health-related policy and practice.

Is there an association between social emotion recognition and moral dilemmas judgement

Martins, Ana Psychology, University of Algarve, Faro, Portugal Reis, Alexandra Psychology, University of Algarve, Faro, Portugal Justo, Mariline Psychology, University of Algarve, Faro, Portugal Simão, Claudia Psychology, University of Algarve, Faro, Portugal Ros, Antónia Psychology, University of Algarve, Faro, Portugal

An interesting question is to understand whether emotion processing, particularly social emotions, has an association with moral judgements. To investigate this association we tested a sample of 36 participants in two tasks. Participants had to recognize three social emotions in a Go-NoGo paradigm and to judge 22 hypothetical dilemmas (amoral, impersonal and personal moral). The results showed a negative association between accuracy in the social emotion task and the proportion of affirmative answers in the judgment of personal moral dilemmas. The results are discussed within a framework suggesting that adequate moral judgements are dependent of a normal social emotions processing.

Gender identity in homosexual subjects

Martxueta, Aitor MIDE, FICE, San Sebastian, Spain Jimenez, Amaia Social Psychology, Psychology, San Sebastian, Spain

Cultural stereotypes support the idea that lesbian women are more masculine than heterosexual women as well as gay men are more feminine than heterosexual men (Kite y Meaux, 1984). There are controversial results of different studies that compare gender identity with homosexual and heterosexual groups. The aim of this study is to examine the differences between gay men and lesbian women with respect to their gender identity. A transversal selective design has been used. In this study participated 110 gay men and lesbian women from Basque Country. Results: The results suggest that

homosexual subjects are not typified sexually and they don't self-describe as masculine as feminine traits.

Stress responses in public speech

Masamoto, Kaori Fuculty of Human Sciences, Matsuyama Shinonome College, Matsuyama, Japan Hayashi, Mikiya Fuculty of Human Sciences, Matsuyama Shinonome College, Matsuyama, Ehime, Japan Mimura, Satoru Guraduate school, Nihon University, Setagaya, Tokyo, Japan

In our daily life, we are often forced to make speeches to be evaluated in public situations. In such situations, various stress responses like complication for making a speech, anxiety, apprehensive about failure, tension, sweating, hot flash, palpitation, and so on, are observed. Previous researches showed that these stress responses alter as phases progress; the anticipation phase and the speech phase. In present research, we examined the change of stress responses throughout the preparation phase, the anticipation phase and the speech phase, via pencil and paper questionnaire.

Factors influencing Japanese patient's communication behavior during medical visits

Matsuda, Yoriko J. F. Oberlin University, Tokyo, Japan Ishikawa, Rie Health Psychology, J. F. Oberlin University, Tokyo, Japan Shibata, Keiko Health Psychology, J. F. Oberlin University, Tokyo, Japan Okuta, Noriko Health and Welfare, YMCA college of Human Service, Kanagawa, Japan Kamba, Naoko Health Psychology, J. F. Oberlin University, Tokyo, Japan

Objectives: To examine the factors influencing Japanese patient's communication behavior during medical visits and to test a hypothetical model of Patient Communication Behavior. Methods: A questionnaire survey was conducted with 103 undergraduates and 460 adults (Mean age: 39.1, SD:15.27). Self-construals, assertiveness, Japanese interpersonal competence, patient communication behavior, and self-efficacy in information exchange were measured. Results: ANOVA revealed women reported more problems in their communication with physicians than men. Path analysis confirmed the validity of the model. Conclusions: Assertiveness increases self-efficacy in information exchange directly or via Japanese interpersonal competence, and which, in turn, leads to less problematic communication behaviors.

Attentional capture does not cause inhibition of return

Matsuda, Yukihisa Grad. School of Info Sciences, Tohoku University, Sendaishi, Japan Iwasaki, Syoichi Graduate School of Info Sci, TOHOKU University, Sendaishi aobaku aramaki, Japan

In this study 94 participants were tested with a spatial cueing task to investigate the relationship between attentional capture (AC) and inhibition of return (IOR). The result showed that there are two separable groups indicating either AC or IOR in 150 msec stimulus onset asynchronie condition in which AC is reported in most previous study. These two groups showed the same amount of IOR. Although participants divided into two groups, faster RT group and slower RT group, the same results were confirmed for each group. These results strongly indicate that AC and IOR are separate phenomena.

The reaction times to the paired personality trait terms by selective response tasks

Matsuda, Kouhei Dept. of Psychology, Bunkyo-Gakuin University, Kanagawa, Japan Sato, Emi Psychology, Shirayuri College, Chofu-City, Tokyo, Japan

The bi-polar paired personality trait terms reflects the one's smallest semantic network model. The reaction time was different in the selecting self-

image from the paired personality traits terms. It hypothesis that personality trait terms ware adjusting myself, reaction time was fast. We measured the reaction times to 10items(version and nerves) in simple RT session and personality self-rating session, when evaluating self-image to the personality traits terms. After classifying personality traits by the personality inventory, we examined reaction times to 10terms in simple RT and personality self-rating session. As a result, adjusted items are more collate than non-adjusted items.

The influence of motivational aspects and experience on intention to enrol in online courses

Mattana, Veronica Dept. of Psychology, University of Verona, San Vito, Italy Bellò, Benedetta Psychology, University of Verona, San Vito, Italy

In this study we investigated the influence of students' experience with computer, online courses attendance, learning expectations and intrinsic motivation on intention to enrol in online courses. A structured questionnaire was administered to 152 students of the post graduate school for assistant teacher. Results showed that: • Motivational aspects, online courses attendance and computer experience predict intention to enrol in online courses. • Intrinsic motivation partially mediates the relationship between expectations and intention. This study stated the significant influence of motivational factors on intention to enrol in online courses. Limitation and suggestions are discussed.

Modulation of alertness and its influence on the spatial distribution of attention and on top-down control based on Bundesens Theory of Visual Attention (TVA)

Matthias, Ellen Inst. für Psychologie, Universität München, München, Germany Bublak, Peter Neurology Clinic, Neuropsychology Unit, Jena, Germany Müller, Hermann J. Psychology, LMU, Munich, Germany Schneider, Werner X. Psychology, LMU, Munich, Germany Finke, Kathrin Psychology, LMU, Munich, Germany

Objectives: We studied the influence of alertness on spatial (distribution of attention) and task-related (top-down control) weighting parameters of Bundesen's 'Theory of Visual Attention' (TVA; 1990). Method: A partial report was administered repeatedly to 16 participants in a normal- or a reduced-alertness state to assess the influence of alertness on the two parameters independently and within the same subjects. Results: A rightward spatial bias appeared under low alertness conditions and was significantly correlated with direct and indirect measures of sleepiness/alertness. Top-down control seemed to be unaffected. Conclusion: The rightward bias might be related to functional lateralization of the alertness system.

Mental health in Spanish women abused by their partners: A comparison of psychological and physical violence

Matud, Pilar Personality, Assessment, La Laguna University, La Laguna, Spain Fortes, Demelza Personality, Assessment an Ps, La Laguna University, La Laguna, Spain

Objective: Analyze differences in mental health between battered women and women who experienced only psychological violence. Methods: Cross-sectional study of a sample of women abused by their partners; 74 of the women experienced physical and psychological abuse and 74 experienced only psychological abuse. Measures: Scaled Version of the General Health Questionnaire; Severity of Symptoms of Posttraumatic Stress Disorders Scale; Physical and Psychological Abuse Scale. Statistical analysis: Analysis of Variance. Results: No statistically significant differences were found between the groups in anxiety, depressive, somatic, social dysfunction and avoidance symptoms. Those who suffered both physical and psychological abuse experienced more posttraumatic symptoms.

Does prejudice and sexism make us vulnerable to HIV?

Mayordomo, Sonia Básica, University of Basque Country, San Sebastián, Spain Landa Ubillos, Silvia Sciences of Education, University of Burgos, Burgos, Spain Páez, Darío Social Psychology, University of Basque Country, San Sebastián, Spain
We have contrasted the negative effects of prejudiced attitudes and sexism in the systematic use of condoms. A representative sample of 2935 Spanish people who answered a questionnaire regarding their sexual behaviours and risk took part in the study. In general, a high level of sexism and homophobia is related to: a) worse information and identification of myths regarding HIV sexual prevention; b) more negative beliefs and attitudes towards condom use; c) less self-perception of control in negotiating its use; d) less intention and actual use of a condom. Sexist and homophobic attitudes should be addressed in HIV prevention programmes.

Different ways to benefit-finding: Introspective reflection and communicative sharing

Mehlsen, Mimi Yung Dept. of Psychology, University of Aarhus, Aarhus, Denmark Thomsen, Dorthe Kirkegaard Dept. of Psychology, University of Aarhus, Aarhus, Denmark Jensen-Johansen, Mikael Birkelund Dept. of Psychology, University of Aarhus, Aarhus, Denmark
Objective: To examine differences in benefit-finding (BF) in positive and negative events. Methods: Students (n=110) were asked to think of an event that changed their lives. They reported if they had talked about the event, and answered questionnaires measuring reflection and BF. Results: Half thought of positive events, half of negative events. Positive events: Talking about the event was associated with greater BF (r=0.43, p<0.01), whereas reflection was associated with less BF (r=-0.32, p<0.05). Negative events: Only reflection was associated with greater BF (r=0.39). Conclusion: Results suggest reflection and sharing experiences are different mechanisms both involved in BF.

Personality factors, self-cognitions and happiness in adolescence

Meleddu, Mauro Dept. of Psychology, University of Cagliari, Cagliari, Italy Scalas, Laura Francesca Education, University of Oxford, Oxford, United Kingdom Guicciardi, Marco Psychology, University of Cagliari, Cagliari, Italy
Happiness is related to extraversion, neuroticism and self-esteem (Hills, Argyle, 2001). In addition to these factors, the study examines the relationships between happiness, emotional autonomy, and self-concept clarity. A group of 400 students (14- to 20-years-old) completed the subsequent instruments: Eysenck Personality Inventory, Emotional Autonomy Scale, Self-concept Clarity Scale, Rosenberg Self-esteem Scale, Oxford Happiness Inventory (OHI). Correlation coefficients and multiple regressions showed significant links between the OHI total score and the other constructs under examination (p < .001). Moreover, hierarchical regressions highlighted differential contributions of the predictors in relation to overall happiness, its subfactors scores and cognitive components.

Dispositional coping with the challenges of surgery

Melo, Maria da Luz Nursing School, University of Azores, Ponta Delgada, Portugal
A research has been down to evaluate how patients react to information. Investigates the interactive effect between information about their clinical situation and the dispositional desire to be given information, valued by coping style monitoring versus blunting. The dispositional desire for information was analysed according to the result of Miller Behavioural Style Scale - MBSS. According to the present research the majority of the patients revel lack of information. The research proved that, in patients with monitoring coping style, when the information given was tailed by the dispositional desire of the patient, he manifests bigger satisfaction and less anxiety.

Cognitive control of memory in a sample of elderly

Menor de Gaspar Pinilla, Julio Psychology, Universidad de Oviedo, Oviedo, Spain Albuerne López, Fernando Psychology, Universidad de Oviedo, Oviedo, Spain Cerezo Menéndez, Rebeca Psychology, Universidad de Oviedo, Oviedo, Spain
This study examines the relationship between executive processes and working memory capacity measures and the performance on item-method directed forgetting task within a sample of elders ranging from 60 to 88 years old (n=50). The results show that in a free recall test restricted to to-be-remembered items the participants intruded high proportion of to-be-forgotten items as well as a reduced directed forgetting effect in a final free recall test. Furthermore, significant correlations among working memory capacity and cognitive flexibility measures and intrusions and directed forgetting effect were obtained. However, measures of inhibition were neither correlated with working memory capacity nor directed forgetting performance.

Adult attachment styles and cognitive vulnerability to depression: The mediational roles of sociotropy and autonomy

Merino, Hipolito Psicologia Clinica, Universidad de Santiago, Santiago de Compostela, Spain Permuy, Beatriz Psicologia Clinica, Universidad de Santiago, Santiago de Compostela, Spain Fernandez Rey, Jose Psicologia Social y Basica, Universidad de Santiago, Santiago de Compostela, Spain
We analyse the mediational role of the personality dimensions of sociotropy and autonomy in the relation between certain styles of attachment and depressive symptoms. In order to do so, a group of university students carried out the Beck Depression Inventory, the Personal Style Inventory and the Relationship Questionnaire. Individuals with attachment styles who have negative models of self obtained significantly higher scores in the BDI than those with attachment styles that imply positive models of self. The data indicated that the influence of the preoccupied style on depression was determined by sociotropy, whilst autonomy partially mediated the relation between the fearful style and depression.

Is it my turn? Preparing for one's death after burying a gay partner from HIV/AIDS

Meris, Doneley HIV Arts Network, New York, USA
This presentation highlights the unique and difficult stories of three gay men who sustained long-term HIV-concordant (both HIV-positive) relationships with their gay partners, cared for and were witnessed to for their partners' agonizing deaths, and now have to confront their own AIDS-related deterioration that follows the exact pattern of their deceased partners. LGBT- and grief-clinicians are provided clinical frameworks on how to meet the challenges of these gay survivors' grieving, healing and dying processes.

Open access: Using the internet for scientific publishing

Mey, Günter Zentrum für Digitale Systeme, Freie Universität Berlin, Berlin, Germany
Since the "Berlin Declaration on Open Access to Knowledge in the Sciences and Humanities" has been released, the claim for open access (OA)—to make publicly funded journal articles available for the public—started to reach a wider audience. But still experiences with OA-publishing are missing to a large extent. Ways to successfully establish an OA-journal will be presented by referring to "Forum Qualitative Sozialforschung/Forum: Qualitative Social Research"(FQS): Traditional and innovative ways of publishing are being discussed which helped FQS—originally coming from German qualitative psychology—to become the most important electronic journal in the field of international qualitative research.

Importance of family in psychiatric patients' recovery from illness

Mfusi, Skhumbuzo Dept. of Psychology, Walter Sisulu University, Umtata, South Africa
Presentation is based on the results of a study that investigated the important role that is played by family members in helping their relatives cope with a variety of psychiatric illnesses. Both the patients and their relatives were interviewed regarding the support available to patients, as well as some of the challenges confronted by both groups. The results were that there is an important role that is played by family members in helping their mentally ill relatives cope and recover from illness. Also, the study found that the South African government needs to provide more mental health specialists, especially in the rural-situated areas of the country.

Sex differences in the in-group bias with minimal groups

Mifune, Nobuhiro Dept. of Behavioral Science, Hokkaido University, Sapporo, Japan Yamagishi, Toshio Behavioral Science, Hokkaido University, Sapporo, Japan
The in-group bias is the tendency to behave altruistically towards in-group members, but competitively towards the out-group. In minimal groups, it has been shown that the in-group bias occurs only when participants know each other's group memberships, suggesting that the bias is an adaptive behavior for generalized reciprocity within groups. According to evolutionary psychology, however, males have a tendency to compete with out-group males, and thus priming participants with same sex partners may lead to intergroup competition among males even when their partner does not know their group membership. To investigate this hypothesis, we conducted an experiment using minimal groups.

The relation between coping styles and posttraumatic stress in a sample of police officers

Mihalcea, Andreea Dept. of Psychology, Titu Maiorescu University, Bucharest, Romania Lita, Stefan Department of Psychology, Romanian Academy, Bucharest, Romania Stoian, Bogdan Centre for Psychosociology, Ministry of the Interior, Bucharest, Romania
Police stress was the focus of many studies all over the world, because this work could be sometimes characterized by brutal problems and impossible problems, with no clear solution and which are not easily solved administratively or technically. The present study investigates the influence of copying styles on the posttraumatic stress of officers involved in special missions. The sample consists of 167 officers who completed the Indices of Coping Responses and the Mississippi Scale for Combat-Related PTSD. The results show that (a) low scores on behavioural coping and high scores on avoidance coping are associated with more posttraumatic stress (Δr=37%), and (b) avoidance is a maladaptive coping style because it accounts for 43% of the PTSD.

Factors influencing old age: A study of institutionalized and non-institutionalized elderly

Mishra, Nidhi Department of Psychology, University of Allahabad, Allahabad, India Dhawan, Nisha Department of Psychology, University of Allahabad, Allahabad, India

A qualitative study was done to explore factors influencing old age among institutionalized and non-institutionalized elderly. Forty elderly persons (20 non-institutionalized and 20 living in religious institutes) of 65-75 years, were asked an open ended question- "What factors influence old age?". Content analysis of the responses indicated following factors - family, economic, health, dependency, spirituality, optimism and functional changes. Responses indicated that non-institutionalized elderly gave importance to family and economic factors while institutionalized elderly gave importance to spirituality and positive thinking. These findings provide an understanding of elderly's perception of ageing and the role of religious institutions in old age.

Stress status among women in teaching profession in Nigeria

Mivanyi, Yuwanna Jenny Education Technical, City University Kaduna, Kaduna, Nigeria Abdulkadir, Asmau Education Technical, City University Kaduna, Kaduna, Nigeria Bamanja, Becky Education Technical, City University Kaduna, Kaduna, Nigeria Makarfi, Amina Administration Section, Teachers Registration Council, Kaduna, Nigeria

Teaching is one of the professions in Nigeria that has a high standard, especially with the establishment of Teachers Registration Council in 1993 backed by Act No. 31. Practicalising this standard could be stressful in the Nigerian acculturated society, much more for the woman who has multiple roles at home. The study examines the stress status of women who are teachers. Guided by null hypotheses, responses to the researcher-designed questionnaire and stress inventory would be subjected to mean difference and chi-square analysis. A workshop for stakeholders would superceed the study to discuss the results for use.

Cognitive interactions between facial expression and vocal intonation in emotional judgment

Mochizuki, Toshiko Dept. of Psychology, Japan Women's University, Kawasaki, Japan

Purpose: We investigated how people integrate emotions of the face and vocal intonation, which are congruent or incongruent. Method: Sixteen elderly people (age: 65–80) and fifteen youth (age: 21–22) participated. Moving images of faces and voices expressing neutral messages were presented simultaneously; observers judged the emotions. Results: When facial and vocal emotions were incongruent, (1) face was a more dominant cue than voice for elderly people, but the youth appropriately used both depending on the emotion, and (2) incongruent expressions were judged more frequently by elderly people as a new fused emotion of neither the face nor voice.

The effects of associative learning on selective attention: The role of implicit verses explicit associations

Money, Sharon Psychology, The University of Kent, Chartham, United Kingdom Sharma, Dinkar Psychology, The University of Kent, Canterbury, United Kingdom

Associative learning is a useful tool for investigating emotionality. Previously neutral stimuli, when paired with emotional stimuli, can acquire an emotional valence though association, enabling the reduction of confounds that stimuli such as words can cause. In four experiments we associate emotional pictures and sounds to nonwords in an initial learning phase. Performance on associated and non-associated non-words was compared in a subsequent colour naming modified Stroop task. Results indicate that interference from associated non-words was reduced when the associative learning was made explicit rather than when it was incidental to the task.

Mental health: Adolescent's beliefs and strategies to access health services

Morais, Camila Psychology, UFRGS, Porto Alegre, Brazil Koller, Silvia Psychology, UFRGS, Porto Alegre, Brazil Bucher, Júlia Psychology, UNIFOR, Fortaleza, Brazil

This study aims to identify beliefs and help-seeking strategies that adolescents hold on mental health. 120 low and high SES elementary/high-school adolescents (12-17 years old) answered a self-report questionnaire. Descriptive statistics and ANOVA showed that beliefs mainly come from family, which represents an important source of social support. It was found a significant gender difference on the strategies to access health services. For girls, parents are responsible for mental illness and should look for help. Boys did not know psychiatrists'/psychologists' roles and had concerns on what people would say. Family context appeared as support for mental illness

Life style and memory impairment in elderly

Morales, Manuel Experimental Psychology, University of Seville, Seville, Spain Luque, Elena EXPERIMENTAL PSYCHOLOGY, UNIVERSITY OF SEVILLE, SEVILLE, Spain Sañudo, Jose Ignacio EXPERIMENTAL PSYCHOLOGY, UNIVERSITY OF SEVILLE, SEVILLE, Spain Moreno, David EXPERIMENTAL PSYCHOLOGY, UNIVERSITY OF SEVILLE, SEVILLE, Spain

Objectives: The aim of this investigation was to study the relationship between cognitive stimulating activities and memory performance in elderly people in a longitudinal research. Methods: 150 elderly were studied in two different moments, existing two-year interval between both measures. All subjects were assessed in episodic and semantic memory. Likewise, they completed a cognitive stimulating activities self-report. Results: The results showed that less active individuals had bigger differences between measures in the Boston naming test. Conclusions: Our study showed that older people engaged in stimulating cognitive activities maintain semantic memory better than older people less interested in these activities.

Do we behave differently as a function of power?

Morales Marente, Elena Dept. of Psychology, University of Huelva, Huelva, Spain Palacios, María Soledad Department of Psychology, University of Huelva, Huelva, Spain Morano, María Department of Psychology, University of Huelva, Huelva, Spain

In this research we investigate the effects of power inequalitites on social relationships at the behavioural level. Specifically, we will use the model entitle "Approach-Inhibition" by Keltner, Gruenfeld and Anderson (2003). Participants were Psychology students and they had different power as a function of the level of their studies. We also manipulated the legitimacy of the power they had. We asked them to participate in a decision about the University policy, and our main dependent variable was the variability of the behaviours they reported. Results suggested the relevance of the asymetry of power in participant's behaviour.

Happiness and mental health in senile people

Mosavi Amiry, Seyed Jalal Medical Clinic, Babol, Islamic Republic of Iran Homayouni, Alireza Dept.Psychology, Medical Clinic, Babol, Islamic Republic of Iran Nikpour, Gholam Ali Dpt.Psychology, Medical Clinic, Babol, Islamic Republic of Iran Golzadeh, Ehsan Dept. Statistics, Payame Noor University(PNU), Babol, Islamic Republic of Iran

The research investigated the role of happiness in reduction of mental illness of senile people. Hypothesis: In senile period happiness can reduce mental illness.84 senile people ranged 50 to 75 were randomly selected and Argyl's Happiness Inventory(AHI) and General Health Questionnaire (GHQ) administered on them. Data analyzed with Pearson correlation formula. Results showed negative and significant correlation between happiness and components of mental illness in GHQ. Because of importance role of satisfaction of life and happiness in old age the plans should be applied for increasing of happiness and satisfaction from life to reduce bad effects of mental illness.

Effect of auditory information processing to brightness judgment

Muroi, Miya Hyogo College of Medicine, Hyogo, Japan

Effect of auditory information processing on brightness judgment was studied. Participants performed both an auditory task and a visual task. In the visual task, they judged the brightness of the target and answered it with brightness scale presented after the target, and in the auditory task, they repeated the sound (Experiment 1), or detected vowels in (Experiment 2). As a result, only in the Experiment 1, participants judged the target brighter than the real brightness when the auditory information was presented simultaneously with the visual target. It suggests that load of the auditory task affects the visual information processing.

What determines 'a meaningful life' for Japanese mothers: The most important factor is 'satisfaction as a mother' and second is 'satisfaction with their personal life' unrelated with 'satisfaction as a wife'

Nagahisa, Hisako Bunkyo Gakuin University, Saitama, Japan

In this study, we examine the developmental change in the relationship between mother's perception of 'a meaningful life (ML)' and self-evaluation through child-raising stages. Mothers in the early stages of child raising (N=88), the middle stage (N=57), and the final stage (N=190) completed questionnaires about (ML), self-evaluation (satisfaction as a mother(SM),as a wife (SW), and as an individual (SI)) and allocation of her personal resources (her time, energy and money). Regression analysis indicated that 1) The significant factor for (ML) change from her mother-role to her personal life. 2) Throughout the stages, (SM) is more significant than (SW) in Japanese mothers.

Predicting students' choices of university majors

Nagy, Gabriel Educational Research, MPI for Human Development, Berlin, Germany Trautwein, Ulrich Educational Research, MPI for Human Development, Berlin, Germany Lüdtke, Oliver Educational Research, MPI for Human Development, Berlin, Germany

Interests and abilities are related to career choices, but there is no consensus on the unique role of these characteristics. The aim of this study was to investigate the role of vocational interests and abilities (mathematics, English, intelligence) in students' choices of university majors in a large sample of students (N=3697). Multinomial regressions showed that abilities and interests were both related to choices when considered in isolation. However, multivariate models demonstrated that abilities (and other characteristics) were no longer predictive when interests were controlled. Results suggest that individual interests are a major force behind self-selection into different academic careers.

Art in a hospital: The role of artists and the effect of the activities

Nakagami-Yamaguchi, Etsuko Graduate School of Medicine, Osaka City University, Osaka, Japan *Hirai, Hironori* General affair section, Osaka City University H, Osaka, Japan *Shintaku, Haruo* Graduate School of Medicine, Osaka City University, Osaka, Japan

The authors had the opportunity to observe art-activities in a general hospital in Osaka where several art programs are put into practice since 2000. These programs were characterized by intensive collaboration with artists, patients and families, and hospital staffs including us. In this study, we focused on these collaborative art activities in the hospital-community. Based on ethnography, text data from the artists' narrative and results of questionnaire surveys, we discussed the role of artists who produced these art-programs as collaborative practice, and the effect of the activities on the people in our hospital-community from the viewpoint of Group Dynamics.

Self-regulation and consistency of interpersonal feeling in emotional control of the children in the United States

Nakata, Sakae Dept. of Psychology, Aichi Gakuin University, Aichi, Japan

It is examined in quality how they controlled emotions and coped with them to maintain smooth communication, from a behavioral response of the children and a change in facial expression to the others on a video recorded on this occasion. As a result, it has become clear that, as for stress coping of three-year-old children, they substituted an accessible thing (a stone) for what they wanted (a ball) in the world of an image and controlled the situation they failed to manipulate when they could not get something in the relationship with the others.

The lower class Brazilian youth and the access to the university

Nascimento, Eduardo Education, University of São Paulo, São Paulo, Brazil

The theme of the research is the reasons and aspirations that the lower class Brazilian youth have about the access to tertiary education. What are the reasons leading the lower class Brazilian youth to aspire to university? The hypothesis is that these aspirations of the lower class Brazilian youth indicate the existence of a life planning through a profession that would both lead to economic improvement and an extended youth condition. Some aspects of social inclusion, color of skin / ethnicity and gender might contribute as social factors in the undertaking of the planning of their lives.

Structure of dysfunctional thoughts in Chinese senior elementary school students and middle school students

Ni, Jie Educational Psychology, Hong Kong, China, People's Republic of : Hong Kong SAR *Sang, Biao* Psychology, East China Normal University, Shanghai, People's Republic of China

The purpose of present studies was to discover the contents and structure of the dysfunctional thoughts -"sick, false, or unreasonable thoughts that cause the appearance of maladjustment and what's more, the emotion disorders"- in Chinese elementary and middle school students. Literature review, interview and questionnaire were employed and 1307 students participated in this research. The results disclosed a five-factor model including "self-defence", "demanding for best treatment", "over-perfectionism", "passive attitude" and "attention-seeking". The significance of the present studies is its primary exploration of the dysfunctional thoughts in Chinese elementary and middle school students. Our findings fill the blank of the study in

dysfunctional thoughts and make a breakthrough in theory.

Dysfunctional thoughts of Chinese senior elementary school students and middle school students: Contents, structure and status quo

Ni, Jie Educational Psychology, Hong Kong, China, People's Republic of : Hong Kong SAR *Sang, Biao* Psychology, East China Normal University, Shanghai, People's Republic of China

The purpose of present studies was to discover the contents, the structure and the status quo of the dysfunctional thoughts -"sick, false, or unreasonable thoughts that cause the appearance of mal-adjustment and what's more, the emotion disorders"- in Chinese elementary and middle school students. Literature review, interview and questionnaire were employed in two studies. More than 2000 subjects altogether participated in. The results showed the structure of the dysfunctional thoughts in Chinese elementary and middle school students was a five-factor model structure and the status quo was beyond optimistic. Our findings gave out instructive suggestion to school counseling, mental health education and learning guidance.

The motivation for success as a personal parameter of innovative activity of students

Nikova-Tsioutsiou, Donka Economic Sociology and Psych., UNWE-Sofia, Sofia, Bulgaria

The work presents the empirical exploration of motivation for success as a personal parameter of the innovative activity of students. The questionnaires for testing the innovative activity and the motivation for success are used in the research. The extract includes 1200 graduating students from three economic universities in Bulgaria. The statistical treatment is done by Correlation, Dispersion, Factor, Regression analyses. Some of the results and the conclusions are: The innovative activity of students correlates with their motivation for success. The motivation for success has influence on innovative activity. The motivation for success is a parameter of innovative activity of students.

Which hemisphere processes the distractor? The effect of cerebral lateralization on selective attention

Nishimura, Ritsuko Psychology & Communication, Aichi Shukutoku University, Mizuho, Japan *Yoshizaki, Kazuhito* Psychology, Aichi Shukutoku, Nagakute, Japan *Kato, Kimiko* Psychology, Aichi Shukutoku, Ngakute, Japan *Haneda, Satoshi* Psychology, Aichi Shukutoku, Nagakute, Japan

This study aimed to investigate whether or not selective attention is modulated by cerebral dominance for letter search. Right-handed 24 participants were asked to discriminate a target letter in a briefly presented letters-array, while ignoring distractors. We manipulated visual-field of the target (left or right visual-field), compatibility between the target and the distractor (compatible or incompatible) and presentation mode (within- or across-fields). Results showed that the compatibility effect was larger when the distractor was presented in RVF than in LVF irrespective of the presentation mode. These results suggested that selective attention is determined by left hemisphere dominance for letter search.

The influence of emotional and non-emotional stimuli on the activation of anterior cingulate cortex using a Stroop paradigm

Nitsch, Alexander M. Biolog. und Klinische Psychol., Universität Jena, Jena, Germany *Miltner, Wolfgang H. R.* Jena, Germany *Straube, Thomas* Biologische und Klinische Psy., Institut für Psychologie, Jena, Germany

Anterior cingulate cortex (ACC) has been distinguished into a "ventral-affective" and a "dorsal-cognitive" subdivision (Bush, Luu and Posner,

2000). Several studies have questioned this appeal. Our purpose was to develop two Stroop-paradigms, which only differ in their emotionality. 15 healthy subjects completed the tasks while brain activation was recorded using functional magnetic resonance imaging (fMRI, 1.5Tesla). Reaction times and error rates displayed a Stroop-effect for both paradigms. FMRI-data shows both in the non-emotional and the emotional task increased activation of dorsal ACC for incongruent compared to congruent trials. These findings contradict the model of ventral-emotional and dorsal-cognitive subdivisions in ACC.

Constructing and testing humor elicitation models

Nomura, Ryota Educational Pcyhology, Kyushu University, Fukuoka, Japan *Maruno, Shun'ichi* Educational Pcyhology, Kyushu University, Fukuoka, Japan

To construct a forecasting model that predicts amount of humor elicited by actual stimuli, 375 Japanese high school and undergraduate students (M = 18.25, SD = 1.76) were instructed to rate humor-relevant variables regarding randomly assigned 16 out of 48 cartoons. With path analysis, predictive powers and goodness of fit indices for 3 models were calculated. The results supported the model assuming that aggressive, sexual, and discriminative components of humor-relevant variables are activated as by-product of elaboration, rather than the one assuming the components to function as an arousal booster. Adaptive functions of a supported model were discussed.

Is threat sufficient to bias attention? An experimental investigation

Notebaert, Lies Ghent University, Ghent, Belgium *van Damme, Stefaan* Exp. clinical and health psych, Ghent University, Ghent, Belgium *Crombez, Geert* Exp. clinical and health psych, Ghent University, Ghent, Belgium

Studies reveal that threatening information captures attention more rapidly than neutral information. However, threat stimuli often differ perceptually from neutral stimuli, leaving the question unanswered whether threat is sufficient to bias attention. Therefore, participants performed a visual search task with equally salient stimuli (coloured circles). One colour (CS+) was fear-conditioned using aversive shocks. Task was responding to a target presented in one of the circles. A repeated measures ANOVA showed faster responses to targets in the CS+ colour compared to the other colours, especially in high-anxious individuals. We concluded that threat is sufficient to automatically bias attention in vulnerable participants.

Influences of the red/blue colour combination presented in the hemifield on human performance

Ohashi, Tomoki Miyagi Gakuin Women's Universi, Sendai, Japan

Many studies have revealed that colour influences human performance. In this research, we presented different colours in the hemifield, and measured the subjects' performances with the Compound Digit Checking Test (measuring attentional switching to global/local objects) and the Block Design Test from WAIS-III (measuring visual abstract processing and problem solving). There were two conditions with respect to the colour combinations: one condition was red in the right hemifield and blue in the left one, while the other condition was the reverse. Twenty-five subjects were randomly divided into two groups, and their blood pressures were measured during the rest periods between the tests. The influences of colour on human performance were discussed.

General and health related quality of life in adolescents with type 1 diabetes

Oles, Maria Inst. of Psychology, Catholic University Lublin, Lublin, Poland

Objectives: To explore the self-perceived quality of life (QOL) and health related quality of life (HRQOL) in adolescents with type 1 diabetes versus healthy youths. Methods A sample of adolescents (K=30, M=30) between 12-18 was investigated by means of The Youth Quality of Life Instrument (YQOL-R) and The KIDSC-REEN-52 instrument. Results The overall QOL and HRQOL of adolescents with and without diabetes differ between the groups. Conclusions The findings suggest need to improve the QOL of adolescents with and without chronic illness and to examine the determinants of the quality of life in the both groups of youths.

Generation of causal attributions for functional and organic pain-analysing the view of children with Rheumatoid Arthritis

Ostkirchen, Gabriele Gerda Inst. für Klin. Neurologie, Universität Duisburg-Essen, Essen, Germany Wiegemann, Eva Clinics of Neurology, University Duisburg Essen, Essen, Germany Cizmowski, Tanja Clinics of Neurology, University Duisburg Essen, Essen, Germany Hachemi, Houyem Clinics of Neurology, University Duisburg Essen, Essen, Germany Howoritsch-Steinberg, Martina Clinics of Neurology, University Duisburg Essen, Essen, Germany Kamberg, Jennifer Clinics of Neurology, University Duisburg Essen, Essen, Germany Konik, Anna Clinics of Neurology, University Duisburg Essen, Essen, Germany Youn, Do Ae Clinics of Neurology, University Duisburg Essen, Essen, Germany Ganser, Gerd Clinics of Neurology, University Duisburg Essen, Essen, Germany Diener, Hans Christoph Clinics of Neurology, University Duisburg Essen, Essen, Germany

Causal attributions for functional and organic pain (AP=abdominal pain; H=headache, RA=rheumatoid arthritis) from 162 children with rheumatoid arthritis (♂29,01%, ♀70,99%, mean age♂:10,21♀:11,22) were categorised (CAT_SYS_PED_PAIN) exhaustively. Overall 1187 causes were named (AP=416,H=390,RA=381). The "illness itself ", the "medical treatment" and the "side effects walking along with it" were generated predominantly (AP12.8%; H14.6%; RA18.6%). Sex-specific preferences were found for headache and rheumatoid arthritis (H:$X2(16)=38,218;p=.001$; RA:$X2(14)=24,983;p=.035$; AP:$X2(17)=18,196,p=.337$). Experiences with a recurrent and progressive disease have a strong impact on functional and organic pain attributions.

Primary headaches and abdominal pain in our school: An academic cooperation with a German grammar school project

Ostkirchen, Gabriele Gerda Inst. für Klin. Neurologie, Universität Duisburg-Essen, Essen, Germany Marco, Grabemann Clinics of Neurology, University Duisburg Essen, Essen, Germany Lotte, Mandy Clinics of Neurology, University Duisburg Essen, Essen, Germany Ostkirchen, Rima Clinics of Neurology, University Duisburg Essen, Essen, Germany Diener, Hans Christoph Clinics of Neurology, University Duisburg Essen, Essen, Germany

This study explores the relationship of primary headaches, functional abdominal pain and life quality. 240 scholars participated in 3 groups (pre, peri and post puberty) each with 80 subjects (40 girls, 40 boys). They completed FSEKB, ROME-III and KINDL questionnaires. Recurrent pain experiences (mean =58,02; SD=1,174) influence the health related life-quality in children (mean=64,94; SD=1,225; F(1,209)=14,332;p<.001). Gender and puberty have no significant effects (headache $\chi2(2)=4,158$, p=.059; abdominal pain $\chi2(2)=1,178$, p=.429). The impact of recurrent pain on health related life-quality measures during school-time is

stressed. Data contradict the hypothesized differences in gender and puberty.

The effect of organizational climate and group identity on perception of socially inconsiderate behavior within organizations

Ozeki, Miki Nagoya University, Nagoya, Japan Yoshida, Toshikazu Graduate School of Education a, Nagoya University, Nagoya, Japan

The purpose of this research was to examine the effect of climate and group identity on the perception of socially inconsiderate behavior within the organization. Organizational climate was assessed through two factors; Management and Frankness. Group identity was composed of two factors, Membership and Pride. A total of 601 students who held membership in varsity clubs at universities participated in a questionnaire survey. Those scoring high on the Membership factor perceived more social inconsiderateness within their club. The Membership factor negatively affected perception of interpersonal inconsiderateness, while conversely, the Pride factor affected it positively, and organizational climate had no influence. These results indicate that the perception of social inconsiderateness is an individual level phenomenon.

Interference of DVD extracts listening on attention while driving

Pêcher, Christelle CLLE-LTC, MDR, Université de Toulouse 2, Toulouse, France Lemercier, Céline CLLE-LTC, MDR, Université de Toulouse 2, Toulouse Cedex 9, France Cellier, Jean-Marie CLLE-LTC, MDR, Université de Toulouse 2, Toulouse Cedex 9, France

Present study investigates the interference of DVD extracts listening on driver's attentional behaviour. DVD extracts used were sound film extracts of 5 genres (drama, comedy, action, horror, sentimental). They were randomly played during a simulated driving task embedding a Peripheral Identification Task (PIT). We hypothesized that each genre of film interferes differently on each driving parameter. Results revealed a degradation of longitudinal control for action films whereas lateral control and RTs to PIT are deteriorated for horror and sentimental films. Implications of the distractive effect of sound and the nature of extracts will be discussed.

The emotional state as a factor of inattention in car driving

Pêcher, Christelle CLLE-LTC, MDR, Université de Toulouse 2, Toulouse, France Lemercier, Céline CLLE-LTC, MDR, Université de Toulouse 2, Toulouse Cedex 9, France Cellier, Jean-Marie CLLE-LTC, MDR, Université de Toulouse 2, Toulouse Cedex 9, France Quaireau, Christophe LPE, Université de Rennes 2, Rennes Cedex, France

This aim of this talk will be to highlight the impact of inattention on the attentional behaviour in driving. At this time, this thematic is just emerging from the driving field of research. One of the major causes of inattention is the degradation of the emotional state (e.g. sadness and anger). Hence, this presentation will firstly review epidemiological and experimental studies about the impact of the emotional state in driving. Secondly, results of 2 experimental studies performed with a driving simulator at the University of Toulouse will be exposed.

The investigation the impact of assertiveness training on assertiveness and happiness of high-school girls

Paeezy, Maryam Tehran, Islamic Republic of Iran

The sample which was comprised of 30 2nd-grade high-school girls in the field of Natural sciences were selected randomly. Gambrill and Richy s Assertiveness Questionnaire (GRAQ) and a self-made open-ended questionnaire to investigate the

reasons for nonassertive and Oxford Happiness Questionnaire (OHQ) were used. The study had five phases; the pilot, the pre-test, the training, the post-test and the follow-up. The results showed a significant difference between both assertiveness scores, basic assertion and opossitional assertion in pre-test and post-test and follow-up for the experimental group. The results showed a significant difference on happiness scores in pre- and post-test and follow-up for the experimental group.

The rehearsal effect of object-based attention on object working memory

Pan, Yi Department of Psychology, Zhejiang University, Hangzhou, People's Republic of China Xu, Baihua Department of Psychology, Zhejiang University, Hangzhou, People's Republic of China Zuo, Wuheng Department of Psychology, Zhejiang University, Hangzhou, People's Republic of China

Under certain conditions, the contents of object working memory can influence the guidance of selective attention. Using nature pictures as the experimental materials, this study tested the hypothesis that object-based attention may play an important role in the rehearsal effect on object working memory for active maintenance of object representations. This study included two experiments in which two different ways of preventing attention-based rehearsal from occurring were separately adopted. The results of the two experiments showed that object-based attention play an important role in the rehearsal effect on object working memory for active maintenance of object representations, and that this attention-based rehearsal effect have some ecological validity.

Counselling men who have sex with men (MSM): Issues and approaches

Pandya, Apurva HDFS, University of Baroda, Vadodara, India

Present paper discusses counseling issues of MSM population addressing the sexuality, mental health and HIV/AIDS issues and explores effectiveness of counseling techniques and approaches. This study is based on 100 case study. Various sexuality and psychosocial issues leads to psychological discomfort or psychiatric morbidities like identity crisis, anxiety, feelings of guilt, substance abuse etc. This study also noted counselling issues around married MSM, female partner of MSM, HIV positive MSM and explores counseling techniques and approaches with sexual and mental health issues. To conclude, HIV/AIDS prevention projects, counseling MSM population is not just restricted to HIV/AIDS and STIs.

Methodology in the study of the burnout syndrome in university professors

Paredes Santiago, Maritza Del Carmen Geografía Humana, Universidad de Los Andes, Merida, Venezuela Viloria Marin, Hermes Antonio Medicion y Evaluacion, Universidad de Los Andes, Merida, Venezuela Avendaño Rangel, Francys Andreina Biología, Universidad de Los Andes, Merida, Venezuela

In this paper we study the incidence of Burnout in a sample of University teachers, using the MBI. Results show level medium of Burnout characterize by levels medium of despersonalization, emotional exhaustion and personal accomplishment. We studied the effects of some variables in the three dimensions of burnout. Sociological and proffesional variables that were related to these subscales were: age, sex, and rank. Other variables for: marital status, have or havent children, and partner with or without work, were not related to burnout levels. As for contour of teacher factor: years of instruction, and academic level, were related to burnout levels neither.

Familial similarity in personality

Parshikova, Oxana *Psychology, Moscow State University, Moscow, Russia*

The main goal of this study is to analyze similarity between parents and their offspring and between spouses as well. At present we have data of 42 families (129 respondents) from Moscow region. Self-completion questionnaires evaluate different personality measures of parents and their offspring (e.g. Big Five, locus of control). The "generation off children" (mean 21 years, st. dev. 3,1) has higher level of Extraversion, Openness and Internal locus of control and lower level of Agreeableness and Conscientiousness than "generation of their parents" (mean 48 years, st. dev. 6,5). Non-random mating is found for Agreeableness and Locus of control.

Cognitive-emotional functioning: Role of emotional intensity in the anxiety

Pasquier, Aurélie *Aix-en-Provence, France* **Bonnet, Agnàs** *Psychologie clinique, Université de Provence, Aix-en-Provence, France* **Pedinielli, Jean-Louis** *Psychologie clinique, Université de Provence, Aix-En-Provence, France*

Anxiety is an emotional trouble very present in the general population and it seems to be linked to depression symptoms. The aim of this study is to test the relations hypothesis between cognitive-emotional functioning, anxiety and depressive symptoms. The study's sample was formed from a group of 50 subjects, aged from 18 to 65. Participants completed Hospital Anxiety and Depression Scale (HAD), Affect Intensity Measure (AIM), Emotional Expressivity Scale (EES) and Levels of Emotional Awareness Scale (LEAS). Our results show strong positive correlations between anxiety symptoms, affect intensity, emotional expressivity and level of emotional awareness. In conclusion, this results point out the importance of emotional variables in the study and treatment of subjects suffering of anxiety symptoms.

Action of specific rhythms on the consciousness attention and reaction rate

Pelageykin, Denis *I.E.A.P., Moscow, Russia*

Were in this work carried out studies of the action of the specific rhythms, including of sonic for the purpose of the impact study of their influence on the consciousness, the cognitive processes, changes in the reaction rate and attention in subjects. The estimation of indices was conducted under laboratory conditions with the application of test programs and systems of the pickups of real time. Tested - students at the age from 20 to 35 years. The result of a study became the development of the dependence of the specific types of specific rhythmical action and by results which demonstrate subjects during the repeated testing. Procedure can be adapted for a change in the objective indices of those indicated above.

Can positive emotions contribute to improving teachers' personal beliefs about their perceived self-efficacy?

Perandones González, Teresa María *Educational Psychology, University of Alicante, Alicante, Spain* **Castejon Costa, Juan Luis** *EDUCATIONAL PSYCHOLOGY, UNIVERSITY OF ALICANTE, ALICANTE, Spain*

The purpose of this study is to examine the impact of positive emotions on teacher self-efficacy. To this end, 55 secondary education teachers responded to four instruments: Teacher's Sense of Efficacy Scale, NEO-FFI, BarOn EQi and Trait Meta-Mood Scale. Data analysis involved the use of Pearson correlation and multiple regression procedure. The results indicated that high levels of positive emotions are related to high levels of teacher self-efficacy and the positive emotions contributed significantly to the prediction of teacher self-

efficacy. The data supported the theoretical expectation of a linkage between positive emotions and teacher self-efficacy (Penrose, Perry and Ball, 2007).

Can dysfunctional attitudes, negative attributional style, pleasant events and personality features predict future depression? A twelve-month follow-up of 483 subjects

Perestelo-Perez, Lilisbeth *Evaluation and Planning Unit, Canary Islands Health Service, Santa Cruz de Tenerife, Spain* **Peñate-Castro, Wenceslao** *Personality, Evaluation and Ps, University of La Laguna, La Laguna, Spain* **Bethencourt-Perez, Juan Manuel** *Personality, Evaluation and Ps, University of La Laguna, La Laguna, Spain*

Objectives: The current study assessed dysfunctional attitudes, negative attributional style, pleasant events and personality failure to predict depression in young adult. Methods: A group of 483 young adult participated in this longitudinal study and they were assessed with self-reported questionnaires. The data analysis consisted of stepwise multiple-regression. procedures. Results: Findings suggest that personality construct of neuroticism and the dysfunctional attitude of dependency play a role in vulnerability to the onset of depressive symptoms, while attributional style did not predict change in self-reported depression symptoms. Conclusions: Analyses supported A.T. Beck's (1976) theory of depression and the big five model but not the hopelessness theory of depression.

Cooperative learning and sociometric status

Perez Sanchez, Antonio Miguel *Evolutive Psychology, University of Alicante, Alicante, Spain* **Poveda Serra, Patricia** *EVOLUTIVE PSYCHOLOGY AND DIDAC, UNIVERSITY OF ALICANTE, ALICANTE, Spain* **Quiros Bravo, Soledad** *EVOLUTIVE PSYCHOLOGY AND DIDAC, UNIVERSITY OF ALICANTE, ALICANTE, Spain*

Objective: verifying that sociometric status and group cohesiveness increase when cooperative learning techniques are used. Method: The participants were 50 students in first year of Compulsory Secondary Education (average age, 12). We used a pretest-postest design with non-equivalent control group. The data was obtained through sociometric test. To analyse the data we used t-Test of difference of means and univaried split-plot analysis of variance. Results: The findings confirmed our hypothesis. Conclusion: Cooperative learning techniques should be included in the classroom dynamics. The enhancement of inter-pair relations improves class atmosphere and academic achievement.

The role of the mediation of dysfunctional attitudes in the relation between adult attachment styles and emotional disorders

Permuy, Beatriz *Psicología Clínica, Facultad de Psicología, Santiago de Compostela, Spain* **Merino, Hipolito** *Psicología Clínica, Facultad de Psicología, Santiago de Compostela, Spain* **Fernandez-Rey, Jose** *Psicología Clínica, Facultad de Psicología, Santiago de Compostela, Spain*

We analysed the mediational role of the dysfunctional attitudes in the relation between attachment and depressive and anxious symptoms. In order to do so, a group of university students carried out the Beck Depression Inventory, the Trait Anxiety subscale of the State-Trait Anxiety Inventory, the Dysfunctional Attitudes Scale and the Relationship Questionnaire. Individuals who had negative models of self obtained significantly higher scores in the BDI and STAI-T than those with positive models of self. The data indicated that the influence of the preoccupied and fearful styles on depression was determined by dysfunctional attitudes, whilst the association of these styles with anxiey was no explained by DAS scores.

Development of the intimacy of Maternal Disclosure Scale (IMDS) using Rasch Analysis

Perrin, Marei *Victoria, Canada* **Ehrenberg, Marion** *Psychology, University of Victoria, Victoria, BC, Canada* **Graves, Roger** *Psychology, University of Victoria, Victoria, Canada*

Objectives: Development of a scale to assess perceived dis/comfort levels of mothers in discussing topics of varying intimacy levels with their adolescent/young adult children. Methods: 55 undergraduates enrolled at a midsize Canadian university completed the newly developed IMDS. One parameter Rasch analysis was used to construct the final scale. Results: Final version of the IMDS possessed good internal consistency (alpha=.97), good response difficulty range, and good spread of retained items. Conclusions: IMDS is a promising scale to assess mothers' perceived comfort levels in maternal disclosure, which may help to identify healthy as well as problematic mother-child relationship dynamics.

Network analysis of respiratory sensations in sports and stress using flowthrough centrality measurements

Petersen, Sibylle *Inst. für Psychologie, Universität Hamburg, Hamburg, Germany* **Mann, Charles F.** *Computer Science/ Engineering, Southern Methodist University, Dallas, USA* **Matula, David W.** *Computer Science/ Engineering, Southern Methodist University, Dallas, USA* **Ritz, Thomas** *Psychology, Southern Methodist University, Dallas, USA*

Patients' self report of respiratory sensations is an important source of diagnostic information. A network analysis method of exploring sensations by a proposed flowthrough centrality measurement based upon hierarchical maximum concurrent flow in networks of descriptors is introduced. 582 individuals rated 25 sensation descriptors regarding situational incidence in sport/exercise and stressful situations. Arrest of breathing (apnea) was the most central sensation in the stressful situations network. For the sport/exercise situations network, the highest flowthrough centrality was observed for being out of breath. These results demonstrate the usefulness of this method in the analysis of self-reported symptoms. Future applications are identified.

The role of friendship on life satisfaction and well-being for aging adults

Pezzuti, Lina *Dep. Clinical Psychology, Universita di Roma, Roma, Italy* **Baiocco, Roberto** *Faculty of Psychology 1, Universita di Roma, Rome, Italy* **Laghi, Fiorenzo** *Clinical Psychology, Faculty of Psychology 1, Rome, Italy* **d'Alessio, Maria** *Clinical Psychology, Faculty of Psychology 1, Rome, Italy*

Objectives. Research of friendship has recently extended to study the importance of friendship role on life satisfaction and well-being for aging adults. Methods. The research examined aspects of friendship initiation and maintenance in aging adults (aged 65-85). The study investigated: a) how aging adults perceive their friendship involvement; b) how friendship support patterns of later life compare with those of earlier stages; c) the way in which friends relate to other source of support; d) the effect of friendship on perceived well-being and life satisfaction. Results support the need of a broadened understanding of friendship in the late adulthood years.

The impact of emotion on memory performance of depressive patients

Pfütze, Eva-Maria *Bochum, Germany* **Lindenberg, Annette** *AG Motivation, Ruhr-Universität Bochum, Bochum, Germany* **Pinnow, Marlies** *AG Motivation, Ruhr-Universität Bochum, Bochum, Germany* **Schweinberger, Stefan** *Psychologie, Universität Jena, Jena, Germany*

Based on various theories of depression and emotion it was tested if the recognition performance of depressive patients relies on the emotional content of to-be-remembered faces. Therefore, probands had to memorize sad and happy faces in a learning phase. Then they had to recognize them in a subsequent recognition phase, where these faces were presented as happy, neutral and sad. The depressive patients recognized the faces they learned as sad better than the faces they learned as happy, while healthy controls recognized the faces learned as happy better than the faces learned as sad. This evidence that memory in depressive patients works better with depression-congruent content confirms the interaction of emotional and cognitive processes.

Ecological momentary assessment of anxiety symptoms: Limited evidence for cognitive theories of panic disorder

Pfaltz, Monique Inst. für Psychologie, Universität Basel, Basel, Switzerland Michael, Tanja Clinical Psychology, University of Basel, Basel, Switzerland Kolodyazhniy, Vitaliy Clinical Psychology, University of Basel, Basel, Switzerland Peyk, Peter Clinical Psychology, University of Basel, Basel, Switzerland Margraf, Jürgen Basel, Switzerland Wilhelm, Frank H. Clinical Psychology, University of Basel, Basel, Switzerland

We tested cognitive theories of panic disorder (PD) by monitoring anxiety symptoms in 20 PD patients, 20 healthy controls, and a clinical control group (15 patients with PTSD), using an electronic diary. Participants rated various bodily, cognitive, and emotional anxiety symptoms five times a day for one week. The relationship between symptoms was assessed using vector autoregression. While for some individuals cognitive factors like expectation of anxiety seem to mediate anxiety, group results only provide limited support for theories assuming a general influence of cognitive factors in the development and maintenance of panic attacks.

Action observation is affected by viewing perspective in dance-novices

Pilgramm, Sebastian Bender Instit. of Neuroimaging, Universität Gießen, Giessen, Germany Zentgraf, Karen Psychology and Sport Science, Universität Giessen, Giessen, Germany Stark, Rudolf Bender Instit. of Neuroimaging, Universität Giessen, Giessen, Germany Munzert, Jörn Psychology and Sport Science, Universität Giessen, Giessen, Germany

Observing someone performing an action activates motor and related regions (Rizzolatti, 2001). Activation can be enhanced, e.g. by motor expertise (Calvo-Merino et al., 2006). It is unknown whether novices' neural networks are susceptible to observing unfamiliar movements from a first- contrasted to a third-person perspective (1PP, 3PP). Ballroom dance videos created by a helmet camera were observed by 15 novices in a functional magnetic resonance imaging study. Results show stronger activation in secondary somatosensory areas and inferior parietal cortex bilaterally during observation of 1PP videos implying agency. Therefore, modulation of motor-related activation also occurs in novices by different viewing perspectives

What drives risky driving behaviour? An analysis based on a proposal for redesigning the theory of planned behaviour

Pimentão, Cristina FCHS, Universidade Fernando Pessoa, Vila Nova de Gaia, Portugal

To better understand risky driving behaviour we are conducting a study based on the Theory of Planned Behaviour (TPB) but also with the intention of redesigning it. To achieve this goal we constructed a questionnaire based on the TPB to apply to drivers between 18 and 50 years old. Trough statistical analysis we want to test the possibility of including an emotional dimension

(e.g., rage) to extend the TPB and to increase its predictive power. We are expecting that the results will show us which dimensions of the model are better predictors of risky driving behaviour. With this knowledge we can propose relevant guide lines to train drivers in the beginning and throughout their driving experience.

Attentional mechanism in depression

Pinnow, Marlies Inst. of Cogn. Neuroscience, Ruhr-University Bochum, Bochum, Germany Karrasch, Natalie Inst. of Cogn. Neuroscience, Ruhr-University Bochum, Bochum, Germany

We consider whether disruption of a specific neural circuit related to self-regulation is an underlying biological deficit in depression. Because depressives exhibit a poor ability to regulate negative affect, we hypothesized that brain mechanisms thought to be involved in such self-regulation would function abnormally even in situations that seem remote from the symptoms exhibited by these patients. To test this idea, we compared the efficiency of attentional networks in a non-clinical high depressive group and a low depressive group. Contrary to the hypotheses we found no deficits in executive attention, but depressive subjects showed a severe deficit in the alerting attention in this pure cognitive task.

Aphasia: Atypical case

Pinto Monteiro das Neves, Maria Teresa Lisbon, Portugal

The author presents a clinical case of a man with 68 years old, who suffered a stoke in April 2007. When evaluating, showed marked difficulty in expressing himself, agrammatic, with spontaneous speech reduced and poor content. The pacient presents a language disorder, nosologically classified in the field of aphasias. However is not a typical case. The author present and discuss (Theory of Luria), the data obtained from neuropsychological assessment process.

Attitudes towards online health care and expected impact on physician-patient-relationship

Pintzinger, Nina Research and Training Practice, Universität Wien, Wien, Austria Stetina, Birgit U. Forschung und Ausbildung, Universität Wien, Wien, Austria Kryspin-Exner, Ilse Inst. für Psychologie, Universität Wien, Wien, Austria

Objectives: Attitudes towards online health care and possible changes of the physician-patient-relationship as a result of using ehealth applications. Methods: A German-speaking online-sample was surveyed using the Attitudes towards Online Health Care Scale (LaCousiere, 2001). Data analysis included statistical inference and descriptive methods. Results: Results demonstrate little positive effects for personal health care as a consequence of using ehealth applications; most participants have negative attitudes to online health care. The expected changes of the physician-patient relationship are still unclear. Conclusion: The patient point of view shows only little impact on personal health care of ehealth applications and physician-patient relationship.

Modeling of cooperative processes of networked teams in critical situations

Pioro, Margarete Naturwissenschaften - EFS, Forschungsgesell. für Angew., Wachtberg-Werthhoven, Germany Duckwitz, Sönke Ergonomics and HMS, RWTH Aachen University, Aachen, Germany Mann, Cindy EFS, FGAN, Wachtberg-Werthhoven, Germany Grandt, Morten Ergonomics and HMS, RWTH - Aachen University, Aachen, Germany

In critical situations teamwork is frequently necessary. This allows for a flatter hierarchy and a greater scope for decision making at lower levels.

However, at the same time each member of the team has an individual and therefore incomplete view of the situation, so that all of the participants are dependent on cooperation to obtain an overview. To evaluate these complex processes and team composition, a simulation approach has been developed. Aiming at the development of a general system model a process assessment based on psychological work analysis has been performed and transferred into an object oriented model description.

Psychometric properties of the Italian version of the Transplant Effects Questionnaire (TxEQ): A study among renal transplant recipients

Pisanti, Renato Dept. of Psychology, University of Rome, Maddaloni, Italy Lombardo, Caterina Dept of Psychology, "La Sapienza" Universi, Rome, Italy Violani, Cristiano Dept of Psychology, "La Sapienza" Universi, Rome, Italy Poli, Luca Dept of Transplants surgery, "La Sapienza" Universi, Rome, Italy Berloco, Pasquale Bartolomeo Dept of Transplants Surgery, University of Rome, Rome, Italy Giordanengo, Luca Dept of Medical Psychology, Hospital "S.Giovanni Batti, Turin, Italy Bennardi, Linda Dept of Medical Psychology, Hospital"S.Giovanni Battis, Turin, Italy

Objective: The Transplant Effects Questionnaire (Ziegelmann et al., 2002) is a well designed instrument to assess several aspect of the emotional representations in transplant recipients. The aim of this study was to examine the psychometric properties of an Italian version of the TxEQ. Method: 125 kidney transplant patients completed the TxEQ, the inventory on coping strategies (CISS-SV) and the Anxiety and Depression scales of the SCL-90. Results: A Confirmatory Factor Analysis supported the hypothesized five-factor model of TxEQ: Worry, Guilt, Disclosure, Adherence, Responsibility. The scales showed acceptable internal consistency and relationships with coping and distress. Conclusion: Results support the construct validity and reliability of the Italian version of the TxEQ.

The measure of engagement at work among Italian health care workers: Factor structure and reliability of Utrecht Work Engagement Scale

Pisanti, Renato Dept. of Psychology, University of Rome, Maddaloni, Italy Paplomatas, Alessia Dept of Psychology, University of Rome, Rome, Italy Bertini, Mario Dept of Psychology, University of Rome, Rome, Italy

Objective: To examine the psychometric properties of the Italian version of the Uthrecht Work Engagement Scale (UWES) among health care workers. Methods: 984 health care workers participated in two studies that included: the Italian version of the UWES, the Multidimensional Organizational Health Questionnaire (MOHQ), and the Maslach Burnout Inventory (MBI). Results: The confirmatory factor analysis supported the hypothesized three-factor model of work engagement, consisting of Vigor, Dedication and Absorption. All of the three dimensions showed acceptable internal consistencies and, consistent to our expectations, showed relationships both with the MOHQ and MBI. Conclusion: The analyses support the construct validity and reliability of the UWES.

The perception of type II diabetes: An Italian adaptation of IPQ-R

Pisanti, Renato Dept. of Psychology, University of Rome, Maddaloni, Italy Lazzari, David Dept of Psychology, Hospital "S. Maria", Terni, Italy Marini, Carla Giulia Dept of Psychology, Hospital "S. Maria", Terni, Italy Fatati, Giuseppe Dept of Diabetology, Hospital "S. Maria", Terni (TR), Italy

Objective: The IPQ-R is a valid and extended instrument to measure illness perceptions. The aim of the study was to validate an Italian version of IPQ-R-Diabetes version. Method: The IPQ-R

Diabetes version was administrated in a sample of 202 type II diabetic patients. Other measures included: HbA1c, Anxiety and Depression scales of the SCL-90. Results: The EFA supported the proposed structures of the IPQ-R. The dimensions showed acceptable internal consistencies and relationships both with HbA1c and distress dimensions. Conclusion: The Italian version of the IPQ-R Diabetes version showed acceptable psychometric properties to be used in clinical practice.

Transplant-related stress, coping strategies and emotional adjustment following renal transplantation

Pisanti, Renato Dept. of Psychology, University of Rome, Maddaloni, Italy *Lombardo, Caterina* Dept of Psychology, "La Sapienza" Universi, Rome, Italy *Violani, Cristiano* Dept of Psychology, "La Sapienza" Universi, Rome, Italy *Poli, Luca* Dept of Transplants Surgery, University of Rome, Rome, Italy *Berloco, Pasquale Bartolomeo* Dept of Transplants Surgery, "La Sapienza" Universi, Rome, Italy *Bennardi, Linda* Dept of Medical Psychology, Hospital"S.Giovanni Battis, Turin, Italy *Giordanengo, Luca* Dept of Medical Psychology, Hospital"S.Giovanni Battis, Turin, Italy
Objective: The influences of transplant related stress and coping strategies on emotional adjustment among renal transplant recipients were examined. Method: 101 patients, selected in two national transplant centres, completed the Scales on Stress and Guilt of the Transplant Effects Questionnaire, the Coping Inventory for Stressful Situations Short Version, and the Anxiety and Depression scales of SCL-90,. Results: Hierarchical regression analyses showed that the combination of stressors and coping strategies explained from 42% to 54% of the variance in emotional adjustment outcomes. Conclusion: Stressors and coping strategies have both additive and interactive effects on emotional adjustment in kidney transplant recipients.

Extending the Job Demands-Control-Support model: The role of curvilinear relationships between psychosocial work characteristics and mental well-being

Pisanti, Renato Dept. of Psychology, University of Rome, Maddaloni, Italy *van der Doef, Margot* Section of Health Psychology, Leiden University, Leiden, Netherlands *Maes, Stan* Section of Health Psychology, Leiden University, Leiden, Netherlands *Lazzari, David* Dept of Psychology, Hospital "S. Maria", Terni, Italy *Bertini, Mario* Dept of Psychology, University of Rome, Rome, Italy
Objective: To examine whether curvilinearity would add explanatory power to the linear relationships between Karasek & Theorell's model job dimensions and mental well-being. Methods: Data were collected by self-report questionnaires including the Leiden Quality of Work Questionnaire for Nurses (LQWQ-N), the MBI, and the psycho-somatic distress dimensions of the SCLR90. The sample consisted of 1385 nurses. Results: Job demands showed the most consistent curvilinear associations across outcomes. Furthermore, all job dimensions were curvilinearly associated with psychological distress. Conclusion: The findings from this study provided partial support for the assumption of curvilinearity in the relationship between psychosocial working conditions and well-being.

Managers' error stories and their impact on learning

Pittig, Diana Work and Organizational Psych, University of Giessen, Gießen, Germany *Bledow, Ronald* Arbeits- und Org.-Psychologie, Universität Gießen, Gießen, Germany
Building on past research on error training, we examined if students can learn from others' errors. We let a sample of 50 psychology and business students listen to managers reporting case studies of either successes or failures. The learning content for both conditions was equal. After listening to the case studies, students in the error training condition performed better in applying what they had learned when working on a transfer task. Furthermore, we found the training condition to interact with participants' error orientation. We conclude that formal and informal learning in work settings can benefit from deliberately focusing on errors.

Children and adolescents beliefs about the main problems in stepfamilies, according to their personal experience

Plasencia, Sonia Psychology, University of La Laguna, La Laguna, Spain *Triana, Beatriz* Psycology, University of La Laguna, La Laguna, Spain
This study attempts to explore what different generations think about stepfamilies and the main problems these have to face, and whether the degree of personal experience of divorce affects these beliefs. In this study there were 448 participants, distributed into age groups (5-6 year-olds; 8-9 year-olds; 11-12 year-olds and 15-18 year-olds) and also according to their personal experience of divorce (50% with experience/ 50% without experience). An open interview was used to explore their explicit knowledge about this topic and ANOVAS were made to analyse the dates. The results show that the age group and the family experience of divorce were to affect beliefs about problems in stepfamilies.

The development of managerial abilities of a person in adolescence

Popova, Galyna of Railway Transport Ukraine, State Scientific-Research Cent, Kiev, Ukraine *Khomulenko, Tamara* Psuchology, Skovoroda Kharkiv NPU, Kharkiv, Ukraine *Podenko, Anton* Psychology, Skovoroda Kharkiv NPD, Kharkiv, Ukraine
The research objective is the analysis of the structure of personal managerial abilities in adolescence and the determination of features and means of their development. Method. The author describes adolescent age abilities to develop managerial abilities. The structure of managerial abilities, which includes formal-dynamic, social-intellectual, emotional-adaptive, regulating and communicative-style characteristics, has been determined by means of factor analysis (the technique of main components with subsequent Varimax-distribution). Results. A complex of methods of psychodiagnostics of managerial abilities of adolescent personality has been suggested: "Social intellect", "Tolerance to ambiguity", "Motivation for success", "Communicative orientation of personality", "Communicative sphere of temperament", "Self-regulation of behavior stile".

The compatibility sequential effect and cognitive capacity

Privado Zamorano, Jesus Madridejos, Spain *Botella Ausina, Juan* Social and Methodology, Universidad Autonoma de Madrid, Madrid, Spain *Colom Marañón, Roberto* Biological and of the Health, Universidad Autónoma de Madrid, Madrid, Spain *Suero Suñe, Manuel* Social and Methodology, Universidad Autónoma de Madrid, Madrid, Spain *Quiroga Estévez, Ángeles* Differential and Work, Universidad Complutense, Madrid, Spain
The Sequential Compatibility Effect (the Compatibility Effect is larger after an Incompatible trial that after a Compatible one) has been mostly linked to the Botvinick et al's Conflict Monitoring Theory. However, some controversy has risen related with an alternative explanation as a methodological artefact of priming effects on the pure repetition trials. In this research, a sample of 478 undergraduate students run three compatibility tasks: an even-odd digit's categorization task; a vowel-consonant letter's categorization task; and a left-right arrow's categorization task. The three tasks showed robust Compatibility Effect, but only the spatial one showed a significant Sequential Effect. The

relationships between this effect and several cognitive capacities are explored.

Outcomes of a social communication enhancement program for individuals with autism within a combined one-to-one and small group setting

Probst, Paul Hamburg, Germany
A social communication enhancement program for individuals with autism was evaluated. The program is based on "structured teaching", play and music therapy and was implemented in 21 weekly one-hour sessions. The findings (based on video time sampling methods) averaged across the 3 participants (two boys and one female adult) indicate that cooperative behaviors occurred in 67%, spontaneous communication in 25%, and reactive communication in 58% of the analyzed time intervals, and that the program was consistently positively rated by the participants' parents. The results of this first evaluation provide some evidence for the clinical validity of the intervention program.

Traumatic events, posttraumatic stress and depressive symptoms among drug users in treatment – preliminary data

Pulcherio, Gilda Graduated Program, PUCRS, Porto Alegre/rs, Brazil *Strey, Marlene* Graduated Program, PUCRS, Porto Alegre, Brazil *Sarti, Paulo* Graduated Program, PUCRS, Porto Alegre/rs, Brazil *Fensterseifer, Daniel* Graduated Program, PUCRS, Porto Alegre/rs, Brazil *Pinent, Carlos* Graduated Program, PUCRS, Porto Alegre/rs, Brazil
Objective: The present study is investigating the posttraumatic stress symptoms (PTSD) and depressive symptoms among male with substance disorder. Methods: All the subjects (n=50) were Brazilian psychiatric outpatients. SPSS 11.5 was used by the statistical analyses. Results: 96,4% of drug-addicted in treatment had experienced to at least 1 lifetime traumatic event. 40% punctuated a total score in the Davidson Trauma Scale which suggests PTSD. Positive correlation between PTSD severity symptoms and severity depressive symptoms (p<0, 005) were found. Conclusions: The trauma evaluation in the addict patients' history is essentially important as a preventive factor of the chronic PTSD and treatment.

Effects of double negation and mismatch in Chinese sentence: Evidence from eye movements

Qingrong, Chen Psychology, Nanjing Normal University, Nanjing, People's Republic of China *Deng, Zhu* Psychology, Nanjing Normal University, Nanjing, People's Republic of China *Tan, Dingliang* Psychology, Nanjing Normal University, Nanjing, People's Republic of China
In the present study, readers' eye movement were monitered when they processed Chinese sentences and pictures. The results revealed that double nagation as a special negation was not more difficutl to be verified than affirmation. The effect disappeared on the total fixation time and fixation times. While the sentence was presented before picture, there was also the mismatch effect. Semantic mismath was inevitable to increase participants' cognitive load and had immediate effects on eye movement. But the mismatch effect was modulated by syntactic complexity. Negation was more difficult to be verified and integrated than affirmation and double negation in the mismatch condition.

Analyzing group performance in navy teams. An application of Graph metodology

Quezada, Ariel Psicología, Universidad Adolfo Ibáñez, Viña del Mar, Chile
The aim of this research is to discover the pattern of relation in small groups that allow the best performances. For this purpose, we generate 10

small groups that work as a functional team, solving problems during 1 hour. Latter, we describe its frequency, direction and type of relation within groups. This description is translated into digraphs, a particular kind of Graph Methodology. After comparing and making a hierarchy of group performance, we suggest a relation between performance and kind of digraph generated, under the hypothesis that in groups uniformly integrated (Chilean Marines), the different performances are associated to different kind of interactions.

The effect of family communication patterns on happiness in high school students of Shiraz

Rahimi, Mehdi Shiraz, Islamic Republic of Iran Jowkar, Bahram Educational psychologh, Shiraz University, shiraz, Islamic Republic of Iran

The aim of study was examining the effect of family Communication patterns on happiness. The sample group included 200 girls and boys students selected by cluster random sampling from high schools of Shiraz. Revised versions of Oxford Happiness and Koerner-Fitzpatrick Family Communication Patterns scales were used. Cronbach alpha coefficient and factor analysis showed acceptable reliability and validity of the instruments. Results of two way ANOVA revealed that consensual and pluralistic patterns in comparison to protective and laissez-faire patterns had higher scores in happiness scale. Gender was a moderator variable.

A study of the relationship between religious attitudes and psychological health of Iranian male and female university students

Rahimi Taghanaki, Changiz Clinical Psychology, Shiraz University, Shiraz, Islamic Republic of Iran Kamranpour, Farideh 4. Stage, Ferdosi Street-Yas Building –, Shiraz, Islamic Republic of Iran

We investigated the relationship between religious views and psychological health of the iranian male (n=232) and female (n=238) students from Shiraz University. They completed General Health Questionnaire (G.H.Q) and a Religious Attitude Questionnaire (R.A.Q). Analyzing the row values using ANOVA and correlation coefficient showed that, the female students had more problems in psychosomatic disorder, behavioral disorder, depression and anxiety, but the difference was only for depression significant (P<0.01). Regarding religious attitudes, the female subjects showed higher averages. There was a positive correlation (P<0.05) between religious attitudes and psychological health, but the girls showed a stronger relationship (P<0.01).

Assessing of psychological causes, social economical divorce in applicants divorce in courts of families at Tehran city (1385-1386)

Rahmani, Narges Kafshgarkola Bozorg, mazandaran, Ghaemshahr, Islamic Republic of Iran Ghasimi, Mitra mirdamad, tehran, tehran, Islamic Republic of Iran mohtashami, jamileh mirdamad, teran, tehran, Islamic Republic of Iran

Articles and methods:The tools of this investigation was questionnaire investigation that it had designed by surveing sources and past studying. Findings:The average and criterion deviation indicators concerned divorcefactor at psychologicall range, parts of the investigation showed that the most of samples investigation for lack of understanding in decision and the range of social factor to have culturall difference by husband and the range of economical factor of divorce too expenses of living it is most important. Discution and result: According to result in this research, the factors of divorce, psychical factor is the first place and social and economical factors are in the second place.

The role of task demands on memory and naming RTs in a transparent orthography

Raman, Ilhan Dept. of Psychology, Middlesex University, London, United Kingdom Hancerli, Sevil Psychology, Middlesex University, London, United Kingdom

The role of orthographic transparency on cognitive processes involved in reading has been debated for nearly three decades. The aim in the present study is to examine the role of task instruction on reading performance and memory in reading a totally transparent orthography, namely Turkish. Previous research in Turkish has shown that reading in a transparent orthography is under the strategic control of readers when task demands are manipulated (Raman et al, 2004). We report a series of experiments whereby the role of task demand is explored on memory and naming of transparent Turkish words.

Differential effects of number of letters on word and nonword naming latency: Revisited

Raman, Ilhan Dept. of Psychology, Middlesex University, London, United Kingdom Kokten, Ozge Psychology, Middlesex University, London, United Kingdom

Previous research conducted in English has shown that number of letters has an impact on RTs in a naming task (Weekes, 1997). The aim of the current study is to explore whether similar effects would be found in Turkish characterized by unique transparent relationship between print and sound. Previous research in Turkish has shown that readers can adopt a lexical strategy in reading (Raman, Baluch & Besner, 2004). Participants named words and nonwords manipulated on length and frequency in naming tasks and data were subjected to regression analyses. The findings are discussed within the dual-route model of reading.

Abstract thought - A challenge for theories of embodied cognition

Rasch, Thorsten Gen. and Educ. Psych., University of Koblenz-Landau, Landau, Germany

The emergent approaches of embodied cognition propose that mental processes and representations are entirely grounded in perception and action. This theory is apparently limited with regard to abstract thought, because abstract concepts are inherently non-pictorial, symbolic representations. However, contemporary cognitive linguistics describes even abstract thought in terms of embodiment: abstract concepts are considered as just metaphorical projections of gestalt-like image schemas, derived from bodily experiences (e.g. blockage, path, container). In fact, our experimental study revealed accelerated reading times and improved recall for abstract sentences, when reading was primed by short visual animations of semantically matching image schemas.

Group ethics in clinical settings

Rasera, Emerson F. Instituto de Psicologia, Uberlândia, Brazil Albino, Emília C. A. Instituto de Psicologia, Univ. Federal de Uberlândia, Uberlândia, Brazil

This study aims to describe the meanings of ethics to psychologists working with groups in clinical settings in a Brazilian city. Data collection consisted on in-depth interviews with ten psychologists about ethical principles and group ethics. Data was qualitatively analyzed and emphasized the meaning-making process. The main results were: an ethical stance characterized by an interaction of professional and personal issues; absence of specific group practice training; confidentiality as the main ethical principle for group practice; and an enhanced sense of ethical commitment when coordinating groups. These understandings invite to reflect about group practice training and its ethical consequences.

Cognition, intuition, creation

Rettenwander, Annemarie Innsbruck, Austria Neuhauser, Gebhard Institute of Psychology, Leopold-Franzens-University, Innsbruck, Austria Lantschner, Ulrike Institute of Psychology, Leopold-Franzens-University, Innsbruck, Austria Walder, Kathrin Institute of Psychology, Leopold-Franzens-University, Innsbruck, Austria Zeillinger, Katharina Institute of Psychology, Leopold-Franzens-University, Innsbruck, Austria Kerle, Carina Institute of Psychology, Leopold-Franzens-University, Innsbruck, Austria Krug, Nadja Institute of Psychology, Leopold-Franzens-University, Innsbruck, Austria Horn, Birgit Institute of Psychology, Leopold-Franzens-University, Innsbruck, Austria Gmachl-Wejbora, Stephanie Institute of Psychology, Leopold-Franzens-University, Innsbruck, Austria

The aim of this study was to investigate how artists' thinking about creative problem solving in their work departs from academic theories on this subject. For instance how do artists cope with difficulties like "fear of the empty sheet"? Do they define phases in the creative process like academic theories do? 112 professional artists (e.g. painters, stage designers, writers) took part in this study (supported by the young researchers fund of Innsbruck University). Qualitative analysis based on Grounded Theory shows, that artists' theories about creative process differ significantly from academic theories – and that there are marked differences between several genres.

About the effect of aesthetics and symbolism on experience and behavior in libraries

Richter, Peter Arbeits-, Organis.-Psychologie, Techn. Universität Dresden, Dresden, Germany Dufter, Michael Psychology, TU Dresden, Dresden, Germany Seeliger, Maria Psychology, TU Dresden, Dresden, Germany

Two contemporary libraries in Dresden (SLUB) and Cottbus (IKMZ) are compared. The research focuses on experience and performance of users, mainly students. The hypothesis suggests that both equally equipped libraries reveal a difference in symbolic effect. Accordingly SLUB is more likely to be a place of concentration and silence, IKMZ a place of work and communication. 200 users each are surveyed, with data collection centered upon the reading areas. Questionaires were implemented regarding the level of activation as well as aestethic and symbolic evaluation. Information on study behavior (continous reading, communication, interaction, etc.) was registered by observation. Variables of social-demography and personality (Big Five) were controlled. The results validate the empirical hypothesis.

Spatial representations in skilled typing

Rieger, Martina Inst. für Psychologie, Max-Planck-Institut, Leipzig, Germany

Spatial representations in skilled typists were investigated by dissociating spatial positions (key-congruence) and names (name-congruence) of keys on a keyboard. Participants responded with crossed hands to the color of colored letters. The keys were either without names (Exp1) or renamed (Exp2). This resulted in effector-congruent, incongruent, and different name/key congruent conditions. In Exp1 participants showed facilitation in the key-congruent/name-neutral condition. In Exp2 participants showed interference in the key-congruent/name-incongruent condition. No effect was obtained in the key-incongruent/name-congruent condition. Thus, key names are neither sufficient nor necessary for the activation of spatial representations in skilled typing; they are however processed.

Elderly drivers' performance in a lane-change task: Dual-task decrement and the investment of effort

Rinkenauer, Gerhard Modern Human-Machine Systems, IfADo, Dortmund, Germany Wilschut, Ellen S. Ageing and CNS alterations, IfADo, Dortmund, Germany

Secondary task demands introduced by driver assistance systems affect driving performance. Especially elderly drivers are vulnerable to dual task interference. We assessed the effect of secondary task complexity on driving performance for young and elderly participants. A lane-change task was used as primary task and a visual search task with different search complexity levels as secondary task. Results revealed a reduced performance of elderly participants. These participants also showed severe and stronger dual task decrements with increasing visual search complexity. Multiple regression analyses of objective and subjective measures suggest that elderly drivers have a better self estimation of invested effort.

Manipulating the frequency of a preview word N+2: Examining lexical parafoveal-on-foveal effects in a boundary paradigm

Risse, Sarah Allgemeine Psychologie I, Universität Potsdam, Potsdam, Germany Kliegl, Reinhold Allgemeine Psychologie I, Universität Potsdam, Potsdam, Germany Engbert, Ralf Allgemeine Psychologie I, Universität Potsdam, Potsdam, Germany

From a distributed parallel processing perspective immediate effects from preprocessing parafoveal word(s) on the current fixation can be predicted (i.e., parafoveal-on-foveal effects). Moreover, these effects should not necessarily be constrained only to low-level visual characteristics but generalized to lexical properties of parafoveal words. In a gaze-contingent display change paradigm (Rayner, 1976) with the boundary set after word N, the frequency of word N+2 was manipulated instead of using random letter strings as incorrect previews. With this manipulation, linear mixed-effect models can be implemented to test different hypotheses about the dynamical origin of preprocessing effects (e.g., the mislocated fixation hypothesis).

Training needs assessment with a focus on best practice: Specification of crew resource management training requirements

Ritzmann, Sandrina Organisationspsychologie, Universität St. Gallen, St. Gallen, Switzerland Hagemann, Vera Lehrstuhl für Organisationspsy, Universität St. Gallen, St. Gallen, Switzerland

Although Crew Resource Management (CRM)-trainings are applied in aviation and other industries and a lot of research exists, little is known about what practitioners actually do. Within a CRM-training project, a training needs assessment is conducted. We investigate best industry and current training practice by interviewing key informants of companies doing CRM- and similar trainings, by observing trainings and by analyzing literature, documents and legal requirements. This data and critical incident interviews will be used to specify training requirements. First results show that practitioners are generally convinced of the importance of CRM-trainings, but that participants still judge CRM as "psycho-babble".

Clinical psychology: Searches and challenges

Rodríguez Sánchez, José Luis Puebla, Mexico

At this moment Clinical Psychology faces different challenges, the answers it give to this challenges, will it allow to continue being the most popular psychological area and with a greater number of practitioners in psychology; to find its identity and over all, to give answers to the social and health demands, necessities and exigencies, that constitutes the reason of their existence. The following work shows a general and personal vision of the challenges that Clinical Psychology faces, of its present state and of answers that are expected of it and of its practitioners.

Adopted teenagers and their vertical and horizontal relationships: Issues and specific characteristics

Rosenfeld, Zoé faculté de psycho et educ, Université Libre de Bruxelles, Bruxelles, Belgium Lotta, De Coster faculté de psycho et educ, Université Libre de Bruxelles, Bruxelles, Belgium Isabelle, Duret faculté de psycho et educ, Université Libre de Bruxelles, Bruxelles, Belgium

The present research explores the parental and non-parental relationships developed by adopted teenagers: do they express specific characteristics or pathological risks linked to the adoption? An interesting way to approach the different representations of the parental and non-parental relationships is to use a "genogramme imaginaire" which can include both vertical and orizontal relationships. The imaginary character of the "genogramme imaginaire" offers adopted teenagers the possibility to represent both their social and biological relationship and to integrate their double origins so as to respect any potential loyalty conflict.

Inhibitory process outside of the attentional focus

Rossini, Joaquim Instituto de Psicologia, Univ. Fed. de Uberlandia, Uberlandia, Brazil Galera, Cesar Psicologia e Educação, Universidade de São Paulo, Ribeirão Preto, Brazil

Purpose: Provide evidence of a spatial inhibitory mechanism of irrelevant information outside of the attentional focus. Method: Thirteen participants were instructed to discriminate a target letter (O or W) that appeared in the center of screen within a rectangular cue. Flanker letters, compatible or incompatible with the targets were displayed inside or outside of the cue. Results: RT shows a reduction of the effect of the incompatible flanker presented outside the cue area and a beneficial effect of congruent flanker inside the cue area. Conclusion: The results are compatible with an inhibitory process outside of attentional focus.

Adolescents' future time perspectives and self-efficacy

Roura Mas, Francesc Departament d'Orientació., Escola Pía., Barcelona, Spain Hernández Encuentra, Eulàlia Psic.ologia i Educació, Univ Oberta de Catalunya, Barcelona, Spain Estaún, Santiago Psicologia Bàsica, Univ. Autònoma de Barcelona, Bellaterra, Spain Cladellas-Pros, Ramon

This study discusses adolescents' future-time perspectives during their final year at secondary school and explores the relationship between these perspectives and their perceptions of self efficacy. Subjects included 280 students (mean age 17.7 years) and four different instruments were used to gather data. A descriptive analysis shows the content, the extension and the perceived control over future plans and fears. And the associative analysis shows that an internal control over projects is significantly and positively related to self-efficacy. Results allow us to identify themes for a tutorial action plan that could contribute to a holistic educational project.

Long-term effects of organizational development in residential care for the elderly focused on the interests of both residents and employees

Roux, Pascale Forschungsgruppe SoWi, Fachhochschule Vorarlberg, Dornbirn, Austria Fredersdorf, Frederic Forschungsgruppe SoWi, Fachhochschule Vorarlberg, Dornbirn, Austria

From 2003 to 2005 corporate culture based on the needs of residents was implemented in two institutions for residential care for the elderly in Vorarl-berg (Austria). Three employee surveys give evidence of the positive effects (Fredersdorf et al., 2006). A follow-up employee survey (105 employees) in 2007 analyzed the sustainability. Distinctions between all employee surveys were determined by Kruskal-Wallis-tests. 12 of the 22 dimensions have improved significantly over 5 years, only one dimension has deteriorated significantly. This result demonstrates that organizational development focused on the interests of residents and employees shows long term effects in addition to the intervention itself.

The management of complex work tasks: The improvement of mental models and performance by applying a spatial planning methodology

Saifoulline, Rinat Universität Bamberg, Bamberg, Germany von der Weth, Rüdiger Business Administration, HTW Dresden, Dresden, Germany Schönwandt, Walter IGP, Universität Stuttgart, Stuttgart, Germany Hemberger, Christoph IGP, Universität Stuttgart, Stuttgart, Germany Grunau, Jens IGP, Universität Stuttgart, Stuttgart, Germany

A methodology for spatial planners has been developed to support complex tasks like the design of traffic concepts. The effects of this methodology were evaluated: Teams had to work on two planning tasks (n=58). Half of the subjects were trained before the first task, the others before the second task. Behaviour was recorded and the results assessed. Knowledge about methodology and their own work processes was examined. Our research showed significant improvement of performance and changes in planning behaviour. Both these findings correlate with a convergence of mental models within teams.

Effect of family-friendly employment policies on applicant attraction: An intergroup relation perspective

Saitere, Sanita Dept. of Psychology, University of Latvia, Riga, Latvia

Study applies intergroup relations framework to examine impact of family-friendly employment policies statement and image emphasizing family identity on perceived organizational attraction to applicants of different parental status. Participants (N=134, age 20-45, 38 males) viewed one of four randomly distributed hypothetic job ads and completed Organizational Attraction Measurement (Highouse, et al., 2003). Conducting 2x2x2 (statement, image and status) MANOVA, the study found no effect of statement on attraction, and effect did not differ by parental status, but found interaction between statement, image and status $F(1,134)=4,27$, $p<0,05$) with statement and image unexpectedly decreasing attraction of parents. Implications for recruitment are discussed.

A developmental process of sense of trust in significant others: An internal working model theory perspective

Sakai, Atsushi Education and Human Sciences, University of Yamanashi, Kofu, Japan Sugawara, Masumi Letters and Education, Ochanomizu University, Tokyo, Japan Tanaka, Mami Letters and Education, Ochanomizu University, Tokyo, Japan

A developmental process of sense of trust in significant others in childhood and early adolescence was examined using data from a longitudinal study of 310 twins. According to the Internal Working Model (IWM) theory (Bowlby, 1973), one's experiences and representations of the relationships with parents predict the quality of relationships with outside of the family members. Results showed that the genetic and environmental factors which affect on the quality of sense of trust in parents in childhood consistently affect on the quality of sense of trust in best friend in early adolescence. Findings are discussed in terms of IWM and behavior genetic perspectives.

Word typicality effect on the conceptual system in bilinguals

Sakaki, Yuko Chikushi Jogakuen University, Fukuoka, Japan

The purpose of the experiment was to investigate the conceptual system in bilinguals. How do the similarity of the two languages and the levels of proficiency of the second language affect the organization of representation? Japanese-English and Japanese-Korean bilinguals were asked to read lists consisting of words with different levels of typicality and instructed to recall words in an arbitrary order. The number of recall and degree of category clustering were submitted to analysis of variance. The results showed that the structures of representation were different between Japanese - English and Japanese-Korean bilinguals as proficiency of the language increased.

The qualitative analysis of conceptual understanding of combinatorial problems during and after the peer interaction

Sakawaki, Takako Dept. of Education, Waseda University, Tokyo, Japan

The study aimed to analyse the conceptual understanding of combinatorial problems (mainly permutations) during and after peer interaction as compared with individual training. The participants were 15 dyads and 11 individuals of 5th graders. During interaction or training, they solved the series of tasks, such as, predicting the number of permutations with justification, checking it by making permutations, justifying the result, etc. (adapted from Piaget & Inhelder, 1951/1975; cf. White, 1982). Their responses to these tasks and related questions in post-tests were qualitatively analysed. The result showed generalized understanding of combinatorial problems wasn't easy even among the peer interaction group.

Children's response biases to sensible and absurd questions

Samuels, Mark Psychology and Education, New Mexico Tech, Socorro, New Mexico, USA

Two experiments compared responses to sensible and nonsensical questions. Two groups of 24 preschoolers (mean age=3:7 and 4:11, respectively) and 24 adults participated in experiment 1. Across participants, questions in a yes/no format (e.g., Is an apple louder than a circle?) and forced choice format (e.g., Which is louder an apple or a circle?) were compared. Despite told to answer "silly" to nonsensical questions, preschoolers consistently answered absurd questions. Younger and older preschoolers performed better on sensible forced choice than yes/no questions, t(23)=2.57, p<.05 and t(23)=3.86, p<.001, respectively. Experiment 2 investigated whether feedback improved the ability to identify nonsensical questions.

Consumption practices and life style of the lesbian, gay, trans (transsexuals, transgenders and cross-dressers) and bisexual population in Bogotá, Colombia

Sandoval Escobar, Marithza Cecilia Psychology, Konrad Lorenz Foundation, Bogotá, Colombia

The objective of the study was to identify the consumption practices and to describe the life style of the lesbian, gay, trans and bisexual population in Bogotá (Colombia). The research had a mixed methodology qualitative and quantitative. In general, it was found that the four populations show consumption that fit with their lifestyle; they spend considerable amounts of money on entertainment and experiential consumption; they prefer high-positioned brands and they represent an important consumption segment for themselves. This study contributes to the knowledge and recognition of the lesbian, gay, trans and bisexual population in Colombia as consumers.

Factorial structure of driver test battery for drivers

Santos, Pablo Granada University, Granada, Spain Catena, Andrés Experimental Psychology, Granada University, Granada, Spain Castro, Ángel Developmental Psychology, Granada University, Granada, Spain Buela-Casal, Gualberto Personality, Assessment and Ps, Granada University, Granada, Spain

OBJECTIVE. Analyze the factorial structure of Driver Test battery for drivers. METHOD. 3773 participants response to Advance Speed task and Bimanual Motor Coordination task. A factorial analysis and logistic regression was done, the latter in order to analyse each item contribution to final puntuation. RESULTS. Three factors explain 53.49% of total variante. First of them (30,68%) means distance desviation in advance speed task, second (15.88%) corresponds to error numbers and time in coordination task, and third (6,93%) is time of desviation in advance task. CONCLUSIONS. This battery shows a good factorial structure, but studies using more heterogeneous samples are needed

Bimanual coordination in tool use: Transformations and targets

Sattler, Christine Psychology, MPI CBS, Leipzig, Germany Massen, Cristina Psychology, MPI CBS, Leipzig, Germany

When a tool is used to touch a target, the required body movement jointly depends on the tool's transformation rule and the target's location. Recent evidence from unimanual tool use suggests that prior information on the transformation rule is more beneficial for movement preparation than prior information on the location. Here, we investigated the relative importance of transformation rules and locations in bimanual tool use. Participants simultaneously operated two tools with congruent versus incongruent transformation rules to touch targets at congruent versus incongruent locations. The results are discussed in the light of research on bimanual reaching without tools.

Will the cat catch the mouse? 5- to 10-year-olds probability judgments and choices in drawing with replacement

Schaub, Simone Inst. für Psychologie, Universität Zürich, Zurich, Switzerland Rapp, Andreas F. Counselling Centre, School Psychological, Stuttgart, Germany Figner, Bernd Psychology, Columbia University, New York, USA

Recent research contrasted the development of intuitive vs. explicit processing in risky decisions. We used a novel board game to assess how 129 children (aged 5, 6, 8 and 10) and adults integrated probability information and aspiration level in their choices and judgments. ANOVAs showed clear improvement in choice with age. Judgments also improved from age 5 to 6, with the latter performing at adult level. However, judgment in 8-10 year olds was oversimplified compared to both 6-year-olds and adults, presumably caused by increased reliance on (suboptimal) explicit strategies. These findings are consistent with developmental dual-process models of decision making.

Prevention of early relational troubles and socialisation of infants: The experience of the "Maison Verte" founded by Françoise Dolto

Schauder, Claude URP/SCLS, Faculté de psychologie - ULP, Strasbourg, France

Places that take in tiny children accompanied by a relative, according to the pattern of the Maison Verte inaugurated in 1979 at Paris, have opened almost all over the world. Anonymous and without appointment, the visitors come to meet and talk. Receiving persons, formed to listen attentively, help young and old to express in words the difficulties and suffering they are lead to live before these

problems transform into symptoms. Illustrated with a short film, our dissertation will explain in what this original experience and its rules, methods, thrusts and limits consists.

Development of professional competencies during students' internships

Scheibner, Nicole FB 12, AB Evaluation, Freie Universität Berlin, Berlin, Germany Hapkemeyer, Julia AB Evaluation, FU Berlin, FB 12, Berlin, Germany Soellner, Renate AB Evaluation, FU Berlin, FB 12, Berlin, Germany

Objective: Assessment of the development of professional competencies during internships within Bachelor programmes. Methods: An online questionnaire for students doing an internship (N~100) was developed. The acquisition of competencies was measured by self-ratings using a retrospective pretest-posttest design. Supporting and inhibitory factors (motivation, self-efficacy, structure of internship) for the gain of competencies are identified using structural equation modelling. Results: The change of students' competency level after internship and factors associated with the success of internships will be reported. Conclusion: To optimize the organisation of internships profile analysis can be used to match levels of competencies of students and requirements of internships.

The Discussion Coding System (DCS): A real time instrument to analyze communication processes

Schermuly, Carsten Inst. für Psychologie, Humboldt-Universität zu Berlin, Berlin, Germany

The DCS aims at coding essential aspects of communication processes in real time or videosupported without much time and effort. This instrument will help researchers to analyze larger samples in an economical manner, and it will help practitioners in quickly diagnosing ongoing discussions and to give timely feedback. A trained observer registers who is speaking what (key phrases) to whom and rates the relationship affect on friendly-hostile and dominant-submissive scales. Additionally, the function of each statement can be categorised. In several studies the DCS demonstrated its reliability and validity. The DCS is especially useful for studies of group decision making.

General causality orientation is associated with positive and negative domain-specific expectation about the future

Schnieber, Anette Department of Psychology, University of Aarhus, Aarhus, Denmark Thomsen, Dorthe Kirkegaard Department of Psychology, University of Aarhus, Aarhus C, Denmark Tønnesvang, Jan Department of Psychology, University of Aarhus, Aarhus C, Denmark Olesen, Martin Hammershøj Department of Psychology, University of Aarhus, Aarhus C, Denmark

Is there a relationship between general causality orientation and expectations about the future? 849 newly admitted students completed measures of autonomous and impersonal causality orientation and expectations about compatibility in 3 domains of life at university: interest in courses' topics, academic skills, social skills. Students with a higher degree of autonomous orientation tended to have higher expectations about social compatibility(r=.22, p<.01) and about interest in courses' topics (r=.25, p<.01). Students with a higher degree of impersonal orientation tended to have lower expectations about all 3 domains (r's=-.21 to -.30, p<.01). Causality orientation seems to pertain to expectations about the future.

The emotional Stroop effect: Disentangling attention and threat

Schupak, Assi Psychology and Education, The Open University of Israel, Raanana, Israel Chajut, Eran Psychology and Education, The Open University of Israel, Raanana, Israel Caspi, Avner Psychology and Education, The Open University of Israel, Raanana, Israel Algom, Daniel Psychology, Tel Aviv University, Tel Aviv, Israel

The emotional Stroop effect shows that people are slower to name the print color of emotional compared with neutral words. Whether the source of the effect is mainly attentional or mainly automatic is debated in the literature. In an attempt at resolution, we presented emotional and neutral words in color along with color words in black. Stroop effects obtained with neutral words but were greatly diluted with emotional words. The results confirm the power of emotional words to capture attention and suggest a new paradigm for probing the sources of the emotional Stroop effect.

The effects of dispositional and situational goal orientation on feedback-seeking behavior

Seijts, Gerard Richard Ivey School of Bus., University of Western Ontario, London, Canada

Individual behavior does not solely depend on preferences for certain goals (that is, goal orientation), but also on situational factors. For example, it is not always possible for individuals to be able to enact on their personal preferences; work settings contain cues (e.g., competitive reward structures) that help determine behavior. Studies directed at predicting behavior should therefore make a concerted effort to understand both the person and the situation. I surveyed MBA students on their dispositional goal orientation and perceptions of the goal climate at their school. Both dispositional and situational goal orientation contributed to the prediction of feedback-seeking.

Is there a person inversion effect that indicates relational information processing from preschool to adulthood?

Seitz-Stein, Katja Inst. für Entw.-Psychologie, Kath. Universität Eichstätt, Eichstätt, Germany Rossmeisl, Uwe Developmental- & Education, Cath. University of Eichstätt, Eichstätt, Germany

Matching a newly seen face to an internal face norm (Expertise-Thesis, Diamond & Carey, 1986) is disturbed by face inversion and causes a decrease of recognition performance. Since the internal norm works more efficiently with increasing experience, experts are impaired to a greater extend. The present study applies the inversion paradigm to whole person recognition. 200 participants from five age groups (six-, eight-, ten-, twelve-years and adults) carried out a recognition task with upright and inverted persons. Results indicate an overall age effect and age dependent differences of stimulus orientation and therefore support the crucial role of relational information in person recognition.

Mechanisms of producing a foreign language text

Sekret, Iryna foreign languages, state technical university, Dnieprodzerzhinsk, Ukraine

The research concerns mechanisms of producing foreign language texts (FLT) at different levels of foreign language competence. Foreign/Native text productions of 500 students were examined by methods of observation, introspection, interview, discourse and statistic analyses. The domination of the mother tongue mechanisms in realization of syntactical relations was proved. Of 32 denotative links (Z. Klichnikova) only 6-14 in FLT were revealed (mostly subjectivity, predication and attribution). Therefore skills of producing FLT should be scanned and developed on the base of the native language and considering mechanisms involved in process of real life writing.

Stress on the phone? Evaluation of a stress management training for call center agents

Semmler, Melanie Münster, Germany Rowold, Jens Psychological Institute, University of Münster, Münster, Germany

The experience of stress is common among employees, with negative side-effects (e.g. absenteeism). Especially in call centres, high stress levels have been reported. Many stress interventions have been developed up to now. It would be economically beneficial to reduce such training programs to relevant contents, but most of them are not specified for a particular target group (Busch, 2004). The present study mainly deals with the evaluation of a stress management training adapted to call center agents. Within a pre-post test design with control group and follow-up measure it is explored whether the intervention has effects on stress scales, such as perceived chronic stress.

Measurement by subjective estimation: Testing for separable representations

Seri, Raffaello Dipt. di Economia, Università dell'Insubria, Varese, Italy Bernasconi, Michele Dipartimento di Economia, Università dell'Insubria, Varese, Italy Choirat, Christine Dept of Quantitative Methods, Universidad de Navarra, Pamplona, Spain

Studying how individuals compare quantitative stimuli is a fundamental problem often addressed through ratio estimation: individuals are asked to give estimates of the ratio of the stimuli. Several psychophysical theories (among which Stevens power-law) claim this process involves cognitive distortions. These theories result in the so-called separable representations (Narens 1996, Luce 2002), including Stevens model. We perform a psychophysical experiment in which 20 subjects answer to 90 questions concerning distance and area ratios. We conclude in favor of the separable representation model, but reject Stevens model. As a byproduct, we provide estimates of the psychophysical functions of interest.

Cognitive therapy alone and combined with pharmacotherapy in the treatment of depression

Shamsaei, Farshid Psychiatric Nursing, Hamedan University, Hamedan, Islamic Republic of Iran Rahimi, Aliraza Psychiatry, Hamedan university of medical, Hamedan, Islamic Republic of Iran Zarabian, M. Kazem Psychology, Hamedan university of medical, Hamedan, Islamic Republic of Iran

Objective: The purpose of this study was to compare the Efficacy of antidepressant medication, cognitive therapy and combination of cognitive therapy and antidepressant medication in the treatment of major depressive disorder. Method: This study was an experimental research. The samples were 120 depressive patients. With random sampling the sample was divided in three groups. Results: Statistical analysis showed cognitive therapy, medication and combination Cognitive therapy intervention and medication were significant effect in depression therapy. ONE WAY ANOVA showed significant difference between cognitive therapy and medication with combination of cognitive therapy and medication. Conclusion: The advantages of combining antidepressants with cognitive therapy are equivocal.

Irritable bowel syndrome: A case study

Sharma, Vandana Dept. of Psychology, Meerut College, Meerut, India

Irritable bowel syndrome: A case study This case is about a female patient(38years) suffering from IBS for the last three years and had undergone various types of treatment and medication. But did not got relief. In depth case study was taken to find out the causes or stressors responsible for this syndrome. As an intervention relaxation technique followed by visual imagery was used. Behavior modification technique was also used in the form of self

monitoring, frequency charts and positive reinforcement schedules. Therapy proved very effective and there was a drastic decrease in her symptoms and discomforts within a month. After two months of regular sessions symptoms were very much in control and very near to normal standards.

An education of entrepreneurships using network based collaboration

Shibuya, Kazuhiko Riken, Saitama, Japan

Internet collaboration and networked activities using PC and mobile devices becomes to be accelerated. Especially, real money trading had appeared the business activities bridging between actual and virtual worlds. So, there are needs to educate appropriately skills and experiences of networking for students. Thereby, the Ubiquitous jigsaw for networked collaborative learning is effective to train anyone who seek to do entrepreneurship coordinating between actual and online activities. Particularly, I applied it to entrepreneur as Limited Liability Partnership. It appears that this learning style is to fit for networked collaboration and partnerships consisted of different backgrounds beyond global and local interconnections.

The effects of specific syntax training on children's false belief understanding

Shu Liang, Mo School of Psychology, HuaZhong Normal University, Wuhan, People's Republic of China Yanjie, Su Department of Psychology, Peking University, Beijing, People's Republic of China

This study aimed to examine the role of specific syntax on false belief understanding in Chinese 3-4-years olds. Eighty-four children were divided into four groups: two syntax-training groups, one misrepresentation-training and one control group. After two training sessions, we found two syntax-training groups performed significantly better on false belief tasks in the post-test than the controls, but not significantly better than misrepresentation-training group. Children's false belief performance was improved by specific syntax training, which may provide an important framework for children representing false belief, although it may not be a necessary condition for children passing the false belief test.

The attachment system and the defensive regulation of attention

Silva, Catarina Dept. of Psychology, ISCTE, Lisboa, Portugal Esteves, Francisco Psychology, ISCTE, Lisboa, Portugal Soares, Isabel Psychology, Universidade do Minho, Braga, Portugal

The attachment system can trigger defensive processes to prevent the processing of emotionally-relevant information. This study investigated such processes using a rapid serial visual presentation of pictures, in which participants searched for a single target. Critical stimuli comprised by emotionally negative/positive, or neutral pictures were included, either two or four items before the target. Preliminary analysis indicated that participants with attachment insecurity, as compared with those with attachment security, showed faster reaction times when the critical distractor is an emotional stimulus. These results may highlight the use of preemptive forms of defense when processing emotionally-relevant information to the attachment system.

The effects of a psychiatric inpatient treatment programme

Simonsen, Inge-Ernald Dept. of Psychology, Norwegian Univ. of Sci. & Tech, Trondheim, Norway Rundmo, Torbjörn Dept. of Psychology, Norwegian Univ. of Sci. &, Trondheim, Norway

The core aim of the present study was to examine the effects of a psychiatric inpatient treatment programme. The programme is based on a biopsychosocial approach. A group of inpatients completed a questionnaire by admission to the ward unit (N=80). They completed the same questionnaire at the time of discharge (N=65). The response rate at pre- and post test was 88%. The results showed a significant positive effect of the treatment programme on degree of subjective satisfaction and overall psychological distress. Model test showed that degree of subjective satisfaction and perceived coping ability was positive associated with overall psychological distress.

Language usage as moral disengagement strategy in post-violent situations

Slawuta, Patricia Dept. of Psychology, New School for Social Research, New York, USA Leidner, Bernhard Psychology, New School for Social Research, New York, USA Castano, Emanuele Psychology, New School for Social Research, New York, USA

Building on research on moral disengagement and language use in intergroup contexts, it is investigated whether communication can serve the purpose of moral disengagement. American participants were confronted with a newspaper article on fictitious incidents of torture and killing of imprisoned Iraqis. The conditions only differed in the responsibility of the wrongdoings (U.S. vs. Iraqi soldiers). High glorifiers gave more external explanations and described ingroup atrocities as less causal, intentional, and goal-driven than outgroup atrocities, whereas there was no such difference for low glorifiers. These findings support the idea that biased language can effectively function as a moral disengagement mechanism.

Attentional capture by feared animal stimuli

Soares, Sandra Dep. CNS, Psychology Section, Karolinska Institutet, Stockholm, Sweden Esteves, Francisco Psychology, ISCTE, Lisbon, Portugal Lundqvist, Daniel Dep. CNS, Psychology Section, Karolinska Institutet, Stockholm, Sweden Ohman, Arne Dep. CNS, Psychology Section, Karolinska Institutet, Stockholm, Sweden

Across two experiments we investigated attentional capture by animal feared stimuli using visual search procedures. The results showed that spider fearful individuals were specifically sensitized by their feared stimuli, detecting a spider faster than snakes or control stimuli. On the contrary, no such effect was found for snake fearful participants, who could not detect snakes faster than spiders. Although the screening, using snakes and spiders fear questionnaires, resulted in two comparable groups, a rating task showed that snake fearful individuals evaluated snakes as negative and arousing as spiders, while spider fearful participants clearly differentiated those two categories.

Chinese Perfectionistic Self-presentation Scale: A validation study

Song, Shanggui Dept. of Academic Affairs, Jinan University of Shandong, Jinan, People's Republic of China Yu, Hairong Psychology Department, Jinan University of Shandong, Jinan, People's Republic of China

Perfectionistic self-presentation is a maladaptive self-presentational style composed of three dimensions: perfectionistic self-promotion, nondisplay of imperfection, and nondisclosure of imperfection. The present study was to examine the reliability and validity of the Chinese Perfectionistic Self-Presentation Scale(CPSPS). Nine hundred and fifty college students in China participated in the study. The factor structure and psychometric properties of CPSPS were explored. The results revealed that the Chinese Perfectionistic Self-Presentation Scale has good reliability and validity and can be used in college students in China.

Transfer effect differs in the positive vs. negative emotional situations

Sozinov, Alexei Lab. Neural Bases of Mind, Institute of Psychology, RAS, Moscow, Russia Laukka, Seppo Learning Research Lab, Oulu University, Oulu, Finland Siipo, Antti Learning Research Lab, Oulu University, Oulu, Finland Alexandrov, Yuri Lab. Neural Bases of Mind, Institute of Psychology, RAS, Moscow, Russia

We studied whether the transfer effect is related to emotions. Two visual discrimination tasks were presented with a 5-minute break to children (mean age of 12 years) in different order and with two emotionally burdening instructions. The negative transfer effect was evident only in the negative emotional situation. We conclude that the proactive effect of learning on formation of previous memory is related to the valence of emotions. The results are discussed in terms of united concept of consciousness and emotion (Alexandrov & Sams, 2005, Cogn.Br.Res., 25:387). Supported: RFH 07-06-00481a

Key competences for apprentices

Stäudel, Thea Wirtschaftspsychologie, Hochschule Harz, Baunach, Germany

As job demands on apprentices in industrial and technical occupational areas are increasing, key competencies (methodological, social, self competencies) become more important. We asked 128 apprentices and 45 instructors from 36 German enterprises to rate the importance of 24 'soft skills' relevant to vocational training and their actual qualification (questionnaires). Results indicate that apprentices know the demands of their jobs and are achievement-oriented. Compared with their instructors' assessment, they overestimate their real key abilities except for social competences. Qualification measures should be taken particularly with regard to problem solving abilities, divergent thinking, initiative and the ability to cope with pressure.

Criterion validity of the multidimensional scale of irrational beliefs with respect to anxiety, depression and life satisfaction

Strobel, Maria Inst. für Psychologie, Universität München, München, Germany Bekk, Magdalena Psychology, LMU München, München, Germany Spörrle, Matthias Dept. for Psychology, Ludwig-Maximilians University, München, Germany

Using a sample of 200 participants, this study seeks to establish criterion validity of the Multidimensional Scale of Irrational Beliefs (MSIB), a newly developed, purely cognitive measure of irrational beliefs. As predicted by Rational Emotive Behavior Therapy, scores on the MSIB are correlated highly and positively with scores on Beck's Depression Inventory and the trait scale of the State-Trait-Anxiety Inventory. Moreover, analyses reveal medium-sized negative correlations with life satisfaction. Each of these relations is shown to be unaffected by age, sex, social desirability, and common method bias. Differential associations between subdimensions of the MSIB with criteria are discussed regarding the separability of irrationality concepts.

Depression and quality of life of Nepalese women

Subba, Usha Kiran Kathmandu, Nepal

The study examines the relationship between depression and quality of life. Both Quantitative and Qualitative methods was used. A questionnaire, QOL, BDI (II) and Diener's Satisfaction with Life scale (SWLS) was applied to a sample of 333 women comprising from general and psychiatric patients of different ecological zones. T-test, ANOVA, Pearson correlation and Regression Analysis were applied for analysis of data. Result shows a mean score of depression was 18.98, QOL was 140.92 and SWLS was 19.85. A significant differ-

ence between caste, social class and depression was found. A negative relationship between depression, QOL and Satisfaction with life was found.

Filial responsibility for parents in adults

Sugiyama, Kanako Nagoya, Japan

The present study examined the relationship of unmarried adults with their parents and filial responsibility. Participants were 126 Japanese adults (30 males and 96 females : age 20-51). They completed a questionnaire concerning their relationship with their parents (10 items) and their filial responsibility on a 5-point scale. Females felt their relationship with their parents was more equitable than their male counterparts. Gender differences were not found in filial responsibility. The adults who had a good relationship with their parents had a more positive filial responsibility in all situations than those who did not have a good relationship.

Pride and self-evaluative emotions: New directions toward a social, linguistic and relational theory

Sullivan, Gavin Brent Berlin, Germany

Insights about positive self-evaluative emotions and pride, in particular, are often described in cognitive appraisal terms. While cognitive appraisal models appear to explain the types of variabilities of emotion that are manifest in experience and expression, the roles of language, relationships and culture are overlooked. This paper reports on theoretical work to contextualize and subsume cognitive features of pride in a new way of understanding important features of the self and identity that occur in conversation-based practices. Empirical work and practical applications are also provided to demonstrate the benefits of rethinking self-conscious positive emotion in linguistic, social and relational terms.

From Chinese teachers' eyes: Factors that enhance educational quality and reduce pressure in schools

Sun, Hechuan RIEEA, Shenyang Normal University, Shenyang, People's Republic of China Feng, Cailing School of Educational Sciences, Shenyang Normal University, Shenyang, Liaoning, People's Republic of China Yang, Xiaolin Education, Shenhe District Committee, Shenyang, Liaoning, People's Republic of China Zong, Feifei RIEEA, Shenyang Normal University, Shenyang, Liaoning, People's Republic of China Ma, Jianyun Students Affairs Office, Xinjiang University, Ulumuqi, People's Republic of China Sun, Yujia FAEM, Beijing Forestry University, Beijing, People's Republic of China

Enhancing educational quality while reducing pressure in schools is a great challenge yet a controversial and paradoxical problem worldwide. Since success of reforms greatly depends upon what teachers believe and what they think, a project has been carried out since 2005. It investigated perceptions of 700 full-time teachers in public senior secondary schools across three provinces in northern China. Both qualitative and quantitative approaches (questionnaires, interviews, SPSS 11.5, factor analysis) were used. The findings show: the ranked influence order looked like a pyramid shape: the relationship closest to the students (the parental level and the teachers level) had the strongest influence. In addition, 45 effective factors at five different levels were identified by the Chinese teachers.

E-mailing as a way of making connections for children using augmentative and alternative communication

Sundqvist, Anett SIDR - IBL, Linköping University, Linköping, Sweden Rönnberg, Jerker ibl, Cidr, Linköping, Sweden

In a 12-week study a symbol-based e-mail client was implemented for children using augmentative and alternative communication (n = 12). Quantitative and qualitative aspects of the e-mails were analyzed. In total, 231 e-mails were sent. The e-mails were analysed post hoc into eight descriptive topic categories, with social etiquette being the dominating category. The results are discussed in relation to Theory of Mind understanding. E-mailing enhanced the social network of the children and gave them a new social arena.

Acquisition of social theory of mind in children using augmentative and alternative communication

Sundqvist, Anett SIDR - IBL, Linköping University, Linköping, Sweden Rönnberg, Jerker ibl, SIDR, Linköping, Sweden
This study focused on the acquisition of Theory of Mind (ToM) in children (aged 7-13) with severe speech impairment using augmentative and alternative communication (AAC). The AAC-group (n = 13) was compared to a typically developing group matched on nonverbal mental age. Tests concerning cognitive and language development, first and second order ToM and social ToM were used. Importantly, no significant difference between the two groups was found on the tests above, suggesting that cognitive ability rather than social experience accounts for the data. Nonverbal intelligence and vocabulary proved to be the best indicators of ToM ability.

The predictability of the cognitive function from the Fagan Test of infant intelligence

Suzuki, Keita Graduate School of Education, Tohoku University, Sendai, Japan Tatsuta, Nozomi Graduate School of Education, Tohoku University, Sendai, Japan Nakai, Kunihiko Graduate School of Medicine, Tohoku University, Sendai, Japan Satoh, Hiroshi Graduate School of Medicine, Tohoku University, Sendai, Japan Hosokawa, Toru Graduate School of Education, Tohoku University, Sendai, Japan
The Fagan Test of Infant Intelligence (FTII) is a standardized test for measuring cognitive function in infancy through a preferential looking technique. The present study was examined the relationship between the FTII and cognitive function in childhood through a longitudinal study. The subjects were 133 mother-child pairs. The FTII was administered when children were 7 months old. Cognitive function was evaluated at 42 months old using the Kaufman Assessment Battery for Children (K-ABC). The results showed no significant relationship between the FTII and the K-ABC. These findings suggest that the FTII is a poor predictor of the later cognitive development.

Temporal training in aphasia therapy

Szymaszek, Aneta Dept. of Neuropsychology, Nencki Inst. of Exp. Biology, Warsaw, Poland Szelag, Elzbieta Laboratory of Neuropsychology, Nencki Inst of Exp Biol, Warsaw, Poland Lewandowska, Monika Laboratory of Neuropsychology, Nencki Inst of Exp Biol, Warsaw, Poland Seniow, Joanna Department of Neurology, IPiN, Warsaw, Poland Fink, Martina Generation Research Program, Ludwig-Maximilian University, Bad Tölz, Germany Ulbrich, Pamela Generation Research Program, Ludwig-Maximilian University, Bad Tölz, Germany Churan, Jan Generation Research Program, Ludwig-Maximilian University, Bad Tölz, Germany Wittmann, Marc Generation Research Program, Ludwig-Maximilian University, Bad Tölz, Germany Pöppel, Ernst Generation Research Program, Ludwig-Maximilian University, Bad Tölz, Germany
Objective: The improvement of auditory speech comprehension (ASC) following a specific temporal training was tested in aphasic patients. Methods: using temporal-order-threshold paradigm timing abilities were measured for either two clicks (monaural presentation) or two tones (400, 3000Hz, binaural presentation), presented in a

rapid sequence. Aphasic patients participated in eight sessions of the specific temporal or non-temporal control training. Results: The temporal training yields improvements both timing and comprehension. The control training did not improve these both abilities. Conclusion: Temporal training improved language abilities. Supported by the KBN grant nos PBZ-MIN/001/PO5/06, BMBF 01 GZ 0301, NN402434633.

The effect of hope therapy on increasing satisfaction in life and happiness in elderly people

Tabaeian, Sayedeh Razieh psychology, Isfahan Univercity, Isfahan, Islamic Republic of Iran Tabae Emami, Shirin psychology, Isfahan Univercity, Isfahan, Islamic Republic of Iran
Objectives: The purpose of this study was to increase the feeling of happiness and satisfaction in life among elderly people through hope therapy. Methods: Thirty 60-70 year old elderly domiciled at Isfahn Elderly House served as two experimental and control groups. Only,the experimental group received ten sessions of hope therapy. The two were pre-tested and post-tested through the Oxford Happiness Scale and Life Happiness Scale. Results: The results of Manova analysis suggests a significant difference between the two groups (p<0.05). Conclusions: The results suggest the positive effect of hope therapy on increasing happiness and satisfaction of life in elderly.

The functions of autobiographical memory and depression

Tagami, Kyoko Faculty of Education, Hirosaki University, Hirosaki, Japan
Relationship between the functions of autobiographical memory and depression was investigated. Nonclinical university students (n=123) remembered the most important episode of their life history and rated their affectivity and functions. They also completed the Beck Depression Inventory, the Trait Meta-Mood Scale, and the Depression-Anxiety Mood Scale. Remembered episodes were categorized as positive or negative and whether their functions were directive, social, or self. Results showed a negative memory bias in depression and indicated functions of autobiographical memory that were characteristic of depression. These results are discussed in terms of the functions of autobiographical memory and emotion regulation in depression.

Antecedents and outcomes of career decision: Based on various types of groups

Tak, Jin-Kook Dept. of Industrial Psychlogy, Kwangwoon University, Seoul, Republic of Korea Lee, Dong-Ha Industrial Psychlogy, Kwangwoon University, Seoul, Republic of Korea
The purpose of this study was to examine the relationships between career decision and its antecedents and outcomes with a sample of various types of youth groups. Data were obtained from panel data. Concerning its relations with the antecedents, sex was not related to career decision. Age and school year were significantly related to career decision. Concerning differences in career decision among the four youth groups, the employed group had the highest score in career decision whereas the high school students had the lowest score. Concerning its relations with the outcomes, career decision was significantly related to experiences of career counselling, vocational training, satisfaction to the major, GPA, job satisfaction, and turnover intentions.

Development of a new emotion recognition task

Takahashi, Tomone Faculty of Education, Shinshu University, Nagano, Japan Nakashima, Mitsuhiko Saku Child Guidance Center, Saku-city, Saku, Japan Hashimoto, Shigune Graduate School of Education,

Shinshu University, Nagano, Japan Nakamura, Akiko Student Councelling Center, Matsumoto University, Matsumoto, Japan Yamamoto, Natsumi Graduate School of Education, Shinshu University, Nagano, Japan
A new emotion recognition task was developed. The task consists of an emotional prosody recognition task and a face-voice recognition task. Sentences used in the task were rated for their emotional contents and were combined with matched and non-matched emotional prosody. A total of 626 university students participated. The results indicated that (1) those who scored high on the new task had lower scores on the Autism Spectrum Quotient and higher scores on the Empathic Experience Scale than those who scored low; (2) females scored higher than males. These results provided evidence for the validity of this new task.

Relationship among unwillingness to attend school, narcissistic tendency and Big 5 in adolescence

Takahashi, Michiko Nagoya, Japan
The purpose of this study was to investigate the relationship among unwillingness to attend school, narcissistic tendency and Big 5 personality model in adolescence. Three Scales were administered to 300 subjects. The result of variant analysis associated : It was revealed that high scores of unwillingness to attend school showed high narcissistic tendency scores and low scores of extroversion, neuroticism, openness and agreeableness. These results suggested that unwillingness to attend school had significant relationships with narcissistic tendency and Big 5 personality model.

Noise improvement in contrast detection is changed by temporal property of stimulus

Takahashi, Tsutomu Psychology, Kwansei University, Nishinomiya, Japan Yagi, Akihiro psychology, Kwansei University, Nishinomiya, Japan
A phenomenon, optimal noise improves detection of subthreshold stimulus compared to no noise stimulus, is called stochastic resonance (SR). However, it is unclear whether optimal noise enhances the subthreshold stimulus above threshold or emphasizes stimulus ON/OFF. In present study, we measured the contrast detection thresholds (CDT) of Gabor patch with/without the stimulus ON/OFF as a function of noise contrast. Result showed that the both CDT were decreased by optimal noise compared to those of without noise. This result shows that noise affected the transient luminance change and couldn't always be explained by previous model of SR.

The examination of functional classification and developmental process of communicative behaviors in infancy

Takeshita, Kanako Human-Environment Studies, Kyushu University, Hyogo, Japan
This study aimed to functionally classify communicative behaviors and examine their developmental associations. A survey was conducted for the caregivers of 351 infants who aged from eight to twenty-two months. The factor analysis indicated that joint attention behavior comprised two factors (understanding of pointing finger and occurrence of pointing finger gestures) and that social attention behavior comprised four factors (showing and imitation, reaction in a novelty situation, understanding other's intention, and noticing other's emotion). Based on the adapted developmental model by structural equation modeling, it was suggested that the behavior of showing and imitation was important in developing communicative behavior.

Error processing and attentional control: ERN/Ne and Pe in a task-switching paradigm

Tanaka, Hideaki Dept. of Psychology, Otemon Gakuin University, Osaka, Japan
The purpose of the present study was to investigate relationship between error processing and attentional control in a task-switching paradigm. The present study studied an error-related-negativity (ERN/Ne) and positivity (Pe), an ERP component reflected error processing. My task-switching paradigm employed the Eriksen flanker task and the color discrimination task. The results indicated that the amplitude of Pe decreased in a task-switching paradigm, but the amplitude of ERN/Ne did not have a change. Thus, the present results support the notion that both error-related components (ERN/Ne and Pe) represent different aspects of error processing. Only Pe reflected attentional control of error processing.

The influence of behavioral interaction on assessment performance in leaderless group discussion

Tang, Linlin I/O Psychology, Zhejiang University, Hangzhou, People's Republic of China
The candidates' behavioral interaction in leaderless group discussion was analyzed in this study. We asked 5-participants-contained groups (N=82) to complete a given problem-solving task in 60 minutes. Divided into two groups, eight experienced assessors either evaluated the content of oral statement or observed and recorded the frequencies of the candidates' movement and expression. It's found that the interaction of behavior (smiles, nods) had an impact on assessment performance, while the fitness of group members' personality operated moderating effects on this relationship. Results showed that the higher fitness was, the stronger influence of behavioral interaction on assessment performance was.

Organizational identification, organizational change orientation and perceived effectiveness of change: A field study

Tang, Ningyu School of Management, Shanghai Jiaotong University, Shanghai, People's Republic of China Ni, Ning School of Law and Politics, Shanghai Normal University, Shanghai, People's Republic of China
Through a field study in a Chinese State Owned Company which is experiencing a big organizational change, the paper studies the relationship among organizational identification, organizational change orientation and perceived effectiveness of change. By surveying 428 employees at different level in the company, it reveals that (1) employees' organizational identification has significant relationship with perceived change effectiveness; (2) employees' change orientations (process-orientation versus result-orientation) have different effect on their perception of the effectiveness of change;(2) employees' organizational identification moderates partially the effect between change orientation and the perceived effectiveness of change.

Emotional memory can modify Posttraumatic Stress Disorder-associated changes in recollective experience

Tapia, Géraldine Saint Julien-en-Born, France Clarys, David Psychologie, UMR CNRS 6215, Tours cedex 1, France El Hage, Wissam Sciences du comportement, EA 3248, Tours, France Bugaiska, Aurélia Psychologie, UMR CNRS 6215, Tours cedex 1, France Belzung, Catherine Sciences du comportement, EA 3248, Tours, France Isingrini, Michel Psychologie, UMR CNRS 6215, Tours cedex 1, France
Objectives. The purpose of the study was to investigate the effects of Post-Traumatic Stress Disorder (PTSD) on emotional recollection. Methods. A group of PTSD patients and a control group were compared on the Remember/Know procedure with negative, positive and neutral words. PTSD patients met the PTSD criteria according to the DSM-IV diagnostic features (APA, 1994). Analysis consisted of two separate analyses of variance for Remember and Know responses. Results. Results showed that for negative words PTSD participants produced more Remember responses than controls. Conclusions. This tendency to recollect negative information more vividly may explain trauma-related memory disturbances in individuals with PTSD.

Factors affecting the early human development

Tatsuta, Nozomi Graduate School of Education, Tohoku University, Sendai, Japan Suzuki, Keita Education, Tohoku University, Sendai, Japan Nakai, Kunihiko Environmental Health Sciences, Tohoku University, Sendai, Japan Satoh, Hiroshi Environmental Health Sciences, Tohoku University, Sendai, Japan Hosokawa, Toru Education, Tohoku University, Sendai, Japan
This study examined how an 18 months-old child development can be predicted from pre/post natal variables including home environment. The Bayley Scales of Infant Development (BSID) was administered to 379 children at 7 and 18 months old. There was a small but significant correlation between the two BSID scores. Step-wise regression analysis selected child sex, maternal IQ and home environment as significant variables for mental development (R2=0.115, p<.001), and birth weight and gestation period for psychological development (R2=0.055, p<.001). These results confirm that various bio-psycho-social factors affect the early human development.

Effects of sleep deprivation on a dynamic visuo-spatial recognition task

Tejero, Pilar Psicología Básica, University of Valencia, Valencia, Spain Chóliz, Mariano Psicología Básica, University of Valencia, Valencia, Spain Pastor, Gemma Psicología Básica, University of Valencia, Valencia, Spain Roca, Javier Psicología Básica, University of Valencia, Valencia, Spain
The effects of sleep deprivation on some short-term memory processes involved in driving a vehicle were studied in habitual drivers. Data were obtained in subjects who performed a dynamic visuo-spatial recognition task while driving in a simulator. Results obtained in analyses of variance on recognition measures suggested that partial sleep deprivation can lead to an impairment in short-term memory processes when memory load is moderate (6 or 7 vehicles), but not when it is low (4 or 5 vehicles). A significant interaction between memory load, sleep deprivation and time on task was found.

Effects of visual-auditory stimulus onset asynchrony on speech discrimination and auditory event-related potentials

Thorne, Jeremy MRC Institute of Hearing Res., Royal South Hants Hospital, Southampton, United Kingdom Debener, Stefan Southampton Section, MRC Institute of Hearing Res, Southampton, United Kingdom
Multisensory investigation often uses synchronous stimuli presentation, although vision (V) usually precedes audition (A) in natural settings. We manipulated VA stimulus onset asynchrony (SOA) in an auditory speech discrimination task (N=17) from 0-100ms. ANOVA revealed a main effect of SOA condition on response time (F=2.2, p=.05), with best performance at SOA=80ms. Analysis of auditory evoked potentials revealed main effects of condition (F=13.7, p<.0001) and mode (AV versus A+V; F=14.9, p<.002) on P2 latency, and a condition-by-mode interaction (F=3.2, p<.02). Shortest P2 latencies were also at SOA=80ms. The similarity of behavioural and physiological effects suggests that non-simultaneous onsets facilitate AV integration.

The emotional modulation of the attentional blink: Effects of taboo and non-taboo arousing stimuli in a dual and single task paradigm

Tibboel, Helen Exp. Clinical & Health Psych., Ghent University, Ghent, Belgium De Houwer, Jan Exp. Clinical & Health Psy, Ghent University, Ghent, Belgium Crombez, Geert Exp. Clinical & Health Psy, Ghent University, Ghent, Belgium
The Attentional Blink (AB) refers to the difficulty in identifying the second of two masked targets (T1 and T2), if these are presented in quick (within 500 ms) succession. The aim of this study was to examine the impact of arousing stimuli on the AB. Our questions were: (1) Can arousing T1 stimuli interfere with processing of subsequent targets? (2) Are arousing T2 stimuli processed more efficiently and can they thus attenuate the AB? (3) Are these effects different when only T2 needs to be reported? (4) Is the AB modulated by any type of arousing stimuli?

Values driving change: A case study

Tiernan, Joan Psychology, University College Dublin, Dublin, Ireland Doddy, Joseph Psychology, University College Dublin, Dublin, Ireland
Schein (2004) notes that basic assumptions hold the key to understanding what drives culture change. These assumptions reshape the values that guide the organisation (Morgan, 1997). This study examined a semi-state, human services organisation that had undergone reorganisation and culture change as a result of a merger. Six core values relevant to organisational development emerged from depth interviews with thirteen managers across thirteen different business units including leadership, integrity, client-centredness, teamwork, unceasing learning, and excellence. Retest at 18 months revealed that new values has been assimilated into existing work practices, indicating evidence of the emergence of a new culture.

Reading behaviour in German school children

Tiffin-Richards, Simon Inst. für Psychologie II, Universität Kaiserslautern, Kaiserslautern, Germany Lachmann, Thomas Psychology Unit II, University of Kaiserslautern, Kaiserslautern, Germany
Proficient reading requires the integration of complex cognitive processes. Causes of failure to achieve proficient reading in school-aged children, despite adequate intellectual and educational parameters, has in the literature been attributed to deficits in phonological, visual and rapid information processing. The present research investigated word and pseudo word reading in young school-aged children. The study was conducted in German, a language with distinct phonological and orthographic regularity. The experimental groups consisted of normally developed readers and participants with specific reading difficulties. Results contrast reading speed and accuracy of German readers with and without specific reading difficulties.

What's in a face? The perception of threat and disfigurement

Tinati, Tannaze School of Psychology, University of Southampton, Southampton, United Kingdom Stevenage, Sarah, V. School of Psychology, University of Southampton, Southampton, United Kingdom
This study examined perceiver reactions toward facial disfigurement. Thirty participants were shown happy, angry, neutral and disfigured faces in a dot-probe task. A face was presented followed by a cue in the same (valid) or different (invalid) location with 250 msecs delay between face and cue. Analysis suggested that angry faces caused aversion of attention on invalid trials for high anxious participants. This reaction was absent with disfigured faces. Instead, subjective feedback indicated a disgust response than a threat response to disfig-

urement. Identifying the behavioural and psychological difference between these responses may facilitate public awareness campaigns in reducing overt reactions.

Being fed up: The impact of task repetitiveness on mental satiation and cardiovascular reactivity

Tomaschek, Anne Arbeits- & Organis.psychologie, Technische Universität Dresden, Dresden, Germany *Schultze, Thomas* Economic and Social Psychology, University of Göttingen, Göttingen, Germany *Mojzisch, Andreas* Economic and Social Psychology, University of Göttingen, Göttingen, Germany *Schulz-Hardt, Stephan* Inst. für Psychologie, Universität Göttingen, Göttingen, Germany *Richter, Peter* Work & Organisational Psyc, TU Dresden, Dresden, Germany
Previous field studies suggest that repetitive work is associated with health risks. However, research has largely neglected the affective experience during repetitive work. In a laboratory experiment simulating an office environment we examined the impact of task repetitiveness on mental satiation (i.e., the feeling of being fed up) and cardiovascular reactivity. As predicted, participants in the high repetitive condition reported an enhanced increase of mental satiation over time and showed a more elevated systolic blood pressure than participants in the low repetitive condition. The increase of mental satiation over time was more pronounced for action-oriented than for state-oriented individuals.

Developing emotion education program for elementary school students in China

Tong, Yuehua Dept. of Psychology, Jinan University of Shandong, Jinan, People's Republic of China *Song, Shanggui* Dept. of Psychology, Jinan University of Shandong, Jinan, People's Republic of China
Social-emotional learning is an important part in psychological health program. However, most psychological health programs in China did not address this issue. Emotion Education Program consists of ten activities which are designed to help children develop the ability to better understand emotions. There are three themes in the program: (a)understanding one's and other's emotions, (b)learning to express and control emotions, and (c)maintaining positive emotion. The activities are carried out in groups for ten weeks, and are based on modeling, role-play, coaching, and discussion. Effectiveness and implications for school counseling are discussed.

Perfectionism and mental health: The mediation role of coping

Tong, Yuehua Dept. of Psychology, Jinan University of Shandong, Jinan, People's Republic of China *He, Guangming* Dept. of Psychology, University of Jinan, Jinan, People's Republic of China
562 university students in China completed measures of perfectionism (concern over mistakes, personal standards, organization, parental expectations), coping (mature coping such as problem-solving and help-seeking, immature coping such as self-blame, avoidance, fantasy), and mental health. Path analyses indicated that mature and immature coping partially mediated the relations between concern over mistakes and mental health. Mature coping partially mediated the relations between personal standards and mental health, but fully mediated the relations between organization and mental health. Immature coping partially mediated the relations between parental expectations and mental health. Implications of the present findings for counseling and intervention are discussed.

Relationships between psychological capital, authentic self and turnover intention: A study of call center tele-consultants

Tong, Jiajin Dept. of Psychology, University of Peking, Beijing, People's Republic of China *Wang, Lei* Psychology, The Peking University, Beijing, People's Republic of China *Guo, Fang* Psychology, The Peking University, Beijing, People's Republic of China
Based on the theory of positive psychology, especially the part of positive organizational behavior and psychological capital, this study explored the relationship among positive capital, authentic self, and turnover intention in 266 tele-consultants. Results showed that hope state (one component of psychological capital) and self-choice (one component of authentic self) predicted lower employee turnover intention. Meanwhile, self-choice mediated the relationship between hope state and turnover intention. Hope state would affect turnover intention more if an individual had a stronger self-choice. These findings help to better understand turnover intention and turnover activities within an organization.

Psychological contract breach: Meta-analytic structural equation modelling

Topa Cantisano, Gabriela Social and Org. Psychology, UNED, Madrid, Spain
Meta-analytic procedures were used to examine relationships between psychological contract perceived breach and outcome variables (organizational commitment, job satisfaction and organizational citizenship behaviors). Our review of the literature generated 41 independent samples in which perceived breach was used as a predictor of these personal and organizational outcomes. Potential moderator variables were examined, and it was found that they explained only a percentage of variability of primary studies. Structural equation analysis of the meta-analytical pooled correlation matrix indicated that the relationships of perceived breach with satisfaction, OCB, intention to leave and performance are fully mediated by organizational trust and commitment.

Profile of socio-affective competences of school children at psychosocial risk

Torres, Alexandra Evolutive Psycology, University of La Laguna, La Laguna, Spain *Rodrigo, Maria Jose* Evolutive Psycology, University of La Laguna, La Laguna, Spain
A differential profile of socio-affective competences between two groups of children from at risk and non at-risk family environments was examined. The sample was 216 children, aged 6 to 12 years. Attachment representations; self concept; locus of control; attributions of peer behaviour; teacher's perception; externalization, internalization and social-cognitive problems were evaluated. A discriminant function analysis was carried out to determine the extent to which the socio-affective competences reliably distinguished between at–risk and non at-risk group. Aggressiveness, externalizations, shyness, and social-cognitive problems for at- risk group and social self-concept for the non at-risk group significantly contributed to the classification.

Behavioral maps in clinical interventions: A proposal

Torres, Carlos CEIC, Universidad de Guadalajara, Guadalajara, Mexico *Becerril, Rodrigo* CEIC, Universidad de Guadalajara, Guadalajara, Mexico
Contingency Analysis it's a methodological framework to identify psychological problems and strategies of behaviour modification. It consisted in 5 steps: a) Analysis of micro-contingencies system, b) Evaluation of macro-contingencies frame, c) Problem development, d) Solutions analysis, and e) interventional procedures. This work show a way to classify and integrate information obtained in the first steps of the contingency analysis in order to the identify one of two kinds of psychological problems: Incongruities between macro and micro-contingencies, or behavioural competences.

First contacts with the adoptive child: Positive and negative experiences on international adoption

Triana Pérez, Beatriz Psicología Evolutiva, University of La Laguna, La Laguna, Spain *Rodríguez Suárez, Guacimara* Psicología Evolutiva y de la E, University of La Laguna, La Laguna, Spain *Plasencia Carrillo, Sonia* Psicología Evolutiva y de la E, University of La Laguna, La Laguna, Spain *Sánchez Gutiérrez, Morerba* Psicología Evolutiva y de la E, University of La Laguna, La Laguna, Spain
The number of children adopted from abroad has increased in Spain in the last decades. Because of the importance of international adoption in our society, it is crucial to know how the adoptive parents' experiences are when they have the first contacts with their adoptive children. 150 adoptive families participated in the study. All of them answered an open interview. Taking into account the information given by the families, we analyzed different experiences, some of them positive and some negative. It is essential to take into account this information in order to give professional advice to future adoptive families.

Temporal acuity, working memory, and the prediction of psychometric intelligence

Troche, Stefan Inst. für Psychologie, Universität Bern, Bern, Switzerland *Helmbold, Nadine* Inst. für Psychologie, Universität Göttingen, Göttingen, Germany *Petras, Christina* Inst. für Psychologie, Universität Göttingen, Göttingen, Germany *Rammsayer, Thomas* Inst. für Psychologie, Universität Bern, Bern, Switzerland
Temporal acuity (TA) of the brain is closely associated with intelligence. The present study investigates mechanisms underlying this functional relationship and asks whether higher TA leads to better temporal organization of capacity-limited resources, e.g., working memory, which are required to perform on intelligence tests. Applying structural equation modelling, TA, assessed by various temporal tasks, was found to reliably predict working memory capacity (WMC) in 200 participants. WMC was highly correlated with psychometric intelligence. The findings support the assumption that the relation between TA and intelligence is due to better temporal organization of capacity-limited resources in individuals with higher TA.

Cross-modal tactile-auditory saltation

Trojan, Jörg Otto-Selz-Institut, Universität Mannheim, Mannheim, Germany *Getzmann, Stephan* Ageing and CNS alterations, IfADo, Dortmund, Germany *Möller, Johanna* Otto Selz Institute, University of Mannheim, Mannheim, Germany *Kleinböhl, Dieter* Otto Selz Institute, University of Mannheim, Mannheim, Germany *Hölzl, Rupert* Otto Selz Institute, University of Mannheim, Mannheim, Germany
Saltation is a spatiotemporal illusion in which the judged position of a stimulus is shifted towards that of a subsequent stimulus. Here, we investigated cross-modal tactile-auditory saltation using a 2AFC paradigm. Sequences of three stimuli (reference, attractee, attractant) were presented as taps on the forehead and/or lateralised sounds via headphones. Participants judged attractee positions relative to references of the same modality. Auditory attractees were mislocalised towards attractants of either modality. Tactile attractees were clearly affected by tactile, but hardly by auditory attractants, demonstrating an asymmetry in tactile-auditory spatiotemporal processing relevant to cross-modal integration.

Children in residential care: Development and attachment representations

Tropa-Alves, Rita Child Protection, Santa Casa Misericórd Lisboa, Lisboa, Portugal *Vieira-Santos, Salomé* Clinical Psychology, Lisbon University-Psychology, Lisboa, Portugal

This study's aim is to characterize development and attachment representations in a group of kindergarten children (aged 4-5) in institutional care. Participants were distributed into two groups: G1 – children in residential care (n=25); G2 – children in a family environment (n=25). Portuguese versions of the Griffiths Mental Developmental Scale and the Attachment Story Completion Task were used. A statistical comparison of the groups was made using the Main-Whitney test. G1 children present lower competence in linguistic expression and comprehension, and display a more insecure attachment type. The results tie in with others referred to in literature, mainly in terms of attachment.

The development of source monitoring in children: Contributions of working memory and binding ability

Turon, Heidi School of Psychology, University of Newcastle, Newcastle, Australia *Chalmers, Kerry* School of Psychology, The University of Newcastle, Newcastle, Australia

The relationship between source monitoring, working memory and binding ability was investigated in 116 children aged between five and nine. Children completed an external source monitoring task (choosing between two soft toys as sources), three measures of working memory, and a visual binding task. Results showed significant effects of age and cue type (perceptual, temporal or both) on source monitoring ability. There were also significant correlations between source monitoring performance, backward digit span and binding ability. In contrast to several previous studies, these results suggest that external source monitoring ability continues to develop beyond the age of 6.

Reshaping of sences: Methaforization as reinterpretation of personal psychological experience

Tymofyeyeva, Nataliya Institute of Psychology, Kiev, Ukraine

Metaphor combines mythopoetic and discource-logic ways of world cognition. Through creating an image and appealing to imagination it helpes to generate new sences perceived and fixed by reason. It shapes notions about objects and presents the way of thinking about them, carrying out a modelling role in cognition process. As a powerful means of receiving, recording and transmission of psychological knowledge, metaphor provides for effectiveness of various interpersonal influences. It facilitates seizure of personal psychological experience (resolving conflicts, overcoming obstacles for personal growth, ets.). Our study focuses on different ways of using metaphorization as an instrument of psychological experience's reinterpretation.

The effect of physiognomical individuality on specific emotional impressions

Ueda, Sayako Dept. of Psychology, Japan Women's University, Kawasaki, Japan *Koyama, Takamasa* Psychology, Japan Women's University, Kawasaki city, Japan

The facial structures vary from face to face. The facial expressions have tendency provided by senders' physiognomy. In the experiment, participants were asked to judge the photographs of neutral and smiling faces from the impression based on positive – negative dimension. It was found that the positive or negative tendency of impression in neutral faces coheres with one in smiling faces. This result suggests that we can divide the faces into two facial types. The positive type, i.e. people with this type provide facial impression in positive way for receiver. And the negative type, vice versa.

The effects of coping methods on guilt over a period of time

Ueichi, Hideo Social System and Management, University of Tsukuba, Tsukuba, Japan *Oishi, Mariko* Policy and Planning Sciences, University of Tsukuba, Tsukuba-shi, Japan

The guilt feeling includes affection with shame and regret that arises when people do what they must not do (action guilt: hurt people and committed a crime) or when they abstain from doing what they must do (inaction guilt: broke a promise and violated a rule). This study classified several situations wherein people feel guilty into two generic categories: interpersonal and rule-breaking situations. Employing the questionnaire method, we examined the changes in guilt, shame, and regret over a period of time and discussed the effects of coping methods (rationalization, self-searching, and self-justification) on the reduction of guilt in each category.

Craving for transcendence: God as substitute for addictive agents?

Unterrainer, Human-Friedrich ARS Addiction Research Society, Gesellschaft "Grüner Kreis", Graz, Austria *Ladenhauf, Karl-Heinz* Pastoraltheology, Karl-Franzens-University, Graz, Austria *Wallner, Sandra* Addiction Research Society, Medical University Graz, Graz, Austria *Liebmann, Peter* ARS Addiction Research Society, Medical University Graz, Graz, Austria

Objectives: Is the desire for religious-spiritual well-being increased in substance dependents living in a therapeutic community? Method: N=504 probands were investigated. Addicts living in a therapeutic community (N=60), general medical patients (N=100), oncological patients (N=81), and healthy controls (N=263). A multidimensional instrument for religious-spiritual well-being (MI-RSB 48) was used together with established questionnaires to assess sense of coherence (SOC-13 scale) and ways of coping (FCQ-LIS). Results: Addicts showed lower bio-psycho-socio-spiritual well-being and less adequate coping strategies than other patient groups and the controls. Conclusions: Religious-spiritual intervention techniques might further improve the treatment in a therapeutic community.

Who knows how much? Sociodemographic profile and general knowledge

Urch, Drazen Zagreb, Croatia *Huic, Aleksandra* Department of Psychology, Faculty of Philosophy, Zagreb, Croatia *Ljubotina, Damir* Department of Psychology, Faculty of Philosophy, Zagreb, Croatia *Tonkovic, Masa* Department of Psychology, Faculty of Philosophy, Zagreb, Croatia *Tomisa, Tia* Department of Psychology, Faculty of Philosophy, Zagreb, Croatia

This study examined relative influence of sociodemographic factors on general knowledge. General knowledge was measured using The Advanced Vocabulary Test (words of Latin and Greek origin).The following sociodemographic data was collected: gender, age, degree of education, profession, current work status, average monthly income, town size. Foreign language knowledge as well as whether or not participants learned Latin or Greek during their schooling was also appraised. Total of 600 respondents participated in the study. Results of a hierarchical regression analysis are discussed. Best predictors proved to be degree in higher education and excellent knowledge of English language.

Puerto Rican women's perceptions and attitudes toward domestic violence

Vàzquez Torres, Hecmary Bayamòn, Puerto Rico

The present study investigated perceptions related to domestic violence within marital relationships. A sample of 112 Puerto Rican female university students between 17 and 26 years of age rated conflicts between husband and wife on a 7-point Likert scale, reacting to cases of physical abuse. Results indicated that a majority of respondents (57%) thought that abuse warranted arrest, although consequences were split between jail time (29%) and counseling (28%). Further aspects of responsibility, justice, and morality are also explored in this study. Conclusions address cultural and gender aspects of marital conflicts and spousal abuse.

Ruminative style predicts motivational changes after a negative mood induction

Vázquez, Carmelo Dept. of Psychopathology, Universidad Complutense, Madrid, Spain *Hervas, Gonzalo* Dept. of Psychopathology, Universidad Complutense, Madrid, Spain *Romero, Nuria* Dept. of Psychopathology, Universidad Complutense, Madrid, Spain

Recent research has shown that ruminative responses may be boosted by a pattern of low BAS (Behavioral Activation System) and high BIS (Behavioral Inhibition System) which may have motivational implications. In this research we explored whether this motivational BIS/BAS pattern, associated to rumination, can be affected by current mood. Ruminators and non-ruminators were assessed with a state version of BIS/BAS scales before and after a negative mood induction procedure. Our results showed that, after induction, participants with a ruminative style had a significantly lower sensitivity to reward whereas levels of sensitivity to punishment remained unchanged. Implications for the understanding the cognitive and motivational nature of rumination are discussed.

What do you expect when you are depressed: An analysis of the effects of mood on sentence completion

Vázquez, Carmelo Dept. of Psychopathology, Universidad Complutense, Madrid, Spain *Moreno, Eva* Pluridisciplinar Institute, Universidad Complutense, Madrid, Spain *Provencio, Maria* Dept. of Psychopathology, Universidad Complutense, Madrid, Spain *Sanchez, Alvaro* Dept. of Psychopathology, Universidad Complutense, Madrid, Spain

Following an extension of the standard 'cloze' probability norming procedure (e.g., Federmeier et al., 2007), this study analyzed whether mood affects the expectation of negative or positive outcomes. Participants (N=179) were presented a series of 70 uncompleted sentences. They were required to complete them with a final word which would imply either a positive or a negative ending as coded by independent raters (Kappa=.85). Participants also completed a number of questionnaires related to positive and negative mood and depression severity. Our results confirmed the hypotheses of a mood-congruent effect on sentence completion which is discussed in terms of current theories of mood and cognition.

Understanding of the new information presented in verbal and visual forms by pre-school children

Vaganova, Natalia Creativity Psychology, Institute of Psychology, Kyiv, Ukraine

The article covers issue of understanding of new information structures by pre-school children, these structures being presented in audio- and visual forms (oral messages – rhymes, notions, tales, stories, pictures, drawings). Theoretical analysis of concept of understanding enabled us to define main psychological indicators and determinants of its manifestations. Elicited were the features specific to the process of understanding of new information by pre-school children through determination of subjective path marks and devising of new image-notions underlying the understanding. Crucial role of the analogy and combinatory mechanisms in development of new semantic constructions was elucidated. Pilot experimental instructional system was developed that is intended for training children in analyzing new information structures and forming relevant skills.

Relation of core self-evaluations, organizational commitment and turn over intention

Valencia, Marshall Dept. of Psychology, De La Salle University, Manila, Philippines
The study tested a structural model that looks at turnover intention as a function of organizational commitment and core self-evaluations (CSE). Survey data from 190 call center agents in the Philippines was analyzed using structural equations modeling. Results indicated negative correlations between CSE and turnover intention. Normative and affective commitment is indirectly related to turnover intentions with CSE as a mediator. Continuance commitment was not related to both CSE and turnover intention. The discussion highlights the viability of the CSE construct as a significant mediator in the turnover intention – organizational commitment nomological network.

Misinformation effect in emotional/neutral pictures

Valeri, Sara Dep.of Psychology, University of Rome, Rome, Italy Candel, Ingrid Dep.of Psychology, University of Maastricht, Maastricht, Netherlands Inguscio, Lucio Dep.of Psychology, University of Rome, Rome, Italy Marucci, Francesco Dep.of Psychology, University of Rome, Rome, Italy Mastroberardino, Serena Dep.of Psychology, University of Rome, Rome, Italy
The aim of this study is to integrate "misinformation effect" and "emotional arousal" paradigms, comparing the memory performance of subjects after a presentation of emotional and neutral pictures. We examine the effect of environmental sounds as misinformation to evaluate the overlap between real picture and post congruent audio stimuli. We explore, furthermore, how different ways to provide misinformation can affect people's memory evaluating the memory performance for misleading/no misleading sounds and leading/no leading questions.

Gay parenthood in The Netherlands

van Balen, Frank Educational Sciences, University of Amsterdam, Amsterdam, Netherlands Bos, Henny Educational Sciences, University of Amsterdam, Amsterdam, Netherlands Van Rooij, Floor Educational Sciences, University of Amsterdam, Amsterdam, Netherlands
This study examines whether planned gay fathers differ from heterosexual fathers on parenting. Twenty-three planned gay fathers were compared with 100 heterosexual fathers. Data were collected through questionnaires, in the Netherlands. Most gay fathers shared child-rearing with the biological mothers of their children and were part-time fathers. Compared to heterosexual fathers, they reported more often happiness as motive for having a child, experienced greater negative parental treatment, felt less competent and more pressure to justify parenthood, and sought more social support. This indicates that gay fathers feel less secure, which might be related to part-time parenting and societal rejection.

Conscious and unconscious proportion effects in masked priming

van den Bussche, Eva Dept. of Psychology, Katholieke Universiteit Leuven, Kortrijk, Belgium Segers, Gitte Psychology, Katholieke Universiteit Leuven, Leuven, Belgium Reynvoet, Bert Psychology, Katholieke Universiteit Leuven, Kortrijk, Belgium
The global neuronal workspace theory (Dehaene & Naccache, 2001) proposes that it is impossible for an unconscious stimulus to be used strategically to enhance task performance (bottom-up effect), while a fully consciously perceived stimulus can be used to improve task performance (top-down effect). These hypotheses were confirmed by the present study. We found that subjects were able to use a manipulation of the proportion of visible Arabic/number word targets to enhance task performance (experiment 1), but they were unable to use a manipulation of the proportion of invisible Arabic/number word primes to enhance task performance (experiment 2).

Job characteristics, self-regulatory skills, goal progress, and employee well-being

van der Doef, Margot Dept. of Health Psychology, Leiden University, Leiden, Netherlands Volkova, Anastasia Dept. of Health Psychology, Leiden University, Leiden, Netherlands
Against the background of the Job demand-control model, this study examines whether demands and control are associated with self-regulatory skills, progress on personal work goals, and well-being. 235 employees completed a questionnaire assessing job characteristics, self-regulatory skills (e.g. planning, attention control), goal progress, and job-related well-being. High skill discretion, and to a lesser extent high decision authority and low demands, were directly related to well-being. Furthermore, skill discretion had an indirect effect on well-being, mediated by self-regulatory skills and goal progress. Skill discretion may influence employee well-being partially through its positive effects on self-regulatory skills and goal progress.

Modality-independent and modality-dependent processing of syntactic gender violations in left cytoarchitectonic BA 44

van Ermingen, Muna Aachen, Germany Heim, Stefan Brain Imaging Center West, Research Centre Jülich, Jülich, Germany Amunts, Kathrin Institute of Medicine, Research Center Jülich, Jülich, Germany Huber, Walter Abt. Neurolinguistik, Universitätsklinikum Aachen, Aachen, Germany
This fMRI study investigates whether left BA 44 supports the processing of gender violations in spoken and written determiner phrases independent of stimulus modality. The gender decision times were longer for violated vs. correct stimuli. A conjunction analysis of decisions for visual and auditory stimuli revealed common activation in left BA 44. Moreover, in BA 44 activation was stronger for violated than for correct stimuli. The data support the view that left BA 44 is involved in the processing of syntactic gender violations.

The self-learning in inline-skating classes at school

Viciana, Jesus Physical Education and Sport, University of Grenade, Granada, Spain Román, Blanca Physical Education and Sport, University of Grenade, Granada, Spain Miranda, M₂ Teresa Physical Education and Sport, University of Grenade, Granada, Spain Martinez, Manuel Physical Education and Sport, University of Grenade, Granada, Spain Martínez, Juan C. Physical Education and Sport, University of Grenade, Granada, Spain
The aim of this research was to promote inline-skating self learning in students through problem-solving tasks. 49 students (13,7 years old) received instruction for 16 days during Physical Education classes. Students and the teacher assessed the

specific skills prior to and after the treatment in a scale of 7 categories (within 2 different items). The data which associates the subjective learning level with an objective teacher's assessment, shows significant differences (p=.005) in dynamic balance, velocity and direction control, jump ability, body and feet laterality. The problem-solving tasks can be used to facilitate the autonomy and self-motivation inline-skating learning process.

Influence of textual coherence in generation of textual and extratextual inferences in university students

Vieiro, Pilar Psicologia Evolutiva, University of La Coruna, La Coruna, Spain
The aim of this work is to analyze the influence of textual coherence in the generation of textual and extratextual inferences in university students. Forty university students were used: twenty read a secuencial text with high coherence and the other twenty read a text with low coherence. We measure the recognition of on-line inferences. Results showed no significant differences in the generation of both types of inferences according to the level of textual coherence. Keywords: inferences, reading comprehension, textual coherence

Design of competencies-based model using the organizational climate survey

Villavicencio Carranza, Miguel Alejandro Mexico City, Mexico
The organizational climate survey is generally used to identify worker's perceptions about different elements that affect their performance. Although these results help to diagnose the organization's main problems, can also be useful to design a competencies-based model for human resource's training and development. Thus, a competencies-based model was designed using the results obtained from an instrument (alpha=.96, factorial analysis=.60) that evaluates 16 organizational climate factor's. The model includes competencies like: human relations, communication and feedback, supervision, support and commitment. Introducing this competencies-based model type, the organization is able to design T&D programs and to incorporate elements for HR performance improvement.

The influence of explicit and implicit goals on the allocation of spatial attention

Vogt, Julia Dept. of Psychology, Ghent University, Ghent, Belgium de Houwer, Jan Department of Psychology, PP05, Ghent University, Ghent, Belgium Moors, Agnes Department of Psychology, PP05, Ghent University, Ghent, Belgium Crombez, Geert Department of Psychology, PP05, Ghent University, Ghent, Belgium
This study examined whether stimuli relevant to a person's current goals influence the automatic allocation of spatial attention. Healthy volunteers responded to targets that were preceded by cues consisting of stimuli relevant to an explicit goal (Experiment 1) or an implicit goal (Experiment 2). Repeated measurement ANOVAs conducted on the reaction times revealed that goal relevant stimuli evoke an attentional bias through holding of attention compared to other activated stimuli. These results support old and recent accounts in attention and motivation that propose an early modulation of attention by the current goals of a person.

Managing injury management performance to improve outcomes for long- term claimants

Volleman, Theodora Premier and Cabinet, Government of South Australia, Adelaide, Australia Heim, Michael
The present study implements a measurement systems approach based on psychological principles to improve case management performance in

resolving long term Workers Compensation claims. A total of 27 case managers handling 150 claims were randomly allocated to either a minimal intervention group or a control group. Participants in the intervention group confidentially rated their own monthly case management performance using a scale developed for this purpose. They then received a graph of the average ratings for the entire group against which they could compare their own performance. The findings are discussed in the context of effective low cost interventions in injury management.

The structure of Inferiority Complex, its expression and levels

Vorone, Santa Social Psychology, Daugavpils Universitaty, Daugavpils, Latvia

In this paper the expression of inferiority complex, its structure and levels of development are analyzed. Attention is given to psychological development of personality in the aspect of dynamics of the inferiority complex concept and to problems in personality development from the perspective of clinical psychology. It was found that the inferiority complex develops dynamically and gradually, and that it has three levels of development: 1) situational; 2) complex as personality feature; 3) clinical. The inferiority complex is composed of complex structure of personality disorders: emotional, social, cognitive and clinical disorders.

How straight are straight people exactly?

Vrangalova, Snezana Human Development, Cornell University, Ithaca, USA Savin-Williams, Ritch Human Development, Cornell University, Ithaca, USA

This study examined different methods of assessing sexual orientation and investigated inconsistencies in the various dimensions of this concept among heterosexually-identified individuals, a finding frequently reported for non-heterosexuals. Three-hundred students aged 18 to 42 (82% heterosexual) completed a web-administered survey. Sexual orientation was assessed using multiple measures. Although sexual behaviors were largely consistent with heterosexual self-identification, sexual attractions and fantasies were strikingly non-exclusive. Consistent heterosexuals differed from inconsistent ones in certain aspects of their sexual histories. Implications for the nature and meaning of sexual orientation components and for the traditional simplistic assessment of sexual orientation are discussed.

A study on the development of 3-6 year-old children's emotion understanding ability from the perspective of the theory of mind

Wang, Xiao Ying Dept. of Psychology, Northeast Normal University, Changchun, People's Republic of China Zhang, Yu Mei Psychology Department, Northeast Normal University, Changchun, People's Republic of China

The purpose of this research is to verifying the age characteristic, the sex difference and the overall development situation of the 3~6year old children's emotion understanding ability development from the Perspective of the Theory of Mind in China. This study employs the experimental method. The research includes four levels?including the emotion exterior performance, the emotion reason understood, the conflict emotion understood and the emotion regulation. The result indicates that:3~6 year-old children's emotion understanding ability from the perspective of the theory of mind is increasing, but there is no significant difference. The development of emotion understanding for children is not straightness, and has the task particularity.

Construct dimension of the employee's content of organizational socialization in China

Wang, Minghui Department of Psychology, Henan University, Kaifeng, People's Republic of China Ling, Wenquan School of Management, Jinan University, Guangzhou,Guangdong, People's Republic of China Fang, Liluo Institute of Psychology, Chinese Academy of Sciences, Beijing, People's Republic of China

Objectives: Organizational socialization is a learning process by which an individual adjusts the attitudes, behaviors he or she needs to participate as an organizational member, the purpose of the study is to explore the construct dimension of the employee's content of organizational socialization in China. Methods: The methods involved literature review, interview, pilot study and survey, The survey data was mainly analyzed with exploratory factor analysis and confirmatory factor analysis. Results: The results showed that organizational socialization content of Chinese employees was comprised of organizational culture, job competency, interpersonal relationship and organizational politics. Conclusions: The four-dimension construct can reflect the contents which Chinese employees should learn in the process of organizational socialization.

Neuroticism, extraversion, emotion regulation, nagative affect and positive affect: The mediating roles of reappraisal and suppression

Wang, Li Inst. of Psychology, Chinese Academy of Sciences, Beijing, People's Republic of China

This study examined the mediating role of emotion regulation between neuroticism and negative affect and between extraversion and positive affect. Participants were 1,000 Chinese undergraduate students. The results of structural equation modeling indicated that neuroticism and extraversion contributed to negative affect and positive affect indirectly through reappraisal beside the direct contribution respectively. Furthermore, neuroticism and extraversion explained 22% of the variance in reappraisal, and neuroticism and reappraisal, extraversion and reappraisal explained 42% and 28% of the variance in negative affect and positive affect, respectively.

Response compatibility effect of gaze and arrow direction

Wang, Hsioa Ling Psychology, ChungYuan Christian University, Chung Li, Taiwan Chao, Hsuan-Fu Psychology, ChungYuan Christian University, Chung Li, Taiwan Kuo, Chun-Yu Psychology, ChungYuan Christian University, Chung Li, Taiwan

From an evolutionary perspective, although both eye gaze and arrow direction are usually classified as central cues of attention, they are believed to have different impacts on human cognition. The current study aimed at investigating the differential effects of eye gaze and arrow direction on attention by studying their response compatibility effects (Experiments 1–4) and by examining the influences of social and nonsocial cues on their effects (Experiments 2–4). The results indicated that eye gaze and arrow direction are different.

The long-term effects of maternal discipline on children's conflict resolution ability

Wang, Lin Dept. of Psychology, Chung Yuan University, Chung Li, Taiwan

This study examined the extent to which maternal disciplinary styles and direct instructions influenced children's goal setting and chosen strategies in conflict resolution one year later. Maternal styles include positive inducement, negative force and non-involvement. The direct instructions are grouped as assertive, prosocial and yielding strategies. Using regression-analysis, data from 568 (275 boys and 293 girls) Taiwanese children from the 2nd to 5th grade and their mothers were analyzed across 2 years. Findings indicated that mothers'

direct instructions of prosocial strategies one year ago influenced daughters', but not sons', setting altruistic goal and using prosocial strategies in peer conflict resolutions.

The time course and source localization of false belief reasoning revealed by an event-related potential study

Wang, Yiwen Research Center for Learning S, Southeast University, Nanjing, People's Republic of China Lin, Chongde School of Psychology, Beijing Normal University, Beijing, People's Republic of China

To investigate the neural substrates of false-belief reasoning, the 32 channels event-related potentials (ERP) of 14 normal adults were measured while they understood false-belief and true-belief used deceptive appearance task. After onset of the false-belief or true-belief questions?N100, P200 and late negative component (LNC) were elicited at centro-frontal sites. False-belief reasoning elicited a significant declined LNC than true-belief in the time window from 400 to 800ms. The source analysis of difference wave (False minus True) at 650ms showed a dipole located in the middle cingulated cortex. These findings suggested that false-belief reasoning probably included inhibitive control.

Dynamic dissociation of person perception and theory-of-mind reasoning investigated by event related brain potentials

Wang, Yiwen School of Psychology, Shandong Normal University, Jinan, People's Republic of China Liu, Yan Research Center for Learning S, Southeast University, Nanjing, People's Republic of China Lin, Chongde Institute of Developmental Psy, Beijing Normal University, Nanjing, People's Republic of China

To investigate the dynamic dissociation of theory-of-mind(tom) reasoning and person perception, event-related potentials(ERP) were recorded from 17 normal undergraduates while they were watching three kinds of cartoons. The amplitudes of P200 and 300-400ms for scene pictures were significantly lower than person perception and tom-cartoons, which the two latter were no difference. From 900ms, the mean amplitudes of tom-cartoons were further dissociated from the person perception. Results reveal that two sub-processes might be involved in theory-of-mind reasoning and person perception.

Effects of presenting mode of reading material on children reading activity

Wang, Aiping Beijing Normal University, Psychology school, Beijing, People's Republic of China

Objective: To study effects of three presenting modes of reading material on children reading activity. Method: 36 fifth-year pupils who have high and low read levels read three articles with three presenting modes: paper, electronic text, and hypertext-format. Results showed: (1) the scores of readers with higher reading level are better than lowers; the scores of schoolgirls are better than schoolboys in conditions of three presenting modes; (2) children reading comprehension don't been affected by different presenting modes of reading materials; (3) children have higher evaluation to hypertext than other presenting modes. Conclusion: most of children can accept and familiar non-linear text quickly.

The role of subtitle in the children's incidental learning

Wang, Aiping Beijing Normal University, Psychology school, Beijing, People's Republic of China

Objective: The role of subtitle in children's incidental learning. Method: three factors: reading levels, pinyin, new word dense, Results: (1) first and three grades children can acquire more new words in high dense condition than low one; (2) the new words first-grade children with low reading level acquired are same as high reading level ones in pinyin subtitles condition, but are lower significantly than high reading level ones in no-pinyin; (3) the new words in pinyin subtitle conditions three-grade children with high reading level acquired aren't different from ones of low and no-pinyin. Conclusion: incidental learning made use of subtitles is a favorable method for children acquiring vocabulary knowledge.

Manipulated facial expressions in relation to subjective emotional reactions

Waterink, Wim Dept. of Psychology, Open Univ. of the Netherlands, Heerlen, Netherlands Van der Laan, Catheleyne Psychology, Open University of the Nether, Heerlen, Netherlands Van Hooren, Susan Psychology, Open University of the Netherl, Heerlen, Netherlands

It was investigated whether specific facial expressions moderate the experience of induced emotions. Sixty subjects participated in a cover story experiment. Different facial expression where brought on by keeping objects between teeth or lips, activating or not activating facial muscles underlying basic emotional facial expressions. Multiple regression analysis led to the finding that for subject where smiling muscles were activated, relatively higher positive emotional reactions on neutral stimuli were accompanied by higher positive emotional reactions on positive stimuli. So, as part of a therapeutic intervention, activating smiling muscles seems more beneficial for subjects who, in general, show initial positive reactions.

Career changers as teachers: Motivations, work perceptions and how it all turns out

Weinmann-Lutz, Birgit Inst. für Psychologie, Universität Trier, Trier, Germany

The purpose of this study was to investigate the positive effect of career change on important professional variables for teachers, like self-efficacy, motivation and work perceptions. Questionnaires of a total of 876 first versus second career teaching students (at the beginning and the end of their training) and experienced professionals were included; 128 thereof were longitudinal data sets. 47 biographical interviews were made. Multivariate analyses of variance, repeated measurement analyses and content analyses were undertaken. Career change has a positive effect on self-efficacy, realistic and idealistic work perceptions; pronounced gender effects were found.

Previous target location and movement direction increase reaction times in a joint movement task

Welsh, Timothy Faculty of Kinesiology, University of Calgary, Calgary, Canada McDougall, Laura Faculty of Kinesiology, University of Calgary, Calgary, Canada Weeks, Daniel Department of Psychology, Simon Fraser University, Burnaby, Canada

Inhibition of return (IOR) refers to longer reaction times to targets appearing in the same location as a previous event. IOR also occurs at the target location of another person's action. Movement direction and target location was confounded in previous between-person IOR research because participants sat across from each other and responded to common targets. Here, participants sat beside each other so we were able to determine if target location repetition or movement direction repetition was responsible for between-person IOR. Results indicate that both location and movement direction are coded in the observer and independently evoke the processes underlying IOR.

Multimethod validation of a screening instrument for job related affective well-being

Wendsche, Johannes Inst. für Arbeitspsychologie, Technische Universität Dresden, Dresden, Germany Uhmann, Stefan Clinical Psychology, TU Dresden, Dresden, Germany Tomaschek, Anne Work and Organizational Psych., TU Dresden, Dresden, Germany Richter, Peter Work and Organizational Psych., TU Dresden, Dresden, Germany

Research has mainly focused on non-specific affective states at the work place: stress and satisfaction. Based on a two-dimensional model of affect (valence, activation) we tested the validity of a more comprehensive, one-click, and semantic-free screening instrument assessing job-related affective states. As proposed, the "affective grid" corresponds to the Positive and Negative Affect Schedule (Study 1). Furthermore, its sensitivity was examined in an experiment inducing different affective states (Study 2) and by applying it before and after oral examinations (Study 3). Studies 4 and 5 showed associations to performance, perceived job strain and cardiovascular reactivity in virtual and assembly-line work.

Cross-modal attention and letter recognition

Wesner, Michael Psychology, CBTC-Lakehead University, Thunder Bay, Canada Miller, Lisa Psychology, CBTC-Lakehead University, Thunder Bay, Canada

Although there is extensive evidence supporting top-down modulation of visual and auditory perceptual processes within the same modality, there remains ambiguity as to how these mechanisms operate on perceptual processes across sensory modalities. Using a letter pairing paradigm, we presented capital letter pairs that were either structurally (e.g., [R] [P]) or phonetically (e.g., [B] [V]) similar and asked participants to indicate the appropriate coding classification, with the added caveat that these letters could be presented unimodally as controls, or concurrently in both modalities. Reaction time and accuracy measurements with different intermodal attentional instructions and letter classifications revealed complex top-down, task-dependent interactions.

My home is my identity: Studies on regional identity

Wiederhold, Uta Prof. für Sozialpsychologie, TU Dresden, Dresden, Germany

The paper proposes a new theoretical concept of regional identification on the background of social identity approach (Tajfel et al.). The main idea is to specify regional identity not by territorial definition like residence but as a shared group membership which rests on processes of intergroup differentiation. An individual feels commited to a region because she/he feels attached to the people who live there. A new scale measuring regional identity (a=.955, N=293,) shows evidence for a membership dimension of regional identity. Furthermore different SEM-models will be tested to fit the database.

Avoidance behaviour of socially anxious women in virtual social interactions

Wieser, Matthias Inst. für Psychologie, Universität Würzburg, Würzburg, Germany Pauli, Paul Department of Psychology, University of Würzburg, Würzburg, Germany Mühlberger, Andreas Department of Psychology, University of Würzburg, Würzburg, Germany

Objectives: Combining virtual reality and eye-tracking allows the investigation of avoidance behaviour in highly controlled social situations. Method: High (HSA) and low socially anxious (LSA) participants and controls were confronted with virtual characters showing averted or direct gaze while eye movements and head posture were recorded. Results: HSA compared to LSA showed more backward head posture in response to male avatars with direct gaze. Furthermore, HSA and controls looked less long at the male avatars with direct gaze than to male avatars with averted gaze. Conclusions: HSA who are confronted with social interaction of opposite sex show avoidance behaviour.

Revisiting age of acquisition effects in Spanish word reading

Wilson, Maximiliano ISTC-CNR, Rome, Italy Cuetos, Fernando Cognitive Neuroscience, University of Oviedo, Oviedo, Spain Burani, Cristina Cogntive Sciences, ISTC-CNR, Rome, Italy

We studied Age of Acquisition (AoA), and its relationship with Frequency and Imageability to evaluate whether lexical-semantic variables influenced word reading in a transparent orthography as Spanish. Fifty-six Spanish adult readers performed Lexical Decision (LD) and Word Naming (WN) tasks, with a fully orthogonal design (AoAxFrequency, AoAxImageability). ANOVAs were conducted. Both AoA and Frequency, but not Imageability, affected LD, with larger AoA effects for Low-Frequency and Low-Imageability words. In WN the effect of Word frequency was stronger than that of AoA. These results are in support of lexical non-semantic reading aloud in transparent orthographies as Spanish.

Evidence for negative automatic evaluation and better recognition of bodily symptom words in health anxiety

Witthöft, Michael Inst. für Psychologie, ZI für Seelische Gesundheit, Mannheim, Germany Schmidt, Erika Clinical Psychology, Centr. Instit. of Ment. Health, Mannheim, Germany Kornadt, Anna Clinical Psychology, Centr. Instit. of Ment. Health, Mannheim, Germany Bailer, Josef Clinical Psychology, Centr. Instit. of Ment. Health, Mannheim, Germany

Objectives: Negative automatic evaluations (NAE) of disorder related stimuli are considered as crucial in various psychopathologies. In health anxiety (HA), NAE might be responsible for the observed memory bias toward health threat stimuli. Methods: Three experimental groups (people with HA, elevated depression scores (D), and controls (C) were compared on an implicit association test (IAT) as a measure of NAE and a recognition task (RT). Results: Focusing on the accuracy data, people with HA demonstrated greater NAE in the IAT and better recognition of symptom words in the RT. Conclusions: NAE of symptoms might maintain health threat representations in memory.

Group-based self-control: The influence of social identification on individual control strategies

Woltin, Karl-Andrew International Graduate College, Universität Jena, Jena, Germany Sassenberg, Kai Knowledge Media Research Cente, Knowledge Media Research Cente, Tübingen, Germany

A self-regulation perspective to (inter)group motivation is applied that combines the action phase model, describing control strategies given a pre- and post-deadline phase of individual goal pursuit, with social identity theory. We expect that the more group members identify with their group, the more they will engage in phase-adequate control strategy usage (i.e., group-based self-control). This hypothesis was supported for behavioural intentions and behavioural measures in a scenario experiment with natural groups and in two laboratory experiments using quasi-minimal groups and manipulating social identification. The findings point to the possibility of applying theories concerning controlled individual self-regulation to (inter)group contexts.

Intergenerational differences in the values of children and family among Korean university students and their parents

Woo, Jo-Eun Dept. of Education, Inha University, Incheon, Republic of Korea *Kim, Uichol* Business administration, Inha University, Inchon, Republic of Korea *Park, Young-Shin* Dept. of Education, Inha University, Incheon, Republic of Korea

The purpose of this study is to examine intergenerational differences in the values of children and family among university students and their parents. A total of 600 respondents (a matched sample of 200 university students and their parents) completed a questionnaire. The results indicate that positive values of children for university students emphasize psychological aspects, such as personal satisfaction and happiness. For their parents, positive values of children emphasize familial and social aspects, such as depending on their children when they are old and continuing the family line. For negative values of children, university students are more likely emphasize constraints in their personal, occupational and social life. Overall, parents are more likely to emphasize traditional familial obligations than university students.

The influence of cognitive holding power, intelligence and mathematical achievement on children's realistic problem solving

Xin, Ziqiang School of Psychology, Beijing Normal University, Beijing, People's Republic of China *Zhang, Li* School of Psychology, Beijing Normal University, Beijing, People's Republic of China

The study aimed to explore whether first and second order cognitive holding power perceived by children in classroom, fluid intelligence, and mathematical achievement can predict their solving standard and realistic problems. Results from an investigation of 119 Chinese 4-6th graders showed that: (1) children's intelligence and general mathematical achievement significantly predicted their performance on both realistic and standard problems, however, second order cognitive holding power predicted their performance on realistic problems but not standard problems; (2) the relationship between first order cognitive holding power and children's correct answers to realistic problems was mediated by second order cognitive holding power.

Fourth to sixth graders representation of area-of-rectangle problems: Influences of relational complexity and cognitive holding power

Xin, Ziqiang School of Psychology, Beijing Normal University, Beijing, People's Republic of China

The aim of the study is to explore 382 4-6 graders' representation level of area-of-rectangle problems belonging to four templates with different relational complexity, and influences of cognitive holding power on it. The results showed that students' representation level improved with grades, and their representation level of four templates had clear hierarchical order. The representation level of each template was significantly predicted by both first and second order cognitive holding power, moreover, the predictive power increased from template 1 to template 4, but the predictive directions were opposite.

Affective aspects of learning: Adolescents' self-concept, achievement values, emotions and motivation in learning mathematics

Xiong, Junmei München, Germany *Tippelt, Rudolf* Department of Education, University of Munich, Munich, Germany

The study aimed at describing adolescents' affective-cognitive processes in learning mathematics. Eleventh graders (n = 464) from two metropolitans in China were administered Motivated Strategies for Learning Questionnaire (Pintrinch et al., 1991), Academic Emotions Questionnaire – Mathematics

(Pekrun, et al., 2005), etc.. Correlation-regression statistics revealed that emotions correlated with Strategies use, Self-concept, and Achievement values positively or negatively based on the valence of the emotions. In addition, Boredom (β = -.27, p < .001), Metacognitive self-regulation (β = .20, p < .001), Performance approach (β = .13, p < .01), and Parental control (β = -.25, p < .001) were predictors of Math achievement. Math achievement is a function of affective-cognitive processes.

2-4 years old children's inhibition and impulsivity

Xu, Qinmei Inst. for Psychology, Zhejiang University, Hangzhou, People's Republic of China *Geng, Fengji* Psychology, Zhejiang University, Hangzhou, People's Republic of China

Objectives?To test children's inhibition and impulsivity. Methods: 53 subjects (23 boys and 30 girls, M = 35.11 months, SD = 6.47) were classified as inhibited, intermediate and uninhibited children based on fearfulness paradigm (Kochanska et al., 2001). The impulsivity was measured by delay tasks (Aksan and Kochanska, 2004). The differences in impulsivity among 3 groups were examined by one-way analysis of variance with post-hoc tests. Results: Differences among 3 types were found (F = 5.97, P < .01); intermediate children's impulsivity was lower than both of inhibited and uninhibited ones. Conclusions: Inhibition was not directly related to implusivity.

Suspicions and the interaction of corporate values with consumer values

Yabsley, Evan Faculty of Business, Central Queensland University, Rockhampton, Australia

This study shows how company values and public statements of corporate social responsibility (CSR), are processed through the prism of the consumer's values and suspicion attributions. A between-within design surveyed 1000 Queensland consumers, utilised stimulus material generated from five Australian brands' CSR statements, a suspicion attribution scale and the Schwartz Value Scale. When controlling for reputation, confirmatory factor analysis and structural equation modelling show mediation of personal values magnifies or suppresses suspicions of corporate egoism. The study both confirms prior studies of individual interaction elements, and also makes a unique contribution with a complete model not confounded by reputation.

A study of socio-psychological characterstics of alcohol abusers among Kurukshetra University boys hostellers

Yadav, Rajender Singh Dept. of Eduction, Kurukshetra University, Kurukshetra, India

The study was conducted on 90 male students(Alcohol Abusers) residing in hostels of Kurukshetra University, Kurukshetra (India) selected through snowball sampling technique using self developed non-directive interview schedule. Percentages and frequencies were calculated for analysis and interpretation of data. The study highlighted general background of alcohol abusers, causes of alcohol coping behaviour. Majority of the alcohol abusers started taking alcohol at the age of 20 yrs & above and developed this habit in the company of friends and significantly large number of alcohol abusers did not want their parents to be informed about their habit of taking alcohol.

Relationship between attitudes toward suicide survivors and views on suicide

Yamanaka, Akira Faculty of Business Administr., Hokkai-Gakuen University, Sapporo, Japan

Attitudes on Suicide Survivors scale (ASS) was developed and the relationship between these attitudes and views regarding suicide was examined. Factor analysis of ASS identified five factors: Rejection of Contact, Finger-Pointing, Confusion

on Contact, Commiseration, and Considering Suicide Taboo. Moreover, factor analysis of responses to the Views of Suicide Scale (Nakamura, 1996) identified three factors that were different from those of previous studies: Connivery, Orientation to Living, and Active Contradiction. Certain factors of the ASS correlated with the three factors in the Views of Suicide Scale.

The study on the development of the spatial-numerical representation in Chinese children

Yang, Tao Research Insitute of Basic Edu, Beijing Normal University, Beijing, People's Republic of China

This study was designed to observe the development of children's spatial representation of numbers, with the bilateral parity response task and the number color response task. 5 to 12 year-old Children and adults were participated in the study. The results showed: (1) Spatial representation of numbers appeared in 5-year-old children and stably existed in children from 5 to 12 year-old. (2) The development of children's spatial representation of numbers was significantly correlative with their ages. As the children's ages increasing, the size of the SNARC effect gradually decreased. (3) The task had different sensitivity to the children in different age.

Experiences of youth about psychological outcomes of substance dependency

Yazdani, Mohsen Nursing Faculty, University of Med Sciences, Isfahan, Islamic Republic of Iran *Fereidooni Moghadam, Malek* Nursing Department, Abadan Nursing Faculty, Abadan, Islamic Republic of Iran *Nasiri, Mahmood* Nursing Faculty, University of Med Sciences, Isfahan, Islamic Republic of Iran *Yazdannik, Ahmad Reza* Nursing Faculty, University of Med Sciences, Isfahan, Islamic Republic of Iran

Objectives: In the recent years young people are the main victims of Substance dependency. Present study was done to describe the experiences of youth about psychological outcomes of substance dependency. Methods: This research is a phenomenological study. Participants were 12 youth with that was selected with purposive sampling method. Data analysis was done via Colaizzi method. Results: The main concept was derived from this study were psychological outcomes that included four sub-themes. Conclusions: The results showed that people after substance dependency showed many negative outcomes. So three approaches of individual, family and community centered in levels of prevention suggested.

The changes of Chinese value orientation: Cross-generation comparisons using Rokeach Value Survey

Ye, Qian Dept. of Psychology, Beijing Normal University, Beijing, People's Republic of China *Yan, Gonggu* Psychology, Beijing Normal University, Beijing, People's Republic of China

Social transition in China, characterized by the Reform and Opening-up policy, impacts Chinese's values greatly. 737 subjects were sampled nationwidely to take Rokeach Value Survey by ranking and rating items. The results indicate that two methods have same function on measuring personal values. Males prefer individual orientated values, while females prefer social/affiliation orientated values. Compared with other generations, the post-80s, born after 1980, pursue various things but value less on Universalism (A world of peace, Equality and National Security). In addition, the young women value more on Salvation and Capable but less on Polite and Self-controlled.

Development and practice of human relations training program for teachers

Yoshida, Michio *Faculty of Education, Kumamoto University, Kumamoto, Japan*

We have developed training programs for teachers to improve human relations skills. This training consists of two courses, namely "Basic training" and "Follow training." Before the "Basic training," teachers ask their students to describe actions they want teachers to carry out and not to carry out. In the "Basic training," teachers analyze students' descriptions and make decisions to change their behavior. After the training, the participants try to achieve their personal goals in their classes. At the end of the school term, teachers conduct survey to get data from their students. Again, the result is analyzed in the "Follow training."

Dual intra-process leading antisocial propensity: The prediction power of social information-processing and self-regulation

Yoshizawa, Hiroyuki *Faculty of Education, Gifu Shotoku Gakuen University, Gifu, Japan* **Harada, Chika** *Graduate School of Education a, Nagoya University, Nagoya, Japan* **Yoshida, Toshikazu** *Graduate School of Education a, Nagoya University, Nagoya, Japan*

The authors examined the prediction power of dual intra-process, which consists of social information-processing (SIP) and self-regulation, for antisocial propensity. Data were collected from 75 male undergraduates in Japan. SIP was assessed by knowledge structures of social rules, normative beliefs about aggression, and cognitive distortion. Behavioral inhibition / approach system, effortful control, and social self-regulation were used as indices for self-regulation. Antisocial propensity was assessed by evaluations of the seriousness and past experience of antisocial behaviors. The results of structural equation modeling revealed the causal antecedent of SIP over self-regulation to predict antisocial propensity.

Coordination of Yin and Yang: Chinese value orientations and their structures

Yu, Guangtao *Business School, CUFE, Beijing, People's Republic of China* **Fu, Pingping** *Department of Management, Chinese Univ. of Hong Kong, Hong Kong, People's Republic of China* **Liu, Jun** *School of Business, Renmin University of China, Beijing, People's Republic of China*

In order to explore the specific traits of Chinese value systems, two studies were conducted following the context-specific approach. At first, 138 Chinese managers were asked to describe ten most important things in life, and 1154 items were collected and sorted into 14 categories after 6 round sorting. Then, Chinese Value Instrument including 79 items was constructed, and 598 undergraduates responded. Results of EFA and CFA indicate Chinese values have ten dimensions: benevolence, universalism, innovation, trust, self-fulfillment, power, familism, comfort, Guangxi?traditionality, being classified into two categories: "He(?)" and "Wei(?)".

Verbal- and non-verbal intelligence tests as measures of cognitive aptitudes: A comparison of privileged and underprivileged elementary school children

Zöller, Isabelle *Inst. für Psychologie, Universität Heidelberg, Heidelberg, Germany* **Treutlein, Anke** *Psychology, University of Education, Heidelberg, Germany* **Roos, Jeanette** *Psychology, University of Education, Heidelberg, Germany* **Schöler, Hermann** *Psychology, University of Education, Heidelberg, Germany*

Verbal intelligence tests are often considered as biased with regard to socio-economic background and prior language-related learning experiences. Nevertheless, intelligence tests continue to be the most widely used measures of cognitive aptitudes. As part of EVES-longitudinal study, cognitive aptitudes as well as reading and spelling skills of 1520 children were assessed at the end of first and second grade (non-verbal test) and fourth grade (verbal test). In all grades underprivileged children are outperformed by children from higher socio-economic background, however, initial results contradict the assumption that these differences are due to unfairness in tests.

Concern for the next generation at work: Generativity and occupational role priorities

Zacher, Hannes *Inst. für Arbeits-Organisation, Universität Gießen, Gießen, Germany*

The purpose of this study was to examine the relationships between Erik Erikson's concept of generativity – the concern in establishing and guiding the next generation – and the priority of various work roles (i.e., job, career, innovator, team member, organizational citizen, and mentor). 130 employees ranked the work roles according to their subjective importance. Results showed that generativity is positively associated with the priority of the innovator and the mentor roles, even after controlling for age, gender, education, and job complexity. This suggests that future research and human resource management should consider generativity as an additional important motive of employees.

The effect of training on citizenship concept learning in 7-8 years old children of Isfahan

Zakerfard, Monir *Isfahan, Islamic Republic of Iran* **Ahmadi, Elaheh** *Psychology, Isfahan university, Isfahan, Islamic Republic of Iran*

The purpose of this study was investigate the effect on citizenship concepts learning in 7-8 years old children of Isfahan. Date of 921 children of Isfahan was obtained with a inventory (researcher made whit alpha=0.72) in pre- and post- stages of the training. T test showed that the training is effective(p<0.05).

Comparison of effective factors on sleeping from aspect of staff nurse in coronary care unit of hospitals of Tehran University of Medical Sciences

Zakerimoghadam, Masoumeh *faculty of nursing, Tehran University, Tehran, Islamic Republic of Iran* **Gadyani, Leila** *faculty of nursing, TEHRAN UNIVERSITY, tehran, Islamic Republic of Iran*

objective: identify of effective factors on sleeping, improves sleeping. Methods & Materials: This research is a comparative descriptive study. The population under research was included 50 nurses who were working in CCU wards .information gathering tools was a questionnaires. Descriptive and perceptive statistical methods (such as t-test, ANOVA test) were used. Results: environmental factors such as turned on light, pain, connection to monitoring systems are the important effective factors on sleeping. Conclusion: According to the research results, the most important effective factors on sleeping are "turned on light", "pain", " connection to monitoring systems".

Emotional lexicon literacy as an index of emotional intelligence and a predictor of well-being and adequate social functioning

Zammuner, Vanda *DPSS, University of Padova, Padova, Italy* **Casnici, Marco** *none, University of Padova, Padova, Italy* **Prencipe, Giuseppina** *none, university of padova, Padova, Italy* **Scapin, Federica** *none, University of padova, Padova, Italy* **Zonta, Silvia** *none, University of padova, Padova, Italy* **Galli, Cristina** *none, University of padova, Padova, Italy*

Hypothesis: emotional literacy, indexed by how emotions are lexicalized and expressed in the language, is a component of emotional intelligence. In two studies about 500 Italian subjects, adoles-cents and young adults, performed various literacy tasks–e.g., produce synonyms for both basic and complex emotions, and quantifiers to modify emotion intensity, duration and hedonic tone. The results showed that emotional lexicon literacy is an important skill, a viable partial index of emotional intelligence, significantly related to other emotional intelligence components (e.g., recogniton of facial expressions), and to measures of well-being and adequate social functioning (e.g., life satisfaction, loneliness).

Leadership, group shift and individual attitudes

Zankovsky, Anatoly *Inst. of Psychology, Russian Academy of Sciences, Moscow, Russia*

The effect of leadership on group and individual attitudes was investigated by having various student groups answer modified Bogart social distance scale 1) individually; 2) after group discussion jointly and 3) individually six month later. Results indicated: (1) seventeen of twenty six groups exhibited a significant group shift, the direction of which was determined by leader's attitudes; (2) significant shifts in post hoc individual decisions were determined by the type of leadership executed in the groups during group discussions; (3) in the groups without distinct leadership a compromising effect, in which group members shifted toward each other, were evident. Findings were related to previous research in the area.

The relationship between family flexibility and cohesion with child goal orientation

Zare, Maryam *Dept. Educational Psychology, Shiraz University, Shiraz, Islamic Republic of Iran* **Samani, Syamack** *Educational psychology, Shiraz University, shiraz, Islamic Republic of Iran*

The aim of study was examining the prediction of goal orientation by family flexibility and cohesion. The sample group included 449 girls and boys students selected randomly from high schools of Shiraz. Goal orientation (Elliot, MacGregor, 2001), flexibility (shakeri, 1381) and cohesion (samani, 1381, 2004) scales were used. Cronbach alpha coefficient and internal consistency showed acceptable reliability and validity of the instruments. Results of multiple regression revealed that cohesion was a positive predictor of Mastery approach and Performance approach and a negative predictor of Performance avoidance. Flexibility was a positive predictor of mastery approach and a negative predictor of mastery avoidance and performance avoidance.

The study of the effect of gender and family communication patterns on spouse selection with regard to process-content model

Zare, Maryam *Dept. Educational Psychology, Shiraz University, Shiraz, Islamic Republic of Iran* **Jowkar, Bahram** *Educational psychology, Shiraz University, shiraz, Islamic Republic of Iran* **Samani, Syamack** *Educational psychology, Shiraz University, shiraz, Islamic Republic of Iran*

The aim of study was examining the effect of Gender and family Communication patterns on spouse selection. The sample group included 200 girls and boys students selected by cluster random sampling from Shiraz University. Samani criteria spouse selection and koerner-fitzpatrick Family Communication patterns scales were used. Reliability and validity of instruments were acceptable. Results of tow way ANOVA revealed that consensual and pluralistic patterns have more emphasis on process and there is no significant diffrences in content dimension. Girls have more scores in process and content and both girles and boys have more emphasis on process. Girls and boys were compared in the rate of importance criteria for spouse selection.

The effects of work-family conflict on Telecom employees' job burnout and general health

Zeng, Chuikai School of Management, Shenyang Normal University, Shenyang, People's Republic of China Shi, Kan School of Management, Chinese Academy of Sciences, Beijing, People's Republic of China

To explore the effects of work-family conflict on job burnout and general health?526 telecom employees were assessed by the questionnaire of Work Interference With Family and Family Interference With Work, Maslach Burnout Inventory-General Survey, and General Health Questionaire-12. Mediating regression analysis indicated that work-family conflict and its two components (WIF?-Work-interference-with family & FIW?Family-interference-with-work) were powerful negative predictors of general health; Job burnout was an important mediator between work-family conflict and general health; specifically, emotional exhaustion and cynicism fully mediated the relation between WIF and general health; Emotional exhaustion, cynicism and diminished personal accomplishment fully mediated the relation between FIW and general health.

On the dimensionality and consequences of hardiness: Development and validation of a measure

Zettler, Ingo Inst. für Psychologie, RWTH Aachen, Aachen, Germany Lang, Jessica no affiliation, no affiliation, Aachen, Germany Lang, Jonas W. Industrial and Organizational, Institute of Psychology, RWTH, Aachen, Germany Friedrich, Niklas Industrial and Organizational, Institute of Psychology, RWTH, Aachen, Germany

Previous research has documented the fruitfulness of hardiness (Kobasa, 1979) as an individual difference variable enhancing stress resilience. However, there is an ongoing controversy concerning the dimensionality of hardiness. Building on previous developments, we describe the development of a new hardiness measure. Two studies using German samples (N = 207, N = 134) indicated that the measure has a stable factor structure with one higher-order (global) hardiness factor and more specific lower-order factors. Additionally, we found discriminant validity regarding other personality traits and social facilitation measures as well as criterion-related validity for the hardiness dimensions.

Preschoolers' decisions in a social interactive game

Zhang, Hui Dept. of Psychology, Peking University, Beijing, People's Republic of China Su, Yanjie Department of Psychology, Peking University, Beijing, People's Republic of China

The current study aimed to examine the preschoolers' social decision making. A two-person interactive game was designed to test their decisions, in which the correct choice could only be made by inferring the opponent's mental state and action. 5 out of 18 6-year-old preschoolers firmly made the correct choices, 6 completely lacked the strategy of considering others, and the other 7 chose randomly. The preliminary result suggests that most of the preschoolers could not make a better decision by inferring other's mental state and action, which is so called Theory of Mind.

The moderate effect of high school students' thinking style on the relationship of physics knowledge and physical creativity

Zhang, Jinghuan Phychology, Shandong Normal University, Jinan, People's Republic of China

The moderate effect of thinking style on the relationship of physics knowledge and physical creativity was explored with 287 high school students. The results verified the moderate effect partially. ① Internal style and local style can mediate the relationship of physics knowledge and originality. ② Judicial style, internal style, global style and internal style mediate the relationship of physics knowledge and appropriateness. ③ The mediation of thinking style to physics knowledge and creativity total scores, flexibility and fluency was not found. The results were discussed further.

Research on the name effect of implicit self-esteem in positive and negative situation in China

Zhang, Xiaozhou Cogn. Neuroscience & Learning, National Key Laboratory of, Beijing, People's Republic of China Chen, Chunhui psychology and social behavior, University of California Irvin, Irvine, USA Lu, Furong psychology, state key Laboratory of cognit, Beijing, People's Republic of China Wu, Xiaolong Psychology, Psychology, Beijing, People's Republic of China Ye, Wenhao psychology, psychology, Beijing, People's Republic of China Xu, Ting psychology, psychology, Beijing, People's Republic of China Wang, Yun Psychology, state key laboratory of cognit, Beijing, People's Republic of China

Name effect is that people prefer letters in their names to letters not in their names. It is a robust effect found in West as an index of implicit self-esteem. We investigated this effect in the East for the first time. 12 male and 17 female Chinese undergraduates from Beijing finished Implicit Association Test (IAT) and the name-letter preferences test both in positive and negative conditions. We found name effect with Chinese students. It was more obviously in positive than negative condition, especially for male students, indicating that people, especially man, had stronger self-esteem in positive condition.

The relation of mathematics anxiety, mathematical beliefs and mathematics achievement

Zhang, Xiaolong Education Develop. & Research, Capital Normal University, Beijing, People's Republic of China Zhang, Risheng College of Psychology, Beijing Normal University, Beijing, People's Republic of China Chen, Yinghe College of Psychology, Beijing Normal University, Beijing, People's Republic of China

Objective: To explore the relation among three factors that are math anxiety, mathematical beliefs and mathematical achievement. Methods: This paper revised some scales and measured the participants whose grade varies from grade 1 in junior high school to grade 3 in senior high school by these scales. Conclusion: Mathematics anxiety is a mediator variable which can mediate the relationship between mathematical beliefs and mathematics achievement; Mathematics had relatively direct effect on mathematical beliefs; There exists a bi-directional influence between mathematics achievement and mathematics anxiety; There also exists a bi-directional influence between mathematical beliefs and mathematics anxiety.

Comparison study on marriage views between christian university students and non-christian university students

Zhao, Ameng Qiqihaer Medical College, Qiqihaer, People's Republic of China Cui, Guangcheng Psychiatry Medicine Department, Qiqihaer Medical College, Qiqihaer, People's Republic of China

Objective: Comparing the sameness and difference on marriage views between Christian university students and non-Christian university students. Approach: carrying out questionnaire and individual interviews on 170 university students and comparing and analyzing the test results between Christian students and non-Christian students. Result: there are obvious differences on marriage objective, marriage view and post-marriage habitation status between Christian students and non-Christian students. Conclusion: most university students are cautious of marriages and emphasizing affection. Non-Christian university students are relatively open-minded to marriage, while Christian university students are relatively traditional and conservative.

Effect of group guidance for effective parenting on child-parent communication and rearing attitude

Zhao, Ameng Qiqihaer Medical College, Qiqihaer, People's Republic of China Liu, Xuanwen Children's Culture Institute, Zhejiang Normal University, Jinhua, People's Republic of China

This study took group guidance for effective parenting to discuss parents' changes on child-parent communication and rearing attitude, in order to promote youth growth in accordance with child-parent relationship improvement. 20 parents were selected to take part in training group, another 20 parents to contrast group. All subjects received pretest, posttest and interview. The results showed that it's feasible and effective to put group guidance of parental effect into parent education. It can make a positive change to rearing attitude and improve child-parent relationship.

Time-personality: A health psychological study

Zheng, Yong School of Psychology, Southwest University, Beibei, People's Republic of China

Yong Zheng School of Psychology, Southwest University, Chongqing, China ABSTRACT Objectives: Classify time-personality types in view of mental health, structure an effective assessment system of time-personality and the coping style of health behavior. Methods: University students participated in the multitrait-multimethod matrix study; Results: Dimensions, as present extension, time relatedness and time direction are significant in health psychology. Conclusions: The model of structural relationship between time-personality and health is primarily constituted.

The competency model and its effectiveness on job attitudes of relationship managers of Chinese Commercial Bank

Zheng, Xiaoming School of Management, Tsinghua University, Beijing, People's Republic of China Yu, Haibo School of Management, Beijing Normal University, Beijing, People's Republic of China Wang, Mingjiao School of Management, Tsinghua University, Beijing, People's Republic of China

In order to construct competency model of relationship managers of Chinese commercial banks and explore the relationship between competencies and job attitudes, the data of 1144 were analyzed with exploratory factor analysis (EFA) and confirmatory factor analysis (CFA). The results showed that the competency model of Chinese relationship managers of commercial banks was composed of customer service, social competency, individual cognition and characteristics. The results of hierarchical regression analysis showed that conscientiousness and cooperation positively related to job satisfaction and emotional commitment; conscientiousness negatively related to turnover intention, but information seeking positively related to turnover intention.

An event-related potential study on implicit attitude processes

Zhong, Yiping Department of Psychology, Hunan Normal University, Changsha, People's Republic of China

Event-related potentials (ERPs) were recorded from adult about the affective priming effects during evaluative categorization task in two stimulus onset asynchrony(SOA) conditions, using Chinese trait words as primes and targets. Experiment showed incongruent trials were faster than affectively congruent trials in each SOA condition., and A

N400 in Frontal lobe and central region that larger negative amplitudes were found for incongruent pairs than congruent pairs. The affective priming affect in evaluative paradigm can be explained by attention model of nonconscious affect.

Psychological capital and transformational leadership behavior: The moderating effect of traditionality
Zhong, Lifeng School of Business, Renmin University, Beijing, People's Republic of China Liu, Yuyu School of Business, Renmin University of China\\, Beijing, People's Republic of China
In the current study, we intended to examine the effect of leader's psychological capital on leader's transformational leadership behavior, and the moderating effect of traditional value on the relationship between psychological capital and transformational leadership behavior. With a sample of 121 supervisor-subordinate dyads from China, hierarchical regression analysis results supported our hypotheses. We found that leader's psychological capital was positively associated with his/her transformational leadership behavior. Leader's traditional value attenuated the relationship between psychological capital and transformational leadership behavior in the Chinese setting. Theoretical and practical applications were discussed. Keywords: psychological capital, transformational leadership behavior, traditionality

Psychological capital and employees' work-related outcomes: The moderating effects of locus of control
Zhong, Lifeng School of Business, Renmin University, Beijing, People's Republic of China Liu, Yuyu School of Business, Renmin University of China, Beijing, People's Republic of China
Based on relevant literature review, we argued that psychological capital would be positively related to employees' job performance and organizational citizenship behavior, and the relationship would depend on employees' locus of control. With a sample of 173 supervisor-subordinate dyads from China, hierarchical and moderated regression analysis results demonstrated that employees' psychological capital was positively associated with their job performance and organizational citizenship behavior. Locus of control moderated the relationship between them. That is, internally-controlled employees had much higher levels of job performance and performed much more organizational citizenship behavior than externally-controlled employees. Limitations and implications were discussed. Keywords: psychological capital, job performance, organizational citizenship behavior, locus of control

Wednesday 23rd July 2008

IA-014: Psychological research on traffic safety in China

Helmut Jungermann (Chair)

Zhang, Kan *Beijing, People's Republic of China*
Car accident killed about 100,000 people every year in China with the dramatically increase of number of cars in China. Traffic safety has drew attention of psychologists for more than 10 years. Some research results suggested approached of reducing traffic accident by psychological methods focusing on training of naïve drivers were done in the past years, but with on clear benefits. A new view focused on licensee was proposed and a series of studies either in lab or by simulations, including tests of licensees' personality, awareness of safety, cognitive features, skills of driving, was done to form a systematic testing approach. The validity of the test was studied.

IA-037: Psychology and human rights in MENA Arab countries: Yemen Psychological Association (YPA) experiences

Jan Strelau (Chair)

Kassim Khan, Hassan *Dept. of Psychology, University of Aden, Aden, Yemen*
In recent years Psychologist and their Professional Organizations in MENA Arab countries became more involved in a number long-short term researches and actions projects on human rights and gender equality. The Objectives of the presentation is demonstrate and discuss roles played by Psycho logists in Arab Region Countries on this major issues. Highlighting their contributions in promoting psychological science knowledge in raising public awareness and attaining positive behavioral changes towards human rights issues in general with more focus on women and child rights movements. Based on the accummulated experiences gained and documented by Yemen Psychological Association (1991-2006), the speaker tries retrospectively to present and discuss roles played by Psychologists in the field, pointing out achievements and also and problems to overcome, concluding his presentation with a list of recommendations for futur activities and effective collaborations between National -International Psychological Organzations and UN -International Organizations of concerns with human rights and welfare.

IA-038: Development of self and competence across cultures: A challenge to psychology

Marcus Hasselhorn (Chair)

Kagitcibasi, Cigdem *Dept. of Psychology, KOC University, Istanbul, Turkey*
Psychological theories of human development reflect (Western) individualistic ethos. Cross-cultural developmental research provides us with insights into possible common paths in the development of children and adolescents. Autonomy and relatedness, as basic human needs, need to be considered. Though not recognized sufficiently by traditional psychological theorizing, the 'Autonomous-Related Self' emerges as a healthy model of universal relevance, since it integrates these two basic needs.

Regarding the development of Competence, global urbanization and converging life styles render the development of cognitive and school like skills increasingly adaptive. Psychology of the 21st Century has to rise to the challenge of becoming more relevant globally.

IA-039: Typical and atypical development: A commentary on the role of genes

Grigorenko, Elena L. *Child Study Center, Yale University, New Haven, USA*
In this presentation, Dr. Grigorenko will discuss a number of concepts from the genomic sciences with regard to their role in understanding typical and atypical development. Developmental illustrations will be drawn from both cognitive (e.g., reading and specific reading disability) and social-emotional (e.g., self-regulation and conduct disorder) domains of maturation and functioning.

IA-040: Doing a psychology of the Chinese people: Discoveries while exploring aboard the Emperor's treasure ships

Joachim Funke (Chair)

Bond, Michael Harris *Dept. of Psychology, Chinese Univer. of Hong Kong, Hong Kong, China, People's Republic of : Hong Kong SAR*
I have spent my last 34 years, researching in Hong Kong, an outpost of the Dragon's Court. My hope has been to bring Chinese culture and its manifestations into international psychological discourse. During this cultural collaboration, my Chinese colleagues and I have explored at least four constructs that might otherwise have remained uncharted: ethnic affirmation, the value dimension of morality versus reputation, relationship harmony and maintenance, and the five dimensions constituting social axioms. In so doing, my theorizing about social behavior has been broadened to include culture, and I have been personally transformed, perhaps Sinicized. This presentation describes how.

IA-041: Psychological well-being of gay men and lesbian women

Hospers, Harm J. *Experimental Psychology, University of Maastricht, Maastricht, Netherlands*
Objectives: To provide an overview of research on psychological well-being of gay men and lesbian women. Methods: Review of available literature. Furthermore, data from our qualitative (N=29) and quantitative cohort (N=185) of young gay men who had their coming-out in the preceding year will be presented. Results: Research on gay men and lesbian women shows elevated risks for mental health problems. This was also found in our cohort of young gay men. Conclusions: These results warrant more research in the factors underlying mental health problems among gay men and lesbian women. Opportunities for interventions are discussed.

IA-042: Global developments in psychology and applied psychology

Carola Brücher-Albers (Chair)

Knowles, Michael *Caulfield, Australia*
This paper examines the nature and origins of psychological thought, the development of its scholarly and scientific traditions, the establishment of psychology as a profession, and the rise of applied psychology to meet the needs of the kinds of problems facing contemporary society. It examines, too, the roles that various international, regional and national associations and societies of psychology play in fostering the development of psychology as a science and a profession. Some of the critical challenges facing psychology in its three major forms are also discussed.

IA-043: Cracking the orthographic code

Arthur Jacobs (Chair)

Grainger, Jonathan *Laboratoire de Psychologie, Université d'Aix-Marseille I, Marseille, France*
I will present a theory of orthographic processing that makes a key distinction between a coarse-grained and a fine-grained orthographic code. The coarse-grained code provides a fast-track to semantics by optimizing use of limited visual information to constrain lexical identity. The fine-grained code provides accurate information about letter sequences that is used to generate a prelexical phonological code. The theory accounts for why it is easy to read words with letters that have been jumbled, insernted, or remved, and explains why such effects arise early in the process of word identification relative to effects of foanology.

IA-044: The Lucifer effect and the psychology of evil

Wolfgang Schönpflug (Chair)

Zimbardo, Philip G. *Dept. of Psychology, Stanford University, Stanford, USA*
Why do good people do evil? How does a social psychological analysis add to our understanding of such human transformations? This slide-based presentation explores such questions on a foundation of classic research, including my Stanford Prison Study, and via a virtual visit to the dungeon at Iraq's Abu Ghraib Prison. In expanding the usual limited dispositional analysis to include the power of situations and of the systems that create and maintain them, we come to appreciate the transformative power of the Nazis over German citizens. Heroism is the antidote to evil, and I propose a new Hero Project to enlist ordinary people into becoming heroes-in-waiting.

IA-045: The new goal psychology: This ain't your grandpa's 'motivation'

Hannelore Weber (Chair)

Kruglanski, Arie *Dept. of Psychology, University of Maryland, College Park, USA*
This address describes a new paradigm in the study of human motivation based on a cognitive approach on goal driven phenomena. Whereas in

prior work motivation and cognition were often juxtaposed to one another, I will describe a new scientific movement in social psychology that explores the cognitive aspects of motivation. Exciting new studies demonstrate that goals be primed outside of individuals' awareness, and that they can exert powerful, albeit unconscious, effects on individuals' choices, thoughts and feelings. The new paradigm addresses the continuous motivational changes that people experience as they move through their environments and react to them.

IA-046: The price of 'privilege': Risks among children of affluence

Robert J. Sternberg (Chair)

Luthar, Suniya New York, USA
Growing up in the culture of affluence can connote various psychosocial risks. Family wealth does not automatically confer either wisdom in parenting or equanimity of spirit; whereas children rendered atypical by virtue of parents' education or wealth are privileged in many respects, there is also, clearly, the potential for some non-trivial threats to their well-being. Dr. Luthar will present empirical evidence from her programmatic research showing that upper-middle class children manifest elevated disturbance in several areas – notably substance use, rule-breaking, and anxiety – and will discuss possible reasons for this; she will also present recent data suggesting parallel adjustment problems among mothers in these communities (i.e., among mothers with advanced educational degrees).

IA-047: Perceptual consequences of threat and prejudice: Misperceiving weapons and other dangerous objects

Peter M. Gollwitzer (Chair)

Larsen, Randy Dept. of Psychology, Washington University, St. Louis, USA Bono, Timothy Psychology, Washington University, Washington, USA
Racial priming effects are interpreted as being due to automatic activation of stereotype-consistent associations (e.g., Black Americans associated with guns). Evaluative priming may also play a role, in that racial primes can 1) influence response compatibility, e.g., pre-activate evaluatively congruent response codes, and 2) influence target encoding, e.g., facilitate encoding of evaluatively congruent targets even in non-evaluative tasks. Across three experiments, results show that racial priming paradigms contain elements of evaluative priming (both target encoding and response compatibility). Theories of stereotype activation need to account for the ubiquitous role of affect in biasing responses to racial out-groups.

IA-048: Early language development as related to the acquisition of reading

Lundberg, Ingvar Dept. of Psychology, Göteborg University, Göteborg, Sweden
Early in development infants start to discover statistical patterns in the surrounding language, and the speech sounds are categorized as phonemic segments. Shared intention, gradually expressed as gaze coordination and declarative pointing pave the way for understanding the meaning of words. Later on, language games, and nursery rhymes facilitate the young child's growing awareness of the phonological structure of language, reaching a critical point in the first stage of reading acquisition. I will review some of my longitudinal and training studies indicating the causal direction of the relationship between phonological awareness and success in learning to read.

IA-049: Visual-spatial working memory in the healthy and damaged brain

Lars-Göran Nilsson (Chair)

Logie, Robert Dept. of Psychology, University of Edinburgh, Edinburgh, United Kingdom
Behavioural studies of healthy and brain damaged adults have indicated that separate, domain-specific resources support temporary memory and on-line manipulation of visual appearance, location, and movement sequences. Studies of temporary memory for feature bindings indicate that working memory representations are integrated, not fragmented across separate systems. Other researchers have argued that working memory comprises temporary activation of long-term memory modulated by focused attention. From behavioural studies of intact and impaired VSWM function, including one study with 90,000 participants, I will argue that integrated temporary representations arise from strategic operation of modality specific systems operating largely independently of long-term stored knowledge.

IA-050: Dissecting the skill of speaking

Christiane Spiel (Chair)

Levelt, Willem for Psycholinguistic, Max Planck Institute, Nijmegen, Netherlands
Speaking is our most complex cognitive-motor skill. I will sketch a 'blueprint' of the speaker, consisting of five basic operations. In conceptual preparation speakers select and order conceptual information, whose expression will reveal their communicative intentions. In grammatical encoding speakers retrieve words and fixed expressions which, in appropriate syntactic combinations, encode the prepared conceptual information grammatically. In phonological encoding speakers retrieve for subsequent words the phonological form codes; these are used to incrementally compute the syllabification and prosody of the utterance. In phonetic encoding and ultimate articulation, stored articulatory gestures are retrieved and executed for each successive syllable, a highly context-sensitive process. Finally, speakers monitor the process and self-repair if deemed necessary.

IA-051: An electrophysiological view on using context or not

Gerd Lüer (Chair)

Kutas, Marta Dept. of Cognitive Science, University of California, La Jolla, USA
Psycholinguistic research over the past two few decades has revealed that language comprehension is incremental in nature – each word incorporated into an ongoing representation of a sentence (or discourse) as soon as it is encountered. In fact, we present electrophysiological evidence not just for rapid incremental interpretation of language input but for active prediction. We further explore the incremental interpretation by examining the online processing consequences of quantifiers (few, most), negation (not) and verb aspect (was –ing, was –ed). Our findings militate against the idea that all possible information from a word is fully and completely activated and incorporated.

IA-052: Cerebral asymmetries: The view from the inside

Anke Ehlers (Chair)

Güntürkün, Onur Ruhr-Universität Bochum, Bochum, Germany
Cerebral asymmetry research has long been pursued with the false premise that lateralization is a uniquely human attribute, associated with language. Therefore, asymmetry research is presently

characterized by a detailed functional understanding but a limited knowledge of its neural basis. Meanwhile time is ripe to focus on animal models for insights into the neuronal processes governing lateralized function. I will show in the asymmetrically organized visual system of birds how minute left-right stimulation differences during ontogeny create functional asymmetries of the developing brain. I then will present evidence for minor physiological left-right-differences that result in major asymmetries of cognitive function.

IA-053: Groups as adaptive devices: Free-rider problems, the wisdom of crowds, and evolutionary games

Peter M. Gollwitzer (Chair)

Kameda, Tatsuya Sapporo, Japan
The behavioral ecology literature has shown that adaptive benefits accrued from group life include the reduction of predation risk, increased efficiency in the acquisition of food and other vital resources, opportunities for social learning, etc. These findings suggest that, despite inherent conflicts of interest among members, groups consequentially serve as adaptive devices for individual survival in natural environments. Although psychological research on small groups has addressed conceptually parallel issues including the efficiency of group performance, the linkage to behavioral ecology has never been explicit. This talk explores the applicability of behavioral ecological theory in the study of human group behavior.

IA-054: Process models for implicit measures of attitudes

James Georgas (Chair)

Klauer, Karl Christoph Freiburg, Germany
Diffusion models are applied to impliciit measures of attitudes, in particular to the so-called Implicit Association Test (IAT). Three process components are thereby disentangled: 1) Ease and speed of information accumulation, 2) speed-accuracy settings, and 3) nondecision components of processing. In several studies, method variance in the IAT is shown to map on individual differences in speed-accuracy trade-offs, whereas construct-specific variance (i.e., the variance that is to be measured) is mapped on the ease and speed of information accumulation. Implications of these dissociations for process theories of the IAT and for applications are discussed.

IA-055: Social interactions: Conceptual reflections and experimental approach

Ribes Inesta, Emilio Centro de Estudios, Universidad de Guadalajara, Guadalajara, Mexico
Contrary to current trends in evolutionary psychology, I assume that social behavior es exclusive of humans. Truly social behavior necessarily involves labor division as well as postponed exchange of labor outomes, possible because of language. Three functional dimensions frame social behavior interactions: power, exchange, and sanction. A theoretical model is proposed to analyze social behavior in terms of interactions framed by different institutional contingencies. An experimental preparation has been designed to evaluate different variables which influence the occurrence of social interactions. Experimental data are shown to support this approach, including some extensions modeling social systems.

IA-056: Motor cognition: What actions tell the self

Frank Rösler (Chair)

Jeannerod, Marc Lyon, France
Self-recognition is far from trivial: It depends upon specific signals, from sensory as well as from central origin. Experiments where self-recognition becomes ambiguous will be used. Two levels of self-recognition, an automatic action identification, and a conscious sense of agency, which both rely on the congruence of the action-related signals, will be identified. The automatic level controls and adapts actions to their goal, whereas the conscious level provides information about the author's intentions. These levels are dissociated in schizophrenic patients. Their automatic self-identification is functional, whereas their sense of agency is impaired: the symptoms of the disease testify to the inability of schizophrenic patients to attribute their own thoughts and actions to themselves.

IUPsyS-007: History of applied psychology in different countries

Helio Carpintero, Bernardo Colorado-Luna (chair)
Applied psychology in the 20th century has had an extraordinary growth, employing new techniques and concepts in order to face an endless variety of social and personal problems. Contributions to this symposium will give an insight of such richness and variety of technical research works, both in European and Latin-American countries, as an example of the complexity of the history of this psychological field.

Psychology facing terrorist attack at Madrid (Spain) the 11-04-2007

Carpintero, Helio Psicol. Basica II, Universidad Complutense, Madrid, Spain
A terrorist attack took place on the 11-M- 2004 in Madrid (Spain). Many people were killed and injured, when bombs exploded in three local trains early in the morning in Madrid. Psychological attention was immediately offered by psychologists, and a vast plan of help was carried out, giving support to victims, families and people suffering from panic and anxiety attacks. Many post-hoc studies have proved the variety of psychopathological effects that followed the catastrophe, and the efficacy of interventions. This had a social echo and positive evaluation of the psychologists' work. Applied psychology, in such cases, add large value to the social acknowledgment attributed to their professionals.

Promoting school achievement and the renewal of teaching methods and educational policies: Recent developments in Portuguese educational psychology

Paixão, Maria Paula Dept. of Psychology, University of Coimbra, Coimbra, Portugal
Contributing to the erradication of school under-achievement continues to be one of the most important themes in Educational Psychology, both at a theoretical and at a pratical level. Several research and intervention programmes were thus developped in Portugal during the second half of the 20th century, namely those funded by the Foundation for Science and Technology that were carried out under our supervision at the University of Coimbra. In line with our main results, promoting strategies of learning motivation, the renewal of teaching methods and, mainly, new directions for educational policies are the main roots proposed for the required developments in this area.

Studies on fatigue: Contributions to psychotechnology in Argentina

Klappenbach, Hugo Facultad de Ciencias Humanas, Universidad Nacional, San Luis, Argentina
The paper analyzes the reception in Argentina of fatigue's research, produced both in Europe and United States (Dockeray, 1920; Strong, 1913, 1914, Seashore, 1904; Squire, 1903; Thorndike, 1900a, 1900b, 1912; Viteles, 1926; Whiting & English, 1923; Yoakum, 1909). Then, original research on fatigue in Argentina are examined, specially the contributions of Alfredo Palacios and Horacio Rimoldi. Those works are analyzed in the context of the development of psychotechics, which strongly increased in the whole country and which reached its majors contributions in the decade of 1940.

Applied psychology: Who was and is supposed to apply it?

Gundlach, Horst Instit. Gesch. der Psychologie, Universität Passau, Passau, Germany
Today, it is understood worldwide, that psychology is applied by psychologists. This concept is, however, hardly one hundred years old, and the beginnings of applied psychology are definitively older. When the concept of an applied psychology originated, it was understood that psychology be applied by members of many different occupations, by judges, by physicians, by teachers, and by others whose main professional training was not in psychology. This concept of applied psychology still exists today, although it is overshadowed by the concept of the professional psychologist. This paper inspects the roots of this relatively new and at first surprising concept.

Reception and development of the psychotechnic applied to the education in the post-revolutionary Mexico (1920-1928) (Part I)

Sanchez Sosa, Juan Jose Dept. of Psychology, UNAM Nat. Auton. University, Mexico City, Mexico
Valderrama, Pablo Escuela de Psicologia, Universidad Latinoamericana, Mexico City, Mexico Colorado-Luna, Bernardo Dept. de Psicologia, UNAM Univ. Nat. Autonoma, Mexico City, Mexico
Applied psychology in Mexico has a long past but a relatively recent history. Historical accounts point out that, professional applied psychology originated in academic settings such as universities and teaching health institutions, but quickly spread to service settings. Early services included "psycho-technicians" who usually did assessment in schools, work environments, correctional facilities and judiciary cabinets. After the early sixties nearly every sphere of human functioning showed the influence of service-providing psychologists whose training is closer to the researcher-practitioner tradition. The fastest growing areas of applications in this context include health service settings and large scale social assessment of programs.

Reception and development of the psychotechnic applied to the education in the post revolutionary Mexico (1920 - 1928) (Part II)

Valderrama, Pablo Escuela de Psicologia, Universidad Latinoamericana, Mexico City, Mexico
Some landmarks of the origin of the psychothecnic are described in the decade of the 20th: the adaptation of the test of intelligence of Binet; the formation of the first specialists in the National University; the collaboration with the University of California to define the Mexican boy's intelligence; the knowledge of the Mexican native's mentality, to determine their capacity of adaptation to the modern nation "mestiza"; the application of psychological tests to diagnose students again entrance to institutions of superior education and the description of the actors, national and foreign that participated in this movement of educational renovation

IUPsyS-009: Human spatial cognition: New avenues of research

Michel Denis (chair)
The cognitive processes underlying navigation and wayfinding are at the core of an increasing number of research programs. Models of spatial cognition have to accommodate the variety of forms of spatial knowledge, as well as the variety of their modes of acquisition and modes of communication. The symposium provides up-to-date information on several important issues of this domain, as currently investigated by cognitive psychology and neuroscience.

Human spatial memory for object location

Janzen, Gabriele for Cognitive Neuroimaging, F.C. Donders Centre, Nijmegen, Netherlands
People spend a great deal of their time navigating through their environment. To be able to find our way home, we need to retrieve spatial information from memory. With different functional Magnetic Resonance Imaging studies, we showed that the human brain automatically organises spatial information by dissociating between places carrying information necessary for wayfinding, and others. Objects occurring at navigationally relevant locations are stored in the parahippocampal gyrus, a region involved in coding object-place associations. The selective neural marking for navigationally relevant objects is rapidly induced and long lasting. This automatic neural mechanism can provide the basis for successful wayfinding.

Sensorimotor interference in spatial reasoning

Avraamides, Marios Dept. of Psychology, University of Cyprus, Nicosia, Cyprus Kelly, Jonathan W.
Spatial cognition studies often require participants to localize objects from different imagined perspectives within a remembered spatial scene. In a series of studies using this paradigm, we found evidence for the presence of sensorimotor interference during the test phase. Our experiments have investigated the conditions under which such interference occurs. Among others, we have contrasted reasoning about immediate vs. remote scenes, and we have examined the effect of verbal instructions and the encoding modality (visual perception vs. language). Our findings will be discussed in the context of a spatial cognition model accounting for sensorimotor interference.

Space and language: How spatial are spatial descriptions?

Pazzaglia, Francesca General Psychology, University of Padua, Padova, Italy
Are visuo-spatial working memory (VSWM) and spatial skills involved in the comprehension and memorisation of spatial descriptions and route directions? The first part of the paper reviews the main results of a series of experiments where a dual-task paradigm is used to investigate the role of VSWM in the encoding and/or retrieval of spatial descriptions. The second part examines the role played by individual differences in VSWM; reading comprehension; and mental visualisation in the memorisation of route and survey descriptions. The results are discussed with reference to theories on spatial text processing, spatial language, and working memory.

Individual differences in object versus spatial mental imagery: The neural mechanisms and applications

Kozhevnikov, Maria Department of Psychology, George Mason University, Fairfax, VA, USA
The visual system processes appearance properties (such as shape and color) and spatial properties (such as location and spatial relations) via separate

subsystems. Using behavioral and neuroimaging data, I will present evidence that such dissociation also exists in individual differences in imagery. That is, some individuals are adept at constructing vivid images of objects but have difficulty representing spatial relations (object visualizers), whereas others are adept at representing spatial relations but have difficulty constructing vivid images (spatial visualizers). Additionally, I will present data showing that such individual differences in object versus spatial imagery affect more complex activities, such as learning and problem solving in science and artistic performance.

Blind people can construct spatial mental models from complex spatial descriptions

Noordzij, Matthijs F.C. Donders Centre, Radboud University Nijmegen, Nijmegen, Netherlands
There is now substantial evidence that visual experience is not an essential feature in the development of spatial representations. However, it remains an open question whether blind people can construct a spatial model from complex spatial descriptions. In our experiments, early blind, late blind and sighted individuals listened to realistic spatial descriptions. We found evidence that both sighted and blind people formed spatial models on the basis of these descriptions. Interestingly, blind people actually performed better than sighted people when the spatial description had a local, route perspective, whereas sighted people performed better when the spatial description had a global, survey perspective.

IS-079: Health behavior change interventions: How do they work?

Aleksandra Luszczynska (chair)
The symposium presents examples of effective health behaviour change interventions. Next, interventions based on a health behaviour change theory (Health Belief Model) are discussed, followed by a comparison of interventions based on different theoretical approaches and a review aimed at evaluating the effects of behaviour change techniques. Finally, formal characteristics of effective obesity treatment programs are discussed.

Promoting a low-fat diet in overweight individuals: Does cognitive functioning moderate the effects of a planning intervention?

Scholz, Urte Inst. für Psychologie, Universität Zürich, Zürich, Switzerland *Kliegel, Matthias* Psychology, Technical University Dresden, Dresden, Germany
Objective: Cognitive functioning is negatively associated with overweight. Planning interventions have been shown to promote health behaviour change. This study examines whether planning interventions are effective independent of individuals' cognitive functioning. Method: At baseline cognitive functioning and nutrition were assessed of 60 controls and 60 planning group participants (sample mean BMI = 31.49; SD = 4.49), nutrition was assessed again four and six months later. Results: The effects of a planning intervention on low-fat diet were not moderated by cognitive functioning. Conclusions: Planning interventions provide an effective means for changing even complex health behaviours independent of cognitive functioning of individuals.

Does the health belief model provide a good theoretical basis for effective behaviour change interventions?

Abraham, Charles Dept. of Psychology, University of Sussex, Brighton, United Kingdom *Sibley, Elissa* Dept. of Psychology, University of Sussex, Brighton, United Kingdom
Objectives: To assess the effectiveness of behaviour change interventions based on the health belief model (HBM). Methods: A systematic review and meta analysis were conducted. Results: Of 441

retrieved abstracts, 36 studies met the inclusion criteria. After removal of outliers, d values ranged from .41 – 1.33 with an overall average, weighted small-to-medium effect size of d=.42. Sources of heterogeneity were explored, including the extent to which interventions were HBM- based. Conclusion: HBM-based interventions have proved to be effective but there is considerable variation in the extent to which interventions reflect the theory.

Are interventions based on theory more effective than those that are not? Development of a method and a synthesis of evidence

Michie, Susan Dept. of Psychology, University College London, London, United Kingdom *Prestwich, Andrew* Psychological Sciences, University of Leeds, London, United Kingdom
Objectives To investigate the associations between theories informing behaviour change interventions, intervention content and impact. Methods Reliable coding frames were developed to assess intervention content and extent of theory application in a systematic review of self-regulation interventions to increase physical activity and/or healthy eating. Results Of the 77% theory-based interventions, there was no association between theory type and intervention content (techniques used). Only 46% studies measured theory-relevant constructs, 42% discussed results in relation to theory and 7% adequately linked intervention techniques to theory. Conclusions Progress in applying theory to intervention development and evaluation is vital for improving behaviour change interventions.

Does changing attitudes, norms, or self-efficacy cause health behaviour change?

Sheeran, Paschal Dept. of Psychology, University of Sheffield, Sheffield, United Kingdom *Armitage, Christopher* Department of Psychology, University of Sheffield, Sheffield, United Kingdom *Mann, Eleanor* Department of Psychology, King's College London, London, United Kingdom *Abraham, Charles* Department of Psychology, University of Sussex, Sheffield, United Kingdom
Health behaviour theories assume that changing attitudes, norms, self-efficacy or intentions will cause changes in health behaviour. The present research tests this assumption by meta-analysing experimental studies that (a) randomly assigned participants to conditions, (b) changed respective cognitions, and (c) asessed changes in subsequent behaviour. Literature searches obtained 214 studies that met the inclusion criteria for the review. Findings indicated that changing attitude, norms, and self-efficacy had effects of approximately medium magnitude on behaviour change. Behaviour change techniques, but not the theoretical basis of the intervention, made an important difference to the effect sizes obtained for behaviour.

Formal characteristics of effective interventions: A systematic review of obesity treatment programs for adults

Luszczynska, Aleksandra Dept. of Psychology, Warsaw School Soc. Psychology, Warsaw, Poland
Objectives: The study tests if the effects of weight loss intervention depend on participants features (e.g., age), intervention features (e.g., duration, number of session, number of targets, individual/group format), and design features (e.g., recruitment method).Methods: The review incorporated trials testing the effectiveness of psychosocial interventions reporting body weight as the main outcome. Results: Larger effects were observed for programs that solely targeted weight control versus other health behaviours, programs evaluated in pilot trials, and programs wherein participants must have self-selected into the intervention. Conclusions: Besides the presence of any theoretical background, the effectiveness of obesity treatment depends on formal characteristics.

IS-080: The design and results of "anti-stress programme" implemented within the cardiovascular disease (CVD) preventive activities (2004-2007)

Miloslav Solc (chair)
The "anti-stress programme" was designed and implemented within the framework of CVD preventive activities. About 60 - 70 individuals were examined every year using a set of psychological (type of behaviour, life events in the past 12 months, daily events in the past month, level of resilience - hardiness), physiological (heart rate variability) and biochemical (total cholesterol, HDL and LDL cholesterol, triacylglycerides, glycemia) variables, as well as using basic demographic data and data from working processes. The same sets of data were used also for intervention. The study was implemented within the project funded by the Grant Agency of the Czech Republic Nr. 406/06/0747.

IS-081: The representation of abstract words

Manuel Carreiras (chair)
The goal of the symposium is to understand how we represent abstract words (e.g., liberty, justice, idea). The five talks will cover different aspects of this uniquely human faculty: a) how abstract works can be learnt and represented from a computational perspective; b) how abstract words can be grounded in perception and action; c) the neural substrate of abstractness; c) evidence from patients and experimental evidence showing dissociations on the representation of concrete and abstract words. A discussion covering the five talks will follow.

The joint contribution of experience and language in shaping meaning representations

Andrews, Mark Dept. of Psychology, University College of London, London, United Kingdom
Evidence suggests that concrete meanings are grounded into our experience (embodiment). However, abstract meanings may be different, as these words may be learnt via language. To test the contribution of experience and language to semantics, we developed Bayesian models that extract statistical patterns from experience-only; language-only or both sources of data combined and we found that the combined model provides best fit to semantic effects. We further developed norms concerning "mode of acquisition" (MoA) tapping into whether words are learnt primarily via experience or language and we found that this variable has good predictive power.

Language processing modulates the activity of the motor system

Buccino, Giovanni Dipt. di Neuroscienze, Università deg. Studi di Parma, Parma, Italy
According to the "embodied language" approach, language processing is mediated by the same neural substrates involved in perception and action. Recent data coming from behavioural, neuroimaging and neurophysiological experiments show that during listening to or reading sentences expressing actions done with the hand, the mouth or the foot, the activity of different sectors of the motor system, overlapping those involved during the actual execution of those same actions, is modulated. Interestingly it has been recently shown that this modulation also occurs during processing language material related to abstract content, thus supporting the idea that even abstract concepts are grounded.

Negation in the brain: Modulating concrete and abstract semantic representations

Cappa, Stefano Dept. of Neurology, Vita-Salute San Raffaele, Milano, Italy *Moro, Andrea* Dept. of Neuroscience, Vita-Salute San Raffaele, Milano, Italy *Marco, Tettamanti* Dept. of Neuroscience, Vita-Salute San Raffaele, Milano, Italy

Sentential negation is a universal feature of languages. In Tettamanti et al (2005) action sentences activated the same action representation as real actions, whereas abstract sentences were associated with posterior cingulate cortex activation. In this fMRI experiment, participants heard sentences of different polarity (affirmative/negation) and concreteness (action-related/abstract). Negation was associated with deactivation of pallido-cortical areas. Negative action-related sentences led to reduction of activations and connection strength within left-hemispheric fronto-parieto-temporal areas. For negative abstract sentences, there was deactivation of posterior cingulate cortex. Negation appears to offer a new perspective on the link between human language and our representation of the world.

Contrasting effects of semantic association and similarity in processing

Crutch, Sebastian Dementia Research Centre, University College of London, London, United Kingdom *Warrington, Elizabeth* Dementia Research Centre, University College of London, London, United Kingdom

A series of experiments are reported which investigate the abstract and concrete word processing abilities of healthy individuals and patients with refractory access dysphasia, deep-phonological dyslexia or deep dyslexia. It is demonstrated that concrete word processing is affected more by semantic similarity than semantic association, whereas abstract word processing is affected more by semantic association than semantic similarity. These contrasting effects of semantic similarity and association are observed in comprehension, reading and odd-one-out judgement tasks. The data provide converging evidence supporting the hypothesis that concrete and abstract concepts are supported by qualitatively different representational frameworks.

Associative and semantic priming: Different findings for abstract and concrete words

Müller, Oliver Psicología Cognitiva, Facultad de Psicología, La Laguna, Spain *Avilés, Alberto* Psicología Cognitiva, University of La Laguna, Tenerife, Spain *Duñabeitia, Jon Andoni* Psicología Cognitiva, University of La Laguna, Tenerife, Spain *Carreiras, Manuel* Psicología Cognitiva, University of La Laguna, Tenerife, Spain

We assessed the semantic organization of abstract and concrete words in a series of priming experiments, contrasting associative with semantic relatedness and varying stimulus-onset asynchrony (SOA). Lexical decision times for abstract words showed only associative priming, starting at SOA 50. Concrete words displayed associative and semantic priming, starting at SOA 100 and 250, respectively. In an event-related potentials experiment (ERP), with associative primes and an SOA of 50, concrete and abstract words both showed an ERP relatedness effect, but with a different scalp distribution. This indicates that associative and semantic relations play a different role for abstract and concrete words.

IS-082: Empirical tests of contemporary utility theories

Anthony A.J. Marley (chair)

A revolution occurred in the 1990s in the development and testing of utility theories, which lead to work that went beyond classic representations such as subjective expected utility. The new work included rank- and sign-dependent utility theories, with cumulative prospect theory an important special case. This symposium presents contemporary work that builds on that framework, including; learning under uncertainty; tests of critical properties of models; probabilistic extensions; the timing of the resolution of uncertainty; and fitting the data of individual decision makers.

"Decisions from Experience" versus "Decisions from Description" under prospect theory: An experimental investigation

Abdellaoui, Mohammed Laboratoire GRID, UMR CNRS-ENSAM, Cachan, France

According to Prospect Theory, decision makers confronted with "description-based" choices under risk overweight low probabilities and underweight middle and high probabilities. Hertwig, Barron, Weber and Erev (2004) report however qualitative experimental results suggesting that this subjective treatment of uncertainty does not hold for "experience-based" decisions, in which decision makers must learn probability distributions from sampling. Our paper reports experimental results based on individual elicitation of Prospect Theory for gains and losses from "description-based" and "experience-based" choice. Despite a few significant discrepancies detected between "description-based" and "experience-based" contexts, our results do not confirm the apparent reversals claimed by Hertwig et al.

Testing critical properties that distinguish descriptive models

Birnbaum, Michael Dept. of Psychology, California State University, Fullerton, USA

Critical properties are theorems that can be deduced from at least one descriptive theory but which do not follow from all of the theories to be compared. If the consequences of the theorem can be falsified, theories that imply those consequences are falsified. In order to design tests, it is helpful to fit a rival theory to previous data to predict where to find new violations of a given theory. This research tactic is illustrated with tests between cumulative prospect theory and Birnbaum's transfer of attention exchange (TAX) model, and with tests between the priority heuristic and the TAX model.

Models of stochastic choice and decision theories: Why both are important for analtyzing decisicians

Blavatskky, Pavlo Inst. for Empirical Research, Universität Zürich, Zürich, Switzerland

This paper compares different combinations of decision theories and models of stochastic choice. We select seven popular decision theories and embed each theory in five models of stochastic choice including tremble, Fechner and random utility models. We find that the estimated parameters of decision theories differ significantly when theories are combined with different models. Depending on the selected model of stochastic choice we obtain different rankings of decision theories with regard to their goodness of fit to the data. The fit of all analyzed decision theories improves significantly when they are embedded in a Fechner model of heteroscedastic truncated errors.

Measuring the impact of uncertainty resolution

Diecidue, Enrico Dept. of Decision Sciences, INSEAD, Fontainebleau Cedex, France

In most real decisions a considerable time between choice and resolution of uncertainty may occur. Individuals may have preferences between gambles that have the same probability distribution over outcomes if they differ in the timing of resolution of uncertainty. These preferences have received relatively little attention in utility theory and decision under uncertainty. We propose an individual elicitation of utility and probability weighting function to understand and measure the impact of delayed resolution of uncertainty. We observed significant differences in probability weighting functions for immediate and delayed resolution of uncertainty.

Data selection for fitting utility theories: Laying the foundations for the cognitive psychometrics of risk

Stott, Henry Dept. of Psychology, University College London, London, United Kingdom

Model fitting in psychology needs to be at the level of individual participants' data in order to avoid misleading single-agent assumptions. This limitation places additional emphasis on experimental data quality. Against this backdrop, the presentation explores methods for optimal stimuli selection in the risky choice paradigm. This is achieved by adopting a parameter space perspective of the stimuli. Fitting Cumulative Prospect Theory to the resultant data shows how this method can be used to decrease modeling errors by, for example, reducing parameter interactions. Various extensions to the technique and the possibility of testing Utility Theories for criterion validity are discussed.

Empirical tests of contemporary utility theories

Marley, Anthony A.J. Dept. of Psychology, University of Victoria, Victoria, Canada

A revolution occurred in the 1990s in the development and testing of utility theories, which lead to work that went beyond classic representations such as subjective expected utility. The new work included rank- and sign-dependent utility theories, with cumulative prospect theory an important special case. This symposium presents contemporary work that builds on that framework, including; learning under uncertainty; tests of critical properties of models; probabilistic extensions; the timing of the resolution of uncertainty; and fitting the data of individual decision makers.

IS-083: From conflict monitoring to control inertia

Pio Tudela (chair)

The view of a unitary and general cognitive control system has been under scrutiny in recent years. In particular, assumptions related to the unity and generality of the system have been seriously challenged. In the present symposium a sample of the current research will be offered. The first three speakers will present experimental evidence suggesting a modular architecture of cognitive control where separate control processes operate and some of them are recruited in a context-sensitive manner. The neural mechanisms associated to particular processes of control will be approached by the last two speakers.

When item specific control bypasses the need for a global control mechanism

Blais, Chris H.Wills Neuroscience Institute, University of California, Berkeley, USA

How control is exerted over the myriad of cognitive operations we have at our disposal and the implementation of that control in the brain has become a major focus for researchers. A popular index of this form of cognitive control is the proportion congruent effect in the Stroop task where the magnitude of the Stroop effect increases as the proportion of congruent trials increases. We provide evidence this effect is driven by an item specific mechanism, not by a global "attend to the word when it helps" mechanism. The implications of this result on the conflict monitoring hypothesis are discussed.

Dissociating between sustained, transient and stimulus driven cognitive control

Funes, Maria Jesús Dept. Experimental Psychology, University of Granada, Granada, Spain *Lupiáñez, Juan* Dept. Experimental Psychology, University of Granada, Granada, Spain *Humphreys, Glyn* Behavioural Brain Sciences, University of Birmingham, Birmingham, United Kingdom

We present relevant dissociations between Gratton and Proportion Congruent effects regarding their ability to generalize across variations in conflict type. We used a combined-conflict paradigm and manipulated the proportion of congruent-to-incongruent trials for one conflict type but not the other. We found that conflict adaptation was highly specific to the type of conflict solved on the previous trial. By contrary, the effect of conflict context generalized across conflict types. This finding suggests the existence of two separate control systems, one transient and responsible of online regulation, and the other sustained and responsible of conflict context effects

Context-sensitive control over attentional orienting

Milliken, Bruce Dept. of Psychology, McMaster University, Hamilton, ON, Canada *Crump, Matthew* Dept. of Psychology, Vanderbilt University, Nashville, USA

Cognitive control is widely conceived as guided by intentional processes engaged in the service of goal-directed behavior. By this view, cognitive control processes can serve a monitoring function over automatic, context-sensitive memory retrieval processes. Here, we suggest that cognitive control itself can be imparted through memory retrieval. Our research strategy introduces a contingency between a task-irrelevant contextual dimension (e.g., spatial location) and the need for cognitive control (e.g., high versus low proportion congruent in a filtering task). Results suggest that distraction from irrelevant stimulus dimensions can indeed vary as a function of context-sensitive retrieval processes cued by the stimulus itself.

Fractionating executive control: Anticipating and reacting to conflict modulates event-related potentials linked to cognitive control differently

Correa, Angel Dept. Experimental Psychology, University of Granada, Granada, Spain *Rao, Anling* Dept. Experimental Psychology, University of Oxford, Oxford, United Kingdom *Nobre, Anna* Dept. Experimental Psychology, University of Oxford, Oxford, United Kingdom

Does our brain comprise a single executive control mechanism, which is commonly triggered when anticipating conflict (proactive control) and reacting to conflict (reactive control)? Event-related potentials associated with conflict detection (N2) were measured during a cued flanker task, and compared for both proactive and reactive control. Proactive control involved anticipating conflict through predictive cues. Reactive control involved experiencing conflict in previous trials (sequential effects). The results showed that proactive control reduced the N2 latency, whereas reactive control attenuated the N2 amplitude over right frontal electrodes. These findings suggest that proactive and reactive control involve partly dissociable neural mechanisms.

Top-down task pre-configuration

Ruz, Maria Dept. Experimental Psychology, University of Oxford, Oxford, United Kingdom *Nobre, Anna C.* Dept. Experimental Psychology, University of Oxford, Oxford, United Kingdom

We investigated the neural mechanisms that prepare for future task requirements. Participants were cued to perform different tasks with words. EEG results showed that cues generated top-down activations that were dissociable across conditions.

Such preparatory states were different depending of whether they required or not a switch from the previous task. fMRI data showed that cues engaged brain areas which were also activated during specific task performance. All this suggests that predictive information settles the brain into highly specific preparatory states, which seems to be mediated by the pre-activation of brain regions that will support subsequent task performance.

IS-084: Computational models of decision making

David Shanks, Peter Juslin (chair)

Although much is known about the psychology of decision making, the development of precise computational models of decision behaviour has only recently begun to make a significant impact in the field. This symposium brings together internationally-renowned researchers with a common interest in developing such models.

A cognitive theory of how people learn to select strategies

Rieskamp, Jörg Max-Planck-Institut, Berlin, Germany

It has been widely assumed that people possess a strategy repertoire for inferences. The strategy selection learning theory specifies how people select strategies from this repertoire (Rieskamp, 2006, JEP:LMC, 32). The theory holds that individuals select strategies proportional to their subjective expectations of how well the strategies solve particular problems and the expectations are updated by reinforcement learning. The theory is compared to a connectionist network, whose weights are modified by error correction learning. Both theories were tested against each other experimentally and the strategy selection learning theory was best in describing the observed learning processes.

Decisions in a changing environment

Speekenbrink, Maarten Dept. of Psychology, University College London, London, United Kingdom *Shanks, David* London, United Kingdom

When learning to make decisions, we must infer how the outcome of our actions depends on the state of the environment. Typically, research investigating decision learning has used stationary environments, in which this dependence is invariant over time. However, as many decision environments are subject to continuous change, learning may be geared towards non-stationarity. We present research which shows participants quickly adapt to changes in the environmental structure, and discuss formal models of how they might do so.

When a learning theory predicts the wrong response: Error of the model or error of the learner?

Meeter, Maarten Dept. of Psychology, University of Amsterdam, Amsterdam, Netherlands

In probabilistic categorization tasks various cues are probabilistically (but not perfectly) predictive of class membership. There are two alternative conceptualizations of learning in such tasks: as rule-based learning, or as incremental learning. Analysis methods based on these conceptualizations can be used to predict responses of categorizers from their responses on preceding trials. They predict responses about equally well, but both suggest that on many trials the response of the categorizer is a toss-up. Here, we investigate whether categorizers on such trials really produce essentially random responses, or whether there are regularities that are not yet captured by learning theories.

Optimal decision making in the cortico-basal-ganglia circuit

Bogacz, Rafal Dept. of Computer Science, University of Bristol, Bristol, United Kingdom

Almost a half century ago, it has been proposed that during simple choice between two alternatives the brain performs a statistically optimal test. This theory, currently known as the diffusion model, describes very well reaction times and accuracies in two alternative choice tasks. It has been recently proposed that the circuit involving the cortex and the basal ganglia performs statistically optimal choice between multiple alternatives. This model helps understand current data and generates experimental predictions concerning both neuro-biology and behaviour. Furthermore, it supplies a bridge between the two disciplines, as it offers a possible neural implementation for the diffusion model.

Sequential and capacity constrained: Taking the constraints on controlled thought seriously

Juslin, Peter Dept. of Psychology, Uppsala University, Uppsala, Sweden

A well-known distinction in cognitive psychology refers to controlled versus automatic cognitive processes. While the capacity constraints of controlled cognitive processing has served as a general rationale for several influential research programs on simplifying heuristics in research on judgment and decision making, detailed explorations of the consequences of these capacity constraints remain rather unusual. In this presentation, I will discuss the consequences of these capacity constraints on controlled cognitive processing for the division of labor between different sorts of knowledge in multiple-cue judgment tasks, but I also illustrate how they provide alternative explanations of several classical phenomena in the heuristics and biases literature, like the conjunction fallacy and base-rate neglect.

IS-085: Psychological approaches to political conflicts

Janusz Reykowski (chair)

The papers in this symposium present empirical research concerning the socio-psychological factors that might contribute to the increase or decrease the destructive political conflicts. Kossowska et al. describe the role of personality factors (RWA and SDO) and their interaction with emotional processes (fear, anger, sadness). Golec et all. discuss the impact of religious orientations and cultural ethno-centrism while Peaz et al. the role of apology for wrong doings. Reykowski describes the socio-psychological mechanisms facilitating the processes of seeking agreements in groups in spite of major conflict of interests or values.

Physiological antecedents of intergroup conflict: Impact of submissive vs. dominant orientation and emotions on outgroup attitudes

Kossowska, Malgorzata Inst. of Psychology, Jagiellonian University, Kraków, Poland *Bukowski, Marcin* Inst. of Psychology, Jagiellonian University, Kraków, Poland *Van Hiel, Alain* Department of Psychology, Ghent University, Ghent, Belgium

Perception of outgroup members is usually seen as important determinants of conflict development and conflict escalation. In the present study we particularly focus on role of negative emotions in the RWA and SDO based prejudice. It is assumed that these emotions should interact with RWA and SDO in different ways and therefore should have different effects on the level of prejudice. In line with recent work, we also expected that these interaction effects would depend on the perceived status of the outgroups. The results of the research will be discussed due to possible ways of conflict reduction.

Religion, ethnocentrism and intergroup hostility intimes of existential threat

Golec de Zavala, Agnieszka Middlesex University, Middlesex, United Kingdom Cichocka, Aleksandra Faculty of Psychology, Warsaw University, Warsaw, Poland

In a number of studies, conducted in different countries (Poland, the U.S. and Iran), we examine the effects of mortality salience on support for international aggression in the context of terrorist threat, with the moderating effects of ethnocentrism and individual religiosity. The belief in the superiority of the European culture is shown to strengthened the inter-group negativity in the context of the Western-Arab world conflict. In mortality salience conditions, people with ethnocentric beliefs support war on terrorism and the Arab world. Moreover, the quest religiosity (Batson, et al, 1986) is shown to mitigate the inter-group negativity in mortality salience conditions.

Apologies as repentance rituals, forgiveness and reconciliation in the case of countries with internal collective violence

Paez, Dario Dept. of Social Psychology, University of Basque Country, San Sebastian, Spain

Societal data was analyzed on the effects of Truth an Reconciliation Commissions on indexes of social and emotional climate. A two (presence of apologies versus absence) between subjects design of independent measures was used. We tested the hypothesis that the salience of apologies, when compared to the absence of them, reinforced national identification, agreement with new reparatory behaviours, higher acceptance of in-group participation in past negative behaviours, agreement with forgiveness as well as decreasing of minimization of frequency of collective violence, reframing of misdeeds and acceptance of the typicality of members involved in collective violence. Also, salience of apologies was supposed to reinforce universal values, social cohesion and a better emotional climate as well as collective guilt and shame. Collective and experimental findings are discussed in relation to the role of rituals of expiation, repentance and collective guilt on the political processes of reconciliation.

Can deliberative procedures suppress antagonistic tendencies in groups?

Reykowski, Janusz Inst. of Psychology, Polish Academy of Science, Warsaw, Poland

According to some normative theories of democracy, the existing discrepancies in interests, values, and action programs should be resolved not merely by power struggle but by rational analysis of differences in debates based on equality and mutual respect of the participants, that is by deliberative procedures. However, it is well known that group discussions take very often an adversarial course - instead of fostering an agreement they lead to escalation of conflicts or to domination of one particular perspective. The question arises under what conditions political debate can meet the deliberative criteria? Theories and research in group behavior suggest that interpretation of the meaning of situation, social identity and group norms are critical factors. The paper will present some specific hypotheses derived from social psychological research and will describe the results of an empirical study where groups of ordinary citizens as well as groups of politicians were trying to solve some ideological differences or conflict of interests existing between them. It was found that in most of the cases it was possible to reach satisfactory agreements in groups. The results of the experiment have some bearing on the problem of reducing antagonistic tendencies in groups.

IS-086: Cross-cultural validation of various measures of emotional intelligence

Vladimir Taksic (chair)

The aim of the Symposium is to discuss about cross-cultural validation of trait and ability approaches in measuring of emotional intelligence (EI). A majority of the communications are about cross-cultural comparison on Emotional Skills and Competence Questionnaire (ESCQ). It consists of 45 items divided in three subscales: a) perception and understanding emotion, b) expression and labeling emotion, and c) managing and regulating emotion. Originally it is developed in Croatian settings using theoretical model of EI established by Mayer & Salovey (1997). At first, it was translated in English, and after that in several languages all ower the World.

Adaptation and validation studies of the ESCQ in the Portuguese context

Faria, Luísa Fac. of Psychology and Educat., University of Porto, Porto, Portugal Lima Santos, Nelson Human and Social Sciences, Fernando Pessoa University, Porto, Portugal

This study presents the adaptation and validation of the ESCQ (Täksic, 2001) in the Portuguese context, using confirmatory factor analysis, with a sample of 730 students, 381 high school 10th and 12th graders, and 349 university 1st and 2nd graders. The ESCQ includes 45 items and 3 dimensions: "ability to perceive and understand emotion" (15 items), "ability to express and label emotion" (14 items), and "ability to manage and regulate emotion" (16 items). The results revealed that the best fitted model has two correlated factors (.55; perception and expression), and integrates only 11 items from the original scale (R2>.30).

Developmental differences in the effects of EI on academic performance in Japanese students

Toyota, Hiroshi Dept. of Psychology, Nara University of Education, Nara, Japan

Developmental differences in the effects of emotional intelligence on academic performance were examined and compared with three habits: life, social, and study habits. Participants were 1,087 Japanese students. Each of them completed a questionnaire that has six revised items in the shorten version of J-ESCQ (Toyota, Morita, & Taksic, 2007) and additional 18 items examined the other three habits. Higher correlations of emotional intelligence scores with academic performances were observed in the third, the fourth, and the fifth graders. The results were interpreted as showing the importance of emotional control in learning setting in elementary school.

Cross-cultural validation of emotional skills and competence questionnaire: Assessing structural equivalence of adapted ESCQ for Argentina

Mikulic, Isabel Maria Faculty of Psychology, University of Buenos Aires, Buenos Aires, Argentina

This study aims to discuss the cross-cultural validation of the Emotional Skills and Competence Questionnaire, consisting of 45 items divided into three subscales: perceiving and understanding emotion, expressing and labeling emotion, and managing and regulating emotion. Classified as a "trait emotional intelligence" or "perceived emotional intelligence" measure, ESCQ has been developed by V. Taksic for Croatian settings using theoretical framework from the emotional intelligence model (Mayer & Salovey, 1997). However, it has been already translated into many languages. Psychometric qualities, structural equivalence and relations with several relevant constructs of translation and adaptation of the ESCQ for Argentina context is analyzed.

Analysis of item bias in the emotional skills and competence questionnaire: A cross-cultural comparison

Holmstrom, Stefan Dept. of Psychology, Umeå University, Umeå, Sweden Molander, Bo Dept. of Psychology, Umeå University, Umeå, Sweden Taksic, Vladimir Dept. of Psychology, University of Rijeka, Rijeka, Croatia

Objectives: To evaluate the Swedish and Croatian versions of the ESCQ instrument (Taksic, 2005) with respect to item bias. Method: ESCQ scores were examined by analyses of differential item functioning (DIF; Zumbo, 1999) in samples of Swedish and Croatian university students. Results: Although DIF-values were low in national comparisons of sex, cross-cultural comparisons revealed a number of items in all scales with values higher than the commonly accepted level (>.035). Conclusions: There is considerable item bias in the present Swedish and Croatian versions when cross-cultural comparisons are performed. Several reasons for this discrepancy are discussed.

Validation of the emotion skills and competence questionnaire in Chinese setting

Xu, Qinmei Inst. for Psychology, Zhejiang University, Hangzhou, People's Republic of China

The Emotion Skills and Competence Questionnaire (Taksic) was translated into Chinese. 1133 Chinese adolescents were asked to complet the Chinese version. Results showed the internal consistency of the scale is 0.91 and the internal consistency of 3 subscales of Perceive & Understand, Express & Label, and Manage & Regulate were 0.74, 0.80, and 0.88, respectively. Item analysis indicated discrimination of each item was good. A three-factor structure of Perceive & Understand, Express & Label, and Mange & Regulate was validated. But there were crossover between Perceive and Express. Sufficient reliability and validity for the ESCQ in Chinese setting were found.

Cross-cultural comparison on ESCQ

Taksic, Vladimir Dept. of Psychology, University of Rijeka, Rijeka, Croatia Mohoric, Tamara Dept. of Psychology, University of Rijeka, Rijeka, Croatia Faria, Luisa Faculty of Psychology and Educ, University of Porto/Portugal, Porto, Portugal Räty, Hannu Dept. of Psychology, University of Joensuu, Joensuu, Finland Avsec, Andreja Dept. of Psychology, University of Ljubljana, Ljubljana, Slovenia Molander, Bo Dept. of Psychology, Umeå University, Umeå, Sweden Extremera, Natalio Dept. of Psychology, University of Málaga, Rijeka, Spain Toyota, Hiroshi Dept. of Psychology, Nara University of Education, Nara, Japan Rashid, Tabassum Dept. of Psychology, Effat College, Jeddah, Saudi Arabia

The Emotional Skills and Competences Questionnaire was developed in Croatian settings, and then translated to Slovene, Spanish, Swedish, Finnish, Portuguese and Japanese. The scale is a measure of trait emotional intelligence and includes three subscales. Sufficient reliability for the total ESCQ score and subscales in all seven countries were found. Results showed significant differences in total scores of ESCQ and scores on all three subscales. The major difference was found in between scores in all European samples on one side, and Japanese sample on the other. Gender differences emerged in Perceive and Understand emotions and Express and Label emotions subscales.

Psychometric properties of Vocabulary of Emotion Test (VET)

Mohoric, Tamara Dept. of Psychology, University of Rijeka, Rijeka, Croatia Taksic, Vladimir Dept. of Psychology, University of Rijeka, Rijeka, Croatia

Emotional intelligence is usually defined as a four-level set of abilities (Mayer & Salovey, 1997). Among these, ability to understand emotions is one that can be best measured with ability test. Vocabulary Emotion Test (VET) was constructed consists of 102 adjectives (short version has 35 items) describing emotional states and mood, and has correct answer, based on a solution from Croatian dictionary (Anić, 1994). Both versions have satisfactory psychometric properties, with reliability coefficient $\alpha=0.91$. Convergent-divergent validity was assessed compared TRE with several traditional intelligence tests showing it has 44% of unique variance. VET was translated in English and Swedish.

IS-087: Work and organizational climate in international perspectives

Andrew A. Mogaji (chair)
Work plays an important role in the lives of people. It is true that apart from providing for the economic and social needs of the individual, work provides some personal values and psychological needs of many workers. Unfortunately, the socio-psychological, economic and the political realities of our work environment have made the satisfaction of these needs to be almost unascertainable. Therefore, in this symposium, there will be an open discussion of the nature of work and how the characteristics of the work environment, often called organizational climate, have impacted on the commitment, involvement, motivation and satisfaction of workers from different nations.

The influence of personal and organisational factors on organisational climate in a large university

Baguma, Peter Inst. of Psychology, Makerere University, Kampala, Uganda
The objective of the study was to assess the influence of personal and organisational factors on organisational climate in a large university setting. Data were collected from 120 randomly selected staff of a large university in Uganda to assess role clarity, respect, communication, reward system, career development, planning and decision making, innovation, relationships, team work and support, quality of service, conflict management, commitment and morale, learning and training and direction. Data were analysed using t- test, ANO-VA and correlation analysis. Results indicated that sex had no effect on all organisational climate variables. Age, position and organisational tenure had significant effects on some of the variables.

Organizational creativity and innovation and psychological well-being among Swedish high-tech workers

Rasulzada, Farida Dept. of Psychology, Lund University, Lund, Sweden
The aims of this paper were to investigate the relationships between organizational factors and organizational creativity and innovation, and between organizational creativity and innovation and psychological well-being of 95 employees working in a high-tech field of industry. The two relationships were tested in a LISREL model that was confirmed. Organizational climate, team climate, gardener leadership, work resources and workload were together related to organizational creativity and innovation, and organizational creativity and innovation was related to the well-being of the employees. One important conclusion was the establishment of the relationship between psychological well-being and organizational creativity and innovation.

Work and organizational climate in the Nigerian manufacturing industries

Mogaji, Andrew A. Dept. of Psychology, University of Lagos, Lagos, Nigeria
This study was aimed at investigating the effects of organizational climate on employees' commitment, involvement, motivation and satisfaction in some Nigerian manufacturing industries. Data were collected from 600 workers randomly selected from some food, shoes and textile industries in Lagos, Nigeria. The test-retest administration of the measures over a 72-day period shows that the organizational climate of the three industries was stable and remained favourable during the time interval between test and retest. The multiple regression analysis shows support for the hypotheses tested about the interaction among interpersonal, intergroup and organizational climate factors facilitating commitment, involvement, motivation and satisfaction among workers.

Organizational safety climate and perceived organizational support in Ghana

Gyekye, Seth Dept. of Social Psychology, University of Helsinki, Helsinki, Finland
The study investigated the link between organisational safety climate and perceived organizational support (POS) among 320 Ghanaian industrial workers. Additionally, it examined the relationship with job satisfaction, compliance with safety management policies, and accident frequency. Perceptions of safety were measured with the 50-item workplace safety (WSS) developed by Hayes et al. (1998). POS was measured with the short version of Eisenberger et al.'s (1990) survey. The responses on the POS items were calculated and a median split was performed to segregate the sample into two groups: participants with high perspective regarding organizational support (n = 166), and participants with low supportive perspectives (n = 154). The linear regression analysis indicated WSS to be a very good predictor of POS. Workers with positive perspectives regarding supportive perceptions equally had positive perceptions on the safety climate scale. Additionally, they expressed greater job satisfaction, were more compliant with safety management policies, and registered lower accident rates. The perceived level of support provided in an organization, apparently, is closely associated with workplace safety perception and other organizational and social factors which are important for safety.

IS-088: Dorsal anterior cingulate cortex: Perspectives on its role in behavior and cognition

Matthew Botvinick (chair)
The dorsal anterior cingulate cortex is widely agreed to play a critical role in decision-making and executive control. Understanding its specific functions is an ongoing challenge. This symposium will bring together a group of cognitive neuroscientists whose work has focused on the cingulate, to review current theories of the area's contribution to cognition and behavior. Among the proposals to be discussed are the idea that the cingulate monitors for error-likelihood or conflict, and the idea that it codes for action outcomes, supporting optimal decision-making. The relations among perspectives will be considered, as will fruitful directions for future research.

Neural systems for error monitoring: Recent findings and theoretical perspectives

Gehring, William Dept. of Psychology, University of Michigan, Ann Arbor, MI, USA **Liu, Yanni** Dept. of Psychology, University of Michigan, Ann Arbor, MI, USA **Orr, Joseph** Dept. of Psychology, University of Michigan, Ann Arbor, MI, USA **Carp, Joshua** Dept. of Psychology, University of Michigan, Ann Arbor, MI, USA
Current theories of the error-related negativity (ERN or Ne), such as the conflict-monitoring and reinforcement-learning theories, propose that the ERN represents a strategic control process that contributes to detecting errors or conflict and adjusting subsequent performance. Largely neglected is the possibility originally proposed by Falkenstein, Coles and others that the ERN is involved in online control–detecting, adjusting or correcting the erroneous action. We review evidence from our laboratory and others that a reformulation of the classic error-detection theory in terms of modern concepts of forward models in motor control is a viable candidate to explain the ERN.

Noticing when things go wrong: Monitoring for conflicts and errors

Yeung, Nick Dept. Experimental Psychology, Oxford University, Oxford, United Kingdom
Activity within medial frontal cortex (MFC) has consistently been observed in two situations: with incorrect responses, and with competition between responses. Conflict-monitoring and error-likelihood theories of MFC function provide contrasting accounts of these findings. According to the former, the MFC functions to monitor for conflict, and shows error-related activity because incorrect responses involve conflict. The error-likelihood theory proposes that the MFC encodes the probability of errors in given situations, and this results in conflict-related activity because errors are likely in situations of conflict. I will describe experimental work that contrasts predictions made by the conflict-monitoring and error-likelihood theories.

Individual differences in medial prefrontal cortex, conflict, error likelihood prediction and risk aversion

Brown, Joshua Psychological & Brain Sciences, Indiana University, Bloomington, USA **Braver, Todd** Psychology, Washington University, St. Louis, MO, USA
The error-likelihood hypothesis suggests that anterior cingulate cortex (ACC) activates in proportion to the perceived likelihood of an error. The same computational model that generated this hypothesis predicts that ACC will also be sensitive to the magnitude of the consequences should an error occur, thus effectively encoding "expected risk." Subsequent fMRI results have confirmed this prediction and further suggest that ACC activity varies with individual differences in risk aversion. We examined whether such differences could be captured in the original error-likelihood computational model. Results strengthen the original theory, showing how it can provide a unified account of multiple individual-difference effects.

The anterior cingulate cortex in learning and reward-guided decision making

Rushworth, Matthew Experimental Psychology, Oxford University, Oxford, United Kingdom **Behrens, Tim** FMRIB Centre, Oxford University, Oxford, United Kingdom **Walton, Mark** Experimental Psychology, Oxford University, Oxford, United Kingdom
When signal changes are recorded in the human anterior cingulate cortex (ACC) during choice behavior, their size varies with the degree to which the choice is unconstrained and with the importance of the outcome. A recent fMRI study suggests that ACC activity changes with the length of the reward history needed to determine the next choice. Such information is critical for setting the rate at which learning occurs. Following ACC lesions, macaques show normal sensitivity to a decrement in reinforcement but the influence of the extended reward history on choice is diminished.

Conflict monitoring and decision making

Botvinick, Matthew Inst. of Neuroscience, Princeton University, Princeton, NJ, USA

According to one influential account, the anterior cingulate cortex (ACC) serves to monitor for conflicts in information processing. According to another influential account, the ACC monitors action outcomes and guides decision-making. A current challenge is to discover how these perspectives might fit together within a larger account. I'll discuss the prospects for such a reconciliation. Juxtaposing the decision-making and conflict-monitoring accounts suggests an extension of the latter, by which conflict would act as a teaching signal driving a form of avoidance learning. The effect of this mechanism would be to bias behavioral decision making toward cognitively efficient tasks and strategies.

Calculating the cost of acting in frontal cortex

Walton, Mark Dept. of Psychology, Oxford University, Oxford, United Kingdom

Whether to persist with a course of action or switch to an alternative is a decision that foraging animals regularly face. Using discrete lesions in animals, we have demonstrated that the anterior cingulate cortex (ACC) may be one crucial component for the cost-benefit calculations guiding such decisions. Rats with ACC lesions show a bias away from persisting in effortful courses of action. Monkeys with ACC lesions update their behaviour in stimulus- or response-switching tasks, but often fail to persist with the correct response. These results will be considered in the light of human neuroimaging studies concerning persistence and flexible decision-making.

IS-089: Research and applications in cultural psychology

Ajit Mohanty, Minati Panda (chair)

Cultural psychological research has examined the processes of the social or cultural construction of the person including thoughts, emotions, motivation, development, identity, and other psychological constructs and for restructuring cultural processes that lead to better psychological functioning both at individual and collective levels. This symposium aims at discussing some empirical research, from different cultural settings and using a variety of theoretical and methodological perspectives, to explore the relationship between culture and human functioning and to demonstrate applications of cultural psychology in education and human development while critically examining theoretical bases of this approach to suggest some shift in emphasis.

Macro cultural psychology: A framework for understanding the relation between culture and psychology

Ratner, Carl Dept. of Psychology, Institute for Cultur. Research, Trinidad, USA

This paper develops macro cultural psychology as a parsimonious, coherent theoretical framework that explains the cultural origins, characteristics, and function of psychological phenomena. It uniquely defines culture as primarily consisting of social institutions, cultural concepts, and artifacts. I show how these macro cultural factors constitute the primary social origins, characteristics, and function of psychology. I explain how macro cultural psychology leads to reforming social institutions, artifacts, and cultural concepts. The scientific and political utility of the theory complement each other. The paper briefly compares macro cultural psychology to micro cultural psychology, cross-cultural psychology, and indigenous psychology.

Reflections on cultural psychology in international and interdisciplinary perspective

Hartnack, Christiane Intercultural Studies, Donau-Universität Krems, Krems, Austria

Increasingly, national, professional and private points of reference dissolve into multiple and seemingly fluid relationships. In the midst of such transformations, cultural psychologists are asked to–and could–play important roles. While striving to have an impact, cultural psychologists themselves face the challenge of keeping pace with constantly changing realities. In order to focus more strongly on the real world, they also need to overcome the constraints of cultural constructs such as national borders and academic disciplines. This presentation highlights, analyses and discusses some of the difficulties and pitfalls of international and interdisciplinary collaboration in cultural psychology.

Multiperspectival methods in cultural historical activity theory: The fifth dimension and playworlds

Lecusay, Robert Lab. of Comparative Human Cogn, University of California, La Jolla, USA

Cultural Historical Activity Theory (CHAT) is an interdisciplinary approach that emphasizes the primacy of social processes in human development. A key component of CHAT methodology is the design of activity systems around questions researchers wish to investigate. Researchers then participate in and simultaneously study these systems. In this paper we present analyses of adult-child interactions from two such systems: The Fifth Dimension and Playworlds. Though our analyses are grounded in concepts central to CHAT, we propose a multipespectival methodology that productively puts CHAT into conversation with complementary approaches from performance studies and distributed cognition.

Home and school mathematics discourse: Epistemological give-and-take

Panda, Minati Zakir Husain Centre, Jawaharlal Nehru University, New Delhi, India

Social and cognitive bases of mathematics learning in two psycho-semiotic environments, considered as two discursive contexts - home and school - are explored to compare mathematical ideas and concepts in everyday discourse in Saora community (a tribe in India) and mathematics discourse carried out in schools which Saora children attend. Presence of "as if discourse" as a special characteristic of modern school mathematics as well as various forms of everyday discourse are highlighted. It is argued that "as if discourse" can be used to connect everyday mathematics in indigenous activities and school mathematics by creating a common recognizable discourse frame.

Application of cultural psychology for intervention in multilingual education program for tribal children in India

Mohanty, Ajit Zakir Husain Centre for Ed., Jawaharlal Nehru University, New Delhi, India

The paper illustrates theoretical and methodological applications of cultural psychology for developing culturally meaningful and effective intervention in an experimental program of multilingual education for Kond and Saora tribal children in primary grades in India. Both critical reality and activity theory perspectives are applied for selection of curricular areas and designing of pedagogic practices for enhancement of children's achievements in school subject and social communicative skills. Ethnographic data on the everyday knowledge of science, mathematics, stories and riddles in the two communities are used by teachers and the MLE workers for guided development of child-focused classroom and individual activities for intervention.

Application of cultural psychology for intervention in multilingual education program for tribal children in India

Panda, Minati Zakir Husain Centre, Jawaharlal Nehru University, New Delhi, India

The paper illustrates theoretical and methodological applications of cultural psychology for developing culturally meaningful and effective intervention in an experimental program of multilingual education for Kond and Saora tribal children in primary grades in India. Both critical reality and activity theory perspectives are applied for selection of curricular areas and designing of pedagogic practices for enhancement of children's achievements in school subject and social communicative skills. Ethnographic data on the everyday knowledge of science, mathematics, stories and riddles in the two communities are used by teachers and the MLE workers for guided development of child-focused classroom and individual activities for intervention.

IS-090: Keeping track of developments in self-regulated learning

Monique Boekaerts (chair)

Writing requires extensive use of meta-cognitive, social, and motivational strategies. It also relies heavily on writing beliefs and affects. Any writing activity is always situated; it involves a dialogue between the writer and a potential reader. Students conceptualize the reader while they write. In order to understand students' successive attempts at SR during the writing process it is essential to know the accessibility and use of various cognitive and affective strategies. The symposium focuses on the interplay between cognitive and affective strategies during SR writing and on the relations between the social and instructional context and students' strategy use.

Investigating the integration of motivational orientations and self-regulation strategies: Employing a stimulated recall methodology

Kaplan, Avi Dept. of Education, Ben-Gurion University, Be'er-Sheva, Israel

I contest a common view of SR as a unitary, distinct, a-contextual construct, and argue that different SR strategies are geared towards different objectives. Different SR strategies become the active manifestation of different motivational orientations for the task. Investigating the embedded meaning of SR strategies within motivational orientations is a methodological challenge. I will describe a stimulated recall methodology which involves a micro-behavioral observation of high-school students' engagement in writing activities followed by a stimulated recall interview in which students report on the strategies they engaged in at different points during engagement and the purpose for employing these strategies.

From self-regulation to socially shared regulation of writing: Different voices in graduate students' writing

Castelló, Montserrat Educational Psychology, Ramon LLull University, Barcelona, Spain

Writing has been traditionally considered an individual and cognitive activity that requires the management of the rhetoric problem as well as issues about planning, translating and revising. Contemporary approaches to the SR of writing study the joint effects of "social" and "cognitive" dimensions on SR in real settings. We will examine the role that communicative situations, context, and interactions play in different models of SR and contrast definitions of writing context, writer's conception and activity, empirical methods, and units of analysis. We present a study with graduate students to illustrate how these aspects are considered from a socially-situated perspective.

Capturing the multiple components of self-regulated writing: A systemic approach

Boekaerts, Monique *Dept. of Educational Studies, Leiden University, Leiden, Netherlands*

Researchers in SR selected a limited set of constructs, measured them, and determined their effect on learning outcomes. This research did not reveal the essential links between the components of SR, mainly due to limitations in research methodology. We explored the patterns of SR in the writing domain. To encompass the multiple facets of the SR of writing, we grafted the 6 component model on the writing domain and included numerous context variables. 1500 vocational students took part in the writing assessment sessions. Our on-line assessment tool captured the SR of writing and predictive methodology detected meaningful patterns in it.

Fictive systems approach in the identification of expected writing performance and the classification and understanding of student performance characteristics

Cascallar, Eduardo *Katholieke Universiteit Leuven, Brussels, Belgium* **Costigan, Tracy Boekaerts, Monique** *Dept. of Educational Studies, Leiden University, Leiden, Netherlands*

We used a predictive systems approach in the prediction of writing performance. These machine-learning techniques offer an iterative methodology that is capable of discovering complex relationships and interactions in the inputs and outcomes. The approach maximizes classification accuracy, and was able to model various outcome patterns from the 1500 students studied. A total accuracy of 96% in the identification of "students-at-risk" was achieved. Techniques developed to explore the classification of students according to patterns detected by the predictive systems in students' individual characteristics will be presented. The implications for the application of these methods in educational studies will be discussed.

IS-091: Parenting prevention programs: An international perspective

Maria Jose Rodrigo, Jan Janssens *(chair)*
The symposium illustrates evidence-based programs from the Netherlands, United Kingdom, Sweden, Germany and Spain. These programs differ from each other in theory of change, intervention goals, target group, type of practitioners, design of evaluation, and outcome measures. However, all programs shared an emphasis to prevent child problems by promoting the quality of parenting and family functioning. The different methods of working with parents will be addressed, as well as their practical implications for the implementation of programs in various countries. The discussion will address these points as well as the quality standards that should be met to improve program effectiveness.

Effects of Triple P

Janssens, Jan *Behavioural Science Institute, Radboud University Nijmegen, Nijmegen, Netherlands*
Objective: Study the effects of Triple P on behavioural and emotional problems in preadolescent children and parenting. Method: Effects of Triple P have been studied by comparing pre- and post tests, and by comparing Triple P parents with parents who received care as usual. Results: Analyses show positive results of Triple P with regard to all dependent variables. Conclusions: Triple P has to be implemented in more Dutch cities as a parenting support program to prevent severe child problem behaviour and to prevent seriously inadequate parenting.

Attachment, marital relationship, care and knowledge: A preventive intervention with first parents

Reichle, Barbara *Educational Psychology, Univ. of Education Ludwigsburg, Ludwigsburg, Germany* **Franiek, Sabine** *Educational Psychology, University of Education, Ludwigsburg, Germany* **Ziegenhain, Ute** *Child & Adolescent Psychia, University of Ulm, Ulm, Germany* **Gebauer, Sigrid** *Child & Adolescent Psychia, University of Ulm, Ulm, Germany* **Kolb, Anne-Katrin** *Child & Adolescent Psychia, University of Ulm, Ulm, Germany*

Objective. The preventive intervention program "The beginning counts" aims to strengthen parents' knowledge and competencies and the marital relationship during the transition to parenthood. Method. Effects were evaluated with a pre-post design comparing trained (n=95) with untrained parents (n=77). Both groups completed questionnaires assessing their knowledge concerning central training issues, relationship satisfaction, self-confidence in interacting with the child and anger management. Results and conclusion. Repeated measures analyses of variance showed positive intervention effects on all variables except marital satisfaction.

The ladybird study: A randomised controlled trial evaluation of the lifestart parenting initiative

Sneddon, Helga *Inst. of Child Care Research, Queen's University Belfast, Belfast, Ireland* **Allen, Sarah** *NFER, Queen's University Belfast, Belfast, Ireland* **Morrison, Nicoli** *Institute of Child Care Resear, Queen's University Belfast, Belfast, Ireland*

Objective. To describe the Lifestart program and evaluation methodology. Method. Lifestart is a parent-directed child-centred programme of child development delivered to parents of children from birth to five years of age. Monthly, during a home-visit, trained Family Visitors bring age-appropriate learning materials and discuss these and the child's development with the parent(s). The programme is open to all parents residing in project areas throughout Ireland. Results. A 5 year evaluation of this programme is just about to begin using Randomised Control Trial (RCT) and qualitative methods. Conclusions: Outcome measures include child cognitive development, parenting knowledge, social support and psychological wellbeing.

"The Incredible Years": Evaluation of the webster Sratton parent management training programme in Sweden

Axberg, Ulf *Dept. of Psychology, Göteborg University, Göteborg, Sweden* **Broberg, Anders** *Department of Psychology, Göteborg University, Göteborg, Sweden*
The Incredible Years is offered to parents whose children display severe disruptive behaviour problems. Its aim is to promote positive parenting and reduce harsh punishment. Parents meet with two trained group-leaders weekly for 12-14 sessions. They practice various parenting skills enlightened by video-vignettes. Objective: To evaluate the effectiveness of the programme in Sweden. Method: Parents of 48 children aged 4-8 participated in the study. A multi-informant, multi-method strategy was used. Results: Preliminary results (pre – post intervention) indicate a statistically significant (p< .01), and clinically relevant (effect sizes >.80), decrease in children's disruptive behaviour. Final results will be presented and discussed.

The "Apoyo Personal y Familiar" program for parents at high psychosocial risk

Rodrigo, Maria Jose *Dept. of Developm. Psychology, University of La Laguna, La Laguna, Spain* **Byrne, Sonia** *Developmental Psychology, University of La Laguna, La Laguna, Spain* **Maiquez, María Luisa** *Developmental Psychology, University of La Laguna, La Laguna, Spain* **Martin, Juan Carlos** *Developmental Psychology, University of La Laguna, La Laguna, Spain*

The objective is to describe the program (APF) aimed at promoting parental competences and positive childrearing in families living under risky psychosocial conditions. APF is a multi-site program delivered through weekly group meetings conducted by social agents. The method combines the parents exposition to other- and self- views with a reflection on the consequences of parental action in concrete child-rearing episodes. Mode of implementation and program results are presented from the last community trial assessing the level of psychosocial risk, social support, and parental functioning. Evidence was found that indicates positive program results on parental functioning and provides futures lines of improvement.

IS-092: Acquisition of control

Wolfgang Prinz, Iring Koch *(chair)*
Control is a multi-faceted psychological concept, which is characterized by the diversity of research fields and theoretical views. This symposium focuses on the control of cognitive processes. Cognitive control needs to be acquired, which can occur both on the short-term, such as in learning and practicing novel skills, and on the long-term, such as in development across infancy. This symposium aims to bring together contemporary views on normal and disturbed development and learning of cognitive control in humans and non-human primates. To this end, international experts discuss how a more integrated conceptual framework for cognitive control can be advanced.

Learning and cognitive control

Koch, Iring *Inst. für Psychologie, RWTH Aachen, Aachen, Germany* **Prinz, Wolfgang** *Inst. für Psychologie, Max-Planck-Institut, Leipzig, Germany*
The concept of cognitive control refers to the ability to recruit cognitive resources and mechanisms required for performing given tasks in a goal-directed and context-sensitive manner. However, performance costs in a task switch suggest that cognitive control is prone to interference arising from competing tasks. The presentation focusses on the role of elementary learning and memory processes implied in cognitive task control. To this end, we present an overview on recent empirical findings suggesting that internal task representations become associatively connected to external cues and stimuli. These findings raise the issue of the dynamic interplay between learning and cognitive control.

The evolution of cognitive control

Call, Josep *Inst. Evolution. Anthropologie, Max-Planck-Institut, Leipzig, Germany* **Amici, Federica Aureli, Filippo**
Humans have evolved a notable ability to inhibit certain responses in favour of others to solve problems. However, it is unclear when this ability may have evolved. We investigated the evolution of inhibitory control by comparing seven primate species in three tasks. One task required subjects to inhibit directly reaching for a visible reward, another required subjects to find a hidden reward and another required selecting the smaller of two quantities to net the larger one. Results suggested that the enhancement of inhibitory skills might be more strongly related to socio-ecological pressures than to common evolutionary history.

Development of understanding the mind and mental control

Perner, Josef *Inst. für Psychologie, Universität Salzburg, Salzburg, Austria*
Developmental investigations during preschool years show persistent correlations between understanding the mind ("theory of mind") and executive

control. We can rule out the methodological explanation that theory-of-mind tasks are simply tacit executive tasks. I argue for a common denominator. Executive control differs from automatic control in that the former requires representation of one's own intentions as intentions, a core element of "theory of mind". It remains open as to whether development of this core ability is primarily driven by advances in executive control or in attributing mental states to self and others, as assessed by theory of mind tasks.

The development of cognitive control: The influence of verbal processes

Karbach, Julia Inst. für Psychologie, Universität des Saarlandes, Saarbrücken, Germany Kray, Jutta Entwicklungspsychologie, Universität des Saarlandes, Saarbrücken, Germany

Recent empirical findings suggest that the development of cognitive control abilities underlie different developmental trends throughout childhood. The first aim of this presentation is to provide an overview of these findings, indicating that some cognitive control abilities are acquired relatively early in development, such as the ability to ignore irrelevant information, while others are acquired relatively slowly, such as the ability to maintain and to select relevant goals. The second aim is to provide some evidence that language influences some of these cognitive control processes and serves as a useful tool to support the regulation of behavior, especially in childhood.

Typical development of cognitve control and abnormal development in ADHD and autism

Konrad, Kerstin Klinische Neuropsychologie, Universitätsklinikum Aachen, Aachen, Germany Kohls, Gregor Herpertz-Dahlmann, Beate

Immature cognition during typical development is characterized by increased susceptibility to interference. Two frequent neurodevelopmental disorders, autism spectrum disorder (ASD) and attention deficit/hyperactivity disorder (ADHD), are both associated with marked deficits in cognitive control abilities. In a series of behavioral and fMRI experiments, we investigated how the neural basis of different aspests of cognitive control (such as interference control and response inhibition) develops in healthy children and in children with ADHD or ASD. Our results indicate some shared behavioral deficits across both disorders but distinct brain abnormalities associated with interference control and response inhibition in ASD and ADHD.

Neurocognitive development of cognitive control: fMRI studies on rule use across development

Crone, Eveline A. Dept. of Psychology, Leiden University, Leiden, Netherlands

The ability to control our thoughts and actions has a long developmental trajectory, not reaching adult-level until late adolescence. Recent advances in developmental imaging indicate that these changes are associated with the maturation of subregions within the prefrontal cortex (PFC), which each contribute to different aspects of control. Using fMRI, we investigated the role of different PFC regions when we adjust our behaviour on the basis of positive and negative feedback. Results of two studies including over 90 participants show that medial PFC and lateral PFC have separate developmental timecourses and that young children use different strategies when learning from feedback.

IS-093: Neuropsychological functioning after exposure to toxic environments

Rosemarie M. Bowler (chair)

Neurotoxic chemicals have been shown to cause adverse health effects in occupational and environ-

mental evaluations across the world. This symposium will illustrate methods used in evaluating the brain function of both children and adults exposed to solvents, heavy metals and other chemicals. Results of investigations in Belgium, the Amazon, the United States and Canada will be presented. Intracellular systems in prenatal life and subsequent psychomotor and cognitive processes and functions in the brain are discussed as recent advances in the field of neurotoxicology. Attending this symposium will contribute to theoretical and applied knowledge on neurotoxicants and neuropsychological methodologies used.

Neuropsychological testing of adults exposed to neurotoxicants

Bowler, Rosemarie M. Dept. of Psychology, San Francisco State University, San Francisco, USA

Selected neuropsychological tests are sensitive and specific to the evaluation of environmental or occupational exposures to neurotoxicants. Extensive research has been published reporting the use of neuropsychological testing in evaluating exposures of adults to organic solvents, pesticides (i.e. organophosphates), gases and heavy metals. Although evaluations of patients exposed to neurotoxicants traditionally requires a lengthy test battery, experience and knowledge gained in the field suggests the efficacious use of a shorter, test battery for adults. This presentation will illustrate the use of clinical tests of cognitive, motor and mood function in a proposed environmental study.

Environmental neurotoxicants and child development

Bellinger, David Dept. of Neurology, Children's Hospital Boston, Boston, USA

The vulnerability of children to compounds that disrupt the development of the central nervous system has raised the specter of a "silent pandemic" of environmental disease resulting from low-level but chronic exposures to chemical contaminants. The evidence is compelling that neurotoxicities occur at environmentally-relevant exposures to lead, methylmercury, and polychlorinated biphenyls, while emerging evidence implicates arsenic, manganese, pesticides, and other chemicals among the other 80,000 chemicals in commercial use. Although the impact of such exposures on an individual child might appear to be modest, their cumulative impact on population health and well-being could be enormous.

Persistence of neuropsychoogical changes in formerly exposed workers: Possible implications

Viaene, Mineke K. Dept. of Occupational, Catholic Universty of Leuven, Leuven, Belgium

Numerous industrial processes relay on organic solvents which causes substantial health problems in the work force. Although the acute neurotoxic potentials of most solvents were known for a long time, only recently investigations documented exposure causing an organic encephalopathy. In a group of 90 formerly exposed workers we demonstrated that even subclinical effects on visuomotor function persist three years after exposure cessation. This implies that neuropsychological tests can be used in secondary prevention. Although controversial, this may imply that aging-related neuronal attrition superimposed on these subclinical effects might cause delayed clinical neuropsychological deficits emerging years after exposure cessation.

Neurotoxic effects of mercury exposure in fish-eating populations of the Brazilian Amazon

Mergler, Donna Dépt. des Sciences Biologie, Université du Québec, Montréal, Canada

In the Amazon, gold-mining and deforestation release mercury into the aquatic systems where it bioaccumulates through the trophic chain, resulting in elevated mercury in carnivorous fish. Studies

have shown mercury-related neurobehavioral deficits in motor, psychomotor, visual and/or cognitive functions. We carried out a follow-up study, which sought to maintain fish consumption while reducing mercury exposure. Re-testing after 5 years showed that persons ate the same quantity of fish, but fewer carnivores; exposure diminished by 39%. Motor functions improved, but visual functions decreased in relation to previous exposure. These findings suggest that some mercury-related deficits, but not visual, may be reversible.

Linking neurotoxicology to cognitive neuroscience: A first attempt

van Thriel, Christoph Neurobehavioral Toxicology, Leibniz-Forschungszentrum, Dortmund, Germany Juran, Stephanie A. Neurobehavioral Toxicology, Leibniz-Forschungszentrum, Dortmund, Germany

During recent year's substantial progress in neurotoxicology and neuroscience have been made. Cognitive processes and functions of the brain can be described at different levels of aggregation: cellular level, neurotransmitter systems, neuronal circuits, and brain areas. Neurotoxic mechanisms have been identified on similar levels. These advances are not sufficiently linked with each other. Hence, we investigated effects of long-term occupational toluene exposure, a chemical suspected to interact with the dopaminergic system, on set shifting task performance. At life-time doses of 50 ppm no diminution of performance were found. More research is needed to bridge the gap between neurotoxicology and –psychology.

Could monoamine and intracellular calcium systems be related to postnatal brain development?

Huel, Guy Dept. of Environmental Health, INSERM U472, Villejuif, France

The monoamine and intracellular calcium systems are two major elements of the nervous system functions. However, their role in human brain development is unclear. Studies on association between the activity of these two systems during prenatal life and subsequent psychomotor performances are relevant. Prenatal factors influencing the monoaminergic and ATPases activities in the early psychomotor development of humans could be demonstrated. It is also suggested that specific psychometric measures such as fine motor tests may be a better developmental measurement to correlate with biochemical parameters than a general cognitive scales. Findings support the use of Ca pump activity as a biomarker of calcium mediated toxicity related to environmental in utero exposures.

IS-094: Leadership and power distance

Kwok Leung (chair)

Effective leadership is important for a group to achieve its goals in any cultural context, but what defines good leadership may show some drastic variation across cultures. Hofstede has identified power distance as an important dimension to characterize cultures, which refers to the extent to which hierarchies and inequalities are accepted in societies. This symposium explores the dynamics of leadership and power distance in several diverse cultural contexts, including Taiwan, Japan, Singapore, Italy, and the U.S. In addition, using data from the GLOBE project, the relationships between power distance and leadership are explored in cultures around the world.

Power distance and authoritative leadership matter: Probing the efficacy: Performance relationship in Taiwan

Wang, An-Chih Dept. of Psychology, National Taiwan University, Taipei, Taiwan Chou, Li-Fang Department of Business Adminis, Yuan Ze University, Taoyuan, Taiwan Cheng, Bor-Shiuan Dept. of Psychology, National Taiwan University, Taipei, Taiwan

While the positive relationship between self-efficacy and performance in the workplace is well-documented, whether this relationship varies with cultural value and leadership has received little attention. Using a sample of 190 supervisor-subordinate dyads from Taiwan, we found that the positive relationship between employees' creative self-efficacy and performance (measured by rated creativity, number of formal suggestions, and overall performance rating) was stronger for individuals low (versus high) on power distance. We also found that authoritative leadership interacted with creative self-efficacy: the relationship between creative self-efficacy and performance was stronger when authoritative leadership was high.

Leader-subordinate relational identity and prosocial organizational behavor: The moderating effects of power distance

Chou, Li-Fang Business Administration, Yuan Ze University, Chung-Li, Taiwan Cheng, Bor-Shiuan Department of Psychology, National Taiwan University, Taipei, Taiwan Jiang, Ding-Yu Department of Psychology, National Chung Cheng Universit, Chia-Yi, Taiwan

Relational identity is significant in Chinese organizations. This study classified leader-subordinate relational identity into expressive and instrumental relational identity. We explored the influence of leaders' leader-subordinate relational identities upon subordinates' prosocial organizational behavior (POB); and further probed into the moderating effect of subordinates' power distance values. Results from a sample of 795 dyadic leader-subordinate data demonstrated that expressive relational identity was positively related to all POB dimensions; instrumental relational identity was negatively related to POB-leader and POB-coworker, but not to POB-organization. Finally, subordinates' powder distance played a moderating role in the relatonshps between relational identity and prosocial organizational behavior.

Culture and power distance effects on norm-enforcement: Intuitive prosecutors as fair but softer toward leaders

Singh, Ramadhar Dept. of Psychology, Nat. University of Singapore, Singapore, Singapore Tasuo, Fujimori Dept. of Psychology, Yokohama Natl Univ, Japan, Japan Yamaguchi, Susumu Dept. of Social Psychology, Univ of Tokyo, Tokyo, Japan Osborne, Chandra Dept. of Psychology, University of Connecticut, Connecticut, USA Srinivasan, Hans Dept. of Marketing, University of Connecticut, Connecticut, USA Fisher, Jeffrey D. Dept. of Psychology, University of Connecticut, Connecticut, USA

In two experiments, Easterners and Westerners recommended punitive actions against those involved in an organizational decision leading to an in-group bias in pay revision. The status of people (chair vs. committee) and the circumstance (control vs. extenuating) of the decision were manipulated. Americans were harsher than Singaporeans or Japanese independent of the status of decision makers. However, situational correction was made in actions against the chair but not against the committee in both the cultures. Mediators of the cultural and circumstance effects were anger and/or the punishment goal of deterrent. Obviously, intuitive prosecutors are fair but softer toward leaders.

Leadership structures, group norms and work motivation in Japanese organizations

Muramoto, Yukiko International Graduated School, Yokohama National University, Yokohama, Japan Yamaoka, Toru International Graduated School, Yokohama National University, Yokohama, Japan

The present research aimed to investigate which factors could be good sensors to detect the decreased motivation to work. Respondents of our panel survey were staff and managers in Japanese chain stores. The questionnaire consisted of several scales, such as work attitude in the previous month, passion for work, perceived quality of working life, leadership structure, and implicit rules in a workplace. Preliminary results suggest that leadership structure (i.e., combinations of formal and Informal leaders) and group norms have a strong impact on work motivation of employees. Further results of longitudinal analysis in a workplace and comparative analysis across workplaces will be presented.

The differential relationship of the immediate supervisor and top management on collective efficacy

Borgogni, Laura Dept. of Psychology, University 'La Sapienza', Roma, Italy Petitta, Laura Dept. of Psychology, University 'La Sapienza', Roma, Italy Dello Russo, Silvia Dept. of Psychology, University 'La Sapienza', Roma, Italy Latham, Gary Rotman School of Management, University of Toronto, Toronto, Ontario, Canada

Professionals (N = 797) in an Italian mail delivery organization were administered a questionnaire measuring self- and collective efficacy, perceptions of their immediate supervisors (IS) and top management (TM), organizational commitment (OC) and job satisfaction (JS). SEM tested the hypothesized nomological net. Self-efficacy, IS and TM were related to CE which in turn was related to JS more so than to OC. Specifically, IS displayed a stronger relationship with CE and JS, while TM was related to OC. This study points to the necessity of intervening on employees' perceptions of leadership at different levels for CE and OC enhancement.

Leadership processes and power distance: A fundamental relationship

Dorfman, Peter Dept. of Management, New Mexico State University, Las Cruces, USA

Leadership Processes and Power Distance: A Fundamental Relationship Peter W. Dorfman New Mexico State University The objectives of this presentation are to explore the cultural effects of Power Distance on various aspects of leadership. Using Hierarchical Linear Modeling (HLM), the GLOBE data set of 62 countries provides evidence to the importance of Power Distance on leadership processes. Charismatic/Value Based and Participative leadership prototypes are endorsed in low power distance societies and organizations whereas Self-Protective leadership is endorsed in high power distance societies and organizations. The implications for managerial leaders and as yet unanswered questions will be discussed.

IS-095: Psychophysiology of hidden memories

Istvan Czigler (chair)

Event-related brain potentials (ERPs) disclosed memory systems capable of representing regularities in auditory and visual stimulation. Mismatch components (auditory and visual MMN) emerge whenever a stimulus violates the established regularities. The function of such implicit memory systems will be discussed in relation to veridical perception and attentional processing. ERP research also indicates that visual stimuli are processed at semantic level by implicit memory systems. Data

will be presented showing the implementation of the auditory memory system.

Automatic and attentional detection of violations in abstract auditory rules

Schröger, Erich Inst. für Psychologie, Universität Leipzig, Leipzig, Germany Bendixen, Alexandra Inst. für Psychologie, Universität Leipzig, Leipzig, Germany Horvath, Janos Inst. für Psychologie, Universität Leipzig, Leipzig, Germany Roeber, Urte Inst. für Psychologie, Universität Leipzig, Leipzig, Germany Trujillo-Barreto, Nelson Brain Dynamics Department, Cuban Neuroscience Centre, Havana, Cuba Prinz, Wolfgang Human Cognitive and Brain Sci, Max Planck Institute, Leipzig, Germany

We investigated the automatic and intentional encoding of abstract rules inherent in sound sequences. Rules concerned within-feature ("ascending frequency between successive tones") or between-feature relations ("short tone is followed by low tone, long tone is followed by high tone"). Initially, none of the subjects acquired explicit knowledge of the rule nor became aware of the presence of rule violations (e.g. infrequent descending frequency with an "ascending" rule). Nevertheless, rules and their violations were automatically detected as revealed by the elicitation of the Mismatch Negativity (MMN) brain wave. It seems that this automatic encoding of rules partly governs the intentional encoding.

The role of implicit memory representation in everyday auditory perception

Winkler, István Dept. of General Psychology, Institute for Psychology, HAS, Budapest, Hungary

In everyday life, multiple sound sources are active in the environment. The mixture of sounds arriving to the ears is sorted into coherent sound sequences (auditory streams) by heuristic algorithms, many of which require information about past behavior of previously detected streams. We suggest that this information is provided by implicit memory representations taking the form of predictive neural models, which have been established by extracting regularities from the auditory input. These models also underlie the deviance detection process reflected by the mismatch negativity event related potential an electric brain response involved resolving competition between alternative sound organizations.

A multimodal look on the neuroanatomy of the auditory mismatch response

Deouell, Leon Dept. of Psychology, Hebrew University, Jerusalem, Israel

Violation of regularities at multiple organizational levels and along every acoustic dimension elicits a distinct set of electrical brain responses, the hallmark of which is the mismatch negativity. Are the responses all elicited by a central 'deviance detector' or are they dependent on diverse processors with some domain specificity? In this presentation, I will review findings concerning the intracranial sources of mismatch responses, from multiple imaging modalities, including inverse solutions of EEG and MEG data, hemodynamic measurements (PET and fMRI), and particularly data from patients with circumscribed brain lesions. These data suggests that diverse brain regions support the mismatch response.

Representation of regularities in visual memory: Event-related potential studies

Czigler, Istvan Budapest, Hungary

As many influential demonstrations (e.g. change blindness) shows, visual changes outside the focus of attention frequently remain unnoticed. However, visual stimuli violating regularities of stimulation may elicit an event-related potential (ERP)component, the visual mismatch negativity (vMMN), even if there are no conscious representations of the regularity/irregularity. VMMN is sometimes preceded by an earlier posterior ERP component. VMMN emerges to deviant stimulus features (color, spatial frequency, motion direction, contrast), to the conjunction of features (objects), and to sequential and temporal irregularities.

Ultra-rapid and involuntary semantic processing of stimuli in rsvp streams
Pesciarelli, Francesca Cognition and Language Lab., Univerity of Padua, Padua, Italy
An Attentional Blink paradigm was used to directly compare and contrast semantic and repetition priming to reported versus missed words. Three target words (T1, T2, T3) were embedded among rapidly black non-word distractors for report at the end of each trial. T1 was never related to T2 and T3, while, T2 and T3 were unrelated, semantically related, or identical. Whether or not T2 was reported, I observed both semantic and repetition priming of T3 in both report accuracy and certain ERP measures. The results suggest that semantic and repetition priming appear to engage at least partially overlapping mechanisms.

IS-096: Evaluation policy and practice in different countries

Thomas D. Cook, Renate Soellner (chair)
Within this symposium our goal is to emphasize the significance of evaluation in today's society, especially in the field of psychology. The symposium will promote the exchange of information and opinions among international evaluation experts. Therefore the policy and practice of evaluation research in different countries will be reflected. Difficulties of applied evaluation research and answers to these problems will be discussed. In particular, specifics when doing evaluation in developing countries will be presented. Furthermore, the issue of educating evaluators will be raised.

Empirically validated non-experimental methods in evaluation
Steiner, Peter M. Dept. of Policy Research, Northwestern University, Evanston, USA
Randomized experiments constitute the gold standard for evaluating treatments and social programs. Since randomized experiments are often hard to implement non-experimental methods are frequently employed to estimate causal effects: regression discontinuity designs, interrupted time series designs, or non-equivalent comparison group designs. Here, we mainly focus on propensity score techniques for balancing non-equivalent groups. Using an experimental within-study comparison of a randomized and quasi-experiment as well as corresponding results from Mexico's PROGRES-SA program we empirically show under which conditions non-equivalent group comparisons can reproduce experimental results. These conditions include the measurement of all covariates related to treatment selection and outcome as well as sufficient overlap, i.e. homogeneity of groups.

Special considerations when doing evaluations in developing countries: The experience of the World Bank and of regional development banks
Cook, Thomas D. Dept. of Policy Research, Northwestern University, Evanston, IL, USA
This paper describes and critically analyzes the more recent evaluation philosophy and practice in international agencies dealing with developing nations, especially the World Bank and regional development banks. An explanation is offered as to why this philosophy was adopted. The explanation emphasizes the perceived failure of strategies predicated on statistical adjustments for selection bias and the growing sense of the viability of

experimental alternatives with which psychologists are familiar.

Institutionalizing the randomized experiment as the praxis model in educational evaluation in the US
Wong, Vivian Dept. of Policy Research, Northwestern University, Evanston, IL, USA
This paper describes the 2001-2007 funding activities of the Institute for Education Sciences (IES) that are designed to privilege random assignment experiments in American educational research. This priority is manifest in IES' research grant programs, evaluation research activities, training programs, founding of a novel professional association, and recruiting psychologists and economists into education research. Although this agenda was initially met with resistance, the process of privileging experiments is now well underway. But will it outlast the Bush Administration, and be incorporated into university teaching curricula and the decisions of journal editors?

Education of evaluation in German-speaking countries
Soellner, Renate FB 12, AB Evaluation, Freie Universität Berlin, Berlin, Germany
The education in evaluation has been part of the academic formation in psychology in Germany for two decades. With an increased demand on evaluators in various social fields in the last years a growing offer of master programs in evaluation emerged. In order to reveal the contents of a psychological based education in evaluation research a web based research of academic courses of 44 German institutes of psychology was conducted. The results of the study will be discussed against the background of master programs' topics in evaluation research in German-speaking countries.

Evaluation policy and practice in German-speaking countries
Spiel, Christiane Inst. für Psychologie, Universität Wien, Wien, Austria
The significance of evaluation and its constant development require a continual dialogue between professionals involved in scientific evaluation, evaluation implementation, and commissioning of evaluation. To meet these demands the DeGEval – Gesellschaft fuer Evaluation was founded in 1997. Central aims of the DeGEval are: (1) professionalization of evaluation by e.g., the "Standards for Evaluation" and the "Guidelines for Evaluation Clients', (2) consolidation of different perspectives, and (3) promotion of information flow and dialogue. The paper presents the DeGEval's contributions to these goals and discusses evaluation policy and practice in the German-speaking countries.

IS-097: Research with Hispanic populations in the Americas

Rolando Díaz-Loving (chair)
Wundt (1916) pioneered both behavioral and cultural psychology. In retrospect, his principal objective of integrating them into an objective, generalizable, yet culturally sensitive science is a project in progress. An ecological or cultural perspective requires direct inclusion or measurement of cultural and structural variables as well as functional relationships of psychological variables within a cultural system. In this symposium we address the contributions that emic studies with Hispanic populations living in the Americas have on the development of further theme selection, theory building, measurement issues, intervention strategies and evaluation. In particular, suicide, family, children and self will be touched on.

Understanding the higher rates of suicide attempts among Hispanic teenage females
Zayas, Luis George Warren Brown School, Washington University, St. Louis, USA
Two decades of national surveys conducted in the U.S. show that adolescent Hispanic females report suicidal behaviors, including suicide ideation and attempts, at higher rates than U.S. youth of other ethnic and racial groups, however only recent research has been focused on Hispanic girls. This paper presents theoretical explanations drawn from cultural psychology, female development, and family functioning. Findings from qualitative and quantitative analyses will be presented. The phenomenology of the suicide attempts suggests a dissociative process not unlike other well-known cultural syndromes. Questionnaire data points to malalignments in the relationship between adolescent females and their parents, especially their mothers.

Mexican ethnopsychology and measurment
Reyes Lagunes, Isabel Facultad de Psicología, Nat. Auton. Univ. of Mexico, México City, Mexico
Assuming that the purpose of all psychological test is to obtain a representative sample of behaviors in which the characteristic, we want to measure is reflected, a series of qualitative-quantitative techniques have been developed to efficiently and ethical evaluate Mexican populations since it allows us to identify the "etic" and "emic" elements of the psychological constructs. The technique of Modified Natural Semantic Networks (Reyes-Lagunes, 1993) is presented as well as diverse examples of its use. Besides, universal instruments and definitions will be contrasted with the peculiarities found in our country.

Assertivness and copying in Mexican children
Flores-Galaz, Mirta Dept. of Psychology, Universidad Autonoma Yucatan, Merida, Mexico
The development of assertiveness is a complex process which occurs through time and is linked to the developmental processes, inserted in a cultural context. The objective of this research is to present studies used to elaborate a scale of measurement assertiveness for children, as well as to explore the relationship among coping styles, attachment styles, and the locus of control. In these studies, participated 1487 children from the city of Merida, Yucatan, Mexico, selected through a non probabilistic sample. The statistic analysis is presented for each one of them and the findings are discussed from the Mexican ethnopsychology.

IS-098: The 2nd century of 'mental tests': Perspectives and prospects on assessment in the 21st century

James Pellegrino (chair)
2008 marks the 100th anniversary of Binet & Simon's publication Le développement de l'intelligence chez les enfants. in L'Année psychologique.. Their seminal work helped spawn the 1st century of mental tests. Without doubt, the assessment of individual intellect has had a profound effect on psychology and education across the globe. As we begin the 2nd century of mental testing, a group of scholars from across the globe has been assembled to consider what we now understand about the nature of human intellect and individual achievement and its implications for theory and practice in the fields of psychological and educational assessment.

Integrating learning theory in an era of accountability testing

Gitomer, Drew *Policy Evaluation & Research, Educational Testing Service, Princeton, USA*
Determining the effectiveness of schools, teachers, and educational interventions has increasingly relied on outcomes of large-scale standardized achievement tests together with increasingly sophisticated analytic evaluative models and research designs. However, the usefulness of these techniques is limited by the quality of assessment instruments that remain relatively divorced from theories of learning and performance. This schism also leads to unfortunate practices in school systems and classrooms. This talk will describe a project being conducted at ETS that builds on advances in cognitive science, technology, and psychometrics to design a new approach to the assessment of student learning outcomes.

Diagnostic testing that just might make a difference

Wiliam, Dylon *Inst. of Education, University of London, London, United Kingdom*
There is appeal in the idea that assessment might support instruction, as well as measuring its effects, but to date the contribution of the psychometric community has been limited. Diagnostic tests are relatively insensitive to instruction, provide instructional guidance that arrives too late to be useful, and are more focused on what students have not learned, rather than what might be done about it. In this paper, I describe a model for the development of single items that can be integrated by teachers into their own classroom practice as "hinge-point" questions, allowing them to make "real-time" adjustments to instruction.

A cognitive architecture framework for the assessment of the human mind: Modular approaches and technical advances

Cascallar, Eduardo *Katholieke Universiteit Leuven, Brussels, Belgium*
The renewed focus on a cognitive architecture as the basic tool to understand the functions of the human mind and its connections to the underlying physical structure, has renewed the emphasis on accurately representing and measuring the functioning of the modular components involved in our "mind's functioning". New measurement approaches and technical developments assess the emergence of and the level of functioning of such cognitive functions through the understanding of the independent modules and their interactions, opening new possibilities in the assessment of mental functions, and the understanding of the role of consciousness and mental workspace in efficient information processing.

Educational assessment and advances in the understanding of human learning

Masters, Geoff *Educational Research, Australian Council for, Camberwell Vic, Australia*
Research into human learning during the 20th century underlined the importance of providing individuals with learning opportunities appropriate to their current levels of readiness and motivation; of developing deep understandings of concepts and principles that provide meaning and structure to knowledge; and of providing supportive learning environments that encourage risk-taking, self-monitoring and a positive view of one's own capacity for learning. This paper will consider the implications of this research for educational assessment in the 21st century. It will be argued that a greater focus will be required on the use of assessments to explore and understand the learning progress of individuals.

IS-099: Advances in evidence-based psychological practice

John Hunsley (chair)
In this symposium we present a sense of the scope of evidence-based practice in psychology and illustrate some of the promises and challenges associated with such practices. Beginning with a focus on assessment, developments in evidence-based psychological assessment and the scientific basis of clinical case formulation will be explored. Turning to evidence-based treatments, the important issues of considering treatment acceptability as part of service delivery and dissemination efforts and evaluating the results of treatment effectiveness studies are examined. The symposium concludes with an illustration of how research can and should inform efforts to develop and implement prevention programs.

Evidence-based assessment

Hunsley, John *Dept. of Psychology, University of Ottawa, Ottawa, Canada*
In recent years there has been growing attention to the importance of ensuring that psychological assessment instruments are firmly supported by scientific evidence. In this presentation, diverse strategies that have been proposed for determining the extent to which an instrument is evidence-based will be briefly reviewed. Additionally, to illustrate the range of evidence-based instruments that are available for both clinical and research purposes, examples will be provided of evidence-based instruments for assessing both youth and adults. Finally, a case will be made regarding the pressing need for research evidence that addresses the clinical utility of psychological instruments.

Empirical foundations of case formulation

Haynes, Stephen N. *Dept. of Psychology, University of Hawaii, Honolulu, USA*
Clinical case formulation is based on the assumption that, compared to standardized treatments, matching treatment mechanisms to causal relations for clients' behavior problems will result in enhanced treatment outcome. The arithmetic and conceptual models underlying the presumed benefits and challenges of clinical case formulation will be presented. Additionally, necessary research designs and data on the incremental outcome of clinical case formulation for several behavior problems (focusing on severe behavior problems) will be presented

Parents' acceptance and use of evidence based treatments for childhood Attention-Deficit/ Hyperactivity Disorder: How to sell what works

Johnston, Charlotte *Dept. of Psychology, University of British Columbia, Vancouver, Canada* *Mah, Janet* *Dept. of Psychology, University of British Columbia, Vancouver, Canada*
Medication and behavior management are evidenced-based (EB) treatments for childhood Attention-Deficit/Hyperactivity Disorder (ADHD). However, parents are frequently reluctant to use these treatments and prefer nonEB alternatives. We present studies examining parents' acceptability and use of these treatments. Parents see medication as less acceptable than behavioral treatment, despite acknowledging medication's greater effectiveness. Acceptability of behavioral treatment predicts short-term, but not longer-term, use. In addition, factors such as parents' beliefs about ADHD and attributions for child behavior predicted aspects of acceptability and adherence to these EB treatments. The implications for increasing parental uptake of EB treatments are considered.

An update on research-informed benchmarks for psychological treatments

Lee, Catherine *Dept. of Psychology, University of Ottawa, Ottawa, Canada*
Hunsley and Lee (2007) conducted a focused review of the treatment effectiveness literature published up until March 2006. A comparison of data from these studies to benchmarks from recent reviews of efficacy trials revealed treatment completion rates comparable to those found in the efficacy benchmarks. Moreover, in most instances, the improvement rates were comparable in effectiveness studies to those reported in randomized clinical trials of treatment efficacy. In this presentation, the review will be updated to include studies published between March 2006 and March 2008. Recommendations for practice and research will be presented.

Systemic challenges facing school based mental health programs

Santor, Darcy *Dept. of Psychology, University of Ottawa, Ottawa, Canada*
School based health centers, early identification screening programs and curriculum based prevention programs are three of the most common delivery modalities for mental health problem identification and intervention in schools. Many of the challenges facing these various initiatives are systemic but may be resolved by embedding them within a health literacy framework emphasizing knowledge acquisition and by implementing these programs with interactive, internet based tools. I illustrate how internet-based approaches can address a number of these challenges, including (a) increasing the availability and accessibility mental health resources, (b) improving knowledge uptake and ensuring on-going evaluation, and (c) maximizing program sustainability.

IS-100: Disaster trauma and intervention

Damodar Suar (chair)
On average, more than two disasters occur everyday somewhere in the world. Natural disasters are most devastating in developing countries and cause widespread human sufferings. Following a disaster, survivors are plunged into psychological and physical sufferings. Survivors need psychosocial care and survival necessities to ameliorate their conditions. With this backdrop, the symposium aims to discuss the disaster trauma, its causes, risk and protective factors of trauma at individual level, and the mass-hysteria and fear psychosis at the community level. It further aims to focus on intervention strategies to ameliorate the trauma at individual level and the symptoms at community level.

Phase-specific intervention for psychosocial sequel of disasters: A longitudinal perspective for improving disaster planning

Kar, Nilamadhab *Dept. of Psychiatry, Wolverhampton City PCT, Wolverhampton, United Kingdom*
Disasters are traumas of such magnitude that the internal existing systems fail to cope with the effects. Psychiatric outcomes vary among individuals and societies depending on their psychosocioeconomic status, resource loss, personal meaning of loss, and adequacy of external intervention. The paper discusses the conceptual framework of different phases relevant to psychosocial sequelae of disasters taking into consideration of manifestations and needs over a period of time. Supporting evidences for predisaster warning phase, during and immediately after, early, recent and remote postdisaster phases based on their manifestations and needs are provided along with suggestions for phase-appropriate interventions.

Exploring the psychological scar of tsunami in children and adolescents

Bhushan, Braj Humanities & Social Sciences, IIT Kanpur, Kanpur, India

A three phase study was conducted to understand the psychological aftereffects of the December 26, 2004 tsunami on children and adolescent victims (primary and secondary). Initially, posttraumatic stress and emotional distress were measured in 101 child victims. This was followed by examining 130 children and adolescents who did not directly experience this catastrophe but had verbal/ pictorial exposure of it. Finally, young volunteers who rushed to one of the sites as relief volunteers were studied. Females reported higher rate of symptoms in the affected group. Non-affected males were higher on intrusion and females on withdrawal symptoms.

Resource loss and trauma

Das, Namita CAS in Psychology, Utkal University, Bhubaneswar, India *Suar, Damodar* Humanities and Social Sciences, IIT Kharagpur, Kharagpur, India

The study examines the impact of resource loss and social support on disaster trauma of tsunami survivors. Data were collected through structured interview schedule 14 months after the tsunami from 416 survivors in Nagapattinum district. The postdisaster trauma was assessed using measures of posttraumatic stress, anxiety, and physical health symptoms. The results reveal that the loss of varied resources increases the postdisaster trauma. Increase in received social support enhances perceived social support and both decrease postdisaster trauma. The internal control, communal mastery, and coping style interacting with the extent resource loss and social support have buffered the post-disaster trauma.

Outgrowing the trauma: Some lessons from disasters in India

Misra, Girishwar Dept. of Psychology, University of Delhi, New Delhi, India

Disasters arrest the normal functioning at individual and community levels by causing unanticipated loss of material and human resources and creating health problems. This presentation examines the various consequences of disasters at individual and community levels and efforts to cope and outgrow from the trauma. The role of socio-economic and psychological sub systems in defining trauma and reconfiguring their lives for healthy development is examined. The results imply an urgent need to evolve culturally embedded comprehensive support systems in the developing countries like India which are becoming more vulnerable in the wake of population pressure, environmental hazards and inadequate technology.

Disaster and trauma: Who suffers and who recovers from trauma, and how?

Suar, Damodar Humanities and Social Sciences, IIT Kharagpur, Kharagpur, India *Das, Namita* CAS in Psychology, Utkal University, Bhubaneswar, India

This study examines the occurrence of disasters, disaster trauma, causes of trauma, and intervention strategies. In India, a disaster occurs in each eight days and natural disasters are most devastating. Disaster trauma manifests in cognitive, affective, behavioural, and physical symptoms. What causes trauma are the reactivation of disaster memory, resource loss, and inadequate social support. Severely exposed victims, children, elderly, poor, lowly educated people, low caste survivors, widows/ widowers, and members from larger families are at risk for trauma. Certain personality characteristics and social support buffer trauma. Intervention strategies are discussed to ameliorate trauma during different phases of natural disasters.

Psychosocial support and intervention in Godhra riots

Nanda Biswas, Urmi Clinical and Health Psychology, Whitelands College, London, United Kingdom

The Godhra riots in 2002 witnessed about 1,000 deaths and large number of families were uprooted and forced to seek shelter in rehabilitation camps. The enormous pain and loss to people was not easy to overcome. Civil societies planned intervention that resulted in the Gujarat Reconciliation Programme launched by CARE India, and also the intervention initiated by Action Aid India. In this paper, case studies of five organizations namely; UTTHAN, OLAKH, UNNATI, SEWA, and Tribhubandas Foundation are covered in riot-affected area. Their intervention in managing emotions, anxiety, support, and lifestyle modification is presented and implications are discussed.

IS-101: Social and cognitive variables related with physical activity practice

Jesús Rodríguez Marín (chair)

The objective of this Symposium is to show the more relevant lines of investigation analyzing theoretical and practical perspectives about the prediction of sport and physical activity practice. Concretely, in this symposium we present results of investigations that have applied different theoretical models that improve the understanding of the processes of acquisition of the exercise behavior. Different models as the Eccles' (1996) expectancy-estimates socialization model and Bronfenbrenner's (1993) ecological systems approach to development, the self-determination theory (Ryan & Deci, 2002), the achievement goals theory (Nicholls, 1989), and the theory of planned behavior (Ajzen, 1991) applied to the study of the acquisition of healthy-lifestyles and the sport dropout, were analyzed.

The role of significant others in the practice of physical activities

Brustad, Robert School of Sport and Exercise, Unversity of Nothern Colorado, Greeley, CO, USA

This presentation will focus on the nature of significant other influence on the physical activity and sport involvement of children and adolescents. The nature and type of significant other influence changes substantially according to the age and developmental status of the individual affected, and according to the context and meaning that characterizes the involvement. Relevant theoretical perspectives will be addressed, most notably Eccles' expectancy-value theory and future directions identified. Current methodological advances will also be discussed.

Motivation, commitment and drop-out in youth elite soccer

Torregrosa, Miquel Psic. BÀsica y Evolut., Universitat Autonoma Barcelona, Bellaterra, Spain *Cruz, Jaume* Psicologia Bàsica, Universitat Autónoma Barcelona, Barcelona, Spain *Sousa, Catarina* Psicologia Bàsica, Universitat Autónoma Barcelona, Barcelona, Spain

The present study explored the relations between motivation, commitment and drop-out in youth soccer players. One hundred and twenty eight young soccer players competing in elite leagues participated in the study. Results show that elite youth players are both highly ego and task oriented, and that they show high levels of sport commitment. At the beginning of the following season 80,4% of the players continued in the same team, and the 19.6% of so-called drop-out split in 16.46% of change of club, 0.60% of changing sport and only a 2.43% of effective drop-out of youth elite soccer.

Motivation and healthy life styles in adolescents

Cervello, Eduardo Art, Humanities and Laws, University Miguel Hernandez, Elche, Spain

This study analyzes the relationships between the motivational climate, goal orientations, the assessment of physical education classes and the behavioral patters of healthy (i.e., practicing sports as extra-curricular activity), and non-healthy lifestyles (consumption of alcohol, tobacco and other drugs) of 502 physical education students. A correlational-descriptive methodology was employed. The results indicated that the perception of a task-involving motivational climate predict positively the student's assessment of the physical education classes. Perception of an ego-involving motivational climate predicts negatively this assessment. Additionally, the assessment of the physical education classes predicts positively the practice of extracurricular sport activity and, such practice predicts negatively the consumption of drugs

---

IS-103: Gene x environment interactions in the life-course development of temperament and attachment

Liisa Keltikangas-Jarvinen (chair)

Interactions between genes and childhood environments in human development have evoked increasing interest. Serotonin system has been suggested to have a special role in a development of personality. Here, an effect of an interaction between serotonin system and childhood environment on adulthood temperament, depression, and attachment have been studied. The findings suggest an obvious role of serotonin in a development of human temperament, however so, that there mostly exists no main effect of serotonin on adulthood outcomes, but serotonin moderates a way how a person experiences his or her environment. In addition, adulthood attachment may be, at least partly, biologically rooted.

The serotonin transporter in emotion regulation and social cognition

Lesch, Klaus-Peter Psychiatrie und Psychotherapie, Universität Würzburg, Würzburg, Germany

Objectives: The gene encoding the serotonin transporter (5-HTT) has been associated with anxiety-related traits and susceptibility for depression. Here we highlight recent discoveries related to allelic variation of 5-HTT function with respect to emotion regulation and social behavior, drawing from an interdisciplinary perspective of behavioral genetics and cognitive neuroscience. Results: We compare two models of 5-HTT-dependent modulation of brain activity and discuss the role of life stress experience in modifying 5-HTT function in the brain. Conclusions: The findings suggest that the impact of the 5-HTT gene on behavior is much broader than is commonly appreciated and may have a role in social cognition.

Temperament in childhood as a predictor of Harm Avoidance in adulthood: Moderation by the 5-HTR2A gene

Pulkki-Råback, Laura Dept. of Psychology, University of Helsinki, Helsinki, Finland *Merjonen, Päivi* Dept. of Psychology, University of Helsinki, Helsinki, Finland *Jokela, Markus* Dept. of Psychology, University of Helsinki, Helsinki, Finland *Salo, Johanna* Dept. of Psychology, University of Helsinki, Helsinki, Finland *Lehtimäki, Terho* Medical School, University of Tampere, Tampere, Finland

Objectives: To study the association of childhood temperament (Emotionality, Sociability, Activity) with adulthood Harm Avoidance and whether the association is moderated by the serotonin receptor 5-HTR2A gene. Methods: 21-year follow-up study of 852 participants from a population-based sample aged in average 10 years at the baseline. Results:

Higher Sociability predicted lower Harm Avoidance over 21 years (B=-0.11, p= .002). However, in a subgroup of carriers of the T/T variant of the 5-HTR2A, higher Sociability was associated higher Harm Avoidance. Conclusions: Early temperament manifests itself in adulthood differentially, depending on genetic factors that regulate the serotonergic system.

Mother's life satisfaction and child's negative emotionality in adulthood: The moderating role of serotonin receptor 2A gene

Merjonen, Päivi *Dept. of Psychology, University of Helsinki, Helsinki, Finland* **Pulkki-Råback, Laura** *Dept. of Psychology, University of Helsinki, Helsinki, Finland* **Lehtimäki, Terho** *Medical School, University of Tampere, Tampere, Finland*

Objectives: We tested whether the interaction between HTR2A gene and maternal life satisfaction affects child's later negative emotionality (NE). Methods: The participants were 706 participants from the Cardiovascular Risk in Young Finns study, being 3-18 years old, when their mothers' life satisfaction was measured. Participants' NE was assessed 12, 17 and 21 years later. Results: Mother's dissatisfaction was associated with child's higher NE, especially its anger component, among carriers of any T allele, but not among carriers of CC genotype. Conclusions: Carriers of T allele are sensitive to environmental effects.

Attachment style in adulthood, the role of interleukin-6 (IL-6) gene and stressful events in early childhood

Salo, Johanna *Dept. of Psychology, University of Helsinki, Helsinki, Finland* **Pulkki-Råback, Laura** *Dept. of Psychology, University of Helsinki, Helsinki, Finland* **Lehtimäki, Terho** *Medical School, University of Tampere, Tampere, Finland* **Keltikangas-Järvinen, Liisa** *Dept. of Psychology, University of Helsinki, Helsinki, Finland*

Objectives: Tentative evidence shows that in addition to environmental effects, individuals may differ in their genetic susceptibility to form attachment bonds. We examined whether the IL-6 -174 G>C genotype, a potential determinant of stress-reactivity, is associated with adult attachment style i) directly ii) by moderating the association between childhood stressful events and adult attachment. Methods: a 21-year, prospective, longitudinal study with a population based sample of 1691 subjects. Results: IL-6 genotype had a main and a moderating effect on dismissing-avoidant adult attachment style. Conclusions: Genes may directly influence the development of attachment, and increase vulnerability to environmental effects.

The association between mother–child relationship in childhood and reward dependence in adulthood is moderated by the serotonin receptor 2A gene

Jokela, Markus *Dept. of Psychology, University of Helsinki, Helsinki, Finland* **Salo, Johanna** *Dept. of Psychology, University of Helsinki, Helsinki, Finland* **Pulkki-Råback, Laura** *Dept. of Psychology, University of Helsinki, Helsinki, Finland* **Lehtimäki, Terho** *Medical School, University of Tampere, Tampere, Finland* **Keltikangas-Järvinen, Liisa** *Dept. of Psychology, University of Helsinki, Helsinki, Finland*

Objective: To examine whether the T102C polymorphism of the serotonin receptor 2A gene (HTR2A) moderates the association between maternal nurturance in childhood and adolescence, and reward dependence (RD) in adulthood. Methods: Cardiovascular Risk in Young Finns study, participants aged 3 to 18 years at baseline and followed for 21 years (n=913). Temperament and Character Inventory (TCI). Results: High maternal nurturance predicted high RD in T/T genotype carriers but not in T/C or C/C carriers, independently of depressive symptoms. Conclusions: The

role of early mother–child relationship in adult attachment-related temperament may depend on allelic variation in the HTR2A gene.

IS-104: Adolescent psychoemotional wellbeing during the period of social change: Actual situation and possibilities of intervention

Andrei Podolskij (chair)

Main purpose of the recent symposium is to consider and compare approaches to the adolescent psychoemotional wellbeing elaborated and tested in the frames of essentially different theoretical outlooks and paradigms - cultural-historical, cross-cultural, and psychoanalytical. The central angle of consideration is to find similarities (phenomena found, intervention technologies implemented, etc.) rather than differences. The emphasis is done on the possibilities of intervention and its efficacy to improve adolescent psychoemotional wellbeing during the period of social change under different social-economic and cultural conditions.

Psychopathology of adolescence as a normal way of being in the post-modern social link

Lesourd, Serge *Faculté de Psychologie, Université Louis Pasteur, Strasbourg, France*

Adolescence is time, structural more than chronological, during which the subject confront to the interdiction to realise entirely and totally the desire. Well our post-modern social link, the liberal one, preaches individualisation of the human relations, so the teenager let be alone in front of his choose and his necessary limits. In this work, we display, with clinical examples, how post-modern society teenagers are controlled by logics who prescribe to thrill (addictions) and to do (consummation, violence, etc.). When use is impossible, then personal fall in value (suicide, depression, etc.) or attacks of our fellow-men (violence, law refusal, etc.) become the normal ways of being.

Testing intervention program to decrease adolescent depressed mood and anxiety

Podolskij, Andrei *Dept. of Developm. Psychology, Moscow State University, Moscow, Russia* **Idobaeva, Olga** *Developmental Psychology, Moscow State Univeristy, Moscow, Russia*

The purpose of the study is to construct and test the intervention program designed to decrease adolescent depressed mood and anxiety. Theoretical and empirical sources of the intervention design are presented and discussed. The key factors that affect an adolescent psycho-emotional non-wellbeing are selected on the base of the big scale data base collected in the sample of Russian and Ukrainian adolescents, their parents, and school teachers. An intervention program has been designed and implemented in accordance with those findings. The results achieved demonstrate strong and weak sides of the intervention program for junior and senior, male and female adolescents.

The role of school environment and family climate in promoting identity change, psychological well-being and integration of immigrant and refugee youth in Canada

Chirkov, Valery *Dept. of Psychology, University of Saskatchewan, Saskatoon, Canada* **de Guzman, Jaquieline** *Dept. of Psychology, University of Saskatchewan, Saskatoon, Canada* **Geres, Koreen** *Dept. of Psychology, University of Saskatchewan, Saskatoon, Canada*

The presentation reports the results of semi-structured interviews of 76 immigrant and refugee families from China, India, Iraq, Sudan, Columbia and other countries regarding their relations within families and consequences of these relations for

children's feeling of ethnic identity, well-being, future life plans and potential for integration into Canadian society. Children's perceptions of school environment will also be reported. Statistical analysis together with the qualitative analysis of the interviews was conducted to reveal direct and moderated relations among the variables. Universal and specific regularities will be reported. The interdisciplinary approach to study immigrant youth will be strongly advocated.

IS-105: Sex and attachment across cultures: A 56-nation study

David Schmitt (chair)

In this symposium, presenters will focus on the systematic distribution of romantic attachment styles and sexual strategies across cultures. Findings from the International Sexuality Description Project—a survey study of over 17,000 people from 56 nations—will be highlighted to reveal, for example, that secure romantic attachment is "normative" in a majority of cultures, preoccupied romantic attachment is particularly prevalent in East Asian cultures, and dismissing romantic attachments are associated with high-stress ecological environments. Research will be presented on sociosexuality, harassment, and sexual jealousy across cultures, as well as using the Internet to effectively collect cross-cultural data on human sexuality.

Sex and attachment across cultures: A 56-nation study

Schmitt, David *Dept. of Psychology, Bradley University, Peoria, USA*

This presentation will focus on the systematic distribution of romantic attachment styles across cultures. Findings from the International Sexuality Description Project—a survey study of over 17,000 people from 56 nations—will be highlighted to reveal, for example, that secure romantic attachment is "normative" in a majority of cultures, preoccupied romantic attachment is particularly prevalent in East Asian cultures, and dismissing romantic attachments are associated with high-stress ecological environments.

Sexuality and attachment: Large scale data collection and cross-validation via the internet

Reips, Ulf-Dietrich *Inst. für Psychologie, Universität Zürich, Zürich, Switzerland*

Internet-based research bears various benefits: (a) studies can be delivered to large numbers of geographically and demographically distributed participants quickly and with low effort; (b) Internet-based research is cost-effective in time, space, administration, and labor; (c) one can recruit large heterogeneous or homogeneous samples, also of individuals with rare conditions of interest (e.g. sexsomnia, Mangan & Reips, 2007). Due to the anonymity of the setting, the Internet is particularly suited for studies on sensitive topics. An Internet-based version of the Internet Sexuality Description Project (ISDP-2) survey created with WEXTOR (http://wextor.eu) is presented, methods and challenges are discussed.

Sociosexuality: Effects of attachment, sex and age in Brazilian samples

Benedetti, José *Dept. of Experim. Psychology, University of São Paulo, São Paulo, Brazil* **Corrêa Varella, Marco Antônio** *Dep. Psicologia Experimental, Universidade de São Paulo, São Paulo, Brazil* **Bussab, Vera Silvia** *Dep. Psicologia Experimental, Universidade de São Paulo, São Paulo, Brazil*

Inter and intra-sexual variation in sociosexuality was investigated regarding attachment and age. 221 undergraduates (Social, Engineering and Biological Areas; 21 years) and 81 adults (38 years) answered the Sociosexual Orientation Inventory (Simpson & Gangestad, 1991) and Relationship Questionnaire

(Bartholomew & Horowitz, 1991). Few researches had been done with non-psychology students and adults. In both age groups, men were more unrestricted (ANOVA). Only unrestricted women had higher model of self (undergraduates) and model of other (adults) styles (r-Pearson). Independently of the cycle in Life History, universal sex differences were confirmed, and attachment style interacted with the sociosexuality differently in each sex.

Sexual development of Lebanese youth: Perceptions and practices of sexuality

Khoury, Brigitte Dept. of Psychiatry, American University of Beirut, Beirut, Lebanon
The purpose of this study was to assess the sexual development of youth in Lebanon: their perceptions, attitudes and practices of sexuality. The study was conducted on a sample (n=500) of Lebanese university students. The topics investigated included sexual development, education and practices, society and sexuality, virginity, masturbation and sexual myths. Results showed that despite the apparent modernization of the Lebanese society, conservatism seemed to be prominent when it came to sexuality. Clear differences were found between men and women. Family and religion, the two pillars of society, were still found to be the main influences of sexual development with the youth group.

Sexual harassment across cultures

DeSouza, Eros Dept. of Psychology, Illinois State University, Normal, USA
This paper will discuss empirical studies that used the Sexual Experiences Questionnaire (Fitzgerald et al., 1988), generally considered one of the most widely used, as well as one of the most valid and reliable instruments that assesses sexual harassment, to highlight frequency rates and outcomes across countries. In addition, studies that investigated perceptions of cross-sex and same-sex sexual harassment, including recommended punishment, will be discussed. Implications will be drawn from the cultural dimensions of high-low power and individualism-collectivism proposed by Hofstede (2001), as well hierarchy-egalitarianism and conservatism-autonomy proposed by Schwartz (1999).

Sexuality and jealousy across cultures

Fernandez, Ana Maria Escuela de Psicología, Universidad de Santiago, Santiago, Chile
Research on jealousy responses to sexual and emotional infidelity supports the universality and sex differentiated nature of this phenomena (in the US, Europe and Asia). A few studies have evaluated jealousy in Spanish-speaking countries, which will be revised in the present discussion, addressing replications conducted in Argentina, Chile, Colombia, Venezuela and Spain. There is also some recent developments and variants of the classical forced-choice methodology, extended to include continuous ratings of jealousy situations, as well as attachment motives for the jealousy response. The implications of the universality of this phenomenon supports the deeper inquire on universal attachment mechanisms that may be sexually dimorphic.

IS-106: Testing and assessment in emerging and developing countries II: Challenges and recent advances

Fanny M. Cheung, Marise Born (chair)
With the growing need for psychological assessment in emerging and developing countries, psychologists encounter many scientific and ethical challenges. This part of the symposium illustrates the challenges of testing and assessment in Vietnam, Indonesia, China and South Africa, and how psychologists contribute to recent advances. In addition to translation and adaptation of imported tests, the combined emic-etic approach of developing indigenous personality assessment measures in China and South Africa are presented as examples of good practice.

Adapting tests for diagnosing learning disabilities in developing countries: The case of Vietnam

Grégoire, Jacques Dept. of Psychology, Université Cathol. de Louvain, Louvain-la-Neuve, Belgium
Vietnam puts strong emphasis children education. As a consequence, the number of children with learning disabilities is growing and there is a need for diagnostic tests. Some French tests were adapted recently in Vietnamese, raising several issues. Unlike achievement tests, diagnostic tests are based on models of cognitive processes involved in reading, writing and calculating. Because of the specificity of the Vietnamese language, the models underlying the tests and the related tasks had to be adapted. Education of test users had also to be organized because an understanding of the models is required to correctly interpret the tests scores.

Challenges of test adaptation and development in Indonesia

Halim, Magdalena Dept. of Psychology, ATMA JAYA Catholic University, Jakarta Selatan, Indonesia
With a growing need for Indonesian-language psychological tests, imported tests are often translated, despite unfamiliarity with cross-cultural assessment methods and copyright requirements. The translation process is not well defined and documented. Standardization and norming of imported tests are inadequate. Developing local tests is not regarded as an important contribution for Indonesian psychologists. I will illustrate the problems of test adaptation and development in Indonesia including the implications on test interpretation with examples from the Indonesian NEO PI-R, MMPI-2, WAIS-R and a local personality test. Possible strategies to stimulate the development of local tests in the future will be discussed.

Etic vs. Emic personality assessment: An integrative approach for deriving an indigenous measure for Chinese personality

Cheung, Fanny M. Dept. of Psychology, Chinese Univ. of Hong Kong, Hong Kong, China, People's Republic of : Hong Kong SAR
In response to the need for culturally relevant personality measures, we adopted a combined emic-etic approach to develop the Chinese Personality Assessment Inventory (CPAI). I will report the program of research that went into the development and validation of the CPAI for adults and for adolescents (CPAI-A). In addition to confirming universal personality dimensions, the interpersonal aspects of personality salient to the Chinese culture are highlighted in the CPAI. Cross-cultural applications of the CPAI showed that these relationally oriented traits are also relevant to non-Chinese cultures, resulting in the renaming of the CPAI to Cross-Cultural Personality Assessment Inventory (CPAI-2).

Uncovering the personality structure of the 11 language groups in South Africa: SAPI project

Meiring, Deon Dept. of Industrial Psychology, University of Stellenbosch, Stellenbosch, South Africa Van de Vijver, Fons Department of Psychology, University of Tilburg, Tilburg, Netherlands Rothmann, Ian Dept. of Industrial Psychology, North-West University, Potchefstroom, South Africa De Bruin, Deon Dept. of Industrial Psychology, University of Stellenbosch, Johannesburg, South Africa
South Africa has 11 official languages and four major ethnic groups. There is a societal and scientific need for comprehensive personality questionnaires that provide reliable and valid measures across all cultural and language groups. Imported questionnaires based on a Western model of independence may not be appropriate for describing African personality in which interdependence (Ubuntu) is more salient. The SAPI project aims to develop a comprehensive personality questionnaire for all South-African language groups. We describe Stage 1 of the project in which person-descriptive terms were gathered and clustered across the 11 languages to come up with a personality structure.

IS-107: Social development, peer relationships and pro-social behaviour

José Eduardo Moreno, Annie Karin Schulz (chair)
The importance of bonding with parents, socialization of the developing child and adolescent within the family and school context, measurement of social skills and the contribution of peer relationships to social development wil be discussed. We present some interesting findings on the relation of peer interaction with their family, social environment and personality. As personality is concerned, psychoticism, neuroticism and extroversion are associated positively with peer negative influence and peer delinquent behaviour. Special attention will be given to the assessment of intervention programs for the development of prosocial behaviour and to the Social Skills Improvement System.

Two decades of social skills research with the social skills rating system

Elliott, Stephen N. Learning Science Institute, Vanderbilt University, Nashville, TN, USA
The Social Skills Rating System has for many researchers become a common lens to capture perceptions of the prosocial behavior of children and youth. Thus, it is important to understand the history of this instrument and what has been learned about children's social behavior over 20 years. This knowledge has played a substantial role in the revision of the SSRS, called the Social Skills Improvement System (SSIS). A co-author of the SSIS will share perspectives on (a) the measurement of social skills, (b) what has been learned about children's social behavior, and (c) what changes lie ahead for persons who wish to use the revised instrument to assess children's social skills.

Methodological perspectives in measuring the effects of an intervention program with adolescents: Pre-post test assessment and questionnaires to evaluate the program

Garaigordobil, Maite Dept. of Clinical Psychology, University Basque Country, San Sebastián, Spain Maganto, Carmen Dept. of Clinical Psychology, University Basque Country, San Sebastián, Spain Pérez, José Ignacio Dept. of Clinical Psychology, University Basque Country, San Sebastián, Spain
The study compared the results obtained when evaluating the program with two assessment methodologies. The sample is made up of 174 adolescents from 12 to 14 years of age (125 experimental and 49 controls). The research uses an experimental multi-group pre-posttest design with repeated measures and control groups. The results suggest that pre-posttest assessment is more suitable when the goal is to validate the intervention, whereas the questionnaires are useful as screening instruments. The results obtained in the questionnaires completed by adolescents and adults were very coherent. The positive effects of the program on diverse factors of socio-emotional development are observed with both methodologies.

The relation of peer interaction to personality and family social environment

Ma, Hing Keung Dept. of Education Studies, Hong Kong Baptist University, Hong Kong, China, People's Republic of : Hong Kong SAR

Overall peer influence and peer's social behavior are associated positively and significantly with good relationship in family. In other words, positive peer interaction is associated with good family relationships. Adolescents came from family with strong cohesion and less conflict tended to have positive peer influences and peer relationships. As far as personality is concerned, psychoticism, neuroticism and extroversion are associated positively and significantly with peer negative influence and peer delinquent behaviour. On the other hand, social desirability is associated positively and significantly with peer positive and negative influences, and peer prosocial and antisocial behaviour. The findings will be interpreted in terms of the cultural context and psychological development.

Promoting prosocial behaviour in school by playground improvement: The effect of supervisors and play materials

Rebolo Marques, Amália Escola Básica Integrada, Faculdade Motricidade Humana, Sesimbra, Portugal

Children in primary school have better relations when the play spaces are improved with material to play freely, and active supervision. We will present three intervention programs that have been held in Portugal. These programs have as main objective the reduction of conflicts and bullying behaviour. We used anonymous questionnaires about peer relations in the playground during recess that children answered before, during and after the intervention to assess this programs. There are statistic differences between aggression and victimisation before and after the intervention, the percentages of children victimised and/or aggressors are lower in the end of all the programs.

Parental styles, self-perception and peer-attributed roles

Moreno, José Eduardo CIIPME, CONICET, Buenos Aires, Argentina Schulz, Annie Karin CIIPME, CONICET, Buenos Aires, Argentina

The main goal of this project was to assess the characteristics of those children who are attributed certain roles as bullies, leaders or isolated. The Argentine Scale of Child Perception of Parental Relationship, Loneliness Scale, Social Competence Scale and RCP of Masten were administered to a sample of 580 children from 9 to 11 years old who attended primary schools in Buenos Aires (Argentina). The results, for example, show that: the bullies have a low perception of their social competence as well as they do not seem to have any difficulties in their relationship with friends and classmates.

IS-108: Aging of the mentally retarded persons in South Asia

Anwarul Hasan Sufi (chair)

Life span of the mentally retarded persons significantly increased in some of the South Asian countries in recent years with the improvement of medical facilities and immunization programs. But new problems are being faced by the families to care them at home. The researcher depicts the life of the aged mentally retarded persons of south Asian countries on the basis of his personal observation of last 25 years. It was observed that the mild and moderate mentally retarded persons live longer than severe and profound mentally retarded persons. Psychosocial conditions are better among the rural than their urban counterparts.

Aging of the female mentally retarded persons in Bangladesh

Nazneen, Sultana Higher Secondary Education, HSTTI, Rajshahi, Bangladesh

In Bangladesh, longer life spans due to improved medical conditions have created new problems to maintain them inside their families. The problems faced by the female mentally retarded persons are more serious than their male counterparts due to socioeconomic conditions and many other drawbacks. The researcher closely observed 12 aged female mentally retarded persons during last 20 years. The researcher studied their health, economy, housing and social security conditions. It was found that though there are many problems they possess excellent subjective well-being. They consider themselves happy to live inside the warmth of their families.

Aging of the mentally retarded persons in Bangladesh: Biological

Haque, Tofazzal Dept. of Pharmacology, Rajshahi Medical College, Rajshahi, Bangladesh

The researcher closely studied 106 mentally retarded cases during 2001 -2006 in the north western part of Bangladesh. He studied the illness and diseases suffered by the cases. Though the major interest was to study the etiology and treatment of convulsive disorders of the cases, the researcher rank ordered the diseases those are barriers to the longer life span of the mentally retarded persons in the country. He also investigated the factors and recommended preventive measures. The researcher also depicts specific geriatric problems of selected 16 cases which project their biological conditions. Finally the researcher recommends some health policy programs.

Residential problems of the aged mentally retarded persons in Bangladesh

Sultana, Sabina Dept. of Psychology, University of Rajshahi, Rajshahi, Bangladesh

In the absence of social welfare networks and residential institutions for the mentally retarded persons in Bangladesh, all the mentally retarded persons are given care by their families. Due to many drawbacks of land and property ownership laws, many wealthy aged mentally retarded persons lead a miserable life inside their own families after the death of their parents. The researcher investigated their living condition, compared the residential accommodation problems and compared these conditions in relation to their degree of retardation, gender and rural-urban residential status.

Social security of the aged mentally retarded persons in Bangladesh

Rahman, Masudur Institute of Bangladesh Studie, University of Rajshahi, Rajshahi, Bangladesh

Though the national constitution of the Bangladesh guarantees that the state will take all the responsibilities of the handicapped persons, yet nothing is being done by the government. All the programs are run by the NGOs. The researcher investigated health, education, employment, housing and social security problems and prospects of several sample in different parts of the country. Finally he recommends that the government should provide monthly financial benefits to the families that the family members are motivated to take the responsibilities instead of sending them to residential homes.

Psychotropic Drug dependence of the aged mentally retarded persons in Bangladesh

Anisuzzaman, M.D. Dept. of Clinical Psychology, Gono Bishwabiddalaya, Dhaka, Bangladesh

Lack of awareness, negligence, healthcare behavioural drawbacks, etc. large majority of the mentally retarded persons are treated as mentally ill and not as mentally retarded. The physicians

prescribe them psychotropic drugs which the family members continue in future without consulting the physicians. Thus a large majority of the aged mentally retarded persons were found completely dependent on psychotropic drugs, especially anticonvulsants. The researcher completed in-depth case studies of 12 aged cases and depicted how and why they were prescribed psychotropic drugs during their childhood and why they are completely dependent on these drugs at their old age.

IS-109: Psychosocial consequences of long-term unemployment

Branimir Sverko (chair)

Despite considerable research during several decades and across various countries, the consequences of unemployment are still at issue. This symposium seeks to take stock of recent research advances and improve our understanding of the psychosocial impact of unemployment. First, the results of two recent long-term longitudinal studies examining the health effects of unemployment will be presented. Meta-analytic findings of the mental-health impact will be given next, followed by a paper discussing how the effects should be explained. The symposium will also address the experiences during job search, and tackle the issues of health impacts of enterprise restructuring.

Unemployment, underemployment and mental health in school leavers: A prospective longitudinal study

Winefield, Anthony H. School of Psychology, University of South Australia, Adelaide, Australia Metzer, Jack School of Psychology, University of South Australia, Adelaide, Australia Winefield, Helen School of Psychology, University of Adelaide, Adelaide, Australia

We report data from a 10-year prospective longitudinal study of school leavers that commenced in 2001. Although the official unemployment rate in Australia is much lower than in the early 1980s, it appears that unemployment is leading to more psychological distress now than it did then. We suspect that this is because young people are more likely to blame themselves for being unable to get jobs when the government keeps insisting (falsely) that jobs are plentiful. The current definition of unemployment in Australia excludes anyone who worked for one hour or more in the week prior to being surveyed.

Health impacts of prolonged unemployment and reemployment: A longitudinal study

Galic, Zvonimir Dept. of Psychology, University of Zagreb, Zagreb, Croatia Sverko, Branimir Dept. of Psychology, University of Zagreb, Zagreb, Croatia Maslic Sersic, Darja Dept. of Psychology, University of Zagreb, Zagreb, Croatia

In a three-way longitudinal survey of initially unemployed persons (N=370), we examined the impact of prolonged unemployment and reemployment on a series of self-assessed measures of both physical and mental health (captured by the SF-36 Health Survey). Already at T1, on most of the health indicators, the participants who remained unemployed scored lower then those who later gained employment. The participants reemployed at T2 and T3 exhibited improved health, but only on the mental-health indicators. The results suggest that poor physical health contributes to prolonged unemployment, while poor mental health both contributes to and results from unemployment.

The impact of long-term unemployment on mental health: Meta-analytic evidence

Paul, Karsten Business und Ökonomie, Universität Nürnberg-Erlangen, Nürnberg, Germany

Objectives: Testing unemployment duration as a moderator of the mental health effects of unemployment. Methods: Meta-analysis of cross-sectional and longitudinal data. Results: Among cross-sectional studies, a linear moderator effect of unemployment duration was identified: The longer the average unemployment duration of the study participants, the more distressed they were. There was no clear evidence for a curvilinear relationship between unemployment duration and distress. In longitudinal studies, however, we found only a weak, non-significant deterioration of mental health among persons who were permanently unemployed and were tested repeatedly. Conclusions: Artificial testing effects may explain the weak agreement between cross-sectional and longitudinal results.

The psychosocial consequences of long-term unemployment: Consequences of what?
Fryer, David Dept. of Psychology, University of Stirling, Stirling, United Kingdom
How should the psychological effects of unemployment be explained? A number of explanatory accounts have been offered by researchers in the unemployment and health literature. Jahoda's Latent Function Deprivation Account has long been influential. In contrast, Fryer's 'Agency Restriction Account' has also received some support. In this presentation, David Fryer revisits the question of what is responsible for the mental health consequences of unemployment drawing upon more recent work in community and critical psychology and suggests a critical synthesis which captures what is important in but also transcends both.

The dynamics of job-search: A daily experience sampling study
Wanberg, Connie 3-300 Carlson School of Mgmt., University of Minnesota, Minneapolis, USA
This repeated measures study applies insights from motivation theories toward the understanding of affect and persistence during job search. Unemployed individuals completed a paper-and-pencil baseline survey, then were sent 15 online surveys every weekday for three weeks. Perceived goal progress positively related to positive affect and reemployment efficacy, and negatively to negative affect. Positive affect related positively to job-search intentions for the next day. Goal progress related negatively to next day job search efforts. The study expands understanding of the dynamics of job search, and the role of goal progress and affect in explaining these dynamics.

Enterprise restructuring, health effects and health promotion
Kieselbach, Thomas Inst. für Arbeitspsychologie, Universität Bremen, Bremen, Germany
Traditional unemployment research has focused on the effects of job loss and unemployment. More recent approaches try to conceive of the process of occupational transitions in a more complex way including the repercussions of unemployment on survivors-of-layoffs and interventions cushioning occupational transitions. Results from a EU project are presented including case studies of companies undergoing restructuring in different EU-countries analyzing health effects and health promotion interventions during restructuring. Preliminary results of a EU Expert Group on "Health in Restructuring" chaired by the author will be outlined aiming at the development of EU-policy recommendations on Occupational Safety and Health.

IS-110: Cognitive functions in aging, psychopathology and social stereotyping

Grzegorz Sedek, Ulrich von Hecker (chair)
The main aim of this symposium is to foster innovative research on cognitive functions. Cognitive functions have become one of the most

important topics in psychology and neuroscience. Among the most intensively studied cognitive functions are working memory and executive attention (the control of one's thoughts and actions), often investigated using neuroimaging techniques. Many populations – among them older adults, persons with emotional disorders, and negatively prejudiced persons – have been shown to demonstrate characteristically different patterns of limitations in cognitive functions. The proposed symposium is aimed at gaining better understanding of cognitive functions, their limitations and possible compensations across specific populations.

Prospective and retrospective memory across the lifespan: An internet study
Maylor, Elizabeth Dept. of Psychology, University of Warwick, Coventry, United Kingdom Logie, Robert Department of Psychology, University Edinburgh, Edinburgh, United Kingdom
Over 89,000 people aged 10-65 years participated in an Internet study that included objective and subjective measures of both prospective and retrospective memory. Generally, performance improved across childhood and declined almost linearly across adulthood. These trends were similar for working memory, binding in short-term memory, and visuo-spatial memory; however, development was more apparent than aging for digit span, with the reverse pattern for prospective memory. One manipulation in the prospective memory experiment benefited younger more than older people whereas another did the reverse. Self-reported prospective and retrospective memory failures varied less across the lifespan and did not correlate with performance.

Development of prospective memory across the lifespan: The impact of inhibitory efficiency
Kliegel, Matthias Inst. für Psychologie, Technische Universität Dresden, Dresden, Germany
Developmental changes in prospective memory (PM) across the lifespan are thought to depend upon the developmental trajectory of executive control. This study applies a PM task to children, young, and older adults. During intention execution, inhibitory requirements were additionally varied. Group differences mirroring inverted U-shaped functions were observed in intention formation, initiation, and execution. Age differences in intention execution were substantially greater when active task interruption was necessary. The current study suggests that the degree of inhibitory control needed to succeed in the task may be one factor underlying lifespan development of PM.

The dynamic relationship between cognition and walking under dual task conditions in healthy aging
Li, Karen Z.H. Dept. of Psychology, Concordia University, Montreal, Canada DeMont, Richard Department of Exercise Science, Concordia University, Montreal, Canada Penhune, Virginia Department of Psychology, Concordia University, Montreal, Canada Fraser, Sarah Department of Psychology, Concordia University, Montreal, Canada Abbud, Gabriela Department of Exercise Science, Concordia University, Montreal, Canada
A growing literature suggests that in healthy aging, more attentional capacity is allocated to motor tasks such as walking and balancing to compensate for age-related declines in physical functioning. Three studies of young and older adults were conducted to evaluate this proposition during concurrent treadmill walking and cognitive performance. Across the experiments we varied the difficulty levels of the walking and cognitive tasks, finding that older adults with poor balance showed prioritization of walking under very easy walking and cognitive conditions. Increasing task difficulty alters poor balancers' ability to prioritize. The

results suggest a boundary condition for compensatory attentional allocation.

Does impaired inhibition for emotional material underlie depressive rumination?
Zetsche, Ulrike Universität Marburg, Marburg, Germany Joormann, Jutta Psychology, University of Miami, Coral Gables, USA
Rumination is an important risk factor for the maintenance and recurrence of depressive episodes. It is still unclear, however, why some people are especially prone to ruminate. The present study investigated whether deficits in cognitive inhibition of emotional material underlie rumination. The sample comprised 25 clinically depressed individuals and 25 healthy controls. Participants completed five computer based reaction time tasks designed to assess the ability to inhibit emotional material (words or face pictures) at different stages of information processing. The Response Style questionnaire was used to assess the level of rumination. Results suggest a link between rumination and inhibitory deficits.

Specific cognitive deficits in subclinical depression
von Hecker, Ulrich School of Psychology, Cardiff University, Cardiff, United Kingdom
In this research, the specificity of functional deficits in subclinical depression is examined. We assume that depressed states are not associated with a general cognitive deficit, but with a highly specific one. In a series of studies we address the hypothesis that depressed individuals have difficulties with generative reasoning, that is, the process of combining piecemeal information into larger, comprehensive mental representations. Two examples are given, one pertaining to the construction of mental models of social cliques out of pairwise sentiment relations, and another with regards to the construction of a linear mental model, based on transitive order information.

Effects of prejudice on memory and linear order reasoning
Sedek, Grzegorz Warsaw, Poland Piber-Dabrowska, Kinga Department of Psychology, School of Social Psychology, Warsaw, Poland
This research examined the impact of individual differences in the strength of negative and positive components of ethnic stereotypes on memory and linear order reasoning. The results of Study 1 indicated that emotional elements (relations with the outgroup) were preserved in the memory of negatively prejudiced participants, but their memory and reasoning concerning ingroup members were significantly impaired. Study 2 replicated these results in a more general positivity x negativity design, including an ambivalent representation. The results suggest a need to integrate theoretical conceptions that encompass an efficiency view of stereotypes and basic research on emotional interference with cognitive processes.

IS-111: Team processes and team effectiveness: Fifty years of progress and prospects for the future

Steve Kozlowski (chair)
The last two decades have witnessed a worldwide shift from work structured around individual jobs to team-based work systems, and there are increasing pressures to enhance team processes, performance, and effectiveness. Although there is a vast research literature relevant to work groups and teams, findings are often contradictory or confusing and actionable information is diffuse. This symposium brings together a panel of experts to summarize the current state of the knowledge-base

on how to enhance team processes, performance, and effectiveness and to highlight promising areas for future theory and research development.

Enhancing team processes and effectiveness: Fifty years of progress and prospects for the future

Kozlowski, Steve Dept. of Psychology, Michigan State University, East Lansing, USA

There is over 50 years of psychological research focused on understanding and influencing the processes that underlie team effectiveness. This presentation will highlight what we know, what we think we know, and what we need to know to improve work group and team effectiveness. Primary attention will be devoted to topics that have well-developed theoretical and empirical foundations to ensure that recommendations are firm. There is a solid foundation for concluding that there is an emerging science of team effectiveness and several means to improve it. Future research and policy implications will be discussed. Emerging research is represented in presentations by other presenters

Team leadership in multicultural teams

Chao, Georgia Dept. of Management, Michigan State University, East Lansing, USA

Cultural diversity presents a challenge for team leadership; diverse team members enhance team resources, but differences can also impede consensus and effectiveness. Chao and Moon (2005) have developed a conceptualization of culture that spans the individual, team, and organizational levels. According to their theory, activation of a specific cultural identity is influenced by the strength of that identity to the person's self-concept, as well as situational characteristics that activate particular patterns of cultural tiles. Leaders can activate specific cultural identities to facilitate team development in diverse teams, creating a unique team identity. Implications for effective team processes, team development, and team leadership in multicultural teams will be discussed.

Shared cognitions, collaboration and team effectiveness

Tannenbaum, Scott Effectiveness, The Group for Organizational, Albany, USA Donsbach, Jamie gOE, Inc, Group for Org. Effectiveness, Albany, USA Beard, Rebecca gOE, Inc, Group for Org. Effectiveness, Albany, USA Nicklin, Jessica gOE, Inc, Group for Org. Effectiveness, Albany, USA

High performing teams collaborate effectively, although teams fail often to collaborate as effectively as they could. A strong contributing factor for collaboration is the extent to which teams possess shared cognitions. This presentation examines and summarizes the research on shared cognitions. There is a growing body of research on shared cognitions with well over twenty empirical studies that have demonstrated their impact on various facets of team performance. We will present a framework of shared cognitions and their relationship with team collaboration and effectiveness. Different types of shared cognitions and ways of enhancing shared cognitions in applied settings will be discussed.

Optimizing resource allocation in teamwork

DeShon, Richard P. Dept. of Psychology, Michigan State University, East Lansing, USA Kozlowski, Steve W. J. Dept. of Psychology, Michigan State University, East Lansing, USA

When working as a member of a team, individuals must allocate resources (effort) toward individual and team goals. As a result, individual and team goals, and feedback related to progress toward these goals, should be potent levers for affecting resource allocation. This presentation will describe ongoing research driven by a multilevel, multiple

goal model of individual and team regulatory processes (DeShon et al., 2004) that affect the allocation of resources across individual and team goals resulting in individual and team performance. Current work is directed toward understanding dynamic, within-person resource allocation processes, formally modeling such processes, and identifying interventions to improve optimal resource allocation.

Twenty-five years of team performance research: Discoveries and developments

Salas, Eduardo Inst. for Simulation, University of Central Florida, Orlando FL, USA

This presentation will focus on outlining what have been the recent discoveries and developments in team performance research since Dyer's (1984) seminal review. Dyer's review covered the literature from 1955-80; our review covered from 1980-2005. So, this presentation will briefly outline what we know about team performance; what have we learned about teamwork, team training and team-level performance assessment; and how the field has changed and evolved over the last two decades.

IS-112: Creating methodological strategies for researching vulnerable populations: Examples from Latin America

Silvia Helena Koller, Marcela Raffaelli (chair)

Psychological researchers working with impoverished and at-risk populations must contend with methodological challenges stemming from their characteristics and the larger context. This symposium will bring together researchers from different Central and South American countries who conduct research and intervention with homeless and impoverished children, adolescents, and their families. The symposium will feature an overview of the Latin American situation, followed by presentations drawing on research conducted in Brazil, Colombia, Peru, and Mexico. Presenters will describe strategies developed to overcome methodological challenges in their work, and the discussant will address the implications of this work for cross-cultural and international research.

Agency and agentic empowerment: Background and measurement of the concepts

Pick, Susan Dept. of Psychology, National University of Mexico, Mexico City, Mexico Lewin, Iwin Evaluación, IMIFAP, Mexico City, Mexico

Most studies in (social) psychology make use of participants of a moderate to high educational level. Accordingly, many recommendations about (quasi-)experimental design and instrument construction take such educated samples as a starting point. Experience with marginalized populations has shown that additional aspects must be included. Here we present some of the lessons we learned during the process of developing programs and conducting research working with (highly) marginalized Latin American populations. These lessons include aspects such as the role of shame and fear, of the unpredictability in their lives, and the use of closed vs. open questions in instruments.

Handling conflicts: From parents to children and from children to parents

Livia Segovia, Jose Dept. of Psychology, Univ. Nac Federico Villareal, Lima, Peru

A psycho-educational program was delivered to families living in a peri-urban zone of Lima. Three groups differing in who received the training (parent only, adolescent only, or parent and child in separate sessions) were compared to each other and to a no-intervention control group. Each group consisted of 8 participants who completed 8 sessions on social abilities, self-control, conflict

resolution, drugs, sexuality, anti-social behaviour and life goals. Results indicated that intervention effectiveness was maximized when either the parent or the adolescent was trained and asked to pass on what they had learned to their (non-participating) child or parent.

Context and development in poor urban sectors in Cali, Colombia

Orozco Hormaza, Mariela Dept. de Psicología, Universidade del Valle, Cali, Colombia Sánchez Ríos, Hernán Dept. de Psicología, Universidade del Valle, Cali, Colombia

Some authors state that children growing up in poor urban settlements generally show some deficit in their cognitive development. The presentation will discuss the use of conventional scales as instruments to evaluate cognitive development, and new methodologies to measure and describe cognitive development. Findings on the relations between cognitive development and characteristics of children's family environment will also be discussed. The application of a social network model to the strategies used by children to solve problems and to dimensions of family contexts, allows the researcher to find affiliation patterns and identify those characteristics in the context that have greater contribution to children's cognitive development.

The situation in Latin America: An overview

Raffaelli, Marcela Psychology and Ethnic Studies, University of Nebraska, Lincoln, USA

Latin America encompasses an array of cultures, reflecting diverse mixtures of the region's original indigenous inhabitants, European colonizers, previously enslaved Africans, and (in recent years) immigrants from around the world. After independence in the early 19th century, many Latin American countries experienced foreign interventions and internal conflicts; more recently, many suffered economic difficulties and political unrest. This history continues to affect the approximately 650 million people who currently live in Latin America. The region is characterized by economic and social inequality, and millions of people live in situations of extreme vulnerability that present challenges and opportunities for psychological researchers.

Naturalistic research on emotional development in at risk Colombian children

Carrillo Ávila, Sonia Dept. de Psicología, Universidad de los Andes, Bogota, Colombia

Developmental studies in natural settings allow researchers to observe behavior in its complexity within the individual's context. However, this approach demands care with measurement, research biases, behavioral disruption and ethical issues, particularly when working with at risk populations. Two studies involving home-visit observations of at risk Colombian children will be presented. In the first study attachment relationships between children, their adolescent mothers and their grandmothers were assessed. In the second, relationships of premature babies with their mothers were analyzed in two treatment programs: a traditional-care and the Kangaroo's program. The role of naturalistic studies in socioemotional research will be discussed.

IS-113: Narrative impact: Foundations and mechanisms

Timothy C. Brock, Melanie Green (chair)

Narratives or stories, even fictional ones, can have profound effects on individuals' beliefs. The research presented in this symposium will explore the underlying mechanisms of narrative persuasion, and the extent to which narrative impact endures over time. Common themes include the role of the self in narrative processing, the importance of mental simulation and transportation, and the limits of narrative influence. Presenters will discuss these topics from perspectives ranging from neuroscience to individual differences. The talks also span a variety of contexts, from consumer psychology to attitudes about social issues.

Understanding narrative persuasion through simulation and self-projection during narrative comprehension
Mar, Raymond Dept. of Psychology, York University, Toronto, Canada

In order to understand how narrative has an impact on our attitudes and beliefs, it is necessary to understand how narratives are understood. Recently, a great deal of evidence has started to indicate that readers undergo a simulation of experience during reading, one that draws upon cognitive and emotional systems normally employed during real-world experience. This evidence is reviewed, including our recent work based on meta-analyses of neuroimaging findings, and its relevance for theories of narrative impact discussed.

'Tis only a novel? Interactive effects of text and reader characteristics on persuasion
Schreier, Margrit School of Humanities, Jacobs Univer. Bremen gGmbH, Bremen, Germany

In a quasi-experimental study, the effects of credibility of a fictional text (credible / lacking in credibility), text focus (inner / outer world), reader involvement (high / low), biological sex, and gender (high / low instrumentality and expressiveness) on persuasion were assessed. Analyses of variance showed that, as predicted, women were more likely to agree with statements concerning protagonists' inner world, whereas men more frequently agreed with statements concerning the outer world. Also as predicted, agreement with textual statements was stronger for readers high in emotional involvement. For text credibility and gender, no significant effects were obtained.

Self-referencing and persuasion: Narrative transportation versus analytical elaboration
Escalas, Jennifer Marketing Dept., Vanderbilt University, Nashville, USA

his research contrasts narrative self-referencing with analytical self-referencing. We propose that narrative self-referencing persuades through transportation, where people become absorbed in a story (Green and Brock 2000). When ad viewers are transported by narrative thoughts, persuasion is not negatively affected by weak ad arguments. Conversely, analytical self-referencing persuades via more traditional processing models, wherein cognitive elaboration is enhanced by relating incoming information to one's self or personal experiences, resulting in a differential persuasive effect of strong versus weak arguments. We also propose that ad skepticism moderates the effect of narrative transportation. These assertions are tested in a series of experiments.

Does media entertainment have a long-lasting impact on its users?
Vorderer, Peter Communication Science, VU University Amsterdam, Amsterdam, Netherlands

According to more recently developed theories of communication, media entertainment can have an effect on its users during exposure as well as shortly after exposure. Little in known, however, about how media users are influenced by entertainment products over an extended period of time. What happens, i.e., to adolescents who grow up with a high exposure to entertainment programming? How do young adults regard and appreciate ethnic diversification if much of their perception of other ethnicities goes back primarily to their playing entertaining video games? On the background of a

recently proposed theory of media entertainment this presentation will derive some hypotheses about the impact continuous exposure to entertainment has on its consumers.

Narrative impact: Effects of fiction and falsehood
Green, Melanie Dept. of Psychology, University of North Carolina, Chapel Hill, USA

Individuals are often equally persuaded by fiction as by fact. There is no moral stigma attached to fiction; it is acceptable to present made-up information if it is appropriately labeled. Do narratives still retain their persuasive power if they are intentionally deceptive? In our research, some participants were first told that a story was factual, and after reading, were informed that the story was inaccurate (either due to intentional deception by the author or a publishing mistake). Individuals in the deception condition still showed narrative-based belief change, even though they derogated the author. Narratives appear to hinder correction efforts.

IS-114: Current directions in apology and forgiveness research

Seiji Takaku (chair)
This symposium presents the most current cross-cultural research on apology and forgiveness. Topics covered in this symposium ranges from cross-cultural examinations of the meaning of apology and responsibility-taking, account-selection bias (i.e., a tendency for both transgressors and victims to perceive their accounts to be more accurate descriptions of the conflicts than their counterpart's), the effects of apology in intergroup conflicts, and two specific case studies dealing with intergroup conflict and forgiveness: (1) intergroup conflict among Angolan, East-Timorese, and Guinean; and (2) intergroup conflict in Northern Ireland.

Can admission of responsibility function as an apology?
Coon, Heather Dept. of Psychology, North Central College, Naperville, USA Matsubara, Fukumi Modern and Classical Languages, North Central College, Naperville, USA

One reason people apologize is to admit responsibility for their actions. Are apologies always necessary following a transgression, or can simply admitting responsibility suffice? In research conducted in Japan and the U.S., students read a scenario where another student ran into them on a bicycle. The cyclist apologized, admitted responsibility for the incident, or did neither. Participants evaluated their satisfaction with his comments, his responsibility for the incident, and his positive and negative attributes. Results indicate that simply taking responsibility may be a good strategy, especially in the U.S.

Forgiveness and intergroup conflict: Northern Ireland a case study
Cairns, Ed Dept. of Psychology, University of Ulster, Coleraine, United Kingdom Hewstone, Miles Dept. of Psychology, University of Oxford, Oxford, United Kingdom

Working from the premise that the conflict in Northern Ireland is best understood in intergroup rather than interpersonal terms (Hewstone & Cairns, 2002) we have explored the possibility that forgiveness can take place at the intergroup (rather than the interpersonal) level. We believe that if the current peace settlement in Northern Ireland is to take root then the historical cycle of revenge will have to be brought to an end. To assist this process we have focused on trying to understand forgiveness in the context of the conflict in Northern Ireland and in particular the factors that promote

or hinder forgiveness and this paper will review our work in that area

What college students say, do and feel as transgressors
Matsubara, Fukumi Modern and Classical Language, North Central College, Naperville, USA Coon, Heather Psychology, North Central College, Naperville, USA

In research conducted in Japan and the U.S., students read two scenarios in which they were a transgressor toward a stranger. In the first scenario they bump into another student while riding a bicycle, causing slight injury. In the second scenario, they are at a fast food restaurant, someone bumps into them and their coffee spills onto a third person. Participants were asked what they would say and do, and how they would feel in each situation, as well as their overall level of responsibility for the incident. Responses were coded qualitatively to examine strategies used in such situations.

Conceptualizations of intergroup forgiveness: Angolan, East-Timorese and Guinean perspectives
Mullet, Etienne Ethics and Work Laboratory, Institute of Advanced Studies, Plaisance, France

We present the results of three studies that examined the significance of intergroup forgiveness among adults in East-Timor, Angola and Guinea-Bissau who had personally been affected by long-term wars and conflicts in their area. Only a small percentage of participants believed that it was not possible for a group of people to forgive another group of people. Participants appeared to have articulated conceptions on what could define intergroup granting of forgiveness. Through structural analyses of the East-Timorese participants' responses, an eight factor model of conceptualizations of intergroup forgiveness was found. Using confirmatory techniques, this model was subsequently tested on the samples of Angolan, and Guinean participants.

A cross-cultural examination on perpetrator: Victim account bias
Takaku, Seiji Social and Behavioral Sciences, Soka University of America, Aliso Viejo, USA

When transgressions occur, victims and perpetrators become victim to their own subjective reality (i.e., naïve realism). As a result, victims often demand apology whereas perpetrators opt for giving accounts that reduce their responsibility (e.g., excuse or justification). In a series of four studies we tested the universality of this so-called perpetrator-victim account selection bias. Study 1 involving the participants' recalling their own past interpersonal conflicts showed that the bias was displayed more by Americans than by Asians; however, the following studies using hypothetical vignettes revealed that the bias was displayed equally by Americans and Asians. Implications of this semi-universal perpetrator-victim account selection bias are discussed.

When outgroup members offer their apology to the ingroup: Perceived suffering and responsibility-taking as predictors of satisfaction and forgiveness
Zebel, Sven Dept. of Social Psychology, University of Amsterdam, Amsterdam, Netherlands Giner-Sorolla, Roger Department of Psychology, University of Kent, Canterbury, Kent, United Kingdom

Recently, psychological research addressed how people experience compunction (e.g. shame, guilt, regret) about their in-group's misdeeds. However, how victimized groups appraise such emotions is yet unclear. We derived a model postulating two distinct inferences from these emotions: the perceived suffering and whether the individual takes responsibility for the in-group's actions. Both should predict satisfaction among victims, but only responsibility-taking may induce forgiveness. We found partial support for this model in four studies in the UK and The Netherlands among non-smokers who read a smoker's compunction for the consequences of passive smoking. The model's external and cross-cultural validity is discussed.

IS-115: Structural equation modeling: State-of-the-art

Helfried Moosbrugger, Karin Schermelleh-Engel (chair)

This symposium deals with state-of-the-art SEM methodology. Rabe-Hesketh presents the generalized linear latent and mixed modeling framework that accommodates different types of responses. Marsh et al. show that the typical multilevel manifest covariate approaches can result in biased estimates of contextual effects. Eid et al. present modern approaches for structurally different methods. Kaplan discusses causal inference within a counterfactual theory of causation. West and Wu show that model fit indices for growth curve models are related to the type of longitudinal data being modeled. Moosbrugger et al. discuss problems of evaluating the fit of nonlinear models.

Multilevel structural equation modeling: Comparing frameworks

Rabe-Hesketh, Sophia Graduate School of Education, University of California, Berkeley, USA

Multilevel structural equation models (SEMs) include latent variables varying at different hierarchical levels such as students and schools. Conventional multilevel SEM partitions the covariance matrix of level-1 variables into between and within components and specifies separate models for each level. Limitations of this approach, and of most generalizations of this approach, include that they do not permit direct specification of cross-level effects of latent variables and that latent variables can be measured by level-1 variables only. We describe the generalized linear latent and mixed (GLLAMM) modeling framework which overcomes these limitations and accommodates ordinal, continuous, and other types of responses.

Multilevel latent covariate models: Controlling for unreliability in contextual studies

Marsh, Herbert Dept. of Educational Studies, Oxford University, Oxford, United Kingdom Lüdtke, Oliver Robitzsch, Alexander Trautwein, Ulrich Zentrum für Bildungsforschung, Max-Planck-Institut, Berlin, Germany Asparouhov, Tihomir Muthén, Bengt

In multilevel modeling, group-level (L2) characteristics are often measured by aggregating individual-level (L1) characteristics within each group to assess contextual effects (e.g., group-average effects of SES, achievement, climate). We show that the typical multilevel manifest covariate approach based on observed (manifest) group means can result in substantially biased estimates of contextual effects and standard errors, depending on sample sizes at L1 and L2, intraclass correlations, sampling ratios, and nature of the data. We introduce a new class of multilevel latent covariate models that provide unbiased estimates and control for unreliability L1 and/or L2, and critically evaluate their appropriate application.

Analyzing multimethod data

Eid, Michael Inst. für Psychologie, Freie Universität Berlin, Berlin, Germany Geiser, Christian Nussbeck, Fridtjof W.

Structural equation modeling has become the most often applied method for analyzing multimethod data. Unfortunately, many applications of structural equation models in this context are affected by identification problems and improper solutions. The main message of this talk will be that different types of methods require different types of models. Modern approaches for structurally different methods will be presented and discussed from a conceptual point of view. In particular, some misunderstandings with respect to the so-called CTC(M–1) model will be addressed and it will be shown how some apparent limitations of this approach can be overcome.

Causality and exogeneity: Implications for structural equation modeling

Kaplan, David Educational Psychology, University of Wisconsin, Madison, USA

This talk will focus on the problem of causal inference in the context of structural equation modeling. I will situate the discussion within a counterfactual theory of causation (Lewis, 1973; Mackie, 198) supplemented with the manipulationist viewpoint of Woodward (2003). I argue that these viewpoints can be imbedded within an improved practice of structural equation modeling based on the probabilistic reduction approach of Spanos (1986) but with special focus on the importance of examining exogeneity assumptions – including weak exogeneity and super exogeneity (including parameter invariance). Both forms of exogeneity are needed to warrant causal claims.

Evaluating fit in growth models for longitudinal data: Insights from SEM and HLM

West, Stephen G. Dept. of Psychology, Arizona State University, Tempe, USA Wu, Wei Dept. of Psychology, Arizona State University, Tempe, USA

Evaluating fit in Growth Curve Models (GCMs) is an important but under studied issue. GCMs involve both mean and covariance structures as well as potential design and missing data issues. The ability to obtain model fit indices for GCMs is directly related to the type of longitudinal data being modeled. Three types of data structures in longitudinal data can be distinguished: balanced, balanced missing at random, and unbalanced. We discuss possible ways of evaluating model fit for each of the three types of longitudinal data in both the SEM and HLM frameworks.

Problems of assessing model fit in nonlinear structural equation models

Moosbrugger, Helfried Inst. für Psychologie, Universität Frankfurt, Frankfurt, Germany Schermelleh-Engel, Karin Inst. für Psychologie, Universität Frankfurt, Frankfurt, Germany Klein, Andreas Dept. of Psychology, University of Western Ontario, London, Canada

In our presentation we will focus on the question how model fit can be assessed for nonlinear structural equation models, as for example, inter-action models. The assessment of overall fit is both a conceptual and practical problem. The conceptual problem is that it is unclear what counts for a saturated model for a nonlinear structure, the practical is related to the fact that nonlinear effects may be difficult to distinguish from data-specific irregularities. New approaches and directions to resolve this problem for nonlinear models are presented and discussed.

S-111: Modulation of automatic social behavior: From an integration of effects towards future research directions

Kai Jonas (chair)

Automatic social behavior is a well established effect in social cognition, with replicated already classic studies. Research has so far mostly focused on general effects. Thus, the aim of this symposium is to present recent findings that provide evidence for moderators and to point to boundary conditions. Schubert et al. suggest incidentally primed category salience as a boundary condition within mimicry effects. Hansen & Wänke address the impact of the self on automatic behavior, a perspective that is broadened and carried further by Cesario. Ferguson as well as Jonas suggest goals and their evaluation as important moderators for automatic behavior.

Category salience kills imitation: The impact of incidental category activation on mimicry

Schubert, Lisa Inst. für Sozialpsychologie, Universität Jena, Jena, Germany Becker, Antje Socialpsychology, University of Jena, Jena, Germany Burmeister, Kerstin Socialpsychology, University of Jena, Jena, Germany Steudel, Anna Socialpsychology, University of Jena, Jena, Germany Jonas, Kai Socialpsychology, University of Jena, Jena, Germany

Automatic interpersonal mimicry is an affiliation strategy used to bond with other individuals. This imitation effect can be moderated by previously activated categories. In our research, we investigated this impact in a running interaction. Therefore, a social category was made salient halfway through an interaction. A strong effect of category salience on automatic behavior was shown in terms of decreased mimicry behavior in case of a negative social category. Further studies investigated alternative explanations (e.g. decrease over time, distraction) for this effect. Based on this dependency of mimicry on category salience, boundary conditions for the imitation effect are discussed.

Stereotype-activation affects the self

Hansen, Jochim Inst. für Sozialpsychologie, Universität Basel, Basel, Switzerland Wänke, Michaela Social Psychology, University of Basel, Basel, Switzerland

The present research investigates whether stereotype-activation influences a person's behavior through altered self-representations (i.e., the active-self account; Wheeler & Petty, 2001). In Experiment 1, priming (young) participants with the stereotype of the elderly caused participants to include stereotype-consistent characteristics into their working self, as assessed with explicit (i.e., self-descriptive) and implicit (i.e., reaction-time based) measures. In Experiment 2, priming (student) participants with the stereotype of professors led participants to be more confident of their own knowledge than participants primed with a less educated profession. These higher self-efficacy beliefs resulted in better performance at a general knowledge test.

A preparatory interaction account of automatic social behavior: Implications and future directions

Cesario, Joseph Dept. of Psychology, Michigan State University, East Lansing, USA

We have proposed that automatic behavior following social category priming results from perceivers preparing to interact with primed category members (Cesario, Plaks, & Higgins, 2006). This motivated preparatory process integrates features of the target, perceiver, and situational opportunities to determine the most effective interaction behavior. I summarize recent research from this perspective, and discuss how considering all three of these input sources makes unique predictions concerning automatic behavior, such as: substitutability of behavioral outputs; identical behavioral output from multiple category primes; multiple behavioral outputs from a single category prime; and effects of the situational constraints unintentionally imposed by researchers.

Goals as moderators of automatic response priming

Jonas, Kai Dept. of Socialpsychology, University of Amsterdam, Amsterdam, Netherlands Sassenberg, Kai Sozialpsychologie, Institut für Wissensmedien, Tübingen, Germany

Interacting with a member of a social category can be relevant to attain ones goals. Thus, automatically activated response behavior (ARP, Jonas & Sassenberg, 2006) can become a mean to a goal. Here, we test whether automatic response priming is moderated by activated individual goals. In Study 1, matching behavior targets were activated faster in a lexical decision task depending on activated goals. Study 2 shows that mere concept activation isn't sufficient to elicit these effects. Taken together, the presented research shows the potential of individual goals to act as a moderator on the selection of automatic response behavior activation.

On the implicit evaluation of goals

Ferguson, Melissa J. Dept. of Psychology, Cornell University, Ithaca, USA

Recent research shows that people's implicit evaluation of an end-state significantly predicted the success of their reported and actual pursuit of that end-state. Across four experiments, people's implicit and quick (less than 150 ms) evaluations of abstract goal words (e.g., "equality," "thin") significantly predicted their success at pursuing those goals, and sometimes did so above and beyond participants' explicit (i.e., intentional, conscious) ratings of the desirability of the goals (Ferguson, 2007). Together, these findings suggest that successful goal pursuit (e.g. refusing a fattening snack), may at times depend on people's "snap" evaluative reactions to abstract words related to their goals.

S-112: Shame: The ugly emotion?

Julien Deonna (chair)

The literature on shame has followed two divergent tendencies: One has been to downgrade the status of Shame as a moral emotion, involving three related claims: (1) shame is social, (2) there is no moral appraisal in shame, (3) shame is maladaptive. Another tendency holds that shame is closely tied to self-protection by adherence to moral values. This interdisciplinary symposium (psychology and philosophy) will bring new data to the debate concerning the social nature of shame (Olthof, Harris, Teroni) and its maladaptiveness (Gilbert, Ferguson), and how they inform the status of shame as a moral emotion.

Myth busting: The science of shame or shame on science?

Ferguson, Tamara Dept. of Psychology, Utah State University, Logan, UT, USA Dansie, Elizabeth J. Dept. of Psychology, Utah State University, Logan, UT, USA

Western science frequently contrasts the "ugly" emotional villain of shame with nobler or heroic guilty feelings. We criticize this prevailing view, stressing that guilt may not be an emotion, shame exists in multiple varieties, and many findings are equivocal due to flawed measurement or manipulations. Recent findings of ours (n > 1000), and uncontaminated published results, supported each criticism among diverse nationalities and methods, particularly in individuals 12 years or older and for shame as an anticipated emotion. Shame's painful affective nature may powerfully motivate appropriate self-criticism, desires to learn from one's past, and the avoidance of similar future mistakes.

What role does social validation play in explaining shame?

Harris, Nathan RegNet College of Asia, Australian National University, Australian Capital Territory, Australia

There has been considerable debate about the role of shame, and whether it is a productive or useful emotion for individuals to feel. Particular emphasis has been placed on comparisons with guilt. In a previous study, which examined the dimensionality of shame-related emotions in drink-driving offenders, shame and guilt formed a single dimension. This research replicates this analysis with 513 juveniles in criminal justice interventions for property and violence offences and shows that the social context in which disapproval of behaviour is expressed has a significant impact on the emotion that is reported.

Shame and morality in school age children

Olthof, Tjeert Faculty of Psychology and Educ, VU University Amsterdam, Amsterdam, Netherlands

In contrast to claims that shame affects moral behavior negatively, I propose that shame in response to a moral transgression functions as a moral emotion if a relevant audience values the individual's adherence to moral norms. To examine this issue we asked 598 10-13 year old children to rate their shame-before-adults and empathy-based guilt in response to imagined acts of bullying. Additional measures reflected other aspects of children's moral attitude and their real life antisocial and pro-social interpersonal behavior. Shame and guilt were similarly related to these measures, which indicates that shame can serve as a moral emotion.

Theoretical underpinnings of shame-related therapy

Gilbert, Paul Mental Health Research Unit, Kingsway Hospital, Derby, United Kingdom

This talk will explore our approach to shame, distinguishing between internal and external shame, and humiliation. The talk will then focus on self-criticism as a form of internal shame. Many people with high shame can be fearful of feelings of warmth and self-reassurance and seem unable to access soothing affect systems. Compassion focused therapy was developed for people who have high shame and self-criticisms and are unable to self-sooth. The talk will outline how compassionate mind training seeks to activate positive affects related to soothing. I will also note some recent data on it effectiveness.

Shame socialism and morality: Some conceptual distinctions

Teroni, Fabrice Center for Affective Sciences, University of Geneva, Genàve, Switzerland

Both in philosophy and psychology, some authors have claimed that, because of its social nature, shame at best plays no role in morality, or at worse promotes immoral behaviour. Others, mainly within philosophy, have claimed that shame, precisely thanks to its sensitivity to social disapproval, is of paramount importance for morality and moral development. In this contribution, we attempt to pin down the role of shame in morality by contrasting it with guilt and argue that the social or non-social nature of shame is not directly relevant to this role. We defend the thesis that the moral relevance of shame is to be ascribed to its function of protecting one's self-respect.

S-113: The higher order factor structure of the big 5: Substance, style or both

Matthias Ziegler (chair)

In recent years there has been a debate on the higher order factor structure of the Big 5. Some results indicate the existence of two stable traits,

alpha and beta. Other researchers have argued that these traits are just signs of social desirable responding. Finally, there also seems to be some evidence for a combination of both trait and response bias. This controversy of substance versus style bears implications for future research in the field of personality psychology. Aim of this symposium is to present all different views and their impact on current and future research.

The two broad factors in lexical studies of personality descriptors

Thalmayer, Amber Gayle Dept. of Psychology, University of Oregon, Eugene, USA Saucier, Gerard Dept. of Psychology, University of Oregon, Eugene, OR, USA

The Big Five do not emerge in lexical studies conducted with wider variable selections or replicate well cross-culturally outside northern European languages. A two-factor model, with factors of Dynamism and Social Propriety, however, appears robust across languages and variable selection strategies. The current study used two-factor outputs from lexical studies in nine languages (eight language-groups) to test this hypothesis and define the most recurrent terms associated with these broader factors. Two-factor solutions were highly consistent and closely resembled higher-order factors of the Big Five. This model might be usefully integrated with models of biological processes and of mental disorders.

The highest order factor of personality and its psychological meaning

Musek, Janek Dept. of Psychology, University of Ljubljana, Ljubljana, Slovenia

The evidence of the strong highest order factor (The Big One) has been established in the recent research of the personality structure. The Big One is characterized by high versus low Emotional Stability, Conscientiousness, Agreeableness, Extraversion, and Openness. It represents a very basic personality disposition that correlates with social desirability, emotionality, motivation, well-being, satisfaction with life, and self-esteem. Quite substantial correlations with the general factor of well-being indicate the existence of a common psychological base of personality dimensions and dimensions of well-being. The possible biological roots of the Big One, evolutionary, genetic, and neurophysiological, are also discussed and analyzed.

Higher order personality factors: What role do states have?

Ziegler, Matthias Inst. für Psychologie, Unversität München, München, Germany Bühner, Markus Inst. für Psychologie, Unverstät München, München, Germany

Some researchers argue for the existence of one or two higher order factors above the Big 5. Whether these factors represent bias or trait remains unclear. In 3 experiments the impact of state on the higher order factor structure was investigated. Study 1 used a Latent State Trait design to evaluate general state impact. In study 2 a faking scenario was used to judge the loading pattern stability of the higher order structure. Finally, study 3 employed an emotion manipulation design to assess the role of emotions. All results will be presented and discussed in the light of existing theories.

Higher-order factors in a five-factor personality inventory and its relation to social desirability

Bäckström, Martin Dept. of Psychology, Lund University, Lund, Sweden

The effort to measure the five factor model of personality has been beset by problems to explain why the factors often are correlated. One possible explanation to this problem is that social desirability (SD) accounts for an important part of personality rating variance. One way of understanding the role of SD is to consider it as a separate factor, more or less uniformly influencing the ratings of the personality factors. This model will be described, scrutinized and compared with other possible models.

Substance and artifact in personality description

Riemann, Rainer Inst. für Psychologie, Universität Bielefeld, Bielefeld, Germany *Ostendorf, Fritz* Abteilung Psychologie, Universität Bielefeld, Bielefeld, Germany *Döbrich, Christian* Abteilung Psychologie, Universität Bielefeld, Bielefeld, Germany
Digman (1997) proposed that the Big Five personality traits showed a higher-order structure with two factors labeled α and β. These factors have been alternatively interpreted as heritable components of personality or as artifacts of evaluative bias. McCrae et al. (2007) showed that artifact models outperformed substance models, but models combining both artifact and substance were slightly better. We extend these analyses to the level of the factor structure of the NEO-PI-R facets, to test the hypotheses that "substance" factors are more important at this level of analysis. Two German data sets (self- and peer reports) are analyzed using SEM.

S-114: Prediction of academic achievement: Theory and practice in different countries

Paul Lengenfelder, Ulrich Schroeders (chair)
Ability and personality measures used in college admission procedures are expected to meet content requirements, assessment standards, and context considerations like institutional utility and legislative risks. The symposium brings together researchers from Austria, Germany, Switzerland and the USA, who are working on admission tools in higher education. The interplay of content, assessment, and context aspects and its effect on admission procedures will be presented and discussed from an international perspective. In the discussion we will focus on the impact of various interventions on the success of admission procedures.

Medical admission test in Switzerland and Austria: Does the same test work similiar in different countries? Experiences regarding fairness, gender aspects and prognostic validity

Hänsgen, Klaus-Dieter Zentrum für Testentwicklung, Universität Fribourg, Fribourg, Switzerland *Spicher, Benjamin* Zentrum für Testentwicklung, University of Fribourg, Granges-Paccot/FR, Switzerland
The "Medical Admission Test EMS", an advancement of the German TMS, has been mandatory in Switzerland since 1998 and at two Austrian universities since 2006. The EMS consists of ten subtests, takes five hours and aims at predicting abilities needed to successfully complete medical studies (duration of study, passing of exams). Due to European mobility, about 50% of candidates in Austria originate from other countries. Success can be predicted equally well for all testees. However, participants from different countries differ in their abilities. This talk will address the question of how to ensure fairness of admission regarding countries and gender.

Validity of a work sample approach in a student admission procedure for psychology

Lengenfelder, Paul Inst. für Psychologie, Universität Salzburg, Salzburg, Austria *Baumann, Urs* Department of Psychology, University of Salzburg, Salzburg, Austria
Access to Austrian universities has changed markedly due to a decision of the European Court of Justice in 2005. For the first time and at short notice, admission procedures had to be introduced in studies like psychology or medicine. The

Department of Psychology (University of Salzburg) developed an admission procedure containing empirically recommended elements as grades and specific measures of aptitude. Additionally, a worksample, which tests learning abilities, was included. The procedure has been applied three times and shows high predictive validity. Conceptual ideas and results are presented and the current status of access in Austrian higher education is discussed.

What you test is what you get: Validity and classificatory efficiency for a new selection tool

Schroeders, Ulrich Iqb, Humboldt-Universität zu Berlin, Berlin, Germany *Formazin, Maren* IQB, Humboldt-Universität zu Berlin, Berlin, Germany *Wilhelm, Oliver* IQB, Humboldt-Universität zu Berlin, Berlin, Germany
In a college admission context, it is advisable to combine a variety of tests, each assessing a specific aspect of proficiency for successfully completing a course. A broader variety of measures reduces method and training effects, allowing for a more precise prediction of academic success. We have developed new tests for the selection of undergraduate Psychology students, assessing reasoning, psychological science comprehension, maths, English, and biology. We will present results from a high-stakes test with 1.191 applicants, focusing on the structure of the tests, their quality and covariance structure and how classification decisions change as a function of the number and variety of subtests.

Do psychosocial factors have a role in promoting college success?

Robbins, Steve Research Dept., ACT, Iowa City, USA
We unravel the differential effects of standardized achievement, grades, status variables (e.g., race and SES), and psychosocial factors (PSF's) when understanding college retention and academic performance behaviors using a longitudinal sample of 14,800 students who entered 48 2- and 4-year postsecondary institutions. We argue that for high stakes testing the issues of coaching, multiple forms, and fakeability preclude use of PSF's. However, we also describe the practical benefits of using PSF's to classify students who are at risk for academic difficulty and dropping out so that interventions can be aimed at improving college success.

What personal qualities are most important for success in higher education?

Kyllonen, Patrick C. Center for New Construct, Educational Testing Service, Princeton, USA
U.S. higher education institutions make admissions decisions based on prior grades, standardized test scores, previous course work, and indicators of noncognitive skills (e.g., leadership, motivation, experience) taken from biographical surveys, personal statements, reference letters, and interviews. Meta-analyses show these variables are predictive of a wide range of academic outcomes, such as grades, completion, comprehensive examinations, research citation counts, and faculty evaluations. I review this evidence along with prospects for new measures we are currently experimenting with, and I discuss the implications of these findings for what they tell about what qualities are most important in determining success in higher education.

Prediction of academic achievement: Theory and practice in different countries

Lengenfelder, Paul Inst. für Psychologie, Universität Salzburg, Salzburg, Austria *Formazin, Maren* IQB, Humboldt-Universität zu Berlin, Berlin, Germany
Ability and personality measures used in college admission procedures are expected to meet content requirements, assessment standards, and context considerations like institutional utility and legislative risks. The symposium brings together researchers from Austria, Germany, Switzerland and the

USA, who are working on admission tools in higher education. The interplay of content, assessment, and context aspects and its effect on admission procedures will be presented and discussed from an international perspective. In the discussion we will focus on the impact of various interventions on the success of admission procedures.

S-115: Interactions with animals and socio-emotional competence

Birgit U. Stetina, Andrea Beetz (chair)
Numerous studies have documented the positive effects of social-emotional competence on personal relations, work life, health and life-contentment. Animals can help people deal with their feelings. They can assist individuals in approaching negative feelings more consciously as well as in coping with these emotions. The positive effects of animals on individuals are shown in many studies and so is their assistance in developing social skills. The overall research question of the presented studies regards the contribution of animal-assisted work to the development of social-emotional competences. Results provide strong evidence for the positive effects of animals on persons of different ages.

Attachment to dogs, emotional intelligence and emotion regulation

Beetz, Andrea Inst. für Bildung, Universität Erlangen-Nürnberg, Erlangen, Germany *Podberscek, Anthony* Clinical Veterinary Medicine, University of Cambridge, Cambridge, United Kingdom
This study investigated attachment to humans and the current dog, Emotional Intelligence (EI), and perceived stress during a stressful task. In 28 female dog-owners and 19 women without a dog (age 18-72) attachment and EI was assessed once and the current emotional state was assessed 5 times during a stressful computer simulation. Interactions with the dog were rated from videotapes. Secure attachment was associated with better EI, and this was linked to less stress during the task. Women attached to their dogs interacted more positively with it, which was linked to less stress. Dogs can be used for emotion regulation, however, its presence alone does not reduce stress.

Quality of relationships to pets and emotion regulation in adolescence

Beetz, Andrea Inst. für Bildung, Universität Erlangen-Nürnberg, Erlangen, Germany *Mayr, Christine* Dept. of Psychology, Universität Salzburg, Salzburg, Austria *Reiter, Alfons* Dept. of Psychology, University Salzburg, Salzburg, Austria
This study investigated the link between the quality of the relationship to humans and animals and emotion regulation (ER) strategies. Questionnaire data (Inventory of Parent and Peer ATtachment; Animal Relations Questionnaire; FEEL-KJ) from 101 Austrian juveniles (56% female, 44% male; age 13-15) were collected. Attachment to the mother, but not father was linked to adaptive ER. Regression analysis showeda positive association between alienation from peers and mother and maladaptive ER. Juveniles with negative representations of animals showed more "over-control" of emotions, while attachment to pets correlated negatively with over-control. Caregiving to animals was related to adaptive ER. Results document connections between attachment to humans and animals and emotion regulation.

Changes in social-emotional behavior and attention span during animal assisted activities with children with psychiatric problems, living in a residential setting

Enders-Slegers, Marie-Jose Faculty Social Sciences, University Utrecht, Utrecht, Netherlands
The present study investigated the effects of animal assisted activities on the behavior, emotions and

attention span of children with psychiatric problems. A treatment group (N=13) was tested before and after 9 weekly interventions with Conners Global Index and Child Behavior Checklist. Interventions were videotaped and evaluated with a Social Behavior Observation list (Kongable et al, 1989). Personal caretakers were interviewed twice. Questionnaire data document positive changes regarding social and emotional aspects of the behavior of 7 children. Positive changes with 13 children were observed during interventions: increasing attention span, new behavior, positive emotions. Animal assisted interventions can improve functioning during the animal visits and even long-term.

Enhancing emotional wellbeing, communications and physical activities with animal assisted interventions with mentally handicapped elderly

Enders-Slegers, Marie-Jose Faculty Social Sciences, University Utrecht, Utrecht, Netherlands von der Linden, L. Geerdink, J.

The study investigated the effects of visiting dogs and their handlers on the emotional wellbeing, communications and activities of mentally handicapped elderly. There was a pre-test and 2 post-tests and 6 repeated measures (videotaped observations) of the visits. Group A was visited by dog and handler (N = 10); Group B was visited by a volunteer (N = 8) and Group C was not visited (N = 7) (age: 47–88). Group A & B showed significant changes in emotional wellbeing and communication during the visits; Group A showed a significant increase in physical activities as well. Visiting dogs can enhance wellbeing, communications and physical activities with mentally handicapped elderly.

Changes in social-emotional competences of adolescents during an animal-assisted-training (MTI)

Stetina, Birgit U. Forschung und Ausbildung, Universität Wien, Wien, Austria Burger, Eva Research and Training Practice, Universität Wien, Wien, Austria Turner, Karoline Research and Training Practice, Universität Wien, Wien, Austria Lederman Maman, Tamara Research and Training Practice, Universität Wien, Wien, Austria Handlos, Ursula SPZ 9, Stadtschulrat für Wien, Wien, Austria Kryspin-Exner, Ilse Research and Training Practice, Universität Wien, Wien, Austria

Objectives: The present study investigated the effects of an animal-assisted-training (MTI) on social-emotional competences of adolescents. Methods: Using a pre-post design a treatment group (27 students aged 11–14 years) and a respective control group were surveyed with questionnaires at two test points. Parameters were among others self-concept and self-esteem. The data was evaluated through statistical inference procedures (GLM). Results: Significant and relevant differences regarding effect sizes were found. A visible development (e.g. more positive self-concept) was documented for the treatment group. Conclusion: Adolescents seem to improve their social-emotional competences during the animal-assisted training (MTI).

Changes in social-emotional competences of first-graders during an animal-assisted-training (MTI)

Stetina, Birgit U. Forschung und Ausbildung, Universität Wien, Wien, Austria Turner, Karoline Lehr- und Forschungspraxis, Universität Wien, Wien, Austria Burger, Eva Lehr- und Forschungspraxis, Universität Wien, Wien, Austria Lederman Maman, Tamara Lehr- und Forschungspraxis, Universität Wien, Wien, Austria Handlos, Ursula SPZ 9, Stadtschulrat für Wien, Wien, Austria Kryspin-Exner, Ilse Lehr- und Forschungspraxis, Universität Wien, Wien, Austria

Objectives: Intention of the present study was to evaluate the effects of the animal-assisted training (MTI) on social-emotional competences of first graders. Methods: In a pre-post design a treatment group of 19 first-graders (aged 5 -7) was evaluated with questionnaires at two testpoints in comparison to a respective control group. Parameters were among others self-concept and emotion regulation. The data was analysed with statistical inference procedures (GLM). Results: Significant and relevant improvements were found (e.g. healthier emotion regulation strategies). Conclusion: The animal-assisted training (MTI) seems to have an enhancing effect on social-emotional competences of young school children.

S-116: Psychobiological consequences of stress

Beate Ditzen, Urs Nater (chair)

There is consistent data from animal research showing that stress might negatively impact health. In line with this, studies in humans suggest that stress might mediate the influences of genes on cognition, emotion regulation, and behavior, with potential implications for clinical conditions such as depression, chronic fatigue syndrome, and obesity. In the symposium, we would like to present and discuss recent findings from international research groups. We will particularly focus on clinical research in humans and discuss cognitive behavioral and non-cognitive treatment options in stress-related disorders.

Serotonin transporter gene variation impact on the Cortisol response to psychosocial stress

Mueller, Anett Biopsychologie, Technical University Dresden, Dresden, Germany

Serotonin has significant links with depression, anxiety and stress responsivity. Here, we studied the impact of the 5-HTTLPR polymorphism on the stress response in three healthy groups (8-12 y., 20-30 y., 60-80 y.) which have been confronted with the Trier Social Stress Test. Additionally, stress responses in infants have been examined by a preventive medical check-up. In these newborns, stress responses did not differ between 5-HTTLPR genotypes. Surprisingly, adults carrying the higher expressing allele of the 5-HTT polymorphism revealed a significantly higher cortisol response than individuals carrying the lower expressing allele. Increased amygdala responsiveness appears to be linked to a relatively low adrenocortical response to psychosocial stress.

Stress, cortisol and memory retrieval in humans: An update on recent findings

Wolf, Oliver Inst. Verhaltenspsychologie, Ruhr-Universität Bochum, Bochum, Germany

Studies in animals and humans have repeatedly observed that stress or treatment with the stress hormone cortisol impairs delayed memory retrieval. This presentation gives an overview about recent findings trying to characterize the brain regions involved in these processes in the human with functional neuroimaging techniques. In addition the relevance of these findings for several clinical groups (e.g. patients receiving glucocorticoid therapy or older subjects with age associated cortisol alterations) is discussed. Here the difficulty to differentiate acute from chronic effects of the stress hormone is illustrated.

The relationship between stress and chronic fatigue syndrome (CFS): A population-based approach

Nater, Urs Chronic Viral Diseases Branch, Centers for Disease Control, Atlanta, USA Reeves, William Chronic Viral Diseases Branch, Centers Disease Control, Atlanta, USA Heim, Christine Psychiatry &

Behavioral Sc, Emory University School of Med, Atlanta, USA

Studies of CFS suggest that stress factors contribute to the development of CFS. We summarize findings from various studies investigating stress factors in persons with fatigue. Subjects meeting the 1994 Research Case Definition of CFS and matched controls were examined using a population-based approach. Early life stress, chronic stress, coping, and salivary cortisol were assessed. Early life stress influences later manifestation of CFS. Attenuated salivary cortisol levels, higher chronic stress levels in adulthood, and maladaptive coping styles are typical of CFS. Stress likely influences central nervous, neuroendocrine and immune systems, resulting in functional changes that lead to CFS symptoms.

Stress and obesity: Is stress reactivity a predictor of weight change?

Messerli-Burgy, Nadine Dept. of Epidemiology and PH, University College London, London, United Kingdom Tunklova, Libuse Dept. of General Internal Med, University Hospital Berne, Bern, Switzerland Znoj, Hansjoerg Dept. of Clin Psychology, University of Berne, Bern, Switzerland Laederach-Hofmann, Kurt Dept. General Internal Med, University Hospital of Berne, Bern, Switzerland

Increasing evidence indicates a relationship between obesity and stress. To date, little is known about the influence of stress reactivity on weight change. We examined 20 obese patients attending a one year weight reduction program and, in parallel, a group receiving diet counselling only. All patients completed autonomic testing sessions at baseline and 12 months follow-up. Stress reactivity did not differ between the treatment groups at baseline. However, results revealed discriminative changes in stress reactivity depending on degree of weight loss. The results provide evidence that stress reactivity may influence weight loss in obese patients.

Treatment options in stress-related disorders

Gaab, Jens Inst. für Klin. Psychologie, Universität Zürich, Zürich, Switzerland Ditzen, Beate Clinical Psychology and PT, University of Zurich, Zurich, Switzerland Hammerfald, Karin Clinical Psychology and PT, University of Zurich, Zurich, Switzerland Nater, Urs Chronic Viral Diseases Branch, Ctrs f. Disease Control (CDC), Atlanta GA, USA Ehlert, Ulrike Clinical Psychology and PT, University of Zurich, Zurich, Switzerland

In a series of studies, we sought to examine the influence of anticipatory cognitive appraisal processes on cortisol stress responses. Using regression analyses we identified anticipatory cognitive appraisal as an important determinant of the cortisol stress response, explaining up to 35% of the variance of the salivary cortisol response. Based on these findings, we examined the ability of cognitive and non-cognitive interventions to influence psychoneuroendocrine responses during acute as well as chronic stress in healthy subjects and patient populations. Results indicate that psychological processes determine neuroendocrine stress responses. Psychotherapeutical interventions may positively modulate these psychobiological interactions in health and disease.

Role of acute versus longterm depressive symptomes in predicting systemic inflammation

Rohleder, Nic Dept. of Psychology, University of British Columbia, Vancouver, Canada Miller, Gregory E. Dept. of Psychology, University of British Columbia, Vancouver, Canada

Depression is a risk factor for coronary heart disease and inflammation has been proposed as mechanism. It is unknown whether long-term or short-term mood changes are responsible. Sixty-five young women provided weekly online ratings of depressive mood over twenty weeks using the CES-

D, and inflammatory mediators were measured before and after. Hierarchical regressions revealed that trait depressive symptoms were not associated with inflammation. In contrast, state depressive symptoms predicted Interleukin-6, but not C-reactive protein. Results suggests that at younger age, fast-reacting inflammatory mediators respond to short-term mood changes, probably mediated by acute changes in stress hormones, rather than long-term endocrine dysregulations.

S-117: New directions in romantic relationship research

Ina Grau, Rainer Banse (chair)
This symposium presents innovative empirical studies in the field of romantic relationships. 1) Culture: Banse investigates the hitherto almost ignored area of arranged marriages in Asia and Arabia. Asendorpf and Penke focus on new trends in Western culture, such as couples living apart, and speed dating to better understand the mechanisms of romantic attraction and relationship maintenance. Neyer uses principles of evolutionary psychology to better understand different family forms. 2) Methods: Dewitte uses latency-based measures and Schönbrodt a virtual reality environment to investigate behavioral aspects of approach-avoidance behavior, and the regulation of intimacy and autonomy.

Speed dating as a paradigm for the study of initial romantic attraction, mate choice and courtship behavior
Penke, Lars Inst. für Psychologie, Humboldt-Universität zu Berlin, Berlin, Germany Asendorpf, Jens Institute of psychology, Humboldt-University Berlin, Berlin, Germany
Research on romantic attraction and mate choice usually relies on self-reports, reactions to isolated cues, or observations in artificial laboratory situations. In contrast, speed dating offers a unique environment to observe initial romantic attraction, mate choice, and courtship in real life. In the Berlin Speed Dating Study, a community sample of 383 singles participated in speed dating events under experimentally controlled conditions. Individual characteristics were assessed, all interactions were videotaped, and two follow-up studies were conducted over a period of 1 year. First results will be presented on what seems to be the first speed dating study including behavioral observation.

Living apart together: Age-dependent faces of a new form of nonconventional couples
Asendorpf, Jens Inst. für Psychologie, Humboldt-Universität zu Berlin, Berlin, Germany Neberich, Wiebke Institute of psychology, Humboldt-University Berlin, Berlin, Germany
We compared living apart together (LAT) couples where two committed partners live in different households with couples sharing a household. A representative German longitudinal study (N>8,000) showed a lower stability of LAT, an increase of LAT over the last 15 years, and a decrease of LAT and the tendency to move together after LAT with increasing age. Two internet surveys (N>2,000) showed a trade-off between more insecure attachment and more intense and satisfactory sexuality with the partner among older LATs. The results suggest that LAT relationships are mainly transitional until midlife but later become a life form of its own.

Differentiating partner from other relationships through emotional closeness and perceived reciprocity
Neyer, Franz J. Inst. für Psychologie, Universität Potsdam, Potsdam, Germany Wrzus, Cornelia Institute of psychology, University of Potsdam, Potsdam, Germany Wagner, Jenny Institute of

psychogerontology, University of Erlangen, Erlangen, Germany Lang, Frieder R. Inst. für Psychogerontologie, Universität Erlangen-Nürnberg, Erlangen, Germany
We propose an evolutionary model of relationship regulation based on 2 mechanisms, the regulation of emotional closeness and reciprocity. Both mechanisms are supposed to differentiate between and within kin, non-kin, and partner relationships. These expectations were confirmed by 2 studies, one online study with 455 young adults and a field study involving 171 middle-age couples from 4 different family forms (i.e., traditional vs. patchwork families, involuntarily vs. motivated childless couples). The associations between closeness and reciprocity differed across family life forms indicating that basic mechanisms of relationship regulation vary also as a function of environmental affordance.

Relationship quality in arranged marriages: First data from Saudi Arabia and India
Banse, Rainer Inst. für Psychologie, Universität Bonn, Bonn, Germany Grau, Ina Institute of psychology, University of Bonn, Bonn, Germany Al Tamimi, Nadia Department of psychology, University of York, York, United Kingdom Jaiswal, Tulika Department of psychology, University of York, York, United Kingdom
Research on marital satisfaction has almost exclusively focused on Western choice marriages, very little is known about predictors and the development of marital quality in arranged marriages. In five studies (total N > 500) in Saudi Arabia and India we measured relationship satisfaction, attachment, and conflict behavior of romantic partners in arranged marriages. The translation of measures into Hindi and Arabic was by and large successful. Marital satisfaction in arranged marriages had similar correlates as in choice marriages, but the level of fearful and preoccupied attachment was significantly higher. Contradicting previous results, relationship quality in arranged marriages did not increase over time.

The role of automatic approach-avoidance tendencies in adult attachment
Dewitte, Marieke Exp Clinical and Health Psych., Ghent University, Gent, Germany De Houwer, Jan Exp Clinical and Health Psych., Ghent University, Ghent, Belgium Buysse, Ann Exp Clinical and Health Psych., Ghent University, Ghent, Belgium
To understand attachment-related behaviour, we conceptualized proximity seeking as an automatic approach-avoidance tendency influenced by context and attachment style. In two experiments, participants made approach and avoidance movements towards/away from attachment figure- and known person-related cues after priming with a distressing or non-distressing context. Results showed that automatic approach responses towards the attachment figure were stronger in a distressing than a non-distressing context. Attachment anxiety heightened the tendency to approach the attachment figure, attachment avoidance reduced this tendency. Findings highlight the utility of indirect measures for understanding attachment processes and provide new evidence on the role of motivational action tendencies in adult attachment.

Intimacy and autonomy in close relationships: Assessment of implicit motives in virtual environments
Schönbrodt, Felix Department of Psychology, Saarland University, Saarbrücken, Germany
In the regulation of distance in close relationships two basal motivational systems are involved: the need for intimacy and the need for autonomy. As it is difficult to satisfy both motives jointly in one situation, a motivational dynamic between both is implied. To assess the dynamics of this process, behavior in virtual environments (VE) is observed.

Therefore an online applicable VE was programmed. Three main advantages are expected from this approach: (a) economical application through online assessment (b) effective instigation of motivational systems and (c) the observation of motivational dynamics. First results of this study will be presented.

S-118: Sexual aggression: Social, individual and professional attitudes

Barbara Krahé, Gerd Bohner (chair)
Misconceptions and stereotypes about sexual aggression are widespread in Western societies. Six papers examine their impact on (biased) information processing and judgments about rape, sexual assault, and sexual harassment. Using data from the United Kingdom and Germany, they examine the influence of extra-legal factors on assessments of victim credibility, victim blame, and perpetrator guilt in rape cases (vs. other crimes), the role of rape-supportive attitudes, circumstances of alcohol-related rapes, effects of media campaigns on rape awareness, and of attractiveness stereotypes on perceptions of sexual harassers. Strategies for reducing the impact of rape stereotypes will also be discussed.

Bad but a beau? Effects of harasser attractiveness on judgments of unwanted sexual attention
Vanselow, Nina Inst. für Sozialpsychologie, Universität Bielefeld, Bielefeld, Germany Bohner, Gerd Inst. für Psychologie, Universität Bielefeld, Bielefeld, Germany
Women's reactions to unwanted sexual attention were studied in a "computer chat" experiment. Female students (N = 152) interacted online with a (virtual) male partner. The male's attractiveness (high, low), the material he sent (remarks, jokes), and its nature (harassing, neutral) were manipulated between participants. The students rated partner and material on several dimensions. Results showed that attractive (vs. unattractive) males and the material they sent were generally rated less negatively. This attractiveness effect was pronounced in the harassing remarks conditions but absent when participants directly judged the material's harassingness. Theoretical and legal implications will be discussed.

Relationship, location and alcohol: Increasing the risk of being raped
Horvath, Miranda London, United Kingdom Brown, Jennifer Department of Psychology, University of Surrey, Guildford, United Kingdom
This paper clarifies that the crucial factors for identifying when a woman has least negotiative space and hence is most at risk of being raped are the relationship she has with the male and the location in which they encounter each other. The findings suggest that different relationships and locations have different etiquettes attached to them and as a result will create different latitudes which affect the amount of space for action women have. Both of these elements interact with the incapacitation or sobriety of the victim. It can be concluded that alcohol can only ever increase risk of being raped and never decrease it.

Rape complainant credibility and expert evidence: Findings of a Mock Jury study
Munro, Vanessa School of Law, University of Nottingham, Nottingham, United Kingdom Ellison, Louise School of Law, University of Leeds, Leeds, United Kingdom
In determining the issue of consent in rape cases, research suggests that jurors are influenced by extra-legal factors relating to the complainant's behaviour before, during and after the alleged

attack. In some jurisdictions, prosecutors may introduce evidence to 'educate' jurors on the realities and impact of rape. Such initiatives (recently proposed for England and Wales) assume that (i) behavioural cues reduce jurors' perceptions of complainant credibility, and (ii) inferential shortcomings in juror understanding are responsive to education. Preliminary findings of a project (drawing on a series of mock jury deliberations) that scrutinised these assumptions will be presented and evaluated.

Effects of irrelevant information on judgments of guilt in a rape case: The moderating role of rape myths and hostile sexism

Bohner, Gerd Inst. für Psychologie, Universität Bielefeld, Bielefeld, Germany Eyssel, Friederike Inst. für Psychologie, Universität Bielefeld, Bielefeld, Germany

We examined how irrelevant information about victim and defendant affects laypersons' judgments in a rape case. After reading a report containing few vs. many irrelevant details about the victim and few vs. many irrelevant details about the defendant, students (N = 106) judged the defendant's guilt and recommended a sentence. They also completed scales of rape myth acceptance (RMA) and hostile sexism (HS). For students high (vs. low) in RMA and HS, many (vs. few) irrelevant details led to lower judgments of guilt and lower sentence recommendations. Rape-related attitudes (RMA, HS) thus caused biased interpretations of case information.

Differences in the attribution of victim blame in cases of sexual assault and robbery

Bieneck, Steffen Inst. für Psychologie, Universität Potsdam, Golm, Germany

Research in legal decision making provides evidence that the evaluation of sexual assault cases is influenced by schematic information processing. To clarify, whether those findings are limited to cases with a sexual connotation, two experimental studies have been conducted. 400 participants were presented with scenarios describing incidents of rape and robbery with the victim being either female or male. Subjects rated perpetrator and victim blame for each case. In addition, stereotypic beliefs about sexual assault were measured. Results indicate that the impact of extraneous information is limited to the processing of cases with a sexual connotation.

Raising rape awareness through mass media campaigns: An experimental evaluation

Krahé, Barbara Inst. für Psychologie, Universität Potsdam, Potsdam, Germany Temkin, Jennifer Sussex Law School, University of Sussex, Brighton, United Kingdom

The study examined the effects of a rape awareness poster campaign on judgements of perpetrator reliability in rape cases differing in defendant-complainant relationship and coercive strategy (force vs. alcohol). N = 2,176 members of the public in the UK rated defendant liability and recommended sentences for six rape scenarios whilst exposed to one of two rape awareness posters, a written paragraph about consent, a combination of both, or a control condition. No effects of the posters or the consent paragraph were found. Recommendations are presented for theory-based media campaigns to raise awareness about sexual assault and to dispel rape myths..

S-119: Service work, emotional labor and emotion regulation

Andrea Fischbach (chair)

Recently, antecedents and consequences of service work have received increased attention in work and organizational psychology. In this international symposium, studies from Europe, China and Australia will be presented allowing for a broad cross-cultural discussion of service work topics. We present empirical studies which focus on specific aspects of antecedents and consequences of service, emotional labor and emotion regulation processes involved in professional social interactions. Studies include customers' perspectives as well as service-employees' perspectives and focus on display rules and their sources, mediators and moderators in the emotional labor-burnout relationship, emotional intelligence, and emotion regulation strategies.

Customer and employee perception of critical incidents in service encounters

Neumann, Christina Arbeits-, Organis.-Psychologie, Universität Rostock, Rostock, Germany Nerdinger, Friedemann W. Org. and Busin. Psychology, University of Rostock, Rostock, Germany

The behavior of frontline service providers determines whether the customer is satisfied or not. In a recently conducted study of brief service encounters in bakery stores we identified out of 105 incidents seven critical behavior-categories (e.g. individual treatment of the customer), representing the perception of customers. In a second study in the same field we ask 40 frontline-employees of bakery-stores for incidents that satisfied or dissatisfied them in the interaction with the customer. The incidents mentioned by employees are compared with those mentioned by customers in the previous study. Similarities, differences as well as conclusions are discussed.

Customers' perception of employees' friendliness in service interactions: Effects of display rules

Fischbach, Andrea Inst. für Psychologie, Universität Trier, Trier, Germany Cillien, Patrick Psychology, Trier University, Trier, Germany

We explored effects of implicit and explicit emotional display rules of a German bank on customers' received friendliness. A sample of 42 tellers reported implicit display rules at work and was explicitly required either expressing friendliness or expressing felt emotions for one week. Their customers (n=160) rated received friendliness. A strong effect of the explicit display rule on customer-ratings was revealed when tellers reported weak implicit display rules for anger-suppression, with maximum ratings in the "friendly"- and minimum ratings in the "felt"-condition. When tellers reported strong implicit display rules, customer-ratings were on average in both conditions. Practical implications were discussed.

Motives for doing emotional labour

Zapf, Dieter Abreits-, Organis.-Psychologie, Universität Franfurt, Frankfurt, Germany

Customer-oriented organisations expect from their service employees to comply with the display rules of the organisation and to show desired emotions in interactions with customers such as being friendly and showing positive emotions. Extending the study of Totterdell and Holman (2003) we hypothesised specific motives such as demonstrating competence, establishing trust, avoiding conflict escalation or motivating a customer to be associated with specific emotion regulation strategies such as attentional deployment, perspective taking or faking emotions. Results from a qualitative study and a diary study with nurses, police officers, salespersons, coiffeurs and flight attendants using hierarchical linear modelling supported our assumptions.

Linking emotional labor and burnout in China

Chen, Xiafang Dept. of Psychology, University of Maryland, Maryland, USA Hanges, Paul Dept. of Psychology, University of Maryland, Maryland, USA

The present study examined the relationship between the emotional labor demands of a job and eventual employee burnout. We also examined the moderating effect of job control and social support on the "emotional labor-burnout" relationship. A survey was distributed to 116 hotel employees, 96 tour guides, and 94 call-center employees in China. Factor and reliability analyses were conducted to confirm scale properties. We found support for our hypotheses. Emotional labor was found to be related to employee burnout. Further, job control and social support moderated this relationship.

Mediating mechanisms among emotional labor, customer related stressors and burnout

Dudenhoeffer, Sarah Inst. of Psychology, Johannes Gutenberg-University, Mainz, Germany Dormann, Christian Psychology, Gutenberg-University, Mainz, Germany

In the present study we investigated emotional labor as a mediator of the relationship between customer related social stressors and burnout. For this purpose we integrated data of 15 studies comprising different service jobs (e.g., flight attendants, nurses, teachers; N = 3155). A series of alternative models involving different types of mediation were tested using latent variable structural equation modelling. By means of multi-group-analysis we also tested if the validity of the overall model could be generalized across occupations.

Upward exaggeration and downward regulation: Emotions felt and emotion regulation in interactions at work

Semmer, Norbert Inst. für Psychologie, Universität Bern, Bern, Switzerland Tschan, Franziska Inst.de Psychologie du Travail, Université de Neuchâtel, Neuchâtel, Switzerland Messerli, Laurence Inst.de Psychologie du Travail, Université de Neuchâtel, Neuchâtel, Switzerland

We try to expand emotion work research by assessing a) 16 different emotions, b) interactions with peers and superiors, and c) fine-tuned upward and downward regulation. Multi-level analyses of more than 1200 interactions of 102 employees with peers and superiors show that appraisal theories predict felt emotions in interactions better than status expectation theories. Negative emotions and self-relevant emotions are more often downplayed, and most positive emotions are more often exaggerated. Hierarchical position and relationship closeness influence emotions felt and displayed. The results suggest that the regulation of emotion display is influenced by display rules, impression management, and protection of face.

Emotion regulation in service

Härtel, Charmine Dept. of Management, Monash University, Clayton, Australia Russell, Kay Director, SJP Financial Services Group, West End, Australia Lloyd, Shannon Management, Monash University, Clayton VIC, Australia Russell-Bennett, Rebekah Advertising, Marketing and PR, QUT, Brisbane, Australia

The link between emotional intelligence and emotional labour has been both theorised and implicitly assumed. The assumption in the literature is that people differ in their abilities to manage their own and others' emotions and this is related to their experiences of emotional labour in service work. To date, little empirical research has been undertaken investigating this link. This paper seeks to address this gap by presenting findings of empirical research undertaken in the complaint handling context. The results suggest that the relationship between emotional intelligence and emotional labour is complex and not entirely parsimonious with current theorisations of emotional intelligence.

S-120: Advances in internet-mediated psychological research

Ulf-Dietrich Reips (chair)
Methods for Internet-based research are currently one of the hot areas in methodology. Within a dozen years, the field has seen a massive increase in the number of studies conducted on the Internet, marking a grass-roots change in how psychological research often is conducted (for examples of Web experiments and surveys see the web experiment list at http://genpsylab-wexlist.unizh.ch/). The present symposium brings together researchers from five countries who present findings on methods, techniques, and tools in Internet-based research and on differences to laboratory research.

Are there effects of color on results of web experiments?

Birnbaum, Michael Dept. of Psychology, California State University, Fullerton, USA Galesic, Mirta ABC, Max-Planck-Institut, Berlin, Germany
Web researchers often use color to make their questionnaires more interesting or easier to navigate. Can color have unintended effects on respondents' answers? A recent study by Elliot, Maier, Moller, Friedman, & Meinhardt (2007, Journal of Experimental Psychology: General, 136, 154-168) suggests that even a brief exposure to the color red may negatively affect performance in achievement tasks, such as IQ tests. If this result replicates on the Web, it would have important implications for the design of Web-based studies. We present results of Web studies in which we manipulated background color and investigated its effect on respondents' answers.

Assessment with visual analogue scales on the internet

Funke, Frederik Kassel, Germany Reips, Ulf-Dietrich Inst. für Psychologie, Universität Zürich, Zürich, Switzerland
Even though visual analogue scales are established instruments for assessing subjective phenomena in self-administered questionnaires, they are rarely used for surveying large samples. One reason is that in a paper and pencil environment, this way of collecting data is burdensome as values have to be read out manually. The burden is reduced in computer-based administration of VAS on the Internet. We conducted two Web experiments to examine data quality of VAS in Internet-based surveys. Findings: There is strong evidence that data collected with VAS are equidistant and on the level of an interval scale, while categorical scales produce ordinal data only.

Spotlight: Validation of an online eye tracking replacement

Schulte-Mecklenbeck, Michael DICE Lab Faculty of Psychology, University of Bergen, Bergen, Norway Murphy, Ryan O. Center for the Decision Scienc, Columbia University, New York, USA Hutzler, Florian Department of Psychology, Univeristy of Salzburg, Salzburg, Austria
In this talk we give an overview of different tools for collecting process data via the Internet. Getting a better insight into the actual actions a participant performs during an experiment gives an additional layer of information that helps building better models of (online-) behavior. The examined methods include recordings of mouse-movements, text-queries to databases or the building processes of knowledge networks. Different methods to visualize gathered data will be discussed. Special focus will be given to Spotlight a new tool that has the potential to mimic laboratory based eye-tracking online.

The effectiveness of the high hurdle technique: Do artificially increased loading times enhance data quality?

Stieger, Stefan BEMAW, Medizin. Universität Wien, Wien, Austria Göritz, Anja Dep Organizational Social Psy, University Erlangen-Nürnberg, Nürnberg, Germany
Two Web-based experiments examined the usefulness of artificially delaying the loading of the first study page. The hope attached to this technique is to filter out less-motivated respondents through a higher respondent burden. Participants who remain in the study are expected to be more motivated and thus to produce data of higher quality. In both experiments the longer the loading time, the lower the likelihood of people responding to the study. However the dropout rate and quality of data were independent of the loading time. Therefore, artificially delaying the loading of the first study page is counterproductive.

Sources of error in response time measurement in the lab and on the web

Czienskowski, Uwe ABC, MPI for Human Development, Berlin, Germany Liske, Nannette Lifespan Psychology, MPI for Human Development, Berlin, Germany von Oertzen, Timo Lifespan Psychology, MPI for Human Development, Berlin, Germany Kaczmirek, Lars Online Surveys, GESIS-ZUMA, Mannheim, Germany Galesic, Mirta ABC, MPI for Human Development, Berlin, Germany Reips, Ulf-Dietrich Psychologisches Institut, Universität Zürich, Zürich, Switzerland
Response time is a frequently used dependent variable in psychological studies, but its measurement can be contaminated by errors originating from different technical sources. We study time delays between the moment the response is made to the moment it is recorded, using Web and lab software applications under various load conditions of computers with varying equipment (CPU, memory, input devices). We find that client-based applications can achieve a reasonable accuracy and precision, and that peripheral devices can be a major source of error. Our results can help researchers to choose the appropriate measurement technology for response time related research questions.

iScience.eu: A toolbox for Internet-based research

Reips, Ulf-Dietrich Inst. für Psychologie, Universität Zürich, Zürich, Switzerland
A free resource for conducting research on the Internet is presented along with usage data, the iScience Server at http://www.iscience.eu/. The iScience Server is a portal that links to a number of tools that fulfill the following functions. 1. create Internet-based studies (WEXTOR, iDex), 2. create visual analogue scales for Web questionnaires (VASgenerator.net), 3. recruitment of participants (web experiment list, web survey list, Web Experimental Psychology Lab), 4. analysis of log files (Scientific LogAnalyzer), 5. inclusion of an Internet-based Big Five personality test with other studies, 6. Automatic interviewing in instant messaging (DIP) 7. teaching of Internet-based research, 8. research in teams and groups (VTT).

S-121: Emotion and behavior

Fritz Strack, Paul Pauli (chair)
In different areas of psychology, explanations of behavior focus on different mechanisms. While social psychologists have long been convinced that people's reflections about the outcomes of their behavior determine what they will do, biological and clinical psychologists have concentrated on the more impulsive impact of emotions (e.g., in addictions). The contributions to this symposium attempt to reconcile the reflective and controlled perspective with the impulsive and automatic accounts of human behavior. They address issues that lie at the intersection of social and clinical psychology and demonstrate the fruitfulness of an integration of both approaches.

Influence of pain on emotion processing

Gerdes, Antje Inst. für Psychologie, Universität Würzburg, Würzburg, Germany Kenntner-Mabiala, Ramona Department of Psychology, University of Würzburg, Würzburg, Germany Alpers, Georg W. Department of Psychology, Universität Würzburg, Würzburg, Germany Andreatta, Marta Department of Psychology, University of Würzburg, Würzburg, Germany Weyers, Peter Department of Psychology, University of Würzburg, Würzburg, Germany Pauli, Paul Inst. für Psychologie, Universität Würzburg, Würzburg, Germany
Emotion modulates pain perception. In order to test whether pain can also influence emotion processing, emotional pictures were presented to 49 healthy volunteers during either a painful pressure stimulation or without pain. Subjective ratings and startle reflex were measured. During pain, positive and neutral pictures were rated more negative and for all pictures arousal ratings were enhanced. Independently of pain, startle reflex amplitudes were reduced for positive and enhanced for negative pictures only when attention was focused on the picture. Thus, pain influences explicit emotion processing, but the startle reflex seems to be more affected by general attentional allocation.

Facial expressions towards food cues are moderated by food deprivation

Deutsch, Roland Lehrstuhl für Psychologie II, Universität Würzburg, Würzburg, Germany Höfling, Atilla Inst. für Psychologie, Universität Würzburg, Würzburg, Germany
This study examined the impact of physiological need states on affective information processing. Facial EMG of forty-six subjects who were satiated or food-deprived was recorded at the zygomatic, corrugator and levator labii muscle while watching pictures of palatable vs. unpalatable foods, and control pictures. Compared to satiated subjects, hungry participants exhibited stronger activity in the zygomaticus region when watching pictures of palatable foods, and weaker activity in the levator labii region when watching pictures of unpalatable foods. These results prompt to an adaptive revaluation mechanism whereby even disgust reactions might be attenuated to facilitate ingestion when being deprived of food.

Do anger stimuli elicit approach or avoidance behavior?

Krieglmeyer, Regina Inst. für Psychologie, Universität Würzburg, Würzburg, Germany Deutsch, Roland Institut für Psychologie, Universität Würzburg, Würzburg, Germany Strack, Fritz Institut für Psychologie, Universität Würzburg, Würzburg, Germany
Emotions and behaviors are regulated by an approach and an avoidance system. However, it is unclear how frustration (obstacles blocking goal pursuit) and anger relate to these systems. Some suggest that these stimuli elicit an approach motivation by arguing that typical behaviors (aggression) imply approaching the target. Others focus on the negativity of the situation and propose that these stimuli elicit an avoidance motivation. Confirming the latter position we demonstrated that goal blocking in an achievement task as well as idiosyncratic anger stimuli facilitate avoidance behavior. These experiments confirm a fundamental relationship between negativity and avoidance motivation.

Mediators of goal effects on facial mimicry

Likowski, Katja Inst. für Psychologie, Universität Würzburg, Würzburg, Germany Mühlberger, Andreas Institut für Psychologie, Universität Würzburg, Würzburg, Germany Seibt, Beate Social and Organiz. Psychology, Utrecht University, Utrecht, Netherlands Pauli, Paul Inst. für Psychologie, Universität Würzburg, Würzburg, Germany Weyers, Peter Institut für Psychologie, Universität Würzburg, Würzburg, Germany

Previous studies demonstrated that the extent to which mimicry is shown depends on actual interaction goals - people with affiliation goals mimic more, whereas people in competition situations show less or even countermimicry. The following study examines the processes underlying these goal effects on mimicry. After manipulating participant's interaction goals (cooperation, competition) they had to look through emotional expressions (happy, angry, sad) while activity of facial muscles was recorded electromyografically. Additionally, potential mediators (cognitive/emotional empathy, self-construal, interpersonal closeness, emotional reactions, strategic concerns) of the expected goal effects on mimicry were assessed. Results are presented at the International Congress of Psychology.

The automatic regulation of basic needs: Food and sexual deprivation prepare us to approach relevant stimuli

Seibt, Beate Dept. of Social Psychology, University of Utrecht, Utrecht, Netherlands Häfner, Michael Dept. of Social Psychology, Utrecht University, Utrecht, Netherlands Strack, Fritz Institut für Psychologie, Universität Würzburg, Würzburg, Germany Deutsch, Roland LS Psychology II, University of Würzburg, Würzburg, Germany

We predicted that immediate reactions towards food and sexual stimuli are tuned to the basic needs of the organism. In Study 1, immediate motivational reactions toward pictorial food stimuli were assessed. As hypothesized, approach reactions were facilitated for participants tested before as compared to after lunch, even in a sample with eating disorders. In Studies 2 and 3, approach reactions towards sexual stimuli were facilitated the longer participants had abstained from sex. This effect obtained independent of gender (although women approached sexual stimuli overall less than men). We conclude that this behavioral readiness is an adaptive reaction serving need fulfillment.

Effects of visual stimuli related to the beginning and the end of the smoking ritual on the reward system

Stippekohl, Bastian Inst. für Psychologie, Universität Gießen, Gießen, Germany Strack, Fritz Institut für Psychologie, Universität Würzburg, Würzburg, Germany Vaitl, Dieter Institut für Psychologie, Universität Giessen, Giessen, Germany

Drug associated stimuli from different temporal stages of drug intake are hypothesized to have different effects on craving in addicts. While cues related to the beginning are shown to be appetitive cues related to the end seem to have a less activating or even inhibitory effect on craving. By means of fMRI we investigated, whether this effect corresponds to differential activation of the brains reward systems. Smokers and non-smokers were presented visual stimuli depicting different temporal stages of smoking. First results show that activation of the reward system and the orbitofrontal cortex differentiate between stimuli related to the beginning and the end of the smoking ritual.

S-122: Applications of eye tracking in research on learning and instruction

Halszka Jarodzka, Tamara van Gog (chair)

Eye tracking, possibly combined with verbal reporting, can be applied to study learners' cognitive processes evoked by different learning materials, which leads to better understanding of why materials are (in)effective. Moreover, it provides input for instructional design (e.g. worked examples) by uncovering experts' cognitive processes when interacting with visual materials. Furthermore, eye movement data can provide detailed insight into the attention allocation and processing demands, therefore eye tracking is a valuable tool for research on learning and instruction – although yet little used in educational research. The studies presented here focus on various applications of eye tracking in instructional research.

Uncovering cognitive processes in learning and instruction: Cued retrospective reporting based on records of eye-movements

van Gog, Tamara OTEC, Open University, Heerlen, Netherlands Brand-Gruwel, Saskia OTEC, Open University, Heerlen, Netherlands van Meeuwen, Ludo OTEC, Open University, Heerlen, Netherlands Paas, Fred OTEC, Open University, Heerlen, Netherlands

The verbal reporting techniques used most in research on learning and instruction, concurrent and retrospective reporting, both have drawbacks. Retrospective reporting often results in omissions/fabrications, and concurrent reporting is difficult to implement when tasks impose high cognitive load or contain auditory information. Cued retrospective reporting (CRR) based on eye-movement records might be able to overcome these drawbacks: while maintaining the retrospective nature, the cue shows both physical (mouse/keyboard) and cognitive (eye movements) actions, thereby presumably leading to less omissions/fabrications. Because a previous study showed promising results, the present study extends the test of CRR to qualitative data (i.e., process coverage).

A process-oriented approach to natural sciences by means of eye-tracking and verbal protocols

Jarodzka, Halszka KMRC, Tübingen, Germany Scheiter, Katharina Cognition and Media Psychology, University of Tuebingen, Tübingen, Germany Gerjets, Peter Knowledge Acquisition with Hyp, KMRC, Tübingen, Germany

In the Natural Sciences, novices have difficulties in recognizing and capturing natural objects when observing their complex and dynamic behavioral patterns. Understanding how experts analyze dynamic scenes will help to overcome these difficulties. Hence, we investigated eye movements and verbal protocols within different expertise levels during a movement classification task. Expertise had no effect on a coarse-grained analysis level, e.g., the number of fixations. Rather, its influence became evident when using more fine-grained methods like scan path analyses, showing that experts are better able to identify and interpret meaningfully relevant patterns. These eye tracking data builds the basis for modelling expert strategies.

Effects of information problem solving skill on judging google search results: An eye-tracking study

van Meeuwen, Ludo Eindhoven, Netherlands Brand-Gruwel, Saskia OTEC, Open University, Heerlen, Netherlands van Gog, Tamara OTEC, Open University, Heerlen, Netherlands

Information-problem solving (IPS) research has shown that many students lack knowledge of how internet search engines work and of the criteria on which to judge search results. In this study, students' eye movements were recorded while they worked on two tasks, in which they had to select one link from a Google search-page with 20 results, that they thought contained reliable answers to the query. It is hypothesized that students with low IPS skill will not consider all results, but select a top-of-page result very fast. The results (currently being analyzed) can contribute to the improvement of IPS training materials.

Are there strategies for visual scanning of diagrams?

Rasch, Thorsten Gen. and Educ. Psych., University of Koblenz-Landau, Landau, Germany Bildungspsychologie, Universität Koblenz-Landau, Landau, Germany Schnotz, Wolfgang Inst. Bildungspsychologie, Universität Koblenz-Landau, Landau, Germany Horz, Holger Inst. Bildungspsychologie, Universität Koblenz-Landau, Landau, Germany

Line graphs display a spatial arrangement of several symbolic and graphic elements, at least labels, numbers, axes, and graphs. A learner is required to look at these elements successively. The visual scanpath of the learner may reflect different linearization strategies. We consider a mapping-strategy (paired x/y-values) versus a tracing-strategy (trends within value ranges). Scanpaths of 36 participants who observed time-to-distance diagrams were analyzed. Results indicate an effect of prior knowledge on gaze durations but no consistent linearization strategies. Obviously an integrated mental representation of the elements succeeds despite of a nearly random visual input.

Animation is not worth ten thousand words

Schneider, Emmanuel LEAD, University of Burgundy, Dijon, France Boucheix, Jean-Michel LEAD, University of Burgundy, Dijon, France

This study analyzed the role of a text explaining the mechanical system comprehension with an animation. The task was to understand a pulleys system with an animation and an explanative text or with an animation only. Results showed that an animation and a text did not improve the comprehension performances compared to an animation only, despite of a more important study time. The eye tracking data showed that the number of fixations in specific areas of the animation and the number of transitions between these areas were less important when participants studied animation with text. When animation is alone learners used more animation display, study time is less, and comprehensions best.

How does the distribution of spatial information across representations affect visual attention in multimedia learning?

Schüler, Anne Inst. of Psychologie, Universität Tübingen, Tübingen, Germany Schmidt-Weigand, Florian Inst. für Psychologie, Universität Kassel, Kasssel, Germany Scheiter, Katharina Cognitive & Media Psycholo, University Tübingen, Tübingen, Germany

Learning with written verbal and pictorial representations challenges students, because they have to decide on how to divide their visual attention across these representations. In an experiment it was investigated how visual attention would be affected by removing the spatial information from the text. Contrary to our expectations that the latter manipulation would induce a more intensive and thus compensatory processing of the visualization, the eye tracking revealed a balanced processing of both representational formats irrespective of the experimental manipulation; however, students' eye movements were affected when applying a more fine-grained and qualitative level of analysis.

S-123: Mechanisms of memory changes across the lifespan

Yee Lee Shing, Marcus Hasselhorn *(chair)*
Memory functioning undergoes reorganization from childhood to old age. This symposium brings together developmental and aging researchers to discuss the mechanisms of memory changes. The five papers examine (i) associations between rehearsal and recall in children; (ii) focus-switching processes and working memory decrements in older adults; (iii) factors of associative deficits in older adults; (iv) associative and strategic components of lifespan episodic memory changes; and (v) determinants of memory functioning (including genetic) from age 11 to 70. Systematic comparisons of different mechanisms contributing to memory changes provide unique opportunities for empirical and conceptual integration of the development and aging of memory functioning.

Tracking down the item's way: Longitudinal study-recall observations in children within a free-recall task

Lehmann, Martin *DIPF, Frankfurt, Germany* **Isemer, Claudia** *DIPF, DIPF, Frankfurt, Germany* **Hasselhorn, Marcus** *Bildung und Forschung, Deutsches Inst. für Internat., Frankfurt, Germany*
With increasing age, children rehearse more actively in a free-recall task, that is they repeat several to-be-learned items together. In our longitudinal study we explored why and when active rehearsal is associated with better recall. We examined children between the ages of 10 and 12 who were mainly using active rehearsal. Within the children's study-recall performance we tracked each item's manifestation from the first rehearsal during the learning phase down to its recall or loss in the recall phase, respectively. The results are discussed with regard to the hypothesis of a common underlying process responsible for rehearsal and recall.

Are age-related decrements in working memory performance caused by differences in focus-switching processes?

Titz, Cora *DIPF, Frankfurt, Germany* **Hasselhorn, Marcus** *Bildung und Forschung, Deutsches Inst. für Internat., Frankfurt, Germany*
Until now there is no consensus on why working memory performance declines in later life. We examined whether age-related performance decrements in a working memory span task are caused by age differences in focus-switching processes. Thirty younger (aged 19-32) and 30 older adults (aged 59-70) performed a number reading task under both high and low focus-switching conditions. Older adults were slower and remembered fewer items than younger, but no interaction emerged for age group by switching condition. The results suggest that while older adults have problems in maintaining items outside the focus of attention, focus-switching processes remain intact.

Assessing potential factors that mediate age-related associative deficits in episodic memory

Naveh-Benjamin, Moshe *Psychological Sciences, University of Missouri, Columbia, USA*
One notion put forth to explain age-related episodic memory decline is the associative-deficit hypothesis, according to which the decline is partially due to older adults' inability to encode separate components of episodes as cohesive units. In the current research, we assessed the role of several factors thought to mediate age-related changes in cognition and evaluated their function in the associative deficit. Several experiments assessed the degree to which speed of processing, attentional resources, inhibitory processes, and sensory loss, may underlie older adults' difficulty in encoding and retrieving of associative information.

Associative and strategic components of episodic memory: A lifespan dissociation

Shing, Yee Lee *Zentrum für Lebenserwartung, Max-Planck-Institut, Berlin, Germany* **Werkle-Bergner, Markus** *Center for Lifespan Psychology, MPIB, Berlin, Germany* **Li, Shu-Chen** *Center for Lifespan Psychology, MPIB, Berlin, Germany* **Lindenberger, Ulman** *Zentrum für Lebenserwartung, Max-Planck-Institut, Berlin, Germany*
We investigate strategic (i.e., elaboration of information) and associative components (i.e., binding mechanisms) of episodic memory and their interactions in a lifespan sample (9-10, 14-15, 20-23, and 70-75 years of age). By varying associative strength and levels of instruction, we examine age differences in recognition memory for word pairs under instructions that emphasize item, pair, or elaborative-pair encoding. Relative to young adults, young children's difficulties in episodic memory primarily reflect lower levels of strategic functioning. In contrast, older adults show impairments in both strategic and associative components. Results support the hypothesis of a lifespan dissociation between associative and strategic components.

Associations with lifetime cognitive ageing in the Lothian Birth Cohort 1936

Deary, Ian J. *Inst. für Psychology, University of Edinburgh, Edinburgh, United Kingdom* **Gow, Alan J.** *Gow Inst. für Psychology, University of Edinburgh, Edinburgh, United Kingdom* **Luciano, Michelle** *Inst. für Psychology, University of Edinburgh, Edinburgh, United Kingdom* **Taylor, Michelle D.** *Inst. für Psychology, University of Edinburgh, Edinburgh, United Kingdom* **Corley, Janie** *Inst. für Psychology, University of Edinburgh, Edinburgh, United Kingdom* **Brett, Caroline** *Inst. für Psychology, University of Edinburgh, Edinburgh, United Kingdom* **Wilson, Valerie** *Inst. für Psychology, University of Edinburgh, Edinburgh, United Kingdom* **Campbell, Harry** *Inst. für Psychology, University of Edinburgh, Edinburgh, United Kingdom* **Whalley, Lawrence J.** *Inst. für Psychology, University of Edinburgh, Edinburgh, United Kingdom* **Porteous, David J.** *Inst. für Psychology, University of Edinburgh, Edinburgh, United Kingdom* **Starr, John M.** *Inst. für Psychology, University of Edinburgh, Edinburgh, United Kingdom*
The Lothian Birth Cohort 1936 comprises over 1000 surviving participants of the Scottish Mental Survey of 1947. They took a valid mental ability test at age 11. They were traced and retested at age about 70, at which time they undertook detailed cognitive testing (including multiple tests of memory), provided blood for DNA extraction and other measures, and also provided a range of other medical, physical and psycho-social data. Here, we describe the association between cognition at age 11 and age 70, and investigate the determinants, including genetic influences, of individual differences in age-related cognitive change over that period.

S-124: Innovative psychological interventions for recurrent headache

Paul Martin *(chair)*
This symposium has been convened to commemorate the first international colloquium on headaches from a psychological perspective, convened in Ulm, West Germany, 25 years ago. The speakers come from four countries and include three of the participants from the Ulm colloquium. The papers challenge traditional methods of managing recurrent headaches such as the advice to avoid trigger factors; and suggest innovative approaches including internet-based interventions, client-treatment matching strategies, preventative programs, how to deliver psychological interventions in primary care, and psychological intervention for medication overuse headache.

Do we need to revise advice/interventions pertaining to headache triggers?

Martin, Paul *Psychological Medicine, Monash Medical Centre, Clayton, Australia*
The traditional clinical advice to headache/migraine sufferers is that the best way to prevent headaches is to avoid the factors that trigger them. This advice is logical but criticisms can be offered, such as: the advice is offered in a theoretical vacuum; there is limited empirical support for avoidance; and it is impractical as triggers are omnipresent. Four recent laboratory studies will be reviewed that show avoidance leads to sensitisation to triggers and exposure leads to desensitisation, in a manner analogous to anxiety. These findings have important theoretical implications and practical implications, including the need to revise traditional clinical advice.

Finding what fits you: Tailoring psychological treatment for headache in a 21st century health care environment

Nicholson, Robert *Community and Family Medicine, Saint Louis University, USA*
Despite being a first-line option for headache prevention, <5% of headache sufferers use psychological treatment for headache. This may be in part due to the "one size fits all" nature of traditional psychological headache interventions. This presentation will discuss how treatment can be tailored to individual needs. The presentation will focus on published and ongoing research looking at how biological, behavioral, cognitive, and social variables can be used to match a treatment to individual needs. Moreover, there will be a discussion of how emerging technologies are being used to increase the accessibility and usability of psychological interventions for headache.

Innovation in delivering headache care

McGrath, Patrick *IWK Health Centre, Dalhousie University, Canada*
The prevalence of headache is such that most health care management, if it is to be available to the majority of headache sufferers, must be given in primary care. Although, many medical treatments originate and are evaluated by specialists, these treatments usually shift to primary care with only the most complex patients being seen in speciality clinics. Psychological interventions have had much more difficulty in making this migration because these interventions require more than writing a prescription. This presentation will examine the strengths and weaknesses of strategies to enhance uptake of psychological interventions and present data on the Family Help approach.

Internet based interventions in recurrent headache

Kröner-Herwig, Birgit *Inst. für Klin. Psychologie, Universität Göttingen, Göttingen, Germany*
Albeit there are effective pharmacological treatments psychological interventions constitute a valuable treatment option. Two meta-analyses on relaxation, biofeedback and multimodal trainings confirmed their efficacy Minimal contact interventions showed comparable effects. This encouraged the development of self-help programs presented via internet, predominantly for adult patients. Not considering the rather large drop-out rates, the improvement reached was significant. In children psychological interventions are even more successful than in adults. Considering that only a fraction of afflicted children have access to psychological treatment, internet based treatment was evaluated in two recent studies. Though the outcome may not be as convincing as in clinic based treatment, it seems to be a viable option of therapy.

Preventative programs in migraine and headaches in children: Basics, description, and effects

Gerber, Wolf-Dieter Inst. für Medizin. Psychologie, Universität zu Kiel, Kiel, Germany *Andrasik, Frank*
Emerging neuro(psycho)physiological data suggest that migraine is a brain stem in-formation processing dysfunction, characterized by cortical hypersensitivity and re-duced habituation to stimuli. From these findings we have developed a two-process biobehavioral model of migraine aetiology: (1) a genetically determined hyperactivity of the central monoaminergic (catecholaminergic) system which could be possibly modulated by learning processes and (2) a homeostatic (counter) regulation and mobilization of reduced (mitochondrial) energy reserve. This talk describes a preventative headache program - MIPAS Family (migraine patient seminar in families)- derived from this model and presents a study comparing this program with a biofeedback training approach.

Headaches and obesity

Nash, Justin Dept. of Psychology, Brown University, USA
Objective – To examine the role of psychological factors and behavioral treatment in medication overuse headache. Methods - Twenty-five individuals with medication overuse headache were evaluated for headache and psychological factors and then participated in a 10-week outpatient behavioral treatment that was hospital-based and delivered in a group format. Results – Participants showed significant improvement in headache frequency, acute medication use, depression, and quality of life. Conclusions – Pharmacologic treatment alone may have limited benefit due to the presence of psychological factors in medication overuse headache. Combining behavioral treatment to pharmacological approaches may help to yield more significant improvement.

S-125: Assessing community violence in a multicultural context

Rafael Javier (chair)
This symposium features 5 different presentations with a discussant covering issues of assessment of community violence in USA and Lebanon. Scholars from these countries will present their research and observations in this regard. Emphasis of the discussion will focus on the specific challenges researchers tend to face in the assessment of violence in individuals coming from different cultural and lingustic communities.

Violence exposure in a diverse community

Clauss-Ehlers, Caroline Educational Psychology, Rutgers University, New Brunswick, USA
Community violence shifts our view from an individualistic notion of violence to consider how violence is experienced on a larger, contextual level where the community, not the individual, is targeted. Community violence occurs in public areas where people live. It does not refer to violence that occurs in someone's home or in a school. While children across diverse racial/ethnic and socio-economic backgrounds are exposed to community violence, research shows that African American and Latino youth are at greatest risk because of the stressors faced by those who live in inner cities. This symposium presentation will further explore the impact of community violence exposure on diverse communities such as the development of post-traumatic stress disorder (PTSD), externalizing behavior problems, and school issues. A review of the limited research that does exist will also focus on prevention and intervention strategies. The author will then present a mediational model that addresses community violence experienced by middle school children from diverse Latino communi-

ties. Barriers to research will be discussed such as ethical guidelines associated with youth who report exposure to community violence when they are research participants as well as school concerns about a critical inquiry process that may ultimately reveal students are more unsafe than expected.

Assessing post-traumatic disorder in a Lebanese context

El-Jamil, Fatimah Dept. of Psychology, American University of Beirut, Beirut, Lebanon
Despite ongoing violence, rates of PTSD in Lebanon remain comparable to estimates reported in Western European WMH surveys. These results may be an indication of protective factors that prevent PTSD as well as an indication of the PTSD diagnosis failing to capture the complexity and variability in the way the Lebanese people perceive the impact of their traumas and the ways in which they are affected by them. Only a narrative approach can address the struggles and symptoms associated with violence in Lebanon. Results will be geared towards developing a culturally relevant understanding of the impact of trauma in Lebanon.

Effects of community violence on children from diverse communities in the USA

Javier, Rafael Dept. of Psychology, St. John's University, Queens, USA
Our study seeks to expand on previous studies on community violence (CV) by providing a much more comprehensive assessment and by assessing such an impact in the context of a culturally/linguistically diverse population. 8-16 year old urban youths exposed to CV in NYC were assessed. Following the General Aggression Model and Hierarchical Linear Model of analysis, our findings are discussed around three basic predictions: 1) Type/nature of CV exposure will have a direct impact on the youth's cognitive/emotional adjustments. 2) The impact of CV will be differentially experienced depending on the youths' characteristics. And 3) this effect will be mediated by the youth's perception of CV, school experience, coping skills, IQ, acculturation, perceived social support, etc.

Effects of community violence on children from diverse communities in USA

Mora, Louis Dept. of Psychology, St. John's University, Queens, USA *Javier, Rafael Art.* Dept. of Psychology, St. John's University, Queens, USA *Kupferman, Fernanda* Dept. of Pediatrics, Flushing Hospital Medical Ctr, Queens, USA *Ford, Sue* Dept. of Pharmacy, St. John's University, Queens, USA *Primavera, Louis* Dept. of Psychology, Touro College, New York, USA
Our study seeks to expand on previous studies on community violence (CV) by providing a much more comprehensive assessment and by assessing such an impact in the context of a culturally/linguistically diverse population. 8-16 year old urban youths exposed to CV in NYC were assessed. Following the General Aggression Model and a Hierarchical Linear Model of analysis, our findings will be discussed around three basic predictions: 1) Type/nature of CV exposure will have a direct impact on that youth's cognitive and emotional adjustments. 2) The impact of CV will be differentially experienced depending on the youths' characteristics. And 3) that this effect will be mediated by the youth's perception of CV, school experience, coping skills, etc.

Evidenced-based treatments for post disaster symptoms in Latino children

Costantino, Giuseppe Dept. of Mental Health, Lutheran Family Health Centers, Flushing, USA *Primavera, Louis* Graduate School of Psychology, Touro College, New York, New York, USA *Meucci,*

Carolina Dept. of Mental Health, Lutheran Family Health Centers, Brooklyn, NY, USA
Background. This study is part of CATS Consortium, the largest youth trauma research related to September 11th terrorist attacks. A 2002 study showed that 75,000 school-age students in NYC exhibited PTSD. Mental health symptoms tend to increase unless immediate postdisaster treatment is provided. Method. In our study, 131 students with PTSD, depression and anxiety were randomly assigned to individual CBT or group TEMAS Narrative Therapy. They underwent 18 therapy sessions. Results. Results indicated that students in both treatments showed significant reduction in PTSD. However, students in TEMAS treatment showed significant greater reduction in depression and in anxiety. Discussion. CBT and TEMAS were effective in reducing PTSD in Latino children. But TEMAS was more effective in reducing anxiety and depression; thus showing the clinical utility of TEMAS as a culturally competent treatment modality.

S-126: Prenatal sex-hormonal programming of behavior: Progress of digit ratio (2D:4D) research and implications for psychology

Martin Voracek (chair)
Currently, there is intense research interest in psychology pertaining to the 2nd-to-4th digit ratio (2D:4D), a probable biomarker for the organizing (permanent) effects of prenatal sex steroids (testosterone and estrogen) on the human brain, body, and behavior. 2D:4D has been shown to be a correlate of a multitude of sex-dependent, hormonally influenced traits and phenotypes, reaching into various domains (ability and cognition, attractiveness, behavioral traits, somatic diseases and mental disorders, personality, physique, physiology, fertility and sexuality, and sporting success). Following an introduction to 2D:4D research, contributors from 4 countries (A, CH, D, UK) will present their novel findings on 2D:4D.

Psychological research on digit ratio (2D:4D): A primer

Voracek, Martin Psychologische Fakultät, Universität Wien, Wien, Austria
The 2nd-to-4th digit ratio (2D:4D) is sexually differentiated: on average, men have lower 2D:4D than women. This inconspicuous anatomical trait has generated much research interest recently (200+ journal articles since 1998), in particular in psychology. Multiple lines of evidence suggest that 2D:4D is a proxy for the organizational (permanent) effects of exposure and sensitivity to prenatal androgens on the human brain, body, and behavior. Individual differences in 2D:4D relate to a variety of sex-dependent, hormonally influenced traits/phenotypes. Preluding 5 specific presentations, this talk presents a general introduction to 2D:4D research and its recent progress for psychologists.

In retrospect: Digit ratio (2D:4D) and manual work

Rösler, Hans-Dieter Inst. für Medizin. Psychologie, Universität Rostock, Rostock, Germany
The aim of this historical study (1957), which evaluated hand outline drawings of 3,237 men and women, aged 14-70 years, was to investigate possible associations between 2D:4D and use of hands. 2D<4D more frequently occurs in people performing heavy physical jobs than in office workers. This difference seems to develop early in the job. Employees in fine handicraft jobs more often exhibit 2D>4D than do academics. This difference is already evident at the beginning of the job training. Such associations between 2D:4D

and manual dexterity, more pronounced for women, point to sex-hormone effects in the development of both traits.

Digit ratio (2D:4D) and child developmental psychopathology

Wolke, Dieter Dept. of Psychology, University of Warwick, Coventry, United Kingdom *Samara, Muthanna* Dept. of Psychology, University of Warwick, Coventry, United Kingdom

2D:4D may be a correlate of child behavior problems (in particular, of attention-deficit hyperactivity disorder, ADHD). We studied a large cohort of children (N>6,000) prospectively from birth (Avon Longitudinal Study for Parents and Children, ALSPAC). 2D:4D, measured at age 11, was positively associated with ADHD and prosocial problems, whereas negatively associated with conduct problems, hyperactivity problems, relational bullying, and family adversity. These associations were, for the most part, confined to boys and diminished with controls for family adversity (except those with ADHD). Family adversity may be a confounder of previously reported assocations of 2D:4D with child behavior problems.

Digit ratio (2D:4D) in adults with gender identity disorder

Krämer, Bernd Abt. Psychiatrie, Universitätsklinik Zürich, Zürich, Switzerland *Noll, Thomas* PPD, Stadt Zürich, Zürich, Switzerland *Delsignore, Aba* Inst. für Psychiatrie, Universitätsklinik Zürich, Zürich, Switzerland *Milos, Gabriella* Inst. für Psychiatrie, Universitätsklinik Zürich, Zürich, Switzerland *Schnyder, Ulrich* Inst. für Psychiatrie, Universitätsklinik Zürich, Zürich, Switzerland *Hepp, Urs* Externer Psych. Dienst, PDAG, Aarau, Switzerland

To examine possible influences of prenatal testosterone on gender identity, we compared 2D:4D of 39 male-to-female (MtF) and 17 female-to-male (FtM) patients with gender identity disorder with data from 176 male and 190 female controls. Group comparisons showed that right-hand 2D:4D of MtF was significantly higher (feminized) than in male controls. Also, comparisons of 2D:4D in biological women revealed significantly higher (feminized) values for the right hands of right-handed FtM. These findings indirectly point to a weak influence of reduced prenatal testosterone as an etiological factor for the development of gender identity disorder.

Digit ratio (2D:4D) and short-term mating orientation

Schwarz, Sascha Inst. für Sozialpsychologie, Universität Wuppertal, Wuppertal, Germany *Mustafic, Maida* Psychologie: Life-Management, Universität Zürich, Zürich, Switzerland *Hassebrauck, Manfred* Inst. für Sozialpsychologie, Universität Wuppertal, Wuppertal, Germany

Schwarz and Hassebrauck (2007) proposed a two-dimensional space of relationship preferences, suggesting that preferences for close relationships (long-term mating orientation) are independent from those for various sexual partners (short-term mating orientation). For both sexes, 2D:4D might be negatively related to short-term mating orientation. Study 1 confirmed this negative association for men (n=94), which was replicated in Study 2 (n=69 men), even with controls for age, relationship status, social desirability, and strength of sex drive. However, there was no association for women (n=149). This sex difference is discussed in terms of flexible female sexual strategies (contingent on the local environment).

Digit ratio (2D:4D), facial attractiveness and facial proportions in frontal and profile view

Offenmüller, Denise School of Psychology, Universität Wien, Wien, Austria *Oechker, Michael* CraniomaxillofacialOralSurgery, Medical University of Vienna, Vienna, Austria *Stieger, Stefan* Unit for Medical Education, Medical University of Vienna, Vienna, Austria *Hofer, Agnes* School of Psychology, Universität Wien, Vienna, Austria *Schwedler, Andreas* Department of Psychology, University of NürnbergErlangen, Nürnberg, Germany *Voracek, Martin* School of Psychology, Universität Wien, Vienna, Austria

Previous research suggests possible permanent developmental effects of prenatal androgens (gauged via 2D:4D) on objective and perceptional features of the face. We examined relations of 2D:4D with frontal-view and profile-view facial proportions or angles (10 each) and 6 perceptional dimensions (including attractiveness), using facial photographs of 124 young adult men and women and 2 rater samples (n=40 each). Although various checks (measurement repeatability, rater consistency, sex differences) indicated data typicality and procedural validity, altogether there was no evidence for relations of 2D:4D with the traits under study, which we chiefly discuss in terms of prior replications failures in 2D:4D research.

S-127: Youth at risk: International interventions and research

Pamela Maras (chair)

This symposium draws together interventions and research for 'youth at risk' in different countries aiming to consider separate and overlapping issues in interventions and research. Presentations focus on behaviour and school failure in England and France (e.g. Maras, Bradshaw & Croft), the involvement of young people in addressing gang issues in South Africa (e.g. Cooper), the inclusion of young people with disabilities in Ireland (e.g. Fleming & Martin) and, in Australia, coping skills training (e.g. Eacott & Frydenberg) and adolescents at-risk of substance abuse (e.g. Gordon). Identification of common themes will enable the development of interventions for young people at-risk.

Psychology and interventions for pupils at risk of underachievement and school exclusion: The year 10 effect

Maras, Pamela Psychology and Counselling, University of Greenwich, London, United Kingdom *Bradshaw, Vicki* Psychology & Counselling, University of Greenwich, London, United Kingdom *Croft, Catherine* Psychology & Counselling, University of Greenwich, London, United Kingdom

Findings are presented from a longitudinal study of over 1,500 adolescents. Some were engaged in interventions aimed at reducing social disaffection. Participants completed measures of social-identification, academic self-concept and motivation, and social, emotional and behavioural difficulties. Consistent with our previous research, developmental trends in identity and self-concept were found - adolescents became more negative about some school-based factors and more positive about aspects of identity. Trends were less clear in the 120 adolescents receiving interventions. Findings demonstrate the importance of psychology in work with young people.

Youth at risk: A model for intervention

Cooper, Saths of South Africa, Psychological Society, Houghton, South Africa

A significant percentage of youth in South Africa are out of school or out of work, reflecting historical patterns that have not been seriously impacted by the country's democratisation. This presentation will primarily focus on the work of a Johannesburg youth organisation, Conquest for

Life, which has developed interventions based on actual youth experience in various black townships in Johannesburg. This model of intervention, and its impact on engaging youth afflicted by gang violence and other self destructive behaviour, will be discussed against personality developmental considerations.

Supporting the inclusion of children with autism

Fleming, Mitchel St. Paul's Services, Beaumont, Dublin, Ireland *Martin, Aoife* St. Paul's Services, Beaumont, St. Paul's Services, Beaumont, Dublin, Ireland

Children with autism have enormous difficulties relating and communicating with others socially. They find it difficult to form relationships and can be excluded from multiple social activities. Over the last decade the Irish education system has evolved and three models of service provision have emerged to address the educational and social needs of these children. This presentation will give an overview of these models and will use illustrative examples to demonstrate the variables which are necessary for successful inclusion and highlight the challenges that lie ahead.

Benefits of the 'best of coping' program for students at-risk of depression

Frydenberg, Erica Faculty of Education, University of Melbourne, Melbourne, Australia *Eacott, Chelsea* Faculty of Education, University of Melbourne, Victoria, Australia

This paper reports on the implementation of the Best of Coping (BOC) program to 114 targeted Year 9 students in a co-educational Catholic school in rural Victoria, Australia. At-risk students were identified according to scores on the Kessler Psychological Distress Scale (K10). Pre-program, at-risk students showed significantly greater use of Non-Productive coping strategies namely self-blame, not cope, tension reduction and keep to self compared to non at-risk students. Positive program effects were reported for the at-risk group with significant reductions in use of Non-Productive coping, including self-blame and a decrease in level of risk for depression.

Austalian adolescents at risk

Gordon, Amanda Society, Australian Psychological, Melbourne, VIC, Australia

Australian Adolescents at risk A snapshot of Australian young people indicates that issues relating to alcohol and drugs (43.5%), bullying/emotional abuse (36.5 %) and coping with stress (35.1%) were the three most common concerns. A recent media campaign using shock tactics to address the dangers of drug use and young people's reactions to such attempts will be presented. The Australian Psychological Society has now entered into a contract with Drug and Alcohol Services to provide clinical placements for psychologists in training, with the hope of being able to present evidence based interventions for health promotion and drug education, which will be acceptable to their target audience.

S-128: Beyond natural numbers: Understanding and processing other categories of numbers

Jacques Grégoire (chair)

A large body of researches is devoted to the development of children's understanding of natural numbers. On the other hand, few researches were conducted on the understanding of the other categories of numbers (e.g., negative integers, rational numbers...). This symposium is devoted to the development of children's understanding of these numbers. Several studies, conducted in Belgium, Greece, Hong Kong and Taiwan, will be presented. These studies emphasize the bias of natural numbers on the learning of new categories of number and the need to reorganize previous knowledge to understand and process these new numbers.

Facilitating the development of fraction concepts in third-grade classrooms: Effects of partitioning and measurement approach

Ni, Yujing Dept. Educational Psychology, Chinese Univ. of Hong Kong, Hong Kong, China, People's Republic of : Hong Kong SAR

This study examined effects of the partitioning and the measurement approach to fraction instruction in third-grade classrooms. Two groups of students received the instruction using one or the other approach. Results of a posttest and a pretest showed a significant improvement in students' understanding of fraction concepts after the instruction using either approach. The performance between the groups also indicated relative benefits of the approaches. The partitioning group performed better on the tasks involving part-whole relation. The measurement group performed better on the tasks about relationship between a given unit and "the whole" and the measure meaning of fraction numbers.

The idea of discreteness and beyond: Aspects of students' reasoning about the dense structure of the rational numbers set

Vamvakoussi, Xenia Cognitive Science Laboratory, University of Athens, Athens, Greece Vosniadou, Stella Cognitive Science Laboratory, University of Athens, Athens, Greece

We conducted a series of studies investigating secondary school students' understanding of the density of rational numbers. We assumed that there would be two constraints a) transfer of natural number knowledge, and in particular of the idea of discreteness, b) students' tendency to treat integers, decimals and fractions as if they were unrelated sets of numbers. According to our results, the idea of discreteness is strong and is not lifted overnight: Students refer to the infinity of numbers in an interval first for integers; they are also reluctant to accept that there can be decimals between fractions and vice versa.

Processing the magnitude of fractions

Meert, Gaëlle Dept. of Psychology, Université Cathol. de Louvain, Louvain-la-Neuve, Belgium Grégoire, Jacques Dept. of Psychology, Université Cathol. de Louvain, Louvain-la-Neuve, Belgium Noël, Marie-Pascale Dept. of Psychology, Université Cathol. de Louvain, Louvain-la-Neuve, Belgium

This study explored the cognitive processes and representations involved in the numerical comparison of fractions. The fractions magnitude could be processed in an analytic way (based on the magnitude of their components) or in a holistic way. In this study, fractions had either a common denominator or a common numerator. To identify the representations involved in the comparison of each category of fractions, we analyzed: (1) the effect of the numerical distance between fractions and between their components and (2) the effect of comparing fractions on subsequent comparison of natural numbers.

The application of the benchmark strategy when comparing fractions

Lai, Meng-Lung Early Childhood Education, National Chiayi University, Minhsiung, Taiwan Yang, Der-Ching Inst. of Mathematics Education, National Chiayi University, Chiayi, Taiwan

The focus of the present research was the application of the benchmark (i.e., transitive) strategy when comparing fractions with different denominators. Little is studied about elementary students' problem-solving strategies on comparing fractions.

Twenty-eight 5th graders were tested to gauge their understanding of fractions. Five types of misconceptions were found and most of which were related to their whole number learning experiences. After the intervention of the benchmark strategy accompanied with pictorial representations, not only most students' misconceptions disappeared but more than half of the participants successfully solved the fraction comparison problem(s). Educational implications for fostering student's fraction understanding are discussed.

Natural numbers and their interference in students' interpretations of literal symbols in algebra

Christou, Konstantinos P. Cognitive Science Laboratory, University of Athens, Ano Ilissia, Greece Vosniadou, Stella Cognitive Science Laboratory, University of Athens, Ano Ilissia, Greece

The purpose of the series of studies we briefly present here is to investigate students' interpretation of literal symbols in algebra. Based on the conceptual change theoretical framework, which admit that prior knowledge can support and also inhibit the acquisition of a new concept, we hypothesized that students' intrinsic knowledge about natural numbers and their privileged role in arithmetic would affect their interpretation of literal symbols in algebra. Our findings support this hypothesis and suggest that students tend to interpret literal symbols to stand only for natural numbers and this affects their performance in mathematical tasks such as functions and inequalities.

Transcoding of decimal numbers

Desmet, Laetitia Dept. of Psychology, Université Cathol. de Louvain, Louvain-la-Neuve, Belgium Grégoire, Jacques Dept. of Psychology, Université Cathol. de Louvain, Louvain-la-Neuve, Belgium

Our first goal was to study the development of transcoding between the Arabic numerical representation (decimals and fractions), the verbal numerical representation, and the analogical representation of rational numbers. Another goal was to enlighten the relationships between transcoding, on one hand, and comparison and addition of decimal numbers, on the other hand. We postulated that transcoding requires more conceptual knowledge than comparisons or additions, both requiring only procedural knowledge (algorithms). Therefore, children should succeed in transcoding tasks later than in comparison or addition tasks. To test this hypothesis, a longitudinal study was conducted from grade 3 to grade 6.

S-129: Unraveling intuitive interference in reasoning: How cognitive-psychological methods can advance science and mathematics education

Wim van Dooren, Reuven Babai (chair)

Human (analytic) reasoning is frequently affected by intuitive/heuristic processes, often accounted for in psychological research by dual process theories. Educational research has shown that intuitive processes are also crucial in reasoning in mathematics and science. The current symposium aims to show that introducing cognitive-psychological methodologies (reaction time measurements, working memory load manipulations, and fMRI data) to the field of education enhance our understanding of reasoning in mathematics and science, enabling to develop and to evaluate improved instructional strategies. It will be shown and discussed how such an interdisciplinary research may cross-feeds both domains, and advance the knowledge in the psychology domain as well.

Interference of primary intuitive concepts in adolescents' reasoning

Babai, Reuven Dept. of Science Education, Tel Aviv University, Tel Aviv, Israel Sekal, Rachel Dept. of Science Education, Tel Aviv University, Tel Aviv, Israel Stavy, Ruth Dept. of Science Education, Tel Aviv University, Tel Aviv, Israel

Previous studies showed that young children tend to classify objects as living or nonliving based on the characteristic of movement. We studied whether this primary intuitive model of living things (moving is living) persists and affects high school students after formal learning of the concept of life, by measuring the accuracy and reaction times of students' classifications. Results showed that student's classifications are interfered by this intuitive model in terms of both accuracy and reaction times. The longer reaction time evident for classification of the "problematic" objects might represent an effortful process needed in order to overcome this intuitive interference.

Proportional reasoning as a heuristic-based process: Time pressure and dual task considerations

Gillard, Ellen Instruct Psych. & Technology, Catholic University of Leuven, Leuven, Belgium van Dooren, Wim Instruct Psych. & Technolo, Catholic University of Leuven, Leuven, Belgium Schaeken, Walter Lab of Experimental Psychology, Catholic University of Leuven, Leuven, Belgium Verschaffel, Lieven Instruct Psych. & Technolo, Catholic University of Leuven, Leuven, Belgium

This study aimed at validating the heuristic-based character of proportional reasoning by focusing on two processing claims of dual-process theories: analytic processes are time-consuming and effortful, whereas heuristic processes are fast and effortless. Participants solved two types of problems: Proportional problems (where proportional strategies are correct) and non-proportional problems (where proportional strategies are incorrect). In experiment 1 we manipulated available solution time. In experiment 2 executive resources were burdened. As expected, for non-proportional problems both manipulations increased proportional and decreased correct answers, whereas for proportional problems no significant effects were observed. This indicates that proportional reasoning relies on heuristic processing.

Characterising intuitive and analytic mathematical reasoning: Intuitive rules and over-use of proportionality

van Dooren, Wim Instruct Psych. & Technology, Catholic University of Leuven, Leuven, Belgium Gillard, Ellen Instruct Psych. & Technolo, Catholic University of Leuven, Leuven, Belgium de Bock, Dirk Instruct Psych. & Technolo, Catholic University of Leuven, Leuven, Belgium Verschaffel, Lieven Instruct Psych. & Technolo, Catholic University of Leuven, Leuven, Belgium

This study aimed at validating whether students applying the 'more A-more B' and 'same A-same B' intuitive rules, and over-using proportionality in mathematical reasoning share the same characteristics: immediacy (intuitive reasoning occurs faster than analytic reasoning) and saliency (salient problem characteristics strengthen intuitions and speed up intuitive reasoning). 129 10th and 11th solved 15 mathematical problems on a computer. Some triggered intuitive rule use, some the over-use of proportionality. Results showed that for all tasks (erroneous) intuitive answers occurred faster than correct answers. Saliency did not affect intuitive reasoning, nor in speeding up answers. Implications for further research are discussed.

The cost of intuitive interference inhibition

Stavy, Ruth *Dept. of Science Education, Tel Aviv University, Tel Aviv, Israel* **Babai, Reuven** *Dept. of Science Education, Tel Aviv University, Tel Aviv, Israel* **Zilber, Hanna** *Dept. of Science Education, Tel Aviv University, Tel Aviv, Israel* **Tirosh, Dina** *Dept. of Science Education, Tel Aviv University, Tel Aviv, Israel*

Numerous examples have shown that application of the intuitive rule 'more A-more B' leads to incorrect judgments. Our previous research suggested that in such cases conflict training could improve participants' performance. In the current study we measured if such training will affect the accuracy rate and reaction times of eight graders. The results showed that conflict training, indeed, improved the success rate. However, these correct responses were obtained with longer reaction times. The reaction times results suggest that the training activated control mechanisms that are effortful and needed in order to overcome the incorrect application of the intuitive rule.

Intuitive rules: The case for and against dual process theories

Osman, Magda *Dept. of Psychology, University of Surrey, Guilford, United Kingdom*

Theories of adult and developmental reasoning propose that reasoning is comprised of two functionally distinct systems that operate under different mechanisms. I will present developmental studies of the formation and application of intuitive rules to argue the following: 1) Although there is evidence that is consistent with dual process theories, there are also limitations within this approach 2) The evidence suggests that what is crucial to understanding how children reason is the saliency of task features 3) The evidence is consistent with a single reasoning system framework that sets out differences in performance according to the saliency of task properties.

S-130: Diagnostic competencies of teachers in assessing students' performance

Sabine Krolak-Schwerdt (chair)

Teachers' diagnostic competencies in assessing students' performance are a major prerequisite to high quality teaching. Though judgment biases and relatively low prognostic validity of diagnostic judgments are well documented, little is known about the causes of low judgment and assessment competencies of teachers. The symposium focuses on diagnostic assessment competencies by interconnecting and broadening perspectives from educational and social psychology. Special topics are teachers' capacities, anchoring and representativeness heuristics in using assessment information as well as reference-group-effects in assessments and judgment stability. Methodologically, contributions cover a wide range of approaches, from experimental to formative classroom assessments and longitudinal measurements.

Stability of primary grade teachers' diagnostic competences

Lorenz, Christian *Inst. für Humanwissenschaften, Universität Bamberg, Bamberg, Germany* **Karing, Constance** *Inst. für Humanwissenschaften, Universität Bamberg, Bamberg, Germany* **Artelt, Cordula** *Inst. für Bildungsforschung, Universität Bamberg, Bamberg, Germany*

Teachers' diagnostic competence is sometimes claimed to be a core competence for high quality teaching. Nevertheless, little is known about the development as well as the stability of teacher judgements related to students' characteristics. Almost all studies in this field are cross-sectional. Based on data from the longitudinal research project BiKS, we will use two measurement points with individual student assessment in different cognitive and non-cognitive domains (N= 2200) as well as corresponding teacher judgements (N=160) for individual students. We will analyse stability of teachers' judgement accuracy related to students' rank order in the domains of the study.

Reference-group-effects on teachers' judgments: A study with the simulated classroom

Südkamp, Anna *Inst. für Psychologie, Universität zu Kiel, Kiel, Germany* **Pohlmann, Britta** *Inst. für Psychologie, Universität zu Kiel, Kiel, Germany* **Möller, Jens** *Inst. für Psychologie, Universität zu Kiel, Kiel, Germany*

In this study with N = 42 University students, reference group effects on performance judgments could be demonstrated, using the computer simulation of a classroom. In the Simulated Classroom, the user poses questions and subsequently assesses the performance of simulated students. Multilevel analysis revealed a negative effect of class average achievement on grades: students were judged less favorable in classes with high average achievement than in classes with low average achievement. Additional analyses of variance showed that this reference group effect on teachers' judgments is stronger for low achieving than for high achieving students.

Assessment for learning: Using assesment formatively in classroom instruction

Pellegrino, James *Learning Sciences Research, University of Illinois, Chicago, USA*

Wise instructional decision making and differentiated instruction depend on teachers taking evidence of what students know and can do, comparing it to expected learning outcomes, and creating learning opportunities that reflect appropriate "next steps" for individual students. Substantial evidence shows that quality formative assessment practices enhance teaching effectiveness and can produce substantial student achievement gains higher. This presentation will focus on two critical issues related to the use of assessment for learning: (a) availability and quality of formative assessment materials within selected U.S. K-8 mathematics curricula, and (b) evidence of teacher capacity to implement such materials in their instructional practice.

Anchor effects in teachers' assessments on student performance: An experimental study with novices and experts in teaching

Dünnebier, Katrin *Inst. für Pädag. Wissenschaft, Universität Wuppertal, Wuppertal, Germany* **Nölle, Ines** *Fachbereich G, ZBL, Universität Wuppertal, Wuppertal, Germany* **Krolak-Schwerdt, Sabine** *Faculty of Humanities, Arts, University of Luxembourg, Walferdange, Luxembourg*

Research on social cognition gives evidence of anchoring effects in decision making: A preceding judgement influences a subsequent judgement of the same target or task. Anchoring effects can be found in different decision and judgement domains, and the consequences may severely affect individual lives, e.g. medical or legal decision making. In our experiments we investigate whether anchor effects can be found in teachers' assessment of student performance. Following the continuum-model of Fiske and Neuberg (1990) we assume that the anchoring effect can be found in novices' (students), but not in experts' judgements.

The impact of assessment goals on representativeness biases in teachers' assessments

Krolak-Schwerdt, Sabine *Faculty of Humanities, Arts, University of Luxembourg, Walferdange, Luxembourg* **Böhmer, Matthias** *Fachbereich Erziehungswissen., Universität Wuppertal, Wuppertal, Germany*

Representativeness biases in judgments involve the use of a social stereotype (e.g., "bloomer") and have been documented in teachers' assessments of students' performance. However, the occurrence of biases may depend on the assessment goal, where goals which increase accountability reduce representativeness biases. Two experiments investigate the effects of teachers' assessment goals on their use of stereotypes in processing of students' information. Results show that attention, memory and assessments of teachers were either biased or relatively unaffected by stereotypes depending on the assessment goal. Thus, assessment goals appear as moderators in teachers' judgments.

S-131: Trauma and Recovery within global contexts

Kate Richmond (chair)

Amidst global crises, PTSD has emerged as a global problem that international psychologists are researching on a variety of fronts. When PTSD was first introduced, it was conceptualized as a response to extreme stress; however, as more reliable methods for detecting the disorder have emerged, researchers have been able to identify pre-morbid factors related to developing PTSD (Yehuda & McFlarlane, 1995). In this symposium, we will highlight the work of several international psychologists who are studying and responding to various experiences of trauma. In particular, we will discuss epidemiology (particularly among cross-cultural contexts), prevention, consequences of and responses to trauma.

Coping with generations of wars: The case of mental health professionals in Lebanon

Kalayjian, Anie *Dept. of Psychology, Fordham University, Cliffside Park, NJ, USA*

The on-going military conflict in the Middle East is a well recognized world problem. The international public's emotional and psychological response to the war was explored. Fifty-five randomly selected participants, ages 15 to 65, were interviewed. Almost three quarters of those interviewed said they felt hopeless or that there was little to no hope for the future, the majority of this group feeling cynical, pessimistic, or disempowered. Israelis were more likely to support their state, but even this group expressed on the apparent unfeasibility of the situation and the desperation of the future. Recommendations will be discussed.

PTSD and natural disasters: A cross-cultural examination

Richmond, Kate *Dept. of Psychology, Muhlenberg College, Allentown, USA*

This presentation aims to describe the psychological effects reported by survivors of three natural disasters: Katrina (New Orleans), 2005 Tsunami (Sri Lanka), and 2006 Earthquake (Pakistan). Cross-cultural analyses demonstrated high levels of PTSD among all participants; however PTSD scores were moderated by education level. Participants' explanations of the disaster varied across cultures, and this had implications for specific trauma responses. Recommendations for developing culture-specific interventions will be highlighted.

PTSD in victims of sex-relating trafficking

Antonopoulou, Christina *Dept. of Psychology, University of Athens, Athens, Greece*

The purpose of this study was to examine the symptoms of PTSD in female victims of trafficking and to establish how they differ than the symptoms of PTSD experienced by other victims of abuse and by females in the general population of Greece. Fifty two females completed the Trauma Syndrome Inventory (TSI) and the Brief Betrayal Trauma Survey (BBTS). The mean scores on the TSI and BBTS for the abused women were significantly higher than the TSI scores of the non-abused women. Recommendations will be made regarding assessment and diagnosis.

Axioprepia (human dignity) and sex trafficking
Pipinelli, Artemis *Dept. of Psychology, Lehman College, New York, USA*
As the population identified as "human trafficking victims" continues to increase, greater attention is being given to ways to improve the lives of the survivors so they can be treated with dignity and respect. Human dignity or Axioprepia, in Greek comes from the word axios (of value or worth) and the verb prepo (means "ought to" signifying a moral value). Human Trafficking victims need "Axioprepia." This presentation will explore the necessary role of social support and empowerment within therapeutic contexts. Specific attention will be given to how axioprepia can effectively inform treatment.

Surviving and thriving after trauma: Reclaiming sexual health in treatment
Needle, Rachel *Dept. of Psychology, Nova Southeastern University, Fort Lauderdale, USA*
Sexual trauma can lead to sexual difficulties (DeSilva, 2001). Sexual functioning and intimacy in adulthood can be significantly affected by child sexual abuse (Courtois, 1979; Finkelhor, 1990). In addition, intimate partner violence (IPV) contributes to poor sexual health. Specifically, IPV has been consistently associated with sexual risk taking, inconsistent condom use or partner nonmonogamy, and sexual dysfunction, particularly chronic pelvic pain (Coker, 2007). Furthermore, intimacy is commonly affected by exposure to trauma. In this presentation, the consequences of trauma on sexual health will be discussed, as well as suggestions for clinicians treating trauma survivors in therapy.

S-132: Occupational health promotion: Interventions on multiple levels

Christian Schwennen, Bernhard Zimolong *(chair)*
Research readily acknowledges that health promotion is a key feature in organizations. Recent investigations on occupational health promotion focus on different/multiple levels of intervention in workplace settings. The scope of the present symposium is to present on-going research and recent results with respect to different intervention levels. Research projects to be presented cover individual, team, organizational, inter-organizational and multi-level approaches. Studies report on workplace health promotion via work design, leadership behavior, occupational health management, health programs to reduce and prevent back pain and increase physical activity as well as on up-to-date qualification needs of safety officers of public authorities.

Evaluating multi-level physical activity interventions in work settings
DeJoy, David M. *Dept. of Health Promotion, University of Georgia, Athens, USA* **Wilson, Mark G.** *Dept. of Health Promotion, University of Georgia, Athens, GA, USA* **Vandenberg, Robert J.** *Dept. of Management, University of Georgia, Athens, GA, USA* **Dishman, Rod K.** *Dept. of Exercise Science, University of Georgia, Athens, GA, USA*
This presentation summarizes outcome and process evaluation results from a randomized12-week physical activity intervention consisting of organizational action and personal and team goal-setting implemented in a sample of over 1400 employees at 16 of a large retail organization in the US. The intervention was effective in increasing moderate and vigorous physical activity and walking among the intervention group (relative to controls). More-

over, the process measures showed generally effective implementation. While this study possessed some important methodological strengths, it also highlights many of the challenges inherent in implementing and evaluating theoretically-driven, multi-level interventions in workplace settings. These challenges will be discussed along with issues related to translation and dissemination of worksite health promotion interventions.

Evaluation of the "Healthy Back" program in a tax administration
Schwennen, Christian *Arbeits- und Org.-Psychologie, Ruhr-Universität Bochum, Bochum, Germany* **Zimolong, Bernhard** *A&O Psychologie, Ruhr-Universität Bochum, Bochum, Germany*
A holistic occupational health management system was implemented at a tax administration. It integrates a multicomponent health program that focuses on back pain prevention. The present study reports results from a health screening of 1043 employees, which measured 13 risk factors followed by individually tailored interventions. Participation rates vary between 36 to 66% for the screening, and between 7 to 59% for the interventions. One half of the participants exhibits moderate to high back pain risk. Results of the pre-post-test evaluation of the interventions will be discussed with regard to the effectiveness of work site health programmes.

The influence of workplace health promotion, leader behavior and team climate on health, attitudes and performance at work
Schraub, Eva Maria *A&O-Psychologie, Universität Heidelberg, Heidelberg, Germany* **Michaelis, Björn** *A&O Psychologie, Universität Heidelberg, Heidelberg, Germany* **Stegmaier, Ralf** *A&O Psychologie, Universität Heidelberg, Heidelberg, Germany* **Sonntag, Karlheinz** *A&O Psychologie, Universität Heidelberg, Heidelberg, Germany*
The present study investigated the impact of workplace health promotion characteristics, leader behavior and team climate on health, attitudes and performance on the individual and team level. Using a multi-source approach, data from 500 blue- and white-collar workers as well as objective performance indicators of a German large-scale enterprise were assessed. As assumed, structural equation analyses revealed that employees' health and attitudes mediate the effects of workplace health promotion characteristics, leader behavior and team climate on performance. Implications for the current need of organizations to establish healthy working conditions besides traditional workplace health promotion programs are discussed.

Healthy leadership: The role of leaders in health promotion
Gurt, Jochen *Arbeits- und Org.-Psychologie, Ruhr-Universität Bochum, Bochum, Germany* **Elke, Gabriele** *Inst. für Psychologie, Ruhr-Universität Bochum, Bochum, Germany*
Several studies indicate that leadership behaviour has a significant impact on employees' health. This contribution will show the foundations of healthy leadership and explain the role of leadership with regard to the implementation of a health management system. Regression models analyzing longitudinal data from two successive health surveys 2005 and 2006 in a German tax administration (N= 1,357) will be presented indicating that specific leadership behaviour indeed influences health related outcome variables. Building on these grounds evaluation results of individual and organisational interventions to promote healthy leadership of middle managers and further possibilities to stabilize such behaviour will be discussed.

Workplace health promotion in a tax office: A participatory approach of work design
Görg, Peter *A&O-Psychologie, Bergische Univ. Wuppertal, Wuppertal, Germany* **Wieland, Rainer** *A&O-Psychologie, Bergische Univ. Wuppertal, Wuppertal, Germany*
Based on the results of five team-oriented workshops on participation and work design in a tax office the present study examines the hypothesis that reduced control due to a new type of workflow management has a significant influence on stress and job satisfaction of the employees. Measures of stress, satisfaction and health are assessed from a group of 35 participants. The intervention consists of variations in control over job characteristics between groups. Finally empirical findings referring to the intervention will be presented.

Effectiveness in occupational health and safety: A longitudinal study of 2000 industrial safety experts
Trimpop, Rüdiger *A&O-Psychologie, Universität Jena, Jena, Germany* **Kalveram, Andreas** *A&O-Psychologie, Universität Jena, Jena, Germany* **Hamacher, Werner** *Consulting, Sytemkonzept, Köln, Germany* **Winterfeld, Ulrich** *Psychology, BGAG, dresden, Germany* **Schmauder, Martin** *Arbeitsingenieurwesen, Technische Universität Dresden, Dresden, Germany*
The 8-year interdisciplinary study maps task changes for safety experts and points out necessary training. 2000 experts are questioned online about activities, effectiveness, occupational and societal frame of their employing company. Individual strategies, roles and effectiveness attributions are assessed and validated by 300 respective managers, works councils and physicans. Results indicate factors for effectiveness in different company sizes, and cultures. Health, personnel and psychological topics are least developed in skills and effectiveness. Research implications are discussed.

S-133: Posttraumatic stress disorder: Theoretical and empirical advances

Andreas Maercker, Anke Ehlers *(chair)*
Posttraumatic stress disorder received much attention recently in psychochological research as well as in the public. The symposium brings together contributions of psychobiology, cognitive and social processes in PTSD research. Ask Eklit discusses a new four-factor PTSD symptom model with re-experiencing, avoidance, dysphoria, and arousal. Tanja Michael focuses on re-experiencing and discusses why triggers are often unaware tpo patients. Kris Kaniasty proposes that both social causation and social selection models account for the causal linkages between perceptions of social support and psychological distress in PTSD. Anke Karl discusses the interaction between psychophysiological correlates of PTSD, of its treatment and genetic polymorphisms. Symposium co-chairs Ehlers and Maercker present new results of their research groups.

Easy triggering of intrusions: Associative learning without contingency awareness in PTSD
Michael, Tanja *Inst. für Psychologie, Universität Basel, Basel, Switzerland*
We examined conditioning to trauma-related stimuli with a paradigm of no unconditioned-conditioned stimuli contingency awareness. Under an attention task, PTSD patients and controls viewed a series of distracters interspersed with pairings of CSs with trauma-related USs. Participants displayed no CS-US contingency awareness, but indicated feeling more anxious when subsequently viewing the trauma-related CS than when viewing the pleasant CS. This conditioning effect was more pronounced in the PTSD group. These findings may explain why reexperiencing is often

triggered by stimuli associated with the trauma although individuals are unaware of the triggers.

Towards a new social facilitation model of posttraumatic stress disorder

Maercker, Andreas Inst. für Psychopathologie, Universität Zürich, Zürich, Switzerland *Nietlisbach, Gabriela* Int. für Psychopathologie, Universität Zürich, Zürich, Switzerland *Gaebler, Ira* Inst. für Psychopathologie, Universität Zürich, Zurich, Switzerland

Complementing to known models of risk and protective factors of PTSD the processes of social facilitation plays a central role in development and maintenance of the disorder and its symptoms. Relevant psychological processes are disturbed empathy in survivors, perceived lack of social acknowledgment as victim or survivor, and emerging processes of anger, hate, and rage in trauma survivors. We present a series of studies focusing on these processes. In result, we propose a comprehensive model of social facilitation that not only explains current signs and symptoms of PTSD but also may serve as framework for (secondary or tertiary) prevention and treatment.

Social causation and social selection models of perceived posttraumatic stress

Kaniasty, Krys Dept. of Psychology, Indiana Univ. of Pennsylvania, Indiana, PA, USA

Authors propose that both social causation and social selection models account for the causal linkages between perceptions of social support in PTSD (and depression). Specifically, it was predicted that the importance of each mechanism would emerge sequentially over time. Structural equation modeling indicated that social causation (more support, less distress) dominated in the early phase of coping with disaster, 6 to 12 months after the impact (Wave 1 and 2). Social selection (more distress, less support) emerged later in time after the event (Wave 3 and 4). Findings demonstrate that causal paths between social support and distress are influenced by interpersonal and social dynamics that are changing across time as coping with a stressor progresses.

Biopsychological risk and protective factors for PTSD and its successful psychotherapeutic treatment

Karl, Anke Dept. of Psychology, University of Southampton, Highfield, United Kingdom

Current models of PTSD postulate that biopsychological factors are involved in the aetiology and maintenance of the disorder. There is also an accumulating body of research that there may also be predisposing biopsychological factors. The aim of this talk is to focus on the interaction with PTSD severity and successful treatment. Based on previous research in treatment-seeking survivors of motor vehicle accidents (MVAs) the interaction between psychophysiological correlates of PTSD, of its CBT treatment and genetic polymorphisms will be discussed. In addition, a framework for future research about the gene person environment interaction will be discussed.

The structure of PTSD symptoms

Elklit, Ask Dept. of Psychology, University of Aarhus, Aarhus, Denmark *Sherlin, Mark* Dept. of Psychology, University of Aarhus, Aarhus, Denmark

Based on previous factor analytic findings and the DSM-IV formulation, six confirmatory factor models were specified and estimated that reflected different posttraumatic stress symptom (PTSD) clusters. The analyses were based on responses from 1116 participants who had suffered whiplash injuries and screened for full or sub-clinical PTSD using the Harvard Trauma Questionnaire. A correlated four-factor model with re-experiencing, avoidance, dysphoria, and arousal factors fitted the data very well. Correlations with criteria measures showed that these factors were associated with other trauma related variables in a theoretically predictable way and showed evidence of unique predictive utility.

Mediators of sex differences in posttraumatic stress disorder and depression after trauma: Results from prospective longitudinal studies

Ehlers, Anke Inst. of Psychiatry, University of London, London, United Kingdom *Böllinghaus, Inga* Inst. of Psychiatry, University of London, London, United Kingdom

After trauma, women have greater risk of developing posttraumatic stress disorder (PTSD) then men. The authors conducted a large prospective longitudinal studies of predictors of PTSD in assault and accident survivors. A range of psychological factors that may mediate sex differences in PTSD rates such as emotional reactions during the trauma and appraisals of the trauma and its aftermath were assessed in the emergency room and at 2 or 4 weeks. Psychological outcome at 6 months was assessed by self-report and diagnostic interview.

S-134: Environmental constraints on cognition

Axel Mecklinger (chair)

There is compelling evidence that environmental affordances, like cultural specific experiences in object or language processing or diversities in schooling and social practice shape cognitive processes in important ways. While environmental influences have been found for basic perceptual and attentional processes, it is largely unexplored how higher order cognitive processes are modulated by environmental factors and how this modulation is reflected in the underlying brain mechanisms. Capitalizing on the diversity of environmental constraints within and between Western and Eastern cultures, the contributors to this symposium explore environmentally adapted visual cognition across a variety of processing domains.

Modulation of spatial-cognitive capacities: Evidence from patients with brain lesions

Kerkhoff, Georg Inst. für Psychologie, Universität des Saarlandes, Saarbrücken, Germany *Groh-Bordin, Christian* Dept. of Psychology, Universität des Saarlandes, Saarbrücken, Germany *Shan, Chunlei* Institute of Psychology, Chinese Academy of Sciences, Bejing, People's Republic of China *Weng, Xuchu* Institute of Psychology, Chinese Academy of Sciences, Bejing, People's Republic of China

Visuospatial perception is important for orientation in space and crucially linked to parietal cortex. Parietal lesions cause visuospatial deficits. Here, we investigated the modulation of such visuospatial deficits in 10 patients with right-parietal lesions, and 10 matched controls under 3 conditions: (1) with a static background of small white dots, (2) with slow clockwise or (3) counterclockwise circular motion of these background stimuli. In conditions 1 and 3 the brain lesioned subjects showed pronounced deficits. However, these were completely normalized in condition 2 with clockwise background motion. Possible cognitive and neural mechanisms as well as implications for therapy are discussed.

Working memory capacity and culture-based expertise

Zimmer, Hubert Inst. für Psychologie, Universität des Saarlandes, Saarbrücken, Germany *Fu, Xiaolan* Institute of Psychology, Chinese Academy of Sciences, Beijing, People's Republic of China

Visual-working memory capacity is a function of the number of objects and of their complexity. We show that not only stimulus characteristics but also the perceiver's expertise influences the capacity. We compared working memory capacity of Westerners with those of the Chinese for colors, Chinese characters, pseudo and nonsense characters that only looked like characters. Both groups had the same capacity for colors. Capacity of Westerners heavily dropped with all characters. As expected, Chinese capacity for characters was the same as for colors, it fall with pseudo and with nonsense characters, but compared to Westerners an advantage remained.

Associative memories: Boundary conditions during encoding and retrieval

Mecklinger, Axel Inst. für Psychologie, Universität des Saarlandes, Saarbrücken, Germany *Weng, Xuchu* Institute of Psychology, Chinese Academy of Sciences, Beijing, Germany *Yang, JiongJiong* Department of Psychology, Beijing University, Beijing, Germany

A key feature of human episodic memory is the creation and retrieval of associations between items and events. Recent neuropsychological studies have suggested that associative memories differ in the degree to which their components can be encoded to form a holistic (unitized) representation. Associative memories with unitized components can be retrieved without hippocampal involvement, whereas the retrieval of associations between arbitrary components depends on the integrity of the hippocampus. We will present event-related potential (ERP) and fMRI studies investigating the brain systems mediating both forms of associative memories as well as the boundary conditions for the formation of unitized memory representations.

Female's situation awareness is better than male during driving: A simulated study

Hao, Xueqin Inst. of Psychology, Chinese Academy of Sciences, Beijing, People's Republic of China *Sun, Xianhong Zhang, Khan*

Drivers' situation awareness (SA) and mental work load (MWL) were tested by applying an A PC-based driving simulator. Both the physiological measures and the subjective assessment were employed to measure MWL. It was found that with the increasing of traffic, the driving performance did not worsen, however participant's MWL increased. At the same time, the participant's SA performance deteriorated. It was also found that female participants got better SA performance than male participants did. No significant effect of driving experience on any dependent variable used in this study was found by the simulated driving.

Lexical interference in logographic and alphabetical writing systems: ERP evidence from a stroop task

Wang, Kui Inst. of Psychology, Chinese Academy of Sciences, Beijing, People's Republic of China *Mecklinger, Axel* Department of Psychology, Saarland University, Saarbrücken, Germany *Hofmann, Juliane* Department of Psychology, Saarland University, Saarbrücken, Germany *Weng, Xuchu* Inst. of Psychology, Chinese Academy of Sciences, Beijing, People's Republic of China

An important issue in psycholinguistic research is how orthographic and phonological information contribute to meaning activation. Therefore, we conducted a Stroop interference experiment with event-related potential (ERP) measures in Chinese and German readers. While the behavioral interference effects were similar across groups, language-specific ERP differences were obtained for color words and color word associates. Congruent Chinese color words elicited a positive component around 400 ms suggesting a facilitated mapping from orthography to meaning in Chinese. Additionally, incongruent Chinese, but not German, color word associates elicited a late negative component that may reflect additional post-lexical processing demands of logographic writing systems.

Familiarity effect in artificial grammars learning
Fu, Xiaolan Inst. of Psychology, Chinese Academy of Sciences, Beijing, People's Republic of China Wan, Lulu Inst. of Psychology, Chinese Academy of Sciences, Beijing, People's Republic of China Dienes, Zoltan Department of Psychology, University of Sussex, Brighton, United Kingdom
Subjects trained on two artificial grammars can control which grammar they use in classifying strings. According to Jacoby, familiarity can not be involved in the control of which grammar to use. In two experiments, participants were trained on two artificial grammars and then used one of the grammars to classify new test strings. After each classification subjects rated the familiarity of the strings. The results showed that when subjects said they were using familiarity, the rated familiarity was greater for test strings consistent with their chosen grammar rather than for strings from the other grammar.

S-135: Offshore and onshore workplaces: The link between safety, wellbeing and health

Torbjörn Rundmo, Stig Berge Matthiesen (chair)
The symposium covers the workplace safety issue, and the link with wellbeing and health. The first presenter demonstrates the effects of working 14 successive 12-hour day shifts. The next presentation compares the health safety culture in Norwegian and UK offshore sector. The third investigates the link between support, commitment and behaviour. Paper 4 studies whether offshore safety may predict mental health. The fifth investigates the associations between participants' experience during skill performance, conducting a safety intervention, and self efficacy. The sixth presentation is aimed to identify which aspects of job insecurity that have impact on turnover intentions and risk behaviour.

Mood and performance changes during 12-hr day shifts over a two-week offshore tour
Parkes, Katharine Dept. Experimental Psychology, University of Oxford, Oxford, United Kingdom
The effects of working 14 successive 12-hr day shifts on sleep, alertness, mood, perceived workload, and reaction time (RT) were evaluated among offshore production operators. Three assessments (using hand-held computers) were made during each of 8 test shifts over the two-week tour. Mood and performance remained relatively stable overall, but alertness decreased across individual shifts. RT variability, but not mean RT, increased across shifts and weeks. Few main effects indicative of cumulative fatigue were observed; this result is consistent with, and extends, published findings for 7 x 12-hr day shifts. However, the more subtle signs of fatigue observed should not be ignored.

A comparative study of HSE-culture on the Norwegian continental and UK continental shelves
Tharaldsen, Jorunn Elise Institute Stavanger, International Research, Stavanger, Norway Mearns, Kathryn Dept. of Psychology, University of Aberdeen, Aberdeen, United Kingdom Knudsen, Knut IRID, IRIS, Stavanger, Norway
The current study is a comparative analysis of HSE-culture as perceived by drilling employees on the Norwegian and UK Continental Shelves. A survey has being carried out on a total of 12 platforms in Norway and UK. Dimensions are extracted from the OSQ, the Trends in Risk level project, a selection of GLOBE organizational culture scales, safety commitment and trust scales and COPSOQ. The results of the questionnaire study are being analysed and will be taken into the company for further analysis, comparing employees' perceptions on the two shelves and defining challenging and risky areas that need to be improved. To be

included into T.Rundmo's and S.B Matthiesen's symposium

Relationships between support, commitment and safety behaviour in the UK offshore industry
Mearns, Kathryn Dept. of Psychology, University of Aberdeen, Aberdeen, United Kingdom Reader, Thomas Psychology, University of Aberdeen, Aberdeen, United Kingdom
Reporting dangers and intervening to protect others are behaviours that help to maintain safety in organizations but perceived organizational support is important for these behaviours to occur. Relationships between support from the organization, supervisors and workmates, organizational commitment, organizational citizenship and reporting dangers and taking action were investigated in a sample of 444 offshore workers on 18 UK installations. The results show no significant relationship between any of the support measures and reporting dangers and taking action, however organizational commitment and citizenship explain 23% of the variance in reporting dangers and 21% of the variance in taking action.

Demand-control, offshore safety and mental health among offshore workers
Søiland, Vibeke Faculty of Psychology, University of Bergen, Bergen, Norway Matthiesen, Stig Berge Faculty of Psychology, Univ. of Bergen, Bergen, Norway Einarsen, Ståle Faculty of Psychology, Univ. of Bergen, Bergen, Norway
A workplace survey study was conducted in offshore oil industry, in which 1022 offshore oil workers participated (response rate= 59%). The questionnaire applied covered various topics amongst others risk perception of their offshore work environment, safety climate, demand-control and mental health. The results showed that the workers' experience of demand and control significantly predicted mental health. Additionally, offshore safety, operationalised as risk perception and safety climate, contributed significantly to the explanation of mental health variance, when controlling for the demand and control aspect. Moreover, an interaction effect between safety climate and risk perception were found.

Is job insecurity related to turnover intentions and risk behaviour?
Rundmo, Torbjörn of Science and Technology, Norwegian University, Trondheim, Norway Emberland, Jan S. Dept. of Psychology, Norwegian Univ. of Sci. &, Trondheim, Norway
This study's aim was to identify which aspects of job insecurity that have impact on turnover intentions and risk behaviour. In addition, the significance of attitudinal (job satisfaction) and psychological outcomes as well as demographic characteristics (gender and age) is accounted for. The results of the study are based on a self-completion questionnaire survey carried out among a representative sample of the Norwegian public (n = 260). Job insecurity indirectly explained turnover intentions and risk behaviour. On this basis it is being discussed whether improvements in management change communication may reduce insecure employees' risk behaviour.

S-136: Workplace and anxiety

Beate Muschalla, Alan M. Langlieb (chair)
Work is an important domain of life. Problems at the workplace and mental health therefore must have interactions. A common final pathway of mental disorders in general and work related anxieties in particular are workplace phobias, with panic when approaching or thinking of the workplace. This is a serious complication with negative consequences for the further course of illness. It makes special therapeutic interventions necessary.

This symposium will present diverse aspects of the interrelations between workplace stress and anxiety, mental health and performance problems, as well as resulting participation disorders, especially appearing as long-term sick leave.

Work stress and anxiety: Epidemiologic findings in a nationally representative sample of working population
Wang, Jian-Li Dept. of Psychiatry, University Calgary, Calgary, Canada
This study was to estimate the 12-month prevalence of depressive, anxiety and substance use related disorders in a representative sample of the Canadian working population, and to investigate the relationship between work stress, work/family balance and anxiety disorders in the population. The data from the Canadian Community Health Survey – Mental Health & Well-being (CCHS-1.2) were used. The CCHS-1.2 was the first Canadian national mental health survey targeting on household residents aged 15 years old and over. It was found that mental disorders are prevalent in the working population. Job insecurity and lack of social support are major work stressors. Work/family imbalance is a significant factor for having an anxiety disorder.

Personal initiative at work and work-related well-being: Why is there no relationship?
Frese, Michael Inst. für Angew. Psychologie, Universität Gießen, Gießen, Germany
Jahoda argued that well-being should include an active approach to things. We tested in our study whether personal initiative was related to well-being. Personal initiative consists of a self-starting, proactive (future oriented), and persistent (overcoming barriers) approach to work. Facets of health and ill-health were measured with depression, negative affectivity, bitterness, self-confidence, and self-efficacy. A longitudinal study on personal initiative and ill-health showed that there are smallish relationships between personal initiative (particularly if measured with a stringent interview measure) and ill-health.

Workplace phobia and work-related participation problems
Linden, Michael Psychosom. Rehabil., Charité Berlin, Teltow, Germany
Background: Workplace-related anxieties appear in different forms. The worst case is a manifestation of a workplace phobia with panic reaction when only thinking of or coming near the workplace. There is a strong tendency of avoidance which does often result in long-term-sick-leave. Method: 230 psychosomatic inpatients were interviewed concerning workplace-related anxieties and resulting work-participation-problems. Results:. 56,8% out of 39 workplace phobic patients were on sick-leave because of the symptoms, and in other 24,3% workplace phobia resulted in job-loss. Conclusion: Workplace phobia is the most severe form of workplace-related anxiety. It has to be taken earnest in primary health care.

Diagnostic instruments for the assessment of workplace-related anxieties
Muschalla, Beate Psychosom. Rehabilitation, Charité Berlin, Teltow, Germany
Background: Workplaces have anxiety-provoking features: failure, mobbing, angry customers, accidents. The quality and quantity of job-anxiety was investigated in patients with mental and somatic illness. Method: 90 psychosomatic and 100 orthopaedic inpatients filled in the Job-Anxiety-Scale. Results: Psychosomatic patients showed significantly higher job-anxiety-scores than orthopaedic patients. Orthopaedic patients score higher in anxiety of functional impairment, whereas psychosomatic patients do more suffer from job-related

generalised worrying, panic, fears of existence and global job-anxiety. Job-anxiety-level was significantly correlated with sick leave-duration. Conclusion: There are differences in quality and quantity of job-anxiety in different clinical groups. This requires consequences for diagnostic and treatment.

Depression, anxiety and substance use disorders and their relation with the workplace
Langlieb, Alan M. Workplace Psychiatry, John Hopkins Hospital, Baltimore, MD, USA
With health care costs rising, many employers are focusing more on the cost of illness and related expenditures of disability and lost productive time. Employers of the new information/technology economy are placing a heightened focus on the prevention of depression, stress and substance use disorders. With this new awareness comes important questions: How many employees suffer from depression, anxiety and/or substance use disorders? What is their impact on productivity? How can employers ensure that their employees are receiving the best treatment, and how can they be measured? What is the emerging role for developing resiliency training among an employed population?

Anxiety and depression in employees returned to work after long-time sick leave
Munir, Fehmidah Dept. of Human Sciences, Loughborough University, Loughborough, United Kingdom
Objectives: Compare psychosocial factors among those returning to work following depression/anxiety (n=65), with those returning following back pain (n=40), cancer (n=40) or heart disease (n=30). Methods: Employers, charities and support groups (n= 60) distributed questionnaires to those meeting participation criteria. Results: Those with depression/anxiety and heart disease reported higher severity of depression symptoms, but only depression/anxiety group reported lower work ability (β=-.22), low self-efficacy in managing ill-health at work (β=-.56) and low workplace support (β=-.35). Conclusions: To enable those with depression to return and maintain work, healthcare professionals and employers should help improve their well-being through workplace support and intervention.

Workplace stress, anxiety and cognitive errors
Harris, Lynne Dept. of Health Sciences, University of Sydney, Sydney, Australia
Objectives: Errors in health care settings have been attributed to failures of cognitive function. This paper examines the relationship between the workplace, anxiety, self-reported cognitive errors, and cognitive performance. Methods: Allied health professionals completed internet-based protocols. Results: Heavy workloads and interpersonal difficulties were associated with elevated anxiety. Anxiety was associated with self-reported workplace cognitive errors, but not with cognitive performance. Conclusions: The findings have implications for the development of stress management approaches for allied health and raise concerns about self-report measures of cognitive errors. Self-reported cognitive errors may reflect a tendency to self-criticism, rather than objective difficulties with cognitive function.

S-137: Future time perspective in adolescence and early adulthood

Toshiaki Shirai, Willy Lens (chair)
Due to their higher cognitive functioning, human beings specify their needs and motives in more or less specific motivational goals, plans, and projects. These motivational goals can be analyzed for their content and for their temporal localization, which is the issue of future time perspective (FTP). Adolescence and early adulthood are the critical period to extend FTP. Each of the presentations will discuss

empirical studies showing the positive effects of a deep and well-structured FTP on present motivation and personality development in different cultural contexts.

Future time perspective, social insertion and risk tendencies among high school and post-secondary students in Peru: A developmental approach
Herrera, Dora Dept. of Psychology, Pont. Universidad Catolica, San Miguel, Peru Lens, Willy Dept. of Psychology, University of Leuven, Leuven, Belgium
During the last ten years the motivational content and the length of Future Time Perspective (FTP) have been measured among 1941 students in Peru. The purposes of this study were (a) providing a better understanding of the role of FTP in adolescents, (b) studying developments in the motivational contents of students' goals over the years and during a transition period in educational institutions. Data has been collected with the Shorter Form of the Motivational Induction Method (MIM). Differences in degree and quality of Social Insertion and in Risk Tendencies were related to FTP. The results and their implications for upcoming social and educational interventions to enhance a more adaptive educational and professional development among Peruvian adolescents are discussed.

Four years longitudinal study on future time perspective during the transition from junior high school to high school
Tsuzuki, Manabu Dept. of Psychology, Chuo University, Hachioji, Japan
In Japan, compulsory education consists of six-year elementary school and three-year junior high school. After graduate from junior high school, students must take an entrance examination to go to high school. Students have a lot of stress during this transition. Based on the four-year longitudinal study, the author has been examined developmental changes concerning future time perspective during the transition from elementary school to junior high school. Analyzing the obtained data, relations between adolescents' future time perspective and other factors (psychological adjustment, academic ability, and self esteem) is examined. The implications for educational support for adolescents' development of future time perspective are discussed.

Considering the future in identity formation: The influence of perceived adult status and a search for mediating variables
Luyckx, Koen Center for Develop. Psychology, Catholic University Leuven, Leuven, Belgium Goossens, Luc Dept. of Psychology, Catholic University of Leuven, Leuven, Belgium Lens, Willy Dept. of Psychology, University of Leuven, Leuven, Belgium Smits, Ilse Center for Develop, Psychology, Catholic University Leuven, Leuven, Belgium
The present paper examined whether perceived adult status influences identity formation, using a recent model of global future-oriented identity formation. Results in a sample of 345 university- and non-university dwelling emerging adults (18-30 years of age) demonstrated that perceived adults scored higher on identity commitments and on identification with these commitments. However, they scored lower on a ruminative (rather than reflective) type of identity exploration than perceived emerging adults did. Mediation analyses demonstrated that these mean differences could be partially accounted for by differences in global need satisfaction and sense of coherence between perceived adults and perceived emerging adults.

Personal goals during educational transitions among adolescence and young adults
Salmela-Aro, Katariina Dept. of Psychology, University of Jyväskylä, Jyväskylä, Finland Riuttala, Elina Dept. of Psychology, University of Jyväskylä, Jyväskylä, Finland
The aim of the present research was to find out, what kinds of groups of adolescents can be formed by the content of personal goals among students at academic and vocational track and how these groups differ in goal appraisals, meaningful life events and subjective well-being. Adolescents in upper secondary education (N=1144) were grouped according to the content of their personal goals using a person oriented approach. Four groups emerged: (1) property-, (2) occupation-, (3) relationships- and (4) self-focused. Those in the self-focused group were exhausted and especially cynical towards their school work and they suffered from almost clinically significant depression.

Longitudinal study of constructing future on the transition from adolescence to adulthood
Shirai, Toshiaki Dept. of Psychology, Osaka Kyoiku University, Kashiwara, Japan
Transition from adolescence to adulthood deals with new life events such as leaving home, financial independence, entrance into work places. This can occur the change of the future prospects. One hundred females were followed to answer the questionnaire on future time perspective in three years after graduation from university in Japan. Results showed that their future prospects played an important role at every wave. This may imply individuals are interacting actively with changing worlds to achieve their transition to adulthood (Lerner, 2002) and to organize their future.

S-138: Exploring the effects of control and value appraisals on emotions within and outside the achievement domain

Anne Frenzel, Thomas Götz (chair)
Grounded in appraisal theoretical thinking, this symposium explores the relationship between control and value appraisals and emotions. In an introductory theoretical input, Pekrun argues these are core appraisals underlying the arousal of emotions in the achievement domain. Frenzel and Lichtenfeld present evidence supporting this claim, using data from experimental and field studies. Goetz widens the perspective and provides evidence that these appraisal dimensions are influential also in non-achievement contexts. Kaufmann reports findings from experimental studies showing that perceived control influences positive and negative affect. Zeidner from the Center for Interdisciplinary Research on Emotions (University of Haifa) integrates and discusses the symposium contributions.

Assumptions of the control-value theory of achievement emotions
Pekrun, Reinhard Inst. für Psychologie, Universität München, München, Germany
The control-value theory provides an integrative framework for analyzing the antecedents and effects of emotions experienced in achievement settings. It is based on the premise that appraisals of control and value are central to the arousal of achievement emotions, including activity-related emotions such as enjoyment and boredom, as well as outcome emotions such as hope, pride, anxiety, or shame. Implications to be discussed pertain to the domain specificity of achievement emotions; their origins, their effects on performance; and the reciprocal linkages between emotions, antecedents, and effects; their relative universality across genders and cultures; and their regulation, therapy, and development.

Girls and mathematics: A "hopeless" issue? A control-value approach to gender differences in emotions towards mathematics

Frenzel, Anne *Inst. für Psychologie, Universität München, München, Germany*

Based on Pekrun's (2006) control-value theory of achievement emotions, gender differences in mathematics emotions were hypothesized due to different levels of control and value beliefs in mathematics among girls vs. boys. Two age groups were analyzed (grades 5/9, N = 2,053/2,528, 49/51 per cent girls). Across age groups, girls reported significantly less enjoyment and pride than boys, but more anxiety and hopelessness. The female emotional pattern was due to girls' low competence beliefs and domain value of mathematics, combined with high mathematics achievement value. Multiple-group comparisons confirmed that structural relationships between variables were largely invariant across genders and age groups.

An experimental test of the control-value theory of achievement emotions

Lichtenfeld, Stephanie *Inst. für Psychologie, Universität München, München, Germany* **Maier, Markus** *Inst. für Psychologie, Universität München, München, Germany*

In the control-value theory, it is assumed that emotional reactions are determined by a multiplicative combination of control and value appraisals. While correlational data support this assumption (Pekrun, Goetz, Titz, & Perry, 2002), experimental evidence on interactive effects of control and value appraisals is still lacking. In three experiments, we manipulated participants' perceived control and value relating to an achievement test, and assessed their anxiety before the test. Experiment 1 used a scenario approach, experiment 2 self-reports of anxiety, and experiment 3 an implicit measure of anxiety. As expected, there was a significant effect of the control x value interaction on achievement anxiety in all three studies.

Emotional experiences and their control and value antecedents

Götz, Thomas *Inst. für Päag. Psychologie, Universität Konstanz, Konstanz, Germany* **Stöger, Heidrun** *Erziehungswissenschaften, Universität Regensburg, Regensburg, Germany*

In the present study, control and value appraisals as well as three positive and three negative emotions were assessed using the experience sampling method. The sample consisted of 50 university freshmen (78% female). Students completed state questionnaires following a signal from a Pocket PC (42 signals, 7 days). In line with hypotheses, we found clear relations between situation-specific state emotions, perceived control, and value appraisals. Despite the overall equivalence of construct relations in non-achievement vs. achievement settings, the correspondence between control/value and negative affect was stronger in situations involving learning and performance.

The causal impact of perceived control in emotional experiences: Evidence on asymmetries on positive and negative affect

Kaufmann, Martina *Inst. für Psychologie, Universität Erfurt, Erfurt, Germany* **Götz, Thomas** *Erziehungswissenschaften, Universität Konstanz, Konstanz, Germany*

According to Pekrun's control-value theory, emotional experiences in achievement contexts should be triggered by appraisals of control over and value of activities and outcomes. Empirical evidence on the impact of value appraisals seems clear cut. Substantiation of the causal role of perceived control is however still scarce, and restricted to the aspect that a sense of uncontrollability elicits negative emotional experience. The present experimental study shows that indeed all emotional

experience, that is both positive and negative emotional experience, varies as a function of perceived control, whether control is actually available (Experiment 1) or merely illusory (Experiment 2).

Stefan Huber (chair)

In recent years religion and spirituality have become topics of psychological interest again. The important role of religion for global developments as well as for individual needs has been rediscovered, and both the beneficial and the critical aspects of religion and spirituality are now regarded as a challenging field for research. Scholars have started to examine the place and role of religiosity and spirituality in personality, to develop well-elaborated measures for religiosity and spirituality and their centrality, and to analyze their impact on ways of meaning-making, coping, health, and well-being. The symposium gives an overview about trends and findings.

Core dimensions, centrality and content: A model for cross-cultural and interreligious research in psychology of religion

Huber, Stefan *KOOM, Universität Mainz, Mainz, Germany*

The paper discusses a model for cross-cultural and interreligious research in psychology of religion (Huber, 2003). This model is characterized by six core dimensions of religiosity (intellect, ideology, experience, private practice, public practice, and consequences in everyday life). The measurement of these dimensions differentiates between centrality and content of religiosity. While the concept of centrality is related to the general relevance of religion in an individual's personality, the concept of content is related to specific behavioural directions of religion. The discussion of the model is empirically based on representative surveys in 21 nations (N>21.000) covering 5 major religious groups (Christianity, Islam, Hinduism, Buddhism, Judaism).

Religiosity and values

Hofmann-Towfigh, Nadi *Potsdam, Germany*

How do religiosity and values relate to each other? Using the data of a study which explored the value priorities and religiosity of members of the Baha'i Faith in Germany (N = 475), some results will be presented to demonstrate how the centrality of religiosity related to values. Further, selected content areas of religiosity, such as fundamentalism and religious reflexivity will be discussed in the framework of the value model (Schwartz, 1992). The measures used for these analyses were the 40-item Portrait Values Questionnaire (PVQ 40; Schwartz, 2000), the "Structure-of-Religiosity-Test" (S-R-T; Huber, 2003), as well as a single-item religiosity measure.

Implicit religiosity: Diversity of life meanings in church members and non-members

Schnell, Tatjana *Inst. für Psychologie, Universität Innsbruck, Innsbruck, Austria*

In contemporary Europe, belonging to a Christian church cannot be equalled with an outlook on life. Similarly, subjective religiosity is not necessarily connected with an institutionalised religion. As research on Implicit Religiosity shows, also secular orientations can be expressed in religious ways and fulfil the 'religious' function of meaning-making. The Sources of Meaning Questionnaire (Schnell&Becker, 2007) was applied to a representative German sample (N=604). With cluster analyses, different types of meaning-orientations among

church members and non-members were identified. Analyses of correlation show diversity in and between sub-samples, but also similarities across sub-samples as regards degree of meaningfulness and other variables.

Worldviews: Form and contents of atheistic, spiritual and religious beliefs and their relevance for four types of well-being

Klein, Constantin *Inst. für Psycholgie, Techn. Universität Dresden, Dresden, Germany*

The paper presents a study about the interplay between worldviews (belief systems) and well-being. Several worldviews have been distinguished, ranging from atheistic positions to traditional Christian positions as well as to alternative spiritual positions. More than 660 respondents represented these diverse worldviews. They completed a questionnaire operationalizing formal characteristics and specific contents of the worldviews. The designed worldview scales identified four types of worldviews whose relationship to mental health was compared. As main results, there are characteristic differences of the level of well-being. The findings illustrate the relevance of belief systems for mental health and emphasize to distinguish between worldviews.

Structure and centrality of religious-spiritual well-being among psychiatric in-patients and healthy controls

Unterrainer, Human-Friedrich *ARS Addiction Research Society, Gesellschaft "Grüner Kreis", Graz, Austria*

AbstractIs the structure and centrality of religious-spiritual well-being associated to personality or psychopathological symptoms?Methods Addicts (N=120), depressive patients (N=100) and healthy controls (N=200) were investigated using a multidimensional inventory for religious-spiritual well-being (MI-RSB 48) in combination with the Centrality scale (C-scale)/ Structure of Religiosity Test (RST) and different personality/ clinical variables.ResultsDifferences in bio-psycho-socio-spiritual well-being were found between the groups. The more central the individual religious construct system is, the more powerful are its effects.ConclusionsThe association between religious-spiritual well-being and psychopathological symptoms might open up new strategies in prevention and therapy of psychiatric diseases.

Religious coping: A resource for personal growth?

Lehr, Dirk *Inst. für Medizin. Psychologie, Universität Marburg, Marburg, Germany*

In the aftermath of crisis some people manage to find benefit, also referred to as personal growth. These studies examined the role of religious coping for personal growth. Sampling included 210 participants with negative life event and 122 patients suffering from chronic conditions. Pargament's religious-coping inventory (RCOPE) allowed close examination of functional and dysfunctional ways of coping. Significant associations of moderate size were found for all dimensions of Tedeschi's and Calhoun's posttraumatic growth inventory. Results suggest positive religious coping to be a resource for personal growth, while the results for negative religious coping are inconsistent and need further discussion.

Siamak Samani, Bruce Ryan (chair)

Family process and content model is a contextual and psychoeducational model. This model tries to provide a valid pattern for family diagnosis and typology for family preparing and repairing. The aim of this symposium is to clarify the different aspects of the model. The concentration of the program in the symposium will be on describing the main dimensions and assumptions of the model, family definition, family social context, methods of family assessment and family typology, experimental evidences, family prescriptive methods, and family therapy. Also the strongnesses and weaknesses of the model will discuss at the end of symposium.

The roles of religion in the family process and content model

Mazidi, Mohammad Dept. Educational Philosophy, Shiraz University, Shiraz, Islamic Republic of Iran
Samani (2006) in his family model, has introduced three interrelated components (processes, contents and social context) through which determine the quality and performance of the family. In this article, I want to concentrate on the effects of "religion", as an effective factor in social context. Religion is not a social institution, as Durkheim and his advocates believe. Rather, it is a system of sacred beliefs, values, ethics and transcendental ideas which impacts all aspects of the family, as Samani has mentioned. Also, a Bio-Rational-Emotional factor will be introduced, as family production, which is affected by family belief system.

A conceptual exploration on family conflicts based on family process and content model

Ryan, Bruce Dept. of Family Relations, University of Guelph, Guelph, Canada Samani, siamak Dept. of Edu. Psychology, Shiraz University, Shiraz, Islamic Republic of Iran
A 21-item marital issues scale, previously developed in a pilot study involving 100 couples, was completed by 600 married adults aged 15 to 54 years. These data were subjected to a principal components analysis using a varimax rotation in order to extract the underlying marital conflict factors. The scree plot indicated a three factor solution: process conflicts (relationship issues), content conflicts (extant family conditions such as employment, income, health), and context conflicts (issues concerning place of family in community and culture). These findings are consistent with the three key components of the Family Process and Contents Model.

Validity and reliability of family process and family content scales

Samani, Siamak Dept. Educational Psychology, Shiraz University, Shiraz, Islamic Republic of Iran
The aim of this research was to study the validity and reliability of family process and family content scales. These two scales were used for family typology in family process and content model. The content of these scales was retrieved from 450 interviews with couples. The sample of this study includes 1258 married persons. Family process scale and family content scale includes 47 and 39 items respectively. Principle component factor analysis revealed that there are 8 factors in family process scale and 8 factors in family content scale. Different technical methods were used to check the reliability of these scales

An analytic point of view on different dimensions of the family process and content model

Jowkar, Bahram Dept. Educational Psychology, Shiraz University, Shiraz, Islamic Republic of Iran
All family models are family intervention models. According to components of each model, Family consultants/therapists analyzing the family system and establishing repair and prepare program for solving family problems. The goal of this article is to analysis different component of family process and content model based on Brofenbrenner's

ecological-system model. Adapting and categorizing the model's components in macro, meso and micro systems could be determine limits and level of interventional programs for family problems. This adaptation provides additional support for applicability of the family model in dealing with family system problems.

Child management strategies in family therapy

Crisante, Lea Sydney West Area Health Serv., Cumberland Hospital, North Rocks, NSW, Australia
Family therapy has traditionally provided broad perspectives regarding the management for child behavioural difficulties resulting in criticisms of a lack of strategies for addressing such issues. This paper considers this by considering current theoretical perspectives with a view to integrating systemic thinking with behavioural family interventions. This discussion is in relation to cultural issues in therapy and how such issues have been addressed in providing services in a transcultural context in Australia. The paper will therefore connect practical and theoretical concerns in family therapy provided in cases in which the child is the identified patient with multicultural service provision in Sydney.

Family typology: Divorced family and family with an addict member

Hashemi, Ladan Arsenjan, Dept. of Psychology, Islamic Azad University of, Arsenjan, Islamic Republic of Iran
The aim of this study was to compare three kinds of family (normal family, family with an addict member and, divorced family) on family process and family content. The sample includes 105 females (35 females for each group). Family process and content scales were used for data gathering. The family process scale includes five subscales (problem solving skills, communication skills, family cohesion, coping strategies and, religious beliefs) and the family content scale has only a general factor. The results of this study revealed that there were significant differences among these families on family process and content

Developing a family needs scale

Nasiri, Habibolah Dept. Educational Psychology, Shiraz University, Shiraz, Islamic Republic of Iran
The aim of this study was develop and to study the psychometric properties of a scale for assessment of basic needs in Iranian family. The sample includes 686 men and women (267 men and 419 women). The results of factor analysis revealed there were 5 factors. The factors named:1- Psychological/Emotional needs, 2-Financial/Economical needs, 3-Physical Health needs, 4-Recreational needs and 5-Educational needs. Alpha Cronbach for these factors and scale were: .92, .90, .77, .88, .75, .95 respectively. In sum, the results showed that the family basic needs scale were reliable and valid scale for assessing family needs for Iranian families.

S-141: From instruction to action: Bridging the gap

Dorit Wenke, Robert Gaschler (chair)
One of the outstanding abilities of humans is their capability to use verbal instructions to guide their behaviour. While non-human primates have to learn new behaviour via effortful and time consuming trial and error learning, humans can use verbal instructions to acquire new behavioural options seemingly effortlessly and very rapidly. This symposium brings together research from cognitive psychology, neuroscience, and volition research investigating how verbal instructions are used to control behaviour.

Implicit learning based on instructed action codes

Gaschler, Robert Inst. für Psychologie, Humboldt-Universität zu Berlin, Berlin, Germany Wenke, Dorit Dept. of Psychology, MPI, Leipzig, Germany Frensch, Peter A.
We investigated how response instructions determine later implicit sequence learning. We instructed participants to either use color or location (e.g. to respond with the green key vs. the outer left key to the diamond-shape; 4 stimuli and responses total). When responses were instructed in terms of color, participants learned the color and the location sequence, as indicated by transfer. With spatial response instructions, they only learned the spatial sequence. These results demonstrate the enormous flexibility of instruction based task-configuration processes and their consequences for automatic skill acquisition processes, with spatial coding as a potential default.

The influence of intentions on behavior

Cohen, Anna-Lisa Psychology, Yeshiva University, New York, USA Gollwitzer, Peter
Recent findings by Cohen et al. (in press) reveal that complex postponed intentions that can be triggered by two or more cues interfere with ongoing task activities (defined in this study as lexical decision latencies). However, simpler intentions that are triggered by only one cue show no such costs. We demonstrate that subjects in the latter condition spontaneously form if-then verbal plans such as those described by Gollwitzer (1999). Such plans clearly articulate a cue + response link (i.e., If I see "X", then I will perform "Y") and thereby free up processing resources for ongoing activities.

Automatic effects of verbally instructed negated relations

de Houwer, Jan Dept. of Psychology, Ghent University, Ghent, Belgium
Participants were to select one of two colors based on the identity of a target letter that was flanked on both sides by a distractor letter. The selection rules stated for each letter which color NOT to select (e.g., if target H, do not select blue). Responses were slower when participants had to select the color that was associated with the distractor in a negative manner. This suggests that, contrary to what is assumed by dual process models, negated relations recently acquired via instructions can be activated automatically.

Dissociating the neural correlates of overcoming interference from instructed and applied stimulus-response associations

Brass, Marcel Dept. of Exper. Psychology, Ghent University, Ghent, Belgium Wenke, Dorit Dept. of Psychology, MPI, Leipzig, Germany Waszak, Florian
Despite the fundamental role of verbal information for our behavioural regulation, the functional and neural mechanisms underlying the transformation of verbal instructions into efficient behaviour are still poorly understood. To gain deeper insights into this transformation, we investigated the neural circuits involved in overcoming interference from merely instructed stimulus-response (S-R) mappings and applied S-R mappings. Here we show that overcoming interference from an instructed S-R mapping involves the preSMA, whereas overcoming interference from an applied S-R mapping involves the ACC, over and above the pre-SMA. These data suggest functional differences and similarities between instructed and applied S-R associations.

How task representations guide attention

Dreisbach, Gesine Inst. für Psychologie, Techn. Universität Dresden, Dresden, Germany *Metzker, Manja Haider, Hilde*

In a series of experiments we compared the effects of stimulus-response (SR) based vs. rule based processing. That is, all participants act upon the exact same stimulus set with the same responses but are instructed to either use direct SR mappings, or one or two simple categorization rule(s). We have been able to show that these task instructions differentially modulate various phenomena such as switch costs, feature binding, and the Simon effect. From this we conclude that instructions form task representations which then guide attention towards relevant stimulus features and shield against irrelevant information.

Re-representating instructed tasks

Wenke, Dorit Dept. of Psychology, MPI, Leipzig, Germany *Gaschler, Robert* Inst. für Psychologie, Humboldt-Universität zu Berlin, Berlin, Germany

Previous research showed that task instructions often determine how humans represent and perform a task. In the present experiments we explored when they would re-represent a task in a way not encouraged by instructions. Participants were instructed to respond to the location of scatter-plots in a spatially compatible manner. We were interested in whether and when participants would use an uninstructed stimulus dimension for responding that was correlated with orientation. First results suggest that subjects strongly rely on and sometimes completely switch to a salient irrelevant stimulus dimension when this dimension facilitates processing.

S-142: Neurophysiological aspects of emotion regulation in borderline personality disorder and implications for treatment

Babette Renneberg (chair)

Recent neurophysiological data support the hypothesis of emotion dysregulation in BPD. The relevance of cognitive aspects, dissociation, anticipation of pain, empathy, and experiential avoidance for processes of emotion regulation are illustrated in the presented studies. Additionally, implications of these results for psychotherapy are outlined.

Cognitive regulation of emotions in borderline personality disorder

Herpertz, Sabine Inst. für Psychiatrie, Universität Rostock, Rostock, Germany *Schulze, Lars* Inst. für Psychiatrie, Universität Rostock, Rostock, Germany *Berger, Christoph* Inst. für Psychiatrie, Universität Rostock, Rostock, Germany *Domes, Gregor* Inst. für Psychiatrie, Universität Rostock, Rostock, Germany

Objectives: Prefronto-limbic dysfunction is thought to underlie emotion dysregulation in borderline personality disorder (BPD). However, we know rather little about prefrontal top-down processing involved in cognitive emotion regulation. Methods: fMRI data were acquired in BPD patients compared to healthy controls during a reappraisal task challenging effortful cognitive suppression of emotion. Results: Data acquired while using cognitive reappraisal strategies showed a differential activation of prefrontal areas between BPD subjects and healthy controls, namely the orbitofrontal and cingulate cortex. Conclusions: Neuroimaging data support the theory of a dysfunctional amygdalar-prefrontal circuit in BPD which underlies emotional instability in BPD.

Pain anticipation: A mechanism involved in affect regulation in BPD?

Schmahl, Christian Klinik für Psychosomatik, ZI für Seelische Gesundheit, Mannheim, Germany *Klossika, Iris* Psychosomatic Medicine, Central Inst. of Mental Health, Mannheim, Germany *Bohus, Martin* Psychosomatic Medicine, Central Inst. of Mental Health, Mannheim, Germany

Objectives: To investigate the interaction between the anticipation of pain, emotional modulation, and pain processing in patients with BPD. Methods: Thermal pain thresholds as well as heat pain fMRI were assessed. Negative and positive mood was induced by IAPS pictures, anticipation of pain was induced by the announcement of an intensive pain stimulus. Results: All emotional pictures increased pain thresholds in healthy controls and in patients. Only in patients, anticipation of pain increased thresholds and led to amygdala deactivation. Conclusions: Pain anticipation was more pronounced in patients with BPD and may be interpreted as a mechanism involved in affect regulation in BPD.

Neuronal correlates of empathy in borderline personality disorder: An fMRI study

Preissler, Sandra Abt. Psychiatrie, Charite Berlin, Berlin, Germany

Objectives: To determine emotional and cognitive empathy in patients with Borderline Personality Disorder (BPD) compared to healthy controls on the behavioural and neuronal level. Methods: We assessed different facets of empathy in 32 female patients with BPD and controls on a new ecologically valid dimensional measure of empathy, the "Multifaceted Empathy Test" (MET). Furthermore, we established neuronal correlates of empathy in both groups using an fMRI adaptation of the MET. Results/Conclusions: Patients with BPD showed significant impairments in cognitive and emotional empathy at the behavioural level. Also, compared to controls, they showed different activations in the fronto-temporal network mediating empathy.

How do patients with borderline personality disorder regulate dissociation and affect?

Ebner-Priemer, Ulrich W. Inst. für Psychosomatiks, ZI für Seelische Gesundheit, Mannheim, Germany

Affective instability and dissociative symptoms are essential in borderline personality disorder (BPD). Studies investigating how BPD patients regulate affect and dissociation are sparse. We assessed emotions, dissociative symptoms and regulation strategies in BPD patients during everyday life using electronic diaries, as well as in the laboratory using psychophysiological and fMRI methods. Heightened affect instability was exhibited and dissociative symptoms were positively related to stress in BPD. Self-injuries and skills were identified as strategies to down-regulate stress and dissociative symptoms. If dissociative symptoms work as emotion regulation strategies, as they inhibit emotional processing and reduce activity in the amygdala, remains unclear.

Hyper-emotionality in borderline personality disorder before and after psychological treatment

Arntz, Arnoud Dept. of Psychology, University of Maastricht, Maastricht, Netherlands

Objectives. To test peripheral and central nervous system emotional responses in Borderline Personality Disorder (BPD), and test whether they normalize after successful psychotherapy. Methods. BPD, Cluster-C control patients, nonpatients, and recovered BPD patients saw emotional and neutral slides during fMRI-scanning. Amygdala, hippocampus, heart rate, and skin conductance responses were assessed. Results. BPD patients showed increased emotional responses to negative stimuli

(p<.05). Recovered BPD patients had normalized responses. Conclusions. BPD is associated with hyper-emotionality to negative stimuli; defensive responses suggest high fear. Psychotherapy normalizes these responses, indicating that amygdala hyper-responsivity is not a simple biological cause, but reflects unsafety in BPD.

The impact of experiential avoidance on changes of depression and anger during treatment for borderline personality disorder

Berking, Matthias Dept. of Psychology, University of Washington, Washington, USA *Neacsiu, Andrada* Psychology, University of Washington, Washington, USA *Comtois, Kate* Psychology, University of Washington, Washington, USA *Linehan, Marsha* Psychology, University of Washington, Washington, USA

Objectives: Given that experiential avoidance is both a putative maintaining factor for core features of borderline personality disorder (BPD) and a potential hindrance for engaging clients into psychotherapeutic treatment, it was investigated whether experiential avoidance has a negative impact on changes in affect-related symptoms during treatment for BPD. Methods: Experiential avoidance, depression and anger were assessed in 81 clients at four points in time during one year of therapy. Results: EA predicted subsequent changes in depression but not in anger. Conclusion: EA impedes progress in at least one crucial outcome of treatment and should therefore be considered an important treatment target.

S-143: Recent developments in selection and guidance in higher education

Oliver Wilhelm, Richard D. Roberts (chair)

The use of psychological assessment in higher education is gaining momentum across the globe. Two primary uses of these assessments are selection and guidance. In this symposium, we present research related to these applications in a number of countries, using large datasets, state-of-the-art statistical modeling, and new technologies. With respect to selection, important developments include a more global perspective of its importance in higher education and the application of advanced psychometric models to ensure fairness. In the realm of guidance, constructs are being extended beyond the evaluation of interests (to domains such as time management and teamwork), with new approaches to intervention (e.g., content validated feedback and action plans).

The assessment of time management

Schulze, Ralf Inst. für Psychologie, Universität Wuppertal, Wuppertal, Germany

Adequate time management (TM) is regarded as an important success factor in various areas of application, including academic success. Many courses and online resources to guide students include some kind of time management assessment and/or recommendations for better TM practices. This presentation focuses on the structure, assessment and corresponding validity evidence of an instrument to assess individual differences in TM. It is concluded that a) TM can be reliably and validly assessed, b) TM is a promising construct for guidance purposes, and c) available TM assessment should not be used in selection contexts due to susceptibility to faking.

Ready edge TM: Evidence and processes supporting a new educational guidance system

Roberts, Richard D. Research and Development, ETS, Princeton, USA *MacCann, Carolyn* Research and Development, ETS, Princeton, NJ, USA *Minsky, Jennifer* Research and Development, ETS, Princeton,

NJ, USA *Jackson, Teresa* Research and Development, ETS, Princeton, NJ, USA *Schulze, Ralf* Research and Development, ETS, Princeton, NJ, USA

Ready EdgeTM is a web-based self-help tool designed to assist students plan and meet educational objectives. Ready EdgeTM comprises assessments, feedback, and action plans for several noncognitive constructs, providing students with advisement that is tailored to their proficiency levels on these constructs. A first version includes measures and feedback concerning Time Management, Test Anxiety, Working with Others, Test-taking Strategies, and Career Planning. In this paper, we discuss data from several large scale studies involving over 2,000 college students that provides validity evidence for the assessments. We also discuss the processes and procedures used to derive content validated feedback and action plans.

Examining the relationships between personality, learning approaches and academic achievement: A longitudinal study

Burton, Lorelle Dept. of Psychology, Univ. of Southern Queensland, Australia

In a longitudinal research project we examined relationships between personality, learning approaches, and academic achievement. Data from 135 psychology undergraduates for a big five measure, an inventory for learning approaches and grade point average for year 1 (GPA1) and year 2 (GPA2) were recorded. Intellect positively predicted GPA1. The surface learning approach negatively predicted GPA1 and GPA2. Conscientiousness and intellect positively predicted use of the deep learning approach. Intellect and emotional stability negatively predicted use of the surface learning approach. Conscientiousness positively predicted use of the Strategic learning approach. The theoretical and practical implications of these findings are discussed.

Success in college: Threats to the utility of admission procedures and neglected guidance and placement issues

Wilhelm, Oliver IQB, Humboldt-Universität zu Berlin, Berlin, Germany

Training success and more specifically success in college are substantially predicted by measures of maximum behaviour. Although the magnitude of the relation between admission measures and college success is pivotal for institutional utility, many admission procedures are more driven by effort-avoidance, marketing, and legislature rather than the attempt to maximize predictive validity. Consequently admission decisions will be poorer then possible. We will review and reanalyze the consequences of various admission procedures and present recommendations. Additionally, we suggest paying more attention to placement and guidance issues in order to maximize learning and minimize attrition in college.

Predictive invariance, measurement invariance and fairness in selection

Wicherts, Jelte Dept. of Psychology, University of Amsterdam, Amsterdam, Netherlands *Borsboom, Denny* Dept. of Psychology, University of Amsterdam, Amsterdam, Netherlands *Romeijn, Jan Willem* Dept. of Psychology, University of Amsterdam, Amsterdam, Netherlands

The fair use of achievement tests for selection purposes demands that these tests are free from measurement bias (i.e., measurement invariant) with respect to sex and ethnic groups. Measurement invariance is defined in terms of measurement models, but measurement bias is studied often by verifying whether a test predicts some criterion (e.g., GPA) equivalently across groups. In this talk, we show that measurement invariance is not to be expected when predictive invariance holds. Next, we show that the use of a measurement invariant

test in selection does not imply that selection is necessarily fair across groups. We discuss the implications.

S-144: Coping with adolescence: Intercultural perspectives

Petra Buchwald, Emilia Lucio Gomez Maqueo (chair)
Adolescence corresponds with critical developmental occurrences in biological, emotional, social, and cultural domains. Teenagers thus live in a context of tremendous and often difficult personal change associated with many problems. Often they are unable to cope with these changes and at high risk for problem behaviors, e. g. substance abuse and suicide. The importance of developing coping skills for adolescents is often underestimated by stress research. However, young people's development of coping strategies and resilience are instrumental in helping them avoid problem behaviors. What adolescents need for social and emotional growth will be analysed in five different studies from different countries.

Coping with joblessness in adolescence: Psychiatric diagnoses in a preselected sample of German unemployed adolescents and young adults

Reissner, Volker Universität Duisburg-Essen, Rheinische Kliniken Essen, Essen, Germany *Rosien, M. Hebebrand, Johannes*

Unemployment in adolescents is related to psychological distress, such as increased levels of anxiety, depression, reduced self-esteem and life-satisfaction as well as alcohol or drug abuse. The Study on Unemployed with Psychosocial Problems Obtaining Reintegration Training under 25 (SUPPORT25) assesses psychiatric disorders, health service utilization and attitudes towards unemployment in Germans aged 18-24. Almost all subjects referred for counselling via the case managers of the unemployment agency met criteria for at least one psychiatric disorder according to DSM-IV. To reduce psychological distress and increase chances of vocational rehabilitation, health behaviours of unemployed adolescents should be improved. Adequate treatment programs are urgently needed.

Teenagers coping with sexual abuse

Schwarzer, Christine Education and Counselling, Universität Düsseldorf, Düsseldorf, Germany *Buchwald, Petra* Education and Counselling, Heinrich-Heine University, Duesseldorf, Germany *Ringeisen, Tobias* Psychology, Univ.of Applied Sc. Münster, Münster, Germany

Empirical studies concerning coping of teenagers are at this point still at the beginning. New research shows however that the choice of reported coping strategies is influenced by sexual abuse that has been experienced. An evaluation of teenagers (N = 367) between the age of 13-17 showed that boys and girls can be differentiated regarding their social and individual coping strategies assessed by the German Strategic Approach to Coping Scale. A grouping of data also revealed that girls that have been sexually abused as opposed to those that did not report such a critical life event significantly decline their social coping and avoid reflection.

Religiosity and suicidal ideation among Arab adolescents

Israelashvili, Moshe School of Education, Tel Aviv University, Tel Aviv, Israel *Kakunda-Mualem, Helen* School of Education, Tel Aviv University, Tel Aviv, Israel

According to Terror Management Theory every person unavoidably faces the question of "why living?". This question is especially bothering for adolescents, who are in the age of establishing their self-identity. Israeli Arab adolescents completed questionnaires on stress, reasons for living, and

suicidal ideation. Findings showed that stress and lack of meaning in life foster suicidal ideation. However, the major sources of differences in suicidal ideation were related to religion. Nevertheless, the buffering role of religiosity against suicidal ideation was found only for Christen but not for Muslim Arab adolescents. Implications for counselling adolescents and features of future studies will be discussed.

Coping, distress, substance abuse and suicide risk in Mexican adolescents

Lucio Gomez Maqueo, Emilia Dept. of Psychology, National University Mexico, Mexico, Mexico *Hernandez-Cervantes, Quetzalcoatl* Dept. of Psychology, National University Mexico, Mexico, Mexico

From within a prevention program in Mexico City a stratified random sample of 1,000 preparatory students (ages 15-19) was screened for substance abuse and suicide risk. Substance abuse was measured with the Drug Abuse Screening Test for Adolescents (DAST-A), the WHO Alcohol, Smoking and Substance Involvement Screening Test (ASSIST) and AUDIT. Coping was assessed following a qualitative approach using Seifge-Krenke's coping categories. Distress and suicide risk were assessed with the Adolescent Suicide Risk Inventory (Hernandez-Cervantes & Lucio, 2003). Different risk levels were considered to determine if adolescents could participate in a school-based intervention strategy or be referred to other programs.

Posttraumatic growth in Romanian adolescents following flood

Kallay, Eva Dept. of Psychology, Babes-Bolyai University, Cluj-Napoca, Romania

Objectives Investigate posttraumatic growth and positive emotional states in Romanian adolescent flood victims. Methods Our study involved 42 Romanian adolescent flood victims assessed regarding: level of depression (BDI), mood states and emotions (POMS), coping (B-COPE), posttraumatic growth (SRGS), and impact of event. Results Significant levels of growth were associated with instrumental support, emotional disclosure, acceptance, humor, and positive emotional states. Nevertheless, we found no significant differences in negative affective states. Conclusions Since 28.2% of the assessed adolescents reported significant levels of growth, our data may represent useful information for developing supportive socio-cultural environments for recovery after disaster by fostering specific coping mechanisms and positive affect.

S-145: Quality assurance for professional assessment by means of an international ISO-Norm: Developments and chances

Lutz F. Hornke (chair)
In March 2006, the German Institute for Standardization (DIN) submitted a proposal to the International Standardization Organization (ISO), to develop an ISO Standard for "Procedures and methods to assess people in work and organizational settings". The goal is to establish a worldwide standard for psychological assessment based on existing national norms like the DIN33430 and other professional standards like those published by SIOP, AERA-APA-NCME, EFPA, BPS, NIP or EAPA. This symposium discusses the needs for such a standard in regard to globally operating organizations / companies as well as the developments and chances of defining and establishing an ISO Standard.

How an ISO standard in occupational assessment provision might improve quality

Bartram, Dave Research Dept., SHL Group Ltd., Thames Ditton, United Kingdom

Key to the success of the ISO standard will be its acceptance by the relevant communities of users of occupational assessment. In this presentation some ways in which the new norm might provide benefits both for consumers of occupational assessment services and their providers will be considered. It will also consider how the ISO standard might act as a general framework for integrating a range of other more specific and more detailed mechanisms for improving assessment quality: such as test user certification schemes and test quality review and registration procedures.

Towards an international ISO-norm for professional assessment: Common themes and varieties among existing professional standards

Hornke, Lutz F. Inst. für Psychologie, RWTH Universität Aachen, Aachen, Germany Kersting, Martin

As a starting point for the ISO initiative, we conducted a systematic review of existing standards for professional assessment like those published by AERA-APA-NCME, DIN, EFPA and ITC. Our review revealed, that these standards have a great deal in common but also some notable differences in both scope and wording of specific requirements. Phrasing of requirements differed on two key dimensions: abstract vs. detailed and normative vs. informative. We discuss how differences between standards are rooted in their cultural and professional context and how universal themes among standards can be integrated into an international consensus for an ISO norm.

Themes in developing an ISO standard for work-related psychological assessment

Born, Marise Inst. of Psychology, Erasmus University Rotterdam, Rotterdam, Netherlands

In a globalized and digitalized world, the necessity of developing an ISO Standard for the work-related assessment of people has become obvious. Tests nowadays are easily available on the internet and more providers of assessment services have become active. By means of a process-oriented view on assessment, several quality-enhancing topics are reviewed which are intended to be to the benefit of the different stakeholders. Among these are the individuals who are assessed, the assessment providers and the assessment users.

Documentation of validity in professional assessments

Sjöberg, Anders Dept. of Psychometric, Assessio International, Stockholm, Sweden

This standard should contain recommendations for procedures and methods used in the psychological assessment of people for work-related purposes. The development of an international ISO-Standard will increase the quality of assessments and encourage an evidence-based approach to assessment. The ISO-Standard should focus on the subsequent decisions that follow the assessments. The interpretation of the assessment should gain support in the documentation provided to the clients. The development and purpose of this ISO-Standard will be discussed and examples of how it can be implemented in organizations.

The international ISO-norm: Chances from the perspective of psychology-practitioners

Lang, Fredi Referat Fachpolitik, BDP e.V., Berlin, Germany

Reasons why the German professional organizations is pursuing an ISO-Standard are described and hypotheses on how the ISO-Standard might foster the quality of psychological assessment in practice are discussed.

S-146: Is there a best way to study acculturation? An examination of conceptualization and measurement of acculturation

Saba Safdar (chair)

In this symposium we examine and compare differences between various conceptualizations of acculturation. Researchers utilize different acculturation conceptualization and measurement. This inconsistency in the literature has yielded different distributions of participants across four acculturation strategies. In other words, different ways of measuring acculturation produce different results and, often, there is poor inter-measure agreement between various conceptualizations. The presenters in this symposium examine these acculturation conceptualizations and their relations with measures of acculturation adaptation. The presenters discuss their empirical data with a particular emphasis on the distinction between these conceptualizations, their relations, and the different results that they produce.

Ask a different question, get a different answer

Berry, John Dept. of Psychology, Queen's University, Kingston, Canada Sabatier, Colette Dept. of Psychology, Universite de Bordeaux, Bordeaux, France

There are two dimensions in the acculturation strategies framework (the degree to which acculturating individuals value their heritage culture and identity; and seek relations with persons in the larger society), allowing four acculturation strategies: assimilation, integration, separation and marginalisation. Alternative operationalisations of the second dimension refer to cultural identity, and adoption of the larger society's culture. We compare the distributions of the four acculturation strategies using all three operationalisations of the second dimension. We conclude that when the questions differ, the outcomes are also likely to. These differences do not undermine the validity of the original operationalisation of the framework.

Method effects in the assessment of acculturation orientations are real, but small

van de Vijver, Fons Dept. of Psychology, Tilburg University, Tilburg, Netherlands

An overview is given of methods to assess acculturation orientations. A study is then described in which three methods, based on a two-dimensional acculturation, are compared in a group of immigrants in the Netherlands. It is concluded that there is evidence for small method effects.

Perceptions of immigrant children on their parents' acculturative strategies

Kurman, Jenny Dept. of Psychology, University of Haifa, Haifa, Israel Roer-Strier, Dorit Social Work, Hebrew University of Jerusalem, Jerusalem, Israel

Acculturation from the child's point of view is investigated. Immigrant children's perceptions of their parents' intents to socialize them into the new culture, or maintain the socialization goals of the culture of origin, as well as the extent to which parents see themselves as effective socializing agents in the new culture are assessed as predictors of immigrant parents' acculturative strategies. The Roer-Strier's four metaphors (the Kangaroo, Cuckoo bird, Chameleon and Butterfly) are studied quantitatively. The relative frequencies of each strategy, as well as their differential relations with adjustment illuminate acculturation processes of children of families who immigrated to Israel.

Exploring acculturation conceptualizations with a sample of international students in Canada

Safdar, Saba Dept. of Psychology, University of Guelph, Guelph, Canada

In the present study, three acculturation conceptualization are examined among international students in Canada. The study has a longitudinal design in which online questionnaires were administered at three points over a two year period. Adaptation of students was measured in relation to psychological well-being, psycho-physical distress, and socio-cultural difficulties. The results of the study indicated that the method used for measurement of acculturation had a considerable effect on patterns of results across outcomes.

Do you get what you ask for? An examination of three operationalizations of acculturation with immigrants in rural and urban Canada

Lewis, Rees Psychology, University Of Guelph, Guelph, Canada Dupuis, Darcy Dept. of Psychology, University of Guelph, Guelph, Canada

In the present study, three popular operationalizations of acculturation: Berry's (1980) framework for intercultural contact, Ward and Kennedy's (1994) operationalization of ethnic and host culture adoption, and the ethnic identity operationalization (Phinney & Devich-Navarro, 1997) were examined. Participants in the study were 212 immigrants to Canada living in rural and urban settings. Acculturation attitudes of the participants were measured using Kim's (1984) 16-item Acculturation Attitudes Scale. Additionally, three different kinds of adaptation were measured: psychological well-being, distress, and socio-cultural difficulties. The three acculturation conceptualizations yielded different distributions of participants across acculturation strategies and had different relations with the three outcome variables.

S-147: Psychology of entrepreneurship - current research and trends: Personal resources and entrepreneurial success (Part I)

Marjan Gorgievski, Ute Stephan (chair)

Recognition of the importance of entrepreneurship for social and economic well-being leads to the questions of how we can attract more people to entrepreneurship and how we can develop entrepreneurial potential (e.g., GEM, 2006). These questions traditionally fall within the field of Work and Organizational Psychology. In two symposia, we want to present novel trends of today's psychology of entrepreneurship research. This is part one of the symposium, which will focus on personal resources (e.g., resiliency beliefs, mood, personal health), both as predictors of entrepreneurial success, and as results of entrepreneurs' job characteristics.

Positive psychological capital and process of business start-up

Laguna, Mariola Inst. of Psychology, Catholic University Lublin, Lublin, Poland

The present study defines entrepreneurship as a goal attainment process and concentrates on the role of positive beliefs within different stages of the process: goal commitment, entrepreneurial intentions and business start-up. More specifically, the role of self-esteem, self-efficacy, optimism, and hope was analysed. Findings from three studies are compared: (1) 332 unemployed attending an entrepreneurship preparation training programme, a longitudinal study; (2) 569 randomly chosen unemployed; (3) 240 adults. Structural equation modeling revealed a web of relationships that impact entrepreneurial intentions and venture creation. Goal commitment had a direct effect on entrepreneurial intentions, and mediated the effects of positive beliefs.

Mood and decision-making: A diary study among starters

Gorgievski, Marjan Industrial and Organisational, Erasmus University Rotterdam, Rotterdam, Netherlands *van Delden, Martijn* IO Psychology, Erasmus University Rotterdam, Rotterdam, Netherlands

The purpose of this diary study among 67 business starters was to test the influence of positive and negative mood on decision-making. Motivation and scope of attention were included as possible mediating variables. Results of mixed linear model analyses showed a strong positive relationship between mood and motivation. However, no relationship between motivation and decision effectiveness was found. Only negative mood, and not positive mood, predicted entrepreneurs' scope of attention. As predicted, negative mood narrowed the scope of attention. In turn, this negatively influenced decision effectiveness and goal attainment.

Fear and primary appraisal in the entrepreneurship context

Spörrle, Matthias Dept. for Psychology, Ludwig-Maximilians University, München, Germany *Welpe, Isabell* Munich School of Management, LMU München, München, Germany *Breugst, Nicola* Wirtschaftswissenschaften, University of Duisburg-Essen, Essen, Germany *Scapin, Kathrin* Munich School of Management, LMU München, München, Germany

Using cognitive theories of emotion, we examine the impact of cognitive and emotional processes on the evaluation and exploitation of entrepreneurial opportunities. We utilized a questionnaire experiment with 344 respondents to analyse the impact of profit margin, personal investment, time to profit, and probability of success on entrepreneurial evaluation and exploitation in a between subjects design. Results indicate that cognitive appraisal is a central determinant of entrepreneurial activity (especially with regard to exploitation) which also fully mediates the relationship between situational characteristics and entrepreneurial behaviour and that fear moderated the relationship between opportunity evaluation and exploitation.

Personal, social and workplace resources of small business owners and their relations to well-being

Dej, Dominika Dresden, Germany *Stephan, Ute* Work&Organisational Psycho, Philipps-University Marburg, Marburg, Germany *Richter, Peter Georg* Work&Organisational Psycho, Technische Universität Dresden, Dresden, Germany

Research on entrepreneurs' well-being has yielded inconsistent results. High work-load, job demands, and long working hours may lead to negative health outcomes. However, entrepreneurs may also experience high job control and autonomy, which may have a positive impact on their well-being (Theorell &Karasek, 1996). To gain a better understanding of the issue, we employed Conversation of Resources Theory (Hobfoll, 1988, 2001). We argue that entrepreneurs' personal, social, and workplace resources compensate potential threats to their well-being. The results of a study, including 120 German entrepreneurs, reveal that high self-efficacy, personal initiative, and self-management skills are important factors in entrepreneur's well-being.

Entrepreneurs' health compared to other occupational groups in a national representative sample

Roesler, Ulrike Inst. für Psychologie, Universität Marburg, Marburg, Germany *Stephan, Ute* Arbeits-, Organis.-Psychologie, Philipps-Universität Marburg, Marburg, Germany *Jacobi, Frank* Klinische Psychologie, Universität Dresden, Dresden, Germany

Prior research has found entrepreneurs to have active jobs. But do they benefit from the potential positive health consequences when compared to other occupational groups? In a national representative sample blood pressure was measured during a clinical examination. Somatic and mental health was assessed with structured clinical interviews. Whilst entrepreneurs showed more favourable blood pressure, lower prevalence of hypertension, mental morbidity, and somatoform disorders, they were not better off concerning other somatic and mental disorders. Referring to the Vitamin model it is suggested that entrepreneurs' jobs could lead to self-exploitation, and that self-management skills moderate the consequences of active jobs.

S-148: Workplace bullying: Antecedents, consequences and interventions (Part II)

Herman Steensma, Stig Berge Matthiesen (chair)

Aggression is one of the most troubling issues facing workers. It can take several forms: homicide,physical assaults, threats, harassment. A distinction should be made between external aggression, caused by organizational outsiders, and internal aggression, i.e. bullying/mobbing committed by colleagues, superiors, or subordinates. To develop successful anti-aggression policies, it is necessary to gain insight into the network of causes and consequences of aggression in the workplace. In the symposium special attention will be paid both to the causes and consequences of workplace bullying and to policies to apply the knowledge to improve the quality of work and social relations.

External aggression, workplace bullying, frustration and the Quality of Working Life (QWL)

Steensma, Herman Soc. and Organizat. Psychology, Leiden University, Leiden, Netherlands

Objectives. To explain relations between external aggression, bullying, absenteeism, turnover, workplace characteristics and frustration. Methods. Employees of hospitals (N = 226) filled out questionnaires with items on leadership, job characteristics, conflict, and aggression between patients, employees, family members of patients. Results. Frustrating job characteristics predicted bullying; bullying predicted absenteeism and turnover. Frequency of aggression toward employees by patients and their family members was higher than the frequency of bullying acts among employees. Bullying correlated relatively strongly with external aggression.l Conclusions. Both bullying and external aggression can be reduced by paying attention to QWL. Bullying is an indicator of low QWL.

Work environment characteristics, mobbing, satisfaction and absenteeism

Lopez Cabarcos, M. Angeles Adm. y Direccion de Empresas, Santiago de Compostela Univer., Lugo, Spain *Vázquez Rodríguez, Paula* Adm. y Direccion de Empresas, Santiago de Compostela Univer., Lugo, Spain *Montes Piñeiro, Carlos* Psicología, Santiago de Compostela Univer., Santiago de Compostela, Spain

ABSTRACT: Objective: To characterize the mobbing processes in a services organization, analyzing some precedent variables (organizational) and some consequence variables. Subjects: 63 persons belonging to a multinational organization of the sector of the hotel and restaurants sector. Methodology: Study of case Results: The obtained results show the importance of the work environment (healthy),

to prevent mobbing processes, influencing these, in turn, variables as the labour satisfaction or the absenteeism. Conclusions: The processes of mobbing present a series of characteristics about which it is difficult to generalise, which supports the theory that its cause cannot be found in one single factor, but in a multiplicity of factors which operates simultaneously.

Victim or Gelotophobic?: How far the pathologic fear of being ridiculous can make people feel victimized in a workplace conflict

Ege, Harald Mobbing e Stress, PRIMA Associazione Italiana, Bologna, Italy

Goals. According to our data (ca 4000 cases), many self-declared victims of workplace conflict are not really subjected to persecution, but just feel victimized (paranoia, manic depression, etc). We assumed that some cases may not suffer from psychiatric pathology, but from a specific adaptive disorder: gelotophobia (definition by Ruch, Zurich University). Method. A group of 50 self declared mobbees was tested with the "LIPT", the "Geloph 46" and guided interviews. Gelotophobia diagnostic criteria and the presence of real workplace conflicts were verified. Results and discussion. Hypotheses were confirmed. Treatment of many victims should be adapted.

The downloading mobbing process at the workplace

Tinaz, Pinar Labour Econ. Indust. Relations, Marmara University, Istanbul, Turkey *Gök, Sibel* Labour Econ. Indust. Relations, Marmara University, Istanbul, Turkey

Objectives. Goals are to determine the mobbing behaviors in downloading mobbing process in Turkey and to reveal the most widespread mobbing behaviors. Methods. A field research was done concerning behavioral signs that refer to mobbing in downloading mobbing process. Data from employees (N =400) in the banking sector were analyzed by standard methods. Results. The behavioral signs according to gender, education, working period within the subsidiary, age, marital status variables are comparatively examined. Conclusions. Continuous criticism of job's outcome and sarcastic speech as the most frequent behavioral signs of downloading mobbing are determined.

Is workplace conflict and workplace bullying the same?

Matthiesen, Stig Berge Psychosocial Science, University of Bergen, Bergen, Norway *Einarsen, Ståle* Faculty of Psychology, University of Bergen, Bergen, Norway *Skogstad, Anders* Faculty of Psychology, University of Bergen, Bergen, Norway

A national representative survey study of workplace bullying was conducted (n= 2539). Workplace bullying was mapped by a 22 items instrument which measure negative acts (NAQ). Interpersonal conflicts were measured by a new 4 items instrument, which explores respectively interpersonal conflicts and conflicts of interests. A significant association were found between workplace conflicts and workplace bullying. However, factor analysis revealed that workplace conflicts and workplace bullying are split into separate factors. The analysis indicates that being exposed to conflicts with leaders can be seen as something different from being exposed to conflicts with colleagues (separate factors were found).

Long term effects of a bullying prevention program in hospitals

Pries, Andrea Inst. für Arbeitspsychologie, Universität Hamburg, Hamburg, Germany *Roscher, Susanne* Inst. für Arbeitspsychologie, Universität Hamburg, Hamburg, Germany *Ostendorf, Pamela Zeh, Annett*

The objective of this study was to evaluate the long term effects of a bullying prevention program that was conducted in three German hospitals (n = 115). The research design included summative and formative evaluation. Having successfully established work - internal conflict counselling services is an achievement of the project. Further results showed some ambiguous effects of the intervention that can be accounted for by various implementation problems. Poor dissemination of information and a lack of management support impeded the efficacy of the measures. Particular methodological issues concerning evaluation and issues raised by the project will be discussed.

S-149: Mechanisms of adaptation: Determining the specific and shared effects of resources, strategies and beliefs

Daniela Jopp (chair)
Throughout the lifespan, individuals attempt to achieve positive outcomes such as high functioning or quality of life. This effort is challenged when confronted with specific difficulties or age-related losses. The present symposium investigates different factors which help the individual in goal pursuit and coping with challenges. The present symposium offers research on three groups of factors: resources – basic individual characteristics such as health, social support, or cognitive structures as self-complexity –, strategies – such as coping, life- or self-management strategies – and beliefs such as perceived control. Findings demonstrate unique and interactive protective effects, suggesting further investigation of concurrent effects for adaptation.

Developmental trajectories for ego-development across the adult lifespan: Evidence from a 12-year longitudinal study
Grühn, Daniel Inst. für Psychologie, Universität Genf, Genf, Switzerland Diehl, Manfred Center on Aging, Colorado State University, Fort Collins, USA Lumley, Mark Department of Psychology, Wayne State University, Detroit, USA Labouvie-Vief, Gisela Department of Psychology, University of Geneva, Genf, Switzerland
Self-complexity is considered as a resource to buffer stressful events. We report data about the developmental trajectory of self-complexity in adulthood and old age measured by Loevinger's ego-development. Data stem from a 12-year longitudinal study (1992-2004) with a lifespan sample from 10 years to 87 years at T1 (M = 44.7 years, N = 400). Analyses (cross-sectional and longitudinal) revealed that ego-development increased considerably until middle-adulthood and reached a peak in late middle-adulthood (40 to 60 years). In old age, ego-development showed small but significant declines. We also report correlates (e.g., well-being) of intraindividual differences and intraindividual change in ego-development.

Complex thinking as a resource in middle-aged and older adults
Leipold, Bernhard Inst. für Psychologie, Universität Hildesheim, Hildesheim, Germany
Traditionally, complex thinking is viewed as a central mean of self-regulation and coping. According to the dual process-model of assimilation and accommodation (Brandtstädter, 1998), complex thinking facilitates accommodative flexibility and enhances disengagement from blocked goals. One hundred and forty eight participants (M = 61.0 years) completed two different measures of complexity, assimilative persistence and accommodative flexibility, and depression. Analyses revealed that subjects higher in complexity show a stronger negative relationship between accommodation and depression. Furthermore, complex thinking seems to be a buffer against depressive mood for older adults. Findings are discussed within the framework of the dual process model.

Valuation of life in old and very old age: Shifting importance of resources
Rott, Christoph Inst. für Gerontologie, Universität Heidelberg, Heidelberg, Germany Jopp, Daniela School of Psychology, Georgia Inst. of Technology, Atlanta, GA, Germany Oswald, Frank Inst. für Psychologie, Universität Heidelberg, Heidelberg, Germany
How much old and very old individuals value their existence has been investigated in the context of quality of life and end of life decisions. Several resources were found to contribute to valuation of life (VOL, Lawton, 1999). The present study investigated whether the importance of resources for VOL varies depending on age, assuming that old and very old age are characterized by differential challenges. Findings showed that for the young-old, the role of health was especially strong, whereas social factors became more significant in the old-old group, suggesting positive adaptation to changing resources far into very old age.

Is better self-management ability associated with smaller resource deficits and with higher well-being later in life?
Steverink, Nardi Dept. of Health Psychology, University Medical Center, Groningen, Netherlands
Self-management ability (SMA) can be conceptualized as a person's generative capacity (i.e. behaviors and beliefs) to achieve and maintain important resources (e.g., health, social relationships). Therefore, better SMA is likely to be related to lower levels of resource deficits, and, indirectly, to higher levels of subjective well-being. Results (N=439, aged 65 and older) showed that SMA was indeed negatively related to resource deficits, and both directly and indirectly – via lower resource deficits – to life satisfaction, positive affect and negative affect. It is concluded that better SMA seems to play a role in successful aging by facilitating resource maintenance and subjective well-being.

Adaptation in adulthood: Which role play resources, strategies and beliefs for well-being?
Jopp, Daniela Institute of Gerontology, Heidelberg University, Heidelberg, Germany Hertzog, Christopher School of Psychology, Georgia Inst. of Technology, Atlanta, GA, USA
How well individuals are able to solve everyday tasks and deal with difficulties is related to several psychological factors. The present study investigates how personal resources, life-management strategies, and control beliefs relate to quality of life based on a sample of 256 young, middle-aged, and older individuals. Structural equation models showed that resources had direct effects on well-being, but also indirect effects mediated by strategies and beliefs. Beliefs also moderated the relation between resources and strategies, as well as between strategies and well-being. Taking the functional interplay between resources, strategies, and beliefs into account adds to our understanding of adaptation.

S-150: Advances in statistical applications for developmental research

Christopher Hertzog (chair)
This symposium presents recent advances in statistical methods for research in life-span development, including the issues of (1) measurement of change, (2) separating intraindividual variability from long-term intraindividual change, (3) separating developmental change from mortality and morbidity processes, (4) use of multi-level models for capturing fixed and random effects of aging, and (5) developmental design issues. The papers highlight the compelling need for statistical applications grounded in theoretical and methodological as-

sumptions about the course and nature of human development and other influences on psychological change.

Placing aging individuals within an aging (and dying) population: A need to connect psychology and demography
Ram, Nilam Human Dev. and Family Studies, Pennsylvania State University, University Park, USA
Research on aging is focused on understanding how individuals change with age and on changes occurring in an aging population. Despite this dual focus, individual-based longitudinal studies are rarely coupled with population- or cohort-level studies, the mainstay of the demography and sociology of aging. The purpose of this paper is to (1) highlight the need for integration across disciplines, (2) illustrate how individual-level change trajectories might be placed within cohort-level changes, and (3) encourage further innovation of modeling, analysis, and data presentation strategies by which we might develop a more comprehensive view of the nature of aging.

Cross-sectional age variance extraction: What's change got to do with
Lindenberger, Ulman Zentrum für Lebenserwartung, Max-Planck-Institut, Berlin, Germany
Psychologists often use cross-sectional age variance extraction (CAVE) to test hypotheses about the number and identity of causes driving behavioral development, with age as the exogenous variable, indicators of developmental mechanisms as mediators of age-related variance, and indicators of to-be-explained developmental phenomena as target variables. By decomposing cross-sectional associations in terms of bivariate growth, we show that longitudinal change in a mediator variable sharing large amounts of age-related variance with the target variable does not have to correlate with longitudinal change in the target variable. We conclude that CAVE provides invalid approximations to the dimensionality and causes of behavioral change.

A multilevel factor analysis perspective on development
Zimprich, Daniel Inst. für Gerontopsychologie, Universität Zürich, Zurich, Switzerland
Objective: To model and structure within-person multivariate longitudinal cognitive changes in old age. Methods: Sample. 221 individuals from the Bonn Longitudinal Study on Aging followed up to 19 years across 7 measurement occasions. Analysis. Multilevel Confirmatory Factor Analysis. Results: 1. More variance between persons than within persons. 2. Stronger indicatr variable correlations between than within persons. 3. A model of three factors (fluid and crystallized intelligence, speed). 4. Equal loadings and equal factor correlations at both levels of analysis. Conclusions: Between-person differences and within-person cognitive changes exhibit the same structure. Hence, they form a functional unity in Cattellian sense.

Comparisons of statistical power for single-indicator and multiple-indicator latent growth curve models
von Oertzen, Timo Life-Span Developm. Psychology, Max-Planck-Institut, Berlin, Germany
We compare the power to detect individual differences in change in latent models with multiple indicators to latent models with one indicator per measurement. We demonstrate the effect of latent residual variance and measurement error to power and give a necessary and complete condition for identical power for models with different numbers of indicators and measurement error. With equally reliable indicators, pooling over K indicators with a measurement error of ?2 is equal to the power of a single indicator with measurement error ?2/K.

However, if the indicators are of different reliabilities, pooling causes a loss of power.

Age differences in cognitive performance variability: Modeling the relation of mean and variance

Schmiedek, Florian Center for Lifespan Psychology, Max-Plnack-Institut, Berlin, Germany

In studies on age differences in cognitive performance variability, strong relations of intraindividual means and variances often lead researchers to perform some linear adjustment of variability measures with measures of mean performance. The underlying assumption of a general linear relationship in this context is questioned and alternative approaches, e.g. variance heterogeneity and overdispersion multilevel models, which allow flexibly modeling variance as a (nonlinear) function of mean performance and other predictors, are discussed. The COGITO study, in which 100 younger and 100 older participants practiced a battery of cognitive tasks over 100 daily sessions, is used to illustrate these methods.

S-151: Effects of the euro changeover on consumer behavior

J. Frederico Marques, Tommy Gärling (chair)

This symposium addresses a number of problems consumers face in their daily economic transactions after the euro changeover or, more broadly, when dealing with a foreign currency. These problems include: learning the value of money in a new currency and the associated mistakes, in particular the effects of the "money illusion"; adaptation to a new currency with special emphasis on conversion strategies and the role of the old currency; and understanding price changes in the new currency with special emphasis on the role of price expectations. Implications for future research and consumer policy will be highlighted.

The "Euro Illusion": Illusion or fact?

Gamble, Amélie Dept. of Psychology, Göteborg University, Göteborg, Sweden

The euro changeover elicited several studies of consumers' conversion strategies, price knowledge, choice, and purchases, using longitudinal surveys, interviews, and controlled experiments. These studies show that the nominal value of the new currency influence the subjective value of money, a bias termed the "euro illusion". Explanations draw on the numerosity heuristic, the anchoring-and-adjustment heuristic, and biased conversion strategies. Here the argument is made that accuracy-effort trade-offs influence the size of the euro illusion. This has been shown in studies varying task importance, time constraints, familiarity and complexity of the conversion strategy, mood, and attitude towards the country or the currency.

Emotional factors in currency perception

Tyszka, Tadeusz Dept. Economic Psychology, LKAEM, Warsaw, Poland Przybyszewski, Krzysztof LKAEM, Warsaw, Poland

People may associate certain currencies with emotional meanings and deeply rooted convictions. Sometimes they become attached to a currency and this attachment may influence their money behavior and price perception. Also, such emotional attachment may cause the resistance to currency changes (e.g. entering euro-zone). In this paper we focus on the influence of positive affect attached to a currency on perception of prices in this currency

Consumer adaptation strategies: From Austrian shilling to the euro

Kirchler, Erich Inst. Wirtschaftspsychologie, Universität Wien, Wien, Austria Hofmann, Eva Inst. Wirtschaftspsychologie, Universität Wien, Wien, Austria Kamleitner, Bernadette School of Business/Management, Queen Mary, Univ. of London, London, United Kingdom

On 1st January 2002, in 12 countries of the European Union euro notes and coins replaced existing national currencies. Citizens had to learn to handle new coins and notes, to evaluate values in the new currency, and to adapt their spending behaviour. Data on how these tasks were performed by Austrians are presented. In particular, Austrian consumers applied four different strategies to establish price intuition for the euro: (a) conversion strategy, (b) intuitive strategy, (c) anchor strategy, and (d) marker value strategy. Data on these strategies shows that their application (a) varies across socio-demographic characteristics, (b) differs with purchase situations, (c) relates to euro attitudes, and (d) changes over time.

The euro illusion in consumers: Price estimation

Del Missier, Fabio Dept. of Psychology, University of Trieste, Trieste, Italy Bonini, Nicolao Dept. of Cognitive Sciences, University of Trento, Rovereto, Italy Ranyard, Rob Dept. of Psychology, University of Bolton, Bolton, United Kingdom

The euro illusion is a transient phenomenon that consists of currency-related asymmetries in the intuitive judgment of product prices made by consumers. In our communication, we will initially present a review of the findings obtained in studies of price estimation, including the result of our own cross-country research involving Italy and Ireland. Then, we will analyze the potential explanations of the euro illusion in price estimation, focusing in particular on the anchoring-and-adjustment accounts. Finally, we will discuss the complex interplay between structural factors (e.g., the currency exchange rate) and psychological mechanisms that produce long-lasting difficulties for consumers after a monetary changeover.

The eurochangeover and numerical intuition for prices in the old and new currencies

Marques, J. Frederico Centro de Invest.em Psicologia, Fundacao Uni. de Lisboa, Lisboa, Portugal

I examine how numerical intuition for prices in euros and in the Portuguese currency escudos developed in Portugal after the euro changeover from estimates of prices collected in the two currencies and at four different times from November 2001 to April 2004. Results for euros show that estimates become progressively more accurate by a process that is related to purchase frequency and suggest that the adaptation is a very slow process. Results for escudos show that the former currency is not simply forgotten but remains as a general benchmark for an extended period.

The EURO changeover and the factors influencing perceived inflation

Belting, Julia Inst. für Psychologie, Techn. Universität Berlin, Berlin, Germany Jungmann, Helmut Institute of Psy. & Ergo., Technical University Berlin, Berlin, Germany Brachinger, Hans Wolfgang Department of Quant. Economics, University of Fribourg, Fribourg, Switzerland Grinberg, Katarzyna Department of Quant.Economics, University of Fribourg,, Fribourg, Switzerland Zacharias, Elisabeth Institute of Psy. & Ergo., Technical University Berlin, Berlin, Germany

In Germany perceived inflation increased after the euro changeover. The official measure of inflation (HCPI) is not adequate for measuring perceived inflation. Brachinger suggests an alternative Index of Perceived Inflation (IPI) to better account for this observation. The IPI is based on several theoretical assumptions derived from Prospect

Theory. In an experimental study we investigated the influence of two factors: purchase frequency and loss aversion. Two additional factors were included. Judgments of inflation were assessed with three different methods. The study provides empirical support regarding the role of the hypothesised factors determining perceived inflation.

Biased price perception after the introduction of the euro: The teuro-illusion

Schulz-Hardt, Stephan Inst. für Psychologie, Universität Göttingen, Göttingen, Germany Traut-Mattausch, Eva Department of Psychology, Ludwig-Maximilians-University, Munich, Germany Greitemeyer, Tobias Department of Psychology, Ludwig-Maximilians-University, Munich, Germany Frey, Dieter Department of Psychology, Ludwig-Maximilians-University, Munich, Germany

The population in Germany as well as other European countries perceived high price increases due to the introduction of the Euro, which stood in contrast to official statistics about price developments and inflation rates. We present evidence from an experimental research program showing that in Germany and Austria the changeover from DM (or Schilling) to Euro led to illusionary price rises: Real price rises were overestimated, stable prices were perceived as having been raised, and a decrease of prices was misperceived as price stability. Expectations of rising prices are shown to be the main cause of this price rise illusion.

S-152: Embodiment

Sabine C. Koch, Simone Schütz-Bosbach (chair)

The traditional problem of body and mind has experienced a revival in recent years. Contrary to Cartesian dualism, recent advances in psychology and neuroscience take the body to be central in the understanding of higher cognitive functions (embodied cognition). Embodiment theories operate on Merleau-Ponty's phenomenological philosophy and a model of knowledge representation that assumes a sensori-motor format of any cognitive activity (Barsalou, 1999). The symposium brings together researchers from various psychological areas with the aim to discuss their findings on body representation, mirror neurons, embodied spatial cognition, body movement, cultural embodiment, and their implications for the body-mind problem.

The role of motor skills in action perception

Knoblich, Günther Dept. of Psychology, Birmingham University, Birmingham, United Kingdom

Embodied Cognition has many facets. One important aspect is the ability to effortlessly perceive others' actions in the light of one's own action repertoire. Comparing the perception of experts and non-experts in a particular motor skill is one important way of studying this ability. I will provide an overview of recent behavioral and brain imaging studies from different labs that have addressed the issue of how motor skills affect perception. These studies suggest that learning a new motor skill does not only affect the human mirror system, but also basic perceptual processes such as visual discrimination and pitch perception.

Embodied spatial cognition

Tversky, Barbara Dept. of Psychology, University of Stanford, Stanford, USA

People have 3 primary axes, two asymmetric, one from head to foot and another from front to back, and a third more or less symmetric axis from left to right. They live in a world with three axes, one of which, the up-down, is asymmetric due to gravity. These facts about their bodies and the world affect people's perception of the world and their behavior in it, and in turn, bias spatial thinking as well as metaphoric spatial thinking. A range of empirical research supporting embodied and situated spatial cognition will be described.

Dynamic movement feedback
Koch, Sabine C. Inst. für Psychologie, Universität Heidelberg, Heidelberg, Germany
Our bodies move in the three dimensions of space, time and gravity. This series of experiments varies aspects of these basic dimensions of movement to investigate dynamic body feedback. It focuses on the influence of movement quality (here: sharp vs smooth movement rhythms), and movement shape, i.e., movement related to the three primary axes (here: approach vs avoidance motor behavior) on affect, attitudes, and cognition. Results suggest systematic influences of movement rhythms on affect, of movement shape on attitudes, and a moderating influence of rhythms on the impact of shape on attitude formation.

Is the body image influenced by primary sensorimotor experiences?
Schütz-Bosbach, Simone Cognitive and Brain Sciences, Max-Planck-Institut, Leipzig, Germany
The term "body image" refers to the conscious visual representation of one's own body, including the structural and geometric details as well as visual and affective aspects. The scientific concept corresponds roughly to the everyday use of the term, namely as the way we see ourselves when we look in a mirror. However, so far little is known on how we learn the (canonical) structure of our own body. A series of experiments will be presented which investigated the possibility that primary sensorimotor experiences may influence the mental representation of one's own body structure.

The conceptualization of body parts
Majid, Asifa Dept. of Psycholinguistics, Max Planck Institute, Nijmegen, Netherlands
According to embodiment theories mental content derives from the body – that we have the concepts we do is due to the particularities of the bodies we have. But little attention has been paid to how people conceptualize the body in the first place. Rather, there is widespread consensus that body parts are based on perception, and thus universal. Cross-cultural experiments, however, show that the body is not conceptualized in the same way by people speaking different languages. The relationship between linguistic and non-linguistic representations of the body need to be re-examined in light of this evidence.

Embodiment in cultures of honour
Ijzerman, Hans Leerstoel Semin, Utrecht University, Utrecht, Netherlands
We tested the hypothesis that cultural orientations have an embodied component. In particular, we investigated the embodiment of honor in two studies, showing that values related to male respect and female 'purity' are affected by erect versus slumped posture directly for individuals from honor cultures, and for individuals from individualist cultures after an honor prime. A third experiment showed that only individuals from honor cultures walked more upright after an honor prime than after a control prime. This demonstration of cultural embodiment is a first experimental support for anthropological suggestions of forming the culturally situated social mind via physical experience.

The subtle effects of writing direction on the perception of human action
Suitner, Caterina DPSS, University of Padova, Padova, Italy
The embodiment approach not only implies that cognition is affected by the body's momentary state, but also by its habitual interaction with its environment. One such habitual interaction is writing and reading which, in our culture, evolves from left to right. We propose that, as a result, people develop a left-right scheme for action, such that action observed with a left-right (rather than right-left) trajectory is (a) imagined and identified with greater ease, (b) perceived as more powerful and impactful. Empirical evidence, including applications to consumer psychology, will be presented.

S-153: Work design for an aging workforce

Ekkehart Frieling, Jürgen Wegge (chair)
In many countries the proportion of elderly employees is continuously increasing. This leads not only to difficulties within social security systems but also to problems within organizations as the whole work force is aging and age diversity is also rising. This symposium investigates the relationship between working conditions and aging processes. The understanding of this link is an important precondition for the implementation of age-differentiated work designs, i.e. age-specific distribution of tasks, age-specific design of work equipment and age-specific personnel development strategies. Recent findings about the effectiveness of such interventions with respect to performance, stress and strain are presented.

Age-differences in work-related motives: Chronological age versus future time perspectives
Grube, Anna Organisationspsychologie, Universität Münster, Münster, Germany Hertel, Guido Psychology III, University of Muenster, Münster, Germany
Considering age-related differences in work motivation is important for successful human resource management, particularly in light of an ageing workforce. Age-related differences in work-related goals, needs, and interests were explored in an online study (N = 358). Age-related differences in the ranking of these motives were observed as expected. However, most of these differences disappeared when participants' future time perspectives were controlled (future work time perspective, date of retirement, work-activities planed after retirement). The results emphasize the importance of perceived time perspectives in comparison to chronological age of employees.

Age and role clarity in the relations between demands, resources and psychological well-being: Results of a complete 2-wave study
de Lange, Annet Experim. and Arbeidspsychology, Rijksuniversiteit Groningen, Groningen, Netherlands De Lange, AH, Van der Heijden, B. Kooij, D., Jansen, PGW In this study (based on a sample of N=2611 Dutch workers) we examine the moderating influence of the age-related variable Role clarity in the relation between (quantitative, emotional) demands, and several types of resources in predicting psychological well-being (measured as emotional exhaustion, job satisfaction and depression). The results revealed that role clarity moderated or buffered the effects of emotional demands in predicting job satisfaction and depression. For emotional exhaustion, role clarity moderated the effects of both emotional and quantitative demands, and for possibilities for development. We will discuss the practical as well as scientific implications of the results found.

Effect of emotion regulation on the health of teachers over time
Philipp, Anja Arbeits- und Org.-Psychologie, Universität Freiburg, Freiburg, Germany Krause, Andreas Schüpbach, Heinz A&O-Psychologie, Universität Freiburg, Freiburg, Germany
Teachers are facing high emotional demands in class. What characterises teachers who manage their emotions well and stay healthy compared to those with burnout? Which emotion regulation strategies have a long-term effect on the health and work ability of teachers? A study (N=91) conducted at two points in time tested these questions in a cross-lagged panel design using structural equation modelling. The results indicate that deep acting has a positive effect on the health of teachers. Surface acting is more frequently used if they feel already burned out. These findings contribute to the development of an age-mixed group supervision.

Supporting older adults to use interactive systems
Sengpiel, Michael Inst. für Psychologie, Humboldt-Universität zu Berlin, Berlin, Germany Wandke, Hartmut Inst. für Psychologie, Humboldt-Universität zu Berlin, Berlin, Germany Struve, Doreen Inst. für Psychologie, Humboldt-Universität zu Berlin, Berlin, Germany
The aging workforce is bound to use new technical systems that will often pose a challenge to use. We investigate ways to support them in using new interactive systems. We focus on areas of training and design of work equipment, exemplified by the use of a ticket vending machine, for which we developed an interactive learning environment for self-learning. Based on Selection-Optimization-Compensation Theory (Baltes) and Social-Learning-Theory (Bandura) we manipulate characteristics of the learning environment, including the simulation, the instruction and the video models, in experimental settings. Results will be presented and integrated in current research. Practical implications will be discussed.

Elderly employees in the automotive industry: Solutions for an age-based work design
Weichel, Julia Inst. für Arbeitswissenschaft, Universität Kassel, Kassel, Germany Buch, Markus Frieling, Ekkehart Inst. für Arbeitswissenschaft, Universität Kassel, Kassel, Germany
The demographic change leads to a continuously rising number of old employees. The focus of our project is on analysing elderly employees working on assembly lines. The sample consists of blue collar workers from two original equipment manufacturers (N=249, N=160). We used objective and subjective data to analyse the current work systems (e.g. decision latitude) as well as the employees' performance (e.g. adaptive performance) and health status (e.g. somatic complaints). We found positive effects of working conditions on the employees' performance which underlines the importance of adaptive work design that promote learning and health over the lifespan.

The impact of age diversity in workgroups on innovation, group performance and health
Wegge, Jürgen Arbeits- und Org.-Psychologie, Technische Universität Dresden, Dresden, Germany Schmidt, Klaus Helmut Universität Dortmund, IFADO, Dortmund, Germany
Age diversity in teams can have advantages (e.g., use of different experiences) as well as disadvantages (e.g., emotional conflicts). Under which circumstances these effects occur has been rarely studied. Therefore, we investigate in two longitudinal studies (N1 = 67, N2= 145 groups) within the administrative sector the influence of age diversity on indicators of work motivation (e.g., satisfaction), group efficiency (e.g., performance) and health (e.g., burnout). Cognitive salience of age diversity, task complexity and diversity mind sets are considered as moderating variables. The results of both studies show that age diversity has positive effects under specific conditions (e.g., complex tasks).

S-154: The psychology of Web 2.0: Personalities, motives and managing impressions

Nicole Krämer, Sabine Trepte (chair)
The buzzword "web 2.0" describes new mechanisms and opportunities: Within the Internet and its platforms like YouTube, MySpace or wikipedia, users are no longer merely recipients but producers of media content. From a psychological perspective, it is open why and how people – despite potential privacy concerns – present themselves in the World Wide Web and publish partly intimate details on their lives. The symposium gives an overview on recent research on social network sites and blogs. The contributions focus on potential the motives and gratifications as well as on the relation of personality factors and the form of self presentation.

StudiVZ - Determinants of social networking and dissemination of information among students
Bosau, Christian Ökonomie und Soz.-Pychologie, Universität Köln, Köln, Germany Fischer, Oliver Personnel Department, Bertelsmann AG, Guetersloh, Germany Koll, Marcus Economic/Social Psychology, University of Cologne, Cologne, Germany
The network community StudiVZ is extremely popular among students in Germany. However, little is known about the reasons underlying students' willingness to participate in that network community and to present information about themselves – and consume information about others – in this manner. What are the motives and gratifications? Do different patterns of media use depend on personality differences or do students just want to have fun? This study, asking StudiVZ-members via online-questionnaires, presents results regarding the reasons for participating in the network, the behaviour within the network as well as the dissemination of private and personal information.

Entering the blogosphere: Motives for reading, writing and commenting
Haferkamp, Nina Inst. für Sozialpsychologie, Universität Köln, Köln, Germany
Weblogs allow authors to develop an individualized web presence that reflects facets of their personal life, opinions and interests. Additionally, the possibility to post comments on the weblog opens a communicative basis for readers and writers. We conducted a survey with 79 bloggers and 172 recipients in order to investigate the motivations for writing, reading and commenting on blogs in consideration of the gender and age of the participants. Results indicate, for instance, that male readers are primarily interested in informative weblogs and that especially male bloggers serve this need while female bloggers prefer to write about personal experiences.

Web 2.0 users' values and concerns of privacy
Trepte, Sabine Inst. für Medienpsychologie, Medienschule Hamburg, Hamburg, Germany Reinecke, Leonard Media Management, Hamburg Media School, Hamburg, Germany Behr, Katharina-Maria Media Management, Hamburg Media School, Hamburg, Germany
Who are the users of web 2.0 services in terms of need for privacy and self-disclosure and what are their values in life? Based on data gathered in an online survey with 702 participants, this study examines issues of privacy for Internet users with high vs. low affinity for the Web 2.0. A cluster analyses identified three groups with different usage patterns of user-generated-content. The statistical analysis revealed significant differences between these groups. For instance, 'producers' of user-generated content show significantly higher scores

in self-disclosure compared to 'recipients' and 'novices'.

The influence of privacy concerns and strategic self presentation motives on self presentation on social networking sites
Utz, Sonja Dept. of Communication Science, VU University of Amsterdam, Amsterdam, Netherlands
Social networking sites have become increasingly popular and many people put a lot of personal information on their profiles. The paper investigates in how far users of social networking sites are concerned with privacy and strategic self-presentation and how these motives influence the amount of personal information that is disclosed on the profile (visible only for friends vs. visible for everybody). An online survey was held among 144 users of Hyves, the largest Dutch social networking site. People who use the internet to influence their image and to maintain personal relationships make more personal information visible to everyone.

Impression management 2.0: Self-presentation on social networking sites and its relationship to personality
Winter, Stephan Inst. für Sozialpsychologie, Universität Duisburg-Essen, Duisburg, Germany Krämer, Nicole Inst. für Sozialpsychologie, Universität Duisburg-Essen, Duisburg, Germany
Social networking sites like MySpace, Facebook or StudiVZ are new, popular means of communicating personality. The aim of this study was to investigate the influence of (offline) personality traits on (online) self-presentation in social network profiles. With a survey among users of the German Web 2.0 site StudiVZ.net and a content analysis of the respondents' profiles we found that self-efficacy of impression management has a strong effect on the number of virtual friends, the detail level of the profile and the style of the personal photo. The results also indicate a slight influence of Extraversion, whereas self-esteem did not have any significant effect at all.

Relevant aspects of successful project-based learning with Web 2.0 tools in schools
Jadin, Tanja Inst. für Kommunikation, Universität Salzburg, Salzburg, Austria Wiesner, Anja Inst. für Kommunikation, Universität Salzburg, Salzburg, Austria Wijnen, Christine Inst. für Kommunikation, Universität Salzburg, Salzburg, Austria Paus-Hasebrink, Ingrid Inst. für Kommunikation, Universität Salzburg, Salzburg, Austria
An evaluation study investigated relevant aspects of successful project-based learning with Web 2.0. 27 teachers and 169 pupils from nine Austrian schools participated in the study. The results show that teacher's attitudes to the Internet as a communication medium predicts the general usage of Web 2.0, the usage of new media in schools, and the usage of Web 2.0 in this project. Significant correlations were found between pupil's learning effects, their use of Web 2.0, and group coherence. Willingness to learn, aspects of class climate, and general satisfaction differ significantly between the project and school. Finally, teacher's actual Web 2.0 usage is discussed.

S-155: Justice and moral behavior

Manfred Schmitt, Claudia Dalbert (chair)
Six studies show that the perception of justice affects moral behavior. Study 1 demonstrates that perceiving justice mediates the effect of the justice motive on rule breaking behavior in schools. Study 2 shows that re-establishing justice is a major goal in revenge. Using an information search paradigm, Study 3 shows that punishment goals are motivated by a desire for justice. Study 4 finds that anti-citizenship behavior at work is driven by the perception of organizational unfairness. Study 5

suggests that justice sensitivity can be increased by priming moral prototypes. Study 6 reveals that civil courage is rooted in justice sensitivity.

Belief in a just world and legal socialization in adolescence
Donat, Matthias Pädagogiches Institut, Universität Halle-Wittenberg, Halle, Germany Dalbert, Claudia Inst. für Pädagogik, Universität Halle-Wittenberg, Halle, Germany
In our study we investigated the hypotheses that rule-breaking behavior of adolescents can be explained by justice experiences at school and also the justice motive. In a questionnaire study on secondary and high school students we assessed general and personal belief in a just world (BJW), justice centrality, just school climate, and several dimensions of rule-breaking behavior. Overall, findings suggest a negative association between BJW and rule-breaking behavior, being mediated by justice experiences at school. We discuss the findings in regard to the adaptive functions of BJW and to implications for further educational and developmental research.

What makes revenge so sweet?
Gollwitzer, Mario Inst. für Psychologie, Universität Koblenz-Landau, Landau, Germany
In two experiments, we investigated under which conditions victims/avengers react with satisfaction to the outcome of an unjust episode. In Experiment 1, avengers were compared with non-avengers. In Experiment 2, the offender suffered from revenge vs. from fateful harm. Additionally, the offender's understanding for his suffering was manipulated. Findings show that (a) offenders' understanding increases victims' satisfaction, (b) taking revenge is satisfactory even when the offender does not understand why he is being punished. Findings are discussed with regard to the question what people hope to achieve when intending to take revenge in the context of a common transgression.

Implicit measurement of punishment goals: Lay people prefer just deserts
Keller, Livia Inst. für Psychologie, Universität Bern, Bern 9, Switzerland
Three Swiss studies investigated lay people's implicit and explicit punishment goals with regard to criminal cases. Implicit goals were assessed using a method applied by Carlsmith (2001, 2006). Participants were asked to assign a sentence and were given the possibility to search for more information. The results for the implicit measure replicated the findings by Carlsmith very closely: Participants were more concerned about just deserts than about deterrence and incapacitation. However, when additional information on restorative justice was given, this information was equally important in determining the sentence. The explicit measure, in contrast, suggested that participants preferred positive special prevention.

Workplace interpersonal deviance (WID) as a reaction to social stressors and organizational justice: The moderating role of personality
Krings, Franciska Business und Wirtschaft, Universität Lausanne, Lausanne-Dorigny, Switzerland Facchin, Stéphanie Department of Psychology, University of Pittsburgh, Pittsburgh, PA, USA
Research on workplace deviance suggest that deviance results from an interaction between organizational and person factors (Judge, Scott, & Ilies, 2006, Penney & Spector, 2005). Building on these models, we studied organizational(distributive/procedural/interactional justice, social stressors) and Big Five personality factors as predictors of work interpersonal deviance (WID) in 265 employees. As expected, social stressors were positively and interactional justice and agreeableness were negatively related to WID. Moreover,

agreeableness acted as a moderator, demonstrating a stronger relation between interactional justice and WID for disagreeable employees. Stressor and agreeableness did not interact, suggesting differential effects of interactional justice and stressors on deviance.

Moral prototypes, moral behavior and justice sensitivity

Osswald, Silvia Inst. für Psychologie, Universität München, München, Germany **Greitemeyer, Tobias** *Inst. für Psychologie, Universität München, München, Germany* **Fischer, Peter** *Inst. für Psychologie, Universität München, München, Germany* **Frey, Dieter** *Inst. für Psychologie, Universität München, München, Germany*

The studies base on the idea of three moral prototypes (just, brave and caring) of Walker and Hennig (2004). It was demonstrated that people relate different moral behaviors to the three prototypes (Studies 1 – 3). Study 4 revealed that the activation of the just prototype promoted moral courage, whereas helping behavior (related to the caring prototype and not to the just) was not affected. Activating the just prototype also affected justice sensitivity on the observer and the perpetrator perspective: Participants became more justice sensitive. For the victim perspective, no differences between the prototype-activation and the control group emerged.

Justice sensitivity and civil courage

Hauer, Johannes Inst. für Psychologie, Universität Koblenz-Landau, Landau, Germany **Krettek, Carmen** *Fachbereich Psychologie, Universität Koblenz-Landau, Landau, Germany* **Baumert, Anna** *Fachbereich Psychologie, Universität Koblenz-Landau, Landau, Germany* **Schmitt, Manfred** *Fachbereich Psychologie, Universität Koblenz-Landau, Landau, Germany*

In a longitudinal study (N = 70), the hypothesis was tested that justice sensitivity contributes uniquely to civil courage over and above empathy, social anxiety, self efficacy, and responsibility denial. At time 1, these traits were measured. At time 2, participants reacted to eight different stories describing cases of innocent victimization. Participants rated for each incident perceived injustice, moral outrage, and the likelihood that they would help the victim, call for support from bystanders, and rebut the perpetrator. At time 3, civil courage was measured in a naturalistic setting. Justice sensitivity affected civil courage conditionally on the type of situation.

S-156: New approaches to item generation for educational and psychological measurement

Carolyn MacCann, Patrick C. Kyllonen (chair)
The generation of test items to assess abilities and aptitudes dates back to Binet, the USA army's alpha and beta intelligence tests, and the Scholastic Aptitude Test (SAT) that followed. Since these beginnings, automatic and rational approaches to item generation more precisely control item complexity and difficulty, important for computerized adaptive testing or large scale standardized testing. In addition, new constructs somewhat orthogonal from cognitive ability require different approaches to item development. This symposium addresses current approaches for item generation for both traditional and new item types, for use in school assessment, educational readiness and training and organizational psychology.

Automatic item generation: Artificial intelligence and transfer learning in physics

Kyllonen, Patrick C. Center for New Construct, Educational Testing Service, Princeton, USA
ETS has developed a system called the Test Creation Assistant (TCA), a template based system for automatic item generation. The system is used to generate many items from a single item "model," and has been applied to both math and physics word problems. In collaboration with Cycorp, Inc. and Northwestern University we added artificial intelligence methods to the system to create problem variants that systematically differ from a "parent" problem, allowing us to test transfer learning. I review the results of a learning experiment and discuss implications for the future of automatic item generation in creating tests and learning materials.

Item development for new measures of cognitive flexibility

Beckmann, Jens F. Accelerated Learning Labratory, University of New South Wales, Australia, Australia **Bowman, David**
While mental flexibility is a central constituent in many theories of intelligence, this capability is insufficiently captured by traditional test scores. Across several studies, a number of novel tasks were constructed comprising a wide variety of item types emphasising the capacity to deal with ambiguity, to switch frames of reference, and to deviate from routine ways of thinking. Results from student and manager samples provide evidence for the differential sensitivities of mental flexibility scores to predict problem-solving behaviours in comparison to traditional metrics. This new approach may serve to redress the existing discrepancy between conceptualisation and operationalisation of intelligence.

New item development approaches for social and emotional intelligence

MacCann, Carolyn Center for New Constructs, Educational Testing Service, Princeton, USA
Item development for social and emotional intelligence (EI) tests requires different processes than those used in conventional intelligence tests, primarily due to the difficulty in scoring EI items. These approaches include: (1) the situational judgment test (SJT) approach; (2) implicit assessments (e.g., the Implicit Association Test); (3) the use of appraisal theories of emotion to develop test items; (4) the use of perceptual tasks to assess emotion recognition; and (5) affective forecasting. The strengths and weaknesses of these approaches (and the convergence between them) are outlined, with empirical illustrations from multivariate data sets.

Selecting sub-items for signal detection indexes

Paulhus, Delroy L. Dept. of Psychology, University of British Columbia, Vancouver, Canada
When maximizing test reliability, standard strategies are to: (1) increase the correlations among items; and (2) increase the number of items. In signal detection theory there are two categories of responses (hits and false alarms), such that these strategies are less straight-forward to implement. Five possible approaches to dealing with this issue are illustrated with a dataset from the Over-Claiming Questionnaire (Paulhus et al., 2003): (1) partition and factor; (2) create sub-accuracy scores; (3) combinatorial approach; (4) crude empiricism; and (5) the ability to discriminate across ability levels.

Using automated text analysis tools to develop verbal ability tests

Gorin, Joanna S. College of Education, Arizona State University, Tempe, USA
A fundamental component of any item generation system is a coding framework used to quantify the relationship between specific features of test questions and associated underlying cognitive processes. In verbal reasoning assessment, ratings of relevant linguistic and semantic variables are typically examined. Natural language processing tools, such as Latent Semantic Analysis, provide an efficient and reliable method to code many of these text-based variables. This presentation describes how such tools could be incorporated into test development and delivery programs to improve the usability and meaning of verbal ability test scores.

S-157: Associative learning of implicit attitudes

Bertram Gawronski, Jan de Houwer (chair)
Behavior is determined not only by explicit attitudes (carefully constructed opinions of what we like or dislike) but also by implicit attitudes (immediate, spontaneous evaluations). Implicit attitudes toward a stimulus can result from pairing it with other stimuli. In this symposium, De Houwer will discuss potential pitfalls when studying associative learning of implicit attitudes. Gawronski shows that newly learned implicit attitudes can be context dependent. Data presented by Ranganath and by Rydell reveal dissociations between the associative learning of explicit and implicit attitudes. Sherman warns that implicit measures of attitudes might not directly reflect underlying associations. Dijksterhuis will be discussant.

Potential pitfalls in the study of associative learning of implicit attitudes

de Houwer, Jan Dept. of Psychology, Ghent University, Ghent, Belgium
Associative learning is an important source of implicit attitudes. However, potential pitfalls complicate the study of associative learning of implicit attitudes. I will discuss four of these pitfalls: One needs to be sure that the measure of implicit attitudes is not contaminated by explicit attitudes. One should realize that different processes might underlie different types of implicit attitudes. Proper controls are needed to exclude the influence of non-associative elements of the procedure. In comparing implicit and explicit attitude formation, results may depend on how explicit attitudes are measured. These pitfalls will be illustrated by referring to new and published data.

I like you, I like you not: Understanding the context-dependency of implicit attitudes

Gawronski, Bertram Dept. of Psychology, University of Western Ontario, London, Canada
Previous research has shown that implicit attitudes can be highly context-sensitive. In the present research, we argue that context effects on implicit attitudes depend on the heterogeneity of prior experiences with the attitude object, leading to cue-dependent activation of evaluative associations. Across 4 studies, implicit attitudes reflected the valence of previously learned information regardless of the context, when this information was evaluatively consistent. However, when the acquired information was evaluatively inconsistent, implicit attitudes became context-dependent, such that they reflected the valence of the information that was associated with a particular context during learning.

Covariation detection and attitude formation

Ranganath, Kate Dept. o fPsychology, University of Virginia, Charlottesville, USA
We investigated the effects of covariation information implicit and explicit attitude formation. Attitudes were induced with an illusory correlation procedure in which participants read twice as many statements about one group (majority) than the other (minority), though the ratio of positive to negative statements was equal. Control conditions

presented an actual correlation between the majority group and positive behaviors or the minority group and positive behaviors. Explicit attitudes showed the illusory correlation effect, implicit attitudes did not. We interpret this as indicating dual-processes wherein implicit attitudes reflect algebraic accounting of covariation and explicit attitudes reflect reflective judgments of that covariation.

The impact of forming discrepant implicit and explicit attitudes: Controlled thought and uncertainty

Rydell, Robert Dept. of Psychology, University of California, Santa Barbara, USA

Discrepant implicit and explicit attitudes toward the same attitude object were formed by concurrently presenting subliminal primes that were inconsistent with the validity of statements about that attitude object. The implications of holding implicit-explicit discrepancies was moderated by ability to perceive them. Normally, people showed decreased attitude certainty but increased cognitive dissonance and implicit ambivalence in response to discrepancies. However, when people could not perseverate because of inability (cognitive load) or lack of motivation (self-affirmation) it was as if no discrepancy existed. Discrepancies did not lead to uncertainty, but controlled thought after the formation of the implicit-explicit attitude discrepancies did.

Implicit attitudes and implicit associations are not the same thing

Sherman, Jeffrey Dept. of Psychology, University of California, Davis, USA

Implicit measures of attitudes often are taken as direct reflections of underlying associations. However, our research shows that these measures reflect a variety of component processes. Motivations to control prejudice, exposure to counter-stereotypic exemplars, and practice at negating prejudicial responses all corresponded with less biased associations. However, these variables also were associated with increased controlled efforts to monitor behavior. Old age and alcohol assumption influenced controlled efforts to inhibit automatic associations, but were not associated with differences in underlying associations. Thus, variance in implicit attitude measures reflects a variety of processes, and may be unrelated to differences in underlying associations.

S-158: Challenges in contemporary research on the assessment and evaluation of collectivism and individualism

Boaz Shulruf (chair)

Over the past three decades collectivism and individualism have been the cornerstone of a large body of cross-cultural research. Most of it, however, used mean scores of scales for collectivism and individualism to classify certain populations as either collectivist or individualists. Recent development in this area suggests that relatively large proportion of any population is either high or low on both collectivism and individualist thus the traditional collectivism-individualism classification of peoples is likely to be determined by only small proportion of any group. This symposium discusses the implication of this development on contemporary research in cross cultural psychology.

Challenges in contemporary research on the assessment and evaluation of collectivism and individualism*Shulruf, Boaz* Faculty of Education, University of Auckland, Auckland, New Zealand

Over the past three decades collectivism and individualism have become the cornerstone of a

large body of cross-cultural research. Most of it, however, used mean scores of scales for collectivism and individualism to classify certain populations as either collectivist or individualists. Recent development in this area suggests that relatively large proportions of any population can be quite varied in their "mix" of collectivism and individualist. This presentation, demonstrates how cluster analysis can reduce the impact of some response biases when collectivism and individualism are compared across different nations and cultures. Implications for further research in this area are discussed.

Culture as situated cognition

Oyserman, Daphna Dept. of Psychology, University of Michigan, Ann-Arbor, USA

Experimental research demonstrates that small and seemingly incidental features of a situation can cue different cultural syndromes and that once cued, a cultural syndrome influences what content and process knowledge seems relevant. Merely reading a short paragraph that primes collectivist or individualist concepts is sufficient to influence people's reasoning strategies in ways that parallel differences between collectivistic and individualistic cultures. Such temporary influences suggest that cultural differences may be better conceptualized within a framework of adaptively tuned situated cognition. I'll present experimental and meta-analytic findings, outline their implications for the conceptualization of culture and discuss basic and applied research implications.

Individualism and well-being: New evidence and theoretical implications

Schimmack, Ulrich Dept. of Psychology, University of Toronto, Toronto, Canada *Diener, Ed* Dept. of Psychology, University of Illinois at Urba, Champaign, IL, USA

Well-being is a culture-free and universally applicable construct because it allows individuals to judge the quality of their lives based on their own, in part culturally determined, ideals. Thus, culture may influence the criteria that individuals use to evaluate their lives, but the outcome of the evaluation process is comparable across cultures. Individualism is a strong predictor of cultural differences in well-being ($N = 50$, $r = .67$). Thus, individualism is an important and valid dimension of cultural variation, and individualistic cultures are better in that they provide better opportunities to maximize well-being.

Adaptation and cross-cultural validation of the Auckland Individualism Collectivism Scale (AICS) in the Portuguese and Romanian contexts

Faria, Luísa Fac. of Psychology and Educat., University of Porto, Porto, Portugal *Ciochina, Laura* Fac. of Psychology and Educat., University of Porto, Porto, Portugal

This study aims to validate, in Portugal and Romania, the AICS (Shulruf, Hattie & Dixon, 2003), to measure Individualism-Collectivism (IND/COL), using a sample of 200 Portuguese and 195 Romanian, 10th and 12th graders. The AICS with 26 items, 15 of Individualism (3 subscales – Uniqueness, Competition and Responsibility), and 11 of Collectivism (2 subscales – Harmony and Advice) was submitted to confirmatory factor analyses that support the use of subscales to measure IND/COL. Further, multivariate analyses evidenced a principal effect of culture on Competition and of gender on Competition, Responsibility, and Advice, and an interaction effect of culture x gender on Harmony.

Individualism-collectivism and school achievement in Italian students

Alesi, Marianna Dept. of Psychology, University of Palermo, Palermo, Italy *Pepi, Annamaria* Dept. of Psychology, University of Palermo, Palermo, Italy

The aim is to study the relationship between individualism-collectivism, personal conceptions of intelligence and school achievement. Participated 222 students attending High School (humanistic, scientific and technique address), distributed according their gender and socioeconomic status. Subjects were given a questionnaire assessing socioeconomic level and school performance, Personal Conceptions of Intelligence Test (Faria, Fontaine, 1997) and Auckland Individualism-Collectivism Scale (Shulruf, Hattie, Dixon, 2007). Significant differences were found on the individualism linked to gender, school address and socioeconomic level. Moreover results show positive correlations between school achievement and individualism in technique students and negative correlations between school achievement and collectivism in humanistic students.

Measuring values and personality traits across cultures: The case of

Norenzayan, Ara Dept. of Psychology, University of British Columbia, Vancouver, Canada *Buchtel, Emma* Dept. of Psychology, University of British Columbia, Vancouver, Canada *Heine, Steven* Dept. of Psychology, University of British Columbia, Vancouver, Canada

Much research inspired by the individualism-collectivism construct contrasts self-reported values and personality traits across cultures. We submit that this enterprise is weakened by significant methodological problems, particularly the reference-group effect, undermining the validity of average country scores of personality traits. Behavioral and demographic predictors of conscientiousness were correlated with different cross-national measures of conscientiousness based on self-reports, observer-reports, and perceptions of national character. These predictors correlated strongly with perceptions of national character, but not with self-reports and peer-reports. Country-level self- and peer-report measures of conscientiousness failed as markers of between-nation differences in personality.

S-159: Science, technology and innovation psychology

Sven Hemlin, Carl Martin Allwood (chair)

In recent years there has been an increased interest in taking a psychological perspective on science, technology and innovation processes. This research area aims at an improved understanding of R&D processes from the perspective of the scientist, groups and organizations were scientists work in academic and industrial settings. This brings together elements of personality, cognitive, social, cross-cultural and industrial/organizational psychology (Feist, 2006; Ford, 1993; Woodman, Sawyer & Griffin, 1996).

The concept of culture and the indigenized psychologies

Allwood, Carl Martin Dept. of Psychology, Lund University, Lund, Sweden

The modern indigenous psychologies (henceforth: indigenous psychologies) are examples of local approaches to psychology (see e.g. Sinha, 1997). They occur in different varieties but they all aim to be culturally and pragmatically relevant to the researcher's own society and are reactions to the dominance of Western or US-American culture in psychological research. This contribution will argue that the concept of culture has not been sufficiently problematized in the literature on the indigenized psychologies and that one of the most basic premises of the indigenous psychologies (culture as a fairly stable, within the "cultural group" singly describable and shared entity) is problematic.

Why are women avoiding the physical sciences?

Feist, Gregory Dept. of Psychology, San José State University, California, CA, USA *Rastogi, Deepika* Dept. of Psychology, San José State University, California, CA, USA

It is not true that women are not going into the sciences, only the physical sciences. We predicted that a preference for people-oriented rather than thing-oriented careers and more flexible working conditions work together to make the physical sciences less appealing to women. The sample consisted of undergraduate and graduate students as well as professors in the physical, social, and biological sciences. As predicted, compared to women in the physical sciences, those in the other sciences scored higher on people-oriented vocational interest and lower on Autism-Spectrum Quotient, and placed higher value on more family-oriented working conditions. Implications are discussed in the context of an emerging new discipline, the psychology of science.

Service science: A case study in the social psychology of science

Gorman, Michael E. Science and Technology, University of Virginia, Charlottesville, USA

The cognitive literature on expertise demonstrates that domain experts develop distinct ways of representing and solving problems; even what is viewed as a problem is unique to specific domains. There is a social studies of science literature that focuses on shared expertise. An interactional expert understands enough of another expertise community to gauge its needs and work with it towards solutions to problems, but cannot do the actual research done by domain experts. This presentation will link these two literatures and apply them to the emerging field of service science.

Creativity stimulating R&D group leaders

Hemlin, Sven Gothenburg Research Institute, Gothenburg University, Gothenburg, Sweden *Olsson, Lisa* Gothenburg Research Institute, Gothenburg University, Gothenburg, Sweden

Group leaders play an important role for creative outcomes of R&D groups. Lately, this issue was reviewed by Mumford et al. (2002) ending in a number of questions. We are currently conducting a study based on the Critical Incident Technique (CIT) to find out what group leader actions are involved in creative situations with R&D groups. Data are collected with three members of each R&D group. We will report the preliminary results of this analysis to answer questions about what situations are involved, why are they considered creative and what conclusions can be drawn about creativity stimulating leadership.

Psychology of science and popper: Some reflections

Kumar, Neelam Sociology of Science, Nistads, New Delhi, India

This paper provides a short note on the evolution of psychology of science. It presents psychology of science as an emerging discipline. The paper also offers some reflections on the links between Popper, one of the most famous philosophers of science, and integration of psychological approaches and methods to study science. Popper had intellectual roots in psychology. His political and scientific views are traced to his early experiences with Marxism and psychoanalysis. Yet Popper not only turned away from psychology as early as 1930 or thereabout, later became one of the most outspoken opponents of psychological approach in science studies.

Innovations in science and technology: A social psychological study

Schulze, Anna Dorothea Inst. für Psychologie, Humboldt-Universität zu Berlin, Berlin, Germany

Innovations in Science and Technology - a Social Psychological Study Most innovation studies in Science and Technology come from the fields of sociology and organization studies. Our study focused on social conflicts within the genesis of innovations in the field of Gene Technology (in basic science, scientist/entrepreneur firms and larger R&D firms). We studied the varieties of conflict and conflict management in innovation processes and their importance for innovation success. Results: An appropriate conflict management is decisive for successful innovation. The scientists adopt a configuration of mode of conflict management. They combine and form patterns. The integrating combined with contending behaviour proved to be more successful than integrating behaviour alone.

S-160: Risk and protective factors of relational aggression in adolescence

Herbert Scheithauer (chair)

Even though in recent years there had been an increasing amount of literature on physical aggression, there is still a lack of studies investigating risk and protective factors for the development of relational aggression in adolescence. This is suprising because studies have shown that in adolescence, relational aggression has especially negative consequences for boys and girls psychosocial development. The studies presented in this symposium investigate contextual or individual risk and protective factors and provide an empirical base for the development of adequate interventions.

Risk and protective factors in the development of (instrumental) relational aggression in adolescence

Ittel, Angela Fakultät für Pädagogik, Bundeswehr Universität München, Neubiberg, Germany

While research has identified multiple motives and forms of physical aggression, relational aggression has not been investigated to identify different subtypes and expressions of this often more subtle form of aggression. This project therefore examines the expression of instrumental relational aggression in 373 male and female adolescents. Results show that factors related to the family, such as parenting, take an effect on boys expression of instrumental relational aggression. For girls individual attitudes and values as well as psychosocial factors are associated with the expression of instrumental relational aggression. Both boys and girls however benefit from a democratic family climate.

The relationship of rejection sensitivity and relational aggression in adolescence

Rosenbach, Charlotte Inst. für Psychologie, Freie Universität Berlin, Berlin, Germany *Bull, Heike Dele* Department of Psychology, Free University Berlin, Berlin, Germany *Renneberg, Babette* Department of Psychology, Goethe University Frankfurt, Frankfurt, Germany

Aim of this study was to analyze the relationship between Rejection Sensitivity (RS), Relational Aggression (RA) and individual problems in adolescence. Longitudinal data from three assessment points (t1, t2=three months later, t3=one year later) are available for 41 adolescents (age 14-18). RS, RA and self-reported strengths and difficulties (SDQ) were assessed. Data from t3 will be presented. A positive correlation between RS and RA was observed. Regression-models for the prediction of individual problems and RA are conducted. The results of this study will contribute to the knowledge of risk factors of Relational

Aggression as well as individual problems in adolescence.

Empathy and perspective-taking: Risk OR protective factors or risk and protective factors in the development of relational aggression in adolescence?

Scheithauer, Herbert Inst. Bildungswissenschaften, Freie Universität Berlin, Berlin, Germany *Bull, Heike Dele* Department of Psychology, Free University of Berlin, Berlin, Germany

The aim of this study was to explore the relationship between empathy (E), perspective-taking (PE) and relational aggression (RA). Data from 126 adolescents (aged 14-16) will be presented. A subsample of 42 adolescents further participated in a longitudinal design over a 15-month-period. PT was assessed with self-reports, E and RA were assessed on the basis of self-, peer- and teacher ratings. We expect both factors to be positively related to RA for extreme groups (high vs. low RA), when the initial measure of RA is controlled. Findings will be discussed with regard to the knowledge about risk and protective factors.

"Fight for me!" Girls' and boys' expectations of defense against same- or other-gender peers

Neuhaus, Janine Inst. für Psychologie, Freie Universität Berlin, Berlin, Germany *Hannover, Bettina* Inst. für Psychologie, Freie Universität Berlin, Berlin, Germany

This research compares male and female 9th graders' expectations (N=900) of an accompanying peer's reaction after being provoked. By using vignettes we also manipulate the companion's gender, consequently resulting in a 2x2 design (gender-target x gender-companion). Referring to the girls-target situation we assume that the same-gender constellation (girl/girl) leads to higher relational aggression and lower overt aggression expectancy rates, whereas the other-gender constellation (girl/boy) evokes an opposite pattern. Furthermore we expect a moderating effect of the subject's agreement to paternalistic-oriented gender roles as described in the culture-of-honor concept (Nisbett, 1993). Results are discussed with respect to preventive school measures.

Longitudinal associations of normative beliefs and relational aggression during middle childhood and early adolescence

Werner, Nicole Dep. of Human Development, Washington State University, Pullman, WA, USA *Lyle, Kelsey* Dep. of Human Development, Washington State University, Pullman, WA, USA

Support for social information-processing (SIP) models of child adjustment suggests that patterns of distal (i.e., latent knowledge structures) and proximal (i.e., on-line) processing of social information predict individual differences in overt and relational aggression (RA) (Werner & Nixon, 2005). The current study utilized a longitudinal design and teacher-ratings of RA to extend our understanding of the role of normative beliefs for RA during middle childhood and adolescence (N=465). Findings indicate that children become increasingly approving of RA, particularly across the transition from elementary to middle school. Moreover, normative beliefs about RA significantly predicted increases in RA behavior across one year.

Ostracism: Effects of being ignored and excluded

Williams, Kipling D. Dept. Psychological Sciences, Purdue University, West Lafayette, USA

Ostracism, being ignored and excluded, is a ubiquitous and powerful form of relational aggression. I present my program of research demonstrating that the initial reaction to ostracism is unmitigated pain; followed by a perceived threat to four fundamental needs, and coping responses aimed at fortifying these needs. Behavioral responses can fortify belonging and self-esteem if they make the individual more open to others and socially attractive; fortifying control and existential needs may be fortified by forcing others to attend to and notice – often resulting in anti-social and provocative acts. Implications for adolescents, for whom belonging needs are very high, are discussed.

S-161: Current perspectives on the concept of wisdom and its development

Judith Glück (chair)
A recent focus in psychological wisdom research is on how wisdom develops through actual life experiences. Current theoretical and empirical work suggests two different, but related conceptions of wisdom: one that views wisdom as a largely cognitive variable acquired through learning and one that emphasizes the integration of cognitive, emotional, and motivational aspects and is acquired through actual experience of life challenges. In this symposium, we present empirical work aiming at understanding (1) how these two types of wisdom are related and (2) how they develop in the course of individual life stories.

Title to be announced
Takahashi, Masami Dept. of Psychology, Northeastern Illinois Univ., Chicago, IL, USA
Our developmental model of wisdom integrates two moments or modes of wisdom: analytical and synthetic mode. The analytic mode concerns the reduction of global systems of wisdom into elementary qualities, and inquiry into this mode primarily entails the exploration of specific knowledge content or information-processing functions. In contrast, the synthetic mode concerns the integration of psychological systems and transformational changes that characterize this integration. In particular, this wisdom mode pertains to cognition/affect integration and a reflective level of conscious experience. It is argued that both analytical and synthetic modes of experience are equally necessary for defining the concept of wisdom.

Christian and Buddhist views on what wisdom is and how it develops
Rappersberger, Stefanie Inst. für Psychologie, Universität Wien, Wien, Austria
Conceptions of wisdom have been shown to be related to culture (Takahashi & Overton, 2005). Spiritual aspects of wisdom, however, though prominent in implicit theories of wisdom, have hardly been studied. In this study, 20 Christian and 20 Buddhist dignitaries were interviewed about wisdom. Content analyses revealed high overlap in conceptions of what wisdom is, although Buddhists put more emphasis on empathy than Christians. Concerning how wisdom develops, Buddhist participants said that wisdom can be acquired through directed learning, while Christian participants emphasized life experience. Both groups viewed reflection as central to the development of wisdom.

Implicit theories of wisdom and its development: Evidence for two different conceptions
Strasser, Irene Inst. für Psychologie, Universität Klagenfurt, Klagenfurt, Austria Glück, Judith Inst. für Psychologie, Universität Klagenfurt, Klagenfurt, Austria Bluck, Susan Department of Psychology, University of Florida, Gainesville, USA
While a number of studies have investigated "lay" theories of what wisdom is, no empirical work exists concerning how people think wisdom develops. In a cooperation with the German GEO-magazine, over 2000 readers completed a brief questionnaire concerning both of these aspects. Data were analyzed in an exploratory way using cluster

analyses. Results showed two different conceptions of wisdom. One focused on cognitive aspects in the definition of wisdom and on learning as the main factor in wisdom development. The other viewed emotional and spiritual aspects as equally important as cognition and focused on challenging life experiences as catalysts for wisdom.

Comparing two different approaches to wisdom
Levenson, Michael R. College of Health, Oregon State University, Corvallis, USA Aldwin, Carolyn Human Development & Family, Oregon State University, Corvallis, OR, USA Taylor, Amanda Human Development & Family, Oregon State University, Corvallis, OR, USA Levaroe, Elizabeth Human Development & Family, Oregon State University, Corvallis, OR, USA Kang, Sungrok College of Health and Hum. Sc., Oregon State University, Corvallis, OR, USA
We contrasted two conceptual and methodological approaches to wisdom, fundamental pragmatics of life (Baltes & Staudinger, 2000) with the liberative model, which focuses on self-transcendence (Levenson et al., 2005), using both qualitative and quantitative measures for both approaches in a sample of 36 women and 14 men (Mage = 71.7). Age was unrelated to self-transcendence, but varied in its relation to pragmatics. Self-transcendence and pragmatics were largely independent, and the vignette measures were uncorrelated with the self-report measures. Self-transcendence related to life satisfaction, practical knowledge inversely to depressive symptoms, and uncertainly management correlated positively with self-report health.

Predictive validity of general and personal wisdom
Staudinger, Ursula M. Zentr. für Lebenslanges Lernen, Jacobs Universität, Bremen, Germany
The paper introduces two measures of personal and general wisdom based on the Berlin Wisdom Paradigm. Reliabilities of both measures are reported from age-comparative samples (young and old adults). Furthermore, similarities and differences in predictive validity of the two measures are reported. Indicators from cognitive and personality functioning are used in the validity analyses.

S-162: Cognition of aesthetics in graphics: The influence of beauty on web-page design and learning

Neil Schwartz, Wolfgang Schnotz (chair)
Scant empirical data exist on aesthetics under the auspices of cognitive theory, and none on learning with graphics. This symposium aims to assemble international researchers to examine the issue. Lenzner explores the aesthetics of scientific graphics on learning physics; Schwartz reports a systematic examination of aesthetics on comprehension of graphic theme; Velesianos reveals aesthetic effects on avatars in virtual learning environments; Tractinsky shows reliable aesthetic effects on web-page design; Lowe traces aesthetics in graphic explanatory communication. Leder presents a model providing deep heuristics in aggregating and advancing the work vis-à-vis the influence of aesthetics on affect and cognition in learning.

Decorative pictures in learning materials: Do they support learning
Lenzner, Alwine Inst. für Psychologie, Universität Koblenz-Landau, Landau, Germany Horz, Holger Inst. für Psychologie, Universität Koblenz-Landau, Landau, Germany Schnotz, Wolfgang Inst. für Psychologie, Universität Koblenz-Landau, Landau, Germany Müller, Andreas Inst. für Psychologie, Universität Koblenz-Landau, Landau, Germany

As already known instructional pictures lead to better learning results, whereas decorative pictures are assumed to be seductive details. We assume an evidence for positive effects of decorative pictures with respect to learners' prior knowledge. Students from 7th and 8th grade (iv1) learned with one of four worksheet versions (iv2: with or without decorative pictures, iv3: with or without instructional pictures). Our results (dependent variables: learning success, eye movements) show a positive effect of decorative pictures for 7th graders and a negative effect for 8th graders. Therefore decorative pictures should only be used for learners with lower prior knowledge.

Empirical findings in studies of visual aesthetics in human-computer interaction
Tractinsky, Noam Informat. Systems Engineering, Ben-Gurion University Negev, Beer-Sheva, Israel
This paper will summarize a recent body of empirical research in the field of human-computer interaction (HCI) that calls attention to the importance of aesthetics in the design of interactive systems. Among other things, this new research demonstrates that people judge the aesthetics of information technology products very rapidly; that although "beauty is in the eye of the beholder," on average users tend to agree about what is beautiful; and that, similar to the effects of beauty on social relations, it influences perceptions of other attributes of the system, such as its usability.

Aesthetic guidelines for the design and development of pedagogical agents
Veletsianos, George Curriculum and Instruction, University of Minnesota, Minneapolis, USA Miller, Charles Curriculum and Instruction, University of Minnesota, Minneapolis, USA Doering, Aaron Curriculum and Instruction, University of Minnesota, Minneapolis, USA
Pedagogical agents are anthropomorphic interfaces used in electronic learning environments for instructional purposes. Such interfaces are often portrayed as virtual humans able to interact, collaborate, and converse with learners. Albeit a growing area of study with high expectations for teaching and learning, prior research has disregarded the visuo-aesthetic properties of pedagogical agents. In this paper, we highlight the importance of such properties and present guidelines for the design and development of aesthetically pleasing pedagogical agents. These guidelines may be used to inform the deployment of virtual characters in learning environments and provide a coherent research agenda for exploring the role of aesthetics in the context of pedagogical agents.

Psychological aesthetics: Basic and applied aspects
Leder, Helmut Inst. für Psychologie, Universität Wien, Wien, Austria
Beauty for long has not been considered particularly important in design. However, growing interest in aesthetics has revealed a number of answers to the question, what the benefits of beauty might be. Basing on our psychological model which describes cognitive and emotional processes and representations involved in processing of art (Leder, Belke, Oeberts & Augustin, 2004) principles of aesthetics are discussed in the realm of design and ergonomics. It is claimed that the consideration of aesthetics can improve the psychological aspects of design in a number of dimensions, such as cognitive fluency, cognitive load and even well-being.

Realism in graphic representation: Aesthetics versus explanatory effectiveness
Lowe, Richard Dept. of Education, Curtin University, Perth, Australia
The degree of resemblance between a referent situation and its graphic representation has long

been considered a key contributor to the aesthetic value of a depiction. Visuospatial realism has traditionally been the main criterion for judging this aspect of aesthetic worth. More recently, technological advances such as computer-based animation have expanded the conception of graphic aesthetics to encompass behavioural realism. For example, both visuospatial and behavioural realism are incorporated at ever increasing levels in computer action games. This paper shows that with education materials however, assumed aesthetic benefits from realism in graphics can occur at the expense of explanatory effectiveness

Learning from graphics: Disentangling the influence of theme and aesthetics

Schwartz, Neil Dept. of Psychology, California State University, Chico, USA Battinich, William Dept. of ExperimentaPsychology, University of Arkansas, Fayettville, USA Lieb, Helmut Faculty of Psychology, University of Koblenz @ Landau, Landau, Germany Mortensen, Chad Dept. of Psychology, California State University, Chico, USA

A tripartite model is debuted showing that thematic relations between web-based graphics and text explains the way graphics effect text comprehension —but only if learners have prior knowledge to induce theme and graphics are immediately perceived as beautiful. We report on three partial-replication studies sampling 500 students in which graphics were manipulated for theme valence, aesthetic quality, and learners' reaction time of aesthetic perception to the aesthetically-controlled graphics. Multiple regression analyses under each experimental condition, and focus-group interviews, revealed that aesthetics evoked emotional responsivity in learners that dictated cognitive access to theme, which in turn, predicted deep thematic text processing.

S-163: Baby signing

Mechthild Kiegelmann, Annette Hohenberger (chair)
While baby signing has recently become popular, little research is available that evaluates potential psychological and linguistic effects of using sign to foster early communication with babies. The presenters in this symposium take two different research perspectives on 1) sign language acquisition in both hearing and deaf children and on 2) symbolic gesturing with hearing children, including evaluating baby signing media. All presenters argue on the basis of empirical research within the context of a controversial debate. An expert in research methodology will serve as a discussant for the presented empirical studies.

Effects of a gestural communication program in Chilean babies

Farkas, Chamarrita Psychology, P. Univers. Catolica de Chile, Santiago, Chile

The research realized explore the benefits of gestural communication program in children', parents' and educators' aspects. Two studies are presented: (a) the effects on the synchronic interactions in 14 dyads mothers-babies of medium socioeconomical level were studied, during three measurements with a Grid to analyze early interactions. The differences in visual, tactile and vocal interactions are discussed. (b) The effects on the stress level in parents and educators of children from social risk families were studied with the Parent Stress Index, Short Form (PSI-SF), during three measurements. The results in each group of caregivers are discussed.

Baby signing with hard of hearing and with hearing children

Kiegelmann, Mechthild IfE, Universität Tübingen, Tübingen, Germany Günther, Klaus-B. Institute for Science of Rehab, Humboldt-Universität zu Berlin, Berlin, Germany

Newer publications on baby signing suggest an increasing number of ASL-signs than early programs. This increase leads us to question whether baby signing can be especially beneficial for deaf children. We hypothesize that baby signing can enhance the development of signing deaf children more directly, because signing is an integral part of their pre-lingual communicative development. Our current research compares the use of baby signing with hearing, hard of hearing, and deaf children. An electronic medium is used in Germany to teach parents and their children baby signs based on the German Sign Language DGS. Preliminary results will be presented.

Baby signing with deaf/blind children

Wolf, Sylvia Inst. für Wissenschaft-Rehabil., Humboldt-Universität zu Berlin, Berlin, Germany

Acredolo and Goodwyn convincingly demonstrated the importance of baby signing for developmental psychology. Yet, the practice of baby signing with disabled children still is a relatively new topic in research. We are especially interested in the effects of baby signing with deaf-blind children, especially any effects on motor and kinaesthetic development. We hypothesize that tactile baby signing fosters the development of the space-time inventory as well as the development of cognitive object permanence. We are presenting a pilot study and research design for a longitudinal investigation.

A longitudinal study investigating the impact on language development of encouraging infants to communicate using signs and gestures

Kirk, Elizabeth School of Psychology, University of Hertfordshire, United Kingdom Pine, Karen School of Psychology, University of Hertfordshire, Hatfield, United Kingdom

We present the first set of findings from a longitudinal study of 40 infants exploring the impact of encouraging gestural communication. Infants were randomly allocated to one of four conditions: Symbolic Gesture training, British Sign Language (BSL) training, Verbal training and a non-intervention control group. At 8m, 12m, 16m, and 20m infants' auditory comprehension and expressive communication (PLS-3 UK) and receptive and productive vocabulary (Oxford CDI) were measured during home visits. Data comparing infants' language development will be reported and the findings will be discussed in relation to notions of gestural communication enhancing early mother-infant interaction and infant language acquisition.

Does baby signing lead to faster language development in hearing children? Evidence from deaf signing babies

Morgan, Gary Dept. of Language and Commu., City University, London, United Kingdom Woll, Bencie DCAL, UCL, London, United Kingdom Woolfe, Tyron DCAL, UCL, London, United Kingdom

If 'baby-signing' classes during 0-36 months speeds language acquisition, children who are native signers should have earlier and faster vocabulary acquisition than their non-signing peers. In a new study on deaf and hearing children's first signs reported through a British Sign Language version of the MacArthur CDI we found no speeded sign language development. Furthermore hearing children of deaf parent's first signs appear at the same age as deaf children's first signs. Observations from 'baby signing' are due to the gesture advantage over speech and sign and not language development gains.

S-164: Cultural psychology and individual agency

Lars Allolio-Naecke, Carl Ratner (chair)
The symposium focuses on power relations, social positioning, and cultural meanings that influence individual action. Neither situations nor persons or things for themselves provoke and guide individual action but the meaning of persons, things and situations do. Moreover people, things and situations are not relevant for everybody in the same manner, because meaning-making itself is a social-historic process that is deep-seated in one's own autobiography. To meet that concern individual action is understood and analyzed as reflecting individual and cultural meanings. The relative influence of these will be discussed by the speakers.

A cultural-historical vs. a romantic view of agency

Ratner, Carl Dept. of Psychology, Institute for Cultur. Research, Trinidad, USA

This paper compares contrasting views of agency. The cultural historical view, pioneered by Vygotsky, Luria, and Leontiev, emphasizes the shared, cultural organization of agency. Agency is a cultural-historical phenomenon that is shaped by social institutions, cultural concepts, social position (class). Idiosyncratic forms of agency are subordinate to culturally shared characteristics that are necessary for culture to persist. Agency is the potential to critically analyze one culture and humanize it to enhance social and psychological life. The romantic view postulates that agency is intrinsically active, creative, and fulfilling. It makes the meanings which guide individual action in society. The individual negotiates with society on his own terms. These positions are evaluated in terms of scientific and political criteria.

How to deal with polyvalence of action

Allolio-Naecke, Lars Inst. für Theologie, Universität Nürnberg-Erlangen, Erlangen, Germany

Everyday activity is structured by ambiguous actions. The question as to the reason why someone did something is not answerable from an outside perspective. But as psychologists, we have to deal with precise models for describing the reasons why someone undertook an action, because from the psychological perspective, we are trying to predict future behaviour. But this is exceptionally difficult, especially in cross-cultural situations. To solve this problem, Ernst E. Boesch proposed the introduction of the polyvalence concept. In my contribution, I show how to use that concept for intercultural trainings.

The norms of culture and the participant's stake

Zielke, Barbara Intercultural Communication, University of Chemnitz, Chemnitz, Germany

The concept of a "dialogical self" is seen as a tool for adapting psychology to the conditions of globalization: all meaningful entities are subject to dialogical processes of meaning construction and the self is one of those entities. More radically, the idea of dialogicality may be employed to deconstruct the individual actor as the object of psychological interest. However, as long we want to distinguish "cultural psychology" from "cultural studies" we should resist the temptation to simply replace identity (of meaning and of self) with plurality. "Dialogicality" calls for a decentered, but not erased concept of self as participant in culture.

Agency, style, and tradition

Baerfeldt, Cor Psychology, University of Alberta, Edmonton, Canada

In recent years, the study of discourse has become a central focus in the cultural psychological study of self. Yet, for lack of an adequate social ontology, discursive psychologies have failed to provide a satisfying account of human agency. This paper turns to the work of the philosopher Merleau-Ponty, who in the last part of his life came to articulate a philosophy of expression and 'style' that could serve as a rich ontological basis for discursive psychology. It is argued that this notion of style provides a way to reconcile the subject of history with the subject of lived experience.

The co-regulation of feelings as social cement
Verheggen, Theo Dept. of Psychologie, Open University Netherlands, Heerlen, Netherlands
From neuropsychology it is known that the human brain has different areas for emotions and feelings (Damasio, 2003). Emotions and feelings are distinguished because the former are directly linked to bodily states whereas the latter leave room for reflection or ideation on those states. This ideational dimension to feelings allows for manipulation, in the sense that what is felt and how it is felt will partially depend on the group one is a member of. It will be argued that being able to express feelings in concordance with what is considered 'proper' or 'right', is one key skill for group membership. It takes feeling for social situations to fit in. That feeling for is learned or trained in everyday situations, and thereby co-regulated with skilled members of the own group. Ref. Antonio Damasio (2003). Looking for Spinoza. Joy, Sorrow, and the feeling brain. Harcourt.

Can the meaning of childhood be changed?
Kleeberg-Niepage, Andrea Psychologie, Freie Universität Berlin, Berlin, Germany
Children are positioned as inferior beings within the western discourse on childhood. Adults posses the power to define a child's development, to regulate children's daily routine (e.g. going to school) and to ascribe a lower social status to children which is justified with the special need of protection children are supposed to have. The implications of this positioning become very obvious when children themselves object to their inferior status which is the case with working children's organisations. These children demand the same rights (i.e. a right to work) as adults have in society. The implications of this objection for a changed meaning of 'childhood' and changed societal power relations will be discussed.

S-165: Evidence-based? Criticism of existing and proposal of new approaches to prevention and treatment of addictive behaviors

Joachim Körkel (chair)
On the basis of existing empirical data the symposium will scrutinize that addiction treatment and policy are evidence-based ("best practice"). Springer reports about attitudes that impede the broad incorporation of opioid maintenance therapy. Based on a RCT Körkel, Becker, Happel and Lipsmeier endorse the implementation of programs for self-controlled drug intake. Verthein advocates heroin-assisted treatment for heroin addicts based on the results of a multicentre RCT. Klein and Schaunig call for a subgroups approach in substance abuse prevention with adolescents based on an epidemiological survey. Uhl puts into question the empirical basis of WHO-guidelines on primary prevention of hazardous alcohol consumption.

Controlled intake of illegal drugs: A randomized controlled trial of a behavioural self-control training
Körkel, Joachim Wissenschaften - Sozialarbeit, Universität für Angewandte, Nürnberg, Germany Becker, Gabi Management, Integrative Drogenhilfe e.V., Frankfurt on the Main, Germany Happel, Volker Social Work and Health, University of Applied Sciences, Frankfurt on the Main, Germany Lipsmeier, Gero Social Work and Health, University of Applied Sciences, Frankfurt on the Main, Germany
Objective: To test the effectiveness of the Behavioral Self-Control Training (BSCT) "KISS" in reducing drug consumption. Method: 144 intravenous polydrug addicts were randomly assigned to 12 KISS sessions or a Waiting List (WL) condition. Ss underwent pre-, post-, and six month follow-up-assessment (including timeline-follow-back for all substances and DSM-IV substance diagnoses). Results: KISS participants show significantly (p < .01) greater reduction in drug intake than WL controls. Pre-assessment self-efficacy and concomitant methadone maintenance treatment are not predictive. Conclusions: BSCT for controlled drug consumption should be considered as treatment option for severely dependent drug addicts not able or willing to live abstinent.

Heroin assisted treatment in Germany, effectiveness and long-term outcome
Verthein, Uwe Universität Hamburg, Hamburg, Germany
In the first 12 months of the German trial on heroin-assisted treatment (HAT) a stratified randomised controlled trial was conducted in order to examine the effectiveness of heroin treatment compared to methadone treatment. Subsequent, a follow-up period was conducted, to assess the long-term effects of HAT. 1,015 patients were included. The central result indicates a significant superiority of heroin treatment over methadone treatment for both primary outcome measures: health and illicit drug use. In the follow up period further improvements took place, a stabilisation of health and social situation was shown. The results confirm the findings of previous international studies. HAT proves to be successful in the long-term treatment of severely dependent heroin users.

Management of opioid maintenance therapy in Austria: A recent empirical study
Springer, Alfred für Suchtforschung, Ludwig Boltzmann-Institut, Wien, Austria Uhl, Alfred Alkohol Information und Co-ord, Anton-Proksch-Institut, Wien, Austria
Objectives: To determine how the situation of oral maintenance treatment for opiate addicts is perceived by physicians and their clients before stricter regulations concerning the use of slow release morphine as substitution drug are enacted. Methods: Interview as well as questionnaire based study involving 176 physicians and 619 of their patients Results: All used substitution medications, i.e. methadone, buprenorphine and slow release morphine have their sound place in the Austrian treatment system and are appreciated by physicians and patients. Conclusions: The newly enacted stricter regulations concerning slow-release morphine endangers the fragile regional system providing maintenance treatment throughout Austria.

Adolescent substance use in relation to school factors: Results of a local monitoring study
Klein, Michael Katholische Fachhochschule, Köln, Germany Schaunig, Ines Centre of Excellence of on App, Catholic University of Applied, Cologne, Germany
Objectives: To determine whether adolescent substance use varies according to school factors such as level of education, social situation and school climate. Methods: More than 3770 pupils from grade 6 to 12 were interviewed concerning their substance use. 35 schools from different school types and districts of Cologne participated. Results: Large differences in patterns of substance use depending on school type, social background and climate factors were found. It was shown that young people from school type "Gymnasium" in favorable districts report higher rates of alcohol and cannabis use. Conclusions: Prevention strategies should be individually implemented in the context of schools and focus more on the identified risk group.

Evidence based alcohol policy: An oxymoron?
Uhl, Alfred Alkohol Information und Co-ord, Anton-Proksch-Institut, Wien, Austria
Objectives: To determine whether it is sensible and/ or possible to base alcohol policy on facts. Methods: Systematic analysis of empirical and theoretical literature concerning evidence based policy development. Results: Speaking logically, practical conclusions cannot be derived from facts solely. The attempt to do so is termed 'Naturalistic Fallacy' in research methodology. The conclusions in the most prominent recent publications on alcohol policy over-simplify the situation from a Northern European alcohol control perspective. Conclusions: We should increasingly discuss ethical considerations involved in policy building and stop to camouflage the decisions as inevitable consequence of evidence.

S-282: Learning from multiple documents embedded in new media

Marc Stadtler, Rainer Bromme (chair)
Learners are frequently required to construct meaning in interaction with multiple documents. E.g., electronic encyclopaedia or Internet websites are used to accomplish learning assignments or to support informed decision making. The skills needed to accomplish such tasks clearly go beyond what is needed in comprehending single and simple documents that have traditionally been investigated in text comprehension research. The symposium brings together researchers that address the crucial question of how readers manage to integrate information across documents and evaluate them in terms of trustworthiness. Thereby, we seek to synthesize and enhance our knowledge of the comprehension of multiple complex documents.

The relationship between source evaluation and comprehension of multiple documents
Bråten, Ivar Dept. of Educational Research, University of Oslo, Oslo, Norway Stromso, Helge Institute for Educ. Research, University of Oslo, Oslo, Norway
We addressed whether source evaluation predicts comprehension of multiple documents containing conflicting information about global warming. After reading, participants rated the trustworthiness of sources and the degree to which they had attended to different source features. Hierarchical regression analyses showed that after controlling for prior knowledge, the degree to which readers trusted information from a research centre and a government office explained additional variance in comprehension. In step three, the degree to which they based their trustworthiness ratings on document type, publisher, and author explained additional variance. Thus, different aspects of source evaluation independently predicted the comprehension of multiple documents.

Remembering who said what: Effects of source credibility and content consistency

Rouet, Jean-François LMDC, CNRS - University of Poitiers, Poitiers, France *Le Bigot, Ludovic* LMDC, CNRS - University of Poitiers, Poitiers, France *Coutieras, Anthony* LMDC, CNRS - University of Poitiers, Poitiers, France

According to the documents model theory, readers integrate information from multiple sources by connecting sources and contents through rhetorical predicates. We investigated the conditions of source separation in the memory for complex messages. We presented pairs of messages about everyday situations. Each message was attributed to a high or a low-authority source. Participants were probed for source-content connections. It was expected that source-content connections would be stronger in the case of (a) discrepant information across messages within a pair and (b) contrasted levels of authority within a pair of sources. The experiment was underway at the time of submitting.

How does that fit together? Fostering structural mapping processes to enhance the integration of information across texts

Stadtler, Marc Inst. für Psychologie, Universität Münster, Münster, Germany *Bromme, Rainer* Psychology Department, University of Muenster, Muenster, Germany

Readers of multiple online-documents are frequently required to pay attention to intertextual relationships to be able to detect inconsistencies or corroborate claims. We tested the hypothesis that readers' attention to intertextual relationships can be enhanced by providing them with ontological salient categories along which they can compare documents. 40 students with low prior knowledge read 15 websites that contained conflicting evidence about a medical topic. Participants were either provided with salient ontological categories or worked without external support. Results show that the availability of ontological categories enhanced knowledge acquisition and the number of intertextual references made while thinking aloud.

Epistemic processing of multiple documents

Richter, Tobias Psychology Department, University of Cologne, Cologne, Germany

Multiple documents dealing with the same issue from different perspectives require comprehenders to identify and evaluate arguments and to integrate conflicting information into a coherent situation model. The present experiments used multiple documents about science topics to investigate how epistemic processes and their representational outcomes are affected by the order in which the documents are received, the presence of evidential markers, and comprehenders' prior knowledge. The results demonstrate that the ability to construct an adequate situation model across multiple documents critically depends on epistemic processes such as monitoring incoming information for plausibility and internal consistency.

Effect of epistemological beliefs on processing complex documents

Vidal-Abarca, Eduardo Dept. of Psychology, University of Valencia, Valencia, Spain *Gil, Laura* Psychology Department, University of Valencia, Valencia, Spain *Salmeron, Lalo* Psychology Department, University of Valencia, Valencia, Spain *Bråten, Ivar* Institute for Educ. Research, University of Oslo, Oslo, Norway *Strømsø, Helge* Institute for Educ. Research, University of Oslo, Oslo, Norway

In two experiments we studied the effect of reader's epistemological beliefs (EB) on the on-line processing of complex documents. In the first study, undergraduate students read various texts on climate change, to either summarizing them or writing an argumentative essay. Students with

sophisticated EB on 'certainty' learnt more from the argumentative task, whereas those with naive EB learnt more from summarizing. In a second study, students read two texts provided with a graphical overview depicting the texts structure. Students with sophisticated EB on 'justification' attended the overview for more time at the beginning of the reading, which improved their comprehension.

S-293: Human-machine-interaction (Part III): Human factors in transportation systems

Mark Vollrath (chair)

Intelligent transportation systems are increasingly introduced in modern vehicles and change the role and tasks of drivers. Mobile (e.g. nomadic devices) and stationary (e.g., navigation systems) information systems contribute to this change. The symposium addresses problems and solutions with regard to the human-machine-interaction in vehicles. On the one hand, assistance and automation may substantially reduce human error. On the other hand, distraction by additional information, system failures and inadequate warnings may lead to new errors and may reduce acceptance of these systems. It will be discussed how to handle these problems by way of the design of the human-machine interaction.

Drivers' mental representation of a traffic situation – Influencing factors

Krems, Josef Allgemeine Psychologie, Psychologisches Institut, Chemnitz, Germany *Baumann, Martin* Allgemeine Psychologie, Psychologisches Institut, Chemnitz, Germany *Roesler, Diana* Allgemeine Psychologie, Psychologisches Institut, Chemnitz, Germany

Situation awareness refers to the perception and interpretation of the current driving situation. If secondary tasks performed while driving impose a significant load on visual attention and WM, then situation awareness should be impaired. In a first experiment we evaluated the visual and WM demand of secondary tasks. In a second experiment these evaluations were further investigated in a simulator study. The results show that both cognitively and visually demanding tasks interfere with the maintenance of a correct situation model in WM. However, visually demanding tasks do not always seem to interfere with visual perception processes.

Online detection of driver distraction

Blaschke, Christoph Human Factors Institute, Universität Bundeswehr, Neubiberg, Germany *Färber, Berthold* Institut für Arbeitswissenscha, Universität der Bundeswehr Mün, Neubiberg, Germany *Limbacher, Reimund* I/EF-56, AUDI AG, Ingolstadt, Germany

Distraction is one of the most common reasons for traffic accidents. Although much is known about the mental processes of distraction, there are only a few attempts to build up a system which is able to detect distraction online. To define functional requirements and find out easy measurable indicators an experiment in a real driving scenario was conducted. Meanwhile behavioural data from the steering wheel, pedals and an eye-tracking system were synchronously captured. Based on these data the potential to recognize a distracted driver of each measured signal was examined, which can serve as good basis for a technical driver-attention-detection-system.

Is cognitive distraction a real problem?

Carsten, Oliver Institute for Transport Studie, University of Leeds, Leeds, United Kingdom

Based on recent studies such as the 100-car study of naturalistic driving carried out in the U.S., it has been argued that the only kind of driver distraction that causes safety problems is visual distraction. In other words non-visual, cognitive distraction is not observed as a precursor to traffic incidents and accidents. This paper argues that, although cognitive distraction may be harder to identify, it is indeed a real problem. It causes different impacts on the driving task, but is clearly identifiable in certain kinds of accidents. It is particularly relevant as a problem for elderly drivers.

Increasing safety may reduce comfort: A dilemma for advanced driver assistance systems

Vollrath, Mark Ingenieurspsychologie, Tech. Universität Braunschweig, Braunschweig, Germany

Advanced driver assistance systems (ADAS) can increase safety by alerts in dangerous driving situations. Early warnings are required so that the driver has sufficient time to react. However, these early warnings may annoy the driver. Two studies are presented to examine this for lane-keeping assistance: a driving simulator and a real driving study with haptic and acoustic lane-keeping assistance, respectively. Driving with both ADAS improved lane keeping quality. However, acceptance of the systems decreased. From the literature, similar effects are known for Intelligent Speed Adaptation systems. Adaptation to drivers' characteristics and the driving situation are discussed as possible solutions.

The effectiveness of multimodal collision warnings

Thüring, Manfred Inst. für Psychologie, Technische Universität Berlin, Berlin, Germany *Fricke, Nicola* Institut für Psychologie und A, Technische Universität Berlin, Berlin, Germany *De Filippis, Mónica* Institut für Psychologie und A, Technische Universität Berlin, Berlin, Germany

Collision warnings must enable drivers to react swiftly and appropriately to an extreme danger they are yet unaware of. To accomplish this, adequate signals must be chosen which prime them on the dangerous object and its relevant features. Empirical studies suggest that auditory icons as well as multimodal signals suit these requirements best. Nevertheless, it still remains unclear which combination of warning features is most effective. To clarify this issue, several combinations were tested in a driving simulator study in which participants were warned about collision dangers. Results showed that particular features of warnings were more effective than others.

Driver reactions to correct and false autonomous emergency braking

Sommer, Fanny CR/AEH3, Robert Bosch GmbH, Stuttgart, Germany *Engeln, Arnd* CR/AEH3, Robert Bosch GmbH, Stuttgart, Germany

To adequately design autonomous emergency braking systems, knowledge is required about the driver reactions that are provoked by such vehicle interventions in correct and false braking scenarios. Tests were conducted at test sites in September/October 2007 to investigate these driver reactions. The tests included correct and false autonomous braking scenarios. CAN bus data and subjective ratings were collected. Results from the driver reactions in correct and false braking scenarios will be presented and discussed.

FP-169: Occupational health promotion

Mental health problems in a large German teacher population and effects of a prevention programm

Zimmermann, Linda Psychosomatische Medizin, Universitätsklinikum Freiburg, Freiburg, Germany Unterbrink, Thomas Psychosomatische Medizin, Universitätsklinikum Freiburg, Freiburg, Germany Pfeifer, Ruth Psychosomatische Medizin, Universitätsklinikum Freiburg, Freiburg, Germany Wirsching, Michael Psychosomatische Medizin, Universitätsklinikum Freiburg, Freiburg, Germany Bauer, Joachim Psychosomatische Medizin, Universitätsklinikum Freiburg, Freiburg, Germany

We applied several inventories (GHQ, SCL, MBI, Effort- Reward- Imbalance Questionnaire) in order to analyze the professional burden and mental health in 949 German teachers and 293 student teachers. Our results indicate high rates of mental health problems (e.g., 29.8% of teachers showed values beyond the GHQ cutoff of >=4). A regression analysis showed that, among a large number of potential influencing factors, adverse events such as aggressive pupil behaviour had the strongest impact on health parameters in teachers. Teachers who took part in an intervention program (CRT, 10 sessions of a manualized group program) responded with a significant improvement on several health- related parameters.

Workplace wellness programs: Investigating the applicability of self-determination theory and achievement goal theory

O'Connor, Christine School of Business, University of Ballarat, Ballarat, Australia

Due to high costs associated with work-time-lost linked to injury and ill health, many companies now offer workplace wellness program to their staff. The aim of this research is to examine two well known motivational theories, self-determination theory and achievement goal theory, and investigate their applicability to the domain of workplace wellness programs. 328 surveys were collected from two organisations with wellness programs. Results showed that more intrinsically motivated individuals scored higher on measures of competence and autonomy, providing support for the tenets of SDT but only partial support was found for the proposed relationship between SDT and achievement goal theory. Further research is discussed.

Stress management means and recreation during work hours in office work environment

Kuznetsova, Alla Faculty of Psychology, Moscow State University, Moscow, Russia

The aim of the empirical study - estimation of stress-management means' and recreation procedures' effects on mental states (MS) in office environment. 300 employees were involved. Methods: the multilevel technology of job analysis, including the stress factors inventory; subjective evaluation of MS was measured by the well-being, acute fatigue and state anxiety scales; coping strategies inventory was used, and the special checklist for investigation of recreation means. The results show the different effects of applied stress-management means on MS dynamics as well as work efficiency: the means targeted directly to the required mental state' achievement are the most effective.

Stress-reduction interventions: Perceived organizational support in Australian universities

Pignata, Silvia Dept. of Psychology, University of South Australia, Adelaide, Australia Winefield, Anthony Psychology, University of South Australia, Adelaide, Australia

Staff at 13 universities were surveyed in 2000 and 2003/04. After the 2000 survey, interventions were recommended to improve employee well-being. In 2003/04, staff were asked whether their university had undertaken any stress-reduction measures among its employees since the 2000 survey. Hierarchical regression analyses compared data from longitudinal participants (N = 872) answering 'yes' or 'no/don't know'. Those answering positively scored lower on psychological strain and higher on job satisfaction, organizational commitment, trust in senior management, and procedural fairness than those answering negatively. We conclude that perceived organizational support in implementing interventions is linked to improved well-being and organizational attitudes.

Stages-of-change in occupational health promotion

Hinrichs, Stephan Institute of Psychology, University of Freiburg, Freiburg, Germany Wilde, Barbara Institute of Psychology, University of Freiburg, Freiburg, Germany Bahamondes Pavez, Carolina Institute of Psychology, University of Freiburg, Freiburg, Germany Schüpbach, Heinz Institute of Psychology, University of Freiburg, Freiburg, Germany

Occupational health promotion often fails because of inadequate interventions. This study examined whether employees' readiness to modify health behavior in the workplace depends on the current stage-of-change (precontemplation, contemplation, action, maintenance) of the individual employee. A questionnaire was used to measure the current stage-of-change of employees and their readiness to modify health behaviour. As expected, stages-of-change predict readiness for behavior modification. The results show that stages-of-change should be recognized as an important factor for occupational health promotion. Companies should use target group-specific strategies for planning health promotion programs in the workplace.

Professional deformations in heads of educational institutions and their prevention

Bondarchuk, Olena Dept. of Psychology, Central Inst. after Pedagog., Kiev, Ukraine

Objectives. To find out professional deformations in heads of educational institutions and ways of their prevention. Methods. The investigation was done on a sample of 215 heads of educational institutions using a specially developed questionnaire. Results. 67% of the respondents were found to be professionally deformed and had the following deformation components: 1) intolerance and aggression (23%); 2) self-sufficiency and slow down of professional and individual development, external locus of control (36%); 3) fixation on a manager's position and expansion of responsibilities beyond the professional competence (41%). Conclusions. A considerable number of the respondents are professionally deformed which calls for a development of a special deformation prevention course.

FP-170: Neuropsychology II

A powerful questionnaire-based screening tool for congenital prosopagnosia

Kennerknecht, Ingo Human Genetics, Westfälische Wilhelms Univ., Münster, Germany Wang, Hui Social Science Department, Chang Chun Taxation College, Chang Chun, People's Republic of China Elze, Tobias Institute for Mathematics, Max Planck Institute, Leipzig, Germany Welling, Brigitte Human Genetics, Westfälische Wilhelms Universi, Münster, Germany Wong, Virginia Department of Pediatrics, The University of Hong Kong, Hong Kong, People's Republic of China Liu, Jia Cognitive Neuroscience, Beijing Normal University, Beijing, People's Republic of China

Objective: Diagnosis of prosopagnosia is generally established by in-depth testing with standardized test batteries for visual cognition. As these time-consuming tests are not suitable for large scale screening, a questionnaire based screening was introduced. Methods: At 2 Chinese universities 2,000 questionnaires with a five-point-rating scale for 21 test items regarding facial and object recognition were distributed. Those students with the highest scores were then invited for diagnostic interview. Results and Conclusions: When starting with the highest scores, every 2nd student was a prosopagnosic. Among a total of 40 students who scored above 2 S.D. more than 1/4 (n=11, 27.5%) were prosopagnosics.

Memory systems during transient global amnesia

Marin, Eugenia Facultad de Psicologia, Universidad Autonoma de Madrid, Madrid, Spain Ruiz Vargas, José María Psicología Básica, Facultad de Psicología (UAM), Madrid, Spain

The aim of this study was to analyze the functioning of different memory systems during Transient Global Amnesia (TGA). Twenty TGA patients and twenty healthy volunteers, matched by age and educational level, were assessed with a broad battery of memory tests. The functioning of episodic, semantic, perceptual representation, and working memory systems was evaluated. Results revealed that episodic, semantic, and perceptual representation systems were significantly affected during the amnesic episode. Only short-term working memory, among the systems evaluated, was spared. Our results suggest that both explicit and implicit retrieval could be affected during TGA episodes.

Neuropsychological features of pathological gambling

Timpano Sportiello, Marco Psychiatry, University of Pisa, Pisa, Italy Conversano, Ciro Psychiatry, University of Pisa, Pisa, Italy Masini, Matteo Psychiatry, University of Pisa, Pisa, Italy

Pathological gambling is a nosographic category, object of many disputes; that is whether it belongs to impulse-control disorders or to obsessive-compulsive spectrum. Recently the role played by frontal functioning in this disease has been often stressed. Twenty-seven subjects suffering from pathological gambling have been examined by a wide-spectrum neuropsychological battery of executive functioning tests; that is WSCT, Gambling task, PM38, Towers of London, Trail Making Test, Verbal Judgments Test, Verbal Fluency Test (Phonetic and Semantic) and Stroop Colour Test. Results show abnormal performances in impulse inhibition skill and verbal abstraction, whereas selective attention and planning appear intact.

Comparison of cognitive disorders in schizophrenic patients with negative symptoms and patients with unipolar andogen psychotic depression

Rahimi Taghanaki, Changiz Clinical Psychology, Shiraz University, Shiraz, Islamic Republic of Iran

We examined whether cognitive disorders related to frontal lobe dysfunctions are specific to schizophrenia. 37 schizophrenic patients with negative symptoms and 27 andogen psychotic depressives completed a series of cognitive tests related to frontal lobe disorders. T test showed that Schizophrenic patients had significantly more problems than depressives only on Stroop (P<0.01) and verbal fluency test (P<0.001), but not on WCST and Turm von Hanoi. It seems such disorders could be seen in any other psychotic disorder. Probably the cognitive disorders in schizophrenia are related to other factors like the severity of clinical symptoms in the patients.

Gingko biloba extract (especially EGb 761®) in cognitive ageing: Specificity of neuropsychological improvement

Kaschel, Reiner Geriatrische Neuropsychologie, Universität Osnabrück, Osnabrück, Germany
Objective: To review the physiological changes underlying the clinical efficacy of Ginkgo biloba. Methods: We selected randomized controlled trials reporting specific neuropsychological changes. Effects in different cognitive domains are listed using a widely accepted taxonomy that further distinguishes dissociable aspects within domains. Results: The broadest database was available for EGb 761®, which shows most pronounced effects in speed-related components of working and long-term memory. Qualitative aspects of performance (e.g. error reduction) are improved in different domains. Conclusion: These findings are compatible with actions on a basic physiological level. Most beneficial effects are exerted on neuropsychological functions usually affected by aging.

Effects of Ginkgo biloba extract EGb 761® on cognition and quality of life in subjects with very mild cognitive impairment

Hoerr, Robert Clinical Research Department, Dr. Willmar Schwabe Pharma, Karlsruhe, Germany Grass-Kapanke, Brigitte Psychogeriatrisches Zentrum, Alexianer-Krankenhaus Krefeld, Krefeld, Germany Tribanek, Michael Clinical Research Department, Dr. Willmar Schwabe Pharma, Karlsruhe, Germany Kaschel, Reiner Geriatric Neuropsychology, University of Osnabrueck, Osnabrueck, Germany
Objective: To assess effects of EGb 761® on cognition and quality of life in subjects with very mild cognitive impairment. Methods: We randomized 296 subjects with cognitive complaints and low functioning in at least one cognitive test to double-blind treatment with 240 mg EGb 761® or placebo once daily for 12 weeks. Results: The intention-to-treat analysis showed significant improvements (p<0.05) beyond placebo effects for EGb 761® in measures of memory (recall and recognition), attention and perceived physical health. Cognitive effects were more pronounced in subjects with lower baseline function. Conclusion: EGb 761® improves cognitve function in very mild cognitive impairment.

FP-171: Neuroimaging

Study of local alterations in blood circulation of the brain in anxious patients before and after cognitive group therapy through radio isotopic studies in SPECT method in Taleghani Hospital, Tehran

Bahrainian, Seyyed Abdolmajid Psychology, Shaheed Beheshti University, Tehran, Islamic Republic of Iran Neshandar, Issa Psychology, Shaheed Beheshti University, Tehran, Islamic Republic of Iran
Abstract: Although anxiety is a factor of motivation, When extending beyond necessary, it becomes a factor of disorder in behavioral system. Methods:. In the present study the method of single photon emission computed tomography (SPECT) was used on patients with anxiety for the first time in Iran, in Taleghani hospital. The research is quasi –experimental with pretest and post-test with a single group, and devices such as: Self Assessment Anxiety Scale, single photon Emission computed tomography (SPECT), diagnosis by psychiatrists, and by clinical psychologists. Findings: There was a meaningful difference between the amount of blood in the left frontal lobe before and after group therapy.

Subcortical responses to colour and luminance in the human visual system as revealed by high-resolution functional imaging at 7T

Grüschow, Marcus Attention & Awareness, Max-Planck-Institut, Leipzig, Germany Stadler, Jörg Non-Invasive Imaging Lab, IfN, Magdeburg, Germany Tempelmann, Claus Neurology II, Otto-von-Guericke University, Magdeburg, Germany Heinze, Hans-Jochen Neurology II, Otto-von-Guericke University, Magdeburg, Germany Rieger, Jochem Neurology II, Otto-von-Guericke University, Magdeburg, Germany Speck, Oliver Biomedical Magnetic Resonance, Experimental Physics, Magdeburg, Germany Haynes, John-Dylan Large Scale Brain Signals, BCCN, Berlin, Germany
Here we investigated subcortical responses to colour and luminance stimuli in the human visual system. We recorded responses using ultra-high-field high-resolution functional imaging at 7T (resolution 1.38x1.38x1.5mm, TR=1s). Visual stimuli were hemifield-checkerboards modulated along two directions in cone-contrast-space with four contrast levels each. Monotonically increasing contrast response functions were obtained for colour and luminance stimuli in LGN and superior colliculus. The LGN was driven more strongly by luminance than colour contrast. The gain of luminance responses was sufficient for separating magno- and parvo-cellular subdivisions of the LGN. Thus, subcortical visual processing can be studied non-invasively in the human brain.

Attending or ignoring similar and dissimilar faces: Neural face selection in the visual stream and Fusiform Face Area (FFA)

Jansma, Bernadette M. Faculty of Psychology, Maastricht University, Maastricht, Netherlands Gentile, Francesco Faculty of Psychology, Maastricht University, Maastricht, Netherlands
We investigated selection of relevant faces among others and tested "biased competition" as a selection mechanism in FFA. We displayed pairs of pictures that either were similar (high competition) or dissimilar (low competition) in perceptual features. Participants either ignored both or attended one of the pictures in a 3T-fMRI blocked-design experiment. Next to an expected attention effect (BOLD-%-signal change attention>ignore in V1-V4-FFA, left/right), we observed a similarity effect in the ignore condition (dissimilar>similar in V4-VP-FFA, right/left), which was reversed in the attend condition (similar>dissimilar in V4 and VP, left). The results seem in line with biased competition and attentional load theories.

Imitation learning of nursing actions: A NIRS study with students and teacher

Saito, Hirofumi Nagoya, Japan Sshiraishi, Tomoko of Nursing and Health, Aichi Prefectural College, Nagoya, Japan Ito, Hiroshi Graduate School of Information, Nagoya University, Nagoya, Japan Oi, Misato Graduate School of Information, Nagoya University, Nagoya, Japan
Using 48 channel near-infrared spectroscopy, we measured the cortical activation in nursing students and their teacher while they observed and imitated videotaped nursing actions under two conditions: with or without a patient (P+, P-). The concentration changes in oxyHb in nursing students and the teacher in the P+ condition showed a significant correlation in Broadman's Area 6, but did not in the P- condition. The results suggest that the existence of a patient induces the upcoming action(s) and modulates the students' action plans to imitate the teacher's.

Task-induced deactivation of the prefrontal and parietal areas in the monkey: A PET study

Watanabe, Masataka of Neuroscience - Psychology, Tokyo Metropol Institute, Tokyo, Japan Kojima, Takashi Psychology, Tokyo Metropol Inst Neurosci, Tokyo, Japan Hikosaka, Kazuo Sensory Science, Kawasaki Univ Medical Welfare, Tokyo, Japan Tsutsui, Kenichiro Systems Neuroscience, Tohoku Univ, Sendai, Japan Tsukada, Hideo Central Research Laboratory, Hamamatsu Photonics, Hamamatsu, Japan Onoe, Hirotaka Functional Probe Research Lab, RIKEN Frontier System, Kobe, Japan
Human imaging studies have well documented that several brain areas are less active during the cognitive task performance than during the resting state. To examine whether similar task-induced deactivation is observed in the monkey brain, we conducted a PET study. We compared brain activity of the monkey during the working memory task performance with that during the resting state. During the task performance, medial and lateral prefrontal, anterior and posterior cingulate, and precuneus areas were less active than during the resting state. Thus, task-induced deactivation was observed in the monkey in similar brain areas as observed in the human.

FP-172: Metacognition, emotion, and problem-solving

"Learn to Think" Project (LTP): Introducing a systematic thinking cultivation curriculum

Hu, Weiping Educational Science Academy, Shanxi Normal University, Linfen, People's Republic of China Han, Qin Educational Science Academy, Shanxi Normal University, Linfen, Shanxi, People's Republic of China Zhang, Lei Educational Science Academy, Shanxi Normal University, Linfen, Shanxi, People's Republic of China Shan, Xinxin Educational Science Academy, Shanxi Normal University, Linfen, Shanxi, People's Republic of China Shi, Quanzhen Educational Science Academy, Shanxi Normal University, Linfen, Shanxi, People's Republic of China
"Learn to Think" Project is a serious of training curriculum intended to help students develop ability to think critically and creatively. The curriculum is designed for primary and secondary school students. Each grade, from first to eighth, has an activity manual detailing instructions for 18 activities and/or exercises specific to thinking skills involving observation, problem finding, concrete and abstract thinking, problem solving, and creative thinking. We started our experiment since 2003. There are more than 100 thousands students participated in the experiment. Preliminary results strongly indicated that the curriculum has very significant impact for all grades on thinking ability, creativity, problem finding ability, learning motivation and study method, and academic performance.

The effectiveness of mindfulness training in mental health promotion in the community

Yu, Nicky K.K. Dept. of Psychology, Chinese Univ. of Hong Kong, Hong Kong, China, People's Republic of : Hong Kong SAR Mak, Winnie W.S. Department of Psychology, The Chinese University of HK, Hong Kong, China, People's Republic of : Macao SAR
The effectiveness of a five-day mindfulness retreat conducted in Hong Kong in May 2007 was assessed. Based on 191 participants, results showed significant increases in the awareness of mindfulness, use of adaptive metacognitive plans, empathy, self actualization, use of cognitive coping methods, and decreases in symptoms of depression, anxiety, and stress. Findings support the effectiveness of using mindfulness to reduce psychological distress in non-therapeutic setting. Possible mechanisms of mindfulness were also tested with partial support in the study.

Use of metacognitive strategies in high and low critical thinking performance: A think-aloud study

Ku, Kelly Yee Lai Dept. of Psychology, University of Hong Kong, Hong Kong, China, People's Republic of : Hong Kong SAR

We examined the role of metacognitive strategies in critical thinking. A total of 138 Chinese undergraduates were assessed on verbal-cognitive ability, critical thinking disposition, and critical thinking performance using Halpern's Critical Thinking Assessment Using Everyday Scenarios (HCTAES). Subsequently ten participants with comparable cognitive ability and critical thinking disposition but with different levels of critical thinking performance (five scoring high and five scoring low on the HCTAES) were retested on thinking tasks with think-aloud procedures. Results indicated that good critical thinkers used more planning, monitoring, and evaluation strategies. Implications for theory development and enhancement of critical thinking are discussed.

Emotion and problem solving: A contribution

Clément, Evelyne Laboratoire Psy.Co (EA 1780), Université de Rouen, Mont Saint Aignan Cedex, France

The present study addresses the effects of failures and successes encountered over the course of a problem on physiological and expressive components of emotion. Nineteen female participants were asked to solve the five-disks version of the Tower of Hanoi problem. The spontaneous skin conductance activity and the facial expressions were recorded without interruption during the problem-solving activity. The specific patterns of emotional manifestations observed during the impasses and the subgoals achievements are interpreted within the framework of the Appraisal Theories and are discussed as reflecting the implication of emotion in a goal-oriented activity such as problem-solving.

Visual imagery and problem solving: Does affective states have any role to play

Singh, Tushar Department of Psychology, Allahabad University, Allahabad, India

Two experimental studies were carried out to explore the effect of affective states and imagery ability on participants' judgment about the usefulness of imagery in problem solving. A 2 * 2 (high and low imagery ability * positive and negative affective state) factorial design was used for the study. In the first study affective states were generated using narrative method and In the second study participants' success and failure on problem solving task resulted in positive and negative affective states. Results showed affective states is particularly important when it is generated from the feeling of success or failure.

Self-regulation and selective exposure: The impact of depleted self-regulation resources on confirmatory information processing

Fischer, Peter School of Psychology, University of Exter, Exeter, United Kingdom Greitemeyer, Tobias School of Psychology, University of Sussex, Brighton, United Kingdom Frey, Dieter Inst. für Sozialpsychologie, Universität München, München, Germany

The present research investigates the impact of self-regulation resources on confirmatory information evaluation and search. Four studies employing different decision cases consistently found that individuals with depleted self-regulation resources exhibited a stronger tendency for confirmatory information processing than non-depleted individuals. Alternative explanations for this effect based on processes of ego-threat, cognitive load, and mood could be ruled out. Mediational analyses suggested that individuals with depleted self-regulation resources experienced increased levels of

commitment to their own standpoint, which resulted in increased confirmatory information processing. In sum, the impact of ego-depletion on confirmatory information search seems to be more motivational rather than cognitive in nature.

FP-173: Moral emotions

Antecedents of moral emotions: An analysis guided by Heider's naive action analysis

Rudolph, Udo Inst. fur Psychologie, Techn. Universität Chemnitz, Chemnitz, Germany Angermann, Nadine Institut fur Psychologie, TU Chemnitz, Chemnitz, Germany Schulz, Katrin Institut fur Psychologie, TU Chemnitz, Chemnitz, Germany

In two studies, the cognitive antecedents of moral emotions are analyzed by means of Heider's (1958) concepts of ought (i.e., normative information), goal attainment and trying. In both studies, participants evaluated situations characterized by different combinations of these concepts. As dependent variables, participants reported whether they experience moral observer emotions (admiration, anger, contempt, disgust, envy, indignation, jealousy, pride, respect, Schadenfreude, and sympathy) and moral actor emotions (embarrassment, guilt, pride, regret, and shame). ANOVAS reveal that Heider's concepts explain impressive amounts of variance in the emotion ratings. Furthermore, cluster analyses confirm that the respective moral emotions map into theoretically meaningful clusters.

Why are we grateful? Pharmacy bonus experiment

Szczesniak, Malgorzata Dept. of Psychology, Catholic University Lublin, Lublin, Poland Zaleski, Zbigniew Dept. of Psychology, Catholic University Lublin, Lublin, Poland

Gratitude is a common emotion that an individual may experience towards a benefactor. In a pharmacy-based real-life experiment and its paper-and-pencil version it was shown that the larger the gift (50% discount on the price of a mediaction vs. 15%) and the greater the effort of the donor (money earned through personal work vs. money received from a wealthy company) then the stronger the gratitude from the recipient. The study provides evidence that gratitude is positively associated with moral and religious values, emotional intelligence, extraversion and agreeableness, while being negatively related to hedonistic values and neuroticism. The results are discussed within the attributional theory.

Moral sphere development in pre-school age

Sharkova, Svitlana Dept. of Foreign Languages, National Metallurgical Academy, Dnipropetrovsk, Ukraine

The specific objective of our study is to research moral sphere development in pre-school age and the factors that influence child's moral choice. Two groups of children (4-5 and 5-6 years old) were suggested eight different situations and the results of the interview revealed the importance of aspects connected with emotional and intellectual sphere development in moral choice. E.g., sometimes children were intent to use their intellect in order to break moral standards and to hide it. As a conclusion we suggest the approaches to improve child's ability to -regulate his/her own emotions, - understand causative factors and others.

Why do I feel so bad?: Autobiographical recollections of moral emotions

Schulz, Katrin Inst. für Psychologie, Techn. Universität Chemnitz, Chemnitz, Germany Angermann, Nadine Institut fuer Psychologie, TU Chemnitz, Chemnitz, Germany Rudolph, Udo Institut fuer Psychologie, TU Chemnitz, Chemnitz, Germany

Two studies analyze the cognitive antecedents and social functions of moral emotions. Autobiographical recollections of moral actor emotions and moral observer emotions were generated by semi-structural interviews, and analyzed by means of ANOVAs and multiple regressions. As dependent variables, participants assessed Heider's (1958) concepts of ought (normative information), goal attainment, and trying, as well as hedonic quality, motivational impact on self-regulation, and regulative social functions (e.g., reward vs. punishment). Results provide strong evidence for a comprehensive classification of moral emotions in terms of Heider's naive action analysis and are discussed with respect to evolutionary explanations of moral emotions.

The psychology of sperm donation: Implications for donor recruitment

Riggs, Damien School of Psychology, South Australia, Australia

Objectives: Little research has been conducted on sperm donor's experiences in Australia. This project aimed to explore the ways in which men who act as sperm donors negotiate their identities in regards to their own families, the families to whom they donate, and their own sense of self. Methods: Individual interviews were undertaken with men in South Australia. Results: A discursive analysis of the interviews highlights the complex range of emotions that shape men's experiences of sperm donation. Conclusions: The results provide clear implications for the recruitment of sperm donors in Australia and the further development of guidelines for ethical practice.

The relation of shame with anger, hostility, physical and verbal aggression between collage students in Tehran

Pourshahriari, Mahsima Dept. of Psychology, Alzahra University, Tehran, Islamic Republic of Iran

The relation of shame, anger, aggression and hostility has been the focus of considerable theoretical discussion, but empirical funding has been inconsistent. Two hundred and seventy undergraduate students of Tehran universities have been chosen according to a multi-stage cluster sampling. The self - conscious Affect Test and the Buss-Perry aggression Questionnaire have been used. The results of seven hypothesis considered Indicated that there were a significant relation between shame, anger, hostility and aggression in both sexes. There were also a positive significant difference between hostility and all other variables in The study except verbal aggression. Key words: shame, hostility, anger, aggression, sex.

FP-174: Human resources and job performance

Reversals in performance evaluation: A range theory perspective

Wong, Kin Fai Ellick Management of Organizations, HKUST, Hong Kong, China, People's Republic of : Hong Kong SAR Kwong, Jessica Y.Y. Marketing, CUHK, Hong Kong, China, People's Republic of : Macao SAR Ng, Carmen K. Management of Organizations, HKUST, Hong Kong, China, People's Republic of : Macao SAR

This paper examines preference reversals in performance evaluation (i.e., one ratee is preferred in one condition and the other one is preferred in the other condition, although all relevant performance information is identical in the two conditions). Results from three studies showed that the perceived difference in performance between two ratees was greater when the information was presented in a narrow range than in a wide range context. This range effect led to evaluation reversals when evaluating two ratees with tradeoffs between performance attributes across ratees. This pattern did not occur when global range information was presented.

Performance in low-quality jobs

Bayona, Jaime Andrés Social Psychology, University of Barcelona, Barcelona, Spain
Low-quality employment is an area that has not been sufficient studied by the Work-Organizational Psychology (WOP) despite around 30% of the world labour force work under these conditions. This study reviews the usefulness of the traditional methods and indicators used by WOP to measure the performance in the low-quality job population (especially for workers outside formal organizations). A comparison is made using subjective and objective measures of job performance at the organizational, group and individual level. Results showed the need to adjust the job-performance assessment methodology for this population. Implications for employability and social policies will be discussed.

A measure of Psychological Capital (PsyCap) and its relationship with work performance, work well-being and social well-being

Siu, Oi-Ling Sociology and Social Policy, Lingnan University, Hong Kong, China, People's Republic of : Hong Kong SAR
This paper aimed to develop and validate a PsyCap measure (Luthans, 2002), and examine its relationships with outcomes. Data were collected among health care workers in Hong Kong and PRC by a longitudinal survey (N = 773 & 287 respectively). The results obtained by CFA supported a 22-item PsyCap scale measuring: self-efficacy, optimism, hope, and resiliency. Hierarchical regression analyses showed that PsyCap (Wave 1) predicted better work performance (job performance, injuries at work), better work well-being (job satisfaction, physical/psychological symptoms), and better social well-being (work-life balance, quality of life) (Wave 2). The construct and criterion validity of PsyCap were demonstrated.

Relation of general aptitudes and job performance in Saipa car company

Oreyzi, Hamid Reza Pschology, Isfahan University, Isfahan, Islamic Republic of Iran Amiri, A. tehran, Saipa car company, iran, Islamic Republic of Iran Moradi, A. tehran, Saipa car company, iran, Islamic Republic of Iran Golparvar, Mohsen psychology, Khorasgan University, iran, Islamic Republic of Iran
Job performance of 300 personnel in saipa car company was obtained as an archival data. Relation between general aptitudes which measure by GATB and performance was significant. Multiple regression analysis show significant relation between certain combination of aptitudes and job performance. Recommendations based on findings presented.

Approaches to developing human capital in manufacturing industries

Muthuraj, Birasnav Management Studies, IIT Roorkee, Roorkee, India Rangnekar, Santosh Management Studies, IIT Roorkee, Roorkee, India
Emphasizing human capital development strategies makes modern organizations being different from the last millennium organizations. The purpose of this paper is to explore the extent to which manufacturing industries give importance to identified factors influencing human capital creation practices with reference to a survey conducted among 70 Indian companies. The survey questionnaire comprises of these factors classified under human resource practices, leadership, and knowledge management. This paper finds that leadership styles and appraising performance play a leading role in human capital development. Companies take major efforts to create such capital by

integrating leadership with knowledge management and human resource practices.

Effects of job attitudes and identity resources on intentions of professional maintenance among women and men in non traditional careers

Vonthron, Anne-Marie Dépt. de Psychologie, Université Bordeaux 2, Bordeaux, France Becker, Maja Département de Psychologie, Université Bordeaux 2, Bordeaux, France Lagabrielle, Christine Département de Psychologie, Université Bordeaux 2, Bordeaux, France Pouchard, Dominique CROP, AFPA, BEGLES, France
This research examined the effects of job attitudes (job satisfaction, organizational and trade affective commitment) and of identity resources (job self-efficacy, perception of gender identity conflict) on intentions of current job maintenance and of trade maintenance. A survey was conducted among 131 women and 61 men (in male versus female-dominated occupations). Regression analyses showed that the intention of staying in the current job was more influenced by the perception of the job context among men than among women. The intention of staying within the trade was more affected by the perception of personal identity resources among women than among men.

FP-175: Human-environment interaction

Lighting for effect: A cross-cultural comparison of the influence of types of light in spiritual and secular environments

Augustin, Sally PlaceCoach, Inc., Holland, USA
Physical environments have a profound effect on human experience, both directly and through nonverbal communication. The psychological influences of daylight and artificial light on people in contemporary spiritual and secular spaces was investigated cross-culturally via in-person interviews of individuals of varied religious orientations and national cultures, site visits, and content analysis of relevant visual and written materials. This investigation revealed that experiencing daylight has a similar expansive effect in both spiritual and secular settings. Conversely, current modes of use of artificial light have more variable influence on mood and symbolic attributions. Designers must consider these diverse effects to optimize place design.

Linking place attachment with social identity orientation: An examination of the relationship between place attachment, social identity orientation and integration to city

Karakus, Pelin Dept. of Social Psychology, Ege University, Izmir, Turkey Göregenli, Melek Social Psychology, Ege University, Izmir, Turkey
The general purpose of the study was to investigate the relations between attachment and social identity orientation as related to city integration. The study was carried out by a field research with a sample of 237 participants. The Urban-Identity Scale (Lalli, 1992), The Aspects of Identity Questionnaire (Cheek, Trop, Chen & Underwood, 1994) and other concerned scales were used in order to collect data. The results revealed significantly different place attachment levels depending on the living area. The main conclusion of the study is the social identity orientation is a significant predictor of the place attachment level. The group who has a higher level of social identity orientation has a higher place attachment.

Physical activities for senior citizens: An analysis of the impacts resulting from the project Academia da Cidade in Camaragibe

Santos, Azenildo Educação Física, Faculdade Maurício de Nassau, Recife, Brazil Menezes, Vilde Educação Física, Universidade do Porto, Recife, Brazil
Our objective was to analyze the impacts resulting from physical activities in open spaces in the city, conducting documentary analysis, semi-structured interviews and focal groups. The results: 1) Civic and grassroot participation is a fundamental element and is relevant in the qualification process; 2) Public users there were a 39% reduction in the use of medication, a 72% increase in people's physical well-being; and 86% increase in the sense of belonging and happiness. Conclusions: a) Civic and grassroot participation is fundamental in the structuring and control of policies: b) There is a growing awareness of the concept of healthy communities.

Mind, body, environment: An integrative approach

Imamichi, Tomoaki Environmental Psychology, City University of New York, Hoboken, USA
This project attempts an integrative approach by examining destination marathon runners, whose activity highlights and integrates mental, physical and environmental components that need to be successfully negotiated. This project also attempts to resolve the apparent paradox of a leisure activity done for fun and pleasure, taken seriously and involving pain. The integrative approach includes quantitative and qualitative measures, investigating how participants have rated their experiences, and why participants have rated their experiences that way. In addition to theoretical and methodological merits, this project hopes to shed light on personal and environmental factors contributing to satisfying and meaningful experiences.

FP-176: Learning in groups

Can advanced digital video technologies support group knowledge processes in complex collaborative design tasks?

Zahn, Carmen Knowledge Media Res. Center, Tübingen, Germany Hesse, Friedrich W. Institut für Wissensmedien, Tübingen, Germany Pea, Roy SCIL, Stanford University, Stanford, CA, USA Rosen, Joe SCIL, Stanford University, Stanford, CA., USA
The research to be presented here relates to the affordances of digital media and their possible implicit impacts on cognitive processing and group discussions during knowledge construction. In an experiment (N=24 dyads), we investigated effects of using an advanced digital video technology as a cognitive tool supporting the accomplishment of a collaborative 'visual design' task. Two conditions were compared, one with activity support by an advanced video tool, one control condition using a comparably simple technology. Results revealed significant effects concerning design strategies, individual knowledge test scores and skills transfer. Practical implications for computer-supported learning at school are discussed.

Impact of culture, personality and digital media on the virtual classroom

Hogg, Jerri Lynn Communication Management, Bay Path College, West Hartford, USA
Language, culture, and personality play a significant role in communication and learning behaviors. The study examined the impact of culture, personality types, and digital media preference on the virtual classroom. A group of African American college students were given the MMPI-2, a demographic information assessment, and an electronic communication survey. Results indicate that certain technologies can facilitate learning and remove some communication barriers across cultures and

personality types. I will demonstrate that, aided with this knowledge, educators can plan more effective ways to utilize technology to reach out to various groups.

Does participation in groups problem solving setting influence individual learning?
Lepage, Beatriz Los Chaguaramos, Centr. University of Venezuela, Caracas, Venezuela
This study examines instructional design model based on cooperative learning focused on the link between cognitive and social processes. Teachers and students from different programs are involved in solve community problems and sharing naive and academic knowledge. Results indicated that 60% of the participants showed cooperative behaviors, 25% presented and solved problems without significant social involvement in cooperative solutions, and 15% showed no interest in solving the problems. This framework has respect for participant's backgrounds, a belief in skills success of all participants, learning as a social process, and learning as an active and constructive process of knowledge acquisition

Behavioral strategies of pupils with high levels of anxiety in the situation of the group interaction
Nechaeva, Raisa Psychology, State University HSE, Moscow, Russia Skatova, Anna Psychology, Lomonosov State University, Moscow, Russia
Anxiety predicts low performance in the variety of educational domains (Sarason, 1960). We aimed to study the relationship between anxiety and behavior in group discussion. 55 high-school students completed MAS (Taylor, 1953) and participated in discussion. We found that both pupils, who demonstrated low and high anxiety levels, can be equally successful in group discussion. It is contradictory to the traditional view that anxious pupils are less prosperous in the situation of group interaction. The findings are discussed in regard to behavioral strategies utilized by pupils with the high anxiety levels in classroom interaction.

Implementing an online monitoring instrument for supporting motivated learning in groups: Experiences from German and Dutch social science students
Martens, Thomas Internation. Bildungsforschung, Deutsches Institut für, Frankfurt, Germany de Brabander, Cornelis Social and Behavior Sciences, Leiden Unversity, AK Leiden, Netherlands Martens, Rob Social and Behavior Sciences, Leiden Unversity, AK Leiden, Netherlands
Previous studies show that an online monitoring tool for reflecting feelings of relatedness, autonomy, competence and interest can compensate motivational loss in learning groups. This hypothesis was tested with social science students learning statistics at university by conducting three studies in Germany and Netherland: a randomized control group experiment (n=128), a comparative study (n=64) and an implementation study (n=100). Statistical analysis shows a significant effect of the instrument regarding motivational outcome just in the first study. Nevertheless, with interview data from the third study guidelines for implementation were identified concerning proper embedding of the instrument in the course framework.

The potentials of ECAM model of mediation in the classroom
Abdul Rahim, Fauziah Dept. of Education, Universiti Utara Malaysia, Kedah, Malaysia
This qualitative study is about building a community of learners that places mediation as central in the learning and teaching of English and Mathematics in a second language context. The study was conducted within a period of three months in Malaysia where I worked with two teachers and two groups of pupils from a Year One class

whereby intense classroom observations, classroom discourse and dialogic discussions with teachers and pupils were gathered. Microgenetic analyses of transcripts revealed four typology of mediation that emerged from the data: environmental mediation, cognitive mediation, affective mediation and metacognitive mediation (i.e. ECAM model of mediation).

FP-177: Gender issues

Distribution of domestic tasks and its perceived fairness: A cross-cultural analysis
Toth, Katalin Social Psychology, University of Nevada, Reno, Reno, USA
The present study examined the cultural effects on the relationship between domestic tasks' distribution and its perceived fairness. Married people from the 2002 ISSP were selected. Hofstede's individualism indices were added. Multilevel modeling was used to analyze two-level variables – cultural and individual variables. Results showed that the higher the level of individualism the bigger the differences between wives' level of perceived fairness and husbands' level of perceived fairness, women always perceiving the division of labor as less fair, even when both contributed equally. In conclusion, culture alone and in interaction with individual characteristics affected people's perception of tasks' distribution fairness.

When Laura and Lukas learn: Stereotype threat and processes of knowledge acquisition
Appel, Markus Bildung und Psychologie, Universität Linz, Linz, Austria Kronberger, Nicole Education and Psychology Dept., University of Linz, Linz, Austria
Stereotypes are harmful when they predict inferior academic performance of a group because victims tend to behave accordingly: stereotype threat affects test performance. Little is known, however, whether and in what ways the phenomenon applies to processes of knowledge acquisition. In this contribution we address this lacuna. While women are seen to be more successful learners in general, they are assumed to underperform when it comes to matters of science and technology (study 1, N = 1058). Multivariate analyses of two further experiments (N = 40; N = 60) document and specify the effect of stereotype threat on learning processes.

Liked women, valued men: Range and limits of the "women are wonderful effect"
Ebert, Irena Dorothee Inst. für Psychologie, Universität Jena, Jena, Germany Steffens, Melanie Caroline Psychological Department, University of Jena, Jena, Germany
On a general evaluative dimension, women are judged more positively than men, both when applying direct (questionnaires) as well as indirect (reaction-time based) measurement tools. The present work aims at illuminating the determinants and generality of the "female preference". In a series of experiments (total N > 500) it was shown that the female preference is partially caused by stereotypic associations of women and warmth. A "male preference" emerges when the general evaluative dimension is replaced by a value based dimension, indicating that women are judged more positively but men are seen as more valuable.

Gender-(a)typical behavior and status: Evaluation of leaders, subordinates, and job-applicants
Michel, Birgit University of Geneva, NCCR Affective Sciences, Geneva, Switzerland Schmid Mast, Marianne Department of Work and Organiz, University of Neuchatel, Neuchâtel, Switzerland
Intending to expand role congruity theory of prejudice toward female leaders (Eagly & Karau, 2002) we hypothesised that (1) in role-incongruent situations individuals are evaluated more favorably when behaving according to their gender role (2)

whereas in role-congruent situations this effect is significantly smaller. 285 students evaluated 16 person descriptions varying on status, gender, and gender-typicality of behavior. Findings support our second hypothesis and yield contradictory results concerning the first hypothesis indicating that for female leaders the gender role but for male subordinates the status role becomes salient. Results of a current study applying this paradigm to job-interview-situations are presented.

Ambivalent sexism in Roman Catholic Poland: where values and equality conflict
Pietrzak, Janina Faculty of Psychology, University of Warsaw, Warsaw, Poland
The subjective positivity associated with being the target of benevolent sexism appears far removed from traditional views of sexism as a negative, devaluing attitude towards women. Benevolent sexism beliefs, however, are based in values that promote and perpetuate gender inequality in society. In Poland, many of these positive attributes of womanhood are emphasized and encouraged by the Roman Catholic Church, an institution that dismisses hostile sexist attitudes while being characterized by strict inequality between the sexes. The studies (Study 1: correlational, Study 2: priming) presented here investigate the relationships between religion, values and ambivalent sexism.

Stereotype threat, intellectual performance and affirmative action in Brazil
Pereira, Marcos Dept. of Psychology, Universidade Federal da Bahia, Salvador, Brazil Silva, Joice Psychology, Universidade Federal da Bahia, Salvador, Brazil
This paper intents to evaluate the intellectual performance of the students favored by affirmative action program. The main hypothesis is that the performance of the students favored by university quotas would be inferior to the others, due to the stereotypes' threat situation. The research was conduced with 120 students. The instrument employed to measure the intellectual performance was a questionnaire with 21 questions about logic. The results demonstrate that the students in stereotypes threat experimental condition achieve a lower performance, but suggests that the negative effects of the stereotypes' threat can be reverted in special conditions.

FP-178: Romantic relationships

The study of the relationship between identity styles, sex roles and sex with spouse selection in single university students
Abedi, Fariba Ward of Psychology, Dr. Hamidiye Clinic, Tehran, Islamic Republic of Iran Shahraray, Mehrnaz faculty of psychology, teacher training university, tehran, Islamic Republic of Iran
the Relationship of Identity Styles, Sex Roles and Sex on Spouse Selection investigated. Three measures of Identity Style (ISI- 6G) Sex Roles (Bem, 1974) and Spouse Selection Criterias were administered to 196 university students. A three way analysis of variance indicated significant interaction effects of identity styles, sex roles and sex on some factor of spouse selection criterias. In the second part of this research, the relationship between sex roles and sex, identity style and sex roles also sex and identity style was investigated. Resuls showed a signsficant relationship in all. Sex differences in Spouse Selection, indicated significant differences between males and females in some factor of spouse selection criterias.

Dating experiences and attitudes towards romantic relationships among Colombians adolescents

Caycedo, Claudia Psychology, Fundación Universitaria Konrad, Bogotá, Colombia Berman, Steven L Psychology, University of Central Florida, Daytona Beach, USA Ovieda, Ana María Psychology, Fundación Universitaria Konrad, Bogotá, Colombia Suarez, Ingrid Psychology, Fundación Universitaria Konrad, Bogotá, Colombia Martin, Angie Psychology, Fundación Universitaria Konrad, Bogotá, Colombia Cubides, Inghry Psychology, Fundación Universitaria Konrad, Bogotá, Colombia

Existing associations between experiences in romantic relationships and attitudes towards love of 223 adolescents aged 15 to 20 years from Bogotá are analyzed. Data were analyzed using correlational statistics and the one-way ANOVA. Significant differences were found among age and gender groups regarding the Beliefs Scale towards love, and gender differences concerning attitudes towards love and involvement. Finally, it was found a positive correlation between identity and intimacy with friendly, altruistic and romantic love as well as a negative correlation between intimacy and ludus love

The study of Iranian couple's love relationship and it's relation with marital satisfaction and demographic variables

Ghamarani, Amir Psychology, University of Isfahan, Isfahan, Islamic Republic of Iran Sharyati, Maryam psychology, university of isfahan, isfahan, Islamic Republic of Iran

The purposes of this study were: 1-The investigation of Iraninan couple's relationship based on sternberg model. Data selected from 66 couples (young and middle years) chosen with availiable sampling method result: 1- there are significant differences between young and middle years couples in commitment and passion, but no in intimacy. 2- in middle years couples, commitment and in young couples, passion were pre-eminent component. 3- love relationship are predicted by level of education, Job and during of marriage, but not with age and nomber of members of couple's family. 5-love relationship predicted the marital satisfaction in terms of following component : marital communication, sexual relation, and personality issue.

Is love blind?: Attractiveness ratings by self, partner and others and the outcome of dating relationships 25 years later

Hill, Charles Dept. of Psychology, Whittier College, Whittier, USA Peplau, Letitia Anne Psychology, UCLA, Los Angeles, CA, USA Rubin, Zick lawyer, private practice, Newton, MA, USA

Physical attractiveness ratings of self and dating partner, plus a panel's ratings of their photographs, were available for both members of 173 couples from the Boston Couples Study. For both sexes, ratings of dating partner were higher than self ratings, which were higher than the panel's ratings. For women only, the difference between their rating of their dating partner and the panel's rating was correlated with their Rubin Love Scale score and with a Romanticism Scale, but not with eventual marriage. However, women with low self ratings were more likely to marry their partner and remain married 25 years later.

Sexual and marital satisfaction in the transition to parenthood

Oronoz, Beatriz Dept. of Psychology, Univ. of the Basque Country, San Sebastian, Spain Alonso Arbiol, Itziar Department of Psychology, Univ. of the Basque Country, San Sebastian, Spain Gorostiaga, Arantxa Department of Psychology, Univ. of the Basque Country, San Sebastian, Spain Balluerka, Nekane Department of Psychology, Univ. of the Basque Country, San Sebastian, Spain

The aim of this study was to analyze the changes experienced by parents in their sexual and marital satisfaction after the birth of the first baby. The sample was composed by 228 married or cohabiting heterosexual individuals (114 women and 114 men) who were assessed with the Spanish version of the MSI-R in two moments: in the last months of their first pregnancy, and four months after the delivery. Results showed that sexual and marital satisfaction diminished for both men and women, and that sexual satisfaction is more related to marital satisfaction for men.

The function of similarity in relationship regulation

Wrzus, Cornelia Inst. für Psychologie, Universität Potsdam, Potsdam, Germany Lang, Frieder R. Inst. für Psychogerontologie, Universität Erlangen-Nürnberg, Erlangen, Germany Neyer, Franz J. Psychology, University Potsdam, Potsdam, Germany

The Evolutionary Model of Relationship Regulation proposes Closeness Regulation and Reciprocity Monitoring as central mechanisms in relationships. Also, similarity correlates positively with emotional closeness and cooperation. The assumed mediational function of similarity was tested in an internet study with 455 young adults and a dyadic study with 171 middle-aged couples. Participants rated the relationships of their ego-centered networks on emotional closeness, reciprocity and three types of similarity. Multilevel mediational analyses confirmed similarity as a mediator in both samples. Physical, skill and subjective similarity mediated large parts of the association between genetic relatedness and emotional closeness, but were of smaller importance for reciprocity.

FP-179: Psychotherapy - Research and treatment methods VI

The case study of Self-Active Relaxation Therapy (SART) for people with physical, developmental and severely mental and physical disabilities

Ki, Heyoung Faculty of Human Relation, Fukuoka Jo Gakuin University, Fukuoka, Japan Ohno, Hiroyuki Faculty of Human Relation, Fukuoka Jo Gakuin University, Fukuoka-shi, Japan

In Japan, Dousa-hou (Naruse, 1975) has been a popular method of psychological rehabilitation for people with disabilities over the past 30 years. SART (Ohno, 2003) is a progressed method based on the theory of Dousa-hou. In this presentation, the characteristics of method and process of SART will be outlined, including outcome data of 30 cases, with 10 physical, 10 developmental and 10 severely mental and physical disabilities. These cases had participated in an intensive SART therapy program, and showed remarkable changes after a week. The effectiveness of SART with 30 cases will be reported with evaluating criteria and visual data.

Family systems coping with threatened illness: The use of therapeutic technique of eye movement desensitization and reprocessing (EMDR), in the psychological treatment protocol

Molero Zafra, Milagros Sintest Psychology, Valencia, Spain Pérez Marín, Marián Faculty of Psychology, C. University of Valencia, Valencia, Spain

When a threatened illness affects a person, the whole family system is seriously affected too. The illness produces deep effects on family members that could be traumatic for some of them. We developed a psychological treatment protocol that includes the EMDR technique that it's effective in the treatment of the emotional symptoms caused by situations of traumatic events. The combined approach that include EMDR and family systems therapy can result in profound changes for both the individual and the family (Kaslow and Shapiro, 2007). We present this protocol that includes both approaches to help families coping with the threatened illness.

The investigating of effectiveness of training relaxation without tension along with Biofeedback and EMDR on war veterans with PTSD

Sahragard Toghchi, Mehdi Dept. of Clinical Psychology, Shahed University, Tehran, Islamic Republic of Iran Roshan, Rasol clinical psychology, shahed university, tehran, Islamic Republic of Iran Ghaedi, Gholam Hosain clinical psychology, shahed university, tehran, Islamic Republic of Iran

Objectives: The aim of this study was to examine the effectiveness of training of Relaxation without tension along with Biofeedback and EMDR on war veterans withPost Traumatic Stress Disorder. Methods: In this research 20 war veterans with PTSD were selected availability sampling and divided into 3 groups of: training of Relaxation without tension along with Biofeedback (n=7), EMDR (n=7) and control group (n=6). Afterthat, experimental groups was attended in treatment sessions while control group didn't attend in any treatment session. Result: experimental groups has been found to be effective on PTSD among Iranian war veterans but there was no significance difference between two treatment method.

FP-180: Dietary behavior I

The dual-motivation model of unhealthy eating behavior

Ohtomo, Shoji Graduate School of Inf.Sci., Tohoku University, Sendai, Japan Hirose, Yukio Graduate School of Env.sStu., Nagoya University, Nagoya City, Japan

This study examined the determinants of dual motivation model of unhealthy eating behavior. 237 undergraduate students responded to a questionnaire measuring intentional motivation, impulsive motivation, descriptive norm, injunctive norm, availability, self efficacy and actual performance of snack eating and instant food eating. Our results indicated that both intentional motivation and impulsive motivation determined unhealthy eating behavior. Moreover, injunctive norm affected intentional motivation. Descriptive norm and availability influenced impulsive motivation and behavior. Furthermore, multiple-sample path analysis suggested that self efficacy moderates the effect of dual motivations on unhealthy eating behavior.

The presentation of 'pro-anorexia' in online group interactions

Gavin, Jeff Dept. of Psychology, University of Bath, Bath, United Kingdom

This project focuses on pro-anorexic identities in an online group setting. Specifically, it examines the presentation of pro-anorexia via an interpretive phenomenological analysis of postings to a 'pro-ana' online discussion forum. Analysis indicates that pro-anorexic identities are normalised and strengthened through the normalization of participants' 'pro-ana' thoughts and behaviours and the group bond created through sharing a 'secret identity'. This process renders participants less likely to reveal their pro-ana identity to friends and family in the real world. The implications of our findings are discussed in relation to the theory of identity demarginalisation.

FP-181: Developmental tasks and challenges in midlife I

Gains and losses related to menopause: An analysis within the framework of conservation of resources theory (COR) by S. E. Hobfoll

Bielawska-Batorowicz, Eleonora Inst. of Psychology, University of Lodz, Lodz, Poland Mikolajczyk, Marzena Institute of Psychology, University of Lodz, Lodz, Poland

Objectives: Menopausal transition was conceptualized within COR theory. It was hypothesized that (1) evaluation of gains and losses correlates with intensity of symptoms, (2) positive attitudes towards menopause correlate with higher evaluation of gains. Methods: Participants were 91 menopausal women. Menopause Representation Questionnaire by Hunter & O'Dea and Questionnaire of Evaluation of Resources by Dudek et al. were administered. Results: Evaluation of gains and losses was related to the use of hormonal replacement therapy. Women perceiving more gains during menopause reported less symptoms and expressed more positive attitudes towards menopause. Conclusions: COR theory provides meaningful framework for analysis of menopause.

Change for the better or change for the worse? Perceived changes as a consequence of an adverse life event and their associations with ruminative thoughts.

Leist, Anja Inst. für Psychologie, Universität Trier, Trier, Germany Filipp, Sigrun-Heide Department of Psychology, University of Trier, Trier, Germany

After the occurrence of an adverse life event, people experience positive and negative changes in their lives (e.g., losses in the occupational domain) and in perceived individual characteristics (e.g., gaining wisdom). In a questionnaire study with N=260 participants (aged 41 to 86 years; temporal distance of the event: one to 52 years), we examined Tait and Silver's (1989) assumption that ruminative thoughts about an adverse life event will persist as long as changes caused by the event are salient for the individual. Ruminative thoughts were not associated with perceived positive changes, but significantly associated with perceived negative changes.

An ecological understanding of stress and self esteem of divorced women in Malaysia

Juhari, Rumaya Human development & Family Stu, Universiti Putra Malaysia, Selangor, Malaysia Yaacob, Siti Nor Human development & Family, Universiti Putra Malaysia, Selangor, Malaysia Baharudin, Rozumah Human development & Family, Universiti Putra Malaysia, Selangor, Malaysia Kahar, Rojanah Human development & Family, Universiti Putra Malaysia, Selangor, Malaysia

The study aimed to determine the influences of family ecological processes on divorced women's stress level and self esteem. A total of 510 divorced women completed self-administered questionnaires measuring the respective variables. The findings indicate that stress level, family functioning, and boundary ambiguity are unique predictors of divorced women's self-esteem, (R2 = 0.38). As for stress level, the predictors are self-esteem, boundary ambiguity, support system, economic hardship and family functioning (R2= 0.39). The study concludes that divorced women's stress level and self esteem are highly influenced by the ecological processes within the self, family and environmental contexts.

FP-182: Dimensions of personality I

Personality and work values

Inceoglu, Ilke The Pavilion, SHL Group Limited, Thames Ditton, United Kingdom Warr, Peter Institute of Work Psychology, University of Sheffield, Sheffield, United Kingdom Bartram, Dave Research, SHL Group, Thames Ditton, United Kingdom

This paper examines conceptual and empirical links between people's values and their personality traits. Personality traits and people's values are often treated separately, with distinct literatures, but they operate together in important ways. Data collected with 294 working adults supported the conceptual propositions: absolute correlations were high when a work value and a personality trait were logically overlapping and low when no such overlap was predicted. Theoretical implications include the development of models of personality structure in terms of networks of values, treating each trait in terms of its mix of those.

The "Little-Five" personality in China: A review of theory, measurement and research

Yu, Yibing Yingdong Building, Room 255, Beijing Normal University, Beijing, People's Republic of China Hong, Zou Ins.Developmental psychology, Beijing Normal University, Beijing, People's Republic of China

This presentation will review the theory, measurement and research about what we have made relating to the "Little Five" personality during the past 10 years in China. It concludes: (1) The issues of culture-specific and age-specific in Chinese "Little Five" Personality; (2) The development of Chinese "Little Five" Personality Scale and its psychometrics qualities; (3) Research relevant to "Little Five" Personality and its distinct findings in the field of educational, Developmental and personality & social psychology et al. The limitation and future directions have also been discussed in the end.

Structure of Russian personality lexicon through the lens of the Cube-in-Globe and Big Five models

Putilov, Arcady Berlin, Germany Putilov, Dmitriy Biology and Biophysics, Research Institute Molecular, Novosibirsk, Russia

We tested whether six bipolar dimensions predicted by the Cub-in-Globe model represent the first six factors revealed by factor analysis of personality-relevant words of everyday language. More than 300 students rated 498 emotion- and personality-referring nouns: whether each term describes herself/himself, someone else whom s/he likes, and someone else whom s/he dislikes. The prediction of the Cube-in-Globe model that any personality trait might be located in three-dimensional space was confirmed. Moreover, the factors of the six-factor varimax solution demonstrate considerable overlap with factors usually referred as the Big Five.

FP-184: Disability and rehabilitation I

Constructing consumer values for community and independent living solutions

Mpofu, Elias Counselor Education and Reha., The Penn State University, University Park, USA

Objective. The study investigated community and independent living solutions preferred by consumers with disabilities. Community and independent living solutions for people with disabilities historically have been service provider rather than by consumer driven. Method. Two-hundred and ten consumers with disabilities participated in the study. Consumer preferred solutions were constructed using concept mapping, a mixed method data analysis approach. Results. Consumer preferences segmented into six clusters weighted mostly to solutions for self-determination and access to enabling resources. Conclusion. Consumer-oriented community and independent living solutions hold great promise for quality of life with a chronic illness or disability.

Forms and senses of everyday space from a wheelchair perspective

Hernandez Anzola, Maria Elisa Cienc. y Tecn. del Comportam., Universidad Simon Bolivar, Caracas, Venezuela

From a Social Psychology interested in the affective dimensions of everyday life, this qualitative study aims to understand how everyday space is configured in narratives (collected through conversational interviews) told by people with motor disabilities who use wheelchairs. Practicing a hermeneutical approach, we identify some forms that everyday space takes in these stories, and analyze expressions which communicate how narrators deal with such space, interpreting from that possible ways to relate to others and to (re)signify senses of coexistence.

Cognitive and psychological rehabilitation in patients with mild and moderate dementia

Agogiatou, Christina Dept. of Psychology, GAADRD, Thessaloniki, Greece Kounti, Fotini Psychology, GAADRD, Thessaloniki, Greece Karagiozi, Konstantina Psychology, GAADRD, Thessaloniki, Greece Bacoglidou, Evaggelia Psysiotherapy, GAADRD, Thessaloniki, Greece Nikolaidou, Evdokia Psychology, GAADRD, Thessaloniki, Greece Nakou, Stiliani Psychology, GAADRD, Thessaloniki, Greece Siampani, Aikaterini Psychology, GAADRD, Thessaloniki, Greece Poptsi, Eleni Psychology, GAADRD, Thessaloniki, Greece Zafeiropoulou, Mirto Psychology, New York College, Thessaloniki, Greece Varsamopoulou, Anastasia Psychology, GAADRD, Thessaloniki, Greece Tsolaki, Magda

Objectives: Improvement of cognitive, functional and emotional performance of patients with mild and moderate dementia. Method: Intervention included 7 therapeutic programs. Participants were 21 demented patients, classified in experimental and control groups. Intervention lasted 4 months. Neuropsychological assessment was administered before and after the intervention. Non parametric tests were used for the statistical analysis. Results: Experimental patients had better cognitive and functional performance than controls at the end of the intervention (MMSE, p = .032) (RBMT, p= .009) (RAVLT, p= .009). Conclusions: The proposed combination of cognitive and psychological interventions was beneficial for patients with mild and moderate dementia.

FP-185: Discipline issues I

The making of prolific faculty researchers in the Philippines: A grounded theory model

Valencia, Marshall Dept. of Psychology, De La Salle University, Manila, Philippines

This study explores variables and socialization processes involved in the shaping of prolific researchers in the context of a developing country. Narrative interviews of six exceptionally productive male scholars were analyzed to come up with a data driven model of pathways to prolific publishing in the context of Philippine realities. Categories and relationships that emerged from the analysis cross-validated previous quantitative investigations on research productivity. Two significant insights are highlighted in the model: the role of a "cognitive contrast" dimension, and the transformations that a set of "core characteristics" undergo throughout critical periods in a scholar's life.

Trends of psychology in a non-Western country

Khaleefa, Omar Dept. of Psychology, University of Khartoum, Khartoum, Sudan

The present study examined trends of psychology in Sudan. Multiple methods were used in collecting data from 21 departments of psychology, 15 centres for special education and 12 psychiatric hospitals. It showed the following trends: (a) psychology is applied and social not pure and biological (b) most psychological services are concentrated in Khartoum State (83%) compared to (17%) to all other 25 ones (c) domination of educational psychology by (39%), (d) majority of students were females (79%), therpsists (88%) and in pre-education (100%), (e) 20% of psychologists were trained abroad, however, they have tremendous contribution (84%) compared to those trained locally (16%).

Becoming a science?: Humboldt University Berlin's Institute for Psychology between World War Two and the construction of the Berlin Wall
Ebisch, Sven Inst. für Psychologie, Humboldt-Universität zu Berlin, Berlin, Germany
After World War II the Institute for Psychology of what was to become Humboldt University Berlin had been largely destroyed. This presentation describes the circumstances of the Institute's postwar reformation and development in the Soviet allied zone and its change, marking the disciplinary direction it was to take, from the Philosophical to the Science Faculty under Kurt Gottschaldt. Based on primary sources, this overview uses Ash's interactive resource-oriented approach to describe the development of psychology at Humboldt University between political upheaval in immediately postwar Berlin and the construction of the Berlin Wall in 1961.

FP-186: Culture and cognition I

Embodied cultural cognition: Psychological perspective and physical body comportment as carriers of culture
Leung, Angela Ka Yee School of Social Sciences, Singapore Management Univers., Singapore, Singapore Cohen, Dov Psychology, University of Illinois, Illinois, USA
Our body is one carrier and perpetuator of culture – cultural assumptions can be embodied in the way we psychologically represent ourselves in mental models (soft embodiment) and the way we physically comport our body (hard embodiment). One study examined the perspective that people embodied as they mapped out time and space metaphors. Euro-Americans were more likely to embody their own (vs. friend's) perspective whereas the reverse was true for Asian-Americans. In another study, Asian-Americans assuming an upright posture endorsed universalistic moral values more strongly whereas those assuming a hugging posture endorsed particularistic values more strongly. We discuss how culture can be implicitly embodied in our imagined and actual actions.

Quizshow knowledge and cultural literacy
Grabowski, Joachim Inst. für Psychologie, Pädagog. Hochschule Heidelberg, Heidelberg, Germany Kiel, Ewald School Pedagogy, University of Munich, München, Germany
Quizshows comprise of scholastic and popular knowledge, which serves as a mirror of cultural participation in a society and allows for some equal opportunity across educational levels. The German and American party game editions of "Who wants to be a millionaire?" (1960 questions each) were classified according to the topic they are drawn from. It turns out that the distribution of questions across topics and the assigned difficulty differs between the two games, supporting existing intercultural stereotypes. Differences are interpreted in terms of the roles of popular knowledge and its composition in the respective cultures.

Conceptualization and measurement of self-efficacy in Malaysian children and young adults
Mohd Zaharim, Norzarina School of Social Sciences, Universiti Sains Malaysia, Malaysia
The study explored sense of self-efficacy in Malaysian children and young adults facing everyday stress. The construct of self-efficacy was reoperationalized into three components: general (across

domains), external (over external events), and internal (over one's self). Consistent with previous research on Asians' versus Westerners' self-efficacy and Asians' stress and coping, the present study found moderate general, external, and internal self-efficacy and higher internal than external self-efficacy across stressful situations. A new conceptualization and measurement of self-efficacy was proposed, taking into account that efficacy beliefs may operate differently in Malaysian and Asian cultures than in Western cultures.

FP-187: Child health I

Sociocultural factors and eating disorders in adolescence: Ealuation of a school-based prevention program
Warschburger, Petra Inst. für Psychologie, Universität Potsdam, Potsdam, Germany Helfert, Susanne Psychology, University of Potsdam, Potsdam-Golm, Germany Bonekamp, Eva Psychology, University of Potsdam, Potsdam-Golm, Germany
Studies indicate a high percentage of adolescents with disturbed eating patterns, which are at risk of developing an eating disorder. To counteract this trend, prevention programs are needed that focus on specific risk and protective factors. The school-based prevention program POPS was developed to improve adolescents general life skills like coping strategies and stress management techniques as well as to brace them for dealing with appearance-related media and social media pressure. Program effects were tested in a random control group design including 1100 high school students from grade 7 to 9. Results from the 3-month follow-up will be reported and discussed.

Health education methods for achieving stable normoglycemia during an educational camp for youth with type 1 diabetes mellitus (DM1)
De Loach, Stan México City, Mexico
Aim: For young persons (age 8—17) with recent-onset DM1 to quickly learn to safely achieve normoglycemia and glycemic stability, through the use of self-directed learning methods, group and individual psychological support, and self-monitored blood glucose (SMBG) levels. Method: 5 international multidisciplinary team members responded to educational and emotional needs of 9 Campers during a 3-day residential diabetes camp. SMBG values furnished statistical data. Results: Mean arrival and departure glucose levels were significantly different (P < .0025]. Mean 3-day euglycemia was uncharacteristically stable. Conclusion: Self-directed diabetologic education and psychological support rapidly and safely produced normal glycemic levels and stability.

A "Children's Hospital of the Future" from the perspective of architectural psychology. An user-needs analysis
Walden, Rotraut Inst. für Psychologie, Universität Koblenz, Koblenz, Germany
Children's hospitals contribute often to experiences of fear in "little patients". A "Little Patients" Association worked to remove the negative effects of conventional hospital design at the Oldenburg Hospital through targeted improvements. The goal of this study, consisting of 59 patients, 65 employees, was to see how hospital design can impact patients' recovery. A questionnaire's "virtual walk-through" gave the observers an overall impression of the building. A five-point rating scale was applied to 171 items by 39 observers. The methods of Building Performance Evaluation, t-tests, and regression analyses were used. In conclusion: child-friendly design gives children's hospitals a competitive advantage. "Quality architecture will give the image of quality care".

FP-188: Clinical / counseling psychology I

Crisis management: How prepared are Australian schools?
Knowles, Ann Dept. of Psychology, Swinburne University, Melbourne, Australia Trethowan, Vicky
There is increasing recognition that traumatic events impact on school communities. This study aimed to develop a school-based crisis management model for traumatic events and to identify the role of school counsellors in managing trauma. One hundred and twenty school counsellors (psychologists and social workers) were surveyed to determine current levels of crisis management training. Results showed 85% of the respondents wanted further training in dealing with traumatic events impacting on their school community. Based on these data a school crisis management training model was developed. It is argued that this model could be applied in school jurisdictions beyond Australia.

Homeostatis reality therapy: A psychological intervention for human welfare
Gairola, Lata Dept. of Psychology, H.N.B. Garhwal University, Srinagar, India Chimbakam, Sebastian Psychology, c/o Dr. Lata Gairola, Srinagar (Garhwal, India
The present study aims to determine the effect of Homeostasis Reality Therapy as a Psychological Intervention for suicidal ideation. It is a model of health and disease based on the Indian Psychology and Culture, developed by Dr. Berkmans Koyical in 1992. The study was conducted on 50 males and 50 females aging 15-30, who had suicidal ideation came to the clinic for the Psychological help. Everyone was administered Homeostasis Reality Therapy individually and found that it was a very effective Psychological Intervention. The study reveals that the major cause for suicidal ideation is the unwanted pregancy.

Dental fear - and how to talk it away. Effects of a training course for dentists
Hagenow, Frank Hamburg, Germany
Research shows that at least 10% of the population suffer from dental fears. Dental fear, whether justified or not, often hinders medical efforts and desirable compliance. A German study from the University of Hamburg among 42 dentists and 168 patients shows a significant reduction of dental anxiety. Their dentists have been trained before in client-centered-counseling. Patients were classified concerning their fear by the Dental-Anxiety-Scale of Corah. It was found that even phobic patients were able to reduce their fear significantly by talking to their dentists before treatment. These effects were not to be found within the group of control.

FP-189: Culture and human development II

Omani teachers' job commitment: Comparisons of personal and organizational variables
Aldhafri, Said Dept. of Psychology, Sultan Qaboos University, Alkhodh, Oman
This study investigated Omani teachers' job commitment. A sample of 450 Omani teachers participated in the study from different school grades. The participants responded to a group of measures related to personal (e.g., teachers' sense of efficacy) and school characteristics (e.g., school climate). The participants also completed a demographic questionnaire. Regression analyses showed that teachers' job commitment could be better predicted using personal characteristics than using school characteristics. I elaborate these findings within the educational and cultural Omani context using a Western framework of job commitment and effi-

cacy beliefs. Implications and suggestions for future research are provided.

The attitude to work and to free time in Poland: The Polish adaptation of the multidimensional work ethic profile

Chudzicka-Czupala, Agata Inst. of Psychology, Silesian University, Katowice, Poland **Grabowski, Damian** Inst. of Psychology, Silesian University, Katowice, Poland

The research is a part of the work on Polish adaptation of the Multidimensional Work Ethic Profile by Miller, Woehr and Hudspeth (2002). The method is a 65-item inventory that measures seven conceptually and empirically distinct facets of the work ethic construct: centrality of work, self-reliance, hard work, leisure, morality/ethics, delay of gratification and wasted time. We collected data from a student sample and a nonstudent working sample. The research results describe the attitude of the members of Polish society to such values like hard work and free time and they show similarities and differences between Poles and other nations.

The personality of circus actors of various ethnic groups as the subjects of creative activity

Dementeva, Kapitolina general and sicial psychology, Mechnikov State University, Odessa, Ukraine

Objective is to study circus actors' personality regarding a genre in which they create scenic images, analyse a circus artist attitude to circus action and national archetype reflection in it. Methodological base: the works of V.Diltej, E.Shpranger, G.Oliort, K.Rogers, A.Maslow; K.K.Platonov's "Personality profile" methodology, biographic method and symbolical interpretation by K.G.Jung. The results show interrelation of actor's personality with genre and creative activity orientation. The belonging to ethnic group is important at the creation of an image. Conclusion: personality features, both typological and ethnic, should be taken into account in individualization of art activity management of a circus actor.

The myth of Chinese modesty: The effect of personal relationships on attribution for achievements

Han, Kuei-Hsiang Division of General Education, Tamkang University, Tamsui County, Taiwan

Using scenario experimental method, this study found that when the achievement was not a threat and the interacting target was an intimate, Taiwanese (people in a Confucian society) would not be modest. On the contrary, they attributed their achievements to ability and efforts. When the achievement would be a threat to others, though Taiwanese would attributed their achievement to luck. The main concern was not modest social norm but empathy. Only when the target was not familiar would Taiwanese be affected by social norm of modesty. Genereally speaking, the results of this study suggested that Chinese (Taiwanese) were not always be modest to their achievements, when situation allowed, Chinese would also be self-enhancing, just like people in Western society.

FP-190: Family issues

Relationships among dimensions of family communication patterns and Iranian children's level of anxiety and depression

Kouroshnia, Maryam university, Shiraz University, shiraz, Islamic Republic of Iran **Latifian, Morteza** university, shiraz university, shiraz, Islamic Republic of Iran

Maryam Kouroshnia Morteza Latifian Shiraz university, Shiraz, Iran ABSTRACT The purpose of this study was to investigate the relationships among dimensions of family communication patterns (conversation orientation and conformity orientation) and children's level of anxiety and depression in Iran. In this study 326 (161 female and 165 male) highschool students completed the Revised Family Communication Patterns Instrument and the short form of Depression Anxiety Stress Scales. The results of multiple regression analysis indicated that family's conversation orientation was a meaningful predictor of children's anxiety and depression and negatively predicted their anxiety and depression. Family's conformity predicted children's anxiety meaningfully and positively but not their depression.

Validity and reliability of the revised family communication patterns instrument in Iran

Kouroshnia, Maryam university, Shiraz University, shiraz, Islamic Republic of Iran **Latifian, Morteza** university, shiraz university, shiraz, Islamic Republic of Iran

Maryam Kouroshnia Morteza Latifian Shiraz university, Shiraz, Iran ABSTRACT The validity and reliability of the Revised Family Communication Patterns (RFCP) instrument were evaluated in a sample of 326 Iranian highschool students. Findings showed that there was a positive relationship between RFCP and Parent-child Bonding Instrument (PBI) which provided evidence to support the criteria validity of the RFCP. Principal component factor analysis was also used to evaluate the construct validity of the instrument. The results showed that two factors of conversation orientation and conformity orientation could be extracted. The RFCP showed a good internal consistency and acceptable test-retest reliability as well as Cronbach alpha coefficient.

The long-term effects of the PREP program: A 10 year follow-up

Markman, Howard Dept. of Psychology, University of Denver, Denver, CO, USA **Stanley, Scott** Dept. of Psychology, University of Denver, Denver, CO, USA **Rhoades, Galena** Dept. of Psychology, University of Denver, Denver, CO, USA **Whitton, Sarah** Dept. of Psychology, University of Denver, Denver, CO, USA

There is a growing interest at National levels in delivering relationship education programs to couples in order to prevent relationship distress and divorce and strengthen marriages, yet very few long-term evaluations of these programs. We present 10 year follow-up data on the long-term effects of the Prevention and Relationship Enhancement Program (PREP) in a sample of 253 couples who received the intervention premaritally and were followed at yearly intervals. We present a new model of relationship health (communication/conflict management, positive connections, commitment, satisfaction, stability) and outcome data on each dimension as couples are entering the highest risk period for divorce and distress. Implications for wide spread dissemination of research-based couples interventions are discussed.

Relationship between childhood attachment quality, adult attachment and attachment to God with family functioning

Shahabizadeh, Fatemeh Birjand Branch, Islamic Azad University, Korasan-Kashmar, Islamic Republic of Iran **Ahadi, Hasan** psychology, Allame Tabataba'ee University, Razavy Khorasan-Kashmar, Islamic Republic of Iran

This study investigated role played by God attachment, adult and childhood attachment in Muslim' reported family functioning. 193 high school students in kashmar, completed questionnaires measuring God attachment, childhood attachment, adult attachment and family adaptability and cohesion (FACES-IV). Results showed at insecure childhood attachment, secure respondents to God had higher mean on family adaptability, cohesion and communication than their insecure counterparts. Also at insecure adult attachment, secure respondents to God had lower mean on family disengaged and chaotically than their insecure counterparts. Family functioning and adult attachment predicted God attachment. Also parental and adult attachment influenced on Family functioning subscales.

FP-191: Education and advanced training I

Instruction monitoring: Implementation of new curricula within a video-based quality circle

Gaertner, Holger Inst. für Schulqualität, Freie Universität Berlin, Berlin, Germany

This study introduces the concept of instruction monitoring (IM) as a way to implement new curricula. IM centres around a content-focused quality circle in which teachers co-operate and discuss videotapes of their own lessons. During one school year, fourteen mathematics teachers took part in two quality circles. Within a quasi-experimental pre-post test design, questionnaires were used to estimate the effects of IM compared with traditional professional development at teacher and student level. The results show that various aspects of instruction changed and that teachers' beliefs shifted towards a cognitive constructivist orientation. At student level, self-assessed subject competence increased.

Assessing beginning teachers: peer to peer teaching and groups of educational reflection in secondary education

Mayoral, Paula Psychology, Ramon Llull University, Barcelona, Spain

Research has shown the main beginning teachers (BT) problems are discipline, behaviour, student's motivation, time and social relations management. Consequently, advice should be pluridimensional and addressed to promote the reflection on practice. The methodology includes the participation of five peer-tutoring in an on-line foro, a tutor observation and groups of educational reflection across five topics in a school year adopting a qualitative approach. The BT problems concern adaptation to school culture and lack of experience, in addition to those mentioned above. The mentors' problems were communication, lack of time and role delivery difficulties. Definitely, classroom tutor observation favours reflective practice in BT and benefit mentors, helping them think about their teaching practice and rethink teaching issues.

The characteristics of deliberate practice in teaching expertise development in China

Hu, Yi Psychology, East China Normal University, Shanghai, People's Republic of China **Zhou, Ruyang** Psychology, East China Normal University, Shanghai, People's Republic of China **Luo, Jiao** Psychology, East China Normal University, Shanghai, People's Republic of China

The study aimed at exploring what kinds of teaching activities can be judged as deliberate practice, and how instructional situations influence them. Ten secondary-school teachers rang from 7 to 30 years teaching were individually at semi-structured interview for 2 hours a week, which last two months. Through protocol analysis, it shows that the time spending on planning and reflective activities in teaching is strongly positive relative to teaching expertise, and which are affected by the academic subject matter and student's achievement level. Then deliberate practice theory is an appropriate way to comprehend the nature and development of teaching expertise.

Effective schools: Evaluation from students, parents and teachers

Koutsoulis, Michalis Dept. of Education, University of Nicosia, Nicosia, Cyprus

The purpose of the research is to define school effectiveness through students, parents and teachers in five schools. The research conducted in two stages. In the first stage participants were asked to define school effectiveness in focus groups. On the second stage participants evaluated their school through questionnaires. Results show that students place attention on the affective domain of school life, parents focus on the buildings and the facilities of the school, while teachers are concern about the results of the educational process.

FP-192: School counseling

A qualitative investigation on ethical and professional issues of school psychological counselors in Turkey

Cetinkaya, Evrim Dept. of Educational Sciences, Middle East Technical Univers., Ankara, Turkey Erdur-Baker, Ozgur Educational Sciences, Middle East Technical Universi, Ankara, Turkey

This study aimed to investigate the ethical/professional issues that Turkish school psychological counselors encounter. The three themes that emerged from semi-structured interviews with twenty school counselors were professional issues (e.g., limited collaborations with other personnel, crowded schools, inadequate physical environment), ethical issues (e.g., confidentiality, multiple relationships, mandatory counseling, and professional competency), and the solution strategies used by psychological counselors. The results indicated that Turkish school counselors were facing with somewhat similar problems as described in the literature of school psychology but with different nature and severity. The results are discussed based on the existing literature and the cultural and economical context of Turkey.

Counseling the culturally different student in the Arabian Gulf region

Hassane, Sofoh Psychology and Counseling, United Arab Emirate University, Al-Ain, United Arab Emirates

The number of foreign students from diverse cultural backgrounds enrolling in schools and colleges in the Arabian Gulf Region is growing rapidly. However, no or very little cross-cultural studies focusing on the needs and attitudes of these students and how they could be effectively helped have emerged in the counseling literature. This presentation will focus on how school counselors can help them adjust to new school climate and culture and develop their learning potentials optimally. It will also focus on the types of concerns they are most likely to bring into counseling and suggest intervention strategies in working with them.

The study of peer counseling effect at school in enhancing the students' level of mental health

Jam, Zahra Tehran, Islamic Republic of Iran Saleh Sedghpoor, Bahram Educational Sciences and Psych, Shahid Beheshti University, tehran, Islamic Republic of Iran Khoshkonesh, Abolghasem Educational Sciences and Psych, Shahid Beheshti University, tehran, Islamic Republic of Iran

The present research studies the effect of peer counseling in increasing the mental health level of the studied statistical society, including 171 female students of high school. After a mental health pretest, they are classified into 3 groups: disorder-free, mild disorder and high disorder; each group is randomly put in the control and experimental groups. Using manova, the results shows firstly dependent variables (physical signs, anxiety, disorder in social function and depression) are independent to each other; secondly the mild disorder group, among all the other groups, is affected just in the variable of anxiety.

Teachers' understanding of children's depressive symptoms

Kleftaras, George Dept. of Special Education, University of Thessaly, Volos, Greece Didaskalou, Eleni Special Education, University of Thessaly, Volos, Greece

The present research aimed at a) estimating the proportion of primary school children experiencing depressive symptomatology and b) exploring teachers ability to recognize their pupils presenting depressive symptoms. Participants were 323 pupils, aged 10-13 years and their classroom teachers. Pupils completed the Children's Depression Inventory, while teachers a questionnaire concerning their perceptions about their pupils' depressive symptoms. A considerable percentage of pupils reach high scores of depressive symptoms especially (negative self-esteem, mood and interpersonal problems). However, teachers identify and report more often behavioural problems and tend to underestimate the incidence and severity of depressive symptoms in their pupils.

Moscow Department of Education: Psychological rehabilitation of younger schoolchildren with delayed psychic development in situation of joint productive activity

Prudnikova, Marina Center, Diagnostics and Consulting, Moscow, Russia

Objective : analysis of factors and conditions ensuring effectiveness of correctional work to improve life standard and restore normal development of families having schoolchildren with psychological impairments. Methods: Neuropsychological diagnostics, Roven's matrixes, projective methodology, parents' questionnaire, mathematical data processing, independent expert evaluation. Results: reorganization of content and direction of interaction between psychologist, family as subject of rehabilitation activity is caused by processes of participation, co-creativity and co-development of all participants of entire system "Rehabilitation-Specialist-Child-Family-Society", ensures family functioning and wholeness as natural and permanent rehabilitation-and-development environment. Conclusion: Quality of Psychologist-Child-Parent interaction in education and rehabilitation process ensures continuous socialization of child on maximal level of his abilities.

Identifying subtypes of career indecision among Portuguese secondary school students: A cluster analytical approach

Santos, Paulo Faculdade de Letras, Universidade do Porto, Porto, Portugal

Career indecision is a complex phenomenon and an increasing number of authors have proposed that undecided individuals do not constitute a group of homogenous characteristics. However, there is some controversy about the different types of career undecided individuals. This study examined career indecision subtypes among a sample of 362 12th grade Portuguese students. Using a battery of scales assessing career and personality dimensions, a cluster-analytic procedure was employed. Several groups of career decided/undecided were identified. Implications for career intervention are discussed.

FP-193: Selective attention

Is sensory processing necessarily affected by exogenous cues?

Niedeggen, Michael Experimentelle Psychologie, Freie Universität Berlin, Berlin, Germany

A visuospatial cueing paradigm was used to examine whether a sensory gain control mediates the effect of covert attention on the appearance of visual stimuli. A short coherent motion signal was embedded in two dynamic random dot kinematograms (RDK) presented left and right of a fixation. Subjects had to decide which RDK was defined by

a higher level of coherence. A short reduction in luminance in one RDK served as a cue. Event-related brain potentials (ERPs) did not indicate that the behavioral effects of valid and invalid cueing are determined by a corresponding modulation of the sensory motion processing system.

Conflict-monitoring and reaction time distributions

Davelaar, Eddy USA

The conflict-monitoring hypothesis of attentional control assumes that conflict is monitored during one trial and affects the attentional control during performance on the next trial. Recently, this hypothesis has been challenged on the grounds of data showing that the sequential dependencies observed in studies using the Eriksen flanker task may be in part due to stimulus or response priming. I will present new data regarding response time distributions that falsifies some possible resolutions to the debate (and produces new questions). I will argue that detailed reaction time distributions should feature more prominently in models of attentional control.

Attentional capture, cueing and the attentional blink

Coltheart, Veronika MACCS, Macquarie University, Sydney, Australia

The attentional blink refers to limits on dual target identification when targets are embedded in a sequence of distractors visually presented approximately 100 ms per item. The second target (T2) is frequently missed when it follows shortly after the first. Recent research has demonstrated evidence for attentional capture by distractors similar to targets. However, similar distractors can also ameliorate the blink by functioning as cues for T2. Two experiments investigated the conditions in which cueing or capture effects occur in single and dual target search. The implications concerning the Temporary Loss of Control and Delayed Engagement accounts are considered.

A dual-phase model of selective attention

Hübner, Ronald Fachbereich Psychologie, Universität Konstanz, Konstanz, Germany Steinhauser, Marco Fachbereich Psychologie, Universität Konstanz, Konstanz, Germany Lehle, Carola Fachbereich Psychologie, Universität Konstanz, Konstanz, Germany

Selective visual attention is an important mechanism of behavioral self-control. First it was thought that selection takes place early in the stream of information processing. Later, it became clear that selection can also occur at later stages. Here, we propose that selection takes place simultaneously at early and late stages. We implemented this idea in a formal dual-phase model and applied it to the Flanker task. By varying spatial uncertainty, we modulated the relative contribution of early and late selection processes. As expected, these modulations were nicely reflected by the variations of the corresponding parameter values of our model.

Crossmodal extinction in neurologically-normal participants: The Colavita effect revisited

Spence, Charles Dept. of Psychology, University of Oxford, Oxford, United Kingdom

Colavita (1974) reported that presenting a light at the same time as a suprathreshold auditory target resulted in people failing to respond to (or be aware of) the sound (a sound that participants were always aware of when presented in isolation). I will describe a number of recent studies on this little-studied, but fascinating, crossmodal phenomenon. I will highlight the spatiotemporal constraints on the Colavita effect and its sensitivity to manipulations of attention/perceptual load. I will highlight the important similarities that exist between the Colavita visual dominance effect and the crossmodal extinction sometimes experienced by stroke patients suffering from neglect.

Attention to graphic cigarette warning labels in non-smokers, smokers and ex-smokers

Hollier, Tanya Dept. of Psychology, Southern Cross University, Orange, Australia Provost, Stephen Psychology, Southern Cross University, Coffs Harbour, Australia

New graphic warning labels form part of a 'fear appeal' strategy to reduce smoking behaviour in Australia. Strength of orientation and disengagement of attention towards warning labels was examined in smokers, ex-smokers and non-smokers (n =48). Non-smokers were not influenced by the warning labels in terms of orientation or disengagement relative to control stimuli. Smokers and ex-smokers showed evidence of both greater orientation to the warning labels, and facilitated disengagement from them. These results suggest either generalised increases in speed of responding following warning label presentation, or the presence of an avoidance response, in both smokers and ex-smokers.

FP-194: Risk, accident and accident prevention

The social representation of traffic accident in Romania: Connections with emotions and decision-making in driving

Holman, Andrei Iasi, Romania Havarneanu, Cornel Psychology, "Al. I. Cuza" Universi, iasi, Romania Havarneanu, Grigore Iasi, Romania Dumitru, Marian Psychology, "Al. I. Cuza" Universi, iasi, Romania

Our research is multi-phased: the first step was aimed at contouring the structure and content of the social representation of traffic accident in the Romanian population, using the method of associative network on various components of this representational object: causes, involved actors, development, consequences, and also emotional determinants and associations. The second stage employed the multidimensional scaling procedure, thus revealing the main dimensions which underpin the social representation of traffic accident. Finally, our results are integrated in an empirical analysis of risk perception, inter-temporal choice and emotional involvement in these decision mechanisms in driving.

Study of mental profile of drivers with hard accident road with use of NEO-PI-R

Aghaei Jeshvaghani, Asghar Khorasgan Branch, Islamic Azad University, Isfahan, Islamic Republic of Iran Abedi, Mohamadreza Psychology, ISFAHAN UNIVERSITY, Isfahan, Islamic Republic of Iran Kanani, Kobra Psychology, University Khorasgan-Isfahan, Isfahan, Islamic Republic of Iran

The objective of this study was to identify mental profile of drivers with hard accident road. The results are based on NEO-PI-R out among a sample of Iranian drivers in year 2006 and 2007 (n=40). Respondents involved in experienced near-accidents and crashes leading to injuries. The questionnaire included big five factor of personality. Results showed that those who scored high on neuroticism (p</05) and those who scored low on openness (p</05), agreeableness (p</01) and conseientiousnessr (p</000) were more involved experienced accidents.kEY wORDS: Mental Profile, Drivers, hard accident road, NEO-PI-R

Unrealistic optimism, impulsiveness and self-construal of Chinese drivers and their relationship to risky driving behaviors

Jiang, Li Institute of Psychology, CAS, Beijing, People's Republic of China Li, Yongjuan Institute of psychology, Chinese Academy of Sciences, Beijing, People's Republic of China Liu, Xueyuan Institute of psychology, Chinese Academy of Sciences, Beijing,

People's Republic of China Zhang, Feng Institute of psychology, Chinese Academy of Sciences, Beijing, People's Republic of China

The aim of the study was to investigate the effect of impulsiveness, self-construal and unrealistic optimism on the risky driving behavior. 108 Chinese drivers were measured their impulsiveness, independent-interdependent self, and self-evaluated their risky driving behaviors as well as their ticket records gotten from policemen. Confirmatory factor analysis testified the constructs of impulsiveness, self-construal and driving behaviors developed in western culture. Results indicated that Chinese drivers also showed significant unrealistic optimism about driving accident; unrealistic optimism mediated the relationship between motor impulsiveness and aggressive driving violations. Implications of the results for traffic safety and future research are discussed.

The influence of cognitive biases on inexperienced, young drivers' risky task performance

Havarneanu, Grigore Iasi, Romania Havarneanu, Cornel Psychology, "A. I. Cuza" Universit, Iasi, Romania Holman, Andrei Psychology, "A. I. Cuza" Universit, Iasi, Romania Dumitru, Marian Psychology, "A. I. Cuza" Universit, Iasi, Romania

We analyze different types of driver's illusions sketching out the difference between drivers' social and cognitive biases, with the focus on the latter. On this recent theoretical base, we conducted an experimental study to asses the adaptation of some young, inexperienced Romanian drivers to a risky task performance. In the second part we also deal with methodological issues, empirical data analysis, main advantages and limits of the study, and draw the main conclusions. Some practical implications are discussed, in particular young drivers' training with regard to the importance of individual differences and feedback during the task.

Effectiveness of warning signs in reducing speed at rural road curves

Weller, Gert Verkehr und Transport, Technische Universität Dresden, Dresden, Germany Voigt, Jana Traffic and Transportation Psy, TU Dresden, Dresden, Germany Schlag, Bernhard Traffic and Transportation Psy, TU Dresden, Dresden, Germany

Inappropriate speed is the most important contributing factor to fatal accidents on rural roads. With the upcoming of the self-explaining road concept (e.g. Theeuwes, 2000) signs that are traditionally used to convey otherwise missing information on the road ahead, seem to lose their attraction. In a simulator study (N=50) we tested different road designs and compared them to the effectiveness of warning signs. A subsequent collection of subjective ratings revealed that the positive effect of signs on reducing speed was due to the respective curves being rated as more dangerous and demanding. These findings have important implications concerning rural road design.

FP-195: Quality of life

Testing a model of health-related internet use and disease coping among individuals living with HIV/AIDS

Mo, Phoenix IWHO, University of Nottingham, Nottingham, United Kingdom Coulson, Neil Institute of Work, Health and, University of Nottingham, Nottingham, United Kingdom

Objectives: To examine factors associated with disease-related Internet use and its effect on disease coping among HIV+ individuals. Methods: 640 HIV+ participants completed an online survey. Measures included: demographic and medical information, HIV-related Internet use, health-related QoL (MOS-SF36), coping (Brief COPE), and physical symptoms (Symptom Checklist). Results:

SEM showed that physical symptoms and disease stage predicted worse health-related QoL, which predicted Internet use. Internet use in turn predicted problem-focused coping and more active discussion about health problems with health professionals. The model achieved a satisfactory fit, CFI=.95, IFI=.93, RMSEA=.06. Conclusions: Health-related Internet use might offer some benefits for HIV+ individuals.

Influence of stigma on quality of life of HIV Positive individuals

Kohli, Neena Psychology, University of Allahabad, Allahabad, India

This study attempts to bring out the influence of stigma on quality of life of 100 HIV positive individuals. Semi-structured interview was used to elicit data on socio-demographics, stigma and quality of life. Results showed a) significant negative correlation between stigma and quality of life and b) age and stigma emerged as significant predictors of quality of life. Findings suggest that PLWHAs should be encouraged to rise above stigma and live a better quality of life and it also cautions health providers and caregivers to help PLWHAs live a life of dignity by being gender sensitive, caring and supportive.

The mediational effect of resilience in relation between emotional intelligence, general intelligence and life satisfaction

Jowkar, Bahram Dept. Educational Psychology, Shiraz University, Shiraz, Islamic Republic of Iran

Abstract This study investigated mediation role of resilience in relationship between Emotional and cognitive intelligence and life satisfaction. Participants were 557 higher education students. Participants completed the Conner-Davidson Resilience scale Shutte emotional Intelligence Scale, Satisfaction With Life scale, and Scale 3 of Cattell Culture Faire Intelligence test. Results showed that (a) emotional and cognitive intelligences directly, were weak predictors of life satisfaction, (b) emotional intelligence in comparison to cognitive intelligence was strong predictor of resilience and (c) resilience was mediator between both kind of intelligence and life satisfaction. Findings also revealed that the relationships between model's variables in girls weren't completely consistent with whole group. Implications and suggestion for future studies are discussed.

Quality of life, self-efficacy, coping and adherence in patients with chronic kidney disease on haemodialysis treatment

Esguerra, Gustavo A. Psicologia, Universidad Santo Tomas, Bogota D.C., Colombia Contreras, Françoise V. Psicologia, Universidad Santo Tomas, Bogota D.C., Colombia Espinosa, Juan C. Psicologia, Universidad Santo Tomas, Bogota D.C., Colombia

The purpose of this study was to identify the psychological variables that can predict the adherence to treatment in chronic kidney disease patients. The Stress Coping Questionnaire (CAE), Spanish versions of SF36 and Generalized Self-efficacy (EAG) was used to assess the coping, quality of life and self-efficacy respectively. The treatment adherence was estimated through biochemical indicators and attendance of haemodialysis sessions. The results indicated that the coping style was the best predictor to adherence and its predicting capacity was improved when interacted with some dimension of quality of life. The implications of these findings are discussed.

Depression and quality of life in cancer patients with and without pain

Tavoli, Azadeh tehran, Islamic Republic of Iran Montazeri, Ali Iranian Institute for Health S, Iranian Institute for Health S, Tehran, Islamic Republic of Iran Roshan, Rasool shahed university, shahed university,

Tehran, Islamic Republic of Iran **Tavoli, Zahra** Arash Institute, Arash Institute, Tehran, Islamic Republic of Iran **Melyani, Mahdieh** Shahed university, Shahed university, Tehran, Islamic Republic of Iran
Objectives: To compare depression and quality of life among Iranian cancer patients with and without pain. Methods: A sample of gastrointestinal cancer patients attending to Tehran Cancer Institute were entered into the study. two standrd instruments were used to measure quality of life (EORTC QLQ-C30), and depression (HADS). Results: 142 patients were studied. Cancer patients with pain (n = 98) reported significantly lower levels of global quality of life and higher levels of depression than patients who did not experience pain (n =44). Conclusions: The findings showed that cancer pain could affect patients' quality of life, and emotional status.

FP-196: Regulation of emotion

A dimensional model of adaptive emotional functioning

Schutte, Nicola Dept. of Psychology, University of New England, Armidale, Australia **Malouff, JOhn** Dept. of Psychology, University of New England, Armidale, NSW, Australia
Objectives: This theoretical paper presents a multi-dimensional model of adaptive emotional functioning that holds that ability and trait conceptualizations of emotional functioning are complementary dimensions. This multi-dimensional model further posits that emotional self-efficacy, states related to positive emotional functioning, and situations that facilitate emotional functioning contribute to adaptive emotional processes. The model sets out how these different dimensions may influence one another and examines how the interaction between dimensions of emotional functioning may lead to positive life outcomes. Some preliminary empirical evidence supports aspects of the multi-dimensional model.

An event-related potential study of implicit attitude to emotion regulation influence on emotional attention performance

Sang Biao, P. R. Dept. of Psychology, East China Normal University, Shanghai, People's Republic of China **Liu, Junsheng** Department of Psychology, Shanghai Normal University, Shanghai, People's Republic of China
Previous research has showen that implicit attitude to emotion regulation could influence emotion regulation without the cognitive costs.However, little is known about how to achieve this. In this study, ERPs were recorded from 15 participants with different implicit attitudes to emotion regulation. The participants were presented slides of International Affective Picture System posing 25 negative and 25 neutral pictures, and the P1 component of the event-related brain potential was used as a proximal index of attention allocation to valanced stimuli.The results indicated that the P1 amplitudes and latencies differ between two different groups, which suggested that implicit attitude to emotion regulation could modulate the early emotional processing.

Getting ready for emotional events: A new paradigm to investigate anticipatory coping

Kazen, Miguel Inst. für Psychologie, Universität Osnabrück, Osnabrück, Germany
Most studies on emotion regulation deal with psychological repair effects after negative events whereas people sometimes are able to psychologically prepare to cope with certain and impending negative and positive emotional events. Does advance warning of an emotional event help or interfere with subsequent task performance? Two studies are reported in which participants were presented with an emotional or neutral prime word shortly before an unrelated imperative cognitive task occurred, under advanced warning about the type of prime (anticipatory coping) or without it (retrospective coping). Results showed that advanced warning influenced coping with emotional events, as indicated by subsequent performance.

Emotional intelligence and its relation to humor styles

Pasupuleti, Subhashini Dept. of Psychology, Osmania University, Hyderabad, India
The purpose of the present study was to examine the relationship between emotional intelligence and humor styles. The study was carried on 200 working professionals from different organizations in India. Standardized questionnaires were used for collecting data. The results of the study showed that emotional intelligence is positively correlated with affiliative humor and self-enhancing humor while it is negatively correlated with aggressive humor and self-depreciating humor. The results also showed that job tenure had an impact on emotional intelligence and certain humor styles. Implications of the study along with suggestions for further research have also been discussed in this study.

The processes of emotional regulation on love dissolution

Sánchez Aragón, Rozzana Dept. of Social Psychology, UNAM, México City, Mexico
When a romantic relationship is finished, its members experience a particular emotional process of mourning. Gross & Thompson (2007) propose five processes in charge to identify the emotional regulation strategies (from selection of situation to action) used for the individual when he/she cope with an emotion. Considering their ideas, the current research was oriented to: a) develop and validate a measure of the processes in the context of romantic relationship dissolution, and b) identify the specific ways to regulate the emotions involved (i.e. sadness, fear and anger). Data from 100 Mexican males and females will be discussed at light of the theory and actual research.

Mindfulness, acceptance, and "meta-emotions": Differentiating processes in experiential avoidance in non-clinical and clinical samples

Mitmansgruber, Horst Department of Medical Psycholo, Medical University Innsbruck, Innsbruck, Austria **Beck, Thomas N.** Department of Medical Psycholo, Medical University Innsbruck, Innsbruck, Austria **Schüßler, Gerhard** Department of Medical Psycholo, Medical University Innsbruck, Innsbruck, Austria
Three studies illuminate the role of facets within the mindfulness/acceptance-spectrum for psychological well-being (PWB): experiential avoidance, mindful awareness, "meta-emotions". Method: Study1 assessed medical students (n=334/n=222) for the development of the Meta-Emotion-Scale. Study2 compared 134 expert paramedics with 105 novices for changes in mindfulness/acceptance with accumulating experience of potentially traumatic incidents. Study3 assessed changes on mindfulness measures in 293 patients in a psychosomatic clinic which were used to predict changes in symptoms and PWB. Results and conclusions: The facets explained large amounts of variance on PWB (52% to 60%). Inclusion of meta-emotions allowed for the identification of important processes in emotion regulation.

FP-197: Psychology and national development I

Scientific disciplines developmental patterns: Psychology in Mexico, 1950-2005.

Morales Nasser, Alejandra Carolina Center for Knowledge Systems., ITESM, Monterrey, Nuevo Leon, Mexico **Carrillo-Gamboa, Francisco Javier** Center for Knowledge Systems., Tecnologico de Monterrey ITESM, Monterrey, Nuevo Leon, Mexico
To describe Psychology development in Mexico, and to identify developmental patterns, a systemic science of science approach, holding interbehavioral theory for interpretation, was achieved. A concurrent triangulation method design was conducted, which included a quantitative methodology (scientometrics), and two qualitative ones (historiography and semi structured interview). 1130 indexed abstracts, authored by Mexican psychologists were analyzed. Nineteen prominent Mexican psychologists were interviewed. Results show five differentiated periods, explained according to historic, economic, political, sociological and psychological dimensions, as well as several patterns related to science development. Data allow planning for better future. Psychology of science double reflexive role is emphasized.

Crisis in psychiatric care in low and middle-income countries: The role to be played by psychology and allied health services

Tsang, Hing Singapore, Singapore
"Every year up to 30 % of the population worldwide has some form of mental disorder, and at least two-thirds of those people receive no treatment, even in countries with the most resources" (Lancet, 2007). The situation is much worse in low and middle-income countries. Psychiatric treatment is not available. While a range of psychological and allied health interventions have been found to be beneficial in improving mental health, focusing on the Lancet Global Mental Health Series 2007, this paper discusses the value of non-medical approaches to mental disorders such as psychological interventions in low and middle-income countries.

A comparative study of historical and philosophical contexts of experimental psychology; philosophical history of psychology in Iran

Hatami, Javad Psychology, University of Tehran, Tehran, Islamic Republic of Iran
modern psychology in Iran is more than eighty years old. In his relatively long period of existence, Iran's psychology couldn't get a worthy position in society of world psychologists. There are different educational & sociological explanations for this failure. In this article we emphasis on historical & philosophical aspects. The aim of this study is comparing philosophical and cultural foundations of modern psychology with philosophical history of psychology in Iran.

30 years of psychological practice in the power industry of Moldavian Republic: Facts, difficulties, goals

Zolotova, Natalia Dept. of Human Resources, GE, Chisinau, Moldova **Podshivalkina, Valentina** General and Social psichology, Odessas State University, Odessa, Ukraine
In this work the history of psychological evolution in the power industry, through the prism of it's historical development, is observed. In 1976 when the power industry was intensively developing psychologists appeared in it. Different types of work where conducted in the following directions: o Personnel selection o Specialist adaptation o The formation of personnel reserve o Sociological survey. This was the period of information gathering. Later the period of stagnation began which consisted in perfection of usable technologies. The power industry was separated in the early 90's. Main tasks these days are: o Use of experience from American and European schools of professional selection. o Work In harmonization of collective and the personality of a specialist.

Promoting school achievement and the renewal of teaching methods and educational policies: Recent developments in Portuguese educational psychology

Viegas-Abreu, Manuel Dept. of Psychology, University of Coimbra, Coimbra, Portugal Paixao, Maria Paula Dept. of Psychology, University of Coimbra, Coimbra, Portugal

Contributing to the erradication of school under-achievement continues to be one of the most important themes in Educational Psychology, both at a theoretical and at a pratical level. Several research and intervention programmes were thus developped in Portugal during the second half of the 20th century, namely those funded by the Foundation for Science and Technology that were carried out under our supervision at the University of Coimbra. In line with our main results, promoting strategies of learning motivation, the renewal of teaching methods and,mainly, new directions for educational policies are the main roots proposed for the required developments in this area.

A series of studies on Chinese farmers' career choice consideration

Zheng, Quanquan Psychology, Zhejiang University, Hangzhou, People's Republic of China

Study 1 The Study of Contemporary Farmers' Work Value and Its Influential Factors The present researchmade a systematic analysis of farmers' work value, work value structure and the influence of different variables on farmers' work value. Study 2 The Study of Contemporary Farmers ' Social Support Using the survey method, taking 1607 farmers coming from Zhejiang and other 14 provinces as the sample, made a systematic analysis of farmers' social support. Study 3 The Influence of Career Cognition and Social Support on Chinese Farmers' Career Choice Consideration The hypothetical model of influences of career cognition and social supports on Chinese farmers' career interest and choice consideration was developed, based on data of 1247 farmers.

FP-198: Progress in creativity research

Investigate the effects of family demographic factors on children creativity development

Khoshnevis, Elaheh Dept. for Psychology, Islamic Azad University, Tehran, Islamic Republic of Iran Ahadi, Hassan Psychology, Allame Tabataba'ee University, Tehran, Islamic Republic of Iran

Using the stratified random sampling, 300 high school students were selected. To evaluate investigated variables, Abedi Creativity Test and 16question researcher made questionnaire were used. The investigation showed: * Creativity mean for the first child was higher than the other children. * Creativity mean for girls was higher than boys. * A significant relationship between fathers'/mothers' education level and children creativity score. * A significant relationship between family economic situation and children creativity score. * A reversed significant correlation between number of children and their creativity score. * A reversed significant correlation between mothers' age and children creativity score. * A direct significant correlation between fathers' age and children creativity score.

A review on psychological research on inventors

Wolf, Katrin Hans-Sauer-Professur, Humboldt-Universität, Berlin, Germany Mieg, Harald A. Hans-Sauer-Professur, Humboldt-Universität, Berlin, Germany

In this lecture we provide a comprehensive review of the international psychological literature concerning the following issues: 1. What is an inventor like? What are personal characteristics of inventors? 2. How can the inventing process be described? 3. What are promising cognitive inventing strategies?

4. Which factors determine the inventor's success? 5. What are differences between inventor experts and novices? 6. How can the performance of an inventor be assessed? We searched PsycINFO and the Psyndex-database from 1990 onwards. The literature on inventors respectively inventing was reviewed with a primary focus on empirical research. An integrated psychological model of invention has been developed and will be presented. It also includes results and data from our own research.

Correlates of creativity in research and development scientists

Misra, Nishi Dept. of Psychology, DIPR, DRDO, Delhi, India

Objectives: Present study was conducted to (i) determine age, discipline and gender differences in scientific creativity, (ii) determine a profile of creative scientists. Method: Sample comprised 100 R&D scientists; aged 25 to 55 years. 'F' ratios and multiple regression analysis were computed. Results: Non-significant differences on gender and age and significant discipline-wise differences were obtained. Creative scientists scored average on neuroticism and extraversion, high on internal locus of control, used a mix of intuitive and systematic cognitive style, scored high on personal accomplishment, were moderately motivated and encountered less workplace barriers. Conclusions: Factors promoting creativity in R&D scientists are discussed.

Fluency, originality and flexibility: Does the scoring method affect the relationship of creativity, intelligence and personality?

Gelleri, Petra Inst. für Psychologie, Hohenheim Universität, Stuttgart, Germany Winzen, Julia Psychology, Universität Hohenheim, Stuttgart, Germany Schwarzinger, Dominik Psychology, Hohenheim University, Stuttgart, Germany Görlich, Yvonne Psychology, Hohenheim University, Stuttgart, Germany Schuler, Heinz Psychology, Hohenheim University, Stuttgart, Germany

In a variety of creativity tests, scoring only accounts for ideational fluency, whereas originality and flexibility of answers are neglected. Preliminary research supports the thesis that fluency can be seen as a sufficient measure of divergent thinking (e.g. Runco, 1986). Indeed, our findings support that there are high correlations between the three measures (ranging from r = .85 to .92, N = 91). However, our results indicate that, depending on scoring method, correlations with other constructs like intelligence and Big Five-factors may vary. Thus, we argue that scoring method has to be accounted for in analyzing relationships to other constructs.

Two paradigms are two vectors of creating the new

Bogoyavlenskaya, Diana Lab. of Diagnostics, Psychological Institute, Moscow, Russia

A comparative analysis of creativity theory has been made in different paradigms. The testological paradigm where vector of development points toward "breadth" and divergent thinking as a creativity factor is represented by the principal "more-or-less." Based on distant associations divergent thinking does not guarantee gaining of a new knowledge. It only provides some possibility for it. The paradigm "process-activity" where we single out the phenomenon based on an identification of the unit of creativity analysis by our method "Creative field". This phenomenon is a result of cognition developing "in depth".

FP-199: Psycholinguistics

Synesthesia and language: Sound/concept and grapheme/concept adequacy evaluation of linguistic signs

Grantyn, Rosemarie Entwicklungspsychologie, Institut für Neurophysiologie, Berlin, Germany Grantyn, Inga Inst. für Romanistik, Humboldt-Universität zu Berlin, Berlin, Germany Betances, David Developmental Physiology, Institute for Neurophysiology, Berlin, Germany Knauer, Gabriele Institute for Romance Studies, Humboldt University Berlin, Berlin, Germany

A central principle of linguistics (Saussure 1916) assumes that the connection between a concept ("signified") and the spoken/written representation of the latter ("signifier") is entirely arbitrary. We have developed a set of tests to address this hypothesis and obtained evidence suggesting that, in contrast to Saussure's principle, an iconic relation between the signifier and the signified may on some occasions exist. We refer to this phenomenon as "iconic synesthesia". Our results lead to the question to what extent iconic synesthesia contributes to early language acquisition, especially in the case of concrete, simple linguistic signs with obvious sensory characteristics.

The shape of words in the brain

Kovic, Vanja Experimental Psychology, Oxford University, Oxford, United Kingdom

Here we present new neurophysiological and behavioural evidence for the psychological reality of sound-symbolism which implies some naturally-biased mappings between linguistic signs and their referents. We designed a categorisation task which captures processes involved in natural language interpretation and found that undergraduate students were faster to categorise novel objects when label-object mappings are sound-symbolic than when they are not. Moreover, early negative EEG-waveforms indicated sensitivity to sound-symbolic label-object associations. This sensitivity to sound-symbolic label-object associations may reflect a more general process of auditory-visual feature integration where properties of auditory stimuli facilitate a mapping to specific visual features.

Idiom syntax: Idiosyncratic or principled?

Tabossi, Patrizia Dept. of Psychology, University of Trieste, Trieste, Italy Wolf, Kinou Psychology, University of Trieste, Trieste, Italy Koterle, Sara Psychology, University of Trieste, Trieste, Italy

Idiom syntax may be represented in superlemmas. Alternatively, one may assume that speakers' competence suffices to constrain the use of an expression. The predictions of these alternatives were tested. In Experiment 1 non-native speakers were better at judging the acceptability of familiar than invented idioms, whereas Italian speakers performed equally well. In Experiment 2, native speakers performed equally well in judging the acceptability of idioms, whether familiar or unfamiliar. In Experiment 3 idiom acceptability increased in pragmatically appropriate contexts. Experiment 4 showed that general rules of Italian limit idiom passivization. The results were interpreted as supporting the competence hypothesis.

What eye-tracking tells about role-name processing

Irmen, Lisa Inst. für Psychologie, Universität Heidelberg, Heidelberg, Germany

Two eye-tracking studies assessed the effect of grammatical gender and gender role typicality on role-name processing. Participants read passages about representatives of social groups (e.g., soldiers, florists) whose gender was later specified through an anaphoric noun phrase (these men/women). A mismatch between the role-name's gender-typicality and the anaphor (florists - men) slowed reading before and after the anaphoric noun. A mismatch between the antecedent's grammatical gender and the anaphor (masculine - women) slowed reading the anaphoric noun itself. These results indicate an effect of gender-cues in early stages of processing and differing time-courses for using grammatical versus conceptual cues.

FP-200: Physical activity

The effects of antenatal exercise on psychological well-being during and following pregnancy and childbirth

Rankin, Jean *Health, Nursing and Midwifery, University of the West of Scot, Paisley, United Kingdom*

Effects of regular exercise during/following pregnancy were investigated with healthy primigravid women (2 separate studies –RCT and self-selected). Aim: Note differences in psychological variables between 2 groups - 1. Control - Routine antenatal care 2. Intervention - Adjunct, structured exercise programme. Psychological variables (early, late, after pregnancy).included positive/negative well-being. Tools: Psychological well-being scale, maternal attitude/adaptation to pregnancy, EPDS. Statitical tests: Repeated measures ANOVAs, follow-up multiple comparisons procedures (95% CI), PPM coefficient of correlations. Findings (both studies): Early pregnancy - No difference; Late/postpartum - significant differences in outcomes - significantly positive findings on all psychological variables for exercising women.

Psychosocial factors associated to physical exercise in undergraduate Mexican students

Rojas Russell, Mario *Mexico, Mexico* **Flórez Alarcón, Luis** *School of Psychology, National U. of Colombi, Bogota, Colombia* **Hernández Prado, Bernardo** *C. of Population Health Res., National Institute of Health, Cuernavaca, Mexico*

OBJECTIVE: To study the association of psychosocial variables to self-reported physical exercise (PE). METHOD: 696 random-selected first-year students answered a questionnaire containing scales to measure Self-efficacy, Readiness to Change for the accomplishment of PE, Attitude, Decisional Balance, and Subjective Norm. Self-Reported PE was estimated in METs. Anthropometric variables were also measured. RESULTS: Men reported practicing significantly more PE than women. On a multivariate logistic model (chi2(9) = 216.59, p = 0.00), volitional stages, self-efficacy, and subjective norm were significantly associated to PE. CONCLUSIONS: Advantages of interventions based on readiness to change are discussed. Limitations of the study are commented also.

Psychosocial determinants are related to exercise adherence during 3-year follow-up of a lifestyle intervention

Hankonen, Nelli *Health Promotion Unit, National Public Health Inst., Helsinki, Finland* **Absetz, Pilvikki** *Health Promotion Unit, National Public Health Inst., Helsinki, Finland* **Haukkala, Ari** *Department of Social Psych., University of Helsinki, University of Helsinki, Finland* **Uutela, Antti** *Health Promotion Unit, National Public Health Inst., Helsinki, Finland*

We sought to identify patterns of exercise adherence and associated psychosocial determinants in participants of a lifestyle counselling intervention based on Health Action Process Approach. Based on physical activity diaries from baseline, and 1-year and 3-year follow-ups, participants (N=260) were grouped into never-exercisers, decliners, late adopters, early adopters and always-exercisers. We found differences in self-efficacy, self-regulation and motivation that predict adherence in ways consistent with theory. BMI of never-exercisers was higher than that of decliners both at baseline and at

3 years. Tailoring of interventions could be useful both in the beginning and during the process.

Development and evaluation of a computer-based counseling system (CBCS) to promote physical activity for patients with chronic disease in general practice

Leonhardt, Corinna *Inst. für Medizin. Psychologie, Universität Marburg, Marburg, Germany* **Herzberg, Dominikus** *Faculty of Informatics, Heilbronn University, Heilbronn, Germany* **Marsden, Nicola** *Faculty of Informatics, Heilbronn University, Heilbronn, Germany* **Jung, Hartmut** *University of Marburg, Inst. f. Medical Psychology, Marburg, Germany* **Thomanek, Sabine** *University of Marburg, Department of General Practice, Marburg, Germany* **Becker, Annette** *Department of General Practice, University of Marburg, Marburg, Germany*

Objectives: This study shows the effects of a Computer-Based Counseling System (CBCS) for health promotion on patients with chronic diseases (Murray et al., 2005) in Germany. Methods: In an interdisciplinary team (psychologists, general practitioners, software engineers) we developed a CBCS. In a pre-post design with N= 50 patients (coronary heart disease or diabetes type 2) we investigate acceptability and effects on attitudes and self-efficacy. Results: Qualitative results show good acceptability and usability. Quantitative data regarding attitudes (Kiveniemi et al., 2007) and self-efficacy are being evaluated. Conclusion: Effectiveness assumed the CBCS should be tested further for the impact on behavioral and clinical outcomes and cost-benefit

A biopsychosocial analysis of a health study in children and youth from Luxemburg

Lämmle, Lena *München, Germany*

A biopsychosocial model was developed to find out the reasons for health and subjective wellbeing. 1253 Participants were assessed in motor skills, health parameters and health behaviours in 2004. The model was analysed using structural equitation modelling. The analysis yielded a good model-fit. A higher social standing leads to better eating habits, more reference persons being active and less sport motivation. Active reference persons enhance sport motivation and both affect positively the physical activity which itself enhances fitness. Fitness leads to better health and less health complaints. A moderator effect of age can be seen as well as biopsychosocial interactions.

FP-201: Positive health psychology

Health psychology and health promotion in settings: The development of a setting-based Sense of Coherence scale (U-SOC)

Graeser, Silke *Gesundheitswissenschaften, Universität Bremen, Bremen, Germany*

This study aimed to develop a theoretically based scale following classical guidelines for test construction. The University Sense of Coherence (U-SOC) scale is based on the concept of salutogenesis (Antonovsky, 1987), operationalized and adapted to a setting perspective. In a German university two surveys examined test-criteria of the U-SOC. Correlations and the comparison of means proved statistically significant differences between the U-SOC score and health status, mental health and psychosomatic complaints. The results of reliability analysis showed a Cronbach's Alpha of 0.90 for the U-SOC. Additional factor and cluster analysis indicated that the scale differentiates between groups. The results of the study underline the relevance of health psychological factors in settings.

Health behaviors: The roles of social integration and ethnic self-identity

Davis, John M. *Dept. of Psychology, Texas State University, San Marcos, USA*

Social integration (SI) and ethnic self-identity (ESI) both relate to health disparities but the underlying processes are unclear. We hypothesized that interpersonal evaluative processes link SI, ESI, and health behaviors. Participants completed measures of health behaviors, SI and ESI. Then, in a 2 X 2 experiment they interacted with a stranger that was attitudinally and ethnically either similar or dissimilar. Finally they evaluated the stranger. Results showed significant effects for attitudinal and ethnic similarity on evaluations, and significant links among SI, ESI, and health behaviors. The present study identified underlying factors linking SI, ESI, and disparities in health behaviors.

Enhancing mental health in youth: Role of positive cognitive states viz. self-efficacy, optimism and hope

Farokhzad, Pegah *Psychology, Panjab University, Tehran, Islamic Republic of Iran* **Askari, Amir** *Psychology, University of mysore, Tehran, Islamic Republic of Iran*

Objective: This study has been conducted to know whether positive cognitive states influence the development of mental health among youth. Method: Sample consisted of 100 males and females in age range of 20 to 25 years who were taken from university students of Tehran, Iran. Participants were given General Self-Efficacy Scale, Life Orientation Test, Hope Scale and psychological Well-Being Scale. Results / Conclusion: Results revealed a positive relationship between psychological well-being and positive cognitive states viz. self-efficacy, optimism and hope among the subjects. Therefore, by enhancing positive cognitive states through various techniques, we can improve mental health.

Spirituality, psychological well-being and subjective well-being among yoga practitioners

Askari, Amir *Psychology, University of Mysore, Tehran, Islamic Republic of Iran* **Farokhzad, Pegah** *Psychology, panjab University, Tehran, Islamic Republic of Iran*

Objective: This study investigated spirituality, psychological well-being and subjective well-being among yoga practitioners. Method: Sample consisted of 30 advanced practitioners of yoga and 30 yoga amateurs in age range of 20 to 60 years. They were 37 males and 23 females from the SVYASA (Deemed University), Bangalore, India. Subjects were given The Psychological Well-Being Scale, Subjective Well-Being Scale, and The Spiritual Transcendent Scale. Results / Conclusion: Significant difference between advanced practitioners of yoga and yoga amateurs was found in Psychological well-being. They do not show significant difference in the level of subjective well-being and spirituality.

The relationships of role ambiguity, role conflict, role overload and mental health with respect to type A and sense of coherence as a moderator variables in employees of a steel company

Neissi, Abdolkazem *Dept. of Psychology, Shahid Chamran University, Ahvaz, Islamic Republic of Iran*

This study was carried out to investigate the simple and multiple correlation of RA, RC, RO and mental healt in employees of a steel company in Ahvaz, Iran. The sample consisted of 196 employees who were selected randomly from the population of the company. RO and RC scale, RO scale, TAQ, SOC scale and GHQ were used to measure the research variables. The results indicated that there are negative correlation between Role Ambiguity, Role Conflict and mental health. Role Ambiguity and Role conflict were the two independent predictors of mental health. Sense of coherence and Type A personality had crucial moderating influence.

The effect of cognitive and metacognitive training on self-esteem of high school female students in Isfahan City

Esmaeili, Maryam Psychology, Isfahan University, Isfahan, Islamic Republic of Iran Moradi, Azam psychology, isfahan university, isfahan, Islamic Republic of Iran Mahdavi, Saeideh medicinece, azad university of najafabad, isfahan, Islamic Republic of Iran

Aim of this research was to determine the effects of cognitive and metacognitive strategies training on self-esteem of the high school female students. Subjects were high school female students in Isfahan who were assigned in two groups randomly. The experimental group was under 10 sessions training of cognitive and metacognitive strategies and evaluated by coopersmith'self-esteem questionnaire. The results of covariance analysis showed that there were significant differences between experimental group and control group regarding to self- esteem(P=0/00). The Results show that training of the strategies effects on self- esteem of female students; therefore teachers must trying for training these strategies.

FP-202: Cross-cultural approaches in psychology I

Process trust: A new concept and its application in intercultural business settings

Clases, Christoph School for Applied Psychology, UAS Northwestern Switzerland, Olten, Switzerland

The conceptual part of the paper will develop our understanding of "process trust" as a new approach to understand the relation between trust and collaborative processes in intercultural settings. Core differences to existing concepts (generalized trust, inter-personal trust, system trust, etc.) will be discussed allowing us to argue for the scientific and pragmatic value of the concept. With "process trust" we focus on the dynamic cognitive-affective evaluation of collaborative processes that may not be grasped with existing approaches. The empirical part will report on outcomes of a study on process trust in Sino-Swiss business settings.

A cross-cultural study about cultural self-efficacy in the preference of acculturation strategies at work

Tabernero, Carmen Dept. of Psychology, University of Cordoba, Córdoba, Spain Briones, Elena Department of Psychology, University of Salamanca, Salamanca, Spain Arenas, Alicia Department of Psychology, University of Sevilla, Córdoba, Spain Cahmbel, M. José Faculty of Psychology, University of Lisbon, Lisboa, Portugal Tramontano, Carlo Department of Psychology, University of Rome La Sapienza, Rome, Italy

Every day, organizations are more competitive and cultural diverse which necessities the development of new skills. From a social cognitive perspective, cultural self-efficacy is defined as a person's perception of their own capability to function effectively in situations characterized by cultural diversity. The present study analysed the role of cultural regulatory and dispositional variables such as self-efficacy, leadership and intelligence to determine acculturation strategies across four experimental scenarios created with fictious newspaper articles. A long sample from different cultural backgrounds participated. Results showed the interactions between three regulatory variables and ethnocultural origin within an ANOVA. Cultural self-efficacy played a main effect on the acculturation strategies adopted.

Attitudes of Chinese commercial pilots toward voluntary reporting systems

von Thaden, Terry Human Factors Division, University of Illinois, Savoy, USA Li, Yongjuan Inst. of Psychology, Chinese Academy of Sciences, Beijing, People's Republic of China

Objective: We compared Chinese pilots' attitudes toward their airline's safety reporting system and a possible anonymous reporting system controlled by their airline, or a third party. Method: We surveyed airline pilots regarding reporting attitude and motivation. Results: Pilots display significant concern about airline peer pressure and punishment. Captains were more reserved about anonymous airline reporting than copilots. Both would utilize a third-party system. Conclusion: Cultural influences and potential biases to reporting cannot be overlooked. Chinese pilots require assurances which can be enhanced by policy not currently present. This will support receiving information from all pilot ranks, consequently promoting system safety.

FP-203: Psychological disorders V

Fibromyalgia and burnout: Same or different types of health problems?

Andersson, Sven Ingmar Dept. of Psychology, Lund University, Lund, Sweden Hovelius, Birgitta Department of Family Medicine, Lund University, Lund, Sweden

Objective. To find out in what ways fibromyalgia and burnout differ or are similar. Methods. Questionnaire study of subjects' cognitive and emotional appraisal, coping intentions and coping, participants (n=300) absent from their jobs for 60 days or more with burnout or fibromyalgia type of diagnoses, the findings related to sociodemographic and medical data. Results and Conclusion. Fibromyalgia and burnout may represent culturally bound ways of dealing with situations that the individuals involved experience as overwhelming. Health-care workers, psychologists included, can serve to reinforce a biomedical perspective on the patients' part, resulting in medicalization, surgery or heavy use of pharmaceutical drugs.

Test anxiety in university students: Harmless tension or disabling mental disorder?

Fehm, Lydia Institute of Psychology, Humboldt-Universität zu Berlin, Berlin, Germany Priewe, Jennifer Institute of Psychology, Humboldt-Universität zu Berlin, Berlin, Germany

Studies on test anxiety are often hampered by selection biases. The present study provides data about symptoms and the extent of test anxiety and associated impairments in an unselected student sample (N = 489; response rate: 93%). The mean score of the university students on the Test Anxiety Inventory (German version) was comparable to those of high school students. Three percent of the sample reported being significantly impaired by their anxiety, thus indicating a possible mental disorder. The participants ask for more information on test anxiety as well as for effective coping strategies, e.g., learning strategies.

Experiential avoidance and eating pathology in a sample of college students in Cyprus

Karekla, Maria Dept. of Psychology, University of Nicosia, Nicosia, Cyprus Kapsou, Margarita Psychology, University of Nicosia, Nicosia, Cyprus

• The present study examined whether higher levels of experiential avoidance are linked to higher rates of eating pathology. Sixty four first year students at University of Nicosia, completed a packet of eating related measures, the Acceptance and Action Questionnaire (AAQ-49), and the Beck Depression Inventory (BDI-II). Multivariate analysis of variance indicated, as predicted, that participants classified as high in emotional avoidance reported higher levels of eating pathology, more uncon-

trolled eating behavior, and higher levels of depression compared to their low avoidance counterparts. Interestingly, individuals high in experiential avoidance reported levels of eating pathology and depression within the clinical range.

The role of superstitiousness on obsessive-compulsive symptomatology

O, Jiaqing Singapore, Singapore Catherine So-kum, Tang Psychology, NUS, Singapore, Singapore

Few studies have elucidated the relationship between superstitiousness and Obsessive Compulsive disorder (OCD), and none has yet explicated the specificities of this relationship. We hypothesized that superstitiousness mediates the relationship between a person's external locus of control and resulting OCD symptoms. Further, the higher the score on "avoiding" aspect (as compared to "achieving" aspect) of superstitiousness for an individual, the higher will be the corresponding incidence of reported obsessive-compulsive symptoms for that individual; vice versa. We expect to observe these phenomena in college students by means of questionnaires, analyzed using factor analyses. Preliminary findings will be presented in the conference.

FP-204: Development in adolescence and young adulthood I

Striving for multiple personal goals: What makes the difference on success in goal management?

Schnelle, Jessica Motivation, Volition and Emoti, University of Zurich, Zurich, Switzerland Brandstaetter, Veronika Motivation, Volition and Emoti, University of Zurich, Zurich, Switzerland

People are generally striving for multiple personal goals. On the basis of theories of self-regulation, we analyzed the antecedents and consequences of goal conflict between work- and private-life goals. Longitudinal field studies with students (N = 283, N = 59), cross-sectional (N = 102, N = 129) studies and an experiment (N = 30) with employees were carried out. Results indicate that goal-conflict is associated with avoidance goal orientation. Additionally, goal-conflict impairs performance and psychological well-being. The generalizability of the outcomes and theoretical implications with respect to conflict in personal goal striving will be discussed.

Occupational aspirations as a device to study Mexican adolescents' development and understanding of socioeconomic organization

Diez Martinez, Evelyn Faculty of Psychology, Univ. Autonoma de Queretaro, Queretaro, Mexico Ochoa, Azucena FACULTY OF PSYCHOLOGY, UNIV. AUTONOMA DE QUERETARO, QUERETARO, QRO.,, Mexico Virues, Ricardo FACULTY OF PSYCHOLOGY, UNIV. AUTONOMA DE QUERETARO, QUERETARO, QRO.,, Mexico

In recent research on social cognitive development, children's and adolescents' understanding about work and employment has been considered as part of socioeconomic knowledge. Students' development of occupational aspirations through different school levels allows an appreciation of their comprehension of social organization and economic expectations and should be considered by developmental psychologists. Occupational aspirations were used as a model of studying Mexican adolescents' comprehension of socioeconomic aspects related to social organization and occupational hierarchy. Questionnaires and individual interviews were conducted with 360 adolescents sampled from 6th, 9th and 12th grades in public and private schools. Results show developmental and socioeconomic differences.

Representation of future profession: Change in professional representation of students from incoming to outgoing in a higher institution
Crescentini, Alberto Scienze dell'Educazione, Alta Scuola Pedagogica, Locarno, Switzerland Antognazza, Davide Scienze dell'Educazione, Alta Scuola Pedagogica, Locarno, Switzerland Donati, Mario Scienze dell'Educazione, Alta Scuola Pedagogica, Locarno, Switzerland Losa, Franco Scienze dell'Educazione, Alta Scuola Pedagogica, Locarno, Switzerland

Teacher education is a debated issue, especially in the current period in which teachers' public representation is getting a gradual weaking. In order to improve our academic programs, it is extremely important to investigate the representation that future teachers have of their job, and how the educational curriculum affects this vision: these were the two goals of our study. We used an "ad hoc" questionnaire, validated in process, and informal interviews. Results show that after three years training, students have modified some aspects of their representation, while others remain unchanged. Several dimensions of this representation show incoherence with reality.

Psychological technologies for businessman potential development
Guseva, Larisa of Business, Ural-Siberian Institute, Ekaterinburg, Russia

The problem of potentiality has always attracted the most rapt attention of those, who deal with human being, behavior and activity. Some natural individual features, capabilities and inclinations, orientation and power of a person are referred to the field of potentiality. The development of potentialities has an overwhelming practical meaning in the context of business undertakings. A businessman is one who takes resources, labor, energy and other assets and combines them in different ways in order to increase their initial costs. At the same time he conducts some changes, makes a new order of activity and develops a new social context etc. The latest achievements in the realm of psychology allow us to mark out the businessman potential as a complex of typical and natural traits of a person and also help us to stimulate its development by means of authentication psychotherapy and leadership education. Applying of these psychological technologies to the practice of psychological consultations and education allows many young businessmen to satisfy their intention to perceive their natural potential, to learn how to manage their lives, to reveal their capabilities and, eventually, to make their dreams come true.

FP-205: Psychotherapy - Research and treatment methods VII

Group psychotherapy for gay men across addictions utilizing gradualism: Theory and practice
Greene, Darrell Darrell Greene, Ph.D., New York, USA
This paper advances a model of addictions treatment called gradualism (Kellogg 2003; Kellogg and Kreek, 2005) within the context of group psychotherapy for gay men. Gradualism attempts to synthesize harm reduction and abstinence-oriented treatment perspectives. A discussion of the benefits of group participation across varying addictions, levels of treatment experience, periods of non-use and psychological commitment to abstinence or behavioral management will be explored according to Yalom's (1995) eleven therapeutic factors. The final section will present illustrations of the model from the author's group experience.

The effectiveness of MBCT group therapy on prevention of relapse in depression
Moradi, Mahnaz Tehran, Islamic Republic of Iran Bahreini, Faezeh psychology, sahiandish counseling center, Tehran, Islamic Republic of Iran Tahmasebi, Siyamak preschool, university of welfare & re, Tehran, Islamic Republic of Iran
Evidence indicates that the risk of depressive as the illness becomes more highly recurrent. MBCT (mindfulness based cognitive therapy) is a meditation based psychotherapeutic intervention designed to help reduce the risk of relapse of recurrent depression. in order to study the effectiveness of MBCT in reducing the relapse, an 8week cource set out for a langitudional investigation with 1year follow up. The analiyses of data indicate that relapse had accured 6.6% in experimental group, and 75%in control group.So it can be concluded that development of mindfulness as a life style can hold a key role in reducing relapse.

The effect of cognitive group therapy and spiritual therapy on depression of teachers training university
Taraghijah, Sadighi Deputy of Students, Ministry of Sciences, Tehran, Islamic Republic of Iran Navabinejad, Shokouh counselling, Teacher,s training University, Tehran, Islamic Republic of Iran Hamdieh, Mostafa Shaheed Beheshti University of, Associated professor of psychi, Tehran, Islamic Republic of Iran
Aim : The main Objective of this study is comparision of effect of two (CGT) and (SGT) among Female depressed students of teachers training university. Method: The sample of the study 24 girls student randomly selected through advertisement. Their depression was confirmed with Beck Depression Inventory BDI and Psychiatric Interview. snbjectsdivided to three groups randomly: group 1 and 2 experimental groups and the three (3) comparing group They were relested with BDI again. The two groups participaled in ten sessions of CGTand SGT. after doing group therapy BDI test was done, then the data was analyzed with (ANOVA). Results:CGT and SGTwere effective significantly in Reducation of depression (p<0/01). .

Experiential / Interpersonal group therapy for chronic pain: An extention of functional analytic psychotherapy
Vandenberghe, Luc Goiânia, Brazil Lemos Barbosa Ferro, Cristina Private Practice, Clinical Psychologist, Palmas, Brazil de Araujo Martins Queiroz, Marilene Psychology, Universidade Católica de Goiás, Goiânia, Brazil
Pain- and stress-related daily-life difficulties experienced by chronic pain patients were identified to also occur during the in-session interactions between participants in group therapy. Aim: Exploring therapeutic possibilities of working in-vivo with these occurrences. Method: In three groups Functional Analytic Psychotherapy (Kohlenberg & Tsai, 1991) strategies were used to ensure in-vivo learning experiences during in-session occurrences of clinically relevant difficulties. Difficulties were categorized and changes monitored. Results: In-vivo occurring difficulties were frequent and diverse. Improvements in Experiential avoidance (trying to avoid feelings), catastrophizing talk and trying to control the behavior of the other were related to changes in reported pain-levels.

FP-206: Issues in priming

Prime retrieval of motor responses in negative priming: Findings in a Go/NoGo task paradigm
Mayr, Susanne Inst. für Exp. Psychologie, Universität Düsseldorf, Düsseldorf, Germany Buchner, Axel Institute of Exp. Psychology, Heinrich Heine University, Düsseldorf, Germany Dentale, Sandra

Institute of Exp. Psychology, Heinrich Heine University, Düsseldorf, Germany
The prime-response retrieval model of negative priming assumes that the transfer-inappropriate prime response is retrieved in ignored repetition (IR) trials. In three auditory identification experiments, a cue in the prime signaled whether participants were to respond (Go) or not (NoGo). Go/NoGo cues were either simple cues presented before or after the prime stimuli or selective cues necessitating a motor discrimination in order to decide upon response execution or suppression. Negative priming was found for all trial types, but an increase in prime response errors to the probes of IR trials was found only when the prime response had been executed. This implies that execution of the prime response is a precondition for prime-response retrieval.

Neural basis for priming of pop-out during visual search revealed with N2pc: An Event-Related Potentials (ERP) study
Cheung, Ching-Kong Dept. of Psychology, University College London, London, Germany Eimer, Martin Psychology, Birkbeck, U of London, London, United Kingdom Kiss, Monika Psychology, Birkbeck, U of London, London, United Kingdom
Repetitions of target-defining features facilitate later reaction times in visual search tasks to discriminate the singleton target among distractors. The effect, termed as priming of pop-out, was proposed to reflect an implicit transient short-term memory, which is essential in focusing attention rapidly. The present study aimed to identify the corresponding event-related potential (ERP). The N2-posterior-contralateral (N2pc) component, which is sensitive to attentional selection, was proposed to reflect priming of pop-out. N2pc latencies corresponded to the behavioural effects. The N2pc onset was delayed in change trials relative to repeat trials, suggesting that priming of pop-out affects target selection.

Viewing static images with implied motion primes action-related stimulus dimensions
Fagioli, Sabrina Dept. of Psychology, University of Rome, Rome, Italy Ferlazzo, Fabio Department of Psychology, University of Rome, Rome, Italy Hommel, Bernhard Department of Psychology, Leiden University, Leiden, Netherlands
Observing grasping or a reaching actions improves the processing of action-related stimulus dimensions (size or location information, respectively). Here, we investigated whether the possibility to predict the course of such actions modulates the dimensional priming effect. Subjects saw static images showing either implied motion or the end state of the actions before discriminating size- or location-defined stimuli. As predicted, the dimensional priming effect was only evident after observing images with implied motion, suggesting that the possibility to infer the further course of the action plays a critical role for directing visual attention.

An ERP investigation of the modulation of subliminal priming by exogenous cues
Marzouki, Yousrii Labo de Psychologie Cognitive, Université de Provence, Marseille, France Midgley, Katherine J Labo de Psychologie Cognitive, Université de Provence, Marseille, France Holcomb, Phillip J Department of Psychology, Tufts University, Massachusetts, Medford, USA Grainger, Jonathan Labo de Psychologie Cognitive, Université de Provence, Marseille, France
Marzouki et al. (2007) demonstrated that masked repetition priming of letter identification is affected by the allocation of spatial attention to the prime location by an exogenous cue. The present ERP study provides a further investigation of such exogenous influences on masked priming. The

electrophysiological data showed a significant modulation of the amplitude of the P3 component generated by target letters as a function of priming and cue validity. Results confirm the influence of exogenous cues on the processing of subliminally presented prime stimuli, and furthermore show that such effects can be obtained in the absence of any eye movements.

FP-207: Dietary behavior II

Adaptation and evaluation of an internet-based prevention program for eating disorders in a sample of women with subclinical eating disorder syndromes

Völker, Ulrike Inst. für Klin. Psychologie, Technische Universität Dresden, Dresden, Germany *Jacobi, Corinna* Inst. f. klin. Psychologie, Technische Universität Dresden, Dresden, Germany *Taylor, C. Barr* Dept. of Medicine, Stanford University, Stanford, USA

Women, reporting initial eating disorder (ED) symptoms are at higher risk for the development of an eating disorder. Preventive interventions should therefore be specifically tailored for this subgroup. Accordingly, the aim of this study was to adapt and evaluate the effects of the Internet-based prevention program "StudentBodies™" for women with subclinical ED syndromes. 90 women, reporting subclinical ED symptoms were randomly assigned to the intervention or a waiting-list control condition and assessed at pre-intervention, post-intervention, and 6-month-follow-up. Results: In a pilot study medium to large effects were found. Pre-post results of the randomized controlled study will be available next year.

Language acculturation and health behaviors in Mexican Americans

Singelis, Theodore Dept. of Psychology, California State University, Chico, USA

This study investigates the effects of acculturation on health promoting behaviors, well being and health in Mexican American adults in California, USA. Participants (N=253) were interviewed by telephone and completed the Bi-dimensional Acculturation Scale, the Health Promoting Lifestyle Profile II, and other measures. Data were analyzed with a series of hierarchical general linear models with education and income as covariates. More than assimilated or separated respondents, biculturals reported better health and performed better on some health behaviors. The high performance and characteristics of the bicultural group are discussed. Supported by a Grant from the National Institute on Aging (#1R15AG19141-01)

Family environment and self-regulation in cardiac patients

Kalavana, Theano Nursing Dept., Cyprus University, Lemesos, Cyprus *Fteropoulli, Theodora* Clinical Health Department, LONDON COLLEGE LONDON, London, United Kingdom

The present study examined the family environment of Greek-Cypriot cardiac patients (N=55, X=60.4), and their self-regulation cognitions in their attempt to improve their health. ANOVA and Regression analyses indicated that the presence of self-regulation cognitions was the most important parameter for their health improvement. Additionally, family factors (cohesion, expressiveness and organization) facilitate self-regulation. In conclusion, this study points out that intervention programs aiming at helping cardiac patients to improve their health and that is of great importance to include family members and/or intimate partners in the whole effort.

FP-208: Dimensions of personality II

Ambivalence phenomenon: Measuring and studying the properties

Lialenko, Anna Psychology, Lomonosov MSU, Moscow, Russia *Mitina, Olga* Psychology, Lomonosov MSU, Moscow, Russia *Osin, Evgeny* Psychology, Lomonosov MSU, Moscow, Russia

This work is devoted to the study and characterization of the personality and social properties of ambivalence toward various concepts. Three groups of subjects were considered: with "creative"(1)/ "noncreative"(2) professions, and those who are currently diagnosed with schizophrenia or depression (3). Several indices of ambivalence were compared. Three aspects of ambivalence are considered: personality, linguistics, and social (concerning human values). The results showed that individuals with "creative" occupation are characterized by a high degree of ambivalence. The high degree of ambivalence is accompanied by the high degree of tolerance to uncertainty but also the high degree of personal anxiety.

Taxonomy and structure of Persian personality-descriptive adjectives

Farahani, Mohammad Naghy Dept. of Psychology, Tarbiat Moallem University, Tehran, Islamic Republic of Iran

This paper describes the development of a comprehensive taxonomy of Persian Personality-descriptive terms, organized in two studies. In the first study six judges searched through a standard dictionary of the Persian language for person-descriptive terms. In the next stage, personality-descriptive adjectives were classified by six Judges into different categories of descriptions. In the second study, the 126 adjectives rated for self-descriptions by 2400 students. Self ratings were factor analyzed and were interpreted to be similar to the Big-Five factors: Agreeableness, Extraversion, Conscientiousness, Intellect, and Emotional Stability.

Using the CPI260 for assessing the personality typology of law enforcement personnel

Lita, Stefan Centre for Psychosociology, Ministry of Interior, Bucharest, Romania *Grigoras, Calin* Centre for Psychosociology, Ministry of Interior, Bucharest, Romania *Stoian, Bogdan* Centre for Psychosociology, Ministry of Interior, Bucharest, Romania *Stoican, Constantin* Centre for Psychosociology, Ministry of Interior, Bucharest, Romania

The California Psychological Inventory has been used in law enforcement settings since 70's for assessing both police cadets and police officers. Our study uses the 3-vector model of personality from the CPI260 in order to investigate the typology of both managers and incumbents working in different law enforcement agencies. The study has three main purposes: (a) to analyze how the Romanian version of CPI260 is working in high stake setting, (b) to compare the typology of semi-military and military personnel with that of civil employees and (c) to perform a latent class analysis on the vector scales. Preliminary results obtained from 250 subjects revealed that the most frequent types are Alpha (54%) and Beta (29%).

FP-209: Disability and rehabilitation II

A systems approach to working with persons with disabilities: A model from the USA

Schiro-Geist, Chrisann Memphis,Tennessee, USA

This will be a demonstration of a systems approach to the adult development of persons with disabilities in the USA. It will be a system that can be applied to moving from dependence to independence,especially in the world of work,but also in independent

living.The model is being re-evaluated in other countries,including China and India by cooperating psychologists. Hopefully,it will also apply to countries such as Germany. It has been used in Ireland. The instrument which has evolved from the model has reliability at the .88-.93 level and might be replicated in other societies.

Health cognitions in Parkinson disease

Glozman, Janna Psychology Department, Moscow State University, Moscow, Germany *Levin, Oleg* Neurology Department, Russian Medical Academy of Po, Moscow, Russia *Sozinova, Helene* Neurology Department, Russian Academy of postgraduat, Moscow, Russia

Objectives: To find out relations between patients' concepts and efficiency of rehabilitation. Methods: 40 patients with PD and their caregivers were assessed through Luria battery; Wylie Self-concept test; Spilberger, Depression, Quality of Life and Inner Representation of disease scales. Results: Patients with less cognitive disturbances, lower depression and anxiety, and balanced type of inner representation of disease show better results in rehabilitation. Internal representation of defects correlates more with emotional disturbances than real motor deficit. Interdependence between quality of life of the patient and his caregiver is revealed. Conclusions: Health concepts should be one of the main orientations in psychological rehabilitation.

Evaluation of the implementation of Corporate Integration Management and the benefit for occupational rehabilitation in Germany

Vater, Gudrun Inst. für Humanwissenschaften, Universität zu Köln, Köln, Germany *Niehaus, Mathilde* Human Science, University of Cologne, Köln, Germany *Marfels, Britta* Human Science, University of Cologne, Köln, Germany

OBJECTIVES AND METHODS Corporate Integration Management (CIM) is an early intervention specifically at work to guarantee tailor-made rehabilitation measures instead of pensions and in order to prevent further work related injuries. The project investigates structures and measures for work related prevention and CIM. There are 630 participants in the nationwide survey. Data has been subjected to univariate as well as multivariate statistics. RESULTS CIM has been applied in 49% of the participating companies. Some of the integration measures are directly connected to a successful return to work, which could be attained in nearly 50% of the CIM-Cases. CONCLUSIONS The results indicate that CIM is an appropriate early intervention for occupational rehabilitation.

FP-210: Child health II

Dental health care and dental anxiety in school children

Margraf-Stiksrud, Jutta Inst. für Psychologie, Universität Marburg, Marburg, Germany *Stein, Stefan* Fachbereich Psychologie, Philipps-Universität, Marburg, Germany *Pieper, Klaus* Kinderzahnheilkunde, Philipps-Universität, Marburg, Germany

Objectives: Children with regular attendance to health care programs before suffering caries and decayed teeth should show less dental anxiety than children visiting the dentist only for treatment reasons. Methods: 300 children aged 6,10, and 12 years were participants of a research program to evaluate the effectiveness of a dental health prevention campaign, 300 received only basic instructions. Dental fear via questionnaire and actual dental health care status were registered. Results: 3x2 analyses of variance revealed lower anxiety levels in children participating the prevention campaign. Further investigations showed interaction effects between sex, anxiety levels an dental status. Conclusions: Regular and intense dental health instructions may reduce dental anxiety levels as a consequence of training to cope with dental tasks.

Coping strategies and quality of life of patients with asthma

Kausar, Rukhsana Applied Psychology, University of the Punjab, Lahore, Pakistan

Study aimed to examine relationship between Coping Strategies (CSs) and Quality of Life (QOL) of asthmatic children. It was hypothesized that: children would use more avoidant CSs; avoidant coping has negative and active coping has positive relationship with QOL. Fifty children with asthma were recruited from a specialized hospital. Pediatric asthma quality of life questionnaire and coping questionnaire were used for assessment. It was found that children employed more CSs and avoidant coping had negative relationship with QOL. There were gender differences in QOL and use of CSs. Findings highlight importance of coping strategies in improving diseased children's QOL.

Stress levels of parents and siblings of disable children

Rauf, Nelofar Dept. of Psychology, Quaid A Azam University, Islamabad, Pakistan Gillani, Nighat Psychology, NIP,Quaid_a_Azam University, Islamabad, Pakistan

The purpose of the study was to assess stress levels of parents and siblings of disabled children. Moderate and severely mentally retarded children were taken as a sample. Results indicate that stress level of parents of mentally retarded children was high as compare to parents of non-disabled children. Mothers of mentally retarded children were more stressed as compared to the fathers. Siblings of non-disabled children feel less stress as compare to siblings of mentally retarded children. Their was no significant difference in stress between sisters and brothers of mentally retarded children. Results also revealed that with increase in family size and income parental stress decreases.

FP-211: Clinical / counseling psychology II

The roles of sensitivity to reward and alcohol expectancies in the relationship between social anxiety and alcohol use

Hasking, Penelope School of Psychology, Monash University, Victoria, Australia Booth, Catherine School of Psychology, Psychiat, Monash University, Victoria, Australia

Objectives To examine whether sensitivity to reward and alcohol outcome expectancies moderate the relationship between social anxiety and drinking behaviour. Methods 454 university students completed an online questionnaire. Results Students with a tendency to avoid social situations drank less even if they held strong tension reduction expectancies and were sensitive to reward. However students whose anxiety was characterised by fear were more likely to drink if they held strong outcome expectancies. Conclusion The relationship between social anxiety and drinking may be better understood by examining different forms of anxiety, and by considering trait characteristics and alcohol-related cognitions.

Nonverbal emotion recognition biases in dual-channel emotion context in the depressed patients

Huang, Yu-Lien Dept. of Psychology, National Taiwan University, Taipei, Taiwan Chen, Sue-Huei Department of Psychology, National Taiwan University, Taipei, Taiwan Tseng, Huai-Hsuan department of psychiatry, National Taiwan Uni. Hosptial, Taipei, Taiwan

This study aimed to empirically investigate the possible nonverbal emotion recognition deficits in dual-channel emotion expression context in the depressed patients. Thirty depressed patients and 39 normal controls completed diagnostic interview, self-report symptom scale, intelligence assessment (WAIS-III-short), and computerized Diagnostic Analysis of Nonverbal Accuracy 2-Taiwan version (DANVA2-TW). Results revealed that, after controlling for IQ, the depressed patients exhibited more accurate for sad and happy emotions in emotion-congruent dual-channel contexts, but displayed positive bias toward happy and negative bias toward fear emotions in emotion-incongruent contexts. Association of depression and potential deficits in nonverbal emotion recognition will be discussed accordingly.

The investigating of effectiveness of cognitive – behavioural group therapy based on Heimberg's model on social anxiety

Melyani, Mahdiyee Clinical Psychology, Shahed University, Tehran, Islamic Republic of Iran Shairi, Mohamad Reza Clinical Psychology, Shahed University, Tehran, Islamic Republic of Iran Ghaedi, Gholam Hosain Psychiatry, Shahed Univresity, Tehran, Islamic Republic of Iran Bakhtiari, Maryam Clinical Psychology, Shahid Beheshti University, Tehran, Islamic Republic of Iran Tavoli, Azadeh Clinical Psychology, Shahed Univresity, Tehran, Islamic Republic of Iran

Objectives: The aim of this study was to examine the effectiveness of cognitive behavioural group therapy (CBGT) with Heimberg's model on social anxiety (SA) among female students. Methods: At first, Social Phobia Inventory (SPI) was administrated to 205 female students of Shahed University. In the second phrase of these 24 students, 16 students were randomly allocated to control (8 subjects) and experimental (8 subjects) groups. Afterthat, experimental group was attended in 12 treatment sessions while control group didn't attend in any treatment session. Finally, experimental and control group were examined by SPI. Result: CBGT with Heimberg's model has been fount to be effective on SA among Iranian female students and the effectiveness could be stable after 1 month

FP-212: Interindividual differences in the experience of emotion I

The achilles' heal of hedonic well-being: Life satisfaction predicts happiness when life is easy, but not during demanding tasks

Vitterso, Joar Dept. of Psychology, University of Tromso, Tromso, Norway Alekseeva, Irina Department of Psychology, University of Tromso, Tromso, Norway Roysamb, Espen Department of Psychology, University of Oslo, Oslo, Norway

Argues that satisfaction is typically felt in effortless (hedonic) situations, but not during demanding tasks. Hypothesized that life satisfaction (LS) is biased towards easiness, making LS a strong predictor of mood in trouble-free situations, but a weak predictor of mood during effortful tasks. Hypothesized that individual tendencies towards personal growth (PG) operate in the opposite direction. Norwegian students (107) completed measures of LS, PG, and then solved a problem. Participants reported mood before and during the task. Path analyses showed that LS predicted mood before, but not during the problem-solving task. PG predicted mood before and during the problem-solving task.

Anxiety trait and death anxiety as predictor variables of student's anxiety reaction in human cadaver disection

Castano, Gloria Diferential & Work Psychology, Universidad Complutense Madrid, Madrid, Spain Casado, Isabel Basic Psychology (Cognitive P), Complutense University, MADRID, Spain Arraez, Luis Human Anatomy & Embriology, Complutense University, MADRID, Spain

The aim is to analyze student's anxiety response to human cadaver dissection and their relationship whit general (trait anxiety) and/or specifics individual characteristics (death anxiety). Participants are 325 students enrolled for the first time in the subject of Human Anatomy. The measurement's instruments are State-Trait Anxiety Inventory, Situations and Responses Anxiety Inventory and Death Anxiety Inventory. STAI-E are completed at the moment just before and immediately after of the first and last dissection of a compulsory course. ISRA and DAI are given a week before the first dissection session. Results show individual differences which leads us to detect students with a propensity to suffer a strong emotional reaction to dissection and to do a preventive intervention.

Does experiential avoidance mediate the relation between anxiety sensitivity and alexithymia?

Pennato, Tiziana Psychiatry, University of Pisa, Pisa, Italy Bernini, Olivia Psychiatry, University of Pisa, Pisa, Italy Berrocal, Carmen Psychiatry, University of Pisa, Pisa, Italy Guazzelli, Mario Psychiatry, University of Pisa, Pisa, Italy

Objective: to test a model in which Experiential Avoidance (EA) mediates the relation between Anxiety Sensitivity (AS) and Alexithymia (AT). Methods: participants included undergraduate students and non-student adults (N=177, males and females, 18-65 yrs.). Measures of AS, EA, and AT were obtained from standardised, self-administered questionnaires. Regression analyses were performed to test for mediational models. Results: while AS significantly predicts EA scores, the effect of AS on AT is not significant when controlling EA scores, whereas the latter predicts AT. Conclusion: EA mediates the relation between AS and AT.

FP-213: Cognitive information processing and learning II

Effects of a cognitive training program for entire school classes

Tiedemann, Joachim Inst. für Pädagog. Psychologie, Universität Hannover, Hannover, Germany Billmann-Mahecha, Elfriede Phil. Fakultät, Universität Hannover, Hannover, Germany

It has been shown that training of inductive reasoning by means of an analytical solving strategy results in transfer effects on intelligence and scholastic achievement in reading and mathematics. As part of the reading literacy program (KOLIBRI) of the Hanover Primary School Study, a five-week cognitive training program for entire school classes was developed for use in a cooperative learning setting. A classroom experiment involving 300 third- and fourth-grade students demonstrated that training to reason inductively results in substantial gains in (CFT-)intelligence in entire school classes. Further evaluation shows high acceptance of the program by both students and teachers.

The effect of distractors on adults' numerical estimation with field independence and field dependence

Si, Ji Wei School of Psychology, Shandong Normal University, Ji Nan, People's Republic of China Xu, Ji Hong School of Psychology, Beijing Normal University, Bei Jing, People's Republic of China

This paper aims to investigate the effect of different disturbing stimulus on adults' numerical estimation with FD and FI cognitive styles. The results showed

: 1) The RT of FIs' was significantly different with that of FDs under the condition of only targets stimulus,2)The accuracy of FIs' estimates was also significant different with that of FDs'estimates when distractors number was twice as targets.3)On the reasonableness of estimates,there was no difference between FIs and FDs among three disturbing conditions and between large and small number groups, respectively.4) As the distractor number increased, FIs altered their representation ways from linear representation to logarithmic representation, but FDs sticked to exert logarithmic representation.

The influence of learning-to-learn on teachers and students' self-assessed academic successes

Sadzaglishvili, Shorena Assessment, National Curric & Assess Cent, Tbilisi, Georgia Janashia, Simon Assessment, National Curric & Assess, Tbilisi, Georgia Berdzenishvili, Tea Assessment, National Curric & Assess, Tbilisi, Georgia Tsereteli, Mzia Assessment, National Curric & Assess, Tbilisi, Georgia

The purpose was to assess "LtL" – whether teachers and students grouped by their self-assessed level of success differ according to their LtL components and to reveal the most influential LtL factors; Our sample comprised of 166 teachers and 1007 students of Georgia. Specially designed likert type questionnaires measured the different components of LtL. Analyzing results by factor analysis, nonparametric measures and regression proved that students as well as teachers having better performance on LtL are disposed to have better self-assessment. The most influential LtL components were revealed. These results show of high importance of evaluation of LtL in school assessment system;

FP-214: Education and advanced training II

Implementation of the project active learning in teachers' pre-service education

Marinkovic, Snezana Faculty of Teacher Education, Uzice, Serbia

Implementation of the original Active Learning (AL) model (developed in Serbia) during the teachers' pre-service education is investigated in this paper. The goals: 1. analysis of the AL model implementation in teaching on the faculty of teachers' education; 2. program evaluation in two directions – to explore the students' understanding of the AL ideas and students' implementation of the AL in teaching. This is an action investigation: it's performed in real social situations; learning practice is realized through the process of change. The sample: the students of Faculty of teachers' education in Uzice, Serbia. The research indicates the possibility of Active learning implementation in university teaching, as well as its effects and problems while being implemented.

Investigating the effectiveness of the short-term educational courses from middle class managers point of view

Sabbaghian, Zahra Education and Psychology, Shahid Beheshti University, Tehran, Islamic Republic of Iran

This research investigated the effectiveness of short-term educational courses. The samples were randomly selected and their knowledge, attitudes and performance were evaluated. Data were analyzed by ANOVA and T- test. The result showed: 1- the short –term courses for middle- class managers increased their knowledge (t=4.38).2- It increased the manager positive attitudes (t=5.34). 3-It improved their performance (t=10.48). 4- Managers attitudes had significant influence on the improvement of their performance (f=56.59). There was no difference in the effectiveness of courses, consider-ing the managers individual characteristics such as gender, education, employment and management background (f=1.31).It can be concluded that short-term courses for managers were effective.

Adaptive design as training wheels for less-experienced, older adults

Bruder, Carmen Inst. of Aerospace Medicine, DLR German Aerospace Centre, Hamburg, Germany Wandke, Hartmut Inst. für Psychologie, Humboldt-Universität zu Berlin, Berlin, Germany Blessing, Lucienne Campus Limpertsberg, Université du Luxembourg, Luxembourg, Luxembourg

Lifelong learning 'just in time' gains in importance. Complex electronic devices require permanent learning. Older users with little experience in using electronic devices need support. Adaptive training application turned out to be promising. Two adaptive principles are researched: the adjustment of complexity to users' experience with electronic devices and adaptive suggestions through program control. In a training study both principles are tested to their effect on older learners' training success. The results show a positive effect of the adjustment of complexity to users' experience. Program control does not affect the learners' success and reduces their self-efficacy.

FP-215: Expression and experience of emotion

Approaching toward or removing from an observer: Is stimulus significance modulated by distance related dynamic contexts?

Neumann, Roland Universität Dortmund, Dortmund, Germany Mühlberger, Andreas Psychology, Universität Würzburg, Würzburg, Germany Wieser, Matthias Psychology, Universität Würzburg, Würzburg, Germany Pauli, Paul Psychology, Universität Würzburg, Würzburg, Germany

We test the assumption that changes in the perceived distance towards emotional charging pictures affect the emotional significance of these stimuli. In our experiments the illusion was induced that IAPS pictures either moved toward or away from the participant. The intensity of the emotional response startle probe and subjective intensity measures were assessed. In two experiments negative IAPS pictures that move toward the observer elicited enhanced arousal ratings and startle responses compared to neutral or positive pictures. Moreover, pictures that seem to remove from the observer or are unmoved exert no influence on subjective arousal or startle responses. These findings replicate earlier reports that movement of emotional pictures enhances their emotional significance.

Emotional coordination in spontaneous infant-father interactions during early infancy

Kokkinaki, Theano Dept. of Psychology, University of Crete, Rethymnon, Greece

This naturalistic study aims to investigate fathers' and infants' emotional expressions in the course of spontaneous paternal infant-directed speech and the preceding / following pauses across infant gender. Microanalysis of infant and paternal facial expressions of emotions of 11 infant-father dyads– within well-defined units and sub-units of analysis – and chi-square analysis (significance level 1%) provided evidence that, in the course of paternal infant-directed speech, but not during preceding / following pauses, fathers and infants (girls and boys) match their emotional states and attune their emotional intensity. This evidence will be interpreted in the frame of the theory of Innate Intersubjectivity.

The expressions of emotion in different relationships

Chu, Ruey-Ling Institute of Ethnology, Academia Sinica, Taipei, Taiwan

This study aims to investigate the "normative" and "ideal" expressions of emotion in different relationships. Study 1 examined the normative expression of emotion of Taiwanese college students in five relationships?parent, sibling, close friend, teacher, and acquaintance. Study 2 investigated the "ideal" expressions of positive/negative, and engaging/disengaging emotions in five relationships. Both results of study 1 and 2 showed that the expression of emotion and the quality of relationship were positively associated, which means the expressions of emotion should be more manifest in a good relationship. In addition to the quality of relationship, this study found that collectivism and interdependent self could predict the expressions of emotion to the family. The cultural moderating effect of emotion is discussed.

Spontaneous facial expressions of emotion: Data on surprise, disgust and anger

Reisenzein, Rainer Inst. für Psychologie, Universität Greifswald, Greifswald, Germany Bördgen, Sandra Fakultät für Psychologie, Universität Bielefeld, Bielefeld, Germany Studtmann, Markus Institut für Psychologie, Universität Greifswald, Greifswald, Germany Weber, Hannelore Institut für Psychologie, Universität Greifswald, Greifswald, Germany

Results of three sets of studies concerned with, respectively the spontaneous facial expression of surprise, disgust, and anger are summarized. The main findings are: (a) spontaneous facial expressions are rare, even when people are alone and inhibitory display rules are thus presumably less important; (b) if facial expressions occur, they are typically only partial; (c) people typically overestimate their facial expressivity. The findings put into question the affect program theory of facial expressions.

FP-216: Cross-cultural comparisons II

Proverbs we work with: Using proverbs in cross-cultural research on the culture of work: A methodological approach

Wolonciej, Mariusz Inst. of Psychology, Catholic University Lublin, Lublin, Poland

Proverbs are pervasive in everyday speech and in human thoughts. The article introduces paremiology – the study of proverbs – as a way to investigate work culture and explore how proverbs can reveal work culture traits of different social groups in the context of features imprinted in about 1900 Polish and German proverbs concerning work. The article describes the operationalisation process of the theoretical term work culture entailed in the brief presentation of the concrete empirical research method. Despite some limitations, necessary to be considered, application of paremiology in work culture research appears to be as a promising field in cross-cultural research.

Dynamic constructivist approach to culture

Hong, Ying-Yi Psychology, University of Illinois, Champaign, USA

The dynamic constructivist approach contends that cultures can be understood as shared knowledge (meaning) among group members, and cultural influences are results of the shared knowledge being (chronically or temporarily) accessible and applicable in certain social contexts. In this talk, I will discuss how this approach (1) sets the stage for a paradigm change in studying cultural influences – from trait-like descriptions to process explanations of cultural similarities or difference; and (2) provides a roadmap to study cultural influences on behaviors. Empirical results from four studies will be used as illustrations.

Does similarity or complimentary bring more satisfaction to Chinese couples?

Lu, Xiaowei Department of Psychology, University College Berkley, Berkeley, USA Peng, Kaiping Department of Psychology, UC Berkeley, Berkeley, USA Gonzaga, Gian eHarmony Labs, eHarmony Labs, Pasadena, USA Wang, Lei Department of Psychology, Peking University, Beijing, People's Republic of China

Results of the researches on matching and marital satisfaction done in West were mixed. But the main patterns seem to be that similarity could probably bring more satisfaction. However, in Eastern Asian cultures (e.g., China), dialectical duality is more appreciated hence complimentary in dyadic relation is more prominent. From the perspective of cultural psychology, the current study explored the impact of matching of Chinese traditional values, personalities, thinking styles and other culture factors to 569 Chinese couples' martial satisfaction. We found that the effect of similarity or complimentary between couples were domain specific dependent on variables that are concerned.

Situated ethnic identity in first and second generation immigrants to Canada

Noels, Kimberly Psychology, University of Alberta, Edmonton AB, Canada Clement, Richard Psychology, University of Ottawa, Ottawa ON, Canada Saumure, Kristie D. Psychology, University of Alberta, Edmonton AB, Canada

This study examined the hypothesis that acculturative change in ethnic identity occurs first in public domains and eventually penetrates intimate domains. Consistent with this hypothesis, the results of a questionnaire survey indicated that, for first-generation immigrants to Canada (N = 266), heritage identity was stronger than Canadian identity in the family and friendship domains, but Canadian identity was stronger than heritage identity in school and public domains. For second-generation immigrants (N = 248) this pattern was attenuated, and in the friendship domain Canadian identity was stronger than heritage identity. A theoretical model of situated ethnic identity is presented.

Social inequality and psychological characteristics: The psychological gap hypothesis

Brenlla, María Elena Observatorio Deuda Social, Universidad Católica Argentina, Buenos Aires, Argentina

This research tries to evaluate if socioeconomic inequality affects the auto-perception of psychological characteristics, suggesting the existence of a psychological gap. For this purpose, a questionnaire was applied annually to 1500 persons living in different urban areas of Argentina from 2004 to 2007 (panel study). Brief versions of tests were included in order to assess locus of control, personal projects, psychological distress and verbal comprehension. The results show significant differences between the people belonging to lower classes and the people belonging to the upper classes. This information would indicate the presence of a psychological gap depending on the socioeconomic level. Key words: Social inequality-Psychological characteristics-Psychological gap

FP-217: Conscious and unconscious processes II

Why good thoughts block better ones: The pernicious "Einstellung" effect

Bilalic, Merim Inst. für Neuroradiologie, Medizin. Universität Tübingen, Tübingen, Germany McLeod, Peter Department of Experimental Psy, Oxford University, Oxford, United Kingdom Gobet, Fernand

School of Social Sciences, Brunel University, Uxbridge, United Kingdom

Experts solve problems quickly because familiar features trigger a pattern of thought that leads to a solution. We show that a good solution that comes to mind can prevent chess experts finding a better one. The experts said they were looking for alternatives but their eye movements showed that they were looking at information relevant to the solution they had already found. The ability of a thought pattern to direct attention to information relevant to itself and away from information relevant to alternatives explains why experts can find it difficult to assimilate information that might make them change their mind.

Playing chess unconsciously: Subliminal priming of conjunction stimuli is restricted to experts

Kiesel, Andrea Inst. für Pschologie, Universität Würzburg, Würzburg, Germany Pohl, Carsten Department of Psychology, Lehrstuhl für Psychologie III, Wuerzburg, Germany Kunde, Wilfried Universität Dortmund, Institut für Psychologie, Dortmund, Germany Berner, Michael P. Department of Psychology, Lehrstuhl für Psychologie III, Wuerzburg, Germany Hoffmann, Joachim Department of Psychology, Lehrstuhl für Psychologie III, Wuerzburg, Germany

Experts in a field process task relevant information more efficiently than novices (Reingold, Charness, Pomplun, & Stampe, 2001). Here we investigated if chess experts are able to detect unconsciously whether a briefly presented chess situation entails a checking configuration. Thereby, check detection required integrating two features – identity and location – of the chess figures. In a subliminal priming experiment, chess experts but not novices revealed unconscious priming effects. We conjecture that experts acquired templates, that is, visual memory episodes for chess configurations in which the respective features are already bound. These templates enable complex visual processing outside of conscious awareness.

How does meditation affect cognition, emotion, behavior and personality?: A meta-analysis

Sedlmeier, Peter Inst. für Psychologie, Techn. Universität Chemnitz, Chemnitz, Germany Jaeger, Sonia Psychology, TU Chemnitz, Chemnitz, Germany Kunze, Sonja Psychology, TU Chemnitz, Chemnitz, Germany Drechsler, Doreen Psychology, TU Chemnitz, Chemnitz, Germany Haarig, Frederik Psychology, TU Chemnitz, Chemnitz, Germany Schenkel, Markus Psychology, TU Chemnitz, Chemnitz, Germany

Numerous studies have examined the effects of meditation. Surprisingly, there exist only a few summaries that looked at specific techniques (TM) or isolated variables (anxiety). The current meta-analysis (n = 136 studies) attempts to give a comprehensive overview of the impact of meditation on psychological (non-physiological) measures in the (non-clinical) adult population. The effect sizes are rather large for all groups of variables showing that meditation can be a powerful means to change aspects of cognition, emotion, behavior and personality. However, different methods of meditation yield different effects and there is a tendency that effects increase with decreasing methodological quality.

"Tell it and you know it – don't tell it, don't know it!": Verbal representation as determinant of conscious knowledge acquisition

Eichler, Alexandra Inst. für Sozialpsychologie, Universität zu Köln, Köln, Germany Haider, Hilde Inst. f. Allg. & Sozialpsy, Universitaet zu Koeln, HF, Köln, Germany

Learning need not necessarily include intention or even awareness. Whereas most studies focus on implicit learning, we consider the development of

conscious knowledge as an important quality of incidental learning. To identify factors that benefit explicit learning, we concentrated on verbal representation by manipulating stimulus type or presence of either articulatory suppression or metronome tones in the serial reaction time task. Reaction times and explicit verbal knowledge were assessed. Results suggest that verbal representation leads to more explicitly expressible knowledge. Furthermore, only subjects with abstract verbal knowledge were able to use their knowledge efficiently and decrease reaction times dramatically.

Intentionality of cognition: A systems-theoretical approach

Tschacher, Wolfgang Psychiatrische Dienste, Universität Bern, Bern, Switzerland

Psychology is frequently confronted with mind-body issues—is there a way by which mentalist and physical approaches to cognition can be integrated? The theory of nonlinear complex systems may offer steps towards a solution to this conundrum: An essential property of self-organized pattern formation lies within its functionality, this being the ability to respond and adapt 'meaningfully' to environmental constraints. Patterns become functional because they consume in a most efficient manner those gradients, which cause their evolution, thereby making synergetic pattern formation appear 'intentional'. We therefore posit that self-organization phenomena may afford basic explanations for the intentionality and purposive behavior.

FP-218: Emotions in interpersonal contexts

Can children's heart rate be used as a marker of differential responsiveness to others' varying emotional states?

Anastassiou-Hadjicharalambous, Xenia Psychology, University of Nicosia, Nicosia, Cyprus Warden, David Psychology, University of Strathclyde, Glasgow, United Kingdom

This study examined whether children's Heart Rate (HR) can be used as a marker of differential responsiveness to others' varying emotional states. Experimental induction was utilised. Children (N=50, aged 7-10) watched a series of filmed emotion evocative episodes (i.e. sadness, anger, fear, happiness) while their HR was recorded. HR was higher in response to others' fear relative to others' anger (p<.01) but no other differences across emotions were significant. Present data suggest that children's HR cannot be used as a consistent marker of differential responsiveness to others' varying emotional states, but rather as an index of unidimensional vicarious affective arousal.

Interpersonal emotion regulation in the dyad: How do couples deal with each other's affective states in daily life?

Horn, Andrea B. NCCR, Clinical Psychology, University of Fribourg, Fribourg, Switzerland Molina, Louella NCCR, University Fribourg, Clin.Psy., Fribourg, Switzerland Rieder, Stefan NCCR, University Fribourg, Clin.Psy., Fribourg, Switzerland Wilhelm, Peter NCCR, University Fribourg, Clin.Psy., Fribourg, Switzerland Reicherts, Michael NCCR, University Fribourg, Clin.Psy., Fribourg, Switzerland Perrez, Meinrad NCCR, University Fribourg, Clin.Psy., Fribourg, Switzerland

Emotion regulation is related with individual health and social functioning, especially in close relationships. This study looks at interpersonal emotion regulation strategies and their effect on one's own and the partner's affective state in couples' everyday life. To asses these constructs couples answered a computer-based diary simultaneously 4 times a day in the run of one week. Emotion regulation strategies are related with affective states of the regulating as well as the perceiving partner, however sometimes in opposite directions. Including actor and partner effects studying health- and relationship-related functional aspects of emotion regulation strategies seems to be highly relevant.

Should I be nice or bad? Effects of discrete emotions on negotiation outcomes

Volmer, Judith Inst. für Sozialpsychologie, Universität Erlangen-Nürnberg, Erlangen, Germany
Emotions are central in social interaction. In two laboratory experiments, we tested the interpersonal effects of discrete emotions (i.e., anger, happiness, surprise, sadness) on negotiation outcomes. In Experiment 1, participants were confronted with an angry, happy, surprised or sad opponent. Results showed that participants interpreted the opponent's emotion and used it strategically. In Experiment 2, we also explored the effects of information on future interactions on negotiation outcomes. Showing negative emotions in single negotiation settings does not pay off in terms of concession making and participants' satisfaction with the negotiation. Implications for strategic display of emotions in negotiations are discussed.

Self appreciation and affective temparaments in psychiatric nurses

Cordeiro, Raul CESM, Escola Sup. Saude Portalegre, Portalegre, Portugal
Self Appreciation and Affective Temperament, have crucial importance, because this fact will influence many phenomena's in nursing practice, like the capacity of develop relationships. 47 nurses, with average age of 38,57 years, working in Mental Health and Psychiatry, were inquired through a Questionnaire of direct application, were introduced measures like: TEMPS-A Scale (Akiskal, 1998), and Scale of Self Personal Appreciation Scale (Ribeiro, 2006).Results indicate a Hyperthymic Temperament. It was verified that women presents a higher Self Personal Appreciation. Affective temperament of nurses seems to be a good predictor of leadership capacity in violence situation at psychiatric services.

Emotional labor and emotional exhaustion: Meta-analysis

Sinambela, F. Christian Dept. of Psychology, University of Surabaya, Surabaya, Indonesia
Supriyanto, Agus Sport Faculty, Jogjakarta State University, Jogjakarta, Indonesia
This study examined the relationship between emotional labor and emotional exhaustion by performing a meta-analysis on research studies that present findings on relationships between emotional labor and emotional exhaustion. Twelve studies involved as a based data in this study. Result indicated that there was a positive correlation between emotional labor and emotional exhaustion (rho = 0,394564; 95% confidence interval, CI = 0,140265 – 0,64886). However we can not do moderator analysis because numbers of studies are limited. Thus, this study can not explain moderator variables that influence effects size variation.

FP-219: Cognition in the business world

Personality and profits of foreign exchange traders

Oberlechner, Thomas Inst. für Psychologie, Webster Universität, Wien, Austria
This study explores the role of personality in the performance of professional traders in the currency market. It explores strategies used by foreign exchange traders to generate profits and determines connections between personality characteristics and trading performance. 416 traders at leading banks in North America provided survey answers regarding their personality and mechanisms used to generate profits. Dependent variables included

objective and subjective measures of trading performance. Results show two main factors of profit generation. Considering subgroups of traders using different profit strategies yields significant connections between personality and trading performance. Personality plays an important role in the decisions taken by actors in financial markets.

Emotions and financial investment decision-making

Wranik, Tanja Psychology, University of Geneva, Geneva 4, Switzerland
Most investors experience strong negative emotions when they lose money, and many overreact to short-term loses and consequently sacrifice long-term gains. We tested the idea that low levels of earnings feedback will lead to fewer subjective losses, fewer negative emotions, and consequently more long-term earnings. Examination of the underlying emotional processes showed that both earnings feedback frequency and individual differences such as personality and emotion regulation skills play a role in predicting emotional experiences, risk-taking behaviors, and long-term investment decisions and earnings. The implications for emotion research and personalized investment strategies will be discussed.

Medical decision making: Contextual and team factors in emergency care departments

Guglielmetti, Chiara Social and Political Studies, State University Milan, Milan, Italy Gilardi, Silvia Welfare and Labour Studies, State University Milan, Milan, Italy Pravettoni, Gabriella Social and Political Studies, State University Milan, Milan, Italy Vago, Gianluca Medicine - Clinical Sciences, State University Milan, Milan, Italy
The presentation illustrates the results of a multimethods study of four Emergency Care Departments, based on the Naturalistic Decision Making approach. The aim was to explore the characteristics of decision-making processes in E.C. departments and to identify the socio-organizational factors that can influence them. Different strategies can be observed in daily work practices with regard to how this task is approached. Where the EC team (physicians/nurses) achieves a shared representation of the role distribution, the continuity and preservation of the patient's safety is guaranteed. Furthermore, interpersonal trust is a critical factor in the process of information sharing, integration and utilization.

Perceived inflation: The impact of experienced frequency of price changes in individual goods

Huber, Odilo W. Psychology Department, University of Fribourg, Fribourg, Switzerland
Perceived inflation refers to the subjective experience of general price development. In contrast to expenditure-weighted official indices, recent models propose the frequency of personal experience with price changes in purchase of goods as determinant for perceived inflation. Three experiments investigate environments with falling, stable, and increasing prices. Different price changes are assigned to two groups of products with identical overall expenditures but different frequency. Products are presented sequentially and prices are compared to learned past reference prices. Final judgments of total expenditure change revealed that in all experiments perceived inflation was dominated by price change of the high frequency group.

FP-220: Cognition and emotion I

Emotion processing stages and variations of EEG theta activity

Leue, Anja Faculty of Psychology, Philipps-Universitaet Marburg, Hamburg, Germany Chavanon, Mira-Lynn Faculty of Psychology, Philipps-Universitaet Marburg, Marburg, Germany Wacker,

Jan Faculty of Psychology, Philipps-Universitaet Marburg, Marburg, Germany Stemmler, Gerhard Faculty of Psychology, Philipps-Universitaet Marburg, Marburg, Germany
Objectives: Self-amplification (i.e., activation of emotional processing) has been suggested as one stage in Lewis' (2005) dynamic emotion processing model. A decrease of theta activity is expected to mirror self-amplification. Method: By conducting repeated measures ANOVA this assumption was assessed in 40 students using pleasant, unpleasant, and neutral pictures. Results: A significant decrease of theta activity occurred 2048 ms after picture presentation. This decrease was significantly larger in high- than low-anxious individuals for unpleasant pictures. Discussion: The results provide evidence for the operationalization of self-amplification and suggest the beginning of the self-stabilisation phase indicating the onset of an emotional appraisal.

Vocabulary Emotion Test (VET): Ability measure of emotional intelligence

Taksic, Vladimir Dept. of Psychology, University of Rijeka, Rijeka, Croatia Mohoric, Tamara Dept. of Psychology, University of Rijeka, Rijeka, Croatia
Emotional intelligence is usually defined as a four-level set of abilities (Mayer & Salovey, 1997). Among these, ability to understand emotions is one that can be best measured with ability test. Vocabulary Emotion Test (VET) was constructed consists of 102 adjectives (short version has 35 items) describing emotional states and mood, and has correct answer, based on a solution from Croatian dictionary (Anić, 1994). Both versions have satisfactory psychometric properties, with reliability coefficient α=0.91. Convergent-divergent validity was assessed compared TRE with several traditional intelligence tests showing it has 44% of unique variance. VET was translated in English and Swedish.

Emotion knowledge: Structure and temporal organization choosen post-cognitive emotions

Jasielska, Aleksandra Inst. of Psychology, Adam Mickiewicz University, Poznan, Poland
This study is based on the conclusion, that representations of emotions can be temporarily manifested in autonarratives. The subjects of this exploratory study are two self-conscious emotions: shame and pride. The participants (N=72) were asked to describe autobiografical emotional episodes. Then the subjects' accounts were categorized by coders and submitted to hierarchical cluster analysis. The result was a prototypical description of these emotions. Derived, exploratory results provide mainly: 1) the descriptions of complex emotions as emotional scripts, 2) the structural characteristics of autonarrative emotions, 3) arbitrate the issue of "potential synthesis" in the field of postcognitive emotions.

Affective interference in temporal perception

Constancio Fernandes, Alexandre Laboratório de Psicologia, ISPA, Lisboa, Portugal Garcia-Marques, Teresa Laboratório de Psicologia, ISPA, Lisboa, Portugal
The presence of an emotion in a human face increases its perceived duration (Droit-Volet et al., 2004). Our study extends this effect to a new set of emotions (happiness, fear, anger) and test the impact that familiarity may exert on it. Participants estimated the duration (between 400-1600 ms) of neutral and emotional faces by comparing them to the extreme durations (short and long) previously learned. The analysis of bisection-points and psychophysical-functions suggest a replication of general overestimation of emotional faces. As expected, familiarity moderates this effect, not because it influences emotional estimations, but

because it bias estimations of neutral-faces durations.

Applying regulatory fit in education setting: The mediating role of prospective and retrospective feeling

Fok, Hung-Kit Division of Social Science, HKUST, Hong Kong SAR, China, People's Republic of : Hong Kong SAR *Yik, Oi-yee Michelle* Division of Social Science, HKUST, Hong Kong SAR, China, People's Republic of : Macao SAR

The present study applied regulatory fit theory to an education setting to demonstrate the ecological validity of the theory. In particular, we test if students experiencing regulatory fit would achieve higher marks in final examination than those who do not experience regulatory fit. Moreover, the present study also investigates the mediating mechanism for regulatory fit effect. Positive prospective feelings and positive retrospective feelings mediated the regulatory fit effect on academic performance.

FP-221: Clinical aspects of cognition I

Automatic processing of familiar and unfamiliar emotional faces on Down syndrome

Morales, Guadalupe Dept. of Psychology, UANL, Monterrey, Mexico *Lopez, Ernesto* Psychology, UANL, Monterrey, Mexico

Down syndrome individuals (DS) were required to recognize familiar (DS faces) and unfamiliar emotional faces (non DS faces), by using an affective priming paradigm. Pairs of emotional facial stimuli were presented with an SOA of 300 ms and an ISI of 50 ms. The goal was to test the hypothesis that recognition deficits on negative information reported by literature on this population includes automatic emotional processing but not necessarily to meaningful negative information. Results showed that not all of the participants have a recognition deficit on negative stimuli and interestingly, positive familiar faces could not be primed by other valenced facial stimuli but they were recognized faster than neutral faces.

Facial expression: The recognition of basic emotions in cocaine dependents: Empirical study with Portuguese

Magalhães, Freitas Facial Emotion Exprssion Lab., Faculty of Health Sciences, Porto, Portugal *Érico, Castro* Facial Emotion Exprssion Lab, Faculty of Health Sciences, Porto, Portugal

This research presents the effect of cocaine in the identification and recognition of the basic emotions (joy, sadness, anger, surprise, disgust, fear and contempt).The sample involved 70 Portuguese participants (25 women, M = 30,5, SD = 4,2;45 men, M = 36,7, SD = 5.6) diagnosised with Induced Disturbances for Cocaine (American Psychiatric Association, 2000). The results confirm that the cocaine dependents present difficulties in the identification and characterization of the universal basic emotions with exception of the sadness and cólera. The results confirm, still, that the women are more spontaneous in the identification and characterization of the basic emotions than men.

Passivity associated to depression protects individuals from the illusion of control

Matute, Helena Dept. de Psicología, Deusto University, Bilbao, Spain *Blanco, Fernando* Psicologia, Deusto University, Bilbao, Spain *Vadillo, Miguel A.* Psicologia, Deusto University, Bilbao, Spain

Depressive realism consists of the correct identification of null response-outcome contingency by depressed participants whereas nondepresed participants usually show an illusion of control. In Experiment 1, we replicated the depressive realism effect with anonymous internet users in an instru-

mental paradigm, and showed that dysphoric participants (who scored higher in the Beck Depression Inventory) gave less responses during the training phase. In Experiment 2, we manipulated the participants' activity level, finding that individuals with lower probability of responding were less affected by the illusion of control. Our results suggest that activity level could explain part of the depressive realism effect.

Emotion understanding deficits and children with learning disabilities

Tong, Yuehua Dept. of Psychology, Jinan University of Shandong, Jinan, People's Republic of China

The present study was to compare emotion understanding in children with and without learning disabilities (LD). Participants were 90 children with LD and 90 children without LD in primary school. Emotion vignettes were used. Children with LD demonstrated significantly lower level of emotion understanding than children without LD. The emotion understanding deficits in children with LD included: (a) poor recognition of facial expressions, (b) delayed recognition of self-conscious emotion, (c) poor understanding of multiple emotions, (d) limited understanding in the causes of emotion, (e) inadequate understanding of hidden emotion, and (f) insufficient development of knowledge about emotion change.

Implicit associations among undergraduate students who self-injure

Cumming, Steve Faculty of Health Sciences, University of Sydney, Lidcombe, Austria

Of 106 students enroled in an Undergradaute Psychology course, 62 were found to participate in deliberate self-injury. Comparisons between the self-injuring and the non self-injuring group suggested differences in emotional regulation, alexithymia and coping resources, although not in coping style. The implicit evaluation of injury-related terms as assessed by the Implicit Association Task (Greenwald et al, 1998) suggested that frequent self-injurers have a slightly more positively valenced view of terms related to injury.

FP-222: Attitudes, beliefs and values

Age differences on attitudes to over 50 workers

Cubico, Serena Psicologia e Antropologia, Università di Verona, Verona, Italy *Ardolino, Piermatteo* Psicologia e Antropologia, Università di Verona, Verona, Italy *Formicuzzi, Maddalena* Psicologia e Antropologia, Università di Verona, Verona, Italy *Venturini, Beatrice* Psicologia e Antropologia, Università di Verona, Verona, Italy

Workers in different life stages live together in organizations. The object of this study is to detect the attitudes to Over-50 workers. The instrument is an on-line ad hoc questionnaire administers to 2,762 Tertiary Sector professionals and managers. A significant relationship with age was found. The older (more so than younger) workers think: competency curves are not linked to age, it is "stupid" to dismiss Over-50 managers, the companies must highlight over-50 competencies, many Over-50 managers are dismissed when they are still valuable workers, and they do not agree that they are in the "waning phase" of their professional lives.

Perception of the potential enemy: How Israeli and Palestinian students see each other's values

Eicher, Véronique Dept. of Psychology, University of Fribourg, Fribourg, Switzerland *Wilhelm, Peter* Department of Psychology, University of Fribourg, Fribourg, Switzerland

In situations of escalated and open conflict the other group tends to be seen as deficient in moral virtue and different from the ingroup in basic values

(Struch & Schwartz, 1989). In order to test these assumptions, we used the Schwartz Value Survey and asked 283 Israeli and 225 Palestinian students to rate the importance of different values from different perspectives (own, typical member of their own nation and typical student from the other nation). Preliminary analyses show, that Israeli and Palestinian students perceive each other to be more different than they really are.

Do age, achieved level of education and demands on personal time influence values, motivation and approaches to learning?

Matthews, Bobbie Dept. of Education, Flinders University, Adelaide, Australia *Hall, Margaret M.* School of Nursing and Midwifer, Flinders University, Adelaide, South Australia, Australia *Darmawan, I Gusti Ngurah* School of Education, Adelaide University, Adelaide, South Australia, Australia

The changing demographic characteristics of students in higher education are of concern to educators. This is particularly evident in the professional education of nursing students where the practical and theoretical aspects are combined in the pursuit of an academic qualification. A longitudinal study has been initiated to measure values, learning approaches and motivation that are extant in undergraduate nursing students at an Australian university. A pilot study has shown that there are two distinct age groups; mature-aged students are more highly motivated despite their lower level of prior learning; universal part-time employment leaves little time for academic endeavour; and older students show a greater incentive to succeed in the program.

The role of appearance and sociocultural models in eating disorders

Santos, Isabel Dept. of Psychology, Universidade Lusófona, Lisboa, Portugal *Simão, Ana* Psychology, ULHT, Lisboa, Portugal *Baptista, Américo* Psychology, ULHT, Lisboa, Portugal *Esteves, Francisco* Psychology, ISCTE, Lisboa, Portugal

The relationship between appearance sociocultural models, eating disorders and body dissatisfaction was studied in sample of 284 young male and female adults. The measures were the Appearance Magazine Exposure, Appearance Culture Among Peers Subscales, Social Cultural Attitudes Toward Appearance Scale-3, Eating Disorder Examination Questionnaire and the Contour Drawing Rating Scale. In general, women are more exposed to magazines, have more conversations with friends about appearance and feel a greater sociocultural pressure and internalization. Appearance culture between peers was positively related with eating disorder symptoms in both sexes, and with body dissatisfaction only in women.

Meaninglessness in Indian context: An existential perspective

Upadhyay, Ishita Department of Psychology, University of Allahabad, Allahabad, India *Dalal, Ajit K.* Department of Psychology, University of Allahabad, Allahabad, India

The mainstream psychology has looked upon meaninglessness as detrimental to one's mental health. The present study is an attempt to trace the nature and occurrence of meaninglessness, as manifestation of an existential crisis. Narratives were taken from the individuals (N=25), belonging to metropolitan cities, who despite being successful, failed to find meaning in what they did/ had been doing. The initial reflection upon the data through the grounded theory approach reveals that meaninglessness paves the ground for a self-enquiry, initiating a search for meaning. This search of meaning begins from looking within playing a pivotal role in resolving the existential crisis.

FP-223: Attachment to the organization: Psychological contract, ownership and organizational identity

Psychological contract and its' formation under the collective culture

Hu, Ping Public Administration School, Renmin University of China, Beijing, People's Republic of China *Liu, Jun* Educational School, Tsinghua University, Beijing, People's Republic of China
This study examined the Chinese teachers' psychological contract context and formatting process(N=308). Results indicated: (1) the generalizability of 3 psychological contract forms: transactional, relational, and balanced was confirmed, (2) The relational obligation was more important than the transactional obligation, (3)Compared to the exchange idea as only mediator in West, career value was playing a significant role in forming Chinese psychological contract, (4) The teachers' perceptual relational support were more positively relative with the psychological contract than the perceptual performance support. The authors discuss the implications of these results for the meaning of psychological contracts under the traditional culture profiles in China and raise issues for future research.

Can self-commitment compensate for communication media effects?

Wittchen, Marion Inst. für Psychologie II, Universität Würzburg, Würzburg, Germany
Computer-supported group work can complicate the development of team trust due to members' physical and temporal separation, thereby reducing individual motivation and performance. Two laboratory studies (N=210) examined whether negative effects of electronic communication on trust, motivation and performance can be prevented by explicit (verbal) self-commitment to team goals. Beyond trust-mediated effects, direct effects on motivation were examined. In line with the assumptions, regression analyses and planned contrasts reveal that trust predicts motivation and performance, and that trust level during electronically-mediated communication resembles trust level during face-to-face communication only if the team partner expressed explicit self-commitment prior to group work.

Antecedents of psychological ownership: Results of a qualitative study with financial traders

Handy, Stephan Frankfurt, Germany *Martins, Erko* Organizational Psychology, University of Rostock, Rostock, Germany *Nerdinger, Friedemann* Inst. für Psychologie, Universität Rostock, Rostock, Germany
Interviews with 36 financial traders were conducted to shed more light on antecedents of psychological ownership (PO) as feeling of possession towards the organization (cf. Pierce et al., 2001). PO has recently been discussed as a decisive state explaining employees work behavior. On the basis of self-assessments of the PO-degree by the interviewed traders we split the interviewees at the median into two groups with high and low PO. Comparisons of the interviewees' expressed implicit theories of how their PO was aroused or not between both groups of traders are discussed to expand and detail the existing models of PO-emergence.

On the nature of the organisational sense-of-identity

Van Tonder, Chris Dept. of Industrial Psychology, University of Johannesburg, Johannesburg, South Africa
The research endeavoured to reaffirm the structure of the organisational Sense-of-Identity instrument that has been used in two previous studies. A convenience sample of 674 respondents hailing from 27 organisations (different industries) completed the questionnaire. Principal factor analysis surfaced four primary factors with good to excellent scale reliabilities. These relate to the relative health, unity, distinctiveness, and development status of the organisation's identity. Results are reviewed in light of other recent studies that used the instrument, and which considered the relevance of the sense-of-identity construct. The implications of the findings for further research and applied organisational management are indicated.

Towards an Eriksonian theory of organisation identity

Van Tonder, Chris Dept. of Industrial Psychology, University of Johannesburg, Johannesburg, South Africa
The purpose of the paper is to consolidate preliminary empirical progress in respect of the Organisation Identity Theory (OIT), proposed by Van Tonder (1999). This theory, which is differentiated from social identity theory and psychoanalytic approaches to organisation identity, is strongly premised on an Eriksonian view of identity. An overview of five empirical studies premised on OIT and completed between 2000 and 2007 are provided. The findings of these studies, which involved both qualitative and quantitative research approaches, converged substantially and provided support for several facets of Organisation Identity Theory. The (significant) implications for organisations are briefly considered.

FP-224: Attachment and relationship from childhood to adulthood

The new criteria of attachment measurement

Matejic Djuricic, Zorica Dept. of Psychology, University of Belgrade, Belgrade, Serbia *Stojkovic, Irena* Psychology, University of Belgrade, FASPER, Belgrade, *Djuricic, Milica* Psychology, University of Belgrade, FASPER, Belgrade,
Exploring the set of changes on the level of global child behaviour in two different contexts of adult-child interaction, the new criteria of attachment have been defined, i.e. " level of activity", considering as the developmental derivation of the baby's complex of vigilence, described in russian child psychology. Analysis of camera recorded data reveals the main indicators of high level of acitivity (during the mother-child interaction) and low level of activity (during the child interaction with the stranger), measured by: motor acitivities engagement, speech production and prosodic features of speech, social participation and social distance.

Attachment and change in adolescence

Podolskij, Andrei Dept. of Developm. Psychology, Moscow State University, Moscow, Russia *Hautamäki, Airi* Swedish School of Social Scien, University of Helsinki, Helsinki, Finland
Attachment theory represents a developmental study of the interaction between many individual and contextual systems and their influences on one another. Change in the individual's working models of attachment concerning the relationship of self to significant others is a developmental process of qualitative stage reorganization. Thus, the working models of attachment are qualitatively reorganized as function of both maturation and context. Normative adolescent development in regard to attachment is analyzed. The attachment patterns represent qualitatively different ways of processing attachment-relevant information. The analysis of adolescent socio-emotional wellbeing is elaborated with the help of Marcia's identity status approach, and Blos' theory of adolescence, paralleling Mahler's work on self-differentiation in infancy.

Partnership and personality in young adulthood

Lehnart, Judith Personality Psychology, University of Potsdam, Potsdam, Germany *Neyer, Franz J.* Personality Psychology, University of Potsdam, Potsdam, Germany *Eccles, Jacquelynne* Personality Psychology, University of Michigan, Ann Arbor, MI, USA
Finding a long-term partner during emerging adulthood is- according to the "social investment principle" of personality development -expected to be related to personality maturation. Using data from the Michigan Study of Adolescent and Adult Development, we compared personality development over 8 years of N=161 "partnership beginners" and N=64 "singles". Transition to a romantic relationship was related to a decrease in depression, whereas self-esteem development was differentially related to relationship experiences for males and females. The predictions of the "social investment principle" could be partly confirmed and implications of the effect of de-investment are discussed.

A cross-cultural typology of antisocial behaviour development during adolescence

Morales, Hugo Faculty of Psychology, San Marcos National University, Lima, Peru
Several causes of the adolescent antisocial behaviour seems to respond to the combination of many risk located along the different levels of human development. This lecture revises the main explicative theories about adolescent antisocial behaviour and tries to reflect them, emphasizing on the Taxonomic theory of the antisocial behaviour proposed by Terrie E. Moffitt (1993, 2003) on two antisocial behaviour main profile among adolescents: i)Life Course Persistent and ii)Adolescence Limited. Some studies are mentioned due to the fact that they confirm the cross-cultural validity of Moffitt's theorical model and its contributions to the design of treatment programs against youth delinquency.

FP-225: Applied social psychology

The social inclusion of people with severe mental disorder through labour insertion processes: designing an integral assessment model from a particular case

Farre, Albert Social Psychology, UAB-FDR, Barcelona, Spain *Pla, Margarida* Chair in Qualitative Research, UAB - Dr. Robert Foundation, Barcelona, Spain *Crespo, Ramon* Chair in Qualitative Research, UAB - Dr. Robert Foundation, Barcelona, Spain *Gonzalez, Inmaculada* Chairmanship, Laboris, Barcelona, Spain *Cardona, Angels* Chair in Qualitative Research, UAB - Dr. Robert Foundation, Barcelona, Spain
This project aims to design and implement an integral assessment model of social inclusion of people with Severe Mental Disorder through labour insertion processes, by analysing the working and intervention method carried out by "Laboris" in Barcelona, Spain. A participatory methodology is implemented throughout its phases in order to achieve its main goals: (a) Contrast systematically the ground principles of the Laboris tasks with the reality and their intervention strategies. (b) Assess the processes that occur in the context of their actions (efficiency, etc.). And (c) Assess their results (effectiveness, impacts, etc.) waited or not, in terms of social inclusion.

Transformation of functions of disaster volunteers in Japan: Action research projects

Atsumi, Tomohide CSCD, Osaka University, Osaka, Japan
Since the 1995 Kobe earthquake, disaster volunteers have become a part of Japanese society. However, their functions drastically changed at the end of the 1st decade due to the 2004 Niigata Chuetsu earthquake. The present study describes the transformation of functions of disaster volun-

teers based on my own long-term action research projects both in Kobe and Niigata. Ethnography reveals that the roles of disaster volunteers changed from efficient disaster response as in Kobe to empowerment toward revitalization of survivors' life as in Chuetsu. Implications of this collective movement are analyzed from the perspectives of group dynamics of the post-industrialized society.

Music to live: Children and young people Venezuelan orchestral system as a constructive space for a citizen ethic

Urreiztieta Valles, María Teresa Ciencias y Tecnología del Comp, Simón Bolívar University, Caracas, Venezuela Hernández, Marisela Ciencias y Tecnología del Comp, Simón Bolívar University, Caracas, Venezuela

The case of Children and Young People Venezuelan Orchestral System is presented as a culture movement that creates opportunities for musical, professional and social-labor development. From a phenomenological perspective, we explored the experience of participating in the orchestral system and its impact on personal, family and socio-educational settings. This movement is guided by values that emphasize conviction ethic -based on merit culture and social commitment-. The meaning of the orchestral system is highlighted as a new social actor that suggest the construction of a different type of leadership, a renewed citizen culture that recreates and challenges the current Venezuelan scenarios.

How AIDS in Africa is framed in the U.S. media: A missed opportunity for agenda-setters to shed light on the link between AIDS and global security, ultimately liable to affect even U.S. citizens

Tobias, Jutta Washington State University, Pullman, USA

The paper's purpose was to examine U.S. media framing of the AIDS epidemic in Africa. Its main hypothesis was that leading U.S. papers significantly under-report the link between AIDS, poverty, social unrest, and ultimately global security. A content analysis of articles on this topic was conducted. Statistical analyses confirmed that reporters rarely cushion AIDS within its larger socio-economic context. This constitutes a missed opportunity for agenda-setters to educate the public about this pandemic, as public attitude change is necessary to generate general support for more effective anti-AIDS policies. Recommendations are provided to re-frame the AIDS crisis in the media.

FP-226: Space, shape, and motion II

Adaptive focusing of spatial attention in the flanker task

Wendt, Mike Fachbereich Psychologie, Universität Hamburg, Hamburg, Germany Luna-Rodriguez, Aquiles Institut für Kognitionsforschu, Helmut-Schmidt-Universität, Hamburg, Germany

Current models of cognitive control assume that frequent conflict evoked by processing irrelevant stimuli results in adaptive focusing on target stimulus information. Consistently, conflict frequency is negatively related to interference elicited by processing irrelevant stimulus features. We investigated whether in the Eriksen flanker task conflict-frequency-related interference reduction reflects focusing of spatial attention. To this end, we intermixed a visual search task and flanker task trials. Search times increased with the distance from the flanker task's target location and this gradient was more pronounced with frequent than with rare flanker-target conflict, thus supporting the idea of conflict-induced focusing of spatial attention.

Towards a unified theory of 3D shape perception

Fleming, Roland MPI for Biological Cybernetics, Tübingen, Germany

Objectives. Unifying theoretical analysis of visual 3D shape cues, including texture, shading and highlights. Experiments test whether we experience illusions of shape predicted by the model. Methods. Model uses the population response of filters tuned to different image orientations (cf. V1 cells). Subjects viewed rendered images of 3D objects and adjusted 'gauge figure' probes to report perceived surface orientation. Results: Model correctly predicts both success and failures of human 3D shape estimation across variations in texture, lighting and surface reflectance properties. Conclusions: For the early stages of 3D shape estimation, seemingly different cues may have more in common than previously believed.

Linear systems investigations of the neural basis of motion perception

Wallisch, Pascal Center for Neural Science, New York University, New York City, USA

The neural basis of motion processing is already well understood in terms of its basic anatomy and physiology. We are using methods from linear systems theory – specifically reverse correlation – to characterize neural responses in area MT. We show that this approach is adequate to evaluate a quantitative model of the MT population response and suggest it as a suitable method for psychological investigations into the neural implementation of computational principles underlying cognitive processes more generally.

FP-227: Children with mental retardation, autism or Down's syndrome I

Assessment and treatment of self-injury in one student with mental retardation

Tang, Jung-Chang Chia-Yi, Taiwan Wang, Ming-Chua Special Education, National Taitung University, ChiaYi, Taiwan Lee, Shu-Hui Special Education, National Kaohsiung Normal Univ, ChiaYi, Taiwan

The purposes of this study were to detect the function of self-injurious behavior (SIB) and to reduce such behavior in one student with mental retardation. An analogue functional analysis was used to assess the function of the student's SIB (Iwata, Dorsey, Slifer, Bauman, & Richman, 1982/ 1994). Results indicated that the student's SIB was maintained by positive social reinforcement. Attention was further provided noncontingently via an ABAB reversal design to compete with the consequence of reinforcement from SIB. Results demonstrated attention could be successfully used to decrease the SIB of this student. Keywords: self-injurious behavior, functional analysis, mental retardation

The effects of goal setting on performance of a motor skill of persons with borderline intelligence and mild mental retardation.

Askita, Maria Thessaloniki, Greece Kokaridas, Dimitris Physical Education and Sport S, Univercity of Thessaly, Trikala, Greece Theodorakis, Yannis Physical Education and Sport S, Univercity of Thessaly, Trikala, Greece

The purpose of this investigation was to examine the effects of goal setting on performance of an unfamiliar motor skill in people with borderline intelligence and mild mental retardation. The empirical studies review lean towards the assigned goals condition. Participants (N = 36) were assigned to one of three goal setting conditions: a) control group, b) assigned group and c) self set group. After the baseline, the groups were provided with different instuctions and tested again.Wilcoxon's analysis indicated a significant improvement on the performance in the assigned goals group (p < .05).

These findings suggest, that expert assigned goals increase performance, in beginners with MR. Relevant methodological and theoretical aspects yielded new research directions.

Steps of social information processing (SIP) in mild intellectually handicapped students across three school levels: based on Crick and Doge' model (1994).

Bashash, Laaya Special Education, Shiraz University, Shiraz, Islamic Republic of Iran

The present study investigates the steps of social information processing (SIP) in mild intellectually handicapped students across three school levels: based on Crick and Doge' model (1994). A sample of 120 students (age 10-18 years old) were randomly selected from the exceptional schools (Shiraz, Iran), and interviewed individually using Tur-Kaspa and Bryan (1994) social stories. The result showed that with increasing school grades, students demonstrated more skills in areas of representing, interpreting social cues, clarifying positive goals and improvement in linking between goals and selected solutions. No significant difference was observed between boys and girls in SIP.

FP-228: Creativity and culture I

How to improve design problem solving?

Hacker, Winfried Inst. für Psychologie, Techn. Universität Dresden, Dresden, Germany Winkelmann, Constance AG, Technische Universität Dresden, Dresden, Germany

Significant improvements of solutions in engineering design problem solving by the application of a question-answering technique (QAT) had so far been shown only for students without any training in engineering design. Therefore, we asked for the effects of this technique used from professional designers (job beginners: N = 42; experts: N = 33). The participants were asked to explain, justify and evaluate their design solution by means of this QAT. The results show significant improvements also for professional designers with significantly higher effects for job beginners. The effects may be explained by processing semantic relationships in answering interrogative questions. Consequences for studies in engineering design are implemented.

What makes bilinguals creative?: A discussion of bilinguals' development factors influencing their creative cognition

Kharkhurin, Anatoliy International Studies, American University of Sharjah, Sharjah, United Arab Emirates

The tested hypothesis is that bilingualism encourages divergent thinking and cognitive flexibility, which together facilitate creative thought. Farsi-English bilinguals from UAE and Farsi monolinguals from Iran were tested on Abbreviated Torrance Test for Adults (ATTA), Invented Alien Creatures (IAC) task, and culture fair intelligence test (CFIT). Bilinguals were classified by their age of English acquisition (AoE) and linguistic proficiency (PNT). A series of correlational analyses, ANOVAs, and regression analyses showed bilinguals' significant advantages on ATTA's innovative capacity, IAC's invariant violation, and CFIT's intelligence. Bilinguals' AoE and PNT had a significant influence on ATTA's generative capacity. The results are discussed in terms of how the specific structure of bilinguals' memory can facilitate their creative thinking.

How does mood influence creative performance

Cervai, Sara Dept. of Political Sciences, University of Trieste, Trieste, Italy Borelli, Massimo Gen. Surg. Int. Care Sciences, University of Trieste, Trieste, Italy

Aim of the research is to explore if and how mood can be associated to creative performance. A sample of students (50% male and 50% female) between 20 and 30 years old were involved answering to POMS – Profile of Mood State (McNair, 1981) and to a paper and pen brainstorming activity. Results show that no strict influence between the two constructs arises in their whole; conversely there is a strong association between the self perception and the creative performance. A more sophisticated model has been created to explain which and how the factors explored through POMS are related with creativity.

FP-229: Culture and human development III

Why Taiwanese students are quiet in class? A cultural analysis of student response to teachers' questions in Chinese classrooms

Fwu, Bih-Jen Center for Teacher Education, National Taiwan University, Taipei, Taiwan

Chinese students are often described by Western academics as quiet and compliant learners. This study intends to investigate why they seldom answer questions in class. A questionnaire of 4 scenarios of answering questions in class was administered to 250 college students in Taiwan. The results show that (1) individuals answering questions voluntarily care more about gaining knowledge, whereas those assigned to answer questions are more concerned about appropriate behaviors in social context; (2) compared with students who answer questions voluntarily, students assigned to answer questions are more likely to be regarded as being humble, a virtue in Chinese culture. The social-cultural mechanisms of these behavioral patterns are discussed.

The study of relation between creativity and social development in adolescents in Tehran

Shafaroudi, Narges Occupational Therapy, Shool of Rehabilitat. Science, Tehran, Islamic Republic of Iran
Rezvan, Zinab Occupational Therapy, Shool of Rehabilitation Scienc, Tehran, Islamic Republic of Iran

The purpose of this study was to examine the creativity and social development in adolescents in Tehran. This paper concerns a descriptive study of creativity and social development in a group of 100 female adolescents of 14-18 years old from high-schools in Tehran. Data were gathered using a demographic questionnaire, Abedi questionnaire and Witzman questionnaire. The data were analyzed by ANOVA. t-test andChi-square. Results showed a positive correlation between creativity and social development. (P<0.05). Moreover there was a significant correlation between mother employment and adolesence social development. (P<0.05). The female adolescents have higher creativity as well as having higher social development.

Remembering in child's play: Historical and cultural perspectives in istomina's experiment and its replications

Yasnitsky, Anton CTL/HDAP, OISE/UT, Toronto, Canada Falenchuk, Olesya Education Commons, OISE/UofT, Toronto, Canada Ferrari, Michel HDAP, OISE/UT, Toronto, Canada

This paper presents a critical review of the numerous attempts to replicate the classical experimental study conducted by Istomina (1947). Specifically, the objectives of this theoretical review were two-fold: 1) to discuss potential failures and successes in replicating the results of the original study; and 2) to present a hypothesis of historical and cultural development of mnemonic processes. To support this hypothesis, we use studies reporting on replications of Istomina's experiment in different cultural settings as well as successful replications of the original experiment at different historical time points but in similar cultural settings (Istomina, 1967, Ivanova & Nevoennaia, 1998).

FP-230: Dysfunctional social behaviors in school: Aggression, anger and violence I

A model of the personality and situational factors in school microviolence

Cocorada, Elena Psychology, University Transilvania, Brasov, Romania Clinciu, Aurel Ion Psychology, University Transilvania, Brasov, Romania Luca, Marcela Rodica Psychology, University Transilvania, Brasov, Romania Pavalache-Ilie, Mariela Psychology, University Transilvania, Brasov, Romania

Studies focused more on general school violence and less on micro-violence occasioned by educational assessment. This study tested a model of assessment-related micro-violence. The participants were 629 students, average age 15.9. Personality variables and assessment-related climate variables were measured. Annual assessment grades were also collected. The statistical method used was regression analysis. A set of variables - intelligence (Bonnardel53), dominance, sociability (CPI), rebel spirit (Clinciu), and assessment climate (Cocoradă & al.) and annual grades were included into a hierarchical regression model with R= .67. Personality variables and assessment climate were found to influence 45% of the level of annual grades.

How to cope with anger in school context?

Maccabez-Arriola, Mónica Dept. of Psychology, University of Fribourg, Fribourg, Switzerland
Retschitzki, Jean Department of psychology, University of Fribourg, Fribourg, Switzerland

The study analyses changes of anger mental representation after the application of the cognitive Anger Control Program (ACP) in school. Pupils with behavioural problems were compared to ordinary pupils (N=31) age 8-11. Changes were measured by the TEC (Pons & Harris, 2000) and the Program Questionnaire. Results show age differences concerning the improvement of anger comprehension, and gender differences. Mental representation scores in Program Questionnaire (score maximum=12) were observed among three groups : ACP group m=8,2; placebo program group m=5; and control group m=5,5. Teaching how to cope with anger in school is possible.

Teachers sense of efficacy mediating the relationship between teachers attributions of bullying and their behaviors towards aggressive students

Stavrinides, Panayiotis Psychology, University of Cyprus, Nicosia, Cyprus

Research has documented how causal attributions predict human behavior in various settings. In this study (N = 216) we examined how teachers explain bullying and the behaviors they adopt in order to deal with the problem. Results have shown that even though causal attributions predict teachers behavior, this relationship is mediated by the teachers sense of efficacy. Specifically, hierarchical regression analysis has shown that both internal and external attributions are mediated by the levels at which teachers believe they can manage their classroom, their instructional strategies, and how well they can engage students in classroom activities.

FP-231: Emotional expression and experience in clinical populations I

Training program in emotional skills for persons with Asperger syndrome

Sixto, Olivar Personality Dept., Valladolid University, Valladolid, Spain

The aim of this study was to show the improvement of the emotional skills of a group of children and teenagers diagnosed with Asperger syndrome, after making use of a specific treatment program. They were assessed via pre- and post- intervention with several questionnaires. The results show an increase in the recognition and expression of emotions, self-regulations and empathy between the pre- and post-test and a decrease in the depression and anxiety. The training program may be adequate for the evaluation and intervention of the emotional needs of individuals with Asperger syndrome.

Comparison of changes in mood: Cartoons vs. mood induction paradigm

Kohn, Nils Department of Psychiatry, UK Aachen, Aachen, Germany Falkenberg, Irina Department of Psychiatry, UK Aachen, Aachen, Germany Schöpker, Regina Department of Psychiatry, UK Aachen, Aachen, Germany Habel, Ute Department of Psychiatry, UK Aachen, Aachen, Germany

Anhedonia can be seen as a major component of depression and describes the decrease or cessation of feelings of pleasure. Thus different moods and a feeling of mirth should be hard to induce in these patients. We compared patients with depression and healthy participants regarding their ability to get into certain moods via an established mood induction paradigm (Habel et al., 2000, Schneider et al., 1994) and humorous stimuli, by recording electrodermal acitivity and facial expressions. Preliminary results point to harder induction of positive emotional states in patients, patients show less autonomic responses and changes in facial expressions.

Association between postpartum depression and emotional changes after delivery

Viegas, Lia Matos Instituto de Psicologia - PSE, Universidade de São Paulo, Cotia, Brazil Andrade da Silva, Gabriela Instituto de Psicologia - PSE, Universidade de São Paulo, São Paulo, Brazil Otta, Emma Instituto de Psicologia - PSE, Universidade de São Paulo, São Paulo, Brazil

To investigate emotional correlates of Postpartum Depression (PPD), 92 Brazilian women screened for PPD using the Edinburgh Postnatal Depression Scale answered questionnaires about their feelings and worries at two days and 2-4 months after delivery. Repeated Measures GLM yielded differences (p<.05) between the two periods. Both depressed and nondepressed mothers increased their worry scores about themselves, their newborns, their other children, and partners. In addition, depressed mothers had more negative feelings regarding the partner and lower scores on emotional welfare. These findings indicate that emotional changes are common after delivery and depressed mothers are more likely to have negative feelings.

FP-232: Families in stress I

Impact of implementation variables on outcome measures in a German application of the family-based primary prevention program FAST (Families and Schools Together)

Fuchs, Irene Lehrstuhl Klin. Psychologie, Universität Siegen, Siegen, Germany Fooken, Insa Lehrstuhl Klinische Psychologi, Universität Siegen, Siegen, Germany

The universal prevention program FAST is a multi-family group intervention that works with the whole family and aims at the improvement of intra- and inter-family relations. FAST is evidence-based and experimentally evaluated in the USA and is implemented in five other countries. This study relates implementation data from about ten program sites in three German cities to target recruitment and/or conduct judgements with about 60 pre-post measurements (including childs behaviour or family climate data) under the hypothesis of a moderate implementation influence. Due to lack of program implementation studies the results will have implications for further German prevention research.

Children of parents with acute central nervous system injuries. Specific mental health risks and protective factors

Stanescu, Dan Florin Comunication and PR, SNSPA, Bucharest, Romania Romer, Georg Klinik für Kinder- und Jugendp, Universitätsklinikum Eppendorf, Hamburg, Germany

To identify factors linked with emotional and behavioral problems in children (4 - 18 year-old) of parents with acute CNS injuries. Instruments: CBCL, YSR, FAD, SF-8, BDI and Karnofsky Index. Risk of problems in children was linked with high levels of family dysfunction, low affective responsiveness, parental over-involvement and depression. Severity of the disease was not associated with child problems. The set of variables, which could predict children problems are health related quality of life (physical), parental depression and affective over-involvement. Targeted treatments, which focus on parental depression and family communication may benefit the children and enhance quality of life.

Protective factors, adaptability and child abuse: An ecological study

Gaxiola, Jose Hermosillo, Mexico Frías, Martha Derecho, Universidad de Sonora, Hermosillo, Mexico

The aim of the study was to analyze the buffering effects of protective factors over risk factors associated with child abuse using the ecological Bronfenbrenner's theory. It is proposed an alternative measure to resilience in parenting called adaptability. 183 mothers living in northwestern Mexico agreed to participate in the study. The data were analyzed with structural equation modeling and indicate that protective factors have negative relation with risk factors; also, the risk factors predict positively the child maltreatment and negatively the construct adaptability. The results confirm the indirect effect of protective factors and the cumulative risk model.

FP-233: Gender differences in work and academic achievement I

Gender differences: Profiles of men and women successful in engineering education

Halpin, Glennelle Auburn University, Auburn, USA Halpin, Gerald EFLT, Auburn University, Auburn, USA Benefield, Larry Engineering, Auburn University, Auburn, USA

That a new generation of problem solvers will be needed is obvious as the world looks for solutions. Among them must be both women and men. The purpose of this study was to identify differential profiles for males and females predicted to succeed in engineering education who did compared/contrasted with those predicted to succeed who did not. From the multivariate and univariate analyses of cognitive, personality, and social variables for >5,000 participants in a longitudinal study in the USA, these profiles emerged. Comparisons and contrasts were made with conclusions leading to a better understanding of differential factors related to success.

Relationship between learning styles and gender

Castano, Gloria Diferential & Work Psychology, Universidad Complutense Madrid, Madrid, Spain

The aim of this study is to show the relationship between Learning Styles and gender Given the diversity of learning styles assessment instruments we choose the Learning Styles Inventory (Kolb, 1985). The results show the existence of individual differences between males and females, though these differences are small. On the one hand, in females the accommodating learning style whereas in men it is predominant the assimilating learning

style. On the other hand, males present a preference to focus the learning from an abstracter focus whereas women prefer to get completely involved in new experiences. Moreover females present more active character at the time of learning, this is, they prefer to employ the theories to make decisions and solve problems.

Gender and negotiation: An empirical study of gender differences in negotiation behaviour

Mura, Giulia Quasi, Università Milano-Bicocca, Milano, Italy Diamantini, Davide Sociologia e Ricerca Sociale, Università Milano-Bicocca, Milano, Italy

This research evaluates the effect of gender in negotiation behaviour, within a working situation. We investigate the: • overbidding; • speed of concessions and log rolling; • impact of an emotional variable. The research was realised in both private and public organizations in Torino on a sample of 73 subjects, using specifically built scenarios simulating a negotiation. The analyses made (T-Test, Anova) show differences in negotiation behaviour between men and women, with women opening the negotiation with lower requests, conceding more during the interaction and reacting more strongly when facing an aggressive counterpart.

FP-234: Memory processes V

Metamemory judgements for faces, nameable pictures and abstract art

Chalmers, Kerry School of Psychology, University of Newcastle, Callaghan, Australia McKay, Phylippa School of Psychology, University of Newcastle, Callaghan, Australia

Fifty eight undergraduate psychology students gave metamemory judgements for three classes of nonverbal stimuli both prior to study and after completing memory tasks. Pre-study judgements were higher than post-test judgements and the difference between pre-study and post-test judgements was greater for faces than for either nameable pictures or abstract art. Positive correlations between metamemory judgements and performance (including correct identification of studied items and false recognition of nonstudied items) suggested that participants who judged their memory as being better were more likely to indicate an item had been studied, whether or not it had been presented during the study phases.

The effects of repression on memory: Are encoding processes involved?

Davis, Penelope Psychology, Griffith University, Brisbane, Australia Harnett, Paul Psychology, University of Queensland, Brisbane, Australia Jovcic, Vedrana Psychology, Griffith University, Brisbane, Australia Krishnamoorthy, Govind Psychology, Griffith University, Brisbane, Australia McClelland, Fiona Psychology, University of Queensland, Brisbane, Australia Walmsley, Karen Psychology, University of Queensland, Brisbane, Australia

Repression is associated with difficulty accessing unpleasant autobiographical memories but the processes underlying the effects of repression on memory remain unclear. This research used the item-method directed forgetting procedure to examine the proposition that repressors are particularly adept at suppressing unwanted material during encoding. Directed forgetting effects for repressors were apparent on both explicit and implicit memory tasks but the intentional forgetting abilities of repressors were no better than those of nonrepressors. These results suggest that autobiographical memory deficits in repressors reflect a greater propensity to use their avoidant encoding skills rather than an enhanced ability to do so.

Ease of recall in memory judgments: How detailed recall undermines the confidence of eyewitnesses

Hellmann, Jens Dept. of Psychology, University of Aberdeen, Aberdeen, United Kingdom Kopietz, René Psychology, University of Bielefeld, Bielefeld, Germany Echterhoff, Gerald Psychology, University of Bielefeld, Bielefeld, Germany

People often use the ease of recalling past events to derive memory judgments, which may lead them to judge their memories as worse despite recalling more. In two experiments we investigated if such an effect can also be found for eyewitness memory. After watching a video depicting a burglary, participants who recalled as many details as possible judged their memory as worse than participants who recalled only a few central details. This effect was mediated by experienced ease of recall and occurred even when attributions to task difficulty were encouraged. Thus, well-intentioned recall attempts may ironically undermine eyewitnesses' confidence.

Head-mounted video cued recall for object- and order memory

Acker, Felix Dept. of Psychology, LaTrobe University, Bundoora, Australia Omodei, Mary Psychology, LaTrobe University, Bundoora, Australia

A set of three studies examined the effect of watching video taken from one's own visual perspective while carrying out naturalistic tasks with respect to recall success. All studies used student populations, one had a between-groups and two had a within-groups design. Confidence intervals and a meta-analytic summary of the studies suggest that watching one's own video enables people to not only remember qualitatively better but also quantitatively more relevant information than comparative video cues. This complements existing results showing head mounted video utility in decision making research. It is a powerful research tool well suited for naturalistic contexts.

FP-235: Issues in attention

Retinotopically independent processing of saliency signals in the near-absence of attention

Bogler, Carsten Attention & Awareness, Max-Planck-Institut, Leipzig, Germany Haynes, John-Dylan Computational Neuroscience, Berstein Center for, Berlin, Germany

It is assumed that a dedicated neural map encodes salient positions in the visual field. According to most models this saliency map is based on integration of feature gradients across multiple feature dimensions. Here we investigated the neural correlates of orientation and colour saliency in humans using fMRI. BOLD activity was significantly increased for the salient positions in early visual cortex and a trend was apparent in intraparietal sulcus. Furthermore the increase in BOLD signals in V3a and V4 was monotonic with increased pop-out. The results point to an independent processing of pop-out signals in the absence of attention.

Modulation of distribution of dots number on strategies and spatial attention allocation during two sequential arrays integration

Ren, Yanju Dept. of Psychology, Shandong Normal University, Jinan, People's Republic of China Xuan, Yuming Institute of Psychology, Chinese Academy of Sciences, Beijing, People's Republic of China Fu, Xiaolan Institute of Psychology, Chinese Academy of Sciences, Beijing, People's Republic of China

In this study, empty cell localization task was employed to investigate the information integration between two sequential dot arrays in two experiments. In the first experiment, the distribution of dots number between two arrays was manipulated to test the image-percept integration hypothesis and convert-and-compare hypothesis. In the second experiment, spatial attention allocation was explored by recording participants' eye movement behavior during the process of integration to further test these two hypotheses. It was found that distribution of dots number between two arrays modulate the participants' strategies and spatial attention allocation during the process of integration.

The impact of heterogeneity along the task-relevant and the: Irrelevant dimensions on feature search

Wei, Ping Dept. of Psychology, Peking University, Beijing, People's Republic of China *Müller, Hermann* Department of Psychology, LMU München, Munich, Germany *Zhou, Xiaolin* Department of Psychology, Peking University, Beijing, People's Republic of China
Objective: To investigate the impact of heterogeneity along the task-relevant and –irrelevant dimensions on feature search. Method: Participants were required to carry out color (or orientation) search while the heterogeneity along the task-relevant and -irrelevant dimensions were orthogonally manipulated. Result: The search times were longer when the task-relevant dimension was heterogeneous than when it was homogeneous. The variation along the task-irrelevant color dimension had an impact upon the efficiency of orientation search, while the variation in orientation had no impact upon color search. Conclusion: The variability of feature values and the relative bottom-up perceptual saliency between dimensions determines search efficiency.

Memory effects in repeated visual search

Körner, Christof Inst. für Psychologie, Universität Graz, Graz, Austria *Höfler, Margit* Institut für Psychologie, Universität Graz, Graz, Austria
Memory effects in repeated visual search In a recent experiment Körner and Gilchrist (in press) had participants search the same ten-letter display consecutively for two different target letters. Using eye movement measurements they found a memory recency effect: A distractor item that was a target during search 1 was found faster in search 2 if it had been fixated more recently. In the presented experiment we introduced retention intervals of 400 ms and 800 ms between searches in order to determine if search information decays in memory. Our results indicate no substantial memory decay. This suggests that search information may be preserved across short intervals.

FP-236: Social support at work

What do expatriates need?: The role of social support networks for successful foreign assignments

Spieß, Erika Psychology, University, München, Germany *Gasteiger, Rosemarie* Psychologie, PricewaterhouseCoopers, München, Germany *Stroppa, Christina* Universität München, München, Germany *Woschée, Ralph* Psychology, University, München, Germany
The aim of the presented research is to shed light on the impact of social support networks on expatriates' success. Based upon a model by Caligiuri and Lazarova (2003) several predictive components affecting cross-cultural adjustment like social interaction and social support were researched. Data were collected from employees working for small and medium-sized enterprises and large-scale enterprises shortly before, during, and after their foreign assignment. Differences and similarities found for employees working for small and medium-sized companies versus major enterprises will be presented. Implications for future research and practical considerations for multinational organizations sending employees abroad will be discussed in the presentation.

A study of the relation between emotional intelligence and leadership styles (Bernard Bass model) of department chairs at University of Isfahan

Mokhtaripour, Marzieh Education, University of Isfahan, Isfahan, Islamic Republic of Iran
The purpose of this study was to investigate the relation between emotional intelligence and leadership styles of department chairpersons at university of Isfahan based on multifactor Bernard Bass model. Research method was descriptive – correlative. Statistical population included all 33 chairs and 454 faculty members whom from was chosen 113 as statistical sample, respectively. Findings showed that:1) There was significant relation emotional intelligence and transformational leadership style $r=0/347$ at $p<0/05$ level., 2) There was a correlation between emotional intelligence and transactional leadership style $r=0/269$ – correlative was not significant at $p<0/05$ level., 3) There was no significant correlation between emotional intelligence and lassies-faire leadership style $r=0/044$ at $p<0/05$ level.

Social identity, personal identity and social support among working and non-working women

Bhatti Ali, Razia Islamabad, Pakistan
ABSTRACT The current study investigated social identity, personal identity and social support among working and non-working women. Working and non-working women (n=80) were purposively selected and assessed on the 2 variables social identity and personal identity. The Aspects of Identity Questionnaire IV (Cheek, 1989) was used to measure social identity and personal identity and the Social Support Scale by Gul & Najam (2001) was used to measure social support. The results of the analysis showed significant differences in personal identity, social identity and social support in working women compared to non-working women. The study illustrates that employed women's personal and social identities are different and stronger compared with non-working women.

Mental health status and social support of young female workers in a joint venture

Han, Buxin Inst. of Psychology, Chinese Academy of Sciences, Beijing, People's Republic of China *Liu, Ying* Dept. of Psych., Beijing Univ., Chaoyang Maternity & Child, Beijing, People's Republic of China
Objectives: Mental health and social support of female workers in joint-venture. Methods: SCL-90 and Social Support Inventory were distributed to 672 workers (mean age 25.18 ± 6.35 years) in a joint venture at Beijing. Results: Young female workers score significantly higher than national norms on each factor of SCL-90, specifically on obsessive-compulsive, anxiety, and interpersonal sensitivity. Those with younger age, shorter working period, middle level of education and income, had poorer mental health status and lower social support which correlated negatively. Conclusion: Young female workers in the joint venture had poorer mental health status correlating with social support negatively.

FP-237: Socio-economic status

Discourse analysis of photographs produced by people living in poverty in Ciudad Juarez, Mexico.

Luna Hernandez, Jesus Rene Dept. de Psicologia Social, Univ. Autonoma de Barcelona, Cerdanyola del Valles, Spain
Most studies on poverty rely on descriptions provided by social scientists of how the poor live, interact and construct their reality. However, such approach denies the opportunity of understanding the poor's version of reality from their perspective. This study aims to get a glimpse on how people living in poverty interact with each other and with others and their environments by providing them with disposible cameras, analyzing the discourse such images produced with the help of Atlas-ti, a software for qualitative analysis. Main topics were family, social problems in their neighboorhoods, and empowering strategies for people and communities.

Psychosocial and structural interventions on self constructed slums: the experiences of their inhabitants

Martín, Yuraima Facultad de Arquitecura, Universidad Central, Caracas, Venezuela *Urreiztieta, María Teresa* Ciencia y tecnología del comp, Universidad Simón Bolívar, Caracas, Venezuela
The objective of this research was to explore and analyse the meaning of psychosocial and structural interventions on self constructed slums located in Caracas, Venezuela, from the experiences of their inhabitants. Between the contributions of Environmental Psychology and the New Dialogic Architecture, the research is oriented by the notion of "place" as "crossroads between human event and structure" developed by Muntañola. Following the procedures proposed by qualitative methodologies, a study case is presented, based on in-depth interviews. The results allowed the understanding of perceptions, cognitions and meanings which guided the behaviour of the subjects involved in those intervention processes.

Perceived risk and public preferences for governmental management of social hazards

Zheng, Rui Social & Economic Behavior, Institute of psychology, CAS, Beijing, People's Republic of China *Shi, Kan* Social & Economic Behavior, Institute of psychology, CAS, Beijing, People's Republic of China *Li, Shu* Social & Economic Behavior, Institute of psychology, CAS, Beijing, People's Republic of China
Risk perceptions are important to the policy process because they inform individuals' preferences for government management of social hazards. A public sample of Chinese (N=524) rated the levels of threat of 20 social hazards. We further use a structural equation model to analyze the influence and effect mechanism of risk perception. It was found that: 1) older participants, less educated and lower-income individuals found the hazards to be more threatening than others 2) Individual character and trust will influence risk perception. Then, greater perceived risk generally produces lower SWB and greater government support. Social support will moderate this relationship.

Intergenerational relations in rural and urban Indian families

Verma, Sunil Department Of Allahabad, University Of Allahabad, Allahabad, India *Satyanarayana, Alturi* Department Of Allahabad, University Of Allahabad, Allahabad, India
This study is directed to comprehend the nature of intergenerational relations and their behavioural manifestations in three socio economic categories (upper class, middle class and lower class) of Indian families. 48 families were taken from Gorakhpur city and Reotipur village in U.P (India). Narratives on day-to-day intergenerational interactions were collected from father and son, mother in-law and daughter in-law. Content analysis reveals that intergenerational relations are affected by changes in terms of power, authority and variations in terms of values and attitude. Results show that intergenerational relations are manifested in terms of conflict, solidarity and ambivalence and the coping mechanisms varied along socio economic categories.

FP-238: Teaching of psychology I

Addressing globalization with feature foreign films

Meiners, Mary Social and Behavior Sciences, San Diego Miramar College, San Diego, USA
Globalization invites many changes in teaching psychology and presents opportunities to prepare students to interact with those different than themselves. Current classrooms often reflect the diversity of world cultures. To acknowledge this diversity and attempt to reduce xenophobia, foreign films have been introduced into the classroom. They are used to illustrate various concepts during class. An additional assignment requires students to view a feature film from a pre-approved list and identify psychological concepts illustrated in the film. The student responses collected in a post assignment survey have been overwhelmingly positive.

Technical support for interactive education in psychology

Vylegzhanin, Vasily IEAP, Moscow, Russia
Interactive laboratory for psychology education will be demonstrated. Technology aspects of education such as unified data collection and processing, scalability, usability, Internet support, data protection will be discussed. Predictor based system supports adaptive curricula for every student just as for groups and courses. This flexible technology makes possible to convert many important themes such as color sense, hearing etc. from text-based lectures to laboratory workshop. Interactive technology supports many classical psychometric procedures and trainings included in personality and social psychology course. Interactive training support is implemented as a form of Internet videoconference.

Psychological types of students and methods of education in psychology

Nedospasova, Veronika Dept. of Clinical Psychology, IEAP, Moscow, Russia
Main methodical issue of psychology teaching is the place of perception theory and cognitive psychology in curriculum. Several variants of curricula for psychology education were compared. The first one is constructed in accordance with the history of discoveries in psychology. Two variants of curricula reflected conceptual sequence, one starts with theory of perception and advances via cognitive process to personality, the other starts with personality and perception theory appears to be lateral in this case. The 4th variant starts with practical studies and theoretical knowledge is introduced in process of experience accumulation. Different variants were more acceptable by different psychological types of students.

Adaptive curricula for interactive education in psychology

Druzhinin, Georgy IEAP, Moscow, Russia
All the potential and actual students in psychology may be divided into 4 main groups. This classification is based on the predictors of their professional interests, social attitudes and mental possibilities. The criteria, methods and technology of such selection and the preliminary income control just as related statistics will be discussed. The optimal variant of curricula for education in psychology and the optimal collection of trainings and interactive components of education technology can be constructed based on the predictors of the future professional success. Some variants of optimal curricula supported by interactive tools will be demonstrated.

FP-239: Teachers' health and well-being: Burnout, professional identity

Burnout differences between primary and secondary education teachers

Merino Tejedor, Enrique Dept. of Psychology, University of Valladolid, Segovia, Spain Rigotti, Thomas INSTITUTE OF PSYCHOLOGY II, UNIVERSITY OF LEIPZIG, LEIPZIG, Germany
Prior empirical studies have shown that teaching is a stressful activity; particularly teachers are prone to suffer from the syndrome of burnout. In this study we will compare the experience of burnout between 106 teachers from primary schools and 181 teachers from secondary schools in Spain. We employed the Brief Burnout Questionnaire to assess antecedents of burnout, the main symptoms, as well as further consequences. Secondary school teachers showed to give higher ratings than teachers from primary schools did. Differences in strain conditions responsible for this result, as well as further actions to prevent teachers from "burning out" are discussed.

Teachers' basic need satisfaction, occupational well-being and adjustment

Kunter, Mareike Zentrum für Bildungsforschung, Mex-Planck-Institut, Berlin, Germany Klusmann, Uta Center f Educational Research, MPI f Human Development, Berlin, Germany
Drawing on self-determination theory, two studies investigated whether teachers' feelings of autonomy, competence, and social relatedness at school were associated with better work adjustment. A cross-sectional study with 124 teachers found substantial correlations between satisfaction of teachers needs and their occupational well-being and maladjustment (i.e., stronger quitting intentions and poorer health). A longitudinal study with a 1-year repeated measurement of 134 teachers showed that teachers' need satisfaction influenced their exhaustion and job satisfaction and even had positive effects on their students' motivation (regression analysis). Teachers' basic need satisfaction thus plays a crucial role in both their professional experience and their performance.

Testing a model of school quality features for promoting and maintaining teachers' health

Altenstein, Christine Inst. für Medizin. Psychologie, Universität Greifswald, Greifswald, Germany Wiesmann, Ulrich Western-Pomerania, Institute of Medical Psycholog, Greifswald, Germany Möbius, Kati Western-Pomerania, Institute of Medical Psycholog, Greifswald, Germany Hannich, Hans-Joachim Western-Pomerania, Institute of Medical Psycholog, Greifswald, Germany
We developed an inventory for the assessment of school resources and deficits from the teachers' point of view. Main objective was the replication of a four factor structure in a representative sample of 556 teachers. Using Confirmatory Factor Analysis, we compared two structural models differing in the number of indicator variables for the latent factors. Both models showed substantial fit; the more parsimonious model was slightly superior. We preferred this solution because it makes the inventory more concise.

FP-240: The development of emotional regulation in adolescence

The development of internalizing problems from age 2 to age 12

Fanti, Kostas Dept. of Psychology, University of Cyprus, Aradippou, Cyprus
The study investigates the development of internalizing problems from age 2-12 using Latent Class Growth Analysis, and tests how temperament, home environment, and cognitive functioning, forecast the differential trajectories of internalizing problems using multinomial logistic regression. The sample consisted of 1232 children (53% male) and was derived from the NICHD Study of Early Child-Care. Groups exhibiting low, moderate, and chronic internalizing problems were identified. The chronic group was characterized by lower cognitive abilities, and a more negative home environment. Findings suggest that interventions need to start early in life and that both personal and environmental characteristics need to be considered.

Adolescents' psychological well-being and memory for life events: Influences on life satisfaction with respect to temperamental dispositions

Siddiqui, Anver Dept. of Psychology, School of Social Sciences, Växjö, Sweden Garcia, Danilo Psychology, Karlstad University, Karlstad, Sweden
The aim of the present study was to explore how the number of recalled life events (positive and negative) predicts psychological well-being (PWB) and how PWB predicts life satisfaction (LS). One hundred and thirty five high school students participated in completing the SWLS (LS), PWB (short-version), PANAS (to create AFT) and the life events recollection task. Results indicated that adolescents with high PA also indicated high PWB. In addition adolescents with low affective profiles had high PWB. Positive and negative life events predicted PWB for self-destructive temperaments; positive life events predicted PWB for low affective temperaments. PWB predicted LS for all temperaments except for the self-actualizing group.

Assesment of self-assertion training in the treatment of stage fright among the Nigerian university girls

Shobola, Adeola Human Resource Development, Covenant University, Ota, Nigeria
Objectives: This experimental study assessed the efficacy of Self Assertion Training (SAT) in the treatment of stage fright among the Nigerian university girls. Methods: 600 girls were selected from two universities using purposive sampling. Self Assertive Training lasted four weeks of four group sessions of 45 minutes was accorded the 315 as experimental group and the rest 285 as control group. Hypotheses were tested with multiple regressions and t-test. Result: Participants exposed to SAT overcame stage fright. Mono sex siblings and course of study of participants had significant effect on the treatment. Conclusions: Self-Assertion is relevant in treating stage fright.

The development of adolescents' implicit attitude to emotion regulation

Liu, Junsheng Dept. of Psychology, Shanghai Normal University, Shanghai, People's Republic of China Sang, Biao Department of Psychology, East China Normal University, Shanghai, People's Republic of China
Previous research has showen that implicit attitude to emotion regulation, as an important aspect of automatic emotion regulation, could influence emotion regulation without the cognitive costs. However little is known about the development of the implicit attitude to emotion regulation. Two hundred 12-18-year-olds were administered the emotion regulation-implicit association test (ER-IAT). ANOVA analyses showed that the older hold much more positive attitude to emotion regulation than the younger, and there is no significant difference between boys and girls. The findings suggested that the emotion regulation practice can help adolescents form more positive implicit attitude to emotion regulation.

FP-241: Substance abuse and addiction II

Illicit drug-consumption: Measuring two cognitive-behavioral risk-factors
Raab, Corina Abt. für Medizin. Psychologie, Universitätsklinik Heidelberg, Heidelberg, Germany Weinhold, Jan Medical Psychology, University Hospital Heidelberg, Heidelberg, Germany Verres, Rolf Medical Psychology, University Hospital Heidelberg, Heidelberg, Germany

Risk- and protective factors play an important role in the consumption of illicit psychoactive substances. Knowledge of and behavior around illicit substances are ignored in the context of psychometric diagnostics. An inventory based on cognitive-behavioral theories containing ten substance-specific modules was constructed to record these two factors. The substances focussed upon were cannabis, amphetamines, ecstasy, hallucinogens and cocaine. The inventory was set up as a web-based record-tool and tested on a sample of 2400 subjects. Scale-reductions have been conducted by means of various statistics. The primary test-theoretical quality-criteria have been calculated and judged as very good.

Onset of tobacco use and transition to other drug use among college undergraduates in north of Iran-2006.
Mohtasham Amiri, Zahra Community Medicine, Guilan University, Rasht, Islamic Republic of Iran Doostdar Sanaye, Mehrnaz Community Medicine, Guilan University, Rasht, Islamic Republic of Iran Jafari Shakib, Abbas Rasht Health Center, Guilan University, Rasht, Islamic Republic of Iran

Background: To estimate the cumulative probability of occurrence of first use of tobacco and the risk of transition to illegal drugs. METHODS: We conducted a cross sectional study of 3958 college students in 2005. Data were collected by using a validated self-applied questionnaire. Results: 722 students (19.5%) were current smokers. The most prevalent substances were Ecstasy (4.3%), opium (2.7%). Tobacco users were at greater risk of starting drug use than nonusers (OR=14.42; 95 % [CI] = 10.62-19.74). Conclusions: The innovative method used in this study yields epidemiologic evidence relating early use of tobacco with initiation of illegal drugs in youth.

Male at-risk and heavy episodic drinkers and their motivation to change drinking
Coder, Beate IES, EMAU Greifswald, Greifswald, Germany Freyer-Adam, Jennis IES, EMAU Greifswald, Greifswald, Germany Bischof, Gallus Psychiatry and Psychotherapy, University of Lübeck, Lübeck, Germany Rumpf, Hans-Jürgen Psychiatry and Psychotherapy, University of Lübeck, Lübeck, Germany John, Ulrich IES, EMAU Greifswald, Greifswald, Germany Hapke, Ulfert IES, EMAU Greifswald, Greifswald, Germany

Objective: At-risk drinkers with heavy episodic drinking (ARHE) have a more problematic drinking style than at-risk drinkers only or heavy episodic drinkers only (AR,HE). With respect to brief interventions, little is known about their motivation to change drinking. Methods: A proactively recruited sample of 425 male general hospital inpatients was used. Results: A lower proportion of ARHE was not ready to change drinking compared to AR,HE (36 vs. 53%). Groups did not differ regarding openness to counseling. Conclusions: Every second male with ARHE and AR,HE is open for counseling. Brief intervention should be tailored to motivation to change drinking.

Female frequent internet gamblers: A qualitative study of their gambling, its impact and their views on treatment and policy
Corney, Roslyn and Counselling, Greenwich Psychology, London, United Kingdom

Aims: to study the gambling history and stories of participants, motivations, impact and helpseeking. Method: Details were advertised on websites and newspapers. 30 frequent gamblers were interviewed over the telephone for approximately one hour. Verbatim transcriptions were analysed using NVIVO and grounded theory. Results/conclusions: Not all women had gambled before. However, internet accessibility meant prolonged periods were spent gambling to the neglect of other life areas. Some were originally motivated by excitement but others gambled to escape from current difficulties. Depression, anxiety, panic attacks and suicide ideation were common. The women were ambivalent towards their gambling and receiving help.

FP-242: Altruism and helping behavior

The emergence of evolutionary altruistic behavior through multilevel selection
Hatori, Tsuyoshi Dept of Civil Engineering, Tokyo Institute of Technology, Tokyo, Japan Fujii, Satoshi Dept of Civil Engineering, Tokyo Institute of Technology, Tokyo, Japan Suminaga, Tetsushi Dept of Civil Engineering, Tokyo Institute of Technology, Tokyo, Japan

This study is aimed to investigate social conditions where an evolutionally altruistic behavior emerges while referring the idea of multilevel selection in the evolutionary theory. For this purpose, we developed a mathematical model describing the evolutional process of altruistic behaviors, which indicated the theoretical hypothesis that group selection could be an important force in the emergence of altruistic behaviors. To test the hypothesis we implemented a questionnaire survey targeting at 300 employees in companies in Japan. The result supported the hypothesis, that indicated that the pressure of group selection was positively correlated with tendency of the emergence of altruistic behaviors.

Pro-social behavior and causal attribution in Brazil
Pilati, Ronaldo Dept. of Social Psychology, University of Brasilia, Brasília, Brazil Leão, Mariana Social Psychology, University of Brasilia, Brasília, Brazil Neves, Julianna Social Psychology, University of Brasilia, Brasília, Brazil Fonseca, Marcus Social Psychology, University of Brasilia, Brasília, Brazil

Pro-social behavior is any act that benefits another person or group. This research tested the influence of causal attribution and helping cost on pro-social behavior intention in a Brazilian cultural context. Simulation experimental design was used with 300 participants. It was developed six scenarios in a factorial design of 2 (controllability X uncontrollability) X 3 (cost: low, medium and high). The data were analyzed through ANOVA and structural equation modeling. The preliminary results indicated that interaction between perceptions of uncontrollability and low helping cost was significantly related to high levels of helping intention (F = 13,11; p ≤ 0,001).

Alter-altruism
Poddiakov, Alexander Dept. of Psychology, Higher School of Economics, Moscow, Russia

Aim of the study is elaboration of egoism vs. altruism opposition by introduction of a new concept, i.e., alternative altruism, or alter-altruism (AA). It is selfless defense of others' interests by doing damage to their competitors, rivals, etc. Classification of various AA types is presented, and cases of AA behavior in various areas are

analyzed. Moral dilemmas of AA are discussed. Experiments, in which children successfully made ethically justified AA decisions to prevent negative characters of a tale and help positive ones, are described. General conclusion is that the concept of alter-altruism creates more differentiated opportunities to analyze social reality.

Civil courage and helping behaviour: Differences between real and anticipated behaviour
Voigtlaender, Denise Inst. für Psychologie, Universität Göttingen, Göttingen, Germany Schulz-Hardt, Stefan Institute of Psychology, University of Goettingen, Goettingen, Germany Schroeder, Sylvia-Maria Institute of Psychology, University of Goettingen, Goettingen, Germany

We conducted three experiments comparing anticipated and real behaviour in situations requiring either help or civil courage. In the civil courage situations participants observed a norm violation (e.g. stealing). In the corresponding helping situations participants perceived a confederate requiring help. Participants either experienced the situation in reality or received a description of the situation and reported their anticipated reactions. While for the help requiring situation anticipated intervention rate was similar to real intervention rate, participants overestimated the intervention rate in civil courage requiring situations. These findings support a theoretical distinction between helping behaviour and civil courage.

Motivations for helping: The moderating role of group membership
Stürmer, Stefan Inst. für Psychologie, Fern-Universität in Hagen, Hagen, Germany Snyder, Mark Psychology, University of Minnesota, Minneapolis, USA

A group-level perspective on helping suggests that salient ingroup/outgroup distinctions play a crucial role in moderating the motivational processes underlying helping (e.g., Stürmer et al., 2005). Common group membership should increase the likelihood of empathy-based helping. When people contemplate offering help to members of outgroups, however, they often may do so in a more systematic and controlled mode of information processing (including cost-benefit analyses). The results of a coordinated series of studies employing different research methodologies (field research vs. controlled experimentation), involving participants of different cultural backgrounds, different helping situations, and different helping criteria provide clear support for these predictions.

FP-243: Self-regulation

The role of spontaneous social comparisons in automatic goal pursuit
Crusius, Jan AG Sozialpsychologie, Universität zu Köln, Köln, Germany Mussweiler, Thomas HF, AG Sozialpsychologie, University of Cologne, Köln, Germany

Automatic goal pursuit has been shown with many goal contents. Despite the importance of these findings, however, little is known about the mechanisms mediating these effects. Drawing upon research showing that representations of significant others and personal goals are strongly related, we suggest that social comparison is a mechanism contributing to goal priming. We assume that the direction of spontaneous social comparisons triggered by goal related stimuli affects the direction of goal pursuit. In internet and laboratory experiments, we found that procedurally priming similarity comparisons before neatness or achievement primes lead to behavioral assimilation, while dissimilarity comparisons resulted in contrast.

Three dimensions of self-regulation

Bak, Waclaw Dept. of Personality, Catholic University Lublin, Lublin, Poland

The paper presents the main thesis of a new theoretical proposition concerning the structure and regulative functions of the self-system. Based on conceptions of Higgins, Markus, and Ogilvie, the self-system is defined as a cognitive structure, composed of different self beliefs (e.g. ideal-self, ought-self, undesired-selves, can-self, impossible-self) and discrepancies between them. It is hypothesized that the self-system one can describe in terms of three dimensions: "negative-self-standards", "positive-self-standards", and "can-self-standards". It is proposed that they can be useful in explaining different aspects of psychological functioning, such as goal realization, self-esteem, and identity. Preliminary results of the research testing the model are presented.

Can self-regulation be truly collective?: Regulatory focus and intergroup behavior

Sassenberg, Kai Institut für Wissensmedien, Tübingen, Germany

Self-regulation approaches such as regulatory focus theory have recently been introduced into the field of intergroup behavior. Research has considered self-regulation as moderator as well as an outcome of intergroup processes. The current presentation gives an overview of intergroup research applying self-regulation approaches from the other's own and other laboratories. Moreover, it answers the question whether self-regulation can be collective. This question is answered by applying the following four criteria: the relevance of group based input (e.g., appraisals), the relevance of group relevant output (e.g., benefits), the impact of social identification, and social sharedness within a group.

Motivational balance at different levels of social complexity: From intrapersonal level to inter-groups level

Mamali, Catalin Dept. of Psychology, Loras College, Dubuque, USA

At the core of the model are the relationships between motivational balance - MB (Mamali, 1981) and levels of social complexity (Hinde, 1979). At the intrapersonal level MB is measured vectorially as a relationship between the intensity and quality of motives (intrinsic/extrinsic) within and across activities. The interaction valence-expectancy-instrumentality (redefined as locus of control) accounts for MB intensity. At dyadic level MB includes also the hierarchical differential between the motives satisfied by each side and varies between co-regressive and co-developmental motives. Empirical results suggest that for each activity there is a certain optimal balance between intrinsic and extrinsic motives.

FP-244: Psychological disorders VI

The automatic and controlled information processing in persons with major depressive disorder

Ghamari Kivi, Hossein Psychology, University of Mohaghegh Ardabi, Ardabil, Islamic Republic of Iran

Objectives: To investigate automatic and controlled information processing and the effects of antidepressant drugs on these variables in major depressive disorder. Methods: 30 persons with major depressive disorder who have been received antidepressant drugs and 30 patients without medication and 30 normal persons have been randomly selected and answered to beck depression inventory, word competition test and words association subscale. data were analysed by one way analysis of variance. Results: there was not significant difference among two participant groups and normal group in automatic processing but there was significant difference($p < 0/05$) in controlled

processing. Conclusion: automatic processing has underling components that are resistant against psychopathplogy but controlled processing is very sensitive.

Interpersonal problem-solving and depression in parents with disabled children

Fotini, Grigoriou Special Education, University of Thessaly, Volos, Greece *Kleftaras, George* Dept. of Special Education, University of Thessaly, Volos, Greece

Depression seems to be one of the most frequent psychological problems of parents with disabled children. Recent research has revealed that the ability of an individual to solve its social and interpersonal problems is associated to various psychopathological conditions. Based on this evidence, the relationship between problem-solving ability and depressive symptomatology of these parents is investigated. 80 parents with disabled children presenting physical/intellectual disabilities participated in this study and were administered: a) Pichot-Questionnaire-of-Depressive-Symptoms and b) Heppner-Social-Problem-Solving-Questionnaire. Significant correlations were found between depressive symptoms and problem-solving ability and specifically problem-solving-confidence, active effort to find alternative-solutions and self-control in problematic situations.

Outcome of postnatal depression screening using Edinburgh Postnatal Depression Scale

Leung, Shirley Department of Health, Hong Kong SAR Government, Hong Kong, China, People's Republic of : Hong Kong SAR *Leung, Cynthia* Department of Educational Psyc, The Hong Kong Institute of Edu, Hong Kong, China, People's Republic of : Macao SAR *Lee, Dominic T S* School of Public Health, The Chinese University of Hong, Hong Kong, China, People's Republic of : Macao SAR *Chan, Ruth* Department of Medicine & T, The Chinese University of Hong, Hong Kong, China, People's Republic of : Macao SAR

Objectives: To evaluate the effectiveness of a postnatal depression screening programme using Edinburgh Postnatal Depression Scale (EPDS), relative to usual clinical practice. Method: 462 mothers with 2-month-old babies attending routine child health service were randomized into postnatal depression screening by EPDS or usual clinical practice. Follow-up counselling was provided by nurses to participants in need. Results: At 6 months postnatal, there was a significant difference in mental health outcome favouring mothers under the EPDS screening programme. Conclusion: The implementation of a postnatal depression screening programme using EPDS, compared with usual practice, resulted in better mental health among the former.

Shame and guilt relationships with depression and anxiety

Motan, Irem Psychology Department, Ondokuz Mayis Uni., Samsun, Ankara, Turkey *Gencoz, Faruk* Psychology Department, Middle East Technical Universi, Ankara, Turkey

The aim of the present study is to underline the relationship of shame and guilt with depression and anxiety. Participants were administered Test of Self-conscious Scale-3, State Shame Guilt Scale, Beck Depression Inventory, Stait-Trait Anxiety Scale. Consequently, shame-proneness, state shame, and lower levels of state pride emerged as common factors for depressive symptoms and trait anxiety. This study addresses the nature of the relationship between self-conscious emotions and depression, anxiety symptoms. Findings of the study are discussed in the frame of Tripartite model. Guilt-proneness and gender factors were interpreted as the differentiating predictors in the light of the literature.

FP-245: Sensory-motor interactions II

Coordination of eye and head movements during visual perception

Altorfer, Andreas Abt. Psych. Neurophysiologie, Universitätsklinik Bern, Bern 60, Switzerland *Käsermann, Marie-Louise* Dept. Psych. Neurophysiology, University Hosp. of Psychiatry, Bern 60, Switzerland *Raub, Ulrich* Dept. Psych. Neurophysiology, University Hosp. of Psychiatry, Bern 60, Switzerland *Thomke, Christa* Dept. Psych. Neurophysiology, University Hosp. of Psychiatry, Bern 60, Switzerland *Würmle, Othmar* Dept. Psych. Neurophysiology, University Hosp. of Psychiatry, Bern 60, Switzerland

As a prerequisite for emotion processing – as a sender or a receiver - one has to use a perceptual apparatus that includes eyes and head. For sending and hiding emotional cues to the environment one has to direct the face to other persons in a way that they can recognize the facial activity. For receiving stimuli out of the environment a distinct orienting is needed if the oculomotor range of about +/- 55° is exceeded. Additionally, for this analysis three-dimensional head movements are involved. Based on the lack of knowledge concerning the perceptual interrelations, several experiments are done to investigate eye-head coordination especially in emotion recognition.

Being conscious of what is reachable in the peripersonal space

Coello, Yann Dept. of Psychology, University of Lille, Villeneuve d'Ascq, France *Bartolo, Angela* psychology, URECA-University of Lille, Villeneuve d'Ascq, France *Amiri, Bastien* psychology, URECA-University of Lille, Villeneuve d'Ascq, France *Bourgeois, Jeremy* psychology, URECA-University of Lille, Villeneuve d'Ascq, France

Perceptually judging what is reachable in the peripersonal space requires integrating information about visual objects with information about the action system. Neuroscientific evidences will be reviewed that suggest that the possibility to anticipate sensory consequences of simulated action might represent the mechanism that provides the perceptual system with information on the limit of peripersonal space. Modifications of the perception of what is reachable when recalibrating the visuo-motor system, in the presence of pathological peripheral deafferentation, or when inhibiting the motor cortex using TMS provide evidences for such mechanism and suggest that motor representations contributes in the perceptual categorisation of external space.

Individual differences in pointing movements under rotated visual feedback

Hellmann, Andreas Inst. für Psychologie, Universität Oldenburg, Oldenburg, Germany *Huber, Jörg W.* School of Human & Life Sci, Roehampton University, London, United Kingdom

We studied the effects of changes of visual feedback on pointing movements of the hand. Participants (n=12) carried out a pointing task using information available on a video display system. Results show systematic spatial errors dependent on the extent and direction of rotation of visual information available to them, supporting and extending our earlier results. The detailed analysis of the performance of individual subjects over repeated trials shows strong individual differences which we interpret as an indication of different abilities and strategies in carrying out precise movements under conditions of altered visual information.

Motor simulation in the observation of tool-use actions

Massen, Cristina Inst. für Psychologie, Max-Planck-Institut, Leipzig, Germany

Visually perceiving others' actions may activate corresponding motor programs in the observer. We investigated the observation of others' tool-use actions. Two participants were taking turns in acting, observing the tool-use action of another person in trial n-1 and executing one in trial n. Previous results indicated that the action rule of the observed action is automatically activated. This study addressed the question, whether these effects are due to the observation of the movement of a human body rather than to the observation of the tool's movement. The results show, that the effects depend on specific characteristics of the human movement.

FP-246: Clinical / counseling psychology III

Triangulation supports a comprehensive understanding of patients' views of their obesity

Metz, Ulrike Inst. für Allgemeinmedizin, Charité Berlin, Berlin, Germany Dieterich, Anja Institut für Allgemeinmedizin, Charité Berlin, Berlin, Germany Heintze, Christoph Institut für Allgemeinmedizin, Charité Berlin, Berlin, Germany

The present study combines quantitative (locus of control, self-efficacy, attribution tendencies) and qualitative (audio-taped preventive consultation in general practices) data as a multi-method approach of examining patients' (N=120) attributions of etiology and therapy regarding their overweight. Significant correlations between physical status (risk score, BMI) and patients' attributions could be found: Patients with BMI between 25 and 35 (kg/m2) differed from patients with BMI>35 (kg/m2) in attributing internally vs. externally. Additionally, differences related to the perceived relevance of support (family, partner, GP) were found. Content analysis of consultations supported and extended quantitative results and maximized validity.

Implicit self-esteem in recurrent depression

Risch, Anne Katrin Klin.-Psych. Intervention, Universität Jena, Jena, Germany Buba, Astrid Psychologie, Friedrich-Schiller-University, Jena, Germany Steffens, Melanie Psychologie, Friedrich-Schiller-University, Jena, Germany Stangier, Ulrich Psychologie, Friedrich-Schiller-University, Jena, Germany

Negative self-relevant cognitions, activated by negative mood, is suggested to play an important role in the recurrence of depressive episodes. Therefore, we investigated implicit self-esteem before and after negative mood induction in patients with remitted depression. We measured implicit self-esteem using the Implicit Association Test. 15 patients, currently depressed, 15 patients, remitted recurrent depressed and 15 controls with no history of depression participated in the study. The results do not support the hypothesis that implicit self-esteem is impaired after negative mood induction in remitted patients. The discussion will focus on the importance of the findings for theories emphasizing cognitive vulnerability factors and implications for maintenance treatment in recurrent depression.

How does empathy influence emotion regulation skills?

Schenkel, Katia Faculty of Psychology, University of Geneva, Genàve 4, Switzerland Wranik, Tanja Faculty of psychology, University of Geneva, Genàve 4, Switzerland Kaiser, Susanne Faculty of psychology, University of Geneva, Genàve 4, Switzerland

Empathy has both an affective and a cognitive component. We investigated the difference between these two in relation to emotion regulation. We hypothesized that people who use affective empathy are less skilled in regulating own emotions and emotions of others. To investigate links between empathy, emotion regulation, and burnout, we conducted a web experiment with helpline volunteers. We found that people who are high in affective empathy have difficulties in emotion regulation and use more maladaptive strategies that people who are high in cognitive empathy. Cognitive empathy is related to more adaptive emotion regulation strategies and less burnout.

FP-247: Social cognition II

Investigation on 340 drug addicts who resume drugs after receiving compulsory treatment

Chen, Zhongyong University, Inner Mongolia Normal, Huhhot, People's Republic of China

In sample of 340 drug addicts who resume drugs after receiving compulsory treatment in the reeducation through labor centers, followed for 2 years, the result showed that slightly more than 50 percent of them relapsed after free from laborer form within one year. The reasons for relapse were drugs available; unable to get rid of psychological dependence on drugs and same social environment as before. A comprehensive, precautionary and controlling measure should be used to control drugs. We should educate the drug abusers through psychological ways and push the whole society to be concerned with the prevention of drug abuse.

The relationship between personality, cognitive and religious with happiness

Khoshkonesh, Abolghasem Education and Psychology, Shahid Beheshti University, Tehran, Islamic Republic of Iran

Abstract The aim of the present research was an investigation on simple and multiple relationships of personality, cognitive, and religious antecedents with happiness feeling: the relationship between happiness feeling, mental health, and academic performance among Shahid Chamran University students, in Ahwaz. A sample of 569 students were selected by stratified ratio random sampling. A variety of measurements including NEO-FFI, cognitive aspects: Psychological Hardiness Inventory, Selfe-esteem, Life Orientation Test-Revised (LOT-R) by Scheier & Carver et al (1994), Oxford Happiness inventory (OHI) by Argyle (2001), GHQ-28, were applied and Grand Total Score (GTS) was taken as index for academic performance and all data were analyzed.

Perceptions of progress towards goal: Can the eye fool the mind?

Kwong, Jessica Y.Y. Marketing Dept., Chinese Univ. of Hong Kong, Hong Kong, China, People's Republic of : Hong Kong SAR Wong, Susanna Y.N. Marketing, The Chinese University of HK, Hong Kong, China, People's Republic of : Macao SAR Ho, Candy K.Y. Marketing, The Chinese University of HK, Hong Kong, China, People's Republic of : Macao SAR

Perceived progress plays a critical role in people's motivation to persist toward a goal. This research demonstrates that the same progress when presented in different formats would alter the perceptions and hence induces different levels of motivation. Using laboratory experiments, we demonstrate that while figure displays exert dominant influences over corresponding numerical displays, this effect is dependent on the relative ease (fluency) in processing the two different modes of information. In addition, perceptions are biased to different degrees when different figures are used. This paper connects our knowledge about the processing of different types of information with goal motivation.

Implementation intentions and artificial agents

Pelta, Carlos Madrid, Spain González Marqués, Javier Basic Psychology II, Universidad Complutense de Mad, Madrid, Spain

We have developed a computer simulation comparing the behavior of two artificial agents (A0 and A1), both of which imitate the use of implementation intentions for achieving a goal R. However, A0 is more balanced for obtaining the goal intention "I intend to achieve R!" while A1 is more balanced for obtaining the implementation intention "I intend to do R when situations L are encountered!" (Gollwitzer, 1996). We have taken as a reference the parameters introduced in (Gollwitzer and Sheeran, 2004). We have accomplished the statistical analysis (including confidence intervals) and A1 improved the global performance of A0. Our simulation confirms partially the results of Gollwitzer and other authors in humans.

FP-248: Stress, coping, and social support

The eustress/distress reaction characteristics influenced by the organizational adult age

Moise, Annemari Dept. of Psychology, Bucharest University, Bucharest, Romania

Many researches reveal the stress in a negative way, but Seyle talked about stress insisting on satisfaction that a person is able to obtain after an out-side tension. We define in a unique manner the concept of eustress/distress and we proposed one specific classification for stress reaction. The hypothesis was: every segment of organizational adult age is having a specific reaction to eustress/distress. We made a complex analysis on the characteristics of eustress and distress on each stage of organizational adult age and we realized the correlation between the two variables. The conclusions are discussed in terms of practical relevance.

The structure of well-being

Musek, Janek Dept. of Psychology, University of Ljubljana, Ljubljana, Slovenia

Multivariate analyses of twelve psychological constructs representing two most integrative theoretical models of well-being (hedonistic and eudaimonic) clearly established a robust hierarchical structure both on the scale as well as on the item level of data. The analyses yielded a very strong highest-order factor (gWB), two higher-order factors (broad factors of happiness and meaning) and five first-order factors (satisfaction, negative emotionaltiy, positive emotionality, relatedness, and growth). The results also confirmed substantial relationships between the dimensions of well-being and dimensions of personality. The gWB is highly correlated with the general factor of personality (gP).

Innovative stress

Nourkov, Valery Dept. of Sociology, RSIIP, Moscow, Russia

Safety and stability is the most common dream for people living in unstable society. Under such circumstances any social innovations meet counteraction and fears. We term it as "innovative stress". Innovative stress leads to social passivity and interferes social development. From our theoretical perspective, traumatic component of innovative stress may be effectively overcome by psychological intervention. The main aim of intervention might be reinterpretation of values underlining innovative processes.

FP-249: The impact of goals, goal-orientation, and volitional processes on learning II

Volition, trait procrastination and motivational interference in university students
Jorke, Katrin Birte Educational Psychology, University of Karlsruhe, Rheinbach, Germany Fries, Stefan Educational Psychology, University of Karlsruhe, Karlsruhe, Germany Winter, Claudia PA Consulting Group, PA Consulting Group, Frankfurt, Germany
Trait Procrastination and the Tendency to Experience Motivational Interference (TMI) are both failures in self-regulation that can have a negative impact on the efficiency of self-regulated learning as well as on students' well-being. In a questionnaire study on 1253 university students Trait Procrastination and TMI were placed in a broader framework of volitional problems. The resulting model demonstrates that insufficient self-regulation (e.g. low persistence, distractibility) in a specific learning context can be caused by the interplay of direct and mediated effects of volitional strategies, Trait Procrastination and TMI. Implications for the development of interventions will be discussed.

Investigating the casual relation ship between perfectionism, motive achievement, text anxiety and academic achievement
Kheradmand Mard Del, Khatereh Tehran, Islamic Republic of Iran
Abstract The objective of this research is specifying the existing relation among the perfectionism, motive achievement, text anxiety and academic achievement sampling method is random proportional classified The data was studied, using the Pierson correlation and the Regression analysis, with the following results: The positive perfectionism with the mediation of the motive achievement has a direct relation with the educational development. The negative perfectionism with the mediation of the test anxiety has an indirect relation with the motive achievement. The negative perfection with the mediation of the motive achievement indirectly has an indirect relation with the academic achievement.

Can measures of students' motivation help predicting school achievement when intelligence and previous knowledge are already known?
Vock, Miriam Inst. IQB, Humboldt-Universität zu Berlin, Berlin, Germany
Former studies showed contradicting results concerning the role of motivation in predicting school achievement when cognitive abilities are controlled. In this study, we analyze the unique contribution of students' motivation beyond intelligence and previous knowledge on school achievement. Cross-sectional and longitudinal data of N = 5,261 high school students from grades 5, 7, and 9 are presented. Measures are several scales assessing motivation (self-efficacy, domain specific self-concept, interests), intelligence (figural and verbal reasoning), standardized achievement tests (maths and German) and grades. Results from classical multiple regression analyses and multi-level analyses (accounting for class and school effects) will be presented and discussed.

Students' and schoolmates' motivation on academic achievement: School-, and student-level analyses in Hong Kong
Zeng, Xihua Educational Psychology, The Chinese University of HK, Hong Kong, China, People's Republic of : Hong Kong SAR
This research examines how schoolmates' motivation moderates the effect of individual students' motivation on academic achievement. Mathematics test scores of 4478 fifteen-year-olds as well as

questionnaires responses in Hong Kong were analyzed via multi-level analyses (School-, and student-level analyses). Despite their grade and family SES, Students scored higher when they had higher interest in mathematics, and when they were in school context with higher mean interest in mathematics. However, the significantly negative effect of individual students' instrumental motivation on mathematics scores was only detected in school contexts with higher mean instrumental motivation.

FP-250: Sexual behaviour

Casual sex: Why and why not?
Vrangalova, Snezana Human Development, Cornell University, Ithaca, USA
Casual sex (CS) is prevalent among university students. The reasons to engage and not engage in it, however, remain unknown. Two hundred students will be asked to list all the reasons they have for (not) engaging in CS. Preliminary measures of motivation for and against CS will thus be constructed. A random sample of 3500 students at a large US university will be invited to participate in an online survey rating their reasons for (not) having CS. Factor analysis will be used to develop a typology of motivations for and against CS. Implications for application of such instruments in future research will be discussed.

Sex puts you in gendered shoes!
Hundhammer, Tanja Inst. für Psychologie, Universität zu Köln, Köln, Germany Mussweiler, Thomas Department of Psychology, University of Cologne, Köln, Germany
A cultural double standard for the sexual experience of women and men prescribes the enactment of different sexual roles. Women's sexual role is submissive-expressive, men's agentic-dominant. We assume that activating the concept of sexuality renders one's own gender and the respective gender stereotype more salient. This should lead to consistent automatic behavior and self-perception. We showed that sex-priming leads to a more gender-stereotypic self-description (Exp 1), a stronger gender identification (Exp 2) and to subservient behavior for women and dominant behavior for men (Exp 3). Sex-primed females hesitated longer before interrupting, indicating a more other-centered social interaction tendency (Exp 4).

Attachment and love: Their influence on sexual behaviour
Garcia Rodriguez, Georgina Mexico City, Mexico Díaz Loving, Rolando Facultad de Psicología, UNAM, México, D. F., Mexico
Attachment and love are both theoretically and empirically linked to sexual behaviour (Fischer, 2004; Bogaert & Sadava, 2002; Frey & Hojjat, 1998). In the context of collectivistic cultures, sexual behaviour is strongly associated to affective aspects of interpersonal bonds (Giraldo, 2000). The purpose of this research was the prediction of sexual behaviour through attachment and love styles. 209 Mexican adults with different relationships status completed three quantitative measures. Multiple regression analysis showed that the frequency of seduction, physical contact, sexual contact and self-eroticism, and the number of life time sexual partners, are reliably predicted by attachment and love styles.

Psychological processes of BDSM: The players perspective
Lopez, David Sociology, California State University, Northridge, USA
This research explores psychological processes associated with BDSM (Bondage and Discipline/ Dominance and Submission/Sadomasochism) based on-depth informal discussions with active

participants in BDSM. In addition, observations were conducted at public venues where BDSM is practiced. Results suggested processes can be categorized at two levels. One, dominant-submissive relationships vacillate in degree of role assumed (Master/Slave or Top/Bottom). Two, emotional responses to BDSM activity are similar to those associated with chemical use/abuse. It is suggested that clinicians be familiar with these processes especially when working with clients addressing dependency, cross-addiction, self-esteem, and self-concept issues.

FP-251: Psychotherapy - Research and treatment methods VIII

ADHD-profile-study in France: First results concerning diagnosis and therapy of ADHD
Jelen, Anna Heidelberg, Germany Huss, Michael Clinic of Child Psychiatry, Charité Berlin, Berlin, Germany Lehmkuhl, Ulrike Clinic of child Psychiatry, Charite Berlin, Berlin, Germany
Objective: The goal of this study is to gain an overview of the current method of care in France for ADHD affected children and adolescents as well as their families. Similar studies have been undertaken in various European countries, inviting comparisons. Method: Until now 54 Questionnaires of 47 boys and 7 girls have been evaluated. The parents were retrospectively questioned about the diagnostics and therapy of the ADHD affected child. Results: The foremost preferred therapy of ADHD is the intervention with psychostimulant medication. Treatments focusing an family, school or behavioral psychotherapy, has been used only in very few cases. An early detection of ADHD and treatments involving school and family are requested from the parents.

Psychocorrection in the context of drawings integral analysis.
Polyanychko, Olena Physical Education, IAPM, Kyiv, Ukraine
The present abstract deals with the specific character of using graphical methods within the framework of theoretical and methodical principles of active socio-psychological training (ASPT) and possibilities of integral vision of the interpretation of the complex of drawings made by one and the same author. While prof. T.S.Yatsenko analyzing drawings, guided by phenomenological approach which stipulates orientation of the understanding of a drawing by the author herself. The diagnostic-correction procedure is made up of concentration attention on systematic characteristics of the unconscious which direct the personality programs of an individual and these are expressed in the tendencies of behaviour.

Dialectical behavior therapy versus cognitive behavior therapy in the treatment of Anorexia and Bulimia Nervosa in adolescents
Salbach-Andrae, Harriet Kinder- und Jugendpsychiatrie, Charité Berlin, Berlin, Germany Bohnekamp, Inga Child and Adolescent psychiatr, Charité, Berlin, Germany Klinkowski, Nora Child and Adolescent psychiatr, Charité, Berlin, Germany Pfeiffer, Ernst Child and Adolescent psychiatr, Charité, Berlin, Germany Lehmkuhl, Ulrike Child and Adolescent psychiatr, Charité, Berlin, Germany
Objectives: Few randomized, controlled trials have examined the efficacy of treatments for eating disorders in adolescents. The aim of the ongoing study is to evaluate the effectiveness of Dialectical Behavior Therapy (DBT) and Cognitive Behavior Therapy (CBT) in adolescents suffering from eating disorders. Methods: Patients with anorexia or bulimia nervosa are randomly assigned to a CBT, DBT or a control treatment including nonspecific supportive clinical management (NCM). Results: CBT and DBT are superior to NCM, while no

significant differences between CBT and DBT were found. Conclusions: CBT and DBT can be effective therapies in the treatment of eating disorders in adolescents.

Learning implementation of exposure therapy for Posttraumatic Stress Disorder: Student perspective and implications for outcome

Meeke, Heidi *Professional Psychology, Pacific University, Portland, USA*

Exposure to caustic events is an all too common human experience, and many go on to develop posttraumatic stress disorder. Treatment markedly shortens suffering but exposure therapy is too often underutilized, leaving many patients chronically impaired. Objectives: "Live" training surmounts obstacles to effective implementation of exposure therapy. Methods: Real-time training with real patients was received. End-state functioning was assessed using clinical significance and reliable change, and treatment adherence was monitored. Results: Patients met "recovered" status and utilization of exposure therapy by student remains high. Conclusions: "Live" training does not interfere with outcome, and may be strongest form of true dissemination.

FP-252: Posttraumatic stress disorders

The scars we can't see: Reducing the onset of Post Traumatic Stress Disorder (PTSD) following traumatic event

Maffia, Anthony J. *Jamaica Hospital, New York, USA*

This presentation will contribute to the evaluation debate by exploring the conceptual and theoretical underpinnings of traumatic stress reactivity and its implications for the development and administration of interventions designed to assist recovery in populations affected by traumatic stress by briefly reviewing the evidence for the effectiveness of psychological debriefing as a means of reducing psychological morbidity following traumatic exposure. Psychological and social influences on response are identified and used to tentatively offer explanations for the differential effectiveness of critical incident stress management in reducing the onset of psychological morbidity.

Development and evaluation of a status quo measuring instrument to assess posttraumatic growth

Barskova, Tatjana *Clinical and Health Psychology, Technische Universität Berlin, Berlin, Germany* **Schubbe, Oliver** *Traumatherapie, Institut für Traumatherapie, Berlin, Germany*

Processes of Posttraumatic Growth reflect beneficial psychological adjustment in persons with traumatic experience. The objective of the study was to develop and to evaluate a status quo measuring instrument of posttraumatic growth, the PGSI. The analysed samples comprised subsamples of 229 adult persons with traumatic experience and 114 parents of disabled children. Exploratory and confirmatory factor analyses revealed a 7-factors solution, corresponding to the following subscales: Relationships to Others, New Possibilities, Personal Strength, Appreciation of Life, Spiritual Changes, Generosity, Openness. Results showed sufficient degrees of reliability, convergent and discriminant validity. The PGSI is recommended particularly for use in longitudinal studies.

The role of posttraumatic growth following terrorism from a terror management perspective

Hall, Brian *Dept. of Psychology, Kent State University, Stow, USA* **Hobfoll, Stevan** *Psychology, Kent State University, Kent, USA*

We conducted a study of terrorism in Israel via telephone surveys that included a national sample of 1,136 Jewish adults. We examined the relationship between posttraumatic growth (PTG) and posttraumatic stress disorder (PTSD) symptom severity, out-group biases against Arabs, and the support for political violence. Findings indicated that PTG was related to greater PTSD symptom severity. PTG was also related to greater threat perception of and exclusionism of Arabs, supporting the mortality salience hypothesis posited by terror management theory. This study suggests that PTG may be a form of defensive coping.

Dependency, self-criticism, social support and posttraumatic stress disorder symptoms in Peruvian university students

Gargurevich, Rafael *Lima, Peru* **Luyten, Patrick** *Psychology, University of Leuven, Leuven, Belgium* **Corveleyn, Jozef** *Psychology, University of Leuven, Leuven, Belgium*

We studied the relationship between Dependency and Self-criticism personality dimensions, social support and posttraumatic stress disorder (PTSD) symptomatology in a sample of 562 Peruvian university students. Results showed that, as expected, Self-criticism was positively associated with PTSD symptoms, and negatively associated with both received and perceived social support. Dependency was associated with intrusion and hyperarousal symptoms, but not with avoidance nor with sleep disturbance symptoms. Dependency was positively associated with perceived social support, while Self-criticism was negatively associated with social support. Results are discussed in light of the differential vulnerabilities for PTSD related symptoms associated with Dependency and Self-criticism.

Psychological reactions and social support in female burn survivors

Gul, Iram *Dept. of Behavioral Sciences, Fatima Jinnah Women University, Rawalpindi, Pakistan* **Idrees, Samreen** *Behavioral Sciences, Fatima Jinnah Women University, Rawalpindi, Pakistan*

The study identified the relationship between post burn psychological reactions and social support in female burn survivors. Sample consisted of 35 female burnt patients (age=18-40 years) with first and second-degree accidental burn injuries. Patients with pre-morbid chronic physical and psychological disorder, serious trauma exposure, intentional burn injuries were not included. Psychological distress, PTSD symptoms and Social Support were assessed with GHQ-12, PTSD Checklist- Specific and Social Support Scale respectively. The results revealed a significant negative relationship between psychological reactions and social support among female burn survivors. The study highlights the importance of psychological assessment of burn victims and role of social support in the rehabilitation programs for these survivors.

Existential trauma: Theoretical novum in psychology of health

Mamcarz, Peter *Dept. of Health Psychology, Catholic University of Lublin, Lublin, Poland* **Popielski, Kazimierz** *Health Psychology, Catholic University of Lublin, Lublin, Poland*

Scientific knowledge of the traumatic impulses consequences has its top discovery in the PTSD. Since in a case of post-trauma a person is reduced by stress to psychophysical functioning, a new attempt of overcoming the old paradigm appeared in defining the new idea on the basis of noopsychosomatic multidimensional model of existence. Moreover the new approach enabled to grasp the temporality of man more broadly, and to change the level of sensitivity to a negative impulse. The new method was arrived Existential Trauma Questionnaire (KTE): (7 factors, 5 grade scale, 139 questions + 4 quality questions) The goal is an attempt to broaden the actual knowledge concerning traumatic impulses consequences, pathological to the subject-personal being of a person.

FP-253: Personality assessment II

Construction and validation of a resiliency scale for Mexican students with low achievement

Esquivel Alcocer, Landy A. *Dept. de Educación, Universidad Autónoma Yucatán, Mérida, Mexico* **Góngora Coronado, Elías A.** *Psicología, Universidad Autónoma Yucatán, Mérida, Yucatán, Mexico*

The objective of this study was the design and validation of a Scale Resilience for Mexican students with low achievement. The participants were 428 students, 214 males and 214 females, with ages between 11 and 17 years old, belonging to a Public High School in Progreso, Yucatan. Exploratory factor analysis resulted in a 10 factors that explains the 41.684 of the total variance. The Alpha Cronbach Reliability Coefficient of the scale was .931. Besides the fact that the scale is psychometrically appropriate for its application, it was identified that the factors agree with the theoretical principles.

Measurement estimation: A coherent construct?

Hogan, Thomas *Dept. of Psychology, University of Scranton, Scranton, USA*

Measurement estimation (ME) involves the rapid, noncalculated estimation of measures (e.g., length, weight, volume, time) of common objects in the environment. Despite ME's long history in psychological assessment and pedagogical practice, our studies call into question its coherence as a construct. In contrast to two other types of quantitative estimation (computational and numerosity), ME shows relatively weak internal consistency; and ME shows no meaningful relationship with a variety of other tests which would be expected to correlate with any quantitative ability. We review this evidence and suggest possible ways to conceptualize several subskills which may possess sufficient internal consistency.

The adequacy of the Irrational Beliefs Inventory (IBI-50) to Arab culture according to psychometric properties

Mohaisen, Khalaf *Psychology, United Arab Emirates Universit, Al Ain, United Arab Emirates*

This research aimed at investigating the adequacy of the IBI (Koopman, et al., 1994) to Arab culture. The researcher was intrigued with the cross cultural findings of the IBI. Sanderman (2002) indicated similarities between American and Dutch samples. Plessis et al (2004) found the IBI is adequate to the white but not to the Black South African students. Findings of this research on 299 university students, using correlations and factor analysis, indicated that IBI is not adequate for Arab culture, since its subscales are not independent from each other and its factor structure is not similar to the original study.

Construct validity of the practical and regulation skills inventory

Rascevska, Malgozata *Dept. of Psychology, University of Latvia, Riga, Latvia*

The aim of this study was to determine the latent structure of Practical and Regulation Skills Inventory (PRSI) in a sample of 209 adults with age M=30.30, SD=13.47 (50% female and 50% male). Principal component confirmatory factor analyses was performed to test hypothetical model previous broached within the framework of qualitative study. The 9 factors were yielded from 195 items: Computer Using, Sports, Household, Foreign Language, Social, Information Interchange, Art and Hobbies, Repair Work, and Regulation Skills (Cronbach's alphas for all scales were above .89). The results support the construct validity of PRSI.

Bradberry-Greevs Emotional Intelligence Test: Norming-process on the high school students in Iran

Seirafi, Mohamad Reza Dept. of Psychology, Islamic Azad University, Karja, Islamic Republic of Iran Sabet, Mehrdad

The purpose is due inspecting the validity, reliability, and finding the norm(totally normig) of the Bradbrry-Greevse EQ test on the high school students in Iran. The sample volume was 600 students (girl&boy), who were studying in the 2006 -2007 academic year. This research performed in2Phase. The statistical analysis was performed using the computer and the software package of spss14. The research findings assured reliability and validity in the Bradberry- Greeves EQ test, then the general norm tables were prepared, which may be used in the field of clinical diagnosis in Iran. Key words: Norming, Test, Emotion Intelligence

FP-254: Perspective taking and joint attention in childhood

Family context and Theory of Mind development in 5-year-olds in the Basque autonomous community

Galende, Nuria Basic Psychological Processes, Basque Country University, San Sebastián, Spain Arranz, Enrique Bernardino Basic Psychological Processes, Basque Country University, San Sebastián, Spain Sánchez de Miguel, Manuel Basic Psychological Processes, Basque Country University, San Sebastián, Spain

The main focus of this study was to analyze the influence of the family context in Theory of Mind development (ToM) in 150 preschoolers. The data was collected through directly interviews with the children at school, interviews with their parents, systematic observation in the home and questionnaires completed by the parents and school counselors. The results showed a significant relationship between some variables within the family context and the children's performance on ToM tasks. Given that intervention can improve the family context, these results have important educational implications.

Comparison of traditional and modern games in Turkey

Dincer, Caglayan Preschool, Ankara University, Ankara, Turkey Gurkan, Tanju Curriculum and Instruction, Ankara University, Ankara, Turkey Sen, Muge Preschool, Ankara University, Ankara, Turkey

This study aims to show to what extent the traditional games are reflected in the modern ones in Turkey. The data were collected through "Traditional Game Form and Modern Game Form" developed by the researchers for this qualitative interview focused study. Traditional Game Form has been created to gather information through interviews from different regions; whereas, Modern Game Form has been filled in with the interview data on the games children play collected from parents of 0-12 year olds from the same region. 50 traditional games from a variety of regions are compared to the modern ones in Turkey.

Joint attention and intersubjectivity in the relation mother–baby

Vieira, Nadja Dept. of Psychology, Univers. Federal de Alagoas, Maceió, Brazil

The statement that "joint attention points out the baby's ability to infer mental estates" was the main problem of this research. Our objective was to analyze the reorganization of activities in the communication mediated by objects, between mother and baby. The analysis was carried out utilizing fifty videos of interaction mother-baby (babies between five and thirty weeks old), in weekly sessions. The baby's comprehension about

the mother's meaningful acts was captured through hierarchical changing in the history of each relation mother-baby. We have concluded that these changing exemplify the way that mental estates introduce itself in the development of the communication, with the support of the joint attention.

The effect of creative drama education on receptive and expressive language developments of 5-6 years old children

Gönen, Mübeccel Preschool Education, Hacettepe University, Ankara, Turkey

This research has been made to analyse the effects of creative drama on receptive and expressive language development of 5-6 years old children groups. 34 children from one kindergarten formed the test group, 34 children from the other kindergarten formed the control group. Language developments were tested as pre-test and post-test by Peabody picture vocabulary test and Denver screening test and then evaluated the effects on creative drama. At the and of statistical analysis, it was found that creative drama education on 5-6 years age group has positive effects on children's receptive and expressive language developments. Key words: language development, creative drama, receptive, expressive.

Comparing children's behavioral and verbal performances: Gender differences in level 1 perspective taking

Zhao, Jing Department of Psychology, Peking University, Beijing, People's Republic of China Wang, Lu Dept. of Psychology, Peking University, Beijing, People's Republic of China Su, Yanjie Department of Psychology, Peking University, Beijing, People's Republic of China

The study aimed to investigate sixty 3-to-5-year-old children's level 1 perspective-taking, and to make a comparison between their behavioral and verbal performances. A hiding game with a one-way mirror and elaborated coding principles was designed. Three-way ANOVA indicated significant interaction among tasks, age and gender $(F(2,48)=3.55, p=0.037, \eta2=0.13)$: girl's behavioral and verbal performances increased from 3 to 5 years old, in the same pattern; boy's behavioral data was similar to girls', while their verbatim improved little across ages. These findings indicated that behavioral task had its advantages to detect more subtle differences about children's level 1 perspective-taking.

Effects of social cues on long-term memory in infancy: An event-related potentials study

Kopp, Franziska Center for Lifespan Psychology, Max-Planck-Institut, Berlin, Germany

This study tested whether the facilitating effect of social cues in infants' object processing could be observed for long-term memory processes as well. 4-month-old and 9-month-old infants were familiarized with visual stimuli while they were engaged in joint attention interactions with the experimenter vs. in a non-joint attention condition. EEG was recorded in two recognition phases (immediately vs. after one week) where familiar items were presented with novel items. Event-related brain potentials (ERP) showed a novelty effect in both recognition phases. Furthermore, 9-month-olds' ERP responses differed between the joint attention and the non-joint attention condition. Results indicate the importance of social interactions for infant learning and long-term memory.

FP-255: Social issues: Children and youth II

Children's drawings reveal the "mondus operandi "of family violence

Simopoulou, Agapi Nursery, University of Ioannina, Rethymno, Greece Zervoudaki, Eleni

This paper is part of a diachronic research which started the year 2005. Studied 270 cases of abused children, in ages 6 to 12, in the island of Crete. The aim was to explore the ways of violence in the families. Information's were taken from interviews with parents, friends, teachers and relatives. The main tool was children's drawings. "Family test", was used to analyze drawings. Results are related with the seven main dimensions of family interaction: Emotional atmosphere, communication, boundaries, alliances, constancy and adaptation, family self efficiency. Also the Study showed that violence in these families has a strong relationship with cruelty experiences of parents. Key words: child abuse, Family focal evaluation, childish drawing

Age differences and development of prejudice among children and adolescents: A meta-analysis

Raabe, Tobias Research Synthesis & Intervent, University of Jena, Jena, Germany Beelmann, Andreas Research Synthesis & Inter, University of Jena, Jena, Germany

This meta-analysis integrates results of studies (N=129) on age differences in prejudice among children and adolescents. Separate data analyses were accomplished concerning the type of prejudice and the method of measurement (ingroup-bias vs. out-group negativity). Several factors (e.g., legitimacy of hostility) were tested as moderators of age-related differences explaining effect size variance. The meta-analysis reveals specific developmental changes regarding prejudice toward different outgroups. Moreover, the results suggest differences between the development of in-group bias and outgroup negativity. In general a need for longitudinal studies and a lack of research on prejudice in adolescents (compared to children) was identified.

The relationship between family communication pattern and child goal orientation

Zare, Maryam Dept. Educational Psychology, Shiraz University, Shiraz, Islamic Republic of Iran Samani, Syamack Educational psychology, Shiraz University, shiraz, Islamic Republic of Iran

The aim of study was examining the prediction of goal orientation by family communication patterns. The sample group included 435 girls and boys students selected randomly from high schools of Shiraz. Goal orientation (Elliot, MacGregor, 2001) scale, and revised version of Koerner-Fitzpatrick Family Communication Patterns scale were used. Cronbach alpha coefficient and internal consistency showed acceptable reliability and validity of the instruments. Results of multiple regression revealed that conversation orientation was a positive predictor of Mastery approach and Performance approach and conformity orientation was a positive predictor of mastery avoidance, performance avoidance and performance approach.

The relationship between parental disciplinary practices and discipline, internalization, social competence and cognitive development problems of children

Gülterler, Derya Bengi Semerci Enstitusu, Istanbul, Turkey Öktem, Ferhunde Cocuk Ruh Sagligi, Hacettepe Universitesi, Ankara, Turkey

In this study, disciplinary practices of Turkish parents and the relationship among these practices and some of personality features of children is examined. The data were collected from 606 Turkish families of 10-11 years old children via 2 questionnaires and Personality Inventory for Children. The results revealed that verbal methods were the most frequently used disciplinary techniques by both mothers and fathers in order to increase the positive and decrease the negative behaviors of children. Especially aggression used by fathers, removal of the reinforcers, neglecting both positive and negative behaviors were related with the problematic personality features of the children.

Motivation, hope, and optimism: Psychological resilience among undocumented immigrant youth in the United States

Perez, William Los Angeles, CA, USA Ramos, Karina Education, Claremont Graduate University, Los Angeles, CA, USA Coronado, Heidi Education, Claremont Graduate University, Claremont, CA, USA Cortes, Richard Education, Claremont Graduate University, Claremont, CA, USA

For many Latino youth, being an immigrant in the United States is not easy—particularly when they lack legal status. The purpose of this study is to explore the factors that influence academic success for undocumented immigrant students. One hundred and seventy two students participated in the study using snowball sampling methodology. Participants completed an online survey and an in-depth one hour interview followed. Understanding risk and resiliency among undocumented Latino immigrant adolescents will help educators, mental health professionals, and policy makers improve the quality of life of current and future generations of families.

FP-256: Personality and well-being I

Attachment style as a predictor to depressive symptoms following in hassles in University students in China

Zhu, Xiongzhao Medical Psychological Research, Second Xiangya Hospital, Changsha, People's Republic of China Abela, John R. Z. McGill University,, Department of Psychology,, Montreal (QC), Canada Tong, Xi McGill University,, Department of Psychology,, Montreal (QC), Canada Yao, Shuqiao Medical Psychological Research, The Second Xiangya Hospital, Changsha, People's Republic of China

Few studies have examined if attachment style would be associated with greater elevations in depressive symptoms following elevation. This study try to examine whether attachment style predict the development of depressive symptoms following increases in hassles in university students. At time1, 635 students (age 16-23 years) from Hunan, China, completed measures assessing depressive symptoms, hassles, attachment styles. Once a month for the next 6 months, participants completed measures assessing depressive symptoms and hassles. Results of hierarchical linear modeling analyses indicated that insecure attachment styles are associated with depressive symptoms, and low secure attachment styles were associated with elevations in depressive symptoms following elevation in hassles. There was a significant interaction between hassles and low secure attachment style.

The development of long-term orientation scale

Zhang, Qi Dept. of Psychology, Peking University, Beijing, People's Republic of China Liu, Xiaoyan Psychology, Peking University, Beijing, People's Republic of China Yang, Qian Psychology, Peking University, Beijing, People's Republic of China Wang, Lei Psychology, Peking University, Beijing, People's Republic of China Lin, Han Psychology, Peking University, Beijing, People's Republic of China Zhang, Xingwei Psychology, Peking University, Beijing, People's Republic of China Xiao, Shanshan Psychology, Peking University, Beijing, People's Republic of China

Long-Term Orientation (LTO) is a tendency towards future planning, influencing many life domains. By means of in-depth interview, brainstorming, and large sample testing, the current research developed a new LTO questionnaire, from a two-dimension perspective rather than from Hofstede and Bond's perspective of thrift and money saving. Significant positive correlations between LTO and criteria such as Initiativitiy, Self-Efficacy, Hope, and Resilience were observed, indicating the good criterion-related validity of the scale. The theoretical constructs of LTO would be further investigated and confirmed in the incoming research and the relationships of LTO with both life and organizational outcomes are discussed.

Coherent approach to the individual differences in subjective well-being: An investigation based on interactionistic research paradigm

Horike, Kazuya Humanities and Social Sciences, Iwate Univesity, Iwate, Japan Matsuoka, Kazuo Humanities and Social Sciences, Iwate Univesity, Morioka, Iwate, Japan Oda, Nobuo Humanities and Social Sciences, Iwate Univesity, Morioka, Iwate, Japan

We investigated the 'coherent' patterns of individual differences (Mishcel & Shoda, 1995) in subjective well-being (SWB) by analyzing the relationships among psychological, social, and emotional well-being (Horike, et al., 2006, AASP). In the present study, we asked 106 participants to rate their SWB on the interaction with the six role persons under the twelve situations. To find the coherent patterns of these ratings, cluster analysis was conducted. Three clusters were elicited. Then, we analyzed the relationships of some cognitive-affective variables (self esteem, optimism, BIS/BAS, and regulatory focus) in each cluster by SEM modeling. The results showed the relationships among these variables differed from these clusters.

Methodological problems if human potential phylogenesis research

Podshyvalkina, Valentyna General and social psychology, Odessa Mechnikov University, Odessa, Ukraine

In this paper the human potential phylogenesis is discussed. The author analyzes the intergeneration differences of attention characteristics in two ways: (1) between three age adults groups and (2) between generations of employees of the beginning of 80s and of the present days. It was shown that the highest indexes of some attention parameters (stability, distribution and concentration) have 30-39 years old employees in both generations. It was found the significant growth of modern aging people's attention indexes. The key goal is to show how the selection practice monitoring can stimulate new research of human potential phylogenesis.

The effect of gender and spirituality differences on SOC among united methodists

Alexandre, Renata Health and Human Performance, MTSU, Murfreesboro, TN, USA Zengaro, Franco Health and Human Performance, MTSU, Murfreesboro, TN, USA

Objectives: Using a salutogenesis framework, this study examined the relationship of gender, spirituality, and SOC to overall health. Methods: Participants were 200 United Methodists. Data were collected through questionnaires. One-way ANOVA and regression analyses were conducted to identify differences in gender, spirituality and SOC. Results: Previous studies have found conflicting results. We hypothesize that males will have a higher SOC. We also hypothesize that a high SOC will correlate with a high level of spirituality. Conclusion: SOC, gender, and spirituality are important in determining effective health care, empowering women, and assisting them in finding value in life's activities.

Sense of coherence, dysfunctional beliefs, automatic thoughts and self-esteem in predicting life satisfaction among Turkish university students

Cecen, Ayse Rezan Psyhological Counselling, Cukurova University, Adana, Turkey

The purpose of this study to determine how university students' life satisfaction are predicted by their level of sense of coherence (SOC), dsysfunctional beliefs, automatic thoughts and self esteem. The study was conducted on 385 university students. To analyse data pearson product moment correlations and regression analyses techniques were used. The findings of this study supported Antonovsky's theoritical frame. The results indicated that there are significant positive strong correlations between life satisfaction SOC, self esteem and, negative correlations between SOC and negative dysfunctional beliefs and negative automatic thoughts. The results of the study has also shown that all independent variables contributed statistically significant (p<.05) in predicting life satisfaction.

FP-257: Memory illusion

The effect of perceptual similarity on false recognition

Hutton, Samuel Psychology, University of Sussex, Brighton, United Kingdom Otero, Samantha Psychology, University of Sussex, Brighton, United Kingdom Weekes, Brendan Psychology, University of Sussex, Brighton, United Kingdom

Participants show increased rates of false recognition to distractors that are semantically related to studied targets, but it is not clear whether this relationship holds for pictorial stimuli. We compared the effects of semantic and perceptual similarity on false recognition and found increased false recognition rates for pictures that were perceptually similar to the learned items. This effect was not observed with written words. A further experiment demonstrated a novel pupillary response to old items during recognition, and an attenuated response to falsely recognized distractors. We conclude that perceptual similarity is important in generating false recognition of pictorial stimuli.

Explaining false recognition in the Deese-Roediger-McDermott paradigma: Spreading, implicit, or global activation?

Brandt, Martin Lehrstuhl Psychologie III, Universität Mannheim, Mannheim, Germany Buchner, Axel Allgemeine Psychologie, Universität Düsseldorf, Düsseldorf, Germany Schmid, Juliane Allgemeine Psychologie, Universität Düsseldorf, Düsseldorf, Germany Undorf, Monika Lehrstuhl Psychologie III, Universität Düsseldorf, Mannheim, Germany

After studying semantically related words, a pronounced false memory effect for related but not studied words is usually observed. Although this effect is under active study, a commonly accepted theoretical explanation is still missing. According to spreading activation theories and implicit activation theories, the representations of critical lures are activated in the study phase, whereas in global activation accounts, critical lures elicit activation during retrieval. In a series of four experiments we test specific predictions of these theoretical accounts. We show that false recognition and false recall are dissociable and that false memories do not depend on pre-existing knowledge structures. Overall, the results favor the global activation account.

Creating false recall and recognition of evolutionary reproduction-related non-presented lure words

Abdollahi, Abdolhossein Psychology, Islamic Azad University-Zarand, Kerman, Islamic Republic of Iran

Two experiments investigated the possibility that high-testosterone adult males would falsely recall and recognize evolutionary reproduction-related lure words in a Deese-Roediger-McDermott list-learning paradigm. in Exp 1, 240 male participants with low and high levels of testosterone received 10 lists of semantically-associated evolutionary reproduction-related words all of which had a non-presented lure word. In Exp 2, another 250 participants with low and high levels of testosterone and under low and high arousal conditions received the same material as in Exp 1. Results indicated that in both experiments, high-testosterone participants falsely recalled and recognized higher levels of non-presented lure words.

Influences of warning and time pressure on false recognition & further evidence for dual-processing theory

Zhou, Chu Department of Psychology, Fudan University, Shanghai, People's Republic of China *Jiang, Yuncheng* Department of Psychology, Fudan University, Shanghai, People's Republic of China *Yang, Zhiliang* Department of Psychology, East China Normal University, Shanghai, People's Republic of China

Adopting Deese-Roediger-McDermott paradigm, the mechanism of false recognition was investigated in a 2 (forewarning) $\times 2$ (presentation time) $\times 2$ (time pressure during recognition) $\times 3$ (types of items) factorial design. ANOVA showed a significant main effect of forewarning, and interaction between item type and time pressure. Using signal detection theory (SDT), further analysis showed that participants had poorer discrimination under time pressure, which indicated that they have no enough time to make judgments. The SDT analysis also showed that participants used more strict response criterion when giving them forewarning. The results are deeply discussed under activation/monitoring theory.

Age differences in the suppression of false memories

Carneiro, Paula Psicologia, Universidade Lusofona, Lisbon, Portugal

The DRM paradigm is one of the most powerful procedures to generate false memories by associative processes. It implies the presentation of lists of associates with the omission of their converging words, thus creating the illusion that those converging words were actually presented. The present study was concerned with the different processes used by adults and children to suppress false memories. The results of a set of experiments using this paradigm showed that although in general adults produced more false memories than children, they are also more able to use monitoring strategies to suppress them.

Observation inflation: Your actions become mine

Lindner, Isabel FG Psychology, AE Methodenl., Universität zu Köln, Köln, Germany *Echterhoff, Gerald* Sozialpsychologie, Universität Bielefeld, Bielefeld, Germany *Brand, Matthias* Physiologische Psychologie, Universität Bielefeld, Bielefeld, Germany *Hussy, Walter* FG Psychologie, AE Methodenl., Universität zu Köln, Köln, Germany

When people repeatedly imagine action performance, they often falsely remember having performed those actions - the imagination-inflation effect (IIE). Based on research showing that the observation of actions can create matching ("mirrored") representations in observers we examined whether a similar effect can be caused by observing someone else's actions. In an IIE-type experiment

(N=60), we found that increasing frequencies of either imagining or observing actions led to increasing false memories of self-performance, and this effect was stronger than in two control conditions. This first demonstration of "observation inflation" is discussed with reference to recent theories of simulation and mirror mechanisms.

FP-258: Medical help seeking

Gender differences in subjective help seeking threshold and health care utilization: Is there an interrelation between both features?

Glaesmer, Heide Inst. für Medizin. Psychologie, Universität Leipzig, Leipzig, Germany *Brähler, Elmar* Medical Psychology, University of Leipzig, Leipzig, Germany *Martin, Alexandra* Clinical Psychology, University of Marburg, Marburg, Germany *Mewes, Ricarda* Clinical Psychology, University of Marburg, Marburg, Germany *Rief, Winfried* Clinical Psychology, University of Marburg, Marburg, Germany

Objectives: Women show an increased health care utilization (HCU) compared to men. We are analyzing the interaction of gender differences in HCU and subjective help seeking threshold (SHST). Methods: A German representative sample of 2511 subjects was face-to-face interviewed using a structured questionnaire. Results: Women show a significantly higher HCU within the last year (number of total/ specialist visits etc.), have a lower SHST and different patterns of complaints triggering help seeking behaviour: Both features are significantly influencing HCU. Conclusions: The meaning of both characteristics will be discussed as a possible reason of the increased HCU in women.

Overlapping relationships of rural and urban providers with their patients

Johnson, Mark Behav Health Research & Svcs, University of Alaska Anchorage, Anchorage, Alaska, USA *Brems, Christiane* Behav Health Research & Sv, University of Alaska Anchorage, Anchorage, Alaska, USA *Mills, Michael E.* Psychology, Loyola Marymount University, Los Angeles, California, USA *Warner, Teddy D.* School of Medicine, University of New Mexico, Albuquerque, New Mexico, USA *Roberts, Laura W.* Psychiatry & Behavior Medi, Medical College of Wisconsin, Milwaukee, Wisconsin, USA

Objectives: Our federally funded study is the first large-scale survey assessing degree to which multiple relationships arise for rural versus urban healthcare providers. Method: We conducted a survey with care providers in Alaska and New Mexico, analyzing responses from 1555 participants. Results: The smaller the community, the more often providers report significant challenges related to overlapping relationships, such as personal, social, and professional contacts with patients. Physical care providers engaged in multiple relationships more often than behavioral care providers. Conclusions: Avoiding multiple relationships in small communities is difficult and occurs at the expense of providers' ability to avoid social isolation.

Patient-doctor-interaction in rehabilitation: The impact of interaction quality on treatment results

Dibbelt, Susanne DRV Westfalen, Klinik Münsterland, Bad Rothenfelde, Germany *Schaidhammer, Monika* DRV Westfalen, Klinik Muensterland, Bad Rothenfelde, Germany *Greitemann, Bernhard* DRV Westfalen, Klinik Muensterland, Bad Rothenfelde, Germany *Fleischer, Christian* DRV Westfalen, Klinik Muensterland, Bad Rothenfelde, Germany

Communication between doctor and patient has a key function in medical care. A new theory-based instrument (P.A.INT-Questionnaire) is presented by which 470 patients and 60 physicians rated the quality of their shared interaction due to affective, instrumental and participation level of interaction (Dibbelt, 2007). There is evidence that the quality of

interaction has influence on outcome parameters like pain, function, control and depressive symptoms.

Knowledge and attitude toward mental health problems as predictor of seeking professional psychological help

Yaghubi, Hamid Dept. of Clinical Psychology, Shahed University, Tehran, Islamic Republic of Iran *Melyani, Mahdiyeh* Dept. of Clinical Psychology, Shahed University, Tehran, Islamic Republic of Iran

Objectives: The purpose of this study was to investigate Iranian college students' attitudes toward seeking professional psychological help. Methods: The sampel (N= 150) are divided to 3 groups:Normal Group = NG, Help Seeking Group= HSG and Non Help Seeking Group= NHSG and evaluated by the GHQ-28 and a researchers-made questionnaire as the Knowledge and Attitude Toward Mental Health Problem and Services Scale (KATMHPSS). Results: 1) NHSG significantly has more mental health problems than HSG. 2) NHSG has less knowledge and more negative attitude than two other groups. 3) HSG has more knowledge and positive attitude than NG. 4) The female students have more favourable attitudes than males.

The role of psychology in community heart failure services: Action research and to influence practice among health professionals

McManus, Jim Dept. of Public Health, Barking & Dagenham NHS PCT, Barking, United Kingdom

An action research programme implemented across East London sought to improve the use of psychological insights in clinical care for people with heart failure. This presentation will report on a multi-professional and multi-phase project to deliver organisational change and increased skills in health professionals, with the aim of preventing death and increasing quality of life in people with heart failure

The role of embarrassment in seeking medical help

Fernandez de Ortega, Hilda Psychology, UAEH, Mexico City, Mexico *Harris, Christine* Psychology, UCSD, La Jolla, USA *Reidl, Lucy* Psychology, UNAM, Mexico City, Mexico *Guzman Saldana, Rebeca* Psychology, UAEH, Tilcuautla, Mexico

Given the importance of embarrassment in seeking medical help, and due to the lack of data about the nature of embarrassment in Hispanics/Latin populations, the specific goal this study was to examine the psychological impact that embarrassment in physician-patient has on a Latin sample. 1057 persons, females and males, completed the embarrassment questionnaire. Participant's answers were analyzed using a factor analysis with varimax rotation. Three factors with appropriate psychometric measures were revealed. First factor related with bodily embarrassment. The second factor accessing comfort with medical examinations, and the third factor indexing concern about negative social. Gender differences were found.

FP-259: Group development

The potential influences of new members on their group life-course and performance

Chang, Kirk Dept. of Applied Psychology, University of Cumbria, Carlisle, Cumbria, United Kingdom

Based on Social Dilemma and Group Socialization theories, this project investigated the influences of new members on group lifecourse and performance. Data were collected via virtual-reality experiments. Experiment One revealed that new members impeded group dynamic by reducing mutual trust and cooperation between members, leading to poorer group performance. Experiment Two discovered that members with higher group-commitment were more likely to be accepted by the group, which encouraged other members to generate contributions to the group. Compared to the implementation of sanction policy (either reward or punishment), higher group-commitment was a better factor to predict group performance. Findings contributed to the theoretical framework of managerial theories.

How important is the time in teamwork: Longitudinal analysis of team members' interdependence and group potency on effectiveness

Mena, Banesa Dept. of Social Psychology, Complutense University, Madrid, Spain Barrasa, Angel SOCIAL PSYCHOLOGY, COMPLUTENSE UNIVERSITY, POZUELO DE ALARCON (MADRID), Spain Gil, Francisco SOCIAL PSYCHOLOGY, COMPLUTENSE UNIVERSITY, POZUELO DE ALARCON (MADRID), Spain

This paper analyzes the influence of time process in cooperative learning situations. A model on the time influence in the development of teamwork is hypothesized using a longitudinal design with 22 university work groups. Results show the different development of team members' interdependence and group potency throughout six months of work and the influence on team effectiveness (performance and satisfaction). Conclusions analyze differences between work groups at three different points of time (beginning, middle, and ending) and teamwork variables' effects during the process of collaborative work

When is it ok to watch over your own? Power, surveillance and social identity.

O'Donnell, Aisling School of Psychology, University of Exeter, Exeter, United Kingdom Jetten, Jolanda School of Psychology, University of Queensland, Brisbane, Australia Ryan, Michelle School of Psychology, University of Exeter, Exeter, United Kingdom

Previous research shows identification affects social influence. We propose that identification affects acceptance of surveillance. In two studies we demonstrate the positive relationship between identification and surveillance acceptance. Shared identity with the powerful led to perceptions of surveillance as ensuring safety, and reduced privacy-invasion, than when identity was non-shared. Paradoxically, when identity between the powerful and others is shared, imposing high surveillance backfires. In two studies, we found leaders using high surveillance while sharing identity with their followers were evaluated less positively and provoked fewer organisational citizenship behaviours and greater privacy infringement than when they used lower surveillance. These studies demonstrate that surveillance may undermine the perception that identity is shared.

Leadership in hospitals' teamwork: Task, relation and change-oriented leadership for different work-groups' areas

Barrasa, Angel Dept. of Social Psychology, Autonoma Univer. of Barcelona, Barcelona, Spain Gil, Francisco Dept. of Social Psychology, Complutense Univer. of Madrid, Madrid, Spain Rodriguez-Medina, Sandra Dept. of Social Psychology, Autonoma Univer. of Barcelona, Barcelona, Spain

In health care, teams have been seen usually as one way to redesign work and to provide better levels of quality in services. Leadership in these teams plays a key role on satisfaction and performance health care work groups' outcome. Sample comprises 406 participants, who are members of 89 healthcare teams at different public hospitals throughout Spain. Results provide parsimonious and meaningful conceptual framework of metacategories with greater explanatory power (task, relation, and change-oriented leadership). Using metacate-

gories will improve the prediction of leadership effectiveness or the explanation of why some leaders are more effective than others in a given situation.

Work values and team's satisfaction and commitment

Porto, Juliana Dept. of Psychology, Catholic University of Brasil, Aguas Claras, Brazil

This study aimed to investigate the impact of personal and perception of team's work values on team's satisfaction and commitment. 105 individuals responded a questionnaire. The intraclass correlation was not significant and analysis was done at the individual level. The results indicated Stability (r=0.266; r=0.318), Interpersonal relations (r=0.322; r=0.375) and Professional Fulfillment (r=0.280; r=0.444) values as positively correlated with team satisfaction and commitment. The perception of these values as the team's values also correlated positively, and perception of Prestige was negatively correlated. The multiple regression analysis yield similar results and models explained 47% and 49% for satisfaction and commitment, respectively.

Culturally diverse work groups as tightly-loosely coupled systems: The role of task and interpersonal social orientations in group performance

Bachmann, Anne Inst. für Psychologie, Universität zu Kiel, Kiel, Germany Simon, Bernd Insitut für Psychologie, CAU zu Kiel, Kiel, Germany

Drawing on the concept of tightly-loosely coupled systems (a concept specifying the quality of interactions among system elements), social identity theory and diversity research we examined the effects on collective task performance of different combinations of task and interpersonal orientations (i.e. coupling) of the interacting group members. Our prediction was that groups composed of members with differing cultural values are most effective when a strong task orientation (tight coupling) is combined with a weak interpersonal orientation (loose coupling). Empirical analyses support our prediction. The utility of the TLCS-concept for social psychological research on diversity and group processes is discussed.

FP-260: Multilingualism II

The resolution of anaphors across languages: Results from monolingual and bilingual speakers

Hemforth, Barbara LPNCog, Université René Descartes/CNRS, Boulogne-Billancourt, France Scheepers, Christoph Department of Psychology, University of Glasgow, Glasgow, United Kingdom Pynte, Joël CNRS/Université René Descartes, LPNCog, Boulogne Billancourt, France Konieczny, Lars Kognitionswissenschaft, Universitaet Freiburg, Freiburg, Germany

Sentences that are superficially highly similar across languages are not necessarily processed the same way. We will present a series of eyetracking experiments applying the visual world paradigm (auditory presentation of the linguistic material plus visual presentation of pictures), showing that anaphor resolution in sentences like "The postman met the street sweeper before he went home." is highly dependent on the language of the listener, in particular on the frequency of the possible interpretations in the language. We will moreover demonstrate considerable L1 to L2 interference effects for late but highly fluent bilingual French-German speakers.

Visual word recognition by trilinguals: Effects of orthographical, phonological and semantic overlaps in language decision tasks

Lavaur, Jean-Marc Dept. of Psychology, Université Montpellier 3, Montpellier, France Aparicio, Xavier Psychology, Université Montpellier 3, Montpellier, France Vandeberg, Lisa Dijkstra, Ton

This research study the role of orthographical, phonological and semantic features of French, English and Spanish translation equivalents during lexical access. We use translation equivalents ranked according to their overlap between languages. Several studies have shown that the representation of cognates in the mental lexicon is different of specific words. 24 trilinguals performed 3 language decision tasks, were french, English and Spanish were compared two by two. Results show that when the degree of overlap is strong between the languages, the response time is lower and there is more errors, according to a non-specific access to the mental lexicon.

Evidence for inhibitory processes in language switching?

Philipp, Andrea M. Inst. Verhaltenspsychologie, RWTH Aachen, Aachen, Germany

In many situations, people have to flexibly switch between languages. We examined whether such language switching goes along with the inhibition of currently irrelevant languages. To do so, we used a cued language-switching paradigm, in which subjects had to name digits or pictures in one of three languages (i.e., German, English, or French). We observed n-2 language repetition costs, indicating the persistence of inhibitory processes. Furthermore, we demonstrated that these inhibitory processes do not affect a specific stimulus or response set only. Rather, we conclude that the language-switching paradigm indeed provides evidence for the inhibition of a competing, irrelevant language.

Effects of semantic ambiguity in bilingual processing: Number, dominance and semantic similarity of translation equivalents

Lavaur, Jean-Marc Dept. of Psychology, Université Montpellier 3, Montpellier, France Laxén, Jannika Montpellier, France

In order to investigate the bilingual semantic memory, we tested words with one or several meanings, one or more than one translation (dominant or not) in two translation recognition experiments. Both number of meanings (which determine, in part, the semantic similarity between its multiple translations) and number of translations (and the relative dominance of the translations) increase the complexity of the representations of the words in the bilingual semantic network, and affect the speed of processing of the words. The interactions are discussed in respect of new tools in the study of the bilingual mental lexicon.

Languages on the screen: Effects of fluency and interlingual subtitles on film comprehension

Lavaur, Jean-Marc Dept. of Psychology, Université Montpellier 3, Montpellier, France Bairstow, Dominique Dept. of Psychology, Université Montpellier 3, Montpellier, France

The aim of this study is to analyse the role of interlingual subtitles on film comprehension. In two experimental conditions (with and without subtitles), the same sequence of a film was seen by bilinguals and monolinguals. Different aspects of comprehension were estimated (images, dialogues and understanding of the situation). The results show facilitatory effects of subtitling (in the native language) for the monolinguals and inhibitory effects for bilinguals. These effects can be extended to different aspects of the sequence. The interpretation of the results is given in the light of text and movie frameworks of comprehension and bilingual information processing

FP-261: Learning strategies II

Learning strategies in the English as a second language (ESL) classroom

Costa-Ferreira, Paula Alexandra Nunes da Carvoeira, Portugal Veiga Simão, Ana Margarida Faculdade de Psicologia e C.E., Universidade de Lisboa, Lisboa, Portugal

The aim of this study is to examine and validate the efficiency of methodology that promotes self-regulation strategies in contextualized settings in the ESL classroom. To accomplish this goal, a case study was done on nineteen elementary school students who participated in behavioral, motivational and cognitive learning tasks in order to accomplish academic goals, such as self-regulatory competency and linguistic skill development. From the qualitative analysis obtained, results suggest that students improved their organizational and self-evaluation competencies as well as their linguistic performance. These findings serve to establish the importance of contextualized self-regulated learning settings in the ESL classroom.

What effects do the integrated format and use of Chinese notes have on learning to read English comprehension as second language?

Chung, Kevin K.H. EPCL, Hong Kong Inst. of Education, Hong Kong, China, People's Republic of : Hong Kong SAR

This study investigated the effects of integrated format and the use of Chinese explanation notes on reading comprehension. One hundred of grade 7 Hong Kong students studied an integrated or a separate format with and without Chinese notes to improve performance in reading. The results showed that the integrated format improved reading comprehension. Learning was improved under the formats in which the English vocabulary was presented with the Chinese notes than it was under those with no notes. It was concluded that the integrated format and Chinese notes could be used in a way to facilitate learning to read comprehension.

An experimental study on reciprocal teaching of seven-grade students' reading comprehension

Yao, Jingjing Psychology, Zhejiang Normal University, Jinhua, People's Republic of China

A mixed-design of three factoral experiment was adopted to assess the effects of reciprocal teaching on reading comprehension, comprehension monitoring and reading attitude of junior middle school students. Results:(1) There were significant differences in questioning, summarizing, reading comprehension monitoring and reading attitude between experimental groups and routine group in both expository and narrative passages. (2) There were significant differences in reading comprehension of expository passages between experimental groups and routine group, but no differences in reading comprehension of narrative passages between experimental groups and routine group except the group with reflection strategy.

Adults' visualization strategies as a tool for text comprehension

Koch, Babette Department of Education, Saarland University, Saarbrücken, Germany Seufert, Tina Department of Education, Saarland University, Saarbrücken, Germany Zander, Steffi Department of Psychology, University of Göttingen, Göttingen, Germany Brünken, Roland Department of Education, Saarland University, Saarbrücken, Germany

Text comprehension can be improved by working out global structures e.g. by constructing a picture. In two experiments we analyzed adults spontaneous picture construction for text comprehension: lear-

ners had to make notes about texts either in any (neutral) or in pictorial (picture) form, and - based on these notes - to answer recall and comprehension questions afterwards. In both studies the picture group constructed significantly more pictures and revealed better learning outcomes. The second study additionally revealed a compensating effect of learners' spatial abilities. Thus, adults need instruction or enhanced abilities to use visualizations strategically for text comprehension.

Making meaningful memory structure comparisons using bootstrap analysis of pathfinder networks

Jennings, Kyle Dept. of Psychology, University of California, Berkeley, USA

Understanding people's memory structures can unlock doors for cognitive, social, and educational psychologists. Pathfinder network scaling is a technique that extracts a network of links between concepts from proximity data, providing a close match to models of semantic memory. Unfortunately, Pathfinder networks lack confidence intervals or obvious points of comparison, making them unsuited to contrasting multiple populations. This research solves these problems by using nonparametric bootstrap analysis. It also presents simulation results that examine how literally the exact structures of the networks can be interpreted and compared. This work reintroduces a valuable tool into the psychologist's toolbox.

Poster Session Wednesday Morning 09:00

The role of family, relatives, and peers in Turkish late adolescents' religious socializations

Özdikmenli Demir, Gözde Psychology Department, Hacettepe University, Ankara, Turkey

As an initial phase of a qualitative research, religious socializations of Turkish University students were investigated. Fifty-one Muslim, middle-class, undergraduate women were asked to write down their childhood and adolescence experiences about their religious socializations with their mothers, fathers, relatives, and peers. For each of the agents, socialization types (e.g.,modelling, instructions, narratives) were grouped and analized. It was found that mothers had a more significant role in their daughters' religious socializations compared to other agents. Among relatives grandparents had the most important role. Expanded sample will be used (50 men) in continious part of this research and gender differences on religious socializations will be discussed.

The concept of self in female psychiatric patients and it's implications for mental health

Abdul Wahab Khan, Rahmattullah Khan Psychology, Int Islamic Univ Malaysia, Kuala Lumpur, Malaysia Khan, Umeed Ali Psychiatry, Int Islamic Univ Malaysia, Kuantan, Malaysia Mat Zin, Nora Psychiatry, Int Islamic Univ Malaysia, Kuantan, Malaysia Ismail, Mohamed Psychiatry, Int Islamic Univ Malaysia, Kuantan, Malaysia

The concept of self has always been an important theme in human sciences. We studied seven female psychiatric patients in whom the theme of self was significantly disturbed in their beliefs: that her physique being rudimentary at birth and subsequently completed with contributions from several male friends; chronological age beginning from the onset of puberty; the very survival of patient absolutely dependent on the male friend and complete forgiveness of her husband's infidelity for the sake of her own survival; and the clinging behavior to severely physically abusive boyfriends; and the delusion of being married to a hundred men and mothering several hundred children.

The effect of leader member exchange (LMX) on organizational climate development

Adibrad, Nastaran Dept. of Counseling Psychology, Shahid Beheshti University, Tehran, Islamic Republic of Iran

In this research 60 employees who where selected randomly of University responded to Organizational Diagnosis Questionnair which assesses seven dimentions of organizational climate(Purpose _ Structure _ Leadership_-Rewards- Helpful _Attitude toward change) as a pre_test. After 8 months all samples responded to ODQ as post _test. The management procedure between that time was Leader Member Exchange which refer to the managing style that every member was looked as an individual The result of this research showed the kind of relationship between leader & memberships could change the Purpose _ Structure _ Leadership-Helpful _Attitude toward change of organizational climate.

Consciousness: What do underwater part of iceberg hides?

Agafonov, Andrey Faculty of Psychology, Samara State University, Samara, Russia

Consciousness is not equal to conscious awareness. Conscious phenomena should include unconscious content of consciousness and its' mechanisms. Microgenesis of conscious awareness can be described as four consecutive steps: 1. Detection of all the incoming information. 2. Comparison of information. 3. Making decision about conscious awareness (or unawareness). 4. Execution of the decision made. At this stage the reflective mechanism joins. Function of the reflective mechanism is to include the information chosen for conscious awareness into content of consciousness that is actually aware. Execution of the decision generates effect of conscious awareness.

Religiosity and marital adjustment

Ahmadi, Khodabakhsh Behavioral Sciences Research, Baqiyatallah Medical Sciences, Tehran, Islamic Republic of Iran Nabipoor Ashrafi, S. Mahdi Behavioral Sciences Research C, Baqiyatallah Medical Sciences, Tehran, Islamic Republic of Iran

This research intends to investigate the role of religiosity in marital adjustment..660 couples from Tehran were studied. Information regarding religiosity and marital adjustment was collected using the researcher's prepared questionnaire, and ENRICH marital satisfaction scale. The results showed that couples who observe religious beliefs have higher rate of marital adjustment. Thus, there is a significant correlation between religiosity and marital adjustment. Regarding the relation between religiosity and the nine subscales of marital adjustment, Communication, Parenting and Religious Orientation account for the highest rate and Sexual Relationship accounts for the lowest rate. Thus, with the increase in religiosity, marital adjustment rate will increase and vice versa. It can be concluded that religiosity develops the grounds for marital commitment

The efficacy of school leadership teams in the context of the Chilean system for the quality assurance of school management

Ahumada Figueroa, Luis Andres Dept. of Psychology, PUCV, Viña del Mar, Chile Montecinos Sanhueza, Carmen Psychology, PUCV, Viña del Mar, Chile Sisto Campos, Vicente Psychology, PUCV, Viña del Mar, Chile

Objectives: Understand how school leadership teams manage their improvement efforts in the context of the System for the Quality Assurance of School Management that is being introduced in Chile's municipals schools. Methods: A questionnaire designed to assess school leadership team's efficacy hypothesized to be related to the capacity to mange improvement was administered to a sample of 135 members of leadership teams from 53 publicly-funded elementary and high schools. Results: Factorial analysis yielded four factors: Trust, Competency, Team Learning, Team Inefficacy. Conclusions: Factors are related with school management in the areas of: Leadership, Curriculum, Resources, Organizational Climate and Results.

HIV/AIDS in Africa: A paradigm shift in control methods

Aire, Justina E. Liberal Studies, St. George's University, St George's, Grenada

The HIV/AIDS pandemic in Africa paints a grim picture. Sub-Saharan Africa is the epicentre where 71% of the world's infections reside. In 1989, almost two decades ago, WHO reported 150 people in South Africa afflicted with AIDS and 2,400 known to be infected with HIV. The numbers have continued to increase tremendously: year 2003, 40 million; today, about 60 million. This rise, despite years of seemingly aggressive control measures, is this researcher's concern. Discussed – Comparative demography and harboured African culture. Suggested - A paradigm shift towards Cognitive restructuring; debriefing faulty assumptions and filling the "void" with appropriate creative materials.

Decision making processes for choosing package holidays to manage anticipated regrets and their resulting experience

Akiyama, Manabu Dept. of Psychology, Kobe Gakuin University, Kobe, Japan

A survey for information requesters to travel argents in Japan was conducted to study how decision-making processes to chose overseas package holidays were linked with anticipated regrets before participating in those tours and with their resulting experience of those chosen tours after finishing them. Participants completed and sent questionnaires back before their departure of purchased package holidays and after their return. The result showed that plentiful experience of overseas tours easily made the chosen package holiday dominant over all the other ones, and that these experiences decreased anticipated regrets of the package holiday.

Microadaptivity in complex learning situations: Integrating competence structures and problem spaces

Albert, Dietrich Inst. für Psychologie, Universität Graz, Graz, Austria *Hockemeyer, Cord* Department of Psychology, University of Graz, Graz, Austria *Kickmeier-Rust, Michael D.* Department of Psychology, University of Graz, Graz, Austria

Adaptive (or personalised) systems have been a hot topic in e-Learning since a number of years. Such systems select learning objects or modify them before presentation according to the individual learner's needs and capabilities. In complex learning situations like simulations or learning games, however, we need adaptivity to the learner within the situation: microadaptivity. We present an approach integrating competence structures from knowledge space theory and problem spaces from the information-processing theory of human problem solving. The resulting system interprets each action of the learner with respect to his/her competence state and intervenes adaptively, e.g. by hinting, whenever appropriate.

Categorization styles among Sudanese gifted and normal children

Ali, Abrahem Islamia Unyversit, Khartoum, Sudan

This study investigates the categorization styles among gifted (N=200) and normal children (N=200) both males (50%) and females (50%) in primary education in Sudan by using chiu (1972) categorization task. The study shows the normal children were more likely to categorize objects according to their relationships (holistic style) while gifted children more likely to categories objects according to their relationship (holistic) and similarities(analytic and abstract style). There is no significant difference between males and females in categorization style, however there is an interaction between abstract style and creativity among gifted children>

The correlation between word familiarity and semantic word familiarity

Amano, Shigeaki Laboratories, NTT Communication Science, Kyoto, Japan

To reveal the relationship between word familiarity and semantic word familiarity, their correlation was calculated for 9449 Japanese multiple-meaning words using a word-familiarity database (Amano & Kondo, 1999) and a semantic-word-familiarity database (Amano, & Kobayashi, in press). The correlation coefficient was 0.571 between word familiarity and the highest semantic word familiarity within each word, but it was 0.168 for the lowest semantic word familiarity. This significant difference indicates that word familiarity has a strong relationship to the most familiar word meaning but not to the least familiar word meaning.

Decision making: When and to whom more information is harmful

Amit, Adi Jerusalem, Israel *Levontin, Sagiv, Lilach* School of Business Administrat, The Hebrew University, Jerusalem, Israel *Caprara, Vauclair, Gebauer,*

People make decisions more easily and confidently choosing from few (rather than many) alternative (Iyengar & Lepper, 2002). Two 2*2 studies examined the effect of few/many attributes and few/many alternatives on choice overload. Findings indicate that in choosing complex products, it is attributes rather than alternatives that cause overload. In Study 1, participants (N=84) experienced more overload when choosing a digital-camera described by 9 (vs. 3) attributes, regardless of the number of alternatives. Study 2 (N=116, studying cell-phones) examined the moderating effect of Need for Cognitive-Closure. The attributes overload effect was replicated – yet only among those high on NFCC.

The costs and benefits of working memory capacity on distraction and mental flexibility

Andres, Pilar School of Psychology, University of Plymouth, Plymouth, United Kingdom *Packwood, Sonia* School of Psychology, Universite Laval, Quebec, Canada *Parmentier, Fabrice* School of Psychology, University of Plymouth, Plymouth, United Kingdom *Barcelo, Francisco* School of Psychology, Universitat Illes Balears, Palma de Mallorca, Spain

The aim of this study was to investigate the hypothesis that the effect of WM capacity on distraction would depend on the status (i. e., relevant or irrelevant) of the extraneous information getting access to it. We tested this hypothesis by comparing low and high WM capacity participants on a Stroop task combining the classical interference condition with a switching condition. The results showed that participants with low WM capacity showed a greater switch cost and a smaller Stroop interference effect than participants with high WM. These results are important to understand the relationship between WM, attention and distraction.

Anxiety in formal and informal caregivers

Aparicio, Marta Diferencial y Trabajo, Universidad Complutense, Madrid, Spain *Sánchez-López, Pilar* Diferencial y Trabajo, Universidad Complutense, Madrid, Spain *Díaz Morales, Juan Francisco* Diferencial y Trabajo, Universidad Complutense,

Madrid, Spain *Fernández Martínez, Teresa* Psicología, Residencia Villaverde-Alzheime, Madrid, Spain *Castellanos Vidal, Beatriz* Psicología, Residencia Villaverde-Alzheime, Madrid, Spain *Tena Fontaneda, Angela* Medicina, Residencia Villaverde-Alzheime, Madrid, Spain

Objectives To analyse how anxiety influences the physical health of formal and informal caregivers. Methods: Those taking part are 100 formal and informal caregivers working or with members of their family in old peoples homes. The instruments used were the ISRA (Miguel Tobal and Cano Vindel, 2002) to measure anxiety and a medical evaluation to analyse physical health. Several MANOVAS were performed to analyse differences between various health variables Results: Caregivers with the highest levels of anxiety are those with the worst measurements of physical health. Conclusions: Psychological treatment in the case of caregivers to control their anxiety would improve their physical health.

Co-construction of affect regulating cognitions: The role of mother's attachment security

Apetroaia, Adela Psychology, SUNY Stony Brook, Stony Brook, USA *Waters, Harriet* Psychology, SUNY Stony Brook, Stony Brook, USA

The co-construction hypothesis (Oppenheim & Waters, 1995) suggests that secure mothers are better at helping their children elaborate affective scripts. To test this hypothesis, 33 mothers and their 4-5 year old children discussed children's hypothetical reactions to six scenarios about positive or negative everyday events, some involving the mother, some not. These conversations were scored on three dimensions of co-construction: focusing on affective content, prompting continued elaboration, and supporting an explanatory framework. Mothers' co-construction skills were correlated with both the Attachment Script Assessment and the coherence scores of the Adult Attachment Interview, showing that secure mothers promoted better co-construction partnerships.

Exploratory study of a possible intergenerational influence.

Aponte, Sandra CCIF,Inc., Guaynabo, Puerto Rico *Altieri, Gladys* Psy. D. Program, Carlos Albizu University, Guaynabo, Puerto Rico *Rosabal-Silva, Ada* Clinical Psychology, Centro de Crecimiento Gaviota, Guaynabo, Puerto Rico

The objective was to compile information to support a possible intergenerational influence. The sample was eighteen grandparents of nine male prison inmates, who were examined with MMSE and then interviewed. Through use of genograms, results were organized and analyzed on a quantitative and qualitative basis. Quantitative results suggested that in families that existed physical or sexual abuse increased the probability of illness related to nervous central system in members of different generations. Qualitative results indicated a consistent pattern of actions with multiplying effects among their family tree. One characteristic of those families was the low incidence of Christian religious practices.

Theories relating to factual findings by Japanese lay people

Arakawa, Ayumu Nagoya University, Nagoya, Japan

In 2009, Saibanin seido (the mixed jury system) will commence. An understanding of the processes used by lay juries will help professional judges, prosecutors, and defense attorneys to prepare deliberations or present evidence. We investigated how lay people consider factual findings using the "Saibanin game". In this game, participants discuss evidence in a manner similar to the fact-finding process undertaken in a real deliberation. The results showed that lay people use specific lay theories for decision-making. For example, lay people consider an accused's irrational behavior in a prosecutor's claim as exculpatory.

Experimental induction of emotional states through music

Arriaga Ferreira, Patrícia Dept. of Psychology, Universidade de Lusofona, Lisboa, Portugal *Franco, Ana* Psychology, UNIVERSIDADE LUSÓFONA, Lisboa, Portugal *Campos, Patrícia* Psychology, UNIVERSIDADE LUSÓFONA, Lisboa, Portugal *Baptista, Américo* Psychology, UNIVERSIDADE LUSÓFONA, Lisboa, Portugal

The present study was conducted to validate musical stimuli for the induction of specific emotional states (sadness, happiness, fear, anger, and neutral). The design was a 10 X 2 mixed factorial with musical stimuli as a within-subjects factor and gender as the between-subjects. Fifty students (29 female and 21 male; 19-30 years) rated their emotions (discrete items to evaluate specific emotions and the self-assessment manikin scales to measure emotional dimensions) immediately after each of the selected musical clips. The stimuli were counterbalanced across participants. The results showed that stimuli used to induce fear, happiness, sadness, and neutral states were successful for both genders, suggesting that these musical clips may be useful for experimental studies.

Bimanual coordination in predicting one's own movements in motor control

Asai, Tomohisa The University of Tokyo, Tokyo, Japan *Tanno, Yoshihiko* Department of Cognitive and Be, The University of Tokyo, Tokyo, Japan

Previous studies have suggested that the left and right hands have different internal models for motor control. We examined motor movement accuracy, reaction time, and movement time in right-handed subjects during a three-dimensional motor control task. In the no-visual-feedback condition, right-hand movement had lower accuracy and shorter reaction time than did left-hand movement, whereas bimanual movement had the longest reaction time, but the best accuracy. This suggests that the two hands have different internal models. Thus, during bimanual movements, both models might be used, creating better planning, but requiring more computation time.

Managerial values in Turkey

Askun, Duysal Degisim Egitim Danismanlik, Istanbul, Turkey *Guneser, Begum* Istanbul, Turkey *Askun Yildirim, Bige* Management & Organization, Marmara University, Istanbul, Turkey

The objective of this study was to explore the effects of certain organizational variables on the managerial values in Turkey. 1023 managers from 7 Turkish regions participated in the study and filled out the questionnaires. Findings were analyzed using regression and ANOVA analyses. A total of three managerial value factors emerged and it was found that organizational tenure had a positive effect on holding proper work values, the number of subordinates a manager is responsible of had a negative effect on holding the proper work values, and a positive effect on holding the improper work values. Educational level of a manager showed a difference in holding proper or improper work values.

Agressive behavior of children as reflection of problem relations on family

Avdeyenok, Lina Borderline States Department, Mental Health Research Institu, Tomsk, Russia

Some families seek for help regarding aggressive behavior in their children. Negative interpersonal relations occur when parents too narrowly imagine fulfillment of parental functions: to clothe, to feed, and to control the child, to punish for deeds. Condition required for establishment of firm spiritual contacts between parents and children is

a high level of information distribution to prevent a difficulty of communication between parents and children and exacerbation of interrelations, aggressive behavior, and verbal insult. Of importance is combination of knowledge of family member about each other with their mutual interest based on empathy, support, maximal benevolence, and delicacy.

Self-esteem and health-compromising behaviors among university students

Büyükgöze Kavas, Aysenur Dept. Educational Sciences, Middle East Technical Univ., Ankara, Turkey

The present study aims to investigate (a) the relationships between self-esteem and health-compromising behaviors related to use of cigarette, alcohol and drug and (b) the gender differences on self-esteem and health compromising behaviors among a group of university students (124 males, 119 females) using a cross-sectional survey design. Participants completed Rosenberg Self-Esteem Scale and a self-report questionnaire. The findings of the study revealed that self-esteem was negatively associated with alcohol and illicit drug use. In addition, cigarette and drug usage were more prevalent among males than females. However, results did not support any gender difference on the self-esteem scale.

Specifics effects of attachment to father on 3-to-5-year-old children's adjustment to school

Bacro, Fabien Nantes, France *Florin, Agnès* Psychology, Université de Nantes, Nantes, France

The purpose of this study is to know, in concordance with studies on fathers'role in child development, if attachment to father has specific effects on 3-to5-year-old children's adjustment to school. Attachment quality to mother and to father was evaluated with a french adaptation of the Attachment Story Completion Task (Bretherton et al., 1990) and school adjustment with a teacher questionnaire (Florin et al., 2002). Results of multiple regression analyses show that if children's adjustment to scholastic rythm and activities is simultaneously linked with attachment to mother and to father, some aspects of school adjustment are specifically linked with attachment to mother and to father.

The role of parents' religious orientation in the formation of their children's religious orientation

Bahrami Ehsan, Hadi Psychology and Education, University of Tehran, Tehran, Islamic Republic of Iran *Pournaghash-Tehrani, Said* Psychology and Education, University of Tehran, Tehran, Islamic Republic of Iran *Rezazadeh, Reza* Psychology and Education, University of Tehran, Tehran, Islamic Republic of Iran *Bahrami Ehsan, zainab* Psychology and Education, University of Tehran, Tehran, Islamic Republic of Iran

In order to determine the relationship between parental religious orientation and their children's, a group of 40 people including father, mother and children was selected. A questionnaire designed by Bahrami Ehsan(2006) to specifically determine Islamic religious orientation was administered to the subjects. The results of the present study showed that there was a relationship between parent's religious orientation and their children's though such relationship included different results and aspects. Specifically, our results revealed that there was no significant relationship between parent's and their children's religiosity; however, there was a significant negative relationship between parent's religiosity and children's subscale of disorganized religiosity. Also, the subscale of parent's religiosity was negatively correlated with the level of hedonism in children.

The role of religious orientation on child rearing styles

Bahrami Ehsan, Hadi Psychology and Education, University of Tehran, Tehran, Islamic Republic of Iran *Pournaghash Tehrani, Saed* Psychology and Education, University of Tehran, Tehran, Islamic Republic of Iran *Gholami Galise, Somaye* Psychology and Education, University of Tehran, Tehran, Islamic Republic of Iran

To determine the role of religious orientation in child rearing styles 180 couples, using a random clustering sample design, were chosen and were administered a revised form of Islamic religious orientation scale (Bahrami-Ehsan, 2001) and child rearing styles questionnaire pertinent to religious orientation and child rearing style. Using descriptive statistics and discriminate analysis, correlation and regression analysis, our results showed that parents with higher religious tendencies resorted to authoritative style of child rearing whereas couples with lower religious tendency adopted authoritarian and permissive child rearing style. These results indicated that religious orientation has a significant effect on the child rearing style.

Psychometric properties and construct validity of the Parents Preference Test (PPT⊚) in the Italian context

Baiocco, Roberto Faculty of Psychology 1, Universita di Roma, Rome, Italy *Westh, Finn* Danish University of Education, Family Research Centre, Copenhagen, Denmark *Laghi, Fiorenzo* Clinical Psychology, Faculty of Psychology 1, Rome, Italy *Rosenberg Hansen, Carsten* Clinical Psychology, Danish University of Education, Copenhagen NV, Denmark *Ferrer, Christian A.* Clinical Psychology, Family Research Centre, Copenhagen O, Denmark *d'Alessio, Maria* Clinical Psychology, Faculty of Psychology 1, Rome, Italy

Objectives. The principal aim of the study was to examine the psychometric properties and construct validity of the PPT in the Italian context. The instrument is a picture-based multiple-choice test with images of parent-child interactions from everyday family activities and it measures the following dimensions: Energy, Focus of Attention, Experiential Modality and Regulation Style. Subjects. The sample was composed of 100 Italian families with children between 5 and 12 years old. Results. PPT showed a good reliability and a convergent validity with different measures of family functioning. Results encourage the use of this instrument in studies concerned with the family.

Psychological counseling and health complaints

Balaceanu, Gheorghe Occupational medicine, Institute of Public Health, Lasi, Romania

Objectives. The influence of psychological counseling on frequency decrease of health complaints. Methods. 151 employees were asked about the frequently felt health complaints, before and after receiving counselings concerning both theirs psychological (temperamental, motivational and of stress resistance) and psychosocial peculiarities, and significant relationships with health complaints. Results. The comparison of frequency from the start with those observed after 5 years, put in evidence a significant diminishion in frequency for a great number of health complaints. Conclusions. The psychological counseling concerning the influence of psychosocial risk factors and psychological peculiarities, can contribute to a significant diminishion in frequency of individual health complaints.

Inhibition of return: A "depth-blind" mechanism?

Barbato, Mariapaola Dipartimento di Psicologia, Sapienza Universität, Roma, Italy *Casagrande, Maria* Dipartimento di Psicologia, Roma, Italy *Mereu, Stefania* Dipartimento di Psicologia, "Sapienza" Università, Roma, Italy *Martella, Diana* Dipartimento

di Psicologia, "Sapienza" Università, Roma, Italy
Marotta, Andrea *Dipartimento di Psicologia, "Sapienza" Università, Roma, Italy*

Four experiments investigated the Inhibition Of Return (IOR), in the three-dimensional and in the two-dimensional space. The first two experiments compared detection and discrimination tasks in eliciting IOR effects in a three-dimensional empty space. Two other experiments assessed the IOR effects in a scene that included two sets of objects (parallelepipeds extending in depth and parallelepipeds located at different depths, extending in the horizontal plane). In each experiment we compared the IOR effects in 2D (both with and without depth clues) and stereoscopic 3D conditions. Results showed IOR in 3D space, confirming that it is not a depth-blind mechanism.

Identity in contemporary scenario and its interaction with art

Barbosa, Cristina Monteiro *Dept. de Psicometria, UFRJ, Rio de Janeiro, Brazil*
Objectives: Identify the different forms of art, aspects of the human soul that are inscribed in our culture to express subjectivity. Method: To study each historical time with signs in order to produce art. Results: Art is a cultural heritage which is constituted by its unique production in the creative act. Restrictive forces imposed to the social norm characterize different ages Conslusions:. Traditions are at the heart of questionings and transgressions carried out by radical movements towards a new order in the modern period. Subversive styles of contemporary art point to the search for an identity in modern times

The impact of a mindfulness training program on managers' stages of consciousness and leadership behaviors

Baron, Charles *Management, Laval University, Quebec City, Canada* **Cayer, Mario** *Management, Laval University, Quebec City, Canada*
This study examined the impact of a mindfulness training program on managers' stages of consciousness and leadership behaviors. The stage of consciousness (Rooke & Torbert, 2005) of 25 managers was evaluated at the beginning and end of a one-year program. A multi-source feedback questionnaire (Cacioppe & Albrecht, 2000) filled out by eight collaborating observers served to evaluate behavioral changes. Compared to the wait-list control group, the experimental group experienced a greater increase in their stage of consciousness (toward the postconventional level) and their collaborating observers reported a greater increase in their visioning, directing and brokering behaviors.

Homogeneity and trends of subordinates' perceptions for leadership in work groups under different team members employment conditions

Barrasa, Angel *Dept. of Social Psychology, Autonoma Univer. of Barcelona, Barcelona, Spain* **Blanch, Josep M.** *Dept. of Social Psychology, Autonoma Univer. of Barcelona, Barcelona, Spain* **Hernandez-Garcia, Laura** *Dept. of Social Psychology, Autonoma Univer. of Barcelona, Barcelona, Spain*
This study tested subordinates perceptions of their team leaders at group level. Different types of teamwork specific data (N= 239 teams, 1099 individuals) were analyzed testing intragroup leadership perceptions homogeneity by rwg(J), ICC(2), and ADM(J). Results provided evidence of aggregate data inside work groups supporting similar trends of leadership perceptions for team members with similar employment conditions. Conclusions indicate that underlying conditions like temporality or job insecurity are mediating the team members' leadership perceptions creating extreme views: higher signification for leadership tasks and idealiz-

ing leaders or lower importance and disapproving them.

Development of objective conscientiousness tasks for student selection

Bath, Anja *Inst. für Sozialwissenschaften, Helmut-Schmidt-Universität, Hamburg, Germany* **Lange, Sebastian** *Social Science, Helmut-Schmidt-University, Hamburg, Germany* **Kluwe, Rainer H.** *Social Science, Helmut-Schmidt-University, Hamburg, Germany* **Beauducel, André** *Social Science, Helmut-Schmidt-University, Hamburg, Germany*
Results of a study requirement analysis at the University of the Federal Armed Forces showed that behavior based conscientiousness is an important predictor of success. New objective paper-pencil-tasks, which measure the degree of systematic conscientious work behavior, were developed. A sample of 158 students aged between 20 and 30 years was examined. First analyses yield significant correlations up to r = -.24 between task performance and intermediate exam. The corresponding structural equation model fitted well. Further results of task development, standardization, and validation are presented.

Drivers' risk assessment under critical driving conditions

Bellet, Thierry *LESCOT, INRETS, Bron, France* **Banet, Aurélie** *LESCOT, INRETS, Bron, France* **Bonnard, Arnaud** *LESCOT, INRETS, Bron, France* **Deleurence, Philippe** *LESCOT, INRETS, Bron, France* **Goupil, Céline** *LESCOT, INRETS, Bron, France*
This research aims at studying drivers' risk assessment cognitive processes. The method consists in combining naturalistic observations while driving, with laboratory experiments. Indeed, a set of critical situations was collected and filmed during naturalistic observations. Then, laboratory experiments were carried out by using these video sequences, and new groups of drivers had to assess their criticality level (from 0 to 100). The presentation will be focused on Laboratory experiment results: 10 car drivers and 10 motorcyclists participated to this experiment, and significant differences have been observed between the 2 groups, concerning risk awareness and the criticality assessment of driving situations.

Scaffolding metacognitive processes in a research environment for web based resources to improve learning quality

Benz, Bastian Frithjof *Inst. für Psychologie, Techn. Universität Darmstadt, Darmstadt, Germany*
This study investigated the effects of integrating scaffolds, which aimed at fostering metacognitive processes, in a computer-based research environment. It was hypothized that scaffolding goal setting, planning, monitoring, (process-)regulation, reflection and modification would enhance the quality of the learning outcome. A closed hypertext environment was searched on a historical period by 24 knowledge workers for about 30 minutes. The experimental group was supported by metacognitive scaffolds. Acquired cognitive models and persisted resources were examined. As hypothized the experimental group outperformed the control group. Additionally log files, questionnaires and interviews were used to evaluate the effectiveness of single scaffolds.

The effect of teaching of Islamic instructions on marital satisfaction of couples

Berah, Zahra *counselling, university of social welfare, Tehran, Islamic Republic of Iran* **Bahrami, Fazel** *counselling, university of social welfare, Tehran, Islamic Republic of Iran* **Younesi, Jalal** *clinical Psychology, university of social welfare, Tehran, Islamic Republic of Iran*
This study was carried out based on Islamic approach for improvement of the relationships of

couples. Many instructions were collected from Islamic sources which to be related to criteria of healthy family, satisfactory relationship and behavior. There are many comments from prophet Mohammad (S) and his followers about these criteria. The techniques of intervention were extracted from the comments. 24 married couples as volunteers were involved in this experimental research. They were divided randomly into two – experimental and control groups. Using Enrich marital satisfaction scales in pretest and posttest stages, the subjects were trained by the techniques. The results showed that the use of Islamic instructions to be able to improve their marital relations and to increase the marital satisfaction.

Change blindness and mnesic processes

Berberian, Bruno *Psychology, SRSC (ULB), Bruxelles, Belgium*
Empirical studies have proven our inability to detect change under a variety of conditions. However, this change blindness does not seem to bias the behavioural adaptations since these adaptations may occur in the absence of conscious awareness. This unconscious change detection also seems to be present in recall tasks (Berberian & Giraudo, in preparation). In this context, we propose to investigate the relation between information structuration in memory and conscious experience of perceptual change by using a gradual flicker paradigm where subjects were asked to memorize and reproduce stimuli which present gradual change. Results and discussion are in preparation.

Effective management by objectives at team leader level in different European countries: The relation between motivational requirements and management related requirements

Berger, Rita *Cerdanyola, Spain* **Gidion, Gerd** *Institut f. Berufspädagogik, University of Karlsruhe, Karlsruhe, Germany* **Font, Antoni** *Basic Psychology, Autonomous University Barcelon, Bellaterra, Spain*
Objectives: Compare the relationship between requirements for Management by Objectives (MbO) (leadership style, autonomy) and motivational requirements (specific, moderate goals, participation, feedback) of team leaders in different countries. Method: Hypothesis: Relationship between MbO and motivational requirements in the countries. Self-established goals will facilitate motivation. 181 team leaders of Germany, United Kingdom, Italy and Spain participated in the study. The employees valued, using questionnaires, the MbO of their superior. Results: Relationship between requirements for MbO and motivational requirements was observed in all participating countries. Conclusion: In some countries increased the participation of group members in goal setting when their autonomy level increased. Goal achievement was perceived as easier.

Reliability and validity of the Italian version of the Anxiety Sensitivity Index

Bernini, Olivia *Psychiatry, University of Pisa, Pisa, Italy* **Pennato, Tiziana** *Psychiatry, University of Pisa, Pisa, Italy* **Berrocal, Carmen** *Psychiatry, University of Pisa, Pisa, Italy* **Guazzelli, Mario** *Psychiatry, University of Pisa, Pisa, Italy*
Objective: to study the psychometric properties of the adaptation into Italian of the Anxiety Sensitivity Index (ASI; Peterson and Reiss, 1987). Methods: participants included 177 undergraduate students and non-student adults. In addition to the ASI, subjects were requested to fill up questionnaires measuring constructs conceptually related with the scale. Statistical analyses for testing the factorial validity, internal consistency, and concurrent validity of the questionnaire were carried out. Results: the ASI is a reliable and valid assessment tool for measuring Anxiety Sensitivity. Conclusion: the

Italian ASI is a valid instrument for measuring Anxiety Sensitivity in population-based studies with Italian samples.

Relationship between leadership style and attitude toward working groups

Berrios Martos, Pilar Dept. of Social Psychology, Universidad de Jaén, Jaén, Spain Lopez Zafra, Esther Dept. of Social Psychology, Universidad de Jaén, Jaén, Spain Aguilar Luzón, María del Carmen Social Psychology, Universidad de Jaén, Jaén, Spain Augusto, Jose Maria Social Psychology, Universidad de Jaén, Jaén, Spain

We wanted to analyze the possible relationship between Leadership Style and Attitude towards working groups. Our sample was compound by 129 individuals (29 men and 100 women), with ages from 19 to 43 años. Our results show that individuals with a transformational leadership style have a positive attitude towards working in groups, whereas laisse-faire style individuals have a negative attitude towards working in groups.

Australian children's learning competence at age 4: The nature and impact of parent involvement in children's education

Berthelsen, Donna Centre of Learning Innovation, Qld University of Technology, Brisbane, Australia Walker, Susan Centre of Learning Innovation, Qld University of Technology, Brisbane, Australia Dunbar, Stephanie Centre of Learning Innovation, Qld University of Technology, Brisbane, Australia

This study investigated the relationship between parental involvement and child outcomes in the early years of school. The analyses use data from The Longitudinal Study of Australian children (LSAC). The analyses use data for 4464 children in the Kindergarten Cohort. The mean age of the children was 6.8 years. Regression analyses, findings support the hypothesized linkages between parent engagement and more positive child outcomes. Outcomes were moderated by family demographic factors, including mothers' education. Implications of the findings focuses on how schools can support involvement, in particular, the extent to which such efforts successfully engage less involved parents

Using music therapy in an intervention to enhance parent-child interaction and the social-emotional functioning of young children

Berthelsen, Donna Centre of Learning Innovation, Qld University of Technology, Brisbane, Australia Nicholson, Jan Royal Children's Hospital, Murdoch Childrens Research Ins, Melbourne, Australia Abad, Vicky Sing and Grow Project, Playgroup Queensland, Brisbane, Australia Williams, Kate Sing and Grow Project, Playgroup Queensland, Brisbane, Australia Hart, Carolyn Sing and Grow Project, Playgroup Queensland, Brisbane, Australia Bradley, Julie Centre of Learning Innovation, Qld University of Technology, Brisbane, Australia Dunbar, Stephanie Centre of Learning Innovation, Qld University of Technology, Brisbane, Australia

This research analyses the impact of a music therapy program on parents' interactional behaviours. The program is a short-term group parenting intervention (10 weeks) to support marginalized parents and their children aged 0-3 years. Analyses are presented for 560 parental participants. Significant improvements were observed from pre to post evaluation in parental sensitivity, engagement with the child, and acceptance of the child. These effects are attributed to the engaging nature of the music intervention and the increased confidence that parents gained through regular participation. The study provides preliminary evidence for the value of music therapy as a parenting intervention.

The third sector in Brazil: Struggles and progresses of program evaluation methods

Berthoud, Cristiana Psychology, University of Taubate, Tremembe - SP, Brazil

The Third Sector has been playing an important role in Latin America in general and particularly in Brazil by developing programs designed to easy the profound social problems related to poverty and urban violence. As the organizations evolve, the need for showing results and impacts promoted by the social interventions has grown as well. Psychology can be of great help by developing research evaluation capable of measuring personal changes and group empowerment. The author will present the results of several evaluations conducted in slums of two major cities in Brazil and will discuss the use of quantitative and qualitative methods.

Discounting of sequences: Form of the process

Bialaszek, Wojciech Dept. of Psychology, University of Warsaw, Warsaw, Poland

The experiment extends traditional research on temporal discounting of single rewards to sequences of rewards. Four models of time discounting were tested by fitting them with nonlinear regression to the sets of indifference points. Analysis of group behavior demonstrated that certain models describe data differently according to delay between rewards. At group level when the delays between rewards are relatively short or very large hyperbolic models fitted the data better than exponential, but at individual level this result is only significant in case of longest delay. Moreover there are no differences when delays between rewards are relatively intermediate.

Cognitive load decreases distractor interference in the Simon task

Biebl, Rupert Inst. für Psychologie I, Universität Nürnberg-Erlangen, Erlangen, Germany Wühr, Peter Psychologie und Sport, Institut für Psychologie I, Erlangen, Germany

The load theory of selective attention and cognitive control claims that cognitive load increases the impact of irrelevant stimulation on performance. We investigated the impact of cognitive load on the Simon effect, which denotes faster responses to spatially corresponding than to noncorresponding stimuli, even when stimulus position is irrelevant. The results from two experiments showed that increasing cognitive load (i.e. letters) decreases the Simon effect, contrary to the predictions of the load theory. The results suggest that the effects of cognitive load on performance depend upon whether the participants select between features of the same object or between different objects.

A metacognitive approach to assess anosognosia in Alzheimer type dementia

Billiet, Caroline Lille, France Antoine, Pascal URECA - équipe FASE, Université Lille 3, Villeneuve d'Ascq Cedex, France Nandrino, Jean-Louis URECA - équipe Fase, Université Lille 3, Villeneuve d'Ascq Cedex, France Cousin, Céline URECA - équipe FASE, Université Lille 3, VILLENEUVE D'ASCQ Cedex, France Roger, Caroline URECA - équipe FASE, Université Lille 3, VILLENEUVE D'ASCQ, France Szafraniec, Claire URECA - équipe FASE, Université Lille 3, Villeneuve d'Ascq Cedex, France

Objectives: To explore unawareness of cognitive deficits in Alzheimer's disease (AD) by using an experimental metacognition paradigm. Methods: 48 patients with AD and 21 control participants asked to predict their own performance at the Dementia Rating Scale (DRS). For each sub-score, the discrepancy between their subjective ratings and the effective test performance was considered. Results: Patients with AD over-estimate their performance in all dimensions of the DRS. However, they show different levels of anosognosia according to the cognitive function. Conclusions:

AD patients shows metacognitive impairments. The results support the assumption that anosognosia is not an unitary concept.

Visual field does not impact the influence of perception on action

Binsted, Gordon Health and Social Development, University of British Columbia, Kelowna, Canada Heath, Matthew School of Kinesiology, University of Western Ontario, London, Canada

Recent examinations have demonstrated a movement execution advantage in the lower visual field (LVF) consistent with a preferential field association to dorsal extra-striate cortex. Two experiments examined the corollary prediction that LVF should show reduced susceptibility to context effects and be less able to access memorial representations of the visual environment. Reaching movements were made after 1-10s delays and to illusory contexts. While a LVF advantage was observed (movement time, error), action was equally influenced by illusory context and memorial delay across fields. These results suggest that field associated performance effects, while present, are not underpinned by a preferential dorsal/ventral stream involvement.

HIV Risk Behavior among vocational school students in St-Petersburg, Russia

Bogolyubova, Olga St. Petersburg, Russia

The purpose of this study was to investigate HIV risk behaviors of youths attending vocational schools in St-Petersburg. The sample consisted of 310 men and women aged 18 – 25, part of the participants were raised in orphanages. Data analyses included frequencies, t tests, chi-squares and correlation analyses. Results: only 31.2% youths reported consistent condom use and 12.9% reported intravenous drug use. Significant correlations were found between various types of risk behavior. Certain differences in risk behavior were found between participants from orphanages vs family background. Further research is necessary to assess HIV risks among young Russians from socially vulnerable groups.

Distributed leadership and team performance in a business strategy simulation

Boies, Kathleen John Molson Sch. of Business, Concordia University, Montreal, Canada Lvina, Elena John Molson Sch. of Business, Concordia University, Montreal, Canada Martens, Martin L. John Molson Sch. of Business, Concordia University, Montreal, Canada

This study aimed to examine the relations between distributed leadership in teams, team processes, and performance. Forty-nine student teams participating in a business simulation game rated their team potency, trust, and team leadership styles. Team potency and trust were positively related to team transformational leadership and negatively related to passive avoidant leadership, but only the latter was significantly negatively related to performance in the business simulation game. These results suggest that teams might not always benefit from transformational leadership qualities, but that "negative" leadership styles might be detrimental to performance and to the trust and confidence in the team.

Effect of GPS sounds on driver's attention (Part 2)

Boujon, Christophe Dept. of Psychology, University of Angers, Angers, France Guillemé, Julien psychology, University of Angers, Angers, France

We formalized attentional model FIDI including four mental states of drivers: Focalisation, Inhibition, Distraction and Inattention (Boujon, Lemercier, Quaireau, 2007). We suppose that distraction effect is less important when sounds are synchronous with visual cue rather than visual target, especially in the ipsilateral localization. Distraction was manipulated by lateralized presentation of realistic sounds extracting from interior of vehicle (GPS vocal commands) while 30 subjects realized a visual cueing task, the Attention Network Test (Fan, Bruce, McCandliss, Sommer, Raz & Posner, 2002). Anova's analysis confirms our hypothesis. These experimental results are particularly fruitful when drivers utilize GPS.

Effect of road traffic sounds on driver's attention (Part 1)

Boujon, Christophe Dept. of Psychology, University of Angers, Angers, France Fuch, Julien psychology, University of Angers, Angers, France Gaillard, Pascal Linguistic, University of Toulouse, Toulouse, France

We formalized model FIDI including four mental attentional states of driver: Focalisation, Inhibition, Distraction and Inattention (Boujon, Lemercier, Quaireau, 2007). We suppose that distraction effect is more important when sounds are synchronous with visual targets rather than cues, especially in the orienting condition. Distraction was manipulated by binaural presentation of realistic sounds extracting from road traffic (fireman's truck siren, bicycle's bell,etc.) while 26 subjects realized a visual cueing task, the Attention Network Test (Fan, Bruce, McCandliss, Sommer, Raz & Posner, 2002). Anova's analysis confirms longer reaction times in this condition. These experimental results will be replicated in car driving simulation.

A psychometric evaluation of a measure of different prayer types among Irish adults

Breslin, Michael J. School of Psychology, University of Ulster at Magee, Londonderry, United Kingdom Lewis, Christopher Alan School of Psychology, University of Ulster at Magee, Londonderry, United Kingdom Shevlin, Mark School of Psychology, University of Ulster at Magee, Londonderry, United Kingdom

Objectives: Recently there has been an increased interest in the use of prayer within empirical research. This study provided a factor analytical evaluation of the Measure of Prayer Type (Poloma & Pendleton, 1991), which measures four different types of prayer. Methods: A sample of 518 Irish respondents completed the Measure of Prayer Type. Results: Three alternative confirmatory factor analytic models were specified and tested. The correlated four-factor model suggested by Poloma and Pendleton (1991) was found to be an acceptable description of the data, and better than the single-factor model and second-order model. Conclusions: Implications of the results were discussed.

The influence of social support in parental practices in psychosocial risk contexts

Byrne, Sonia Psicología Evol. y Educ., University of La Laguna, La Laguna, Spain Rodrigo Lopez, Mª José Psicología evol. y educ., University of La Laguna, La Laguna, Spain

Families experiencing negative psychosocial conditions receive many forms of social support. But it is important to know to what extent is social support effective in promoting adequate parenting in at-risk families. Participants were obtained from a sample of 1150 mothers attending a parenting program. The results of ANOVA analyses indicate that the formal sources of support have a negative effect in at-risk families; they were associated to increases in permissive practices and decreases in inductive practices. In sum, formal support providers should revise the way they convey their help, because they are affecting negatively to those families that need them more.

Effects of time pressure and motivation on the use of the priority heuristic

Cüpper, Lutz Inst. Experiment. Psychologie, Universität Mannheim, Mannheim, Germany Undorf, Monika Experimental Psychology, University of Mannheim, Mannheim, Germany

Brandstätter, Gigerenzer, and Hertwig (2006) proposed the priority heuristic to account for violations of expected utility theory. However, evidence that people use the priority heuristic for their decisions is rare. In our experiment, participants chose repeatedly between pairs of lotteries that differed in their expected value. The priority heuristic predicted choice behavior more accurately than expected value. Additionally, time pressure increased the number of choices in favor of the priority heuristic. High motivation decreased the number of optimal choices. Although the first findings lend support to the priority heuristic, the last one needs further clarification.

Youth gang: COoncept of masculinity and their vulnerability to HIV and Aids

Cabanela, Noriel Peer Education Dept., PRRM, Quezon City, Philippines Acaba, Jefrry Peer Education Dept., PRRM, Quezon City, Philippines

Youth gangs in the philippines have a critically high regard towards "pagkalalaki" or masculinity. The Study It aims to identify the knowledge, attitudes, and behaviors, and practices among youth male gang members with regards to masculinity, gender, sex, and STIs including HIV and AIDS. Specifically, this study aims to know and recognize the perceptions of young male gang members toward masculinity; identify attitudes and behaviors among gang members which directly expose them to vulnerability and risk of acquiring STI, HIV and AIDS; This study was employs a multi-stage sampling.

Age-of-Acquisition norms for a large set of Portuguese nouns and their relation with other psycholinguistic variables

Cameirão, Manuela Speech Laboratory, FPCEUP - UP, Porto, Portugal Vicente, Selene Speech Lab, FPCEUP - UP, Porto, Portugal

We collected Age-of-Acquisition estimates for a set of 916 frequent Portuguese nouns that vary in orthographic length (1 to 5 ortographic syllables). The words were divided in 11 different paper questionnaires, using a nine-point scale as first proposed by Carrol and White (1973). A total of 491 under-graduate students participated in this study (Mean Age = 20,47; SD= 2,98). Correlations between AOA and other psycholinguistic variables were analyzed. The results show that words learnt earlier in life tend to be shorter in phonological and orthographic length. They are also more frequent and have more dense phonological and orthographic neighbourhoods.

Child Sexual Abuse characteristics, attributions of responsibility and disclosure

Canton Cortes, David Developmental Psychology, University of Granada, Granada, Spain Canton Duarte, Jose Developmental Psychology, University of Granada, Granada, Spain

The aim of the study was to analyse the relation of CSA characteristics and attribution of responsibility for the abuse with the occurrence of disclosure. Our sample comprised 91 female College students from the University of Granada, who had suffered CSA before the age of 13. Regression analyses showed that the disclosure of the abuse in a public way was related to the relationship with the aggressor and blaming the family for the abuse, while the child telling to someone about the abuse was related also to its duration. We can conclude that the disclosure is related to the CSA characteristics and attributions of responsibility for the abuse.

Elementary development of perfectionism scale for Chinese college student

Cao, Guanghai Faculty of Education, Jining University, Jining, People's Republic of China Li, Jianwei Faculty of Education, Qufu Normal University, Qufu, People's Republic of China

By analyzing and sorting answers to the open questionnaire, the scale including 66 items were compiled. Then exploratory and confirmatory factor analysis was applied to the data. The Scale consisted of 42 items, six subscales: Perfect Expectation, Personal Standards, Concerns with Mistakes, Organization, Introspection, Parents' Expectation and Control. The six factors explain 55.71? of the variance with loading between 0.49~0.85,and had internal consistencies with split-half reliabilities 0.77~0.86,Cronbach's alphas 0.78~0.92, and test-retest reliabilities of 0.77~0.91?p<0.01?. The Scale for Chinese Students has satisfying validities and reliabilities.

A development research about the influence of endogenous and exogenous attention on number processing

Cao, Xiaohua Dept. of Psychology, Zhejiang Normal University, Jinhua, People's Republic of China

The study was conducted to investigate the stages and the distance effect of number processing with equipment of EYELINK II. Participants were children and adults in China. The findings were as follows: Perceptual representation stage on number processing was significant influenced by the exogenous cue validity rather the endogenous cue validity; Both of two attention condition, the influence of subjects type on perceptual representation stage was significantly different; The ability of reaction execution on number processing had no significant difference between the 9 years old children and the adults; The distance effect was occurred in perceptual representation stage, and was independent of the motor execution stage.

Are technological tools efficient for training and update on domestic violence?

Cardenas Lopez, Georgina Dept. of Psychology, UNAM, Mexico City, Mexico Berra, Enrique Psychology, UNAM, Mexico city, Mexico Ramirez, Ana Paola Psychology, UNAM, Mexico city, Mexico Torres, Carolina Psychology, UNAM, Mexico city, Mexico Labrador, Francisco Psychology, Univ Complutense de Madrid, Madrid, Mexico

Due to the increasing levels of domestic violence in Mexico, the need of personnel for intervention and prevention of this problem, and the increasing use of computer-based teaching modes for professional competencies formation, several tutorials have been developed to support the teaching of design and application of intervention programs for domestic violence. The presented results were obtained from students trained by VR and face-to-face training, from three tutorials that incorporate hypertext, virtual simulation and digital video for professional competencies teaching focused on diagnosis and planning for psychological intervention and prevention of: couple violence, dating violence and witness to violence.

Relations between parental attitudes and childrens temperament to reactive and proactive aggression

Carrasco, Miguel Personalidad, Universidad UNED, Madrid, Spain González, Paloma Personalidad, Universidad UNED, Madrid, Spain del Barrio, Victoria Personalidad, Universidad UNED, Madrid, Spain Gordillo, Rodolfo Personalidad, Universidad UNED, Madrid, Spain

Relations between self-reported parental reactions, childrens temperament and reactive-proactive aggression were examined. Evidence was consistent with the conclusion that relations between childrens aggression, parental reactions and childrens temperam!ent depends on both: the age of children and the type of aggression (proactive and reactive). A sample of 274 children (54% boys) whose ages ranged from 4 months to six years old, were studied. Multiple regression analysis were conducted and the results showed the existence of a specific pattern according the hypothesis proposed.

Learning and students' behavior in audio conferencing versus face-to-face classroom

Caspi, Avner Education and Psychology, Open University of Israel, Ra'anana, Israel

In two studies the differences between audio conferencing and traditional face-to-face learning were examined. We investigated whether the medium richness, medium naturalness, and visual anonymity determine students' learning efficacy, perception, satisfaction, participation, risk-taking, immediacy and disinhibited behavior. As hypothesized, audio conferencing was as effective as face-to-face learning. Face-to-face communication was perceived as better than audio conferencing in the emotional-experiential aspects of learning: amount of students' attention and interest, learning satisfaction, and enjoyment from the interaction. These results are explained in terms of media naturalness and as an effect of visual anonymity, and suggest a distinction between the cognitive and the emotional-experiential aspects of perceived learning.

Differences in the locus of control for HIV/AIDS between the adolescent natives and immigrants

Castro, Ángel University of Granada, Granada, Spain *Bermudez, Maria Paz* Psychology, University of Granada, Granada, Spain

OBJECTIVE. The objective was to compare the native Spanish adolescents and the adolescent immigrants who live in Spain according to the locus of control for HIV/AIDS infection. METHOD. The sample consists of two groups. One of them of 100 native Spanish adolescents and the other of 100 adolescent immigrants who live in Spain, with the ages between 14 and 19 years. The Spanish adaptation of the scale about the locus of control for the health modified for AIDS was utilized. RESULTS. The significant differences which depend on the country origin are presented and discussed.

Peer group rules perception for HIV prevention in terms of psychopathological variables

Castro, Ángel University of Granada, Granada, Spain *Bermudez, MariaPaz* Psychology, University of Granada, Granada, Spain *Paniagua, Freddy A.* Psychology, University of Texas, Granada, Spain *Buela Casal, Gualberto* Psychology, University of Granada, Granada, Spain *OBoyle, Michael* Psychology, University of Texas, Granada, Spain

OBJECTIVE. Evaluate the peer group rules perception for the adoption of HIV prevention behaviours in normal adolescents and in adolescents with psychological disorders. METHOD. This is an "ex post facto" study, cross-sectional type. The scales were applied of a collective way under the same conditions for the 620 participants who formed the sample. RESULTS. We find statistically significant differences between the normal adolescents and the adolescents with psychological disorders. CONCLUSIONS. Psychopathological variables of a group must be considered in order to design a HIV prevention program.

Meta-platform for building e-learning environments

Ceglie, Flavio Pathological Anatomy, University of Bari (Italy), Bari, Italy *Gentile, Enrichetta* Informatics, University of Bari (Italy), Bari, Italy *Monacis, Lucia* Psychology, University of Bari (Italy), Bari, Italy

Our paper aims at building the architecture of federating e-learning environments based on the Problem Solving paradigm in order to develop

meta-cognitive abilities of the task executive control, of the cognitive components monitoring, and therefore of cognitive self-regulation. This meta-platform is equipped with all the necessary services giving life to a virtual community, and it allows the users to access, through Problem Solving model, competences and formative materials available in the network-adhering centres. This model has been tested on 146 students enrolled at humanistic and scientific faculties. Data show an improvement of students' productivity in the virtual system.

Whether or not negative beliefs about worry is the mediator between intolerance of uncertainty and generalized anxiety disorder?

Chang, Ben-Sheng Psychology, Soochow University, Taipei, Taiwan *Wang, Chun-Hui* Psychology, Soochow University, Taipei, Taiwan

Why does intolerance of uncertainty (IU) develop generalized anxiety disorder (GAD)? Many published papers have supported that the negative belief about worry (NBW) is the necessary factor for developing GAD. The purpose of the present study is to test whether NBW is the mediator between IU and GAD. Taiwanese college students (333 students) were recruited to fill out Intolerance of Uncertainty Scale, Meta-cognitions Questionnaire, and Generalized Anxiety Disorder Questionnaire. Simple regression and setwise multiple regression were used to analyze data in accordance to Baron and Kenny's mediator formula. The result supports that NBW is the mediator between IU and GAD.

Psychometric validation of the Chinese version of Metacognitions Questionnaire (MCQ-30): A test of metacognitive theory of worry and obsessive compulsive symptoms

Chang, Sue-Hwang Department of Psychology, National Taiwan University, Taipei, Taiwan

Metacognition is critical to the pathogenesis of emotional disorders. This study reports psychometric properties and validation of the short form of Metacognitions Questionnaire-Chinese version (MCQ-30; Cartwright-Hatton & Wells, 2004). MCQ-30 along with STAI, BDI, MOCI and PSWQ were administered to 203 college students. The results showed good internal consistency and test–retest reliability. Factor analysis replicated the original five-factor structure. Positive associations between metacognitions and measures of worry and obsessive–compulsive symptoms further confirmed the metacognitive theory of intrusive thoughts. Chinese MCQ-30 may serve as an efficacious tool in assessing metacognitive domains considered important in conceptualizing psychopathological processes.

Relief of suppressed emotion in forbearance: The effect of empathy and the way to promote it

Chen, I-Fen Taipei, Taiwan *Lin, Yi-Cheng* Department of psychology, National Taiwan University, Taipei, Taiwan *Huang, Chin-Lan* Department of Psychology, National Taiwan University, Taipei, Taiwan

For Chinese, forbearance (?) has been considered as a common and valued coping tactics in interpersonal conflicts in daily lives. However, forbearance implies an unwilling or unpleasant suppression of emotions. To maintain one's psychological well-being, it is important to adopt some transforming strategies to relieve the suppressed emotions. This study examined the effectiveness of various transforming strategies. Furthermore, a revised expressive diary writing (PDDP) was used to improve participants' abilities of perspective taking. Results showed being empathetic was the most effective strategy to relieve discomfort, and PDDP increased empathy toward others. Indigenous implications were discussed.

Children's grade, gender and their questions

Chen, Pei-Lan Taichung, Taiwan *Tzeng, Yuhtsuen* Center for Teacher Education, NationalChungChengUniversity, Chia-Yi, Taiwan

The purpose of this study was to examine children's questions generated from different grades and gender. Taking a revised taxonomy of questions (twenty types) as our analytical framework, we use ANOVA with grade and gender as between-subjects variables and type of question as a within-subjects variable to analyze questions generated from eighty-nine children. The results indicated a statistically significant two-way interaction (F (38, 1577) = 3.95, MSE = 8.79, p < .01). Children's questioning types were different by their grade level, whereas children's gender did not influence their questions. The results will contribute to children's questioning development.

Uncovering the configurational performance with resource-based view: A test of the relationships between Board capital composition and firm performance

Chen, Ling-hsiu Information Management, Chaoyang University of Tech., Taichung County, Taiwan *Lin, Shang-Ping* Business administration, NYUT, Douliou, Taiwan

The BOD (board of directors) is the heart of corporate governance. Different types of capable directors not only formed different profile of BOD capital composition but also reflect different power status among BOD members. The present study proposed that: Different compositions of BOD have different effects on firm performance; the more balance composition in BOD capital, the better firm performance. 482 listing companies included in this study and the result indicated that there is not significant difference in firm's market performance in different type of BOD capital composition, but the "Balance BOD" had a highest ROA. That is, firm with the equivalent distributed type of capable directors had highest internal performance.

Web-based personalized learning system, based on learner's knowledge structure

Chen, Ling-hsiu Information Management, Chaoyang University of Tech., Taichung County, Taiwan *Lin, Shang-Ping* Business Administration, NYUT, Douliou, Taiwan

Personalized service is important in the context of e-learning service. However learner's ability was always neglected in previous research. The present study applied the Pathfinder Network and developed a Web-based personalized system to elicit and diagnosis learner's knowledge structure. This system also can provide learning recommendation to learner by using a modified "C" index. The experiment results indicate this Web-based personalized learning system can provide personalized learning progress based on learner's ability and learner has higher satisfaction with this personalized learning system.

Ambivalent sexism, marriage, and power-related gender-role ideology

Chen, Zhixia Huazhong University of Science, Department of Sociology, Wuhan, People's Republic of China *Fiske, Susan* Princeton University, Department of Psychology, Princeton, USA *Lee, Tiane* Princeton University, Department of Psychology, Princeton, USA

Using Glick and Fiske's (1996) Ambivalent Sexism Inventory, a new Gender Roles in Marriage Inventory examined the relationship of ambivalent attitudes toward women and power-related gender-role ideology about marriage. We hypothesized that ambivalent sexism influences marital power through two mechanisms: enacting male dominance at the beginning of a marriage by mate selection criteria, and maintaining male dominance during the marriage by power-related gender-role norms for marriage. Results from Chinese and American samples indicate that ambivalent sexism relates both to male dominance and to traditional gender role ideology in mate selection criteria and norms in marriage. Cultural similarities and gender differences are also discussed. Key words: hostile sexism, benevolent sexism, mate selection, gender role marriage norms

The development of "Chinese Christians' Religiosity Scale"

Chen, Yongsheng *Dept. of Psychology, Zhejiang Normal University, Jihua, People's Republic of China*
The aim is to develop "Chinese Christians' Religiosity Scale "(CCRS). The hypothesis is that elements of Chinese Christians' religiosity are divinity belief, transcend experience, morality pursuit, and institutional participation. Subjects were 711 Chinese Christians(male 296, female 415; 12-76 years of age). The CFA supported the hypothesis of four-factor. CCRS had 19 items(divinity belief, 4 items; transcend experience, 6 items; morality pursuit, 5 items; and institutional participation, 4 items). A significant correlation was found between CCRS and Santa Clara Strength of Religious Faith Questionnaire (r=0.698, p<.01). The internal consistency and two-week test-retest reliability were 0.860, 0.876, respectively.

Time management disposition and gender differences: A study based on Chinese population

Chen, Ying *Dept. of Psychology, Jinan University of Shandong, Jinan, People's Republic of China* **Tong, Yuehua** *Dept. of Psychology, Jinan University of Shandong, Jinan, People's Republic of China*
Time management disposition reflects how individuals control and make use of their time. Time management disposition is composed of three dimensions such as the sense of time value, the sense of time control, and the sense of time efficacy. This variable is considered as a personality trait with multi-dimensions. The study aims at exploring gender differences in time management disposition. 300 university students completed the Time Management Disposition Scale. Results indicated that females scored significantly higher in all three dimensions. Implications of the findings are discussed.

The relationships among Chinese children's home literacy experiences, early literacy acquisition and their later reading performance at school: A longitudinal study

Chen, Xiao *Educational School, Beijing Normal University, Zhuhai, People's Republic of China* **Zhou, Hui** *Psychology, Sun Yat-sen University, Guangzhou, People's Republic of China*
In Study One, 97 first graders' (Mean age =6.5 years, SD = .28) early literacy acquisition (oral vocabulary, Chinese character recognition) were tested before formal school instruction began, and parents reported children's informal and formal literacy experiences at home. Results showed that only informal home literacy experiences predicted oral vocabulary significantly and only formal home literacy experiences predicted Chinese character recognition significantly. In Study Two, 64 children were followed up to the end of the first semester. Results showed that only children's character recognition predicted both of children's final Chinese exam scores and usual performance on the Chinese lessons significantly.

Disappointment in decision-making: Evidence from an ERP study

Chen, Manqi *Dept. of Psychology, Capital Normal University, Beijing, People's Republic of China* **Fang, Ping** *psychology, Capital Normal University, Beijing, People's Republic of China* **Jiang, Yuan** *psychology, Beijing Sport University, Beijing, People's Republic of*

China Li, Yang *Dept. of Psychology, Capital Normal University, Beijing, People's Republic of China*
Previous decision-making researches mostly focus on P300 and feedback negativity(FRN)'s sensitivity to gains-and-losses, but neglect to discuss the relationship between emotion and decision-making. In order to probe it, present study investigates the ERPs' differences between disappointment induced by losses and elation by gains in disappointment study paradigm. Research shows:1)elation's ERPs is wholly more positive than disappointment within 200 milliseconds;2)disappointment elicits greater FRN than elation;3)elation elicits greater P300 than disappointment;4)disappointment increases late positive complex(LPC)'s amplitudes during 400-800 milliseconds at anterior brain. Those results suggest P300 and FRN mainly reflect decision-making's processing, and LPC mostly reflect the relationship between emotion and decision-making.

Temporal cross modal capture of audition and tactile apparent motion

Chen, Lihan *Inst. für Psychologie, Universität München, München, Germany* **Shi, Zhuang hua** *Psychology, Ludwig Maximilian University, Munich, Germany* **Mueller, Hermann** *Psychology, Ludwig Maximilian University, Munich, Germany* **Zhang, Zhijun** *Psychology, Zhejiang University, Hangzhou, People's Republic of China*
In cross modal capture of audition and tactile apparent motion,asynchronous audio captures the apparent tactile apparent motion direction,change the bistable motion to be one dominant direction(-left or right).We have launched three experiments to investigate the audition captures tactile apparent motion in temporal domain.In the first experiment,we use 500ms SOA and 9 levels of delay between audition and tactile stimuli. We replicated this cross modal capture in 400ms SOA condition and eliminate the initial bias with a revised method.In the third experiment,we adopted an adjustment procedure,after adjustment,the one dominant direction of tactile apparent motion is changed to be bi-stable again.

The development of 5-9 years old children's intuitive knowledge about horizontal projectile motion

Chen, Guang *School of Psychology, Beijing Normal University, Beijing, People's Republic of China* **Li, Xiuxun** *School of Psychology, Beijing Normal University, Beijing, People's Republic of China* **Chen, Huichang** *School of Psychology, Beijing Normal University, Beijing, People's Republic of China*
The present study investigated 40 5-9 years old children's intuitive knowledge about the trajectory of horizontal projectile motion through prediction, perceptual judgment, and observation tasks, and found that (1) Children's knowledge can be properly classified as four models, including straight-down model, inverted-L model, slope model, and quasi-parabolic model. (2) 7- and 9-year-olds perform significantly better on perceptual judgment task than they do on prediction task, and this superior performance can be transferred to the following prediction task; 7-year-olds benefit most from perceptual judgment task. (3) Observations of the real dynamic event do result in substantial progress of 5-year olds' performance.

The structure of transactional leadership in China

Chen, Wenjing *and Management, School of Economics, Beijing, People's Republic of China* **Shi, Kan** *Chinaese Academy of Science, institute of psychology, CAS, beijing, People's Republic of China*
Researchers in China found the different structure of transformational leadership, but have not developed the transactional leadership. This study examines data collected from 3,500 manager-subordinate paired participants. EFA, CFA, HRA and

partial correlations were used. The major finings are?firstly, inductive methods showed that transactional leadership is a four dimensions structure includes contingent reward, contingent punishment, process control and anticipated investment. Secondly, the effects of transactional and transformational leadership are different. Transactional leadership could significantly predict intention to leave controlling for transformational leadership, while transformational leadership could significantly predict in-role performance, extra-role performance, satisfaction and leadership effectiveness controlling for transactional leadership.

Performing a concurrent visual task enhances (not impedes) standing stability

Cherng, Rong-Ju *Department of Physical Therapy, National Cheng Kung University, Tainan, Taiwan* **Chao, Wan-Jiun** *Department of Physical Therapy, National Cheng Kung University, Tainan, Taiwan* **Chen, Jenn-Yeu** *Institute of Cognitive Science, National Cheng Kung University, Tainan, Taiwan*
The effect of a concurrent task on standing stability was examined in fourteen adults who performed a visual search task while standing barefooted with feet together on a fixed or compliant support surface. The search task involved eight different set sizes. Results showed that performing the search task improved standing stability. The improvement did not vary with the set size of the search, neither with the type of foot support. The results suggest that standing as a postural task does not compete with a cognitive task. Rather, it is maintained at a level needed for performing the cognitive task.

A new framework for understanding concept

Cheung, Chi Ngai *Dept. Educational Psychology, Hong Kong Chinese University, Hong Kong, China, People's Republic of : Hong Kong SAR*
Concept is not a basic unit of idea, not just representation and algorithm, and much more than categorization. Concept is a phenomenon that should be understood from perspectives like evolution, biological structure and cultural-historical background. I propose a framework attempting to integrate these perspectives, to resolve controversies between existing theories about concept, and to create bridges for these existing theories. In the proposed framework, two external sources of concept are identified, namely immediate environment and external knowledge system. Internal psychological processes are differentiated into explicit and implicit concept levels. How this framework exemplifies a new conceptualization of concept will be discussed in detail.

The effects of immigrant mothers' adjustment on young children's family experiences and learning behaviors

Chin, Jui-Chih *Early Childhood Education, Taipei Municipal Uni. of Educ., Taipei, Taiwan* **Chen, Yin-Ying** *Early Childhood Education, Taipei Municipal Uni. of Educ., Taipei, Taiwan* **Lu, Wen-Yueh** *Early Childhood Education, Taipei Municipal Uni. of Educ., Taipei, Taiwan*
The current study was to investigate life adjustment of immigrant mothers and its effects on family processes and children's learning behaviors. Immigrant mothers of 445 Taiwanese preschool children filled out a questionnaire. Children's learning behaviors were assessed by teachers. Structure equation modeling was conducted. The model indicated that immigrant mothers' self-efficacy in childrearing, perceived support, and cultural accommodation positively influenced the engagement of qualified parent-child interactions. However, all family factors exerted no influence on children's learning behaviors. The results manifested that mothers' adjustment to motherhood and migrant life was influential to children's family experiences. Furthermore, the discontinuity be-

tween family and school experiences deserved educators' efforts for bridging the two in order to empower minority children.

Factor structure and psychometric properties of the Symptom Assessment-45 Questionnaire

Chorot, Paloma Psychology, Universidad Nac. Educ. Dist., Madrid, Spain Sandin, Bonifacio Psychology, Universidad Nac. Educ. Dist., Madrid, Spain Valiente, Rosa M. Psychology, Universidad Nac. Educ. Dist., Madrid, Spain Santed, Miguel A. Psychology, Universidad Nac. Educ. Dist., Madrid, Spain

Psychometric properties of the Spanish Symptom Assessment-45 Questionnaire (SA-45) were examined in a sample of undergraduates. The SA-45 is a 45-item self-report instrument of psychiatric symptomatology derived from the original Symptom Checklist-90 (SCL-90) which assesses each of the same symptom domains as its parent instrument with no item overlap across domains. As expected, exploratory factor analysis supported a structure of 9 factors which corresponds with the nine proposed subscales. Normative data, reliability (internal consistency) and validity were also examined supporting sound psychometric properties. Findings provide support for the use of the SA-45 as a measure of dimensions of psychopathology.

The association among self-injury behavior, emotional intensity, and cognitive processes in patients with mood disorders

Chuang, Ya-Jen Psychiatry, Tri-Service General Hospital, Taipei, Taiwan Huang, San-Yuan Psychiatry, Tri-Service General Hospital, Taipei, Taiwan Lee, Shu-Fen Psychiatry, Tri-Service General Hospital, Taipei, Taiwan Hsia, Yi-Hsin Psychiatry, Tri-Service General Hospital, Taipei, Taiwan

This study explored the association among self-injury behavior, emotional intensity, and cognitive processes in patients with Mood-related Disorders. Subjects completed Emotional Visual Analogue Scales and Stroop Test. Data were analyzed by T-test and Pearson Correlation. In SIB group, intensity of irritability and anxiety was significantly correlated to color interference of reading word (CIRW). In non-SIB group, intensity of euphoria was significantly correlated to CIRW and word interference of naming color. For SIB group, intensity of irritability and anxiety worse function of linguistic process. For non-SIB group, linguistic and non-linguistic processes competed with and interfered each other, following intensity of euphoria.

Sympiified voice fundamental frequency contour as indicator of stress at work

Cicevic, Svetlana Faculty of Transport and Traff, Beograd, Serbia

Voice fundamental frequency contour is (the F0 contour) plays an important role in conveying prosodic, as well as para- and non-linguistic information, and in numerous investigations was proven as an good indicator of physical and emotional state of speaker. In the present study, the simplified F0 contour of air traffic controllers' voice was presented, as a parameter of stress induced by time on duty. Multisyllabic word was chosen as a test-word, thus F0 contours for two basic syllabic nuclei has to be shown. Generally, the end of the working session is characterized by increasing F0 values, as well as ones of the contour realizations. It seems that syllable nuclei are sensitive to various duration of working session.

The influence of place of residence and gender on the self-concept and social skills of Portuguese middle school students

Coelho, Vítor Costa de Caparica, Portugal

This study analyzes the influence of gender and place of residence on self-concept and social skills of Portuguese middle school students (N = 209: 93

male, 116 female; 115 from rural settings, 94 from urban settings). Results showed that students from rural schools presented higher levels of social isolation, social anxiety and lower levels of self-control in social situations, academic, social and family self-concept. Regarding gender girls reported higher levels of consideration for others, social anxiety and family self-concept while boys reported higher emotional self-concept. These extensive differences should be taken into consideration when designing intervention programs for these communities.

Unwanted intrusive thoughts and daily hassles

Combaluzier, Serge Dépt. de Psychologie, Université de Rouen, Mont-Saint-Aignan, France Bouteyre, Evelyne Departement de Psychologie, Universite de Rouen, Mont-Saint-Aignan, France

INTRODUCTION : On a phenomelogical way, there are two kinds of disturbances of the mind : internal phenomena as unwanted intrusive thoughts (UIT) and external phenomena as daily hassles. On an experimental approach, each of these paradigms have been explored in their relationships with mental health and disorders. But the relationships between UIT, daily hassles and mental health have not been explored yet. It will be the aim of this communication.

Variations on maternal control and support practices according to the childs sex

Contreras, Carolina Pruebas y Medición, INEE, México City, Mexico Reyes, Isabel Unidad Investigaciones Psicoso, UNAM, México City, Mexico

The purpose of the study was to determine whether there are significant differences due to the sex of the children on maternal control and support practices. A sample of 302 children attending a public elementary in southern Mexico City and their mothers was evaluated using two scales with 18 items each and alphas of .77 and .92. Significant differences were found for the three factors of the supporting scale, (t=2.429, p=.016; t=2.410, p=.017; t=2.475, p=.014). The control scale showed significant differences only for the inductive factor (t=2.343, p=.020). In both cases, differences were only found in the mothers reports.

Parental restriction and toddlers' intake of unhealthy snacks: The moderating influence of snack food availability

Corsini, Nadia CSIRO Human Nutrition, Adelaide, Australia Wilson, Carlene Human Nutrition, CSIRO, Adelaide BC SA, Australia Kettler, Lisa School of Psychology, University of Adelaide, Adelaide BC SA, Australia Danthiir, Vanessa Human Nutrition, CSIRO, Adelaide BC SA, Australia

Objective: To examine whether snack food availability moderates the relationship between restriction and snack food intake. Method: Sixty-six toddlers (2.3 ± 0.3 years old) were given free access to low energy dense (LED) and high energy dense (HED) snack foods; intake (KJ) of the latter was measured. Parent report questionnaires measured restriction and availability. A hierarchical multiple regression analysis was used to test the interaction. Results: Restriction was a significant predictor of toddlers' ad libitum intake of HED snacks only when availability was high. Conclusions: Research on restriction and children's eating behaviour should examine the context in which restriction occurs.

Parental divorce and depression: The role of the family environment

Cortes Arboleda, Maria Rosario Developmental Psychology, Faculty of Psychology, Granada, Spain Cantón Duarte, José Developmental Psychology, Faculty of Psychology, Granada, Spain Cantón Cortés, David Developmental Psychology, Faculty of Psychology, Granada, Spain

The study investigated the relation of the family system variables with the depression, depending on the home structure. The participants, 147 College student children of divorced families and a comparison group, completed the BDI and the FES. Pearson correlations and logistic regressions analyses were carried out. The Conflicts were related to the scores on depression in all the families. The Organization was related only in the case of children of divorced families, and the Recreational Orientation in the intact families. Explained variance was higher in the case of the divorced families. In summary, some characteristics of the family environment are related to the scores on depression of the children, although these relationships vary depending on the family structure.

Profiles of marital partners' agreement across various areas of the relationship

Cubela Adoric, Vera Dept. of Psychology, University of Zadar, Zadar, Croatia Jurkin, Marina Department of Psychology, University of Zadar, Zadar, Croatia Jurevic, Jelena Department of Psychology, University of Zadar, Zadar, Croatia Ivos, Erma Department of Sociology, University of Zadar, Zadar, Croatia Kamenov, Zeljka Department of Psychology, Faculty of Philosophy, Zagreb, Croatia

The aim of this study was to develop an empirically derived typology of couples using the scores of partners' agreement in the evaluation of various areas of the relationship. Both partners from 183 couples completed a newly developed multidimensional inventory (UPBKO, Cubela Adoric & Jurevic, 2006), which assesses perception of the relationship along twelve dimensions. Cluster analysis of the agreement scores yielded five different patterns or types of marital couples: vitalized, balanced, traditional, disharmonious, and conflicted. In evaluating the present results, comparability with the typologies that were established in previous research programs will be discussed.

The consistency of grammatical gender effect in bare noun production. New evidence from the picture word interference paradigm

Cubelli, Roberto DISCOF, University of Trento, Rovereto (TN), Italy Paolieri, Daniela DISCOF, University of Trento, Rovereto (TN), Italy Lotto, Lorella DPSS, University of Padova, Padova, Italy Job, Remo DISCOF, University of Trento, Rovereto (TN), Italy

The selection of grammatical gender in bare noun production is a controversy issue. In a new series of experiments with the picture-word interference paradigm we confirmed a reliable effect of gender congruency in Italian: Naming times were slower to picture-word pairs sharing the same gender. This effect was independent from the morphological transparency of the distracters, but responses were significantly slower when the distracters were transparent for gender. Overall, the pattern of results of the present study support the notion that grammatical gender is always selected when needed to access the correct nominal ending and the associate inflectional paradigm.

Relation between child's personality characteristics and his/her attachment to kindergarten teacher

Cugmas, Zlatka Slov. Konjice, Slovenia

The purpose of this study was to examine the associations between child's personality characteristics and his/her attachment to kindergarten teacher. 101 children participated in the research. Children's ages ranged from 24 to 74 months. Trained observers filled-in the Child's attachment to his/her kindergarten teacher (Cugmas, 2007) and the Inventory of child individual differences (Zupančič & Kavčič, 2004). More security expressed children, higher scores they had on the subscales considerate, positive emotion, achievement, and compliant. More resistance they expressed, higher scores they had on subscales antagonistic and negative affect. More avoidance they expressed, higher scores they had on antagonistic-subscale.

The role of perceived susceptibility and worry as predictors of helmet and condom use by Spanish adolescents

Cunill Olivas, Monica Dept. of Psychology, University of Girona, Girona, Spain

This study investigated the perceived susceptibility and concern about being infected with the HIV virus or involved in a motorcycle crash in 489 secondary students, and tested whether these were predictors of helmet and condom use. Adolescents felt more susceptible to having a motorcycle crash than becoming infected with HIV, but they felt more worried about becoming infected with the HIV virus than about having a motorcycle crash. Only the level of concern about HIV infection predicted the intention to engage in preventative behaviour. Perceived susceptibility seems to increase with the frequency of the problem, and the degree of concern increased with the perceived seriousness.

Facts and illusions of self-presentational impact of cigarette smoking

Czarna, Anna Kraków, Poland

Objective of the study was to research the influence of gender and smoking status on private naïve theories of female perceptions of male cigarette smokers. The purpose behind it was to indirectly address the issue of self-presentational motives directing potentially addictive behaviours. The online research allowed to cast light upon both solid knowledge, awareness of the self-presentational impact of smoking as well as positive illusions about outcomes of cigarette smoking, held by smokers and nonsmokers. Discussion highlights those among the illusions which might be particularly motivating to enter smoking habit for each of the sexes.

Managerial motives and transformational leadership

Dörr, Stefan Organizational Psychology, A47-Consulting, München, Germany Maier, Günter Organizational Psychology, University of Bielefeld, Bielefeld, Germany

The purpose of this study was to examine the linkage between motives of leaders and perceptions of their transformational leadership behavior. We assessed explicit achievement, power and affiliation motives of leaders (N=81) as well as perceived transformational leadership behavior, influence tactics and employee effectiveness from direct subordinates of the leaders (N=359). Results showed that power motive is positively and achievement motive is negatively related to transformational leadership. The relationship between motives and transformational leadership are moderated by the influence tactic rational argumentation. Finally, transformational leadership is a mediator for the relationship between power motive and employee effectiveness.

The relationship between attitude toward premarital sex and marital satisfaction among married females and males in Tehran.

Dadkhah, Asghar Dept. of Clinical Psychology, University of Welfare & Rehab., Tehran, Islamic Republic of Iran Ghaffari, Fateme ghaffari Dept. of Clinical Psychology, University of Welfare & Re, Tehran, Islamic Republic of Iran Haji Seyd Razi, Hamideh Dept. of Clinical Psychology, University of Welfare & Re, Tehran, Islamic Republic of Iran Ramin, Somayyeh Dept. of Clinical Psychology, University of Welfare & Re, Tehran, Islamic Republic of Iran Asgari, Ali Dept. of Clinical Psychology, University of Welfare & Re, Tehran, Islamic Republic of Iran

The purpose of this research was survey of the relationship between attitude toward premarital sex and marital satisfaction. Four hundred forty six married persons (222 females & 224 males) were selected randomly through multistage sampling from Tehran. The instrument was premarital sex attitude scale created by researches with Chronbach s alpha of 0.91. The second instrument was the revised short form of ENRIC (relied by Asgari & Bahmani for Iranians population in 1385) with Chronbach s alpha of 0.92. Factor analysis validity of attitude scale lead to extraction three factors: premarital simple relationship, positive & negative effects and consequences.

Effects of nonverbal communication in social skills training

Daibo, Ikuo Dept. of Social Psychology, Osaka University, Osaka, Japan Iso, Yukiko Dep of Child Psychology, Tokyo Future University, Tokyo, Japan Tniguchi, Junichi Psychology and Communcation, Osaka International University, Moriguchi, Osaka, Japan

Many people do not possess sufficient skills in daily communication. Therefore, they have little social support each other and have some interpersonal conflicts. They need to improve communication skills. When we encode own messages and decode others' messages in appropriate manner, those communication behaviors lead to activate not only our selves' adaptation but the high performance of many partners in own society. We examined university students' encoding and decoding skills in detecting types of interpersonal relationships in natural settings. The closed and unfamiliar relations- strangers, best friends- than relatives and coworkers were recognized accurately. The accuracy of decoding was correlated positively with encoding skill.

Associations between body dysmorphic symptoms, body image and self-consciousness in a representative population sample

Daig, Isolde Inst. für Med. Psychologie, Charité Berlin, Berlin, Germany Albani, Cornelia Universität Leipzig, Psychosomatic Medicine, Leipzig, Germany Brähler, Elmar Universität Leipzig, Institute of MedicalPsychology, Leipzig, Germany

Body dysmorphic symptoms are characterized by a distressing and impairing preoccupation with an imagined or slight defect in appearance. The study investigates the association between body image and body dysmorphic symptoms by taking self-consciousness into account. A sample of 1621 persons (14-99 years), participated in a German nationwide survey. Women reported more body dysmorphic symptoms and higher self-consciousness than men. People with body dysmorphic symptoms reported a more negative body image and higher self-consciousness. Aspects of self-consciousness moderated the association between body dysmorphic symptoms and negative body image. Results are discussed towards hypotheses of affect modulation and depression tendency.

Error-related responses supporting grammatical plasticity

Davidson, Douglas F. C. Donders Center, Nijmegen, Netherlands Indefrey, Peter Language and Multilingualism, F. C. Donders Center, Nijmegen, Netherlands

The objective of this study was to investigate whether feedback-related electrophysiological activity during language learning is related to improved grammatical discrimination. Twenty native-Dutch speakers classified German noun phrases presented with and without feedback. Without feedback, participants' classification was near chance and did not improve. During training with feedback, P600 responses appeared to declension and gender but not case violations, and classification improved.

A feedback-related negativity appeared in training and later decreased. The results show that error-related responses change during learning, suggesting that they index decision-making processes that occur during grammar acquisition.

Parenting and socio-personal development in contexts of social vulnerability

de la Caba Collado, M. Angeles Methods and Diagnosis in Edu., University of Basque County, San Sebastian, Spain Bartau Rojas, Isabel M.I.D.E., Facultad F.I.C.E., Universidad del País Vasco, San Sebastian, Spain

The aim is to assess an educational program for improving the socio-personal development of minors living in situations of social vulnerability, and the parenting skills of their parents. The sample group comprised both fathers, mothers and minors. 10 families participated in the first phase and 6 participated in the second phase. A pretest-posttest design was used, assessing the process using questionnaires and diaries. Improvements were found in the emotional and cooperation skills of the minors, as well as in parents' ability to respond to their children's needs. The educational intervention helps develop values such as 'learn to care for' in contexts of social vulnerability.

Musical abilities and their relation to cognitive skills and self-concept in 11-to 14-year-old children

Degé, Franziska Inst. für Entw.-Psychologie, Universität Gießen, Gießen, Germany Wehrum, Sina clinical psychology, Justus-Liebig-University, Gießen, Germany Ott, Ulrich BION, Justus-Liebig-University, Gießen, Germany Stark, Rudolf clinical psychology, Justus-Liebig-University, Gießen, Germany Vaitl, Dieter BION, Justus-Liebig-University, Gießen, Germany Schwarzer, Gudrun developmental psychology, Justus-Liebig-University, Gießen, Germany

It is assumed that musical abilities influence non-musical abilities (e.g. intelligence) positively. Our study tested effects of musical abilities on children's specific cognitive abilities and on their self-concept. 63 children (34 girls; 11,7 to 14,6 years) were tested in music perception and production, spatial sense, phonological awareness, attention, sensorimotor-functions, verbal-, visual- and auditory memory and self-concept. Significant associations were found for musical abilities and spatial ability, phonological awareness, attention, visual memory and self-concept. For sensorimotor-functions, verbal and auditory memory no significant relations could be revealed. Our results suggest that musical activity enhances specific cognitive abilities as well as children's self-concept.

Cognitive evaluation in Parkinson's disease

Delgado Suárez, Iván Clinical Neurophysiology, Santiago General Hospital, Santiago de Cuba, Cuba

Background: The cognitive dysfunction in Parkinson disease is still incipient and the reports have been showed contradictory ones. Aims: Objective evaluation the cognitive fuctions in PD recording ERP P300, determing correlations between clinical and electrophysiological variables Methods: Twenty PD patients classified wiht eged bettween 40 and 65 yeasr old, and neurophysiological evaluation by Mini Mental Test. Results: The results are compatible with delay in cognitive processing of the information, a decrease in the intensity of the processes of selective attention and asynchrony in the activation of generators of this potentials in the PD We concluded that ERP P300 is very useful test in objective evaluation of cognitive functions in PD

The role of child care center directors in teachers' return to school

Deutsch, Francine Dept. of Psychology, Mount Holyoke College, South Hadley, USA **Tong, Taryn** Psychology, Mount Holyoke College, South Hadley, USA

Telephone interviews with seventy-eight childcare center directors examined their role in encouraging preschool teachers to pursue higher education. Although directors' educational values and mentoring attitudes were associated with self-reported mentoring, contrary to prediction, mentoring did not mediate teachers' enrollment in college classes. Nonetheless, logistic regressions showed that the more directors valued higher education and the more confident directors were in a targeted teacher's ability, the more likely she was to be taking college classes. Directors' impact on the educational pursuits of their teaching staff suggests that the workplace is an under-researched, critical context for the educational trajectories of nontraditional students.

Trauma and positive health: The complete state model of health

Diaz, Dario Dept. of Social Psychology, Universidad Autonoma de Madrid, Madrid, Spain **Blanco, Amalio** Social Psychology, Universidad Autonoma de Madrid, Madrid, Spain

Objetives. The Complete-State-Model of Health (CSMH) considers mental health as a syndrome of symptoms of hedonia and positive functioning. In this study we have take the CSMH as theoretical framework for the study of traumatic events. Methods. 42 victims of 11-M terrorist attack filled in questionnaries assessing PTSD and positive health. Results. Exploratory-confirmatory factor analyses support that PTSD and mental health form two different factors. Only one victim was diagnosed as healthy although 9 participants did not show the disorder. Conclusion. Rather than forming a single bipolar dimension, health and illness are correlated unipolar dimensions. The presence of mental health require a positive personal and social functioning.

Depression in epilepsy

Diaz Martinez, Carina Clinical Neurophysiology, General Hospital, Guantanamo, Cuba **Diaz Martinez, Annia** Internal Medicine Department, General Hospital, Guantanamo, Cuba

OBJECTIVES: Estimate the frequency of depression in patients with epilepsy and to correlate patient characteristics with the degree of depression. METHODS: 51 patients were asked to complete a questionnaire. Depression scores were assessed. ANOVA test was used in statistical analysis. RESULTS: 39% had major depression. Seizure-free patients had lower depression scores. Depression scores were not related to the number, type of antiepileptic drugs or epilepsy type. One-half of depressed patients were not on antidepressant medication. CONCLUSIONS: Depression is a common condition in epilepsy patients. A better diagnosis and treatment of should be reached.

Visual-spatial layout contributes to unimanual coordination

Dietrich, Sandra Inst. für Psychologie, Max-Planck-Institut, Leipzig, Germany **Rieger, Martina** Psychology, Max Planck Institute CBS, Leipzig, Germany **Prinz, Wolfgang** Inst. für Psychologie, Max-Planck-Institut, Leipzig, Germany

Is unimanual coordination of movements with external events based on the actual movement or on the way movement effects are embedded in the environment? Participants coordinated their movements with a circular moving stimulus. The relation of movement effects to external events was varied by placing movement effect and stimulus trajectory either next to each other (Experiment 1) inside each other (Experiment 2) or on top of each other (Experiment 3). In the experiments different co-ordination modes were of advantage. We argue that the way movement effects are embedded in the environment is crucial for unimanual coordination with external events.

Criteria for choosing romantic partners relative to gender and relationship status

Dinic, Bojana Novi Sad, Serbia

The aim of this research was to examine gender and relationship status (in a relationship or not) differences considering the criteria for choosing romantic partners, which were assessed by the KIP110 questionnaire (Dinic, 2005). Combining gender and relationship status, four groups of participans were created. Two discriminant functions were singled out: 1. separates female from male participans, showing that females prefer more similar interests and competence in their partners; 2. showing that the participans who are in a relationships prefer more emotions and connivance and social status and similar origin from those who are not.

Generalized quantifiers in natural language

Druzhinin, Georgy IEAP, Moscow, Russia

In any language some words reflect the idea of graduation. Such words as "almost", "most of..." etc. that express the idea of some part of any thing or group can be named as generalized quantifiers. Such words as "very", "too", "rather" etc. reflect the idea of multiplication of certain feelings or efforts. Simple experiments (made with Russian-language and bilingual subjects) show the statistically stable qualitative interpretation of such quantitative graduation values and individual trends in it under certain changes in psychological state (fatigue etc.). These results could explain the actual subjective significance and correct the evaluations by psychometric scales.

Transformations of students; mental state in students years

Druzhinina, Elena IEAP, Moscow, Russia

Longitude study of Russian university students' mentality showed systematic transformations during education time. Some aspects of students' motivation to professional education under conditions of modern information and education technologies in various periods of students' years will be discussed as important factors of these transformations. Many of these transformations are caused by cognitive dissonances that appear after gained information verification with the modern information technologies. Variants of cognitive-based neurotization, its predictors and its manifestations in aberrant and deviant behavior as frequent results to certain motivation issues will be discussed just as recommendations for coping such negative consequences and after-effects.

How social influence in leadership dyads is mediated by self-determination when subordinates are treated with consideration

Eckloff, Tilman Inst. für Sozialpsychologie, Universität Hamburg, Hamburg, Germany **van Quaquebeke, Niels** Social Psychology, University of Hamburg, Hamburg, Germany

The results of the Ohio Studies suggest that considerate leadership behaviour is one important source of leadership effectiveness (for recent review see Judge, Piccolo, & Ilies, 2004). Moreover, empirical research in the framework of Self-Determination Theory shows that increasing subordinates' self-determination will lead to positive outcomes, such as performance enhancement (Deci & Ryan, 2000). In the present study, we link both perspectives and, specifically in two field studies (N1 = 563 and N2 = 596), we show that the relation between consideration and subordinates' openness towards leader influence is partially mediated by the satisfaction of subordinates' intrinsic needs for self-determination.

Rhythmic closure in music perception

Edelman, Laura Dept. of Psychology, Muhlenberg College, Allentown, USA **Helm, Patricia** Allentown, USA **Kussmaul, Clif** Psychology, Muhlenberg College, Allentown, PA, USA

A series of studies investigated the role of rhythmic patterns on the perception of closure in music. Percussive sounds were presented in patterns that varied by the number of repetitions, whether the pattern ended in a long or short note, whether each measure was begun by a dynamic accent, and the placement of a triplet within the measure. We compared the results of trained musicians with non-musicians. We found a greater degree of closure for even numbers of repetitions, for patterns ending in longer notes, and generally stronger results for musicians than non-musicians. The dynamic accent had no effect

Relationship between thyroid hormones and obesity in 15 to 49 years old depressed women

Eftekhari, Mohammad Hassan Nutrition, Shiraz University, Shiraz, Islamic Republic of Iran **Ahmadi, Mehdi** Nutrition, Shiraz University, Shiraz, Islamic Republic of Iran **Firoozabadi, Ali** Psychology, Shiraz University, Shiraz, Islamic Republic of Iran **Soveid, Mahmood** Endocrinology, Shiraz University, Shiraz, Islamic Republic of Iran

Background: The involvement of the thyroid hormones is generally believed to be important in the aetiopathogenesis of depression and obesity. Aim: To investigate thyroid profile in depressed women and depressed obese women. Methods: A total 60 subjects (depressed women and depressed obese women) were selected. Serum samples were collected and assayed for thyroid indices. Results: Comparison of thyroid hormone indices revealed no significant differences between two groups. Conclusion: There were not any significant association between thyroid profiles and obesity in depressed obese women.

The entry point of face recognition: The basic level and/or the subordinate level?

Endo, Mitsuo Dept. of Human Sciences, University of the Ryukyus, Nishiharacho, Japan

We addressed the entry point in face recognition. If the entry point in face recognition would not be at the basic level but at the subordinate level of unique identity, face recognition at the basic level could be achieved by a search through semantic memory. The results of experiment did not yield a significant positive correlation between naming pictures and words at the basic level for faces, suggesting that the same process was not used to name pictures and words at the basic level for faces. Thus the entry point at the basic level of faces should still exist.

Motor learning affects neural processing of visual perception

Engel, Annerose Allg.Physiologische Psy., Philipps-Uni. Marburg Psy., Marburg, Germany **Burke, Michael** Psychology, Philipps-University Marburg, Marburg, Germany **Fiehler, Katja** Psychology, Philipps-University Marburg, Marburg, Germany **Bien, Siegfried** Neuroradiology, Philipps-University Marburg, Marburg, Germany **Rösler, Frank** Psychology, Philipps-University Marburg, Marburg, Germany

We investigated whether motor learning has an influence on how observed movements are later processed by neural networks dedicated to movement execution and perception. While watching artificial object movements, ten participants imitated the trajectories with their hands and ten participants solved a working-memory task. After that, the hemodynamic responses were recorded while participants observed artificial object movements. Motor-related brain areas (supplementary motor area, inferior parietal lobe) responded more in the motor experienced than in the memory group. This shows that movement training affects movement perception, and that neural networks related to motor execution are also triggered by artificial, non-biological movements.

Autonomous agents with personality

Enz, Sibylle Inst. für Allg. Psychologie, Universität Bamberg, Bamberg, Germany Zoll, Carsten Inst. für Allg. Psychologie, Universität Bamberg, Bamberg, Germany Ho, Wan Ching School of Computer Science, University of Hertfordshire, Hatfield, United Kingdom Schaub, Harald Human Sciences, University of Bamberg, Bamberg, Germany Lim, Mei Yii School of Mathematical and Com, Heriot-Watt University, Edinburgh, Germany

The presented work aims at enhancing an existing agent architecture with a set of basic needs in order to reflect personality differences on the level of autonomous agent behaviour. The model is implemented and evaluated in the context of a virtual learning application ("ORIENT") for small groups of users (teenagers), providing them with the opportunity to learn about commonalities and differences between cultures, about reasons for intercultural and interpersonal conflicts and how to resolve them, and thus enhancing their intercultural sensitivity. Moreover, the evaluation focuses on the cooperative learning process while interacting with the software.

Love styles and relationship longevity

Erwin, Philip Social and Psycholog. Science, Edge Hill University, Ormskirk, United Kingdom

Objective: to examine the relationship between love styles and the longevity of romantic relationships. Method: 82 participants provided details of their current personal relationships and completed the Hendrick et al. (1998) Love Attitudes Scale. Partial correlations, controlling for age, showed that relationship longevity was correlated with scores on the Pragma love style for males ($r = .37$, $p < .05$) and the Mania love style for females ($r = -.29$, $p < .05$). Conclusions: The results will be interpreted with reference to existing literature on gender differences in styles of interaction and behaviour in close romantic relationships.

Psychological Obstacles' contributing to recruiting female employees into managerial positions at companies affiliated to Energy Ministry of Iran

Esbati, Zinat Psychology and Education, Tehran University, Tehran, Islamic Republic of Iran Gharavian, Ahmad Human Resource Development, Energy ministry, Tehran, Islamic Republic of Iran

The purpose of present research was to ascertain the most important psychological and sociological obstacles contributing to recruiting women employees in managerial position in companies affiliated to Energy Ministry (EM) of Iran. 1180 female employees and 171 men managers from companies affiliated to EM completed Women Employees Questionnaire ($\alpha=0.82$), and Managers' Questionnaire ($\alpha=0.92$). The results indicated that women' level of being extrovert and achievement motivation were low. The results also revealed managers' negative attitude toward women' power at work, and their positive attitude toward traditional roles discrimination between men and women. The level of being extrovert and achievement motivation could be interpreted in terms of sociological obstacles.

Psychological wellbeing's model in the vision of Islam's prophet and holly infallibles

Faghihi, Ali Naghi Human Sciences' Faculty, Qom University, Qom, Islamic Republic of Iran

Aim is, to discover psychological wellbeing's model from Islamic hadiths. Method is hermeneutic with analyzing of Islamic hadiths' content for reaching to above aim. Findings: Psychological wellbeing has some levels. First is inexistency of any disorder in his psychological system and next is, optimizing and upgrading the vision and affection, and developing of personality in all aspects related to self and Allah Almighty and people and nature. Conclusion: Each person that has more human perfection, has more psychological wellbeing.

The comparison of dysfunctional thoughts and social adjustment among infertile employed and unemployed women in Iran

Fatemi, Azadeh Sadat family counseling, Welfare and Rehabilitation Uni, Tehran, Islamic Republic of Iran

In this research the effects of occupation on dysfunctional thoughts and social adjustment among infertile women were explored. We chose 240 infertile women utilizing cluster random sampling method. Women filled dysfunctional thoughts and social adjustment questionnaires. MANOVA analysis was performed to analyze data. Results demonstrate that dysfunctional thoughts in infertile unemployed women were far more than those in employed women. Also social adjustment in infertile women with occupation was more than those without occupation ($F=42.9$, $P<0.01$). Occupation status of infertile employed women in interaction with their education, affects rate of dysfunctional thoughts ($F=5.5$, $P<0.01$), whereas it does not have significant effect on social adjustment.

The pride of Chinese urban poverty adolescents

Feng, Xiaohang Chang Chun, People's Republic of China Zhang, Xiangkui Psychology Department, Research Center of Child Devel, Chang Chun City, People's Republic of China

Abstract: Objectives This study aims to explore the feeling of pride and the other related factors about the Chinese urban poverty adolescents.Methods 400 Chinese urban poverty students and 334 urban common students were tested through three questionaries. Analysis of variance and stepwise regression were adopted. Results The experiencing level on pride of urban poverty adolescents was lower than urban common adolescents. Regression analysis showed that global self-esteem, academic self-esteem and social self-esteem played significant prediction effects on pride. Conclusions The positive emotions such as pride can improve the development of mental healthy of Chinese urban poverty adolescents.

The dyadic regulation of closeness and reciprocity in couples living in different family types

Flaig, Katherina Humboldt-Universität zu Berlin, Berlin, Germany Neyer, Franz J. Persönlichkeitspsychologie, Universität Potsdam, Potsdam, Germany Wrzus, Cornelia Persönlichkeitspsychologie, Universität Potsdam, Potsdam, Germany

Marital relationships in middle adulthood provide a basis for differential parental care and mutual cooperation. Longitudinal dyadic approaches were used in this research to investigate the dynamics of interdependence between spouses from traditional families, patchwork-families, motivated childless and involuntary childless couples. The 171 couples were studied twice over a 12 months interval. Due to diverging necessity of cooperation and parental care the dyads showed differential relationship patterns, with couples in patchwork-families showing the highest levels of interdependence in emotional closeness and reciprocity.

Analysis of artificial concepts formation in children of different socio-cultural levels

Flores, Dulce Dept. de Psicología, Universidad Autónoma de Puebla, Puebla, Mexico Talizina, Nina Psicología, Statal University of Moscow, Moscow, Russia

339 mexican school children of both sexes from different socio-economic levels (6-9 years), were evaluated with The Protocol of formation of new concept (Flores 2002). The statistical and cualitative analysis shows differences. 105 children (30.97%) had acquired the action of formation of concept: 11 native children have it (15.94%), 20 rural children (22.22%), 30 lower urban children (33.33%), and 44 urban children (48.89%). The analysis of variance shows significant differences between the four groups analized (One way ANOVA F (8.048) p<=0.000). Discussion realized on the terms of the social context, of the characteristics of each population and the intellectual development.

A comparison of family content and processes of families with and without handicapped children

Fooladchang, Mahboobe Dept. Educational Psychology, Shiraz University, Shiraz, Islamic Republic of Iran Zakerian, Mojtaba Dept of Exceptional Children, Shiraz University, Shiraz, Islamic Republic of Iran

The aim of this study was to compare family content and processes of Iranian families with and without handicapped children. 120 families (27 families with handicapped & 93 families without handicapped children) responded to the scales of Family Content and Processes. The results of One-way ANOVA revealed that families with handicapped children scored significantly lower than families without handicapped children on family processes. For family content, the results were the same as family processes. Overall, this study showed the effects of the presence of handicapped children on family content and processes. Keywords: family processes, family content, handicapped children's family, handicapped children.

EEG alpha oscillations and object recognition

Freunberger, Roman Department of Psychology, University of Salzburg, Salzburg, Austria Klimesch, Wolfgang Department of Psychology, University of Salzburg, Salzburg, Austria

In the present study, we investigate the role of upper alpha oscillations for semantic access and retrieval processes. Subjects were presented trains of distorted pictures (with decreasing levels of distortion), and were asked to respond as quickly as possible when they recognize the meaning of the picture. Preliminary results show that during the time window of picture recognition, upper alpha power decreased but inter-areal phase synchronization increased as compared to meaningless control pictures. We assume that synchronous alpha oscillations might reflect topographically specific neural network activity that is related to the access of semantic information in LTM.

Mental disease perception for psychotic patient families

Frischenbruder, Sandra Servico Psicologia - Clinica, Feevale - UFRGS, Poa, Brazil

Objective In Brazil, the programs regarding family support in public mental health services are not enough to provided information and emotional support. The study investigated the conceptions and the meanings about the mental disorder of the parents of patients with psychosis. METHOD This was a qualitative, descriptive study. The content of semi-structured interviews was interpreted in psychoanalytic perspective. RESULTS: The results revealed that the family conception about the mental disease is related to a problem of social and the synonym of incapacity. The cure conception is related to the recovery of productive abilities and the remission symptoms.

Color activation of non color words through Spanish idiomatic expressions

Fuentes, Luis Jose Murcia, Spain Bretones, Carmen Filología Inglesa y Alemana, Universidad de Almería, Almería, Spain

Perceptual symbol systems predict that perceptual information is represented in language comprehension. When referents change, their representations are affected accordingly. Here we extended the predictions of the perceptual symbol hypothesis to linguistic material whose referents do not have perceptual properties in real world but they do through association with idiomatic expressions. We used a Stroop-like task in which target words that were indirectly associated to colors (e.g., royalty is blue because its association with "blue blood"), appeared in congruent or incongruent colors. Results showed Stroop interference effects, supporting the perceptual symbol account and extending it to representation of idiomatic language

How do players decide rational strategies in actual games?

Fukuda, Ichiro Faculty of Business Administra, Setsunan university, Neyagawa, Japan Shimizu, Jun Department of Psychology, Konan Women's university, kobe, Japan Yamamoto, Masayo Faculty of Human studies, Jin-ai university, takefu, Japan Monden, Kotaro Faculty of Industrial Society, Ritsumeikan university, kyoto, Japan

We conducted two-person zero sum games which have different equilibriums and mixed strategies to explain how players decide their strategies, and to examine psychological effects of minimax and maximin strategies. Method: College students (N=352) were divided into two groups and played different games 30 times. Result: Players planned on using maximin strategies, not minimax strategies, as expected according to game theories. Conclusion: Minimax strategies are difficult to use because they depend on the opponent's payoff. The students seemed to be in conflict about using maximax and minimax strategies, and to hesitate in changing their strategies while playing games.

The relationship between Mobile phone mail and cognition of interpersonal relationship-Perceived social support as a mediator-

Furutani, Kaichiro Social and Clinical psycholofy, Hijiyama University, Hiroshima, Japan Nishimura, Takashi Dep.of Clinical psychology, Hiroshima International univ., Higahihiroshima, Japan

In this research, we considered the relationship between Mobile phone mail use and cognition of interpersonal relationship by mediate factor social support. Scholar discussed relationship of interpersonal relationship and mobile phone use (e. g., Furutani & Sakata, 2006). Furutani and Sakata (2006) showed mobile phone use was correlated fulfillment of interpersonal relationship. We focused on three interpersonal cognition elements (fulfillment, intimacy and trust) and cognition of received social support as mediate factor. A pass analysis showed that Mobile phone mail use intimacy and social support directly. And, Cognition of received social support mediated Mobile phone use and fulfillment and trust.

Relationship between PTSD symptoms, physical health and pain diagnosis: The role of hyperarousal symptoms and depression

Gómez Pérez, Lydia Personalidad, Evaluac. y Trab., Universidad de Málaga, Málaga, Spain Flor, Herta Department of Clinical and Cog, University of Heidelberg, Cent, Mannheim, Germany Wessa, Michàle Department of Clinical and Cog, University of Heidelberg, Cent, Mannheim, Germany

Three-hundred- thirteen subjects with a history of traumatic experience were interviewed (1) to explore the contribution of PTSD symptoms in the prediction of physical health and pain diagnosis and (2) to test the hypothesis that depression mediates the relationship between PTSD symptoms and physical health, likewise the relationship between PTSD symptoms and pain diagnosis. Regression analysis showed that, after controlling for depression, only hyperarousal symptoms predicted physical health. Mediation analysis indicated that hyperarousal was directly and indirectly (through depression) related with physical health. The effects of PTSD symptoms on pain diagnosis were fully mediated by depression. These results support the suggestion that in its relation with PTSD, pain seems different from other health outcomes.

The effects of supervisor – subordinate personality similarity and role behavior on team performance

Gabrane, Liva Dept. of Psychology, University of Latvia, Riga, Latvia

Aims of the study are, to examine the effect of supervisor – subordinate personality trait similarity and complementarity on team performance and test, whether role behavior mediates the relationship between supervisor - subordinate personality similarity and team performance in client service teams within a finance organization. The measures: NEO PI-R for personality traits, SYMLOG Adjective Rating Form for role behavior and organizational performance criteria for team performance. Statistical method: multilevel regression analysis. Expected results: team performance can be predicted by supervisor – subordinate complementarity on extraversion and similarity on conscienscious-ness, agreeableness and neuroticism. Roles mediate the relationship between personality and team performance.

Family context and the development of theory of mind in a sample of 5-year-old children from the Basque country

Galende, Nuria Basic Psychological Processes, Basque Country University, San Sebastián, Spain Sánchez de Miguel, Manuel Basic Psychological Processes, Basque Country University, San Sebastián, Spain Arranz Freijo, Enrique Basic Psychological Processes, Basque Country University, San Sebastián, Spain

The objective of this study was to analyse the influence of family context in the development of 50 preschoolers Theory of Mind (ToM). Data were collected through interviews with children in the school, interviews with parents, systematic observation at home and questionnaires filled in by parents and tutors. Results show a significant relationship between family context variables and performance in ToM tasks. These results have important educative implications, as far as family context can be improved through intervention.

Stepping out of an American context: Defining spirituality and religiousness from a French Canadian perspective

Gall, Terry Lynn Faculty of Human Sciences, Saint Paul University, Ottawa, Canada Malette, Judith Faculty of Human Sciences, Saint Paul University, Ottawa, Canada Guirguis Younger, Manal Faculty of Human Sciences, Saint Paul University, Ottawa, Canada

This qualitative study explored 25 French Canadians' definitions of spirituality and religiousness. Spirituality was defined in more positive, personal, "secular" humanistic terms that encompassed 5 themes: connection to God, guide to life, meaning, sense of self and sense of universality. Religiousness was narrowly confined to three aspects of organized religion: adherence to a religion, the use of religious gestures and connection to God. As such, religious-

ness provoked more negative connotations of authority, control, and oppression. In comparison to American studies, French Canadians make a clearer distinction between their experience of a personal spirituality and the "man-made" laws of religions.

The effect of age, gender and education on the attitude of ethnicity in Golestan Province, Iran

Ganji Jamehshoorani, Ghorbanali Humanity, Islamic Azad University, Azadshahr, Islamic Republic of Iran Ganji, Mohamad Reza Humanity, Islamic Azad University, Azadshahr, Islamic Republic of Iran

The main objective in this paper was to study the effect of age, gender, and education on the attitude of these ethnics towards one another. Distribution Tables, Chi-Square, and Z-Test were analytical tools in this paper. Cluster sampling and Cochran formula were employed in the selection of sample and sample size for each ethnic group Major conclusions reached are as follow: 1) Age does not pose statistically significant effect on the attitude of ethnics towards one another. 2) Neither gender nor education exerts statistically significant influence on the ethnic attitudinal changes towards one another.

Relations between interparental discord, problem behaviors and peer adaptation in school of 7-year-old Chinese children

Gao, Wen Psychology School, Beijing Normal University, Beijing, People's Republic of China Chen, Hui-chang Psychology School, Beijing Normal University, Beijing, People's Republic of China

Few researches pay attention to occasional, moderate interparental discord's influences on children in average families. In a longitudinal study to a higher-income sample of China's urban children from 1995, 103 children's problem behaviors, peer adaptation in school and parental disagreements were investigated when they were 7 years old, separately based on parents' and teachers' reports on scales. Although less frequent and intense interparental discord in average families predicted children's internalizing and physical problems, it didn't predict children's externalizing problems and had positive relations with peer adaptation in school. These could be explained by children's limited cognition ability and specific content of interparental disagreement, and provide some implications for family intervention and peer adjustment.

Jealousy, relationship and infidelity: Modulated variable

García Leiva, Patricia Psicología Social, Uniservidad de Málaga, Málaga, Spain Canto, Jesús Psicología Social, Uniservidad de Málaga, Málaga, Spain Gómez-Jacinto, Luis Psicología Social, Uniservidad de Málaga, Málaga, Spain

This study aims the understanding of differences between woman and men in situations of hypothetic infidelity (emotional or sexual) and how this emotion is influenced by characteristics envolved in couple relationship. 372 subjects choose which of two possible infidelity situations causes a larger emotional distress. They have completed a questionnaire about theirs relationships characteristics too. The data show that women experienced a higher intensity of emotional distress when they think about the emotional and sexual infidelity. The results also revealed that both men and women are more worried about emotional infidelity, although these results are modulated by relationships characteristics. Keywords: jealousy, emotional infidelity, sexual infidelity, emotions

The measurement of drivers' mental workload and physiological state: A simulation-based study

Ge, Yan *Institute of Psychology,CAS, Beijing, People's Republic of China* **Zhang, Kan** *Psychology, Institute of Psychology,CAS, Beijing, People's Republic of China*

The purpose of this study was explored the probability of using physiological indices as feedback of different driving conditions. 43 drivers completed a simulated car-following task which was used to evaluate how a secondary task affected their response to a periodically braking lead vehicle. A baseline condition with no secondary task was compared to a simple and a complex secondary task conditions. The results showed some physiological indices (HRV and HR) reflected drivers' conditions. Subjective workload ratings also indicated secondary task introduced a significant cognitive load. This study provided support for developing devices monitoring drivers' physiological and psychological conditions.

Effects of chromatic distributions and pedestal contrast on chromatic discrimination

Giesel, Martin *Inst. für Allg. Psychologie, Universität Gießen, Gießen, Germany* **Hansen, Thorsten** *General Psychology, Justus-Liebig-University, Giessen, Germany* **Gegenfurtner, Karl** *Inst. für Psychologie, Universität Gießen, Gießen, Germany*

We investigated the interplay between the effects of chromatic distributions and adaptation on chromatic discrimination thresholds. Using a four-alternative forced-choice procedure increment and decrement threshold vs. contrast curves were measured for various pedestals along one test direction in DKL color space. The stimuli were either homogeneously colored disks, or stimuli whose chromaticities were modulated along the test direction symmetrically around the mean chromaticity of the pedestal. The results indicate that the effects of the pedestals and of the chromatic distributions are additive. We show that a model with multiple higher level chromatic mechanisms can describe the data well.

Guilty, altruism and self-esteem in the helping behavior

Goncalves, Gabriela *Psicologia, Universidade do Algarve, Faro, Portugal* **Santos, Joana** *Psicologia, Universidade do Algarve, Faro, Portugal* **Gomes, Alexandra** *Psicologia, Universidade do Algarve, Faro, Portugal* **Viegas, Mélanie** *Psicologia, Universidade do Algarve, Faro, Portugal* **Boeiro, Helena** *Psicologia, Universidade do Algarve, Faro, Portugal*

This study intended to observe if the manipulation of guilt has an effect on helping behaviour. It was also our interest to observe if the level of altruism and the state self-esteem have an effect in helping behaviour. It was congregated a sample of 136 participants. It was used the self report altruism scale, a task and the state self-esteem scale. The results allowed us the observation of an effect of guilt in helping behaviour. Likewise, the female participants were the one's that helped more. We observed also meaningful differences at the altruism level in state self-esteem.

The writing superiority effect: Advantages of written knowledge recall

Grabowski, Joachim *Inst. für Psychologie, Pädagog. Hochschule Heidelberg, Heidelberg, Germany*

The writing superiority effect says that knowledge diagnosis has higher content validity in the written than in the oral recall mode. We report on two experiments demonstrating the effect's range and strength. A group of high-performing, highly selected air-force candidates recalled the states of the U.S.A., a group of students recalled Germany's national holidays either orally or written. In both studies, written recall was superior (ANOVA; p < .05) to oral recall, compared to a cued-recall post-

test for maximal knowledge assessment. Thus, it is generally important to consider the verbal recall mode in exams and knowledge assessment contexts.

Dietary restraint, eating behaviour and food palatability: Implications for binge eaters

Griffin, Tara *Toormina, Australia* **Provost, Stephen** *Psychology, Southern Cross University, Toormina, Australia*

200 non-diabetic participants' (26-30 yrs, SD = 2.10; 59 male & 137 female) dietary restraint and food palatabilty was measured by the Restraint Scale (Herman & Polivy, 1975), Three-Factor Eating Questionnaire (Westenhoefer et al., 1994) and the Food Palatability Questionnaire (Griffin, 2006). It was expected that people high in dietary restraint will have a greater finickiness to unpalatable food types, compared to low restrained eaters. The main findings from a factor analysis, were that they did not differ in the liking for the six food types, but between certain individual foods from a range of the taste types.

Desirable leadership behaviours in Romanian gendarmerie

Grigoras, Mihaela *Centr. for Psychosociology, Ministry of Interior, Bucharest, Romania*

The rationale of this paper was to identify perceptions of successful leadership behaviours in Romanian Gendarmerie, given the specific of the organization and the kind of service provided. The study reports and compares preferred leadership traits and traits actual exhibited by leaders in a Gendarmerie unit, as defined by responses to the Leader Behaviour Description Questionnaire XII (Stogdill, 1963). The sample consisted of 96 commissioned and non-commissioned officers. Factor scores showed significant differences (p<0.01) between preferred and actual leader behaviours, except for scales Role Assumption and Production Emphasis. Results indicate that Gendarmerie leaders are not perceived as generally exhibiting desired behaviours and can be used in leadership training.

Behavioral strategy at divorce

Grishunina, Elena *Moscow, Russia*

The goal - gender features of behavior at divorce, distinctions of strategies divorce initiator. Methods - the phenomenological analysis of personality-situational interaction, the interviewing, the content-analysis, the correlation analysis. The examinees: 105 clients of Hot line «Divorce» and medical centers'. Results (statistically significant, p<0,01) - the behavior of divorces initiators' differs in stability more often, consciousness of behavior is extremely high; men's strategy are socially comprehensible (acceptable), however they are not aimed at core of situation, they estimate own behavior as habitual. While women unstable strategy, the range of activity is small.

Anorexia and bulimia nervosa in Mexican high school students

Guadarrama, Rodalinda *CU UAEM Temascaltepec, UAEM, Tejupilco, Mexico*

The objetive was to determine the anorexia and bulimia nervosa that are present in highschool students, so that, it was worked with the whole population. These were 316 people, both sex, of Mexico. The instruments: the Bulit Test, wich is used to detect bulimia's symptomatology. And the Eating Attitudes Test, wich is used to detect anorexia's symptoms. The results show that a considerable percentage of 17% from population presented eating disorders symptoms, predominating anorexia. This facts allows to conclude that due the expose in the literature, a considerable percentaje of teenagers from exterios zones to the large cities are beging prone to these kind of disorders.

The book as mediator in the study of insult: A Mexican experience

Guerra, Elida *Psychology, UAQ, Queretaro, Mexico*

This article suggests an empirical approach to raise awareness of the problem of bullying at schools through the use of disturbed readings. A children's tale, a wooden boy who mutilate himself in order to be accepted by others, encouraged children and teenagers from 6 to 14 years old to talk about the pressure to conform an "ideal" identity. Our findings showed that whereas insults received inside family hurt children the most, insults between peers regarding to physical characteristics and those made by teachers about students intelligence and attitudes, force individuals to change themselves in order to conform.

Structure and measurement of Taoist personality

Guo, Yongyu *School of Psychology, Huazhong Normal University, Wuhan, People's Republic of China*

This study proposed Taoist Personality, and explored the correlation between Taoist personality and well-being. College students were invited to grade five Taoists' characters on the revised personality adjective scale, and six dimensions of Taoist Personality were found through exploratory factor analysis. Then, Taoist Personality Inventory was compiled to further explore the structure of Taoists' typical personality. The inventory has 25 items scattered on the six factors named as wisdom, charity, maturation, sturdiness, straightforwardness and glamour. Multiple regression analysis showed a relatively high correlation between Taoist personality and well-being. Sturdiness and straightforwardness were shown to directly affect well-being.

Teacher leadership and attitude toward education reform in Indonesia

Hadjam, M. Noor Rochman *Psychology, Gadjah Mada University, Yogyakarta, Indonesia* **Widhiarso, Wahyu** *Psychology, Gadjah Mada University, Yogyakarta, Indonesia*

Teachers become more aware of and concerned about school-wide issues. They discuss possible solutions and act to make changes. All of these behaviors where teachers are going above are forms of leadership. Leadership, then, does not only refer to administration. This study was conducted to investigate relationship between leadership characteristics and attitude toward change within context education reform. A data was collected to 180 teachers from 45 province in Indonesia. Research suggest that leadership had an effect on the teacher positive attitude toward education reform and their commitment to professional learning community.

Religious coping and adjustment to stressful life events

Hagemann, Tim *Fachhochschule der Diakonie, Bielefeld, Germany* **Caston, A. T.** *Department of Psychology, University of Denver, Denver, USA* **Shallcross, A. J.** *Department of Psychology, University of Denver, Denver, USA* **Mauss, I. B.** *Department of Psychology, University of Denver, Denver, USA*

The study was designed to test the hypothesis that religious coping is associated with positive adjustment to stressful live events (SLE). Eighty females aged 18-60 who had recently experienced SLE (divorce, illness, or death of a relative) took part in the study. Participants completed several questionnaires, including impact of recent SLEs, depressive symptoms, affective states, and religious coping. Results indicate that religious coping has a protective effect on self-reported depressive symptoms and on affective states in the aftermath of SLEs, such that no religious coping was associated with lower well-being than all other levels of religious coping

A longitudinal study for adolescents' parent-oriented self construal in China

Haimei, Wang Center for Deaf Children, China Rehabilitation Research, Beijing, People's Republic of China

354 junior-high-school students in grade 7 (171 male and 183 female) as the subjects were selected from two high schools in Beijing. Three waves tests have been taken in one year longitudinal study which included a series tests for the students and their teachers. Results: (1)Both the parent-oriented self-construal have the ascend trend from grade 7 to grade 8. (2)There was no significant difference between boys and girls in the two kinds of students' self-construal. (3)The developmental trend of different parent-oriented self-construal levels' students are different, which the high level group was ascending, the low level group was descending, and the middle level group keep stable development.

How can justice conflicts be deescalated? Evaluation of two intervention techniques

Halmburger, Anna Inst. für Psychologie, University Koblenz-Landau, Landau, Germany *Baumert, Anna* Psychology, University Koblenz-Landau, Landau, Germany *Nazlic, Tanja* Psychology, Ludwig-Maximilians University, München, Germany *Schmitt, Manfred* Psychology, University Koblenz-Landau, Landau, Germany

We evaluated two intervention techniques for deescalating social conflict: In a conflict about the distribution of tuition fees among two university faculties, general empathy induction was compared with a specific justice intervention aiming at reducing feelings of injustice. Ninety students filled in questionnaires on how their tuition fees should be used. Mediated by decreased anger, general and specific intervention increased the willingness to share tuition fees with the other faculty. After empathy induction, participants perceived the request to keep tuition fees for the own faculty as more unjust while after specific intervention, participants perceived the requests of both faculties as equally justified.

The effect of abacus and mental arthimetic on intelligence development among primary school pupils in Khartoum state

Hamza, Alya Faculty of Arts- Psychology, khartoum University, khartoum, Sudan

This study aimed at examining the effect of abacus training and mental arithmetic on intelligence development among primary school pupils in Khartoum State. The sample comprised (3085) pupils both males and females. The number of control group is (1144).Experimental (1) (593) and experimental (2) (1340). The researcher used the standard progressive matrices test designed by John Raven. The study revealed that the controlled group obtained in pre test (16.84) and (19.84) in post test. Experimental group (1) (33.54) in the post test. While experimental group (2) obtained (16.89) in pre test and (25.05) in the post test.

Nonverbal responses to the restriction on moving hands

Hanaya, Michiko Dept. of Education, Hirosaki University, Hirosaki, Japan

In this study, each of 10 subjects, 20-21 years old female students, was told to talk with a female student who was quite familiar. The experiment consisted of two parts. On one part, they talked as usual, and on the other part, the subject's movements of the hands were limited. Their movements of the head, arms, legs, eyelids, gaze directions, etc. were tape-recorded for 3 minutes in each condition. The record was analyzed and revealed that the duration of head movements and the number of blinks increased as the movements of the hands were limited.

Music improves sleep quality

Harmat, Laszlo Institute of Behavior Sciences, Semmelweis University, Budapest, Hungary *Takács, Johanna* Institute of Behavior Sciences, Semmelweis University, Budapest, Hungary *Bódizs, Róbert* Institute of Behavior Sciences, Semmelweis University, Budapest, Hungary

Objectives: Investigation of the effects of relaxing classical music on students' sleep quality. Methods: We used a three group repeated measures design. 94 students (ages 19-28) with sleep complaints. Participants listened to classical music or audiobook at bedtime for 3 weeks. In the control group there was no intervention. Sleep quality was measured by Pittsburg Sleep Quality Index. Results: Repeated measures ANOVA revealed a main effect of GROUPS (P=0·0028) and TIME (P<0·0001). There was an interaction between TIME and GROUPS (P<0·0001). Post-hoc Bonferroni-test showed that music significantly improved sleep quality (P<0·0001). Conclusion: Classical music is useful intervention for sleeping problems.

Predictors of BII fears in people receiving intravenous chemotherapy

Harris, Lynne Dept. of Health Sciences, University of Sydney, Sydney, Australia *Jones, Mairwen* Faculty of Health Sciences, University of Sydney, Sydney, Australia *Catherine, Carey* NCHECR, University of New South Wales, Sydney, Australia

Objectives: Previous findings concerning predictors of BII concerns have come from student samples and samples undergoing single blood draws. This study extended this work to examine predictors of BII concerns among outpatients receiving chemotherapy. Method: Outpatients receiving chemotherapy for cancer (n=187) completed a questionnaire. Results: Fifteen percent had scores on the Mutilation Questionnaire comparable to samples with BII phobia. The predictors of BII concerns in this sample were consistent with those from general population samples and from samples with BII phobia. Conclusions: The findings have implications for understanding and reducing distress associated with provision of necessary care in oncology settings.

The influence of self-esteem on psychological distance between self and other

Hasegawa, Koji Faculty of Arts, Shinshu University, Matsumoto, Japan

Sociometer theory suggests that self-esteem functions as a monitor of social acceptance. According to this theory, we predicted that low self-esteems would percept the psychological distance between self and one's friend more far than high self-esteems. 183 undergraduates participated in the investigation. The results consisted with the prediction. Moreover, low self-esteems suffered from the dilemmas that they didn't want to approach (or part) too much though they wanted to approach (or part) their friend. To resolve the dilemmas, low self-esteems wanted to reassure whether their friend accepted them, but they had frozen to worry about evaluation from their friend.

Dimensions of relationship quality: An international comparison

Hassebrauck, Manfred Inst. für Sozialpsychologie, Universität Wuppertal, Wuppertal, Germany *Fehr, Beverley* Department of Psychology, University of Winnipeg, Winnipeg, Canada *Schwarz, Sascha* Social Psychology, University of Wuppertal, Wuppertal, Germany

Based on the prototype of relationship quality (Hassebrauck, 1997) we examined the dimensions of relationship quality. In a first study with a German sample based on a principle components analysis, four dimensions – Intimacy, Agreement, Independence, and Sexuality – underlying the prototype of relationship quality were identified.

This four factorial structure was replicated with samples from Australia, Brazil, Canada, Greece, Hungary, Italy, Poland, Spain and Turkey. Scales based on the four factorial structure of relationship quality showed satisfactory reliability. Hassebrauck, M. (1997). Cognitions of relationship quality: A prototype analysis of their structure and consequences. Personal Relationships, 4, 163-185.

The exploratory study on the assessment of the facilities in a Japanese campus

Hatakeyama, Akifumi Psychological Sciences, Health Science Univ. of Hokkai, Sapporo, Japan

This study deals with the exploratory investigation on the assessment of the facilities in a Japanese university campus. The subjects were consisted of undergraduate students. At first, they were required to discuss and give the items they thought they were necessary to use the facilities in the campus. After that, they strolled around the inside of their own campus, and assessed it in reference to the given items in their discussion. The main results showed that the students were highly assessed them, because they liked their university itself. Base upon the results, how and why they attached it were discussed.

Silence within dyadic conversations and interpersonal affect

Hatanaka, Miho Tsukuba, Japan

Relationships between silence within conversations and interpersonal affect were investigated. In a questionnaire study, 214 undergraduates reported affects in three conversational settings. Results indicated that when the relationship with the partner was close, silence was not rated negatively. However, when the relationship was not close, in response to silence the participants reported more embarrassment when the conversational partner was more attractive, whereas they reported more apathy and irritation when the conversational partner was less attractive. These results suggest that the effect of silence within a conversation on interpersonal affect is different according to the relationship between the conversational partners.

The effects of cognitions of joking relationship on joking behaviors to friend

Hayama, Daichi Dept. of Psychology, University of Tsukuba, Tsukuba, Japan

The purpose of this study was to examine whether cognitions of joking relationship affect joking behaviors. undergraduates (n = 208) were examined (a) difference in their joking behaviors between the best friend and an ordinary friend, and (b) the effect of cognitions regarding the joking relationship (understanding the friend and being accepted by the friend) on joking behaviors. Results indicated that participants significantly more used aggressive jokes with the best friend. furthermore, the sense of being accepted by a normal friend promoted aggressive jokes, whereas the sense of being accepted by the best friend reduced the need for other-enhancing jokes.

Patients' personality and spouses' ways of giving support: which contributes more to the recovery after first Acute Coronary Syndrome (ACS)?

Haze-Filderman, Liat Psychology, Bar-Ilan University, Ramat-Gan, Israel *Vilchinsky, Noa* Bar-Ilan University, Ramat-Gan, Israel *Leibowitz, Morton* Cardiology, Meir Medical center, Kefar Saba, Israel *Reges, Orna* Cardiology, Meir Medical Center, Kefar Saba, Israel *Khaskia, Abid* CARDIOLOGY, MEIR MEDICAL CENTER, KEFAR SABA, Israel *Bental, Tamir* cardiology, Meir medical center, kefar saba, Israel *Mosseri, Morris* CARDIOLOGY, MEIR MEDICAL CENTER, Ramat-Gan, Israel *David, Daniel* Sackler Medical school, Tel Aviv University, Tel Aviv, Israel

Objective: to explore the interaction, between the spouses' ways of giving support and the patients' attachment style, to recovery outcomes six months after first ACS. Method: 77 patients and spouses completed the Ways of Giving Support Questionnaire and the Experiences in Close Relationships scale during hospitalization. Outcomes measured at six months were: depression, anxiety, BMI, blood lipids, Hs-CRP, smoking, rehabilitation attendance and resuming work Results: Active engagement predicted decrease in patients' BMI and Overprotectiveness predicted non attendance in rehabilitation programs. Ten significant interactions were found. Conclusions: The interpersonal dynamics determining appropriate behavior following a medical crisis are complex

The animate/inanimate distinction in visuomotor coordination

Hegele, Mathias Bewegungskoordination, Insitut für Arbeitsphysiologie, Dortmund, Germany Heuer, Herbert Movement coordination, Insitut f. Arbeitsphysiologie, Dortmund, Germany

The present experiment aimed to elucidate some of the conditions that trigger the action observation-execution system when humans coordinate their actions with objects in their environment. Subjects performed sinusoidal movements in temporal synchrony with a human model or a dot moving in the same (congruent) or the orthogonal (incongruent) direction presented as static postures or dynamic displays of continuous motion. Results revealed visuomotor interference for simultaneously observing a human incongruent action, but only for continuous motion displays. Thus, it seems that movement information is required to be present in order to trigger specific interference effects related to the animate/inanimate distinction.

The effects of marriage preparation program on changing beliefs about spouses

Heidari, Mahmood Psychology and Education, Shahid Beheshti University, Tehran, Islamic Republic of Iran Mazaheri, Mohammad A. Psychology & Education, Shahid Beheshti University, Tehran, Islamic Republic of Iran

This study aims to evaluate the effects of educating cognitive skills of marital life in changing the relationship beliefs of the university students. A sample of 16 Males and 36 femails approaching to get married recruited from an established marriage preparation program at the Family Research Institute. All filled a battery of questionnaires at baseline and after training. It was found that irrational relationship beliefs were significantlt decreased as a result of the intervention. Detailes are discussed in the light of findings.

What neuroimaging can tell us about cognition: fMRI reveals access to syntactic gender information in German bare noun production

Heim, Stefan INB3 - Medizin, Forschungszentrum Jülich, Jülich, Germany Eickhoff, Simon B. INB3 - Medicine, Research Centre Jülich, Jülich, Germany Friederici, Angela D. Neuropsychologie, MPI f. Kognit.- u. Neurowiss., Leipzig, Germany Amunts, Katrin INB3 - Medicine, Research Centre Jülich, Jülich, Germany

Is syntactic gender information available in German bare noun production? We investigated this question with fMRI using gender priming during overt picture naming. The speech latencies showed no priming effect. In contrast, fMRI revealed priming in left BA 44 known to support gender processing. This priming effect in fMRI indicates that gender was available during bare noun production. The present study has implications for the ongoing discussion what neuroimaging may tell us about cognition. Neuroimaging data may be more sensitive than behavioural data and thus useful dependent variables providing information

for the specification of cognitive models (e.g., of language production).

Cognitve processes underlying simple heuristics: The recognition and the fluency heuristic

Heister, Julian Berlin, Germany Marewski, Julian ABC, MPIB Berlin, berlin, Germany

The recognition heuristic and the fluency heuristic are prime examples of simple heuristics for inferential judgments. Inferences are based solely on recognition and processing fluency, respectively. Even though these heuristics have stirred a lot of research examining the conditions under which they are employed, surprisingly, until today the lower level cognitive processes involved in their use are unexplored. Combining eye movement data with reaction time data and outcome measures, we examine these processes. In particular, we compare situations in which people are instructed to consciously apply the heuristics to situations without explicit instructions about strategy use.

Identity styles, commitment, and religiosty among moslems students

Hejazi Moughari, Elaheh Educational Psychology, University of Tehran, Tehran, Islamic Republic of Iran

The purpose of this study was to investigate the relationship between identity styles (information, Normative, Diffuse/avoidance), identity commitment and religiosity (orthodoxy, external critique, relativism, second naiveté). For this, reason 419 Moslems first and second year undergraduate students were chosen randomly. 2 questionnaires were administrated :ISI(identity style inventory, Berzonsky,1992)and PCBS(post- critical belief, Duriez, and al,2000). For analyzing the data, multivariate regression was used. The result indicated that: identity styles were able to predict the religiosity, commitment had a significant relation with orthodoxy, external critique and relativism and nonsignificant with second naiveté.

On the influence of intention-based and stimulus-based actions on action-effect associations

Herwig, Arvid Inst. für Psychologie, Max-Planck-Institut CBS, Leipzig, Germany Prinz, Wolfgang Psychology, Max Planck Institute CBS, Leipzig, Germany Waszak, Florian Psychologie de la Perception, Université Paris Descartes, Paris, France

Humans either carry out actions to produce effects in the environment (intention-based) or to accommodate to environmental demands (stimulus-based). Until now, little is known about the functional differences between these two types of action. We investigated how the type of action influences the formation of short-term (assessed in a prime-probe stimulus-response task) and long-term (assessed in a separate test phase) associations between actions and their auditory effects. Whereas short-term bindings occurred for both types of action, long-term action-effect learning was observed only for intention-based actions. The findings suggest that intention-based and stimulus-based actions are accompanied by different types of learning.

Trias of trust in patients with mental disorders and its implications for the therapeutic processes

Hewig, Martina Inst. für Klin. Psychologie, Universität Trier, Trier, Germany Hank, Petra Psychologie, Universität Trier, Trier, Germany Krampen, Günter Klinische Psychologie, Universität Trier, Trier, Germany

Interpersonal trust, trust in oneself (i.e., self-efficacy) and trust in the future (i.e., hopefulness vs. hopelessness) are the central components of the salutogenetic action-theory based "Trias of Trust Model" (TTM). The present study investigated characteristic patterns in the trust trias in 143 inpatients with distinct mental disorders. Multivariate analysis methods revealed significant differ-

ences between the groups concerning trust in oneself and hopelessness. Patients with somatoforme disorders showed significantly higher trust in themselves than depressive patients. Patients with personality disorders got significantly higher scores in hopelessness compared to other mental disorders. Practical implications of these findings for therapeutic processes are discussed.

Bad decisions in Blackjack activate anterior cingulate cortex.

Hewig, Johannes Biological and Clinical Psych., Friedrich-Schiller-University, Jena, Germany Straube, Thomas Biological and Clinical Psych., Friedrich-Schiller-University, Jena, Germany Trippe, Ralf H Biological and Clinical Psych., Friedrich-Schiller-University, Jena, Germany Hecht, Holger Biological and Clinical Psych., Friedrich-Schiller-University, Jena, Germany Kretschmer, Nora Biological and Clinical Psych., Friedrich-Schiller-University, Jena, Germany Miltner, Wolfgang H R Biological and Clinical Psych., Friedrich-Schiller-University, Jena, Germany

Recently we reported on medial frontal negativities in the event related potentials in response to negative outcomes in a computer version of Blackjack. The present study examined decision making in Blackjack using functional magnetic resonance imaging. 17 participants had to decide at a certain point score whether to take another card or not at different degrees of risk (13-18 points). Participants had to get closer to 21 than a computer opponent, and had to avoid getting over 21 points. The participants showed increased activity in the anterior cingulate cortex after taking a decision which was extremely risky or extremely cautious.

Ethnography of science cafe: A function of a facilitator in the communication between scientists and citizens

Hidaka, Tomo Dept. of Literature, Ritsumeikan University, Kyoto, Japan

In this study I focused on the communication between scientists and citizens in Science Cafe. Discourse of the people in the field was analyzed. By using the KJ method and discourse analysis, the result was summarized into the following point. Citizens can hold a conversation with scientists more actively when a facilitator is there. The facilitator supports the conversation by "correcting" the words of the citizens. Knowledge difference between scientists and citizens can be flattened by the facilitator's support, and citizens get more chance to talk. This indicates the bidirectional communication between professional and non-professional can be achieved by the presence of a facilitator.

Processing and weighting of information affecting escalation of commitment

Hiemisch, Anette Inst. für Psychologie, Universität Greifswald, Greifswald, Germany Schelske, Stefan Institut of Psychology, University of Greifswald, Greifswald, Germany

Theory clearly indicates task dimensions affecting escalation of commitment However, which dimensions do people spontaneously, perceive and consider in realistic situations? Within a complex scenario 200 students choose a field of study, received failure feedback and finally decided if they wanted to continue. Commitment for the chosen topic, the cognitive representation of the decision problem as well as motivational variables were assessed. Regression analysis revealed that after controlling for commitment certain aspects of the cognitive representation (e.g. thinking about incentives of termination) explained additional variance of the probability to continue. The motivational basis for representing those aspects is discussed.

Attentional capture and stimulus saliency in a selective reaching task

Higgins, Laura Dept. of Kinesiology, University of Calgary, Calgary, Canada Welsh, Timothy Kinesiology, University of Calgary, Calgary, Canada

The present experiment determined the relative influences of four different dynamic stimulus properties (onset, offset, blink and motion) on attentional capture and movement organization. Participants were required to make aiming movements to a target while ignoring a distracter that was characterized by one of the other three stimulus properties. It was found that movement trajectories deviated towards the distracter. Importantly, movement deviations were only present in conditions in which interference effects in reaction time were observed - conditions in which the distracter afforded a highly salient competing response. These results have implications for current models of selective reaching movements.

Age differences of anxiety and depression in cancer patients

Hinz, Andreas Inst. für Medizin. Psychologie, Universität Leipzig, Leipzig, Germany Schwarz, Reinhold Dept. of Social Medicine, University of Leipzig, Leipzig, Germany Krauss, Oliver Dept. of Social Medicine, University of Leipzig, Leipzig, Germany

The objective of this study was to investigate the prevalence of anxiety and depression in cancer patients using the Hospital Anxiety and Depression Scale (HADS). Participants were 1529 cancer patients and 2037 persons from the German general population. In the cancer patients, the risk of psychiatric distress was nearly twice that of the general population. However, for older age groups there were only small differences between cancer patients and the general population The results show that large sample sizes are necessary to evaluate the psychological situation of cancer patients, and that age and gender differences must be taken into account.

Cross-modal interactions between visual brightness and image of consonants

Hirata, Sachiko Dept. of Psychology, Kwansei Gakuin University, Nishinomiya Hyogo, Japan Ukita, Jun Psychology, Kwansei Gakuin University, Nishinomiya Hyogo, Japan

Voiced consonants (VC) are considered to be darker than voiceless consonants (LC). Garner's speeded classification was used to test the assumption that this effect is caused by cross-modal interactions between visual brightness and image of consonants. We adopted four pairs (VC and LC) of Japanese Hiragana letters as stimuli and manipulated their colors to either white or black. Supporting our hypothesis, results of 32 participants indicated significant differences between congruent (VC/black, LC/white) and incongruent (LC/black, VC/white) conditions in brightness and consonant discrimination. However, issue related to the formation of stimuli remains to be clarified.

Effects of varied risk values in risk messages and the number of sources on receivers' response under ambiguity

Hirota, Sumire Musashi Inst. of Technology, Yokohama, Japan

This study examined how varied risk values and the number of sources in risk communication influenced the receivers' response, using a 2nd order probability model; the 1st and 2nd being risk values and number of sources, respectively. College students participated in two experiments (n = 187 and 105). Analysis performed using a general linear model revealed number of sources as the strongest factor. Persuasive effect was the largest in a low-conflict condition, where variances of risk values in messages were moderate compared to those in high-

and no-conflict. Although frequent risk format was the most effective, its size was small.

Anxiety and perceptual load modulate the degree of attentional resources required to process emotional bimorphemic words

Ho, Ming-Chou Dept. of Psychology, Chung-Shan Medical University, Taichung, Taiwan Yang, Nien-Ying Psychology, Chung-Shan Medical University, Taichung, Taiwan Pan, Jia-Chi Psychology, Chung-Shan Medical University, Taichung, Taiwan Chen, Hui-Tzu Psychology, Chung-Shan Medical University, Taichung, Taiwan Chu, Yi-Chen Psychology, Chung-Shan Medical University, Taichung, Taiwan Liu, Yi-Ling Psychology, Chung-Shan Medical University, Taichung, Taiwan Li, Shuo-Heng Psychology, Chung-Shan Medical University, Taichung, Taiwan

Whether the threat stimuli (e.g., fearful face) drives attention involuntarily without controlled attention is a long debate. We suggest that threat detection requires controlled attention and test two hypothesis. First, perceptual load (e.g., Lavie, 1995) could modulate the detection of the threat stimuli (Chinese bimorphemic words). Namely the performance of threat detection is better in low load condition than in high load condition. Second, load-modulated threat detection is less effective for individuals with high level of anxiety. In conclusion, this study shows that the selection of the threat stimuli requires controlled attention and anxiety modulates the detection of the threat stimuli.

Can attention shift between objects in a discrete mode?

Ho, Ming-Chou Dept. of Psychology, Chung-Shan Medical University, Taichung, Taiwan Li, Shuo-Heng Psychology, Chung-Shan Medical University, Taichung, Taiwan Hsu, Chen-Chia Psychology, Chung-Shan Medical University, Taichung, Taiwan Kuo, Chung-Yang Psychology, Chung-Shan Medical University, Taichung, Taiwan Yang, Nien-Ying Psychology, Chung-Shan Medical University, Taichung, Taiwan Chen, Hsiao-Heng Psychology, Chung-Shan Medical University, Taichung, Taiwan

As early debate regarding the mode of attentional shift in space (i.e., analog vs. discrete), the mode of attentional shift between objects requires further investigation. We employed the same/different judgment task similar to Kwak, Dagenbach and Egeth (1991) to examine the mode debate. Participants judged two letters (TT, LL, or TL) that appear briefly on two of eight outlined squares with three different distances between these two squares. Result showed comparable judgment times across three distances (a discrete mode). Further, a horse racing model ensured a serial process in such task. This study has critical implications in object-based attention literature.

Object-based attention: A between-object cost or within-object benefit?

Ho, Ming-Chou Dept. of Psychology, Chung-Shan Medical University, Taichung, Taiwan Hou, Chi-Chung Psychology, Chung-Shan Medical University, Taichung, Taiwan Shin, Ya-Ling Psychology, Chung-Shan Medical University, Taichung, Taiwan Huang, Wan-Ru Psychology, Chung-Shan Medical University, Taichung, Taiwan Kuo, Hui-Tzu Psychology, Chung-Shan Medical University, Taichung, Taiwan

Object-based attention (OBA) is attributed to a between-object cost or within-object benefit. Atchley and Ho (2001) added a spatial baseline to reaction time (RT)-based OBA paradigm and found that OBA is best described in terms of the cost to switch attention between objects. The accuracy (ACC) and RT measures reflect qualitatively different aspects of processing, attentional allocation vs. decision process. By employing the ACC measure and the similar design to Atchley and Ho, we found similar patterns of attentional allocation on a display when objects were present

or absent. This result could shed some light on the debate of cost/benefit issue.

Choice deferral arising from two different types of processing

Hoffrage, Ulrich HEC, University of Lausanne, Lausanne, Switzerland White, Chris M. HEC, University of Lausanne, Lausanne, Switzerland Reisen, Nils HEC, University of Lausanne, Lausanne, Switzerland

To explain why people often defer making a choice, we developed the Two-Stage, Two-Threshold model. It assumes that people defer choice because no option reaches an acceptable level of attractiveness or because there is uncertainty regarding which option is best. Preferential choice therefore involves two stages of processing, one that computes the absolute attractiveness of each option independently of the others, and another that computes their relative attractiveness. In our experiment, participants' self reported reasons for their deferrals depended on whether it was important to find the best alternative, or a good alternative regardless of whether it was the best.

Shared representations in coacting individuals

Holländer, Antje Inst. für Psychologie, Max-Planck-Institut, Leipzig, Germany Prinz, Wolfgang Inst. für Psychologie, Max-Planck-Institut, Leipzig, Germany

Common coding theory claims that perceived events and planned actions share a common representational domain. There is evidence that these representations may be shared between self and others. Investigating task sharing is one way of studying real-time social interactions. In this paradigm two individuals take care of a certain aspect of a common task. There is evidence that although no interpersonal coordination is required, the task aspect of the other agent is taken into account as well. The present study investigates the underlying neural mechanisms of co-representation in task sharing using EEG. The findings provide evidence that similar neural mechanisms are involved in monitoring one's own actions and the actions of others.

Software features and their influence on extraneous cognitive load in a comparison task when analysing videos for the purpose of learning

Hollender, Nina Hochschuldidakt. Arbeitsstelle, TU Darmstadt, Darmstadt, Germany Schmitz, Bernhard Hochschuldidakt. Arbeitsstelle, TU Darmstadt, Darmstadt, Germany

The study tested the influence of software design on cognitive load when classifying sequences of a video and comparing own classifications with classifications made by an expert. 36 students took part, with one group being able to compare the classifications integrated within the same screen and one group having to switch between two separate screens. A control group conducted no comparisons. Cognitive load was measured by subjective rating and by means of a secondary task. Results yielded significant higher cognitive load (p<0.05) for the separate comparison group. However, there were no differences in the performance in a post-test.

E-accessibility for the disabled persons in Bangladesh

Hossain, Mahjabeen Khaled Inst Of Hazrat Mohammad (SAW), Dhaka, Bangladesh

There is a general social stigma attached to disability, which is virtually inescapable for many religion, society and nation. Bangladesh as a third world country can not ignore this issue. Here it is estimated 3.4 million children and 10 million adults living with disabilities. Disable person face a cycle where they become the poorest of the poor. Providing e-accessibility should be required with the combined commitment & contribution of government, non-government & private organizations. The paper will reflect the problems encountered, and the future course of action for creating access of visually impaired persons to technologies.

The effects of exercise on physical fitness and cognitive function in elderly who need a care

Hotta, Ryo Human Environmental Studies, Kyushu University, Kasuga, Japan
Objectives: The purpose of this study was to investigate the effect of regular exercise on physical fitness and cognitive function in elderly who need a care Methods: Subjects were 22 elderly aged 67-86 years. Physical fitness was assessed by 7-item test battery of physical performance and cognitive function was measured by Stroop task. Data was analyzed using one-way analysis of variance. Results: Once a week exercise made some improvements in physical fitness and cognitive function. Conclusions: This study indicates that some functions of elderly can be changed by regular exercise. We must consider about the reason of them.

The research of emotion: EEG activation induced by musical mode and tempo

Hou, Jian Cheng Psychology, Lab of Cognitive Neuroscience, Nanjing, People's Republic of China
Using Polygraph to explore the emotion induced by different music patterns. Oscillations were induced by 6 music patterns in 20 subjects. Drew out appointed oscillations and analyzed through ANOVA. The major is striking in parietal, central and frontal; minor energies are higher than major. The gender in temporal is striking and males are higher than females. Both major and gender are remarkable in parietal and central with Band β and γ— they are attributed to brain's physiological difference between genders, meanwhile reflects the differences of information conformity. Major and gender can induce widespread oscillations during musical mental activity.

Analysis on family environment of the heroin addicts

Huang, Mei Dept. of Social Science, Hainan Medical College, Hainan, People's Republic of China Liu, Yumei Dept. of Social Sciences, Hainan Medical College, Haikou, People's Republic of China
Objective: To evaluate family environment of the heroin addicts and investigate a novel rehabilitation therapy in psychology and society for persons who rely on opium maternal. Methods: By using FES CV, a comparative study was performed on 50 heroin addicts and 50 normal controls. The generalized cases of dependants were investigated. Results: Family environment of the heroin addicts was characterized by indifferent familiarization, cool sensibility. Conclusions: The methods of integrated intervention on drug addicts were provided.

When she is prettier than me: A neuro-scientific evidence of social comparison

Huang, Xu Management and Marketing, Hong Kong Polytechnic Univ., Hong Kong, China, People's Republic of : Hong Kong SAR Zhang, Zhijie Department of Psychology, South-West University, Chongqing, China, People's Republic of : Macao SAR Yuan, Hong Department of Psychology, South-West University, Chongqing, China, People's Republic of : Macao SAR Lam, Wing Management and Marketing, Hong Kong Polytechnic U, Hong Kong, China, People's Republic of : Macao SAR Xiang, Nan Public Administration, Sichuan University, Cheng Du, China, People's Republic of : Macao SAR Wang, Yongli Business Management, Zhong Shang University, Guangzhou, China, People's Republic of : Macao SAR
Social comparison can occur and influence self-evaluations unconsciously, even based on information received at 90-110ms after stimulus onset. However, it is not known whether social compar-ison occurs at 90-100ms or afterwards. We examined the amplitudes of event-related potentials (ERPs) responses to attractive and unattractive face images at 100ms using data collected from 33 participants. We found that the amplitudes of ERP responses to attractive faces were lower than unattractive faces when social comparison was not present, but higher than unattractive faces when the participants compared these face images with their own. We conclude that social comparison occurs at around 100ms.

Family communication process influences adolescent attachment style: The moderating effect of self-esteem

Huang, Yunhui Dept. of Psychology, Peking University, Beijing, People's Republic of China Shi, Junqi Psychology Department, Peking University, Beijing, People's Republic of China Wang, Lei Psychology Department, Peking University, Beijing, People's Republic of China
The present study aimed at investigating how family communication process (including socio-orientation dimension and concept-orientation dimension) influenced adolescent attachment style. Parents reported family communication process while their adolescent children reported self-esteem and attachment style. Although concept-orientation was believed "better" than socio-orientation, results showed that concept-orientation tended to reduce the attachment avoidance and anxiety but only in high self-esteem adolescents. Socio-orientation tended to increase attachment anxiety only in low self-esteem adolescents, and it even tended to decrease attachment avoidance in high self-esteem adolescents. Self-esteem moderated how family communication process influenced adolescent attachment style.

Psychological characteristics of Japanese young workers who experienced early retirement.

Igarashi, Atsushi Division of Career Development, Fukushima University, Fukushima, Japan Saito, Noboru Division of Career Development, Fukushima University, Fukushima, Japan Amano, Mikiko Division of Career Development, Fukushima University, Fukushima, Japan
We investigated psychological characteristics of young employees who experienced early retirement. Participants were 756 Japanese young employees who had graduated a university during 2003 to 2006. Over twenty percent (21.6%) of all the participants experienced early retirement. We found no significant relationship between the experience of early retirement and a level of reality shock, which they faced at the workplace. Multiple regression analysis revealed that the person who retired early had higher anxiety during their process of deciding their jobs before their first employment, and they felt higher level of 'busyness' about their jobs after the employment.

Attention effects on auditory brainstem responses during contralateral noise masking

Ikeda, Kazunari CRSEP, Tokyo Gakugei University, Tokyo, Japan Sekiguchi, Takahiro Educational Psychology, Tokyo Gakugei University, Tokyo, Japan Hayashi, Akiko CRSEP, Tokyo Gakugei University, Tokyo, Japan
Attention-related modulation of auditory brainstem response (ABR) was determined in humans during continuous and contralateral masking. Employing an oddball procedure, two tone pips (0.5 and 1 kHz) with intensity at 80 dB SPL were delivered to the left ear. Participants each conducted two tasks either ignoring sounds or attending to 1-kHz tones. When a white noise with sufficient intensity was continuously exposed to the right ear, significant amplitude differences between the two tasks were found for both tones within the ABR latency. Therefore, the intensity of contralateral masking might be critical to reveal attention-related modulation of the ABR.

Effects of self-consciousness and the feelings of guilty on the coping behaviors after being caught lying

Imagawa, Tamio Psychology for Well-Being, Hokusei Gakuen University, Sapporo, Japan
In this study, the author examined the effects of self-Consciousness and the feelings of guilty on the coping behaviors which people adopted when they were caught out in a lie. Self-Consciousness, the feelings of guilty and the coping behaviors were asked to 250 participants(86 male students and 164 female students). Results were obtained by path-analysis. The feelings of guilty contributed to distinguish between apologing and the other coping behaviors and to distiguih among the settings. Self – Consciousness contributed to distinguish among the settings. Implications of these findings in the Self-consciousness literature were discussed.

Change of computer anxiety in first-year students taking a course of informatics and computer training

Inoue, Takeshi Cognitive Information Science, Shiga University, Otsu, Japan
The purpose of this study was to investigate the change of computer anxiety in first-year students taking a course of informatics and computer training. Two kinds of questionnaire: one is measured for information literacy and the other for computer anxiety, were executed for 29 students in April (immediately after matriculation in a university), May, June, and July. The results showed that computer anxiety was significantly higher in April than in May, June, or July, independent of information literacy of the students. This fact suggests that computer anxiety decrease rapidly after students have started to learn information literacy.

Influence of state anxiety on body sway with visual target changing in size

Ishida, Mitsuo Dept. of Physiology, Enviromental Sciences, Yamanashi, Japan Nagai, Masanori Department of Physiology, Yamanashi Inst., Fuji-Yoshida, Yamanashi, Japan Wada, Maki College of Law, Nihon University, Chiyodaku, Tokyo, Japan
In the present experiment, relationship between the body sway and the degree of anxiety was explored in 11 healthy participants while standing with a visual target changing in size. The size of visual target continuously varied between 5.34 degree and 8 degree in visual angle with a frequency of 0.3 Hz. Body sway recorded was analyzed by FFT analysis, and correlation were examined between the power and score of state-anxiety. The results indicated the significant negative correlation (r= -0.68) between the power of the frequency band of 0.1-0.21 Hz and the degree of anxiety in the left-right axis.

Family relationship in the rural areas of Bangladesh: A comparative study on Muslim and Santal community

Islam, A.K.M. Shafiul Dept. of Sociology, Rajshahi University, Rajshahi, Bangladesh Islam, AKM Shafiul Dept. of Sociology, Rajshahi University, Rajshahi, Bangladesh
This study will provide a detail perspective of family relationship pattern between Muslim and Santal communities, and explore the family relationship norms, marriage relationship and developing bond. This study also compares the sexual behaviour, marriage relationship pattern and marriage role relationship among these communities. Family relationship pattern depends on various influencing factors in Bangladeshi culture. It will try to depict factors which influence the relationship pattern among the Muslim and Santal communities in rural Bangladesh. It's based on a significant sample of

Muslim and Santal families collected through survey and participant-observation methods from selected study areas in Bangladesh.

The effectiveness of listening to Al-Quran recitation to improve driver performance

Ismail, Rozmi School of Psychology, Universiti Kebangsaan Malaysia, Bangi Selangor, Malaysia Mohd Nor, Mohd Jailani School of Psychology, Universiti Kebangsaan Malaysia, Bangi Selangor, Malaysia Kurniawan, Yohan School of Psychology, Universiti Kebangsaan Malaysia, Bangi Selangor, Malaysia

This study aimed to asses how far listening to Al'Quran recitation help drivers to concentrate while driving a vehicle. This experiment was carried out in a driving simulator where physiological changes were measured. 20 male volunteers participated in the study. They were asked to drive without time limit and they could stop when they felt tired. The result of this experiment shows that the duration for driving while listening to the Al'Quran recitation treatment is longer than driving without Al'Quan recitation condition. Subjects' reaction time when driving with Al'Quan treatment condition was also faster. This study suggested that Al' Qur'an recitation therapy could be implemented to increase safety and comfortness for drivers.

The effect of videotape feedback of a dyadic interaction on metaperception

Iso, Yukiko Dept. of Child Psychology, Tokyo Future University, Tokyo, Japan Kasagi, Yuu Dept. of Social Psychology, Osaka University, Suita, Osaka, Japan Daibo, Ikuo Dept. of Social Psychology, Osaka University, Suita, Osaka, Japan

This study examined the hypothesis that observing oneself in videotape would improve the accuracy of metaperception (prediction of how others viewed oneself). Seventy female students participated in conversations with unacquainted partners twice, of which were videotaped, and estimated the metaperceptions after both conversations. Before the second conversations, two-thirds of participants observed the videotape of either themselves only or participants and partners in the first conversations. Another third observed a videotape which wasn't related to conversations. As the results, although the hypothesis wasn't confirmed, social skills correlated with improvement of meta-accuracy. We discussed the relationships between social skills and the effectiveness of videotape feedback.

Transition to parenthood: A comparison between the perceptions of adolescents, emerging adults and expecting parents

Israelashvili, Moshe School of Education, Tel Aviv University, Tel Aviv, Israel Moldavsky, Michal School of Education, Tel Aviv University, Tel Aviv, Israel

The current study compared the perceptions regarding the transition to parenthood among three groups of Israeli Jews - (1) 94 adolescents, (2) 116 emerging adults and (3) 88 expecting parents. The participants completed questionnaire related to their level of idealization, motivation, and future parental self-efficacy. Study findings indicated that the level of idealization and the level of parental self-efficacy are higher among males than females. However, the level of motivation to parenthood was higher among females. Differences among the three study groups were found only for females but not for males. The study findings' implications will be discussed.

Bimanual coordination between individuals: Do we represent the task of a coacting partner?

Jäger, Christina Inst. für Psychologie, Max-Planck-Institut CBS, Leipzig, Germany Holländer, Antje Psychology, MPI CBS, Leipzig, Germany Prinz, Wolfgang Psychology, MPI CBS, Leipzig, Germany

When two individuals take care of a certain aspect of a common task they do not have a representation of his/her own task alone. Recent findings show that one takes the aspects of a coacting partner's task into account as well. Participants were required to perform symbolically cued reaching movements varying in movement amplitude. The experiment was conducted in a partial (single) and shared (joint) condition. We predicted a disadvantage in RT for dissimilar cued movement amplitudes in the shared but not in the partial condition. Results are discussed with respect to the processes of joint action and task sharing.

The role of quality social support in university student achievement attitudes: A Chilean sample

Jacoby, Brian Eugene, USA McWhirter, Benedict Counseling Psychology, University of Oregon, Eugene, OR, USA

The purpose of this study is to investigate adolescent social risk and protective factors, and identify variables that may influence self-evaluation and achievement outcomes. We collected surveys from 130 students (aged 18-20) attending two Chilean universities, which measured quality of communication and level of connection with family, friends, peers, and school; and educational and attitudinal outcome measures: self esteem, hope, connection to self, and attitudes toward the future. Participants also reported demographic variables, such as family cohabitants and socioeconomic status, which may play a role in positive educational outcomes and social support factors. Early evidence reveals a connection between family social support and positive achievement attitudes.

Differential rehabilitation outcome in eating disorder patients

Jagsch, Reinhold Inst. für Psychologie, Universität Wien, Wien, Austria Wiesnagrotzki, Stefan Psychiatry and Psychotherapy, Medical University of Vienna, Vienna, Austria Gombas, Wolfgang Psychotherapy, Psychosocial Strategies, Vienna, Austria

Objective: Using a differential research paradigm we evaluated treatment success in eating disorder patients. Methods: Fifty-one patients were treated for eight weeks on basis of an inpatient psychoanalytic-based procedure. Four groups built on concordance or discrepancy of subjective and objective ratings of symptoms severity were compared using health-related quality of life as outcome measure. Results: Using a pre/post comparison design huge improvements could be found for two groups while no changes over time occurred for the other two. Conclusions: Results emphasize the importance of subjective ratings of symptoms as they seem to play an important role for treatment success.

Categories encapsulate causal properties, influencing similarity

James, Nathalie Dept. of Psychology, UCLA, Venice, USA Cheng, Patricia Psychology, UCLA, Venice, CA, USA

To demonstrate that categories form during causal reasoning, participants examined objects whose features predicted certain outcomes. The features of half the objects were confounded with an extraneous variable. Participants formed clearer categories around objects whose features were unconfounded, indicating that they took the objects' causal context into account instead of generating categories around the objects' similarity alone. Additionally, participants formed different categories to meet different goals set by the experimenter, indicating that categories are purpose-driven rather than merely descriptive. Finally, unconfounded, goal-relevant features were disproportionately weighed in similarity judgments indicating that similarity is a product of causal category formation.

Effects of task parameters on individual differences in pursuit tracking performance

Jerneic, Zeljko Department of Psychology, University of Zagreb, Zagreb, Croatia Palekcic, Jasenko Department of psychology, University of Zagreb, Zagreb, Croatia

The aim was to explore the effects of some task parameters on individual differences in tracking performance. 16 pursuit tracking tasks representing all possible combinations of four task characteristics (control dynamics, input regularity, input form, and track preview) were selected for the experiment. Factor analysis of performance data revealed three factors indicating that the extent of correlations between tracking tasks depends on whether the input function is continuous or step one, and in the case of tracking step function whether the track is displayed or not. Besides, between-factor correlations suggested the existence of a second-order tracking factor.

A case study of chords and their inversions recognition by mental rotation or sound character

Jiang, Cong Inst. für Musik, Universität halle-Wittenberg, Halle, Germany

This study is an attemptable research of recognition of chords and their inversions. Music is a kind of auditory spatial art, so it is hypothesized that there might be mental rotation when we hear chord and inversions. The subject, a post-graduate major in musicology, is asked to listen to 20 pairs of triads and seventh chord with their inversions, and report that the second chord in each pair is of which inversion. The reaction time of inversions is not significantly but longer than that of original chords. It can be concluded that mental rotation plays a part in the recognition of chords and their inversions.

Intrinsic, extrinsic religiosity and well-being

Joshi, Shobhna Psychology, Banaras Hindu University, Varanasi, India Kumari, Shilpa Psychology, Banaras Hindu University, Varanasi, India

The terms intrinsic and extrinsic religion currently represent the backbone of empirical research in the psychology of religion. An intrinsic orientation (I) involves internal religious motives within a person whereas extrinsic orientation (E) involves external motives outside the religion, using the religion for unreligious ends. Similarly, well-being comprises people's evaluation, both affective, and cognitive, of their lives. The study of I, E and well-being, is still an emerging area in psychology and has to mature as an independent enterprise in India. Thus future work would be focused on examining the relationship between religiosity and well-being.

Role of family environment in behavioural problems and self-esteem amongst Indian adolescents

Joshi, Renuka PG Department of Psychology, D.A.V.(PG) College, Dehradun, India

The present study evaluates the effect of family environment on behavioural problems and self esteem amongst adolescents. 200 school children (10 - 14 years) were administered standardized Family Climate Scale, Child Psychopathology Measurement Schedule and Self Esteem Inventory. The children of unfavorable family environment (UFE) scored significantly higher on conduct disorder, anxiety and somatization than favorable family environment (FFE) subjects. On self esteem also UFE children possessed significantly low level of personally perceived self (PPS). Significant gender differences were observed on conduct disorder, depression, physical illness with emotional problems, somatization, PPS and socially perceived self amongst the subjects.

The correspondence of the adult romantic attachment between sibblings and romantic partners

Kamenov, Zeljka Department of Psychology, University of Zagreb, Zagreb, Croatia Jelic, Margareta Department of Psychology, University of Zagreb, Zagreb, Croatia

The aim of the study was to compare the adult romantic attachment of persons grown up in the same family. The prototypic perspective claims that the attachment representations formed in childhood remain stable and have the defining influence on relationships in adulthood. From the revisionist perspective, a person's attachment to a particular other could be also a function of the experiences with this particular partner. Dyadic analyses were conducted on young adults, their siblings and their romantic partners, comparing the degree of correspondence of the romantic attachment between siblings in relation to the attachment style of their current romantic partners.

Adult attachment dimensions, emotion, and evaluation toward relationships: Similarity between mother-child dyads and romantic relationships in adolescents

Kanemasa, Yuji Faculty of Human Sciences, Osaka University of Human Scie, Osaka, Japan

This study was conducted to reveal the similarity between mother-child dyads and romantic relationships in adolescents, based on the relationships between adult attachment dimensions, emotion, and evaluation toward relationships. Participants were 209 pairs of late-adolescent children and their mothers and 104 romantic couples in adolescents. The main results were as follows: in both relationships, Anxiety dimension was positively correlated to own and partner's negative emotion and negatively related to own and partner's evaluation toward relationships. Moreover, the relations between Anxiety dimension and own and partner's evaluation toward relationships were mediated by own and partner's negative emotion respectively in both relationships.

How to guarantee transfer?

Kaps, Silvia Christina Pädagogische Psychologie, Tech. Universität Braunschweig, Braunschweig, Germany Juergens, Barbara Paedagogische Psychologie, TU Braunschweig, Braunschweig, Germany

Companies invest nearly 2 percent of labor costs in trainings (State of Industry Report, 2004). But trainings are only profitable if there is successful trainings-transfer. Georgenson (1982) states that probably only 10 percent of the training-contents are effectively transferred. An internet-based support should significantly increase transfer of training. Using a social skills training and the internet-based support, a 160 participants will be tested in a 4 x 4 Design (training + internet-support, training only, internet-support only, no intervention and four measuring times). It is supposed that participants in the training + internet-support condition will significantly increase transfer of training. First results will be presented.

Organization heads' well-balanced orientations toward personnel and task as turnover prevention

Karamushka, Liudmyla Organizational Psychology, Institute of Psychology, Kyiv, Ukraine Fil, Alena Lab. of Organiz. Psychology, Institut of Psychology, Kiev, Ukraine Liplyanska, Oksana Organisational Psychology, Institut of Psychology, Kyiv, Ukraine

Objective. Investigation of organization employees' orientations toward tasks and personnel. Methods: The investigation was done on a sample of 248 educational organization heads using R.Blake-J.Mouton Inventory and SPSS. Results. 1) 77.1% of the respondents were highly task-oriented and 31.9% personnel-oriented. 2) Turnover in organizations along with material and organizational factors (low salary, uncomfortable work conditions, etc.) may be caused by personality factors (lack of managers' attention to employees' individual and professional interests, self-realization, and career promotion, etc.). Conclusion. The investigation findings call for organization heads' paying more attention to 'the human factor' being an important turnover preventing and performance improving measure.

Anxiety and depression in an outpatient clinical sample in Cyprus

Karekla, Maria Dept. of Psychology, University of Nicosia, Nicosia, Cyprus Kapsou, Margarita Psychology, University of Nicosia, Nicosia, Cyprus Constantinou, Marios Psychology, University of Nicosia, Nicosia, Cyprus Adonis, Marios Psychology, University of Nicosia, Nicosia, Cyprus

The present study aimed to examine the reported levels of anxiety and depression in a sample of individuals seeking treatment in an outpatient clinic, in Cyprus. Fifty four clients (39 females, Mage = 31) completed the State and Trait Anxiety Inventory (STAIS-T) and the Beck Depression Inventory (BDI-II) at intake. The majority (61.1%) reported not receiving any psychiatric help or taking medication. This population presented high levels of anxiety, both state (M=50.76) and trait (M=52.22), and overall moderate levels of depression (M=20.02). In general males and females did not differ in terms of anxiety and depression (p > .05).

Effects of working circumstances on processes of work-family conflicts in dual-career couples

Kato, Yoko School of Human Sciences, Sugiyama Jogakuen University, Nisshin, Japan Tomida, Makiko Graduate School of Education, Nagoya University, Nagoya, Japan Kanai, Atsuko Graduate School of Education, Nagoya University, Nagoya, Japan

This study examined a model of work-family conflicts processes in which working circumstances affect depression directly and/or indirectly. The circumstances mean family-unfriendly climates, unmanageable conditions, and supports from leaders. A survey of Japanese dual-career couples covering 103 males and 186 females was analyzed. Results showed that all three circumstances increased depression indirectly, and only family-unfriendly climates and unmanageable conditions affected it directly. In consideration of indirect effects, the climates and the supports influenced depression via work-family conflicts, while unmanageable conditions influenced it via coping behaviors.

Conflict management about cats-breeding in urban community: Case of community cats activity in Yokohama City

Kato, Kensuke Nobeoka, Japan

In this study, I investigated the case of community conflict caused by cats-breeding in urban area, Yokohama, Japan (case of "community cats" activity), and considered the features of this practice from the perspective of activity theory. In this activity, residents treated "cat problem" as "residents-relation problem" thoroughly to manage community conflict, and established "guideline" including two divided claims (like/dislike cats). I conducted participant observation toward this activity for 3 years, and interviewed with residents. It was considered that the activity system concerned with this practice transfigured and expanded toward other daily activities in the community through residents' narratives and activities.

Japanese parenting through gendered lenses: Expectations and behaviors towards sons and daughters

Katsurada, Emiko Psychology, Kwansei Gakuin University, Nishinomiya, Japan

This study examined whether parents' developmental expectations and parenting behaviors were different with respect to their sons and daughters. Mothers and fathers of 352 children (163 boys and 189 girls) aged 4 to 6 answered the questionnaire on developmental expectations and their responses to difficult parenting situations. The results showed that both mothers and fathers expected sons to be emotionally mature earlier than daughters are. It was also found that, in general, fathers' behaviors toward daughters were gentler than those towards sons. It is concluded that parents have different expectations and behaviors toward sons and daughters.

Lay theories of depression among Japanese undergraduates: Text mining analyses

Katsuya, Noriko Fujisawa, Japan Oka, Takashi Department of Psychology, Nihon University, Setagaya-ku, Japan Sakamoto, Shinji Department of Psychology, Nihon University, Setagaya-Ku, Japan

We examined lay theories of depression among Japanese undergraduates. It is thought that people have lay theories of depression. For example, people have their images of depressive behavior, symptoms, and the causes and remedies of depression. We investigated lay theories of causes and remedies of depression. The total of 313 Japanese undergraduates answered their images of depression in an open-ended format. We analyzed text data participants answered using text mining method. Correspondence analyses indicated that participants described causes of depression as rumination, cognitive styles, and stressful events. Also, participants mentioned remedies of depression as difficulties, positive thinking, and distractions.

The test-retest reliability of the autokinetic illusion by tracking the appared movement

Kaul, Gerlinde Berlin, Germany Keitel, Jürgen Federal Institute for Occupati, Berlin, Germany

Individuals in complete darkness, observing a fixed point-source of light, will report seeing the light move, thats known as autokinetic illusion, and its beyond of somebodys control. Everybody has an individual kind of percepted movement similarly provocable everytime. When the autokinetic illusion starts by itself the person keeps track of that movement by mouse connected with a digitizer. The investigation aims at checking the reliability of the tracks of autokinetic illusions reproduced by each person. We determine the intraindividual variation of repeated autokinetic illusions and the interindividual differences in that variation from persons who have several stress in their lifes.

Self concept and emotional intelligence of Pakistani adolescents from orphanages and intact families

Kausar, Rukhsana Applied Psychology, University of the Punjab, Lahore, Pakistan Rasheed, Asima Behavioural Sciences, Fatima Jinnah Women University, Rawalpindi, Pakistan

Study compared adolescents from orphanages and intact families on self-concept (SC) and emotional intelligence (EI). It was hypothesized that intact family adolescents have positive SC and high EI than those from orphanage. Hundred adolescents were recruited from public schools (N = 50) and orphanage (N = 50). Analysis revealed that two groups of adolescents did not differ on self concept and EQ. Boys scored higher on self-concept and emotional intelligence as compared to girls and there was positive relationship between self-concept and emotional intelligence. Findings did not support the notion that adolescents in orphanage differ in self concept and emotional intelligence.

The role of feedback in temporal coordination
Keller, Peter Max-Planck-Institut, Leipzig, Germany Ishihara, Masami Psychology, Max Planck Institute, Leipzig, Germany Prinz, Wolfgang Psychology, Max Planck Institute, Leipzig, Germany

Rhythmic actions performed alone or in concert with others (e.g., dancing) generate receptive feedback when one's own and/or others' effectors impact upon the body. To investigate the role of such feedback in temporal coordination, people synchronised with an auditory metronome by finger tapping on different regions of their own and others' forearms. Movement timing variability increased with the sensitivity of the region irrespective of forearm identity. Increased sensitivity may affect timing accuracy by attenuating receptive feedback when tapping on one's own body, while analogous effects may emerge through the simulated attenuation of feedback when tapping on another's body.

Fitness to drive under the influence of psychoactive medication
Kenntner-Mabiala, Ramona Lehrstuhl Psychologie 3, IZVW, Universität Würzburg, Würzburg, Germany Kaußner, Yvonne Lehrstuhl Psychologie 3, IZVW, Universität Würzburg, Würzburg, Germany Hoffmann, Sonja Lehrstuhl Psychologie 3, IZVW, Universität Würzburg, Würzburg, Germany Krüger, Hans-Peter Lehrstuhl Psychologie 3, IZVW, Universität Würzburg, Würzburg, Germany

Psychoactive medications are known to cause cognitive side effects, considered to be partly relevant for fitness to drive. However, there is only few empirical data providing information about the dangers of driving when taking psychoactive medications. An encouraging approach for testing fitness to drive under the influence of psychoactive medications is the implementation of driving tests in a high-fidelity driving simulator. Sensitivity and validity of certain parameters assessing driving performance for evaluation of driving fitness are discussed. Results are based on N=30 subjects, being treated with two different psychoactive drugs in a double-blind crossover-design.

Psychometric evidence on individual differences in conflict adaptations for the Simon and the Eriksen Flanker task
Keye, Doris IQB, Humboldt-Universität zu Berlin, Berlin, Germany Wilhelm, Oliver IQB, Humboldt-University, Berlin, Germany Oberauer, Klaus Experimental Psychology, University of Bristol, Bristol, Germany

Conflict- and context slow-down have been proposed as indicators of a conflict-monitoring system that initiates cognitive control to resolve conflicts in information processing. We investigated individual differences in conflict-monitoring and correlates. Besides working memory capacity (WMC) and impulsivity measures, 167 adults completed a Simon and an Eriksen flanker task. We obtained conflict- and context slow-down independent of stimulus repetition. Individual differences in conflict slow-down but not context slow-down could be identified as unique sources of variance. WMC and impulsivity were not differently correlated with conflict or non-conflict trials. Costs of conflict-monitoring are discussed from a binding perspective on working memory.

The relation between university student's religiosity and their demographical features
Khodayarifard, Mohammad Dept. of Psychology, University of Tehran, Tehran, Islamic Republic of Iran
Objective: The purpose of this study was to measuring university students' religiosity and their demographical characteristic. Method: 1911 uni-

versity students were studies in a survey which used stratified random sampling. The student religiosity scale developed by Khodayarifard (2006) was used. Results: As the level of parents' education increases, the degree of religiosity increases among university students, Discussion: It can be concluded that instruction and practice of religious beliefs and acts in the family has a considerable effect on internalization of the principles and beliefs by the family members through modeling and identification with the parents.

Forgiveness and its relationship with life satisfaction, mental and physical health, and family relatioships.
Khullar, Sangeeta Psychology, MKP (PG) College, Dehra Dun, India
150M and 150F Ss of age groups 18-35, 36-55, and 56-80 completed Williams Forgiveness, CMI Health, Life Satisfaction and Family Relatioship Scales. Results: The two sexes do not differ on Forgiveness and Life satisfaction at any age level; middle aged females are more forgiving than younger ones. Life satisfaction increases with age For men who enjoy greater physical health. Forgiveness correlates positively with mental health and life satisfaction. Physical health and forgiveness are not correlated. Forgiveness correlates significantly with the eight areas of family relatioships. Forgiveness has important interpersonal and health implications.

Parental involvement and expectations and their relationship with academic anxiety and achievement and self expectations of students of residential and day schools
Khullar, Sangeeta Psychology, MKP (PG) College, Dehra Dun, India
200Ss each from day and residential schools completed the Parental Expectations(PE), parental Involvement(PI), Self Expectations(SE), and Academic Anxiety(AA) Scales. Percentage on last school examination costituted Academic Achievement(Ac Ach). Results showed significant differences in PE in the two schools and no difference in PI, AcAch,and AA. SE and PE correlated highly in both cases. For day schools AA was positively correlated with PE and SE and negatively With PI. For residential schools AcAch correlated negatively with with PI and SE and positively with AA. Implications: day and residential schools may differ but children are still living their parents' dreams.

Treasure every meeting, for it will never recur: The effects of expectancy of an ongoing relationship on interpersonal communication
Kimura, Masanori Dept. of Social Psychology, Osaka University, Suita, Japan Iso, Yukiko Child Psychology, Tokyo Future University, Adachi-ku, Tokyo, Japan Daibo, Ikuo Social Psychology, Osaka University, Suita, Japan
This study investigated the effects of expectancy of an ongoing relationship on interpersonal communication through two experiments. In experiment 1, 23 dyads unacquainted with each other were assigned to "expectancy of an ongoing relationship" or "no-expectancy" condition, and they participated in either conversation. Spontaneous motivations to continue the relationship were measured before conversations in experiment 2. Results were consistent. When participants hadn't expected the relationship to continue, participants whose social skills were high talked with partners more actively more than those who had lower skills. Social skills would make us possible to 'treasure every meeting which never recurred'.

Emotional irresponsiveness toward the social events and emotions for close others.
Kino, Kazuyo English and Communication, Hiroshima International Univ., Higashi-hiroshima, Japan
The effect of positive/negative emotions for close others on the emotional reactions toward social events, i.e. news, was investigated in this study. A set of questionnaire, about the emotional reactions toward three different kinds of social events and positive/negative emotions for close others, was administered to 249 adolescents (mostly undergraduates). It was shown that the positive emotion for others negatively correlated, but negative emotions for others had no correlation with emotional irresponsiveness toward social events. Positive concerns for close others tend to lead the emotional reactions towards the wider social world and contribute to enrich adolescents' emotional world.

Advanced digital video technologies for collaborative design tasks in school classes: Empirical evidence on the conditions for effective cooperation and learning
Klages, Benjamin Knowledge Media Res. Center, Tübingen, Germany Zahn, Carmen Cognitive Psychology, Knowledge Media ResearchCenter, Tübingen, Germany Hesse, Friedrich W. Cognitive Psychology, Knowledge Media ResearchCenter, Tübingen, Germany
We investigate the educational value of visual design tasks involving advanced digital video technologies as cognitive tools in German language and history lessons. Based on the theoretical background of "visual design as collaborative problem solving", we examine the specific conditions necessary for effective collaboration and learning in a 2x2 field study design. Results from previous lab studies suggest that student groups who are supported by advanced video technology (as compared to a control group) elaborate on video information in more detail during group interaction, thereby also acquiring more knowledge and visual literacy skills. Our current field data support this assumption.

The effects of mating motivation on women's sense of humor
Koeppl, Julia Inst. für Sozialpsychologie, Universität München, München, Germany Greitemeyer, Tobias Social Psychology, LMU Muenchen, Muenchen, Germany
Empirical research on mating preferences has emphasized that sense of humor is an important characteristic for both sexes. While men are attracted to women who respond appreciatively to their humor, women prefer partners who actively generate humor. Considering these findings from an evolutionary point of view, one may suggest women primed on mating to be more receptive to funny situations when the actor is male. In contrast, mating motivation should not affect a man's rating of a joke. In study 1 these hypotheses were corroborated by presenting funny caricatures. Currently the findings are replicated for real behavior.

Using VEs in teaching historical chronology
Korallo, Liliya Dept. of Psychology, Middlesex University, London, United Kingdom
Questionnaires revealed that people have problems with historical chronology and teachers reported that children had difficulty learning it. The current study investigated benefits of using VEs in the teaching of academic disciplines with strong chronological components. Events were sequentially displayed in a virtual fly-through that a user could navigate as though using a time-machine. The hypothesis was that more would be learned about sequences from a VE version than in control conditions – paper-printed or PowerPoint versions

– especially when challenge was incorpoprated. Different age groups were compared. The findings were mixed, but some supported the hypothesis for particular groups.

Companionate love, passionate love and safe sex in dating relationships

Kordoutis, Panos Dept. of Psychology, Panteion University, Athens, Greece

We hypothesized that type of love in intimate relationships is associated with safe sex behaviors. University students (272 men, 295 women, aged M=21.76) rated their recent dating relationship on companionship and passion and indicated frequency of, condom-use, condom-use negotiation scripts, and reasons for non-use. Analyses of variance showed that women in passionate relationships used condoms less often and their proposal for condom–use was denied more frequently, than women in companionate ones and men generally. Non-use was attributed more strongly to relationship anxiety in passionate and to risk-denial in companionate relationships. Protective behavior, particularly women's, appears sensitive to love type.

Antecedents for transformational leadership: The role of leader's task perceptions

Korek, Sabine Arbeits- und Org.-Pschologie, Universität Leipzig, Leipzig, Germany Mohr, Gisela Work and Organizational Psycho, University Leipzig, Leipzig, Germany

The literature on contextual factors for transformational leadership suggests, that complex, changing and flexible organizational structures further the emergence of transformational leadership. Transferring this notion to leaders' task characteristics, we investigated, whether these factors are related to transformational leadership ratings of followers. Multi-level-analyses of self-report data from 134 leaders and 427 direct followers from different organizations showed, that leaders, who rated their main tasks as complex and changing, were evaluated more transformational by their followers. Results suggest, that challenging work tasks may enable leaders to show more transformational leadership behaviour, which is beneficial for personal and organizational outcomes.

Rules vs. examples based learning in German noun plurals

Kovic, Vanja Experimental Psychology, Oxford University, Oxford, United Kingdom

The present behavioural study examines learning morphology of German-noun-plurals based on rules, examples or on both, rules and examples. Three experimental conditions: learning German-noun-plurals based on rules, via associations or by both, rules and associations, were conducted. The results suggest that the morphological patterns are learned more easily in the form of rules and thus, seem to be more easily captured by dual-route than single-route theories. However, error patterns across the: e, -n, -er, Û, -s rules revealed results confronting dual-route theories and suggested the existence of two mechanisms rather than one for learning regular inflection in German-plural-nouns.

Organizational and psychological consequences of influence regulation: The concept of deinfluentization

Kozusznik, Barbara Pedagogy and Psychology, University of Silesia, Katowice, Poland

To answer questions about metamorphic effects of power /Kipnis/, satisfaction and effectiveness of managers in the context of new models of organizations /Handy, Peters, Drucker/ which require deinfluentization - ability of influence regulation /Kozusznik/. 325 managers data were collected about deinfluentization, influence tactics, self and other perception, satisfaction and effectiveness. Managers with high level deinfluentization

have more positive perception of themselves and other people and are the most effective group. Women managers made up half of this group. Managers should enrich their knowledge about influence regulation tactics. Women managers should enrich their managerial role with deinfluentization behaviour and make it part of their own strengths.

Collaboration across distance: A management model for virtual teams in production networks

Kraemer, Bjoern W & O Psychology, Ruhr-University Bochum, Bochum, Germany Zimolong, Bernhard W & O Psychology, Ruhr-University Bochum, Bochum, Germany

Virtual teams face a number of management challenges. The purpose of this study is to examine the differing effects of explicit control (process management, information management, cooperation rules) and implicit control (shared mental models, trust) on team processes (communication, cooperation, coordination) and outcomes (satisfaction, time-to-market, performance) in virtual teams. Data from a questionnaire survey show the impact of explicit control on implicit control, team processes and different outcome variables in 26 interorganizational product development teams. The results will be discussed with regard to the effectiveness of the suggested management model to improve processes and outcomes in virtual teams.

Distinctive features of employees' task and personnel orientations in business organizations

Kravtsova, Julia Organizational Psychology, Institut of Psychology, Kiev, Ukraine

Objectives. To find out distinctive features of employees' task and personnel orientations in business organizations. Methods. The investigation was done on 150 employees from different specialization business organizations using the R.Blake & J.Mouton Managerial grid. Results. 1. The area of organization's activity statistically significantly (r<0.001) correlated with employees' orientation toward task (public services - 85.4%, production - 58.0%, and trade - 54.2%). 2. The area of organization's activity statistically significantly (r<0.001) correlated with employees' orientation toward personnel (trade - 70.8%, public services - 26.8%, and production – 26.0%). Conclusion. Enhancement of organizational performance requires balancing of employees' orientations toward task and personnel.

Role of visualization, gesture of the hand and verbal comments at presentation of the objekt

Kuchinskaya, Nataly Department of Psychology, Belarusian State Pedagogical U, Minsk, Belarus Shamal, Diana Department of Psychology, Belarusian State Pedagogical U, Minsk, Belarus

Researches by B.Tversky,G.Gibson,V.Zinchenko at the choice of effective means for presentation of a object or idea are known. We have carried out own researches by method perception actions on specification of a role of gesture of a hands. Results of experiments have shown efficiency of gesture only if it will be with the next conditions: one-coordinate, rapid, realized without noise. Conclusion: it is necessary to add the conclusions received earlier Barbara.Tversky.- with a severe constraint which is necessary for efficiency of gesture by a hand in a direction of object at its presentation: one-coordinate, rapid, realized without noise.

Anticipating distracted addressees: How speakers' expectations and Aaddressees' feedback influence storytelling

Kuhlen, Anna Katharina Dept. of Psychology, Stony Brook University, Stony Brook, USA Brennan, Susan E. Psychology, Stony Brook University, Stony Brook, USA

Speakers tell better stories to attentive than distracted addressees. Is this due to reduced feedback, or to speakers' expectations about whether addressees are engaged? In 39 dyads we had speakers tell stories to addressees who were either attentive or else distracted; half the speakers in each group were told (accurately or inaccurately) that their addressee was distracted by a secondary task. Speakers with attentive addressees told more vivid stories, but only when they expected attentive addressees. We conclude that storytelling is shaped not only by addressee feedback, but also by how speakers construe a lack of addressee feedback.

Gender stereotype priming on reaching and grasping actions

Kuria, Emily Ngubia Dept. Cognitive Neuroscience, SISSA, ISAS, Trieste, Italy Sartori, Luisa General Psychology, University of Padova, Padova, Italy Castiello, Umberto General Psychology, University of Padova, Padova, Italy Rumiati, Raffaella Ida Cognitive Neuroscience, SISSA/ISAS, Trieste, Italy

The study investigated whether gender-stereotype priming alters behavior in a reach-to-grasp paradigm. Participants (N=15) reached towards, grasped and placed the stimulus in a concave container (Non-social condition) or the experimenter's hand (male/female – Social condition). The critical variable used as a measure of possible behavioral differences for contrasting social attitudes was the grasping aperture (Becchio,et al,2007). The key result is that gender-priming modified the kinematics. During reach, participants displayed faster velocity with members of the opposite sex. During grasp, longer RT's for grasp aperture with members of the opposite sex were observed. These changes reflect how gender stereotypes affect motor action.

Affective disorders in cancer patients

Kuznetsova, Anna Psychological faculty, Northern State Medical Univers, Arkhangelsk, Russia

The purpose of study was to examine anxiety and its components in cancer patients. The participants were 120 women with breast and ovarian cancer treated by different form of therapy. They were evaluated using psychological tests. The high level of anxiety was found in patients. The most common symptoms were: fatigue, fear about future and nervousness about social contacts. Different components of anxiety were found in groups according to form of therapy. In this study the most common components of anxiety in cancer patients were found. Patients treated be different therapy need to get different type of psychological support.

Attachment, alexithymia and anxiety

Láng, András Dept. Educational Studies, University of Pécs, Pécs, Hungary

Rooted in early caregiver-infant relation, people with different attachment styles deal differently with emotional issues. In this study connection between attachment dimensions, alexithymia and anxiety was investigated. Correlation between avoidance and alexithymia, and between anxious attachment and anxious symptoms was expected and tested on a sample of university students (n=90) using self-report measures. Correlational analysis partially confirmed hypotheses. Alexithymic features and anxiety correlated with both dimensions showing an expected pattern based on theory of AAI and connection between attachment styles and internalizing and externalizing syptoms revealed in several studies.

Best friends: Intimacy and self-disclosure

López Becerra, Claudia México, Mexico Rivera Aragón, Sofia Social Psychology, UNAM, México, D. F;, Mexico

Specially, interactions among friends, display greater closeness, expressions of affection, pro-social behaviour, intimacy, support, trust, so forth (Blieszner & Adams, 1992) which allow its members to be authentic and feel belongingness to the other. In order to know the amount of intimacy and self-disclosure exist among best friends we applied the Intimacy and Self-Disclosure Scales to 505 adult females and males from Mexico City. Among the main findings, we found females are more empathic, supportive and express their feelings than males and younger participants also showed more friendship (p.e. sharing activities and emotional aspects, giving affection, etc.) than older people.

Relationship of adaptive behavior disorders and codependence level and parents attachment for 16-18 years old adolescents

Laizane, Ilona Psychology, University of Latvia, Riga, Latvia

The research investigates relationship between behavioral disorders, codependence level and parents attachment. The observed sample includes 250 adolescents from the contemporary and professional secondary schools, age group 16-18 years. Research methods included codependency level evaluation tool "Spann-Fischer Codependency Scale" (SFCDS, Fischer, Spann & Crawford), family relationship evaluation tool "Inventory of Parent and Peer Attachment" (G.Armsden, M.T.Greenberg) and Youth Self-Report (T.Achenbach). The observation results confirmed positive correlation between behavioral disorders and codependence level and parents attachment. Behavioral disorders Withdrawal/ Depression, and Somatic Complaints correlate more in the female group, whereas Anxiety/ Depression, Aggressive Behavior and Rule-Breaking Behavior are more common in the male group.

Social workers' and welfare recipients' attributions for poverty from two perspectives

Landmane, Dace University of Latvia, Riga, Latvia

Objective of the study is to examine social workers' (observer) and welfare recipients' (actor) attributions for poverty from two perspectives (the explainers' own perspective and imagined out – group members' perspective). In this study the socio - demographic variables and attributions for poverty is assessed. The Attributions for Poverty Questionnaire was adapted from Nasser and Abouchedid (2001). From own perspective social workers incline to attribute poverty to individualistic factors, but welfare recipients incline to structural factors. From the perspective of out – group social workers incline to attribute poverty to individualistic and structural factors, but welfare recipients incline to individualistic factors.

Empowering the practitioners in their daily educational work: Developpement and use of the AcReDi e-diary

Langers, Christian EMACS, Université du Luxembourg, Walferdange, Luxembourg Meyers, Christian EMACS, Université du Luxembourg, Walferdange, Luxembourg Koenig, Vincent EMACS, Université du Luxembourg, Walferdange, Luxembourg

The results produced by a scientific research analyzing the Luxembourgian school system together with teacher's and researcher's needs led to the creation of software, helping the practitioners in their daily educational work. This cognitive tool leads to user empowerment by providing him with a methodology for doing his research as a critical and reflexive social actor. More precisely, the practitioner can rely on this tool for data gathering, its formalization and analysis. The software's underlying concepts are derived form the theories and methods of action research, ICT and the praxeology. This communication summarizes the user oriented design and in-field validation.

Family stress, parenting skills and socio-cognitive competences of retarded children siblings

Larcan, Rosalba Scienze dell'Educazione, University of Messina, Messina, Italy Cuzzocrea, Francesca Scienze dell'Educazione, University of Messina, Messina, Italy Oliva, Patrizia Scienze dell'Educazione, University of Messina, Messina, Italy

This study aims to verify if the presence of a child with mental retardation affects family functioning, parent and children stress, and social skills of non-disabled siblings. Twenty-four families were selected. Half of these had a mental disabled child, in the others neither child had disabilities (control group). Parents, non-disabled siblings and their teachers were asked to complete several questionnaires. Many differences were found in family functioning between groups. Parents and non-disabled child think they have more caregiving difficulties and more stress. The presence of a disabled child affects non-disabled siblings' social skills both at home and at school

Attentional capture by color in red/green color blind people

Larsen, Janet Dept. of Psychology, John Carroll University, University Heights, USA Kenner, Frank Psychology, John Carroll University, University Heights, OH, USA

In two experiments the attention of red/green colorblind participants was affected by color in the same way as participants with normal color vision. Participants located an X in an array of nine angular or round grey letters. Across 360 trials, a colored target letter facilitated responding, and a colored distractor letter slowed responding compared to trials with no color. The effect was larger for angular than for round non target letters. In experiment one, red, green and blue had similar effects. In experiment two, green had the same effect even when non-target letters were in eight different shades of grey.

Personal and dispositional predictors of nurse manager burnout: A time-lagged analysis

Laschinger, Heather School of Nursing, University of Western Ontario, London, Canada Finegan, Joan PSYCHOLOGY, UNIV OF WESTERN ONTARIO, LONDON, Canada

This study examined the influence of effort-reward imbalance, a situational variable, and core self-evaluation, a dispositional variable, on nurse managers' burnout levels over a 1-year period. Nurse managers (n=134) responded to a mail survey at 2 time points. The results supported the hypothesized contribution of both personal and situational factors to nurse manager burnout over a one year time frame. Although burnout levels at Time 1 accounted for significant variance in emotional exhaustion levels one year later (B = .355, nurses' effort-reward imbalance (B = .371) and core self-evaluations (B = -.166) accounted for significant additional amounts of explained variance (p<.05).

Intrusiveness in romantic relationships: A combined qualitative-quantitative cross-cultural study

Lavy, Shiri Dept. of Psychology, Univ. of Californiain Davis, Ramat Gan, Israel Mikulincer, Mario Psychology, Bar Ilan University, Ramat Gan, Israel

Objectives: Intrusiveness is a core manifestation of autonomy-proximity/dependence imbalance. Definitions of autonomy, interdependence, and their "balance" vary across cultures. This study among Americans, Indians and Israelis explores intrusiveness through its cultural variations and beyond them. Methods: Sixty participants from each culture described intrusiveness. Their answers were analyzed and yielded 38 kinds of intrusive behaviors. Participants from each culture then rated the

prototypicality of these intrusive behaviors. Results and Conclusions: Cultural and gender differences that were found in ratings of certain intrusive behaviors are discussed in terms of 'core' vs. culture-specific aspects of autonomy and interdependence.

Organizational retaliation behavior: The role of the authority representation on interactional justice

Le Roy, Jeanne UFR SPSE, département de psych, Université Paris 10 Nanterre, Nanterre, France Finkelstein, Remi UFR SPSE, département de psych, Université Paris 10 Nanterre, Nanterre, France

The relationship between interpersonal injustice and hostile leadership was explored to study Organizational Retaliation Behavior (ORB). Two studies examined the influence of negative leadership on interpersonal justice feelings among a sample of 340 French students. People who had a negative leadership priming (study 1) or who had to remember a negative past leadership experience (study 2) engaged more in ORB than people in other conditions when they read a text with an unfair authority. Practical implications, limitations, and suggestions for future research will also be discussed.

A new coding method of dyadic love expression and its correlations with attachment styles and relationship qualities

Lee, Kit Ling Dept. of A. Social Studies, City University of Hong Kong, Hong Kong, China, People's Republic of : Hong Kong SAR Freeney, Brook

Expressions of love messages can be implicit or explicit. Tools available for these measurements are limited. Using existing expressive behavioral measurement, validity of a new coding method for these two forms of expressions is studied. Ninety-two married couples completed questionnaires measuring expressive behaviors, attachment styles and relationship satisfaction. Avoidant and anxious attachment ratings were negatively associated with the two forms of expressions and positively with secure attachment ratings. Explicit expression had stronger associations with relationship satisfaction and conflict than implicit expression. The result suggested that the new coding method is valid and complementary to other communication measurements.

Learning styles of gifted learners on e-leaning environment

Lee, Hyunjoo Dept. of Education, Seoul National University, Seoul, Republic of Korea Shin, Jongho Dept. of Education, Seoul National University, Seoul, Republic of Korea Kim, Yongnam Dept. of Education, Seoul National University, Seoul, Republic of Korea

The purpose of this study was to identify e-learning styles of gifted learners and to suggest effective e-learning environments for them. The participants were 1012 4th to 8th graders including 432 gifted students and 580 average-achieving students. Cluster analysis was performed to classify students on the basis of cognitive, affective, and behavioral characteristics on the e-learning environment. Gifted students were clustered into three subgroups which showed different learning characteristics: 'leading learner', 'individual learner', and 'passive-learner' types. The results of the study suggested guidelines for developing effective e-learning systems suited for educational needs gifted students.

Romantic relationship style, coping, identity development and mental health among Chinese and Australian adolescents

Leung, Cynthia Educational Psychology, Counse, The Hong Kong Institute of Edu, Tai Po, China, People's Republic of : Hong Kong SAR Karnilowicz, Wally Dept. of Psychology, Victoria University, Melbourne, Australia Moore, Susan School of Life and Social Scie,

Coping in relation to the big five personality factors

Morán, Consuelo Psychology, Sociology and Ph., University of León, León, Spain

Objectives: To examine the relationship between coping strategies and the "Big Five" personality factors in a sample of Spanish human services. Methods: A descriptive study was performed with 248 participants. They completed two self-report questionnaires, Ways of Coping and NEO-FFI. Pearson correlation analysis. Results: Extraversion and conscientiousness was positively correlated with planning, active coping, reframing, and seeking social support. Neuroticism was positively correlated with escape-avoidance and negatively with planning. Conclusions: Into the association between coping and personality, extraversion and conscientiousness are the most important factors. Implications of these findings in relation to previous research are discussed.

Big five personality factors and coping strategies in university students

Morán, Consuelo Psychology, Sociology and Ph., University of León, León, Spain

Objectives: To study the relationship between the personality five factors and coping strategies in university students. Methods: In a descriptive study, 334 participants completed: Ways of Coping and NEO-FFI. Pearson correlation analysis and t-test. Results: Extraversion, openness, and conscientiousness correlated positively with planning, active coping, positive reframing, and seeking social support, and negatively with escape. Neuroticism correlated positively with escape and negatively with planning and active coping. Conclusions: Into the relationship between coping and personality, in young people, extraversion, openness, and conscientiousness are the most important factors. Implications of these findings in relation to previous research are discussed.

Maintenance of and recovery from post-traumatic stress disorder among civilian war survivors

Morina, Nexhmedin Department of Psychology, Friedrich-Schiller-University, Jena, Germany Priebe, Stefan Social & Community Psychia, Queen Mary, U. of London, London, United Kingdom CONNECT group, The Social & Community Psychia, Queen Mary, U. of London, London, Germany

Little is known about the factors affecting the long-term course of PTSD. The present paper describes the results of the CONNECT project (funded by Commission of the European Union) that has investigated long-term clinical and social outcomes among more than 4.000 people with war experiences in countries of Ex-Yugoslavia and refugees in Western Europe. Preliminary results of the follow-up interviewing show that a significant number of people who met criteria for PTSD at t1 have recovered from PTSD at t2 (one year later). This presentation will focus on the risk and recovery factors related to the course of PTSD.

Means for developing spirituality: Different for classic religiosity and modern spirituality?

Muñoz-García, Antonio Educ. and Developm. Psychology, University of Granada, Granada, Spain

Although from a traditional perspective traditional means (eg reading of sacred texts), are considered goods means for developing spirituality (classical), other elements are significant when we ask people whether proposed, no traditional means (eg. see a beautiful landscape), are good means for developing spirituality. A previous study related traditional spiritual means with measures of traditional religiosity (Muñoz-García, 2007), but they were negatively related with dimensions of modern spirituality. These were positively associated with new age practices and elements of sexuality. Help-

ing behaviours were significant for persons with traditional and modern spirituality. This work will try to replicate these results including new means (e.g. arts), and doing more detailed analyses of dimensions of religion and modern spirituality.

How do Spanish students of educational sciences perceive religion and spirituality?

Muñoz-García, Antonio Educ. and Developm. Psychology, University of Granada, Granada, Spain

The purpose of this study is to investigate how students of educational sciences perceive religion and spirituality. This topic is interesting because of the significance of spirituality in last years. The university students were asked to give their meanings of religion and spirituality and after analyzing the written expressions on them. We put attention to the result observing whether the dimensions obtained are the same that produced by Ubani and Tirri (2006): the institutional dimension, the humanistic dimension, and the supernatural dimension, and whether there are non traditional meanings of spirituality in a classical religious-cultural context.

An exploration of leader's emotional intelligence within a top international financial institution

Mullally, Ruth Executive Talent Management, AIB, Dublin 6, Ireland

This study aims to explore trends and differences across Emotional Intelligence scores of AIB executive leaders. The sample consists of 595 AIB executives from Ireland, UK and Poland from 2002 – 2008 that completed the ECI (an emotional intelligence 360♂ instrument from Hay McBaer that looks at self, manager, direct reports and peer scores). Using SPSS, various statistical analysis was conducted to identify differences and trends within the sample. Research is presently being conducted with final results expected in early March.

Relationship between cognitive and physical functions in the community living elderly

Murata, Shin Faculty of Health Care Science, Himeji Dokkyo University, Hyogo, Japan Oyama, Michie NPO Hukusiyogunet, Non-Profit Organization, Hyogo, Japan Murata, Jun Graduate School of Biomedical, Nagasaki University, Hyogo, Japan Mizota, Katsuhiko Faculty of Rehabilitation, Nishikyushu University, Hyogo, Japan Tsuda, Akira Department of Psychology, Kurume University, Hyogo, Japan

The cognitive and physical functions of 192 elderly people who are living in the local community were evaluated. By simple correlation and multiple regression analyses, the educational background, finger dexterity, and time of walking in a 10-m course with obstacles were extracted as factors related to their cognitive function. Statistically, cognitive function was correlated with the duration of education, finger dexterity, and reduced walking time in a 10-m course with obstacles. These results suggest that intervention to increase finger dexterity and training to improve walking ability in different situations are Effective for the prevention of should be initiated to prevent age-related decreases in cognitive function in the elderly.

Necessary and received social support in times of economic crisis

Muzdybaev, Kuanyshbek Psychology of Morality, The Institute of Sociology, St. Petersburg, Russia

Purposes of researches were to establish dynamics of necessary and received social support (SS) by representatives of different social groups during economic crisis. Results of two researches are informed. In everyone of sample were 700 persons. It is established: in the middle of 90th years over 83% of respondents were required in several kinds of SS, however, need for help less than half requiring was satisfied. Basic obstacle of a low level of granting of SS was not only scarcity of economic resources but significant disintegrations of society.

Main sources of rendering of SS were relatives and friends of respondents.

Distinctive manifestations of innovative teamwork skills in civil servants

Mykhailenko, Viktoria Organizational Psychology, Institut of Psychology, Kiev, Ukraine

Objectives: Finding out main types and manifestations of civil servants' teamwork skills and their place among innovative skills. Methods: Managerial skills questionnaire, Team-building behavior questionnaire, Wetten and Cameron Orientation toward innovations Scale. The investigation was done on a sample of 118 civil servants. Results: Using the factorial and cluster analyses it was found that 81.9% of the respondents had basic team work skills (cooperation skills and positive self-esteem) and only 19.0% had innovative teamwork skills (orientations toward a creative team-leader and team development). Conclusion: Civil servants' basic teamwork skills are more developed compared to innovative skills which calls for their special innovative skills development training.

Self-efficacy and leadership: Identifying a process variable mediating the effects of leadership on employees' performance

Nölting, Hanna Psychologisches Institut II, Universität Münster, Münster, Germany Hell, Wolfgang Psychologisches Institut II, WWU Münster, Münster, Germany Rowold, Jens Psychologisches Institut II, WWU Münster, Münster, Germany

Exploring the effects of different leadership styles on organisational criteria is a prominent research field. The present study compared the simultaneous effects of two leadership styles (transformational leadership and LMX) on employees' subjective performance. Followers rated these leadership styles of their respective supervisor in a sample of German non-profit organisations. Employees' occupational self efficacy was assessed as a potential mediator of the anticipated effects. Results revealed that LMX had a positive effect on employees' performance and that this effect was mediated by self-efficacy. Surprisingly, transformational leadership did not affect performance but self-efficacy. Implications for leadership theory and practice are discussed.

Characteristics of body sway during stance in pregnant women and influences of anxiety during pregnancy on body sway

Nagai, Masanori Dept. of Physiology, Yamanashi Inst. Environm. Sci., Fujiyoshida, Japan Ishida, Mitsuo Physiology, Yamanashi Inst. Environm. Sci., Fujiyoshida, Japan Arii, Yoshie Nursing, Yamanashi Prefectural Universi, Kofu, Japan Natori, Hatsumi Nursing, Yamanashi Prefectural Univ., Fujiyoshida, Japan Wada, Maki College of Law, Nihon Univ., Tokyo, Japan

Pregnant women experience great changes in body alignment and mental state. In pregnant women, we have explored characteristics of body sway during stance and influences of anxiety on body sway. The area of body sway was greater in pregnant women than that in age-matched, non-pregnant women. There was no difference in path-length of body sway between pregnant and non-pregnant women. A fast Fourie's transform (FFT) analysis of body sway has shown that pregnant women rely on somatosensory inputs to maintain standing posture more greatly than non-pregnant women. Higher anxiety during pregnancy increased the area and path-length of body sway.

Leadership of managers as a facilitator of good safety management: A unique contribution of the Japanese association of traffic psychology

Nagatsuka, Yasuhiro Niigata, Japan

Objectives: Current findings of a road safety campaign study commenced in 1996 by the

Japanese Association of Traffic Psychology are reported. Methods: The campaign was aimed at removing "Looked But Failed To See" (LBFTS) error bcause it was "LBFTS" that headed accident statistics. Company president and/or other top executives of ten companies actively participated in action research with their colleague drivers. Results: In various transportation companies group cooperation in organizations was facilitated depending on the leadership of managers. As results accidents reduced in most companies. Conclusions: The campaign was considered to be informative for developing advanced safety management in company.

Comparative study of memory deficits in younger and older adults

Najam, Najma Applied Psychology and Psychol, Punjab University, Lahore, Pakistan Noor, Fatima Behaviorual Sciences, Fatima Jinnah Women University, Rawalpindi, Pakistan

Objectives: To assess and compare verbal and working memory, visuomotor abilities and verbal fluency of older and younger adults. Methods: A sample of 40 adults was administered Weschler Memory Scale, Benton Visual Retention Test (BVRT) Controlled Word Oral Association Test (CWOAT) Results: Older adults have deficits in working and visual memory with significant decline age. No significant difference in verbal memory were found. Conclusion: Evaluation of memory / cognitive functioning is needed for intervention

The influence of perceptions of retirement on psychological well-being

Nakasu, Yuka human sciences, Osaka University, Suita-shi, Osaka-hu, Japan

This study examined the effects of perceptions of retirement on marital relationship and life satisfaction after retirement. The questionnaires consisted of perceptions of retirement, marital companionship, marital satisfaction, and psychological well-being. They were administered to 200 retired men and women, whose ages ranged from 60 to 70 years old. Perceptions of retirement were categorized into three types (positive, neutral and negative). The results indicated that positive perceptions of retirement influenced marital satisfaction and psychological well-being mediated by marital companionship. In contrast, negative perceptions of retirement were associated with marital and life dissatisfaction.

Are normal narcissists psychologically healthy in stressful daily life?

Nakayama, Rumiko Nagoya University, Yokkaichi, Japan

This study was to examine correlation between narcissism and psychological health considering amount of daily (life event) stress. Participants were 239 undergraduates, and they completed narcissism scale at Time1, and scale of anger and depression, life event stress at Time1, 2 (Time 1: October, 2006, Time 2: January, 2007). There was noticeable difference between low stress and high stress group. That is, in the low stress group, narcissistic grandiosity lessens depression in 3 month (-.20, p<.001), however, in the high stress group, such impact was not showed (.06, n.s.). Results indicate that impact of narcissistic grandiosity is situation-dependent.

Graphomotoric and vocal expression in the stress condition

Nesic, Milkica DEpartment of Physiology, Faculty of Medicine, Nis, Serbia Nesic, Vladimir DEpartment of Psychology, Faculty of Phisiolophy, Nis, Cicevic, Svetlana DEpartment of Management, Faculty of Transport and Traff, Belgrade,

The aim of this investigation was to explore the effects of stress on the graphomotoric behaviour.

One hundred students of medicine participated in this study in two conditions: control condition and and just before exam. They solved mental subtracting serial seven arithmetic task. The subjects had to pronounce aloud and simultaneously to write the results. The results of digitalized voice showed higher intensity of voice and longer pauses, but shorter duration of the utterance due to anticipation stress. Changes of graphomotoric expression in the magnitude and distance of written units coresponded the changes of voice caracteristics.

Personality characters and emotional intelligent in students of distance education university

Nikpour, Gholam Ali Dept. of Psychology, Medical Clinic of Dr. Mosavi, Babol, Islamic Republic of Iran Allahyari, Abbas Ali Dept. of Psychology, University of Tarbiat Modares, Tehran, Islamic Republic of Iran Homayouni, Alireza Dept. of Psychology, Islamic Azad University, Babol (Amirkola), Islamic Republic of Iran Mosavi Amiri, Seyed Jalal Dept. of Psychology, Dr.Mosavi Clinic, Babol (Amirkola), Islamic Republic of Iran

The study investigated this research question that are there specific personality characters that related to emotional intelligent ? Method research is causative-comparative (Ex post facto).73 students of distance education university were randomly selected and Mokioly's Characterlogy Inventory (MCI) and Shutt Emotional Intelligent Inventory(SEII) were administered on them. The inventory assesses personality based on eight characters: sanguine, indifferent,nervous,indolent,indignant,-passionate,sentimentee, amorphous. Data analyzed with ANOVA. Results showed significant differences between grades of emotional intelligent in personality caracters that most of students with high in emotional intelligent are indignant and nervous. Conclusion: The finding can be used for predicting and increasing of social interaction and academic performance in university in regard to individual differences specially personality factors.

Incidence of anxiety in students of Azad Islamic University

Noughani, Fatemeh Faculty of Nursing and Midwife, Tehran University, Tehran, Islamic Republic of Iran

Introduction: Approximately so percents of adults with 15-45 years old have experienced a psychiatric problem. Methods and materials:This study is an analytic-descriptive research that examines students' anxiety of Azad University, Varamin- Pishva Branch.The samples were 400 students.Data collection tool was questionnaire including two sections: First section consist 17 questions about demographic data, Second section consist SCL-90 test anxiety. Findings:The results of this research showed that prevalence of anxiety in students were 22.2 percents. Conclusion:Because high prevalence rate of mental disorders in students of university, we recommended advices for promotion of anxiety in university such as consultation centers.

The relation between intolerance of uncertainty and worry about ambiguous situations in older adults

Nuevo, Roberto Psychiatry Service, Hospital de la Princesa, MADRID, Spain Márquez-González, María Psicologia Biologica y de la S, Universidad Autónoma de Madrid, MADRID, Spain Cabrera, Isabel Psicologia Biologica y de la S, Universidad Autonoma de Madrid, MADRID, Spain Montorio, Ignacio Psicologia Biologica y de la S, Universidad Autonoma de Madrid, MADRID, Spain

Objective: to explore the relations between Intolerance of Uncertainty (IU) and Worry about Ambiguous Situations (WAS) in older adults. Method: 111 community-dwelling older adults completed measures of IU, WAS, severity of worry, trait-anxiety, and depression. Results: A hierarchical regression analysis revealed that IU explained a

significant (p=.004) percentage of variance in WAS after controlling for gender, age, severity of worry, trait-anxiety, and depression (total adjusted R2=.169). IU was the only significant predictor in the final equation. Conclusions: these results highlight the potential role of intolerance of uncertainty in the explanation of excessive worry in the old age.

Are differences in reading performance between students with or without LD better explained in terms of IQ or reading-related cognitive deficits?

O'Shanahan, Isabel Didácticas Específicas, Facultad de Educación, La Laguna, Spain Jiménez, Juan E. Psicología, Facultad de Psicología, La Laguna, Spain

The focus of the study reported here was to explore the effects of the IQ and reading-related cognitive deficits in the explanation of differences in reading performance between students with or without LD. A sample of 443 Spanish children (264 Male, 179 female) were classified into four groups according to IQ as measured by the Culture Fair (or Free) Intelligence Tests Raven (<80, 81-90, 91-109, 110-140) and into two groups based on reading level (LD and NLD). Our findings indicate that IQ does not explain the differences between children with LD and NLD children in reading-related cognitive deficits.

An investigation of the source(s) of conscious awareness of action

Obhi, Sukhvinder Dept. of Psychology, Wilfrid Laurier University, Waterloo, Canada

Participants made judgments about the initiation times of active and passive key-presses that varied in their force. Judgments were made by reporting the position of a rotating clock hand. Results showed that awareness of action for both active and passive movements was anticipatory and identical, and that judgments of forceful movements were less anticipatory than judgments of softer movements. This suggests that the signal underlying conscious awareness of movement initiation was not premotor, but instead related to sensory feedback arising from the movement. Thus, the brain can use efferent and afferent information sources for conscious decisions about action timing.

Effects of horticultural therapy activities on mood in students of occupational therapy department

Ogawa, Noriyuki Occupational Therapy, Kyushu University of H&W, Nobeoka, Miyazaki-Prif., Japan Koura, Seigo Occupational Therapy, Kyushu University of H&W, Nobeoka, Miyazaki-Prif., Japan Oshikawa, Takeshi Occupational Therapy, Kyushu University of H&W, Nobeoka, Miyazaki-Prif., Japan

It is usual in the student of the Occupational Therapy Department to often feel the stress by the clinical training. These researches were an investigation into changing attitudes among their students that participated in horticultural therapy activities. The 'Profile of Mood State' was used to measure changes in students' moods and emotions. Consequently, the values for negative factors decreased after the horticultural therapy activities. The benefits of horticultural activities with occupational therapy technique can be seen not only in the area of general therapeutic effect but also in the positive effects on all related peoples' emotional health.

Incessant unrest in Kaduna state, Nigeria: Youths involvement and its implication for their educational development.

Ohidah, Eunice Ozavive Education, Kaduna Polytechnic Kaduna, Kaduna, Nigeria Kato, Rosemary EDUCATION (TECHNICAL), KADUNA POLYTECHNIC, KADUNA, KADUNA, Nigeria Ornengala, Arikeola EDUCATION (TECHNICAL), KADUNA POLYTECHNIC, KADUNA, KADUNA, Nigeria

Kaduna State occupies a very strategic position in the academic development of Nigerian Nation. Premiere universities, polytechnics and monotechnics in Northern Nigeria are located there. It is known as centre of learning. But crises of different nature have bedeviled it and distorted its prospect for fast educational development, especially among the youths. This study looked at the involvement of youths in such crises as most of the time they were blamed for the unrest. How has this affected their educational development? How can they be engaged in targeted activities towards their educational development? Samples are drawn from both Urban and Rural centers. BY: E. O OHIDAH; R. KATO AND A. A. OMENGALA KADUNA POLYTECHNIC, KADUNA NIGERIA

Odor identification impairment predicts cognitive decline and Alzheimer's disease

Olofsson, Jonas Dept. of Psychology, Stockholm University, Stockholm, Sweden Rönnlund, Michael Department of Psychology, Umeå University, Umeå, Sweden Nordin, Steven Department of Psychology, Umeå University, Umeå, Sweden Hedner, Margareta Psychology department, Stockholm University, Stockholm, Sweden Nilsson, Lars-Göran Psychology department, Stockholm University, Stockholm, Sweden Nyberg, Lars Dept. of Radiation Sciences, Umeå University, Umeå, Sweden Larsson, Maria Psychology department, Stockholm University, Stockholm, Sweden

Assessment of odor identification ability (ODID) has been proposed to improve early detection of Alzheimer's disease (AD), since olfactory structures are affected in early stages of AD. We investigated the relationship between ODID and cognitive functioning (MMSE) to AD conversion within a five-year test interval using data from the large-scale, longitudinal Betula study. Preliminary results indicate that ODID impairment is associated with AD conversion, as well as to cognitive decline in non-demented elderly, at five years post-test. The results suggest that olfactory deficits are indicative of changes in the aging brain.

The Road to Happiness? Car use and subjective well-being

Olsson, Lars E. Center for Consumer Science, Gothenburg University, Gothenburg, Sweden Jakobsson, Cecilia Center for Consumer Science, Gothenburg University, Gothenburg, Sweden Gamble, Amelie Center for Consumer Science, Gothenburg University, Gothenburg, Sweden Gärling, Tommy Center for Consumer Science, Gothenburg University, Gothenburg, Sweden

Are there any interactions between, on the one hand, motives for car use and access to a car, and on the other hand, everyday travel and activity patterns, satisfaction with transportation, and subjective well-being? A questionnaire containing (i) cognitive and affective evaluations of life satisfaction, (ii) transportation satisfaction, as well as (iii) different measures associated to everyday activities, will provide answers. Responses from (i) 3000 randomly selected households (autumn 2007), and (ii) 100 families agreeing to change their transport behaviour, will be analysed. The latter families will answer questionnaires repeatedly, both before their changes (autumn 2007) and after (spring 2008).

Epidemiology of mental disorders in urbanized areas of Natanz in Iran

Omidi, Abdollah Dept. of Health, Kashan Medical University, Kashan, Islamic Republic of Iran

Abstract Objectives: The present study was an epidemiological assessment of mental disorders among 15 years or older residents of urbanized areas of the Natanz. Methods: 650 families randomly were selected, then randomly one person from each family. After General Health Questionnaire 62 man and 107 women were above cut off point, evaluated by clinical interviews according to DSM-IV criteria. Results: The rate of mental

disorders is 17.2% for men and 31.3% for women. Significant correlations was between mental disorders and age, sex, education, marriage, employment, family history. The most prevalent disorders were Dysthymic disorder(5.8%),generalized anxiety(5.3%),and depression(3.3%). Conclusion: Prevalence of mental disorders is (24.2%).

Phonological advance planning in sentence production

Oppermann, Frank Inst. für Psychologie I, Universität Leipzig, Leipzig, Germany Jescheniak, Jörg D. Institut für Psychologie I, University of Leipzig, Leipzig, Germany Schriefers, Herbert NICI, Radboud University Nijmegen, Nijmegen, Netherlands

Our study addressed the scope of phonological advance planning, extending previous work on phrase production (Jescheniak et al., 2003, JEP:HPP). Participants decribed visual scenes by producing sentences in various formats, while ignoring auditory distractors phonologically related or unrelated to either the depicted agents or patients. Distractors related to a noun in the utterance-initial phrase consistently facilitated the naming response, while distractors related to a non-initial noun interfered with it. This interference effect was modulated by the serial position of the second noun. Overall, our findings suggest that the scope of phonological advance planning might well span over a complete sentence.

The development and validation of Dichotomous thinking scale

Oshio, Atsushi Dept. of Psychology, Chubu University, Kasugai, Japan

Dichotomous thinking is to think things as binary opposition. This thinking style is helpful for us to understand things easily. But it is also related to some negative psychological constructs such as borderline personality disorder and perfectionism. The purpose of this study was to develop useful and well-validated inventory of dichotomous thinking. Participants were 386 Japanese undergraduates. Factor analysis of Dichotomous Thinking Inventory revealed two factors; preference for dichotomy and dichotomous belief. Both subscales positively related to borderline personality disorder scale. People who score high on the inventory were rated as chary and open-and-shut person by their friends.

Frequency effects in reading words mixed with nonwords in the Italian transparent orthography

Paizi, Despina ISTC-CNR, Rome, Italy Zoccolotti, Pierluigi Psychology, University of Rome La Sapienza, Rome, Italy Burani, Cristina ISTC, CNR, Rome, Italy

When in transparent scripts words are mixed with nonwords, word frequency effects can be eliminated. Readers either de-emphasise the lexical route (route de-emphasis) or homogenise reaction times for all stimuli by adjusting a time criterion for articulation (time criterion account). With four list manipulations we assessed frequency effects in reading aloud words and nonwords in Italian. No list context effect was found, but frequency effects remained constant irrespective of list manipulation. These results pose a challenge for the route de-emphasis and the time criterion accounts. Reading nonwords may be easier in Italian than in English, therefore strategic control is unnecessary.

Woman and leadership: Steps towards authentication

Palumbo, Gabriella Dept. of Ontopsychology, A.I.O., NGO in UN Cons. Status, Rome, Italy Bermabei, Pamela A.I.O. - F.A.i.L., Italy, Roma, Italy

The aim of the work is : 1)to describe how to analyse and advice psychologically, socially and economically woman from adolescence to maturity; 2) to present the application of ontopsychological approach to evolve female leaderistic attitude; 3)to identify and discuss concrete suggestions to facil-

itate woman leadership. In particular the following aspects will be discussed: a)partner realtionship; b)woman and family; c)sexual understanding; d) strategies for woman leadership in our times.

Assessing the equivalence of computerized vs. face-to-face leaderless group discussion:A task-technology fit perspective

Pan, Lushan School of Management, Zhejiang University, Hangzhou, People's Republic of China Fan, Wei

This study compared the predictive validity between computerized and face-to-face leaderless group discussion (LGD) in different tasks. Seventy-two 5-person groups of university students worked in either computerized or face-to-face LGD on both cooperation and competition situation. ANOVA of test data showed that there is no significant difference between medium when applicant performed in the cooperation task. However, difference in the competition task, with computerized LGD reporting lower predictive validity. Furthermore, to investigate the effect mechanism of medium on applicant performance, this study found that socioemotional communication as well as task-oriented communication plays important mediating roles between medium and criterion.

The contribution of sex-role identity to vocational interests and occupational preference in Greek adolescents

Paraskevopoulou, Polyxeni Athens, Greece Kontoulis, Ioannis PSYCHOLOGY, UNIVERSITY OF ATHENS, ATHENS, Greece Pischos, Charalampos PSYCHOLOGY, UNIVERSITY OF ATHENS, ATHENS, Greece

Measures of sex-role orientation, vocational interests and occupational preference are obtained from adolescents pupils. The aim of the study is to define the orientation between sex-role identity (masculinity and androgyny) and vocational interests (Holland's vocational types), as well as, the relation between sex-role identity and adolescents' occupational interests. Additionally, interaction of parents' occupation to adolescents' vocational interests and occupational preference is examined.

Effects of concept mapping on nursing students learning retention

Parsa Yekta, Zoreh Medical-Surgical Nursing, Tehran Univ. of Medical Scienc, Tehran, Islamic Republic of Iran Parsa Yekta, Zohreh MEDICAL-SURGICAL NURSING, TEHRAN UNIVERSITY OF MEDICAL S, TEHRAN, Islamic Republic of Iran Taghavi, Taraneh MEDICAL-SURGICAL NURSING, TEHRAN UNIVERSITY OF MEDICAL S, TEHRAN, Islamic Republic of Iran

Objective:determination of concept mapping's effects on nursing students learning retention.Material&Methods:a quasi-experimental research :experimental(n=106)control(n=99)was designed(lecture for case and concept mapping for control group,data collection by a questionnaire).Results:The scores of the case was considerably higher than the control group(p<0.005).There was a significant statistical difference(p<0.05)between the mean score of cumulative post-test(case=73.29/100&control=68.69/100)as well as scores of retention test(case=72.40/100&control53.30/100). Conclusion: The concept mapping as a teaching method has significant effects on nursing student learning and their retention.

Problem-based learning and graduates' competencies

Patria, Bhina INCHER, Universität Kassel, Kassel, Germany

This paper investigates differences in competencies among graduates. Two groups were compared, group of graduates who studied in higher education with a high emphasis on problem-based learning (group 1); and group of graduates who studied in higher education institution with less emphasis on problem-based learning (group 2). CHEERS data which consist of 2000 graduates from 13 countries in Europe and Japan were analysed. The result of t-test analysis indicates that there are significant differences of competencies between graduates in group 1 and 2. Group 1 have higher competencies in Leadership, Personal working skills, Organisational skills, Interpersonal skills and Field-related knowledge.

The effectiveness of the leadership: The feedback of the collaborators like element of comparison and increase for the manager

Pellegrini, Matteo Psychological Department, Università di Verona, Verona, Italy Nocera, Antonio Psychological Department, Università di Verona, Verona, Italy Tronchet, Stefano Psychological Department, Università di Verona, Verona, Italy Bellotto, Massimo Psychological Department, Università di Verona, Verona, Italy

The aim of this research is to explore the perceptions of managers and those of their collaborators about the most-effective leadership-styles (optimal-style) to put them in relationship each others and with behaviours (really) used. The sample consists in 100 European managers and 600 collaborators. The survey instrument is a questionnaire on Leadership-style (Blake-Mouton-Managerial-Grid-Model). Analysis of data highlights strong correspondences, in the two groups, about the perception of the optimal leadership-style. In both groups, however, there are significant differences between optimal leadership-style and really-used style and between self-perception of managers about their behaviours and perception of the collaborators about manager behaviours.

Empirical evidence of the relationship between impulsivity and aggression

Pereda, Noemi Assess. and Psych. Treatment, University of Barcelona, Barcelona, Spain Gallardo Pujol, David Pers., Assess. & Psych. Tr, University of Barcelona, Barcelona, Spain García Forero, Carlos Pers., Assess. & Psych. Tr, University of Barcelona, Barcelona, Spain Maydeu Olivares, Alberto Pers., Assess. & Psych. Tr, University of Barcelona, Barcelona, Spain Andrés Pueyo, Antonio Pers., Assess. & Psych. Tr, University of Barcelona, Barcelona, Spain

Introduction: There is a misconception in the literature about the impulsive aggression concept. Objective: Our aim was to provide empirical evidence of the relationship between impulsivity and aggression. Methods: BIS and AQ-R were administered to 768 healthy respondents. Pearson's and canonical correlations were then calculated. A Principal Components Analysis was also conducted to explore whether impulsive aggression can be defined phenotypically as a single component. Results: The common variance between impulsivity and aggressiveness was never higher than 42%. The PCA reveals that one component is not enough to represent all the variables. Conclusion: Our results show that impulsivity and aggressiveness are two separate, although related constructs.

Socio-emotional and intellectual correlations in children's attitudes about conflict

Perez Fernandez, Jose Ignacio Personality and Psychological, Faculty of Psychology, San Sebastian, Spain Garaigordobil Landazabal, Maite Personality and Psychological, Faculty of Psychology, San Sebastian, Spain Maganto Mateo, Carmen Personality and Psychological, Faculty of Psychology, San Sebastian, Spain

The purpose of this study is two-fold: a) to study the concomitant relationships between children's attitude about conflict and different factors of their intellectual and socio-emotional development; and

b) to identify the predictive variables of positive attitudes about conflict. The sample consists of 90 children aged 7 to 9. The study uses correlational methodology. Pearson coefficients show strong relationships between positive attitudes about conflict and higher levels of intellectual and socio-emotional development. Through multiple regression analyses, the following variables were identified as predictors of positive attitudes about conflict: self-evaluation as a creative person, low aggressiveness, and high non-verbal intelligence. The ANOVA results do not reveal gender or age differences in attitudes about conflict.

Does life satisfaction change over a year?: Different answer among different age groups

Pezzuti, Lina Dep. Clinical Psychology, Universita di Roma, Roma, Italy Artistico, Daniele Baruch COllege, The City University of New Yor, New York, USA Picone, Laura Dep. Clinical Psychology, Faculty Psycology, ROMA, Italy

Objectives. The objective of this work is to study life satisfaction among older adults. Methods. To accomplish this goal we designed a longitudinal study by recruiting 80 older adults that were tested twice (average follow-up 408 days). Life Satisfaction scores were analysed in conjunction with indices of education, health, and age. Results. After follow-up life-satisfaction scores decreased overall. However, significant interactions with age, education, and health were found to explain part of the variance. Specifically, life satisfaction did not decrease among the "young-older" adults (65-75 yrs) with a higher level of education and the "old-older" adults (76+) in good health.

Prevalence of pain in veterans suffering from post-traumatic stress disorder

Poundja, Joaquin Research Centre, Douglas Hospital, Montreal, Canada Fikretoglu, Deniz Research Centre, Douglas Hospital, Montreal, Canada Brunet, Alain Research Centre, Douglas Hospital, Montreal, Canada

Objectives: To assess for the prevalence of physical pain in veterans suffering from post-traumatic stress disorder (PTSD), and to compare this prevalence to other samples of pain suffering patients. Methods: We administered the Brief Pain Inventory and the PTSD Checklist at a Veterans Affairs Canada PTSD clinic (N=130). Confidence intervals were used for pain prevalence comparisons. Results: Nearly 87% of these veterans were suffering from pain; these rates were similar/higher than most of those reported by populations suffering from a physical disability/illness or cancer pain. Conclusions: Pain is a major issue in PTSD suffering veterans and should be screened for.

Nightlife leisure of people between 15 and 35 years old: A case study in a Spanish city

Prado Gascó, Vicente Javier Psicologia Social, Universidad de Valencia, Valencia, Spain Quintanilla Pardo, Ismael Psicologia Social, Universidad de Valencia, valencia, Spain

Objectives: Describe and analyze "Nightlife Leisure" perception of people involved in the phenomenon. Show the Generalized profile of that people. Compare the profile with other groups. H1: People of the generalized profile are less aware of the "Nightlife leisure" drawbacks than others H1.1:Women are more aware H1.2:Old People are more aware H1.3:Post-university are more aware H1.4:People that go out more than 8 times are more aware H1.5:People that spend less than 20 Euros a night are more aware Methods Administration of the DSM. Factor analysis, correlations, regression, ANOVA, (SPSS14). Sample=1022 subjects. Results The hypothesis have been partially confirmed

The effet of sadness and age on components of attention

Quaireau, Christophe Lab. of Exp. Psychology, University of Rennes 2, Rennes, France Lemercier, Celine Lab. travail et cognition, University of Toulouse, Toulouse, France Boujon, Christophe Lab. of Psychology -, University of Angers, Angers, France

Driver inattention is thought to cause many automobile crashes. Inattention appears when information, non pregnant and non relevant mobilize our mind, like negative emotion and rumination. This study explore the effect of sadness and the effect of age on three components of attention (alert, orientation and executive control) measured with the attention network test – ANT (Fan 2002). Subjects are assessed by a computerized ANT task without or after a negative mood induction (Mayer, 1995) and instruction to get gloomy thoughts. Anova is used to put forward the effect of sadness and the effect of age on the three components of attention.

Basic level as the pattern of activation in the conceptual system

Radchikova, Nataly Dept. of Psychology, BSPU, Minsk, Belarus

It is proposed to explain cognitive privilege of some categories in taxonomy (basic level effect) by a higher activation of corresponding concepts in the conceptual system of individual. Three consequences of this explanation are experimentally checked and allow to make the following conclusions: 1. Basic level(s) could be easily shifted or added because the mechanism of activation has to be quick and efficient to serve for adaptation purposes. 2. There is no connection between basic level and typicality: both typical and atypical members of categories may show basic level effect. 3. Some abstract concepts could show basic level effect.

Return to work after major depression: A 5-year naturalistic follow-up study

Raitasalo, Raimo Research Department, The Social Insurance Institut, Helsinki, Finland Toikka, Tuula Research Department, The Social Insurance Instituti, Helsinki, Finland Salminen, Jouko Research Department, National Public Health Institu, Turku, Finland Saarijärvi, Simo Department of Psychiatry, Turku University Hospital, Turku, Finland

Objectives. Do baseline psychiatric and psychological factors predict return to work of depressive outpatients? Methods. The study group comprised 131 depressive outpatients, who were on sick leave due to their illness. Several psychological measures as the Beck Hopelessness Scale and WAIS-R were used. Statistical tests were Students t, chi-square and logistic regression analysis. Results. Return to work after five years was associated with sel-efficacy and motivation to stay at work. Conclusions. When palnning treatment for depressive patients, it is important to support their ability to sustain hopefulness and motivation.

Autobiographical memory in remitted bipolar disorder

Ramos, Ines Psicologia Aplicada, ISPA - Instituto Superior de, Almada, Portugal Cláudio, Victor Clínica, ISPA, Lisboa, Portugal

Memory processing and recall in bipolar disorder were studied analysing the valence and structure of evoked autobiographical memories. A group of subjects with bipolar disorder (n=15) was compared with a group without psychopathological symptoms (n=15). The individuals were evaluated using the Autobiographical Memory Task, Beck Depression Inventory, Hamilton Depression Scale, Hipomania Scale, Positive and Negative Affect Schedule, and State-Trait Anxiety Inventory. The bipolar group reported a frequent recall of negative and categorical autobiographical memories. This study suggests that the predominance of general autobiographical memories maintains and increases symptoms in bipolar disorder.

Psychological practices in public health services in Brazil

Rasera, Emerson F. Instituto de Psicologia, Uberlândia, Brazil Goya, Ana Carolina A. Instituto de Psicologia, Univ. Federal de Uberlândia, Uberlândia, Brazil

This study aims to describe the psychological practices developed in public health services in a Brazilian city. The data was collected by semi-structured interviews with nineteen psychologists and analyzed through the constructionist perspective. The main results were: emphasis on individual psychotherapy; group activities as a response to the increasing mental health demand; absence of activities related to health promotion and prevention; lack of social-political involvement; unfamiliarity with the directions of the National Health System. These results point to the need to promote changes in Psychology training in Brazil in order to offer a better response to public health needs.

With a little help from my spouse...: Shared everyday-life knowledge facilitates collaboration in old age

Rauers, Antje Lifespan Psychology, MPI for Human Development, Berlin, Germany Riediger, Michaela Lifespan Psychology, MPI for Human Development, Berlin, Germany Schmiedek, Florian Lifespan Psychology, MPI for Human Development, HU, Berlin, Germany Lindenberger, Ulman Lifespan Psychology, MPI for Human Development, Berlin, Germany

Older adults may compensate for individual losses in cognitive performance by collaborating with others. We predict that using shared everyday knowledge with a familiar partner facilitates this collaboration, especially for older adults. In an experimental paradigm based on the game Taboo, participants had to explain target words to another person using as few hints as possible. 76 younger (20-30 years), and 84 older adults (70-80 years) worked once with an unfamiliar partner, and once with their spouses. As predicted, especially older adults profited from collaborating with their spouses, and from the strategy of using shared everyday-life knowledge.

To identify the health status and social interaction of the elderly in earth quake areas of Pakistan

Rauf, Nelofar Dept. of Psychology, Quaid A Azam University, Islamabad, Pakistan Akbar, Asma public health trainer, Helpage International, Islamabad, Pakistan

It was a baseline study conducted in 38 IDP camps of Muzaffarabad and Hatian Bala. Results identified that Athritus is more commonly indicated illness in IDP camps that is 497 cases were identified. While second to arthritis are eye Problems 9.9%. Out of 2190 caretakers/family members of elderly 1155 (52.7%) replied that they are aware of the illness/disease of the elderly in their home. Before earthquake most of the elderly population (63.1%) in the IDP camps daily socialize with other people in their area while after the disaster this percentage reduced to 47.6%.

Bimanual distractor interference

Ray, Matthew Kinesiology, University of Calgary, Calgary, Canada Welsh, Tim Kinesiology, University of Calgary, Calgary, Canada Weeks, Daniel Psychology, Simon Fraser University, Burnaby, Canada

Previous research has shown that during a bimanual selective reaching task in which the left hand responded to targets in left space and the right hand responded to targets in right space, distractors presented in contralateral space caused the greatest

amount of interference. In the present study, the left hand responded to targets in the bottom of the screen and the right hand to targets in the top of the screen to determine if the contralateral effect is based on conflict between hands or space. Results suggest that side of space is key to the effect.

The effectiveness of stage-matched interventions in promoting multiple health behaviours

Remme, Lena Berlin, Germany Lippke, Sonia Health Psychology, FU Berlin, Berlin, Germany Wiedemann, Amelie Ulrike Health Psychology, FU Berlin, Berlin, Germany Ziegelmann, Jochen Phillip Health Psychology, FU Berlin, Berlin, Germany Reuter, Tabea Health Psychology, FU Berlin, Berlin, Germany Gravert, Christian Gesundheits- und Sozialpolitik, Deutsche Bahn AG, Berlin, Germany

Objectives: Testing the effectiveness of a stage-matched intervention in promoting physical activity and healthy nutrition in a randomized controlled trial. Methods: Participants (N=442) were randomized to stage-matched or standard-care treatments. Multivariate analyses in a longitudinal design (1-month follow-up). Results: Physical activity: The stage-matched intervention was superior to the standard-care intervention in increasing goal-setting and behaviour. Nutrition: The stage-matched intervention was superior in behaviour promotion, and as effective as the standard-care intervention in enhancing goal-setting. Conclusions: Compared to standard-care, stage-matched interventions are effective interventions to promote a healthy lifestyle. Stage theories serve as a valid theoretical backdrop when designing interventions.

To be or not to be at risk: Spontaneous reactions to risk information

Renner, Britta Inst. für Psychologie, Universität Konstanz, Konstanz, Germany

The present study examined spontaneous responses after cholesterol and blood pressure risk feedback in South Koreans (N = 951). Most spontaneous responses were related to four types of reactions: Emotions, feedback valence, expectedness, and lifestyle change. This pattern emerged consistently across different threat levels (low, borderline high, high risk) and across different types of risk feedback (cholesterol, blood pressure). Importantly, three out of the four most often generated types of reactions (emotions, expectedness, and lifestyle change) are comparably underrepresented in previous research. Moreover, the results suggest that predominantly adaptive response patterns were generated in the face of personally consequential feedback.

Prideful self-reliance: older men's account of masculinity in caregiving

Ribeiro, Oscar M. ICBAS - UP, UNIFAI, Porto, Portugal Paúl, Constança ICBAS - UP, UNIFAI, Porto, Portugal

Literature on older men as family caregivers has been increasing as it has the efforts in understanding later life masculinities. This qualitative study relied on a sample of 50 men aged 65+ (mean age 78 years) caring for their dependent wives, and aimed to identify their major difficulties and coping strategies used to deal with the situation. Main burdening consequences are related to changes in interpersonal relationship dynamics, the presence of sub-clinical depressive symptoms and self-negligent health behaviors. The influence of strong views of masculinity on the expression of psychological burden and on the use of community services are discussed along with its implications for professional practice.

Intervention-engagement and its role in the effectiveness of stage-matched interventions: Evidence from an online study on physical activity

Richert, Jana Inst. Gesundheitspsychologie, Freie Universität Berlin, Berlin, Germany Lippke, Sonia Health Psychology, Freie Universität Berlin, Berlin, Germany Ziegelmann, Jochen Health Psychology, Freie Universität Berlin, Berlin, Germany

Objectives To test whether stage-matched treatments are superior to mismatched and control treatments in the promotion of physical activity. To investigate the relationship between intervention-engagement and the different interventions. Methods N=427 participants were randomized to a stage-matched, mismatched or control treatment. Multivariate analyses; baseline, 1- and 6-months follow-up measures. Results Stage-matched interventions were superior to all other conditions with regard to motivational and volitional variables. Intervention-engagement was a marginally significant moderator. Type of intervention had no effect on level of intervention-engagement. Conclusions Interventions are most effective in promoting physical activity when they are stage-matched and when intervention-engagement is high.

Integrated diagnostic and health prevention for nursing staff in elderly care

Richter, Peter Arbeits-, Organis.-Psychologie, Techn. Universität Dresden, Dresden, Germany

The work-place situation of nurses is characterised by high work demands and vulnerability for stress-related health outcomes (Schaufeli, 2007). Risk-models require the combined analysis of psychological and physical workload. This study, consisting of 194 nurses in elderly care (response rate: 85, 6 %), intended to identify risk factors at work by use of questionnaires and objective method. Muscle pain and reduced psychological health were associated with high psychological job demands, non- permanent work contracts, and increased physical workload. In addition, poor ergonomic conditions, reduced social support, and information deficits, jointly, are correlated with higher muscle-skeletal complaints.

Willingness to support the elderly: The view of adult children and the elderly

Ries, Thierry FLSHASE, Universität Luxemburg, Walferdange, Luxembourg Ferring, Dieter INSIDE, University of Luxembourg, Walferdange, Luxembourg

An over-ageing of European societies will have consequences in several domains especially with respect to social expenditures, health provision and education. People may live longer but this does also imply that they will sometimes be longer in need of health care. The present study picked up the notion of supporting the elderly in case of sickness and disability. In a first study on 2.175 subjects (60-90 years), the view of the elderly concerning the willingness of their offspring to support them was analyzed; in a second study this willingness was investigated in a sample of 1.208 adult children (40-50 years).

A behavioural intervention program to prevent HIV/STI and unwanted pregnancies among Mexican adolescents

Robles Montijo, Silvia Susana Investigación-UIICSE, FES Iztacala-UNAM, Tlalnepantla, Mexico Moreno Rodríguez, Diana Investigación-UIICSE, FES IZTACALA-UNAM, Tlalnepantla, Edo. de México., Mexico Rodríguez Campuzano, Lourdes Investigación-UIICSE, FES IZTACALA-UNAM, Tlalnepantla, Edo. de México., Mexico Díaz González y Anaya, Eugenio Investigación-UIICSE, FES IZTACALA-UNAM, Tlalnepantla, Edo. de México., Mexico Frías Arroyo, Beatriz Investigación-UIICSE, FES IZTACALA-UNAM, Tlalnepantla, Edo. de México.,

Mexico **Rodríguez Cervantes, Martha** *Investigación-UIICSE, FES IZTACALA-UNAM, Tlalnepantla, Edo. de México., Mexico* **Barroso Villegas, Rodolfo** *Investigación-UIICSE, FES IZTACALA-UNAM, Tlalnepantla, Edo. de México., Mexico* **Castillo Nava, Pilar** *Investigación-UIICSE, FES IZTACALA-UNAM, Tlalnepantla, Edo. de México., Mexico*

This paper reports a study that assessed the effectiveness of a behavioural program to prevent sexual risk behaviours among two hundred adolescents of 14.5 years mean age, with and without sexual experience. A pre-test-post-test experimental design with control and experimental groups was used. During pre and post evaluation phases participants completed self-report questionnaires assessing psychosocial (beliefs, attitudes, self-efficacy, norms, and intentions toward condom use) and behavioural (communication about sex, condom use negotiation styles, the type of partner and sexual practices, frequency of condom use and correct condom use skill) variables. The results show differences between the experimental and control groups, and among teenagers with and without sexual experience after behavioural training phase.

Aged people and Sense of Community (SC)

Rodriguez Feijoo, Nelida *Dept. de Psicología, CONICET - CIIPME, Buenos Aires, Argentina* **Vignale, Paula** *Psicología, CONICET - CIIPME, Capital Federal - Buenos Aires, Argentina*

The aim of this research is to analyze the relationship between aged people and SC. A Personal Data Questionnaire and a SC Scale were given to 350 Argentinean of different age, gender and social and economical level. Factor and Variance Analyses were used. Results suggest that some social and demographic variables considered have a statistically significant influence on the respondents' SC. Given the longevity growth and the need to maintain the quality of life, aged people' SC is a piece of information that must be taken into account when considering moving to a new neighborhood or a geriatric institution.

Depression and medical conditions in a probabilistic Puerto Rican elderly sample

Rodriguez Gomez, Jose *PhD Psychology Program, Carlos Albizu University, San Juan, Puerto Rico* **Quintero, Noel** *PhD Psychology Program, Carlos Albizu University, San Juan, Puerto Rico* **Auger, Carmen** *PhD Psychology Program, Carlos Albizu University, San Juan, Puerto Rico*

In PR, a Caribbean island under the government of the USA, a total of 425,137 elderly have been identified representing an increase of 11.2 percent in comparison with the 1990 Census(Hetzel & Smith, 2001). In this study, a causal-comparative, cross-sectional design was used; comparing older adults (n = 410, mean age 75.6 years) according to their depressive symptoms level in terms of the number of medical conditions reported by them. Our findings suggest that a mild moderate but significant relationship exists between depression and medical conditions (rho = .31, p < .05). Public Health implications are presented and discussed

Frequency of word-use predicts behavior in patients with Alzheimer disease

Rohlfs Dominguez, Paloma *Personalidad y Evaluacion, Universidad de Granada, Granada, Spain*

We have studied the impact of the frequency effect on the word production deficit commonly manifestad by patients with mild Alzheimer disease when performing an object naming task. We speculated that patients (N= 10), would commit more errors than controls (N= 26) and that both spanish groups would show significantly the frequency effect. The results of statistical error analysis for intergroup comparison indicated that, overall, controls performed the task better than patients, but while the

control group showed a significant frequency effect, the patients showed only a trend to a significant inverse frequency effect. Further research is needed to explain this last result.

Caregiving and personal growth: Two irreconcilable concepts?

Rohr, Margund K. *Inst. für Psychogerontologie, Universität Erlangen-Nürnberg, Erlangen, Germany* **Lang, Frieder R.** *Inst. für Psychogerontologie, Universität Erlangen-Nürnberg, Erlangen, Germany*

Psychological research on caregivers of older adults focusses on burden emphasizing risks of stress, depression and loss. Only recently attention is paid to the possible rewarding aspects of caregiving tasks and the process itself. However, longitudinal studies assessing changes in the caregiver process are still rare. The current study aims at caregiving transitions using data from the German Socio-Economic-Panel (SOEP, N = 8804). Resilient and burdened caregivers are differentiated based on indicators of personal growth and competence in everyday activities and social participation. Findings point to opportunity benefits of the caregiving situation and determinants of personal growth among caregivers.

Synergetic approach to integration of liberal and technical education

Romanovsky, Aleksandre *Psychology, National Technical University, Kiev, Ukraine* **Irina, Vasilyeva** *Psychology, National Technical University, Kiev, Ukraine* **Irina, Yuryeva** *Psychology, National Technical University, Kiev, Ukraine* **Olga, Ignatyuk** *Psychology, National Technical University, Kiev, Ukraine* **Nataliya, Usyk** *Psychology, National Technical University, Kiev, Ukraine*

Objective To find out general laws of building individual education algorythms Methods The research was done on a sample of 5000 (the experimental group included 500) third- and fourth-year students of informatics department at Kharkiv Polytechnics using mathematic modelling, testing, interviewing, and a laboratory experiment. Results The experimental group's performance increased by 16.2% due to the application of the found algorithm of adaptation to studying the integrated arts and technical course. Analytical correlations between components of individual training allowed to receive data necessary for successful knowledge acquisition. Conclusions Analytical laws of the adaptation can be used in building self-improving intellectual computer systems. The findings can be helpful in developing various training courses.

Leadership relationship with unit climate and soldiers' motivation for task accomplishment in military structures

Rozcenkova, Andzela *Dept. of Psychology, University of Latvia, Riga, Latvia*

Abstract Leadership relationship with unit climate and soldiers' motivation for task accomplishment in military structures Andzela Rozcenkova University of Latvia Riga, Latvia The study explores transformational leadership in military structures: (1) if there is significant relationship between commanders' leadership and unit climate, soldiers' motivation for task accomplishment; (2) if there is significant relationship between commanders' self-esteem leadership and soldiers' estimate. Methods: Unit Climate profile (U.S. Army Research Institute, 1990), Leadership profile (Nissinen, 2001), Groups' motivation of task accomplishment (LV National Defence Academy, 2004). Participants: platoon officers (N=25) and soldiers (N=500). Theoretical and methodological implications are discussed in the research.

Motor bottleneck or central response monitoring in temporally overlapping tasks?

Ruiz, Susana *Psychologisches Institut, Universität Tübingen, Tübingen, Germany* **Ulrich, Rolf** *Psychologisches Institut, Universität Tübingen, Tübingen, Germany*

Although there is strong evidence for a central bottleneck process in temporally overlapping reaction time tasks, recent psychological refractory period (PRP) studies indicate that bottleneck processes may also include the response execution stage, or alternatively, processes of response monitoring. This experiment was designed to disentangle these two alternatives. To this end, we manipulated the temporal demand for Task 2 execution in a PRP paradigm. A clear effect of Task 2 manipulation on Task 1 reaction time was obtained even when the execution processes of the two tasks did not temporally overlap. This result supports the response execution hypothesis.

Schizotypal personality and the five-factor model: Two aspects of openness make opposite predictions

Ryder, Andrew *Dept. of Psychology, Concordia University, Montreal, Canada* **Ring, Angela** *Department of Psychology, Concordia University, Montreal, QC, Canada* **Lavigne, K.** *Department of Psychology, Concordia University, Montreal, QC, Canada* **Bagby, R. Michael** *Department of Psychiatry, Univ, Centre for Addiction and Menta, Toronto, Ontario, Canada*

The five-factor model of personality can characterize many personality disorders, but a dimensional understanding of Schizotypal Personality Disorder (STPD) remains elusive. We hypothesized that Openness-to-Experience (OE) consists of two aspects (Openness and Intellect) that make opposite predictions regarding STPD. STPD and OE measures were administered to 233 university students and 100 psychiatric outpatients, and results analyzed with hierarchical multiple regression. In both samples, Openness and Intellect were inter-correlated, but the former was positively related to STPD (B=.154,.298) whereas the latter was negatively related (B=.170,.214). This complex relation may explain previous difficulties in identifying clear personality trait correlates for STPD.

The emotional experiences and subjective well-being of the elderly in Korea: The Hallym Longitudinal Study of aging

Ryu, Kyung *Dept. of Psychology, Hallym University, Chuncheon, Republic of Korea*

Objectives: To investigate the changes of subjective well-being(SWB) and emotional experiences and analyze the effects of emotion experiences and regulations on the SWB in old age through the longitudinal study from 2003 to 2007. Methods: PANAS, PGCMS, and the emotion regulation scale were used and HLM, SEM were performed. Results: SWB was not dramatically decrease with age and the elderly experienced more positive and less negative emotions. Experiencing more positive, less negative emotions and using self-protective strategies had positive effects on the SWB in old age. Conclusion: Emphasis of positive aspect of aging and the meaning of emotional life.

Using comparison to promote young children's concepts of material kind

Saalbach, Henrik *Inst. of Behavioral Sciences, ETH Zürich, Zürich, Switzerland* **Hardy, Ilonca** *Inst. of Behavioral Sciences, ETH Zurich, Zurich, Switzerland*

The process of comparison is a crucial mechanism underlying young children's categorization of objects. We investigated children's ability to construct conceptual categories of material kind by having 73 preschoolers make inferences about the behaviour of different items in water after they had observed objects of a given material to float or sink. Objects of extreme mass, volume, and shape served as distractors. In a 2x2 within-groups design, we prompted comparison by varying the number of observed objects and by using material labels. Both prompts significantly increased children's material choices and accompanying verbal explanations thus facilitating their conceptualizations of material kind.

Image of God and style of religious education

Sadeghi, Mansoureh Alsadat *Psychology, Family Institute, Tehran, Islamic Republic of Iran* **Mazaheri, Mohammad Ali** *psychology, family institute, tehran, Islamic Republic of Iran*

The goal of the present research is investigation relationship between style of religious education and image of God in University students. 374 students were chosen and completed questionnaires measuring image of God (rebuilted scale of Lawrence, 1997), style of religious education inventory: parenting style scale (Naghashan, 1979) and parental religiousness (Granqvist, 1998). Data were analyzed Two way anova. The results showed that parenting styles has a main effect on the scores of the total subscales of God image (P< 0.05). Interpretation of results focouses on the parent-child relationship with regared to theories of object relations, attachment and learning social.

Aftereffects of response inhibition in the stop-signal task

Sakajiri, Chie *Dept. of Disability Sciences, University of Tsukuba, Tsukuba, Japan* **Maekawa, Hisao** *Disability Sciences, University of Tsukuba, Tsukuba, Japan*

We conducted the stop-signal task to examine the aftereffects of the response inhibition. The participants were engaged into a choice reaction time task as the primary task, but were required to stop the reactions when stop-signals were occasionally presented after go-signals at some delays. We showed that the reaction times in the present trials became longer as the delays in the last trials increased. As for the trials after successful response inhibition, the reaction times in repetition condition of go-signals were longer than of non-repetition. These results can be explained by the priming effect.

Women and aging: The case of a bus driver retired

Sanchez de Miguel, Manuel *Dept. of Psychology, Univ. of the Basque Country, San Sebastian, Spain* **Lizaso, Izarne** *PSYCHOLOGY, UNIVERSITY OF THE BASQUE COUNT, SAN SEBASTIAN, Spain*

Actually number of women working at traditional male jobs is increasing. This study claims to reveal some difficulties (i.e. reconciling family and professional life) of a women bus driver (n=1) retired (62 year old) along his work and life history. After doing several semi-structured interviews, Interpretative Phenomenological Analysis (IPA) was conducted on full verbatim transcripts to investigate in particular the transitional experience at retirement. Driver's several reflections about his health condition, interpersonal relations and care of ill parents showed most of one dilemma concerning membership of traditional family and out of a typical male job after 40 years employed.

The Spatial Visualization Dynamic Test- Revised: An experimental approach.

Santacreu, Jose *Personalidad,, Universidad Autonoma de Madrid, Madrid, Spain* **Contreras, Maria Jose** *Psicología Básica I, UNED, Madrid, Spain*

Visualization (Vz) refers to the ability to mentally manipulate visual patterns. This work presents the Spatial Visualization Dynamic Test-Revised (SVDT-R). In this visualization task the participant must simultaneously direct two moving dots towards a given destination. The destination changes from trial to trial and, in order to direct

the two moving dots, participants must use a digital compass linked to each of them. In the SVDT-R, the moving dots disappear from the computer screen and participants must imagine their movement. Authors report that the study applied to 274 participants, shows the high validity and reliability of the spatial test considered.

Effects of social intention on the control of action

Sartori, Luisa *Dipt. di Psicologia, Università di Padova, Padova, Italy* **Becchio, Cristina** *Dipartimento di Psicologia, Università di Torino, Torino, Italy* **Bulgheroni, Maria** *Dipartimento di Psicologia, Università di Padova, Padova, Italy* **Castiello, Umberto** *Dipartimento di Psicologia, Università di Padova, Padova, Italy*

We investigated how social goals are incorporated into action plans. In Experiment 1 participants grasped an object and located it within a container (blocked trials). In 20% of trials a human agent seated next to the participant unfolded the hand to ask for the object (perturbed trials). In Experiments 2 & 3 the agent was replaced by a robotic device or performed an action not conveying a social request, respectively. Results indicate that motor response varied depending on the nature of the perturbation. Only human gestures conveying a social request modified pre-planned action by on-line integration of other's actions.

The relationship of gesturing, cognitive ability, and personality

Sassenberg, Uta *Psychology, Humboldt University of Berlin, Berlin, Germany* **van der Meer, Elke** *Psychology, Humboldt University of Berlin, Berlin, Germany*

Gestures are produced to communicate information to the listener, facilitate the speaker's thinking and learning, and regulate interpersonal relationships and emotions. Individuals differ in the frequency of gesture production. However, its relationship to cognitive ability and personality is yet unclear. High school students judged and described their strategies for geometric analogies. Frequencies of different gesture types were analysed in relation to participants' performance and pupil responses, cognitive ability, and personality. Individuals' cognitive ability and personality predicted production of different gesture types. The results are discussed in relation to theories of the functions of gesture production.

The relation between personality traits and reaction times to personality trait terms: Personality traits of extraversion-introversion, nerves-toughness

Sato, Emi *Dept. of Psychology, Shirayuri College, Tokyo, Japan* **Matsuda, Kouhei** *Psychology, Bunkyo-Gakuin University, Fujimino-shi, Saitama, Japan*

There was individual difference of the autonomous nerves system in the study of neurosis tendency (Eysenck,1967). Therefore, it's difficult to examine experimentally personality traits. It hypothesized reaction times (RT) to personality trait terms would change with the personality traits in this study. We examined RT to 10 terms in each session. As a result, though RT to 10 terms in self-rating session didn't reveal personality traits, it was demonstrated that the rate of change that based on personal RT in simple session was changed by Extraversion-Introversion, Nerves-Tough. This result suggested that RT would be able to show personality traits as behavioral evidence.

New latent-variable approach to actual-ideal discrepancy theory: Actual and ideal appearance, physical self-concept and global self-esteem

Scalas, L. Francesca *Dept. of Education, University of Oxford, Oxford, United Kingdom* **Marsh, Herb W.** *Education, University of Oxford, Oxford, United Kingdom*

Actual-ideal discrepancy (AID) theory of self-concept is heuristic, dating back to William James, but has received limited empirical support. We introduce a new latent-variable methodology (structural equation models with multiple indicators on all constructs), testing gender and age invariance (adolescents and young-adults; N=1693). In support of theoretical predictions, we confirmed the joint effect of actual and ideal appearance, we found contributions of actual (positive) and ideal (negative) appearance on Physical Self-Concept and Global Self-Esteem (partly mediated by Physical Self-Concept) that varied slightly with gender. Success of our innovative methodological approach supports AID theoretical predictions, confirming the importance of substantive-methodological synergies.

Influence of pursuit velocity on the enhancement of chromatic sensitivity during smooth pursuit eye movements

Schütz, Alexander C. *Inst. für Allg. Psychologie, Universität Gießen, Gießen, Germany* **Braun, Doris I.** *Allgemeine Psychologie, Universität Gießen, Gießen, Germany* **Gegenfurtner, Karl** *Inst. für Psychologie, Universität Gießen, Gießen, Germany*

Recently we showed that visual sensitivity for chromatic stimuli is enhanced during smooth pursuit eye movements. Here we investigate the influence of pursuit velocity on this enhancement. We measured contrast sensitivity for peripheral, color modulated stimuli during fixation and during smooth pursuit. We tested three different pursuit velocities: 3.5, 10.5 and 14.1 deg/sec. Results show that the sensitivity for chromatic stimuli is improved in all pursuit conditions, even for the slow velocity. Higher pursuit velocities result in stronger improvements of chromatic sensitivity. A similar relationship has bee shown for the amplitude of saccades and the magnitude of saccadic suppression.

Age-related effects on working memory performance and P300

Schapkin, Sergei A. *Berlin, Germany* **Freude, Gabriele** *Mental workload, Fed. Inst. for Occup. Safety &, Berlin, Germany*

Elderly employees were hypothesised to involve a broader neuronal network into the task performance than younger to compensate the working memory decline. In the high memory load condition (HML) they had to memorize a letter sequence and to respond when a letter was repeated. In the low memory load condition (LML) they had to respond when the letter "X" appeared. The RT and number of errors were larger in HML than in LML, while P300 was smaller and delayed in HML. Elderly made more errors than younger in HML condition. The P300 was delayed and more frontally distributed in elderly.

Perceptual learning of force control in pointing movements

Schinauer, Thomas *Inst. für Psychologie II, Universität Kaiserslautern, Kaiserslautern, Germany* **Kalveram, Karl Theodor** *Psychology, University of Düsseldorf, Duesseldorf, Germany* **Lachmann, Thomas** *Psychology Unit II, University of Kaiserslautern, Kaiserslautern, Germany*

The content of motor memory is called an "internal model" and comprises both knowledge of physical properties of the body and the environment. Pointing requires conversion of perceived distance into force commands, and neural information of both vision and proprioception to be actively coordinated as well. Although the control of isometric force production cannot be generalised to the control of kinematic variability, our experiments show retention of an acquired model in such a difficult task to be satisfying when being learned visually open-loop. The results shed light on the discussion of the force control hypothesis in motor control.

A neuro-physiological model of the evolution of goal-oriented behavior based on the development of agency

Schmidt, Tino Psychology, TU Dresden, Dresden, Germany Lehmann, Hagen Computer Science, University of Bath, Bath Spa, United Kingdom

Our cognition creates a sense of authorship for our actions to differentiate them from actions done by other agents, called "sense of agency". We describe a dynamical, neuro-physiological model, which focuses on two types of internal neural-temporal information-loops. The "forward loop" uses efference copies to predict the sensory consequences of motor commands whenever movements are made. The "feedback loop" provides the current action program with corrections of the motor commands to achieve the state desired by the action. Our model describes how the interaction of "feedback-" and "feedforward-loop" forms a "sense of agency" and shows neuro-physiological evidence for this phenomenon.

Predictors of health behavior within the nutrition sector

Schnitzspahn, Katharina Groß-Gerau, Germany Scholz, Urte Psychologisches Institut, Universität Zürich, Zürich, Switzerland Kliegel, Matthias Institut für Psychologie, Technische Universität Dresden, Dresden, Germany

Acquisition and maintenance of health behaviors are often poorly predicted by behavioral intentions. To close this intention-behavior-gap volitional constructs are needed. The present cross-sectional, web-based study on nutrition behavior investigates a prediction model that includes planning and action control as postintentional mediator variables. Participants were 381 women and 88 men (aged 18 to 79; BMI from 19 to 57), who took part in a web-based program. Structural equation modeling showed that only action control was a proximal predictor of the nutrition behavior assessed. Practical implications and suggestions for future research are discussed.

When less is more: Negative outcomes of discrepancies between explicit and implicit self-esteem

Schröder-Abé, Michela Inst. für Psychologie, Techn. Universität Chemnitz, Chemnitz, Germany Rudolph, Almut Psychology, Chemnitz University, Chemnitz, Germany Schütz, Astrid Psychology, Chemnitz University, Chemnitz, Germany

Implicit self-esteem (SE) can be used to distinguish discrepant (high explicit/low implicit or high implicit/low explicit) and congruent (high/high or low/low) forms of SE. Assuming that SE discrepancies are dysfunctional irrespective of their direction, we conducted four studies to investigate their relation to health and defensiveness (assessed by self- and observer ratings). Multiple regression analyses revealed significant interactions between implicit and explicit SE. When occurring in combination with low explicit SE, high implicit SE is related to defensiveness and impaired health. Thus, SE discrepancies can be regarded as stressors and high implicit SE is not necessarily advantageous.

Family caregivers' quality of life and the impact of incontinence

Seither, Corinna Grad.-Kolleg Multimorbidität, Charité Universitätsmedizin, Berlin, Germany

Frail elderly persons living at home are often cared for by a family member. Despite the high prevalence of urinary and fecal incontinence in old age its impact on family caregivers has been relatively unexplored. This study investigated to what extent care receivers' incontinence affects - among other stressors - different dimensions of quality of life of family caregivers (N=620) using multiple regression methods. Also the moderating role of social support, self-efficacy and quality of the relationship were explored. First results will be presented. Implications for interventions focussing family caregiver's quality of life will be discussed.

Psychosocial variables associated to diet adherence in obese patients: A longitudinal study

Serrano-Alvarado, Karina Chimalhuacan, Mexico Rojas-Russell, Mario School of Psychology Zaragoza, National U. Mexico, Mexico, Mexico

Objective: Study the prospective association of self-efficacy and readiness to change to diet adherence (DA) in obese patients. Method: Four measurements, one month apart, were performed in 93 patients participating in a drug trial. Self-efficacy and readiness to change related to diet, were measured. Adherence to diet was assessed through a one-month retrospective log. Results: Multivariate analysis showed a significant association of self-efficacy and volitional stages to adherence. Perceived stress and health affected adherence also. Conclusions: Interventions to strengthen DA in obese patients should take into account motivational readiness and build up perceived self-efficacy.

Survey of mental health needs of Hamedanian people

Shamsaei, Farshid Psychiatric Nursing, Hamedan University, Hamedan, Islamic Republic of Iran

Objectives: The aim of this study is to identify the mental health needs of Hamedanian people. Methodology: This was a descriptive cross-sectional study. The participants consist of 1300 individuals who were selected by stratified sampling. Results/Conclusions: Results showed that the Hamedan city people believed that mental health services are inadequate (45%), they did not access services near their home (74%) and media information about services was poor (34%). The expressed needs of people were: mental health education (72%), established mental health centers in schools and factories (<50%) and expanding the comprehensive mental health centers in the city (58%). The paper provides a rationale for providing mental health service delivery that are easily accessible, to promote mental health.

The relationship between mental health and quality of life of hemodialysis patients

Sharif, Farkhondeh Psychiatric and Mental Health, Shiraz University, Shiraz, Islamic Republic of Iran Vedad, Fariba psychiatric and mental health, Shiraz University of Medical S, Shiraz, Islamic Republic of Iran

The purpose of this study was to investigate the relationship between mental health and quality of life of hemodialysis patients. Methods: The sample consisted of 90 hemodialysis patients. They were assessed by a demographic questionnaire, General Health Questionnaire, Short form questionnaire (SF-36). Mental Health was assessed in four domains and the SF-36 questionnaire are summed into eight scales. The data were analyzed using t-test, spearman's correlation, ANOVA. Results: The findings revealed that many quality of life domains were correlated significantly with mental health domains. The result of this study indicated that many quality of life domains were correlated with mental health domains and hemodialysis has effect on different aspects of patient's life.

Psychological principles of foreign language teaching management in preschool

Sharkova, Nataliya Dept. of Psychology, Dnipropetrovsk Nat. University, Dnipropetrovsk, Ukraine

The presentation reveals complex analysis of foreign language teaching- learning process. An empirical study has been carried out to test with statistical methods the main principles underlying psychologically safe and pedagogically grounded conditions of foreign language teaching and learning. The evidence was found that the learning efficacy results from the activity approach where non-verbal activity covers the teaching-learning process thus leading cognitive development of children and maintaining their learning motivation. An experiment has demonstrated that specific language activities based on the young learner's actual interests and needs significantly impact on memorizing of the foreign language vocabulary.

Gender effects on the activation of parent-child attachment

Shen, Lierong Institute of Psychology, Chinese Academy of Sciences, Beijing, People's Republic of China Liu, Huashan School of Psychology, Huazhong Normal University, Wuhan, People's Republic of China

Three studies examined the gender effects of college students' working models of attachment and emotional and social loneliness on the activation of parent-child attachment. Results showed that father-child attachment activation led to higher self-models in relationships with male friends than that of mother-child attachment; mother-child attachment activation led to higher models of others in relationships with female than that of father-child attachment; same-sex parent-child attachment activation led to lower social loneliness, while different-sex parent-child attachment activation led to lower emotional loneliness, than control conditions. The findings expand attachment theory, emphasizing gender effects on the influence of parent-child attachment.

Constructive study on the evaluative index system of guidance activity lesson

Shi, Lijun School of Teacher Education, Zhejiang Normal University, Zhejiang Jinhua, People's Republic of China Sui, Guang Yuan School of Teacher Education, Zhejiang Normal University, Zhejiang Jinhua, People's Republic of China

Objectives: Constructing an evaluative index system of guidance Activity lessons taken in a class. Method: An inventory was constructed after 78 professional guidance teachers were interviewed. The explorative factor analysis method was employed and 12 mental health education theorists and experienced school guidance practitioners were conducted to discuss the validity and the distribution of relative weight. Analytical Hierarchy Process was used. Results: The evaluative index system was established, including three first-degree indices and nine secondary indices. Each hold respectively the relative weight. After applied into practice, it had been proved that this index system was of correspondingly high quality.

Why do kindergarten teachers need to smile?

Shimizu, Masuharu Dept. of Literature, Kobe Women's University, Kobe, Japan Mori, Toshiaki Graduate School of Education, Hiroshima University, Higashi-Hiroshima, Japan

This study investigated the developmental differences in face identification. Sixty-nine kindergarten children and 41 college students were presented with 11 pairs of woman's portrait and were asked to judge whether they are the same woman's faces or not for each pair. Three pairs had the same woman's face: two serious faces, serious face vs. smiling face, and two smiling faces. Children judged more correctly for two smiling face pair than for two serious face pair. Younger children judged less correctly for two serious face pair. These results were discussed in relation to the neuronal development and the teacher education system.

Relationships among neuroticism, coping styles, academic stressors and reactions to stressors of male and female college students in Iran: Structural equation modeling

Shokri, Omid psychology, Teacher Training University, Tehran, Islamic Republic of Iran
This study examined the relationships among neuroticism, coping styles, academic stressors and reactions to stressors. SEM was used to assess the relationships among latent and measured variables in the conceptual model. The MANOVA indicated significant difference in neuroticism, coping styles, academic stressors and reactions to stressors by gender. Higher levels of academic stressors were predicted by higher scores of neuroticism and emotion oriented and by lower scores of task oriented. Higher academic stressors predicted greater reactions to stressors. All of the regression weights were statistically significant, and models' predictors accounted for 75% of the variance in reaction to stressor.

Influences of spatiotemporal conditions of feature-change on visual object representation continuity

Shui, Rende Dept. of Psychology, Zhejiang University, Hangzhou, People's Republic of China Shen, Mowei Dept. of Psychology, Zhejiang University, Hangzhou, People's Republic of China
Visual object representation continuity, i.e. the perception of a changed visual object as the same one, is an essential cognitive ability. Two different types of theories have been proposed: focuses on the object spatiotemporal continuity and the importance of feature change. The effects of object's feature-change were examined by 5 experiments of multiple-object-tracking (MOT) task with manipulating spatiotemporal conditions of feature-change. The results showed that feature change has great effects on the maintenance of object representation continuity when 2 collided objects exchange their features; the effects of color- and shape-change are larger than that of orientation-change.

Parents' education predicts their school-related beliefs and practices with their children

Silinskas, Gintautas Department of Psychology, University of Jyväskylä, Jyväskylä, Finland Lerkkanen, Marja-Kristiina Department of Psychology, University of Jyväskylä, Jyväskylä, Finland Poikkeus, Anna-Maija Department of Psychology, University of Jyväskylä, Jyväskylä, Finland Niemi, Pekka Department of Psychology, University of Turku, Turku, Finland Siekkinen, Martti Department of Psychology, University of Joensuu, Joensuu, Finland Nurmi, Jari-Erik Department of Psychology, University of Jyväskylä, Jyväskylä, Finland
This longitudinal study investigated how parents' education contributes to parental school-related beliefs and practices with their kindergarten children. A total of 1024 mothers and 713 fathers filled in a questionnaire measuring their educational level, school-related beliefs and practices. The performance in reading and math of 1024 children was also examined. The results indicated that parents with a low educational level instructed their children in reading and math more than those with a high education. By contrast, less educated parents were less involved in shared-reading and reported more negative beliefs about children's performance on academic skills, compared to higher educated parents.

Satisfaction with friends, intimacy, family and social activities: Are there differences between women with obesity reporting distint eating behaviours?

Silva, Isabel FCHS, Universidade Fernando Pessoa, Porto, Portugal Pais-Ribeiro, Jose Faculdade de Psicologia e de C, Universidade do Porto, Porto, Portugal Cardoso, Helena Endocrinology, ICBAS-UP; HGSA, Porto, Portugal
OBJECTIVES: To analyse social support satisfaction differences between women with obesity reporting distinct eating behaviours and yo-yo phenomena. METHODS A cohort of 168 women with obesity answered to the Social Support Satisfaction Scale in the context of a clinical interview. RESULTS: Women reporting yo-yo phenomena show lower family satisfaction. Women presenting binge eating disorder show lower satisfaction with friends, family, intimacy and total social support. There are no significant differences concerning sweet/fat food craving, seasonal pattern of eating behaviour, night eating syndrome and continuous nibbling. CONCLUSIONS: Social support revealed to be an important variable in the distinction of women with obesity presenting distinct eating behaviours.

The forms of the present time orientation and well-being in the context of the full time perspective

Sobol-Kwapinska, Malgorzata Faculty of Social Sciences, Catholic University of Lublin, Lublin, Poland
Objectives: The objective was to examine the relationships between the forms of the present time orientation (hedonism, fatalism and active concentration) and well-being. Methods: The data on three time orientation measures and two well-being measures from participants aged from 19 to 65 years were analyzed using multiple regression analysis and cluster analysis. Results: The active present time orientation, unlike hedonism and fatalism, was associated with high well-being, positive evaluation of time, and effective realization of goals. Conclusions: Beside hedonism and fatalism, the present time orientation can also take the form of the active, engaging concentration on the current moment.

The training of reading according to invariant method in Mexican children

Soloviova, Yulia Dept. of Neuropsychology, University of Puebla, Puebla, Mexico Quintanar, Luis Neuropsychology, University of Puebla, Puebla, Mexico
Educational system in Mexico is facing strong difficulties, especially in teaching of reading. The objective of our study is to show the possibilities of Training of Reading created on the bases of the theory of Historic and Cultural Development and Activity Theory. The Method was applied to Mexican school and pre-school children during application of programs of individual correction and in classroom groups. The results show special achievements in writing, reading and general linguistic abilities after application of method during a school year. The conclusions stress important possibilities of application of new invariant methods in modern education.

Team orientation and attitudes towards different forms of teacher-collaboration

Soltau, Andreas FB 11 - Psychologie, Universität Bremen, Bremen, Germany Mienert, Malte FB 11, Psychology, University of Bremen, Bremen, Germany
We report on an empirical online survey conducted in 2007 with N=223 teachers from primary and secondary schools. The aim of the study is to verify the impact of the so-called "pursuit of autonomy" which the scientific literature mentions as an explanation for the absence of teacher collaboration in schools. The collected data comprises the frequency of implementation of 15 forms of teacher collaboration; attitudes towards these forms and teachers' general team orientation. The study concludes that although ambitious forms of teacher collaboration are rarely implemented, team orientation and attitudes towards these forms are surprisingly positive.

Perfectionism and depression: Testing the specific vulnerability and diathesis-stress model in a Chinese population

Song, Shanggui Dept. of Academic Affairs, Jinan University of Shandong, Jinan, People's Republic of China Tong, Yuehua Dept. of Psychology, University of Jinan, Jinan, People's Republic of China
So far, research results in testing the specific vulnerability and diathesis-stress model were inconsistent. The present study examined whether perfectionism acts as a vulnerability factor for distress in response to life events. A cross-sectional study and a longitudinal study were conducted to test these tow models in 426 college students in China. The findings were that concern over mistakes and doubt about action both interacted with negative life events to predict depression symptoms at Time 1 and Time 2. No support was obtained for a perfectionism specific vulnerability model.

Gender differences in perfectionism and type a behavior: A Chinese perspective

Song, Shanggui Dept. of Academic Affairs, Jinan University of Shandong, Jinan, People's Republic of China Xu, Jun Dept. of Academic Affairs, Jinan University of Shandong, Jinan, People's Republic of China
Objective: To investigate the gender differences in perfectionism and Type A behavior of Chinese university students. Method: Perfectionism Scale for Chinese College Students and Type A Behavior Personality were administered to 258 university students in China. Results: (1) Males scored significantly higher than females in Concern over Mistakes, Organization, Parent Expectation, and in the total score of perfectionism. (2)Type A Behavior and Type B Behavior of females manifested significant differences in dimensions of perfectionism and total score. Conclusion: Gender differences were identified in perfectionism and Type A behavior.

Optimism and pessimism in relation with goal orientations in classroom settings

Soric, Izabela Department of Psychology, University of Zadar, Zadar, Croatia Penezic, Zvjezdan University of Zadar, Zadar, Croatia Vulic-Prtoric, Anita Department of Psychology, University of Zadar, Zadar, Croatia
There are a number of different models of goal orientations in classroom settings that propose two general goal orientations labelled as learning vs. performance goals. The current study investigated whether students' optimism and pessimism, self-esteem, values and intrinsic motivation predict their goal orientations and academic achievement. The participants were 220 secondary school students which completed the questionnaires anonymously during a regularly scheduled classroom period. Gender, optimism and values in learning were negative predictors of work-avoidance goal orientation; pessimism and values predict performance goal orientation while values and intrinsic motivation predict learning goal orientation. Learning goal orientation was a predictor of students' academic achievement. Optimism and pessimism could have an important role in forming students' goal orientations.

Identifying learning disabilities: Psychometric Characteristics of the McCarney Learning Disability Evaluation Scale (LDES), based on a Greek sample

Souroulla, Andry Dept. of Psychology, University of Cyprus, Nicosia, Cyprus Panagiotou, Georgia PSYCHOLOGY, UNIVERSITY OF CYPRUS, NICOSIA, Cyprus Kokkinos, Konstantinos PSYCHOLOGY, UNIVERSITY OF CYPRUS, NICOSIA, Cyprus

The study aimed to field test a Greek translation of the Learning Disability Evaluation Scale (LDES, McCarney, 1996) and to examine its factor structure, reliability and validity. 165 educators completed the LDES for one of their students, aged 5 -14 years. Results revealed that the Greek LDES generally maintains the original factor structure (7 subscales) and high reliability. The significant associations between the LDES, the Reading Ability Test (Trigka, 2004) and school grades, supported its validity. Logistic regression analyses indicated that the LDES could identify our sample and children with learning difficulties, with an accuracy of 81.3%. Results are discussed

Age effects on parafoveal processing in reading Kathrin Spitzer

Spitzer, Kathrin Coswig, Germany Sawyer, Kathryn Psychology, Florida State University, Tallahassee, USA Charness, Neil Psychology, Florida State University, Tallahassee, USA Sachs-Ericsson, Natalie Psychology, Florida State University, Tallahassee, USA Radach, Ralph Psychology, Florida State University, Tallahassee, USA

Prior research in the domains of visual search and driving has suggested that elderly adults have a smaller functional field of view. We used a sentence reading task including saccade contingent display manipulations to directly test the hypotheses that benefit from parafoveal word preview is reduced in this population relative to college age controls (Laubrock, Kliegl & Engbert, 2006). Results indicate that elderly readers are not only substantially slower but also show a more pronounced word frequency effect (Rayner et al., 2006). Critically, preview benefit was greatly attenuated in the elderly group, suggesting a significantly reduced perceptual span.

Head movement during requesting

Srisayekti, Wilis Dept. of Psychology, Padjadjaran University, Bandung, Indonesia

This study was intended to see whether a difference in provided channels caused differences in the nonverbal behavior in dyadic communication. 8 persons were involved with their partners, for the face-to-face situation and the telephone situation. A video system was employed to gather the data of their head-movement during requesting. Results showed that there was more head-movement in the face-to-face situation as compared to the head-movement in the telephone situation, both for the mobility and the complexity of movement. The head-movement went in line with the whole-body movement, and went in the opposite direction of the eye movement.

Ethnic self labels as promotive factor in the change of language usage among adolescent ethnic German immigrants

Stößel, Katharina Inst. für Entw.-Psychologie, Universität Jena, Jena, Germany Silbereisen, Rainer K. Inst. Entwicklungspsychologie, Universität Jena, Jena, Germany

This longitudinal study on Ethnic German immigrants to Germany examines whether ethnic self labeling as majority (German) or minority member (Russian or Ethnic German) relates to frequency of German language usage. Growth Curve Models on 585 adolescent first generation immigrants reveal that indeed level of language usage relates to levels of ethnic self labels, and change of language usage

to change of self labels. A higher level and a growth of self labeling as German relates to more German language usage, and vice versa for self labeling as minority member. Results reveal the interrelatedness of these change processes during acculturation.

Neural correlates of simulation during action prediction

Stadler, Waltraud Inst. für Psychologie, Max-Planck-Institut, Leipzig, Germany Schubotz, Ricarda Cognitive Neurology, MPI Cognitive & Brain Scie, Leipzig, Germany Springer, Anne Department of Psychology, MPI Cognitive & Brain Scie, Leipzig, Germany Graf, Markus Department of Psychology, MPI Cognitive & Brain Scie, Leipzig, Germany Prinz, Wolfgang Department of Psychology, MPI Cognitive & Brain Scie, Leipzig, Germany

Action prediction is assumed to be a major purpose of activating the motor system during action observation. If an observed person is transiently occluded, internal models are used to predict disrupted visual action information. Accordingly, fMRI during action occlusion indicates increased activity in BA 44, premotor cortex, parietal regions and the posterior superior temporal sulcus (pSTS) which were previously associated with action simulation. Provided that the observed action is of relevance for the observer, internal simulation of disrupted actions is a highly automated process. By varying task instructions, however, activity can be modulated in parts of this network.

Different leaderships and aspects of personality of leading politicians versus electional success

Stallony, Marc Oliver Recklinghausen, Germany Rowold, Jens Psychologisches Institut II, WWU Münster, Münster, Germany

This empirical study follows the question to which extent leadership and different aspects of personality of leading politicians may be possible predictors for electional success of these politicians. At first this study follows the question how far charismatic leadership (Konger & Kanungo, 1998), moral-based ledership (Yukl, 2002) and transactional leadership (Bass, 1985) take influence of the electional success. Results show significant effects for moral-based and transactional leadership. At second study this study follows the question which aspects of personality take significant influence on the electional success. Significant results were shown and correlations between leadership and aspects of personality will be discussed.

Optimism and self-efficacy: Psychological and psychosocial aspects

Stanculescu, Elena Faculty of Psychology, Universoty of Bucharest, Bucharest, Romania

The purpose of the study was to examine the psychological correlates of self – efficacy and optimism. We supposed that self – efficacy and optimism are positively correlated with psihosocial well – being, life satisfaction, happiness, self – esteem, perceived social support. We expected that students that volunteering are more optimistic and have high level of self – efficacy. The sample consisted of 403 university students. Statistical analysis included: bivariate correlations, Mann Whitney U Test, One Way ANOVA. The hypothesis were confirmed. The results highlight that optimists and self – efficacious people have a high quality of life.

Psychological correlates of schoolchildren loneliness

Stanculescu, Elena Faculty of Psychology, Universoty of Bucharest, Bucharest, Romania

The aim of this research was to investigate some psychological aspects of loneliness. We supposed that loneliness is negatively correlated with self – esteem, optimism, social skills, perceived social support. We assumed that there are more cross –

classifications LL & LM level of perceived social support and optimism in the case of high scores of loneliness. The sample consisted of 289 schoolchildren (7th & 8th grade). We used Multidimensional Scale of Perceived Social Support, Teacher Estimation of Social Skills Scale, Life Orientation Test, Loneliness and Social Dissatisfaction Scale. The hypotheses were confirmed. We concluded that teachers must modeling appropriate social relations.

Psychological comorbidity and coping strategies in patients with chronic tinnitus

Stege, Uta Medizin und Rehabilitation, Charité Berlin - Physikalische, Berlin, Germany Joachim, Ricarda CC12 Internal Medicine, Universitaetsmedizin Berlin, Berlin, Germany Stege, Kathrin CC12 Internal Medicine, Universitaetsmedizin Berlin, Berlin, Germany Graf, Markus Department of Psychology, Germany Kischkel, Eva CC12 Internal Medicine, Humboldt University Berlin, Berlin, Germany Mazurek, Birgit CC16 Otorhinolaryngology, Universitaetsmedizin Berlin, Berlin, Germany Reißhauer, Anett CC12 Internal Medicine, Universitaetsmedizin Berlin, Berlin, Germany

Tinnitus associates with psychological distress. In the presented study, we examined psychological comorbidity and coping strategies in a population of patients with chronic tinnitus. We used established questionaires for scoring the tinnitus symptoms, psychopathology, depression, and coping behavior. Severely affected tinnitus sufferers (decompensated tinnitus) reported higher levels of psychosocial distress and somatic impairment. Further, patients with decompensated tinnitus showed dysfunctional coping strategies like depressive coping, trivialisation, and wishful thinking. We propose the early assessment of psychological comorbidity and dysfunctional coping strategies to apply timely a psychological treatment, which, in end effect might prevent further progression of tinnitus.

A professional evaluation scale for middle level managers

Stoica, Mihaela Dept. of Psychology, University Dimitrie Cantemir, Tirgu Mures, Romania

The aim this study is: to make a scale with behavioural references for managerial performance. The procedure followed in 5 steps: defining the professional dimension; obtaining the behavior references for each dimension; retro-version, all the items to be distribute at initially dimension; the experts should note the level of competence for each item and finally making the scale (Smith & Kendall, 1963). The scale's validity was achieved by comparing it to a parallel scale, the mixed standard assessment scale by accomplishing the multitrait-multimethod matrix.

Effects of a combined nutrition and stress-management training to life-quality, coping skills and eating-behaviour of elementary school kids

Stoll, Oliver Inst. für Sportwissenschaften, Universität Halle-Wittenberg, Halle, Germany Reinhardt, Christian Sports Science, Martin-Luther-University Halle, Halle (Saale), Germany

Objectives: The aim of the study was the evaluation of a combined nutrition and stress-management training to life-quality, coping skills and eating-behaviour of elementary school kids. Methods: We used a longitudinal, randomised experimental study-design, comparing a treatment group (n=75), getting the intervention and a non-intervention control group (n=75). The dependant variables were life-quality (KINDL), stress appraisal and coping (SSKJ-R) and eating behaviour (IEG-Kind). The statistical analysis was performed using a GLM with repeated measurements. Results: We found seven significant interaction-effects group x time based on improvements of the treatment-group individuals. Conclusions: Based on these results, we recommend to implement this intervention into future health promotion interventions of school kids.

Differences among some social groups in Bulgaria in their extraversion, neuroticism, psychotocism and social desirability

Stoyanova, Stanislava Dept. of Psychology, SWU, Blagoevgrad, Bulgaria
This paper presents the results from a study carried out in 2005-2006 among 378 respondents in Bulgaria by using Eysenck's Personal Questionnaire. The prisoners sentenced for theft and the secondary students were the most extraverted ones, the civil servants and the pensioners were the least extraverted ones. The social workers and the prisoners sentenced for theft were the most emotionally unstable, the teachers and the civil servants were the most emotionally stable. The university students and the policemen had the highest score on the Psychotocism, the teachers and the social workers had the lowest score on the Psychotocism.

Self-efficacy, health risks and work behavior in Indian families

Sud, Shonali St. Bede's College, Dept.of Psychology, Shimla, India
Self-efficacy combating health risks, initiating the desire for physical exercise and facilitating effective work behavior in a family was studied on 158 subjects (92 adults, 44 females and 48 males, mean ages=38.90 and 42.89 years, and 66 children, 36 female and 30 male, mean ages=18 years). The hypotheses that self-efficacy predicts exercise(r= .25) as well as efficient work behavior(r=.67) within a family stands accepted. Older males were better workers than females. Educated professionals showed greater concern for health risks and motivated for lifestyle changes, their children are linking effective work performance with good health in practically every home in India

Self-efficacy, stress and interpersonal relations of employees in India

Sud, Shonali St. Bede's College, Dept.of Psychology, Shimla, India
Self efficacy-stress effect on Interpersonal relations in India was examined on 155 (94 male, mean age =39.64 years, and 64 female, mean age =38.97 years) employees. The hypotheses that self-efficacy predicts good interpersonal relations (R=.430) more for women in comparison to men as well as moderates stress (r=.-311) stands verified in this study. Results show that self-efficacy predicted good interpersonal relations only among older males (> 48 years of age) and they therefore showed better understanding and adjustment towards their female colleagues. The stress buffering effect of self-efficacy stands verified in this study.

A research on relationship among learning burnout, self-esteem and subjective well-being of college students

Sun, Lili School of Management, Shenyang, People's Republic of China Zhang, Shuhua school of management, Shenyang Normal University, Shenyang, People's Republic of China Yi, Weijing school of management, Shenyang Normal University, Shenyang, People's Republic of China
Abstract Objective? To explore the relationship among learning burnout, self-esteem and subjective well-being. Method: 446 college students were investigated.Results :(1) Gender difference was significant, male students were higher than female at the level of reduced personal accomplishment;(2) juniors were lower than seniors at the level improper behavior, and freshmen at the level reduced personal accomplishment; (3) Dejection had partial indirect effect on SWB mediating through self-esteem, and reduced personal accom-

plishment had absolute indirect effect on SWB mediating through self-esteem. Conclusion: self-esteem had a mediated effect on learning burnout and subjective well-being. (Key words) Learning burnout, Self-esteem, Subjective well-being

Lifestyle factors, genetics and cognitive aging

Sundström, Anna Dept. of Psychology, Umeå University, Umeå, Sweden
As the population in most industrialized countries ages rapidly, a major challenge is to understand what factors enhance successful cognitive aging. A number of lifestyle factors have been associated with cognitive function in elderly people. However, less is known about whether changes in lifestyle factors late in life have an effect on cognitive aging. Therefore, the aim of this study is to examine whether changes in lifestyle factors in late life, for example social activities, and physical activities, affect cognitive aging and, furthermore, whether these factors interact with genetics (e.g. APOE). Data from a longitudinal cohort study will be used.

Personal "secret ingredients" that predict satisfaction in romantic relationships

Sverko, Dina Department of Psychology, University of Zagreb, Zagreb, Croatia Lovrencic, Katarina Department of psychology, University of Zagreb, Zagreb, Croatia Mimica, Bartul Department of psychology, University of Zagreb, Zagreb, Croatia Okrosa, Jelena Department of psychology, University of Zagreb, Zagreb, Croatia Ostovic, Ines Department of psychology, University of Zagreb, Zagreb, Croatia
Both theory and previous research suggested a link between emotional intelligence, self-esteem and success in interpersonal relationships. Romantic relationships should also benefit from mentioned personal characteristics. The aim of the present study was to examine the associations between emotional intelligence, self-esteem, Stenberg's components of love, duration of the romantic relationship and perceived satisfaction with it. Participants were 294 students from the University of Zagreb. The results of multiple regression analysis showed that predictors accounted for 38% of variance in romantic relationship satisfaction. Intimacy emerged as the best predictor.

Relationship between musical abilities and foreign word pronunciation

Takahashi, Yuwen Faculty of Education, Shishu University, Nagano, Japan Ishimoto, Yoko Oise Junior High School, Nagoya-city, Nagoya, Japan Takahashi, Tomone Faculty of Education, Shinshu University, Nagano, Japan
The relationship between musical abilities and the ability to pronounce foreign words was examined. Musical discriminatory tasks, English and Chinese pronunciation tasks, a digit span test, and a questionnaire on the experience in music, English and Chinese were administered to 41 Japanese university students who have learned English in schools but had no experience in Chinese. Results from correlation and regression analyses showed that after controlling working memory span, there was a positive correlation between musical abilities and the ability to pronounce foreign words. People who were good at discriminating sounds were better able to reproduce sounds in foreign languages.

Subjective and situational conditions of choosing coping strategies among adolescents

Talik, Elzbieta Inst. of Psychology, Catholic University Lublin, Lublin, Poland
The main problem of the following research concerned subjective and situational conditionings to choose religious and nonreligious coping strategies. Situational variables are specific stressors for adolescents that are family, school, peer and personal stressors. Subjective variables are: sense of self-efficacy and intensity of religious attitude.

There is one more variable, interactive one, which is sense of controllability of stressors. The research was conducted using a sample of 451 adolescents. Multiple regression analysis and contrast analysis were conducted. Exemplary results show that adolescents with low sense of controllability more often choose religious passive deferring strategy and those with high sense of controllability – nonreligious planful problem solving.

The effect of interesting introduction and interest value on children's motivation to learn

Tanaka, Etsuko Dept. of Human Science, Osaka University, Kobe, Japan
This study examined whether interesting pre-activity and an emphasis on interest value positively influence their motivation to learn. In this study, experimental science lessons were administered to 4 classes (100 children, 3 grades, ages from 8 to 9). The lesson consisted of a pre-activity designed to attract students' interests and an emphasis on interest value of the subject task by the teacher. As a result, the students in the experimental classes were more motivated to learn the subject task than the students in the control classes.

Which of the pathological severity of mental disorders or the state of symptoms determine a patient's subjective well-being?

Tanaka, Yoshiyuki Isesaki, Japan Tsuda, Akira dept. of Psychology, Kurume University, Isesaki City, Japan Horiuchi, Satoshi Graduate school of Psychology, Kurume University, Isesaki City, Japan Murayama, Hiroyoshi Graduate school of Psychology, Kurume University, Isesaki City, Japan Tomita, Masaru Psychiatry department, Kurume University Hospital, Isesaki City, Japan Jingu, Sumie Health Promotion Foundation, Fukuoka, Isesaki City, Japan
The aim was to investigate which of mood disorders' pathological severity or its symptoms' general state influenced more upon subjective well-being (SWB). SWB was measured with the Psychological Lively Scale-revised in 61 patients having mood disorder. Each patient's pathological severity was estimated from clinical equivalency of his/her antidepressants' dosage and his/her general state of symptoms. The statistical results revealed that patients' SWB was related to his/her general state of symptoms but not to his/her pathological severity itself. The results suggested the importance for a patient's SWB to control his/her represented symptoms more than the pathological severity of mood disorder itself.

Seeing how you act: Motor interference in action simulation

Tausche, Peggy CBS - Inst. für Psychologie, Max-Planck-Institut, Leipzig, Germany Springer, Anne Psychology, MPI CBS, Leipzig, Germany Prinz, Wolfgang Inst. für Psychologie, Max-Planck-Institut, Leipzig, Germany
Recent findings suggest that perceiving action activates corresponding motor programs in the observer. This is ascribed to the mental simulation of observed actions. We aimed to investigate the functional relationship between action perception and action execution more detailed. Participants watched transiently occluded actions and had to predict the action course after occlusion (i.e., simulation task). While some performed only the simulation task, others received a secondary motor task or a secondary sensory task. We predicted a break-down of simulation performance only under motor task conditions. Results are discussed with respect to differentiation between perceptual and motor functions in action prediction.

Comparative investigation for coping strategies in Islamic and modern psychology

Tavakoli, Mahgol Psychology, Isfahan University, Isfahan, Islamic Republic of Iran Torkan, Hajar Psychology, Isfahan University, Isfahan, Islamic Republic of Iran

Stress can be assumed as one of the most important consequence of Modern period. It not only is effective on developing many kinds of Physical and Mental Disorders, but also it causes Personal and Social dysfunctions in individuals and wastes economic and humanistic recourses of individual and his family and society. Because of importance of this phenomenon, we need effective strategies to cope with it. Many of studies stated that one of the important factor in success of therapy method is accordance of it with culture of target population. So the goal of this research is comparative study of therapeutic methods in Islamic and west cultures.

The relationship between the different dimensions of religiosity and moral identity

Tavakoli, Mahgol Psychology, Isfahan University, Isfahan, Islamic Republic of Iran Neshat Doost, Hamid Taher Psychology, Isfahan University, Isfahan, Islamic Republic of Iran Latifi, Zohre Psychology, Isfahan University, Isfahan, Islamic Republic of Iran

Objective: Purpose of this research was study of relationship between the different dimensions of religiosity and Moral Identity in students of Isfahan University. Method: In a quasi-experiment design, a sample of 78 members (41 males, 37 females) was been selected by random sampling, then Religiosity Measure Scale (Serajzade,1377) and Moral Identity Scale(Aquino,2002) were administered. Result: The results showed that there is a significant correlation between religiosity and moral identity total scores. Conclusion: The significant correlations between symbolization and application and ritual in female group, and significant correlation between internalization and belief in male group, showed the differences of male and female that can be assumed as a important factor.

Coping with distress due to locomotor disability

Tewari, Shruti Department of Psychology, Allahabad University, Allahabad, India

The present study aims to understand the process of adjustment to disability within the framework of stress research. It promotes the idea of emotional rehabilitation. A questionnaire exploring distress, disability appraisal, coping and adjustment to disability was administered on an incidental sample of 100 individuals with locomotor disability (18-50 years) along with 10 in-depth interviews. The statistical and content analysis revealed physical, attitudinal, economic barriers and future concerns as the major domains of distress due to locomotor disability. Problem focused coping was significantly correlated with low distress and adjustment to disability (manifested in term of personal achievement and wellbeing).

Promoting sustainable mobility: Soft policies for newcomers

Thronicker, Ines Urban Ecology, Environ. Planni, Helmholtz-Centre of Environmen, Leipzig, Germany Harms, Sylvia Urban Ecology, Environ. Planni, Helmholtz-Centre of Environmen, Leipzig, Germany

The study examines the behavioral efficacy of a soft-policy measure when applied during a residential relocation. How does habitual mode choice temporarily turn into rational mode choice due to context changes, and how do interventions at this very moment take effect? Conducted as a pre-post field experiment in Leipzig, Germany, in 2008, newcomers and habitants participate in a two-wave survey. Between the surveys, subsamples of newcomers and habitants receive information and incentives to use public transport, car sharing, or bike. With special concern to the new approach of a pre-move intervention, we present procedure and first results of the study.

Not only explicit self-esteem influences memory bias for self-relevant information

Tian, Lumei School of Psychology, Shandong Normal University, Jinan in Shandong Province, People's Republic of China

To date, research on effects of implicit self-esteem on memory bias for self-relevant information is very sparse. This study assessed implicit self-esteem using Implicit Association Test and explicit self-esteem using Rosenberg Self-Esteem Scale in 184 undergraduates. Later, the participants were asked to free-recall the self-relevant words just seen before as many as possible. Stepwise multiple regressions showed that explicit self-esteem and its interaction with implicit self-esteem significantly influenced the amount of positive words correctly recalled, but did only implicit self-esteem influence that of negative words recalled. It suggests not only explicit but implicit self-esteem influence memory bias for self-relevant information.

An idiographic study of health behavior change from insulin dependence to independence

Toise, Stefanie C. Dept. of Psychology, Clark University, Worcester, USA

This idiographic study examines how psychological and behavioral changes allowed a diabetic to go from insulin dependence to insulin independence in treating her type 2 diabetes mellitus. Following the process of her change with specific relevance to diagnosis and insulin use, her psychological intra-variability and dynamics for change were expressed in measurable physiological outcomes. Yoga served as an important catalyst for lifestyle changes and maintenance. Using theories of self-perception, self-compassion, family, and field theory, the participant's successful changes were examined in intraindividual contexts. Finally, use of the partnership model allowed participant and researcher to discuss the study from their perspectives.

Faking personality measures in the setting of a traffic-psychological assessment for regaining the driving license: Explicit self-report questionnaire versus Objective Personality Test versus Implicit Association Test

Torner, Felix Sicher Unterwegs GmbH, Vienna, Austria Litzenberger, Margarete Faculty of Psychology, University of Vienna, Vienna, Austria Schützhofer, Bettina Wissenschaft und Forschung, sicher unterwegs GmbH, Vienna, Austria

The susceptibility to faking of the explicit Inventory of Driving Related Personality Traits (Herle et al., 2005), the Objective Personality Test Vienna Risk-Taking Test Traffic (Hergovich et al., 2006) and the self-developed Implicit Association Test (IAT – Risk-Taking) was explored. The quasi-experimental design included the comparison between real-world examination-candidates of traffic-psychological assessments with a guaranteed faking-intention and a honest control group. For the statistical analysis a sequential testing design was used. While the explicit self-report measure as well as the "Objective" Personality Test were sucessfully faked by the real-world examination-candidates, the conscious distortion of the IAT failed. Implications are discussed.

School resiliency building: Greek in-service and student teachers assessment

Tsakalis, Panayiotis Dept. of Psychology, University of Crete, Rethymno, Greece

This study aims at examining the evaluations of the resiliency-building elements (Belonging, Competence, Empowerment, and Usefulness) that Greek schools provide to teachers and students. Approximately 150 in-service and 250 student teachers participated in this survey, responding to the School Resiliency-Building Assessment Inventory (Henderson & Milstein, 1996:114-116) adjusted in Greek (1=done, 2=enough done, 3=much to be done, 4=nothing done). Factor analysis confirms the original elements/factors and reliability analysis appears adequately high (a>0.73) in the Greek sample. Assessment is not sufficiently positive, though in service teachers' evaluations are significantly (p<0.001) more favorable/school-defending (M=2.2) than student teachers' evaluations which appear more strict/negatively-biased (M=2.6).

The Diagnostic Analysis of Nonverbal Accuracy 2-Taiwan version (DANVA2-TW): A computerized dual-channel instrument of nonverbal emotion recognition

Tseng, Huai-Hsuan Dept. of Psychiatry, NTU Hospital, Taipei, Taiwan Chen, Sue-Huei Department of Psychology, National Taiwan University, Taipei, Taiwan Huang, Yu-Lien Department of Psychology, National Taiwan University, Taipei, Taiwan

Objectives: To establish a culture-suitable instrument with Han faces and voices for assessing the accuracy and the intensity of non-verbal emotions. Methods: 109 college students received computerized tests presenting emotional stimuli randomly. 30 photos and 30 voice clips across 5 emotional categories (happy, sad, angry, fearful and neutral) with highest agreement level were selected from 600+ stimuli. Results: High agreement level in both facial (0.73) and paralanguage subtest (0.81). The test-retest reliability among 35 college students with 2-weeks interval is also good (Kappa = 0.77). Conclusion: DANVA2-TW is a culture-suitable, reliable computerized instrument for nonverbal emotion recognition in Han populations.

Affective disorders in children with learning disabilities

Tsouma, Stauroula- Melina Athens, Greece Michopoulou, Alexandra Psychology Department, General Children's Hospital, Palaia Penteli, Greece Belesioti, Barbara Psychology Department, General Children's Hospital, Palaia Penteli, Greece Goula, Vasiliki Psychology Department, General Children's Hospital, Palaia Penteli, Greece

The aim of this study is to identify psychological problems in children with learning difficulties. The sample consisted of 421 children, aged 7-14, categorised into 3 groups: a) slight learning difficulties, b) dyslexia and c) mental disabilities. Children completed Beck Youth Inventory (BYI). Parents filled Ascenbach's questionnaire. According to BYI, 29% of children mentioned low self-esteem, 32,3% anxiety, 22,1% depression symptoms, 21,6% anger and 20,9% disruptive behavior. According to Ascenbach's questionnaire, 21,4% of parents mentioned: anxiety, 21,4% depression symptoms, 18,5% aggressiveness and 16,2% delinquent behaviour.

Odours affects hand posture when grasping

Tubaldi, Federico Dept. of General Psycholoy, University of Padova, Padova, Italy Ansuini, Caterina General Psycholoy, University of Padova, Padova, Italy Tirindelli, Roberto Neuroscience, University of Parma, Parma, Italy Castiello, Umberto General Psycholoy, University of Padova, Padova, Italy

We investigated hand shaping kinematics when grasping large or small targets in the presence or absence of odours evoking large or small objects. We found that 'small' odours rendered hand shaping for the large targets similar to that for small targets presented in isolation. Conversely, 'large' odours rendered hand shaping for the small targets similar to that for large targets presented in isolation. When the odour 'size' matched the target size, kinematics was facilitated by the olfactory stimulus. We contend that chemosensory representations of objects contains highly detailed information about the action that the objects require.

Later life depression: Life satisfaction, level of functioning and free time activities

*Tzonichaki, Ioanna Occupational therapy, Techn. ed. inst. of athens, Volos, Greece **Kleftaras, George** Dept. of Special Education, University of Thessaly, Volos, Greece **Malikiosi-Loisos, Maria** Faculty of Early Childhood Ed., University of ATHENS, Volos, Greece*

Quality of life is directly related to an individual's life satisfaction and is partly influenced by his/her engagement in satisfying free time activities and subjective perception of his/her level of functioning in significant life areas. The aim of the present research is to study the impact of older adults' quality of life on their depressive symptomatology. 250 community-living elderly persons fulfilled: a) the Life-Satisfaction-Questionnaire, b) the Pichot-Questionnaire-of-Depressive-Symptoms, c) the Satisfaction-from-Performance-in-Activities-of-Daily-Living-Scale and d) the Leisure-Time-Scale. Significant correlations were found between depressive symptoms, level of functioning in significant life areas (specifically the every day activities), leisure time and life satisfaction.

Relationships between categorization tasks and the categorical structures

Ueda, Takashi Waseda University, Tokyo, Japan

It is often said that participants in a categorization task tend to classify the exemplars based on single dimensional information. This tendency suggests there would be a discrepancy between a categorization task performance and the mental representation of categorical structures inferred from the task. So in this study I investigated the task-representation relationships by using several conceptual tasks including two-class classification, free sorting / clustering, and similarity judgment, to several natural or artificial concepts. Results and analyses re-confirmed the participants' general tendencies of one-dimensional categorical judgments, and also suggested the variety of inferred representations of categories or concepts.

Zen Buddhist monk's meaning of life

Urata, Yu Sakai Minami-ku, Japan

The issue of meaning of life has received more attention in recent years, and a variety of research has showed a wide variety of sources of meaning of life. Meaning is constructed within his or her sociocultural context such as religion and cultural worldview. This study examined the question about the meaning of life by analyzing the narratives of Zen Buddhist monks. Semi-structured interview were conducted with Zen Buddhist monks. Then using the Kawakita Jiro (KJ) method, the data were analyzed qualitatively, focusing on how the participants constructed their life meanings from the perspective of Buddhism.

Central assumptions in paranoia: Do paranoid patients believe in a just world?

*Valiente Ots, Carmen Psicología Clínica, Univ. Complutense Madrid, Madrid, Spain **Espinosa López, Regina** Psicología Clínica I, Universidad Complutense Madrid, Pozuelo de Alarcón, Spain **Cantero, Dolores** Psicología Clínica, Univ. Complutense Madrid, Madrid, Spain **Hervas, Gonzalo** Psicología Clínica, Univ. Complutense Madrid, Madrid, Spain **Provencio, María** Psicología Clínica, Univ. Complutense Madrid, Madrid, Spain **Romero, Nuria** Psicología Clínica, Univ. Complutense Madrid, Madrid, Spain **Vázquez, Carmelo** Psicología Clínica, Univ. Complutense Madrid, Madrid, Spain*

We examined whether deluded paranoid patients show 'shattered assumptions' (Janoff-Bulman, 1992). Although PTSD studies (Otto et al., 2006) have convincingly shown that traumatic experiences may often negatively affect commonly shared beliefs about the world, there are no studies that have addressed that issue in paranoids. We compared paranoid, depressive, PTSD and control subjects that completed the WAS (Janoff-Bullman, 1989) and BJW (Dalbert et al., 1997) as well as clinical measures. Clinical groups have more extreme view of world justice than normal controls. Controls have a higher sense of benevolence of the world, and together with paranoids have higher levels of self-worth and personal control. Depression and trauma was associated to a lower sense controllability of the world.

Mechanisms of subliminal semantic priming: A meta-analysis

*van den Bussche, Eva Dept. of Psychology, Katholieke Universiteit Leuven, Kortrijk, Belgium **Reynvoet, Bert** Psychology, Katholieke Universiteit Leuven, Kortrijk, Belgium **van den Noortgate, Wim** Educational Sciences, Katholieke Universiteit Leuven, Kortrijk, Belgium*

The conditions under which subliminal semantic priming effects can or can not be observed remains an important object of discussion that has produced numerous inconsistent research results. Therefore, this meta-analysis was conducted to expose the mechanisms underlying subliminal semantic priming. By statistically combining the research results on subliminal semantic priming conducted throughout the years we unravelled some of the factors that significantly moderate the emergence of subliminal priming effects (for example: the task used in the experiment, the use of novel versus repeated primes, the use of number versus word primes, the category size of the stimuli, etc.).

Aging and verbal working memory capacity

*Van den Noort, Maurits Biological and Medical Psych., University of Bergen, Bergen, Norway **Bosch, Peggy** NICI, Radboud University Nijmegen, Nijmegen, Netherlands **Van Kralingen, Rosalinde** Foodstep, Foodstep B.V., Wageningen, Netherlands*

Objectives The development of verbal working memory capacity over time was investigated. Methods Four different age groups were tested with the new standard computerized version of the reading span test (Van den Noort et al., 2006, 2008). Results Compared to the young adults, the old adults showed a significant decrease in verbal working memory capacity, a significant slowing down in mental processing, made significantly more intrusion errors, and had no recency-effect. Conclusion Interestingly, the results show that there are larger age-related effects in short term verbal memory span than was expected on the basis of aging theories so far.

Vigilance and attention defects as human failure contributing factors

*Van Elslande, Pierre INRETS, Salon-de-Provence, France **Jaffard, Magali** Accident Mechanisms, INRETS, Salon de Provence, France **Fouquet, Katel** Accident Mechanisms, INRETS, Salon de Provence, France*

Problems relating to drivers' vigil and attentional state have a recognized incidence in accidentology, but little is known about their relative influence in accident mechanisms. This paper apprehends the various facets which these problems cover, by exploitation of an important sample of in-depth accident studies, according to a model of typical human error-generating scenarios analysis. The results show that attentional problems have a frequency of occurrence more important than problems of vigilance, among the elements which contribute to the genesis of a human functional failure. In contrast, vigilance deficits present a higher degree of impact than the defects of attention, in the cause of accidents.

Depression, burnout and the impact of events among volunteer counsellors in South Africa

Vawda, Naseema Dept. of Behavioural Medicine, King George V Hospital, Durban, South Africa

This pilot study assessed psychological distress among volunteer counsellors. 16 subjects completed a demographic questionnaire and the Beck's Depression Inventory (BDI), Maslach's Burnout Inventory (MBI) and Impact of Events Scale (IES). 25% reported moderate/severe Depression on the BDI. 18.75% reported high and 43.75% moderate Depersonalization on the MBI. 43.75% reported low Personal Accomplishment(MBI) while 12.5 5 reported high Emotional Exhaustion(MBI). Positive correlations existed between the BDI and Emotional Exhaustion (MBI) (p<0.05)and the Avoidance and Intrusion subscales of the MBI with Personal Accomplishement (MBI)(p<0.05). Implications of the findings are discussed.

Asymmetries in speech perception: Perceptual salience at lexical level?

*Vera Constan, Fatima Psicologia Basica, Universitat de Barcelona, Barcelona, Spain **Sebastián-Gallés, Núria** Psicologia Bàsica, Universitat de Barcelona, Barcelona, Spain*

Perceptual salience is an important dimension in the configuration of the vocalic space during development, but its relevance in adult speech perception has been neglected. We present data from two auditory lexical decision tasks to Spanish stimuli. Non-words were generated by exchanging phonemes /e/ and /i/ from real words (ventana (window) - * vintana; camisa (shirt) - *camesa). Both behavioural and ERP measurements indicated an asymmetry in the processing of non-words: differences in the reaction times and in the N400 component were observed for both non-word types. The results indicate that perceptual salience effects extend into adult speech perception.

Structure factorial of the maslach burnout inventory: A comparative study España-Venezuela

*Viloria Marin, Hermes Antonio Medicion y Evaluacion, Universidad de Los Andes, Merida, Venezuela **Paredes Santiago, Maritza Del Carmen** Geografía Humana, Universidad de Los Andes, Merida, Venezuela **Avendaño Rangel, Francys Andreina** Biología, Universidad de Los Andes, Merida, Venezuela*

We study the stability of the latent structures of the MBI in subsets of the overall sample and offer a comparative study of two groups of University professors, one of them Spanish (762) and the other Venezuelan (194). Overall we observed that for the subsets of men, women, not burnt out, extremely burnt out and those with two subscales with extreme values, the trifactorial structure with the factors associated with Emotional Exhaustion, Self-esteem and Depersonalisation is apparent in these collectives for both studies. However, in some cases, such as Venezuelan women, the axes do not have such a clear interpretation.

Sleep related car crashes in young drivers: Risk perception and sleepiness at wheel coping strategies

*Violani, Cristiano Dept. of Psychology, Sapienza. University of Rome, Rome, Italy **Lucidi, Fabio** of Psychology, Sapienza. University of Rome, Rome, Italy **Mallia, Luca** of Psychology, Sapienza. University of Rome, Rome, Italy*

The aim of the study is to examine which factors are associated with the risk perception to have night-time car crash in young drivers and to evaluate the strategies most commonly used to counteract sleepiness at the wheel. 1123 young drivers with at least 6 months driving experience participated to the study. Males are less worried about night-time car crashes than females. Risk perception is negatively related to night-time driving and positively related with the episodes of driving sleepiness. To counteract sleepiness at the wheel, the 51,47% of the participants "would continue driving but do something", whereas 48% of them "would stop driving and do something".

Motor fitness is related to executive control processes in older adults

Voelcker-Rehage, Claudia JCLL, Jacobs University Bremen, Bremen, Germany Godde, Ben JCLL, Jacobs University Bremen, Bremen, Germany Staudinger, Ursula M. JCLL, Jacobs University Bremen, Bremen, Germany

We analyzed the relationship between older adults' motor and cognitive performance. 116 older participants worked on a flanker task inside and outside of a 3T Siemens Headscanner and completed a heterogeneous battery of 12 motor tests. Results revealed a significant positive correlation between motor and cognitive performance. Particularly, motor balance, fine coordination, and speed showed the highest association with flanker performance. 35.1% of the total variance in cognitive performance was explained by these factors. Furthermore, participants with low motor performance showed more wide-spread brain activation patterns than older adults with high motor fitness during the flanker task, indicating compensation processes.

Interaction between object characteristics and spatial language processing

Vorwerg, Constanze SFB 673, Universität Bielefeld, Bielefeld, Germany

In order to verify linguistic spatial relations, such as 'in front' or 'behind', with respect to seen object pairs, a frame of reference (FoR) has to be activated. This study examined the influence of reference-object characteristics and FoR repetition vs. contrast in successive trials. Participants decided as quickly as possible whether a sentence described a 3D picture presented simultaneously in a head-mounted display. Results reveal influences of object shape (compact, e.g. a dolphin, vs. "looking-through" objects, e.g. a bicycle), and category (animals vs. vehicles vs. manipulable objects). Most subjects switched easily between both FoRs; there were no sequential effects.

Salutogenetic approach and diabetic patient

Voseekova, Alena Hygiene and Preventive Medici, Faculty of Military Health Sci, Hradec Kralove, Czech Republic Burdová, Veronika Hygiene and Preventive Medici, Faculty of Military Health Sci, Hradec Králové, Czech Republic Grossmann, Petr Hygiene and Preventive Medici, Faculty of Military Health Sci, Hradec Králové, Czech Republic Halajčuk, Tomáš Hygiene and Preventive Medici, Faculty of Military Health Sci, Hradec Králové, Czech Republic Hrstka, Zdeněk Hygiene and Preventive Medici, Faculty of Military Health Sci, Hradec Králové, Czech Republic

Salutoprotective factors of lifestyle influence the ability to manage stress and by this the course of the disease. We pay detailed attention to S.O.C. type resistance and percentage representation of the usual psychological state components in type 2 diabetic patients. Knowledge of these factors enables us to estimate the extent of vulnerability of the patient and his ability to cope with his disease, to accept a change in treatment, and to keep the treatment regimen. The possibility of strengthening the resistance of an individual by psychological means creates space for targeted psychological intervention (counselling, psychotherapy).

Anxiety affects body sway during orthostatic standing in college students

Wada, Maki College of Law, Nihon University, Tokyo, Japan Nagai, Masanori Physiology, Yamanashi Inst. Environm. Sci., Fujiyoshida, Japan

We have examined whether anxiety affects body sway during stance in college students. Using a within-subject paradigm, we have found that anxiety level positively correlates with the area and length of body sway. A fast Fourie's transform (FFT) method was further performed in order to examine whether anxiety influences sensory processing for maintaining standing posture. In high anxiety group, percentile power of low frequency components, which is under the influence of visual and vestibular inputs, was greater and percentile power of high frequency components, influenced by somatosensory inputs, was smaller in comparison to those of low anxiety group.

On the flexibility of the planning scope for lexical access in sentence production

Wagner, Valentin Inst. für Psychologie, Universität Leipzig, Leipzig, Germany Jescheniak, Jörg D. Department of Psychology, University of Leipzig, Leipzig, Germany

A series of picture-word interference experiments explored whether the planning scope for lexical access is structurally fixed or rather flexible, depending e.g. on the cognitive load currently imposed on the system. When participants produced SVO-sentences under standard conditions, subject and object nouns were found to be lexical-semantically activated to similar degrees at speech onset, as indexed by similarly sized interference effects from semantic distractors. When the same sentences were produced in a situation requiring additional conceptual processing, the interference effect for object nouns was strongly attenuated, supporting a flexible view of lexical retrieval.

Cross-language activation in bilingual processing of compound words: The effect of semantic transparency

Wang, Min Human Development, University of Maryland, College Park, USA Cheng, Chenxi Human Development, University of Maryland, College Park, USA

Objective: We aimed to examine the effect of semantic transparency in processing compound words among adult Chinese-English bilinguals. Method: A lexical decision task in English was administered. A design of 2 (semantic transparency in English: transparent vs. opaque) X 2 (lexicality of the translated compounds in Chinese: real word vs. nonword) was employed. Twenty-five Chinese-English bilingual speakers were tested. Results: We predict a significant interaction between semantic transparency of English compound words and the lexicality of the translated Chinese compounds. Conclusion: Cross language activation of compound words in bilinguals is affected by semantic transparency of the target compounds.

Age differences of prefrontal cortex activation in encoding process of item memory

Wang, Dahua Inst. of Developm. Psychology, Beijing Normal University, Beijing, People's Republic of China Tang, Dan Beijing Normal University, Institute of Developmental Psy, Beijing, People's Republic of China Peng, Huamao Beijing Normal University, Institute of Developmental Psy, Beijing, People's Republic of China Shen, Jiliang Beijing Normal University, Institute of Developmental Psy, Beijing, People's Republic of China

This study aimed at examining the universality of Hemispheric Asymmetry Reduction of Older Adults (HAROLD) model of item memory indicated by cued-recall task. 25 old adults (60-78 years old) and 15 young adults (20-29 years old), who were both at same educational level, took part in

the study. The participants were required to complete cued-recall tasks at two difficult levels during fMRI scanning. Results suggested that, during the encoding process, the HAROLD model was non-universal. It was found presenting only in difficult task rather than simple task of cued-recall memory.

The development of children's conflict resolution abilities

Wang, Lin Dept. of Psychology, Chung Yuan University, Chung Li, Taiwan

This study traces the developmental trajectory of children's conflict resolution abilities. Four-year longitudinal data have been collected from final 130 (64 boys, 66 girls) Taiwanese children since the 3rd grade. Using correlation and ANOVA, results showed that children's abilities remained stable in each sequential year. The developmental trajectory of altruistic goal-setting and prosocial strategies declined, while its instrumental goal-setting and assertive strategies went up over the four years. The assertive strategies specially increased for girls when they were in the 4th and 6th grades. This phenomenon may reflect the assertive need in puberty, while girls reach their puberty earlier than boys.

Applicability of five-kind of personality inventory for college students' personality measurement: Comparison study with 16PF

Wang, Aiping Beijing Normal University, Psychology school, Beijing, People's Republic of China Xu, Yan Beijing Normal University, Psychology school, Beijing, People's Republic of China

Objective: Applicability of five-kind of personality inventory (FKPI, Xue, Chongcheng etc., 1988) for college students' personality measurement. Methods. Using FKPI and 16PF measured 237 college students; Results: (1) man students' mean is higher significantly than woman in Taiyong (strength) and Yinyangpinghe (equilibrium) dimensions of FKPI, and perfectionism and creativity dimensions of 16PF. But their score of warmth, privateness and tension dimension of 16PF are lower significantly than woman ones; (2) Except reasoning, abstractedness, privateness, openness and creativity dimensions of 16PF, all dimensions of FKPI correlated with other dimensions of 16PF on corresponding content. Conclusion FKPI is available for measurement of college student's personality.

Similarity comparisons affect children's interpretation of sentences with contrastive focus

Wang, Yatong Dept. of Psychology, Kaifeng University, Kaifeng, People's Republic of China

Three experiments were designed to investigate the effects of similarity comparisons on children's interpretation of contrastive focus in sentence with "only". Experiment 1, similar to one of experiments of Paterson et al's study (2006), employed a sequential sentence-picture verification task in which subjects were asked to hear sentences and indicated whether they correctly described the events depicted in each of six pictures. The results in another two experiments showed that two-example learning by comparison rather than one-example learning can better promote children's comprehension of ambiguous focus in sentences with only.

Stages and cognitions in physical activity: A theory-guided investigation

Warner, Lisa Marie Berlin, Germany Lippke, Sonia Health Psychology, FU Berlin, Berlin, Germany Wiedemann, Amelie Ulrike Health Psychology, FU Berlin, Berlin, Germany Reuter, Tabea Health Psychology, FU Berlin, Berlin, Germany Ziegelmann, Jochen Philipp Health Psychology, FU Berlin, Berlin, Germany

Objectives: Investigating the relationship of social-cognitive predictors and stages derived from the Health Action Process Approach (HAPA) for different types of physical activity. Methods: Responses of N=103 blue collar-workers were analysed via regression (mediation hypothesis) and ANOVA. Results: Social-cognitive variables predicted leisure-time physical activity (planning mediated relations). Participants different mindsets across stages supported stage-assumptions. Physical activity due to household chores, blue-collar work or locomotion could not be explained by HAPA variables. Conclusions: Type of physical activity has to be considered when testing theoretical models. Both stage and continuous assumptions of the HAPA build a useful basis for designing interventions.

Is it me? Motor resonance effects after observation of one's own and others' actions

Weiß, Carmen Inst. für Psychologie, Max-Planck-Institut, Leipzig, Germany Tsakiris, Manos Psychology, Royal Holloway, egham, United Kingdom Haggard, Patrick Psychology, ICN, University College London, London, United Kingdom Schütz-Bosbach, Simone Psychology, MPI CBS, Leipzig, Germany

A converging body of evidence indicates that both the execution and observation of actions activates overlapping cortical networks. This implies a shared, agent-neutral representation of self and other. We compared motor facilitation after observation of one's own and others' actions presented in an ambiguous situation to investigate whether the human motor system equates or differentiates self and other. Furthermore, subjects were required to make an explicit judgement about the ownership of the hand performing the action. The results will be discussed with respect to a sensorimotor and explicit self-representation and the possible interrelation between them.

Sense of coherence and healthy aging

Wiesmann, Ulrich Inst. für Medizin Psychologie, Universität Greifswald, Greifswald, Germany Niehörster, Gabriele Institute for Medical Psycholo, University of Greifswald, Greifswald, Germany Hannich, Hans-Joachim Institute for Medical Psycholo, University of Greifswald, Greifswald, Germany

We tested two hypotheses derived from Antonovsky's (1987) salutogenic model: Resources co-vary with the sense of coherence (SOC), and the SOC is a mediator of resource effects on subjective health. 387 seniors (26.6% men) filled out a comprehensive questionnaire assessing subjective health, SOC, and 19 biopsychosocial resources. The SOC was predicted by optimism, self-esteem, low depressive mood, self-efficacy, and expected social support. The SOC strongly mediated resource-effects on psychological health and symptom reporting, but not on physical health. With respect to gerontological practice and intervention, the SOC is an important estimate of idiographic strengths in health matters.

Older spouses' dyadic problem solving performance

Wight, Melanie Inst. für Gerontopsychologie, Universität Zürich, Zürich, Switzerland Martin, Mike Gerontopsychology, University of Zurich, Zurich, Switzerland

Collaboration with the spouse may be an important resource for successful problem solving, especially in old age. To examine individual versus dyadic problem solving performance of older adults, we present data from an ongoing study of elderly spouses (N = 50; minimum age 60 years). The comparison of individual versus dyadic problem solving abilities provides a better understanding of older couples' dyadic adaptation processes when faced with a problem solving task. Our results suggest that older familiar dyads are expert collaborators who might be able to compensate for individual cognitive deficits through dyadic cognition.

Ability perceptions, perceived control and risk avoidance among male and female older drivers

Windsor, Tim Centre for Mental Health Res., Australian National University, Canberra, Australia Anstey, Kaarin Centre for Mental Health Res., Australian National University, Canberra, Australia Walker, Janine Centre for Mental Health Res., Australian National University, Canberra, Australia

Associations between perceived control over driving, driving ability perception (an index of unrealistic optimism) and self-reported avoidance of high-risk driving situations were examined in a sample of 304 older drivers. Associations between perceived control over driving, ability perception and indices of well-being (life satisfaction and depressive symptoms) were also investigated. Results indicated that perceived control over driving and perceived driving ability were associated with reduced risk avoidance and increased well-being, with these associations moderated by sex. Results are discussed in terms of adaptive and maladaptive consequences of perceptual biases and the importance of effective self-regulation for aging well.

Companion animals, attachment and health in the elderly

Winefield, Helen Dept. of Psychology, University of Adelaide, Adelaide, Australia Chur-Hansen, Anna Psychiatry, University of Adelaide, Adelaide, Australia

The scientific literature is equivocal regarding the possible health benefits of companion animal ownership in older people. Adults aged 60+ years (N = 314) responded to standardised scales, then qualitative interviews explored further the connections between companion animal ownership, the human-animal bond, and owner well-being. Pet ownership failed to explain variance in health after taking account of health habits such as smoking. Some older people gain the potential health benefits of pet ownership in other ways, and some with deep attachment to their pet but few other attachments may be at risk of psychological distress and other health problems.

What factors impact on mainstream teachers' beliefs about children with learning difficulties?

Woolfson, Lisa Dept. of Psychology, University of Strathclyde, Glasgow, United Kingdom Brady, Katy Psychology, University of Strathclyde, Glasgow, United Kingdom

Objectives: To explore teachers' beliefs about teaching children with learning difficulties. Method: Data were gathered from 199 teachers on attributions, self-efficacy and coping with learning difficulties, attitudes to disabled people, and general optimism. Results: Multiple regression analyses found efficacy was a positive predictor of external locus of causality attributions (p =.007), stability (p = .003) and controllability (p = .059). Sympathy was a negative predictor of external locus of causality (p = .002) and stability (p = .046). Conclusions: Teachers with high self-efficacy and those whose attitudes to disabled people were not overwhelmed by sympathy used more positive attributions about the possibilities for learner progress.

Why some chronic disease patients felt more negatively than others? A study in Taiwan

Wu, Chih-Hsun Psychology (S115), National Taiwan University, Taipei, Taiwan Huang, Yun-Hsin Psychology (S115), National Taiwan University, Taipei, Taiwan Huang, Yang-Wen Psychology (S115), National Taiwan University, Taipei, Taiwan Cheng, Yih-Ru Psychology (S115), National Taiwan University, Taipei, Taiwan Wu, Yin-Chang Psychology (S115), National Taiwan University, Taipei, Taiwan

Many studies had found that chronic disease patients had experienced more negative emotions. However, some patients adapted well to their disease. This study aimed to explore the psychological factors that could affect chronic patients' emotion. Negative emotions, disturbed level, and subjective evaluation of health were measured by questionnaires. The results showed that chronic patients who were more disturbed by "increased daily hassles" and "changes in one's functions" reported more negative emotions. These results implied that comprehensive health education programs, especially those helped patients to change their life styles, might be useful to dealing with chronic patients emotional problems.

Upright Chinese characters grab attention second to faces

Wu, Shengjun Dept. of Psychology, Fourth Military Medical Univ., Xi'an, People's Republic of China Zhu, Xia Psycology, Fourth Military Medical Univer, Xi'an, People's Republic of China Miao, Danmin Psycology, Fourth Military Medical Univer, Xi'an, People's Republic of China

Objectives: To investigate whether Chinese characters have the similar ability to capture attention as human faces for native Chinese. Methods: Twenty-four undergraduates participated in the go/no-go and inhibition of return (IOR) experiments. Results: In the go/no-go experiment, upright Chinese characters significantly delayed target response times in comparison with other stimuli categories except upright faces. In the IOR experiment, delayed responding of saccade to a location that previously contained Chinese characters or faces was observed. Conclusions: These results supported the hypothesis that Chinese characters have the similar ability to attract attention as faces for native Chinese.

Risk of depressive reaction and its prevention in chronic disease patients

Wu, Yin-Chang Psychology (S115), National Taiwan University, Taipei, Taiwan Chien, Liang-Lin Psychology (S115), National Taiwan University, Taipei, Taiwan Huang, Yun-Hsin Psychology (S115), National Taiwan University, Taipei, Taiwan Wu, Chih-Hsun Psychology (S115), National Taiwan University, Taipei, Taiwan Huang, Yang-Wen Psychology (S115), National Taiwan University, Taipei, Taiwan

The study aimed to establish intervention programs for probable emotional and suicidal problem of chronic disease patients in primary care settings. To explore the influential psychological factors, researchers examined the interrelationships between personal disease-related construct, cognitive adjustment, self-efficacy, coping and emotional reactions by inventories. The result suggested: (1) most patients could reconstruct their cognitive appraisals to chronic diseases and reported less threatening feelings; (2) high self-efficacy related with more problem-focused coping and less depressive mood; (3)low self-efficacy increased both avoidant coping and negative mood. According to the results, we proposed tentative programs to enhance adjustment of chronic disease patients.

An ERP study on the time course of top-down control of visual attention

Wykowska, Agnieszka Inst. für Psychologie, Universität München, München, Germany Schubö, Anna Psychology, LMU, Munich, München, Germany

Stimuli are very salient might capture attention in a bottom-up manner. However, top-down control can modulate processing enabling selection of relevant input. Using ERP methodology, we examined how top-down and bottom-up mechanisms interact throughout the process of visual selection. Our paradigm combined visual search with post-display probe presentation. Probes followed search displays with two different time delays. In line with behavioral results, ERPs locked to probes presented after a longer delay revealed effects on the P1 component likely reflecting top-down control of focal attention. We concluded that with time, top-down control guides focal attention efficiently to the relevant target.

Effects of driving fatigue on mental workload in real road condition

Xu, Xianggang Chinese Academy of Sciences, Institute of psychology, Beijing, People's Republic of China Sun, Xianghong Chinese Academy of Sciences, Institute of psychology, Beijing, People's Republic of China Zhang, Kan Chinese Academy of Sciences, Institute of psychology, Beijing, People's Republic of China

Objectives: Drivers' performance in driving secondary tasks, and relationship between physiological indices and subjective mental workload (MWL) were investigated between two different driver conditions. Methods: Ten taxi drivers were required to do oral calculations during driving in the morning and in the afternoon, respectively. Performance of secondary task, physiological indices, subjective MWL and subjective feeling of fatigue were compared. Results: Difference of calculation errors was significantly found, with more errors in the morning than in the afternoon. Physiological indices showed different results. The other two subjective measurements were also compared. Conclusions: The results shows practice effects and verified the Yerkes-Dodson Law.

On the relationship between the mere exposure effect and the contextual cuing effect

Yagi, Yoshihiko Comprehensive human sciences, University of Tsukuba, Ibaraki, Japan Kikuchi, Tadashi Comprehensive human sciences, University of Tsukuba, 8572, Japan

We investigated the relationship between the mere exposure effect in which previous exposures to stimuli increased participants' preference for those stimuli, and the contextual cuffing effect (CC) in which visual search performance was faster for targets appearing in previously exposed configurations than for targets appearing in new configurations. Participants were asked to search T -target among rotated L-distractors. The mean reaction time showed a typical CC. Then, participants were asked to evaluate how much they like the repeated or new configurations. The results showed that the liking ratings for the repeated configurations were lower than those for the new configurations.

Perceived pain and anxiety before and after amniocentesis among Turkish pregnant women

Yalcinkaya-Alkar, Özden Psychiatry, SB Etlik Ihtisas Hospital, Ankara, Turkey Yalvac, Serdar Ethem OBSTETRICS AND GYNECOLOGY, SB ETLIK MATERNITY HOSPITAL, ANKARA, Turkey

The main objective of this study was to examine the Turkish pregnant women's perception of pain and anxiety before and soon after the amniocentesis. A total of 294 pregnant women from the obstetrics clinics of SBEtlik Maternity Hospital who had amniocentesis performed were interviewed at hospital before and soon after amniocentesis. Demographic, obstetrics and other related variables, which may affect pain and anxiety perception, were included into the study. After descriptive statistics presented, paired samples t tests and analysis of variance conducted. The results revealed that although there was a decrease in perceived pain and anxiety after the procedure, perceived anxiety was still higher than the perceived pain level after the amniocentesis. Implications of these results were discussed.

Attentional Control in Visual Search with Singletons: Effects of Spatial Information

Yamaoka, Kao Psychology, Sophia University, Tokyo, Japan Umeda, Satoshi Psychology, Keio University, Tokyo, Japan

When there exists one salient stimulus (singleton) in a visual field among others, whether attention can be controlled in a top-down fashion is still controversial. Our present study investigated whether attentional control can be observed when participants have the advanced knowledge about spatial locations of the upcoming targets, by manipulating their probabilities. Our results indicated that when participants were capable of predicting the locations of the upcoming targets, the performance was enhanced and it was not affected by irrelevant singleton. Our findings suggest that advanced spatial information enables participants to ignore the irrelevant singleton and make top-down attentional control possible.

An event related potential study of accessing word meaning in two languages for Chinese-English bilinguals

Yang, Runrong teacher's college, Dalian University, Dalian, People's Republic of China

This study was to investigate the representation and processing of first and second language words of Chinese-English bilinguals. A semantic categorization task was employed, while ERPs were recorded and behavioral data were also collected. The results were: first language repetition and second language repetition produced a significant reduction than control condition respectively, between-language repetitions were different for different language order: the priming effects from L2 to L1 were larger than from L1 to L2. The results suggested within-language repetition facilitated the decision at both lexical (orthography and phonology) and conceptual (meaning) level, while between-language repetition had different priming mechanism.

Effect of performing arithmetic and reading aloud on memory tasks in the elderly

Yoshida, Hajime Dept. of Psychology, Ritsumeikan University, Kyoto, Japan Furuhashi, Keisuke psychology, Fukuoka prefectural University, tagawa, Japan Ookawa, Ichiro psychology, tukuba University, tukuba, Japan Tsuchida, Noriaki psychology, ritsumeikan University, kyoto, Japan Nakamura, Yoshiro psychology, ritsumeikan University, kyoto, Japan Son, Kin psychology, ritsumeikan University, kyoto, Japan Takahashi, Nobuko psychology, ritsumeikan University, kyoto, Japan Ishikawa, Mariko psychology, ritsumeikan University, kyoto, Japan Miyata, Masako psychology, ritsumeikan University, kyoto, Japan Hakoiwa, Chiyoji psychology, ritsumeikan University, kyoto, Japan

Recent studies demonstrated that solving easy arithmetic and reading aloud activated prefrontal lobe more than other cognitive tasks by using fMRI. Two experiments were conducted to examine effect of performing these tasks on memory performances such as working memory, short-term memory, or long-term memory in the elderly. A total of 70 elderly were given tasks of simple arithmetic or reading aloud over 35 sessions in Exp.1 with feedback to their responses and in Exp.2 without feedback. Results in the long-term memory task showed significant difference between Experimental and control groups in post-test. These results were discussed in terms of activation theory of prefrontal lobe.

The role of Islamic ceremony (Taazizyeh) on development of moral judgment among adolescents in Iran

Younesi, Jalal counselling, University of social welfare, Tehran, Islamic Republic of Iran Amirjan, Sarah counselling, University of social welfare, Tehran, Islamic Republic of Iran Soltani Abad, Mojtaba counselling, University of social welfare, Tehran, Islamic Republic of Iran

The purpose of this research was to study the effect of Taaziyeh on development of moral judgment among adolescents. Taaziyeh is an impressive traditional Islamic ceremony in Iran for memory of grand son of prophet Mohammad (s) who to be martyred thirteen centuries ago. 75 male adolescents (15-17) participated in Taziyeh whom to be selected randomly and answered moral judgment development questionnaire after end of the ceremony. The same number of subjects were selected as control group. Findings revealed a significant difference between two groups (p≤0.05). This means that the participation in Taaziyeh can enhance moral judgment development. The results indicate the positive role of some religious ceremony on development of moral judgment ofadolescents.

Effects of response style on the personality and self-esteem

Yu, Yibing Yingdong Building, Room 255, Beijing Normal University, Beijing, People's Republic of China Hong, Zou Inst.Developmental psychology, Beijing Normal University, Beijing, People's Republic of China Kejia, Qu Ins.Developmental psychology, Beijing Normal University, Beijing, People's Republic of China

Are the relationships of personality and self-esteem "real" ? This study examines the response style effects on the "Little Five" Personality and Global Self-Esteem(GSE) with 1654 Chinese students. Preliminary analysis shows that the simple correlation between GSE and "Little-Five" personality or response styles are all significant at the 0.05 level above and beyond. After controlled the effects of response styles, the combined variance explanation ratio and the partial regression coefficients of personality factors on the GSE decrease for some extent respectively. It implies that the relationship between personality and self-esteem may be inflative partially.

The psychology of waiting

Zakay, Dan Dept. of Psychology, Tel-Aviv University, Tel-Aviv, Israel

Waiting is a common daily behavior. A model, based on time perception processes and on social factors like social justice, is suggested for explaining waiting behavior. The model can account for phenomena like abandoning of waiting, feelings of stress while waiting and other typical waiting behaviors. Implications of the model for the design of real and virtual waitings' environment as well as implications for marketing are discussed.

The correlation between social support, coping style and subjective well-being of college students

Zhang, Jianren Department of Psychology, Hunan Normal University, Changsha, People's Republic of China

Objective: To explore college students' relations among social support?coping style and subjective well-being(SWB). Methods: Two hundred and fourteen college students were evaluated with Index of Well-being?Affect Scales?Simplified Coping Style Questionnaire(SCSQ)and Social Support Rating Scale(SSRS). Results: Social support correlated with SWB significantly and positively. Positive coping style was positively correlated with SWB?but negative coping style was positively correlated with negative affect. Positive coping style was positively correlative with social support?and negative coping style was negatively correlative with subjective support.Conclusion: SWB had significant correlations with social support and coping style.

Tracking the time course of segmental and tonal encoding in Chinese spoken production: an event-related potential study

Zhang, Qingfang Institute of Psychology, Beijing, People's Republic of China

This study investigated the time course of segmental and tonal encoding during Chinese spoken production. Participants were shown pictures and carried out a go/nogo decision based on either segmental or tonal information. The segmental decision was to determine whether the picture name started with a specific phoneme (i.e., /j/) or not. The tonal decision was to determine whether the picture name was of tone 1 (tone 2, tone 3 or tone 4) or not. Analyses of N200 effects indicated that segmental and tonal information was retrieved simultaneously. It provides evidence for Levelt et al.'s (1999) language production model.

How negative numbers cause spatial shifts of attention if they can

Zhang, Yu Psychology, Shaanxi Normal University, Xi'an, People's Republic of China

Studies have shown that processing magnitude of positive numbers can cause spatial shifts of attention, for negative numbers, however, there's rare evidence for whether processing negative numbers can cause such shifts. The present experiments was to investigate if processing negative numbers can cause spatial shifts of attention, and whether it depends upon magnitude or absolute value. Experiment1 reveals spatial shifts of attention depending upon absolute value, whereas upon magnitude in Experiment2. The study suggests that processing negative numbers can cause spatial shifts of attention, how it does, however, seems to depend upon the inter-influence from other involving numbers on them.

Negative attentional set based on abstract conceptual level: Evidence from the suppressed N2pc in the attentional blink

Zhang, Dexuan Department of Psychology, Hangzhou Normal University, Hangzhou, People's Republic of China Martens, Sander BCN Neuroimaging Center, University of Groningen, Groningen, Netherlands Zhou, Xiaolin Department of Psychology, Peking University, Beijing, People's Republic of China

The attentional blink (AB) is a deficit in reporting the second of two targets when it occurs 200-500 ms after the first. Here we investigate how a distractor stimulus presented prior to the first target can alter the attentional set, the amount of resources allocated as indexed by the N2pc ERP component, and behavioral performance for the second target. Suppression effects were found when the critical distractor matched the second target, either at the level of perceptual features, or the level of conceptual features. Possible implications for existing theoretical models of the AB are discussed.

Does saccade inhibition of return severed as a foraging facilitator: Evidence from two behavior studies

Zhang, Yang Dept. of Psychology, Northeast Normal University, Changchun, People's Republic of China Ming, Zhang Psycology, NortheastNormal university, Changchun, People's Republic of China

Objective: The goal of current study was to determine whether saccade inhibition of return (IOR) served as a foraging facilitator or an intrinsic aspect of shifting attention (Hooge et al, 2005). Methods: Thirteen and fourteen students served as participants in experiment 1 and 2 respectively. The spatial working memory (SPWM) load was manipulated by have the SPWM load or not (experiment 1) or varying the memory set size between one and four (experiment 2). Results and Conclusions: The saccade IOR wasn't modulated by SPWM. Therefore, saccade IOR is not served as a foraging facilitator.

On relations between pupils, mental health, personality and parental rearing patterns

Zhang, Jianren Department of Psychology, Hunan Normal University, Changsha, People's Republic of China

Objective:To explore the interaction among mental health, personality and parental rearing patterns in 6-13 years old children. Methods:273 children aged in 6-13 years old were assessed by Egna Minnen Barndoms Uppfostran (EMBU) Scale, Eysenck Personality Questionaire (EPQ) and SCL-90. Result:The N and P of EPQ were correlated positively with each factors of SCL-90. Negative correlation between parent's affective warmth and the scores of factors of SCL-90. Positive correlations exist between parent's punishments, overprotection, rejection and the scores of factors SCL-90. Conclusion:Parental rearing patterns may effect childern's mental health through the Mediation effect of childern's personality.

How contextual characteristics in organizations enhance employee creativity? A dynamic model

Zhang, Kai School of Business, Renmin University of China, Beijing, People's Republic of China

This paper systematically reviews and integrates theoretical and empirical research on contextual characteristics enhancing employee creativity in the workplace and explores the dynamic mechanism of the effects of these ones on employee creativity. Based on a self-organizing theory of human motivation, a new theoretical model is put forward through including interest into the dynamic mechanism. It is suggested that employees' interest in work mediates the impact of the contextual characteristics on their creativity. Implications of this theoretical model for future research and management practices are discussed.

Cognitive development of 3~6 years old Chinese children's beliefs on the relationship between gender-role and aggression

Zheng, Lijun Dept. of Psychology, Hangzhou Normal University, Hangzhou, People's Republic of China Hu, Jun Law School, Hangzhou Normal University, Hangzhou, People's Republic of China

Cognitive development of 3~6 years old Chinese children's beliefs about the relationship between gender-role and aggression were systematically examined via 3 personal interviews (N=376). In Interview 1, children aged from 3 have obtained the ability of reasoning out certain aggression forms across gender-role information. In Interview 2, both of preschoolers and pupils have enabled to infer gender types from given aggression behavioral labels. In Interview 3, it found out 3-4 years old children were more apt to make systematical mistakes and memory distortion. These findings suggest Chinese children aged from 3 have organized schemata about the relationship between gender-role and aggression that affect their cognitive activities, the development of such schemata patterns tends to be stable.

Development of internet-related behavior questionnaire for adolescents

Zhou, Shijie Second Xiangya Hospital, Central South University, Changsha, People's Republic of China

Objective:To develop an instrument for assessing the internet-related behavior characteristics of adolescents. Methods:The initial questionnaire consists of 70 items, which involve the assessment of cognitive, emotional, and behavioral characteristics related to internet usage. A total of 1096 valid data samples of college students were collected. Results:Exploratory factor analysis resulted in a 9-factor solution, which can be specified as information seeking and technological mastery, cybersexual and game, and so on. 9 factors could explain 51.651% of the total variance. Confirmatory factor analysis(C-FI) showed that the 9-factor construct was across-

sample confirmed. Conclusion:The Internet Behavior Questionnaire for Adolescents had acceptable construct validity.

Mental health in a German teacher sample at the beginning of their occupational career

Zimmermann, Linda Psychosomatische Medizin, Universitätsklinikum Freiburg, Freiburg, Germany Wangler, Jutta Psychosomatische Medizin, Universitätsklinikum Freiburg, Freiburg, Germany Unterbrink, Thomas Psychosomatische Medizin, Universitätsklinikum Freiburg, Freiburg, Germany Pfeifer, Ruth Psychosomatische Medizin, Universitätsklinikum Freiburg, Freiburg, Germany Wirsching, Michael Psychosomatische Medizin, Universitätsklinikum Freiburg, Freiburg, Germany Bauer, Joachim Psychosomatische Medizin, Universitätsklinikum Freiburg, Freiburg, Germany

In order to analyze how early mental health problems arise in the occupational career of German teachers, we applied several inventories (GHQ, MBI, AVEM) in 470 German student teachers (students after having completed their university studies, but teaching under supervision). With respect to the GHQ, 45 % of the student teachers sample showed values beyond the cutoff >=4 (compared to "only" 29.8 % in teachers) reflecting a high level of job strain. One of the causes for this surprisingly high rate might be that a majority of the student teachers indicated that they felt insufficiently prepared for their job.

The simple and multiple relationship of personality characteristics and mental health with blood type system (ABO) in students

Zirak Moradlou, Hossein Dept. of Psychology, Shahid Beheshti University, Tehran, Islamic Republic of Iran

The aim of this study was, identification and determination of simple and multiple relationship of personality characteristics and mental health with blood type system (ABO), with causal-comparative method, random cluster sampling, NEO-FFI, SCL 90-R, and confident evidence indicator blood type, in 169 students of Shahid Beheshti University. According to t-tests, one way analysis of variance and analysis of regression: 1- There is significant relationship between neuroticism with global severity index and Conscientiousness with mental health. 2- There is no causal effect between bLood type system (ABO), with personality characteristics and mental health. 3- There is no effect gender on mental health, but it effects agreeableness.

Poster Session Wednesday Afternoon 14:00

Parental perspectives on mental retardation and their interaction with their children

Abdurahman, Feruz Special Needs Education, Addis Ababa University, Addis Ababa, Ethiopia

This study aimed to assess how parents understand mental retardation, and their interaction with the mentally retarded child at home. The effect of " mother-to mother" interaction program, under the support of a non-governmental organization called Medical Missionary of Mary's Counseling Center, based in Addis Ababa, was also assessed. 6 parents and 2 project coordinators from the organization were purposely selected. Semi-structured interview and were the main tools for data collection. Qualitative method of analysis was employed The parents described mental retardation as a natural phenomenon given by God as a punishment. Further research has to be conducted in this regard and awareness of parents on mental retardation and early intervention should be enhanced.

Socioemotional violence prevention program in Puerto Rican preschool children

Abelleira Martinez, Mayra A. Dept. of Psychology, University of Puerto Rico, Mayaguez, Puerto Rico Hernandez, Giselle 7066, Bo. Maria, Moca, Puerto Rico Alicea Cuprill, Giselle Marie Psychology, University of Puerto Rico, Bayamon, Puerto Rico Armstrong Rivera, Nicole M. Psychology, University of Puerto Rico, Mayaguez, Puerto Rico Nunez Zapata, Mayra A. Biology, University of Puerto Rico, Mayaguez, Puerto Rico

This investigation assessed the response of very young children to a culturally adapted violence prevention program. The "Second Step" program was adjusted according to the Puerto Rican culture and implemented with a classroom of 37 preschool children, whose social skills, along with teacher perception of the program, were evaluated. Qualitative findings indicated that the material adaptations required further alterations to make them more amenable to teacher schedules and systemic limitations within the school. Quantitative analyses indicated significant behavioral change from pre- to post-test in 46% of the participants. Implications for cultural adaptation of curricula and the implementation context are discussed.

Emotional Labour; Job stress in call centres: Does emotional intelligence matter?

Agrawal, Rakesh Kumar OB&HR, Ins. of Management Technology, Ghaziabad, India Misra, Renu OB&HR, Ins. of Management Technology, Ghaziabad, India

Most studies available in literature implicitly or explicitly conclude that emotional labour has negative and dysfunctional consequences, such as job stress and emotional exhaustion, for workers. However, they do not examine the role of emotional intelligence in the relationship. In this study, we examine the mediating effect of emotional intelligence in the relationship between emotional labour and job stress by analysing data collected through standard instruments from 150 customer service agents in call centres in India. Since it is an ongoing research and data collection is in progress, the findings would be available only at the time of submission of full paper.

Parents as partner: A study of problems affecting parents in training their children with intellectual deficits

Ahlawat, Sangeeta Dept. of Education, University of Krukshetra, Kurukshetra, India

Parents play an important role in the education and training of a child with intellectual deficit. However, the scenario w.r.t. parents' participation in India is not very encouraging. The study was conducted to find the parents' problems in training their intellectually challenged wards. Parents of 50 children studying in special schools in two districts of Haryana were administered questionnaires. The parents revealed various problems; mothers reported more problems than fathers; parents of female children had greater problems; less educated endorsed more problems; low income and severity of the condition were positively related to problems faced.

Reading difficulties among dyslexics: Efficacy of a remedial programme

Ahlawat, Sangeeta Dept. of Education, University of Krukshetra, Kurukshetra, India

The study was planned to see the effectiveness of an intervention programme in remediating reading difficulties among children with dyslexia. The study employed pre-test post test control experimental design. Forty respondents (20 each in experimental and control group) in the age range 8-10 years and studying in public schools in Panipat district of Haryana were selected purposively. A six weeks programme comprising of different activities was administered. The programme was found to be effective in improving sound-symbol association, phonic analysis, semantic closure, lexical processing, language internalization, grapheme phoneme association, verbal visual correspondence, listening comprehension and reading comprehension.

Life values inventory (LVI): Studies with Portuguese college students

Almeida, Leonor Dept. de Psicologia, Universidade Lusofona, Lisboa, Portugal Tavares, Patricia Psicologia, Universidade Lusofona, Lisboa, Portugal

The use of the Life Values Inventory (LVI) – Portuguese Version (Almeida, 2006) -in the higher education context was the goal of a research with a group of 271 college students. Following a summary of the bibliography's revision about the importance of the values in the career development, it is presented the analysis of the scores obtained with the Life Values Inventory: means and standard deviations; internal consistence coefficients, by the alpha of Cronbach method; factor analysis and groups differences analysis defined by field of studies, gender, geographic area and public vs. private universities.

Linkage of job characteristics and depression in a national health survey in the United States

Alterman, Toni NIOSH-DSHEFS-SB, CDC, Cincinnati, USA Grosch, James CDC/NIOSH/DART, National Institute for Occupat, Cincinnati, USA Chen, Xiao CDC/NIOSH/DSHEFS, National Institute for Occupat, Cincinnati, USA Chrislip, David CDC/NIOSH/DART, National Institute for Occupat, Cincinnati, USA Petersen, Martin CDC/NIOSH/DSHEFS, National Institute for Occupat, Cincinnati, USA Muntaner, Carles CAMH, University of Toronto, Toronto, Canada

Associations between depression and proxy measures for workplace psychosocial factors and work organization were examined. Job characteristics from the Occupational Information Network (O*NET) were linked to the U.S. National Health Interview Survey. Scales were developed through factor analyses and linkage was done using occupational titles. Logistic regression showed that several O*NET variables (e.g., guiding work of others, gaining knowledge, and positive management relations) were protective for depression after adjustment for gender, race, ethnicity, education, and age. Additional analysis using this linkage technique is warranted, and may suggest other important job characteristics associated with worker well-being.

Can a painful stimulus induce either conditioned avoidance or conditioned approach?

Andreatta, Marta Inst. für Psychologie, Universität Würzburg, Würzburg, Germany Mühlberger, Andreas Psychology, University of Würzburg, Wuerzburg, Germany Kenntner-Mabiala, Ramona Psychology, University of Würzburg, Wuerzburg, Germany Pauli, Paul Psychology, University of Würzburg, Wuerzburg, Germany

The study investigated how the timing between unconditioned stimulus (US) and conditioned stimulus (CS+) influences the valence of the CS+. A between design was used: 22 participants were forward conditioned (CS preceded US) and 22 were backward conditioned (CS followed US). Valence and arousal ratings as well as startle reflex were measured as dependent variable. CS+ was rated more negative and more arousing after conditioning compared to CS-. Furthermore, the startle response after conditioning was enhanced during CS+ presentation than during presentation of the control. In summary, CS+ acquired aversive qualities after being both forward and backward conditioned.

Self-esteem and communication in adults

Armas Vargas, Enrique Person., Evaluat. & Psychology, Psychology Faculty, Tenerife, Spain

This study investigated the relationship between the Self-Esteem Questionnaire (CAE, Armas-Vargas, E.) with adults and the relationship with a Communication Index (father, mother, brothers, couple; friends and labor environment). 100 adults (49 men & 51 women, age 23-54 years). Factor analysis and reliability was conducted on CAE: 4 factors (58% variance): He himself (alpha=.90); Negative Comparison with Others (alpha=.90); Valuation of Ineffectiveness (alpha=.78); The Others (alpha=.73). We obtained a significantly correlation between the factors Negative Comparison with others & valuation of Ineffectiveness, and a difficult communication with brothers, couple, boss & mother. When Self-evaluation and the evaluation of the others are positive, communication with friends, brothers and boss is easy.

Relationship of participation in decision-making, trust, and organizational citizenship behavior with organizational identity and justice from personnel's point of view in an industrial complex

Ashja, Arezoo i/o Psychology, Isfahan University, Isfahan, Islamic Republic of Iran Nouri, Abolghasem i/o psychology, isfahan university, isfahan, Islamic Republic of Iran Oreyzi, Hamid Reza i/o psychology, isfahan university, isfahan, Islamic Republic of Iran Samavatian, Hossein i/o psychology, isfahan university, isfahan, Islamic Republic of Iran

This paper investigated The relationship of participation in decision-making, trust, and organizational citizenship behavior with organizational identity and justice from personnel's point of view in an industrial complex. data gathered from 200 company's employee through relative questionnaire. correlations, reggressions and path analysis indicated significant relationship between variables.

Animal-assisted play therapy for children suffering from emotional stress

Axelrad-Levy, Tamar Animal Assisted Therapy, David Yallin Colage, Jerusalem, Israel

This new intervention is derived from D. W. Winnicott's theory and has two basic objectives: 1) the animals, as represented in their life cycle, serve as intermediaries between the child's external-inner reality. 2) the child relates to his/her inner contents indirectly, through projection and transference. The therapy sessions take place in a special space called the Animal-Corner. There the child is free to choose the type of animal and the character of the relationship with the animal and the therapist. Two examples are presented, demonstrating how to work through topics such as self-identity and conflict related to mother- child bonding.

Psychological assessment and management of lower back pain among orthopaedic patients

Ayeni, Esther Dept. of Psychology, University of Lagos, Lagos, Nigeria

This study with two phase-assessment and treatment examined the orthopaedic, social and psychological causes of lower back pain in orthopaedic and non-orthopaedic patients in Lagos, Nigeria. PSE, PRS ans SCL-90 were administered on the two sets of participants, 80 patients and 90 non-patients. Independent T-test, Pearson Product Moment Correlation and, ANOVA were the stastical methods used. The study reveled; significant difference in the pain manifestiation and psychopathology of patients and non-patients; psychopathology differences between female and male participants; significant correlation of pain and psychopathology. Results emphasized the need to complement chemotherapy and physiotherapy with psychotherapy

Humiliation, embarrassment and guilt in Japanese part-time job

Azami, Ritsuko University of the Sacred Heart, Tokyo, Japan

In western society, shame is maladaptive and guilt is adaptive. This study is to examine whether or not shame and guilt are adaptive for Japanese. Participants were 92 Japanese undergraduates who had part-time job experiences. They were semi-structured interviewed about the degree of shame and guilt they felt when being rebuked by their boss, customer, or co-worker. Factor analysis of self-ratings on shame and guilt extracted three factors; humiliation, embarrassment, and guilt. Humiliation was related to maladaptive characteristics such as anger, while guilt was related to adaptive characteristics such as apology.

Eco-cultural influences on pictorial depth perception

Babu, Rangaiah Maharaja's College, University of Mysore, Mysore, India

Influence of eco-cultural contexts on pictorial depth perception with special reference to domestication of livestock studied using Hudson's pictorial depth perception test. Five groups of tribes and non-tribes were selected for the study. It was expected that the tribes with domestic livestock would preceive more three dimensions in pictures compared to the tribes without domestic livestock. The effect of livestock domestication was not found in the present study. Men perceived significantly more three dimensions in pictures. The study showed clear trend in the scores on three-dimensional perception with urban literates on the top, followed by urban illiterates, rural illiterates and tribes (both groups) fitted the eco-cultural model.

Repetition priming effects caused by consciously perceived versus unconsciously perceived primes are dependent on qualitatively different aspects of a visual stimulus

*Bacon, Benoit A. Dept. of Psychology, Bishop's University, Sherbrooke, Canada **McCabe, Eric** Psychologie, Université de Montréal, Montréal, Canada **Gosselin, Frédéric** Psychologie, Université de Montréal, Montréal, Canada*

Conscious and unconscious visual encoding differ in quantitative activation (threshold) but we argue that they also differ qualitatively. A repetition priming paradigm (stimuli: ten faces; half females) is used in conjunction with Bubbles, a method that partially and randomly reveals aspects of the prime (x, y coordinates and spatial frequency). We introduce two masking conditions so that primes are encoded consciously or unconsciously. Following 3072 gender discrimination trials, linear regression (bubble masks and response times) show that conscious priming depends on well defined elements of the prime whereas unconscious priming depends on qualitatively different low-frequency global aspects of the prime.

Electrophysiological measurements indicate operation of internal forward models of self-agency in the auditory modality

*Baess, Pamela Inst. für Psychologie I, Universität Leipzig, Leipzig, Germany **Jacobsen, Thomas** University of Leipzig, Institute of Psychology I, Leipzig, Germany **Schroeger, Erich** University of Leipzig, Institute of Psychology I, Leipzig, Germany*

Discriminating between the source of agency as self-generated or externally generated is an essential ability. Internal forward models of self-generated actions are assumed to underlie such processes using comparisons between motor command (efference copy) and sensory feedback (reafference) information. Using human electroencephalography, we observed attenuated responses for self-generated sounds compared to externally generated sounds. These attenuation effects occurred during early auditory cortical processing (prior 50 ms after stimulus presentation), even for variable sound input with respect to sound's quality and onset. Our data support the existence of internal forward models, which have been proposed for other modalities, also in audition.

The nature and outcomes of work-family enrichment amongst South African employees.

*Bagraim, Jeffrey School of Management Studies, University of Cape Town, Cape Town, South Africa **Jaga, Ameeta** School of Management Studies, University of Cape Town, Cape Town, South Africa*

This study examined the nature and outcomes of work-family enrichment amongst South African employees (N = 336) who responded to a self-report questionnaire from multiple sites of a retail organization. Factor analysis was used to examine the dimensionality of work-family enrichment, its bi-directionality, and its distinctiveness from work-family conflict. Hierarchical multiple regression evidenced that work to family enrichment helps predict organisational commitment and job satisfaction, even when controlling for demographic and work variables, and that the affect component of family to work enrichment helps predict family satisfaction. The implications of the results are discussed.

Efficacy of metacognitive therapy on maladaptive metacognitive believes and post-traumatic stress disorder symptoms, in Iraq-Iran war.

*Bakhtavar, Essa Clinical Psychology, Isfahan University, Isfahan, Islamic Republic of Iran **Neshat–Doost, Hamid taher** clinical psychology, isfahan university, isfahan, Islamic Republic of Iran **Molavi, Hossain** clinical psychology, isfahan university, isfahan, Islamic Republic of Iran **Bahrami, Fateme** clinical psychology, isfahan university, isfahan, Islamic Republic of Iran*

The aim of this study is examine the efficacy of metacognitive therapy on maladaptive metacognitive beliefs and PTSD symptoms. From the war handicaps were diagnosed on the basis of DSM-IV and the Mississippi Scale for PTSD, 34 subjects were randomly selected. The experimental group beside resaving drug which was performed in an identical condition whit control group, underwent metacognitive therapy was carried out in 8 sessions (90 minutes) for the experimental group. Than post-test a 2 month follow-up were administered. The results showed that the experimental group scored significantly less the control group did on the maladaptive metacognitive and PTSD scale on the post-test and follow-up (p<0.01). Keywords: metacognitive therapy, PTSD, war handicapped.

The study of relationships between organizational justice and organizational climate with counterproductive behaviors in one of the companies of Isfahan City.

*Barati, Hajar I/o Psychology, Isfahan University, Isfahan, Islamic Republic of Iran **sadeghiyan, kave** I/o psychology, Isfahan University, Isfahan, Islamic Republic of Iran*

The aim of this study was to investigate the relationship between organizational climate and organizational justice with counterproductive behaviors. The sample consist of 112 employees who were selected randomly from one of the Isfahan city's companies. The instruments used in this research consist of Organizational Climate Questioner, Organizational Justice Questioner and Counterproductive Behaviors Cheklist. The result showed that there was a negative relationship between counterproductive behaviors to individual and climate And there was a negative relationship between counterproductive behaviors to organization and cooperative climate and, procedural Justice.

Limits and possibilities in psychotherapeutic treatment of patients from poor communities

*Barbosa, Cristina Monteiro Dept. de Psicometria, UFRJ, Rio de Janeiro, Brazil **de Freitas Perez, Lucia Maria** Dept. de Psicologia, UNESA / FAMATh, Rio de Janeiro, Brazil*

Aim: make clear the limits and possibilities of psychotherapy in institutions that comprise social clinic care. Method: it is a clinical research that consisted of psychological treatment of patients from poor communities in Rio de Janeiro, Brazil. Result: based on patients' speech, the conclusion is that besides the scarcity due to serious social factors, we verified a significant difficulty of symbolization. Conclusion: it was verified that psychological clinic is bonded with social and cultural issues.

The diagnoses and the intervention in the symptoms of learning disabilities

*Barbosa, Cristina Monteiro Dept. de Psicometria, UFRJ, Rio de Janeiro, Brazil **de Castro, Ana Carolina Policarpo** Dept. de Psicometria, UFRJ, Rio de Janeiro, Brazil **de Carvalho, Patrycia Nazaré** Dept. de Psicometria, UFRJ, Rio de Janeiro, Brazil **Mahmud, Larissa Lopes** Dept. de Psicometria, UFRJ, Rio de Janeiro, Brazil **Gonçalves, Karla Pinto Baptista** Dept. de Psicometria, UFRJ, Rio de Janeiro, Brazil*

OBJECTIVES: Present a discussion about the psychological evaluation of children with learning disabilities' complaint. METHODS: Interviews, the diagnostic hours game and a battery of psychological tests (projectives and objectives). RESULTS: The evaluations produced um effect of knowledge's construction about the hidden symptoms of learning disabilities. CONCLUSION: The psychological diagnoses has being an important field of diagnoses and intervention of learning disorders.

The double and the cracked mirror

Barbosa, Cristina Monteiro Dept. de Psicometria, UFRJ, Rio de Janeiro, Brazil

Objectives: To verify a link between psychoanalysis and modern art. Method: This study intends to discuss narcissism and its relation with modern art. Results: In Cubism, Picasso and Braque represent the cracked mirror. They tear the canvas, allowing a fragmented image to be viewed, destroying the unified illusive space of the image by showing the tragic: the real. Conclusios: In psychoanalysis, the ego is constituted by an image in the mirror, whereas the other as specular image reflects a narcissistic illusion of wholeness. This imaginary reflection is "cracked" as the subject is constituted by the access to the symbolic.

Parental acceptance-rejection, internalizing and externalizing behavior problems in children with learning disabilities

Batum, Petek Istanbul, Turkey

The aim of this study was to examine the levels of parental acceptance-rejection and behavior problems in children with learning disabilities (LD).Results revealed that children with LD were more rejected by their parents and showed higher levels of behavior problems than children without LD. Gender x Group interaction effect indicated that LD girls' mothers perceived higher rejection than mothers of girls without LD. Regression analyses indicated that for both groups of children, children's perception of maternal rejection predicted internalizing problems while mothers' perceptions of rejection towards their children predicted externalizing problems. Overall, findings of the study shed light to the importance of parental rejection in learning disabilities and draws attention to including parents in the treatment plan.

Accuracy of professional evaluation

Baturin, Nikolay General psychology, Southern Ural State University, Chelyabinsk, Russia

The problem of the accuracy of evaluation that is maked by specialists in very different fields of the social activity is highly actual. It influences the quality of managerial decisions and as well results of organization activities. Evaluation and its accuracy are observed from the position of the Evaluation Theory (1997, Baturin). The cycle of experimental researches indicated that accuracy of evaluation is a derivative of the reflection accuracy of the object evaluation; the quality of evaluation base, the adequacy of the comparison object with base and accuracy of evaluation expression. Different components of context, personal features of estimator and evaluation style also influence the evaluation accuracy. Special trainings are designed for compensation of factors that reduce evaluation accuracy.

Psycho-social and developmental determinants of health risk behavior

Bazillier, Cecile Psychology, Universite ParisX Nanterre, Nanterre, France Mallet, Pascal Psychology, Université ParisX Nanterre, Nanterre, France Verlhiac, Jean-François Psychology, Université ParisX Nanterre, Nanterre, France

The aim of our communication is to present the first results of a longitudinal study, which is designed: (a) to measure the effects of a program intended to prevent children from smoking and eating misbehaviors; and (b) to examine several factors that are expected to mediate the effects of this prevention program. We used a pre-test, post-test and control group method. The participants are 1,000 eight-to-eleven -year-old children leaving in the suburb of Paris. The research is in progress and we will be able to communicate the first results during the congress.

Psychological factors of diagnostic condition: students' perception of the movie "Nell"

Becker, Elisabeth CCBS - PPGDD, Univ. Presbit. Mackenzie, São Paulo, Brazil Lacerda, Carla Renata CCBS - PPGDD, Univ. Presbit. Mackenzie, São Paulo Sp, Brazil Guimarães Germano, Renata CCBS - PPGDD, Univ. Presbit. Mackenzie, São Paulo Sp, Brazil Ormenese Gomes, Millena CCBS - PPGDD, Univ. Presbit. Mackenzie, São Paulo Sp, Brazil Mariano, Fabiana CCBS - PPGDD, Univ. Presbit. Mackenzie, São Paulo Sp, Brazil Alves, Bianca CCBS - PPGDD, Univ. Presbit. Mackenzie, São Paulo Sp, Brazil

Interdisciplinarity is a research field in Brazil, particularly when the diagnostic condition is considered. For both, health professionals and patients, specific psychological factors take place. It is meaningful to know the perceptions involved, so a qualitative study has been conducted, in order to describe it, and the preliminary results are presented. A class of nineteen students of physiotherapy has been interviewed after watching the movie "Nell"; their perceptions and attributions to the meaning of the normality were recorded, as well as the ethical issues observed on the interactions between professionals and patient shown in that movie.

The role of cognitive appraisels in elderly population with chronic pain

Beja da Costa, Ana Santiago do Cacém, Portugal Ros, Antónia Psicologia, Universidade do Algarve, Faro, Portugal Martins, Ana Psicologia, Universidade do Algarve, Faro, Portugal

The aim of this study is to understand the relationship between one's experience of pain, cognitive appraisals, some emotional variables and coping strategies. The participants (36 elderly subjects suffering from chronic pain) were asked to answer to the MPQ (Melzack, 1975), the HADS (Zigmond & Snaith, 1983), CAD (Soriano &

Monsalve, 2002) and to 20 cognitive appraisals. We found significant relationships between the cognitive appraisals and the pain experience, coping strategies and emotional variables in study. These results are discussed based on the theoretical models of Lazarus and Folkman (1984) and Sharp (2000). Key words: pain, cognitive valorisations, copin, emotional variables.

Public politics of management and social representations about its managerial instruments

Bellico da Costa, Anna Edith Mestrado em Educação, FAE / UEMG, Belo Horizonte, Brazil Cabral de Vasconcelos Neto, Milton Microbiologia, FUNED/, Belo Horizonte, Brazil

It was investigated social representation (SR) of the Sanitary surveillance's servers about: Agreement of Results (AR) and individual performance evaluation(IPE) while managerial instrument in the public administration and implications of its in the public politics. Likert's questionnaire was used on perceptions, beliefs and values associates AR and IPE with instructions for the research. The speech pro AR and its importance was better understood than IPE for to servers and integrated their SR. There was a conflicting SR of the servers on the effectiveness of the managerial instruments propagated by the official speech making the management difficult.

Emotional wisdom: Its effects on employees' emotion regulation and relationships at work

Belschak, Frank HRM-OB, Amsterdam Business School, Amsterdam, Netherlands Verbeke, Willem Marketing, Erasmus University Rotterdam, Rotterdam, Netherlands Bagozzi, Richard Marketing, University of Michigan, Ann Arbor, USA

Emotional wisdom is defined as a set of seven dimensions concerning how to regulate emotions within specific domains in such a way that the individual's and the collective's well-being are tied together. Using operationalizations of emotional wisdom for employees working in a sales environment in two studies covering an intra-organizational (among colleagues) setting and an inter-organizational (customer-salesperson) setting, we discover that salespeople who score high on emotional wisdom cope better with emotionally challenging situations and achieve better social relationships than those who score low on emotional wisdom. The results hold even when controlling for the effects of emotional intelligence.

Beyond the Barbie-Matrix: School based primary prevention of eating disorders

Berger, Uwe Inst. für Psychosoz. Medizin, Universitätsklinik Jena, Jena, Germany Bormann, Bianca University Hospital Jena, Institute of Psychosocial Med, Jena, Germany Brix, Christina University Hospital Jena, Institute of Psychosocial Med, Jena, Germany Sowa, Melanie University Hospital Jena, Institute of Psychosocial Med, Jena, Germany

Objective: More than 25% of the 12 year old girls in Thuringia (Germany) show problematic eating behaviour. This was the starting position of a newly developed program for the prevention of anorexia nervosa in girls ("PriMa"). Method: We describe the program evaluation (controlled study using a pre-post-design including 1.006 girls), and development of follow-up programs, including an intervention for boys. Results: Using standardized measures, the girls in the intervention group reported significant improvements in body self esteem, figure dissatisfaction, knowledge and eating attitudes. Conclusions: Based upon the PriMa evaluation, we established a comprehensive health promotion program at 60 Thuringian schools.

Overcoming consequences of family violence in Latvian women: Attachment perspective.

Bite, Ieva Dept. of Psychology, University of Latvia, Riga, Latvia

The aim of this study is to examine connections between changes in trauma symptoms, coping strategies, social adaptation, and adult attachment after psychotherapy for women survivors of childhood abuse and domestic violence. 80 women who participated in 12 sessions' trauma focused treatment groups or 20-25 individual therapy sessions completed several self report measures. Adult attachment interviews were analyzed for 10 women. Respondents who participated in treatment indicated significant changes in trauma symptoms and social adaptation. No changes in coping strategies were found. There are positive changes in the attachment security. Changes are more significant after group therapy than after individual treatment

Causal, preparation, and prediction judgments are not based on the same information

Blanco, Fernando Bilbao, Spain Matute, Helena Psychology, University of Deusto, Bilbao, Spain Vadillo, Miguel Ángel Psychology, University of Deusto, Bilbao, Spain

Most of human contingency learning literature relies on the participants' judgments of contingency between a cue and an outcome. However, variations in the specific wording of the test question produce different patterns of contingency judgments. This is due to a flexible use of the information when participants answer one type of question or another. In two experiments with college students and Internet users, we manipulated the relationship between a cue and an outcome in order to asses its effect on causal, preparation, and prediction judgments. We conclude that sensitivity to covariational manipulations is different for each type of judgment.

The daily dynamics of personal initiative at work

Bledow, Ronald Arbeits- und Org.-Psychologie, Universität Gießen, Gießen, Germany Schaupp, Kerstin Work and Organizational Psych, University of Giessen, Gießen, Germany

Whereas the nomological network of antecedents and consequences of personal initiative has received a great deal of attention, the daily micro processes that promote or inhibit personal initiative have only rarely been studied. To close this gap we have just completed a diary study with 100 employees over 5 consecutive days with data collected twice a day. We examine how daily events, affect and expectations impact on initiative directed at different goals (short term vs. long term goals, individual vs. team goals). Using HLM we further examine how individual trait differences moderate day-level relationships.

Attractiveness of employers offering possibilities to corporate volunteering

Blohm, Gesche Social Psychology, LMU Munich, München, Germany Traut-Mattausch, Eva Social Psychology, LMU Munich, München, Germany Frey, Dieter

Corporate Volunteering – employees community involvement – is for companies a highly visible action to meet their social responsibility. But are companies who offer their employees possibilities to participate in volunteering more attractive to potential job applicants? To investigate this question we conducted studies with students and managers. Participants were given job announcements of two virtual companies, one of them giving employees opportunities to engage in volunteering projects. Results demonstrated that companies offering volunteering are significantly more attractive, so that participants would rather apply for and recommend them. Moreover, the company offering volunteering was significantly rated more positive on different organizational variables.

Intergroup differences in values and thinking styles in relation to intercultural experience

Bobowik, Magdalena *Psychology Department, Univ. of the Basque Country, Donostia-San Sebastian, Spain* **Zawadzki, Roman** *Psychology Department, Warsaw University, Warsaw, Poland* **Bilbao, Maria Angeles** *Psychology Department, Univ. of the Basque Country, Donostia-San Sebastian, Spain*

The purpose of the study was to investigate the relation between experience of studying abroad, thinking styles and values. 70 students participated in the study, forming two groups of comparison (with or without intercultural experience). Participants were asked to answer Schwartz Personal Values Questionnaire and Sternberg Thinking Styles Inventory. Results showed significant differences in values and tendential differences in thinking styles. Students with intercultural experience preferred creativity-related and flexible styles, valued more self-direction, stimulation and achievment, but less security and tradition in comparison to those without such experience. Significant correlations between values and thinking styles were also found.

Mother And Child Play In Down Syndrome and typically developing dyads

Bornstein, Marc *NIH / NICHD / CFR, Bethesda, USA* **Esposito, Gianluca** *rovereto (TN), Italy* **deFalco, Simona** *DiSCoF - Cognitive Science, University of Trento, rovereto (TN), Italy* **Venuti, Paola** *DiSCoF - Cognitive Science, University of Trento, rovereto (TN), Italy*

Objective: This study aimed to investigate mother-child play in children with Down syndrome (DS) as compared with typically developing (TD) children. Method: 21 children with DS (M developmental age = 20 mo) were videorecorded during solitary and collaborative play with mothers. A group of mental age-matched typically developing (TD) children served as control. Results: During solitary play, DS children showed less exploratory play than TD children, but the two groups did not differ in symbolic play. During collaborative play with mothers, no differences were found between the two groups either in exploratory or symbolic play. Conclusions: Mother-child interaction during play exerts a unique and positive influence on children's play development in both TD and DS group.

Neurotransmitters in acupuncture research: A solid indication for further psychiatric research

Bosch, Margaretha *Support & Psychose, ggnet Groenlo, Groenlo, Netherlands* **Van Den Noort, Maurits** *biological and medical psychol, University of Bergen norway, bergen, Norway*

Objectives Recent results indicate that the neurotransmitters that are involved in acupuncture are the exact same neurotransmitters that are involved in many psychiatric disorders. Methods An extensive literature review was conducted on acupuncture and its related neurotransmitters. Results Acupuncture was found to normalize dopamine-, and increase melatonin levels. Furthermore, acupuncture was found to influence neuropeptide Y, which is involved in eating disorders. Acupuncture can therefore support other therapeutic measures like psychotherapy. It might be used as an add-on treatment. Conclusions Since strong indications for results have come forward, we plead for further research on mental illnesses in combination with acupuncture.

Cerebral activations during a long lasting pain stimulation

Brand, Gerard *Neurosciences Lab., Universite de Franche-Comte, Besancon, France* **Brand, Gérard** *Neurosciences Lab., Universite de Franche-Comte, Besancon, France* **Buron, Gaëlle** *Neurosciences Lab., Universite de Franche-Comte, Besancon, France* **Hacquemand, Romain** *Neurosciences Lab., Universite de Franche-Comte, Besancon, France* **Jacquot, Laurence** *Neurosciences Lab., Universite de Franche-Comte, Besancon, France*

Functional brain imaging research has revealed a large distributed network of brain regions involved in pain. However, the relationship between the temporal aspects of perceived pain and cortical activities is greatly unknown. Especially, the temporal profile of fMRI signals in tonic experimental pain has been poorly understood. Thus, this study was designed to characterize BOLD signal intensity time course during a continuous pain. Results showed strong differences in relation to gender, bilateral activations whether hemispheric contralateral activations to the side of stimulation were maximal and a cycle of BOLD effects with successive higher and lower activations during the stimulation.

Bolivian adolescent risk behaviors and protective and risk factors in relation to ethnic self identification

Camacho, Carmen *Psychology, Resear Institute of Psychology, La Paz, Bolivia* **Uriioste, Rodrigo** *Psychology, Resear Institute of Psychology, La Paz, Bolivia* **Ciairano, Silvia** *Psychology, University of Turin, Turin, Italy* **Setanni, Michele** *Psychology, University of Turin, Turin, Italy* **Sappa, Viviana** *Psychology, University of Turin, Turin, Italy*

The study aimed at investigating the risk behaviour of bolivian adolescents. It is aimed at individuating protective factors and risk, with teenagers from La Paz and El Alto, using a self-report and anonymous questionnaire, controlling ethnicity, gender, and age. 1,719 Bolivians adolescents participated from 10 to 18 yrs. With respect to Self-identification ethnicity, 27% were Mestizo, 24% Aymara, 17% Hispanic-Latino, 9% White, 3% Quechua, 3% Amazon, and 1% African American; 16% did not self identified. The analyses showed strong relationship between ethnic self-identification and both levels of risk behaviour and protective and risk factors.

Biofeedback assited relaxation, hypnosis and music as a control procedure in panic disorder

Campos, Patricia *Mexico, Mexico*

Panic disorder has been widely studied, nevertheless testing the effectiveness of psychological interventions have relevance in clinical settings. The main objective of the present study was to evaluate the impact of brief interventions in patients with panic disorder who attended the National Institute of Psychiatry in Mexico City.18 men and 12 women aged 20-55 years were evaluated before and after different procedures. Results shows important clinical implications for hypnosis and biofeedback *National Institute of Psychyatry México City **Milton Erickson Institute of Mexico City ***National University Mexico City

Evaluation of online therapy as a tool for the development of clinical skills in a university community site

Cardenas Lopez, Georgina *Dept. of Psychology, UNAM, Mexico City, Mexico* **Flores Plata, Lorena** *Psychology, UNAM, Mexico city, Mexico* **De la Rosa, Anabel** *Psychology, UNAM, Mexico city, Mexico* **Duran, Ximena** *Psychology, UNAM, Mexico city, Mexico*

Recently, computer-based treatment systems have been published with successful results. These new modalities are increasingly applied for depression and anxiety disorders. These systems have not only reduced time and financial costs of evaluation and analysis, but have also facilitated an alternative for helping psychologists to learn new competencies for practice in telehealth field. This paper will present results of the implementation and evaluation of a teaching program, aimed at 17 Psychology students, that provides psychological services through Internet. Additionally, it will focus on clinical outcomes and the impact among participants of this innovative therapeutic modality.

Influence of pregnancy related worries on childbirth

Carmona Monge, Francisco Javier *Ciencias de la Salud II, Universidad Rey Juan Carlos, Alcorcón (Madrid), Spain* **Marin Morales, Dolores** *Servicio de Obstetricia, Hospital de Fuenlabrada, Fuenlabrada (Madrid), Spain* **Peñacoba Puente, Cecilia** *Psicología, Universidad Rey Juan Carlos, Alcorcón (Madrid), Spain* **Carretero Abellán, Isabel** *Psicología, Universidad Rey Juan Carlos, Alcorcón (Madrid), Spain* **Moreno Moure, Amparo** *Servicio de Obstetricia, Hospital de Fuenlabrada, Fuenlabrada (Madrid), Spain*

Objectives The purpose of this study is to analyze the relationship between worries related to pregnancy and mode of delivery. Methodology Sample: 39 pregnant women from Fuenlabrada Hospital. Measurement instruments: Cambridge Worries Scale, SCL90-R and NEO-FFI. All questionnaires were cumplimented during the first trimester of pregnancy. Results There were 18 eutocic deliveries and 21 non eutocic deliveries. A general linear model analysis was conducted controlling SCL-90 score and NEOFFI scores. Significantly higher scores in CWS were found in non eutocic deliveries $(F(1,35)=4,73, p=0,037)$. Conclusions The diminution of worries could help improving labour outcomes and in the prevention of non eutocic deliveries.

Sleep deprivation and suppression of a prepotent response

Cavallero, Corrado *Dept. of Psychology, University of Trieste, Trieste, Italy* **Jugovac, Davide** *Psychology, University of Trieste, Trieste, Italy*

Goal: To evaluate the impact of sleep deprivation on dominant response inhibition Method: 30 participants. Two conditions: Baseline (testing after a regular night of sleep at home); Deprivation (testing after one night of total sleep deprivation). Results: After sleep deprivation, Stop Signal RT (estimate of the inhibition process efficiency) was significantly worse (p<.05) than in Base-line. Conclusions: Results suggest a considerable impairment of the efficiency of the inhibition process following sleep loss. This is in agreement with the hypothesis of an impairment of the frontal lobe functions when normal architecture of sleep is disrupted.

White middle-class boys as "children-at-risk": Biographical literacy of teachers in primary schools

Chamakalayil, Lalitha *Inst. für Pädagogik, Universität Oldenburg, Oldenburg, Germany*

Who are "pupils at risk"? The term, ambiguously used in Germany, lacks a unified definition. Qualitative case reconstruction interviews, recounting biographies of challenging 2nd grade pupils, were conducted with teachers to assess their perception of students. Surprisingly, teachers chose to talk about white, middle class boys, similar to their own socioeconomic and ethnic background. Parents were described as displaying attitudes supporting or mirroring their children's difficult behaviour: competitiveness, masculine, sexualised behaviour and defiance of rules seems to be interpreted by them as an advantage in a globalized, competitive marketplace. Teachers did not take resilience-oriented development approaches for boys into consideration and were unaware of options for professional support; instead, doing class and doing gender processes were perpetuated.

Innovation implementation in the public sector: An integration of institutional and collective dynamics

Chang, Jae-Yoon Dept. of Psychology, Sungshin Women's University, Seoul, Republic of Korea Choi, Jin-Nam Business Adminisration, Seou National University, Seoul, Republic of Korea

This study integrates institutional factors and employee-based collective processes as predictors of the implementation and innovation effectiveness. We propose that institutional factors shape employees' collective implementation efficacy and innovation acceptance, and that these employee-based collective processes mediate the effects of institutional factors on implementation outcomes. We tested this framework in the context of 47 agencies of the Korean Government. Three-wave longitudinal data were collected from 60 external experts and 1,732 government employees. The results reveal the importance of management support for collective implementation efficacy, which affected employees' collective acceptance of the innovation, and these collective employee dynamics mediated the effects of institutional enablers on successful implementation as well as the amount of long-term benefit.

Advance organizers on learning and retention of facts and concepts

Chang, Moon K. Mathews AL, USA

OBJECTIVES. This study examined the effect of advance organizers (AOs) on acquisition and retention of facts and concepts presented in a science film and the interaction of AOs and ability levels. METHODS. Sixteen undergraduate students were randomly assigned to four groups. A 2x2 factorial design was utilized and ANOVA (equal n) was performed separately on the immediate-and delayed-retention test data. RESULTS. The results indicated that AOs increased learning and retention of facts and concepts. However, no interaction between AOs and the ability levels was found. CONCLUSIONS. Ability was non-significant but AOs were significant on performance.

Spiritual, value-based leadership and job insecurity: The role of employees' work affects

Chen, Chin-Yi Business Administration, National Yunlin University, Toulin City, Taiwan

ABSTRACT "Spiritual leadership"—a concept integrating leader values, attitudes, and behaviors, has been recently proposed and measured by Fry et al. (2005). This study examines whether spiritual leadership buffers the negative side of organizational behavior, e.g., job insecurity, and how affects play a role in the process. Questionnaire responses were collected from a sample of 458 Chinese employees from a variety of work settings in Taiwan. Results showed that spiritual leadership was mediated by positive affects to influence the "quantitative" type of job insecurity, and by negative affect to influence the "qualitative" job insecurity. Cultural issues and practical implications were discussed. KEY WORD: spiritual leadership, value-based leadership, job insecurity, work affect, Chinese employees

The development of emotional intelligence in high school students in Taiwan

Chen, Lee-Chou Eduation and Counseling, NTNU, Taipei, Taiwan

The purposes of this study are to conduct the indexes of emotional intelligence in high school students, and to explore the differences of EI among different background subjects. Using EI Scale to survey 2029 high school students, All results are as follow: (1) EI Scale is a valid and stabled battery used to test emotional cognition, emotional expression, positive inspiration, emotional regulation, and emotional reflection in high school students. (2) There are significant differences of EI among gender, birth order and age. This standard test will be used to study the trend of psychological and behavioral performance in high school students.

An analysis of the association between emotional expressivity and emotional labor

Cheung, Francis Department of Psychology, CUHK, Hong Kong, China, People's Republic of : Hong Kong SAR

Objective: To examine the associations between different emotional expressivity dimensions (i.e. positive expressivity, negative expressivity, impulse strength) and emotional labor strategies (i.e. surface acting, deep acting, expression of naturally felt emotions). Method: A total of 476 Chinese human service employees were recruited (Male = 123, Female = 353) in this questionnaire survey. Results: Hierarchical regression analyses showed that even when work characteristics were controlled, negative expressivity was still a significant predictor of surface acting and deep acting while positive expressivity was a significant predictor of expression of naturally felt emotions. Conclusion: Future research should adopt the multi-dimensional approach to delineate the effect of emotional expressivity on emotional labor.

Not distraction but intentional suppression can lead to long-term forgetting

Chie, Hotta Dept. of Psychology, University of Nagoya, Nagoya, Japan Kawaguchi, Jun psychology, university, nagoya, Japan

Recent research indicates that intentionally suppressing retrieval of an unwanted memory impairs its later recall. In the current study, we examined whether a similar type of memory impairment can be observed when people simply divert attention away from an unwanted memory. This issue was investigated by using a modified Think/No-Think task, designed to prevent remembering the unwanted memories, instead of intentionally suppressing themselves. Although both intentional suppression and distraction impaired memory for to-be-avoided traces on an immediate test, only distraction caused the deficits in later recall. These findings suggest that intentionally suppressing retrieval, rather than distracting attention is crucial for the long-term forgetting regulation of unwanted memories

Episodic memory inhibition and spreading activation: Evidence of episodic memory inhibition using the Think/No-Think task

Chie, Hotta Dept. of Psychology, University of Nagoya, Nagoya, Japan Hidetsugu, Tajika psychology, university, nagoya, Japan Nwumann, Ewald psychology, university, nagoya, New Zealand

We examined whether to suppress an event intentionally could also impair memory for related events to the avoided one. After study unrelated pairs, participants were asked to avoid repeatedly thinking of the target words to a cue or recall it. Then, they were asked to recognize as accurately and quickly as possible. The test materials included the target words and two kinds of nonstudied words. The result showed that spreading activation was found to the nonstudied words relating semantically and orthographically to the target words. This finding suggests episodic inhibition can be widespread to the related representation to avoided memories.

Humour in psychotherapy: A theoretical overview

Chiotis, Georgios Dept. of Psychology, City University, London, United Kingdom

In the present paper, the intricate interrelationship between the use of humour and psychotherapy is discussed, along with the possible outcomes of this application. This is achieved by a brief literature review and examination of the concept of humour (types, definitions, theories), and how major figures in philosophy and psychology are incorporating it in their theories of personality. Afterwards, a brief image of the use of humour in therapy is presented, while discussing how it is applied in different schools of psychotherapy. Finally, the positive and negative aspects of the application of humour in psychotherapy are presented and discussed.

Feelings of young people in acute postsuicide towards significant others

Chistopolskaya, Ksenia Moscow, Russia

Aim of the study was description of feelings of young people in acute postsuicide towards their nearest relatives and aquaintances. Main hypothetic feelings were alienation and despair. 20 young people (15-25 years) after recent unsuccessful suicidal attempt were given modified PRISM (Buchi & Sensky, 1998) and repertory grid technique (Kelly, 1955). Descriptive, correlation and factor analyses were used for interpretation. Subjects reported to experience negative feelings in all their contacts. Alienation was seen through placing subjects against others or with least significant for them people. The results are useful for therapy of young people in acute postsuicide.

Validation of the diagnostic test for dependent and avoidant personality disorder

Choi, Jin-Hoon Dept. of Psychology, Chungbuk National University, Chongju, Republic of Korea

The purpose of this study is to test reliability and validity of dependent personality disorder(DPPD) scale and the avoidant personality disorder(AVPD) scale in Diagnostic test for Personality Disorder (Seo & Hwang, 2006). Two PD scales, Interpersonal Dependency Inventory, Schema Questionnaire, Social Avoidance and Distress Scale, Dysfunctional Beliefs Test, Fear of Negative Evaluation Scale, and Inventory of Interpersonal Problems were administered to 566 college students and adults. Two PD scales were retested to sixty participants. Test-retest reliabilities of two PD scales were r=.82, and .84 and Chronbach Alpha .74, and .73. Two scales were positively correlated with criterion related dependency and avoidance.

The curriculum development for remediating basic skills of learning among primary school children with learning disabilities

Chookhampaeng, Chowwalit Curriculum and Instruction, Mahasarakham University, Maha-Sarakham, Thailand

The purpose to develop a remedial curriculum for improving the basic skill of learning. Divided into four steps : Step one : The studying fundamental data. As the result, the curriculum for children with learning disability that consist of four steps: input, process, memory, and output. Step two : The developing curriculum. As the result, the curriculum was to remedial the perceptional skill, language skill, and cognitive skill. Step three : The implemntation was conducted with the primary school children. The result was the all children's learning skill were higher than before at 0.01 of significant statistical level, but the language learning skill were lower than the criteria. Step four : The curriculum evaluation. The result from the parent seminar was satisfaction.

The effects of organizational policies supportive of gay and lesbian employees on job involvement

Church, Robin *Human Resources Management, Ryerson University, Toronto, Canada*

This study examined the effects of organizational policies supportive of gay and lesbian employees (policies) on the job involvement of gay and lesbian employees (involvement). A survey was administered to 551 gay men and lesbians (182 in Canada, 369 in the United States). Structural analysis was used to assess relationships and mediation. There was no direct relationship between policies and involvement but discrimination on the basis of sexual orientation was found to mediate the relationship between policies and involvement. This study underscores the importance of policies in reducing discrimination ensuring a workplace in which gay and lesbians can fully contribute.

Two different extinction processes in the Barnes Maze

Claro La Rotta, Silvana *Psychology, Universidad Nacional, Bogota, Colombia* **Vargas, Viviana** *Psychology, Universidad Nacional, Bogota, Colombia* **Cuestas, Marcela** *Psychology, Universidad Nacional, Bogota, Colombia* **Lamprea, Marisol** *Psychology, Universidad Nacional, Bogota, Colombia* **Troncoso, Julieta** *Psychology, Universidad Nacional, Bogota, Colombia* **Múnera, Alejandro** *Psychology, Universidad Nacional, Bogota, Colombia*

It was compared the extinction process in the Barnes maze after two acquisition protocols. Sixteen subjects acquired a spatial preference and twenty four hours later eight of them received a reinforced trial as test, while the others received two reinforced trials separated for a non-reinforced trail followed for seven extinction trials (for both groups). Statistical analysis showed a treatment x trial interaction, indicating a resistance to the extinction process in the group with the two reinforced trials separated for a non-reinforced one. Differences may be explained in terms of partial reinforcement during the tests.

Treatment outcomes from 41 years of conducting psychotherapy in private practice

Clement, Paul *Private Practice, South Pasadena, USA*

Of 2042 cases seen by a clinical psychologist, 126 came for assessment only, 249 dropped out during intake, and 76 were still in treatment at the time of data analysis. The patients fell into 186 diagnostic categories and ranged in age from 6 months to 88 years at intake. Of 1591 treated patients, 69% were improved at termination. Success rate varied greatly across diagnostic categories. There was a significant negative correlation between age and outcome. The correlation between number of sessions and percentage of cases imrpoved was positive and significant. Treatment effect sizes were large.

Pragmatic Case Studies in Psychotherapy (PCSP): A new on-line journal

Clement, Paul *Private Practice, South Pasadena, USA*

Describes how to prepare manuscripts for PCSP, an on-line journal of systematic case studies in psychotherapy from a wide range of approaches. Usually two experts write comments about a given case study. Then the author of the primary article prepares a reply. The main article, the comments, and the reply appear as a set. PCSP began publication in 2005. Over time it will develop a very large database of case studies. Researchers and clinicians can access these articles on-line at no cost. The journal's editorial board comes from nine countries. The web address is http://pcsp.libraries.rutgers.edu

Localizing psychological usability evaluation methods

Clemmensen, Torkil *Dept. of Informatics, Copenhagen Business School, Fredriksberg, Denmark*

We investigated if, in the think aloud usability test, the moderator's cultural cognitive style (Nisbett, 2003) have to be similar to the user's to get valid results. Localized clipart was used in experiments in Copenhagen, Beijing and Guwahati. 33 university students and professors participated as test users. Anova analysis of problem detection rates and communication events suggested that cross cultural test conditions created a 'tourist' effect that emphazised the non-important problems with the product. More focus is needed on the cultural cognitive style of moderators versus users. The application of the think aloud method benefits from insight from cultural psychology.

Behavioral, electrophysiological and pharmacological Oxytocin action on sensorial perception of pain

Condés Lara, Miguel *Dipt. de Neurofisiologia, Instituto de Neurobiología, Querétaro, Mexico* **Martinez Lorenzana, Guadalupe** *Neurofisiologia, Instituto de Neurobiología, Querétaro, Mexico* **Rojas Piloni, Gerardo** *Neurofisiologia, Instituto de Neurobiología, Querétaro, Mexico* **Rodríguez Jiménez, Javier** *Neurofisiologia, Instituto de Neurobiología, Querétaro, Mexico*

Recently, we described that electrical stimulation of the hypothalamic Paraventricular Nucleus (PV) as well as the intrathecal Oxytocin (OT) administration inhibits nociceptive dorsal horn neuronal responses (Brain Res. 2006, 1881: 126-137) and produced analgesia in neuropathic rats (Pain 2006,122: 182-189). In the spinal cord OT inhibits sensory glutamatergic transmission between afferent fibers and dorsal horn neurons. Our results suggest that OT action indirectly inhibits sensory transmission in dorsal horns neurons by spinal inhibitory GABA-a interneurons. This work reveals the importance of neuronal endogenous mechanisms involved in analgesia as well as their importance related with sensorial perception.

Automatic processing of intergroup information as a mechanism of subjective culture

Contreras Ibáñez, Carlos C. *Dept. of Social Psychology, UAM, Mexico City, Mexico* **Cruz, Christian E.** *Sociology, Social psychology, UAM, Mexico City, Mexico*

Several phenomena associated with subjective culture are expressed as cognitive contents externally elaborated and acquired without mental effort, supervision, awareness and mindfulness, just features defining automaticity or unconscious processing. This work objective is to correlate scores of cultural orientation with heuristic use frequency, spontaneous attribution habits, self-monitoring and implicit stereotyping, under the hypothesis that interdependent self-construal use more often this processing way, due to social norm fulfillment habit. This was tested with 152 Mexico City university students who responded appropriate instruments and participated in implicit association test studies. Correlations generally follow the hypothesized pattern, which are interpreted within culture-cognition framework.

The development and initial validation of a revised attributional style questionnaire

Creed, Peter *School of Psychology, Griffith University, Gold Coast, Australia* **Travers, Katrina** *Applied Psychology, Griffith University, Gold Coast, Australia* **Morrissey, Shirley** *Applied Psychology, Griffith University, Gold Coast, Australia*

Despite its wide use, the internality subscale of the Attributional Style Questionnaire (ASQ) rarely correlates with depression and ill-health, and its factor structure does not reflect the three dimen-

sions of explanatory style. To address these shortcomings, we rewrote items, provided individual item-stems, and administered the revised ASQ to 320 adults. EFA identified six factors, representing positive and negative aspects of the three dimensions of explanatory style. We then administered the scale to 409 adults. CFA confirmed a good fit, indicating support for an improved measure. Future studies need to examine construct validity and determine scale's suitability to measure explanatory style.

Work values and small business behaviour

Cubico, Serena *Psicologia e Antropologia, Università di Verona, Verona, Italy*

Small businesses (SMEs) are very dependent on little groups of decision-makers. This research intends to highlight the link between the decision-maker's work values and organizational behaviour. The instruments used are the Italian version of the Questionnaire Work Importance Study/Work Values Scale and an in-depth interview; subjects are 47 SME owners. We found that specific orientation work values emerged which are significantly correlated to specific organizational choices: Materialistic-Orientation with (negative) spin-off behaviour in employees, Self-Orientation with presence of company's web page, Other-Orientation with presence of company's web page and membership in Entrepreneurial Associations, Independence-Orientation with hiring of foreigners (negative).

Some relevant aspects in negotiation efficacy and rationality

Cunha, Pedro *Faculty of Human and Social Sc, University Fernando Pessoa, Porto, Portugal* **Pereira, Pedro** *Faculty of Human and Social Sc, University Fernando Pessoa, Porto, Portugal*

Our research studies the relation between negotiation efficacy and rationality. We have followed Mastenbroeks integrative model (1987, 1989) for negotiation efficacy and the Bazerman and Neales perspective (1993) about rational negotiation. These variables are measured by the CEN II (Negotiation Efficacy Questionnaire) with a sample (N=204) divided in four subgroups according to their different negotiation experiences. We have crossed a set of socialdemographical variables with negotiation efficacy and negotiation rationality. We have confirmed the existence of differences in negotiation efficacy associated to marital status, academic qualifications, age and profession. Concerning negotiation rationality, age, academic qualifications and profession seem to play an important role.

Organizational commitment in Spanish and Italian volunteers: A comparative study.

Dávila, Celeste *Social Psychology (Sociology), Complutense University of Madr, Madrid, Spain* **Díaz-Morales, Juan Francisco** *Work and Individual Difference, Complutense University of Madr, Madrid, Spain* **Pasquini, Marianna** *Psychology, University of Florence, Florence, Italy* **Giannini, Marco** *Psychology, University of Florence, Florence, Italy*

The attitudes toward the organization have important in the explanation of the continuity of the volunteers in the organizations. We compared Spanish and Italian volunteers using the Organizational Commitment Questionnaire (OCQ) to assess organizational commitment. Confirmatory and multiple-groups confirmatory factor analysis were used to assess factor structure and structural invariance across countries. The results showed that a two-factor model of organizational commitment best characterizes the OCQ structure of both samples. Factorial invariance across countries was demonstrated for both factors "strong involvement" and "strong acceptance". These findings are discussed in relation to previous research on organizational commitment and volunteerism.

Revised behavioral rating scales on infant temperament: A description of the scales

D'Ocon, Ana Department of Psychology, University of Valencia, Valencia, Spain Simó Teufel, Sandra Dept. of Psychology, University of Valencia, Valencia, Spain
This study is focused on the measurement of infant temperament in a structured episode. It was carried out through behavioral rating scales on ten temperament dimensions grouped in: Emotional tone, Interaction, Action and Self-regulation. The purpose of the study is to describe the scales and to analyze how they adjust to the construct they are supposed to measure. Subjects in the study were 40 children. They were assessed at 6 and 12 months. Results are a preliminary analysis of these infant temperament dimensions, and include reliability and validity aspects of this observational instrument.

Introduction to Japanese Psychological Rehabilitation Therapy and its application on aged people

Dadkhah, Asghar Dept. of Clinical Psychology, University of Welfare & Rehab., Tehran, Islamic Republic of Iran
Psychological treatment in rehabilitation often deals not only with the stresses imposed by disability and altered life circumstances but also with issues of aging, hospitalization and medical tests and procedures. PTSD may be an aspect of patients' emotional responses as they relive the accidents or traumas, sometimes in the form of flashbacks or nightmares. Naturally in the course of continuing treatment, psycho-rehabilitationists may deal with range of evolving and changing responses to the whole spectrum of effects of disability and its life-altering impact. In this report we try to introduce Japanese Psychological Rehabilitation Therapy and its Application on aged people

Get better social skills: Computerized theory of mind training for children with intellectual disability

Danielsson, Henrik SIDR - IBL, Linköping University, Linköping, Sweden Sundqvist, Anett IBL, SIDR & Linköping Universit, Linköping, Sweden Rudner, Mary IBL, SIDR & Linköping Universit, Linköping, Sweden Hofer, Nina IBL, SIDR & Linköping Universit, Linköping, Sweden Rönnberg, Jerker IBL, SIDR & Linköping Universit, Linköping, Sweden
The effect of a computerized theory of mind training program was investigated in children with intellectual disability with a mean age of 12 years. The training time was 15 minutes every school day for 5 weeks and took place in the participant's school. Compared to an age matched control group with intellectual disability, who performed computerized training not related to theory of mind, there were training effects for some theory of mind measures, but not for all. The results are promising and form a basis for further research.

Cross-cultural differences in attention, mood, and behavior problems: Japanese and U.S. post-secondary students

Davis, J. Mark School of Liberal Arts, Georgia Gwinnett College, Lawrenceville, USA Takahashi, Tomone Education, Shinshu University, Nagano, Japan Shinoda, Haruo Psychology, Rissho University, Tokyo, Japan
This presentation reflects initial results of a larger collaboration between researchers in Japan and the U.S. comparing self-report of attention, mood, and behavior problems in post-secondary students. Counter to initial hypotheses, results (t-tests) indicated that Japanese students reported more past (elementary school) and recent attention problems on a DSM-IV-TR-based ADHD checklist. Differences in past problems were primarily due to greater report of inattention than hyperactivity or impulsiveness for the Japanese students. Com-

parisons (correlations) between ADHD checklist scores and mood and behavior problems (Achenbach scales) will also be reported. Future studies will examine differences in the factor structure of ADHD symptoms.

Latin American foreign students in Rio Grande do Sul: Adaptation strategies in acculturation process

de Alencar Rodrigues, Roberta Dept. de Psicología, UAB, Barcelona, Spain Neves Strey, Marlene Psicologia, PUCRS, Porto Alegre, Brazil
This paper presents the migration process of Latin American foreign students in Rio Grande do Sul. We have tried, through interviews with six Latin American foreign students, to identify the easiness and the hardships found by that group in the acculturation process and their adaptation strategies. We have also sought to verify if men and women of this study experienced migration in different ways. The findings points out that the greatest difficulties are related to housing, food, climate and language, while the easiness refers to interpersonal communication and attitudes such as persistence. Due to the globalization scenario, we propose that universities be prepared to received such a group, facilitating their access to housing and language courses.

The rapid effects of psychoanalysis in the children' clinic

de Barros, Rita Maria Manso Psicologia Clinica, UERJ / PGPSA, Rio de Janeiro, Brazil
Objectives: Starting from in inquiry on the situations of clinic experience in the current times, it points to analyze the rapid effects of psychoanalysis nowadays. The psychoanalysis can help children and his parents Method: The method employed was the analyses of various clinical reports on a university clinic of psychology; consider the suffering and the results in a short time. Results: Many children and his parents were found that the pain is reverted in pleasure and the suffering changes in satisfaction on the life experiences. Conclusions: The psychoanalysis is one of the best treatments to help children and his parents.

A study on the consequences of within-organization staff homogeneity on an organization's creativity and innovativeness

de Cooman, Rein Dept. of I/O Psychology, Vrije Universiteit Brussel, Brussel, Belgium de Gieter, Sara Work & Organizational psyc, Vrije Universiteit Brussel, Brussel, Belgium Pepermans, Roland Dept. of I/O Psychology, Vrije Universiteit Brussel, Brussel, Belgium Jegers, Marc Work & Organizational psyc, Vrije Universiteit Brussel, Brussel, Belgium
Within I&O psychology, high person-organization fit resulting from value congruence is mostly mentioned for its positive consequences on employee attitudes. However at the organizational level, theoreticians often warn for negative outcomes. As put in the ASA theory, at the long term organizations are occupied by a set of like-minded employees. It is predicted that this homogeneity has negative effects on innovativeness and creativity. To test this hypothesis, the present study questions a group of teachers as well as their principals. Using mixed-method technique, respondents are asked to evaluate their person-organization fit, as well as the school's creativity and innovativeness.

Questing for social identity after merger organization

Deng, Zhiwen School of Art & Law, Changsha Uni.of Science&Techn., Changsha, People's Republic of China
Questing for social identity after merger organization Base on Tajfel' SIT and a social identity model of postmerger identification (Daan Van Knippenberg, et al), a social identity model of Chinese

merger-university was constructed by us. According to the model, we have workout a social identity measuring scale for merger-university. There are four components in the "scale", namely organizational identity strength, organizational emotion, interpersonal and person-organization relationship, leadership. After measuring 437 teachers who come from 14 postmerger colleges and interviewing with 32 teachers, four findings are discovered. It is the most ravishing that interpersonal relationship is the most effective factor for individual's identification and behavior in postmerger organization.

Miniature saccades mimic as neural oscillations: Revisiting the induced gamma band response

Deouell, Leon Dept. of Psychology, Hebrew University, Jerusalem, Israel Greenberg-Yuval, Shlomit Psychology, The Hebrew U. of Jerusalem, Jerusalem, Israel Tomer, Orr Psychology, The Hebrew U. of Jerusalem, Jerusalem, Israel Keren, Alon Psychology, The Hebrew U. of Jerusalem, Jerusalem, Israel Nelken, Israel Neurobiology, The Hebrew U. of Jerusalem, Jerusalem, Israel
Objectives: To test the view that human induced gamma band EEG response (iGBR) reflects neural oscillations related to object representation. Methods: We recorded iGBRs induced by visual stimuli, together with video eye-tracking and single-trial analysis; Results: We show that individual iGBRs are time-locked to the onset of miniature saccades (MS) and reflect spike potentials likely of ocular muscles origin. The characteristic average 200-300 ms iGBR latency is related to a post-stimulus increase in MS probability, which depends on stimulus features. Conclusions: The typical 200-300 ms broadband iGBR is not related to neural oscillations but to an increase in MS rate.

The organisation of number facts in memory

Depestel, Isabel Experimental Psychology, KULeuven Campus Kortrijk, Kortrijk, Belgium Verguts, Tom Experimental Psychology, Ghent University, Gent, Belgium
A recent connectionist model of retrieval in single digit multiplication that tries to explain the organisation of number facts in memory, was examined. The model states that candidate answers to an arithmetic problem cooperate or compete, which causes the well-known five, tie and size number effects. Additionally, it predicts a new number effect which would increase with aging, while the other effects would decrease. The presence and development of all effects were tested with children and adults of various ages. The predictions were confirmed, which offers new insights for current arithmetic models and allows a better understanding of human memory.

Prosociality does not moderate the relations between severe levels of psychopathic traits in children and poor parent-child relationships

Diamantopoulou, Sofia Dept. of Psychology, Uppsala University, Uppsala, Sweden Rydell, Ann-Margret Department of Psychology, Uppsala University, Uppsala, Sweden
We examined the unique and shared relations between prosociality, psychopathic traits, i.e., symptoms of Oppositional/Defiant/Disorder (ODD) and callousness/unemotionality (CU), and parent-child relationships (PCR). Parents rated ODD, CU, prosociality, parent-child conflicts (PCC), and parental involvement (PI) for 1199 ten-year-old children. Effects were examined by hierarchical regression analyses. With control for the other variables, prosociality was negatively related to poor PCR; ODD were uniquely, positively related to PCC; both ODD and CU were negatively related to PI. Moderating effects of prosociality indicated that it may not act as a protective factor against poor PCR among children with severe levels of psychopathic traits.

Cardiovascular risk factors, MRI-lesion patterns and the development of Mild Cognitive Impairment

Dlugaj, Martha Neurologie, Universitätsklinikum Essen, Essen, Germany Mönninghoff, C. Dragano, N. Wilhelm, Hans Neurologie, Universitätsklinikum Essen, Essen, Germany Möbus, S. Todica, Olga Neurologie, Universitätsklinikum Essen, Essen, Germany Siegrist, J. Jöckel, K. H. Erbel, R. Weimar, Christian Neurologie, Universitätsklinikum Essen, Essen, Germany

Objective: The objective of this study was to examine the influence of 12 medical and psychosocial cardiovascular risk factors on the development of a Mild Cognitive Impairment (MCI) and the relationship between MCI and MRI-lesion patterns within the context of the Heinz Nixdorf RECALL (HNR)-Study. Methods: Participants were 74 men and women from the HNR-Study cohort, who showed a reduced performance in a dementia screening. MCI was diagnosed by cognitive tests. Results: First analyses indicate an influence of some cardiovascular risk factors on the development of MCI. Conclusions: Controlling cardiovascular risk factors can reduce the risk of developing MCI.

The cub of psychotherapy

Dorofte, Tatiana Dept. of Education, Technical University of Iasi, Iasi, Romania

Objectives: The presentation of a methodological-analytic model for the systematization of the existing psychotherapies and the forecast of future models, that was published in 1986. The methodology, ressembling to that of Guilford model of the intellect, leaded us to the creation of a three-dimensional model whose referential axes allowed us to obtain 30 categorised cells and the delimitation of an evolutionary corssbar from 1.1.1. cell to 3.2.5. cell. Results: With this instrument we classified a great number of the 200 knowned psychoterapies up to nowadays and we forecasted the emergence of the integrative orientation in psychotherapy.

Nap now, profit later: Memory consolidation in gifted adolescents with sleep debt

Dresler, Martin Inst. für Psychiatrie, Max-Planck-Institut, München, Germany Genzel, Lisa Psychiatrie, Max-Planck-Institut, München, Germany Steiger, Axel Psychiatrie, Max-Planck-Institut, München, Germany

Chronic sleep deprivation has been repeatedly shown to impair neural functioning. We tested the effects of daytime naps on verbal learning in 64 gifted adolescents who had experienced moderate to severe sleep loss for 10 days. The subjects were tested on two consecutive days with a story-learning and a word-learning task. The stories and words had to be recalled 5 hours after learning with or without a 45 minutes nap, and in a retest session one week later. The daytime naps had a beneficial effect on verbal learning which became even more pronounced after one week.

Standardization of novel questionnaire for autobiographical memory (AM) and evaluation of emotional stimuli

Drobetz, Reinhard Clinical Psychology, Faculty of Psychology, Vienna, Austria Derntl, Birgit Clinical Psychology, Faculty of Psychology, Vienna, Austria Kryspin-Exner, Ilse Clinical Psychology, Faculty of Psychology, Vienna, Austria

Aim of study 1 was the preclinical standardization of an AM-questionnaire, which consists of 22 visual stimuli. A population of 180 students and non-students participated. Additionally, we focused on the AM-specificity. Prior to the AM-investigation, 100 other healthy subjects rated each AM-picture for 6 possible triggered primary emotions (study 2). It is intended to use the material in fMRI-studies. Significant effects of gender and education on the ratings of both studies will be presented. Data

analysis of the investigation of AM-specificity indicates that gender and education are the significant factors of AM-retrieval. Therefore, further AM-studies should consider both variables.

Development of inspection time: The role of accelerated education for gifted children

Duan, Xiaoju Institute of psychology, Beijing, People's Republic of China Shi, Jiannong developmental and educational, Institute of psychology, Beijing, People's Republic of China Zhou, Dan research, Beisen measurement company, Beijing, People's Republic of China

185 gifted children aged from 9 to 13 years old (94 in accelerated education and 91 in normal education) were tested individually on a typical visual inspection time task. Children in accelerated education outperformed their age peers slightly in normal education by shorter IT. But the main effect of education was not significant, $F(1,179)=2.27$, $P?.05$. The result suggests that experience doesn't play an important role in the development of processing speed and is consistent with the prediction of global trend hypothesis. The implications of this for wider theoretical interpretations of the development of processing speed are discussed.

Group norms and group identification: The application of social identity constructs to childhood bullying

Duffy, Amanda Coombabah, Australia

This study explored whether group norms and group identification were relevant to the explanation of childhood bullying. Participants (N = 169), aged 5 to 12 years, were asked to pretend that they had been placed in a team for a drawing competition. The norms of the team were then manipulated (bullying versus helping) and the child's identification with the team also assessed. An analysis of variance revealed that group norms and identification interacted to influence children's bullying intentions. This finding has important implications for our understanding of bullying, as well as for the development of anti-bullying interventions.

Relationship between moral development and altruism and coping style in personality factors of the students in Tehran

Ebrahimy, Azam Psychology, Shahid Beheshti University, Tehran, Islamic Republic of Iran

This study investigates the relationship between moral development and altruism and coping style in personality factors. 360 subjects were selected through multi- stag cluster sampling. D.M.T, Big(5) and (C.S.Q) as well as the statistical methods of Anova, HSD and regression used. results indicated that the emotional coping has a reverse relationship with neuroticism and altruistim in speech freedom situation:(RDT), but it have a direct relationship with gender and moral development at 4 stage l. Avoidant –detached style has a direct relationship with the moral development at 4 stage. The rational style has a direct relationship with openness, agreeableness, conscientious, neuroticism and altruistic tendencies of speech freedom situation :(RDT) but it reverse with gender.

Exhaustion in the evening as a function of workday and social stressors: A multilevel analysis

Elfering, Achim Department of Psychology, University of Bern, Bern, Switzerland Grebner, Simone Department of Psychology, University of Michigan, Bern, USA Semmer, Norbert Karl Department of Psychology, University of Bern, Bern, Switzerland

Objectives: This field study related social stressors at work to psychological recovery from work. Methods: During three working weeks 34 male employees reported their recovery status after work and in the evening at 9 p.m. Results: In multilevel analysis of 482 evening measurements sleep quality,

recovery status after work, weekdays, and social stressors were related to recovery status. An interaction between social stressors at work and weekdays indicated a more progressive decline in those reporting a high level of social stressors at work. Conclusions: Social stressors at work accelerate the loss of resources across consecutive work days.

Removal of front vs back office work in call centre: An intervention study

Elfering, Achim Department of Psychology, University of Bern, Bern, Switzerland Bestetti, Marco Department of Psychology, University of Bern, Bern, Switzerland Schade, Volker Centrum für PersonalManagement, CPMO, Bern, Switzerland

Objective: Evaluation of work intervention in call centre. Taks of former front and back office work were unified. Methods: Within a pre- and posttest design including a control group, 265 agents reported data on work characteristics, well-being, and subjective performance. Objective data on performance were also collected. Results: There were positive effects of the intervention on former front office agents in all dependent variables. Former back office agents however, showed mixed results, including a decline in quality of work and well-being. Conclusions: Interventions in Call Centre should carefully consider differential effects depending on former work design.

Understanding workers' perception of bullying in the workplace: A cross-cultural study

Escartin, Jordi Social Psychology, Barcelona University, Barcelona, Spain Arrieta Salas, Carlos Psychology, Costa Rica University, San Jose Costa Rica, Costa Rica Rodriguez-Carballeira, Alvaro Social Psychology, Barcelona University, Barcelona, Spain

The main objective is to analyze the workers perception about bullying in the workplace, comparing 4 different samples (two from Central-America and two from Southern Europe). The data was obtained from employees who attended mobbing prevention courses and from employees who didn't. A single open question was used: "What do you understand when you think about bullying at work? Significant differences (p <, 001) were found for the type and direction of abuse when comparing the different sub samples. Friedman chi-square revealed differences (p<, 001) between the categories of mobbing, however, Kruskall-Wallis showed non-significant differences between sub samples. Results and limitations are discussed

Psychophysiological reactions to fear and disgust pictures

Esteves, Francisco Dept. of Psychology, ISCTE, Lisbon, Portugal Ruiz Padial, Elisabeth Psychology, Universidad de Jaén, Jaén, Spain Reyes del Paso, Gustavo Psychology, Universidad de Jaén, Jaén, Spain Mata, José Luis Psychology, Universidad de Granada, Jaén, Spain Ferreira, Ana Cláudia Psychology, ISCTE, Lisbon, Portugal

The aim of the present study was to compare psychophysiological responses to pictures associated with fear and disgust. Participants were exposed to a series of 40 emotional pictures, previously classified as fearful, disgust, pleasant or neutral. Skin conductance, heart rate, startle response, and levator labii superioris EMG-activity were recorded continuously. Each picture was also evaluated in two dimensions – affective valence and arousal. The results showed a clear differentiation between pleasant, unpleasant and neutral images on all measures, however, only the levator EMG-activity, with larger responses to disgust pictures, could differentiate fear from disgust.

Alphabet book reading by senior kindergarteners: Does their letter knowledge dictate their eye movements?

Evans, Mary Ann Psychology, University of Guelph, Guelph, Canada Saint-Aubin, Jean Psychology, Université de Moncton, Moncton, New Brunswick, Canada

Twenty children ages 59 to 71 months read an alphabet book while their eye movements were monitored. Results revealed that children spent significantly more time on the illustration than on the letter or the word, which did not differ one from the other. Most importantly, after controlling for vocabulary knowledge, the number of letters known by a child accounted for a significant amount of variance in the latency before fixating the letter, and the time spent fixating the word. Thus, children must have acquired a critical mass of letter knowledge in order for alphabet books, to elicit attention to print.

Effects of a brief behavioral treatment for insomnia in individuals with HIV: A pilot study

Fair, Christine BBHH-Scottsdale, Scottsdale, USA Ramstad, David 116B, Carl T Hayden VAMC, Phoenix, USA

Insomnia is associated with HIV impacting quality of life and medical outcome. This pilot study explored the effectiveness of a brief behavioral treatment for HIV infected individuals. Six adults with HIV participated in a behavioral treatment utilizing sleep education, restriction, and modified stimulus control to improve length/quality of sleep. Measures including sleep diaries, sleep quality, sleep drive, and insomnia severity were completed at baseline, week one, and post-intervention. Improvements in sleep drive and recognized sleep habits impacting sleep quality were observed post-intervention. Significant reductions in Insomnia were not observed. Future research recommends increased number of sessions and adherence to protocol.

A longitudinal study on the development of theory of mind understanding in Chinese children

Fang, Fuxi Institute of Psychology CAS, Beijing, People's Republic of China Wellman, Henry Center for Human Growth and De, University of Michigan, Ann Arbor, USA Liu, Yujuan Developmental Psychology, Institute of Psychology CAS, Beijing, People's Republic of China Liu, Guoxiong Developmental Psychology, Institute of Psychology CAS, Beijing, People's Republic of China Kang, Rong Developmental Psychology, Institute of Psychology CAS, Beijing, People's Republic of China

Cross-sectional, scaling methods with children raised in Western societies show theory-of-mind understandings develop in consistent sequences. Do longitudinal data confirm the same sequences? And, do children from quite different sociocultural circumstances evidence the same sequences? To address these questions we used a theory-of-mind scale with 140 Chinese preschoolers from Beijing and 135 English-speaking children from the US and Australia. Focally, we followed 31 Chinese children longitudinally, with multiple scale assessments. Longitudinal results confirm the cross-sectional findings of a common sequence of understanding (with the same steps longitudinally and cross-sectionally), as well as sociocultural differences in children's developing theories of mind.

The development of the operational thinking in Chinese school children

Fang, Fuxi Institute of Psychology CAS, Beijing, People's Republic of China

How does operational thinking develop in school children and which factors effect its development? We addressed these questions by assessing children longitudinally at ages 7, 9 and 12 who come from various qualities of schooling on four Piagetian's

cognitive tasks. A horizontal and vertical decalage for the acquisition were found. Concrete reasoning was manifested in some general stagelike manner combined with individual variations. A phenomenon of error-of - growth was identified in the process of acquiring conservation-of -volume. The inter-individual differences in development were constrained by the interaction of internal factors and external factors. Low- level ability children gained more benefits from schooling.

Anger assessment with the STAXI-2: Psychometric properties on Iranian university students

Farahani, Mohammad Naghy Dept. of Psychology, Tarbiat Moallem University, Tehran, Islamic Republic of Iran

The aim of this research is preliminary report of Spielberger's State-Trait Anger Expression Inventory –2 (STAXI-2) for students (aged 20-29 years old) of Isfahan University in Iran. This study presents initial data on a Persian version of the inventory. The subjects were 600 students from Isfahan University and 30 psychiatric patients from Esfahan Farabi hospital. The results provide initial support for Spielberger's factorial model of anger in a Persian sample, also was indicated an acceptable validity and reliability for the inventory. The results of this study are in consisting with the spielberger, s report (1999).

A and B Personality types: Which effect on mental health?

Fathi-Ashtiani, Ali Behavioral Sciences Research C, Baqiyatallah University of Med, Tehran, Islamic Republic of Iran Mahdavian, Alireza Department of Psychology, Science and Culture University, Tehran, Islamic Republic of Iran Ziglari, Hamideh Department of Psychology, Science and Culture University, Tehran, Islamic Republic of Iran

The study, investigates the relationship between the mental health and personality types of university students. 170 students (85 females and 85 males) were selected. The instruments used comprised General Health Questionnaire, and A and B Personality Questionnaire. The t-test and multiple regression coefficient were used to analyze the data. There was a significant difference between students with A and B personality types in somatic symptoms, anxiety, social dysfunction and depression. That means that the students with B personality type have better mental health. Moreover A and B personality types have 12% and 6% of variance of mental health.

Qualitative methods in pre-post-evaluation of a group psychotherapy for chronic pain: An exploratory study

Fernández Puig, Victoria Faculty of Psychology, University Ramon Llull, Barcelona, Spain Semis, Ricard Pain Clinic, Hospital Germans Tries i Pujol, Barcelona, Spain Bakaikoa, Maika Pain Clinic, Hospital Germans Tries i Pujol, Badalona, Spain Borrell, Dani Pain Clinic, Hospital Tries i Pujol, Badalona, Spain Farriols Hernando, Nuria Faculty of Psychology, University Ramon Llull, Barcelona, Spain Palma Sevillano, Carolina Faculty of Psychology, University Ramon Llull, Barcelona, Spain Segura Bernal, Jordi Faculty of Psychology, University Ramon Llull, Barcelona, Spain Monerris, Mar Pain Clinic, Hospital Germans Tries i Pujol, Barcelona, Spain

Objectives: The aim is to compare perceptions, coping strategies and disabilities in chronic pain experience as a way to describe patients improvement. Methods: Subjects are patients at the Pain Clinic which have assisted to a 12 weekly sesions of group psychotherapy and fullfilled a set of quantitative tests and an open questionnaire related to chronic pain experience before and after the treatment. In addition with quantitative measures,

qualitative methods shed new light to pre-post-treatment evaluation. Data analyses procedures are specified according to grounded theory guidelines with support of the computer-based ATLAS/ti instrument. Results and conclusions are in a processing stage.

Differences between immigrant and non immigrant origin families in paternal stress during the hospitalization of a son

Fernandez Castillo, Antonio Develop.-Education. Psychology, University of Granada, Granada, Spain Vílchez-Lara, María José Anesthesiology and reanimation, Hospital Complex of Jaen, Jaén, Spain Sada-Lazaro, Emilio Develop.-Education. Psychology, University of Granada, Granada, Spain

We studied some of the variables that have been related to paternal stress during pediatric hospitalization, seeking for differences between indigenous and immigrant parents. In our study participated 137 parents with hospitalized children in the region of Andalusia (Spain). 85 of them were non immigrant parents and 52 immigrants. Our data indicate that no significant differences exist, in the general level of stress, between the two groups of parents. Nevertheless, it was observed differences among the associated variables with stress in the two groups. We discuss the important implications of our results for hospital context health care and institutional politics.

Anxiety in immigrant parents during hospitalization of their children

Fernandez Castillo, Antonio Develop.-Education. Psychology, University of Granada, Granada, Spain Sada-Lazaro, Emilio Develop.-Education. Psychology, University of Granada, Granada, Spain Vílchez-Lara, María José Anesthesiology and reanimation, Hospital Complex of Jaen, Jaén, Spain

Our first objective is to analyze the presence of anxiety in immigrant parents during the hospitalization of a son or daughter, looking for differences in function of the geographical origin. Gender differences are looked for in second place. In our study there participated 75 immigrant and 75 non immigrant parents randomly selected. All of them had children hospitalized in Andalucia, Spain. We found anxiety in immigrant population like in non-immigrants but no significative differences between the two groups. No gender differences were found in immigrants. The emotional alterations of parents are important for the achievement of wellbeing during pediatric hospitalization.

Comparative analysis of on-line versus traditional tutorship use in a university educational innovation project

Fernandez Castillo, Antonio Develop.-Education. Psychology, University of Granada, Granada, Spain

The objective of this work is to carry out a comparison analysis between the main systems of tutorship in high education. 312 students of the Faculty of Educational Sciences of the University of Granada, aged between 18 and 38, answered voluntarily the assessment instruments. A cluster analysis indicated two large groups of subjects: those that show a preference for the use of traditional tutorship, and those that prefer the virtual tutorship. A majority of the students prefer traditional tutorial action. None of the two main alternatives is clearly better than the other, each one of them have advantages and objections.

"The story of my life": Analysing homeless' and professionals' perspectives on homelessness

Ferreira, Joaquim Armando Fac.of Psychol. and Ed. Scienc, University of Coimbra, COIMBRA, Portugal Mairos Nogueira, Sónia Fac.of Psychol. and Ed. Scienc, University of Coimbra, Coimbra, Portugal

The main goal of this research was to study factors that enhance the probability of becoming homeless, being homeless over time and successful (re)insertion in society. To do so, we developed a multi-method qualitative approach that included participant observations during street interventions (n>50) and semi-strutured interviews with currently and formerly homeless (n=20). From their life stories it became clear that some dimensions coexist in the three situations (e.g., social policies, job instability, relations, vocational volatility). However, only some of them are essential to the process of successful reinsertion, namely: relationships, training and work opportunities, counseling and specific intervention strategies.

Assessing the locus of task-switch costs within the processing stream

Fiedler, Anja Inst. für Psychologie, Universität Tübingen, Tübingen, Germany *Schröter, Hannes* Psychologisches Institut, Eberhard-Karls-Universität, Tübingen, Germany *Ulrich, Rolf* Psychologisches Institut, Eberhard-Karls-Universität, Tübingen, Germany

When participants are required to switch from one task to another task, switch-costs are usually observed in reaction time (RT). It is unclear, however, where these costs occur within the processing stream. We employed the lateralized readiness potential (LRP) to localize this switch-cost effect within the RT processing stream. The experiment required participants to switch between tasks, which differed in their response sets. As expected, RT increased when participants had to switch from one to another task. Most importantly, however, the LRP results indicate that this increase is associated with slower premotor and motor processing compared to a non-switch condition.

Emotional expression and leadership effectiveness: A study of Singaporean Chinese workers

Fu, Jeanne Ho Ying Nanyang Business School, Nanyang Technological Univers., Singapore, Singapore

The current research explores the effect of emotional expression on perceived leadership effectiveness. Past research (Tiedens, 2001) has shown that for Euro-Americans, angry emotion conferred more power to leaders than sad emotion. I propose that East-Asians perceive angry emotion differently than do Euro-Americans. East-Asians perceive angry emotion as less conducive to effective leadership because anger is perceived as manifesting loss of emotional control. Singaporean Chinese workers first viewed video clips in which a leader conducted a meeting expressing either angry, calm or sad emotion. Participants then rated effectiveness of the leader. Results showed that calm leaders were perceived as better leaders than angry and sad leaders.

Japanese life-patterns in the 2000's: Student volunteering in Japan, China and the UK

Furukawa, Hideo Dept. Intercultural Studies, Ryukoku University, Ohtsu, Japan *Yorifuji, Kayo* Research Institute, International Economy and Work, Osaka, Japan *Yamashita, Miyako* graduate school of humanities, Okayama University, Itami, HYOGO, Japan

Volunteering is one of the most important activities which enhance the quality of life for students as well as company employees. So as to explore the differences of volunteering among three countries, a preliminary survey was conducted on campus. Interim findings indicated by analyzing the questionnaire data of three universities are follows. Firstly, students in the UK are more often engaged in volunteering than any of the others. Secondly, students in Japan are willing to participate in volunteering potentially. Thirdly, students in China are sometimes mobilized to so-called compulsory volunteering. Some lessons learned from volunteering in the UK were discussed.

Changes of reward system in Japanese management and the effect on the contextual performance

Furukawa, Hisataka Human-Environment Studies, Kyushu University, Fukuoka City, Japan *Ikeda, Hiroshi* Human Sciences, St.Thomas, Amagasaki, Japan

Success of Japanese organizations has been attributed to employees' higher organizational commitment and teamwork caused by 'equality' based on seniority reward system. Recently, almost all Japanese organizations altered seniority system to outcome-based one. This study examined, using path analysis, the effect of outcome-based system on employee's task and contextual perfomance through survey for 6 Japanese organizations. Results revealed the introduction of outcome-based system did not have necessarily direct and negative effect on employees' contextual performance. Specifically, new reward system had impact first on the employees' procedural and distributional justice perception. Justice perceptions influenced employees' teamwork orientation, and then contextual performance.

Inhibitory mechanisms in verbal and emotional processing in early Parkinsons Disease: Global or specific impairments?

Fusari, Anna Basic Psychology II, UNED Univ. Nac. Ed.a Distancia, Madrid, Spain *García Rodríguez, Beatriz* Basic Psychology II, UNED Univ.Nac.Ed.a Distancia, Madrid, Spain *Ellgring, Heiner* Psychology, Julius Maximilian University, Wurzburg, Germany *Molina Arjona, José Antonio* Neurology, Hospital XII de Octubre, Madrid, Spain

In this study we have tested inhibitory abilities in early and unmedicated Parkinsons patients (PD). We compared performance of a group of PD patients and controls on a verbal Stroop test, an emotional facial identification cued task and an emotional inhibitory task with congruent and incongruent trials (emotional expressions/corresponding nouns). Results showed an impaired performance of PD patients in the three tasks, although this deficit was more pronounced in the Stroop and the emotional inhibition task. We did not find correlation between these two inhibitory tasks, suggesting that inhibition is a multidimensional process and is not affected by stimulus type.

Prevalence of sexual coercion against dating partners by male and female university students worldwide

Gámez Guadix, Manuel Universidad Autonoma de Madrid, Madrid, Spain *Straus, Murray A.* Family Research Laboratory, University of New Hampshire, Durham, USA

Objective: The purpose of this study was to provide information on the extent to males and females perpetrated sexual coercion against a dating partner in 32 national contexts around the world. Method: This research is part of the International Dating Violence Study. Samples were collected at 68 universities in all major world regions. Results: Overall, about 26% of the men and 19% of the women reported perpetrating some form of verbal sexual coercion, and 2.4% of men and 1.8% of women admitted to some form of physically forced sex. Conclusions: Findings showed that there were large differences between nations in the rates of sexually coercive behavior and that women as well as men engage in sexual coercion.

Psychological variables related to treatment outcome perception in chronic pain patients

Gómez Pérez, Lydia Personalidad, Evaluac. y Trab., Universidad de Málaga, Málaga, Spain *López Martínez, Alicia Eva* Personalidad, Evaluación y Tra, Universidad de Málaga, Málaga, Spain

The aim of this study is to examine the simultaneous predictive power of personality factors, pain coping and medical adherence, in order to explain how patients evaluate their medical treatment outcomes. 73 non- malignant chronic pain patients were assessed using the Clinical Millon Multiaxial Inventory, the Vanderbilt Coping Strategies Questionnaire, the Participant Compliance Reporting Scale, a self-reported measure of medication adherence and the Patients' Treatment Outcomes Perception Questionnaire. Canonical correlation analysis revealed that are patients with a less adjusted personality and which tend to use more active pain coping responses those which perceived the medical treatment as less effective.

What do we think about when we compare two Japanese Kanji numbers?

Gan, Qingwei Cognitive Psychology Lab., Ochanomizu University, Tokyo, Japan *Ishiguchi, Akira* Cognitive Psychology Lab, Ochanomizu University, TOKYO, Japan

Multi-digit Arabic numeral system is a place-value system which contains both shape and position information, but Japanese Kanji numeral system only uses shape information to represent the base and power dimension of a number. Three experiments were conducted to investigate what we think about when comparing two multi-digit kanji numbers simultaneously. The results show that (1) the multi-digit kanji number is represented compositionally in comparison; (2) the length of kanji number influence the decision time; (3) the shape information works internally regardless of whether it is used to represent base or power.

Analyzing the safety climate and safety behavior relationship on aircrew

Gao, Juan Shanghai, People's Republic of China *You, Xuqun* Department of Psychology, Shaanxi Normal University, Xi'an, People's Republic of China

On the assumption that the relationship between safety climate and safety behavior is mediated by perceived barrier and situation awareness, we propose four structural equation models. Factor analysis is applied to test the instruments and to verify the goodness of fit of the proposed models, and an optimal model is thus picked out. Three conclusions are drawn: (a) Safety climate has indirect effect on safety behavior via perceived barrier and situation awareness; (b) Safety climate has indirect effect on situation awareness via perceived barrier; (c) Safety climate has strong direct effect on perceived barrier, which indicates it is necessary to eliminate the excursive attitude of aircrew to further ensure aviation safety.

Loyalty to supervisor in Chinese context: Antecedents and outcomes

Gao, Yan Dept. of Psychology, Beijing Normal University, Beijing, People's Republic of China *Zhang, Peng* Human Resource, Huawei Technologies Co., Ltd., Shenzhen, People's Republic of China

The paper is to test that Loyalty to supervisor is a more effective predictor of job-related outcomes than organizational commitment in China, a highly relationship-oriented context. 389 subjects from 3 companies answered questionnaire measuring 7 constructs including Loyalty to Supervisor, Organizational commitment, and job satisfaction. Their OCB and task performance was rated by supervisors. Result from regression analysis indicates that loyalty to supervisor was more strongly associated with in-role performance, organizational citizenship behavior than organizational commitment. The data also indicate that "Guanxi", interactional justice, perceived supervisor's Personal Morality, and Goal Efficiency are the important antecedents of subordinate's loyalty to supervisor.

11-M as seen by children

García Renedo, Mónica Oficina de Cooperación, Universitat Jaume I, Castellón de la Plana (Spain), Spain **Valero Valero, Mar** *Oficina de Cooperación, Universitat Jaume I, Castellón de la Plana (Spain), Spain* **Gil Beltrán, José Manuel** *Oficina de Cooperación, Universitat Jaume I, Castellón de la Plana (Spain), Spain* **Caballer Miedes, Antonio**

Our aim is to analyse the graphic representations made by schoolchildren on the 11-M terrorist attack (Madrid, 2004). The sample is made up of 116 students of a state school in Castellón (Spain). Ages range between 8 and 12, with an average age of 9.78 (s.d.=1.29). The drawings and writings were analysed descriptively through an inter-rater analysis. This study offers knowledge on the emotional and cognitive world of children with regard to large-scale human tragedies. This knowledge may prove very useful to devise intervention strategies that allow parents, teachers and psychologists to understand and help children after the event of traumatic situations of this kind.

The role of the universitat Jaume I in emergencies and disasters

García Renedo, Mónica Oficina de Cooperación, Universitat Jaume I, Castellón de la Plana (Spain), Spain **Valero Valero, Mar** *Oficina de Cooperación, Universitat Jaume I, Castellón de la Plana (Spain), Spain* **Gil Beltrán, José Manuel** *Oficina de Cooperación, Universitat Jaume I, Castellón de la Plana (Spain), Spain*

Unfortunately, there is a piece of news about floods, earthquakes and terrorist attacks on a daily basis. As well as material and personal damages, these situations have a psychosocial impact in the population. By taking into account all these factors, the Universitat Jaume I has a new work area: the "Disasters Intervention and Humanitarian Aid Area". There are two specifics projects in this area: a) A course in International Humanitarian Aid b) Psychosocial Observatory on Resources in Disaster Situations (OPSIDE-UJI) The main objective in this poster is to show the main two projects in this area that our University is currently working on.

The risk and protective factors of behavior and emotional problems of children with bronchial asthma: The role of parents personality and family context

Garckija, Renata Klinical and Organizational ps, Vilnius University, Vilnius, Lithuania

Bronchial Asthma (BA) is diagnosed to 1 of 50 Lithuanian children. It is suggested that the psychopathology among BA children is by great degree related to parental and family context. By our research we seek to evaluate the impact and interplay of parental and family variables, such as parents personality, parenting styles and conflict resolution strategies, to psychological adjustment of children with BA. We will compare the the clinical group with controls and make our conclusions on the basis of Structural Equation Modeling analysis.

Application of NEO-PI-R test and analytic evaluation of it's characteristics and factorial structure among Iranian university students

Garousi Farshy, Mirthagy Dept. of Psychology, Tabriz University, Tabriz, Islamic Republic of Iran

This study investigates the existence of Five-factor model of personality in Iran. A Persian translation of revised NEO personality inventory was prepared. Content validity and cultural relevance of it, were assessed. Final version of test was administered to a sample of students from Iran universities(N=1717, aged 18-24). Separate principal component analyses with varimax rotation were conducted on the intercorrelations of 30 facet scores. Results showed existence of five major factors. A sixth factor was also extracted and called "Narcissism". This factor was different within groups, males and females.

Concurrent validity and reliability of Persian form were acceptable.

Beyond cultural Specific: Cross- cultural management in the context of globalization: General trends and psychological implications

Genkova, Petia Inst. für Psychologie, Universität Passau, Passau, Germany

The Study tries to pinpoint the extent to which a given corporate culture is applicable in a different cultural context. These Studies present the results from really HR- Audits. One study is about an establishment of an American company in Germany (supply industry). The second study is about a German establishment in the United States (mechanical engineering industry). The results clearly reveal that the acceptance of a corporate culture in a foreign cultural context is very low among the employees of the host country. The attempt to implement a given concept of motivation programs and human resources development measures has held negative effects instead of positive effects on work efficiency and on the commitment of staff. General trends are discussed.

"Short-term" neuropsychological interventions on children and adolescents with Attention Deficit Hyperactivity Disorder (ADHD) and learning disabilities

Giger, Elisabeth Kinderpsychologie, Z.E.N., Biel, Switzerland **Hassink, Ralph-Ingo** *Kinderpsychologie, Z.E.N., Biel, Switzerland* **Giugliano, Sara** *Kinderpsychologie, Z.E.N., Biel, Switzerland*

Aim of this study is to evaluate the outcome of "short-term" neuropsychological interventions on children and adolescents with ADHD and comorbid learning disabilities. Up to now we followed 25 patients, aged 10-18 years with ADHD diagnosis for a short neuropsychological treatment. After a detailed neuropsychological examination, specific individual academic success-strategies were implemented. Parents and teachers were also specifically instructed. Questionnaires of change of behaviour and academic achievement assessment were used to evaluate the success. All patients improved significantly their academic, learning and attitudinal characteristics and they were able to sustain these improvements after intervention.

ADHD and learning disabilities

Glozman, Janna Psychology Department, Moscow State University, Moscow, Germany

Objectives: To prove relationship of ADHD with learning disability, to find out its neuropsychological mechanisms and efficient methods of neuropsychological remediation. Methods: Luria battery, Conners ADHD questionnaire. Results: ADHD was revealed in 81% of learning disable children. Neuropsychological assessment proved its relation with decreased brain activation and underdeveloped executive functions. A complex program of motor and cognitive remediation aimed to activate the child ("saturation" with activity instead of prohibit it) and to form an ability of self-control Conclusion: The proposed system of neuropsychological remediation does not look for a "button" to switch off child's hyperactivity, but it forms strategies to control it. It favors both child attention and success in learning.

Relational reasoning in the abstract and motor domains: An fMRI study

Golde, Maria Cognitive Neurology, MPI CBS, Leipzig, Germany **Schubotz, Ricarda I.** *Cognitive Neurology, MPI CBS, Leipzig, Germany* **von Cramon, D. Yves** *Cognitive Neurology, MPI CBS, Leipzig, Germany*

The study aimed at differentiating brain correlates of relational processes in the motor and abstract domains using fMRI. A reasoning paradigm adapted from Raven's Progressive Matrices was employed with subjects performing in an "abstract"

condition and an "action" condition. Integration of relations was either required or not. Results showed a broad, predominantly left-lateralized fronto-parietal network to be activated for relational integration in both domains. Reasoning with abstract as compared to reasoning with action stimuli activated distinct networks. More detailed analyses revealed differential involvement of regions within the frontal cortex. Results underline functional relevance of premotor cortex in purely cognitive tasks.

Dimensions of symbolic brand image perception in Poland

Gorbaniuk, Oleg Experimental Psychology, Catholic University of Lublin, Lublin, Poland

With the goal of identifying dimensions of brand personality among Polish consumers, 870 people were tested from 16-34 years of age. Respondents described 37 brands from various product categories (utilitarian, symbolic/utilitarian, symbolic). The results confirm a five factors structure obtained in previous research studies (Aaker, 1997, 2001). The isolated dimensions are Competence, Excitement, Openness to others, Sophistication, and Snobbery. The result of the carried out research is the Polish Brand Personality Scale composed of the presented five dimensions, thirteen facets and thirty nine personality traits. Particular scales obtained good internal and test-retest reliability.

Dimensions of symbolic brand image perception in Poland

Gorbaniuk, Oleg Experimental Psychology, Catholic University of Lublin, Lublin, Poland

With the goal of identifying dimensions of brand personality among Polish consumers, 963 people were tested from 16-34 years of age. Respondents described 24 brands from various product categories (utilitarian, symbolic/utilitarian, symbolic). The results confirm a five factors structure obtained in previous research studies (Aaker, 1997, 2001). The isolated dimensions are Competence, Excitement, Openness to others, Sophistication, and Snobbery. The result of the carried out research is the Polish Brand Personality Scale composed of the presented five dimensions, thirteen facets and thirty nine personality traits. Particular scales obtained good internal and test-retest reliability.

Performance anxiety during a musical performance and a non-musical, social performance situation

Gorges, Susanne Inst. für Psychologie I, Universität Würzburg, Würzburg, Germany **Alpers, Georg W.** *Department of Psychology I, University of Würzburg, Würzburg, Germany*

Literature reports mixed results on the relationship between musical performance anxiety and social anxiety. Only few studies compare them in an experimental design. In the current study we compared subjective performance anxiety, cortisol, and heart rate in 31 music students while playing in a concert and while giving a speech in front of an audience. We expected that the level of performance anxiety is similar for the musical and non-musical performance. Conclusions with respect to the nature of musical performance anxiety and its relationship to social anxiety disorder are discussed.

Why do Polish students learn English and how do they perceive this language? Psychological image of English language and motivation for learning English at Polish students.

Grabarska, Anna Lublin, Poland

Investigating reasons for learning English and connection between the type of motivation and "personality" of English and its similarity with ideal I. 160 students filled in the questionnaire of motivation and the ACL. ANOVA and post hoc test were used. Individuals with high or medium level of intrinsic and high level of extrinsic motivation perceive English more positively and perceive their ideal I as more similar to personality of English than individuals with low level of intrinsic and medium level of extrinsic motivation. English is becoming "world language". The personality of English is supposed to be one of the factors influencing the motivation for learning English.

Two points of view on motives for learning English and on psychological image of this language. A cross-cultural study involving Poland, United Kingdom and the United States of America.

Grabarska, Anna Lublin, Poland
Investigating reasons for learning English by Polish students given by themselves and by native speakers from UK and the USA. Also an attempt at describing the "personality" of English by Poles and native speakers. 180 subjects filled in the questionnaire of motivation and the ACL. Descriptive statistics were used. Both groups (Poles and native speakers) indicated definitely more extrinsic than intrinsic motives for learning English by Polish students. In description of the "personality" of English Poles chose only positive adjectives while native speakers also some negative ones. English is becoming "world language". The language and motivation for learning it may be perceived differently by various nations.

Psychological models of social inference

Grant, Malcolm Dept. of Psychology, Memorial University, St. John's, Canada Snook, Brent Psychology, Memorial University, St. John's, Canada Button, Cathryn Psychology, Memorial University, St. John's, Canada
A matching heuristic model of social inferences was compared with two integration models, an unweighted-cue model and a weighted-cue model. University students saw pictures of targets (coded for gender, age, attractiveness, smiling, ethnic identity, and ethnic garb) and judged their liberalness (Study 1) or intelligence (Study 2). In both studies, the weighted-cue model significantly outperformed the unweighted model. The heuristic model, using in most cases just one or two cues, was as accurate as the weighted-cue model in predicting intelligence judgments and significantly better for liberalness judgments. We discuss the psychological plausibility of these models and their susceptibility to overfitting.

The study on the personality of pupils in China

Gu, Liqun School of of Management, Dalian Polytechnic University, Dalian, People's Republic of China Liu, Wen Department of Psychology, Liaoning Normal University, Dalian, People's Republic of China
Elementary school is a critical phase in which children form and develop their own personality. It is also a key link in carrying out quality education. In order to scientifically grasp the characteristics and law of pupils' personality development and make feasible policies, targeted at 489 pupils in China, and based on research and data in «Evaluation Scale of Children's personality Development». This research sums up the characteristics in age and differences in sex concerning pupils' personality development in urban areas of China .

Cognitive modeling of in-group preference effects in an implicit association task

Gula, Bartosz Inst. für Pychologie, Universität Klagenfurt, Klagenfurt, Austria Höbart, Bernhard Department of Psychology, Klagenfurt University, Klagenfurt, Austria Vitouch, Oliver Department of Psychology, Klagenfurt University, Klagenfurt, Austria
Two different accounts of the cognitive processes involved in the Implicit Association Test (IAT) were examined. In this study (N = 84) a new IAT capturing ethnic group preferences was applied and

yielded IAT effects in good accordance with the literature. Mierke & Klauer's (2001) probabilistic task switch neglect model accounted for the IAT effects (though moderated by age) while the QUAD model (Conrey, et al. 2005) did not fit the data. In light of the QUAD models' capability to independently estimate in-group preference and out-group derogation, possible explanations for the misfit are discussed and plausible extensions of the original model's parameter assumptions are suggested.

Changes in Body Mass Index (BMI) and eating disorder symptomatology over the life cycle in western Canadian men and women: ethnic contrasts

Harrell, Andrew Population Research Laboratory, University of Alberta, Edmonton, Canada Boisvert, Jennifer A. Population Research Laboratory, University of Alberta, Edmonton, Alberta, Canada
Objectives. Changes in BMI and disordered eating over the life cycle of men, women, whites and non-whites were investigated. Methods. A representative survey (n = 1200) of Western Canadians. Drive for Thinness, Bulimia and Body Dissatisfaction were analyzed with ANOVA. Results. Differences in Bulimia between whites and non-whites were due to BMI variations. Drive for Thinness was higher for women at every age except for those 65 + years. Body Dissatisfaction was greatest in the obese and in whites. Conclusions. Canadian ethnic differences in disordered eating are unique. Gender differences become minimal with advanced age.

The mass man as defector: Implications of Ortega's "The rebellion of the masses" on social dilemma research

Hatori, Tsuyoshi Dept of Civil Engineering, Tokyo Institute of Technology, Tokyo, Japan Fujii, Satoshi Dept of Civil Engineering, Tokyo Institute of Technology, Tokyo, Japan Komatsu, Yoshihiro Dept of Civil Engineering, Tokyo Institute of Technology, Tokyo, Japan
The objective of this study is to develop measurements of spiritual vulgarity of the masses based upon Ortega's "the revolt of the masses"(1930) and to investigate relations between the measurements and defective behaviors in various social dilemmas. For this purpose, we implemented two questionnaire surveys targeting at 200 university students and 1000 households in Japan, respectively. The factor analysis on the vulgarity measurements produced two subscales; autistic attitude and contumelious attitude. Furthermore, obtained data from both surveys indicated that the vulgar scales were correlated with tendency of defective behaviors in social dilemmas, e.g. anti-environmental behavior and destructive behavior of landscape.

Studies on Yips(2)

Hayashi, Kiyoshi Dept. of Psychology, Shiraume Gakuen College, Tokyo, Japan Ogino, Nanae Psychology, Shiraume Gakuen College, Ogawacho Kodairasi Tokyo, Japan Yagi, Takahiko Psychology, Chuo Gakuin University, Kujike Abikosi Chiba, Japan
Objectives Hayashi and Yagi(2006) suggested that the yips were relevant to characteristics of perfectionism. This survey has been carried out to show some relationship between perfectionism and other personality traits. Methods Survey with perfectionism scale, obsessional inventory and MMPI to 99 university students(2007). Results We found Concern over Mistakes and Doubting of Actions scales are more correlate to MMPI and LOI sub-scales than Desire for Perfection and Personal Standard scales. Conclusions We suggested such negative factors of perfectionism more affected to activate neurotic conditions. To reduce such conditions we suggested it is useful to apply several relaxation programs.

Is self-leadership more than volitional efficacy?

Heiss, Christian Lehrstuhl für Sportspsychologie, Technische Universität München, München, Germany Beckmann, Jürgen Lehrstuhl für Sportspsychologie, Technische Universität München, München, Germany Ehrlenspiel, Felix Lehrstuhl für Sportspsychologie, Technische Universität München, München, Germany
Volitional efficacy can be separated into self-regulation and self-control (Kuhl, 1998). Questionnaires assessing volition seem to show a high overlap to the measurement of self-leadership (Neck & Manz, 2002). This was tested in a study with a sample of 323 students using an exploratory factor analysis. The results indicate that both concepts load on distinct factors. This could be explained by theoretical distinctions between self-control, which is mainly a descriptive whereas self-leadership is mainly a normative construct. Based on these findings it is hypothesized that self-leadership skills are necessary to show self controlled behaviour.

Implicit and explicit memory in ADHD

Heubeck, Bernd School of of Psychology, Australian National University, Canberra, Australia Clapham, Laura School of of Psychology, Australian National University, Canberra, Australia McKone, Elinor School of of Psychology, Australian National University, Canberra, Australia
Aloisi, McKone and Heubeck (2004) reported that children with ADHD showed problems in explicit memory performance but not in implicit memory compared to matched controls. Their memory tasks were of a visual nature. The current study asked if similar findings can be obtained presenting auditory memory tasks. Boys with ADHD were matched by age to boys without a diagnosis and given working memory, category exemplar generation and category cued recall tests. Poorer results on the digits backwards test of working memory were obtained as well as the expected explicit/implicit dissociation in ADHD. Implications for theory and learning with ADHD are considered.

Sibling numbers and age at menarche

Hinobayashi, Toshihiko School of of Human Sciences, Osaka University, Suita, Japan Minami, Tetsuhiro School of of Human Sciences, Osaka University, Suita, Japan Akai, Seiki School of of Human Sciences, Osaka University, Suita, Japan Yasuda, Jun School of of Human Sciences, Osaka University, Suita, Japan Shizawa, Yasuhiro School of of Human Sciences, Osaka University, Suita, Japan Itoigawa, Naosuke School of of Letters, Mukogawa Women's University, Suita, Japan Yamada, Kazunori School of of Human Sciences, Osaka University, Suita, Japan
The association of sibling numbers and age at menarche was evaluated in 48,905 Japanese schoolgirls. The material was collected in February,2005. Status quo data on menarche was analyzed by probit analysis with the number of children in a family.The median age at menarche tended to increase significantly (p<0.001)with each increasing sibling, up until 3 or more siblings. While the total age at menarche was 12.22 years old, the age at menarche among a one-child-family was 12.0 years old. But, the influence of sibling numbers was less than that of so-called secular trend.

Work-family conflict: Reducing conflict and enhancing gain with a behavioral family intervention

Holdstein, Doreen Inst. für Psychologie, Tech. Universität Braunschweig, Braunschweig, Germany Hahlweg, Kurt Institut für Psychologie, TU Braunschweig, Braunschweig, Germany
Working parents encounter a variety of conflicting duties in their work and family lives. The present study examined the efficacy of a parenting program especially designed to their needs, including topics such as positive parenting, stress management, and

balancing work and family life. For this purpose 87 parents have been randomly assigned to an experimental group and a waitlist-control condition. Effect sizes for individual, family-related, and work-related outcome variables, such as work-to-family and family-to-work conflict, stress, and life satisfaction are presented. The results will be discussed with regard to implications for the work-family research and workplace health promotion.

Children's rejection sensitivity for intimate relationships in Japan

Honda, Junko child and family welfare, Den-en-Chofu University, Kawasaki-shi Kanagawa-ken, Japan
Children high in rejection sensitivity (RS) anxiously expect rejection and are at risk for interpersonal and personal distress. In this study, we developed a measure to pick up children high in rejection sensitivity in Japan. Japanese children(9-12 years-old) high in rejection sensitivity avoided intimate relationships with same-sex friends. They didn't want the relationships with firends to continue for a long time. The result implicated that children high in rejection sensitivity seek security through avoiding proximity to their firends.

Deliberation or Intuition?: The impact of decision modes with regard to efficiency of simple versus complex probabilistic inferences

Horstmann, Nina Research on Collective Goods, Max-Planck-Institut, Bonn, Germany
Recent studies suggest advantages of unconscious information processing compared to deliberation with regard to decision quality (Unconscious Thought Theory; Dijksterhuis, 2006). Glöckner and Betsch (in press) conduct with the Parallel Constraint Satisfaction Rule a mathematical specification of these processes and show that individuals are able to integrate complex information automatically in an astoundingly narrow time frame. Combining these approaches an experiment based on probabilistic inferences is designed to investigate the efficiency of intuitive and deliberate decision modes depending on low vs. high complexity. It is expected that intuition yields good decisions regardless of complexity level, while deliberation results in suboptimal decisions under high complexity.

Psychological Information Engineering (PIE)

Hu, Zhan Dept. of Psychology, East China Normal University, Berlin, Germany
PIE is an interdisciplinary field that relates to psychology, information science, automation technology and other applied sciences. In order to realize the informationization for psychology, PIE fully applies contemporary information technology to the research and application of psychology. Simply speaking, we can regard PIE as two main parts: theoretical and engineering. The former focuses on the psychological methodology based on the information technology. The latter strives for developing practical information system, tools, products that aim to accelerating the research and application of psychology. The integration and interaction of the two parts certainly will lead psychology to a new situation.

A modified paradigm in P300-based lie detection using autobiographical information

Hu, Xiaoqing Dept. of Psychology, Zhejiang Normal University, Jinhua, People's Republic of China
This current study used a modified paradigm of P300-based lie detection to examine its efficiency. Unlike the previous researches which combined deceit and recognition together, this paradigm separated these two cognitive processes. 14 participants were instructed to press the button by a signal displayed on the screen which indicate "be honest" or "be deceptive" after a name. The results showed

a significant difference on P300's amplitude between recognition/nonrecognition regardless of the participants' overt behavior at site Pz(p <.005) and Cz(p <.000). Subsequent MANOVA(stimulus × sites) revealed the recognition/nonrecognition cognitive process had significantly different P300 amplitude topographies.

Individual differences in causal reasoning development

Hwang, Hye-Young Dept. of Education, Seoul National University, Seoul, Republic of Korea Kim, Jung-Ha Dept. of Education, Seoul National University, Seoul, Republic of Korea Lee, Hyun-Joo Dept. of Education, Seoul National University, Seoul, Republic of Korea Shin, Jong-Ho Dept. of Education, Seoul National University, Seoul, Republic of Korea
The purpose of the paper was to investigate individual differences in the development of causal reasoning ability and to identify correlates with the differences. Specifically, gender, working memory capacity, and background knowledge were investigated as correlates in the study. Inter- and intra-individual differences were also investigated among contents of causal reasoning: Psychological, behavioral, and physical contents. Participants were about 1,000 students in grades 1 to 6. Results of the study showed that gender and background knowledge were significant correlates with causal reasoning, and that inter- and intra-individual differences were found in the different content areas of causal reasoning.

Four-aspect model of resilience: Cognition and utilization of personal and environmental resources

Ihaya, Keiko Human-Environment Studies, Kyushu University, Fukuoka, Japan Nakamura, Tomoyasu Human-Environment Studies, Kyushu University, Fukuoka-city, Japan
Resilience is the capacity of people to cope with harmful events. We classified the resilience in regard with four aspects of resource: cognition and utilization of personal and environmental resources. As this classification, four scales measuring these resources were developed. Next, we estimated the difficulty and discrimination of each item in these scales using Item Response Theory. The results showed the middle to low difficulty and the middle discrimination. Therefore, we suggest that four scales are adequate for measuring resilience of normal people and promote the clarification of the resilience more than to date.

Revelation effect on autobiographical memories

Inan, Asli Dept. of Psychology, Atilim University, Ankara, Turkey Tekman, Hasan Psychology, Uludag University, Bursa, Turkey
We investigated the revelation effect for autobiographic memories under two different conditions: Either one of the words in half of the items of a Life Event Inventory (LEI) was presented as an anagram or an unrelated word was presented as an anagram before half of the LEI items. Participants were asked to solve the anagram and then rate their certainty that the event described in the LEI sentence happened to them before the age of ten. The responses of 92 undergraduate and graduate students showed that solving an anagram before a sentence did not affect the ratings for any lists although revealing a word in the sentence by anagram solution resulted in higher ratings for one list.

Age differences in work motivation

Inceoglu, Ilke The Pavilion, SHL Group Limited, Thames Ditton, United Kingdom Segers, Jesse Department of Management, University of Antwerp, Antwerpen, Belgium Bartram, Dave Research, SHL Group, Thames Ditton, United Kingdom Vloeberghs,

Daniël Dept. Management, University of Antwerp, Antwerpen, Belgium
To date there are very few empirical studies, especially with larger samples, which have investigated the relationship between employee age and levels of motivation. This paper examines age differences in work motivation in a UK sample of more than 9000 individuals who completed a comprehensive motivation questionnaire for selection or development purposes. Age differences were examined separately for men and women and by considering whether relationships between age and motivation are non-linear. Results generally support propositions from the literature which suggest a shift in people's motivators rather than a general decline in motivation with age.

Comparing social anxiety in Chinese, Spanish and North American adolescents

Ingles, Candido J. Dept. of Health Psychology, Universidad Miguel Hernandez, Elche, Spain Zhou, Xinyue Psychology, Sun Yat-Sen University, Guangzhou, People's Republic of China La Greca, Annette Psychology, University of Miami, Miami, USA Hidalgo, Maria D. Psychology, University of Murcia, Murcia, Spain
This study examined the differences in social anxiety between adolescents from China, Spain and US. The results revealed that: (a) Chinese adolescents scored significantly higher than North American and Spanish adolescents on the on the SAS-A total and its subscales; (b) Chinese adolescent – both boys and girls – scored higher on the SAS-A and its subscales than both North American adolescents (boys and girls) and Spanish adolescents (boys and girls), and (d) Chinese adolescents – both 10th grade and 12th grade - scored higher on the SAS-A and its subscales than North American adolescents (10th grade and 12th grade).

Decisions under ambiguity: Effects of sign and magnitude

Inukai, Keigo Behavioral Science, Hokkaido University, Sapporo, Hokkaido, Japan Takahashi, Taiki Behavioral Science, Hokkaido University, Sapporo, Hokkaido, Japan
Decision under ambiguity (uncertainty with unknown probabilities) has been attracting attention in cognitive science and behavioral economics. However, recent neuroimaging studies have mainly focused on gain domains while little attention has been paid to the magnitudes of outcomes. In this study, we examined the effects of the sign (i.e. gain and loss) and magnitude of outcomes in ambiguity aversion and the additivity of subjective probabilities in Ellsberg's urn problems (Camerer & Weber, 1992). We observed that (i) ambiguity aversion was observed in both signs, and (ii) subadditivity of subjective probability was not observed in negative outcomes.

Mere exposure to face increases social attention: Vocal stroop interference effect as revealed in N400

Ishii, Keiko Behavioral Science, Hokkaido University, Sapporo, Japan Kobayashi, Yuki Evolutionary Cog Sciences, University of Tokyo, Tokyo, Japan Kitayama, Shinobu Psychology, University of Michigan, Ann Arbor, USA
Automatic attention to a partner's vocal affect is likely to index interpersonal sensitivity in social interaction. We demonstrated that exposure to a schematic face reliably increases this sensitivity. Participants were asked to listen to emotional words spoken in emotional tones of voice, and judge the meaning of each word as positive or negative while ignoring the attendant vocal tone. Half of the participants viewed schematic faces during the judgment. As predicted, greater interference from vocal tone was found in the face condition than in the no-face condition as measured

by response time (Study 1) and electro-encephalography (Study 2).

Psychoeducational intervention to maintain flow activities in everyday life: Improvement in stress response and affective state

Ishimura, Ikuo University of Tsukuba, Tsukuba, Japan *Kawai, Hideki* C&C Innovation Research La, NEC Corporation, Ikoma, Japan *Kunieda, Kazuo* C&C Innovation Research La, NEC Corporation, Ikoma, Japan *Yamada, Keiji* C&C Innovation Research La, NEC Corporation, Ikoma, Japan *Kodama, Masahiro* Institute of Psychology, University of Tsukuba, Tsukuba, Japan

The purpose of the study was to examine the improvement in stress response and affective state by the intervention to increase flow activities for non-autotelic group. Prescreening non-autotelic group (N=28) according to no flow activity in everyday life, 15 experiment participants consented to execute flow activities in two weeks. After one month interval, intervention group reported more flow activities than control group. The ANOVAs on Depression (Anxiety), Liveliness, and Cognition-thought of helplessness in two groups before and after intervention showed significant differences. The intervention indicates to be important for promoting flow activities and improvement in stress response and affective state.

The relationship between relational aggression and social intelligence of preschool children

Isobe, Miyoshi Meiji University, Kyoto, Japan

Relational aggression harms others through damage to their relationships. Previous studies suggest that having a high social intelligence could facilitate the use of such aggressive behavior. This study investigated the relationship between relational aggression and social intelligence among preschool children. The social intelligence of 64 preschool children was assessed in terms of their knowledge of peer relationships and peers' preference in toys and in activities by means of an interview using a small scale replica of their classroom and preschoolers' figures as props. As expected, the results revealed several differences in social intelligence between relational aggressive and non-aggressive children.

Development and evaluation of the Japanese version of the DVD: Bandura's social cognitive theory: An introduction

Itoh, Hideko Research and Development, Nat. Inst Multimedia Education, Chiba, Japan

Effects of verbal and visual presentations on learning the DVD, "Bandura's social cognitive theory: An introduction," were investigated and effective Japanese captions were developed. Graduate students with little knowledge of the theory responded to tests using texts and images. All the topics were rated as interesting. Comprehension tests on aggressive modeling, moral disengagement, and efficacy, showed high correct responses. Test of applying acquired knowledge to daily life revealed that the social cognitive theory could be helpful to the participants. These results are discussed in relation to the development of learning and instructional guides to increase the effects of the DVD.

Prosocial personality, USA vs Buddha teaching, the similarity and differences

Jarernvongrayab, Anu Public Administration, Prince of Songkla University, Hat Yai, Thailand

The objective of this study was to compare the similarities and differences between prosocial personality concept that developed in the united state and Buddha teaching. The meaning of each concept will be discussed. The researcher hypotheses that prosocial personality in Buddha teaching has had wilder meaning than prosocial personality developed in united state. Two concepts were measured to test the similarities and differences by canonical correlation statistic with 200 Thai people. The results and discussion will be followed in the proceeding.

Reasoning about spatial and nonspatial relations in Nonverbal Learning Disabilities (NLD)

Jiang, Zhao-ping Philosophical School, Wuhan University, Wuhan, People's Republic of China *Yu, Guo-liang* Research Institute of Psycho, Renmin University, Beijing, People's Republic of China

The study investigated the reasoning about spatial and nonspatial relations in three groups of children aged 11-14: children with NLD, children with verbal learning disabilities (VLD), and children without learning disabilities who served as controls. Besides figure-nonspatial problems, the other three reasoning tasks (figure-spatial, verbal-spatial, and verbal-nonspatial) were four-term series problems. The results found the NLD group didn't differ from control group on nonspatial reasoning and experienced specific difficulties with spatial problems. The VLD group developed well in figure-nonspatial problems, but showed deficits in other three tasks. The results indicated a dissociation between spatial and non-spatial relation reasoning in NLD.

Distinct brain plasticity and mechanism of language and perception: A longitudinal case study

Jin, Hua Center for Studies of Psychol., South China Normal University, Guangzhou, People's Republic of China *Lin, Xueying* MR section, Guangzhou Overseas Chinese Hos, guangzhou, People's Republic of China *Chen, Zhuoming* neurology department, Guangzhou Overseas Chinese Hos, guangzhou, People's Republic of China *Liu, Shirun* MR section, Guangzhou Overseas Chinese Hos, guangzhou, People's Republic of China *Leng, Ying* Center for Studies of Psychol, South China Normal University, guangzhou, People's Republic of China *Wang, Ruiming* Center for Studies of Psychol, South China Normal University, guangzhou, People's Republic of China *Zhong, Weifang* Center for Studies of Psychol, South China Normal University, guangzhou, People's Republic of China *Cai, Mengxian* Center for Studies of Psychol, South China Normal University, guangzhou, People's Republic of China *Xu, Guiping* Center for Studies of Psycho, South China Normal University, guangzhou, People's Republic of China *Mo, Lei* Center for Studies of Psycho, South China Normal University, guangzhou, People's Republic of China

It is well known that children with early brain lesion can acquire nearly normal cognitive function. However, the underlying mechanism of such plasticity is still unclear. We addressed this question with multiple methods. 5 years after haematoma removal under left endocranium, the 11-year-old boy acquired fully normal vision and basically normal language skill. MRS data showed the left cortex has less neuron than the right one. FMRI data indicated normal activation in left occipital area but abnormal one in other left cortex in visually language task. These results suggested distinct brain plasticity and mechanism of visual perception and language.

Comparison between MMPI and MMPI-2

Jo, Hye-Seon Dept. of Psychology, Chungbuk National University, Chungbuk, Republic of Korea *Hwang, Soon-Taeg* Psychology, Chungbuk National University, Cheongju, Chungbuk, Republic of Korea *Moon, Kyung-Joo* Psychology, Maumsarang, Cheongju, Chungbuk, Republic of Korea

The purpose of this study is comparing T-scores of subscales and code types between the MMPI and MMPI-2. MMPI and MMPI-2 were administered to college students(N=156, age=22.8±2.1) divided two group for counterbalancing the order effect. Time interval of administration of two tests was one week. Paired T-tests were calculated to compare on the 3 validity scales and 10 clinical scales of the MMPI and MMPI-2. Comparisons of mean T-scores for validity scales and clinical scales showed differences on scales L, K, Hs, Pd, Pa, Pt. The concordance rate for highest scale was 37.8%; for 2 code types, 19.2%.

Comparision of relaxation and respiration training in the treatment of headache: The importance of the cost effectiveness

Jodar, Rafael Psychology, Universidad Comillas, Madrid, Spain *Prieto, Maria* Psychology, Universidad Comillas, Madrid, Spain *Espinar, Isabel* Psychology, Universidad Comillas, Madrid, Spain *Carrasco, Maria Jose* Psychology, Universidad Comillas, Madrid, Spain *Oliva, Beatriz* Psychology, Universidad Comillas, Madrid, Spain

Despite the well-known success of some behavioural treatments for management of headache, new approaches with lower training times and higher adherence are needed. Thus, the main goal of the current study is to study the efficacy of a respiration training treatment, with higher costs effectiveness, in a sub-clinic sample. Using an experimental approach, the respiration procedure, muscular relaxation, and placebo condition are compared. Intensity and frequency of headaches, as well as the impact of headache in daily life are compared in the three experimental groups. Implications for headache treatments are discussed.

Social role perceptions in Romanian female students and a group of eating disordered patients

Joja, Oltea Clinical Psychology, Institute for Endocrinology, Bucharest, Romania *Berar- Hasigan, Anca* Clinical Psychology, Institute for Endocrinology, Bucharest, Romania

Key words: gender roles, Romanian, female students, eating disorders The study attempts to enlarge the perspective of risk for eating disorders (ED) in Romania, a culture that is progressively subscribing to Western social norms. We compared 202 young female students and 37 ED patients, using a grid questionnaire for social roles. Investigated groups displayed significant differences between the social ideal and and the female gender stereotype and they both showed discrepancies between self-image and ideal-self. Students perceived themselves as more goal oriented and feminine and their ideal-self disclosed more career related features, as compared to ED patients. Data contribute to extending evaluation of promoted social models in Eastern Europe.

Myself in the mirror: Comparison of Korean and Saudi Arabian young women's self-construction while trying on lipstick

Joo, Yoon-Keang Worcester, USA

Self develops in constant interaction with the socially meaningful environment. Young women (18-25 years of age) in South Korea and Saudi Arabia were interviewed in an individual experimental setting where they first put on a given lipstick (13 trials with different shades) in front of a mirror while explaining their feelings about each stimulus. Highly differentiated positively valued meaning complexes concerning shades of bright red were found in all cases in Saudi Arabia. Korean women were hesitant to accept comparable colors in their social contexts. The results are discussed within the cultural psychology of Ernest Boesch (Fernweh/Heimweh dialectics).

Behavioral and emotional problems of preschoolers: Results of epidemiological study in Lithuania

Jusiene, Roma General Psychology, Vilnius University, Vilnius, Lithuania *Barkauskiene, Rasa* Psychology, Mykolas Romeris University, Vilnius, Lithuania *Bieliauskaite, Rasa* General Psychology,

Vilnius University, Vilnius, Lithuania **Bongarzoni-Dervinyte, Asta** Institue of Community Health, Vilnius University, Vilnius, Lithuania **Raiziene, Saule** Psychology, Mykolas Romeris University, Vilnius, Lithuania

The aim of the present study is to find out the prevalence of behavioral and emotional problems of children aged 2 to 5 years old in Lithuania. More than one thousand parents and about seven hundred caregiver-teachers rated the preschoolers'- with Strengths and Difficulties Questionnaire (SDQ, Goodman, 1997). The environmental and familial risk and protective factors related to the preschoolers' emotional and behavioral problems (such as parental education, social-economic status, urban vs. rural residence, etc.) are presented and analyzed. The prevalence of the psychological problems is also discussed in the developmental and cultural perspective. This study is supported by Lithuanian State Science and Studies Foundation

Zimbardo time perspective inventory: The adaptation process of the Lithuanian version

Kairys, Antanas Dept. of General Psychology, Vilnius University, Vilnius, Lithuania **Liniauskaite, Audrone** Department of Psychology, Klaipeda University, Klaipeda, Lithuania

ZPTI is one the mostly used method of time perspective research which is translated to many languages. The aim of this report is to present the ZPTI adaptation process in Lithuania and psychometric qualities of ZTPI Lithuanian version. The sample consisted of 353 students. The factory analysis that was performed showed that the same factors as in original inventory can be distinguished, though some items fall to other scales (especially many items from Present Fatalistic Scale). Cronbach's alphas range from 0,647 (Present Fatalistic) to 0,813 (Past Negative Scale), these indices from original method differ marginally.

Reading the face: Comparing the Facial Action Coding System (FACS) as a video-based method and the Electromyogram (EMG) as a biophysiological method

Kaiser, Anna Inst. für Neurowiss. Systeme, Universität Hamburg, Hamburg, Germany **Büchel, Christian** Dep. of Systems Neuroscience, University of Hamburg, Hamburg, Germany **Rose, Michael** Dep. of Systems Neuroscience, University of Hamburg, Hamburg, Germany

Facial muscular reactions can be assessed either with the Facial Action Coding System (FACS) or the Electromyogram (EMG). In the present study, these two methods were compared with respect to their similarities, differences and ability to differentiate basic emotions. Bipolar EMG recordings and video recordings for FACS analysis were conducted simultaneously while subjects underwent emotion elicitation. Results indicate that EMG is as reliable as FACS in differentiating both positive and negative emotions and within negative emotions. Furthermore, EMG provides additional information on low level changes that are not detectable by FACS, a procedure that relies on observable changes.

Social structure and causal attribution: The influence of relational mobility

Kamaya, Kengo Dept. of Behavioral Science, Hokkaido University, Sapporo, Japan **Yuki, Masaki** Behavioral Science, Hokkaido University, Sapporo, Japan

Prior research has revealed cross-cultural differences in attribution styles. East Asians tend to make more external attributions, whereas North Americans tend to make more internal attributions.. This research aims to unpack the underlying mechanism of these cultural differences in terms of different social structures across culture. In particular, we focus on the relational mobility, defined as "the

amount of opportunities to form new relationships, when necessary in a given society/social context". As predicted, participants who found themselves living in a more relationally mobile environment made stronger internal, as contrasted with external, attribution than those in a less mobile environment.

Development of a Japanese version of the BIS/BAS scale

Kamide, Hiroko Osaka University, Osaka, Japan **Daibo, Ikuo**

This study aimed to develop a Japanese version of the BIS(behavioral inhibition system)/BAS(behavioral activation system) scale to assessing two general motivational systems that underlie behavior and affect. 169 students evaluated a Japanese version of the BIS/BAS scale, MAS (Manifest anxiety Scale), and MPI (Maudsley Personality Inventory). Factor analysis revealed that the Japanese version of the BIS/BAS scale consisted of four factors and corresponded to an original scale (Carver and White, 1994). Correlations among scales also corresponded to the original result. And convergent and discriminate validity in the form of correlations with alternative measures were reported.

Implicit affect influence and explicit judgments: Role of reflective system of evaluation

Karwowska, Dorota Dept. of Psychology, University of Warsaw, Warsaw, Poland

In two studies the impact of implicit affect on judgments was limited by activation of reflective system of evaluation. In Study 1, 90 subjects were randomly assigned to one of two conditions: neutral (subjects compared symbols and decided if they were the same or different); reflective (subjects evaluated "good and bad" aspect of patriotism). In Study 2, we repeated the procedure using different manipulations. In both Studies "the affective priming paradigm" was used as a measure of implicit affect influence. The results show less implicit influence in reflective conditions than in neutral and control ones.

Examination of maintenance factors in school attendance through text mining

Kato, Akiko Faculty of Human Sciences, Waseda University, Saitma, Japan **Katsuragawa, Taisuke** Faculty of Human Sciences, Waseda University, Saitma-Ken Tokorozawa-shi, Japan **Kanno, Jun** Faculty of Human Sciences, Waseda University, Saitma-Ken Tokorozawa-shi, Japan

Unlike the traditional concept of truancy support which focuses on promoting individual's academic adaptation abilities and improving academic maladjustment, the purpose of this study was to investigate the positive factors which promote school attendance from a total point of view, including environmental adjustment. Combination of 319 college students participated in a Correspondence analysis along with a questionnaire on the reason for continuously attending school. As a result, males showed clusters associated with will and growth, while females showed clusters associated with personal relationships and situational control, as the factor for continuous school attendance.

Aimed movement of the arm in individuals with the mental retardation: The role of speed - accuracy trade off

Katsuyoshi, Shinya Dept. of Education, University of the Ryukyus, Okinawa, Japan **Nagato, Kiyoshi** Education, Univ. of the Ryukyus, Okinawa, Japan **Tanaka, Atsushi** Education, Univ. of the Ryukyus, Okinawa, Japan **Ushiyama, Michio** Education, Kyoto Univ. of Education, Kyoto, Japan **Okuzumi, Hideyuki** Education, Tokyo Gakugei Univ., Tokyo, Japan

The purpose of this study was to investigate the role of speed-accuracy in aimed arm movement in

individuals with mental retardation by measuring movement time and accuracy. The subjects were measured on how quickly and accurately they pored liquid into a cup to red line. There were 39 individuals without mental retardation and 38 individuals with mental retardation in the study. In addition, the subjects were classified according to the clinical type (Down's syndrome, autism, and the other mental retardation) and four types which added the individuals without mental retardation there compared and examined.

To aggregate or not to aggregate? Subject areas on judgment achievement: A critical meta-analytic approach

Kaufmann, Esther Inst. für Psychologie, GESS, Mannheim, Germany **Sjödahl, Lars** Malmö School of Education, Lund University, Lund, Sweden **Athanasou, James A.** Faculty of Education, University of Technology, Sydney, Australia **Wittmann, Werner W.** Department of Psychology, Chair II, Mannheim, Germany

Judgment achievement in the framework of SJT (Tucker, 1964) was estimated with the Hunter and Schmidt method (2004) to correct for errors. 29 studies, encompassing 1 041 persons who judged 43 tasks were considered. The overall judgment achievement across different tasks was moderate (.42), but judgment achievement in different topic areas varied from a low (.22, psychological science) to a high (.58, other research areas) level. Finally, the analysis evaluated the influence of single judges, possible moderating factors and critiqued the value of a meta-analysis across tasks or separating in areas on judgment achievement in SJT.

Approaches to direct mailing in fundraising: Argumentative structure and image choice

Keller, Raphaela Inst. für Kommunikationswiss., Universität München, München, Germany **Fahr, Andreas** IfKW, Ludwig-Maximilians-Universität, München, Germany **Brosius, Hans-Bernd** IfKW, Ludwig-Maximilians-Universität, München, Germany

A two-by-three factorial experiment tested how the argumentative structure and choice of images influence the affective, cognitive and motivational reaction of direct-mail recipients. 288 persons were sampled and allocated by quota (sex and age). Two different text versions representing two argumentative structures (exemplification vs. base-rate information) were combined with three different images of a boy in a developing country: One showed the outcome of potential help (positive), another the challenging circumstances (negative) and a third clearly indicated the child's misery (very negative). The findings are interpreted along theoretical assumptions of the exemplification theory and motivational psychology. Approaches for fundraisers are derived: Direct mailings with exemplifications and positive images are particularly influential.

Implicit learning of semantic category sequences

Ketels, Shaw Dept. of Cognitive Science, University of Colorado, Boulder, USA **Healy, Alice** Cognitive Science, University of Colorado, Boulder, USA

Following the work of Goschke and Bolte (2007), we isolated implicit learning and application of abstract information. Participants watched movies of a cursor clicking on 9, 12, or 15 individual clip art images in a random spatial array. They then immediately reproduced the sequences. These sequences were either randomly ordered or consisted of items from 5 categories in a repeating order. Regardless of instruction condition, participants showed an accuracy advantage when the sequences were determined using a set ordering of categories, as compared to randomly generated sequences. The results suggest that individuals can acquire and apply abstract information implicitly.

Investigating the casual relation ship between perfectionism, motive achievement, text anxiety and academic achievement

Kheradmand Mard Del, Khatereh Tehran, Islamic Republic of Iran

Abstract The objective of this research is specifying the existing relation among the perfectionism, motive achievement, text anxiety and academic achievement sampling method is random proportional classified The data was studied, using the Pierson correlation and the Regression analysis, with the following results: The positive perfectionism with the mediation of the motive achievement has a direct relation with the educational development. The negative perfectionism with the mediation of the test anxiety has an indirect relation with the motive achievement. The negative perfection with the mediation of the motive achievement indirectly has an indirect relation with the academic achievement.

A requirement analysis of study specific demands: What requirements of ability and personality do students need to be successful?

Khorramdel, Lale Inst. für Psychologie, Universität Wien, Wien, Austria Maurer, Martina Faculty of Psychology, University of Vienna, Vienna, Austria Kubinger, Klaus D. Faculty of Psychology, University of Vienna, Vienna, Austria

Using Flanagan's Critical Incident Technique different university subjects such as Medicine, Psychology, Sociology, Architecture, Public and Communication, Mechanical Engineering, Business Administration, Economics, and Law were analyzed: The aim was to establish the requirements of ability and personality of adherents for mastering the study specific demands but avoid to drop out. Once these requirements are given, either an obligatory assessment-based selection could be applied or a qualified consulting could be given, even using self-assessments. Students and persons of the academic faculty were interviewed, the respective general results will be given.

The relation between popularity and Theory of mind in school-age children

Kim, Areum Department of Psychology, Chungbuk National University, Chungbuk, Republic of Korea Ghim, Hei-Rhee Department of Psychology, Chungbuk National University, Chungbuk, Republic of Korea

This research investigates the relationship between popularity and Theory of mind in school-age children. Children's popularity were assessed with perceived popularity nominations in a sample of 74 fifth, and sixth grade elementary school students. A sample of 74 children were given measures mind-reading tasks and social behaviors, Index of empathy for Children. Popularity correlated most strongly with their social score, empathy scores, and then with their mindreading ability. Theory-of-mind understanding was related to higher scores of aggressive behavior for boys and prosocial behavior for girls. The results are discussed that being perceived boys and girls as popular is a key determinant of social skills.

Post-error performance optimization by modulation of goal-relevant information processing

King, Joseph Cognitive Neurology, MPI-CBS, Leipzig, Germany von Cramon, D.Y. Cognitive Neurology, MPI-CBS, Leipzig, Germany Ullsperger, Markus Cognitive Neurology, MPI Neurological Research, Köln, Germany

The neural mechanisms underlying the reinstatement of goal-directed behavior following error commission are relatively unknown. The current fMRI study tested the hypothesis that post-error performance is optimized by top-down modulation of goal-relevant information processing. To this end, 21 healthy volunteers performed a high error-rate inducing version of the Simon task comprised of stimuli known to activate a specific region of the ventral visual stream. By weighting post-error related hemodynamic responses with individually observed degrees of post-error behavioral adjustments, we found a dissociation between cognitive control mechanisms selectively amplifying goal-relevant visual attention and inhibiting motor responses primed by goal-irrelevant spatial information.

Gaze following among toddlers

Kishimoto, Takeshi Human Sciences, Osaka University, Suita, Osaka, Japan Shizawa, Yasuhiro Human Sciences, Osaka University, Suita, Osaka, Japan Yasuda, Jun Human Sciences, Osaka University, Suita, Osaka, Japan Hinobayashi, Toshihiko Human Sciences, Osaka University, Suita, Osaka, Japan Minami, Tetsuhiro Human Sciences, Osaka University, Suita, Osaka, Japan

We experimentally investigated whether 3-year-old toddlers could follow their peers' gaze. In the experimental trials, an experimenter induced a child (looker) to look at a doll on display, and observed the reaction of another child (follower) in front of the looker (and not looking at the doll). In the control trials, the experimenter displayed the doll in an identical manner when the follower was alone. The followers followed the gaze of the lookers, looking at the doll in approximately 90% of the experimental trials, compared with 20% of the control. These results indicate that 3-year-olds can follow their peers' gaze.

Perceived caregiver barriers in the management of children's asthma: A qualitative study

Knestel, Andrea Institute of Psychology, Syracuse, USA Raymond, Kimberly P. Psychology, Syracuse University, Syracuse, USA Fiese, Barbara H. Psychology, Syracuse University, Syracuse, USA

Research suggests that poor management of a child's asthma is associated with higher levels of wheezing, activity limitations, and more missed school days. This study investigated caregiver barriers in managing a child's asthma. Primary caregivers of 150 children, ages 5 to 12, with mild to severe asthma, provided narrative responses to a semi-structured interview. Open coding revealed the emergence of five barrier categories: Knowledge, Time, Finances, Healthcare, and Control. With this information, healthcare professional and therapists will be better equipped to help caregivers develop social and emotional coping strategies that will increase effective asthma management.

Decisions below uncertainty: Intuitive and deliberated decision-making and their information processing influenced by the amount of information

Komes, Jessica Erfurt, Germany Ulshoefer, Corina Psychology, University of Erfurt, Erfurt, Germany Geiger, Antje Psychology, University of Erfurt, Gotha, Germany

This study should clarify the opposed hypotheses concerning (1) which is the decision-making style – intuition or deliberation – that leads to more accurate decisions and (2) which kind of information processing – heuristic or automatically-holistic – serve which kind of decision-making style. 49 subjects estimated the prices of menus using Paper-Pencil-Method and a computer animated presentation; while manipulating decision-making styles and the amount of information. The results, using One-way-ANOVA (GLM with repeated measurement), indicate that intuitive decisions are preferable, and that the amount of information and experience are influential on the accuracy of decision making and on the selection of information processing method.

The role of imagination in decision making

Konstantinidis, Andreas Jakovos IPA, Technical University Berlin, Berlin, Germany Jungermann, Helmut IPA, Technical University Berlin, Berlin, Germany

People often base their decisions on the anticipated potential outcomes of the given options and their utilities. Sometimes, however, the presentation of options includes features of the options which seem to be relevant for the decision outcome although they are clearly not relevant at all. But the decision makers imagination is stimulated, evoking an extra utility which determines their choices. Data from an internet-based study with 360 participants support this hypothesis and show the specific influence of the concreteness and the intensity of the (experimentally evoked) imagination. The findings have both theoretical and practical significance for marketing and advertising.

The neuromotor antecedents of emotion regulation in the face

Korb, Sebastian CISA, Université de Geneve, Geneve, Switzerland Grandjean, Didier Faculty of psychology, CISA/Université de Geneve, Geneve, Switzerland Scherer, Klaus Faculty of psychology, CISA/Université de Geneve, Geneve, Switzerland

One form of emotion regulation is the voluntary suppression of one's emotional facial expression. By using Electroencephalography (EEG) and facial Electromyography (EMG) we investigated the neural correlates of spontaneous, posed, and suppressed smiles. In three experimental conditions healthy participants (1) looked at amusing stimuli and freely expressed their feelings; (2) looked at amusing stimuli but suppressed their facial expressions; or (3) looked at neutral stimuli while smiling. Our analyses focused upon the Readiness Potential (RP), which precedes movement-onset. We expected to find a RP before all three types of smile. Preliminary results will be presented.

The dual nature of priming: Logic and associations jointly influence indirect measures of evaluation

Kordts, Robert Inst. für Psychologie, Universität Würzburg, Würzburg, Germany Deutsch, Roland Lehrstuhl Psychologie II, University of Wuerzburg, Wuerzburg, Germany Gawronski, Bertram Department of Psychology, University of Western Ontario, London, ON, Canada Strack, Fritz Lehrstuhl Psychologie II, University of Wuerzburg, Wuerzburg, Germany

Previous research found that implicit measures such as the affective priming assess only valence associations, but not logical reasoning (e.g., negation, Deutsch et al., 2006). As there is evidence that implicit measures vary with respect to underlying processes (e.g., Gawronski et al., in press), we looked at a different priming measure, the affective misattribution procedure (AMP, Payne et al., 2005). Surprisingly, all other conditions being equal, the AMP reflects logical reasoning (valence negation), in contrast to the affective priming paradigm. We further looked at boundary conditions: Negation was not reduced by time pressure, but it was reduced by cognitive load.

Diagnostics of consequences of social deprivation in early childhood

Kostadinova, Krasimira Child&School Health Protection, Nation.Center PublicHealthProt, Sofia, Bulgaria

Creating tools for measurement of the consequences of social deprivation in young children reared in risk environment is important in overcoming them. Objective: To establish approach, dimensions, diagnostic proceedings for assessment of social deprivation process and result. The study covered 266 infants, 120 toddlers, 142 caregivers in institutions applying Developmental scale, experimental assessment of relationships with adults and peers, case study, longitudinal observation, JSS of Spielberger, MBI, and others. The results show a delayed mental development and leading activities, typical somatic symptoms, deprived personality development, and related social characteristics. Social deprivation in early childhood is a complicated phenomenon and needs personality-based complex diagnostic method.

The psychological effects of horticutural therapy on aged people that was implemented every day concentrically
Koura, Sigo Occupational, Kyushu University of H&W, Nobeoka, Miyazaki-Prif., Japan Ogawa, Noriyuki Occupational, Kyushu University of H&W, Nobeoka, Miyazaki-Prif., Japan Oshikawa, Takeshi Occupational, Kyushu University of H&W, Nobeoka, Miyazaki-Prif., Japan
An attempt was made to develop a geriatric care technique characterized and investigate the psychological effects by the use of horticultural therapy that stimulates the senses in nursing homes. The effects of every day activities on horticultural therapy evaluation sheet, the face scales and PGC morale scales were improved more than every week activities. Even if the object person and clients changed, it was suggested that horticultural therapy activities be suitable as a nursing care for elderly people technology because neither atmosphere nor the smile changed. These results suggested that horticultural therapy for aged people improved psychological and behavioral aspects.

Individual differences in decision making about investing money for future pension
Kovalev, Yuri Dept. of Psychology, St. Petersburg University, St. Petersburg, Russia
Objectives – main goal of research was - how different people make decision about investing pension money in governmental asset management company (with low income) or private asset management company (with high income). Methods – was used original questionnaire designed for Russian sample and socioeconomic data. Participants 76 male and 83 female in age 28-32 with higher education (half in economics and half in humanities); Results - the evidence of this study suggests that not type of education but sex and marital status should dictate choice for people. Conclusions - decision about most conservative investment is most typical for married men and women.

Comparison of typological and dimensional approaches in business focused measurement of personality
Krüger, Claudia Zentrum für Testentwicklung, Universität Fribourg, Granges-Paccot, Switzerland
Based on the widespread agreement on the Five Factor Model as dimensional approach to personality, research on typological approaches has increased recently. This study focuses on the merit of this perspective for occupational personality assessment. The BIP-6F (Business Focused Inventory of Psychology - 6 Factors; Hossiep & Krüger, in prep.) measures 6 global dimensions of personality, relevant in the professional context. Using the BIP-6F, personality types are extracted from a working sample (N=3169) and compared to Big-Five based cluster solutions. The criterion validity of types compared to dimensions is tested and incremental insights using the typological approach are presented.

The Janus face of self-selection and self-generation in source monitoring: Early abilities and late inabilities in 3-, 4- and 5-year-old children
Kraus, Uta Inst. für Psychologie, Universität zu Kiel, Kiel, Germany Koehnken, Guenter Inst. für Psychologie, Universität zu Kiel, Kiel, Germany
Source attributions to real-person-sources were examined. Forty-eight children (M=38, M=45, M=56, M=65) were presented 4 sticker book pages. On each page, two person-sources (child-adult/child-child) per source term (reality-monitoring familiar; realty-monitoring unfamiliar; external; internal source monitoring) chose two wildlife-stickers, pasted them into the book and described what each animal was doing. Source recall was examined immediately afterwards. Results showed source attributions above chance in all age groups in the reality-monitoring terms and in the external terms in older 3-, 4- and 5-year-olds (t-tests). Results indicate that children conceptualized the internal sources as a sole source and failed to attribute them correctly.

Because it matters to me: Differential emotion elicitation by experimental manipulation of self-relevance and goal conduciveness appraisals
Kreibig, Sylvia D. Inst. für Psychologie, Universität Genf, Geneva, Switzerland Gendolla, Guido H. E. Dep't of Psychology, University of Geneva, Geneva, Switzerland Scherer, Klaus R. Dep't of Psychology, University of Geneva and Swiss, Geneva, Switzerland
Based on Scherer's (2001) Component Process Model and Gendolla's (2004) elaboration of Motivational Intensity Theory, we investigated the prediction that motivation-based appraisals differentially determine emotional responding. Participants' appraisal of self-relevance (low/high) and goal conduciveness (low/high) was experimentally manipulated using the success-failure manipulation (Nummenmaa & Niemi, 2004). Self-report indicated increased disappointment and embarrassment in the high-self-relevance/low-goal-conduciveness condition and increased amusement and pride in the high self-relevance/high-goal-conduciveness condition. Autonomic nervous system reactivity showed sympathetic discharge in response to self-relevance manipulation and respiratory and facial expressive changes in response to goal-conduciveness manipulation. Implications of results regarding motivational processes in emotion elicitation are discussed.

Prevalence of disturbed eating behaviour in girls with insulin dependent diabetes mellitus and the influence of disturbed eating behaviour on metabolic control (HbA1c)
Kristensen, Lene Juel Dept. of Psychology, University of Århus, Århus C., Denmark Thastum, Mikael Department of psychology, University of Århus, Århus C., Denmark Schnieber, Anette Department of psychology, University of Århus, Århus C., Denmark Mose, Anne Hvarregaard Departments of Paediatrics, Aarhus University Hospital, Århus N., Denmark Birkebæk, Niels Department of Paediatrics, Aarhus University Hospital, Århus N., Denmark
Girls with diabetes mellitus (DM) (N = 21, age 11-17 years) completed measures of objective overeating episodes (OOE) and objective bulimic episodes (OBE) from the EDE-Q. Data regarding metabolic control (HbA1c) were obtained through a national diabetes register. 41 % of the girls had one or more episodes of OOE, and 29 % had one or more episodes of OBE in the preceding month. Significant higher HbA1c were found among girls with than without episodes of OOE (9.1 versus 8.1, p = .033), and among girls with than without episodes of OBE (9.4 versus 8.1, p = .013).

Effects of the number and the order of syllables in the articulatory suppression effect
Kroneisen, Meike Lehrstuhl für Psychologie III, Univerität Mannheim, Mannheim, Germany Erdfelder, Edgar Lehrstuhl für Psychologie III, Universität Mannheim, Mannheim, Germany
Short-term memory is known to deteriorate if irrelevant syllables are articulated during retention. The working memory model posits that this articulatory suppression (AS) effect is unaffected by what is being articulated. We tested whether the number of syllables (0 to 4) and their order (word-like vs. inverted sequences) affects the strength of the AS effect on immediate serial recall of letter sequences. The AS effect increased with number of syllables and was smaller for word-like sequences of three or more syllables. Results are most parsimoniously explained by assuming that the episodic buffer supports retention of verbal information under AS.

The effects of task instruction on P300 amplitude in a concealed information test
Kubo, Kenta Graduate School of Integrated, Hiroshima university, Higashi-Hiroshima, Japan Nittono, Hiroshi Integrated Arts and Sciences, Hiroshima university, Higashi-Hiroshima, Japan
Event-related brain potentials were recorded in a concealed information test to examine the effect of task instruction. Eighteen participants selected one playing card from five and were told that the experimenter would detect the card on the basis of their physiological responses. In the suppress condition, participants were instructed to make their responses smaller to leave the card undetected. In the enhance condition, they were instructed to make their responses larger to allow the experimenter to detect the selected card. Regardless of the instruction type, the P300 amplitude was significantly larger for the selected card than for the not-selected cards.

Comparison of identification procedures for intellectually gifted preschool children
Kuger, Susanne BiKS-Forschungsgruppe, Universität Bamberg, Bamberg, Germany Ebert, Susanne BiKS research group, University of Bamberg, Bamberg, Germany Dubowy, Minja BiKS research group, University of Bamberg, Bamberg, Germany Weinert, Sabine BiKS research group, University of Bamberg, Bamberg, Germany
Regarding concept and realization, integrative and comparable research about early intellectual giftedness and its adequate promotion is rare. Identification procedures for scientific and educational purposes are commonly based on Spearman's theory of a general factor of intelligence or else on Gardner's theory of multiple intelligences sometimes expressed as 'cognitive profiles'. Using data of 547 children in the longitudinal study BiKS-3-8, which surveys children and their environments (family and preschool) from their entry to preschool, this analysis compares different identification procedures and their validation throughout one year. Results will be discussed focusing on implications for the educational practice.

Functions of autobiographical remembering in situational and cultural contexts
Kulkofsky, Sarah HDFS, Texas Tech University, Lubbock, USA Wang, Qi Human Development, Cornell University, Ithaca, USA Hou, Yubo Psychology, Peking University, Beijing, USA
The present research examined functions of remembering across situational and cultural contexts. In study 1, European-American and Asian-American undergraduates described memories in two hypothetical contexts: thinking about an event alone, or sharing an event with friends. In study 2, European-American and Chinese students reported memories in response to cue-words. For

each memory students reported when and why they thought about and talked about the memory. In both studies, students reported remembering for social, directive, and self functions. Situational and cultural contexts influenced the functions that were reported. The results are discussed in light of the influence of context on remembering.

Cross-correlation functions demonstrate offset effects in the covariance of endocrine and subjective-psychological responses to psychosocial stress

Kumsta, Robert School of Psychology, University of Southampton, Southampton, United Kingdom Schlotz, Wolff School of Psychology, University of Southampton, Southampton, United Kingdom Entringer, Sonja Psychiatry and Human Behavior, University of Irvine, Orange, USA Jones, Alexander MRC Epidemiology Resource Cent, University of Southampton, Southampton, United Kingdom Hellhammer, Dirk Department of Psychobiology, University of Trier, Trier, Germany Wüst, Stefan Department of Psychobiology, University of Trier, Trier, Germany

Although stress response theories typically assume substantial correlations of psychological and endocrine stress responses, studies of psycho-endocrine covariance produced inconsistent results. To examine if this is due to different dynamics of the systems, we repeatedly and synchronously measured hypothalamus-pituitary-adrenal (HPA) axis activity and tense and energetic arousal in response to a psychosocial laboratory stressor in 221 subjects. Cross-correlation analyses showed significant time lagged correlations of tense arousal with HPA-axis responses. These results demonstrate offset effects in the covariance of psycho-endocrine stress responses and suggest that analyses of psycho-endocrine covariance need to take different dynamics of response systems into account.

Depression association between dysmenorrhea and menstrual distress in adolescence girls

Kuo, Chin-Jung College of Public Health, Environmental Health, Taichung, Taiwan Kuo, Hsien-Wen College of Public Health, Environmental Health, Taichung, Taiwan

Abstract Objective?We investigated the relationship between levels of depression and primary dysmenorrheal among adolescent girls. Method?Cross-sectional study design was performed a senior high school in Taiwan. All subject (n=680) were interviewed using a questionnaire including 18 Moos Menstrual Distress question (MMDQ) and the Center for Epidemiologic Studies-Depression Scale (CES-D). Results?A significant effect of depression status on the MMDQ score was found using a logistic regression model adjusted for covariance. Conclusion?The data show that association dose-depended between depression status and MMDQ score.

Relationship between gonadal steroids and brain activation patterns during emotion processing in women

Lamplmayr, Elisabeth Inst. für Psychologie, Universität Wien, Wien, Austria Kryspin-Exner, Ilse Faculty of Psychology, University of Vienna, Wien, Austria Bauer, Herbert Faculty of Psychology, University of Vienna, Wien, Austria Derntl, Birgit Klinik für Psychiatrie und Psy, Universitätsklinikum Aachen RW, Aachen, Germany

Findings concerning sex differences in neuropsychological functions are contradictory. One possible explanation for these inconsistencies is the influence of gonadal steroids on neural functions. In females gonadal steroids underlie profound fluctuations. Different levels across the menstrual cycle could either cause or mask sex differences in neuropsychological functions and brain activation. In the present study hormone levels at different points in the menstrual cycle are assessed and correlated with neuropsychological functions on the one hand and electrical brain activation during emotional processing on the other hand. Preliminary results will be presented.

Sexual behaviour, drug abuse and tobacco abuse among the street children

Lamsal, Shyam Community Health Nursing, B. P. Koirala Inst. of Health, Dharan, Nepal Walia, Indarjit Community Health Nursing, Post Grad Inst od Med Edu and, Chandigarh, India

Among the 100 children, Forty-two subjects had sexual exposure at various age with either girlfriend or prostitute in which two subjects were homosexual. Seventy subjects were substance/s abusers, which included 49 alcohol abusers, 48 smokers, 42 tobacco chewers, 3 injectable drug abusers and 51 various other types of substance/s abusers. Majority of the children were uncertain about the amount and frequency of the substance/s they abuse except the tobacco chewers where majority i.e. 28 chew one or two packets of tobacco per week.

Explaining the entrepreneurial intentions of young people: A cross-cultural study

Lanero, Ana Social Psychology, Faculty of Psychology, Salamanca, Spain Sánchez, José C. Social Psychology, Faculty of Psychology, Salamanca, Spain Villanueva, José J. Social Psychology, Faculty of Psychology, Salamanca, Spain Yurrebaso, Amaia Social Psychology, Faculty of Psychology, Salamanca, Spain

The aim of this study was to analyze the differences between Spanish and Mexican young people in entrepreneurial intentions and other psychological variables frequently linked with entrepreneurship, such as entrepreneurial self-efficacy, risk-taking propensity and proactiveness. We collected self-report data from 150 Spanish and 165 Mexicans, all of them University students. MANOVA was carried out in order to prove cross-cultural differences in entrepreneurial intentions and the other psychological variables. According to expected, Mexicans showed higher levels of entrepreneurial intentions, self-efficacy, risk-taking propensity and proactiveness than Spanish. The study suggests several ways of promoting self employment, specially directed to Spanish university students.

The relationship among creativity, motivation and well-being of children

Lee, Mina Child Education and Psychology, Sung Kyun Kwan University, Seoul, Republic of Korea Um, Jee-Hong Child Education and Psychology, SungKyunKwan University, Seoul, Republic of Korea Choe, In-Soo Child Education and Psychology, SungKyunKwan University, Seoul, Republic of Korea

The purpose of this study was to investigate the relationship among motivation (intrinsic, material, social), creativity (creative thinking, creative personality) and well-being (emotional, social, psychological). 'Motivation scale'(Choe,2002), 'Creativity Inventory for young Students'(Choe, 2005) and 'Well-being scale'(Keyes, 2005) were administered to 155 6th grade elementary students. Correlation analysis demonstrated that intrinsic motivation and material motivation, but not social motivation, were significantly related to creativity and well-being. Also, creativity was significantly related to emotional and psychological well-being except social one. Using multiple regression analysis, intrinsic motivation, material motivation and creativity revealed a significant contribution to the prediction of psychological well-being.

The Lee cross-cultural anxiety dream scale: An extended study

Lee, Sang-Bok Pastoral Counseling Graduate, Kangnam University, Yongin, Republic of Korea

This study analyzed anxiety dream scale as represented in dream contents of both 476 Korean college students and 165 Korean-American college students. A total of 258 dreams were collected and evaluated by using the Lee Cross-cultural Dream Scale, for which the intensity of anxiety was coded. A two-sample t test on the Lee Cross-cultural Anxiety Dream Scale means (Korean Group: M=1.8; Korean American Group: M=2.4) showed significant difference between the two groups (p<0.001). Two-sample t test on anxiety by gender (Female: M=2.3/ Male: M=1.8) was significant (p<0.01). The author designed this scale to explore cross-cultural comparisons of anxiety dream scales.

Context-dependency of information as a function of task experience

Leon, Samuel P. Psychology, University of Jaen, Jaen, Spain Ramos Alvarez, Manuel Miguel Dept. of Psychology, University of Jaen, Jaen, Spain Abad, Maria J.F. Psychology, University of Jaen, Jaen, Spain Rosas, Juan M. Psychology, University of Jaen, Jaen, Spain

Attentional theories of learning and memory suggest that there is a reversal relationship between the experience with the task and the attention participants pay to the context. A human instrumental conditioning experiment was conducted in which the influence of the training level (3, 5 or 8 trials) on the magnitude of the context-switch effect was evaluated. Performance was impaired by the context switch only after 3 training trials. Experience with an incidental context seems to lead participants to stop paying attention to it, and to quit using the context as a relevant factor for their performance in the task.

The psychometric properties of the Depression-Happiness Scale short-form and the Oxford Happiness Questionnaire short-form among Slovak students

Lewis, Christopher Alan School of Psychology, University of Ulster at Magee, Londonderry, United Kingdom Adamovová, Lucia Institute of Experimental Psyc, Slovak Academy of Sciences, Bratislava,, Slovak Republic

Objectives: To facilitate cross-cultural research in the psychology of happiness, the present aim was to examine the psychometric properties of the Slovak translation of the 6-item Depression-Happiness Scale and the 8-item short-form of the Oxford Happiness Questionnaire. Method: A sample of 151 Slovak university students completed the two translated measures. Results: Support was found for the internal reliability, unidimensionality and convergent validity of the two translated measures. Conclusions: These results suggest that both of these short measures could be commended for further use among Slovak respondents when a brief measure of happiness is required. Limitations of the present study are discussed.

Importance of ratings in self-estimated intelligence: A means of validation?

Lewis, Christopher Alan School of Psychology, University of Ulster at Magee, Londonderry, United Kingdom Cruise, Sharon Mary Department of Psychology, University of Chester, Chester, United Kingdom

Objectives: Previous research has examined the influence of beliefs about intelligence on how individuals estimate their own intelligence. However, no research has examined importance ratings of self-estimates of intelligence as a means of validating self-ratings. Method: 455 participants provided self-estimates in ten domains of intelligence, and rated the degree to which they endorsed the importance of each domain of intelligence. Results: Correlation analyses indicated small to moderate significant positive associations between importance ratings and self-estimates of domains of intelligence. Conclusion: These findings attest to the role of importance as a means of establishing the construct validity of self-estimated intelligence.

The test and revision of Hewitt Multi–dimensional Perfectionism Scale for Chinese college students

Li, Na Faculty of Education, Qufu Normal University, Qufu, People's Republic of China Li, Jianwei Faculty of Education, Qufu Normal University, Qufu, People's Republic of China

1959 college students were tested, and then the exploratory and confirmatory factor analysis was applied to the data, at last the α coefficients, 1 month interval test-retest reliabilities and other factors were computed. The revised Scale consisted of 15 items, and explained 49.55? of the variance with loading between 0.49~0.77. And x2,RMSEA,NFI,CFI,GFI met requirements of psychological assessment. The α coefficients of the scale and sub–scales and test-retest reliabilities were over 0.65. The revised Scale for Chinese college students is more suitable for use among the native students.

Effects of 1+2 training pattern for phonemic awareness on English words decoding

Li, Tsingan School of Psychology, Beijing Normal University, Beijing, People's Republic of China Li, Xin Cui School of Psychology, Beijing Normal University, Beijing, People's Republic of China Lin, Chongde School of Psychology, Beijing Normal University, Beijing, People's Republic of China

To investigate effects of 1+2 training for phonemic awareness on English words decoding, a pretest-posttest comparison group quasi-experimental design was adopted, 89 grade 3 pupils were assigned to three groups: Scheme A, Scheme B and comparison groups. Schemes A and B were characterized by integrated training of phonemic awareness with phonetic symbol and letter-sound correspondences (1+2), nonetheless, Scheme A involved phonemic segmentation and blending, whereas Scheme B involved phonemic identification, segmentation, blending, deletion and substitution. It was found that both Schemes A and B could significantly enhance decoding skills, however, there was no significant differences between two Schemes.

The inactivation of the basolateral amygdala disrupts contextual, but not discrete cue conditioned association in morphine-induced cue preference

Li, Jie KLMH, Institute of Psychology, Beijing, People's Republic of China Wu, Yan KLMH, Institute of Psychology,CAS, Beijing, People's Republic of China Li, Yonghui KLMH, Institute of Psychology,CAS, Beijing, People's Republic of China Sui, Nan KLMH, Institute of Psychology,CAS, Beijing, People's Republic of China

The authors examined the effects of the basolateral amygdala (BLA) in morphine related contextual and discrete cue conditioning. The apparatus for conditioned cue preference paradigm was consisted of three compartments (contextual conditioning) or one compartment (discrete cue conditioning). Prior to conditioning sessions rats received intra-BLA injections of lidocaine. Time in the morphine-paired side minus saline-paired side was analyzed by using two-way analyses of variance. The results show BLA inactivation selectively impaired acquisition of context-morphine association without interfering with discrete cue-morphine association. These observations are compatible with the view that BLA contributes to contextual, but not elemental conditioning in fear conditioning.

The development and validation of the Chinese clinical multi-axial inventory

Li, Xixi Department of Psychology, Chinese University of HK, Hong Kong, China, People's Republic of : Hong Kong SAR Leung, Freedom Department of Psychology, Chinese University of HK, Hong Kong, China, People's Republic of : Macao SAR

Large scale self-report personality inventory is the most frequently used tool in psychological assessment. However, there has not yield an indigenous and theoretically sound clinical instrument for Chinese clinicians. The present study intends to develop the Chinese Clinical Multiaxial Inventory (CCMI) that corresponds closely to modern conceptualization of psychopathology with the multiaxial DSM system. The CCMI is designed to assess: 1) Axis-I clinical symptoms; 2) Axis-II disordered personality features; and 3) psychosocial adjustment. The reliability and construct validity of the CCMI scales will be examined and the standardization will be conducted using a large data-set of psychiatric and normal samples.

PTSD and chronic pain: Development, maintenance and comorbidity

Liedl, Alexandra BZFO, Berlin, Germany Knaevelrud, Christine Research Department, Center for Torture Victims, Berlin, Germany

Objectives: In addition to Posttraumatic Stress Disorder (PTSD) 30-80% of traumatized individuals also suffer from chronic pain1. Methods: A review of the current literature on mechanisms of development, maintenance and comorbidity of PTSD and chronic pain will be provided. Results: Based on the review the "Perpetual Avoidance Model" was developed. Consequential treatment implications will be presented. Conclusions: The presented model helps to understand the development and maintenance of these two disorders and the way how they interact, which is of crucial importance for treatment. 1 Otis JD, Keane TM, Kerns RD (2003) An examination of the relationship between chronic pain and posttraumatic stress disorder. J Rehabil Res Dev 40:397-406

Mobile phones use in classroom activities: A psycho-social educational approach

Ligorio, Maria Beatrice Psychology, University of Bari, Bari, Italy Tateo, Luca Education Sciences, University of Salerno, Fisciano (SA), Italy

The contribution presents a positive model of mobile phones use in educational context, based on empirical evidences of technologies supporting reflexive thinking, meta-cognition and collaborative problem solving into classroom activities. Within a EU funded project, 40 high school students have been involved in a collaborative problem solving activity and asked to video-record the relevant moments of the work with their own mobile phones. The videos constitute the stimulus for a classroom discussion which have been video re-corded and analyzed by researchers. Results show that mobile technology can effectively support collaborative learning activities.

Race, culture and psychotherapy

Lijtmaer, Ruth Ridgewood, USA

In the US, race and culture are used stereotypically; therefore we have chasms that go unacknowledged. Therapists may misjudge the verbalizations of the patient, attributing the patient's behavior only to pathology if they are unaware of the significance of race and culture in people's lives. Even if both members of the dyad are of similar background, we cannot take the patient's conflicts for granted. The clinician's ethnic biases and psychodynamic beliefs influence identifying what is pathological and consequently the therapeutic process. The presentation will focus on the challenges therapist's face when working with patients different from them.

Children's conceptions of death and suicide

Lin, Siu-Fung Dept. Applied Social Studies, City University of Hong Kong, Kowloon, China, People's Republic of : Hong Kong SAR Yuen, Tracy Applied Social Studies, City University of Hong Kong, Kowloon, China, People's Republic of : Macao SAR

Irreversibility, nonfunctionality, and universality of Death and the concept of suicide are considered understood by most children by age 7-10 years. A total of forty 4 to 5-year-olds and 7-8 year olds were recruited to examine whether education programme would foster the development of death concept and thus affect children's attitude towards suicidal behaviour in later life. A local popular video clip extracted from an animation "My life as McDull" was used for exploring the concept of death among very young children in HK while a short story "The poisonous apple" was used to investigate children's dis/approval of killing oneself.

The compilation of perfectionism scale for Chinese adolescents and youths

Lin, Yanyan Faculty of Education, Jining University, Jining, Jingning, People's Republic of China Li, Jianwei Faculty of Education, Qufu Normal University, Qufu, People's Republic of China

We compiled a Native Perfectionism Scale for Chinese adolescents and youths that fits the Chinese cultural background. The Scale consisted of 38 items, six subscales?Perfect Expectation, Personal Standards, Concerns with Mistakes and Doubts, Organization, Introspection, Parents' Expectation and Control?. Factor analysis indicated that the six factors explain 55.35? of the variance with loading between 0.52~0.82.The seven subscales had internal consistencies with split-half reliabilities 0.78~0.87,Cronbach's alphas 0.82~0.92, and test-retest reliabilities of 0.80~0.91?p<0.01?. The Scale is well practical.

Hydration and cognitive performance of secondary school children

Ling, Jonathan Dept. of Psychology, Keele University, Newcastle-under-Lyme, United Kingdom Stephens, Richard Psychology, Keele University, Newcastle-under-Lyme, United Kingdom Hodges, Katie Psychology, Keele University, Newcastle-under-Lyme, United Kingdom

Objectives: Research has suggested a relationship between hydration and cognitive performance. While evidence for this relationship is robust for adults, the data for children is unconvincing. Methods: The cognitive performance of children hydrated with 500ml of water was compared with those hydrated with 50ml of water in a randomised cross-over design. After a short interval, children completed 4 tests measuring cognitive function. Results: Performance on 3 of 4 tests was improved in the 500ml hydration condition compared to the control (p<.002). Conclusions: Increased hydration in children can lead to improvements in performance, specifically short- and long-term memory and executive function.

Effect of epistemic motives on group creativity under different cultures

Liou, Shyhnan Dept. of Labor Relations, National Chung Cheng Uni., Chia-Yi, Taiwan

This study proposes that need for cognitive closure(NFC)influence group creativity under different cultures through dual routes which include promoting group centrism and motivating cultural conformity. Experiment 1 tests the effects of NFC on divergent and convergent performance of group creativity under different cultures (interdependent vs. independent) (H1 & H2). Experiment 2 examines the moderating function of dissent expression (promote divergent thinking, H3)and transformational leadership(promote divergent and convergent thinking, H4)on NFC effects, thus functional dissociate those dual routes. Results support H1 to H3, and H4 partially.

The study of emotional intelligence and interaction between peers for elementary students

Lo, Pin-Hsin and Counseling, Dept. of Education. Psychology, Taipei, Taiwan

We try to edit a scale to evaluate the interactions among schoolchildren, and then to explore the relationship between schoolmates' interaction and emotional intelligence. We use questionnaire for 1393 elementary students. Data gathered is processed with "confirmatory factor analysis", "reliability analysis", "one-way MANOVA", and "t-test". We find: First, schoolgirls interact more positively, compared with schoolboys. Second, the development of positive and negative interaction between peers for the sixth grade is more obvious than other grades. Third, schoolchildren who score high in emotional intelligence interact more positively with each other than those who score low in emotional intelligence.

Attention modifies gender differences in face recognition

Lovén, Johanna Karolinska Institutet, Aging Research Center, Stockholm, Sweden Rehnman, Jenny Karolinska Institutet, Aging Research Center, Stockholm, Sweden Herlitz, Agneta Karolinska Institutet, Aging Research Center, Stockholm, Sweden

Women recognize more faces than men do. This advantage is more prominent for female faces and may depend on women directing more attention to female than to male faces. To assess this, participants completed two face recognition tasks: one with full and one with divided attention at encoding. Gender differences, favouring women, were reduced when attention was divided, as compared to the full attention condition. Preliminary results suggest that gender differences for female faces vary as a function of the degree of available attention. Thus, women may attend more to female than to male faces, resulting in more accurate recognition.

Can "less" be "more" in group decision making?

Luan, Shenghua School of Social Sciences, Singapore Management Univ., Singapore, Singapore Katsikopoulos, Konstantinos Human Development, Max Planck Institute, Berlin, Germany Reimer, Torsten Communications, University of Maryland, College Park, Maryland, USA

We compared the decision performance of two groups in this study: one with members using the Take-the-best (TTB) strategy and the other with members using the Minimalist (MIN) strategy. While TTB requires members to have precise knowledge about the task environment, MIN requires them to know nothing. It turned out that the ignorant MIN group can beat the knowledgeable TTB group in environments where information is more evenly distributed among the cues. Moreover, this group-level less-is-more effect will be magnified when group size is large, knowledge has to be acquired through learning, and cues' information is subject to errors.

Industrial psychology in the (sometimes) contradictory context of workplace- and lifestyle-enhancement

Lueken, Kai Prevention, Unfallkasse Rheinland-Pfalz, Andernach, Germany Simon, Wenke Prevention, Unfallkasse Rheinland-Pfalz, Andernach, Germany Stoewesandt, Antje Prevention, Unfallkasse Rheinland-Pfalz, Andernach, Germany

Industrial psychological research traditionally resorts to workplace enhancement methods. On the one hand it is obvious that activities focussing the working conditions are in the long term more effective and efficient than behavior-related train-

ings. But on the other hand more health related approaches focussing on individual ressources might be more accepted by the focus group and the social partners. Progressive Workplace Health Management allows for both approaches. The results of several employee attitude surveys in the public sector (n $\asymp$ 17.000) are presented and show in which way the approaches are combined. They provide support for a modern interpretation of reliable psychological knowledge.

The importance of the type of information in the misinformation paradigm

Luna, Karlos Basic Psychological Processes, Univ. of the Basque Country, San Sebastián, Spain Migueles, Malen Basic Psychological Processes, Univ of the Basque Country, Donostia-San Sebastián, Spain

Using the misinformation paradigm we investigated the type of contents that are more conducive to generating false memories. In three experiments the participants watched a video about a bank robbery and received false misinformation through a questionnaire. The misinformation could be about an action or a detail (Exp. 1), central or peripheral information (Exp. 2) and high or low typicality (Exp. 3). In general, there were more false alarms with details, with peripheral information and with high typicality contents. This results suggest the importance of the type of information in the creation of false memories with ecological materials.

The development of Adolescent Authentic Happiness Questionnaire

Luo, Yueh-Chuan National Taiwan Unversity, Taipei, Taiwan Lin, Yicheng Department Psychology, National Taiwan Unversity, Taipei, Taiwan

Based on the model of authentic happiness (Seligman, 2000), this study aims to develop adolescent authentic happiness questionnaire. Taiwan Adolescent Authentic Happiness Questionnaire was developed with 978 subjects recruited from five junior and senior high schools. The principal component analysis with Varimax rotation and confirmatory factor analysis were used to examine the factor structure of the scale. The results showed that 18 items were grouped into 4 dimensions: self-actualization, altruistic happiness, interpersonal relationship, and family happiness, that accounted for 53?of the total variance explained. All of the18 items had factor loadings higher than .40 and external validities were pretty good.

Career choice and apprenticeship. Do migrant and native students differ?

Müller, Romano Inst. für Bildungspsychologie, Pädagog. Hochschule Bern, Bern, Switzerland

Six independent variables were supposed to be of importance for the vocational process of adolescents from different cultural background, SES and sex: educational prerequisites; intelligence; vocational goals, self-efficacy; proximal barriers and support. The dependent variable was defined by "level of the assigned profession". Variables were modelled following the guidelines of the socio-cognitive career theory SCCT. An electronic questionnaire was submitted to 5201 apprentices in 64 professions (Swiss-natives: 4208; migrants: 993; age: 19;2). Analyses by SEM. Independently of cultural, social background and sex 48% of the variance of the assigned level of profession can be explained by the SCCT-model. The impact of proximal variables remains negligible. Apprentices from a migrant background are disadvantaged.

Students' handling of graphs in university

Marín Oller, Cristina San Sebastián de Los Reyes, Spain Pérez Echeverría, María del Puy Psicología Básica, Universidad Autónoma de Madrid, Madrid, Spain Postigo Angón, Yolanda Psicología Básica, Universidad Autónoma de Madrid, Madrid, Spain

The fundamental aim of this research is to analyse psychology students' skills to read and interpret graphic information, and more concretely: to analyse the possible differences between recognition (selection) and interpretation of graphs and to study the influence of familiarity with graph's content (psychological-non psychological), in relation with the participant's amount of instruction in psychology. We found significative differences according to the following variables: familiarity with content; kind of task (selection/ interpretation) and instruction level of participants.

Dimensionality and correlates of the social dominance orientation scale on Croatian sample

Maricic, Jelena Institute of Social Sciences, Zagreb, Croatia Franc, Renata Psychology, Institute of social sciences, Zagreb, Croatia Sakic, Vlado Psychology, Institute of social sciences, Zagreb, Croatia

The aim of the study is to explore structure and correlates of the SDO Scale on Croatian nationally representative sample (N=1004). Factor and correlational analysis, and ANOVAs were conducted. Results confirm two-dimensional factor structure, named oppositions to equality and group-based dominance. Opposition to equality is higher among males, less religious and right politically orientated people (p<0,01). Higher group-based dominance orientation is more characteristic for low income group and low education level, older age (p<0,01), and males (p<0,05). Results are discussed in relations to Croatian social context and to results from previous studies about SDO scale in different countries.

How are we including our pupils with Emotional and Behavioural Difficulties (EBD)?

Martin, Ana Educational Psychology, Universidad Autonoma de Madrid, Madrid, Spain Martin, Elena Educational Psychology, Universidad Autonoma de Madrid, MADRID, Spain Sandoval, Marta Educational Psychology, Universidad Autonoma de Madrid, MADRID, Spain

The aim of this study is to understand the problems faced by the educative system in Madrid when trying to include pupils with EBD (Wagner et al., 2006; Clough et al., 2005). The method used combines questionnaires that assess characteristics and resources of schools and individual variables, which are answered by pupils, their parents, teachers, school counsellors, head teachers and professionals from Mental Health Services; and focus groups with a smaller sample. Some of the obstacles described by participants are: lack of training, difficulties in collaboration with external services, or negative attitudes towards their inclusion. Guidelines for educative-policies are offered.

Differential outcomes: Improving memory in five and seven-year-old children

Martinez, Lourdes Neurociencias y CC de la Salud, Universidad de Almeria, Almeria, Spain Plaza, Victoria Neurociencias y CC de la Salud, Universidad de Almería, Almería, Spain Ortega, Elena Neurociencias y CC de la Salud, Universidad de Almería, Almería, Spain Fuentes, Luis Psicología Básica y Metodologí, Universidad de Murcia, Murcia, Spain F. Estévez, Ángeles Neurociencias y CC de la Salud, Universidad de Almería, Almería, Spain

Until recently, no one had explicitly addressed the issue of whether the differential outcomes procedure (DOP) might improve memory performance in humans. To explore this issue, in the present study children were trained on a conditional discrimination task and then they were tested after 1 day, 1 hour and 1 week from this training phase. The results indicated that participants showed higher performance and persistence of learning when DO were arranged. This finding demonstrated that the use of the DOP facilitate long-term memory in children and suggest its use as aid to memory in people with memory impairments.

Suppression of the pain experience enhances interpretation biases of ambiguous stimuli

Masedo, Ana I. Personalidad, Evaluación, Universidad de Málaga, Málaga, Spain Masedo Gutiérrez, Ana I. Personalidad, Evaluación y Tra, Universidad de Málaga, Málaga, Spain Esteve Zarazaga, M. Rosa Personalidad, Evaluación y Tra, Universidad de Málaga, Málaga, Spain

Objectives We wanted to study if suppression of the pain experience could play a role in the development of cognitive biases. Method Participants were randomly allocated to one of the next conditions: suppression, acceptation and spontaneous coping strategies. After the intervention participants completed the cold pressor task while engaging in the relevant coping strategy. Cognitive biases were assessed at the end of the follow up session. Results and conclusion There was a significant effect of the experimental condition on bias towards affective vs sensory pain words. Participants in the suppression condition showed a stronger bias towards sensory and affective pain.

How to control epistemic uncertainty fifty-fifty

Masuda, Shinya Nursing and Medical Care, Keio University, Fujisawa, Japan Sakagami, Takayuki Psychology, Keio University, Minato-ku, Tokyo, Japan Hirota, Sumire Environmental and Information, Musashi Inst. of Technology, Tsuzuki-ku,Yokohama, Kanagawa, Japan

We examined the joint effect of anchoring and epistemic uncertainty (Bruine de Buin et al., 1998) in an experimental survey. 101 respondents estimated eight personal risk questionnaires which followed one of three different probabilities (20, 50, and 80%) as an exemplar for answering a questionnaire. Results from the open-ended responses showed that frequencies of the 50% response disappeared when probability of the exemplar was 20% or 80%, but they were highest in six out of eight questionnaires when it was 50%. Epistemic uncertainty seems to be controlled not only by answering methods, but also by anchoring items.

Psychological mechanisms in the development of chronic headache in patients with migraine or tension type headache

Matatko, Nadine Klinik für Neurologie, Universitätsklinikum Essen, Essen, Germany Fritsche, Günther Klinik für Neurologie, Universitätsklinikum Essen, Essen, Germany

Objectives: Our prospective, population based longitudinal study investigated the interaction of biological factors, psychiatric comorbidity, stress exposure and headache-coping in transformation of episodic to chronic headache (CH). Methods: 1) Cross-sectional comparison (CH (n=43) vs. non-CH (n=344)); 2) longitudinal regression (baseline and 1-year follow-up; in n=325 headache remained episodic, n=19 developed CH); 3) matched pairs for chronic patients. Dependent variables: Stress exposure, social support, emotional, cognitive and coping reaction to headache. Results: CH-patients are impaired in depression (p=.000), stress experience (p=.005) and seeking social support (p=.002). Discussion: CH-prevention could be possible by training patients in functional stress coping and social skills.

The present conditions of the dysuria patients in Japan

Matsuda, Hisao Sakai, Japan

In Japan, careworkers and healthcare practitioners in the field are devising countermeasures against future caring in Japan. In this research, especially, the social effects of difficulties in urinating after spine injuries and cerebral infarctions are discussed.

The effects of treatments of urination disorders on mental and psychological states of the patients and their families were investigated. The research showed that burdens of nursing cares by families included a lot of mental factors. The results contributed to supporting practices of staff members in the field of nursing cares from mental and psychological viewpoints.

The effects of home environment on parenting and child development

Matsumoto, Satoko Ochanomizu University, Tokyo, Japan Sugawara, Masumi Department of Psychology, Ochamomizu University, Tokyo, Japan Sakai, Atsushi Division of School Education, University of Yamanashi, Kofu, Japan

Children experience various effects of environment throughout their developmental trajectory. Therefore, it seems necessary to find out the process which explains the relationship between environment and children's development. The objective of present study is to examine this mechanism by using the data collected from Japanese families with infants. In this study, home environment will be the focus of consideration. The specific aspects of home environment examined are conditions of inside/outside the house. The indirect effects of these environmental conditions on children's development are examined, where the variables measuring parenting placed as the mediator, and children's characteristics placed as outcome variables.

The role of response mode on Stroop and reverse Stroop interference in the group version test

Matsumoto, Aki Human-Environment Studies, Kyushu University, Fukuoka, Japan Hakoda, Yuji Human-Environment Studies, Kyushu University, Fukuoka, Japan Watanabe, Megumi Human-Environment Studies, Kyushu University, Fukuoka, Japan

We developed the group version of the Stroop Color-Word Test, which measures both Stroop and reverse Stroop interference (Hakoda & Sasaki, 1990). This test was performed by matching response, where participants selected the appropriate word and color patch from the provided choices printed on paper. In this study we conducted this test using two response modes: oral and matching. Results showed salient Stroop interference in oral response. However, both types of interference were recognized and statistically significant in matching response. It is proposed that this test might be a valuable tool for measuring individual differences in human information processing.

Why playing games is better than living lifes

Mayer, Monica Inst. für theor. Psychologie, Universität Bamberg, Bamberg, Germany

The objective of this research was to realise why people get so absorbed in computer games that they forget everything outside. To figure out how and why these people get addicted some people were very deeply examined, using the case study method. 27 persons aged 8 to 68 were interviewed, 22 males and five females. The four gaming types based on Bartle (Explorer, Achiever, Socializer and Killer) were ratified and their psychic mechanisms as well as the motivational and cognitive base of the addiction as part of the psychic anatomy were elucidated based on the Theory of Action Regulation.

Timing emotional sounds: Contingent negative variation modulation predicts modulation of subjective duration

Mella, Nathalie Neuroscience, CNRS, Paris, France Pouthas, Viviane neuroscience, CNRS, Paris, France

The influence of emotion on time processing has been investigated in previous studies, showing that negative events generate a lengthening of subjective

duration. The present experiment aimed at determining electrocortical correlates of such an effect. Twelve participants estimated the duration of neutral and negative sounds varying in arousal level, when attending to time and when attending emotion. Highly arousing sounds were judged longer than less arousing ones. This effect was stronger when attending to emotion than when attending to time. Subjective duration modulations were reflected by right frontal negativity (CNV), which suggests that CNV in an index of experienced duration.

Do physicians inform themselves and their patients in a balanced manner?

Mendel, Rosmarie Inst. für Psychiatrie, Technische Universität München, München, Germany Traut-Mattausch, Eva Department of Psychology, Ludwig-Maximilians-Universität, München, Germany Hamann, Johannes Psychiatric Department, Technische Universität München, München, Germany Jonas, Eva Department of Psychology, Universität Salzburg, Salzburg, Austria Frey, Dieter Department of Psychology, Technische Universität München, München, Germany Kissling, Werner Psychiatric Department, Technische Universität München, München, Germany

Objective: To determine whether physicians making a treatment decision inform themselves and a patient about the benefits and risks of antipsychotic drugs in a balanced way. Methods: Subsequent to a brief case history, physicians indicated which benefits and risks of antipsychotics they will inform themselves or their patients about respectively. Results: Physicians informing themselves looked for more risks than benefits; physicians informing a patient presented significantly more benefits than risks. Conclusions: A risk-related information search can lead to a neglect of potential benefits and thus cause suboptimal decisions; a benefit-related information presentation to patients can entail legal actions against physicians.

Development of a screening tool for the identification of psychooncological treatment needs in breast cancer patients

Meraner, Verena Biologische Psychiatrie, Univ.-Klinik für Psychiatrie, Innsbruck, Austria Giesinger, Johannes Biologische Psychiatrie, Univ.-Klinik für Psychiatrie, Innsbruck, Austria Seiwald, Elisabeth Biologische Psychiatrie, Univ.-Klinik für Psychiatrie, Innsbruck, Austria Kemmler, Georg Allgemeine Psychiatrie, Univ.-Klinik für Psychiatrie, Innsbruck, Austria Sperner-Unterweger, Barbara Biologische Psychiatrie, Univ.-Klinik für Psychiatrie, Innsbruck, Austria Holzner, Bernhard Biologische Psychiatrie, Univ.-Klinik für Psychiatrie, Innsbruck, Austria

Purpose In order to facilitate identification of patients with psychooncological treatment needs we developed a suitable screening instrument based on patient-reported outcome. Methods 105 breast cancer patients participated from Innsbruck Medical University. Assessment instruments used were EORTC-QLQC30, HADS, DT and HQ. Statistical methods included logistic regression and ROC-curves. Results Stepwise forward-selection showed that EORTC-QLQC30 subscales Role-Functioning and Emotional-Functioning as well as former psychological treatment were the optimal predictor set for the need of psychooncological treatment. The AUC for this predictor set was 0.88(CI95%0.82-0.95). Conclusion Assessment of patients QOL appears useful for prediction of psychooncological treatment needs in breast cancer patients.

Instruction based modulation of the Simon effect

Metzker, Manja Dresden, Germany Dreisbach, Gesine Allgemeine Psychologie, Technische Universität Dresden, Dresden, Germany

In a series of experiments we compared the effects of stimulus-response (SR) based vs. rule based processing on the Simon effect. That is, all participants received the same stimulus set, but were instructed to either use direct SR mappings or one categorization rule. The Simon effect, i.e. faster reaction times when stimulus and response location correspond, was only present when participants used a categorization rule, but disappeared when participants used SR mappings. This result contradicts classical theoretical accounts of the Simon effect, such as dimensional overlap model and other dual route models. Implications for Simon effect theory will be discussed.

Assertive style in the deaf student: A comparative study
Mies i Burrull, Àngels Psicologia Evolutiva, UAB, Bellaterra /Cerdanyola, Spain Fornieles, Albert Psicobiologia i Metodologia, UAB, Bellaterra / Cerdanyola, Spain
This researh analyses awareness of social-competency skills in deaf students on the basis of their auto-perception and that of their school peers. Differential aspects amongst deaf and non-deaf students are also studied in this respect. The sample consists of 10 deaf subjects, currently undertaking primary education, with an oral communicative mode. A questionnaire on social interaction skills and the CABS scale (Michelson, 1987) are used. The results to date show a lesser tendency in the use of an assertive style in the resolution of conflicts. The conclusions allow us to gain which aspects merit greater attention for future intervention.

Achievement motivation and leadership between the gifted children.
Mohamed, Hiba Psychology, Niel West, Khartoum, Sudan
This Study aims at investigating the relationship between achievement motivation and the characteristics of leadership in the gifted children. The sample constitutes of (418) pupils (212) are males and (206) females. And (23) primary school teachers. Three tools were used in the study: achievement motivation, leadership, behavioral characteristics of gifted children.There is no correlation the study showed achievement motivation and leadership. There are no differences between males and females in achievement motivation and leadership. There are according to assessment of the teacher UC MAS students are motivated, while the students gifted school is less motivation.

Emotional functioning and sleep disorders in children aged 6-12 yrs
Mojs, Ewa Dept. of Health Sciences, Poznan University, Poznan, Poland Glowacka, Maria Dept. of health Sci, Poznan Univ. of Medical Sci, Poznan, Poland Zarowski, Marcin Chair and Dept of Dev. Neurol., Poznan Univ. of Medical Sci, Poznan, Poland Samborski, Wlodzimierz Clinic of Physiotherapy, Rheum, Poznan Univ. of Medical Sci, Poznan, Poland
The aim of the study was the estimation of the emotional processes in children aged 6-12 yrs. of age. 84 boys and girls participated in the study. They fulfilled a questionnaire of the SD. Next 30 patients from the examined group with diagnosed SD participated in the psychological and neurological examination. The STAI and STAIC scale, scale of impulsivity, control expression of emotions and depression used in the study. The statistical analysis shows the significant correlation between SD and the prevalence of emotional disorders. There was no correlation between the duration of SD and the results of psychological tests.

Motivations for promotion and prevention in the initiation and maintenance of close relationships
Molden, Daniel Psychology, Northwestern University, Evanston, Illinois, USA Finkel, Eli Psychology, Northwestern University, Evanston, Illinois, USA Johnson, Sarah Psychology, Northwestern University, Evanston, Illinois, USA Eastwick, Paul Psychology, Northwestern University, Evanston, Illinois, USA
Desires for advancement (promotion) and security (prevention) are both fundamental human motivations. The present research investigates how such motivations influence the initiation and maintenance of close relationships. Two longitudinal studies, one involving people seeking romantic relationships and one involving people already in romantic relationships, assessed the pursuit of possible partners and commitment to existing partners, respectively. Correlational analyses revealed that stronger motivations for promotion predicted increased pursuit of potential partners and decreased commitment to current partners whereas stronger motivations for prevention predicted the opposite pattern of results. Relationship satisfaction may therefore depend upon different motivations at different stages of relationships.

Double dissociation between reading and spelling
Moll, Kristina Inst. für Psychologie, Universität Salzburg, Salzburg, Austria
We investigated the dissociation between reading and spelling deficits in 110 German speaking children based on four groups: children with isolated reading deficits, children with isolated spelling deficits, children with both deficits and controls. Children read words and pseudohomophones derived from these words. We expect intact orthographic representations reflected by a lexicality effect for reading disabled and controls, but not for spelling disabled children. Furthermore, we assume a deficit in access to phonology reflected by reduced naming speed in rapid digit naming tasks for reading disabled in contrast to controls and spelling disabled children. The data are currently being analysed.

Adult attachment styles and attitudes towards sharing time with one's partner
Monteoliva, Adelaida Social Psychology, University of Granada, Granada, Spain Garcia-Martinez, J. Miguel A. SOCIAL PSYCHOLOGY, UNIVERSITY OF GRANADA, GRANADA, Spain Calvo Salguero, Antonia SOCIAL PSYCHOLOGY, UNIVERSITY OF GRANADA, GRANADA, Spain Aguilar-Luzon, Maria del Carmen PSYCHOLOGY, UNIVERSITY OF JAEN, JAEN, Spain
This study examines if people with different attachment styles differ in their attitudes towards sharing time with one's partner. The study was carried out using 746 university students. The Relationship Questionnaire (RQ) was administered to determine the adult attachment style. Direct measures of their attitude towards sharing time with one's partner were also collected. Variance analyses show significant differences according to adult attachment style in their attitudes towards this interpersonal behaviour. Scheffé tests revealed that participants with a secure and preoccupied attachment style showed the most positive attitudes towards sharing their time with one's partner, whilst both types of avoidant individuals showed the less positive attitudes. Dismissing individuals reported the lower average score.

Construction of the conflict attribution scale in Mexican couples
Montero Santamaria, Nancy Faculty of Psychology, Nat. Aut. University of Mexico, Mexico City, Mexico Rivera Aragon, Sofia PSYCHOLOGY FACULTY, UNAM (MEXICO), DF - MEXICO, Mexico Diaz Loving,

Rolando PSYCHOLOGY FACULTY, UNAM (MEXICO), DF - MEXICO, Mexico
Unlike interaction with strangers (a major criticism to the experimental study on Attribution), marriage consists in constant observation of the other's behavior. Hence, this study was aimed at constructing an instrument that could provide integral measurement of attribution to conflict in Mexican couples. The Attribution and Emotions Scale (Betancourt, Flores and Cortes, 2004) was therefore applied. It was answered by volunteers living with their partners (474 males and 491 females). Results obtained through the psychometrical analysis included in the instrument show that Intentionality predominates and that Causality Locus and Stability are also identified, giving a greater active role to the other in the relationship.

The role of demographic variables in predicting mental health among physically disables in Isfahan City
Moradi, Azam Psychology, Isfahan University, Isfahan, Islamic Republic of Iran Ghamarani, Amir Psychology, University of Isfahan, Isfahan, Islamic Republic of Iran
The purpose of this research was to determine the share of employment status, marital status,education level, intensity of disability, and gender in predicting the mental health of physically disables. Subjects were consisted of 100 members of Isfahanian Society of Disables who were selected randomly. For assessing the mental heath GHQ - 28 was used. Results of stepwise regression analysis showed that employmentstatus and marital status are best predictors for mental health respectively, but adding education level, intensity of disability, and gender to former variables can't increase the predicting power of the mental health in physically disables significantly.

Preschool children's interactive play: Individual differences and their antecedents
Morino, Mio Early Childhood Education, Shokei College, Kumamoto, Japan
The aim of this study was to examine how children's understanding of mental states, language ability and peer interactions at the age of 3 (Time1) were related to the quality of their play after the transition to the new class of 4-year-olds (Time2). A sample of 57 children (Time1) completed the tasks of theory of mind, understanding of emotions and Picture Vocabulary Test. The observations were also made when children (Time1 and 2) were free to choose their own playmates and activities. As a result, the role of language ability was important in the interactive play.

How does informative and non-informative feedback influences learning in children?
Moschner, Barbara Inst. für Pädagogik, Universität Oldenburg, Oldenburg, Germany Anschütz, Andrea Institut für Pädagogik, Universität Oldenburg, Oldenburg, Germany Thiel, Christiane Institut für Biologie, Universität Oldenburg, Oldenburg, Germany Özyurt, Jale Institut für Biologie, Universität Oldenburg, Oldenburg, Germany Parchmann, Ilka Institut für Chemie, Universität Oldenburg, Oldenburg, Germany
The influence of feedback in relation to individual differences and brain activity in learning tasks was investigated. The combination of an educational and a neuroscience study showed interesting results. 230 children (age 10 to 13) completed a learning task (with informative or non-informative feedback) and measures for individual differences. 37 children in a functional neuroimaging study completed the same task while their brain activity was assessed. When the learning material was structured the informative feedback group performed slightly better than the non-informative feedback group. Positive feedback was associated with stronger

activity in visual brain regions and the caudate nucleus.

Mikhail Bakhtin's dialogue approach combined with Gestalt approach as a means of improving the group work in workshops, group psychotherapy and team building

Mstibovskyi, Illia Rostov-on-Don, Russia

Objective: to elaborate theoretical basis and practical tools for the group leader in the form of unique methods of maintaining a group dialogue. Methods: 1. modeling the essential features of Mikhail Bakhtin's Dialogue Approach (MBDA) in relation to group work. 2. using Gestalt Approach to make group members experience the dialogue during specially organized exercises. 3. assessing group work in the dialogue mode basing on Kurt Levin's field theory. Results: A rapid natural increase of group cohesiveness, member's sincerity and activeness, which is achieved primarily by means of encouraging both their autonomy and participation in the group.

Construct validity of employment interviews - Do they assess, whatever you ask for?

Mussel, Patrick Inst. für Sozialwissenschaften, Universität Hohenheim, Stuttgart, Germany Schuler, Heinz Institute for Social Sciences, University of Hohenheim, Stuttgart, Germany Höft, Stefan FH für Arbeitsmarktmanagement, Bundesagentur für Arbeit, Mannheim, Germany

The present study investigated construct validity of employment interviews in light of their dimensions, i.e. the constructs they aim to assess. Based on a sample of 282 candidates applying for a clerical apprenticeship, a multimodal interview was applied. Comprehensive exploratory and confirmatory construct analyses indicated correlations with social competence as assessed via self reports (.17-.30) and assessment center tasks (.51-.57, uncorrected); however, as expected, construct saturation was moderated by the dimensions underlying the interview. It is concluded that, in addition to the typical, dyadic situation of the interview, construct validity is determined by the content of questions and rating scales.

Pre-selection methods for employment interviews – A reference model

Mussel, Patrick Inst. für Sozialwissenschaften, Universität Hohenheim, Stuttgart, Germany

Even though employment interviews are quite expensive, they represent one of the most often used methods for personnel selection. The present paper reviews a total of seventeen methods regarding their utility for pre-selecting candidates prior to the interview according to two dimensions: process efficiency and diagnostic gain. Based on an extensive literature search and data from meta-analytic and primary studies, a reference model was established reflecting the utility of these methods for pre-selection. As such, this model integrates the literature concerning construct and criterion related validity of the interview and can be used as guideline for practitioners designing selection processes.

Reconsolidation in human episodic memory

Nadel, Lynn Dept. of Psychology, University of Arizona, Tucson, USA Hupbach, Almut Psychology, University of Arizona, Tucson, USA Hardt, Oliver Psychology, McGill University, Montreal, Canada Gomez, Rebecca Psychology, University of Arizona, Tucson, USA

Reactivated memories can be modified and subsequently require reconsolidation. We reported reconsolidation effects in human episodic memory: Memory for an object set was modified by presentation of a new set if participants were reminded of the first set before learning the second set. The reminder involved three components: the

experimenter, a reminder question, and the spatial context. We now show re-instating the spatial context is crucial for obtaining the reminder effect. An additional study looked at the boundary conditions for contextual reminders. We found that the spatial context triggers reconsolidation only in unfamiliar but not in familiar contexts.

Relationship between depression and hostility among teachers

Naderi, Mohamad Mehdi Azadshar, Islamic Republic of Iran

Objective: The purpose of the present study was to examine the relationship between depression and hostility among teacher. Method: Participants were 531 teachers of education organization of Golestan province in Iran. The mean age of the participants was 37.49 years (SD = 5.58). There were 215 men and 316 women. Measures: All participants completed a questionnaire booklet containing one self-report measures: The Symptom Checklist-90-R (SCL-90-R). Results: The results of the present study demonstrate that:Correlation between depression and teacher's hostility is meaningful and positive (r = 0.714, p<0.001). Conclusions: The present study revealed that a more depression is associated with a high level of self-reported hostility.

Birth weight is associated with antenatal maternal cortisol diurnal rhythm

Nagamine, Mitsue Adult Mental Health, NCNP, NIMH, Nishi-tokyo, Tokyo, Japan Saito, Satoru Fundamental Research, Joso Research Center, Tsukubamirai, Japan Okabayashi, Hideki Psychology and Education, Meisei University, Hino, Tokyo, Japan Kim, Yoshiharu Adult Mental Health, NIMH, Kodaira, Tokyo, Japan

In this study, an influence of the antenatal maternal activity of hypothalamus-pituitary-adrenal axis on birth weight was investigated by measuring diurnal cortisol rhythm in 20 midterm and 24 late pregnant women (mean age 29.3±4 yrs). The participants were classified into non-decrease, low level decrease and high level decrease groups, according to their cortisol decrease rate (from 8:00 to 11:00). Birth weight was significantly lower in midterm than late pregnant in non-decrease group (p<.05). This finding suggests the effect of the antenatal maternal flattened diurnal cortisol rhythm on birth weight differs between midterm and lateterm.

Effects of instructions in individuals with the mental retardation

Nagato, Kiyoshi Education, Univ. of the Ryukyus, OKINAWA, Japan Katsuyoshi, Shinya Education, Univ. of the Ryukyus, Okinawa, Japan Tanaka, Atsushi Education, Univ. of the Ryukyus, Okinawa, Japan Ushiyama, Michio Education, Kyoto Univ. of Education, Kyoto, Japan Okuzumi, Hideyuki Education, Tokyo Gakuei Univ., Tokyo, Japan

The purpose of this study was to investigate the role of instructional effects in individuals with mental retardation by measuring movement time and accuracy. The subjects were measured on how quickly and accurately they pored liquid into a cup to red line. There were 39 individuals without mental retardation and 38 individuals with mental retardation in the study. In addition, the subjects were compared and examined the four types which were classified according to the three clinical types and healthy person.

Redressing inequities in third-partner relationships

Nakajima, Makoto Education & Human Development, Nagoya University, Nagoya, Japan Yoshida, Toshikazu Education & Human Developm, Nagoya University, nagoya, Japan

This study examined whether an individual maintain equity in trans-relational relationships(Austin & Walster, 1975). A total of 129 undergraduates

completed a questionnaire that contained two hypothetical exchange situations. The respondents were initially either over-rewarded or under-rewarded, and then they were given a chance to distribute the rewards between themselves and their partners. In each situation, the respondents worked with different partners. In addition, respondents were informed that their partners worked with someone at another time. The results indicate that over-rewarded people redressed those inequities from third parties only when they knew that their first and second partner worked together.

Relative importance of expressive behavior in emotion judgment with contexts: The effects of situation, sex of judges, and nationality of expressers on Japanese judges

Nakamura, Makoto International Studies, Utsunomiya University, Utsunomiya, Japan

The present study focused on the effects of situational information (situation where expressions occurred: public versus private), nationality of expressers (Japanese versus American), and sex of participants on the judgment of emotion by 78 Japanese college students. Multilevel analysis revealed that expressions were more important than elicitors in the emotion judgments and that expressions of American expressers were more weighted than those of Japanese. The relative importance of expressions in emotion judgment was replicated in the present study and the findings were discussed in terms of the relative effectiveness of contextual information in the judgment of emotion.

Emotional control of the children in stress coping and the process of the resolution

Nakata, Sakae Dept. of Psychology, Aichi Gakuin University, Aichi, Japan

It is an important and interesting subject to study which behavior is taken associated with which emotion, in order to control emotions in stress coping and to maintain smooth communication. This study covers toddlers in the United States and emotional control seen among multiage members surrounding three-year-old children is examined. Stress coping seen in interpersonal relations with multiage children is taken up here.

The assessment of risk propensity through a dilemmas task

Narváez Rullán, María Dept. of Psychology, Autónoma University of Madrid, Madrid, Spain Botella, Juan Department of Psychology, Autónoma University of Madrid, Madrid, Spain Martínez Molina, Agustín Department of Psychology, Autónoma University of Madrid, Madrid, Spain Rubio, Víctor J. Department of Psychology, Autónoma University of Madrid, Madrid, Spain Santacreu, José Department of Psychology, Autónoma University of Madrid, Madrid, Spain

Risk Propensity (RP) is a trait characterized by an increased probability of engaging in behaviors that involve some potential harm, but also an opportunity for some benefit. A sample of 892 people participated in a study in which a new RP task, composed of several dilemmas, was explored. Each dilemma includes the initial set plus sequential approximations for estimating the Indifference Value between a Secure and the expected value of an uncertain Game. The scores showed good internal consistency, reasonably test-retest reliability, and good validity as reflected in the correlation with other Risk Propensity task.

Influence of learning techniques on information processing

Navaneedhan, Girija Chennai, India Saraladevi, Krishnan Physical Science, Meston college of education, Chennai, India

Objective of the study: To establish the fact that effective information processing is dependent on the learning techniques one adopts. Methodology of the study: A sample of 100 students in the age group 13 to 17 were chosen. They were divided in to two groups control and experimental. To experimental group certain specific learning methods were taught.For the same group neuro transmitter serotonin was tested taking blood samples of the students before and after adopting learning techniques. Expected results : Increase in serotonin levels in the blood sample establishes the relationship between information processing and learning techniques.

The role of visual imagery as mind tool in information processing

Navaneedhan, Girija Chennai, India

Objective : To understand the significance of visual imagery in the information processing of individuals. Methodology: Visual imagery is one of the mind tool which enables an individual to experience the perception of some object event or scene that occurs when the relevant object, event, or scene is not actually present to the senses. The sample consists of boys and girls of the age group 17 years chosen and given training in visual imagery to learn chemical bonding in chemistry. Their confidence level and achievement ability were tested before and after the application othe tool. Expected results : Calculation of "t" test value revealed a markable improvement in achievment test scores and also boosted the confidence level of the students

Parents' child-feeding practices: A comparison between two towns Mexico City and Morelia, Michoacán

Navarro, Gabriela Social Psychology, UMSNH, Morelia, Michoacan, Mexico

The objective of this study was to compare Parents' feeding attitudes and practices in two Mexican samples of mothers from different towns. Participants: 300 mothers of 4 to 11-year-old girls and boys from Mexico city and 300 from Morelia, completed the Mexican adaptation of the Child Feeding Questionnaire MACFQ, Cronbach's alpha =.8383 (Navarro, 2006), a self-report measure of parental attitudes, beliefs and practices about child feeding and obesity proneness. It will be presented Factor structure of the MACFQ by town. Means of the seven factors of the MACFQ were compared between towns by Student t- test.

Unobserved heterogeneity in trauma patients desire for autonomy in medical decision making in an emergency department

Neuner, Bruno Anesthesiology and Intensive M, Charité - Universitaetsmedizin, Berlin, Germany Weiss-Gerlach, Edith Anesthesiology and Intensive M, Charité - Universitaetsmedizin, Berlin, Germany Neumann, Tim Anesthesiology and Intensive M, Charité - Universitaetsmedizin, Berlin, Germany Schoenfeld, Helge Anesthesiology and Intensive M, Charité - Universitaetsmedizin, Berlin, Germany Miller, Peter Drug and Alcohol Prevention, MUSC, Charleston, USA Schlattmann, Peter Biometry and Clin Epi, Charité - Universitaetsmedizin, Berlin, Germany Braehler, Elmar Medical Psychology and Sociolo, University Leipzig, Leipzig, Germany Spies, Claudia Anesthesiology and Intensive M, Charité - Universitaetsmedizin, Berlin, Germany

Objectives: To evaluate unobserved heterogeneity in trauma patients' desire for autonomy in medical decision-making (DAD). Methods: Study in 1,009 emergency department patients (median age 32 years, 62% male). A covariate adjusted finite mixture model was established. Results: Three latent subpopulations (low DAD in 53.3 % / medium DAD in 35.6 % / high DAD in 11.1 % of patients), a positive association of female gender respectively school education, and a negative association of higher age respectively substance use with patients' DAD was evaluated. Conclu-

sions: Trauma patients' DAD showed unobserved heterogeneity which could not be explained by established explanatory variables.

The influence mechanism of the small or middle-size enterprise owners' charismatic leadership toward followers

Nie, Xue Lin Hangzkou Dianzi University, Hang Zhou, People's Republic of China Ye, Yujian College of Management, Hangzhou Dianzi University, Hangzhou, People's Republic of China He, Quan Department of Psychology, Zhejiang University, Hangzhou, People's Republic of China

This study investigated 206 employees who come from small or middle-size enterprises, to explore the relationships between owner's charismatic leadership, the employee's self-efficacy, self-esteem, self-structure and organizational citizenship behaviors(OCBs). The results showed that self-efficacy mediated the relationship between strategic vision and non-conventional behavior of charismatic leadership and OCBs, self-esteem mediated the relationship between sensitivity to environment and non-conventional behavior of charismatic leadership and OCBs, but the effect of the non-conventional behavior is negative. Finally, strategic vision and personal risking influence the self-construal, but the self-construal did not influence the OCBs, the influence of sensitivity to followers is not significant.

The dependence of emotional child's reactions on methods of punishment and reward in family

Nikolaeva, Elena Dept. of Child's Psychology, State University, St. Petersburg, Russia

The problem of this research was to analyze a variety of children cardiac reactions on emotional stimuli (remembering of the reward and punishment in family). 162 children (7 yr. old) were participants. Programs SPSS and Surface have been used. We showed, that system of interaction of children and parents at which children believe, that them do not encourage or seldom praise, promotes change of cardiac reaction not only in a situation of the reward, but also punishment when their vegetative reaction under stress decreased.Research was supported by Grant 07-06-00576a by RGSF

Comparison of normative beliefs between Japanese and U.S. students to group abusive activities

Nishida, Kimiaki Nursing Dept., University of Shizuoka, Shizuoka, Japan Almendros, Carmen Psychology, Madred Autonoma Unversity, Madred, Spain Yamaura, Kazuho Business Admin. and Inform., University of Shizuoka, Shizuoka, Japan Watanabe, Namiji Letters, Ferris women University, Shizuoka, Japan Kakuyama, Takashi Human Social Science, Tokyo International Univ., Tokyo, Japan

The purpose of this study is to investigate cross cultural communalities and differences of normative beliefs to group abusive activities between Japanese and U.S. students. For, we developed Group Health Scale which is consisted of 51 items for what activities are abusive psychologically against personal human rights. The students of the both countries responded to the questions: If you belonged to a group, or an organization that is characterized by each of the following items, how would you feel? It is found that the U.S. students have two cognitive structures which are classified into seven sub-structures in the Japanese.

Effect of self-esteem on reselecting interactional partners in persuasion games: An investigation using the Settoku Nattoku Game (2)

Nishimura, Takashi Dept. of Clinical Psychology, Hiroshima International Univ., Hiroshima, Japan Yanagisawa, Kuniaki Graduate school of I.A.S., Hiroshima Univ., Higashi-Hiroshima, Japan

Effect of self-esteem on selecting interactional partners was investigated using a persuasion game named the Settoku Nattoku Game (SNG; Sugiura, 2003). In this study, we focused on the effect of self-esteem on repeated selection of interactional partners by using data from two SNGs. Freshmen at a university (n = 24) participated in the SNG game twice. The results were consistent with prior studies and indicated that high self-esteem people tended not to select the same partners, whereas low self-esteem people tended to repeatedly select the same people.

Effects of attachment on interpersonal relationship development

Niwa, Tomomi School of Education, Nagoya University, Nagoya, Japan

The aim of the present study was to examine the different contact frequency and amount of interaction in the early stage of relationship to favorable or unfavorable person arising from the features of attachment to parents. Four hundred and sixteen undergraduates and 587 undergraduates were surveyed on the contact frequency and amount of interaction with unfavorable or favorable person respectively. The main result showed those low on avoidance of parental attachment had less interaction with favorable person than those who scored high. However, there was no difference in contact frequency between those who were high on avoidance of parental attachment and those who were low.

Psychometric properties of the obsessive beliefs questionnaire: Children version in a non-clinical Spanish sample

Nogueira, Raquel Personalidad y Evaluación, University of Málaga, Málaga, Spain Godoy, Antonio Personalidad, Evaluación y Tto, University of Málaga, Málaga, Spain Gavino, Aurora Personalidad, Evaluación y Tto, University of Málaga, Málaga, Spain Valderrama, Lidia Personalidad, Evaluación y Tto, University of Málaga, Málaga, Spain Fernández, Rosa Personalidad, Evaluación y Tto, University of Málaga, Málaga, Spain Quintero, Carolina Personalidad, Evaluación y Tto, University of Málaga, Málaga, Spain Romero, Pablo Salud Mental, Hospital de Jaén, Jaén, Spain

The Obsessive Beliefs Questionnaire (OBQ, Obsessive Compulsive Cognitions Working Group, 2001) is a self-rated scale that is used for measure cognitive aspects of obsessive - compulsive disorder (OCD). The aim of this work is evaluate the dimensionality, reliability and validity of the children version of this questionnaire in a Spanish sample of children, the Obsessive Belief Questionnaire - Children Version, (OBQ – CV, Godoy, unpublished work). The results indicate that the OBQ - CV is a reliable measure in this sample and that it has a good convergent and discriminant validity with different measures of anxiety and depression.

On the syndromological approach to studying the personality aspects of teaching stress

Nosenko, Eleonora Dept. of Psychology, National University, Dnipropetrovsk, Ukraine

The aim of the study was to assess the adequacy of the approach. 60 young teachers were assigned to groups differing(t-test) on the level of anxiety and depression as an index of burnout. Correlation analysis (r-Pearson)of the scores on burnout and those on Cattell 16 PF revealed six symmetrical factors the opposites of which characterised low (1)and high (2) burnout groups : B,E,G,L,O,Q2 (p<.01) Five nonsymmetrical factors also had significant correlations in group 2: H,I,Q3,Q4,N. Factor C had positive correlation in group 1. The findings prove the adequacy of the approach and prompt the ways of improvement in training teachers.

Verbal memory in experienced actors and controls

Notthoff, Nanna Dept. of Psychology, Stanford University, Stanford, USA Jonides, John Department of Psychology, University of Michigan, Ann Arbor, USA

Objectives: How do actors remember verbal material? Hypothesis: Actors extract the meaning first, then remember details. They are successful recalling meaningful stories, less with unrelated words. Methods: We tested experienced actors' (nA=21) and controls' (nC=24) memory for unrelated (RAVLT) and related pre-categorized word lists (CVLT) and their ability to recognize themes (Roediger & McDermott False Recall Paradigm). Results: No significant differences were found in RAVLT and CVLT. Actors identified more themes in the False Recall Paradigm (meanA=4.14,S-DA=2.17; meanC=1.79,SDC=1.25; p=0.0001). Conclusions: Actors are better at extracting gist than controls, resulting in better performance when remembering meaningful materials using their own categories.

Recollective states as predictors of academic success

Nourkova, Veronika Psychology, Moscow State University, Moscow, Russia Yeremenko, Victoria Psychology, Moscow State University, Moscow, Russia

Can verbs, that students use starting their exam answers with, predict their grades? In the study 250 participants rated those verbs which mean states of consciousness accompanying recollection. Cluster analyses extracted 3 types of such states: type 1 - "know, remember", type 2 - "recollect", type3 - "think, suppose, feel". Comparing verbs by which students start their exam answer and grades they got we found out that verbs forming the first group predict the highest proportion of excellent grades, verbs from the second group predict the highest proportion of medium grades and verbs from the third group predict the highest proportion of lowest grades.

Electroencephalographic correlates of cognitive development in children aged 5 to 6 years

Novikova, Svetlana Developmental Psychophysiology, MSUPE, Moscow, Russia Posikera, Irina developmental psychogenetics, PIRAE, Moscow, Russia Tsetlin, Marina developmental psychophysiology, MSUPE, Moscow, Russia Pushina, Natalya developmental psychogenetics, PIRAE, Moscow, Russia Malakhovskaya, Elena developmental psychophysiology, MSUPE, Moscow, Russia Stroganova, Tatiana developmental psychogenetics, PIRAE, Moscow, Russia

Objective: To estimate the relationships of electroencephalographic (EEG) spectral parameters under attention load on cognitive functioning in preschoolers. Methods: EEG was recorded in 82 5-to-6-year-old children under three conditions: "Closed eyes", "Visual attention", "Attention-to-speech". Intelligence (IQ) was measured using Kaufman Assessment Battery for Children. Multiple regression was applied. Results: EEG spectral amplitudes under "Closed eyes" condition did not relate to IQ parameters. In contrast, theta rhythm spectral amplitudes registered under attentive states explained up to 34% of IQ scores variance. Conclusions: The findings showed the contribution of EEG theta under attentional load in the individual diversity of IQ in children.

The effect of an audience on cortisol response to a speech task

Oda, Yayoi Toyko, Japan Endo, Kenji Department of Psychology, Aoyama Gakuin University, Toyko, Japan

Although many studies demonstrate that cortisol increases during speech, few studies demonstrate the effect of an audience. To examine the effect of an audience upon cortisol response, undergraduates participating in groups of 10-12 were divided into audience and non-audience conditions. Each participant of the audience condition group delivered a 5-minute speech to the experimenter and the rest of their group, whereas the participants of the non-audience condition performed the same task in another room without an audience. The result demonstrated that the salivary cortisol level only increased in the audience condition group and not in the non-audience condition group.

Making clinical psychology accessible to people with intellectual disabilities

Ogi, Laura Learning Disabilities, National Health Service, Birmingham, United Kingdom

Aim This is a unique initiative to promote access of information around psychological care, facilitate informed consent and support the education of related professionals. Method A 37 min DVD in which psychologists introduce the approach they use at work in a way that is easy to understand and a booklet for related professionals. Results Outcomes assessed through five service user focus groups and two professionals focus groups. Conclusion The results will be discussed in relation to the proposed aims such as facilitating access to psychological care, the education of related professionals and informed consent.

Self-regulation in early childhood: The relations to social skills and problem behaviors

Ohuchi, Akiko University of Tsukuba, Tsukuba, Japan Sakurai, Toyoko Faculty of Human Welfare, Den-en Chofu University, Kawasaki, Japan Sakurai, Shigeo Inst. of Psychology, University of Tsukuba, Tsukuba, Japan

The purpose of this study was to examine the relations of self-regulation to social skills and problem behaviors in Japanese preschool children. We considered four aspects of self-regulation: self-assertiveness, self-inhibition, attention shifting and attention focusing. Four hundred and fifty-two children's self-regulation were rated by their parents. Two hundred and sixty-two of them were rated social skills and problem behaviors by their teachers. We made a cluster analysis of the standardized scores of four aspects of self-regulation and found six clusters. The results of analysis revealed the different characteristics of social skills and problem behaviors in each cluster.

Classification of Ibasho "Person who eases your mind" in female undergraduates

Okamura, Toshimitsu Nara Nersery College, Kyoto, Japan

Ibasyo (the comfortable place) is an idiosyncratic word to Japanese culture. Ibasyo referred to the space, the time and the person that ease your mind. Especially the person who eases your mind was critical. Participants were asked to choose alternatives of answers to the questions, "Who is the person that eases your mind in situations (high or low anxiety)?" Multiple correspondence analyses were performed to the choices of person mentioned above. The results indicated that the person who eases your mind were categorized to three groups by two axis in both situations, namely "myself", "family" and "friend" groups.

Improving autonomy in mentally retarded children by precision teaching method

Oliva, Patrizia Scienze dell'Educazione, University of Messina, Messina, Italy Cuzzocrea, Francesca Scienze dell'Educazione, University of Messina, Messina, Italy Larcan, Rosalba Scienze dell'Educazione, University of Messina, Messina, Italy

The aim of study is to verify the effectiveness of the software, based on Precision Teaching (PT), for increasing, in mentally retarded subjects, knowledge and correct use of money. It was compared the fluency and accuracy of answering between two groups (mental disabled and non-disabled subjects). It was investigated the gender differences in learning. The results showed an improvement of knowledge for all the groups, and, in the post-training, there aren't differences among the students. Precision Teaching method seems to have enhanced significantly the accuracy and fluency on answering, and, in general, the learning of correct use of money.

Emotional support reduces social pain and anterior cingulate cortex activation during ostracism

Onoda, Keiichi Psychiatry and Neurosciences, Hiroshima University, Hiroshima, Japan Ura, Mitsuhiro Integrated Arts and Sciences, Hiroshima University, Hiroshima, Japan Nittono, Hiroshi Integrated Arts and Sciences, Hiroshima University, Hiroshima, Japan Nakashima, Kenichiro Integrated Arts and Sciences, Hiroshima University, Hiroshima, Japan Mishima, Shoko Integrated Arts and Sciences, Hiroshima University, Hiroshima, Japan Okamoto, Yasumasa Psychiatry and Neurosciences, Hiroshima University, Hiroshima, Japan Yamawaki, Shigeto Psychiatry and Neurosciences, Hiroshima University, Hiroshima, Japan

To examine the effects of emotional support on social pain caused by ostracism, we conducted an fMRI study in which participants played a virtual ball-tossing game (Cyberball task). They were initially included and afterward excluded. In the latter half of the excluded session, they received emotionally supportive text messages on the screen. The emotional support reduced subjective social pain and the activation of anterior cingulate cortex associated with ostracism. The results suggest that anterior cingulate cortex is involved in representation of psychological pain.

Interference and overshadowing in contingency learning

Orgaz, Cristina Bilbao, Spain Vadillo, Miguel Angel Psychology, University of Deusto, Bilbao, Spain Matute, Helena Psychology, University of Deusto, Bilbao, Spain

The aim of this experiment is to study the relationship between interference and cue competition in contingency learning. These effects were explored by testing 62 college students with a standard preparation for the study of human contingency learning. Inferential analyses show that a cue that has been overshadowed loses its ability to interfere with another cue. Interestingly, current models of associative learning predict no interaction between these phenomena. These results also suggest that interference can be used as an indirect measure for cue competition effects

Hungarian and French students' social representation on competition

Orosz, Gábor Reims, France

The purpose of the present study is to compare Hungarian and French students' social representation of competition. Words associated to competition were collected. Vergàs's process of analysis was carried out to show the structrure and content of the representations. According to our results Hungarian and French students' representations are basically similar, containing mainly sport. However among peripheral elements some differences appear: French students concentrate on the motivating factors of competition, but success and economic concepts play a central role in the representation of Hungarians. These results can be explained by the countries' different historical and cultural backgrounds.

Subjective alienation: Measurement and correlates

Osin, Evgeny School of Psychology, University of East London, Moscow, Russia

The aim of the study was to develop a Russian-language psychometric tool measuring subjective alienation based upon the Alienation Test (Maddi, Kobasa & Hoover, 1979). A pool of 120 items was administered to adult and student samples (N=452). Item-total correlations, factor analysis and structural equation modeling were used, yielding a 60-item questionnaire measuring 4 patterns of subjective alienation over 5 different domains. The alienation scale and its subscales demonstrate high internal consistency and significant negative correlations with a number of subjective well-being measures. An original scale of alienation in educational setting was also developed, demonstrating similar results.

Emotional intelligence and structures through designing scale suitable to the Sudanese environment

Osman, Habab Psychology, Adrak Private Company, Khartoum, Sudan osman, habab psychology, adrak private company, Khartoum, Sudan

This study examines the identification of emotional intelligence and structures through designing scale suitable to the Sudanese environment. To achieve this aim, two scientific methods were employed, namely, documentation and descriptive method. The questionnaire and the scale was applied to a group of 410 participants both males and females. The study shows that items and dimensions of the constructed scale enjoyed adequate level of reliability and validity. The result of factor analysis shows that there is a high saturation of emotional intelligence with five sub structures including (Self-awareness & Motivation, Managing Emotion, General Mood, Emotion Facilitation of Thinking, and empathy).

The influence of repetition on the change of cue-validities

Ostermann, Tanja Bonn, Germany

Inconsistent with the common assumption of unidirectional reasoning from cues to options, it was recently shown that subjective cue-validities are changed during the process of decision making (Simon et al., 2004). The observed bidirectionality in reasoning is explained by automatic processes of maximizing consistency (Glöckner & Betsch, in press). Based on these results an experiment was conducted to test whether repeated in comparison with singular presentation of decision tasks influences the strength of these changes in cue-validities. It was furthermore examined whether these changes also influence subsequent decisions.

Altruism with price as a signal: On intrinsic motivation and crowding-out

Otto, Philipp Inst. für Mikroökonomiks, Europa-Universität Viadrina, Frankfurt, Germany Bolle, Friedel Microeconomics, Europa-Universität Viadrina, Frankfurt (Oder), Germany

In this paper we provide an explanation why and how external intervention can undermine intrinsic motivation. It is hypothesized, that the offered price is taken as a proxy for the "market value" of the corresponding activity. By including an "altruism parameter" in our simple model of intrinsic motivation, we can make straight forward predictions about changes in intrinsic motivation and resulting observed behavior like crowding-in or crowding-out, correspondingly with or without persistence. Which of these effect is observable on the aggregated level, fully depends on the constitution of the two variables "altruism" and "income" in the group.

Examining the effects of mother's socialization goals, developmental expectations, and psychological control in Turkish preschool children's social competences

Ozturk, Pinar Psychology, Abant Izzet Baysal University, Bolu, Turkey Kumru, Asiye Psychology, Abant Izzet Baysal University, Bolu, Turkey

This study examines the effects of mothers' socialization goals, developmental expectations, and psychological control in preschool children's prosocial behaviors, thoughtfulness, verbal intelligence, and hostility. The total of 175 children aged 4-6 years old, their mothers and teachers were recruited in Turkey. Results revealed that older children scored higher on prosocial behaviors and verbal intelligence; girls scored higher on prosocial behaviors; and boys scored higher on hostility. Also, socialization goal of child's self development positively predicted prosocial behaviors and verbal intelligence; inconsistent control behavior negatively predicted verbal intelligence and thoughtfulness; and developmental expectations about social skills negatively predicted prosocial behaviors.

Quantifying and delimiting the proliferation of executive functions

Packwood, Sonia Quebec, Canada Tremblay, Sébastien École de psychologie, Université Laval, Quebec, Canada

The proliferation of executive functions (EF) makes this concept unclear and difficult to operationalize. The purpose of the present study is to estimate the extent of the proliferation and the degree to which EF overlap conceptually and psychometrically. A meta-analysis and exhaustive literature review have enabled us to identify the most frequent EF as well as the neuropsychological tests typically used to measure them. A semantic network analysis revealed clusters of EF and also indicated several overlaps across EF. These results are very informative about the organisation of EF and promote a holistic view of executive control.

Predicting risk factors of attachment disorders in school age children with respect to parents' attachment styles

Paivastegar, Mehrangis Dept. of Psychology, Alzzara University Tehran, Tehran, Islamic Republic of Iran

Attachment disorders of all degrees are a significant and growing feature of all society. These disorders not only damage individual children, but also society at large.If these disorders in children are not recognized and adressed, it is difficult to treat and prevent them. In this study, We investigated the relationship between parents attachment style and Children's attachment disorder.Parent 's attachment style was tested. It was also found that girls presented attachment disorder more than did boys. The final analysis of data indicates the insecure/ anxiety attachment and marital conflict as major predictors of children attachment disorders.

The effects of obligation of role on marital conflicts in Chinese couples

Pan, Chun Feng Department of Psychology, National Taiwan University, Taipei, Taiwan Hwang, Kwang Kuo Department of Psychology, National Taiwan University, Taipei, Taiwan

Most of past researches attempting to investigate why conflicts happened in marital relation highlighted personal trait or the characteristics of the marital relation per se. However, the authors employed "methodological relationalism" to stress the obligation of different roles between persons-in-relation to explore the cause of Chinese marital conflict. Results supported the authors' expectation that obligation of role base on different relationship between the subjects and other significant others such as mother or father in law was determinant of the cause of the marriage conflicts. The issue of mending the marriage relationship is worthy to discuss further.

Cross-cultural adaptation of overseas Chinese students in Japan

Pan, Hong Graduate School of Integrated, Hiroshima University, Higashi-Hiroshima, Japan Ura, Mitsuhiro Integrated Arts and Sciences, Hiroshima University, Higashi-Hiroshima, Japan

Effect of support acquisition strategy of overseas Chinese students (n=177) on cross-cultural adaptation was examined by focusing on social-networking skills. The result of a pass analysis indicated that the relationship between social networking skill and adaptation was mediated by emotional/informational supports from Japanese people. Specifically, empathy/conflict-resolution skill was effective in eliciting support from Japanese and this support facilitated social cross-cultural adaptation, which in turn led to better mental adaptation. In addition, it was revealed that for Chinese students with high network maintenance skill, academic/informational supports from Chinese people which were affected by empathy/conflict-resolution skill facilitated mental adaptation.

Relationship quality and health: The moderating effect of community involvement

Paprocki, Christine Dept. of Psychology, Columbia University, New York, USA Patton, Matthew Psychology Department, University of Chicago, Chicago, USA Visser, Penny Psychology Department, University of Chicago, Chicago, USA

Individuals who are unsatisfied in their marriages are at heightened risk for negative physical health outcomes (see Burman & Margolin, 1992 for review). The current study examined moderators of this relationship using data from 4,242 married individuals who participated in the National Survey of Midlife Development in the United States (MIDUS). Regression models indicated a significant interaction between measures of community involvement and relationship quality on physical health: higher community involvement predicted better health ratings, especially for those in low quality relationships. This implies that community involvement may be particularly beneficial or therapeutic for individuals unhappy in their marriages.

Construct validity of Paulhus' Comprehensive Inventory of Desirable Responding (CIDR)

Parmac, Maja Department of Psychology, University of Zagreb, Zagreb, Croatia Galic, Zvonimir Department of Psychology, University of Zagreb, Zagreb, Croatia Jerneic, Zeljko Department of Psychology, University of Zagreb, Zagreb, Croatia Prevendar, Tamara Department of Psychology, University of Zagreb, Zagreb, Croatia

The aim of this study was to test the construct validity of the Croatian version of Paulhus' Comprehensive Inventory of Desirable Responding (2006). The CIDR comprises four subscales intended to measure components of social desirability: agentic management, agentic enhancement, communal management and communal enhancement. For this purpose independent samples of participants were tested in three situations with different instructions for self-presentation: one honest (N1=224) and two different "fake good" instructions (N2=249, N3=196). Conducted analyses revealed different factor structures in three situations, giving partial support to the model. Further studies are needed.

When are predictions self-fulfilling?

Peetz, Johanna Dept. of Psychology, Wilfrid Laurier University, Waterloo, Canada Buehler, Roger Psychology, Wilfrid Laurier University, Waterloo, Canada Griffin, Dale Sauder School of Business, University of British Columbia, Vancouver, Canada

We examined under which conditions people's predictions of task completion dates carry over to their actual completion times. We randomly assigned students to predict an early or a late completion date of an experimental task, using an anchoring procedure. In the task, participants were asked to write three short essays in the 14 days following the session. These essays were either sent by email (easy condition) or by letter mail (difficult condition). Our results show that, in the domain of task completion, predictions carry over to behavior only for easy but not for difficult tasks.

How are causal powers combined?
Perales, Jose Cesar Dept. Psicología Experimental, Universidad de Granada, Granada, Spain **Maldonado, Antonio** Psicología Experimental, Universidad de Granada, Granada, Spain **Candido, Antonio** Psicología Experimental, Universidad de Granada, Granada, Spain **Contreras, David** Psicología Experimental, Universidad de Granada, Granada, Spain **Catena, Andres** Psicología Experimental, Universidad de Granada, Granada, Spain
Generative causes make the probability of their effects grow beyond zero or a certain base rate. But how do naïve reasoners compute the expected probability of an effect when two causes of such an effect are simultaneously present? And how is the power of a single cause discounted from a compound? Several experiments are presented in which people failed to combine or discount causal powers in accordance with normative probability calculus. Instead, they seem to use simple additive and subtractive combination rules that can give rise to judgment biases (over- and under-expectation) with significance in daily life.

Culture and coaching
Perkins, Patrick Scott New York-Presbyterian Hopsital, Weill Cornell Medical College, New York, USA **Cronan, Kerry Richard** Counselling Centre Ltd., Professional Consulting and, Eagle Farm, Australia **Aidman, Eugene Vladimir**
Coaching, in particular in the area of leadership, has become a regular practice in consulting psychology. Strategies will only be effective if they fit the cultural context in a way that does not mix the change in interpersonal process with a possible unnecessary change evolving in the cultural context. This presentation will draw upon studies in coaching that alert practitioners to the issue of the appropriate recognition of culture both within and surrounding the context of organizations, as well as the harmonizing of the interactions between branches of organizations of the one company.

An investigation of multiple predictors of bulimia nervosa
Pfost, Karen S. Psychology, Illinois State University (110, Normal, Illinois, USA **Westendorf, Christina** Normal, Illinois, USA **Meadows, Brooke A.** Psychology, Illinois State University (110, Normal, Illinois, USA **Philippe-Albrecht, Nona** Psychology, Illinois State University (110, Normal, Illinois, USA
Bulimia nervosa seems associated with body objectification, perfectionism, impulsivity, low self-esteem, and avoidant coping, with feminism being a potential buffer. This study extends research on determinants of bulimia nervosa by assessing predictors using the Objectified Body Consciousness Scale, Multidimensional Perfectionism Scale, Barratt Impulsiveness Scale, Rosenberg Self-Esteem Scale, the COPE, and the Feminist Identity Development Scale. These measures, along with the BUILT-R (a measure of bulimic symptoms), will be administered to 250 females at a public university in the U.S. A hierarchical regression analysis will be conducted to asses the contribution of these predictors.

The personal styles inventory: A measure of normal-range personality traits
Pfost, Karen Dept. of Psychology, Illinois State University, Normal, USA **Kunce, Joseph** Psychology, Educational & Psychologica, Columbia, USA **Newton, Russel** Psychology, Educational & Psychologica, Columbia, USA
The Personal Styles Inventory (PSI-120; Kunce, Cope, & Newton, 1999) is a measure of normal-range personality characteristics which is a unique assessement tool. Profiles take the form of an eight-component circumplex with underlying axes of introversion/extroversion and preference for stability/change. Feedback describes both personality as a whole and the three domains of cognition, affect, and behavior. The discrepancy between basic and current behavior serves as a barometer of current stress in response to environmental demands. A considerable body of research attests to the PSI-120's concurrent and discriminant validity

The role of competitiveness and social comparison in youth's health behaviors
Piko, Bettina Dept. of Behavioral Sciences, Universtity of Szeged, Szeged, Hungary **Skulteti, Dora** Dept. of Behavioral Sciences, Universtity of Szeged, Szeged, Hungary **Gibbons, Frederick** Dept. of Psychology, Iowa State University, Ames, USA
Objectives: The main goal of the present study is to investigate the role of competitiveness and social comparison in health-compromising and health-promoting behaviors. Methods: Data were collected from high school students (N = 548) in the Southern Plain Region, Hungary, using self-administered questionnaires. Multiple regression analysis was used in the statistics. Results: The role of social attitudes may be quite different depending on the situation they are used: competitiveness may act as a risk factor for substance use, social comparison may act as a protection. Conclusions: These results suggest that learning to be more socially oriented should be a part of children's socialization.

Machiavellianism and the characteristics of friendship in same-sex couples of friends
Pilch, Irena Inst. of Psychology, University of Silesia, Katowice, Poland
The aim of this study was to examine the associations of Machiavellianism with the characteristics of friendship. The data were obtained from the sample of 81 same-sex couples of friends (aged 17–49). Mach IV and a set of self-descriptive measures of a relationship's characteristics (closeness, satisfaction, support, influence, control, self-disclosure, trust, attractiveness) were used. Correlational, regression and cluster analysis were performed. Machiavellianism was negatively related to closeness, satisfaction and trust, and positively to control, but mainly for men. The results imply that Machiavellianism may reduce the quality of manly friendship. The implications are discussed in terms of evolutionary psychology.

Psychometric properties of WISC-IV verbal subtests (Latvian version) in individual versus group testing situation
Pivovarovs, Andrejs Dept. of Psychology, University of Latvia, Riga, Latvia **Rašvska, Małgožata** Psychology Department, University of Latvia, Riga, Latvia
The purpose of this study was to evaluate the differences of psychometric properties of WISC-IV five Verbal subtests (Latvian version) between individual and group (writing) testing. The participants, 470 students aged 11 through 16 were divided in 5/5 matched samples. Analysis showed that discrimination indices in individual testing are somewhat higher than in group testing. Mean scores in individual testing are higher than in group testing, yet only two subtests have statistically significant differences. There are also other persistent differences of subtests psychometric properties

between individually and group administered testing. Key words: psychometric properties, WISC-IV, discrimination index, verbal subscales

Anxiety profile as indicator of child psychological wellbeing in different life spheres
Podolskij, Andrei Dept. of Developm. Psychology, Moscow State University, Moscow, Russia **Karabanova, Olga** Developmental Psychology, Moscow State University, Moscow, Russia
Anxiety is considered to be an indicator of child psychological wellbeing. Different types of anxiety are described in contemporary studies besides traditionally selected personal and situated ones. It's fruitful to describe also an anxiety profile, which represents a combination of different types of anxiety as anxiety level in different life spheres varies very much. Using the A. Prihozhan Anxiety test it has been shown that anxiety profile is determined by such important variables as child's interrelations with parents, peers, teachers, and also school achievements. Results achieved allows to work out a correction work for children with high level of anxiety

Construct validity: How to prove it by theory-based item generating rules and IRT model-based analyses
Poinstingl, Herbert Inst. für Psychologie, Universität Wien, Wien, Austria **Kubinger, Klaus D.** University of Vienna, Faculty of Psychology, Vienna, Austria
The Family Reasoning Test (FRT) is a new verbal reasoning test. The testee has to find the right relationship of two persons when a short story is given as an item of a more or less complex family description. The items are built by using theory-based item generating rules, the latter stated according to some cognitive operations. The linear logistic test model (LLTM; Fischer, 1972), a specialization of the Rasch model, is used in order to test the construct validity of the test. If the LLTM holds then the hypothesized cognitive operations actually determine the difficulty of an item.

The ability to detect egoism: Social distance matters
Pradel, Julia Wirtschafts- u. Sozialpsychol., Universität zu Köln, Köln, Germany **Fetchenhauer, Detlef** Economic and Social Psychology, University of Cologne, Cologne, Germany
From an evolutionary point of view the ability to distinguish altruistic from egoistic interaction partners is highly adaptive - especially in close relationship with high interdependence. To find out whether humans are in fact capable to read signs of prosociality we examined 328 students of elementary and secondary school classes. We initially tested the true degree of altruism of each individual by asking subjects to divide some money between themselves and another person anonymously. Afterwards subjects had to predict their classmates' decisions. Indeed, estimates were much better than chance. Furthermore, social closeness (e.g. friendship) influenced the accuracy of predictions positively.

Behavioral analysis of sexuality in relation to HIV/AIDS: Commitment in sexual behavior
Pramod, D. S. Community Counselling, Health Alert Organsiation, Deopur, Dhule, India **Vaishali, P.S.** Community counselling, Health Alert Organsiation (NGO, Deopur, Dhule, India
Objectives: To assess Behavioral analysis of Sexuality in relation to HIV/AIDS. Methods: feedback questionnaire available to all consultants. Results: 35 consultants addressed for study, 68% allopathic, 20% Ayurvedic & 12% traditional-healers. couples screened 21% reported talk about HIV/AIDS affection. 79% kept silence. 78% of agreed to be screened after counseling. Conclusion:HIV/AIDS

affection often comes into private conversations of many couples [68 We need to permanent sensitization and information and adequate care taking of the already affected Lessons learned: Rural/tribal population an iceberg phenomenon. need to shift our focus form urban to rural areas where AIDS is epidemic.

Academic achievement in relation to depressive symptomatology, intelligence and neuropsychological variables

Preiss, Marek Dept. of Psychology, Prague Psychiatric Center, Prague, Czech Republic *Franova, Lenka* Psychology, Institute of Psychology, Prague, Czech Republic

Project examined relations between academic achievement, depressive symptomatology, neuropsychological variables and intelligence in children sample (N=814), from elementary schools in Prague. Neuropsychological tests, depressive scale, academic performance and intelligence were administred. Significant relations between school grades and intelligence, depressive symptomatology and partially neuropsychological variables was found. Common variance of used psychological variables for the overall average grades was 25.8% (p<.0001), for boys 25.7 and for girls 30.1. When examining problematic academic achievement it is necessary to control for depressive symptomatology. Psychological variables can explain only 1/4 of academic achievement, 3/4 are necessary to be explained with other information.

Development of the Types of Intuition Scale (TIntS)

Pretz, Jean Dept. of Psychology, Illinois Wesleyan University, Bloomington, USA *Brookings, Jeffrey* Psychology, Wittenberg University, Springfield, OH, USA

The TIntS was developed to measure three types of intuition identified in a recently-published literature review (Pretz & Totz, 2007): holistic, inferential, and affective. Holistic intuitions integrate diverse sources of information in a Gestalt-like and non-analytical manner, inferential intuitions are based on previously-analytical processes which have become automatic, and affective intuitions are based on feelings. Items for each type of intuition were administered to 170 undergraduates. Reliability and factor analyses supported the distinction among the three predicted types of intuition, and the scales were validated by examining correlations with existing measures of intuition and personality.

Does incentive strength affect response force?

Puca, Rosa Maria Inst. für Bildung, Ruhr-Universität Bochum, Bochum, Germany *Rinkenauer, Gerhard* Modern Human-Machine Systems, IfADo, Dortmund, Germany

In two experiments we assessed whether behavioral strength is modulated by incentive strength. Participants had to press a force key, whenever a number appeared on the screen. Positive, negative numbers and zero indicated the amount of points they could either win or loose. Experiment 1 revealed that response force increased with the amount of points. In Experiment 2 this finding was replicated. An additional control group, however, in which participants were instructed just to respond to the presented numbers, did not show any response force effects. Thus, our findings strongly suggest that incentive strength affects response force.

Equotherapy: Health professionals speaks on their motivations for the exercise of this work

Pugas, Mirela Mackenzie University, São Paulo, Brazil *Yabuki, Renata* Psychology Course, Mackenzie University, São Paulo, Brazil *Becker, Elisabth* Pós-graduation, Mackenzie University, São Paulo, Brazil

The horse is an animal applied as a therapeutic resource for its useful characteristics. The objective of this research was describing the present factors in the heath professional chosen to work with 'Equotherapy'. The method had as procedure of five semi structure interviews. The result ('content analyses') allowed to consider for this group the motivation say about liking the animal and the interaction with it and the opportunity to work in nature conditions. These professionals find in the direct observation of therapeutics benefits and the experience of humanity help are the most important motivational link of continuity of this activity.

The neural basis of syllogistic reasoning: An event-related potential study

Qiu, Jiang School of Psychology, Southwest University, Chongqing, People's Republic of China *Zhang, Qinglin* School of Psychology, Southwest University, Chongqing, People's Republic of China

The spatiotemporal analysis of brain activation from syllogistic reasoning and one baseline task (BST) execution was performed in 14 normal young adult participants using high-density event-related brain potentials (ERPs). Results mainly showed that (see figure 1): a greater negativity in VSR and ISR as compared to BST developed 600-700 ms. Dipole source analysis of difference waves (VSR-BST and ISR -BST) indicated that the negative components were mainly localized near the medial frontal cortex/the anterior cingulate cortex, possibly related to the manipulation and integration of premise information.

The relationship between socio-economic status and mental health

Rajaei, Yadollah Zanjan, Islamic Republic of Iran

The aim of this study was to investigate the relationship between socio-economic status (income, education, and occupation) and mental health. 150 employees in Zanjan comprising university heads, professors, teachers, civil servants, laborers, and farmers completed the Mental Health Inventory (MHI) and demographic information form. Data were analyzed using One- Way ANO-VA and Chi- Square. Results revealed that there were significant relation between indexes of SES, distress and well -being. Significant differences were found between men and women in distress and well -being. Finding can be helpful in providing appropriate policies for preventive programs and promoting public health.

Hypnosis in the alleviation of procedure-related pain in children with cancer

Ramírez Zamora, Laura Mriam Queretaro, Mexico

Although cancer is not always painful in its own right, these patients undergo numerous painful procedures including lumbar puncture (LP) and bone marrow aspiration (BMA) Objectives 1) Examine the efficacy of a hypnotic intervention in reducing procedure-related pain and anxiety during PL and BMA among patients with leukemia 2) Adapt a coping pain questionnaire, a distress behavioral scale and the Stanford Hypnotic Clinical Scale for Children to Mexican population. 3) Explore changes in coping and hypnotic responsiveness after hypnotic intervention Methods 20 pediatric leukemia patients undergoing regular LP and BMA in a cuasiexperimental design with repeated measures. Pilot results will be presented

Relationship of gatekeepers' attitude toward condom use and condom use behavior of female sex workers in China

Ran, Zhao and Economy, Central University of Finance, Beijing, People's Republic of China *Fang, Xiaoyi* Institute of developmental Psy, Beijing Normal Univery, China, Beijing, People's Republic of China *Li, Xiaoming* medical school, Wayne State University, USA, Detroit, USA

To explore gatekeepers' attitudes toward condom use, and to assess their association with FSWs' consistence condom-use, condom use intention and sexual disease infection. Condom use specific support from gatekeepers was rather low in establishments. Gatekeepers' attitudes toward condom use were positively associated with condom use frequency (OR, 1.326; 95%CI: 1.048-1.678) and intention (ß, 0.127; P?0.001; R2adj, 0.096; F, 23.728***) among 454 establishment-based FSWs in Guangxi, China. However, they were not associated with sexual disease infection. Health workers should work together with gatekeepers to create a supportive local environment for condom use in establishments. In addition, treatment of sexual disease will be necessary.

Pecularities of ethnic identity and ethnic stereotypes of young people from mono and multicultural families in Latvia

Raschevskis, Vitalijs Social Psychology, Daugavpils University, Daugavpils, Latvia *Vorobjovs, Aleksejs* Social Psychology, Daugavpils University, Daugavpils, Latvia *Ruza, Aleksejs* Social Psychology, Daugavpils University, Daugavpils, Latvia

The objective of the research is to study peculiarities of ethnic identity and ethnic stereotypes of young people from mono and multicultural families in Latvia. Theoretical background is based on Tajfel's and Turner's social identity theory, Berry's theory of acculturation, Ericsson's and Murcia's theory of identity formation, etc. Two methods have been used in the research: Phinney's Multi Ethnic Identity Method (MEIM), and Soldatova's Types of Ethnic Identity Method (TEIM). The results let to make a conclusion peculiarities of ethnic identity and ethnic stereotypes of young people from mono and multicultural families in Latvia.

Epidemiology of postpartum anxiety and depressive disorders

Reck, Corinna Inst. für Psychiatrie, Universität Heidelberg, Heidelberg, Germany

Objectives: Depressive and Anxiety Disorders are the most frequent mental disorders in the postpartum period. This is the first study on postpartum anxiety disorders in Germany. Methods: In a two-stage screening procedure a population-based representative sample of 1024 postpartum women were studied over the first three months postpartum using DSM-IV-criteria. Results: The estimated rate of anxiety disorders was 11.1% and of depressive disorder was 6.1%. Young mothers (< 25 years) with a high education level had a heightened risk of developing depression following delivery. Conclusions: Controlled studies comparing postpartum and non-postpartum prevalence of anxiety disorders are required, as well as specialized programmes for prevention and treatment.

Impact of violent computer games on memory consolidation and concentrativeness

Rehbein, Florian KFN, Universität Hannover, Hannover, Germany *Mößle, Thomas* Medienn. und Schulleistung, KFN, Hannover, Germany *Kleimann, Matthias* Medienn. und Schulleistung, KFN, Hannover, Germany

Objectives: To test the hypothesis whether the perception of media violence especially videogames results in lower performances in memory, learning and attention. Methods: Experiment (between-subjects design). 360 participants aged 18-25. Treatment: Non-violent filmlets, violent filmlets, non-violent videogames, violent videogames and non-media leisure activities. Outcome measures: School related memory and learning performance (VVM: Visueller und Verbaler Merkfähigkeitstest; WERNICKO: Fictional language acquisition), attention performance (KLT-R: Konzentrations-Leistungs-Test). Results: Statistical evaluation indicating impairment of concentrativeness in violent videogame usage but no impairment of memory performance. Conclusion: Our findings are strengthening the "Modified-Information-Processing-Hypothesis" rather than the "Delition-Hypthesis".

Coping strategies and personal strengths and difficulties in internationally adopted children

Reinoso, Marta Dept. de Personalitat, Universitat de Barcelona, Barcelona, Spain Forns, Maria Personalitat, Universitat de Barcelona, Barcelona, Spain

This study analyzes the type of coping strategies used by international adopted children and their relationship with personal strengths and difficulties. The Kidcope (Spirito et al., 1998) and the Strengths and Difficulties Questionnaire (SDQ; Goodman, 1997) were administered to a sample of 50 internationally adopted children (50% boys and 50% girls) and their parents, respectively. The subjects were recruited from several adoptive parents associations of Barcelona (Spain). Self-reported problems were categorized and their relationship to coping strategies and psychological adjustment was explored. The results are discussed within the framework of Lazarus and Folkman's stress and coping model (1984).

Love addiction: The role of personality in its understanding

Retana, Blanca Mexico City, Mexico Sánchez, Rozzana Psychology Social, UNAM, Distrito Federal, Mexico

The addiction to love is in our days, a pathological consequence of many personal and situational variables that are related (Retana-Franco, 2007). Among these, the personality traits play an important role in the way the lover feels, thinks and behaves being close and far from his/her object of love. Based on this, the purpose of this research was to measure persistence, anxiety, obsessiveness, despair, sense of emergency, and others traits in order to identify the personality profile of these lovers. Findings will be described in terms of the literature of love, passion, addictions to substances and gender differences.

The emotional regulation process of jealousy: The case of homo and heterosexuals lovers

Retana, Blanca Mexico City, Mexico Sánchez, Rozzana Psychology Social, National Autonomous University, Distrito Federal, Mexico

Jealousy is an emotion that emerges when the individual perceives a real or imaginary threat to the exclusivity with a love one (Diaz-Loving, Rivera- Aragón & Flores-Galaz, 1989). In this context of romantic jealousy, the experience evokes high vulnerability. Due to its intensity and the strong consequences in the emotional life, it appears necessary to explore the processes involved in the way the individual cope with the emotion and with the object of love (Gross & Thompson, 2007). The present research studied in 200 Mexican adults (50% homo & 50% heterosexual) the five processes that allow examine the main mechanism to regulate the emotion and the particular strategies.

Is there a common construct underlying the need for cognition, perfectionism, industriousness and persistence?

Reyes Lagunes, Isabel Facultad de Psicología, UNAM, México, Mexico García-y-Barragán, Luis Felipe Facultad de Psicología, UNAM, México, Mexico Correa-Romero, Fredi E. Facultad de Psicología, UNAM, México, Mexico

In this poster is presented the adaptation and validation of five scales from four different theoretical approximations and the relation between them, the constructs evaluated were Need for cognition, Perfectionism (2 different scales), industriousness and Persistence. The sample was no probabilistic, intentionally conformed by 446 participants (male = 47%; Age M=23, SD=9) from

Mexico City. The scales present Cronbach's Alpha values from 0.78 to 0.91, factor and structural equation modeling analysis were performed, the results shows an underlying theoretical construct to the four constructs referred previously.

Disentangling the working memory impairment in ADHD

Rhodes, Sinead Psychology, University of Stirling, Stirling, United Kingdom Park, Joanne Psychology, University of Stirling, Stirling, United Kingdom Seth, Sarah Psychiatry, University of Dundee, Dundee, United Kingdom Coghill, David Psychiatry, University of Dundee, Dundee, United Kingdom

Research investigating the specific nature of the working memory (WM) impairment in Attention Deficit Hyperactivity Disorder (ADHD) is lacking. Here we investigated executive and non-executive aspects of verbal and spatial WM functioning in children with ADHD. Twenty-seven drug naïve boys with ADHD (age range 7-13) and matched controls performed a range of specifically designed and standardized WM tasks. Children with ADHD were impaired on visuo-spatial but not on a non-executive verbal WM task requiring the ability to maintain information in memory. The current data disentangles the WM impairment in ADHD suggesting particular difficulties in executive aspects of visuo-spatial WM.

Is genetic information helpful or harmful? A randomised clinical trial

Rief, Winfried Inst. für Psychologie, Universität Marburg, Marburg, Germany

The emerging success of genetic research leads to more and more knowledge about the heredity of several disorders. However, the question arises whether this genetic information is helpful or harmful for affected people. We investigated 300 people with obesity, and they received either a psychological consultation including information on genetic determinants of obesity, or a psychological consultation without genetic information. Group allocation was per randomisation. Results indicated that the inclusion of genetic information is only warranted for a subgroup of people with obesity, namely those with clear individual evidence for genetic determinants (family history of obesity or MC4R-mutation).

Questionnaire for Obsessive Compulsive Disorder Diagnoses (Q-OCDD): Psychometric properties in a clinical group

Rivas Moya, Teresa Psychobiology and Methodology, University of Málaga, Málaga, Spain Gavino, Aurora Psychobiology and Methodology, Málaga University, Málaga, Spain Planas, Amanda Psychobiology and Methodology, Málaga University, Málaga, Spain

This study focuses on the validation of the Questionnaire for Obsessive Compulsive Disorder Diagnoses (Q-OCDD; Planas, Rivas and Gavino, 2004; Rivas, Planas and Gavino, 2004) in a Clinical Group. 17 subjects aged 16-57 answered the Q-OCDD, Yale-Brown Obsessive-Compulsive Scale (YBSR(A); Baer, Brown-Beasley, et al., 1993) and underwent a Clinical Interview based on DSM-IV-R. Agreement between raters is 0.87. Convergence/Divergence between the classification of Q-OCDD and YBSR(A) scores are shown. Criterion validity of Q-OCDD categories in relation to DSM-IV-R criteria shows moderate sensitivity (78.6) and high specificity (100) in detecting OCD. The clinical and theoretical implications of these results are discussed.

Thinness and beauty: When food becomes the enemy

Robles, Delma Center for Counseling Services, De La Salle-College of St. Ben, Manila, Philippines

The study examines self-construal variables (perfectionism, body image, ideal body shape, and

socio-cultural pressure) and their path leading to bulimia, anorexia and binge eating as mediated by self-esteem and well-being among 137 college women. Three models were tested using path analysis. Model 1 showed that body image significantly affects self-esteem and well-being. When the model was constricted, perfectionism had a significant effect on self-esteem and well-being in addition to the effects of body image. The third model shows the best fit. Self-esteem and well-being mediates the effect of body image and perfectionism to bulimia.

Romantic love, physical attraction and sexual behaviour in Mexican adolescents

Robles Montijo, Silvia Susana Investigación-UIICSE, FES Iztacala-UNAM, Tlalnepantla, Mexico Díaz Loving, Rolando Investigaciones Psicosociales, Facultad de Psicología, UNAM, México, D.F., Mexico

This study evaluated the relationship between physical attraction and romantic love with the intention of having sex and using condoms in adolescents with and without sexual experience. The participants were 300 Mexican teenagers (mean age of 15.2 years), 50% with sexual intercourse experience. The results indicated that intention of having sexual intercourse was related to physical attraction in adolescents with no sexual experience and only with intense sexual desire in those who already have had sexual experience. The intention to use condoms was related to romantic love in adolescents with no sexual experience and it was related to physical attraction and passionate love only in sexually experienced teenagers.

Beliefs about the future

Rocca, Claudia Psychology, Carleton University, Ottawa, Canada Thorngate, Warren Psychology, Carleton University, Ottawa, Canada

In a world that is undergoing change, it's important to determine young adults' expectations about the future. Here we examine what students from different countries think about their own futures and that of the world. Participants from Canada and Iran completed a questionnaire assessing future expectations for themselves and the world. The results give insights about cultural differences in individual's personal views and expectations of their futures the world's. We want to determine if beliefs about the future are related to gender and age, and see if the methodology is useful for exploring cultural differences in images of the future.

Conflict emergence and conflict management in developing scientific innovations

Rocholl, Anne Berlin, Germany Schulze, Anna Dorothea Organizational Psychology, Humboldt Universität zu Berlin, Berlin, Germany

The genesis of scientific innovation is characterized by conflicts and controversies. If they are handled constructively, the process of innovation proceeds more constructively, too. In 50 problem-centred interviews with researchers in basic research and applied research in the field of genetic engineering, we analyzed the process of innovation from an early stage to the implementation in new products and methods. In longitudinal studies we followed the development of six projects. Based on this, we created a model which shows the main steps of innovation development. We demonstrate how these accompany the handling of conflicts.

Effects of psychotherapy and exercise-training on psychosocial and physiological parameters of HIV-1 positive persons

Rojas, Roberto Station B3, Klinik Roseneck, Prien am Chiemsee, Germany Hautzinger, Martin Abteilung Klinische Psychologi, Universität Tübingen, Tübingen, Germany Schlicht, Wolfgang Institut für

Sportwissenschaft, Universität Stuttgart, Stuttgart, Germany

The present study was designed to compare the effects of a psychotherapy intervention and an exercise-training program on psychosocial and physiological parameter in a sample of HIV-1 positive persons. A pre-, post-test design with two experimental groups (psychotherapy, n= 20; exercise, n= 19) and a control group (n= 14) was carried out. Health-related quality of life improved significantly in the exercise and in the psychotherapeutical group relative to the control group. Coping strategies, as well as immune indices remained invariable in the three groups. Findings suggested that exercise and psychotherapy interventions enhance health-related quality of life in HIV-1 positive individuals.

Internal structure of the DBAS-18 in a sample of Spanish elderly

Rojas, Antonio Facultad de Psicologia, Universidad de Granada, Granada, Spain Sierra, Juan Carlos Facultad de PsicologÂ-a, Universidad de Granada, Granada, Spain López, Carmen AEPC, AEPC, Granada, Spain Sanchez, Arturo AEPC, AEPC, Granada, Spain

This study analysed internal structure of the Spanish DBAS-18 using the sample of 433 Spanish elderly (age: M = 68.25; SD = 8.99). Four factors yielded by Sierra et al. (2006) in a Spanish shift-workers sample obtaining different values of internal consistency: Consequences of the insomnia on the diurnal yield/functioning (α = .73), Control and prediction of the sleep (α = .50), Consequences of the insomnia on the physical and mental health (α = 0.75), and Expectations on the association sleep-age (α = .50). The factor analysis conducted afterwards drew out another four factors but not with hardly any coherence.

Psychometrics properties of Athens Insomnia Scale-5 in a Spanish sample

Rojas, Antonio Facultad de Psicologia, Universidad de Granada, Granada, Spain Sierra, Juan Carlos Facultad de PsicologÂ-a, Universidad de Granada, Granada, Spain Sanchez, Arturo AEPC, AEPC, Granada, Spain

This work shows the psychometric properties of Athens Insomnia Scale-5 (Soldatos et al., 2000) in Spanish sample of 237 adults (mean age = 50.89; SD = 20.67) (41.8% for men and 58.2 for women). The exploratory factor analysis has yielded only one factor that explains 49.43% of the variance, showing internal consistency of .74, better than the values obtained by Guilera et al. (2006) using Spanish university students sample. The scale did not show the capacity to differentiate between men and women, but the results indicated significant correlation with the age (r = .20; p < .01).

The implications of depression and the main impact on the human body

Romero Molina, Adriana Metepec, Mexico

The present work has the objective to analyze the main implications of depression and its impact in the bodies of the five subjects; for this end it was implemented a qualitative study. Autobiographical techniques, semi structured interviews and a projective technique was applied to this investigation, such techniques were implemented to the five adult women that attended psychological attention regarding depression. The results that were obtained show that the subjects present symptoms such as insomnia, gastrointestinal difficulties, headaches, pain on the neck area and finally, weakening of the psychomotor functions. These symptoms make identifiable the body's implications that its brings with itself a depression.

What do people with disabilities desire from their service organizations of personal assistance?

Roos, John Magnus Inst. of Psychologie, University of Gothenburg, Göteborg, Sweden Hjelmquist, Erland Department of Psychology, Göteborg University, Göteborg, Sweden Thoren-Jönsson, Anna-Lisa Neuroscience and Physiology, Göteborg University, Göteborg, Sweden

The present study investigated what adult users of Swedish personal assistance desire of their service organizations. Qualitative analysis of interviews with 12 users gave five categories: (1) Interact with the user in a service-minded way, (2) mediate between users and personal assistants, (3) provide good work conditions for personal assistants, (4) represent the user politically and (5) have a proper ideology of personal assistance. The results were discussed in relation to theories of customer desires. The first category corresponds to desires of service customers in general, while the other four categories are more specific for personal assistance.

Developmental study about textual and extratextual inferences and its relationchip with working memory

Rosende, Marta PSICOLOGÍA EVOLUTIVA Y DE LA E, UNIVERSITY OF LA CORUÑA, LA CORUÑA, Spain Vieiro, Pilar Psicologia Evolutiva, University of La Coruna, La Coruna, Spain

The aim of this work is to analyze the relationship between textual vs. extratextual inferences and working memory. One hundred and twenty subjects were used (40 from 4th primary grade; 40 from 2nd Primary grade and 40 from University). three on-line proofs were used to measure inferences and three different versions of Reading span Test were used to measure working memory as independent variable. Results showed:a) significant differences according to WM in 2nd grade students in the use of textual inferences; b) significant use of textual generation in 3rd garde group; c) significant developmental differences between three groups in generation of both inference types. Keywords: inferences, reading comprehension, working memory.

Enemies: Their purpose in our Lives

Rourke, Jessica Victoria, BC, Canada Gifford, Robert Dept. of Psychology, University of Victoria, Victoria, Canada

The need for enemies was examined. We hypothesized that participants would report a need for enemies, having previously had enemies, and that enemies serve a purpose. The participants were 141 undergraduates at a Canadian university. On openended and checklist items, 15% expressed a need for enemies, 79% had experienced at least one enemy in their lifetime, and 41% believed that enemies serve a purpose (e.g., motivating them to improve and as a means of social comparison). Those with higher self-esteem reported a greater need for enemies. Perhaps counter-intuitively, enemies may often play a valuable role in people's lives.

The psychology of internet activity

Rudnicka, Patrycja Inst. of Psychology, University of Silesia, Katowice, Poland

Despite the Internet becomes important part of everyday life, significant differences in its dispersion and use are being observed. Demographic, environmental and individual factors are mentioned as key issues. However their relationships and influence on internet activity is still to be explored from psychological perspective. Based on data gathered from over 1000 students, cluster analysis and structural equation modeling (SEM) were used to identify and estimate causal relationships between psychological factors and patterns of internet use. Study results show self-efficacy, anxiety and attitudes significant factors shaping internet activity.

Changes in the cognitive restructuring technique during the psychological treatment

Ruiz, Elena Biological & Health Psychology, Universidad Autónoma de Madrid, Madrid, Spain Calero, Ana Psidologia Biologica y Salud, Universidad Autonoma de Madrid, Madrid, Spain Montano, Montserrat PSICOLOGÍA BIOLÓGICA Y SALUD, UNIVERSIDAD AUTÓNOMA DE MADRID, MADRID, Spain Frojan, María Xesús PSICOLOGÍA BIOLÓGICA Y SALUD, UNIVERSIDAD AUTÓNOMA DE MADRID, MADRID, Spain

The aim of the present work is to analyze the changes in the restructuring technique as the treatment progresses. We observed 10 recorded sessions of a single case who requested treatment in a private centre. 6 segments of restructuring were randomly selected and analyzed with The Observer XT and a coding system for the verbal behaviour of therapists and clients. Results show changes in the verbalizations of the therapist and the client during the application of the technique. In the long term it means an advance in a general model which will guide a more systematic use of the technique.

Relation between verbal recall memory and facial affect perception in schizophrenia

Ruiz, Juan Carlos Facultad de Psicologia, University of Valencia, Valencia, Spain Dasí, Carmen FACULTAD DE PSICOLOGÍA, UNIVERSITY OF VALENCIA, VALENCIA, Spain Soler, María José FACULTAD DE PSICOLOGÍA, UNIVERSITY OF VALENCIA, VALENCIA, Spain Fuentes, Inma FACULTAD DE PSICOLOGÍA, UNIVERSITY OF VALENCIA, VALENCIA, Spain Jaramillo, Paola FACULTAD DE PSICOLOGÍA, UNIVERSITY OF VALENCIA, VALENCIA, Spain Tomás, Pilar CRIS - VELLUTERS, CRIS - VELLUTERS, VALENCIA, Spain

Patients with schizophrenia have a consistent deficit in facial affect perception. This deficit might underlie the poor adaptive functioning of schizophrenic patients and could be attributed to impairments in basic neurocognitive domains. This study explores the relationship between emotion perception measured using the Face Emotion Identification Test (FEIT) and the Face Emotion Discrimination Test (FEDT) (Kerr & Neale, 1993), and two verbal recall tests: immediate and delayed recall in a sample of 45 patients. Results show a significant association between recall tasks and the FEDT. The implications of the results in the study of neurocognition and social cognition are discussed.

Collective efficacy, civic culture, fear to crime, perception of police, emotional climate and victimization: A exploratory study in Bogota

Ruiz Pérez, Jose Ignacio Psychology, Universidad Nacional de Colomb, Bogotá, Colombia Cepeda Gómez, Diana Magaly Psychology, Universidad Nacional de Colomb, Bogotá, Colombia

Recent research show collective efficacy is a relevant variable in community impact of delinquency, fear to crime and health problems. In this paper relationships between collective efficacy, civic culture, and perception of police, victimization and emotional climate and crime victimization is presented. Data were obtained from a non-randomized sample of university students (three institutions) and neighbors of Bogotá.

Psychosocial subgroups in patients with chronic pain: Evidence for maladaptive pain-related coping within the dysfunctional group based on the Multidimensional Pain Inventory

Rusu, Adina Carmen Inst. für Medizin. Psychologie, Ruhr-Universität Bochum, Bochum, Germany Hasenbring, Monika Med. Psychology & Sociolog, Ruhr-Universitat Bochum, Bochum, Germany

Background: To examine the relationship between the Dysfunctional group, based on the Multidimensional Pain Inventory (MPI), and dysfunctional pain-related coping strategies. Methods: 120 chronic pain patients were assigned to MPI groups and compared on pain-related fear-avoidance coping (FAC) and endurance coping (EC) measured by the Kiel Pain Inventory. Results: Dysfunctional patients reported more anxiety/depression, help-/hopelessness, catastrophizing and thought suppression than did adaptive copers. However, subgroups did not differ with regard to endurance behaviour and avoidance of social and physical activity. Conclusions: Future studies should investigate the contribution of thought suppression and endurance behaviour within the MPI groups and unravel the complex relationship between pain-related FAC and EC.

Self-concept, attachment security and motivation of achievement in university students

Sabelnikova, Natalia Pedagogical Institute, Barnaul State Pedagog. Univer., Barnaul, Russia

The purpose of the study was to investigate relation between peculiarities of young adults' motivation of achievement, attachment and the particular aspects of their self-concepts (self-respect, self-interest, self-acceptance, etc.). Subjects were 147 university students. The following instruments were employed: Motivation Questionnaire by Kubyshkin; Experience in Close relationships Inventory (ECR) by Brennan, Clark and Shaver and Self-Attitude Questionnaire by Stolin. Results show differences in attachment of the subjects with different levels of aspiration for competition and social prestige. The level of aspiration for competition differs also in students with different peculiarities of self-concepts. Self-concepts of students with different attachment styles are also examined. Implications of the results are discussed.

Image is everything?: The effects of industry groups images on private investors willingness to invest

Sachse, Katharina Inst. für Psychologie, FR 2-6, Technische Universität Berlin, Berlin, Germany Jungermann, Helmut Psychologie, FR 2-6, TU Berlin, Berlin, Germany

According to traditional theories of finance the willingness to invest in stocks is determined by risk and return. Yet, studies have shown that other factors like e.g. the "home" of the company also affect investment decisions. We hypothesized that another factor is the image of industry groups, such as Software or Media. 140 participants were asked to invest (hypothetically) 50.000 € in funds of different industry groups. Subjects also had to assess the image of these industries. A regression analysis showed that the amount invested was best predicted by the image. Perceived risk and benefit were significant predictors as well.

The role of emotions in conflict resolution strategies in cross-sex friendships of adolescents

Salanga, Maria Guadalupe Corpuz Counseling & Educational Psych, De La Salle University, Manila, Philippines

A between-groups experiment was conducted to examine the effect of appeasement and supplication emotions evidenced by the target on conflict resolution strategies utilized by the other individual in the conflict exchange. One hundred eighty-six participants were randomly assigned to vignettes depicting their involvement in a conflict with an opposite sex friend evidencing either appeasement or supplication emotions. Participants then rated the strategies they would likely utilize to handle the conflict. Results of one-way analysis of variance reveal that appeasement emotions led the other individual to use proactive resolution strategies while supplication emotions led to the use of passive resolution strategies.

Prevalence of dissociation among German adolescents and the relations to academic achievement and media use

Sann, Uli Inst. für Pädagog. Psychologie, Universität Frankfurt, Frankfurt, Germany

Objectives: The study aimed at examining the prevalence of dissociation and its connection to academic achievement. Methods: 1784 German secondary school students were surveyed. Data was analyzed by means of hierarchical regression and path analysis. Results: 12,6% of the students (response rate 88 %) showed high dissociation scores signifying pathological dissociation. This prevalence was higher than that for antisocial behaviour and emotional distress. While dissociation showed no relation with academic achievement, it was related with the use of media. Conclusions: The high prevalence of severe dissociation suggests continuing research on the relation between dissociation and social functioning.

Gender and hierarchical level effects in using interpersonal influence tactics in Brazilian organizations

Santille, Alexandre Experimental Psychol, Universidade de São Paulo, São Paulo, Brazil Andrade da Silva, Gabriela Experimental Psychol, Universidade de São Paulo, São Paulo, Brazil Otta, Emma Experimental Psychology, Universidade de São Paulo, São Paulo, Brazil Samartini, André IMQ, Fundação Getúlio Vargas, São Paulo, Brazil

To investigate gender and hierarchical level effects in using interpersonal influence in Brazilian organizations, 141 agents and 274 targets (subordinates, peers and bosses) filled a questionnaire evaluating 11 influence tactics. Results showed that influence tactics usage were affected by hierarchic level of the target more than by the gender of the target. Nonetheless, male agents reported greater usage than their targets of most of the tactics, while female agents evaluated themselves similarly to their targets. Also, we found that there were differences between self and others evaluations concerning tactics usage, suggesting the importance of conducting both analysis in future research.

Mood congruence effects in depressed patient's childhood memories

Santos, João Barreiro, Portugal Cláudio, Victor Clínica, ISPA, Lisboa, Portugal

The objective of this study was to ascertain whether or not depressed individuals show a mood congruency effect when remembering their childhood memories. The results of two groups – one with fifteen subjects without a previous history of psychopathology and the other composed of fifteen subjects with a depression diagnosis – were compared using an Autobiographical Memory Task, the Beck Depression Inventory, State-Trace Anxiety Inventory and a Schema Questionnaire. The results showed the inexistence of a mood congruency effect, which suggests that childhood memories aren't as biased as more recent ones. This discrepancy can be useful in therapeutical work.

Reliability and factor structure of the Hurlbert Index of sexual assertiviness from a transcultural study

Santos, Pablo Granada University, Granada, Spain Sierra, Juan Carlos Personality, Assessment and Ps, Granada University, Granada, Spain Ortega, Virgilio Psychology, Granada University, Granada, Spain Gutierrez, Ricardo Psychology, Granada University, Granada, Spain Maeso, María Dolores Psychology, Behavioral Psychology Spanish, Granada, Spain Gomez, Pilar Psychology, Behavioral Psychology Spanish, Granada, Spain

OBJECTIVE. Reliability and factor structure of the Hurlbert Index of Sexual Assertiviness (HISA; Hurlbert, 1991) were examined in two Spanish-speaking women samples with different cultures. METHOD. HISA was administered to 300 Salvadorian women and 227 Spanish women. RESULTS. For the Salvadorian sample, items 14, 19, 20, and 22 showed lower item-total correlations; the hypothesized one-factor solution accounted for 31.50% of the variance and alpha coefficient was .89. For the Spanish sample, items 8, 20, and 22 obtained lower item-total correlations; the one-factor model accounted for 31.97% of the variance and alpha coefficient was .90. In addition, similar results were reported from both samples

Emotional labor and impression management in the local tourism industry

Sarabia - Ridad, Chizanne Psychology Dept., Negros Oriental State Univ., Dumaguete City, Philippines

ABSTRACT This research is considered to be a prime study in the Philippine context. This study attempted to establish the relationship between emotional labor and impression management in the local tourism industry. A total of 160 respondents working as frontline staff were asked to answer the questionnaires. Two sets of questionnaires were used to gather the data: (1) Emotional Labor Instrument; and (2) the Balance Inventory of Desirable Responding (BIDR), which included impression management. Emotional labor is evident, regardless of reported impression management strategies. The results also serve as a tool to increase awareness about the tendencies towards job exploitation and psychologically hazardous working environments.

Cognitive behaviour therapy on emotional and personality factors

Saraladevi, K.K. Dept. of Physical Science, Mesten College of Education, Chennai, India

This investigation focusses on emotional and personality factors among college students. 200 college students from 18 to 25 years age group were selected and their emotional and personality factors were tested and pre-test scores were noted. They were given cognitive behaviour therapy were given for three weeks along with deep muscle relaxation. Then their anxiety, anger, depression states, happiness, self confidence, concentration and emotional intelligence were measured. Data were statistically analysed through 'C.R', correlation coefficicient and 'F' test. conclusions. There were significant differences between pre-test and post-test scores of anxiety, anger, depression states happiness, self confidence, concentration and emotional intelligence among college students before and after applying CBT

Study on the evolution of the personality disorders in a day hospital

Sarmiento Luque, Teresa Barcelona, Spain Aguirre, Candida PSYCHIATRY, FUNDACION HOSPITAL DE MOLLET, BARCELONA, Spain Sanchez, Jose Maria PSYCHIATRY, FUNDACION HOSPITAL DE MOLLET, BARCELONA, Spain Fabregat, Vicente PSYCHIATRY, FUNDACION HOSPITAL DE MOLLET, BARCELONA, Spain Borrego, Raquel PSYCHIATRY, FUNDACION HOSPITAL DE MOLLET, BARCELONA, Spain Corominas, Antoni PSYCHIATRY, FUNDACION HOSPITAL DE MOLLET, BARCELONA, Spain

OBJETIVE: To determine the predictive factor of response in patients with personality disorders. DESIGN & METHOD: 40. Sociodemographic, historical and clinical variables (SCL-90/GSI) were collected at the admission. The following variables were assessed throughout the treatment: Social Adaptation Self-evaluation Scale, Coping Orientations to Problems Experienced and the Simplified questionnaire of adhesion and therapeutic compliance. Data collected at discharge: SCL-90/GSI, personality (SCID-II), intelligence (WAIS-III) and questionnaire of satisfaction with treatment. The analyses: bivariant test and logistic regression.

RESULTS: The variables "suppression of competing activities and venting of emotions" are positively related and "religion" is negatively. CONCLUSIONS: Perception and coping strategies are predictors of improvement.

Face validity in personality tests: Psychometric instruments and projective techniques in comparison

Sartori, Riccardo Dept. of Psychology, University of Verona, Verona, Italy

Objectives: Face validity differentiates personality tests such as projective techniques and psychometric instruments. People were asked to compare the two kinds of tests on the mere basis of their surface. Methods: 238 participants were administered an ad hoc tool. Data were analyzed using techniques of Correspondence Analysis. Results: Personality tests are judged in two dimensions: the aesthetic and the efficacy. Although participants acknowledge that psychometric instruments are credible and scientific, there is a clear preference for projective techniques, principally by females, people younger than 22 and participants with lower education (p < .05). Conclusions: The aesthetic dimension seems to prevail over the efficacy dimension.

Acquiescence and social desirability in the Italian version of the Balanced Emotional Empathy Scale (BEES) by Mehrabian

Sartori, Riccardo Dept. of Psychology, University of Verona, Verona, Italy

Objectives: The study has investigated the effects of acquiescence and social desirability in the Balanced Emotional Empathy Scale (BEES) by Mehrabian, which is a self-report instrument for the measurement of emotional empathy. Methods: 204 participants were administered the 30 items of the BEES together with 9 items from the Social Desirability Scale (SDS) by Marlowe and Crowne. The data were analyzed using techniques of Linear Correlation and Analysis of Variance. Results and Conclusions: Results show that the responses to the items of the BEES are not affected by acquiescence, but, though not in a particularly marked way, by social desirability (r between BEES and SDS = .21, p < .001).

Prediction of psychiatrists on the incidence of Egorrhea symptoms among university students in Japan

Sasaki, Jun Dep.Cogn.Behav.Sci., University of Tokyo, Tokyo, Japan Tanno, Yoshihiko Dep.Cogn.Behav.Sci., University of Tokyo, Tokyo, Japan

Objectives: People with "egorrhea" symptoms (ES: Kasahara, 1972) feel that private information (i.e. emotions and thoughts) "leak out," and it is regarded as a serious clinical condition. The aim of the present study was to investigate the predictions of psychiatrists on the incidence of ES among university students. Methods: Using a twelve-item instrument designed to assess ES, the prediction of psychiatrists on the incidence of egorrhea and its actual incidence were compared. Results: The actual incidence of egorrhea was higher than the predicted incidence. Conclusions: Japanese psychiatrists might tend to diagnose ES as a clinical problem.

The role of the visuospatial sketchpad in associative learning

Sasaki, Takashi Department of Education, Keio University, Japan, Tokyo, Japan

Three experiments were conducted to investigate the role of the visuospatial sketchpad in associative learning. Experiment 1 demonstrated that spatial tapping was more disruptive than articulatory suppression during an associative learning task. This effect was confirmed in Experiment 2 using the relearning method to examine the effect of the spatial tapping task. In Experiment 3, the set size of the primary task was reduced and the secondary spatial tapping task resulted in faster RTs during the relearning session: a finding consistent with a contextual interference effect. These results suggest that the visuospatial sketchpad plays a crucial role in associative learning.

Evaluation of Japanese college students with ADHD-related problems: A comparison between morningness and eveningness groups

Sato, Toshihiko Health and Social Services, Tohoku Bunka Gakuen Univ., Sendai, Japan

To evaluate a relationship between ADHD and nocturnal life, or continuous phase-shifting of the circadian rhythm to the later hours, 497 students answered a questionnaire, which included items from the Japanese versions of the Morningness-Eveningness Questionnaire (MEQ) and the College-level ADHD Questionnaire (CAQ). The students were divided into three subgroups based on their MEQ scores: Morning, Intermediate, and Evening types. One-factor ANOVAs and post-hoc tests revealed that the Evening group reported a significantly higher score on inattention and hyperactivity than other groups (p < 0.05), and also reported a higher score on impulsivity than the Intermediate group.

Performance monitoring and decision making in patients with borderline personality disorder

Schürmann, Beate Inst. für Klin. Psychologie, Humboldt-Universität zu Berlin, Berlin, Germany Kathmann, Norbert Clinical Psychology, Humboldt-University of Berlin, Berlin, Germany Renneberg, Babette Psychology, University of Frankfurt a. M., Franfurt am Main, Germany Endrass, Tanja Clinical Psychology, Humboldt-University of Berlin, Berlin, Germany

Patients with borderline personality disorder (BPD) are characterized by marked impulsive behaviour associated with diminished action monitoring and deficits in decision making. Despite its relevance for goal directed behaviour little is known about the neurobiological correlates of these processes in patients with BPD. In the present study, decision making was examined in patients with BPD and matched healthy controls while performing a modified version of the Iowa Gambling Task. Performance monitoring was obtained by measuring the error-related negativity after erroneous responses and negative feedback. The results reveal alterations of performance monitoring and decision making in patients with BPD.

Is it always better to share?: Differential associations of couples' shared possible selves with psychological well-being as a function of marital quality

Schindler, Ines Dept. of Psychology, University of Utah, Salt Lake City, USA Berg, Cynthia A. Psychology, University of Utah, Salt Lake City, UT, USA Butler, Jorie M. Psychology, University of Utah, Salt Lake City, UT, USA Fortenberry, Katherine T. Psychology, University of Utah, Salt Lake City, UT, USA Wiebe, Deborah J. Southwestern Medical Center, University of Texas, Dallas, TX, USA

We examined effects of sharing possible selves with one's spouse for psychological well-being, which we hypothesized to depend on marital quality. Both members of 61 couples (38-84 years) coping with the husband's prostate cancer completed assessments of possible selves, marital quality, and psychological well-being. Using our coding system for shared selves, we found that a higher percentage of couple's shared selves was related to greater purpose in life and self-acceptance in happily married spouses. Unhappily married spouses reported less environmental mastery with more shared selves. We concluded that sharing possible selves is an asset only for happily married couples.

Validation and standardization of the test of every day attention for children in Flanders and the Netherlands

Schittekate, Mark Dept. Psychology, Ghent University, Gent, Belgium Fontaine, Johnny Testpracticum PPW, Ghent University, Ghent, Belgium de Clerck, Stefaan Testpracticum PPW, Ghent University, Ghent, Belgium Groenvynck, Hans Testpracticum PPW, Ghent University, Ghent, Belgium

The Test of Everyday Attention for Children (TEA-Ch) is a promising battery to measure attentional processes developed in Australia (Manly et al., 1999). The test consists of nine subtests which are mend to measure three functionally separable attention systems, namely Selective Attention, Sustained Attention and higher level "executive" control. The test was validated and standardized on a sample of 293 healthy Australian children between the ages of 6 and 16. However, generalizability of psychological instruments to other cultural groups cannot be merely assumed. The focus of the cross cultural current research is the need for 'local' norms.

Relevance of spatial frequencies for the attentional bias to threatening faces

Schmidt-Daffy, Martin Biopsychologie/Neuroergonomics, Technische Universität Berlin, Berlin, Germany

Three experiments investigated whether an attentional bias to threat is mediated by information contained in low spatial frequencies. In each experiment 24 male students completed a visual-dot-probe-task with low- and high-pass filtered pictures of different facial expressions. Confronted with neutral expressions angry expressions (threatening) attract more attention than happy expressions, especially when low-pass filtered pictures were used. However, attention towards angry and happy expressions did not differ when directly confronted. Results are in line with the assumption that a threatening signal contained in low spatial frequencies increases attention to salient perceptual information independent of its emotional valence.

An improved scoring procedure for the name Letter task

Schmukle, Stefan Inst. für Psychologie, Universität Leipzig, Leipzig, Germany Krause, Sascha Department of Psychology, University of Leipzig, Leipzig, Germany Back, Mitja Department of Psychology, University of Leipzig, Leipzig, Germany Egloff, Boris Department of Psychology, University of Leipzig, Leipzig, Germany

In the name letter task participants report their liking for all letters of the alphabet. Conventionally, a score of implicit self-esteem is computed for each participant as the difference between the evaluation of her/his initial letters and the corresponding evaluation by participants whose initials did not include those letters. We introduce a new scoring procedure that additionally controls for differences in evaluation tendencies between participants. We could demonstrate its superiority by showing that the improved but not the conventional scoring leads to a theoretically predicted moderation effect: Implicit and explicit self-esteem were positively correlated only for participants low in deliberation.

Retraumatization: A review

Schock, Katrin Research, Behandlungszentrum Folteropfer, Berlin, Germany Knaevelsrud, Christine Research Department, Center for Torture Victims, Berlin, Germany

Objectives: Retraumatization is a frequently cited but ill-defined condition. In general the term is used to describe aggravations of PTSD symptoms due a stressor related to the initial traumatic experience. Aim of this presentation is to give an overview of current concepts of retraumatization. Methods: Review of research literature. Results: Based on the literature review dimensions were identified which provide a coordinate system for the definition of retraumatization: 1) duration/intensity of initial symptoms 2) duration/intensity of current symptoms 3) nature of the retraumatizing event. Conclusion: Current research is characterized by very heterogenic definitions of retraumatization. The proposed dimensions allow a comparison of these diverse approaches.

Effects of psychosocial stress on working memory: Is there an influence of task difficulty and emotional valence?

Schoofs, Daniela *Inst. Verhaltenspsychologie, Ruhr-Universität Bochum, Bochum, Germany* **Preuß, Diana** *Inst. für Psychologie, Ruhr-Universität Bochum, Bochum, Germany* **Wolf, Oliver** *Inst. Verhaltenspsychologie, Ruhr-Universität Bochum, Bochum, Germany*

Objectives: To examine the influence of stress on working memory. Methods: The performance in an n-back task varying in difficulty and stimuli employed (digits vs. neutral and emotional pictures) was assessed after psychosocial stress or a control-condition. Results: Analysis revealed significant impairments of stressed subjects in the digit version of the n-back task. This effect was not modified by task difficulty but decreased in size the longer the task was performed. Conclusions: Stress associated endocrine changes produce working memory impairments in a neutral n- back version. Findings will be compared with results obtained with the emotional working memory task.

Motivation and knowledge acquisition during computer supported collaborative learning

Schoor, Cornelia *Technische Uniersität Chemnitz, Chemnitz, Germany* **Bannert, Maria** *Professur Päd. d. E-Learning, TU Chemnitz, Chemnitz, Germany*

This study investigated the influence of motivation on knowledge acquisition and learning activities during computer supported collaborative learning (CSCL). Based on findings on motivation during individual learning, we hypothesized that motivation has a positive influence on CSCL outcomes. We therefore measured motivation before, during and after a CSCL task. We found that self efficacy, a positive attitude towards collaboration and flow during the session had a significant positive influence on knowledge acquisition. Performance avoidance goal orientation and work avoidance showed negative relationships with knowledge acquisition. Thus, motivation is important in CSCL while the mediating processes still have to be analysed.

Affect control theory: Linking social cognition to symbolic interactionism

Schröder, Tobias *Inst. für Psychologie, Humboldt-Universität zu Berlin, Berlin, Germany*

Affect Control Theory (ACT; Heise, 1979, 2007) holds that people control social interactions by striving to maintain feelings about the situation. Stemming from sociology, ACT predictions have rarely been tested in psychological experiments. We asked 60 Ss to manage a computer simulated company by communicating with different virtual employees. Preliminary results of the experiment support ACT: predicted specific actions correlated with observed Ss' actions (ρ=.40), predicted specific emotions correlated with Ss' reported emotions (ρ=.49). We discuss these results in terms of overcoming the gap between the "two social psychologies" via using ACT for linking Social Cognition to Symbolic Interactionism.

Positive faces, words and scenes facilitate approach

Schulz, Stefan M. *Inst. für Psychologie 1, Universität Würzburg, Würzburg, Germany* **Gerdes, Antje B.** *Department of Psychology 1, University of Würzburg, Würzburg, Germany* **Alpers, Georg W.** *Department of Psychology 1, University of Würzburg, Würzburg, Germany*

Facilitation of compatible movements (approach vs. avoidance) in response to emotional stimuli (positive vs. negative) has been found with different tasks, stimuli, and outcome variables. We resolved issues of referential ambiguity, feedback, and different response measures in a novel task. In 26 participants, we compared times needed for initiation and execution of compatible vs. incompatible arm movements in response to emotional faces, words, and scenes. Initiation was slower for scenes. Execution was faster when stimulus valence and response were compatible, particularly for approaching positive stimuli. The results validate our task, but suggest moderating factors for response facilitation by valence evaluation.

Emotional and cognitive correlates of social skills in middle childhood: A preliminary study

Schulz, Annie Karin *CIIPME / CIPCA, Buenos Aires, Argentina*

It is a well known fact that development of social skills in childhood is closely related to later social, academic and psychological performance. The purpose of this study was to evaluate some of the most important emotional and cognitive correlates of social skills, such as positive emotions, loneliness, depression, and coping styles in Argentinean children from 8 to 12 years old (n = 300). Methods of data collection consisted in different behaviour rating scales (parent and teacher report) and self reports. Results of multivariate analysis of variance between social skills and the other variables are consistent with previous findings and theory.

Acquaintanceship effect and judgement accuracy in well-acquainted dyads

Schweinberger, Kirsten *Inst. für Psychologie, Universität Fribourg, Fribourg, Switzerland* **Vollmann, Manja** *Department of Psychology, University of Konstanz, Konstanz, Germany* **Renner, Britta** *Department of Psychology, University of Konstanz, Konstanz, Germany* **Weber, Hannelore** *Department of Psychology, University of Greifswald, Greifswald, Germany*

This research examines to what extent the acquaintanceship effect (Funder, 1999) can be shown among well-acquainted dyads and whether qualitative or quantitative facets of acquaintanceship are better predictors for judgement accuracy. 90 students rated their own degree of optimism and were assessed by 3 acquaintances using the Life Orientation Test-Revised and the Generalized Self-Efficacy Scale. Accuracy was determined by inter-judge agreement between peer ratings and target self-ratings. Analyses show that only qualitative aspects of acquaintanceship such as closeness of friendship are associated with self-peer agreement. These findings suggest that qualitative aspects of relationships were underestimated in previous studies.

Students' preferential helpers in facing various areas of concerns

Setiawan, Jenny Lukito *Universitas Ciputra, Surabaya, Indonesia*

This paper describes a study designed to investigate preferential helpers on various areas of concern among Indonesian students. A questionnaire consisted of 14 areas of concerns and 14 choices of helpers was distributed to 1,279 students. Findings showed that friend, mother and self was the most preferred helpers across areas of concerns. Specifically, friend was mostly chosen in 7 areas of concerns, mother was the most preferred helper in

3 areas of concerns. Self was the most common choice in 4 areas of concerns. The study confirms that preferential helpers are conditional to the nature of problem.

The study of hand function in chronic schizophrenia

Shafaroudi, Narges *Occupational Therapy, Shool of Rehabilitat. Science, Tehran, Islamic Republic of Iran* **Dori, Fatemeh** *Occupational Therapy, Shool of Rehabilitat.ion Scien, Tehran, Islamic Republic of Iran*

This study was conducted to compare the hand function in Schizophrenics with healthy controls. Jebson Taylor was used to assess the hand function of 27 schizophrenic patients as well as 27 controls. There was a significant difference between the schizophrenic group and the healthy group. The scores of seven subtests of Jebson in schizophrenics were lower than the healthy group.(p<0.05) Altered hand function often limits the person's capacity to perform effectively to complete daily tasks. Based on the results, hand dysfunction has to be considered in schizophrenic patients so the treatment and planning for improvement of these deficits are important.

Effects of Sildenafil (Viagra) on inhibitory cognitive task in the rats

Shahidi, Siamak *Physiology, Medical Sciences, Hamadan University of Medical, Hamedan, Islamic Republic of Iran* **Arjipour, Mahdi** *Physiology, Medical Sciences, Hamadan University of Medical, Hamedan, Islamic Republic of Iran* **Komaki, Alireza** *Physiology, Medical Sciences, Hamadan University of Medical, Hamedan, Islamic Republic of Iran* **Mahmoodi, Minoo** *Biology, Islamic Azad University,Hameda, Hamedan, Islamic Republic of Iran*

Sildenafil (Viagra) is an inhibitor of phosphodiestrase type 5 which has been demonstrated in the brain cortex and hippocampus. The effects of pre-training, post-training or pre-retrieval administration of sildenafil on the inhibitory cognitive task in the rats were tested using shuttle box apparatus. Pre-training administration of sildenafil decreased the number of trials to acquisition. Post-training and pre-retrieval of sildenafil increase time spent in the dark compartment. Sildenafil facilitate acquisition, consolidation and retrieval of inhibitory avoidance task. Therefore, it seems sildenafil acts as a memory enhancer in the simple inhibitory cognitive task in the rats.

The moderated effect of trait and state self-control on framing effect

Shan, Jing *Psychology Department, Peking University, BeiJing, People's Republic of China* **Wang, Haini** *Psychology Department, Peking University, BeiJing, People's Republic of China* **Wang, Lei** *Psychology Department, Peking University, BeiJing, People's Republic of China*

Three studies demonstrated that trait and state self-control ability moderated framing effect. Study 1 and Study 2 used different tasks (risky choice problems and Balloon Analogue Risk-taking Task) to examine the moderation effect of trait self-control ability on framing effect. We manipulated the state self-control ability to test the moderation effect of state self-control ability in Study 3. As predicted, participants high (vs. low) in trait and state self-control were less likely to be influenced by frame and their choices were more consistent across different frames. These results suggest that self-control is an important moderating variable for framing effect.

Comorbidity in teacher rated ADHD children

Sharma, Vandana *Dept. of Psychology, Meerut College, Meerut, India*

Objective : to examine prevalence rate of comorbidity and gender differences in the expression of comorbidity in teacher rated ADHD-Children.

Design: socially varied, mainly urban children centered in the city of meerut in U.P., India. 222 ADHD children aged between 6-12yrs, were rated by teacher on Vanderbilt scale. Result : Almost 50% ADHD children show comorbidity. Gender difference is not significant in the rate of comorbidity, but significant difference is found in the expression. Conclusion: the results suggest that gender influences the type of comorbidity. Boys show more oppositional defiant disorder, while girls show more anxiety.

The effect of the attitudes shown by the respondent in self-disclosure on the evaluation for general self and general others.

Shiomura, Kimihiro *Iwate Prefectural University, Iwate, Japan* **Moribe, Masato** *Toyogaoka-Gakuen, Reformatory Institution, Toyoake, Japan* **Ohashi, Sanae** *Nanyo Senior High School, Kyoto Prefectural High School, Kizugawa, Japan*

Forty-eight female university students participated in this experiment. The participants were asked to disclose themselves to the respondent. The attitude of the respondent was experimentally manipulated as two conditions, the one is acceptable condition and the other is non-acceptable condition. The implicit associations of Self and Others with good-bad connotation measured by GNAT are implicit self-esteem. The GNAT is a conceptually quite similar technique to the IAT. We analyzed the degree of change in these indexes before and after the self-disclosure. The results in implicit indexes suggested that the boundary between Self and Others was made unclear by self-disclosure.

The relationship between self-effacement for in-group/out-group members and self-related concepts

Shiomura, Kimihiro *Iwate Prefectural University, Iwate, Japan* **Funakoshi, Risa** *Faculty of Social Welfare, Iwate Prefectural University, Iwate, Japan* **Noguchi, Kenji** *Department of Psychology, University of Florida, Gainesville, USA*

The purpose of the research is to investigate how self-related concepts predict self-effacement for in-group/out-group members. Participants were 211 Japanese university students (male 83, female 128). Multiple regression analyses were conducted on self-effacement for in-group members and out-group members. Self-effacement for in-group members was significantly predicted by independent self (β= -.15*), extraversion (β= -.33**), other-directedness (β= .13*), and IOS for in-group members (β= -.25*). The results for out-group members are quite different. Based on these findings, we discussed about the differences between in-group/out-group members and its involvement for Japanese adolescents.

How can Japanese-specific positive automatic thoughts predict future depressive states?

Shiraishi, Satoko *Tokyo, Japan* **Koshikawa, Fusako** *Department of Psychology, Waseda University, Tokyo, Japan* **Sugamura, Genji** *Department of Psychology, Kansai University, Osaka, Japan*

This study examined how Japanese-specific positive automatic thoughts (PATs) could affect future depressive states. Volunteers (N=204) completed assessments of PATs, negative automatic thoughts (NATs), negative events (NEs), and depression twice in a month. Hierarchical multiple regression analysis showed that the frequency of NEs and PATs directly predicted future depressive cognition. It was also revealed that the interactions between NEs and NATs, and ones between NEs and PATs affected future depressive mood in the same direction. Although reducing the degree of future depressive cognition, PATs increase future depressive mood via NEs.

Investigate the test of the colored progressive matrices upon those with special needs of hearing impairment in Khartoum

Siddig, Zahra *Khartoum, Sudan*

The present study aims to investigate the test of the Colored Progressive Matrices upon those with special needs of hearing impairment in Khartoum state between the ages of 6 to 12 year old. The amount of the sample chosen for the study was 170 children both gender from the educational institutions in Khartoum State. The most essential recommendation of this research is orienting research makers and post-graduate students to focus on and use this idea in doing psychological Tests, and measuring the ability of hearing impaired patients to be used in research works as well as in scientific applications.

Developmental delay: The meaning of a term

Silva, Elisabete *Faculdade de Psicologia, Universidade de Coimbra, Coimbra, Portugal* **Petrucci Albuquerque, Maria** *Centro de Psicopedagogia, Faculdade de Psicologia, Coimbra, Portugal*

The present research addresses the precision and theoretical delimitation of the term developmental delay. Since it is a commonly used term amongst Portuguese child care professionals, the study examines different professionals conceptions of this term. For this purpose, a questionnaire was designed, which amongst other items, asked professionals to identify the criteria used to diagnose developmental delay; to characterize the child with a developmental delay; to enunciate the areas most affected in this condition. The analysis of the answers obtained in a group of 100 professionals, showed the absence of a common meaning amongst professionals using the term.

A multidimensional view of temperament: Correlation between parental reports and observational methodology

Simó Teufel, Sandra *Dept. of Psychology, University of Valencia, Valencia, Spain* **DOcon, Ana** *Department of Psychology, University of Valencia, Valencia, Spain* **Banacloche, Diana** *Department of Psychology, University of Valencia, Valencia, Spain*

This study is focused on the measurement of infant temperament and analyzes the correspondence between two different assessment techniques: on one side temperamental data obtained by parental reports and, on the other side, observational assessment made by a trained observer on several rating scales on infant temperament dimensions. Subjects in the study were 40 assessed at 6 months. Parents fill out the Infant Behavior Questionnaire (IBQ-R; Gartstein and Rothbart, 2003) and children were observed during a structured episode through the Revised Behavioral Rating Scales on Infant Temperament (DOcon and Simó, 2007). This instrument evaluates ten infant temperament dimensions: irritability, sadness, pleasure; social orientation, cooperativeness, activity; attention, reactivity, soothability and stability.

Study of self-destructive phenomenon

Sokolova, Elena *Psychology, Moscow State University, Moscow, Russia*

Study of suicide phenomenon is presented; their emotional, regulatory, cognitive, interpersonal determinants are examined. Rorschach test with scales (Lerner, Blatt, Ilizur), Marlens-Witkin scale for cognitive style; test for coping strategies Plutchik-Kellerman, SCL-90 was used. 200 patients were examined - with depressive disorder and suicide attempts. Results demonstrate connection between structural-functional organizations of the defense mechanisms, differentiation - integration, dependency - autonomy, hostility - cooperation. Results specify the role of deficiency symbolic processes in lowering effectiveness of self-regulatory systems,

allows differentiating borderline and narcissistic types of personality, level of suicide risk

The effect of network overlaps on roommates' perceived legitimacy with regard to conflicts

Soma, Toshihiko *Faculty of Humanities, Kyushu Women's University, Kitakyusyu, Japan*

This study aimed to examine the effect of network overlaps outside roommate relationships on the perceived legitimacy of roommates and their partners when a conflict arises in the relationship. Based on Klein & Milardo (2000), I hypothesized that roommates having larger networks that only support their own positions will perceive themselves as more legitimate than their counterparts. Sixty-one female boarding students participated in this survey. The path analysis revealed that roommates coping with a conflict find it difficult to consider their behaviors as legitimate when they have more networks supporting both theirs and the partners' positions.

Effects of general mental ability and emotional intelligence on self-assessed career-related abilities

Song, Jiwen Lynda *School of Business, Renmin University, Beijing, People's Republic of China* **Law, Kenneth S.** *Department of Management, The Chinese University of Chin, Hong Kong, People's Republic of China* **Chen, Zhijun** *Department of Management of Or, Hong Kong University of Scienc, Hong Kong, People's Republic of China* **Huang, Emily G.** *Department of Management, Hong Kong Baptist University, Hong Kong, People's Republic of China*

The present study investigated the relationship between emotional intelligence and self-assessed career-related abilities. 506 college students in a large university in eastern China participated the survey. A two-wave longitudinal design (with a 3-month interval) was adopted to avoid the threat of common method variance. Through hierarchical linear regression analyses, we found that on top of General Mental Ability, emotional intelligence measured in Time 1 had incremental predictive power for students' self-assessed career-related abilities (including social abilities and enterprising abilities) in Time 2. Theoretical contributions and implications were discussed.

Emotional intelligence, evaluation and development in bachelor students

Sosa Correa, Manuel *Psicología, Universidad Autónoma de Yucatá, Mérida Yucatán, Mexico* **Gamboa Ancona, Lorena** *Psicología, Universidad Autónoma de Yucatá, Mérida Yucatán, Mexico* **Peniche Aranda, Cyntia Cristina** *Psicología, Universidad Autónoma de Yucatá, Mérida Yucatán, Mexico*

This experimental investigation had as main objective the evaluation and development of Emotional Intelligence (EI) for which two groups were used, an experimental and a control one. An EI and NEO personality pretest was applied to both. A workshop designed to develop EI was given to the experimental group afterwards, lastly EI and personality posttest was applied to both groups. Results allowed to develop a personal growth protocol, which can be used as guidance to utilize thoughts for our own psychological well being.

Prenatal stress during war: Findings and outstanding questions

Sosic, Bojan *Research and Development, HealthNet International, Sarajevo, Bosnia and Herzegovina*

A quasi-prospective study is being conducted in Sarajevo, Bosnia and Herzegovina, aiming to explore the existence, mechanisms of onset, appearance, and the extent of childhood-expressed effects of maternal exposure to stressors during war. Children born during war are screened for several putative markers of prenatal stress in comparison to children born before and after the war. Preliminary findings, and problems relating to certain nuisance variables, especially nutritional, are discussed. Special attention is given to the duration of war-related stressors during gestation. The relation of prenatal stress to the so-called 'transgenerational PTSD' is examined.

Development and validation of an instrument to measure planning competence and problem solving capacity: The Gate-Card Test (GCT)

Spijkers, Will Inst. für Psychologie, RWTH Aachen, Aachen, Germany

The Gate-Card-Test (GCT) was developed to measure planning- and problem solving capacity. Contruction of the GCT is based on classical maze-tests (e.g., Porteus Maze Test). The GCT consists of 60 (single) maze-tasks. There are two advantages over the classical maze-tasks. First advantage is, that the test considers different standardized levels of difficulty. Second advantage means, that an objective evaluation is guaranteed, because one optimal solution for every task was implemented. The instrument was validated by tests measuring cognitive skills, like organisational ability, intelligence, working memory, conceptualisation skills and cognitive flexibility (n=81). Results confirmed the hypothesized correlations.

Networks in Nigeria: A pilot study on network characteristics and their relation with life satisfaction in a Nigerian sample

Stadler, Christian Psychologische Praxis, Dachau, Germany Strobel, Maria Psychology, LMU Muenchen, Muenchen, Germany Spörrle, Matthias Dept. for Psychology, Ludwig-Maximilians University, München, Germany

Social relationships are a central determinant of life satisfaction. The collectivity of individual social relationships form a social network. This study examines such networks in a Nigerian sample (N = 108). Network size, proportions of positive and negative relationships within those networks, and structural characteristics (e.g. network centrality) were assessed. Furthermore, network characteristics were examined concerning their association with life satisfaction. Results indicate overall positive relations of network size with life satisfaction and differential relations of network characteristics with life satisfaction. Results are discussed in terms of (1) cross-cultural assessment of network characteristics, (2) life satisfaction as related to social structural characteristics, and (3) differential associations between network types and different aspects of life satisfaction.

Confidence bias: An instance of systematic irrationality?

Stankov, Lazar International Testing Service, Princeton, USA Kleitman, Sabina Psychology, The University of Sydney, Sydney, Australia

This paper explores the nature of miscalibration as assessed by the over/underconfidence bias score and links it to another instance of non-normative (irrational) responding - the lack of awareness of the additivity principle of probability theory. Four studies employed a multiple-choice test of Verbal Reasoning to assess these two tendencies. The results indicate that over 60% of participants tend to violate the '"additivity"' postulate of probability theory. The manner in which participants violate the additivity principle – neglect of non-focal alternatives - is related to measures of confidence and miscalibration bias. There exist tendencies towards irrationality that are independent of overall ability level.

Dissociation of decisions in ambiguous and risky situations in obsessive-compulsive disorder

Starcke, Katrin Inst. für Physiol. Psychologie, Universität Bielefeld, Bielefeld, Germany Tuschen-Caffier, Brunna Clinical Psychology, Albert-Ludwig-University, Freiburg, Germany Markowitsch, Hans Physiological Psychology, University of Bielefeld, 33501 Bielefeld, Germany Brand, Matthias Physiological Psychology, University of Bielefeld, 33501 Bielefeld, Germany

Patients with obsessive-compulsive disorder (OCD) often have problems in everyday decision-making and previous investigations found deficits in the Iowa Gambling Task (IGT) measuring decisions under ambiguity. In the present study, OCD patients' performance on a decision-making task with explicit and stable rules, the Game of Dice Task (GDT), was investigated. Twenty-three patients with OCD and 22 comparison subjects were examined with the GDT, the IGT, and further neuropsychological tasks. Patients performed poorly in the IGT, but were unimpaired in the GDT and executive functioning, indicating reduced decision-making under ambiguity commonly linked to orbitofrontal dysfunctions, but intact decision-making under risk conditions.

Comparison of a card and a computer version of the Wisconsin card sorting test

Steinmetz, Jean-Paul Dept. of Psychology, University of Luxembourg, Walferdange, Luxembourg Houssemand, Claude Psychology, University of Luxembourg, Walferdange, Luxembourg

The Wisconsin Card Sorting Test (WCST) has been frequently used to assess prefrontal cognitive functioning. The aim of this study was to evaluate the validity of the computer version of the test in comparison to the card version. A total of 106 healthy subjects received either the card version or the computer version during the first followed by the card version or the computer version during the second part of the experiment. Repeated measures MANOVA have been conducted in order to analyze within-subjects variations depending on the assignation. Results will be discussed.

The impact of self-efficacy and collective efficacy on kindergarten students' emotions and achievement

Stephanou, Georgia Early Childhood Education, University Western Macedonia, Thessaloniki, Greece

This study examined (a) the effects of kindergarten students' pre- domino game emotions, self-efficacy and collective efficacy in the formation of their performance in the games, and (c) the role of efficacy beliefs in emotions, and in the impact of emotions on performance. The participants (n=200) completed the scales at the middle of a school year. The results showed that (a) students' experienced a variety of emotions (mainly, encouragement), (b) emotions, self-efficacy and, mainly, collective efficacy positively influenced performance, (b) collective efficacy, compared to self-efficacy, was a more powerful formulator of emotions, and of the impact of emotions on performance.

Insulin, brain and gender: Effects of intranasal insulin in male and female humans

Stockhorst, Ursula Inst. für Psychologie, Universität Osnabrück, Osnabrueck, Germany Blicke, Maren Inst. of Medical Psychology, University of Duesseldorf, Duesseldorf, Germany Folly, Maria Inst. of Medical Psychology, University of Duesseldorf, Duesseldorf, Germany Romanova, Daria Inst. of Medical Psychology, University of Duesseldorf, Duesseldorf, Germany Scherbaum, Werner A. Endocr., Diabetol., Rheumat., University of Duesseldorf, Duesseldorf, Germany

Objective: Effects of acute intranasal insulin on food-intake, memory, blood-glucose, hormones and symptoms were examined in healthy males

and females. We expected an anorexic effect of central insulin in males only, and memory-improvement in both genders. Methods: Under double-blind conditions, 30 female and 30 male students were administered six times either intranasal insulin (20 iU) or placebo. Blood-glucose, hormones, memory and symptoms were repeatedly assessed, food-intake was measured in a single test-meal. Results: After insulin, only males reduced food-intake and showed respective blood-glucose and hormonal changes, females tended to improve specifically spatial memory. Discussion: Gender-specifity is discussed. (DFG STO 323/1-2).

Alexithymia: State, trait, diagnosis or?

Stoimenova-Canevska, Emilija Communication, New York University Skopje, Skopje, The former Yugoslav Republic of Macedonia

Objective: The aim of the study was to determine what alexithymia is. Method: The study was conducted in Macedonia in a year period, on 100 psychosomatics and 100 healthy subjects. NEO-PI-R, info from GP record and interview with each participant was preformed. The results were analyzed with descriptive statistics, correlation method and factorial analysis. Results: There is connection between alexithymia and neuroticism, agreeableness, conscientiousness on the level of the whole sample, but there is difference between two sub-samples. Conclusion: Still unclear what really alexithymia is; it seems that it has chameleonic attributes depending of the angle of view.

Conflict when religiosity and sexual orientation collide: Reconciliation through resilience

Subhi, Nasrudin School of Education, The University of Queensland, St. Lucia, Australia

The purpose of this study was to explore processes of resilience among gay men who currently or previously identified with the Christian faith and their experiences of conflict between religiosity and sexual orientation. A qualitative study was conducted via in-depth semi-structured interviews with purposively selected gay men. Three distinct resilience strategies emerged, specifically embracing religiosity, altering religious beliefs and abandoning religion to reconcile conflict. Religiosity was considered within a resilience framework developed in the study. The resilience framework proved to be a viable means of exploring the conflict and indicated that multiple pathways towards resilience exist.

The importance of test-item sensitivity on stereotype threat effects

Suen, Mein-Woei Taichung, Taiwan Wang, Jui Sing China Medical University Hospi, China Medical University Hospi, TAICHUNG COUNTY, Taiwan

Keller (2003) indicates stereotype threat effects (STEs) reveal while participant' ability have been push to limit. Two experiments were drawn out to know the importance of test-item sensitivity on gender STEs. Experiment 1 used Whites (n=36) for a 2(stereotype:threat vs.non-threat) × 3 (test-item difficulty:low vs.moderate vs.high) design. Results reveal gender STEs just occur on the moderate test. Experiment 2 occupied Asians (n=40) for a 2(stereotype) × 2 (difficulty:moderate vs.high) design. The results showed STEs just reveal on high difficulty test. Thus, test sensitivity for inducing STEs is according to the ability of participant group. More details and findings are discussed.

Eye movement performance under endogenous and exogenous cue in learning disabilities

Sui, Guangyuan Zhejiang Normal University, Jinhua, People's Republic of China

Classical cue paradigm was employed to examine the endogenous and exogenous attention in learning disability group and control group with EYE-LINKII.The results indicated that under the conditions of low endogenous cue predictivity and long SOAs (onset of a target) of exogenous cue, no cue-validity effects was found in all groups; participants in grade 6 performed better than those in grade 3; there were no differences on response time and cognitive speed between learning disabled and matched groups but with significant differences on cognitive span and strategy. These results demonstrated that the attentive quality of learning disabled children differed from matched group to some extent.

Age-related changes in voluntary and reflexive saccades in children with learning disabilities

Sui, Guangyuan Zhejiang Normal University, Jinhua, People's Republic of China
Experiments were conducted using eye movements to investigate age-related changes in reflexive saccades and voluntary control of saccadic eye movements in children with learning disabilities(LD). The results indicated that (1)in pro-saccade task, there were no significant differences in reflexive saccades between LD and normal children; (2)in anti-saccade task, the LD groups showed significantly higher percentage of errors than the control groups, the rate of errors got no significant age-related changes in LD children(9-12years old); (3)in memory-guided saccade task, LD children took longer saccadic reaction time than normal children. These results demonstrated that LD children's inhibitory control abilities were not improving with their aging.

Cross-cultural study on peer experience and loneliness of Chinese and American children

Sun, Xiaojun Psychology, Hua Zhong Normal University, Wuhan, People's Republic of China Zhou, Zongkui Psychology, Hua Zhong Normal University, Wuhan, People's Republic of China Zhao, Dongmei Psychology, Hua Zhong Normal University, Wuhan, People's Republic of China Cohen, Robert Psychology, University of Memphis, Memphis, USA Hsueh, Yeh College of Education, University of Memphis, Memphis, People's Republic of China
With the thriving of ecology movement and cross-cultural research, the influence of peer interaction on loneliness in the comprehensive ecological background was taken into consideration. 430 Chinese children and 165 American children in elementary school from grade four to six participated in this investigation.A hypothesized structural equation model was applied to test the relations between peer experience(e.g., peer relationship) and loneliness. The results indicated that there was no significant cultural difference on the functioning pattern between peer experience and loneliness, but some path coefficents of the model have difference.

Response control ability through error processing

Suzuki, Kota Graduate School of Sports, University of Tsukuba, Tennodai, Japan Shinoda, Haruo Faculty of Psychology, Rissyo University, Sinagawa, Japan
The relationship between motor impulsivity due to task performance and error-related negativity (ERN) was examined. In experiment 1, subjects were classified according to their performance on the arrow flanker task. This resulted in an impulsive group (shorter response time (RT) and higher error rate), an average group (average RT and error rate), and a prudent group (longer RT and lower error rate). In experiment 2, ERN was recorded in the impulsive and average groups, and results showed that ERN decreased in the impulsive group. Overall, differences in ability of response control may stem from differences in response conflict monitoring.

Effects of the reasons for hiding the inner self on verbal strategy arising from a sense of unwanted transparency

Tabata, Naoya Dept. of Psychology, University of Tsukuba, Tsukuba, Japan
The purpose of this study was to investigate the reasons for hiding the inner self on verbal strategy arising from a sense of unwanted transparency, the sense that another person seemingly notices something that they would rather conceal. Undergraduate participants were asked to pretend to be graduate students and to interview confederates. The experimental conditions were manipulated by the reason for hiding that they were really undergraduate students. After a sense of unwanted transparency was manipulated, participants were asked a contrived question. As expected, verbal strategy for the question was affected by the reason for hiding the inner self.

The development of the innovative leadership scale

Tak, Jin-Kook Dept. of Industrial Psychlogy, Kwangwoon University, Seoul, Republic of Korea Kim, Chan-Mo Management Study Center, POSCO Research Institute, Seoul, Republic of Korea Cho, Eun-Hyun Industrial Psychlogy, Kwangwoon University, Seoul, Republic of Korea
The present study investigates the reliability and validity of the innovative leadership scale. With a sample of 177 employees in a large company, the results of factor analyses showed that the five-factor model with 14 items had a high fit to the data. These factors were innovation pursue, problem solving, vision presentation, risk-taking, and showing initiative. All of these factors were significantly related to various criteria such as identification with the group, attachment to the group, organizational commitment, and supervisor satisfaction, confirming criterion-related validity of the scale. Results of multiple regression analyses showed that risk taking and showing initiative were more important predictors in explaining criteria.

The development of the friendship-behavior scale and the relation of intimacy

Takagi, Mami Kansai University, Nisinomiya, Japan Takagi, Osamu Faculty of Sociology, Kansai University, yamate-cho,suita-city,oosaka, Japan
The main purpose of this study was to develop the friendship-behavior scale and to investigate the relation of intimacy. 207 participant completed questionnaire regarding their friendship-behavior of friend or close-friend. According to factor analysis of the friendship-behavior, four factors were revealed: "self-disclosure", "gathering the information of the friend", "forming relations" and "observation". In addition, the level of intimacy caused the difference in the friendship-behavior. The analysis found that "self-disclosure" and "forming relations" were increased to close-friend compared with friend. However, to the friend, observation behavior was increased. That is, the criterion validity was confirmed.

Effects of attaciment on interpersonal relationship development

Takagi, Kuniko School of Social Work, Seirei Christopher University, Hamamatsu, Japan Niwa, Tomomi Education and Human Developmen, Nagoya University, Nagoya, Japan
The effect of parental attachment on Interpersonal Affect's (IA) changes in the early stage of relationship was examined. This longitudinal study was conducted at a 3-month interval at the beginning of a university year, where each time 1027 freshmen were asked to rate IA for favorable or unfavorable person. From the result of the multiple regression analysis, the effects of "Anxiety to Parental Attachment" were prominent in the relationship to favorable person. That is, the more they had

anxiety to parental attachment, the higher they rated "hatred", "threat", and "envy" to favorable person, but there were no significant relation to the changing amount of IA.

Recognition memory for cars and identification of location

Takahashi, Masanobu Dept. of Psychology, University of the Sacred Heart, Tokyo, Japan Kawaguchi, Atsuo Fine Arts and Music, Aichi Prefectural University, Aichi, Japan Kitagami, Shinji Department of Psychology, Nagoya University, Nagoya, Japan
We investigated how accurately people can remember the locations in which the cars were present. Participants were shown each of 10 photographs of cars, of which 5 were in one location and 5 in another location. In the two-alternative forced-choice recognition test, they were shown 20 photographs of cars, displayed in pairs. Immediately after that, two-alternative forced-choice test for the location, in which each of the target cars had initially appeared, was administered. The results showed that people recognize cars much better than they remember where the cars were encountered. These results are discussed in terms of source monitoring framework.

Big loss in gamble situation and impulsivity

Takano, Yuji Dept. of Psychology, Senshu University, Kawasaki, Japan Takahashi, Nobuaki Shimojo project, JST ERATO, Atugi-shi, Kanagawa, Japan Hironaka, Naoyuki Shimojo Project, JST ERATO, Atsug-shi, Kanagawa, Japan
Forty-four collage students underwent the Iowa Gambling task and impulsivity test, Matching Familiar Figures Test (MFFT). In general, the participants gradually shifted the choices from high-risk to low-risk. However, the impulsive participants with high scores of MFFT made more risky choice than the reflective participants. They tended to continue risky choices after big loss and the tendency enhanced as the loss cumulated. On the other hand, the reflective participants avoided risky choices after big loss. Cognitive impulsivity is related to the sensitivity to monetary loss.

Reciprocal relation between rumination and depression

Takano, Keisuke The University of Tokyo, Tokyo, Japan Tanno, Yoshihiko Graduate School of Arts and Sc, the University of Tokyo, Tokyo, Japan
Rumination is characterized as a negative repetitive thinking style. Previous researches have suggested rumination might be a risk factor of depression. On the one hand rumination may contribute to increasing depression, but at the same time depression may intensify rumination. In the present study, such a reciprocal relation between rumination and depression was investigated. Two-time points assessment was conducted on 160 undergraduates. Cross-lagged effects model and Synchronous effects model showed that rumination intensified depression and that depression intensified rumination. This result indicates that there may be a reciprocal relation between rumination and depression, which can maintain and exacerbate depressive disorders.

Does "Nostalgic feelings" influence the recall of autobiographical memory?

Takigawa, Shinya Dept. of Psychology, Hokkaido University, Sapporo, Japan Naka, Makiko Psychology, Hokkaido University, Sapporo, Japan
The present study examined the influence of nostalgic feelings on recall of autobiographical memory. Fifty-seven undergraduates were asked to give their autobiographical memory in their childhood and nostalgic music they listened to when they were in elementary school. A month later, they were asked to decide whether episodes shown on a screen were from their elementary school days or from junior high school days. In one condition,

nostalgic music was accompanied whereas in another conditions no music or non-nostalgic music were given. Results showed those who experienced nostalgic feelings in music condition recalled elementary school episodes with shorter reaction time.

Perceptions of teaching technology, professors' effectiveness in applying technology and business students' learning performance

Tang, Thomas Li-Ping Management and Marketing, Middle Tennessee St University, Murfreesboro, USA Austin, Jill Management and Marketing, Middle Tennessee St University, Murfreesboro, USA

This study examined business students' perceptions of four objectives (i.e., fun, learning, motivation, and career application) across five types of teaching technology (i.e., Projector, PowerPoint, Video, Internet, and Lecture), business professors' teaching effectiveness in using these technologies, and students' learning performance (self-reported GPA). Results revealed that younger students preferred video, whereas older students favored lecture. Further, the use of video for learning, projector and lecture for fun, PowerPoint for career and motivation, and Internet for learning all contributed to professors' overall teaching effectiveness. Finally, professors' effectiveness in using the lecture method and low expectation for the use of a projector were related to high GPA.

Allocation of attention to the prisoner's dilemma payoff matrix

Tanida, Shigehito Graduate School of Letters, Hokkaido University, Sapporo, Japan Yamagishi, Toshio Graduate School of Letters, Hokkaido University, Sapporo, Japan

According to social value orientation, people with a pro-social value orientation cooperate in the one-shot prisoner's dilemma game because they internalize payoffs to other people as a part of their social utility. To examine the validity of this model, we used an eye-tracker to determine whether cooperators pay more attention to other player's payoffs than defectors. Results of the experiment revealed no difference between cooperators (n=43) and defectors (n=72) in attention to other's payoffs. A time series analysis revealed that defectors spent more time looking at their own outcomes early in the experiment when first understanding the payoff structure.

The effect of the self-enhancing presentations on the appraisals from friends

Taniguchi, Junichi Kawanishi, Japan

The present study examined the effect of the self-enhancing presentations toward their friends on the evaluations from friends. 120 pairs of same-sax friends answered the questionnaire. Main findings were as follows: 1) Participants with low self-esteem presented themselves in more self-enhancing ways to their friends than participants with high self-esteem. 2) Participants got more positive appraisals from their friends than their self-views. 3) Only if the closeness of participants with their friends were low, on dimensions of competence, the more self-enhancing participants' self-presentations toward their friends were, the more positive they got actual appraisals from their friends.

The impact of executive functioning on the personality of air traffic controllers

Taukari, Atish Bombay, India

The study looked at the relationship between executive functions and personality facets in air traffic controllers. Fifty psychologically and physically healthy controllers were assessed on the Behavioral Assessment of Dysexecutive Syndrome Battery and NEO Five-Factor Inventory. Results reveal that controllers' ability to plan actions ahead in order to solve problems predicts agreeableness

and neuroticism. Further, spontaneous planning ability and minimizing errors by using feedback predicts agreeableness. Thus, planning ability enhances cooperativeness and reduces maladjustment in controllers.

The study of emotional intelligence in women who attempted suicide with the poisoning

Tavakoli, Mahgol Psychology, Isfahan University, Isfahan, Islamic Republic of Iran

Objective: In this study the EQ in women who attempted suicide with the poisoning method was investigated. Method: In a semi-experimental research, 80 women who attempted suicide from poisoning agency in Isfahan Nour hospital as an experimental group and 80 Normal women as a control group were randomly selected and Bar-On EQ questionnaire was administered. Result: Total EQ scores and its items in an experimental group in compare with control group were very low (p<0/0001). Also the cut-off point for 2 groups was reported in the paper. Conclusion: EQ in women who attempted suicide significantly was lower than normal women and low EQ can be considered as a risk factor for suicide.

The association between quality of life and pain beliefs in cancer patients

Tavoli, Azadeh tehran, Islamic Republic of Iran Montazeri, Ali Payesh, Iranian Institute for Health, Tehran, Islamic Republic of Iran Roshan, Rasool shahed university, shahed university, Tehran, Islamic Republic of Iran Tavoli, zahra Arash hospital, Arash hospital, Tehran, Islamic Republic of Iran

Objectives: The purposes of this study was to determine the relationship between pain beliefs and quality of life(QOL) in Iranian cancer patients. Method: A consequence sample of gastrointestinal cancer patients attending to Tehran Cancer Institute were assessed for QOL(the EORTC QLQ-C30) and pain beliefs(the PBPI). Results: 98 patients were studied. higher scores on pain consistency were negatively and significantly associated with QOL. Conclusion: This study has supported the multidimensional notion of the cancer pain experience in Iranian patients. Although these data are correlational, they provide additional support for a biopsychosocial model of chronic pain.

A laboratory study of upward emotional contagion: How followers influence leadership effectiveness

Tee, Eugene Brisbane, Australia

In a laboratory study, we tested hypotheses that followers' mood states influence leaders' performance though emotional contagion processes. Twenty-eight (28) Australian undergraduates assumed the roles of leaders and supervised teams of trained confederates who were instructed to portray either positive, negative, or neutral moods during a car-building task. Leader mood and performance were assessed by trained observers. Results supported our hypotheses. Leaders were found to 'catch' both positive and negative mood from followers. Leaders in a positive mood were also found to perform more effectively than leaders in a negative mood, suggesting that followers' moods have the ability to influence leadership effectiveness.

Gender aspects of deputy school principals' conflict management competence

Tetyana, Dzuba Organizational Psychology, Institute of Psychology, Kiev, Ukraine

Objectives. To find out links between deputy school principals' gender and their conflict management competence. Methods. The investigation was done on 158 deputy school principals using Karamushka Conflict management competence survey and SPSS. Results. Men and women deputy statistically significantly differed in levels of development of

cognitive and personality components of conflict management competence (r<001 and r<0.05 respectively). No statistically significant distinctions were found between males and females in levels of development of the operational component of the conflict management competence. Discussion. The findings can be used in conflict management training at institutions of post-graduate pedagogical training.

Introducing heterogeneous form item sets in general mental ability tests the case of the problem test

Tonkoviæ, Maša Department of Psychology, Faculty of Philosophy, Zagreb, Croatia Huic, Aleksandra Department of Psychology, Faculty of Philosophy, Zagreb, Croatia Urch, Drazen Department of Psychology, Faculty of Philosophy, Zagreb, Croatia

The Problem Test, a new general mental ability test, is introduced. The lack of specific instructions and variety of test item forms make it suitable for measuring the capacity to adapt to new problems, reducing the exercising effect to minimum. The aim of this research was to make a psychometric validation of the test. The results of 1200 participants were examined in a real employment testing context. Although the test consists of items heterogeneous regarding form and content, the Cronbach alpha index points to high test reliability (α=0,87). The issue of compiling heterogeneous instead of homogeneous item forms is discussed.

We cannot force intuition

Topolinski, Sascha Inst. für Psychologie II, Universität Würzburg, Würzburg, Germany Strack, Fritz Institut für Psychologie, Universität Würzburg, Würzburg, Germany

Intuitive judgments about whether a word triad has a common associate or not without retrieving the common associate depend on the partial semantic activation of the common associate. We show that this activation runs automatically and is even hampered by reasoning. In Experiments 1-3 the mere presentation as well as the incidental reading of a triad activated the common associate, while an intentional search for the common associate did not. Memorizing of the word triad even inhibited the common associate. In Experiment 4, searching for the CA decreased the accuracy of intuitive coherence judgments compared to merely reading the triad.

Psychometric study of the reading comprehension test for children of first grade of Lima, Peru

Torres, William Callao, Peru Delgado Vasquez, Ana Esther Psychology, URP, Lima, Peru Escurra Mayaute, Luis Miguel Psychology, URP, Lima, Peru

Presents the psychometric study of the reading comprehension test for children elaborated by Alliende, Condemarín, and Milicic. The participants were 734 students of first grade of public and private schools of seven school districts (UGEL) of Lima, Peru. The reliability of the test was calculated using Cronbachs alfa coefficient (0.65 to 0.85), which shows that the test is up to the standards. It was used the CFA to validate the instrument and it was find that the test has one factor. The test instructions, the answer sheets, the scoring norms, were adapted. Its pointed out the work of the graduate students on LD at the Universidad Ricardo Palma

Individual differences in emotional intelligence and incidental memory of words

Toyota, Hiroshi Dept. of Psychology, Nara University of Education, Nara, Japan

Participants were required to complete the Japanese version of emotional skills and competence questionnaire to assess the level of emotional intelligence. Then they were asked to rate pleasantness of the episode that each target reminded it of followed by unexpected free recall tests. Participants with high emotional intelligence recalled targets with pleasant, neutral and unpleasant episodes equally. Whereas for participants with low emotional intelligence, targets with neutral episodes were recalled less than those with pleasant and unpleasant ones. These results were interpreted as showing that the level of emotional intelligence determined the effectiveness of episodes on targets as retrieval cues.

E-teaching skills approach enhancement in health psychology e-learning: The role of a decision-making approach under visual-analogical scenarios

Trovato, Guglielmo *Internal Medicine & Health Psy, University of Catania, Catania, Italy* **Pace, Patrizia** *Health Psychology, University of Catania, Catania, Italy*

E-Learning is encouraged in health professions education considering that this new educational technology efficiently delivers educational materials at reduced costs, with increased access, clear learning-process accountability. An e-learning course was developed with the goals of improving students knowledge and skills. Health psychology issues and problem-solving skills in decision-making under specific case-studies were included in the learning object delivered to students. This approach, mainly visual-analogical, depends on skills and potential of student self-teaching, i.e. in their capacity of re-building a correct case-study and/or a decision-making tree. The developed e-learning tool was effective and improved knowledge/skills achievement of medical and psychology students.

Disease representation and contextualization as critical associated components of clinical decision making: A preliminary study

Trovato, Guglielmo *Internal Medicine & Health Psy, University of Catania, Catania, Italy* **Catalano, Daniela** *Internal Medicine & Health, University of Catania, Catania, Italy* **Pace, Patrizia** *Internal Medicine & Health, University of Catania, Catania, Italy* **Aprile, Giuseppe** *Surgery & Endoscopy, University of Catania, Catania, Italy* **Magro, Gaetano** *Pathology, University of Catania, Catania, Italy*

Objective:Context factors in medical decision-making are commonly considered negligible components of errors and/or medical interventions complications. Effects and mutual relationship, if any,of physician's disease representation and personal contextualization,not only on diagnosis but also on treatment-choice of patients. Method:A questionnaire addressed to decision making in gastroenterology was developed and validated. Comparison of models of different disease representation and pathways of contextualization in some categories of medical specialists(pathologists, gastroenterologists, internists, family doctors)was done. Results:different disease representation were observed: contextualization issues were associated with different features in decision making and professional behavior. Conclusion:physician's contextualization and disease representation are important features in clinical decision-making.

The role of various moods play in facial emotion recognition

Tseng, Huai-Hsuan *Dept. of Psychiatry, NTU Hospital, Taipei, Taiwan* **Chen, Sue-Huei** *Department of Psychology, National Taiwan University, Taipei, Taiwan* **Huang, Yu-Lien** *Department of Psychology, National Taiwan University, Taipei, Taiwan*

Objectives: To examine the negative effects of depression and interpersonal sensitivity on perception of facial emotions. Methods: 88 college students received assessment of computerized Diagnostic Analysis of Nonverbal Accuracy 2-Taiwan version (DANVA2-TW) and SCL-90-R. Results:

Concerning facial emotion recognition accuracy, no significant differences among groups with various levels of depress mood, but interpersonally sensitive subjects make more mistakes. Conclusion: Person with higher interpersonal sensitivity, but not depression, tends to make more mistakes in perceiving facial emotions. Discussion will center around the role of various moods play in facial emotion recognition.

Gender stereotypes implicit in language: A cross-cultural comparison of gender ascriptions in German and Chinese interpersonal verbs

Tumasjan, Andranik *Inst. für Psychologie, Universität München, München, Germany* **Bekk, Magdalena** *Department of Psychology, Ludwig-Maximilians University, München, Germany* **Klaas, Hannah Sophie** *Universität München, München, Germany* **Spörrle, Matthias** *Dept. for Psychology, Ludwig-Maximilians University, München, Germany*

Two samples (N = 386) from Germany and China were compared in order to investigate intercultural specifics of gender stereotypes in language. Using the Revised Action-State Distinction (Rudolph & Försterling, 1997) 24 interpersonal verbs were selected to examine verb type effects on gender ascriptions to persons involved in social interaction. Consistent with previous research, German respondents perceived interpersonal actions (e.g. support) as being caused by men whereas interpersonal states (e.g. surprise) were perceived as being induced by women. Additionally, results provide first evidence that Chinese participants perceived both types of interpersonal interaction to be caused by men. Implications for intercultural communication are discussed.

The role of music in young adults' emotional lives

Udovicic, Martina *Dept. of Psychology, Faculty of Philosophy, Sesvete, Croatia* **Banozic, Adrijana** *Department of psychology, Faculty of Philosophy, Zagreb, Croatia* **Vojnic Tunic, Ana** *Department of psychology, Faculty of Philosophy, Zagreb, Croatia* **Prot, Sara** *Department of psychology, Faculty of Philosophy, Zagreb, Croatia* **Stamenkovic, Barbara** *Department of psychology, Faculty of Philosophy, Zagreb, Croatia* **Plosnic, Fani** *Department of psychology, Faculty of Philosophy, Zagreb, Croatia*

This study explored the links of emotions and moods with listening to music in a sample of Croatian young adults (N = 250). Survey data was collected, measuring participants' habits of listening to music and their moods before, during and after listening. The participants reported their predominant mood while listening to music is happy, relaxed and inspired. The majority of participants (89%) reported feeling better after listening to music, and positive mood induction was one of the most common motives for listening to particular types of music. No reliable differences in mood were found between fans of different music genres.

Emotional intelligence evaluation using the BarOn (I-CE) Inventory in a sample of Lima, Peru

Ugarriza-Chavez, Nelly *Psychology, Universidad Ricardo Palma, Lima, Peru*

The BarOn Emotional Quotient Inventory was used with a representative sample of 1996 participants form the urban area of Lima, Peru, The age of all men and women included in the sample were over 16 years old. A second-order confirmatory factor analysis was performed on the composite scales of the EQ-I which verified the 5-1 factorial structure proposed by the eclectic model of the emotional intelligence of Bar-On (1997). It was found that emotional intelligence increases with age, and that significant gender differences do exist for many factorial components. The alpha coefficient was .93 for the Total CE, revealing the internal consistency of the inventory. Administration, scoring and interpretation norms were elaborated.

Effects of attending to or away from pain depend on the level of catastrophic thinking about pain

van Damme, Stefaan *Clinical Psychology, Gent University, Gent, Belgium*

We investigated the effects of spatial attention on pain experience. During short pain stimulation attention was directed to (focus) or away from (distraction) the stimulated hand using a cueing task. ANOVA's showed lower fear ratings in the focus relative to distraction group. Also less pain was reported in the focus group but only in participants low in catastrophic thinking about pain. However, for high catastrophizers, pain ratings were lower in the focus group. It is concluded that focusing to pain helps controlling affective responses to pain, whereas distracting from pain diminishes sensory pain perception, particularly when appraised as threatening.

Enhancement of emotional clarity: An intervention study

van de Loo, Kirsten *Inst. für Psychologie, Techn. Universität Darmstadt, Darmstadt, Germany* **Schmitz, Bernhard** *Institut für Psychologie, Techn. Universität Darmstadt, Darmstadt, Germany*

The aim of the study was to enhance emotional clarity as it is an important variable within learning. 108 students were assigned to two experimental and a control group. Experimental group A was trained to experience and describe specific emotions, experimental group B got a mindfulness training. Emotional clarity was measured by the Trait Meta-Mood Scale (Salovey et al., 1995), an emotion recognition task and a questionnaire measuring the accuracy of emotion descriptions. Multivariate analyses of variance showed expected effects on some of the dependent variables. Results are discussed regarding effect sizes and the character of future interventions.

Comparing web-based and face-to-face memory testing

van Hooren, Susan *Dept. of Psychology, Open University Netherlands, Heerlen, Netherlands* **Franssen, Marielle** *Psychology, Open University Netherlands, Heerlen, Netherlands* **Waterink, Wim** *Psychology, Open University Netherlands, Heerlen, Netherlands*

The aim of this study is to examine the validity of web-based testing. Performance on a web-based memory test was compared to a face-to-face memory test, taking into account differences in computer attitude, computer experience and motivation. A counter balanced within subjects design was used. After accounting for the intrinsic factors, scores on the web-based test are lower than scores on the face-to-face test. These differences were more pronounced in older age. In spite of the advantages of web-based testing, it is crucial to consider that web-based neuropsychological testing is not comparable to face-to-face testing, especially among older age groups.

Psychometric properties of motivation for choice of study program inventory

Vanags, Martins *Dept. of Psychology, University of Latvia, Riga, Latvia*

The Motivation For Choice Of Study Program Inventory (Voitkāne, Miezīte, Raščevska & Vanags, 2006) was designed to measure motivation of choice for study program in high-school graduates entering university. This study extended the previous psychometric findings (Vanags, 2006) to a bigger sample. The questionnaire construction was done on two independent samples (first stage N=145, both males and females, age 18-20; second stage N=300, both males and females, age 17-20). Factor analysis exposed three dimensions with high internal consistency: external motivation, motivation for knowledge, motivation for career development. Divergent validity of SPCI was tested. Keywords:

study motivation, first-year student adjustment, inventory, SPCI

Acute stress has not effect on long-term object recognition memory in rats

Vargas, Viviana Psychology, Universidad Nacional de Colomb, Bogotá D.C., Colombia *Torres, Angelica* Psychology, Universidad Nacional de Colomb, Bogotá D.C., Colombia *Múnera, Alejandro* Physiology, Universidad Nacional de Colomb, Bogotá D.C., Colombia *Lamprea, Marisol* Psychology, Universidad Nacional de Colomb, Bogotá D.C., Colombia

A previous experiment developed in our laboratory showed a deleterious effect of acute stress on the acquisition of short-term memory measured by an object recognition task. Present experiment evaluated the effect of acute stress at long-term memory in 24 male Wistar rats randomly assigned to one of three groups: a) One hour motor restriction b) Four hours motor restriction and c) no restriction, followed by the acquisition of the task, and evaluated 24 hours latter. A one way ANOVA test showed no significant differences between groups, indicating that acute stress do not affect the acquisition of long-term object recognition memory.

Interference and facilitation effects on the recall of a list of words induce by presented or self-generated verbal information

Vargas, Viviana Psychology, Universidad Nacional de Colomb, Bogotá D.C., Colombia

It was compared the effect of self-generated verbal information with externally presented verbal information over the recall of a list of words. A factorial design was used with independent variables of: a) moment of presentation, and b) kind of information; it was also a control group. 63 students were randomly assigned to the groups. Multiple ANOVA analysis was used to see the effects over the number of right and wrong answers in free recall and key recall. Presentation of external information, before and after recall, produced an interference effect; on the contrary, self-generated information produced a facilitation effect.

Emotion regulation difficulties and adjustment in newlyweds couples

Velotti, Patrizia Dynamic and Clin. Psychology, University of Rome, Rome, Italy *Castellano, Rosetta* Dynamic and Clinical Psycholog, University of Rome, Rome, Italy *Zavattini, Giulio Cesare* Dynamic and Clinical Psycholog, University of Rome, Rome, Italy Objective: Although researchers have examined the link between marital adjustment and different personality's aspect, the precise role of emotion remains unclear (Snyder, 2006). The current study explores the link between individual's difficulties in emotion regulation and dyadic adjustment in the context of newlyweds couples. Methods: Partecipants. 100 couples participated. Measures.. The Difficulties in Emotion Regulation Scale (DERS, Gratz & Roemer, 2004). The Dyadic Adjustment Scale (DAS, Spanier, 1976). Results: We tested two main effects: actor effect and partner effect and we found that difficulties in emotion regulation had a negative impact on dyadic adjustment.

The effects of leadership practices and perceived organizational support on maritime crew team performance: The mediating role of affective commitment

Viranuvat, Parinda I/O Psychology, Thammasat University, Bangkok, Thailand

This study tested the influence of team leadership behaviour and perceived organizational support (POS) on team performance. Affective commitment to leader was proposed to mediate the relationship between leadership and team performance, as measured by objective measurement of team performance. Affective commitment to organization was also proposed to mediate the effects that POS had on team performance. The mediation test was done by using Baron and Kenny's (1986) method. The results indicated that only POS, not leadership behaviours, positively affects team performance. No mediating relationship was found in the hypothesized model. This anomalous results lead to questions pertaining subjective vs. objective criteria

The impact of an osteopathy treatment on chronic pain intensity

von Fischern, Iris Praxis Evost, Wiesbaden, Germany *Deichmeier, Frank* Praxis Evost, Praxis Evost, Wiesbaden, Germany *Spörrle, Matthias* Psychology, LMU, Munich, Germany

Treatment of chronic pain patients is of increasing relevance in clinical research. Our study investigates potential reduction of patients' levels of pain intensity due to an osteopathy treatment. Thirty-six persons with chronic pain diagnosis participated in a two-stage treatment process and repeatedly filled out established measures (e.g. Numerical Rating Score) of pain localization and intensity. In a first stage participants received no intervention, in the second stage a maximum of six osteopathy treatments was given. Analysis revealed significant reductions of pain intensity in the waiting period as well as in the treatment period. The improvement during the treatment period was significantly larger than the one during the waiting period.

Gender and educational differences in shame in adolescents

Vrij-Hoogendoorn, Lida PACT, Mediant Mental Health, Enschede, Netherlands *Christenhusz, Lieke* Department of Psychology &, University of Twente, Enschede, Netherlands *Drossaert, Constance* Department of Psychology &, University of Twente, Enschede, Netherlands *Baneke, Joost* Department of Psychology &, University of Twente, Enschede, Netherlands

Shame is one of the important causal factors in psychological pathways and becomes particularly prominent from the period of adolescence. In this study 954 high school students, mean age 16 year, filled out a questionnaire on three specific areas of shame. Higher educated adolescents reported significantly more general shame than lower educated adolescents, and females reported more characterological, behavioural and bodily shame compared to males. The largest gender difference was found in bodily shame. As a conclusion, gender and educational differences should be taken into account in future research of shame related issues in adolescents.

Evidence of prenatal transfer of testosterone in humans?: Decreased left-handedness in females from opposite-sex twin pairs

Vuoksimaa, Eero Dept. of Public Health, University of Helsinki, Helsingin Yliopisto, Finland *Kaprio, Jaakko* Department of Public Health, University of Helsinki, Helsingin Yliopisto, Finland *Pulkkinen, Lea* Department of Psychology, University of Jyväskylä, University of Jyväskylä, Finland *Rose, Richard J.* Psychological & Brain Scie, Indiana University, Bloomington, Finland

Objectives: Female twins from opposite-sex pairs might be exposed to prenatal transfer of testosterone. Testosterone is suggested to play role in the formation of handedness. Earlier singleton studies have shown that right-handers have higher levels of testosterone than left-handers. Methods: We studied handedness in population based FT12 study, which includes all Finnish twins born in 1983-87. We used cluster corrected chi2 statistics. Results: the prevalence of left-handedness was significantly lower in females from opposite-sex pairs compared to females from same-sex pairs. Conclusion: Results support the prenatal testosterone transfer hypothesis and are very unlikely to be caused by postnatal socialization effects.

Formal complexity, real cognitive complexity and reaction time

Vylegzhanin, Vasily IEAP, Moscow, Russia *Druzhinin, Yury* Experimental Psychology Dept., IEAP, Moscow, Russia

The problem of complexity is to be discussed as intermedial between computer and cognitive science. Formal computational complexity of solved tasks evaluated by well-known formal methods was compared with neurophysiological and psychophysical data. Formal evaluation of complexity was graduated by differences in reaction and solving time that were interpreted as indicators of real cognitive complexity. Degrees of fatigue level evaluated by instrumental methods and interpreted as addition cognitive complexity showed approximately monotonic dependency between computational complexity and real subjective complexity.

Use of patient-self-assessments in emergency care to predict mortality for heart failure patients

Wahl, Inka Psychosomatik, UKE Hamburg, Hamburg, Germany *Rose, Matthias* Psychosomatic Medicine, UKE Hamburg, Hamburg, Germany *Weinrich, Daniel* Dept. of Cardiology, Charité Berlin, Berlin, Germany *Strohm, Sebastian* Dept. of Cardiology, Charité Berlin, Berlin, Germany *Vollert, Jan-Ole* Dept. of Lab Medicine, San Francisco General Hospital, San Francisco, Germany *Müller, Christian* Dept. of Clinical Chemistry, Charité Berlin, Berlin, Germany *Möckel, Martin* Dept. of Cardiology, Charité Berlin, Berlin, Germany

Objective: Evaluate the potential of patient-self-assessments predicting mortality of heart failure (HF) patients. Methods: 99 patients with decompensated HF were included. New-York-Heart-Association classification (NYHA), B-type-na-triuretic peptide (BNP), Minnesota Living with Heart Failure Questionnaire (MLHFQ) have been determined within 24h after admission. Results: 17 patients died due to HF within 12 months. Those with BNP-values >600pg/ml or MLHFQ-scores > 70 had an increased mortality-ratio (p<0.05, Kaplan-Meier-analyses). Patients with both risk factors had a 54 percent likelihood of dying within one year in contrast to nine percent for patients without both risk factors. Conclusion: Self-assessments help to predict mortality for HF patients.

Representations and motivations to breastfeed: A comparison between French and German mothers.

Walburg, Vera Université Toulouse le Mirail, CERPP, Toulouse, France *Conquet, Marlene* Université Toulouse le Mirail, CERPP, Toulouse, France *Callahan, Stacey* Université Toulouse le Mirail, CERPP, Toulouse, France *Chabrol, Henri* Université Toulouse le Mirail, CERPP, Toulouse, France *Schölmerich, Axel* Fakultät für Psychologie, Ruhr-Universität Bochum, Bochum, Germany

Objectives: The purpose of this study was to investigate the potential reasons for the dissimilarity in breastfeeding rate between German (90%) and French (56.3%) mothers. Methods: Representations about breast and bottle feeding so as motivations to breastfeed or not were collected and compared in 126 French and 80 German primiparous mothers. Results: Results show significant differences between these two populations in terms of breastfeeding representations and motivations to breastfeed or not. Erroneous and irrational beliefs are more representative in French mothers. Conclusion: This study provides insight for understanding breast-feeding rate differences between these two countries.

Revision of the "Wiener Matrizen Test"

Waldherr, Karin *Inst. für Psychologie, Universität Wien, Wien, Austria* **Formann, Anton K.** *Faculty of Psychology, University of Vienna, Vienna, Austria* **Piswanger, Karl** *Personal- und Managementpartne, Pendl & Piswanger, Vienna, Austria*

Objective: Does the Wiener Matrizen Test (WMT; Formann & Piswanger, 1979) show Rasch Model (RM) properties despite the huge changes since its first publication (social changes, extensive research on RM with development of new model tests)? Methods: The WMT was given to n=2495 persons (14-64 years). Psychometric properties of the WMT were analysed by means of various model tests. Results: Despite extensive model testing and high test power only six items were excluded. Reliability and validity of the shorter WMT are comparable with the original. Conclusion: The results further indicate that the WMT is independent of cultural contexts.

Gratitude, relationship quality and life satisfaction in friendship pairs

Walker, Simone *Psychology, UTM, University of Toronto, MIssissauga, Canada*

The current study examined gratitude within best friendships. Ninety-two best friend pairs reported their own dispositional gratitude, friendship quality and life satisfaction. Participants also reported three gratitude-related memories which were reliably coded for the emotional response and expression of the beneficiary. Main results showed that participants rated the friendship as more companionable, nurturing, and intimate, and were more satisfied with life when the beneficiary experienced and expressed grateful emotion. In conclusion, results suggest that both the experience and expression of gratitude within a friendship are important for the quality of the relationship and the life satisfaction of the pair.

Research on Chinese puberty sexual morals structure

Wang, Yuan *School of Teacher Education, Shenyang Normal University, Shenyang, People's Republic of China* **Guo, Li-Yan** *School of Teacher Education, Shenyang Normal University, Shenyang, People's Republic of China*

Based on the literature review on sexual morals, a structural interview and an open-ended questionnaire were designed to measure sexual morals of puberty, and then a Chinese Puberty Sexual Morals Scale were developed. The results showed that the scale was of good reliability and validity, which consisted of four components, the brink sex behavior morality, process sex behavior morality, purpose sex behavior morality, sex information dissemination morality.

The experimental research on time pressure affecting decision strategy

Wang, Dawei *Psychology, Shandong Normal University, Jinan, People's Republic of China*

The study examines how decision-makers make decision strategy, using Information Board and Eye- Movement technique. During the study process, the researcher explored the problem by introducing time pressure (high/moderate/low) and task (important/unimportant) variable. By analyzing Eye-Movement data, the results were as follows: (1) Time pressure and task had more effects on decision making;(2) When encountering time pressure, decision makers were inclined to choosing linear strategies to cope with tasks of great significance, vice versa.

The structure, developmental characteristic of adolescents' interpersonal competence

Wang, Yingchun *Beijing, People's Republic of China* **Zou, Hong** *Institute of developmental psy, shcool of psychology, Beijing, People's Republic of China*

Interpersonal competence referred to the tendency to behave effectively and appropriately, which made him in harmony with others. The present research defined the structure of interpersonal competence, and then developed the "Interpersonal Competence Questionnaire(ICQ)" and explored the general characteristic of adolescent' interpersonal competence. Results indicated: (1)Interpersonal Competence Questionaire included 3 factors: interpersonal motivation, interpersonal cognition and interpersonal skills; (2)There were significant grade difference in interpersonal motivation, grade and gender difference in interpersonal skills and interaction between gender and grade in interpersonal cognition.

Affective and facial responses to tastes in human adults

Weiland, Romy *Inst. für Psychologie, Universitätä Würzburg, Würzburg, Germany* **Macht, Michael** *Institute of Psychology, University of Würzburg, Würzburg, Germany*

Objectives: We examined the influence of tastes on affective and facial reactions. Methods: Thirty-two subjects rated intensity, pleasantness, and mood in response to taste solutions differing in concentration and quality. Facial reactions were recorded and were analysed by the Facial Action Coding System. Results: Facial reactions were differentially affected by tastes. With increasing concentration, subjects rated tastes as more intense, and some tastes (bitter, salty, umami) as less pleasant. Conclusion: Facial responses in human adults are similar to those found in human newborns. Moreover, taste concentration plays a key role in the quantity of facial reactions.

Personal light: Evaluation of dynamic lighting by Philips in Hamburg schools

Wessolowski, Nino *Abt. Psychosomatik, UKE Hamburg-Eppendorf, Hamburg, Germany* **Schulte-Markwort, Michael** *Abt. Psychosomatik, UKE Hamburg-Eppendorf, Hamburg, Germany* **Barkmann, Claus** *Abt. Psychosomatik, UKE Hamburg-Eppendorf, Hamburg, Germany*

Positive effects of lighting on performance in workplaces indicate that optimizing lighting in classrooms is a promising approach to improve the performance of students. This study compares seven programs differing in illuminance and colour temperature. Main objectives are to investigate effects on attention, aggressiveness and hyperactivity in students. Therefore, in a controlled field trial, six natural classes are observed cross-sectionally and longitudinally. First results point to positive effects on work speed and accuracy, assessed by the "d2". The findings will lead to conclusions on effects, usability and acceptance of Dynamic Lighting in the school setting.

Human amygdala habituation during the presentation of auditory stimuli

Wieckhorst, Birgit *Psychiatrie - Psychologie, Universität Basel, Basel, Switzerland* **Mutschler, Isabella** *of Psychiatry / Psychology, University of Basel, Basel, Switzerland* **Schulze-Bonhage, Andreas Speck, Oliver Hennig, Jürgen** *Medical Physics, University Hospital Freiburg, Freiburg, Germany* **Seifritz, Erich** *of Psychiatry, University Hospital Bern, Bern, Switzerland* **Ball, Tonio** *Epilepsy-Center, University Hospital Freiburg, Freiburg, Germany*

The human amygdala has been reported to habituate in response to visual stimuli (e.g., Fischer et al., 2003). It is less clear, however, whether and in which amygdala subregion habituation also occurs in response to auditory stimuli. Using functional

MRI, brain responses to piano pieces were investigated in 18 healthy subjects. We find that the relative magnitude of responses in the latero-basal amygdala, defined using a probabilistic map (Amunts et al., 2005), significantly declined over time (p<0.05). These results indicate that habituation is not specific to visual amygdala responses but represents a more general property of human amygdala function.

Who benefits from planning?: The road to action is paved with high intentions

Wiedemann, Amelie *Gesundheits-Psychologie, Freie Universität Berlin, Berlin, Germany* **Schüz, Benjamin** *Lifelong Learning / Institutio, Jacobs University Bremen, Bremen, Germany* **Schwarzer, Ralf** *Health Psychology, Freie Universität Berlin, Berlin, Germany* **Sniehotta, Falko F.** *School of Psychology, University of Aberdeen, Aberdeen, United Kingdom* **Scholz, Urte** *Social and Health Psychology, University of Zurich, Zurich, Switzerland*

Objectives If-then planning facilitates the translation of intentions into action. Mediation effects of planning are assumed to be stronger in individuals with high intentions. Methods Moderated mediation analyses in two longitudinal studies on physical activity and oral hygiene (follow-up 3 months, respectively 4 months after baseline). Results The strength of the indirect effect of intentions on behavior via planning increased along with levels of intentions (moderator). The sufficient level of intentions is different for the two behaviors. Conclusions Small changes in intentions might determine whether planning translates intentions into action. The importance of intentions should be considered when developing planning interventions.

The effect of process improvement on coordination success in work teams

Wiedow, Annika *Inst. für Psychologie, Universität zu Kiel, Kiel, Germany* **Ellwart, Thomas** *School of Applied Psychology, University of Applied Science, Olten, Switzerland* **Konradt, Udo** *Dep. of Psychology, University of Kiel, Kiel, Germany*

In two studies we examined the effect of process improvement (i.e. reflection, adaption) on team coordination as well as its mediating mechanisms on a cognitive level (shared mental models) as well as on a motivational level (team trust). In an experimental control group design study with 32 three-student groups process improvement was manipulated by reflecting previous performance. In a cross-sectional field study, members of 116 organizational teams rated process improvement activities and coordination. ANOVA and Partial Least Square analyses indicated that process improvement led to better team coordination. This effect was partially mediated by shared mental models and team trust.

Religiosity and substance use in a community sample of adults

Wills, Thomas *Dept. of Epidemiology, Einstein College of Medicine, Bronx, USA* **Walker, Carmella** *Epidemiology, A Einstein College of Medicine, Bronx, USA* **Ainette, Michael** *Dept. of Epidemiology, Einstein College of Medicine, Bronx, USA*

OBJECTIVE: To better understand the effect of religiosity. METHOD: A sample of 330 adults (M age 41 years) reported on behavioral aspects of religiosity [e.g., belonging, attendance] and personal aspects [e.g., value on religion, nonreligious spirituality, forgiveness]. RESULTS: Religiosity was inversely related to smoking and alcohol use. The effect of personal religiosity was mediated through lower risk-taking tendency and less coping motives for smoking and alcohol use, also with a direct effect to (less) alcohol use. The effect for behavioral aspects was mediated through less coping motives for alcohol use and heavy drinking. CONCLUSIONS: The protective effect of religiosity for substance use is partly mediated through psycho-social factors.

Are female leaders more transformational?: Transactional and transformational leadership of historical male and female leaders
Wohlers, Christina Münster, Germany Rowold, Jens Institute of Psychology II, University of Muenster, Münster, Germany
Although research found that female supervisors and managers exhibit more transformational leadership than their male counterparts, considerable more male than female leaders can be found. Empirical research comparing male and female leaders at the CEO- or world-class level is virtually nonexistent. The present study utilized a sample of 35 historical leaders from various fields such as politics, military, and business. Subjects were students of psychology who were presented a biography of one of the historical leaders. Results revealed that female leaders exhibited more transformational leadership than male leaders. These results were stable across historical period and subject's gender.

Anxiety and depression show opposite patterns of associations with Glucocorticoid receptor expression in children
Wolf, Jutta Dept. of Psychology, University of British Columbia, Vancouver, Canada Chen, Edith Psychology, University of British Columbia, Vancouver, Canada
The present study tested whether the overlapping constructs depression and anxiety might predict different patterns of activation at the molecular level. Glucocorticoid-receptor expression was assessed repeatedly in 36 healthy children and 50 children with asthma. Child anxiety and depression were measured at baseline. Only healthy children showed decreases in glucocorticoid-receptor expression in response to anxiety and increases in response to depression (beta=-.64,p<.001; beta=.56,p=.004, resp.). The present results suggest that in healthy children, depression and anxiety do show distinctive features at the molecular level. Children with asthma, however, may have an immune system that responds less dynamically to negative psycho-social states.

Are all anger experiences the same?
Wranik, Tanja Psychology, University of Geneva, Geneva 4, Switzerland Fiori, Marina Psychology, University of Chicago, Chicago, Ilinois, USA
We examined similarities and differences between anger at another person and anger at the self. Participants responded to questions about recent anger experiences, including their evaluations, behaviors, and regulation strategies. We also measured emotion regulation styles, personality, and well-being. The two anger experiences differed in important ways, including intensity, length, evaluation structure, and resultant behaviors. Moreover, although social sharing was frequent in both types of anger, it was only positively associated with anger intensity when angry with another person. We will discuss anger experiences in terms of emotional intelligence and functionality for the work environment and in social relationships.

Measuring susceptibility to emotional contagion. Preliminary analysis of psychometric properties of a Polish adaptation of the Emotional Contagion Scale
Wrobel, Monika Inst. of Psychology, University of Lodz, Lodz, Poland
Objectives: The aim of the study was to adapt the Emotional Contagion Scale (ECS) to Polish conditions. Methods: The ECS was translated into Polish with the use of back translation procedure and then completed by 186 participants aged 19 to 31.

Results: The analysis of the psychometric properties of Polish version (factor structure, homogeneity and test-retest reliability) revealed that the parameters of the adaptation are satisfactory and comparable with the characteristics of the original scale. Conclusions: The preliminary results indicate that Polish ECS can be treated as a useful and reliable tool for measuring individual differences in susceptibility to emotional contagion.

The competing value framwork (CVF) presidential leadership behavior in technology universities in Taiwan
Wu, Ming-Hsun International Business Admi., Chien Kuo Technol. University, Chang Hua, Taiwan Lai, Ying-Chun applied foreign Languages, Chung Shan Medical University, ChangHua, Taiwan Shiah, Yung-Jong General Education Center, ChienKuo Technology University, ChangHua, Taiwan
The purpose of this research was to investigate the presidential leadership behaviors in 29 technology universities in Taiwan based on the Competing Values Framework (CVF) presidential leadership behavior.It includes four second-order factors-relating to people, leading change, managing processes, and producing results. Each second-order factor includes 3 first-order factors. 651 valid samples were collected from 29 technology universities in Taiwan. MANOVA were applied to determine if there are significant differences between/among the categories in each demographic variable. Participants' gender, whether they participate in administrative duties, age, and whether they were homeroom teachers influenced teachers' perceptions on their president's leadership behaviors.

The theoretical construct and measurement of college students' interpersonal interaction efficacy
Xie, Jing Dept. of Psychology, Beijing Normal University, Beijing, People's Republic of China
Based on investigation about more than 1000 college students' interpersonal interaction,we compile a scale to analyse the college students' interpersonal interaction efficacy.Through this research,we want to discuss the internal structure of the college students' interpersonal interaction and bring the concept of self-efficacy into the area of interpersonal interaction.The result demonstrates the sense of college students' interpersonal interaction efficacy consists of six aspects:intimation efficacy,impression management efficacy,benefit-other efficacy,connection efficacy,mood-control efficacy,self-value efficacy.

Emotional reactions of parents to their child's aggression and withdrawal
Xu, Qinmei Inst. for Psychology, Zhejiang University, Hangzhou, People's Republic of China Xu, Linfen Psychology, Zhejiang University, Hangzhou, People's Republic of China Xie, Lincong Social Sciences, Zhejiang Police College, Hangzhou, People's Republic of China
Objectives: This study aimed to assess emotional reactions of parents to their child's aggression and withdrawal in China. Methods: 302 parents having one child aged 4 to 8 were interviewed with a structural questionnaire developed from Mills and Rubbin (1990). Results: (1) Parents' dominant emotional responses to both of aggression and withdrawal were concern. (2) Child's aggression mainly evoked parents' anger and embarrassment whereas child's withdrawal caused their disappointment. (3) Parents reported more negative emotions to 6-year-old and 8-year-old child's problematic social behavior than to 4-year-old child's. Conclusion: Parents' emotional reactions to aggression were different from to withdrawl.

Regulatory focuses and co-worker preferences
Yamagami, Makiko Educational Program, Ochanomizu University, Wakoh, Japan
This study examined the influence of regulatory focuses on interpersonal attraction. 117 undergraduate students read the behavior descriptions of two different persons who use promotion focus vs. prevention focus, respectively. They selected one of them as a future co-worker, and responded to the Regulatory Focus Questionnaire (RFQ: Higgins, et al., 2001). A 2 (high vs. low promotion focus) x 2 (high vs. low prevention focus) ANOVA revealed the significant interaction effect: when the promotion focus is low, highly prevention focused participants tend to choose prevention focused target. The result suggests that the preferences of the self-regulation affect the interpersonal preferences.

The difference of evaluation apprehension among diverse cultures
Yamagiwa, Yuichiro Inst. for Extended Study, Tokyo Metropolitan University, Hachioji, Japan Kawana, Yoshihiro Faculty of Education of Inform, Kawamura Gakuen Woman's Univer, Abiko, Japan
The comparative survey was conducted in terms of the degree of evaluation apprehension. 357 Japanese, 90 Chinese, and 105 American were asked how much they apprehended others' evaluations in 26 situations. Five factors were extracted, and Japanese apprehended others' evaluations more than two other countries on four factors which were Misbehavior in Public, Mistakes in Public, Evaluation for Ability and Public Attention, and they were related to negative emotions. But there was no difference on Public Appearance relating to pleasant emotion. These results may be derived from the differences of relative values of self-assertiveness and the evaluation from others.

Characteristics of paranoid thoughts in a non-clinical population
Yamauchi, Takashi The University of Tokyo, Japan, Tokyo, Japan Sudo, Anju Graduate School of Medicine, The University of Tokyo, Japan, Tokyo, Japan Tanno, Yoshihiko Graduate School of Arts and Sc, The University of Tokyo, Japan, Tokyo, Japan
Objectives: We examined the characteristics of paranoid thoughts compared with social anxious thoughts in Japanese student sample. Methods: Participants were 148 undergraduates. Nine characteristics were assessed on both paranoid thoughts and anxious ones: resistance, distress, absurdity, conviction, corrigibility, controllability, perception of intended harm, anger and frequency. Results: A multivariate analysis of variance (MANOVA) indicated that patterns of the characteristics differed depending upon two kinds of thoughts (Wilks' F (9, 125)=9.12, p<.001). Conclusions: Paranoid thoughts were characterized by higher absurdity, perception of intended harm and anger, and lower frequency and conviction compared with social anxious thoughts in non-clinical samples.

The study on social support network to accelerate thriving from career crisis: In the case of researchers at early career developmental stage
Yamaura, Kazuho University of Shizuoka, Shizuoka, Japan Sakata, Kiriko Integrated Arts and Science, Hiroshima University, Higashi-hiroshima, Japan Nishida, Kimiaki Nursing, University of Shizuoka, Shizuoka-City, Japan
The purpose of this study was to figure out the relationship between the characteristics of social-support-networks, which Japanese researchers hold at early developmental stage, and thriving from their career crisis. An in-depth interview of 28 researchers indicated 4 types of network: some sincere admirer, old and trusted labmates, informants as quarry of excited idea, remotely related

persons. We found that they had happened to be acquainted with informants in the struggling process to recover from their career crises. Also, continuous joint studies with informants, largely consisting of a few, had an important role to their thriving and career development.

SAKURA – Pseudo-personality construction of virtual patients in scenarios of a simulated dental clinic

Yamazaki, Haruyoshi School of Dentistry, Nihon University, Tokyo, Japan Matsuno, Toshio School of medicine, Nihon University, Itabashi-ku Tokyo, Japan Yamada, Hiroshi College of Humanities and Scie, Nihon University, Setagaya-ku Tokyo, Japan Nakajima, Ichiro School of Dentistry, Nihon University, Chiyoda-ku Tokyo, Japan

Newly developed role-playing software, Sakura, graphically represents clinical scenarios to enhance students' manners and dental knowledge. The student plays the dentist and three animation patients receive utterances the student chooses from five, prepared on the Transactional Analysis. Each choice affects the patient's two emotional factors – anxiety and anger, which are graphically represented real time to show the effect of choice immediately. The student can graphically understand how his choice affected the patient's emotional conditions in a good/bad way. As a result of the above simulation course, students' understanding of the importance and tact in dentist-patient communication was greatly improved.

Comprehension and application of verbal communication strategies characterized by Chinese primary school children with learning disabilities

Yan, Rong English Department, BISU, Beijing, People's Republic of China Yu, Guoliang Institute of Psychology, Renming University of China, Beijing, People's Republic of China

The present research aims to explore the development of verbal communication strategy characterized by Chinese learning-disabled children in primary schools. 241 third-, fourth-, fifth- and sixth- grade students (117 LD & 124 Non-LD) participated in this study. Repeated measure was used to examine the differences between the two groups. The results indicate that LD children were developmentally retarded than those without LD at both comprehension and application levels. The aforementioned findings were helpful to the interventions for the improvement of LD children's social skills.

Effect of self-esteem on negotiation time when selecting interactional partners in a persuasion game: An investigation using the Settoku Nattoku game (1)

Yanagisawa, Kuniaki Hiroshima University, Higashihiroshima, Japan Nishimura, Takashi Dep. of clinical Psychology, Hiroshima International Univ., Higashihiroshima, Japan Ura, Mitsuhiro Graduate school of I.A.S., Hiroshima University, Higashihiroshima, Japan

People with low self-esteem may take longer to negotiate when selecting partners for interactions. The effect of self-esteem on negotiation time was investigated using a persuasion game named the Settoku Nattoku Game (SNG; Sugiura, 2003). Freshmen at a university (n = 26) participated in a study that focused on data of "persuasion players" in the SNG. The results were consistent with the hypotheses suggesting that people with low self-esteem tend to spend more time negotiating than people with high self-esteem. The author has discussed the possibility that people with high and low self-esteem take different approaches when interacting with others.

A study of relation between team leaders' in-degree centrality in networks and the corresponding team effectiveness

Yang, Hui Beijing, People's Republic of China Ji Ming, Zhang Center of Psychology counselin, Beijing Normail University, beijing, People's Republic of China Ran, Bian school of psychology, Beijing Normail University, beijing, People's Republic of China Xuanhui, Lin school of management, Beijing Normail University, beijing, People's Republic of China

This paper investiagtes that, against a background of Chinese culture, the impact of team leaders' in-degree centrality in the corresponding team advice networks and friendship networks, on team effectiveness (including subjective task performance, team viability, and cooperation satisfaction). Fifty-three team leaders and their team members from various organizations(totally 369 persons)have participated in this study. The outcome of regression analysis shows that team leaders' in-degree centrality in team advice networks has a significantly positive impact on team effectiveness, whereas team leaders' in-degree centrality in friendship network fails to have a significant impact on team effectiveness.

An investigation of team social capital as a mediator between transformational leadership and team effectiveness

Yang, Hui Beijing, People's Republic of China Luo, Fang Department of Psychology, Beijing Normal University, Beijing, People's Republic of China

This paper investigates, against the background of Chinese culture, if and how team social capital plays as a mediator between transformational leadership and team effectiveness. Fifty-three team leaders and their team members, with a total of 369 people, have participated in this study. An analysis via structural equation model (SEM) shows that, team social capital indeed acts as a mediator between two dimensions of transformational leadership—individualized consideration and professional skills—and team effectiveness, whereas it fails to act as a mediator between other two dimensions of transformational leadership—moral influence and inspirational motivation—and team effectiveness

Study on mathematics learning disability children's solving complex arithmetical problems

Yao, Jingjing Psychology, Zhejiang Normal University, Jinhua, People's Republic of China

Protocol method was employed to study the process of complex arithmetical problem-solving of grade four students, while easy of learning and judgment of confidence were tested. Result: (1)LD children's problem-solving process is consistent with the general pattern of problem-solving, but each process has its own characteristic, appearing different error types. (2)LD children were distinctly lower than learning gifted students in easy of Learning develop level and in Judgment of Confidence of math problem solving. (3)There is no distinct difference in Easv of Learning and Judgment of Confidence between boys and girls.

The role of speech rate and gaze in persuasion

Yokoyama, Hitomi Dept. of Social Psychology, Osaka University, Suita, Japan Daibo, Ikuo Social Psychology, Osaka University, Suita, Japan

Two experiments were conducted whether slow speech rate and/or a high amount of gaze affected the perceptions of speaker persuasiveness, using a videotaped message by a female speaker. In Experiment 1, one of three speech rate messages (slow, moderate or fast) was presented by an audio player. The result indicated that the effect of the speech rate was not significant. In Experiment 2, speech rate (slow / fast) and a amount of gaze (low / high) were manipulated and presented. The result

suggested that the slow speech rate and high amount of gaze affected the positive perceptions of speaker persuasiveness.

Visual-spatial representations in mathematical problem solving among children with and without learning difficulties in mathematics

Yu, Guoliang Inst. of Psychology, Renmin University, Beijing, People's Republic of China Yan, Rong English, BISU, Beijing, People's Republic of China

The present study aims to explore how schematic and pictorial representations were used and associated with spatial ability in mathematical problem solving among 30 MD and 31 Non-MD Chinese primary school children, using Mathematical Processing Instrument. The results indicate that MD Children reported less use of schematic representations but more use of pictorial representations and showed less successful performance on mathematical tasks than Non-MD children. In addition, there was a decrease and tendency to use pictorial representations by the children without MD, but no decreasing tendency was found among those with MD. The aforementioned findings were helpful to the interventions for LD children's mathematical problem solving.

Resilience and mental health among people living with HIV/AIDS and their spouses in a rural area of central China

Yu, Xiaonan School of Public Health, Chinese Univ. of Hong Kong, Hong Kong, China, People's Republic of : Hong Kong SAR Lau, Joseph T. F. School of Public Health, ChineseUniversityofHongKong, Hong Kong, China, People's Republic of : Macao SAR Cheng, Yimin Social medicine, National Research Institute fo, Beijing, China, People's Republic of : Macao SAR Xu, Shuqin Shangcai Services Station of F, Shangcai Services Station of F, Zhumadian, China, People's Republic of : Macao SAR Lu, Yanhong National Research Institute fo, National Research Institute fo, Beijing, China, People's Republic of : Macao SAR Tsui, Hiyi School of Public Health, ChineseUniversityofHongKong, Hong Kong, China, People's Republic of : Macao SAR Zahng, Jianxin Institute of Psychology, Chinese Academy of Sciences, Beijing, China, People's Republic of : Macao SAR Mak, Winnie W. S. Department of Psychology, ChineseUniversityofHongKong, Hong Kong, China, People's Republic of : Macao SAR

This cross-sectional study examines resilience and mental health of people living with HIV/AIDS (PLWHA) and their spouses in a rural county of Central China. 200 PLWHA and their spouses were interviewed separately. The measurements included resilience, depression, anxiety, and stress etc.. The prevalence of mental problems, factors associated with mental health (e.g. HIV symptoms, medication and side effect), and the relationship between resilience and mental health were investigated. The interaction between the psychological status of the PLWHA and their spouses was also explored. The implications of providing psychological service and conducting intervention to promote resilience and mental health were discussed.

The effects of associative direction and strength on metacognitive illusions for children with learning disabilities

Yu, Guoliang Inst. of Psychology, Renmin University, Beijing, People's Republic of China Hou, Ruihe Psychological Counselling, Renmin University, Beijing, People's Republic of China

Metacognitive illusions refered to the absolute defferences between judgments of learning (JOLs) and recall because individuals were misguided by invalid cues. Both children's with and without learning disabilities (LD) (3-6 graders) metacognitive illusions and group differences were examined. Paired-associate direction and strength tasks (Koriat & Bjork, 2005) were used to find aspects of the cue-target relationships contributing to metacognitive illusions. Results indicated children exhibited metacognitive illusions for weak, especially backward word-pair. It was higher metacognitive illusions for children with LD than normal children. We argued backward word-pair enhance learners sensitive to metacognitive illusions, which could distinguish sensitively from two groups.

Social information processing in Chinese children with and without LD

Yu, Guoliang Inst. of Psychology, Renmin University, Beijing, People's Republic of China Dong, Yan Institute of Psychology, Renmin University of China, Beijing, People's Republic of China

The present study aimed to examine social information processing in Chinese children with and without learning disabilities (LD). Children were placed into three different social interactive situations associated with peers and adults using Dodge's SIP in two sub-situations: the blurry situation and the clear one. The results demonstrated that children with LD had more difficulties in blurry and clear authority-compelling situations; LD children demonstrated significantly lower performance in encoding accuracy and completeness. Under blurry peer situations, the total number of reactions and the number of negative and aggressive responses in LD children were significantly greater than those of non-LD children.

How to lead Chinese organizational learning: Relationship between paternalistic leadership and organizational learning

Yu, Haibo School of Management, Beijing Normal University, Beijing, People's Republic of China Xiaoming, Zheng Tsinhhua University, School of Economic and Managem, Beijing, People's Republic of China Liluo, Fang Institute of Psychology, Chinese Academy of Sciences, Beijing, People's Republic of China Wenquan, Ling School of Management, Jinan University, Guangzhou, People's Republic of China

In order to explore the relationship between paternalistic leadership and organizational learning, four hundred and ninety one surveys from ten Chinese enterprises were collected by surveying. The results of HRA (hierarchical regression analysis) showed that benevolence leadership and moral leadership were positively correlated with organizational learning; however, authoritarianism leadership were negatively correlated with organizational learning. The results also showed that there were positive interaction effects of moral and benevolence leadership on individual learning, authoritarianism and benevolence leadership on explorative learning, benevolence and authoritarianism leadership on exploitation; and there were negative interaction effects of moral and authoritarianism leadership on collective learning, moral and authoritarianism leadership on exploitation learning.

Advanced digital video technologies as "design tools": Conditions for effective collaboration and self-regulated learning in the classroom

Zahn, Carmen Knowledge Media Res. Center, Tübingen, Germany Hesse, Friedrich W. Institut für Wissensmedien, Tübingen, Germany Klages, Benjamin Knowledge Communication, Knowledge Media Research Cente, Tuebingen, Germany Pea, Roy Wallenberg Hall, Stanford University/SCIL, Stanford, CA., USA Rosen, Joe Wallenberg Hall, Stanford University/SCIL, Stanford, CA., USA

Advanced digital video technologies can support new types of self-regulated collaborative learning in school. In our DFG-funded research, we investigate the instructional method of using video as a "design tool" for knowledge and visual skills acquisition in German/history lessons. Based on cognitive theories of writing and design, a field study (N = 234) was conducted to test impacts of digital video technology and media-related concepts on pupils' colla-

boration, knowledge/visual skills acquisition and motivation. Results reveal a general effectiveness of the instructional method and a significant superiority effect of an advanced technology over a more simple solution on pupils' task interest.

The "Forest" project: Learning biology by multimedia design in primary education

Zahn, Carmen Knowledge Media Res. Center, Tübingen, Germany Rau, Thomas Lerngruppe Blau, Französische Schule Tuebingen, Tuebingen, Germany

A pilot study on computer-supported learning in primary school compared writing a researchers' notebook (paper & pencil) to designing a multimedia presentation (computer) in biology lessons with 24 pupils. Analyses of the notebooks and design products revealed significant positive correlations between information structuring in the notebooks and performance in multimedia design for all pupils. Moreover, girls wrote significantly more text into their notebooks than into their computer-based multimedia presentations. No similar effects were found for computer-based writing and visual design activities. Results will be discussed in relation to their practical implications for elementary instruction.

The comparison of family functioning in depressed patients and patients without psychiatric disorders in Isfahan

Zargar, Fatemeh Clinical Psychology, Tehran Psychiatric Institute, Tehran, Islamic Republic of Iran

The purpose of this study was comparing the family functioning between depressed patients and patients without psychiatric disorder in Isfahan. from 3 clinics of psychotherapy in Isfahan city, 30 depressed patients were randomly selected. The control group was consisted of 30 non-psychiatric patients who were referred to one hospital in Isfahan. The Bloom's Family Functioning Test (FFT) was administered to both groups The results of analysis of covariance showed that family cohesion, family sociability, family idealization (amount of family pride) of depressed patients and total of family functioning was significantly lower than control group.

Cross-cultural gender attitudes: Hostile and benevolent sexism to men in Poland, South Africa and Great Britain

Zawisza, Magdalena Dept. of Psychology, University of Winchester, Winchester, United Kingdom Luyt, Russell Department of Psychology, The University of Winchester, Winchester, United Kingdom Zawadzka, Anna Maria Department of Psychology, The University of Gdansk, Gdansk, Poland

Cross-cultural studies exploring gender attitudes indicate that those in Great Britain (GB) and South Africa (SA) lie at opposite ends of the liberal-conservative continuum. None of these studies includes Polish (PL) participants. It was hypothesized that gender attitudes in PL would lie between those in GB and SA. Attitudes, hostile and benevolent sexism to men, among students from each country (n = 120) were compared. One way ANOVAs partially confirmed the hypothesized pattern. Attitudes in PL and GB were less sexist and hostile than those in SA but SA and PL attitudes appeared equally more benevolent than those in GB.

Metabolic syndrome, but not major depression itself influences Cytokine levels in depressed inpatients.

Zeugmann, Sara Klinik für Psychiatrie, Charité-CBF, Berlin, Germany Anghelescu, Ion-George Klinik für Psychiatrie, Charité-CBF, Berlin, Germany Schwarzer, Ralf Gesundheitspsychologie, Freie Universität Berlin, Berlin, Germany

OBJECTIVE: To assess how depression and metabolic syndrome modulate proinflammatory cytokine production. METHODS: Severity of illness

(HAMD-17), metabolic syndrome (International Diabetes Federation criteria) and cytokine concentrations (CRP, IL-6, adiponectin, resistin and fibrinogen) were assessed in 69 depressed inpatients. RESULTS: Analyses of variance revealed that depressed patients with the metabolic syndrome had significantly higher levels of CRP and IL-6, and significantly lower levels of adiponectin. Correlational analyses did not reveal a relationship between severity of depression and proinflammatory cytokine activation. CONCLUSIONS: According to the present data, cytokine dysregulation is amplified in depressed inpatients with metabolic syndrome.

Are they really self-confident: The influence of concealing learning-relevant information on the self-concept of students with learning disabilities

Zhang, Bao-shan Institute of Psychology, Chinese Academy of Science, Beijing, People's Republic of China Zhao, Jun-yan Institute of Psychology, Chinese Academy of Science, Beijing, People's Republic of China Yu, Guoliang Institute of Psychology, Renmin University of China, Beijing, People's Republic of China

Through the experiment context of individual interviews with strange authorities, the influences of concealing learning-relevant information on the self-concept of LD children are tested on both the conscious and unconscious level. In the study, LD children and NLD children are distributed respectively to the interview context with disclosing learning information and that with concealed learning information. The results indicate that, the state self-esteem of LD children under the condition of concealing learning-relevant information has improved dramatically; LD children under the condition of concealing learning information has a tendency of suppressing negative self-image.

A research of the relationships between leadership behavior and job satisfaction in hospital

Zhang, Hui Dept. of Humanities, Capital Medical University, Beijing, People's Republic of China

Objective This research is designed to explore the relationship between the leadership behavior style and job satisfaction in the primary community hospital. Methods Let 173 medical staffs complete the questionnaire including leadership behavior scale and job satisfaction scale anonymously. Results Leadership behavior styles of hospital administrators have made significant difference in job satisfaction. Of the four leadership styles, doctors and nurses in the leader of PM style perceive greater extent of job satisfaction than those who under other leadership styles. Conclusion PM leadership style is the best one, and the worst is pm style.

Consumers' multiattribute decision-making of search engine

Zhang, Lirong Institute of Psychology, CAS, Beijing, People's Republic of China Wang, Yong CSEB, Institute of Psychology, CAS, Beijing, People's Republic of China Fan, Chunlei CSEB, Institute of Psychology, CAS, Beijing, People's Republic of China

This study explored the consumers' multiattribute decision-making of search engine. 201 adjectives of attributes collected by surveys and former studies were divided into 3 categories: functional, symbolic and experiential. Subjects were asked to decide the importance of these attributes, presented randomly with E-Prime software, and to respond as quickly as possible when choosing search engine. Results show a negative correlation between importance and RT (reaction time) and functional attributes have the shortest RTs, which are significantly faster than those of symbolic/experiential attributes. The results suggest that consumers focus more on functional rather than symbolic/experiential attributes when choosing search engine.

Influences of event-valence, time-pressure, description and reference on subjective probability judgments

Zhang, Qin Dept. of Psychology, Capital Normal University, Beijing, People's Republic of China **Qiu, Xiaowen** *Department of Psychology, Capital Normal University, Beijing, People's Republic of China*

The present study investigated whether the subjective probability judgments were influenced by event-valence (positive or negative), time-pressure (with or without), description (in detail or in general) and reference (self or others). 31 participants were asked to estimate the probability of 136 events with or without time-pressure. Results showed that participants gave higher probability estimate for positive other-reference events than self-reference events. In addition, higher probability was related to positive events described in detail without time-pressure and positive events described in general with time-pressure. These results were discussed in the context of the culture difference between the east and west world.

Effect of cue location compound letter processing: An ERP study

Zhang, Xuemin School of of Psychology, Beijing Normal University, Beijinig, People's Republic of China **Li, Yongna** *School of Psychology, New York State University, New York, Armenia* **Bai, Siyu** *School of Psychology, Beijing Normal University, Beijinig, People's Republic of China*

In the present study, we recorded event-related potentials both for pre-cued and post-cued compound letter processing. The results suggested that the processing of post-cued was distinguished from that of pre-cued condition. The hierarchical processing for a compound letter followed after a pre-cue cause frontal and parietal hemispheric asymmetry in early negativity (N1) and long-latency positivity (P3); Global and local processing showed difference in both early negativity (N1) and long-latency positivity (P3). The congruency of the compound letter showed effect only in long-latency positivity (P3). One interesting finding was the significant effect in left hemisphere, no such effects in right hemisphere.

Study on mental healthy improvement of woman in climacteric period by Yoga

Zhao, Ameng Qiqihaer Medical College, Qiqihaer, People's Republic of China **Liu, Haiyan** *Psychiatry Medicine Department, Qiqihaer Medical College, Qiqihaer, People's Republic of China*

Objective: To discuss the influence of Yoga on mental healthy of woman in climacteric period. Method: 64 voluntary women in climacteric period were attended Yoga training while another 64 as contrast group. Results: obvious improvement on the anxiety level, the sleeping quality and physiologic indexes were found in the training member. Conclusion: Yoga can improve the state of mental healthy of woman in climacteric period.

Explicit and implicit measures of intimate relationships and their influential factors

Zhou, Le Dept. of Psychology, Peking University, Beijing, People's Republic of China **Su, Yanjie** *Department of Psychology, Peking University, Beijing, People's Republic of China*

In order to investigate whether social relationships shape the selves of Chinese in the same way as with German's (Pohlmann & Hannover, 2006), we measured explicit and implicit closeness of Chinese's relationships with their lovers, mothers and best friends, as well as their self-construal. Results indicated that the interdependent showed lover-reference effect and higher implicit closeness of lover than the independent, which did not show this effect. Moreover, we found that the more interdependent the independent subjects were, the higher their explicit closeness with their lovers and best friends. The results suggest that Chinese construct their relationships differently from Germans.

Effects of entrepreneur's characteristics on performance in Chinese small high-tech firms

Zhu, Jiping Enterprise Management, Zhejiang University, Hangzhou, People's Republic of China **Qi, Zhenjiang** *enterprise management, Zhejiang University, Hangzhou, People's Republic of China*

This empirical research focuses on the relationships between entrepreneur's characteristics, organizational fitness and firm performance in Chinese small firms. MANOVA and multiple regression were used in analyzing questionnaire data from 251individuals in 35 small high-tech firms. The results indicate that: (1) The abilities to make decision, foresee and innovate varied among the entrepreneurs in small high-tech and non high-tech enterprises; (2) fitness between organizational elements significantly correlated with the entrepreneur's characteristics; (3) the entrepreneur's abilities to make decision, foresee and innovate had significant effects on small high-tech firms' performance. Practical implications and future research direction are discussed.

Problematic mobile phone use and psychological health of college students in Malaysia

Zulkefly, Nor Sheereen Fac. of Med. & Health Sciences, Universiti Putra Malaysia, Selangor, Malaysia **Baharudin, Rozumah** *Fac of Med. & Health Scien, Universiti Putra Malaysia, Selangor, Malaysia*

The relationship between problematic mobile phone use (PMPU) and psychological health was explored in a sample of college students in Malaysia. PMPU was measured using a 27 items scale (Bianchi & Phillips, 2005), whilst the psychological health was assessed using the 12 items, GHQ (Goldberg, 1978). Results revealed that the students do not exhibit problem mobile phone use behavior, and were at a moderate level of psychological health. Nonetheless, students with higher scores on the PMPU scale appeared to be more psychologically disturbed. This study adds to the limited information about mobile phone use amongst young people in Malaysia.

Thursday 24th July 2008

IA-017: Priming, feeling of knowing and recognition: A new perspective on their interrelationship

David Shanks (Chair)

Reder, Lynne Dept. of Psychology, Carnegie-Mellon University, Pittsburgh, USA

Midazolam is a benzodiazepine commonly used as an anxiolytic in surgery. A useful attribute of this drug is that it creates temporary, reversible, anterograde amnesia. Studies involving healthy subjects given midazolam in one session and saline in another, in a double-blind, cross-over design, provide insights into memory function. Several experiments will be described to illustrate the potential of studying subjects with transient anterograde amnesia. This talk will also outline how this drug can be used in combination with fMRI to provide more insights about brain functioning than either method in isolation.

IA-057: Can causal structures be tested with correlations?

Jochen Ziegelmann (Chair)

Bentler, Peter M. Los Angeles, USA

Historically, interesting psychological theories have been phrased in terms of correlation coefficients, which are standardized covariances, and various statistics derived from them. Methodological practice over the last 40 years, however, has suggested it is necessary to transform such theories into hypotheses on covariances, and statistics derived from them. This complication turns out to be unnecessary, since the methodology now exists to test hypotheses on latent structures of correlations directly. Some examples are given. Limitations of correlation structures are also noted.

IA-058: Learning 'about' versus learning 'from' other minds: Natural pedagogy and the role of ostensive communicative cues in cultural learning in human infants

Erik de Corte (Chair)

Gergely, György Budapest, Hungary

Infants fast-learn many types of cultural knowledge from observing others, even when they cannot grasp their relevant properties. Simulation-based imitation cannot explain the transmission of such cognitively 'opaque' cultural forms due to its 'relevance-blindness': its lack of selection mechanisms to differentiate relevant from non-relevant aspects of observed behaviors. Humans evolved a specialized cognitive adaptation, an inferentially-based social-communicative learning system for cultural transmission: 'Natural Pedagogy'. Ostensive-communicative cues play a crucial role in guiding inferences about relevance. The design structure of NP is presented together with supporting evidence from infancy studies testing the theory's assumptions in different knowledge domains.

IA-060: Culture of conflict: Evolvement, institutionalization and consequences

Pierre L.-J. Ritchie (Chair)

Bar-Tal, Daniel School of Education, Tel Aviv University, Tel Aviv, Israel

Intractable conflicts are defined as being protracted, irreconcilable, violent, of zero sum nature, total, and central, and parties involved have an interest in their continuation; they are demanding, stressful, painful, exhausting and costly both in human and material terms. These experiences require adaptation to the conditions of intractable conflict in order to meet three fundamental challenges: Satisfying the needs of the society members, coping with stress, and withstanding the rival. In trying to confront them successfully, societies develop appropriate socio-psychological infrastructure, which includes collective memory, ethos of conflict and collective emotional orientations. This infrastructure fulfills important functions, on both the individual and collective levels, including the important role of formation, maintenance and strengthening of a social identity that reflects this conflict. Special attempts are made to disseminate this infrastructure via societal channels of communication and institutionalize it. This infrastructure becomes hegemonic, rigid and resistant to change as long as the intractable conflict continues. Eventually this infrastructure becomes the foundation for the development of culture of conflict. Its major themes appear in public discourse, cultural products, school books, and societal ceremonies. Society members make attempts to maintain them and impart them to the new generations. The themes of the infrastructure become a prism through which society members construe their reality, collect new information, interpret their experiences and then make decisions about their course of action. The emerged culture of conflict ends up serving as a major fueling factor to the continuation of the conflict and as an obstacle to its peaceful resolution.

IA-061: Perception, attention and memory: A free-energy formulation

Ulman Lindenberger (Chair)

Friston, Karl J. for Neuroimaging London, Welcoe Trust Centre, London, United Kingdom

Formulating Helmholtz's ideas about perception, in terms of modern theories furnishes a model of perceptual inference and learning that can explain many aspects of cortical organisation and responses. Using constructs from statistical physics, the problems of inferring the causes of sensory input and learning the causal structure of their generation can be resolved using exactly the same principle. Furthermore, inference and learning can proceed biologically. The ensuing scheme rests on Empirical Bayes and hierarchical models. The use of hierarchical models enables the brain to construct context-sensitive prior expectations and provides a principled way to understand perception, attention and perceptual learning.

IA-062: The research and the practice of organizational psychology in Brazil: Challenges and perspectives for the new millennium

Michael Knowles (Chair)

Ferreira, Maria Christina Salgado de Oliveira University, Nitéro, Brazil

Aiming to present the state of art of the research and practice of organizational psychology in Brazil, the paper begins with a brief description of the undergraduate and graduate courses on organizational psychology and then characterizes the situation of labor market for organizational psychologists nowadays. After that, it makes a synthesis of the main research lines in organizational psychology, with a special focus on organizational behavior, and discusses the gaps that are still present in the area. It ends with a discussion on how these investigations may contribute to the improvement of the organizational environment and to employee well being.

IA-063: Higher-order cognitive processes in pseudo-automatic associative processes of priming and conditioning

Géry d'Ydewalle (Chair)

Fiedler, Klaus Psychologie, Universität Heidelberg, Heidelberg, Germany

Basic-level associative processes – such as priming, conditioning, or implicit associations – are considered automatic and independent of volition. In contrast to this popular notion, a growing number of findings demonstrate that these phenomena are subject to similar strategic influences as controlled cognitive processes. To illustrate this phenomenon, I present recent findings from three experimental paradigms, evaluative priming, evaluative conditioning, and the implicit association test (IAT). In all three paradigms, deliberate encoding instructions can be shown to eliminate the allegedly automatic effects, and strong strategic effects are sensitive to the baserates and contingencies observed across the stimulus series.

IA-064: From psycho-analysis to culture-analysis: A culturally sensitive revision of psychology

Sabine Sonnentag (Chair)

Dwairy, Marwan Nazerat Ellit, Israel

Psychotherapy aims to reveal unconscious drives or promote self actualization. When this is done with a client from a collective culture it may lead to confrontations with the family and the social environment. Metaphor therapy and culture-analysis are suggested to help such client. In metaphor therapy the inner world is addressed and dealt indirectly and symbolically without bringing unconscious content to the consciousness. In culture-analysis therapist identifies subtle contradictions within the belief system of the client and employ cultural aspects that may facilitate change. Similarly to how a psychoanalyst analyses the psychological domain and brings conflicting aspects to the consciousness (e.g. aggression and guilt) in order to mobilize change, a culturanalyst analyses the client's belief system and brings contradicting aspects to the consciousness in order to mobilize revision in attitudes and behavior.

IA-065: Risk, resources and academic resilience in immigrant youth

Rainer K. Silbereisen (Chair)

Motti-Stefanidi, Frosso Dept. of Psychology, University of Athens, Athens, Greece
Immigration is a taxing experience for immigrants. Immigrant youth, in particular, has to contend with both immigration related and normative developmental challenges. School is a salient acculturative and developmental context where they actually need to deal with such challenges. Based on evidence from over 2000 immigrant adolescent students living in Greece and their native peers, as well as from the international literature, some of the most important barriers and some of the promotive/protective factors for immigrant youth's school competence will be presented. A resilience approach to immigrant youth's adaptation will be adopted, and acculturation will be examined within a developmental framework. It will be argued that a better insight into these issues is the key to the successful promotion of productive immigrant youth development.

IA-066: Posttraumatic stress disorder: From theoretical model to effective treatment

Norbert Kathmann (Chair)

Ehlers, Anke Inst. of Psychiatry, University of London, London, United Kingdom
In the immediate aftermath of traumatic events, most survivors show some symptoms of posttraumatic stress disorder (PTSD), but the majority recover without intervention. The Ehlers and Clark (2000) cognitive model specifies factors that explain why some survivors do not recover on their own and develop chronic PTSD. The presentation will give an overview of the model and recent experimental and prospective longitudinal studies testing its predictions. The model has led to the development of a novel psychological treatment programme for PTSD. Four randomised controlled trials showed that the treatment is highly acceptable, and more effective than wait list, self-help or an equally credible psychological treatment.

IA-067: Psychotherapists at work: Exploring the construction of clinical inferences

Hans Westmeyer (Chair)

Leibovich de Duarte, Adela Buenos Aires, Argentina
This presentation addresses the way in which psychoanalysts and cognitive psychotherapists construct their clinical inferences, the kind of data they base their hunches, their technical-clinical criteria and the theories that mediate and facilitate the organization and comprehension of the material offered by patients. The clinical inferential work includes the production of propositions that convey a meaning beyond the manifest immediately available information. Aspects of systematic empirical study concerning similarities and differences in the ways in which psychoanalysts and cognitive psychotherapists arrive at clinical inferences and the part played in this process by prior experience and theoretical orientation will be presented.

IA-068: Agency and communion as fundamental dimensions of social cognition

Ralf Schwarzer (Chair)

Wojciszke, Bogdan Dept. of Social Psychology, Warsaw School, Sopot, Poland
We propose agency and communion as two basic content dimensions of social judgments, and that these dimensions are differently related to the actor vs. observer perspective. Actors being agents and observers being recipients of an action differ in their objectives (completing vs. understanding the action) and hence focus on different content. We present a series of studies showing that: (1) agentic and communal content is prevalent in the perception of both individuals and social groups; (2) agency, individualism, masculinity, and competence constitute one class of person descriptors which is relevant and desired in the actor perspective; (3) communion, collectivism, femininity, and morality constitute another class which is relevant and desired in the observer perspective; (4) within the actor perspective agentic content is more important than communal one; (5) within the observer perspective communal content is more important than agentic one.

IA-069: Race, racism, knowledge production and South African psychology

Duncan, Norman Dept. of Psychology, University of Witwatersrand, Johannesburg, South Africa
The aims of this paper are to present an examination of the history of South African psychology from its formal establishment in the 1920s to date and the intersection between this history and the development of the ideologies of 'race' and racism in broader South African society. Specifically, the paper argues that the formal establishment of South African psychology was strongly propelled by the South African academy's commitment to white hegemony during the early 1920s. Indeed, this commitment was sustained for the better part of the twentieth century. The paper also explores the various forms that opposition to this commitment assumed over the years.

IA-070: Behavior genetics: Quasi-experimental studies of environmental processes

Marc Richelle (Chair)

D'Onofrio, Brian Psychological & Brain Sciences, Indiana University, Bloomington, USA
Objective: The presentation will highlight how behaviour genetic methods, such as sibling-comparison, co-twin control, and children of twin approaches, can explore environmental risk factors. Methods: A review of specific studies that have disentangled co-occurring genetic and environmental processes when exploring how family risk factors influence child and adolescent adjustment. Results: The use of quasi-experimental designs has allowed researchers to draw strong causal inferences about some family risk factors, whereas the use of such approaches suggest that some putative risk factors do not have causal influences on offspring adjustment. Conclusions: Behaviour genetic methods can be powerful tools for studying environment risks.

IA-071: Early childhood development in Southern Africa

Merry Bullock (Chair)

Zimba, Roderick F. Windhoek, Namibia
All over the world Early Childhood Development focuses on the concepts of child survival, growth, devlopment, care and protection. In Southern

Africa, the current understanding of these concepts is supposed to inform theory and practice in the field. The main purpose of this presentation is to review the provision of Early Childhood Development programmes in the Southern African Region and assess their impact on the developmental well-being of children. Southern African policies on Early Childhood Development and some research findings based on the Region will provide literature for the review. The review will communicate the role of the psycho-social and social cultural contexts in the development of children in Southern Africa.

IA-072: The role of executive control in the task switching paradigm

Iring Koch (Chair)

Vandierendonck, André Experimental Psychology, Ghent University, Gent, Belgium
The task-switching paradigm used to study cognitive control in task planning reveals a task execution cost when switching to another task is required. Theoretical accounts attribute this cost either to interference between current and previously executed tasks or to the need to reconfigure the cognitive system for applying the new task. Typically, these accounts are supported by findings which cannot be explained by the opposite theoretical position. The present talk will defend the thesis that a single unified theory assuming task switching conflicts arise at different stages and levels of task processing can account for the findings in task switching.

IA-073: Perspectives: Theory of mind and identity in pre-school

Perner, Josef Inst. für Psychologie, Universität Salzburg, Salzburg, Austria
The mind represents the world, thus characteristically takes a point of view (perspective). An important step in understanding the mind (theory of mind) comes with the metarepresentational ability to understand perspectives. This ability is also involved in an explicit understanding of identity (e.g., "Cicero is Tully") because it requires an understanding that two terms denote a single entity. Children have problems with such statements up until 4 years, the age at which they master related problems, e.g., alternative naming games, and acquire explicit understanding of other metarepresentational problems, e.g., understanding false beliefs, visual perspectives.

IA-074: Temperance and the strength of personality: Evidence from a 35-year longitudinal study

Kan Zhang (Chair)

Pulkkinen, Lea Jyväskylä, Finland
Peterson and Seligman (2004) have made a step toward a vocabulary of measurable positive human traits by distinguishing 24 specific character strengths, classified under six broad virtues that consistently emerge across history and culture. The fifth virtue is temperance referring to strengths that protect against excess. It is indicated by, for instance, forgiveness, modesty, prudence, and self-regulation (self-control). I started my research work in the late 1960s with the concept of self-control used as a synonym for self-regulation. It refers to how a person exerts control over his or her own responses (thoughts, emotions, impulses, performances) so as to pursue goals and live up to standards (ideals, norms, targets, and expectations of other people). I developed a model on impulse control and tested it with 369 school children in 1968. The results showed that the model could be applied to the analysis of individual differences in

positive and negative social behavior. The cross-sectional study transitioned into a long-term long-itudinal study (the Jyväskylä Longitudinal Study of Personality and Social Development, JYLS) in which the same individuals have been studied from the age of 8 to age 42 with intervals of 6 to 8 years. Data have been collected on five developmental lines: 1) Socioemotional behavior and personality; 2) Education and work; 3) Family of origin and one's own family; 4) Health behavior and health; and 5) Social integration. The results have shown that high self-control assessed in childhood and early adolescence and indicated, particularly, by constructive, prosocial behavior is associated with positive adult development in all lines. It is linked to higher emotional stability in adulthood, longer education, higher income, lower divorce rate, more controlled health behavior and better health, and lower likelihood of delinquent behavior. Thus temperance as indicated by self-control - although it may not be a fashionable virtue in the Western world at present - has evidenced its role in the strengths of personality.

IA-075: Development of social cognition

Wolfgang Stroebe (Chair)

Meltzoff, Andrew Inst. for Learning & Brain, University of Washington, Seattle, USA
Important advances in cognitive science have come from discoveries within developmental psychology. Infants are born with the ability to connect to other people. They have an extraordinary capacity for imitation, and in the first year can follow the gaze of the adults around them. I suggest that imitation provides a foundation for the later development of theory of mind. Infants recognize that other people are 'like me' in their actions (behavioral imitation) and develop the idea that others are 'like me' in their mental states (theory of mind). New findings concerning developmental social cognition will be discussed in the context of modern work in cognitive science.

IA-076: New perspectives on moral emotions: An electro-physiological study in normal and violent subjects

James Georgas (Chair)

Ostrosky-Solis, Feggy Mexico, Mexico
Objective: To study the brain correlates of basic and moral emotions in a group of controls and of criminal offenders. Method: Event Related Potentials were recorded while viewing pictures of emotionally charged scenes with and without moral content as well as emotionally neutral pictures. Results: In normal subjects unpleasant pictures with and without moral content prompt a marked negative going slow wave, with higher amplitude at frontal, parietal and temporal sites of the left hemisphere. In the criminal offenders no significant differences between the stimuli were found. Conclusions: In criminal offenders the emotional components of cognition are disturbed and poorly integrated.

IUPsyS-010: Flexibility in arithmetic: Theoretical, methodological and instructional challenges

Patrick Lemaire, Lieven Verschaffel (chair)
Flexibility in the use of arithmetic strategies, models, and representations plays an increasingly important role in current theories of arithmetic thinking, learning, and teaching. The overall aim of this invited symposium is to discuss theoretical, methodological, and instructional aspects of this flexibility issue. The five studies that will be presented address various aspects of flexibility in topics like one- or two-digit arithmetic, numerosity judgement, arithmetic word problem solving, and decimal fractions. Besides analyses of flexibility per se, relations with with cognitive development, intelligence, and instruction will be addressed.

The use of logical-mathematical principles in solving arithmetical operations
Nunes, Terezinha Dept. of Education, University of Oxford, Oxford, United Kingdom Peter, Bryant Dept. of Education, University of Oxford, Oxford, United Kingdom
If a child does not know a number fact, it does not follow that the child cannot solve the operation. The child might know other number facts and some logical principles that combined can lead to a correct solution. If a child does not know what is 42–39 but counts from 39 to 42, the child could combine this knowledge with the understanding of the inverse relation between addition and subtraction. We will review studies on the development of children's understanding of the inverse relation to analyse whether this understanding can give children more flexibility in solving arithmetic problems.

Strategic changes in children's two-digit addition problem solving
Lemaire, Patrick Dept. of Psychology, Université de Provence, Marseille, France Calliàs, Sophie Dept. of Psychology, Université de Provence, Marseille, France Vitu-thibault, François' Dept. of Psychology, Université de Provence, Marseille, France
Thirty adults, 30 third graders, and 30 fifth graders solved two digit-subtraction problems under choice and no-choice conditions. In the choice condition, they could use either an N10 strategy (i.e., doing 73-10=63-9=52) or a 1010 strategy (i.e., doing 60-10=50, 13-9=4, 50+4=54) on each problem. In the no-choice condition, participants were required to use each strategy on all problems. Data showed that mean percent use of each strategy as well as strategy performance changed with age, problem type, and presentation format. Interactions indicated increased strategy flexibility and adaptivity to problem, situation, and strategy characteristics with cognitive growth.

The effect of intelligence and feedback on children's strategic competence
Luwel, Koen Dept. of Education, University of Leuven, Leuven, Belgium Foustana, Ageliki Dept. of Primary Education, University of Athens, Athens, Greece Verschaffel, Lieven Dept. of Education, University of Leuven, Leuven, Belgium
A test-intervention-test design was used to investigate the effect of feedback and intelligence on children's strategic competence in a numerosity judgement task. In both test sessions (TS), we used the choice/no-choice method to assess strategy repertoire, frequency, efficiency and adaptivity in children of three intelligence groups. During the intervention, half of the children from each group received outcome feedback (OFB), whereas the other half received strategy feedback (SFB). We observed large differences between the three groups on all strategy parameters in TS1. At TS2 these differences became smaller, whereby SFB was more beneficial than OFB.

The strategic use of alternative representations in arithmetic word problem solving
Thevenot, Catherine Dept. of Psychology, University of Geneva, Geneva, Switzerland Oakhill, Jane Dept. of Psychology, University of Sussex, Sussex, United Kingdom
Multiple-step arithmetic problems can be solved by diverse strategies depending on the mental representation. This representation will determine the organization of sub-goals. The studies presented here aim at determining the conditions under which specific strategies are set up by adults. We show that adults usually organize their sub-goals as they are explicitly mentioned in the problem, even though a less working memory demanding strategy could have been used. However, increasing problem difficulty leads individuals to set up more economic strategies and this is even more likely when the cognitive cost of the construction of the underlying representation is low.

Is flexibility based on the integration of conceptual and procedural knowledge? The case of decimal fractions
Schneider, Michael Inst. Verhaltenswissenschaften, ETH Zürich, Zürich, Switzerland Stern, Elsbeth Inst. Verhaltenswissenschaften, ETH Zürich, Zürich, Switzerland
It has been suggested that procedural flexibility results from the integration of (flexible but inefficient) conceptual knowledge and (efficient but inflexible) procedural knowledge. Tests of this hypothesis are hampered by the fact that it is unclear how conceptual and procedural knowledge can be measured validly and partly independently of each other. We investigated these questions in the domain of decimal fractions using a multimethod approach in an experimental design (Study 1) and a longitudinal design (Study 2). The results, obtained with 288 fifth- and sixth-graders, indicate that conceptual and procedural knowledge were inseparably intertwined. We discuss methodological and theoretical implications

IUPsyS-011: Internationalising qualifications in psychology: Challenges and opportunities

Ingrid Lunt (chair)
The symposium will focus on the challenges faced by psychologists living and working in an increasingly globalised and mobile world. Within Europe a project over the past 10 years has developed a European qualification system which aims to set a common framework and standard for qualifications in psychology across the European Union and beyond. This qualification, the EuroPsy, has excited considerable interest across Europe, and more widely, and is being used as a yardstick for considering a more international framework for psychology qualifications. The EuroPsy will be presented, challenges facing the projects piloting the qualification in Finland and the United Kingdom will be considered, and the wider implications of the EuroPsy for the rest of the world will be discussed.

Internationalising psychology qualifications: the example of the EuroPsy and the challenges for wider internationalisation
Lunt, Ingrid Dept. of Education, University of Oxford, Oxford, United Kingdom
The EuroPsy qualification has been developed over 10 years and has now been accepted by EFPA and indirectly the European Union. This provides a major opportunity for psychology in Europe, both in relation to standards and quality, and to facilitate mobility. However it also poses challenges. The challenges and opportunities will be discussed in this paper.

EuroPsy - proceedings in Finland
Tikkanen, Tuomo Finnish Psychol. Association, Helsinki, Finland Niemienen, Pirrko Nieminen, Pirrko University of Tampere, Tampere, Finland
Finland has been a partner in EuroPsy - project from the beginning and is now one of the pilots experimenting the EuroPsy system as an "experimental garden". In a country where the degrees and qualifications of the psychologists are regulated by law and where there are only six departments

educating psychologists the experiment has started favourably. During the experiment the following steps have been taken: translating the EuroPsy report, the ethical commitment to national and European ethical codes, the application forms; preparing the supervised practice evaluation forms and the instructions for supervisors; evaluating the curricula and establishing the National Awarding Committee NAC. The Finnish EuroPsy website was opened www.europsy.fi and all the Finnish psychologists were invited to apply for the EuroPsy certification. So far over hundred applications have been accepted by the NAC. The proceedings and experiences will be described and discussed.

Implementing the EuroPsy certificate. Experience and learning gained from Spain
Peiro, Jose M. Dept. of Social Psychology, University of Valencia, Valencia, Spain
In the present paper the work carried on in Spain to launch the Europsy ECP will be reported. Special attention will be paid to all the work done to develop a system of supervised practice attuned to the competencies model established in Europsy. Moreover, a pilot experience carried on in cooperation with the Erasmus Mundus Master on Work and Organizational Psychology to use the competences model in the evaluation of the internship will also be reported.

Implementing the EuroPsy in France: An added difficulty or a good opportunity for the profession?
Lécuyer, Roger University Paris-Descartes, Paris, France
The implementation of the EuroPsy is a challenge for national organisations in every country in Europe. This challenge is somewhat more difficult when there are many organisations, many students, many qualified psychologists and significant unemployment. The French Federation, therefore, has a particular need for the EuroPsy as a means of cooperation between the different organisations, and as a means to regulate the annual number of qualified, or at least the number of EuroPsy certificated psychologists, which need to be harmonized in Europe. If the French awarding committee is wise, the EuroPsy is therefore a good opportunity for French psychologists.

IUPsyS-012: Challenges for psychology in the developing / majority world

Saths Cooper (chair)
Utilising their involvement in national and international psychology organisations, the presenters will illuminate the historical, current and future dilemmas confronting psychology in parts of the majority/developing world. Representing African, Latin American, Middle and Far Eastern perspectives on the new terrain of psychology that has been and is likely to continue to be fought in the 21st century, insights into the form and content of the dilemmas faced by organised psychology in these regions will be shared. The presenters contend that the outcome of the contestations occurring in these non-mainstream regions of the world are likely to determine the worth of psychological science and practice beyond their regions and impact on psychology globally.

Psychology in Latin America
Ardila, Ruben Dept. of Psychology, National Univ. of Colombia, Bogota, Colombia
Psychology in Latin America comes from European and U.S. sources, but has also reached a stage of relative maturity in which original contributions have been made. In all Latin American countries there are psychology training programs, labora-

tories, scientific journals, applications, community involvement, and the perceived need to be socially-relevant. At the beginning of the XXIth. century, the main issues facing Latin American psychology are: scientific research, contextual relevance, political involvement. Psychologists in Latin America are very concerned with scientific issues and also with big social issues such as poverty, discrimination, social participation and the role of minorities. Key words: Latin American psychology, science, social relevance, professional development.

Psychology as science and profession in Mexico: Background, challenges and perspectives
Sanchez Sosa, Juan Jose Dept. of Psychology, UNAM Nat. Auton. University, Mexico City, Mexico
Although not consistent with the contemporary western conception of our discipline, psychological-type interventions in Mexico can be traced as far back as the fifteenth century. Its inception as formal scientific discipline in the late nineteenth century marked simultaneously a faster development within the context of contemporary science and an identifiable link with socially relevant problems. The presentation will analyze some of the key factors leading to the current status and perspective of Mexican psychology as scientific discipline and as profession as well as some challenges ahead, mainly in the context of a developing nation.

Promoting international perspectives
Farah, Adnan Jordan Psychological Society, Irbid, Jordan
Psychology in developing countries needs to meet the challenges of the Twenty First century. By examining some cultural and multicultural considerations, Psychologists are encouraged to move closer to bridge the gap in the field and move toward a global vision for profession. With the increasing recognition that the world has become a global village, psychologists must move forward to progress the status of psychology locally and internationally. To achieve this goal, some suggestions and initiatives are presented.

Psychology in Yemen and the Arab World: Obstacles and challenges
Saleh, Maan A. Bari Dept. of Behavioral Sciences, Aden University, Aden, Yemen
In Yemen and the Arab world psychological and mental health issues have close connections with myths, superstitions and distorted religious concepts, thus stigmatising psychology as a science. The ghost of wars, internal struggles, poverty, increases in the rate of reproduction and illiteracy persist. Despite this, psychology benefited through study abroad programs from the sixties. This presentation will discuss the positions of and obstacles to psychological science at the main Arab Universities and Psychological Associations in the Mideast, as well as their implications for development.

Majority world contributions for universal psychological science
Pandey, Janak Behav. and Cognitive Sciences, University of Allahabad, Allahabad, India
Scientific mainstream psychology originating in minority world intellectual soil proliferated in majority world countries, overshadowing rich knowledge existing for centuries regarding nature of mind, consciousness, society, people and behaviour in their own cultural context. One way export of psychology and uncritical acceptance of western theories and methods scuttled integration of social, economic, political and cultural variables in understanding psychological processes and facilitating psychology to develop as a truly universal science. Western psychology has faced formidable challenges recently and there are concentrated efforts for "decolonization" and establishing a universal

scientific psychology by changing its character from exclusive to inclusive.

Measuring attitudes, values and personality across the world: Again the emperor has no clothes
Nair, Elizabeth Dept. of Psychology, Work & Health Psychologists, Singapore, Singapore
Present day scientific psychology has its roots in the Americas and Europe, where originated much of the theorizing and postulations in social and developmental psychology, and personality. A much favoured approach in many fields of international psychology today is to use single "universal" instruments to measure attitudes, values, and even personality across countries, and attempt to draw seemingly meaningful comparisons from this exercise. This paper will examine where we are heading with this trend, and how it should be shaped to be relevant.

IS-116: Brain mapping of syntax and semantics

Yosef Grodzinsky (chair)
This symposium will discuss recent results from experiments that use advanced methods and techniques in order to map the language regions of the human brain. We will present the current picture on brain/language relations, as it emerges from recent syntactic, semantic, and discourse comprehension studies in fMRI with healthy adults, from experiments with patients suffering from aphasic syndromes, subsequent to focal lesions in the language regions of the brain, and from precise anatomical investigations of these regions.

Syntax in aphasia
Alexiadou, Artemis Institut für Linguistik, Universität Stuttgart, Stuttgart, Germany
A large number of studies in aphasia literature deals with the production of verbs, searching to identify the semantic, syntactic and other non-linguistic factors (e.g. word frequency) that influence verb production. In this presentation I examine the moprho-syntactic properties of verbs with alternating transitivity and investigate how argument structure complexity influences the performance of Greek aphasic patients. In particular, I examine how the presence vs. absence of an external argument, its syntactic representation as well as its morphological realization influence aphasic performance.

Discourse deficits in aphasia
Huber, Walter Neurolinguistik - Neurologie, RWTH Aachen, Aachen, Germany
New data from a series of fMRI experiments are presented which aim at disentangling underlying mechanisms of online story segmentation by comparing normal and impaired story comprehension under varying recipient conditions. The central hypothesis is that recurring narrative shifts during natural story comprehension – irrespective of spoken, signed or filmed form of presentation – are reflected by synchronous brain activations across frontal, temporal and cingular areas of both hemispheres. First results demonstrate the precunues in combination with the posterior cingulum to be crucially involved in online detection of narrative shifts.

Anatomy of the language regions in the brain
Amunts, Karin Institut für Medizin, Forschungszentrum Jülich, Jülich, Germany
Broca's and Wernicke's regions are crucial for language processing, and cover several cytoarchitectonic areas, and the involvement of each area in particular components of language processing is still widely unknown. From an anatomical perspec-

tive, the assignment of these components based on functional imaging and electrophysiological studies to distinct cortical areas is difficult. Data from cytoarchitectonic analysis of Broca's and Wernicke's regions, examples of the comparison of probabilistic maps with activations obtained in functional MRI for structure-functional analyses, and data from quantitative receptorautoradiography of classical neurotransmitter systems will be presented.

IS-117: Attention and action: Cognitive neuroscientific evidence for interactions and dissociations

Glyn W. Humphreys (chair)
Emerging work from cognitive neuroscience indicates a close coupling between attention and action. Attention is influenced by action relations between objects and by the potential of objects for action. These effects extend to include the social possibilities of action between agents. In this symposium we bring together recent research that uses a variety of techniques (neuropsychological studies, evopken potentials, fMRI) to investigate the interaction between action and attention. The implications of the work for understanding attentional operations in the brain will be discussed.

Introduction to attention and action
Humphreys, Glyn W. School of Psychology, University of Birmingham, Birmingham, United Kingdom
Recent studies demonstrate that attention can be influenced by action - with effects emerging based on the action planned in a task and on the visual possibilities for action in the environment. I will summarise recent data and highlight how talks in the symposium illustrate the importance of understanding action constraints for models of attention

Interactions between attention and action
Buxbaum, Laurel Moss Rehabilitation Unit, University of Pennsylvania, Philadelphia PA, USA
Objects may automatically activate the responses associated with them. At the same time, the intention to perform a specific action affects the salience of objects affording that action. We present a series of investigations exploring the interaction of object and task factors in determining response interference. These studies enable several key conclusions. First, distinctly different patterns of interference by distractor objects are associated with different motor responses. Second, there are reliable relationships between the presence or absence of a specific plan of action and the salience of different objects. Taken together, these findings suggest a mutually constraining relationship between the processes underlying object selection and action selection that is expected to reproduce across objects and tasks.

Binding objects through action
Riddoch, Jane Dept. of Psychology, University of Birmingham, Birmingham, United Kingdom
Patients with parietal lesions have shown recovery from extinction when pairs of objects share an action relative to when they do not (Riddoch et al. 2003, 2006). In investigating the visual constraints on this effect, we found that the action relation advantage is reduced when the objects are inverted, while inversion does not affect unrelated objects. The effect is also reduced by changing the size of objects relative to one another. We suggest that the effects of action relation are based on high-level grouping of stimuli which reduces spatial competition between the stimuli in patients with parietal damage.

Attending to other's actions
Bekkering, Harold Nijmegen, Netherlands
In Posner-like attentional cueing tasks, we investigated the extent to which the observation of other's action intentions influences attentional orientation of the observer. Interestingly, we found that the effect of gaze orientation of the model was modulated by the fact if the model only oriented to a certain target region, or could really perceive an object at that specific region. In addition, cueing effects were found for meaningful hand-target interactions, but not for similar meaningless control stimuli. Together, the data reveal new insights in higher order mechanisms involved in aligning your attention to somebody else's action intention.

Action-related influences on the orienting of visuospatial attention: Evidence from
Handy, Todd Dept. of Psychology, University of British Columbia, Vancouver, Canada
The covert orienting of visuospatial attention has long been tied to perceptual facilitation in the ventral visual pathway. Yet anatomical and functional considerations suggest that covert visuospatial attention may also facilitate action-related processing in the dorsal visual pathway. Here I present the results of two event-related potential studies supporting this hypothesis. The first study demonstrates that visualspatial attention can be automatically drawn towards graspable objects, while the second indicates that it can also be automatically drawn towards one's heading point during visually-simulated selfmotion. Taken together, this evidence suggests that visual spatial selection may play a key role in visuomotor planning.

IS-118: Visual perception: From experiments to modeling

Henrikas P. Vaitkevicius, Galina V. Paramei (chair)
The first symposium will focus on internal representation of features of visual image. It will address mechanisms of color coding by human visual system, overview mechanisms of identification of veridical line orientation and visual illusions. Speakers will also focus on mechanisms of perceptual changes in space and time and address dynamic processes (attention) in perception. The second symposium will focus on psychophysics of chromatic vision, on discrimination of bimodality stimuli (color and line orientation), and on comparative perspective on mechanisms of achromatic vision mathematical modeling of various functions of achromatic vision. The symposium will be concluded by a presentation on mathematical meta-approach to coding of visual discrimination.

Binocular rivalry and neural dynamics
Blake, Randolph Dept. of Psychology, Vanderbilt University, Nashville, TN, USA
Conflicting monocular images compete for access to consciousness in a dynamical fashion, a phenomenon called binocular rivalry. Rivalry entails competitive interactions at multiple neural sites, including those where eye of origin information is retained. Rivalry attenuates visual adaptation to form and motion, but some information about the suppressed stimulus still reaches higher brain areas. Top-down influences can promote perceptual grouping during rivalry, and selective attention can extend the local dominance of a stimulus over space and time. Neural circuits responsible for the dynamical properties of rivalry may shed light on the neural dynamics of visual awareness.

Are there universals in mental timing?
Geissler, Hans-Georg Inst. für Psychologie, Universität Leipzig, Leipzig, Germany
Timing of perception and perception of time are commonly considered as disparate psychological manifestations of time. From experimental evidence in motion perception, visual categorization and duration discrimination, we suggest that various facets of mental timing are governed by the same universals, an elementary time-lattice unit Qo that provides absolute anchoring of time scales, a relative upper bound M and a "stretch parameter" q which jointly determine maximum extension of discrete temporal ranges. Discussing possible physiological implications, we conclude that temporal-range organization reflects a hitherto overlooked fine-tuned coordination of wave-like and delay-like constituents required to guarantee stability of brain processes.

Stages for extracting colour information
Kulikowski, Janus Faculty of Life Sciences, University of Manchester, Manchester, United Kingdom Parry, Neil Manchester, United Kingdom
Colour information is processed by many stages of the visual system. Primate colour vision relies on 3 cone types which sample visible light and send signals to second stage cone-opponent units. Surprisingly this stage determines not only the threshold detection for chromatic patches, but also matching surface colours under various illuminants. Hue discrimination at detection thresholds reveals contribution of the third stage, colour-opponency, which determines colour categories, or unique hues. These hues remain constant for paracentral locations providing veridical vision. However, more challenging tasks of colour identification require contributions from higher colour centres (V4) and complex spatio-temporal interactions.

Visual illusions in perception
Bertulis, Algis Dept. of Biology, Kaunas University of Medicine, Kaunas, Lithuania Bulatov, Aleksandr Dept. of Biology, Kaunas University of Medicine, Kaunas, Lithuania Bielevicius, Arunas Dept. of Biology, Kaunas University of Medicine, Kaunas, Lithuania
In psychophysical experiments, subjects report a bent axis of the three-dot stimulus when a contextual spot is present above or below the central dot and the other two below or above the end-dots with the same spot-to-dot gap size. The contextual spots produce distortions of perceived length when situated on the axis of the three-dot stimulus and generate distortions of perceived angle size when the three-dot stimulus is arranged in the right angle shape. The experimental data can be interpreted in terms of the local positional averaging of profiles of excitation evoked by the stimulus parts in the visual pathways.

The perception of chromatic stimuli in the peripheral human retina
McKeefry, Declan Dept. of Optometry, University of Bradford, Bradford, United Kingdom Parry, Neil Manchester, United Kingdom Murray, I.J. Faculty of Life Sciences, University of Manchester, Manchester, United Kingdom
We have studied the changes that occur in human colour perception in the peripheral retina. By modelling the magnitude of activation produced in the L-M and S- cone opponent systems for matched para-foveal and peripheral chromatic stimuli, we have found that variations in perceived appearance are mirrored by a reduction in function of the L-M opponent system. The operation of the S-cone opponent system is affected to a much lesser degree, implying that there is a changing pattern of predominance between the two cone-opponent mechanisms in the peripheral retina. We will explore possible retinal and cortical bases for these changes.

Hue and saturation shifts induced by spatial contrast

Paramei, Galina V. Dept. of Psychology, Liverpool Hope University, Liverpool, United Kingdom Bimler, David Massey University, Wellington, New Zealand
We modulated monochromatic test fields by varying the intensity of a broadband annulus to induce spatial contrast. The resulting changes in test appearance – quantified by collecting colour-naming responses – are represented as a 4D colour space. Two dimensions describe independent achromatic qualities, identified as Desaturation and Induced Darkness. Both are functions of the luminance of the surround and the brightness of the test field. Induced darkness affects the perceived hue of the field, in a similar way to changing a colour's objective intensity. These non-linearities place constraints on possible loci within colour processing for the lateral interactions responsible for spatial contrast.

Evolutionary models of color categorization under population heterogeneity and nonuniform environmental color distributions

Jameson, Kimberly A. Inst. for Mathematical Beh., University of California, Irvin, USA Komarova, Natalia Mathematics, University of California, Irvine, USA
We present computational modeling results that bear on a classic controversy in psychology: The factors contributing to human color categorization across individuals and cultures (Jameson 2005). We investigated specific processes by which shared color lexicons evolve from interactions in societies of communicating agents (Komarova, Jameson & Narens 2008), using evolutionary game-theory to examine constraints appropriate for simulated individual agents and societies of agents. A new pattern of results is found regarding robust agent-based color categorization solutions. Implications for theories of human color naming and categorization, and the formation of human semantic categories that are shared cross-culturally, are discussed.

Achromatic vision in invertebrate and vertebrate retina: Comparative research and modeling

Chernorizov, Alexandr Dept. of Psychophysiology, Moscow State University, Moscow, Russia
Intracellular recording in the retina of a snail Helix lucorum L. indicates two types of cells responding to flashes of achromatic light: D-type cells, with sustained depolarization, and H-type cells, with sustained hyperpolarization. Within a proposed two-channel model of snail achromatic vision, responses of the D- and H-cells are represented by a two-dimensional 'excitation vector'; its length is constant and the direction codes perceived light intensity. The vector model of light encoding in snail is discussed in relation to models of achromatic vision in vertebrates – fish, rabbit, monkey, and humans, based on psychophysical and neurophysiological data.

Influence of adaptation on a perceived orientation of line

Vaitkevicius, Henrikas P. Dept. of Psychology, University of Vilnius, Vilnius, Lithuania Viliunas, Vilius Dept. of Psychology, University of Vilnius, Vilnius, Lithuania Bliumas, Remigijus Dept. of Psychology, University of Vilnius, Vilnius, Lithuania Stanikunas, Rytis Dept. of Psychology, University of Vilnius, Vilnius, Lithuania Svegzda, Algimantas Dept. of Psychology, University of Vilnius, Vilnius, Lithuania Kulikowski, Janus Faculty of Life Sciences, University of Manchester, Manchester, United Kingdom
J.Gibson observed that during prolonged viewing, a line perceptually rotates towards the nearest vertical or horizontal orientation (normalization effect), and moreover the perceived orientation of subsequently presented line depends on the orientation of adapting one (tilt after-effect). The mechanisms of both phenomena (especially of normalization) remain poorly understood. According to our experimental results adapting line perceptually rotates to the nearest three lines: vertical, horizontal and diagonal. We propose a simple neuronal model of orientation detectors, whose responses are determined by the cardinal detectors. It is shown that both normalization and tilt-after-effect could be explained by adaptation of these cardinal detectors.

Discrimination of bimodality stimuli in the visual system

Izmailov, Chingis Dept. of Psychology, Moscow State University, Moscow, Russia
Perception of color and shape are practically independent research areas. Theories in either take no account of findings from the other. Presumably this is a corollary of the independence of an image's optical characteristics (intensity; spectral distribution) and contour characteristics (borders between areas of different color or brightness). Here I present results of a comparative experimental study on discrimination of bimodality visual stimuli: lines varying in color and orientation. Data obtained psychophysically in humans are related to those gained from frog electroretinograms. The experimental data are considered within a geometrical model, whose dimensions represent color- and shape-processing modules.

IS-119: Recognition and reconciliation - Dedicated to Professor Bernhard Wilpert

Henry P. David, Czarina Wilpert (chair)
The Holocaust ended more than six decades ago. Its impact continues to be felt today: in the unhealed traumas of survivors and their children, the shame of perpetrators and the incomprehension of descendants. What have we learnt from this? This symposium takes the opportunity of the Berlin 2008 Congress, to inspire a systematic reflection on the conditions and consequences of the Holocaust and other genocides. Few of the generations involved are still alive. Questions are: learning from the experience of genocide, implications for the second generation and others, individual and collective victimization, conditions for achieving recognition and reconciliation, implications for psychology.

Personal reflections of a survivor

Lustiger, Arno Frankfurt, Germany
Being one of the few living survivors of several Nazi concentration camps and death marches, the internationally known historian will analyze what has helped him personally to overcome the terrible atrocious experience of his youth and to become politically and intellectually a highly involved citizen in Germany. He will draw the lessons from his own biography for representatives of the discipline of Psychology which focus on human experience, development, thinking and acting. Further he will formulate conditions political and societal institutions must meet to prevent similar horrors in the future.

Dialogue between descendants from opposite sides: of Holocaust survivors and of Nazi perpetrators

Bar-On, Dan Ben Gurion University, Beer-Sheva, Israel
Having been active in the field since many years Daniel Bar-On has through his practical work and scientific publications achieved a remarkable international reputation. He will illustrate his approach by showing a documentary in which one of his groups was filmed during their second encounter. Further, he will report on his work with families of holocaust survivors in Israel and his interviews with descendants of Nazi perpetrators and how he succeeded in bringing the two sides into dialogue. In concluding his intervention he will highlight the role of storytelling to develop dialogue in current social conflicts.

The Second Generation of the Shoah: Taking on the trauma and the opportunity for post-traumatic growth

Spiegel, Miriam Victory MSW, Zürich, Switzerland
Each survivor develops individual coping mechanisms for dealing with the trauma of the Shoah part of which is often the strong wish to protect their own children from ever being vulnerable to this kind of danger. The many, sometimes complex reasons for survivors not to tell their stories to family members induced a self-imposed silence serving as an invisible protective shield. However, the survivors were not able to prevent the legacy of their own trauma from being passed on. One can observe a "conspiracy of silence" separating parents not willing or able to speak and children unable or willing to speak. The children face a double bind with no possibility of either succeeding to alleviate the excruciating pain of their parents or of having the belief that they could give new meaning to their lives. Nevertheless, the Second Generation collectively bears the potential for healing familial wounds and for post-traumatic growth, paving the way for reconciliation and for a future without violence.

Post-conflict socio-emotional obstacles to reconciliation

Ajdukovic, Dean Dept. of Psychology, University of Zagreb, Zagreb, Croatia
Massive traumatization and genocide do not happen in a social vacuum, they are pre-planned and designed to destroy another human group. Findings from a series of studies of obstacles to social reconstruction in the city of Vukovar, which once had an important Serbian minority, will be presented. Several surveys helped to identify individual predictors or social factors that are obstacles to reconciliation. Qualitative studies and interviews investigated interpersonal processes that lead to loss of trust, disruption of norms, decreasing quality of in close social interactions and breaking of cross-ethnic close friendships when atrocities were committed in the city. Even after 12 years the Croats were convinced that their Serb friends withheld information that meant life and death. Serb respondents insisted that they never had such information. Such conflicting narratives block the potential for reconciliation. A model for community social reconstruction will be presented.

IS-120: Why is IQ a predictor of death?

Ian J. Deary, Beverly A. Roberts (chair)
People with higher IQ test scores from early life are more likely to survive to old age, and less likely to have illnesses such as cardiovascular disease. These important findings have been replicated in large samples in a number of countries. The new field of cognitive epidemiology attracts researchers who are extending and trying to explain these findings. In this symposium, leading researchers in the field present new findings from five different nations. They investigate a number of variables and constructs that might help to explain the IQ-death and illness associations, including personality traits, reaction times, socio-economic status, and genes.

Intelligence, personality and the death of the Scottish Nation

Deary, Ian J. Inst. für Psychology, University of Edinburgh, Edinburgh, United Kingdom

The 6-Day sample of the Scottish Mental Survey 1947 contains almost all (1208) people born on the 1st day of the even-numbered months of 1936 and at school in Scotland at age 11. The following measures were taken at about age 11: IQ, teacher's ratings of conscientiousness/mood stability, childhood illnesses, detailed information on parental/home background, and their occupation in their mid-20s. They were linked to Scottish public and health records to obtain information about illnesses and deaths up to 2001. Here we describe how childhood IQ and personality combine to predict morbidity and mortality up to half a century later.

Reaction time and mortality in the UK health and lifestyle survey

Roberts, Beverly A. Dept. of Psychology, University of Edinburgh, Edinburgh, United Kingdom

We investigated the association of reaction time performance and reaction time change with mortality over 21 years of follow-up in 9003 members of the UK Health and Lifestyle Survey. After controlling for socioeconomic status, health behaviours and health status, slower and more variable reaction times and greater declines in reaction time performance across 7 years were significantly related to increased risk of death from all-causes and death from cardiovascular disease, stroke and respiratory disease. The cognition-mortality relationship may be explained in part by the brain's efficiency of information processing. However, issues with regard to reverse causality must be considered.

Socio-economic position in childhood, cognitive performance in young adulthood and mortality in CHD or stroke in later life: Swedish conscripts study

Rasmussen, Finn Child Adolescent Public Health, Karolinska Institutet, Stockholm, Sweden

The aim was to study associations between IQ and mortality in all causes, coronary heart disease (CHD) and stroke and the possible modifying/mediating role of social factors. One million Swedish men born 1950-76 who underwent IQ testing at age 18 were followed until middle-age. Data on parental and own education and social position and mortality were derived from Swedish national registers. Twenty years of follow-up generated 15,000 deaths. Inverse associations were seen between IQ, all-cause, CHD- and stroke mortality. These associations were of similar strengths within socio-economic groups. This study showed robust step-wise relations between early adult IQ and mortality.

IQ in early adulthood: associations with somatic and psychiatric health outcomes in the Vietnam experience study

Batty, G. David Social Public Health Sciences, Medical Research Council, Glasgow, United Kingdom

We examine the associations between IQ and later disease in a cohort study of 4157 US men with IQ scores in early adulthood, clinical data with repeat IQ testing in middle-age, and subsequent mortality follow-up. Higher IQ scores were associated with a reduced risk of later total mortality, cardiovascular disease, homicide, the metabolic syndrome, depression, and generalised anxiety disorder. IQ change between early adulthood and middle aged also predicted future mortality risk. Some of these effects were mediated via socioeconomic status.

Is SES a surrogate for IQ in predicting health?

Gottfredson, Linda S. School of Education, University of Delaware, Newark, USA

The SES-health gradient is the remarkably pervasive and linear relation between socioeconomic indicators and health behavior, health, and longevity. The IQ-performance gradient is the remarkably pervasive and linear relation between intelligence and performance in school, jobs, and functional literacy. IQ and SES are correlated, so the SES gradient may actually be a weak form of the IQ gradient. IQ at induction and self-reported education, occupation, income, and diverse health outcomes in midlife for 15,288 Vietnam-era veterans are used to test Gottfredson's (2004) IQ-surrogacy hypothesis: SES-health gradients steepen when SES indicators correlate more highly with IQ (income, then occupation, then education).

Genetic and environmental links between brain and body in old age: Findings from the Longitudinal Study of Aging Danish Twins

Johnson, Wendy Dept. of Psychology, University of Minnesota, Minneapolis, USA

In old age, cognitive and physical functions are correlated, but the basis for this correlation is not understood. In a large, population-representative sample of elderly Danish twins, genetic influences on latent variable representations of cognitive and physical functions were substantially correlated (r=.56), as were nonshared environmental influences (r=.48). We discuss three explanations for these correlations as possible mechanisms through which IQ predicts death. First, many physical illnesses common in late life also have cognitive consequences. Second, general ageing processes may affect both cognitive and physical functions. Finally, lifelong cognitive function may contribute to healthy lifestyle benefiting late-life physical function.

IS-121: Pathways to resilience across cultures: Lessons from studies of positive development under adverse circumstances

Michael Ungar (chair)

The International Resilience Project (IRP) brings together researchers from more than a dozen countries from six continents seeking to understand the processes and outcomes associated with positive development under adverse circumstances. Together, team members are breaking conceptual ground identifying homogeneity and heterogeneity in the social and psychological factors associated with resilience across cultures and contexts. This symposium reports on a number of studies and their findings, as well as methodological challenges associated with the study of resilience. It raises theoretical, methodological and practice issues related to the pathways to resilience found among high-risk children and youth globally.

Pathways to resilience: Results from a mixed-method 14-site international exploratory study of the psychosocial determinants of health

Ungar, Michael Dept. of Social Work, Dalhousie University, Halifax, Canada

Objective: Resilience researchers face challenges in conceptualizing and developing standardized metrics of resilience that are representative of adolescent experiences across cultures. Methods: An 11 country pilot study, the International Resilience Project, sought to develop a culturally and contextually relevant measure of youth resilience, the Child and Youth Resilience Measure (CYRM). Results: Employing a culturally sensitivity iterative research design introduced to the study a number of problems: ambiguity in the definition of positive outcomes; a lack of predictability of models across cultures; and measurement design challenges. Con-

clusions: Understanding resilience across cultures requires sensitivity to the tension between homogeneity and heterogeneity.

'Day in the life' of resilient adolescents in eight diverse communities around the globe

Tapanya, Sombat Dept. of Psychiatry, Chiang Mia University, Chiang Mai, Thailand Lau, Cindy Psychology, University of British Columbia, Vancouver, BC,, Canada Cameron, Catherine Ann Psychology, University of British Columbia, Vancouver, BC,, Canada

"Day in the life" of resilient adolescents in eight diverse communities around the globe. This ecological study documents daily experiences of adolescents, determined by their communities in varying global locations, to thrive despite adversity. Our method for investigating youth in context adapts Gillen, Cameron, et al (2007)'s "day in the life" methodology, video-recording one entire "day" of two resilient immigrant youths in Vancouver, Canada. Preliminary analyses of these data include examination of the teenagers' determination of appropriate locations for independent and collaborative leisure and cultural engagement and characteristics of peer and familial interactions. Cross-cultural comparisons of these case studies of youths in varying locations broaden understanding of the daily specifics of positive adolescent adaptation.

Capturing resilience: Is it possible and are there similarities across cultures?

Hjemdal, Odin Dept. of Psychology, Norwegian University, Trondheim, Norway

Objective: Identifying central protective factors associated with resilience is essential. Instruments for measuring resilience factors among adolescents and adults have been developed demonstrating satisfactory psychometric properties in Norwegian samples. The results have also demonstrated predictive qualities for both adolescents and adults. Methods: Samples from Belgium (N =364), and Brasil (N = 222), and others are compared to Norwegian samples. Results: The confirmatory factor analyses indicated that the resilience measures remained psychometrically acceptable across these cultures. Conclusion: Resilience Scale for Adults and Resilience Scale for Adolescents has shown indications of cross-cultural validity, and may be of interest across several cultures.

Resilience among Russian youth

Makhnach, Alexander Inst. of Psychology, Russian Academy of Science, Moscow, Russia Laktionova, Anna Inst. of Psychology, Russian Academy of Science, Moscow, Russia

Russian teenagers from special schools (n=74) have been tested. Child and Youth Resilience Measure has been used [Ungar, et.al. 2005]. In the factor 1 "Personal characteristics" such characteristics as self-realization, independence, confidence have entered. In the factor 2 "Relationships" a role of a family environment, attitudes with peers have entered. The factor 3 "Teen's culture" describes the attitude of teenagers to the influence of culture and formation of their own cultural environment. In the factor 4 "Community" the questions estimating socialization of teenagers have entered. In the factor 5 "The Country" the questions showing on the importance of the attitude of teenagers to the country have been included. Data about Russian teenagers resilience are discussed.

Uphenyo ngokwazi kwentsha yasemalokishini ukumelana nesimo ensinzima: A South African study of resilience among township youth

Theron, Linda School of Educational Sciences, North-West University, Vanderbijlpark, South Africa

Objectives South African township youth face multiple risks. This paper: 1. provides understanding of antecedents to township youth resilience; 2. highlights the protective role of Life Orientation classes and culture. Method Research surveying the importance of lifeskills classes was conducted with 934 black youth. The survey data were ranked using the SAS program. Follow-up focus-group interviews were conducted with 80 youth. Results Youth prioritised lifeskills that foster health promotion and personal development. The youths attributed resilience to personal, familial and environmental (school / cultural) factors. Conclusion The study underscores resilience as a dynamic, reciprocal person-context transaction in which culture and school play pivotal roles.

Resilience from birth to 40: A comparison of Japanese immigrants and indigenous Hawaiians

McCubbin, Laurie Dept. of Psychology, Washington State University, Pullman, USA McCubbin, Hamilton Social Work, university of Hawaii at Manoa, honolulu, USA

The longitudinal study of resilience of individuals from birth to adulthood have been negligible and absent when applied to children of diverse ethnic backgrounds and histories. Continuing the classic work of Werner and Smith in their study of all children born on the island of Kauai in the Hawaiian Islands, cohorts consisting predominantly of immigrant Japanese and indigenous Hawaiians, the investigators in this symposium examined and present previously unreported analyses and findings revealing risk and protective factors related to their adaptation at age 30. The results emphasize common to as well as culturally unique predictors. Implications for research and practice will be discussed.

IS-122: Visual attention

Claus Bundesen (chair)
A wealth of empirical evidence on the nature of visual attention is being accumulated. Behavioral studies show a huge range of attentional effects in human performance on visual tasks, neurophysiological studies show attentional effects in firing rates of individual cells in the visual system of primates, and brain-imaging and lesion studies document the functional anatomy of visual attention. The symposium focuses on attempts to integrate the findings theoretically in terms of biased competition, the theory of visual attention called TVA, and extensions of TVA.

Modeling visual attention by TVA

Kyllingsbæk, Søren Dept. of Psychology, University of Copenhagen, Copenhagen, Denmark
Visual attention is a major field within cognitive psychology with many papers published every year. Bundesen (1990) proposed a computational theory of visual attention (TVA) which contrary to most other theories yields direct quantitative predictions in different paradigms. Lately, the model has been applied to data from neuropsychological patients with deficits such as visual neglect and simultanagnosia. Quantitative modeling of data from psychological experiments is a promising line of research. In this presentation I will review our work on modeling visual attention with TVA drawing on examples from studies of neurologically intact subjects as well as brain damaged patients.

Neural mechanisms of visual attention in NTVA

Bundesen, Claus Dept. of Psychology, University of Copenhagen, Copenhagen, Denmark
The neural interpretation of TVA (Bundesen, 1990) called NTVA (Bundesen, Habekost, & Kyllingsbæk, 2005) accounts for attentional effects in both human performance and firing rates of individual cells in the primate visual system. In NTVA, there are two basic mechanisms of attention: filtering and pigeonholing. Filtering (selection of objects)

changes the number of cortical neurons in which an object is represented so that this number increases with the behavioral importance of the object. Pigeonholing (selection of features) scales the level of activation in individual neurons coding for a particular feature.

TVA-based patient studies

Habekost, Thomas Dept. of Psychology, University of Copenhagen, Copenhagen, Denmark
In the last few years quite a number of studies have used Bundesen's Theory of Visual Attention (TVA; Psychological Review 1990) to investigate attention disturbances after brain damage. A wide variety of neuropsychological conditions including visual neglect, alexia, and neurodegenerative diseases have been studied. The talk presents a review of this emerging research field and discusses four main strengths of the TVA based test method: sensitivity, specificity, reliability, and validity.

The attention blink and the theory of visual attention: Evidence from the dwell time paradigm

Schneider, Werner X. Inst. für Psychologie, Universität München, München, Germany Kambeitz, Joseph Inst. für Psychologie, Universität München, München, Germany
When two targets (T1, T2) are presented in short intervals and are masked, subjects are often unable to report T2 - a phenomenon named 'attentional blink' (AB). Inspired by the 'theory of visual attention' (TVA, Bundesen, 1990), we studied how the 'attentional weighting' of T1 influences T2 processing and the time course of the AB function. Results from several experiments relying on a 'dwell time' version of the AB paradigm developed by Duncan et al. (1994) show weighting-based effects of T1 manipulations on T2 accuracy.

IS-123: Psychological well-being: When coping makes a difference

Daniela Sacramento Zanini, Maria Forns (chair)
Coping involves the cognitive and affective actions used when we are confronted with life circumstances that may be regarded as stressful or traumatic events. Studies have demonstrated that the type of stressful events that the individual is coping with, and the coping response itself, can affect individual well-being and adaptation to life. Furthermore this influence seems to vary depending on sex and age and the specificity of the stressful event. The aim of this symposium is to promote a discussion on different ways of coping and how its related concepts can affect individual well-being as demonstrated by recent research.

Wellbeing and coping in adolescent populations

Frydenberg, Erica Faculty of Education, University of Melbourne, Melbourne, Australia Lewis, Ramon Faculty of Psychology, La Trobe University, Melbourne, Australia
Coping involves cognitive and affective actions as a response to the demands of a situation. Some coping responses are perceived as effective and others not. With young people, coping is particularly important because it is related to current and future wellbeing. The current paper examined the frequency of use and perceived efficacy of two coping styles, namely Positive Active and Negative Avoidant on both adolescent wellbeing and dysfunction in a sample of 870 adolescents. To maximize wellbeing it appears more important to assist adolescents to minimize their use of negative avoidant coping strategy than to increase use of positive active coping.

Positive functions of coping: Implications for

Greenglass, Esther Dept. of Psychology, York University, North York, Canada
In contrast to traditional coping strategies that tend to be reactive, proactive coping is oriented more towards the future. The Proactive Coping Inventory (PCI) assesses separate aspects of coping including proactive coping, preventive coping, strategic planning, reflective coping, and instrumental and emotional support seeking. The idea that coping may have positive functions parallels recent research highlighting the significant role of positive beliefs in the promotion of health. Recent findings are presented showing the relationship between psychological well-being, social support and coping in a variety of different contexts.

Stressful and traumatic life events in Spanish university students

Pereda, Noemi Assess. and Psych. Treatment, University of Barcelona, Barcelona, Spain Forns, Maria PETRA, University of Barcelona, Barcelona, Spain
The purpose of this study was to establish the prevalence of stressful and traumatic events in Spanish university students. The sample was composed by 1,033 undergraduate students, ranging from 18 to 30.6 years old. Data was obtained by The Traumatic Life Events Questionnaire (Kubany & Haynes, 2001). Ninety two percent of the students have been exposed to at least one stressful life event. Exposure varied by sex. Also, sex differences were found in the appraisal of the events as traumatic and causing major distress. The results suggest the need to increase prevention programs, taking into consideration the important gender variation.

Antecedents and consequences of coping

Sacramento Zanini, Daniela Dept. de Psicologia, Universidade Catolica de Goias, Goiânia, Brazil
Studies have demonstrated that coping responses can be related with some variables such as personality traits, type and intensity of stress, perceived social support, gender and age. Beside that, depending on the relationship established with these antecedents variables different consequences can be observed in means of the implication for individuals' mental health and well-being. The objective of this study is to demonstrate some of the relations related by different studies assessing coping response in different countries and its implication for individuals' well-being.

IS-124: Clinical case formulation

Stephen N. Haynes (chair)
Clinical case formulation (CCF) is one of the most important and challenging tasks in psychological assessment. This symposium will address examples of CCF with children and adults, the application of CCF at an institution level, the costs and benefits of CCF, models for evaluating the reliability and validity of CCF, the functional analysis as one approach to CCF, methods of constructing a CCF, a relational conception of CCF, and methods of validating a cognitive-behavioral case formulation.

Analysis and treatment of clients with ADD/ADHD with substance use: Two case examples

Timonen, Tero Dept. of Psychology, University of Joensuu, Joensuu, Finland
Two cases are presented to show how the use of a functional analysis case conceptualization model can help in therapeutic decision-making. The first case involved a youngster with ADD/ADHD, leaning disability, epilepsy, and violence behavior problems. The second case involved a young married man, with two children, with a life-long history of ADD/ADHD, prior drug use, and impulse control problems. Both cases show some

of the risks persons having ADD/ADHD. Although the situation in both cases is different, there are some similarities. Thus the cases will be used to illustrate that there can be common factors in the analysis of these kinds of persons and what could be the major therapeutic components

Reliability of clinical case formulation: The case of functional analysis

Virués Ortega, Javier Nation. Center of Epidemiology, Carlos III Health Instituto, Madrid, Spain

Research and application of functional analysis has been limited to individuals with developmental disabilities because of methodological and practical limitations to the experimental verification of contingencies through multi-element designs. To overcome these restrictions, an indirect approach to functional analysis will be suggested. This approach uses multiple clinical methods such as clinical interviewing, self-recording and observation. The methodology that will be proposed is focused on clinical practice and is driven by experimental research on (a) empirically-based repertoires of causal variables associated to the behavior-problem being analysed and (b) empirically-based repertoires of signs of such causal variables that could be identified through indirect methods. Examples of this application and methods to test its reliability will be discussed.

A relational conception of case formulations

Westmeyer, Hans Inst. für Psychologie, Freie Universität Berlin, Berlin, Germany

The basic structure of a case formulation, considered from a relational point of view, is very simple: x (a person or group of persons) constructs y (the case) as z (the case formulation) at t (a certain point in time) within tc (a certain theoretical context). This reflects the fact that a certain case could be formulated in various ways dependent on the constructing persons, the point in time at which they formulate the case, and the theoretical context within which the formulation is embedded. The consequences of this relational conception for appropriate formulations of a case will be discussed.

Testing cognitive behavioral case formulations

Mumma, Greg Dept. of Psychology, Texas Technology University, Lubbock, TX, USA

A cognitive-behavioral case formulation (CBCF) tailors CB treatment to the particular needs of the patient. Although treatment manuals often consider CBCFs essential, there have been few empirical tests of the validity of CBCFs. This presentation focuses on two methods to test CBCFs: (a) Tests for the construct validity of measures of idiographic constructs and (b) Tests of structural relationships – variables that trigger or maintain distress. Topics include developing a sampling plan within an intensive longitudinal assessment to obtain multivariate times series data to sensitively test both substantive and dynamic (temporal) hypotheses; and the statistical analyses of the data.

Systems-level case formulation: Functional analysis of patient aggression at a psychiatric hospital

Iruma Bello, Stephen Haynes Dept. of Psychology, University of Hawaii, Honolulu, HI, USA

Most case formulations, particularly functional analyses, address immediate antecedent events, consequent events, and environmental contexts. However, many of the causal variables for behavior problems reside with distal events and social systems. We will present an example of a systems-level functional analysis of aggression by patients in a psychiatric inpatient unit and discuss methods of acquiring systems-level data. In addition to social contexts, triggering factors, and responses of staff members, the functional analysis identified staff

supervision, rotation and training, inconsistent administrative policies, insufficient measurement and record keeping, poor communication among staff, and insufficient inter-discipline communication.

IS-125: Individual differences in executive control functions

Daniel Gopher (chair)

Executive control processes are the class of processes that guide, coordinate and synchronize the execution of goal directed performance, and monitor the conduct of tasks. The five presentations of the session will examine a wide perspective of individual differences in executive control, across several dimensions: Life span (infants, young and old adults); control functions (self regulation, decision making, attention control and cognitive reserve); manifestations and correlates (behavioral, neurophysiological, genetic antecedents). A concluding discussion will address the many facets of differences in executive control and determinants of their development.

Individual differences in executive attention and effortful control in early childhood

Sheese, Brad E. Illinois Wesleyan University, USA *Posner, Michael* Dept. of Psychology, University of Oregon, Eugene, USA *Rothbart, Mary K. Voelker, Pascale*

Findings from a four-year longitudinal study using anticipatory looking to trace the development of executive attention from infancy into early childhood will be presented. Results link anticipatory looking to patterns of overt self-regulatory behaviors in infancy and early childhood. Results also show that genes that are linked to executive attention in adulthood are also linked to anticipatory looking in infancy and early childhood. For example, both the common val158met COMT allelic distinction and COMT haplotypes predicted anticipatory looking. These results suggest that the rate of dopamine metabolism is important for the development of executive attention in early childhood.

Individual variability in cognitive performance in aging

Stern, Yaakov Taub Institute, Columbia University, New York, USA

The concept of cognitive reserve (CR) posits that individual differences in how tasks are processed provide differential reserve against age-related changes. Using the response signal method, healthy young and older adults completed a nonverbal delayed response task with 5 different deadlines. Hintzman & Curran's three-parameter compound bounded exponential model of speed-accuracy tradeoff was used to describe changes in discriminability associated with total processing time for each subject. Aging impaired the maximum capacity, but not the temporal threshold, for discriminability. Individual variability in rate was mediated by variables associated with CR (e.g. IQ). fMRI data from this task will be presented.

Using cognitive models for understanding individual differences in decision making and neuropsychological disorders

Yechiam, Eldad Behavioral Science Area, Technion, Haifa, Israel

Findings from a complex decision making task (the Iowa gambling task) show that individuals with neuropsychological disorders are characterized by maladaptive risk-taking behavior. A cognitive model is presented which decomposes performance in this task into three underlying components: the impact of rewards and punishments; the impact of recent versus past payoffs; and choice consistency. Findings from 15 studies are organized by classify-

ing the observed decision deficits using these three components. The results improve the sensitivity of the task to differences between neurological patients with different brain lesions, chronic abusers of different drugs, and criminals incarcerated for diverse crimes.

On the interplay of emotion and cognition: Individual differences, executive control and performance under stress

Beilock, Sian Dept. of Psychology, University of Chicago, Chicago, USA *DeCaro, Marci S.*

How motivational and emotional factors combine with executive control processes to produce skilled performance is of fundamental importance to understanding human cognition. Yet, it is only recently that the interplay of emotion and cognitive control has received much attention in human performance research. In this presentation I will show how emotion-filled, high-stress testing situations impact executive control processes such as the working memory capacity needed for successful performance in tasks such as math problem solving. Moreover, I will provide evidence that unwanted skill failures in high-stress situations are dependent on variations in the cognitive abilities of the performer.

The factorial structure of the differences between individuals in their ability to focus on a task and switch between tasks

Gopher, Daniel of Technology, Technion- Israel Institute, Haifa, Israel *Chuntunov, Olga*

Individual differences in task focusing and switching were investigated using the task switching paradigm. A digit or a letter classification tasks were performed in 40 trial blocks. Tasks switched in 0%, 10% or 50% probability. Other manipulations were Flankers of the same or other task, and 2 versus 4 responses. All manipulations had strong effect on performance. Correlations showed high and reliable individual differences. Factor analysis obtained a single factor in the two response condition, accounting for both focusing and switching performance. In the separate, 4 responses conditions, focusing and switching were mapped into two correlated factors. All other manipulations did not influence the factorial structure. It appears that the requirement to change responses involves a different control mechanism, which is not taped when switch probability, perceptual interference, stimulus type or S-R mapping rules change.

IS-126: Lexical and phonological aspects of bilingual language processing

Nuria Sebastian Galles, Alberto Costa (chair)

Recent bilingual studies have shown that both languages are engaged when only a single language is required. The goal of our study was to identify the scope of cross-language competition and the mechanisms that allow it to be resolved during the planning of speech. Our aim was to examine cross-language activity using converging evidence from response times (RTs), event-related potentials (ERPs), and acoustic measurements of speech. We report a series of experiments that show that not only are both languages active briefly during the earliest stages of planning, but that cross-language activity extends into the execution of the speech plan.

Bilingualism and cognitive control: Neural perspectives

Abutalebi, Jubin Psychology, University San Raffaele, Milan, Italy

A key question in bilingual language production research is how individuals control the use of their two languages (i.e., in order to prevent unwanted interferences from the non-target language). The psycholinguistic literature concerning language control is indecisive and it is debated whether control constitutes a main feature of bilingual language processing. During my talk, I will first show that neuroimaging data does, indeed, support the notion that cognitive control is an active component of bilingual language processing. Moreover, I will present new fMRI data providing neural evidence that this unique "control faculty" may lead to some cognitive advantages in everyday life.

Brain structure and language processing: Individual differences and expertise-related brain differences
Golestani, Narly Inst. Cognitive Neuroscience, University College London, London, United Kingdom
I will present results of several studies in which we show that individual differences in how quickly people learn to hear foreign speech sounds, and in how well they can articulate foreign speech sounds, predict brain structure. We show that brain structural variability in brain regions that are thought to functionally underlie phonetic perception and production partly predict variability in these very behavioral skills. I will also describe results of work on expertise-related brain structural differences. Results illustrate how the study of brain structure can be informative, and specifically, how information about brain structure can inform brain function.

Language switching and the bilingual interactive activation model
Grainger, Jonathan Laboratoire de Psychologie, Université d'Aix-Marseille I, Marseille, France
Current accounts of language switching effects during language comprehension in bilinguals often appeal to task control mechanisms, when in fact there is no task to control. Recent language priming experiments using ERPs have shown that language switching effects arise with very brief prime durations (60 ms) and appear relatively early in the ERP waveforms, starting around 200 ms post-target onset. This is the first evidence for fast-acting automatic language-switching effects occurring in the absence of overt task switching, therefore implying that language-switching effects in comprehension cannot completely be the result of executive control processes.

Cross-language competition begins during speech planning but extends into bilingual speech
Kroll, Judith Dept. of Psychology, Pennsylvania State University, University Park, USA *Gerfen, Chip* Spanish, Pennsylvania State University, University Park, PA, USA *Guo, Taomei* Cognitive Neuroscience, Beijing Normal University, Beijing, People's Republic of China *Misra, Maya* Comm Sciences and Disorders, Pennsylvania State University, University Park, PA, USA
Recent bilingual studies have shown that both languages are engaged when only a single language is required. The goal of our study was to identify the scope of cross-language competition and the mechanisms that allow it to be resolved during the planning of speech. Our aim was to examine cross-language activity using converging evidence from response times (RTs), event-related potentials (ERPs), and acoustic measurements of speech. We report a series of experiments that show that not only are both languages active briefly during the earliest stages of planning, but that cross-language activity extends into the execution of the speech plan.

Individual differences in non-native phoneme perception: Linguistic or acoustic origins
Sebastian Galles, Nuria Barcelona, Spain *Díaz, Begoña* Parc Cientific & Dept Psic, Universitat de Barcelona, Barcelona, Spain
When learning a second language one domain particularly difficult to master is that of the phoneme inventory. Factors like age of acquisition, amount of exposure and motivation account for a lot of the variability in final attainment. However, even when these factors are controlled, important variability remains. Data from two different populations: Spanish-Catalan and Dutch-English bilinguals are presented. Participants's performance in a battery of behavioral is used to classify participants as good and poor L2 perceivers. Electrophysiological recordings on different acoustic and L1 phoneme perception tests show that poor L2 perceivers are also worse at perceiving some native contrasts.

IS-127: Basic associative learning and the human condition

Richard Thompson (chair)
Here we focus on basic associative learning: Classical conditioning of discrete responses (e.g., eyeblink) and classical conditioning of fear. Brain organization and behavior are strikingly similar between animal models and humans in these basic forms of learning. We will examine effects of stress on measures of learning and memory in humans: the hormonal bases of stress; the nature of learned fear; basic learning impairments in the fetal alcohol syndrome and schizophrenia; and early diagnosis of Alzheimer's disease, fragile X syndrome, autism and obsessive-compulsive disorder.

Effects of stress on eyeblink conditioning in humans
Daum, Irene Inst. für Kognitive Neuro., Ruhr-Universität Bochum, Bochum, Germany
We studied the effects of psychosocial stress (as induced by the Trier Social Stress Test) on classical eyeblink conditioning. In a tone-airpuff delay procedure, male subjects of the stress group showed a significant increase in cortisol levels compared to a control group, lower overall conditioned response rates during both acquisition and extinction and a flatter learning curve, suggesting a conditioning impairment presumably related to temporary hippocampal dysfunction. This effect was not seen in females. Parallels and differences to the findings in animals will be addressed.

Stress, learning and the anatomy of a sex difference
Shors, Tracey Dept. of Psychology, Rutgers University, Piscataway, NJ, USA
Sex differences in learning and the response to stress are well established. Despite these differences, it is usually assumed that males and females use similar brain structures and anatomical circuits to respond to stressful life experience. In this symposium, I will present data showing that males and females can respond in opposite ways to stressful experience and use distinctive anatomical circuitries to do so. Such differences may explain, at least in part, the high incidence of PTSD and depression in women. [Supported by NIH (NIMH 59970) and NSF (IOB – 0444364)]

Cortical auditory fear conditioning pathway conveys predictive CS information
Kim, Jeansok Dept. of Psychology, University of Washington, Seattle, WA, USA
Objectives: We investigated the role of auditory cortex (AC) in the predictive value of the tone CS in fear conditioning. Methods: Adapting Rescorla's (1968) design, control and AC lesion rats were divided into Groups I and II. Both groups received (5 daily sessions of) 6 tone-shock and 6 tone-alone

presentations; GI additionally received 6 unpaired shocks (lowering the predictive value of the CS). Results: Control GII froze more than control GI to CS, but no difference was observed in AC lesion rats. Conclusions: The cortical CS pathway is critical in evaluating the predictive value of the CS for the US.

Eyeblink classical conditioning as a model system for exploring brain correlates of fetal alcohol syndrome and schizophrenia
Steinmetz, Joseph College of Liberal Arts, University of Kansas, Lawrence, USA
Because much is known about the behavioral and neural correlates of eyeblink classical conditioning, this associative learning procedure has recently been used rather extensively as a model system to explore a variety of human clinical disorders. In this presentation, I will summarize recent data from non-humans and humans we have collected concerning two clinical disorders; Fetal Alcohol Syndrome and Schizophrenia. Deficits in eyeblink conditioning have been noted for both clinical disorders. Furthermore, our data suggest that cerebellar pathologies may be involved in both disorders.

Utility of associative learning in early diagnosis and evaluation of therapeutic outcome
Woodruff-Pak, Diana Dept. of Psychology, Temple University, Philadelphia, PA, USA
Delay eyeblink classical conditioning is of demonstrated utility in the early diagnosis of Alzheimer's disease (AD), and this form of associative learning differentiates AD from other forms of neurodegeneration such as Parkinson's and Huntington's disease. Patterns of conditioning also characterize a number of disorders including fragile X syndrome, autism, obsessive-compulsive disorder, and schizophrenia. Results from the rabbit model system have generalized to humans in demonstrating that eyeblink conditioning is sensitive to pharmacological manipulations. In this manner associative learning is a potential tool for the assessment of therapeutic interventions.

IS-128: Western theories in the Thai practices

Ubolwanna Pavakanun (chair)
This symposium particularly focuses on the effectiveness of Western theories/ ideas in the Thai practices. Therefore, all paper of presentation are only the studies in Thailand. Private and Academic organizations are emphasized studying in theoretical and applicable aspects. The meta and the inferential analysis are the methods in these studies. People in the management level are the focus groups in the theoretical and survey studies. GLOBE, Hertzberg, McClelland, AQ, EQ are the ideas in these types of studies. Teachers, students, including parents, are the main subjects for the academic and experimental studies. Each paper have their own theory to prove.

Thai social culture, organizational culture and effectiveness leadership in 2000's-now
Pavakanun, Ubolwanna Pranakorn, Thailand
This study was synthesized 12 researches of 1,668 middle manager in difference types of Thai organizations; during 2000's and now. The results show that, although the situation in Thailand had been fluctuated and affected followed the crisis of politic and economic during these 1900s and 2000s; Social culture, Organizational culture, and Effectiveness Leadership of Thailand emphasize least on Individualism, Organizational culture and Effectiveness Leadership of Thailand emphasis on Future Orientation but Social culture emphasis on Power Distance. Social culture is related to Organizational culture. These results can use to

guide the management to improve system of other business in Thailand.

The relationships between adversity quotient, emotional quotient, business ethics and stress of Small and Medium Entrepreneurs (SMEs) in Bangkok

Kumbanaruk, Thirasak Dept. of Psychology, Thammasart University, Bangkok, Thailand
The purpose of this research is to study how factors such as adversity quotient, emotional quotient and business ethics relate to the stress of 1,000 SMEs in Bangkok. In conclusion, the SMEs generally has high AQ, EQ and business ethics while the level of stress is normal. However, the high scores of AQ, EQ and business ethics may be due to the "Self Assessment" research methodology. Nevertheless, evidence that business ethics has a negative correlation with the level of stress is remarkably impressed. Moreover, an apparent reverse relationship between AQ, EQ and the level of stress is demonstrated within this study.

The meta-analysis of job-satisfaction as a predictor for worker performances in Thai academic studies

Arisa Samrong, Mookda Sriyong Dept. of Psychology, Ramkhamhaeng University, Bangkok, Thailand
There were many differences in Thai research findings concerned Hertzberg 's theory of job satisfaction. The meta-analysis of job-satisfaction as a predictor for worker performances in Thai academic organization, was applied to be the method in this research. Two trends of this analyzing are : all studies which focused on the relationship between job - satisfaction and organizational committment, turn-over, and job performances. The other is all studies which used job - satisfaction as predictor for job performance. The results show that the most effective factor was found relating to intrinsic motivator as suggested in Hertzberg's theory of motivation.

Subjective well-being of children the relations with parents and teachers

Chuawanlee, Wiladlak Behavioral Science Research, Srinakharinwirot University, Bangkok, Thailand
Supparerkchaisakul, Numchai
This research aimed to examine 1) the relation between two types of parental rearing practices and the parent-child relationship, 2) the relation of parental and teacher nurturing practices and children's subjective well-being, and 3) the variation of structural relationship of variables between boys and girls. Five questionnaires were administered to 1,687 sixth graders in Bangkok. The findings suggested that love and reason orientations of parents had an indirect impact on the children's well-being via the parent-child relationship and this relationship together with teachers' caring practice had cast certain influence on the children's well-being. Moreover, structural relationship did not vary in sex.

A study of the relations between administrators' leadership and perception towards the academic administrative effectiveness in Buddhist university

Srikhruedong, Siriwat Dept. of Psychology, Mahachulalongkornrajavidyalaya, Bangkok, Thailand
One hundred and seventy one administrators in Mahachulalongkornrajavidyalaya University were studied of the perception and the relations of administrators' leadership style, department conditions, and the effectiveness of administrations. The comparison among the variables was also analyzed. The results show that the administrators' style compounds between the affiliation and the achievement styles; the perception of department conditions concerning the interrelationship between administrator co-workers were at a high level, the

condition of work-structure and administrators' power the effectiveness of and administrations were at moderate level. The relationships showed in the perception of administrator – co-workers, work structure, power, and the effectiveness of administrations.

A study of relationship between socio-psychological factors and academic achievement of students of Mahachulalongkornrajavidyalaya University

Theerawongso, Phramaha Prayoon Dept. of Psychology, Mahachulalongkornrajavidyalaya, Bangkok, Thailand
The purposes were to study the relationship between psychosocial factors and academic achievement of students of Mahachulalongkornrajavidyalaya University. Samples used to research were 200 higher students of the first year, academic 2005 from Mahachulalongkornrajavidyalaya University. The results were summarized as follows: Appearance psychological factors, achievement motivation internal locus of control, future –orientation, environments in University, Relationship between students and friends, positive relationship and an aggregate academic achievement of students in goodness, excellence and significantly happiness at .01 level, unless Mental health level, there was no relationship with an aggregate academic achievement and can separate each other, having statistical significant.

Teacher's participation on enhancing intelligence faculties of Thai youth

Boonprakob, Pannee Behavioral Science Research, Srinakharinwirot University, Bangkok, Thailand
Boonprakob, Manat Behavioral Science Research, Srinakharinwirot University, Bangkok, Thailand
Chuawanlee, Wiladlak Behavioral Science Research, Srinakharinwirot University, Bangkok, Thailand
Tongpakdee, Tasana Behavioral Science Research, Srinakharinwirot University, Bangkok, Thailand
Vihokto, Panthanee Behavioral Science Research, Srinakharinwirot University, Bangkok, Thailand
Tansuwannon, Chintana Behavioral Science Research, Srinakharinwirot University, Bangkok, Thailand
The main objectives of this action research were to construct and develop teaching activities and formats appropriate to enhancing intelligence faculties of the sixth graders, and to investigate the results from applying such activities and formats in the classroom. Research methodology was based on quantitative and qualitative approaches using PAR technique. The subjects were 155 students and 10 teachers in total.
Key findings revealed that 1) the effects of teaching activities showed improvement in the students' total scores on intelligence faculties at .05 significant level. 2) Positive changes were found in teachers' teaching activities and formats management, personality, and their perception towards students.

IS-129: Media effects on attitudes and behavior

Lucyna Kirwil (chair)
The symposium presents recent findings on characteristics and psychological mechanisms of negative and positive effects of the old and new media. Speakers from three countries will show results from laboratory and field studies on: (1) relationships between exposure to TV violent contents and identification with aggressors, negative stereotyping and prejudice formation; (2) role of arousal and emotional desensitization to media violence on aggression approval, aggressive thoughts and behavior; (3) conditions under which the TV, Internet use and online games playing have a positive effect on users' social capital and well-being. Results are

discussed in terms of social-cognitive theories and General Aggression Model.

Relations between Arab-American and Jewish-American adolescents' exposure to media depictions of middle-eastern violence and their ethnic stereotypes about the violent propensities of ethnic groups in America

Huesmann, L. Rowell Inst. for Social Research, University of Michigan, Ann Arbor, USA Dubow, Eric Psychology Department, Bowling Green State University, Bowling Green, USA Boxer, Paul Psychology, Rutgers University, Newark, USA Ginges, Jeremy Psychology, New School for Social Research, New York, USA Souweidane, Violet ISR, U of M, Ann Arbor, MI, USA O'Brien, Mureen ISR, U of M, Ann Arbor, MI, USA Hallman, Samantha ISR, U of M, Ann Arbor, MI, USA Moceri, Dominic ISR, U of M, Ann Arbor, MI, USA
We examined the relation between exposure to media depictions of violence in the Middle East and the social-cognitive responses (e.g., ethnic stereotypes) of Jewish-American and Arab-American youth. Participants were recruited from three schools in an ethnically diverse large U.S. mid-western city. Students completed self-report and computerized implicit stereotyping the school day. As hypothesized, we found that exposure to news media depictions of mid-east violence perpetrated by the other ethnic group was significantly related to higher levels of identifying with aggressors from one's own ethnic group and to more negative stereotypes about American teenagers from the other group.

Some consequences of the media linking Islam to terrorism

Bushman, Brad Inst. for Social Research, University of Michigan, Ann Arbor, USA
News media frequently link the religion Islam to terrorist acts. Such news reports may have serious side effects on the Arab population, such as increasing prejudiced feelings toward Arabs. Some recent studies on the effects of terrorism news on implicit and explicit prejudiced attitudes towards Arabs will be described.

Desensitization to media violence as a predictor of aggressive cognitions and behavior

Krahé, Barbara Inst. für Psychologie, Universität Potsdam, Potsdam, Germany Möller, Ingrid Inst. für Psychologie, Universität Potsdam, Potsdam, Germany
A key mechanism linking media violence to aggression is desensitization to violent media images. In this study with 231 men, skin conductance level (SCL) was recorded during exposure to a violent film scene. Speed of return of SCL to baseline was used as a measure of habituation, recognition of aggressive words in a lexical decision-task and delivering noise blasts were measures of aggressive cognition and behavior. As predicted, the faster participants habituated to the violent film, the faster they recognised aggression-related words and the more aggressive behavior they showed. The findings are discussed in relation to the General Aggression Model.

Effects of violent media consumption on emotional arousal and proactive/reactive aggression in young adults

Kirwil, Lucyna Social Psychology, Warsaw School of, Warsaw, Poland
Proactive aggression (PA) is premeditated, controlled action. Reactive aggression (RA) is not fully controlled angry reaction. The hypothesis that violent media consumption (VMC) in adult age serves a different role for PA than for RA was confirmed in two studies in young adults (N1=122, N2=120). VMC predicted PA (together with diminished anxious arousal, violence approval and

readiness to aggressive thoughts), but not RA, that was predicted by trait anger, violence approval and readiness to aggressive thoughts. The findings are discussed in terms of desensitization theory, cognitive and emotional mechanisms of PA and RA and need for justification of own behavior.

Media and social capital: The specific role of TV and internet use

Skarzynska, Krystyna Dept. of Psychology, Polish Academy of Sciences, Warsaw, Poland *Henne, Kamil* Dept. of Psychology, Warsaw School of Social Psych, Warsaw, Poland

We examined whether the TV and Internet usage enhances social capital and increases psychological well-being in three surveys conducted in: nationwide representative sample (N=9625), schools (N=124) and on-line games players (N= 165). The Internet users had more social capital (trust, social support, number of friends, social and political participation) that increased with duration of usage. Media use mediated between kind of school and social capital. Beginners in on-line gaming showed lower social capital than non-players but the difference decreased with time. The findings indicating positive media effects on social capital are explained by the way the media are used.

S-166: Intergroup relations: From hostility to social justice (under the auspices of the International Network of Psychologists for Social Responsibility; INPsySR)

Christopher Cohrs, Ferdinand Garoff (chair)
We constantly witness conflict and social injustice all over the world. From the perspective of a socially responsible science, psychology has to do its best to alleviate these conditions: to contribute to the reduction of direct and structural violence and the development of peaceful and socially just conditions. INPsySR aims to facilitate this goal with this symposium on conditions of hostile and harmonious intergroup relations. Contributions look at the phenomenology and the roots of right-wing extremism and hostile intergroup relations as well as possibilities and strategies to develop positive intergroup relations and social justice and peace more generally.

Right-wing attitude in Germany: Results of a representative study

Geißler, Norman Medizin. Universität Leipzig, Germany *Brähler, Elmar* Medizinische Psychologie, Medizin. Universität Leipzig, Leipzig, Germany *Rothe, Katharina* Medizinische Psychologie, Medizin. Universität Leipzig, Leipzig, Germany *Weissmann, Marliese* Medizinische Psychologie, Medizin. Universität Leipzig, Leipzig, Germany *Decker, Oliver* Medizinische Psychologie, Medizin. Universität Leipzig, Leipzig, Germany

Based on the definition of a consensus conference, a right-wing attitude is a multidimensional concept. Our presentation is based on the data of a representative study in Germany with 4872 participants (2006). We will discuss the results, especially regarding age, sex and education. Besides a Leipzig version of a right wing attitude questionnaire, used by members of the consensus conference, this study included questionnaires on sexism, social dominance, authoritarism, deprivation, resilience, depression, personality and parental educational methods. A model of factors, which may have an impact on the development of a right wing attitude, will be discussed.

Group-focused enmity: Its expressions and roots

Zick, Andreas Inst. für Sozialpsychologie, Universität Jena, Jena, Germany *Küpper, Beate* Mathematics & Natural Scie, TU Dresden, Dresden, Germany

The construct of a syndrome of group-focused enmity is introduced. It is conceptualized as a syndrome of significantly related prejudices against several outgroups which rests on a generalized ideology of inequality, has common predictors and common outcomes representing the destruction of equal worth of individuals and groups. By representative German cross-sectional and panel data (2002 – 2007) the construct is validated (SEM). It will be shown that Allport's (1954) basic idea of interrelated prejudices was adequate. The syndrome approach has many implications for research on prejudice and discrimination as well as for intervention and policy making.

Group-based victim consciousness and its effects on intergroup relations

Vollhardt, Johanna University of Massachusetts, Amherst, USA

Salient beliefs regarding group-based victimization often fuel intergroup conflict. However, they can also motivate individuals to help other victimized groups. The present experiment tests whether this may be explained by perceived similarities between ingroup and outgroup victimization. In a lab-setting, 60 Vietnamese-American college students read about refugees to the US. The salience of similarities versus differences between Vietnamese and other refugees was manipulated. In support of the hypothesis, results revealed that salient similarities increased support for outgroup victims, whereas salient differences decreased it. In conclusion, the cognitive representation of group-based victimization is important in explaining positive and negative intergroup relations.

Discovering the 'Virus' of dehumanization: A radical change in approach to war and peace research

Netzer, Olek Tel Aviv, Israel

Blind Areas were discovered in belief-systems of fanatics of conflict, covering fundamental human facts: individuality of all people including "Them", "We" and "I" as a responsible human who may be wrong in any of his/her beliefs. That condition is defined as "Dehumanization". Blind Areas and their corresponding Patterned Beliefs are organized in a Syndrome that serves as the analytical and diagnostic tool for identification of Dehumanization in language. Applications in Education and Political Analysis bring Blind Areas to awareness thus undermining the self-justification system that avoids cognitive dissonance. Interventions apply to Direct Causes that make dehumanized orientation possible.

Where on earth is social justice and peace? Challenges for psychology

Degirmencioglu, Serdar M. Istanbul, Turkey

Social justice and peace are still marginal constructs in most areas of psychology. An examination of introductory textbooks reveals that very little or no space is devoted to social justice and peace. Psychology is presented as a value-free effort with little connection to daily life or to efforts to secure rights and peace for humans around the world (e.g., most developmental psychology textbooks do not mention children's rights). An analysis of forces that push social justice and peace to the margins, and dynamics that pull them centerstage is presented. Challenges in training, practice, advocacy/organizing, and policy-making are highlighted. A set of recommendations is discussed.

S-167: Internal and external influences on the Implicit Association Test (IAT)

Konrad Schnabel, Wilhelm Hofmann (chair)
At age 10 of the IAT, this symposium brings together recent research exploring how method effects and various external manipulations influence IAT measures. Teige-Mocigemba & Klauer, and Schmitz & Klauer show methodical influences on the validity of IATs. Maliszewski presents group priming effects on implicit prejudice. Kobayashi et al. explore effects of implicit-explicit consistency. Hofmann, Deutsch, Banaji & Lancaster show the influence of mental control strategies on implicit preferences, and Schnabel & Asendorpf the influence of evaluative conditioning on implicit social anxiety. Together, the findings help to get a better understanding of the malleability and validity of IAT measures.

Effects of compatibility-order on the IAT's validity

Teige-Mocigemba, Sarah Inst. für Sozialpsychologie, Universität Freiburg, Freiburg, Germany *Klauer, Karl Christoph* Social Psychology/Methodology, Albert-Ludwigs-Universität, Freiburg, Germany

Since its publication, the IAT is known to be affected by compatibility-order: IAT effects tend to be larger if the so-called compatible block precedes the so-called incompatible block than vice versa. As compatibility is a function of interindividual differences in the attitude, compatibility-order might influence the rank order of IAT effects and thus, the IAT's validity. In two studies, validity was estimated by means of predicting group membership (Study 1: smokers vs. non-smokers; Study 2: left-wing voters vs. right-wing voters) and implicit-explicit correlations. Validity estimates were better, if participants first completed the compatible block indicating the crucial role of compatibility-order.

Attitude accessibility in the implicit association test

Schmitz, Florian Inst. für Sozialpsychologie, Universität Freiburg, Freiburg, Germany *Klauer, Karl Christoph* Social Psychology, Albert-Ludwigs-Universität, Freiburg, Germany

In the past decade, implicit attitudes research has become increasingly popular (Fazio & Olson, 2003), with the Implicit Association Test (IAT, Greenwald, McGhee & Schwarz, 1998) as the most prominent research tool. It is argued that completion of compatible and incompatible IAT blocks can result in differential changes in automatic attitude accessibility. This notion was derived from the Task Switching Account of the IAT (Mierke & Klauer, 2001) and was in part made responsible for the observed IAT effects and differential malleability of IAT blocks. In a series of 7 experiments the predictions were confirmed and defended against alternative explanations.

One person plus his/her several identities: One or several implicit attitudes?

Maliszewski, Norbert Department of Psychology, University of Warsaw, Warsaw, Poland

The aim of 4 studies was to explore whether the activation of people's different social in-group categories (e.g., Poles, victims of Word War II) affects implicit preferences for the in-group compared to an out-group (e.g., Jews). Study 1 showed that focusing attention on Polish national identity increased participants' implicit preferences for Poles compared to Jews. In Study 2, the activation of the common group "we victims" (Poles and Jews together) weakened participants' implicit preferences for Poles compared to Jews. Study 3 and 4 replicated these results for attitudes towards football fans.

Relationships between the type of implicit and explicit self-esteem and social adaptation

Kobayashi, Chihiro Dept. of Psychology, Kobe College, Hyogo, Japan *Yamaguchi, Susumu* Dept of Social Psychology, University of Tokyo, Tokyo, Japan *Masumoto, Kouhei* Dept of Law & Literature, Shimane University, Matsue, Shimane, Japan *Tabuchi, Megumi* Department of Human Sciences, Osaka University, Suita, Osaka, Japan *Arai, Ryujun* Department of Human Sciences, Osaka University, Suita, Osaka, Japan *Hirai, Kei* Department of Human Sciences, Osaka University, Suita, Osaka, Japan *Fujita, Ayako* Department of Human Sciences, Osaka University, Suita, Osaka, Japan

The present study examined relationships between the type of implicit and explicit self-esteem and people's social adaptation, such as loneliness and subjective well-being. Participants were 84 adults. They completed a self-esteem IAT (implicit self-esteem) and the Rosenberg Self-Esteem Scale (explicit self-esteem). Analyses revealed that participants with both low explicit and low implicit self-esteem displayed the lowest degree of adaptation, whereas participants with low explicit and high implicit self-esteem displayed higher degree of adaptation. The findings show that low explicit self-esteem itself is not maladaptive as along as implicit self-esteem is high.

Mental resistance to temptation: Self-control strategies and implicit attitude change

Hofmann, Wilhelm Psychologie, LS Psychologie II, Würzburg, Germany *Deutsch, Roland* Department of Psychology, University of Würzburg, Würzburg, Germany *Banaji, Mahzarin R.* Psychology, Harvard University, Cambridge, MA, USA *Lancaster, Katie* Department of Psychology, Harvard University, Cambridge, MA, USA

Do mental self-control strategies influence the automatic evaluation of tempting stimuli? In a first study, we found that participants who reappraised a chocolate product by using non-affective "cool" reconstructions exhibited weaker implicit attitudes toward the chocolate than participants who used affective "hot" reconstructions by thinking about the consumption experience. These findings were replicated and extended in a web-based IAT study in which we found that the highest reduction in implicit positivity towards the temptation resulted in an implementation intentions condition. These results suggest that mental control strategies influence the degree of automatic affect elicited when a tempting stimulus is encountered.

Malleability of automatic rejection associations in social anxiety

Schnabel, Konrad Persönlichkeitspsychologie, Humboldt-Universität zu Berlin, Berlin, Germany *Asendorpf, Jens* Persönlichkeitspsychologie, Humboldt-Universität zu Berlin, Berlin, Germany

Three internet studies explored whether automatic rejection associations can be reduced by evaluative conditioning tasks. Study 1 showed that repeated measures designs are suboptimal when studying intervention effects on Implicit Association Tests (IATs) due to the general decline of IAT effects in IAT retests. Study 2 showed that the conditioning task was able to decrease implicit but not explicit social anxiety. First analyses of Study 3 revealed that this reduction effect can be stabilized if the conditioning task is repeated on a daily basis in a diary study. Discussion focuses on the stability of intervention effects on IATs.

S-168: Social psychology online: Connecting methodologies for qualitative inquiries

Jesus Rene Luna Hernandez (chair)

Social practices on Internet have developed in multiple ways. This symposium offers a review of different methodologies used to explore how people relate with each other and with non-human agents both online and offline. Even though each paper represent different topics, the common issue in all of them is that new forms of social interaction have been developing which require less orthodox ways of re-conceptualizing society and social psychology.

Network analysis of metaphors about technoscience in immigrants' everyay discourse

Luna Hernandez, Jesus Rene Dept. de Psicologia Social, Univ. Autonoma de Barcelona, Cerdanyola del Valles, Spain *Muñoz Justicia, Juan Manuel* Psicologia Social, Univ. Autonoma de Barcelona, Bellaterra (Cerdanyola), Spain

Access to information is one of the basic Human Rights. However, the digital/informational divide has been growing. Unequal access to digital information affects people who already have severe disadvantages in the social, economic, and political areas, such as those who have emigrated from Third World countries to economically developed countries such as Spain. A research strategy is described which analyzes discursive networks of metaphors about science and technology (technoscience) produced by recent sub-saharian immigrants in Spain. Narrative data about metaphors of technoscience in the life of the immigrants is analyzed in the context of recent incorporation to Spanish society.

Individualized connectivity: A review of the community concept in cyberspace

Georgieva Ninova, Maya Dept. de Psicologia Social, Univ. Autonoma de Barcelona, Cerdanyola del Valles, Spain

The technological advances in the society affects the everyday life and change our traditional forms of organization, are also consequence of the necessities to interact with others. Internet not only supports the preexisting relations but it makes possible the emergency of new forms of being and acting together. Therefore, it is argued that it is necessary to review the community concept, oppossing three perspectivas (psychological, anthropological and sociological) that define it spatially. Its proposed to study the community as networks of relations that don't necessarily belong to the same local unit. This way, the contemporary community becomes an individualized network of relations.

Playing games with boring technologies: An essay on wireless networks and collective action

Bona, Yann Psicologia Social, Univ. Autonoma de Barcelona, Cerdanyola del Valles, Spain

In this article we trace a path through the relations between play, innovation and free wireless networks. Drawing on our research results, we will examine how the everyday engagements with wireless technologies are lived and developed by their producers. In this sense, we need to take into account informal practices, such as play, in order to understand why anyone would bother to build free city-wide wireless networks without making business. Instead of an understanding based on political commitments or existing frustrations with conventional Internet Service Providers, this networking collective action may be better understood under a "play paradigm" regarding technology.

Free practices in a private world: Critical analysis of creative processes in contemporary societies

Farre, Albert Social Psychology, UAB-FDR, Barcelona, Spain

This work raises the study of creativity and creative processes as a relevant field for the sociological Social Psychology. The main goal of this work is to consider the creativity and the creative process as social processes. Considering therefore the need to analyse them in the social-cultural-historical context in which they occur, opening a new scenario to think about creativity and the creative process in the present time. In this new scenario, the dominant forms of knowledge circulation based on an individualizing "ontology of creative works" are no longer unique. And their pertinence and legitimacy can be reraised.

Reticular discourse analysis of the structure and meanings in collective action on the internet

Aceros, Juan Carlos Dept. de Psicologia Social, Univ. Autonoma de Barcelona, Cerdanyola del Valles, Spain

The web data analysis has recently become one of the forms to study social and collective online action. This paper proposes two ways of studying the contents using social network analysis. The first one allows the construction of a study field and texts selection for the analysis. The second one allows representing a discourse network structure of previously selected texts. Taking a concrete case as an example, every step to realize two proposed types of the web data analysis is shown in detail.

S-169: Evolution, motivation and mood

Randolph M. Nesse (chair)

This symposium reviews the rapid recent progress in understanding how natural selection shaped the mechanisms that regulate motivation and mood. The presentations will bring together work on animal behavior with new studies of human motivation and mood regulation. Participants will hear the results of new laboratory and longitudinal studies that test several closely related theoretical models about how mood and motivation regulate goal pursuit. The symposium will compare and contrast those models and apply the results to the urgent problem of understanding the evolutionary origins and functions of mood as a basis for understanding its disorders and finding better treatments

Paradise lost: Costs and benefits of uncoupling the brain hemispheres

Kuhl, Julius Inst. für Psychologie, Universität Osnabrück, Osnabrück, Germany

In accordance with a neuropsychological model of the motivational significance of hemispheric function, discrepancies between explicitly perceived and actual self-choices (self-infiltration) should be removable by experimental induction of right-hemispheric activation (squeezing a soft ball with one's left hand). Experimental findings supporting this claim are reported along with findings demonstrating better performance at a remote-associates task involving right-hemispheric parallel processing (Bowden et al., 2005) after presentation of affiliation-related compared to power-related primes. These two motivational domains have been related to right versus left hemispheric processing in previous research. Findings are discussed from an evolutionary point of view comparing possible costs and benefits of an increasing trend toward hemispheric separation.

Positive and negative affect as resource and information for goal-engagement and disengagement

Heckhausen, Jutta Dept. of Psychology, UC Irvine, Irvine, USA *Carmody, Carrie* Dept. of Psychology, UC Irvine, Irvine, USA *Haase, Claudia* Dept. of Psychology, University of Jena, Jena, Germany *Poulin, Michael* School of Medicine, University of Michigan, Ann Arbor, USA

The regulation of goal engagement and disengagement is discussed from a functionalistic and lifespan encompassing perspective that views positive and negative affect as means rather than ends of action regulation. Two experimental studies are reported on the interface of positive and negative affect, individual control-related orientations, and the time taken to engage in and disengage from difficult solvable and unsolvable tasks. Findings indicate that negative and positive affect serves as a resource for ongoing commitment to controllable goals. After repeated and prolonged failure, decreases in positive affect trigger goal disengagement. Individual differences in control orientation interact with this pattern.

Depression can be an adaptation: Benefits in the development of goal disengagement capacities in adolescence

Wrosch, Carsten Dept. of Psychology, Concordia University, Montreal, Canada Miller, Gregory E. Dept. of Psychology, University of British Columbia, Vancouver, Canada

Objectives. This study examined whether depression can serve adaptive functions by enabling a person to disengage from unattainable goals and thereby promote the person's quality of life. Method. A multi-assessment longitudinal study was conducted, following 104 adolescent women over approximately 19 months. Results. Baseline depression scores predicted an increase in goal disengagement capacities over time. Moreover, increases in goal disengagement capacities predicted low levels of subsequent depression scores, controlling for previous depressive symptoms. Conclusions. The findings demonstrate that depression can be an adaptation by facilitating the development of adaptive goal disengagement capacities in adolescence.

An evolutionary model of low mood states

Nettle, Daniel Dept. of Psychology, Newcastle University, Newcastle, United Kingdom

Objectives: Low mood is induced by worsening situations, and is characterised by reduced lethargy and risk aversion. This study examines why such a suite of responses should be adaptive. Methods: An optimality model was constructed where organisms have a baseline condition, a minimum condition for viability, and fluctuations in state. Results: When state drops a below base-line, the optimal response is energy-minimisation and risk-aversion. When state deteriorates further, towards minimum viability, there is an abrupt transition to risk-proneness. Conclusions: This approach sheds light on depression and low mood, and possibly, through prediction of a risk-prone low mood state, mania too.

Methods for measuring individual motivational structures

Nesse, Randolph M. Inst. for Social Research, University of Michigan, Ann Arbor, USA

Objectives This study investigates strategies for measuring important personal life goals and progress towards them to find methods that can be used for clinical and epidemiological populations. Methods Three different approaches to measuring motivational structure were compared. Results A method that elicits subject's descriptions of personal life goals in a nomothetic framework, combined with a narrative description of progress or lack of progress, and emotional reactions provided useful information about individual motivational structures. Conclusions Idiographic narrative data on motivational structures can be combined with nomothetic data on goals and resources to gather data on the crucial factors that influence mood

S-170: How to foster self-regulated learning? Different methods to support cognitive and metacognitive learning strategies

Sandra Hübner, Meike Landmann (chair)

Strategies of self-regulated learning (SRL) are supportive to cope with many requirements in context of learning and studying. However, students often fail to apply beneficial cognitive and metacognitive strategies of SRL. This symposium

deals with the question how SRL could be fostered effectively. Firstly, effects of SRL-interventions are summarized and effective aspects of such interventions are identified within a meta-analysis. Furthermore, cognitive and metacognitive prompts in multimedia learning, in concept-mapping as well as in writing learning journals are examined. Finally, effects of self-regulation diaries on individual reference norm are presented. The studies are using various methodological approaches (e.g. think-aloud, process-analysis).

The effectiveness of pedagogical agents in prompting cognitive and metacognitive self-regulatory processes during multimedia learning

Azevedo, Roger Dept. of Psychology, University of Memphis, Memphis, USA Baker, Shanna Department of Psychology, University of Memphis, Memphis, USA Witherspoon, Amy Department of Psychology, University of Memphis, Memphis, USA Lewis, Gwyneth Department of Psychology, University of Memphis, Memphis, USA West, Stacie Department of Psychology, University of Memphis, Memphis, USA

In this multi-method study we examined the effectiveness of cognitive and metacognitive SRL prompting by a pedagogical agent (APA) on college students' multimedia learning of a science topic. Fifty university students were randomly assigned to either effective prompting (EPC) or no prompting (NPC) condition. Learners were either prompted by the APA to read the multimedia content (NPC) or to deploy key SRL processes (EPC) during learning. Learners in the EPC gained statistically significantly more knowledge than those in the NPC. Think-aloud protocols indicated that those in the EPC deployed statistically significantly more key SRL processes related to multimedia learning.

Self-regulated learning and academic achievement: A meta-analysis

Benz, Bastian Frithjof Inst. für Psychologie, Techn. Universität Darmstadt, Darmstadt, Germany

To quantitatively summarize the effect of SRL-interventions on academic achievement and to identify effective features of SRL-interventions, a meta-analysis was performed. Conducting a computerized literature search in the databases "ERIC", "PsycINFO " and "Psyndex", 2190 abstracts were examined and narrowed down to 28 studies, which met integration criteria. Information was extracted from the studies by two independent raters (IR: .96). Study effect sizes (Hedges' g) were calculated and integrated applying a random effects model. The overall effect of SRL-interventions on academic achievement was .78. Metacognitive content, computer-based scaffolding and a sample age of 16-20 were identified to be effective features.

Enhancing self-regulated learning by writing learning journals: What type of instructional support is helpful?

Hübner, Sandra Inst. für Psychologie, Universität Freiburg, Freiburg, Germany Nückles, Matthias Department of Psychology, University of Göttingen, Göttingen, Germany Renkl, Alexander Department of Psychology, University of Freiburg, Freiburg, Germany

Learning journals are a medium for self-regulated learning. Nevertheless, instructional support is required to fully exploit this potential. In this study, secondary school students (N = 70) received cognitive and metacognitive prompts when writing learning journals. To enhance consideration of the prompts, they received: (a) "informed prompting" providing meta-knowledge about the prompted strategies; (b) a journal example that modelled the use of strategies; (c) "informed prompting" and an example; or (d) no such support. "Informed prompting" increased learning outcomes in the short- and medium-term. The example fostered

the application of strategies in the short-term and learning outcomes in the medium-term.

Self-regulation diaries to Foster individual reference norm?

Landmann, Meike Inst. für Psychologie, Techn. Universität Darmstadt, Darmstadt, Germany Schmitz, Bernhard Inst. Psychology, Techn. Universität Darmstadt, Darmstadt, Germany

This study aimed to proof the impact of self-regulation diaries on a competence related individual reference norm in adulthood. Participants at a self-regulation-training filled out a diary over 42 days. Reference norm orientation was not exercised in the training but assessed in the diary. Trend analyses proofed the effects. The results evidenced a significant linear improvement of the individual reference norm. Interestingly, the social reference norm remained stable. These effects could be verified in three studies (N=91). Moreover, 22 participants filled out the diary without taking part in the training. Under this condition the effects could be confirmed as well.

Concept mapping for learning from texts: The effect of cognitive and metacognitive prompts

Hilbert, Tatjana School and Instrut. Psychology, Universität Göttingen, Göttingen, Germany

Concept maps consist of nodes representing concepts and links representing the relationships between concepts. This study investigated the benefits of cognitive and/or metacognitive self-regulation prompts on learning outcomes when learning by concept mapping. Compared to a control group without prompts, participants who were prompted while concept mapping achieved a significantly better learning outcome. However, mixed prompts were not more beneficial than solely cognitive or metacognitive prompts. Although prompts had a positive effect on using a new learning technique, prompting learners once was not sufficient to help learners to successfully use this learning technique on their own.

S-171: Visual and cognitive determinants of reading development

Ralph Radach (chair)

The symposium combines cognitive views on early literacy development with new experimental approaches to the role of visual processing and visuomotor control. The traditional gap between these perspectives is narrowed, as the contributions targeting visuomotor deficits are based on analyses of natural reading (or close approximations), thus avoiding problems associated with more basic tasks. The research to be reported uses two languages, English and German, which have substantial similarities, but also differ in important ways. Perhaps the most important difference is the degree of orthographic transparency, leading to language specific patterns of problems in mastering the task of reading.

Young children's early literacy skills and their significance for later reading

Lonigan, Christopher J. Center for Reading Research, Lerning Systems Institute, Tallahassee, FL, USA

Prior research has revealed that skills developing during the early childhood period have significant consequences for learning to read. To date, however, little is known concerning the comparative significance of these skills for children who are English-language learners. In this study, we examined the growth of phonological processing (phonological awareness, phonological memory, and rapid naming), print knowledge, and oral language skills in both first and second language learners (N = 500) during preschool and the predictive significance of children's skills in these three areas for learning to read in English. Results revealed common patterns of development and predictive significance across groups.

Non-phonological predictors of learning to read in German

Hippmann, Kathrin Sprache und Kommunikation, RWTH Aachen, Aachen, Germany
Prior research suggests that difficulties in learning to read English are mainly caused by phonological deficits. Our goal was to test the validity if this claim for a language with a more transparent orthography. A sample of preschool (kindergarten) students were asked complete tasks examining phonological awareness, working memory, naming speed, visual attention, print knowledge, intermodal integration and symbolic understanding. Standardized tests of reading and writing during 1st grade served as criterion variables. Elementary symbol acquisition measured assessed via visual-verbal paired associate learning turned out to be one oft the best predictors, while the impact of phonological awareness measures was modest.

The non-phonological components of rapid serial naming

Schatschneider, Christopher Dept. of Psychology, Florida State University, Tallahassee, USA
Some researchers have argued that the cognitive abilities that underlie Rapid Serial Naming (RSN) that are related to reading ability lie outside the domain of phonology (Wolf and Bowers, 1999). However, the evidence cited for this position is relatively weak. We will briefly review published evidence surrounding RSN and reading, and present data from a large-scale individual differences study providing an alternative line of evidence regarding the non-phonological components of RSN. A related experiment used saccade contingent display manipulations to restrict the perceptual span during RSS. Results indicate that parafoveal processing is a powerful determinant of performance in this task.

Tracking non-linguistic visual processing demands critical for early reading

Radach, Ralph Dept. of Psychology, Florida State University, Tallahassee, USA Vorstius, Christian Dept. of Psychology, Florida State University, Tallahassee, FL, USA Günther, Thomas Department of Child Psychiatry, RWTH Aachen Medical Center, Aachen, Germany
Prior attempts to study attentional and visuomotor deficits in early reading have often used laboratory tasks remote from reading. Our goal was to capture the spatiotemporal dynamics of continuous reading while avoiding confounding from ongoing linguistic processing. A task was designed in which strings of ooooooo are arranged like a line of text and participants are asked to detect stings that contain a target c, like ooocooo. We report results obtained using several samples of elementary school students, demonstrating striking similarities with fixation patterns found in normal reading. Relations to measures of reading performance and theoretical implications will be discussed.

Eye movements in dyslexic and normal reading in grades 3, 4 and 5

Thaler, Verena Inst. für Experim. Psychologie, Freie Universität Berlin, Berlin, Germany
We assessed the eye movements and vocal reaction times of 50 dyslexics (7 – 11 years) and 48 age-adequate readers (7 – 10 years) in third, fourth and fifth grade during reading single words and non-words of different length and consonant cluster density. Dyslexic readers showed stronger effects of lexicality, length and density. Gaze duration, mean fixation duration, number of fixations and vocal reaction times were affected. Unimpaired readers

showed a significant development toward shorter fixation durations and fewer fixations whereas dyslexic readers showed only a slight trend toward shorter fixation durations. Implications for cognitive development of dyslexics are discussed.

Visual word recognition and sentence processing of dyslexic readers

Hawelka, Stefan Inst. für Psychologie, Universität Salzburg, Salzburg, Austria
Eye movements of young adult dyslexic readers and controls (N=18/18) were recorded during reading the Potsdam-Sentence-Corpus. Main finding were the short forward saccades length and massively increased effects of word length, frequency and predictability for dyslexic readers. A further critical observation was that even when dyslexic readers recognized a word with a single fixation, its duration was substantially prolonged. The short saccades may reflect a reduced number of letters which can be processes in parallel and/or a reduced number of whole-word recognition units. The increased duration of single fixations may reflect impaired speed of access to phonology and meaning from visual word representations.

S-172: The cross cultural research on children's creative personality

Wen Liu, Aimin Wang (chair)
Six speakers are from China and USA;Wen Liu will present Chinese preschool children's structure and types of creative personality. Jiliang Shen will discuss the structure of adolescents' creative personality and the cross-cultural study of adolescents' creative personality. Lizhu Yang will discuss a follow-up study of 4-year-old self-imposed delay of gratification as a predictor of children's school-based social competences at age 9. Lihua Zhang will present studies on explicit and implicit self-esteem of junior middle school students with different Levels of test anxiety. Doris Bergen & Aimin Wang will discuss effects on children's creativity of super-realistic technology-enhanced toys.

A Follow-up study of 4-year-old self-imposed delay of gratification as a predictor of children's school-based social competences at age 9

Yang, Lizhu Dept. of Psychology, Liaoning Normal Universtiy, Dalian, People's Republic of China Wang, Aimin Dept. of EducationalPsychology, Miami University, Oxford, Ohio, USA Wang, Jiangyang Dept. of Psychology, Shenyang Normal University, Shenyang, People's Republic of China
Self-imposed delay of gratification is the core of the ability of self-control in that is the important part of creative personality. Fifty-four 4-year-old children were examined with the self-imposed delay of gratification task. When they were 9, school-based social competences were measured by combining the methods of teachers' structure interview and assessment, peer nomination, children's self-report about social anxiety and loneliness. The results suggested that children's early self-imposed delay of gratification was a force to predict future school adjustment. The children who were high with self-imposed delay of gratification at 4 would develop well in school-based social competences at 9.

Effects on children's creativity of super-realistic technology-enhanced toys

Bergen, Doris Dept. Educational Psychology, Miami University, Oxford, USA Wang, Aimin Dept. Educational Psychology, Miami University, Oxford, USA
Children's creative expression has been most evident in their play with toys such as blocks and dolls, which encourage elaborative, imaginative pretense and/or social games, unique to the personality of the particular child. Now, however, toys for young children are often enhanced with

computer chips that enable the toy to elicit specific language or actions from the child. Many such toys are exaggerated replicas of theme characters. This presentation will review a number of research studies of children's play with super-realistic technology-enhanced toys and discuss the potential effects of such toys on children's creative play.

A study on the structure of adolescents' creative personality

Shen, Jiliang Inst. Developmental Psychology, Beijing Normal University, Beijing, People's Republic of China Wang, Xinghua Inst. Developmental Psychology, Beijing Normal University, Beijing, People's Republic of China Zhou, Ji Inst. Developmental Psychology, Beijing Normal University, Beijing, People's Republic of China
This study explored the structure of creative personality with a sample of 1300 senior and junior high school students and college students aged from 15 to 29 from China. Confirmatory Factorial Analysis indicated that adolescents' creative personality consisted of three dimensions, which were internal, external and self. Internal factor consisted of Self-confidence, Internal motivation, Persistence and Norm-doubt; External factor consisted of Curiosity, Openness, Independence and Risk-taking; Self factor contains only one sub-dimension which was Self-acceptance. In the both groups of middle school students and college students, the applicability of this three-factor model of creative personality was acceptable.

A study on one trait of creative personality: Self-esteem and test anxiet

Zhang, Lihua Dept. of Psychology, Liaoning Normal University, Dalian, People's Republic of China Han, Huimin Dept. of Psychology, Liaoning Normal University, Dalian, People's Republic of China
The study explored the relationship between self-esteem and test anxiety of junior high school students. 78 high-level and 92 low-level test anxiety subjects received The Self-Esteem Scale and Implicit Association Test, which were designed to measure explicit and implicit self-esteem. Results show that :The explicit self-esteem level of high-level test anxiety subjects was significantly lower than the low-level ones, they had the same level of implicit self-esteem. The disparity between implicit and explicit self-esteem was different between the two groups. Junior high school students tend to engender test anxiety when their explicit self-esteem level was lower than the implicit one.

The study on Chinese preschool children's structure and developmental characteristics and types of creative personality: Based on teachers' perceptions

Liu, Wen Dept. of Psychology, Liaoning Normal University, Dalian, People's Republic of China Qi, Lu Dept. of Psychology, Liaoning Normal University, Dalian, People's Republic of China
The purpose of this research is to investigate the structure and characteristics of children's creative personality and find the potential and tendency of special area. Observation, interview and questionnaires were used to explore the creative personality of children. By EFA and CFA, we got nine traits: novelty, independence, and sense of humor, sense of achievement, cooperation, self-confidence, sensitivity, curiousity, and aesthetic ability. The creative personality of preschoolers has significant difference among ages. Chinese children's creative personality can be divided into three types: cooperation, science, and art.

A cross-cultural study of adolescents' creative personality

Shen, Jiliang Inst. Developmental Psychology, Beijing Normal University, Beijing, People's Republic of China Wu, Yue Inst. Developmental Psychology, Beijing Normal University, Beijing, People's Republic of China Hu, Xingyi Inst. Developmental Psychology, Beijing Normal University, Beijing, People's Republic of China

This cross-cultural study examines the impact of different cultures upon adolescent creative personality, in which 1257 senior and junior high school students aged from 13 to 22 from China, Japan and Germany participated. Results indicates that, German adolescents performed better than the other two countries' on the internal factor of creative personality, however, they got lower score on the external factor; There was no significant difference between Chinese and Japanese students on the dimension of internal and external factors. On the self factor, Chinese students got the lowest score, and the difference between German and Japanese students was not significant.

S-173: Emotional regulation of learning: Psychobiological and comparative studies

Alba Elisabeth Mustaca, María del Carmen Torres Bares (chair)

The devaluation in the quality of an expected appetitive reinforcer, triggers a series of responses know as frustration. Also is well known that emotions can affect our perceptions and learning processes. We present a set of results that include procedures of consummatory and instrumental negative contrast, consummatory extinction, partial reinforcement effect and magnitude of reinforcement extinction effect using Wistar rats, Roman rats, dogs, birds and quails subjects; and how emotions of different affective valence can bias causal learning in humans. These studies show that the negative contrast effect is an accurate model for the study of anxiety.

Emotional effects of extinction on sexual instrumental behavior in birds

Gutierrez, German Lab. Psicologia Exper., Universidad e Bogotá, Bogotá, Colombia Baquero, Alejandro Psychology, Universidad Nacional de Colomb, Bogotá, Colombia Montoya, Bibiana Psychology, Universidad Nacional de Colomb, Bogotá, Colombia

Divergence in instrumental learning in vertebrates seems to be mediated by emotional factors. Partial Reinforcement Extinction Effect (PREE) and Magnitude of Reinforcement Extinction Effect (MREE) covary in different vertebrate species. In birds, however, a dissociation is observed: PREE and reversed MREE are observed, when food is used as reinforcement. We present studies of MREE using quail and copulatory access as reinforcement. A reversed MREE was demonstrated. Other results of studies on the manipulations of reinforcement magnitude are also presented. The results are discussed within the context of the paradoxical reinforcement effects and divergences in learning processes in birds.

Frustration effect on interspecific communication responses in dogs

Bentosela, Mariana CONICET-IDIM-UBA, Lab. Psicología Experimental, Buenos Aires, Argentina

The effect of frustration on domestic dogs' communicative behavior was investigated. Instrumental successive negative contrast (SNC) and extinction were used. Initially, subjects received a preferred reward (liver) for gazing towards the experimenters face in a situation where food was visible but out of reach. Next, dogs unexpectedly obtained dry food (a less-preferred reward) instead of liver and in the extinction group a reward omission. Experimental subjects significantly gazed less, rejected more the devalued reward and increased the distance from and back position towards the experimenter. We also discuss possible mechanisms involved in interspecific communication responses.

Emotion in reward-reduction paradigms: A study with Roman High (RHA) and Roman Low (RLA) Avoidance rats

Torres Bares, María del Carmen Dept. of Psychology, Universidad de Jaen, Jaen, Spain Gómez, José de la Torre Vacas, Lourdes Callejas, José Enrique Escarabajal, Dolores Rosas, Juan Manuel Aguero, Angeles Tobena, Adolfo Fernández-Teruel, Albert

Animals models of reward reduction consist of emotionally aversive experimental situations where an expected reinforcer is suddenly omitted, reduced in magnitude or degraded in quality. In this presentation a series of experiments show that strain of rats psychogenetically selected on the basis of their emotional reactivity (low in RHA and high in RLA rats, respectively) exhibit behavioural differences in reward reduction paradigms such as instrumental and consummatory successive negative contrast, instrumental extinction and partial reinforcement extinction effect. These results are discussed within the framework of those theories proposed to explain the emotional modulation of these phenomena

Memory and emotion in frustration

Mustaca, Alba Elisabeth CONICET-IDIM-UBA, Lab. Psicología Experimental, Buenos Aires, Argentina

In the consummatory successive negative contrast (cSNC), rats downshifted from 32% to 4% sucrose solution exhibit a temporary reduced consumption in comparison with rats that experience only the 4% solution. The present experiments show that corticosterone strengthens an aversive emotional component of the response elicited by the surprising reduced reward magnitude during the initial downshift trial, and that there is a renewal frustration effect (RFE) after the recovery from cSNC. In addition, other results indicate a correspondence between the intensity of the negative contrast effect in the first downshift trial and the inconditional fear measured in a light/dark test.

Emotion and causal learning

Cándido, Antonio Psicología Experimental, Universidad de Granada, Granada, Spain Maldonado, Antonio Psicologia Experimental, Universidad de Granada, Granada, Spain Catena, Andrés Dept. of Experimen. Psychology, University of Granada, Granada, Spain García-Retamero, Rocio Dept. of Experimen. Psychology, University of Granada, Granada, Spain Serrano, Jesús Dept. of Experimen. Psychology, University of Granada, Granada, Spain Perales, José César Dept. of Experimen. Psychology, University of Granada, Granada, Spain

Is well known that emotions can affect our perceptions and learning processes. In this talk, we present data showing how emotions of different affective valence can bias causal learning. Results when emotions are induced both while participants learn non-emotional cause-effect relationships, and when the causes and effects have a strong affective valence are reported. From a theoretical point of view, which causal learning mechanisms are influenced by emotional factors are discussed

S-174: Distributed cognition: A framework for understanding learning with technology

Charoula Angeli (chair)

In this symposium, five empirical studies examine the extent to which the framework of distributed cognition can effectively inform and illuminate issues regarding the design and outcomes of technology-enhanced learning. The results show that distributed cognition serves well as an analytic framework for explaining human aspects of cognition related to design or problem-solving tasks with technology. But, when students are involved in learning and not information or design tasks, then more detailed and theoretical accounts of distributed cognition are needed to explain how learning is distributed and how change occurs from novice to expert thinking.

Distributed cognition in technology-enhanced foreign language learning: Creating a web-based tourist guide for London

Narciss, Susanne Psych. Learning & Instruction, Technische Universität Dresden, Dresden, Germany Körndle, Hermann Inst. für Psychologie, Technische Universität Dresden, Dresden, Germany

This paper aims at investigating the benefits and constraints of using technology in socio-constructive language learning on the basis of the distributed cognition (DC) framework. To this end it (a) describes how the multimedia tools TEE (The Electronic Exercise) and EF-editor (Exercise Format Editor) can serve socio-constructive language learning from a DC point of view, (b) reports how TEE and EF-editor have been used in a foreign language classroom with 25 7th grade students for creating a web-based tourist guide to London, and (c) presents data revealing the benefits and constraints the teacher and students experienced through this learning scenario.

Distributed cognition in a sixth-grade classroom: An attempt to overcome alternative conceptions about light and color

Angeli, Charoula Dept. of Education, University of Cyprus, Nicosia, Cyprus

The purpose of the study was to examine how nine dyads of sixth-grade students engaged in a distributed collaborative inquiry with ODRES™, a computer tool, to learn about light and color. The data were analyzed using qualitative and quantitative methods and the results showed that learning with ODRES™ positively affected students' understandings and promoted a lasting effect on their conceptions. Moreover, the results showed that in complex distributed social systems such as a technology-rich elementary school classroom, technology-mediated collaboration may not always lead to intellectually productive interactions for learning. Implications for designing distributed educational systems for children are discussed.

Collaborative virtual environments as means to increase the level of intersubjectivity in a distributed cognition system

Ligorio, Maria Beatrice Dept. of Psychology, University of Bari, Bari, Italy Cesareni, Donatella Dept. of Psychology, University of Rome, Rome, Italy

Virtual environments extend the space of interaction beyond the classroom. In order to analyze how distributed cognition functions in such an extended space, we focus on the architecture of intersubjectivity. The Euroland project– a virtual land similar to Second Life – was analyzed with the aim of tracking down the process and the structure of intersubjectivity. Participants were located in different cities in two countries – Italy and the Netherlands. A group of ten 13-years old students was observed. Seven videotapes were analyzing. A set of episodes revealing intersubjectivity was captured and discussed. Three progressively phases were found.

Scientific investigations with primary school children: A distributed cognitive system
Valanides, Nicos Dept. of Education, University of Cyprus, Nicosia, Cyprus
Twenty dyads of sixth-grade students participated in the study. students in each dyad interacted with a device to investigate its functioning. The device consisted of a box having on its surface eight light bulbs in a line and five switches underneath. The bulbs and the switches were connected in a hidden circuit inside the box. Students were instructed to form and test hypotheses. Data were collected with observations and think-aloud protocols. Qualitative methods were employed to analyze the interactions among students and the device. The results report on the underlying cognitive processes operating when learning in a distributed cognitive system.

Coercing collaborative learning processes by online feedback and instructional design strategies
Zumbach, Jörg Bildungswissenschaften, Universität Salzburg, Salzburg, Austria
Two methods for fostering collaborative learning in dyads are compared: a feedback-mechanism to scaffold collaborative behavior, and use of distributed learning resources to force process of negotiating knowledge. In a web-based collaboration environment for learner dyads instances of collaboration are examined and combined with online feedback. In addition, resources available to the partners were varied. The influence of these interventions on outcomes related to knowledge acquisition, problem-solving, group climate and collaborative behavior was examined. Results suggest there are benefits in providing a feedback approach in fostering collaboration and enhancing problem-solving quality.

S-175: Constructing dynamic mental models from external representations

Tamara van Gog, Wolfgang Schnotz (chair)
The studies presented in this symposium focus on the effects on learning, more specifically, on students' acquisition of dynamic mental models, from different types of external representations, such as text and pictures, animations, and video-based modelling examples. Effects of sequencing representations, redundancy of information, presentation speed, attention guidance, and dynamics of the representations are investigated, and in several studies eye tracking is used to study effects on learning processes directly. These studies contribute to our understanding of the effects of different types of representations on students' mental model acquisition, and provide guidelines for the design of more effective instructional materials.

Effects of presentation speed on learning dynamic information from animations: An eye-tracking study
Meyer, Katja Inst. für Psychologie, Universität Koblenz-Landau, Landau, Germany Rasch, Thorsten Inst. für Psychologie, Universität Koblenz-Landau, Landau, Germany Schnotz, Wolfgang Inst. für Psychologie, Universität Koblenz-Landau, Landau, Germany
Due to the transient nature of animations and limitations of human information processing, the animation speed has an important influence on what is learned. Our question was how different animations speeds affect the perception and cognitive processing of dynamic information. 20 students learned how a 4-stroke-engine works with an animation. During learning eye-tracking was applied. Analyses of fixation times and frequencies of fixations show that there are different patterns of fixation depending on the animation speed. The

results indicate that the animation speed affects the salience of the different dynamic levels and cognitive processing of the corresponding dynamic information.

Using snapshots with animation to facilitate understanding dynamic systems
Rebetez, Cyril Tecfa, University of Geneva, Carouge, Switzerland Betrancourt, Mireille Tecfa, University of Geneva, Geneva, Switzerland
This contribution reports a study investigating the effect of using snapshots highlighting the critical steps to facilitate the processing of animation explaining the functioning of dynamic systems. Two factors were used: the display of snapshots of critical steps (with or without) and the type of graphics (static or animated). Eyetracking data were recorded, along with off-line measures of memorization and comprehension, in order to investigate the consequence of the presence of snapshots on visual attention. We expect that only active visual exploration of the snapshots by the learner during presentation will be linked with higher comprehension scores.

Learning from text and pictures: Effects of sequencing and redundancy
Ullrich, Mark FB8: Psychologie, Universität Koblenz Landau, Landau, Germany Schnotz, Wolfgang Inst. für Psychologie, Universität Koblenz-Landau, Landau, Germany
Many studies have shown that adding pictures to text can improve learning, provided that picture and text are presented at the same time. Sometimes this is not possible and temporal contiguity cannot be realized. We ran three experiments to investigate the effects of sequencing and redundancy on learning outcomes when picture and text are presented in succession. Results indicate that learners perform better when the picture is presented before the corresponding text and if picture and text are informationally redundant. We also found an interaction that refers to interferences between pictorial and textual information when the text is presented first.

Including eye movements in modelling examples: Effects on learning and transfer
van Gog, Tamara OTEC, Open University, Heerlen, Netherlands Paas, Fred OTEC, Open University, Heerlen, Netherlands
This study investigates whether the effectiveness of multimedia modelling examples can be further improved by incorporating the model's eye movements. Modelling examples usually show only how a model solves a problem (solution steps), without explicating the underlying thought and attention processes. Eye movements reflect attention allocation and studies have shown that more experienced individuals focus their attention faster and more on relevant information. Hence, a discrepancy in attention allocation between the model and the novice studying the example is likely. Including the model's eye movements in examples could diminish this discrepancy, by guiding the learner's attention through the problem-solving process.

Effects of consecutive presentation of text and picture on learning
Sarti, Julia Inst. für Psychologie, Universität Koblenz-Landau, Landau, Germany Rasch, Thorsten Inst. für Psychologie, Universität Koblenz-Landau, Landau, Germany Schnotz, Wolfgang Inst. für Psychologie, Universität Koblenz-Landau, Landau, Germany Horz, Holger Inst. für Psychologie, Universität Koblenz-Landau, Landau, Germany
This study investigates the influence of consecutive presentation of text and picture on learning processes and learning outcomes based on the assumption that cognitive processing of information sources depends on previously presented

information. In a learning experiment, 105 psychology students were randomly assigned to seven conditions. In three conditions, subject studied only one information source (text, map, diagram). In four further conditions, subjects had to study text and picture consecutively (text-map, text-diagram, map-text, diagram-text). An ANOVA shows an impact of sequence on learning time as well as on learning outcomes. These findings may help to create more effective instructional designs.

S-176: Advances in research on the cognitive determinants of intelligence

Karl Schweizer (chair)
The symposium concentrates on research concerning the cognitive basis of intelligence. A number of determinants of higher-order cognitive abilities have been identified in past research. The symposium presentations focus on these established and also on novel determinants that are either cognitive units or general cognitive characteristics. Accordingly, the presentations address the following topics: attention, capacity for complexity, learning processes, temporal acuity of mental processing and working memory. They include innovations resulting from conceptual elaborations, new and improved assessment techniques and novel research methodology especially in the field of data analysis. Furthermore, new results are presented in support of the determinants.

The capacity for complex mental permutations as a source of individual differences in fluid intelligence
Bowman, David Accelerated Learning Labratory, University of New South Wales, UNSW, Australia
The complexity of cognitive tests is a well established feature of the taxonomy of mental capabilities. We report on an investigation of the capacity to deal with increasing numbers of mental permutations in the swaps task, the figure-exchange task, the letter-exchange task, and the number-ordering task, across three studies. These mental permutation tasks (MPT) require participants to mentally manipulate the order of elements, maintain intermediate orders, and perform further permutations on these part-solutions to provide a final response. The complexity metric is evaluated from both broad (loadings on a Gf factor) and narrow (loadings on a MPT specific factor) perspectives.

Exploring the nature of individual differences in working memory capacity
Unsworth, Nash Dept. of Psychology, University of Georgia, Athens, USA
Previous work has conceptualized individual differences in working memory capacity (WMC) as differences in active maintenance of information. Recently Unsworth and Engle (2007) suggested that individual differences in WMC are due to both differences in active maintenance and differences in controlled search processes. This claim is examined in terms of tasks that require active maintenance (e.g., antisaccade) and tasks that require controlled retrieval in the absence of active maintenance (e.g., delayed free recall). It is argued that both components are necessary for understanding individual differences in WMC and their relation to higher-order cognitive abilities.

Beyond simple storage: Which working memory related cognitive functions predict reasoning?
Krumm, Stefan Inst. für Psychologie, Universität Marburg, Marburg, Germany
This study examined cognitive abilities related to the concept of working memory (WM) including executive functions, short-term memory, sustained attention. Tasks were selected from established

models and administered to 199 students. WM models were systematically compared and applied to predict reasoning. Analyses also considered mental speed as a predictor. A model with a latent short-term storage and manifest coordination as predictors of reasoning showed the best fit and explained 59% of reasoning variance. Coordination mediated the contribution of mental speed. Executive functions did not add unique contributions. In sum, short-term storage and coordination were relevant for the prediction of reasoning.

On neurocognitive processes underlying psychometric intelligence: Contrasting the mental speed approach with the temporal resolution hypothesis

Troche, Stefan Inst. für Psychologie, Universität Bern, Bern, Switzerland Helmbold, Nadine Inst. für Psychologie, Universität Göttingen, Göttingen, Germany Rammsayer, Thomas Inst. für Psychologie, Universität Bern, Bern 9, Switzerland

Two hypotheses on sources of general intelligence were compared: Temporal resolution hypothesis predicts that temporal acuity of the brain is an important aspect of intelligence whereas mental speed approach claims higher speed of information processing accounting for higher intelligence. Structural equation modelling revealed that performance on timing tasks – but not reaction times derived from the Hick paradigm – predicted intelligence in 260 participants. Mental speed and intelligence were found to be associated indirectly – mediated by temporal acuity. These results are interpreted as support for both, mental speed and temporal resolution hypotheses with temporal resolution being more fundamental than mental speed.

The role of intelligence in learning an executive attention task: A Latent Growth Curve (LGC) approach

Goldhammer, Frank Internat. Bildungsforschung, Deutsches Institut für, Frankfurt, Germany Rauch, Wolfgang Institut für Psychologie, J.W. Goethe-Universität, Frankfurt, Germany Schweizer, Karl Institut für Psychologie, J.W. Goethe-Universität, Frankfurt, Germany Moosbrugger, Helfried Inst. für Psychologie, Universität Frankfurt, Frankfurt, Germany

Intraindividual differences in attention performance are investigated over the course of a 6-minute testing session. A sample of 193 subjects completed the Frankfurt Adaptive Concentration Test (FACT), a measure of executive attention, as well as intelligence tests and a perceptual speed test. LGC models demonstrate an increase of speed and accuracy in FACT performance following a linear trajectory. The covariates intelligence, perceptual speed, and age show different effects on initial performance (latent intercept) and performance growth (latent slope). Furthermore, covariate effects obtained for speed and accuracy differ substantially. Results are discussed with respect to skill acquisition theory.

Gf/Gc theory and complexity-enhancing manipulations

Stankov, Lazar International Testing Service, Princeton, USA

This presentation will briefly review some of the issues that led to the development of the theory of fluid and crystallized intelligence, early work with competing tasks and subsequent attempts to manipulate task complexity. In the second part I shall elaborate on my own experiences in doing this kind of research, what have we learned and where can we proceed from here.

S-177: Anger assessment: New developments

Georges Steffgen, Hannelore Weber (chair)

The major goal of this symposium is to discuss new developments in anger assessment. Hannelore Weber (D) presents results on the validity of the Anger-related Reactions and Goals Inventory–Revised (ARGI-R). Thomas Kubiak (D) reports results from a study about anger experiences in daily life based on an ARGI diary-version. Sophie Recchia (L) presents a French adaptation of the ARGI-R. Georges Steffgen (L) resumes results from a study of a German adaptation Deffenbacher's Driving Anger Scale. Claire Lawrence (UK) presents a new inventory designed to measure sensitivity to frustration and provocation: The Situational Triggers of Aggressive Response (STAR) scale.

The anger-related reactions and goals inventory revised

Weber, Hannelore Inst. für Psychologie, Universität Greifswald, Greifswald, Germany Kubiak, Thomas Inst. für Psychologie, Universität Greifswald, Greifswald, Germany

This paper presents the Anger-related Reactions and Goals Inventory Revised (ARGI-R) that was designed to measure habitual functional and dysfunctional strategies as well as habitual goals in regulating anger. The seven reaction subscales and the seven goal subscales (containing four items each) were rationally derived from theory and research on anger. Results from two cross-sectional studies demonstrate good psychometric properties of the ARGI-R and attest to its construct and criterion validity. In Study 1, expected relationships with trait-anger, psychological and social well-being were found. Results from Study 2 show substantial convergence between self- and other-reports on anger-related reactions and goals.

Daily life anger assessment

Kubiak, Thomas Inst. für Psychologie, Universität Greifswald, Greifswald, Germany Freese, Ankre Institute of Psychology, University of Greifswald, Greifswald, Germany Jonas, Cornelia Institute of Psychology, University of Greifswald, Greifswald, Germany Weber, Hannelore Institute of Psychology, University of Greifswald, Greifswald, Germany

We examined every day anger episodes focusing on the functionality of anger-related reactions. 63 participants took part and completed diaries for one week, assessing anger episodes, anger-related reactions, anger-related goals, and the degree to which these goals were attained. We found significant differences with regard to reaction-goal patterns that differed, in turn in the degree of goal attainment indicating differences in these patterns' functionality. The diary method proved to be useful to capture the facet of functionality, which otherwise is difficult to assess with conventional questionnaires. Our results suggest further examining interindividual differences in reaction-goal patterns and functionality in responses.

French adaptation of the anger-related reactions and goals inventory revised

Recchia, Sophie Dept. of Psychology, University of Luxembourg, Walferdange, Luxembourg Steffgen, Georges Psychology, University of Luxembourg, Walferdange, Luxembourg Weber, Hannelore Psychology, University of Greiswald, Greifswald, Germany

The presented study validated a French adaptation of the Anger-related Reactions and Goals Inventory-Revised (Kubiak, Wiedig-Allison, Zgoriecki & Weber, 2007) with a sample of 184 students of the University of Luxembourg. The postulated 7 factor structure could be found for the reaction subscales,

but not for the goal subscales in confirmatory factor analyses. Correlations with the German State Trait Anger Inventory- II (Schwenkmezger, Hodapp & Spielberger, 1992) confirm the construct validity of the questionnaire, nevertheless further item reformulations are necessary. The translation procedure as well as the related analyses to verify the equivalence of the two versions will be discussed.

Deffenbacher driving anger scale: Psychometric properties of a German version

Steffgen, Georges Dept. of Psychology, University of Luxembourg, Walferdange, Luxembourg Recchia, Sophie Psychology, University of Luxembourg, Walferdange, Luxembourg Ludewig, Jean-Luc Psychology, University of Luxembourg, Walferdange, Luxembourg

Driving anger is defined as more frequent and intense anger while operating a motor vehicle. The presented study (n=115) examined the reliability and validity of a German version of the Driving Anger Scale (Deffenbacher, Oetting & Lynch, 1994). According to the original version the results from exploratory and confirmatory factor analysis approved the six factor solution. Internal reliability was also satisfying. All subscales correlated positively and confirmed a general dimension of driving anger. Overall findings of the German version of the Driving Anger Scale replicated findings of earlier findings.

New inventory to measure sensitivity to frustration and provocation: The Situational Triggers of Aggressive Response (STAR) scale

Lawrence, Claire Dept. of Psychology, University of Nottingham, Nottingham, United Kingdom

Objectives: This paper presents the development of the self-report Situational Triggers of Aggressive Responses (STAR) scale. Methods: Four studies use a mixture of cross-sectional, quasi-experimental and experimental methods (N range between 100-849) to test the predictive and discriminant validity of the STAR scale facets: sensitivity to frustrations and sensitivity to provocations. Results: Sensitivity to frustrations are related to trait anger, hostility and lower self-esteem, sensitivity to provocations are linked to physical and verbal aggression and narcissism. STAR facets predict perceptual bias in interpreting ambiguous aggressive behaviour. Conclusions: The applications for the STAR scale in clinical and forensic settings are discussed.

S-178: Social axioms: Recent advances across cultures

Sylvia Xiaohua Chen (chair)

Leung and Bond have proposed the construct of social axioms - defined as generalized beliefs about how the world functions - and conducted studies round the world to examine its factor structure and predictive validity. In this symposium, researchers from the U.S., Italy, Malaysia, the Philippines, and Poland will present their work on its recent development and functional utility. They confirm its five-factor structure and examine differences of social axioms across demographic variables. Social axioms are found to associate with coping style and moral judgment development, moderate the effects of personal convictions on hope, and account for low levels of subjective well-being.

Social axioms in the USA

Singelis, Theodore Dept. of Psychology, California State University, Chico, USA

Dimensionality of the Social Axioms Survey (SAS) was assessed in a sample of college students and non-student adults across eight locations in the USA (N = 2164). Ethnic and regional differences in social beliefs were also assessed. Exploratory and confirmatory factor analyses supported the five-factor structure found previously in international samples. African Americans held stronger spiritual beliefs than Asian- or Euro-Americans. Asian-Americans were more inclined toward cynical social beliefs than were other groups and believed more in fate control than Euro- or Hispanic-Americans. Implications for comparisons of samples from the USA with other countries are discussed.

Validity of the Italian social axioms survey
Comunian, Anna Laura Dept. of Psychology, University of Padua, Padova, Italy
Validity of the Italian version of the Social Axioms Survey (SAS-I, Comunian, 2004) is tested in two respects. Firstly, the purported five dimensional structure of the SAS-I was tested. Secondly, the relations of the axioms dimensions to coping style and moral judgment development were analysed. The SAS-I was given to a sample (N= 181) with two-specific scales: the Coping Scale (Comunian, 2005) and the Padua Moral Development Scale (Comunian; 2004). Results supported both the purported five-dimensions structure and hypothesized relationships to coping and moral judgment development. Implications for further studies about situational influences on social axioms studies were discussed.

Social axioms among students in Sabah, Malaysia
Ismail, Rosnah Psychology & Social Work, Universiti Malaysia Sabah, Kota Kinabalu, Sabah, Malaysia
This study examined social axioms among Malay, Chinese, and Kadazan students enrolled in the Universiti Malaysia Sabah (UMS). The sample comprised 272 students (77 Malay, 81 Chinese, 77 Kadazan, and 38 others). Each student completed 82-item of Social Axioms Survey (SAS) on a 5-factor structure: Social Cynicism, Social Complex, Reward for Application, Fate Control, and Religiosity. The results indicated significance differences between gender on Social cynicism and Fate control. There are also significant differences between Malay, Chinese, and Kadazan on Fate control, Religiosity, and Social cynicism. Correlations between the Dimensions of the SAS and between the demographic variables and social axioms were examined.

Social axioms moderate the influence of positive "I"-convictions on hope
Bernardo, Allan B.I. Counseling and Edu. Psychology, De La Salle University, Manila, Philippines Kintanar, Niel Steve M. Department of Psychology, Ateneo de Manila University, Quezon City, Philippines
Two studies investigate the influence of personal convictions and social beliefs on trait hope (Snyder, 2000). Using transactional analysis theories of personality, Study 1 investigated how positive and negative convictions about oneself (I-convictions) and others (You-convictions) predict trait hope in Filipino students. Results showed that I-convictions positively predicted hope. Study 2 considered whether social axioms moderate the relationship between I-convictions and hope. The results indicate that social complexity amplifies the influence of I-convictions on hope, whereas social cynicism diminishes the same. The results indicate how appraisals of the social environment tapped by social axioms can modulate how personality dimensions influence positive cognitions such as hope.

Unraveling mysteries of the post-communist world: Cynicism that breeds mistrust and unhappiness - A cultural analysis of a cross-cultural phenomenon
Boski, Pawel Dept. of Psychology, Polish Academy of Sciences, Warsaw, Poland
Since early 1990s, there has been a flow of data showing extremely low levels of SWB in the post-communist world These findings are not sufficiently explained by objective indicators such as HDI or GDP. Indeed, this regional niche itself is responsible for 26% of variance in Diener's SWLS. This paper will present evidence that social cynicism is responsible for this phenomenon. The essence of the Communist rule which stayed in power for the length of 50-70 years, was creating a gap between official propaganda and experienced reality, i.e. cynicism generating potential. Macro-level data will be analyzed and cultural interpretations elaborated.

S-179: The rise of national intelligence in the Sudan

Fadi Al-Mawla El-Shiakh (chair)
This study provides data for the possible rise of national intelligence in the Sudan. The Draw Man Test was applied between 1964 and 2006, WISC-R and WISC-111 between 1988 – 2005, and WAIS – R between 1978 – 2007. This study shows that the national rise of intelligence per decade for the above test is 2.40, 2.04, and 5.66, respectively Various explantions were discussed regarding Flynn's effet.

The rise of national intelligence in the Sudan
Khaleefa, Omar Dept. of Psychology, University of Khartoum, Khartoum, Sudan
The rise of national intelligence in the Sudan This study provides data for the possible rise of national intelligence in the Sudan. The Draw Man Test was applied between 1964 and 2006, WISC-R and WISC-111 between 1988-2005 and WAIS-R between 1987-2007. The study shows that the national rise of intelligence per decade for the above tests is 2.90, 2.04 and 5.66, respectively. Various explantions were discussed regarding Flynn' effect.

S-180: Special features of self-regulated learning

Michaela Schmidt, Charlotte Dignath (chair)
Self-regulation is an important competence for learning. Therefore, in this symposium we present five approaches that examine important aspects of self-regulated learning and possibilities to support them. - Whitebread: The measurement of metacognition and self-regulation in young children. - Nurmi: Children's learning at primary school: Role of motivation and feedback - Perels et al.: Self-regulation interventions - Cardelle-Elawar & Sanz de Acedo Lizarraga: Shaping Teacher Identity Through Self-regulation - Lapka et al.: Fostering beneficial self-related cognitions as essential components of self-regulation in a challenging learning context Discussant: U. Trautwein, Germany.

The measurement of metacognition and self-regulation in young children
Whitebread, David Faculty of Education, University of Cambridge, Cambridge, United Kingdom
Observational approaches were developed to explore the development of self-regulatory and metacognitive abilities in young children (3-5 years). First, an observational coding scheme was constructed, which identifies verbal and non-verbal behaviours of self-regulatory and metacognitive abilities. Second the CHILD 3-5 checklist was developed, which could be used to assess the self-regulation of the children. 32 early years teachers collected evidence of metacognitive abilities evidenced by children during learning activities which were constructed to provoke metacognitive or self-regulatory behaviours. The data suggested that this scale can be used reliably, that it has external validity and a high level of internal consistency.

Children's learning at primary school: Role of motivation and feedback
Nurmi, Jari-Erik Department of Psychology, University of Jyväskylä, University of Jyväskylä, Finland
Learning consists of recursive interactions between the learner and his or her learning outcomes. On the one hand, learning is directed by students' motivation and interests, which then, being reflected on various self-regulation activities (e.g. planning, metacognition, avoidance, etc), contribute to learning. On the other hand, the outcomes of learning impact students' motivation and self-regulation, by modifying their interests, beliefs andvalues. The present presentation will test the described model by using several data sets in which children's motivation, task-focused behavior and academic skills is modeled across the first years of primary school.

Self-regulation interventions
Perels, Franziska Inst. für Pädag. Psychologie, Techn. Universität Darmstadt, Darmstadt, Germany Otto, Barbara Educational Psychology, University of Frankfurt, Frankfurt, Germany Schmitz, Bernhard Educational Psychology, TU Darmstadt, Darmstadt, Germany
The aim of the study is the implementation and evaluation of training programs to improve the self-regulated learning of students. These trainings are based on a process adaptation of Zimmerman's model of self-regulation and aim at enhancing self-regulation by specific strategies. The strategies are taught by means of contents of a specific subject, in our case mathematical problem solving. The trainings are evaluated regarding self-regulation as well as mathematical problem solving. The results show significant improvement of self-regulative competence as well as of mathematical problem solving. Important implications for research and practice can be drawn from these results.

Shaping teacher identity through self-regulation
Cardelle-Elawar, Maria Dept. Educational Psychology, College of Teacher Education, Glendale, USA Sanz de Acedo Lizarraga, María Luisa Psychology and Pedagogy, Public University of Navarre, Pamplona, Spain
This qualitative study describes the outcomes of in-service teachers enrolled in graduate classes. Teachers engaged a in self-regulated narrative-inquiry process that allowed them to situate themselves within their educational and historical context. They followed an interview protocol in pairs where they asked each other a series of questions related to their experiences on what keeps them on teaching. Meaningful descriptive narratives summarizing the interview results were analyzed for generative themes. Implications for research and teaching are discussed in regard the value of this self-regulatory inquiry process to better know themselves, learn about their students and improve their professional growth.

Fostering beneficial self-related cognitions as essential components of self-regulation in a challenging learning context
Lapka, Dominik Faculty of Psychology, University of Vienna, Wien, Austria Schober, Barbara Faculty of Psychology, University of Vienna, Wien, Austria Wagner, Petra Department of Psychology, University of Applied Sciences, Linz, Austria Reimann, Ralph Faculty of Psychology, University of Vienna, Wien, Austria Gradinger, Petra Faculty of Psychology, University of Vienna, Wien, Austria Spiel, Christiane Faculty of Psychology, University of Vienna, Wien, Austria
Efficient self regulated learning comprises also beneficial self-related cognitions. Because of demonstrable positive effects of self-efficacy, flexible implicit personality theory and functional causal

attributions on learning results, these aspects should be fostered especially in challenging learning contexts. Therefore the promotion of beneficial self-related cognitions regarding methodology is one aim of a learning program for psychology students called Vienna E-lecturing (VEL), which will be presented in this contribution. VEL was evaluated within a matched control group design with repeated measurements (n=168). We collected quantitative and qualitative data. First analyses show promising results about the effectiveness of VEL promoting beneficial self-related cognitions.

S-181: Learning and strategy selection in multi-attribute decision making

Arndt Bröder, Tilmann Betsch (chair)
The multiple strategy view has prevailed in decision research since Beach's and Mitchell's (1978) contingency model. Recent approaches also emphasize that decision strategies are selected contingent on environmental demands. The nature of the strategy selection process, however, is still undefined. Whereas the contingency model conceptualizes it as a deliberate cost-benefit analysis, other approaches are less explicit about bottom-up or top-down processing in this domain. The contributions to this symposium discuss various attempts to identify and model relevant processes in the strategy selection problem, such as reinforcement learning, intuition, associative processes, evidence thresholds, and effects of the learning regime.

How to replace multiple strategies by multiple representations: Simulations and evidence
Glöckner, Andreas Research on Collective Goods, Max-Planck-Institut, Bonn, Germany **Betsch, Tilmann** Sozial- und Organisationswiss., Universität Erfurt, Erfurt, Germany
In contrast to multi-strategy models, the parallel constraint satisfaction rule (PCS; Glöckner & Betsch, in press) proposes that decision making is based on one unique consistency-maximizing mechanism. Differences in choices result from different representations of decision tasks. One of the distinct predictions of the PCS rule is that the interpretation of information is changed within the decision process. Three experiments were conducted to test this hypothesis by comparing subjective cue validities before and after decisions. Results converge in showing that decision making is an inherently constructivist process, as suggested by the PCS rule.

Evidence accumulation: The "desired level of confidence" as a stopping rule in sequential information acquisition
Hausmann, Daniel Department of Psychology, University of Zürich, Zürich, Switzerland **Läge, Damian** Department of Psychology, University of Zürich, Zürich, Switzerland
Judgments and decisions under uncertainty are frequently linked to a prior search for relevant information. Evidence accumulation models assume an active and sequential information search until enough evidence has been accumulated to pass a decision threshold (stopping point of information search). With an information board and an attractive scenario (horse race betting) an individual evidence threshold ("desired level of confidence") was measured and tested against a fixed stopping rule (one-reason decision making) and the class of multi-attribute information integrating models. The results clearly favour the evidence threshold model. Implications and other influencing factors for modelling decision making processes are discussed.

The importance of learning when making inferences
Rieskamp, Jörg Max-Planck-Institut, Berlin, Germany
Previous experimental findings on probabilistic inferences are reexamined from a learning perspective. The observed learning process is modeled with the strategy selection learning (SSL) theory (Rieskamp & Otto, JEP:General, 135), which assumes that people select strategies according to the strategies' subjective success expectations, which are updated on the basis of experience. For both previous studies it is shown that people did not anticipate strategies' success from the beginning of the experiment. Instead, the behavior observed at the end of the experiments was the result of a learning process that can be well described by the SSL theory.

Influence of learning regime and cue format on decision strategies and exemplar-based judgment
Bröder, Arndt Inst. für Psychologie, Universität Bonn, Bonn, Germany **Newell, Benjamin** School of Psychology, University of New South Wales, Sydney, Australia
Strategy approaches of multiple cue decisions assume that cue-criterion relations are represented in memory which are later integrated in judgments. Two objections might be raised: First, often during learning it is not yet clear which information will later be cue or criterion. Second, rather than integrating cues during judgment, participants might retrieve exemplars of cue constellations to infer a criterion without using abstract cue-criterion relations. A series of experiments is reported which showed no support for the first objection when the learning regime was changed, whereas the latter view is supported for a specific kind of cue information format.

Towards an integrative model of automatic and deliberative decision making
Betsch, Tilmann Sozial- und Organisationswiss., Universität Erfurt, Erfurt, Germany **Glöckner, Andreas** Research on Collective Goods, Max Planck Institute, Bonn, Germany
We claim that the automatic and the deliberate system guide different operations when making a decision. Specifically we posit that the integration of information and the application of a selection rule are governed by the automatic system. The deliberate system is assumed to be responsible for information search, inferences and the modification of the set of information the automatic processes act on. We outline a theoretical framework that integrates automatic and deliberate processes and is able to model choices among both behavioural options and search strategies.

S-182: Psychology of excellence

Ai-Girl Tan, Jürgen Wegge (chair)
The papers address an essential theme in learning, thinking and creativity toward excellent performance. The underlying theories of excellence identified for the studies are Bandura's self-efficacy and Zimmerman's self-regulation, as well as Amabile's componential model of creativity, and creative cognition of Finke, Ward and Smith. These theories developed in the West are validated and applied in the Euro-Asian contexts. The existing theories related to psychology in excellence and learning seem to recognize the essentiality of contextual variables, and take task specificity as a focal and departure point of research.

The use of peer consensual technique to assess inventive ideas during generative and explorative phases
Lee Pe, Madeline Psychological Studies, Nanyang Techn. University, Singapore, Singapore
Using peer consensual assessment technique (Amabile, 1982) the inventive ideas (for a 'silent' alarm clock) generated during the generative (n = 690) and exploratory (n = 32) phases (Finke, Ward & Smith, 1992) were evaluated in groups of three among Singapore university students. The products were evaluated on two qualities: practicality and originality. High inter-rater reliability for practicality (r>.50) and moderate for originality (r=.30 - .49) were observed. The above seemed to suggest that moderate-high range of reliability may be sufficient to distinguish between the generative and exploratory phases (practicality: p =.018, Cohen d = .46; originality: p =.014, d=.50; creativity index: p=.007, d=.57).

High school students' creativity efficacies
Ho, Valerie Psychological Studies, Nanyang Techn. University, Singapore, Singapore **Tan, Ai-Girl** Psychological Studies, Nanyang Techn. University, Singapore, Singapore
High school students' creativity efficacies were measured based on the componential model of creativity (Amabile, 1983) and Bandura's (1997) self-efficacy: Creativity-relevant, domain-relevant, and affect (which signifies the presence of task motivation). A total of 389 students in Singapore rated on a Likert scale their efficacies. The students in the study perceived themselves with moderate creativity efficacies (M = 3-3.5). The efficacy scales were found to be significantly and positively correlated with domain-relevant efficacies and positive affect but negatively correlated with negative affect. Females rated significantly higher of perceived creativity efficacy (cognitive) and perceived creativity efficacy (affect) than did males.

Affectivity and performance among high school students
Yong, Lim-Chyi Psychological Studies, Nanyang Techn. University, Singapore, Singapore **Lee Pe, Madeline** Psychological Studies, Nanyang Techn. University, Singapore, Singapore **Tan, Ai-Girl** Psychological Studies, Nanyang Techn. University, Singapore, Singapore **Ow, Steve** Psychological Studies, Nanyang Techn. University, Singapore, Singapore
A total of 270 high school students' affectivity and performance were measured before (Time 1) and after (Time 2) service learning using Positive Affect and Negative Affect Schedule (PANAS) and task specific performance (e.g., interacting with the host and people in the receiving country). For comparison, their perceived creativity characteristics were measured using the Khatena-Torrance Creativity Perception Inventory (KTCPI). After a two month interval there was significant increase in PA (T2, mean difference .13, p<.003, Cohen, d = .20), and task specific performance – interaction (mean difference .35, p < .001 level, d = .36). Ratings of KTCPI at T1 and T2 remained. PA seemed can be a predictor for task specific performance interaction (17% of variance).

Self-efficacy and success in English as a foreign language
Özcan, Güzide Dünya Bankas Konutlar, Kocaeli, Turkey **Wegge, Juergen** Organisational&Social Psyc, TU Dresden, Dresden, Germany
We examined the relationship between English self-efficacy beliefs and English proficiency among gifted and average students in Turkey. A total of 231 high school students (105 gifted; 126 average) answered a self-efficacy questionnaire and took a foreign language aptitude and an English proficiency test. T-tests revealed a significant difference

in terms of perceived self-efficacy and performance (all p < .01), with gifted students having higher levels than average students. Controlling for several variables, self-efficacy was also found to be a significant predictor of English proficiency in both groups. The results support Bandura's claim that self-efficacy contributes independently to performance rather than simply reflecting cognitive skills.

S-183: Neurofeedback: Clinical applications in mental disorders

Stephan Mühlig (chair)
Whereas a robust body of research documents that there are biological predispositions jointly responsible for various mental disorders like attention deficit disorder, depression, anxiety, and obsessive compulsive disorder, on the other hand new research has shown that medication is only mildly more effective than placebo. Advances in EEG technology have given rise to a promising new alternative in treating these conditions with non-invasive behavioral methods: "EEG Biofeedback" or "Neurofeedback". This symposium intends to review new findings on the neurofeedback treatment of substance use disorders and to present new study results from application in the treatment of depression and ADHD.

Neurofeedback for treating substance abuse disorders: A review

Neumann-Thiele, Anja Inst. Klinische Psychologie, Tech. Universität Chemnitz, Chemnitz, Germany
Context: Neurofeedback (NFB) is a promising adjunctive psychophysiological approach for treating various mental disorders (e.g., ADHD, emotional and addictive disorders) enabling individuals to control their neuroelelctrical brain activity. Objective: The aim of the review is to determine the clinical potential capacity of NFB in the treatment of substance abuse disorders (SUD). Methods: We got the data by electronic literature search (Medline, Web of Science, Cochrane Library databases) supplemented by manual reference checks (important journals, references of most important articles) and included studies conducted between 1980 and 2007. Results of the meta-analysis are discussed and drawn conclusions are presented.

Exploring the effects of EEG-alpha-asymmetry-biofeedback in depressive disorders

Schneider, Sabine Inst. Klinische Psychologie, Tech. Universität Chemnitz, Chemnitz, Germany
Six patients with major depression were trained by a neurofeedback protocol within 15 sessions to influence neuronal asymmetrical activation of the PFC, as Davidsons MAAE (1995) proclaimed. EEG alpha measuring was standardized at frontal positions F3, F4 and Cz. Following Rosenfelds Protocol (1997), the protocol at hand got reward, if patients were able to increase left frontal activation. In result concentration, mood and relaxation were improved, depressive symptoms were reduced. Remarkable, the learning process showed a variable pattern and the frontal asymmetry was not significantly modified. Factors of the protocol, beeing effective in reduction of depressive symptoms, are critically discussed.

Feedback of slow cortical potentials and theta/beta ratio in ADHD results from a long term follow up

Gani, Cihan Institute of Medical Psycholog, University of Tuebingen, Tübingen, Germany Strehl, Ute Institute of Medical Psycholog, University of Tuebingen, Tübingen, Germany
Objective: To assess long term effects after cortical self-regulation-training. Methods: 52 children were randomly assigned to a training of slow cortical potentials (SCP), or to a Theta/Beta training.

Eleven children of the SCP group and 12 children of the Theta/Beta group took part in booster sessions more than 2 years after the last training session. Parents rated behavioral symptoms. Attention was measured with the Testbatterie zur Aufmerksamkeitsprüfung (TAP). Results: All improvements that had been observed at previous assessments turned out to be stable. In each group, 50% of the children no longer met the ADHD - criteria.

Neurofeedback in ADHD promising options and constraints from 30 years research

Strehl, Ute Inst. für Medizin. Psychologie, Universität Tübingen, Tübingen, Germany
Objective: Review of the results of 30 years neurofeedback for children with ADHD. Method: Neurofeedback in ADHD refers to the hypotheses of cortical underarousal. In the Electroencephalogram increased Theta and decreased Beta activity has been reported. Event-related potentials exhibit longer latencies and smaller amplitudes. Training protocols therefore aim at self regulation of e.g. Theta/Beta ratios, the Sensory-Motor-Rhythm or Slow Cortical Potentials. Results: Although promising results have been reported from the beginning, neurofeedback has not been accepted as a standard treatment. Shortcomings were small groups, no thoroughgoing diagnosis, lack of prospective studies, no control groups and no follow-up reports. Recently a number of studies promise to bring about a rebound.

S-184: Chronic pain in children and adolescents: From epidemiology and maintaining factors to treatment

Tanja Hechler (chair)
Chronic pain is a common childhood experience with headache and abdominal pain as the most frequent occurring pain experiences. Psychosocial and psychobiological mechanisms are thought to play a pivotal role in the development and maintenance of chronic pain (Kröner-Herwig, Thastum, Hermann). The important role of the parents and their impact on the child's pain behaviour has recently been demonstrated (Goubert). Effective treatment is essential to break the vicious cycle of pain, disability and emotional distress particularly for those children who display extensive disability (Hechler). The present symposium gives an overview on five vital topics explaining the development, maintenance and treatment of chronic pain in children and adolescents.

The burden of multiple pains in children and adolescents - Psychosocial correlates: Findings from an epidemiological study in Germany

Kröner-Herwig, Birgit Inst. für Klin. Psychologie, Universität Göttingen, Göttingen, Germany Steur, Hester Inst. für Klin. Psychologie, Universität Göttingen, Göttingen, Germany Vath, Nuria Inst. für Klin. Psychologie, Universität Göttingen, Göttingen, Germany
In an epidemiological study on more than 3600 German children and adolescents self-report data on pain in multiple locations was assessed. Ss were asked for the frequency of pain in 10 different locations. About 18% reported recurrent pains in at least 3 body regions. A combined score was used to create three groups (low, medium, high pain). First analyses of various biopsychosocial variables demonstrated an association of multiple pains with parental pain, psychosomatic symptoms, depressiveness, dysfunctional coping, negative climate within the family and school stress. Thus juveniles with high pain scores are characterized by various environmental stressors and emotional strains.

The role of pain coping strategies and pain-specific beliefs in pain experience in children and adolescents suffering from chronic pain: Findings from an epidemiological study in Denmark

Thastum, Mikael Dept. of Psychology, University of Aarhus, Aarhus, Denmark
Pain is one of the primary symptoms in children with arthritis (JCA) and has been shown to be a significant predictor of impaired psychosocial function. Possible modulators of pain perception in JCA children may be their use of pain coping strategies and health beliefs. Based on finding from a longitudinal study it will be discussed whether these factors can assist in understanding the different levels of pain and participation in social and physical activities, and whether it could be possible to identify and to focus interventions on the subgroup of children where the pain experience is in discordance with the disease activity.

Psychobiological aspects of the development of chronic pain in children and adolescents: Findings from experimental research studies in Germany

Hermann, Christiane Inst. für Neuropsychologie, ZI für Seelische Gesundheit, Mannheim, Germany
The development of chronic pain in children and adolescents involves the formation of pain memory and concomitant changes in the neural processing of pain-related stimuli. In a series of studies in children with recurrent pain of different origin using quantitative sensory testing and EEG recordings we have shown that recurrent pain is associated with altered pain sensitivity, however the observed changes depend on the type of pain problem. By contrast, hypervigilance to pain may evolve during the development of chronic pain regardless of its origin. The implications for the understanding and treatment of chronic pediatric pain will be discussed.

Chronic pain in children and adolescents: How much suffering in the families? Findings from studies in Belgium and the U.K.

Goubert, Liesbet Dept. Experimental Psychology, Ghent University, Ghent, Belgium Vervoort, Tine Department of Experimental and, Ghent University, Ghent, Belgium Eccleston, Christopher Psychology, University of Bath, Bath, United Kingdom Crombez, Geert Department of Experimental and, Ghent University, Ghent, Belgium
Objective: The studies presented in this presentation examined the effects upon parents of observing their child in pain. Methods: Findings will be presented of studies in parents of schoolchildren participating in a cold water test, and of a study in parents of children with chronic pain participating in a "speeded walking test". Results: Multiple regression analyses showed that catastrophizing about their child's pain was significantly related to more distress when observing their child in pain, both in parents of schoolchildren and parents of children with chronic pain. Discussion: The findings are discussed within a theoretical model of empathy and pain.

When pain is severe: Findings from a specialised German inpatient treatment for children and adolescents suffering from chronic headache and abdominal pain

Hechler, Tanja Vestische Kinderklinik Datteln, Vodafone Foundation Institute, Datteln, Germany Dobe, Michael Vestische Kinderklinik Datteln, Vodafone Foundation Institute, Datteln, Germany Kosfelder, Joachim Vestische Kinderklinik Datteln, Vodafone Foundation Institute, Datteln, Germany Damschen, Uta Vestische Kinderklinik Datteln, Vodafone Foundation Institute, Datteln, Germany Hübner, Bettina Vestische Kinderklinik Datteln, Vodafone Foundation Institute, Datteln, Germany Marbach, Sonja Vestische Kinderklinik Datteln,

Vodafone Foundation Institute, Datteln, Germany
Schroeder, Sandra Vestische Kinderklinik Datteln,
Vodafone Foundation Institute, Datteln, Germany
Zernikow, Boris Vestische Kinderklinik Datteln,
Vodafone Foundation Institute, Datteln, Germany
The present study investigated the effectiveness of an inpatient program for children with chronic pain by analyzing i) statistically significant changes in pain-related variables and emotional distress, and ii) the clinical significance of these changes. 200 children (7 - 18 years) were evaluated at baseline and 3 months post-treatment. Patients demonstrated significant changes in all variables. Seventy-seven percent, 49% and 20% demonstrated clinically significant changes in pain intensity, pain-related disability, and emotional distress. Results are promising in two ways: 1) an inpatient program might interrupt the negative effects of chronic pain; 2) the exploration of clinical significance has demonstrated utility and can be applied to future effectiveness studies.

S-185: Neural bases of autobiographical memory and the self

Pascale Piolino (chair)
Autobiographical memory has long been regarded as episodic in nature defined by a sense of the self in time and the mental reliving of subjective experiences from the encoding context. However, autobiographical memory is multifaceted, consisting of a set of self semantic information as well as episodic memories specific to an individual, which allow one to construct a feeling of identity and continuity. Yet, the neural bases of autobiographical memory remain debated. The aim of this symposium is to shed light on this issue by emphasizing its common and unique substrates compared to episodic and semantic memory, and the self.

In search of autobiographical memories: Neural bases of retrieval mechanisms
Piolino, Pascale CNRS - LPNCog, Institut of Psychology, Boulogne Billancourt, France
We aimed at identifying the cerebral structures whose synaptic function subserves the recollection of lifetime's episodic autobiographical memory and its breakdown. A correlative method was used between a sophisticated autobiographical memory test where the nature of memories could be strictly controlled across several time periods and resting-state brain metabolism using PET in healthy aged subjects, Alzheimer's disease and frontotemporal dementia. The findings revealed different mechanisms of deficits according to the group of patients. They mainly highlighted the distinct role of left prefrontal structures and right hippocampus in generative processes and in the recollection based on reliving of episodic details.

The self and its brain's subcortical-cortical midline system
Northoff, Georg Inst. für Psychiatrie, Medizin. Universität Magdeburg, Magdeburg, Germany
Recent concepts of self in neuroscience and psychology seem to consider the self an "inner entity" or as illusory. I here suggest a different concept of the self, a process-based concept that avoids either assumption. I characterize the self by subjectivity which empirically is supposed to be traced to a specific process, self-related processing. Based on current empirical imaging data, self-related processing is assumed to be mediated by neuronal activity in a subcortical-cortical midline system. In conclusion, I here present empirical evidence for neuronal mechanisms underlying our self which therefore can neither be considered an entity nor illusory.

Neural correlates of envisioning emotional events in the near and far future
D'Argembeau, Arnaud Dept. Cognitive Sciences, University of Liàge, Liàge, Belgium
Adaptive decision making depends crucially on the ability to mentally simulate emotional situations that might happen in the future. In this talk, I will present an fMRI study that investigated this process, focusing on the influence of the perceived temporal distance of positive and negative imagined episodes. The results suggest that the ventromedial prefrontal cortex might assign emotional values to mental representations of future events that pertain to long-term goals. On the other hand, striatal regions such as the caudate nucleus might support more concrete simulations of action plans to achieve rewarding situations in the near future.

Exploration of autobiographical memory: Modeling of a common and unique neural network compared to episodic and semantic memory
Burianova, Hana Dept. of Psychology, University of Toronto, Toronto, Canada Grady, Cheryl Dept. of Psychology, University of Toronto, Toronto, ONT, Canada
The objective of this study was to delineate a functional network common to autobiographical, episodic, and semantic types of retrieval, as well as a functional network unique to autobiographical retrieval. 12 healthy young adults participated in a visual fMRI experiment. The common network consisted of neural areas that covaried in activity across all three memory conditions, suggesting shared memory processes. The unique autobiographical network consisted of neural areas that give rise to processes of highly contextualized recollection and personal re-experiencing of events. These data contribute to our understanding of the neural organization of declarative memory.

Autobiographical memory after unilateral temporal lobe resection: Relation with volumes of medial temporal lobe structures of medial temporal lobe structures
Noulhiane, Marion CNRS - LPNCog, Institut of Psychology, Boulogne Billancourt, France
Medial Temporal Lobe (MTL) structures are crucial in episodic autobiographical memory (AM) retrieval. Their distinct involvement however still needs to be clarified. The recollection of episodic AMs covering the whole lifespan was assessed (TEMPau task) in patients after MTL resection to treat refractory epilepsy. MRI volumetric analysis of postoperative medial and lateral temporal structures were performed and related to performance. Patients with right and left MTL resection had impaired episodic AM across all time periods. A permanent and bilateral MTL network contributes to episodic AM, the MTL right structures being particularly responsive in reliving the encoding context regardless of remoteness.

Hippocampal activation for autobiographical memories over the entire lifetime in healthy aged subjects: An fMRI study
Viard, Armelle Inst. Cognitive Neuroscience, University College London, London, United Kingdom
We tested the two concurring theories of memory consolidation which propose either a temporary (standard model; Squire and Alvarez, 1995) or a permanent (multiple-trace model; Nadel and Moscovitch, 1997) role of the hippocampus in episodic memory retrieval. In the MRI, 12 healthy aged females recalled episodic autobiographical memories across 5 time-periods (from childhood and adolescence to the last 12 months) from cues selected by questioning a family member. Activation was detected mainly in the superior frontal gyrus, precuneus and hippocampus for all time-periods, thus supporting the multiple-trace model.

Moreover, bilateral hippocampal activation was particularly sensitive to rich episodic recollection characterized by autonoetic consciousness.

S-186: Testing neuropsychological models across populations: the advantages of examining measurement equivalence

Noel Gregg (chair)
In this symposium, a method for testing the generality of neuropsychological models will be described. Unfortunately, very few studies are available in which the measurement equivalence of commonly used assessment tools have been investigated with clinical populations. Five papers will be presented to illustrate the broad application of tests of measurement equivlence in the field of neuropsychology. Implications for the diagnosis and accommodation of clinical populations will be discussed.

Latent mean and covariance differences with measurement equivalence in college students with developmental difficulties versus the WAIS-III/WMS-III
Gregg, Noel Dept. of Psychology, University of Georgia, Athens, USA
Intelligence measures are usually part of the assessment battery for the diagnosis of adults with LD and/or AD/HD. The hypothesis of measurement equivalence was examined in two samples of college students with developmental difficulties, namely, a sample of students with LD (n= 186), and a sample of students with AD/HD (n=170). Scores on the third editions of the Wechsler Intelligence and Memory Scales were compared with an age-matched subset of the co-norming sample (n= 375). Results supported the assumption of measurement equivalence, but revealed marked differences across samples in latent variable variances and covariances, and latent variable means.

Latent mean and covariance differences with measurement equivalence in college students with LD and AD/HD versus the beck depression inventory normative sample
Bowden, Stephen Psychology, University of Melbourne, Victoria, Australia Weiss, Larry The Psychological Corporation, Harcourt Assessment, San Antonio, USA
Objective: Measurement equivalence was examined in college students with Learning Disability (LD: n=297) or Attention-Deficit/Hyperactivity Disorder (AD/HD: n=217). Methods: Scores on the Beck Depression Inventory-II (BDI-II) were compared with a representative, normative sample (n=528). A nonparametric confirmatory factor analysis was used to evaluate measurement equivalence across the groups. Results: A three factor model of BDI-II scores was found to fit best in each of the groups examined. Measurement equivalence was shown to hold across groups for this model. Conclusions: The same psychological constructs underlie mood symptoms in all groups.

Errors to avoid when comparing CFA models
Bandalos, Deborah Educational Psychology, University of Georgia, Athens, USA
A common type of measurement validity evidence is factorial validity, in which the researcher demonstrates that the number and nature of the factors underlying test items is consistent with theory. However, such studies are often conducted with a norming sample, and may not hold in for all subgroups within the population. Such differences are sometimes referred to as test or item bias, and are considered to be weaknesses of the test. However, in many cases differences in factor structure can yield important information about

how people in different groups understand and respond to items or stimuli.

Higher order factor analysis of the Reynolds intellectual assessment scales with a referred sample

Nelson, Jason School Psychology, University of Montana, Missoula, USA

The purpose of this presentation is to discuss the results of an investigation of the Reynolds Intellectual Assessment Scales (RIAS) using a referred sample (N=1163). More rigorous factor extraction criteria, in addition to those used in RIAS development, were investigated. Exploratory and higher-order factor analyses using the Schmid and Leiman procedure were conducted. All factor extraction criteria indicated extraction of only one factor. The proposed three-factor solution was not supported. Higher-order factor analyses indicated the majority of variance was accounted for by the general intelligence factor. Implications for the use of the RIAS with similarly referred individuals will be discussed.

Role of extended time on the SAT reasoning test for students with disabilities

Lindstrom, Jennifer RCLD, University of Georgia, Athens, USA

This study examined the latent structure of Scholastic Aptitude Reasoning Test (SAT®, 2005) across groups of examinees without disabilities tested under standard time conditions (N=2,476) and examinees with disabilities tested with extended time (N=2,476). First, CFA was used to assess the fit of a single-factor structure model for the Critical Reading, Math, and Writing sections. Next, a study of factorial invariance examined whether a common factor model for the three sections holds across the two groups at increasingly restrictive levels of constraint. Invariance across the two groups was supported for factor loadings, thresholds, and factor variances.

Application of measurement invariance in the field of neuropsychology

Coleman, Chris 335 Milledge Hall, UGA RCLD, Athens, GA, USA Bandalos, Deborah REMS, UGA, Athens, GA, USA

Neuropsychological tests are typically used to assess the functioning of people with a wide range of cognitive complaints (e.g., head injury; dyslexia; amnesia; attention problems). It is important to consider whether available tests measure the same constructs across these diverse populations. This presentation will address the principles of measurement equivalence and demonstrate how an extension of familiar confirmatory factor analytic (CFA) techniques can be used to evaluate measurement equivalence across groups.

S-187: Introduction to Japanese psychological rehabilitation therapy and its application on aged people

Asghar Dadkhah, Surender Kumar (chair)

Psychological rehabilitation therapy is the application of psychological knowledge and understanding on behalf of individuals with disabilities and society through such activities as research, clinical practice, teaching, public education, development of social policy and advocacy. Although the process of rehabilitation has traditionally been viewed as 'physical' in nature, it is now considered a multifaceted process involving not only the services of surgeons, occupational therapists, physiotherapists, and speech therapists but also exercise scientists, dieticians, and psychologists. Psychological treatment in rehabilitation often deals not only with the stresses imposed by disability and altered life

circumstances but also with issues of aging, hospitalization and medical tests and procedures.

Aging and rehabilitation

Teymouri, Fariba Dept. of Clinical Psychology, University of Welfare & Rehab., Tehran, Islamic Republic of Iran

Rehabilitation is designed for the individual who has individual needs. The one thing that must be understood is that it takes time to regain the functions that have been lost. In many cases most functions can return. It is essential that aged people survivors and their families recognize that many people recover from strokes to live long and rewarding lives. Medical, psychosocial, and vocational outcomes associated with rehabilitation interventions in multiple settings are being investigated among aged patients, TBI patients, end-stage renal disease patients, and stroke survivors. Prevention of secondary disability is a central focus of rehabilitation.

Aged people and relaxation

Roudsari, Moloud Pourmohammadi Dept. of clinical psychology, Kherad Roshangar Institute, Tehran, Islamic Republic of Iran

The society and surrounding often causes aged people to push their minds and bodies to the limit, often at the expense of physical and mental well-being. Relaxation techniques are helpful tools for coping with stress and promoting long-term health by slowing down the body and quieting the mind. Such techniques generally entail: refocusing attention (by, for example, noticing areas of tension); increasing body awareness; and exercises (such as meditation) to connect the body and mind together. Used daily, these practices can over time lead to a healthier perspective on stressful circumstances

Dohsa-hou and empowerment

Dadkhah, Asghar Dept. of Clinical Psychology, University of Welfare & Rehab., Tehran, Islamic Republic of Iran Pirmoradi, Mohammad Reza Dept. of Clinical Psychology, University of Welfare & Re, Tehran, Islamic Republic of Iran Masjedi, Abbas Dept. of Clinical Psychology, University of Welfare & Re, Tehran, Islamic Republic of Iran Asadi Bedmeski, Fariba Dept. of Clinical Psychology, University of Welfare & Re, Tehran, Islamic Republic of Iran Esbati, Mehrnoush Dept. of Counceling, University of Welfare & Re, Tehran, Islamic Republic of Iran

The purpose of the report is to study the efficacy of a Dohsa–hou, a Japanese Psycho rehabilitation method, in the treatment of major depression in adults. Each subject had 12 sessions of 45 minutes training over 4 weeks. Post-assessment and follow-up assessment was done. Findings from analyzing pre- and post-data from these tests indicated that depression was reduced. The Dohsa-hou method was followed by lower depression for these men, mainly evident in cognitive, somatic and affective symptoms.

Aging and tele rehabilitation

Dadkhah, Sajjad Dept. Information Technology, Multimedia University Malaysia, Kuala Lumpur, Malaysia

Tele-rehabilitation services are home-based, utilize a combination of traditional psychological rehabilitation and advanced technologies, and promote independence and the maintenance of skills necessary to remain living at home to reduce complications, hospitalizations, and unscheduled clinic and emergency room visits. The role of the patient is central, and through the use of communications technology, they are able to become actively involved in the process of managing their care and treatment interventions.. The integration of mental and physical care coordination and high technology for home monitoring provides for improved patient

compliance, improved service delivery to the home, early intervention of medical complications.

Aging and tele medicine

Dadkhah, Sepideh Medicine management, North Corolina University, Raleigh, USA Beiknejad, Mehdi Medicine management, North Corolina University, Raleigh, USA

The crowd is about to witness "tele-medicine,". Medical and educational specialists call it a virtual reality-like advancement that can enable doctors, researchers or medical students to witness procedures from afar via the Internet. Telemedicine and home monitoring. devices could be useful in treating the growing elderly population, according to doctors and home health experts. Technology may be one of the solutions for the looming aging crisis. The remote monitoring systems can track: Blood pressure; Heart rate; Temperature; Oxygen saturation Restlessness; and Weight gain. The technology is evolving and that he expects the devices to eventually include more features.

S-188: Advances in leadership research: The structure of leadership behavior and its influence on performance, strain, organizational cynicism and the role of the context

Joerg Felfe (chair)

In this symposium, the issue of leadership effectiveness is addressed. Taking an occupational health perspective, results indicate that sub dimensions of transformational leadership specifically influence followers' well being (Franke & Felfe). As Schilling shows leadership may influence cynicism even after controlling for other antecedents. Hoch and Wegge focus on participative and team shared leadership as predictors for performance in virtual conditions. Results from Heinitz and colleagues provide support for a 5 factor model of leadership that integrates transformational-transactional and Ohio State models. Using critical incident technique Pundt and colleagues found specific leader follower interactions in different types of organizations.

Transformational leadership and followers' well being

Franke, Franziska Inst. für Psychologie, Technische Universität Dresden, Dresden, Germany

Although transformational leadership has received much empirical attention over the last years, there is little research linking it with well-being. Moreover, the few existing studies only used combined measures of transformational leadership. Therefore, we examined the relationships between transformational and transactional leadership and perceived strain on the level of sub dimensions in two (industrial, administrational) samples (N = 710). As expected, we found specific relations for the leadership sub dimensions. Individualized consideration (IC) appeared to be the most important predictor. Moreover, it could be shown that the relation between leaders' IC and perceived strain is mediated by organizational climate.

Does leadership matter? Analyzing antecedents of organizational cynicism

Schilling, Jan Inst. für Psychologie, RWTH Aachen, Aachen, Germany

In times of rapid change, many employees develop cynical attitudes towards their company. The objective of the present study was to investigate the influence of leadership on organizational cynicism in comparison to other variables focused at organizational issues (procedural justice, trust in management, affective commitment). In a survey study with employees of a facility management company (n=190), leadership was shown to be related to organizational cynicism even though other variables (especially procedural justice) seem to be more important antecedents. The results give first evidence that personal leadership might impact employees' organizational cynicism beyond the influence of organizational variables.

The effectiveness of empowering leadership in virtual working conditions
Hoch, Julia Inst. für Psychologie, Technische Universität Dresden, Dresden, Germany Wegge, Jürgen Arbeits- und Org.-Psychologie, Technische Universität Dresden, Dresden, Germany
We investigate the impact of participative goal setting and team shared leadership on performance. In study 1 (N = 126, N = 120) participative goal-setting was significantly related to performance only when it takes place via video conferencing (compared to face-to-face conditions). In study 2 (N = 496) moderated regression analysis showed that shared leadership is more strongly related to performance in virtual teams than in face-to-face teams. In sum, the results suggest that participative and empowering leadership have a particular strong impact on work motivation and achievement in virtual working conditions.

Examining a five-factor model of leadership behavior
Heinitz, Kathrin Inst. für Psychologie, Freie Universität Berlin, Berlin, Germany Piccolo, Ronald F. College of Business Administra, University of Central Florida, Orlando, USA Bono, Joyce E. Dep. of Psyochology, University of Minnesota, Minneapolis, USA Rowold, Jens Psycholog. Institut, Westfälische Wilhelms-Universi, Münster, Germany Judge, Timothy A. Department of Management, University of Florida, Gainesville, USA
Four distinct but related studies were conducted to systematically examine overlap between the trans-formational-transactional and Ohio State models of leader behavior. In study one, we reviewed studies that measured both models and drew general conclusions about the uniqueness of five sets of leader behavior. In studies two, three, and four, we collected original data in diverse organizational settings to 1) test a five-factor model of leader behavior, and 2) generalize the model across several outcomes and cultures. Results provide support for a model of leadership that recognizes overlap across two popular models and uniqueness in the prediction of work outcomes.

The critical incident technique: A complement for questionnaires in leadership research?
Pundt, Alexander Inst. für Psychologie, Universität Rostock, Rostock, Germany Martins, Erko Inst. für Psychologie, Universität Rostock, Rostock, Germany Horsmann, Claes S. Inst. für Psychologie, Universität Rostock, Rostock, Germany Nerdinger, Friedemann W. Inst. für Psychologie, Universität Rostock, Rostock, Germany
We exemplify the application of the critical incident technique (CIT) in leadership research studying leader behavior in face-to-face interactions. As a result of interviews two years ago, seven different organizations were assigned to one of three types of organizational culture of participation (OCP). For this study, 29 employees from these organizations were asked to describe one face-to-face interaction with their leader which they perceived to be proceeding either well or badly. Results show qualitative differences between the types of OCP with regard to the characteristics of the reported interactions. Results imply that investigating leadership by CIT may complement questionnaire research.

S-189: Worksite health promotion: Measuring worksite health and work-life-balance

Christine Busch, Julia Grunt (chair)
Worksite health promotion should be designed on a sound health-related work-analysis. Most well-established instruments for the health-related work-analysis were developed for skilled industrial workers. They fail to address relevant characteristics and demands of new forms of work, e.g. freelancer, and of traditional target groups such as physicians, unskilled or migrant workers. In the course of this symposium recently developed and validated measures for health-related work-analysis will be presented. An additional focus will be on the analysis of work-life-balance and work-family-conflict. Particular methodological challenges will be discussed.

Development and validation of an instrument for the stress-related analysis of freelance work
Grunt, Julia Arbeits- und Org.-Psychologie, Universität Hamburg, Hamburg, Germany
A standardized self-report instrument for the stress-related analysis of freelance work was developed in order to improve the current scarcity of knowledge regarding the nature of this type of work. Reliability and construct-validity were analysed in 2 consecutive studies with German freelancers (N=147, N=226). The majority of measures were found to be satisfactorily valid, consistent and stable. Rating scores from freelancers with comparable working-conditions accorded to a promising degree; a finding which suggests a degree of objectivity in the measures used. Major challenges with regard to the analysis of complex work-activities (e.g. analyzing intellectual work, variability of conditions) are discussed.

Work-life balance of freelancers: Empirical results
Janneck, Monique Work and Org. Psychology, University of Hamburg, Hamburg, Germany
Freelance work is of growing significance for the job market as standard employment relationships wane. However, many freelancers face high levels of job insecurity and heavy workloads. In this study, the work and life situation of freelance knowledge workers (n=126) was investigated by means of a web survey, which was developed on the basis of a qualitative pilot study. Results show that work-life balance is an important predictor of economical success. While overall work-life balance is good, many freelancers fear work-family conflicts due to long and irregular working hours and severe job pressure, resulting in a high childlessness rate.

Stress-related job analysis for hospital physicians: Development and validation of an instrument
Keller, Monika Arbeits- und Org.-Psychologie, Universität Hamburg, Hamburg, Germany Bamberg, Eva Work and Org. Psychology, University of Hamburg, Hamburg, Germany Gregersen, Sabine Prävention u. Rehabilitation, BG Gesundheitsdienst u. Wohlf., Hamburg, Germany
High job-stress in hospitals leads to negative effects for the physician's health and for the quality of patient care. The aim of this study is to develop an instrument for stress-related job analysis for physicians in multiple steps. First, the current situation of German physicians was analysed in 13 interviews and 3 observations. Based on these studies, an instrument – a self-report questionnaire and an observational measure – was developed and tested in 13 interviews and 18 observations. In the last step, the instrument is tested statistically. The methodical approach and the benefit of the instrument will be discussed.

How to analyse work and health of the semi- and unskilled worker
Busch, Christine Inst. für Psychologie, Universität Hamburg, Hamburg, Germany Roscher, Susanne Work and Org. Psychology, University of Hamburg, Hamburg, Germany
In a German state project dealing with resource and stress management for the semi- and unskilled worker, we tested analysis and evaluation instruments: a screening instrument including interview and observation methods, a short questionnaire, including amongst others effort-reward-imbalance (ERI), and physiological parameters (e.g. cortisol saliva). The results (n= 60) show that well-established questionnaires do not fit this target group. Difficulties occurred in understanding and not being familiar with questionnaires. The found results point to the recommendation of focusing on observation and interview methods and physiological data.

Work-related risk factors for migrant workers' well-being in Germany: The role of work-family conflict
Grimme, Jennifer Arbeits- und Org.-Psychologie, Universität Hamburg, Hamburg, Germany Hoppe, Annekatrin Stanford Research Center, Stanford University, Stanford, CA, USA
The number of migrant workers in low-skilled labor is continuously increasing in Germany. This study examined whether migrant workers in a mailing company (n=89) encountered more work-related risk-factors in the psychosocial work environment than their German colleagues (n=149). Validated work analysis measures were linguistically and culturally adapted. As expected, migrant workers reported higher levels of work-related risk-factors; social isolation was the main predictor for physical strain. For both groups work-family conflict was the main predictor for psychological well-being, especially for female migrant workers. These findings may serve as a basis for future interventions.

The EFQM model: An instrument for worksite health promotion?
Vincent, Sylvie Work and Org. Psychology, University of Hamburg, Hamburg, Germany
The EFQM (European Foundation for Quality Management) Model is the most widely used framework for total quality self-assessment in Europe. The central question of the study is whether this instrument integrates concepts of worksite health promotion. The analysis is based on interviews pertaining to the EFQM-criteria "leadership" and "employee orientation" conducted among 25 employees of a Swiss service company. 15 constructs were extracted from the data using qualitative content analysis. The verification of the construct validity was conducted by means of the Multitrait-Multimethod approach. The results indicate that concepts of worksite health promotion constitute an integral component of the model.

S-190: Experiences with artistic production in different populations: Research and psychotherapy

Sonia Grubits (chair)
Presentation of three studies in Brazilian center west: analysis of indigenous children's drawings, study of children's drawings of the Pantanal region and reflections on therapeutic riding, bringing a historical background, symbols analyses and the horse representation. Other studies at French institutions propose the psychosemiotic approach of the act of creation in psychotherapy and the exact nature of the factors operators of changing. A study analyses primitive art work with psychological interpretations. The other study discusses the

changes in the way in which the Europeans perceived other people and their art over the course of time, particularly Brazil's indigenous people.

Kadiwéu children's drawings
Grubits, Sonia Dept. of Psychology, Dom Bosco Catholic University, Campo Grande, Brazil
Researches developed in the Kadiwéu Reserve in Brazilian center west based on children from two to nine years old drawings was aimed to observe the influence of the culture in the environment of the infantile development. The children's drawing is deeply marked by the basis of the culture and reflect the social values. In reference to the evolution of the infantile drawings, observed by the search of similarities between the drawings of the Kadiwéu children and the no Indian children had identified common subjects and traces as well as significant differences, mainly in the use of colors and forms.

Art and therapy: A psychosemiotic approach
Darrault-Harris, Ivan Lettres et Sciences Humaines, Université de Limoges, Limoges, France
One of the most important foundations of Art-Therapy consists in recognizing the power of transformation of creation. The psychosemiotic approach of the act of creation in psychotherapy proposes spotting the place of the patient-creator and the exact nature of the factors operators of changing. Two possible places must inter-act in art-therapy: a very commun place where the patient is speaking about his/her troubles and the place of creation, in a good distance from the precedent spot, where he/she creates a genuine work (perhaps belonging to Art) source of transformation.

Therapeutic riding and the symbols related to the horse
Grubits Freire, Heloisa Bruna Dept. of Psychology, Dom Bosco Catholic University, Campo Grande, Brazil
Therapeutic Riding involves people suffering with many kinds of disorders or deficiencies by stimulating self-esteem, self-confidence, developing space orientation, balance, laterality, communication; besides offering physical gains it also favours sensibility, corporeal scheme perception, and socialisation. The horse in the therapeutic context can be experienced as a symbol of primitive illustrations and with this symbolic dimension represents the domain of adverse forces revealing dreams and the horseman's desires. The representation of the horse is linked to imaginative activity and along the History many of them became famous and immortalized in the mythology and artistic manifestations representing characteristics or man's aspirations.

Works of primitive art: Psychological interpretations and cultural variations
Novello Pagliant, Nanta Lettres et Sciences Humaines, Université de Limoges, Limoges, France
Our intervention suggests wondering about the productions of Brazilian Primitive Art, stored in the Museum of Unconscious in Sao Paulo, Brazil. It will be clear that this artistic production, henceforth declared as national patrimony, is asking interesting questions. Can we give the status of artist to schizophrenic patients inmate in medical structures ? How can we know what means that huge production of written and plastic works ? We will see that the cultural influence has acted an important part in the production of these artists. Is it possible that an universal disease as schizophrenia elaborates again cultural features in its outside manifestation ?

Identity construction of pantanal children *Arantes, Michele Brazil*
This research aimed to investigate the identity construction process of some pantaneira school

children, MS – Brazil, through drawings, and also some psychosocial aspects involved in the process. The results of the analysis of the drawings show some aspects which are influencing the construction of the identity of the pantaneira children such as the habits, the tradition, the beliefs, the difficulties to access that region, imposing the isolation due to shyness of the pantaneiro man.

The representation of "The Other": The Images of the New World created by the Europeans
Pedroso, Maira CeReS - C.Sémiotique, IUFM du Limousin, Limoges, France
The purpose of this study is to discuss the changes in the way in which the Europeans perceived other people and their art over the course of time, particularly Brazil's indigenous people after what we call "The Discovery of the New World." The idea of "The Other," established in both the narrative and visual imagination, evolved over time — from the bizarre to the seductive, from disgust to exoticism, from the savage to the purely human — and we can see that these images were created by European society also to define themselves the way they wanted to be.

S-191: Career adaptability during the transition to adulthood

Vladimir Skorikov (chair)
In modern, post-industrial societies characterized by rapid social, economic and technological changes, career adaptability becomes progressively important as a factor of occupational success and satisfaction, particularly in young workers. Nevertheless, despite considerable interest in the issues of career adaptability among theorists and practitioners over the past 30 years, there has been almost no corresponding empirical research. Thus, the goal of this symposium is to bring together researchers from three continents, Australia, Europe, and North America, to discuss the results of their ongoing studies of career adaptability during the transition to adulthood in relation to career development theory.

Dimensions and criteria of career adaptability
Skorikov, Vladimir Dept. of Psychology, University of Hawaii, Hilo, USA
A review of the literature on career adaptability has been conducted to identify approaches to describing its dimensions and criteria. Career adaptability has been described as readiness to cope with both unexpected career changes and normative career transitions. The construct of career adaptability can be viewed as a set of interrelated, adaptive dispositions and behavior, such as planfulness, goal directedness, self-efficacy, self-regulation, exploration and decisiveness. Direct criteria of adaptability include career success and satisfaction, whereas indirect criteria comprise psychosocial adjustment and well-being. There is a clear need for empirical research on the relationships between career adaptability dimensions and its criteria.

Testing a self-regulation model of career adaptability in late adolescents
Creed, Peter School of Psychology, Griffith University, Gold Coast, Australia Fallon, Tracey School of Psychology, Griffith University, Gold Coast, Australia
Objectives: We viewed career adaptability in late adolescence as management of career concerns about future career, and hypothesised that concerns were the product of person and situation, and mediated by self-regulatory strategies. Method: We assessed concerns, self-regulatory strategies, goal orientation and social support in a large sample of university students. Results: We found that goal orientation and social support were associated with concerns, that self-regulation was associated with

concerns, and that self-regulation mediated between disposition, support and concerns. Conclusions: Career adaptability at this age can be fruitfully viewed as the application of self-regulation strategies to the management of career concerns.

Effects of career planning on occupational fit, satisfaction and self-perception in young adults
Porfeli, Erik Dept. of Behavioral Sciences, NEOUCOM, Rootstown, USA Skorikov, Vladimir Psychology, University of Hawaii at Hilo, Hilo, USA
The goal of this study was to test a hypothesis that career planning represents a positive factor of career adaptability in young adulthood manifested in occupational satisfaction and positive self-perception. Longitudinal relationships between career planning, attitudes toward work and college, work and school satisfaction, self esteem, self-efficacy and happiness were examined in a sample of 370 young adults using a three-wave, longitudinal design. Career planning was a significant predictor of each criterion of adaptability studied even controlling for previous levels of adaptation. The results suggest that career planning is an important component of career adaptability in young adulthood.

Achievement and social strategies during university studies and career characteristics 10 year later
Salmela-Aro, Katariina Dept. of Psychology, University of Jyväskylä, Jyväskylä, Finland Nurmi, Jari-Erik Dept. of Psychology, University of Jyväskylä, Jyväskylä, Finland
The aim of this longitudinal study was to examine the impact of achievement and social strategies during university studies on work career 10 years later. 297 university students completed the Strategy and Attribution questionnaire four times while in college and measures of career adaptation and success, such as employment status, burnout and engagement, 10 years later. Pessimistic and avoidant strategies during university studies predicted an unsuccessful transition from college to work, while high success expectations predicted a successful transition. The results suggest that functional achievement and social strategies are significant factors of career adaptability in young adulthood.

Career indecision and adjustment during the transition to adulthood
Skorikov, Vladimir Dept. of Psychology, University of Hawaii, Hilo, USA
The goal of this study was to test the hypothesis that career indecision represents a career adaptability problem during the transition to adulthood. In the course of a 6-year, longitudinal study, career indecision and various indicators of adjustment were assessed twice a year in high school and annually thereafter in a sample of 312 youths. Adolescent career indecision was predictive of distress in young adulthood. Different patterns of change in career indecision throughout adolescence were associated with different outcomes in terms of occupational adjustment. The findings suggest that career indecision and indecisiveness are indeed important, negative factors of career adaptability.

S-192: Applications of personality: Expanding construct, criterion and cultural horizons

Brian S. Connelly (chair)
Personality is alive and well across the globe as a central determinant of behaviors at work, at school, and at play. Amidst old-fangled challenges to applied uses of personality, our first two papers show that personality traits are closely linked to both work criteria and many counterproductive college behaviors, such as academic dishonesty and substance abuse. Next, two papers meta-analyti-

cally examine the structure and measurement of two Five Factor traits central to work and school, conscientiousness and agreeableness. Our final two papers show that culture moderates Five Factor traits and Core Self-Evaluations prediction of expatriates' job performance and adjustment.

Personality variables in industrial, work and organizational psychology: Current and new applications

Ones, Deniz S. *Dept. of Psychology, University of Minnesota, Minneapolis, MN, USA* **Dilchert, Stephan** *Dept. of Psychology, University of Minnesota, Minneapolis, MN, USA*

In this presentation, we draw on meta-analytic evidence to comprehensively summarize (a) the optimal and unit-weighted multiple correlations between the Big Five personality dimensions and behaviors in organizations, including motivation, job satisfaction, leadership, and job performance; (b) the generalizable bivariate relationships of conscientiousness and its facets with job performance constructs; and (c) the incremental validity of personality measures over cognitive ability. We also provide an evaluation of the merits of alternatives that have been offered in place of traditional self-report personality measures for organizational decision making.

Counterproductive college behaviors: Using personality to predict violence, theft, drug abuse and academic dishonesty among students

Dilchert, Stephan *Dept. of Psychology, University of Minnesota, Minneapolis, USA* **Ones, Deniz S**. *Dept. of Psychology, University of Minnesota, Minneapolis, MN, USA*

A comprehensive scale of Counterproductive College Behaviors was developed to measure destructive and illegal behaviors. Six hundred students answered questions about cheating on exams, lack of effort, substance abuse, illegal activities on campus (including violence), as well as other criminal behaviors (e.g., theft, fraud). A Big Five personality inventory was used to predict who would engage in such behaviors while in college. Agreeableness and conscientiousness facets predicted both admitted incidents as well as peer-ratings of deviance. While agreeableness predicted interpersonal deviance (e.g., violence toward other students), conscientiousness related to deviance targeted at the institution (e.g., theft of university property).

Conscientiousness: Investigation of its facet structure through meta-analytic factor analysis

Connelly, Brian S. *Dept. of Psychology, University of Minnesota, Minneapolis, USA* **Davies, Stacy E**. *Dept. of Psychology, University of Minnesota, Minneapolis, MN, USA* **Ones, Deniz S**. *Dept. of Psychology, University of Minnesota, Minneapolis, MN, USA* **Birkeland, Adib** *Carlson School of Management, University of Minnesota, Brooklyn, NY, USA*

The Big Five personality factor of conscientiousness has been recognized as an important determinant of behavior in health, clinical, work, and educational psychology. However, debate continues about the structure of conscientiousness's defining facet traits. We meta-analyzed the relationships between conscientiousness measures on seven major personality inventories. We factor-analyzed this meta-analytic intercorrelation matrix to sort conscientiousness's facet traits. We then meta-analytically estimated the relationships among these conscientiousness facet traits and their relationships with Big Five personality factors. Our results identify compound personality traits (traits composed of Conscientiousness and other Big Five Factors) and offer new insights into the structure of conscientiousness.

Agreeing on agreeableness: Interrelations among agreeableness constructs

Davies, Stacy E. *Dept. of Psychology, University of Minnesota, Minneapolis, MN, USA* **Connelly, Brian S**. *Dept. of Psychology, University of Minnesota, Minneapolis, MN, USA* **Ones, Deniz S**. *Dept. of Psychology, University of Minnesota, Minneapolis, MN, USA* **Birkland, Adib** *Carlson School of Management, University of Minnesota, Minneapolis, MN, USA*

Personality theorists have generally convened on recognizing the Five Factor Model as an organizing structure for personality traits, but the lower level facet structure of these facets remains nebulous. We examined the facet structure of agreeableness. Raters independently sorted agreeableness measures into facet categories, and we meta-analyzed the relationships within facet categories and with measures of the other Big Five personality factors. Our results highlight the need to convene on agreeableness's structure and suggest that further attention to facet taxonomies may improve agreeableness measures.

European big five findings of the iGOES (international Generalizability of Exaptriate Success) project

Albrecht, Anne-Grit *Business Psychology, Leuphana University Lueneburg, Lüneburg, Germany* **Paulhus, Frieder** *Inst. für Business Psychologie, Leuphana Universität, Lüneburg, Germany* **Dilchert, Stephan** *Department of Psychology, University of Minnesota, Minneapolis, MN, USA* **Ones, Deniz S**. *Department of Psychology, University of Minnesota, Minneapolis, USA*

The large European expatriate body is underrepresented in present studies, typically including US-American expatriates working in Asia. Likewise, the Big Five, being well-explored in domestic settings are understudied in expatriate settings. Big Five personality data from the iGOES project covering 550 expatriates and seven European countries is presented. Mean level differences of personality scores were computed. The predictive validity of the Big five for expatriate job performance and adjustment was analyzed. Analyzes suggest some variance in personality scores and effect sizes after statistical artifacts have been taken into account. Hence, analyses were conducted testing the moderating effect of culture.

The role of core self-evaluations in the success of European expatriates

Paulus, Frieder *Inst. für Business Psychologie, Leuphana Universität, Lueneburg, Germany* **Albrecht, Anne-Grit** *Inst. für Business Psychologie, Leuphana Universität, Lüneburg, Germany* **Dilchert, Stephan** *Department of Psychology, University of Minnesota, Minneapolis, USA* **Ones, Deniz S**. *Department of Psychology, University of Minnesota, Minneapolis, USA*

Core Self-Evaluations (CSE) as defined by Judge, Locke, Durham, and Kluger (1998) has been shown to be a valid predictor of different job-related criteria in domestic settings (e.g., Judge & Bono 2001). Even though studies considered some constituent traits of CSE to be relevant for adjustment and job performance during international assignments, the higher order personality construct has mostly been neglected in the field of expatriate research. Within the iGOES project we examined the role of CSE for adjustment and performance in a sample of 500 German expatriates working across Europe and analyzed moderating influences of host-country cultures.

S-193: Integrative Analysis of Longitudinal Studies on Aging (IALSA)

Scott Hofer, Andrea Piccinin *(chair)*

The IALSA research network is comprised of substantive and statistical researchers for innovative and coordinated analysis of over 25 of longitudinal studies on aging. The initial program of research focuses primarily on changes in cognition and in health, and in explaining cognitive change in the context health-related change with age. Collaborations across research teams lead to decisions regarding measurement and analysis protocol which permit integrative analysis, synthesis of results, and sensitivity analysis within and across studies. In this symposia, we describe the research network and process and present new results from several studies that exemplify IALSA research aims.

Integrative analysis of longitudinal studies on aging: A coordinated analysis process for cross-validating and extending results on aging-related change

Hofer, Scott *Human Dev. and Family Science, Oregon State University, Corvallis, USA* **Piccinin, Andrea** *Human Dev. and Family Science, Oregon State University, Corvallis, USA* **Spiro III, Avron** *MAVERIC, VA Medical Center, Boston, USA* **Martin, Mike** *Dept. of Gerontopsychology, University of Zurich, Zurich, Switzerland*

The IALSA research network is an open international network of people, data and methods to collaborate in the analysis and synthesis of existing longitudinal data on aging. The network features 1) Simultaneous evaluation of longitudinal data, to test, replicate, and extend prior findings and theories of aging; 2) Harmonization of variables, leading to more robust measurements with broader validity; and 3) Coordinated analysis of existing data with state-of-the-art methods to ask new and old questions emphasizing within-person changes in contrast to between-person age differences. This program of coordinated longitudinal research will build integrative models of aging through the evaluation and extension of existing theoretical models.

Cognitive decline as an index of subsequent dementia and death

Johansson, Boo *Dept of Psychology, University of Gothenburg, Gothenburg, Sweden* **Thorvaldsson, Valgeir** *Psychology, University of Goteborg, Goteborg, Sweden*

Acceleration in cognitive decline is observed several years prior to clinical diagnosis of dementia and subsequent death in an initially non-demented, population-based sample. The sample was drawn from the Göteborg H70 study, Sweden. Individuals were assessed at age 70 and on up to 12 subsequent occasions over 30 years or until death. Data were analyzed using mixed linear change-point analysis, using a profile likelihood approach. We identified a substantial acceleration in decline prior to diagnosis of dementia and death across cognitive domains. Normative change can be discerned from pre-clinical change and terminal decline long before a dementia diagnosis or death.

Impact of vascular disease on cognitive aging

Spiro III, Avron *MAVERIC, VA Medical Center, Boston, USA* **Brady, Christopher** *MAVERIC, VA Boston Healthcare System, Boston, USA*

The role of health in cognitive aging deserves detailed examination. We consider the impact of vascular diseases on cognitive trajectories. Since 1993, over 1000 older men (aged 50-90) from the Veterans Affairs Normative Aging Study completed a cognitive assessment at each medical exam. We compared age trajectories on cognitive tasks among men with different prevalent vascular conditions, adjusting for education. Men who had experienced an MI did worse on 2 of 5 tasks (MMSE, Animal Fluency) than those with no vascular disease, or those with hypertension or angina. Age-related trajectories vary depending on disease prevalence, suggesting the importance of considering health in cognitive aging.

The effect of depressive symptoms on cognitive decline in a population-based sample of older adults followed for 11 years
Anstey, Kaarin Center for Mental Health Res., Australian National University, Canberra, Australia Luszcz, Mary Psychology, Flinders University, Adelaide, Australia
Objectives: To evaluate the effect of depression on cognitive decline. Methods: A population based sample (n=2078 at baseline, aged 65-101) was followed for 11 years. Multilevel models evaluated the effect of change in depression (the Centre for Epidemiological Studies Depression Scale) on change in memory (picture recall task) and processing speed (digit symbol substitution test), adjusting for covariates. Results: Increase in depressive symptoms was associated with faster rate of decline in Memory (β = -.04, p = .004) and Processing Speed (β = -.12, p < .001). Conclusion: Prevention of late-life depression may reduce cognitive decline at the population level.

The modelling of individual trajectories of cognitive decline from studies with missing data
Matthews, Fiona MRC Biostatistics Unit, Cambridge, United Kingdom Muniz, Graciela MRC Biostatistics Unit, Institute of Public Health, Cambridge, United Kingdom
Objectives: We aim to measure individual cognitive decline in the presence of potentially informative missing data. Methods: Latent growth mixture and Bayesian random effects models were fitted to MMSE scores from individuals in the MRC Cognitive Function and Ageing Study, where 13,004 individuals were followed over 10 years with continuous monitoring death data. Results: Classes of individuals with similar development were identified in addition to class specific risk factors. The role of the missing data on the modelling process was investigated. Conclusions: Missing data play a key role in longitudinal studies, its adequate modelling is necessary to assure accurate results.

Twelve-year correlated longitudinal changes in cognition in old age
Zimprich, Daniel Inst. für Gerontopsychologie, Universität Zürich, Zurich, Switzerland Martin, Mike Dept of Gerontopsychologie, Universität Zürich, Zurich, Switzerland
We will describe 12-year correlated changes in cognitive abilities—fluid and crystallized in-telligence, memory, processing speed—in old age. Data of three measurement occasions and 313 individuals (age at T1: 63 years) come from the Interdisciplin-ary Longitudinal Study of Adult Development (ILSE). After having established strong measure-ment invariance, across the 12 years all four abilities showed a decline. Decline was strongest in memory (d = -.97), followed by processing speed (d = -.61), fluid intelligence (d = -.57), and crystallized intelligence (d = -.14). Correlated changes ranged from .72 (fluid intelligence and processing speed) to .41 (memory and processing speed).

Longitudinal change of individual differences in verbal learning in old age
Rast, Philippe Bern, Switzerland Zimprich, Daniel Dept. of Gerontopsychology, University of Zurich, Zurich, Switzerland van Boxtel, Martin School of Mental Health, Maastricht University, Maastricht, Netherlands Jolles, Jelle Dept. of Neurocognition, Maastricht University, Maastricht, Netherlands

Verbal learning is adequately described by three individually varying parameters: Initial level (beta), potential maximum performance (alpha), and learning rate (gamma). We present structured latent growth curve models that capture six-year long-itudinal changes of these parameters in old age. Data come from the Maastricht Aging Study (N = 327, Mean age at T1: 68 years). Results show a significant increase in beta across time. All change variances were significant. Changes in learning parameters were correlated (beta-alpha: .21; beta-gamma: .49; alpha-gamma: -.42), showing that initial performance develops together with max-imum performance and learning rate, while the latter two tend to develop apart.

S-194: Psychology at the United Nations: What psychologists do and how you can influence global policies and events

Judy Kuriansky (chair)
Participants at the current ICP meeting are presenting important work on varied topics which can be important contributions to multi-stake-holders in international issues, including govern-ments, NGOs, civil society, the business sector, and the United Nations and its agencies. The presenters cover how participants can make their expertise known at the UN; current issues facing the UN; work psychologists are doing as UN representatives (e.g. on climate change); the first Psychology Day at the UN; steps for advocacy on local and interna-tional levels; models of partnerships among psy-chological researchers, clinicians and governmental organizations; and how students can be involved.

Psychologists making a difference at the UN and on the global stage: Specific advances in ageing and violence against women and establishing the First Psychology Day
Denmark, Florence Pace University, USA
Dr. Denmark is the Main Representative for ICP and for APA at the UN and a member of the Executive Committee of the UN /NGO Committee on Mental Health. Serving her third term as Chair of the UN /NGO Committee on Ageing, she attends meetings of CONGO, and is a member of the Committee on the Status of Women and two of its subcommittees (on older women and on violence against women). She will describe how she worked with other NGO psychologists to establish the first-ever Psychology Day at the UN, held October 10th and 11th, 2007. She would be happy to make arrangements for anyone coming to NY to visit the UN.

Psychologists at the United Nations: Advocacy, activities, and opportunities to impact world governments, policies and events on human rights, climate change, AIDS, poverty and other global issues
Kuriansky, Judy Clinical Psychology, Columbia Univ Teachers College, New York, New York, USA
As a main representative to the UN for IAAP for many years, and on the board of the UN Committee on Mental Health, Dr. Kuriansky will present an overview of what psychologists do at the United Nations and give guidelines as to how ICP attendees can get involved in various projects and activities of the UN from wherever they live. These include providing their research relevant to UN issues, joining committees, and advocating on local and national levels. Sample advocacy action will be presented (e.g. regarding disaster risk reduction) as well as upcoming projects of the NGOs accredited at the UN about human rights.

Addressing climate change and disaster: Examples of service learning partnerships between educational institutions, the UN and civil society
Weissbecker, Inka Dept. of Psychology, University of Louisville, Louisville, USA
As a specialist in disasters and climate change, Dr. Weissbecker will describe several international projects involving the United Nations, educational institutions, and civil society. She will discuss ways in which multiple stakeholders such as governmen-tal and international agencies, academics, and students can come together and address issues that we face as a global community. Specifically, she will talk about a service learning project on disaster mental health preparedness in Belize, a high school project on climate change in Tanzania, a class on global perspectives in psychology and about her work as an NGO representative of IUPsyS at the United Nations.

S-195: Social and individual responses to terror and trauma (under the auspices of the International Network of Psychologists for Social Responsibility; INPsySR)

Ferdinand Garoff, Miriam Schroer (chair)
We constantly witness conflict and social injustice all over the world. From the perspective of a socially responsible science, psychology has to do its best to alleviate these conditions: to contribute to the reduction of direct and structural violence and the development of peaceful and socially just conditions. InPsySR aims to facilitate this goal with this symposium on social and individual responses to terror and trauma. Contributions look at media representations of terrorism and public responses to the threat of terror, expert recommen-dations for alleviating the impact of mass-casualty events, and individuals' and communities' coping with traumatic events.

The Jena terrorism study: Media data
Haußecker, Nicole Inst. für Psychologie, Universität Jena, Jena, Germany Frindte, Wolfgang Department of Psychology, Friedrich-Schiller-University, Jena, Germany Schneider, Johannes Department of Psychology, Friedrich-Schiller-University, Jena, Germany
First results of a two-year qualitative and quanti-tative content analysis of the news coverage about terrorism are summarized in this paper. Newscasts of TV-channels ARD, ZDF, RTL, Sat1, N-TV and Arte will be analyzed from mid-august 2007 on, over a first period of nine month. Content-related aspects, e.g. presentation of terrorist threats, causes, results and attempts of assertion, as well as Emotionalization and Stereotypization of the cov-erage will be levied with the codebook. Commu-nications-scientific approaches serve as theoretic background, to clarify how and why News coverage could strengthen the saliency of associations to terrorism and advance causal interpretations and assessments.

The Jena terrorism study: First interview data
Schneider, Johannes Inst. für Komm. Psychologie, Universität Jena, Jena, Germany Frindte, Wolfgang Institut für Psychologie, Abt. für Komm.Psychologie, Jena, Germany Haußecker, Nicole Inst. für Psychologie, Universität Jena, Jena, Germany
Our research program contains a three-wave long-itudinal study including interviews and short questionnaires focussing on individual construc-tions about the phenomenon of terrorism (Duration 2 years, N=100). This paper presents results of the first and second wave. Of specific interest are the general attitude towards terrorism as the acceptance

of anti-terror operations or the acceptance of terror groups and causal explanations, the impact of terrorism on daily life, intra- and intergroup behaviour. Also the influence of social and individual mediator variables (e.g. sociodemographic and socioeconomic characteristics, xenophobia, social dominance orientation, authoritarianism, personal values and religious beliefs, media reception) will be investigated.

Managing the psychology of fear and terror: Results from an assembly of experts

Seyle, Conor *Psychology Beyond Borders, Austin, USA* **Ryan, Pamela** *Psychology Beyond Borders, Austin, TX, USA* **Naturale, April** *N/A, Psychology Beyond Borders, Austin, TX, USA*

In 2004 an International Assembly brought together experts in the fields of fear, terror, and trauma to develop guidelines for how societies can reduce the impact of terror attacks and natural disasters. Based on research in the psychology of trauma, terrorism, and related fields, attendees developed five recommendations for mediating the impact of mass-casualty events: facilitation of informed dialogue about terrorism; building societal resilience through preparedness, treatment, and community support; facilitation of collaborations across people working in different domains related to terrorism; exploring and modeling conflict resolution methods; and encouraging and supporting moderates over extremists. Recommendations are discussed in detail.

Does collective trauma affect individual processing of traumatic crises?

Garoff, Ferdinand *Helsinki, Finland* **Lähteenmäki, Virpi** *FiPSR, Espoo, Finland*

Traumatic crises are sudden and unexpected events resulting in serious loss and happen universally. In Collective cultures insecure political situations, as in Palestine can create collective traumas. This presentation examines the effects of collective traumas on individuals processing traumas. The study is based on interviews and simulated debriefing groups of 28 traumatized Palestinians. There were changes in what was considered normal and in defense mechanisms: heroism and nationalism and too early comforting limited the room from normal grief. Too much emphasis was given to religion, lessening the subjectivity of individuals. People became easily irritated or isolated and revengeful. The conclusion is that the collective traumas significantly influence the process of traumas.

Listening to children's experiences of war and evacuation

Palonen, Kirsti *Helsinki, Finland*

The first phase of the case study took place in four refugee camps during and after the summer war 2006. The second part took place in Beddawi and Shatilla camps during and after the armed clashes in Nahr el-Bared camp in summer 2007. The staff of a Palestinian NGO asked the children to tell stories using the Storycrafting method. Although the choice of the theme was free the children told about their traumatic experiences. Children's experiences, reactions and means of coping were analysed. The predominant reaction was a fear to be killed. Playing helped children to cope. The storycrafting procedure creates an interaction between child and adult, which has therapeutic effect.

S-196: Protective factors and supportive environments for lesbian, gay and bisexual adolescents

Carol Goodenow (chair)

Lesbian, gay, or bisexual (LGB) adolescents are more likely than heterosexual youth to experience victimization, suicidality, and other negative outcomes, so it is important to identify personal and environmental factors that may reduce their risk. This symposium addresses several of these factors: LGB adolescents' perceptions of social support and other protective characteristics; the attitudes, beliefs and behaviors of school staff and heterosexual peers toward sexual minority youth; and specific interventions and school features associated with more positive environments for these adolescents. Discussion of the five papers will focus on opportunities for nurturing healthy development of LGB young people.

Factors protective against self-harm in gay, lesbian and bisexual youth

Goodenow, Carol *Northboro, USA*

Recent research has documented elevated rates of suicidal ideation and attempts among gay, lesbian, and bisexual adolescents. Identifying factors that may protect against suicidality and other self-harm among these youth is critical. Logistic regression analyses examined predictors of self-harm among sexual minority adolescents (n=219) participating in a larger statewide population-based survey of 50 high schools. Perceiving social support from key adults, doing well in school, and attending a school with a gay/straight alliance were significantly associated with lower rates of suicide attempts and other self-harming behavior. Protective effects were stronger for male than female gay/lesbian/bisexual adolescents.

The role of protective factors in reducing the odds of teen pregnancy Iinvolvement among bisexual adolescents in Canada and the U.S.

Saewyc, Elizabeth *School of Nursing, University of British Columbia, Vancouver, Canada* **Homma, Yuko** *School of Nursing, University of British Columbia, Vancouver, Canada* **Skay, Carol** *School of Nursing, University of Minnesota, Minneapolis, USA* **Pettingell, Sandra** *School of Nursing, University of Minnesota, Minneapolis, USA* **Poon, Colleen** *Research, McCreary Centre Society, Vancouver, Canada*

Population surveys of youth in school have consistently found higher rates of teen pregnancy among bisexual vs. heterosexual adolescents, but few studies have examined predictors of teen pregnancy for sexual minority youth. This study examined whether protective factors similarly reduced the odds of pregnancy involvement for sexually active bisexual and heterosexual male and female students in 3 cohorts of high school surveys in both British Columbia and Minnesota (Cohort Ns=21,560 to 70,561). Age-adjusted odds ratios, separately by gender and orientation group, found key protective factors were similar for all cohorts and orientations, but fewer protective factors for bisexual youth overall.

The relationship between school context and heterosexual students' attitudes about homosexuality

Horn, Stacey *School of Education, University of Illinois, Chicago, IL, USA*

This study investigated the impact of school context on ninth- through twelfth-grade heterosexual students' (n = 1070) attitudes about homosexuality and sexual prejudice. Using a self-report questionnaire participants responded to items regarding their beliefs about homosexuality, whether they had a gay or lesbian (GL) friend, comfort with GL peers, and hypothetical scenarios regarding exclusion and teasing of GL peers in two schools that differed in the number of safe school practices implemented. Analyses found that school context predicted most measures of attitudes toward homosexuality: students in the school with more safe schools practices exhibited more tolerant attitudes.

Safer sexual diversity climates: An evaluation of Massachusetts' safe schools program for gay and lesbian students

Szalacha, Laura *College of Nursing, University of Illinois, Chicago, USA*

This paper investigates faculty, staff and administrators' perceptions of the sexual diversity climate (SDC) in Massachusetts secondary schools, based the implementation of recommendations of the Safe Schools Program for Gay and Lesbian Students (SSP). Data were collected from 683 professional staff members from a stratified random sample of 35 schools. There were statistically significant positive differences in SDC where one or more of the SSP recommendations were implemented, especially with regard to teacher training, with differential effects by gender. This study provides valuable information on ways to establish safer sexual diversity climates in secondary schools to benefit all members.

Attitudes and behaviors of school staff regarding health promotion services for lesbian, gay and bisexual youth

Anderson, Clinton *Lesbian, Gay, Bisexual Issues, American Psychological Ass., Washington, USA* **Tomlinson, Hank** *Lesbian, Gay, Bisexual Issues, American Psychological Assn., Washington, DC, USA*

This paper examines the self-perceived roles of school counselors, nurses, psychologists, and social workers regarding delivery of health promotion services to lesbian, gay, bisexual and questioning (LGBQ) youth. Results include information gathered from a preliminary needs assessment and from data collected before and after participation in a training workshop designed to increase intentions to provide services—particularly related to HIV prevention—to LGBQ youth. Discrepancies between school professionals' attitudes about their roles and their actual delivery of services existed across all health-promotion behaviors. Participation in the training was associated with intentions to provide more and better services to LGBQ youth.

S-197: Cultural patterns of family relationships and value orientations

Gisela Trommsdorff, Cigdem Kagitcibasi (chair)

This interdisciplinary symposium brings together an international group of scholars from five countries on the basis of the cross-national "Value of Children and Intergenerational Relations Study". The papers deal with cultural patterns of family relationships, integrating sociological, anthropological and psychological perspectives. They entail comparative studies of exchange in kinship systems, parenting, adolescents' family models, values, religious and future orientations, and variations in family relations across generations. The contributions serve to demonstrate the usefulness of a cross-cultural approach for the theoretical and methodological advancement of studies on family and values.

Cultural patterns of exchange in kinship systems: Results from a comparative survey in eleven societies

Nauck, Bernhard *Inst. für Soziologie, Techn. Universität Chemnitz, Chemnitz, Germany*

The paper integrates the institutional approach of social anthropology and the interactionist approach of family sociology and social gerontology, in relating the institutional settings in societies to the major interaction dimensions "opportunity", "communication and emotional closeness" and "mutual help". A data set of 7.475 standardized interviews with mothers from 11 societies, comprising 38.539 kinship relationships, is used to describe cross-societal variations of kinship interaction types.

Multivariate regression analysis on "closeness" and "mutual help" show that the institutional settings have a stronger effect on kinship relationships than the positioning of the respondents in the social structure or their individual attitudes.

Values of children and family models of adolescents: An eleven-culture study

Mayer, Boris Inst. für Psychologie, Universität Konstanz, Konstanz, Germany Trommsdorff, Gisela Inst. für Psychologie, Universität Konstanz, Konstanz, Germany

Starting from Kagitcibasi's (2007) conceptualization of family models, this study compared N = 2961 adolescents' values across eleven cultures and explored whether patterns of values were related to the three proposed family models through cluster analyses. Three clusters with value profiles corresponding to the family models of interdependence, emotional interdependence, and independence were identified on the cultural as well as on the individual level. Furthermore, individual-level clusters corresponded to culture-level clusters in terms of individual cluster membership. The results largely support Kagitcibasi's proposition of changing family models and demonstrate their representation as individual-level value profiles across cultures.

Adolescent future orientation and the role of maternal parenting: A German-Turkish comparison

Albert, Isabelle Faculty of Humanities, University of Luxembourg, Walferdange, Luxembourg Klemenz, Cordelia Department of Psychology, University of Konstanz, Konstanz, Germany Trommsdorff, Gisela Department of Psychology, University of Konstanz, Konstanz, Germany

The aim of the present study was to investigate cultural similarities and differences in the future orientation of German and Turkish adolescents regarding future partnership and family and the impact of maternal parenting. The sample is part of the cross-cultural study "Value of Children and Intergenerational Relations" and included 619 German and Turkish mother-adolescent dyads. Results showed that German adolescents were more insecure about the realisation of their plans, while Turkish adolescents had more hopes. Additionally, control had a negative impact on future orientation in Germany. The results are discussed in a theoretical framework of culture-specifics of family and development.

Values, family relationships and religiosity of adolescents in two European countries: France and Germany

Brisset, Camille Dept. of Psychology, Université Victor Segalen, Bordeaux Cedex, France Sabatier, Colette Dept. of Psychology, Université Victor Segalen, Bordeaux Cedex, France Trommsdorff, Gisela Inst. für Psychologie, Universität Konstanz, Konstanz, Germany

This study explores the role of religiosity on adolescents' future perspective on family, their perception of the quality of their family life and their societal values in two European countries which have strong dual anchorages Christian (Catholic / Protestant) and laic, France and Germany taken in account the parents- adolescent 's concordance on religiosity. Results with 172 French and 268 German indicate that religiosity has a clear modest effect in both countries on their view of their future family life (number of children, marriage), on their family values and their perception of their parents' implication but not on societal values.

Family model in Poland

Lubiewska, Katarzyna Inst. of Psychology, Kazimierz Wielki University, Bydgoszcz, Poland

The present study strives to investigate the predominating family model in Poland. The sample is part of the cross-cultural study "Value of Children and Intergenerational Relations" and includes 300 three generational families from Western, Central and Eastern Poland. The family structure, cultural context, socialization values and family interactions were assessed to describe the predominating family model in different parts of Poland. The study revealed some interesting results regarding family structure and family values. Results are discussed in the theoretical framework of family models in social change (Kagitcibasi, 2002).

S-198: Basic processes of film perception and cognition

Stephan Schwan, Markus Huff (chair)

At first sight, films present information in ways that differ considerably from natural viewing conditions, for example in terms of abrupt viewpoint changes or occurrences of temporal gaps. Nevertheless, empirical findings suggest that film principles are not mere arbitrary conventions, but instead take basic perceptual and cognitive mechanisms into account, thereby allowing the mind to adapt to such "unnatural" viewing conditions with apparent ease. The six studies of the symposium will examine this assumption in more detail, including attention mechanisms (e.g. eye movements, multiple object tracking), perception of basic film rules (e.g. 180 degree system), and event cognition.

Tracking multiple objects across abrupt viewpoint changes

Jahn, Georg Inst. für Psychologie, Tech. Universität Chemnitz, Chemnitz, Germany Huff, Markus Cybermedia, KMRC, Tübingen, Germany Schwan, Stephan Cybermedia, KMRC, Tübingen, Germany

The reported experiment tested the effect of filmic cuts on the attentional tracking of multiple objects in dynamic 3D-scenes. Observers tracked targets that moved independently among identically looking distractors on a rectangular floor plane. Rotational viewpoint changes of 20° and 30° impaired tracking performance considerably, whereas tracking across a 10°-change was comparable with continuous tracking. Thus, tracking seems dependant on a low-level process saved against small disturbances by the visual system's ability to compensate for small changes of retinocentric coordinates. Tracking across large viewpoint changes succeeds only if allocentric coordinates are remembered to relocate targets after displacements.

Do film illiterates understand basic cinematographic principles?

Ildirar, Sermin Faculty of Communication, Istanbul University, Vezneciler-Istanbul, Turkey

In this experimental field study in Turkey we have compared the comprehension of some of the formal features of cinema like cut, pan, establishing shot, ellipse, and parallel montage by adult first-time viewers with viewers who had up to five years and more than ten years TV viewing experience. The differences between the five years and more than ten years experienced participants were bigger than the differences between the first-time and five years experienced viewers. Whereas the comprehension of cut, pan and establishing shot was dependent of viewing experience, this was not the case for ellipse and parallel montage.

Semantic, aesthetic and cognitive effects of flashbacks in film

d'Ydewalle, Géry Dept. of Psychology, University of Leuven, Leuven, Belgium Sevenants, Aline Dept. of Psychology, University of Leuven, Leuven, Belgium

Principles of film editing were investigated by assessing the consequences of inserting flashbacks. In Experiment 1, the gravity of acts committed by the main actors was perceived to be more salient in the linear than in the flashback version. Aesthetic assessment did not vary. In Experiment 2, pupil size of the viewers, as a measure of mental load, was registered on-line. Mental load was heightened due to the flashbacks. In discussing distinctive advantages of intellectual versus narrative editing, flashbacks appeared not to enhance aesthetic judgments; linearity emphasized the semantic features of the leading actors with less consumption of mental resources.

Questioning the rules of continuity editing

Hecht, Heiko Inst. für Psychologie, Universität Mainz, Mainz, Germany Kalkofen, Hermann Inst. für Psychologie, Universität Göttingen, Göttingen, Germany

When a change of perspective is used in the midst of a dynamic event, film directors tend to agree that a straight-match cut is not advisable. Such a cut would instantaneously transition from one camera angle or position to the next. However, they disagree on how to accomplish subjective continuity. We empirically tested competing continuity hypotheses. We systematically varied the temporal parameters of a dynamic scene that continued across a camera jump. Computer-animated sequences had to be adjusted until they looked maximally smooth and temporally correct. Observers very consistently preferred gaps (ellipses). Implications for film theory are discussed.

Crossing the line: Understanding the 180° system of continuity editing

Huff, Markus Cybermedia, KNOWLEDGE MEDIA RES. CENTRE, Tübingen, Germany Schwan, Stephan Cybermedia, KMRC, Tübingen, Germany

Hollywood cinema has developed the system of continuity editing which tends to avoid confusion of the spectator. A central rule out of it is the 180 degree rule which specifies the positions of cameras. By using ambiguous scenes we explored this rule in two experiments. Participants were shown movies each consisting of two shots both depicting a car driving by. Subjects had to rate whether the cars were driving in the same direction. Results confirm the central message of the 180 degree system according to which the cameras have to be on the same side of the line of action.

S-199: Values, culture, and developmental tasks: Clashing or conforming with academic involvement of adolescents?

Ursula Kessels, Stefan Fries (chair)

The symposium addresses the question how doing well at school is related to other crucial aspects of a student's identity. From different theoretical backgrounds, the papers examine which aspects of students' identities might enhance or diminish academic involvement and the valuing of achievement. Specifically, they study the impact of value orientations, ethnic as well as cultural background, and gender) on academic involvement. They highlight the importance of the perceived fit between an individual's identity related variables on the one hand and academic demands on the other hand, and how this congruence varies with the context a person is found in.

Aspiring for achievement in the family and school contexts during adolescence

Daniel, Ella Psychology department, Hebrew University of Jerusalem, Jerusalem, Israel Knafo, Ariel Psychology department, Hebrew University of Jerusalem, Jerusalem, Israel Boehnke, Klaus School of Human. & Social, Jacobs University Bremen, Bremen, Germany

We examine the importance adolescents ascribe to achievement values, an important topic due to the relevance of values to achievement behaviors. 500 German and Israeli Adolescents reported their values of achievement, both in general and in their roles as students and family members. The importance of achievement is compared between cultural groups, as well as within individuals, between roles. We test the hypothesis that values correlate positively between contexts, revealing stable individual differences. However, achievement is more important at the student than at the family context. Inter-individual differences in value importance can be predicted using values prevalent in adolescents' environments (school, family).

Learning motivation, leisure experience and value orientations in Italian students

Hofer, Manfred Inst. für Bildungspsychologie, Universität Mannheim, Mannheim, Germany Schmutz, Stefan Educational Psychology, University of Mannheim, Mannheim, Germany Marta, Elena Social Psychology, Università Cattolica Milano, Milano, Italy

In this paper, the impact of motivational interference experienced during leisure time resulting from school-leisure conflicts on value orientations is studied. An Italian sample is used because Italy has got one of the few half-day schooling systems in the world and embodies a post-industrialized country with a wide range of leisure attractions. In a cross-sectional self-report study, impairment of experience during leisure is analysed as dependent on extrinsic/intrinsic learning motivation and acting upon students' value orientations (achievement and well-being). Structural equation models show that motivational conflict is inversely related to intrinsic learning motivation and positively to well-being value orientations.

Value development in the transition from school to university

Husemann, Nicole Educational Research, MPI for Human Development, Berlin, Germany Trautwein, Ulrich Educational Research, MPI for Human Development, Berlin, Germany Luedtke, Oliver Educational Research, MPI for Human Development, Berlin, Germany Nagy, Gabriel Educational Research, MPI for Human Development, Berlin, Germany

Stability and change of values in the transition from school to university were investigated in a large-scale 4-year longitudinal study with students in various fields of study (N = 1091). Results show that value orientations affected the choice of majors (self-selection processes). The perception of the fellow students' values in a certain major was associated with change in values (socialization processes). In addition, the congruence between students' individual value profiles and the perceived value profiles of their fellow students was positively related to subjective well-being, interest in the study field, and negatively related to the dropout intentions.

When academic achievement clashes with developmental tasks of adolescents

Kessels, Ursula Edu. Studies und Psychologie, Freie Universität Berlin, Berlin, Germany

Two experiments tested the assumption that positive feedback about academic performance threatens important aspects of adolescents' identity (being autonomous; conforming to gender role expectations), leading to a rejection of the positive feedback. Study 1 (N=132) found that students downplayed their academic effort after the ascription of being very close to the teacher (compared to control group). Study 2 (N=135) found that boys reported relatively more interest in physics related topics and less in typical sex-typed teenager topics after very positive feedback on talent for physics (compared to average feedback), while girls reported more interest in feminine topics after positive feedback.

Avenues to overcoming the achievement gap: The interplay of classroom composition, clique norms, and educational values of immigrant students

Zander-Music, Lysann Bildung und Psychologie, Freie Universität Berlin, Berlin, Germany Hannover, Bettina School and Teaching Research, Freie Universität Berlin, Berlin, Germany

This study focuses the role of peers in facilitating educational achievement examining the intersection of value and status homophily. Combining social network analysis and multilevel methods data of 900 adolescents in 42 classrooms was analyzed. Assessed measures include students' social networks, educational values, test performance as well as contextual classroom variables. Results indicate that clique formation follows common academic values and ethnic background depending on the salience of these criteria and the distribution of achievement in the classroom context. Gender differences were found depending on the type of network (social support/academic advice). Implications for educational practice will be discussed.

S-200: Constructing spatial models from various sources

Valérie Gyselinck (chair)

This symposium is dedicated to the question of the construction of a spatial model from different sources or perspectives. Understanding the similarities and differences among representations should have important theoretical implications to understand the nature of the spatial models. In most of the studies presented, spatial information derives from visual or verbal inputs. The experiments presented can directly confront two modes of presentation of spatial information, or various perspectives within a single mode of presentation. The role of individual differences and the role of working memory components are also considered. The discussion will allow us to confront the diverse results to answer the question of the functional equivalence (or not) of the representations built.

Functional equivalence of spatial representations derived from vision and language

Avraamides, Marios Dept. of Psychology, University of Cyprus, Nicosia, Cyprus Koushiou, Maria Dept. of Psychology, University of Cyprus, Nicosia, Cyprus

Spatial representations are formed through our senses but also through symbolic media such as maps and language. Understanding the similarities and differences among representations derived from different sources is important from both a theoretical and practical perspective. Here, we review empirical evidence suggesting that spatial representations from various sources are functionally equivalent. First, we present findings from a series of experiments that compared reasoning about locations encoded through visual perception or spatial language. Second, we report indirect evidence for functional equivalence from a series of perspective-taking experiments that used either vision in virtual environments or language as the input source.

Remembering locations on the basis of spatial actions and spatial language

May, Mark Faculty for Mind & Social, Helmut-Schmidt University, Hamburg, Germany Gall-Peters, Alexandra Faculty for Mind & Social, Helmut-Schmidt University, Hamburg, Germany

We will report about ongoing research on memory access after real and imagined perspective switches in space. Of special interest is whether spatial actions and spatial language lead to the same or to different kinds of location memory. Assuming that actions (e. g., haptic explorations) dominantly lead to sensorimotor codes, while language (e. g., verbal descriptions) dominantly leads to propositional codes, differences in the behavioral consequences and/or neural activity following both types of learning are expected. Experimental results obtained so far are in line with a parallel activation of sensorimotor and propositional representations, confirming a dual code hypothesis.

Following a route in a virtual environment or hearing a verbal description of that route: What changes?

Gyselinck, Valérie LPNCog, Université Paris Descartes, Boulogne-Billancourt, France

We investigated how people create spatial models of routes as a function of the source through which spatial knowledge is acquired. Routes in a city within a virtual environment and verbal descriptions of the same routes were used. Results on verification tests about spatial relations and sketch maps suggest that the encoding source influences the way the spatial model can be explored on time of testing, but that the spatial models are equally accurate. In addition, the involvement of the visuo-spatial and the verbal working memory has been explored with a dual-task paradigm, and results suggest a differential involvement as a function of the source.

Visuo-spatial individual differences in spatial text processing

Meneghetti, Chiara Dept. of General Psychology, University of Padua, Padua, Italy

Using a dual-task paradigm, studies have evidenced the role of visuo-spatial (VSWM) and verbal working memory systems in the processing of spatial descriptions. A question that remains unclear is whether visuo-spatial individual differences affect the involvement of WM systems. Individual differences in the strategies used (verbal or visuo-spatial) and in spatial abilities were investigated in two researches. Participants listened to spatial descriptions and performed or not at the same time a spatial or a verbal concurrent task. Results showed that individuals with good spatial abilities were able to process the spatial texts efficiently also during the spatial secondary task performance requiring the VSWM support.

Working memory and spatial descriptions: Insights into mental model form and function

Brunyé, Tad Cognitive Science & Applic, US Army Res, Dev & Enginee, Natick, USA Taylor, Holly Psychology, Tufts University, Medford, USA

Work in our lab using secondary tasks targeting working memory subsystems during retrieval has elucidated the form and function of mental models derived from spatial descriptions. We discuss the independent and interactive roles of three working memory subsystems towards the application of mental models formed from survey and route descriptions: visuospatial sketchpad, articulatory loop, and central executive. Results suggest that mental model form and the operations performed upon them vary both by input perspective and extent of experience with that perspective. Ultimately, however, readers develop models that are far abstractions from the perspective and ordering of the spatial descriptions themselves.

S-201: Conflicts as signals: Adaptation based on top-down control and bottom-up signaling

Birgit Stürmer (chair)

Conflicts can be seen as signals optimizing information processing within the cognitive system. Current research starts to unravel the processes mediating between signals indicating discrepancies in information processing and subsequent optimization. Most often such adaptation processes are based on interactions between bottom-up signals and top-down control effects. Although separate brain networks can be distinguished for bottom-up alerting, orienting and top-down executive control, top-down effects on information processing might be overrated. The studies presented here will fathom the scope and limits of top-down and bottom-up adaptation in information processing.

The relation between expectancy violations and the optimization of task strategies

Schwager, Sabine Inst. für Psychologie, Humboldt-Universität zu Berlin, Berlin, Germany

A number of incidental learning experiments investigate the relation between expectancy violations and optimization of participants' task strategy. Previous studies showed that computer-generated premature responses increase the probability of strategy shifts. Premature responses violate timing expectancies (too fast response) and sequencing expectancies (response before stimulus). The current experiments were designed to disentangle the effects of both expectancy violations. Results are discussed in terms of the "Unexpected-Event hypothesis": Conflicts caused by violations of one's expectations about task processing (unexpected events) trigger a search for an explanation, which might lead to the detection of task-inherent redundancies and the formation of optimized strategies.

Bottom-up adaptation versus top-down control in the Simon task

Alpay, Gamze Inst. für Psychologie, Humboldt-Universität zu Berlin, Berlin, Germany Stürmer, Birgit Inst. für Psychologie, Humboldt-Universität zu Berlin, Berlin, Germany

Although cognitive control gains much interest in cognitive neuroscience, the contribution and interplay of top-down and bottom-up processes in conflict adaptation and resolution are still not elucidated. To address this issue, we inserted precues that triggered top-down control in a Simon task. Here, reaction times are typically slower when the response location does not match the task-irrelevant stimulus position. However, the Simon effect vanishes after preceding incompatible trials. Our behavioural and psychophysiological data reveal that sequential modulations of the Simon effect were not affected by precuing, hence, narrowing down the role of top-down control on bottom-up adaptation processes.

The functional integration of the anterior cingulate cortex during conflict processing

Fan, Jin Dept. of Psychiatry, Mount Sinai School of Medicine, New York, USA

Although functional activation of the anterior cingulate cortex (ACC) related to conflict processing has been studied extensively, the functional integration of the subdivisions of the ACC and other brain regions during conditions of conflict is still unclear. We will discuss about our new findings of the physiological response of several brain regions in terms of an interaction between conflict processing and activity of the anterior rostral cingulate zone of the ACC, and the effective connectivity between this zone and other subdivisions of ACC as well as other cortical regions such as the lateral prefrontal, primary and supplementary motor areas.

Adaptation processes after different types of conflict in a combined Simon/Go-NoGo-paradigm

Nigbur, Roland Inst. für Psychologie, Humboldt-Universität zu Berlin, Berlin, Germany Stürmer, Birgit Inst. für Psychologie, Humboldt-Universität zu Berlin, Berlin, Germany

In three electrophysiological studies we combined a Simon task with a threefold probability manipulated NoGo task to investigate whether different types of cognitive conflicts trigger distinct adaptation processes. The Simon effect was modulated by the preceding trial type with significant reductions following incompatible trials and a weaker reduction after NoGos and errors. Moreover, the N2 to NoGos and incompatible trials varied in scalp distribution and showed differential context sensitivity. We, hence, conclude that incompatible Simon trials trigger adaptation processes that differ from those after NoGo trials and errors engaging distinct but interacting neural networks for cognitive control.

Cognitive control mechanisms in the human brain

Egner, Tobias Feinberg School of Medicine, Northwestern University, Chicago, USA

The term 'cognitive control' describes the ability to flexibly adjust one's behavior in the pursuit of internal goals. I will argue that cognitive control does not constitute a unitary 'general resource' that is applied whenever behavioral adjustments are required, but that cognitive control should rather be thought of as a collection of multiple, specialized neural mechanisms that address different types of challenges. I will present data showing that different types of conflict in information processing engage different cognitive control resources (and distinct associated neural mechanisms), and that conflict-driven control mechanisms are distinct from, and independent of, expectancy-based control mechanisms.

S-202: Healthy lifestyles consisting of different behaviors: Understanding mechanisms for designing effective interventions

Sonia Lippke (chair)

Lifestyles incorporate not only one behavior but the orchestration of different risk factors such as inactivity, unhealthy eating, smoking and sunbathing. What are mechanisms of multiple behaviors and complex behavior change? Interventions targeting one behavior can impact on other domains, and programs addressing more than one behavior may be less effective. What are evidences and mechanisms? This symposium provides the platform for a debate with international experts who have investigated this area from different perspectives. Studies on different behaviors with their interrelations and mediating variables will be presented. Interventions targeting one vs. multiple behaviors will be compared, future directions will be discussed.

Intercorrelations between cognitions, intentions and multiple health behaviors

de Vet, Emely Dept. of Health Sciences, Vrije Universiteit, Amsterdam, Netherlands

Objectives: To examine interrelations between comparable, hierarchical, and sequential behaviors. Methods: Three questionnaire studies among adults (Study 1 N = 1055; Study 2 N = 709) and undergraduates (Study 3: N = 587). Results: Interrelations were weak for comparable behaviors (fish, fruit and vegetable intake). For hierarchical behaviors, performing a specific act (walking) and a behavioral category (physical activity) were related, but only weak with the end goal (weight-control). Finally, buying vegetables predicted preparing vegetables, which in turn predicted eating vegetables (sequential behaviors). Conclusions: Interrelations were more profound for sequential than for hierarchical or same level health behaviors.

Sun protection versus sunbathing: Additional positive effects of intervening on one aspect of a risk behavior

Aiken, Leona Dept. of Psychology, Arizona State University, Tempe, USA

Objectives. Skin cancer prevention involves two distinct behaviors—increased sun protection and decreased sunbathing. Given powerful norms supporting sunbathing, we examined whether an intervention only emphasizing use of sunscreen could also reduce sunbathing. Methods. Caucasian young women (n=201) participated in a randomized trial of the intervention. Outcomes were assessed with ANCOVA and mediational analysis. Results. Sun protection increased and sunbathing decreased ($p < .05$ in both cases). Distinct factors mediated the intervention effect on sun protection versus sunbathing. Conclusions. Appropriately designed interventions emphasizing one behavioral component of a health threat may positively influence other more change-resistant behavioral components of the same threat.

The earlier the better and the more broad effects: A Randomized Controlled Trial (RCT) to prevent behavioral disorders among children

Schmid, Holger School of Social Work, Univers. of Applied Sciences, Olten, Switzerland

Objectives: To test the effectiveness of health promotion programs preventing juvenile behavioral disorders. Methods: RCT with random assignment of school-classes to four conditions: (1) combination of family-school-based ("Fit-For-Life" + "Triple-P"), (2) family-based ("Triple-P"), (3) school-based ("Fit-For-Life"), and (4) control-group (waiting-list). Teachers and parents observed strength and difficulties of students. Results: 78 school-classes (78 teachers, 1466 students, 901 parents) participated. The follow-up shows reductions in behavioral problems as well as reduced smoking onset in the combined family-school-based condition. Conclusions: Educational programs for health promotion are effective if applied on different levels and prior to problem manifestation, and focusing on multiple behaviors.

Behavior matters: What works in self-regulation interventions?

Michie, Susan Dept. of Psychology, University College London, London, United Kingdom Abraham, Charles Department of Psychology, University of Sussex, Falmer, United Kingdom Whittington, Craig Psychology Outcomes Research, University College London, London, United Kingdom McAteer, John Psychology Outcomes Research, University College London, London, United Kingdom

Objectives: To compare effectiveness of self-regulation interventions across healthy eating (HE) and physical activity (PA) interventions. Methods: The effect of behavior change techniques (BCTs) and a BCT set derived from self-regulation theory on effectiveness was investigated using meta-regression with 21 HE and 24 PA evaluations. Results: Time management explained 59% of the variance for HE whilst teaching people to review behavioral goals and use prompts/cues explained 49% of the variance for PA. The theoretical technique set accounted for 70% of variance for HE and none for PA. Conclusion: Understanding more about the targeted behaviors may be essential to intervention effectiveness.

Challenges in multi-behavior intervention and theory-based research: From single theories to integrations

Lippke, Sonia Gesundheits-Pschologie, Freie Universität Berlin, Berlin, Germany *Ziegelmann, Jochen P.* Gesundheits-Psychologie, Freie Universität Berlin, Berlin, Germany
Objectives: To merge stage models and transfer theories, to test whether stage-matched interventions are more successful than no intervention and stage-mismatched intervention, and self-regulatory resources from one behavior are transferred to other behaviors. Methods: Experimental online-study following-up N=701 individuals after four weeks. Results: Stage-matched interventions helped individuals more to increase their intentions and plans than no treatments and stage-mismatched interventions. Having planned how to exercise facilitated intentions and plans to eat healthy. Behavior change depended on successful increases in mediators (self-efficacy, intention and plans). Conclusions: Transfer effects should be targeted when designing healthy lifestyle interventions with more than one behavior.

S-203: Psychological perspectives on chronic pain

Birgit Kröner-Herwig (chair)
The symposium presents 2 studies on chronic pain in children and adolescents with either a perspective on its epidemiology or respectively its treatment, in particular internet based treatment of paediatric headache. Another intervention study focusses on headache in adults, with the specific directive to prevent further medication overuse which is a common problem in migraine. Two papers target the process of developing chronic pain under a risk factor perspective. They focus either on back pain respectively on postoperative pain. An experimental study investigates the highly important issue of pain control and the consequences of losing it.

The epidemiology of chronic pain and its burden on children and adolescents

Passchier, Jan Dept. Medical Psychology&Psych, Erasmus Medical Center Uni., Rotterdam, Netherlands
Objective: To present the state of art on prevalence of chronic pain in children, its burden and psychological treatment. Method: Narrative review of existing literature Results: Chronic pain is highly prevalent in children and particularly in adolescents. The quality of life of children and adolescents with chronic pain is significantly diminished. Psychological interventions have found to be effective. Use of mobile telephones and internet increases its cost-effectiveness - and possibly its attractiveness. Conclusions: A subgroup of youngsters with chronic pain needs help. Effective cognitive behavioral interventions are available. Support by e-health techniques are recommended.

Internet based selfmanagement interventions for paediatric headache

Trautmann, Ellen Inst. für Klin. Psychologie, Universität Göttingen, Göttingen, Germany *Kröner-Herwig, Birgit* Inst. für Klin. Psychologie, Universität Göttingen, Göttingen, Germany
Objectives: The present study aimed at the evaluation of internet-based interventions for recurrent headache in children and adolescents (10-18 yrs.). Method: Efficacy of two internet-based programs (cognitive-behavioural treatment, CBT, applied relaxation, AR) with psychoeducation was compared in a RCT (n=68). As main outcome measures headache activity and pain catastrophizing were assessed. Results: Significant reductions in headache activity were found in the two treatment groups from pre- to post-treatment. Especially CBT lead to a significant decrease in pain catastrophiz-

ing. Changes were maintained at 6-month follow-up. Conclusions: The internet format appears to be a viable treatment option, particularly when clinical face-to-face treatment is not available.

Secondary prevention of medication overuse in migraine patients

Fritsche, Günther Inst. für Neurologie, Universität Essen, Essen, Germany
Objectives: The study evaluated a cognitive-behavioural minimal-contact program for prevention of medication overuse headache (MOH) in a multi-centre-design. Method: 168 migraine-patients in seven German Headache-Centres and with high intake frequency of migraine medication were included. Half of the participants obtained a 5-session-training for restrictive drug intake; the other half served as a control group by only obtaining an educational booklet. All recruited participants continued usual medical treatment during the whole investigation period. Results: The number of migraine- and intake-days declined significantly at post and follow-up. The contents of the training and the data for evaluation will be presented.

Hypervigilance and postoperative pain

Lautenbacher, Stefan Inst. Physiolog. Psychologie, Universität Bamberg, Bamberg, Germany
Objectives: Hypervigilance, which is a rigid focus of attention on pain observed in many chronic pain conditions, was tested for prognosis of postoperative pain. Methods: 60 young men were investigated prior to cosmetic chest surgery and four times afterwards. Hypervigilance to pain were assessed by the dot probe task (implicit measure) and questionnaires (explicit measures). Outcome variables were postoperative pain intensity and disability as well as intake of analgesics. Results and Conclusions: Hypervigilance appeared to be apt for prognosis of acute and persistent pain. Furthermore, it adds on the explanatory power of the other psychological predictors (pain sensitivity, mood, cortisol).

Pain related fear avoidance and endurance in the development of individually tailored, risk based interventions

Hasenbring, Monika Inst. für Medizin. Psychologie, Ruhr-Universität Bochum, Bochum, Germany
Objectives. Pain-related fear-avoidance (FAC) and endurance coping (EC) represent predictors of chronic back pain. Methods. 141 patients with subacute back pain were studied in a prospective cohort at baseline, at 3 and 12 months follow-up. Multiple regression analyses calculated the predictive power of Catastrophizing, Help-/hopelessness, Thought Suppression, Avoidance and Endurance Behaviour, assessed by the Kiel Pain Inventory and the Tampa Scale of Kinesophobia. Results. FAC as well as EC were seen as significant independent predictors of recurrent pain at both follow ups (R-Square .29 and .47). Conclusion. The need of cognitive-behavioral interventions targeted individually on FAC and EC was suggested.

Consequences of losing control over pain: An experimental investigation

van Damme, Stefaan Experim. Clinical Psychology, Gent University, Gent, Belgium *Crombez, Geert* Experim. Clinical Psychology, Gent University, Gent, Belgium *Eccleston, Christopher* Pain Management Unit, University of Bath, Bath, United Kingdom
Objectives This study experimentally investigated the effects of losing control over previously controllable pain. Methods Healthy volunteers gained control over pain stimuli and subsequently lost it (N=37), or never had control over the pain (N=37). Task behaviour and pain ratings were assessed. Results ANOVA's showed that losing control over pain was associated with persistent attempts to regain control, increased fear and

attention to pain. Conclusions Blocking attempts to control further intensifies attempts to control. This is accompanied by increased fear and attention at the cost of other demands. The findings suggest that persisting attempts to control uncontrollable (chronic) pain may have negative consequences.

S-204: Cognitive, social and emotional processes in creative teams

Kristina Lauche, Petra Badke-Schaub (chair)
The quality of team performance depends upon three core processes: 1) cognitive processes of problem solving, 2) social interaction and development team mental models, and 3) emotional and motivational processes. So far relatively little is known for reactive, complex and protracted tasks such as design. This symposium investigates how design teams address ill-defined problems, deal with complexity and uncertainty, and develop communication and cooperation strategies over time. The contributions show that variety of methodological approaches such as longitudinal field studies, interviews and experiments is required to enhance our understanding.

Success factors for teamwork in design

Zamel, David Ben Data and Process Management, Daimler AG, Ulm, Germany
In this study, 16 semi-structured interviews on critical success factors for collaborative projects were conducted with designers from different hierarchical levels. Based on these interviews, contents and processes that predict successful team work in design and innovation projects were found. Team mental models are needed for task, roles and responsibilities, and decision process. The results fit well to a system with four basic teamwork functions that have been derived from system theory. A measurement system for teamwork mental models is proposed and methodological issues are discussed.

Social skills in design teams

Bierhals, Reimer Inst. für Psychologie II, Universität Bamberg, Bamberg, Germany *Schuster, Ilona* Inst. für Psychologie, Universität Bamberg, Bamberg, Germany *Geis, Christian* Product Development Machine E., Darmstadt University of Techno, Darmstadt, Germany *Badke-Schaub, Petra* Product Innovation Management, Delft Technical University, Delft, Netherlands
This study presents a behavioural marker system for design teams covering all relevant aspects of group behaviour and illustrates the system's development process. After an extensive literature review on non-technical skills, half-standardized interviews with 39 designers from 15 companies were conducted in order to assess decisive behaviour in the daily working life of the participants. These statements were categorised into a complex system composed of three hierachical levels. Finally, the categories were integrated into a model explaining group effectiveness. It turned out that behaviour patterns facilitating the development of shared understanding in teams play a key role regarding team performance.

Shared mental models in practical application: Benefits and limitations

Kohler, Petra Research, Daimler AG, Ulm, Germany *Schnall, Julia* Automotive Technical Engineeri, MB-technology GmbH, Sindelfingen, Germany *Bergholz, Wencke* Data and Process Management, Daimler AG, Ulm, Germany
A field study was conducted with 30 engineers from an automotive company to compare shared mental models (SMMs) and group performance of product development in a local meeting and a distributed

groupware meeting. The teams had to solve two different tasks. No significant difference for the cost-optimizing task was found, while groups solving the design task still had more complete SMMs and a better group result in the local meeting. The elucidation of SMMs was validated by the known correlation between mental models and information-acquisition. In light of these results, current methodological limitations of measuring shared team knowledge are discussed.

The development of shared mental models in design teams: An experimental analysis

Neumann, Andre Product Innovation Management, Delft University of Technology, Delft, Netherlands *Badke-Schaub, Petra* Product Innovation Management, Delft University of Technology, Delft, Netherlands *Lauche, Kristina* Product Innovation Management, Delft University of Technology, Delft, Netherlands

Shared mental models of the task but also of the team have been proven to positively influence team performance. However, it is not clear whether these general assumptions hold for creative teams where diverse ideas are desirable. In an experimental study of eleven teams of design master students we investigated the development of shared mental models. We used protocol analysis and questionnaires to assess mental models within the teams. Results show that shared representations of the team but also of the process positively influenced the outcome. Using the same approach, supporting evidence was found in two engineering meetings in industry.

Emotion-dynamics in multi-disciplinary design teams

Jung, Malte Center of Design Research, Stanford University, Stanford, CA, USA *Ade, Mabogunje* Center of Design Research, Stanford University, Stanford, CA, USA

Gottman (2000) showed that emotions predict relationship satisfaction and divorce in married couples. This study aims at finding correlations between emotions communicated within a design team and team performance. In an exploratory study of 10 teams of students of a three quarter long graduate course in mechanical engineering, the role of emotions was investigated. A laboratory protocol was developed, to obtain 15-minute video segments of each team solving a problem that occurred within their process. The video data was coded for emotions in order to explore how emotions influence team performance.

Comparing actions of creative designing

Sachse, Pierre Inst. für Psychologie, Universität Innsbruck, Innsbruck, Austria *Englisch, Ulrike* ZLB, Universität Erfurt, Erfurt, Germany

Presuming designing could be described as a central aspect of human actions the action of designing is regarded as a continuum: Its poles are characterized by the technical and the non-technical (artistic) design process. This is accompanied by the thesis that differences (e.g. criteria for breaking off the process) as well as common features (e.g. complex, multiple problem solving) could be abstracted from technical and artistic design processes. On this theoretical foundation and based on empirical data from an interview study (n=100) and an experimental study (n=60) necessary recommendations for designing and supporting the process will be deduced and discussed.

S-205: Practice advances in clinical psychology

John Norcross (chair)
Professions must proactively direct their futures and fluidly adapt to the evolving needs of their clients as well as the larger society. This symposium

features six practice advances in clinical and counseling psychology: primary care psychology, ethics in emerging areas, multicultural competence, the invisible psychologist, evidence-based practices, and prescription privileges. A distinguished panel of health-care psychologists will describe and illustrate these practice advances and place them in an international context.

Primary care psychology

Bray, James Family & Community Medicine, Baylor College of Medicine, Houston, TX, USA
Primary care psychology is an exciting new area for the profession. The opportunities in primary care psychology necessitate additional knowledge of primary care and different skills in caring for primary-care patients. This expansion of knowledge and skills reflects the evolution of psychology from being a mental health profession to a full partner in the health professions. For many years psychologists have collaborated with physicians and other healthcare providers; however, this has mainly been in the mental health arena. Work in primary care has been more recent. This paper describes practice opportunities in primary care and methods for collaborative practice.

Ethics in emerging areas

Campbell, Linda Counselling & Human Develop., University of Georgia, Alpharetta, USA
Abstract: Psychology is a continuously growing and evolving profession. With each new area of practice, the standards of practice are revised, updated, or are developed in the case of emerging areas. Ethical principles and standards then too must continually be reconsidered and applied to psychological services in an educative process meant to assist psychologists in their decision making. This presentation will present emerging areas of practice such as telehealth, geropsychology, sports, wellness, and executive coaching. Often, practice emerges while the profession is crafting the standards of care for that area. Decision making in emerging areas will also be discussed.

Multicultural competence

Kelly, Jennifer Psychology, Atlanta Center for Behavioral, Atlanta, USA
As society becomes more diverse, the probability that a psychologist will have the opportunity to treat a person of a different cultural background is highly likely. As such, the race, culture, ethnicity, and lifestyle of both the psychologist and the client do matter. The American Psychological Association approved Guidelines on Multicultural Education, Training, Research, Practice, and Organizational Change for Psychologists (Multicultural Guidelines) in 2003, which represented a major accomplishment in advancing multiculturalism in psychology. This presentation will highlight the Multicultural Guidelines and the relevance of them to the practice of psychology around the globe.

Ethics and the invisible psychologist

Koocher, Gerald Dept. of Health Studies, Simmons College, Boston, USA
Psychologists have historically conducted research, taught, and provided human services directly with and for people who could readily identify the providers as psychologists. Increasingly, many psychologists find themselves engaged in supplying consulting services that affect many people, but take place away from public view. In these situations the client may be a non profit agency, corporation, or government entity, but the effects of the psychologist's work may have rippling consequences that reach many individuals. The ethical responsibilities of such invisible psychologists working in such roles may extend to members of the public not typically considered clients of the psychologist.

Evidence-based practice in psychology

Norcross, John Dept. of Psychology, University of Scranton, Scranton, USA
Evidence-based practices (EBP) have emerged as one of the most contentious and consequential advances in health-care psychology. Originally starting in Great Britain, EBPs are becoming a dominant force around the world in determining what will be taught, practiced, funded, and researched. This paper will review the nascent definitions of EBPs as the integration of the best available research, clinician expertise, and patient characteristics, culture, and values. I will summarize the central controversies surrounding EBPs in psychology and then discuss their new sets of skills and attitudes.

Prescription privileges

Resnick, Robert Dept. of Psychology, Randolph-Macon University, Ashland, USA
In 1984, a discussion began within organized psychology in the USA concerning the feasibility of adding prescriptive training to our training. Was it good for the public and/or the public? In 1995 the American Psychological Association formally endorsed prescriptive authority to appropriately trained psychologists. Interest in this issue has now become international. Countries world wide have come to recognize the benefits of such authority on quality of care. This presentation will review the common progression that national societies usually follow and the risks/benefits of adding prescription privileges to psychologists' competencies.

S-206: Self-regulated learning in mathematics and science classes

Franziska Perels, Barbara Otto (chair)
Self-regulation is an important competence. Therefore, in this symposium we present five approaches that examine important aspects of self-regulated learning in school and university. - Zeidner et al.: Student Conscientiousness, regulated Learning, and science Achievement - Hascher et al.: Emotion regulation as important feature of self-regulated learning in school - Dignath et al.: Investigating mathematics teachers' promotion of self-regulated learning - a multi-method approach. - Labuhn et al.: Fostering self-regulated learning in science education. Evaluation of a classroom-based intervention. - Minnaert: Dissonances in self-regulated learning among freshmen: integrated versus disintegrated learning patterns. Discussant: E. Souvignier, Germany.

Student conscientiousness, regulated learning and science achievement

Zeidner, Moshe Dept. of Psychology, University of Haifa, Haifa, Israel
Student Conscientiousness, Regulated Learning, and Science Achievement Moshe Zeidner, Billie Eilam, & Irit Aahron University of Haifa Presenter: Moshe Zeidner This prospective field study examined the nexus of relations between the five-factor model (FFM) trait of Consciousness (C), self-regulated learning, and science achievement in junior high school students. In addition, we tested the mediating role of self-regulated learning (SRL) in the relationship between C and academic achievement. This study supported the hypothesis that SRL mediates the frequently observed relationship between C and academic performance.

Emotion regulation as important feature of self-regulated learning in school

Hascher, Tina Inst. für Bildung, Universität Salzburg, Salzburg, Austria *Hagenauer, Gerda* Department of Education, University of Salzburg, Salzburg, Austria *Kriegseisen, Josef* Department of Education, University of Salzburg, Salzburg, Austria *Riffert, Franz*

Department of Education, University of Salzburg, Salzburg, Austria

The study focuses on the effects of "learning cycles" sensu Alfred North Whitehead in a 8th grade science classroom. The objectives were to test the cognitive, emotional and motivational potential of the three instructional steps (romance, precision, generalization) of this program. During a school year the students of the experimental group (N = 24) went trough six learning cycles which were evaluated in terms of interest, emotion, learning outcomes in comparison to a control group (N = 25). Results indicate the potential of learning cycles; however they also point to the specific challenges of self-regulation, especially on an emotional level.

Investigating mathematics teachers' promotion of self-regulated learning: A multi-method approach

Dignath, Charlotte Inst. für Pädag. Psychologie, Universität Frankfurt, Frankfurt, Germany **Büttner, Gerhard** Educational Psychology, University of Frankfurt, Frankfurt, Germany **Veenman, Marcel V.J.** Educational Psychology, University of Leuven, Leiden, Netherlands

This study should provide an insight into direct and indirect ways of strategy instruction in real mathematics classroom settings by comparing multimethods of assessment and multi-perspectives of teachers and students. For this purpose, an assessment instrument was developed to register teachers' strategy instruction and their creation of learning environments which are conducive to self-regulated learning. Observation data was compared with data from questionnaires asking teachers about their promotion of self-regulated learning, as well as asking students how they judge their teachers' promotion of self-regulated learning.

Fostering self-regulated learning in science education

Labuhn, Andju Sara Graduiertenkolleg 11, Universität Göttingen, Göttingen, Germany **Bögeholz, Susanne** Educational Psychology, G.-A. University of Goettingen, Göttingen, Germany **Hasselhorn, Marcus** Educational Psychology, G.-A. University of Goettingen, Göttingen, Germany

The study addresses the integration of a self-regulation intervention into regular science classes. A quasi-experimental design was used to evaluate the effectiveness of a unit on nutrition that was designed to improve seventh graders (N=199) self-regulation. Results confirm that self-regulated learning can be enhanced through this brief intervention. A follow-up testing revealed that although self-regulation had slightly decreased, students who received training still scored higher than control students and outperformed them on a knowledge test. The authors conclude that self-regulated learning can be enhanced within regular classes. Students benefit both in terms of self-regulation and acquisition of content knowledge.

Dissonances in self-regulated learning among freshmen: Integrated versus disintegrated learning patterns

Minnaert, Alexander Dept. of Educational Sciences, University of Groningen, Groningen, Netherlands

Learning patterns were addressed in both a traditional and a student oriented curriculum. Subjects were 244 law and 244 social science students. Both groups were matched on GPA. All freshmen were administered twice on learning strategies, orientations, and conceptions. The structure of learning patterns was stable over time in the traditional environment. It was not stable in the student oriented one: dissonances in learning patterns appeared. Analysis of repeated measurements revealed a significant increase of self-regulation and a significant decrease of external regulation in the student oriented learning environment. The

importance of dissonances in learning patterns will be discussed.

S-207: Psychology of entrepreneurship – current research and trends: Social and cultural aspects of entrepreneurship (Part II)

Ute Stephan, Marjan Gorgievski (chair)

Recognition of the importance of entrepreneurship for social and economic well-being lead to the questions of how we can attract more people to entrepreneurship and how we can develop entrepreneurial potential (e.g., GEM, 2006). These questions traditionally fall within the field of Work and Organizational Psychology. In two symposia, we want to present novel trends of today's psychology of entrepreneurship research. This is part two of the symposium, which will focus on social and societal, i.e. cultural aspects of entrepreneurship.

Adolescents' entrepreneurial orientation predicted by personality traits and entrepreneurial family background

Schroeder, Elke Inst. für Entw.-Psychologie, Universität Jena, Jena, Germany **Schmitt-Rodermund, Eva** Lehrstuhl für Entwicklungspsyc, Friedrich-Schiller-Universität, Jena, Germany

Entrepreneurial activities are likely to be related to personality traits and early entrepreneurial experience. In this study, personality and entrepreneurial family background were hypothesized to predict adolescents' entrepreneurial orientation (e.g. entrepreneurial interests, self-rated competencies). The data of 623 high school students were analyzed using structural equation modeling. Results show that adolescents with high levels of achievement orientation and need for social dominance had a strong interest in entrepreneurial activities. Moreover, growing up in a family business predicted high levels of entrepreneurial orientation. Factors stimulating adolescents' entrepreneurial orientation, e.g. family values, role models, are discussed.

Correlates of networking in a German sample of entrepreneurs

Grau, Andreas Inst. für Sozialpsychologie, Technische Universität Dresden, Dresden, Germany **Dej, Dominika** Work&Organisational Psycho, University of Technology, Dresden, Germany **Hering, Cornelia** Work&Organisational Psycho, Philipps-University Marburg, Marburg, Germany **Stephan, Ute** Work&Organisational Psycho, Philipps-University Marburg, Marburg, Germany

Networking includes behaviors aimed at building and maintaining informal relationships, that possess the (potential) benefit to ease work related actions by voluntarily granting access to resources and by jointly maximizing advantages of the individuals involved (Wolff & Moser, 2006). Networking is an important strategy for entrepreneurs but little is known about those entrepreneurs who engage in networking behaviors. The results of the present study on 118 Entrepreneurs show significant correlations of networking with social competence, social support as well as self efficacy and personal initiative. Implications of these results and directions for future research on entrepreneurs' networking behavior are discussed.

Success of small business owners in Peru: Strategies and cultural practices

Unger, Jens Uniton Management, Universität Gießen, Gießen, Germany **Rauch, Andreas** Department of Management, ERASMUS University Rotterdam, Gießen, Netherlands **Lozada, Maria** Unit on Management, Universität Gießen, Gießen, Germany

Gielnik, Michael Uniton Management, Universität Gießen, Gießen, Germany

The study investigates moderating effects of owners' cultural practices on the relationships between strategic orientations/actions and small business success. We argue that success relationships are higher if strategy variables are aligned with the cultural practices that owners support in their business. Based on interview and questionnaire data of 112 small business owners in Peru we found positive success relationships for planning, personal initiative, entrepreneurial orientation, and innovation. These relationships were generally higher if there was a match between strategic variables and cultural practices. The study shows the usefulness of a moderator approach to the understanding of small business success.

National culture and innovation

Lukes, Martin University of Economics, Prague, Czech Republic

In the current business climate, it is important to understand how innovation processes vary across cultures. However, the cross-cultural research focused on universal dimensions and specific connections to innovations remained underdeveloped. On the other hand, the majority of innovation studies are culturally biased. We found in peer-reviewed journals in Proquest database only five empirical and four theoretical studies directly relating national culture and innovation. Only one researched innovative behaviour of acting individuals. We recommend specific research design using representative samples in four European countries, focusing on innovative behaviour, and combining results with the existing data from European Social Survey.

Societal legitimation: Cultural practices and entrepreneurship in 35 countries

Stephan, Ute Fachbereich Psychologie, Philipps-Universität Marburg, Marburg, Germany **Uhlaner, Lorraine** Center for Entrepreneurship, Nyenrode Business Universiteit, Breukelen, Netherlands

The societal legitimation hypothesis (Etzioni, 1987) states that the perception of a supportive environment, i.e. entrepreneurship-favourable cultural practices, will be related to national entrepreneurship rates. This hypothesis was tested in 35 cultures based on data from project GLOBE (House et al., 2004) and GEM (Bosma & Harding, 2007). Cultural practices of high humane orientation and low assertiveness were positively associated with entrepreneurship rates (controlling for GDP). Furthermore, meditation analyses indicated an indirect effect of cultural practices, which are related to national wealth (individualism, power distance, uncertainty avoidance, future and performance orientation) via GDP on entrepreneurship rates.

S-208: Prospective memory development across the lifespan

Matthias Kliegel (chair)

Prospective memory refers to the interplay of cognitive abilities associated with the planning of intended actions and their self-initiated realisation at the appropriate moment. Six presentations from five international groups will discuss studies which investigated the development of prospective memory from childhood into old age. Besides the identification of developmental trends, a paradoxical and so far unresolved pattern of findings regarding the age-related execution of intended actions in the laboratory and in everyday life is discussed. In addition to describing the age-related patterns in performance, all talks will discuss potential mechanisms underlying the development of prospective memory across the lifespan.

Preschool children and prospective memory: Delaying the execution of an intention affects performance
Rendell, Peter Dept. of Psychology, Australian Catholic University, Fitzroy, VIC, Australia Vella, Melissa School of Psychology, Australian Catholic University, Fitzroy, VIC, Australia Terrett, Gill School of Psychology, Australian Catholic University, Fitzroy, Victoria, Australia Kliegel, Matthias Developmental Psychology, Dresden University, Dresden, Germany Henry, Julie School of Psychology, University of New South Wales, Sydney, Australia
Previous studies of preschooler's prospective memory have required minimal working memory resources and have shown that preschoolers are able to perform an event-based prospective memory task. The present study used a paradigm requiring working memory processes. Sixty preschoolers (4.3 – 5.6 years) while playing a computer driving-game, were required to carry out a delayed intention either immediately a target cue appeared or after a 10 s or 20 s additional delay. While the length of this delay did not have an effect, the delay itself reduced performance by around 50% but did not result in complete prospective memory failure amongst preschoolers.

Temporal processing of multiple intentions
Mäntylä, Timo Dept. of Psychology, Umea University, Umea, Sweden
Temporal information processing is involved in a variety of cognitive constructs, including prospective memory, and sense of time is a prerequisite to different goal-directed activities, such as planning and task coordination. I will summarize experimental studies in which participants viewed events comprising multiple elements with different temporal trajectories (cf. a play in which the actors enter and leave the scene at different times). These findings suggest that memory for temporal patterns is related to individual and developmental differences in executive functioning. I will relate these findings to research in cognitive timing and time-based prospective memory.

A busy week: Task setting, motivation and age differences in prospective memory
Aberle, Ingo Inst. für Psychologie, Technische Universität Dresden, Dresden, Germany
Older adults outperform younger adults in naturalistic prospective memory tasks, while being outperformed in laboratory tasks. The aim of the present study was to investigate the role of motivation and task setting in this paradox. A realistic laboratory task (virtual week-board game) and a naturalistic task (write short messages by mobile phone) were applied. Motivation was manipulated by lottery participation. Forty younger and 40 older adults took part in the study. While performance in the naturalistic tasks was equal between age groups, older adults were outperformed in the lab-based task. When controlling for processing speed, the age effect disappeared.

The realisation of delayed intentions: Age differences and potential mechanisms
Ellis, Judi Dept. of Psychology, University of Reading, Reading, United Kingdom Pereira, Antonina Dept. of Psychology, University of Reading, Reading, United Kingdom
We report findings from experiments that explore the benefits of enactment at encoding and semantic relatedness between a retrieval cue and its associated action on prospective memory (PM) performance. Studies indicate higher performance (i) when physical enactment was used during encoding than when encoding was merely verbal and (ii) when cue-action pairs are semantically related. These beneficial effects were maintained under high attentional demands. The benefits of these manipulations for people diagnosed with Mild Cognitive

Impairment will be addressed with a view to the development of a rehabilitation technique for a population at risk for the development of Alzheimer's disease.

The role of social importance in adult age differences in prospective memory
Altgassen, Mareike Inst. für Psychologie, Techn. Universität Dresden, Dresden, Germany
Young adults tend to outperform old adults in laboratory-based prospective memory (PM) tasks, whereas in naturalistic settings old adults perform better. It is possible that old adults regard the naturalistic tasks as more important than young adults. However, if a PM task is perceived as more important more attentional resources should be allocated to that task resulting in increased PM performance at the expense of ongoing task performance given older adults limited processing resources. This currently ongoing study varied the social importance of a laboratory-based PM task; first results indicate effects on age-related performance in young and old adults.

S-209: Individual differences in work-related transitions across the life span

Bärbel Kracke, Bettina S. Wiese (chair)
People vary in how they cope with normative and non-normative life transitions. Our symposium addresses aspects of individual agency and received environmental support in different phases of working life across five countries. Three presentations investigate predictors of the normative school-to-work transition: occupational exploration (Kracke & Dietrich), work- and family-related goals (Wiese & Freund), and cohort membership (Schoon). Three papers focus on individual characteristics in specific non-normative transitions: risk taking in entrepreneurship (Korunka), proactive strategies during the return to work after maternity leave (Seiger & Wiese), and retired adults' goal foci with respect to voluntary work (de Lange et al.).

Preparation of the school-to-work transition in adolescence
Kracke, Bärbel Inst. für Entw.-Psychologie, Universität Erfurt, Erfurt, Germany Dietrich, Julia Psychology, University of Erfurt, Erfurt, Germany
To become certain about a future occupational career is a major developmental task in adolescence. Adolescents vary a lot in the intensity with which they engage in activities, which provide them with information about their interests and abilities as well as about the world of work. Previous studies have shown that adolescents explore more intensely when they already have at least a vague occupational goal. Our study on 252 German high-school students investigated how individual occupational exploration changes after a six-month intervention. The adolescents were trained in setting goals and seeking information about educational possibilities after leaving high school.

School-to-work transitions in times of social change
Schoon, Ingrid Inst. of Education, University of London, London, United Kingdom
Objective: To examine variations in school-to-work transitions in times of social change. Method: Drawing on data collected for two British Birth Cohorts born in 1958 and 1970 we examine variations in transition patterns and their antecedents. A latent class approach is adopted to establish a typology of how work and family related roles combine within individuals. Result: Findings illustrate a differentiation into fast and slow track transitions with variations between as well as within subgroups of the population.

Conclusion: Findings are discussed in terms of destandardisation, differentiation, and individualisation of life course transitions in times of social change.

From high school to university: Do family plans influence career decisions in adolescence?
Wiese, Bettina S. Inst. für Psychologie, Universität Zürich, Zürich, Switzerland Freund, Alexandra M. Inst. für Psychologie, Universität Zürich, Zürich, Switzerland
Students graduating from high school face the task of deciding about whether or not to continue higher education at a university. We investigate this decision and the actual transition to university in a longitudinal study with 556 high-school graduates (M = 19 yrs) in Switzerland. Data from the first wave show that plans to enter university are associated with professional motives of achievement and power. For females also extra-professional goals are predictive: Life plans of early marriage and parenthood keep them from the university track and foster the decision for a less prestigious higher education at the college level.

The transition process into entrepreneurship: Results from the Vienna Entrepreneurship studies
Korunka, Christian Fakultät für Psychologie, Universität Wien, Wien, Austria
Psychological research focuses on individual predictors of a (successful) transition into entrepreneurship. In the interdisciplinary "Vienna Entrepreneurship studies" we analyzed this transition process from different starting points. Economic knowledge in high school students was found to be a resource for the transition process. In another longitudinal study we tested a model consisting of (1) indicators related to the entrepreneurial person, (2) resources/environment indicators, (3) their interactions and (4) founding process indicators to predict founding success (who went into business?) and business success/failure (who survived?). We found that characteristics of the person (risk taking) affect founding success but do not affect business survival.

Successfully re-entering the workforce after maternity leave
Seiger, Christine P. Inst. für Psychologie, Universität Zürich, Zürich, Switzerland Wiese, Bettina S. Institute of Psychology, University of Zurich, Zurich, Switzerland
The re-entry of mothers into working life after maternity leave is a common transition for many women. Surprisingly, however, this transition has largely been overlooked by psychological research. Women's own behavioral and self-regulatory strategies as well as social support by the work and family environments are currently being investigated in a four-wave longitudinal study with 100 Swiss women as potentially important determinants of successful re-entry. We will present results concerning the relative impact of support and proactive strategies on re-entry success from two weeks before to six months after the transition.

The role of time perspective in relations between achievement goals, work engagement and performance of post-retired workers
de Lange, Anna H. Social and Organ. Psychology, University of Groningen, Groningen, Netherlands van Yperen, Nico Social and Organ. Psychology, University of Groningen, Groningen, Netherlands Bal, Matthijs Management and Organisation, Free University Amsterdam, Amsterdam, Netherlands Van der Heijden, Beatrice IJM Organizational Behavior, Maastricht school of Managemen, Maastricht, Netherlands
In this study, we test a theoretical model that applies insights of socioemotional selectivity theory

(Carstensen, 1995) and the achievement goal approach (Dweck, 1986) to work motivation and behavior of older workers. As known from life-span psychology, both the tendency toward affiliation and avoidance goals increase with age. We expect older workers to have a tendency to adopt mastery-avoidance instead of mastery-approach goals, and will present data from N = 172 post-retired workers (aged 61 to 79) who voluntarily continue to work to illustrate relations between time perspective, work goals, and outcomes such as work engagement and job performance.

S-210: Psychology in a global era: Challenges, opportunities and responsibilities

Wade Pickren (chair)
The impact of globalization represents both a challenge and an opportunity for the future of psychology. As a product of the EuroAmerican intellectual tradition, psychological science and practice have enjoyed significant growth in many parts of the world, especially since World War II. In recent years, tensions between the EuroAmerican tradition in psychology and local traditions and practices grounded in specific cultural contexts have emerged. In this symposium, scholars from three countries address some of the key concerns— curriculum and training, media impact, research ethics, barriers to women, the need to incorporate feminist perspectives——and offer workable solutions.

Internationalizing psychology: Organizational, curriculum and epistemological changes for a global era
Marsella, Anthony Dept. of Psychology, University of Hawaii, Honolulu, HI, USA
With few exceptions, psychology, as an academic discipline, is driven by Western cultural assumptions rooted within individuality, materialism, competition, reductionism,scientism, and empiricism. The global era in which we now live requires we alter this approach both within the Western world and across the globe. It is not only the inherent biases of ethnocentricity that must be resolved, but also the critical issue of the invalidation and decontextualization of experience and behavior among non-Western people. In so many ways, this represents a hegemonic imposition and privileged positioning that has political, economic, and moral consequences. This presentation will recommend changes in psychology's professional, scientific and academic organizations and in psychology's curriculum content, training, and supervision.

Women and psychology in a global era
Cheung, Fanny M. Dept. of Psychology, Chinese Univ. of Hong Kong, Hong Kong, China, People's Republic of : Hong Kong SAR
Women share many common concerns across nations and cultures. Despite major strides in improving women's status and equal opportunities in many parts of the world in the 20th century, the gender gap still prevails. In this presentation, I will focus on two key underlying barriers, violence against women and work-family interface, which may be exacerbated in the globalization trend. The global perspective of these issues poses challenges for psychological theories and research. Understanding the cross-cultural similarities and differences in the conceptualization, manifestation and responses to these issues will enhance the contribution of psychology in addressing these gender issues.

Cross-cultural research ethics: Challenges and dilemmas
Leong, Frederick T.L. Dept. of Psychology, Michigan State University, East Lansing, USA
While the APA has its own Code of Ethics with guidelines regarding research, these guidelines do not specifically address international and cross-cultural research. The purposes of this paper is to (a) provide a review of some of major ethical challenges and dilemmas in conducting cross-cultural research and (b) issue a call to the APA Committee on International Relations in Psychology (CIRP) and the Division of International Psychology to begin to assess and evaluate the nature and extend of ethical problems in conducting cross-cultural research among its members while guided by the Resolution on Culture and Gender Awareness in International Psychology.

Psychology, media and the world
Wedding, Danny Dept. of Psychiatry, Missouri Ins. of Mental Health, St. Louis, USA
The implications of new developments in technology and media have not been fully explored by psychologists. For example, initiatives currently underway propose to ensure that every child on the planet will have access to the internet; if this goal can be achieved, what will it mean for education? China has approximately 1.3 billion people; this means that the country has at least 42,000 citizens with an IQ of 160 or greater. This talent will have to be harnessed if we are to address the global challenges confronting humanity, and psychologists will have important roles to play in facilitating this development.

Feminist psychology in global context: Challenges, opportunities, concerns
Rutherford, Alexandra Dept. of Psychology, York University, Toronto, Canada
Since the 1970s, feminist psychologists have consistently proposed an alternative to traditional psychology. This alternative rejects the essentializing of gender and the primacy of intrapsychic factors, and asserts the importance of social, cultural, and other structural variables in understanding women's lives. Despite this common base, feminist psychology takes different forms depending on its regional contexts. I will show how these forms reflect variations in the roles and status of women, the issues women face, and the politics of gender by drawing examples from the work of feminist psychologists in Canada, the United States, Latin America, Western Europe, and the United Kingdom.

S-212: Ethics, psychology, torture: Conflicts of interest

Jancis Long (chair)
Involvement of psychologists in treating and interrogating prisoners of the US military is of concern to many. Despite making strong resolutions against torture, the American Psychological Association has allowed psychologists to be participant consultants at sites and for practices that violate international law, human rights, and professional ethics "to do no harm". We describe this conflict as context for opening discussion of how psychologists world-wide may find themselves using psychological knowledge for unethical ends. a New Code of Ethics for resposible psychologists is presented for discussion and adaptation.

Torture: Historical perspectives, contemporary issues, future implications
Marsella, Anthony Dept. of Psychology, University of Hawaii, Honolulu, HI, USA
Continued endorsement and use of torture today by numerous nations under the guise of national security has profound political, cultural and moral implications for our global community. Torture's prevalence in myriad forms throughout human history raises serious questions about its roots in human nature. Its legitimation, overt and covert, within political systems and national cultures reveals deep contradictions of attitude to persons and values. At stake in our efforts to define torture, prevent it, heal its victims, criminalize its practice, and prosecute its perpetrators is the very nature of the world we choose to envisage for ourselves and future generations

Interrogating the American Psychological Association, collaborations, resistances and psychology's role in US military-intelligence
Reisner, Steven Dept. of Medicine, New York University, New York, USA
This presentation details the three-part story of US Psychology and detainee abuses. Part One. After September 11th 2001, the US Administration demanded enhanced techniques for interrogating foreign detainees. Military psychologists responded. Part Two. The American Psychological Association co-sponsored conferences with the FBI, the CIA, and Homeland Security to secure a central position for psychologists as counter-intelligence Behavioral Science experts, putting military and intelligence psychologists in charge of determining ethical limits. Part Three. A growing group of psychologists began investigating, protesting and working to change APA's abrogation of its principles in collaborating with Bush Administratiion policies on detainee interrogations

Vulnerability of psychologists world-wide to unethical requests
Mangrulkar, Latika Fresnius Medical, Car-North America, Santa Rosa, USA **Long, Jancis** Extension, UCalifornia Berkeley, Berkeley, CA, USA
Psychologists have inexact, but powerful, tools for affecting human behavior, feelings and decisions. Psychologists have been used extensively to consult on how best to influence people's buying habits, work tolerances, voting preferences, fear levels, military efficiency as killers, and willingness to give up information and values in response to pain. As with all science, knowledge gained can be put to benign or malignant use. This presentation extends the US torture and abuse debate to encourage discussion of many other moral problems psychologists encounter worldwide, in governments, NGO's or commerce, when they are asked to design the means for ethically questionable ends.

Psychosocial work in Iraq under military protection: Ethical dilemmas and dangers
Agger, Inger Private Consulting Company, Psychosocial Consultation, Copenhagen, Denmark
Working as a psychologist on a democratization project in Iraq in 2005 that was financed by the British government involved this author in a number of ethical dilemmas. Though familiar with post trauma and peacebuilding work in many war torn societies, she found the anomalies of working for human rights and democracy while under the protection of an occupying force, for womens' rights in a profoundly male oriented culture, and for political inclusiveness in a setting where the "other", however conceived, was seen as a threat to survival, presented daily challenges to her professional and humanitarian ethics.

A new ethical code for responsible psychologists
McConochie, William Dept. of Psychology, Political Psych. Research Inc., Eugene, USA
Psychologists for Social Responsibility has drafted an Ethics Code to address situations where psychologists are requested to research or apply psychological knowledge that causes harm to others. The Code also provides guidelines for psychologists working at sites where violations of

human rights and international law occur, or where (as in military training) harm is said to be for a legitimate cause. Highlights of this Code will be presented, and the draft made available for discussion and adaptation to specific ethical dilemmas. The Code takes into consideration human vulnerability to behave inhumanely (e.g. administer simulated electric shock) under authoritarian leadership.

S-213: Interventions for autism spectrum disorders: Concepts and outcomes

Paul Probst (chair)
ASD are caused by neurodevelopmental factors and characterized by complex cognitive, emotional, and behavioral deficits. Correspondingly, both individuals with autism and their social environments face multiple demands and have complex needs for social support. In the symposium the focus will be on the outcomes of some family-, school, and center-based intervention programs for ASD, which were carried out in Italy, the UAE, Canada, and Germany. Common key components of the programs examined are: "Visually Structured Teaching", "Naturalistic Format" and "Broad-Spectrum Counselling". The findings consistently show clinical evidence for their effectiveness. Further, practical implications resulting from theory-of-mind and personality research are discussed

Temperament and internalizing disorders in children with Asperger's disorder: Implications for interventions

Konstantareas, Mary Dept. of Psychology, University of Guelph, Guelph and Toronto, Canada
Anxiety and depression are well documented in children with Asperger's Disorder. In this study we examined how three dimensions of temperament might predict parent-reported and self-reported depression in a sample of children and adolescents with Asperger's Disorder. The dimensions were: flexibility/rigidity, approach/withdrawal and mood. Of them, a regression analysis revealed that only flexibility/rigidity was a significant, unique predictor of depression. Thus, children with Asperger's Disorder unable to adapt flexibly to their environment are more likely to experience depression. The implications of these findings for early prevention and intervention are discussed.

Central coherence in autistic children and its links with theory of mind: Implications for interventions

Sang Biao, P. R. Dept. of Psychology, East China Normal University, Shanghai, People's Republic of China *Ren, Zhen* Dept. of Psychology, East China Normal University, Shanghai, People's Republic of China *Deng, Ciping* Dept. of Psychology, East China Normal University, Shanghai, People's Republic of China
Central Coherence and its links with Theory of Mind were investigated on 12 autistic and 28 normally developed children with the same verbal ability. Central Coherence was assessed by the Block Design Test (WAIS) and the Embedded Figures Test, and Theory of Mind by five belief tasks. The results indicated: performance on Theory of Mind was unrelated to Central Coherence; Central Coherence in the autistic group was significantly lower than in the normal group; there was a medium high correlation between the two measures of Central Coherence. The practical implications of Theory of Mind and Central Coherence research are discussed.

Outcomes of a parent group training and a teacher group training for autism spectrum disorders in Germany

Probst, Paul Hamburg, Germany *Leppert, Tobias* Therapy, Autism Treatment Center, Hamburg, Germany
A three full-day parent group training and a three half-day teacher group training, followed respectively by family or classroom-based individualized short-term support, were evaluated. 23 parents with 24 children (M= 9 yrs) participated in the parent and 10 teachers with 10 students (M= 10 yrs) in the teacher training. Both trainings focused on antecedent interventions based on the "structured teaching" method of the TEACCH approach and consequence-based interventions based on contemporary behavioral methods within the naturalistic paradigm. The summative evaluation based largely on the perspectives of parents and teachers suggests some evidence for clinical validity of both programs.

Implementation of structured teaching methods in a classroom for pupils with autism in the United Arab Emirates (Shajah Autism Center)

Leppert, Tobias Inst. für Klin. Psychologie, Autism Treatment Centre, Hamburg, Germany *Bagh, Muna* Inst. für Klin. Psychologie, Sharjah Autism Center, Sharjah, United Arab Emirates
In a 5-day teacher training (40 hours) structured teaching methods were implemented in a classroom (7 boys with autism; age 9-12) in a school for pupils with Autism Spectrum Disorders in the United Arab Emirates. The training consisted of an introduction to the TEACCH approach followed by instructions for implementing routines and instruments to improve the physical and temporal orientation of pupils and the organization of tasks. Group and individual effects are assessed. Preliminary analysis shows significant decreases in pupils' challenging behaviors. First results of the pilot study, including effect sizes and individual improvements, are presented.

Outcomes of two TEACCH-based educational programs and an integration program: An Italian comparison study

Panerai, Simonetta Special Education, IRCCS Oasi Maria SS, Troina, Italy *Trubia, Grazia* Special Education, IRCCS Oasi Maria SS, Troina, Italy *Zingale, Marinella* Special Education, IRCCS Oasi Maria SS, Troina, Italy *Finocchiaro, Maria* Special Education, IRCCS Oasi Maria SS, Troina, Italy *Zuccarello, Rosa* Special Education, IRCCS Oasi Maria SS, Troina, Italy *Buono, Serafino* Special Education, IRCCS Oasi Maria SS, Troina, Italy
This study compared the "Integration Program", an Italian program for children with disabilities, and the international program for children with autism TEACCH, which was implemented at the Oasi Institute as two different programs: a TEACCH-residential program (for children residing at the institute) and a TEACCH-family training. Pre- and post-intervention PEP-R and VABS scores were compared over three years in matched groups of children with autism and mental retardation. TEACCH-based programs were most effective, especially the TEACCH-family training. Significant differences were found in imitation, cognitive-verbal performance, daily living skills and socialization, providing evidence for the clinical validity of the TEACCH program.

Lessons learned from supporting individuals with ASD having complex needs

Rampton, Glenn Dept. of Clinical Psychology, Kerry's Place ASD Services, Aurora, Canada
Kerry's Place Autism Services (KPAS) supports more than 2000 individuals with Autism Spectrum Disorder and their families across Southern Ontario, Canada. We have found that, if the underlying,

often environmentally based reasons for "challenging behaviour" can be identified and resolved, treatment becomes easier. Data from case studies will be presented that demonstrate how application of "best practice" principles inherent in the biopsychosocial model have led to significant decreases in challenging behaviour and to improved quality of life for many individuals that had not been able to be supported adequately at home or by other medical or social services agencies.

S-214: Attentional and mental control processes across different psychological disorders

Ralph Erich Schmidt, Jonathan Smallwood (chair)
Mental disorders may be analyzed in two fundamentally different ways: in terms of particularities or commonalities. Research on attentional biases (e.g., Mathews & MacLeod, 2005), thought suppression (e.g., Rassin, 2005), and on mind-wandering (e.g., Smallwood & Schooler, 2006) has contributed to the latter approach. The aim of this symposium is to offer an integrative view of clinically relevant insights from these lines of research. Scientists from five different countries will present and discuss new findings about the implications of attentional and mental control processes in childhood sexual abuse, anxiety, dysphoria/depression, suicidality, and insomnia.

Linking thought suppression to recovered memories of childhood sexual abuse

Geraerts, Elke School of Psychology, University of St. Andrews, St Andrews, United Kingdom
In the current study, we employed a thought suppression paradigm, with autobiographical experiences as target thoughts, to test whether individuals reporting spontaneously recovered memories of childhood sexual abuse (CSA) are more adept at suppressing positive and anxious autobiographical thoughts, relative to individuals reporting CSA memories recovered in therapy, relative to individuals with continuous abuse memories, and relative to controls reporting no history of abuse. Results showed that people reporting spontaneously recovered memories are superior in suppressing anxious autobiographical thoughts, both in the short term and long term. This superior ability was related to a reduced meta-awareness of the intrusions.

Attentional retraining procedures: Manipulating early or late components of attentional bias?

Koster, Ernst H.W. Dept. of Experim. Psychology, Ghent University, Ghent, Belgium
According to cognitive models of anxiety disorders, attentional bias for threatening information play a causal role in vulnerability to and maintenance of anxiety. Methodology to reduce attentional bias has been found to reduce emotional reactivity and anxiety. The present study was aimed at identifying the effects of this attentional bias reduction on early and later stages of threat processing. Undergraduates were allocated to an attentional bias reduction versus control condition. It was found that attentional bias reduction influenced late but not early stages of threat processing. These effects are related to the vigilance-avoidance hypothesis and indicate that the attentional bias reduction procedures need further improvement.

Studying the stream of consciousness: The psychophysiolological, emotional and cognitive correlates of the wandering mind

Smallwood, Jonathan Dept. of Psychology, University of Aberdeen, Aberdeen, United Kingdom
Nothing attests to the dynamic nature of the stream of consciousness more effectively than does the experience of mind wandering. This talk reviews a

growing body of evidence that explores the objective correlates of a wandering mind (see Smallwood & Schooler, 2006, Psychological Bulletin). Using behavioural and physiological measures, studies have documented the cost of mind wandering on the analysis of the task environment and have provided indirect evidence of the emotional salience of these experiences. Finally, this talk will discuss recent evidence that links the experience of wandering mind to the development of clinical disorders such as depression.

Future expectancies and suicide risk: The interplay between personality and cognition
O'Connor, Rory C. *Dept. of Psychology, University of Stirling, Stirling, United Kingdom*
Objectives. Pessimistic future expectancies (hopelessness and future thinking) and perfectionism are related to suicidality. The present paper will determine the extent and nature of their relationship. Methods. The findings from a number of studies of clinical (suicidal patients) and non-clinical participants will be reported. Results. Impaired positive future thinking predicts short-term outcome following a suicidal episode. Positive future thinking is a better predictor of outcome following a suicidal episode than global expectancies of the future (hopelessness). The pernicious effects of social perfectionism are exacerbated by the lack of positive future thinking. Conclusions. The theoretical and clinical implications will be discussed.

Sleep disturbances set the stage for daytime dysfunctions in mental control and vice versa
Schmidt, Ralph Erich *Inst. für Psychologie, Universität Genf, Genf, Switzerland*
An emerging line of research investigates the impact of impaired sleep on mental control processes operating during the day—and the consequences of dysfunctional daytime control strategies for sleep quality. The present paper reports the results of a multi-method approach to the relations between sleep quality and mental control processes using a battery of questionnaires, a computerized mental-control task and physiological measures of effort mobilization. Results indicate that (a) insomniacs tend to rely on dysfunctional thought-control strategies, (b) lack mental resources when compared to good sleepers, and (c) try to mobilize extra effort to compensate for their deficits.

S-215: Quality assurance in the assessment process

Karl Westhoff (chair)
Different approaches to quality assurance in the assessment process are presented from Spain (1), The Netherlands (2), Austria (3), and Germany (4-6): 1.) A Multimedia System for teaching the assessment process. 2.) Assessment revisited: a systemic approach. 3.) An instruction guide for non-psychologists to administrate a test: Experiences of a large scale assessment using teachers. 4.) The Instrument for the Description of Interviewer Competence in Proficiency Assessment: Quality assurance in training and practical work. 5.) The Task-Analysis-Tools - an instrument for practitioners: psychometric properties and experiences of application. 6.) Knowledge about Emotional Stability and Conscientiousness in summarizing an in-depth interview.

A multimedia system for teaching the assessment process
Fernández Ballesteros, Rocio *Faculdad de Psicologia, Universidad Autónoma de Madrid, Madrid, Spain*
A Multimedia System for Teaching the Assessment Process (Sitema Multimedia para el Aprendizaje del Proceso de Evaluación, SIMAPE) has been developed. The SIMAPE consists in a DVD in where a

case is presented following the steps of the assessment process. The case deals with memory problems introduce by the patient's brother Several interviews with the patient and her brother are preformed. SIMAPE contains also all the information regarding hypotheses formulation and testing hypothesis and, finally, reporting results phases. Along these phases, through an interactive system, students are trained.

An instruction guide for non-psychologists to administrate a test: Experiences of a large scale assessment using teachers
Frebort, Martina *Inst. für Psychologie, Universität Wien, Wien, Austria* **Khorramdel, Lale** *Fakultät für Psychologie, Universität Wien, Wien, Austria* **Kubinger, Klaus D.** *Fakultät für Psychologie, Universität Wien, Wien, Austria* **Maurer, Martina** *Faculty of Psychology, University of Vienna, Vienna, Austria*
Within the national standard tests for mathematics and reading in Austria an instruction guide was developed to train non-psychologists for test administrators. School teachers were trained by professional test psychologists and the profit for the resulting test administration was evaluated. The importance of developing instruction guides very carefully and of coaching non-psychologists by intensive trainings is exemplified.

The instrument for the description of interviewer competence in proficiency assessment: Quality assurance in training and practical work
Strobel, Anja *Inst. für Psychologie, Technische Universität Dresden, Dresden, Germany*
To assess the psychometric features of the Instrument for the Description of Interviewer Competence in Proficiency Assessment (DIPA) 51 practicing assessors and 80 psychology-students (retest: 63) evaluated an interview-process on the basis of the DIPA-items and assessed economical and practical aspects of the instrument. Kappa-coefficients for objectivity were in the mid range, coefficients for retest-reliability were over .50 for all parts of the DIPA. Validity, assessed as percent agreement with a master solution, was satisfactory (58 to 86 percent). Economical and practical aspects were evaluated as promising. Further new results, prospects and limits using the DIPA are presented and discussed.

The task-analysis-tools: An instrument for practitioners
Koch, Anna *Inst. für Psychologie, Technische Universität Dresden, Dresden, Germany*
The Task-Analysis-Tools (TAToo) intend to bring scientifcally proven approaches into practical work. The basics of the instrument are: (1) Critical Incident Technique, (2) KSAO-approach, (3) future-oriented analysis. Questionnaire, workshop and interview are three included parallel versions. Psychometric properties were assessed by applying the TAToo in pracitcal work. First results showing that the combined methods are necessary conditions for the validity of task analyses. Economic and practical aspects were assessed positive by the participants and the users. Results on interrater-reliability (importance ratings) and retest- reliability will follow. The instrument and four current studies on the psychometric properties will be presented.

Knowledge about emotional stability and conscientiousness in summarizing an in-depth interview
Liebert, Claudia *Inst. für Psychologie, Technische Universität Dresden, Dresden, Germany*
To have full knowledge about the meaning of a trait and its behavior descriptions is crucial for detecting the respective statements in an in-depth interview. We developed category systems for the traits Emotional Stability and Conscientiousness which

show the facets and the respective behavior descriptions. 67 students of psychology in their 3rd year of study were trained in one of the two category systems. Results show a clear improvement of summarization of in-depth interview transcripts with respect to the use of category systems containing relevant trait knowledge. Trained users detected more relevant statements and had less irrelevant statements.

S-216: The practitioner-scientist: Answering research questions grounded in practice

Jeannette Milgrom (chair)
The growing movement of Evidence Based Practice has encouraged clinical psychologists to integrate empirical research into their daily clinical work. They draw on published scientific knowledge as applicable to regular clinical practice. An interesting additional source of knowledge is being provided from clinical practice itself. Clinical psychologists, by virtue of their university training, are increasingly contributing to the knowledge base of their own profession and providing 'hands-on' research grounded in the reality of practice. It is the research that emerges from the 'practitioner-scientist' that melds the papers presented in this symposium.

Current issues in perinatal depression: Screening, treatment and prevention
Milgrom, Jeannette *Clinical and Health Psychology, Heidelberg Repatriation Hospit, Heidelberg Heights, Australia*
This paper will discuss issues pertinent to large-scale management of perinatal depression in the community. Current controversies, including the debate over screening, will be discussed in the context of our experience in the beyondblue National Post-natal Depression Program, an Australian public health initiative. This involved over 40,000 pregnant women being screened directly for depression over four years and followed-up postnatally, and included educational and/or resource materials. Psychosocial risk factors, the effectiveness of treatments, the challenge of developing pathways to care and our Toward Parenthood prevention program (offered in a randomised trial to 100 women) will also be presented.

Can social support be enhanced? Results from a randomized control trial
Martin, Paul *Psychological Medicine, Monash Medical Centre, Clayton, Australia*
Over the last three decades, a vast literature has accumulated showing that inadequate social support can have pathological consequences, affecting the development and progression of a range of disorders from potentially lethal diseases such as cardiovascular disease and cancer, to high prevalence, disabling disorders such as depression and chronic headache. Relatively little attention, however, has been devoted to how to help individuals increase the size of their social support networks and derive more support from them. Described here is a randomized control trial designed to evaluate a newly developed, ten session, group program called Promoting Social Networks and Support.

Generalized self-efficacy: Process and outcome in cognitive-behavioural therapy for depression
Nathan, Paula *Centre Clinical Interventions, Perth, Australia* **Watson, Hunna -**, *Centre Clinical Interventions, Northbridge, Perth, Australia*
Objectives: To examine the mechanisms of change in CBT and the role of generalised self-efficacy (GSE). Methods: Pre and post-treatment depressive symptomatology was examined in patients with unipolar depression treated with CBT (N= 159). A

hierarchical regression model sought to determine whether GSE comprised a unique contributor to improvement. Results: Significant improvement occurred, covarying with increased GSE. Controlling for relevant covariates, change in GSE uniquely accounted for 12% of the variance. Conclusions: CBT involves the application of skills, which impacts on symptomatology. The study demonstrates the importance of GSE and recommends that treatment include strategies to help patients take action.

Transdiagnostic CBT for eating disorders: Predictors and outcomes of treatment
Fursland, Anthea Centre Clinical Interventions, Perth, Australia
Objective: To investigate transdiagnostic CBT at an Australian clinic. Method: Fifty-one patients received a diagnostic work-up. Baseline measures were repeated at post-treatment. Results: Both completer and intention-to-treat outcome data are presented (N= 51). 69% completers recovered and 81% showed improvement to within 1 SD of community norms on eating pathology. Despite no significant predictors of recovery, higher eating pathology and lower distress tolerance were predictive of less improvement. Drop-outs (31%) evidenced lower self-esteem, lower self-efficacy, lower levels of distress tolerance, greater interpersonal difficulties and greater eating pathology. Conclusion: CBT-E is an effective treatment in an out-patient public health service.

Strategy and innovation: Linking government policy and service delivery
Patterson, Yvonne Dept.of Education and Training, Policy and Review Directorate, East Perth, Australia
Objectives: To create innovative approaches which link research, government and human services planning. Methods: Western Australian case studies of actual strategies were compared. Results: Case studies reflecting research and policy partnerships are examined. These include government agencies, specialist research institutes and community groups. Challenges and benefits are presented. Conclusions: The paper describes how research bridging human service providers and government policy makers reciprocally benefit both domains. This approach has enhanced the effective delivery of high quality human services in Western Australia through a concerted approach of complementary strategies.

The practitioner-scientist: Answering research questions grounded in practice
Watson, Hunna Centre Clinical Interventions, Northbridge, Perth, Australia Milgrom, Jeannette Clinical and Health Psychology, Heidelberg Repatriation Hospit, Heidelberg Heights, Australia
The growing movement of Evidence Based Practice has encouraged clinical psychologists to integrate empirical research into their daily clinical work. They draw on published scientific knowledge as applicable to regular clinical practice. An interesting additional source of knowledge is being provided from clinical practice itself. Clinical psychologists, by virtue of their university training, are increasingly contributing to the knowledge base of their own profession and providing 'hands-on' research grounded in the reality of practice. It is the research that emerges from the 'practitioner-scientist' that melds the papers presented in this symposium.

S-217: Insecure attachment style and depression in adolescents and adults: The impact on parenting and partner roles

Antonia Bifulco (chair)
The symposium aims to examine how insecure attachment style relates to depressive disorders in adolescents and adults, and across cultures. The

emphasis is on women and girl's experience, although sons and husbands are also included in some samples. All studies use the standardised Attachment Style Interview (ASI) in UK, Malaysian, Portuguese and Italian samples. The presentations look at attachment style in the key roles of parent or partner and how insecure styles increase risk of disorder. Implications for lifespan interventions and service-use are discussed.

Marital relationship, insecure attachment style and poor parenting of the next generation in the UK
Bifulco, Antonia Health and Social Care, Royal Holloway University, London, United Kingdom
Objective: To examine intergenerational transmission of risk of psychological disorder using an attachment model. Methods: 146 high-risk London mothers and their adolescent children were interviewed, with. attachment style, marital history and parenting competence (in mothers), and childhood neglect/abuse (in adolescents) measured, with clinical disorders measured in both. Results: Mothers' marital difficulties were associated with her incompetent parenting and with her neglect/abuse of offspring. This latter related to emotional disorder in the young people. Conclusion: An ecological approach is important in understanding the mechanisms by which maternal insecure attachment style influences transmission of risk to the next generation.

Deliberate self-harm among high-risk adolescents in the UK: The significance of attachment and role reversal
Rusu, Adina Carmen Inst. für Medizin. Psychologie, Ruhr-Universität Bochum, Bochum, Germany
Background: There is little research on self-harm behaviour and attachment style. Aims: To examine the relationship between self-harm, childhood maltreatment, attachment style and later disorders outcomes. Methods: 146 high-risk community-based adolescents were interviewed on their psychological disorder, childhood maltreatment, self-esteem, school experience and attachment style. Results: 21% of adolescents exhibited self-harm behaviours. These related to problem relationships with parents, particularly role reversal, insecure attachment style and internalising disorder. These factors and felt incompetence as a student were important predictors of self-harm behaviours. Conclusions: There are important Implications of these findings for assessment and treatment of adolescents with deliberate self-harm.

Attachment style in relation to depressive-risk among single and married Malaysian mothers
Abdul Kadir, Nor Bayah Health and Social Care, Royal Holloway, Univ. London, Egham, United Kingdom
Background: Insecure attachment style as a predictor of depression has not been studied in Malaysia. Method: A questionnaire study of 1,002 mothers (half single and half married) was conducted in Johor. A subset of 61 with depression were interviewed for attachment style (ASI) and depression (SCID). Results: Loglinear regression showed that insecure attachment, negative evaluation of self, poor support, life events and single parent status provided the best model for depression. Fearful attachment style was most prevalent with dual styles among single mothers. Conclusion: The attachment and depression model was confirmed in Malaysian women with single mothers at particular risk.

Teenage pregnancy, attachment style and depression in a Portuguese series.
Figueiredo, Barbara Psychology, University of Minho, Braga, Portugal Bifulco, Antonia Health and Social Care, Royal Holloway, London, United Kingdom Pacheco, Alexandra Psychology, University of Minho,

Braga, Portugal *Costa, Raquel Psychology, University of Minho, Braga, Puerto Rico Margarino, Rute Psychology, University of Minho, Braga, Portugal*
Objective: To examine the experience of pregnancy in teenage years and adulthood in a Portuguese series, using an attachment model Method: The Attachment Style Interview and the Edinburgh Postnatal Depression Scale were administered to 66 pregnant adolescents and 64 pregnant adult women. Results: Pregnant teenagers were significantly more likely to have insecure attachment styles and prenatal depression. Logistic regression showed Enmeshed style and poor partner support provided the best model for prenatal depression. Age at pregnancy did not add to the model. Conclusion: Insecure attachment style should be addressed in prevention and intervention strategies with teenage mothers.

Insecure attachment style, support and depression among couples in Italy having their first baby
Valoriani, Vania Dept. of Clinical Psychology, University of Florence, Florence, Italy Vaiani, Serena Clinical Psychology, University of Florence, Florence, Italy Ferrari, Maria Gabriella Clinical Psychology, University of Florence, Florence, Italy Benvenuti, Paola Clinical Psychology, University of Florence, Florence, Italy Bifulco, Antonia Health and Social Care, Royal Holloway, Uni London, London, United Kingdom Vanni, Claudia Clinical Psychology, University of Florence, Florence, Italy
Background: Both mothers and fathers need investigation in attachment studies of postnatal depression during transition to parenthood. Method: 40 couples expecting their first baby were interviewed using the Attachment Style Interview. EPDS for depression was administered pre and postnatally. Results: Depression rates were higher in the pregnant mothers than their partners, and this related to poor support, avoidant attachment style and higher rates of depression. Gender effects were found. Conclusion: Women's transition to parenthood required high felt attachment to their partners and trust in their emotional support for wellbeing. Without this there is higher risk of pre and postnatal depression.

Attachment style in carers and use of filial therapy in enhancing foster placement
Thomas, Geraldine Lifespan Research, Royal Holloway, London, United Kingdom
Background: filial therapy is acknowledged as an effective method for enhancing children's adjustment to foster-care placement. Less is known about the impact of carers attachment style. Method: A small pilot project using the ASI prior to training in filial therapy with foster carers was undertaken. Effects on the stability of placement and child/carer interaction were examined. Results: Initial case examination shows the foster carer's attachment style can play a critical role in the effectiveness of the filial therapy. Conclusion: Attachment Style Interviews can help predict foster carer's quality of interaction with children placed and be an aid to childcare services.

S-218: Antecedents and outcomes of school motivation in different contexts

Burkhard Gniewosz (chair)
The goal of this symposium is to bring together five papers from three continents that share the same framework: students' school motivation. Academic values, goals, and motivation will be the central constructs of all papers – treated as dependent as well as independent variable. Six different samples (Malaysian, Taiwanese, Canadian, American, and German) will serve as empirical base for the investigation of antecedents as well as outcomes

of this motivation related group of variables. Adopting an ecological perspective, the effects of family and school context as well as moderations of effect patterns by macro contextual variations will be presented.

Teachers' practices and student motivation
Archambault, Isabelle *École de psychoéducation, Université de Montréal, Montreal, Canada* **Janosz, Michel** *Ecole de Psychoéducation, Université de Montréal, Montréal, Canada* **Chouinard, Roch** *Département d'Éducation, Université de Montréal, Montréal, Canada*
Teachers' practices can contribute differently to student achievement motivation. Using cluster analysis and hierarchical linear modeling, the goals of this study were 1) to identify patterns of practices teachers use in class and, 2) to test how these patterns influence student achievement motivation over time. Data were collected for 683 teachers and their 25,000 students who participated in two waves (2004-2005) of the New Approach New Solutions Study (Québec, Canada). Results demonstrated that different patterns of teachers' practices have differential effects on the development of student achievement motivation. Our findings have multiple implications for teachers' training.

The effects of parental values and activities on student's achievement-related values
Gniewosz, Burkhard *Inst. für Psychologie, Universität Jena, Jena, Germany* **Noack, Peter** *Inst. für Psychologie, Universität Jena, Jena, Germany*
Following the tenets of expectancy × value models and social learning theory, the present study investigates the parent-to-child transmission of achievement-related task values, as mediated through parents' school related activities. Based on a sample of ~1000 German students and their parents, structural equation model analyses showed a complete mediation of the parental value effects on the student's own values, as mediated through the perceived parental values. These perceptions themselves were based on the actual parental activities as well as their perceptions. Discussing the results in terms of observational learning and value transmission, the role of the perceived values will be emphasized.

The roles of perceived classroom goal structures and achievement goals in academic help seeking behaviours among Malaysian adolescents
Awang-Hashim, Rosna *Dept. of Cognitive Sciences, University Utara Malaysia, Sintok, Malaysia* **Md. Ali, Ruzlan** *Faculty of Cog Sc & Educat, University Utara Malaysia, Sintok, Malaysia*
The study hypothesized that perception of classroom goal structures influenced students' help seeking behaviors through their achievement goals. Survey data were collected from 2192 Malay and Chinese secondary school students (14-16 years old) from 30 schools in northern Malaysia. Structural equation modeling was used to test model invariance between the two ethnic groups. Findings were consistent with the western literature for the Malay data but two non-invariant paths were observed in the Chinese data whereby performance avoidance goal was not related to help seeking behaviors. Discussion will center on cross-cultural differences in these motivational variables.

Is high motivation in academic performance or effort always good to adolescent development? School contexts as moderating variable
Chen, Kun-Hu *Dept. of Clinical Psychology, Fujen Catholic University, Hsinchuang, Taiwan* **Lay, Keng-Ling** *Dept. of Psychology, National Taiwan University, Taipei, Taiwan*
As an old Chinese proverb says, "All occupations rank low, only book-learning is exalted." It implies working hard and getting high academic perfor-

mance are important in Chinese society. However, the relationship between high motivation in academic performance/effort and mental health has received little attention. To examine the relationship, the study applied large-sample survey in six junior-high and high schools in Taiwan. The results of hierarchical regression analyses indicated that some interaction effects between academic/effort motivations and school contexts had positive effects on adolescent depression. This study suggests academic motivation in different school contexts plays different roles to adolescent mental health.

S-219: International cognitive competence levels: Causes, consequences and development

Heiner Rindermann (chair)
International cognitive ability studies measuring thinking abilities, knowledge and the intelligent use of knowledge and known as student assessment or intelligence test (IQ) approaches have attracted a lot of scientific and public interest (e.g. European Journal of Personality, 21, 667-787). But what are the causes for different national levels of cognitive abilities? Is there an ongoing upward process ("Flynn-effect")? Or will the secular rise stop and even turn around at least for the most modern countries? Which effects have high cognitive ability levels and their possible future rise or fall for the development of societies? These are subjects dealt by a symposium composed of researchers with different theoretical viewpoints.

IQs of nations and their correlates
Lynn, Richard *Dept. of Psychology, University of Ulster, Bristol, United Kingdom*
This paper presents mean IQs for approximately 120 nations and their correlates. These include (1) per capita income (r= approximately .7); educational attainment (r= approximately .8); fertility (r= approximately -.6); longevity (r= approximately .6); religious belief (r= approximately -.6); and happiness (r= approximately 0). Causes and consequences of the national differences for the development of societies and individuals are discussed. These include the question of whether national cognitive levels are an important factor in economic development and whether the intelligence of the world's population is declining.

Is IQ a determinant of income inequality?
Meisenberg, Gerhard *Dept. of Biochemistry, Ross University, Portsmouth, Dominican Republic*
The average intelligence of the population is related to the distribution of wealth within societies. A high IQ of the country's population reduces the Gini index independent of GDP, educational exposure, political freedom and other plausible predictors. This otherwise strong effect is no longer present at IQs above 90 to 95. The variance of intellectual ability within the country is less important. The spread of student performance on standardized international school assessments (TIMSS, PISA) is not consistently related to the Gini index, although a trend in the expected direction is observed in some regression models.

Psychometric and piagetian approach in comparison
Oesterdiekhoff, Georg *Institute for Soziologie, Universität Karlsruhe, Karlsruhe, Germany*
Populations of different societies differ in their average scores on intelligence tests. As a general rule, people from developed countries perform better than people from less developed countries. One reason for this is that IQ test scores of populations in industrialized countries have been rising more or less continuously for more than 100 years. The mental capacities of pre-modern popula-

tions rarely develop to the stage of abstract thinking. Psychometric research results can be understood in the context of Piagetian cross-cultural psychology. The two theoretical approaches complement each other, and together they explain the cognitive dimension of social change and cultural modernization.

Educational policy and international cognitive competence levels
Rindermann, Heiner *Inst. für Psychologie, Universität Magdeburg, Magdeburg, Germany*
Previous international studies of student performance have provided results regarding abilities of students and various aspects of educational systems. Analyses indicate positive relationships (in correlations, partial correlations and path analyses) between student ability and educational levels of adults, preschool education, discipline, quantity of institutionalized education, attendance at additional schools, early streaming and the use of central exams and tests. Rather negative relationships are found with high repetition rates, late school enrolment and class sizes. A high ratio of migrants has not been found to be negatively associated except when migrant families show a lower educational level than the native population.

Culture-mediated motivational influences on international student assessment and intelligence means
Steppan, Martin *Inst. für Psychologie, Universität Innsbruck, Innsbruck, Austria*
Previous research (e.g. Boe et al., 2002a, b; Woschek, 2005; Rindermann, 2006) has shown that general competence and motivation (e.g. "student task persistence"), rather than specific knowledge, are relevant for success in international student assessment studies. These factors could distort (bias) test results, rankings and their internal correlations (g, or G-factor), and they can influence (develop) the measured ability levels. Different motivations (test-taking, learning, "I want to be better" etc.) depend probably on cultural factors such as religion. Models adjusting test results for motivation and models explaining cognitive ability differences at the national level by motivational factors are presented.

S-220: School failure in the Portuguese and Spanish speaking world

Edgar Galindo (chair)
School failure is a main problem in the Portuguese and Spanish speaking countries; In Africa, it is a social problem together with mental and sensorial deficiencies. School failure is a result of a wide range of factors, some of psychological nature. Psychology must be able not only to identify the causes of school failure, but mainly to explore adequate solutions for every context. These papers analyze different aspects of the topic in Portugal, Spain, Mexico, Angola, Mozambique and Cape Verde, with an emphasis on 1) the relation between previous skills and the onset of school failure and 2) the development of training procedures for children in school age.

The game and its influence in academic achievement
Damián Díaz, Milagros *Dept. of Psychology, University National Autonomus, México City, Mexico*
Play has been shown to have a direct influence on the psychological development of children, affecting learning, creativity, emotional & social aspects, encouraging new skills, and fostering participation in decision-making processes. Consequently, play has been utilized as a teaching resource. This research aims to analyze the play preferences in

Mexican elementary school 6-years-old children (N= 1500), from medium and low socioeconomic levels. It also identifies preferential playing games at home and at school, by boys and girls. Results of a questionnaire and the corresponding quantitative analysis are presented (SPSS, 12.0), showing favorite play places (at school, at home or outdoors), preferences and playing styles.

School failure in Mexican children: Effects of pre-academic and linguistic behavioral levels
Guevara, Yolanda Dept. of Psychology, National University Mexico, Mexico City, Mexico Lopez, Alfredo Dept. of Psychology, National University Mexico, Mexico City, Mexico Huitrón, Blanca Dept. of Psychology, National University Mexico, Mexico City, Mexico Delgado, Ulises Dept. of Psychology, National University Mexico, Mexico City, Mexico Hermosillo, Angela Dept. of Psychology, National University Mexico, Mexico City, Mexico

Several studies have proved that, adequate levels of preacademic and linguistic behaviors (Previous knowledge or entry cognitive behaviors) are necessary to avoid school failure. Our research had two phases. 1): 262 children from low socioeconomic status were assessed through behavioral tests to determine linguistic and preacademic skills level, and reading, writing, and math skills, at the beginning, in the middle and at the end of the first school year. Results show a narrow relationship between entry repertoires and level of developed academic skills, with academic problems related to preacademic and linguistic skills. 2): Ten such children were trained in linguistic and preacademic skills, with encouraging results in school achievement.

Treatment of school failure with a program of discipline in the classroom
Vidal Lucena, Margarita Dept. de Investigación, Instituto Calasanz Educación, Madrid, Spain

School failure has been related to problems of conduct, among other causes. In this paper we present the first results of a program of discipline in the classroom, that has been designed on the basis of several pilot studies carried on in a Spanish school. This program is based on cognitive theory; it introduces explicit, simple, contextualized rules, according to a series of sequenced levels at school. The goal is to reduce the incidence of factors that are directly related to school failure, by introducing rules of behaviour that decrease the time of conflict and increase instructional time.

Treatment of school failure with behavioral techniques
Galindo, Edgar Dept. of Psychology, Universidade Lusofona, Lisboa, Portugal

School failure, a main problem in Portugal (http://www.min-edu.pt), is due to many factors, including psychosocial deficiencies. Behavioral procedures have been widely applied to help deficient persons, like Galindo (1999, 2001) with children in Latin-American slums. This experience is here applied in Portugal to 6 - 12 years old children, failing school because of family problems or social exclusion (poverty or ethnic minority). First, a quasi-experimental study (Multiple Baseline) was carried out, with 8 children. Results are evaluated in terms of % of attained objectives, time, and school satisfaction. Procedures were later applied to 20 children.

Treatment of school failure in Portuguese children: Case studies
Marcelino, Lilia Dept. of Psychology, Universidade Lusofona, Lisboa, Portugal Galindo, Edgar Dept. of Psychology, Universidade Lusofona, Lisboa, Portugal

Selected case studies of 6-12 year old children living in Lisbon slums, participating in the project "Treatment of school failure with behavioral techniques" are presented. Behavioral diagnostic and treatment procedures were designed according to teachers' aims and consistent with the particular social and/or learning problems of each child. Causes of failure are multiple: family instability, child neglect, lack of Portuguese language (immigrants) or social skills. Results are evaluated by % of attained behavioral objectives, time of training and degree of school/family satisfaction. In most cases, treatment was successful. Nevertheless, remarkable differences were found between objective criteria and the degree of satisfaction.

School failure in Angola, Mozambique and Cape Verde: A project for Africa
Guerra Marques, Sónia Dept. of Psychology, Universidade Lusofona, Lisboa, Portugal Sardinha, Erika Dada, Catia Dept. of Psychology, Universidade Lusofona, Lisboa, Portugal Centeio, Denise Dept. of Psychology, Universidade Lusofona, Lisboa, Portugal

African students participating in the project "Treatment of school failure with behavioral techniques" analyze the problem in their countries, where it is associated with mental, sensorial, motor or psychosocial deficiencies and the consequences of war. Percentages of primary school repeaters and survival rate to grade 5 are respectively 10% - 62 % in Mozambique, 15% -93% in Cape Verde and 29%-(unknown) in Angola, a country where additionally about 1,5 million children live in difficult conditions (3,000 on the streets) and 750,000 (310,784 in Mozambique) suffer deficiencies, mostly without attention. A project is presented, which includes a "Training Center for Children at Risk" managed by parents and depending from the local University, whose students apply behavioral techniques.

S-221: Dementia therapy: What can psychology contribute?

Gabriele Wilz, Katja Werheid (chair)

Due to the raising prevalence of dementia worldwide, there is a pressing need to develop supportive intervention strategies for patients affected by dementing disorders and their caregivers. However, research on clinical application and efficacy of psychological interventions in these populations is scarce. The present symposium gathers evidence on a variety of psychological treatments for patients with dementia as well as caregivers, ranging from psychotherapy to focused psychological and social interventions. Scientists from different European countries will present latest evidence on the evaluation of psychological treatments and discuss future developments in this area.

Description and outcomes of a psychological and occupational therapy intervention for dementia family caregivers
Losada, Andres Dept. of Psychology, Universidad Rey Juan Carlos, Madrid, Spain Márquez González, María Biological and Health Psycholo, Universidad Autónoma de Madrid, Madrid, Spain Peñacoba, Cecilia Dept. of Psychology, Universidad Rey Juan Carlos, Madrid, Spain Gallagher Thompson, Dolores School of Medicine, Stanford University, San Francisco, USA Knight, Bob G. Clinical Psychology, University of Southern Califor, Los Angeles, USA Cigarán, Margarita Dept. of Psychology, Universidad Rey Juan Carlos, Madrid, Spain Moreno, Ricardo Dept. of Psychology, Universidad Rey Juan Carlos, Madrid, Spain

Preliminary results of a multicomponent and interdisciplinary (cognitive-behaviour-therapy and occupational-therapy) intervention for dementia caregivers are presented. Caregivers were randomly assigned to an intervention condition (n = 40) or a control condition (n = 50), and blind interviews were conducted. The results show a significant reduction from pre-intervention to post-intervention of depression (p < .01), anxiety (p < .05) and dysfunctional thoughts (p < .01), and a significant increase in pleasurable activities (p < .01) and satisfaction with these activities (p < .01) in those caregivers that participated in the intervention condition. These changes were not significant in the control group.

Evaluation of health effects of assisted vacations for persons with dementia and their spouses
Wilz, Gabriele Inst. für Klin. Psychologie, Technische Universität Berlin, Berlin, Germany Fink-Heitz, Margit Institute of Public Health Res, Technische Universität München, Munich, Germany

Objective: An evaluation of assisted vacations for persons with dementia and their caregivers was conducted for the first time in caregiving research. Method: A quasi-experimental, 2-group design with two measuring times was used to examine whether assisted vacations lead to a reduction in physical complaints and depression in family caregivers (N=29). Results: The overall emotional and physical state of the participants in the intervention group showed significant improvements in comparison with the control group three months after the first interview. Conclusions: Assisted vacations can be seen as a way of diminishing the risk of stress disorders for family caregivers.

Dyadic exchange and well-being in couples with one spouse suffering from dementia
Braun, Melanie Sozial.- und Gesundheitspsy., Universität Zürich, Zürich, Switzerland

Objective: Dementia prevalence increases due to growing life expectancy. Equity and a balanced exchange predict relationship quality and well-being. In couples with dementia, equity should be impaired by a modified dyadic exchange. Method: Thirty couples (N=60) with a demented husband participated in the study. Social exchange, equity, and well-being are assessed longitudinally. Objective and subjective methods are combined to analyse dyadic processes. Results: Caregiving wives experience more depression and inequity, and lower satisfaction with life than their husbands. Despite their impairment, the demented subjects participated actively. Conclusions: Relations between exchange, well-being, and health decline comprise essential information for couple interventions.

Evaluation of a cognitive behavioural group intervention program for caregivers
Kalytta, Tanja Fachbereich I, Techn. Fachhochschule Berlin, Berlin, Germany Wilz, Gabriele Inst. für Klin. Psychologie, Technische Universität Berlin, Berlin, Germany

Objectives: The effect of a cognitive behavioural group program was examined in caregivers of dementia patients. Methods: The participants were 71 caregivers who were assigned to either a group receiving treatment or a group receiving usual care (control group). We measured caregivers' resources, body complaints, and depressive symptoms. MAN-OVAs allowed for examination of short-term effects of the intervention. Results: Caregivers who attended the intervention report a raised awareness and understanding of the illness. The participation at the intervention program was significantly associated with in changes body complaints. Conclusions: The findings confirm the importance of interventions for caregivers of dementia patients.

Effective factors in psychosocial interventions in dementia care
Vernooij-Dassen, Myrra Dept. of Clinical Psychology, University of Nijmegen, Nijmegen, Netherlands

Many psychosocial interventions in dementia care have been developed over the last decades. Meta-analyses provide evidence on effectiveness of some interventions. No single intervention can address the complexity of needs of dementia patients and their carers. Factors that contribute to effectiveness are tailor made care and opportunities to make choices between interventions. The evidence on effectiveness so far should be used in conceptual models helping to explain which support is helpful for who and why this support is effective. A conceptual model will be proposed not only focussing at the benefits, but also at the costs of receiving support.

Cognitive behavioral therapy in depressed patients with mild cognitive deficits

Werheid, Katja Inst. für Psychologie, Humboldt-Universität zu Berlin, Berlin, Germany *Ehlers, Birka* Inst. für Psychologie, Humboldt-Universität zu Berlin, Berlin, Germany *Kischkel, Eva* Inst. für Psychologie, Humboldt-Universität zu Berlin, Berlin, Germany

Cognitive behavioral group therapy (CBT-G) is a well-established psychological treatment of depression in healthy elderly – but evidence regarding elder adults with reduced cognitive capacities is scarce. We investigated elder patients with Major Depression and mild cognitive deficits, yet not dementia. Apart from standard geriatric day care treatment, half of them participated in a CBT-G program, while the others joined unspecific group activities. Our current results show reduced depression in both groups immediately after treatment. For the six-months follow-up, we expect CBT-G to be associated with an increased level of self-guided physical and social activities.

S-222: New directions in multinomial modeling

Christoph Stahl (chair)

This symposium is about a class of stochastic models that are tailored to specific research paradigms and allow the measurement of latent cognitive processes underlying observed responses, like memory judgments or reasoning decisions. The talks will present novel applications of this family of models, for example to prospective memory and to binding in episodic memory, and current developments in the statistical framework, including the consideration of interindividual differences, comparisons with signal-detection models, and extensions to hierarchical stochastic models. The symposium thereby highlights the use and further development of the family of stochastic models for the focused analysis of substantive research questions in cognitive psychology.

The multinomial model of event-based prospective memory

Bayen, Ute Inst. für Psychologie, Universität Düsseldorf, Düsseldorf, Germany *Smith, Rebekah E.* Dept of Psychology, Univ. of Texas at San Antonio, San Antonio, TX, USA

Prospective memory is remembering to perform an action in the future. The multinomial processing tree model by Smith and Bayen (2004, 2006) is the first formal model of event-based prospective memory and allows us to separately measure prospective and retrospective components of performance in event-based prospective memory tasks. After reviewing experimental validation of core model parameters, the presentation will demonstrate the usefulness of the model in localizing age related differences in prospective memory task performance in studies on child development and cognitive aging.

Signal detection versus threshold models of recognition and source memory

Bröder, Arndt Inst. für Psychologie, Universität Bonn, Bonn, Germany *Schütz, Julia* Department of Psychology, University of Bonn, Bonn, Germany

Conventional measures of recognition and source memory often confound memory processes and response biases. To solve this problem, multinomial models have been proposed. These assume finite

sets of latent states and hence imply a threshold concept. Critics have suggested signal detection models (SDT) with normally distributed probability densities on a familiarity continuum as a viable alternative. Analyses typically show curved ROCs for rating data which is interpreted in favour of SDT. However, this conclusion is invalid. We report experiments and arguments that challenge the conclusion.

Signal detection theory in the dark: Measuring sensitivity and response bias without being able to separate hits and false alarms

Erdfelder, Edgar Lehrstuhl Psychologie III, Universität Mannheim, Mannheim, Germany *Cüpper, Lutz* Lehrstuhl Psychologie III, Universität Mannheim, Mannheim, Germany *Bernstein, Daniel M.* Department of Psychology, Kwantlen University College, Surrey, BC, Canada

Signal Detection Theory (SDT) is normally used to disentangle memory strength and response bias in recognition memory tests. There are some fields of research, however, in which SDT cannot be applied because the answer key required to separate hits and false alarms is unknown (e.g., autobiographical or eyewitness memory research). We suggest a finite mixture extension of SDT to cope with this problem. The model is presented and tested using (a) computer simulations and (b) episodic recognition data. It is shown that the new mixture model can approximate SDT results well if the assumptions underlying SDT hold.

The latent-class hierarchical approach to parameter heterogeneity in multinomial models: First applications

Stahl, Christoph Inst. für Psychologie, Universität Freiburg, Freiburg, Germany

Multinomial processing tree (MPT) models are a flexible family of stochastic models for experimental paradigms. In applications of MPT models to aggregated data, parameter homogeneity across participants is a precondition that is often violated. A hierarchical extension to multinomial models – the latent-class hierarchical framework – has been proposed that can detect and model parameter heterogeneity. It is demonstrated that this framework is successful in detecting and in modeling parameter heterogeneity in a variety of paradigms. It is further demonstrated that the latent-class framework can be used to investigate interindividual differences in performance in several experimental paradigms.

Testing for and specifying individual participant and item differences in multinomial processing tree modeling

Batchelder, William Dept. of Cognitive Sciences, University of California, Irvine, USA *Smith, Jared* Dept. of Cognitive Sciences, University of California, Irvine, CA, USA

Multinomial Processing Tree (MPT) models, as well as many other types of formal models in cognitive psychology, apply to data where each participant makes categorical responses to a fixed set of item events, e.g. memory items, choice trials, or absolute judgments. This paper presents computationally easy, non-parametric, hypothesis tests for detecting the presence of participant and/or item heterogeneity in such data. When heterogeneities exist, it is important to specify random effects in an MPT model. The paper provides a general approach to modeling heterogeneities in MPT models using psychometric concepts from item response theory modeling.

Analyzing contingency tables with multinomial processing tree models

Hu, Xiangen FedEx Institute of Technology, University of Memphis, Memphis, USA *Batchelder, William* Cognitive Psychology, UC Irvine, Irvine, USA

Log-linear models incorporating quasi-independence are frequently used to analyze contingency table data with structurally missing cells. There are some limitations with the log-linear approach, and these limitations can be overcome with Multinomial Processing Tree (MPT) models. MPT models are a family of non-linear, graphical models for categorical data that have been used widely for analyzing categorical data in the psychological sciences. MPT models will be specified for contingency tables with structurally missing cells, and these models will be shown to handle a wider class of hypotheses than the ones that can be specified within the log-linear approach.

S-223: Preventing emotional disorders: European research activities with the GO!-Program

Simon-Peter Neumer, Juliane Junge-Hoffmeister (chair)

The GO!-Program (Junge et al., 2002) is a prevention program with the specific target of depression and anxiety disorders. The program combines cognitive-behavioral disorder-specific treatment components with other more general health promoting factors. It has been used in Germany, Switzerland, Austria and Norway since 1998. Its effectiveness has been originally evaluated through controlled studies with adolescents and in an adopted version with young adults. Recently several new studies within different settings have been conducted. The aim of this symposium is to give an overview concerning ongoing research and to discuss perspectives for prevention research and practice in Europe.

Prevention of anxiety and depression in adolescents: How does GO! work within a universal school setting? Results from Germany and Switzerland

Junge-Hoffmeister, Juliane Clinical Psychology, Technical University Dresden, Dresden, Germany *Neumer, Simon-Peter* RBUP East and South Norway, Center for Child Mental Health, Oslo, Norway *Bittner, Antje* Psychosomatic Clinic, University Hospital, Dresden, Germany *Balmer, Katharina* Clinical Psychology, University of Basel, Basel, Switzerland *Manz, Rolf* Fed. Ass. Accident Insurances, Fed. Ass. Accident Insurances, München, Germany *Margraf, Jürgen* Clinical Psychology, University of Basel, Basel, Switzerland

The GO!-Program was developed to prevent the potential negative impact of anxiety and depression in adolescence. The short- and long-term effectiveness of this cognitive-behavioral intervention was investigated within two controlled studies using schoolbased, universal settings in Germany and Switzerland. A comprehensive questionnaire battery and structured interviews were used for a differential efficacy and process evaluation. Results: GO! was well accepted. Program effects could be shown concerning knowledge and potential risk factors for the development of anxious and depressive symptoms. However, results regarding a symptom reduction were limited within the universal settings. Implications for a setting specific application will be discussed.

Chances and limits of GO! within a selective setting: Results from Austria

Wieser, Alexandra Inst. Bildungswissenschaften, Universität Graz, Graz, Austria *Jauk, Marlies* Educational Sciences, University Graz, Graz, Austria *Reicher, Hannelore* Educational Sciences, University

Graz, Graz, Austria *Peer, Andrea* Educational Sciences, University Graz, Graz, Austria

The following research findings are based on our experiences as GO!-coaches. 96 adolescents (grades 5-11) took part in 7 GO!-courses within different settings: grammar school vs. secondary general school, gender-homogeneous vs. gender-heterogeneous. The efficacy of GO! was evaluated in a training-control-group-design with repeated measurement; for 3 GO!-courses 3-month-follow-up data are reported. In an additional research project 8 randomly drawn GO!-participants were administered a qualitative evaluation interview. In general, the present studies give evidence to the effectiveness of GO, at least regarding short-time effects. Implications of quantitative results and qualitative interviews for prevention work in different school settings are discussed.

GO! for young women. Results of the evaluation of the adopted GO!-Program for young women and in progress developments for the specific target group of pregnant women

Bittner, Antje Psychotherapy and Psychosomat., University Hospital TU Dresden, Dresden, Germany *Neumer, Simon* Mental Health (R.BUP), Centre for Child + Adolescent, Oslo, Norway *Junge-Hoffmeister, Juliane* Inst. of Clinical Psychology, Technische Universität Dresden, Dresden, Germany *Manz, Rolf* Bundesverband der Unfallkassen, Bundesverband der Unfallkassen, München, Germany *Margraf, Jürgen* University of Basel, Inst. of Clinical Psychology, Basel, Switzerland

Aims of this study were the implementation and evaluation of the cognitive-behavioural prevention programme GO! for anxiety disorders and depression in young women. 110 women (mean age 24.7 years) participated in the quasi-experimental intervention study with a 6- and a 12-month follow-up. Results show that the treatment group had significantly fewer depressive symptoms and dysfunctional cognitions, showed significantly less avoidance behaviour, and had significantly greater improvements concerning general self efficacy and perceived social support than the control group. Implications for a prevention programme to reduce stress, anxiety, and depressive symptoms in pregnant women will be discussed.

Smart parents: First results of a Norwegian pilot study with parents of children and adolescents with emotional disorders

Gere, Martina Prevention Research, RBUP East and South Norway, Oslo, Norway *Neumer, Simon-Peter* Prevention Research, RBUP East and South Norway, Oslo, Norway

In this pilot study, the Norwegian version of GO! has been adapted for parents of anxious or depressed children (age 7 to 15 years). Our objectives were to ensure the feasibility of SMART PARENTS; to evaluate user-satisfaction; and to confirm earlier obtained effects with the GO! program. Pre- and post measures included symptoms of anxiety, depression and stress, resilience and gain of knowledge. Pre-Post-Comparison and Reliable Change Index (RCI, Truax, 1991) were used for analyzing the whole group and single cases. Results of the pilot study will be presented and discussed.

How to solve power problems in prevention research: Examples from the women's study

Müller, Johannes Inst. of Psychology II, Technical University Dresden, Dresden, Germany *Neumer, Simon-Peter* Mental Health, Centre f. Child and Adolescent, Oslo, Norway *Hoyer, Jürgen* Clinical Psych. and Therapy, Technical University Dresden, Dresden, Germany *Manz, Rolf* (BUK), Bundesverband der Unfallkassen, München, Germany

Unsatisfactory statistical validity is a common problem in clinical research settings. Using the

example of a pre-post evaluation of the GO! program conducted with young women the problematic issue of statistical power is introduced. Several possible ways to increase power are discussed, e.g. Erdfelder's (1994) compromise power analysis and ways to reduce error variance or the amount of tests. In case of small sample and effect sizes significance tests should not be used. Here, e.g. the reliable change index of Jacobson and Truax (1991) might be a reasonable alternative.

Future directions for the prevention of anxiety and depression in research and practice with the GO!-Program and its adoptions

Neumer, Simon-Peter RBUP East and South Norway, Oslo, Norway *Junge-Hoffmeister, Juliane* Clinical Psychology, TU Dresden, Dresden, Germany

The final discussion will provide an overview of all studies conducted with the GO! Program based on an integrative model linking prevention and treatment, proposed by J. R. Weisz and colleagues in 2005. The presentation covers a wide range of the program's applications targeted at different areas, with attempts to highlight challenges and changes concerning the future development of the GO! program.

S-224: Beyond a universal personality structure: Recent research on the cross-cultural (Chinese) personality assessment inventory

Fanny M. Cheung (chair)

The Cross-cultural (Chinese) Personality Assessment Inventory (CPAI) was developed using a combined emic-etic approach which includes universal and culturally relevant personality constructs. The CPAI research program aims to establish not only the reliability and validity of an indigenously derived assessment measure, but also to promote understanding of personality beyond that of a universal personality structure. This symposium presents the latest research on the CPAI-2 and the adolescent version, CPAI-A. The papers highlight the value of indigenously derived personality scales in understanding vocational interest, career exploration, life satisfaction, adjustment, and self-other congruence in personality ratings among Chinese adults and adolescents.

Joint analysis of the UNIACT and the CPAI-2: A cross-cultural investigation of vocational personality types and general personality traits

Cheung, Shu Fai Dept. of Psychology, University of Macau, Macau, People's Republic of China *Leong, Frederick T. L.* Dept. of Psychology, Michigan State University, East Lansing, MI, USA *Cheung, Fanny M.* Dept. of Psychology, Chinese Univ. of Hong Kong, Hong Kong, People's Republic of China

This study investigates the relationship between UNIACT's vocational personality types and an indigenous Chinese personality inventory, the CPAI-2. The UNIACT and the CPAI-2 were administered to 371 college students in the United States and 412 students in Hong Kong. The structures of the two inventories in the two samples were examined using joint factor analysis and canonical correlation to study the relationship between the Western model of career-related personality and the general personality model with Chinese origin. The contribution of the CPAI-2 to understanding the Western model of vocational personality types from the Chinese perspective will be discussed.

The contributions of personality traits and parenting styles to career exploration

Fan, Weiqiao Dept. of Psychology, Chinese Univ. of Hong Kong, Hong Kong, China, People's Republic of: Hong Kong SAR *Cheung, Fanny M.* Dept. of Psychology, Chinese Univ. of Hong Kong, Hong Kong, China, People's Republic of: Hong Kong SAR *Leong, Frederick T.L.* Dept. of Psychology, Michigan State University, East Lansing, USA *Cheung, Shu Fai* Dept. of Psychology, Macau Univiversity, Macao, China, People's Republic of: Macao SAR

The study investigated the contributions of personality traits and parenting styles on career explorations. 412 Hong Kong and 371 American university students took part in the study. Significant cross-cultural differences were found on the direct influences of personality traits (especially the culturally relevant personality dimensions assessed by the CPAI-2) and parenting styles on career explorations. Furthermore, significant mediating effects of some universal (e.g., Leadership) and indigenous (e.g., Family Orientation) personality scales on the relationships between parenting styles and career explorations were obtained. The implications of the results on vocational counseling and development among university students were discussed.

Personality and work-family interface as predictors of job and life satisfaction among female teachers in Hong Kong

Wan, Sarah Lai Yin Dept. of Psychology, Chinese Univ. of Hong Kong, Hong Kong, China, People's Republic of: Hong Kong SAR *Cheung, Fanny M.* Dept. of Psychology, Chinese Univ. of Hong Kong, Hong Kong, China, People's Republic of: Macao SAR

This study investigated the role of personality variables, including Self-Acceptance, Optimism, Family Orientation and Harmony, in the prediction of relationships between work-family interface and job and life satisfaction among 528 Hong Kong Chinese female teachers. Results from regression analyses showed that among the four personality variables, Optimism best explained both job and life satisfaction, while Self-Acceptance and Family Orientation also explained job and life satisfaction respectively. Significant moderating effects of Optimism and Family Orientation in explaining life satisfaction were found only among married women. The meaning of work-family balance and its relationship to subjective well-being for women were discussed.

The role of personality on the relationship between violence exposure and adjustment outcomes among Chinese adolescents

Ho, Man Yee Dept. of Psychology, Chinese Univ. of Hong Kong, Hong Kong, China, People's Republic of: Hong Kong SAR *Cheung, Fanny, M.* Dept. of Psychology, Chinese Univ. of Hong Kong, Hong Kong, China, People's Republic of: Macao SAR

This study aims to examine the relationship between exposure to violence and psychosocial adjustment in adolescents, and to explore the protective influences of interpersonal related personality traits. A sample of 800 adolescents aged 12 - 14 years in Hong Kong were surveyed about their exposure to violence, interpersonal related personality and adjustment outcomes using the Children's Report of Exposure to Violence (CREV), the Youth Self Report (YSR), and the Adolescent Version of Chinese Personality Assessment Inventory (CPAI-A), respectively. The effects of different forms of violence exposure (victimization and witness) and perpetrators (strangers and familiar person) on outcomes were also investigated.

S-225: Binge eating behavior: Basics and therapy outcome

Tanja Legenbauer, Silja Vocks (chair)

Binge eating behaviour is a frequent symptom that is often associated with obesity. To date, the knowledge about triggers for binge attacks is limited, making it difficult to develop effective treatments for this kind of psychopathology. Therefore, in this panel, recent findings on cognitive, emotional, and psychophysiological antecendents and correlates of binge eating will be presented. Furthermore, the symposium will focus on research concerning the outcome of various therapeutic approaches for binge eating behaviour and obsity such as cognitive behavior therapy, body image therapy and surgery. At the end of the panel, the presented findings will be integrated and discussed.

Triggers of binge eating before and after short-term CBT (based on EMA assessment)

Munsch, Simone Inst. für Psychologie, Universität Basel, Basel, Switzerland Meyer, Andrea H. Inst. für Psychologie, Universität Basel, Basel, Switzerland Wilhelm, Frank Inst. für Psychologie, Universität Basel, Basel, Switzerland

Objectives: To identify antecendents and consequences of binge eating before and after short-term CBT based on EMA. Methods: Twenty-eight individuals were randomly allocated to treatment or wait-list. Binge eating was studied using EMA (7 days) before wait-list, before and after treatment. Results: Before and after treatment, binge eating was triggered by interpersonal conflicts, negative mood, or situational antecedents. Most prominent consequences of binge eating were cognitions of low self-efficacy. Conclusion: Training of interpersonal problem solving, coping with negative mood, restructuring of low self-efficacy cognitions could represent moderators of change. Using EMA, treatment protocols could be tailored specifically to patients.

Effects of body image therapy: A randomized-controlled study with obese individuals

Vocks, Silja Inst. für Klin. Psychologie, Universität Bochum, Bochum, Germany Nasrawi, Nadia Clinical Psychology, Universität Bochum, Bochum, Germany Trojca, Dorothea Clinical Psychology, Universität Bochum, Bochum, Germany

Objective: Effects of a cognitive-behavioural body image therapy for obesity were analysed. Methods: 34 females were randomly assigned to either a manualized body image therapy or a waiting condition and answered several self-report questionnaires and the "photo distortion technique". Results: A 2x2 ANOVA revealed a strong reduction of body dissatisfaction, weight/shape concerns, depression and body checking and avoidance behaviour among participants of the therapy, whereas no pre-post-changes were found in the control group. Additoionally, participants estimated their own figure to be slimmer after the treatment. Conclusions: Cognitive-behavioural body image therapy is a promising intervention for body image improvement in obesity.

Psychophysiological effects of binge eating severity

Vögele, Claus School of Human Life Sciences, Roehampton University, London, United Kingdom

It has been suggested that up to 80% of patients with eating disorders are affected by cardiac complications. There is recent evidence that changes in autonomic cardiac control associated with alternating periods of starvation and bingeing may contribute to this scenario in eating disordered patients. The present study investigated cardio autonomic regulation and stress reactivity in relation to endocrinological parameters of dietary restriction status and binge eating severity in women diagnosed with bulimia nervosa. The results confirm the notion of cardiac sympathetic inhibition during caloric restriction and increased activity during periods of bingeing.

Binge eating behavior before and after obesity surgery

Mühlhans, Barbara Psychosomatik u. Psychotherap., Universitätsklinik Erlangen, Erlangen, Germany de Zwaan, Martina Abt. für Psychosomatik, Universitätsklinikum Erlangen, Erlangen, Germany

Binging behaviour is common among severely obese patients prior to bariatric surgery, after surgery in a small proportion of patients binge eating reoccurs. With the Eating Disorder Examination (EDE) Interview we assessed eating behaviour among patients prior to surgery and at a 1&2 year follow up. We were especially interested in the frequency of binging behaviour, the prevalence of Binge Eating Disorder (BED), and the influence of binge eating behaviour on weight reduction. Pre surgery binging episodes did not predict amount of weight loss after surgery, only the re-occurrence of disordered eating seems to have an effect.

Predictors and moderators of treatment outcome in individuals with BED

Schlup, Barbara Inst. für Psychologie, Universität Basel, Basel, Switzerland Munsch, Simone Inst. für Psychologie, Universität Basel, Basel, Switzerland Meyer, Andrea Inst. für Psychologie, Universität Basel, Basel, Switzerland

Objective: This study compared treatment outcomes of two cognitive-behavioral treatments (CBT) of differing length. Implications for stepped care and cost-effectiveness are discussed. Method: 76 participants with BED participated in a 16- or 8-session CBT. Remission and recovery from binge eating, reduction of binge episodes and body mass index were compared at posttreatment and until 1-year follow-up. Results: The longer treatment was generally superior to the shorter intervention at the end of treatment, but less so at the end of follow-up. Conclusion: CBT, short or long-term, was efficacious. Short-term CBT could be a cost-effective initial intervention for BED patients.

Longterm weight change after different treatments in obese individuals: Associations to disturbed eating behaviors and psychiatric comorbidity

Legenbauer, Tanja Psychosomat. Medizin, Ruhr-Universität Bochum, Dortmund, Germany Herpertz, Stephan Psychosomat. Medizin, Ruhr-Universität Bochum, Dortmund, Germany

Objective: To investigate the impact of binge eating on longterm weight change in obese individuals undergoing different weight loss treatments. Method: Participants of a conventional weight loss treatment (N=219) and obesity surgery patients (N=127) were investigated with a structured interview (SIAB-EX) and questionnaires at baseline and after four years. Percentage of excess weight loss was calculated. Results: Binge eating was no predictor for weight loss, but the degree of disinhibition after four years explained 45.8% of weight loss in the conventional treatment group. Conclusions: Not pre- but posttreatment disturbed eating patterns are of predictive value for the extent of weight loss in conventional but not in surgical weight loss treatment.

S-226: Cultural influences on mental health and illness behaviors

Winnie Mak, Sylvia Xiaohua Chen (chair)

The influences of culture on mental health and illness behaviors are examined through the application of theoretical frameworks, the support of empirical data, and case examples in the counseling context in a series of five studies. Moving beyond culture, the studies unpackage cultural influences by examining the relationships of specific culturally salient variables on well-being and help-seeking intentions and practices. It is hoped that the

symposium can offer a forum among researchers to understand how culture can impact the illness experience of individuals and how interventions can be adapted to cater to the needs of cultural diverse individuals.

Understanding distress and help-seeking: The role of face concern among Chinese Americans, European Americans, Hong Kong Chinese and Mainland Chinese

Mak, Winnie Dept. of Psychology, Chinese Univ. of Hong Kong, Shatin, China, People's Republic of : Hong Kong SAR

The role of face concern in distress and help-seeking was examined. In Study 1, the single-factor structure of face concern was confirmed among Chinese Americans and European Americans. Face concern was found to be positively related to distress and help-seeking, above and beyond age, gender, and ethnicity. Study 2 deconstructed face concern into a two-factor model among Hong Kong Chinese and Mainland Chinese. In Study 3, two factors of face concern were supported among community Hong Kong Chinese and Mainland Chinese. Self-face was positively associated with distress and help-seeking. These findings highlighted the importance of specific cultural values in counseling.

Seeking help from mental health professionals: Cross-cultural comparisons among four cultural groups

Chen, Sylvia Xiaohua Applied Social Sciences, Hong Kong Polytechnic Univ., Hong Kong, China, People's Republic of : Hong Kong SAR

The present study examined the contributions of psychological distress and lay beliefs about the etiology of mental illness to seeking help from mental health professionals among four cultural groups: European Americans, Chinese Americans, Hong Kong Chinese, and Mainland Chinese. Group differences were found in help-seeking history and likelihood, with European and Chinese Americans more likely to seek help than Hong Kong and Mainland Chinese. Multiple-group path analysis showed that psychological distress, causal attributions, and prior help-seeking history significantly predicted help-seeking likelihood. Our findings demonstrate the importance of culture in understanding psychopathology and how cultural norms shape help-seeking propensities.

Using an extended theory of planned behavior to understand help-seeking for mental health problems among Chinese

Mo, Phoenix IWHO, University of Nottingham, Nottingham, United Kingdom Mak, Winnie Psychology, Chinese Univ of Hong Kong, Shatin, China, People's Republic of : Hong Kong SAR

The study applied and extended Ajzen's Theory of Planned Behavior (TPB) to understand intentions to seek professional help for mental health problems among Chinese. 941 Chinese were recruited using a randomized household design in Hong Kong. Results from structural equation modelling showed that attitude, subjective norm, and perceived behavioural control significantly predicted help-seeking intention. Model comparisons showed the extended model, with subjective norm indirectly predicted help-seeking intention through influencing attitude and perceived behavioural control, achieved better fit than the original TPB model. Results suggested that subjective norm might be a more important component in understanding help-seeking in Chinese population.

Application of the theory of planned behavior to acculturation: A longitudinal study on mainland Chinese students in Hong Kong

Wu, Ellery Dept. of Psychology, Chinese Univ. of Hong Kong, Shatin, China, People's Republic of : Hong Kong SAR *Mak, Winnie* Psychology, Chinese Univ of Hong Kong, Shatin, China, People's Republic of : Macao SAR *Teng, Yue* Dept. of Psychology, Chinese Univ. of Hong Kong, Shatin, China, People's Republic of : Macao SAR

The present study uses the Theory of Planned Behavior as a theoretical framework to examine the role of social cognitive factors on acculturation. Using a longitudinal design, the study also explores changes in cultural adjustment and associated psychological and socio-cultural consequences over the course of one year. 775 mainland Chinese students from three major universities in Hong Kong participated in the present study. Findings illustrated the importance of acculturative factors in the adjustment of students over time. Implications to counseling services at the university are discussed.

Seeking counseling in Hong Kong: Reflections from a practicing psychologist

Dorcas, Allen Applied Social Sciences, Hong Kong Polytechnic Univ., Kowloon, China, People's Republic of : Hong Kong SAR

Psychological consultation behaviors are examined and compared between Chinese and expatriates in Hong Kong. Data was collected informally over a 10 year period by a Western psychologist providing counseling in English, French and Chinese. It is observed, among other things, that Chinese clients are more hesitant to seek out professional services and often wait until the severity of the problem becomes unbearable. This is not reflected as strongly with expatriate clients who seem more relaxed about consulting a psychologist and often see counseling as an opportunity for self-awareness and understanding.

S-227: Internet-based interventions in clinical psychology

Birgit Wagner (chair)
Internet-based psychotherapeutic interventions are an emerging area of research concerned with treatment efficacy. Meta-analyses (Barak et al, in press; Spek et al., 2007) provide strong support of the effectiveness of online psychological interventions. A large number of studies have shown that Internet-based interventions are as effective as or even more effective than routine face-to-face clinical care. The presentations in this symposium will present results of treatment interventions for the following psychological disorders: Social Phobia, depression, panic disorders, PTSD in post-war countries, complicated grief and eating disorders. The results of the RCTs and future implications of Internet-based interventions are discussed.

Protocolled treatment through the internet, research and practice

Lange, Alfred Dept. of Clinical Psychology, University of Amsterdam, Amsterdam, Netherlands *Ruwaard, J. Schrieken, B.*

The paper starts with the general structure and elements of the Interapy treatment site and provides a brief overview of the effect sizes of five randomized controlled trials, on: PTSD, Chronic Stress, Depression, Panic Disorder and Bulimia Nervosa. Subsequently, the paper describes clinical outcome data on 1000 patients that were treated after the effectivity was proven in the RCT's. Extra information on personal Websites: www.alfredlange.nl

Internet-based treatment for complicated grief: A longitudinal study

Wagner, Birgit Inst. für Psychopathologie, Universität Zürich, Zürich, Switzerland

Bereaved individuals with complicated grief diagnosis (n = 50) were randomly assigned to either the treatment group or a waiting list control condition. 58.8% of the participants lost their child, 11.8%, their partners, 11.8% their sibling. The 5-week intervention consisted of three modules: (1) self-confrontation with the circumstance of death of a significant person, (2) cognitive reappraisal and (3) sharing and farewell ritual. The participants in the experimental group (n = 25) improved significantly compared with the participants in the waiting control condition maintained the symptom reduction at a 1.5-year follow-up. An increase of posttraumatic growth at post-treatment was found.

Es[s]prit - Prevention of eating disorders through the internet

Kordy, Hans Forschungszentr Psychotherapie, Universität Heidelberg, Heidelberg, Germany *Bauer, Stephanie* Zentrum für Psychotherapie, Universität Heidelberg, Heidelberg, Germany *Mößner, Markus* Forschungsstelle für Psychoth., Universität Heidelberg, Heidelberg, Germany *Wolf, Markus* Forschungsstelle für Psychoth., Universität Heidelberg, Heidelberg, Germany

Es[s]prit is an Internet-based eating disorders (ED) prevention program for college students. It follows a stepped-care approach and combines support components of increasing intensity (e.g. forums, moderated chats). Participants who develop substantial ED symptoms during their participation in the program are referred to the University Counseling Center. Compared to traditional prevention programs, the main advantage of Es[s]prit is the monitoring system which allows for timely interventions in case of negative developments. The underlying concepts and various components of this complex prevention program will be introduced, and experiences with the approach in a sample of German college students will be reported.

A virtual treatment center for trauma victims in Iraq

Knaevelsrud, Christine Research, Center for Torture Victims, Berlin, Germany *Wagner, Birgit* Department of Psychopathology, University of Zürich, Zürich, Germany

Due to widespread human right violations and current terror in post-war Iraq a large percentage of the population suffers from psychological consequences. However an adequate psychiatric and psychotherapeutic infrastructure is lacking. In ccoperation with the Iraqui Kirkuk Center a virtual treatment center was implemented. The contact between patient and therapist occurs exclusively via email. The treatment is based on a clinically evaluated culturally adapted treatment protocol (Interapy). Preliminary evidence suggests that this treatment approach is well-accepted and effective. To our knowledge this is the first approach which provides psychological support through Internet in a post-war country. Currently a RCT is conducted to examine this approach empirically.

A web-based cognitive-behavioral approach to social phobia: Results of a randomized controlled trial

Caspar, Franz Dept. für Psychologie, Universität Bern, Bern, Switzerland *Berger, Thomas* Dept. für Psychologie, Universität Bern, Bern 9, Switzerland *Hohl, Eleonore* Dept. für Psychologie, Universität Bern, Bern 9, Switzerland

This study evaluates a web based cognitive behavioral approach to social phobia. The intervention consists of a 10 week use of an Internet platform including an interactive self-help guide, a module for contacts with a therapist, a monitoring and feedback system of patient's response, and collaborative elements, offering patients opportunities to share experiences with other patients. The sample: 50 subjects (treatment group n=30; wait-list control n=20) suffering from moderate to severe social phobia (assessed with SCID and several questionnaires). Final results of the controlled trial are positive and will be presented along with findings related to predictors of outcome.

S-228: Developmental aspects in cognitive neuroscience

Jacqueline Zöllig (chair)
This symposium presents current directions in neuropsychological aspects of cognitive development. The first contribution approaches this issue from an anatomical perspective focusing on the rostral prefrontal cortex and it's implications for development. The following talks address the subject from a functional perspective concentrating on development-related changes in encoding of future actions, time estimation, and item, source, and prospective memory. These changes are studied from different perspectives using fMRI, EEG, and behavioural data with healthy participants from different age groups and a group of patients with schizophrenia. Consequently, the symposium integrates relevant findings for developmental approaches in cognitive neuroscience.

Cognitive and social functions of rostral prefrontal cortex: Implications for development

Gilbert, Sam Inst. Cognitive Neuroscience, University College London, London, United Kingdom

Rostral prefrontal cortex, approximating Brodmann Area 10, is one of the slowest-developing regions of the human brain. This region does not reach maturity until late adolescence or adulthood, suggesting its importance for developmental cognitive neuroscience. However, until recently, virtually nothing was known of its precise functions. Here, I will discuss some recent studies exploring its cognitive and social roles, especially in prospective memory and mental state attribution. I will relate these studies to an overarching theory, the 'gateway hypothesis', which describes these functions in terms of the need to direct attention towards self-generated versus perceptual information.

Age differences in brain activation during the encoding of future actions

Eschen, Anne Inst. für Psychologie, Universität Zürich, Zürich, Switzerland

Objectives: The purpose of the study was to investigate age differences in brain activation during encoding of future actions. For young adults, a differential activation of motor brain regions in the left and for old adults in both hemispheres is expected. Methods: fMRI data was acquired while 17 young (18-30 years) and 17 old (60-75 years) adults encoded 24 actions for later execution and 24 actions for later verbal report and watched 24 actions. Actions were presented as words and videos. Results: Data analysis is still ongoing. Conclusions: The findings will extend previous knowledge on age-specific activation patterns during encoding.

Age-related deficits in timing performance: Electrophysiological evidence

Wild-Wall, Nele Inst. für Berufsphysiologie, Universität Dortmund, Dortmund, Germany

Aging affects fronto-striatal brain circuits being also important for timing behaviour. Therefore, young and old participants performed a time-production and a time-discrimination task. The Contingent Negative Variation (CNV) was measured. Time production was deficient in old compared to young participants; an increased frontal CNV suggested increased effort. In contrast, performance did not differ across groups for time discrimination; the frontal CNV was comparable between age-groups. Hence, an age-related decline was only evident in time production when demands on timing and motor processes were high. Thus, a time-production task seemed a sensitive test for subtle age-related changes in fronto-striatal circuits.

The impact of negative emotion on item and source memory in healthy aging: An ERP approach
Gruno, Maria Department of Psychology, Humboldt University Berlin, Berlin, Germany Wilhelm, Sophia Department of Psychology, Humboldt University Berlin, Berlin, Germany Werheid, Katja Department of Psychology, Humboldt University Berlin, Germany Kathmann, Norbert Department of Psychology, Humboldt University Berlin, Berlin, Germany

We investigated event-related potential (ERP) correlates of the negativity-induced enhancement (NIE) of item and source memory in healthy aging. Young and elderly adults studied negative and neutral faces along with context information. In a later recognition test they were asked to classify faces as studied or non-studied and assign them to their proper context. Results showed that NIE effects on item and source memory varied as a function of age and were mirrored by age-dependent changes in the ERP old/new effects. Findings suggest that the action point of negative emotion on memory is subject to age-related change.

Learning of sequences improves prospective memory performance in older adults
Zöllig, Jacqueline Inst. für Psychologie, Universität Zürich, Zürich, Switzerland Sutter, Christine Institute of Psychology, University of Zurich, Zurich, Switzerland Helg, Andrea Institute of Psychology, University of Zurich, Zurich, Switzerland Martin, Mike Institute of Psychology, University of Zurich, Zurich, Switzerland

The study investigates whether learning the sequence of stimuli in which a prospective task is embedded increases prospective memory performance of older adults. Behavioural data revealed fewer prospective false alarms and a faster reaction time in correct cue detection in the training group. Electrophysiological data showed differences in the amplitude of the FSW, associated with the disengagement from the ongoing activity following the detection of a prospective cue. Source localization in this time window with sLORETA revealed a higher activation of frontal regions in the control group suggesting that more resources are needed to successfully perform the prospective task.

Execution of delayed intentions in schizophrenia
Altgassen, Mareike Inst. für Psychologie, Techn. Universität Dresden, Dresden, Germany
Prospective memory refers to the ability to form intentions and to realize them on one's own initiative after a time delay. This study explored event-based prospective memory performance in individuals with schizophrenia and healthy controls. To disentangle the relative contribution of the retrospective and prospective component on prospective remembering, retrospective memory load was varied. Overall, a general prospective memory impairment was observed in schizophrenia. Significant deficits even emerged when retrospective memory demands were reduced to a minimum. Both the retrospective and the prospective component seem to contribute to the impaired prospective memory performance in schizophrenia.

S-229: Need assessment and public health

Uwe Rose (chair)
Need assessment is a useful tool for tailoring services and ressources in public health. Nowadays the main focus is on expert-defined operationalizations of need assessment (e.g. prevalences of disorders, levels of disability or the availability of effective treatments). But there is a gap between expert-defined need and the actual use of services. This can partly be explained by integrating motivational or volitional determinants as indicators for subjective need. Methods and studies concerning the relationship between need and real use of services in public health will be in focus of the symposium.

The use of psychological determinants for tailoring workplace health promotion
Walter, Stefanie Prevention, IGP, Bernau, Germany
The study on need asssessment takes place in the field of workplace health promotion. This surveillance makes a contribution to the question which determinants influence utilisation. A first screening of 875 employees shows a subjective need of 57% attending courses reducing backache. In the end only 12% of the amployees have participated. The data analysis indicates the occupational status as one of the most obvious barriers. This surveillance once more clarifies, that the expert-defined need does not correlate with the real participation. The subjective need as well as barriers, e.g. occupational status, do influence the objective demand.

Intended self-selection as an indicator for need: A new pathway to need assessment?
Rose, Uwe Mental Workload, Stress, FIOSH, Berlin, Germany Zimmermann, Linda Psychosomatice Medicine, Univ. Medical Center Freiburg, Freiburg, Germany Pfeifer, Ruth Psychosomatice Medicine, Univ.Medical Center Freiburg, Freiburg, Germany Unterbrink, Thomas Psychosomatice Medicine, Univ. Medical Center Freiburg, Freiburg, Germany Bauer, Joachim Psychosomatice Medicine, University Med. Center, Freiburg, Germany
Objectives - Intention to take part in a coaching program was used for predicting utilisation. Methods - A census of 2484 public school teachers were requested to fill in mental health questionnaires and invited to participate. Logistic regression analysis was used to regress the binary outcome variable of attendance on mental health scales and intention to take part. Results – Stratifying for gender and adjusting for mental health scales did not alter the strong association (crude OR = 85.5) between intention and utilisation. Conclusion – Indicators for the burden of diseases or disorders are not sufficient for defining need for health services.

Workplace health management for drivers in transport companies: Need of workplace health management for professional drivers
Michaelis, Martina Inst. für Sozialmedizin, FFAS, Freiburg, Germany Rose, Uwe Mental Workload, Stress, FIOSH, Berlin, Germany
Objectives: The focus is on the relationship between intention and real implementation of workplace health management (WHM) for drivers in small transport companies. Methods: A probability sample of decision makers (10%-sample, n=5.500) was asked by means of a standardized telephone interview and by questionnaires Results: Response rate was 11% (n=603). One third (n=197) demonstrates general intention for participation at a model program. Conclusions: There is only evidence for a low need level despite a low response rate. Above this, the study illustrates some unresolved issues regarding unmet need for WHM.

Determinants for using psychotherapy: Barriers, expert-defined and subjective need
Harfst, Timo BTPK, Berlin, Germany Koch, Uwe Medical Psychology, University Clinic of Hamburg, Hamburg, Germany Dirmaier, Jörg Medical Psychology, University Clinic of Hamburg, Hamburg, Germany Schulz, Holger Medical Psychology, University Clinic of Hamburg, Hamburg, Germany
Objectives - Intention to take part in an outpatient psychotherapy, recommendation for psychotherapy, subjective barriers and psychopathology was used for predicting mental health care utilisation. Methods – A consecutive sample of 1642 inpatients of four different psychosomatic hospitals were requested to fill questionnaires on different aspects of psychopathology and health care utilization at pre, post and 6-months-follow-up. Logistic regression analysis was used to identify predictors of mental health care utilization after inpatient treatment. Results – Quality of aftercare preparation and contact to outpatient therapists were the strongest predictors of utilization. Conclusion – Psychopathology and expert defined need insufficiently predict utilization.

Subjective need and the utilisation of medical inpatient rehabilitation
Hüppe, Angelika Inst. für Sozialmedizin, Universität Lübeck, Lübeck, Germany Schlademann, Susanne Inst. für Sozialmedizin, Universität Lübeck, Lübeck, Germany Mattis, Christine Institute for Social Medicine, University of Luebeck, Luebeck, Germany Raspe, Heiner Institute for Social Medicine, University of Luebeck, Luebeck, Germany
The practice of needs assessment in health care is challenging. A screening algorithm to objectify and assess individual rehabilitation needs was developed. Empirical data of more than 10.000 members of statutory pension funds and health insurances were analysed, originating in two surveys and three RCTs on chronic disorders (mainly back pain, rheumatoid arthritis, and type 2 diabetes mellitus). Subjective needs highly agreed with the ratings following the algorithm. Unexpected few patients (between 11% and 25%), with both high objective and subjective needs, utilised an explicitly offered rehabilitation, stating manifold obstacles. Although appropriate and necessary, currently available interventions are substantially underused.

S-230: Emotion regulation in borderline personality disorder: New findings regarding sensitivity and reactivity to emotional stimuli

Christian Stiglmayr (chair)
Affective instability and problems with emotion regulation are central to borderline personality disorder. An assumption is that these problems are related in part to greater emotional sensitivity a low threshold and faster reactions to emotional stimuli as well as heightened reactivity and longer lasting reactions. Different studies using various paradigms as well as multi-level assessments of emotional sensitivity and reactivity are presented.

Disorder specificity of aversive tension and dissociation in borderline personality disorder: A computer-based controlled field study
Stiglmayr, Christian AWP-Berlin, Berlin, Germany
Objective: Recent studies have demonstrated that patients with Borderline Personality Disorder (BPD) experience more frequent and more intense episodes of aversive tension and dissociative features compared with healthy controls. Disorder specificity of these findings for BPD however remained unclear. Method: Aversive tension and dissociative symptoms were assessed in 63 patients with BPD, 13 depressive patients, 14 patients with anxiety disorders and 40 healthy controls under open field conditions for 48 hours. Results: Borderline patients reported significantly higher levels and a steeper rise of aversive tension compared to the other groups of patients and healthy controls. In all investigated groups there was a positive correlation between experienced tension and dissociation.

Psychophysiology of emotion regulation in borderline personality disorder

Kuo, Janice Dept. of Psychology, Stanford University, Stanford, USA

Objectives: Investigate Linehan's theory that BPD is characterized by heightened sensitivity and reactivity across emotions and contexts. Methods: Twenty BPD, 20 social anxiety disorder, and 20 normal controls engaged in two emotion induction contexts (imagery and film viewing) eliciting sadness, fear, and anger. Dependent variables were respiratory sinus arrhythmia, skin conductance response, and self-report. Results: BPD participants displayed heightened emotional sensitivity but not reactivity compared with the other two groups, as indicated by baseline physiological and self-report measures. Conclusions: BPD individuals appear to be characterized by emotional sensitivity, but not reactivity, suggesting that treatments should target emotional sensitivity in BPD.

Exploring emotional sensitivity in borderline personality disorder and healthy controls using facial affect paradigm

Lynch, Thomas School of Psychology, Exeter University, Exeter, United Kingdom *Schneider, Kristin* Psychology, Duke University, Durham, NC, USA

Objectives: Greater emotional sensitivity in Borderline personality disorder (BPD) is tested using facial affect morphing tasks. Methods and Results: BPD correctly identified facial affect at an earlier stage than normals, regardless of valence. Second study, 90 non-clinical participants randomized to: 1) Expressive Suppression 2) Expressive Mimicry 3) No-Instruction control. Expressive Mimicry was superior at correctly identifying facial affect at an early stage compared to participants of both other conditions (all ps < .05). Physiological data (facial electromyography, skin conductance, heart-rate, respiration rate) will be presented. Conclusions: Emotional sensitivity in BPD may partly be influenced by emotion contagion/mimicry of facial affect.

Facial emotional expressions and behavioral intentions as reactions to social exclusion in borderline personality disorder

Renneberg, Babette Berlin, Germany *Stäbler, Katja* Inst. für Psychologie, Universität Heidelberg, Heidelberg, Germany *Fiedler, Peter* *Röpke, Stefan* Department of Psychiatry, Charité - University Medicine, Berlin, Germany

Facial emotional reactions during and behavioral intentions after social exclusion were examined in 35 women with BPD and 35 female healthy controls. Participants played a virtual ball-tossing game "Cyberball" (Williams, 2001) which has proved to induce social exclusion (randomly assigned experimental condition) in a reliable way. While playing Cyberball participants were videotaped and facial emotional expressions were analyzed using EMFACS (Ekman & Friesen, 1984). BPD patients displayed less positive and more negative and mixed facial emotional expressions compared to healthy controls. BPD patients reported more aggressive intentions and escape than controls after the game.

Emotional reactivity to auditory stimuli in borderline personality disorder

Rosenthal, M. Zachary Cognitive Behavioral Research, Duke University, Durham, NC, USA *Ahn, Roianne* Cognitive Behavioral Research, Duke University, Durham, NC, USA *Rivinoja, Clark* Cognitive Behavioral Research, Duke University, Durham, NC, USA

Objectives: The purpose of this study is to examine emotional reactivity to auditory stimuli in BPD. Methods: In four experiments using different kinds of pleasant and unpleasant sounds (pure tones, real-world sounds, music, personally-relevant sounds),

healthy controls (n = 20) and individuals with BPD (n = 20), emotional reactivity is assessed using psychophysiological (e.g., heart rate), self-report, and motoric (facial affect) methods. Results: Dependent variables are magnitude of emotional response, number of emotional responses to pleasant/unpleasant stimuli, and habituation. The study is ongoing. Conclusions: Results will indicate whether there are specific kinds of stimuli associated with differential emotional reactivity in BPD.

Impulsivity and emotion dysregulation in borderline personality disorder

Chapman, Alexander Dept. of Psychology, Simon Fraser University, Burnaby, BC, Canada *Leung, Debbie* Dept. of Psychology, University of Washington, Seattle, WA, USA

Objective: To examine the association of borderline personality disorder and emotional states with impulsivity in the laboratory. Methods: Participants who were high (n = 39) and low (n = 56) in BPD features completed measures of emotional state before a laboratory measure of impulsivity. Results: High-BPD participants committed a greater number of impulsive responses than did low-BPD participants. High-BPD participants who were in a negative emotional state committed fewer impulsive responses than high-BPD participants who were not in negative emotional state. Fear, nervousness, and shame negatively correlated with impulsivity among high-BPD participants but not among low-BPD participants. Conclusion: Certain emotional states attenuate impulsivity among persons with BPD features.

S-231: Advancements in leadership theory and practice

Jens Rowold (chair)

Over the last five decades, several theories of leadership developed independently from each other, although considerable theoretical overlaps between these theories exist. This symposium tries to shed light on the theoretical and empirical interrelationships of the main leadership theories. The first three presentations will contribute to the factorial, convergent, discriminant and criterion-oriented validity of seven leadership styles (i.e., transactional, transformational, and ethical leadership, delegation behavior, leader-member exchange, initiating structure and consideration). The next two presentations provide evidence for the effectiveness of transformational leadership training and coaching. Finally, the interrelationship between transformational leadership, communication competence, and conflict management abilities is addressed.

Nomological network of leadership constructs: Results from a multi-sample study

Rowold, Jens Inst. für Psychologie 2, Universität Münster, Münster, Germany *Heinitz, Kathrin* Institute of Psychology, Free University of Berlin, Berlin, Germany

Since 1950, various leadership theories developed independently from each other, although considerable theoretical overlaps between these theories exist. Moreover, empirical research demonstrated that several leadership constructs (e.g., transformational leadership and LMX) intercorrelate strongly. Do we really need more than one leadership theory? Consequently, by comparing and contrasting several leadership theories, the present study contributes to the nomological network of five leadership styles: Transactional and transformational leadership, LMX, initiating structure and consideration. Based on empirical data from samples from the CoLeS (Context and Leadership Styles) project, evidence for factorial, convergent, discriminant and criterion-oriented validity of these leadership styles is presented.

Psychometric properties of a scale for the assessment of ethical leadership

Staufenbiel, Kathrin Inst. für Psychologie 2, Universität Münster, Münster, Germany *Rowold, Jens* Institute of Psychology 2, University of Muenster, Muenster, Germany

Ethical leadership is an emerging construct in organizational research. However, tools for the assessment of ethical leadership have been virtually nonexistent. One notably exception was the English scale developed by Brown and colleagues (2005). The present study provides evidence for adequate psychometric properties of a German version of this scale. Two independent research studies (total N = 1430) explored the factorial and criterion-oriented validity of this scale. Several subjective (e.g., followers' satisfaction) and objective (e.g., branch-level profit) criteria were chosen in order to gain a fuller picture of the effects of ethical leadership. The results confirmed adequate psychometric properties.

Leadership and innovative behavior in organizations: An empirical investigation on transformational leadership, leader-member exchange and delegation

Nerdinger, Friedemann Inst. für Psychologie, Universität Rostock, Rostock, Germany *Pundt, Alexander* Institute of Psychology, University of Rostock, Rostok, Germany

We investigated the relationships between three types of employee innovative behavior (employee creativity, voice behavior, and taking charge) and transformational leadership, leader-member exchange, and delegation behavior in a questionnaire field study. Findings from 150 employees from different organizations indicate that all three leadership constructs are related to voice behavior and taking charge. However, in a simultaneous test, only delegation behavior is related to all three types of innovative behavior, given controls for individual variances in job demography and perceived need for organizational change. These findings imply that delegation behavior should have a comeback in theories on leadership and innovative behavior.

Transformational leadership training and its effect on follower perception of transformational leadership and value congruency and leaders perception of commitment and proactivity

Radstaak, Jens Angew.- und Arbeitspsychologie, Universität Münster, Münster, Germany *Rowold, Jens* Institute of Psychology 2, University of Muenster, Muenster, Germany

The impact of transformational leadership training on followers' perceptions of transformational leadership and the value congruency was tested. Additionally, the moderation effect of leaders' proactivity was investigated. Experimental group leaders received transformational leadership training and coaching. Two samples (total N = 45) with control group (N= 12) were utilized. Results indicated that the training increased transformational leadership. Also, followers ratings for value congruency indicated a decrease in the value discrepancy for the experimental group, which has implications for transformational leadership theory. Results suggest that the training was more effective for trainees' scoring high on proactivity.

Effects of transformational leadership training and coaching on follower perception of transformational leadership, commitment and organizational citizenship behavior

Mönninghoff, Martina Inst. für Psychologie 2, Universität Münster, Münster, Germany *Rowold, Jens* Institute of Psychology 2, University of Muenster, Muenster, Germany

The impact of transformational leadership training on followers' organizational citizenship behavior

(OCB) and commitment was tested. Additionally, and for the first time, the moderation effect of leaders' self-monitoring was investigated. Experimental group leaders received transformational leadership training (2 days) and coaching (4 days). Three samples (total N = 60) from German Industries with control group (N= 20) were utilized. Results from covariance analysis indicated that the training increased OCB and commitment. Also, results suggest that the training was more effective for leaders' scoring high on self-monitoring, which has implications for transformational leadership theory.

Transformational leadership and social competence

Torjus, Nicole *Wirtschatpsychologie, Freie Universität Berlin, Berlin, Germany* **Heinitz, Kathrin** *Wirtschaftspsychologie, Free University of Berlin, Berlin, Germany* **Proch, Sascha** *Wirtschaftspsychologie, Freie Universität Berlin, Berlin, Germany*

Leaders are attributed with a higher level of social competence. Conflict management and thereby the ability to communicate openly as well as the competence to build up positive relationships are fundamental leadership tasks. The concept of transformational leadership targets the establishment and maintenance of a positively experienced communication culture. Leaders with highly developed communicative abilities are seen as being more transformational. This study examines the relationship between communication competence, conflict management abilities and transformational leadership. With a sample of N = 451 the two-way relationships of these concepts are highlighted and their high correlations are examined in detail.

S-232: Self-regulation: Key factor in health behavior change?

Benicio Gutiérrez-Doña, Amelie Wiedemann (chair)
Self-regulation strategies facilitate initiation and maintenance of health-enhancing behaviors. However, questions about the effectiveness of specific self-regulatory techniques in particular contexts and working mechanisms of self-regulation interventions remained unsolved. Aim is to identify whether and how different self-regulatory strategies contribute to sustained intervention effects on health behavior and well-being. Results of a meta-analysis (S. Maes), randomized controlled trials (C. Carver, A. Wiedemann), a systematic review (C. Abraham), and longitudinal studies (B. Gutiérrez-Doña) provide empirical evidence on how key self-regulatory strategies facilitate health behaviors. Suggestions are made how health promotion efforts and theories can be enhanced by integrating evidence-based self-regulatory strategies.

Specifying self-regulation intervention techniques in the context of healthy eating

Abraham, Charles *Dept. of Psychology, University of Sussex, Brighton, United Kingdom* **Michie, Susan** *Deptartment of Psychology, University College London, London, United Kingdom* **Whittington, Craig** *Dept. of Psychology, University of Sussex, Brighton, United Kingdom* **McAteer, John** *Dept. of Psychology, University of Sussex, Brighton, United Kingdom*
Objectives To define self-regulatory behaviour change techniques (SR-BCTs) and relate their application to the effectiveness of healthy eating (HE) interventions. Methods Meta-regression was used to link coded intervention content to effectiveness in a set of 22 HE intervention evaluations, identified by means of a systematic review. Results Intervention content was categorised according to inclusion of SR-BCTs. Interventions which included five specified SR-BCTs were significantly more effective (d = .43) and those not including these BCTs (d =.19). Conclusion Self-regulatory

techniques may be critical to the effectiveness of healthy eating interventions.

Self-regulation and psychological interventions for rheumatoid arthritis: A meta-analysis

Maes, Stan *Dept. of Psychology, Leiden University, Leiden, Netherlands* **De Gucht, Veronique** *Dept. of Psychology, Leiden University, Leiden, Netherlands* **Shoval, Hilla** *Dept. of Psychology, Leiden University, Leiden, Netherlands* **Boyle, Catherine** *Dept. of Psychology, Leiden University, Leiden, Netherlands*
Objectives To examine the effectiveness of psychological interventions in RA. Interventions were assessed in terms of self-regulation (SR) principles such as goal setting, ownership, planning, feedback, outcome expectations, emotion and attention control, self-monitoring, self-reinforcement and anticipatory coping. Methods Thirteen studies were included. Data were extracted on study design, sample, disease and intervention characteristics, and direction and nature of the outcomes. Results Psychological interventions produce weak effect sizes for wellbeing, pain and disability, but the effectiveness increases if interventions make use of SR principles. Conclusions SR interventions are an important adjunctive form of therapy in the medical management of RA.

Stress management, self-regulation and adaptation to breast cancer

Carver, Charles S. *Dept. of Psychology, University of Miami, Coral Gables, USA* **Antoni, Michael H**. *Dept. of Psychology, University of Miami, Coral Gables, FL, USA* **Lechner, Suzanne C**. *Dept. of Psychology, University of Miami, Coral Gables, FL, USA*
We examined benefits of a 10-week cognitive-behavioral stress management intervention on well-being among women undergoing treatment for breast cancer. Participants were assessed before randomization, 3 months after conclusion of treatment (6 months after recruitment), and 6 months later (a year after recruitment). Measures included distress, social disruption, and positive experiences. Also assessed were self-perceptions of skills taught by the intervention. Effects of the intervention were substantial and long-lasting on most outcomes. Also affected was participants' confidence of being able to relax at will (a self-regulatory skill). Mediational tests suggest that enhancement of that skill may underlie the intervention's beneficial effects.

Effects of self-regulation on healthy dietary behavior and physical activity tested in a randomized controlled trial

Wiedemann, Amelie *Gesundheits-Psychologie, Freie Universität Berlin, Berlin, Germany* **Lippke, Sonia** *Gesundheits-Psychologie, Freie Universität Berlin, Berlin, Germany* **Reuter, Tabea** *Gesundheits-Psychologie, Freie Universität Berlin, Berlin, Germany* **Ziegelmann, Jochen P**. *Gesundheits-Psychologie, Freie Universität Berlin, Berlin, Germany* **Schüz, Benjamin** *Jacobs Center Lifelong Learnin, Jacobs University Bremen, Bremen, Germany*
Objectives: Testing the effects of computer-tailored interventions targeting self-regulatory techniques (e.g., goal setting, action planning) to enhance healthy dietary behavior and physical activity in a randomized controlled trial (RCT). Methods: Interventions were delivered to 317 participants with one-month follow-up measures (use of self-regulatory techniques, goal behaviors). Results: Multivariate analyses indicated that the interventions led to significant increases in both goal behaviors, which were mediated by the use of self-regulatory techniques. These effects were moderated by participants' motivation. Conclusions: Cognitive changes produced by self-regulation interventions lead to significant increments in health behavior. However, intervention effectiveness largely depends on people's underlying motivation.

From intentions to actions: Self-efficacy and self-regulation in the adoption and maintenance of health behaviors in Costa Ricans and Germans

Gutiérrez-Doña, *Benicio Sistema Estudios de Posgrad., Universidad Estatal Distancia, San José, Costa Rica* **Renner, Britta** *Jacobs Center on Lifelong Lear, Jacobs University Bremen, Bremen, Germany* **Schwarzer, Ralf** *Department of Health Psycholog, Freie Universitaet Berlin, Berlin, Germany*
This longitudinal study examined the mediator model postulated in the Health Action Process Approach (HAPA). Specifically, the study emphasizes the impact of self-efficacy beliefs and self-regulation processes on the adoption and maintenance of health-related behaviors (i.e., healthy diet, and physical exercise). Data were gathered at two measurement points in time, 6-months apart, from a longitudinal sample of about 500 Costa Ricans. Results supported assumptions and offer new insights regarding the prediction of health-related intentions (motivation phase) and health-related actions (volitional phase). Findings are compared with previous results and discussed in light of cross-cultural validation and implications for health promotion.

S-233: Multidisciplinary models to the study of resilience today's societies

Rafael Javier (chair)
This symposium features five presentations with a discussant covering issues of assessment of resilience in general and in Latinos in the USA. Five scholars will present their research and will provide unique insights as to the specific challenges in assessing resilience in a multicultural and interdisciplinary context.

A view of resilience in the Latino context

Camacho-Gingerich, Alina *Dept. of Psychology, St. John's University, Queens, USA*
In this presentation we will address the relevant issues related to the definition and assessment of resilience and risk factors when dealing with Latinos. Part of the presentation will include a discussion of how cultural influences interact with normal developmental pathways to give rise to what we then call the 'Latino individual.' Understanding what factors are involved in making possible for an individual to excel even in the face of challenges and for another to flounder in the face of stress has been of great interest to behavioral scientists and other scholars. When dealing with the Latino population, this issue is further complicated because we are not dealing with a monolithic population with the same experience.

Developing a culturally sensitive measure of resilience

Clauss-Ehlers, Caroline *Educational Psychology, Rutgers University, New Brunswick, USA*
This presentation will discuss the role of culture in resilience and explore the developmental of a cultural resilience measure. A review of the literature will focus on the role of resilience and adversity among youth from diverse cultural backgrounds. A review of current resilience measures will also be provided. The finding that many current measures of resilience do not address the role of culture in resilience will be reviewed. The author will then describe the development of her own measure of cultural resilience, the Cultural Resilience Measure (CRM). The CRM was tested on 305 college-aged women. The CRM proved to be psychometrically sound. Findings indicated that childhood stressors were found to be differentially experienced by individuals from different racial/ethnic and socioeconomic status backgrounds, suggesting that ecological aspects of the environment influence the development of resilience within

a cultural framework. A conceptual framework that illustrates how culture contributes to resilience and coping is presented.

On the myth of trauma and resilience

Lewis, Jeffrey Dept. of Psychology, St. John's University, Flushing, USA

To investigate the collapse of resilience both intersubjectively; why if 2 people live through similar traumatic experience one emerges psychologically intact while the other may undergo failures not self evident in the circumstances; and secondly intrasubjectively; why does someone who has demonstrated elasticity in numerous life crises, suddenly breakdown in a recent episode. Is it the idiosyncratic "meaning" of this particular trauma; is it due to cumulative effect; does it tap the "fault-line" of a tenuous defensive infrastructure? The author's organizing tenet is that things happen to actual people with individual histories, so that the reaction can be understood only through the analysis of the specific individual and not the proximal trauma and its expected outcome.

A look at proctive factors of children expose to violence

Mora, Louis Dept. of Psychology, St. John's University, Queens, USA

We sought to assess the resilience factors in 8 to16-year-old urban youths exposed to community violence in New York City, following a multi-influence model of development and a mediational model. Such factors include but are not limited to religious involvement, level of acculturation, children's psychopathology, and children's intellectual functioning. Children and parents completed a series of scales in interview format as administered by doctoral students. This study is set apart from most previous work, as children were recruited from pediatric medical units in ethnically diverse communities. Thus, our findings will be discussed in the context of these factors.

S-234: Individual and organisational variables of career related continuous learning

Niclas Schaper, Sabine Hochholdinger (chair)
Career related continuous learning activities in organisations are important to keep up with actual and future job demands. Besides well designed training measures certain individual and organisational variables and the use of other kinds of learning activities (e.g. self-organized learning, e-learning) contribute to the effectiveness of career related learning. With reference to models of training effectiveness and career related development activities the role of certain individual (e.g. self management abilities, learning attitudes) and organisational variables (organisational learning culture, failure management culture) concerning continuous learning motivation and behavior and transfer of learning are analysed in the different contributions of the symposium.

The role of individual characteristics in self organized learning activities

Mann, Jacqueline Inst. für Psychologie, Universität Paderborn, Paderborn, Germany Schaper, Niclas Inst. für Psychologie, Universität Paderborn, Paderborn, Germany Hochholdinger, Sabine Inst. für Psychologie, Universität Paderborn, Paderborn, Germany

Organizations need to know in which ways "Career-related-continuous-learning" can be supported. Focusing on personal characteristics results of a longitudinal field study covering 3 measuring points with a sample size of 80 participants will be presented. More specifically the relevance of attitudes toward learning and development, per-

ceived benefits and individual learning skills in predicting the intention to engage in self-organized learning activities, the commitment to chosen learning activities and self-reported learning results, considering a hypothesized moderating influence of attitudes toward the learning method and the perceived need for development, are examined.

Prediction of individual e-learning success by organisational learning culture and individual transfer motivation

Hochholdinger, Sabine Inst. für Psychologie, Universität Paderborn, Paderborn, Germany Schaper, Niclas Inst. für Psychologie, Universität Paderborn, Paderborn, Germany

Objectives: This study investigated the role of organisational learning culture as predictor of individual transfer of e-learning-success mediated by individual transfer motivation. These variables were employed testing a research framework drawn from literature on occupational training. Methods: The study's participants were 146 apprentices of electro-technical occupations, who rated organizational learning culture, individual transfer motivation, and individual effects of learning and transfer after several e-learning periods. Results: Learning culture correlated positively with learning and transfer through the mediation of transfer motivation. Conclusions: The results confirmed the relevance of organisational learning culture for individual transfer motivation and transfer of learning.

Organisational learning culture and it's effects on continuous learning motivation and behavior

Schaper, Niclas Inst. für Psychologie, Universität Paderborn, Paderborn, Germany Hochholdinger, Sabine Inst. für Psychologie, Universität Paderborn, Paderborn, Germany Mann, Jacqueline Inst. für Psychologie, Universität Paderborn, Paderborn, Germany

Organisational learning culture refers to expectations, guidelines, and pratices to support continuous learning on the job. A questionnaire study with 307 persons from different organisations and jobs was conducted to analyse, if these variables are related to continuous learning motivation and behavior. In a regression model direct relations of organisational learning culture with continuous learning motivation and behavior were analysed. It was also examined if effects of learning culture on continuous learning behavior are mediated by learning motivation. Results show that learning culture variables are positively related to learning motivation and behavior. Also, the assumed mediation effect could be confirmed.

Transfer of training as citizenship performance

Solga, Marc Inst. für Psychologie, Universität Bonn, Bonn, Germany Solga, Jutta personnel diagnostics, personal point GmbH, Bonn, Germany

In this rather programmatic contribution, we propose to conceive of transfer of training as a special kind (or manifestation) of citizenship performance, namely job dedication. We substantiate this approach and highlight theoretical aspects that allow for the explanation of training transfer by employing concepts from the research on contextual and citizenship performance (i. e., fairness perceptions, psychological contract).

Learning from mistakes and innovation

Putz, Daniel Indust. und Organ. Psychology, RWTH Aachen, Aachen, Germany Ujma, Maja Human Resources Development, QIAGEN GmbH, Hilden, Germany Schilling, Jan Dep. of IO Psychology, RWTH Aachen University, Aachen, Germany

Innovativeness has become an important competitive factor in times of increasing customer needs and rapid market shifts. Therefore, many companies try to boost innovative behaviors of their

employees through trainings and conductive job designs. The present study investigates the relationship between the work environment, innovative behaviors and related variables based on a survey of 171 German, Swiss and US-American employees of a biotechnology enterprise. Results highlight the impact of organizational climate for innovation and learning from errors on innovative behaviors, personal initiative and group performance, thereby pointing at some critical aspects to support creativity and innovation in everyday work life.

S-235: Assessment centers: Organizational practices, individual differences correlates and influencing factors on construct validity

Klaus G. Melchers, Martin Kleinmann (chair)
Assessment centers (ACs) are widely used for personnel selection as well as for training and development purposes. Therefore, it is important to identify factors that affect candidates' performance in an AC or that influence the prediction of later job performance on the basis of ACs. It is also essential to consider ways to ensure that ACs generate valid assessments of candidates' strengths and weaknesses. The papers in this symposium assess to which degree organizational practices reflect the current state of the art, which individual differences correlates predict AC performance and also factors that influence construct measurement in ACs.

State of the art of assessment centres: Survey results from Austria, Canada, France, Germany, Netherlands, Sweden, Switzerland, and U.S.A.

Krause, Diana Dept. of Social Science, University of Western Ontario, London, Canada Thornton, George Department of Psychology, Colorado State University, Fort Collins, USA

Given the challenges of implementing assessment centers (ACs) in international organizations, we develop a model that explains cross-cultural variability in AC practices due to cultural conditions (i.e., extent of uncertainty avoidance and power distance) and institutional conditions (i.e., differences in institutionalized collectivism, employment laws, and legal norms). The model is used to explain differences in the design, execution, and evaluation of ACs in organizations located in eight countries in Western Europe and North America. We also identify trends in AC practices over time and discuss implications for improvement of AC practices, and directions for future AC research.

Adequate problem perception: A passport to successful assessment center performance?

Andreßen, Panja Aviation and Space Psychology, German Aerospace Center (DLR), Hamburg, Germany Höft, Stefan FH für Arbeitsmarktmanagement, Hochschule der Bundesagentur, Mannheim, Germany Scholl, Johanna Aviation and Space Psychology, German Aerospace Center (DLR), Hamburg, Germany

It is hypothesized that accurate perception of the actual interpersonal problem, clear understanding of desirable results, and knowledge about suitable solution strategies are necessary but not sufficient elements to successfully complete AC exercises. To test these hypotheses, the content of 120 structured forms used by pilot trainee applicants in preparation for a role play exercise (lead questions: "What is the problem? What is your intention? What are your plans for the talk?") was analysed. The results show limited support for the supposed interlink between perception and performance. Consequences for related selection methods (situational interviews, situational judgement tests) are discussed.

Predictor interactions in determining assessment center performance

Dilchert, Stephan Dept. of Psychology, University of Minnesota, Minneapolis, USA Ones, Deniz S. Dept. of Psychology, University of Minnesota, Minneapolis, MN, USA

Recent research supports the idea that various noncognitive variables interact in the prediction of important work behaviors, including job performance (Witt et al., 2002; Judge & Erez, 2007). We examined whether several personality traits interacted in the prediction of assessment center (AC) dimension and exercise scores. In two samples of managers (Ns = 2,924 and 1,848) replicable interactions between agreeableness and conscientiousness as well as emotional stability and extraversion predicted AC dimension ratings such as motivation and leadership. Similar patterns were not found for predicting AC exercise scores. Implications of these findings for AC theory and practice will be discussed.

Self-assessor congruence in an assessment center for personnel selection

Höft, Stefan FH für Arbeitsmarktmanagement, HS der Bundesag. für Arbeit, Mannheim, Germany Bath, Anja Dep of Personality Psychology, University of the Armed Forces, Hamburg, Germany Bürger, Hella Dorothea Dep of Aviation and Space Psy, German Aerospace Center, Hamburg, Germany

The study investigates the utility of self-assessments in an assessment center used for personnel selection. 1315 applicants for pilot trainee positions assessed their own performance regarding four dimensions in three different interpersonal assessment center exercises using retrospective behavioral inventories. Congruencies between self- and assessor-ratings show a consistent pattern across dimensions and exercises and add relevant information for the prediction of the final selection outcome. Substantial relations exist with self-peer ratings collected 18 month later in flight training school. It is concluded that self-assessments used in the proposed way are a useful complementing diagnostic approach for personnel selection.

Do assessors have too much on their plates? Measurement quality and the number of to-be-observed candidates in an assessment center group exercise

Melchers, Klaus G. Inst. für Psychologie, Universität Zürich, Zürich, Switzerland Kleinmann, Martin Inst. für Psychologie, Universität Zürich, Zürich, Switzerland

Assessment centers (ACs) often lack construct validity. A factor that has been suggested to contribute to these problems are the assessors' large cognitive demands during the observation of AC participants. As previous research concerning this factor is limited and inconclusive, we evaluated whether the number of participants assessors have to observe at the same time during a group discussion affects measurement quality in this discussion. 1081 participants in a selection AC were evaluated by assessors who concurrently observed either four or five participants. Significant improvements of discriminant validity and interrater-reliability were found when assessors observed four instead of five participants.

The effects of exercise instructions on the observability of assessment center behavior

Schollaert, Eveline Dept. de Psychologie, Universiteit Gent, Gent, Belgium Lievens, Filip Dept. de Psychologie, Universiteit Gent, Gent, Belgium

Role-plays are popular exercises in assessment centers and leadership development programs. However, research on role-plays and exercise (role-player) instructions is sorely lacking. This is surprising as potential lacks of inter-role-player consistency in evoking behavior or the use of specific exercise instructions might influence the standardization of the assessment procedure. In this study we use trait activation theory to develop exercise instructions which might activate behavior relevant to specific traits. A group of final year students (N = 150) participate in an assessment center simulation, we examine the effects of the exercise instructions on the observability of assessment center behavior.

S-236: Psychological research with the German socio-economic panel

Gisela Trommsdorff, Frieder R. Lang (chair)

The interdisciplinary symposium brings together an international group of scholars, who use the representative data set of the GSOEP (established more than 20 years ago as household panel) in their work. The papers integrate psychological and economic perspectives with regard to psychological and developmental issues: age-, cohort- and period-related effects on life satisfaction, effects of economic strain and parenting on future orientation, national differences in trust, and the validation of a test for cognitive abilities in adolescents. The contributions serve to demonstrate the usefulness of the GSOEP for theoretical and methodological advancement in psychology.

Future expectation and subjective well-being across adulthood

Lang, Frieder R. Inst. für Psychogerontologie, Universität Erlangen-Nürnberg, Erlangen, Germany Weiss, David Psychology and Sport Science, University Erlangen-Nürnberg, Erlangen, Germany

The study explored future well-being in relation to changes in current life satisfaction, health, and socioeconomic resources across a 12-year time interval of the German Socio-economic Panel (1993-2004; N = 6636, 16 – 88 years). Results of growth curve analyses show a dedifferentiation of current and future life-satisfaction with increasing age. Socio-economic resources and health were found to moderate the associations. High SES is re-lated to lower age differences in future well-being as compared to low SES. The findings underscore the impact of contextual resources on subjective well-being and psychological resilience across adulthood.

Using the german socio-economic panel study to assess age-related changes in life satisfaction

Lucas, Richard E. Dept. of Psychology, Michigan State University, East Lansing, USA

Objectives: The goal was to determine whether life satisfaction changes with age. Methods: Panel data from the GSOEP were analyzed. Cross-sectional analyses and multilevel modeling techniques were compared. Results: The two analyses provided different pictures of age-related change. After controlling for apparent instrumentation effects, life satisfaction was stable from young adulthood until age 70, after which it declined steadily. Conclusions: Panel studies with refreshment samples provide a strong method for separating age-related change from confounding effects. Intuitive models about the link between age and satisfaction were supported: During the time of life when objective circumstances decline, satisfaction drops.

It's time!: Psychologists can and should start unraveling age, period and cohort effects in studying temporal change

Denissen, Jaap Inst. für Psychologie, Humboldt-Universität zu Berlin, Berlin, Germany

The current study revisits an issue that was first raised by Schaie and Baltes by simultaneously analyzing age, period, and cohort (APC) effects on life satisfaction using multi-cohort panel data from the German SOEP. Results obtained by the application of an interactive, bifactorial statistical framework indicated small but significant period and age effects, and no replicable cohort effects. It is hoped that applying this framework to the analysis of temporal changes in other psychological variables will result in a more accurate picture of age, period, and cohort effects on human development.

Relations among parental economic strain, supportive parenting and adolescents' future orientation

Agache, Alexandru Inst. für Psychologie, Universität Konstanz, Konstanz, Germany Trommsdorff, Gisela Inst. für Psychologie, Universität Konstanz, Konstanz, Germany

In this study we analyzed the relations between economic strain, supportive parenting, and adolescents' future orientation and the impact of future orientation on adolescents' academic achievement. We used cross-sectional data from the German Socioeconomic Panel (2001-2005; n = 1598, 17 years old adolescents and their parents). Results of the structural equation modeling showed: Perceived parental economic strain and supportive parenting are negatively correlated and mediate the influence of the objective economic hardness on adolescents' future orientation. Furthermore, adolescents' future orientation is a strong predictor of their academic achievement. Implications for theory and policy interventions are discussed.

Decomposing trust: Explaining national trust differences

Naef, Michael Inst. für Empirsche Forschung, Universität Zürich, Zürich, Switzerland Fehr, Ernst Inst. Empirical Res. Economics, University of Zurich, Zürich, Switzerland Fischbacher, Urs Department of Economics, University of Konstanz, Konstanz, Germany Schupp, Jürgen German Socio-Economic Panel, German Inst. for Economic Res., Berlin, Germany Wagner, Gert G. German Socio-Economic Panel, German Inst. for Economic Res., Berlin, Germany

Objectives: We measure and explain potential differences in representative trusting behaviour in terms of preferences, demographics and belief variables. Methods: We combined an interactive behavioural experiment with representative surveys in Germany and the U.S.A. Results: Americans trust strangers much more than Germans, a trust gap we explain almost entirely. Americans are less risk and betrayal averse and exhibit higher levels of selflessness. Moreover, they expect both a high payoff and equality between truster and trustee at much higher trust levels than Germans. Conclusions: Risk and social preferences and belief variables deserve increased attention in future survey research.

Validating a test of general reasoning ability adequate for the inclusion in SOEP

Schneider, Michael Inst. Verhaltenswissenschaften, ETH Zürich, Zürich, Switzerland Stern, Elsbeth Inst. Verhaltenswissenschaften, ETH Zürich, Zürich, Switzerland

In 2006 for the first time all 835 persons in the SOEP panel between 16 and 18 years of age completed a newly developed short form of the Intelligenz-Struktur-Test 2000 as a measure of their general reasoning ability. We evaluated the validity and reliability of this test by comparing its distributional characteristics and factor structure to those of the original test and by relating the test scores to other SOEP variables. Given its short length, the test has satisfactory validity and reliability. It will be useful for future research, e.g., on the impact of cognitive abilities on labor market chances.

S-237: Psychological foundations of cognitive technical systems

Berthold Färber, Heiner Deubel (chair)
The aim of the cluster of excellence "Cognition for Technical Systems" (CoTeSys) is to provide technical systems with cognitive capabilities such as perception, reasoning, learning, and planning in order to act and interact with humans in a natural way. Because this cannot be done without psychological input, several partners from psychology are engaged in the cluster to integrate basic psychological knowledge, advanced user interface ideas and evaluation procedures in the cluster. The symposium brings together experts from Psychology and Neurology contributing to the development of technical systems of the future on the basis of their specific expertise.

Enhancing automatic saliency computations by dynamic weighting of feature dimensions
Müller, Hermann Inst. für Psychologie, Universität München, München, Germany Zehetleitner, Michael Psychology, Ludwig-Maximilians-University, München, Germany
The dimension weighting account (DWA) explains performance differences for intertrial transitions of target-defining visual dimensions by assuming that pre-attentive computations of saliency are modulated by weighting of previously relevant feature dimensions. Here we investigate the pre-attentive nature of dimensional intertrial effects by varying strength of feature contrast and congruency of the stimulus-response mapping. Although both manipulations decrease performance, from a decision perspective the DWA predicts only the perceptual manipulation to affect the cost of cross-trial changes in dimensions. The results support this view, thus strengthening the assumption of the DWA that dynamic changes of dimensions affect pre-attentive salience computations.

Movement coordination in human-human interaction
Schuboe, Anna Inst. für Psychologie, Universität München, München, Germany Vesper, Cordula Psychology, Ludwig-Maximilians-University, München, Germany Stork, Sonja Psychology, Ludwig-Maximilians-University, München, Germany
Coordinating one's own movements and actions with movements and actions of another person is an ability that is relevant in everyday social life as well as in professional work environments. The present contribution investigated human movement coordination in an interaction task with the intention to extract coordination rules that may be transferred to human-robot interaction. Movement parameters of two humans were recorded in a simple construction task using a six degree-of-freedom magnetic motion tracker. Results showed that participants dynamically coordinated the timing of their movements both in movement onsets and during execution. Results are discussed with respect to their relevance and applicability to human-robot interaction.

Recognition and prediction of pedestrian intentions from a moving vehicle
Schmidt, Sabrina Human Factors Institute, Universität der Bundeswehr, Neubiberg, Germany Perez-Grassi, Ana Distributed Measurement System, Technical University Munich, München, Germany
Aim of the project is a system that is able to recognise action intentions and by means of that predict pedestrian behaviour, i.e. to be able to warn a driver of a possibly hazardous situation. A video experiment with naïve participants was conducted to get first hints about the parameters by which humans are able to recognise pedestrians' intentions. Further experiments and measurements (with

Lidar and infrared camera) help to decide which of the found parameters are necessary and which sufficient as well as finding the critical limits for the parametrisation in a model of pedestrian behaviour.

Handing over: Anticipation in joint action
Glasauer, Stefan Inst. für Neurologie, Universität München, München, Germany Huber, Markus Neurology, Ludwig-Maximilians-University, München, Germany Knoll, Alois Robotics and Embedded Systems, Technical University Munich, Garching bei München, Germany Brandt, Thomas Neurology, Ludwig-Maximilians-University, München, Germany
Successful joint action requires the seamless coordination between partners. Here we investigated how such coordination is achieved. We chose a handing-over task, which, despite its simplicity, requires agreement upon certain basic prerequisites and boundary conditions. Over the first three trials, the duration necessary to perform one handover decreased significantly due to a combination of reduced reaction and joint manipulation times. Thus, our preliminary results show that basic parameters of joint action are determined indirectly and adaptively while cooperating. The outcome of this implicit negotiation is used to anticipate the partner's next action and, thereby, to achieve higher efficacy.

Emotion in human-robot interaction: Recognition and display
Wendt, Cornelia Human Factors Institute, Universität der Bundeswehr, Neubiberg, Germany Kühnlenz, Kolja Automatic Control Engineering, Technical University of Munich, München, Germany Popp, Michael Human Factors Institute, University of the Bundeswehr, Neubiberg, Germany Karg, Michelle Automatic Control Engineering, Technical University of Munich, München, Germany
Given the importance of emotional aspects for natural human-robot interaction, we aim at providing cognitive systems with the ability to recognize and to display emotional states. In order to establish an emotion recognition system, we induced non-extreme emotions typical for interaction scenarios (e.g. over- versus underchallenge), which can be distinguished due to the underlying physiological signal patterns (ECG, SCR, BVP). Emotion display as another major concern is realized by the robot head EDDIE (23 degrees of freedom). User studies indicate that six basic emotions can reliably be recognized.

Modeling user stress in a cognitive architecture
Neumann, Hendrik Universität der Bundeswehr, Neubiberg, Germany Deml, Barbara Human Factors Institute, University of the Bundeswehr, Neubiberg, Germany Halbrügge, Marc Human Factors Institute, University of the Bundeswehr, Neubiberg, Germany
Cognitive architectures are powerful tools to test hypotheses about human-machine interaction efficiently. In order to create realistic user models, the architecture must be able to simulate the whole range of human behavior. To this end, we are extending the architecture ACT-R (Adaptive Control of Thought – Rational) to include both the formation and the effect of stress. The extension is based on appraisal theories developed in emotion psychology. By comparing empirical data of human drivers to those of a cognitive driver model, we are able to demonstrate how the ACT-R appraisal module enhances the realism of user models in technical settings.

Psychological foundations of cognitive technical systems
Deubel, Heiner Psychology, Experimental Psychology Unit, München, Germany Färber, Berthold Human Factors Institute, Universität der Bundeswehr, Neubiberg, Germany

The aim of the cluster of excellence "Cognition for Technical Systems" (CoTeSys) is to provide technical systems with cognitive capabilities such as perception, reasoning, learning, and planning in order to act and interact with humans in a natural way. Because this cannot be done without psychological input, several partners from psychology are engaged in the cluster to integrate basic psychological knowledge, advanced user interface ideas and evaluation procedures in the cluster. The symposium brings together experts from Psychology and Neurology contributing to the development of technical systems of the future on the basis of their specific expertise.

S-238: Reading development in languages with transparent orthographies: From local models to universal theories

Timothy Papadopoulos, George Georgiou (chair)
The identification of early precursors to word reading and reading comprehension by and large, was and remains an Anglo-Saxon endeavor. Significant research, however, has been also conducted in many other languages, particularly of transparent orthographies, aiming to either validate these models or introduce new ones. The present symposium argues that the future of reading development and disability research lies extensively in its ability to build new universal theories that would integrate various stances into an overarching framework, providing more thorough explanations of reading development and relevant difficulties.

Examining the home literacy model of reading development in Greek
Manolitsis, George Preschool Education, University of Crete, Rethymno, Greece Georgiou, George Educational Psychology, University of Alberta, Edmonton (AB), Canada Parrila, Rauno Educational Psychology, University of Alberta, Edmonton-AB, Canada
The purpose of the present study was to examine the Home Literacy Model of reading development in an orthographically transparent language. Seventy Greek children were followed from kindergarten until grade 3 and were administered measures of general cognitive ability, phonological awareness, letter knowledge, rapid naming, vocabulary, reading fluency, and comprehension. The parents of the children responded also to a questionnaire on home literacy activities. The results indicated that the Home Literacy Mode is overly simplistic and should be expanded to include relationships with RAN and letter knowledge.

Antecedents of reading in a transparent orthography (Finnish)
Leppänen, Ulla Dept. of Psychology, University of Jyväskylä, Jyväskylä, Finland Aunola, Kaisa Dept. of Psychology, University of Jyväskylä, Jyväskylä, Finland Nurmi, Jari-Erik Dept. of Psychology, University of Jyväskylä, Jyväskylä, Finland
This study examined various cognitive and social antecedents (kindergarten, Grades 1 and 2) of technical reading and reading comprehension in Grade 4. Also, the role of task-focused behavior was examined. In this Jyväskylä Entrance into Primary School Study (JEPS; Nurmi & Aunola, 1999-2007) around 207 children were followed from kindergarten (6-year olds) to Grade 4. The preliminary results showed that high levels of letter knowledge, visual attention, metacognitive awareness and mothers' education predicted grade 4 reading. In addition, teacher assessed task-focused behavior predicted both beginning reading and later reading comprehension even after controlling for earlier reading skills.

Gender ratio and cognitive profile in dyslexia: A cross-national study

Jiménez, Juan E. Dept. of Psychology, University of La Laguna, Tenerife, Spain

The purpose of this study has been to analyze the gender-related differences in the prevalence of dyslexia across different cultural contexts in a consistent orthography. A second purpose of this study was to analyze whether there are cross-national patterns of differences on cognitive processes involved in reading and spelling between Guatemalan and Spanish males and females groups with dyslexia. The log-linear analysis was used to analyze the interaction between nationality, gender and reading level in order to know if the number of dyslexics detected is different across the countries independently of gender. Likewise, analyses of covariance (ANCOVA) were conducted on the reading and cognitive processes measures.

A local model to teach phonetic sensitivity in Dutch

van der Kooy-Hofland, Verna Social and Behaviour Sciences, Leiden University, Leiden, Netherlands Bus, Adriana G. Social and Behaviour Sciences, Leiden University, Leiden, Netherlands

In Dutch, children's proper names play a special role in the development of phonetic sensitivity. In joint attentional activities such as name writing, the fact that grown-ups stimulate children to reflect on their elementary writing activities may be the start of phonetic sensitivity. In order to test this model experimentally we designed a computer program with 40 tasks, imitating adult instruction: after practicing name writing, kindergarten children did tasks with their first letter and practiced recognition of this sound in their own name and other words. The experimental children (N = 90) outperformed the control group (N = 45) in phonetic sensitivity and writing skills.

A longitudinal appraisal of the development of passage comprehension in Greek

Papadopoulos, Timothy Dept. of Psychology, University of Cyprus, Nicosia, Cyprus Kendeou, Panayiota Educational & Counselling, McGill University, Quebec, Canada

We sought to identify early correlates of word reading and passage comprehension in 289 Greek-speaking children. In kindergarten and grade 1, children were administered measures of phonological awareness, nonverbal ability, speech rate, working memory, RAN, word reading, and passage comprehension (grade 1 only). The analysis showed that in kindergarten RAN, phonological awareness, and working memory directly predicted word reading. In grade 1, phonological awareness, working memory, and nonverbal ability predicted word reading, whereas passage comprehension was predicted by phonological awareness, nonverbal ability, and word reading. These findings indicate that phonological measures have higher predictive power than RAN measures in passage comprehension.

S-239: Traffic Psychological Assessment - Bridging the gap between theory and practice

Gernot Schuhfried (chair)

The symposium deals with contemporary topics of traffic psychological assessment and the retention of mobility, ranging from formal guidelines for the assessment of fitness to drive to a variety of validation studies for several traffic psychological questions, including the fitness to drive of (1)elderly persons, (2)after a traumatic brain injury or (3)of physically handicapped clients in adapted vehicles. The symposium concludes with a presentation of computerized methods for cognitive rehabilitation and training which could be applied in order to help

clients to regain their fitness to drive and maintain their mobility.

The role of cognitive performace testing in the assessment of driving aptitude

Brenner-Hartmann, Jürgen Abt. Psychologie, TÜV SÜD Life Service GmbH, Ulm, Germany

Driving fitness can be defined as a time-enduring ability and willingness to adopt safe driving behavior. Doubts about suitability are: • physical-mental fitness (health, cognitive ability) when applying, • development, change, adjustment and stabilization of an illness or problematic behavior • formation of insight, behavioral disposition, motivation and habituation processes. This shows the significance of ability assessment in the overall context of the judgment of driving fitness. These dimensions play a role in the evaluation of results. The dependence of currently displayed performance on current fitness and motivational factors must be considered when evaluating test results.

Predictive validity of the expert system traffic in healthy adults

Häusler, Joachim Psychological Assessment, SCHUHFRIED GmbH, Mödling, Austria Sommer, Markus Psychological Assessment, SCHUHFRIED GmbH, Mödling, Austria Schützhofer, Bettina Traffic Psychology, Sicher unterwegs GmbH, Wien, Austria Risser, Ralf Traffic Psychology, FACTUM, Wien, Austria

The present study investigates the predictive validity of the ability tests of the Expert System Traffic, applying linear multivariate statistics and artificial neural networks. A standardized on-road test served as criterion measure. A total of 222 healthy adults participated in this study. The predictive validity was evaluated using linear multivariate statistics and artificial neural networks. The results indicate that artificial neural networks yield practically relevant classification rates (80%) and validity coefficients (.68) and enable a clear distinction to be made between safe and unsafe drivers at the individual level. The results have been cross-validated using a smaller independent data set.

Predicting fitness to drive after traumatic brain injury or stroke

Schauer, Susanne Generation Research Program, Ludwig-Maximilians-Universität, Bad Tölz, Germany

The present study investigates the predictive validity of the Expert System Traffic in patients who sustained traumatic brain injuries or strokes. A standardized on-road test served as criterion measure. A total of 119 patients participated in this study. The predictive validity was evaluated using linear multivariate statistics and artificial neural networks. The results indicate that artificial neural networks (classification rate: 95%, sensitivity: 88%, specifity: 98%) outperform linear multivariate methods (classification rate: 74%, sensitivity: 46%, specifity: 89%); indicating the presence of more complex relations between psychometric tests and actual driving behavior.

Conditional driving license for elderly drivers

Dorfer, Max Führerschenkommission, Sanitätsbetrieb Bozen, Bozen, Italy

Respondents exhibiting safe driving behaviour in simple, well known traffic situations while failing in more complex ones are commonly classified as conditional fit to drive. Despite the common use of this procedure little research has been conducted on the cognitive abilities which separate conditional safe drivers from safe and unsafe drivers. Respondents were classified as safe, conditional safe or unsafe according to their performance in a standardized on-road test containing simple as well as complex traffic situations. Using the Expert System Traffic a set of cognitive and perceptual ability

traits was identified which best distinguished these three groups.

Compensational effects regarding the fitness to drive of handicapped drivers in adapted vehicles

Grünseis-Pacher, Edith CLUB MOBIL, Andorf, Austria Risser, Ralf Traffic psycholgy, FACTUM, Wien, Austria

In the framework of traffic-psychological examinations, compensations for singular deficiencies in relevant ability dimensions are to be considered. Methods of judgment formation are typically based on information derived from a normal population, whereas compensatory mechanisms in physically handicapped respondents could be radically different. The present study investigates those compensatory mechanisms in handicapped persons, based on test data from the Expert System Traffic and two independent standardized driving samples in adapted vehicles, concluding that traditional models of fitness to drive cannot be generalized to these clients - necessary modifications are suggested.

Computerized cognitive training: Theory and possible applicability in traffic psychology

Sturm, Walter Neurologische Klinik, Universitätsklinikum Aachen, Aachen, Germany

Attention functions are an important component of fitness to drive. The computerized training of attention has proved to be an effective method of treating attention disorders after cerebral injury; the specific training of attention can also have a positive impact on fitness to drive. The new attention training program CogniPlus builds on these findings and makes use of professionally designed computer gaming software. It comprises training modules for the six most important attention functions (alertness, vigilance, spatial attention, selection attention, focused attention, divided attention) and automatically adapts the difficulty of the task to the client's ability level and reaction times.

S-240: Informal learning in museums with media: Perspectives from cognitive, media and educational psychology

Eva Mayr, Daniel Wessel (chair)

This symposium provides insight in current international projects on learning with media in museums. Museums as prototypical informal learning settings attract visitors of all ages and backgrounds. Thus, they are extremely important for life-long learning. However, museums were widely neglected by contemporary psychology, missing out on opportunities to study learning in a highly self-regulated naturalistic setting. Conversely, psychological insights can explain and improve learning in museums. The presented studies address the question how media can be used to stimulate, support, and improve learning processes in museums.

Supporting learning processes in museums with personalised labels

Mayr, Eva Virtual PhD Program, Universität Tübingen, Tübingen, Germany Zahn, Carmen Knowledge Media ResearchCenter, Knowledge Media ResearchCenter, Tuebingen, Germany Hesse, Friedrich W. Knowledge Media ResearchCenter, Knowledge Media ResearchCenter, Tuebingen, Germany

When people visit informal learning settings like museums, they often do not give priority to learning. This could be due to reduced cognitive capacities available for information processing. To enhance elaboration of information presented and learning in museums it is assumed that information presentation should be adaptive and match visitors' interests. To address the effect of adaptive information presentation an experiment is conducted. Information is adapted to visitors' goals. Visitors, who are provided with adaptive information, invest less time in exhibit selection. This indicates reduction of cognitive demands. However, they are superior to visitors without adapted information in knowledge transfer.

Supporting situational interest and knowledge exchange with mobile media

Wessel, Daniel AG Wissensaustausch, Institut für Wissensmedien, Tübingen, Germany *Zahn, Carmen* AG Wissensaustausch, Institut für Wissensmedien, Tübingen, Germany *Hesse, Friedrich Wilhelm* AG Wissensaustausch, Institut für Wissensmedien, Tübingen, Germany

Situational interest and continuing engagement with contents of exhibitions are of crucial importance in informal learning settings like museums. We analyze how visitor learning can be supported by providing additional information in moments of situational interest in an exhibit and by allowing bookmarking of interesting exhibits for post-visit reflection. These questions were addressed in a 2x2 design (additional information available, bookmarks accessible after the visit) in an exhibition. Logfiles and questionnaire results showed that additional information improved the evaluation of the exhibit and post visit engagement with the topic although post-visit use of the bookmarks was rare.

Evaluating a learning-by-design approach in a technology museum

Reimann, Peter CoCo Research Centre, University of Sydney, Sydney, NSW, Australia *Mann, Susanna* CoCo Research Centre, University of Sydney, Sydney, NSW, Australia

This work addresses the problematic relation between formal school curriculum and activities school classes perform in museum settings. In co-operation with Australia's largest technology and design museum (The Powerhouse Museum, Sydney), we have developed an approach to learning in a museum settings that builds on the learning-by-design pedagogy developed by Kolodner and co-workers, and employs various technologies (multimedia authoring tools, collaboration software, and tablet PCs) to link pre-visit and post-visit activities to the museum visit. We will report observations and outcomes from a first study using a mixed-method approach.

Do reconstructions influence familiarity and dating of past ages?: A preliminary study

Glaser, Manuela AG Cybermedia, Institut für Wissensmedien, Tübingen, Germany *Garsoffky, Bärbel* AG Cybermedia, Institut für Wissensmedien, Tübingen, Germany *Schwan, Stephan* AG Cybermedia, Institut für Wissensmedien, Tübingen, Germany

We suggested that reconstructions (re-enactments, VR) in archaeological television documentaries should enhance the feeling of familiarity with past periods and should result in dating the periods more forward in time. We tested four measures of familiarity and three dating measures in a between-subject-design (n=40). Subjects watched 8 clips, half of them with and the other half without reconstructions. After each clip subjects rated familiarity and dated the depicted period. ANOVAs showed that reconstructions tend to result in decreased familiarity and interact significantly with content on dating. Type of measure and other characteristics of film seem to influence the results.

Learning science at museums: A media terminal as scaffold for critical thinking and opinion formation about nanotechnology

Knipfer, Kristin Virtual PhD Program, Universität Tübingen, Tübingen, Germany

Today, science museums are challenged to present the ambivalence of current scientific topics and to support visitors' reflective judgement about socio-

scientific issues. As scaffold, a discussion terminal was implemented within the context of an exhibition about nanotechnology. We examined whether or not support for critical evaluation of arguments pro/con nanotechnology, expressing one's own opinion, and social comparison information about other visitors' opinion foster knowledge acquisition and opinion formation. The results show that support for critical thinking is crucial for integration of controversial information and formation of well-founded opinions. Own opinion expression and social comparison information further enhances reflective judgement.

FP-262: Language and thought

Role of inner speech in written generation of ideas and in written communication of them: Mutual influence of joint and individual brainwriting

Janoušek, Jaromír Faculty of Philosophy, Charles University, Praha 1, Czech Republic

The aim was to examine role of inner speech in written idea generation under conditions of interpersonal and intrapersonal written communication. Two types of triadic groups were scheduled. One type (30 groups) started with joint brainwriting and changed to individual brainwriting. Other type (30 groups) proceeded in opposite direction. Manifestations of inner speech appeared in different forms of connections among idea proposals and in lack of them. Individual brainwriting after joint one brought significantly more connections of higher complexity than individual brainwriting alone. Joint brainwriting after individual one brought significantly more contentually linked-up turns than joint brainwriting alone.

Verb factivity, complementation and theory of mind

Tang, Suki K.Y. Dept. of Psychology, CUHK, Hong Kong, China, People's Republic of : Hong Kong SAR *Cheung, Him* Department of Psychology, CUHK, Hong Kong, China, People's Republic of : Macao SAR *Tam, Kandix T.Y.* Department of Psychology, CUHK, Hong Kong, China, People's Republic of : Macao SAR *Szeto, Ching Yee Lovenner* Department of Psychology, CUHK, Hong Kong, China, People's Republic of : Macao SAR

To investigate the relationship between language and theory-of-mind (ToM), thirty-eight kindergartners were tested twice over 3 months on ToM, the complement syntax, and the understanding of verb factivity. We found that early ToM predicted late factivity, only when the ToM tasks involved belief reasoning. While early factivity did not predict late ToM, it did predict late complement syntax. We argue that belief-related ToM is fundamental to understanding the factivity of complement-taking (mental) verbs, which in turn constitutes the foundation for developing a full complement syntax. Our conclusion is more consistent with the hypothesis that thought precedes language.

Design and evaluation of a methodological alternative for studying referential behavior using a computer assisted task

Hurtado-Parrado, Camilo Dept. of Psychology, University of Manitoba, Winnipeg, Canada *Peña-Correal, Telmo* Psicología, Universidad Nacional Colombia, Bogotá, Colombia

Some interactions are characterized by the possibility of the listener to respond in a conventional manner to the relation between what a "speaker" says or what a "writer" writes and objects/events absent, not apparent or future novel situations – named "transference tests"- (e.g., someone is describing another person events/objects not present. The research question was: "Does the experience of being trained to generate references (i.e. training for producing coherent "phrases"

which refer past occurred relations between objects, using a very simplified artificial conventional system) produce a differential effect over the performance during a transference phase?

I hear and I forget?: A comparison of the implicit causality effect in language between a German and a Chinese sample

Tumasjan, Andranik Inst. für Psychologie, Universität München, München, Germany *Spörrle, Matthias* Dept. for Psychology, Ludwig-Maximilians University, München, Germany

Implicit causality in verbs (i.e. causal attribution of interpersonal events to either the subject or the object) is a robust phenomenon across different languages (see for review: Rudolph & Försterling, 1997). However, most previous research used European languages, thus lacking intercultural generalizability. Our study is the first to investigate verb causality in two parallelized samples (N = 386) from Germany and China by using the respective national languages. Results demonstrate implicit causality in both languages. However, consistent with previous research indicating increased variability and situational consideration in Asian respondents' attributions, the causality effect was much weaker in the Chinese sample.

Developing language and social understanding in the early years

Thelander, Mary Speech and Language, University of Toronto, Toronto, Canada *Falenchuk, Olesya* OISE, University of Toronto, Toronto, Canada

To become literate, a child must be able to reason: to find meaning in facts known or assumed. In Toronto, most children who start school speak different languages, come from different cultures, and view differently the meaning of others' actions and communications. Lacking both knowledge of the language of instruction and culturally shared social understanding of what is in others' minds, minority language children are at risk of not becoming literate. The study aim is to determine whether the literacy of minority language children can be improved if they are taught narrative skills and social reasoning in an explicit fashion.

Language influence on image and emotion generation during text comprehension

Yerchak, Mikalai Dept. of Psychology, Minsk Linguistic University, Minsk, Belarus

Text comprehension was studied. 30 advanced second language learners were asked to listen to four English stories and signal every moment they had images (two stories) and emotions (two stories). The Russian equivalents were offered to another similar group. The indices of the two groups were alike: the maximum and the minimum amounts of signals fell on the same elements both in English and Russian texts. In many cases the texts in Russian stimulated 2-3 times as many images (emotions) as the English ones. So the native language remains more closely linked to the image and emotion components of our thoughts.

FP-263: Attitudes in context

Health attitude as behavioral disposition: Why do you eat fast-food if you say it is not healthy?

Byrka, Katarzyna Technology Management, Eindhoven Univ. of Technology, Eindhoven, Netherlands *Kaiser, Florian G.* Technology Management, Eindhoven Univ. of Technology, Eindhoven, Netherlands

Intuitively, health attitudes, expressed as evaluative statements, seem to determine health behavior. However, empirical research rarely confirms a strong attitude-behavior relationship. With our model, we argue that attitudes underlie both evaluative statements and behaviors, but that the former are easier to endorse than the latter. With survey data (N=391), we assessed evaluative statements and self-reported behaviors in various health domains. As predicted, evaluative statements proved easier to endorse than behaviors. Also, various health behaviors were interdependent and could be collapsed into a single dimension. We conclude that the attitude-behavior inconsistency results from not considering difficulties of various behavioral records.

Why TPB doesn't seem to work in México?: The role of culture in distinguishing intention, volition and desire

Contreras Ibáñez, Carlos C. Dept. of Social Psychology, UAM, Mexico City, Mexico Bedolla, Berenice Facultad de Psicología, UNAM, UNAM, Mexico City, Mexico

Theory of planned behavior (TPB) establish worthwhile models with specific predictions about conduct; however several studies find lower explicative power in Mexican samples. We have found that a cultural orientation measurement mediates the separability of intention into two components: volition (cognitive) and desire (affective). With the objective of comparing adjustment of culture sensitive TPB models, we apply appropriate instruments on recycling behavior to 270 adult women, inhabitants of Mexico City, and analyze the data with Lisrel. Findings supports separation hypothesis and boost explained variance from .20 to .70. We discuss these results remarking the role of culture in cognitive process.

The relationships among developmental goals and machiavellian personality beliefs among Iranian college students

Latifian, Morteza Dept. Educational Psychology, Shiraz University, Shiraz, Islamic Republic of Iran Bashash, Laaya Educational Psychology Dep., Shiraz university, Shiraz, Islamic Republic of Iran

Shiraz University Shiraz, IRAN The aim of this study was to investigate the relationships among college-students' goals and their machiavellian personality beliefs. 315 university students were selected by random cluster sampling method. Mean age and standard deviation were 20.1 and 1.8 year respectively. Two scales; Kiddie Mach Scale and Developmental Life Goals Scale (Brandtstadter's model), were used. Regression analysis indicated that students' machiavellian beliefs predicted six main developmental goals (social security, esteem, social relation, personal security, avoidance security, and survival). In general, the pattern of relationship illustrates a unique combination of machiavellian beliefs and developmental goals for Iranian youth.

Women's gender identity and their attitudes towards feminists

Kwiatkowska, Anna Cross-Cultural Psychology, Warsaw School of Social Psycho, Warsaw, Poland

Feminism entails a commitment to breaking down the structures that keep women lower in status and power. Because feminism seeks social change, e.g. challenges traditional gender roles, there is a wide array of attitudes towards feminists – from positive to negative. The research question concerns the role of gender identity (i.e. conceptualization of herself as a woman, and conceptualization of women as a social category) in attitudes formation. In two studies gender identity was measured with Hoffman Gender Scale (N=74), and Crocker and Luhtannen Collective Self-Esteem Scale (N=60). Results showed significant role of gender self concept, and public image of women (the higher, the less positive attitudes).

The male attitude norms Inventory-III (Afrikaans, English and Xhosa versions): Measures of masculinity ideology in South Africa

Luyt, Russell Dept. of Psychology, University of Winchester, Winchester, United Kingdom

Afrikaans, English and Xhosa versions of the Male Attitude Norms Inventory-III (MANI-III) are introduced as multidimensional measures of South African masculinity ideology. Evidence surrounding the cross-cultural content and construct validity of their predecessor, the Male Attitude Norms Inventory-II (MANI-II), suggested and guided measurement revision. Exploratory factor analysis rendered a three-factor model of traditional masculinity across language sub-samples (n = 1497). Factorial invariance across sub-samples was not supported. It was therefore considered appropriate to develop separate measures for each language group. A particularising approach to measurement was also deemed appropriate given their theoretical grounding within the social constructionist perspective.

Effort counts more than performance: The value of effort in pursuit of academic achievement in Confucian society

Wang, Hsiou-Huai Center for Teacher Education, National Taiwan University, Taipei, Taiwan

Traditionally, effort is regarded as the means to achieving high performance, that is, effort has its instrumental value. This study intends to investigate that under the influence of traditional Chinese-Confucian thought, effort not only has an instrumental value, but also has moral and social value. A group of 521 high school and college students in Taiwan were administered a questionnaire with four scenario varying in the degree of effort and performance. The results show that effort counts more than performance in judging a student's moral salience and social popularity. Cultural roots to these beliefs and implications for education are discussed.

FP-264: Instructional media: Multimedia learning, e-learning, computer-based learning

Help design in a computer-based learning environment the effect of perceived understanding and support of meta-cognitive processes

Schworm, Silke Inst. für Pädagogik, Universität Regensburg, Regensburg, Germany

Computer-based learning-environments offer on demand help which should enable the learners to cope with occurring problems. However, learners are not using those help facilities effectively. Help seeking requires learners' awareness of need for help. In an experiment we compared two conditions (n = 70 students of educational sciences) that differed with respect to whether learners' were given the opportunity to diagnose their own understanding. Preliminary results show that results in learning-tasks which enable learners to better judge their own understanding are related to their perceived certainty about understanding the learning-content as well as to their help seeking behaviour.

Transforming and leveraging knowledge gained in e-learning "roadmap to e-learning @ ETH Zurich"

Troitzsch, Heide Inst. für Angew. Psychologie, Fachhochschule Nordwestschweiz, Olten, Switzerland Clases, Christoph School of Applied Psychology, FHNW, Olten, Switzerland

Knowledge gained from teaching in e-learning settings is usually linked to specific projects and individuals. At ETH Zurich a manual was developed that makes this knowledge accessible for beginners in the area of e-learning. The tool

integrates two knowledge management strategies: codification and coordination. By applying knowledge management techniques, existing experiences were documented. The resulting manual helps lecturers throughout the developmental stages of their e-learning projects and within the complex socio-technical environment (e.g. stakeholder, projects and technologies). Extensions towards an interactive web-based tool will be presented, which encourages further learning and knowledge building within the organisation.

Transitioning from the classroom to fully online courses

Meiners, Mary Social and Behavior Sciences, San Diego Miramar College, San Diego, USA

Tools of emerging technologies challenge us and bring new opportunities simultaneously. The response is for some to resist and criticize; others allow the tools to drive pedagogy. The ability to teach fully online courses also presents issues around design, development, infrastructure, assessment, delivery, quality control and student support. This paper will focus on challenges faced in converting a highly interactive classroom course to a fully online course, describing some of the strategies involved in the design, development and implementation of an exemplary course with learning theory underpinnings. Included will be factors that contribute to student retention and success.

Multimedia learning: Influence of a reset button and interactive seductive details on retention and comprehension in interactive animations

Rey, Günter Daniel Allg. und Kognit. Psychologie, Universität Trier, Trier, Germany

In two experiments (N = 107, N = 45), students received an interactive animation that explained a special type of neural network (self organizing map) followed by retention and transfer tests. The existence of seductive (= interesting but irrelevant) details and a reset button, used for a specific form of learning control, did not influence retention and transfer performance. However, analysis of click frequency with a multilayer feedforward network and inferential statistics analysis with bootstrap indicate that an adequate use of a reset button improves retention and transfer, while too much or too little use lead to lower learning performance.

Multimedia-learning in mathematics: Inducing cognitive conflicts

Sander, Elisabeth Inst. für Psychologie, Universität Koblenz, Koblenz, Germany Heiß, Andrea Psychology, University of Koblenz, Koblenz, Germany

According to Piaget's theory, inducing cognitive conflicts in general is an effective teaching method. Aim of our study was to find out whether this method is effective in multimedia-learning, too. A conflict-inducing, learner-controlled trigonometry-programme was developed and compared with a programme-controlled version. Each of the programmes was applied to a group of seventeen-years-old pupils (n=66). Results indicate that pupils learning with the learner-controlled version showed more cognitive conflicts and deeper comprehension in a post-test and in a follow-up. It is concluded that inducing cogntive conflicts is effective in multimedia-learning.

Computer assisted and multidimensional learning: A teaching model for assisting Iranian university students to learn better

Hameedy, Mansoor Dept. Educational Psychology, Alzahra University, Tehran, Islamic Republic of Iran Rastgoo Moghadam, Mitra Educational Psychology, Alzahra University, Tehran, Islamic Republic of Iran Akhavan, Mahnaz Educational Psychology, Alzahra University, Tehran, Islamic Republic of Iran Kiamanesh, Alireza

Based on the social constructivist principles of learning and teaching, a multidimensional teaching model has been developed to help the Iranian university teachers in assisting students to learn problem solving skills through co-learning and computer use. The model emphasizes both lower and higher cognitive skills needed in problem solving while highlighting the affective and behavioral aspects of learning through cooperation and utilization of new technologies. Two groups of university sophomores were matched academically in order to help with the testing of the developed model. The preliminary results indicate the effectiveness of the model compared to the common approach to teaching.

FP-265: Leader-member exchange

The relationship of organizational justice, social exchange relationship to psychological contract breach: Evidence from China

Jin, Yanghua School of of Management, Zhejiang Gongshang University, Hangzhou, People's Republic of China Nie, Biao school of management, Zhejiang Gongshang University, hangzhou, People's Republic of China Jiang, Xin school of management, Zhejiang Gongshang University, hangzhou, People's Republic of China

Using two different samples, this study examined the relationship of social exchange, organizational justice to psychological contract breach under Chinese settings. Results demonstrated that perceived organizational support and leader-member exchange were antecedent variables of organizational justice. Procedural justice, interactional justice partially mediated the relationship between perceived organizational support and psychological contract breach; the effect of leader-member exchange was fully mediated by organizational justice variables. Except for distributive justice, procedural justice and interactional justice were significant predicators of employee's psychological contract breach perception. Research results supported the relational model of organizational justice under Chinese "Guanxi" culture.

Relationship between job-demand, job-control and work-family conflict: The moderating role of leader-member exchange

Zeng, Chuikai School of Management, Shenyang Normal University, Shenyang, People's Republic of China Shi, Kan School of Management, Graduate University of CAS, Beijing, People's Republic of China

To explore the moderating effects of LMX on the relationship between job–demands, job control and work-family conflict, 526 employees were assessed by the questionnaire of Work Interf erence With Family and Family Interf erence With Work, Job–Demands and Decision Latitude, and Leader-Member Exchange 7. Moderating regression analysis indicated that job–demands, job control and LMX were powerful predictors of work-family conflict (both work interference with family and family interference with work); Leader-Member Exchange was an important moderator between job demands and work-family conflict (both WIF and FIW); but not between job control and work-family conflict in this research

The antecedents of trust in management in Chinese organizations: An empirical analysis to the effects of contract and LMX

Yan, Jin School of management, Zhejiang University, Hangzhou, People's Republic of China Zheng, Mei International Co., Zhejiang Materials Industrial, Hangzhou, People's Republic of China Miao, Lingling School of management, Zhejiang University, Hangzhou, People's Republic of China

Trust is a psychological state comprising the intention to accept vulnerability based on positive expectations of intention or behaviors of another.

The trustors often adopt varied approaches to control the risks caused by trust, such as contracts and personal relationships. We supposed that the interaction of contracts and LMX will be meaningful in explaining the trust behaviors. 154 of effective questionnaires was collected in survey. The results showed that a contract would enhance the trust in management significantly when the subordinates have low LMX with their supervisors. When the LMX is high, effects of contract is not significant.

The impact of the emotional intelligence of employees and their manager on the job performance of employees

Yuan, Denghua Dept. of Psychology, Jiangxi Normal University, Nanchang, People's Republic of China Yu, Qiong psychology department, HRM research centre, Nanchang, People's Republic of China

Yuan Denghua YuQiong (Jiangxi Normal University, Nanchang, China 330027) Using a sample of 218 managers and 640 employees from 30 firms, the present study examined whether leader-member exchange (LMX) mediate the relationship between manager's emotional intelligence (MEI) and the job performance of their employees by applying the structural equation modeling analysis. The results indicated that employee's emotional intelligence (EEI) and MEI positively impacted both task performance (TP) and contextual performance (CP) of employees, the LMX perceived by the employees partially mediate the relationship between MEI and their employees' TP and CP. Results highlight the importance of MEI, EEI and LMX in enhancing the job performance of employees.

Aspirations of female leaders at workplace: The impact of perceptions of gender congruency between family and work

Lopez Zafra, Esther Dept. of Social Psychology, Universidad de Jaén, Jaén, Spain García Retamero, Rocio Social Psychology, Universidad de Granada, Granada, Spain Berrios, Maria del Pilar Social Psychology, Universidad de Jaén, Jaén, Spain

The increase of working women is not followed by an increase in women leaders. Critical is the congruency between women's roles in their personal and professional lives. Ease of attainment of a leadership position is affected by age and structural factors. These factors might also affect women's perceptions of compatibility of family and work roles. We examined the influence of people's expectations about the compatibility of family and work roles on their evaluations of a possible promotion into a leadership role. We differentiated between a female- and a male-congenial environment. Our results show that people's expectations affected their promotion possibilities in work environments that were either congruent or incongruent with the leader's gender role.

The effect of relationship quality in Taiwanese military teams: Investigating the interaction of leader-member exchange and team members' exchange

Huang, Min-Ping Business Administration, Yuanze University, Chungli, Taiwan Cheng, Bor-Shiuan Psychology, National Taiwan University, Taipei, Taiwan Liang, Wei-Chun Graduate school of Management, Yuan Ze University, Chung-Li, Taiwan Chou, Li-Fang Business Administration, Yuan Ze University, Chung-Li, Taiwan

The objective of this study was to investigate the effects of leader-member exchange (LMX) and team members' exchange (TMX) on individual member's work performance and organizational citizenship behavior (OCB). The interaction effect between LMX and MMX was also investigated. We conducted a network questionnaire survey to collect empirical data from Taiwanese military teams. In

total we got 214 batteries troops, including 214 leaders and 642 team members' data. Results show that the positive effect of LMX is stronger than TMX's. Specifically speaking, the work performance and OCB of in-group team members (regarding to the team leader) are significantly higher. Besides, there is complicated interaction between LMX and TMX.

FP-266: Implicit learning and memory

Implicit learning in multiple faces tracking

Chen, Wenfeng Institute of Psychology, Chinese Academy of Sciences, Beijing, People's Republic of China Ren, Dongning Institute of Psychology, Chinese Academy of Sciences, Beijing, People's Republic of China Fu, Xiaolan Institute of Psychology, Chinese Academy of Sciences, Beijing, People's Republic of China

It was evident implicit learning is invoked when exposed to face (Burton et al., 1999). This study examined implicit face learning during multiple faces tracking. Experiment 1 found significant priming for target faces in MOT task. Experiment 2 found implicit face learning impaired tracking performance. Experiment 3 found similar performance for multiple identical faces and inverted faces while performance decreased for upright faces. Results showed both inverted and upright faces in MOT caused implicit learning, but more intensive for upright faces. It suggested while structural encoding was disrupted by inversion, learning was sufficient to abolish the effects of configural manipulation.

Inferences in the comprehension and learning from refutation text

Diakidoy, Irene-Anna Dept. of Psychology, University of Cyprus, Nicosia, Cyprus Shamounki, Christina Psychology, University of Cyprus, Nicosia, Cyprus Ioannides, Christos Philosophy &History of Sci, University of Athens, Athens, Greece Mouskounti, Thalia Psychology, University of Cyprus, Nicosia, Cyprus

This study compared recall, inferencing, and learning from refutation and expository texts. Undergraduate students (N=37) were pretested on their knowledge of a scientific concept, read the assigned text on the same topic, and completed a recall task and a posttest. ANOVA indicated that both high- and low-knowledge students who read the refutation text drew more valid integrative and elaborative inferences than students who read the expository text (p<.01). Differences in posttest and recall scores were in the same direction but non-significant. Therefore, any positive learning effects obtained with refutation texts can be attributed to the facilitation of inferential processing.

Can we know what we can control in sequence learning?

Fu, Qiufang Institute of Psychology,CAS, Beijing, People's Republic of China Dienes, Zoltan Department of Psychology, University of Sussex, Brighton, United Kingdom Fu, Xiaolan Institute of Psychology, Chinese Academy of Sciences, Beijing, People's Republic of China

This paper combines the Process Dissociation Procedure (PDP) and subjective measures to explore whether unconscious knowledge emerges early or later in sequence learning. The results showed that sequential knowledge was detectable either early or later in training but the control over knowledge only emerged later, indicating that subjects acquired unconscious knowledge early. Moreover, the control over knowledge was expressed even when subjects gave intuition attributions, suggesting that the ability to control could be based on unconscious structural knowledge. Combining the PDP with subjective measures may be a good way to measure the conscious states of both structural and judgment knowledge.

Models of artificial grammar learning

Kinder, Annette Inst. für Psychologie, Universität Potsdam, Potsdam, Germany

Two connectionist models of sequential learning are contrasted, the Simple Recurrent Network (SRN) model and the Competitive Chunking (CC) model. Two experiments tested the predictions of these models in Artificial Grammar Learning. Experiment 1 showed that when judging test stimuli participants apply knowledge of the positions of single elements in the training stimuli. Experiment 2 demonstrated that participants apply knowledge of bigram frequency when judging the test stimuli. As demonstrated by computer simulations, only the SRN model and not the CC model explains these effects, which shows the superiority of the SRN as a model of Artificial Grammar Learning.

Implicit learning of phrase-structure grammar in language and music

Rohrmeier, Martin Faculty of Music, University of Cambridge, Cambridge, United Kingdom Fu, Qiufang Institute of Psychology, Chinese Academy of Sciences, Beijing, People's Republic of China

Phrase-structure grammars (PSG) play a central role in linguistic and musical syntax (Patel, 2003) both of which are acquired implicitly throughout early development. Using the same artificial PSG in language and music, four cross-cultural experiments investigate implicit learning of complex syntax involving features of recursion, hierarchicality, and long-distance dependencies. Preliminary results showed that subjects could acquire the hierarchical structure of the artificial grammar and performed significantly above chance in recognizing grammatical categories. Final results are expected to yield insight on differences in efficacy of PSG acquisition between the two domains, and which levels of recursive structure people can acquire.

Cue facilitation in contingency learning when there is no time to think

Vadillo, Miguel A. Dept. de Psicología, Universidad de Deusto, Bilbao, Spain Matute, Helena Departamento de Psicología, Universidad de Deusto, Bilbao, Spain

Experimental studies on contingency learning have shown that cues tend to compete to become associated with an outcome. The present series of experiments was designed to test whether the opposite effect, cue facilitation, can be observed in a standard contingency learning task with college students and Internet users as participants. Simple inferential analyses show that these facilitation effects can be observed (Experiment 1) and that they are highly dependent on time pressure (Experiment 2). These results suggest that cue facilitation is better understood in terms of basic encoding and retrieval mechanisms, rather than in terms of reasoning processes.

FP-267: Juridical decision making

Decision making processes in experts and novices

Garcia Retamero, Rocio Experimental Psychology, Granada, Spain Dhami, Mandeep K. Institute of Criminology, University of Cambridge, Cambridge, United Kingdom

We compared the decision strategies and cue use of experts and novices. The task was to decide which of two residential properties would be more likely to be burgled based on eight cues such as the location of the property. Participants were 36 imprisoned burglars that had committed residential burglary between 1-3,000 times (expert group 1), 36 police officers with 5-28 years of experience (expert group 2), and 36 University students that were not

victims of residential burglary (novice group). Results showed that experts and novices differed in the strategies they used to make inferences and the cues they considered important for making such inferences.

Legal decision making in euthanasia: The impact of victim's consent, psychological evaluation and judge's instructions on responsibility and culpability judgments

Denàve, Catherine Nord, Université de Lille 3, Lille, France Alain, Michel Dept. of Psychology, Universite du Quebec, Trois-Rivieres, Canada

Legal decision-making in euthanasia has been rarely studied regarding the victim's consent in a social psychological perspective. This study investigated the impact of this consent (present/absent), the type of psychological evaluation (victim's suffering/defendant's suffering) and judge's instructions (standard/nullification) on jurors' judgments. Participants (N=122) read a summary of a trial, rated the responsibility of the defendant and rendered a verdict. Results confirm the significant main effect of victim's consent: more lenient judgments are made with the victim's informed consent. Results are discussed in terms of attribution of responsibility taking into consideration the issue of consent in the law of crime.

A series of studies on the role of apology in law: A psycholegal perspective

McKillop, Dianne School of Psychology, Edith Cowan University, Joondalup, Australia Allan, Alfred School of Psychology, Edith Cowan University, Joondalup, Australia Allan, Ricks School of Psychology, Edith Cowan University, Joondalup, Australia Drake, Deirdre School of Psychology, Edith Cowan University, Joondalup, Australia

Although there is a history of concern with the role of apology in law, the concept has not been well defined. Our social and clinical psychological research has indicated that the received meaning of apology in legal and other contexts is complex and multidimensional. For example, a subjective sense of justice is impacted by the perceived motivations and intent of the apologist. Associated constructs include remorse, forgiving and reconciliation. This presentation will describe the evolution of a psycholegal model of apology. The model has important implications for justice in criminal and civil law, and for actual and proposed law reform.

Tension between psychological research findings and civil law (family-rights) in Germany

Baumgärtel, Frank Institut für Rechtspsychologie, Universität Bremen, Bremen, Germany

Since publication of Goldstein et al. (1973) and followers the law agents in germany tend to reform the familiy regulations in law. It seemed to be a good adaptation of rules to modern forms of familiy constructs. After 10 years there tend to be a greater difference between psychological research findings and the basis of juridically judgement in one site, at the other site jugdements there will be have influences of the psychological consultants, not based of rules to experts in law.

Crime scene analysis and issues of validity and methodology: A case study

Knight, Zelda Gillian Dept. of Psychology, University of Johannesburg, Johannesburg, South Africa

Criminal profiling or crime scene analysis is defined as the process of using behavioural evidence left at a crime scene to make inferences about the offender, including inferences about the personality characteristics and psychopathology as well as the relationship between the offender and the victim. However, it seems that serious questions have been raised with regard to the validity and methodology of profiling work based on crime scene analysis. This article examines the current literature on the

validity and methodological issues of crime scene analysis and a case study, based on a crime scene analysis, presented in court, is documented. A critique of this case study highlights the need to be cautious about crime scene analysis.

FP-268: Interpersonal relationships

Becoming friends by chance: Random seat assignment predicts friendship formation

Back, Mitja Psychologisches Institut, Universität Leipzig, Leipzig, Germany Schmukle, Stefan Psychologisches Institut, Universität Leipzig, Leipzig, Germany Egloff, Boris Psychologisches Institut, Universität Leipzig, Leipzig, Germany

Since the days of the ancient Greek philosophers, friendship has been conceived of as a result of our free will. In contrast, this study addresses the question as to whether friendship development is influenced by pure chance upon initially encountering others. We investigated psychology freshmen upon first meeting and after their first year of study. Random seat assignment during a one-off introductory session was predictive of friendship formation: Students who coincidentally sat in neighboring seats or in the same row during the initial session reported greater friendship intensities one year later. Becoming friends may thus indeed be due to chance.

Adolescents' self-efficacy beliefs and quality of experience in interpersonal relationships with friends and parents

Steca, Patrizia Psychology, University of Milan, Milan, Italy Bassi, Marta Scienze Precliniche, University of Milan, Milan, Italy Caprara, Gian Vitttorio Psychology, University of Rome, Rome, Italy

This study investigated interpersonal relationships and associated quality of experience of 130 Italian adolescents with different levels of perceived self-efficacy in managing relationships with friends and parents. Participants provided self-evaluation of perceived self-efficacy, quality of their friendships and communication with parents, and were monitored with experience sampling method for one week during their daily life. Compared with low self-efficacy adolescents, high self-efficacy participants reported higher quality of their friendships and better communication with parents. They also spent more time with friends and parents, and reported more frequently engaging and rewarding experiences (optimal experiences) in family and peer interactions.

Social competence as a mediator between peer relationship and loneliness in middle childhood

Zhou, Zongkui School of Psychology, Huazhong Normal University, Wuhan, Hubei, People's Republic of China Sun, Xiaojun School of Psychology, Huazhong Normal University, Wuhan, Hubei, People's Republic of China Fan, Cuiying School of Psychology, Huazhong Normal University, Wuhan, Hubei, People's Republic of China

Relationships among social preference, friendship quality, self-perceived social competence, loneliness and mediating effects of the variables were examined in this study. 571 Chinese elementary school children from Grades 3 to 5 were investigated. The results indicated that, the relationships among social preference, friendship quality, self-perceived social competence and loneliness were significant, and there were significant gender differences; self-perceived social competence had mediating effect between peer relationship and loneliness; there were indirect and direct relation between loneliness and social preference or friendship quality through the mediating effect of self-perceived social competence; loneliness and social preference were indirectly correlated.

I have a crush on you! Development and validation of the index of having a crush (Index C)

Rodrigues, David *Sala 224, ISCTE, Lisbon, Portugal* **Garcia-Marques, Teresa** *Social & Organizational Ps, ISPA, Lisbon, Portugal*

Interpersonal attraction is complex and vast, reaching different types of relationships. We focus the concept of initial attraction defined as having a crush. Using both prototype and subjective experience approaches, we analyzed this construct's attributes. Here is presented the process of developing a new measure, designed to tap these feelings: Index of Having a crush (Index C). The measure's psychometric properties were studied, either considering an attraction target (Study 1) or an unknown target (Study 2). We discuss the importance of this kind of measures to interpersonal relationships and interpersonal attraction knowledge.

The function of filial piety: Defense against mortality anxiety

Chuang, Yao-Chia *Educational Psychology, PingTung Uni. of Education, PingTung, Taiwan*

Terror management theory suggests that people cope with awareness of death by defending their cultural worldview. The study examined whether filial piety serves this function of cultural worldview. Five-hundred adult Taiwanese answered a questionnaire that sequentially included the measurement of filial piety belief, the manipulation of mortality salience or dental-pain, and the judgment of un-filial transgression. It was found that after reminded of mortality, people who scored high in filial piety belief were more critical of the un-filial behavior supposedly displayed by the children of others. The findings have implication for the role of filial piety in Chinese culture.

Experimental peace psychology: Priming compassion eliminates aggression toward outgroups under mortality salience

Abdollahi, Abdolhossein *Psychology, Islamic Azad University-Zarand, Kerman, Islamic Republic of Iran*

Following a Terror Management Theory experimental paradigm, two experiments examined the effect of priming compassion-inducing images on mitigating aggressive attitudes toward outgroups. In Exp 1, 200 adult participants (under mortality salience or dental pain salience) watched 10 images depicting compassion-inducing scenes. They, then, responded to a series of items on aggression toward an outgroup. In Exp 2, 100 adult participants (under mortality salience or dental pain salience) were subliminally primed with the same pictorial stimuli and responded to the same items. Results revealed that in both experiments, participants in the mortality salience conditions showed less aggressive attitudes toward an outgroup.

FP-269: Intergroup attitudes

Intergroup attitudes in the post-apartheid South Africa

Bornman, Elirea *Communication Science, University of South Africa, Pretoria, South Africa*

In the deeply divided South African society, race has become the primary unit of social analysis. The struggle against apartheid furthermore enhanced interest in South African race relations. The 1994 advent of a new political dispensation has been accompanied with expectations of improved intergroup relationships. The current study investigating intergroup attitudes after 1994 formed part of a 2001 countrywide survey among a random sample of 2530 respondents. The results indicate negative relationships between blacks and Afrikaans-speaking whites. Noteworthy is the dislike expressed by blacks towards Afrikaans-speaking whites. Possible reasons for the findings and directions for future research are discussed.

Extending the Stereotype Content Model: The Mainland Chinese stereotype of the Hong Kong Chinese

Guan, Yanjun *Psychology, Chinese University Hong Kong, Hong Kong, China, People's Republic of : Hong Kong SAR* **Bond, Michael** *Psychology, Chinese University, Hong Kong, China, People's Republic of : Macao SAR* **Zhang, Zhiyong** *Psychology, Peking University, Beijing, People's Republic of China* **Deng, Hong** *Psychology, Peking University, Beijing, People's Republic of China*

The study explored the content of the stereotype held by Mainland college students in China towards the Hong Kong Chinese and the relations of various components of stereotypes to other intergroup variables. The results showed that perceptions of the higher status and greater Westernization of Hong Kong society were related to Westernized values and beliefs judged to be held by Hong Kong people, which in turn predicted the degree of perceived similarity of the two groups of Chinese. In addition, perceived similarity predicted the intention to interact with Hong Kong Chinese through the mediation of reflected prejudice.

Effects of intergroup similarity/dissimilarity on majority attitudes towards immigrant groups

Lopes, Rui *Social and Organ. Psychology, ISCTE, Lisboa, Portugal* **Vala, Jorge** *Social Psychology, ICS, Lisboa, Portugal*

Our studies aim at addressing the effects of intergroup similarity/dissimilarity on intergroup attitudes and intends to conciliate two competing approaches, considering that the dimension to which intergroup similarity/dissimilarity refers to serves to reconcile those approaches. Experimental studies were run and regression analysis of the data allowed to conclude that when intergroup similarity/dissimilarity refers to a symbolic dimension, as ingroup identification goes up, the more negative is the attitude toward a similar group; when intergroup similarity/dissimilarity is in terms of instrumental aspects, a similar group is targeted with more negative attitudes only in a condition of competition.

When "real men" derogate men: The role of ingroup projection in antigay discrimination

Reese, Gerhard *DFG Forscungsgruppe, Universität Jena, Jena, Germany* **Jonas, Kai J.** *Social Psychology, University of Jena, Jena, Germany* **Steffens, Melanie C.** *Social and Cognitive Psych., University of Jena, Jena, Germany*

According to Self Categorization Theory (SCT, Turner et al., 1987), intergroup comparisons occur within the context of a superordinate category. Based on SCT, the Ingroup Projection Model (Mummendey & Wenzel, 1999) predicts that ingroup members are perceived as more prototypical for the superordinate category than outgroup members, which in turn is related to more outgroup derogation. In a series of experiments, these predictions were tested with gay and heterosexual men given the superordinate category men. The hypothesized relationship between ingroup prototypicality and outgroup derogation emerged. These findings shed new light on antigay discrimination processes.

Knowledge of the out-group as an antecedent of perceived threat to the in-group: A test of integrated threat theory in India

Singh, Purnima *Humanities and Social Sciences, IIT Delhi, Delhi, India* **Tausch, Nicole** *Department of Psychology, University of Cardiff, Cardiff, United Kingdom* **Hewstone, Miles** *Experimental Psychology, Oxford University, oxford, United Kingdom* **Ghosh, Emmanual** *Department of Humanities, University of Allahabad, Allahabad, India*

Extending integrated threat theory, we tested a theoretical model which considered realistic and symbolic threats as proximal predictors of prejudice, and knowledge of the culture of the out-group and quantity and quality of prior contact with out-group members as antecedents of threat in the context of Hindu-Muslim relations in India. Structural equation modelling revealed that realistic, but not symbolic, threat significantly predicted out-group attitudes. Out-group knowledge was positively associated with perceived realistic and symbolic threat. Contact quantity was positively associated with realistic and symbolic threat, and contact quality was negatively associated with both. The implications of these findings are discussed.

Conflict, identity, and narrative: The process of intergroup contact between Israeli and Palestinian youth

Hammack, Phillip *Dept. of Psychology, University of California, Santa Cruz, USA* **Pilecki, Andrew** *Psychology, University of California, Santa Cruz, USA*

Responding to the need for studies of intergroup contact that are both naturalistic and process-focused (Dixon, Durrheim, & Tredoux, 2005; Pettigrew, 1998), we used both qualitative and quantitative methods to examine the process of intergroup contact for Israeli and Palestinian youth. Findings revealed that youth tend to reproduce the polarizing discourse of their respective national narratives as they engage in dialogue with one another. The process participants underwent was consistent with social identity theory (Tajfel & Turner, 1979), which argues that contact results in a greater identification with ingroup identity. We present narrative data to illustrate this process, with particular attention to issues of power and social structure in the encounter.

FP-270: Interindividual differences in cognitive performance

Studies on individual differences with intellectually gifted children in mainland China for 20 years

Shi, Jiannong *Institute of Psychology, Beijing, People's Republic of China*

Several hundred intellectual gifted children with different ages were involved in the project during the last two decades. Their cognitive performances, school achievement, non-intellectual aspects, neural indices, and hormonal level at different ages were investigated and compared with their average peers. It has been found that gifted individuals have significant better cognitive performance and school achievement, more realistic self-concept, relatively lower hormonal level than the normal individuals. And the ERP studies found that gifted children on P300 or P600 were shorter on latency but higher on amplitude than average children.

Gender-difference in cognitive control

Zhou, Haotian *Inst. of Psychology, Chinese Academy of Sciences, Beijing, People's Republic of China* **Ren, Dongning** *Institute of Psychology, Chinese Academy of Sciences, Beijing, People's Republic of China* **Fu, Xiaolan** *Institute of Psychology, Chinese Academy of Sciences, Beijing, People's Republic of China*

Though past research on gender-differences has demonstrated that the psychological discrepancies between men and women are significant and reliable, rarely have the possible gender-differences in more fundamental cognitive processes been explored. This study examined the hypothesis that there might exit a gender-disparity in terms of cognitive control. 40 undergraduates (20 males) participated in an Eriksen flanker task with reaction-time data submitted to a mixed-design ANOVA. The results show that compared to males, females were more susceptible to flanker interference at both featural and categorical levels, suggesting a more relaxed inhibitory control which permitted contextual yet task-irrelevant information to be processed.

Gender-fairness of a knowledge test: Testing for differential item functioning and criterion validity

Steinmayr, Ricarda *Inst. für Psychologie, Universität Heidelberg, Heidelberg, Germany* **Heene, Moritz** *Institute of Psychology, LMU, Munich, Germany* **Spinath, Birgit** *Inst. für Psychologie, Universität Heidelberg, Heidelberg, Germany*

The present studies aimed at testing a knowledge test (KT) for gender-fairness. Study 1: N = 645 (387 female) students (11th and 12th grade) were tested. Items of the KT were checked for differential item functioning (DIF). Several items showing DIF were identified. Study 2: N = 342 students (204 female) were tested by means of the same KT. Predicting school performance (SP) by the KT with and without biased items was tested for gender differences by means of multi-group analysis. Both the KT with and without DIF proved to be fair in the prediction of SP.

A note on the development of sex differences in three-dimensional mental rotation

Geiser, Christian *Psych. and Educational Science, Freie Universität Berlin, Berlin, Germany* **Lehmann, Wolfgang** *Psychology, University of Magdeburg, Magdeburg, Germany* **Eid, Michael** *Psychology, Free University of Berlin, Berlin, Germany*

Three-dimensional mental rotation problems are among the cognitive tasks that show the largest sex differences in favor of males. However, there is still an uncertainty as to the emergence and development of these differences. We tested N = 1624 individuals between 9 and 23 years of age with the Mental Rotations Test (Vandenberg & Kuse, 1978; Peters et al., 1995). Males outperformed females in all age groups ($0.52 < d < 1.49$). Structural equation modeling analyses revealed that the sex difference slightly increased with age. Our findings are discussed within a nature-nurture interactionist framework of sex differences in spatial abilities.

Something unknown is doing we don't know what!: Discrepancies between explicit and implicit representations of the intelligence self-concept

Dislich, Friederike *Universität Koblenz-Landau, Landau, Germany* **Gschwendner, Tobias** *Personality&Psych.Assessme, University of Koblenz-Landau, Landau, Germany* **Hofmann, Wilhelm** *Psychology II, University of Würzburg, Würzburg, Germany* **Zinkernagel, Axel** *Personality&Psych.Assessme, University of Koblenz-Landau, Landau, Germany* **Schmitt, Manfred** *Personality&Psych.Assessme, University of Koblenz-Landau, Landau, Germany*

In a series of studies we investigated how discrepancies between implicit and explicit representations of the intelligence and mathematical self-concept are related to negative feedback and stereotype threat. In a first study (N=150) we examined whether a discrepant intelligence self-concept was related to more vulnerability after receiving negative feedback for an attended intelligence test. In a second study (N=120) we examined the moderating role of implicit and explicit representations of the mathematical self-concept on performance deficits typically associated with stereotype threat. The empirical findings are discussed with regard to the potentially underlying mechanisms of implicit-explicit consistency and implicit-explicit moderation.

Positive effects of concern over mistakes: A relativization of a so called maladaptive facet of perfectionism

Altstötter-Gleich, Christine *Inst. für Psychologie, Universität Koblenz-Landau, Landau, Germany* **Brand, Matthias** *Physiological Psychology, University of Bielefeld, Bielefeld, Germany*

We report two studies (N = 58 and 72, respectively) in which we examined the link between specific behavioral data (decision-making and test performance) and perfectionism. In both investigations persons who scored high on concern over mistakes (CoM) and low on personal standards showed the best performance. This finding is inconsistent with reports on the dysfunctional character of CoM. We argue that high CoM is maladaptive for psychological health, as previous research demonstrated, but it might be functional for several aspects of behavioral or cognitive effectiveness. The results are discussed in the context of motivational variables, self-concept and mood data.

FP-271: Interindividual differences in social and emotional performance

Are conscientious individuals less innovative? On the interplay of personality and innovation potential

Inceoglu, Ilke *The Pavilion, SHL Group Limited, Thames Ditton, United Kingdom* **Gasteiger, Rosina Maria** *Advisory People & Change, PricewaterhouseCoopers, Munich, United Kingdom* **Anderson, Neil** *Business School, University of Amsterdam, Amsterdam, Netherlands* **Bartram, Dave** *Research, SHL Group, Thames Ditton, United Kingdom* **Port, Rebecca** *DDI UK Ltd, DDI UK Ltd, Stoke Poges, United Kingdom* **Zibarras, Lara** *Organisational Psychology Grou, City University London, London, United Kingdom* **Woods, Stephen** *Work & Organisational Psyc, Aston Business School, Birmingham, United Kingdom*

Although conscientiousness proves to be the best personality indicator for predicting successful job performance, findings in the literature point to a negative relationship with innovativeness. This paper examines the interplay between innovation potential and facets of conscientiousness in two studies conducted with MBA students and employees of a food manufacturing company (total N=376). Results indicate that the achievement and dependability facets of conscientiousness show differential relationships with innovation potential: individuals with high innovation potential are more likely to be vigorous, forward thinking and achieving but less consciousness and detail-conscious. Implications for future research and Human Resource Management are discussed.

Emotional intelligence: Individual differences

Sosa Correa, Manuel *Psicología, Universidad Autónoma de Yucatá, Mérida Yucatán, Mexico* **Iuit Briceño, Jorge** *Psicología, Universidad Autónoma de Yucatá, Mérida Yucatán, Mexico* **Duarte Briceño, Efrain** *Psicología, Universidad Autónoma de Yucatá, Mérida Yucatán, Mexico*

The objective in this investigation is to know the differences by age, sex and academic level in Emotional Intelligence. 185 subjects; senior high school and undergraduate students with average age of 19.61 years old answered the Emotional Intelligence Test (Sosa Correa 2007). A scale type Likert was designed which presents affirmations on perceived abilities regarding emotions handling. A 0.986 Alfa Cronbach coefficient. there were no significant differences by age nor academic level, but significative differences by sex in six factors.

Emotional intelligence: Confirmatory and exploratory factor analysis

Rezaeian Faraji, Hamid *Dept. of Psychology, Arak University, Arak, Islamic Republic of Iran*

The relationship between emotional intelligence and academic adjustment in three hundred freshman student arak university was examined. Student completed the Bar-on emotional intelligence inventory(EQ-I) and Borow academic adjustment inventory. confirmatory factor analysis suggest four factor for assessment of E.Q in Iranian student. Stepwise regression suggest that there is meaningful relation between E.Q and academic adjustment dimension. Analysis of variance suggested meaningful relation between sex and E.Q with academic adjustment dimension.

Social intelligence in the context of the theory of fluid and crystallized intelligence

Seidel, Kristin *Methoden, Diagnostik, Evaluat., Universität Magdeburg, Magdeburg, Germany* **Weis, Susanne** *Methoden, Diagnostik, Evaluati, University Magdeburg, IPSY, Magdeburg, Germany* **Süß, Heinz-Martin** *Methoden, Diagnostik, Evaluati, University Magdeburg, IPSY, Magdeburg, Germany*

This paper addresses the question of how social understanding (SU), the core dimension of social intelligence, is related to the theory of fluid (gf) and crystallized (gc) intelligence (e.g., Horn & Noll, 1994). 175 participants (age: M=28.61; SD=5.54) worked on the performance-based Social Intelligence Test of Magdeburg (Süß, Seidel, Weis, 2007) focusing on nonverbal material as well as on gf/gc markers. Results: In confirmatory factor analyses SU was separable from both gf and gc, but more highly correlated with gc (.31) than with gf (.05). The findings indicate that SU should not be subsumed under either gf or gc.

Predicting academic success with self-rated, faked and peer-rated personality facets

Ziegler, Matthias *Inst. für Psychologie, Unversität München, München, Germany* **Bühner, Markus** *Psychology Department, Ludwig Maximilian University, Munich, Germany* **Heene, Moritz** *Inst. für Psychologie, Unverstät München, München, Germany*

Predictive power of noncognitive tests in academic settings is widely discussed. This longitudinal study explored which personality facets predict academic success. Personality was assessed under honest conditions, applicant conditions and peer ratings were also obtained (N = 147). All measures were taken in the first weeks of the first semester. The statistics grade was used as criterion. Five facets predicted performance (11%) while faked scores did not. However, peer ratings added another 14%. Controlling for intelligence only slightly reduced the effect sizes. Practical implications for student counselling will be discussed as well as theoretical considerations regarding the assessment of personality.

Interpersonal flexibility as a facet of social-emotional intelligence: Conceptual and measurement issues

Cheng, Cecilia *Dept. of Psychology, University of Hong Kong, Hong Kong, China, People's Republic of : Hong Kong SAR*

The present research adopted a theory-driven approach to address conceptual and measurement issues in the study of interpersonal flexibility. A situation-based measure was designed to assess interpersonal flexibility. Consistent with theories of social and emotional intelligence, results revealed that interpersonal flexibility was conceptually similar to coping flexibility, but was conceptually distinct from cognitive flexibility. Interpersonal flexibility was also found to mediate the relationship between social competence and interpersonal adjustment. Interpersonal flexibility was found to predict flexibility in leadership behaviors in a laboratory setting, and interpersonal adjustment to their first full-time job for recent university graduates.

FP-272: Interindividual differences in social behavior

Personality traits as mediators of the relationship between opinion leadership and expertise

Gnambs, Timo Inst. für Bildungspsychologie, Universität Linz, Linz, Austria Batinic, Bernad Education and Psychology, University of Linz, Linz, Austria

Opinion leader are exceptionally influential people, who informally shape attitudes and behaviour of their social reference group (e.g. friends or relatives). Frequently expertise (self-perceived knowledge) is viewed as a necessary precondition for an opinion leadersinfluence; although in the past strongly varying correlations between opinion leadership and expertise have been reported. This study examines the influence of personality traits as mediators of the relation between opinion leadership and expertise. A convenience sample (N = 200) completed a questionnaire containing scales for opinion leadership, expertise, Big Five and various additional personality constructs. Mediation analysis revealed a strong mediating effect of extraversion and typical intellectual engagement, suggesting a specific personality profile of opinion leaders.

Individual differences in types of humour according to basic cognitive and affective abilities and membership in social groups

Toroj, Malgorzata Dept. Experimental Psychology, Catholic University of Lublin, Lublin, Poland

The main aim of the study was to find cognitive, affective and social correlates which may help to account for a particular type of humour. Students from different social organisations (religious, scientific, social, and artistic) were examined. On the basis of the data collected, different types of humour were distinguished and correlated with cognitive, affective and social variables. There are specific relations between single variables, grouped in different types of humour. Members of specific organizations differ according to the level and type of humour.

Who teases nerdy smarties?: Multilevel analyses on big five and self-esteem in grade eight students

Rentzsch, Katrin Inst. für Psychologie, Techn. Universität Chemnitz, Chemnitz, Germany Schröder-Abé, Michela Psychology, TU-Chemnitz, Chemnitz, Germany Schütz, Astrid Psychology, TU-Chemnitz, Chemnitz, Germany

"Nerd" is one of the most feared labels among adolescents. High-achieving students are at risk of being stigmatized. The present study focuses on those who label others a nerd (so-called teasers). 317 students from grade eight completed questionnaires on behavior in class, the Big Five, and self-esteem. Multilevel analyses show that teasers are more extraverted, less conscientious, and less agreeable than other students. They exhibit lower self-esteem in achievement and in handling criticism, but higher self-esteem in social interaction. Schooltype and grades are moderators. Results are discussed with regard to causes of labeling and possibilities to prevent against discrimination.

The role of personality in blame attribution and perceived emotions for hypothetical incidences of victimisation

Heym, Nadja School of Psychology, University of Nottingham, Nottingham, United Kingdom Lawrence, Claire School of Psychology, University of Nottingham, Nottingham, United Kingdom

Objectives: This study investigated the relationship between personality and (i) blame attribution, and (ii) anticipated emotions during victimisation. Method: 212 students completed measures of Psychoticism (EPQ-R), BIS/BAS, impulsivity, trait aggression, perspective taking and empathic concern scales. Results: Psychoticism predicted lack in remorse and anticipated fear during victimisation. Trait aggression predicted increased anticipated anger. Empathy was not related to anticipated emotions. The relationships of Psychoticism with (i) lack in remorse, and (ii) lack in fear were moderated by BIS-anxiety. Conclusions: Global factors of personality but not facet levels predicted blame attribution. The anxiety and Psychoticism interaction mirrors findings in psychopathy research.

Personality profiles of the hated and intimate friends

Mastor, Khairul Center for General Studies, Universiti Kebangsaan Malaysia, Selangor, Malaysia

The general aim of this study is to determine the personality profiles' similarity and differences between persons with they like and hate. Samples are 60 Malaysian Chinese respondents of equal number of gender (mean age = 22.08, SD = 1.31). Instrument used is the 60 items of the FFM Inventory (Costa & McCrae, 1992) and a self-designed interpersonal scale (α = 0.80). Findings indicate that all respondents' personality types are significantly correlated with the person that they like, in a positive direction, except Neuroticism. Differences among gender's personality profiles of person they like and hate are also observed.

Combining social axioms with personality measures and self-reported driving behavior in predicting traffic accidents

Renge, Viesturs Dept. of Psychology, University of Latvia, Riga, Latvia Austers, Ivars Department of Psychology, University of Latvia, Riga, Latvia Muzikante, Inese Department of Psychology, University of Latvia, Riga, Latvia

Social axioms are a set of beliefs about the world in which individuals function (Leung et al., 2002). We tested whether these beliefs may be combined with traditional predictors of road traffic accidents, namely, driving behavior self-reports (measured by Drivers Behavior Questionnaire, DBQ), and personality trait Hostility (measured by the corresponding NEO-PI-R subscale). To test this assumption 324 drivers filled in a questionnaire containing DBQ, NEO-PI-R Hostility subscale, and Social Axioms Survey. Hierarchical regression analysis showed that social axioms added predictive power to explaining traffic accidents over that provided by measures provided by DBQ and NEO-PI-R Hostility subscale.

FP-273: Interindividual differences in stress, emotionality, and coping I

A computer-based information-processing technique of predicting proneness to emotional stress

Nosenko, Eleonora Dept. of Psychology, National University, Dnipropetrovsk, Ukraine Arshava, Irina psychology, National University, Dnipropetrovsk, Ukraine

The study was aimed at testing the validity of the learned helplessness elicited under simulated information- processing failure conditions as a predictor of subjects' proneness to emotional stress. 110 subjects participated in the study simulating oral exchange of visually displayed information between air flight controllers and pilots. After unexpected exposure to failure caused by the demand to convey information exceeding short-term memory capacity some subjects experienced learned helplessness manifested by statistically significant differences in

performance and hesitation in speech prior to failure and after it. Given the vulnerable subjects also appeared to prefer emotion-focused coping the suggested technique proved valid.

Generality vs. specifity of coping with stress

Erdmann, Gisela Biopsychology, Institute of Psychology, TUB, Berlin, Germany Janke, Wilhelm Institute of Psychology, University of Wuerzburg, Würzburg, Germany

Most authors in the field of stress and coping agree with Lazarus transactional stress theory, according to which the assessment of coping needs the conjoint consideration of the person and its actual environment. Results with the German Stress Coping Inventory (Stressverarbeitungsfragebogen) demonstrate that – at least when assessed by self-report – the kind of coping remains relatively constant over (1) time, (2) different kinds of stressors, and (3) different states or responses. Importantly, a stressor-specific in comparison to an unspecific assessment of coping does not significantly improve the prediction of responses to this stressor or the kind of coping with it.

Validation of stress coping instruments: Differences between groups

Janke, Wilhelm Institute of Psychology, University of Wuerzburg, Würzburg, Germany Erdmann, Gisela Biopsychology, Institute of Psychology, TUB, Berlin, Germany

The paper discusses validation strategies for stress coping scales emphasizing differences between groups. Groups were defined by (1) subject characteristics (e.g. sex, age, ethnic), (2) profession (e.g. pilots, journalists, police man) or (3) clinical criteria (e.g. depressive or not, kind of disorder). Data were gathered with the German Stress Coping Inventory SVF (Stressverarbeitungsfragebogen). The observed group differences demonstrate a remarkable validity of the SVF. This contrasts with results on the criterion-oriented validity of the test. Possible reasons for these discrepancies and conclusions with regard to validation strategies for assessment methods of coping are discussed.

Relationship between moral development and altruism and coping style in personality factors of the students in Tehran

Ebrahimy, Azam Psychology, Shahid Beheshti University, Tehran, Islamic Republic of Iran Khoshkonesh, Abolghasem Psychology, Shahid Beheshti University, Tehran, Islamic Republic of Iran Saleh Sedghpoor, Bahram Psychology, Shahid Beheshti University, Tehran, Islamic Republic of Iran

this study investigates the relationship between moral development, altruism and coping style in personality factors. 360 subjects were selected through multi- stag cluster sampling. The instruments were (D.M.T), Goldberg Big(5) and C.S.Q. statistical methods of Anova, HSD and regression. results indicated the emotional coping has a reverse relationship with neuroticism and altruistic tendencies of speech freedom :(RDT) and it have a direct relationship with gender and moral development at 4 stage. Avoidant –detached style has a reverse relationship with the moral development at 4 stage and the rational style has a direct relationship with openness, agreeableness, conscientious, neuroticism and altruistic tendencies of speech freedom situation :(RDT) but a reverse with gender

How coping mediates the effect of Type D personality on psychosomatic functioning: A study of Chinese patients with coronary heart disease

Yu, Xiaonan School of Public Health, Chinese Univ. of Hong Kong, Hong Kong, China, People's Republic of : Hong Kong SAR

This study examines the particular coping strategies of coronary heart disease (CHD) patients with Type

D personality, and tests the mediating effect of coping in relation to Type D personality and psychosomatic health. 96 CHD patients completed the Chinese version of measurements on Type D Personality, medical coping styles, severity of CHD, and morale. The results showed that the Type D personality ones used less confrontation and more acceptance-resignation as coping. Coping functioned as the mediator to transfer the effect of Type D personality on psychosomatic health. Implication for integrating coping modification into the Type D personality intervention is discussed.

Gender-specific differences in occupational stress and coping strategies among low qualified workers: A qualitative approach

Kalytta, Tanja Fachbereich I, Techn. Fachhochschule Berlin, Berlin, Germany *Ducki, Antje* Fachbereich I, TFH Berlin, Berlin, Germany

Objectives: The study is a contribution to our understanding of low skilled women's and mens work and family lives. Methods: Drawing on qualitative data from interviews with 40 women and men who do "unskilled" work, we explore the sources of their job satisfaction and their daily management of work and private family life. Results: First results emphasize the impact of gender. For instance, women having children report work-family-conflicts. Conclusions: The major issue of low skilled workers, especially men, is not the management of work and family life, but the availability and quality of resources, such as social support or wages.

FP-274: Psychotherapy - Research and treatment methods IX

Evaluation of the effectiveness of a cognitive/behavioral program with disruptive and depressed children in Puerto Rico

Cabiya, José Research Dept., Carlos Albizu University, San Juan, Puerto Rico *Padilla, Lymaries* Research, Carlos Albizu University, San Juan, Puerto Rico *Manzano, Joel* Research, Carlos Albizu University, San Juan, Puerto Rico *Sanchez, Jovette* Research, Carlos Albizu University, San Juan, Puerto Rico *Gonzalez, Karelyn* Research, Carlos Albizu University, San Juan, Puerto Rico

This study evaluated the effectiveness of a school-based, cognitive/behavioral intervention with Puerto Rican children diagnosed with disruptive disorders and depressed mood. 174 children were assigned to the intervention and 104 children to wait-list group. The intervention was administered in groups of 6-8 children in 12 sessions. Outcome measures were administered before, 1-week and 6-months after treatment. Results indicate that the intervention was effective in reducing self-reports of depressed mood and teacher ratings of disruptive disorders. This study provides evidence that a well manualized cognitive/behavioral intervention can be successful implemented in school settings in Puerto Rico.

Do dysfunctional beliefs predict therapy outcome?

Ertle, Andrea Psychother. und Somatopsychol., Humboldt-Universität zu Berlin, Berlin, Germany *Joormann, Jutta* Dept. of Psychology, University of Miami, Miami, USA *Wahl, Karina* Psychiatry and Psychotherapy, University Hospital Lübeck, Lübeck, Germany *Kordon, Andreas* Psychiatry and Psychotherapy, University Hospital Lübeck, Lübeck, Germany

Dysfunctional beliefs are the core element of the cognitive behavioral model explaining the etiology and maintenance of psychological disorders. In a longitudinal study we assessed dysfunctional beliefs and symptoms of 77 outpatients (N=45 Obsessive Compulsive Disorder, N=21 Major Depression,

N=11 Panic Disorder) prior and after a completed cognitive-behavior therapy course. Data were analyzed using hierarchical linear modeling to see if dysfunctional beliefs prior to therapy accounted for differences in clients' rates of their symptoms after the therapy course. The results provide empirical support to the hypothesis that cognitive changes precede improvement. Clinical implications are discussed.

Planning little goals: Expectancies and motivation in depressed mood

Miller, Robyn School of Psychology, Deakin University, Geelong, Australia

This study explored how the habitual use of simple daily goals may protect against depressed mood, particularly by influencing sense of control and optimism. Participants were 203 Australian community adults. They completed an anonymous questionnaire containing four personality and mood scales together with goal-setting items. Data were analysed by factor analysis and the testing of simple path models. The goal-setting items formed two separate factors. Each factor significantly influenced optimism both directly and indirectly via sense of control. The findings demonstrate an alignment of different theoretical perspectives on depressed mood and implicate new strategies for the treatment of mild depression.

Positive emotion treatment group for depression: The evaluation of its treatment effects and change factors

Shieh, Bi-Ling Department of psychology, Kaohsiung Medical University, Kaohsiung, Taiwan *Fu, Weining* Department of psychology, Kaohsiung Medical University, Kaohsiung, Taiwan *Lin, Jiaru* Department of psychology, Kaohsiung Medical University, Kaohsiung, Taiwan

The study was to investigate effects of emotion-focused group treatment programs for depression – designed to enhance patients' emotion awareness, regulation, and reflection and utilization, as well as the ability to experience positive emotions. A 2 (pretest vs. posttest) x 3 (positive emotion vs. non-positive emotion vs. control group) factorial mixed design was used; 22, 24, and 15 patients in each group. It was found that patients who received positive emotion enhancement showed significantly better results than the other two groups, both in symptom reduction and emotion competence improvement. Positive emotions with relevant emotion abilities are important change factors for depression.

FP-275: Aesthetic preferences

Aesthetic preferences for individual colors and color combinations

Schloss, Karen Dept. of Psychology, UC Berkeley, Berkeley, USA *Palmer, Stephen E.* Psychology, UC Berkeley, Berkeley, CA, USA

Forty-eight participants evaluated 37 colors in 32 color-related tasks, including various preference ratings, colorimetric assessments, and emotional associations. Average ratings of single-color preference were a smooth function of hue: highest at blue and lowest at yellow-green. Rated blueness/yellowness explained 88% of this variance. Preferences for figure-ground color pairs depended on both figure and ground color, but were poorly predicted by preferences for the two individual colors (only 19% of the variance). Adding ratings of color harmony for the color pairs increased the total to 71% of the variance. No evidence was found that complementary colors were perceived as harmonious.

Tactile and visual influences upon aesthetic evaluation of unfamiliar stimuli

Jansson-Boyd, Cathrine Psychology, Anglia Ruskin University, Cambridge, United Kingdom

This study explored if tactile information can influence overall visual aesthetic evaluation of unfamiliar stimuli. Participants aesthetically rated thirty-six cards that comprised a square-wave tactile grating, with ridge widths 1,2,3.2mm. All combinations of textures on the front (visual stimulus) and reverse (tactile stimulus) were used. The gratings on the reverse were orthogonal to those on the front. Participants had to: -Haptically explore the reverse sides of 2 cards to identify which had a convex surface. -Place their hand on the tactile pattern and slide the card up a ramp until the card could be seen through an aperture. Results show that when we like what we see, we allow ourselves to like what we feel.

Aesthetic preferences for spatial composition

Palmer, Stephen E. Dept. of Psychology, University of California, Berkeley, USA *Gardner, Jonathan* Dept. of Psychology, University of California, Berkeley, CA, USA

Artists and graphic designers continually face the problem of composing their works in aesthetically pleasing ways. Our results show strong, consistent preferences in the spatial composition of simple images containing familiar objects and configurations of objects in rectangular frames to be positioned at/near the center of the frame (the "center bias") and to face into the frame (the "inward bias"). Further results show strong preferences in vertical composition (a "lower bias" for objects generally seen from above and an "upper bias" for objects generally seen from below) as well as for the size of objects.

An aesthetic assessment of art works of different modalities

Pejic, Biljana Dept. of Psychology, Faculty of Philosophy, Belgrade, Serbia

The research had the aim to determine the following: how art works of different modalities (paintings and music) are arranged in a semantic space considering the stages of development and whether there are any similarities in the assessment of different modalities within the same stages of an art movement. Forty psychology students assessed 108 reproductions of paintings and music compositions, within the period of early, middle and late baroque, according to the dimensions of the following: a. regularity, b.dynamism, c. aesthetic evaluation and d. affective evolution. The results show that both baroque paintings and music compositions are different, and this is assessed in different development stages. The largest differences were obtained in the dimensions of aesthetic evaluation and dynamism.

FP-276: Acquisition of language III

Literacy development in at-risk children: Outcomes of the Stanislaus County school readiness program

Stanislaw, Harold Dept. of Psychology, California State University, Turlock, USA *McCreary, Jamie* Dept of Psychology, Calif State Univ, Stanislaus, Turlock, USA *Esterly, Jennifer* Dept of Psychology, Calif State Univ, Stanislaus, Turlock, USA

Objectives: To assess literacy development in at-risk children. Methods: 2,500 children in California's Stanislaus County had their literacy assessed longitudinally in grades K, 1, and 3. Multiple regression was used to predict literacy from such factors as demographics and participation in government programs designed to improve readiness to learn. Results: Literacy scores varied with months of formal instruction, age, native language, and the classroom instructional language. School readiness programs seemed to help English learners overcome the literacy gap they would otherwise have exhibited relative to native English speakers. Conclusions: School readiness programs may facilitate literacy development in at-risk children.

Linguistic environment and language development of pre-school children

I., Anjali Department of Psychology, Allahabad Degree College,A.U., Allahabad, India
The objective of the present study is to investigate quality of linguistic environment in home and its role in predicting the language development of preschool children. 24-37 months old boys and girls (n=84) and their mothers were taken from joint families of three social classes. A semi-structured interview schedule consisting of 7 categories was used to measure linguistic environment. Grammar Comprehension Test, Word Meaning Test and expressive skill Test were used to assess language development. A Multiple Regression Analysis performed on Linguistic Environment Inventory showed their significant contribution in language development. Linguistic environment had moderating effect on relationship between social class and language development.

Language transfer through word order for bilingual infants

Wanner, Peter Tohoku University, Sendai, Japan
This paper examines a Bilingual First Language Acquisition (BFLA) Infant's productive use of Japanese word order in a sentence using English vocabulary (i.e. What that is?) Findings of this study over 30 months do not provide significant creative utterances of the BFLA infant using word order of one language to express themselves using vocabulary from another language. However, if this type of construction is evaluated during the short time interval within which it occurs (i.e. 3 months), it takes on more significance. Hence, the important stage of this type of development in a BFLA infant language is defined.

FP-277: Accuracy of personality judgements

The influence of the similarity in personality profiles on the accuracy of personality judgments

Weis, Susanne Inst. für Psychologie I, Universität Magdeburg, Magdeburg, Germany Seidel, Kristin Institute of Psychology I, Otto-von-Guericke University, Magdeburg, Germany Süß, Heinz-Martin Institute of Psychology I, Otto-von-Guericke University, Magdeburg, Germany
The present study investigates whether the actual similarity of personality profiles and the assumed similarity predict the accuracy of personality judgments. A heterogeneous sample of 182 adults rated the personality traits of eight target persons on nine dimensions as well as their assumed similarity with the targets. Additionally, the actual similarity of the personality profiles of the subjects with the targets was assessed. Results: The assumed similarity was consistently negatively correlated with the accuracy of the judgments across the different targets, whereas the actual similarity had no impact on the judgmental accuracy. Assumed and actual similarity were not related.

Effects of the prosodic features of speech sound upon the personality impressions

Uchida, Teruhisa Research Division, NCUEE, Tokyo, Japan Uchida, Chiharu Faculty of Literature, Nagoya Women's University, Nagoya, Japan
This study investigates the formation of personality impressions along with speech sound. Prosodic features such as speech rate, pitch, pauses, and intonations were manipulated to synthesize the continua of speech stimuli. Participants were asked to rate their impressions on these stimuli using Big

Five personality traits. The results indicated that each trait had a distinctive change pattern, while reversed U-shape patterns were their common characteristics. Each personality trait could be estimated with a quadratic regression equation. By integrating these five equations, the whole personality impression could be re-constructed. This procedure can be applied to synthesize speech sounds with artificial personalities.

Cross-cultural consistency and differences in perception of expressive behavior: An American-Chinese comparison

Zhang, Fang Dept. of Psychology, Assumption College, Worcester, USA
The present study examined naïve personality judgments of expressive behavior made by American and Chinese judges. Forty-seven American undergraduates and forty-nine Chinese undergraduates were shown snap-shots of extraverted and introverted American targets behaving in the everyday environment and asked to rate the targets on extraversion and friendliness. Even though American and Chinese judges both were able to use expressive cues to make similarly accurate personality judgments, American judges showed a perceptual bias in favor of extroverted targets, whereas Chinese judges showed a perceptual bias in favor of introverted targets.

Informant-ratings of personality are systematically affected by the relationship between target and informant

Leising, Daniel Inst. für Psychologie, Universität Halle-Wittenberg, Halle, Germany Paelecke-Habermann, Yvonne Psychology, University of Halle-Wittenberg, Halle (Saale), Germany Paelecke, Marko Psychology, University of Halle-Wittenberg, Halle (Saale), Germany
Four-hundred and eight participants judged a target of their choice on the Big Five, and reported how much they liked the target. Liking predicted socially desirable descriptions of the targets. Liking also led to reduced variance in the personality variables, lowering correlations with external criteria. As targets tend to nominate informants who like them, the resulting informant-ratings are likely to be biased. Therefore, the recruitment of informants should be made independent of the targets' preferences. The hypothetical advantage of informant-ratings (incremental validity in comparison to self-ratings) has yet to be demonstrated empirically.

FP-278: Cognition and emotion II

Emotion perception for faces and music: Is there a link?

Yong, Chi King Bauhinia Dept. of Psychology, Chinese Univer. of Hong Kong, Hong Kong, China, People's Republic of : Hong Kong SAR McBride-Chang, Catherine Department of Psychology, The Chinese University of HK, Hong Kong, China, People's Republic of : Macao SAR
Relations between perception abilities of emotions in music and facial expressions, as well as relations between music training and emotion perception abilities were investigated. One hundred Chinese second graders were tested on perceptions of both emotions in music and facial expressions. Face emotion perception ability was significantly and positively associated with music emotion perception ability (r=.41). In addition, children who had received music training previously scored significantly higher on emotion perception for both facial expressions and music. Results suggest an intriguing link between music training and emotion perception across modalities.

Developmental features of emotional prosody recognition from vocal cues

Dmitrieva, Elena Inst. of Evol. Physiology, Russian Academy of Science, St. Petersburg, Russia Gelman, Victor ICT, Med. Acad. for Postgrad.Stud., St-Petersburg, Russia
This study investigates the developmental changes in speech emotional prosody processing at noise background and signals' acoustic parameters important for recognition of emotional valence. The sample consisted of 105 listeners (7-65 years old). The Linear Regression analysis of the data revealed fundamental frequency, first two formant frequencies, signal-to-noise ratio and age to be the main factors influencing the recognition of emotional prosody valence. The age-related changes in speech emotional information perception at noise were shown to be most significant for positive valence and to depend on different set of acoustic cues. Support by grants: RFH 07-06-00821à, DFG GZ 436RUS 17/45/06

Auditory adaptations of the dot probe task and the emotional cuing paradigm: How does the emotional valence of spoken words influence the orienting of attention in healthy subjects?

Bertels, Julie UNESCOG, Université Libre de Bruxelles, Brussels, Belgium Kolinsky, Régine UNESCOG, Université Libre de Bruxelles, Brussels, Belgium Morais, José UNESCOG, Université Libre de Bruxelles, Brussels, Belgium
Attentional biases linked to negative written words are rarely observed in healthy individuals using the dot probe task (DPT). Since audition is considered as the main alerting system, we adapted the DPT to the auditory modality. Attentional biases to taboo, positive and negative words were indeed observed in that situation, but were not systematically replicated in other experiments using variants of the auditory cuing paradigm. We will present the results of the latter studies, and attempt to understand these divergences.

An acoustical explanation of the perception of musical harmony (Resolved and unresolved chords, major and minor chords)

Cook, Norman D. Dept. of Informatics, Kansai University, Osaka, Japan
Contrary to popular arguments concerning Western harmony, the perception of the "stability" of musical chords and the positive/negative affective "valence" of major/minor chords is not primarily culture-dependent, but is a consequence of acoustical factors. The key to a quantitative understanding of harmony is consideration of 3-tone psychophysics. By adding the effects of interval consonance/dissonance (a 2-tone factor) and a quantitative measure of triadic symmetry/asymmetry (a 3-tone factor), the empirical results on harmony perception and chord usage in classical music is reproduced without recourse to traditional harmony theory (Cook, Tone of Voice and Mind, Benjamins, 2002; Music Perception, 24, 315, 2007).

FP-279: Stereotypes and categorization II

How sensitive are stereotypes to the salient context?

Santos, Ana Sofia Faculdade de Psicologia, Universidade de Lisboa, Lisboa, Portugal Garcia-Marques, Leonel Faculdade de Psicologia, Universidade de Lisboa, Lisboa, Portugal
Stereotypes are no longer seen as fixed-representations. Manipulation of context-stability affected stability of stereotype-assembling across-sessions (Garcia-Marques et al., 2006). Recent conceptual processing views predict that heuristic-judgments derived from mnesic-activation can occur without being complemented by a monitoring-based component (Schunn et al., 1997). Applied to stereotypes

those mechanisms predict contextually-salient non-stereotyped information to be incorporated in assembled-stereotype. Study 1 primed a non-stereotyped concept (unrelated linguistic-task) immediately before stereotype-assembling. Non-stereotyped concept was more frequently chosen as a relevant-attribute of the group when prime matched the non-stereotyped concept. When a counter-stereotyped concept was primed (Study 2), average distribution choices (perceived-dispersion measure) were flatter.

The effect of stereotype suppression on memory
Kudo, Eriko Psychology, Tokyo Christian Woman's Univ., Tokyo, Japan *Numazaki, Makoto*

We examined the effect of stereotype suppression on memory. Participants were asked to write a typical holiday of a business woman or a home-maker. Half the participants were told to exclude any stereotypic description. Then as a second task, they were given a description of a woman and asked to rate the impression. The description contained both of stereotypical traits of businesswomen and homemakers. About twenty minutes later, participants were asked to recall the description. They recalled stereotype inconsistent descriptions more if they had suppressed the stereotype at the beginning of the study. Consequences of stereotype suppression were discussed.

Black single mothers in the US: A contextualized look at the impact of negative stereotypes and myths on parenting
Taylor, Sunday Roxbury, USA

An examination of the impact of stereotype acceptance/rejection on Black Single mothers' parental efficacy, and parenting practices. Survey data collected from Black Single mothers in large NE US city, measuring stereotype endorsement, parenting practices and parental efficacy. Regression analyses indicate that stereotype acceptance is associated with lower parental efficacy, and a decrease in nurturing parenting practices. Using an ecological framework, findings are discussed and approaches to addressing these issues are suggested.

FP-280: Stress and mental health II

Exploring the pattern of stress and personality type among forest personnel
Upadhyay, Bal Krishna Psychology, Bhopal School of Social Scienc, Bhopal, India

With the objective to identify types of stressors and examining the effect of designation and personality on stress in the forestry sector, participants from Madhya Pradesh Forest Department, i.e., Forest Officers- FOs- (N=63) and Field Staff- FS- (N=168), were selected for this study. Six stressors were identified using the factor analytic study and personality scale by Beech et al. was adapted to assess personality type. Results of 2(designations) x 3(personality) factorial design indicated that FS experienced more stress than FOs. Interestingly, more FS than FOs demonstrated possessing type A personality. Results have been discussed in the light of available literature.

Stress, coping and mental health in rural and urban settings
Joshi, Jyotsna Dept. of Psychology, S.N.G.G.P.G. College, Bhopal, India

The study aims to examine the variations in experience of stress, coping, social support and mental health through self-report measures in sample of rural and urban (N=360) male and female adolescents. Females displayed higher stress as compared to males. Rural and elder participants experienced higher stress as compared to urban and younger participants. Females and young adults used cognitive coping more frequently. Younger participants' mental health was reported superior

than elder group but the reverse was true for emotional health. Male and younger participants displayed higher social support. The results are discussed in the context of transactional approach to stress.

Stress, mental disorders and IBS
Solati Dehkordi, Seyed Kamal Psychology, Isfahan University, Isfahan, Islamic Republic of Iran *Kalantari, Mehrdad* psychology, isfahan university, isfahan, Islamic Republic of Iran

Objectives: the aim of this study was to find relationship between life events stress, mental disorders and IBS. Methods: this descriptive and cross- sectional study was performed during six months on the 76 patientsIBS.the life events stress or Paykel, GHQ-28 and Rome[22] criteria and clinical interview was used assessment. Results: the differences were statistically significant between life events stress or sand mental disorders with IBS (P < 0/05). Conclusion: psychology distress and life events stressors is important component of the IBS symptom experience and should be considered when treatment strategies are designed.

FP-281: Substance abuse / epidemiology, course and intervention II

Time since cannabis use cessation: Implications for mood and IQ performance
Murphy, Philip Social & Psychological Science, Edge Hill University, Ormskirk, Lancashire, United Kingdom *Erwin, Philip G.* Social & Psychological Sci, Edge Hill University, Ormskirk, Lancashire, United Kingdom *Wareing, Michelle* Centre for Public Health, Liverpool JMU, Ormskirk, Lancashire, United Kingdom *Blackman, Linda* Social & Psychological Sci, Edge Hill University, Ormskirk, Lancashire, United Kingdom *Yanulevitch, Kate* Social & Psychological Sci, Edge Hill University, Ormskirk, Lancashire, United Kingdom *Keane, Emma* Social & Psychological Sci, Edge Hill University, Ormskirk, Lancashire, United Kingdom *Fisk, John E.* Psychology, UCLAN, Preston, Lancashire, United Kingdom *MacIver, Linda* Social & Psychological Sci, Edge Hill University, Ormskirk, Lancashire, United Kingdom *O'Connor, Tina* Social & Psychological Sci, Edge Hill University, Ormskirk, Lancashire, United Kingdom *Montgomery, Catharine* Psychology, Liverpool JMU, Liverpool, United Kingdom

Objectives. To explore the relationship between cannabis use, self-reported mood, and IQ test performance. Method. Time since last cannabis use for 61 current or former users was a dependent variable (DV) in a hierarchical linear regression where measures of self-reported anxiety, arousal and depression formed Model 1. For Model 2 scores from Ravens Matrices Set E were added. Results. Model 2 predicted 23.1% of (DV) variability. All the predictors were negatively related to the DV. Conclusions. Depression and anxiety may be relatively unproblematic over time since cannabis cessation compared to a decline in arousal and IQ related performance.

Trauma and addiction: Diagnostics and treatment
Feselmayer, Senta Frauenabteilung, Anton Proksch Institut, Wien, Austria *Andorfer, Ute* Frauenabteilung, Anton Proksch Institut, Wien, Austria *Scheibenbogen, Oliver* Frauenabteilung, Anton Proksch Institut, Wien, Austria *Beiglböck, Wolfgang* Frauenabteilung, Anton Proksch Institut, Wien, Austria

Addicts frequently experienced traumatic events in their childhood. Below we will examine the relationship between addiction, trauma and growing up in a family with an addiction history. 100 in-patients (50 men and 50 women) participated in a survey using the following test instruments (MPSS; Modified PTSD Symptom Scale) and CAST (Children of

Alcoholics Screening Test). First results show that 38% of the male patients and 51% of the female patients grew up in a family with addiction problems (Chi-Square=3,316; df=2). In their youth 78% of all patients experienced violence and 50% felt subjectively neglected. Based on this data a specific treatment approach has been developed which will be presented here.

The knowledge of college students about substance abuse in Iran
Javadian, Reza Khomeinishahr Branch, Islamic Azad University, Esfahan, Islamic Republic of Iran *Gorji, Usef* social work, Islamic Azad University, Esfahan, Islamic Republic of Iran *Behzadmanesh, Maryam* social work, Esfahan Welfare Organization, Esfahan, Islamic Republic of Iran

This research examines the knowledge and attitudes that Islamic azad university students hold about substance abuse. A total of 3449 students from eighteen colleges who completed questionnaire, were randomly selected. The data analyze was done by T-test and multiple regressions. The results revealed that students knew the factors of addiction and prevention methods of substance abuse (79.1% and 89.6%, respectively). The authors explored the differences between male and female college students' attitudes toward factors of addiction (p<.01), treatment (p<.05) and prevention methods of substance abuse (p<.001). Multiple regressions analysis showed, 1.5% of knowledge variance was predicted by demographic indices (p<0.01).

FP-282: Developmental tasks and challenges in midlife II

Personal networks, social interaction, and developmental transitions: The social impact on family formation.
von der Lippe, Holger Institute of Psychology, University of Magdeburg, Magdeburg, Germany

The structure of and interaction processes within people's personal networks form an important background for developmental pathways throughout the life span. However, the motivational function of networks – beyond "support" – is hardly understood. We conducted mixed-methods interviews with 69 young adults (egos), aged 28 to 30 years, and some of their network members (alters) in two different regions of Germany. Our results show that network partners are a crucial source of motivation and orientation for young adults concerning parenthood. However, network influence does not unfold uni-directionally, but people also regulate their networks in order to correspond with their motivational processes.

World War II children coming of age in Germany: The impact on attachment and marital careers
Fooken, Insa FB 2, Psychologie, Universität Siegen, Siegen, Germany

World War II experiences in childhood turned out to have a lasting but often hidden impact on adult developmental processes and aging. This phenomenon became evident in a qualitative, in-depth interview study on 'late divorces' with 111 participants representing three different birth cohorts (1930, 1940, 1950). Other than the pre-war (1930) and post-war (1950) cohorts the participants born during the war (1940) showed far mor defence than coping while dealing with marital and relational problems. Thus, life-span developmental processes need to be related to the concomitant historical context in order to understand how and why people maintain mental health.

Body image following menopause
Rubio Ardanaz, Eduardo Psicología Social, University of Basque Country, Leioa, Spain *Fang, Xiao* Director, Chinese Studies Center, Bilbao, Spain *del Hierro, Máite* Enfermería, University of Basque Country,

Leioa, Spain *Rubio Ardanaz, Juan Antonio*
Antropología Social, University of Extremadura,
Bilbao, Spain *Vallejo, Gorka* *Enfermería, University of*
Basque Country, Leioa, Spain *Reglero, Leire*
Enfermería, Servicio Vasco de Salud, Galdakao, Spain
The discourses of different women on the changes
caused by menopause, and how their personal views
on life itself evolved were collected by looking at
various topic areas using qualitative data compila-
tion techniques. Topics covered included the meaning of life, power relationships, sexuality, self-
control,self-efficiency, to name a few. Findings
show a profound change in the feeling of control
over one's own life, as well as in some of its specific
areas and other basic feelings, arrived at by
experiencing and acknowledging the physical
changes and modified body image.

FP-283: Clinical / counseling psychology IV

Do patients with visual field defects show changes in their personality traits?

Jobke, Sandra *Inst. für Medizin. Psychologie,*
Universität Magdeburg, Magdeburg, Germany *Sabel,*
Bernhard *Institute of Medical Psycholog, Otto-von-*
Guericke-University, Magdeburg, Germany *Kasten,*
Erich *Institute of Medical Psycholog, University of*
Schleswig Holste, Lübeck, Germany
We investigated if patients show changes in their
personality or a reduced quality of life as a result of
their visual field defect (VFD). 15 patients with
VFD filled out the revised version of the Freiburger
Persönlichkeitsinventar (FPI-R) and the National
Eye Institute Visual Function Questionnaire (NEI-
VFQ). In the total sample all FPI-R scales were in
the inconspicuous standard range. The size of their
VFD does not correlate with the satisfaction with
life but with the dependency on other. Patients with
VFD show no changes in their personality.
Presumably they have learned it well to compensate
their reduced visual functions.

Psychotherapy in cross cultural perspective

Narasappa, Kumaraswamy *School of Medicine,*
University of Malaysia Sabah, Kotakinabalu, Malaysia
. Psychiatrist and Psychologists working in Asian
countries are trained in these countries followed the
western model of Psychotherapy and when they
enter into profession, the societies belief culture
comes in the way of treatment. Unless the therapist
is fully aware of the "Belief system" existed in
society, s/he could not be a successful therapist. I
would like to report my experiences as a clinical
psychologist in India, Malaysia and Brunei quoting
examples of patients seen for psychotherapy and
highlighting why psychotherapy is not so successful
in Asian countries and suggesting the ways to
improve the Psychotherapy by adopting certain
measures which are relevant to cultural context.

Using virtual characters to study gaze perception in high-functioning autism

Schwartz, Caroline *Universität zu Köln, Köln,*
Germany *Bente, Gary* *Department of Psychology,*
University of Cologne, Köln, Germany *Vogeley, Kai*
Department of Psychiatry, University of Cologne,
Köln, Germany
Adults with high functioning autism were compared
to a non-clinical control group regarding their
capability to identify directed social gaze. Animated
virtual characters were used as social stimuli in two
different tasks, one asking for the adjustment of
gaze direction and one asking for the judgement of
simulated gaze. Response time, error rates and
physiological arousal served as dependent measures. In addition participants' gaze was measured
by means of a remote eye tracker to account for
variations in reactive gaze aversion related to
directed gaze of the virtual characters. The novel

research paradigm and first results will be discussed.

FP-284: Interdisciplinary issues

Management of interdisciplinary research networks: New models, new challenges

Scheuermann, Michael *Psychology, University of*
Freiburg, Freiburg, Germany *Defila, Rico* *IKAÖ,*
University of Berne, Berne, Switzerland *Di Giulio,*
Antonietta *IKAÖ, University of Berne, Berne,*
Switzerland
The contribution presents new findings from a
broad international questionnaire study on inter-
and transdisciplinary processes and some insights
from the project "Forschungsmanagement" sponsored by the DFG. The findings of these projects
confirm the conditions and major tasks of successful inter- and transdisciplinary research and of
professional management of such research that
have been formulated before, but they emphasize
the importance of developing common goals and
questions and of developing a shared theoretical
basis in order to arrive at a synthesis. Based upon
these findings a new coherent management-model
of large-scale interdisciplinary research networks
will be presented.

ECOS-UADY: A model for interdisciplinary community work at universities

Castillo León, Teresita *Facultad de Psicología, Univ.*
Autónoma de Yucatán, Mérida Yucatán, Mexico
Echeverría, Rebelín *Facultad de Psicología, Univ.*
Autónoma de Yucatán, Mérida, Mexico
The purpose of this paper is to analyze the plural
and participatory construction of the Collaborative
Spaces Society-Autonomous University of Yucatan
(ECOS-UADY) as an interdisciplinary model to
facilitate the conjoint work society-university. It's
based in a participatory action research methodology with the participation of undergraduate students, professors, and community and academic
programs administrators of a public university in
Mexico. The results are discussed based on
conception, objectives, politics, strategies, resources
and the methodological and theoretical frame that
will guide the actions considering the integral
formation and social pertinence of the universities

Beliefs about the scientific community: Sociology of science and technology

Vázquez Alonso, Angel *Dept. of Psych. Education,*
Univ. of the Balearic Islands, Palma de Mallorca,
Spain *Manassero Mas, Maria-Antonia* *Psychology, U.*
of the Balearic Islands, Palma de Mallorca, Spain
This communication identifies some consensual
beliefs about the internal sociology of science
through empiric evidence. A 16-expert panel
assesses about one hundred sentences from the
Views on Science, Technology, and Society Questionnaire. Two kind of beliefs emerge from experts'
consensus: appropriate beliefs, which describe
appropriately and realistically the scientific community, and naïve beliefs, whose description is not
adequate, for instance, the myth about scientists'
isolation and absorption around their research).
These consensual beliefs on the sociology of science
could be used as nature of science contents in the
school science curriculum, which is finally discussed.

Effective factors and indicators that enhance educational quality at the national level

Sun, Hechuan *RIEEA, Shenyang Normal University,*
Shenyang, People's Republic of China *Yu, Wenming*
RIEEA, Shenyang Normal University, Shenyang,
Liaoning, People's Republic of China *Sun, Miantao*
RIEEA, Shenyang Normal University, Shenyang,
Liaoning, People's Republic of China *Sun, Yujia*
FAEM, Beijing Forestry University, Beijing, People's
Republic of China

This study explored the important factors and
indicators which might enhance educational quality
at national contextual level. Based on the findings
of a large European Commission project, it has
drawn on insights from four areas of research:
organizational culture and psychology; school
effectiveness; school improvement and public
choice, which yielded a "goal-pressure-support"
conceptual model accompanied by ten national
contextual factors and forty-eight indicators. These
ten factors and forty-eight indicators gained empirical support of thirty-one case studies contributed by eight European countries. Given the
original conceptual model and the empirical support of thirty-one case studies, this study may have
important implications for both educational policy-
makers and practitioners.

FP-285: Competence development and competence management I

Learning in a dynamic job environment: Deliberate practice of software engineers

Sonnentag, Sabine *Universität Konstanz, Konstanz,*
Germany *Volmer, Judith* *Dept of Psychology,*
University of Erlangen-Nurembe, Erlangen, Germany
Niessen, Cornelia *Dept of Psychology, University of*
Konstanz, Konstanz, Germany
Continuous learning at work is important for
employees in fast changes business contexts. This
study examined if deliberate practice (i.e., regular
purposeful activities aiming at competence improvement) are related to job performance in the
domain of software development. More than 130
software engineers participated in this study and
provided reports on deliberate practice. Job performance was assessed by supervisor ratings and self-
report data. Deliberate practice via internet activities and consultations with co-workers were
positively related with job performance suggesting
that continuous learning is one important correlate
of high performance in dynamic job environments.

Relations between work values and professional competence

Hetze, Anna-Maria *Methoden der Psychologie, Techn.*
Universität Dresden, Dresden, Germany
In recent years, some authors in the field of work
and organizational psychology have been required
for greater emphasis on values or goal content. The
study examined bivariate and canonical correlations between work values and the self-concept of
professional competence. Based on samples of
white-collar-workers in various occupational fields
work values and facets of the self-concept of
professional competence have been measured with
standardized questionnaires. The results show
medium kanonical correlations between the constructs. From the results can be concludes that
work values and so the directional aspect of work
motivation are important for developing professional competence.

Competence management in product design

Debitz, Uwe *Inst. für Psychologie, Technische*
Universität Dresden, Dresden, Germany *Hacker,*
Winfried *Psychology, TU Dresden, Dresden, Germany*
Stöckert, Henryk *Machine Tools, TU Berlin, Berlin,*
Germany
The scarcity in design experts requires their well-
organised placement in order to achieve innovative
products and thereby competitive advantages.
Therefore the management of staff competencies
is gaining in importance. In an interview study 38
enterprises predominantly with project work in
engineering design were analysed. Mainly the
available competencies of the designers and the
competence requirements of design orders are not
systematically identified and documented and, thus,
are assigned to designers due to organizational
constraints and subjective impressions only. There-

fore a tool for competence management of designers was developed and evaluated.

FP-286: Emotion I

Cultural background and emotional responding: Differential effects on different aspects of emotion

Mauss, Iris Dept. of Psychology, University of Denver, Denver, USA Butler, Emily Family Studies & Human Dev, University of Arizona, Tucson, USA Roberts, Nicole Psychology, Arizona State University, Denver, USA

The literature on cultural influences on emotion is riddled with inconsistencies. We argue that some of these inconsistencies might be resolved by differentiating between trait and state emotion, and by separately considering different aspects of state emotion (experience, behavior, and physiology). In order to do so, we examined these aspects of emotions in the context of Asian-American (AA) versus European-American (EA) cultural backgrounds. Results from two negative emotions (sadness and anger) suggest that cultural background was not associated with trait emotion or physiological responses, but that EAs exhibited greater state emotion experience and behavior than AAs.

Emotional climate, civic culture and fear to crime in four Latin American nations

Ruiz Pérez, Jose Ignacio Psychology, Universidad Nacional de Colomb, Bogotá, Colombia Turcios, Luis Alfredo Psychology, Universidad Tecnologica, San Salvador, El Salvador Fariña, Francisca Psychology, Universidad de Vigo, Vigo, Spain

Psychology students from Spain, El Salvador, Colombia and Mexico answered a survey on emotional climate, perceived civic culture (e.g.: consideration between neighbors), fear to crime, satisfaction with police and crime victimization. In previous research, civic culture was negatively associated with fear to crimen, and positively with satisfaction with police. In the present paper, relationships between emotional climate and civic culture and satifaction with police were analyzed, like dependent and independent variable.

Multicultural personality, performance and strain of Chinese managers

Yan, Wenhua Dept. of Psychology, East China Normal University, Shanghai, People's Republic of China

The objective of the present study is to explore the relationship between multicultural personality and performance, strain of native managers in mainland China. 185 managers from government, private companies and joint ventures in Shanghai answered the questionnaire. 56.8% were male, 91.3% were between 25 - 35 years old, and 62.4% had no any experience to go abroad. The regression analysis results showed that four dimensions of multicultural personality could predict work performance: Cultural empathy, Social initiative, Emotional stability, and Flexibility; only Emotional stability could predict both psychological and physical strain. The conclusion is that MPQ can be used in selection and training for the Chinese expatiates in the future after more specific localization based on Chinese culture.

FP-287: Factors of influencing stress and coping behavior I

Gains and costs of work stressors: Challenge and hindrance stressors predict differentially subjective success

Grebner, Simone Dept. of Psychology, Central Michigan University, Mount Pleasant, USA Mauch, Ivo Department of Psychology, University of Bern, Bern 9, Switzerland Zehnder, Cölestin Department of Psychology, University of Bern, Bern 9, Switzerland

Baumgarten, Joy Department of Psychology, University of Bern, Bern 9, Switzerland

Challenge stressors (CS) were expected to predict success positively and hindrance stressors (HS) to predict success negatively (LePine et al., 2005). The ISTA (Semmer et al., 2005) was used to measure task-stressors, the BITE (Grebner et al., in prep.) to assess social stressors, and the SUCCESS (Grebner et al., 2007) to measure subjective success (N = 307 employees of 2 organizations). Using regression analysis, time pressure (CS) predicted positively career success, role ambiguity (HS) predicted negatively goal attainment, and social stressors (HS) predicted negatively positive feedback and career success. CS can lead to gains while HS seem to have preliminarily costs.

Proactive behavior as a reaction to job stressors: Stressor-specific proactive behavior and general proactive behavior

Spychala, Anne Inst. für Psychologie, Universität Konstanz, Konstanz, Germany Sonnentag, Sabine Universität Konstanz, Konstanz, Germany

Contrary to what one might expect, earlier research showed repeatedly that job stressors are positively related to proactive behavior at work. We assumed that employees show different kinds of proactive behavior and developed separate measures for stressor-specific proactive behavior and general proactive behavior. In two cross-sectional studies (190 employees, 363 student assistants) CFAs confirmed construct validity. Both measures showed positive relationships with job control, self-efficacy and job involvement, although relationships were stronger for general proactive behavior. More, we found positive relationships for both scales with time pressure and work interruptions, negative correlations with overload, but no correlations with situational constraints.

Organizational and personal values impact on occupational well-being

Silva, Leticia Sao Paulo, Brazil Porto, Juliana Dept. of Psychology, Catholic University of Brasil, Aguas Claras, Brazil

This study aimed to investigate the organizational and personal values impact on occupational well-being. The sample was composed by 102 employees of a food company in São Paulo, Brazil. The instruments of measures used were the Profiles of Organizational Values Inventory, the Portrait Values Questionnaire and the Occupational Well-Being Scale and the data were analyzed by hierarchical multiple regression in three blocks using the software SPSS v.13. The results pointed that organizational values impact on occupational well-being and personal values moderate this relation. The regression model explained 27% of variance.

FP-288: Interindividual differences in stress, emotionality, and coping II

Subjective well-being: The role of humour and coping

Carballeira, Monica Personalidad, Eval. y T. Psic., Universidad de La Laguna, La Laguna, Spain Marrero, Rosario J. Personalidad, Eval. y T. Psic., Universidad de La Laguna, La Laguna, Spain

The main purpose of this study was to investigate the relationships among humour, coping and subjective well-being. 500 participants completed the Humour Styles Questionnaire (Martin et al. 2003), the COPE (Carver et al., 1989), the Happiness Scale (Lyubomirsky and Leper, 1999), the Satisfaction with Life Scale (Diener et al., 1985), and the PANAS Scales (Watson et al., 1988). The dimensions of humour maintained significant relationships with coping and well-being, but the tendencies of Affiliative and Self-Enhancing hu-

mour were different from Aggressive and Self-Defeating humour ones. Multiple regression analyses predicted 19% of the variance for both Happiness and Life Satisfaction.

Components of affective vigilance: Separating binding, attraction and interference effects of threat-related stimuli

Hock, Michael Inst. für Psychologie, Universität Mainz, Mainz, Germany Peters, Jan H. Psychology, University of Mainz, Mainz, Germany Krohne, Heinz Walter Psychology, University of Mainz, Mainz, Germany

An extended version of the visual dot-probe paradigm is introduced that allows to separate three facets of affective vigilance: binding (prolonged fixation of threatening stimuli), attraction (frequent orientation towards threat), and interference (response interruption). Associations between anxiety-related personality variables and attentional measures were examined in a nonclinical sample (N = 104). For individuals with an repressive coping style, threat stimuli had weak binding, but strong attracting effects. For anxious individuals, strong binding effects were found. Finally, individuals with an sensitive coping style manifested strong interference effects. The results support the proposed differentiation of three components of vigilance.

Procrastination and emotion regulation

Gröpel, Peter Piestany, Slovak Republic

In the present article, we examine the role of emotion regulation by predicting procrastination. Regulation of positive affect was expected to be beneficial for overcoming procrastination whereas regulation of negative affect should not have a strong effect. Using samples of students (N = 73), managers (N = 510), and general population (N = 9,351), our hypothesis was supported: The regulation of positive affect showed a strong effect on procrastination whereas the regulation of negative affect showed no effect, when testing both forms of emotion regulation simultaneously. The findings suggest the importance of positive affect regulation by initiating and maintaining actions.

Explicit and implicit assessment of emotional expressivity

Tausch, Anja Inst. für Psychologie, Universität Mainz, Mainz, Germany Krohne, Heinz Walter Psychologisches Institut, Johannes Gutenberg-Universität, Mainz, Germany

Based on the extended model of emotional expressivity, relations between three central expressivity facets (core expressivity, other-directedness, public performing) were tested. Each facet was assessed by an Implicit Association Test (IAT) and two explicit measures: ratings of IAT words and expressivity scales. Word ratings correlated significantly with both IATs and scales, whereas scales and IATs correlated significantly for other-directedness and public performing but not for core expressivity. For most correlations women exhibited higher coefficients than men. It is proposed that associations between implicit and explicit measures of emotional expressivity are moderated by the degree of social orientation during emotion expression.

Disgust sensitivity as an antecedent and a consequence of disgust behavior

Zinkernagel, Axel Universität Koblenz-Landau, Landau, Germany Dislich, Friederike Institute of Psychology, University of Koblenz-Landau, Landau, Germany Gschwendner, Tobias Institute of Psychology, University of Koblenz-Landau, Landau, Germany Hofmann, Wilhelm Institute of Psychology, University of Würzburg, Würzburg, Germany Schmitt, Manfred Institute of Psychology, University of Koblenz-Landau, Landau, Germany

We tested the double dissociation model and the self-perception theory in the domain of disgust. Study 1 (N = 79) tested whether implicit and explicit disgust sensitivity indicators are specific predictors of automatic and controlled disgust behavior. In contrast to the double dissociation model, we found that controlled disgust behavior was predicted both by explicit and implicit disgust sensitivity measures. In line with self-perception theory, Study 2 (N = 85) showed that the self-observation of automatic disgust behavior feeds into the explicit disgust sensitivity self-concept. However, this effect depends both on personality moderators and the framing of the self-perception task.

Effects of gender role on personal resources and coping with stress

Lipiñska-Grobelny, Agnieszka Inst. of Psychology, University of Lodz, Lódz, Poland
This study investigates the relationship between gender role in accordance with Bem's indices and both personal resources and coping. The Bem Sex Role Inventory, Coping Inventory for Stressful Situations, Satisfaction with Life Scale, Life Orientation Scale-Revised, Generalized Self-Efficacy Scale and Personal Competence Scale were completed by 123 females and 185 males. Results reveal that androgynous, masculine women and masculine men possess stronger psychological resources. Moreover satisfaction with life, femininity, and personal competences are significant predictors of coping. Masculinity is a positive predictor only in problem-oriented coping. These findings have implications for the conservation of personal resources as well as for stress management interventions.

FP-289: Children with mental retardation, autism or Down's syndrome II

Mothers of Down's Syndrome babies: Implications for early intervention

Bolsanello, Maria Augusta University Federal do Parana, Curitiba-Paraná, Brazil
The research examines how mothers of Down's syndrome babies, aged 0-2 years, conceive their participation in the early intervention, in Curitiba, Brazil. Methods: interviews with mothers, content analysis in a qualitative approach. Results: The mothers do not follow the instructions given by the professionals because they are afraid of hurting their children. They do not receive practical instructions that teach them how to stimulate and play with their infant in the daily routines. Conclusions: The early intervention programs, in Brazil, do not provide an effective participation of the mother, and thus, new alternatives that favor the child-family interaction are needed.

Reducing behavioral problems through a communicative instructional model for preschool children with autism

Chano, Jiraporn Speech Clinic, ENT 6, Srinagarind Hospital, Khonkae, Khonkaen, Thailand *Sarnrattana, Unchalee* Special education, khonkaen University, Khonkaen, Thailand *Pinpradit, Neon* Curriculum and instruction, Khonkaen university, Khonkaen, Thailand
Objectives: To Developing of a communicative instructional model to reduce behavioral problems in preschool autistic children in the Thai context. Methods: Ten male children diagnosed with autism were included. The subjects were between 3 and 6 years of age. The Single - Subject Designs were used. Results: Based on what we already know about the various strategies that can help behavioral problems of children with autism. PAT Model is an attempt to draw from and combine techniques used PESC,ABA,TEACCH. This model can control behavioral problems. Conclusions: The model

is a comprehensive, educational approach and multidisciplinary framework.

The effects of pivotal response training on communicative behavior of preschoolers with autism

Tang, Jung-Chang Chia-Yi, Taiwan *Lee, Shu-Hui* Special Education, National Kaohsiung Normal Uni, ChiaYi, Taiwan *Wang, Ming-Chua* Special Education, National Taitung University, ChiaYi, Taiwan
The purposes of this study were to assess the efficacies of pivotal response training (PRT) to three children with autism. A multiple baseline design across participants of single case methodology was used to examine the treatment effects of PRT on children's communicative behavior (Koegel, Schreibman, Good, Cerniglia, Murphy, & Koegel, 1989). Visual inspection was conducted to assess the effects of PRT. Results indicated that after PRT was implemented for one month, the frequency of communicative behavior increased to high levels in these children. The treatment effects of PRT could be maintained for two weeks and be generalized to different persons.

Face processing in children with autism spectrum disorder: Independent or interactive processing of facial identity and facial expression?

Krebs, Julia Inst. für Psychologie, Universität Gießen, Gießen, Germany *Biswas, Ajanta* Psychology, University of Sheffield, Sheffield, United Kingdom *Pascalis, Olivier* Psychology, University of Sheffield, Sheffield, United Kingdom *Schwarzer, Gudrun* Psychology, University of Giessen, Giessen, Germany
Typically developing children process face identity independently of facial expression but process facial expression in interaction with identity. Our study investigated whether such an asymmetric pattern of processing can also be found in autistic children, who are thought to process faces atypically. 8- to 15-year-old autistic children (N=26) were asked to sort faces as fast and accurate as possible by identity or emotional expression. In contrast to normal individuals, autistic children processed both, facial expression and identity, independently of each other. The results suggest face processing in autistic individuals to be less integrative than face processing in typically developing children.

FP-290: Learning disabilities, intellectual disabilities

A study of effects of parent's attitude on self-image and social development of learning disabled students

Baiat Mokhtary, Leila Mashhad, Islamic Republic of Iran
lerning disability has negetive effects on mental-emotional aspects of a child and leads to negetive self concept and low social development of the child.therefor the role of parents attiude is very important.positive attitude of parents lead to a more positive self concept and social growth of learning disabled children and vice versa.the available sample including all 20 boys (7-12 years old)refrd to mashhad exceptional students school were selected.the hypothesewas accepted by comparing the effects of parents positive and negative attitude on the self consept and social growth of children.

Overt attention orienting vs covert attention orienting in children with learning disabilities

Sui, Guangyuan Zhejiang Normal University, Jinhua, People's Republic of China *Wu, Yan* Learning Research Center, Southeast University, Nanjing, People's Republic of China
To extend the ecological validity of covert attention, Experiments were conducted to investigate the overt attention in Learning Disability(LD) groups and control groups. The results indicated that

endogenous cue-validity was found both in the LD groups and control groups of grade 3 and grade 6; under shortest SOA, no exogenous cue-validity was found in grade3, regardless of groups; when SOA was increased, the exogenous cue-validity was stable in all groups, with weakest effect in LD group of grade 6. These results demonstrated that LD children who had attention deficit may partly be because of ineffective use of the cued information, a generally slow cognitive processing speed, and lack of proper cognitive strategies.

The curriculum development for remediating basic skills of learning among primary school children with learning disabilities

Chookhampaeng, Chowwalit Curriculum and Instruction, Mahasarakham University, Maha-Sarakham, Thailand
The purpose to develop a remedial curriculum for improving the basic skill of learning. Divided into four steps : Step one : The studying fundamental data. As the result, the curriculum for children with learning disability that consist of four steps: input, process, memory, and output. Step two : The developing curriculum. As the result, the curriculum was to remedial the perceptional skill, language skill, and cognitive skill. Step three : The implemntation was conducted with the primary school children. The result was the all children's learning skill were higher than before at 0.01 of significant statistical level, but the language learning skill were lower than the criteria. Step four : The curriculum evaluation. The result from the parent seminar was satisfaction.

Coding and processing difficulties of children with mathematics learning disabilities: A study based on PASS theory

Deng, Ci-Ping Psychology Department, East China Normal University, Shanghai, People's Republic of China
In the study, simultaneous processing tasks and successive processing tasks from Das-Naglieri: Cognitive Assessment System were employed to assess coding processing of 30 pupils with only mathematics learning disabilities (MLD) and 30 pupils with mathematics and reading disabilities (MRD) from elementary schools. Results showed that, two groups of children got lower scores on both types of coding tasks than normal children, and children with MRD performed significantly worse on successive processing tasks than those with MLD. It seems that successive processing may be one of indicators based on which researchers could discriminate MLD from MRD

Work your memory: Computerized working memory training for children with intellectual disability

Danielsson, Henrik SIDR - IBL, Linköping University, Linköping, Sweden *Sundqvist, Anett* IBL, SIDR & Linköping Universit, Linköping, Sweden *Rudner, Mary* IBL, SIDR & Linköping Universit, Linköping, Sweden *Hofer, Nina* IBL, SIDR & Linköping Universit, Linköping, Sweden *Rönnberg, Jerker* IBL, SIDR & Linköping Universit, Linköping, Sweden
The purpose of the present study was to investigate the effect of a computerized working memory training program for children with intellectual disability. The participants had a mean age of 12 years. The training took place in the child's school environment for 15 minutes every school day for 5 weeks. There were training effects for some working memory measures, but not for all, compared to an age matched control group, also with intellectual disability, who also performed computerized training, but not related to working memory.

Cognitive and social problem solving in adults with intellectual disability
Nota, Laura Dept. of Develop. Psychology, University of Padova, Padova, Italy Sgaramella, Teresa Maria Psicologia dello sviluppo, Università di Padova, Padova, Italy Ferrari, Lea Psicologia dello sviluppo, università di Padova, padova, Italy Soresi, Salvatore Psicologia dello sviluppo, università di Padova, padova, Italy

The ability of thirty young adults with intellectual disability to solve cognitive and social problems was examined. Problem solving was measured by asking participants to produce a response to eight hypothetical real life situations. A spared ability to choose the most adaptive solutions was found in both cognitive and social problem solving, although not to the same extent. A relationship was found only between cognitive problem solving and intelligence level; both components were not related to language development and organization The study shows the relevance of studying problem solving in real life but separately assessing both cognitive and social dimensions

FP-291: Intelligence I

Estimation of multiple intelligences in Kordofan State
Elhaj, Ali Psychology, University of Kordofan, Elobied, Sudan Mohammednour, Obeidallah psychology, university of kordofan, elobied, Sudan

Abstract Estimation of multiple intelligences in Kordofan State This study investigates the estimation of multiple intelligences (MI) in Kordofan State, Sudan. A constructed measure of nine multiple intelligences was applied to a group of 562 pupils in primary education (11-15 years), both males (50%) and females (50%) from urban (64%) and rural areas (36%). The study showed that there was a significant difference in most aspects of MI between male and female participants, favoring the later. Furthermore, it showed that there was a significant difference in the estimated MI between rural and urban areas favoring the later. Finally, many suggestions and recommendations were reached.

Validity of the Base Intelligence Quotient test (BaslQ)
Sjöberg, Anders Dept. of Psychometric, Assessio International, Stockholm, Sweden

A nested confirmatory factor analysis (CFA) was applied to data (N=2740) in an attempt to identify a hierarchical model of general mental ability. The nested factor analysis is described as a "top down"-approach, i e that the lower-strata factors are separated from the variance derived from the higher strata. This means that the general factor is not contaminated by the variance in the lower order factors. The CFA shows a good fit between the hypothesized model and the data. Evidence based on relationships with external variables supports the interpretation of both the general factor and the lower-strata factors.

Factors affecting Khon Kaen University students' multiple intelligences
Pinpradit, Neon Educational Psychology, Khonkaen University, Khonkaen, Thailand Wongpinunwatana, Wirat Humanity, Khonkaen University, Khonkaen, Thailand

This study investigated factors affecting students' Multiple Intelligences development from familial, social, and psychological aspects. Khon Kaen University students were populations. Sample were five hundred students. The data were collected in the 2006 academic year. Stepwise multiple regression and path analysis were used for data analysis. It was found that the university environment, reasoning child-rearing practice, self-efficacy and achievement motivation can predict students' Mul-

tiple Intelligence at 32.8 percent. The result of path analysis indicated that students' Multiple Intelligence was directly affected by achievement motivation and self-efficacy. It is recommended that achievement motivation and self-efficacy be developed simultaneously for the growth of students' Multiple Intelligences.

Processing style, emotional Intelligence and well-being
Schutte, Nicola Dept. of Psychology, University of New England, Armidale, Australia Thorsteinsson, Einar Dept. of Psychology, University of New England, Armidale, NSW, Australia Hine, Donald Dept. of Psychology, University of New England, Armidale, NSW, Australia Foster, Roxanne Dept. of Psychology, University of New England, Armidale, NSW, Australia Cauchi, Avril Dept. of Psychology, University of New England, Armidale, NSW, Australia Binns, Caroline Dept. of Psychology, University of New England, Armidale, NSW, Australia

This research examined a model proposing that experiential and rational dual processing styles influence level of emotional intelligence, which in turn influences subjective well-being. One hundred and fifty-four adult participants completed measures of rational and experiential processing, emotional intelligence, affect and life satisfaction. Structural equation modeling identified a best fit model for predicting latent well-being. Experiential and rationale processing both significantly predicted level of emotional intelligence. Emotional intelligence in turn was strongly associated with well-being. Emotional intelligence mediated between the processing styles and well-being, with experiential processing contributing some variance not accounted for by emotional intelligence.

The relationship of the Berlin intelligence structure model and the three stratum theory
Süß, Heinz-Martin Inst. für Psychologie, Universität Magdeburg, Magdeburg, Germany Seidel, Kristin Psychology, Otto-von-Guericke-University, Magdeburg, Germany Weis, Susanne Psychology, Otto-von-Guericke-University, Magdeburg, Germany

This paper investigates the relationship of the Berlin Intelligence Structure Model (BIS; Jäger, 1982) and the Three Stratum Theory (TST; Carroll, 1987). The BIS is based on an almost representative sample of tasks found in the literature, TST on a reanalysis of 460 data sets. The tasks of the BIS-Test (Jäger, Süß, & Beauducel, 1997), a measure of the BIS model with high structural validity, were classified in the TST. Confirmatory factor analyses of BIS-Test data of 910 students confirm eleven TST-factors. The results help to interpret the BIS constructs in terms of Carroll's theory and vice versa.

Predictability of item parameters for automatically and manually generated figural matrices items
Hofer, Stefan Psychologischer Dienst, Bundesagentur für Arbeit, Nürnberg, Germany

Automatic item generation is of growing interest, hence the predictability of item parameters is a key research question. The present study compares various statistics, e.g. basic parameters of the Linear Logistic Test Model (Fischer, 1974), of items from different figural matrices tests with regard to their generalizability and stability. Results of studies for automatically generated items (n=350 persons) are contrasted with those of manually developed items (n>600 persons). Within instruments generalizability and stability are rather satisfactory, between instruments substantial distinctions can be found. Implications for the development of predictor sets for this item type are discussed.

FP-292: Indigenous and ethnopsychology

Culture and colour concepts
Groh, Arnold Sekr. FR 6-3, Technische Universität Berlin, Berlin, Germany

Objectives: Follow-up examination of former research on verbal factors of visual memory and the assumption of a lack of colour concepts in indigenous societies. Methods: Field research with indigenous participants in South East Asia and West Africa. Ishihara- and Pflügerhaken-Test, standardised colour tablets, retranslations. Results: All of the investigated indigenous societies had names for any colour presented. However, cultural factors of being indigenous vs. globalised were reflected by the use of reference objects for naming colours. Conclusions: Cognitive categorisation of visual perception takes place regardless of the cultural context. Former misunderstandings resulted from inappropriate methodological designs.

The attitudes of the Sudanese universities student towards female genital mutilation and their relationship with some demographic variables.
Altalib, Mohammed Psychology, Omdurman Islamic University, Khartoum, Sudan

the sample size was (1000) : (500) male and (500) females, including (250) circumcised and (250) non. The research finded many results, the more important of it: The attitudes towards F. G. M are negative. And there was positive correlation between it and the age, and inverse correlation with mother's and father's level of education, socio-economic status. And there were differences on it between males and females, infibulated females and non, rural and urban, those who get married and single, Muslims and Non – Muslims) successively. The most important and predictive variables for attitudes were : mother's education .

Co-authorship networks and power relations in the production of Mexican psychological research
Luna Hernandez, Jesus Rene Dept. de Psicologia Social, Univ. Autonoma de Barcelona, Cerdanyola del Valles, Spain

The development of indigenous psychology requires the integration of views coming from diverse contexts. However, very few researchers from universities outside of the main metropolitan areas (i.e. Mexico City and Guadalajara) collaborate with each other in the production of psychological research in Mexico. This study is an update of previous research (Luna, 2004) which shows, by using text network analysis of co-authored papers, that UNAM is still the center of research networks in Mexican psychology, at least as presented in proceedings of recent Mexican Psychological Society congresses. This centrality may slow the development of a really indigenous mexican psychology.

Ethnopsychological training as a method of interethnic competence teaching
Sangadiyev, Chingis Ulan-Ude, Russia

In modern society psychological training is considered to be more universal method of interethnic competence teaching. It helps overcome ethnical egotism and negative stereotypes. The program of ethnopsychological training of communication is aimed at seizing necessary skills for successful interethnic cooperation in polyethnic educational sphere. The effectiveness of the training program is statistically proved. It is aimed at the perception of man's behavior and communication as ethnically conditioned. It helps smooth ethnic prejudice and ethnic egocentrism. Taking into consideration the polyethnic character of Russian schools ethopsychological training is an important component of young generation educational program.

Ethnopsychology of modern teenagers' orientation

Tudupova, Tuyana Ulan-Ude, Russia

The study of personality's orientation is viewed as an important theoretical, experimental and applied problem in modern multicultural world. Ethnopsychological and inner psychological character and the structure of personality's orientation are studied. It is shown that ethnopsychological factor is one of the basic elements in orientation structure. The conception of ethnopsychological training is aimed at forming personality's tolerant orientation. The specifics of working with teenagers are shown with the help of ethnopsychological training, which was implemented in ethnically homogeneous forms of national schools and in ethnically combined groups (Buryat and Russian pupils). The results showed the effectiveness of the training.

Yin Yang dynamic thinking style and social judgment

Sun, Chien-Ru Department of Psychology, Chung Yuan University, Chung-Li, Taiwan

Yin Yang dynamic thinking style is rooted in the Chinese culture. In the present study, we created a Yin Yang index to measure the degree of Yin Yang dynamics that people possess in their thinking style. We then investigated how the index related with social judgment, and found that people who are high in Yin Yang dynamic tend to make less extreme decisions and rate outcome state as less stable. Moreover, although the result showed that people tend to have more Yin-Yang turns (i.e., negatives turn to positives), yet Yang-Yin turns (i.e., positives turn to negatives) are more influential.

FP-293: Individualism / collectivism I

Enhancing intercultural competence of Chinese students studying in Germany and German students studying in China

Hansen, Miriam Inst. für Psychologie, Universität Freiburg, Freiburg, Germany *Song, Jie* Department of Psychology, University of Freiburg, Freiburg, Germany *Spada, Hans* Department of Psychology, University of Freiburg, Freiburg, Germany

We are developing theoretically and empirically grounded training elements improving the intercultural competence of Chinese and German exchange students. Initially, we carried out a study at several Chinese and German universities to identify the main problems actually faced by the students. A questionnaire asked for experienced differences in cognition, emotion, and communication as well as for behavior in specific, experimentally varied situations. In contrast to some naïve clichés and scientific conjectures, only a few cultural differences (e.g. the style of communication) were crucial for students, while others (e.g. the presentation of negative emotions) were no source of intercultural problems.

Intending as an individual and as a cultural process

Adamopoulos, John Dept. of Psychology, Grand Valley State University, Allendale, USA *Furgerson, Luther* Psychology, Grand Valley State University, Allendale, Michigan, USA

Models of intention formation have typically assumed that intraindividual processes mediate culture's influence. Recent applications of such models have indicated that intending follows divergent paths in individualistic and collectivist cultures, with attitudes influential in intention formation in the former and norms in the latter. This investigation explored the contributions of these two components along with moral obligation in predicting intentions in a within-subject, as opposed to the typical between-subject, design in US and Greek samples. Results suggested that attitudes and moral obligations are important determinants of intentions in the two cultures in ways that go beyond standard individualism-collectivism theory.

Conceptions of individualism and collectivism in contemporary India and China

Alfoldy, Sarka Faculty of Arts, Charles University, Prague, Czech Republic

Objectives: Comparative study of contemporary India and China. Our objective is to elucidate primarily changes in the traditional collectivism related to the current trends of the rapid economic development of these two Asian giants. Method: Qualitative phase: • In-depth structured interviews • Content analysis Quantitative phase: • Testing of hypotheses Results: • Current changes in collectivism/individualism in India and China. • Manifestation of these changes in individuals' behaviour, approaches, values, communication, etc. in groups (families and work teams). • The impact of these changes on the creation of these cultures' global character. Conclusion: Identification and understanding of the changes in the traditional collectivism of India and China, will provide us with valuable knowledge for communication with these countries in all spheres.

Conservatism: A major dimension of individual and cross-cultural differences?

Stankov, Lazar International Testing Service, Princeton, USA

Recent studies employing self-report measures of four broad psychological domains - personality, social attitudes, values and social norms - point to the existence of a Conservatism factor that cuts across these domains. A person scoring high on this factor is also likely to score somewhat lower on measures of cognitive abilities and intelligence. Broad Conservatism factor can be identified when countries are used as units of analysis. This broad factor correlates with countries' investment in education, measures of school achievement and Failed States Index. Conservatism may be a more useful dimension of cultural differences than, say, individualism/collectivism or presentation styles.

Self construal, ethnic orientation and motivation in Indian and British young adults

Tripathi, Kailas Nath Psychology, Barkatullah University, Bhopal(M.P.), India

Variations in self-conception, goal orientation, ethnic identification, and academic motivation were assessed through self report measures in comparable samples of British White (N=50), British Indian, (N=35) and Indian (N=100) young adults. The British white group displayed significantly stronger relational self and mastery goal than the other groups and Indians displayed significantly stronger performance goal, ethnic orientation toward group and higher intrinsic and extrinsic motivation than the other groups. The British Indians selectively overlapped with its Indian and British counterparts. Implications of the findings for an increasingly globalizing world are discussed using the process of cultural contact and individualism - collectivism

The role of value orientations in individual innovation process

Dang, Junhua Shenzhen, People's Republic of China *Wang, Lei* Psychology, Peking University, Beijing, People's Republic of China *Yao, Xiang* Psychology, Peking University, Beijing, People's Republic of China *Yang, Ting* Psychology, Peking University, Shenzhen, People's Republic of China *Qiu, Chengfu* Psychology,

Peking University, Shenzhen, People's Republic of China

This study separately measured idea generation and idea implementation as two components of innovation and examined how they were impacted by individual value orientations. The results showed that both horizontal individualism and collectivism had positive influences on idea generation; vertical collectivism had a negative effect on idea generation but a positive one on idea implementation; although vertical individualism was not correlated to either idea generation or idea implementation, it moderated the relationship between the two components: idea generation would predict idea implementation quite well among high vertical individualists, while this prediction disappeared among low vertical individualists.

FP-294: Health cognition and risk behavior

Is there a reciprocal relationship between health behaviour and psychological and somatic distress?

De Gucht, Veronique Health Psychology, Leiden University, Leiden, Netherlands *Maes, Stan* Health Psychology, Leiden University, Leiden, Netherlands *Heiser, Willem* Methodology, Leiden University, Leiden, Netherlands

Objectives: Examine the relationship between health behavior and distress. Methods: 318 primary care patients completed questionnaires at baseline (T1) and 6 months follow-up (T2). Regression analyses were conducted to explore the relation between: (1) health behavior at T1 and (psychological and somatic) distress at T2, and (2) distress at T1 and health behavior at T2. Results: Patients reporting a less healthy lifestyle at T1 reported more distress at T2 (p<.01). The interaction between psychological and somatic distress at T1 was the best predictor of health behavior at T2 (p<.01). Conclusions: A reciprocal relationship between health behavior and distress was found.

Cognitive resources of perceived control, stress-recovery state and affective malaise in Fibromyalgia

Velasco, Lilian Dept. de Psicología, Universidad Rey Juan Carlos, Alcorcón, Spain *Peñacoba Puente, Cecilia* Departamento de Psicología, Universidad Rey Juan Carlos, Alcorcón, Spain *González Gutiérrez, José Luis* Departamento de Psicología, Universidad Rey Juan Carlos, Alcorcón, Spain *Mercado Romero, Francisco* Departamento de Psicología, Universidad Rey Juan Carlos, Alcorcón, Spain *López López, Almudena* Departamento de Psicología, Universidad Rey Juan Carlos, Alcorcón, Spain *Fernández Sánchez, Maria Luisa* Departamento de Psicología, Universidad Rey Juan Carlos, Alcorcón, Spain *Moreno Rodríguez, Ricardo* Departamento de Psicología, Universidad Rey Juan Carlos, Alcorcón, Spain *Barjola Valero, Paloma* Departamento de Psicología, Universidad Rey Juan Carlos, Alcorcón, Spain *Bullones Rodríguez, Ma. Angeles* Departamento de Psicología, Universidad Rey Juan Carlos, Alcorcón, Spain *Jimenez, Paul* Departament of Psychology, Graz University, 8010, Austria *Kallus, Wolfgang* Departament of Psychology, Graz University, Alcorcón, Spain

This study evaluates a causal model of linkages among cognitive resources of perceived control, stress-recovery state, and affective malaise using structural equation modelling. Data were obtained from a sample of 130 fibromyalgia patients. Results were consistent with the proposition that the stress-recovery balance mediates the relationship between cognitive resources and affective malaise. Direct effects of cognitive resources on function limitation were observed, while pain intensity and symptoms were direct predictors of the affective malaise. It is indicated the possible interpretation of several techniques employed in the treatment of Fibromyalgia as strategies orientated to the equilibrium between stress and recovery.

High school students' attitudes towards premarital relations between boys and girls and its effects on their mental health

Faghihi, Ali Naghi Human Sciences' Faculty, Qom University, Qom, Islamic Republic of Iran Ghobary Bonab, Bagher Psychology and education Facul, Tehran University, Tehran, Islamic Republic of Iran

The aim of the current study was to investigate the attitude of senior high school students towards unlawful premarital relationships between boys and girls. To this end, 120 students (males and females) were selected based on the cluster sampling and, questionnaire about this matter were distributed among them. Findings indicated that high school students believed that premarital relationships can jeopardize their health. They also believed that in addition to negative health effects, premarital relations can have a negative impact on students' self-esteem making them feel guilty and also leads to the abuse of girls by boys most of the times.

Card-sorting as a diagnostic approach and an evaluation tool for caregiver interventions in chronic stroke care

Beische, Denis Geriatrische Rehabilitation, Robert-Bosch-Hospital, Stuttgart, Germany Hautzinger, Martin Klin.Psych. und Psychotherapie, Universitaet Tuebingen, Tuebingen, Germany Becker, Clemens Geriatrische Rehabilitation, Robert-Bosch-Hospital, Stuttgart, Germany Heyl, Ruth Geriatrische Rehabilitation, Robert-Bosch-Hospital, Stuttgart, Germany Lindemann, Beate Geriatrische Rehabilitation, Robert-Bosch-Hospital, Stuttgart, Germany Pfeiffer, Klaus Geriatrische Rehabilitation, Robert-Bosch-Hospital, Stuttgart, Germany

Defining and analysing the specific problem areas are the important first steps for an effective problem solving in caregiver counselling. To facilitate this process a set of 40 cards has been developed for family caregivers of stroke survivors. Beyond the use as an assessment tool as part of the problem solving approach the card procedure gives a better understanding of relevant burdensome areas that are responsive to this kind of intervention. The development of the card-set and the results with data from 30 participants of an ongoing RCT study are presented and compared with other established diagnostic approaches.

Multiple health-risk behaviour of prescription drug users

Otto, Christiane Psychiatrie - Psychotherapie, Uni-Klinik Schleswig-Holstein, Lübeck, Germany Bischof, Gallus Klinik f.Psychiatrie/-therapie, Uni Klinik-SH, Campus Luebeck, Luebeck, Germany Crackau, Brit Klinik f.Psychiatrie/-therapie, Uni Klinik-SH, Campus Luebeck, Luebeck, Germany Loehrmann, Ira Klinik f.Psychiatrie/-therapie, Uni Klinik-SH, Campus Luebeck, Luebeck, Germany Zahradnik, Anne Klinik f.Psychiatrie/-therapie, Uni Klinik-SH, Campus Luebeck, Luebeck, Germany Rumpf, Hans-Jürgen Klinik f.Psychiatrie/-therapie, Uni Klinik-SH, Campus Luebeck, Luebeck, Germany

Objectives: Dependence and misuse of prescription drugs are highly prevalent. Analyzing multiple health-risk behaviour, the use of different kinds of substances as well as other lifestyle and health-related characteristics are of importance. Methods: 6020 general hospital patients (18 to 69 years old) were screened for their use of prescription drugs, alcohol, nicotine and mental health. Results: Chances are that prescription drug users smoke. Patients using regularly medicaments are more likely smokers and more probably risky alcohol consumers. Conclusions: The results will be discussed. The perspective of multiple health-risk behaviour can give important information for planning interventions.

Is sexism a barrier for HIV/Aids sexual prevention?

Landa Ubillos, Silvia Sciences of Education, University of Burgos, Burgos, Spain Goiburu, Eider Sexology, Lahia-Nahia Elkartea, San Sebastián, Spain Martín, Mónica Sexology, Lahia-Nahia Elkartea, San Sebastián, Spain

We will test how sexism and sexual double standards affects Aids prevention. 517 Spanish students took part in the study. Measures used were: Double Standard Scale, Ambivalent Sexism Inventory, Neosexism Scale, and scales regarding knowledge, attitudes and behaviour towards Aids sexual prevention. Measures were answered before and after an Aids sexual prevention programme. Those participants with higher levels of sexism and sexual double standards were those who presented less knowledge and more negative attitudes towards condom use. They also had less skill in resolving situations with high sexual risk. Sexism can be a barrier in acquiring knowledge for Aids prevention.

FP-295: Applications of item response models in educational and psychological measurement

Many-facet Rasch modeling of rater-mediated performance assessments

Eckes, Thomas TestDaF Institut, Hagen, Germany

The many-facet Rasch measurement model (MFRM or facets model; Linacre, 1989) extends the basic Rasch model to incorporate more variables (or "facets") than the two that are typically included in a paper-and-pencil testing situation (i.e., examinees and items). The present paper summarizes findings from recent applications of the facets model in a variety of psychological and educational measurement settings, discusses the rater dependence problem caused by multiple ratings, and reviews alternative approaches advanced to deal with this problem. Finally, implications of the facets model for analyzing and monitoring rater behavior in large-scale performance assessments are pointed out.

Assessing listening comprehension in the first language: Some psychometric perspectives

Robitzsch, Alexander IQB, Humboldt-Universität zu Berlin, Berlin, Germany Neumann, Daniela Philo IV, IQB, B, Germany Köller, Olaf Philo IV, IQB, B, Germany Behrens, Ulrike Institut für deutsche Sprache, Universität Hildesheim, Hildesheim, Germany

Since 2004 educational standards have been established in Germany for German, Maths and the first Foreign Languages French or English to measure what core competencies students have acquired when leaving school. For German as first language the competencies reading comprehension, writing, orthography, grammar awareness, speaking and listening comprehension are relevant. Comparing the mean growth pattern (grade 8 to 10 across different school types) a multidimensional Rasch model was used to determine the competencies' dimensional structure. We focus on the assessment and dimensional analyses of listening tasks. Special attention was given to the influence of the listening stimulus and predictors of item difficulty on student achievement which was researched with testlet models and LLTM models.

Measuring writing skills in French as a foreign language: The reliability and validity of analytic versus global ratings

Oehler, Raphaela IQB, Humboldt-Universität zu Berlin, Berlin, Germany Vock, Miriam IQB, Humboldt Universität, Berlin, Germany Tesch, Bernd IQB, Humboldt Universität, Berlin, Germany

After developing writing tasks based on the Common European Framework for Languages and the Educational Standards a representative study of German students (N = 3000) from grade 8 to 10 was conducted in Spring 2007. The texts were coded using analytic and global ratings based on a uni-level approach. In this presentation, results concerning the relationship between analytic ratings and a single global rating (across different raters) as well as their relation to grades and to students' performances in reading and listening comprehension will be given. Implications for coding writing tasks in a foreign language are discussed.

Measuring the effect of multiple choice response format by some IRT models

Hohensinn, Christine Inst. für Psychologie, Testzentrum Universität Wien, Vienna, Austria Kubinger, Klaus D. Faculty of Psychology, Centre of Testing & Consul, Vienna, Austria Holocher-Ertl, Stefana Faculty of Psychology, Centre of Testing & Consul, Vienna, Austria Reif, Manuel Faculty of Psychology, Centre of Testing & Consul, Vienna, Austria Khorramdel, Lale Faculty of Psychology, Centre of Testing & Consul, Vienna, Austria Sonnleitner, Philipp Faculty of Psychology, Centre of Testing & Consul, Vienna, Austria Gruber, Kathrin Faculty of Psychology, Centre of Testing & Consul, Vienna, Austria Frebort, Martina Faculty of Psychology, Centre of Testing & Consul, Vienna, Austria

The Centre of Testing and Consulting develops the national standard tests for Reading and Mathematics. There a design of test booklets is used where the same item content is administered with different response formats. Under discussion are the free response format and at least two different multiple choice formats: "1 from 6" (a single correct response option plus five distractors) and "2 from 5" (two solutions plus three distractors). Using two different IRT approaches discloses the effect of the response format on item solving probabilty. That is Fischer's LLTM and the "Difficulty plus Guessing PL-model" (Kubinger & Draxler, 2006).

Confidence testing as a diagnostic tool

Musch, Jochen Inst. für Exp. Psychologie, Universität Düsseldorf, Düsseldorf, Germany Ullrich, Sebastian Inst. f. Exp. Psy., University of Duesseldorf, Duesseldorf, Germany Szekeres, Istvan Head Office Cologne, psychonomics AG, Cologne, Germany Goeritz, Anja Organizat. & Social Psycho, Univ. of Erlangen-Nuremberg, Nuremberg, Germany

Multiple choice tests encourage guessing and provide limited information if test takers have partial knowledge. By contrast, multiple evaluation tests make partial knowledge count by asking for the confidence in all answer alternatives. Confidence in the correct answer is rewarded by positive payoffs; confidence in wrong answers is punished by negative payoffs. If logarithmic scoring functions are used, test takers can maximize their final score only by honestly reporting their true knowledge. We report experiments showing that confidence testing based on logarithmic scoring helps discriminating more reliably between members of groups with known differences in aptitude, and also allows a better prediction of external criteria.

Block versus mixed-order item presentation in personality inventories: An IRT analysis

de Bruin, Gideon Human Resource Management, University of Johannesburg, Johannesburg, South Africa Taylor, Nicola Psychology, University of Johannesburg, Johannesburg, South Africa

Objectives Investigation of the effects of blocked versus mixed order item presentation in personality inventories. Methods Participants completed a personality inventory with items presented in blocks (493 participants) or in mixed order (810 participants). Data were analysed using the Rasch rating scale model. Results Block presentation produced more reliable measures, better fit, and less extreme-response tendency. The Rasch dimension accounted for more variance in the block presentation method. However, block presentation produced more violations of the assumption of local independence. Conclusion Block presentation of items in personality inventories is likely to produce better psychometric properties than mixed-order item presentation.

FP-296: Hierarchical positions and performance

Does CEO personality matter? Implications for financial performance and corporate social responsibility

Jacquart, Philippe Dept. of Management, University of Lausanne, Lausanne-Dorigny, Switzerland Antonakis, John Fac. of Business & Economi, University of Lausanne, Lausanne-Dorigny, Switzerland Ramus, Catherine Donald Bren School, University of California, CA - Santa Barbara, USA

We investigate whether CEO implicit motives predict corporate social performance and financial performance. Using longitudinal data on 258 CEOs from 118 firms, and controlling for country and industry effects, we found that motives significant predicted both financial performance (Tobin's Q and the CAPM) and social responsibility. In general, need for power and responsibility disposition were positively predictive whereas need for achievement and affiliation were negatively predictive of outcomes. Contrary to previous theorizing, corporate social responsibility had no link to financial performance. Our findings suggest that executive characteristics have important consequences for corporate level outcomes.

The influence of leadership empowerment on employee silence

Gao, Liping social & organizational center, school of management, Beijing, People's Republic of China Shi, Kan social & organizational ce, school of management, Beijing, People's Republic of China

Within organizations, employee silence has been a noticeable phenomenon these days. In this study, the data from 40 groups and 314 pairs of supervisor- employee were used to explore the influence of leadership empowerment behaviors on employee silence in China. The results were that trust did not mediate the relationship between leadership empowerment behavior and employee silence, but the level of trust had impact on the relationship. Employees with the highest level of the trust on supervisor remain silence rarely; while whether employees with moderate and low trust on supervisor remain silence or not is influenced by leadership empowerment behavior.

Power dynamics, leadership and ingratiation: A study on Indian public sector

Pattanayak, Biswajeet Asian School of Business Mgt, Bhubaneswar, India Niranjana, Phalgu Organisational Behaviour, Asian School of Business Mgt, Bhubaneswar, India Ganguly, Somdutta Psychology, Utkal University, Bhubaneswar, India

The study intends to find out the effects of age of organization (old & new) and hierarchical positions (executives & supervisors) of employees on bases of power, leadership styles and ingratiation in Indian public sector organisations & to explain their interrelationships. It follows a 2x2 factorial design with 400 samples. Standardized questionnaires are used to measure the dependent variables. The findings reveal that inter group difference exist with regard to all variables. An integrated analysis shows that leadership is a power function and contributes to influence strategies of ingratiation. Based on the findings OD interventions are suggested.

Morphology of organizational vision

Vlasov, Peter Applied psychology institute, Kharkov, Ukraine

Objectives: research structure entrepreneur's organizational vision in transitional environment, identifying structure of intentions and differences between entrepreneur's and manager's visions. Methods: sample – 50 owners-initiator, 107 top-managers; methods – interview, intent-analyses, actual sentences articulation. Results: self-conception, conception of environment and organizational activity underpin the organizational vision and conception. Self-conception actualize in initiator's work. The values of security and benevolence have the main significance and conflict with values of development. Initiators avoid the uncertainty by managing of relations and recourses. Initiators and top-managers have different values and personification of results. Cognitive complexity provides specified estimation of situation and flexible criteria for decision-making, orientation, openness and adaptation.

Professor = leader? An investigation of faculty roles

Peus, Claudia Inst. für Psychologie, Universität München, München, Germany Weisweiler, Silke Department of Psychology, Ludwig-Maximilians-University, Munich, Germany

Role set analysis (Merton, 1957) has been frequently used in research on managerial roles (e.g. entrepreneur, leader). However, empirical studies have neglected a detailed analysis of faculty roles – beyond research, teaching, and service. We conducted qualitative interviews focusing on faculty roles and in particular the leader role with 25 senior professors of different departments of a large German university. Analyses revealed that professors have very different perceptions of their leader role: e.g. patriarch, team coach, or even denied being a leader. Results are discussed against the background of a large-scale survey currently undertaken with the professors' employees.

Perceived power distance as mediator of reciprocal trust between supervisor and subordinate

Seppälä, Tuija Social psychology, University of Helsinki, Helsinki, Finland Lipponen, Jukka Social psychology, University of Helsinki, Helsinki, Finland Pirttilä-Backman, Anna-Maija Social psychology, University of Helsinki, Helsinki, Finland

Trust is assumed to be reciprocal. However, few studies have explored trust as truly interpersonal. The current paper examined trust in supervisor-subordinate dyads. We explored how the supervisor's trust was related to the subordinate's perceptions of power distance, and subsequently how perceptions of power distance are related to the subordinate's trust. Path analysis revealed that power distance mediated the relationship between the supervisor's trust and the subordinate's trust. Meanwhile, the supervisor's trust was not directly related to the subordinate's trust. We concluded that power distance contributes to trust because it implies position in the work group, and the supervisor's trust and the subordinate's trust were not associated because trust is differently salient for the parties.

FP-297: Higher education, university education in specific subject domains

Socio-cognitive differences between novice and expert tutorial functions at university

Roselli, Néstor Faculdad de Education, CONICET / UNER, Rosario, Argentina Borgobello, Ana IRICE, CONICET, Rosario, Argentina Peralta, Nadia IRICE, CONICET, Rosario, Argentina

This presentation aims to compare the teaching function of both the expert (professor) and the novice (assistant) in experimental situations. Twelve groups of university students were tested in teaching situations with a professor and an assistant. Results show that assistants attend more than professors the social and psychopedagogical support of learning; professors focuse specially on the epistemic dimension (knowledge by itself). The difference regards also the linguistic context. Finally there is a great difference concerning specifically the cognitive construction of knowledge and the learning results. Answers to a questionnaire applied to students are coincident with these conclusions.

Office hours in higher education: The case of Qatari university students

Semmar, Yassir Dept. of Psychology, Qatar University, Doha, Qatar

Over the past decade, a number of research studies have pointed to the pedagogical and educational benefits related to the regular attendance of office hours. However, there seems to be a tendency among Qatar University students to avoid going to their instructors' office hours. The purpose of this study is to gain a better insight into the reasons that make students resistant to attending office hours. Factor analysis was first conducted to reveal the components underlying this resistance; Multivariate Analysis of Variance was then employed to analyze the effects of gender, GPA, and year of enrollment on those factors.

The blurring between strict and fluid demands at the Umeå Dentistry Programme

Schéle, Ingrid Dept. of Psychology, Umeå University, Umeå, Sweden Hedman, Leif Psychology, Umeå University, Umeå, Sweden

The objective was to study elements forming students' professional identity and experience of dental education. Focus was on how students cope with conflicting demands and the interaction between a male dentist norm and predominantly female students. Semi-structured interviews were conducted with three teachers and ten students from the Umeå dentistry programme. The Grounded Theory method used generated a model centred on "Experiencing ambiguity" – ambiguity about actual effort needed and actual demands to be met. Also central were "Experiencing stress", time related as well as strain related, and "Demands lead to quality". The consequences of this ambiguity will be further explored.

Can learning approaches mediate the effect of engineering dispositions on achievement?

Magno, Carlo Counseling and Educational Psy, De La Salle University-Manila, Manila, Philippines Mamuag, Marife CLPA, De La Salle-College of Saint B, Manila, Philippines

The study investigates whether learning approaches can mediate the effect of engineering dispositions on ability. A scale was constructed to measure engineering disposition that includes practical inclination, analytical interest, intellectual independence, and assertiveness. Learning approaches includes monitoring, deep strategy, shallow-processing, persistence, and environmental structuring. A standardized achievement test for engineering students was also used. The measures were administered to 500 engineering students using a longitudinal design. The Structural Equations Modeling was used to test the model. The results show that possessing the engineering disposition enables the use of better approach to learning which consequently results to better achievement and aptitude.

Case-based learning with worked-out examples in medicine: Effects of errors and feedback
Stark, Robin Universität des Saarlandes, Saarbrücken, Germany *Kopp, Veronika* Faculty of Medizine, University of Munich, München, Germany *Fischer, Martin* Faculty of Medicine, University of Munich, Munich, Germany
Objectives: To facilitate medical students' diagnostic competence, case-based worked-out examples were implemented in a computer-based learning environment and enhanced with errors and feedback. Methods: 153 students were randomly assigned to four conditions of a 2x2-factorial design (errors vs. no errors, elaborated feedback vs. feedback of correct result). Results: The acquisition of diagnostic competence was especially supported by errors in combination with elaborated feedback. This effect was independent from prior knowledge and time-on task and proved to be sustainable. Conclusion: The results demonstrate that the implemented instructional method which combined example-based learning with elements of situated learning is successful in medicine.

FP-298: History

Early twentieth-century research in Italy on the perception of time
Degni, Silvia Dip. dei Processi di Sviluppo, Università La Sapienza, Roma, Italy *Cimino, Guido* Social & Developmental Psych., University of Rome 1, Rome, Italy
In the first decades of the twentieth century, following the tradition of the psychophysics studies carried out in the German laboratories, two Italian psychologists, Vittorio Benussi and Enzo Bonaventura, conducted experimental research on temporal judgments and on their conditions of variability. They studied the "subjective" and "objective" factors that intervene in the evaluation of the temporal duration of specified time intervals. In this way, they succeeded in formulating two laws of a general kind: 1) the evaluation of the duration varies with the variation of the representative and affective content; 2) the greater qualitative richness of the representation results in an underestimation of the duration. Their innovative experiments found confirmation in analogous research conducted in those years in European laboratories.

Are colours subjective?: The Fechnerian rediscovery
Sinatra, Maria Dept. of Psychology, University of Bari, Bari, Italy
In the first half of the nineteenth century, the dichotomy interpretation of the subjective or objective nature of colours constituted an important research topic within the large field of physio-psychological optics. This paper deals with the reconstruction of the 1840s Osann-Fechner debate over the origin of phenomena such as afterimages, contrast colours, and coloured shadows. This subjective origin, often related to Anschauung, a recurring term used by Helmholtz, was the basis for the guidelines of Fechner's project, which increasingly distanced itself from materialism to arrive at the discovery both of unconscious knowledge and of the fundamental formula of psychophysics.

The relevance of Pierre Janet's dynamic psychology for current cognitive and social psychological research.
Saillot, Isabelle Institut Pierre Janet, Paris, France
Pierre Janet (1859-1947) was the founder (1901) and first President (1901-1902) of the French Psychological Society (SFP). Although acknowledged in the field of psychopathology (dissociation), his experimental psychology remains under-appreciated. Janet's model addresses the impact of fatigue/force on the link between action and thoughts. Our objective is to show that this « dynamic psychology » is still relevant today for cognitive and social psychology. As an illustration, recent experiments on cognitive dissonance and Just World Theory will be discussed from a Janetian perspective. We hope that recognising Janet's relevance in this area will stimulate further experimental research.

Intelligence and politics: The history of Binet's intelligence test
Foschi, Renato Facoltà di Psicologia1, Roma, Italy *Cicciola, Elisabetta* Dynamic and Clinical Pychology, University of Rome, Rome, Italy
Alfred Binet was a controversial scholar whose eclectic scientific production represents a milestone in modern psychology. This paper aims at providing fresh insights into Binet's work by trying to capture the intersections between Binet, his naturalistic culture and the political context in which he created the intelligence test. In using original archive's data, the presentation reconstructs the political and institutional background of Binet's research and shows how the naturalism and experimentalism he promoted were complementary to the solidarist conceptions that were particularly prevalent among those who supported his work during the Third Republic.

Shadows on the genesis of psychology in Germany in the 20th century: New results towards political efforts based on changes of "Völkerpsychologie" in favour of the totalitarian system
Guski-Leinwand, Susanne Bad Honnef, Germany
The genesis of psychology in Germany in the 20thCentury show, that psychology in Germany finally contains a hidden mix of scientific and political efforts. Psychology in Germany was early instrumentated for hostile aims and influenced from outside: Psychological theories and approaches – like the "Völkerpsychologie" of Wilhelm Wundt - were abused and turned into a "differentielle Völkerpsychologie": This changed theory and contributions under the name "Völkerpsychologie" were generated as hostile approaches against selected folks under various names. The consequences which show a support of rassistic concepts for the SS and other cruel parts of the NS-System will be discussed.

How to prevent railway and road accidents? The pioneering Italian investigations
Monacis, Lucia Dept. of Psychology, University of Bari, Bari, Italy
In 1908 H. Münsterberg stressed the importance of the use of a preventive test for tramway drivers, and during the Congress of Psychology held in Berlin in 1912, he presented a study on the selection of streetcar drivers. In Italy, in 1907 P. Petrazzani and in 1909 M. L. Patrizi had already urged the need for psychophysiological selection of drivers. This paper describes their investigations carried out in the laboratory of psychology of the psychiatric clinic in Reggio Emilia and in the laboratory of psychology in Turin in order to establish how much time and distance drivers required to avoid unexpected obstacles.

FP-299: HIV risk perception

Cultural context of HIV/AIDS reduction strategies with Caribbean adolescents
Baird, Donna Behavioral & Social Science, University of Maryland, Adelphi, USA *Yearwood, Edilma* School of Nursing, Georgetown University, Washington, DC, USA *Jones, Lisa* School of Nursing, Georgetown University, Washington, DC, USA
Problem: In the Caribbean, women and young girls are becoming infected with HIV at a rate six times greater than men. Our study examined effective methods for reducing HIV/AIDS risks among adolescent girls in the Caribbean. Methods: One hundred females, ages 15-21 were randomly assigned to a control or intervention group. Subjects were assessed at baseline and post-intervention. Results: ANOVA analysis revealed significance post-intervention on items measuring feelings about self, perceived risk and sexual attitudes. Conclusion: Sustainable HIV/AIDS prevention programs that address the cultural context of stigma, promote HIV testing, and reinforce safer sex practices are needed with vulnerable populations.

Development of a health behaviour model for HIV/AIDS prevention
Gräser, Silke Psychologie, Universität Oldenburg, Oldenburg, Germany *Krischke, Norbert R.* Psychologie, Universität Oldenburg, Oldenburg, Germany
Current results of research show that migrants do not profit sufficiently from HIV/AIDS prevention, treatment and care, therefore the Bremer Public Health Services offer a cultural sensitive approach for Sub-Saharan migrants. Aim of this study is to identify barriers and to develop a cultural sensitive model to optimize the accessibility of HIV/AIDS prevention programs. Interviews with a sample of African key persons, multiples and community-leaders were analysed by qualitative content analysis (Mayring, 2003). Preliminary results concerning cognitive and motivational barriers in terms of accessibility of HIV/AIDS preventive measures based on Health Action Process Approach Theory (Schwarzer, 2001) will be presented.

Intuitive judgments of HIV risk: An event related brain potential study
Schmälzle, Ralf FB Psychologie, AG Schupp, Universität Konstanz, Konstanz, Germany *Renner, Britta* Psychology, University of Konstanz, Konstanz, Germany *Schupp, Harald* Psychology, University of Konstanz, Konstanz, Germany
Recent models of health risk perception emphasize the role of intuitive affective processes. To study the neural correlates of the intuitive perception of health risks, event-related brain potentials (256 channels) were measured while participants judged the risk of HIV-infection of 120 persons' based on facial appearance. Results showed enlarged positive brain potentials for 'risky' faces over centro-parietal sensor locations in a time window from 350 – 600 ms. Considering previous findings in affective neuroscience, we propose that faces judged as risky attain higher saliency already very early during information processing and guide selective attention processes.

Condom use among romantic partners: An integrative model of individual and relationship factors
Leung, Stephanie Yat Chi Psychology, CUHK, N.T., China, People's Republic of : Hong Kong SAR *Mak, Winnie Wing Sze* Psychology, CUHK, N.T., China, People's Republic of : Macao SAR
This study tested the effectiveness of a condom use model that incorporates individual cognitions and relationship level factors in understanding condom use among romantic partners. It is found in a sample of sexually active dating individuals in Hong Kong that on top of individual attitudes, subjective norms and perceived behavioral control over condom use, greater relationship power and sexual communication are associated with greater control over condom use and in turn actual condom use, while relationship commitment hinders condom use. Findings of the study are of theoratical as well as practical significance to the research on condom use.

Decision making and risk perception-assessment of donors undergoing living donor liver transplantation (LDLT)

Papachristou, Christina Psychosomatiche Medizin, Charite Universitätsmedizin, Berlin, Germany Schmid, Gabriele Department of Psychology, Basel University, Basel, Switzerland Walter, Marc Department of Psychiatry, University of Basel, Basel, Switzerland Frommer, Joerg Psychiatry, Psychotherapy, University Otto-Von-Guericke, Magdebrug, Germany Klapp, Burghard F. Psychosomatic Medicine, Charite University Medicine, Berlin, Germany

Objectives. LDLT increasingly performed over the last years, raises medical-ethical issues due to the high donor risk. Methods. Qualitative research study based on semi-structured clinical interviews with 28 donors before LDLT, analysed using the method of Grounded Theory. Results. All donors initially immediately agreed to donation. Later two donor groups were identified; these who consciously think through their decision and these who avoid rethinking it, suppressing ambivalence or anxiety. Surgery risks are perceived and processed in different ways, including risk awareness, denial, limited acceptance and fatalism. Conclusion. The concepts of informed consent and decision autonomy in LDLT are being questioned.

HIV/AIDS knowledge and sexual behaviors among college students in Jakarta

Suci, Eunike Dept. of Psychology, Atma Jaya Catholic University, Jakarta, Indonesia

Objectives: to measure the HIV/AIDS knowledge, sexual behavior, and drug use among college students Methods: cross-sectional study with 320 students of Atma Jaya Catholic University as the sample Results: Students' knowledge on HIV/AIDS was not high, 64% had experienced sexual relationships. As for the sexual behavior, of the 33 males and 25 females who were sexually active, 66% and 68% reported to be unprotected. Only three students reported to be IDUs. Conclusion: The university needs to provide better information on HIV/AIDS and safe sexual behavior. Few students reported as IDUs due to the crimimal penaltiy for them.

FP-300: Discipline issues II

Study of scientifical network collaboration between researchers: The academic female psychologists

Penaranda, Maria Psicologia Basica y Metodologi, Universidad de Murcia, Espinardo, Spain Quiñones Vidal, Elena psicologia basica y metodologi, universidad de murcia, Espinardo (Murcia), Spain

Women have less visibility and presence in some fields, overall in those positions including certain influence and power (Prpic, 2002). Regarding the case of scientific women, we observe that their network of scientific publications is quiet damaged compared to male networks. Based on Floyd's algorithm, differences between men and women are analysed. The network of collaboration and work between authors in psychology is nearly inexistent for female psychologies.

Multiple jobholding and portfolio careers in psychology

Olos, Luiza Inst. für Arbeitspsychologie, Freie Universität Berlin, Berlin, Germany Hoff, Ernst-H. Arbeits-, Berufspsychologie, Freie Universität Berlin, Berlin, Germany

Drawing on data from retrospective written and oral surveys, the occupational trajectories of German psychologists (N=585) and physicians were analyzed and compared. Results show that multiple jobholding occurs only in psychology, where it is the most prevalent career pattern (N=104). Portfolio careers result from conditions prevailing in the profession, a restrictive labor market, and indivi-dual choices. They can generally be considered positive for the profession, with "specialized generalists" promoting knowledge exchange and networking. Most psychologists also have positive attitudes toward portfolio careers, which further the goals of variety, autonomy, flexibility, and work-life balance. They are, however, associated with career insecurity.

Constructing community educational psychology in higher education institutions

Pillay, Jace Faculty of Education, University of Johannesburg, Johannesburg, South Africa

This paper constructs the notion of community educational psychology by drawing on the main tenets of community and educational psychology. Based on theory and research it is argued that there has to be a critical review of teaching, learning and research of community educational psychology in Higher Education Institutions (HEIs) if it is to add any value to local communities. Furthermore, it is argued that community engagement should be an essential component of the vision and mission of HEIs. Based on the arguments several suggestions on reconstructing teaching, learning and research in community educational psychology in HEIs are proposed.

FP-301: Culture and cognition II

The power of simplification

Williams, Kinga Agnes Psychological Consultancy, MENSANA Intercultural, Goring-on-Thames, United Kingdom

The presentation sets out to explore what provides the persuasive power to various world-views. At times of danger (e.g. war, terrorism), world-views with a clear vision of an orderly world-structure (e.g. fundamentalism, communism) become increasingly attractive (Salzman 2006). It is suggested that their appeal is due to their simplicity. The presentation proposes that individual cognitive simplifications and socio-cognitive simplifications are very similar: both resorted to as temporary labour-saving devices to free up capacity - a process that results in cognitive errors. These simplifications are as powerful as they are dangerous. To counteract the tendency, targeted intercultural communication is proposed.

Epistemological clash: Tensions and conflicts in the Zambian mathematics classroom

Panda, Minati Zakir Husain Centre, Jawaharlal Nehru University, New Delhi, India Ndhlovu, Zanzini B. Zakir Husain Centre for Educat, Jawaharlal Nehru University, New Delhi, India

This paper examines the epistemological clash between out-of-school and in-school mathematics practices in a rural government Zambian school resulting from the interface between a version of "Western" mathematics, sufficiently recontextualized in Zambian cultural context which emphasised obedience, discipline, memorization and rejection of home knowledge and the everyday mathematics. It analyses the classroom observation data and the case study of four class VI Ngoni/Tumbuka students using discourse analysis technique. The results show that while the school systematically works towards undermining and eradicating the local community's mathematical practices and epistemological knowledge, at the same time, it keeps school mathematics truncated and generally inaccessible.

Can deterministic thinking predict marital satisfaction?

Younesi, Jalal counselling, University of social welfare, Tehran, Islamic Republic of Iran Younesi, Maryam counselling, University of social welfare, Tehran, Islamic Republic of Iran Askari, Ali counselling, University of social welfare, Tehran, Islamic Republic of Iran

One of major cognitive distortions is deterministic thinking. This type of thinking ignore any possibility or probability in conclusion about the events. In religious perspective, the distortion is seen as destructive factor for ruining balance of fear and hope which to be an important sign of people's faith. The questionnaire with 50 items were developed. Its validity and reliability were maesured among 500 hunderds people and to show reasonable validity and reliability. Results of factor analysis indicated five factors which to be involved in this kind of thinking. Moreover in another study, 300 couples answered the questionnair and Enrich marital satisfaction inventory. Analysis of regression showed that determinstic thinking can predict marital satisfaction of subjects significantly (P<.05).

FP-302: Cross-cultural approaches in psychology II

Is optimism universal? A meta-analytical investigation of optimism levels across 23 nations

Fischer, Ronald School of Psychology, Victoria University Wellington, Wellington, New Zealand Chalmers, Anna School of Psychology, Victoria University Wellington, Wellington, New Zealand

A meta-analysis of dispositional optimism levels as measured by the Life Orientation Test (LOT, Scheier & Carver, 1985) across 23 countries (k = 305; N=108,071) is reported. The impact of cultural differences on optimism is examined. Using mixed-effect modeling, overall culture differences were small and only marginally significant. Greater individualism and higher femininity (Hofstede, 1980) were associated with greater optimism (explaining 3% of the variance). Greater egalitarianism (versus hierarchy, Schwartz, 1994) was consistently associated with higher optimism (explaining 2% of the variance). Claims of fundamental cultural differences were not supported. Implications for cross-cultural research and health applications are discussed.

Situational judgment integrity in decision-making: A comparison study of the U.S. students and Chinese students

Chen, Lijun Government Department, Zhejiang University, Hangzhou, People's Republic of China

The study aimed to compare the different understanding of integrity under differnt culture via response to the business integrity dilemma. After developing a Situational Judgment Integrity Test (SJIT) ; we completed a survey to 336 Chinese universtiy students and 271 the U.S. universtiy students. The study showed the score level of Chinese students was significant lower than that of the U.S. students; and there were different dimensions of integrity construct between two countries. These differences could be explained by Chinese Guanxi's culture. It also revealed that the situational judgment integrity was positively related to Big Five's personality dimension both with two samples. Further research, applications and the limitations were discussed too.

Cross-cultural universality and variation of causal attribution: A comparative study of attribution of social events among Chinese, Korean and American

Wu, Shengtao The Institute of Psychology, Beijing, People's Republic of China Zhang, Jianxin Laboratory of Mental Health, The Institute of Psychology, Beijing, People's Republic of China Lai, Jianwei culture psychology, The Institute of Psychology, Beijing, People's Republic of China

Growing cross-cultural evidence suggested that the fundamental attribution error(FAE) in East-Asian culture was often obscured. The present study tested Cross-cultural Universality and variation of Causal Attribution. Study 1, through quality analysis of medias in China, Korea and USA, found that both Chinese and Korean medias tended to attribute in-group events to internal factors(-FAE), while Chinese and American medias attributed out-group events to external factors. Study 2 found that both Chinese and Korean participates revealed significant FAE in constructed-question condition, but revealed no FAE in open-question condition. At last, the authors discussed the cultural origin and variation factors of FAE.

FP-303: Task switching

Task switching with and without response-set switching

Konde, Zoltan Dep. of General Psychology, University of Debrecen, Debrecen, Hungary Barkaszi, Irén Institute of Psychology, Hungarian Academy Of Sciences, Budapest, Hungary

The contribution of response related processes to the difficulty of task switching was investigated using predictable and random task switching paradigms. In four experiments we contrasted task switching condition in which the reconfiguration of Stimulus-Response mapping was required with condition in which task switching was required without S-R reconfigurations and with condition in which S-R reconfiguration was required without task switching. Again response-stimulus interval was manipulated in all experiments. The results will be discussed in terms of controversy between reconfiguration account and response selection account of task switching.

Control failures and error processing in task switching

Steinhauser, Marco Inst. für Psychologie, Universität Konstanz, Konstanz, Germany Hübner, Ronald Fachbereich Psychologie, Universität Konstanz, Konstanz, Germany

The task-switching paradigm is used to investigate executive control involved in task-set reconfiguration and the resolution of task conflicts. Task errors occur when these control processes fail and an unintended task elicits its response. In a series of experiments, we examined the consequences of task errors and their detection for subsequent processing. Our results indicate that task errors imply associative strengthening of the wrong task even when errors are detected. However, error detection triggers processes that compensate the aftereffects of error learning. Together with a connectionist model, our data demonstrate how error processing compensates the negative consequences of control failures.

FP-304: Persuasion and communication II

The impact of gendered role models on self-efficacy and behavioural intention, as mediated by observers' goal orientation and models' speech-acts

Radu, Miruna ENTREPRENEURSHIP, ADVANCIA, Paris, France Popescu, Cristian POLITICAL THEORY, IEP, Le Perreux sur Marne, France

We conducted a 2*2*2 experiment in order to measure the effects of goal regulatory focus (promotion vs. prevention), exposure to feminine vs. masculine role models, and incentives vs. warnings on entrepreneurial intention and self-efficacy. We tested the gender congruence hypothesis (same-gender models are more effective) and the correspondence hypothesis (incentives are effective with promotion goals – warnings with prevention goals). 160 undergraduate students were exposed to role model testimonials and results, analyzed through ANOVA, largely confirm both hypotheses. Moreover, role models' impact is mediated by goal regulatory focus and speech-acts such as incentives or warnings.

What makes online word-of-mouth referrals effective? Impact of relationship aspects and senders' characteristic

Wiesner, Anja E-Learning, Education and Psychology, Linz, Austria Batinic, Bernad E-Learning, Education and Psychology, Linz, Austria

This study examines how word-to-mouth communication and their antecedents influence behaviors at different stages of the decision-making process. The reactions of 617 recipients were observed after receiving an e-mail from an acquaintance asking them to complete an online-survey. Consistent with expectations, logistic regression analyses show that aspects of the relationship between the sender and the recipient (tie strength, importance of relationship) and senders' personality traits (opinion leadership, expertise) influence recipients' responses. However, the extent of influence greatly varies at different stages. We discuss the potential of a multi-staged model in comparison to a single-outcome model regarding online marketing.

Corporate reputation and its impact on consumers' word-of-mouth behavior

Liu, Yuyu School of Business, Renmin University of China, Beijing, People's Republic of China Liu, Jun School of Business, Renmin University of China, Beijing, People's Republic of China Song, Jiwen School of Business, Renmin University of China, Beijing, People's Republic of China

Going beyond the existing literature of corporate reputation with two components (cognition and emotion), this study put forward a new component: behavior. The three components construct of corporate reputation has satisfactory validity, according to factor analysis using a sample of 253 consumers in the P. R. China. We also hypothesized that corporate reputation has positive impact on consumers' word-of-mouth referral behavior. Structural Equation Modeling (SEM) results demonstrated that the emotion component of corporate reputation had the highest predictive power on consumers' word-of-mouth behavior. Limitations and practical applications were offered.

Predicting the explicit and implicit effects of round and thin advertising models on product evaluations

Häfner, Michael Social and Organ. Psychology, Utrecht University, Utrecht, Netherlands Trampe, Debra Marketing, University of Groningen, AK Groningen, Netherlands

Remarkably, the bulk of research dealing with the effects of thin and round advertising models focuses on comparison processes and thus on the self-evaluative consequences of exposure to such models. Rarely any studies are devoted to investigating product evaluations as a function of different models. The present work aims to fill this void by systematically investigating the effects thin and round models exert on implicit and explicit product evaluations. In line with our hypothesis, results from three experiments suggest that round models yield only more positive explicit product evaluations but more negative implicit product evaluations as compared to thin models.

FP-305: Personality and well-being II

Empirical verification of a multidimensional appraisal-based resilience measure

Velichkovsky, Boris Psychology, Moscow State University, Moscow, Russia

The aim of the study was to develop and to verify empirically a state-trait multidimensional resiliency measure based on situation and coping resources appraisals. Anxiety, anger, and depression scales, scales of functional resources exhaustion, and various measures of adaptational outcomes were collected on 751 Russian subjects. Factor validity was tested with confirmatory factor analysis. Construct validity was shown with a derived composite resiliency index. High index scores correlated with more somatic and psychological health, dominance of positive emotions, less distress and less involvement in "stress spirals". Resiliency index moderated the stressor-stress relationship and identified individuals who thrive under stress.

Intentional model of emotional well-being: Measurement and convergent, divergent and incremental validity study

Simsek, Omer Dept. of Psychology, Izmir University of Economics, Izmir, Turkey

The major problem with current emotional well-being scales was that they lacked intentionality (being about something). A new emotional well-being scale was developed addressing intentionality. It focused on individuals' affective evaluations of their life and was showed to have good psychometric quality. In the second study, this new scale was shown to be structurally different from extraversion and neuroticism dimensions, a shortcoming of current emotional well-being scales, namely Positive and Negative Affect Scales (PANAS). This new measure was correlated with neuroticism and extraversion moderately. Moreover, it had better predictive and incremental validity than PANAS with regard to satisfaction with life.

Forgiveness of self and others and mental health: The search for causal explanations

Macaskill, Ann Dept. of Psychology, Sheffield Hallam University, Sheffield, United Kingdom

While there has been considerable growth in forgiveness research, the literature still contains many assumptions, frequently data is correlational, and causal links are missing. This research aims to explore possible causal links between forgiveness of self and others, mental health and life satisfaction using mediational analysis with large samples of undergraduate students. In the first study, trait anger and anger expression are found to be mediators of forgiveness of others and symptomatic mental health and subjective well-being. This is not the case for self-forgiveness confirming the distinctiveness of the processes. The second study examines other possible mediators of self-forgiveness.

The effects of work-related situational cues on intraindividual variation in the emotional and motivational states of managers

Minbashian, Amirali Accelerated Learning Labratory, University of New South Wales, UNSW, Australia Beckmann, Nadin Accelerated Learning Lab, University of New South Wales, Randwick, NSW, Australia Wood, Robert Accelerated Learning Lab, University of New South Wales, Randwick, NSW, Australia

The present study investigates the sensitivity of emotional and motivational states experienced by managers in their everyday work lives to work-related situational cues. Sixty managers were asked to report situational characteristics (e.g., people present, task difficulty, etc.) and emotional/motivational states at five random times each day over several weeks. We use hierarchical linear modelling to show that the typical manager experiences high amounts of variability in psychological states, and that this variability can be linked to various situational cues. The findings provide insights into how managers differentially react to work-related situations and guide the development of interventions for the effective functioning of managers at work.

FP-306: Personality and temperament from infancy to young adulthood

A study on preschool children's structure of sense of humor and its developmental characteristics and relationship with temperament: Based on teachers' perceptions

Liu, Wen Dept. of Psychology, Liaoning Normal University, Dalian, People's Republic of China Zou, Lina Department of Psychology, Liaoning Normal University, Dalian, People's Republic of China

A long term research has indicated that sense of humor(SOH) is closelyrelated to children's development of congniton,personality,social skill and emotions. In the preliminary studies we developed a sense of humor questionnair for preschoolers and explored the construct of children's SOH by means of the questionnaire by EFA and CFA. The construct of SOH for preshoolers has three elements:humor appreciation, humor production and humor coping. Significat age and gender differences of preschoolers' SOH were found.And temperament has obvious influence on SOH.

Temperament dimensions related to self-control in a community sample of children

Wills, Thomas Dept. of Epidemiology, Einstein College of Medicine, Bronx, USA Ainette, Michael Dept. of Epidemiology, Einstein College of Medicine, Bronx, USA Walker, Carmella Epidemiology, A Einstein College of Medicine, Bronx, USA

OBJECTIVE: To better understand how temperament dimensions are related to self-control characteristics. METHOD: The sample was 330 children (M age 9.3 years). Temperament scales were from Buss and Plomin, Rothbart, and Windle. Composites were assessed for good self-control (e.g., planfulness, problem solving, future time perspective) and poor control (e.g., distractibility, impulsiveness, nondelay of gratification). Temperament dimensions correlated with good self-control were persistence, attentional focusing, positive emotionality, low intensity pleasure, and sociability. Poor control was correlated with activity level, negative emotionality, irritability, rigidity, and frustration. Cross-correlations were minimal. CONCLUSIONS: The results support epigenetic models of development (Rothbart & Ahadi, 1994) and the two-factor model of impulse and constraint (Carver, 2005).

Continuity versus discontinuity of temperament between 3 months and 15 years of age: Results of a longitudinal study

Rollett, Brigitte Inst. für Entw.-Psychologie, Universität Wien, Wien, Austria Werneck, Harald Developmental Psychology, University of Vienna, Vienna, Austria Hanfstingl, Barbara Psychology, University of Klagenfurt, Klagenfurt, Austria

In the relevant literature, the stability of temperament from infancy to adolescence is controversially discussed. To study trajectories, we reanalysed the data of the longitudinal study "Family development in the course of life" (FIL), originally including 175 families (6 waves: pregnancy, child's age 3 months, 3, 8, 11, 15 years). Temperament of the target children was assessed at each wave. Clusteranalysis evinced highly variable proportions of children's groupings into types of temperament at the different age levels. Using Wold's PLS procedure, we developed a model of individual and family related indicators predicting temperament in adolescence.

FP-307: Clinical / counseling psychology V

Comorbid substance use disorder in patients with bipolar disorder

Mühlig, Stephan Inst. Klinische Psychologie, Tech. Universität Chemnitz, Chemnitz, Germany

Substance use disorders - SUD are significantly overrepresented in individuals with bipolar spectrum disorders. Comorbid SUD generally predicts poorer outcome and higher morbidity and mortality (suicide rate) in bipolar disordered patients. This presentation systematically reviews the common problems associated with establishing a bipolar disorder diagnosis in patients with concomitant SUD, as well as the treatment options that have been studied in this area. Although there are growing needs for developing special treatment approaches for this challenging patient population, only few clinical trials have been conducted to examine the efficacy of integrated programs to treat simultaneously the dual affected patients.

Stop, think and assess psychotherapy: Contributions from research on Portuguese dyads of therapists and clients

Soares, Luísa Psicologia e Estudos Humanisti, Universidade da Madeira, Funchal, Portugal

This study observed process and therapeutic result of 39 dyads of therapists and clients at 1st, 3rd, 5th and 8th session. The results suggest interesting considerations concerning the style of therapist and client. Help therapists to recognize his style, perceive his compatibility and levels of higher success with certain style of clients can improve his performance. Women and externalised profile of clients seemed to remain more in therapy than man and internalized profile. Also, identify levels of self-determination for therapy in client, could increase therapeutic success. Evaluation of therapeutic result (CORE-OM) could be implemented as regular practice in psychotherapy.

Perfectionistic self-presentation in relation to self-handicapping behavior and self-esteem in chinese college students

Song, Shanggui Dept. of Academic Affairs, Jinan University of Shandong, Jinan, People's Republic of China Yu, Hairong Psychology Department, Jinan University of Shandong, Jinan, People's Republic of China

The present investigation was to examine the relation of perfectionistic self-presentation to self-handicapping behavior and self-esteem. Five hundred and thirty-one college students in China participated in the study. The Chinese Perfectionistic Self-Presentation Scale, Chinese Self-Handicapping Scale, and Chinese Self-Esteem Scale were administered. Correlation analysis and regression analysis were conducted in the study. The results indicated: (1)Perfectionisctic self-presentation was positively associated with self-handicapping behavior; (2) Perfectionisctic self-presentation was negatively associated with self-esteem; (3) Perfectionisctic self-presentation and self-esteem were positive predictors of self-handicapping behavior. The implications of the study are discussed.

FP-308: Sensory-motor interactions III

Cognitive and neural mechanisms involved in goal inference

Liepelt, Roman Cognitive Neurology, Max Planck Institute, Leipzig, Germany von Cramon, D. Yves Cognitive Neurology, Max Planck Institute, Leipzig, Germany Brass, Marcel Experimental Psychology, Ghent University, Gent, Belgium

The observation of an action directly activates the internal motor representation in the observer. Although direct matching is simple it might underlie higher order cognitive processes, such as inferring other's goals. We tested behaviorally if goal inference and intention attribution modulates motor priming and found evidence for both. Further, we tested with functional magnetic resonance imaging which neural circuits are involved in goal inference. In line with mentalizing accounts, inferring goals from other's actions seems to be the outcome of a set of low-level computational processes taking place in right superior temporal sulcus (STS), the right temporo-parietal junction area (TPJ) and parts of the inferior parietal lobule (IPL).

Attentional biases toward the dominant hand during bimanual reaching

Buckingham, Gavin Dept. of Psychology, University of Aberdeen, Aberdeen, United Kingdom Carey, David P. Psychology, University of Aberdeen, Aberdeen, United Kingdom

Despite both hands being utilised in a huge array of tasks, there is little research into how attention interacts with the hands during bimanual reaching. Peters (1981) proposed that attention is biased toward the right hand of right handers during bimanual coordination, which may account for unimanual asymmetries in both performance and selection. In a series of studies investigating this hypothesis, the direction of attention during the performance of fast bimanual reaches was inferred from the performance in a following unimanual reach. The right hand consistently outperformed the left hand in conditions which suggest an attentional, rather than motoric asymmetry.

Perceptive invariants in autokinetic phenomenon

Druzhinin, Georgy IEAP, Moscow, Russia

Autokinetic apparent movement was recorded by subjects with no serious perceptive or cognitive anomalies. In fact the subjects recorded sequences of tangent vectors to the seen movement. The results show that each subject has his own stable strategies in geometrical transformations of visuo-motor space structure (parallel transfers, left and right rotations, waiting time etc.). Certain sound stimulation (music, speech, noise) changed the collection of used geometrical patterns, but these changes were test-retest stable. This fact yields the hypothesis about relatively stable perceptive styles that may be described in terms of local maps and manifolds in sensomotor space.

The impact of working memory load on eye-gaze cueing

Law, Anna Dept. of Psychology, John Moores University, Liverpool, United Kingdom Langton, Stephen Psychology, University of Stirling, Stirling, United Kingdom

Objectives: Two experiments investigated whether attentional cueing by eye-gaze is modulated by secondary tasks. Methods: In experiment 1, undergraduate participants were given a digit pre-load to hold in working memory during each gaze-cueing trial. In experiment 2, participants performed an auditory n-back task (0-back or 2-back). Results: In experiment 1 the secondary task did not modulate eye-gaze cueing – there was no effect of low load (1 digit) or high load (5 digits). However, eye-gaze cueing was reduced in experiment 2. Conclusions: Eye-gaze cueing is a powerful process and it is not easily disrupted, but it may not be entirely reflexive.

FP-309: Individualism / collectivism II

Culture, family and cognitive style

Arab-Moghaddam, Narges Behavioral Sciences, Iranian Academic center, Shiraz, Islamic Republic of Iran Jamshidy, Behnam Behavioral Sciences, Iranian Academic center, Shiraz, Islamic Republic of Iran Lartifian, Morteza

Behnam, Jamshidy; Morteza, Latifian; and Narges, Arab - moghaddam The aim of this research was to compare cognitive style of nomadic and urban students in interaction with parenting styles. Four hundred and five nomadic (N=200) and urban (N=205) students were selected via cluster random sampling method. Group Embedded Figure Test and Parenting Style Inventory were administrated. The analysis of co-variance (school grade was controlled) indicated that cognitive style and association between parental control and cognitive style is affected by cultural differences. It could be concluded that in collective cultures, parental control can have positive effect on cognitive style. Corresponding Author: Narges Arab - moghaddam; narabmoghaddam@yahoo.com

Cultural perspectives on school motivation: The relevance and application of goal theory within individualist and collectivist societies

McInerney, Dennis OER, Nation. Institute of Education, Singapore, Singapore Liem, Arief NIE, Nanyang Technological Universi, Singapore, Singapore

This paper reports a study with six cultural groups (Anglo-Australian, Anglo-American, Lebanese, Chinese, Aboriginal, and Navajo), reflecting individualism and collectivism in which the aim is to demonstrate the cultural relevance and applicability of goal theory to explaining and interpreting motivation in school settings. The paper describes the use of SEM to develop motivational scales representing achievement goals that have validity and reliability in cross-cultural settings, and the use of these scales for describing and explaining academic attitudes and achievement across these six cultural groups. Particular attention is paid to similarities and differences between groups based on the Individualism-Collectivism typology.

Is individualism and collectivism discernible by nonverbal behavior?

Pennig, Sibylle Social and Media Psychology, University of Cologne, Köln, Germany Bente, Gary Social and Media Psychology, University of Cologne, Cologne, Germany Senokozlieva, Maria Social and Media Psychology, University of Cologne, Cologne, Germany Krämer, Nicole Social Psychology, University of Duisburg-Essen, Duisburg, Germany

Individualism and collectivism are central dimensions for the comparison of cultures. The current study focuses on nonverbal behavior exhibited by different cultures and investigates the recognizability of individualistic and collectivistic values by these signals. Dyadic interactions with participants from the United Arab Emirates, the United States, and Germany were shown to a German sample. The use of a novel computer animation tool allowed masking the particular cultural background of the dyads. The results provide evidence that collectivism is discernible by nonverbal behavior and are discussed with respect to theoretical concepts of individualism and collectivism.

Conflict resolution of Sundanese and Chinese children in Bandung, Indonesia

Srisayekti, Wilis Dept. of Psychology, Padjadjaran University, Bandung, Indonesia

This study was aimed to describe the conflict-resolution-pattern of children from two subcultures in Bandung-Indonesia, and its relationship with the mother's value-orientation toward social relation. Subjects were 80 children (male and female, 9-12 year old, 40 Sundanese and 40 Chinese), with their mother. Their self-report on their conflict-experiences and the solutions were obtained through an interview. The individualism-collectivism tendency of mother's value orientation was classified from their reactions to the vignettes contained hypothetical situations. Results indicated that there was a similar description from both subcultures, for the

conflict-resolution-pattern of children and for its relationship with the mother's value-orientation.

FP-310: Competence development and competence management II

The relationship between competency model and the performance of human resource professionals in Chinese enterprises

Zheng, Xiaoming School of Management, Tsinghua University, Beijing, People's Republic of China Deng, Xiaofeng School of Management, Tsinghua University, Beijing, People's Republic of China Ulrich, Dave Ross School of Business, University of Michigan, Ann Arbor, USA Brockbank, Wayne Ross School of Business, University of Michigan, Ann Arbor, USA

Based on Michigan Human Resource Competency Study, our research focused on exploring the relationship between competency model and the job performance of human resource professionals in Chinese enterprises. The 1987 samples of 138 companies from HR professionals and their associates were collected through 360 degree feedback, and analyzed with exploratory factor analysis, confirmatory factor analysis and multiple regressions. The results showed that the competency model for HR professionals was composed of individual quality, human resource management skills, strategic contribution and business knowledge. HR competencies explain 43% of the overall performance of human resource professionals. There was the significant impact of HR competencies on HR professionals' performance.

Evaluation of the development of intercultural competence by culture-specific intercultural training

Behrnd, Verena Dresden, Germany

The evaluation of the development of intercultural competence in its sub domains by didactic versus experimental intercultural training is examined. The sample consists of students participating in an additional education program about Latin America and a control group. The culture-specific instrument consists of critical incidents in the sub domains individual, social and strategic intercultural competence and the use of problem solving strategies that have been proved successful in business proposals. Statistical analysis shows significant enhancement of social and individual intercultural competence and problem solving after experiential training and shows the necessity of including intercultural trainings in skill development programs.

Ethnotolerance as orientation of professional behavior of railway transport workers

Popova, Galyna of Railway Transport Ukraine, State Scientific-Research Cent, Kiev, Ukraine Samsonkin, Valeriy Director, SSRCofRT, Kiev, Ukraine

Purposes: determining the role of ethnic factor of conflicts nature in the limited space conditions (passengers transportation on railways), analyzing cognitive and affective components of railways' workers and policemen aims in relation to passengers of other nationality. Methods: modification of the Rozenzweig test, Bogardus scale, questioning, mathematical statistics. Results. Examinees aims have stereotype: the more personality perceived by a worker differs on external parameters from the own ethnic group, the more negative opinion and relation is expressed in relation by him/her. Conclusions. The program of aim forming for ethnotolerance consciousness and prophylaxis of extremism is based on teaching to the base techniques for inter-group communication and conflicts control.

Gender and development of self esteem in professional context: The case of teachers

Piperini, Marie Christine ISPEF, Université Lyon 2, Lyon, France

Working life and personal characteristics interact on self-esteem and its facets. 219 teachers and 219 students who would be teaching (313 women, 125 men), was examined with the S. Coopersmith's inventory. The results make it possible to state that there are differences inter-gender on the feeling of professional competence and self-esteem is an ambiguous and a little weak quality of teachers, evolving during career.

FP-311: Emotion II

Evaluation of a training program to increase emotional well-being among immigrants

Brenk, Charlotte Inst. für Psychologie, Universität Koblenz-Landau, Landau, Germany Schmitt, Manfred Psychology, University Koblenz-Landau, Landau, Germany

Rigid culture specific schemata in social situations can lead to wrong interpretations and to negative emotion. We propose that these consequences can be avoided by increasing the flexibility of situation perception. This idea was implemented in an intercultural training program. To test the effectiveness of the program, N = 39 immigrants were trained. Effectiveness was tested using several cognitive, emotional, and behavioral criteria as outcome variables. Comparisons between baseline, post test, and follow up test as well as between experimental and control group via analysis of variance procedures suggest effectiveness of the program regarding the measured outcomes (p < .05).

Emotion within or between people: Emotion expression and emotion inference across cultures

Uchida, Yukiko Kawanishi, Hyogo, Japan Townsend, Sarah Psychology, UC Santa Barbara, Santa Barbara, CA, USA Markus, Hazel Psychology, Stanford University, Stanford, CA, USA

Studies tested the hypothesis that in European American (EA) contexts, emotions are understood as primarily subjective, whereas in Japanese (JA) contexts, emotions are understood as inter-subjective. JA participants, relative to EA, were more likely to infer that an athlete was experiencing emotions when they read a self-description in which the target mentioned her relationships. Furthermore, when shown a photograph of athlete either alone or with teammates, JA participants inferred that he was experiencing more emotions when shown with his teammates, while EA participants inferred that he was experiencing more emotions when alone.

Measuring adolescents subjective well-being. How many items and dimensions are required? A Rasch-based item-reduction study

Erhart, Michael School of Public Health, Bielefeld University, Bielefeld, Germany Ravens-Sieberer, Ulrike School of Public Health, Bielefeld University, Bielefeld, Germany Europe, KIDSCREEN Group School of Public Health, Bielefeld University, Bielefeld, Germany

To test how far the 10-dimensional KIDSCREEN-52-item subjective well-being instrument could be reduced without loosing crucial information, reliability and validity. 20000 children and adolescents from 13 European countries answered the mailed KIDSCREEN-52. Parallel item reduction strategies (Rasch, differential item functioning, factoranalysis) were applied. A 6-dimensional 31-item short-version captured 71,9% of the original variance (canonical correlation) and achieved similar reliability (0.79-0,89) and validity (0,20-0,57). A 15-item index represented 39.3% variance (reliability=0.87) with inferior validity (0.14-0.52). Reducing items and dimensions to 3/5 enabled comparable assessment. The short-index could be applied for screening for psychological aspects of subjective well-being.

FP-312: Factors of influencing stress and coping behavior II

Locus of control as a moderator in personality and occupational stress linkage: A case study of telecommunication personnel
Das Swain, Rasmita Dept. of Psychology, University of Jammu, Jammu, India
This study investigated the personality, occupational stress and locus of control of government and private telecommunication personnel. Results indicated that there was no significant difference between personality and locus of control of personnel belonging to government and private organisations except occupational stress. The effect of age was insignificant. There were negative co-relation between personality, occupational stress and locus of control. The path analysis revealed that locus of control as a moderator could establish positive linkage between personality and occupational stress. Implications for how telecommunication organisations might work more effectively with different age group personnel are discussed. Keywords: Locus of Control, Personality, Occupational Stress

Sense of coherence in military medical students
Grossmann, Petr Military Hygiene, FVZ UO, Hradec Kralove, Czech Republic Burdova, Veronika Military Hygiene, FVZ UO, Hradec Kralove, Czech Republic Voseekova, Alena Hygiene and Preventive Medici, Faculty of Military Health Sci, Hradec Kralove, Czech Republic
Sense of Cohence (SOC) is a basic quality of a human personality. It is one of the salutoprotective factors (like coping styles, percieved social support etc.) The position on the scale of vulnerability – coherence indicates the capacity of coping with stress. The emotional quality of SOC moderates the potential pathophysiological reaction to stress. Monitoring of SOC can be widely used in psychological work with performers of stress exposed professions (firemen, rescue workers etc.). A high rate of SOC was found in students of military medicine, i.e. young adults preparing for work in stressful situations (caring profession in battle conditions). Their avarage SOC value is 151. A qualitatively assessed case study is consistent with quantitative assessment of SOC.

Challenge and hindrance job demands, job resource and their relationships with vigor and exhaustion: A two-wave study
Siu, Oi-Ling Sociology and Social Policy, Lingnan University, Hong Kong, China, People's Republic of : Hong Kong SAR Lin, Lin Chinese Academy of Sciences, Institute of Psychology, Beijing, People's Republic of China Shi, Kan Graduate University of CAS, Chinese Academy of Sciences, Beijing, People's Republic of China
This study focused on job demands (JDs), job resource (JR), and their relationships with vigor and exhaustion. Results of SEM of a two-wave survey of 200 nurses indicated that: a) JR enhanced vigor exclusively; b) hindrance JD decreased vigor, while challenge JD increased vigor; c) both forms of JDs aggravated exhaustion. In addiction, it was also found that vigor fully mediated the relationship between job characteristics and job performance, whereas exhaustion fully mediated the relationship between JDs and health problems. Results suggested research and practice on engagement could benefit by distinguishing among challenge and hindrance JDs.

FP-313: Instruction, construction, and learning: Specific trainings, teaching practices, text-books I

Constructivism and the US classroom in the 21st century
Flattau, Pamela Ebert IDA STPI, Washington, USA
Among theories of cognitive development, constructivism reveals the most "conspicuous psychological influence on curriculum thinking" in the late 20th century (Fensham, 1982). More recently, contemporary debates have centered around the appropriate balance between "direct instruction" and more guided learning typical of constructivist thinking for science and mathematics education. In 2007, the IDA Science and Technology Policy Institute explored trends in pedagogical research and national support in that area.

Self-generated drawings for supporting comprehension of complex dynamics
Mason, Lucia Dept. DPSS, University of Padova, Padova, Italy Coral, Valentina DPSS, University of Padua, Padova, Italy Lowe, Richard K. Education, Curtin University of Technolog, Perth, Australia
Learner transformation of content from one representation to another is a common educational strategy. However, this strategy is largely associated with "writing to learn" approaches. Educational effects of transforming content by generating drawings remain largely unexplored. Students watched an animation of Newton's Cradle, a dynamic device that is visuospatially simple but temporally complex, and drew sets of pictures to explain its operation. Immediate and delayed written posttests required students to explain the Newton's Cradle dynamics. Comparison with pretests indicated that although self-generated drawings can be effective in helping students extract relevant information from the animation, the benefit obtained is short-lived.

Theoretical and reflective thinking: Effects of different instructional approaches
Krause, Ulrike-Marie Inst. für Bildung, Universität des Saarlandes, Saarbrücken, Germany Stark, Robin Education, Saarland University, Saarbruecken, Germany
We investigated effects of situated direct instruction and scaffolded situated learning on theoretical and reflective skills of preservice teachers. Two seminars on anxiety and aggression in school were implemented by the same lecturer. Students should be encouraged to deal with the topic in a scientific way instead of relying on naïve theories. Seminar 1 (N = 22) consisted of direct instruction with exercises, seminar 2 (N = 30) focussed on self-regulated case work and moderated discussions. In both seminars, the same theories and authentic cases were addressed. Preliminary analyses (ANOVA) revealed a significant superiority of situated direct instruction.

FP-314: Self perception

Mediating processes Involved in the relationship between rejection sensitivity, aggressive responses and self-silencing behaviors
Goncu, Asli Inst. of Psychology, Middle East Technical Univ., Ankara, Turkey Sumer, Nebi PSYCHOLOGY, MIDDLE EAST TECHNICAL UNI., ANKARA, Turkey
The aim of the research is to provide an empirical test of the mediating role of attributions in the relationship between Rejection Sensitivity (RS) and aggressive responses and self-silencing behaviors. The link between RS, violence and hostility is suggested to be mediated by negativity attributed to partner intentions as well as responsibility and blameworthiness attributions to self and partner. On the other hand, RS is proposed to be associated with self-silencing behaviors through the mediation of self-attributions. The proposed model is tested

with SEM. The results will be discussed in terms of implications for future research and practice.

Curiosity from two perspectives: Self- and other-ratings
Hartung, Freda-Marie Inst. für Psychologie, Universität Konstanz, Konstanz, Germany Renner, Britta Psychology, University of Konstanz, Konstanz, Germany
Curiosity is a basic driver for learning and development. The present study (N=182) assessed curiosity as a personality trait from two perspectives: self-ratings and observer ratings. The results indicate that self and observer ratings were based on different information. Observer relied on appearance-related cues of the target and projected their own personality traits onto the target. Conversely, self-ratings were more related to other traits such as emotional sensitivity rather than specific appearance-related cues. The findings suggest that curiosity represents a "visible" trait. However, self- and other conceptions diverge systematically.

The perceived self-consistency influences self-esteem, subjective well-being and psychology well-being
Huang, Yunhui Dept. of Psychology, Peking University, Beijing, People's Republic of China Wang, Lei Psychology Department, Peking University, Beijing, People's Republic of China
Individuals perceived self-consistency influenced their self-esteem and well-being. Under time pressure, participants reported weather 67 adjectives were good descriptions of themselves in the eyes of themselves and in the eyes of others randomly. One point was given once evaluations in the eyes of self and others were consistent for the same adjective. Participants' self-esteem, subjective well-being (including general life satisfaction, subjective vitality, positive and negative affect), and psychological well-being were also assessed. Results showed that such perceived self-consistency positively related with participant's self-esteem and well-being. Moreover, the self-esteem was the mediator between perceived self-consistency and well-being variables.

Stages in the help-seeking decision-making process and factors involved
Setiawan, Jenny Lukito Universitas Ciputra, Surabaya, Indonesia
This paper describes a study designed to investigate stages in the help-seeking decision-making process and factors involved. Multimethod design was adopted which involved 1,279 respondents. Results found that there was a hierarchical system in coping behaviour. Respondents tried to face their problems on their own before seeking help. Internal resources and problem perceived, social impacts, and personal characteristics were involved in help-seeking decision process. Personal qualities of and familiarity with the potential helpers, perceived capacity to help, social role and the accessibility of the potential helpers, guarantee of confidentiality were considered in the selection of helpers.

FP-315: Affective neuroscience

Inhibition dysfunction in depression: Event-related potentials during negative affective priming
Liu, Mingfan Nanchang, People's Republic of China
The study aims to investigate neurophysiological correlates of inhibition deficit for negative materials using event-related potentials in depressed patients. Data collected from 18 patients with unipolar depression and 18 controls was analyzed in a negative priming affective task. ERPs revealed the neurophysiological correlate of this deficit. In addition to reduced P2 amplitude for negative trials and reduced late positive component amplitude for positive and negative trials in patients, the ERP

differences of different conditions were also found in response to negative experimental targets. Inhibition dysfunction of negative affect influences the earlier attention allocation and the later evaluation in patients.

Autonomic and self-reported responses to emotional pictures in anorexic, alexithymic and depressed participants

Nandrino, Jean-Louis Dept. of Psychology, University Lille 3, Villeneuve d'Ascq, France *Hot, Pascal* Psychology, University Chambery, Chambery, France *Dodin, Vincent* Psychiatry, Saint Vincent de Paul Hospital, Lille, France *Latree, Julie* Psychology, University Lille3, Villeneuve d'Ascq, France *Decharles, Sandra* Psychology, University Lille3, Villeneuve d'Ascq, France *Bouwalerh, Hammouh* Neurosciences, University Lille1, Villeneuve d'Ascq, France *Berna, Guillaume* Psychology, University Lille3, Villeneuve d'Ascq, France *Sequeira, Henrique* Neurosciences, University Lille1, Villeneuve d'Ascq, France

Recent findings concerning anorexia allow us to hypothesize that anorexic patients can express a disconnection between physiological and cognitive self-reported responses to emotional stimulations. Therefore, the present study compared skin conductance responses (SCRs) and subjective variables (valence, arousal ratings) induced by emotional pictures (pleasant, unpleasant) in anorexic (AN), alexithymic (AL), depressed (DEP) and control participants (CONT) during a categorization and an activation ratings tasks. Main findings showed that, in AN, the SCRs amplitude did not increase according to the self-reported activation ratings. In conclusion, preliminary results suggest that AN develop a specific emotional processing distinct from alexythimia and depression.

Changes of hemisphere-specific cognitive performance after manipulation of valence, motivational direction and intensity of affect by emotionally contagious film clips

Papousek, Ilona Inst. für Psychologie, Universität Graz, Graz, Austria *Lang, Brigitte* Psychology, Karl-Franzens University Graz, Graz, Austria *Schulter, Günter* Psychology, Karl-Franzens University Graz, Graz, Austria

In the framework of the models on (prefrontal) laterality and affect, we examined if relative performance in verbal and figural fluency tests changed after the induction of specific affective states. Using a within subjects design (n=70), affective states were experimentally induced by specially developed film clips. Results of repeated measures analyses of variance / planned comparisons indicate that changes in hemisphere-specific performance are attributable to the emotional dimensions that were varied. To advance research in this field, attempts to disentangle the effects of different emotional dimensions seem to be valuable, even if it might not be possible to accomplish the task in a perfect way.

Neural correlates of emotion processing under working memory demands

Schäfer, Axel Inst. für Klin. Psychologie, Universität Graz, Graz, Austria *Bischoff, Matthias* Clinical Psychology, University of Giessen, Giessen, Germany *Hermann, Andrea* Clinical Psychology, University of Giessen, Giessen, Germany *Vaitl, Dieter* Clinical Psychology, University of Giessen, Giessen, Germany *Schienle, Anne* Clinical and Health Psychology, University of Graz, Graz, Austria

Interactions of negative emotions (fear, disgust) and working memory (WM) are not well understood. We studied 29 females who performed 0- and 2-back tasks with fear and disgust inducing visual stimuli during fMRI scanning. While behavioural data remained largely unaffected, increased neural activity occurred in the anterior cingulate in both fear and disgust conditions compared to neutral

control stimuli under high workload demands. Also, correlations with trait measures of anxiety, disgust sensitivity, and behavioral inhibition with typical WM and emotion processing regions were observed. Results point to increased effort counterbalancing interference of emotional processes with WM.

Individual differences in disgust imagery: An fMRI study

Schienle, Anne Inst. für Klin. Psychologie, Universität Graz, Graz, Austria *Schäfer, Axel* Clinical Psychology, University of Graz, Graz, Austria *Hermann, Andrea* Clinical Psychology, University of Giessen, Giessen, Germany *Pignanelli, Roman* Clinical Psychology, University of Giessen, Giessen, Germany *Vaitl, Dieter* Clinical Psychology, University of Giessen, Giessen, Germany

This functional magnetic resonance imaging (fMRI) study investigated individual differences in visual disgust imagery. Twenty-four females were asked to first view and subsequently visualize disgust- and happiness inducing pictures. Relative to disgust perception, disgust imagery provoked activation in the bilateral insula, the ACC and the inferior parietal cortex. The reported vividness of imagery was positively correlated with activation in the aforementioned brain regions. Negative correlations were observed between trait disgust and inferior parietal activity. Altogether, disgust-sensitive individuals tended to report less clear disgust visualizations and showed reduced activation in brain areas that are relevant for vivid disgust imagery.

FP-316: Neuropsychology III

Asymmetries in prism adaptation and unilateral neglect

Redding, Gordon Dept. of Psychology, Illinois State University, Normal, USA

Proprioceptive adaptation only transferred from exposed (dominant) right hand to unexposed left hand, indicating lateralized limb control and only right hemisphere mapping of both left and right body space. Visual adaptation only transferred from exposed (non-dominant) left hand to unexposed right hand, suggesting directional right-to-left hemispheric control supplements left hemisphere representation of right space. Results are interpreted to indicate that right hemisphere damage disrupts inter-hemispheric control, leaving left body space unavailable for right hand action. Damage may also disrupt lateralized control of the left hand with further neglect of left body space and may produce concomitant bias of eye movement control leaving only right space in the left hemisphere available for intentional visual action.

Hemispheric asymmetries in discourse processing: Evidence from false memories for lists and texts

Benartzi, Elisheva Dept. of Psychology, Kinneret College, Emek Hayarden, Israel *Faust, Miriam* Psychology, Bar-Ilan University, Ramat-Gan, Israel

Objectives: To examine whether the right-hemisphere coarse semantic coding extends to memory for text-related meanings. Method: Thirty-five participants were tested on the word-lists false memory paradigm (Roediger & McDermott, 1995) to examine susceptibility of the left (LH) and right (RH) hemispheres to unpresented target words following the presentation of semantically related words appearing in either word lists or short texts. Results and Conclusions: The RH produced more false alarms than the LH for unpresented target words. However, this hemispheric difference was more pronounced for texts than for word lists, supporting the RH coarse semantic coding theory (Beeman, 1998).

Seeing without one or both cerebral hemispheres

Werth, Reinhard Inst. für Neuropsychologie, LRZ - Universität München, München, Germany

The visual functions of nine children who had suffered the loss of one or both cerebral hemispheres, were examined using a specially designed arc perimeter. The results show that even after complete hemispherectomy in early life the visual field may have a normal extent. After the destruction of both cerebral hemispheres, two children were still able to follow a stimulus that was shown in the foveal region with eye and head movements. One cerebral hemisphere may represent the whole visual field receiving input from both hemiretinae. Neural structures in the midbrain are able to mediate visual functions in the fovea.

Exploring the high dimensional semantic space in the brain

Sikström, Sverker Dept. of Cognitive Science, Lund University, Lund, Sweden *Kallioinen, Petter* Cognitive Science, Lund University, Lund, Sweden

Processing of words from semantic word classes activates networks of semantic representations in the human brain, which has been investigated by subtracting brain activity evoked from two semantic word categories. Here we show that arbitrary semantic representations in the brain can be investigated by utilizing high dimensional semantic spaces, generated from LSA. We correlate estimates of semantic distance with ERP potentials recording during word processing to study semantic representations in the brain. The results show that a large number of different semantic categories show specific topographical patterns across time. This method has several advantages compared to the subtraction method.

FP-317: Nonverbal communication

The role of masculinity, femininity, androgyny and sex on nonverbal decoding accuracy among Czech college students

Trnka, Radek Dept. for Research, Faculty of Humanities ChU, Prague 5, Czech Republic *Panama, Jose* Department of Ethology, Research Institute of Animal P, Prague, Czech Republic *Blažek, Vladimir* Department of Anthropology, West Bohemia University, Pilsen, Czech Republic

College students (f=101, m=100) judged slides of 7 basic facial expressions. Afterwards, students filled out the Czech version of the Personal Attributes Questionnaire. Groups of masculine, feminine, androgynous and undifferentiated persons were created by median split method. Data were assessed in GLM with decoding accuracy for facial expressions as a dependent variable and sex of subjects and M-F types as effects. Biological sex was found to be significant for correct recognition of facial expressions. M-F types had no significant influence to accuracy of decoding of facial expressions. Females reached significantly higher accuracy scores for facial expressions than males.

Designing an international knowledge system on the meaning of facial behavior

Merten, Jörg Clinical Psychology, Psychology, Saarbrücken, Germany

Among the nonverbal channels the facial behavior has the capacity to send the most specific information about emotional states and cognitive appraisal processes. The board of the "International Society for Facial Expression"(www.facial-expression.org) starts a WWW-based knowledge system to gather and evaluate empirical studies in a database to further research and practical applications in the realm of facial behavior. Especially effects of contextual information on the meaning of the facial behavior like gender and cultural differences will be addressed in the database. In the presentation the design of the database (inclusion criteria, content structure) and first results will be presented.

Brain mechanisms underlying human communication

Noordzij, Matthijs F.C. Donders Centre, Radboud University Nijmegen, Nijmegen, Netherlands *Newman-Norlund, Sarah* F.C. Donders Centre, Radboud University Nijmegen, Nijmegen, Netherlands *De Ruiter, Jan Peter* MPI Psycholinguistics, Max Planck Institute, Nijmegen, Netherlands *Hagoort, Peter* F.C. Donders Centre, Radboud University Nijmegen, Nijmegen, Netherlands *Levinson, Stephen* MPI Psycholinguistics, Max Planck Institute, Nijmegen, Netherlands *Toni, Ivan* F.C. Donders Centre, Radboud University Nijmegen, Nijmegen, Netherlands

Human communication involves more than language abilities or symbolic codes: it relies on the attribution and anticipation of communicative intentions. We isolate this ability by using a task requiring communication without prior conventions. Planning communicative actions and recognizing their communicative intention relied on the same brain region, the right posterior superior temporal sulcus (measured with fMRI). The response of this region was lateralized to the right hemisphere, modulated by the ambiguity in meaning of the communicative acts, but not by their sensorimotor complexity. This finding supports that our communicative abilities are distinct from both sensorimotor processes and language abilities.

Constituent order in communication

Langus, Alan Dept. Cognitive Neuroscience, SISSA, Trieste, Italy *Nespor, Marina* Scienze Umane, Università d. Studi d. Ferrara, Ferrara, Italy

A consistent order of constituents is presumably the easiest way to guarantee the clarity of non-linguistic communicative messages. The present study investigates whether there is an underlying order in communication. In Experiment 1, Italian native speakers had to describe simple scenarios using only gestures. The results show a strong preference to place gestures of Subjects and Objects before those of Actions – a non-canonical order in Italian. Experiment 2 measured participants' reaction times to video-taped gesture strings that differed only in their constituent order. The results are discussed in the light of emerging (sign-)languages, language change as well as language acquisition.

Gesture as effective teaching tools: Are students getting the point?

Rumme, Paul Dept. of Information Science, Nagoya University, Nagoya, Japan *Saito, Hirofumi* Information Science, Nagoya University, Nagoya, Japan *Ito, Hiroshi* Information Science, Nagoya University, Nagoya, Japan *Oi, Misato* Information Science, Nagoya University, Nagoya, Japan *Lepe Garza, Alberto* Information Science, Nagoya University, Nagoya, Japan

To examine the effectiveness of human pointing gestures and laser pointer in teaching English prepositions to L2 learners, we assigned three school classes to conditions illustrating prepositions of place with 1) pointing gestures, 2) laser pointer, or 3) without additional support. The students' task was to complete a pretest to evaluate knowledge of prepositions, watch a video describing the use of prepositions, and complete a posttest to evaluate the learning effect of the video. Results showed students in the gesture condition scored higher than the laser condition and the control condition, suggesting gestures are effective attractors for presenting prepositional concepts.

FP-318: Computers in psychological research

The game of mind-reading: Online-poker as a research tool

Breuer, Johannes Sozial- und Medienpsychologie, Universität zu Köln, Köln, Germany *Eschenburg, Felix* Sozial- und Medienpsychologie, Universität zu Köln, Köln, Germany *Bente, Gary* Sozial- und Medienpsychologie, Universität zu Köln, Köln, Germany *Aelker, Lisa* Sozial- und Medienpsychologie, Universität zu Köln, Köln, Germany

The process of mind-reading is essential for many social interactions and also a central element of playing poker. The characteristics of online-poker can be used to study skills like mind-reading, deception and hiding, since it offers control over cards, high involvement, recording possibilities, objective performance measures and a standardized course. The lack of social cues in online-poker could be compensated by feeding back data from different measurements (e.g. gaze or arousal) into the game. In a first exploratory study we recorded galvanic skin response, pulse volume amplitude, eye-movement, mimics and game events to identify relevant social cues in this context.

The use of mouse and keyboard in response time researches

De Marchis, Giorgio P. CAP2, Universidad Complutense, Madrid, Spain *Trespalacios, José Luis F.* Básica II, UNED, Madrid, Spain *Rivero, María del Prado* Básica II, UNED, Madrid, Spain

The three most common ways to collect data in experiments measuring response time (RT) with computers are keyboard, verbal responses, and mouse. The aim of this research is to elucidate the differences due to the use of keyboard or mouse devices. Groups of twenty subjects each and various blocks have been compared. Ceteris paribus. Data were analysed with ANOVA. In the keyboard results exists an order (learning) effect. Such effect does not appear using the mouse device. The mouse shows more meaningful differences than the keyboard in the interference among blocks. As a criterion validity we have used the semantic gradient. Both devices give similar, although not identical, results.

Measuring social desirability in web surveys through client-side paradata

Van Acker, Frederik AROR, Vrije Universiteit Brussel, Brussels, Belgium *Theuns, Peter* AROR, Vrije Universiteit Brussel, Brussels, Belgium

In some situations people tend to answer questions in a socially desirable manner. Several instruments have been developed to measure the extent to which respondents do this (e.g. Crowne, & Marlowe, 1960; Stöber, 2001), however some of these scales can be faked (Furnham, & Henderson, 1982). There is some evidence that socially desirable answering is reflected in response times (Holtgraves, 2004; Holden, Wood, & Tomashewski, 2001). In this study a method is tested to assess social desirability in online surveys basing on client-side paradata, namely item response time and response changes. Social desirability is induced in one group, and response behavior is compared to a control group.

EQUIWORD: A software application for the automatic creation of truly equivalent word lists

Lahl, Olaf Inst. für Exp. Psychologie, Universität Düsseldorf, Düsseldorf, Germany *Pietrowsky, Reinhard* Inst. of Exp. Psychol., University of Düsseldorf, Düsseldorf, Germany

Word lists are most commonly used in the investigation of human memory. To prevent transfer effects, repeated measures require multiple lists of different words. Yet, the psycholinguistic properties of all lists should match as closely as possible to avoid confoundings. EQUIWORD is a Windows program that completely automates the creation of word lists that are truly parallel with respect to an arbitrary set of attributes. EQUIWORD takes existing or user-defined psycholinguistic databases as input and computes several coefficients of distance for all possible word pairs or tuples. On that basis, creating equivalent word lists is simply done by selecting the pairs/tuples with the lowest distance coefficients.

FP-319: Justice and fairness

Reactions to Injustice: Analysis of different social contexts

Pandey, Kavita Psychology, University Of Allahabad, Allahabad, India *Pande, Namita* Psychology, University Of Allahabad, Allahabad, India

The idea of Negative Justice (how people react when harm has been done) is the recent trend in justice research. The present study explored the role of different social contexts and the relationship between the offender and the victim in determining the reactions to injustice. An experiment was conducted using DirectRT where participants (N=60) responded for eight hypothetical scenarios of unfair incidence (offender being relative/known person or stranger) followed by four reactions (withdrawal, retribution, legal action, forgiveness) to unfairness. Taking legal action was the general trend. The later responses significantly determined by the intensity of harm and relationship with the offender.

Intelligence, belief in a just world, and the choice of strategies to restore justice

Spranger, Thomas Sangerhausen, Germany *Maes, Jürgen* Inst. für Bildung, Universität der Bundeswehr, München, Germany *Schuster, Julia* Faculty of Education, Bundeswehr University Munich, Munich, Germany

According to justice motive theory we defend our BJW using rational (e.g. attempts to restore justice, acceptance of personal limits) and irrational strategies (e.g. denial, blaming victims). We conducted an online-vignette study in which subjects were confronted with cases of violence that had happened to stimulus persons. Whereas subjects' IQ predicted the choice of rational strategies, BJW was the best predictor for the choice of irrational strategies. Using the recently developed multidimensional Just World Inventory (by Maes, Montada, and Schmitt) we were able to show that the choice of strategies is differentially connected to different facets of BJW.

Authority preference, individual/group setting and recipient merit or disadvantage as determinants of perceived distributive fairness in an Indian sample

Pandey, Vijyendra Dept. of HSS, Indian Institute of Technology, Kanpur, India

The present study examined the effects of High/ Low Authority preference, Individual/Group setting and Allocator/Recipient Role on the perceived distributive fairness of reward allocation to a non-disadvantaged meritorious recipient versus a low-merit disadvantaged recipient. Responses of a sample of Indian college students to a reward allocation scenario revealed that allocation to a Meritorious recipient was perceived to be more fair than that to a Disadvantaged recipient. The significant interactions between the variables deviated from expectations based on higher power distance, and relative collectivism among Indians. The findings were interpreted in terms of the changed perception of deservingness in the context of socio-economic development.

When illegitimacy make you act: Powerlessness and goal pursuit

Willis, Guillermo Byrd Psicología Social, Universidad de Granada, Granada, Spain Rodríguez-Bailón, Rosa Psicología Social, Universidad de Granada, Granada, Spain

Recent Models in Social Psychology state that power and its nature (i.e. legitimacy) have important consequences. It has been argued that power-holders, when compared with powerless people, have greater accessibility of their goals and tend to set them more quickly. In this paper we argue that when power differences are illegitimate, the opposite pattern can be found. For probing this hypothesis, two experiments were conducted. Results showed that powerless illegitimate participants, when compared with powerless legitimate ones, had their goals more accessible and needed less information for setting them. The implications of these findings for social change are discussed.

Trust does matter in social networks: A longitudinal study

Igarashi, Tasuku Dept. of Social Psychology, Osaka University, Osaka, Japan

A year-long survey was conducted to investigate the impact of generalized trust on a social network of 70 Japanese first-year undergraduates. Those with high generalized trust were less likely to nominate friends at the first semester, but this trend was reversed throughout the summer vacation, and continued until the end of the school year. In other words, although those with high generalized trust might be active in relationship formation, they might be careful to form relationships at an initial stage so as to distinguish others to be trustworthy or not. These results imply the role of trust as social intelligence.

FP-320: Child and adolescent psychopathology IV

A comparative study on organization-planning executive function in adolescents with and without conduct disorder

Alizadeh, Hamid School of Psychology, Allameh Tabataba'i, Tehran, Islamic Republic of Iran Hashemi Azar, Janet School of Psychology, Allameh Tabataba'i, Tehran, Islamic Republic of Iran Askari, Marzieh School of Psychology, Allameh Tabataba'i, Tehran, Islamic Republic of Iran

This study was conducted to examine organization-planning executive function (EF) in adolescents with and without conduct disorder (CD). Sixty-nine adolescents aging 12-14, including 38 with CD, and 31without CD were recruited from schools in Tehran. The Child Symptom Inventory-4 and Diagnostic and Statistical Manual of Mental Disorders (2000) criteria were used for screening and diagnosis of the adolescents with DC. The Rey-Osterrieth figure test was administered to evaluate organization-planning EF. The findings revealed that there exists a significant difference between adolescents with and without CD (X2 = 15.56; p<.05This study provides evidence that adolescents with CD have considerable deficits in EFs.

Considerations regarding the under identification of children with Attention Deficit/Hyperactivity Disorder (AD/HD)

Zournatzis, Vaggelis Psychological Center 'ARSI"ARSI, Athens, Greece Karaba, Rania Psychological Center, Athens, Greece Badikian, Marilina Psychological Center "ARSI, Psychological Center, Athens, Greece Dalapa, Paraskevi Psychological Center "ARSI, Psychological Center, Athens, Greece Chatzaki, Voula Psychological Center "ARSI, Psychological Center, Athens, Greece

The study investigates adult perceptions that may lead to the underdiagnosis of AD/HD. Parents of 170 children diagnosed with AD/HD aged 6-17 completed the "AD/HD Rating Scale IV" (DuPaul, 1998). Rates of contact with mental health services were also examined.Two thirds of parents with children with AD/HD have already visited another specialist, but only half of them reported receiving adequate help. Most of them failed to recognize AD/HD symptomatology. Learning and behavioural difficulties were reported as the key problems rather than AD/HD symptoms. Improved training about AD/HD for mental health specialists and parents becomes a matter of the utmost importance in Greece, in order to minimize underdiagnosis of the disorder.

The effect of Social Skills Training (SST) on improving peer relationships in primary school boys with Attention Deficit/Hyperactivity Disorder (ADHD)

Tabaeian, Sayedeh Razieh psychology, Isfahan Univercity, Isfahan, Islamic Republic of Iran Amiri, Shole psychology, Isfahan Univercity, Isfahan, Islamic Republic of Iran Kalantari, Mehrdad psychology, Isfahan Univercity, Isfahan, Islamic Republic of Iran Neshatdoost, Hamid Taher psychology, Isfahan Univercity, Isfahan, Islamic Republic of Iran Karahmadi, Mojgan psychology, Medical Univercity of Isfahan, Isfahan, Islamic Republic of Iran

Objectives: The aim of this study was to investigate the effect of social skills training through direct training and parental training on improving peer relations in primary school children with attention deficit hyperactivity disorder. Methods: The subjects were 45 primary school boys who were diagnosed as having such disorder. Results: The results show the effectiveness of social skill training on improving peer relations (p<0.05). Conclusions: The pair comparisons showed that the combined social skills training (direct and parental training) together with medical therapy presented to the second experimental group had far more effects compared to just direct training.

Expressive and receptive language abilities in Spanish-speaking children with Attention Deficit/ Hyperactivity Disorder

Velez-Pastrana, Maria C. Clinical Psychology - Ph.D., Universidad Carlos Albizu, San Juan, Puerto Rico Figueroa, Mayra Speech-Language Pathology, Universidad Carlos Albizu, San Juan, Puerto Rico Bustillo, Maria Speech / Language Pathology, Universidad Carlos Albizu, San Juan, Puerto Rico Gonzalez, Francisco Clinical Psychology - Ph.D., Universidad Carlos Albizu, San Juan, USA Rodríguez, Samarí Clinical Psychology - Ph.D., Universidad Carlos Albizu, San Juan, USA Palou, Ana Clinical Psychology - Ph.D., Universidad Carlos Albizu, San Juan, USA Ilarraza, Tayra Clinical Psychology - Ph.D., Universidad Carlos Albizu, San Juan, USA Martinez, Julio Clinical Psychology - Ph.D., Universidad Carlos Albizu, San Juan, Puerto Rico

Study examines receptive and expressive language in Spanish-speaking children with Attention Deficit/Hyperactivity Disorder (ADHD). Sixty school children in Puerto Rico (ages 9 – 12), including 30 diagnosed with ADHD and a "normal" comparison group will be administered the Clinical Evaluation of Language Fundamentals® - 4th ed. (CELF® - 4) and Vocabulary and Block Design subtests from the Weschler Intelligence Scale for Children - Puerto Rico Revision). Student's t tests will compare the 2 groups' scores on all measures. We will discuss the study's results and implications, as they relate to the study of language and neuropsychological deficits among children with ADHD.

FP-321: Management styles and organizational culture I

Organizational culture perception and management satisfaction: A case study of a Spanish software development organization

Prado Gascó, Vicente Javier Psicologia Social, Universidad de Valencia, Valencia, Spain Quintanilla Pardo, Ismael Psicologia Social, Universidad de Valencia, valencia, Spain

Objectives: Analize the links between organizational culture and management satisfaction. Hyp: Some dimensions of a constructive style have a direct and positive relation with management satisfaction of workers Methods Administration of the Organizational culture inventory (OCI) and job satisfaction inventory. Analysis: Factor analysis correlations, regression (SPSS 14). Between OCIs dimensions and different dimensions of job satisfaction Sample=196 subjects from 270 workers. Results Self-Actualizing and Humanistic-Encouraging (constructive style dimensions) have a positive and direct influence on management satisfaction. Conclusions Other organizational or demographic variables may modulate the relation between organizational culture perception and job satisfaction. It has been considered in other works.

Culture and leadership styles in South Korean multinationals in India

Tripathi, Anand Prakash Dept. of Psychology, University of Delhi, New Delhi, India

Cultural contexts have differential effects on the perceptions of management practices by managers and professionals. This study explored the perceptions of the management styles and the organizational culture in both Indian and Korean organizational settings (n=165) and examined its relationship with leadership styles in Korean multinational organizations operating in India. The study employed qualitative and quantitative strategies for data collection. Findings revealed linkages between cultural context and dominant leadership styles. Also, changes in cultural perspectives and beliefs about effective leader behavior between Indian and Korean participants were noted. The implications for evolving culturally sensitive effective management practices are suggested.

Cultural intelligence: Construct and criterion related validity

Tang, Ningyu School of Management, Shanghai Jiaotong University, Shanghai, People's Republic of China Fu, Jia School of Management, Shanghai Jiaotong University, Shanghai, People's Republic of China Dai, Naling School of Management, Shanghai Jiaotong University, Shanghai, People's Republic of China Li, Xiaofei School of Management, Shanghai Jiaotong University, Shanghai, People's Republic of China

Based on Earley and Song's 4-dimension CI model, this paper studied the construct and criterion-related validity of CI in Chinese context. Study 1 surveyed 250 managers in Shanghai, Beijing and Shenzhen with CI, emotional intelligence (EI) and role-based performance questionnaires.The results showed that(1) CI could be differentiated from EI via EFA;(2) the four-dimension construct of CI was proved by CFA and (3) CI had significant effects on role-based performance. Using self-reports of CI and EI and supervisor-ratings of performance, Study 2 sampled managers and professionals in a Chinese company. The result also supported that CI could predict performance well.

FP-322: Neural bases of behavior I

Dependence of neuronal activation and trial-and-error behaviour during new skill acquisition on prior learning history

Svarnik, Olga Lab Neuronal Bases of Mind, Institute of Psychology, Moscow, Russia Fadeeva, Tatiana Lab Neuronal Bases of Mind, Institute of Psychology, Moscow, Russia Alexandrov, Yuri Lab Neuronal Bases of Mind, Institute of Psychology, Moscow, Russia

To study how prior learning history influences current acquisition of a new skill we analyzed neuronal activation, measured by c-fos gene expression, and animals' behavior during learning. Rats were trained an appetitive lever-pressing task on one side of the experimental chamber either by five-stage shaping procedure or by one-stage unsupervised procedure. After animals' performance reached the plateau level, they were retrained for similar operant behavior on the other side of the chamber. Although animals of both groups demonstrated outwardly similar behavior, learning strategies and neuronal activation in the cortical areas of animals of the two groups were different.

Limbic system is hyperactivated in readiness for speech moment in persons who stutter

Kiselnikov, Andrey Department of Psychology, Moscow State University, Moscow, Russia

Objectives. Stuttering is a frequent and stable disorder of speech. Our purpose was to study the psychophysiological mechanisms of stuttering with a cross-disciplinary set of neuroscientific methods. Methods. 23 subjects with stuttering and 18 fluent speakers were assessed through studying of visual, auditory and speech-related ERPs with dipoles localization and comprehensive Lurian neuropsychological examination. Results. We revealed hyperactivation of left limbic system during preparation to pronounce a word and neuropsychological defects (especially in memory, motor and neurodynamic spheres) concerned with weakness of the postfrontal and deep structures. Conclusions. The hyperactivated emotions generating limbic system interfere with normal preparation to speech.

Quasi-movements: Implications of a novel motor-cognitive phenomenon

Hohlefeld, Friederike U. Berlin, Germany

Can you do a movement without doing it? This paradoxical task constitutes the novel motor-cognitive phenomenon of "quasi-movements", which we define as volitional movements which are minimized by the subject to such an extent that finally they become undetectable by objective measures. Quasi-movements were explored with electroencephalography, electromyography, and rating scales. Despite the absence of motor responses, quasi-movements were associated with a sense of movement and strong neuronal activation over sensorimotor cortices. Our findings are applicable to neurocognitive studies of motor imagery, motor intention, and movement control. Furthermore, quasi-movements represent a new conceptual, effective approach for brain-computer interfacing.

FP-323: Creativity and culture II

Decoding the bilingual mind: Thinking and feeling in two languages

Javier, Rafael Dept. of Psychology, St. John's University, Queens, USA

Language is used to categorize and organize a wide range of experiences in ways that make possible for the information to be remembered and retrieved. In the case of bilinguals where two languages are involved, this process becomes complicated. In this paper I will examine the evidence for the bilingual mind and will discuss the implication of such a phenomenon on cognition, memory and emotional

development of those with more than one linguistic code to organize information.

Cultural influences on artistic creativity : A comparison between German and Chinese

Yi, Xinfa Bereich Gesundheitspsychologie, Freie Universität Berlin, Berlin, Germany Schwarzer, Ralf Freie Universität Berlin, Health Psychology, Berlin, Germany Lin, Chongde Beijing Normal University, Institute of Developmental Psy, Beijing, People's Republic of China Yu, Guoliang Renmin University of China, Institute of Psychology, Berlin, People's Republic of China

Objectives: (a) the rated creativity of artworks created by German and Chinese college students,(b) the criteria used by German and Chinese judges to evaluate these artworks. Methods: 45 German students and 61 Chinese students were recruited in the Experiment with two tasks. Results and conclusions: The study demonstrated that the two groups of students differed in their artistic creativity. German participants produced more creative and aesthetically pleasing artworks than did their Chinese counterparts, and this difference in performance was recognized by both German and Chinese judges. The results seem to support the hypothesis that an independent self-oriented culture is more encouraging of the development of artistic creativity than is an interdependent self-oriented culture.

The hermeneutics of acculturation: An analogical mapping strategy and six domains

Lee, Sang-Bok Pastoral Counseling Graduate, Kangnam University, Yongin, Republic of Korea

An analogical mapping perspective is applied to interpreting acculturative processes. The acculturation processes are interpreted from the analogical mapping perspective, more specifically, six domains for the analogical thinking. Lee reported Korean-American college students' rates of behavioral acculturation (Lee, 2006A), values acculturation (Lee, 2006B), and of unconscious acculturation represented in Korean-American college students' dreams (Lee, 2005). Lee (2005) designed "The Lee Acculturation Dream Scale" to analyze the location of each dream by evaluating the dream content, and reported that Korean-American college students' acculturation processes were represented in the unconscious dream images. The self has a capacity to adapt to different cultures.

The creation of substitutes: Social correlates for affective decoding in artwork

Andrews-McClymont, Jenna Decatur, USA Duke, Marshall Psychology, Emory University, Atlanta, USA

A relationship between social competency and the affective decoding of artwork was hypothesized since interpersonal studies have revealed a link between social skills and nonverbal, receptive abilities. A series of tasks matching emotion label or facial expression to art as well as social and mood measures were administered to sixty university undergraduates. Additionally, participants were randomly assigned to one of two treatment environments to test for ambient stimuli effects. Results supported the relationship between social competency and art decoding, and an interaction between environment and participant mood on decoding abilities was also discovered as the result of a regression analysis.

FP-324: Dysfunctional social behaviors in school: Aggression, anger and violence II

Conception, implementation and evaluation of a social and emotional learning program

Raimundo, Raquel FPCE-UL/ FCT, Costa de Caparica, Portugal Marques Pinto, Alexandra Psychology, FPCE-UL, Lisboa, Portugal Lima, Maria Luísa Social Organizational Psycholo, ISCTE, Lisboa, Portugal

This study analyses the conception, implementation and evaluation of a social emotional learning program, applied to 157, 4th grade students from 8 classes. Social competences, aggressive behaviour, academic behaviour, social isolation, social problems and anxiety were analyzed. The program was efficient on improving social competences and avoiding the increase of aggressive behaviours. Although in the correct direction, no significant differences were found regarding academic behaviour, social isolation and social problems. The intervention group presented more anxiety in the post-test. The results support the need to apply the program with a larger sample and to focus more on the internalised problems.

Peer relationship and school violence

Pulido, Rosa Dept. Educational Psychology, Alcala University, Madrid, Spain Martin Seoane, Gema Educational Psychology, Alcala University, Madrid, Spain

This study examines the relation between the social adjustment in the classroom and the role of aggressor or victim, in school violence situations. The general aim was to determine the relevance of different protective and risk factors in Secondary school students Participants were 1.635 students (aged 14-18 years), from a representative sample of Spanish high school students. The variables measured were: frequency of school violence (exclusion, psychological violence and physical violence) and adjustment to the classroom environment (rejected, controversial, neglected,...). From among the results we can point out the importance of these variables in the school violence situations. The implications of these findings and the relevance for preventive programs are discussed.

The effectiveness of multimedia learning in children with dysfuntional behavior

Castro, Nancy ITHM, University of Santo Tomas, Marikina City, Philippines

This study helps children maintain their well being despite of life difficulties. Multimedia learning is an instructional message in form of animation (Mayer, et al, 2004). It attempts to answer the following questions: What is the demographic profile of the participants in terms of: age, gender, and type of dysfunctional behavior? and Is there a significant difference between the posttest results of the control and experimental group? It was based on Bandura's Social-Cognitive Theory. The True Experimental Design was used. The two (2) groups were given a posttest of Children's Depression Inventory and Feelings, Attitudes, and Behaviors Scale for Children. It shows that multimedia learning has a significant effect to children with dysfunctional behavior.

Demographic influences on learners' disposition to violence in an African society

Ojo, Olubukola Educ. Found. and Counsell, Obafemi Awolowo University, Ile Ife, Nigeria Ajibike, Lawani EDUC. FOUND.$ COUNSELLING, OBAFEMI AWOLOWO UNIVERSITY, ILE-IFE, Nigeria

This study investigated the level of disposition to violence of learners from monogamous and polygamous African marriage forms and the influences of parental occupation and level of education. Six hundred learners were randomly selected from six local government areas of Osun state, Nigeria. The Students' Disposition to Violence Scale was used to collect information. The results revealed that that the percentage of learners from polygamous homes who were disposed to violence were higher than those from monogamous homes. It was also discovered that fathers occupation and mothers educational level were significant influences on the disposition to violence of learners.

FP-325: Emotional expression and experience in clinical populations II

Interactive regulation of affect in postpartum depressed mothers and their infants

Reck, Corinna Inst. für Psychiatrie, Universität Heidelberg, Heidelberg, Germany
Objectives Postpartum depression is associated with impaired mother-infant interaction in the first months of life which is thought to lead to later compromises in infant affect regulation and development. Methods A sample of 34 depressed dyads and 34 healthy dyads comparable for infant age and sex were videotaped in the Face-to-Face Still-Face Paradigm. Infants' ages were between 2 and 8 months. Results Healthy dyads had higher levels of positive affect and interactive coordination than depressed dyads (p=0.004, z=2.63). Conclusions These differences are likely to have long term compromising effects on the development of the mother-child relationship and the child's development.

Frequencies and effects of emotional crying in 415 psychosomatic patients: Are there two types of crying?

Rottler, Veronika Psychosomatische Medizin, Uniklinikum, Freiburg, Germany Brodner, Judith Psychosomatische Medizin, Uniklinikum, Freiburg, Germany Wirsching, Michael Psychosomatische Medizin, Uniklinikum, Freiburg, Germany Bauer, Joachim Psychosomatische Medizin, Uniklinikum, Freiburg, Germany
We investigated the frequencies and effects of crying in psycho- somatic outpatients. We applied an inventory asking the patients about (i) how often they cried and (ii) whether or not they felt relieved after crying. In addition to the clinical diagnosis, we applied a dissociative symptom and a somatoform disorder questionnaire. Predictors of frequent crying were female gender, dissociative symptoms, an affective disorder, and low education. Contraintuitively, high crying frequencies were not negatively, but rather positively related to dissociative symptoms. The proportion of patients feeling worse after crying was higher in the frequent crying group, compared to patients who cried less.

Deficits in the different components of empathy in schizophrenia patients

Derntl, Birgit Psychiatry and Psychotherapy, RWTH Aachen, Aachen, Germany Falkenberg, Irina Psychiatry and Psychotherapy, RWTH Aachen, Aachen, Germany Toygar, Timur Psychiatry and Psychotherapy, RWTH Aachen, Aachen, Germany Hülsmann, Anna Psychiatry and Psychotherapy, RWTH Aachen, Aachen, Germany Schneider, Frank Psychiatry and Psychotherapy, RWTH Aachen, Aachen, Germany Habel, Ute Psychiatry and Psychotherapy, RWTH Aachen, Aachen, Germany
Objectives: The ability to empathize with other people is an important prerequisite for successful social interaction. Patients with schizophrenia demonstrate deficits in perspective taking (Langdon et al., 2006) and emotion recognition (Gur et al., 2002), thus suggesting a dysfunctional emotional competence. Methods: To further clarify this deficit in schizophrenia patients, the different components of empathy were investigated with separate paradigms in patients and healthy controls. Results/Conclusion: Results indicate a significant empathy

deficit in patients in particular emotion experience is strongly impaired and should be further explored with respect to its neural correlates. Gur, R.E. et al. (2002). Am J Psychiatry 159, 1992-1999. Langdon, R., Coltheart, M. & Ward, P.B. (2006). Cognit Neuropsychiatry 11, 133-155.

Roles: Object-oriented vs. cognitive modeling

Sekharaiah, Chandra, K. College of Engineering, Jawaharlal Nehru Tech. Univ., Kakinada, A.P., India Gopal, U. Rakesh, U.G. Swapna, U.
In this paper, we investigate object schizophrenia problem (OSP), as relevant to role-related patterns such as bureaucracy pattern and some of the GOF patterns. Further, we present the computational details of the complexity of OSP in terms of degree of OSP. We present the details of the ongoing work to relate the software schizophrenia and the cognitive theories such as cognitive dissonance, Kelly's conceptualization of roles as cognitive constructs and psychological health. Our investigations in the form of a unique analogy of the problems in human cognitive systems Vs. software schizophrenia problems give some deeper insights in understanding the human schizohprenia-related issues in psychological health.

FP-326: Families in stress II

What do pediatricians and mothers talk about in the well-child program visits?

Nunes, Cristina Dept. de Psicologia, Universidade do Algarve, FCHS, Faro, Portugal
In Andalusia, pediatricians are the main counseling formal source about children's development and education, through the "Well-Child Program". Unfortunately, there is a limited knowledge about their practices and skills to guide parents and evaluate child's psychological development. In this study we analyzed, through content analysis, 49 pediatricians' visits from Seville. We described the visits' characteristics (format, length and communication patterns), discussed topics and pediatricians' recommendations to mothers. The results show that pediatrician's agenda focuses mainly on bio-medical issues. Child development and education are not priorities. We discuss the implications of the variability between professionals and strategies to improve the program.

Childhood attachment quality and coping with stress in married and single adults

Sepahmansour, Mojgan Dept. of Psycology, Islamic Azad University, Tehran, Islamic Republic of Iran Khoshnevis, Elaheh Psycology, Islamic.Azad.Unive.Teh.Central, Tehran, Islamic Republic of Iran Shahabizadeh, Fatemeh Psycology, Islamic.Azad.Unive.Teh.Central, Tehran, Islamic Republic of Iran
This study investigated how married adults cope with stress as a function of their childhood attachment style in compare with singles. Data were gathered from 104 adult individuals (M.A. university student of Islamic Azad University Central Tehran Branch) included measures of attachment to parents and ways of coping with stress. Single participant insecure respondent to mother had higher mean on confronting coping and escape – avoidance, and secure respondent to father had higher mean on confronting coping and seeking social support.

Participation in online infertility support groups: An exploratory qualitative study

Malik, Sumaira Nottingham, United Kingdom Coulson, Neil S Work, health & organisatio, University of Nottingham, Nottingham, United Kingdom
Objectives: The purpose of this study was to explore the online experiences of individuals accessing online infertility support groups. Method: 95 participants completed an online questionnaire

consisting of a series of open-ended questions exploring their reasons for and experiences seeking online support. Responses were analysed using thematic analysis. Results: Analysis revealed 5 themes: 'Information and empowerment', 'Reduced sense of isolation', 'Improved relationship with partner', 'Unique features of online social support', and 'Negative effects of online communities'. Conclusions: Although participants gained a range of benefits from participation, there were also a number of potential negative effects identified, which require further investigation.

A systematic review of infertility - psychology related aspects - in Sudan

Khalifa, Wisal School of Psychology, Ahfad University for Women, Omdurman, Sudan
Infertility – psychology related aspects - in Sudan Wisal Khalifa, PhD candidate, Ahfad University for Women, Khartoum - Sudan. The paper aims to present the results of an ongoing review on Psychology related aspects to infertility in Sudan. Coming up with psychological issues addressed or overlooked is the primary objective for the review in addition to review research methods and gender issues covered. Computer and hand search are methods for the data collection. Content analysis will be used to analyze the data collected. Conclusion and recommendation on the study will be drawn later based on the findings of this study.

FP-327: Gender differences in work and academic achievement II

Career development of young physicians: A follow up study

Alfermann, Dorothee Inst. für Sportpsychologie, Universität Leipzig, Leipzig, Germany Busse, Cindy Medical Psychology, University of Leipzig, Leipzig, Germany Stiller, Jeannine Medical Psychology, University of Leipzig, Leipzig, Germany Brähler, Elmar Medical Psychology, University of Leipzig, Leipzig, Germany
Objectives: To discover determinants of young physicians' career development and work-life balance with special emphasis on gender. Hypotheses: A masculine gender self-concept and male gender should facilitate a successful career. Methods: Participants completed questionnaires immediately after graduation from medical school and again four years later. Participants described and evaluated career development, family life, gender self-concept, and career success. Results: Though we found gender differences in career development gender self-concept was far more important. Masculinity was an important predictor for occupational success. Conclusions: In line with other research career development is influenced by gender and by gender self-concept, masculinity in particular.

Gender values and governance

Mukhopadhyay, Lipi Centre for HRD and Beh Studies, Indian Inst. of Public Adm., Delhi, India
Gender equity as a norm for sustainable development is accepted across the world. But in development projects and implementation the results are not very encouraging. This study examines gender role stereotypes, cultural diversity, religious and community influences on gender values and governance in North India of a local self government. Women elected members (25) and villagers (130) were interviewed on gender role stereotypes and values. Gender values are influenced by religion, cultural practices and stakes of the dominant group. Change in belief systems and values of the dominant group in a community is imperative for meaningful and proactive governance.

Gender differences in work and well-being: Signs of progress?

Fiksenbaum, Lisa Dept. of Psychology, York University, Toronto, Canada *Burke, Ronald J.* Business, York University, TORONTO, ON, Canada *Koyuncu, Mustafa* School of Tourism, Erciyes University, Turkey, Turkey

Women continue to enter the workforce in increasing numbers, yet few women reach the ranks of upper management. This research examines gender differences in work experiences and levels of psychological well-being in three different occupations in Turkey. Similar findings were noted in all three samples. First, significant gender differences were found on personal demographic and work situation characteristics, which is consistent with previous studies. Second, there were few differences on measures of work and career outcomes and psychological well-being, again consistent with recently reported research findings. We interpret the absence of difference on important work and well-being outcomes as signs of women's progress.

Research on factors influenced professional development of female teachers in university

Li, Yijing Organization Management, Shanghai Jiao Tong University, Shanghai, People's Republic of China *Tang, Ningyu* Organization management, Shanghai Jiao Tong University, Shanghai, People's Republic of China

With the rapid development of Chinese higher education, more female teachers work in the university, however they also encounter some so-called "glass ceiling" problems. Research indicates that woman's role orientation, work-family conflict and organizational support are closely related to the phenomenon. This article examined factors using questionnaire, interview and statistic analysis. The main conclusions indicated that? 1) Both male and female teachers pursue high career goals; 2) female teachers suffer more work-family conflicts than male teachers; 3) both male and female teachers consider the organizational support is very equal.

FP-328: Biopsychology

Sex hormonal modulation of interhemispheric interaction

Bayer, Ulrike Dept. of Psychology, University of Durham, Durham, United Kingdom *Hausmann, Markus* Psychology Department, University of Durham, Durham, United Kingdom

Previous neuropsychological and neurophysiological research has shown that changing sex hormone levels across the menstrual cycle affect interhemispheric interactions. The present study tested postmenopausal women with either estrogen replacement (n = 15), estrogen-progesterone replacement (n = 19) or with no hormone replacements (HRT) (n = 31) using tasks which cannot be performed without interhemispheric interaction. Saliva levels of estradiol and progesterone were analyzed using chemiluminescence assays. Results showed a HRT-related modulation in the efficiency of interhemispheric integration. Interhemispheric transfer time was not effected by HRT. The results suggest that estrogen affects specific aspects of functional cerebral organisation in older women.

Modulation of the desire for specific foods with transcranial direct current stimulation

Boggio, Paulo Psychology, Universidade Mackenzie, Sao Paulo, Brazil *Macedo, Elizeu Coutinho* Psychology, Universidade Presb. Mackenzie, Sao Paulo, Brazil *Orsati, Fernanda* Psychology, Universidade Presb. Mackenzie, Sao Paulo, Brazil *Nitsche, Michael* Psychology, Georg-August-University Goetti, Göttingen, Germany *Pascual-Leone, Alvaro* Neurology, Harvard Medical School, Boston, USA *Fregni, Felipe* Neurology, Harvard Medical School, Boston, USA

To assess whether modulation of the dorsolateral prefrontal cortex (DLFPC) with transcranial direct current stimulation (tDCS) modifies food craving in healthy subjects. We performed a randomized sham-controlled cross-over study in which 23 subjects received sham and active tDCS of the DLPFC. Subjects were exposed to food and also watched a movie of food. Craving for viewed foods as indexed by VAS was reduced by active tDCS. Moreover, after active stimulation, subjects fixated food-related pictures less frequently and consumed less food. The effects of tDCS on food craving might be related to a modulation of neural circuits associated with reward and decision-making.

Reduced cortisol secretion in response to psychosocial stress in patients with generalized anxiety disorder

Fries, Eva Inst. für Biolog. Psychologie, Techn. Universität Dresden, Dresden, Germany *Ebert, Daniela* Psychology, TU Dresden, Dresden, Germany *Kling, Ricarda* Psychology, TU Dresden, Dresden, Germany *Beesdo, Katja* Psychology, TU Dresden, Dresden, Germany *Kirschbaum, Clemens* Biological Psychology, TU Dresden, Dresden, Germany

Hypothalamus-pituitary-adrenal (HPA) axis reactivity was investigated in Generalized Anxiety Disorder (GAD), a condition characterized by excessive worries. We hypothesized that GAD-patients show, compared to healthy subjects, increased endocrine response to a psychosocial stressor, the Trier Social Stress Test (TSST). Cortisol was determined in saliva (TSST -30, -2, +1, +10, +20, +30, +45, +60 min) and participants rated agitation, tiredness and anxiety (TSST -5, +5 min). ANOVA for repeated measures revealed a blunted cortisol response to the TSST with increased perception of agitation, tiredness and anxiety in GAD. Studies are underway to elucidate mechanisms underlying blunted HPA axis reactivity in GAD.

Auricular acupuncture and its effects on vagal activity

La Marca, Roberto Psychology, University of Zurich, Zürich, Switzerland *Nedeljkovic, Marko* Psychologie, University of Zurich, Zürich, Switzerland *Yuan, Lizhuang* Psychology, University of Zurich, Zürich, Switzerland *Maercker, Andreas* Psychology, University of Zurich, Zürich, Switzerland *Ehlert, Ulrike* Psychology, University of Zurich, Zürich, Switzerland

The nervus vagus (NV) is associated with several psychiatric and somatic disorders. Some studies show a potential role of acupuncture to affect the activity of the NV. The purpose of our study was to examine acute effects of auricular acupuncture on vagal acitivity and mood. 14 healthy subjects participated single-blind and in randomized order to a (1) control condition without intervention, (2) placebo, (3) manual and (4) electrical acupuncture. Mood was maesured before and after each intervention and cardiorespiratory data was collected continuously (LifeShirt). Analyses of cardiorespiratory and mood data are in progress and will be presented at the meeting.

FP-329: Intelligence II

Not so natural after all: Intelligence always matters

Navarrete, Gorka Psicologia Cognitiva, Universidad de La Laguna, La Laguna, Spain *De Neys, Wim* Departement Psychologie, KULeuven, Leuven, Belgium *Santamaría, Carlos* Psicologia Cognitiva, Universidad de La Laguna, La Laguna, Spain

Ecological Rationality proponents suggest a special evolutionary status for natural frequencies. We used the classical Breast Cancer problem and divided our sample in two groups according to the Cognitive-Reflection-Test score. We found the higher CRT-score group was twice more accurate in this task than the low CRT-score. The strong relation between a general intelligence measure and the accuracy in this task is hard to explain from the Ecological-Rationality perspective, as it put into question the claim for the existence of an isolated module specifically tuned to work with natural frequencies. On the contrary, it's congruent with General-Purpose or Dual Processes explanations.

Prognostic validity of high ability assessment by the Viennese model of high achievement potential

Holocher-Ertl, Stefana Psychologische Diagnostik, Universität Wien, Wien, Austria *Hohensinn, Christine* Psychologische Diagnostik, Universität Wien, WIen, Austria *Kubinger, Klaus* Psychologische Diagnostik, Universität Wien, Wien, Austria *Schubhart, Sivlia* Psychologische Diagnostik, Universität Wien, WIen, Austria

The Viennese model of high achievement potential abandons the IQ-based criterion (IQ > 130) for high ability assessment but focusses on various surrounding conditions like achievement motivation, emotional stability, and family background. That is, high achievement potential might be given even if there is no high, but a well-levelled intelligence; and high achievement potential might be not given even if there is high giftedness. Applying this model it is of interest, whether the psychological consulting diagnosis of high achievement potential is prognostical valid. For this, a follow-up study was done with the clients of our Centre of Testing and Consulting.

Structural knowledge, fluid intelligence and control performance in complex problem solving tasks

Goode, Natassia Accelerated Learning Labratory, University of New South Wales, UNSW, Australia

This study investigates whether there is a causal relationship between structural knowledge and system control in complex problem solving tasks, which is moderated by fluid intelligence. 60 students received either complete, partial or no instructions regarding the structure of the system, and controlled the system to reach specific goals. ANCOVA revealed that control increased with structural knowledge, although performance was better than random across conditions. Fluid intelligence was a significant predictor of control only under complete and partial knowledge conditions. It appears that problem solving is limited by participants' fluid intelligence only when structural knowledge is acquired.

FP-330: Interpersonal processes and relationship I

Diversity training and the coaching of managers in a multi-layered organization: A case study

Stones, Christopher Dept. of Psychology, University of Johannesburg, Johannesburg, South Africa

This paper reports on the outcomes of a series of dynamic interactive workshops dealing with issues of diversity in the workplace in a premiere anti-fraud and corruption investigation unit where the project managers have to confront complex approaches to the commission of fraud while simultaneously having to deal effectively with their team members in an increasingly changing investigation environment given ongoing socio-political, technological and funding changes. Workshop participants reported greater self-insight and more willingness to exercise cautious innovation while also exhibiting fewer stress-related symptoms.

Effect of affective stimulation on cognitive-affective impairments of autism

Banerjee, Mallika Dept. of Psychology, University of Calcutta, Kolkata, India

The study purports to establish an intervention method to combat with affective bluntness of autism. The base level emotional, social and cognitive impairments of 16 autistic children were assessed. Two basic emotions were chosen for intervention, viz., pleasure & pain. Each child was exposed individually to a series of 20 sessions of affective stimulation containing (1) mock show of adult and child, (2) dolls (3) motion pictures (a software) (4) still pictures (5) sketches - of two basic emotions. The abovementioned dependent variables were reassessed. Pre-Post statistical analyses revealed a significant positive effect of affective stimulation on the triad impairments to combat with AUTISM.

FP-331: Organizational justice and cultural values

Antecedents and consequences of the needs for organizational justice

Muck, Peter Wirtsch.- u. Org.-Psychology, Universität Bielefeld, Bielefeld, Germany Stumpp, Thorsten W & O Psychology, University of Bielefeld, Bielefeld, Germany Maier, Günter W & O Psychology, University of Bielefeld, Bielefeld, Germany

Antecedents and consequences of a new construct in organizational justice research are analyzed in two studies. In the first study, the need for procedural justice predicted student satisfaction as well as university citizenship behavior (civic virtue) across a seven-week interval in contrast to the need for distributive justice (N = 116 students). In the second study, different antecedents were analyzed simultaneously in the work context (N = 112 employees). The needs largely depend on different antecedents, e.g., specific dispositions, the level of perceived organizational justice, the stimulation by other work aspects, and the compensation for deficiencies apart from organizational injustice.

Personnel compensation: Background and analysis of consequent variables

Grueso, Merlin Patricia CIDI, Univ. Pontificia Bolivariana, Palmira, Colombia Anton, Concha Psicologia Social, Universidad de Salamanca, Salamanca, Spain

The purpose of this research was to identify the cultural values associated with the implementation of a system of fair compensation from gender perspective and its effect in the development of organizational commitment. The sample was 425 employees. The administered questionnaire measured five values of the corporate culture, best practices for personnel compensation from gender perspective and organizational commitment. The results indicated that a best human resources compensation practices are related with uncertainty tolerance value and these affect the development of affective, continuance and normative commitment to the organization.

Value-orientation as extension of psychological contracts: Parish volunteers and pastors

Scheel, Tabea Work/Organizational Psychology, University of Leipzig, Berlin, Germany

In line with recent literature, the common distinction of transactional and relational Psychological Contracts (PC) will be extended for a value-oriented dimension. Value-oriented Psychological Contracts should be specifically relevant for volunteers on honorary posts. Aim of this qualitative study is the exploration of value-related PC categories as well as PC breach and its attribution. In Protestant parishs of Berlin, Germany, semistructured interviews with volunteers and pastors were conducted. Interviews were analysed by qualitative content analysis.

Results indicate a value-oriented dimension of volunteers and pastors PC. Implications of this new dimension for further quantitative research will be discussed.

Creating performing organisation through optimistic culture: An Indian experience

Niranjana, Phalgu Asian School of Business Mgt, Bhubaneswar, India Pattanayak, Biswajeet OB & HR, Asian School of Business Mgt, Bhubaneswar, India

This study attempts to understand dynamics of learned optimism, and organisational ethos across types of organisations, hierarchical positions and gender of employees and to examine functional relationship between learned optimism and organisational ethos. It's a 2x2x2 factorial design with 600 samples. The study has thrown many interesting results. There is a significant difference among the independent variables on organisational ethos and learned optimism. Manufacturing sector has better organisational culture in terms of openness, autonomy, collaboration and experimentation whereas service sector has high learned optimism. Based on the findings, OD interventions are suggested for performance improvement in the organisations.

Organizational justice and job satisfaction: Does culture moderate the relationship?

Jain, Neha Humanities and Social Sciences, IIT Dehli, New Delhi, India

This paper examines the moderating role of autocratic culture on organizational justice- job satisfaction relationship. The sample consisted of 138 employees from private and public sector organizations having autocratic culture. The analysis focused on measuring the differential effect of organizational justice on job satisfaction as a function of the moderator. The hypothesis proposed that the positivity of the relation between organizational justice and job satisfaction would be higher for low autocratic organizations than for high autocratic organizations. Regression analysis carried out across two sectors i.e. private and public showed no differences..

FP-332: Quality assurance in higher education

Educational standards in vocational higher education institutions in Austria

Pächter, Manuela Inst. für Pädag. Psychologie, Universität Graz, Graz, Austria Lunger, Sigrun Educational Psychology, Psychology/University of Graz, Graz, Austria Manhal, Simone Educational Psychology, Psychology/University of Graz, Graz, Austria Macher, Daniel Educational Psychology, Psychology/University of Graz, Graz, Austria Fritz, Ursula Unterricht, Kunst und Kultur, Bundesministerium, Wien, Austria

In 2007 educational standards were introduced for the "Higher Education and Vocational Education and Training Institutions" in Austria. For five core subjects educational standards and models of competences were defined. Based on these models examples were developed which illustrate the educational standards and can be used by teachers in their lessons. In a nation-wide empirical investigation more than 100 teachers applied the examples in their courses. The teachers and approximately 1700 students evaluated the quality of the examples with regard to their difficulty, their adequacy to the students' age, their adequacy for the respective educational standard and other aspects.

National student survey of teaching in UK universities: Dimensionality, multilevel structure, convergent and discriminant validity and relations to other indicators

Cheng, Jacqueline Green College, University of Oxford, Oxford, United Kingdom Marsh, Herbert W. University of Oxford, Department of Education, Oxford, United Kingdom

In a UK-wide university-benchmarking exercise, all graduating undergraduates completed a multidimensional course satisfaction survey in 2005 and 2006 (171,320 and 157,371 students; 140 universities; 41 disciplines). Multilevel analyses demonstrated a well-defined 8-factor structure at the student level and reliable differentiation between universities and disciplines within universities (despite modest variance components). Diverse student background variables had only very small effects on differentiation between universities and disciplines. Research performances (UK Research Assessment Exercise) of universities and departments within universities were only modestly related to corresponding student satisfaction aggregates. Across the two years (two different cohorts), results and university rankings were highly consistent.

Academic course evaluation: Competences versus satisfaction

Leidner, Bernhard Dept. of Psychology, New School for Social Research, New York, USA Braun, Edith Psychology, Free University of Berlin, Berlin, Germany

This presentation clarifies the conceptual distinction between satisfaction, as measured by academic course evaluation instruments, and competence acquirement, as measured by the "Berliner Evaluationsinstrument für selbst eingeschätzte, studentische Kompetenzen" (Berlin Evaluation Instrument for self-reported student competences). Against the background of the Bologna Process, a sample of 1,403 students from 54 interdisciplinary courses at nine German universities was used to show the empirical distinction between satisfaction and competence acquirement by means of structural equation modeling. The relevance and importance of outcome-(competence-)oriented, compared to 'traditional', input-oriented academic course evaluations will be discussed.

How do university students evaluate and use e-learning?

Manhal, Simone Inst. für Pädag. Psychologie, Universität Graz, Graz, Austria Maier, Brigitte Educational Psychology, Psychology/University of Graz, Graz, Austria Pächter, Manuela Inst. für Pädag. Psychologie, Universität Graz, Graz, Austria

2196 students from 16 universities and 13 colleges of higher education in Austria, studying a wide range of subjects, took part in a questionnaire survey. All students were enrolled in an e-learning course. They were asked about their course experiences and expectations on e-learning with regard to various didactic components (tutorial support, peer collaboration, learning outcomes, etc.). Furthermore, they compared e-learning to learning in face-to-face courses. The statistical analyses reveal distinct (and partly unexpected) differences in students' evaluations and comparisons of e-learning and face-to-face courses. They advocate blended learning and a combination of the advantages of both forms of learning.

FP-333: Clinical / counseling psychology VI

Examination of depression, anxiety, stress scales (DASS) factor structure in Iranian population

Dehghani, Mohsen Family Research Institute, Shahid Beheshti University, Tehran, Islamic Republic of Iran Ganjavi, Anahita Family Research Institute, Shahid Beheshti University, Tehran, Islamic Republic of Iran

DASS has been proven as a reliable tool to discriminate between three related but different constructs of depression, anxiety, and stress. This scale has been used in different countries including Iran. However, factor structure of the test is yet to be examined in the culture. A large sample was recruited randomly (N=760). In addition to the scale, demographics were collected as well. It was found that 3 constructs with 34 items could assess the three domains.

Psychiatric and personality disorder diagnoses in parents of eating disordered adolescents

Klinkowski, Nora Kinder- und Jugendpsychiatrie, Charité Berlin, Berlin, Germany *Woldt, Lea* Child and Adolescent Psychiatr, Charité, Berlin, Germany *Pfeiffer, Ernst* Child and Adolescent Psychiatr, Charité, Berlin, Germany *Lehmkuhl, Ulrike* Child and Adolescent Psychiatr, Charité, Berlin, Germany *Salbach-Andrae, Harriet* Child and Adolescent Psychiatr, Charité, Berlin, Germany

Objectives: To determine the occurrence of psychiatric and personality disorder diagnoses in parents of eating disorder patients. Methods: To date, 64 parents (Mage = 45.8 + 5.6 years) of acute eating disorder patients were administered structured diagnostic interviews (CIDI-DIA-X; SCID-II) and a personality inventory (PSSI). To compare them with respect to gender and their daughter's diagnosis, Chi square analyses and ANOVA were conducted. Results: The most frequent general psychiatric diagnoses were substance abuse (36.9%) and affective disorders (26.2%). 17% were diagnosed as having a personality disorder (avoidant, obsessive-compulsive, depressive and borderline). Conclusions: The findings underline the importance of giving full clinical attention to the impact of parental psychiatric illnesses.

Computer based diagnostics with illiterate traumatized refugees: Potential and challenges

Mueller, Julia Psychiatric Department, University Hospital Zurich, Zurich, Switzerland *Knaevelsrud, Christine* Research, Center for Torture Victims, Berlin, Germany

Assessing traumatized refugees is challenging. Illiteracy and multilinguality makes standardized psychological assessment difficult and resource consuming. We therefore developed an audiovisual computer based diagnostic tool (MultiCASI) which allows illiterate individuals to answer questionnaires without the help of interpreters. In our study we examined the feasibility of MultiCASI in traumatized refugees and compared the collected data with paper/pencil approaches. We randomly assigned 40 participants to either "paper/pencil" or "MultiCASI" questionnaires. Psychopathology and the number of reported traumatic events did not differ within both conditions. MultiCASI was accepted well. Implications and further possibilities to apply this new diagnostic approach will be discussed.

Improving the psychometric properties of the Hospital Anxiety and Depression Scale (HADS)

Winter, Jeanette School of Psychology, University of Aberdeen, Aberdeen, United Kingdom *Johnston, Marie* School of Psychology, University of Aberdeen, Aberdeen, United Kingdom *Sniehotta, Falko F.* School of Psychology, University of Aberdeen, Aberdeen, United Kingdom *Pollard, Beth* School of Psychology, University of Aberdeen, Aberdeen, United Kingdom

OBJECTIVES The present study proposes a methodology to improve psychometric properties using confirmatory factor analysis (CFA) and item response theory (IRT) models. METHODS Cross-sectional HADS data from disabled populations were analysed and compared to a sample of non-clinical adults in the UK. CFA and IRT models were used to identify sensitive items relative to three different factor models. RESULTS Two HADS items showed poor discrimination across all three tested models using IRT. Removing these two non-sensitive items improved model fit using CFA. CONCLUSIONS The present study showed improved psychometric properties of the HADS by identifying and discarding two items.

FP-334: Time perception

Spatial cues' effects on temporal judgments: Mandarin speakers' spatiotemporal metaphors

Wang, Ying Inst. of Psychology, Chinese Academy of Science, Beijing, People's Republic of China *Zhang, Kan* HumanFactors&EngineeringPs, Institute of Psychology, CAS, Beijing, People's Republic of China *Zhang, Zhijie* School of Psychology, Southwest China University, Chongqing, People's Republic of China

Metaphors are frequently used for abstract conceptions. Horizontal and vertical metaphors are two different spatiotemporal ways for time conception. No definite conclusion on English speakers' preference. Little research on Mandarin speakers is found. This study examines two spatial cues' effects on temporal judgments among Mandarin speakers, tying to figure out which way they prefer. Results show that when they think about time, they equally use both. There is no prior spatiotemporal metaphor between the horizontal and the vertical ones when Mandarins think about time and make temporal judgments. Possible reasons including language and culture influences and future research are discussed.

Individual time representations and philosophical concepts of time

Svynarenko, Radion Odessa, Ukraine

The paper examines the psychological importance of existing in philosophy four time concepts: substantial, relational, static and dynamic. Basing on their particular time properties description the specific questionnaire was constructed. The research revealed that individuals in general more often mark dynamic and substantial properties of time and much less often static and relational. Moreover, the individuals can be divided in four typological groups, which differ in dominating representations about properties of time. Thus, the main idea of this paper is to show that philosophical time concepts reflect individual time representations.

The time line is mapped onto the visual field

Polunin, Oleksii Kiev, Ukraine *Holmqvist, Kenneth* The Humanities Lab, Lund University, Lund, Sweden *Johansson, Roger* The Humanities Lab, Lund University, Lund, Sweden

The mapping of general and local time direction onto the visual field was studied in two experiments. The hypothesis was that the left hand side of the visual field is associated with the past, and the right hand side with the future. Subject's attention was directed to the biographical past or future and the corresponding eye movements were recorded. Eye fixation analyses revealed that the past, compared to the future, was mapped significantly further to the left in the visual field (p<.001). Additionally, the past was mapped higher along the vertical axis than the future (p<.001).

An experimental investigation of involuntary, uncued remembering of prospective memory

Imai, Hisato Dept. of Psychology, Tokyo Woman's Christian Univ., Tokyo, Japan *Ishii, Yukiko* Psychology, Tokyo Woman's Christian Univ., Tokyo, Japan

We conducted an experiment on involuntary, uncued remembering of event-based prospective memory (PM). Twenty-six undergraduates were instructed to answer a questionnaire in an envelope when a photograph of envelopes (remembering cue) was presented while performing category judgment; however, the cue wasn't presented actually. The results showed that 88.5% of the participants correctly performed the PM task, indicating that they involuntarily remembered the PM task without the remembering cue. In addition, the frequency of involuntary remembering was gradually increased toward the end of the experiment, which is similar to the time-based PM performance. Nature of involuntary remembering of PM will be discussed.

Event- and time-based prospective memory: An experimental investigation

Khan, Azizuddin Humanities and Social Sciences, IIT Bombay, Bombay, India *Sharma, Narendra K.* Humanities and Social Sciences, Indian Institute of Technology, Kanpur, India *Dixit, Shikha* Humanities and Social Sciences, IIT Kanpur, Kanpur, India

An experimental study was conducted on 80 subjects to investigate the role of time monitoring and cognitive load in prospective memory (event-based and time-based). Cognitive load and task conditions (Event vs. Time-based) were the independent variables. Accuracy in prospective memory was the dependent variable. Analysis of variance and regression analysis were conducted to analyze the data. All the main effects and interactions were significant. Significant differential effects were obtained under event-based and time-based task. However, the effect cognitive load was more detrimental in time-based prospective memory. Results also revealed time monitoring is critical in the successful performance of time-based prospective memory.

FP-335: Experimental psychotherapy

Now you see it now you don't: Change blindness is ameliorated by phobic cues

Alpers, Georg W. Inst. für Psychologie, Universität Bielefeld, Bielefeld, Germany *Gerdes, Antje B.M.* Psychology, Universität Würzburg, Würzburg, Germany

Fear-relevant stimuli are thought to boost attention in phobic patients. This is the first study to examine whether change blindness, which disrupts visual awareness, is ameliorated by phobia-related cues. 23 phobic and 20 non-anxious participants viewed two successive displays which were briefly interrupted by a blank. On some trials an object was changed. Participants were to indicate if a change occurred and to identify the changed object. Overall, the groups did not differ in their response criterion and tendencies to indicate a change. However, only patients were significantly more accurate when the change involved a spider compared to neutral objects.

Seeing the silver lining: Reappraisal ability moderates the relationship between stress and depression

Caston, Allison Dept. of Psychology, University of Denver, Denver, USA *Shallcross, Amanda* Dept of Psychology, University of Denver, Denver, USA *Mauss, Iris* Dept of Psychology, University of Denver, Denver, USA

There is a robust relationship between stressful life events (SLEs) and depression. It is unclear, however, why some are resilient in the aftermath of SLEs, while others experience depression. We argue that one's ability to down-regulate negative emotions using cognitive reappraisal may be an important protective factor against depression. To test this hypothesis, we assessed reappraisal ability (RA) using a laboratory procedure in women who had recently experienced a SLE. Results indicate that stress was positively associated with depression three months later. RA was indeed protective such that high-stress women who possessed high RA were indistinguishable from their low-stress counterparts.

Structure and dynamic of semantic memory in schizophrenic patients

Lepilkina, Taissia Mental Health Research Center, Moscow, Russia

Objectives. The structure of semantic memory abnormalities in schizophrenic patients was studied. We hypothesized that patients' disturbances in retention and reproduction of texts arise from derangements of syntactical structure of clause. Methods. 61 patients diagnosed schizophrenia performed subtests VII and V of WMS, 23 of them who had met criteria of stable remission were tested in a year later. Test texts were analyzed syntactically. Results. Significant improvement (p<.05) of semantic memory in patients with remission was related to quantity of key semantic units (subjects and predicates) increase and wasn't related to short-term memory storage extension. We conclude that improvement of semantic memory in schizophrenic patients relates to recovery of syntactical structure of sentence.

Comparison of adult ADHD symptoms between a substance abusers sample and a community sample

Socarras, Joel Dept. of Clinical Psychology, Carlos Albizu University, San Juan, Puerto Rico Velez, Maria Clinical Psychology, Carlos Albizu University, San Juan, Puerto Rico

The purpose of this investigation was to compare symptoms of Attention Deficit/ Hyperactivity Disorder (ADHD) in adults between two samples: subjects with Substance Abuse and/or Dependence and a community sample. Symptoms were assessed using the Wender Utah Rating Scale (WURS) and the Adult Self Report Scale. Using analysis of variance, significant statistical differences were found between both samples for the WURS. Results suggest a higher incidence of ADHD in substance-users when compared to individuals with no history of drug-misuse. These results remind us to consider the co-existing psychiatric disorders and to re-think effective treatment for substance abusers in Puerto Rico.

FP-336: Cognitive aging: Memory processes, decision making, and cognitive interventions

A fMRI study of age differences in encoding of source memory

Peng, Huamao Psychology School, Beijing Normal University, Beijing, People's Republic of China Tang, Dan Psychology School, Beijing Normal University, Beijing, People's Republic of China Wang, Dahua Psychology School, Beijing Normal University, Beijing, People's Republic of China Shen, Jiliang Psychology School, Beijing Normal University, Beijing, People's Republic of China

To examine the hemispheric asymmetry reduction of older adults (HAROLD) model of source memory, 25 old adults (60-78 years old) and 15 young adults (20-29 years old) from Beijing were recruited as subjects. During the fMRI scanning, the subjects were asked to finish two difficult levels location-recall task, which is the index of source memory. The encoding process was recorded. Results showed that the HAROLD was founded in old adults in encoding of location-recall task at the simple level rather than the difficult level. It was concluded that HAROLD was a task difficulty specific phenomena.

Age-related differences in the disruption of prose recall by irrelevant speech

Bell, Raoul Inst. für Exp. Psychologie, Universität Düsseldorf, Düsseldorf, Germany

Inhibition deficit theory predicts that older adults are more susceptible to distraction than younger adults. Two experiments tested this hypothesis by examining age-related differences in the disruption of prose recall by irrelevant speech. Participants were required to read visually presented texts. During reading, they ignored auditorily presented distractor speech. Older adults were more susceptible to the disruption of prose recall by irrelevant speech and made more intrusion errors than younger adults. The results are novel in showing age-related differences in the susceptibility to interference even when target and distractor stimuli are presented in different modalities.

Memory changes in healthy older adults: Objective and subjective changes

Preiss, Marek Dept. of Psychology, Prague Psychiatric Center, Prague, Czech Republic Stepankova, Hana Psychology, Prague Psychiatric Center, Prague, Czech Republic Steinova, Dana Psychology, Prague Psychiatric Center, Prague, Czech Republic Lukavsky, Jiri Psychology, Academy of Sciences, Prague, Czech Republic

We expect that memory training effects positively both objective and subjective changes. Participants (N=120) of a 5-week memory training course, were tested before, after and six months later. We examined the "transfer effect of first order"(memory tests), "transfer effect of second order" (other performance tests), "transfer effect of third order" (daily living) and "transfer effect of fourth order" (proxy measures). Comparison with controls was made. The results are discussed with respect to changes in quality of life and possibility of sustaining of the training effect. Memory functions training may be a meaningful part of free-time activities in ageing population.

FP-337: New technology and instruments

Qualitative methods for improving standardized questionnaires

Baasch, Stefanie Inst. für Psychologie, Universität Magdeburg, Magdeburg, Germany Ittner, Heidi Psychology, OvGU, Magdeburg, Germany Bamberg, Sebastian Psychology, OvGU, Magdeburg, Germany Welsch, Janina Project MAX-SUCCESS, ILS NRW, Dortmund, Germany Linneweber, Volker Präsident der Universität, Universität des Saarlandes, Saarbrücken, Germany

While testing a new model of behavior change (Affect-Goal-Desire-Intention Model) with a standardized European-wide questionnaire on travel mode choice, some critics emerged about the comprehensibility of questions. Though the statistical data seemed to be valid, the questionnaire was tested with a qualitative method to find out, if and how people did understand and interpret the questions. A mixture of "aloud thinking" while filling out the questionnaire and routing questions delivered information about the revision of the questionnaire. The answers and notes were recorded and analyzed with a short form of Mayrings Qualitative Content Analysis.

The effect of motivational factors on the elaboration of differentiated road pricing charges

Schade, Jens Verkehrspsychologie, TU Dresden, Dresden, Germany Roessger, Lars Verkehrspsychologie, Technische Universität Dresde, Dresden, Germany Wagner, Christiane Verkehrspsychologie, Technische Universität Dresde, Dresden, Germany Bonsall, Peter Institute for Transport Studie, University of Leeds, Leeds, United Kingdom

In the transport sector differentiated pricing is increasingly used to influence behaviour in order to manage the demand for infrastructure. This leads to the question up to what degree of differentiation are people able and willing to understand and to respond to transport charging structures? We hypothesise that besides cognitive limitations acceptability of road pricing influences the responses to differentiated charges. We conducted a two-factor variance analytical design, where we varied the complexity and the acceptability of road pricing. Dependent variables are latency time and error rate in price estimation. Results emphasize that motivational factors effect the cognitive elaboration of prices. The implications will be discussed.

Advanced driver assistance systems: Two different actor groups and their acceptance of modern car technologies

Müller, Stefanie Inst. für Psychologie, Universität Magdeburg, Magdeburg, Germany Ittner, Heidi Institut für Psychologie, Otto-v.-Guericke-Universität, Magdeburg, Germany Linneweber, Volker Präsidium, Universität des Saarlandes, Saarbrücken, Germany

Advanced Driver Assistance Systems (ADAS) shall support the human regarding several driving tasks. These systems are designed to inform or warn the driver or even operate autonomously. Therefore a changing in the driving process is expected and the question of acceptance of ADAS arises. Our project aims to support the benefits and also usage of ADAS focusing on two actor groups, drivers and professional bodies working in the automotive sector. Two studies have been conducted (Ndrivers = 7687; Nprofessionals = 517) in order to identify psychologically essential variables to explain and enhance the acceptance and therefore adequate usage of ADAS.

Detecting safety relevant driver-states by using acoustic speech features: A pattern recognition based measurement approach

Krajewski, Jurek Inst. Wirtschaftspsychologie, Universität Wuppertal, Wuppertal, Germany Wieland, Rainer Work & Organizational Psyc, Univ. Wuppertal, Wuppertal, Germany Golz, Martin Work & Organizational Psyc, Univ. Wuppertal, Wuppertal, Germany

This paper gives an overview of the application area, procedure and added-value of acoustic speech analysis. The study of safety relevant internal driver states (e.g. sleepiness, stress, anger, fear) requires non-interrupting, and sensor application-free, measurements. After a decade of rapid development within the speech processing area, acoustic speech analysis reaches classification accuracies of over 85%. The procedure of the pattern recognition based speech analysis includes the following steps: (1) recording speech material, (2) preprocessing (noise filtering, segmentation), (3) computing speech features (articulatory, speech quality and prosodic features), (4) reducing dimensionality, (5) using machine learning algorithms (MLP, SVM, K-NN), and (5) evaluating the prediction on unseen data.

FP-338: Psychology and national development II

Indicator development and the millennium development goals

Flattau, Pamela Ebert IDA STPI, Washington, USA

In September 2000, over 190 members of the United Nations adopted the Millennium Declaration and formulated eight Millennium Development Goals which have become a "universal framework for development and a means for developing countries and their partners to work together in pursuit of a shared future for all." Measurement of progress towards those goals requires the development of indicators of social and economic progress. Drawing on recent work for the US National Science Board ("Digest of Key Science and Engineering Indicators 2008"), this paper will outline challenges confronting effective social indicators development including: item specification and data availability, comparability of measures internationally, and the presentation of "readily usable" findings through data visualization strategies.

Psychological maintenance of education for sustainable development

Shmeleva, Irina International Relations, S. Petersburg State University, Saint Petersburg, Russia
The goals of UN Education for Sustainable Development - encouraging ecological consciousness activation, pro-environmental behavior, environment knowledge acquisition, personal and community participation in solving environmental problems - need psychological support and maintenance. Development of competences in quick adequate response, future oriented anticipation of challenges of the globalizing world, system and interdisciplinary thinking, understanding influences of the interactive environmental actions, democratic governance and leadership is seen as interconnected efforts of scientific, practical and psycho-pedagogical accompaniment of SD education, ecological consciousness development and values changing. Cases from Saint-Petersburg University curriculum in SD education and research results from Values Survey would be presented.

The viewpoint of individuals from different professional groups on the rights of children under risk

Kargi, Eda Preschool Education, Hacettepe University, Ankara, Turkey *Akman, Berrin* Preschool Education, Hacettepe University, Ankara, Turkey
This research is carried out to find out the viewpoints of 180 people from different professional groups (parliamenters, artists, journalists and practitioners from NGOs) striving for the well-being of children. The researchers conducted interviews with the participants where they asked questions about the definition of children under risk, general health status, the factors which drive children to these risks, policies which may improve the situation. Categorical analysis technique was used to analyze the data collected. It was found out that the opinions of different professional groups vary about the concept of children under risk and the establishment of policies about the involvement rights of children.

Structuring and restructuring strategies for science education: The National Defense Education Act of 1958

Flattau, Pamela Ebert IDA STPI, Washington, USA
In 1958, the US Congress enacted the National Defense Education Act (NDEA) to ensure the security of the nation through "the fullest development of the mental resources and technical skills of its young men and women." Originally described by then-President Eisenhower as "short-term emergency legislation" in response to the Soviet launch of Sputnik, NDEA had a lasting effect in two areas of US education: student financing strategies and availability of guidance, counseling and testing at the secondary school levels for the identification of talent. The IDA Science and Technology Policy Institute documented some of these effects in a report to the White House Office of Science and Technology Policy in 2006.

FP-339: Innovation II

Perceived role breadth and individual role innovation of technical service employees

Dettmers, Jan Arbeits- und Org.-Psychologie, Universität Hamburg, Hamburg, Germany *Stremming, Saskia* W&O-Psychology, University of Hamburg, Hamburg, Germany *Marggraf-Micheel, Claudia* W&O-Psychology, University of Hamburg, Hamburg, Germany *Bamberg, Eva* W&O-Psychology, University of Hamburg, Hamburg, Germany
Service employees with customer contact are expected not only to perform the core technical service delivery tasks but also tasks regarding customer relationship, information processing and organizational change. Whether employees feel responsible for these additional tasks is a matter of perceived job or role breadth. 241 technical service employees and their supervisors of 49 enterprises were asked about their perceived job breadth. Regression analyses revealed significant statistical links between perceived job breadth and individual role innovation. Multi-level analysis points at organizational and supervisor characteristics. Results underline the importance of individual role definitions as a predictor for organizational behaviour of employees.

The impact of team innovation climate, climate strength, and locus of control on innovative behavior: A multi-level analysis

Cao, Jiyin Dept. of Psychology, Peking University, Beijing, People's Republic of China *Wang, Lei* Psychology, Room 209, Peking University, Beijing, People's Republic of China
Using a sample of 658 employees constituting 86 proximal work groups from a variety of multiple organizations and occupations, the authors investigated the relationships among team innovation climate, climate strength, locus of control, and innovative behavior. Cross-level results of hierarchical linear models indicated that team innovation climate was positively related to individual innovative behavior. Further, the cross-level effect was moderated by locus of control; the positive cross-level effect of team innovation climate was found to be more significant for those higher on external locus of control. In addition, climate strength was positively associated with team innovation behavior.

Moderating cognitions in the relationship between fairness perceptions of feedback and personal initiative and innovative behavior

Sparr, Jennifer L. Arbeits- und Org.-Psychologie, Universität Konstanz, Konstanz, Germany *Sonnentag, Sabine* Psychology, University of Konstanz, Konstanz, Germany
This field study examined the moderating effects of three types of cognitions (task-, motivation-, and person-centered) on the relationship between perceived fairness of informal supervisor feedback and personal initiative and innovative behavior. Data from 122 employees working in project teams or small agencies were used. Personal initiative and innovative behavior were peer rated. Hierarchical regression analyses showed that fair feedback is positively related to personal initiative and innovative behavior if individuals concentrate on task-related thoughts and on personal relevance of the feedback. Thus, the relationship between fair feedback and valued behaviors seems to depend on cognitions about the feedback.

Differential approach to workplace innovation factors facilitating New Idea Generation do not necessarily support their implementation

Fay, Doris Institute of Psychology, University of Potsdam, Potsdam, Germany *Urbach, Tina* Institute of Psychology, University of Potsdam, Potsdam, Germany *Goral, Agata* Aston Business School, Aston University, Birmingham, United Kingdom
It is widely acknowledged that workplace innovation is the result of two activities: new idea generation and their implementation. Even though those activities differ substantially from each other, research trying to identify differential predictors is still scarce. This study explores the role of individual- and unit-level variables to predict the two innovation activities. Self and supervisor ratings were obtained from 142 software designers (22 supervisors) which were analysed with hierarchical linear modelling. Results reveal differential cross-level interaction effects. For example, individuals' external communication compensated for a low level of proactive climate with regard to idea generation; other processes, however, were relevant for idea implementation. Implications for theory development and the management of innovation will be discussed.

The simple and multiple relationship of leadership style, problemsolving style, and work group relationships with innovative organizational climat and innovative behavior in an industrial company.

Afshari, Ali Daran Isfahan, Islamic Republic of Iran *Haghighi, Jamal* psychology, chamran university, ahvaz, Islamic Republic of Iran
this study explored the simple and multiple relationship of leadership style, problem solving style and work group relationships with innovative organizational climat and innovative behavior in an industrial company.to this end 200staff were selected by tratified random sampling model.the research quationnairs were completed with them.according to the result of this research there is significant positive correlation between all antecedent variable and innovative climat except for role expectation of leadership.also innovative behavior had significant positive relationship with all antecedent variable except for intuitive problemsolving and work group relationships.

FP-340: Psychological theories II

Thomas Willis's 17th century neuroscience

Barone, David Dept. of Psychology, Illinois State University, Normal, USA
Thomas Willis is recognized in medical history as the father of neurology. John Locke, his student, discredited Willis's psychology as speculative, and Boring and other historians of psychology after Brett dismissed it as prescientific. This paper revisits Willis's work, especially De Anima Brutorum (1672), as a progenitor of today's neuroscience. His discoveries in brain anatomy informed his understanding of conscious vs. unconscious functioning, subcortical reflexes, automaticity of skills, sleepwalking, instinct vs. learning, cognitive-emotional conflicts, etc. Locke, foreshadowing Watson and Skinner, advocated descriptive empiricism, thereby supporting introspective psychology and delaying research on brain localization of psychological functioning until the 19th century.

Ladygina-Kots: Russian pioneer in evolutionary psychology

Mironenko, Irina Dept. of Social Psychology, SPb Univers. Humanities, St. Petersburg, Russia
Russian psychology is now facing the challenge to join international mainstream. A survey of its history should help to promote mutual understanding and to facilitate integration. Ladygina-Kots (1889-1963) was an expert in Comparative Psychology. As a Darwinist, she emphasized the evolutionary nature of human cognition and emotion like modern western evolutionary psychologists do. However, she stressed the dialectics of human nature and highlighted alongside with similarities fundamental differences between ani-

mals and human beings. She raised infant chimpanzee in her family thus providing comparative study of chimpanzee development and that of a human child reported in the book published in 1935.

FP-341: Psychological disorders VII

Eating disorder symptomatology and young women: Sex role orientations, achievement concerns, social comparison and gendered high school milieu

Jones, Mairwen Behav. & Community Health, University of Sydney, Sydney, Australia Davey, Zoe School of Psychology, The University of Sydney, Camperdown Sydney, Australia

Objectives: Examined the relationship between high school gender composition and eating disorder symptomatology, and the extent to which sex role orientation, achievement concerns, and differential rates of appearance based social comparison may be predictive of differences in maladaptive eating. Methods: Measures were completed by 95 female university students. Results: No significant differences were found in eating disorder symptomatology as measured by three subscales of the Eating Disorder Inventory 3, figure preferences, sex role orientations and role concerns, or social comparison between the two high school groups. Conclusions: Previous high school gender composition was not associated with current levels of eating disorder symptomatology.

A combination of cognitive-behavioral therapy and pharmacy therapy in delusional disorder

Khodayarifard, Mohammad Dept. of Psychology, University of Tehran, Tehran, Islamic Republic of Iran

The purpose of present study was treatment of a subject with delusional disorder, erotomatic type, by using a combination treatment method (Cognitive Behavioral and pharmacotherapy). The method of current study was single-subject design (ABA). The techniques which were used were including: cognitive-reconstructing by correcting subject's beliefs, interpretations about events, reinforcing logical thinking, evaluating of evidences, teaching of problem solving, behavioral cognitive copying strategies, relaxing, positivism and pharmacotherapy. The results indicated that the combining method was highly effective in eliminating the symptoms and preventing from it's recurrence in a 6 months period. Consistency and inconsistency of the results was discussed.

Adolescents and eating disorders: Risk factors

Maganto, Carmen Dept. of Clinical Psychology, University Basque Country, San Sebastián, Spain Garaigordobil, Maite Dept. of Clinical Psychology, University Basque Country, San Sebastián, Spain Maganto, Juana Mary Dept. of Clinical Psychology, University Basque Country, San Sebastián, Spain

The goal of this research is to investigate the prevalence of the following risk factors in Eating Disorders and the significant relationships between them: age, sex, Body Mass Index, body satisfaction, anxiety level, obsession with thinness, fear of maturity, and perfectionism. The non-clinical sample is made up of 400 adolescents (14-18) Several assessment instruments were employed. The most important results revealed significant differences related to sex, with scores and percentages higher in women than in men in the EAT (31.25% and 9.5% respectively), in Trait Anxiety, in bulimia (9.3% and 1.9% respectively), and in obsession with thinness (14.5% and 2.9% respectively).

The therapy of eating disorders in the ANAD therapeutic living communities: An evaluation of clinical effects

Wunderer, Eva Wohngruppen bei Essstörungen, ANAD e.V., München, Germany Weis, Sabine Wohngruppen bei Essstörungen, ANAD e.V., München, Germany Schnebel, Andreas Wohngruppen bei Essstörungen, ANAD e.V., München, Germany

Eating disorders are usually treated in specialised clinical settings. However, it is difficult for patients to transfer their achievements into everyday life. Therapeutic living communities offer an alternative as their setting is close to everyday life. Patients remain integrated in school or work, live largely independently and are continuously cared for by a multidisciplinary team. When evaluating the ANAD therapeutic living communities' concept, several professional disciplines were taken into consideration: psychotherapy, nutritional therapy and social work. Standardised outcome measures(e.g. EDI2, BDI, SCL90R) were used to assess 38 patients with eating disorders in a pre-post design. Data analysis reveals significant improvements in multiple areas.

FP-342: Job satisfaction

Investigating the relationship between personality traits and job satisfaction among Iran track manufacture

Garousi Farshy, Mirthagy Dept. of Psychology, Tabriz University, Tabriz, Islamic Republic of Iran

370 employers of the Track Manufacture were completed NEO-FFI & JDI to evaluate personality & job satisfaction. Results showed that there was a positive relation between Conscientiousness, Extraversion & Agreeableness with job satisfaction and a negative relation between neuroticism & job satisfaction. A positive relationship between amount of salary & education with job satisfaction was observed. Regression Analizing revealed that conscientiousness, neuroticism and openness could predict job satisfaction. Monthly salary was significant predictor of job satisfaction.

Personnel effectiveness in a security-service organization: Contributors and consequences

Sinha, Arvind Humanities & Social Sciences, Indian Institute of Technology, Kanpur, India Srivastava, Sweta OB and HR Area, Indian Institute of Management, Kozhikode, India

Abstract: Some "antecedent" variables of effectiveness and relationship of effectiveness with some of the organizationally relevant "consequences" were explored, using questionnaires and a sample of 270 male lower and middle level respondents from a government security-service (police) organization. Data were analyzed using correlations, factor analysis, and regression analyses. The "antecedent" variables contributing to the dimensions of effectiveness were: internal motivation, lesser organizational politics, supervisors' support, and perception of organizational justice. Dimensions of effectiveness were found associated with job satisfaction and employees' happiness. Implications toward effective service organization functioning were discussed and future directions for research were identified. Keywords: Effectiveness on Conceived Roles, Happiness, Job-accomplishment, Job-satisfaction, Organizational Justice, Organizational Politics, Personal Effectiveness, Supervisors' Support.

The mediating effects of organizational justice and trust on the relationship between leadership styles and job satisfaction

Wu, Weiku School of Economics Management, Tsinghua University, Beijing, People's Republic of China Song, Jiwen Department of OB and HR, School of Business, Beijing, People's Republic of China Zhang, Dongying Department of Management,

Sinopec Corp., Beijing, People's Republic of China Tan, Shuang Department of OB and HR, School of Business, Beijing, People's Republic of China

In this paper we developed an integrated model based on theories of leadership, organizational justice, and organizational trust. We sampled 240 employees of a state-owned enterprise in China. The hierarchical regression results showed that: (1) trust, distributive and procedural justice fully mediated the relationship between the two leadership styles transactional leadership and employees' job satisfaction; (2) trust, distributive and procedural justice only partially mediated the relationship between transformational leadership and job satisfaction. We further discussed the practical implications in Chinese context (Supported by NSFC 70572012, 70702024).

The relationship between quality of life and job satisfaction in nurses of different wards

Janatian, Sima Psychology, University of Isfahan, Isfahan, Islamic Republic of Iran Yoosefi, Zahra Psycology, University of Isfahan, Isfahan, Islamic Republic of Iran Kasaei, Rahim Psycology, University of Isfahan, Isfahan, Islamic Republic of Iran

This study aimed at determining the relationship between some work-related, and demographic aspects in nurses at four general hospitals in Isfahan, Iran. 50 female and 50 male nurses were selected randomly and the three research questionnaires were administered to measure job satisfaction, quality of life, as well as demographic variables. The multivariate analysis of variance of data indicated the kind of significant relationships such as quality of life with job satisfaction and its sub-scales ($p < .05$), education and gender with job satisfaction ($p < .01$), and education with job satisfaction of colleagues ($p < .001$). Keywords: quality of life, job satisfaction, nurses, demographic variables.

FP-343: Language and action

'Step back and lead': Communicative strategies of managers and supervisors in critical conversations

Pullwitt, Tanja School of Psychology, Aberdeen University, Aberdeen, United Kingdom Mearns, Kathryn Dept. of Psychology, University of Aberdeen, Aberdeen, United Kingdom Lauche, Kristina The Design Methodology Group, TU Delft, Delft, Netherlands

This qualitative study evaluates managers' and supervisors' performance during critical conversational situations with subordinates. It explores which communicative strategies define participants' dynamic movement in the 'social space' (Danziger, 1976) and how these movements impact on the conversational outcomes (i.e. agreement to change). Ten conversations with 20 participants were analysed using discourse analysis techniques. Status reducing strategies and increased solidarity between interlocutors led to positive conversation outcomes. Strategies that increased the intervener's status with unchanged or decreased solidarity led to negative conversation outcomes. These findings illustrate how managers' and supervisors' defensive communication strategies allow for positive outcomes in critical conversational situations.

Alignment of object naming in a dialog-experiment

Weiß, Petra SFB 673, Universität Bielefeld, Bielefeld, Germany Hellmann, Sara Maria SFB 673, Universität Bielefeld, Bielefeld, Germany Herzig, Cornelia SFB 673, Universität Bielefeld, Bielefeld, Germany

To investigate how people build up shared knowledge for coordination in communication we developed a flexible experimental setting, the Jigsaw Map Game, permitting to examine interactive language processing in natural face-to-face dialogs.

We report an experiment on the coordination of object naming. Results show that people easily coordinate on common names especially when referring to objects as indirect reference objects and that nearly know explicit negotiations concerning names occur. We conclude that the setting has proved its applicability and that lexical coordination is achieved in an automatic and resource-sensitive way as proposed by Pickering & Garrod (2004) within their alignment approach.

Processing sentences in desiderative mood affects approach/avoidance actions

Claus, Berry Inst. für Psycholinguistiks, Universität des Saarlandes, Saarbrücken, Germany *Bader, Regine* Psycholinguistics, Saarland University, Saarbrücken, Germany

This study investigated whether processing desiderative-mood sentences facilitates approach related actions (pulling) compared to avoidance related actions (pushing). Participants listened to sentences and made sensibility judgments. Response times for desiderative-mood sentences (Lea wants to rest in a hammock) were significantly shorter when the judgment had to be indicated by pulling compared with pushing a joystick. In contrast, response times for factual-mood control sentences (Lea has rested in a hammock) did not differ between the two response-mode conditions. The finding that sentences in desiderative mood are associated with particular motor actions is in line with embodied theories of language comprehension.

FP-344: Career success

Social representations of the effort, luck and merit as criteria of professional promotion: A case of the health public servers

Bellico da Costa, Anna Edith Mestrado em Educação, FAE / UEMG, Belo Horizonte, Brazil *Cabral de Vasconcelos Neto, Milton* Microbiologia, FUNED, Belo Horizonte, Brazil

It was investigated the social representations (SR) of the Effort, Luck and Merit as criteria of professional promotion to the health public servers and the influence of those SR in the recognition of the individual performance evaluation (IPE) as valid instrument for professional assessment in Minas Gerais. Likert's questionnaire was used on perceptions, beliefs and values associates to the factors of professional recognition. Belief of that luck in the life as main factor for advance in the career. Antagonistic SR to the promotional factors of the professional valuation were observed as reason for those servers reject IPE as managerial instrument.

Personal, academic and labour factors as antecedents of job quality of university graduates

Gamboa Navarro, Juan Pablo Dept. of Social Psychology, University of Valencia, Valencia, Spain *Peiró Silla, José María* Social Psychology-OPAL, University of Valencia, Valencia, Spain *González Romá, Vicente* Social Psychology-OPAL, University of Valencia, Valencia, Spain

The aim of this study was to test the role of subject degree, personal characteristics, competences, instrumental knowledge and labour experience during and after university studies in the prediction of different indicators of job quality of university graduates, such as occupational fit, status, pay and job satisfaction. The study was carried out using a sample of 6988 Spanish young graduates, and hierarchical multiple regression analysis was used to investigate the relationships. Controlling for some demographic variables, results showed an important predictive power of subject degree, the effect of other predictors depended on the criterion. Theoretical and practical implications are discussed.

The proactive personality relation with entrepreneurialism and career success

Zareie, Fahimeh Psychology, Isfahan University of Iran, Isfahan, Islamic Republic of Iran *Nouri, Abolghasem* Psychology, Isfahan University of Iran, Isfahan, Islamic Republic of Iran *Ayati, Mohammad Mehdi* Psychology, Isfahan University of Iran, Isfahan, Islamic Republic of Iran

The purpose of this study is to determine relationships among proactive personality and entrepreneurialism and career success. Data have been collected on 150 supervisors in 3 companies. Proactive personality has been measured with Bateman and Crant's (1993) 17-item proactive personality scale (PPS), and career success has been assessed with Greenhaus, Parasuraman, and Wormley's (1990) 5-item career satisfaction scale. Results show that there are significant relationships among some variables. Key words: proactive personality, career success and entrepreneuriality

Relations between work commitment and career success: Are some dimensions more important?

Parts, Velli Psychology, Tallinn University, Tallinn, Estonia

The purpose of these two surveys (n= 2000) was to compare the role of various dimensions of work commitment (work and job involvement; affective, normative, and continuance organizational commitment) in objective and subjective career success (operationalised via salary level and promotions, and career and job satisfaction respectively). Results of OLS regression in study 1 revealed that, (i) affective organizational commitment and job involvement are most important commitment dimensions for both aspects of career success, (ii) gender and position in organization (rank-and-file employee, specialist, manager) mediate commitment–career success relationships. Study 2 largely replicated these findings.

FP-345: New challenges and approaches in work-organizational psychology

Perceived flexibility demands and work strain

Höge, Thomas University of Innsbruck, Institute of Psychology, Innsbruck, Austria

Economies and organizations of most industrialized countries are transforming towards increased flexibility (Rousseau, 1997). The reported questionnaire study analyzed flexibility demands of N=407 workers from a broad variety of branches. Controlling for socio-demographic variables, aspects of the work arrangement and working conditions as well as individual work orientations the results of hierarchical multiple regression showed evidence for a significant relationship between flexibility demands and emotional as well as cognitive irritation. The findings are discussed against the background of the entreployee-concept (Voß & Pongratz, 1998) and the distinction between organization- vs. human-oriented flexibility at work.

The excluded jobs in work-organizational psychology

Bayona, Jaime Andrés Social Psychology, University of Barcelona, Barcelona, Spain

The Work-Organizational Psychology (WOP) has done a great advance in the understanding of the people at the work context; nevertheless, WOP has put aside the research and intervention of jobs outside formal organizations. This study shows some of the historical factors that took the WOP to focus almost exclusively on jobs inside organizations and "forget" other work categories (i.e. informal jobs, low-quality jobs, self employment, employment hardship and underemployment). It is discussed that this attention on organizational jobs will be against both the fully psychological under-

standing of the workers' conditions and the actual labour market in the non-industrialized economies.

Successful volunteering: The impact of job and organisational characteristics on satisfaction and commitment

Güntert, Stefan Tomas Organ.- u. Arbeitswissenschaft, ETH Zürich, Zürich, Switzerland *Wehner, Theo* Zentr. f. Org.- u. Arb.-Wiss., ETH Zürich, Zürich, Switzerland

This research on volunteering integrates the perspectives of social psychology and work and organisational psychology to explain satisfaction and commitment of volunteers. Questionnaire data were obtained from 961 people volunteering for a non-profit organisation providing services for the elderly. SEM and regression analyses were conducted. Satisfaction is best predicted by task characteristics and the extent to which beneficiaries appreciate volunteers' work. Satisfaction, recognition by the organisation, and professional and social support predict volunteers' commitment. There is evidence for conflicts between organisational commitment and task-related involvement. Moderating effects of different motives support functionalist theorizing and integrate an activity theory perspective.

Globalization as a challenge for traditional leadership: Stress-leaders are wanted

Zankovsky, Anatoly Inst. of Psychology, Russian Academy of Sciences, Moscow, Russia

Globalization demands a new type of leader, whose leadership potential hidden in everyday activities is revealed exclusively under stress conditions. His specific self-regulation pattern thus becomes the most important competency that integrates other personal and professional qualities. Under stress and usual conditions the following parameters of 243 managers were analyzed: expert judgements of leadership behaviour, leaders' efficiency, psychophysiology and job satisfaction. Stress-leaders group under standard conditions demonstrated midlevel efficiency/job satisfaction and low level of leadership. Under stress they showed high levels of leadership, efficiency and job satisfaction. This group was also characterized by the highest in job mobility and carrier pace, i.e. was the most demanded at modern labour market.

FP-346: Psychotherapy - Research and treatment methods X

Evaluation of solution-focused brief therapy outcome: Methods and case example

Pakrosnis, Rytis Dept. of General Psychology, Vytautas Magnus University, Kaunas, Lithuania *Cepukiene, Viktorija* General Psychology, Vytautas Magnus University, Kaunas, Lithuania

The aim of the presentation is to illustrate the original methodology for evaluation of therapeutic changes in the course of Solution-Focused Brief Therapy by presenting a case example. The case presented is of a 14 year male, living in foster care facility for 12 years, diagnosed for emotional-behavioral disorder. The case illustration covers: techniques used in each session; content of the conversations; step by step changes of client's perception of the problem situation, behavior and problem severity; the results of formal evaluation of positive changes using subjective and standardized measures. The materials demonstrate how presented methodology allows grasping significant changes of client's problem severity and psychosocial adjustment thus can be used for clinical and research purposes.

Counseling physically disabled individuals: The concept of loss

Kleftaras, George Dept. of Special Education, University of Thessaly, Volos, Greece

The concept of loss is of central importance to the disabled individual. It is a painful process, where basic assumptions, views, behaviors, principles and values may have to be abandoned and new ones developed. In this article, special attention is paid to the concept and meaning of loss as well as the counseling significance of the individual's soul-searching-for-meaning of life and personal life meaning in disability and loss. Priority is placed on the existential perspective of loss-of-control and independence, dependence and "transition". A combination of humanistic-existential models and cognitive-behavior approaches is proposed as more appropriate for counseling individuals with disabilities.

Psychotherapy at a university counseling center: Students' symptoms and progress

Lucas, Margaretha Counseling Center/CAPS, University of Maryland, College Park, USA Hunt, Patricia Counseling Center, University of Maryland, College Park Maryland, USA

Psychotherapy at a University Counseling Center: Students' Symptoms and Progress. Margaretha S.Lucas Patricia F. Hunt University of Maryland College Park, Maryland Topic List: 21.6 Psychotherapy Research and Treatment Methods The study investigated help-seeking university students' distress and progress in therapy. Data from 3000 help-seekers were collected at a counseling center at a large American university. A survey was used to collect intake and progress data on help-seeking students' functioning. Factor analyses, Chi-square analyses, and Analyses of Variance measured gender and cultural differences at different times. Results and Conclusions: Groups presented unique symptoms. Progress in functioning depended on initial symptom presentation.

Integrative psychosomatic therapy in genitourology

Michailov, Michael Ch. Inst. für Physiologie, Inst. Umweltmedizin/ICSD e.V., München, Germany Schumitz, Heidrun Dept. Physiology, Inst. Umweltmedizin/ICSD e.V., Muenchen, Germany Neu, Eva Dept. Physiology, Inst. Umweltmedizin/ICSD e.V., Muenchen, Germany

Objectives: High complex interaction of psychic, neuro-hormonal, drug factors in urogenital pathology needs new therapy-models considering also psychotropic hormones/drugs (Acta-Physiol.-Scand.-191/S.659:49/2007; Br.-J.-Urol.-94:24-5/258-9/2004). Method: Psychic ("polar-attitude-list")/physiological-effects by occidental/oriental practices (genito-urological patients/probands[Urol. 70/3A/232-3/2007]. Results. Respiratory/music-psychotherapy: Increased psychological-items. Physical-yoga-therapy: Voluntary-apnoe-duration-increase/10-25%, respiratory/heart-rate-decrease/10-30% (n=51,p<0.05-0.01). Conclusions: Integrative psychosomatic-therapy by implication of combined physical, pharmaco-, psychotherapies based on occidental/oriental medicine/psychology in genitourology in context of integralanthropology could help for better health acc.-to UNO-Agenda-21.

FP-347: Attribution and related issues

Attribution of responsibility, social skills and self-esteem: Perception of prisoners and non-prisoners in Malaysia

Subhayya, Nirajs Murti Medic. and Behavioral Science, Internat. Medical University, Kuala Lumpur, Malaysia Nair, Elizabeth Psychology, Work & Health Psychologist, Singapore, Singapore

This study examines the attribution of responsibility, social skills and self-esteem among prisoners and non-prisoners in Malaysia. Responsibility and Self-Esteem Questionnaire (RSEQ) was analyzed using SPSS. T-test and one-way ANOVA were used to determine the significant difference between prisoners and non-prisoners. The finding showed a significant difference between prisoners and non-prisoners on attribution of responsibility for present status, perception of social skills and level of self-esteem. The Chinese attributed more external responsibility for change compared to Malays. The perception of social skills for Malays was reported to be higher. An implication for rehabilitation programmes for both groups was discussed.

Ethical justification as a parallel to causal attribution: Outlining and investigating the concept of prescriptive attribution.

Gollan, Tobias Dept. of Social Psychology, University of Hamburg, Hamburg, Germany Witte, Erich H. Dept. of Social Psychology, University of Hamburg, Hamburg, Germany

This presentation introduces a conceptual framework to investigate how people construe ethical justifications of their behaviour, while presenting first empirical findings and sketching a future research program. It is argued that ethical justification is parallel to the concept of causal attribution regarding logic, and thus can be conceived as a 'prescriptive attribution': While in classic attribution events are attributed to causal sources, in prescriptive attribution behaviour or ethical decisions are attributed to ethical principles. Further conceptual similarities are discussed, an empirically supported taxonomy of ethical principles is presented, and strategies for future research on prescriptive attribution are outlined.

An examination of attribution theory in the context of natural disasters

Marjanovic, Zdravko Psychology, York University, Toronto, Canada Greenglass, Esther R. Psychology, York University, Toronto, Canada Struthers, C. Ward Psychology, York University, Toronto, Canada

Although Weiner's (1995) attribution theory has been applied in numerous contexts, it has not been tested with groups of natural-disaster victims. We hypothesized that judgments of victim responsibility would predict greater anger and less sympathy, which in turn would predict decreases in helping intentions and helping behavior. Weiner's model was tested in two studies using experimental and nonexperimental designs. Across studies, path analysis validated Weiner's model, demonstrating that judgments of responsibility predicted lower levels of sympathy, which in turn predicted decreases in helping intentions and helping behavior. The utility of Weiner's model in predicting helping toward disaster victims is discussed.

Action/inaction sequence, near - miss and consensus effects in regret and disappointment

Krishnan, Lilavati Humanities and Social Sciences, IIT Kanpur, Kanpur, India

Two studies involving subjects in India examined regret and disappointment. The first study investigated action/inaction and high/low consensus using a scenario depicting an unfair outcome. In the second study, the action-inaction sequence, a near/far miss, and high/low consensus were investigated in the context of a hypothetical quiz contest. Findings indicated that regret and disappointment may not be correlated, and that the action/ inaction effect on future likelihood of action may vary depending on the action-inaction sequence, high/low consensus and the margin by which a goal was missed. Cultural factors such as a collectivistic orientation might also play a role.

FP-348: Conceptual change and cognitive complexity across the lifespan

Development of young children's counterfactual reasoning and its influencing factors

Chen, Yinghe Dept. Development. Psychology, Beijing Normal University, Beijing, People's Republic of China Wang, Jing Beijing Normal University, Developmental Psychology,DPI, Beijing, People's Republic of China

This study was conducted to explore the development of counterfactual reasoning of 3-to 5-year-old children as well as the effects of cognitive complexity and domain knowledge on their performance. Verbal protocol and story-telling (3 stories each including 4 pictures) were implemented to test 94 participants who came from a preschool in Beijing. Repeated-measures MANOVA was used and the results revealed: the development of counterfactual reasoning was influenced mainly by cognitive complexity (length of causal chain and the difficulty of question). Domain knowledge had indirect effect on counterfactual reasoning at different ages, whereas its effect was weaker than that of cognitive complexity.

Construction skills in chimpanzees (pan troglodytes) and human children (homo sapiens sapiens)

Poti, Patrizia CNR, ISTC, Rome, Italy Hayashi, Misato Kyoto University, Primate Research Insitute, Inuyama City, Aichi, Japan Matsuzawa, Tetsuro Kyoto University, Primate Research Institute, Inuyama city, Aichi, Japan

We compared construction skills in chimpanzees and human children. Chimpanzees were three youngsters and five adults. Humans were thirty children ages 24, 30, 36, 42, and 48 months. Subjects were given model constructions to reproduce and their constructions were rated for accuracy to the model. Two-way Analyses of Variance were conducted. Chimpanzees were advanced in constructing support relations in stacks, but only adults made accurate copies of model constructions. Adult chimpanzees and children age 24 months copied one-spatial-relation models. Human children from age 30 months also copied two-spatial-relation models. In conclusion, construction skills partially differ in the two species.

Temporal relations of personal events in life: How correct are four-year-old children?

Goertz, Claudia Developmental Psychology, Institute of Psychology, Frankfurt, Germany Krömer, Regina Developmental Psychology, Institute of Psychology, Frankfurt, Germany Knopf, Monika Developmental Psychology, Institute of Psychology, Frankfurt, Germany

50 four-year-olds had to place pictures of personal life events on a "street of life". Events differed in distance to the presence. Afterwards the children had to sort the pictures on two stacks: "past" and "future". Whereas most of the participants failed to place the life events correctly on the street almost all were able to sort the pictures correctly into past and future events. Therefore it is assumed that children of that age are not able to transfer temporal relations into spatial relations using the "street of life" as a methaphor for the passage of time.

Age-differences in the transfer of task-switching training

Karbach, Julia Inst. für Psychologie, Universität des Saarlandes, Saarbrücken, Germany Kray, Jutta Psychology, Saarland University, Saarbruecken, Germany

This study investigated age differences in the transfer of task-switching training in young and older adults. We examined near transfer to structurally similar tasks and far transfer to structurally dissimilar 'executive' tasks (e.g., Stroop task), and to other task domains. Participants were tested with an internally cued switching paradigm in a pretest–training–posttest design. Results showed near transfer, especially in older adults, and far transfer to other 'executive' tasks and fluid intelligence. Thus, the training promoted several executive control abilities, pointing to its usefulness for numerous clinical and educational applications. Long-term effects from a one-year follow-up will be presented.

FP-349: Human factor engineering

Effects of expertise and case complexity on anaesthetists' mental representation during pre-operative consultation

Neyns, Valérie Clle-LTC, UTM - MDR, Toulouse Cedex 9, France
This research explores the construction of anaesthetists' mental representation. Two variables were studied: anaesthetists' expertise and case complexity. Twenty participants performed 2 tasks: a categorization of patients' files and a simulation of patient consultation. Results indicate that experts categorize files using information about surgery and patient's state whereas novices categorize using general risk factors. The analysis of information gathering shows that, whilst novices explore files according to their complexity, experts follow the presentation order, no matter the case complexity. Results contribute to expert planning research and, in a computerization context, may help to design compatible interfaces.

Evaluating user interface effects on situation awareness within the Mission to Means Framework (MMF) approach

Bassan, David Human Research & Engineering, Army Research Laboratory, Aberdeen Proving Ground, USA
Evaluating user interface effects on situation awareness must take into account the context in which the behavior will occur. The Mission and Means Framework (MMF) approach allows one to concisely state the military mission and to operationally evaluate the military utility of alternative approaches. Mission threads developed using a top-down MMF process provide a warfighter's concept of the operation which the materiel developer, human system integrator, and comptroller can use for their work. In this approach, one compares element capabilities affected by user interfaces to element task requirements to place assessments of situation awareness in context.

Improving synthesized Chinese speech alarm design in emergency evacuation: Quantifying and predicting effects of different parameters on perceived urgency, intelligibility and impact on behavior

Li, Huiyang Inst. of Psychology, Chinese Academy of Sciences, Beijing, People's Republic of China Sun, Xianghong Institute of Psychology, Chinese Academy of Sciences, Beijing, People's Republic of China Zhang, Kan Institute of Psychology, Chinese Academy of Sciences, Beijing, People's Republic of China
Three experiments were held to optimize the acoustic and semantic parameters of synthesized speech alarms in emergency. Experiment 1, 2 investigate effects of speaker gender, speaking rate, noise and SNR on perceived urgency and intelligibility of speech alarms. The more fast and loudly the signals are spoken, the more urgent they are rated. They are not intelligible at the rate of 7 characters/second. Experiment 3 studies how the alarms influence participants' behavior in a 3-D virtual reality environment. People tend to evacuate when they know the fact of fire, than when they were only told to evacuate or more information.

Earcon blood pressure displays: Comparisons between auditory and visual BP display usability in an operating theatre context

Spring, Peter School of Safety Science, University of New South Wales, Sydney, Australia Watson, Marcus O.
Investigated was which Blood Pressure (BP) display modality: earcon auditory (BPE) or visual (BPV), would be most effective in a dual-task paradigm simulated operating theatre context. Eighteen undergraduates participated in a repeated measures design study. BP monitoring objective user performance and subjective user experience DV measures were compared after manipulating the IV - BP display modality - in either a cross-modal (BPE and visual), or intra-modal (BPV and visual display secondary task) condition. BP monitoring was superior for the earcons in terms of BP display update detection and response reliability and timeliness. Subjective user experience predictions were mostly supported.

Discourse analyses of a computer-mediated trust study

Qu, Weina Beijing, People's Republic of China Zhang, Qiping CICS, Palmer School, Long Island University, Brookville, USA Zhang, Kan Institute of Psychology, Chinese Academy of Sciences, Beijing, People's Republic of China
Trust in computer-mediated communication is increasingly attracting researchers' attention yet unexplored extensively in social / organizational psychology. The objective of this study is to empirically examine the effect of media and task on people's trust perception. A total of 42 pairs of Chinese undergraduate participated in the study by performing either negotiation or brainstorming task through either video channel or Instant Messenger. Particularly this paper reported our discourse analyses. It revealed that when no prior personal relationship existed (strangers) in a virtual environment, video does not always increase people's trust perception. It helps only when the task involves conflicts.

How to improve human performance technology?

Burov, Oleksandr Kiev, Ukraine Samsonkin, Valeriy Director, SSRCofRT, Kiev, Ukraine Burova, Olena patent Search, Ukrainian Institute of Industr, Kiev, Ukraine
Objectives Revealing reasons that confine accuracy of operator performance prediction, ways to improve level of performance, identifying the drivers for the performance gap. Methods Methods and regression models developed for operators' capacity prediction at: professional selection, professional aging monitoring, day-to-day check. Results Validity of results was checked on 500+ operators. Regression models built and investigated in relation to number of variables included into models. Conclusions Number of indices included into model has an optimum. Significance of the presentation: demonstration of reasons why traditional ways cannot ensure the high level of prediction and control of human performance.

FP-350: Human resource practices

Sustainable human capital management in Swiss companies

Eberhardt, Daniela Embrach, Switzerland
Objective of the study was to identify the state-of-the-art of Human Capital Management (HCM) in applying concepts of Corporate Social Responsibility (CSR) and Sustainability. The framework of sustainable HCM includes the employee-related content of twelve international standards and regulations (i.e. United Nations Global Compact, Standard for Social Accountability) as well as topic-specific survey-data. N=112 annual reports of Swiss companies have been analysed using the framework of sustainable HCM with its ten content categories. Sustainability in HCM is not systematically applied and used in Swiss companies. The kind of activities varies within companies and industries.

Relationship between human resources practices and performance: Mediating effect of job insecurity, organizational support and job satisfaction

Latorre, M. Felisa Social Psychology, University of Valencia, Valencia, Spain Ramos, José Social Psychology, University of Valencia, Valencia, Spain Estreder, Yolanda Social Psychology, University of Valencia, Valencia, Spain
This study analyses relationships between human resources practices and performance. Analysis includes organizational support, job insecurity and job satisfaction as mediating variables. The sample is composed by 835 Spanish employees from 47 companies of food, sales and education sectors'. Our results show a double mediation by two ways. Human resources practices show significant relationships with job insecurity as well as organizational support. In turn, job insecurity and organizational support are both related with job satisfaction. Finally, job satisfaction is related to performance. Our findings prove how human resource practices influence performance, giving support to the theories of human resource management.

Are 'Hybrid' HRM practices really good for local employees in developing countries?

Yavuz, Serap Middlesex University, London, United Kingdom Jackson, Terence Business & Management, Middlesex University, London, United Kingdom
This study aims at understanding local employees' perceptions of appropriateness as well as effectiveness of hybrid HRM practices in multinational companies (MNCs). It is hypothesized that as an HRM practice is perceived to be more hybrid by local employees, it will also be perceived as more appropriate and effective. While the appropriateness is conceptualized as the perceived ethicality of that practice, effectiveness is conceptualized in terms of employees' satisfaction with HRM as well as higher organizational commitment and lower turnover intentions. Data collection via surveys from employees working in MNCs, in Turkey, is in progress. Findings and implications will be presented.

The mediate effect of multidimensional perceived organizational support in the relationship of supportive human resource practices and Chinese employees' job performance

Chen, Zhixia Huazhong University of Science, Department of Sociology, Wuhan, People's Republic of China Eisenberger, Robert Department of Psychology, University of Delaware, Newark, USA
A model investigating antecedents of multidimensional perceived organizational support (multi-POS) and the role of multi-POS (affective POS and instrumental POS) in predicting job performance was developed and tested via structural equation modeling. 626 Chinese employees completed attitude surveys that were related to job performance. Results suggest that perceptions of supportive human resources practices (supervisor support, participation in decision making, organizational fairness) contribute to the development of multi-POS, and Multi-POS mediates their relationships with job performance. Key words: perceived organizational support, human resources practices, job performance

Human resource management practices in family business: Reflexes of psychological contract?
Casimiro, Mafalda Social Sciences, Polythecnic Institute of Leiri, Leiria, Portugal
The main goal of this study is to understand what type of psychological contract predominates in family business and the consequences it has in human resource management practices in that kind of companies. We are studying 12 family companies of Marinha Grande, one of most important industrial cities of Portugal. Psychological contract was measured by the instrument developed by Rousseau (Rousseau, D. M. (2000). Psychological contract inventory (Tech. Rep. No. 2000-02). Pittsburgh, PA: The Heinz School of Public Policy and Management. Carnegie Mellon University) and Human Resource Management will be identified by an in instrument under construction.

FP-351: Behavior genetics

Serotonin transporter gene: Brain-derived neurotrophic factor gene interaction and signs of depression and anxiety in parents of psychotic patients
Alfimova, Margarita Preventive Genetics, NMHRC, Moscow, Russia Korovaitseva, Galina preventive genetics, NMHRC, Moscow, Russia Lezheiko, Tatyana preventive genetics, NMHRC, Moscow, Russia Golimbet, Vera preventive genetics, NMHRC, Moscow, Russia
An interaction between the 5-HTTLPR polymorphism and Val66Met polymorphism of the brain-derived neurotrophic factor (BDNF) gene was reported to moderate the development of depression in response to environmental stress. To investigate whether this interaction contributes to distress in subjects experiencing a burden of having a mentally-ill offspring, 235 parents of psychotic patients and 102 controls were genotyped and administered MMPI. Significant 5-HTTLPRxBDNF interaction effects on Depression and Psychasthenia scores were found in parents only. These results support the view that 5-HTTLPRxBDNF interaction might moderate the level of anxiety and depression caused by stressful situation. This work was funded by RFH08-06-0086a.

Gene environment interaction for COMT on emotional processing
Herrmann, Martin Klinik für Psychiatrie, Universitätsklinik Würzburg, Würzburg, Germany Würflein, Heidi Klinik für Psychiatrie, Universität Würzburg, Würzburg, Germany Schreppel, Theresa Klinik für Psychiatrie, Universität Würzburg, Würzburg, Germany Mühlberger, Andreas Psychologisches Institut, Universität Würzburg, Würzburg, Germany Reif, Andreas Klinik für Psychiatrie, Universitätsklinik Würzburg, Würzburg, Germany Canli, Turhan Department of Psychology, Stony Brook University, Stony Brook, USA Lesch, Klaus-Peter Klinik für Psychiatrie, Universitätsklinik Würzburg, Würzburg, Germany Fallgatter, Andreas Klinik für Psychiatrie, Universitätsklinik Würzburg, Würzburg, Germany
The interaction between genes and environment is highly relevant for our understanding of the development of psychiatric disorders. Here we tested whether life stress, as an environmental factor, modulates the COMT genotype effect on emotional processing. Therefore we measured the event-related brain potentials in 81 healthy subjects during the processing of positive and negative emotional pictures. We found that high and low life stress modulates the effect of the COMT genotype on the neural correlates of positive stimuli processing in contrary manner. High life stress diminishes the positive evaluation of stimuli but only in subjects with the Met/Met genotype.

Stress-related negative affectivity and genetically altered 5-HTT function: Evidence for synergism in shaping risk for depression
Jacobs, Nele Dept. of Psychology, Open University Netherlands, Heerlen, Netherlands Kenis, Gunter Psychiatry and Neuropsychology, Maastricht University, Maastricht, Netherlands Peeters, Frenk Psychiatry and Neuropsychology, Maastricht University, Maastricht, Netherlands Derom, Catherine Center for Human Genetics, Catholic University Leuven, Leuven, Belgium Vlietinck, Robert Population Genetics, Maastricht University, Maastricht, Netherlands
Some people are biased towards negative emotionality but never develop depression; others do. In a large female cohort study, it was found that a functional polymorphism of the serotonin transporter gene (5-HTTLPR) moderated the tendency of negative affectivity in daily life to contribute to the onset of symptoms of depression. It was showed that this finding may explain previous reports suggesting a moderating effect of 5-HTTLPR genotype on the depressogenic effect of stressful life events. These findings indicate that genotype-stress interactions in depression may be better understood in terms of mechanisms more proximal to the processing of negative emotion itself.

Cognitive-behavioral profiles of children with subtelomeric deletions
Roubertoux, Pierre Dept. of Medical Genetics, INSERM, Marseille, France Fisch, Gene Dept. of Epidemiology & He, NYU, New York, USA
Cognitive-behavioral features of children with subtelomeric deletions have not been systematically assessed. We examined 15 children with either del2q37, del8p23, del11q25, or 4p-, using a neuropsychological battery to evaluate cognitive ability, adaptive behavior, emotionality, attentiveness/hyperactivity, and autistic-like features. We found an unusually high proportion of our sample (4/15 or 27%) could be diagnosed as autistic-like. In addition, each disorder was associated with a different cognitive-behavioral profile. In particular, among children with del2q37, strengths in abstract/ visual reasoning and weaknesses in expressive speech/language were found. Additional findings about adaptive behavior, attention deficits, emotionality will also be presented.

Etiology of motivation in elementary school children: Self-perceived ability and fear of failure
Spengler, Marion Inst. für Psychologie, Universität des Saarlandes, Saarbrücken, Germany Spinath, Frank M. Psychology, Saarland University, Saarbrücken, Germany Spinath, Birgit Inst. für Psychologie, Universität Heidelberg, Heidelberg, Germany Wolf, Heike Psychology, Saarland University, Saarbrücken, Germany
The present study is part of CoSMoS, a twin study investigating Cognitive Ability, Self-Reported Motivation and School Achievement (Spinath & Wolf, 2006). Data was available from more than 400 pairs of monozygotic and dizygotic twin children. We examined the role of genetics for individual differences in motivational variables (self-perceived ability, intrinsic values, fear of failure, hope for success). To elucidate sources of individual differences in motivation, we investigated the relationship among the four variables in univariate and multivariate genetic analyses and found evidence for significant genetic and non-shared environmental effects on all motivational variables. Implications for future research are discussed.

FP-352: Judgement and decision making

Illusory correlation: Distinct events or distinct baserates?
Vogel, Tobias Institute for Psychology, University of Heidelberg, Heidelberg, Germany Freytag, Peter Institute for Psychology, University of Heidelberg, Heidelberg, Germany Fiedler, Klaus Institute for Psychology, University of Heidelberg, Heidelberg, Germany Kutzner, Florian Institute for Psychology, University of Heidelberg, Heidelberg, Germany
In the original publication on illusory correlations, Hamilton & Gifford (1976) showed that participants link frequently observed behaviour to majority-members and rare behaviour to minority-members. According to the authors, the overestimation of distinct events (i.e. minority-members show rare behaviours) causes the effect. Following the pseudo-contingency-framework (Fiedler & Freytag, 2004), we show that the distinct alignment of baserates causes illusory correlations. In 2 experiments with 104 undergraduate students, participants produced illusory correlations, even if the stimulus-set did not contain observations of the distinct cell.

Motivated perception: Evidence for a positivity bias in early perceptual processes
Voss, Andreas Inst. für Psychologie, Universität Freiburg, Freiburg, Germany Klauer, Christoph Psychology, Universität Freiburg, Freiburg, Germany
Interpreting ambiguous situations is not a purely data-driven process but can be biased by top-down influences. In the present studies, motivational influences on perception were investigated with a color discrimination paradigm in which ambiguous stimuli had to be classified according to their dominating color. One of two colors indicated a financial gain (or a loss, respectively) whereas the alternate color remained neutral. Results indicate an overestimation of the "positive" color. To separate perceptual and judgmental biases, Ratcliff's (1978) diffusion model was employed. These analyses revealed positivity biases both on perception and on judgment.

Situational familiarity and the use of nonverbal and verbal information in judgments of veracity
Reinhard, Marc-Andre Inst. für Sozialpsychologie, Universität Mannheim, Mannheim, Germany Sporer, Siegfried L. Social Psychology, University of Mannheim, Mannheim, Germany Marksteiner, Tamara Social Psychology, University of Mannheim, Mannheim, Germany
According to the assumptions of the situational-familiarity hypothesis, only high familiarity with a situation leads to the use of verbal information when making judgments of veracity. Under low situational familiarity, people predominantly use nonverbal information for their judgments. In both Experiments 1 and 2, as predicted, when familiarity was low, only the nonverbal cues influenced participants' judgments of veracity. In contrast, participants in the high familiar condition used only the verbal cues. Experiments 3 and 4 furthermore found that participants with high situational familiarity achieved higher accuracy in classifying truthful and deceptive messages than participants with low situational familiarity.

Duplex-response: Punishment and repompense in contrast to univariate judgments
Hommers, Wilfried Inst. für Psychologie, Universität Würzburg, Würzburg, Germany
Harmdoers may be punished or required to give recompense for the harm. These modes of treatment may be used concurrently in the legal system and in everyday morality. In contrast to this duplex response, most psychological research on morality

used univariate responses either studying these modes of treatment separately or employing e.g. good-bad judgments. The study reported compared ratings on the badness of the action of the wrongfully acting person with ratings on the duplex response. Overall, results with the duplex response showed individual differences, developmental trends and supported the concepts of Andersons Information Integration Theory.

FP-353: Attitudes and attitude change

Implicit verb causality influences attitude transference effects

Walther, Eva Inst. für Psychologie, Universität Trier, Trier, Germany

Previous research has demonstrated that people's evaluations of other individuals can recursively transfer to themselves, such that people who like others acquire a positive valence whereas people who dislike others acquire a negative valence. The present studies tested whether this effect is influenced by implicit verb causality implied in the evaluative statements. Experiment 1 provided first evidence that transference effects were depending on the linguistic category (interpretative action verb vs. state verb). Specifically, transference effects are more pronounced when interpretative action verbs instead of state verbs were used. Experiments 2 replicated this finding and ruled out alternative explanations.

The effects of attitudinal structural consistency on attitude, intention, behavior and their relationships

Zhou, Jie Inst. of Psychology, Chinese Academic of Science, Beijing, People's Republic of China Wang, Erping Institute of Psychology, Chinese academic of science, Beijing, People's Republic of China Yu, Guangtao Business School, Central University of Finance, Beijing, People's Republic of China

This study explored the effects of attitudinal structural consistency on attitude, intention, behavior and their relationships. MONOVA analysis and chi-square test indicated: (a) the interactions of attitude base and affective-cognitive consistency (ACC) on attitude and intention were significant, but neither attitude base nor ACC had any effects on behavior. The difference test of correlation coefficient and T-Test indicated: (b) the interactions of attitude base and ACC on attitude-intention and intention-behavior relationships, but not on attitude-behavior relationship, were significant. Regression analysis indicated: (c) only under low ACC or high ACC and cognitive-based attitude condition, intention was the mediator of attitude-behavior relationship.

Study on the assertive behavior, locus of control and subjective well-being of Bulgarians using internet

Georgieva, Svetoslava Varna, Bulgaria

There are revealed 23 correlations between assertive behavior, locus of control and subjective well-being in Bulgarians using internet. Three tests were used – for assertive behavior, locus of control and subjective well-being in an online form, filled by 220 Bulgarians. The hypothesis more assertive Bulgarians will have higher level of subjective well-being was not proved. The hypothesis that there is significant difference in the locus of control of both sexes was proven, as women have more often external locus of control. There was also significant correlation showing people with higher level of subjective well-being have more often internal locus of control.

A qualitative study of the attitude towards social market economy in Germany: Justice aspects and the comparison with alternative economic systems

Kaminski, Simone Inst. für Psychologie, Universität München, München, Germany Frey, Dieter Department of Psychology, Ludwig-Maximilians-Universität, Munich, Germany Traut-Mattausch, Eva Department of Psychology, Ludwig-Maximilians-Universität, Munich, Germany Greitemeyer, Tobias Department of Psychology, Ludwig-Maximilians-Universität, Munich, Germany

Within a study using semi-structured, in-depth interviews we explored the attitude of the German population towards the social market economy (SME). 24 adults covering a range of ages and educational attainment were interviewed in summer 2007. Main topics were the understanding of the SME in general, the comparison with alternative economic systems and the role of justice aspects in context of the SME. We found that most people had little knowledge about the SME. A lot of aspects of the SME were criticised, but all in all respondents judged it as fair, especially in comparison with other economic systems.

Statements on opinion change as result of comparison processes: The relation between size of opinion change and the direction of comparison

Sklad, Marcin ACC, Roosevelt Academy, Middelburg, Netherlands

Three experiments explore the possibility that people's statements about their opinion changes aren't expressions of implicit theories of change (Ross, 1989), but outcomes of comparison processes. In two experiments, 194 undergraduates declared opinion changes. ANOVA confirmed the hypothesis: subjects declared significantly larger opinion change comparing presence to past than comparing past to presence, as predicted by Tversky's (1977) feature-matching model of comparison. Analysis of declared opinion changes of 90 adult Warsawians, confirmed the finding. Moreover, regression analysis showed that direction-size relationship was moderated by respondents' concentration on the past measured by the time perspective inventory (Zimbardo & Boyd, 1999).

Attitudes toward marriage: Embeddedness and outcomes in personal relationships

Riggio, Heidi Dept. of Psychology, CSU Los Angeles, Los Angeles, USA Weiser, Dana Alyssa Human Dev./ Family Studies, University of Nevada, Reno, Reno, Nevada, USA

Marriage attitudes, attitude embeddedness, personal relationship outcomes, and parental marital conflict and divorce are examined using 400 undergraduate students. More embedded marriage attitudes are more predictive of evaluations of general marriage issues and relationship scenarios than less embedded attitudes. Consistent with findings that marriage attitudes influence relationship quality (Amato & Rogers, 1999), more embedded attitudes are predictive of relationship conflict, commitment, satisfaction, desirability of alternatives, and expectations of relationship success. Individuals with divorced parents report more negative marriage attitudes. Future research on relationship attitudes, their strength, and consequences of parental divorce and conflict for offspring marriage attitudes are discussed.

FP-354: Attachment styles

Attachment style and relationship quality: The mediating effect of dyadic coping

Dinkel, Andreas Psychosomatische Medizin, Techn. Universität München, München, Germany

Objectives: Investigated the hypothesis that dyadic coping mediates the effect of attachment style on relationship quality. Methods: Cross-sectional study with N = 192 persons from the general population who were living in an intimate relationship. Mediation was analyzed using the standard regression approach. Results: The results confirmed the hypothesis. However, only positive dyadic coping acted as mediator, no such effect was observed with negative dyadic coping. Furthermore, mediation effects only occurred when relationship quality was the criterion variable, and not relationship satisfaction. Conclusion: Coping with stress in couples can be seen as one process by which attachment style exerts its influence on relationship quality.

Attachment: A comparison of young offenders and their parents with control groups

Kõiv, Kristi General Education, University of Tartu, Tartu, Estonia

This research addresses the question of whether juvenile offenders and non-offenders and also their parents can be distinguished by current attachment styles and attachment history. Two groups of adolescents (offenders and matched controls) and adults (parents of offenders and non-offenders) were required to complete the Three Attachment Style Measure and the Parental Bonding Instrument. Findings revealed significant differences in: (1) attachment styles of adolescents and adults: offenders and their parents had insecure attachment style; (2) attachment history: offenders and their parents perceived contradictions in maternal over-protection during their childhood, reflecting distortions of cross-generational transmission of attachment.

Do attachment anxiety and avoidance suppress accurate partner perception of investment model variables?

Macher, Silvia Department of Psychology, University of Graz, Graz, Austria

Adult attachment is associated with relationship specific expectations and experiences, with secure attachment coming along with higher relationship satisfaction, more investments and stronger relationship commitment than insecure attachment. I assumed that attachment is also associated with the perceptions of investment model variables at one's partner, and that the accuracy of these perceptions is reduced by the perceiver's attachment insecurity. Partners of 77 couples completed questionnaires assessing self reported investment model variables, the respective partner perceptions, and attachment insecurity. Results from hierarchical regression analyses show that attachment insecurity is associated with underestimated partner satisfaction, investments, and commitment, and overestimated partner alternatives.

Attachment and depressed affect: The mediating effects of social support on depressed affect

Mak, Miranda Chi Kuan Psychology, Chin. University of Hong Kong, Hong Kong, China, People's Republic of : Hong Kong SAR Bond, Michael Psychology, ChineseUniversity of Hong Kong, Hong Kong, China, People's Republic of : Macao SAR Friedman, Mike Psychology and Education, Catholic University of Louvain, Louvain-la-Neuve, Belgium Simpson, Jeffry Psychology, University of Minnesota, Minneapolis, USA Rholes, Steve Psychology, Texas A&M University, College Station, USA Chan, Clare Psychology, ChineseUniversity of Hong Kong, Hong Kong, China, People's Republic of : Macao SAR

The purpose of the study is to examine the mediating effects of perceived social support and relationship satisfaction on attachment styles and depressed affect cross-culturally (America and Hong Kong). We hypothesize that attachment styles, perceived social support and relationship satisfaction will have similar impact on depressed affect in the two cultural groups. However, the linkage strength between avoidant attachment to romantic partner and perceived social support will be different in America and Hong Kong. We recruited 350 American and Hong Kong college students to test out the hypotheses. The results supported our hypotheses. Further implications were discussed.

Transfer of attachment functions and adjustment among young adults in China

Zhang, Hong Psychology, The Chinese Uni of HongKong, Hong Kong, China, People's Republic of : Hong Kong SAR Chan, Darius K-S. Psychology, The Chinese Uni of HongKong, Hong Kong, China, People's Republic of : Macao SAR

A total of 147 Chinese college students, aged 21.44, completed a questionnaire which was designed to measure attachment-related functions fulfilled by various figures, loneliness, positive/negative affects, and self-esteem. Major findings of the current study are: a) Hazan and Shaver's (Hazan & Shaver, 1994) sequential model of attachment transfer, which has been shown to be valid among Western samples, was replicated; and b) both attachment supports from parents and peers were found to be associated with participants' self-esteem and emotional states (e.g., loneliness and negative affect). However, these effects were moderated by gender and dating experience.

Couple or trouble: Attachment dimensions and problem-solving task in dating heterosexual couples

Wang, Ya-Ling EPC, NTNU, Taipei, Taiwan Tsai, Shung-Liang

This study examined how couples with different degree of attachment dimensions interact with each other and analyzed with continuous scales rather than categories. 30 dating heterosexual couples completed questionnaires, and self-classification and cluster-based methods are also used to compare with each other. Each couple was asked to discuss a top problem area in their relationship, which they had previously identified. The problem discussions were videotaped for 10 minutes and coded with the Interaction Dimensions Coding System. The findings indicated that different attachment-pairing couples interact diversely while discussing their top problem area.

FP-355: Students' beliefs, expectations, learning and memory strategies

Investigation the role of learning styles and cognitive styles in learning English, mathematics and physics

Homayouni, Alireza Dept. of Psychology, Islamic Azad University, Bandargaz, Islamic Republic of Iran Taghypour, Hassan Dept. of Psychology, Izlamic Azad University of Ban, Babol, Islamic Republic of Iran Nikpour, Gholam Ali Dept. of Psychology, Izlamic Azad University of Ton, Babol, Islamic Republic of Iran Mosavi Amiri, Seyed Jalal Dept. of Addiction studies, Dr mosavi Clinic, Babol, Islamic Republic of Iran

The research aims to study the question that is there relationship between learning styles and cognitive styles and student's learning of English, mathematics and physics?300 son grade II high school students were randomly selected and Kolb's Learning Styles Inventory, LSI, and Witkin's Group Embedded Figures Test, GEFT, were administered on them. For analyzing the data, Pearson correlation coefficient was used. The results showed that there are significant and positive relationship between field independent cognitive styles, abstract conceptualization, analytical learning styles and learning of English,mathematics and physics. The findings can be used for predicting and assessing of academic performance in high schools in regard to

individual differences and increasing of learning of English, mathematics and physics.

Students' mathematical dispositions: The interrelated role of classroom culture and students' beliefs

de Corte, Erik Center for Instruc. Psychology, University of Leuven, Bierbeek, Belgium Depaepe, Fien Center for Instructional Psych, University of Leuven, Leuven, Belgium Verschaffel, Lieven Center for Instructional Psych, University of Leuven, Leuven, Belgium

The paper reports a year-long study in two sixth-grade classrooms, which differed in teachers' approach towards mathematical problem solving (i.e., traditional vs reform-based). Tests and questionnaires were used to measure mathematical achievement, problem-solving skills, and mathematics-related beliefs at the beginning and end of the school year. Classroom cultures were unravelled through analyses of videorecordings of all problem-solving lessons during the year. Interviews with teachers and students focused on their perception of the norms in their classroom. The results document the complexity of the relatioships between the classroom culture and students' beliefs.

Beliefs about knowledge and knowing of Thai university students: Personal epistemology and the undergraduate education

Fujiwara, Takayoshi International College, Mahidol University, Nakhonpathom, Thailand

Objectives: This research investigates how students develop their beliefs about knowledge and knowledge acquisition during their undergraduate education. Methods: Two groups of students in a Thai university completed a questionnaire: first-year students (n = 1,755) and students finished their undergraduate study (n = 1,767). Results: A five-factor structure is identified for their beliefs. Significant differences are identified between the first-year and the graduates in four factors out of the five identified factors. The differences are more noticeable in some majors than others. Conclusions: The undergraduate education could have an influence on students' epistemological developments in some aspects.

Metacognition component and performance: An analysis to student work

Escorcia, Dyanne Sciences de l'éducation, Université PARIS X, Carrières sur seine, France

This study explores the metacognitive processes that students bring to the task of producing written work. It was hypothesized that the writers who produce better-quality texts would demonstrate a higer level of metacognitive processes. Fifty students in their freshman university study completed a questionnaire and were interviewed. A metacognitive level was established and the data was correlated with a measure of written performance designed by the author. The Breavais-Person indicated that only metaknowledge and planning and self-instruction strategies are correlated with the writing quality. The findings identified which metacognitive components are most associated with performance.

Metacognitive strategies used by university students in the process of mathematical problem solving

Farias, Mariana Desarrollo Humano, Ins. Univers. de Tecnologia, Caracas, Venezuela

The purpose of this study was to analyze the use of metacognitve regulating strategies by university students, when they face up mathematical problems, through the five steps Shönfelds approach (1992), reading to analysis, exploration, planning, and implementing-evaluation. A 27-items questionnaire was constructed to measure the student's metacognitive processes in mathematical problem

solving, in 205 both male and female individuals, 19 year old average, from a Venezuelan Technological Superior Institute, before, during and after they solve mathematical problems. In order to evaluate the psychometric properties of the questionnaire it was applied only in its preliminary version seeking implications in the educational practice.

"I've been told that's a good textbook": Does quality information about an instructional medium influence achievement?

Fries, Stefan Inst. für Pädag. Psychologie, Universität Karlsruhe, Karlsruhe, Germany Haimerl, Charlotte Ed;ational Psychology, University of Mannheim, Mannheim, Germany

Following research on the Pygmalion effect and on persuasive communication, an experiment assessed the effect of quality information about an instructional medium on students' achievement alongside potential moderating conditions. 81 students were tested after having learned with a hypertext on statistics in four different conditions. They demonstrated higher achievement in response to positive compared to negative information, but no moderating effect of content relevance (moderate vs. high). Attitudes towards computers (measured using the FIDEC) moderated the effect: Only the achievement of students with positive attitudes was affected by the quality information. Practical implications of the results are discussed.

FP-356: Advances in factor analysis and structural equation modeling

Choosing the number of factors based on simplicity

Okada, Kensuke Cognitive & Behavioral Science, The University of Tokyo, Tokyo, Japan Shigemasu, Kazuo Cognitive & Behavioral Sci, The University of Tokyo, Tokyo, Japan

Choosing the number of factors is one of the traditional problems in factor analysis, which is a widely used statistical technique in psychology. The existing methods include the use of Kaiser-Guttman criterion, scree plot, parallel analysis, fit index such as AIC and standard error scree. Here, the authors propose a different approach based on the idea that the number of factors that maximize the simplicity of resultant factor loading matrix should be chosen. A new rotation method that maximizes the simplicity is utilized. We show the usefulness of our method by applying this method to real psychological data.

A simulation study on parallel analysis with ipsative data

Beauducel, André Inst. für Sozialwissenschaften, Helmut-Schmidt-Universität, Hamburg, Germany Kusch, René Faculty of Hum. and Soc. Sci., Helmut-Schmidt-University, Hamburg, Germany

Special caution is necessary when PCA is performed with ipsative data. On the other hand, it has been shown in several studies that parallel analysis (PA) is a reasonable method in order to ascertain the number of components to extract. The present simulation study investigates whether PA can be performed with ipsative data. The results show that PA based on normative data leads to a substantial amount of overextraction when applied to ipsative data. However, even PA based on ipsative data tends to a slight amount of overextraction. Recommendations for an optimal use of PA with ipsative data are given.

How to analyze data getting from semantic differential technique (SD)

Mitina, Olga Dept. of Psychology, Moscow State University, Moscow, Russia

SD and modifications are powerful in studying implicit stereotypes. Subjects evaluate concepts using the scales. Developing 3-mode data analysis is important in these cases. We suggest new way of such analysis. For each subject we calculate a vector of correlation between each pair of the concepts. Then we use traditional 2-mode factor analysis. To interpret the factors we use graphs. The vertexes of the graph are the concepts. The pair of the concepts are connected by an edge if the pair has a high loading on the factor. We will illustrate this method using examples from study of selfconception, ethnopsychology and geo-psychology.

Estimating and testing average causal effects by conditioning on latent covariates: The application of non-standard structural equation models

Kroehne, Ulf Inst. für Methodologie, Universität Jena, Jena, Germany Steyer, Rolf Department of methodology, FSU Jena, Jena, Germany

The theory of individual and average causal effects motivates the estimation and testing of average causal effects by conditioning on all covariates relevant for causal interpretation. If covariates are latent, the constrained structural equation models are "non-standard" because of a) the interactions between covariates and treatment, b) the likely heteroscedastic error variances and c) the stochastic nature of the covariates. Three different structural equation models (a random slope model, a mixture model and a corrected wald test statistic based on a multi-group model) are presented and compared with respect to convergence rates, type-I error rates and statistical power.

The utility of structural equations models in detecting adaptation equivalence: A study of the accuracy of estimation, power and type-1 error rate of multigroups confirmatory factor analysis with mean structure as a special case of structural equations models

Purwono, Urip Dept. of Psychology, Universitas Padjadjaran, Bandung, Indonesia

Three simulation studies to investigate the accuracy of estimation, Type-1 error rate, and the power of Multigroups Confirmatory Factor Analysis with Mean Structures in identifying parameters invariance across groups when Wald's statistics was employed were carried out. Results indicated that sample size of 600 was required to detect .35 standardized units difference in Kappa parameter with a probability of .75. A difference of .2 in Lambda parameter was detectable with probability of .9 when the sample size was 300 or more. It was concluded that the procedure has the potential utility for investigating equivalence between adapted versions of a test.

A model for integrating fixed-, random-, and mixed-effects meta-analyses into structural equation modeling

Cheung, Mike W.-L. Psychology, National Uni. of Singapore, Singapore, Singapore

Meta-analysis and structural equation modeling (SEM) are two important techniques in the behavioral, social and medical sciences. The present study proposes a model for integrating fixed-, random-, and mixed-effects meta-analyses into SEM. By applying an appropriate transformation on the data, studies in meta-analysis can be analyzed as subjects in SEM. This study also shows the benefits of using the SEM approach to conducting a meta-analysis. Examples are used to illustrate the equivalence between the meta-analytic and SEM approaches. Future directions on and issues related to this approach are discussed.

FP-357: Advances in item response modeling

Item calibration error in Computerized Adaptive Testing (CAT)

Yousfi, Safir Research and Development, Federal Employment Agency, Nürnberg, Germany

Computerized Adaptive Testing is aimed at optimizing measurement precision by real-time item selection during the ongoing test session. The respective item selection algorithms rely on the values of the item parameters. Estimates of item parameter are usually based on observed item responses in a calibration sample. The item calibration error is usually not taken into account by the adaptive item selection algorithms. This might lead to flawed estimates of person parameters and their standard errors. The effects item calibration errors in the context of adaptive testing are analysed theoretically and by simulation studies. Strategies to deal with problem are discussed.

A new equating method for nonequivalent groups design under nonrandom assignment

Miyazaki, Kei University of Tokyo, Tokyo, Japan Shigemasu, Kazuo Cognitive & Behavioral Sci, University of Tokyo, Tokyo, Japan Hoshino, Takahiro Cognitive & Behavioral Sci, University of Tokyo, Tokyo, Japan

In this paper we propose a new equating method for a common-item nonequivalent groups design in item response theory (IRT). The scores of the tests that the examinee of each group doesn't answer can be regarded as missing data. In the situation where the examinees can select test forms, a mere application of multiple group IRT modeling can yield biased results because missing data are non-ignorable. In order to solve this problem, we modeled the test form selection behavior. Through the simulation study, we showed that the proposed method can provide adequate estimates of the parameters.

Comparison of three approaches to missing response data for binary items in item response theory

Zeng, Li Dept. of Mathematics, Beijing Normal University, Beijing, People's Republic of China Xin, Tao psychology, beijing normal university, beijing, People's Republic of China Zhang, Shumei mathematics, beijing normal university, beijing, People's Republic of China

Missing response data is common in educational assessment surveys. This paper explored the relatively performance of three representative algorithms: EM Algorithm, MH within Gibbs and DA-T Gibbs Sampler in the estimation of the 2PL item parameters. An extension was made to the EM Algorithm: previous applications deleted the incomplete cases which contain missing response data, while we utilized the information of these cases in this study. Simulation studies and real data examples were used in the comparison. Within the simulation, the factor effect of sample size and missing rate are investigated. The result reveals that DA-T Gibbs Sampler is better.

Comparison of three non-parametric approaches to attribute characteristic curve estimation

Yu, Na Psychology, Beijing Normal University, Beijing, People's Republic of China Xin, Tao psychology, beijing normal university, beijing, People's Republic of China

The ACC (attribute characteristic curve) which was put forward by Tatsuoka and Xin tao (2006) describes the relation between the attribute mastery probability and the latent trait. It demonstrates great potential on both theory and practice. The estimation of ACC is essentially a nonparametric issue since there is no prior function for the curve.

This paper explored the relative efficiency of three widely used smoothers: kernel, spline and loess with Pearson statistic, Deviance and as criteria. The result reveals that spline demonstrate better than kernel and loess on model-data fit.

The effect of sample size ratio on the power and type I error of the mantel-haenszel and logistic regression procedures in the detection of differential item functioning

Herrera Rojas, Aura Nidia Dept. de Ciencias Humanas, Universidad Nacional, Bogotá, Colombia Gómez, Juana Facultad de Psicología, Universidad de Barcelona, Barcelona, Spain

Two of the more used method for detecting differential item functioning DIF are Mantel-Haenszel (MH) and logistic regression (LR). This paper describes a Monte Carlo experiment that was carried out in order to analyse the effect of sample size ratio on the power and Type I error of the MH and LR procedures. The design was fully-crossed factorial with 168 experimental conditions and the dependent variables were power and the rate of false positives calculated across 1000 replications. The results enabled the significant factors to be identified and practical recommendations are made regarding use of the procedures by psychologists interested in the development and analysis of psychological tests.

FP-358: Advances in psychological measurement and research methods

Cognitive diagnostic models

Yan, Duanli Research and Development, Educational Testing Service, Princeton, USA Almond, Russel Mislevy, Robert

There is growing interest in psychology and assessments that coordinate substantive considerations, learning psychology, task design, and measurement models. This paper extends the research on the design and analysis in a cognitive assessment (Yan, presentation at 28th ICP) and on the examples from our book Bayesian networks in Educational Assessment, and provides a comparison of several cognitive diagnostic models including fusion model and Baye net for their characteristics and uses. This 'evidence centered' perspective to assessment holds promise for meeting the challenge Cronbach raised in his famous 'two disciplines of psychology' address to the American Psychological Association in 1957.

Selection of optimum psychological communication dyad strategies based on a Fuzzy MCDM process

Liu, Fangyi Business Administration, NTUST, Mituo Township, Taiwan Hung, Yi-Jung Operation and Marketing, Swire Coca-Cola (S&D) Ltd., Mituo Township, Kaohsiung Coun, Taiwan

The selection of communication dyad psychological strategies is a typical multiple criteria decision-making (MCDM) problem. This paper aims to evaluate them for different personal psychological cognition. To deal with the uncertain judgment of decision makers, uncertain and imprecise judgments of communicate senders and receivers are translated into fuzzy numbers. This fuzzy prioritization method can derive crisp priorities from a consistent or inconsistent fuzzy judgment matrix by solving an optimization problem with non-linear constraints. The result shows that fuzzy MCDM method proposed is a simple and effective tool for tackling the uncertainty and imprecision associated with optimum communication dyad psychological problems, which might prove beneficial for plant marketing managers.

Optimal design of signal detection theory studies

Stanislaw, Harold Dept. of Psychology, California State University, Turlock, USA

Objectives: To determine how response bias and the number of signal and noise trials affect sensitivity measures in signal detection theory (SDT) applications. Methods: Exact probability spaces for SDT measures were calculated for various sample sizes, sensitivities, and response biases. Power was calculated from the slope of the probability function. Biases in sensitivity measures were calculated by comparing parameter estimates to actual values. Results: Designs that increase power also tend to increase biases in sensitivity measures, but some regions of the probability space reduce these problems. Conclusions: Optimal designs have false alarm rates near 30% and hit rates near 75%.

Biases in frequency reports: Effects of response format, time unit and reference period on reported behavioural frequencies

Klaas, Hannah Sophie Universität München, München, Germany *Stich, Jennifer* Psychology, LMU München, München, Germany *Pösl, Miriam* Psychology, FH Erding, Erding, Germany *Spörrle, Matthias* Dept. for Psychology, Ludwig-Maximilians University, München, Germany

Based on previous research regarding the assessment of frequency reports we conducted a questionnaire experiment to assess the temporal dimension of student media consumption. As in precedent studies we used a low and a high frequency scale and an open response question format. Expanding this, we simultaneously manipulated the time unit of response (minutes, hours) as well as the reference period (day, week, month). Results replicate existing findings regarding the influence of frequency scales and reference periods. Findings indicate that the effect of the response format on subsequent self-assessment questions is smaller when using an open response format. Respondents systematically underreport media consumption when asked to give answers in minutes rather than in hours.

Latent semantic analysis reveals higher valence for ingroups than outgroups

Gustafsson, Marie Psychology, Stockholm University, stockholm, Sweden *Sikström, Sverker* Dept. of Cognitive Science, Lund University, Lund, Sweden

A new data-driven method for automatic extraction of stereotypes and values in written text is suggested: A semantic space was created from 120 K news articles using Latent Semantic Analysis (LSA). The distances in the semantic space were analyzed and interpreted. The results show that several types of ingroups are higher valued than outgroups. First- and second person pronouns are higher valued than third-person pronouns. The same patterns were found for nations showing higher valence for home-countries and national neighbours. This is the first study using the LSA method to study ingroups and outgrups. Methodologically important issues are discussed.

FP-359: Acquisition of language IV

Pragmatic-semantic factors and input influence Danish children's comprehension of passive constructions

Jensen de López, Kristine Dept. of Psychology, University of Aalborg, Aalborg, Denmark *Sundahl, Lone* Department of Psychology, University of Aalborg, Aalborg, Denmark

We investigate the production and comprehension of Danish passive constructions by 3-6 year-old children. We analysed spontaneous production of passive constructions in 19 Danish child-adult discourse dyads and tested 50 children on their comprehension of active and passive constructions. The results indicate that passive constructions are infrequent in production, however the periphrastic passive is more frequent than the morphological passive. Periphrastic passives are also comprehended significantly earlier than morphological passives. This acquisition pattern challenges the maturation hypothesis and the non-canonical structure hypothesis suggesting that pragmatic-semantic aspects also play a role in children's acquisition of passive constructions.

Comprehension vs. production in language acquisition

Prat-Sala, Merce Department of Psychology, The University of Winchester, Winchester, United Kingdom *Hahn, Ulrike* School of Psychology, Cardiff University, Cardiff, United Kingdom

Four studies are presented that examine comprehension and elicited production of three syntactic structures (i.e. active, passive and dislocated-active clauses) by 293 Catalan-speaking children, aged 3-12 years. Results show that all children produce and comprehend 'actives'. Interestingly, however, they show that while children comprehend 'passives' before they produce them; the same children also produce 'dislocated-actives' before they comprehend them. Hence, for 'passives', comprehension precedes production, but for dislocated-actives, production precedes comprehension. These results occurred even when the verbs presented to participants were systematically varied. They are explained within the general framework of a cue based approach to acquisition.

Canonical and symbolical uses of objects and development of language: A case study

Moro, Christiane Institute of Psychology, Lausanne University, Lausanne, Switzerland

Vygotski argues for a conception of development in terms of semiotical constructions. He poses the crucial role of meaning to approach the co-constitutive development of language and thought. In our paper, we point out another socio-historical and semiotic argument. It concerns the links between development of language and forms of socio-semiotic activities related to the canonical and symbolical uses of objects appropriated at pre-linguistic level. To approach the development of language, we consider that it is necessary to take into account this previous socio-semiotic development in which language is produced. This argument will be examined through a case study.

Relationship between reading/writing development in English and cognitive abilities amongst Japanese junior high school pupils: Normal vs. poor readers

Wydell, Taeko Dept. of Psychology, Brunel University, Uxbridge, Middlesex, United Kingdom *Uno, Akira* Comprehensive Human Sciences, University of Tsukuba, Tsukuba, Japan

The relationship between phonological-awareness-skills and reading abilities in English/Japanese was investigated using 180 Japanese 2nd-Grade Junior-High-School Pupils (aged 14). 14 different tests including I.Q., Reading in English/Japanese-Kanji, and other phonological-awareness-tests, e.g., Rapid Automatised Naming were administered. No significant difference over the IQ-scores was found between the normal-group and reading-disabled (RD) group, but the RD-group showed significantly poorer performance than the normal-readers on the tests tapping phonological- awareness skills. The results also revealed that the RD-group showed much worse performance on reading English than Japanese compared to the normal-group. The language universality and specificity of reading processes are discussed.

Cognitive behaviours and connectivity mental system in second language context: Declines in sensitive period?

Figueiredo, Sandra Dept. of Educational Sciences, Campus Universitário Santiago, Aveiro, Portugal *Silva, Carlos* Educational Sciences, Campus universitário Santiago, Aveiro, Portugal

Regarding the lack subsisting in the second language acquisition research, related with the cognitive processing, it was developed a screening instrument to observe the linguistic behaviour on the several levels. Findings in what concerns the decoding competence will be discussed, regarding the performance of monolinguals and second language learners (130 individuals) in tasks such as the dichotic hearing test. Will be suggested a mental linguistic system of connectivity that could fossilize even in the younger learners. The concept of phonological awareness is not necessarily involving the consciousness level, influencing judgement behaviours in the linguistic task and compromising the phonological representations.

Poster Session Thursday Morning 09:00

Partners' attitudes in the process of group psychotherapy of vaginismus

Yslam, Serkan Psychiatry, Istanbul University, Istanbul, Turkey *Aslantas Ertekin, Banu* Psychiatry, Istanbul University, Istanbul, Turkey *Berkol, Tonguc Demir* Psychiatry, Istanbul University, Istanbul, Turkey *Kayir, Arsaluys* Psychiatry, Istanbul University, Istanbul, Turkey

Vaginismus is a major cause of unconsummated marriages. Besides women, partners' characteristics also have an important role for the maintenance of this condition. Partners' motivations and attitudes towards treatment are key issues in both individual and group psychotherapy. We are conducting group psychotherapy with vaginismic women using psychodrama and behavioral techniques in Istanbul Medical Faculty since 1989. In this presentation, we will remark some observations on partner's attitudes and behaviors at the beginning of the therapy and the changes we observed regarding these issues throughout the therapy process.

A survey of Iranian regular education teacher's knowledge of Learning Disabilities

Abdi, Beheshteh Social sciences, National Organization for Educ, Tehran, Islamic Republic of Iran

This study examines Iranian regular education teacher's knowledge of learning disabilities. A thirty-four multiple choice item questionnaire about learning disabilities was designed which had adequate psychometric properties in pilot study. The final sample consisted of 409(245 women and 164 men)Iranian regular education teachers. A Mean Confidence Interval Estimation showed that the extent of teacher's knowledge of learning disabilities was low (42 percents).Using t- test and Analisis of Variance tests showed that Female teachers, teachers with higher education qualifications (BA and higher) and teachers with lower teaching experience (less than 10 years) were found to be significantly more knowledgeable about learning disabilities. These findings address the imprtance of providing in service training for Iranian regular education teachers.

Effects of a cognitive-behavioural treatment on activities of daily living and quality of life in elder adults

Acosta Quiroz, Christian Mexico City, Mexico

The purpose of this study is to increase frequency of activities of daily living and life satisfaction level associated with it in 40 elder adults through a cognitive-behavioural treatment. Two focal groups of 12 people each were developed to elaborate an inventory on instrumental activities of daily life and quality of life, and psychometric properties of Yesavage Geriatric Depression Scale in its short version in Spanish (alpha=.8496) as well as the Mexican version of Beck Anxiety Inventory (alpha=.8860) were assessed in 82 retired persons to exclude subsequently patients with dementia, besides a neuropsychological evaluation. Further results will be presented.

Joint procrustes component analysis for exploring the perceptual and semantic structures in three-way semantic differential data
Adachi, Kohei Dept. of Human Sciences, Osaka University, Suita, Japan
I consider performing principal component analysis (PCA) separately for each of the stimuli by scales matrices obtained from participants with the semantic differential method. This PCA shows better fit to a dataset than three-way component analysis, but the former solution has indeterminacy on nonsingular transformation. To determine it, I propose joint Procrustes analysis (JPA). Differently from the existing Procrustes analysis, both component scores and loadings are transformed jointly without a constraint on transformation matrices in JPA. I present its algorithm and illustrate that JPA allows us to capture the inter-participant agreement and differences in perceptual and semantic structures.

Determinants of compassion fatigue, burnout and compassion satisfaction among mental health professionals
Agcaoili, Suzette SWIDB, Dept. of Social Welfare & Devt, Quezon City, Philippines Mordeno, Imelu Dept. of Psychology, University of San Carlos, Cebu, Cebu City, Philippines Decatoria, Johnny Graduate School, University of Santo Tomas, Manila, Philippines
Objectives: This study identified the determinants of compassion fatigue, burnout and compassion satisfaction among mental health workers relating to socio-demographic profile and dimensions of psychological well-being. Methods: 216 mental health professionals from the Philippines participated in the study. Standard multiple regression data analysis was utilized at 0.05 level of significance. Results: Multiple regression analysis demonstrated that higher Compassion Fatigue was predicted by lower level of self-acceptance. Burnout is negatively associated with positive relations with others and self-acceptance. Compassion Satisfaction was predicted by longer years of working as mental health professional and higher level of positive relations with others.

Designing the in-service training
Akbari, Soheila education and Psychology, Shahid Beheshti University, Tehran, Islamic Republic of Iran Sabbaghian, Zahra education and Psychology, Shahid Beheshti University, tehran, Islamic Republic of Iran
In this research the training design as one of the main processes of training approach have been concentrated A questionnaire with 13 variables was used. Samples were 291 representatives and staff Insurance Training Center. To analyze the data, ANOVA and t-test were used. The most distance between the present (2.07) and optimum status (4.31) was for "the amount of practical activities of the course." there was a significant difference concerning the education and optimum status of program design (F: 3.15 p=0/009). The courses which had no effect on job promotion were not suitable for training.

Developmental capacities of Nigerian infants and children: Are they precocious?
Akinsola, Esther Dept. of Psychology, University of Lagos, Lagos, Nigeria
The Denver Pre-screening Developmental Questionnaire was adapted and used to establish trends in developmental capacities of Nigerian Infants and Children and also determine their precocity. 1153 Infants and Children, consisting of 613 males and 540 females, randomly selected, and presumed to be normal served as participants. Their ages ranged between 2 and 72 months. The questionnaire administered covered four developmental functions namely: gross motor, language, fine motor adaptive, and personal social. Results obtained revealed sequential developmental capacities of the participants, and provided evidence for their precocity on some of the questionnaire items.

Occupational stress of young physicians
Alfermann, Dorothee Inst. für Sportpsychologie, Universität Leipzig, Leipzig, Germany Busse, Cindy Medical Psychology, University of Leipzig, Leipzig, Germany Stiller, Jeannine Medical Psychology, University of Leipzig, Leipzig, Germany Braehler, Elmar Medical Psychology, University of Leipzig, Leipzig, Germany
Objectives: To gain insight into perceived stress and coping mechanisms among young physicians. Methods: Participants completed questionnaires immediately after graduation from medical school and again four years later. Participants evaluated occupational stress, work load and effort-reward imbalance. Results: The young physicians reported work overload, which lay above that of more experienced physicians. The effort-reward-imbalance increased significantly during the first years of professional life and was greater than that of more experienced physicians. Conclusions: Young physicians should be better prepared to decrease work load and to cope with stress in order to prevent health problems.

Psychometric properties of the test for creative thinking – drawing production: Studies with the Portuguese samples
Almeida, Leonor Dept. de Psicologia, Universidade Lusofona, Lisboa, Portugal Ibérico Nogueira, Sara Psicologia, Universidade Lusofona, Lisboa, Portugal Urban, Klauss Psicologia, Leibniz University of Hannover, Hannover, Germany
We present some results concerning the psychometric characteristics of the TCT-DP (Test for Creative Thinking- Drawing Production by Urban & Jellen, 1996) for the Portuguese adult sample (646 subjects), based on the exploratory factorial analysis and on the analysis of the Reliability with Cronbach's Alpha method. The results reveal a good level of internal consistency. From the factorial analysis seven dimensions emerge, in contrast to the 6 dimensions from the German sample. We discuss the implications of the results for the evaluation of creative thinking for the Portuguese population.

Exploratory Factor Analysis of the Dimension of Self Efficacy about Teaching (DSEBT)
Almoziraee, Abdullah Psychology, Qassim University, Buraidah, Saudi Arabia
The purpose of this study was to investigate the factor structure of the Dimension of Self Efficacy about Teaching (DSEBT) Scale using exploratory factor analysis techniques. Preservice teachers (N= 509) from a middle province university in Saudi Arabia participated in the current study. The principle axis with promax rotation yielded four out of seven factors specified by the DSEBT scale: classroom management and discipline, community and parent involvement, special education, and decision making.

The influence of work-related stress and lifestyle on atherosclerotic cardiovascular disease risk factors among Japanese male workers
Ando, Mikayo Okayama University, Okayama, Japan Asakura, Takashi Lab.Health & Social Behavi, Tokyo Gakugei University, Koganei, Japan Giorgi, Gabriele Dep. Psychology, University of Firenze, Firenze, Italy
The purpose of this study is to identify how work-related stress and life styles are related to cumulative atherosclerotic cardiovascular risk factors. Japanese male workers (N=490) participated in a cross-sectional survey using self-reported questionnaires. A best fit path model on cumulative atherosclerotic cardiovascular risk factors was constructed using a lifestyle variable as a mediator. Depression and over-tasking were significantly associated with binge eating. Binge eating and age were significantly associated with cumulative atherosclerotic cardiovascular risk factors. These findings suggest that workers' mental health and over-tasking, as well as unhealthy eating behaviors, may be important factors in preventing atherosclerotic cardiovascular disease.

Teaching efficacy, interpersonal, intrapersonal skills and teaching performance in the Tertiary School
Angeles, Marie Paz Psychology Department, Tarlac State University, Tarlac City, Philippines, Philippines
This study investigated the relationship between interpersonal, intrapersonal skills and teaching efficacy, teaching performance and teaching efficacy as perceived by the teachers, peers and student samples. The following are the research problem : Is there a relationship between interpersonal skills and teaching efficacy ? ; Is there a relationship between intrapersonal skills and teaching efficacy ?; Is there a relationship between teaching efficacy and teaching performance? Descriptive statistics, item analysis, pearson correlation coefficient were the tools for evaluation. Results of the study shows that teachers interpersonal and intrapersonal are related to teaching efficacy.Teaching efficacy do not show significant relationship with teaching performance. Analysis of data suggests that teaching efficacy be explored deeply in different settings in the Philippines.

Physical activity determinants: Do they differ amongst normal weight, overweight and obese individuals?
Araujo-Soares, Vera Health and Social Care, The Robert Gordon University, Aberdeen, United Kingdom Skar, Silje Molloy, Gerard Aucott, Lorna Dombrowski, Stephan Sniehotta, Falko Aberdeen, United Kingdom
Targeting weight-loss implies addressing physical activity (PA). Behavioural interventions should address evidence-based determinants of behaviour-change. We test if the role of cognitive, behavioural and social-geographical determinants of PA differs between normal-weight, overweight and obese. 1155 university students reported on BMI, vigorous PA, social deprivation, habit, TPB variables and social support at the beginning and end of the year. SEM was used. No systematic differences in the predictive power of the determinants tested ($\Delta \chi 2$ (df;p)= 52.2 (38; .06)=NS) were found. Evidence on the determinants of PA can be used in designing interventions to increase PA regardless of BMI.

A reflected behavioral manifestation of the human emotional stability
Arshava, Iryna Dept. of Psychology, Dnipropetrovsk National Univ., Dnipropetrovsk, Ukraine
The study tested the hypothesis about the prognostic value of the preferred coping strategies as a form of the reflected manifestation of the human emotional stability. A group of 62 parents of chronically sick children were split into subgroups of problem-focused and emotion-focused copers. It

was found out that the latter changed their behavioral patterns under the impact of the child's illness in the direction of narrowing the scope of their social functions previously maintained while problem-focused copers retained a simultaneous-intuitive mode of pursuing personality aims. The findings open up new prospects for predicting human emotional stability.

Negative life events, cognitive coping strategies and psychological distress among Indonesian maids in Malaysia

Avicenna, Mohamad Dept. of Psychology, State Islamic University, Tangerang, Indonesia
This study will focus on the relationship between the use of specific cognitive coping strategies and psychological distress among Indonesia maids who suffer from physical and sexual abuse in Malaysia. The specific cognitive strategies they use to handle distress will be measured by the Cognitive Emotion Regulation Questionnaire (CERQ), whereas psychological distress will be measured by Depression Anxiety Stress Scales (DASS). Relationships between variables will be measured by Pearson correlations. Expectantly, there will be positive relationships between psychological distress and unadaptive cognitive coping strategies. The results of this study will be discussed.

"Fear of creativity" phenomenon

Babaeva, Julia Dept. of General Psychology, Lomonosov MSU, Moscow, Russia
Creativity takes great courage, openness to challenge and ability to overcome stereotypes, hardships and mistakes. Absence of these qualities attenuates creativity. Author's research allowed to indicate various factors which subjectively appear as "fear of creativity" and to classify them. Sample group included 175 participants aged 7-16 years. We used original questionnaires, modeling of "creative risk" situations, special educational tasks and psychological trainings, tests of creativity. Results: "fear of creativity" aggravates development and exhibition of creativeness. Means for overcoming this fear among schoolchildren were described. Using of them leads to considerable increase of creativity index.

The self-image and the creative potential of the polytechnic students

Balgiu, Beatrice of Social Sciences, University Poltechnica, Bucharest, Romania
The study is proposing itself the research of the relations between the self-image and the creativity. Starting from the theoretical premises that reveal the fact that the self-image is a factor of the creativity dynamics, we have discovered students technicians with different levels of creativity. These ones were analyzed from the perspective of the personality features (Berkeley Inventory) of the abilities and of the creative attitudes. It reaches the conclusion that the subjects highly creative have an self evaluation superior to the majority of the dimensions of the self-image as well as a structure more consistent of this.

Neuroimaging of human amygdala subregions?

Ball, Tonio Epilepsie-Zentrum, Universität Freiburg, Freiburg, Germany Mutschler, Isabella Freiburg, Germany Eickhoff, Simon Speck, Oliver Hennig, Jürgen Schulze-Bonhage, Andreas
The major subdivisions of the amygdala - the laterobasal group, the superficial group, and the centromedial group - have been extensively studied functionally and anatomically in animals and have also been anatomically delineated in humans, but the functional characteristics of these amygdala subregions in humans are still unclear. Here we present results from functional MRI (fMRI) investigations of subregional response properties of the human amygdala. Our findings indicate that

probabilistically defined anatomical subregions of the human amygdala show distinctive fMRI response patterns. Methodological limits and further directions for neuroimaging of human amygdala subregions are discussed.

The relationship of cognitive functions to the duration of alcohol abstinence in individuals with alcohol dependence syndrome

Bapat, Radhika Dept. of Behavioral Sciences, Sahyadri Specialty Hospital, Pune, India Chauhan, Ashutosh Behavioral Sciences, Sahyadri Specialty Hospital, Pune, India
The present study attempted to explore the recovery of neurocognitive functions in males with alcohol dependence syndrome but currently abstinent for varying lengths of time: 1-2 weeks, 1-2 months, > 6 months. The three groups (n1=13, n2=11, n3=9) did not differ on age, education and quantity of ethanol consumed in the lifetime and were interpreted as homogenous. Statistical analysis using ANOVA was done and results indicated a clear improvement on certain neuropsychological measures with protracted abstinence. Variables like age, education, lifetime consumption of ethanol and total lifetime years of consumption of alcohol correlated with the rate of recovery.

Joint attention in mental development

Baraldi Sobral, Renata Psychology, Alagoas Federal University, Maceió, Brazil Vieira, Nadja Psychology, Alagoas Federal University, Maceió, Brazil
This study is an approach of the communicative processes in early life as constitutive of the mental development. The mother-baby joint attention for the same object is used to explain the production of meaning that emerges from the interdependence between human beings and the social environment. This research presents a microgenetic analysis of longitudinal videos of mother-baby interaction. The results point to different configurations of the mother-baby communication mediated by object, showing the relation between joint attention and mental development, emerging as processes that are present from the first weeks of life, not only from the 9 months (TOMASELLO, 1999).

Interpersonal intelligence enhancement through cooperative learning

Baysara, Lyudmila Dept. of Psychology, National University, Dnipropetrovsk, Ukraine
The hypothesis of the research lies in the assumption that learners acquire communication skills in the course of cooperative learning which enhances interpersonal intelligence and lays the foundations for effective interaction with the community. Being the state-of-the-art research of interpersonal intelligence cooperative learning is considered to be the key factor for strengthening it. The following methods of research have been used: test of flexibility in communication, multiple intelligences tests and readiness to team work test. The availability of positive interaction, face-to-face interaction, individual accountability and stress on interpersonal skills contributed to the positive results of the research.

The effects of perfectionism and stress on mood: An experimental approach

Bender, Jens Fachbereich 8, Universität Koblenz-Landau, Landau, Germany Blattner, Mark Fachbereich 8, Universität Landau, Landau, Germany Ott, Mareike Fachbereich 8, Universität Landau, Landau, Germany Altstötter-Gleich, Christine Inst. für Psychologie, Universität Koblenz-Landau, Landau, Germany
A multitude of quasi-experimental studies reveal that perfectionism is associated with lower well-being. An important mediator of this association is perceived stress. Until now, there is only one experimental study (Wirtz et al., 2007) that analyzes the interrelation of perfectionism and stress. This

study, however, focuses on neurophysiological measures. We present two studies (N = 72 and 90) realizing three stress conditions: no stress, task related stress and interpersonal stress. Results of path analysis emphasize the important role of perfectionism concerning the exposure to stress. Further results to mood and control variables like test-anxiety and self-efficacy are reported and discussed.

Prospective memory and rostral prefrontal cortex: Involvement of a system mediating stimulus-oriented and stimulus–independent attending?

Benoit, Roland G. Inst. Cognitive Neuroscience, University College London, London, Germany Gilbert, Sam Inst. Cognitive Neuroscience, University College London, London, Germany Frith, Chris D. -, UCL & University of Aarhus, London, Germany Burgess, Paul W. Inst. Cognitive Neuroscience, University College London, London, Germany
Using fMRI, we investigated whether the oft-reported rostral prefrontal cortex (PFC) activations during prospective memory paradigms might reflect the demands that such tasks make for selection between stimulus-oriented (i.e., environmentally prompted) and stimulus-independent (i.e. environmentally decoupled) attending. Using a 2x2 factorial design, we crossed (i) a prospective memory vs. ongoing task only manipulation with (ii) a stimulus-oriented vs. –independent manipulation. Common regions of activation within rostral PFC provoked by both manipulations supported the hypothesis. However, additional rostral PFC recruitment outside these areas suggested that this is not a complete explanation of the rostral PFC haemodynamic changes during prospective memory performance.

Lottery selection: Choosing for oneself and advising others

Bereby-Meyer, Yoella Dept. of Psychology, Ben Gurion University, Beer-Sheva, Israel Moran, Simone School of Managment, Ben Gurion University, Beer-Sheva, Israel
We examined peoples' coordination in a lottery selection task, where they made choices for themselves or advised choices of others. 160 participants chose (or advised others to choose) between participating in a low or high prize lottery (e.g., 100 NIS versus 200 NIS). The prize in both lotteries was contingent on own (or on advised person's) performance in identifying celebrities' distorted faces. In both conditions, despite correct beliefs about the distribution of choices, participants who considered themselves more skillful chose the high prize lottery significantly more than participants who considered themselves less skillful. Consequently, the former obtained lower expected gains.

Creative thinking in understanding of painting

Berezanskaya, Natalya Dept. of Psychology, Moscow State University, Moscow, Russia
Does the level of creativity influence on process of thinking while the object of thinking is painting? Participants were divided into group with high level of creativity and group with low level of creativity. They were asked to describe verbally eight Gauguin's works and entitled them. Guilford's Alternative Uses Task and Remotes Associations Task (Mednick) were employed. We obtained significant higher number and diversity of answers in high creative group. Qualitative analysis showed existence of three levels of interpretation: intellectual, empathic and "invention of new meaning". Contrary to expectations, there were no significant correlations with the level of participant's creativity.

A comparative study of risk perception, risk willingness and risk sensitivity

Bergly, Tone Helene Dept. of Psychology, Norwegian Univ. of Sci.&Techn., Trondheim, Norway Rundmo, Torbjörn Dept. of Psychology, Norwegian Univ. of Sci.&Te, Trondheim, Norway

The core aim of this study is to examine if there are cross cultural differences in risk perception and risk willingness among people in Norway, India and Ghana. Data collection was carried out among 742 respondents spring 2006. This study showed that there were cross cultural differences in risk perception in Norway, Ghana and India. Ghanaians perceived the risk as higher then all the other respondents. There were also evidence supporting people being risk sensitive. The study also found some predictors of perceived risk of violence, the strongest one were country and perceived natural risks.

Culture, traditions and tied-up sexuality of women with vaginismus

Berkol, Tonguc Demir Psychiatry, Istanbul University, Istanbul, Turkey Aslantas Ertekin, Banu Psychiatry, Istanbul University, Istanbul, Turkey Islam, Serkan Psychiatry, Istanbul University, Istanbul, Turkey Kayir, Arsaluys Psychiatry, Istanbul University, Istanbul, Turkey

Contrary to the Western countries, vaginismus is a frequent condition and the most common reason for applications to sexual dysfunction treatment units in Turkey. This fact suggests that the social, cultural and religious factors may play an important role in the etiology of vaginismus. In this presentation we will report our impressions of these topics particularly from a psychotherapy group involving 14 women with vaginismus using psychodrama and behavioral techniques, but also from our group psychotherapy experiences in The Treatment Center for Sexual Dysfunction of Psychiatry Department in Istanbul Medical Faculty since 1989.

The relationship between approaches to learning and expected efficacy for teaching young children

Berthelsen, Donna Centre of Learning Innovation, Qld University of Technology, Brisbane, Australia Brownlee, Joanne Centre of Learning Innovation, Qld University of Technology, Brisbane, Australia Boulton-Lewis, Gillian Centre of Learning Innovation, Qld University of Technology, Brisbane, Australia Dunbar, Stephanie Centre of Learning Innovation, Qld University of Technology, Brisbane, Australia

Teachers' personal self-efficacy is related to learning outcomes of children. This study investigated relationships between self-efficacy beliefs for teaching young children and the approaches to learning held by students enrolled in a vocational course in preparation for work in child care settings. Questionnaires were completed by 180 students. Students who held adult-oriented, as opposed to child-oriented efficacy beliefs, were more likely to have reproductive approaches to their own learning. Students with a contextual approach to learning were more child-oriented. The importance of a relational and contextual approach to learning are discussed in order to enhance teaching practices with young children.

Analogy strategies development in senior pre-school-age children

Bila, Iryna Kamyanets-Podilskiy University, Kamyanets-Podilskiy, Ukraine

The research covers issues of analogy strategies development in senior pre-school-age children. Conceptual inferences were made regarding level of development of creative intellectual actions in senior pre-school-age children; prerequisites of their development elicited. Experiment was conducted, intended for study of specificity of analogy strategies manifestation in creative activity of senior pre-school-age children. In research developed and experimentally tested the conceptual model and all-embracing technique of analogy strategies development. The creative tasks that underlie the creative training technique are aimed at development of positive emotional attitude of senior pre-school-age children towards creative activity, formation of sensory experience, and improvement of analogy skills.

Have you been here before?: Decoding memory traces for visual scenes from brain signals

Bles, Mart BCCN - Berlin, Berlin, Germany Haynes, John-Dylan BCCN - Berlin, BCCN - Berlin, Berlin, Germany

When humans perceive visual scenes they were previously exposed to, an extensive cortical memory network is activated. Here, we investigate whether it might be possible to decode from brain signals whether a subject covertly recognizes a visual scene. After navigating a set of 3D environments, subjects viewed videos of "old" or "new" environments during fMRI scanning. A pattern classifier was trained to categorize brain activity patterns as "old" or "new". Above-chance classification was possible from the medial temporal lobe and parietal cortex. Our results show that neuroimaging can be used to reveal memory traces with potential use in forensic sciences.

Evaluation of subjective representation of stability of motivational constructs (RSM)

Blinnikova, Svetlana Psychology, Moscow State University, Moscow, Russia Mitina, Olga Psychology, Moscow State University, Moscow, Russia

A method for evaluation of RSM was created. Subjects were given different patterns of behaviors and were asked to evaluate probabilities of following them two others. One of them has the same motivational basis as the initial one and the second has an opposite motivational basis. Using RSM we found out that a person admits possibility of motivational changing in a greater degree depending on an individual characteristic and less on motivational content. Four different strategies of answers according of combination of the two probabilities which subjects gave to the consequences are: full restricted, incomplete restricted, unrestricted and overlapping choices.

On the role of motivation in teaching

Bogoslovskaya, Zarifa Psychology Faculty, Moscow State University, Moscow, Russia

The aim is empirical study of motivation impact on teaching and learning process. The importance of raising the quality of education is emphasized. The accent is made on moral values, development of internal motivation, mutual understanding between the teacher and a student, and the place of teacher's own skills in this process. Peculiarities of teaching foreign language to the students of psychology are given.

Why mixed models are so few used?

Borelli, Massimo B.R.A.I.N., University of Trieste, Trieste, Italy Cervai, Sara Dept. of Political Sciences, University of Trieste, Trieste, Italy Battaglini, Piero Paolo B.R.A.I.N., University of Trieste, Trieste, Italy

A simple research in the most known databases of scientific literature in psychology (PsycInfo, PsycLit) shows that just the 4% of the empirical studies uses a mixed model/multilevel approach. On the other side more than 60% still uses a linear regression approach, often in an uncritical way. Despite the Generalized Linear Models (GLM) have been published in the early '70 and their strengths have repeatedly been demonstrated in different fields, their use is still neglected. The present paper aims to clarify their effectiveness in the psychological field and how they can overcome linear regression limits.

Emotional false memories in mild cognitive impairment

Brückner, Katja Hamburg, Germany Moritz, Steffen Inst. für Psychiatrie, Universität Hamburg, Hamburg, Germany

Three groups of participants (healthy older adults, mild cognitive impairment [MCI] and Alzheimer's disease [AD]) underwent an emotional variant of the Deese-Roediger-McDermott-(DRM)-task. They studied four lists that were strongly converged semantically on a non-presented critical theme word. These were either depression-relevant (i.e., loneliness), delusion-relevant (betrayal), positive (holidays) or neutral (window). The results points out that the MCI-group shows despite on a normal overall emotional memory performance in many but not in all features very similar performance as patients with AD. The diagnostic potentials of the emotional valente DRM-task are discussed and results of older depressed patients are considered.

A case of history repeating: Investigating the effects of distractor repetition on social categorization.

Brebner, Joanne School of Psychology, University of Aberdeen, Aberdeen, United Kingdom Macrae, C. Neil School of Psychology, University of Aberdeen, Aberdeen, United Kingdom

Objectives: Does social categorization continue to occur following repeated presentation of a to-be-ignored face? Methods: Participants were required to classify target names while ignoring faces presented either as primes, flanking stimuli or central distractors. These faces appeared either once, or several times, and their influence on reaction times were measured. Results: Response times were slower on mismatching than on matching trials regardless of distractor repetition. Conclusions: Perceivers are unable to ignore task-irrelevant sex-cues from faces, even when they are presented multiple times. While neuroimaging research suggests that distractor repetition would attenuate interference, social categorization appears to be immune to such effects.

Reaction time and fractional anisotropy

Bringas, Maria Luisa Dept. of Neuropsychology, CIREN, Havana, Cuba Valdes, Pedro Neurophysics, Cuban Neurosciences Center, Havana, Cuba Ojeda, Alejandro Neuropsychology, Cuban Neuroscience Center, Havana, Cuba Rodriguez, Lupe Neuropsychology, CIREN, Havana, Cuba Lage, Agustin Neuroinformatics, Cuban Neuroscience Center, Havana, Cuba

Diffusion tensor imaging DTI was used to investigate the relationship between white matter and reaction time RT. DTI allows calculating the fractional anisotropy FA (indirect measure of presence of myelin in the axons). 45 normal and young subjects performance in a continuous performance test (single and complex RT task) was correlated with the FA voxel matrix of the group over the white matter mask of the Montreal Neurological Institute. The localization, using Mori 2005 DTI atlas, of RT-AF correlation with significant coefficients ($p < 0.03$) were corona radiata bilateral, right inferior and superior longitudinal fasciculus and the left thalamic radiation.

The influence of resilience beliefs as a resource in the interaction with customers

Buchczik, Nana-Rosa Mainz, Germany Dormann, Christian Psychology, JohannesGutenbergUniversity, Mainz, Germany

As yet the phenomenon of resilience as a resource has mainly been investigated in the field of developmental psychology. In the present online and questionnaire study with 160 human service providers resilience has been investigated as a positive belief in psychological coping with stress. Results indicate 4 factors (emotional rebounding, verbal offence, psychological stabilisation, balance), which could reduce the negative impact of customer-related social stressors on the psychological condition variable (burnout). The results give reason for further considerations regarding resilience as a belief in ones own psychological resistance to stress.

Contextualized reasoning: Testing for medium specificity and relations with fluid and crystallized intelligence

Bucholtz, Nina *IQB, Humboldt-Universität zu Berlin, Berlin, Germany* **Formazin, Maren** **Wilhelm, Oliver**
Reading and audiovisual comprehension are prominent instances of contextualized reasoning. Such measures can be conceptualized as a linear function of fluid and crystallized intelligence. In two studies (n=94; n=216) with 10th graders reading comprehension was measured with paper-pencil tests and audiovisual comprehension was measured on laptops and PDA's respectively. In both studies reading and audiovisual comprehension were correlated very close to unity. The relations of both comprehension measures are very high with fluid intelligence and crystallized intelligence. We conclude that individual differences in comprehension measures are not medium specific and are primarily due to fluid intelligence.

Communal coping styles and observable coping behaviour

Buchwald, Petra *Phil. Fakultät, Universität Düsseldorf, Düsseldorf, Germany* **Schorn, Nicola** *Educational Science, University of Duesseldorf, Willich, Germany*
Aims of the study were the conceptual integration of the multi-axial coping model and the model of interaction in groups in order to analyse the influence of individual and communal coping styles on observable coping behaviour in rescue situations. Fifteen paramedics filled in the German Strategic Approach to Coping Scale (Hobfoll, 1998) and were video-observed while acting in real rescue situations. The interactions were marked on the basis of Systematic Multiple Level Observation of Groups (Bales & Cohen, 1982). Stepwise regression analyses confirmed significant effects of coping styles on observable coping behaviour and the conceptual integration of the two models.

When younger adults have worse memories than the elderly: An investigation of adult age differences in the formation of false memories.

Bucur, Barbara *Saint Peters, USA*
To investigate age differences in the formation of false memories, healthy older and younger adults completed an incidental encoding task using words which were semantic associates of a word that was never presented, the critical lure. Independent groups t-tests revealed that older adults recalled significantly fewer of the lures than younger adults. Thus, older adults do not always show memory impairments compared to younger adults and, under incidental encoding conditions, are actually less susceptible to the influence of false information. This could be due to various individual difference variables that are more important predictors of cognitive decline than increased age.

The correlations between academic achievement and Mc. Clelland's motivation. A study on university students

Budi Taruna, Zamralita *Psychology, Tarumanagara University, Jakarta, Indonesia*
According to McClellands's theory of motivation (1987), motivation consists of n-ach, n-aff, and n-pow. A student who has academic achievement supposes to also have high level of the n-ach Two hundred (200) university students, (age 17-22) participated in this study. Their GPA scores were recorded and compared to their responses on questionnaire based on McClellands's. Students

with high GPA scores were not necessarily high on n-ach. Some students with lower n-ach do not necessarily have lower GPA than their classmates. Discussions include the possibility of differences between the concepts of academic achievement. Gender and cultural aspects may influence the variability of the needs which give impact to the variability of the academic achievement.

Finders and seekers: Creativity as a function of college major

Burshteyn, Dmitry *Dept. of Psychology, Siena College, Loudonville, USA* **Martin, Kayleigh** *Psychology, Siena College, Loudonville, NY, USA* **Geer, Jordan** *Psychology, Siena College, Loudonville, NY, USA*
The purpose of this study was to investigate differences in creativity on finding-seeking dimensions, specifically the differences between business, liberal arts, and science majors. In this study a representative random sample of 55 Siena College students of 20 different majors was administered a 40-item inventory based on Durmysheva's (2006) instrument. The Analysis of Variance (ANOVA) indicated no statistically significant differences in seeker dimension F (2, 52) =1.559 p<.220. Also, no significant differences were observed on the finder dimension F (2, 52) =.165 p<.848.

Personality and coping with a low-control situation: Cross-lagged latent variable analysis

Busko, Vesna *Department of Psychology, Faculty of Philosophy, Zagreb, Croatia*
The study aimed to test the hypothesized nature and directions of personality, appraisals, and coping relationships. The data were collected on a sample of 421 basic military trainees within a follow-up study of coping with low-control stress. Structural equation models used to test hypothesized mediation effects of cognitive appraisals were specified within a 2-wave cross-lagged panel design, with stationarity assumed on theoretical grounds. Partial mediation effects of event stressfulness were confirmed for emotion-focused coping only. The results were compared with those obtained by structural equation analyses done within different methodological framework but tested against the same data sets.

Who's smart, who's not? The nature of snap judgments about intelligence.

Button, Cathryn *Psychology, Memorial University, St. John's, Canada* **Grant, Malcolm** *Psychology, Memorial University, St. John's, Canada* **Snook, Brent** *Psychology, Memorial University, St. John's, Canada* **Arvidsson, Martin** *Psychology, Memorial University, St. John's, Canada*
This study examined the nature of snap judgments that perceivers often make about the cognitive abilities of others, including strangers, with comparatively little information. College students were asked to rate the intelligence of a series of people presented in pictures. These had previously been rated by different participants on a number of visually prominent characteristics, such as age, attractiveness and ethnicity. Intelligence inferences were related to attractiveness and age, with the nature of the inference varying across ethnic groups. Results are discussed in terms of the nature of social inferences and the cues used to make them.

The metaphor: A necessary cognitive device in didactic texts

Calderon, Gabriela *Psychology, UAQ, Queretaro, Mexico*
The metaphor is an important cognitive device in texts (orals and written) created to illuminate some shared features between source and target making easier to understand new concepts and ideas. The aim of this study was to detect and analyse which kind of metaphors Mexican university students

used when they write didactic texts for children between 6 to 8 years old. Our findings show that the schematic metaphors were the most used to explain topics like mind, black holes and friendship, though students did not realise they were using metaphors.

Agent-based modeling design for policy-making support: Using the findings of questionnaire surveys

Cao, Yang *Kansai University, Osaka, Japan* **Maeda, Taiyo** **Arikawa, Hiroshi** **Murata, Tadahiko**
In conventional multi-agent simulation (MAS) studies, agent parameters have been arbitrarily set by researchers. The Policy Grid Computing Laboratory (PG Lab) of Kansai University aims, however, at the construction of more realistic social simulation models, and accordingly gives greater emphasis to the design of agent types. A method for classifying agent types has been devised based on the clarification, through questionnaire survey results, of the relations between agents' basic characteristics (demographic variables such as gender, age, and occupation) and their psychological outlooks (variables of personal involvement or attitude regarding particular policies or other matters).

Short-term cognitive training increases activation in mesocorticostriatal circuits in ADHD and mimics effect of psychostimulant medication

Carmona, Susanna *Psiquiatria i Medici, URNC UAB, Barcelona, Spain* **Hoekzema, Elseline** *Psiquiatria i Medicina Legal, URNC UAB, Barcelona, Spain* **Bielsa, Anna** *Unitat de Paidopsiquiatria, Hospital Vall d'Hebron, Barcelona, Spain* **Tremols, Virginia** *Departament de Pediatria USP, Institut Universitari Dexeus, Barcelona, Spain* **Valencia, Joana** *Psiquiatria i Medicina Legal, URNC UAB, Barcelona, Spain* **Rovira, Mariana** *Psiquiatria i Medicina Legal, CRC Corporacion Sanitaria, Barcelona, Spain* **Soliva, Joan Carles** *Psiquiatria i Medicina Legal, URNC UAB, Barcelona, Spain* **Ramos, Antonio** *Departament de Psiquiatria, Hospital Vall d'Hebron, Matadepera, Spain* **Casas, Miquel** *Departament de Psiquiatria, Hospital Vall d'Hebron, Barcelona, Spain* **Vilarroya, Oscar** *Psiquiatria i Medicina Legal, URNC UAB, Barcelona, Spain*
Our work studies the impact of short-term cognitive training on brain activity, and provides a neural account of the effects of cognitive training in Attention Deficit and Hyperactive Disorder (ADHD). Results indicate that cognitive training increments activity in core components of mesocorticostriatal circuits, which are structures known to be severely affected in ADHD pathophysiology. Interestingly, our cognitive-training neural effects mimic those of methylphenidate administration, suggesting that cognitive training and psychostimulant medication elicit their effects via the same neural circuitry.

Validating pedagogy graduating examination constructs through structural modelling

Castañeda Figueiras, Sandra *Postgraduate Psychology, National Autonomus University, México City, Mexico*
Using 669 answers of pedagogues to a national major graduating examination, construct validity of cognitive demands and cultural background was established through confirmatory factorial analysis. The resulting model ((χ2=6, 14 gl, p = .48; IBBAN=0.99, IBBANN=.99, IAC= .99 and RMSEA=0.000) constituted three factors: cultural background, understanding and applying knowledge. The last two influenced directly and positively to the global proportion of correct marks (.51 and .42, respectively), the first one influenced the correct marks indirectly. The relationship between cognitive level demand and cultural background was .25, and all factors explained 68% of the variance among examinees. Implications to foster and

evaluating quality in complex learning are discussed.

Epidemiology of HIV/AIDS in Europe: Comparative analysis by countries

Castro, Ángel University of Granada, Granada, Spain Bermudez, María Paz Psychology, University of Granada, Granada, Spain Buela Casal, Gualberto Psychology, University of Granada, Granada, Spain
OBJECTIVE. The aim of this study is to analyze the current situation of HIV/AIDS in European countries. METHOD. This research uses a descriptive by observation design (document analysis). The most recent data about HIV/AIDS published by OMS (2007) and UNAIDS (2007) was used. RESULTS. This study shows that in the East of Europe, Estonia has the highest prevalence index in the range of age between 15 and 49 years old, and in the West, Spain has the highest prevalence index. CONCLUSIONS. In the fight against AIDS, measures of prevention must been done and these must to go towards youth, because of the vast majority of infections is during or few after adolescence.

Infant simulator projects with disadvantaged girls: Marginalizing with the best of intentions?

Chamakalayil, Lalitha Inst. für Pädagogik, Universität Oldenburg, Oldenburg, Germany Spies, Anke Institut für Pädagogik, Carl von Ossietzky Universität, Oldenburg, Germany
Computerized infant simulators have been used since 2000 with increasing popularity by pedagogical practitioners in and out of school. To assess concepts and aims, pre- and post-project group discussions with girls, a quantitative questionnaire (N=90) and 27 problem-centered interviews with practitioners were conducted Germany-wide. Results showed that these parenting projects strengthen the marginalisation of disadvantaged girls (doing class, doing ethnicity, doing gender processes), fail to fulfil the promise of rescuing (not yet conceived!) children from neglect and maltreatment and argue by wrongly presuming dramatically rising rates of 'teenage pregnancy', resulting in mothers under 20 being portrayed as failures, doomed to neglect their parenting responsibilities – disastrous, if early pregnancy becomes biographical reality for participating young women.

User satisfaction, community participation and quality of life among Chinese wheelchair users with spinal cord injury

Chan, Sam Chi Chung Occupational Therapy Dept., Tai Po Hospital, Hong Kong, China, People's Republic of : Hong Kong SAR Chan, Alice Po Shan Occupational Therapy Dept., Tai Po Hospital, Hong Kong, China, People's Republic of : Macao SAR
The study aimed to explore relationships among spinal cord injury (SCI) wheelchair users' satisfaction, community participation and quality of life. Thirty-one SCI wheelchair users completed Quebec User Evaluation of Satisfaction with assistive Technology (C-QUEST), World Health Organization Quality of Life Questionnaire (WHOQOL-BREF (HK)), and items of International Classification of Functioning Disability and Health (ICF). Spearman correlation revealed C-QUEST services and device sub-scores were weakly correlated with ICF human environmental factor and WHOQOL-BREF (HK) domain-scores, respectively. Social relationship and leisure participation were moderately associated with WHOQOL-BREF (HK) scores. Results suggest that community participation and human environment were more related to QOL.

Results of the "Program to prevent underage smoking in Peruvian teenagers"

Chau, Cecilia Psychology, PUCP, Lima, Peru Torres Llosa, Cecilia Educational Programmes, Instituto APOYO, Lima, Peru Calonge, Denisse Educational Programmes, Instituto APOYO, Lima, Peru
The Smoking Prevention Program aims to delay the onset of tobacco use by informing on its components and consequences and increasing social skills and decision-making. 674 male and female students participated in the program. Non-parametric statistics were used for Wilcoxon related samples (p<.05) and the U Mann-Whitney test. The results of the pre- post-test were: the percentage of those who had used tobacco at least once increased by 5%, availability increased by 10% and current use increased 2% in one year. However, the students have learned about the components of cigarette smoke and its consequences, have increased their social skills and have maintained a negative attitude towards tobacco use.

Task difficulty: Could it moderate the relationship of implicit cognition and explicit cognition?

Chen, Honghua Chengxian College, South-East University, Nanjing, People's Republic of China Liwei, Zhang applied psychology, BeiJing Sport University, Banjing, People's Republic of China
Does task difficulty moderate the correlation between implicit self-esteem (ISE) and explicit self-esteem (ESE)? Assuming it will do. 105 college students completed Rosenberg Self-esteem Scale, Implicit Association Test and Task Difficulty Selection. Correlate and paired-sample T test in SPSS contributed to the date analysis. Task difficulty could not moderate the relationship between ISE and ESE. However the ISE of extreme difficult task was really higher than that of medium difficult task. It was found that the low correlation between ISE and ESE was very stable and the people with high ISE may choose the most difficult or easiest task.

The relationship between body image measured by different methods, general self-esteem and life satisfaction

Chen, Li West District of Siping, Jilin Normal University, Siping, People's Republic of China Zhang, Liwei Haidian District of Beijing, Beijing Sport University, Beijing, People's Republic of China
Taking BMI, subjective physical self-worthiness, behavioral intention of body change, general self-esteem and life satisfaction as the validity criterion, compared four body image measures including questionnaire(Q), figure selection(FS), figure adjustment(FA) and implicit attitude(IA). 160 university students(97 males, 63 females, mean age 21.21)participated. Factor analysis indicated that Q, FS and FA were grouped into explicit category while IA was grouped into implicit. There was only a low correlation between explicit body image and general self-esteem. Hierarchical regression analysis showed that after controlling the contribution of general self-esteem body image still made added contribution to the prediction of life satisfaction.

Neurobehavioral disturbances in a patient of olfactory groove meningioma

Chen, Pin-Hao Psychology, National Taiwan University, Taipei, Taiwan Yang, Chi-Cheng Psychology, National Taiwan University, Taipei, Taiwan Tseng, Han-Ming Neurosurgery, NTU Hospital, Taipei, Taiwan Tu, Yong-Kwang Neurosurgery, NTU Hospital, Taipei, Taiwan Mau-Sun, Hua Psychology, National Taiwan University, Taipei, Taiwan
Olfactory groove meningioma may cause dysfunctions of orbitofrontal cortex (OFC). We presented a case whose pre- and post-operation neurobehavioral changes. Before surgical treatment, multiple behavioral changes, including negative behaviors,

such as aspontaneity and loss of insight, and disinhibited behaviors, such as impulsivity and hyperorality were noted. Meanwhile, the patient also showed executive dysfunctions including conceptual formation and mental shifting. Dramatically improvements in behavioral and emotional control with only a mild executive dysfunction were observed after tumor excision. Thus, the OFC is closely related to regulation of social conducts and behavioral control.

A survey of Taiwan universities on the conducting of formal courses in creativity

Chen, Chao Yi Dept. of Special Education, National Taiwan Normal Univer., Taipei, Taiwan
The purpose of this study was to explore the nature of creativity courses taught at the university level. This study analyzed the content of fifty-eight creativity course syllabi, collected from a variety of courses taught in thirty college and universities. And the professional field contains education, business, psychology, management, engineering, communication, design, drama and art etc... All syllabi were analyzed and inspected its purpose, content, teaching method, document reading, assignment and assessments. Finally, put forward three suggestion and inspections: the teachers should write syllabus attentively to meet students' right to know, the suggestion of the university creativity curriculum design and teaching attitude, and the aspect of future research.

Evaluation of design through eye movements while viewing packages of Japanese canned coffee beverages

Choi, Jeong-Seo Dept. of Design Psychology, Chiba University, Chiba, Japan So, Moon-Jae Chiba University, Chiba, Japan Koyama, Shinichi konakadai, inage, chiba univ., chiba, Japan Hibino, Har konakadai, inage, chiba univ., chiba, Japan
Packages of Japanese canned coffee beverages contain design elements such as brand names and logos designed to catch consumers' attention. In order to investigate how each element catches consumers' attention, we recorded eye-movements while the subjects viewed the cans. The results were as follows: (1) The subjects view larger elements for a longer duration; (2) The subjects view graphics for a longer duration than characters, when they were of similar size; and (3) The eyes move from graphics to letters. We will further investigate how much attention is paid to those elements.

Evaluation of the effects of a memory rehabilitation programme on neurological patients

Chouliara, Niki Nottingham University, Nottingham, United Kingdom
Few studies assess effectiveness of memory rehabilitation (MR) at disability level and the measures used might not reflect functional outcomes. This study explores qualitatively participants' experience in a MR group. Eleven interviews were conducted with neurological patients after completion of a MR programme and analysed using thematic analysis. Five main themes emerged : a) gaining insight, b) self-efficacy, b) benefits of the group setting, d) use of memory aids, e) changes in cognition/.everyday life. Important changes took place following memory rehabilitation which were not detected by existing measures. There is a need for an appropriate sensitive outcome measure.

The relationship between teachers' achievement goal orientation and their creativity fostering behavior

Chu, Yuxia educational phycology, Shandong Normal University, Jinan, People's Republic of China Zhang, Jinghuan educational phycology, Shandong Normal University, Jinan, People's Republic of China

This study investigated the relationship between primary school teachers' achievement goal orientation (learning goal orientation and performance goal orientation) and their creativity fostering behavior and the mediating role of creative teaching self-efficacy. Data were collected from 486 primary school teachers in Shandong province, China. Results showed that primary school teachers' achievement goal orientation was significantly positively correlated to their creativity fostering behavior and creative teaching self-efficacy(r?.482**, p<.01; r?.182**, p<.01);Teachers' creative teaching self-efficacy was the mediator between teachers' learning goal orientation and creativity fostering behavior. Key words Teachers' Achievement goal orientation, teachers' creativity fostering behavior, teachers' creative teaching self-efficacy, mediating regression

Neuro-cognitive mechanism of English language learning anxiety modulating language production

Conghui, Liu *Institute of psychology, Beijing, People's Republic of China* **DanLing, Peng** *School of psychology, institute of cognitive neural, Beijing, People's Republic of China* **Chunming, Lu** *School of psychology, institute of cognitive neural, Beijing, People's Republic of China* **Yanhui, Yang** *Department of Radiology, Department of Radiology, Beijing, People's Republic of China* **Guosheng, Ding** *school of psychology, institute of cognitive neural, Beijing, People's Republic of China*

The neural basis of foreign language anxiety and its modulating speech production was investigated among selected 24 young subjects (12 high and 12 low foreign language anxious subjects) using functional magnetic resonance imaging. We found that, compared to high anxious group, the low anxious group showed greater activation in ventral striatum and weaker activation in left temporal lobe in the English verb generation task. Our findings of enhanced ventral striatum responses suggested that there is more effective self-reward mechanism in low anxious group. The pattern of activation in temporal lobe might reflect the mechanism of anxiety modulating speech production.

Comparative thinking styles in group and person perception

Corcoran, Katja *Köln, Germany* **Mussweiler, Thomas** *Social Psychology, University of Cologne, Köln, Germany*

Perceptions of individuals and groups are intertwined in either an assimilative or a contrastive way (e.g. in stereotyping or projection). I hypothesize that these effects are related to different comparative thinking styles (searching for similarities versus dissimilarities). If primed to search for similarities, participants perceive an individual more similar to the group s/he belongs to (Study 1) and a group more similar to an individual member (Study 2) than if primed for dissimilarities. Such assimilative and contrastive effects in person and group perception are replicated in Study 3 and point toward a comparison process between the individual and the group.

Loss processes: Where's the help?

Cunill Olivas, Monica *Dept. of Psychology, University of Girona, Girona, Spain* **Clavero, Pedro** *PSYCHOLOGY, UNIVERSITY OF GIRONA, GIRONA, Spain* **Gras, Eugenia** *PSYCHOLOGY, UNIVERSITY OF GIRONA, GIRONA, Spain* **Sullman, Mark** *Shool of PSYCHOLOGY, University of Hertfordshire, Hatfield, United Kingdom*

This study investigated the perceived efficacy of an intervention program designed to reduce suffering associated with oncological illness and bereavement. Also it is measured the degree to which patients can share their concerns about illness or death and express feelings with their family or friends.This cross-sectional research surveyed 100 oncology patients and people who had lost an important person.The participants reported that the professional support received was very helpful.- However, they reported shortcomings in the help received from their social support network.The therapeutic context turns into an essential space for emotional expression. Results can be used to improve the adaptation processes in the case of traumatic life events.

Interindividual differences in neuroticism and partnership adaptation matters for the timing of parenthood – but only for men

Dörnte, Mareike *University of Rostock, Rostock, Germany* **Ötsch, Berit** *KJPP, University of Rostock, Rostock, Germany* **Reis, Olaf** *KJPP, University of Rostock, Rostock, Germany* **von der Lippe, Holger** *Institut of Psychology, University of Magdeburg, Magdeburg, Germany*

The timing of first parenthood during emerging adulthood usually is explained by demographic variables, such as age, education and gender. The model tested here introduces neuroticism and partnership adaptation as additional predictors. Hypotheses were tested with time-to-event data from the Rostock Longitudinal Study (n=212). The analyses include measures from four waves at respondents ages 14, 20, 25, and 32 years and apply hazard regression models. Neuroticism and low partnership adaptation reduced the probability of parenthood only for men. For women, the prediction of first parenthood was not enhanced by adding measures of neuroticism and partnership adaptation to the model.

Impact the organization activity involvment to improve the softskill on the adolescence

Dariyo, Agoes *Psychology Faculty, Tarumanagara University, Jakarta, Indonesia* **Elisati Waruwu, Fidelis** *Psychology Faculty, Tarumanagara University, Jakarta, Indonesia*

Student Organizationis as the part of education process which will give chance to get the experience for the university student. They want to improve thei intellectual, aptitute, creativity, inisiative, management skill and social skill in the organization. Every member will face and handle the problem of adjustment with the others. Therefore, they has to improve and enhance the capacity and ability to solve the social problem in order to reach the good adjustment. Findings of this qualitative research wast here was the impact the organization activity involvement to the softskill on the adolescence.

Perception and control of goal-directed grasping movements in 6-month-old infants

Daum, Moritz *Inst. für Psychologie, Max-Planck-Institut, Leipzig, Germany* **Prinz, Wolfgang** *Psychology, Max Planck Institute, Leipzig, Germany* **Aschersleben, Gisa** *Psychology, Saarland University, Saarbrücken, Germany*

In the present study, 6-month-olds' understanding of a grasping action was directly compared to their level of grasping performance. In a perception task infants were presented with expected and unexpected final states of grasping movements towards differently sized objects. In an action task, infants grasping towards different graspable objects was coded. Results indicate that only infants who performed a scissor grasp differentiated between the two final states in the perception task while infants who only used radial palmar grasps did not. This supports the assumption that action perception and control are closely linked already early in infancy.

The difficulties of the homosexual students: A case study

De Leon, Aurna *Guidance and Testing Center, Notre Dame of Dadiangas Univ., General Santos City, Philippines*

This study was made to find out the difficulties of the homosexual students to themselves, family, school and society.The informants of the study were the homosexual students. The study used the qualitative-descriptive case study using personal observations and records, interviews and focus group discussions. The study revealed that the difficulties of the homosexuals were confusion of their sexual identity, not being accepted by their own family, verbal abuses were experienced in school, and also humiliation was experienced because of their sexual orientation. With these findings, the researcher recommends that a program be developed for homosexuals to help them cope and adjust to their difficulties. This is an enormous contribution to a growing literature on homosexuality.

Identity and personality: The creativity

De Santis, Elisa *A.I.O., NGO in UN Cons. Status, Roma, Italy*

The pivotal point of the evolution of psychology is the research of the creative personality (F. Barron, A. Matiushkin). The work will focus on the path of creativity. The point of creativity is grasped from a continuum of egoic maturation in the hisotry of the environmental becoming (A. Meneghetti). The authors will discuss the results of the XI International Congress of Ontopsychology on Education and Politics: The creativity and of the International seminar on the Psychology of Creatvity (F. Barron, A. Matiushkin, A. Meneghetti) as well as the applications in different Countries: Brazil Europe, Russia.

Influencing partner modelling processes by providing collaborative learners with partner knowledge awareness

Dehler, Jessica *Applied cognitive & media psy, University of Tübingen, Tübingen, Germany* **Sangin, Mirweis** *CRAFT, EPFL, Lausanne, Switzerland* **Bodemer, Daniel** *Applied cognitive & media, University of Tübingen, Tübingen, Germany* **Buder, Jürgen** *Applied cognitive & media, University of Tübingen, Tübingen, Germany*

Collaborative learners benefit from models about their partners knowledge. We investigated whether providing information about partners knowledge supports partner modelling processes. This experimental study engaged 39 peer dyads in computer-mediated knowledge communication. Subjects in the knowledge awareness condition were provided with external representations about their partner's knowledge while control condition subjects were not. Subjects estimations of own and partner knowledge were used to calculate partner modelling accuracy for each individual. Accuracy did not differ between conditions. However, a significant intraclass correlation of accuracy values in knowledge awareness condition dyads suggests that they accomplished partner models by interaction rather than individually.

Human amygdala responsivity to masked fearful eyes: Fact or artefact?

Dietrich, Caroline *Biological&Clinical Psychology, Friedrich-Schiller-University, Jena, Germany* **Mothes-Lasch, Martin** *Biological&Clinical Psycho, Friedrich-Schiller-University, Jena, Germany* **Miltner, Wolfgang H. R.** *Biological&Clinical Psycho, Friedrich-Schiller-University, Jena, Germany* **Straube, Thomas** *Biological&Clinical Psycho, Friedrich-Schiller-University, Jena, Germany*

Recently, it was proposed that fearful eyes that are backwardly masked by neutral faces, and thus not consciously perceived, induce stronger amygdala activation than masked happy eyes (Whalen et al., Science 306, 2061, 2004). However, with the present fMRI - study we show that this effect is rather due to an interaction between the masked eyes and the eyes of the mask. We observed no differential amygdala responsivity to masked fearful and masked happy eyes when another mask than a face was used or when the masked eyes were positioned beyond the eye region of the mask.

Educational Psychology: The professional development of the teacher of the rural area
Drobot, Loredana D.P.P.D., Resita, Romania Ileana, Rotaru D.P.P.D., "Eftimie Murgu" Univer, Resita, Romania
The study propose is to identify a psycho-sociological and pedagogical profile of the rural area teacher.Our research hypothesis is: if there is identified the learning style, the level of rational and irrational subjects' cognitions, then the teachers learning process is realized by the particular learning and teaching strategy in the most adequate manner. The research sample consist of 126 persons.The research instruments used are: the questionnaires of identifying the teaching stiles, the questionnaire of Accentuated Personality Karl Leonhard, the dysfunctional attitudes scale (DAS, A type), the questionnaire of automatic thoughts and the scale of self-efficacy (SES).The research interpretative findings represents items in elaborating further programmes of continuing forming.

Using of the T-factor analysis at data processing the psychomotor tapping-test
Dubinina, Anna biology, MSU, Moscow, Russia
Purpose- to investigate psychomotor displays in the tepping-test a method of the T-factor analysis. As a material of research 101 young man and 102 girls psychomotor testing students of Moscow State University. Development of high-speed abilities was defined under Ilyin's tepping-test. Data are processed with T-fector analysis. Results. The first T-factor a parameter of total reactance. The second T-factor describes dynamics of fatigue. The third T-factor defines character of mobilization. The revealed laws do not find out sexual distinctions. The conclusion. This method in comparison with a classical method is more self-descriptiveness and yields authentic statistical results.

Aging in Chocó: Life span, aging and quality of life in Chocó, Colombia
Dulcey-Ruiz, Elisa Research, AIG de Colombia & Cepsiger, Bogotá, Colombia Izquierdo de Castro, María Elvira Research, AIG de Colombia & Cepsiger, Bogotá, Colombia Franco-Agudelo, Martha Inés Research, AIG de Colombia & Cepsiger, Bogotá, Colombia
Objectives: to identify perceptions and beliefs about: different stages of life, with emphasis on old age; the quality of life; and the future of the Chocó, the poorest province of Colombia, located on the Pacific coast and inhabited mainly by afro-descendants. The methodology included surveys and individual and group interviews. The main concerns of the elderly were the family, the community and keeping their culture and traditions alive. The perception of the own ageing process was more positive than the perception of other's people aging. Living peacefully, health, job opportunities and food were considered high-priority aspects for quality of life.

Validation of a test for predicting resilient adolescents: Youths in Medellin, Colombia
Duque, Luis F School of Public Health, University of Antioquia, Medellin, Colombia Montoya, Nilton School of Public Health, University of Antioquia, Medellin, Colombia Restrepo, Alexandra School of Public Health, University of Antioquia, Medellin, Colombia

Objectives: Validation in Colombia of Child and Youth Resilience Measure (CYRM) from International Resilience Project. Methods: We tested Reproducibility (22 persons 14 to 23 years). Content and internal consistency validated in 39 resilients, 43 youth with deviant behaviors and 66 controls matched by sex and age. Internal consistency was estimated by non-parametric factorial analysis, validity of content using U of Man-Withney, logistic regression and ROC curves. Results: Reproducibility: 75 - 86%. Correlation between measurements: 75%. Best predictive model has seven questions (sensitivity 96%, specificity 76%, power 80%) Conclusions: A simplified CYRM test predicts resilients amongst Medellin, Colombia, adolescents and youth.

Personality traits as mediators of stress in the presence of sexual risk behavior in adolescents
Duran, Consuelo Mexico City, Mexico Lucio, Emilia Postgraduate Studies, UNAM, Mexico City, Mexico Meave, Sonia Postgraduate Studies, UNAM, Mexico City, Mexico
The purpose of this research was to examine the relation of personality traits with sexual risk behavior in Mexican adolescents. Personality traits were measured by the MMPI-A and sexual risk behaviors were assessed through the Adolescents Development Questionnaire (Meave & Lucio, 2006). Participants were 403 adolescents, ages 13 to 18 (X=15.1, S.D=1.2). Discriminatory analysis suggests that girls in higher risk show anxiety, depression, family and alcohol problems, in contrast to boys in higher risk who show behavior and school problems, and drug and alcohol use. Results suggest the importance of considering prevention strategies in relation to mental health in adolescents.

Peer education in HIV prevention: A comparison of two models
Dwertmann, David Inst. für Psychologie, Universität Mannheim, Mannheim, Germany Völkle, Manuel Psychology, Chair II, University of Mannheim, Mannheim, Germany
Results of the evaluation of a community based Peer Educator Project for HIV prevention among high school students are reported. N = 405 teenagers from three different schools participated in the program. The evaluation was designed as a (quasi-experimental) pre-post test with a three-month follow-up questionnaire. Positive ratings of the program, a significant increase in knowledge, and a small but significant improvement in intention to protect oneself against HIV were found. Special emphasis is put on the comparison of Ajzen's (1991) "Theory of PLAnned BEhavior" and the "Information-Motivation-Behavioral-Skills" model of Fisher & Fisher (1992; Fisher, Fisher, & Williams, 1994).

Optimistic and pessimistic biases and comparative judgmental processes in Japan
Endo, Yumi Dept. of Social Psychology, Kansai University, Suita, Japan
Several studies on the above-average effects have recently claimed that these biases are consequences of uneven focus on self-relevant and underutilization of peers-relevant information. However, there would be some possibilities that these tendencies are prevalent only in Western cultures. The present study was conducted on comparative judgments in Japanese students. The results showed that participants tended to focus on their own abilities without paying much attention to their peers. These findings suggest that people tend to place more weight on the self and refer less to normative standards when considering their comparative position in a group.

Phonological awareness and process oriented literacy approaches: A comparative study of didactic resources aimed at populations with and without special education needs
Espinosa, Karla Psicologia Evolutiva, Univers. Complutense Madrid, Madrid, Spain
Phonological awareness (PA) as a prerequisite of the reading development has been questioned by the whole language literacy approach and its current derivative views. In this study, 113 literacy didactic resources oriented to both populations with and without special education needs, were compared based on 3 analytical points: a) teaching method, b) teaching method and publication date and, c) didactic resources' specific purpose. The results demonstrated that regardless of the publication date, the mainstream literacy proposals are focused on traditional methods, prioritizying and stressing decoding processes such as PA above those related to comprehension, significance, and reading and writing use for authentic purposes.

Investigating differences in burnout and engagement for primary and secondary teachers: Is grade level taught important?
Extremera, Natalio Social Psychology, University of Málaga, Malaga, Spain Durán, Auxiliadora Social Psychology, University of Málaga, MALAGA, Spain Rey, Lourdes Personality Psychology, University of Málaga, MALAGA, Spain
The purpose of this study was to investigate the relationship between levels of engagement and burnout teacher and grade level taught. Responses from Spanish 245 teachers (117 primary teachers and 128 secondary teachers) were analyzed. Analyses of Variances showed that secondary teachers reported higher levels of Depersonalization and lower levels of Personal Accomplishment, Vigor, Dedication and Absorption than their primary counterparts. It is suggested that working with adolescents in high school context might generate higher levels of burnout and less sense of engagement.

To be or not to be disabled: Priming effects on perceptions of warmth and competence
Eyssel, Friederike Sozialpsychologie, Universität Bielefeld, Bielefeld, Germany Zebrowitz, Leslie A. Psychology, Brandeis University, Waltham, MA, USA
The notion that disabled persons are often perceived as warm but incompetent was tested experimentally: 73 participants were primed with warmth or incompetence and then watched a video depicting an interaction between two targets, where one of the targets either did or did not appear disabled. We hypothesized that stereotype priming should affect judgments of the disabled, but not those of the nondisabled target. As predicted, the disabled (but not the nondisabled) target was rated as extremely warm following warmth priming. For perceived competence, no significant effects were observed. This study provides partial support for the mixed stereotype content hypothesis.

Which attributes affect the success of psychotherapy – and how accurate can these be measured during therapy process?
Fäh, Jolanda Zentrum für Testentwicklung, Universität Fribourg, Granges-Paccot, Switzerland Zollet, Nadine Zentrum für Testentwicklung, Universität Fribourg, Granges-Paccot, Switzerland Hänsgen, Klaus-Dieter Zentrum für Testentwicklung, Universität Fribourg, Granges-Paccot, Switzerland
The questionnaire QMP-ZM (Qualitätsmanagement Psychotherapie – Moderator- und Zielvariablen) measures patient- and therapist-specific features relevant for successful psychotherapy, e.g. motivation, social support and therapeutic alliance. It consists of a pre- and a post-therapy version and is implemented in a system for psychotherapy quality management. Statistical calculations based

on a sample of German inpatients (N=155) show good psychometric properties and revealed a factor structure consistent with the theoretical model. In this paper, the sensitivity of change of scales and items are analysed. In addition, based on the two measurement times a model is presented with a special look to predictability of success.

Socio-moral reasoning and socio-historical change: A study in China

Fang, Fuxi Institute of Psychology CAS, Beijing, People's Republic of China **Keller, Monika** *für Bildungsforschung, Max-Planck-Institut, Berlin, Germany* **Edelstein, Wolfgang Fang, Ge** *Institute of Psychology CAS, Beijing, People's Republic of China*

The study analyzes the effects of socio-historical change in Mainland China on the development of socio-moral reasoning. The design includes a cross-sectional study of different age groups tested in1990, follow-up longitudinal studies, and assessment of the same age groups in 2007. Participants were asked about decision-making, moral judgment and feelings in a friendship dilemma. The longitudinal samples revealed similarities, but also differences in the use of content categories. An increase in self-interest and a decrease in other-oriented and normative reasons can be seen as due to cultural change towards individualism. The replication samples serve to follow up on this effect.

The effects of councelor theoretical orientation and gender differences on the preference of psychotherapeutic theoretical orientation

Farsati, Sophia Dept. of Psychology, American College of Greece, Athens, Greece

This experiment examined the effects of gender differences and councelor theoretical orientation on the preference of psychotherapeutic orientation. Twenty four undergraduate students were presented with a series of statements depicting either Cognitive-behavioral or Psychodynamic theoretical orientation. It was hypothesized that females prefer Psychodynamic orientation to councelling practice due to emphasis that is placed on feelings and expession of affect. On the other hand males prefer Cognitive-behavioral orientation due to emphasis that is placed on logical reasoning. The results revealed that females stated their agreement more frequently when the psychodynamic statements were presented. Males when the psychodynamic statements were presented they moderately preffered them more frequently than the cognitive-behavioral ones.

Competitive attitudes as mediator of educational experience on sadness

Fernandez, Itziar Dept. of Social Psychology, Open University Madrid, Madrid, Spain **Carrera, Pilar** *Social Psychology, Universidad Autonoma de Madri, Madrid, Spain*

This research analyzed competitive attitudes as mediator of emotional experience in 29 countries. The cross-cultural sample (N=5436) responded to competitive attitudes' Triandis (Green, 2003), and emotional experience on sadness (Fernández, 2001). We examined the relationship between culture dimensions of Hofstede (2001) with competitive attitudes, and emotional experience on sadness. Results showed that subjects living in individualist and egalitarian cultures reinforce verbal expression of sadness, and decrease self-modification. Finally, the competitive attitudes as a mediator variable explaining why individualist report higher sadness. Furthermore, competitive attitudes mediate hierarchical values: Participants in hierarchical cultures report low verbal expression and high secondary coping.

Improving Mild Cognitive Impairment (MCI) diagnosis by further decomposing memory components

Ferreira, Daniel Dept. de Psicobiología, Universidad de La Laguna, La Laguna, Spain **Barroso, Jose** *Departamento de Psicobiología, Universidad de La Laguna, la laguna, Spain* **Nieto, Antonieta** *Departamento de Psicobiología, Universidad de La Laguna, la laguna, Spain* **Correia, Rut** *Departamento de Psicobiología, Universidad de La Laguna, la laguna, Spain* **Bueno, Jose** *Departamento de Neurología, Hospital La Candelaria, lSanta Cruz de Tenerife, Spain* **Sánchez, María del Pino** *Departamento de Psicobiología, Universidad de Murcia, Murcia, Spain*

Amnestic MCI criteria require low performance in a memory test. Furthermore, we propose that memory impairment must be differentiated in two components: consolidation (related to medial temporal structures) and acquisition/retrieval (related to frontal cortical-subcortical connections). In this way, only the medial temporal subtype must be considered as "amnestic". We compared both classification criteria in 26 MCI patients. Memory impairment was present in all patients, but it only was related to the consolidation process in the half of the subjects. Therefore, differentiating between consolidation and acquisition/retrieval components could increase the diagnostic accuracy in amnestic / non-amnestic differentiation.

Mild Cognitive Impairment (MCI): Cognitive impairment characterization in multiple-domain subtypes

Ferreira, Daniel Dept. de Psicobiología, Universidad de La Laguna, La Laguna, Spain **Barroso, Jose** *Departamento de Psicobiología, Universidad de La Laguna, la laguna, Spain* **Nieto, Antonieta** *Departamento de Psicobiología, Universidad de La Laguna, la laguna, Spain* **Correia, Rut** *Departamento de Psicobiología, Universidad de La Laguna, la laguna, Spain* **Ruiz Lavilla, Nuria** *Departamento de Neurología, Hospital La Candelaria, Santa Cruz de Tenerife, Spain* **Sánchez, María del Pino** *Departamento de Psicobiología, Universidad de Murcia, Murcia, Spain*

Our purpose was to describe the pattern of cognitive impairment in multiple-domain MCI subtypes (n=28). Executive functions were the most affected (93%), followed by motor functions (61%) and acquisition/retrieval in memory (75% verbal, 54% non-verbal). Attention impairment and cognitive slowing were more frequent in a-MCI MD (73%) than in na-MCI MD (46%). Memory consolidation was impaired in a-MCI MD. The rest of the functions were affected in fewer than 30% of participants. In conclusion, both subtypes shared frontal affection, with larger predominance of the cortical-subcortical type in na-MCI MD, and they differed in a-MCI MD medial temporal lobe affection.

Social facilitation and information-processing

Fonseca, Ricardo UIPCDE, Inst. of Applied Psychlgy, Lisbon, Portugal **Garcia-Marques, Teresa** *UIPCDE, Sup. Inst. of Applied Psychlgy, Lisbon, Portugal*

This study, addresses the relation between passive presence of others and less elaborative information-processing. Participants assigned to isolation, coaction or mere-presence condition performed a decision-making task (see Ferreira et al. 2006) framed by Jacoby's PDP. Results revealed no differences regarding the automatic component of processing and a significant linear trend for controlled processing, suggesting that the presence of others is associated with more elaborative information-processing and not with less. Data is discussed focusing the specific role that the nature of the task can have on this pattern of results

Psychoenergetic drawing: A psychotherapic proposal combining analysis of the depth, imaginary and drawing

Fontana Sartorio, Marialfonsa Associazione Qualita e Formazi, Milano, Italy **Gnocchi, Nicoletta** *Associazione Qualita e Formazi, Associazione Qualita e Formazi, Milano, Italy* **Raiola, Elda** *Associazione Qualita e Formazi, Associazione Qualita e Formazi, Milano, Italy* **Chiaia, Olga** *Associazione Qualita e Formazi, Associazione Qualita e Formazi, Milano, Italy* **Duga, Marina** *Associazione Qualita e Formazi, Associazione Qualita e Formazi, Milano, Italy*

Psychoenergetic Drawing™ balances analytical formulation with image, drawing and body (psychic energy, energetic signal, resonance and analytical concepts). In presence of an energetic signal from the patient, the psychotherapist invites him to assemble on the predominant emotion, to let flow on the paper sheet with unconscious movements of his hand, the colours that he feels, in an almost sub-vigilant state; afterwards he expresses feelings that drawing arouses in him, also within its spatial component. Then follows the analytical interpretation. This abreaction material is integrated in the psychotherapeutic development. Good results for insight, psychic development, also with frail and traumatized patients.

Preference for mode of delivery of cognitive behaviour therapy among people with social phobia.

Foster, Lisa Health Science, University of Sydney, Sydney, Australia

Computer-assisted cognitive behaviour therapy (CCBT) has demonstrated effectiveness for people with social anxiety; however little literature has identified characteristics of people most likely to access CCBT. Computer use may perpetuate symptoms by reducing frequency of personal interactions. Objectives: In people with social anxiety, identify 1. characteristics (e.g. age, internet use, avoidance) associated with CCBT preference; 2. advantages of CCBT (e.g. cost, access, anonymity). Method People with social anxiety recruited from clinics and internet sites completed a questionnaire about their characteristics, computer use, anxiety and depression symptoms, and treatment preferences (stated preference discrete choice modelling). The findings have implications for delivering effective therapy to those experiencing social anxiety.

Implementation of an evaluated multidisciplinary functional restoration treatment for patients with chronic back pain in further rehabilitation-clinics

Fröhlich, Stephanie M. Abteilung Bad Rothenfelde, Institut für Rehaforschung, Bad Rothenfelde, Germany **Greitemann, Bernhard** *Abteilungsleitung, Klinik Münsterland, Bad Rothenfelde, Germany* **Niemeyer, Ralph** *I.f.R., Abtlg. Bad Rothenfelde, Klinik Münsterland, Bad Rothenfelde, Germany*

Objectives: The integrated orthopaedic-psychosomatic concept has proven to be lastingly effective in the treatment of chronic back pain. How and with which results can this concept be established in further rehabilitation-clinics? Methods: The treatment consisted of 14 multidisciplinary moduls and multiprofessional anamneses. It was implemented in 5 rehabilitation-clinics. 343 Patients have received the program, 308 are part of the control group. Results: Three month after rehabiliationend the treatment group was characterized by a significant stronger decrease in pain and more health behaviour than the control group. Conclusions: The implementation was time-consuming but worthwhile. Long-term studies are work in progress.

Madness returns to city: Therapeutic residence as a strategy of constructing the substitutive web in Brazilian mental health

*Freire, Flávia Helena Rio de Janeiro, Brazil **Merhy, Emerson** Clínica Médica, UFRJ, Rio de Janeiro, Brazil*
Objective: To discuss concept of therapeutic residence as a device to help de de-institutionalization in Brazil. Method: Cases studies with three distinguish therapeutic residences. There were interviewed users/households; caregivers and managers. Results: Observed that residences, which were inserted in community, provide an approximation of households in circulation spaces at everyday life. This care aims to offer development of ordinary skills required on daily life at home and improves the autonomy in and outside home. Conclusion: Therapeutic residences are strategic devices in Brazilian Psychiatric Reform process affording the inversion of assistencial mode of mental health.

Support Groups in institutional context

Frischenbruder, Sandra Servico Psicologia - Clinica, Feevale - UFRGS, Poa, Brazil
OBJECTIVE The use of group psychotherapy in mental health care systems has been increasingly growing in Brazil. This paper aims to investigate the influence of support groups on the family of children who have cognitive and emotional disorders. METHODS The study was conducted in Novo Hamburgo, Brazil and used a qualitative approach. Protocols were applied to 12 parents before and after the sessions. Each protocol consisted of questions concerning feelings and beliefs about the cognitive disorders as well as children-parent interactions. RESULTS The study indicates that this group may have been an effective treatment modality for these families provided information and emotional support

Acculturation model based culture identity: A study framework

*Fu, Jia Antai College of Management, Shanghai Jiao Tong University, Shanghai, People's Republic of China **Tang, Ningyu** Antai College of Management, Shanghai Jiao Tong University, Shanghai, People's Republic of China*
Firstly, the author introduces the concept of acculturation, and compares different acculturation models. Then, analyze culture intelligent which is the new development of acculturation. At last, we propose a new acculturation model based culture identity, and the dynamic constructivist approach is conducted, we intend to use the culture priming experiment to evaluate the structure and validity of Culture Intelligent. This paper propose the study framework for the future, if the result of the experiment is suitable for this new model, we can make conclusion that Culture Intelligent is availability.

The effects of presentation size and color to natural scene recognition

*Fujii, Tetsunoshin Dept. of Letters, Hokkaido University, Sapporo, Japan **Kawabata, Yasuhiro** Department of Letters, Hokkaido University, Hokkaido, Japan*
This study investigated the influence of presentation size of images and chromatic contrasts on recognition memory of natural scenes. 3 presentation size (Large, Middle, Small) conditions were used in this experiment. In order to contain the same amount of spatial information between each condition, the range of spatial frequencies (SF) involved images were regulated. For example, the stimuli in Large conditions have large presentation sizes but are composed of the low-SF. Large presentation size images composed by the low-SF were recognized better than small presentation size images composed of the high-SF. These images were also affected by the change of chromatic contrasts.

Personality-dependent dissociation of absolute and relative loss processing in orbitofrontal cortex

*Fujiwara, Juri Div Sys Neurosci, Tohoku Univ Grad Sch Life Sci, Sendai, Japan **Tobler, Philippe** Dept Physiol, Develop Neurosci, Univ Cambridge, Cambridge, United Kingdom **Taira, Masato** ARISH, Nihon Univ, Tokyo, Japan **Iijima, Toshio** Div Sys Neurosci, Tohoku Univ Grad Sch Life Sci, Sendai, Japan **Tsursui, Ken-Ichiro** Div Sys Neurosci, Tohoku Univ Grad Sch Life Sci, Sendai, Japan*
A negative outcome can have motivational and emotional consequences on its own (absolute loss) or in comparison to alternative outcomes (relative loss). The consequences of incurring a loss are moderated by personality factors such as neuroticism and introversion. However, the neuronal basis of this moderation is unknown. We investigated the neuronal basis of loss processing and personality with fMRI in a choice task. We found a correlation of relative loss with neuroticism and absolute loss with introversion in distinct regions of the lateral orbitofrontal cortex. These results suggest a dissociation of personality dimension and loss type on the neuronal level.

Cognitive linkage between trait information about self and other

Fukushima, Osamu Psychology, Niigata University, Niigata, Japan
The present study applied the task facilitation paradigm and examined the hypothesis that trait information about the relational self would link to trait information about the corresponding person. Thirty-seven participants initially judged both their father and mother on personality traits and on frequency of use of daily necessities, then judged trait about self-with-father or self-with-mother. Overall, the initial judgments about father and mother speeded the trait judgment about the corresponding relational self. This facilitation was stronger for women than men especially when they initially judged about parents' personality traits. Implications for the structure of social self-representation are discussed.

The contribution of the noradrenergic system to memory consolidation during sleep in humans

*Gais, Steffen Neuroendocrinology, University of Lübeck, Lübeck, Germany **Rasch, Björn** Neuroendocrinology, University of Lübeck, Lübeck, Germany **Wagner, Ullrich** Neuroendocrinology, University of Lübeck, Lübeck, Germany **Born, Jan** Neuroendocrinology, University of Lübeck, Lübeck, Germany*
Brain noradrenaline regulates arousal and information processing. Here, we investigated whether noradrenergic activity is related to memory consolidation during sleep. Subjects performed an odour recognition task, requiring them to learn six unfamiliar odours and, 24-h later, to recognize them among twelve odours. In a placebo-controlled design, they received the alpha2-adrenergic agonist clonidine, which prevents noradrenalin release. The substance was administered post-learning during sleep or wakefulness. We show a significant performance increase when subjects slept as compared to subjects staying awake. This sleep-related increase was eliminated by clonidine. Thus, noradrenergic activity during sleep might have a functional role in memory consolidation.

The application of unfolding IRT model in personality assessment

Gao, Pengyun Dept. of Psychology, Beijing Normal University, Beijing, People's Republic of China
This research aims to construct a compulsive symptom inventory basing on unfolding item response modal, a newly developed but theoretically robust method in constructing personality questionnaire. The study compiles several estab-

lished questionnaire to build a comprehensive item pool such as 16PF, MMPI et al. The item pool comprises 145 items of different level of severity of compulsive symptom. Subjects of 525 colleage students accomplish all the items and the data are input into GGUM software. After the item location and person location are work-out, the researcher picks out items according to their location and constitute an inventory.

University students' misconceptions about statistics: What are they?

Gao, Yu-Jing Education and Human Resource, Hsuan Chuang University, Hsinchu, Taiwan
Many students have expressed difficulties in learning statistical concepts. However, traditional approaches of assessment such as multiple-choice questions and word problems often fail to identify their misconceptions. The study examines Taiwan's university students' misconceptions about fundamental statistics by using a concept map tool (IHMC Cmap Tools). Student scores on concept maps are compared with scores on a formal assessment. Some aspects of the concept map scores are positive correlated with the formal assessment. Diagnostic information concerning students' errors can also be gained from an investigation of student concept maps, which enables clarification of student misconceptions.

Intercultural comparison of meaning in life

*Gapp, Sabine Personality-Psychologie, Universität Innsbruck, Innsbruck, Austria **Schnell, Tatjana** Personality Psychology, University of Innsbruck, Innsbruck, Austria*
The study investigated differences in sources of meaning between the collectivistic Peruvian and the individualistic German culture. The SoMe-Questionnaire (Schnell & Becker, 2007) was applied to a Peruvian (N=110) and a German (N=604) sample. Analyses of Variance, multiple regressions, correlations, t-tests, and an explorative factor analysis were calculated. Inter alia, results show that explicit religion as well as clearly socially focussed sources of meaning attribute more to the experience of meaningfulness in Peru than in Germany. Factor analysis shows a correlational pattern which informatively differs from the German structure.

Neuropsychological assessment in dementias and neurodegenerative diseases in processes of legal incapacity

*García Rodríguez, Beatriz Dept. of Basic Psychology II, UNED, Madrid, Spain **Fuentes, José Carlos** Desarrollo Sanitario, FUDESAN, Madrid, Spain **Fusari, Anna** Basic Psychology II, UNED, Madrid, Spain*
Recent investigations have highlighted the validity of some neuropsychological tasks in the assessment of cognitive impairment which leads to several legal incapacities. In cognitive assessment, inhibition and executive control tasks are extremely sensitive detecting mental deficits. We have tested performance of three groups of participants (early Alzheimer, early Parkinson, healthy elderly) in four tasks aimed to detect early impairments: verbal Stroop, emotional inhibitory task, Wisconsin Card Sorting Test and n-back task. Results have shown an impaired performance of Alzheimer and Parkinsons patients in all tasks, suggesting the convenience of this neuropsychological assessment in processes of legal incapacity due to mental impairments.

Gender and sexual education

*Garcia Vega, Elena Dept. of Psychology, University of Oviedo, Oviedo, Spain **Rosana, Rico** Psychology, University of Oviedo, Oviedo, Spain **Paula, Fernández** Psychology, University of Oviedo, Oviedo, Spain*
The aim of this work was study the influence of sex and gender variables in the sexual attitudes. A sample of 411 university students completed the

Bem Sex Role Inventory (BSRI Short version, Bem, 1974; Fernandez, García-Vega y Rico, 2006), Sexual Opinion Survey (SOS, Fisher at al, 1988; Carpintero, 1994) and a interview. Correlational analyses revealed many significant associations among sexual attitudes and biological sex. Analyses of variance showed effects for both sex of subjects and gender role orientation on several of the dependent measures. Knowing the differences, we will be able to elaborate appropriate sexual educational program for this population.

The campus sexuality of the post-1980s college students in China today

Geng, Wenxiu Department of Psychology, East China Normal University, Shanghai, People's Republic of China

Objectives: To explore the reality of the campus sexuality of the post-1980s college students in China today and the relative influenced factors. Methods: 476 boys, 1059 girls from 10 universities of Shanghai and 288 mothers were recruited in the survey. Data from questionnaire and deep interviews. Results: Virginity is still the most treasure viewed by most of the post-1980s college students. Yet they reported premarital intercourse much more than before. The post-1980s college students accepted cohabitation from passively to actively. Conclusions: These findings provide strong evidense that there are general gap between the parents and their post-1980s children, who are open-minded regarded sexuality. Key words: Campus Sexuality, the post-1980s College Students, general gap

Cultural factors on life satisfaction: A cross-cultural study

Genkova, Petia Inst. für Psychologie, Universität Passau, Passau, Germany

A culture comparing study of China, Germany, France and Bulgaria was set to review the impact of cultural patterns on the subjective well-being. Individualism/ collectivism (Triandis, 1996) and the specification of authoritarian attitude (Altemeyer, 1988) were included as cultural patterns. The results show that there are emic (cultural specific) as well as etic (cross-cultural- valid) tendencies. A paradisiacal meaning of happiness exits cultural universally, but its contents are culture specific. Performance and community were determined as a factor for a culture specific satisfaction of life. As a moderator the subjective culture (Triandis, 1994) was determined for subjective satisfaction of life cultural universally. As a further universal predictor self-esteem was identified (SEM-modelling and hierarchical regressions).

Do diabetes prevention programs increase somatization in healthy subjects at risk?

Giel, Katrin Psychosomatische Medizin, Universitätsklinik Tübingen, Tübingen, Germany Schrauth, Markus Psychosomatic Medicine, University Hospital Tübingen, Tübingen, Germany Fritsche, Andreas Internal Medicine IV, University Hospital Tübingen, Tübingen, Germany Zipfel, Stephan Psychosomatic Medicine, University Hospital Tübingen, Tübingen, Germany Enck, Paul Psychosomatic Medicine, University Hospital Tübingen, Tübingen, Germany

Objectives To investigate potential negative psychological side effects of a diabetes prevention program such as increased somatization. Methods During a two-year lifestyle intervention program to prevent diabetes type II in adults at risk, psychological symptoms were assessed with the SCL-90-R. A repeated measure ANOVA compared symptoms at baseline and after 9 months for complete data sets available (n = 118). Results Somatization scores did not change, and total SCL scores indicating overall psychological burden did significantly decrease over the course of 9 months of program participation. Conclusions The data suggests that

prevention results foremost in beneficial psychological outcomes.

Quality of life and post-partum depression

Gili, Margarita Dept. of Psychology, University of Balearic Islands, Palma de Mallorca, Spain Serrano, Jesus Psychology, University of Balearic Islands, Palma de Mallorca, Spain Bauzá, Natalia Psychology, University of Balearic Islands, Palma de Mallorca, Spain Monzón, Saray Psychology, University of Balearic Islands, Palma de Mallorca, Spain Roca, Miquel Psychology, University of Balearic Islands, Palma de Mallorca, Spain

There are a few studies linking depression and quality of life in postpartum depression. Follow-up Cohort-study at 2-3 days, 8- week and 32-week. Sociodemographic data, personal history, labour data and data from the newborn were collected. The Edimburgh Post-natal Depression Scale and The Nottingham Health Profile were administered to a sample of 297 volunteers. Comparison of the levels of depression obtained with the Edimburgh Post-natal Depression Scale were performed by the analysis of variance (ANOVA) for repeated measures showing significative statistical differences in decreasing depressive symptomatology at 32-week. Energy, pain, physical motility and sleep are the quality of life dimensions that show significative differences.

Barriers to teaching about sexual orientation minorities in the classroom

Gillis, Joseph Roy Dept. Counselling Psychology, University of Toronto, Toronto, Canada

Qualitative analysis of 52 interviews with teachers-in-training addressed their attitudes related to sexual orientation and pedagogical strategies. A two-stage analysis categorized narrative data using Riddle's Attitudes Toward Difference scale, and analysed discourses framing anticipated classroom strategies. Four attitude categories emerged that shaped their pedagogy. These were Repulsion, Pity, Conditional Support and Active Support/Advocacy. These attitude categories were further modified by narratives of discourses of invisibility, implicit/explicit curriculum, and safety and support. The findings suggested the importance for inclusive teaching strategies to recognize that the discussion of sexual minorities in the classroom is limited by individual and institutional constraints.

Academic - student interaction and student's emotional tension

Gintere, Erika Liepaja Pedagogic Academy, Liepaja, Latvia

Interaction between a lecturer and a student during studies can facilitate lowering of students' stress as well as its increasing above the allowed norm. In the process of interaction between a lecturer and a student, the Level of students' stress before an exam is influenced by the following factors: • domineering transactions between a lecturer and a student; • lecturer's communicative culture; • communication barriers during studies; • lecturer's stereotypes; • lecturer's leadership style; • determination of the most appropriate learning style for a student; • lecturer's individual qualities. Analyzing the factors mentioned above it is possible to determine several ways to prevent the increasing Level of student's stress before testing knowledge.

Theory of mind in healthy subjects: An independent cognitive domain?

Giovagnoli, Anna Rita Neuropsychology Laboratory, C. Besta National Neurol Inst, Milano, Italy Reati, Fabiola Neuropsychology Laboratory, C. Besta National Neurol Inst, Milano, Italy Aresi, Anna Neuropsychology Laboratory, C. Besta National Neurol Inst, Milano, Italy

Objectives To determine the mechanisms of theory of mind (ToM) in healthy subjects. Methods ToM

was evaluated in 74 subjects using the Faux Pas task (FPT) that requires the recognition or exclusion of faux pas in 20 stories, providing two detection and four analysis scores. Results Separate Pearson coefficients, Student t tests, and factor analyses showed no relationship of the FPT scores to age, education, gender, and language, memory and executive functions scores. Conclusions ToM represents a specific domain distinct from other cognitive functions, independent from demographic variables. This suggests a fundamental survival-related nature, resistant to ageing and culture deprivation.

Resilience and psychological resources in children

Gonzalez-Arratia, Ivonne Posgrado, Facico-Uaem, Toluca, Mexico Valdez-Medina, Jose Luis POSGRADO, FACICO-UAEM, Toluca, Mexico Dominguez Espinosa, Alejandra POSGRADO, U. IBEROAMERICANA, D.F., Mexico

The purpose of this research was knowing the degree of prediction of variables integrated in the multidimensional model, denominated internal factors (self-esteem, locus of control, coping with problems, functions of the self) and external (intra-family relationships) on the resilient behavior of institucionalized children and children from integrated families (N=355). The study demostrated differences by sex, group, life condition and risk level. According to the multiple regression analysis, intra-family and self-esteem are the factor to contribute most to the explanation of the proposed model. These findings invite to think of integral program oriented toward promoting infant resilience.

Does organisational identification predict organisational commitement behaviours at different levels of hierarchy in the organisation?: A study on the Romanian organisations.

Goras, Maura Cluj-Napoca, Romania

The present study intends to address the problem of the turnover behaviour of the employees as a result of their low commitment to the organisation. This is to be studied from the perspective of Social Identity Theory. The study verifies if organisational commitment varies in connection with the level of identification with the organisation, the position occupied in the hierarchy of the organisation, the initial expectations toward the organisation and the organisational culture. Both qualitative and quantitative methods will be employed. A different pattern of relations between the variables under study is expected due to the lack of a well-defined and stable culture of the Romanian organisations.

The memory of predictive inferences

Gras, Doriane Malakoff, France Tardieu, Hubert Cognitive psychology, University Paris Descartes, Boulogne-Billancourt, France Nicolas, Serge Cognitive psychology, University Paris Descartes, Boulogne-Billancourt, France

We aimed to follow the path of read words and predictive inferences in the different memory systems of the SPI (serial, parallel, independent) model of Tulving (1995) during and after the reading of the text. A first set of experiments using a naming task and a stroop-like task shows that the words read in the texts are present in PRS (perceptual representation system) and working memory, while the predictive inferences are placed only in working memory. Then, a recognition task shows that the words presented and the predictive inferences are stored in long-term memory, probably in semantic and episodic memories.

Value component of psychological culture of higher education students

Grushevsky, Valeriy Organizational Psychology, Institute of Psychology, Kiev, Ukraine

Objective. To find out factors that shape the value component of higher education students' psychological culture. Methods. The investigation was done on 230 students of humanitarian institutions of higher education using interviews, factorial analysis, and SPSS. Results. Seven factors that influence formation of the value component of students' psychological culture (the total dispersion 62.5%) were identified: responsibility (12.6%), family (11.2%), financial welfare (10.8%), hedonism (7.7%), friends (7.6%), altruism (7.6%), and egocentrism (5.0%). Conclusions. The investigation findings can be used in developing effective trainings to shape students' psychological culture.

The development of early attachment: An observation study on an infant throughout the first year

Gu, Chuanhua Dept. of Psychology, School of Psychology, Wuhan, People's Republic of China

Sunshine, a healthy female infant was observed naturally by a professional developmentalist throughout the first year to investigate the micromechanism of attachment development. The observation indicated that Sunshine developed from the first stage of "uterus attachment" to the second stage of "uterus-like attachment" (including generalized attachment and differentiated attachment), and then to the third stage of "social uterus attachment", and with each stage supported by the correspondent typical behavioral mode. The author concluded that the developmental process of early attachment is essentially characterized by the gradual promotion of socialization extent.

The role of neighborhood activity in restoration of vision

Guenther, Tobias Inst Medical Psychology, Otto von Guericke University, Magdeburg, Germany Mueller, Iris Inst Medical Psychology, Otto von Guericke University, Magdeburg, Germany Sabel, Bernhard A. Inst Medical Psychology, Otto von Guericke University, Magdeburg, Germany

By comparing baseline campimetric charts and charts which were assessed after vision stimulation training was applied, topographic areas of improvement (hot spots) and without improvement (cold spots) are identified in the baseline chart. We compared the spatial topographic neighborhood in the baseline chart of those hot and cold spots and observed that the neighborhood around hot spots has been more active than around cold spots. The difference in the activity around hot and cold spots is reduced at larger distances. We hypothesize that the mediation of restoration is partially mediated by activation coming from the undamaged spatial surround. The observed spatial limitations of activation propagation is comparable to results from animal experiments.

A population-based, multi-level study of interactions of socio-cultural neighborhood and child characteristics on children's early development

Guhn, Martin Dept. Educational Psychology, University of British Columbia, Vancouver, Canada Gadermann, Anne Educational & Counseling P, University of British Columbia, Vancouver, Canada Hertzman, Clyde Health Care and Epidemiology, University of British Columbia, Vancouver, Canada Zumbo, Bruno D. Educational & Counseling P, University of British Columbia, Vancouver, Canada

This study examines interactions between socio-cultural neighborhood and child characteristics on development at a population level. Developmental data, obtained via the Early Development Instrument (Offord & Janus, 1999) for 41,834 kindergar-

ten children were linked to Canadian census data for all 465 neighborhoods in British Columbia, and analyzed via multi-level modeling. Controlling for demographic variables, a (positive) relationship between neighborhood income and children's development was significantly moderated by gender and English-as-a-Second-Language (ESL) status: Boys had lower, steeper gradients than girls (p=.003), ESL children lower, flatter gradients than non-ESL children (p=.033). These findings indicate differentiated, context-dependent resiliency patterns for sub-populations of children.

Research on sexual moral development characteristics of 13~18 adolescents

Guo, Li-Yan School of of Teacher Education, Shenyang Normal University, Shenyang, People's Republic of China Wang, Yuan School of Teacher Education, Shenyang Normal University, Shenyang, People's Republic of China

The study explored the psychological development characteristics of the sexual morals of adolescents whose ages ranged from 13 to 18. Results showed significant age and gender differences for the overall development of adolescents' sexual morals. Overall, level of sexual morals of adolescents increased first and then declined, which indicated that ages of 14 and 17 were the key period to the development of adolescents' sexual morals. Compared to girls, boys tended to be more liberal and open. Implications for sexual moral education of adolescents were discussed.

The road to success

Gupta, Parvinder Organizational Behavior, Indian Institute of Management, Ahmedabad, India

An individual's success by societal yardstick is mostly evaluated in terms of money, status, awards, and similar criteria. Using qualitative approach, this study aimed at exploring the concept of success and identifying factors leading to success. Six people from varied fields who were considered successful by societal yardstick were included in the sample. They were interviewed using a semi-structured schedule. Data were organized into categories such as definition of success, early years, personal characteristics, and role models. Findings revealed that success was viewed differently by different people. Further, respondents had certain striking similarities indicating key common factors responsible for success.

Creativity in "theory of mind" tasks.

Guskova, Anna psychology, Moscow state university, Moscow, Russia

The objective was to study Guilford's creativity characteristics (fluency, flexibility, originality, readiness) in TOM tasks. For the investigation we created tasks of following types: understanding, explanation, evaluation and prediction the specific of other's mental world tasks. Participants were 194 students of different departments of university, including psychologists. Data were analyzed with Spearmen's coefficient of correlation. No significant correlations were found between creativity characteristics in Uses tests and the ones in TOM tasks, and also between the same characteristics in different TOM tasks. Results can be explained by the fact that different representations of individual knowledge were used: cultural stereotypes, individual experience, complicated models and theoretical knowledge of psychology.

An analysis of treatment effects: Using the EB-45 for providing feedback to therapists on their outpatients psychotherapy outcome.

Häußinger, Constanze Therapie- und Beratungszentrum, Georg-Elias-Müller-Institut, Göttingen, Germany Bernadi, Cornelia Georg-Elias-Müller-Institut, Universität Göttingen, Göttingen, Germany Ruhl, Uwe Georg-Elias-Müller-Institut,

Universität Göttingen, Göttingen, Germany Kröner-Herwig, Birgit Georg-Elias-Müller-Institut, Universität Göttingen, Göttingen, Germany

Objectives: Studies have shown that providing therapists with feedback about their outpatients' treatment progress improves treatment outcome. We describe and illustrate our system of measuring and of feedback information about outpatient treatment. Methods: This study used the German version of the Outcome Questionnaire – the Ergebnisfragebogen (EB-45). All outpatients who took up psychotherapy (N=220) in our outpatient University Psychotherapy Unit completed a standardized form of the EB-45 twice (diagnostic and 10th session). Results and discussion: The study examines the treatment outcome and the feedback to therapists. The data is yet to be analysed and will be presented on the congress.

Predicting the causal agent in verbally described social interactions

Höjvig, Mette Dept. of Psychology, Aarhus Universitet, Århus C, Denmark Tumasjan, Andranik Psychology, Ludwig-Maximilians-Universität, München, Germany Spörrle, Matthias Dept. for Psychology, Ludwig-Maximilians University, München, Germany

Implicit causality in interpersonal verbs (i.e. causal assumptions about the initiator of a social interaction) has been extensively investigated, especially in English and German language (cf. Rudolph & Försterling, 1997). The present study is the first to investigate verb causality in Danish language using a student sample (N = 96) while simultaneously examining consensus (i.e. to what extent others besides the grammatical subject treat the object like this) and distinctiveness (i.e. to what extent solely the object person is treated by the subject like this) as predictors of causal attribution to subject or object. A strong verb causality effect in Danish language emerged. Consensus proved to be a better predictor than distinctiveness for causal attribution.

Psychometric properties of a civics knowledge measure developed for immigration and naturalization purposes

Hülür, Gizem IQB, Humboldt-Universität zu Berlin, Berlin, Germany Greve, Anke Wilhelm, Oliver Köller, Olaf

In many countries with higher immigration rates immigrants are required to demonstrate language skills and general knowledge about the country in order to apply for immigration or naturalization. We will report research on the assessment procedures of civics knowledge currently developed for Germany. We will report results for competing measurement models, differential item functioning across ethnicities, comparisons between migrants and non migrants with and without matched background variables, relations with German language proficiency and aspects of differentiation and dedifferentiation of factor space in more or less skilled groups of participants.

Measuring implicit motives in romantic partner relationships: A domain-specific approach

Hagemeyer, Birk Inst. für Psychologie, Universität Potsdam, Potsdam, Germany Neyer, Franz Department of Psychology, University of Potsdam, Potsdam, Germany

Contrasting the common view of implicit motives as fundamental, domain-unspecific needs, we experimentally developed an operant measure of the implicit needs for intimacy, autonomy, and affiliation in the domain of partner relationships. In a 4-group-between-subjects-design, 400 participants were primed with autobiographical memories related to need-specific vs. neutral experiences and completed a TAT-like picture-story task. Group differences in contents of participants' answers were analysed to define and validate motive-specific thematic categories. Stimulus materials, a new scoring system, and validation results are presented. Future applications are discussed.

Scientistic Attitude as a tool for improving achievement motivation among Iranian students: Development and trial of a model

Hameedy, Mansoor Dept. Educational Psychology, Alzahra University, Tehran, Islamic Republic of Iran Akhavan, Mahnaz Rezabakhsh, Hossein Raheb, Ghoncheh Educational Psychology, Alzahra University, Tehran, Islamic Republic of Iran

From a social constructivist perspective, school learning is much like scientific inquiry in all its aspects except level! Thus students must be helped to gradually develop characteristics similar to those of scientists. Among such characteristics is the assumed attitude that scientists have toward learning, knowing, and knowledge. If students develop a scientistic attitude, i.e. one similar to that of a scientist, they would be self regulated corroborating learners with high measure of self-efficacy. Assuming that attitudes are more of a determining factor in achievement motivation than aptitude, a model has been developed and is currently being tried on Iranian students.

Individual differences in cognitive abilities: A component processes account

Hannon, Brenda Dept. of Psychology, Univ. of Texas at San Antonio, San Antonio, USA Daneman, Meredyth Psychology, The University of Toronto, Mississauga, Canada

We examined the extent to which integrating prior knowledge with new information can account for the variance typically shared among tests of cognitive abilities. Participants completed a measure of knowledge integration ability as well as a battery of cognitive tests that assessed general fluid intelligence and specific abilities (verbal, math, spatial). Not only was knowledge integration an excellent predictor of performance on all the abilities tests, but it tended to have better predictive power than two measures of working memory capacity. We argue that knowledge integration is a fundamental process that underlies skill on a range of complex cognitive tasks.

Effect of relaxation techniques on self-care ability for hemodialysis patients

Haramaki, Yutaka Clinical Psychology, kagoshima University, Kagoshima, Japan

If hemodialysis patients have a pain, they often feel fear, anxiety and depression. They also need high quality medical care but also involves self-care abilities. We examined the effect of relaxation techniques (Dohsa-hou) on pain for hemodialysis patients. 7 patients received 6 sessions of relaxation using Dohsa-hou from medical staff during dialysis for 1 month. Patients evaluated their pain/feeling, and were interviewed about self-care on post relaxation. 7 patients performed relaxation techniques alone at home as self-care ability. These findings suggest that the effects of relaxation techniques on pain correlate with inducing the will to perform self-care in hemodialysis patients.

Predicting learning outcomes using multilevel analysis of behavioral data from learning experiments

Hartig, Johannes Educational Quality, DIPF, Frankfurt am Main, Germany Meyer, Katja Department of Psychology, University of Koblenz-Landau, Landau, Germany

Multilevel analysis is increasingly often applied to data from repeated measurements. Typically, an outcome variable is predicted by person-level predictors, time-varying predictors, or time itself (growth curve modeling). However, trends in time-varying variables may also be used as predictors for person-level variables. We used a multilevel model to predict learning outcomes by repeatedly measured behavioral variables from a multimedia learning experiment (N=57). It can be shown that individual trends in learning behavior provide additional information above the mere aggregated frequencies of these variables. Generalization of the application to other experimental data is discussed.

Psychological factors affecting Japanese university students' food selection for lunch of either convenience store or department store riceballs

Hasegawa, Tomoko Tokyo, Japan Sakai, Nobuyuki Department of Life Sciences, Kobe Shoin Wemen's Universiy, Kobe City, Japan Imada, Sumio Department of Psychology, Hiroshima Shudo University, Hiroshima City, Japan

Objective: Two experiments examined psychological factors affecting the selection of 'riceballs'. Method: Fifty-six students selected convenience store or department store riceballs. At the selection and after consuming the selected riceballs, participants assessed their appearance and taste (experiment1). One week later, participants conducted blind tastings of both riceballs (experiment2). Result: Forty-five students selected convenience store riceballs due to their availability, whereas the others selected due to taste or safety. In Experiment1, participants selecting department store riceball gave more positive assessments though there was no difference in the assessment in experiment2. Conclusion: Participants selected and consumed with an image of the source.

The path model of influential factors on organizational safety

Hasegawa, Naoko Human Factors Research Center, CRIEPI, Tokyo, Japan Hayase, Ken-ichi Human Factors Research Center, CRIEPI, Tokyo, Japan Takano, Ken-ichi Human Factors Research Center, CRIEPI, Tokyo, Japan

The purpose of this study is to develop a path model of influential factors on organizational safety. For the development, path analysis was applied to the questionnaire data obtained from five industries, i.e., electric utility, contracting (principal and sub-contractor), chemical, and food production. As a result of the analysis, path models were developed for each industry and several important factors were extracted by comparing the models, e.g. 'Mutual trust between a leader and followers'. These results will be utilized to draw up a road map toward enhancement of organizational safety by prioritizing safety measures which help them overcome organization's weaknesses.

Reversal learning with different type of stimuli in patients with unilateral hemisphere damage.

Hashimoto, Yukari Psychology, Fukuyama University, Fukuyama, Japan Sawada, Kozue Psychology, Hiroshima Prefectural Rehabiri, Higashihiroshima-vity, Japan Maruishi, Masaharu Higher Brain Function Center, Hiroshima Prefectural Rehabiri, Higashihiroshima-city, Japan Toshima, Tamotsu administration officer, Prefectural University of Hiro, Hiroshima, Japan

In the present study employed reversal learning paradigm using several kinds of stimuli to assess the performance of patients with unilateral hemisphere damage and investigate the role of stimuli which could affect on discrimination shift learning.

Equating item parameters under the graded response model

Hattori, Tamaki Comprehensive Human Sciences, University of Tsukuba, Tsukuba, Japan

This paper presents two item characteristic curve methods of estimating equating coefficients for the item parameters of the graded response model under the common-item design. The first is one in which the criterion function is defined on the both target and new scales like the Haebara's criterion function for the dichotomous response model. The second is one in which the criterion function is defined only on the target scale. The results of simulation experiments suggest that the item characteristic curve, the test characteristic curve and the Mean & Sigma methods are preferable to the category characteristic curve and the Mean & Mean methods in terms of standard errors.

ERP correlates of list-method directed forgetting

Hauswald, Anne Inst. für Psychologie, Universität Konstanz, Konstanz, Germany

Instructing subjects to forget items of a previously learned list and then presenting another to-be-remembered list leads to less recall of the first list than without a forget instruction. Using electrophysiological measures during encoding, we explored underlying processes of list-method directed forgetting of words (neutral or unpleasant). Directed forgetting was found for both neutral and unpleasant words. Additionally, electrophysiology showed an activity increase in frontal regions during the presentation of words that followed the forget instruction (450 - 650 ms after stimulus onset). As frontal areas are associated with inhibitory processes, they seem to be involved in list-method directed forgetting.

Effect of pride and respect on the occupational identity and cooperative behavior of nurses

Hayase, Ryo Graduate School of I. A. S., Hiroshima University, Hiroshima, Japan Sakata, Kiriko Graduate School of I. A. S., Hiroshima University, HIgashi-Hiroshima, Japan Kohguchi, Hiroshi Department of sociology, Ryutsu Keizai University, Ryugasaki, Japan

The effect of pride in the nursing profession and the sense of being treated respectfully by colleagues on the occupational identity and cooperative behaviors, including in-role and extra-role cooperation of nurses were investigated. Participants in the study were 124 nurses. As predicted, a path analysis indicated that pride and respectful treatment by colleagues, increased occupational identity, which in-turn increased the willingness to engage in cooperative behaviors. Furthermore, respectful treatment by colleagues increased the willingness to directly engage in extra-role cooperation. The authors discussed a possibility that the quality of the medical service depends on the identification of nurse's profession.

Who profits?: Predictors for therapy outcome of cognitive-behavioral therapy in patients with somatoform symptoms

Heider, Jens Campus Landau, Universität Koblenz-Landau, Landau, Germany Zaby, Alexandra Campus Landau, Universität Koblenz-Landau, Landau, Germany Schröder, Annette Campus Landau, Universität Koblenz-Landau, Landau, Germany

Objectives: As of today it has not been possible to identify predictors for therapy outcome of cognitive-behavioral therapy in patients with somatoform symptoms. Methods: In a longitudinal design the predictive relevance of sociodemographic variables, comorbidity and other disorder specific variables for shortterm therapy-outcome was investigated in 78 out-patients attending a cognitive-behavioral group intervention. Results: Sociodemographic variables as well as comorbid anxiety and depression were not associated with therapy outcome. Multiple regression analysis indicated a positive relation between symptom count and therapy outcome. Conclusion: Particularly strongly impared out-patients with numerous somatoform symptoms profit from shortterm therapy.

The effect of COMT Val158Met on neural correlates of delay discounting: An fNIRS study

Heinzel, Sebastian Psychiatrie und Psychotherapie, Universität Würzburg, Würzburg, Germany Lesch, Klaus-Peter Psychiatry and Psychotherapy, Psychobiologie, Würzburg, Germany Fallgatter, Andreas J. Psychiatry and Psychotherapy, Psychophysiology/fct.Imaging, Würzburg, Germany Schecklmann, Martin Psychiatry and Psychotherapy, Psychophysiology/fct.Imaging, Würzburg, Germany Plichta, Michael M. Psychiatry and Psychotherapy, Psychophysiology/fct.Imaging, Würzburg, Germany
Processing of inter-temporal choice uniformly activates the right dorsolateral prefrontal cortex (DLPFC) independent of the rewards' delay-to-delivery whereas the orbitofrontal cortex (OFC) is preferentially activated by immediately available rewards. The present functional near-infrared spectroscopy (fNIRS) study examines dopaminergic influence on this neural correlate of delay discounting and its relation to impulsivity measurements. The results show that particularly high impulsive subjects according to a delay discounting task exhibited increased neural delay discounting in the OFC. Furthermore, analyses on the COMT genotype affecting brain processing revealed that the homozygote Met-allele carriers showed increased neural delay discounting compared to subjects of other genotypes.

Familiarity or conceptual priming: Event-related potentials in name recognition

Hellmann, Johan Dept. of Psychology, Lund University, Lund, Sweden Stenberg, Georg Johansson, Mikael Rosen, Ingmar
The present study examined the ERP components of recognition memory using an episodic memory task with stimulus material consisting of names, half of which were famous, all varying in frequency. These dimensions, frequency and fame, exerted powerful effects on memory accuracy and dissociated the 2 recognition processes. The ERPs corresponded fully to the behavioural data. Frequency affected the frontal component exclusively, and fame affected the parietal component exclusively. Moreover, a separate behavioural experiment showed that conceptual priming was sensitive to fame, but not to frequency. Our data therefore indicate that the FN400 varies jointly with familiarity, but independently of conceptual priming.

Emotion regulation and the ventromedial prefrontal cortex in spider phobia

Hermann, Andrea Bender Institute of Neuroimag., University of Giessen, Giessen, Germany Schäfer, Axel Clinical and Health Psychology, University of Graz, Graz, Austria Walter, Bertram BION, University of Giessen, Giessen, Germany Vaitl, Dieter BION, University of Giessen, Giessen, Germany Schienle, Anne Clinical and Health Psychology, University of Graz, Graz, Austria
The aim of this study was to identify the role of the ventromedial prefrontal cortex in the automatic vs. effortful regulation of emotions in spider phobic subjects. In an fMRI study, 16 spider phobic females were asked to up- and down-regulate their emotions elicited by spider and aversive pictures. First results show a diminished hemodynamic response in the ventromedial prefrontal cortex towards spider vs. aversive pictures independent of the regulation instruction. Since this region is critically involved in the automatic regulation of emotions, strong emotional reactions towards phobic objects may be due to a deficit in automatic emotion regulation mechanisms.

Cognitive-behavioral treatment of aggressive children: Outcome research

Hernández-Guzmán, Laura Psychology, National University of Mexico, Mexico City, Mexico
A randomized trial design was used to investigate the efficacy of cognitive-behavioral therapy of aggressive children, with or without the participation of their parents. Two groups of aggressive children were exposed to manualized cognitive-behavior therapy during 12 sessions. But only in one of the groups parents were trained to deal with their aggressive children. Improvements were observed after treatment in both groups; however the effect was maintained three and six months later only when parents participated. Results are discussed in terms of the importance of parental involvement during CBT interventions for the treatment of aggressive behavior.

Implications of revisions to Gray's personality model for the measurement of individual differences in approach and avoidance behaviour

Heym, Nadja School of Psychology, University of Nottingham, Nottingham, United Kingdom Lawrence, Claire School of Psychology, University of Nottingham, Nottingham, United Kingdom Ferguson, Eamonn School of Psychology, University of Nottingham, Nottingham, United Kingdom
Objectives: Recent revisions of Gray's RST were examined by (i) comparing Carver and White's 1-factor BIS scale with a 2-factor solution separating BIS and FFFS, and (ii) mapping the revised RST onto the Eysenckian space. Methods: 212 participants completed Carver and White's BIS/BAS scales and the EPQ-R. Results: Using confirmatory factor analysis and path analysis, the results showed that (i) the two-factor model separating BIS and FFFS best fitted the data, and (ii) Eysenck's Psychoticism was located between BIS and BAS, Neuroticism between BIS and FFFS, and Extraversion between BAS and FFFS. Conclusions: Implications for personality assessment are discussed.

Complex span versus binding tasks of working memory: The gap is not that deep

Hildebrandt, Andrea IQB, Humboldt-Universität zu Berlin, Berlin, Germany Schmiedek, Florian Lövdén, Martin Wilhelm, Oliver Lindenberger, Ulman Zentrum für Lebenserwartung, Max-Planck-Institut, Berlin, Germany
How to measure working memory capacity is an issue of ongoing debate. Complex span tasks, which combine short-term memory demands with secondary tasks, compete with paradigms characterized by requiring building, maintaining, and updating of arbitrary bindings. With latent variable analysis based on content-heterogeneous operationalizations, we find a correlation between a complex span factor and a binding factor that is not statistically different from unity (r = .96). Both factors predict reasoning equally well. Processes involved in building, maintaining, and updating arbitrary bindings may constitute the common working memory ability underlying performance on reasoning, complex span, and binding tasks.

The effect of group supportive psychotherapy on decreasing depression and increasing marital adjustment women who suffer from multiple sclerosis

Hodjatzadeh, Farahnaz Binesh Kara, Tehran, Islamic Republic of Iran Ghalkhani, zahra counseling, Binesh Kara, Tehran, Islamic Republic of Iran
Objective-this study assess the effectiveness of group Supportive Psychotherapy on decreasing Depression and increasing Marital Adjustment women who suffer from Multiple Sclerosis METHOD AND RESEARCH: In order to conduct this research 70 women from 6500 women were selected who were memberships of M.S Association, live in Tehran, at least have diploma and married. The method of this research was random. They answered SCL-90-R and Marital adjustment test as pre-post test. 16 patients were selected and replaced in two groups-controls and experimental. In order to analyze was used T test. CONCLUSION: there was a significant difference between Supportive Psychotherapy and decreasing Depression. Zahra Ghalkhani

Does the bee give you malaria?: The dimensionality of and sex differences in general knowledge in high-school students

Hofer, Agnes A. Scheiblingkirchen, Austria Formann, Anton K. Basic Psychological Research, University of Vienna, Vienna, Austria Voracek, Martin Basic Psychological Research, University of Vienna, Vienna, Austria
In a large sample (N=1088) of Austrian high-school students (grades 10-12), scores on 18 primary knowledge domains (163-item adaptation of Lynn's [2001] General Knowledge Test) were invariably positively interrelated. This positive manifold suggests a higher-order semantic memory factor (general knowledge/information that is culturally valued, but on-specialist). Sex differences in general knowledge, favoring boys, were large (d=0.8). Boys excelled girls in 14 out of 18 domains (except for Fashion, Medicine, Nutrition/Cookery, Popular Music), with effect sizes up to d=1.0 (Finance, Physics/Chemistry, Sport). Implications of these findings and psychometric shortcomings (fairish internal scale consistencies, lack of Rasch scalability) are discussed.

Performing at our best: The impact of optimal experiences at work

Hofslett Kopperud, Karoline Leadership,Organizational Mgt., Norwegian School of Management, Oslo, Norway
Within work and organizational psychology, the happy/productive worker thesis has received much attention. However, it has been a source of confusion and controversy. Some argue this is caused by the way happiness has been understood. In the current study, happiness is suggested to include experiences such as work engagement and flow, which in turn are expected to have important effects on performance. Questionnaires were distributed to Norwegian employees and students (N = 158). Regression analyses indicate strong relationships between engagement, flow and performance. The importance of including such variables when studying the happy/productive worker thesis is supported.

Creative processes in conceptual combination: Emergence of original concepts

Horng, Ruey-Yun Dept. Industrial Engineering, National Chiao Tung University, Hsinchu, Taiwan Lu, Po-Hui Dept. Industrial Engineering, National Chiao Tung University, Hsinchu, Taiwan Liao, Chia-Ning Dept. Industrial Engineering, National Chiao Tung University, Hsinchu, Taiwan
Objective: Conceptual combination involves joining of two concepts to produce new concepts which satisfy the representation of each constituent concept. Original concepts may emerge from conceptual combination. In this study, the effects of the ontological category of noun-noun pairs on interpretative mechanisms and originality of new concepts were examined. Methods: Three lists of 9 noun-noun pairs were administered to 90 participants. Results: Eight interpretation mechanisms were identified. Noun pairs of the same ontological category produced less original ideas, whereas natural or artifact nouns paired with abstract nouns produced more original ideas. Conclusions: Cross-domain search or abstraction is conducive to Creativity.

The Impact of the interaction context and gender-role-selfconcept on communication behaviour

Horvath, Lisa Kristina Inst. für Psychologie, KF Universität Graz, Graz, Austria Athenstaedt, Ursula Institut für Psychologie, KF Universität Graz, Graz, Austria

The Gender role self-concept (GRS) is the amount of feminine and masculine stereotypes people ascribe to themselves. Concerning communication behaviours there is evidence that women and men differ. In interactions men speak and interrupt more than women and women show more verbal reinforcement and nodding than men. In the present study, we expected that the GRS and communication behaviours will vary with the social context. 120 mixed-sex and same-sex dyads discussed a gender-typical or gender-neutral topic. The GRS was measured before the discussion and communication behaviours were observed during the interaction. The GRS and the interaction context predicted communication behaviours.

Brain imaging of cognitive development: A meta-analysis of 36 fMRI studies

Houde, Olivier Paris, France Rossi, Sandrine Joliot, Marc

Over the past decade, functional magnetic resonance imaging (fMRI)has made it possible to map brain functions safely in the human child in vivo. Here,we offer the first meta-analysis of these fMRI data in three cognitive and school-dependent systems: numerical abilities, reading, and executive functions. 36 fMRI studies including 591 healthy children and adolescents with mean ages of 4 to 17 years were included in this meta-analysis by the Activation Likelihood Estimation (ALE) technique. Three distinct neural networks were identified. This meta-mapping of the children's brain would provide a reference point for cognitive developmental and educational psychology.

Organismal behavior of organization: A new perspective of OB

Hu, Zhan Dept. of Psychology, East China Normal University, Berlin, Germany

Simply different from the traditional Organizational Behavior("behavior" here just implies the individual behavior in organization), the research for Organismal Behavior of Organization conducts systemic psychological research on organization as a whole. Actually, an organization is an artificial "intelligent system" and can be regarded as a "thinking-organism". Then it has its own feeling, thinking, personality and etc, so one organization is known from others because of its specifically psychological characteristic and behavior. Hence we can safely say that an organization is worthy of a particularly important object of psychological research.

The modified analytical steps for multilevel latent growth modeling and Its applications

Huang, Xiaorui Faculty of Education, Chinese Univers. of Hong Kong, Hong Kong, China, People's Republic of : Hong Kong SAR Chang, Lei Faculty of Education, Chinese University of HongKong, Hong Kong, China, People's Republic of : Macao SAR Gao, Ding-Guo Department of Psychology, Sun Yet-Sen University, Guangzhou, China, People's Republic of : Macao SAR

The purpose of the present study is to modify MCA analytical procedures so that it can be used to analyze multilevel growth data. The modification is based on Mplus procedures that are combined with those defined by multilevel latent growth modeling. Real data were used to demonstrate the modified MCA procedures. These data are from the social developmental research that examines such social behaviors as externalizing, internalizing problem behaviors, and various emotion regulation strategies of children and adolescents across three time points.

How acculturated cultural orientation is filtered through bi-directional parent-child interactions: Taking Chinese immigrant parents as examples

Huang, Elenda Y.J. Dept. of Psychology, Peking University, Beijing, People's Republic of China Su, Yan-Jie Department of Psychology, Peking University, Beijing, People's Republic of China

This study aimed to illustrate how Chinese immigrant parents bi-directionally interact with their young children in Canada. Immigrants' maternal and paternal bid types in response to children's agency under bi-culturally ecological system were analyzed upon parents' acculturations. Parent-child interactive assessment game, half-structured interviews, and cultural-orientation questionnaires were applied. 18 families, 52 parent-child dyadic interactions were analyzed. Results showed parents with vertical-collectivism orientation tended to guide, raise attention and interrupt for further dutifulness on children, while horizontal-collectivism parents with abundant responsiveness and significant cooperative supports. It is suggested how Chinese immigrant parents filter their acculturated cultural orientation to next Canadian-born generation.

Reciprocity between Chinese employers and employee

Huangfu, Gang School of management, Beihang University, Beijing, People's Republic of China Zhang, Gangying Department of Psychology, Shaanxi Normal University, Xi'an, People's Republic of China Dai, Hang China Aviation Industry Corpor, China Aviation Industry Corpor, Beijing, People's Republic of China

This study used Fehr and colleagues'(1993) paradigm to investigate the attitudes of 186 Chinese managers and 382 employees and students. Results showed that in the Chinese labor market, there was reciprocity between employers and laborers, i e., the employers would like to pay above average salaries in the market, while employees would like to devote more effort than expected for their salary level. Results also showed that there were differences between areas with different economic levels, between laborers of different educational backgrounds, and between state-owned, private and joint ventures on the expected salary level and employees' devotion.

Comparison of different software programs for the parameter estimation of the Linear Logistic Test Model

Ihme, Jan Marten Inst. für Psychologie, Universität Jena, Jena, Germany

The Linear Logistic Test Model (LLTM) is a model, which can refer the difficulty of an item to its components, e.g. cognitive steps which are necessary to solve the item. Various software packages contain modules for the estimation of LLTM parameters. This study compares the LLTM parameter estimations of several software programs for real and for simulated data. Large differences were found between the estimations of the software programs, which were only partly due to different estimation algorithms. Recommendations are given for choosing a program and an estimation algorithm for different data constellations.

The interactive effects of group goals and job characteristics on task and contextual performance in Japanese organizations

Ikeda, Hiroshi Dept. of Human Sciences, St. Thomas University, Amagasaki, Japan Furukawa, Hisataka Faculty of Human-Environment S, Kyushu university, Fukuoka City, Japan

This study examined the effect of setting group goals on team member's activities in terms of task and contextual performance. A survey was conducted for 140 Japanese employees. Moderated regression analyses revealed that, for teams which need higher interdependence among members, setting group goal was positively related to contextual performance, but not to task performance. Higher interdependence was not necessarily required, however, setting group goal has no relation to contextual performance, and even negatively to task performance. These findings suggest that in order to facilitate team activities, setting group goal is effective for the job requiring close interdependence among members.

Developmental transition of "Meta-Social Skill"

Ishii, Yukako Education, JPSP, University of Tokyo, Toyono-Gun Osaka, Japan

In this study, I did comparing investigation about social skill (both expression skill and non-expression skill) and meta-cognition from adolescent to adult. 150 high school students as middle adolescence group, 224 undergraduate students (mean age 19) as later adolescence group and 295 as adult group were participated in a questionnaire survey. As a result of anova, significant differences were partly seen. Later adolescence group's score of non-expression skill was significantly low to both middle adolescence group and adults. As to meta-cognition, it was shown that mean score increase pro rata to developmental level. There were no significantly differences about expression skill score.

Changing times for the university: The new role of the university teacher as a manager of learning resources

Isidro, Ana Isabel Social Psychology&Anthropology, University of Salamanca, Salamanca, Spain

In the present communication, we will discuss about the entering of the information and knowledge society in the university teaching process and what fittings in both attitudes and habits have to be done as a consequence of such irruption. The new technologies suppose new abilities but mean new formation, qualification, improvement and motivation challenges. Hence, the university teacher role must be redefined. Besides, the university student, as a passive recipient, cannot be imagined. Not everything in the cyberspace is valid, fair, and neutral. The information evaluation demands a decision that will implicate capability to discern the essential to the accessory.

Asymmetries in hemispheric control of attention in schizotypy

Ito, Shinya Nihon University, Tokyo, Japan

It seems unclear that schizotypy have the same difficulty which is like as the attentional deficits schizophrenia frequently shows to some extent. The present study investigated attentional performance in volunteer participants with "high" and "low" scores in Schizotypal Personality Questionnaire Brief. In Posner task high group was distinguished from low group by a slower response to a target in the right visual field than to a target in the left visual field when attention was not first directed to the target location. This result is one of the evidence that schizotypy and schizophrenia exist on a continuum.

Motivational factors in the treatment of agoraphobia and panic disorder

Ivert, Petra Maria Psychosomatische Klinik, Klinik Roseneck, Prien, Germany Mander, Johannes Roseneck, PsychosomaticHospital Roseneck, Prien Am Chiemsee, Germany Geissner, Edgar Roseneck, PsychosomaticHospital Roseneck, Prien Am Chiemsee, Germany

Previous studies showed that anxiety patients can fail to succeed when participating in therapies in an only passive, mechanical way. To examine in detail which motivational factors can help (and therefore must be stressed in therapy) to overcome insufficient improvement, we analysed motivational dimensions of change and of maintenance. 180 patients were tested four times during therapy. FA revealed three factors of change (Initial Awareness; Specific Intention to Act; and – in contrast – Problem Denial) and three factors of maintenance (Learning Attitude; Perseverance; and Confidence). Scales derived from those proved to be reliable, valid and useful instruments to control therapeutic change.

What makes your lesson a success? A qualitative study on teachers' goals for mathematics

Jacob, Barbara Psychology, University of Munich, München, Germany Frenzel, Anne Psychology, University of Munich, München, Germany Becker, Sabine Psychology, University of Munich, München, Germany Pekrun, Reinhard Psychology, University of Munich, München, Germany

Teaching quality is one of the major concerns in instructional psychology. It is an open question whether teachers actually seek to achieve the goals identified by researchers as relevant. This qualitative study explored if teachers' goals for their own teaching reflect theoretically proposed dimensions of teaching quality. In an open questionnaire, 300 mathematics teachers were asked to describe their goals for successful teaching. Six major dimensions were extracted to categorize their answers. "Student cognitive growth" was named most frequently, followed by "student affective-motivational involvement". An unexpected finding was the frequent reference to external feedback. Implications concerning outcome-based policies are discussed.

Justice perceptions of performance appraisals: Effects on counter productive and proactive behavior at work

Jacobs, Gabriele Personnel and Organisation, Erasmus University, Rotterdam, Netherlands Belschak, Frank Amsterdam Business School, University of Amsterdam, Amsterdam, Netherlands Den Hartog, Deanne Amsterdam Business School, University of Amsterdam, Amsterdam, Netherlands

Performance appraisals are a widely used HR-instrument. This study among 356 police officers examines the effects of performance appraisals from an organizational justice perspective. We expected that justice perceptions of performance appraisal influence proactive and counterproductive behaviour at work via two mediators (support and commitment). Results show that procedural and interactional justice affected perceptions of supervisory support. Supervisor support affected commitment which, in turn, was related to proactive and counterproductive work behavior. Support and commitment fully mediated the relationship between justice perceptions and work behaviors. Thus, even a single yearly performance appraisal strongly affects perceptions, attitudes, and behaviors at work.

Zone of proximal development in the context of the first-year transition

Jakkula, Kaisa Centre of Developm. Teaching, University of Oulu, Kajaani, Finland Helenius, Aili Department of Teacher Educatio, University of Turku, Rauma, Finland

The purpose is to find out how the zone of proximal development is being constructed in mother-child interaction in the child's first-year transition, from 6 to 18 months. The longitudinal follow-up was carried out as multiple case study in free-play situations in which 6 mother-child dyads participated in laboratory and another 6 pairs in family situations. Video episodes were analysed micro-analytically. The communicative meanings, development of the child's self, delayed imitation and later the adoption of speaking skills are analysed. Interaction quality seems to affect the timing of the aspects of transition. The crucial influence of parents at the turning points of development is based on perceiving and respecting the child's initiative.

Basic life tasks

Janakov, Blagoja Dept. of Psychology, Skopje University, Skopje, The former Yugoslav Republic of Macedonia

People everyday assign tasks and are engaged in their realization. Human life is primarily realization of tasks and preparation for that. Tasks are numerous and various (social, private, official etc.). Part of the tasks are general for all people, but the ways of their realization less or more vary,which is socially and personally determined. Task realization has consequences and effects. Four life tasks are considered in this paper. (1) Well-being, good living. It is probably the most general and the most basic task. (2) Loving and partnership/togetherness. (3) Working and doing. (4) Personal development, self-realization and self-perfection.

Commitment to the supervisor, organizational commitment, and supervisor's organizational commitment: A balance perspective

Jiang, Ding Yu Department of Psychology, National Chung Cheng Uni., Min-Hsiung, Chia Yi, Taiwan Wang, Yu-Hsuan Department of Psychology, National Chung Cheng Uni., Min-Hsiung, Chia Yi, Taiwan Wu, Hsu-Chu Department of Psychology, National Chung Cheng Uni., Min-Hsiung, Chia Yi, Taiwan

This study investigated the relationship among subordinates' commitment to the supervisor (CTS) and organizational commitment (EOC), and supervisors' organizational commitment (LOC) based on Heider's balance theory. Study 1 and 2, each sampling 70 Taiwanese undergraduate students, used scenario method to investigate the triadic commitment relationship. The analytic results supported balance perspective that the interaction of CTS and LOC significantly predicted EOC. Study 3, using questionnaire survey method, collected 421 Taiwanese employees sample. The analytic results supported the balance perspective as well. Moreover, in contrast to imbalance group, balance group had higher job performance and intention to stay.

Group identity in Chinese organizations

Jiang, Ding Yu Department of Psychology, National Chung Cheng Uni., Min-Hsiung, Chia Yi, Taiwan Yan, Zong-Yi Department of Psychology, National Chung Cheng Uni., Min-Hsiung, Chia Yi, Taiwan Lin, Pei-Hua Department of Psychology, National Chung Cheng Uni., Min-Hsiung, Chia Yi, Taiwan

The goal of this study is to identify the construct and establish the measurement of group identity. In study 1, using induction approach from 36 Taiwanese employees of various work groups, the study generated ten main contents of group identity, for example trustworthiness, high group performance, and competent group members. Based on study 1's finding, Study 2 aimed to develop a group identity measure. Exploratory factor analysis indicated an 8-factor measure with 37 items. The subsequent group-level analysis, using 55 Taiwanese work groups, indicated that group identity strength positively associated with group cooperation and coherence.

Business moral value among supervisors and subordinates

Jiang, Ding Yu Department of Psychology, National Chung Cheng Uni., Min-Hsiung, Chia Yi, Taiwan Lin, Yi-Chen Department of Psychology, National Chung Cheng Uni., Min-Hsiung, Chia Yi, Taiwan Chang, Yung-Han Department of Psychology, National Chung Cheng Uni., Min-Hsiung, Chia Yi, Taiwan

This study investigated the relationship between supervisors' and subordinates' business moral value (BMV) and the moderating effects of supervisors' moral leadership and subordinates' identification to the supervisor. Using a questionnaire survey, this study collected a sample of 264 supervisor-sub-

ordinate dyads from various Taiwanese business organizations. Regression analytic results are as follows: (a) supervisors' BMV is positively associated with subordinates' BMV, such as political integrity, preservation of company resources, and honesty to customers; (b) higher supervisor's moral leadership and subordinates' identification to the supervisor increased the association between supervisors' and subordinates' BMVs; (c) subordinates' BMV is positively associated with work motivation.

Organizational commitment correlates of transformational leadership: A meta-analysis

Jin, Jing Dept. of Psychology, Peking University, Beijing, People's Republic of China Cham, Heining Department of Psychology, Peking University, Beijing, People's Republic of China

Objectives A meta-analysis of 13 articles involving transformational leadership and organizational commitment, covering various countries and jobs, was conducted to compute an average effect of transformational leadership on organizational commitment. Results Transformational leadership was found to have a moderate correlation (r = .38) with organizational commitment. And correlations between the 3 subscales (Charismatic Leadership, Individualized Consideration, and Intellectual Stimulation) in Multifactor Leadership Questionnaire (Bass, 1985) and Meyer and Allen's (1991) 2 facets of organizational commitment (affective and normative commitment) ranged from .15 to .45. Conclusions Transformational leadership is a good predictor of organizational commitment, especially of affective commitment.

Chinese undergraduates' sexual attitude: The application of multidimensionality of sexual attitudes scale in China

Jin, Can Can Department of psychology, Beijing Normal University, Beijing, People's Republic of China Zou, Hong Department of psychology, Beijing Normal University, Beijing, People's Republic of China He, Shan Shan Department of Social Work, HongKong University, HongKong, China, People's Republic of : Hong Kong SAR

To explore Chinese College Students' sexual current situation and to apply Multidimensionality of Sexual Attitudes Scale developed by Hendrick?a sample of 1050 Chinese students was examined in Internet. Results indicated that there are significant differences in Permissiveness, Instrumentiality, Comunion and Pleasure for subjects with different love frequency, and there are significant differences in Instrumentiality, Comunion and Pleasure for subjects in the different love stage; The conclusion is that sex centered on self (Permissiveness and Instrumentiality)and sex center on the relationship(Comunion, Pleasure and Responsibility)-change and develop alternately with the development of love.

Influence of fair and supportive leadership behavior on commitment and organizational citizenship behavior

Jonas, Klaus Inst. für Psychologie, Universität Zürich, Zürich, Switzerland Rietmann, Brigitte Department of Psycho, University of Zurich, Zurich, Switzerland Meierhans, Diana Department of Psycho, University of Zurich, Zurich, Switzerland

The study examines the influence of fair and supportive leadership behavior on employees' self-reported organizational citizenship behavior. 260 bank employees completed a questionnaire in which they rated their supervisor's behavior, their commitment (toward organization and supervisor) and the degree to which they engaged in organizational citizenship behavior. Structural equation analysis provides support for the assumption that the impact of fair and supportive leadership is mediated by employees' commitment to the organization as well as to the supervisor.

The influence of retention interval and emotional arousal on recognition memory and its neural correlates

König, Stefanie Experiment. Neuropsychologie, Universität des Saarlandes, Saarbrücken, Germany Mecklinger, Axel Experimental Neuropsychology, Saarland University, Saarbruecken, Germany

Emotion has been suggested to influence the memorability of events. We investigated to what extent encoding and retrieval processes are affected by an item's emotional arousal and how retention duration modulates these processes. We found that high-arousing negative pictures were remembered better than low-arousing negative and neutral pictures after a 24 hour retention interval. Event-related potential measures revealed that the retrieval of high-arousing events was qualitatively richer especially at long retention duration and that these negative pictures gain prioritized processing already at encoding. The latter mechanism may account for the enhanced recognition memory performance for those pictures.

Prevention with depressed mothers and their children in German mother-child health resorts

Kötter, Charlotte Präventionsfoschung, Institut für Therapieforschung, München, Germany Stemmler, Mark Jaursch, Stefanie

Children of depressed mothers are at high risk to develop internalizing or externalizing disorders (Goodman, 2007), partly caused by parental impairments (Gelfand & Teti, 1990). Our study aims to develop, implement and evaluate a prevention program, EFFEKT-E, which focuses on maternal parenting and children's problem-solving skills. We conduct a quasiexperimental time-sample study at 13 mother-child health resorts. There are currently 275 mothers in the control group and 270 mothers are anticipated in the intervention group. Mothers complete a questionnaire about parenting, parental stress, social support as well as behaviour problems and anxiety/depression symptoms of their children. Post effects of the programme will be presented.

The effects of a decoy's position in consumer choice

Kamada, Akiko Dept. of Human Sciences, Bunkyo University, Saitama, Japan

Preferences between two alternatives (X and Y) are different when a third choice (Z) that is inferior to the two alternatives is added as a decoy. This phenomenon is known as the attraction effect. The decoy's inferiority was manipulated by changing its quality and price. The results showed that when the quality of Z was fixed as equivalent to that of Y and the price of Z was close to that of X, Y was perceived as less attractive as its price went up. In contrast, when the price of Z was fixed and its quality was manipulated, the choices were not varied much.

Intercultural expertise in international military missions

Kammhuber, Stefan Business und Social Management, RheinAhrCampus Remagen, Remagen, Germany

German soldiers have been involved in many international missions since the 90s. In order to avoid unnecessary conflicts, intercultural expertise is essential. Building up on a decade of intercultural research in the German Bundeswehr, I will present a study about the connection of specific cultural standards and hostile action in international missions. Theoretical background includes Intercultural Expertise and Action Theory. 30 experts of the German Bundeswehr were interviewed by means of critical incident technique. The analysis was conducted by means of qualitative content analysis. Conclusions can be drawn regarding both, the preparation and the on-mission-coaching of soldiers.

Organization-based self-esteem in an international context: Results of a validation study in six languages

Kanning, Uwe Peter Inst. für Psychologie, Universität Münster, Münster, Germany

We report on a study in which the English-language original of a scale on the measurement of organization-based self-esteem was translated into five further languages (German, Polish, Hungarian, Spanish, Malay) and validated. The employees of an international company were surveyed in seven countries (USA, Canada, Germany, Poland, Spain, Hungary and Malaysia). For purposes of validation, the job satisfaction, the self-rated job performance and the support of the employees in implementing the company values (commitment) were used. The results show that the translations proceeded successfully. In all cases, a reliable scale emerges, which correlates positively with the validity criteria.

Emotion regulation in Japan and US

Karasawa, Mayumi Communication, Tokyo Woman's Christian Univ, Tokyo, Japan Hirabayashi, Hidemi Psychology, Tokyo Woman's Christian Univ, Tokyo, Japan Tardif, Twila Psychology, University of Michigan, Ann Arbor, USA

In this study, we examined behavioral difference in emotion regulation and explored the role of executive functioning and emotional understanding abilities together with parent emotionality and emotional socialization strategies to their children. Sixty Japanese and 57 American preschool children (4 years old) participated in two emotional challenging task and other 9 tasks. We found that basic differences in emotionality-behavioral and cognitive level of emotion regulation as well as parents factors. Individual and cultural aspects of these differences and the coordination of emotional responses across multiple levels of responding will be discussed in terms of a complex systems perspective.

Evaluation of therapy and therapist: Comparison of client-centered therapy, gestalt therapy, and rational-emotive psychotherapy

Kashibuchi, Megumi Department of Psychology, Gakushuin University, Tokyo, Japan Takahira, Mieko Research and Development, NIME, Chiba, Japan

The purpose of this study was to examine the image and the preference of therapy and therapist by university students not majoring in clinical psychology. In the experiment, the students watched Client-centered therapy, Gestalt therapy, and Rational-emotive psycho-therapy in the video "Three Approaches to Psychotherapy," then evaluated each therapy and therapist. The results showed that Rational-emotive psycho-therapy was evaluated as the most typical and positive therapy and therapist by the students. The gap of evaluation that might exist between the experts on clinical psychology and the students, had to also be considered.

Where does a feeling of nostalgia come from? The interaction of memory and the feeling of nostalgia

Kawaguchi, Jun Department of Psychology, Nagoya University, Nagoya, Japan

Reflecting past events sometimes make people to have a strong feeling of nostalgia. What type of processes underlies the emergence of nostalgia? Retrieval of episodic memory should be related to nostalgia, but it has not been investigated yet. This study examined the influence of factors of memory attributes, including accuracy of memory for past events, the years of interval of past events, and so on, upon the feeling of nostalgia. The results showed the relation between the memory attributes and the strength of nostalgia. The processes to make nostalgia are discussed.

An explanatory model of physicians for suicide prevention: Analysis of physicians' statements made to suicidal patients

Kawashima, Daisuke Tokyo, Japan Koyama, Tatsuya School of Nursing, TokyoWomen'sMedicalUniversity, Ogawa-Higashi, Kodaira, Tokyo, Japan Kawano, Kenji NIMH, NCNP, Ogawa-Higashi, Kodaira, Tokyo, Japan Ito, Hiroto NIMH, NCNP, Ogawa-Higashi, Kodaira, Tokyo, Japan

This study examined an explanatory model of primary care physicians for suicide prevention by considering statements made by physicians to patients with suicidal ideation. Physicians with experience of communicating with suicidal patients were asked to describe their statements. A total of 166 responses to the open questions were used for text-mining analysis, and frequently used words were identified. In addition, five clusters were confirmed by correspondence analysis, i.e., sympathy and account-making, referral to psychiatrists, prospects of diagnosis and recovery, no-suicide contracts, and the meaning of life and consideration to others.

A reevaluation of canonical categories in flashbulb memories

Kaya Kiziloz, Burcu Dept. of Psychology, Bogazici University, Istanbul, Turkey Tekcan, Ali I. Psychology, Bogazici University, Istanbul, Turkey

We aimed to reevaluate the canonical categories in flashbulb memories, reported thirty years ago by Brown and Kulik (1977). One hundred and thirty five participants reported - in as much detail as possible - how they first learned about three significant public events in recent history: the attacks of 9/11 in New York, USA, a bombing attack in Turkey, and the last minute cancellation of a nationwide university entrance examination, again, in Turkey. Results showed that canonical categories differed for the three events and that personal consequentiality influenced the number and type of canonical categories.

Personality traits of team members: A forgotten factor influencing the performance of diverse teams

Kearney, Eric Bremen, Germany Voelpel, Sven JCLL, Jacobs University Bremen, Bremen, Germany

Organizational teams are becoming increasingly diverse with respect to demographic variables and experiential backgrounds. We extend recent attempts to identify the moderators and mediators that influence the diversity-team performance relationship. Specifically, we propose that the balance between the positive and the negative effects of team diversity depends in no small measure on the personality traits of the team members. We present the results of three empirical studies confirming our hypothesis that team member traits such as need for cognition and need for cognitive closure affect both processes and outcomes in diverse teams.

Judgments of preferences are only "partial measures" of memory

Kellen, David FPCE-UL, Lisbon, Portugal Garcia-Marques, Teresa UIPCDE, ISPA, Lisbon, Portugal

Following a dual-process approach to recognition memory we assume that two independent components, an automatic familiarity and controlled recollection, underlie a recognition judgment (Jacoby, 1991). Our approach extends this duality to other type of judgments such as liking. Doing so, we assume that both recognition and preference are partially derived from a feeling of familiarity activated in face of familiar stimuli. Their sometimes found independence derives from the other variability components that are not shared between recognition and preference. In this paper we present preliminary evidence for this assumption, by showing that under inclusion or list-indifference conditions, the association of both measures is higher than under exclusion or list-discrimination conditions.

The bidirectional relationship of depression and physical functioning after coronary artery bypass graft surgery

Kendel, Friederike Inst. für Med. Psychologie, Charité Berlin, Berlin, Germany *Lehmkuhl, Elke* Thor and Card surgery, Deutsches Herzzentrum Berlin, Berlin, Germany *Regitz-Zagrosek, Vera* CCR, Charité, Berlin, Germany *Hetzer, Roland* Thor and CardSurgery, Deutsches Herzzentrum, Berlin, Germany

Objectives: To examine the predictive relationship of depression and subjective Physical Functioning after bypass surgery. Methods: The sample of this longitudinal study consisted of 579 patients (22% women) undergoing bypass surgery at the Deutsches Herzzentrum Berlin in 2005. Patients filled out questionnaires (depression: PHQ-9; Physical Functioning: SF-36) 1 day before surgery, 2 months and 1 year after surgery. Results: A cross-lagged path analytic model demonstrated predictive priority of depression over Physical Functioning for both men and women. Conclusions: The results underline the importance of depression – a modifiable risk factor - for the course of recovery for both men and women.

Arizona Sexual Experience Scale (ASEX): Patients with depression

Kesicky, Dusan Bratislava, Slovak Republic *Novotny, Vladimir* Psychiatry, Medical School, Bratislava, Slovak Republic *Kesicka, Melinda* Psychiatry, Medical School Hospital, Bratislava, Slovak Republic

It is often necessary to find out what phase of sexual cycle is affected in depressed patients. In the sample of 67 participants was found out the influence of depression depth on changes in desire, arousal, coital readiness, orgasm and satisfaction. By statistical analysis the significant influence of depression depth was found out most on decrease of desire, less on arousal and coital readiness. The influence on extent of sexual desire is significant in men. In women the depression influences arousal and coital readiness, less influences desire. ASEX is useful tool for specifying the influence of depression on sexual cycle.

Interaction between introversion-extroversion and self-confidence on changing taste sexuality

Khalatbari, Javad Dept. of Psychology, IAU of Tonekabon Branch, Tonekabon, Islamic Republic of Iran *Ghorbanshirodi, Shoreh* PSYCHOLOGY, IAU OF TONEKABON BRANCH, TONEKABON, Islamic Republic of Iran

The studied population is single and married women and men in tehran, and a sample of 200 single and married women and men were choosed. First exmamines answered the variety seeking sexuality test (cts), then the rosenbers self-esteem scale and after that eysenck personality inventory. The results indicate that mens variety seeking sexuality is more than womens, in addition, singel people have more variety seeking sexuality. Moreover, introversion-extraversion and neurotiicism charactierstics can predict the variety seeking sexuality, but self-confidence is not a proper predictor for this variable. It means that the interaction between introversion-extraversion and self confidence does not have any effect on changing taste sexuality.

Using the measurement's method of the reflexive representations in cross-cultural researches

Khromov, Anatoly Dept. of Psychology, KGU, Kurgan, Russia *Basimov, Mikhail* Psychology, KGU, Kurgan, Russia

Method of multilevel reflexive measurements of cultural peculiarities, minimizing mistakes of etic methods is suggested. The assessment performed in three levels - as mutual direct, as own mutual reflexive, and as mutual reflexive representations from the standpoint of other cultures' subjects. Method was applied in cross-cultural research of Russia, India and USA. Multiple pair comparisons of "parameter- group" relations for thirty six estimations based on Student's criterion are transforming in continuous scale with reference frame common for all measurements - zero point of comparative ponderability and are geometric representing their attitudes in space of cross-cultural assess.

Analysis of the psychological transformation by women's makeup behavior self to pretend to be and self to be seen from another person

Kido, Ayae Education, Kyoto University, Kyoto, Japan

In modern Japanese society, makeup behavior is considered important for a female's appearance, because makeup plays an essential role in interpersonal relationship. Whenever women wear makeup, they imagine another person who exists in their Assumptive World. This study aims to figure out the structure of the Assumptive World, and how the Assumptive World is constructed in women's mind. 4 women who engage in post of beauty were interviewed, and analyzed by Narrative analysis. As a result, nest of boxes structure was figured out. In addition, this study found the way of dialogue with others in their Assumptive world.

Infant febrile seizures: Influence on hippocampus volume and declarative memory

Kipp, Kerstin H. Inst. Exper. Neuropsychologie, Universität des Saarlandes, Saarbrücken, Germany *Becker, Martina* Experimental Neuropsychology, University of the Saarland, Saarbrücken, Germany *Mecklinger, Axel* Experimental Neuropsychology, University of the Saarland, Saarbrücken, Germany *Reith, Wolfgang* Department of Neuroradiology, Saarland University Hospital, Homburg, Germany *Gortner, Ludwig* Department of Neonatology, Saarland University Hospital, Homburg, Germany

More than 50% of temporal sclerosis patients also suffered from infant febrile seizures. Therefore, we suspect that febrile seizures may be the cause of temporal lobe lesions, in particular in the hippocampus. We compared hippocampus volumes and declarative memory of children (7-9 years) with and without infant febrile seizures. The volume distributions of both groups largely overlap, the febrile seizures group has only a marginally lower volume. At first sight, the effects of febrile seizures seem to be negligible. But essential impairments are observed in verbal episodic memory performance which correlates with the hippocampus volume. Further results will be discussed.

Instruction of self-regulated learning in mathematics lessons

Kistner, Saskia Inst. für Psychologie, Universität Frankfurt, Frankfurt, Germany *Rakoczy, Katrin* Bildungsqualität u. Evaluation, DIPF, Frankfurt, Germany *Dignath, Charlotte* Psychology, Goethe-University, Frankfurt, Germany *Büttner, Gerhard* Psychology, Goethe-University, Frankfurt, Germany *Klieme, Eckhard* Bildungsqualität u. Evaluation, DIPF, Frankfurt, Germany

This study investigates the instruction of self-regulated learning in classroom settings. 60 videotaped mathematics lessons (ninth-grade) are analysed using two new observation instruments. A low-inferent coding instrument is used to assess the implicit or explicit instruction of cognitive, meta-cognitive, and motivational strategies. A high-inferent rating scale is used to assess features of the learning environment that foster self-regulated learning. Preliminary results indicate that explicit

strategy-instruction is rare in classrooms. However, if implicit strategy-instruction is considered, a high amount of strategy-instruction takes place. Further analyses will concern e.g. correlations between the instruction of self-regulated learning and performance.

The effects of emotion on verbal overshadowing.

Kitagami, Shinji Dept. of Psychology, Nagoya University, Nagoya, Japan *Yamada, Yohei* Department of Psychology, Nagoya University, Nagoya, Japan

The verbal overshadowing effect is the phenomenon in which describing a previously seen face impairs its recognition (Schooler & Engstler-Schooler, 1990). The primary purpose of this study was to investigate whether emotional states influences verbal overshadowing. In order to induce emotional states, unpleasant or neutral pictures selected from the International Affective Pictures System (IAPS) were presented at the beginning of the experiment. As a result, we found that emotional states could influence the emergence of the verbal overshadowing effect. The implications of these findings for research and practice are discussed.

Program development on prevention skills against sexual assault among school aged children

Kittipichai, Wirin Faculty of Public Health, Mahidol University, Bangkok, Thailand *Klatthong, Sutida* Faculty of Public Health, Mahidol University, Bangkok, Thailand *Majang, Chutichai* Faculty of Public Health, Mahidol University, Bangkok, Thailand *Charupoonphol, Phitaya* Faculty of Public Health, Mahidol University, Bangkok, Thailand *Nanthamingkolchai, Sutham* Faculty of Public Health, Mahidol University, Bangkok, Thailand

This study aimed at investigating the effects of a program of prevention skills against sexual assault of school aged children. 72 students were equally divided into an experimental and control group. The program based on participatory learning in five lessons: knowledge of sexual assault, critical thinking, self-awareness, decision making and communication skills as well some techniques to promote the self-efficacy were employed to all lessons. The differences of mean scores of life skills and self-efficacy to prevent sexual assault before and after implementation of study group were significantly higher than those of control group. The program was an effective tool used to promote prevention to student's sexual assaults.

Internet-dependence as the problem of interpersonal communication among technical and humanities students

Klyewa, Aljona Samara, Russia

The objective of the study is to describe the impact of educational environment on forming of Internet-dependence among technical and humanities students. Using E.A. Schepelina's 'Perception of Internet' survey (sample N=90) we found that technical students are better involved in the Internet subculture; have more definite goals of behavior in Internet; are better motivated to use Internet as communicative means, first of all, for communication with the persons of opposite gender; try to transfer the norms from virtual to real world. Humanities students have a stronger disposition to animate computer than technical students.

Clinical approaches to occupational stress management: Development and evaluation of a job-related group-therapy programme for inpatient rehabilitation

Koch, Stefan Zentrum für Verhaltensmedizin, Klinik Roseneck, Prien am Chiemsee, Germany *Luckmann, Judith* Department Medical Psychology, Philipps-University Marburg, Marburg / Lahn, Germany *Hillert,*

Andreas Center of Behavioural Medicine, Clinic Roseneck, Prien am Chiemsee, Germany

The objective of this longitudinal study was to evaluate a specific job-related group-therapy programme in a sample of inpatients with cardiological and orthopaedic diseases. In a controlled design 1338 inpatients in somatic rehabilitation were allocated to two treatment conditions. Both contained standard symptomatic therapy. In addition, the intervention-group received job-related group-therapy (5 sessions: work motivation, stress management, social skills at work and job perspectives). The experimental group reported a high acceptance of their CBT-based job-related treatment. Other outcome measures were return-to-work, inability-to-work, job-related coping skills (AVEM) and work satisfaction, demonstrating positive effects of job-related therapy in addition to standard rehabilitation.

Singaporean Chinese parents' and children's conceptualization of childhood anxiety

Koh, Jessie Bee Kim Human Development, Cornell University, Ithaca, USA Chang, Weining C. Psychology, Nanyang Technological Uni, Singapore, Singapore Fung, Daniel S.S. Child Guidance Clinic, Institute of Mental Health, Singapore, Singapore Kee, Carolyn H.Y. Child Guidance Clinic, Institute of Mental Health, Singapore, Singapore Woo, Bernardine S.L. Child Guidance Clinic, Institute of Mental Health, Singapore, Singapore

The present study examined Asian parents' and their children's conceptualization of anxiety. Ninety-two Singaporean Chinese parent-child pairs (aged 27-58; 78 mothers; aged 6-12; 19 girls) responded to the parents' and child's versions of the Asian Children Anxiety Scale respectively. Based on parents' responses, two culturally-salient interpersonal dimensions of anxiety: Over-Concern-with-Losing-Face and Over-Concern-with-Authority-Approval, in addition to two internationally-recognized dimensions: Affective-Manifestations and Bodily-Symptoms-and-Arousal were found. Convergent validity of parents' and children's operationalization of anxiety was supported by the moderate positive correlations between parents' and children's ratings. Findings are discussed with respects to parental cognition and the socialization of emotion in Asian cultures.

The role of affective states in interpreting thoughtless behaviors taken by peers

Koike, Haruka Tsu, Japan

The role of affective states in interpretation of peers' behaviors was examined. A total of 206 participants were induced to positive, neutral, or negative mood and were presented with vignettes describing several behaviors that lacks in interpersonal considerations, taken by their peers. The participants were asked to rate to what extent they felt the behaviors lacked in interpersonal considerations. The results of ANOVA revealed no significant relationships between the affective states and the behavior evaluation. It was concluded that the importance of peer relationships made the participants to avoid relying on their temporal affective states when interpreting their peers' behaviors.

Japanese life patterns in the 2000s V: Leadership

Kokubo, Midori Business Administration, Ritsumeikan University, Nara, Japan Nakashima, Wataru Psychology + connect, Institute of Applied Social, Osaka, Japan Furukawa, Hideo Intercultural Studies, Ryukoku University, Ohtsu, Japan

The objective of this study is to investigate whether leadership effectiveness is influenced by hierarchy and task uncertainty. 3767 employees of a Japanese communication-related company responded to a questionnaire. The targeted sample consists of the lowest class workers, the lowest managers and the middle managers. The results show PM-type leadership (Misumi, 1984) is useful to increase the lowest class workers' motivation in the high task uncertainty and the lowest managers' motivation in the low one. It is not useful to increase the middle managers' motivation. I conclude that PM-type leadership can be affected by hierarchy and task uncertainty.

The narrative self as multiplex cinema

Kolga, Voldemar Dept. of Psychology, University Nord, Tallinn, Estonia

The new self under different names – empty, liquid, fragmentated, protean self – is emerging instead of solid self. The narrative self can be expressed in self-stories. The function of narratives are to synthesise reality (Ricoeur, 1984). Participants were asked to tell stories about their lives. Results: 8 women and 6 men, ages 25 – 88, 1 – 11 stories per person. Self-stories are presented on the time axis from childhood to present, or as life events with special meanings, e.g. my love stories. Self-story movie theatres may be well-organized or as unique happenings without commensurability.

Description of self and other in child-mother daily conversation: Comparison of longitudinal trajectories

Komatsu, Koji School Education, Osaka Kyoiku University, Kashiwara, Osaka, Japan

In this study, we examined two cases of daily conversations between 4 to 6 years old children and their mothers (recorded over 1 year, with more than 100 recordings each). The analysis concentrated on the commonalities in dyadic negotiation and construction of the child's 'relational self'- the network of perceptions about everyday interactions as revealed in mother-child conversations. Investigation of recurrent episodes revealed that the child's comparison between self and others, guided by the mother, had the function to constantly clarify the position of the child in interpersonal relationships. A developmental trend towards mastery of positioning skills was demonstrated.

Motivation of choosing the profession of teacher

Koren, Lyudmila Organizational Psychology, Institute of Psychology, Kiev, Ukraine

Objectives: To find out main types of motives of choosing the profession of teacher. Methods: The investigation was done on 368 teachers using Ye.Ilyin Motives of choosing the profession of teacher questionnaire and SPSS. Results: Three types of motivation were identified: 1) internal motivation (creative work (+0.797), interest in teaching (+0.795), wish to share knowledge (+0.790), importance of teacher's work (+0.759), communication need (+0.702), wish to be among the intellectuals (+0.678); 2) external-situational motivation (long holiday (+0.866); external circumstances (+0.520)); 3) external-status motivation (research work and scientific degrees (+0.850), need of power (+0.786)). Conclusion. The findings can be used in teachers' training.

Effects of value orientations on managerial decision-making in organizations

Korol, Olga Organizational Psychology, Institut of Psychology, Kiev, Ukraine

Objectives: Finding out effects of value orientations on managerial decision-making in organizations. Methods: The investigation was performed on 300 industrial and civil service employees using M.Rokeach Value survey, L.Laptev Rating of employees' value orientations, and Spearman criterion. Results: The Level of professionalism scale positively correlated with High work outcomes and recognition scale (L.Laptev, R= 0315, p<001), Productive life scale (R=0.290, p<0.01), and Creativity scale (M.Rokeach, R= 0.235, p<0.01). At the same time employees' uncertainty of positive work outcomes and fear of work intensification result in their resistance to decision implementation. Conclusion: Employees' value orientations influence managerial decision making and implementation.

Psychological help and infertility treatment

Kossakowska-Petrycka, Karolina Institute of Psychol, University of Lodz, Lodz, Poland Chanduszko-Salska, Jolanta Institute of Psychol, University of Lodz, Lodz, Poland

Objectives: In Poland every sixth couple have a problem with procreation and year after year there are more and more couples that experience difficulties related to impeded procreation. Poster shows a role of psychological help in infertility treatments Methods: A literature review Results: Poster presents a model of interactions of psychological treatments developed by the authors. Conclusions: Psychological factors play an important role not only in etiology but they also modify the course and effectiveness of infertility treatment, even when it is thoroughly explained medically.

Implicit learning and other cognitive predictors of expert stage of career development: Fuzzy logic modeling of professional success

Kostrikina, Inna Inst. of Psychology, Russian Academy of Sciences, Moscow, Russia Kenig, Vitaliy Psychology faculty, Moscow State University, Moscow, Russia

The hypothesis that performance on implicit learning tasks is related to professional success on different jobs was examined in a sample of 238 specialists (IT, economic, and school teaching). The psychometric intelligence, creativity, and cognitive style of field-dependence/independence were measured also. We used WizWhy-system from Data Mining methods to data. This system allowed discovering the maximum "if-then" rules. The rules were defined by pattern's predictors of successful and non – successful. The fuzzy logic model demonstrated more reliability and forecasting compared with structural equation models.

Dialectical behavioral therapy for borderline personality disorder: A meta-analytic review

Kröger, Christoph Inst. für Klin. Psychologie, Tech. Universität Braunschweig, Braunschweig, Germany Kosfelder, Joachim Clinical Psychology, University Düsseldorf, Düsseldorf, Germany

Objective: Dialectical Behavioral Therapy (DBT) is considered as being 'possibly efficacious' in the treatment of Borderline Personality Disorder (BPD). What is the overall empirical evidence for DBT? Are there specific areas of differential effectiveness? Method: A review of the literature revealed 10 studies investigating DBT' effectiveness. Effect sizes (ES) were calculated across all measures as well as specifically for impulsivity, social adjustment, and general psychopathology. Results: The overall mean ES is 0.62. No differences in effectiveness were found between inpatient and outpatient DBT treatments. Conclusions: DBT seems to be generally effective. There is a need for more controlled studies especially for inpatient DBT.

A new conceptualization of the bases of trust

Krause, Diana Dept. of Social Science, University of Western Ontario, London, Canada

Previous classifications of the bases of trust published between 1953 and 2007 distinguish between one and 10 trust bases (e.g., competence, openness, predictability, fulfilment of promises, delegation, benevolence, fairness, loyalty). In light of some weaknesses of N = 48 previous classifications of the bases of trust (e.g., lack of differentiability), we argue that it would be advantageous with respect to theory and methods to reduce the number of the trust bases to a distinguishable amount. A new classification of the bases of trust is proposed that distinguishes between benevolence, consistency, and integrity.

Investigation of entrepreneurs' readiness to take business risks

Kredentser, Oksana Organizational Psychology, Institut of Psychology, Kiev, Ukraine

Objectives. Finding out entrepreneurs' readiness to take risks in business activity. Method. The investigation was done on a sample of 108 owners of small commercial businesses in 2007 using observation, interviews, and GET TEST. Results. 33.3% of the respondents preferred working risk-free, 28.6% didn't like taking risks, and 21.4% preferred minor and mid-level risks. Only 5% of the entrepreneurs had positive attitudes toward business risks. 47.6% of the businessmen rated present business risks extremely high. Conclusions. In their work entrepreneurs frequently come across various psychological problems. A special psychological training can help businessmen manage risky situations.

The cognitive orientation of creativity

Kreitler, Shulamith Dept. of Psychology, Tel-Aviv University, Tel-Aviv, Israel

The purpose was to test the predictive validity of the Cognitive Orientation Questionnaire of Creativity (COQC) in architecture. The hypothesis was that the COQC scores - beliefs about self, reality, norms and goals - would predict creativity in architectural design. A design task and the COQC were administered to 52 architecture students. The designs were assessed independently by five architects on criteria representing major creativity variables. Multiple regression and discriminant analyses showed that the COQC predicted most of the creativity variables. The results highlight the role of motivation concerning creativity and provide insights into the conditions supporting creativity and its promotion.

Neural correlates during imagery of social situations in social phobia (SP)

Kretschmer, Nora Biolog. und Klin. Psychologie, Universität Jena, Jena, Germany Mohr, Alexander Biological&Clinical Psycho, Friedrich-Schiller-University, Jena, Germany Miltner, Wolfgang H. R. Jena, Germany Straube, Thomas Biological&Clinical Psycho, Friedrich-Schiller-University, Jena, Germany

Imagination of social phobia related situations induces pronounced symptoms in patients suffering from social phobia. In this fMRI study, we investigated brain activation and subjective and peripherphysiological responses during script-driven symptom provocation in individuals with SP. Compared to healthy persons, individuals with SP showed stronger subjective anxiety ratings and increased heart rate. Furthermore, analysis of the fMRI data showed significantly increased activation in ACC, right posterior insula and, most pronounced, in the medial prefrontal cortex. These results suggest specific neural networks associated with anxiety during script-driven imagery in subjects with social phobia.

Does stress differentially affect recall of situation-related and -unrelated information?

Kuelzow, Nadine Psychologie und Ergonomiks, Techn. Universität Berlin, Berlin, Germany Erdmann, Gisela Biopsychology, Psychology and Ergonomics, Berlin, Germany

Two consecutive experiments investigated whether acute stress differentially affects recall for situation-relevant and -irrelevant information. One week after initial learning free recall was tested in 40/30 male students under stress or control condition (anticipation of solving a problem-task with or without public evaluation). In experiment 1 words, half related, half unrelated to the stress context, in experiment 2 information units from two texts,

providing instructions for the problem-task or another task, had to be remembered. In both studies, stress effects were limited to an enhanced recall of situation-unrelated items, indicating an increased retrieval of less relevant information under acute stress.

Neural correlates of decision making based on explicit information about probabilities and incentives in healthy subjects

Labudda, Kirsten Inst. Physiolog. Psychologie, Universität Bielefeld, Bielefeld, Germany Woermann, Friedrich G. MRI Unit, Bethel Epilepsy Center, EvKB, Bielefeld, Germany Mertens, Markus MRI Unit, Bethel Epilepsy Center, EvKB, Bielefeld, Germany Pohlmann-Eden, Bernd MRI Unit, Bethel Epilepsy Center, EvKB, Bielefeld, Germany Markowitsch, Hans J. Physiological Psychology, University of Bielefeld, Bielefeld, Germany Brand, Matthias Physiological Psychology, University of Bielefeld, Bielefeld, Germany

To date little is known about the neural correlates of subcomponents of decision making under risk conditions with given information about probabilities and potential outcomes. We investigated activation changes during decisions based on such explicit information using functional magnetic resonance imaging in twelve healthy subjects. The integration of the information presented leads to activations within the dorsolateral prefrontal cortex, the posterior parietal lobe and the anterior cingulated gyrus (all Z < 4.34, p corrected < .05). This activation pattern might indicate the involvement of executive functions, conflict detection mechanisms and arithmetic operations during decision processes in explicit risk conditions.

Impact of activation of optimistic cognitions on information processing

Lai, Julian Dept. of Psychology, City University of Hong Kong, Hong Kong, China, People's Republic of : Hong Kong SAR

Optimistic cognitions were activated using a priming procedure adapted from the Scrambled Sentence Test in 38 Chinese undergraduate students and the effect on processing words with positive and neutral valence was assessed by a Chinese version of the Emotional Stroop Task. A control group (n = 40) exposed to non-optimistic primes was also include to form a 2 x 2 design with repeated measures (positive vs. neutral words). Results of ANOVA showed a significant interaction effect: response latency in the experimental group was larger for positive than neutral words but a reverse pattern was observed in the control group.

The moral competence of Slovak students

Lajciakova, Petra Dept. of Psychology, Catholic University, Ruzomberok, Slovak Republic

Considering frequent discussions about the issue of influence of education on moral behavioural decision-making the purpose of this study is to illustrate the theoretical as well as the empirical approaches to moral judgment competence. Using Moral Judgement Test – Questionnaire on Ethical Problems, the aim was to investigate the relationship between moral judgment maturity and education and physical age. Research sample was formed by 392 university and secondary school students. The results indicate that education has positive influence on moral judgment competence.

Testing a central presumption of Holland's model by analysing circumplex data structures

Langmeyer, Alexandra Fakultät für Pädagogik, Universität der Bundeswehr, Neubiberg, Germany Tarnai, Christian Fakultät für Pädagogik, Universität der Bundeswehr Mün, Neubiberg, Germany Van Schuur, Wijbrandt Methodologie & Statistiek, University of Groningen, Groningen, Netherlands

In Holland's theory persons and environments can be characterised according to their six predominant orientations. Persons aspire to environments which correspond with their orientations. Therefore, we can deduce that students consider fields of study from the point of view of their dominant orientations. It is investigated which fields of study students (N=499) had taken into consideration when selecting their subjects. Also, the content-adjacency of other subjects to their own course of study is examined. Furthermore, we analyse whether the subjects constitute a circumplex by using the method of the nonparametric circular unfolding. The data can be depicted by circumplex structures.

Participatory research in a school setting: An acculturation process

Leblanc, Raymond Dept. d'Education, Université d'Ottawa, Ottawa, Canada Ducharme, Daphne Schoof of Rehabilitation scien, Université d'Ottawa, Ottawa, Canada

The purpose of the study was to measure the impact of a training program in phonological awareness that was offered to 64 grade 1 and grade 2 teachers in a francophone school board of the province of Ontario, Canada. An action research and training framework guided the collaborative work between university researchers and teacher participants. Findings suggest that teacher training in phonological awareness did produce better achievement in reading for at-risk students in grade one and even more significant progress for reading disabled second grade students. We will discuss more fully the constraints of conducting participatory research in a school setting where traditional methods and conservative values dominate.

Between passion and attachment: Why young adults wish to teach young children?

Lecocq, Gilles Dept. of Psychology, ILEPS, Cergy, France

The purpose of this communication is to reveal the paradoxical feelings and the contradictory motivations which accompany 30 young adults during their training allowing them to become teacher with young children. So, with the Five-Factor Model of Personality and with three conversations spread out over a period of twelve months, we shall highlight four main configurations which consuisent of young adults to teach young children: The young secure and passionate adults, the young secure and amotivated adults, the young insecure and passionate adults, the young insecure and amotivated adults

Language situates thoughts and feelings

Lee, Spike W.S. Dept. of Psychology, University of Michigan, Ann Arbor, USA Oyserman, Daphna Institute for Social Research, University of Michigan, Ann Arbor, Michigan, USA Bond, Michael Harris Department of Psychology, Chinese University of Hong Kon, Hong Kong, China, People's Republic of : Hong Kong SAR

Behavioral and cognitive effects of language are well documented (Oyserman & Lee, 2007). To test whether these effects are mediated or paralleled by language effects on motives, this research manipulated language of instruction and response (between subjects: English vs. Chinese) among 200 Chinese university undergraduates. ANOVA found that language shifted both self-concept content and self-esteem maintenance motives: English heightened independence and self-esteem concern. Importantly, mediation analyses revealed that cognitive and motivational effects of language operated independently. Results argue for the role of language as a broad-stroke tool that activates multiple—even conflicting—culturally-relevant thoughts and motives.

The research of ethnic tolerance, social identity and social communicative competence among teachers in Russian, Latvian and Estonian schools

Leppik, Tatjana Higher School of Psychology, Tallinn, Estonia Plotka, Irina psychology, Higher School of Psychology, Riga, Latvia

Empirical study of social communicative competence, ethnic tolerance and social identity among Teachers in Russian, Latvian and Estonian schools. Methods: πThe questionnaires of the social-communicative competence evaluation (Kalininsky, L.); π Types of Ethnic Tolerance (Soldatova, G., Shaigerova, L.); π Self attitude test (Kun, M., Mc Partlend, E.). Participants: 94 adults, aged 22-50. Was revealed some distinctions in structure of tolerance, identity and communicative competence at considered groups of teachers. The general tendency shows that at a low level of communicative competence, increases intolerant attitude to representatives of own and other ethnic groups.

The motivational sphere of creative workers

Leybina, Anna Psychology, Yaroslavl State University, Yaroslavl, Russia

Purpose - motivational sphere of workers with differing levels of creativity. Seventy-nine creative and eighty-three non-creative workers took part in this research. Russian scientific methods were used to investigate motivational sphere and creativity. Both groups of subjects displayed similar components of pragmatism, prestige and activity, but significant differences were found in the areas of communication, comfort, accomplishment and feelings of societal usefulness. The structure of the motivational sphere and the common and differing attributes in relationship to creativity levels of workers was discovered. The program to improve creative motivation and creativity itself based on these results is created.

A study on spare time management structure and features of college student

Li, Jian-Wei Qufu Normal University, Faculty of Education, Qufu, People's Republic of China

College students' spare time occupies a large part of their lives, and plays an important role in their development. In order to explore the psychological structure of college students' spare time management, a College Students' Spare Time Management Scale including two dimensions ——positive dimension and negative dimension was developed according to the correlative theories of time management disposition at home and abroad.. A time management model of college students' spare time was established by a survey of 1250 college students after items selection and road correction. The results showed : 1) three factors ——sense of spare time control, sense of purpose and sense of effectiveness could be drawn out from the first dimension, and the second dimension was consisted of sense of chaotic spare time. 2) The reliability and validity of this scale had reached basic measurement requirements. 3) There were significant differences in college students' spare time management between gender, rural and urban, liberal arts and science, grades and academic achievements.

Jingye in the Chinese context: A construct has been neglected by OB research

Li, Chaoping School of Public Admin., Renmin University, Beijing, People's Republic of China

JINGYE was a widely used concept in Chinese management practices, however little empirical studies pay attention to it. The present study explores the indigenous concept of JINGYE in the Chinese context. Data was collected from a diverse sample of 268 mangers and employees from different companies using open questionnaire, and then were subjected to content analysis to identify major forms of JINGYE in China. Results revealed 9 dimensions of JINGYE. Finally the difference

between JINGYE and Job Engagement, Job Satisfaction, Organizational commitment and Job Involvement was further discussed. Key Words: JINGYE, Job Engagement, Job Satisfaction, Organizational Commitment, Job Involvement

Work resources and burnout: The moderating effect of psychological capital

Li, Chaoping School of Public Admin., Renmin University, Beijing, People's Republic of China

We examined the moderating effect of psychological capital on the relations of work resources and job burnout in China. Using moderated multiple regressions with data collected from 468 employee, we found that the relationship between work resources and burnout was significantly moderated by employee's psychological capital. As predicted by the conservation of resources model, psychological capital moderated the impact of work resources typically under conditions in which the resources were low. Theoretical and practical applications were discussed. Keywords: psychological capital, job burnout, work resources

Feelings of metacognitive accuracy influence judgments of learning: Evidence for a second meta-level

Li, Weijian Dept. of Psychology, Zhejiang Normal University, Jinhua, People's Republic of China Li, Libo Department of Psychology, Zhejiang Normal University, Jinhua, People's Republic of China

Feeling of metacognitive accuracy(FMA), monitoring metacognitive judgments, may function as a second meta-level. Present research aimed to examine how accurate FMA was, and whether FMAs influence judgments of learning(JOLs). 43 undergraduates were instructed to complete two study-test trials. FMA was elicited after test for each item by asking the participants how accurate the JOL was. Friedman One-way ANOVA showed the absolute accuracy for items with high FMA was significantly higher; Wilcoxon Signed Ranks Test indicated items with low FMA changed significantly more between two trials. FMA was accurate to some extend, and individuals might base their JOLs partly on FMAs.

Cross-cultural stability of a faceted structure for fluid and crystallized intelligence

Liepmann, Detlev Wirtschafts- u. Sozialpsychol., Freie Universitaet Berlin, Berlin, Germany Horn, Sierk East Asian Studies, University of Leeds, Leeds, United Kingdom Brocke, Burkhard Differentie- und Persönlichkei, Technische Universitaet Dresde, Dresden, Germany Beauducel, André Differentiell & Diagnostik, Helmut-Schmidt Universitaet, Hamburg, Germany

The faceted model of fluid and crystallized intelligence, developed in the German culture, has been investigated for English and Japanese speaking countries. The model is based on the German Intelligence-Structure-Test (IST 2000 R) and comprises a facet for verbal, numerical, and figural intelligence. The present study investigates the similarity of the faceted structures based on German (N=660), British (N=1205), and Japanese (N=524) participants. The significant differences found for the parameters do not affect the overall structure substantially. Differences between samples are found for (figural) matrices and verbal analogies as well as for the measure of crystallized intelligence.

Parasocial interaction with game characters: Gender-specific influences

Linek, Stephanie Department of Psychology, University of Graz, Graz, Austria Marte, Birgit Department of Psychology, University of Graz, Graz, Austria Albert, Dietrich Department of Psychology, University of Graz, Graz, Austria

Para-social interaction (PSI) with game-characters is one of the main determinants of gameplay within single-player and serious games, respectively. To date most video games are designed for male players and thus, gender-specific effects of PSI are largely unknown. To investigate this issue, an educational adventure game with male and female game-characters (created within the EC-project ELEKTRA) will be presented to male and female players. The dependent measurements include PSI and identification as well as motivational and cognitive (cognitive load and learning) variables. The according data assessment will took place in November; results and conclusions will be reported at the congress.

Game-based learning: Motivational and cognitive impact of background music

Linek, Stephanie Department of Psychology, University of Graz, Graz, Austria Marte, Birgit Department of Psychology, University of Graz, Graz, Austria Albert, Dietrich Department of Psychology, University of Graz, Graz, Austria

Background music is a core design-element of serious games. However, research in this field led to rather inconsistent results about its impact on learning. To investigate this issue in the proposed study an educational adventure game on optics (created within the EC-project ELEKTRA) was presented either with or without background music to 59 school pupils (38 males & 21 females). The dependent measurements included motivational as well as cognitive variables. The findings reveal that background music can be used to enhance the intrinsic motivation and the so-called flow-experience without influencing cognitive load and learning success.

Travel perceived risk and communication enforcement: An empirical study in Taiwan

Liu, Fangyi Business Administration, NTUST, Mituo Township, Taiwan Hung, Yi-Jung Operations and Marketing, Swire Coca-Cola (S&D) Ltd., Mituo Township, Kaohsiung Coun, Taiwan

Perceived risk reduction is the most important motive of psychological cognition to seek word-of mouth (WOM) communication. The authors use the membership grade of 'possibility' of sender's intention of WOM and 'significance' of WOM's influencing of the receiver's purchase decision to get the weights of travel perceived risks and establish the analysis matrix of WOM communication enforcement. Finally, we use the Taiwan consumers of abroad group inclusive tour (G.I.T.) as an example to do empirical study. This implies that consumers have the personal characteristic of higher travel perceived risks and they prefer the communication enforcement strategy of buying travel assurance.

Using Fuzzy MAUT to analyze the effects of perceived risk based on word-of-mouth theory

Liu, Fangyi Business Administration, NTUST, Mituo Township, Taiwan Lin, Tom M.Y. Business Administration, NTUST, Taipei, Taiwan

Because of the subjective cognition on risk attributes and the fuzziness on perceived-risk judgment, consumers feel psychological uncertain. This study examined the effects of personal perceived risk on word-of mouth (WOM) communication. In this paper, through comparison, the authors found that the fuzzy multi-attribute utility theory (FMAUM) had a more reliable prediction outcome that the general linear regression model. The result shows that the WOM senders think the social and psychological risks attributes are higher and more significant, and the WOM receivers think the financial risk and functional risks attributes are higher and more significant.

A study on the development of preschooler's false-belief understanding and deceptive strategies

Liu, Xiuli Dept. of Psychology, Northeast Normal University, Changchun, People's Republic of China
The purpose was to explore the development of preschooler's false-belief understanding and deceptive strategies.The study adopted two standard false-belief tasks and the deceptive task. 121 subjects aged 3-6 were included. Results showed that: (1) 3-year-olds could succeed on the unexpected-content task, but it was not until 4 that children could understand the unexpected-location task; (2)3-year-olds could use the strategies of lying and destroying proof, but it was not until 4 that children could use the strategy of "making false mark"; (3) there wasn't the significant correlation between false-belief and deceptive strategies for children aged 3 and 6, but there was the significant correlation for children aged 4-5.

Emotional intelligence: Information behind multidimensional construct

Liu, Bangcheng Public Administration, Shanghai Jiao Tong University, Shanghai, People's Republic of China Yang, Wensheng Center for Consulting, Shanghai Jiao Tong University, Shanghai, People's Republic of China
There had been attentions paid to emotional intelligence, which was a critical variable to individual development and leadership. Though literatures insisted it be appropriate to study emotional intelligence in a multidimensional perception, most of current researches just focused on the holistic effects of emotional intelligence, and few analyzed the issues of specific dimensions. Based on sampling in public servants in China, the study used MANOVA and SEM techniques to analyze the demographical variables' effects on the multidimensional construct, and particularly pay attentions to emotional intelligence's holistic effects and specific dimensions' effects on individual performance.

Disagreement of organizational justice perceptions: An empirical test

Liu, Jun School of Business, Renmin University, Beijing, People's Republic of China
Since managers and employees play unequal roles in organizations, they would have distinct perceptions regarding managerial practices. Understanding such distinctions and investigating the underlying causes help improve business administration and motivate organizational members as well. Employing survey data obtained from in a large Chinese SOE (State Owned Enterprise) and SEM (Structural Equation Modeling) analytical technique, the study evaluated rating disagreement between managers and employees in terms of their perceptions of organizational justice. Possible causes of the disagreement and managerial implications were discussed in the paper.

A validity study of the pay satisfaction questionnaire in the Mainland of China

Liu, Bangcheng Public Administration, Shanghai Jiao Tong University, Shanghai, People's Republic of China Tang, Ningyu Organizational Administration, Shanghai Jiao Tong University, Shanghai, People's Republic of China Zhu, Xiaomei Department of Management, Shanghai Jiao Tong University, Nanchang, People's Republic of China
Pay satisfaction questionnaire (PSQ) has become a popular instrument to evaluate attitudes to pay. Unfortunately, during past more than 20 years since PSQ was developed in 1985 by Heneman and Schwab, the factor structure of pay satisfaction remains equivocal and there is inconsistency in the number of dimension. To further investigate the dimensionality of PSQ, especially in Chinese context, we conducted a study in a large organization in the northwest China. We found the unique or two-factor model fit the data well with a high internal reliability according to using different rotation techniques (such as varimax or direct oblique).

Two-component model of verbal intelligence

Lobanov, Alexander Dept. of Psychology, BGPU, Minsk, Belarus
In the presented research intelligence is considered as a form of organization of individual mental experience. Two-level model of intelligence (A.Jensen) distinguishes two types of intelligence: concrete intelligence (associative abilities) and abstract intelligence (cognitive abilities). We propose a new method called "Leading Grouping Mode" to diagnose these two types of intelligence. This method includes a list of scientific notions that should be grouped in one of two possible ways – associative or conceptual. Conceptual grouping mode corresponds to the level of formal operations. Correlational and cluster analyses of the data obtained allows to specify the structure of verbal intelligence.

Gifted students and school achievement

Lopez Alacid, Maria Paz Alicante, Spain Perez Sanchez, Antonio Miguel EVOLUTIVE PSYCHOLOGY AND DIDAC, UNIVERSITY OF ALICANTE, ALICANTE, Spain Quiros Bravo, Soledad EVOLUTIVE PSYCHOLOGY AND DIDAC, UNIVERSITY OF ALICANTE, ALICANTE, Spain
Objective: To analyse the content of the articles published in scientific magazines from 1992 to 2006, determine which years have seen a greater number of publications and establish the number of articles devoted to the study of school enrichment and gifted students. Method: Bibliometric analysis of ERIC (Educational Resources Information Center) data base from 1992 to 2000, using "gifted" and "school enrichment" as key words. Results: Most authors are in favour of school enrichment procedures in the teaching of gifted students. Conclusions: School enrichment procedures are very effective to improve creativity, motivation and level of achievement of gifted students.

Pedagogic practice and supervision in the process of training nursery school teachers

Ludovico, Olga Escola Superior de Educação, Universidade do Algarve, Faro, Portugal Gonçalves, José Escola Superior de Educação, Universidade do Algarve, Faro, Portugal
The study, qualitative in nature, focuses on the eighteen students from a class in the final year of their course of Nursery School Teachers, in the school year 2006/2007. The main objective is to understand the importance of pedagogical practice and of supervision in their training process. One of the instruments used in the collection of data was a survey by questionnaire, whose open questions indicates that these curricular units are considered very important because of reflection, sharing and individual accompaniment. It warns also of the necessity to favour a model of training that promotes the positivity of an affective-relational atmosphere.

Three different analysis to study confidence-accuracy relationship on memory of a bank robbery and on general knowledge

Luna, Karlos Basic Psychological Processes, Univ. of the Basque Country, San Sebastián, Spain Martín Luengo, Beatriz Basic Psychological Processes, Univ of the Basque Country, Donostia-San Sebastián, Spain
In this study the confidence-accuracy relationship was examined using three different analysis. After watching a video about a bank robbery, participants answered cued recall questions about general knowledge and then questions about the robbery. They also rated their confidence in answers in a 0-100% scale. With both materials the correlations were high, the correct answers were evaluated with more confidence than the incorrect ones, and the calibration was good. It is argued that the correlation could not be the more informative method to study the confidence-accuracy relationship.

Occupational health and safety analysis in olive oil industries

Luque, Pedro Jesus Jaen, Spain Palomo, Antonio Psychology, Universty of Jaén, Jaén, Spain Pulido, Manuel Psychology, University of Jaén, Jaén, Spain
General objective: Study of the causes of accidents related to the human factor in olive oil industries. Specific objectives: (1) Statistical analysis of occupational injuries; (2) Exploration of human factors underlying accidents; (3) Analysis of the suitability of the existing system of recording and notification of occupational injuries and diseases from the human factor perspective. Methods: Different methods are used depending on the specific nature of the objectives (statistical analysis, focus groups, experts panel...). Results: Preliminary data is presented related to the first specific objective, based on the statistical analysis of occupational accident reports from 2004 to 2006.

Psychic change of children that undergo psychotherapy and emotional holding of adults in charge and teachers

Luzzi, Ana Dept. de Psicología, Universidad de Buenos Aires, Buenos Aires, Argentina Padawer, Maria Psicología, Universidad de Buenos Aires, Buenos Aires, Argentina Bardi, Daniela Psicología, Universidad de Buenos Aires, Buenos Aires, Argentina Jaleh, Marcela Psicología, Universidad de Buenos Aires, Buenos Aires, Argentina Freidin, Fabiana Psicología, Universidad de Buenos Aires, Buenos Aires, Argentina Wainszelbaum, Dina Psicología, Universidad de Buenos Aires, Buenos Aires, Argentina Slapak, Sara Facultad de Psicología, University of Buenos Aires, Buenos Aires, Argentina
Objective: To study the relationship between the change process of children who undergo psycho-analitical psychotherapy and the emotional holding of parents and teachers. Method: Codification of group psychotherapy sessions and of orientation groups for parents; construction of matrixes and reports per child and his/her parent. Design of an instrument which collects teachers s perceptions. Results: The study of psychotherapeutic process and the research about the capacity of parents and teachers to offer emotional holding contribute to improve the therapeutical change processes. Conclusions: The results allow to improve the therapeutical strategies of an assistance center that attends a vulnerable population.

Effects of psychosocial stress on neural correlates of selective attention

Mühlhan, Markus Inst. für Psychologie, Technische Universität Dresden, Dresden, Germany Weerda, Riklef Psychology, University of Oldenburg, Oldenburg, Germany Wolf, Oliver T. Psychology, University of Bielefeld, Bielefeld, Germany Thiel, Christiane M. Psychology, University of Oldenburg, Oldenburg, Germany
Prior studies have shown an attentional modulation of the fusiform face area (FFA) and the para-hippocampal place area (PPA) when attention is directed to faces and scenes respectively. The present study aimed to investigate the effects of psychosocial stress on such attentional modulations of neural activity. We used functional magnetic resonance imaging employing a selective attention paradigm with faces and landscapes. Prior to scanning participants (n=41) underwent the Trier Social Stress Test or a control procedure in a between subject design. In preliminary data analysis we found a stress-induced suppression in FFA and PPA which suggests reduced top-down modulation under psychosocial stress.

Early adolescents' well-being and their preference for the use of instant messaging: A cross-lagged regression analysis

Ma, Liyan Psychology, Capital Normal University, Beijing, People's Republic of China Lei, Li Institute of Psychology, Beijing, People's Republic of China

The correlation between Well-being (IWB) and the preference for the use of Instant Messaging (IM) for early adolescents was identified by using Cross-lagged Regression design. With questionnaires, a longitudinal study was done with 103 students from 7 grades in China. It was found that the preference for the use of IM at time 1 could positively predict IWB (after about one year) significantly; and that the index of affect at time 1 could significantly predict the preference for the use of IM at time 2. There was some stability in early adolescents' IWB and the use of IM.

The moderate effect of perceptions of control on the relation between life events and pathological internet use of early adolescents

Ma, Liyan Psychology, Capital Normal University, Beijing, People's Republic of China Lei, Li Institute of Psychology, Beijing, People's Republic of China

In order to explore the moderate effect of perceptions of control on the relation between life events and Pathological Internet Use (PIU) of early adolescents, a survey was carried out with 192 students in China. The results indicated that the moderate effect of internal control and unknown sources of control on the association between life events and PIU were significant, namely, the positive relation of them for the participants of high internal control was higher than that for the low internal control; life events could predict PIU positively for students of high unknown sources of control, but not for low.

The sense of justice, organizational behaviour and well-being

Maes, Jürgen Inst. für Bildung, Universität der Bundeswehr, München, Germany Wade, Diana Faculty of Education, Bundeswehr University Munich, Munich, Germany Gerlach, Tanja Faculty of Education, Bundeswehr University Munich, Munich, Germany Schuster, Julia Faculty of Education, Bundeswehr University Munich, Munich, Germany Müller, Florian IUS, Alpen-Adria-Univ. Klagenfurt, Klagenfurt, Austria

According to justice motive theory (JMT) being treated fairly by others is a primary concern of human beings. It can be hypothesized from JMT that the experience of injustice (e.g. by performance appraisals or other personnel measures) will affect organizational behaviour and individual well-being. We conducted an online survey in a large company (N = 330). As expected well-being as well as behavior at the workplace were considerably affected by the experienced procedural justice: The higher the experienced injustice the less identification with one's company, the more inner withdrawal from the job and the more antisocial behaviour (mobbing) we found.

Efficacy of a stepped-care program as compared to a standard cognitive therapy for patients with social phobia

Mall, Anna Psychosomatische Medizin, Zentralinstitut für Gesundheit, Mannheim, Germany Kiko, Sonja Psychosomatic Medicine, Centr. Instit. f. Ment. Health, Mannheim, Germany Steil, Regina Psychosomatic Medicine, Centr. Instit. f. Ment. Health, Mannheim, Germany Bohus, Martin Psychosomatic Medicine, Centr. Instit. f. Ment. Health, Mannheim, Germany

Objectives The aim of the study is to examine the efficacy of a stepped-care program (SCP) as compared to an established therapist-guided treatment (Clark et al., 2003; standard therapy, ST). Methods In a blinded randomized-controlled trial, 102 out-patients with social phobia (SP) are assigned either to the ST or the SCP which starts with a computer-based self-help phase. Remission rates and effect sizes (Cohen's d) will be reported. Results Preliminary results suggest that the self-help program seems to reduce social anxiety symptoms and depressive symptoms (n = 17). Conclusions Preliminary conclusions concerning the efficacy of self-help interventions for patients with social phobia will be drawn.

Statistical properties of a restricted randomization test

Manolov, Rumen Behavioral Sciences Methods, University of Barcelona, Barcelona, Spain Solanas, Antonio Behavioral Sciences Methods, University of Barcelona, Barcelona, Spain

A previous investigation identified a fraction of ABAB data divisions (triplets) for which the corresponding randomization test was robust against the violation of the independence assumption. The present study uses Monte Carlo methods to analyze the robustness and power of a restricted randomization test based on 52 triplets for Mean difference and 51 triplets for Student's t. Autocorrelation did not distort Type I error rates for half of the data divisions and a common pattern was found among those triplets. Power was not sufficient for small and medium effects. The technique studied does not seem an appropriate solution.

Data-division-specific robustness and power of randomization tests for ABAB designs

Manolov, Rumen Behavioral Sciences Methods, University of Barcelona, Barcelona, Spain Solanas, Antonio Behavioral Sciences Methods, University of Barcelona, Barcelona, Spain Bulté, Isis Centre Method. Educational Res, Katholieke Universiteit Leuven, Leuven, Belgium Onghena, Patrick Centre Method. Educational Res, Katholieke Universiteit Leuven, Leuven, Belgium

The statistical properties of a randomization test for single-case ABAB designs are studied. Conditional Monte Carlo methods were used to estimate the Type I and Type II error rates for each data division (triplet). The robustness against the violation of the independence assumption was investigated for different degrees of serial dependence. Autocorrelation had slight influence only for some triplets, contrasting with previous findings based on common randomization distributions. The randomization test was sufficiently sensitive only for effect sizes d ≥ 1.7. The application of the technique can lead excessive risk of incorrect statistical decisions according to the data division chosen.

Against violence and harassment in the workplace

Manz, Rolf Prävention, DGUV, München, Germany

Violence and harassment in the workplace have become important problems during the last decades. We have developed a program to help affected companies to deal with these situa-tion. Employers and employees can work together in order to prevent violence and harassment. The program includes several steps: Starting with a survey the companies are trained to use these measures in order to get self control over the process. First results are presented that describe the situation in job centres, the process of program implementation and primary effects of the program.

Social representations of psychologists: An exploratory study among French people

Marchetti, Elise GRC University of Nancy 2, Nancy Cedex, France Lafrogne, Claude Lorraine, EPME La Fédération, Stenay, France Schoenenberger, Sandrine Lorraine, Université P. Verlaine, ETIC, Metz cedex 1, France

The aim of this study is to explore and to compare the contents of social representations of psycholo-gist, among psychologists themselves, their collea-gues, and general population. Three different groups (N= 30 participants per group) were asked to give associated words to the word "psychologist" - the method we used is the "associative maps" one (Abric, 1994). Data analysis shows that there are some differences. General population talks more about emotions, problems and body, whereas colleagues of psychologists regard them as thera-pists and as testing people. The psychologists evoke a lot ethics and deontology, and also care, therapy and counselling.

A personal organization skills and a study methods intervention on university students

Martins, Alda Olhão, Portugal Saul, Jesus Psychology, University of Algarve, Faro, Portugal

University students have frequently adaptation problems that they couldn't solve by themselves. To prevent and solve these problems was developed a personal organization skills and a study methods program. The goal of this program was to develop strategies to solve personal and academic problems in university students. This program was applied on 21 students of the Algarve's University. For a control group, it was also selected 21 students with similar characteristics. The program participants have significantly improved their personal organi-zation and study methods skills, when compared with the control group. Levels of anxiety have decreased and students became more motivated.

Do people help those who helped a free-rider in indirect reciprocity settings?

Mashima, Rie Inst. für Behavioral Science, Hokkaido University, Sapporo, Japan Takahashi, Nobuyuki Behavioral Science, Hokkaido University, Sapporo, Japan

Indirect reciprocity is one mechanism that allows for altruistic behaviors among n-persons. Using analytical method and computer simulations, pre-vious studies have concluded that the key to make indirect reciprocity possible is excluding not only free-riders but also indiscriminate-givers who help free-riders. In order to determine the validity of this conclusion, we conducted a laboratory experiment to examine people's actual strategies in indirect reciprocity settings. Results clearly supported the theoretical conclusion—people excluded not only free-riders but also indiscriminate-givers. Addi-tional analysis suggested that this exclusion is not a result of intentional punishment but an unin-tended consequence of genuine behaviors toward discriminate-givers.

When repeated reminders lead to forgetting: Spontaneous suppression of negative associations

Mather, Mara Dept. of Psychology, University of California, Santa Cruz, USA Mangold, Stefan Dept. of Psychology, University of Göttingen, Göttingen, Germany

In this study, re-exposure to a cue led either to memory suppression or enhancement of associated memories, depending on whether those memories were aversive or pleasant. Participants first learned face-picture pairings, in which neutral faces were paired with positive, negative or neutral pictures. Next, in the re-exposure phase, the face cues appeared alone, either zero, one or six times each. Finally, participants saw each face again and tried to recall its associated picture. Re-exposure to the face cues had opposite effects on memory for positive and negative associations, reducing mem-ory for negative associations and enhancing mem-ory for positive associations.

Impact of CBT on adjustment of patients suffering from social phobia

Mathur, Shachi *Psychology, Jamia Millia Islamia Univ., Delhi, India* **Khan, Waheeda** *PSYCHOLOGY, JAMIA MILLIA ISLAMIA UNIV., DELHI, India*
Objective was to assess adjustment in social phobia patients. It was hypothesized that CBT with medication would yield significant improvement than medication alone. Methods: 10 Social phobia patients from AIIMS hospital, Delhi equally assigned to Group I (CBT intervention & medication), Group II (medication) and were administered 120 item Global Adjustment Scale (PSY-COM Services, Delhi, 1994). Results: CBT with medication was effective in improving the level of social, emotional, family and occupational adjustment in social phobia patients, while only health and sexual adjustment improved with medical treatment. Conclusion: CBT with medication seems more useful treatment intervention in social phobia patients.

Digital divide and stereotype boost: Self-stereotypes as barometer of performance

Mauch, Martina *Berlin, Germany*
Bridging the gender gap two studies examined the relevance of self-categorization while performing on computers. It was hypothesized that whilst self-categorizing a stereotype is used to predict performance expectancies and influences performance using computers. Quasi-experimental studies with male and female students revealed when women's gender-related collective self is accessible, the negative gender stereotype led to worse performance (stereotype threat). When the gender-related relational self is accessible, the positive gender stereotype led to improved performance (stereotype boost) compared to women with no gender-related self-categorization and compared to men. These results with medium effect sizes are seen as having implications for interventions improving women's computer competence.

Art therapeutic technique of collages as a tool of professional identity development

Mazehoova, Yvona *Psychology, University of South Bohemia, Ceske Budejovice, Czech Republic* **Kourilova, Jana** *Psychology, University of South Bohemia, Ceske Budejovice, Czech Republic* **Stuchlikova, Iva** *Psychology, University of South Bohemia, Ceske Budejovice, Czech Republic*
The study presents the technique of collages used for mapping of anticipated professional roles in future teachers. The roles which are foreseen by student teachers are analyzed and a typology of the professional identity collages is proposed.

Islands of memory: Amnestics remembering autobiographical experiences

Medved, Maria *Dept. of Psychology, University of Manitoba, Winnipeg, Canada* **White, Caelin** *Psychology, University of Manitoba, Winnipeg, Manitoba, Canada* **Hirst, William** *Psychology, The New School, Winnipeg, Manitoba, USA*
In people with anterograde amnesia, memories of post-onset autobiographical experiences are typically impoverished. However, there have been sporadic reports of vivid islands of memory that are both specific and detailed. The aim of this study was two-fold: 1) to verify the presence of such memories by interviewing amnestics and 2) to code these post-onset memories of events for both quality and quantity. Results revealed over half of the amnestics had an island of memory–a memory significantly different from their other barren memories. This finding suggests that in some amnestics there is more variability in memory performance than previously believed.

Effects of motivational orientation on negotiations in virtual teams

Melchior, Stefan N. *Universität Rostock, Rostock, Germany* **Pundt, Alexander** *Organizational & Business, University of Rostock, Rostock, Germany* **Nerdinger, Friedemann** *Inst. für Psychologie, Universität Rostock, Rostock, Germany*
Although a large body of research has examined virtual teams, little is known about negotiations in virtual teams. This study examined the effects of motivational orientation. Two types of teams were created on the basis of social motives, egoistic and prosocial. Four hundred twenty-three business students solved a three-issue, three-person-team negotiation task via computer-mediated, text-based communication. Prosocial teams exchanged more information and less opinion, and showed more positive and less negative social-emotional reactions than proself teams did. Information exchange mediated the relationship between motivational orientation and team outcome. Prosocial teams exchanged more information and therefore reached higher outcomes.

The relationship between locus of control and type A/B behavior patterns with job satisfaction among secondary school male teachers

Memar, Mohammad Ali *Shahid Beheshti University, Tehran, Islamic Republic of Iran*
The purpose of this study was to investigate the relationship between locus of control and Type A/B behaviour patterns with Job Satisfaction. The work locus of control Scale, the Bortner Type A Scale and the Minnesota Satisfaction Questionnaire (MSQ) was given to A sample group contain 151 male secondary school teachers. Results showed a significant relationship between locus of control and Type A/B behaviour with job satisfaction. Teachers with internal locus of control and Type B behaviour tended to have higher job satisfaction scores than others. In addition locus of control was a powerful predictor of job satisfaction.

Multiple Sclerosis patients' subjective uncertainty and social identity complexity during the treatment

Metra-Ozolina, Solvita *Dept. of Psychology, University of Latvia, Riga, Latvia* **Gritane, Egita** *Psychology, University of Latvia, Riga, Latvia*
The study assessed the process of coping with subjective uncertainty (Hogg, 2000) and social identity complexity (Brewer & Roccas, 2002) after being diagnosed Multiple Sclerosis. The Multiple Sclerosis patients who had just received a positive diagnosis were compared to the patients who have had a course of treatment for one year. After the introduction of the diagnosis to Multiple Sclerosis patients they have a high level of subjective uncertainty, as well as a low level of Social Identity Complexity. A one year treatment of Multiple Sclerosis patients reduces their subjective uncertainty and raises complexity of their social identity.

The psychological mechanism of entrepreneurial decision making: Causal model validation

Miao, Qing *Scholl of Public Admin., Zhejiang University, Hangzhou, People's Republic of China* **Wang, Zhong-Ming** *Department of Psychology, ZheJiang university, Zhejiang Hangzhou, People's Republic of China*
According to 277 entrepreneurial questionnaires, this article testified the causal model of psychological mechanism on the entrepenrual decision making. The result of structural equation modeling indicated entrepreneurial alertness and prior knowledge were the direct factor to the entrepreneurial opportunity recognition. They influenced the entrepreneurial decision via the variables of opportunity recognition. Thus, opportunity recognition played a mediating role in the full model.

Distinguishing between social, communal, and interdependent types of in-group identification

Milanov, Milen *School of Psychology, University of Newcastle, Callaghan, NSW, Australia* **Rubin, Mark** *School of Psychology, University of Newcastle, Callaghan, NSW, Australia* **Paolini, Stefania** *School of Psychology, University of Newcastle, Callaghan, NSW, Australia*
Three studies distinguished between social, communal and interdependent types of in-group identification and tested a new scale that measures these constructs. Participants completed an on-line questionnaire consisting of the Social, Communal, and Interdependent Identification Scale (SCIIS) together with a range of previously validated measures of attachment style and relationship orientation. Cross-cultural differences in types of identification were found. Relative to secure individuals, avoidant individuals had lower social and communal identification. The research provides evidence for the validity and reliability of SCIIS and supports the idea that there are types of in-group identification distinct from those proposed by social identity theory.

An experimental approach model based on simulating competition and conflict

Milcu, Marius *Psychology, University of Sibiu, Sibiu, Romania*
Objectives: The intention of our study is to simulate a conflict experimental situation. Precisely, we try to discriminate between two experimental situations: interpersonal competition and interpersonal conflict, using a computerized test, in order to identify the specific circumstances for this easy conversion from one to another, under strictly surveyed lab circumstances. The whole study is developed on the notion of power, which we are thus trying to give back to social psychology. Sample: 244 participants, 18-31 years old. Results: When getting control over the other is essential for the partners, moreover, if control is either the very purpose, or the only means to be employed for reaching the purpose, then we have to do with conflict.

Psychological factors contributing to unsafe behavior in medical staff

Misawa, Ryo *Human Environment Studies, Kyushu University, Fukuoka, Japan*
This study investigated the effect of psychological factors on unsafe behaviors in medical staff. 238 medical staff (physician, nurse, pharmacist, etc.) completed questionnaires. Based on previous findings, I hypothesized the causal model that organizational factors may affect unsafe behaviors indirectly through personal factors. Path analysis demonstrated that the hypothesized model fit the data, with all fit indices meeting the criteria. Concerning personal factors, evaluated cost (e.g., increased workload) and ineffectiveness of safety rules increased the frequency of unsafe behavior. Concerning organizational factors, organizational management and norms increased the frequency of unsafe behavior indirectly through their effects on personal factors.

Changes in the ability of practice teachers to observe classes before and after practice teaching

Mishima, Tomotaka *Education, Hiroshima University, Higashi-Hiroshima, Japan*
This study investigates the effects of practice teaching on the development of practice teachers' "observational skills." Fifty-three practice teachers reported their impressions of a videotaped math class before and after experiencing their own practice teaching. The "observational skills" were analyzed from three different perspectives, using written reports from the practice teachers. Major findings were: (1) both the number of "problems

identified" and "alternative proposals" increased after practice teaching; (2) experienced teachers have better "class evaluation skills" than practice teachers. These findings are discussed in relation to the effects of practice teaching on practice teachers' "observational skills."

Developmental therapy supervision of beginning, intermediate and advanced therapists

Miyazaki, Rie Kyushu Univercity, Fukuoka, Japan
This study examined contents and strategies of supervisions toward therapists in different levels of expertise (beginner, intermediate, and advanced) in Dohsa-Hou (a developmental therapy) for cerebral palsy children. After watching videos where each therapist training the child, 9 supervisors participated in the survey study that asked what (open-end format) and how (multiple questions) they would supervise to each of the therapist. Results of contents were as expected; skill focus for beginners, contingency engagement for intermediates, empathetic engagement for advanced would be supervised. However, strategies did not show any differences. Modeling would be most likely used regardless of therapists' expertise levels.

Compassionate therapy for sexual dissatisfaction

Montgomery, Bob Dept. of Psychology, Univers. of the Sunshine Coast, Southport, Australia Morris, Laurel Psychology, Uni of the Sunshine Coast, Southport, Australia
Compassionate therapy (CT) combines mindfulness and cognitive behavioural therapy to reduce self-criticism and self-blame to facilitate enjoyment of life. Successful sexuality is often hindered by intrusive shame or guilt or by excessive performance-consciousness, risk factors for all of the common sexual disorders, of interest, arousal, orgasm, and pain, and common causes of sexual dissatisfaction. CT aims to counter this by encouraging people to give themselves permission to enjoy sexual feelings and interests, by correcting misinformation, and through behavioural exploration and strengthening of sexual responsiveness. This approach will be outlined and briefly illustrated.

Health promotion and illness prevention by focussing on self-efficacy

Montgomery, Bob Dept. of Psychology, Univers. of the Sunshine Coast, Southport, Australia Morris, Laurel Dept. of Psychology, Univers. of the Sunshine Coast, Southport, Australia
Research prompted by Protection Motivation Theory identifies self-efficacy for making healthier behavioural change as a major determinant of the initiation and maintenance of such change. The four factors known to build self-efficacy can all be utilised to build motivation for healthier behaviour, particularly helping people to experience successful changes by teaching effective goal-setting, a commonly misunderstood strategy. Modelling of successful behaviour change, verbal persuasion especially by oneself, and a balanced approach to stress management are also utilised. This approach, applicable with individuals or groups, will be outlined and briefly illustrated.

The effect of stress and context on reconsolidation of episodic hippocampally-based memory in humans

Moore, Jennifer Psychology, National University of Ireland, Kildare, Ireland Roche, Richard AP Psychology, National University of Ireland, Kildare, Ireland
This project elucidated the impact of stress during reconsolidation, unravelling the phenomenon whereby reactivated memories can be weakened/erased by inhibited hippocampal protein synthesis. Visual-paired associates were presented with local contextual backgrounds which were reinstated 24 hours later in a filler task, thereby reactivating the consolidated memory trace. A stress or control task was given immediately following reinstantiation. Recall of original pairs was tested without context presentation. As predicted, the stress group exhibited impaired recall. Indeed, continuous retrieval/reconsolidation of traumatic memories in PTSD patients is what enables their persistence. By inhibiting retrieval, stress-induced cortisol may weaken memory traces, thus reducing symptoms.

Etiology and therapy of mental disorders based on a cognitive-religious model

Moradi, Azam Psychology, Isfahan University, Isfahan, Islamic Republic of Iran Ghamarani, Amir psychology, isfahan university, isfahan, Islamic Republic of Iran
Theoretically basic of Cognitive –Religious Model can be showed in a figure as follow and named" The Cognitive – Religious Model Cognitive- religious therapy can be administrated in both individual and group manners. The preference of group method as compared with individual method is that in group therapy there isn't need to direct induction of therapist's opinion to clients.

Employees' and managers' values and OCB: Conflicting employee values lead to the same work behavior

More, Keren Vered Rehovot, Israel Sagiv, Lilach Business school, Hebrew university Jerusalem, Mount Scopus, Jerusalem, Israel
The current study examined how Organizational Citizenship Behavior (OCB) is affected by values at two levels: We studied employees' values reflecting an individual characteristic, and managers' values expressing a situational characteristic. We furthered studied the interaction between the two. Respondents were 166 employees and their 53 direct supervisors in three branches of an international pharmaceutical company. Reports of employees' values and individual initiative OCB and of managers' values were analyzed using Polynomial regressions. As hypothesized, emphasizing achievement, universalism and benevolence values positively predicted OCB, whereas managers' values had no effect. Surprisingly, employee-manager fit effects were insignificant.

On the magnitude of publication bias in studies of the therapeutic efficacy of hypnosis

Moshagen, Morten Inst. für Exper. Psychologie, Universität Düsseldorf, Düsseldorf, Germany Musch, Jochen Institute of Experimental Psy, University of Düsseldorf, Germany
Meta-analyses are widely used to evaluate the efficacy of interventions, but may be biased due to the selective publication of studies reporting favourable results. We employed a variety of methods to test for the presence of publication bias in a meta-analysis of 57 randomized controlled trials investigating hypnosis as a therapeutic tool. Our results show that publication bias contributes considerably to the effect size estimate. However, we also show that while the use of an uncorrected estimate may be overly optimistic, the efficacy of hypnosis is substantial and may not be explained on the basis of publication bias alone.

Individual learning and collaborative knowledge building with Wikis: An experimental study

Moskaliuk, Johannes Applied Cognitive Psychology a, University of Tuebingen, Tübingen, Germany Kimmerle, Joachim Applied Cognitive Psychology a, University of Tuebingen, Tübingen, Germany
The study aims at empirically testing a theoretical model of collaborative knowledge building with wikis. This model assumes that individual learning and collaborative knowledge building are based on the interplay between people's knowledge and the information available in the wiki. Individual learning is considered as happening through internal processes of assimilation and accommodation. Collaborative knowledge building happens through activities of external assimilation and accommodation. This study demonstrates these four processes in an experimental setting. The results show that a medium level of incongruity between people's knowledge and a wiki's information supports individual learning and collaborative knowledge building.

Mechanism of retrieval inhibition in directed forgetting: Retrieval success produces inhibition

Mu, Defang Institute of Developmental Psy, School of Psychology,BNU, Beijing, People's Republic of China Song, Yaowu Department of Psychology,, Hebei University, Baoding, People's Republic of China Chen, Yinghe Institute of Developmental Psy, School of Psychology,BNU, Beijing, People's Republic of China
Two experiments tested the possibility that retrieval-induced forgetting is responsible for directed forgetting with the list-method paradigm using Chinese unrelated material by 120 university students. In two experiments, different additional list 2 retrieval practices were given to determine whether this would increase directed forgetting. In Experiment 1, free recall test was given without cuing. While in Experiment 2, stem completion test was required to ensure the success of retrieval. The results show the magnitude of the directed forgetting effect was increased only by retrieval success in Experiment 2, rather than in Experiment 1. This indicates that retrieval success can explain the retrieval inhibition in directed forgetting.

Predictors of motivation and job satisfaction

Mudra, Gyan CHRD, NIRD, Hyderabad, India
The purpose of this study is to investigate predictors of motivation and job satisfaction among employees.To analyse the factors influencing motivation and job satisfaction, data from government employees were collected. Predictors of general job satisfaction were tested by controlling statistically for gender, job tenure, and current job. Analysing the responses with respect to motivation and job satisfaction, quite interesting findings were observed. Job satisfaction can be improved if money is not the reason for working. Another way must then be found to intrinsically motivate them. This would be best achieved if the workers enjoy what they do and can become wrapped up in it, thus achieving flow.

The modification of TV recipients' perception of time units duration

Myronenko, Hanna ISPP, Kyiv, Ukraine
The influence of duration of TV consumption on the recipients' subjective duration of time unit was studied by an adapted technique for free subjective measurement (O.Polunin). This technique provides the most adequate design of influence of videotape recording on time presentations of teenagers. Sample: 110 schoolchildren of age 14-15 years, among whom psychological TV-recipients' typological groups were selected ("indifferent", "interested", "dependent"). Results: in case of long-term TV watching a loss of the control is accompanied by the maladaptive loss of time feeling and reality alienation. To optimize the person's time existence in conditions of intensive mass-media influence, training was developed.

Are there interindividual and situational moderators of the truth effect?

Nadarevic, Lena Lehrstuhl Psychologie III, Universität Mannheim, Mannheim, Germany Erdfelder, Edgar Lehrstuhl Psychologie III, Universität Mannheim, Mannheim, Germany
Several studies have demonstrated that repeatedly presented statements receive higher truth ratings than new statements. We examined whether this "Truth Effect" is moderated by different person-

ality traits. In Experiment 1, participants rated the validity of repeated and non-repeated trivia statements in two phases. These judgment phases were separated by a retention interval in which different personality questionnaires were completed. In Experiment 2, by contrast, personality questionnaires were not provided until the final judgment phase was finished. The results indicate that truth ratings depend on both, personality characteristics and aspects of the experimental setting.

Relations of the gender-related personality traits and stress to sexual behaviors among college students
Nagurney, Alexander Psychology, Texas State University, San Marcos, TX, USA Bagwell, Brandi Psychology, Texas State University, San Marcos, TX, USA
The present study sought to examine the relationship between the personality traits of agency, communion, unmitigated agency (UA) and unmitigated communion (UC), and sex behaviors (specifically, the number of partners and the frequency of engaging in safe sex practices). Additionally, perceived stress was examined as a potential moderator of these relationships. Participants were college students (n = 142) who completed a questionnaire that evaluated the traits and behaviors of interest. Regression analyses revealed significant relationships between both UA and UC and sex behavior, with perceived stress serving as a significant moderator of the UC and behavior relationships.

Hopelessness, depression and social support amongst tuberculosis (TB) patients attending a public health clinic in South Africa
Naidoo, Pamela Dept. of Psychology, University Of the Western Cape, Cape Town, South Africa
Objectives: In South Africa (SA) there is a high prevalence of TB. In this study it is hypothesized that there is a high prevalence of hopelessness and depression amongst TB patients, and inadequate social support. Methods: Over a 4-month period, adult TB patients attending a public clinic are being recruited. A series of questionnaires assessing hopelessness, depression and social support are being administered. Descriptive statistics, correlational and regression analyses will be conducted. Conclusions: This study is current and will be completed in December '07. It is hoped that a strategy to alleviate the burden of TB will be devised based on the findings of this study.

Does in-group identification not always lead to positive mental health? The moderating effect of trait self-esteem on the relationship between in-group identification and depression
Nakashima, Kenichiro Graduate School, Hiroshima University, Hiroshima, Japan Isobe, Chikae behavior Science, Hiroshima University, Higashi-Hiroshima, Japan Ura, Mitsuhiro behavior Science, Hiroshima University, Higashi-Hiroshima, Japan
Social Identity Theory research indicates in-group identification can lead to positive mental health. However, from the viewpoint of Sociometer Theory, this is not always so. We hypothesized that individuals with low trait self-esteem would experience positive mental health through in-group identification, whereas individuals with high trait self-esteem would not. We conducted a longitudinal questionnaire survey at 3-month intervals (n = 163). Results of a hierarchical multiple regression analysis revealed that in-group identification lowered depression tendency for individuals with low self-esteem, but not individuals with high self-esteem. These results are consistent with the hypothesis based on Sociometer theory.

Music: An effective tool for preventing drug use among teenagers
Narváez Rullán, María Dept. of Psychology, Autónoma University of Madrid, Madrid, Spain Fouce, Guillermo Madrid, Psicólogos Sin Fronteras, Madrid, Spain Fossoul, Mónica Madrid, Psicólogos Sin Fronteras, Madrid, Spain Izquierdo, Eva Madrid, Psicólogos Sin Fronteras, Madrid, Spain
Music occupies a privileged position among teenagers' hobbies. A variety of topics related to drugs are present in many songs (Fouce, 2003). In Psicólogos Sin Fronteras, Madrid, we have designed a program called "Prevenir en otra Onda", where music stops being part of the problem and becomes a prevention tool. Our objective was to assess prevention effectiveness and satisfaction with the experience. A sample of 160 teenagers participated in the program. We used a quasi-experimental design with pre and post-test assessments. The results suggest that "Prevenir en otra onda" is an effective tool that teens value favorably.

The role of self-esteem within the organizational context
Nebel, Claudia Inst. für Arbeitspsychologie, Technische Universität Dresden, Dresden, Germany Wolf, Sandra Work Psychology, TU Dresden, Dresden, Germany Richter, Peter Work Psychology, TU Dresden, Dresden, Germany
A multitude of authors emphasize the important role of resources in the organizational context. The study investigated the role of the personal resource organization-based self-esteem (OBSE, Pierce et al., 1989) within the Job Demands-Resources (JD-R) model (Demerouti, Bakker, Nachreiner, & Schaufeli, 2001) among 364 workers of different German organizations, who answered a questionnaire. Analysis of correlations, regressions analysis and structural equation modeling (SEM) analyses were performed. Findings suggest the important role of OBSE for workers health und engagement, implications of these findings are discussed.

The relationship between employee's commitment to change and work outcomes: The role of trust in the supervisor
Neves, Pedro Department of Psychology, University of Évora, Évora, Portugal Caetano, António Department of Psychology, ISCTE, Lisboa, Portugal
Herscovitch and Meyer's (2002) model of commitment to change focuses on employee commitment and its relation to behavioral support for change initiatives. We conducted a field study (N=221) with employees from several organizations in order to examine if and how affective commitment to change influences work outcomes. Using SEM, we found support for a full mediation effect of trust in the supervisor in the relationship between affective commitment to change and three work outcomes: perceived performance, OCBs and turnover intentions. These results support the claim that the impact of employee's affective commitment to a particular change may extent to other situations and relationships, and as such, influence work outcomes.

Wanting acceptance and fearing rejection: Consequences of social approach and avoidance motivation for processing of social stimuli
Nikitin, Jana Inst. für Psychologie, Universität Zürich, Zürich, Switzerland Freund, Alexandra M. Department of Psychology, University of Zurich, Zurich, Switzerland
Two studies investigated differences between social approach and avoidance motivation regarding the information processing of social stimuli. In Study 1, partially masked facial expressions were presented and had to be categorized as positive or negative. Implicit approach motivation was associated with a positivity bias, while avoidance motivation was not. Using an arm-flexion-tension paradigm, Study 2

showed that a combination of high explicit avoidance and approach motivation was associated with participants' pushing negative stimuli away from themselves more slowly than they pulled positive stimuli toward themselves. These results can be interpreted as dissociation of implicit and explicit motivation.

Effective strategy learning for higher performance in work organization
Nogami, Makoto Human Environment Studies, Kyushu University, Fukuoka, Japan Furukawa, Hisataka Human Environment Studies, Kyushu University, Fukuoka, Japan Yanagisawa, Saori Marketing and Distribution, Nakamura Gakuen University, Fukuoka, Japan
Recent research revealed the importance of members' strategy learning as a source of higher performance in organizations. This study, based on 6 month sequential questionnaire survey for 164 employees, investigated the relations of members' effort consciousness, feedback acquisition, and leader's guidance to members' strategy learning. Results showed members' effort consciousness and feedback acquisition had direct and significant positive influence upon their strategy learning. Guidance by leaders, such as vision presentation and strategy presentation, showed only indirect effect through members' effort consciousness and feedback acquisition upon members' strategy learning. These findings suggest the significance of employees' self-regulation to promote learning.

Implicit assessment of proneness to emotional stress through foreign language anxiety
Nosenko, Eleonora Dept. of Psychology, National University, Dnipropetrovsk, Ukraine Arshava, Irina psychology, National University, Dnipropetrovsk, Ukraine Nosenko, Dina psychology, National University, Dnipropetrovsk, Ukraine
The hypothesis about foreign language anxiety(-FLA) as an implicit manifestation of the individual's proneness to stress was tested on two subgroups of 50 undergraduate students diagnosed with the Classroom FLA Scale (Horwitz & Young,1991) and the frequency of hesitation phenomena in speech (Nosenko,1981) as possessing high or low FLA levels. Since the subgroups appeared to differ (ϕ^* Fisher at p<.05) on proportions of state- vs. action-oriented individuals (Kuhl's ACS-90) and emotion- vs. problem- focused copers (Endler and Parker, 1993), i.e. on personality predictors of proneness to stress, the hypothesis was considered to be proved.

Perceived organizational communication and its relationship with four psychological and organizational variables
Nouri, Aboulghasem Psychology, University of Isfahan, Isfahan, Islamic Republic of Iran Samavatyan, Hossein Psychology, university of Isfahan, Isfahan, Islamic Republic of Iran Oreyzi, Hamid reza Psychology, university of Isfahan, Isfahan, Islamic Republic of Iran Sanati, Javad Industrial Medicine Center, Industrial Medicine Center, Isfahan, Islamic Republic of Iran
This study aimed at investigating the relationship between organizational communication as perceived by employees and four psychological as well as organizational variables. By applying the research questionnaire, the relationships of organizational communication with organizational climate, organizational support, job satisfaction and psychological stress were significant (P<0.01). Implications of the findings for managers, employees and organizations are also discussed.

Clinical case formulation as a path coherent with psychological well-being-oriented psychotherapy

Novoa-Gómez, Mónica Maria Psicologia, Pontificia Univ. Javeriana, Bogotá, Colombia *Caycedo, Claudia* Psicologia, Pontificia Univ. Javeriana, Bogotá, Colombia *Ballesteros de Valderrama, Blanca Patricia* Psicologia, Pontificia Univ. Javeriana, Bogotá, Colombia

A validation based on the Behavioral-Analytic theoretical perspective was carried out in order to contribute to organization of the information obtained in the evaluationin a way that is coherent and cosistent with certain analysis categories belonging to the field of Psychological Well-being. Validity was defined as a function of the use of Single Case Design and ime-series methodology.- Validity criteria for the finished cases was theefficacy of intervention. Results point out the high level of inferences and hypotheses based on clinical judgment, rather than on empirical evidence. Application of results in three levels will be discussed: professional, Clinical Psychologist education plan and conceptual level.

Creativity and competitiveness study of characterization of creativity based on life stories from small businessmen

Nunes, Florbela Dept. de Psicologia, Universidade de Evora, Evora, Portugal

The work presented the results of research about the understanding of the process of creativity in business context. The present discussion about the creativity process (Martinez, 1997; Goleman, 2003; Csikszentmihalyi, 2004) our proposal is focused on the identification of factors facilitators or inhibitors to the expression of creativity, from small businessmen. Following a methodology of ball of snow to select the sample, the data come from interviews conducted with 10 entrepreneurs, in order to do a qualitative analisys. Finally, we discuss the contributions of the identification of factors facilitartors/ inhibitors of creativity, from small businessmen in terms of its sustainability.

A possible origin of self-esteem: The finger length ratio (2D:4D) negatively correlates with implicit self-esteem

Oe, Tomoko University of Tokyo, Tokyo, Japan *Hirabayashi, Sayuri* Graduate School of Humanities, Tokyo Metropolitan University, Tokyo, Japan *Numazaki, Makoto* Graduate School of Humanities, Tokyo Metropolitan University, Tokyo, Japan *Shigemasu, Kazuo* Grad Sch of Arts and Sciences, University of Tokyo, Tokyo, Japan

The second-to-fourth finger length ratio (2D:4D) is thought to be an index of prenatal sex hormone exposure, with low 2D:4D associated with high testosterone levels and associated with low oestrogen levels. We tested the associations between 2D:4D and implicit attitudes toward self and others. Participants (N=105) completed three single-category Implicit Association Tests as measures of implicit attitudes toward self and others. We found that participants with lower 2D:4D had stronger implicit positive attitude toward self and made more difference between self and others. These results suggest that the prenatal sex hormone exposure is one of determinants of implicit self-esteem.

The impact of explicit references in computer supported collaborative learning: Evidence from eye movement analyses

Oehl, Michael Universität Lüneburg, Lüneburg, Germany *Pfister, Hans-Rüdiger* LueneLab, University of Lüneburg, Lüneburg, Germany *Gilge, Anja* LueneLab, University of Lüneburg, Lüneburg, Germany

Chat-based Computer Supported Collaborative Learning (CSCL) often suffers from limitations due to the communication medium. A frequently reported consequence is the lack of discourse coherence and by this a lack of cognitive coherence in the learning process. To overcome these deficiencies, the implementation of explicit references with chat messages caused higher learning results. However up to now, we do not know enough about the responsible cognitive processes. In this experimental study, we analysed eye movements during a chat-based CSCL scenario to gain indications of learners' use of references. The results allow implications for a modified design of (chat-based) CSCL.

A coding scheme to analyse global text processing in computer supported collaborative learning: What eye movements can tell us

Oehl, Michael Universität Lüneburg, Lüneburg, Germany *Pfister, Hans-Rüdiger* LueneLab, University of Lüneburg, Lüneburg, Germany

Studies in research on Computer Supported Collaborative Learning (CSCL) usually gain their scientific findings from pre-/post-tests, video or logfile analyses. Although eye movements have proved to be a valuable source of information for the study of cognitive processes, they are hardly regarded in the field of CSCL. A crucial reason for this is the lack of suitable observational schemes. To bridge this gap, we propose a categorial coding scheme for global text processing in CSCL on the base of established well-defined eye movement measures. The empirical examination showed its high inter-rater reliability ($\kappa M = 0.91$). Implications for CSCL are discussed.

A new approach to psychology: Neural correlates of emotional meaning, a brain imaging study

Ofek, Einat Neuropsychology, Mind Epos, Yokneam, Israel

This study addresses neurophysiological correlates of subjective emotional experience. Previous brain correlate studies have not evaluated the degree or characteristics of subjective emotional significance nor specifically the importance of people in the subject's life to the subject. EEG was measured while normal subjects heard names. A post-experiment validated questionnaire was performed to evaluate emotional significance. A robust, specific brain response to emotional stimuli was found. Many brain correlates of emotions such as love, hatred, trauma, longing and early memory were described. These findings may enhance psychotherapy methods; especially PTSD, autism, depression and anxiety treatment/diagnosis, among other conditions.

Factors affecting semantic similarity among Jukugo neighbors

Ogawa, Taeko Faculty of Human Relations, Tokai Gakuin University, Kakamigahara, Japan *Kawakami, Masahiro* Faculty of Human Science, Osaka Shoin Women's University, Kashiba, Japan

Japanese two-kanji compound words (Jukugo) have two sets of neighbors: Front-neighbors that share the same front-kanji and Rear-neighbors that share the same rear-kanji of the Jukugo. We investigated factors affecting semantic similarity among Jukugo neighbors. In a neighbor recall-task, participants were presented with single kanji, and asked to recall Jukugo neighbors (Front-neighbors or Rear-neighbors depending on the condition) as many as possible in a minute for each kanji. This task consists of twenty items. The results were analyzed in terms of how factors such as number of neighbors and recall frequency of neighbors affect the semantic similarity rating among neighbors.

Effectiveness of Self-Active Relaxation Therapy (SART): Analysis of POMS and STAI changes

Ohno, Hiroyuki Faculty of Human Relation, Fukuoka Jo Gakuin University, Fukuoka, Japan *Ki, Heyoung* Faculty of Human Relation, Fukuoka Jo Gakuin University, Fukuoka, Japan *Haramaki, Yutaka* Professional Graduate School, Kagoshima University, Kagoshima-shi, Japan *Noi, Mica* Faculty of Mental Health and W, Seinan Jo Gakuin, Kitakyusyu-shi, Japan

The effectiveness of SART (Ohno, 2003) was evaluated. The SART is a modified version of Dosa-hou (Naruse, 1975), which has been a popular method of psychological rehabilitation for disables over the past 30 years in Japan. The changes seen among 41 adults in the mood and anxiety assessment, POMS and STAI, before and after the session were analyzed by ANOVA. Remarkable changes toward positive categories in POMS and STAI were evident(Experiment 1). In Experiment 2, 27 adults who received continuous sessions of SART also showed positive changes in the assessment of POMS and STAI checked in every sessions.

Effect of communicative modes and intention of self-presentation on the perception of communication qualities and the communication behavior.

Okamoto, Kaori Gifu, Japan

The present study examined the validity of a model assuming that physical-context factor and social-context factor determine their social-information-processing, and that the social-information-processing determines their communication behaviors. As the physical factor, two communication modes, different in an amount of non-verbal communication (face-to-face and cellular-phone-mail), was manipulated. As the social-context factor, two messages (a self-enhancing presentation message and a self-deprecating presentation message), different in intention of self-presentation was manipulated. As the social-information-processing factor, the perception of communication qualities was measured. As the communication behavior, interpersonal impression to the sender of presentation message was measured.

The distribution of the sum of independent random variables can be calculated exactly - almost always

Oldenbürger, Hartmut A. Universität Göttingen, Göttingen, Germany

There is a widespread belief that the solution of the problem stated in the title inevitably leads to combinatorial explosion. This erraneous mindset should be eliminated as it is a thinking-barrier. Therefore this contribution fosters possible developments of statistical distributional modelling and testing for various application domains. The presentation describes the mathematical bases of convolution and demonstrates building several general Galton-Boards by successive distribution construction. Even more complex architectures and situations can be handled, e.g. planned comparisons. When calculations are done exactly, approximation or estimation by simulation is obsolete. - Statistics textbooks need a chapter on convolution, and beyond.

The relationship between mood and affect in individual and group level and organizational prosocial behavior and job absenteeism in workplace

Oreyzi, Hamid Reza Pschology, Isfahan University, Isfahan, Islamic Republic of Iran *Omidi Arjenaki, Najmeh* Pschology, Isfahan university, isfahan, Islamic Republic of Iran *Jahanbakhsh Ganjeh, Madineh* Pschology, Isfahan university, isfahan, Islamic Republic of Iran *Goudarzi, Saied* Pschology, Isfahan university, isfahan, Islamic Republic of Iran

The purpose of this study was to investigate the relationship between mood and affect in individual and group level and organizational prosocial behavior and job absenteeism in workplace via within analysis and between analysis (WABA).Statistical population was all of absent personnel from their work frequently without permission and were belonging to work group.147 participants(35 groups)were selected randomly. Findings indicated improvement of determination coefficient that explained variance in group level relative to individual level. Keywords: Mood, Affect, Prosocial behavior, Absenteeism

Cross-cultural validity of the infant-toddler HOME inventory in application to the developmental context of Turkish-German toddlers

Otyakmaz, Berrin Özlem Inst.
Bildungswissenschaften, Universität Duisburg-Essen, Essen, Germany

In this study the cross-cultural validity of the Infant-Toddler HOME Inventory was proofed for its use in the assessment of the developmental context of Turkish-German toddlers. The original HOME (Caldwell & Bradley, 1984) and culture-specific additional items, developed by the author, were administered to 36 Turkish-German immigrant and 35 German families. Findings obtained from the supplement items and the original HOME items suggest that there are different environmental aspects which have a specific relationship with the cognitive outcomes of Turkish-German and German toddlers, repectively. As SES and cultural background of the both samples are confounding further studies should control these variables.

Managing mobile availability: Experimental verification of a model of interdependence

Pöschl, Sandra Inst. Media und Kommunikation, Technische Universität Ilmenau, Ilmenau, Germany

Ubiquitious mobile communication is two edged: we profit by possibilities of contact, but public mobile phone use can be disturbing. A theoretical model based on interdependence theory was worked out: It can be used to explain reactions to mobile phone calls interfering in an existing face-to-face interaction. The model is tested by a laboratory experiment with student participants, including structural aspects of interdependence situations, role of the subject (witnessing or receiving a call) and gender as independent variables, and individual behaviour and perceived quality of outcome as dependent variables. The presentation will include the results of the study in progress.

Comparison of the strategies used to train new researchers in chemistry, physics and mathematics

Padilla Vargas, María Antonia Centro de Estudios e Investiga, University of Guadalajara, Guadalajara, Mexico Loera Navarro, Verónica de Fátima Centro de Estudios e Investiga, University of Guadalajara, Guadalajara, Mexico Matsuda Wilson, Hitomy Edith Centro de Estudios e Investiga, University of Guadalajara, Guadalajara, Mexico Arteaga Flores, Georgina Margarita Centro de Estudios e Investiga, University of Guadalajara, Guadalajara, Mexico

The objective was to compare training strategies used by researchers in Chemistry, Physics and Mathematics to train their apprentices. In each area six investigators of three different generations participated: 2 with 25 years of research experience, 2 with 12 years of experience, trained by the first ones, and 2 trained by the seconds. Three instruments designed to fit the present research purposes were used to collect data. Results showed that the most frequently used strategy was specific training of manual abilities, regulated by constant feedback. The implications that these results have for teaching sciences are discussed. Key Words: Training strate-

gies, experts, novices, Chemistry, Physics, Mathematics.

The effect of self-care programs on psycho-social and cognitive functioning of multiple sclerosis patients

Pahlavanzadeh, Saeid Psychiatric Nursing, Isfahan University, Isfahan, Islamic Republic of Iran Alimohammadi, Nasrollah Medical-Surgical Nursing, Isfahan University of Med Sci, Isfahan, Islamic Republic of Iran Soltani, Mohammad Hosein Medical-Surgical Nursing, Isfahan University of Med Sci, Isfahan, Islamic Republic of Iran

Objectives: Multiple sclerosis may make acute disabilities influencing life trend. Self care programs can improve quality of life. So this study was done by above aim. Methods: This study was quasi-experimental. Twenty eight MS patients were selected by convenient sampling. The subjects were asked to attend three educational sessions and after three weeks started self-care programs, then questionnaire was filled by patients. Results: Findings showed a noticeable increase in mean score in psycho-cognitive (P<0.00l) and social function (P<0.00l) after self care programs. Conclusions: The findings showed that self-care activities resulted in promoting psychosocial functioning, improving self-esteem and quality of life.

Outcome of solution-focused brief therapy working with adolescents in foster and health care settings

Pakrosnis, Rytis Dept. of General Psychology, Vytautas Magnus University, Kaunas, Lithuania Cepukiene, Viktorija General Psychology, Vytautas Magnus University, Kaunas, Lithuania

The aim of the study was to evaluate the outcome of Solution-Focused Brief Therapy for adolescents in foster and health care settings. The treatment manual, standardized and subjective measures evaluating changes of problem situation and psychosocial adjustment were used. Foster care treatment and control groups each consisted of 47 adolescents. Health care treatment group consisted of 65 while control group of 44 adolescents. The average number of sessions was 3.5. Result analysis revealed significant decrease in the severity of the problems presented for the therapy and significantly more positive changes of psychological functioning in both treatment groups compared to controls. Factors best predicting better outcome were revealed for both settings.

Shaping the thinking and learning styles according to the task and academic specialization

Palos, Ramona Department of Psychology, West University of Timisoara, Timisoara, Romania

Purpose: "to surprise the way the learning tasks students confront in comparison with their academic specialty shape their thinking and learning styles". Objectives: to identify the thinking, learning and teaching styles of the content students prefer, considering their specialization. Sample: 120 students (the IVth year of Medicine, IT, Literature Faculty). Used test portofolio: "thinking style inventory", "learning style inventory", "teaching style questionnaire". We expect to surprise the way learning tasks shape students thinking and learning styles, and to see the outlining of a preference for teaching styles, considering their specialization. Pragmatic value: designing educational materials, choosing efficient teaching methods.

Indian youth and habit of drug

Pandey, Ugrasen Dept. of Social Science, SRK PG College Firozabad, Firozbad, India

The paper examines the association of various socio-economic factors with the use of drugs by indian youth in India. Data were collected from a large sample, using a self-reporting questionnaire. It

was found that analgesics, tobacco and alcohol were the most commonly used drugs amongst some 30 per cent of the students. Factors such as age, urbanity, sex, marital status as well as the family's educational and economic status were seen to be relevant. Inter-parental and inter-generational tensions in the family also had a bearing.

Creativity: It's relation to self-esteem and music talent in Greek adolescents

Paraskevopoulou, Polyxeni Athens, Greece Gkritzalis, Nikitas PSYCHOLOGY, UNIVERSITY OF ATHENS, ATHENS, Greece

The aim of the study is to examine the level of creativity and self-esteem in Greek adolescents in relation to music talent. The participants are adolescent pupils of "Music Schools" and "Standard Schools" (control group). Inventories and questionnaires examining level of several domains of self-esteem and levels of creativity, are administered. relation of creativity and talent, as well as, self-esteem and talent is examined. Are talented pupils more creative than control group students? Are there any differences in self-esteem between the two groups of pupils (control and talented)? Demographic data are also included in the analyses.

Creativity and reading behavior

Park, Mi-Cha BK21 Group of Multi-Cultural, Sung Kyun Kwan University, Seoul, Republic of Korea Lee, Mi-Na Child Psychology & Educati, SungKyunKwan University, Seoul, Republic of Korea Choe, In-Soo Child Psychology & Educati, SungKyunKwan University, Seoul, Republic of Korea

The possibility of a relationship between creativity and reading habit was investigated. A creativity test consisting of creative thinking, creative motivation, and creative personality was administered to 151 elementary school students. A reading behavior test was also taken. The results showed that creativity was significantly correlated with reading behavior. Efficient and strategic reading was correlated with creativity(r(140)=.572, p<.001). Also, children who were more interested in reading showed higher creativity(r(143)=.448, p<.001). The results invite a speculation that good reading habit might facilitate creativity.

Relationship between temperament and personality disorder

Park, Mi-Jung Dept. of Psychology, Chungbuk National University, Chungbuk, Republic of Korea Hwang, Soon-Taeg Psychology, Chungbuk National University, Cheong Ju, Chungbuk, Republic of Korea Lee, Joo-Young Psychology, maum-sarang, Cheong Ju, Chungbuk, Republic of Korea

The purpose of this study was to examine the relationship between temperaments and Personality Disorders. 753 college students(mean age=21.46 ± 2.42) completed the Diagnostic Test for Personality Disorders(DTPD) and the Temperament and Character Inventory(TCI). Correlational analysis of temperaments and Personality Disorders revealed that NS(Novelty Seeking) was positively correlated with antisocial, borderline, histrionic, narcissistic, schizotypal, dependent and paranoid PDs, and negatively correlated with obsessive-compulsive and schizoid PDs. HA(Harm Avoidance) was positively correlated with avoidant, paranoid, schizoid, dependent, schizotypal, and borderline PDs, and negatively correlated with the score of histrionic PDs. RD(Reward Dependence) was positively correlated with histrionic, dependent, and narcissistic PDs, and negatively correlated with schizoid, paranoid PDs.

Similarities between clients and counselors: What kinds of preferences have potential clients?

Pauliukeviciute, Klaudija Dept. of General Psychology, Vytautas Magnus University, Kaunas, Lithuania *Zardeckaite-Matulaitiene, Kristina* General Psychology, Vytautas Magnus University, Kaunas, Lithuania *Dirsiene, Jurgita* General Psychology, Vytautas Magnus University, Kaunas, Lithuania

The aim of the study was to evaluate clients' preferences for counselor and relationship between clients and counselors socio-demographical and psychological characteristics. Non-random convenience sampling was used in this study. 196 participants ranged in age from 18 to 68 years were surveyed. Questionnaire, generated on previous research in the field, consisting of 42 items on preferences about counselors' socio-demographical and psychological characteristics was used in the study. The findings indicated that participants expressed preference for counselor woman. Participants expressed preference for older, married, healthy, the same sexual orientation and language speaking counselor with the greater working experience. Participants expressed no preferences for counselor religion, ethnicity and social status.

Effectiveness and cost-effectiveness of antidepressants and psychological interventions

Perestelo-Perez, Lilisbeth Evaluation and Planning Unit, Canary Islands Health Service, Santa Cruz de Tenerife, Spain *Garcia-Perez, Lidia* Evaluation and Planning Unit, Canary Islands Health Service, Santa Cruz de Tenerife, Spain *Peñate-Castro, Wenceslao* Personality, Evaluation and Ps, University of La Laguna, La Laguna, Spain *de las Cuevas-Castresana, Carlos* Psychiatry, School of Medicine, University of La Laguna, La Laguna, Spain

Objectives: To provide an update review of the best quality evidence for the clinical effectiveness and cost-effectiveness of antidepressants and psychological interventions in depressed patients. Methods: A systematic review of the literature and an economic evaluation were undertaken. We reviewed electronic databases (Medline, Embase...) until July 2007. Four reviewers considered studies for inclusion and extracted data; conflicts were resolved through consensus. Results: Selective serotonin reuptake inhibitors, serotonin-norepinephrine reuptake inhibitors and psychotherapy (primarily cognitive behaviour and interpersonal therapies) were more effective at promoting remission than control conditions. Conclusions: Antidepressants and psychotherapy may both be effective first-line treatments for patients with mild to moderate depression.

Reliability and factor structure of the thinking styles inventory in a Italian sample

Picconi, Laura Biomedical Studies, University of Chieti-Pescara, Chieti, Italy *Chirumbolo, Antonio* Biomedical Studies, University of Chieti-Pescara, Chieti, Italy

According to Sternberg's mental government theory, there are 13 thinking styles. In this paper we investigated the validity of the Italian version of Thinking Styles Inventory (TSI) in a sample of 373 students (49% of males). Analysis of internal consistency and factor structure indicated that the TSI is reliable and valid. The first factor was loaded by functions styles; the II factor was loaded by forms styles. The III factor contrasted the internal with the external styles; the IV factor contrasted the global with the local styles. At last, the V factor contrasted liberal and conservative styles.

Defining monogamy

Planes, Montserrat Psicologia, Facultat de Psicologia, Girona, Spain *Cunill, Mónica* psicologia, facultat de psicologia, girona, Spain *Gomez, Ana Belen* psicologia, universitat de girona, girona, Spain *Gras, Eugània* psicologia, universitat de girona, girona,

Spain *Font-Mayolas, Sílvia* psicologia, universitat de girona, girona, Spain *Sullman, Mark* school of psychology, university of hertfordshire, herts, United Kingdom *Aymerich, Maria* psicologia, universitat de girona, girona, Spain

Objectives: This study investigated the signification, for young people, of the term "monogamy", which is one of the recommendations to avoid the sexual transmission of the HIV. Method: This cross-sectional research surveyed 750 Spanish university students (67.7% female) and asked them to define monogamy. Results: The majority of the definitions of "monogamy" were only partially correct (61.9%) and some were completely wrong (6.8%). A large number of students did not answer or provided digressive responses. Conclusions: The term "monogamy" is not well understood by university students. If they do not fully understand this recommendation, which is one way to prevent the sexual transmission of the HIV, it is unlikely to be practiced correctly.

Adaptation of Defense Style Questionnaire in Latvia

Plaude, Alla of psychology, University of Latvia, Riga, Latvia *Rascevska, Malgozata* of Psychology, University of Latvia, Riga, Latvia

The purpose of the project is to test psychometric properties of Latvian version of Defense Style Questionnaire (DSQ) (Bond, 1983). DSQ was translated into Latvian by the back-translation method, questioning 100 adults and 100 psychiatry patients. The Cronbach's alpha for Non-adaptive scale was .85, Image-distorting scale - .77, Self-sacrifice scale - .63, Adaptive scale - .37. The confirmatory factors analysis of the questionnaire items showed that the Latvian version of DSQ corresponds to the structure of factors of original version only partially. There was not obtained 4 defense mechanism styles according to original combination of items, but only two factors. Key words: defense mechanism

The difference between creativity of mathematicians and psychologists

Plháková, Alena Dept. of Psychology, Palacký University Olomouc, Olomouc, Czech Republic *Reiterová, Eva* Dept. of Psychology, Palacký University Olomouc, Olomouc, Czech Republic

The authors will present the results of the preliminary study on the implicit theories of creativity. In this study, 50 students of mathematics and 50 students of psychology at Palacký University in Olomouc described typical behaviors and mental activities of a highly creative person, psychologist, or mathematician. From the contents of the replies, a list of characteristics was created, describing behaviors and mental activities of a creative person, mathematician and psychologist. The differences among these three types of creative people will be discussed.

Unconscious emotional priming and self-reported ethnical attitudes: Aspect of measurements correspondence

Plotka, Irina Higher School of Psychology, Riga, Latvia *Igonin, Dmitry* Psychology, Latvian University, Riga, Latvia *Bluminau, Nina* Psychology, The Higher School of Psycholog, Riga, Latvia

The relation between explicit and implicit ethnic attitudes (EA) measures was studied. Was used the unconscious emotional priming paradigm, in which the visual presentation of target evaluative adjective was preceded by prime stimulus - the names of three ethnic groups at varying stimulus onset asynchronies (SOAs) – 200, 500, 1000 ms. Participants (80 adults), preliminary divided into groups depending on self-reported EA, estimated emotional valence of the adjectives. Responses latencies were registered. Repeated-measures $2 \times 3 \times 3$ factorial analysis of variance for latency and within-subject design were

used. The effect of primes-targets valences and SOAs intervals on responses latencies was demonstrated.

Hindsight bias as a consequence of interference and poor inhibitory control?

Pohl, Rüdiger F. Inst. Verhaltenspsychologie, Universität Mannheim, Mannheim, Germany

In hindsight, people tend to overestimate the quality of their foresight estimates. This hindsight bias could stem from interference between outcome and previous knowledge, which in turn could result from the inability to effectively inhibit the outcome knowledge. In a study with 60 participants, interference was manipulated by the degree of similarity between participants' original estimates and outcome information. Inhibitory control was measured by established test scales. The results showed effects of interference on recalled estimates, but not on the amount of hindsight bias. Moreover, individual hindsight bias was not related to the amount of inhibitory control.

Peculiarities in using thematic drawings set for group psychocorrection .

Polyanychko, Olena Physical Education, IAPM, Kyiv, Ukraine

Diversity of techniques for using the psychodrawings is aimed at finding such techniques that would give opportunity to cognize the peculiarities of the unconscious sphere of psychics. It is free drawing (one draws whatever one wants) that just serves this purpose, as well as additional drawing (the sheet of paper goes round and each participant adds his own detail to the drawing), team-drawing when the whole group is drawing on one and the same sheet of paper. We have noticed that drawings contain images which expose the character of the author's relations with the surrounding world (with people, objects, nature).

When a bad strategy is worse than no strategy at all: The interaction of implicit vs. explicit processing with problem complexity

Pretz, Jean Dept. of Psychology, Illinois Wesleyan University, Bloomington, USA *Zimmerman, Corinne* Psychology, Illinois State University, Normal, IL, USA

We replicated and extended previous work on implicit and explicit approaches to problem solving in the balance-scale task paradigm. In two studies, the interaction of strategy and problem complexity was observed. The explicit, rule-seeking strategy led to rule induction among few participants. Among nondiscoverers, implicit participants (who did not seek the rule) were faster and more accurate on high-complexity problems than explicit participants. Implicit processing led to better transfer than explicit processing. We argue that rule seeking may fixate participants on inappropriate hypotheses. For highly complex problems, an implicit approach may allow passively acquired knowledge to be expressed.

The information and subjective time as result of processing of stimulus by memory

Prisnyakova, Lyudmila Dnipropetrovsk, Ukraine *Prisniakov, Volodymyr* Mechanics, NAS of Ukraine, Dnipropetrovsk, Ukraine

Objective is definition of information and time as reactions of person to an external or internal signal. Method is the analysis of experimental data confirming the proposed hypothesis. Results. The size of quantum of information is determined, which is 1.6 104 times more of quantum Planck. Fluctuations of an alpha-rhythm determine subjective time. Dependence between objective time as by irritations and between internal time as by sensation is received. Conclusion. The unit of measurements of information is the regulated subjectively complete formation. Information is result of activity of memory in reply to external perturbations in maintenance of nonequilibriumness of an alive organism

Influence of the internet on the psychological activity of a human being: Personality of internet users

Przepiorka, Aneta JP II, Catholic University of Lublin, Lublin, Poland Blachnio, Agata Psycho. Emotion and Motivation, Catholic University of Lublin, Lublin, Poland

The objective of this study is to reveal the features of an individual's personality and how that may be connected with how often they use the Internet. The data was used to test these hypotheses: (i) individuals of external LOC are more prone to be negatively affected by the Internet, (ii) individuals of internal LOC are more resistant to being negatively affected by the Internet, and (iii) extraverts and individuals with a higher level of social support have a positive experience when using the Internet and, therefore, take advantage of using it more often.

Effects of a prolonged and voluntary hyperventilation procedure in a psychotherapeutical context

Puente, Iker Psicologia Basica y Evolutiva, UAB, Barcelona, Spain

The study explore the effects of a hiperventilation procedure in certain personality properties, meaning of life and levels of distress. Two groups of 31 subjects each (aged 18-35 years) were compared using a repeated measures design (pre-post). The experimental group participate for first time in a workshop where the hiperventilation procedure is used. The test used were the SCL-R-90, the Purpose in Life Test (PIL) and the Temperament and Caracter Inventory-revised (TCI-R). The statistical analysis shows a significant reduction in the Global Severity Index (SCL-R-90), and a significant increase in the meaning of life (PLT), SelfDirection, Cooperativeness and SelfTrascendence (TCI-R) in the experimental group.

Mechanization and social relationships in olive harvesting

Pulido, Manuel Psychology, University of Jaén, Jaén, Spain Luque, Pedro Jesus Jaen, Spain Palomo, Antonio Psychology, University of Jaén, Jaén, Spain

Objective: Studying the impact of mechanization of olive harvesting processes on organized activity and, particularly, on social relationships. Method: A qualitative methodology based on discursive production was used to obtain social representations. Interviews were conducted with 28 olive harvesting incumbents using a semi-structured format. Results: New mechanized jobs impair staff communication and cause more social isolation than traditional non-mechanized jobs.

Psychophysics of the taste process of virgin olive oil

Ramos Alvarez, Manuel Miguel Dept. of Psychology, University of Jaen, Jaen, Spain Paredes Olay, Maria C Psychology, University of Jaen, Jaen, Spain Moreno Fernández, Manuela Psychology, University of Jaen, Jaen, Spain Callejas Aguilera, Jose E. Psychology, University of Jaen, Jaen, Spain Abad, Maria J.F. Psychology, University of Jaen, Jaen, Spain Rosas, Juan M. Psychology, University of Jaen, Jaen, Spain

A methodology to approach the taste process of virgin olive oil is proposed, based on a nonparametric variant of the Signal Detection Theory, and the robust approach of the exploratory data analysis. This approach provides appropriate detection-discrimination-recognition-memory indexes together with decision indexes. Additionally, it uses robust inferential statistics that allow for an optimization of the statistical significance decisions around descriptive indexes. This method is illustrated with detection and discrimination experiments.

In the eye of the beholder: Implicit theories of happiness among Filipino adolescents

Ramos III, Rufino College Guidance Center, Ateneo de Naga University, Naga City, Philippines

This qualitative research was designed to gain an understanding of the concept of happiness among Filipino adolescents. To probe into their conceptions of happiness, descriptions of a typical happy Filipino adolescent, and perceived sources of happiness, ten (10) Focus Group Discussion sessions were conducted among sixty-eight (68) urban-based university college students from Metro Manila and the Bikol Region. Overall, the findings of the study reveal that when using the cross-cultural perspective, the implicit theories of happiness for Filipino adolescents are predominantly consistent with the ideas/conceptions of happiness from those of the collectivist cultures.

Young children of mentally handicapped mothers: How do they develop?

Rauh, Hellgard Inst. für Psychologie, Universität Potsdam, Postdam, Germany Sass, Grit Institute for Psychology, University of Potsdam, Postdam, Germany Simo Teufel, Sandra I, University of Valencia, Valencia, Spain

Young children (10 – 80 months, n=22) of mentally (non-genetically) deficient mothers (IQs 40-90), living with their mothers in supervised arrangements, were, mostly, themselves mentally retarded. Neither maternal IQ, nor maternal family risk, nor kind of living arrangement (institution or community), nor maternal sensitivity in mother-child play, did predict child MDI (Bayley) or IQ (K-ABC). Rather, infants and toddlers, especially those of very low functioning mothers, seemed to fare better in institutional, but preschool-age children of moderately and better functioning mothers in community living arrangements. Institutional all-day supervision seemed to impede parenting abilities and to delimit the range of children's experiences.

Does reading of womens magazines influence mood and body image?: An experimental study

Rettenwander, Annemarie Innsbruck, Austria Humer, Lisa Institute of Psychology, Leopold-Franzens-University, Innsbruck, Austria

The aim of this experimental psychological study was to investigate whether reading beauty and fashion magazines influences mood and body image more negatively than popular science magazines. 143 girls aged 13 to 15 were assigned randomly to one of two groups – one group reading beauty and fashion magazines, the other popular scientific magazines (both for 15 minutes). After that reading all girls answered the same standardized questionnaires regarding body image, eating behaviour and actual mood. The results show that reading beauty and fashion magazines has a statistically significant negative influence on the mood and body image, compared to science magazines.

Comparing the drawing characteristic in Draw-A-Person Test between middle mental retarded and nonmetal retarded children

Rezaei Dehnavi, Sedigheh Isfahan, Islamic Republic of Iran

The purpose of this study was comparing the drawing characteristic related to personality and existence abnormalities in Draw- A-Person Test between Middle Mental Retarded and Nonmental Retarded children.15 MMR children paired (ages,-sex) with NMR children. Each child was wanted to draw a person.Paird-sample T and McNemar tests Applied to Analyze the Data. The Findings show no significantly Differences (exclude in ratio of body to leg)in MMR and NMR Children in personality relates, But in existence abnormalities Indicators the differences between two groups was Significant (sig:.05). These results suggest that draw- a person test can be used to investigate abnormalities in MR children.

The "Mozart Effect": Fact or artifact? A critical test using IRT-scaled item material and active controls

Rieder, Alexandra Inst. für Psychologie, Universität Klagenfurt, Maria Saal, Austria

Does listening to Mozart increase spatiotemporal test performance? This "Mozart effect" has fueled a heated debate for almost 15 years now. Following Gittler et al. (2006), we implemented an improved experimental design using IRT-scaled spatial test material, extended by four active control groups. Data from N = 208 participants (musicians vs. non-musicians) show that listening to self-selected music had mildly positive effects on post-test performance, while listening to Mozart did, along with other conditions, not lead to significant improvement. Results are consistent with the arousal-mood hypothesis, and not with a Mozart effect account. They reveal additional insight into preference effects.

Effects of video game violence on social information processing (SIP)

Riesner, Lars Institut für Psychologie Kiel, Kiel, Germany Schartenberg, Marcus Entw.- Pädag. & Rechtspsyc, Institut für Psychologie Kiel, Kiel, Germany Staude-Müller, Frithjof Entw.- Pädag. & Rechtspsyc, Institut für Psychologie Kiel, Kiel, Germany

This experimental study tested whether playing violent video games induces changes in SIP. After screening for trait aggressiveness to form three groups (high, medium, low), 137 young men were randomly assigned to one of two versions of a "first-person-shooter" game differing only in level of violence. Following play, dependent variables were assessed using a lexical decision task to measure aggressive priming, a face categorization task to measure hostile affect processing bias, and a punishment paradigm to measure aggressive behavior. As predicted, results showed that video game violence influenced several stages of SIP, and revealed a general shift toward greater hostility.

Effects of a behavioral training in the correct use of condoms in high school students

Robles Montijo, Silvia Susana Investigación-UIICSE, FES Iztacala-UNAM, Tlalnepantla, Mexico Rodríguez Cervantes, Martha Investigación-UIICSE, FES IZTACALA-UNAM, Tlalnepantla, Edo. de México., Mexico Frías Arroyo, Beatriz Investigación-UIICSE, FES IZTACALA-UNAM, Tlalnepantla, Edo. de México., Mexico Barroso Villegas, Rodolfo Investigación-UIICSE, FES IZTACALA-UNAM, Tlalnepantla, Edo. de México., Mexico Moreno Rodríguez, Diana Investigación-UIICSE, FES IZTACALA-UNAM, Tlalnepantla, Edo. de México., Mexico Díaz González y Anaya, Eugenio Investigación-UIICSE, FES IZTACALA-UNAM, Tlalnepantla, Edo. de México., Mexico Rodríguez Campuzano, Lourdes Investigación-UIICSE, FES IZTACALA-UNAM, Tlalnepantla, Edo. de México., Mexico Castillo Nava, Pilar Investigación-UIICSE, FES IZTACALA-UNAM, Tlalnepantla, Edo. de México., Mexico

This study assessed the effectiveness of a behavioural training in the correct use of condoms in high school students. A pre-test-post-test experimental design with control and experimental groups was used. Participants included 225 students (average age of 14.5 years); the experimental group received training in the behavioural ability to place and to remove a condom on a penis model for teaching. Direct and indirect measures of condom use were obtained. The results showed differences favouring the group that received training, but there was no correlation between the measures of condom use. The importance of considering in prevention programs for HIV, STI and unwanted pregnancies a behavioural training in the correct use of condoms is discussed.

Parent-partner-adolescent communication about sex: Effects of an HIV/STI and pregnancy prevention program

Robles Montijo, Silvia Susana Investigación-UIICSE, FES Iztacala-UNAM, Tlalnepantla, Mexico Frías Arroyo, Beatriz Investigación-UIICSE, FES IZTACALA-UNAM, Tlalnepantla, Edo. de México., Mexico Moreno Rodríguez, Diana Investigación-UIICSE, FES IZTACALA-UNAM, Tlalnepantla, Edo. de México., Mexico Barroso Villegas, Rodolfo Investigación-UIICSE, FES IZTACALA-UNAM, Tlalnepantla, Edo. de México., Mexico Rodríguez Cervantes, Martha Investigación-UIICSE, FES IZTACALA-UNAM, Tlalnepantla, Edo. de México., Mexico Rodríguez Campuzano, Lourdes Investigación-UIICSE, FES IZTACALA-UNAM, Tlalnepantla, Edo. de México., Mexico Díaz González y Anaya, Eugenio Investigación-UIICSE, FES IZTACALA-UNAM, Tlalnepantla, Edo. de México., Mexico

This study assessed the effects of an HIV/STI and pregnancy prevention behavioural program on the frequency of communication about sex with parents and partners, determining their relationship with the intention of having sex and using condoms in the next sexual encounter. Two hundred and twenty-five teenagers participated in the study. A pre-test post-test experimental design with control and experimental groups was used. The results showed that talking with parents about sexual issues was positively correlated with the intention to use condoms but not with the intention of having sex, whereas talking with sex partners was positively correlated with the intention to having sexual intercourse and condom use at their next sexual encounter.

Polish adaptation of the Hoffman Gender Scale

Roszak, Joanna Dept. of Psychology, Warsaw School of Social Psych., Warsaw, Poland

The purpose was to introduce a new gender identity measure. The Hoffman Gender Scale (Hoffman et al. 2000) represents an approach, which is not focused on sex stereotypes, but shifts to personal significance of gender identity. The translated 14-item HGS was employed in a series of studies aimed to verify the translation, explore the possible two-factor structure proposed by Hoffman, and provide data on discriminant validity by comparing the BSRI, NEO-FFI and HGS scores. The Polish HGS is a relatively reliable (Alphas > .868) and valuable tool of one-factor structure, designed to tap the intrapersonal aspect of one's gender.

Status of outpatient neuropsychological care in Germany

Rother, Aline Jahnsdorf, Germany Mühlig, Stephan Inst. Klinische Psychologie, Tech. Universität Chemnitz, Chemnitz, Germany

The present study, designed as a national survey, focused on determining the current status of outpatient neuropsychological care in Germany, which was assumed to be suboptimal. In June 2006 a 13-page questionnaire was sent out to n=232 neuropsychologists offering non-hospital treatment in Germany. At present the response rate amounts to 61.32%. By means of a descriptive analysis numerous questions concerning therapist, office and patient characteristics as well as various structural facts have been evaluated. The results show an inappropriate provision of healthcare in this field.

Relationships between gambling addiction and sensations seeking in casino customers and university students from Bogota

Ruiz Pérez, Jose Ignacio Psychology, Universidad Nacional de Colomb, Bogotá, Colombia

A non-randomized sample (n=45) of casino customers and university students answered a survey about gambling frecuency, demographic data and two scales: South Oaks Gambling Screen (SOGS) and Sensation Seeking Scale (V) (SSS-V). Results showed a 58% of people with probable addiction to gambling, and only four items of SSS-V showed significative correlations with SOGS score.

Affect, conceptual evaluation standards and the readiness to focus on others

Rutkowska, Dorota Faculty of Psychology, Warsaw University, Warsaw, Poland Szuster, Anna Faculty of Psychology, Warsaw University, Warsaw, Poland

Prosocial behavior is connected with evaluation processes based on affect as well as on conceptual, reflective standards. Other-focused standards seem particularly important for prosocial behavior as they allow to decide what is advantageous or disadvantageous for others. It was expected that that the situational activation of affect vs reflective evaluation as well as subjective accessibility of other-focused standards can modify prosocial behavior. The results of two experimental studies show that affect is a significant factor determining prosocial activity of people with low accessibility of other-focused standards, whereas people with high accessibility of other-focused standards remain independent of situational evaluative conditions.

A study on effect of giving massage and acupuncture for abused children

Saito, Mami Human Life and Environment, Keisen University, Tama, Japan

This report is the examination on the effect that abused children are treated with massage during psychotherapy. Often they are given acupuncture for children. Abused children who live residential children's home are subjects. They are 10 persons the age of 6-15 years. They are treated with massage for about 25 minutes. Giving massage lets them relaxed. Sometimes they took a nap and told their feelings. The way of touching body is efficacious for being relaxed. It is supposed that relaxation allows them to rely on a particular person and the effect of their feelings release.

The conceptual components of hope in two languages: The case of English-Filipino bilinguals

Salanga, Maria Guadalupe Corpuz Counseling & Educational Psych, De La Salle University, Manila, Philippines Yabut, Homer J. Psychology Department, De La Salle University-Manila, Manila, Philippines

The present study inquired into the conceptual components of hope in two languages, English and Filipino. Participants from tertiary-level institutions provided written narratives of experiences wherein they felt hope (or pag-asa) and experiences wherein they felt the loss of hope (or kawalan ng pag-asa). Twenty-eight participants completed the Filipino language version of the questionnaire and 29 completed the English language version. Core ideas were extracted from the narratives and subjected to thematic analysis. Findings reveal that narratives in English and Filipino share similarities in the role of actual or perceived social support in inducing and sustaining feelings of hope.

Disturbed eating behaviour and attitudes in children: The effect of BMI, pubertal development and gender.

Sand, Liv VASSØY, Norway Stormark, Kjell Morten Unifob helse, University of Bergen, Bergen, Norway

The purpose of this study was to investigate the connection between eating problems, weight, and puberty in a community sample (n=5160) of

children aged 10-13 years. Children's self-report on Eating Disturbance Scale (EDS-5) were compared with Body Mass Index (BMI) and pubertal state. The results support the hypothesis that eating disorders symptoms are most frequent in girls, and that pubertal development might increase the risk of such problems. The predictive value of reported weight is low, and the relevance of pubertal state is different in girls and boys. This gender effect highlights subjective elements of children's body self perception that should be further adressed.

Spanish version of the Anxiety Sensitivity Index-3

Sandin, Bonifacio Psychology, Universidad Nac. Educ. Dist., Madrid, Spain Chorot, Paloma Psychology, Universidad Nac. Educ. Dist., Madrid, Spain Santed, Miguel A. Psychology, Universidad Nac. Educ. Dist., Madrid, Spain Valiente, Rosa M. Psychology, Universidad Nac. Educ. Dist., Madrid, Spain

The Anxiety Sensitivity Index—3 (ASI-3) is a new 18-item self-report multidimensional instrument designed to assess the three best replicated dimensions of anxiety sensitivity, i.e., Physical, Cognitive and Social Concerns. In the present study we examined the factor structure of the Spanish version of the ASI-R in a nonclinical sample. Exploratory and confirmatory factor analyses indicated a hierarchical factor structure consisting of 3 lower-order factors and 1 higher-order factor; the 3 lower-order factors were identical to the ones reported by Taylor et al. (2007) and support the three anxiety sensitivity dimensions. Suggestions for the clinical usefulness of the scale are reported.

Pretend play of children from Brazilian Communities

Santos, Ana Dept. Experimental Psychology, Universidade de São Paulo, São Paulo, Brazil

This work investigated pretend play of Brazilian children of three communities: a rural village, Xocó Indians and Mocambo Black.This study was based in naturalistic observation of 92 children from 2 to 12 years old in their free outdoor activities. Results indicated that: Symbolic play is a very close representation of their parents life. Realistic subjects prevailed over fantasy ones, and a strong gender stereotype was detected. These results were consistent with our hypotheses about some existing particularities in the development, that are associated with the cultural and familiar enviroment of the children.

Effects of the imagery rehearsal therapy in the posttraumatic stress disorder's symptoms of women victims of intrafamiliar violence

Santos, Pablo Granada University, Granada, Spain Argueta, Linda Psychology, Technological University of El, Granada, Spain Miró, Elena Personality, Assessment and Ps, Granada University, Granada, Spain

OBJECTIVES. To analyze the efficacy of the imagery rehearsal therapy (IRT) for the nightmares and the main symptoms presented by women victims of intrafamiliar violence with postraumatic stress disorder (PTSD). METHOD. Twenty women (n=10 control group and n=10 treatment group) fulfilled several questionnaire about PTSD and emotional disturbances. RESULTS. The evaluation post-intervention (one month of therapy with one semanal session) shows significant decreases in the frequency and malestar due to nightmares and also in the main symptoms of PTSD (reexperimentation, activation and avoidment). CONCLUSIONS. IRT can be an affective and efficient treatment not only for nightmares but also for PTSD.

The early education and the development in the pre-school years at the children of Romania: Pilot study of the PROMESED project, financed by CNMP, nr. 91064/18.09.2007

Sassu, Raluca Dept. of Psychology, University, Sibiu, Romania Giurgiu, Laura Dept. of Sport, University, Sibiu, Romania Bobarnea, Amfiana Dept. of Psychology, University, Sibiu, Romania

Objectives: - Localization of the conditions of the early education in the institutions of pre-school instruction in Romania; - Evaluation of the levels of cognitive, social-emotional and psycho-motor development, on age groups; - Determination of a connection between the programs of early instruction and the levels of development; Methodology: the NEPSY battery, questionnaires for the parents and teachers, observation protocols, etc. Subjects: a representative sample of the institutionalized, pre-school population from the city of Sibiu; Debates: the localization of profiles of development, the connections between different fields of development to assure the support for the growth of the educational ability.

Home based psychological intervention for disaster affected children

Satapathy, Sujata PPCCI, NIDM, New Delhi, India

Psychological reactions and behaviour of 45 children aged 7-11 years were observed and assessed on Impact of Events Scale, Beck Anxiety Inventory, General Health Questionnaire, and Amritsar Depression Inventory. 15 children sustaining fire injuries and having stress, anxiety and depression symptoms underwent an intensive ten-day homebased psychological intervention program, comprising of play therapy, psycho-education, counseling, and community-based outreach programs. Although for each case, depending on the individual need, little flexibility was adopted in the intervention, children showed significant improvements in their behaviour, emotional expressions and overall social interaction. Significant mean differences were found between pre and post-intervention scores on different scales. The wider applicability of this could be tested across countries and across disasters.

The "openness" of a society determines the relationship between self-esteem and subjective well-being (1): A cross-societal comparison

Sato, Kosuke Dept. of Behavioral Science, Hokkaido University, Sapporo, Japan Yuki, Masaki Behavioral Science, Hokkaido University, Sapporo, Japan Takemura, Kosuke Behavioral Science, Hokkaido University, Sapporo, Japan Schug, Joanna Behavioral Science, Hokkaido University, Sapporo, Japan Oishi, Shigehiro Psychology, University of Virginia, Charlottesville, USA

From the evolutionary/adaptationist perspective, we propose that the difference in the impact of self-esteem on subjective well-being (SWB) between North Americans and East Asians can be explained by the societal difference in relational mobility, a socio-ecological factor reflecting the amount of opportunities to form new relationships, if necessary. We, as predicted, found that (1) the association between self-esteem and SWB was stronger in the US than in Japan, (2) perceived relational mobility was higher in the US than in Japan, and (3) the cultural difference (1) disappeared when perceived relational mobility was entered into the regression model.

The effects of anonymity of the self and the other on self-disclosure

Sato, Hirotsune University of Tsukuba, Tsukuba, Japan Yoshida, Fujio Comprehensive Human Science, University of Tsukuba, Tsukuba-city, Japan

The effects of anonymity on self-disclosure were investigated in a CMC situation by separately manipulating anonymity of the self and the other. Sixty female undergraduate students were randomly assigned to a 2 (self: anonymous or non-anonymous) $\times$ 2 (other: anonymous or non-anonymous) experimental design. The anonymity was manipulated by presenting information such as the photo, name, and sex of the self or the other on the computer screen. Results indicated that the anonymity of the self had no effects on disclosure, whereas anonymity of the other decreased disclosure.

The implicit - explicit achievement motive congruence: A condition of flow experience

Schüler, Julia Inst. für Psychologie, Universität Zürich, Zürich, Switzerland

Flow conditions were analyzed by referring to implicit-explicit motive congruence research. This research assumes that achievement motive congruent individuals are more able to bring themselves into situations that fit their motives. We suppose that this motive-situation fit facilitates involvement in an activity (a flow characteristic). A correlational study confirmed that achievement motive congruence is related to flow. An experimental study revealed that achievement motive congruent participants only reported more flow than incongruent participants, when they were in a motive-situation fit condition (achievement), but not in non motive-situation fit conditions (neutral, affiliation).

Investigating the validity of the modality and redundancy principle in multimedia learning for complex texts

Schüler, Anne Inst. of Psychologie, Universität Tübingen, Tübingen, Germany Scheiter, Katharina Media Psychology, University of Tuebingen, Tübingen, Germany Gerjets, Peter Knowledge Acquisition with Hyp, KMRC, Tübingen, Germany

We investigated if the modality and the redundancy principle (Mayer, 2001) also hold for longer, complex texts and if the pacing of the presentation acts as a moderating variable. 122 students were tested in a 3 (audio vs. visual vs. both) x 2 (system vs. self paced) design. The conducted ANOVAs show no modality or redundancy effect for recall and transfer performance neither in the system-paced nor in the learner-paced condition. Currently we explore via eye tracking why the principles may not be valid when presenting long and complex texts and if the prerequisites for finding the principles are fulfilled.

BEFKI - Berlin Test of Fluid and Crystallized Intelligence

Schipolowski, Stefan IQB, Humboldt-Universität zu Berlin, Berlin, Germany Schroeders, Ulrich Wilhelm, Oliver

The BEFKI (Berlin Test of Fluid and Crystallized Intelligence) is a newly developed psychometric test which measures fluid (45 minutes) and crystallized (20 minutes) intelligence. The fluid intelligence part differentiates between three content aspects (verbal, numerical, figural) using relational reasoning, mathematical reasoning and Charkow-style items. The crystallized intelligence scale assesses general knowledge in humanities, social and natural sciences across 16 domains. We report empirical findings of a study with 599 lower secondary pupils. The factor structure of the measures and the relations with criteria (a vocabulary task, two traditional measures of fluid intelligence, and school grades) are evaluated.

Cross-modal interference in object recognition

Schmid, Carmen Inst. für Neurowissen. Systeme, Medizin. Universität Hamburg, Hamburg, Germany Büchel, Christian Dep for Systems Neuroscience, University med center Hamburg, Hamburg, Germany Rose, Michael Dep for Systems Neuroscience, University med center Hamburg, Hamburg, Germany

This fMRI-study aimed to investigate cross-modal interference between visual and acoustic object recognition areas. Stimuli were presented under two levels of recognizability (with and without visual/acoustic noise). Participants were instructed to alternately attend to one of the two modalities and perform an object recognition task while simultaneously being exposed to stimuli in the other modality. We found increasing activity with increasing recognizability in visual and acoustic object processing related areas. Within these regions reduced activation under conditions of high compared to low cross-modal recognizability was observed.

Psychological and neural foundations of the emotional Stroop effect in social phobia

Schmidt, Stephanie Biolog. und Klin. Psychologie, Universität Jena, Jena, Germany Miltner, Wolfgang H. R. Jena, Germany Straube, Thomas Biological and Clinical Psych., Friedrich-Schiller-University, Jena, Germany

Slowing of reaction times to disorder-related words was repeatedly demonstrated in individuals with anxiety disorders in emotional Stroop tasks. However, the psychological and neural basis underlying this interference effect is not well understood. For its investigation, social phobics and healthy volunteers performed an emotional Stroop task while subjects were scanned with functional magnetic resonance imaging. The used paradigm provided the possibility to investigate slow and fast interference effects. The results indicate a dominant contribution of fast interference effects to the emotional Stroop phenomenon. Furthermore, this effect was positively correlated with activation of dorsomedial prefrontal cortex and rostral anterior cingulate cortex.

What is the fundamental principle of information or knowledge?: Looking for a useful definition and universal properties - An interdisciplinary view

Schott, Franz Dresden, Germany

Information processing is omnipresent in human beings, e. g. during immune defense, metabolism, actions, thinking, and philosophizing. Is there a common fundamental principle of these different manifestations of information? The answer proposed is: in all forms of information processing appear schemata of changing states. The advantage of the interdisciplinary view is demonstrated with different problems: Looking for a useful definition and universal properties of information; the differentiation between knowledge, emotion, and motivation, between human used and machine used information. In contrast to growing conceptual diversification in psychology the proposed view offers a parsimonious and universal approach of the concept "information".

Mental health help-seeking after interpersonal violence: An integrative model

Schreiber, Viola Inst. für Psychologie, Freie Universität Berlin, Ingolstadt, Germany Renneberg, Babette Psychology, FU Berlin, Berlin, Germany Maercker, Andreas Inst. für Psychopathologie, Universität Zürich, Zürich, Switzerland

A model integrating empirical data and theory was developed describing why survivors of interpersonal violence refrain from, delay or engage in mental-health help-seeking. It delineates individual, interpersonal and sociocultural parameters relevant for seeking psychosocial care. To verify the model an online-survey of survivors of interpersonal violence was conducted in a German speaking sample from the general population (age range 17-66). The model was tested with structural equation modeling and the adjusted model is presented along with inferences about its clinical implications.

An extended 4-phases-testmodel for clinical trials and its application on clinical psychology publications in the German-speaking countries

Schui, Gabriel ZPID - Universität Trier, Trier, Germany Krampen, Günter Direktor, ZPID - Universität Trier, Trier, Germany

Objectives: Classification of clinical psychology publications to an extended 4-phases-testmodel for clinical trials. Methods: Assignment of clinical psychology publications from the German psychology database PSYNDEX to the different phases using a combined automatic/intellectual procedure. Results: Most of the assigned 16,467 empirical papers refer to test-phases 0,1,4 and 5 (developmental-phase, screening- phase, therapeutic-use-studies, and prevention/quality-of-life- trials). Studies assigned to test-phases 2 and 3 (randomized-controlled-trials, multi-center studies/meta-analyses) were published less frequently. Conclusions: German clinical psychology has an extensive reservoir of publications on empirically supported psychotherapy at its disposal. Deficits are in publications on randomized-controlled-trials, multi-center studies, and meta-analyses.

Flow painting: The connection between flow experience and graphic talent among children

Schulz, Nina Universität Hildesheim, Hildesheim, Germany

Flow experience is seen as an important element of optimal motivation, therefore plays an important role in the support of talent. Different motivational factors (flow, self concept etc.) while painting were investigated in an empirical longitudinal study (three measurement times) with 123 primary school pupils (self assessment). The results show a meaningful connection between the graphic talent of children and the flow experience when painting. Therefore, in order to encourage graphically talented children, the motivation, especially the flow, should always be taken into account along side the teaching of more advanced techniques.

Functional integration in a language network during orthographic word processing in normal and dyslexic readers: A dynamic causal modelling study

Schurz, Matthias Inst. für Psychologie, Universität Salzburg, Salzburg, Austria Kronbichler, Martin Psychologie, Universität Salzburg, Salzburg, Austria Wimmer, Heinz NW Fakultät, Universität Salzburg, Salzburg, Austria

This functional magnetic resonance imaging study investigated differences in the reading related brain response of 20 dyslexic and 19 matched nonimpaired German readers. Brain activation was measured for 180 items (words, pseudohomophones, pseudowords). Dyslexic readers exhibited lower activation in a left occipitotemporal and higher activation in a right occipital region and also in several left frontal regions. Dynamic causal models (Friston et al, 2003) were constructed for brain areas involved in normal and dyslexic reading. We found that functional coupling of brain areas depended highly on letter string familiarity and differed markedly between dyslexic and nonimpaired readers.

Why distribution anomalies unveil an error in psychology

Schwarz, Michael Bad Brückenau, Germany

Distribution anomalies are usually explained by independent variables. However, the analysis of more than 8000 patients and 27 bio-psycho-social scales suggests an alternative explanatory approach, which is of considerable methodological and application-oriented importance. The author arrives at the conclusion that a meaningful monitoring of subjective health factors can be realized only, if scientific importance is ascribed to distribution-generating, item-related self-regulatory processes of the "measuring equipment 'man'" independently from the "measuring equipment 'questionnaire'". Hence, to correct error theory as the basic axiomatic premise of psychometrical methodology, a psychologically well-founded theory of fluctuation of validity is proposed.

Training coherence and problem-solving skills in video conferences

Schweizer, Karin Psychology III, University Mannheim, Mannheim, Germany Pächter, Manuela Inst. für Päd. Psychologie, Universität Graz, Graz, Austria Maier, Brigitte Inst. Pädagogische Psychologie, Universität Graz, Graz, Austria

Compared to face-to-face communication, communication in video conferences suffers im-pairments which may lead to difficulties in achieving a common ground of mutual under-standing and in maintaining coherence. Consequently, groups may show a lower perform-ance especially in complex group tasks such as problem-solving tasks. In an experimental study the effectiveness of different trainings was investigated (problem-solving training, co-herence training, combination of problem-solving and coherence training, no training). 24 groups of three members each were analysed. All trainings influenced the discourse and the groups' means to establish a common ground. However, only the problem-solving training lead to a higher group performance.

Is memory performance in the stem-completion task related to executive measures?

Sebastian, Maria Victoria Psicologia Basica I, Univ. Complutense de Madrid, Madrid, Spain Menor, Julio Psicologia, Univ. Oviedo, Oviedo, Spain

This study examined performance in the stem-completion task (SCT) of Alzheimer patients (AD), elderly control (C), and young students. It was found a disease effect in SCT. Furthermore, some AD and C carried out two tasks, a Brown-Peterson (B-P) task, and a dual task. AD had a lower performance than C in both tasks. Correlations between priming effect in SCT, and the scores in the two tasks (B-P task and dual task), were obtained in AD y C groups. Negative correlation was found between priming and perseverations scores only in AD. Data were explained in terms of executive problems in AD.

The promotion of mental health in primary care: Preliminary results of a group therapy program

Segura, Jordi Psychology, Blanquerna Faculty, Barcelona, Spain Cebrià, Jordi Psychology, Blanquerna Faculty, Barcelona, Spain Farriols, Núria Psychology, Blanquerna Faculty, Barcelona, Spain Palma, Carol Psychology, Blanquerna Faculty, Barcelona, Spain Cañete, Josep Psychiatry, Mataro's Hospital, Mataró, Spain Vidal, Raquel Psychology, Blanquerna Faculty, Barcelona, Spain Ger, Sandra Psychology, Blanquerna Faculty, Barcelona, Spain Ferrer, Marta Psychology, Blanquerna Faculty, Barcelona, Spain Segarra, Gerard Psychology, Blanquerna Faculty, Barcelona, Spain Vázquez, María Psychology, Mataró's Hospital, Mataró, Spain Fernández, Victoria Psychology, Blanquerna Faculty, Barcelona, Spain

Objectives: To observe changes in psychopathology and quality of life in patients that take part in psychotherapy groups integrated in primary care. Method: A randomized longitudinal study was developed with 32 patients with adaptive disorder and anxious-depressive symptomatology. Clinical assessments were carried out at pre and post-treatment by Symptom Check List, Subjective Quality of Life, Self-esteem. Results: Changes in the global severity of symptoms (p= 0,021, Wilcoxon test). Especially in anxiety(p= 0,008), hostility(p= 0,007) and in subjective quality of life(p=0,014). Conclusions: We observed the improvement in psychopathology and the perception of wellbeing in patients who were attended in primary care.

Neuronal correlates of facial emotion discrimination in adolescence

Seiferth, Nina Y. Department of Psychiatry, RWTH Aachen University, Aachen, Germany Pauly, Katharina Department of Psychiatry, RWTH Aachen University, Aachen, Germany Kellermann, Thilo Department of Psychiatry, RWTH Aachen University, Aachen, Germany Shah, N. Jon Institute of Neurosciences, Reseach Center Jülich, Jülich, Germany Schneider, Frank Department of Psychiatry, RWTH Aachen University, Aachen, Germany Kircher, Tilo Department of Psychiatry, RWTH Aachen University, Aachen, Germany Habel, Ute Department of Psychiatry, RWTH Aachen University, Aachen, Germany

Introduction: It is known that facial emotion discrimination is still developing during adolescence, although the underlying changes in brain activity are unclear to date. Hence, the aim of this study was to explore and to compare the emotion discrimination ability and its neural correlates in adolescents and young adults. Methods: An emotion discrimination task was applied while fMRI data were acquired. Results: Data analysis revealed that during adolescence predominantly subcortical and occipital brain areas participate in emotion discrimination in faces, whereas in adulthood the participation of prefrontal areas increases. Discussion: The activation of the frontal cortex might reflect the advanced 'policing' influence on other brain structures and its relevance in regulation of emotions.

Global-local interface in advertising: Construction of desire of Bengali consumer

Sengupta, Amitava PSYCHOLOGY, UNIVERSITY OF CALCUTTA, Kolkata, India De, Sonali PSYCHOLOGY, UNIVERSITY OF CALCUTTA, Kolkata, India

Multiplicity of product availability has made it obligatory to make advertisements more penetrating so that they can make the products more meaningful in terms of their social-cultural connotation increasing their need. In the present study 180 advertisements representing four product-categories from Bengali periodicals of four time-periods were content-analyzed to see how feature-attribution to products changed over time. Analyses show that feature attribution to products changed over time to make them more culturally meaningful to the Bengali consumers in terms of their desire and thus signified object-choice. Through advertising the 'object choice' is now calculatively constructed by the logic of consumption.

Faces of power. Face-ism and poltical leadership in the TV news of Germany, USA and UAE.

Senokozlieva, Maria Social and Media Psychology, University of Cologne, Köln, Germany Pennig, Sibylle Social and Media Psychology, University of Cologne, Cologne, Germany Bente, Gary Social and Media Psychology, University of Cologne, Cologne, Germany

The concept of "face-ism" implies that pictures of people showing more face than body convey impressions of dominance. Based on this assumption the study addresses cultural differences in the presentation and the perception of political leaders in the TV-news from Germany, USA and UAE. Face-ism is measured by means of a novel software tool. Perceptual effects were analysed on the bases of selected clips from the three countries representing different face-ism scores. To avoid stereotype activation the study uses computer animations of neutral characters instead of the original videos. The novel methodologies as well as first results will be presented.

The effect of training life skills on social adjustment, self esteem and achievement motive

Sepahmansour, Mojgan Dept. of Psycology, Islamic Azad University, Tehran, Islamic Republic of Iran
the aim of this study was to examine the effect of training life skills on social adjustment,self esteem and achievement motive. the sample of 40 students university was selected and randomly placed in control and exprerimental group. using pre-post experimental group design. the results showed that there was a statistically significant at(Alfa= 0/05). the experimental group had gotten higher score that control group. suggested that such training programmes should be more support.

A statistical theory of estimation in psychophysical experiments

Seri, Raffaello Dipt. di Economia, Università dell'Insubria, Varese, Italy Bernasconi, Michele Dipartimento di Economia, Università dell'Insubria, Varese, Italy Choirat, Christine Dept of Quantitative Methods, Universidad de Navarra, Pamplona, Spain
We propose a general statistical framework for psychophysical experiments. The answer of a subject depends on the stimuli through an unknown function f. f is customarily studied in an experiment in which J subjects are gathered, the same I questions are proposed to each individual who provides a set of I responses. This rises the point whether a large J or I is more important for the design of an experiment. We propose an estimator of f and consider several cases in detail. Properties of tests and model selection are also considered.

Different correlations between sex steroids and fluid intelligence in prepubertal and pubertal boys

ShangGuan, FangFang Center of Human Development, Institute of Psychology, Beijing, People's Republic of China
Recently hormones were believed to remodel brain structures involved in learning and memory, as well as intelligence. The aim of this paper is to investigate the possible difference between hormone effects on fluid intelligence of prepubertal and pubertal boys. 49 prepubertal boys and 63 pubertal boys were recruited for fluid intelligence test. In the prepubertal group, no correlation was found between salivary testosterone levels and fluid intelligence, while in the pubertal group, significantly negative correlation was found. It is implicated from these results that sex steroid surge in puberty play an important role in fluid intelligence development.

Social facilitation in the Stroop task and the role of strategic inhibition

Sharma, Dinkar Psychology, University of Kent, Canterbury, United Kingdom Massey-Booth, Rob Psychology, University of Kent, Canterbury, United Kingdom Brown, Rupert Psychology, University of sussex, Brighton, United Kingdom Huguet, Pascal Laboratoire de Psychologie Cog, Aix-Marseille Université, Marseille, France
The presence of a 'naïve' confederate can reduce the Stroop interference shown by participants (Huguet, Galvaing, Monteil & Dumas, 1999). We present evidence that social facilitation in the Stroop task is caused by strategic inhibition of the distracter word. Huguet et al.'s (1999) social facilitation finding was replicated, and delta plot analyses revealed that participants in the mere presence condition were strongly inhibiting distracter information. This assertion is supported by the fact that no distracter inhibition, and indeed no social facilitation, was found when the RSI was decreased so that participants were less able to prepare for every trial.

The relationships between migration and children's creative thinking

Shi, Baoguo Dept. of Psychology, Capital Normal University, Beijing, People's Republic of China Shen, Jiliang Institute of Developmental Psy, Beijing Normal University, Beijing, Haidian District, People's Republic of China Plucker, Jonathan A. Center for Evaluation & Ed, Indiana University, Bloomington, Indiana, USA Lin, Chongde Institute of Developmental Psy, Beijing Normal University, Beijing, Haidian District, People's Republic of China Xu, Jingjing Counseling Center of Mental He, Chinese University of Politica, Beijing, Haidian District, People's Republic of China
Using test and questionnaire method, investigated the relationship between migration from rural area to city and 909 elementary school students' creative thinking. Study 1 compared creative thinking among migrant children, rural children and urban children. Study 2 compared creative thinking among short-term, mid-term and long-term migrant children. Study 3 examined the path from migration to creativity. The results showed: 1). Migrant children obtained significant higher score than rural children on creative thinking. 2).Short-term migrant children got significant lower score than mid-term and long-term migrant children on creative thinking. 3). Migration related factors have both direct and indirect effects on creativity.

Chinese version of the paranormal belief scale

Shiah, Yung-Jong General Education Center, Chienkuo Technology University, Changhua, Taiwan Chiang, Shih-Kuang Clinical Psychology, Yu Li Veterans Hospital, Yuli town, Taiwan Wu, Ming-Hsun International Business Adminis, Chienkuo Technology University, Changhua, Taiwan Tam, Wai-Cheong Carl Psychology, ChungYuan Christian University, Chung Li, Taiwan
Many studies have explored the relationship between paranormal belief, religiosity, cognitive abilities and mental health. It is also of interest to explore theses topics in Chinese society, since it has not been studied so far. The first goal of the present study therefore is to construct the Chinese version of the Revised Paranormal Belief Scale (RPBS) with back-translation procedure. Participants were 300 college studies. The data has being analyzed. The construct validity and reliability of the RPBS will be reported.

Preschooler's appraisals of other's emotions and emotional dissemblance toward the other person

Shibata, Toshio Dept. of Psychology, Hokusei Gakuen University, Brookline, USA
This study examined preschooler's appraisal of other's emotion and emotional dissemblance. Sixty children listened to stories in which the protagonist would hide his/her emotion toward the other person. Children were asked how would the protagonist really feel, how would the protagonist appraise the other person's emotion, and why the protagonist hid his/her own emotion. The results indicated that children recognized adequately the protagonist's emotion and his/her appraisal of the other's emotion. Though even 6-year-olds could not understand the reason of the protagonist's emotional dissemblance, children interpreted the protagonist's emotional dissemblance coherently in their own way.

Reproducibility of cortical activation in expert motor skill: A NIRS study with nursing actions

Shiraishi, Tomoko Nagoya, Japan Oi, Misato Graduate School of Information, Nagoya University, Nagoya, Japan Ito, Hiroshi Graduate School of Information, Nagoya University, Nagoya, Japan Saito, Hirofumi Graduate School of Information, Nagoya University, Nagoya, Japan
Using 48 channel near-infrared spectroscopy, we measured the cortical activation in a nursing teacher who repeated nursing actions twice. Three

factors were manipulated to construct three experimental conditions: observing videotaped own nursing actions with a monitor or recalling one's own actions without (M+/M-), imitating 'with-patient' action or 'without-patient' (P+/P-), and with verbal-communication or without (C+/C-); M+P-C-, M-P+C-, M-P+C+ conditions. Based on the concentration changes in oxyHb in the teacher between the first and the second trials, the number of positively correlated channels are relatively high: M+P-C-(43/48-channels), M-P+C-(39/48), M-P+C+(42/48). This suggests cortical activation patterns in the teacher are reproducible.

Interpersonal perceptions as predictors of group performance

Sierra, Vicenta Dept. of Quantitative Methods, ESADE, Barcelona, Spain Solanas, Antonio Behavioral Sciences Methods, University of Barcelona, Barcelona, Spain Andrés, Amara Behavioral Sciences Methods, University of Barcelona, Barcelona, Spain
In the present research, dyadic global measurements of interpersonal perceptions were used to forecast groups' performance. Specifically, groups of students were studied in a real situation of educational assignment and marks were gathered as an indicator of groups' performance. Our results show that final marks are accounted for an only global measurement of interpersonal perceptions. By means of linear regression analysis we respectively obtained R2 = .219 and R2 = .457 for group sizes equal to four and five. These results partially support that dyadic approaches can be useful to predict groups' performance in social environments.

Male domination as an obstacle to AIDS prevention for women in the Sub Saharan African culture

Simeone, Arnaud ISPEF, Université Lyon 2, Lyon, France Diakite, Mariam ISPEF, Université LYON 2, LYON, France
Objective: The research aims to identify the obstacles to AIDS prevention for Sub Saharan African women perceived by AIDS prevention activists. This research is based on male domination theory. Method: Fourteen interviews were conducted with French AIDS prevention activists working with migrants from the sub Saharan area. The interviewees are from different organizations in the city of Lyon (France). Results: Only female activists consider Male domination as a key factor of Sub Saharan African women HIV infection and as an obstacle for AIDS prevention. No interviewee uses this concept in theirs practices. Male domination is perceived as a cultural fact not to be questioned.

T-data measures as valuable alternatives in personality assessment

Singh, Umed Deptt. Of PSychology, Kurukshetra University, Kurukshetra, India Verma, Nidhi Deptt. Of PSychology, Kurukshetra University, Kurukshetra, India
Most of the studies to date by psychologists in the field of personality have depended on Q- (Questionnaire) and L-data (Life record). Both L- data & Q-data are easy to gather,& make good sense to the psychologists because of their face validity. However, L-data and Q-data are liable to various distortions such as judgmental errors, ignorance or dishonesty by subjects. T-data measures (objective tests) refer to the direct measurement of behavior in a standard situation. T-data measures are not dependent on the subjects' evaluation, but measure direct reactions. This paper is aimed to identifiy various apects of personality by T-data.

Personality structure of Hindi speaking Indians

Singh, Jitendra K. Singh Starategic Behaviour, DIPR, DRDO,, New Delhi, India

Extending the cultural approach to personality this study adopted lexical analysis to uncover the structure of personality in India. Focusing on Hindi language spoken by a majority segment of Indian population the relevant adjectives were analyzed. Based on this analysis the structure and taxonomy of personality in Hindi speaking Indians was examined. The data were factor analyzed from 1 to 7 factor solutions using varimax rotation. The best solution emerged at six factors. The finding indicates the presence of a six factor structure of personality which is broader than what is proposed in big five factors' theory.

Mother's sense of competence and child's behavior in response to parent training program encouraging child's emotional development in Latvia

Skreitule-Pikse, Inga Dept. of Psychology, University of Latvia, Riga, Latvia Miltuze, Anika Department of Psychology, University of Latvia, Riga, Latvia Sebre, Sandra Department of Psychology, University of Latvia, Riga, Latvia

The goal of the study was to assess the effectiveness of the parent training program. 60 mothers of preschool children ages one to five participated in the program. The mother's sense of competence and child's behavior was assessed before and after participation in the parent training program and 6 months later. The children's behavior was evaluated by both their mothers and teachers. Mothers participating in the parent training program during the post-training evaluation reported higher ratings of parenting sense of competence and less child's externalizing behavior problems.

Method of evaluation of the psychic change of children who undergo group psychoanalytical psychotherapy

Slapak, Sara Psicología, Universidad de Buenos Aires, Buenos Aires, Argentina Luzzi, Ana Dept. de Psicología, Universidad de Buenos Aires, Buenos Aires, Argentina Cervone, Nelida Psicología, Universidad de Buenos Aires, Buenos Aires, Argentina Ramos, Laura Psicología, Universidad de Buenos Aires, Buenos Aires, Argentina Grigoravicius, Marcelo Psicología, Universidad de Buenos Aires, Buenos Aires, Argentina Nimcowicz, Diana Psicología, Universidad de Buenos Aires, Buenos Aires, Argentina

Objective: To describe a method for the evaluation of the psychic change in children who undergo group psychoanalitical therapy. Method: Development of analitical codes and subcodes which are assigned to observational records of group psychoanalitical psychotherapys sessions; construction of a data matrix for qualitative data analysis, which collects codes grouped in families and comprises the period and the sequence of the sessions that are being studied. Elaboration a report for each template. Results: Reconstruction of the psychotherapeutic process of each patient in the group psychotherapy context. Conclusions: the method can be extended to individual psychotherapies and to other conceptual frames.

A system for scoring motive imagery in pictures

Slavova, Iva Allg. und Angew. Psychologie, Universität Tübingen, Tübingen, Germany Puca, Rosa Maria Insitute of Pedagogy, University of Bochum, Bochum, Germany Üstünsöz-Beurer, Dörthe General and Applied Psychology, University of Tübingen, Tübingen, Germany

Achievement, Affiliation/Intimacy and Power belong to the most important human needs, affecting virtually any aspect of human behavior. Winter (1991) developed a system for scoring these three motives in running texts. To date however no such

system for pictures exists. On the basis of Winter's manual we developed a new system for identifying motive imagery in pictures. It contains categories referring to possible manifestations and implications of the three motives in any kind of pictorial material. First applications of this instrument in a cross-cultural context indicate that it can be reliably used to determine the motivational contents of pictures.

Interhemispheric interaction during perception of words of different emotional valence and nonwords

Sommer, Werner Inst. für Psychologie, Humboldt-Universität zu Berlin, Berlin, Germany Olada, Ella Psychology, Humboldt-University, Berlin, Germany Schacht, Annekathrin Inst. für Psychologie, Humboldt-Universität zu Berlin, Berlin, Germany

What is the role of interhemispheric interaction in processing words of different emotional valence and nonwords? 12 males performed structural decision tasks with right or left hand to nonwords (NW) and words of positive, negative, and neutral emotional valence (Wpos, Wneg, and Wneu) presented to left and right visual fields (RVF, LVF). We calculated the so-called FMN score, which increases as mean RT or the variance of the RT distribution decreases. In contrast to Wneg and NW, the FMN showed RVF/Left Hemisphere superiority for Wpos, which was independent of directness of access, that is, inter- or intrahemispheric transfer.

Perfectionism scale on interpersonal relation for Chinese college students

Song, Guangwen Research Center of Psychology, Qufu Normal University, Qufu, People's Republic of China Li, Jianwei Faculty of Education, Qufu Normal University, Qufu, People's Republic of China

We compiled a native multi–demension perfectionism scale from the perspective of interpersonal relation for Chinese college students that fits the Chinese cultural background well. The scale consisted of 34 items, five Dimensions:compared with the others, self-oriented, others orientation, other-other oriented, community-oriented. Five dimensions can explain 57.168% of the total variance, the items load is 0.403 to 0.822. The homogeneity reliability of the scale is 0.734 ~0.844, the retest reliability is 0.730~0.836, p<0.05, p<0.01, and RMSEA, RMR, NFI, CFI, GFI is 0.062, 0.070, 0.823, 0.814 .

Using the LLTM for the determination of item generating rationals for the comprehension of reading

Sonnleitner, Philipp Inst. für Psychologie, Universität Wien, Wien, Austria

Even though the need for assessing reading comprehension (rc) is increasing, a theory-based construction of rc-items is very rare. For that reason, an item generating rational has been developed in consideration of the CI-model of Kintsch (1998) and the inference-classification of Graesser et al. (1994) and finally validated by using Fischer's LLTM on an approved reading comprehension test. The study provides much information for further test-developments in this field and demonstrates once more the usefulness of the LLTM to verify construct-validity and analyze task-requirements.

The interaction of cognitive and social factors in creativity

Sousokolova, Irina Lab. of Diagnostic, Psychological Institute, Moscow, Russia

To overcome the common difficulties in the testing of creativity, we use the "creative field method" (D.Bogoyvlenskaya) which diagnoses creativity as a quality and measures it as a quantity in a single experimental framework. Assuming that "intellectual self action" (ISA), defined as an individual's

cognitive initiative to go beyond the limit of a given task, represents the core of creativity, we study the genesis of ISA via different types of family relations. Our results show that ISA is determined by social factors, and that the cognitive and social initiative of an individual have common roots.

An exploration of masculinity, femininity, sexual fantasy and masturbation as predictors of marital satisfaction

Soyer Ozer, Asli Bengi Semerci Enstitusu, Istanbul, Turkey

The major problems that this study adressed were the identification of group differences on masculinity, femininity, monthly frequency of sexual fantasy, monthly frequency of masturbation, and marital satisfaction, as well as the investigation of which predictor variables account for a significant proportion of the criterion variables monthly frequency of sexual fantasy, monthly frequency of masturbation, and marital satisfaction.Results revealed that, gender, frequency of sexual intercourse, and age found to be the predictors of monthly frequency of sexual fantasy. Also, monthly frequency of sexual intercourse and monthly frequency of masturbation contributed to the prediction of marital satisfaction. The findings were discussed in the light of the relevant literature.

Effect of frequency in the fragment completion task with unique and multiple solutions

Spataro, Pietro Dept. of Psychology, University Sapienza, Rome, Italy Rossi-Arnaud, Clelia Psychology, University Sapienza, Rome, Italy Pazzano, Paola Psychology, University Sapienza, Rome, Italy Salutari, Manuela Psychology, University Sapienza, Rome, Italy

Previous research has almost invariably found an advantage of low-frequency words (LF) in the Fragment Completion Task when only unique solutions were allowed. In two experiments frequency effects were assessed on unique and multiple-solution fragments using the same methods of construction. In the first experiment priming was greater for high-frequency (HF) words with multiple fragments, but slightly better for LF-words with unique fragments; however, in the second experiment the advantage of HF-words was evident with both types of fragments. This effect was independent from test-awareness. A generate/recognize model was applied to explain these results.

Controlling automatic imitation recruits key processes involved in social cognition

Spengler, Stephanie Cognitive Neurology, MPI for Human Cog. & Brain, Leipzig, Germany von Cramon, D. Yves Cognitive Neurology, MPI for Human Cog. & Brain, Leipzig, Germany Brass, Marcel Dept. of Exp. Psychology, Ghent University, Ghent, Belgium

In neuroimaging studies the control of imitation (CI) activated regions (anterior-fronto-median-cortex (aFMC), temporo-parietal-junction (TPJ)), implicated in social-cognitive processing (SC). This suggests that IC requires mechanisms needed in SC. Here, overlapping functions of CI and SC were investigated in a within-subject fMRI study with four tasks tapping these functions. Commonly activated regions occurred in aFMC and TPJ. CI was further related to behavioural and neural correlates of SC. This supports the idea that CI recruits processes involved in SC, including the ability for representing one's own or others' intentions, and the capacity to differentiate between self- and other-related actions or perspectives.

Becoming hostile through gaming?: Longitudinal investigation of the influence of violent video games on aggression *Staude-Müller, Frithjof Inst. für Psychologie, Universität zu Kiel, Kiel, Germany*

This study was designed to identify antecedents and effects of violent video game use. About 600

German secondary school students (aged 12-16 years) completed a survey twice with an interval of one year assessing the relationships between video game habits and aggression-associated variables (aggressiveness, delinquency, aggressive attitudes, sensation seeking, empathy). Results of hierarchical regression analysis and structural equation models revealed concurrent and lagged effects of violent video game use on aggression variables. It is concluded that theoretical models need to be expanded to also include internal (e.g., motivational variables) and external (e.g., parental control) conditions of video gaming.

Intraindividual reaction time variability as a measure of circadian rhythms in cognitive control

Steinborn, Michael Inst. Verhaltenspsychologie, Universität Tübingen, Tübingen, Germany Rolke, Bettina Cognitive Psychology, University of Tübingen, Tübingen, Germany Bratzke, Daniel Cognitive Psychology, University of Tübingen, Tübingen, Germany Ulrich, Rolf Cognitive Psychology, University of Tübingen, Tübingen, Germany

We examined circadian rhythm effects on choice reaction time (RT) performance. To this end, 12 participants performed a digit comparison task in a 40-hour constant routine protocol. In addition to mean RT, we calculated intraindividual RT variability which is considered to reflect noise within the brain's neural control circuits. Circadian rhythm effects were observed for mean RT and variability, whereas RT variability was more sensitive to circadian effects than mean RT. This result is consistent with the current view of RT variability as a highly sensitive and task-independent signature of executive control functioning, which is influenced by the circadian rhythm.

Valence asymmetries in implicit and explicit social information processing

Stenberg, Georg Bunkeflostrand, Sweden Faraon, Montathar Psychology, Kristianstad University, Bunkeflostrand, Sweden

Does implicit social cognition fall prey to the same biases as explicit attitudes do? Participants in two experiments made forced-choice responses concerning the behaviours of a fictional protagonist, about whom information was successively revealed. Attitudes were probed by explicit evaluations and by the Implicit Association Test (IAT), and information processing models were fitted to the choice responses. An initial positivity bias and a negative attentional bias were found in explicit attitudes and choice behaviour. Implicit attitudes exhibited the same biases, although with less sensitivity.

Cointegration methodology

Stroe-Kunold, Esther Heidelberg, Germany Werner, Joachim Department of Psychology, University of Heidelberg, Heidelberg, Germany

Cointegration methodology allows treating non-stationary (i.e., integrated) time series as a multi-variate system if their linear combination is stationary. Despite its potential for psychological process research, it seems unfamiliar to most psychologists. This approach enables the investigation of non-stationary processes that are mutually interconnected (feedback and causal relations). Additionally, error-correction modeling allows analysing long- and short-term dynamics within a system consisting of various psychological processes. Furthermore, cointegration tests are instruments to detect spurious correlations between integrated time series. After a brief introduction, these methodological findings gained by means of Monte Carlo simulations as well as empirical analysis are further described.

The development of deaf children with cochlear implants: The parents' point of view

Suarez, Maria Developmental Psychology, University of La Laguna, La Laguna, Spain Rodríguez, Carmen RESEARCH IN EDUCATION, UNIVERSITY OF LA LAGUNA, LA LAGUNA. TENERIFE, Spain

The aim of the study was to assess the outcome of deaf children with cochlear implants (CI) from a broader perspective of quality of life or of the effects on the child and family from the point of view of parents. Participants included 15 mothers with typical hearing whose children were present users of CI. The parental views and experiences were surveyed using a Closed Format Questionnaire developed by O'Neill et al. (2004). The areas assessed were: communication, general functioning, well-being, social relationships, education, process and effect of implantation. The discussion will be focused on the overall effectiveness of implantation.

Influence of auditory feedback on speech output monitoring

Sugimori, Eriko Komaba, Japan

We investigated the influence of auditory feedback on speech output monitoring by using white noise mask. In the learning phase, we presented words to participants who then read aloud, lip-synched, or imagined reading them with or without white noise. In the monitoring phase, we asked participants whether each word had been read aloud or not. Lip-synched word were more likely to be misattributed to "Read aloud" in the white noise condition than in the not noise condition, suggesting that participants monitor whether they really read aloud or not on the basis of their mouse movement in the white noise condition.

The validity of "word of mouth" on the web: The nonverbal cues can interfere with consumers' memory.

Sugitani, Yoko Hitotsubashi University, Yokohama, Japan

The purpose of this study was to demonstrate that Computer-Mediated Communication (CMC), such as e-mail, online chat and bulletin board would be more suitable for "Word-of-Mouth" than face to face communication. CMC can't convey communicators' facial expression, voice, and gestures, therefore, we tend to think it less effective tool than face to face. But, in the experiment, the subjects memorized less information when they saw the video tape in which a woman was talking about her new mobile phone than when they read the same script as video presented by papers. The reason of this result was discussed.

Temporarily established self-referential information can modulate attention

Sui, Jie Changchun, People's Republic of China Wang, Lingyun Department of Psychology, Northeast Normal University, Changchun, People's Republic of China Zhang, Ming Department of Psychology, Northeast Normal University, Changchun, People's Republic of China

The purpose of this study was to explore whether temporarily established self-referential information can modulate attention. Participants were given a spatial cuing task, where they had to judge the orientation of a cued target presented to the left or right visual field. Before the experiment, participants learned to associate self with one colour cue and friend with another colour cue. We found that participants' responses were faster when the cue was self-referential relative to friend-referential. The results suggest that self-referential information can modulate attention by increasing the cue effect when self-referential information is relevant to the task.

Influence of self-related information on attention

Sui, Jie Changchun, People's Republic of China Liu, Chang Hong Department of Psychology, The University of Hull, Hull, United Kingdom

Two experiments were conducted to investigate how self-related information affects attention. Participants were asked to judge whether the horizontal or vertical line of a cross was longer, while ignoring task-irrelevant materials. The task-irrelevant materials were faces (Experiment 1) or personal information such as participant's birthday (Experiment 2). We found that participants' responses were slower when the task irrelevant materials were self-related, suggesting that self-related information automatically captures attention and competes with another ongoing task. Our experiments also demonstrate that this effect can be generated by different types of self-related materials.

Emotional intelligence in schools: Perspectives of Malaysian teachers

Syed Hassan, Syed Najmuddin Pusat Pengajaran Pembelajaran, Univ. Teknikal Malaysia Melaka, Melaka, Malaysia

This study aims to 1) understand the concept of emotional intelligence, 2) identify components of emotional intelligence, 3) explore patterns that contribute to emotional intelligence, 4) what affect their emotional stability and, 5) how they overcome those challenges. Samples consists of 31 secondary school teachers. Three in-depth interviews and three focus groups protocol are done. Data gathered was analyzed using NUD*IST software. The findings are a combination of what Goleman (1995,1999) posit and a few new sub-domains emerged. These findings might be the emotional intelligence framework of Malaysian teachers.

Personality resources in schizophrenia

Szirmak, Zsofia Inst. für Psychologie, Freie Universität Berlin, Berlin, Germany Jockers-Scherübl, Maria C. Campus Benjamin Franklin, Charite-Universitätsmedizin, Berlin, Germany

This study investigates the applicability and relevance of the Big- Five Model of personality to the study of schizophrenia. Two short Big Five personality measures in their self-rating form were administered to 27 patients with a schizophrenic disorder. Personality data were analyzed together with results of five widely used cognitive and neuropsychological tests. In addition, participants were asked about their opinion on the applicability and comprehensibility of the measures, and about their preferences regarding item formulations and response formats. The results underline the importance of the combination of quantitative and qualitative methods in clinical personality research.

Trait self-esteem as a protector against threats from the past

Tabata, Takuya Graduate School of Literature, Osaka City University, Osaka-si, Japan Ikegami, Tomoko Graduate School of Literature, Osaka City University, Osaka-si, Japan

This study examined whether trait self-esteem serves as a protector against threats from past instances of relationship distress. Japanese university students with high and low trait self-esteem were instructed to recall and write down their most painful experience of interpersonal rejection. The amount of degradation in state self-esteem by such threatening memories was much smaller for participants with high trait self-esteem than for those with low trait self-esteem, although the perceived painfulness of the experience did not differ between the two groups. Results were discussed in terms of the high resilience of people with high trait self-esteem.

A cross-cultural study of figure drawing movements between Germans and Japanese

Taguchi, Masanori Language and Culture, Dokkyo University, Soka, Japan Hirai, Seiya Human Sociolpgy, Nagsaki International Univ., Sasebo, Japan

The present study aimed to examine the differences in figure drawing movements of students from different cultural settings. Forty-one right-handed university students in Germany and Japan were asked to draw a circle and a triangle in one stroke. The results showed that Japanese drew a circle clockwise starting from the downside of the figure while Germans drew it counterclockwise from the upside. In the triangle-drawing-task, Japanese drew a triangle from top to left-down direction, while Germans drew from left-down to top. These differences in figure drawing movements were attributed to the differences in the writing systems between Germany and Japanese.

Episodic memory inhibition and spreading activation duration: Further evidence of episodic memory inhibition using the Think/No-think task

Tajika, Hidetsugu Psychology and Education, Kobe Shinwa Women's University, Kobe, Japan Hotta, Chie Environmental Studies, Nagoya University, Nagoya, Japan Neumann, Ewald Psychology, University of Canterbury, Christchurch, New Zealand

We examined whether inhibiting memory material intentionally could impair memory for related material after a week. Participants studied unrelated paired-associates, and had the Think/No-Think phase. After one week, participants were asked to respond as quickly and accurately as possible whether a presented word was among those previously studied. Test items included (1) studied target words; (2) nonstudied words sematically related to target words, and (3) nonstudied words unrelated to target words. Results indicated that both studied target words and words sematically related to them required longer to respond to than unrelated words. Apparently, the episodic inhibition of "No-Think" items can spread to semati-cally related items, and be manifested after a week.

Money as a cultural tool and east asian children: Toward a cultural theory of children's social development

Takahashi, Noboru Dept. of School Education, Osaka Kyoiku University, Kashiwara, Japan

Children who live in consumer society begin to know money at an early age. While parents give money as an allowance to their children, they rigorously control how to use it as well. Children use the money to construct social relationships with their friends, such that they buy fashion goods, eat together with friends, and so on. Money is, therefore, a cultural tool which mediates between children and others. In this symposium, we will discuss how east asian children from Japan, Korea, China, and Vietnam become to use money in culturally appropriate way on the basis of our questionnaire research.

Personality and psychopathological profiles in individuals exposed to mobbing

Talamo, Alessandra Dept. of Psychiatry, S. Andrea Hospital, Rome, Italy Tatarelli, Roberto II Facoltà Medicina Chirurgia, University of Rome La Sapienza, Rome, Italy Girardi, Paolo II Facoltà Medicina Chirurgia, University of Rome La Sapienza, Italy

Increasingly, mental-health professionals have been asked to assess claims of psychological harm arising from harassment at the workplace, or mobbing. This study assessed the personality and psycho-pathological profiles of 146 individuals exposed to mobbing using Minnesota-Multiphasic-Personality-Inventory-2. Profiles and factor-analyses were obtained. Two major dimensions emerged among those exposed to mobbing: 1- depressed mood, difficulty in making decisions, change-related anguish, and passive-aggressive traits 2- somatic symptoms, and need for attention/affection. This cross-sectional study provides evidence that person-ality profiles of mobbing-victims and psychological damage resulting from mobbing may be evaluated using standardized assessments, though a long-itudinal-study is needed to delineate cause-and-effect relationships.

Structure of self and psychological adjustment among adolescents

Talik, Wieslaw Inst. of Psychology, Catholic University Lublin, Lublin, Poland

Structure of self is defined by self-certainty, self-concept stability, self-concept clarity, self-concept compartmentalization, self-concept differential im-portance, self-complexity, self-concept differentia-tion. This report presents results of individual research which was conducted using a sample of 160 adolescents. The main problem of this research is formulated in the following question: what is a structure of self-system in adolescence and what kind of connection is between this structure and psychological adjustment? The following methods were used: "Who am I with different people" (own constructed inspired by Harter, 1999), SCC, SES, TPI, PANAS. The research was conducted in correlation model. There is specific connection between psychological adjustment and structure of self among adolescents.

ERPs discriminate true from false memory in a film-watching paradigm

Tamm, Sascha Kognitive Neuropsychologie, Freie Universität Berlin, Berlin, Germany Galow, Anett Forensic Psychiatry, Charité Berlin, Berlin, Germany Niedeggen, Michael General Psychol.&Neuropsyc, Freie Universitaet Berlin, Berlin, Germany Bösel, Rainer Cognitive Neuropsychology, Freie Universitaet Berlin, Berlin, Germany

After watching a short film about a robbery, 27 participants had to answer 35 yes-no-questions. In order to distort participants' memory of the scenes, 25 of these questions contained misleading informa-tion. Seven days thereafter, participants were answering the same questions a second time. Questions without misleading information were correctly answered in 87% of the cases (hits), misleading questions were erroneously accepted in 37% (false alarms). Event-related potential (ERP) of false alarms parallel the time course of hits with the exception of a transient negativity (400-500 ms). This effect is related to a covert detection of semantic incongruency.

The effects of words and facial expressions on perception of apology in children

Tamura, Ayana Kyoto University, Kyoto, Japan

This study examined how the wrongdoer's words and facial expressions affect the perception of apology, and how the effect develops in childhood. 346 children (1st, 3rd, and 5th graders) were required to read a hypothetical story in which a wrongdoer employed one of four types of apolo-gies: 2(words; apology or no-apology) × 2 (facial expressions; guilty or no-guilty). Children were asked to answer some questions. The results showed that it was in no-apology with guilty face conditions that the biggest difference was found. There were at least 2 steps of developmental changes of perception of apology in childhood.

Cultural identities of adolescent immigrants: A three-year longitudinal study including the pre-migration period

Tartakovsky, Eugene Ramat Gan, Israel

Changes in cultural identities of immigrants were investigated in a three-year longitudinal study. Adolescents immigrating from Russia and Ukraine to Israel filled out questionnaires four times: half a year before their departure from their homeland and for three consecutive years after immigration. Three stages were distinguished: Devaluation of the homeland and idealization of the host country in the pre-migration period, disillusionment with the host country and strengthening of the homeland identity in the first years after immigration, and the formation of an inconsistent bi-cultural identity in the later post-migration period. Pre-migration psychological well-being and perceived social con-ditions in the host country predicted post-migration psychological well-being.

Mothers' networks of social support in Italian and German cultural groups in South Tyrol

Taverna, Livia Faculty of Education, Free University of Bozen, Bolzano, Italy Farneti, Alessandra Faculty of Education, Free University of Bozen, Bolzano, Italy

Objective: The purpose of this study was to verify if in South Tyrol the organization of mothers' networks of social support differ in the Italian and German linguistic groups. Method: We admi-nistered to 88 Italian and 96 German mothers of children aged 2 to 5 years a Social Network Questionnaire in which indicate who help them in childcare. Results: Germans declare to obtain social support in childrearing mostly from their friends (32.4%), while Italians relay on the support offered by their own family (35.3%). Conclusion: Cultural differences in the way mothers organize their networks do exist.

Development of eating behavior scale and study on the factors related to BMI

Tayama, Jun Tohoku-Rousai Hospital, Sendai, Japan

The purpose of this study is to develop eating behavior scale and to investigate the eating behavior factor structure associated with BMI. The subjects consisted of 950. The subjects com-pleted the questionnaire consisting of 30 items. Factor analysis was carried out and five dimensions were identified. The abnormality level of eating behavior was higher in the female group than in the male group. We found that the abnormality level of eating behavior was higher in the very under weight group, slightly under weight group, over weight group and obese group than in the healthy weight range group.

Moral disengagement mechanisms in software piracy

Thatcher, Andrew PDept. of Psychology, University of Witwatersrand, Witwatersrand, South Africa Mathews, Mary Psychology, University of the Witwatersran, WITS, South Africa Wentzell, Alethea Psychology, University of the Witwatersran, WITS, South Africa Fridjhon, Peter Statistics & Actuarial Sci, University of the Witwatersran, WITS, South Africa

Objectives: The development of a measure to assess moral disengagement mechanisms as predictors of software piracy intentions. Methods: Forty ques-tionnaire items developed based on Bandura's eight moral disengagement mechanisms. Draft question-naire distributed to five international experts in moral disengagement then pilot-tested on 402 South African workers. Item and factor analyses reduced questionnaire to 20 items and three factors. Revised questionnaire administered to independent sample of 193 South African and Zambian workers; compared to software piracy attitudes and inten-tions. Results: Significant positive correlations (moderate/high effect sizes) found between the three stages and attitudes and intentions towards soft-ware piracy. Conclusion: Results discussed in relation to the contribution of Social Cognitive Theory towards understanding and reducing soft-ware piracy in emerging countries.

Safer sex through entertainment education: Realizing the entertainment education approach with a computer game about HIV/AIDS and condom use for female adolescents

Thies-Brandner, Yvonne SHSS, R IV, Jacobs University Bremen, Bremen, Germany

Entertainment education is a strategy to educate people through entertainment. Research has shown that it can have positive effects on people's behavior, attitudes, knowledge, and interpersonal communication. It works with various media (products) such as radio, TV soap operas, street theatre, or comics. The question is whether this strategy also works for computer games. To test this, an entertainment education computer game about HIV/AIDS education was developed. The computer game led to a significant increase in knowledge about HIV/AIDS, but no increases in interest and communication could be observed. Possible explanations and suggestions for future research are discussed.

Cultural differences and the relationship between eating habits and mental health of Japanese, Korean, and Austrian female university students

Tominaga, Mihoko Nursing and Nutrition, Siebold University of Nagasaki, Nagayo Nagasaki, Japan *Taguchi, Masanori* Interdisciplinary studies, Dokkyo University, Soka-shi Saitama, Japan *Yoon, Ho-Sook* Japanese, Cyber University of Foreign St, Dongdaemun-gu Seoul, Republic of Korea *Roth, Roswith* Psychology, University of Graz, Graz, Austria

To investigate the cultural differences and the relationship between eating habits and mental health, a questionnaire survey was performed among Japanese (N=276), Korean (N=103) and Austrian (N=127) female university students. The mental health of Austrian students tended to be better than that of Japanese or Korean. In eating habits, numerous significant differences established by analyses of variance were recognized among the three countries and some habits were extracted which indicated a relationship with mental health. Results suggested that securing enough sleeping time and enhancing the awareness of healthy eating behavior were important to maintain the good mental health conditions.

What is family? in four East Asia: Cultural comparison of "family" displayed in Japanese, Korean, Chinese and Taiwanese

Tomo, Rieko Contemporary Social Studies, Doshisha Women's College, Kyoto, Japan

The purpose of this study is to consider the relationship of the transformations of the family styles displayed in texts, and fluctuations of society and economy, by statistical analysis of the "Family" displayed in four East Asian (Japanese, Korean, Chinese and Taiwanese) elementary school texts published 1960-2000. The results were as follows: 1) Economic fluctuations like recessions upgraded woman's position in a family. 2) Social changes like the employment rate for women influenced the relationship between husband and wife. These results indicate that it is important to study the relationship between family styles and socio-economic cultural changes in these societies.

The role of implicit theories of personality in selective attention to person-related information

Tong, Jennifer School of Social Sciences, Singapore Management Universit, Singapore, Singapore

Research has shown that Implicit Theory of Personality guides the way we understand other people's behavior. Compared to those who believe that personality is malleable ("incremental theorists"), people who believe in fixed personality traits ("entity theorists") are more likely to make global evaluative trait judgments on the basis of a small sample of recently occurred behaviors. Extending on this idea, entity theorists will attend more to trait-confirmatory rather than trait-inconsistent information, while incremental theorists will show the reverse pattern. This hypothesis is tested in a computerized person perception task by measuring information choice and reading time.

The role of naive theories in causal explanation

Toyama, Midori Psychology, Gakushuin University, Tokyo, Japan

Classical attribution theories placed great emphasis on traits and dispositional properties in causal explanation, but recently, the importance of more transient mental states has been widely noticed. This study attempted to examine the nature of naive explanation of behavior. Participants were first required to describe one major cause for each of several events, and then, they were asked to choose plausible causes from the alternatives for the same set of events. Results showed that desires and emotions were most frequently mentioned in free descriptions but choice responses were predominantly dispositional. The differences between two response modes are discussed.

Factors influencing the accuracy of item parameter estimates in the two-parameter logistic model

Tran, Ulrich Faculty of Psychology, University of Vienna, Vienna, Austria *Formann, Anton* Faculty of Psychology, University of Vienna, Vienna, Austria

Item parameter estimation in the two-parameter logistic model independently of the latent distribution via conditional maximum likelihood (CML) is not feasible without imposing specific constraints on the parameters. Commonly used marginal maximum likelihood (MML) algorithms either rely on distributional assumptions or estimate the latent distribution from the data. As previous research showed, accuracy of item parameter estimation depends on the correctness of assumptions and on the adequacy of implemented methods (cf. Woods & Thissen, 2006). Here, we present preliminary results of a simulation study concerning the power of specific algorithms to detect differences of various sizes in true item parameters.

Electrophysiological correlates of the control of emotional memories

Treese, Anne-Cecile Dept. of Psychology, Lund University, Lund, Sweden *Johansson, Mikael* Psychology, Lund University, Lund, Sweden *Lindgren, Magnus* Psychology, Lund University, Lund, Sweden

This event-related potential (ERP) study investigated memory control processes for emotional and neutral faces. 30 participants performed repeated runs of a continuous recognition task. Participants had difficulties to distinguish relevant from currently irrelevant memories, and these were highest for positive faces. The ERP data suggest that different retrieval monitoring processes contributed to the successful control of neutral and negative memories. For neutral faces early reality monitoring was effective while for negative faces later strategic retrieval monitoring was engaged. Attempts for strategic retrieval processes were also made for positive faces, however the information retrieved seemed non-diagnostic for rejecting irrelevant memories.

Inappropriate emotional illness representation in fibromyalgia patients

Trovato, Guglielmo Internal Medicine & Health Psy, University of Catania, Catania, Italy *Catalano, Daniela* Internal Medicine, University of Catania, Catania, Italy *Pace, Patrizia* Internal Medicine & Health, University of Catania, Catania, Italy *Martines, Giuseppe Fabio* Internal Medicine, University of Catania, Catania, Italy

Objective: To assess difference on illness perception, quality of life and anxiety and depression level of patients with rheumatoid arthritis (RA) and fibro-myalgia (FM). Methods: twenty RA patients and twenty FM patients completed the IPQ-r, the SF36 and HADS. Results: RA patients have a significantly worse general health and perceive illness as longstanding disease with severe consequence. FM patients have a higher levels of anxiety and a worse emotional representation. Conclusion: FM patients feel more emotional dysfunction than patients with a clearly defined and potentially disabling medical condition do. Data support importance of patients' illness perceptions in perpetuating this disorder.

The effect of the emotion on the size of human figures in children's drawings

Tsiakara, Aggeliki Preschool Education, University of Thessaly, Volos, Greece

The purpose of this research is to study the relation between the factor of size of drawing and the emotion. It has been considered that factors such as emotion, gender, age and family will affect the factor of size in children's drawings. Children aged 6, 8 and 9 took part and were asked to design a football player of their favorite team and of another team. The analysis showed that the size of human figure is larger when children's emotions are positive towards it, however is smaller when emotions are negative.

Do you like this car? Neural encoding of object valence and intensity

Tusche, Anita Attention and Awareness, MPI CBS, Leipzig, Germany *Haynes, John-Dylan* Attention and Awareness, MPI CBS, Leipzig, Germany

How is the valence of objects encoded in brain activity? We presented subjects with images of different cars and asked them to rate their valence. Simultaneously we recorded brain activity using fMRI. Neural activation in the medial prefrontal cortex and in early visual areas was correlated with valence ratings, a result that was confirmed by multivariate pattern classification. In contrast, regions of the temporal lobe, including amygdala and insula, were correlated with both extremely negative and extremely positive ratings, suggesting a rectified valence response. The results thus reveal a dissociation between neural encoding of valence and intensity.

Attitudes of Japanese adolescents toward comic magazines: Characteristics of "Boys Love" ("shonen-ai", "m/m slash") readers

Ui, Miyoko Dept. of Psychology, University of Tsukuba, Tsukuba, Japan *Fukutomi, Mamoru* Education, Tokyo Gakugei University, Musashikoganei, Japan *Kamise, Yumiko* Sociology, Edogawa University, Nagareyama, Japan

For Japanese adolescents, comic magazines are one of sources for getting information about romantic love and sexual behavior. Since the 1990s, "Boys Love"("shonen-ai", "m/m slash") comic, which portrays romantic or sexual relationships between men, appeared in Japanese comic market. "Boys Love" comic is characterized as description of radical sexual behavior and excessive gender role, in contrast to comic which portrays romantic or sexual relationships between men and women. First, we reviewed the history of "Boys Love" comic since 1970s. Second, the questionnaire survey for Japanese university students was conducted. We examine how much "Boys Love" comic is widespread and what is attractive to adolescent readers.

A pilot study about assessment of relational representation in preschool children: Self, attachment and interpersonal schemas

Uluc, Sait psychology, Hacettepe University, ANKARA, Turkey *Öktem, Ferhunde* Child Psychiatry, Hacettepe University, ANKARA, Turkey

In the frame of Attachment Theory, it is assumed that there is a strong relationship among the Working Model of Attachment, the Working

Model of Self and Interpersonal Schemas. This study examines the relation among Attachment, Self and Interpersonal Schemas in a sample of 60 preschool children which contain 33 boys and 27 girls. Results indicated that mental representation of the Self in the preschool children occur at the relational content and it's closely related to Model of Attachment that they have. Based on this research's results, it is also assumed that Attachment has an important role in the formation of interpersonal expectations.

Identifying methods of parental support for improving children's emotional intelligence

Ulutas, Ylkay Child Development Education, Gazi University, Ankara, Turkey *Omeroglu, Esra* Child Development Education, Gazi University, Ankara, Turkey

The development of children's emotional intelligence depends on parents' emotional intelligence, their emotional attitudes and the support they give to children at home. Parents with high emotional intelligence consider it important to have quality time with their children through activities such as reading books or engaging in artistic and social tasks. The study consists of parents with 6-year-old children. Parents were evaluated by "Emotional Intelligence Assessment Scale" and "Parental Attitude Scale". Their home observed according to "Home Environment Assessment Scale". The results revealed a relationship between parents' emotional intelligence, parental attitudes and the home environment they offer to their children.

Form matters (?): Effects of presentation mode and editing on the emotional processing of TV-news

Unz, Dagmar Inst. für Medienpsychologie, Universität des Saarlandes, Saarbrücken, Germany *Schwab, Frank* Media Psychology, Saarland University, Saarbruecken, Germany

Formal features of audiovisual media like film cuts are known to elicit orientation reactions and increase attention, thus we assumed that changes in camera work affect the emotional interpretation. The study utilized a 2 (cutting frequency) x 2 (size of shot) repeated measure design (n=57). As dependent variables certain components of emotions were recorded. The results indicate that presentation modes have an impact on emotions, e.g., negative events are appraised as more unpleasant, if close up shots are used. Cutting frequency seems to influence the feeling of sadness. Above that, the results indicate interaction effects of content and presentation mode.

The Spanish version of the disgust scale-revised

Valiente, Rosa M. Psychology, Universidad Nac. Educ. Dist., Madrid, Spain *Sandin, Bonifacio* Psychology, Universidad Nac. Educ. Dist., Madrid, Spain *Chorot, Paloma* Psychology, Universidad Nac. Educ. Dist., Madrid, Spain *Santed, Miguel A.* Psychology, Universidad Nac. Educ. Dist., Madrid, Spain

The Disgust Scale–Revised (DS-R) is a new version of the original Disgust Scale by Haidt et al. (1994) designed to measure individual differences in sensitivity to disgust. Although there have been suggested three main dimensions for the scale [i.e., core disgust (food, animals and body products), animal-remainder disgust (death and envelope violations) and contamination disgust], the structure of the DS-R is poorly known yet. In this work we examine the factor structure, reliability and validity of the Spanish version of the DS-R in a nonclinical sample. Results are discussed in terms of the usefulness of the scale in the field of the anxiety disorders.

Emotional discomfort in women and men at the start of an assisted reproducion techniques program in outpatients at the University Hospital in Florence (Italy)

Valoriani, Vania Dept. of Clinical Psychology, University of Florence, Florence, Italy *Vanni, Claudia* Clinical Psychology, University of Florence, Florence, Italy *Ferrari, Maria Gabriella* Clinical Psychology, University of Florence, Florence, Italy *Cardillo, Emanuela* Clinical Psychology, University of Florence, Florence, Italy *Vaiani, Serena* Clinical Psychology, University of Florence, Florence, Italy *Benvenuti, Paola* Clinical Psychology, University of Florence, Florence, Italy

OBJECTIVES: The dynamics of mental health in couples during treatment with assisted reproduction techniques (ART) were the focus of our research. We assessed the differences between women and men regarding the infertility problem, investigating emotional state, psychological wellbeing, neurotic traits and marital satisfaction.. METHOD: We assessed 230 couples administering them: STAY Y-1 to evaluate the anxiety state, EPDS to evaluate mood state, GHQ-12 to evaluate psychological wellbeing, C-CEI to evaluate neurotic symptomatology and GRIMS to evaluate perception of the marital state. RESULTS: We found significant differences between women and men and we assume a difficult in men's expression of emotions

Me, myself and I: The effects of self in social cognition

van Bussel, Kim Aberdeen, United Kingdom *Turk, Dave* Psychology, University of Aberdeen, Aberdeen, United Kingdom *MacRae, Neil* Psychology, University of Aberdeen, Aberdeen, United Kingdom

Information encoded in relation to self is better remembered than information encoded in relation to others (the self-reference effect, SRE). In this fMRI-experiment, participants sorted pictures of shopping items into baskets that were either their own or someone else's. Afterwards, memory was assessed by conducting a surprise recognition test. The results showed that items sorted into one's own basket are better remembered than items assigned to someone else's basket. fMRI-results showed greater activation in the insular cortices and bilaterally in the parietal cortex for owned items compared to not-owned items, suggesting an emotional and attentional component underlying the SRE.

Implicit false memory: A cognitive neuropsychological approach

van Damme, Ilse Dept. of Psychology, University of Leuven, Leuven, Belgium *d'Ydewalle, Géry* Department of Psychology, University of Leuven, Leuven, Belgium

In three experiments, it was investigated whether Korsakoff patients would show diminished implicit false memory for semantically related words in the Deese/Roediger-McDermott (DRM) paradigm. This was done to examine whether previous findings of reduced false memory were due to problems at encoding, recollection, or both. Stem completion was tested either at the end of the experiment (Experiment 1) or immediately after study (Experiments 2 and 3). Both study instructions and study duration were manipulated. Results revealed that Korsakoff patients' veridical and false memory scores were only impaired when explicit recollection was required, but not when memory was tested implicitly.

Acculturation and nationality

Varela Macedo, Victoria Facultad de Psicología, Universidad Nacional de México, Mexico City, Mexico

Goal in this study was to analyze the influence of nationality as a variable in the process of acculturation of international students. College and post-graduate students, from Mexican universities participated as subjects. An acculturation scale and a battery of tests were applied to 396 students, in order to get information about the way acculturation was taking place. 209 females (52.8%), 187 males (47.2%) participated. Nationality was shown as a quiet important variable regarding acculturation. Significant differences were shown in ANOVA among groups' means. Latino and Europeans groups' means were the highest.

Idleness as a psychological phenomenon

Varvaricheva, Yana Dept. of Psychology, Lomonosov MSU, Moscow, Russia

Idleness is a part of common-sense psychology but its scientific analysis is important. The research based on A.N. Leontiev's concept of activity shows that idleness is a complex multidetermined phenomenon, with structure which is homogenous to the activity structure. Its reasons are located on 4 levels: 1)physiology; 2)operations; 3)acts; 4) motivation. Individual and situational idleness may be distinguished. The research included 6 questionnaires and 205 participants. The conclusion: all the criteria of idle situations form 3 categories: "Self view" (e.g.tiredness) "Task view" (e.g.monotony) and "Circumstances view" (e.g.noise). These results and new questionnaires may be used in research and practical work.

Sensation seeking, sexual risk behaviors and ADHD characteristics in Puerto Rican young adults

Velez-Pastrana, Maria C. Clinical Psychology - Ph.D., Universidad Carlos Albizu, San Juan, Puerto Rico *Carradero, Hector* Clinical Psychology - Ph.D., Universidad Carlos Albizu, San Juan, Puerto Rico *Bernier, Lucyann* Clinical Psychology - Ph.D., Universidad Carlos Albizu, San Juan, Puerto Rico *Torres Vecchini, Ana* Clinical Psychology - Ph.D., Universidad Carlos Albizu, San Juan, Puerto Rico *Ramos, Birla* Clinical Psychology - Ph.D., Universidad Carlos Albizu, San Juan, Puerto Rico *Perez, Carilu* Clinical Psychology - Ph.D., Universidad Carlos Albizu, San Juan, Puerto Rico *Vega, Janira* Clinical Psychology - Ph.D., Universidad Carlos Albizu, San Juan, Puerto Rico

Study examines relation between sensation-seeking personality traits, symptoms and behaviors associated with Attention Deficit Hyperactivity Disorder (ADHD) and sexual risk behaviors among Puerto Rican young adults. 200 Puerto Rican adults complete the Zuckerman Sensation Seeking Scale V, the Wender Utah Rating Scale and a questionnaire assessing sexual risk-behaviors. Sensation seeking has been linked to sexual risk behaviors. ADHD has been associated with risky behaviors such as reckless driving and gambling. People with ADHD who present high sensation seeking tendencies may engage in sexual behaviors that place them at higher risk of HIV/STD infection or unwanted pregnancy. Clinical implications are discussed.

Self-report assessment of impulsivity in children

Vigil, Andreu Psicologia, Universitat Rovira i Virgili, Tarragona, Spain *Cosi, Sandra* psicologia, universitat rovira i virgili, Tarragona, Spain *Canals, Josepa* psicologia, universitat rovira i virgili, Tarragona, Spain *Codorniu, Maria Jose* psicologia, universitat rovira i virgili, Tarragona, Spain

Given the difficulties assessing impulsivity in children using self-report questionnaires we evaluate the factorial structure and internal consistency of two measures: Dickman Impulsivity Questionnaire (DIIc) for children and the children's adaptation of Barrat's impulsivity scales (BISc) Questionnaires where translated into Spanish by an English native speaker and administered to two samples of 377 and 446 individuals. Data was analysed by Exploratory Factor Analysis. DIIc had neither a clear factorial structure nor sufficient reliability. BISc showed a three factor structure similar to adults' version and good psychometric properties. BISc appears as a good questionnaire to assess impulsivity in children

The developmental dynamics between task-motivation and competence beliefs during elementary school years

Viljaranta, Jaana Department of Psychology, University of Jyväskylä, University of Jyväskylä, Finland Aunola, Kaisa Department of Psychology, University of Jyväskylä, University of Jyväskylä, Finland Nurmi, Jari-Erik Department of Psychology, University of Jyväskylä, University of Jyväskylä, Finland

Previous research has shown that children's competence beliefs in certain school subjects are associated with related task-motivation. Since there is little research on the lagged relationships between motivation and competence beliefs, a longitudinal data from first to seventh grade was gathered from 211 children to examine this topic. The preliminary results showed that task-motivation and competence beliefs in literacy and mathematics declined during elementary school years. Moreover, task-motivation and competence beliefs showed prospective associations across time.

How Hellene pupils use time: A time diary study

Vleioras, Georgios Volos, Greece

What we do defines what skills we develop. Thus, in order to study child development, it is essential to know what children do during the day. This study investigated the time use of Hellene 3rd and 4th graders. A hundred seventy-one pupils described a school day by means of a time diary. On average, they spent 9h09 for rest, 8h31 for school-related activities, 3h25 for discretionary activities (1h24 for television viewing), and 2h47 for activities such as getting dressed, eating, moving, etc. These results raise concerns about the cognitive, emotional, and social development of Hellene pupils.

Attentional distraction by auditory stimuli as intervention for reducing breathlessness during exercise in patients with COPD

von Leupoldt, Andreas Department of Psychology, University of Hamburg, Hamburg, Germany Taube, Karin Atem-Reha GmbH, Atem-Reha GmbH, Hamburg, Germany Schubert-Heukeshoven, Stephan Atem-Reha GmbH, Atem-Reha GmbH, Hamburg, Germany Magnussen, Helgo Pulmonary Research Institute, Hospital Grosshansdorf, Grosshansdorf, Germany Dahme, Bernhard Department of Psychology, University of Hamburg, Hamburg, Germany

We examined the influence of attentional distraction on exercise-induced breathlessness and affective state in twenty patients with chronic obstructive pulmonary disease. Patients performed two 6-min-walking-tests of similar exercise-intensity. Under one exercise-condition, distractive auditory stimuli were presented. The other condition was performed without distraction. During auditory distraction, the global level of breathlessness and the perceived unpleasantness of breathlessness were smaller while positive affectivity was higher compared to the non-distraction condition. Perceived intensity of breathlessness remained stable across conditions. The results suggest that auditory distraction might serve as intervention for reducing breathlessness and increasing positive affectivity during exercise in this patient group.

The effects of verbal supports on diversification and sophistication of visual images in "As if" drawings by four- and five-year-old children: Focus on the developmental difference of strategies to integrate concrete objects and prior knowledge

Wakayama, Ikuyo Dept. of Education, Hiroshima University, Hiroshima, Japan

The purpose of this study is to examine the effects of verbal supports on"as if" drawings of four-year-old and five-year-old children. Children performed "as if" drawing in three different conditions, i.e., Contour, Parts, and Control. The major finding is that the drawings of four-year-old children in Contour were more diversified and sophisticated than those in the other two conditions, and the drawings of five-year-old children in Parts were more diversified than those in Control condition. These results were discussed in terms of developmental theories on conceptual development.

Movie taste as a reliable indicator of personality structure

Wallisch, Pascal Center for Neural Science, New York University, New York City, USA

Most classical personality tests suffer from lacking reliability. Those that are reliable, like the NEO-PI are often inadequate to predict behavior in different situations. We propose that this is mostly due to items that are too unspecific and that rely on introspective self-reports. We instead suggest to use the liking of specific movies. These items are very specific and have strong affective components. Our analysis shows that such a test of movie taste has surprisingly high reliability. Moreover, we were able to extract stable factors using principal component analysis. Finally, we propose a metric of like-mindedness based on this approach.

Gender differences in early adolescents' academic motivation: A longitudinal investigation in America and China

Wang, Qian Department of Psychology, Chinese Univ. of Hong Kong, Hong Kong, China, People's Republic of : Hong Kong SAR Pomerantz, Eva Department of Psychology, Univ. of Illinois, Champaign, China, People's Republic of : Macao SAR

This research examined gender differences in academic motivation among 374 American and 451 Chinese early adolescents. Four times over the seventh and eighth grades, children and their teachers reported on multiple dimensions of children's motivation. Structural equation modeling revealed: In America, generally, girls reported higher motivation than did boys; both genders reported declining motivation over time. In China, generally, girls and boys reported similar motivation, which declined in quality but not intensity over time. In both countries, teachers rated girls less helpless than boys. Over time, teacher-rated helplessness remained stable in America but increased in China (more so for girls).

Emotion regulation and executive function of Chinese preschoolers

Wang, Li Dept. of Psychology, Peking University, Beijing, People's Republic of China Ji, Meng Psychology, Peking University, Beijing, People's Republic of China Tardif, Twila Psychology, University of Michigan, ann arbor, USA

Emotion regulation involves coordination across behavioral, psychological, and physiological sub-systems that develop over time. The Purpose of this study is to examine the relation between emotion regulation and executive function in Chinese preschooler. Sixty 4-year-old Chinese children were tested during 3 successive days at their preschools. Emotion regulation was coded in boring task, disappointment task and frustration task, as well as their abilities to regulate and control their behavior were measured in a number of "executive

functioning" tasks. It was found that children's emotional reactions in the challenge tasks significantly correlated with their executive function

Culture and hostile attribution: Analytic vs. holistic judgments of intents and causes in China and the US

Wang, Yilan School of Educational Science, Huzhong University, Wuhan, People's Republic of China Peng, Kaiping Psychology, University of California, Berkeley, USA Zhou, Zhijing School of Educational Science, Huzhong U. of Science & Te, Wuhan, People's Republic of China

We tested the hostile attribution in cross-cultural contexts. 20 scenarios involve three intentional states (benign, ambiguous, and hostile) and two types of agents (individual vs. group) were presented to 200 college students from two elite universities in China and the US. We found that American participants made stronger intentionality judgments, and attributed more internal dispositional causes than situational causes. There was a significant main effect by intents that hostile behavior to be more intentional than both benign and ambiguous behaviors. Surprisingly, we didn't find culture by agent interactions. Implications to culture and cognition research and international politics are discussed.

The time course and source localization of false belief reasoning revealed by an event-related potential study

Wang, Yiwen School of Psychology, Shandong Normal University, Jinan, People's Republic of China Liu, Yan School of Psychology, Shandong Normal University, Jinan, People's Republic of China Lin, Chongde School of Psychology, Beijing Normal University, Beijing, People's Republic of China

To investigate the neural substrates of false-belief reasoning, the 32 channels event-related potentials (ERP) of 14 normal adults were measured while they understood false-belief and true-belief used deceptive appearance task. After onset of the false-belief or true-belief questions?N100, P200 and late negative component (LNC) were elicited at centro-frontal sites. False-belief reasoning elicited a significant declined LNC than true-belief in the time window from 400 to 800ms. The source analysis of difference wave (False minus True) at 650ms showed a dipole located in the middle cingulated cortex. These findings suggested that false-belief reasoning probably included inhibitive control.

Study of discriminant validity between cultural intelligence and emotional intelligence

Wang, Gigi Organization and Management, Shanghai Jiao Tong University, Shanghai, People's Republic of China Tang, Ning Yu Organization and Management, Shanghai Jiao Tong University, Shanghai, People's Republic of China

Objective: To prove if Cultural Intelligence (CI) structure accords with Ang Soon's Four-Factor CI model, CI and EQ are independent in Structural Dimension. Method: 351 college students were assessed with EQ?CI questionnaires in Chinese. Result: The reliability analysis of CI reveals 0.86 to 0.93 α coefficient. Exploratory Factor and Confirmatory Factor Analysis indicates that four-factor model of CI is the most suitable model. The same analysis measurement on 36 items of CI and EQ shows they accord with two-factor model, which proves CI and EQ are structurally independent. Conclusion: Four-factor CI model has cross-cultural similarity in China. CI and EQ are related but independent concepts.

How do Chinese newspapers report on Japan: A comparative study between national organs and local papers

Wang, Ge Social Psychology Lab., Ochanomizu University, Tokyo, Japan Sakamoto, Akira Social Psychology Lab, Ochanomizu University, Tokyo, Japan

Objectives: Finding out how China's newspapers report on Japan and the differences between national organs and local papers. Method About 1657 articles were analyzed from two papers from 2001 to 2004. We investigated credibility, content and manner of reporting, e.g. tone. We also calculated agreement of each measure. Results: The reporting in both newspapers was insular and lacking in topicality. There was a lot of positive information about Japan and Japanese people in articles. Significant differences between these two newspapers in the manner of reporting were found. Conclusion: Chinese newspapers' reporting on Japan is limited and needs more topicality.

Investigating the processing of musical syntax violations in 7th grade children using fMRI

Wehrum, Sina Psychology, Justus-Liebig-University, Gießen, Germany Stark, Rudolf Psychology, Justus-Liebig-University, Gießen, Germany Ott, Ulrich Psychology, Justus-Liebig-University, Gießen, Germany Degé, Franziska Psychology, Justus-Liebig-University, Gießen, Germany Schwarzer, Gudrun Psychology, Justus-Liebig-University, Gießen, Germany Vaitl, Dieter Psychology, Justus-Liebig-University, Gießen, Germany

Aim of the study was to identify differences in the neuronal processing of musical syntax errors in children with varying degrees of musical experience. Forty-two 7th graders were investigated using fMRI while listening to music pieces with and without errors of different intensities. First results indicate associations between error intensity and musical experience. While high musical experience was related to stronger brain activity in response to slight errors, low experience was associated with stronger activity in response to heavy errors. Activity was found in structures known to be involved in musical (inferior frontal gyrus) and emotional (medial prefrontal cortex) processing.

Effort beliefs and role obligation

Wei, Chih-Fen Department of Psychology, Chung-Yuan C. University, Chung-Li, Tao Yuan County, Taiwan

Chen et al. (in press) found that Taiwanese students tended to showed self-serving attribution pattern for personal goals based on autonomous interest, but attribute failure to pursue to vertical goals based on social expectation to lack of effort. Because vertical goals were closely associated to role obligation, it was inferred that there was positive correlation between effort beliefs and role obligation. In other words, the more one thought life goals were parts of role obligation, the more he would attribute success or failure to effort.

Neural correlates of resilience to trauma

Westphal, Maren Psychiatry, Mount Sinai Medical School, New York, USA New, Antonia Psychiatry, Mount Sinai Medical School, New York, USA Charney, Dennis S. Psychiatry, Mount Sinai Medical School, New York, USA

Background Investigating neural correlates of post-traumatic stress disorder (PTSD) and resilience is important for understanding differential risk to trauma. This fMRI study examined brain activity during effortful emotion regulation in female survivors of sexual assault with and without PTSD. Methods 12 women with PTSD, 13 without PTSD (stress-resistant), and 14 healthy non-traumatized controls performed a cognitive reappraisal task while in the scanner. Results and Conclusions Stress-resistant participants showed significantly greater activation in anterior insula and anterior cingulate gyrus than PTSD and control participants when asked to deliberately enhance their emotional responses to unpleasant images, which may reflect better regulatory ability.

Center-surround patterns emerge as optimal predictors for human saccade targets

Wichmann, Felix Modellierung Kognit. Prozesse, Techn. Universität Berlin, Berlin, Germany Kienzle, Wolf Empirical Inference, MPI for Biological Cybernetics, Tübingen, Germany Franz, Matthias Empirical Inference, MPI for Biological Cybernetics, Tübingen, Germany Schölkopf, Bernhard Empirical Inference, MPI for Biological Cybernetics, Tübingen, Germany

Much of a visual scene is perceived after a few saccades despite the rapid drop-off in sensitivity away from the fovea. This suggests an effective strategy for selecting saccade targets. Local image structure is known to influence saccade target selection. Which visual features are most important is still under debate, however. We show that center-surround patterns emerge as optimal solution for predicting saccade targets using modern machine learning techniques. Our model is surprisingly simple compared to previously suggested models and is consistent with neurophysiological hardware in superior colliculus. Bottom-up visual saliency may thus be computed sub-cortically.

Washing powder advertisement: The final curtain in gender equality?

Winiewski, Mikolaj Institute for Social Sciences, Warsaw University, Warsaw, Poland Majcher, Malgorzata Faculty of Psychology, University of Warsaw, Warsaw, Poland

The presented research concerns the problem of gender perception. Ads using their specific, easy language present gender issues symbolic way therefore often are biased by gender stereotypes. Main aim of this study was to "catch" the influence of stereotypic content of ads on persistence and enforcement of gender stereotypes. Two stages of research have been conducted. The first stage was set to create a method of recording stereotypic gender content. Second stage of research was an experiment. The dependent variables were the evaluation of average men and women. The independent variables were stereotypical and non stereotypical ads. Research results show that the influence of stereotypical advertisement content enforces gender stereotypes.

Transformational leadership in the context of effort–reward-imbalance and occupational health

Wolf, Sandra Arbeits- und Org.-Psychology, Technische Universität Dresden, Dresden, Germany Nebel, Claudia Inst. für Arbeitspsychologie, Technische Universität Dresden, Dresden, Germany

Referring to the augmentation–effect (Bass & Avolio, 1994) high rates of transformational leadership would also imply a balanced effort-reward-ratio. But probably both concepts concentrate on similar aspects. The current issue analysed the structure of effort-reward-modell (ERI, Siegrist, 1996) and transformational leadership-components (MLQ, Felfe & Goihl, 2006) using factorial analyses. Furthermore the contribution of transformational leadership on employees health in addition to effort-reward-balance is shown for a sample of N= 364 blue- and white-collar workers by regressional modells. Implications for the prevention of psychosocial health risks are introduced.

The MMPI-2 Gender-Masculine and Gender-Femininescales: Gender roles as predictors of psychologicalhealth in clinical patients

Woo, Matthew Dept of Psychology, Institute of Mental Health, Singapore, Singapore Oei, Tian School of Psychology, University of Queensland, Brisbane, Australia

The present study assessed the personality constructs of masculinity and femininity and hypothesized that the Gender-Masculine (GM) scale of the MMPI-2 would be more effective than the Gender-Feminine (GF) scale in predicting psychological well-being. This hypothesis stems from previous research that has indicated the dominance of the masculinity model. One hundred and seventy-seven psychiatric patients from Australia and Singapore completed the MMPI-2. Hierarchical multiple regression revealed significantly stronger masculinity effects, with significance achieved on measures of ego strength and low self-esteem. Overall, the results are consistent with an interpretation that GM is a better correlate of psychological well-being as compared to the GF scale

Constraints and support in work/family domains, work/family conflict and their consequences: A Taiwanese-British cross-cultural comparison

Wu, Hsin-Pei Inst. of Human Resource, National Central University, Jhongli, Taiwan Lu, Luo Dept. of Business Administrati, National Taiwan University, Taipei, Taiwan

The aim of this research was to explore relations between work/family constraints and resources, work/family conflict (WFC), and work- and non-work related outcomes in a cross-cultural comparative context involving Taiwanese and British employees. For Both Taiwanese and British employees, work and family constraints were positively related to WFC, whereas work resources were negatively related to WFC. Furthermore, WFC was negatively related to work and family satisfaction. More importantly, we found that nation moderated the relationship between WFC and work/family satisfaction: WFC had a stronger detrimental effect on both domain satisfaction for British than Taiwanese.

The Influence of Stimulant Material Category on the Stroop Dilution Effect

Xu, Baihua Psychology, Zhejiang University, Hangzhou, People's Republic of China Xu, Lin Psychology, Zhejiang University, Hangzhou, People's Republic of China

The counting Stroop was adopted to investigate if the domain of the materials or the nature of the target material was the main cause of Stroop dilution effect?with Chinese characters or characters from top of keyboard as targets, and with Chinese numerals or Arabic numerals as distracters respectively. The result suggested that whether materials were from the same domain was the main cause of the Stroop dilution effect. The result supported domain-specific, limited-capacity processing. It also proposed that there could be two kinds of information processing systems, language and non-language, in cognitive control of attention.

Images of turning points: Cultural-historical representations in the contemporary drawings termed "Image Map of my Life" and traditional folk pictures

Yamada, Yoko Graduate School of Education, Kyoto University, Kyoto, Japan Strohmeier, Dagmar Faculty of Psychology, University of Vienna, Vienna, Austria Grabner, Anna Faculty of Psychology, University of Vienna, Vienn, Austria

The purpose was to understand how people represent the life course of their own life stories. We have collected over 1,000 freehand drawings called "The Image Map of my Life" (IML) by Japanese, British, and Austrian adults, by means of questionnaires. The typical symbols of transition, such as "Boundary", "Bride", "Landmark", "Gate", and "Guide", were compared with images in traditional Japanese folk pictures from the Edo era (16th-19th centuries): "Life Slope of Aging in Kansin-Jukai Mandara" and "Life Backgammon". Although the cultural, historical and religious backgrounds differed markedly, these symbols were common across cultural and historical contexts.

Appreciating art verbally: Verbalization can make a work of art seem to be either trash or a masterpiece

Yamada, Ayumi Dept. of Psychology, Gakushuin University, Tokyo, Japan

This study tested whether appreciating art verbally would aesthetically confuse viewers. Participants verbalized why they either liked or disliked two paintings: one was representational art; the other, abstract art. While it was easy to describe reasons for liking and disliking the representational art, the same proved difficult for abstract art. Those who verbalized reasons for liking the works were more likely to prefer the representational painting, whereas those who verbalized reasons for disliking them were less likely to prefer the same. The findings suggest that verbalization caused people to base their evaluations on the reportable aspects of their aesthetic experience.

Japanese life-patterns in the 2000s I: Life-pattern and work/family/leisure balance

Yamashita, Miyako Okayama University, Itami, HYOGO, Japan Yagi, Ryuichiro Research Institute, International Economy and Work, Osaka, Japan Abe, Shingo Fuculty of Contemporary human, Baika Women's University, Ibaraki, Osaka, Japan Miyata, Minako Psychology +connect, Institute of Applied Social, Osaka, Japan

This study introduces 'Life-pattern', a new psychological model, as a tool to measure changing pattern of life. The model represents the concept that covers both developmental and life-style/career changes over the lifetime. It can depict some common patterns of people's lives by integrating various aspects and developmental stages of life. By using this model, this study examines relationships between the work/family/leisure balance and life satisfaction, based on the data collected from 1500 Japanese workers. The results indicated that 'perceived happiness' was mainly affected by the home domain, whereas 'perceived life worth living' by both the home and the work domains.

Personality characteristics analysis of freshmen students

Yang, Xiaoling Psychology Faculty Office, Changsha University of Science, Changsha, People's Republic of China

AIM: To understand personality characteristics of freshmen students and to determine the personality characteristics of varied groups METHODS: The students are tested online under the network.. CONCLUSION? There exist differences between male and female students?between students of various disciplines in many aspects of their personality factors.There is a gap between personality traits of urban students and rural students. Personality traits differentiate insignificantly between the only child and the non-only-child. Economical conditions do not exert so much influence over the personality development. Among the various influential factors social environment and cultural background comprise the two basic elements in shaping the personality of the students.

Reliability and validity of the Chinese love attitude scale

Yang, Yang Psychology, Harbin Normal University, Harbin, People's Republic of China
The research aims to explore the usability of Love Attitude Scale in Chinese college students. 1009

subjects were investigated by 42-item Love Attitude Scale in which their love experiences were examined. In result, the six factors were proved by CFA and 22 items were included in LAS which had good structural validity, $\chi2(df)$: 666.42(200); RMSEA: 0.048. The internal consistency was 0.706 to 0.818 respectively. The attitudes towards love are a multidimensional psychological value, and the six love styles—Eros, Ludus, Storge, Pragma, Mania, and Agape are cross-cultural. The developed scale in the present study is available to assess the love attitude tendency of Chinese college students.

Children's drawings analyzed by the digital pen

Yato, Yuko Dept. of Psychology, Ritsumeikan University, Kyoto, Japan
This research was conducted in order to investigate the developmental changes in children's drawing activities during the scribbling stage, using the high technology interface device, the digital pen (Hitachi Maxell Ltd.). It converts handwritten analog information created by the pen and paper into digital data and stores it in its built-in memory. Twenty 2-to 4-year-old children were asked to draw pictures with the digital pens, and their drawing styles (speed, pressure, and strokes) were analyzed. The results revealed that the digital pen was technically feasible for analyses of drawing activities and developmental changes were found in children's scribbles.

The Event-related potentials characteristics of affective priming effect in alexithymia

Yi, Jinyao Central South University, Second Xiangya Hospital, Changsha, People's Republic of China Yao, Shuqiao Central South University, Second Xiangya Hospital, Changsha, People's Republic of China Zhong, Mingtian Central South University, Second Xiangya Hospital, Changsha, People's Republic of China Ling, Yu Central South University, Second Xiangya Hospital, Changsha, People's Republic of China

Objective: To analyze the characteristics of emotional automatic processing in alexithymia. Methods: 23 alexithymic and 23 nonalexithymic finished subliminal and supraliminal affective priming tasks, while the Event-Related Potentials were recorded. Results:(1) In subliminal affective priming tasks, there were no significant differences of correct rates and latencies between alexithymic and nonalexithymic, while in supraliminal tasks, the mean response latencies of alexithymic were longer than those of nonalexithymic. (2) In subliminal tasks, there were no significant differences of P2 and P3 between alexithymic and nonalexithymic, while the alexithymic was characterized by a decreased P2 peak amplitude and a P3 peak amplitude in supraliminal tasks. Conclusion: Alexithymic have deficit in automatic processing for emotional information that is aware of.

Effect of individual differences in working-memory capacities on schematic processing in impression formation

Yoshida, Ayano Dept. of Welfare Psychology, Tohoku Fukushi University, Sendai, Japan
This study examined the effect of individual differences in working memory capacity on processes for interpersonal information processing. In the Experiment, the paradigm proposed by Canter and Mishel (1977) was used. Fifty-two participants made impression judgments on the stimulus person who vitalizes the extroverted schema.The individual differences in WMC was measured by reading-span test. The amount of cognitive resources was manipulated by restricting time for judgment. Results showed that, only when cognitive resources were not restricted, the tendency to evaluate the stimulus person as "extroverted" was weaker in the high-WMC subjects than in the low-WMC subjects.

Level of processing and stimulus presentation time affects false memory

Yoshimura, Hiroki Letter, Hokkaido University, sapporo, Japan Shiotsubo, Ikuko Letter, Kochi University, Kochi, Japan Naka, Makiko Letter, Hokkaido University, sapporo, Japan

False recall and recognition memory were examined using DRM paradigm. Eighty-three participants were shown 120 words from eight DRM list.those in deep condition were asked to create sentences, and those in shallow condition were asked to counted vowels. Stimulus presentation time was 1.5 sec or 3sec. Then they were given recall and recognition tests. Results showed in both recall and recognition tests, list and critical words were more remembered in deep condition than in shallow condition. Although there was no effect of presentation time, semantic processing increased correct memory performance and false memory.

Challenging of deterministic thinking (cognitive therapy based on Islamic culture)

Younesi, Jalal counselling, University of social welfare, Tehran, Islamic Republic of Iran Younesi, Maryam counselling, University of social welfare, Tehran, Islamic Republic of Iran

One of cognitive distortions which has eminent role in developing depression and Anxiety, is deterministic thinking. This distortion emerges in the process of conclusion which is able to direct individual's mind in rigidity way and prevent him to consider any alternative in interpretation of events. In religious perspective, the distortion is seen as destructive factor for ruining balance of fear and hope which to be an important sign of people's faith. In this article, development of deterministic thinking and its role in creating mental disorders have been explained. Moreover as a basic cognitive therapy, the techniques of reality testing for challenging of this distortion have been described.

Visual perspective taking in autistic children and its relationship with gesture imitation

Yu, Yue Dept. of Psychology, Peking University, Beijing, People's Republic of China Su, Yanjie Psychology Department, Peking University, Beijing, People's Republic of China

Autistic children's visual perspective taking (VPT) ability was generally believed to be intact, but a particular response pattern during their imitation cast doubt on this idea. The current study compared 15 autistic children and 15 matched typically developing children on a Level-2 VPT task and a gesture imitation task. The results showed that autistic children performed worse in both tasks; the two scores correlated with each other and they also correlated with a specific type of error during imitation. These findings suggest a deficient of VPT skill in children with autism, and it might relate to their imitative deficit.

Factors produce changes of evaluations

Yusupova, Yulia Dept. of General Psychology, Southern Ural State University, Chelyabinsk, Russia
Variability is an attribute of the evaluation from the position of the Evaluation Theory (Baturin, 1997). Variability is unavoidable and necessary for support the evaluation adequacy. Researches (Baturin) show that evaluations change under the influence of numerous factors. These factors divided into internal and external. Internal factors are subject psychic phenomena. External factors are factors that influence the subject and process of evaluation from external environment. Also factors that influence the evaluation variability are natural and unnatural. These factors influence following evaluation components: subject, evaluation base, comparison object with base and evaluation expression. The problem of the variability of evaluation is actual for professional estimator as well other specialists.

The validity and reliability coefficients of Iranian adolescents risk-taking (IARS)

Zadeh Mohammadi, Ali Shahid Beheshti University, Fanily Research Institute, Islamic Republic of Iran Ahmad Abadi, Zohreh Fanily Research Institute, Shahid Beheshti University, Tehran, Islamic Republic of Iran Heidari, Mahmood Pychology Department, Shahid Beheshti University, Tehran, Islamic Republic of Iran Jeie Tehrani, Najmieh Deputy of Culture, Ministry of Culture, Tehran, Islamic Republic of Iran

The study evaluated the validity and reliability coefficients of scale and subscales of Iranian Adolescents Risk-taking (IARS). IARS contains 38 items in 7 subscales. The sample was 807 high school students (371 boys and 436 girls) were randomly selected from Tehran city and all subjects completed the IARS. The validity of IARS were (KMO = .949 and X2 = 16789.044, df = 703, p = .001). The alpha of scale obtained more satisfactory averaging .938 and for risky driving .715; violence .782; smoking .931; drug use .906; drinking .907; sexual relationship and behavior .856 and hetero-sexual attitude.809.

Interpersonal factors in empathic accuracy

Zaki, Jamil Dept. of Psychology, Columbia University, New York, USA Bolger, Niall Psychology, Columbia University, New York, USA Ochsner, Kevin Psychology, Columbia University, New York, USA

Paradoxically, perceiver empathy has failed to consistently predict empathic accuracy (EA). This disparity may be explained by variability in the expressivity of social targets; the current study addressed this possibility. Targets were videotaped while talking about emotional events, and then rated those videotapes for the affect they had felt while talking. Perceivers viewed these videotapes while inferring target affect. EA was operationalized as the correlation between target and perceiver ratings of target affect. Multilevel modeling revealed an interaction: perceiver empathy predicted EA only when target expressivity was high. This finding suggests that both target and perceiver factors contribute to EA.

Socially desirable responding or favorable personality?

Zaltauskas, Katrin Inst. für Psychologie, Universität Halle-Wittenberg, Halle, Germany Borkenau, Peter Department of Psychology, MLU Halle-Wittenberg, Halle (Saale), Germany

Social desirability scales ask for unlikely virtues to identify persons presenting themselves in a too favorable light on personality questionnaires. Thus their scale means should be higher for self-descriptions (e. g., "I never lie") than for descriptions of knowledgeable informants (e.g., "he/she never lies"). We obtained evidence that just the opposite might be true. On several personality questionnaires, including six scales to measure socially desirable responding, 304 pairs of students mutually described themselves and the peer. Self-reports means were compared to the peer reports means.

Perceived self-competence vs. fiscal expectations in success and in failure

Zawadzka, Anna Maria Inst. of Psychology, University of Gdansk, Gdansk, Poland

The existing research shows that whether it is success or failure that motivates the individual to perform an action depends on self-esteem. Self-competence and success of the individual reflect their fiscal aspirations. Self-esteem is linked to perceived self-competence. A series of experiments was carried out (N=500). The following hypotheses were tested and confirmed by ANOVA: fiscal expectations are raised in a situation of success in persons with high perceived self-competence and fiscal expectations are raised in a situation of failure in persons with low perceived self-competence.

The family model in the mass-media of Latvia

Zekova, Natalja Dept. of Social Psychology, Daugavpils Universitate, Daugavpils, Latvia Zekova, Natalia Social Psychology, Daugavpils Universitate, Daugavpils, Latvia

The mass-media play an important role in the social model development of society.The object of the research-the presented model of the family in the mass-media of Latvia.. The gualitative analysis of the family model will give the comprehension of the changes tendency in the modern family.

Extension of EM algorithm for finite mixture in item response theory for missing response data

Zeng, Li Dept. of Mathematics, Beijing Normal University, Beijing, People's Republic of China Xin, Tao psychology, beijing normal university, beijing, People's Republic of China Zhang, Shumei mathematics, beijing normal university, beijing, People's Republic of China

The traditional EM Algorithm for Item Response Theory treated latent trait (theta) as missing and deleted the incomplete cases to estimate the item parameter. Woodruff etc (1997) changed latent trait into discrete variable and applied EM Algorithm for finite mixture in parameter estimation. Based on Woodruff's work, we kept the incomplete cases and regard missing response data as "missing" like the latent trait. In our simulation, we investigated the relative performance of these two methods under different sample size and missing rate. The result reveals that our method is better, especially in the situation that the missing rate is large.

Thematic or taxonomic? Object categorization in children and adults

Zhang, Jiayu Dept. of Psychology, Peking University, Beijing, People's Republic of China Su, Yanjie Department of Psychology, Peking University, Beijing, People's Republic of China

The study aimed to investigate conceptual preference for either thematic or taxonomic relationships by manipulating the way presenting the materials. 39 7-year-olds and 37 undergraduates were presented with pictures or words of three objects and asked to pick two of them that went together. The way of presenting the materials has little to do with the preference, however, adults grouped the objects more on the basis of relationships than did children, $F(1,72) = 9.38$, $p = 0.003$, $\eta2 = 0.12$. It indicated that individuals show a preference for thematic relations as the development, suggesting the effect of culture and experiences.

The responsibility judgment and criticism decisions from an atributional perspective

Zhang, Aiqing School of Business, Central University of Finance, Beijing, People's Republic of China Yu, Guangtao School of Business, Central Univ of Finance&Ec, Beijing, People's Republic of China Qian, Zhenbo School of Business, Central Univ of Finance&Ec, Beijing, People's Republic of China Xia, Feifei College of education, Illinois State University, Illinois, USA

When someone failed to achieve his or her goals, decisions related with responsibility and criticism judgment often made by onlookers to motivate and reprimand the target. 196 sophomore participants attended this research. A structural equation model that reflected the relationships among attributional variables, affect responses and criticism decision was tested in Chinese culture. The results suggested that the participants assigned behavior responsibility according to causal locus as well as the perception of controllability. Afterward, responsibility inference elicited anger and sympathy and contributed to criticism decisions. Findings were discussed in terms of related culture and social values.

The newlyweds' conformity of marriage role expectation and performance during the first three intimate relationship phases: A U-shaped curve

Zhang, Yaofang Department of Psychology, Beijing Normal University, Beijing, People's Republic of China

We hypothesis that the inner process of newlyweds' accommodation is one's marriage role expectation is getting close with the other's role performance. At first three phases of intimate relationship, newlyweds' perceptive conformity of role expectation and performance shows a U-shaped curve. Using the questionnaires to measure marriage role conformity and intimate relationship phase. At romance stage, the real role conformity is low, but the perceptive conformity is high. During power struggle stage, real and perceptive one are both low. And during stability stage, real and perceptive one are both high. There is a pseudo-harmony during romance stage.

A study of initialization trait value in computerized adaptive personality testing

Zhang, Qinghua Scientific Research Office, Beijing Educ. Exam. Authority, Beijing, People's Republic of China

Typically, the approach to set initialization trait value has no effect on measurement accuracy if the length of computerized adaptive testing is enough. However, it would influence personality trait estimation in computerized adaptive personality testing (CAPT), since there are relatively few items for each trait. A new approach of initialization value estimation was proposed. The regression model of θ (the initialization value) to examinees' self-evaluation was used. Results indicate that compared with the common method of CAPT that assumes the initialization value of all examinees' to be zero; the new method reduced the deviation in trait estimation.

Development of China vocational interest card sort

Zhang, Zhe Education College, Zhejiang Normal University, Jinhua, People's Republic of China Liu, Xuanwen Children's Culture Institute, Zhejiang Normal University, Jinhua, People's Republic of China Zhang, Yingping Children's Culture Institute, Zhejiang Normal University, Jinhua, People's Republic of China

Vocational Interest Card Sort is a uniquely constructive and interactive assessment. The paper is to develop China Vocational Interest Card Sort (CVICS) on the basis of Holland theory. 607 Chinese secondary school students (male 231, female 367) were investigated. Item analysis found that CVICS had stability in time and people. CVICS Cronbach's a coefficient was .94, split-half correlation coefficient was .93 and retest reliability was .52. Validity analysis showed that CVICS was fitted to Holland's hexagonal model. The correlation coefficient between VICS and satisfaction is 4.66, p<.05. The correlation coefficient between VICS and satisfaction is 3.98, p<.05.

Study on the translation process from a cognitive-psychological perspective

Zhao, Yushan School of Foreign Language, North China Electric Power Uni, Beijing, Haidian District, People's Republic of China

Psychology of language and cognitive psychology are widely used in language studies. Based on human information-processing theory, the paper probes into the a translator's mental mechanism when translating with the aim to contribute to a better understanding of the cognitive process implied in translating. A new model of translating is constructed to establish an account of how the information-processing faculties of the translator's mind enable him to comprehend the source language text. A TAP is used to make a case study describing translators' mental state through the contrastive analysis. Keywords: cognitive psychology; translating process; model

The characteristic of representational model in different word problem-solving processing phase of children primary 4~6

Zhong, Ningning social work, Beijing youth politics college, Beijing, People's Republic of China

Rewrite task and abbreviate task were administered to children in primary 4~6 grade, in order to research the representational difference between comprehensible phase and executive phase. The results indicated: (1) Situation model was used in comprehensible phase and problem model was used in executive phase; (2) With entering the higher grade, situation model was used consistently, problem model was used more often; (3) The situation information in abbreviate task was chosen less in superior pupils, in another word, inferior pupils were worse than superior pupils in identifying redundant information; (4) Representation model was influenced by representation level.

Ending romantic relationships: The role of relationship characteristics, personality and compassionate love

Zimmerman, Corinne Dept. of Psychology, Illinois State University, Normal, USA *Sprecher, Susan* Sociology and Anthropology, Illinois State University, Normal, USA *Hesson-McInnis, Matthew* Psychology, Illinois State University, Normal, USA

We studied how compassionate (e.g., other-oriented) individuals are when disengaging from romantic relationships. Hierarchical regression revealed that relationship characteristics (e.g., seriousness, length), personality (Costa & McCrae, 1995), and Compassionate Love Scale (Sprecher & Fehr, 2005) scores each accounted for unique variance in the degree to which compassionate strategies were chosen to disengage from a relationship, total R2 = .39, F(12, 85) = 4.52, p < .0005. Although prior research has focused on the role of compassionate love in contributing to aspects of ongoing relationships (e.g., social support), we found compassionate love is also important in easing the dissolution of relationships.

Poster Session Thursday Afternoon 14:00

Examining the positive and negative developmental outcomes among Turkish adolescents with high and low trust beliefs

Özdikmenli Demir, Gözde Psychology Department, Hacettepe University, Ankara, Turkey *Kandap, Yeliz* Psychology Department, Hacettepe University, Ankara, Turkey *Sayl, Melike* Psychology Department, Hacettepe University, Ankara, Turkey *Kumru, Asiye* Psychology Department, Abant İzzet Baysal Univer, Bolu, Turkey

This study examined the effect of the level of trust beliefs toward parents, peers, and teachers in prosocial and agressive behaviors, types and the quality of friendship, and self-perceptions. Participants were 782 adolescents from 7th to10th grades in Turkey. Results indicated that adolescents with high trust beliefs had higher scores in belonging to school, positive friendships, altruism, and positive self perception. However, adolescents with low trust beliefs had higher scores on having deviant friendships, aggressive behaviors, loneliness, negative self-perception, and lower friendship quality. Trust belief to different targets' interactions with gender were especially observed on being bully/victim and positive/negative friendship quality.

The effect of stereotype threat on physician trust

Abdou, Cleopatra Psychology, UCLA, Los Angeles, USA *Fingerhut, Adam F.* Psychology, Loyola Marymount University, Los Angeles, USA *Davies, Paul G.* Psychology, University of British Columbia, Kelowna, Canada

We examined whether stereotype threat affects the health behaviors and decisions of minority women. Evidence suggests that African American females are more mistrustful of European American male physicians than their European American counterparts. In addition, when exposed to negative stereotypes of African American female sexuality (e.g., from Hip Hop album covers), African American females seem to exhibit a heightened sense of susceptibility to gynecological health problems, whereas European American females seem to gain a sense of immunity from gynecological health problems by this exposure.

Severity of life stress as a function of imagined social support

Acuna, Laura Psychology, National University of Mexico, Mexico City, Mexico *Gonzalez, Diana Alejandra* Psychology, National Univeristy of Mexico, Mexico City, Mexico *Bruner, Carlos A.* Psychology, National Univeristy of Mexico, Mexico City, Mexico

Adults (N=697) judged the severity of four well-known stressful-life situations as a function of two combined variables. One variable was the support of an increasing number of imaginary people. The other variable was whether the respondent had experienced or not the specific stressful situation. In accordance with Social Impact Theory, the severity of the stressful situation was a negatively-accelerated decreasing function of the number of imaginary supporters. When experienced, stressful events were judged as less stressful than when not experienced.

Promoting reading comprehension by teaching expository text structure

Adam-Schwebe, Stefanie Inst. für Pädag. Pschologie, Universität Frankfurt, Frankfurt, Germany *Souvignier, Elmar* Educational Psychology, Westfälische Wilhelms-Universi, Münster, Germany

Aim of the present study was to investigate, whether a short instruction in identifying and using structural aspects of expository texts would promote reading comprehension. A total of 298 5th graders were examined in a control group design with repeated measures. Statistical analyses (ANOVAs) revealed no group differences in a standardized reading test, while the instructed group outperformed the control group with respect to answering short essay questions. Results indicate that even a short instruction on expository text structure can promote reading comprehension. However, more instructional time seems to be needed to bring about transfer effects on a standardized test.

Psychosocial predictors of human trafficking in south west Nigeria

Adejumo, Gbadebo Human Resource Development, Covenant University,Ota, Ogun, Ota, Nigeria

Objective This study investigated psychosocial predictors of child involvement as victims of human trafficking. Methods 604 participants were randomly selected for this study. Four survey instruments were adopted; The Interpersonal Support Evaluation List, Coping Orientation to Problems Experienced, Rosenberg Self-Esteem Scale, and Domain–Specific, Risk-Taking Attitude Scale. Involvement in Trafficking in Person Scale was developed. Multiple regression analysis was used to analysis data collected Results Poor social support, avoidant coping, risk propensity, and poor self-esteem combined to predict child involvement as victims of human trafficking. Conclusion Findings indicated that children should be empowered

through functional social support, active coping strategy reasonable risk attitude and high self - esteem

Self-concept of identified gifted pupils

Adlesic, Irena Crnomelj, Slovenia

In Slovenia we execute identification of gifted pupils in primary schools (Slovenian concept of discovering and working with gifted pupils). I did a research about self-concept of identified gifted pupils in comparison with other pupils at the school. I used SDQ-1 (Self Description Questionnaire; Marsh, Parker and Smith, 1983). With statistical methods Iestablished differences between identified gifted pupils and other pupils in academic and non-academic self-concept and the components of self-concept. Results of the study help us make programmes for developing real positive self-concept of gifted pupils. Results show that these pupils need additional academic knowlwdge: more contents, deep proceedings and programmmes for personality growth-first of all on self-concept.

Cross-cultural research of Russians and Kazakhs ethnical identity processes in multi-ethnical Kazakhstan

Aimaganbetova, Alnara Dept. of Psychology, Kazakh National University, Alma-Ata, Kazakhstan

Study of transforming ethnical identity basic levels and forms was conducted with the help of methodical workouts modified up to multi-ethnical Kazakhstan conditions. The research object were students representing three regions of the republic with different dominancy of Russian and Kazakh population. Empirical study revealed cognitive and affective components of ethnical identity and its forms scaling from positive ethnical identity up to ethno-fanatical states. Tolerance and intolerance level was indicated by assessment of person's relation to his own or other national-ethnical groups, scaling the threshold of emotional reacting towards "foreign language" environment and the level of aggressiveness towards alien people.

A survey of the most frequent problems of school children in UAE using three forms of assessment

Alghorani, Mohammad Adnan Dept. of Psychology, United Arab Emirates Univ., Al Ain, United Arab Emirates

This study investigated the perspectives of teachers, administrators, social specialists, and psychological specialists, regarding the prevalence of various children's problems. When participants were asked to list children's problems in order with regard to frequency, lack of motivation and low academic achievement were at the top of the lists. Comparing frequencies of paired categories of problems indicated that the most frequent problems are behavioral. When participants were asked to rate how spread is each of the 61 problems identified in the survey, more than half of the problems were rated between moderately-spread and vary spread.

The rekindling of the community principle: A way for conceptualizing community

Almeida, Eduardo Educación y Psicología, Univ. Iberoamericana Puebla, Puebla, Mexico *Sánchez, María Eugenia* Educación y Psicología, Univ. Iberoamericana Puebla, Puebla, Mexico

This presentation is a mix between description and reflection. The life of the authors is rooted both in practice and academics. They will pick up examples from their thirty years of community experience in Mexico that highlight a new way of conceptualizing community. In their understanding the concept claims to be partial, process oriented, and it is not free of dilemmata and contradiction. The community processes contain particular dilemmas related to interaction, conflict and utopian components. The objective is to contribute to the rekindling of the neglected community principle supposed to regulate modernity

Does perspective taking reduce cultural stereotypes and prejudice?

Alvarez, Jose Luis Educación, Universidad de Cordoba, Cordoba, Spain Gonzalez Castro, Jose Luis Ciencias de la Educación, Universidad de Burgos, Burgos, Spain Ubillos, Silvia Ciencias de la Educación, Universidad de Burgos, Burgos, Spain González González, Hugo Educación, Universidad de Córdoba, Cordoba, Spain Palmero, Carmen Ciencias de la Educación, Universidad de Burgos, Burgos, Spain Jiménez, Alfredo Ciencias de la Educación, Universidad de Burgos, Burgos, Spain

Research on stereotyping and prejudice has important applications in the explanation of interpersonal and intergroup behaviour in the classroom context. It is important to develop the ability to gain some control over the use of stereotypes and prejudice. Our study evaluated the effects that perspective taking exerted on implicit stereotyping and prejudice, and on explicit prejudice in a Spanish educator students sample. Results obtained from data collected with the Implicit Association Test showed that stereotyped associations and prejudiced evaluations were reduced through the use of such a strategy, but only in some conditions linked to personal attributes

The effect of chess playing on problem- solving skill

Aminranjbar, Mahnaz Karaj, Islamic Republic of Iran
In order to investigate the effect of chess playing on problem-solving skills,in this research that was done through exprrimental pretest -posttest design,it was hypothesized that chess playing improves p-s skills. for this purpose 54 college student were selected and divided randomly into two groups.after conducting pretest (test numer one of 8-part test of Eysneck logical reasoning) experimental group recived 8 session of two chess play instruction.at the end of 8th session, posttest (test 2 of 8-part test)was performed in two groups.the mean of score differences in evry group in pretest and posttest were compared.calculated t was 1/745 .cocequently,the alternative hypotesis was approved.

Conflicts and resolution strategies in a school context: Girl students and woman teacher's perspective

Andrés Gómez, Maria Soledad Dept. de Psicopedagogía, Universidad de Alcalá, Madrid, Spain Martín Ortega, Elena Psicología Evolutiva y Educ., Universidad Autonoma (Madrid), Madrid, Spain Barrios, Angela Psicología Evolutiva y Educ., Universidad Autónoma (Madrid), Madrid, Spain

We present data, part of a wider empirical study about school climate, that show the gender variable strong influence in the perception of the conflicts and in the strategies to confront them. The work took place in two Secondary Schools in a hard social area in the boundary of Madrid, during the academic years 2000/2002. The questionnaires, specially designed, were distributed between students (N= 1240) and teachers (N=118). We used Anovas and Chi-Square (p≤ 0,05 and 0,01), Scheffe and DMS. In a general sense, the results show better competences of girls and women in order to maintain positive relationships.

Life and health conditions of a worker in a rural settling

Aparecida, Rosemeire Scopinho Department of Psychology, Federal Uni. of San Carlos, San Carlos, Brazil

Studying the organizational process of a rural settling, I have tried to understand the meaning given to health-illness by workers and health practices being developed, comparing information obtained from documentary analysis, interviews and observation of the daily routine of life and work in the settling. The contrast between urban and rural life way is a strong feature in the meaning of health-illness. Between idealized concepts and feasible practices, the attempt to solve problems and make health a social right, came up against the fragmentary and inarticulate way that public policy involved in the land reform has been implemented in Brazil.

Overprotective Latin-Americans mothers against children development: Case of study

Arias Galicia, Fernando Dept. of Psychology, Morelos University, Cuernavaca, Mexico Melgarejo, María Dept. de Psicotherapia, Morelos University, Temixco, Mexico

Objective: To demonstrate that overprotection process has a negative influence in children development. Methods: case of study Results: The person involved, who is 40 years old, paralyzed his life project because of this problem, he attended therapy to solve it, but after wards he stopped it, because he was not able to live by himself, separated from his mother. Conclusions: culturally spoken, Latin mothers are overprotective and this process is a limitation to a healthy adult development.

Psychosocial variables as correlates of University Maladjustment behaviour

Arogundade, Odunayo Dept. of Behavioural Studies, Redeemer's University, Ogun, Nigeria

The goal of the study was to examine the influence of some psychosocial variables like personality factors (extraversion, agreeableness, neuroticism, conscientiousness and openness), gender and age in predicting university maladjustment. The participants, 134 students in the age range 16-30 years randomly selected from a private University in Nigeria. The Big Five Personality inventory (BFI) and University Maladjustment Scale (UMS) were used to collect data. Multiple regression analysis and t-test statistics were used to analyze the data. The result showed that all the psychosocial variables jointly predicted 87% of the University Maladjustment variance. The implications were also discussed in terms of screening fresh intakes into University and minimizing student unrest.

Break-up of romantic relationships changes sense of coherence: A strategy for stress coping

Asano, Ryosuke Dept. of Social Psychology, Osaka University, Suita, Japan Daibo, Ikuo Social Psychology, Osaka University, Suita, Japan Horike, Hiroko Faculty of Arts, Tohoku Gakuin University, Sendai, Japan

The present study examined the changeability of sense of coherence (SOC; a way of seeing the world that is comprehensive, manageable, and meaningful) in relation to a stress coping with dissolution of romantic relationships. A questionnaire was administered to 403 undergraduates, including those who had experienced terminations of romantic relationships (N=234). Structural equation modeling revealed that hostile coping and regretted coping decreased the levels of SOC. These results suggested that SOC might be negatively changed according to stressful events of interpersonal relationships. The association between SOC and social acceptance in close relationships was discussed.

Are spatial body processing so special?

Auclair, Laurent LPNCog - CNRS, Université Paris Descartes, Boulogne-Billancourt Cedex, France
Spatial representations are different for human bodies and other spatial objects. However, this difference could be articulated on the human/non human axis or on the living/non living axis. We tested these two possibilities in a matching experiment using an inversion paradigm, with human bodies, puppets (simplified body representation), familiar animals and non-living objects. Like Reed (2003), we found that the inversion effect was smaller for non-living objects than for human bodies. Most importantly, the inversion effect was smaller for puppets and animals than for human bodies, a result which is in favour of the human/non human difference of representation.

"To be honest, your suffering makes me hate you": Being reminded of ongoing suffering of historical victims increases prejudice

Awanesjan, Arthur Social and Legal Psychology, University of Bonn, Bonn, Germany Clemens, Sarah Inst. für Sozialpsychologie, Universität Bonn, Bonn, Germany Imhoff, Roland Social and Legal Psychology, University of Bonn, Bonn, Germany

Being confronted with ongoing victim suffering after ingroup atrocities can elicit group-based guilt which may evoke negative views of the victims. We developed an indirect test measuring whether the manipulation of activated historical representation had an impact on prejudice against the victim-group. Manipulating historical representation (ongoing harm vs. not) and social desirability (bogus pipeline vs. off) we found an interaction effect (ANOVA; N=63). Compared to a baseline measure ongoing harm priming led to an increase of victim derogation for participants in the bogus pipeline condition. Forced to be honest, perpetrator group members react to ongoing harm with victim disparagement.

Campus Violence: A case study of University of Lagos

Ayenibiowo, Kehinde Dept. of Psychology, University of Lagos, Lagos, Nigeria

This research is an attempt to investigate the incidence of violence among university students using University of Lagos as a case study. A questionnaire on different kinds of violence was administered to 446 students of the university. In addition, four focus group discussion sessions were conducted. Most of the respondents were aged 21-25 years. The results show the prevalence of verbal violence. However, physical violence was recorded more among the students in the first year than the higher levels. The findings show the need for proper orientation and guidance on social interaction for new students of tertiary institutions

The dimension of playing and the symbolic reachability

Barbosa, Cristina Monteiro Dept. de Psicometria, UFRJ, Rio de Janeiro, Brazil Maia Pereria, Andreza Dept. de Psicometria, UFRJ, Rio de Janeiro, Brazil Cavgias Martins Fraga, Madellon Dept. de Psicometria, UFRJ, Rio de Janeiro, Brazil Muruci Abreu, Michelle Dept. de Psicometria, UFRJ, Rio de Janeiro, Brazil

Objective- Show that the child symbolizes his pain through the act of playing. Methodologu- This study consisted in the analyses of a group of 6 children from poor communities in Rio de Janeiro/ Brazil, using psychoanalyti theories, privileging free and ludic sessions. Result- that the act of playing give the child psychic preparation for unpleasent events. At clinic, through ludic activities, the child builds a narrative about its own life. Conclusion- through of act of the ludic playing the children tell event and his life's pain; the analyst would have the role of interlocutor, listener and interpreter the psychic elaboration.

The use of physical discipline in parenting practices: Predictors in a Portuguese sample

Barroso, Ricardo Psychology, University of Trás-os-Montes, Vila Real, Portugal Gonçalves, Miguel Psychology, University of Minho, Braga, Portugal Machado, Carla Psychology, University of Minho, Braga, Portugal

The present study has the objective to observe the effect of cultural and psychopathological variables (beliefs on physical punishment and parental psychiatric symptomatology) in the disciplinary practices. Through the corresponding analyses of regression we look explanations in the analysis of the ratio of variance for the most predictor. For the accomplishment of the study we requested to a sample of 126 citizens (parents or mothers) the schedule of VBS Scale, PI, CBCL 4-18 and the BSI. The variables Obsessive-Compulsive, Anxiety and Hostility have greater ratio in the prediction of the potential use of physical abuse in the children.

Interpreter Competency Exam: Mental Health (Revised)

Barsukov, Sergiy Dept. of Clinical Psychology, George Fox University, Newberg, USA *Pearson, Melinda* Clinical Psychology, George Fox University, Newberg, USA *McMinn, Mark* Clinical Psychology, George Fox University, Newberg, USA *Roid, Gale* Literacy, Language, Learning, Southern Methodist University, Dallas, USA *Adams, Wayne* Clinical Psychology, George Fox University, Newberg, USA

One of the most important aspects of culture is language, making it essential for psychological services to be offered in a language suited to the client's needs. There are no validated tests to assess interpreters' competence in mental health interpretation. Interpreter Competency Exam in Mental Health (revised) was developed to assess competence of Russian interpreters in mental health setting. It was normed on 32 subjects of professional interpreters, and its revised version contains 98 items with 3 subtests. It tests interpreter's mental health terminology, concepts, and interpreter ethics. Reliabilities range from .84 to .98 on its subtests.

Impact of computer-supported collaboration and knowledge awareness on analogical problem solving

Baumeister, Antonia Inst. für Medien-Psychologie, Universität Tübingen, Tübingen, Germany *Engelmann, Tanja* (IWM-KMRC), KnowledgeMedia Research Center, Tuebingen, Germany *Hesse, Friedrich W.* (IWM-KMRC), KnowledgeMedia Research Center, Tuebingen, Germany

An experimental study investigated whether computer-supported collaboration enhances source problem retrieval and transfer of solution to target problems compared to individual analogical problem solving, and whether an external representation for supporting knowledge awareness regarding the source problem the partner has remembered additionally supports collaborative analogical problem solving. Collaborating dyads with an external representation for supporting knowledge awareness were compared to collaborating dyads without such an external representation and to a baseline of nominal dyads. Both collaborative conditions developed knowledge awareness. Nominal dyads solved more target problems, but collaborating dyads were more confident when they had solved the target problems correctly.

Disabling the able: Stereotype threat and women's deductive reasoning

Bedynska, Sylwia Dept. of Psychology, School of Social Psychology, Warsaw, Poland *Dreszer, Joanna* Psychology, Nicolaus Copernicus University, Torun, Poland

Gender differences in standardized math can be explained according to the Stereotype Threat Model (Steele & Aronson 1995) It suggests that stereotype may influence performance of able group members in the situation of test taking. The stereotype may interfere with test accuracy by blocking ability to strategize. In the presented study generative reasoning task was used to assess the ability to build a mental model. Results showed that under stereotype threat women were unable to integrate information and those generative thinking deficits were due to the problems in cognitive strategy but not the shortage of the working memory capacity.

Pro social Behavior in adolescents: Content validation of the scale VMS with Brazilian sample

Bellico da Costa, Anna Edith Mestrado em Educação, FAE / UEMG, Belo Horizonte, Brazil

Objective: to investigate the understanding of the content scale Visions of Morality (VMS) (Mc Adams & Shelton, 1990) - subscale: social morality, by adolescents' samples due the low adhesion of them to the pro social actions. It was proceeded content analysis of that subscale and about the answers of adolescents. Results: the majority's items describes specific situations of the US culture without correspondence here; situations with similarity those lived in Brazil are committed for our circumstances partner-politics that modify the sense of pro social actions. Conclusion: it will have to modify some items or to exclude them to guarantee reliability.

Personal determinants of the pupil's rowdyism at school: Test of a structural model

Bennacer, Halim Université d'Orléans, Tours, France

This work aims at studying, in a causal theoretical model, the role of some personal features and some dynamical mechanisms of the personality in the determination of the pupil's rowdyism at school. Conducted on a sample of 336 elementary school pupils, it allows us to develop a structural model accounting for 43 % in the pupil's rowdyism variance (Path analysis). The results show that the dynamical mechanisms of the personality, relating to the affective entry characteristics (Bloom), play an important mediating role as dependent and independent variables.

"In" or "Out"? The Impact of minimal & maximal goal orientations on reactions towards norm deviants

Berthold, Anne DFG Unit, Universität Jena, Jena, Germany *Mummendey, Amelié* DFG Unit, Universität Jena, Jena, Germany *Kessler, Thomas* DFG Unit, Universität Jena, Jena, Germany *Luecke, Bastian* DFG Unit, Universität Jena, Jena, Germany *Schubert, Thomas* Social Psychology Department, Free University Amsterdam, BT Amsterdam, Netherlands

We expect individuals to evaluate others with reference to different types of goals. Evaluations relative to minimal goals vary in an all-or-none-fashion as either acceptable or unacceptable; maximal goals imply graded evaluations, ranging from more to less positive (Brendl & Higgins, 1996). Consequently, violations of minimal goals are assumed to elicit more easily explicit negative treatment (e.g. punishment) than violations of maximum goals. Participants saw pictures showing a smoker in different distances to a smoking area, that was marked by yellow bars (min) or was not (max). Identical behaviors were evaluated more negatively under minimal than maximal goal orientations.

The impact of a gratitude ritual in subjective well-being: An experiment

Bilbao Ramírez, Maria Angeles Psicología Social, Universidad del Pais Vasco, San Sebastian, Spain *Páez, Dario* Psicología Social, Universidad del Pais Vasco, San Sebastian, Spain *Campos, Miryam* Psicología Social, Universidad del Pais Vasco, San Sebastian, Spain *Bobowik, Magdalena* Psicología Social, Universidad del Pais Vasco, San Sebastian, Spain

The aim of this study was to evaluate the impact of a gratitude ritual on subjective well-being. 103 students were divided into two experimental and one control groups. Participants were asked to answer a brief questionnaire, complete a cognitive exercise to elicit emotional reaction (positive or negative experience) and write a Christmas card to a person they were grateful. After Christmas vacations a post-assessment was conducted. Preliminary results show interesting differences between controls and experimental participants. The impact of positive and negative salience in gratitude ritual on SWB will be presented, and also the effect of family variables and celebrations.

Analysing time differences in isochronous sequences: Holistic or analytic encoding?

Blaschke, Stefan BCCN, Universität Göttingen, Göttingen, Germany *Hass, Joachim* BCCN, University of Göttingen, Göttingen, Germany *Herrmann, Michael* BCCN, University of Göttingen, Göttingen, Germany *Rammsayer, Thomas* Pers. & Diff. Psy. & D, University of Bern, Bern, Switzerland

Sussman and Gumenyuk (2005) found that a series of sound intervals is processed holistically if presented in rapid succession. This questions the validity of pacemaker-counter timing mechanisms that assume an analytic processing. The goal of the study was to clarify if a rapid presentation of intervals leads to a holistic or analytic processing in a time perception task. We varied the total duration of a sequence of intervals using different durations and numbers of intervals. Weber fractions increase with longer durations but not with an increasing number of intervals indicating analytic rather then holistic processing.

Poverty: Survey on a sample of young people - Cross-cultural analysis Spain-Italy

Bonechi, Francesca Dept. of Social Psychology, Universidad Autónoma de Madrid, Madrid, Spain *Cavallero, Paola* Social Psychology, University of Florence, Florence, Italy

Objective: to explore basic elements constituting the Social Representation of poverty of young people belong to different social-economic contexts. Method: 346 spanish and italian students; mesures of central and peripheral elements of Social Representations. Results: Osgood's Semantic Differential shows the Representation's field. "Average position" and "Frequency apparition" identifies central and peripheral elements. A hierarchical Cluster analysis reveales negative attitud towards poverty, but not towards poor people. External attribution prevails. Descriptive statistics reveals low knowledge about poverty, especially in the italian group. Conclusions: the central core of Social Representation is similar in the both groups, with big differences in peripheral elements.

Emotional state changes and risk-taking: The example of scuba-diving

Bonnet, Agnàs Dep. of Psychology, University of Provence, Aix-en-Provence, France *Fernandez, Lydia* Psychology, University of Picardie, Amiens, France *Piolat, Annie* Psychology, University of Provence, Aix En Provence, France *Pedinielli, Jean-Louis* Psychology, University of Provence, Aix En Provence, France

Risk-taking implies a cognitive evaluation process to determine the level of risk involved in an activity. Emotional phenomena affect behavioural choices. This study examines how emotional responses to the perceived risk of a scuba-diving injury, in turn, affects emotional states, contribute to divers' behaviour. The study sample consisted of 131 risk-takers and non-risk-takers divers. The emotional states before and after the behavior were assessed using the Differential Emotion Scale (Izard, 1977). Results indicated presence of subjective emotional experiences that are specific to whether a risk has been taken. Emotional states and emotional arousal appear to act as on emotional self-regulation by way of risk-taking behavior.

Practices and beliefs in Italian mothers of 5-month-old infants

Bornstein, Marc H. *Nichd, Nih, rovereto (TN), Italy* *Esposito, Gianluca* *rovereto (TN), Italy* **de Falco,** *Simona* *DiSCoF - Cognitive Science, University of Trento, Rovereto (TN), Italy* **Venuti, Paola** *DiSCoF - Cognitive Science, University of Trento, rovereto (TN), Italy*

A common assumption is that the manner in which one rears a child will depend on the practices and beliefs of the respective culture into which the infant was born. In this study, we compared beliefs and behaviors in mothers of 5-month-old infants. As beliefs, we analyzed ideas that mothers hold about their own actual childrearing, in two parenting domains: social and didactic. As practices, through the Emotional Availability Scales (EAS) we assess mother behavior during a 1-hr interaction with the child. We found consistent correlations between practices and beliefs.

Job satisfaction cross-culturally: Is it just acquiescence what we measure?

Bosau, Christian *Ökonomie und Soz.-Pychologie, Universität Köln, Köln, Germany* **Fischer, Lorenz** *Economic/Social Psychology, University of Cologne, Cologne, Germany* **Meyenschein, Kerstin** *Economic-/Social-Psychology, University of Cologne, Cologne, Germany*

Job satisfaction (JS) is regularly measured in international organizational surveys and compared across cultures. While research has noted that different cultures show different degrees of response tendencies, there have been almost no results how JS-measurements are influenced by response tendencies e.g. aquiescence. Researching exactly this, our results interestingly show that the JS-level is lower in cultures showing high aquiescence. Furthermore, we can show that acquiescence is able to almost fully mediate the often reported individualism-JS-relation: Culture leads to acquiescence that in turn leads to the JS-level. Intercultural JS-measurements are therefore rather an expression of communicational norms than of true variation.

Teachers' and children's perceptions of childhood behaviour difficulties: Comparison of two different school and social environments

Bouchafa, Houria *IPSA, UCO, Angers Cedex 01, France* **Déry, Michàle** *Special Education, University of Sherbrooke, Sherbrooke, Canada* **Jousseau, Aline** *IPSA, UCO, Angers cedex 01, France*

Childhood behaviour difficulties have major consequences on school and adult life adaptation. This study compared children and teachers perception of children's behaviour difficulties from two contrasted school and social environments. The population was composed of 40 children, half of them attending mainstream elementary schools while the others living in underprivileged districts, and their teachers. Structured diagnostic interviews based on DSM-IV criteria were used for teachers and children answered to the Dominique Interactive, a computerized pictorial questionnaire. Main results showed no difference between teachers' evaluations, whatever the environment. They overestimate exteriorized behaviours compared to children who revealed more interiorized problems.

Asymmetry of attention shifting in healthy very low birth weight infants

Burdukova, Julia *Clinical & special psychology, MGPPU, Moscow, Russia* **Tsetlin, Marina** *Clinical & special psychol, MGPPU, Moscow, Russia* **Stroganova, Tatiana** *behavioral genetics, PIRAO, Moscow, Russia*

Objective: To investigate putative asymmetry of spatial attention in healthy preterm very low birthweight infants(VLBW). Methods: A-not-B task was administered to 16 VLBW and 16 full-term (FT) infants aged 13–14 months. The error rate for left and right target locations separately was used as a measure of performance. Repeated-measures ANOVA was used for data analysis. Results: Unlike symmetrical task performance in FT infants, VLBW demonstrated significant rightward asymmetry of A-not-B errors. They also made more errors than FT in trials with right target only. Conclusions: The results imply that healthy preterm infants have sub-clinical rightward attentional deficit.

Economic behaviour and imperfectly choices: Experts and ordinary people on the same wrong way?

Bustreo, Massimo *Istituto di Consumi, IULM University, Feltre, Italy* **Castelli, Luciana** *Consumi, comportamento e comun, IULM University, Milano MI, Italy* **Russo, Vincenzo** *Consumi, comportamento e comun, IULM University, Milano MI, Italy*

The individual behaviour is largely work of making decisions and solving problems. It is work of choosing issues that require attention, setting goals, designing courses of action, and evaluating and choosing among alternative actions. Spending, earning, and investing are actions not "risk-free" from an irrational or unnecessary behaviour. This quali-quantitative research aims to highlight the differences of the «bounded rationality» (Simon, 1982; Gigerenzer e Selten, 2002) between experts (bank operators) and ordinary people (undergraduate students). The results want to show the connection between the economic behaviour between experts and ordinary people, both on a cognitive and an emotive level.

Personal values, family socialization and coping styles related to emotional regulation in hispanic context

Campos, Miryam *Social Psychology, Basque Country University, San Sebastian, Spain* **Basabe, Nekane** *Social Psychology, Basque Country University, San Sebastian, Spain* **Zubieta, Elena** *Social Psychology, Buenos Aires University, Buenos Aires, Argentina* **Páez, Darío** *Social Psychology, Basque Country University, San Sebastian, Spain*

The objective of this study is to explore the relationships between Schwartzs Individual Values, family adaptative functioning, perceived parental socialization styles and functional - dysfunctional personal ways of Coping using a optimal emotional regulation indicator. A descriptive correlation study was carried out based on a convenience sample of 220 Spanish and Chilean university students. Results show higher endorsement of Hierarchical values related to dysfunctional family climate and less optimal parental socialization styles in order to cope with anger and sadness. Benevolence shows more relevance than conservation values in perceived familiar social climate promoting adaptative coping styles in positive cognitive reevaluation.

The temporal-spatial strategy of children on sampling traits for irregular figure recognition

Cao, Xiaohua *Dept. of Psychology, Zhejiang Normal University, Jinhua, People's Republic of China*

An eye movements study on the temporal-spatial strategy for irregular geometric figure recognition was conducted. The design of the experiment as a 2×2 mixed model. The factors were grade type(grade 6 or grade 3) and display type(rotated or not rotated). It was found that, The students of grade 6 always were good at spatial strategy of adding the number of fixations, and then adjusting the duration on each fixation; but the students of grade 3 were good at using temporal strategy of adding duration on each fixation, and then adding the number of fixations on sampling. The interaction between grade and display style had a significant effect on the spatial strategy in the figure recognition.

The Career Orientation Program (COP) experience

Carvalho, Renato Gil *Dept. de Psicologia, DRE/UMa, Campanário, Portugal*

The COP intends to develop a higher vocational maturity and a more extended future time perspective (FTP) in students, especially when they're at the end of compulsory school. It was implemented during the school year and consisted in three types of activities: a program of thematic group sessions involving vocational dimensions, individual counseling, and parallel activities such the participation in conferences, information and study/experimental activities. Results have shown an increase in vocational maturity and in the extent of students' FTP, suggesting the program effectiveness and sustaining the necessity of orientation policies in educational organizations.

Pluralistic ignorance and deviance: Perceptions solid facts of reality

Chadee, Derek *Psychological Research Centre, University of the West Indies, St. Augustine, Trinidad and Tobago*

Data from a survey of 760 secondary school students (14 – 16 years) are used to assess the relationship between the propensity to observe social norms and pluralistic ignorance. Measurements are taken of students' perception of their peers on deviant and illegal behaviour including usage of tobacco, alcohol, marijuana, cocaine, sexual behaviour, use of obscene language/swearing, and bulling. Students' were also asked about the frequency of their own behaviour/usage. The results are discussed in the context that much of people's behaviour are influenced by their perception of how other members of their group behaviour and the implications of such misperception. Findings are analyzed based on socio-econmic status and ethnic background of respondents and other factors.

Inhibition of return facilitates location selection

Chao, Hsuan-Fu *Dept. of Psychology, Chung Yuan Christian Unives., Chung Li, Taiwan*

Inhibition of return (IOR) refers to slowed responses to a target that appears at a cued location. In the current study, a location selection task was used to demonstrate the facilitatory effect produced by IOR. A target and distractor were presented at the same time, and participants were instructed to indicate the location of the target. The results showed that it took a shorter time to respond to the target when the distractor was presented at the cued location. These results support the idea that an exogenous cue can facilitate target selection by inhibiting distractor location.

Toilet training process: A psychological perspective

Chen, Bin-Bin *Department of Psychology, Shanghai Normal University, Shanghai, People's Republic of China* **Rugolotto, Simone** *Department of Pediatrics, University of Verona, Verona, Italy*

OBJECTIVE: To review the literature on toilet training process (TTP) based on psychological development. METHODS: Through a literature review method, all theories and viewpoints on psychological development for TTP were reviewed. RESULTS & DISCUSSIONS: Two main psychological views for TTP have been described: Erik Erikson's first two stages of psychosocial development, and behaviorist viewpoints. The former emphasized the role of psychosocial influences including parental responsiveness on TTP. The latter is applied to actively teaching toileting behaviors. How evidenced-based toilet training practices meet the requirements of infant and toddler's psychological development and help them learn toilet training skills was presented.

Cross-model pre-attentive processing and audio-visual modality effect of time perception as indexed by mismatch negativity

Chen, Youguo School of of Psychology, Chongqing, People's Republic of China *Huang, Xiting* School of Psychology, School of Psychology, Chongqing, People's Republic of China
Objectives: The present study investigate the neural basis of cross-model pre-attentive processing and audio-visual modality effect of time perception within 200 ms. Methods: The auditory and visual temporal mismatch negativity (MMN) was obtained in the "cross-modal delayed response odd-ball paradigm" from 15 healthy subjects. Results: Attention affected amplitude of visual MMN but not auditory MMN; The latency of auditory MMN was significant shorter than that of visual. Conclusions: The auditory time perception is mainly automatic processing, while visual time perception includes automatic and controlled processing; Audio-visual modality effect is result from a latency difference and maintaining attention difference.

A preliminary test of a three-dimensional model of performance anxiety in the context of sports performance

Cheng, Wen-Nuan Kara Recreation & sports management, Taipei Physical Education Coll, Taipei, Taiwan *Hardy, Lew* School of health, sport &, University of Wales, Bangor, United Kingdom
To reflect the adaptive potential (producing positive effects) of anxiety more explicitly, a three-dimensional model of performance anxiety was proposed, with a third regulatory dimension in addition to the intensity-oriented dimensions of cognitive and physiological anxiety. The predictive validity of this model was initially examined in the context of elite level of tae-kwon-do sports performers (N = 99) in Taiwan. Data including ratings of pre-competitive anxiety and assessment of performance were collected using self-report instruments and analyzed via moderated hierarchical multiple regression. The findings showed support for the three predictions of anxiety variables with single and interactive effects upon sports performance.

The accountability of schooling-related experiences for learning behaviors of minority students

Chin, Jui-Chih Early Childhood Education, Taipei Municipal Uni. of Educ., Taipei, Taiwan *Lu, Wen-Yueh* Early Childhood Education, Taipei Municipal Univ. of Ed, Taipei, Taiwan *Chen, Yin-Ying* Early Childhood Education, Taipei Municipal UnivEducation, Taipei, Taiwan
The purpose of the study was to explore the relationships between schooling-related experiences and minority students' learning behaviors. Teachers of 1128 first- and second-grade Taiwanese students with immigrant mothers filled out the survey questionnaire. The analysis of hierarchical multiple regression revealed that, with demographic variables controlled, more preschool experiences and more participation in supplementary learning programs could predict adaptive learning behaviors. However, parent involvement in school became the most powerful predictor when entered, whereas supplementary program participation and SES were ruled out. These findings manifested that more parent involvement and more preschool experiences would facilitate minority students' adaptive learning behaviors, regardless of SES and supplementary resources to which they had accesses.

Coping responses as mediator to type-A personality in promoting general health: A path analysis of predictive factors

Chinaveh, Mahbobeh Dept. of Psychology, Islamic Azad University, Shiraz, Islamic Republic of Iran
This study examines the Goodness-of-fit of the moderating effect of coping responses on Type-A personality in promoting general health among Iranian university students. Three hundred and twenty-six students took part in the study. The students completed Type-A behavior, Coping Responses and General Health questionnaires. Findings from the study show that the fit indices for this model are excellent. The RMSEA was 0.05, and the GFI and AGFI were 0.95 and 0.94, respectively. Approach responses (r = -0.43) and avoidant responses (r = 0.39) were shown to have direct effects on general health. The findings also show that Type-A personality has small direct and indirect effect (r = 0.14) on general health. All paths were significant at p

The conditions of activity of elderly people

Chudzicka-Czupala, Agata Inst. of Psychology, Silesian University, Katowice, Poland *Popiolek, Katarzyna* Institute of Psychology, Silesian University, Katowice, Poland
The problem of our research were conditions of activity of elderly people. We tried to find out why some elderly people cope better with everyday problems than others. The variables we measured were: activity, coping, time perception, social relations, hope and transgression. The results indicate the most common forms of activity of elderly and they describe the connections between the variables. They show how elderly people perceive time and how they judge the way they function in time (we explored for example: acceptance, social adequacy, effectiveness). Time perception appeared an important factor which influences human activity and determines life satisfaction.

Media representations of people with disabilities: An intercultural approach

Ciot, Melania-Gabriela DPPD, Univers. Tehnica Cluj-Napoca, Cluj-Napoca, Romania
Objective: Identifying certain particularities in media's portrayals of people with disabilities in Eastern European area (Romania) that could be associated with political, socio-economical and cultural factors. Method: content analysis (investigative), which will surprise the type of social representations of disability. Sample of publications: publications between 1989-1999 and 2003 at central and local level with daily, weekly and monthly appearance, with a circulation level more than 500.000 and with a specific for social and political elements. Results: specific Romanian media images of disability. Conclusions: there are connections between Romanian media portrayals of disability and the political, socio-economical and cultural factors that characterized each period of investigation, influenced by the Western media models of disability.

Occupational stress arising from workplace bullying between nurses

Clarke, Darren Dept. of Health and Ageing, Office of Aged Care Qua.&Compl, Adelaide, Australia *Jones, Mairwen* Behav. & Community Health, University of Sydney, Sydney, Australia *Adamson, Barbara* Behavioural & Community Hl, The University of Sydney, Lidcombe Sydney, Australia
Objectives: Examined incidence and effects of bullying between nurses. Methods: Health consequences of exposure to workplace bullying were examined in a sample of 352 nurses using a questionnaire adapted from the Occupational Stress Indicator (Cooper et al, 1988) to measure the type and frequency of distress experienced. Results: The effects of bullying on the wellbeing of victims were widespread. They included 'fatigue (52%)', 'insomnia (45%)' and 'headaches (45%)'. Conclusions: Bullying was a significant occupational stressor impacting on victim's health and their ability to function adequately. Ref:Cooper, C. L., Sloan, S. J. and Williams, S. (1988). 'The Occupational Stress Indicator'. Windsor: ASE.

Positive Attitude: The impact of two social and emotional learning programs on social skills

Coelho, Vitor Costa de Caparica, Portugal *Sousa, Vanda* Projecto Atitude Positiva, Académico Torres Vedras, Oeiras, Portugal
This study analyzes the impact of two social and emotional learning programs upon elementary and middle school student's social skills. It contemplates both students (1312) and teachers (91) perspectives regarding results. Subjects filled in 4 questionnaires in the program's beginning and end. A paired sample comparison and analysis of variance were conducted regarding scores reported in three years of program application. Results showed changes in several social skills dimensions (3 for middle school, 4 for elementary school). Teacher ratings mostly confirm results obtained by self-report. As such we can conclude that both programs proved effective in promoting several social skills.

Project 'Atitude Positiva': Analysis of the first 3 years

Coelho, Vitor Costa de Caparica, Portugal *Freitas, Rute* Projecto Atitude Positva, Academico de Torres Vedras, Torres Vedras, Portugal *Gomes, Ana* Projecto Atitude Positiva, Académico de Torres Vedras, Torres Vedras, Portugal *Sousa, Vanda* Projecto Atitude Positiva, Académico de Torres Vedras, Torres Vedras, Portugal
This presentation analyzes the first three years of Project 'Atitude Positiva', whose main objective is promoting social skills in elementary and middle school students. The analysis follows the steps taken in establishing the project, in which 5367 students have already taken part. Activities were added as result of suggestions or needs identified by staff, other activities were changed, due to over-lapping and low levels of attendance. Results, from student and teacher ratings, demonstrate that 3 programs proved to be effective in promoting targeted skills, while achieving high levels of satisfaction. Project 'Atitude Positiva' has, during these years, achieved its goals.

'Positive Attitude': The impact of two social and emotional programs on self-concept and self-esteem

Coelho, Vitor Costa de Caparica, Portugal *Freitas, Bárbara* Projecto Atitude Positiva, Académico de Torres Vedras, Lisboa, Portugal
This study analyzes the impact of two social and emotional learning programs upon elementary and middle school student's self-concept and self-esteem. The sample was composed of 1312 (425 elementary, 887 middle school) students who participated in weekly programs with evaluation questionnaires in its beginning and end. A paired sample comparison and an analysis of co-variance were conducted analyzing three years of program application. Results showed significant increases in social self-concept and self-esteem (both intervention groups) and emotional self-concept (elementary group). No changes were found neither in other dimensions of self-concept nor in control groups. These results support continuing the programs.

Barriers to seeking help for mental health problems in rural Australia

Collins, Joanne Dept. of Psychology, University of Adelaide, Adelaide, Australia *Winefield, Helen* Psychology, The University of Adelaide, Adelaide, Australia *Ward, Lynn* Psychology, The University of Adelaide, Adelaide, Australia *Turnbull, Deborah* Psychology, The University of Adelaide, Adelaide, Australia
Objectives: This study used mixed methods to explore barriers to the use of mental health services in rural Australia. Individual, psycho-social and cultural aspects of the rural context that impact on help seeking behaviour were examined. Methods:

Semi-structured interviews (N=16) and questionnaire data were obtained from adult rural residents recruited from General Practice surgeries (N= 40). They were asked about attitudes towards help-seeking for mental health. Results/Conclusions: Thematic analysis identified stigma, stoicism, lack of services, awareness and lack of psychological mindedness as barriers. Preliminary quantitative results will be discussed, as well as their implications for effective implementation and use of rural mental health services.

Caregiver-child interactions during meals: Eutrophic children in comparison with mild to moderate undernourished children

Cortés-Moreno, Assol DIP Aprendizaje Humano, UNAM FES Iztacala, Tlalnepantla, Mexico *López Ramírez, Miriam* DIP Aprendizaje Humano, UNAM FES Iztacala, Tlalnepantla, Edo. Mex, Mexico *Avilés Flores, Ana Laura* DIP Aprendizaje Humano, UNAM FES Iztacala, Tlalnepantla, Edo. Mex, Mexico *Romero Sánchez, Patricia* DIP Aprendizaje Humano, UNAM FES Iztacala, Tlalnepantla, Edo. Mex, Mexico

This study compares social interactions in feeding situation between dyads caregiver-child with different child nutritional condition. Thirty 18-month-old children and their caregivers participed, half of children were undernourished. Adult-child interactions during meals were analyzed using an observational system with three categorical levels: proximity/orientation, presentation/food intake, and vocalizations. Undernourished children's caregivers were less oriented to child activity and they displayed fewer vocalizations; whereas, eutrophic childrens caregivers changed food when child refused to intake, and their vocalizations were refered to organoleptic properties and child behavior. Children behavior showed not differences. Results suggest a regulator role of adult behavior for child intake.

Are dental anxiety online support groups helpful?: Self-ratings of efficacy, anxiety and pain

Coulson, Neil I-WHO, University of Nottingham, Nottingham, United Kingdom *Buchanan, Heather* I-WHO, University of Nottingham, Nottingham, United Kingdom

Objectives This study explored whether group participation was associated with lower pain ratings and dental anxiety. Methods An online questionnaire was completed by 91 members of Dental Fear Central who provided ratings of group efficacy, past and anticipated dental pain and completed the Modified Dental Anxiety Scale (MDAS). Results Sixty percent reported that the support group had 'somewhat' or 'greatly' lessened their anxiety, a finding confirmed by their MDAS scores. Lower anticipatory pain scores were reported for those whose anxiety had lessened. Conclusions The results suggest that online support may be effective in reducing anxiety and anticipated pain for some individuals.

Personal and psychological profile of separated couple's adolescent children: A basis for a proposed proactive values program

Crisostomo, Golda Aira College of Liberal Arts & Scie, Colegio de San Juan de Letran, Quezon City, Philippines

The purpose of this study was to describe the personality characteristics and coping strategies of adolescent children of separated couples. The study employed a descriptive comparative research design with sixty-eight (68) high school students from a catholic school in Nueva Ecija, Philippines. Results revealed that adolescent participants often employed both negative coping strategies (avoiding problems, being humorous) and positive coping strategies (seeking spiritual support, investing in close friends) in order to deal with the experience of parental separation. High-average scores on personality areas (dominance, sensitivity and withdrawal) were also evident. Findings became the basis for the development of a proactive values program.

The role of value orientations in individual innovation process

Dang, Junhua Shenzhen, People's Republic of China *Wang, Lei* Psychology, Peking University, Beijing, People's Republic of China *Yao, Xiang* Psychology, Peking University, Beijing, People's Republic of China *Yang, Ting* Psychology, Peking University, Shenzhen, People's Republic of China *Qiu, Chengfu* Psychology, Peking University, Shenzhen, People's Republic of China

This study separately measured idea generation and idea implementation as two components of innovation and examined how they were impacted by individual value orientations. The results showed that both horizontal individualism and collectivism had positive influences on idea generation; vertical collectivism had a negative effect on idea generation but a positive one on idea implementation; although vertical individualism was not correlated to either idea generation or idea implementation, it moderated the relationship between the two components: idea generation would predict idea implementation quite well among high vertical individualists, while this prediction disappeared among low vertical individualists.

The role of types of valence for the automatic activation of intergroup prejudice

Degner, Juliane Department of PSychology, Saarland University, Saarbrücken, Germany

In social cognition, it is typically assumed that negative intergroup attitudes and prejudices are represented as direct and strong associations of a group with a (predominantly negative) evaluation. This conception bases on a unipolar understanding of valence, varying between positivity and negativity. In contrast, we propose that a differentiation into types of evaluations, termed possessor- vs. other-relevance, can be found already at this basic level. Using a masked version of the affective priming paradigm, we could show that automatic prejudice activation in response to different outgroups follows a systematic pattern in accordance with the societal status of the respective groups.

Comparison of reading comprehension on first and second grade high school students of public and private schools of Lima Peru

Delgado-Vasquez, Ana Esther Psychology, UNMSM, Lima, Peru *Escurra-Mayaute, Luis Miguel* Psychology, UNMSM, Lima, Peru *Atalaya-Pisco, Maria Clotilde* Psychology, UNMSM, Lima, Peru *Pequeña-Constantino, Juan* Psychology, UNMSM, Lima, Peru *Torres, William* Psychology, UNMSM, Lima, Peru

It is presented the comparison on reading comprehension on first and second grade high school students considering public and private schools. The participants were 597 students of seven school district (UGEL) of Lima, Peru. The instrument was the reading comprehension test. Previously, it was done a Psychometric study. It was found differences on RC considering public and private schools. The first grade students of private schools have grater reading comprehension of narrative and descriptive texts. Considering students of second high school level it was find differences on students belonging to each kind of school. The second grade high school students of private schools have developed more their lexical, syntactic and pragmatic abilities.

Multiple roles of well-being in terrorist attack survivors

Diaz, Dario Dept. of Social Psychology, Universidad Autonoma de Madrid, Madrid, Spain *Blanco, Amalio* Social Psychology, Universidad Autonoma de Madrid, Madrid, Spain *Bonechi, Francesca* Social Psychology, Universidad Autonoma de Madrid, Madrid, Spain

Objetives. Different researchers have shown that traumatic event shatters the victim's basic assumptions. H1: In severe trauma, post-traumatic cognitions mediate the relationship between trauma and symptoms of health. H2: In not severe traumas basic assumptions are not enterely broken. Symtoms of health mediate the relationship between trauma and post-traumatic cognitions. Methods. 96 victims of 11-M terrorist attack filled in questionnaries assessing PTSD, post-tramautic cognitions and positive health. Results. The analysis (Sobel Test and bootstrapping) confirmed the two complete mediations. Conclusion. Consistent with the Notion of Multiple Roles, the same variable (health operationalized by measures of well-being) can be a procces or a consecuence depending of trauma severity.

Sequential-distributed strategy on dynamic spatial tasks

Diaz, David Universidad Autonoma de Madrid, Madrid, Spain *Santacreu, Jose* Psychology, Universidad Autonoma de Madrid, Madrid, Spain *Lopez Almeida, Patricia Ines* Psychology, Universidad Autonoma de Madrid, Madrid, Spain *Martinez Molina, Agustin* Psychology, Universidad Autonoma de Madrid, Madrid, Spain

The objective of this study is to identify the solving strategy on dynamic spatial tasks by means of the analysis of the executing sequence. In order to do so we counted on a sample of 4559 university graduated. Each participant executed all three tasks on a computerized system. The data were analyzed with the graph theory and with a variance analysis. The result for the ANOVA was: $F=1102.03$, $p<.000$. The main conclusion was that the solving strategy for the task can be described in a scale variable (Sequential-Distributed) with effect of the feedback of the task.

The cooperative game and assertive behaviour.

Diaz Martinez, Francisca Dept. of Evolutive Psycology, University of Alicante, Alicante, Spain *Perez Sanchez, Antonio Miguel* EVOLUTIVE PSYCHOLOGY & DID, UNIVERSITY OF ALICANTE, ALICANTE, Spain *Quiros Bravo, Soledad* EVOLUTIVE PSYCHOLOGY & DID, UNIVERSITY OF ALICANTE, ALICANTE, Spain

Objective: Our research was aimed at verifying the following hypothesis: the student's assertive behaviour increases when the cooperative game is used in the classroom setting. Method: The participants were 90 students in fourth year of primary education (average age, 9). To analyse the data we used t-Test of difference of means and univaried split-plot analysis of variance. Results: The hypothesis formulated was confirmed. Conclusions: The use of the cooperative game increases the students' assertive behaviour. Students learn to respect themselves and the others: the classroom atmosphere improves and the academic achievement increases.

Psychosocial factors and their role to depressive symptomatology in primary school children receiving special educational support

Didaskalou, Eleni Special Education, University of Thessaly, Volos, Greece *Kleftaras, George* Dept. of Special Education, University of Thessaly, Volos, Greece

This research aims at a) estimating the incidence of depressive symptomatology in ordinary primary school students receiving special educational support in resource settings and b) exploring the relationships between depression and certain psychosocial factors. 134 fifth and sixth grades pupils with general learning difficulties, completed the Children's Depression Inventory and a questionnaire including a number of psychosocial factors. Approximately 55% of students attending resource rooms display high levels of depressive symptoms. Furthermore interesting associations were identified between children's depressive symptomatology and certain psychosocial factors, such as relations with parents and siblings, friends in school and neighbourhood and satisfaction in class.

An ERP study on visual illusory motion

Ding, Xiaopan Psychology,School of Education, Zhejiang Normal University, Jinhua, People's Republic of China Yu, Xiumei psychology,shool of education, Zhejiang Normal University, Jinhua, People's Republic of China Ma, Jianhong psychology, Zhejiang University, Hangzhou, People's Republic of China Hu, Huamin psychology, Zhejiang University, Hangzhou, People's Republic of China Fu, Genyue psychology,shool of education, Zhejiang Normal University, Jinhua, People's Republic of China
Objective: To explore the neural basis of the visual illusory motion by using event-related potential. Methods: 100 stimulus (duration 2000ms) of a visual illusory motion figure and a static figure were randomly presented with equal probability. Ten healthy participants were asked to judge the pictures being motional or not. The EEG was recorded from 128 scalp sites using electrodes mounted in HydroCel GSN cap(Electrical Geodesics Incorporated, Oregon,USA)Results: The figures can evoke different C1 component in POz and P100/P200 component in O2/t3/. Conclusion: The visual illusory motion forms at the primary visual cortex not the high-level one.

The interdependence of cohesion mode, compatibility and performance in youth football teams

Dombrovskis, Valerijs Dept. Educational Psychology, Daugavpils University, Daugavpils, Latvia Guseva, Svetlana Daugavpils University, Daugavpils, Latvia Lapina, Lasma Social Psychology, Daugavpils University, Daugavpils, Latvia Ilisko, Dzintra Educational Psychology, Daugavpils University, Daugavpils, Latvia
The aim of the research is to study the peculiarities of forming cohesion and compatibility among Latvian youth football teams. The aim of the research is to study the correlation between teams' cohesion mode in the beginning of a season and their general performance in the end of it. The methods used in the research are Group Environment Questionnaire and Obozov's Compatibility Test. The significant correlation was found by calculating coefficients both in the beginning and in the end of the season. The authors discuss results of cohesion and compatibility, found to be higher in the beginning of the season.

Gender identity and sexist women's position: Impact of masculine priming

Domenech-Dorca, Gwenaël Dept. de Psychologie, Université Paris X, Nanterre, France
This study examines the different links which can exist between gender's identity evaluation and sexist women's position towards their own group whether they were primed or not with a masculine prototype. Their gender identity was measured by the B.S.R.I. scale (Bem, 1974) and their sexist evaluation collected thanks to the A.S.I scale (Glick & Fiske, 1996). Regression analyses were performed. Mainly, we observe that "benevolment sexism" significantly decreases in strong masculine gender women's group when they were primed with the masculine prototype. This result and other identitary and context sights will be discussed.

An investigation of mental-social stress-inducers based on the fourth axis of DSM-IV among students of Islamic Azad University, Quchan Branch

Dorostkar Moghadam, Hossein Psychology, Azad University of Quchan, Quchan, Islamic Republic of Iran Jabari, Khatereh Psychology, Azad University of Quchan, Quchan, Islamic Republic of Iran
The purpose of this research is to recognize and grade life's stress-inducing phenomena of Iraninan students. This research is in survey form in which 360 students were randomly chosen through cluster sampling;and 81-item questionaire measuring stress-inducing events was performed. Gathered information was analyzed by t-test and f-test. Based on obtained results, the most important life's stress-inducing phenomena from students' viewpoint were ranked as followings. Mother's death, death of family member, father's death, unfaithful spouse, uncurable desease of family member, spouse's death, university lay-off, being raped and committing murder. The results pinpoint that female students confronting stress-inducers show lower threshold level of sensitivity.

Perception of temporal order and intellectual giftedness

Dreszer, Joanna UMK in Torun, Torun, Poland Szelag, Elzbieta Laboratory of Neuropsychology, IBD, Warsaw, Poland
Objectives: The relationship between auditory temporal order judgment (TOJ) and intellectual giftedness was tested. Methods: Gifted (GI) and non-gifted individuals (NI) reported the order of two tones presented in a rapid sequence. Results: More efficient performance was observed in GI individuals in comparison with NI ones (lower order threshold values). Conclusions: These results support the notion that TOJ may depend on both timing and cognitive functioning.

Academic and psychosocial factors associated to performance anxiety in adolescents

Dumont, Michelle Psychology, Univers. QuébecTrois-Riviàres, Trois-Riviàres, Canada Leclerc, Danielle Psychology, Universit QuébecTrois-Riviàres, Trois-Riviàres, Canada Massé, Line Psychology, Univers. QuébecTrois-Riviàres, Trois-Riviàres, Canada Potvin, Pierre Psychology, Univers. QuébecTrois-Riviàres, Trois-Riviàres, Canada McKinnon, Suzie Psychology, Univers. QuébecTrois-Riviàres, Trois-Riviàres, Canada Grégoire, Martin Psychology, Univers. QuébecTrois-Riviàres, Trois-Riviàres, Canada
Introduction : The relation between performance anxiety related to exams and the observed performance is relatively well known whereas the relationship between this anxiety and certain other psychosocial factors is fairly less documented. Method. 542 grade 10 students completed many questionnaires. Results. A multiple regression analysis indicates that performance anxiety is positively associated to psychological stress, internalized behaviour, unproductive coping or social coping whereas it would be negatively related to arithmetic marks, externalized behaviour, self-efficiency and self-esteem. Conclusion. These results suggest that the development of intervention tools is necessary so that students to do not become even more anxious though the course of their development when put in a situation where they must achieve.

Evolution of the academic achievement and psychosocial resources of five psychological distress profiles observed during adolescence

Dumont, Michelle Psychology, Univers. QuébecTrois-Riviàres, Trois-Riviàres, Canada Leclerc, Danielle Psychology, Univers. QuébecTrois-Riviàres, Trois-Riviàres, Canada McKinnon, Suzie Psychology, Univers. QuébecTrois-Riviàres, Trois-Riviàres, Canada
Few studies have analysed the individual differences and the effect of time on the academic and psychosocial adaptation of adolescents depending on their variable degrees of distress. 181 students in grade nine and 144 in grade 11, totalling a longitudinal sample of 81 students. The best trajectory for the adaptation was associated to the group of students whose distress levels decreased between the middle and end of high school. The trajectories the least favourable for adaptation corresponded to the group of students whose distress levels increased or remained high during the same period of time. Considering that behaviour problems tend to maintain themselves over time, therapists and researchers must examine the nature of the interventions that are offered to students.

Rape perpetrated by the intimate partner: The influence of rapist's ideology information and observer ideology in judgments about denouncing rape to police

Duran Segura, Maria Mercedes Dept. of Social Psychology, Faculty of Psychology, Granada, Spain Moya, Miguel Dep. of social Psychology, Faculty of Psychology, Granada, Spain L. Megias, Jesus Dep. of Experimental Psycholog, Faculty of Psychology, Granada, Spain
The main aim of this work was to study the influence of giving information of rapist's ideology and observer ideology, in judgments about denouncing rape. 206 students read two hypothetical rape scenarios in a heterosexual intimate relationship where the man was the assailant. In one scenario he was described as a "benevolent sexist man" and in the other not. Participants answered the Ambivalent Sexism Inventory and the Rape Myth Acceptance Scale, and emitted their judgments about the convenience for the victim to denounce her partner. Judgments were affected by an interaction between information given about sexist ideology of rapist and sexist ideology of the observer.

Quality of life of persons with chronic mercury intoxication in postcontact period

Dyakovich, Marina and Human Ecology, Industrial Medicine, Angarsk, Russia Kazakova, Polina clinic of occupational desease, Industrial Medicine & Huma, Angarsk, Russia
The influence of mercury on the workers in Chemical manufacture has resulted in chronic mercury intoxication (CMI). The social value CMI is great, this disease amazes of the persons of able-bodied age, quite often proceeds hardly, progresses and is the reason of proof loss of work capacity. After termination contact with mercury grow progressively worse psychoneurological changes, narrowing of social contacts because lossing of professional work capacity are capable to complicate social adaptation and reduce quality of life. It causes necessity of development of the programs of social - psychological support of such patients for optimization of their social functioning.

Age related dynamics of experiencing difficult situations with blind adolescents.

Dzyakau, Dzmitry Dep. of psychology, BGPU, Minsk, Belarus Martysevich, Hanna philosophy and social science, BGU, Minsk, Belarus
Goal: age related dynamics of experiencing difficult situations with blind adolescents. Methods: genetic modeling experiment, descriptive statistics, dispersion analysis. Results. A functional structure of experiencing difficult situations includes correlations goal-motif, goal-objective conditions. Blind children correlate only goal and objective conditions. The specification has been interpreted with the conception of M. Merlo-Ponty. A model of psychological correction of the structure of experiencing the situations has been suggested. Conclusion. The results obtained can be used in the

practice of diagnosing the level of experiencing difficult situations; in the design of correctional programs, duaring academic training at schools for blind children.

Being hedonic and becoming prudent

Ein-Gar, Danit Managment Dept., Tel-Aviv University, Tel Aviv, Israel
The current research suggests that peoples' choices and preferences shift depending on their time-oriented mindset. More specifically, we show that when individuals think about their current selves (i.e. are in a "being" mindset) they are more likely to be hedonic. However, when individuals think about their future selves (i.e. are in a "becoming" mindset) they are more likely to be prudent. We examine this notion in 3 studies (testing spending preferences, gift-receiving preferences, and a choice setting) and find a consistent pattern, in which "being" leads to more hedonic preferences and choices whereas "becoming" leads to more prudent ones.

Pooling unshared information: An experiment comparing two different type of computer-mediated group discussions with face-to-face group discusison

Eisele, Per School of Managment, Blekinge Inst. of Technology, Ronneby, Sweden
The aim of the study was to examine effects of computer-mediated information on the use of unshared information during group discussions. The participants (N=77) were psychology students (37 men and 40 women with a mean age of 28,4) that were randomised into three different conditions, IT based on writing, IT based on talking and face-to-face interaction. The result indicate that IT based on writing affect the use of unshared information but not IT based on talking, as compared to face-to-face interaction. Discussions of this result are being provided.

Studying factors causing dissatisfaction in couples of Qom City

Faghihi, Ali Naghi Human Sciences' Faculty, Qom University, Qom, Islamic Republic of Iran Ghobary Bonab, Bagher Psychology and education Facul, Tehran University, Tehran, Islamic Republic of Iran
The aim of the current study was to investigate the factors of dissatisfaction in couples. Ex-post facto design was used and 150 couples were selected as samples by means of random sampling. Results show that the 3 factor of 1-difference in social level of spouses ($P < 0.05$), 2-cognitive skills ($P < 0.01$), and 3- communication skills ($P < 0.01$) all are related to dissatisfaction levels of couples. It could be concluded that levels of marital satisfaction is a function of socio-economic status, stress level of couples, problem or deficiency in cognitive and communication skills, and some other factors in couples' life.

The effect of attention orienting on stereopsis

Fang, Huicong Department of Psychology, East China Normal University, Shanghai, People's Republic of China Shen, Mowei Department of Psychology, Zhejiang University, Hangzhou, People's Republic of China
By adopting a 3D spatial cueing paradigm, this research explored how different kinds of attention orienting influenced stereopsis. The results showed that:(1)At the short SOA, the uninformative peripheral cue produced a facilitative effect on the subsequent discrimination task in the 3D condition; At the long SOA, it showed the inhibition of return spread across different depth planes.(2)At both the short and the long SOA, the predictive central symbolic cue produced a facilitative effect on the subsequent discrimination task in the 3D condition, the difference between the two treatments was not statistically significant.

Grandparents and new communication's technologies

Farneti, Alessandra Faculty of Education, Free University of Bozen, Bressanone, Italy Cadamuro, Alessia Faculty of Education, Modena Reggio University, Reggio Emilia, Italy Taverna, Livia Faculty of Education, Free University of Bozen, Bressanone, Italy Quadri, Tatiana Faculty of Psychology, Goldsmiths College, London, Italy
New technologies, particularly mobile phones and computer-based communication, have actually changed the ways used for staying in contact. This involves a lot of difficulties for elderly persons, but can also stimulate them to find new ways to be nearer to the young generations. This study, based on a questionnaire created by P.K. Smith, asks 97 grandparents and 200 grandchildren (range 10-14) about their way to communicate. Results demonstrate that the most part of grandparents use mobile phones to communicate with their grandchildren but don't use neither sms and computer. Grandmothers are more involved than grandfathers in intense relationships with grandchildren.

Traditional healing practices sought by Muslim psychiatric patients in Lahore, Pakistan

Farooqi, Yasmin Applied Psychology, University of the Punjab, Lahore, Pakistan
This research explored the type of traditional healing practices sought byPakistani Muslim psychiatric patients. The sample composed of 87 adult psychiatric patients. Those suffering from somatoform; personality/conduct disorders; and schizophrenia sought multiple traditional healing methods more than those with anxiety and affective disorders. Female patients used more traditional healing practices; whereas male patients visited Islamic Faith Healers and Sorcerers more frequently. These findings may be attributed to gender discrimination in mobility and taboos attached to women's consultation of male traditional healers. Islamic religious traditions and Pakistani cultural norms affect the health care choices of the Pakistani psychiatric patients.

Overcoming of emotional communicative problems in students

Fedosova, Anna Organizational Psychology, Institut of Psychology, Kiev, Ukraine
Objectives. Overcoming of emotional difficulties in students' interpersonal contacts can improve both psychological climate in groups and organizational culture of the university. Methods. We studied 300 students' emotional problems using The Boyko Emotional Problems in Communication Inventory. Results. 56.0 % of the respondents were found to have difficulties in managing their emotions. After a special training the problems with managing emotions decreased from 64.0 % to 39.0 %. The number of students with dominant negative emotions went down from 45.0 % to 21.0 %. Conclusions. The results confirmed the effectiveness of training for overcoming emotional difficulties in students.

The speech of youth from Febem/SP about their reality

Feffermann, Marisa Health Institut of São Paulo, São Paulo, Brazil Figueiredo, Regina Young and Health, Health Institut of São Paulo, São Paulo, Brazil Abramovay, Miriam Education, OEI, São Paulo, Brazil
Objectives: understanding the quotidian of interned youths to use as psycho-pedagogical and organizational basis for intervention strategies by the institution. Methods: two focal groups and 16 semi-structured interviews, with interned youths. Indicators: personal profile; sexuality; drugs; violence. Results: these youngsters lived situations of much vulnerability in communities, mainly the police violence; they have sexual information, what isn't enough to have a secure sexual life; they use illicit drugs and preferably the licit ones; inside the

institution the reports are of many aggressions and disrespect. Conclusions: youngsters' very vulnerable situations before the imprisonment are reproduced inside the institution, which has the function of re-socialization

Research on the effects of achievement goals on self-regulated learning of the fifth grade students

Fei, Wang Psychology, Beijing Normal University, Beijing, People's Republic of China
The present study investigates the goals and outcomes of the school work of elementary students to discuss the effects of perceptions of classroom goal structures and individual achievement goals on self-regulated learning of Grade 5 students. The questionnaires include Perception of Classroom Goals Structure Questionnaire- for Chinese subject (PCGSQ-C) and Individual Achievement Goals Questionnaire (IAGQ). A field-test was conducted to examine the effects of intervening teachers' behavior on students' perceptions of classroom goal structures, individual achievement goals and self-regulated learning. The results implied that students' perception of classroom mastery structure can been improved with active participation from the teacher, but did not found significant change of individual achievement goals and self-regulated learning.

Sensitivity to high frequency tones and word recognition in young and older adults

Feitosa, Maria Angela Inst. of Psychology, University of Brasília, Brasília, Brazil Silva, Isabella M. C. Psychology Institute, University of Brasília, DF, Brazil
The purpose of this work was to relate sensitivity to 0,250-16kHz tones to word recognition in four competition conditions (silence, S/N +10, S/N 0, and S/N -10) in younger (25-35) and older (45-55 years old) adults. All participants presented clinically normal thresholds for 0,250 to 8 kHz, but older individuals presented statistically higher thresholds for all frequencies, especially in the 8-16kHz range. With competitive noise, word recognition deteriorated for all participants, but especially for the older adults. Omission errors prevailed in noisier, and replacement by other words in quieter conditions. Phonetic analysis showed greater preservation of vowels than of consonants.

The effect of two-sided advertising depends on how grave the second side is

Felser, Georg Wirtschaftspsychologie, Hochschule Harz, Wernigerode, Germany Lichters, Marcel Wirtschaftspsychologie, Hochschule Harz, Wernigerode, Germany Müller, Kristina Wirtschaftspsychologie, Hochschule Harz, Wernigerode, Germany Willebrandt, Charlotte Wirtschaftspsychologie, Hochschule Harz, Wernigerode, Germany
Advertising can be more effective when the message also admits flaws in the offer. This strategy, however, not only communicates truthfulness. By conversational norms any disadvantage which is disclosed will be regarded as being more serious than any other disadvantage which is not communicated. In our research we presented participants (N > 200) two-sided advertisings for a hotel in which the disclosed disadvantage varied in the degree of seriousness. Participants expected unmentioned flaws to be much more likely, when a relatively serious disadvantage was communicated as opposed to the disclosure of a minor flaw.

Psychological research on graduates' job-search behavior in China

Feng, Cailing College ofPsychology, Shenyang Normal University, Shenyang, People's Republic of China Fan, Lisan College of Business, Shandong Institution of Busine, Yantai,Shandong Province,China, People's Republic of China Shi, Kan

School of Management, Chinese Academy of Sciences, Beijing,China, People's Republic of China the relationships between self-efficacy, job-search expectation, job-search intention and job-search behavior were discussed by questionnaire for 1000 university graduates in China. The important findings include: beyond gender and family background, there was a statistically significant relationship between self-efficacy and job-search intention, so was the relationship between job-search expectation and job-search intention; graduates with higher job-search intention apperceived more job-search expectation than those with lower job-search intention; job-search intention was an supplement for the relationship between self-efficacy and job-search behavior; job-search intention was a substitute for the relationship between job-search expectation and job-search behavior.

African students in Coimbra: Some distorted stories

Ferro, Maria Jorge Fac. Psicologia Ciencias Educ., University of Coimbra, Coimbra, Portugal Ferreira, Joaquim Armando FPCE Univ Coimbra, Fac. Psicologia Ciencias Educa, Coimbra, Portugal Ribeiro Santos, Eduardo João FPCE Univ Coimbra, Fac. Psicologia Ciencias Educa, Coimbra, Portugal

The main purpose of our research was to establish knowledge about African students' life conditions in Coimbra. We tried to find if they felt injustice towards them from city inhabitants and particularly from other students or staff from the University. A participatory research study was carried out with fifty participants during two school years. A set of initial interviews was prepared to listen to students' voices and to give them time and space to talk about their problems and expectations. Results on processes, outcomes and implications for intentional multicultural counseling interventions with African students living in Portugal will be discussed.

How to cook a SNARC: Number placement in text changes spatial-numerical associations

Fischer, Martin School of Psychology, University of Dundee, Dundee, United Kingdom Mills, Richard Psychology, University of Dundee, Dundee, United Kingdom

BACKGROUND: Why do Western people associate small/large numbers with left/right space (SNARC effect)? OBJECTIVE: To determine if SNARC depends on the positioning of numbers in texts. METHOD: 22 normal adults read cooking recipes for comprehension. Numbers in these text appeared left/right on the monitor to be congruent/ incongruent with SNARC (between groups); regression analyses of parity decision times evaluated SNARC before and after reading. RESULTS: The congruent group showed reliable SNARC before and after reading; the incongruent group's SNARC was significantly reduced. CONCLUSIONS: Number identities become rapidly associated with spatial positions. SNARC is thus only a temporary aspect of number representation.

Styles of communication and assertiveness as predictors of marital satisfaction

Flores Galaz, Mirta Margarita Facultad de Psicologia, Universidad Autonoma Yucatan, Merida, Mexico Marentes Castillo, Maria Salette FACULTAD DE PSICOLOGIA, UNIVERSIDAD AUTONOMA YUCATAN, MERIDA, YUCATAN, Mexico Cauich Pasos, Addy Elizabeth FACULTAD DE PSICOLOGIA, UNIVERSIDAD AUTONOMA YUCATAN, MERIDA, YUCATAN, Mexico

The objective of this study was to determine a prediction model of marital satisfaction begining with communication styles and assertiveness in men and women. 250 people from the city of Merida, Yucatan, Mexico answered to the Multidimensional Scale of Assertiveness (Flores & Díaz-Loving, 2004), the Inventory Communication Styles of the Couple (Sánchez & Díaz-Loving, 2003), and

the Multiphasetic Inventory of Marital Satisfaction (Cañetas, Rivera & Díaz-Loving, 2000). Multiple regression analysis by sex is presented. The findings are discussed by proportioning assertive abilities to the couples, and with that, promote the communication and the satisfaction in the relationship.

What does it mean to be identified as mentally ill? Social representations, unification and differentiation

Foley, Catherine Coffs Harbour, Australia

Catherine Foley & Gail Moloney (Southern Cross University, Coffs Harbour, Australia). This study examined Foster's (2001) claim that all mental illnesses are associated with a representation of general mental illness, whilst also being differentiated from each other. Australian students (n = 115) completed one of three randomly assigned versions of a self-report questionnaire about stereotypical beliefs and social distance. One-way between-groups multivariate analysis of variance revealed a distinction between depression and schizophrenia. However, a distinction was also found between depression and general mental illness. The dynamic nature of social representations and the role of the media are discussed, as are the implications for how mental illness is understood in Australia today.

Effects of gap-saliency in human interval timing: Extension of subjective time depends on complexity and not emotion of visual gaps

Folta, Kristian Cogn. Neuroscience, German Primate Center, Göttingen, Germany Wolf, Oliver T. Cognitive Psychology, Ruhr-University, Bochum, Germany Treue, Stefan Cognitive Neuroscience Lab, German Primate Center, Göttingen, Germany Schoofs, Daniela Cognitive Psychology, Ruhr-University, Bochum, Germany

Objectives: Analysis of misperceptions of temporal durations induced by gap-stimuli presented within 8s-intervals while varying gap-saliency. Methods: Emotion, arousal, and complexity were rated to assign stimuli to 3 subsets: 1) Simple & neutral gaps of low arousal, 2) Complex & neutral gaps of medium arousal, 3) Complex & negative gaps of high arousal. Timing-performance in 21 subjects was measured in baseline- and gap-trials with 2s-gaps. Results: Simple & neutral gaps of low arousal induced no misperceptions. Only complex gaps induced 1.5s-extensions of subjective time. Conclusion: Complexity (rather than arousal or emotional content of gaps) determines gap-saliency in human interval timing.

School dropout in Portuguese adolescents

Formosinho, Maria Faculty of Psychology, Coimbra University, Coimbra, Portugal Taborda, Maria C. Faculty of Psychology, Coimbra University, Coimbra, Portugal

School dropout and antisocial behaviour among portuguese adolescents Maria da Conceição Taborda- Maria Formosinho l. Objectives. The authors investigated the relationship between school dropout and anti-social behaviours in adolescence. 2. Method In this study, the number of pupils that took part were 445. Beyond a personal meeting set up, there were also used psychometric tools: CBCL (Achenbach, 1991a) TRF (Achenbach, 1991b) – YSR (Achenbach, 1991c) – SRA (Loeber et al, 1989) 3. Results Among the pupils in the sample, the rate of dropout is about 18 %. These adolescents showed higher rates of delinquency, more aggressive behaviour, higher consumptions of different kinds of drugs, as well other kinds of antisocial behaviours.

Retirement planning: Differences between managerial and non-managerial ocuppational categories

Franca, Lucia Graduate Studies in Psychology, UNIVERSO, Rio de Janeiro, Brazil Verónica, Carneiro Graduate Studies in Psychology, UNIVERSO, Niterói, Brazil Shirley, Bernardino Graduate Studies in Psychology, UNIVERSO, Rio de Janeiro, Brazil

Brazilian Social Welfare has just been reformed bringing a change in early retirement by postponing the retirement age. As a consequence workers will have to work longer as well as having reduced pensions. This study compared the differences amongst Brazilian top executives and non-executive workers when they plan for retirement. Different dimensions were found when the scale of Key Factors for Retirement Planning was analysed by occupational category. The findings from this study have important implications for education and human resources development, in determining the key factors for retirement planning, retaining older workers and second career preparation.

Designing reorganization by studying professional situated practice: An ethnomethodological perspective

Frascaroli, Daniela Dipt. di Psicologia, Università Cattolica Milano, Tortona, Italy Scaratti, Giuseppe Psychology, Catholic University of Milan, Milan, Italy Ripamonti, Silvio Gorli, Mara

Objectives: The paper discusses an intervention of reorganization conducted in a complex organization that manages networks of services for child education.The main issue was to introduce a new professional role to sustain the link between the two original ones (the pedagogical and the administrative axes): a "unique co-ordinator" able to run the services with less superimposition and with better proximity with the stakeholders. Methods: The paper underlines the ethnomethodological device and tools applied in making knowledge concerned the ways through which the new professionals shape a situated practice in dealing with new role. Results: The paper highlights the poignant points of the new professional practice, obtained through ATLAS.Ti and T-LAB analysis of data base collected.

Phonological traces in early speech recognition

Friedrich, Claudia Inst. für Biolog. Psychologie, Universität Hamburg, Hamburg, Germany Schild, Ulrike Biological Psychology, University of Hamburg, Hamburg, Germany Röder, Brigitte Biological Psychology, University of Hamburg, Hamburg, Germany

Word fragments (primes) alter neurophysiological processing of following complete words (targets). A left-lateralized Event-Related Potential (ERP) between 300 and 400 ms (the P350) has been related to the activation of modality-independent word form representations. Formerly, we tested ERPs for written targets preceded by spoken primes. In the present experiment we investigated ERP responses to spoken targets following spoken primes. Early ERP differences starting at 100 ms appear to reflect speech sound processing. Together with the P350 effect we found a Phonological Mismatch Negativity (PMN) that might be related to the rapid testing of phonological expectancies in speech recognition.

The bullying in junior high schools in Japan (2): The effect bullying has on future friends and relationships

Fujiwara, Tamae Dept. of Humanities, Nagasaki Junshin University, Nagasaki, Japan Yoshitake, Kumiko Humanities, Nagasaki Junshin University, nagasaki, Japan

This study looks at how the experience of being a victim of bullying at junior high school effects future friends and relationships. The following is the result of a questionnaire targeting 72 femaile undergraduates. The students who had many experiences of being bullied at junior high school showed the following tendencies: 1) storong inferiority complex, 2) low sense of trust in friends, 3) little self-disclosure with frends, 4) low satisfaction with friends. Therefore, students lose confidence by becoming a victim of bullying, so they defend themselves against human relationships.

Childhood and adolescent victimization and sexual coercion by male and female university students in 32 nations

Gámez Guadix, Manuel Universidad Autonoma de Madrid, Madrid, Spain Straus, Murray A. Family Research Laboratory, University of New Hampshire, Durham, USA

Objective: This study examined the relationship of neglect history, sexual abuse, and corporal punishment to sexual coercion against a dating partner. Method: The participants are a convenience sample of 13,877 students in 32 nations. Multinomial logistic regression was used to test the hypotheses. Results: The results showed that experiencing prior victimization as a child or adolescent was related to perpetrating sexual coercion in dating relationships either directly or indirectly through antisocial traits and behaviors. Conclusions: The findings suggested a high level of similarity between men and women in the paths linking prior victimization experiences to sexual coercion against a dating partner.

Ultrasound triggered mental representations of the infant at 20 weeks of pregnancy: Presentation of the assessment tool TC_sono20

Gürber, Susanne Klinische Forschung, Universität Bern, Bern, Switzerland Jaussi, Chantal Department ofClinical Research, University of Berne, Bern, Switzerland Lemola, Sakari Personality & Develop. Psy, University of Basel, Basel, Switzerland Stadlmayr, Werner Obstetrics and Gynecology, University Hospital Berne, Bern, Switzerland Surbek, Daniel Obstetrics and Gynecology, University Hospital Berne, Bern, Switzerland Meyer-Wittkopf, Matthias Obstetrics and Gynecology, University Hospital Bern, Bern, Switzerland Boukydis, Zack Erikson Institute, Erikson Institute, Chicago IL, USA

Background: Ultrasound in pregnancy is assumed to have an impact on the representational world of the parents-to-be. To date ultrasound-triggered perceptions have not been explored with respect to the couple's triadic capacity (TC), i.e. the capacity to anticipate an appropriate level of family functioning. Objective: To explore an ultrasound-based setting to assess TC. Method: 40 parents were assessed with the TC_sono20 at 20 weeks of gestation. Results and conclusions: A variety of emotional and cognitive reactions, and of the capacity to share their experience was found in couples, confronted with their ultrasound-conveyed baby. Basic categories will be presented.

Within stability of representations and stimuli influence in a categorization task

Gaillard, Audrey Laboratoire de Psychologie, Université Paris 8, Saint Denis, France Urdapilleta, Isabel Laboratoire de Psychologie, Université Paris 8, Saint Denis, France Richard, Jean François Laboratoire de Psychologie, Université Paris 8, Saint Denis, France

The goal of our study was to examine stability of subjects' representations during a categorization task of concrete objects. Hundred fifty participants (Mean: 24.04; SD 8.7) took part to three sessions, each session being separated by a two weeks' delay. The subjects were divided into three experimental conditions : "foods", "animals" and "bathroom". They accomplished a sorting task on 45 names and a Properties Production Task (PPT) to explain their groupings. The results demonstrate that, in a sorting task, the concrete objects' type does not influence the representations stability. However, in

a PPT the within stability is related to the level of objects' description: the within stability of specific properties is weaker than when categories of properties were considered.

About saints and superheroes: A test of Paulhus' model of social desirability

Galic, Zvonimir Dept. of Psychology, University of Zagreb, Zagreb, Croatia Jerneić, Željko Dept. of Psychology, University of Zagreb, Zagreb, Croatia Parmač, Maja Dept. of Psychology, University of Zagreb, Zagreb, Croatia

The aim of this study was to test Paulhus' model which states that there are two social desirability factors (egoistic and moralistic bias), both of which have conscious and unconscious aspects (management and enhancement). In our study participants completed the Comprehensive Inventory of Desirable Responding (Paulhus, 2006) in three situations: honest (N=224), "fake good-agency" (N=249) and "fake good-communion" (N=196). As expected, egoistic bias increased most in "fake good–agency", and moralistic bias in "fake good–communion" situation. However, the increase was present on enhancement as well as on management scales. Thus, the new model was only partially confirmed.

Vatiations on the MMPI scales in relation to acculturation of women of migratory zones of Veracruz, Mexico

Garcia, Camilo Dept. de Psicología, Universidad Veracruzana, Veracruz, Mexico Clairgue, Erika Nayeli Psicología, Universidad Veracruzana, Xalapa, Veracruz, Mexico Rivera, Natanael Psicología, Universidad Veracruzana, Xalapa, Veracruz, Mexico Medina, Esteban Psicología, Universidad Veracruzana, Xalapa, Veracruz, Mexico Herrera, Rodolfo Psicología, Universidad Veracruzana, Xalapa, Veracruz, Mexico Jaimes, Esteban Psicología, Universidad Veracruzana, Xalapa, Veracruz, Mexico

Following previous research (Chavez, 2007), this study is a comparison of the degree of acculturation and their performance on the MMPI-II of 50 women from migrants areas in Mexico. The MMPI-II and Ethnicity Questionnaire (Tsaj,1998) showed a positive correlation between the degree of assimilation to globalization and consumption and the T scores in the Es, PA, and D scales. Results suggest that the less assimilated share lower expectations for economic gains, less consumption and stress. For those who score higher, tension between desires may generate stress and higher scores on MMPI-II. These results show consistency with previous literature (Padilla, 1979).

Latinos' evaluations of outgroup and ingroup dating couples

Garcia, Amber Dept. of Psychology, The College of Wooster, Wooster, USA Riggio, Heidi Psychology, California St. University, LA, Los Angeles, USA

Latinos represent the largest ethnic minority group in the United States, yet relatively little research examines Latinos' attitudes toward ingroup and outgroup dating. Participants were asked to report evaluations of and feelings about a dating couple. The racial composition of the couple was manipulated between subjects, such that participants read about either a same-race or interracial couple. Results indicate a significant interaction between sex and racial composition of the couple on affective responses. Latino men reported feeling more positive emotions toward the Latino couple compared to the other couples. Suggestions for future research and implications for intergroup relations are presented.

Family TV patterns effects on children socialization in a sample of Spanish pupils of Málaga City

Garcia Martin, Miguel Angel Dept. of Social Psychology, University of Malaga, Malaga, Spain Hombrados Mendieta, Maria Isabel SOCIAL PSYCHOLOGY, UNIVERSITY OF MALAGA, MALAGA, Spain

The aim of the paper is to investigate the children TV patterns of use, the permissiveness/control that parents exercise and the potential relationship among these factors and antisocial attitudes and aggressive behaviours. The results showed that the pattern of use of television (e.g., number of hours watching TV per day, content type watched, permissiveness/control of parents over children television consumption, etc.) affects several aspects of the observed socialization and aggressive behaviours of children. Watching some TV programmes, especially those with violent content, had some negative influences on children, who show higher levels in aggressiveness-stubbornness measures such as disruptive behaviours, lack of discipline and no respect for rules.

Family stress and coping strategies used by adolescents in single and dual earning families

Garg, Saloni Child Development, Govt. Home Science College, Chandigarh, India

The study examined family stress and coping strategies of early adolescents in single and dual-earning families. Students, 75 boys and 75 girls, from schools of Gobindgarh, Punjab, India completed tools that measured family stress (frustration, conflict, pressure, and anxiety) and coping strategies (e.g. distancing, escape avoidance, and self-control). Results, using t-test, indicated adolescents in dual-earning families to experience more family stress in areas of conflicts and anxiety as compared to their counterparts. Coping strategies of self-control, seeking support, and reappraisal were more significantly used by adolescents in dual-earning families. Implications focus on programs promoting resiliency among adolescents from dual-earning families.

Coping with macro-social uncertainty: Results from a study designed as methodological triangulation

Gerhold, Lars Erz.-Wiss. und Psychologie, AB Erz.Wiss. Zukunftsforschung, Berlin, Germany

Transactional stress paradigms focus on processes of cognitive appraisals and coping. Based on this theoretical model this contribution shows that macro-social uncertainties (societal-political events) in comparison to personal uncertainties need a 'demographic freedom' to be perceived as meaningful. Furthermore it is shown that collecting information and social exchange are the most commonly used coping strategies when direct control is impossible. These results (based on questionnaire data) are complemented by findings from qualitative interview data and discussed against the theoretical background and the methodological triangulation approach. The conclusion is that macro-social uncertainty does not have negative effects on satisfaction with life.

Gaining respect: Do competence, status and power lead to respect?

Ghanbari, Dominic Experimental Psychology, University if Oxford, Oxford, United Kingdom

The aim of the current research was to study the different characteristics that have been said to lead to respect for an individual, and to examine whether the possession of competence, status and power lead to greater respect. Perceived competence and perceived status both lead to higher scores on the respect action tendencies and to lower scores on the disrespect action tendencies. Unlike competence, status was also related to a stronger tendency to pretend to admire and agree with the target person. Possession of power was unrelated to respectful behaviour, but was related to pretence.

Scientific productivity on the field of test adaptation
Gomez Benito, Juana Metodologia C. Comportamiento, Universitat de Barcelona, Barcelona, Spain Padilla, José Luis Metodologia C. Comportamiento, Universidad de Granada, Granada, Spain Guilera, Georgina Metodologia C. Comportamiento, Universitat de Barcelona, Barcelona, Spain Hidalgo, M. Dolores Metodologia C. Comportamiento, Universidad de Murcia, Murcia, Spain

This study seeks to offer a wide-ranging overview of the state of scientific literature regarding Test Adaptation by means of a bibliometric study. The analysis makes use of the Web of Science database as well as ERIC, Medline, Psychinfo and Psychology and Behavioral Sciences Collection. The adaptation of evaluation instruments makes sense in the framework of transcultural assessment. The search is restricted to the terms "cross-cultural assessment", "cross-cultural testing", "test adaptation", "test translation". The results emphasize that since the 90's, the number of publications on the topic has increased dramatically and should continue to increase with only intermittent changes.

The perception family on multiple intelligences of children in infant and primary
Gomis Selva, Nieves Educativonal Psychology, University of Alicante, Alicante, Spain Valero Rodriguez, Jose Evolutive Psychology and Didac, University of Alicante, Alicante, Spain Pérez Sánchez, Antonio Miguel Educativonal Psychology, University of Alicante, Alicante, Spain Castejón Costa, Juan Luís Educativonal Psychology, University of Alicante, Alicante, Spain

The aim is to Know the perception of parents on their children's multiple intelligences expressed outside school. Assumptions: 1.Member parents highlight some areas mainly as strengths and weaknesses in their children. ; 2. Parents do not indicate ability or trait in their children that may have influence in schools. Methodology: Attendance: 144 parents of children in infant or primary education. Instruments: Questionnaire taken from SPECTRUM. Procedure: Individual application in a May 2007 meeting. Data Analysis: analysis of frequency with SPSS (12.01). The results confirm the first hypothesis and reject the second one. Conclusions: Parents provide valuable information about the skills and traits expressed by students outside school which may influence the development in the classroom.

"Team's best match" and "team's worst match": The handball coaches' prototypical narratives
Gonzaga, Luís Dept. of Psychology, University of Algarve, Faro, Portugal

This study intends to compose the prototypical narrative of handball coaches from their personal experiences. The dichotomised approach ("best" and "worst" matches) suggests our intentional option for "critical incidents" approach focussing on coaches' experiences characterized by high emotional involvement. The sampling and analysis methodology draws on Grounded Theory. Our sample includes 81 handball coaches, aged 23 to 55. Each coach was invited to post their autobiographical "small stories" in an online discussion group, anonymously, or sending them by email. Data was coded using MAXQDA2007, software for qualitative analysis. Results will be presented and their relevance to psychological practice discussed.

Sex differences in general knowledge revisited: Academic versus popular knowledge makes the difference
Grabowski, Joachim Inst. für Psychologie, Pädagog. Hochschule Heidelberg, Heidelberg, Germany Schmitt, Markus Psychology, Univ. of Education Heidelberg, Heidelberg, Germany Weinzierl, Christian Psychology, Univ. of Education Heidelberg, Heidelberg, Germany

Males were frequently shown to perform better than females in many knowledge domains. Referring to cultural literacy studies, however, the distinction between academic and popular knowledge is considered relevant rather than domain-specificity. 99 German 12th-graders completed a 132 item questionnaire, systematically constructed from academic and popular quiz show items. No sex-related main effect was observed: boys only perform better on academic items, revealing an interaction between sex and knowledge type. Thus, when comparing the sexes with respect to knowledge, the cultural status of the items plays a role beyond specific domains: Females aren't simply less knowledgeable!

Adolescent girl's coping: Sexual abuse trauma versus imprisonment trauma
Grigutyte, Neringa Dept. of Psychology, Vilnius University, Vilnius, Lithuania

The aim of the study was to investigate the consequences and coping strategies of sexually abused incarcerated teenager girls' (13-17 year old). Clinical interview, structured questionnaires and projective techniques were used. The data showed that sexually abused victims have more emotional and behavioural problems and their formation of identity is more distorted. Different coping strategies are used for coping with different types of trauma. Active coping strategies are used significantly often and positive reframing or acceptance is used significantly rare for sexual abuse trauma in comparison with imprisonment trauma. Finally, the results and practical implementations are discussed.

Professional segregation and gender stereotypes: A study of four industries in Latvia
Gritane, Egita Pedagogy and Psychology, University of Latvia, Riga, Latvia Austers, Ivars Pedagogy and Psychology, University of Latvia, Riga, Latvia

Gender stereotypes attributed to employees of four industries and their relation to professional segregation were assessed. The representative samples of Latvian population and four industries answered questions on four predefined stereotype dimensions (Fiske et al., 2002), on gender differences in professional abilities, and on professions suited to each of the genders. The results indicate shared beliefs regarding professions that are considered to suite females and males. Males have a privilege to be more flexible in their professional choice. The results are discussed from the perspective of self-categorization motives and the process of intergroup stereotyping.

Investigation of comparative judgement regarding job and living preferences
Groh, Arnold Sekr. FR 6-3, Technische Universität Berlin, Berlin, Germany

Objectives: Investigated lifestyle preferences of indigenous subjects in Africa vs. Europe. Methods: Subjects in Nigeria (University of Ibadan) and in Switzerland (UNO, Geneva) filled out a forced-choice questionnaire. Preferences were calculated (Law of Comparative Judgement). Results: In Nigeria, a high-class job in a major African city was preferred, whereas in Switzerland, preferences of the indigenous representatives tended towards more traditional lifestyles. Conclusions: Findings conform to the Theory of Symbolic Self Completion. Within the "dominant-dominated" spectrum

of cultures in the presently globalising world, subjects of a dominated cultural background show complementary/compensatory patterns of lifestyle preferences in a dominated vs. dominant context.

The influence of regular physical exercises on the body image: Imaginary or real
Grubits, Sonia Dept. of Psychology, Dom Bosco Catholic University, Campo Grande, Brazil Nunes, Paulo Ricardo Dept. of Psychology, Dom Bosco Catholic University, Campo Grande, Brazil Freire, Heloisa Bruna Grubits Dept. of Psychology, Dom Bosco Catholic University, Campo Grande, Brazil

Aim: to analyze the perception of the benefits of physical exercises on the body image. Participants: ten women whose age ranged from 35 - 49 years old were chosen according to the criteria of accessibility from the Health and Physical Activity Project in Campo Grande. Research: qualitative investigation using Phenomenology as theoretical methodological referential with participants' interviews. The statements were evaluated using the ideographical and nomothetical analysis. Result: the practice of regular physical activity is an important alley for the people to have a better understanding of its usefulness which was configured in a better perception of the body image.

Are implicit and explicit self-esteem dissociated?
Grumm, Mandy Inst. für Psychologie I, Universität Leipzig, Leipzig, Germany Nestler, Steffen Institute of Psychology I, University of Leipzig, Leipzig, Germany von Collani, Gernot Institute of Psychology I, University of Leipzig, Leipzig, Germany

This study analysed the changeability of self-esteem in terms of the Associative-Propositional-Evaluation Model (APE-Model). In particular the APE-Model postulates two qualitatively different modes of information processing. It is assumed that changes in associative structures lead to changes in indirect measures whereas changes in propositional knowledge lead to changes in direct measures. This study explored whether a subliminal evaluative conditioning procedure influences self-esteem. It is analysed if changes in implicit self-esteem can be transferred to explicit self-esteem if participants think about their momentary feelings toward themselves. Results are mainly in line with our expectations and corroborate the APE-Model's assumptions.

Filipino perspective of effective counselors: A model that works
Guarino, Aime Counseling Center, Brokenshire College, Davao City, Philippines

This qualitative study investigated the qualities of effective counselors as perceived by counseling stakeholders. The responses were content analyzed and categorized, constructing an empirically derived Model of Effective Counselors. It yielded four thematic clusters: knowledge and attitude, affective, interpersonal and spiritual qualities. It then examined how these identified qualities operate among those peer-nominated effective counselors through a case study. Ten effective counselors nominated by their peers served as subjects. All nominees possessed the qualities identified in the model. The study found that Filipinos view effective counselors as possessing an integrated set of cognitive, affective, interpersonal, and spiritual qualities.

Effectiveness of relaxation training, communicative skills and its effects on teachers health
Guerrero Barona, Eloisa Psicología y Antropología, Universidad de Extremadura, Badajoz, Spain Pajuelo, Carlos Psicología y Antropología, Universidad de Extremadura, Badajoz, Spain López, Manuel Psicología y Antropología, Universidad de Extremadura, Badajoz, Spain Fajardo, Blanca Psicología y Antropología, Universidad de

Extremadura, Badajoz, Spain **Sánchez, Javier** *Psicología y Antropología, Universidad de Extremadura, Badajoz, Spain* **Acquadro Maran, Daniela** *Psicología y Antropología, Universidad de Extremadura, Badajoz, Spain*

A program focused on stress control has been applied to 152 non university teachers. Its object has been to develop emotional and personal competences to manage stress situations and check their effects on health. Trained strategies have been relaxation, breathing, and communicative skills. Results indicate effectiveness due to assertive skills enhancements, as anxiety has been reduced. Training on relaxation has not been that effective and after the program, mental health probability has been doubled, as psychopathological risk has been reduced.

Electrophysiological marker of referential integration processes

Gugler, Manfred *Max-Planck-Institut, Leipzig, Germany* **Rossi, Sonja** *Berlin Neuroimaging Center, Berlin, Germany* **Friederici, Angela D.** *CBS, Max-Planck-Institut, Leipzig, Germany* **Hahne, Anja** *Neuropsychology, MPI Hum Cog and Brain Sciences, Leipzig, Germany*

Referential connections within a sentence define the relations between different sentence units. The present ERP study compared word category violations embedded in sentences with and without a reference structure. Reference was created between a noun and a following prepositional phrase. In both sentence structures, an anterior negativity reflecting phrase structure building processes and a P600 indicating processes of syntactic reanalysis were observed. Importantly, an additional negativity was only elicited in sentences with a reference structure. We hypothesize this negativity reflects referential integration processes between the two sentence units.

Crawling infants' use of perceived width of a doorway to plan a locomotion path

Gunawan, Ronald *Inst. für Psychologie, Max-Planck-Insitut, Leipzig, Germany* **Daum, Moritz M.** *Psychology, Max Planck Insitute, Leipzig, Germany* **Prinz, Wolfgang** *Psychology, Max Planck Insitute, Leipzig, Germany*

The present study investigated infants' ability to integrate the width of a doorway to the planning of their locomotion. Infants aged seven, eight, and nine months had to choose between a passable and an impassable doorway in order to crawl towards their mother who was located behind a barrier. Results showed that nine-month-olds as well as more experienced eight-month-old crawlers planned their locomotion path correctly. Hands-and-knees-crawlers performed better than belly-crawlers. These findings provide further evidence that not only age but also locomotor experience plays an important role in infants' implementation of environmental information into their planned and executed actions.

Different strategies employed by native speakers and L2 learners in sentence processing

Guo, Taomei *Institute of Cognitive Neurosc, Beijing Normal University, Beijing, People's Republic of China* **Jiang, Nan** *Department of Applied Linguist, Georgia State University, Atlanta, USA* **Yan, Yan** *Institute of Cognitive Neurosc, Beijing Normal University, Beijing, People's Republic of China* **Guo, Jingjing** *Institute of Cognitive Neurosc, Beijing Normal University, Beijing, People's Republic of China*

Readers have to use both semantic and syntactic information to understand the sentence correctly when reading a sentence,. Since native speakers and L2 learners use different ways to learn a language, an interesting issue is which kind of information plays a more important role in sentence reading.

Using the ERP technique, we investigated whether native English speakers and English learners use different strategies to comprehend sentences. Our results indicated that native speakers processed sentences more automatically than learners, and that the latter were more sensitive to the local syntactic errors.

The SWS-survey II of stress, work and mental health: Concluding 15 years of research in Mexican population on stress and support

Gutiérrez, Rodolfo E *Psychology, National University of México, Mexico, Mexico*

This work recapitulates studies on psychometric grounding, predictive power and refinement of constructs that originates the SWS-Survey-II. Dimensions were clarified and some items abridged or rephrased in comparison with its 15-year-old preceding version. The studies included 4,450 Mexican workers who responded the original version of SWS allowing us to gather health and job-performance indicators. The results show reliability coefficients for the 8 dimensions running from .82 to .93, structural fitting indices around .92 for unidimensional solutions, supporting discriminant/convergent validity. Performance and physiology relationships are shown as well. SWS–Survey (Gutiérrez & Ostermann,1994) is suggested as a strong, practical and effective tool for this population.

The influences of classroom interaction on creative question-asking ability

Han, Qin *Educational Research Academy, Shanxi Normal university, Linfen, Shanxi, People's Republic of China* **Hu, weiping** *Educational Research Academy, Shanxi Normal university, Linfen, Shanxi, People's Republic of China* **Zhou, Zongkui** *School of Psychology, Center China Normal University, Wuhan, People's Republic of China*

Several studies had been done in this paper. First, a peer interaction questionnaire for classroom learning was developed. 1660 grade 4 and grade 5 primary school students took part in the test. The results suggested that classroom interaction can be divided in thinking interaction, affection interaction, group coherence, and attitude to the group. The questionnaire has satisfied reliability and validity. Second, the influences of classroom interaction on creative question-asking ability were studied by laboratory experiment and classroom experiment. The result indicated that group structure influences the creative question-asking ability of students, and there are different influential pattern for different learning task difficulty. Third, the influential Structure Model of Creative Question-asking Ability was constructed by using LISREL software.

Comprehension: The relative contributions of three sources of individual differences

Hannon, Brenda *Dept. of Psychology, Univ. of Texas at San Antonio, San Antonio, USA*

Everyone knows that measures of lower-level word processes, higher-level processes, and working memory predict comprehension ability. Further, a number of comprehension theories suggest how some of these sources might relate. Yet, many of these relationships have gone untested and so it is unclear whether one or all of the sources make separate and important contributions to comprehension performance. The present study focuses on this issue. The results replicated a number of previous findings; however they also revealed that although the three sources made unique contributions to comprehension performance, lower-level and higher-level processes were the most important contributors.

Spontaneous transfer of a problem solution without a hint

Hannon, Brenda *Dept. of Psychology, Univ. of Texas at San Antonio, San Antonio, USA*

To date, many studies have demonstrated that spontaneous analogical problem solving rarely occurs across different domains of knowledge (e.g., Gick & Holyoak, 1980). In the present study we attempted to increase the frequency of spontaneous analogical problem solving across different domains of knowledge by enhancing the qualities of participants' mental representations of both the source problems and target problems. The results showed increases in spontaneous analogical problem solving across different domains of knowledge to a level that was equivalent to a non-spontaneous hint condition. We interpreted our findings within Kintsch's (1988) construction-integration framework for comprehension.

Native and non-native segmentation of continuous speech

Hanulikova, Adriana *Department of Linguistics, Humboldt University Berlin, Berlin, Germany* **Mitterer, Holger** *Psycholinguistics, Max Planck Institute, Nijmegen, Netherlands* **M. McQueen, James** *Psycholinguistics, Max Planck Institute, Nijmegen, Netherlands*

How do second language learners cope with two different languages during comprehension of spoken language? Previous research suggests that even proficient learners are influenced by both their native language and the second language when segmenting continuous speech. The present work investigated the degree to which sublexical cues (stress) and lexical cues (possible words) can be adopted or suppressed by Slovak listeners in German spoken input. The results show that non-native listeners can acquire segmentation procedures that differ from their native language but at the same time they might not be able to prevent interference from their native lexicon.

Studies of the influence of parents and teachers' interaction on students' learning qualities

Hao, Ruoping *Dept. of Education, Taiyuan Teachers College, Taiyuan, People's Republic of China*

Abstract We invite 1,581 people to take part in this experiment. The result is: the parents' three-dimensional interactions (cognition, emotion and strategy) of the experimental class are much better than those of the ordinary class; the psychological health, learning qualities and every other factor of the experimental class are higher than the ordinary class; and the relationships between teachers and students, parents and children and ways of teaching and training of the experimental class are better. Key words: parents and teachers' interaction; psychological health; learning qualities; training

The impact of student-teacher relationships and classroom climate on stress reactivity at the end of the first semester in school

Harwardt, Elena *Human Science, University of Cologne, Cologne, Germany* **Ahnert, Lieselotte** *Human Science, University of Cologne, Cologne, Germany*

The present study uses saliva cortisol in order to explore how and under what conditions children display patterns of stress after the first semester in school. Children (n=100) were administered tests for maths and reading/writing skills, and were observed in their classrooms. Teachers filled out the Student-Teacher-Relationship Scale. On Monday and Friday, saliva was taken from each child. Results showed clear patterns of increasing stress levels from Monday to Friday which were related to the quality of the child-teacher relationship, teachers' emotional support as one of the aspects of classroom climate and levels of skills in maths, reading and writing.

Why do people show the self-effacing tendency?
Hashimoto, Hirofumi Graduate School of Letters, Hokkaido University, Sapporo, Japan Yamagishi, Toshio Graduate School of Letters, Hokkaido University, Sapporo, Japan

Our purpose in this study is to consider the self-effacing tendency which has been explained in terms of self-construal as a "default adaptive strategy" to avoid accruing negative reputation. The results from a series of studies we conducted suggest that when a reason to accurately report self-judgment was provided, the self-effacing tendency completely disappeared in both American and Japanese students. But when they lacked the reason, the self-effacing tendency was stronger among Japanese than Americans and women than men. We propose that these differences are due to the cost of offending others in acquiring resources from outside current relationships.

Helping professions and normality
Havigerova, Jana Marie Inst. of Primary Education, University of Hradec Kralove, Hradec Kralove, Czech Republic Haviger, Jiri D. of infor. and quant.methods, University of Hradec Kralove, Hradec Kralove, Czech Republic Janebova, Radka D.of social work and politics, University of Hradec Kralove, Hradec Kralove, Czech Republic Zikl, Pavel Institute of primary education, University of Hradec Kralove, Hradec Kralove, Czech Republic

This study focuses on the implicit (tacit, subjective, lay, intuitive) concepts of normality. Attention is paid to the question: Which descriptors are crucial for the description of a normal individual given by helping professions (psychologists, special educators, social workers), and to what extent do they differ when the description is given by IT specialists? A new projective method was constructed (an adaptation of Kelly's Repertory grid test) to obtain these answers. The article presents partial results of the research.

The Psychophysics of Pictorial Depth Perception: The role of 2-visual-cue and 3-visual-cue factors
Hayashi, Takefumi Informatics, Kansai University, Takatsuki, Osaka, Japan Cook, Norman D. Dept. of Informatics, Kansai University, Osaka, Japan

The mechanisms of stereoscopic depth perception are well-understood, but the mechanisms underlying "pictorial" depth perception remain obscure. We have found that pictorial depth cues can be classified as essentially 2-cue processes (occlusion and relative retinal-size) or 3-cue processes (linear perspective and shading/shadows), while texture gradients can be defined as multiple 2- and 3-cue processes. We have studied the importance and brain localization of these cues in psychophysical, behavioral and fMRI studies of the perception of depth using 2D and 3D visual stimuli (Brain Research 1163, 72, 2007; Empirical Studies of the Arts 26, 67, 2008; Spatial Vision, in press).

Does it pay to be nice? Personality and earnings in the UK
Heineck, Guido Economics, University of Erlangen-Nurembe, Nuremberg, Germany

Objectives: Examine the relationship between personality, as measured by the Five Factor Personality Inventory, and wages in the UK, based on data drawn from the British Household Panel Survey (BHPS), 2005. Methods: Multiple regression analysis, correcting for sample selection as well as accounting for endogeneity and testing for non-linearity. Results: No clear patterns for openness, conscientiousness and extraversion; wage penalties for neuroticism and agreeableness. Conclusions: Non-cognitive skills modestly contribute to the variation in earnings of both male and female workers in the UK.

Representation and processing of negated information
Hemforth, Barbara LPNCog, Université René Descartes/CNRS, Boulogne-Billancourt, France Shuval, Noa LPNCog, Université René Descartes/CNRS, Boulogne-Billancourt, France Rigaut, Catherine LPNCog, Université René Descartes/CNRS, Boulogne-Billancourt, France

A good way to tap into the representation of negated information is to see how accessible this information is, e.g. for anaphoric reference. We will present a series of eyetracking experiments applying the visual world paradigm (auditory presentation of the linguistic material plus visual presentation of pictures) as well as reading techniques, showing that the position of the negated constituent as well as the exact form of the negation influences accessability, from highly accessible (when the negated information is in focus) to nearly inaccessible (when the information is unfocused and part of a linguistic repair).

Novelty preference: Effect of feedback level.
Hernández, Mayra University of Guadalajara, Guadalajra, Mexico Burgos, José Experimental Analysis, University of Guadalajara, Guadalajra, Mexico Morando, Areli Experimental Analysis, University of Guadalajara, Guadalajra, Mexico Padilla, Ma. Antonia Experimental Analysis, University of Guadalajara, Guadalajra, Mexico de la Torre, Carolina Experimental Analysis, University of Guadalajara, Guadalajra, Mexico Maciel, Roberto Experimental Analysis, University of Guadalajara, Guadalajra, Mexico

The present study sought to determine the effect of the level of feedback (no feedback, medium feedback, or high feedback) for interacting with certain stimuli on the preference for novel stimuli. Students were given five trials where left-clicking with a mouse on a colored geometric figure that was presented on a computer screen was followed by either no feedback, or a medium or high level of feedback. Then, all participants were given a choice between the figure that had been previously given and a new figure that was different in color and shape. The results show that substantially more participants preferred the not novel stimulus in the medium- and high-level conditions.

Indicators of vulnerability in a sample of women: Health, loneliness and self-esteem
Herrera, M. Carmen Social Psychology, University of Granada, Granada, Spain Valor-Segura, Inmaculada Social Psychology, University of Granada, Granada, Spain Expósito, Francisca Social Psychology, University of Granada, Granada, Spain

Roles developed traditionally by the women imply lifestyles with some risk factors in their health and in consequence it can produce a high use of medical services. This research aim is analyzes implications for physical and psychological health of women derived from the conditions of isolation and lack of social recognition in domestic work. The results show that housewives have a lower self-esteem, feel more loneliness and they have a higher vulnerability to suffer a health problem (psychological or social) compared to women working outside home.

Fostering teachers counseling competence: Terms of effective interventions for teacher education and training
Hertel, Silke Biqua, Dipf, Frankfurt, Germany Bruder, Simone Educational Psychology, TU Darmstadt, Darmstadt, Germany Schmitz, Bernhard Educational Psychology, TU Darmstadt, Darmstadt, Germany

The counseling of parents and students is a main subject of teachers activity that is constantly gaining importance. Researchers and practitioners point out the necessity of optimizing teachers training in the field of counseling (e. g. Grewe, 2005). Based on an empirical definition of teachers counseling

competence (see Hertel & Schmitz, 2006), a training programm for (preservice) teachers was developed and evaluated (multimethodological assessment approach). MANOVAS and MANCOVAS were conducted. For participating teachers (n=88) improvement of all competence facets and counseling specific knowledge was observed. Preservice teachers (n=85) did improve in terms of personal resources and counseling specific knowledge.

A person-centered perspective on intimate relationships
Herzberg, Philipp Yorck Inst. für Medizin. Psychologie, Universität Leipzig, Leipzig, Germany

The links between personality dimensions and various indicators of intimate relationships functioning has been investigated in numerous studies using a variable-centered approach. Although this approach yielded valuable insights into the personality-relationship transactions, these neglect the configuration of different variables within the person. As a completion, the person-centered approach offers advantage over the variable-centered approach. For instance, the whole configuration of characteristics within a person is taken into account which is more suitable than pursuing complex interactions analyses. The aim of the presentation is to demonstrate the potential of the person-centered approach for studying the interplay between personality and personal relationships.

Temperament as a moderator of emotional state and coping strategies
Heszen, Irena Health Psychology, Warsaw School of Soc. Psychol., Warsaw, Poland Gruszczynska, Ewa Health Psychology, Warsaw School of Soc. Psychol., Warsaw, Poland

The hypothesis of temperament as a moderator of stress phenomena was tested. Subjects were 224 cardiac infarction patients. Three questionnaires were applied to measure temperament, an emotional state and coping behavior. The measurement was repeated under different intensity of stressor. In series of variance analyses main effects of temperament and stressor intensity on emotional state and coping were found, whereas all the interactional effects revealed to be insignificant. Thus, although temperament had a direct influence on emotional and behvioral reactions to stressor, its moderating role was not confirmed.

Pulling the strings: The role of illness-related control perceptions in emotional adjustment to cancer
Hoffmann, Martine INSIDE/Psychology, University of Luxembourg, Walferdange, Luxembourg Ferring, Dieter INSIDE/Psychology, University of Luxembourg, Walferdange, Luxembourg

The present study aimed at exploring illness-related beliefs in cancer patients by analyzing the extent to which self-generated feelings of control over the illness relate to emotional adjustment. The sample consisted of 126 patients. Clusteranalyses resulted in a three-cluster solution regrouping patients with 'low', 'moderate' and 'high' levels of illness-related perceived control. Analyses of variance indicated that the clusters differed significantly on measures of coping strategies and subjective well-being. The cluster displaying highest levels of illness-related control perceptions showed significantly higher levels of 'threat-minimization', and it was associated with significantly lower levels of state- and trait-anxiety than the other clusters.

Is there a difference in syntactic processing when comparing German and Spanish speakers: Overlapping tasks and ERPs yield language-independent effects.

Hohlfeld, Annette Deutsche Sprache der Gegenwart, Universität Potsdam, Potsdam, Germany Martin-Loeches, Manuel Cognitive Neuroscience, Instituto Salud Carlos III, Madrid, Spain Sommer, Werner Institut für Psychologie, Humboldt-Universität, Berlin, Germany

We present data from 16 German and 16 Spanish native speakers, who had to assess the acceptability of visually presented correct or incorrect sentences. Additional task stimuli were presented 100, 400, or 700 ms before the target word. Whereas the LAN, elicited by gender incongruence, was not modulated by SOA, peak latency of the P600 component was delayed when SOA was short. These findings were equal in both languages. In addition we observed a delay in the offset of the P600 component for Spanish relative to German sentences. This effect is discussed with respect to gender access and preparation intervals.

Comparisonal investigation of personality traits and mental health in athletes and nonathletes students

Homayouni, Alireza Dept. of Psychology, Islamic Azad University, Bandargaz, Islamic Republic of Iran Homayounnia, Morteza Dept. of Sport Sciences, Shahid Rajaii University, Tehran, Islamic Republic of Iran Nikpour, Gholam Ali Dept. of Psychology, Medical Clinic of Dr. Mosavi, Babol (Amirkola), Islamic Republic of Iran Mosavi Amiri, Seyed Jalal Dept. of Psychology, Medical Clinic of Dr. Mosavi, Babol (Amirkola), Islamic Republic of Iran Pourabdoli, Mohammad Dept. of Psychology, Izlamic Azad University, Hashtroud, Tabriz, Islamic Republic of Iran Mohammadzadeh, Rajab Ali Dept. of Psychology, Payame Noor University, Babol (Bandepeye Gharby), Islamic Republic of Iran

The purpose of this research is to compare personality traits and mental health in athletes and non athletes students. Hypothesis: Athletes students have better mental and psychological health than non athletes students. 67 athletes and 64 nonathletes students were randomly selected and NEO-PIR inventory and General Health Questionnaire (GHQ)were administered on them. Data were analyzed with independent T formula. Results showed significant differences between variables. Non athletes have more neuroticism personality trait and were high in components of mental illness. It is concluded sport rehearsals and physical fitness have positive effects on temperament and mood and reduce mental illness symptoms and give sense of happiness and newness in life.

Task-set decay: Facts and fictions

Horoufchin, Himeh Inst. für Kogn. Psychologie, RWTH Aachen, Aachen, Germany Philipp, Andrea M. Cognitive Psychology, RWTH Aachen, Aachen, Germany Koch, Iring Inst. für Psychologie, RWTH Aachen, Aachen, Germany

Current theories suggest that the implementation of a task set is needed to execute cognitive tasks. In the task-switching literature, a decrease of switch costs with increasing RCI (i.e., response-to-cue interval) is typically attributed to the decay of task sets: Decay of previously established task sets is assumed to facilitate the next task in case of a task switching. Yet, we present experimental data using the cuing-version of the task-switching paradigm suggesting that decay mainly refers to a loss of task-repetition benefit which occurs under certain conditions only. Theoretical implications for the assumption of decay in task switching are discussed.

Independent – interdependent self-schemas and Taijin kyofusho symptoms in Japan: Cultural factors in social anxiety variants

Hoshino, Takatoshi Dept. of Arts and Sciences, University of Tokyo, Meguro, Japan Tanno, Yoshihiko Arts and Sciences, University of Tokyo, Meguro-Ku, Japan

It is said that the characteristic of Taijin kyofusho symptom is the fear of offending others or causing discomfort to others. By contrast, the feature of Social Anxiety Disorder is the fear of being embarrassed. The difference mentioned above is said to be derived from cultural factors in Collectivism (in Japan culture)-Individualism (in Western culture). The purpose of this study was to investigate the relationship between collectivism (interdependent self-schema) and Taijin kyofusho symptoms. The multiple regression analyses suggested that individuals with interdependent self-schema (and without independent self-schema) endorsed much Taijin kyofusho symptoms, but individuals with independent self-schema did less.

Differential responses of infants interacting with a live video image of either the self or the other in real and masked image conditions

Hosokawa, Toru Human Development, Tohoku University, Sendai, Japan Suzuki, Keita Human Development, Tohoku University, Sendai, Japan Sasaya, Takashi Human Development, Tohoku University, Sendai, Japan Tatsuta, Nozomi Human Development, Tohoku University, Sendai, Japan China, Aoko Human Development, Tohoku University, Sendai, Japan Chua Yi-Lynn, Stephanie Human Development, Tohoku University, Sendai, Japan Hongo, Kazuo Human Development, Tohoku University, Sendai, Japan

The purpose of this study was to elucidate how infants are sensitive to the temporal contingency between visual and proprioceptive feedback in masked specular images. Sixteen to 24 month-old infants were placed facing a video image either of themselves or of another infant in real and masked image conditions, and were required to play the "janken" (rock-scissors-paper) game with the specular images on a video screen. Infants' responses such as gazing, emotional and verbal expressions, and heart rate during the play were observed. The results suggested a dominant role of concurrent synchronization of movement for visual self-recognition.

Where do I see me?: Evaluation of a new emotional writing method of psychological displacement and its beneficial effects

Huang, Chin-Lan Division of General Education, NTU of Science and Technol., Taipei, Taiwan Lin, Yicheng Department of Psychology, The National Taiwan University, Taipei, Taiwan Chang, Jenho Department of Psychology, National Taiwan University, Taipei, Taiwan Seih, Yitai Department of Psychology, National Taiwan University, Taipei, Taiwan

This study examined a new emotional writing paradigm, i.e., PDDP. PDDP instructs participants to write diary in first-person pronoun first, and then narrate the same event from a different perspective using second-person pronoun. Finally, the participants write it again with third-person pronoun from yet another perspective. These three narrations were written in a consecutive sequential order. 108 participants kept their diaries using PDDP three times a week for 6 weeks. Their psychological adjustments, life satisfaction, and emotional experiences were measured before and after the diary keeping period. The beneficial effects and mediating mechanisms of PDDP were both evaluated.

Visual short-term memory: The effect of presentation time and fixations

Huebner, Gesche Inst. für Allg. Psychologie, Universität Gießen, Gießen, Germany Gegenfurtner, Karl R. Allgemeine Psychologie, JLU Giessen, Giessen, Germany

We examined the influence of presentation time and fixations on performance in a visual short-term memory task. Participants viewed a display containing eight photographs of natural objects for between 250 and 3000 ms. Memory for one object was tested subsequently. During stimulus presentation, participants either fixated the center of the circle or looked around freely. Unlike many recent reports of object memory we found that neither presentation time nor fixating objects influenced performance. We calculate that a capacity of about 3 items in visual memory is reached within 250 ms of viewing and does not increase with prolonged viewing.

Content analysis of suicide in Pakistan: Preliminary study

Hussain Kanwal, Rabia Behavioral Sciences, Fatima Jinnah Women University, Rawalpindi, Pakistan Naz, Sajida Behavioral Sciences, Fatima Jinnah Women University, Rawalpindi, Pakistan

The present study was conducted to analyze the suicidal rate in Pakistan and to explore different aspects of committed suicide during the period of one year from October 1, 2006 to October 1, 2007. The objectives of study were assessed through the information/news given in two newspapers (The daily Jang and Dawn) of Pakistan. The findings indicated increased incidence of suicide in youngsters as compared to adults. The significant mean difference of suicides was found among males as compared to females. As it was preliminary study, committed suicidal rates in last five year would be analyzed through newspapers in future.

Event-related potential correlates of Delboeuf illusion

Imai, Akira Psychology, Faculty of Arts, Shinshu University, Matsumoto, Japan Goto, Takuo Design, Nagoya University of Arts, Kitanagoya, Japan

Event-related potential (ERPs) correlates of the Delboeuf illusion were obtained under a psychophysical setting. Using the constant method, undergraduates judged a briefly flashed comparative stimulus by "large" or "small" response in comparison with a standard stimulus. ERPs to the comparative stimulus were collected separately for the large and the small responses. The small response evoked larger P3 amplitudes compared to the large response at frontal sties (Fz and Cz), but did not at posterior sites (Pz and Oz). This tendency disappeared at near threshold level. The P3 amplitudes seem to be related to judgment processes and the magnitude of illusion.

Effect of outcome imagery on motor planning and control in dart throwing: An analysis of motor preparation time and fluctuation of dart landing points

Imai, Fumihito Sapporo, Japan Hishitani, Shinsuke psychology, Hokkaido University, Sapporo, Japan

The effects of outcome imagery on motor planning and control in dart throwing were investigated in two experiments. In experiments 1 and 2, 16 and 15 participants, respectively, generated one of three outcome images before each throw. These were that the trajectory of dart to hit on, above, or below the target. Motor preparation time was shown to be longer under the latter two conditions in experiment 2. However, the images showed no bias effect on the dart landing points in both experiments. It was suggested that outcome imagery has a role in motor planning and control in dart throwing.

Message order effects, self-relevance and need for cognition in persuasion

Imai, Yoshiaki Faculty of Sociology, Toyo University, Tokyo, Japan

The hypothesis that self-relevance and need for cognition moderate order effects in persuasive messages was examined. Students read messages including strong and weak points of exams as a graduation requirement, and answered their attitudes toward the exams and the need for cognition scale. An analysis of variance showed that low self-relevance students were more favorable toward the exams after receiving strong points first than after receiving weak points first, while there were no order effects for high self-relevance students. Furthermore, those who are high in need for cognition agreed with the exams more than the low need for cognition.

Personality and regulation determinants of rational decision making in political voting situations

Indina, Tatiana Self-Regulation Psychology, Psychological Institute RAE, Moscow, Russia
Morosanova, Varavara Self-Regulation Psychology, Psychological Institute RAE, Moscow, Russia

Personality, cognitive and regulation determinants of rational decision making in political voting situations are investigated. Sample: 290 subjects (18-65 yrs). Methods: Political voting model, expert estimations and content-analysis, Raven Standart Progressive Matrices, Personality decision making factors, (Kornilova, 2003), Keirsey Temperament Sorter, Self-regulation Profile Questionnaire (Morosanova, 2000). Results: Subjects with high rationality level are characterized by high level of general intelligence and conscious self-regulation. They also have higher exponents of Introvertion, Sensation, Judging and Thinking personality traits. Among the main determinants of Rational decision making high level of general intelligence, Thinking and Judging personality traits and conscious self-regulation are distinguished.

Development of dimension-based processing in visual search in children

Indino, Marcello Inst. für Psychologie, Universität Zürich, Zürich, Switzerland Grubert, Anna Psychologisches Institut, Universität Fribourg, Fribourg, Switzerland

Visual search is highly efficient for targets differing from distractors in salient features. However, reaction times are affected by the dimensional definition of the target in previous trials: Benefits are observed with repetitions, costs with changes. As the cognitive function of these dimensional-based modulations remains unclear we investigated, in a developmental approach, if dimension-based processing emerges gradually or is related to a specific developmental step. Search reaction times of participants aged four to 20 years revealed dimension-based effects to occur not before age eight. This finding suggests that the emergence of the effect is associated with a developmental step.

Planning and problem solving skills in children: Tower of London, age, and IQ

Injoque-Ricle, Irene Instituto de Investigaciones, CONICET - F. Psicología, UBA, Ciudad de Buenos Aires, Argentina Wilson, Maximiliano ISTC-CNR, Rome, Italy Burin, Débora Instituto de Investigaciones, CONICET - F. Psicología, UBA, Ciudad de Buenos Aires, Argentina

Objectives: To explore the relationship among Tower of London (TOL) task performance, IQ, and Age, in an Argentinean sample. Methods: 107 children, aged 6 (n=26), 8 (n=27), 11 (n=24), and 13 (n=30) years-old completed a version of the TOL task, Vocabulary, and Block Design subtests (WISC-R). Pearson correlations among TOL, IQ, and Age were conducted. Results: Moderate,

positive and significant correlations between TOL and Age (r= .435; p < .001), and between TOL and IQ (r= .282; p = 0.003), were found. Conclusions: Planning and problem solving increase with age in childhood, and are related to total IQ.

Spatial representations of time in action

Ishihara, Masami Inst. für Psychologie, Max-Planck-Institut, Leipzig, Germany Keller, Peter Department of Psychology, Max Planck Institute for CBS, Leipzig, Germany Rossetti, Yves Espace et Action, INSERM Unit 864, Bron, France Prinz, Wolfgang Department of Psychology, Max Planck Institute for CBS, Leipzig, Germany

Temporal periodic stimuli have spatial characteristics and responses to such stimuli are biased by mental representations of their onset timing: left-side responses to early onsets are faster than those to late onsets, whereas right-side responses to late onsets are faster than those to early onsets [spatial-temporal association of response codes (STEARC) effect]. This supports the existence of a 'mental time line' in action. We investigated whether this congruity effect was influenced by the amount of preceding temporal information. Results showed that the effect does not depend on this factor, suggesting that space-time associations affect action independently of expectancy strength.

Left-right spatial bias and reading habits: The inter-task relationship among left-right spatial bias tasks

Ishii, Yukiko Sakamoto-Kata, Tokyo, Japan

This study examined spatial bias tasks to 64 Japanese undergraduates whether reading habits work to 7 left-right spatial biases similarly. We found that aesthetic-picture-preference tasks and thematic-role tasks were significantly correlated with each other, while line-bisection task and location-of-drawing task were correlated significantly. Inhibition-of-return task wasn't correlated with other tasks. Interestingly, first correlation group showed right-left reading habit's biases and the second showed left-right reading habit's biases as well. These results suggested that reading habits might differently affect in Japanese which has both vertical top-to-bottom and horizontal left-to-right reading habits in daily life. Reading mechanism with movement will be discussed.

Negotiations in social dilemma settings: A more ecologically valid approach

Ittner, Heidi Department of Psychology, Otto-von-Guericke-University, Magdeburg, Germany

Negotiations around the provision of public goods are an established object in social psychology. Laboratory-experimental methods are the dominant approach although, these settings are rarely subjectively meaningful: Participants distribute "gift goods" and rarely get in contact with the negotiation partner. Therefore, the ecological validity of most studies is questionable. An alternative experimental design is presented, in which the subjective meaningfulness of the setting is manipulated. Within that, the configuration and influence of justice judgements on (un-)cooperative behavior will be analysed. From the results important theoretical and practically relevant insights for justice psychology and social dilemma- and negotiation research are expected.

Relations between happiness-increasing strategies, personality traits and happiness in Croatian youth

Ivanusevic, Sanja Primary School Ludbreg, Primary School Ludbreg, Ludbreg, Croatia Brajsa-Zganec, Andreja Institute of Social SciencesIP, Zagreb, Croatia Kaliterna-Lipovcan, Ljiljana of Social Sciences, IVO PILAR Institute, Zagreb, Croatia

The main goal of this study was to explore the relationship between happiness-increasing strate-

gies, personality traits and happiness level in 573 undergraduate students. The participants completed self-report measures assessing their happiness increasing strategies, happiness, and personality traits. The results showed that females are generally happier than males, and that they use almost all happiness-increasing strategies more often. Hierarchical multiple regression analyses revealed that extraversion and emotional stability, and in the second analysis, four of eight examined happiness-increasing strategies were significant predictors of happiness. In addition, after controlling for students' individual characteristics, happiness-increasing strategies were significant predictors of happiness

Determinants of career attitudes: Developmental differences

Janeiro, Isabel Centro de Investigacao, Universidade de Lisboa, Carcavelos, Portugal

Super's (1990) model of the bases of career maturity indicates time perspective, self-esteem and causal attributions as psychological determinants of career attitudes. The objective of this study was to analyse the effects of those determinants on career attitudes. 320 students from grade 9 and 300 from grade 12 participated in the study. The analysis of results, based on the methodology of structural equations modelling (LISREL), revealed, in both grades, only one determinant, the future time perspective, to affect directly career planning. However, some developmental differences also emerged. The implications for career counselling are further discussed.

When teachers treat me well, I think I belong: School belonging and the psychological well being of adolescent girls in India

Jethwani-Keyser, Monique Bayside, USA

This study explores Indian girls' experiences of belonging in school and how those experiences shape psychological adjustment. Semi structured interviews (n=16) with girls at an urban, government-aided high school in southern India reveal that feelings of belonging are defined by perceptions of teacher support, encouragement and care. Separate hierarchical regression analyses (n=141, mean age = 13.48) reveal that belonging is a significant correlate of self esteem and depression over and above person level factors (caste) and the experience of competition and stress in school. These results suggest that positive teacher relationships in school are critical for belonging and the psychological well-being of adolescent girls in India.

Study on childhood abuse, parenting styles and antisocial personality disorder

Jiang, Jiang School of Psychology, Beijing Normal University, Beijing, People's Republic of China

The relationship between childhood abuse, parenting styles and antisocial personality disorder (APD) was examined in a sample of 866 prisoners with related scales. Significance test of difference, correlation analysis, and regression analysis revealed that prisoners with APD were treated with more emotional and physical abuse, less care and autonomy by their parents; Childhood abuse had significant positive correlation with APD, less care with more APD, less encouragement of behavioral freedom and mother's denial of psychological autonomy with less APD; Childhood abuse and parenting style predicted APD significantly and emotional abuse and mother's denial of psychological autonomy had positive predictable effect, while care is the reverse.

Influence of illustration on reading comprehension for field-dependent and field-independent children

Jiao, Lihua Department of Psychology, Capital Normal University, Beijing, People's Republic of China *Zhang, Qin* Department of Psychology, Capital Normal University, Beijing, People's Republic of China

The present experiment investigated influence of illustration on reading comprehension of field-dependent and field-independent children using difficult and easy texts. 52 children (26 field-dependent, 26 field-independent) read two texts with or without illustrations and then completed reading comprehension tests. Results showed that field-dependent children got better result in reading comprehension test when they read easy text without illustration than with illustration. However, no significant effects of illustration and/or degree of difficulty were found for field-independent children. The result suggested that illustration interfered with reading comprehension of field-dependent children when they read easy text.

Gastric carcinoma: Treatent adherence influenced by perceived social support

Jidveian, Mara Dept. of General Medicine, UMF, Bucharest, Romania *Pantelimon, Iuliana* General Medicine, UMF, Bucharest, Romania

Objectives: to identify the degree to which patients' gender, residence and social support may influence their adherence to treatment. Methods: 120 patients, 27-59 years, with gastric carcinoma and evenly divided by residence and gender. They were administered the MARS and Perceived Social Support Questionnaire. Results:All patients showed a high level of adherence to treatment (mean score = 42.3). Urban men under 40 years old were more compliant and with higher level of social support (45.5 vs. 37, p=0.01). (42.7 vs. 36.5, p=0.01). Conclusions:Gender and residence could have relevance for long-term prognosis, as the social support influences the adherence.

Personality traits as predictors of residential mobility within and between U.S. states: Midlife in the United States survey

Jokela, Markus Dept. of Psychology, University of Helsinki, Helsinki, Finland

Objective: To examine whether personality traits prospectively predict migration propensity within and between U.S. states. Methods: The participants were 3711 women and men from the Midlife in the United States survey, who were followed for 7 to 11 years. Personality traits were assessed on a "Big Five" inventory at baseline. Results: High openness to experience and low agreeableness increased migration propensity within and between states, while high extraversion increased migration propensity within but not between states. Conclusions: With regards to personality, open-minded, extraverted, and self-interested individuals may be most likely to change residential location in the United States.

The effects of motivation for bullying on frequency of bullying

Kaneko, Yasuyuki Dept. of Psychology, Chuo University, TokyotoTamashi, Japan

The purpose of this study was to compare differences in relationships among motivation for bullying and frequency of bullying by contrasting them between groups. 1306 junior high school students were administered conformity, motivation for bullying, frequency of bullying, and levels of norm-consciousness. Cluster analysis was performed. We classified the students into 3 groups based on conformity and norm-consciousness. A motivation for bullying affected frequency of bullying directly. Based on the model aforementioned, multiple regression analyses were conducted

every 3 groups. As a result, even though conducted bullying itself looked same, motivation for the bullying was different among groups.

Impulsivity in layperson's mind

Kangro, Eva-Maria Psychology, Tallinn University, Tabasalu, Estonia

There exists a lack of consensus about what constitutes impulsivity. Impulsivity as a nonreflective behavior could refer to a deficit in knowledge or skills. Another orientation is that impulsivity is a response to social or personal conditions involving frustration. It could also refer to weak self-control or tendency to respond quickly. Although the term impulsivity is usually reserved for maladaptive behavior, it may also possess both functional and dysfunctional meanings. In turn, orientation and behavior are understandable in consideration of a context. Laypersons' understanding reflects a variety of meanings (control, reflection etc) and antecedents (dispositional, social, and stress-related).

To leave or not to leave: Social mobility and social exclusion in Chinese culture

Kao, Joey Dept. of Psychology, Chung Yuan University, Chungli, Taiwan *Sun, Chien-Ru* Psychology, Chung Yuan Christian U., Chung Li, Taiwan

The present research investigates the different social exclusion conditions and possible responses after social exclusion in Chinese culture. In experiment 1, the effects of group status (high vs. low) and the probability of re-acceptance by the group (20% vs. 50% vs. 80%) are investigated. We predict that participants will try their best in the high status and 50% probability social exclusion condition. In experiment 2, we prime different self-construals (independent vs. interdependent self), and manipulate the reasons of exclusion (ability vs. interpersonal aspect). We predict that interdependents who are excluded for interpersonal reasons, will be most unwilling to leave and make the most effort to reverse the situation.

Cultural construction of self and identity among Sikhs in India

Kapur, Preeti New Delhi, India

Using qualitative approach this study explores how selves emerge and are transformed in the course of changing experiences,socio-cultural and historical circumstances in the Sikh community. The making of Sikh identity in terms of its emergence, its style of articulation, process of trandformation and regeneration, consolidation and maintenance are documented. It is observed that in the Sikh way of life the person's individuality is instrumental in achieving unity and harmony amongst self-aspects. A Sikh is expected to live and serve in society, a stable and well-adjusted identity arises not by segregation of one's self, but by living in society, that is, by serving and sharing.

The cultural meaning of identity construction in disease state

Karnilowicz, Wally Dept. of Psychology, Victoria University, Melbourne, Australia

An examination of the construction of self-identity within psychological ownership when confronted by disease state (Prostate Cancer). Meanings associated with the impact of disease state are identified and reflected upon within the social context. The study argues for the construction of identity within unique interpretations of the cultural meanings of symbols and artefacts embedded within and outside of the individual. It investigates human experiences and aims to determine the meanings people attach to a particular lived experience. It examines perspectives of their world and details content and structure of consciousness

to account for diversity within unique yet shared essential meanings.

The effect of the multiple audience problem on self-presentation

Kasagi, Yuu Dept. of Social Psychology, Osaka University, Suita, Japan *Daibo, Ikuo* Social Psychology, Osaka University, Suita, Japan

How successfully can people solve the "multiple audience problems" (Fleming et al., 1990)? Female participants were asked to talk with the opposite or same sex confederate in the situation where the other female participant was observing on side (either multiple audience condition or same sex observer condition, respectively). Also, we set the control condition in which no participants were observing on side was present. Results showed that participants in the multiple audience condition presented themselves more attractive in scores on social-desirability and intimacy than others. We discussed these findings in terms of compensatory self-presentation.

The social interactions of 2-year-old infants toward a crying infant

Kato, Mayuko Suita, Japan *Minami, Tetsuhiro* Human science, Osaka University, Suita, Japan *Hinobayashi, Toshihiko* Human sciense, Osaka University, Suita, Japan *Yasuda, Jun* Human science, Osaka University, Suita, Japan *Shizawa, Yasuhiro* Human science, Osaka University, Suita, Japan

The present study examined the social interactions of 2-year-old infants toward a crying infant. The participants were 10 infants at a day-care center, and the observations were conducted on infants aged 24 months. The behaviors of the infants toward a crying infant were coded to pulling or pushing, teasing, glaring, approaching, soothing, no reaction, and play interactions. The results revealed that the closer the interactions during daily life, the more sympathetic were the behaviors of the infants engaging in soothing behaviors. This suggests that the social interactions of infants are influenced by closer interactions with peers in daily life.

Effect of guidance for stress management on frustration and feeling of burnout of mothers of Mentally Challenged (MC) children

Kaur, Kiranpreet Popular Jewellers, Yamunanagar, India *Ravneet, Chawala* Govt. Homescience college, panjab university, India

The study was carried out to study the level of stress, frustration and feeling of burnout, to examine and compare the effect of with and without treatment of 'guidance for stress management' on selected variables on mothers of MC children. Purposive sampling technique was used to select the sample of 40 mothers of MC children from Utthan.The data was collected by administering: Family Stress Scale,Frustration test, Burnout Inventory, Group Guidance Schedule. The findings of present study revealed that effect of guidance for stress management on frustration and feeling of burnout was seen among the mothers of MC children.

Difference threshold modification of middle tone hues under unique hue perceptual learning task

Kawabata, Yasuhiro Dept. of Psychology, Hokkaido University, Sapporo, Japan *Nishikawa, Rintaro* Dept. of Psychology, Hokkaido University, Sapporo, Japan *Kawabata, Miho* Dept. of Psychology, Hokkaido University, Sapporo, Japan

Memory task for the location of a target hue in a 4*4 colored matrix was performed. Each of the 16 squares within a matrix was assigned one of four unique hues, and observers were asked to report the location of a target hue. The initial frame rate was 2 matrices per second and it was increased as observers' performance improved to as high as 25 matrices per second. Observers performed the color hue discrimination task before and after the memory task. Attending to a particular target hue influenced discrimination of middle tone hues which contained the primal hue.

The relationship between epistemological beliefs and reading comprehension in Japanese

Kawasaki, Eriko University, Kawamura Gakuen Woman's, Chiba, Japan Iseki, Ryuta Psychology, University of Tsukuba, Ibaraki, Japan

Epistemological beliefs of students have been proved to affect their academic achievements. However, there can be different structure of epistemological beliefs in Asia. This research focuses on the relationship between epistemological beliefs and reading comprehension in Japanese undergraduates. The Japanese Epistemological Beliefs Scale (Tomita & Nakano, 2006), which was restructured based on the Epistemological Questionnaire (Schommer, 1998) and the Epistemic Belief Inventory(Schraw et al., 2002), correlated with performance on reading test. One subscale of JEBS, the dialogical nature of knowledge, had the strongest relationship to reading and this factor was absent in prior researches in the United States.

A qualitative study of cohesion in amateur soccer team

Kawazu, Keita Human Environmental Studies, Kyushu University, Kasuga, Japan Sugiyama, Yoshio Institute of health science, Kyushu university, Kasuga city, Fukuoka, Japan

The purpose of this study is to reexamine the conceptual model of group cohesion. The subjects consisted of some male amateur athletes who belong to high competitive level soccer team. The data acquisition method was the problem-centered interview. In order to analyze the data, the qualitative content analysis was used. To the qualitative content analysis, 90 cords and 29 subcategories was extracted. Some sub-categories were applied to conceptual model of group cohesion, other were not applied to it.

Survivors of communism regime in Lithuania: Post-traumatic effects of the past

Kazlauskas, Evaldas Dept Clin Psychology, Vilnius University, Vilnius, Lithuania Gailiene, Danute Dept Clin Psychology, Vilnius University, Vilnius, Lithuania Domanskaite-Gota, Vejune Dept Clin Psychology, Vilnius University, Vilnius, Lithuania

OBJECTIVES: 300,000 Lithuanians were imprisoned or displaced to Siberia for political reasons during communism regime. Purpose of this study was to assess posttraumatic reactions and predictors of posttraumatic health of survivors. METHODS: Survivors of political repression (n=1404) were randomly selected from Lithuanian national registry. We assessed life-time traumatic experiences, exposure to political violence, posttraumatic reactions, and mediating factors between trauma and current health. RESULTS: Posttraumatic reactions were predicted by trauma exposure, female gender, lower level of education, lower Sense of Coherence. CONCLUSIONS: Long-term posttraumatic effects of political violence are prevalent among survivors even after the collapse of Communist regime, and strongest predictor of current health is life-time traumatic experiences.

Trauma transmission to second generation: Are there any links between long-term post traumatic stress reactions of political violence survivors and post-traumatic stress of their adult offspring?

Kazlauskas, Evaldas Dept Clin Psychology, Vilnius University, Vilnius, Lithuania Gailiene, Danute Dept Clin Psychology, Vilnius University, Vilnius, Lithuania Domanskaite-Gota, Vejune Dept Clin Psychology, Vilnius University, Vilnius, Lithuania

OBJECTIVES: Purpose of present study was to investigate links between posttraumatic stress reactions of prolonged political violence survivors and posttraumatic stress of their adult offspring. METHODS: Non-clinical sample of 50 pairs of political violence survivors and their adult offspring (mean age = 41.8) participated in study. We used Lithuanian versions of Trauma Symptom Checklist, Impact of Event Scale - Revised, and Beck Hopelessness Scale. RESULTS: No significant correlations between parent and children measures were found. CONCLUSIONS: There are limitations due to a small sample in this study. Results confirmed that long-term posttraumatic stress reactions of survivors have no direct impact on posttraumatic stress reactions of their adult offspring.

Innovations and innovativeness at school

Keskinen, Soili Turku, Finland Siltala, Reijo Department of teacher training, University of Turku, Rauma, Finland Hakala, Jenni Department of teacher training, University of Turku, Rauma, Finland Luoto, Anna department of teacher training, University of Turku, Rauma, Finland Tenhunen, Anu Department of teacher training, University of Turku, Rauma, Finland

According to our earlier studies concerning business innovations, shared knowledge, trust and positive dependency of colleagues, networking, skills and expertise are significant in developing innovations. Our study goal is to describe typical features of innovative school work. We interviewed 6 school principals and asked them to define the innovativeness at school and to name the most innovative teacher of their school. Then we interviewed those 6 named teachers. We asked them to describe innovativeness at school work, their pedagogical thinking and teaching manners. After qualitative analyses we found that same features are typical for school innovativeness as to business innovations.

Efficacy of stress inoculation training in smellioration of post partum depression in women

Khalatbari, Javad Dept. of Psychology, IAU of Tonekabon Branch, Tonekabon, Islamic Republic of Iran

The aim of this study was to evaluate the efficacy of stress-inculation training (SIT)relieving of distress,-depression post partum symptoms in women.First 70 definitly diagnosed post partum depressions were selected from clinic of different in city of tehran.In second step they were tested by given two questionnarires of depression of Beck, psychiatric distress of Markham..It was found that the SIT gruop was significantly less depresses, anxious and distressed than control subjects(a<0.05).The study results suggest that SIT can be effectively applied as a therapeutic to in püst partum depression.

Psychological aspects od students' attitudes to money

Khodakevych, Olga Organizational Psychology, Institute of Psychology, Kiev, Ukraine

The objective of the piloting study was to reveal students' attitudes to money. Method: The data from the self-completion questionnaire developed by the researcher were processed by content analysis. The research took place in Kyiv; the sample consisted of 100 students, age 19 - 20 years, male and female. Results: 1). Money associates both with positive emotions (joy (53.7%); happiness (35.1%); respect (27.7%) and negative ones (shame (30%); envy (29.6%); anxiety (27.7%); panic (25.9%); anger (24%); fear (20.1%). 2). Many students work (46.3 %) expressing positive attitude to earning money (82.2%). 90.6% of students depend on their parents, receiving pocket money. Conclusion: students' money attitudes are ambivalent.

Effectiveness of a simulation game as a disaster drill for young children

Kikkawa, Toshiko Business and Commerce, Keio University, Tokyo, Japan

This study evaluated the effectiveness of a simulation game called 'Bosai-duck' as a disaster drill for children aged 3 to 5 years old. 'Bosai-duck' was originally designed as a card game for children to teach them the 'First move' when faced with various disasters. In the game, players are asked to take the first action for the hazard appearing on each card, as quickly as possible. By analyzing pictures drawn by nursery school children, the author found that the game was effective for teaching children about disasters.

Frames of reference in the measurement of academic self concepts

Knigge, Michel Qualitätsent. im Bildungswesen, Humboldt-Universität zu Berlin, Berlin, Germany

Most instruments designed to measure the academic self concept are not varying the frame of reference explicitly (Marsh, 1988). Dickhäuser et al. (2002) developed an instrument that distinguishes between four reference frames for general academic self-concept. The aim of this study was to investigate if differences regarding the big fish little pond-effect (bfple, Marsh & Hau, 2003) occur. Also comparisons for different school type populations where conducted. The analyzed sample consists out of 1278 students. Results shows variation for bflpe over the different subscales and differential school type effects are found. Further efforts on development of such instruments are discussed.

Qualitative reasoning in physics: Use of inquiry, ICT-tools and social interactions

Kohler, Alaric Psychologie et Education, Institut, Neuchâtel, Switzerland

This poster presents a design-based research with physics classrooms at college, using simulative and argumentative ICT-tools. The case design is based on inquiry and social interactions to foster learning. The main results concerning learning within discussion, overcoming preconception, and the role of media and teacher support in knowledge construction will be exposed. More precisely, results show analyses of individual or social processes happening during the construction of a solution to physics problems. Written, audio and video data give a precise recording of pupils progression during the whole teaching session.

The effects of sensitivity of other's opinion and induced-anxiety on interests in nuclear power

Koike, Fumiyo Faculty of Sociology, Kansai University, Osaka, Japan Tsuchida, Shoji Faculty of Sociology, Kansai University, Suita-shi, Japan Tsujikawa, Norifumi Graduate School of Sociology, Kansai University, Suita-shi, Japan Tanigaki, Toshihiko Social awareness research, INSS, Mikata-gun, Fukui, Japan Nagaoka, Yutaka Social awareness research, INSS, Mikata-gun, Fukui, Japan

We examined that individuals' interests in nuclear power were affected by their sensitivity of other's opinion about nuclear power and induced - anxiety. Three hundred and twenty-three people who lived in Osaka area, Japan participated in the laboratory experiment. They were asked to watch a video to induce anxiety about future energy supply(experiment condition), or to watch a video explaining the history of energy with neutral feelings(control condition). Then, participants freely searched information about nuclear power on a database. The number of informations that participants read and the time to read it were recorded and analized

Monochronic-Polychronic attitudes toward time in Ukrainian, American and French cultures

Kovalchuk, Olena *Psychology and Pedagogics, National Technical University, Kiev, Ukraine*

Objectives: To assess attitudes toward time in Ukrainian, American and French cultures. Methods: Five groups of college students, including two groups of exchange students, were surveyed using the "Monochronic-Polychronic Self-Test" by G. Hofstede. Results: Representatives of the American culture demonstrated a highly monochronic level of perception of time. Ukrainian students and students who studied in France and French students showed moderately polychronic level. Exchange students placed between the Ukrainian students and the representatives of the host countries. Conclusions: Our results can be applied to cross-cultural interaction in educational, business and political spheres as well as for designing adaptation programs.

The mental transformation of body parts in development: Imagery and motor processes - when are they connected?

Krüger, Markus *Inst. für Psychologie, Universität Greifswald, Greifswald, Germany*

Effects of anatomical constraints on the mental rotation of body parts have been reported as being more pronounced in children than in adults, suggesting a stronger link between motor processes and imagery in childhood. In a recent series of experiments, we were able to replicate effects of anatomical constraints on the mental rotation of hands, but only under certain conditions. When such effects occurred, they were not stronger in children than in adults. Therefore our results cast doubt on the assumption that imagery derives from sensorimotor processes ontogenetically.

The relationship between sense of coherence, Buddhist practice, work-family conflict and job burnout among working women

Kreausukon, Pimchanok *Psychology, Chiangmai University, Chiang Mai, Thailand*

This study investigated the level of job burnout and the relationship between Sense of coherence, Buddhist practice, Work – family conflict and Job burnout among working women. Samples were 181 married female university lecturers. Research instruments were Sense of coherence scale, Buddhist practice scale, Work – family conflict Inventory and Maslach Burnout Inventory. Data were analyzed using descriptive statistics and Pearson's correlation coefficient. Results indicated that; there was a moderate level of job burnout among samples. Sense of coherence and Buddhist practice were negatively related to job burnout while Work – family conflict was positively related to job burnout.

The benefits of social support: For whom?

Kreitler, Shulamith *Dept. of Psychology, Tel-Aviv University, Tel-Aviv, Israel*

The goal was to identify in cancer patients psychological correlates of readiness to use social support. The participants were 167 patients of both genders, with different cancer diagnoses and in different disease stages. They were administered questionnaires assessing the use of different kinds of social support and a cognitive orientation questionnaire assessing motivational tendencies for using social support. Discriminant and multiple regression analyses showed that the cognitive orientation variables provided good predictions of the use of social support. The results enable identifying patients who can benefit from social support and those who need help for using this coping resource.

The mental health of working female in Japan, Taiwan and Thailand

Kuang, Mei-Fun *Nippon Heart Support Network, Fukuoka, Japan*

This is a study of the mental health of working females in Japan, Taiwan and Thailand using semi-structured interview, GHQ-30 and 2 hours support group. The mental healht status, stress coping method and PMS were analyzed and discussed according to different culture and social-economic envrionments. The stress coping model was proposed and examed.

Effects of vocational trainings on coping with long-term unemployment

Kuhnert, Peter *Organisationspsychologie, TU Dortmund, Dortmund, Germany* **Blankermann, Heike** *Organisationspsychologie, TU Dortmund, Dortmund, Germany* **Seifert-Friedel, Nadine** *Organisationspsychologie, TU Dortmund, Dortmund, Germany* **Kastner, Michael** *Organisationspsychologie, TU Dortmund, Dortmund, Germany*

The study was part of the Project SUMAS (Social and multimedia-based work and social assistance) in EQUAL II (2005 – 2007) concerning the relationship between coping strategies and vocational trainings. The participants of the survey were 215 people with different vocational trainings (55% women, 45% men). Over 50% of the participants have a low level of education and were unemployed for more than two years. Results: Productive coping decreases with length of unemployment while emotion-focused coping increases with length of participation in vocational trainings. This also corresponds with results of other European studies.

Components of listening skills among Japanese college students and their relation to social adjustment

Kukiyama, Kenichi *Dept. of International Studies, Kyushu Sangyo University, Fukuoka, Japan*

In Japan, it is thought that listening skills play an important roll in social adjustment. But most of the studies regarding listening skills have been conducted in counseling or English education settings, and they have been scarcely examined in the context of social adjustment. Questionnaires were administered to 221 college students. Exploratory factor analysis revealed that Listening Skills Scale had eight sub-scales (creating a comfortable atmosphere, empathy, advice, understanding facial expression, interests, eye contact, attending, and genuineness). Subscales were moderately reliable and valid, and had relation to friendship satisfaction and positive attitude toward peers.

The Influence that the children's reactions give to classroom discourse

Kuroda, Mayumi *Kyoto, Japan*

In the classroom, there are not only communications that center on the teacher but also communications that center on children. Child's communications play an important role in the class. Children are learning through child's communications and adjust their attitude. The purpose of this research is to clarify the process that the children's discourse approved. Child's space might be formed not only by the teacher's intention but by the children's responses to the utterance according to situation. The child's reaction is related child's daily relation and to the content of the utterance of child. Two or more children's spaces are concomitant.

A study for testing the construct validity of personal permeability of the group

Kurokawa, Masayuki *Graduate School of Education, Nagoya University, Nagoya, Japan* **Yoshida, Toshikazu** *Graduate School of Education a, Nagoya University, Chikusa-ku, Nagoya, Japan*

This study examined the construct validity of personal permeability of the peer-group by investigating correlations with relevant scales and interpersonal skills. A total of 174 fifth- and sixthgraders participated in this study. Personal permeability of the group had significantly positive correlations with openness in friendship and interpersonal skills, and negative correlations with self-protection in friendship and sensibility to friendship-threatening stressors, but sensibility was found negative only among girls. On the other hand, personal permeability of the group had no significant correlation with perceived group cohesiveness. These results confirmed the construct validity of personal permeability of the group.

The structure, stability and age trends of temperament in a Japanese sample

Kusanagi, Emiko *Kokugakuin Junior College, Kitahiroshima City, Japan* **Nakano, Shigeru** *Developmental Psychology, Hokkaido Health Science Univer, Sapporo City, Japan* **Sekine, Megumi** *Developmental Psychology, Hokkaido Health Science Univer, Sapporo City, Japan* **Kondo-Ikemura, Kiyomi** *Developmental Psychology, Hokkaido Health Science Univer, Sapporo City, Japan*

The structure, stability and age trends of temperament were explored longitudinally in a Japanese sample. Temperament was assessed using the Japanese Infant Behavior Questionnaire-Revised (IBQ-R) at 3 (n=49), 10 (n=38), and 16 months (n=35). The factor structure varied with the age of the infants. This result suggested that the structure of temperament might be influenced by the developmental level of infant. The scores on the temperament scales showed stability from one time of measurement to the next. Although no strong gender differences were found, there were significant age trends. Most of the scales increased with age.

A cross-cultural study on social monitoring and reputation on interpersonal trust: What does it takes to trust the out-group?

Kwan, Letty *Dept. of Psychology, University of Illinois, Champaign, USA* **Hong, Ying-Yi** *Psychology, University of Illinois UC, Champaign, USA*

We hypothesized that interpersonal trust in East-Asian culture build on whether an individual belongs to a highly monitored/reputable group, while trust in North-American culture builds on similarities to the self. 157 and 102 participants in Singapore and US respectively participated in this within subject design questionnaire. Participants have to indicate their trust level on a likert scale towards four targets from the in-group, out-group, reputable out-group or a stranger. Univariate ANOVA showed that American participants show high in-group trust while Asian participants displace same level of trust towards in-group and the reputable out-group targets [F(1,257) = 3.98, p < .047].

Self-efficacy moderates the relationship between work stress and depressive symptoms

László, Krisztina *Inst. of Behavioural Sciences, Semmelweis University, Budapest, Hungary* **Salavecz, Gyöngyvér** *Inst. of Behavioural Sciences, Semmelweis University, Budapest, Hungary* **Kopp, Mária** *Inst. of Behavioural Sciences, Semmelweis University, Budapest, Hungary*

Objective: To investigate whether self-efficacy moderates the relationship between job stress and depressive symptoms. Methods: Self-reported data about effort-reward imbalance at work, overcommitment, self-efficacy and depressive symptoms of 2252 working subjects was analyzed using multivariate logistic regression models which controlled for sex, age, education and occupational class. Results: In multivariable-adjusted analyses employees with both high effort-reward imbalance and low self-efficacy had a 1.91-fold (1.10-3.31) risk for mild to severe depressive symptoms. The interaction term between overcommitment and self-efficacy was not significant (odds ratio: 1.21, 0.77-1.91) Conclusions: Enhancing self-efficacy may attenuate the detrimental effect of work stress on mental health.

Personal resilience and mental health among Chinese undergraduates in Hong Kong

Lai, Julian Dept. of Psychology, City University of Hong Kong, Hong Kong, China, People's Republic of : Hong Kong SAR

The moderating effect of personal resilience (a composite of optimism, self-esteem and mastery) on the mental health impact of daily hassles was examined in a group of N = 237 Chinese undergraduates in Hong Kong. Results of multiple regression analyses showed that the mental health (operationalized by the GHQ-30) of the more resilient participants was less negatively affected by daily hassles than that of their less resilient peers. The direct effect of resilience on mental health was also significant. These findings clearly demonstrate the mental health benefits of resilience in a relatively young and healthy population.

Virtual togetherness: A grounded theory investigation of the experience of companionship in computer-mediated friendships among adolescents

Lajom, Jennifer Ann Psychology, De La Salle University-Manila, Manila, Philippines

The study explored how adolescents make sense of companionship in computer-mediated friendships using grounded theory. Ten adolescents with online friends were interviewed and data were analyzed using open, axial, and selective coding. Peer debriefing, member-checking, and inquiry audit ensured trustworthiness of theory. Findings showed that the experience of virtual togetherness (online companionship) is composed of online interactivity, means for online interactivity (avenues for interaction and perceptive envisioning), time, sense of gut-feel, perceived degree of friendship closeness, and consequences arising from friendship closeness. These elements contribute to the understanding of adolescent online friendship formation and maintenance despite the variation in context.

The possible effect of published preelection poll results on the electoral behavior

Lamza Posavec, Vesna Dept. of Public Opinion, Ivo Pilar Institute, Zagreb, Croatia

The research of influence of published preelection poll results on the electoral behavior stems from the hypothesis that such an effect is possible under the following conditions: (1) that a person has seen or heard the poll results, (2) is able to reproduce them correctly, and (3) trusts their accuracy. Two public opinion polls were carried out on nationally representative samples. Observed differences in intended voting preferences were not linked to the indicators of possible preelection poll influence. Such results compare favorably to those of previous researches, stating that there are no convincing scientific proofs of the possible effect of published preelection poll results on the electoral behavior.

Abridged or not abridged: The issue of factor loadings on big five trait dimensions revisited

Larsson, Magnus R. Dept. of Psychology, University of Lund, Lund, Sweden Bäckström, Martin Psychology, Lund University, Lund, Sweden

The aim of this study was to investigate the validity of the Abridged Big Five Dimensional Circumplex model (AB5C; Hofstee, de Raad, & Goldberg, 1992) in 930 Swedish participants responding to an Internet based version of an AB5C-test from the Interpersonal Personality Item Pool (IPIP). Using a factor analytical approach our results supported the

AB5C model in that the investigated adjectives had a primary loading on one of the Big-Five personality dimensions and a secondary loading on another dimension. Based on this finding we argue that the AB5C model deserve a renewed attention in trait psychology.

Relationship between students' life goals and their personal values

Lavshuk, Yelena Dept. of Psychology, State Education School, Moscow, Russia

We hypothesized that subjects used different strategies for ranging of life goals and personal values. Rokeach Value Survey and Emmonce Inventory were used. 40 students took part in experiments. 7 experts have chosen from the list with personal goals produced by participants those which mostly related to each Rokeach Value Survey point in accordance with similarity of meanings. Data analysis showed that ranks of Rokeach values indicated by participants did not correspond with volumes of mentioned categories (counted as a number of personal goals included into each semantic category). Results could be used in counseling and career development.

Role and dynamic of cortical structures in different duration ranges process: A behavioral and event-related potential study

Le Dantec, Christophe U.F.R. Psychologie Rouen, Mont Saint Aignan, France Gontier, Emilie Psychologie, U.F.R. Psychologie Rouen, Mont Saint Aignan, France Paul, Isabelle Psychologie, U.F.R. Psychologie Rouen, Mont Saint Aignan, France Ghazouani, Ismahain Psychologie, U.F.R. Psychologie Rouen, Mont Saint Aignan, France Bernard, Christian Psychologie, U.F.R. Psychologie Rouen, Mont Saint Aignan, France Lalonde, Robert Pharmacologie, INSERM Rouen, Mont Saint Aignan, France Rebaï, Mohamed Psychologie, U.F.R. Psychologie Rouen, Mont Saint Aignan, France

A behavioral and electrophysiological (ERPs) evaluation was conducted on the role of the dynamics between the prefrontal and posterior cortex in the processing of temporal information. Duration trios lasting between 250 and 2000 ms were presented and the subjects had to recognize if the second or the third duration was equal to the first one. The results shows a strong correlation between prefrontal and parietal activities which reveals a functional link involved in the necessary cognitive processes (attention, memory, decision) to achieve the task. Furthermore, the collaboration seems to be more important with the long durations than the short ones.

The injury in the sport fields : A way to meet a meaningful life

Lecocq, Gilles Dept. of Psychology, ILEPS, Cergy, France

The main purpose of this communication will be to reveal the benefits living by injured athletes. While identifying configurations associating the notions of transcendence, passion and attachment we shall clarify the stages to be proposed to an athlete so that this one renforcent its fragile physical zones and soften its stiff physical zones. It will be an opportunity to reveal a connection between the Scylla of normality and the Charybdis of pathology.

Spirituality, wisdom and transcendence: Psychological perspectives

Lecocq, Gilles Dept. of Psychology, ILEPS, Cergy, France

How to reduce the gap between two human realities: The mind and the spirit ? It is from this question that we shall clarify of which manners the narrative psychology allows for one person possessing an unstable identity to open in the fundamental human experiences, beliefs, meaning and feelings.

So, we shall identify the stages which facilitate the access to a know-how that requires not less than being aware of the virtual nature of oneself.

The death of an Old European Rugby: Psychological perspectives

Lecocq, Gilles Dept. of Psychology, ILEPS, Cergy, France

Since the rugby became professional in 1995, new economic practices influenced the behavior of the players, the sponsors, and the spectators. The purpose of this communication is to show of which manners two psychological processes condition the investment of the new professional players of rugby: the excellence and the exclusion. Then, two questions allow us to construct some psychological perspectives about the twilight of an old european Rugby : How to manage the players during a great social tranformation? How to manage the marketing of the human experiences in the fied of economy?

Public representations of genomics: An analysis of British mass-media and government literature

LeCouteur, Amanda Dept. of Psychology, University of Adelaide, Adelaide, Australia

Objectives: To investigate the coherence/ambivalence of public attitudes towards genomics in the UK. Method: A discursive analysis of government and mass-media documentation. Results: Government reports were more positive and optimistic about genomics than mass-media representations. The former repeatedly mobilized narratives of national scientific success and shared national ownership of genomics 'advances'. Explanations involving government regulation and expert control were routinely deployed to account for the 'challenges' associated with genomics. Science's legitimacy was warranted in terms of an empiricist repertoire that omitted mention of knowledge producers and interests. Conclusions: The findings highlight the importance of analysing public discourse for understanding how outcomes for new biotechnology are negotiated in society.

Respect for parents and grandparents: Indigenous psychological analysis

Lee, Sang-Mi Dept. of Education, Inha University, Incheon, Republic of Korea Park, Young-Shin Dept. of Education, Inha University, Incheon, Republic of Korea Kim, Uichol Business administration, Inha University, Inchon, Republic of Korea Tak, Soo-Yeon Education, Inha University, Inchon, Republic of Korea

The purpose of this study is to examine the basis of respect for their parents and grandparents among Korean high school students and their parents using indigenous psychological analysis. A total of 600 participants (a matched sample of 200 high school students and their parents) completed an open-ended questionnaire developed by Park and Kim (2007). The results indicate that respondents respect their father and due to their sacrifice, followed by sincerity and being a role model. For their mother, sacrifice, sincerity and raising them were listed as the most important reasons. For grandparents, sacrifice, benevolence, and consanguinity were listed as the most important reasons. These results indicate that sacrifice is the basis of respect for elders in Korea.

A study on stress, coping strategies, intelligence and attention of adolescent depression in Taiwan

Lee, Shu-Fen Psychiatry, Tri-Service General Hospital, Taipei, Taiwan Liao, Cheng-Tsung Rehabilitation, Mackay Memorial Hospital, Taipei, Taiwan

Introduction and Purpose? The current study is aimed at understanding the relations between life pressure events, coping strategies, severity of depression, IQ, and attention performance in clinical adolescents. Material & Methods?65 depressed adolescents (12-18 years old) completed the

Beck Depressive Inventory, the Stress Inventory, the Coping Strategies Inventory, the Gordon Diagnosis System and the Wechsler Intelligent Scale for Adult-Revised or Children-Third Edition. The obtained data was analyzed by descriptive statistics and t-test. Results & Conclusions? The main stressors in depressed adolescents in Taiwan were schoolwork(43%). Their often use emotion-focused strategy(57%). Their IQ in the average degree, impulse inhibition abilities lie in normal range(60%), sustained attention lie in abnormal range(80%).

Job-related dysfunctional attitudes and mental health in school teachers

Lehr, Dirk Inst. für Medizin. Psychologie, Universität Marburg, Marburg, Germany Trageser, Carolin Medical Psychology, Philipps-University Marburg, Marburg, Germany Hillert, Andreas Center of Behavioral Medicine, Roseneck Center, Prien am Chiemsee, Germany

While coping with job-stress is well investigated, less is known about cognitive appraisal. Therefore, 574 teachers were examined using three established measures of job-related dysfunctional attitudes (DA) simultaneously. Additionally, new scales were developed to assess DA towards requesting social-support. A satisfying fit was found for a hierarchical six-factorial model of DA in a confirmatory-factor-analyses. Regression analyses revealed two dimensions of DA to be most important for affective disorders: strong overlap between job-related and general self-esteem; DA towards requesting social-support. Cognitive-behavioral therapy showed significant effects of moderate size for the reduction of each DA dimension in a subgroup of 120 inpatient-teachers.

Attitudes reflecting national identity in Lithuanian young people population

Lekaviciene, Rosita Dept. of Psycology, Kaunas University, Kaunas, Lithuania Antiniene, Dalia Dept. of Psychology, Kaunas University, Kaunas, Lithuania

The aim of the research is to determine the content and peculiarities of national identity among Lithuanian youth. The goals of the research are: to analyze from the phenomenological point of view the structure of their national identity and to determine indicators representing the cultural context of the country. National identity attitudes were investigated employing an original, anonymous close-type questionnaire. The structure of the national identity was established with the help of multistage factorial validation. We discovered that the attitudes rather clearly polarize into the components reflecting modern and traditional attitudes towards nationality. Multidimensional Scaling was used to obtain the model of gradation of national identity expression. The typological variety exists among young people in sense of national identity.

Auditory evoked potentials related to the perception of temporal order

Lewandowska, Monika Dept. of Neuropsychology, Nencki Inst. of Exp. Biology, Warsaw, Poland Bekisz, Marek Neurophysiology, Nencki Inst of Exp Biology, Warsaw, Poland Szymaszek, Aneta Neuropsychology, Nencki Inst of Exp Biology, Warsaw, Poland Medygral, Justyna Neuropsychology, Nencki Inst of Exp Biology, Warsaw, Poland Szelag, Elzbieta Neuropsychology, Nencki Inst of Exp. Biology, Warsaw, Poland

Objectives: Electrophysiological correlates of temporal order (TO) perception were tested. Methods: 21 subjects reported the order of two different tones presented with a pause of 10ms or 60ms (difficult or easy condition, respectively). Pearson correlations between N1 and P2 amplitudes or latencies and correctness level were computed separately at each electrode. Results: negative correlations at the Fz and Cz electrodes were found between P2 amplitude and correctness level for the difficult condition. Conclusions: P2 component constitutes an electrophysiological correlate of TO perception.

Do newborns suffer from weather?

Lewe-Kayser, Mirjam Potsdam, Germany Rauh, Hellgard Psychology, University of Potsdam, Potsdam, Germany Ziegenhain, Ute Pädagogik, Jugendhilfe, Klinik für Kinder- und Jugendp, Ulm, Germany

To assess early climate and weather sensitivity, 76 healthy newborns were examined with the Brazelton Neonatal Behavioral Assessment Scale at the days 3, 10, and 30 of their life. Orientation to animate and inanimate stimuli, alertness, motor maturity, physiological and state control clearly improved with age, whereas irritability, peak of excitement, consolability, self-quieting, smiles, and reinforcement value were unrelated to age in the first month of life. Hot outdoor temperature (over 25° Celsius, no air conditioning) negatively affected the newborns' alertness and motor tonus – with age controlled -, high levels of pollution affected physiological and motor robustness.

Infusing cultural horizons: The Nova Acculturation Scale

Lewis, John Center for Psychological Studi, Nova Southeastern University, Ft. Lauderdale, USA Gloria, Gallegos Center for Psychological Studi, Nova Southeastern University, Ft. Lauderdale, USA Cifci, Seda Center for Psychological Studi, Nova Southeastern University, Ft. Lauderdale, USA Jihan, Elhage Center for Psychological Studi, Nova Southeastern University, Ft. Lauderdale, USA

Studies have shown that low levels of acculturation negatively affect quality of life and mental health in individuals from different ethnicities in the United States. This is due to the fact that there is no unique acculturation scale that evaluates acculturation among ethnicities within the USA. This study introduces the newly developed Nova Acculturation Scale to examine quality of life and acculturation across different cultures. The present paper reveals preliminary reliability and validity data among different cultures and ethnicities. This presentation will bring forward results from a pilot study in South Florida recently completed.

Personality, situation, and mood-congruent judgment: Interactive effects of self-esteem and time pressure

Li, Chongliang Xili, Nanshan, People's Republic of China Wang, Lei Psychology, Peking University, Beijing, People's Republic of China

The aim of the present research was to explore the interactive effects of self-esteem and time pressure on mood-congruent judgment. Results revealed that, under time pressure condition, when negative mood was induced, participants either high or low in self-esteem exhibited the typical mood-congruent judgment. However, under no time pressure condition, when negative mood was induced, high self-esteem participant did not exhibited mood-congruent judgment, while low self-esteem participant showed the same mood-congruent judgment as they did under time pressure condition. The results were discussed in terms of integrating personality and situational factors in research of mood-congruent effects.

Developmental changes in visual Chinese character perception-An ERP study

Li, Su Institute of Psychology,CAS, Beijing, People's Republic of China Zhao, Jing Labo for Higher Brain Function, Institute of Psychology,CAS, Beijing, People's Republic of China Weng, Xuchu Lab for Higher Brain Function, Institute of Psychology,CAS, Beijing, People's Republic of China

Objective: We investigated the developmental changes of event-related potential in rapidly processing visual Chinese character during early years. Methods: Subjects were pre-schoolers (5–6 years). We used a revised "one-back" paradigm and selected four types of stimuli (line drawings, cartoon faces, stroke combinations and Chinese characters). EEG data were recorded from 32 electrodes. Results: ERPs elicited by Chinese characters showed clear early negativities like N170. Chinese characters elicited larger N170 amplitudes than other types of stimuli at occipito-temporal channels in high-reading ability children. Conclusion: Findings suggested that rapidly characters processing is linked to increased reading skill, rather than increased age per se.

Early access and integration of meaning indicated by accentuation: A mismatch negativity study

Li, Xiaoqing Speech Cognition, Institute of Psychlogy, Beijing, People's Republic of China Yang, Yufang Speech Cognition, the Institute of Psychlogy, Beijing, People's Republic of China Wang, Lin Speech Cognition, the Institute of Psychlogy, Beijing, People's Republic of China Li, Weijun Speech Cognition, the Institute of Psychlogy, Beijing, People's Republic of China

The mismatch negativity was used to examine the on-line processing of accentuation aligned with words of different information states. An odd ball design, with Chinese spoken sentences and concomitant picture context as materials, was applied. It was found that, for males but not for females, the mismatch responses were significantly larger for inconsistent accentuation deviants as compared with mere acoustic or mere picture context deviants. The results indicated that listeners could access and integrate the meaning indicated by accentuation into semantic context in the very early stage; there were gender differences in the sensitivity to the meaning extracted from prosody.

Mental health studio in the universities of Shanghai: Self-help and mutual help of students

Li, Zhengyun Psychological CounselingCentre, Shanghai, People's Republic of China Zhou, Yuan Shnaghai Normal University, Psychological CounselingCentre, Shanghai, People's Republic of China

The mental health studio(MHS)which developed newly is a way, by which counseling centre extends its services to the students' community or dormitories. As a propaganda base, an activity base and a training base, the MHS settling in students' community (dormitories) is to make mental health education near to students; raising the levels of students' knowing, accepting and using the function of mental counseling and the knowledge of mental health. It seems that more and more students are interested in MHS and get to used it. The universities with MHS are increasing.

A survey on the generalized problematic internet use in Chinese college students and its relations to stressful life events and coping style

Li, Huanhuan department of psychology, Sun Yat-Sen university, Guangzhou, People's Republic of China Jiaqi, Wang department of psychology, Sun Yat-Sen, Guangzhou, People's Republic of China Li, Wang Center for Studies of Psycholo, South China Normal University, Guangzhou, People's Republic of China

Objective: To examine the prevalence of generalized problematic Internet use (GPIU) and its relations to stressful life events and coping style. Methods: Six hundred and fifty-four college students completed self-reported measures of GPIU Scale, China College student Stress Questionnaire, and Coping style questionnaire. Analysis of Structural Equation Model was used to explore the interactive effects of stress and coping style on GPIU. Results: Among the samples, 13.6% was diagnosed as GPIU. The GPIU group experienced more stressful life events and used more negative coping strategies than nonaddicts. Conclusion: Stressful life events would contribute to GPIU indirectly through negative coping strategies.

Infants produce communicative acts based on the common ground they have shared with their interlocutors

Liebal, Kristin Developmental Psychology, Max Planck Institute EVAN, Leipzig, Germany Carpenter, Malinda Developmental Psychology, Max Planck Institute EVAN, Leipzig, Germany Tomasello, Michael Developmental Psychology, Max Planck Institute EVAN, Leipzig, Germany

The ability to rely on shared experience or common ground when communicating is an essential pragmatic skill. Here we investigated this skill in infancy. After sharing a different game with each of two experimenters, 18-month-old infants went to a test room with one of those experimenters (counterbalanced). There they faced posters representing each game. We scored infants' communication about the posters for the adult. Results showed that infants communicated appropriately, based on the experience they had previously shared with the accompanying adult (Fisher's exact, N=24, p<.02). Thus, infants are competent with this pragmatic skill even before being competent with language.

Post-traumatic stress disorder (PTSD), strategy of coping and social support in French women victims of domestic violence

Lignon, Saba Touluse, France

In this study we explore the PTSD, coping and perceived social support of French women victims of domestic violence. Seventy one participants were recruited in a service of legal medicine. A psychologist leads an interview to measure PTSD's diagnosis, social support and coping. 50% of participants present a PSTD. They show more active coping, instrumental support, emotional support and acceptance, and less humor and substances. Usually they seem satisfied by 3,63 people supporting them. We notice correlation between types of violence (psychological, physical and sexual) and PTSD's, coping's and social support's items. We'll discuss clinical and research implications.

The relationship between the Vividness of Visual Imagery Questionnaire and the egoistic form of social desirable responding tested using the Over-Claiming Technique

Ling, Jonathan Dept. of Psychology, Keele University, Newcastle-under-Lyme, United Kingdom Allbutt, John Psychology, University of Salford, Salford, United Kingdom

Objectives: Paulhus (2002) proposed a multifactorial model of social desirable responding (SDR), dividing it into egoistic and moralistic types. Our previous research found scores on self-report measures of visual imagery correlate primarily with egoistic bias. However, this research only used subjective measures of SDR. Methods: Correlations between the VVIQ, subjective and objective measures of the egoistic bias were investigated. Results: The main finding was that the pattern seen in previous studies was replicated with subjective measures and importantly also with the objective measure. Conclusions: This provides further support that self-report measures of visual imagery correlate primarily with egoistic bias.

Evaluation apprehension effect in group creativity: A cultural comparison

Liou, Shyhnan Dept. of Labor Relations, National Chung Cheng Uni., Chia-Yi, Taiwan

This study tested the hypothesis that Asians are less productive than Westerners in interactive groups than nominal groups due to their higher evaluation apprehension. Besides, Asians are hypothesized to generate more useful ideas whereas American are likely to generate more original ideas because Asians are more pragmatic and conformity oriented, and Westerners are more independent and uniqueness oriented. The study used a 2 (Culture) X 2 (Group Type) X 2 (Criticism) factorial design. The result indicated that Asians generated fewer ideas than their American counterparts, and American showed higher original but less useful ideas than Asians in interactive groups.

An investigation of college students' implicit ideas of narcissism

Liu, Yanlou Research Center of Psychology, Qufu Normal University, Qufu, People's Republic of China Li, Jianwei Faculty of Education, Qufu Normal University, Qufu, People's Republic of China

By using the method of social validity on 378 college students, we found that college students' narcissism personality consists of five factors: self-superiority feeling, self-opinionated, obstinacy and insistence, authority and inferiority feeling. The most representative and consistent ones are self-opinionated, showing-loving, commanding others, pity, obstinacy, selfishness, pain, ability feeling and inferiority. The age has no significant impact on implicit ideas of narcissism(F =.592, p =.986), but the profession and gender do (F =3.073,p =.040; F =2.408, p =.026). Narcissism personality is a compound of overt narcissism and covert narcissism.

The joint functions of personal self, relational self and collective self on self-autonomy

Liu, Yan School of Psychology, Beijing Normal University, Beijing, People's Republic of China

Based on the three-level self-construal theory, this research is aimed to explore the relationship between self-construal and self-autonomy. 477 college students completed the "Three-level self-construal Questionnaire" and the "Self-regulatory Questionnaire". Results showed: (1) Personal self can significantly promote the realization of self-autonomy; (2) From the direct effect, relational self has some negative effect on self-autonomy, but can act as a moderator, enhancing the effect of personal self on self-autonomy; (3) Collective self has ambivalent effects on self-autonomy: on one hand it can significantly enhance self-autonomy; on the other hand, it may weaken the effect of personal self on self autonomy.

The relationship between parental rearing behavior and mental health of undergraduates

Liu, Yingjie University, Inner Mongolia Normal, Huhhot, People's Republic of China He, Jiaofei Class 15, Grade 1, Hainan Middle School, Haikou City, Hainan Province, People's Republic of China

Objective: To research the relationship between parental rearing behavior and mental health of undergraduate. Methods: 400 undergraduates were investigated with self-made questionnaire, SCL-90 and EMBU. Results: More than 20% undergraduates have the prevalence problems of mental. Correlation analysis showed that the total score and factors cores of SCL-90 had positive correlation with fathers' punishment, over interference, over protection, rejection, preference and mothers' over interference, rejection, punishment, preference. Parental warmth had negative correlation with the total score and factors cores of SCL-90. Conclusions: Parental rearing behavior is closely related to mental health in the medicinal undergraduate.

Distributive justice and cooperative behavior in social dilemmas

Liu, Chang-Jiang School of Management, Shenyang Normal University, Shenyang, People's Republic of China Hao, Fang Insitute of Psychology, Renmin University of China, Beijing, People's Republic of China

The study examined the effect of distributive justice in explaining cooperation in social dilemmas. Participants were presented with each of four kinds of distributive justice principle in educational policies, and then a social dilemma. Resulted showed that individuals judged equality-based educational policies to be fairer than equity-based policies. Regression analyses showed that need principle contributed more to cooperative behavior than equality principle when participants confronted with an educational social dilemma. The finding indicated a realistic rationality when facing with realistic social dilemmas. (Note: The research is supported by "Humanities and social science project of the Ministry of Education (06JCXLX003)")

Actions involved in goal attainment

Lopez-Suarez, Ana Delia PhD Program, Univ Nal Aut de México (UNAM), Coatepec, Veracruz, Mexico Uribe-Prado, Jesús Felipe Psycholoy, Univ Nal Aut de México (UNAM), Mexico City, Mexico

This preliminary study determined the actions people carry out to attain a desirable goal. Some theoretical bases were: Little's four stages of personal projects' structure and organization, Gollwitzer's Action Model (1990) and Bandura's Social-Cognitive Theory of Agency (2001). Seventy Mexicans answered the questionnaire. By cuantitative and cualitative techniques (content analysis, multidimensional scaling), results were: absorption, planning, trying hard, use of resources and finding support. These actions were similar to those described by the authors mentioned above.

Confirmatory factor analysis of the Spanish version of the revised scale for caregiving self-efficacy in a sample of dementia caregivers

Losada, Andres Dept. of Psychology, Universidad Rey Juan Carlos, Madrid, Spain Peñacoba, Cecilia Dept. of Psychology, Universidad Rey Juan Carlos, Madrid, Spain Lopez, Javier Dept. of Psychology, Universidad San Pablo Ceu, Madrid, Spain Marquez Gonzalez, Maria Dept. of Psychology, Universidad Autónoma de Madrid, Madrid, Spain

The Revised Scale for Caregiving Selff-Efficacy consists in three factors: self-efficacy for obtaining respite, self-efficacy for responding to disruptive behaviors and self-efficacy for controlling upsetting thoughts. Confirmatory Factor Analysis (CFA) of the scale was tested in a sample of 165 Spanish Caregivers. The fit indexes of the full factor model were adequate ($\chi 2$/df = 2,03; IFI = .90; CFI = .90; RMSEA = .08). Negative and significant associations between the RSCSE and depression, burden and dysfunctional thoughts were found. These results provide support for the factor structure of the RSCSE and for its utility as a research and clinical tool.

Validation of the Spanish version of the Anxiety Control Questionnaire Revised (ACQ-R)

Losada, Andres Dept. of Psychology, Universidad Rey Juan Carlos, Madrid, Spain Márquez González, María Biological and health psycholo, Universidad Autónoma de Madrid, Madrid, Spain Peñacoba, Cecilia Dept. of Psychology, Universidad Rey Juan Carlos, Madrid, Spain Velasco, Lilian Dept. of Psychology, Universidad Rey Juan Carlos, Madrid, Spain Romero, Rosa Dept. of Psychology, Universidad Rey Juan Carlos, Madrid, Spain

The psychometric properties of the Spanish version of the ACQ-R, a 15 item questionnaire measuring perceived control about three dimensions (emotional, threat, and stress), are analyzed (N = 370; age =21.8; SD=5.2; 77.3% women). The three-factor structure was supported trough Confirmatory-Factor-Analysis (CMIN/DF = 1.96; CFI = .975; TLI = .965). Internal consistency (.65-.85), test-restest-reliability (.83-.90) was adequate for subscales and total score. Negative associations were found between subscales and anxiety (-.47 to -.72) and depression (-.24 to -.43). The Spanish version of the ACQ-R presents good psychometric properties and appears as a useful tool for clinical and research purposes.

Desirability of control and job control in professionnal health service: Effects on burnout
Lourel, Marcel Dept. of Psychology, University of Rouen, Mont Saint Aignan, France *Gueguen, Nicolas* Department of Psychology, University of Bretagne Sud, Lorient, France *Mouda, Farida* Department of Psychology, University of Rouen, Mont Saint Aignan, France
OBJECTIVES: The aim of the research was to study desirability of control (DC), job control (JC) and Burnout among 108 professional health (aged 41.14, sd 10.08). METHODS: The desirability of control was assessed by Burger and Cooper's scale, the subscale's of Karasek were used to assess job control, and burnout by Maslach and Jackson's scale. RESULTS: the analysis of variance showed that high desirability of control and low JC was effect to emotional exhaustion and depersonalisation. Low JC was effect to personal accomplishment. CONCLUSION: The difference between DC and JC and implications for personnel and organization were discussed.

Alternative medicine in the Philippines among Indigenous-Filipinos and Chinese-Filipinos
Lu, Yung Chang Quality Control, Sophia Mineral Services, Quezon City, Philippines
The paper wanted to look at the complementary therapies used by Filipinos and Tsinoys, the Filipino-Chinese residents, in dealing with health issues, including obstetrics and gynecology. Here are some observations and analytic constructs like: Filipino Chinese residents have always been engaged in traditional medicine combining herbs, barks of trees, roots and plant parts in curing certain illnesses. The difference however is the mix of religion among indigenous Filipinos, not evident among Chinese. The study shows a great bearing on the link to health and wellness which can be traced to the contribution of psychosomatic effects.

The elimination-by-aspects rule as a practical method to support health experts' decision making
Lueken, Kai Prevention, Unfallkasse Rheinland-Pfalz, Andernach, Germany
There is an unmanageable amount of instruments analyzing mental workload. So a software tool is developed to improve the accuracy and speed of the selection process. This software is free available for health experts. Several stress inventories were analysed in view of 23 selection criteria (e.g. branch of trade, costs, scientific background, reliability,...). Based on these data the software tool enables a step-by-step elimination of "non-fitting" stress inventories by considering individual user priorities of the selection criteria (Tversky's EBA-rule). Besides scientific considerations the consultancy performance of health experts becomes more related to practical considerations.

School counselors and teachers: Expert professionals' strategies to collaborate
Luna, Maria Educational Psychology, Universidad Autonoma de Madrid, Madrid, Spain
School counselors and teachers have to collaborate to prevent and solve problems in high schools. In Spain, as in other countries, this joint task seems to be difficult in itself. The work of two highly efficient and expert school counselors was observed during one academic year. We recorded their discourse in the different meetings they held with teachers. The discourse analysis showed the kind of strategies they use to fragment the problems and to establish an atmosphere of trust. Illustrating the strategies used by efficient and expert school counselors might help us improve the training processes of these professionals.

Intervening strategy to junior students' learning motivation by group counseling
Luo, Lijing Dept. of Social Sciences, Hainan Medical College, Haikou,Hainan, People's Republic of China *Li, Chunbao* Department of Social Sciences, Hainan Medical College, Haikou,Hainan, People's Republic of China
Objective: What's the intervening strategy to junior high school students' learning motivation by group counseling? Methods: Choosing a certain junior high school students as studying samples by Group Counseling, selecting 40 members who have bad learning motivation, coaching the group and 40 members to contrast. Results: The intervention method by group counseling to the learning motivation of the junior high school students is effective. Conclusions: Intervening strategy to junior high school students' learning motivation is encouragement and support of important person, WDEP system, reading, drawing, short lectures, psychological drama and write exercise.

Infant behavior diaries: Assessment with electronic and written methods
Müller, Silvana SESAM, Universität Basel, Basel, Switzerland *Hemmi, Mirja* sesam, University of Basel, Basel, Switzerland
Introduction: An individual project within sesam assesses how accurate parents remember important life events of their children, such as sleeping-, feeding-, crying- and fussing behavior, during their course of development. Paper-and-pencil diaries and electronic diaries are used as methods of assessment of infant behavior. Method: 120 German-speaking women with an infant at the age of 6 months are asked to complete the diaries within three days. Additionally, actigraphs will be used for obtaining information about the infants and mothers sleep/wake pattern. First results of the pilot study and their implications will be presented and discussed.

Psychosocial support (PS) system in Japan Red Cross Society (JRCS) and next research points in disaster
Maeda, Jun Common Subject, Muroran Inst. of Technology, Muroran, Japan
Objective:PS is needed to affected persons and also to helpers in disaster.I would like to examine of system of PS through JRCS's activities during about a decade. Activities and next point of issues:JRCS's trained trainers who educated based on the manual of International Federation of Red Cross/Cresent practiced PS activities in several areas and types of disaster in Japan.It was revealed a couple of difficulties of PS:Coordination with other organization, long terms and continuing support and support to PS members.More serions problems are delegation system and way of coordination of PS members. Conclusion:For more practical PS,not only individual massive educatuion and also aritifices as organization of relief activities is needed.

Reading competence at tertiary level
Manchen Spörri, Sylvia Angewandte Linguistik, Sprache in Beruf und Bildung, Winterthur, Switzerland *Landert, Karin* ISBB, ZHAW, Winterthur, Switzerland *Suter Tufekovic, Carol* ISBB, ZHAW, Winterthur, Switzerland *Schütz, Hans* ISBB, ZHAW, Winterthur, Switzerland *Müller Längerich, Viviane* ISBB, ZHAW, Winterthur, Switzerland *Weinzinger, Caroline* ISBB, ZHAW, Winterthur, Switzerland
Reading competence is generally considered a key competence in mastering communicative tasks. To examine the reading competence of students at universities of applied sciences two reading tests were developed for tertiary level German and English, using multiple choice questions. The aim is to provide a standardised reading test for students at this level and thus to help establish educational standards. In November 2007 the reading tests will be tested on approximately 1,000 first and fifth semester students. After evaluating the results regarding demographic factors and reading habits the test will be further optimised. First results are expected for January 2008.

The prevalence of puberty related psychological problems among the first grade high school boys
Mansour, Ladan Counseling (psychology), University of Shahid Beheshti, Tehran, Islamic Republic of Iran *Abdi Zarrin, Sohrab* Counseling(psychology), University of Shahid Beheshti, tehran, Islamic Republic of Iran
In this research, the prevalence of puberty related psychological problems were determined among 100 first grade high school boy students from the educational district 1 in Tehran. Sampling was cluster type. Data was collected by means of mental health questionnaire and researcher-made questionnaire. SPSS was used for analyzing data. Results of the study indicated that the prevalence of psychological problems during puberty was about 39% and they were significantly related to variables such as: having problems with parents, suicidal tendency and flee from home. Considering the high prevalence of psychological problems during puberty in students, paying more attention by parents, counselors and also school authorities in order to find and help these students is necessary.

The effects of social skills training program that considering Chinese cultural characteristics: View-point from participants, interactional partners and observers
Mao, Xinhua Dept. of Human Science, Osaka University, Suita, Japan *Daibo, Ikuo* Human Science, OSAKA UNIVERSITY, Suita, Japan
The purpose of this research is to examine the effects of a social skills training(SST) program that considering Chinese cultural characteristics by using the evaluations from participants themselves, interactional partners and observers. The programs that connected / not connected with social skills were carried out to experimental and control group which constructed by 39 Chinese undergraduates. In the result, there were improvements of evaluation in behavior from participants themselves, interactional partner and observers in experimental group. No changes were found in control group. The effects of SST program were confirmed in behavioral levels.

Electrophysiological evidence for early case invariance in word recognition using an adaption paradigm
Mariol, Marina CODE, Université de Louvain, Louvain-la-Neuve, Belgium *Jacques, Corentin* CODE, Université de Louvain, Louvain-la-Neuve, Belgium *Rossion, Bruno* CODE, Université de Louvain, Louvain-la-Neuve, Belgium
Our experiment attempts to evaluate the time course of invariant word recognition using an adaptation paradigm. We recorded brain potentials during repeated stimulation. By manipulating orthogonally the identity and case of primes and targets we evaluate the invariance of this code. The results show that with the same stimulus (RAGE/RAGE; rage/RAGE) a reduction in the electrophysiological signal is observed, at the N170 level, whereas another stimulus do not produce any signal reduction. Our findings are threefold: we observed adaptation both for identity and for cross-case in occipital regions around 170 ms in left but not right regions.

Twins' psychology: Imitation and emotions in a pair of dizygotic twins

Markodimitraki, Maria Pre-School Education, University of Crete, Rethymnon, Greece

The aim of the present longitudinal and naturalistic study was to explore and describe several basic aspects of early imitative exchanges in twins' intrapair, parents'-twin infants' and grandparents'-twin infants' free interactions and the emotional state of the partners during the imitative sequences. A pair of non-identical twins of different gender was observed with their parents and grandparents at home from the 2nd to the 10th month of their life. It was found that several basic aspects of imitation did not differ significantly in interactions of non twin infants with adult partners, although there were significant differences in twins' intrapair interactions and individual differences.

Stress, coping and health in doctors of Spanish healthcare organizations

Martinez, Fermin Health Psychology. Edf. Altami, University Miguel Hernandez, Elche, Spain Benavides, Gemma Health Psychology. Edf. Altami, University Miguel Hernandez, Elche, Spain Solanes, Ángel Health Psychology. Edf. Altami, University Miguel Hernandez, Elche, Spain Orgiles, Mireia Health Psychology. Edf. Altami, University Miguel Hernandez, Elche, Spain Pastor, Yolanda Health Psychology. Edf. Altami, University Miguel Hernandez, Elche, Spain

The purpose of this paper is to analyze the effects of stress and coping in physical health of doctors who work in Spanish healthcare organizations. A sample of 112 doctors (Age average=42.01 years, SD=10.23) was examined using correlation analysis. Results show that good physical health measured by SF-36 is inversely related with the use of avoiding strategies of coping and related with planning strategies; and that stress is inversely related with some aspects of physical health. We can conclude that programs directed to improve physical health in doctors have to take into consideration the role of stress and coping in physical health.

Culture, human development and violence

Matos Coelho, Maria Inês Mestrado em Educação, UEMG, Belo Horizonte, Brazil

This paper analyses the relationships between violence at schools, culture and human development in brazilian contexts. The research survey draw a picture of the leading modes of violence such as acts against property, vandalism, graffiti, and interpersonal aggression, mainly among the pupils. The violence at school has been examined both as a consequence of a set of inadequate school practices, and as one of the aspects that characterizes the contemporary society. In conclusion, the perspectives of culture and human development and the adoption of an ethnography approach have been a significant foundation to develop effective practices against violence at schools.

Risk and protective factors related to behavioral problems of students in Japanese school.

Matsuo, Naohiro Dept. Educational Psychology, Tokyo Gakugei University, Tokyo, Japan

The purpose of this study is to investigate the risk and protective factors related to behavioral problems of student in Japan. 382 elementary, junior high and senior high school teachers answered the questionnaire that included the items about possible risk and protective factors (individual, family, school and community level), and behavioral problems (fight, violence, bullying, interpersonal conflict and disobedience to teachers) of their students. Result indicated that some risk and protective factors were significantly related to behavioral problems of students. Outcome of this study might help educators and researchers to develop programs to prevent behavioral problems of Japanese school.

Adopting psychological technology in indigenous work settings: Experiences from psycho-legal services in Cameroon

Mbebeb, Fomba Emmanuel Psychology Unit, F.L.S.S., University of Dchang, Cameroon

This paper examines the use of psychology, a "Eurocentric product" in African indigenous work settings. The study is focused on the Mbororo Fulanis, an indigenous group in Cameroon; excluded from mainstream citizenship participation, and reconstructing its personality due to changing socio-economic and political pressures. Analysis is based on the use of Psycho-Legal Extension model; an extension paradigm designed to build competence, restore psychic loss and reinforce citizenship behavior. In this exploration, adopting and assessing the social relevance of psycho-technology involved the intricacies of manipulation and indigenalisation. Challenges inherent in developing culture-fit paradigms have been discussed within the context of African development.

Adolescence, post traumatic stress disorder and resilience: Interdiscipline in a catastrophe

Meinardi Mozej, Teresa Dept.de Adolescencia, Hospital Ramos Mejia, Buenos Aires, Argentina

On December 30 th, 2004, a catastrophe occurred in Argentina. A closed disco caught fire during a rock concert by the use of sparklers that produced fire and toxic smoke. This event caused the death of 194 persons, most of them adolescents were assisted in Psychological Service in Ramos Mejia Hospital. From a psychological perspective we mainly observed Acute Post Traumatic Stress Disorder. However, we could prove that some adolescents emerged stronger from the experience, showing resilient traits that preserved them phisically and psychologically, impeding the development of pathology. In this presentation we will describe PTSD and its therapeutical approach, articulating it with the concept of resilience.

Standardization and validity of a scale that measures family functionality: A study made in Mexico with 40 Mexican families

Melgarejo, Maria Dept. de Psicotherapia, Morelos University, Temixco, Mexico Arias Galicia, Fernando Dept. of Psychology, Morelos University, Cuernavaca, Mexico

Objective: To create and validated a scale that measures family functionality and to prove its effectiveness. Methods: Extraction Method: Principal Component Analysis. Rotation Method: Varimax with Kaiser Normalization a Rotation converged in 11 iterations. Results: The scale had 3 dimensions: problem resolution, organization and family structure and emotional climate and it was used with 40 families and even though the objective was not the relation between family functionality and years of marriage there was not a difference among them. Conclusions: as the scale could be validated, it can be used as an important tool for therapists, to diagnose and help families.

An examination of the effects of structured group counseling method on dealing with emotional difficulties

Meng, Li Department of Psychology, Shaanxi Normal University, Xi'an, People's Republic of China Cen, Jian Affiliated Middle School of SNU, Shaanxi Normal University, Xi'an, People's Republic of China

This study explored the effects of structured group counseling method, using a sample of junior high middle school students who had difficulties of adaptation into the school life. 10-person groups were formed and rational emotional therapy method was adopted. We also measured coping ways and self-harmony before and after the one-week therapy. Other students who didn't attend the therapy were used as a control group. We found that structured group counseling of this study was useful in helping student adaptation, especially in dealing with emotional difficulties.

Students and teachers perceptions of socio-emotional well-being within Chilean primary schools

Milicic, Neva Dept. de Psicología, Universidad Católica de Chile, Santiago de Chile, Chile Alcalay, Lidia Psychology, Universidad CatÃ³lica de Chile, Santiago, Chile Berger, Christian Dept. of Psychology, Alberto Hurtado University, Santiago, Chile Torretti, Alejandra Psychology, Universidad Catolica de Chile, Santiago, Chile Arab, María Paz Psychology, Universidad Catolica de Chile, Santiago, Chile Justiniano, Bernardita Psychology, Universidad Catolica de Chile, Santiago, Chile

The present study focuses on socio-emotional learning processes in schools. It intends to learn those factors that foster or inhibit socio-emotional learning and consequent well-being, both from the students and teachers' perspectives. The following dimensions are considered: self-consciousness and consciousness of others, self-regulation, coping strategies, communication skills, and social integration. Preliminary results based on focus groups conducted with both 3rd and 4th grade students and teachers identify as influential factors attitudes and actions of others (teachers, peers and family) and school characteristics (infrastructure, after-school programs, teachers' competencies and curricular methodologies). Implications for intervention programs will be discussed.

The influences of the degree of a reader's interest in the Japanese haiku poem on the rating of affective meaning of each haiku

Minagawa, Naohiro Human Development, Naruto University of Education, Naruto, Japan

The purpose of this study was to examine the influence of the degree of a reader's interest in the Haiku on the rating of affective meaning of each haiku. Five groups of 20 university students rated 8 haikus which was selected from textbook with the semantic differential scale composed of 15 adjective pairs. As a result, rating by the participants who take great interest in the Haiku discriminated clearly between haikus by rating. Contrastively, rating by the participants who take no interest in the Haiku was obscure. Thus, affective meaning of a haiku varies with the degree of the reader's interest.

Young children's understanding of false sadness

Mizokawa, Ai Graduate School of Education, Kyoto University, Kyoto, Japan

This study examined whether young children understand that it is possible to express sadness even when one does not really feel sad. Forty 4- and 6-year-old children listened to eight stories in which it was appropriate for the protagonist to hide his/her real emotions because of either pro-social or self-protective motivation. Children were asked to infer the protagonist's real and expressed emotions. The results showed that 6-year-olds recognized real and apparent emotional expressions more accurately than did 4-year-olds. Most importantly, this study revealed the ability of 6-year-olds to recognize others' false expression of sadness from a self-protective motivation.

Relationships between definition and expression of love: A focus on Malay adults

Mohd Hoesni, Suzana School of Social Sciences, Universiti Sains Malaysia, Pulau Pinang, Malaysia Hashim, Intan H.M. School of Social Sciences, Universiti Sains Malaysia, Pulau Pinang, Malaysia

Love is important in predicting well being of married couples (Jungsik & Hatfield, 2004) and the environment of family life (Cui, Conger, & Lorenz, 2006). Yet, existing studies mainly focus on western culture and single young adults. This study aims to gain understanding on the issue of marital love within eastern culture by focusing on how 260 Malay adults who were about to get married view and express love. Result show specific relationships between definitions and expressions of love. Finding also suggests a new dimension of love termed as "interpersonal harmony". Findings are discussed within current theories on love.

PAS and parental mobbing relationship

Monacis, Lucia Dept. of Psychology, University of Bari, Bari, Italy D'Angelo, Anna Servizio sovradistrettuale, ASL Foggia, Foggia, Italy Cocco, Ornella Servizio di Riabilitazione, ASL Foggia, Foggia, Italy Pinto, Franca Human Sciences, University of Foggia, Foggia, Italy Terrone, Grazia Human Sciences, University of Foggia, Foggia, Italy Sinatra, Maria Psychology, University of Bari, Bari, Italy

Our research analyzes the psycho-affective development of 0-14 aged children, by verifying the influence of both the Parental Alienation Syndrome and the Parental Mobbing. 104 families were tested by: 1. T.A. Achenbach's Child Behaviour Check List to measure the psycho-affective development; 2. R. Gardner's PAS to assess the Parental Alienation Syndrome; 3. G. Giordano's questionnaire to examine the Parental Mobbing. Empirical findings revealed: alienating parents are mainly the guardian ones; guardian-children show somatic complaints, manipulative behaviours, as well as aggressive and rule-breaking behaviours. These factors are stressed when a commorbility occurs between the PAS diagnosis and the parental mobbing one.

An event-related potential investigation of the mere categorization effect on the orthographic stage in visual word processing

Montalan, Benoit Psychology, Universite de ROUEN, Mont-Saint-Aignan, France Personnaz, Bernard Psychologie, Université de Rouen, Mont-Saint-Aignan, France Bernard, Christian Psychologie, Université de Rouen, Mont-Saint-Aignan, France Lalonde, Robert Médecine, Université de Rouen, Rouen, France Rebaï, Mohamed Psychologie, Université de Rouen, Mont-Saint-Aignan, France

The present study used event-related potentials (ERPs) to investigate the mere categorization effect on the orthographic stage, indexed by the N170, in visual word processing. During a social evaluation task, two minimal group labels were presented as supraliminal primes, and twenty positive and negative adjectives as targets. Results indicated for subjects with a minimal group membership a larger N170 in the left hemisphere for the same adjectives preceded by an in-group prime rather than an out-group prime. These findings reflect the existence of a top-down influence due to social categorization on the orthographic stage in visual word processing.

Effect of counterfactuals and rules on a risk choice

Morando, Areli Experimental Analysis, University of Guadalajara, Guadalajara, Mexico Burgos, José Experimental Analysis, University of Guadalajara, Guadalajara, Mexico Hernández, Mayra Experimental Analysis, University of Guadalajara, Guadalajara, Mexico Padilla, Antonia Experimental Analysis, University of Guadalajara, Guadalajara, Mexico

Using a proprietary fantasy computer game where participants role-played a virtual character, participants were first given a choice between fighting against an easy monster (no-risk choice) and fighting a hard monster (risk choice). Unbeknownst to the participants, the probability of vanquishing the monsters was 1.0 for de easy and 0.0 for the hard one. Then, participants were given a feedback consisting of either a rule or a counterfactual. Then,

participants were given a second choice of the same kind. The results indicate that the rule was more effective in reducing the number of participants who made the risk choice.

Consequences of the child abuse on the development of the language

Moreno Manso, Juan Manuel Psicología y Antropología, Universidad de Extremadura, Badajoz, Spain Garcia-Baamonde Sánchez, María Elena Psicología y Antropología, Universidad de Extremadura, Badajoz, Spain

The study contributes a major knowledge on the consequences of the child abuse in the development of the language. Tries to value if the skills psycholinguistic of the children are below his age; establish which are the most affected linguistics competitions; and to verify if significant differences exist according to the age and the sex. The results confirm that the institutionalized children demonstrate a development of the language lower than the awaited thing, being major the difficulties in pragmatics that in the rest of components of the language. The children lack competent strategies in the solution of interpersonal problems.

Child negligence: Repercussions of the ill-treatment on the personality

Moreno Manso, Juan Manuel Psicología y Antropología, Universidad de Extremadura, Badajoz, Spain García-Baamonde Sánchez, María Elena Psicología y Antropología, Universidad de Extremadura, Badajoz, Spain

The investigation analyzes the degree of social, school and family, personal failure to adapt of 47 children of ages included between 6 and 18 years, in situation of negligence. The results indicate that the children demonstrate such features of the personality as anxiety, insecurity, introversion and low self-esteem, that they impede their personal and social adjustment. The personality of the children in situation of ill-treatment is characterized by the presence of an anxiety superior to the average, emotional instability, insecurity, introversion and apprehension. The children have difficulty to relate to the others, have minor tolerance to the frustration.

Cultural and discipline differences within a two-factor model of moral types

Munro, Don School of Psychology, University of Newcastle, Callaghan, Australia Miles, Bore School of Psychology, University of Newcastle, Callaghan, NSW, Australia Powis, David School of Psychology, University of Newcastle, Callaghan, NSW, Australia

We developed two measures: the Mojac scale measures a Libertarian–Communitarian dimension of moral orientation (valuing the needs of individuals versus the needs of society), and the NACE measures Involvement with others versus Detachment (empathy and confidence versus narcissism and aloofness). These tests were administered to medical school applicants and students of medicine, psychology and other caring professions from several countries, including Australia, Taiwan, Japan, Israel, Sweden, UK, and Canada (more than 27,000 people in total). We will present the cultural and disciplinary differences found on our two-factor model of moral types.

Ethnic aspects of choosing a spouse in Latvia: Identity factors and ethnic typology of families

Murasovs, Vadims Daugavpils University, Daugavpils, Latvia

This study aims to uncover the influence of nationality aspects on building families in Latvia in 2005-2007. The research is based on twenty statements test and sociological survey. The results indicate the increasing significance of culture (+8%), race (+11.9%), religion (+17.6%), citizenship (+3%), and the decreasing significance of language

(-1.2%) factors. The willingness to form ethnically homogeneous families has grown (+19.2%), (ethnically heterogeneous families +2.2%), while the percentage of respondents saying ethnicity doesn't matter has fallen from 80% to 58.1%. These results, supplemented by the analysis of identity statements (ethnicity +5.5%, citizenship -10.1%), clearly indicate the influence of identity issues.

The relation among working memory, short-term memory, phonological processing and reading comprehension in children

Muroya, Naoko Disability Sciences, University of Tsukuba, Tsukuba, Japan Maekawa, Hisao Comprehensive human sciences, University of Tsukuba, Tsukuba, Japan

To investigate association among working memory (WM), phonological short-term memory (STM), reading comprehension, and possible reading related skills and/or abilities, complex memory spans, serial word recall, reading comprehension, phonological awareness, color naming, and non-verbal cognitive ability were measured in children of 3rd and 4th grade. Reading comprehension was shown to be associated significantly with WM, STM, and phonological awareness but correlation between STM and comprehension was not significant if WM was partialed out. Results may suggest that WM and phonological processing fundamentally contribute to reading comprehension performance.

The development of causal explanation mode about physical phenomenon caused by unobservable intermediate

Nagamori, Yoshihiro Tokyo, Japan

The purpose of this study is to examine the developmental change of causal explanation mode. In this study, we asked ninety 5-, 7-, 9-, and 12-year-old children to explain the physical phenomenon that bent paper(10cm × 20cm) was moved by wind blown by pulling board made of the corrugated cardboard. This phenomenon was caused by a property of unobservable air, that is, the property that air maintains the same density. As a result, there are the significant age differences in causal explanation modes between 5-, 7-year-olds and 9-, 12-year-olds. The result indicated the existence of Piaget's precausality in young children.

The psychological effect of the motivation video to team sports players

Nagao, Yuichi Human Environmental Studies, Kyushu University, Kasuga, Japan Sugiyama, Yoshio Human-Environment Studies, Kyushu University, KASUGA CITY, FUKUOKA, Japan Yamazaki, Masayuki Human-Environment Studies, Kyushu University, KASUGA CITY, FUKUOKA, Japan Kawadu, Keita Human-Environment Studies, Kyushu University, KASUGA CITY, FUKUOKA, Japan

The purpose of this study is to investigate the effect of watching "Motivation Video" before a competition on psychological states of group sports athletes. DIPS-B.1 (Tokunaga, 1998) and STAI-state (Spielberger, 1970) were used to evaluate psychological states. In addition, the subjective measurement was used to assess motivational changes. As a result, most of members reported the surge of the motivation after watching Motivation Video. However, the difference was not seen in psychological states measured by questionnaires. It's recommended to conduct the experimental study for the evaluating the effect of Motivation Video in order to control the biases in the future.

Baby care experiences and set for baby care

Nakatani, Katsuya Psychology and Sociology, Kinki University, Nara, Japan

Set for baby care would involve perception of baby, drive for contact with baby, motivation of care taking, etc.. In the audio visual experiment, pictures and voices of babies were presented and their prettiness and drive for contact were evaluated by female students. The same participants answered to a questionnaire on their experiences of baby care. Baby care experiences, especially those before sexual maturation, correlated with the positive perception of babies and drive for contact. A kind of sensitive period can be assumed for the onset of set for baby care.

Ethnography of laughter in TV entertainment programmes in Japan

Nameda, Akinobu Dept. of Psychology, Ritsumeikan University, Kyoto, Japan

This research focuses on laughter in TV entertainment programmes. The purpose of this research is to describe the scene which laughter begins and generates itself. The data are collected by observing TV entertainment programmes and organised by using the KJ method (Kawakita 1986) to depict the moments. As the result, it is shown that there are four concepts including laughter caused by 'the way separating from ordinary context', 'recognising feelings', 'repeating' and 'rhythms and actions'. From the four groups, a hypothesis that there could be the rules for people to laugh is constructed.

Risk-taking in preschoolers

Nikiforidou, Zoi Ioannina, Greece pange, jenny of early childhood education, university of Ioannina, ioannina, Greece

Risky decision-making reveals an understanding of the underlying concepts of risk and probability. In the current two-stage decision task, preschoolers were tested on whether they show a risky or riskless preference for gains and/or losses. Each condition (gain vs loss) was consisted of 3 trials with differences in the probability level (50:50, 33:66, 25:75). Overall, preschoolers showed a significant preference towards the risky option and made more significant risky choices in order to avoid a loss than to achieve a gain (t= 0.032> 05); these findings support the preference shift. The gender and the probability level were found not to affect children's risky preference.

Individual cultural orientation as predictor of job satisfaction in Chinese and Norwegian managers

Nilsen, Wendy Dept. of Psychology, University of Trondheim, Trondheim, Norway Rundmo, Torbjörn of Science and Technology, Norwegian University, Trondheim, Norway

The aim of the study was examining the role of individual cultural orientations (allocentrism and idiocentrism) for job satisfaction and the Job Demand-Control (JDC)-model. 194 Chinese and Norwegian managers participated in a quantitative survey study, with a response rate of 81.6 % and 63.3 %. When conducting separate hierarchical regression analysis, individual cultural orientation emerged as predictors of job satisfaction in both samples. Though several differences emerged in the separate regression analysis, when significance-testing these differences only allocentrism appeared as significantly different in the two samples. The study suggests further examination of job satisfaction and the JDC-model when used cross-culturally.

Social support and the timing of parenthood

Oetsch, Berit Clinic Child/Adol. Psychiatry, University of Rostock, Rostock, Germany Dörnte, Mareike Child/Adol. Psychiatry, University of Rostock, Rostock, Germany Reis, Olaf Child/Adol. Psychiatry, University of Rostock, Rostock, Germany von der Lippe, Holger Institute of Psychology, University of Magdeburg, Magdeburg, Germany

Social networks provide support during stressful life events. Our study predicts the timing of parenthood by introducing social networks as covariates into time-to-event models controlling for demographic variables (age, gender, education). Data stem from the Rostock Longitudinal Study

(n=206) including four points of measurement (age 14, 20, 25, 32). As expected, gender and education have a strong influence on fertility behavior. The experience of good support by friends in earlier life (age 14, 20) increases, in later life (age 25) decreases the risk of parenthood after age 29. Furthermore, the family of origin serves as an important role-model for men.

The influence of subgroup derived from cluster analysis on adolescents' delinquency: With the cluster variable of parental attachment, emotional autonomy, and conflict parents

Oh, Ji Eun Psychology, Chungbuk National University, Cheongju, Republic of Korea Kim, Sang Hee Psychology, Chungbuk National University, Cheongju, Republic of Korea Lim, Sung Moon Psychology, Chungbuk National University, Cheongju, Republic of Korea

The purpose of this study was to examine the relationship between adolescent's latent delinquency and clusters of parent attachment, emotional autonomy, and parent-adolescent conflict with data from 1,344 middle and high school students. An analysis of cluster and two-way analysis of variance were conducted. As a result, first, four clusters (low and high conflict, high and low attachment) were found. Second, 'high conflict' cluster was revealed to associate with latent delinquency most and 'high attachment' cluster least. Also, it was found that high school student have a greater association with latent delinquency than middle school student do, and that the interaction variance between clusters and school level have influence on latent delinquency.

Effects of different social networks on changes in the subjective well-being of Japanese elders over three years

Okabayashi, Hideki Dept. of Psychology, Meisei University, Tokyo, Japan

Objectives: Effects of different social networks on the changes in the subjective well-being of Japanese elders over three years were examined. Methods: Valid responses (498) at the initial mail-survey and two- and three-year follow-up surveys were analyzed using Hierarchical Linear Modeling. Results: Social participation, interaction with friends, conversation with spouse, and number of children were beneficially related to both initial levels of depression and life satisfaction. Among female elders with more children, depression had been deteriorating over the duration. Conclusions: While the importance of social network was confirmed, the relations of female elders to children need to be examined further.

Self-determination theory fails to explain additional variance in well-being

Olesen, Martin H. Dept. of Psychology, University of Aarhus, Aarhus, Denmark Schnieber, Anette Psychology, University of Aarhus, Aarhus, Denmark Tønnesvang, Jan Psychology, University of Aarhus, Aarhus, Denmark Thomsen, Dorthe K. Psychology, University of Aarhus, Aarhus, Denmark

This study investigates relations between the five-factor model (FFM) and self-determination theory in predicting well-being. Nine-hundred-and-sixty-four students completed e-based measures of extroversion & neuroticism (NEO-FFI); autonomous- & impersonal general causality orientation (GCOS) and positive- & negative affect (PANAS). Correlation analysis showed moderate positive relationships between extroversion, autonomous and positive affect; neuroticism, impersonal and negative affect. Regression analysis revealed that autonomous explained additional 2% of variance in positive affect, when controlling for extroversion (P<0,001). However impersonal did not explain variance in negative affect when controlling for neuroticism. Self-Determination Theory seems in-

adequate in explaining variance in well-being supporting an integration with FFM.

Predictors of satisfaction with life: A comparative study of undergraduate and graduate students of the University of Coimbra

Oliveira, Albertina Dept. of Educational Sciences, Faculty of Psychology, Coimbra, Portugal

Abstract: Recently studies concerning the domain of well-being or happiness have been multiplied, framed by the recent movement of positive psychology. In this poster, we looked for to establish the predictive value of four blocks of variables (self-esteem, personality variables of conative-motivational scope, learner self-directedness and demographic variables) in undergraduate (N=222) and graduate students (N=158) of the University of Coimbra. Using hierarchical regression analysis, only self-esteem and self-discipline have showed positive influence on satisfaction with life concerning the undergraduate students, while only self-esteem revealed such impact among the graduate students. This data allows implications for the counselling of university students.

What the Nigerian adolescents say about sexuality

Oluwatula, Cordelia Omozehi-Esther Guidance and Counselling, Redeemer's High School, Mowe, Nigeria

This study examines the perceptions of Nigerian adolescents about their sexualityas related to some psychosocial variables. Perspectives from Health Belief Model were used. 200 adolescents were randomly selected from a high school. Data were collected with Adolescent Sexuality Questionnaire and analysed with Parson Correlation Coefficients and Regression Analysis. The results show that the major dimensions of sexuality include communication, dressing, attraction to the opposite sex and friendliness. Some relationships were observed between the dimensions and the psychosocial variables. The study concludes that the adolescents do have script for their sexuality.

The aggressive behavior among college athletes: A qualitative approach

Omar Fauzee, Mohd Sofian Sports Academy, Universiti Putra Malaysia, Selangor, Malaysia Asmuni, M. Nizam

The objective of this study is to examine the factors that contribute to aggressive behavior among college athletes. A sample of 20 athletes aged between 21 to 25 years old are invited to participate. All of them are college athletes who have represented their respective university in sports. They have to sign an inform consent letter to enable the interviews to be tape recorded. The interviewed are transcribed and were content analyzed by a group of sports panel. Three major themes emerged. The themes are Unable to control emotions, external factors, and individual natural instinct. Recommendations are also suggested.

Intrafamiliar similarity of social attitudes

Oniszczenko, Wlodzimierz Faculty of Psychology, University of Warsaw, Warsaw, Poland

The study examines intrafamiliar similarity between mothers, fathers and their young adult children in two types of social attitudes examined on two separate dimensions – moral conservatism – liberalism (MC-L) and free market economy – state interventionism (FM-SI). Participants were members of 358 full families, including mothers aged from 35 to 61, fathers aged from 36 to 64 lat, and their children (178 males and 180 females) aged from 17 to 25. Correlation analysis as well as linear regression analysis confirmed, that for MC-L fathers are mostly agreed with their sons and daughters, while mothers mostly influenced their children's attitudes to economical affairs.

Fundamental study on the place-of-work norm of the nurse in connection with medical safety
Onizuka, Kanako Kansai University, Ibaraki-shi, Osaka, Japan Takagi, Osamu sociology graduate course, Kansai University, Suita-sity, Japan
The purpose of this study is to examine whether the group norm can be treated as a factor of place-of-work level by using the agreement index (rwg).333 nurses were responded to the questionnaire of group norm about communication. As a result of judging based on the index, it was suggested that the injunctive norm and the descriptive norm that aimed at safety should be treated as a factor of the place-of-work level shared among members. However, the injunctive norm and the descriptive norm that gives priority to efficiency are not shared among members.

Feedback frequency and pre-contact description effects on instrumental and verbal performances in 10 to 12-years-old elementary school students
Ortiz, Gerardo CEIC-CUCBA, Universidad de Guadalajara, Guadalajara, Mexico Gutiérrez, Faviola Psicología-CUAltos, Universidad de Guadalajara, Tepatitlán, Mexico Gutiérrez, Elizabeth Psicología-CUAltos, Universidad de Guadalajara, Tepatitlán, Mexico Márquez, Viridiana Psicología-CUAltos, Universidad de Guadalajara, Tepatitlán, Mexico Ramírez, Denisse Psicología-CUAltos, Universidad de Guadalajara, Tepatitlán, Mexico Razo, Rebeca Psicología-CUAltos, Universidad de Guadalajara, Tepatitlán, Mexico
In the present study, we assessed the effects both of feedback frequency and presence or absence of generic instructions with respect to the Response component on instrumental (i.e. response accuracy) and verbal performance (i.e. post-contact descriptions or rules) on sixteen students of elementary school, using a first order matching-to-sample task. Contrary to the results obtained in similar studies with pre-grade students, we observed a greater number of generic and non-pertinent post-contact descriptions, which suggest both an effect of instructional precision and the change in the feedback frequency, as well as effects related to the individual experience of subjects.

Role of the family in drug abuse
Pandey, Ugrasen Dept. of Social Science, SRK PG College Firozabad, Firozbad, India
A simple random survey of 9863 population out of the total 70,000 population is one slum pocket of agra revealed drug dependence in 104 persons. Out of 104, 83.65% smoked 'brown sugar' 10.68% used cannabis and 5.77% opium. Most of the addicts (95.2%) belonged to large families. Family history of alcoholism and drug abuse was present in 41.35%. Parental deprivation was additional contributing factor in 30.7%.

Perceived social support in adolescence: Gender and grade differences
Pastor, Yolanda Dept. of Health Psychology, Miguel Hernández University, Elche, Spain
This paper examined differences on perceived social support by gender and grade in a sample of 648 Spanish adolescents (M age=13.4, SD=1.7, Range = 11-16 years) from three academic levels. A validated Spanish version of "Social Support Scale for Children" (Harter, 1985) was used (Pastor, Benavides, et al., 2004). MANOVA and Bonferroni test were used for data analyses. Results showed a significant interaction gender by grade [Wilks = .96, p<010; Pillai = .03, p<.001, Squared Eta= .018]. Oldest girls have higher scores on friendship and classmate perceived social support that those of the rest of boys and girls aged groups. Parents and teachers perceived social support decreased by grade.

An exploratory study about psychosocial profile of adjustment in early adolescence
Pastor, Yolanda Dept. of Health Psychology, Miguel Hernández University, Elche, Spain Benavides, Gemma Health psychology, Miguel Hernández University, Elche, Spain
The aim of this paper was to describe a psychosocial profile of adjustment versus maladjustment's adolescents. Sample consisted of 648 adolescents (52% boys and 48% girls) between 11 to 16 years from Elche (Spain). The variables considered were gender, academic level, self-concept dimensions, self-esteem, perceived social support, family cohesion, school integration, community satisfaction, aggressive thoughts and troubled behavior. Two-Step Clustering Procedures were used to determine the natural adolescent's groupings. Results showed 4 adolescent's groups as the best clustering, attending BIC. The included variables discriminated among 4 groups and they were relevant to locate characteristics of risk adolescents' group as well as adjusted adolescents' groups.

Parents as facilitators in choosing vocational education for their children. Training for school career counsellors focused on co-operation with parents for their children
Paszkowska-Rogacz, Anna Occupational Psychology, Academy of Management, Lodz, Poland
The poster present results of the research conducted among the young people (106) and their parents (91) who suggest that children tend to refer to their parents as vocational advisors in opposite to parents who complain that they feel excluded from the process of vocational assistance offered to their children. In their opinion in most cases it results from the skeptical attitudes of teachers and advisors as far as parents' competences in this field are concerned. Additionally there are no trainings for parents which would teach them to influence positively the vocational orientation of their children. The poster also presents the second objective of the research which was to develop a training addressed to school vocational advisors which would teach them how to cooperate with parents of schoolchildren's facing the choice of the future vocational career. This aim promoted active participation of a new actor – parents, in the process of vocational assistance, this actor, thanks to the cooperation with professional advisors will gain proper knowledge to necessary to provide professional help to the children facing making a career decision.

A cross-cultural study of forgiveness and emotional intelligence
Patil, Kanak Pune, India Akrivos, Dimitris Students Affairs, Hellenic American University, Athens, Greece
The present research is an exploratory study comparing forgiveness and emotional intelligence between Greek and Indian students. Heartland Forgiveness Scale (2005) and Schuttes Emotional Intelligence scale (1998), were administered to 88(44 males and 44 females) Indian students and 88 (44 males and 44 femles) Greek students. Preliminary data analysis using the Pearson's Product Movement Correlation revealed significant positive correlation (p<0.01)of forgiveness (total),(HFS -total), forgiveness of self(HFS-S), forgiveness of situation (HFS-Sit), forgivness of others(HFS-O) to Emotional Intelligence(total). While significant positive correlation (p<0.05) of HFS (total), HFS-S, HFS-Sit to EI (total) were revealed in the Greek sample. Thus the study aims at contributing to theory and cross-culture counselling.

Organizational Citizenship Behavior (OCB) of workers in Mahasarakham University of Thailand
Peemanee, Jindarat Management Dept., Mahasarakham University, Mahasarakham, Thailand
Study Objectives. First, to study behavior of Organizational Citizenship Behavior (OCB) of Workers in Mahasarakham University(MSU) of Thailand. Second, to create tools for measuring the OCB of Workers in MSU. Third, to compare the OCB of Workers from the opinion of students, staffs and lecturers. (N= 795) Questionnaires as instrument. Analyses the data included Descriptive statistic, Principal Component, Varimax Method, and F-test. The results of the OCB for lecturers has 5 components which are "Sportsmanship", Courtesy, Altruism, Conscientiousness and Civic virtue. Moreover, the OCB for staffs has 3 components which are Responsibility, Courtesy organization and Altruism.

Parents' and adolescents' perceptions of their relationships: A cross-national comparison in Canada, France and Italy
Perchec, Cyrille Psychologie - CRPCC, Université Rennes 2, Rennes, France Michel, Claes Psychologie, University of Montreal, Montreal, Canada Bariand, Francoise Psychologie - CRPCC, Université Rennes 2, Rennes, France Miranda, Dave Psychologie, University of Montreal, Montreal, Canada Benoit, Amélie Psychologie, University of Montreal, Montreal, Canada Lanz, Margherita Psychology, Università Cattolica del Sacro, Milano, Italy Marta, Elena Psychology, Università Cattolica del Sacro, Milano, Italy
The objective of the present study is to examine similarities and differences between parents' and adolescents' perceptions of their everyday life relationships such as communication. A cross-sectional sample was made up of more than 600 adolescents – aged from 11 to 19 years (M=15.04 years; SD=1.9) – who filled out a self-report questionnaire about relationships with both mother and father respectively. Parents also filled a questionnaire regarding their own perception of the relationships with their child. This paper will focus on the comparison of parents/adolescent similarities and discrepancies across the three cultural contexts.

Exploring the Aggression Questionnaire cross-culturally
Pereda, Noemi Assess. and Psych. Treatment, University of Barcelona, Barcelona, Spain Garcia-Forero, Carlos Pers., Assess. & Psych. Tr, University of Barcelona, Barcelona, Spain Gallardo-Pujol, David Pers., Assess. & Psych. Tr, University of Barcelona, Barcelona, Spain de-la-Piedra, Mar Pers., Assess. & Psych. Tr, University of Barcelona, Barcelona, Spain Suso, Carlos Pers., Assess. & Psych. Tr, University of Barcelona, Barcelona, Spain
Objective: The aim of the present study is to cross-culturally explore the differences between Catalan and American samples with regard to an aggression questionnaire. Methods: Aggression Questionnaire-Refined has been used to obtain aggressiveness measures. A total sample of 733 sophomore students was recruited in Spain and United States of America. Results: There are some differences in the expression of hostility and verbal aggression and in the structure of both questionnaires. Discussion: Implications and possible causes of the differences are discussed herein.

Reading nonwords aloud: The "changed letter" effect varies as a function of reading abilities
Peressotti, Francesca DPSS, University of Padova, Padova, Italy Mulatti, Claudio DPSS, University of Padova, Padova, Italy Job, Remo DISCOF, University of Trento, Rovereto (TN), Italy
Mulatti et al. (2007) showed that reading times of nonword derived from words by changing a letter

varied as a function of the position of the changed letter. Changes in initial position letters lead to longer responses than in final position. This study investigated the developmental trend of this effect. Nonwords were derived by changing either the 1st or the 4th letter of Italian words. Seven-year old children showed longer RTs and more errors when the changed letter was the 4th than the 1st. The effect disappeared for 8-year old children. Nine-year old's performance was adult-like. The results are discussed with respect to the recent computational models of reading.

The locus of the sound-to-spelling consistency effects

Petrova, Ana Psychologie, Université Paris Descartes, Boulogne-Billancourt Cedex, France Ferrand, Ludovic Psychology, Universite Blaise Pascal, Clermont-Ferrand, France

Two experiments investigated the locus of sound-to-spelling consistency effect. Experiment 1, using an auditory lexical decision task, showed strong sound-to-spelling consistency effect with words but not with nonwords. In Experiment 2, the same words were used in an auditory lexical decision task and in a task less reliant on lexical information - rime detection. The same pattern of results as Experiment 1 was found for the lexical decision task while rime detection led to less clear effects, and no interaction between frequency and consistency. These observations imply a lexical locus on the influence of spelling in the phonological processing of adult speakers.

Better than expected: Decision making with correct answers

Pfabigan, Daniela Fakultät für Psychologie, Universität Wien, Wien, Austria Sailer, Uta Brain Research Labor, Faculty of Psychology, Vienna, Austria Bauer, Herbert Brain Research Labor, Faculty of Psychology, Vienna, Austria

The topic of the present study is the positive reward prediction error following decision outcomes which are better than expected. We investigated whether it's possible to find event-related potential components in the ongoing electroencephalogram corresponding to the error-related negativity after error commission. Using DC-EEG, subjects had to learn stimulus-response-contingencies in a combined probabilistic learning gambling task. The better they performed the more money they could win. Some trials had an unexpected positive outcome, thus inducing a positive reward prediction error signal. Source localization methods were applied for statistical analysis. Results and further implications are presented.

Determination of the self-perception of students of different groups of subjects with respect to the Big Five and Big Six

Pfuhl, Nadja Fachgebiet Gymnasialpädagogik, Technische Universität München, München, Germany Guglhör-Rudan, Angelika Fakultät für Pädagogik, Universität der Bundeswehr Mün, Neubiberg, Germany Tarnai, Christian Fakultät für Pädagogik, Universität der Bundeswehr Mün, Neubiberg, Germany

The person's personality is the most significant factor for deciding in favour of a field of study. Persons aspire to environments corresponding to their orientations (Holland 1997). In an online-survey students (N=1464) evaluate their fellow-students regarding their personality (BigFive). Equally, they characterise fields of study according to the six dimensions of Holland (BigSix). By means of cluster- and discriminate-analyses, common and differing features of the students and fields of study are tested. It is possible to differentiate between various groups of study adequately on the basis of the students' personality evaluations together with the characterisation of the fields of study.

Effects of age, sentence context and noise-vocoding on word identification: Behavioural and electrophysiological findings

Pichora-Fuller, M. Kathy Dept. of Psychology, University of Toronto, Mississauga, Canada Dupuis, Kate Psychology, University of Toronto, Mississauga, Ontario, Canada Sheldon, Signy Psychology, University of Toronto, Mississauga, Ontario, Canada Phillips, Natalie Psychology, Concordia University, Montreal, Quebec, Canada

Off-line behavioural and on-line event-related brain potentials were used to investigate age-related differences in how listeners identify acoustically intact or distorted (noise-vocoded) words presented in high- or low-context sentences, either with or without priming by sentence context. Both age groups identified more words in high- compared to low-context sentences, especially when primed. Importantly, older adults benefited at least as much as younger adults from sentence context and priming. The pattern of ERPs suggests that on-line lexical activation is affected by the use of context in both age groups, with patterns of activation varying according to the degree of distortion.

Wishful thinking: Meta-analysis reveals publication bias, lab differences and nonspecificity in the Mozart effect

Pietschnig, Jakob Inst. für Psychologie, Universität Wien, Wien, Austria Voracek, Martin School of Psychology, University of Vienna, Wien, Austria Formann, Anton School of Psychology, University of Vienna, Wien, Austria

The Mozart effect (alleged transitory gains in spatial abilities, merely through listening to specific classic music) is a highly publicized, but scientifically contested finding. To resolve this debate, we conducted the so far largest meta-analysis on the topic (>50 studies, >3,500 subjects). Results show clear evidence for publication bias in this literature and quite dramatic (almost threefold) effect-size differences obtained by Mozart effect proponents versus other researchers. The Mozart effect seems amazingly nonspecific, generalizing to other types of music and possibly to any exposure to vivifying experience. Hence it may be sufficiently explained through the well-known effects of general arousal.

Cognitive abilities and stress associated with reading acquisition in Zulu speaking children

Pillay, Cecilia Dept. Behavioural Medicine, University of KwaZulu-Natal, Durban, South Africa

Objective: To understand reading related skills in isiZulu; establish whether these are similar to other languages, and identify correlates with the stress response Methodology: Participants were isiZulu speaking, grade four learners (N=250) from three different primary schools. A segmentation measure, rapid automatised naming test, mono-and poly-syllabic real word reading, the mono-and polysyllabic non-word reading tests and a stress symptom checklist were administered. Results: There were significant relationships between the reading tests skills and self-reported stress measures. Conclusion: The implications of these results are considered in teaching reading to non-English speaking children and understanding stress response and reading in school children.

Sibling relationship when a child has a rare disease: Comparative study of Cornelia de Lange Syndrome (CdLS) and Prader-Willi Syndrome (PWS)

Pimentel, Maria João Child Development Centre, Hospital de Dona Estefânia, Lisboa, Portugal

This study approaches the relationship between the child with a rare disease and its healthy siblings. Siblings of children with CdLS (G1; n=21) and with PWS (G2, n=13) participated. Family drawings and the Family Relations Test were used to assess the dynamics of the sibling relationship. Groups were compared through statistical analysis. Results indicate a special dynamic in these sibling relationships. Differences between groups are related to specific aspects of each disease. This study shows the specificity of sibling relationship when a child has a rare disease and indicates the importance of attending to the sibling's need of support.

The mixed elderly stereotype in the Brazilian context

Pinheiro de Paula Couto, Maria Clara Department of Psychology, Psychology Institute, UFRGS, Porto Alegre, Brazil Koller, Silvia Helena Departamento de Psicologia, Instituto de Psicologia/UFRGS, Porto Alegre, Brazil Novo, Rosa FPCE, Universidade de Lisboa, Lisboa, Portugal

According to the stereotype content model many out-group stereotypes are mixed into two dimensions, warmth and competence. Older-persons, for example, are perceived as warm but not competent in many countries. This study aims to investigate whether these kind of mixed elderly stereotype exist in Brazil. Participants were 120 divided in two samples (60 adults and 60 older-persons) and surveyed about society's perceptions of older-persons. Matched pair t-tests revealed significant differences between competence and warmth for both samples being warmth higher than competence. These results show that mixed elderly stereotype exist in the Brazilian context and is manifested from both adults and older-persons.

The functional meaning of the N400 and the P600 associated with thematic integration processing

Pizzioli, Fabrizio UCL, Louvain-la-Neuve, Belgium Rossion, Bruno Psychology, UCL, Louvain la neuve, Belgium Nakano, Hiroko School of Science, Saint Mary's College of Califo, Moraga, USA

In this study event related potentials were used to investigate auditory thematic integration processes in the sentences where verbs were either congruent, incongruent and Semantically-Unrelated, (e.g., The tree read the old man) or Thematically-Reversible (e.g., The newspaper read the old man). The plausibility of the subject noun as a theme was also manipulated. The Semantically-Unrelated condition elicited both a P600 and a N400 effects while the Thematically-Reversible condition elicited only the P600 effect, modulated by the degree of plausibility. The nature of P600 and N400 effects are discussed in terms of thematic attraction, semantic-association, thematic-structural violation, and animacy.

Strategies of emotion regulation in the Ainsworth Strange Situation: Typically developing toddlers and toddlers with Down Syndrome

Poltz, Nadine Werder, Germany Biermann, Katharina Institute of Psychology, University of Potsdam, Potsdam, Germany Rauh, Hellgard Institute of Psychology, University of Potsdam, Potsdam, Germany Thiel, Thomas Institute of Psychology, University of Potsdam, Potsdam, Germany

Ainsworth Strange Situation videotapes of 11 children with Down Syndrome at Mental Ages of 12-14 months, and 23 non-DS infants at CA 12 months, matched for gender and quality of attachment, were analyzed with respect to emotion regulation strategies. Down Syndrome children tended to outperform the typically developing children in number and variety of orientation, referencing, searching, and self-calming strategies. With increasing stress, securely attached DS children increased the number and frequency of self-calming strategies, even more than did avoidantly insecure non-DS children, and securely attached non-DS children showed only very few strategies, and these primarily in less stressing situations.

Child abuse allegations and the parental alienation risk

Poundja, Joaquin Research Centre, Douglas Hospital, Montreal, Canada Cyr-Villeneuve, Catherine Psychologie, Université de Montréal, Montreal, Canada Prégent, Manuel Psychologie, Université de Montréal, Montreal, Canada

To study the frequency of child abuses allegations professed by a parent towards the other, in divorced and conflicting families, for which Parental Alienation risks are estimated very high or very low. We have studied the frequency of neglect, physical, sexual, and psychological abuses, in 82 families. The $\chi 2$ analysis indicates that the neglect allegations have a higher frequency in the very low risks group, but that no significant difference is found in other kinds of abuse allegations. The studied allegations are not part of the common characteristics of the cases in which the Parental Alienation risks are very high.

Contributing emotional responses to scholar aggressive relationships (I)

Prado Delgado, Victor Manuel National Office of Research, Antonio Nariño University, Bogotá, Colombia Botia Sanabria, Maria Lucero National Office of Research, Antonio Nariño University, Bogotá, Colombia

This descriptive study inquiries emotional responses, jargon and communicative styles as factors related with scholar context aggressive behaviors. From a constructivist view were designed, validated and applied two structured questionnaires. Results show aggressive responses as ways to demand (personal) debts, communicate emotions, defend oneself of others agression, clearly associated with a victim role; see someone else suffering cause emotional reactions but dont move helping or caring behaviors. The 54 evaluated kids (12-14 age) dont seem be aware of their emotional responses and dont think they can manage it positively; sadness, anger and loneliness are the most frequent reported emotions.

Student's quality of life (Rerearch at Islamic school in Indonesia)

Pramadi, Andrian Dept. of Psychology, University of Surabaya, Surabaya, Indonesia Yuliana, Lily Psychology, University of Surabaya, Surabaya, Indonesia

We found that a lot of problems of children in Indonesia.All of these problem can be the cause of decreasing quality of life. Research objective is Student's quality of life at school based Islam religion. Research samples are 180 Islam (moslem) students. The results are 20 % elementary students has a very high and 20% has low grades of quality of life. And 22 % of junior high students has a high quality of life and 22% has a very low quality of life. And the senior high school students that 23 % has a low quality of life. The result is interesting to take discussion that how relation school based religion and quality of life.

Generative parents and their children's socialization memories: Stories of family teaching moments by young children and adolescents

Pratt, Michael Psychology, Wilfrid Laurier University, Waterloo, Canada Norris, Joan Psychology, Wilfrid Laurier University, Waterloo, Canada Lawford, Heather Psychology, Wilfrid Laurier University, Waterloo, Canada Cressman, Kate Psychology, Wilfrid Laurier University, Waterloo, Canada

Generativity is Erikson's midlife personality construct of concern for future generations, and predicts to more effective styles of parenting. Two studies examined the narratives that 8 year-olds (30 families) and 18 year olds (35 families) told about parents' value teaching. Parent generativity was measured on the Loyola Generativity Scale (LGS) of McAdams. Results showed significant positive relations of parental LGS scores to children's direct quotations of parent voices in their stories, to rated story quality, and to child acceptance of story message. Generative parents' greater effectiveness as teachers thus is reflected in more memorable family socialization moments for their children.

The effects of personal space invasions on anxiety, performance and time

Proestou, Paula Athens, Greece

An experiment was conducted to examine whether personal space invasion affects participants anxiety level, number of errors at the IQ test and the time they spend in the room. For the purpose of this experiment 24 participants were asked to fill out an Anxiety Self-Rating scale, and then to answer some IQ questions while someone else was sitting very close to them, or far away from them or with nobody else in the room. A Multivariate Analysis of Variance was conducted and showed that the hypothesis was partially confirmed. It was confirmed for the time they spend in the room and for the no effect of proximity on anxiety.

Music preferences of Croatian young adults

Prot, Sara Dept. of Psychology, Faculty of Philosophy, Zagreb, Croatia Udovicic, Martina Department of psychology, Faculty of philosophy, Zagreb, Zagreb, Croatia Vojnic Tunic, Ana Department of psychology, Faculty of philosophy, Zagreb, Zagreb, Croatia Banozic, Adrijana Department of psychology, Faculty of philosophy, Zagreb, Zagreb, Croatia Stamenkovic, Barbara Department of psychology, Faculty of philosophy, Zagreb, Zagreb, Croatia Plosnic, Fani Department of psychology, Faculty of philosophy, Zagreb, Zagreb, Croatia

This study tested a newly constructed survey of music-listening habits and genre preferences on a sample of 250 Croatian urban young adults. Results show that young adults spend an average of 1-2 hours a day listening to music and see music as an important part of their lives. The most frequently preferred music genre was rock (41%). Principal component analysis revealed a four-factor structure of music preferences, explaining 54% of the variance. Common motives for listening to a particular type of music were inducing a good mood, enjoying the performer's technique and finding deeper meaning in lyrics and melodies.

The processing of words primed by polite formulas or abusive words

Qiu, Xiaowen Department of University, Capital Normal University, Beijing, People's Republic of China Zhang, Dexuan Department of University, Hangzhou Normal University, Hangzhou, People's Republic of China Liao, Yu Department of University, Capital Normal University, Beijing, People's Republic of China Zhang, Qin Department of University, Capital Normal University, Beijing, People's Republic of China

The present study investigated behavioral responses to positive, negative and neutral target words primed by polite formulas or abusive words in a valence decision task. 27 participants were asked to decide whether the valence of each target word was pleasant or unpleasant under SOA of either 200 or 600ms. Results indicated faster responses to affective words primed by polite formulas than by abusive words under both SOA conditions. Under SOA of 600 ms, neutral words primed by abusive words were easier to be viewed as positive ones. These results were interpreted as the effects of arousal and culture.

The impact of school organizational creative climate on teachers' creative motivation and teachers' innovative instructional capability: A hierarchical linear model

Quan, Yuetong School of of Psychology, ShanDong Normal University, Ji'nan ShanDong, People's Republic of China Zhang, Jinghuan School of Psychology, ShanDong Normal University, Jinan, People's Republic of China

Questionnaire survey was used on 1459 teachers from 38 junior high schools in Shandong province, China?to investigate the impact of school organizational creative climate (SOCC) on teachers' creative motivation(TCM) and teachers' innovative instructional capability (TIIC). The Hierarchical Linear Model was used to analyze the data. The result showed that SOCC strengthened the positive correlation between TCM and TIIC, weakened the positive correlation between the synergic extrinsic motivation and TIIC. The negative correlation between the non-synergic extrinsic motivation and TIIC was not affected significantly by SOCC. Key words: school organizational creative climate(SOCC), teachers' creative motivation (TCM), teachers' innovative instructional capability(TIIC)

The relationship between ego identity status and locus of control in college students

Rahiminezhad, Abbas psychology, University of Tehran, Tehran, Islamic Republic of Iran

For the purpose of studying concurrent validity of ego identity the relationship of Persian versions of ego identity status scales and locus of control scales of Levenson(1972) were studied on 40 female undergraduate students in Tehran. In this preliminary study the correlation of the identity diffusion scale of ego identity status(EOM-EIS 2) and internal locus of control(I)scale was-0.48,and chance scale(C)was 0.32 both were significant.The correlationof foreclosure scale of EOM-EIS2 and chance Scale(C) was 0.42 that was significant. The correlation of ideological foreclosure scale and internal locus of control was -0.33 that was significant.

Mental representation of temporal information in event sequences

Raisig, Susanne Berlin, Germany Welke, Tinka Institut für Psychologie, Humboldt Universität, Berlin, Germany Hagendorf, Herbert Institut für Psychologie, Humboldt Universität, Berlin, Germany van der Meer, Elke Inst. für Psychologie, Humboldt-Universität zu Berlin, Berlin, Germany

Temporal relations between events are crucial in the performance of event sequences. In order to make inferences on the underlying representation, we investigated the cognitive strategies during the processing of temporal information. In a temporal order judgment task, participants were presented event triplets where the temporal order was manipulated. Reaction times indicated a sequential, self-terminating decision strategy. However, pupil data and error rates indicated that the temporal information of the complete sequence is available and affects the decision. It was concluded that event sequences are represented sequentially but are processed holistically where the cognitive system integrates all temporal information.

Documenting emotion: The cultural construction of anger

Rajaram, Srividya Dept. of Humanities, Indian Institute of Technology, New Delhi, India Nair, Rukmini Humanities, Indian Institute of Technology, New Delhi, India Srinivasan, Anupama Humanities, Indian Institute of Technology, New Delhi, India

Though emotion research in psychology is dominated by the use of quantitative measures, such objective measures do not capture the role that culture plays in constructing a social world. The current paper uses the medium of a 15 minute documentary film (Hindi, English subtitles) made by Indian adolescents on the basic emotion of anger to demonstrate how cultural dimensions of feeling may be finely analyzed using qualitative methods. This paper is part of a larger project which aims to show how such films made by children on emotions like shame, rage and joy aid our understanding of complex emotional cognitions.

Predictors of subjective well-being among Filipino adolescents

Ramos III, Rufino College Guidance Center, Ateneo de Naga University, Naga City, Philippines

This study was conducted to assess the salience of personality (self-esteem, extraversion, neuroticism) and psychosocial (family satisfaction, relationship harmony, and social support) variables in the prediction of subjective well-being (SWB) among urban university-based Filipino adolescents. College students (n = 305) from two state universities and two private universities in the Philippines were recruited for this study. Results of the study revealed that self-esteem emerged as the strongest and the most reliable predictor when the cognitive and affective measures of SWB are utilized. Implications of the findings on the formulations of SWB in the Philippine context are presented.

Effects of the familiarization and power functions in children's obedience

Rangel, Nora Universidad de Guadalajara, Zapopan, Jalisco, Mexico *Ribes, Emilio* CEIC, Universidad de Guadalajara, Zapopan, Jalisco, Mexico *Ponce, Raquel* CUCS, Universidad de Guadalajara, Zapopan, Jalisco, Mexico

Prescription, regulation, administration and monitoring of interactions are four different functions involved in any power relation. The purpose of this experiment was to evaluate the effects of the time of familiarization with the experimenter, and the exercise of each one of the functions of power in children's obedience. Each child was exposed to one, two, three or four sessions of familiarization. In a second part of the experiment, children were exposed to each one of the power functions. Results showed differential effects on children's obedience due to both, familiarization time, and the type of power function exercised.

The investigation of spillover between work and private life and domain-specific outcomes referring to personality and coping

Reichl, Corinna Saarbrücken, Germany *Wolf, Heike* Psychologie, Universität des Saarlandes, Saarbrücken, Germany *Spinath, Frank M.* Psychologie, Universität des Saarlandes, Saarbrücken, Germany

While research on the interface between work and private life is increasing, comprehension of inter-individual differences as well as the systematic examination of domain-specific outcomes are still deficient. Focusing on physicians (N=417) and a heterogeneous sample of other occupational groups (N ≍ 400), study 1 investigates the influence of personality (five-factor-model) on the experience of positive and negative spillover and its moderating role between spillover and burnout/work engagement. Study 2 relies on the examination of domain-specific affective and behavioural outcomes of spillover and coping. Results underline the importance of considering individual variables concerning the experience of and reaction to spillover.

Modulation of distribution of dots on strategies and spatial attention allocation during two sequential arrays integration

Ren, Yanju Dept. of Psychology, Shandong Normal University, Jinan, People's Republic of China *Xuan, Yuming* Institute of Psychology, Chinese Academy of Scieneces, Beijing, People's Republic of China *Fu,*

Xiaolan Institute of Psychology, Chinese Academy of Sciences, beijing, People's Republic of China

In this study, we employed empty cell localization task to investigate the information integration between two sequential dot arrays in two experiments. In the first experiment, we manipulated the distribution of dots between two arrays to test the image-percept integration hypothesis and convert-and-compare hypothesis. In the second experiment, we explored spatial attention allocation by recording participants' eye movement behavior during the process of integration to further test these two hypotheses. It was found that distribution of dots between two arrays modulate the participants' strategies and spatial attention allocation during the process of integration.

Clarifying lexicality effects in the left occipitotemporal cortex

Richlan, Fabio Inst. für Psychologie, Universität Salzburg, Salzburg, Austria *Kronbichler, Martin* Psychologie, Universität Salzburg, Salzburg, Austria *Wimmer, Heinz* NW Fakultät, Universität Salzburg, Salzburg, Austria

Objectives: Functional neuroimaging studies on visual word processing yielded inconsistent lexicality effects in left occipitotemporal cortex. To clarify, two meta-analyses were computed. Methods: GingerALE software was run on 232 coordinates extracted from 22 published studies. Results: A large cluster in the left occipitotemporal cortex with higher activity for pseudowords than words was identified. However, a small lateral inferior temporal cluster exhibited higher activity for real words. This pattern was also found in an fMRI study from our lab which presented words and pseudowords and contrasted standard lexical decision with a phonological syllable counting task.

Work-family conflict differences between post-war generation and pre-war generation in Korean women

Rie, Ju-Il Dept. of Psychology, Hallym University, Chuncheon, Republic of Korea *Ryu, Kyung* Psychology, Hallym University at Korea, Chuncheon, Republic of Korea

We collected data about work-family confilcts from about 350 womens in korea. They consists of students, housekeepers, working women, and the retired. After then we divided data into post korean war generation and pre korean war generation. we anticipated that work and family duty would be most important factors in their life in pre-war generation, but personal life and quality of life would be most important factors in post-war generation. And work-family conflicts would be more greater in post war generations than in pre war generations. Data showed that our anticipation were right. we discussed about meaning of work-family conflicts in korean womens.

Household responsibilities in the family of origin and self-efficacy in young adulthood

Riggio, Heidi Dept. of Psychology, CSU Los Angeles, Los Angeles, USA *Garcia, Amber* Psychology, College of Wooster, Wooster, Ohio, USA *Valenzuela, Ann Marie* Psychology, CSU Los Angeles, Los Angeles, USA

A central empirical question is how and to what extent family of origin experiences contribute to offspring self-efficacy, beliefs about one's competence (Bandura, 2000; Schneewind, 1995). Using self-report responses of 191 undergraduate students, we examined how household responsibilities while growing up related to young adults' general and work self-efficacy. Results indicated that frequency of household chores was positively related to self-efficacy, and that young adults beginning regular chores and "looking after yourself" at an earlier age reported greater self-efficacy. Implications of other family features (parental

divorce, maternal employment, and poverty) are discussed in relation to household chores and offspring self-efficacy.

Judgement accuracy of teachers concerning basic reading capacities

Rjosk, Camilla Freie Universität Berlin, Berlin, Germany *McElvany, Nele* Human Development, Max Planck Institute, Berlin, Germany *Grabbe, Yvonne* Human Development, Max Planck Institute, Berlin, Germany *Becker, Michael* Human Development, Max Planck Institute, Berlin, Germany

This study investigates the diagnostic competence of German teachers concerning basic reading capacities of sixth graders with and without migration background on different judgement levels (achievement of sixth graders in general [N=46 teachers], of their own class [N=33 t.] and of individual children [N=33 t.]) by means of different accuracy measurements and achievement level matched pairs. The outcomes indicate, among others, an overestimation of achievement and no difference in accuracy related to children with and without migration background. The findings have theoretical and practical implications for teachers' initial and continued education in the domain of diagnoses of pupils' achievement.

Building family integrity in later life

Rodrigues, Sofia Dept. of Health Sciences, University of Aveiro, Aveiro, Portugal *Silva, Ana Raquel* Health Sciences, University of Aveiro, Aveiro, Portugal *Marques, Filipa* Health Sciences, University of Aveiro, Aveiro, Portugal *Santos, Liliana* Health Sciences, University of Aveiro, Aveiro, Portugal *Sousa, Liliana* Health Sciences, University of Aveiro, Aveiro, Portugal

This study aims at contributing to a better understanding of family integrity in later life (based on Erickson's psychosocial development theory). A semi-structured open interview (based on King & Wynne, 2004) was administered to 8 participants aged over 64 years old. Main results suggest that family integrity is influenced by: strong family relations; perception of available support; and a philosophy of life that dispose a positive attitude even beyond negative events. Family integrity does not exclude negative current or past events, but involves the acceptance of life as it is/was, integrating all life in a peaceful meaning.

The self-learning in inline-skating classes at school

Roman, Blanca Physical Education and Sport, University of Granada, Granada, Spain *Martínez, Juan Carlos* Physical Education and Sport, University of Granada, GRANADA, Spain *Martinez, Manuel* Physical Education and Sport, University of Granada, GRANADA, Spain *Miranda, Mª Teresa* Physical Education and Sport, University of Granada, GRANADA, Spain *Viciana, Jesús* Physical Education and Sport, University of Granada, GRANADA, Spain

The aim of this research was to promote inline-skating self learning in students through problem-solving tasks. 49 students (13,7 years old) participated in Physical Education classes. Students and the teacher assessed the specific skills prior to and after the treatment in a scale of 6 categories (within 2 different items). The data which associates the subjective learning level with an objective teacher's assessment, shows significant differences (p=.005) in dynamic balance, velocity and direction control, jump ability, body and feet laterality. The problem-solving tasks can be used to facilitate the autonomy and self-motivation in inline-skating learning process.

Familial approach of the emotional awareness in obesity

Rommel, Delphine Psychologie URECA, Université Lille 3, Villeneuve d'Ascq Cedex, France *Nandrino, Jean-Louis* Psychologie URECA, Université Lille 3, Villeneuve d'Ascq Cedex, France *Victor, Laetitia* Psychologie URECA, Université Lille 3, Villeneuve d'Ascq Cedex, France *Antoine, Pascal* Psychologie URECA, Université Lille 3, Villeneuve d'Ascq Cedex, France *Delecourt, Francois* endocrinologie et diabétologie, GHICL Saint Philibert, Lomme Cedex, France *Dodin, Vincent* Psychiatrie Adulte, GHICL Saint Vincent, Lille Cedex, France
Objectives: The aim of the study was to explore the emotional disturbances and the link between them and the family organization in obesity. Methods: Patients suffering from obesity and controls answered questionnaires about alexithymia (TAS-20), emotion regulation (ERQ), emotional awareness (LEAS), family cohesion and adaptability (FACES-III) and parental bonds (PBI). Results: We find a positive correlation between alexithymia and paternal overprotection. Conclusion: We discuss the idea of emotional disturbances as a characteristic of the family interaction rather than the patient's sole concern.

Doing favours

Ruscito, Francesca Psychology, Carleton University, Ottawa, Canada *Thorngate, Warren* Psychology, Carleton University, Ottawa, Canada *Esbati, Zinat* Psychology, Tehran University, Tehran, Islamic Republic of Iran
This research examined cross-cultural differences in social interdependence for daily problem solving using a diary method. People solve daily problems on their own, and also solve problems with other people's help. These acts of unpaid assistance are called favours. We are interested in learning about favours in different cultures, like Canada and Iran. We asked students to answer questions about favours and disfavours they have done for others yesterday and that were done to them. The results give insights about cultural differences in the kinds of favours done, and suggest that the methodology is good for exploring such differences.

Psychological contract assessment and organizational dimensions: Evaluation in a non-profit organization

Russo, Vincenzo Consumer, Behavior and Org., Iulm University, Milan, Italy *Crescentini, Alberto* Dep. Psychology, Cattolica University of Milan, Milan, Italy
Italian non-profit field is changing. Purpose of our work was to promote a change in a non-profit organization consistent with the quality system through a research-intervention process. An abridged version of Psychological Contract Inventory (Rousseau, 2000); a contract breach scale and a satisfaction scale, a climate questionnaire and 10 interviews to stakeholders has been used to collect data. The middle manager grew up from the bottom of organization is used as a reason for the not taking in care of responsibility and to stop any Organizational change. Our data, using two different non-profit organizations as comparison, were used to encourage improvements defining the main criticism, attributing causes and solutions to each professional family.

Effects of a manualized cognitive behavioral treatment for childhood obesity

Sørebø Danielsen, Yngvild Department of Psychosocial Sci, University of Bergen, Bergen, Norway *Pallesen, Ståle* Department of Psychosocial Sci, University of Bergen, Bergen, Norway
Objective: This report presents preliminary results from an ongoing clinical trial investigating the effects of a 12-session cognitive behavioral intervention for childhood obesity (age 8-12) (N=22). The outcome variable was BMI. Results: ANOVA with one within subjects factor (Time) and one between group factor (Group) was used. Neither the main effect for Time nor for Group was significant. The interaction effect was however significant (F1,20=10.3, p<.01). The children in the treatment group had reduced their BMI with 1.19 points compared to a 0.78 points increase in the control group from pre- to post-treatment. Conclusion: The intervention shows promising effects.

When the leash constrains the dog: Investigating the impact of semantic associations and processing modalities on sentence production

Saß, Katharina Psychiatrie und Psychotherapie, Universitätsklinikum Aachen, Aachen, Germany *Theede, Katharina* Universiteit Maastricht, Faculteit der Psychologie, Maastricht, Netherlands *Sachs, Olga* Psychiatrie und Psychotherapie, Universitätsklinikum Aachen, Aachen, Germany *van der Lugt, Arie* Universiteit Maastricht, Faculteit der Psychologie, Maastricht, Netherlands *Heim, Stefan* Research Center Juelich, Institute of Neurosciences, Jülich, Germany *Kircher, Tilo* Psychiatrie und Psychotherapie, Universitätsklinikum Aachen, Aachen, Germany
The present study investigated the production of sentences with respect to associatively related concepts (car-garage), different modalities (auditory, visual) and different stimulus onset asynchronies (-150ms, 0ms) using an adapted picture-word interference task. The results revealed that (a) associatively related concepts were active during speech production and led to semantic interference, (b) semantic interference was only detected for the first noun of the sentence and (c) modality did not have an impact on performance. Altogether, we could show that sentence production is incremental and associations play an important role in speech production.

Music complexity effect on its semantic metaphoricity versus aesthetic appreciation relationship

Sabadosh, Pavel Psychology of Abilities, Institute of Psychology RAS, Moscow, Russia
Objective of the study was to investigate how musical structure influences the depth of aesthetic appreciation. Stimuli represented 8 instruments' timbres repeated in 3 sets differing in melodic feature: the first representing isolated tones, the second and the third – simple and more complex melodies. 56 adult subjects of both sexes performed free description task of each set' most and least preferred stimuli. Unlike isolated tones, two melodic sets revealed stimulus semantic metaphoricity level significant increase with preference; similarly, melodic complication yielded semantic metaphoricity growth in preferred stimuli only. Apparently, melodic complication modifies aesthetic appreciation quality inducing higher levels of interpretation.

The investigation relationship between cognitive factors and counterproductive work behavior

Sabahi, Parviz psychology, isfahan university, isfahan, Islamic Republic of Iran *Nouri, Aboulghasem* psychology, isfahan university, isfahan, Islamic Republic of Iran *Oreyzi, Hamid Reza* psychology, isfahan university, isfahan, Islamic Republic of Iran
The aim of this study was to investigate the relationship between cognitive factors and counterproductive work behavior. A random sample of including 135 from an industrial company in Tehran completes research questionnaires. Result indicates that there are significant relationships between the dimensions of organization cognition (including job satisfaction, interactional, procedural and distributive justice), with total counterproductive work behavior, counterproductive work behavior towards organization and counterproductive work behavior towards persons (p<0.01). Result of regression model showed that cognitive factors better predict counterproductive work behavior towards persons rather than counterproductive work behavior towards organization. keywords: job cognition, counterproductive work behavior.

Styles of parenting across the three subcultures of India

Sachdeva, Neeti Dept. of Psychology, Jesus and Mary College, New Delhi, India
The study investigated the Style of Parenting across the three communities settled in Delhi, India. A sample of 135 parents (mothers, fathers, grandmothers and grandfathers) from the three communities was taken. The sample was equally drawn from the joint and nuclear families having children below five years of age. A structured measure on the Parenting style was used. A 3 x 2x 2 Factorial ANOVA was computed for Community x Generation x Gender. Significant results were found. The results are discussed in the cultural context of parenting.

Influencer and/ or manipulator: The analysis of situational and personal mediators and moderators of social influence

Safron, Magdalena Social Psychology D., SWPS, Warsaw, Poland
The aim of the study was to investigate differences between a manipulator and an influencer. Participants (140 employees of commercial institutions, whose work could be characterized by various levels of interpersonal contact and position in power hierarchy) answered some questionnaires (i.e. scales of machiavellianism, psychopathy, preferences and sense of control) and declared their behaviour in interpersonal situations. Answers were classified into 22 forms of influence and described on 3 dimensions of impact. Their relations with personal and situational variables (as possible predictors and mediators) were objects of the structural equation modelling procedure. Results verified existing approaches to actors and situations of social influence.

Is migrational background of older Turkish people living in Germany a risk faktor for mental health?

Sahyazici, Fidan für Altersfragen, Deutsches Zentrum, Berlin, Germany *Huxhold, Oliver* Altersfragen, Deutsches Zentrum für, Berlin, Germany *Herbrich, Ina* für Gerontologie, Deutsches Zentrum, Berlin, Germany *Tesch-Römer, Clemens* Deutsches Zentrum Gerontologie, Berlin, Germany
Former migrant labourers are double burdened due to social disadvantage and a lack of coping strategies. This study investigates the mental health of older Turkish migrants living in Germany. Data from the 2nd wave of the nationally representative German Ageing Survey are used for analyses. By comparing a sample of Turkish migrants (N=101, mean age=54 years) and a German sample (N=2795, mean age=61 years) with ANOVA and ANCOVA we corroborate our hypothesis, that Turkish migrants, on average, suffer from more depressive symptoms. Contrary to our expectations, this effect was largely diminished after controlling for socioeconomic status. Implications are discussed.

An evaluation of the preconditions of emotional intelligence in 0-1 year old children

Saiz Manzanares, Maria Consuelo Education Sciences, Universidad de Burgos, Burgos, Spain *Ortego, Jesus* EDUCATION SCIENCES, BURGOS UNIVERSITY, BURGOS, Spain
Cognitive development allows us to better understand emotions which as they turn into more complex features develop emotional control and regulation. The expression of emotions is linked to the interactions a child establishes with rearing

figures. In this study we will analyze the preconditions of emotional intelligence in 0-1 year old children enrolled in a primary school. Results will show that these children are capable of establishing spontaneous visual contact, show shared attention and bodily contact patterns. They are also able to respond to processes of emotional understanding, and start processes of emotional relationship.

Imageability ratings for a large number of written and spoken Japanese words

Sakuma, Naoko *Tokyo Metro. Inst. of Gerontol, Itabashi-ku, Tokyo, Japan* **Tatsumi, Itaru F.** *Research group, LD Dyslexia center, Ichikawa, Chiba, Japan* **Fushimi, Takao** *Faculty of Rehabilitation, Kitasato University, Sagamihara, Kanagawa, Japan* **Ijuin, Mutsuo** *Dementia Intervention, Tokyo Metro. Inst. of Gerontol, Itabashi-ku, Tokyo, Japan* **Tanaka, Masayuki** *Primate Research Institute, Kyoto University, Inuyama, Aichi, Japan* **Amano, Shigeaki** *Cognitive Language Information, NTT Communication Science Labo, Souraku-gun, Kyoto, Japan* **Kondo, Tadahisa** *Human and Information Science, NTT Communication Science Labo, Atsugi, Kanagawa, Japan*

Imageability ratings were collected for a large number of Japanese words, including nouns, verbs, adjectives, and adverbs. Each word was presented in written forms (n=48,714) and/or spoken forms (n=39,447). For 21,690 words having neither homograph nor homophone, the correlation coefficient between visual and auditory ratings was .913. Despite our imageability and familiarity from Amano and Kondo (1999) were highly correlated (r=.796 for visual ratings and r=.782 for auditory ratings), different correlation values across word classes were obtained ranging from r=.804 (nouns) to r=.666 (adverbs). These results suggest that imageability and familiarity reflect different aspects of word attributes.

A comparative study of perception of child abuse among junior and senior college students: Indian perspectives

Samantaray, Sudhir K. *Psychology, Govt. College, Sector-11, Chandigarh, India*

A comparative paradigm was adopted to study 359 samples consisting of school children and young adults were selected randomly from schools and colleges of Chandigarh, India. Standardized questionnaire on four types of abuse namely physical, sexual, emotional and neglect was adopted and the data were analyzed by parametric tests. The analysis of data clearly indicates that the obtained "t" value for children and young adults is 2.09 which are significant at 0.05 levels. This indicates that there is difference among children and young adults with regard to child abuse and violence against children. Protection of child rights and prevention of abuse and violence against children require joint venture at all levels starting from home to Government.

The repercussion of lying on trust and collaboration in the work place

Sanchez, Flor *Dept. de Psicologia Social, Universidad Autonoma de Madrid, Madrid, Spain* **Caballero, Amparo** *Psicología Social, Universidad Autónoma de Madrid, Madrid, Spain* **Suárez, Tatiana** *Psicología Social, Universidad Autónoma de Madrid, Madrid, Spain*

The effects of the type of lie and objectives for lying on the work environment are explored through measures of acceptability, graveness, and perception of consequences through staff evaluations. Results show the objective for lying has greater repercussions on social appraisal for the behaviour, perception of the consequences on the work environment, with varying effects according to objective type. Lies that benefit others are considered more acceptable, less grave and harm trust and collaboration to a lesser extent. Meanwhile, lies that look for personal gain while harming others are scored less acceptable and deteriorate work processes requiring collaboration and trust

Women bus drivers: Transference of competences and innovative behaviours

Sanchez de Miguel, Manuel *Dept. of Psychology, Univ. of the Basque Country, San Sebastian, Spain* **Lizaso, Izarne** *PSYCHOLOGY, UNIVERSITY OF THE BASQUE COUNT, SAN SEBASTIAN, Spain* **Larranage, Maider** *PSYCHOLOGY, UNIVERSITY OF THE BASQUE COUNT, SAN SEBASTIAN, Spain* **Arrospide, Juan Jose** *PSYCHOLOGY, UNIVERSITY OF THE BASQUE COUNT, SAN SEBASTIAN, Spain*

According to the theoretical model of Almudever et al. (2005), the aim of this study is to describe and analyze the transfer of competences and innovative behaviours in traditionally male-dominated professions. In this study took part 29 female bus drivers from two metropolitan (Bilbao and San Sebastián) bus companies in Spain. The data was collected by individual interviews and were analyzed using Interpretative Phenomenological Analysis (IPA) to identify three master themes: competences, mediators and innovative behaviours. The study shows that women bus drivers are developing a new professional identity based on distinctive behaviours and intentionality addressed to organizational change.

A training program for improving logical communication skills of Japanese high school students

Sannomiya, Machiko *School of Education, Naruto University of Education, Naruto, Japan* **Kawaguchi, Atsuo** *music, Aichi pref. Univ. of FA.&, Aichi, Japan*

Not a few Japanese university students have difficulty constructing and expressing their own opinions. They seem to be lack of logical communication training before entering university. The present study reports a training program of logical communication for high school students, and its evaluation. The lessons (16 class-hours) contained writing, discussion, and reflection as students' activities. Comparison of performance between training and non-training group with pre vs. post design revealed the effectiveness of this program. Students' free reports showed their development of metacognition and motivation for constructing opinions, which is considered to be a key for successful training.

The influence of local context on explanatory inferences during expository text comprehension

Saux, Gaston *Programa Estudios Cognitivos, CONICET - Univ. Buenos Aires, Buenos Aires, Argentina*

Readers ability to integrate unfamiliar concepts into explanations during expository text reading was explored. In two experiments, reading times for target sentences placed at different loci and consistent or inconsistent with previous information were measured. Experiment 1 assessed inference generation in long and short scientific passages, presenting target sentences immediately after their explanatory antecedent. In Experiment 2, intervening sentences between target sentence and its explanatory antecedent were manipulated. Results indicated better detection of inconsistencies when presented immediately after their explanatory contexts. When explanatory contexts shifted, integration of consequents into an explanation was diminished, impairing the construction of a coherent representation.

Arousal and music preference: Does the body move the soul?

Schäfer, Thomas *Department of Psychology, Chemnitz University of Technol, Chemnitz, Germany* **Sedlmeier, Peter** *Department of Psychology, Chemnitz University of Technol, Chemnitz, Germany*

People often report feelings of subjective arousal when listening to their preferred music. Can this subjective impression be related to objective physiological measures? And if so, does preference induce arousal or is the reverse true? In a first study, we found that when listening to music, preference and physiological arousal (e.g., heart rate, skin conductance) are indeed highly correlated. In a second study we manipulated arousal and found strong effects on preference: for the same piece of unknown music, higher arousal yielded higher preference ratings. The results indicate that arousal might be a potent determinant of the strength of music preference.

The impact of persons' hierarchical level and on-the-job experience on skill at detecting deception

Scharmach, Martin *Social Psychology, University of Mannheim, Mannheim, Germany* **Reinhard, Marc-André** *Social Psychology, University of Mannheim, Mannheim, Germany* **Müller, Patrick** *Social and Organizational Psyc, Utrecht University, Utrecht, Netherlands*

In an internet study the impact of persons' hierarchical level and on-the-job experience on skill at detecting deception was examined. Participants judged the veracity of 14 video recordings of stimulus persons in job interviews. Half of the stimulus persons had given accounts of their actual most recent job, the other half had been instructed to report on a bogus job. In line with studies showing no effect of expertise on skill at detecting deception, we found no relationship between hierarchical level and on-the-job experience and accuracy of veracity judgments.

Persistence in the face of failure: Positive and negative effects of neuroticism

Schelske, Stefan *Universität Greifswald, Greifswald, Germany*

Previous research on persistence in a failing course of action found only small effects of neuroticism. The present study was designed to investigate the contrary roles of neuroticism in dysfunctional persistence depending on situational factors. 91 participants were randomly assigned to a good chance and a bad chance situation and tested for persistence at an insoluble task. A 2 (neuroticism) x 2 (situation) ANOVA revealed a significant main effect of situation and a significant interaction effect. In summary, participants high in neuroticism, compared to low ones, show low persistence in good chance but high persistence in bad chance situations.

Contralesional crossing over in chronic neglect reveals disregard of the ipsilesional hemispace

Schmidt, Michaela *Inst. für Medizin. Psychologie, Universität Madgeburg, Magdeburg, Germany* **Guenther, Tobias** *University of Magdeburg, Inst. of Medical Psychology, Magdeburg, Germany* **Sabel, Bernhard A.** *University of Magdeburg, Inst. of Medical Psychology, Magdeburg, Germany* **Gall, Carolin** *University of Magdeburg, Inst. of Medical Psychology, Magdeburg, Germany*

Paradoxically, neglect patients frequently bisect short horizontal lines (2–2.5 cm) to the left of the objective midpoint crossing over towards the otherwise neglected space. 53 patients with chronic hemispatial neglect performed bisection of long lines (30 cm) combined with recording of eye-fixation. Crossing over was observed in 6 patients. Patients with crossing over spent more time fixating to the left of the objective midpoint of the line (M=69.4%, SE=4.9) than to the right (M=30.6%,

SE=4.9), t=3.9, p<.01, revealing a disregard of the ipsilesional hemispace. Crossing over of long lines is supposed to be a frequent phenomenon in chronic neglect.

Existential indifference: Attributes of a new category of meaning in life

Schnell, Tatjana Inst. für Psychologie, Universität Innsbruck, Innsbruck, Austria

With the advance of Positive Psychology, the experience of meaningfulness has gained much attention. Its absence is usually equalled with a crisis of meaning (CoM). Empirical research reveals that a high percentage of people neither experience meaningfulness, nor suffer from a CoM. In a representative German sample, this subsample– named 'existentially indifferent'–made up 35% of the population. Results of a study applying the NEO-PI-R, HSWBS, and SoMe in a student sample (N=135) show the existentially indifferent to be clearly distinguishable from people with high meaningfulness and CoM, respectively, as regards sources of meaning, well-being/satisfaction with life, and personality traits.

Evaluation of a training program for children with developmental constructional disorders: Preliminary results

Schroeder, Anne Inst. für Psychologie, Werner Otto Institut, Hamburg, Germany *Probst, Paul* Psychology, University of Hamurg, Hamburg, Germany

Visual-constructional disorders are discussed in context of different developmental disorders. A modular training program was developed to improve visual spatial abilities such as spatial perception, imagery, construction, and orientation, focusing individual metacognitive skills. 14 children aged 5 to10 years with severe constructional disorders and an IQ higher than 70, participate in the training for 20 hours on average. Data are collected at 5 time points in a fixed schedule before and after training. Effect sizes and long term effects will be assessed. Preliminary analysis showed high effect sizes. First results of the pilot study are presented.

Young people and self-growth: The ontopsychological residence

Schutel, Soraya FOIL, Brazil, Sao Paulo, Brazil *Bernabei, Barbara* A.E.O., Rome, Italy

The work will describe: a) the socio-psychological analysis on the results to train young persons to be aware of their inclinations, ambitions, limits and potential; b)the residence methodology by ontopsychology. In particular, the five indicators of verification: 1)psychological analysis of the subject; 2) environment: an ecologically healthy, simple, culturally humanistic place for serene conviviality; 3) the close participation of the professional psychologist; 4) ecological conviviality; 5) to individuate subject's specificity, according to the form of her/his ontic in-itself. Results will be discussed through case studies from Germany and Brazil.

Predicting preschool behavior problems by parenting style: Sense of parenting satisfaction and efficacy

Sebre, Sandra Psychology, University of Latvia, Riga, Latvia *Skreitule-Pikše, Inga* Psychology, University of Latvia, Riga, Latvia *Miltuze, Anika*

This study examined associations between factors predictive of preschool children's behavior problems. Mothers and fathers of 210 preschool children completed questionnaires concerning their child's externalizing and internalizing problems, their parenting style, sense of satisfaction, efficacy and overall parenting competence. Most prominent effects were found in regard to preschoolers' aggressive behavior, which was predicted by lower levels of parenting satisfaction, and higher levels of

guilt-inducing psychological control, behavioral control and physical punishment. Preschoolers' mean aggression scores in Latvia were found to be higher than in the United States. These results imply an accelerated need for additional preventive, educational parent training programs.

Tolerance to bullying and the bullying tactics: Differences between Korean and British workers

Seo, Yoo-Jeong Nadine Lenton & Wortley Hall, University of Nottingham, Nottingham, United Kingdom

Objectives: The study aimed to compare Korean and British workers' degrees of tolerance towards bullying and to investigate whether the kind of bullying tactics used in the UK are also used in Korea. Methods: Survey design was used. 93 employees completed a questionnaire developed by the author. ANOVA was employed. Results: Koreans, particularly males, showed greater tolerance towards negative acts and were more likely to respond that the listed bullying acts would never occur around them. Conclusions: Cultural differences were found in the attitudes towards bullying. To investigate bullying in Korea, a new questionnaire should be developed with different items.

Fostering reading comprehension in English and German through peer-assisted learning strategies

Seuring, Vanessa Pädagogische Psychologie, Universität Gießen, Gießen, Germany *Schünemann, Nina* Pädagogische Psychologie, Universität Gießen, Gießen, Germany *Spörer, Nadine* Pädagogische Psychologie, Universität Gießen, Gießen, Germany

This study investigated how the reading comprehension of 7th-grade German students can be improved through peer-assisted learning strategies (High school PALS). The sample consisted of 74 students who were assigned either to one of three conditions: (a) PALS in German, (b) PALS in English (which was a foreign language) or (c) control condition. Training success was assessed with standardized and experimenter-developed tests. At posttest and at maintenance only students of the German PALS condition attained higher scores on measures of reading comprehension and strategy knowledge than control students. Modifications are discussed to foster the effectiveness of PALS in a foreign language.

Relationship between perceived childhood attachment and adult attachment and its relationship with attachment to God

Shahabizadeh, Fatemeh Birjand Branch, Islamic Azad University, Korasan-Kashmar, Islamic Republic of Iran *Sepahmansour, Mojgan* psychology, Azad university,central tehra, tehran, Islamic Republic of Iran *Koshnevis, Elahe* psychology, Azad university,central tehra, tehran, Islamic Republic of Iran *Ahady, Hasan* psychology, Allame Tabataba'ee University, Khorasan Razavy-Kashmar, Islamic Republic of Iran

To examine relationship between perceived childhood attachment and adult attachment and role played by adult attachment and childhood attachment quality in Muslim subjects' reported attachment to God, 193 students of high school in Iran completed questionnaires measuring childhood attachment, Adult Attachment, and attachment to God.. results showed insecure attachment to parents was positively related to insecure adult attachment and insecure adult attachment positively related to insecure attachment to God. results showed if adult attachment was insecure, secure respondents to parents had secure attachment to God. if student had secure adult attachment, insecure students to parent reported secure attachment to God.

The measurement of organizational culture: An explorative study in Mainland, China

Shi, Wei LHR, Renmin University of China, Beijing, People's Republic of China

This study uses the research methods of Delphi Technique,factor analysis and so on to look for a set of culture measuring instrument which suits the Chinese actual situation, and is convenient for the operation. The results demonstrate the organizational culture includes 4 levels, 11 dimensions and 67 items. Social level includes these dimensions: The customer-oriented, the enterprise character; organizational level includes: Strategic system, organization atmosphere, organization composition of forces, cultural approval; the group level includes: The innovation and changes, team cooperation; and individual level includes: staff development, the salary rewards and punishment, and leader behavior.

Effect of peer supervising on training of normal school students' counseling skill

Shi, Lijun School of Teacher Education, Zhejiang Normal University, Zhejiang Jinhua, People's Republic of China

Objectives: To investigate whether the practice model of peer supervising may play a role in the development of students' counseling skill. Method: 60 sophomores of department of psychology, zhejiang normal university, took part in this study, with 30 under the peer supervising group and 30 as control group undertaking the teaching-practice training. Field study and involvement observation methods were employed. The data were analyzed with a one-way ANOVA. Results: Compared to ordinary training model, Peer supervising has a significant influence on consultants' case conceptual and self-observation skill level; a big difference between cases' evaluation about the two types of consultants.

Memory and recognition of vocal quality

Shigeno, Sumi Psychology, Aoyama Gakuin University, Tokyo, Japan

Vocal quality of several speakers who speak sentences in their native and foreign language was investigate. The speakers were Japanese and Americans. They uttered several sentences in both Japanese and American English. The results indicate that the memory of vocal quality was rather rubust and could be retained for several weeks. The results further indicate that the memory of vocal quality was dependent on the spoken languages.

Description of Iranian elite soccer players' motivational traits

Shojaei, Masoumeh School of Physical Education, Al-Zahra University, Tehran, Islamic Republic of Iran *Danesh Far, Afkham* School of physical education, Al-Zahra University, Tehran, Islamic Republic of Iran

The purpose of this study was to describe Iranian elite male soccer players' motivational characteristics. 61 soccer players of senior, youth under 19 and under 23 years old national teams completed the sports attitude inventory. The data were analyzed by descriptive statistics. On the basis of results, the elite players' motivation to achieve success was twice as much their motivation to avoid failure. Moreover, senior national team players and midfielders had more competitive motivation than other players. The fact indicated a tendency to be more sensitive to what adults thought than the younger players.

Effects of observational and mental practice on learning of serve volleyball

Shojaei, Masoumeh School of Physical Education, Al-Zahra University, Tehran, Islamic Republic of Iran *Danesh Far, Afkham* School of physical education, Al-Zahra University, Tehran, Islamic Republic of Iran

The purpose of the present study was the comparison of the effect of modeling and imagery on learning of volleyball simple serve. 48 novice female students were randomly selected and matched in 4 groups (control, modeling, internal and external imagery). Data of performance were analyzed by 4*4 ANOVA with repeated measures of test factor. Results indicated that the performance of modeling group and after that internal imagery were significantly better than external imagery and control groups in last retention and transfer tests. These findings suggest that modeling is more effective than imagery for learning a disceret motor skill.

The effect of age on motivational traits of Iranian elite soccer players
Shojaei, Masoumeh School of Physical Education, Al-Zahra University, Tehran, Islamic Republic of Iran
Danesh Far, Afkham School of physical education, Al-Zahra University, Tehran, Islamic Republic of Iran
The purpose of this study was to investigate the effect of age on their competitive motivation. 60 soccer players of senior, youth U-19 and U-23 national teams completed the sports attitude inventory. The data analyzed by MANOVA. The statistical analysis indicated the players of senior national team were significantly more motivated to avoid failure than youth U 19 national team players. The fact indicated that those players may have had a tendency to be more sensitive to what adults thought than the younger players.

Modulating the right visual field advantage in reading: A study in children and adults
Siéroff, Eric Institut de Psychologie, Université Paris Descartes, Boulogne-Billancourt, France Riva, Miléna Institut de Psychologie, Université Paris Descartes, Boulogne-Billancourt, France Régnier, Angélique Institut de Psychologie, Université Paris Descartes, Boulogne-Billancourt, France
Identification of parafoveal words was investigated in 6- to 10-year-olds and in adults. The classical right visual field advantage (RVFA) was equivalent in different groups when words were presented unilaterally. When distracters were simultaneously presented with words (in opposite visual fields), performance decreased in children more than in adults, showing a stronger capture of attention by irrelevant information in children. Finally, when words were bilaterally presented (one in each visual field), inducing a left-to-right strategy of report, performance was symmetrical in adults, but showed a RVFA in children (as with unilateral displays), suggesting less efficient endogenous orienting of attention.

Development of a Portuguese self-efficacy measure of Holland's vocational personality types
Silva, José Faculty of Psychology, Universidade de Coimbra, Coimbra, Portugal
Social Cognitive Career Theory proposes that several cognitive constructs are implicated in the formation of career interests. Career self-efficacy is considered to be one of the most important predictors of a person's pattern of vocational preferences. The purpose of this study is to present the development of a Portuguese self-efficacy measure of six vocational personality types. A questionnaire containing 60 items was administered to a sample of 300 high school students. The validity and reliability of the scale scores was analysed and the results show that the measurements made have acceptable psychometric properties.

Assuming the identity of the drug-addict
Simache, Daniela Study and Survey, Nat. Agency f Supporting Youth, Bucharest, Romania
The research sets out to analyze the way in which drug addiction influences the psycho-social profile of personality. The research methods used were the interview, the associative-verbal experiment followed by introspection and the experiment of continuing a text, the dynamic-contextual calitative analysis and semnificativ statistical analysis. The research subjects were heroine users: 100 for the interview and 30 for the experiments. The results we obtained showed inside orientation, with negative connotation, of the user's image and his assuming the status and social role of a drug-addict. To conclude, heroine addiction leads to a process of characterized by self-stigmatization and self-exclusion.

How French social workers make their judgment about the necessity to admit somebody to a homeless shelter.
Simeone, Arnaud ISPEF, Université Lyon 2, Lyon, France Michalot, Thierry ISPEF, Université LYON 2, LYON, France
Objective : The research investigates how social workers take into count objective eligibility requirements, but also subjective elements, to judge about the necessity to admit somebody to a homeless shelter. This research is based on the Functional Theory of Cognition. Method : 40 French social workers evaluated the necessity to accept an applicant to a homeless shelter using five information : gender, lack of housing, perceived hygiene, perceived aggressiveness, perceived inebriation (2 x 2 x 2 x 2 x 2). Results : The results show 1) that the subjective elements are largely taken into consideration, and 2) that the objectively poorest applicants are also the least favourably evaluated.

Identifying the eligibility criteria used by French social workers to accept a person in a C.H.R.S (homeless shelter and social reintegration centre)
Simeone, Arnaud ISPEF, Université Lyon 2, Lyon, France Michalot, Thierry ISPEF, Université LYON 2, LYON, France
Objective: The research investigates what eligibility requirements (objective or not) social workers take into account to evaluate the necessity to admit somebody to a homeless shelter. It is based on the social representation theory. Method: This research is done with 150 students in their last year of social studies and 50 experienced professionals. The free association and the search for the central core method is used. Results: The results describe the central systems of the representation for the necessity of admission, as well as the peripheral ones of these representations. The opposition Objective- non operant / Subjective – operant criteria is central for these representations.

Children's drawings reveal the "mondus operandi "of family violence
Simopoulou, Agapi Nursery, University of Ioannina, Rethymno, Greece Zervoudaki, Eleni
This paper is part of a diachronic research which started the year 2005. Studied 270 cases of abused children, in ages 6 to 12, in the island of Crete. The aim was to explore the ways of violence in the families. Information's were taken from interviews with parents, friends, teachers and relatives. The main tool was children's drawings. "Family test", was used to analyze the drawings. Results are related with the seven main dimensions of family interaction: Emotional atmosphere, communication, boundaries, alliances, constancy and adaptation, family self efficiency. Also the Study showed that violence in these families has a strong relationship with cruelty experiences of parents. Key words: child abuse, Family focal evaluation, childish drawing

Mediating effect of employee empowerment on organizational factors of empowerment and organizational performance of service employees
Sison, Christina CLPA, DLS-College of St. Benilde, Manila, Philippines
This investigates the effect of employee empowerment on organizational empowerment and organizational performance. A multiple-part survey questionnaire was accomplished by 315 employees. Results revealed that both measures of employee empowerment partially mediate between empowering organization and organizational performance.

Shift work, stress, and employee well-being: A meta-analytic investigation.
Skowronski, Mark Business, McMaster University, Hamilton, Canada Baba, Vishwanath DeGroote School of Business, McMaster University, Hamilton, Canada
Objective: As 25% to 30% of North American workers work non-standard hours, the authors sought to summarize the existing literature of shift work's effects on employee well-being empirically. Methods: A meta-analysis (N=27190, 27 Studies) comparing shift workers and non-shift workers was conducted. Dependent variables included job satisfaction, commitment, turnover intention, and stress. Results: A small but significant reduction in well-being across studies exists for shift workers. These negative effects are stronger for employees working fixed as opposed to rotating shifts which is counter-intuitive. Conclusion: Although shift workers report more stress and negative attitudes than non-shift workers, the effect is small and moderated by the stability of work patterns.

Received social support in relation to job search behaviour
Slebarska, Katarzyna Inst. of Psychology, University of Silesia, Katowice, Poland
The main goal of this work was to investigate the relation between social support received by unemployed people and its influence on their job search behaviour. The study was conducted among German and Polish unemployed adults. We analysed the adequacy of received social support as an important moderator in the investigated relation. The conclusions of the study are based on the hypothesis that individuals receiving more adequate support from others might be more active in searching for employment. The study also shows, when given support could decrease one's tendency to search for a job.

The impact of parenting on self-esteem, self-efficacy, homesickness and adjustment to college
Smith, Gregory Dept. of Psychology, Dickinson College, Carlisle, USA
Three months before starting college assessments of parenting styles, self-esteem, and self-efficacy were made on 203 students and their parents. After starting college, homesickness and college adjustment were assessed. Authoritative parenting related to higher self-esteem and self-efficacy, less homesickness, and better emotional and behavioural adjustment to college. Authoritarian parenting had an opposite effect. Five months later students were re-tested on homesickness and adjustment to college. Differences in homesickness and emotional adjustment, but not behavioural adjustment, persisted. Further analysis suggested that parenting impacted self-esteem and self-efficacy. Those variables then affected homesickness and college adjustment.

The moderating effect of situational strength on the relationship between personality traits and counterproductive work behavior

Smithikrai, Chuchai *Dept. of Psychology, Chiang Mai University, Chiang Mai, Thailand*

This study investigated the extent to which the strength of situations moderates the relation between personality traits and counterproductive work behavior (CWB). It was hypothesized that the relations between personality traits and CWB would vary across strong and weak situations. In addition, there would be an interaction between conscientiousness and agreeableness in predicting CWB. As predicted, the results showed that the effect of personality on CWB depended on the strength of the situation. The result also indicated that, in a weak situation only, conscientiousness has a stronger, negative relation to CWB when agreeableness is high than when agreeableness is low.

Cognitive needs and predispositions in daily practice and preference for sports

Smits, Tim *Centre for Ethics, Katholieke Universiteit Leuven, Leuven, Belgium* **Pattyn, Bart** *Centre for Ethics, Katholieke Universiteit Leuven, Leuven, Belgium*

From a psychological perspective, the present study supplements the ongoing sociological research on cultural practices such as physical activity. Fitting a series of studies about cognitive needs (e.g., closure) and daily practices, we demonstrate that cognitive needs and interpersonal predispositions (e.g. essentialist beliefs, types of national identification) predict preferences about sports. Using questionnaire data collected among adolescents we focus on crucial preferences and attitudes: team versus solo, structured training and objective progression measures, regulations, ... We conclude that these attitudes and preferences moderate the relation between psychological variables and eventual preferences for sports as such.

Experimental evidence that the theory of planned behaviour does not explain behaviour change

Sniehotta, Falko *Aberdeen, United Kingdom*

This study aimed to test the TPB experimentally. Design: 2(behavioural-belief-intervention (BBI) or not)*2(normative-belief-intervention (NBI))*2(control-belief-intervention (CBI)) factorial. N=659 students were randomised to receive messages addressing salient beliefs. Primary outcome: objectively recorded attendance to university sports-facilities; secondary outcomes: post-intervention TPB. Main effects of the BBI on attitudes and of the NBI on subjective norm, PBC, attitudes and intentions were found. The CBI did not alter post-intervention cognitions, but was the only intervention to change behaviour (F(1,564=4.980; p=.026; eta2=.009) not mediated by cognitions. While the findings support the TPB's assumptions on intention formation, behaviour change results are not in line with the TPB.

A profile of mental health care users presenting at hospitals in Limpopo Province (South Africa)

Sodi, Tholene *Dept. of Psychology, University of Venda, Thohoyandou, South Africa*

Objective The aim of the study was to investigate the characteristics of assisted and involuntary mental health care users (MHCUs) presenting at various hospitals in one health district in Limpopo Province (South Africa). Method Using the archival method, the authors accessed and studied over 800 files submitted to Capricorn Mental Health Review Board by various health establishments in Limpopo Province. Results More than 60 percent of the MHCUs were males who were in the age category of 20 to 30 years. Most of the MHCUs were given the diagnosis of schizophrenia and related psychotic conditions. Conclusion The limitations associated with archival method are highlighted.

Determinants of perceptions of poverty in Turkey

Solak, Nevin *Social Psychology, Ege University, Yzmir, Turkey* **Göregenli, Melek** *Social Psychology, Ege University, Yzmir, Turkey*

The aim of this study was to investigate relationships among causal attributions for poverty, perceived socioeconomic status, sociopolitical ideologies (as measured by the Economic System Justification, Personal Belief in a Just World and Group-Based Dominance Scales) and attitudinal support for poverty policies. In our student sample (N = 592), perception of the causes of poverty was found to be more structural than individualistic and fatalistic. Structural equation modeling results showed that sociopolitical ideologies mediated the relationships of the perceived socioeconomic status and attributions for poverty. In addition, higher individualistic attributions for poverty and economic system justification predicted decreased attitudinal support for poverty policies.

An inductive study on the innovative corporate culture in the P. R. China

Song, Jiwen Lynda *School of Business, Renmin University, Beijing, People's Republic of China* **Zhang, Kai** *School of Business, Renmin University of China, Beijing, People's Republic of China* **Zhu, Chaowei** *School of Business, Renmin University of China, Beijing, People's Republic of China*

The present study applied Denison and Mishra's framework of corporate culture to the study of innovative corporate culture in the P. R. China. In an inductive study, 30 out of 48 MBA students in PRC were invited to write out characteristics of innovative corporate culture in accordance with our definition. The sorting results based on 224 entries showed that China's innovative corporate culture includes four major dimensions: innovation adaptability, innovation goals and vision, innovative atmosphere, and incentive systems. The study may lay a foundation for future theory development of innovative corporate culture and corresponding measure validation (Supported By RUC Research Grant 2006031751).

The characteristics of subject well-being of LIUSHOU children and its relation with social support

Song, Shujuan *School of Psychology, Huazhong Normal University, Wuhan, People's Republic of China* **Liu, Huashan** *School of Psychology, Huazhong Normal University, Wuhan, People's Republic of China* **Chen, Xuelian** *School of Psychology, Huazhong Normal University, Wuhan, People's Republic of China*

To explore the characteristics of subject well-being (SWB) of LIUSHOU children in China who are cared by people other than parents as their parents chronically worked away from home and its relation with social support. 264 LIUSHOU middle school children and 279 non- LIUSHOUers children were investigated with SWB Scale and Social Support Questionnaire. SWB of LIUSHOU children was lower than non- LIUSHOUers, but there was no significant difference. SWB of LIUSHOU girls was significantly lower than that of LIUSHOU boys. Subjective support and support utilization were significantly positive predictors for well-being. Comparatively, the LIUSHOUers with higher-level social support reported more happiness.

Inertia to change?: The moderating role of traditionality on the relationship between CEO leadership styles and middle manager responses

Song, Jiwen Lynda *School of Business, Renmin University, Beijing, People's Republic of China* **Tsui, Anne S.** *W.P. Carey School of Business, Arizon State University, Arizona, USA* **Liu, Jun** *School of Business, Renmin University of China, Beijing, People's Republic of China* **Wang, Yang** *Engineering Department, Nortel Comm Engineering Ltd., Beijing, People's Republic of China*

This study investigates how middle managers' cultural value of traditionality acts as the inertia to change in response to CEO's leadership styles of risk-taking and benevolence-showing. The moderating role of traditionality is examined in 45 Chinese firms using a series of Hierarchical Linear Modeling analyses. Contrasting the rule of social exchange, we find that traditional middle managers have a low level of affective commitment and high intention of turnover when CEOs are risk-taking. Traditional middle managers also exhibit a low level of task performance and OCB when they are led by benevolent CEOs. (Project supported by NSFC 70702024)

The comparison of 3 types of therapy in major depression

Sotodeh, Namat *Psychology, Isfahan University, Isfahan, Islamic Republic of Iran* **Behnam, Behnaz** *psychiatrist, semnan university, semnan, Islamic Republic of Iran*

The purpose of this study was to determine the effect of cognitive, Drug and combine therapy in major depression treatment. In this experimental study, we study 56 depressed patients in available sampling that admitted in Psychiatric wards in Semnan University in Iran. The patients were assignment groups randomly. The tools in this study were the BECK and a demographic questionnaire. We completed beck questionnaire for all groups in pretest. Then we intervention. 1 month after, post test was completed. Results showed that combine therapy was more effective in male. Cognitive therapy and drug therapy was statistically significant in Experimental groups (P= 0.001). Drug therapy was better on females and Cognitive Psychotherapy on male.

Efficacy of cognitive therapy vs. interpersonal psychotherapy in the treatment of social phobia.

Stangier, Ulrich *Psychology, University of Jena, Jena, Germany* **Heidenreich, Thomas** *Soziale Arbeit, Gesundheit, Fachhochschule Esslingen, Esslingen, Germany* **Schramm, Elisabeth** *Psychiatry, University of Freiburg, Freiburg, Germany* **Berger, Matthias** *Psychiatry, University of Freiburg, Freiburg, Germany* **Clark, David M.** *Psychology, Institute of Psychiatry, London, United Kingdom*

Cognitive therapy for social phobia is an efficacious treatment for social phobia. In addition, Interpersonal Psychotherapy has proven to be an effective treatment of depression and might be a promising alternative. The efficacy of both treatment approaches was compared in a randomized controlled trial. 121 patients meeting DSM IV criteria for social phobia were randomly allocated to Cognitive Therapy, Interpersonal Psychotherapy, or waiting list control group. At post-treatment, both treatments archieved significantly better results in all outcome variables than WCL. With respect to clinician-rated social phobic symptoms, CT was significantly superior to IPT at post-test and at 1 year follow-up.

Regulatory focus and strategy use in professional goal setting and planning

Steidle, Anna *Inst. für Psychologie, Techn. Universität Chemnitz, Chemnitz, Germany* **Werth, Lioba** *Department of Psychology, Chemnitz Uni. of Technology, Chemnitz, Germany*

In order to clarify the relation between self-regulation strategies (Higgins, 1997) and motivational skills in planning professional goals, we examined how employees set and planned their professional goals depending on their regulatory focus. Growth-oriented promotion-focused employees used more strategies during goal agreement (e.g. set more ambitious goals) than duty-oriented prevention-focused employees. During goal planning, promotion-focused employees concentrated more on focus-compatible approach strategies and less on focus-incompatible prevention strategies than prevention-focused employees. Implications concerning soft skills such as employees' self-management within organizations, management by objectives, leadership, and self-management training are discussed. Higgins, E. T. (1997). Beyond pleasure and pain. American Psychologist, 52, 1280-1300.

Possibilities and obstacles of moral education in school as a field of educational and school psychology: Results from a survey of heads of secondary schools in Bavaria/Germany

Stein, Margit Lehrstuhl für Sozialpädagogik, Kathol. Universität Eichstätt, Eichstätt, Germany

Schools are obliged not only to help pupils to build up academic competencies but also to develop and form a stable value system. Within the value project a value questionnaire for educational goals in schools was formed basing on the PVQ (Portrait Values Questionnaire) of Shalom Schwartz. On the basis of a representative sample 576 secondary schools in Bavaria answered to the value questionnaire for educational goals and also reported about their projects within the domain of moral education. The educational goals and experiences with moral education were correlated with the school's problems with violence, school life, and moral training for teachers. Within the next year an international perspective is planned. The survey will also be carried out in Poland.

Parents' verbal comments in relation to their child's diagnosis and language level: Comparing children with Down syndrome, autism and typical development

Strid, Karin Dept. of Psychology, Göteborg University, Göteborg, Sweden Tjus, Tomas Department of Psychology, Göteborg University, Göteborg, Sweden Heimann, Mikael Dept. of Behavioural Science, Linköping University, Linköping, Sweden

Parents' verbal comments were investigated during a free play situation with their child: whether the comments were synchronized or unsynchronized with their child's' focus of attention. Three groups of children were compared: Down syndrome (DS), autism and typical development (TD). Parents of children with autism used fewer synchronized comments than the other two groups, and DS parents used more unsynchronized comments compared to TD parents. Furthermore, the language level of the child had an impact on type of parent's comments when comparing the different groups. Results are discussed in terms of individual differences between children with the same diagnosis.

Who's able to disengage from blocked goals? The role of core self-evaluations in goal self regulation

Stumpp, Thorsten Organizational Psychology, University of Bielefeld, Bielefeld, Germany Maier, Günter W. Organizational Psychology, University of Bielefeld, Bielefeld, Germany

It is most important for well-being to experience favourable situational resources for attaining one's goals. The purpose of this study was to investigate the role of core self-evaluations (CSE) in the disengagement process of unattainable personal goals. At the end of the final year at school, 141 job newcomers provided a list of three personal work and leisure goals. Goal commitment, attainability and CSE were assessed. Longitudinal results revealed that persons with high core self-evaluations disengaged from low attainable goals whereas individuals with low core self-evaluations strengthened their goal commitment for blocked goals. Thus core self-regulations supports self regulatory competence.

Preliminary construction of the mental health scale with an adaptive orientation for secondary school students

Su, Dan School of Psychology, Southwest University, Beibei, Chongqing, People's Republic of China Huang, Xiting School of Psychology, Southwest University, Beibei, Chongqing, People's Republic of China

Dan Su, Xiting Huang School of Psychology, Southwest University, Chongqing, China AB-STRACT Objectives: Construct a scale with an adaptive orientation, which can effectively assess secondary school students' mental health. Methods: Following an open-question survey, the initial version of Mental Health Scale for Secondary School Students (MHS-SSS) was established, 1,567 students participated in the test of the initial scale. Items of the final scale were determined by item analysis and exploratory factor analysis. Results: Secondary school students' mental health includes five dimensions: Life well-being, Study satisfaction, Interpersonal harmony, Exam calmness, Emotional stability. Conclusions: The MHS-SSS is a valid and reliable assessment for secondary school students' mental health.

The role of sense-of-identity and fact-of-identity in predicting organisational performance

Sugreen, Gulshan The Human Concept, Johannesburg, South Africa Van Tonder, Christian Louis Industrial Psychology, University of Johannesburg, Johannesburg, South Africa

The principal objective of the study was to examine the role of organisation identity and more specifically the constructs of organisational Sense-of-Identity and Fact-of-Identity, in predicting organisational performance, as measured by the Performance Index (PI). Factor analysis of data obtained from 265 respondents, representing three companies, yielded several key factors with strong reliabilities. Correlational analyses revealed strong relations between the more subjective Sense-of-Identity and the more "objective" Fact-of-identity factors on the one hand and organisational performance on the other. Regression analyses further conveyed the strong predictive capability of these identity constructs and underscored their importance and meaningfulness in organisational settings.

A cross-cultural study of personality traits in 4- and 5-year-old children between China and Australia

Sun, Xiaojie Intern. Business Communication, Dongbei University, Dalian, People's Republic of China Lizhu, Yang Department of Psychology, Liaoning Normal University, Dalian, People's Republic of China

This cross-cultural study examines the impact of different cultures upon child personality formation. Using Child Personality Teachers' Assessment Questionnaire and employing collectivism/individualism theory, 4- and 5- year-old children from China and Australia participated in the study. Result of multivariate analysis indicates that the personality characteristics of Chinese children are in agreement with collectivism, while those of Australian children are in agreement with individualism. Findings highlight the influence of cultural values upon child personality formation. Keywords: culture, collectivism/individualism, child personality

Organizational culture and organizational development: A Chinese case study

Sun, Hechuan RIEEA, Shenyang Normal University, Shenyang, People's Republic of China

Organizational culture plays a powerful role in changing organizations. It is the cultural change that supports the teaching-learning process which leads to enhanced outcomes for students. The importance of organizational culture and in parti-

cular a school's guiding value system is enabling change and enhancing educational provision. Inevitably, understanding organizational culture is a crucial factor in both transforming an organizational culture and reconstructing it. A case study will be presented. It focused on the relationship between organizational culture and its behavior and development. Two universities in China were closely observed and compared for more than three years.

The personality features of Chinese students in Japan

Sun, Yi Psychology Department, Ochanomizu University, Tokyo, Japan

To clarify the personality features of Chinese students in Japan, the study compared 4 groups of Chinese students (17-23 yrs, A: local Chinese without will to study abroad; B: local Chinese with will to study abroad; C: Chinese staying in Japan ≤1y; D: Chinese in Japan >1y) using Temperament & Characteristic Inventory. By one-way ANOVA, the results showed Group-D had significant higher Persistence than Group-B and lower Cooperativeness than the other three; Group-C and Group-D had higher Persistence than Group-A, and higher Novelty-Seeking than the other two, significantly. The characteristics are original attribution or production of acculturation was discussed.

Research on attribution bias in listed companies' annual reports in China

Sun, Manli Business School, Renmin University of China, Beijing, People's Republic of China Zhou, Ting business school, Renmin University of China, beijing, People's Republic of China

we test whether performance attribution bias exists in Chinese listed companies' annual reports. We selected companies from 6 industries which have been affected greatly by environment changes for the year 2004 and 2005. Further, we test if the attribution behavior could explain the future stock price trend. T-test and multivariate regression analysis are employed in the paper. We find that, companies with excellent performance tend to attribute the success to the management, while companies with poor performances are more likely to lay blames on environment. Only internal attribution has a positive correlation with stock price, which indicates that investors are not misled by external attribution bias.

Transfer into a new culture and cultural identity Kazuyo Suzuki (Saitama Gakuen University, Kawaguchi, Japan)

Suzuki, Kazuyo Humanities, Saitama Gakueu University, Kawaguchi, Japan

This study aims to clarify a process of identity formation of interculturally married women living in a new culture. The subjects are 16 middle-aged Japanese women married to Indonesian men living in Bali. Repeated interviews were carried out during 1991-2006. It is inferred that identity crisis brought by a cultural contact reaches reintegration through psychological moratorium, and that the identity formed while living in Japan is spirally reconstructed at each cultural contact. Furthermore, the mechanism of "wavering" of cultural identity between Japanese and Indonesian (Balinese) culture is hypothetically illustrated by relationship between two cultures with time.

Exploitation of child worker: Social problem issue in Pekanbaru, Riau, Indonesia

Syarifah, Farradinna Pekanbaru-Riau, Riau, Indonesia

Many children work in Indonesia, they work with dangerous tools. The aims of this study were to show exploitation of child worker as a social problems issue in Pekanbaru, Riau, Indonesia. Child worker entails strong potential for exploitation and abuse, harsh working condition and deprivation of rights. This study were designed as observation type and the data collection were involved a set of questionnaire and interview to child worker between ages twelve-sixteen years old. As a conclusion, the higher level of exploitation of child worker happened to girls, less education to children, high potential exploitation and abuse.

Goal orientation predicts professional burden

Tönjes, Britt *Psychologie und Sport, Universität Erlangen-Nürnberg, Nürnberg, Germany* **Dickhäuser, Oliver** *Psychology and Sports, Univ. Erlangen-Nürnberg, Nuremberg, Germany* **Kröner, Stephan** *Psychology and Sports, Univ. Erlangen-Nürnberg, Nuremberg, Germany*

We examined whether goal orientations according to Dweck (1986) and Harackiewiecz (2002) relate to teachers' professional burden. In a first cross-sectional study (N = 84 teachers) learning goal orientation was negatively related and performance avoidance orientation was positively related with the dimensions of Maslachs burnout inventory. A second longitudinal study (N = 101 teachers) demonstrated that the direction of this relation is rather from goal orientation to burnout than other way round. We discuss that goal orientations should be examined more intensively in the explanation of burnout.

Antecedents of person-job fit and its relation to turnover intentions: Based on a sample of newcomers

Tak, Jin-Kook *Dept. of Industrial Psyclogy, Kwangwoon University, Seoul, Republic of Korea*

This study was intended to examine the relations of a person-job fit to three antecedent variables and turnover intentions. Three antecedent variables such as realistic job preview, career planning, and core self-evaluation were included. Using on-line survey, data were collected from 901 newcomers who had been in the organization less than 6 months. AMOS was used to test the causal model. Various fit indices showed that the model had the high fit to the data. Also, all the hypotheses were supported. Three antecedent variables directly influenced person-job fit, which directly influenced turnover intentions. Realistic job preview also directly influenced turnover intentions.

Life-patterns of Japanese in the 2000s VI: Effectiveness of the scale of Inappropriate leadership behaviors

Takahara, Ryuji *International Economy & Work, Osaka, Japan* **Yamashita, Miyako** *the graduate school of humanit, Okayama University, Itami, HYOGO, Japan* **Kokubo, Midori** *Business Administration, Ritsumei University, Nara, Japan*

Many leadership theories applied to the work site use the amount of leadership behaviors as the assessment scale. However, if the leader's attempt to increase followers' certain behaviors fails or was misunderstood, behavior rating of the leader by the followers remains low. This may encourage the leader's inappropriate behavior. In this study, a scale for inappropriate leadership behavior was investigated. The results showed that improper leadership behaviors can be evaluated by another independent scale and the followers' satisfaction with the leader and enjoyment of work are affected not only by appropriate leadership behaviors but also by inappropriate ones.

Factors regulating citizen participation of community activities in Japan

Takahashi, Naoya *Inst. of Psychology, University of Tsukuba, Tsukuba, Japan*

In Japan, the importance of civil participation is argued. However, the lowness of interest for politics and society is pointed out. This study performed the survey for randomly sampled 600 adults in Musashino-city to examine factors regulating civil

participation for problem solution activity in community. Women, 40's, and having a schoolchild in one's family had high participation rate. Multiple discriminant analysis (discriminant rate 60.2%) indicated that participation was determined by the number of organizational affiliation in community. Intention to participate was promoted by communication with neighbors and profit for oneself or one's family brought by activity.

Gender harassment and achievement motivation in Japanese organizations

Tanaka, Kenichiro *Graduate School, Nihon University, Tokorozawa, Japan* **Kobayashi, Atsuko** *Graduate School, Nihon University, Tokorozawa, Saitama, Japan*

The present study examined the model in which egalitarian attitudes towards sex roles either facilitated, or did not facilitate the perception of gender harassment, and tested the relationship between the perception of harassment and the enhancement of achievement motivation in female victims. Respondents were 137 adult Japanese women working in public organizations in Saitama Prefecture. The results of hierarchal multiple regression analysis revealed that female workers who had an egalitarian attitude toward sex roles were apt to perceive gender harassment, and that women who did not perceive gender harassment were apt to enhance competitive achievement motivation.

Developmental trend and gender differences in inventive creativity among children and adolescents: A cross-sectional study from China

Tang, Min *Psychologie und Päd. Wiss., Universität München, München, Germany*

Inventive creativity (IC) as measured by Scientific Creativity Test for Children and Adolescents (SCTCA, Shen et. al., 2002) and an adapted version of Invent Iowa Evaluation Rubic (IIER, Colangelo et. al., 2000), was tested among 1109 participants (663 boys and 446 girls) of the "1st Inventive Creativity Contest for Children and Adolescents in China". Results revealed a significant increase of IC among the participants from the lower grades to the upper grades. Gender differences existed in originality dimension of creative problem solving ability and the quality of product improvement. The participants' academic ranking was found negatively related to their IC.

The good samaritan effect: Motives of helping behavior, the love of money, and culture

Tang, Thomas Li-Ping *Management and Marketing, Middle Tennessee St University, Murfreesboro, USA* **Sutarso, Toto** *Management and Marketing, Middle Tennessee St University, Murfreesboro, USA* **Davis, Grace Mei-Tzu Wu** *CEO, Eureka Globalization & Dev, 29160., USA* **Dolinski, Dariusz** *School of Social Psychology, Warsaw University, Wroclaw, Poland* **Ibrahim, Abdul Hamid Safwat** *Department of Psychology, Iman University, Riyadh, Saudi Arabia* **Wagner, Sharon L.** *Research and Analytics, Genentech, Inc., South San Francisco, CA, USA*

We test a model of employee helping behavior (a component of Organizational Citizenship Behavior) with a direct path (Intrinsic Motives ? Helping Behavior, the Good Samaritan Effect) and an indirect path (the Love of Money ? Extrinsic Motives ? Helping Behavior). Results supported the Good Samaritan Effect. Further, the love of money was positively related to extrinsic motives that were negatively related to helping behavior. We test the model across four cultures (the USA, Taiwan, Poland, and Egypt). The Good Samaritan Effect was significant. The love of money may cause one to help in one culture (Poland) but not to help in others.

Corporate entrepreneurship change management process model and it's effectiveness validation

Tang, Suping *School of Management, Zhejiang University, Hangzhou, People's Republic of China* **Zhongming, Wang** *college of management, Zhejiang University. China, Hangzhou, People's Republic of China*

This is a field study of corporate entrepreneurial transition using contextual embedded study. A transformation time framework of corporate entrepreneurial transition is put forward based on the above proven relationship and prior theories on transformation time framework. Action research is conducted in a real estate company. Based on the comparison of change management process and effectiveness of Lenovo, Litie, Jincheng Groups, the time framework adapting with transition features of Chinese enterprises is developed. Meanwhile, some problems are found in the transition process of Chinese enterprises, and this time framework is significant for guiding the entrepreneurial transition of Chinese enterprises.

Big Five Model in relation to the circumplex structure of the Holland Model

Tarnai, Christian *Fakultät für Pädagogik, Universität der Bundeswehr, Neubiberg, Germany* **Langmeyer, Alexandra** *Fakultät für Pädagogik, Universität der Bundeswehr Mün, Neubiberg, Germany* **Guglhör-Rudan, Angelika** *Fakultät für Pädagogik, Universität der Bundeswehr Mün, Neubiberg, Germany*

Based on the theory of Holland (1997), the structure of a person's interests can be described by six orientations, which are arranged in a hexagon. The current study examined the relation between the Holland Model and the Big Five Model in a sample of students from different fields of study at the Universität der Bundeswehr (N=600) using online versions of the AIST (Bergmann & Eder, 2005) and the NEO-PI-R (Ostendorf & Angleitner, 2004). The results show that the facet scales of the BigFive-Model can be integrated into the hexagonal structure of the Holland Model represented by a circumplex.

Understanding teacher professional identity in educational contexts

Tateo, Luca *Education Sciences, University of Salerno, Fisciano (SA), Italy* **Mollo, Monica** *Education Sciences, University of Salerno, Fisciano (SA), Italy* **Marsico, Giuseppina** *Education Sciences, University of Salerno, Fisciano (SA), Italy* **Iannaccone, Antonio** *Education Sciences, University of Salerno, Fisciano (SA), Italy*

The contribution presents a psico-social model in which personal biography, social representations, situated educational practices and relationships with significant Others are taken into account to understand teachers professional identity construction process. The results of 2 studies conducted by a research team (PRASSI and LEAD projects) of the University of Salerno with semi-structured narrative interviews on 2 groups of 43 and 53 Italian teachers will be presented. Such interesting results draw a model with respect to the teachers professional identity as an ongoing process throughout professional trajectory, involving personal biography, practices, artefacts, representations of teaching and organisational culture.

Mother's strategies for making new interaction with their first child after having second-born child

Terui, Yuko *Tokyo, Japan*

This study investigated that what mothers become awareness of changes of interactions with firstborn child after having second-born child and what they have as strategies for making interactions with firstborn children. Most mothers reported that was difficult for maintaining same interaction with first born child as before having second-child. In the case of reporting guilt feeling with first-born child for changing interactions with them, mothers' guilty related to a notion of equality between siblings. And purposeful bringing firstborn child into caretaking for second-born child which is one of mothers' strategies in their childrearing promoted new interactions mothers and firstborn children.

Causes of resistance to change at institutions of higher education

Tolkov, Olexandre *Organizational Psychology, Institute of Psychology, Kiev, Ukraine*
Objective: To determine causes of resistance to change at institutions of higher education. Methods: The research was done on 125 managers and employees at institutions of higher education using L.Karamushka Resistance to change questionnaire. Results: The most important causes of resistance to change included unclear work that required extra intellectual and emotional efforts (36.9%), unawareness of rewards produced by new activities (26.2%), misunderstanding of organizational importance of new activities (25.4%), and fear of losing prestige due to inability to do new work (21.3%). Conclusion: The findings can be used in making change at institutions of higher education.

Fault belief, aptitude, natural leadership and peer relations in preschool children

Tong, Jiajin *Dept. of Psychology, University of Peking, Beijing, People's Republic of China* **Wang, Lei** *Psychology, The Peking University, Beijing, People's Republic of China* **Man, Jing** *Educational Psychology, Beilei Kindergarten, Shenzhen, People's Republic of China* **Deng, Huijun** *Educational Psychology, Beilei Kindergarten, Shenzhen, People's Republic of China* **Sun, Xiaoxin** *Educational Psychology, Beilei Kindergarten, Shenzhen, People's Republic of China* **Shen, Ruina** *Educational Psychology, Beilei Kindergarten, Shenzhen, People's Republic of China* **Ren, Lihong** *Educational Psychology, Beilei Kindergarten, Shenzhen, People's Republic of China* **Yu, Li** *Educational Psychology, Peking University Kindergarten, Beijing, People's Republic of China* **Zhang, Ruifeng** *Educational Psychology, Beilei Kindergarten, Shenzhen, People's Republic of China*
The present research aimed to explore the relationship among fault belief, aptitude, natural leadership, and peer relations in preschool children. We surveyed 286 preschool children with researchers rating fault belief and aptitude of each children, and kindergarten teachers rating the natural leadership and peer relations. Regression analysis showed that natural leadership and aptitude predicted prosocial behaviors, while natural leadership, fault belief, and aptitude predicted the aggressive behaviors, shy, and asking for help behavior. We discussed the implications and applications of these findings on kindergarten education.

The efficacy of transactional analysis group therapy on marital satisfaction

Torkan, Hajar *Psychology, Isfahan University, Isfahan, Islamic Republic of Iran* **Tavakoli, Mahgol** *Psychology, Isfahan University, Isfahan, Islamic Republic of Iran*
Objective: Purpose of this study was to investigate the efficacy of Transactional Analysis group therapy on marital satisfaction. Method: 16 couples referred to 4 psychological clinics in Isfahan were randomly selected and assigned to the experimental and control group. Index of Marital Satisfaction was administered. Result: The results showed that the experimental group significantly measured higher on marital satisfaction both in the post-test and the follow-up than the control group did (P< 0.05). Conclusion: Instructions of Transactional Analysis increase communication, problem solving and emotional skills of couples and helping them for arriving at autonomy and being free from ineffective models of communication e.g. games

through a process of personal-interpersonal improvement.

Using clients' complaints as starting point for innovation - Predictions from the two-by-two model of complaining reactions

Traut-Mattausch, Eva *Inst. für Psychologie, Universität München, München, Germany* **Jonas, Eva** *Department of Psychology, University of Salzburg, Salzburg, Austria* **Frey, Dieter** *Department of Psychology, Ludwig-Maximilians-University, Munich, Germany*
Complaints often contain important information on how services can be improved. However, they are rarely used as a source for innovation. Based on Kruglanski's lay epistemic theory we developed a two-by-two model of reactions to complaints. According to our model, the type of reaction (open-minded, avoidant, insulting, or pacified) displayed when faced with a customer complaint depends on the existing motivation ("closure approach/avoidance", "high/low defense motivation"). Results of two studies in which we varied the closure motivation and the defense motivation of our participants in the laboratory and in the field show evidence for the predicted four reactions to complaints.

The source of sport confidence among secondary school athletes in Hong Kong

Tsang, Eric C. K. *Cape, HK Institute of Education, Tai Po, China, People's Republic of : Hong Kong SAR*
The aim of the present study was to examine the source of sport confidence among secondary cross-country athletes. Ninety four athletes (47 males and 47 females) with a mean age of 15.26 (S.D. = 1.87) completed the Sources of Sport-Confidence Questionnaire (SSCQ) after a major competition. It was found that athletes perceived that "social support" was the major source of sport confidence. Significant gender difference was observed that males perceived "demonstration of ability" as more important. Also, significant age differences were found that younger athletes perceived that "mastery" was more important, whereas, older athletes believed in "ability". The findings of this study allow coaches to develop confidence among young athletes.

Effects of anxiety and disposition to trust in others on attitudes and information exploring behaviors in risk communication

Tsuchida, Shoji *Dept. of Psychology, Kansai University, Osaka, Japan* **Tujikawa, Norifumi** *Psychology, Kansai University, Osaka, Japan* **Koike, Fumiyo** *Psychology, Kansai University, Osaka, Japan* **Tanigaki, Toshihiko** *Social Research, INSS, Fukui, Japan*
Effects of anxiety and disposition to trust in others on risk perception, and information exploring behaviors were examined. Three hundred and twenty-three individuals between 20 and 59 years old were randomly sampled and participated in an experiment. The participants watched a video putting fear of future insufficient energy supply into them or a video explaining energy supply with no fear, and then they explored a database of nuclear power. Participants' information exploring behaviors, risk perception of nuclear power, trust in people who made the video and the database, and disposition to trust in other persons were measured and analyzed.

Inhibitory function in stimulus-response compatibility task and aging

Tsuchida, Noriaki *Dept. of Psychology, Ritsumeikan University, Kyoto, Japan* **Yoshida, Hajime** *Psychology, Ritsumeikan University, Kyoto, Japan* **Okawa, Ichiro** *Psychology, University of Tsukuba, Tokyo, Japan* **Son, Kin** *Psychology, Ritsumeikan University, Kyoto, Japan* **Takahashi, Nobuko**

Psychology, Ritsumeikan University, Kyoto, Japan **Ishikawa, Mariko** *Psychology, Ritsumeikan University, Kyoto, Japan* **Miyata, Masako** *Psychology, Ritsumeikan University, Kyoto, Japan* **Sakaguchi, Yoshie** *Psychology, Ritsumeikan University, Kyoto, Japan* **Hakoiwa, Chiyoji** *Psychology, Ritsumeikan University, Kyoto, Japan* **Nakamura, Yoshiro** *Psychology, Ritsumeikan University, Kyoto, Japan* **Furuhashi, Keisuke** *Psychology, Fukuoka Prefectural University, Tagawa-city, Japan*
This study examined the effect of aging on location-based inhibitory function using Stimulus-Response Compatibility tasks. Stimulus-Response Compatibility tasks set up different compatibility conditions between a stimulus and response. In this study, we gave 50 young adults and 42 elderly adults color discrimination dual-tasks, and then analyzed the Stimulus-Response Compatibility effect. Our results showed that in the young adult group only, incorrect response rates and Stimulus-Response Compatibility effect both decreased under the dual task conditions. These results were discussed based on Goodale's theory on the relationship between inhibitory function and the two visual pathways.

Anxiety, interest and inference to others were influence the intent to transmit the risk information about nuclear power

Tsujikawa, Norihumi *Graduate School of Sociology, Kansai University, Osaka, Japan* **Tsuchida, Shoji** *Faculty of Sociology, Kansai University, Suita, Osaka, Japan* **Koike, Fumiyo** *Graduate School of Sociology, Kansai University, Suitashi, Osaka, Japan* **Tanigaki, Toshihiko** *Social awareness research, INSS, Mihama-cho, Mikatagun, Fukui, Japan* **Nagaoka, Yutaka** *Social awareness research, INSS, Mihama-cho, Mikata-gun, Fukui, Japan*
This study was examined that anxiety, interest and inference to others influenced the intent to transmit the risk information after risk communication about the Nuclear power. 323 individuals were randomly sampled and participated in the experiment. At the experiment, participants watched a video putting fear of future insufficient energy supply into them (experiment condition) or a video explaining energy supply with no fear (control condition), and then they explored a database of nuclear power which consisted of agreeable, opposite and neutral information. The results showed that participants whose anxiety and inference to others were high had the highest communicative intent about the agreeable information.

Personal control as a moderator of perceived organizational support on turnover intentions

Uysal Irak, Doruk *Psychology, Carleton University, Ottawa, Canada* **Mantler, Janet** *Psychology, Carleton University, Ottawa, Canada*
Employees who feel unsupported by their organization are more likely to quit; however, little is known about variables that moderate this association. Personal control is a buffer for people in stressful environments and may moderate the effect of perceived organizational support on turnover intentions. Based on surveys of 798 hospital nurses, consistent with past research, greater organizational support was associated with lower turnover intentions, but only for nurses with higher personal control. For nurses with lower personal control, organizational support did not affect turnover intention. Although it is commonly accepted that turnover should be lower in a supportive organization, individual differences moderate this association.

Some peculiarities of time perspective among students in Russia

Valieva, Faina *Dept. of Foreign Languages, State Polytech. University, St. Petersburg, Russia* **Panfilova, Anna** *Foreign Languages, Polytechnic University, St-Petersburg, Russia*

The focus of this paper is on construct of time perspective, which is viewed as an individual's way of relating to the psychological concepts of past, present and future. The aim of this work was to find out in what time perspective students from different cultural and regional backgrounds live and if their backgrounds influence their decision making ability and success. Another aspect that we were interested in was how time perspective of individuals from different cultural backgrounds may influence the process of communication. Our research was based on the sample of more than 500 students studying at Saint-Petersburg Universities.

The differential impact of positive and negative affectivity on affective organizational commitment

Vantilborgh, Tim Psychology and Education, Vrije Universiteit Brussel, Brussel, Belgium **Pepermans, Roland** *Psychology and Education, Vrije Universiteit Brussel, Brussel, Belgium*

In this study a survey (N=230) has been set up to investigate the relationship between the dispositional factors positive and negative affectivity and the affective component of organizational commitment including several of its antecedent variables. Structural equation modeling revealed an indirect effect of both negative and positive affectivity on affective commitment through the antecedent variables as well as moderator effects. The antecedent variables feedback, interaction, autonomy, role ambiguity, role conflict and the frequency of experiencing positive moods at work played a key role. We therefore conclude that dispositional factors cannot be neglected when studying organizational commitment.

Developmental status of preterm infants

Vasilyeva, Marina Dept. of Biology, St. Petersburg University, St. Petersburg, Russia

Assessments of personal-social, motor, adaptive, language, cognitive and general developmental skills were administered to 23 preterm and 28 full-term infants at 2; 3,5; 4,5; 6; 8; 10, 12 months using Battelle Developmental Inventory. Regressions for age-equivalent total BDI scores revealed significant irregularities in neurobehavioral outcomes of preterm infants. These specific features in development of preterm infants may be associated with heterochrony of maturational processes during the sensitive brain developmental periods as well as with preterm infant's early sensory experience that may alter brain function and structure.

IMPAC: A five phase existential treatment model for mood disorders

Venter, Henry Dept. of Psychology, National University, Fresno, USA

The objective of this paper is to determine the efficacy a newly developed five-phase psychotherapeutic model based on the core tenets of existential theory. The model was utilized in the treatment of a Caucasian female with depression. The efficacy was evaluated by a single-case (N=1) Experimental Design with a baseline followed by a post-treatment assessment. The results showed a significant decrease in symptoms based on the baseline data and the post-treatment assessment. The newly developed model effectively translated existential theory into a practical counseling process more readily accessible for practitioners and it provided a measurable impact on the counseling outcome.

Neighborhood density and the special role of Age-of-Acquisition in spoken word recognition in Portuguese

Vicente, Selene Faculty of Psychology, University of Porto, Porto, Portugal **Castro, São Luís** *Faculty of Psychology, University of Porto, Porto, Portugal* **Walley, Amanda** *Department of Psychology, University of Alabama, Birmingham, USA*

We examine the role of Age-of-Acquisition (AOA) and neighborhood density (ND) on spoken word recognition in Portuguese. Sixty-three adults and forty-six adolescents performed a task of identifying words in a background of noise. The stimuli were disyllabic CVCV words varying in AOA and ND. Accuracy analyses revealed that the advantage of sparse over dense neighborhoods reported in the literature was found only for the early-acquired-words (adults = 86 vs. 79%, adolescents = 82 vs. 74%; for late-acquired words, ns). Thus, the ND effect depends on AOA, which is a major factor influencing the recognition process.

The challenge of the beginning: A methodological proposal to analyze the communication mother-baby

Vieira, Nadja Dept. of Psychology, Univers. Federal de Alagoas, Maceió, Brazil

The difficulty to analyze the outset of human communication was the main problem of this investigation. In this analysis one included the mother-baby relationship as a co-regulated and self-organizing system. The model Establishment, Extension and Abbreviation – EEA is a completely conceptual approach of the Dynamic Systems. Following longitudinal data recorded in video, it was possible to identify different hierarchic processes and to characterize distinct microgenetic dimensions in the mother-baby interchanges, named as levels of immediateness, gentleness and talking turn. One concluded that the EEA model put forward resources that help to clarify the emergent processes in a dynamic of reorganization, which express the communication development in early life.

The impact of goals in Portuguese teachers subjective well-being

Vieira, Luís Sérgio Dept. de Psicologia, Universidade do Algarve, Faro, Portugal **Saul Neves, Jesus** *Departamento de Psicologia, Universidade do Algarve, Faro, Portugal*

Recent researches show the predictive power of the personal goals in the subjective well-being (SWB) and the top-down theories or temperamental model describe the importance of the person-environment fit. This work examines the association between personal goals (professional project, initial motivation, intrinsic motivation and professional commitment) with the teachers' subjective well-being. Regression analyses showed that the intrinsic motivation and the professional commitment are the more important variables associated with SWB. The results showed that the personals factors explain 14%, the pedagogic relation factors explain 8.1%, and the school environment variables explain 3.4% of the variance of the SWB.

Mothers of children with developmental problems: Characterization of parenting stress

Vieira-Santos, Salomé Dept. of Clinical Psychology, Faculty of Psychology, Lisboa, Portugal **Pimentel, Maria João** *Child Development Center, Hospital de Dona Estefânia, Lisboa, Portugal* **Santos, Vanessa** *Child Development Centre, Hospital de Dona Estefânia, Lisboa, Portugal* **Vale, Maria do Carmo** *Child Development Centre, Hospital de Dona Estefania, Lisboa, Portugal*

This study aims to characterize parenting stress in mothers of children with developmental problems, a dimension that has been insufficiently studied among this population in Portugal. Mothers of children (aged 6-12) with (n=80) and without (n=80) developmental problems participated in the study. The Portuguese adaptation of the Parenting Stress Index was used. Groups were compared through independent samples t-test. The results show that mothers of children with developmental problems present higher levels of parenting stress (Total, Domains, and specific subscales). In spite of

the reduced dimension of the samples, results accentuate the need to consider parenting stress in intervention programs.

Parenting stress and behavioral problems in mothers of children with developmental problems

Vieira-Santos, Salomé Dept. of Clinical Psychology, Faculty of Psychology, Lisboa, Portugal **Pimentel, Maria João** *Child Development Centre, Hospital de Dona Estefânia, Lisboa, Portugal* **Vale, Maria do Carmo** *Child Development Centre, Hospital de Dona estefânia, Lisboa, Portugal*

This study aims to characterize the parenting stress experienced by mothers of children with developmental problems, and to analyze the relationship between this dimension and the perception of their child's behavior. Portuguese adaptations of the Parenting Stress Index and of the Child Behavior Checklist were used. Participants were mothers of children (aged 5-11), with (G1, n=80) or without (G2, n=80) developmental problems. Mothers of G1 perceive significantly higher levels of parenting stress in different areas. A positive relationship between parenting stress and behavioral problems was found. Results highlight critical stress areas for maternal functioning and reinforce a relationship between parenting stress and child behavior.

Early social communication and attachment

Vogt, Anika Neuseddin, Germany **Schellhas, Bernd** *Potsdam, University of Potsdam, Potsdam, Germany* **Rauh, Hellgard** *Potsdam, University of Potsdam, Potsdam, Germany*

The relationship between communication skills and attachment was examined in 30 toddlers in two three-minutes' situations with their mothers at 12 and 18 months, based on categories of the Early Social Communication Scales (ESCS, Mundy et al. 2003). At 12 months, children with insecure patterns of attachment (A or D vs. B) (Strange Situation Procedure at 12 months) produced significantly more communication activities whereas children with secure patterns of attachment at 12 months (B vs. A or D) significantly more often initiated, or responded to, eye contact, joint attention, and behavioral requests at 18 months.

Personal determinants of alpine skiers' fear manifestations

Volyanyuk, Nataliya Institute of Psychology, Lutsk, Ukraine **Podlyashanyk, Wasiliy** *Psychology, Institute, Lutsk, Ukraine*

Research objective lay in identifying personal determinants of alpine skiers' fear development. Methods: free self-description questionnaire; State-Trait Anxiety Inventory by C. D. Spielberger; multiple-factor personality determination technique by R.Cattell. Results. It was determined that skilled alpine skiers have the following personal determinants of fear manifestations: rigidity of thinking ("B"-factor), dependence upon the others ("I"), carelessness ("F"), conformism ("Q2"-factor), disposition towards risk ("N"), orientation upon the inner world ("M"), tenseness and frustration ("Q4").

Injury risk in sport: A matter of overconformity?

Würth, Sabine Sport Psychology, Universität Wien, Wien, Austria

Overconformity in sport involves high sport identity, excessive effort, and seeking for social approval. The present study set out to examine whether overconformity is associated with the injury risk of young athletes. In a cross-sectional study, 212 athletes were asked to report their individual history of sport injuries, and to fill in scales measuring excessive effort, goal orientation, and sport identity. Regression analyses revealed that tying one's identity to sport is related to the number of injuries athletes contract during their career. Follow-up data will show whether overconformity might also predict injury risk of athletes in a prospective way.

A pound of lead feels heavier than a pound of feathers...but only at first

Wagman, Jeffrey Dept. of Psychology, Illinois State University, Normal, USA Zimmerman, Corinne Dept. of Psychology, Illinois State University, Normal, IL, USA Orr, Jeremiah Dept. of Psychology, Illinois State University, Normal, IL, USA

We investigated whether the naïve answer to the riddle "Which weighs more: a pound of feathers or a pound of lead" has a basis in perception. Blindfolded participants hefted boxes containing a pound (453.6g) of lead and a pound of feathers and reported which felt heavier. Participants reported that the box containing lead felt heavier at a level above chance, but this effect dissipated over time. This pattern occurred regardless of whether participants were aware of the possible contents of the boxes. The naïve answer to the riddle seems to have some basis in perception.

Intergroup dynamics in goal contagion: Cultural group membership and salience in the adoption of others' goals

Wan, Ching Dept. of Psychology, Nanyang Technological Univ., Singapore, Singapore

Goals can be contagious, as people automatically adopt a goal after observing others engaging in behaviors that imply the goal. The current research proposes that goal contagion effect depends on the intergroup dynamics present in the social perception context. Singaporean Chinese participants were presented with the goal-directed behaviors of either a Singaporean Chinese (ingroup) or a Singaporean Malay (outgroup) person. The salience of cultural group membership was also manipulated. Results showed that goal contagion was a function of both cultural group membership and the salience of such membership. Implications of the findings for intergroup relations will be discussed.

An experimental study on competence trap in organizational decision making in China

Wang, Zhongming School of of Management, Zhejiang University, Hangzhou, People's Republic of China Ren, Xulin School of Management, Southwest Univ of Finance, Chengdu, People's Republic of China Li, Kai School of Management, Zhejiang University, Hangzhou, People's Republic of China

In the areas of organizational decision making, competence trap is regarded as being determined by organizational routines and the adaptive features in decision makers' choices. In a study supported by NSFC, the experimental design of resource distribution decision-making paradigm was adopted. A decision task of organizational resource coordination was used while the decision makers' searching behavior was observed under the changing decision rules. Altogether, 132 management students participated in this study. The results indicated that the decision makers' searching behavior showed two modes: dynamic adaptability and competence trap. This adaptive process demonstrated the construction and change of organizational decision-making competence.

Organizational change-based leadership modeling: An ASD perspective

Wang, Zhongming School of Management, Zhejiang University, Hangzhou, People's Republic of China

In a field study supported by NSFC on organizational change among Chinese entrepreneurial firms, a change leadership model was tested. Four key dimensions of leadership competencies were constructed: vision-driven, culture-shaping, creative breakthrough, framework innovation. Situational and critical incident measures were developed and the multi-stage change process was formulated.

With the perspective of adaptation-selection-development, the organizational change-based leadership model was validated and proved to be significantly correlated with indicators for organizational effectiveness. Implications of this change leadership model to the organization development of Chinese entrepreneurial firms were highlighted on the basis of person-organization interactive fit.

Some evaluation factors inducing teachers' job burnout in Chinese primary and middle school

Wang, Jinsu School of Psychology, Shandong Normal University, Jinan, People's Republic of China

Currently, job burnout is considerably prevalent in Chinese primary and middle school teacher group. The author analyzed those factors that would aggravate burnout in criterions, subjects, proofs and outcomes of teacher evaluation, and gave the following suggestions to improve the quality of teacher evaluation. One should be 1) exerting the action of manager, 2) involving teacher in the process, 3) attaching importance to teacher professional development, 4) putting portfolio assessment into practice, 5) praising teachers' excellence. In addition it was pointed out that only utilizing the positive leading function of teachers' evaluation could avoid job burn effectively.

Research on the relationship between middle-school students' participation and teacher's behavior in classroom

Wang, Yun Beijing, People's Republic of China Zhang, Xiaozhou Psychology, State Key Lab of Cognitive Neu, beijing, People's Republic of China zhu, zhe Psychology, State Key Lab of Cognitive Neu, beijing, People's Republic of China Chen, Fumei Psychology, State Key Lab of Cognitive Neu, beijing, People's Republic of China Xu, Shaogang Psychology, State Key Lab of Cognitive Neu, beijing, People's Republic of China Li, Li Psychology, State Key Lab of Cognitive Neu, beijing, People's Republic of China

Student's participation plays a special role in their academic achievement. The relationship between student's participation and teacher's behavior in classroom was examined. 7th (n=190) and 10th (n=186) grade students from Beijing were asked to complete Student Participation Questionnaire (a=.86) and Perception of Teacher's Behavior Questionnaire (a=.76). Exploratory Factor Analysis indicates students' participation can be divided into behavior participation, thoughts participation, and emotional experience, while teachers' behavior are consisted of emotion management, teaching organization, asking questions and class management. Regression analysis shows teaching organization significantly predicts students' behavior participation and emotion experience, while teacher's asking questions best predicts students' thoughts participation.

A review of researches on physical self-concept of college students in China

Wang, Cuiping University, Xijian Physical Education, Xi an, People's Republic of China

The paper aims to summarize the current research situation of physical-self of college students in China. We analyzed researches on physical self-concept of college students from three aspects including research quantity, research status and research results. On the basis of literature reviews, We found some limitations in present studies, put forward some effective methods to solve these problems.

Job burnout among university faculty: The causes and the internal relationship of the MBI's three dimensions

Wang, Fang Beijing, People's Republic of China Xu, Yan School of Psychology, Beijing Normal University, Beijing, People's Republic of China

The study examined the antecedents of job burnout and the internal relationship of the MBI's construction among a cross-sectional sample of 481 university teachers, then among a 10-lagged longitudinal sample of 22 faculties from the same university through a diary study. With regard to the causes of burnout, job demand and job resource were two key predictors of burnout. As far as the internal relationship of the three dimensions of burnout is concerned, there was a strongly positive relation between exhaustion and cynicism, and explanatory style strengthened the relation. The professional efficacy, however, had null relation with exhaustion and cynicism.

Third-person advantage of mental rotation

Wang, Peng Psychology, East China Normal University, Shanghai, People's Republic of China You, XuQun Psychology, ShaanXi Normal University, Xian, People's Republic of China

This study compared first-person with third-person mental rotation of imagined environments in the transverse plane (Experiment 1), coronal plane (Experiment 2) and median sagittal plane (Experiment 3) respectively. Each experiment was a 2 (first- and third-person rotation) × 4 (degree) mixed-design. 116 right-handed undergraduates took part in the experiments at the age between 19 and 21. Reaction times and accuracy in the three experiments all indicated that it was easier for observers to spatially update displays from third-person perspective versus from first-person perspective, namely third-person advantage of mental rotation.

Attitudes towards organizational wrongdoing and intention of whistle-blowing in Japanese employees

Wang, Jinmin School of Risk and Crisis, Chiba Institute of Science, Chiba, Japan

This study examined the determinants of attitudes towards and intention to whistle -blowing on organizational wrongdoing. Organizational commitment, collectivism, type of employment, and other individual factors were examined based on survey data collected from 465 employees from Japan. Findings showed that: components of organizational commitment had different effects on intention of whistle-blowing according to types of employment; collectivism had negative relationship with intention of whistle-blowing; full-time workers were more willing to blow the whistle, had more self-efficacy in reporting, and paid more attention to co-workers opinions than temporary workers. Implications on prevention of organizational wrongdoing were also discussed.

The relation between parental educational practices and the self-esteem of Brazilian teenagers

Weber, Lidia Dept. of Psychology, Federal University of Parana, Curitiba, Brazil Richartz, Marisa Psychology, Federal University of Parana, Curitiba, Brazil Richartz, Mariana Psychology, Federal University of Parana, Curitiba, Brazil

This research investigated the relations existing between parental educational practices and the self-esteem of Brazilian teenagers. 1,252 students aged between 12 and 18 took part in the study, providing replies in a collective and anonymous manner to three different scales, namely: the Family Interaction Quality Scales - FIQS (Weber et al., 2003); the Responsiveness and Demandingness Scales (Lambom et. al., 1991); and the Self-esteem Scale (Rosenberg, 2003). Statistical analysis revealed that relations exist between positive parental educational practices and high self-esteem, whilst it was also observed that low self-esteem is related to negative parental practices.

Parental practices in one parent and two parent adoptive Brazilian families

Weber, Lidia Dept. of Psychology, Federal University of Parana, Curitiba, Brazil Pereira, Cristina Psychology, Federal University of Parana, Curitiba, Brazil Dessen, Maria Auxiliadora Psychology, Federal University of Parana, Curitiba, Brazil

The purpose of this study was to compare the self-esteem and the parental practices perceived by children adopted by one parent and two parent families in Brazil. The results showed that, regardless of the marital status of the parents, the children perceived family interaction in a similar way, and did not present differences in relation to the feelings they have for their parents or in relation to perceived parental involvement and monitoring. No significant differences were found with regard to self-esteem and parental styles. In both kinds of family, the children have an adequate concept of themselves and there is a predominance of the participative parental style, which is more favourable for healthy child development.

The influence of sport type on the development of the sport specific achievement motive in young elite athletes

Wenhold, Franziska Inst. für Sportpsychologie, Universität Potsdam, Potsdam, Germany

The following study longitudinally assesses the development of the sport specific achievement motive using the Achievement Motives Scale-Sport (Elbe & Wenhold, 2005) in a sample of 115 young elite athletes from three elite sport schools in the state of Brandenburg, Germany. The study indicates that the sport specific achievement motive is a fairly stable personality factor, however, when considering the sport type a developmental difference can be found. The motive hope for success decreased only in team players and not for individual athletes. The results indicate that attention should be paid to the motivational development of young athletes performing a team sport when switching to an elite sport school.

Regulatory focus affects goal pursuit: An example focusing on expectancy x value–effects

Werth, Lioba Social- & Organizational Psych., Chemnitz University Technology, Chemnitz, Germany Steidle, Anna Social- & Organizational P, Chemnitz University Technology, Chemnitz, Germany

Relating self-regulation to goal theories, this study aimed to identify the influence of stable self-regulation strategies (Higgins, 1997) in the context of professional goal pursuit. Growth-oriented promotion-focused employees evaluated the efficacy of their goal behavior more positively and tended to evaluate the instrumentality of their goal achievement slightly more positively than prevention-focused employees. Regulatory focus moderated the interactive influence of outcome expectancy and goal value on goal commitment: in the case of prevention focus and an attractive goal, the effect of outcome expectancy on goal commitment was reduced. Implications concerning leadership, goal agreement, and commitment in organizations are discussed. Literature Higgins, E. T. (1997). Beyond pleasure and pain. American Psychologist, 52, 1280-1300.

Application of the Kaufman assessment battery for children second edition on Frenchspeaking children in Switzerland

Wicht, Caroline Dépt. de Psychologie, Université de Fribourg, Fribourg, Switzerland Retschitzki, Jean Dept. of Psychology, University of Fribourg, Fribourg, Switzerland

The purpose of this study was to evaluate the usefulness of the K-ABC II on Swiss french-speaking children. The test has been constructed to reduce cultural differences in intelligence assessement. Our research consists in assessing 35 children

of age 7-8 with 10 subtests of the battery. The analyses of the results indicate that 7 of the 10 subtests give the same results for the Swiss and the Amercian children of the same age. The goal of Kaufman & Kaufman (2004) to reduce cultural differences in the scores of the test seems to be partially achieved with our population.

The roles of parental involvement and social capital in children's learning motivation

Wild, Elke Inst. für Psychologie, Universität Bielefeld, Bielefeld, Germany

In view of strong associations between family socioeconomic status and German students' school performance this study examines to what extent SES affects amount and quality of parental involvement (PI) and whether PI mediates the relationship between SES and students' attitudes toward learning. Data stem from a longitudinal study starting with 304 German 3rd graders and their parents. Regression analyses indicated that a significant amount of the variance in a four-dimensional measure of PI could be accounted for by SES. In addition, structural equation modelling validated the mediational model. School policy implications will be discussed.

Rejection of naturalized players during the FIFA World Cup: Ideology, prejudice or convenience?

Willis, Guillermo Byrd Psicología Social, Universidad de Granada, Granada, Spain Rodríguez Bailón, Rosa Psicología Social, Universidad de Granada, Granada, Spain Moya, Miguel Psicología Social, Universidad de Granada, Granada, Spain Morales Marente, Elena Psicología, Universidad de Huelva, Huelva, Spain

The last FIFA World Cup had an interesting phenomenon: 21 teams involved players that did not were born in the country, but have its nationality. This research tried to explore some factors that lead supporters to accept/reject the inclusion of those players. For doing so, some ideological variables (i.e. SDO, patriotism, prejudice, etc.) were considered in two different international samples (Spain and Mexico). Results showed that the main variables that predict rejection of naturalized players are: prejudice towards immigrants and the belief that those players will not improve team's performance. Data will be discussed on the light of intergroup relations.

A study on the effects of supervisors' technical skills and emotional intelligence on subordinates' job satisfaction

Wu, Weiku School of Economics Management, Tsinghua University, Beijing, People's Republic of China Yu, Tianliang School of Economics&Manage, Tsinghua University, Beijing, People's Republic of China Song, Jiwen Department of OB and HRM, Renmin University of China, Beijing, People's Republic of China

Equipped with theories of emotional intelligence, leadership and power, the paper investigated the impacts of supervisors' technical skills and emotional intelligence (EI) on subordinates' job satisfaction. Based on the data analyses of 124 leader-follower dyads in a hospital in the P. R. China, we found that supervisors' other-evaluated technical skills and emotional intelligence, and subordinates' self-evaluated emotional intelligence had significant impacts on subordinates' job satisfaction. Managerial implications were provided. (Supported by NSFC 70572012, 70702024, 50539130)

The procedure of authentication translation instruments in cross-culture research

Wu, Ming-Hsun International Business Admi., Chien Kuo Technol. University, Chang Hua, Taiwan Lai, Ying-Chun Department of Applied Foreign, Chung Shan Medical University, Taichung, Taiwan Shiah, Yung-Jong International business admi., ChienKuo Technology University, ChangHua, Taiwan

The three stages of experimental design to figure out the problems of maintain valid translation when piloting a small group with English and Chinese version instruments. When differences occurred their reasons were three: (a) they did not understand the English word, (b) they felt differently about the item at the time, or (c) The translations were to blame. The final authoritative version of the instrument was produced thorough interviews and negotiations. Therefore, the researcher devised a procedure to improve the translation accuracy. The "Figure" shows the process of authentication translation and test-retest between Chinese and English version instruments in using bilingual pilot sample to come to consensus about the translations.

Character frequency effect confounded by number of different words a character generates

Wu, Jei-Tun Department of Psychology, National Taiwan University, Taipei, Taiwan Yang, Si-Cyun Department of Psychology, National Taiwan University, Taipei, Taiwan

Character frequency is confounded by character's ability to combine with others to generate different words. Compared to characters with lower frequency, characters with higher frequency generate more different words embedding them. To investigate their effects on character lexical decision and naming, character frequency and number of different words embedding a particular character with character frequency balanced were simultaneously manipulated in this study. Ninety college students participated. A two-way nest design analysis of variance was conducted. Results showed that besides character frequency effect, number of different words generated from a low frequency character exhibited a significant facilitating effect.

We make the team: The effect of team social capital on team effectiveness

Wu, Xin School of Economics & Managemt, Beihang University, Beijing, People's Republic of China Wu, Zhiming School of economics & mana, Tsinghua University, beijing, People's Republic of China

This study examined the relationship between team social capital and team potency, team performance, and organizational citizenship behavior (OCB). Survey data were collected from 288 team members and their supervisors in 52 knowledge work teams in China. The results showed that the relational dimension of team social capital was positively related to team potency and team performance rated by external supervisors. The cognitive dimension of team social capital and the relational dimension of social capital were positively related to different domains of OCB. Team social capital partially mediated the relationship between OCB and team performance.

An empirical research on relationships among processing speed, executive function and fluid intelligence

Wu, Xiaodong School of PublicAdministration, Northwest University, China, Xi'an, People's Republic of China Zheng, Zijian School of PublicAdministration, Northwest University, China, Xi'an, People's Republic of China Gao, Xiaocai School of PublicAdministration, Northwest University, China, Xi'an, People's Republic of China Wang, Shuzhen School of PublicAdministration, Northwest University, China, Xi'an, People's Republic of China Zhang, Fuchang School of PublicAdministration, Northwest University, China, Xi'an, People's Republic of China

This paper explores relationships among processing speed, executive function (EF) and fluid intelligence. Six texts were completed by 84 children subjects in Qinba Mountains. Spearman correlation shows that the correlation between inspect time (IT) and EF is not significant, but significant between IT and fluid intelligence; the correlation between recognition speed and fluid intelligence is not significant, but significant between recognition speed and EF. Meanwhile, stepwise regression shows that IT and memory updating enter the equation, which explain 34.9% and 30.5% of total variances respectively. Consequently, IT and memory updating are strong predictors of fluid intelligence.

The dangerous myth about outsourcing: Implications for supply chain management

Xia, Amy Yu Management and Marketing, Middle Tennessee St University, Murfreesboro, USA Tang, Thomas Li-Ping Management and Marketing, Middle Tennessee St University, Murfreesboro, USA

In the wake of globalization, many organizations in the developed countries have outsourced their production of components, products, and services to developing or underdeveloped countries in order to take the advantages of cheaper land, natural resources, human resources, labor rates, and the exchange rates. Although the products' unit rates may be cheaper, executives may face many risks/challenges, especially from the supply chain management perspectives. This paper attempts to examine critical risks regarding suppliers' quality of products/service, total cost, product delivery, new product development, and the management system when considering the effectiveness and efficiency of outsourceing in supply chain management.

A research on the relationship of parental rearing patterns, self-concept and internet addiction behavior

Xie, Jing Dept. of Psychology, Beijing Normal University, Beijing, People's Republic of China

Based on investigation about 1,317 undergraduate student to research the relationship between parental rearing patterns, self-concept and internet addiction behavior. The result demonstrated that the parental rearing patterns, especially the paternal rearing patterns, will influence the internet addiction behavior, and the self-concept is an important mediator between parenting styles and internet addiction behavior. These findings suggest that parental rearing patterns can indirectly influence internet addiction behavior.

A qualitative study: Chinese bereaved adolescent's grief process and influencing factors

Xu, Jie Institute of Developmental Psy, BeiJing Normal University, Beijing, People's Republic of China Zhang, Risheng Institute of Developmental Psy, BeiJing Normal University, beijing, People's Republic of China Zhang, Wen Institute of Developmental Psy, BeiJing Normal University, beijing, People's Republic of China

To explore the Chinese adolescent's grief process and its influencing factors. One to 1.5 hour in-depth interviews were conducted for thirty-two 11-17 year old adolescents, half male, half female, half of the participants had lost their mother, and half had lost their father. The transcribed interview data was analyzed by thematic analysis.The interviewee's grief process and its influencing factors resulted in different categories, themes and sub-themes in grief stage, cope style, family value etc.Chinese adolescents had the same bereavement processes and its influencing factors as that found in western, but some important cultural specifics were found.

Corporate social responsibility of Chinese firms and its impacts on corporate social capital: An empirical study based on 1268 manufacture firms investigation

Xu, Shangkun Business School, Remin University of China, Beijing, People's Republic of China Yang, Rudai China Center for Economic Rese, Peking University, Beijing, People's Republic of China Dai,

Xiang Business School, Remin University of China, Beijing, People's Republic of China

This study collects data on social responsibility and social capital of Chinese businesses based on a 1268-firm questionnaire covering 12 cities. First we define the scope of corporate social responsibility, and then construct a measuring tool for 5-dimension corporate social responsibility and 4-dimension corporate social capital. The research proposes econometric verification formula in the framework of OLS Model and Ordered Probit Model respectively. The empirical process indicates that when businesses take more social responsibility, more social capital will be generated accordingly; additionally the impact of individual dimension of the corporate social responsibility on social capital varies significantly.

The corporate culture of China: An inductive analysis involving the conceptual dimension and the development of a measuring scale

Xu, Shangkun Business School, Remin University of China, Beijing, People's Republic of China Dai, Xiang Business School, Xiangtan University of China, Xiangtan, People's Republic of China

In the Chinese firm-based study I, 180 top managers have been interviewed and questioned. From the qualitative data, twelve dimensions of China's corporate culture have been identified. A further research conducted from the study of corporate culture documents for 20 leading Chinese enterprises is employed to examine the above mentioned dimensions, and some peculiar elements within Chinese corporate culture are also addressed against the Western practice. In Study II we develop corporate culture scale with 1200 employers from 60 firms as the sample, and the exploratory factor analysis and confirmatory factor analysis are executed to form the corporate culture scale.

Study of the relation among social withdrawal type, self-perceived social competence, peer relationship and loneliness in middle childhood

Xu, Wei Social Science Dept., HBTCM, Wuhan, People's Republic of China Zeng, Yanya social science department, hbtcm, wuhan, People's Republic of China

This study tried to examine the function of social withdrawal behavior, peer relationship and self-perceived social competence to loneliness. Sociometric nomination, sociometric rating and questionnaire method were applied in this survey. The results showed:Significantly negative correlation was found between social preference, self-perceived social competence, positive friendship quality and loneliness;In active withdrawal type children, There were no significant loneliness difference between high self-perceived social competence, normal and low self-perceived social competence children.;Results from SEM indicated that social withdrawal behavior has impact on loneliness through 3 type mediator effect;Cross-lagged analyses indicated that when the influence of self-perceived social competence was controlled.

Effect of cognitive-behavioral group counseling on university students of anger management

Xu, Yun Shanghai Pudong Software Park, Shanghai, People's Republic of China Liu, Xuanwen Children's Culture Insititute, Zhejiang Normal University, Jinhua, People's Republic of China

The study included two parts. The first part focused on the revise of State-Trait Anger Expression Scale. Its reliability and validity was examined. The second part was to develop cognitive-behavioral group counseling. Eleven students randomly in experiment group were arranged to attend eight sessions (16 hours in total) of cognitive-behavioral group counseling. The control group of another 11 students received no treatment. Results showed that the reliability and validity of STAXI reversion is

good. Cognitive-behavioral group counseling had an immediate and six weeks follow-up effects on decreasing state anger, trait anger and irrational belief, but no effects on constructive anger expression.

Combined neurofeedback with Ritalin treatment for attention-deficit / hyperactivity disorder in children: comparison with each alone

Yaghubi, Hamid Dept. of Clinical Psychology, Shahed University, Tehran, Islamic Republic of Iran

Objectives: The aim is compared the effectiveness of combined treatment made of Neurofeedback(low beta and beta training) together with Ritalin vs. each of them alone, in reduction the "ADHD" symptoms. Methods: Participants were 16 children with ADHD aged 8–9.5 years that equally were assigned to 3 interventional situations and a waiting list for 10 weeks treatment or assessment. Results: The results showed that the Combined Group has better effect other than 3 groups in two subscales of the TOVA (Omission and Commission) and also behaviors related to the disorder were rated as significantly reduced by parents on the Conners Scale- Parent Form. Conclusion: These findings emphasizes of the combination method as a better choice.

Japanese life-patterns in the 2000s IV: Work motivation and corporate culture

Yagi, Ryuichiro IEWRI, Osaka, Japan Yamashita, Miyako graduate school of humanities, Okayama University, Itami, HYOGO, Japan Tanaka, Daisuke Psychology + connect, institute of Applied Social, Osaka, Japan

The so-called 'Japan's lost decade' affected Japanese companies, and their traditional strength has been weakened. This study investigates the phenomenon from the viewpoint of relations between corporate cultures, work motivation and corporate performance. The research was conducted by surveying 140 Japanese labor unions and companies including Toyota and Canon, with the total number of respondents 160,000. The intrinsic/extrinsic work motivation indices, used to analyze the data, were helpful in predicting the company performance and operating profits per employee. The results reconfirmed the effects of the traditional Japanese corporate culture on the work motivation and the corporate performance.

Creativity in group context: How ideas exchange influences individual creative ability

Yagolkovsky, Sergey Applied Psychology, Moscow State Hum. University, Reutov, Russia

Our study focuses on cognitive and social aspects of creativity. Effects of ideas sharing on parameters of creativity were assessed in an idea generation paradigm. Stimulus ideas were grouped into 4 semantic categories: high creative, with low level of novelty, aggressive, and "silly" ideas. Creativity parameters (productivity, flexibility, and originality) were assessed using the Russian version of the Guilford Unusual Uses Test. Experimental data showed the most intensive changes ($p<0.05$) of originality in the group where "silly" stimulus ideas had been exposed. Results of the study can be used for the enhancing the individual creativity.

Time perception and time orientation: An exploratory study of their relations to interpersonal relationship.

Yaksina, Irina General and Experimental Psych, Higher School of Economics, Krasnogorsk, Russia

The problem of time is a central and fundamental psychology question. Our inner clocks are postulated as basic to our sense of internal time. Past, present, future orientation influenced on all aspects of human being. The aim of our investigation is to examine relation between individual habits of time perception (τ- type, B.Tsukanov, 1991, 2000), time orientation and peculiarities of interpersonal relationship. Participants were 286 adults (aged 18 to 53 years). The factor analysis indicated the bi-directional link between individual habits of time perception (τ- type) and peculiarities of interpersonal relationship (empathy, level of communication control and so on).

How difference in presentation styles of uncertainty affects on risk perception and trust?

Yamazaki, Mizuki Fac. of Environmental Studies, Musashi Inst. of Technology, Tokyo, Japan

This study examined how presentations of uncertainty in risk estimates affect public risk perceptions and citizens' trust in risk-assessing agencies. 460 participants read a fictitious scenario of emerging infectious disease with varying risk magnitudes: 25% vs. 15-35%, 50% vs. 45-65%, and 75% vs. 65-85%. The result showed that in high threat magnitude, a point-estimate caused more anxiety than a range-estimate; while in low risk magnitude, a range-estimate led to more anxiety than a point-estimate. The level of trust in risk-assessing agency did not differ significantly with varying conditions. These findings would have important implications for risk communication.

Self-regulated learning using MBO

Yanagizawa, Saori Business, Marketing & Distr., Nakamura Gakuen University, Fukuoka, Japan

This study's purpose is to examine the effect of MBO (management by objectives) on self-regulated learning. Participants were 164 factory employees in a Japanese drug maker company. This company required employees to set not only performance goals but also learning goals in MBO. Participants answered the questionnaire about self-regulated learning activities. Employees, who were fully conscious of the need to learn by setting goals, tried to transfer the learning to improved job performance, frequently seek feedback, and evaluate the degree of learning. These results suggested that self-regulated learning activities were carried out by using MBO designed to encourage employees' learning.

Research on counseling concept based on traditional chinese culture

Yang, Wensheng Psychological Counseling, Shanghai Jiao Tong University, Shanghai, People's Republic of China

This article tries to construct a new counseling concept, which has absorbed ideas from Buddhism and ZongHengism, based on traditional Chinese culture. The research believes counseling goal is to help clients get rid of their worries and disturbance and lead a free life. The causes of clients' problems are rooted in their hearts, which are their greed, anger, stupidity, arrogance and doubt. Therefore, it is the counselor's responsibility to help them overcome and defeat these weaknesses in their hearts. So the counselor has to employ special canvass, which is similar to ancient Chinese persuasion art mentioned in literature of ZongHengism.

The apprehension of implement: Moderating effect of the thinking manner Zhong Yong on relationship of creativity ability and innovation behavior

Yang, Qian Dept. of Psychology, Peking University, Shenzhen, People's Republic of China Wang, Lei Psychology Department, Peking University, Beijing, People's Republic of China Peng, Jing Psychology Department, Peking University, Shenzhen, People's Republic of China Qiu, Chengfu Psychology Department, Peking University, Shenzhen, People's Republic of China

This study discussed one possible reason for Needham's Paradox through examining the moderating effect of the thinking manner ZHONG YONG on the relationship between creativity ability and innovation behaviors. The results showed that for those high on ZHONG YONG, innovation behaviors are not closely related to creativity ability; nevertheless, for those low on ZHONG YONG, high creativity ability predicted high innovation behaviors while low creativity ability implied low innovation behaviors. These results suggested that ZHONG YONG as a thinking manner is somewhat the apprehension factor for creativity ability to develop into innovation behaviors.

The influence of work values and achievement motivation on professional school teachers' job burnout

Yang, Dianxia Psychology Department, Jinan, People's Republic of China

The aim of this research was to explore the influence of work values and achievement motivation on professional school teachers' job burnout. By testing 304 teachers of 4 professional schools with job burnout questionnaire in primary and secondary teachers, work values questionnaire and achievement motivation questionnaire, we found that among the four factors of job burnout, personal accomplishment had positive correlations with achievement motivation and work values, the other three factors (emotional exhaustion, cognition drought, and depersonalization) had negative ones with achievement motivation and work values. Both achievement motivation and work values had significant predictable effects on teachers' job burnout.

R&D performance: Work motivation and team innovation climate

Yang, Yann-Jy Technology & Innovation Manag., National ChengChi University, Taipei, Taiwan

The R&D performance is crucial for high technology industries in an increasing competitive environment. The study explored the relationship between the R&D performance, the work motivation, the creativity, and the group innovation climate. The performance data of the merit system and a questionnaire survey for 247 R&D professionals of 11 groups were analyzed from a large multinational electrical company. Result of cluster analysis indicated that the members of high R&D performance teams were creative and with the high enjoyment and outward motivations, moreover, the high R&D performance teams were high task oriented. However, the relationships between the work motivations of challenge and compensation were not significant.

Shyness influence the relationship between employee's creativity and their innovation behaviors

Yao, Xiang Dept. of Psychology, Peking University, Beijing, People's Republic of China Wang, Lei Department of Psychology, Peking University, Beijing, People's Republic of China

Shyness as a personality trait has been generally conceptualized as the presence of inhibition and discomfort in social situations. The current research aims to investigate the impact of shyness on the relationship between employee's creativity and innovation behaviors in workplace. Two-hundred and eighty-nine Chinese employees completed questionnaires including creativity, innovation behavior and shyness. Regression analysis revealed that creativity is an important predicator for innovation behavior ($p<.01$), shyness has a significant moderating effect upon this relationship ($p<.05$). These findings underline the importance of personality trait for predicating employee innovation behavior.

Multi-level model of entrepreneurial team comprehensive competency

Ye, Yujian College of Management, Hangzhou Dianzi University, Hangzhou, People's Republic of China Nie, Xue Lin Hangzkou Dianzi University, Hang Zhou, People's Republic of China Wu, Zhangge Department of Hotel Management, Zhejiang Tourism College, Hangzhou, People's Republic of China

This study wants to build a three-level model of Entrepreneurial team comprehensive competency. Competency at team leader level includes adapting the teamwork, sharing leadership and integrating team; competency at team level team knowledge?-skill and attitude; competency at team member level individual position competency and inter-individual complementary competency. Data of 60 teams which are less than 6 years old was collected by questionnaire survey and the multi-level construct is tested. And every dimension can significantly predict financial, growth and competitive performance in high-technology companies but no for low-tech industry, which indicts entrepreneurial teams are especially important for high-tech entrepreneurship.

Can we have culture free and universal self esteem? Report of study of self esteem inventory among Iranian children

Younesi, Jalal counselling, University of social welfare, Tehran, Islamic Republic of Iran Younesi, Maryam counselling, University of social welfare, Tehran, Islamic Republic of Iran

With the aim of standardization, Culture Free Self Esteem Inventory (CFSEI - Form A) was studied at two phases of pilot and main in Iran. The results showed acceptable reliability and validity of the scale among children. Some items of the inventory were modified or revised based on Iranian culture. According to the results of factor analysis which was carried out in main study among 1300 children, this scale can measure factors of self esteem among Iranian population which is not able to measure them in Canadian population.. The findings have indications for challenging of notion which emphasize on existing of universal self esteem among children with different cultures.

Organizational symbols in workplace settings: An ethnographic approach

Yusof, Norhafezah Dept. of Communication, Universiti Utara Malaysia, Kedah, Malaysia

This study investigated selected organizational symbols in workplace settings. The findings were based on a six month ethnographic fieldwork of several Information Communication Technology (ICT) based corporations in one of the Malaysian Multimedia Super Corridor cities. Using ethnographic methods – participant observation, ethnographic interviewing, structured interviewing and official documentation, the researcher discovered two main organizational symbols i.e., black sofas and staff identity cards which affected organizational culture in the corporations. Thus, discussion will center on these two key organizational symbols in relations to work practices in organizations.

A study on relationship between family factors and academic achievement of Ghom province high school students

Zadeh Mohammadi, Ali Shahid Beheshti University, Fanily Research Institute, Tehran, Islamic Republic of Iran Heidari, Mahmood Psychology Department, Shahid Beheshti University, Tehran, Islamic Republic of Iran

The objective of this study was to investigate the relationship between family function, family conflict, parenting styles, and economic-educational level of family and academic achievement of high school students. A sample of 505 students was randomly (251 female) from high schools of Ghom Province. Parents of students were asked to complete the Family Assessment Device, Marital conflict, and Parenting styles. The results revealed that family functioning is significantly related to academic achievement (p=%3). No significant difference was found between marital conflict and academic achievement. Families with high educational and economic level had significantly children with better involued in academic achievement..

Applying a non-validated personality test in a cross-cultural investigation: A pilot study
Zand, Faezeh Inst. of Psychology, University of Copenhagen, Copenhagen K, Denmark
Many psychologists avoid the use of personality tests with individuals who come from cultures where the tests have not been culturally validated. A group of 120 Iranians were tested with Millon Clinical Multiaxial Inventory – III; an inventory that is not validated in Iran. The sample consists of university students, clinical clients, psychiatric patients, and immigrants. The experiences related to culturally relevant issues will be discussed. An initial conclusion seems to be that thorough knowledge of the test's structure, as well as of the target group's language and socio-cultural background, seem to be of utmost importance in achieving the correct scores.

Study of teachers' ability to diagnose teaching problems in elementary secondary schools
Zeng, Tuo Department of Education, Jiaying College, Meizhou GuangDong Province, People's Republic of China
A research of elementary and secondary school teachers' ability to diagnose teaching problems and the factors in it was launched by means of investigation and experiment. One hundred and seventy five teachers participated in the present study. The data obtained was submitted to repeated-measure analysis of variance(ANOVA) and stepwise-liner regression analysis by SPSS12 and the result shows: (a) On the whole, the teachers' ability to diagnose teaching problems was poor. (b) The ability to diagnose teaching problems could be significantly predicted by pedagogical and psychological knowledge as well as practical knowledge. The findings suggest that a teacher's pedagogical and psychological knowledge as well as practical knowledge are fundamental to his ability to diagnose teaching problems.

A case study of cognitive-behavior training on a primary school student with Attention Deficit Disorder (ADD)
Zhang, Yingping Children's Culture Institute, Zhejiang Normal University, Jinhua, People's Republic of China Liu, Xuanwen Children's Culture Institute, Zhejiang Normal University, Jinhua, People's Republic of China Zhang, Zhe Education College, Zhejiang Normal University, Jinhua, People's Republic of China
Objective: To explore the effect of Cognitive-Behavior Training on promoting the class attention behavior of a student with attention deficit disorder. Method: The subject received pretest, posttest and follow-up test after she received 4 times of Cognitive-Behavior Training. Results: Frequencies of class attention deficit behavior in posttest and follow-up test are significantly fewer than the frequencies in pretest. Conclusion: The Cognitive-Behavior Training is effective on attention deficit behavior of the case; the self-instruction training based on behavior rectifies technology has significantly follow-up effect compared with behavior technology.

The effect of solution-focused group counseling on secondary vocational school students of career maturity and career self-efficacy
Zhang, Yingping Children's Culture Institute, Zhejiang Normal University, Jinhua, People's Republic of China Liu, Xuanwen Children's Culture Institute, Zhejiang Normal University, Jinhua, People's Republic of China
Objective: To analyze the immediate and follow-up counseling effects and the therapeutic factors of solution-focused group counseling on secondary vocational school (SVS) students. Method: 48 SVS students with low career maturity received pretest, posttest and follow-up test with Career Development Scaling and Career Self-Efficacy Scaling. 24 students in experiment group attended eight sessions of solution-focused group counseling. Results: Solution-focused group has immediate effect on increasing career maturity and career self-efficacy of SVS students. But follow-up effect only find in career self-efficacy. Conclusion: Solution-Focused Group Counseling is an effective career guidance model and the mechanism is to increase the members' self-efficacy.

A study on the cognitive characteristics of the graduates with trait anxiety
Zhang, Xiaolong Education Develop. & Research, Capital Normal University, Beijing, People's Republic of China Chen, Yinghe College of Psychology, Beijing Normal University, Beijing, People's Republic of China
This research combines the affect structure with the cognitive-content specificity together by the theory of Effortful Control. And we also use the production system of the cognition architecture to merge the different theory. The research uses scale and executive tasks to investigate the cognitive characteristics of the graduate students with trait anxiety. The results shows that some of indexes of the EC(Efforful control) are significant predictive factors of symptoms of trait anxiety and level of impulse.

The psychological clinic and the development of sandplay therapy in China
Zhang, Risheng Inst. of Developm. Psychology, Beijing Normal University, Beijing, People's Republic of China Xu, Jie Institute of Developmental Psy, Bei Jing Normal University, BeiJing, People's Republic of China Zhang, Wen Institute of Developmental Psy, Bei Jing Normal University, BeiJing, People's Republic of China
Sandplay therapy as a psychotherapy from the West had deep theory source from the East culture. It had been for 10 years since Zhang Risheng introduced sandplay therapy to China by 2008, In China Sandplay therapy rooms had been set up in many universities, middle schools, kindergartens and special schools. Sandplay therapy had been used as an effective psychotherapy for children who are the autistic, abused, aggressive, traumatic and also for improving adults' interpersonal relationship and a training method for counselor's supervision. It can be seen sandplay therapy would have a better development in Chinese clinical practice field in the future.

Sandplay therapy for an undergraduate girl with obsessive-compulsive disorder
Zhang, Wen Dept. Developm. Psychology, Beijing Normal University, Beijing, People's Republic of China Zhang, Risheng Developmental Psychology, Beijing Normal University, Beijing, People's Republic of China Xu, Jie Developmental Psychology, Beijing Normal University, Beijing, People's Republic of China
To explore the psychotherapeutic process and effect of sandplay therapy for Obsessive-compulsive Disorder. Method: an undergraduate girl diagnosed using criteria from the DSM-IV with Obsessive-

compulsive Disorder was given 12 sessions of individual sandplay therapy. Result: The theme of the girl's sandtrays changed from traumatic to healing, from disrupted to centered. The Obsessive-compulsive symptoms of her became less severe and the social functioning improved after therapy. Conclusion: Sandplay therapy is effective as psychotherapy for Obsessive-compulsive Disorder, there are special characteristics in the therapeutic process and sandtrays of Obsessive-compulsive Disorder.

Paternalistic leadership and followers' outcomes: The mediating effects of leader-member exchange
Zhang, Kai School of Business, Renmin University of China, Beijing, People's Republic of China Huang, Ying School of Business, Renmin University of China, Beijing, People's Republic of China Song, Jiwen School of Business, Renmin University of China, Beijing, People's Republic of China
Paternalistic leadership (PL) had been found to be prevalent in Chinese context. Authoritarianism, benevolence, and moral leadership styles were regarded as its three dimensions. This study explored the effects of these dimensions of PL on followers' organizational citizenship behavior (OCB) and organizational commitment. The mediating effects of leader-member exchange (LMX) on the relationships between PL and followers' outcomes were tested. Two hundred and fourteen employees participated in this study. Correlation and hierarchical regression analyses were employed to test the hypotheses. The results showed that LMX fully mediates the relationships between PL and followers' OCB and partially mediates the relationships between PL and organizational commitment.

Cultural differences in attitudes towards mode of delivery: Elective caesarean sections in China and Germany
Zhao, Zengmei Experimentelle Psychologie, Universität Düsseldorf, Düsseldorf, Germany Zhou, Renlai EEG/ERP Laboratory, Beijing Normal University, Beijing, People's Republic of China Yin, Hengchan Physical Education and Sports, Beijing Normal University, Beijing, People's Republic of China
Considerable cultural differences in the preference for different birth modes have been observed. As a mode of delivery, elective caesarean sections are much more frequent in China than in Germany. To explore the background of this imbalance, attitudes towards mode of delivery were surveyed among pregnant Chinese and German women, as well as nonpregnant control women in both countries. The results show that Chinese women are more inclined to opt for an elective caesarean delivery. Significant cultural differences were observed in general attitudes toward elective caesarean sections and vaginal delivery, fear of pain, anxiety over childbirth, and anxiety over loss of control during birth.

A longitudinal study of children's peer acceptability and the effect of social behaviors from middle to late childhood
Zhao, DongMei Management College, Wuhan, People's Republic of China Zhou, ZongKui School of Psychology, HuaZhong Normal University, Wuhan, People's Republic of China Cohen, Robert Department of Psychology, University of Memphis, Memphis, Armenia Hsueh, Yeh Department of Psychology, University of Memphis, Memphis, People's Republic of China Sun, XiaoJun School of Psychology, HuaZhong Normal University, Wuhan, People's Republic of China
To explore the development of children's peer acceptability and the effect of social behaviors on their acceptability, 285 students of Grade 3 and 4 participated in a 3-year longitudinal study. Hier-

archical Linear Model was conducted. Results indicated that (1) children's peer rating scores both from girls and boys significantly ascended during the 3 years. There is gender difference in peer rating score. (2) Children's passive withdrawal negatively affected children's peer rating scores both from boys and girls significantly. Overt aggression negatively impacted children's peer rating scores from girls significantly. The passive withdrawal became maladaptive from middle childhood in Chinese culture.

Exploring loss aversion in 14 areas of P. R. China

Zheng, Rui Social & Economic Behavior, Institute of psychology, CAS, Beijing, People's Republic of China Li, Shu Social & Economic Behavior, Institute of psychology, CAS, Beijing, People's Republic of China Ren, Xiaopeng Social & Economic Behavior, Institute of psychology, CAS, Beijing, People's Republic of China Bai, Xinwen Social & Economic Behavior, Institute of psychology, CAS, Beijing, People's Republic of China

Loss aversion, the fact that losses have a greater impact than gains, is a fundamental property of behavioral accounts of choice. In this paper, we explored loss aversion among different classes. A public sample (N=4475) which from 14 area in China was tested. It found that : 1) there is a systematic individual difference among risk aversion.λvalue of older, less educated and lower-income individuals are higher than others; 2) The λ value of Public who came from city, town and rural area are significant different. 3) Interestingly, we show that higher life satisfaction decreased loss aversion.

The characteristic of obsessive-compulsive symptoms and the correlation with defense mechanisms in undergraduates

Zheng, Yin Zhanjiang, People's Republic of China Li, Jie Department of Psychology, PEKING UNIVERSITY, Zhanjiang, People's Republic of China

By means of investigation with questionnaires and interview of individuals, the characteristics of obsessive-compulsive special for undergraduates were analyzed and discussed in thiresearch. Meanwhile, the correlations between defense mechanisms and obsessive-compulsive symptoms of undergraduates were further investigated. The approach of questionnaires was employed to investigate the obsessive-compulsive symptoms of undergraduates and the defense mechanisms, based on an Obsessive-Compulsive Symptoms Questionnaire of Undergraduates. The result shows that there is significant correlation between obsessive-compulsive symptoms and the defense mechanisms of undergraduates. Especially, the usage of some immature and intermediate defense mechanisms is very meaningful in explaining the obsessive-compulsive symptoms of undergraduates

The relationship between working memory and representional level of children primary 4~6

Zhong, Ningning social work, Beijing youth politics college, Beijing, People's Republic of China

Working memory tasks (central executive task, Phonological loop task and visuospatial pad task) and representional task were administered to 161 students from the fourth to sixth grade, in order to explore the relation between working memory and representation. The results showed that: (1) Representational level was influenced by visuospatial pad, and representational level was the mediating variable between visuospatial pad and mathematical achievement; (2) Visuospatial pad capacity was greater, children' achievement difference between MPI test and MPI drawing test was less; (3) Phonological loop capacity was greater, children' achievement in MPI test improved but not significant.

The feature of elementary fourth to sixth graders' representational level in math word problem and its influence on problem-solving

Zhong, Ningning social work, Beijing youth politics college, Beijing, People's Republic of China Chen, Yinghe psychology department, Beijing Normal University, Beijing, People's Republic of China

Rectangle area task and MPI test were administered to 161 students from the fourth to sixth grade by experiment method, in order to explore the representational level in math word problem and its influence on problem-solving. The results showed that: (1) representational level improved with children entering the higher grade, and the gender difference was unsignificant on representational level; (2)Regardless of grade, superior pupils were highest on representational levels. When the representational level was higher, the test achievement was better; (3)With the items got more difficult, the difference of test achievement between representational levels got greater.

The effects of clues on Chinese anagram problem solving

Zhou, Zhijin Dept. of Psychology, Central China Normal Univers., Wuhan, People's Republic of China Li, Ruiju Psychology, Central China Normal Universit, Wuhan, People's Republic of China

Two experiments were conducted to explore the effect of clues on Chinese anagram problem solving, which used two kinds of clues that include answer-related words (semantic clues) and rules for guessing anagram problems. The results show that: (1) valid rule clues in both the subliminal and the supraliminal conditions can facilitate problem solving ; (2) valid supraliminal semantic clues can facilitate problem solving, whereas invalid supraliminal semantic clues have interference with problem solving; (3) both invalid semantic clues and rule clues under the liminal do not show any negative effect on problem solving.

The development of children's mutual friendship and the prospective effect of social behaviors: A three-year longitudinal study

Zhou, Zongkui School of Psychology, Huazhong Normal University, Wuhan, Hubei, People's Republic of China Zhao, DongMei Management College, South-Central Univ. for Nation, Wuhan, Hubei, People's Republic of China Liu, Jiujun School of Psychology, Huazhong Normal University, Wuhan, Hubei, People's Republic of China Cohen, Robert Department of Psychology, University of Memphis, Memphis, USA Hsueh, Yeh College of Education, University of Memphis, Memphis, USA

The current research aimed to investigate the development of children's mutual friendship and the effect of social behaviors on mutual friendship. 285 students of Grade 3 and 4 participated in a 3-year longitudinal study. Hierarchical Linear Model was conducted. Results indicated (1) children's mutual friends' number with boys and girls both significantly ascended during the 3 years. (2) Passive withdrawal had a significantly negative effect on children's mutual friends' number with boys; overt aggression had a significantly negative effect on children's mutual friends' number with girls, while relational aggression had a significantly positive effect on mutual friends' number with girls.

Friday 25th July 2008

IA-077: The architecture of emotion: Synchronisation of component processes

Werner Sommer (Chair)

Scherer, Klaus R. CISA, Universität Genf, Genf, Switzerland
Emotions are flexible response preparation mechanisms allowing organisms to adapt optimally to events of major significance for well being. Their key feature is the variable degree of coupling or synchronization of subsystems driven by the appraisal of the pertinence of events and the individual's ability to cope with consequences. This process is recursive (with sequential, cumulative effects) and occurs at several levels of automaticity, effort, and consciousness. The continuously varying response configurations, synchronized across motivational, expressive, and somatovisceral components, provide the organism's best estimate of an optimal action readiness. This architectural blueprint will be complemented by pertinent empirical findings.

IA-078: Neurological bases of counterfactual meaning

Rainer Kluwe (Chair)

de Vega, Manuel La Laguna, Spain
Counterfactual sentences like "If Mary had bough the lottery ticket, she would have won the prize" involve a dual meaning: The real world state (Mary did not buy the ticket nor won the prize) and an alternative "as if" world state (Mary bough the ticket and won the prize). We use behavioral methods as well as ERP and fMRI techniques to explore how people understand counterfactuals, focussing on two issues: Is counterfactual meaning embodied? That is, could it activate sensorimotor processes in the brain? And which is the role of prefrontal structures in processing the dual meaning of counterfactuals?

IA-079: Cultural cognition

Michael Knowles (Chair)

Tomasello, Michael Leipzig, Germany
Human beings are biologically adapted for cultural life in ways that other primates are not. Humans have unique motivations and cognitive skills for understanding other persons as intentional agents like the self with whom one can share emotions, experience, and collaborative actions (shared intentionality). The motivations and skills involved emerge in human ontogeny at around one year of age, as infants begin to participate with other persons in various kinds of collaborative and joint attentional activities (cultural practices), including linguistic communication.

IA-080: An evolving perspective on affects and self-regulation

Herbert Scheithauer (Chair)

Carver, Charles S. Dept. of Psychology, University of Miami, Coral Gables, USA
Models of separate systems for approaching incentives and avoiding threats typically incorporate ties to dimensions of affects. It is argued here that both systems relate to affects of both valences.

Frustration and anger enhance effort in incentive pursuit (as does eagerness), depression reflects disengagement from incentives perceived as unattainable, and happiness and joy promote relaxation of current effort toward the incentive to which the affect relates. These properties facilitate pursuit of incentives that are within reach, permits abandoning incentives that cannot be reached, conserves resources, and fosters attainment of multiple goals within a given time frame, via satisficing and multitasking.

IA-081: Developmental dyslexia: The visual attentional span hypothesis

Valdois, Sylviane Grenoble, France
The connectionist multitrace memory model of reading (Ans, Carbonnel & Valdois, 1998) predicts that developmental dyslexia might follow from a visual attention span (VAS) disorder. We will provide evidence from both group and single case studies showing that phonological and VAS disorders typically dissociate in developmental dyslexia. The cerebral correlates of VAS abilities will be identified and evidence reported for a selective dysfunction of parietal regions in the participants with a single VAS disorder. These overall findings support the existence of distinct dyslexia subtypes, in particular one subtype characterised by a VA span disorder resulting from a parietal cortex dysfunction.

IA-085: Reflection and impulse: Predicament and promise

Helio Carpintero (Chair)

Strack, Fritz Institut für Psychologie, Universität Würzburg, Würzburg, Germany
Depending on external requirements, the adaptation of human behavior involves accuracy and speed. These criteria require different psychological processes that operate in harmony or conflict. Recently, social psychologists have described a number of dual-systems models specifying the cognitive mechanisms that are linked with the two processes. The reflective-impulsive model (RIM) has added motivational and emotional components to explain how behavior is generated under different conditions. Specifically, the model claims that behavior is a joint function of reflective and impulsive mechanisms and describes their interaction at different sequential stages. It has implications for diverse manifestations of human thinking, feeling and acting.

IA-086: Multisensory processes and how they emerge

Dietrich Manzey (Chair)

Röder, Brigitte Hamburg, Germany
Events that stimulate more than one sensory system are usually processed faster and more accurate than unisensory events. Animal studies have suggested that although multisensory neurons exist in primates at birth, more specific multisensory processes develop during the first year of life. In animals but recently in humans as well it has been demonstrated that visual deprivation from birth causes changes in multisensory interactions. If vision is restored after

some months of congenital blindness, audio-visual integration capacities do not fully recover. These and other results suggest that multisensory functions in humans are acquired based on experience during ontogeny.

IA-087: The psychology of dieting and overweight: Testing a goal conflict model of the self-regulation of eating

Meinrad Perrez (Chair)

Stroebe, Wolfgang Social and Organ. Psychology, Utrecht University, Utrecht, Netherlands
Obesity has increased dramatically in developed countries. A theory will be presented which explains why self-regulation of weight can be difficult for chronic dieters in food-rich environments. According to this theory, the eating behaviour of chronic dieters (restrained eaters) is dominated by a conflict between two incompatible goals: enjoying palatable food and losing weight. While the dieting goal normally curbs the desire for eating enjoyment, this fragile balance is easily disturbed by attractive food cues resulting in inhibition of the dieting goal. Supportive research is presented. It is argued that this theory can integrate earlier theories of self-regulation of eating.

IA-088: The impact of mirror neurons on cognition

Frank Rösler (Chair)

Rizzolatti, Giacomo Parma, Italy
We live in a word full of objects, sounds and movements. Among these stimuli, the actions of our conspecifics are particularly important for survival. How do we understand the actions of others, their intentions and emotions? There is growing evidence that this capacity is largely based on a mechanism that directly transforms visual information on motor acts into a motor representation of the same acts. In my presentation I will review the properties of this mechanism ("mirror mechanism") and discuss its implications for cognition. I will conclude discussing the relationship between the impairment of mirror mechanism and autism.

IA-089: A cross-cultural perspective on the development of sharing behaviour: Integrating behavioural economics and psychology

Zhu, Liqi Institute of Psychology, Chinese Academy of Sciences, Beijing, People's Republic of China *Keller, Monika* Max-Planck Institute for human, Max-Planck Institute for human, Berlin, Germany
This study compared the development of sharing behavior among Chinese and German 8-, 11- 13- and 18-years-olds, by adopting classical economic games, the Dictator (DG) and Ultimatum Game (UG). Children's offers as proposers in both games were collected. Results showed that: In DG, there was no significant difference between Chinese and German children. However, in UG Chinese and German children showed different trajectories. As they got older, Chinese children were more likely to offer less, while German children's offers showed a U-shape. Cross-culturally, the majority of children

revealed a fairness orientation by preferring an equal split in both conditions.

IA-090: Emotion regulation and the social sharing of emotion: Interpersonal and collective processes

Ralf Schwarzer (Chair)

Rimé, Bernard Louvain-la-Neuve, Belgium
People talk recurrently about their emotions. It is commonly assumed to be relieving. Correlative and experimental studies assessed how far simply sharing an emotion reduced its impact. No such effects occurred, but participants reported benefits from sharing. Examining sharing interactions revealed them to elicit empathy. Little room is left to cognitive processing, which is critical to emotional recovery. It was then predicted that sharing an emotion with an empathic partner would not reduce the shared emotion, but would entail marked positive effects for socio-affective variables. Reverse predictions were formulated for a partner stimulating cognitive responses. Experiments successfully tested these predictions.

IA-091: New social identities and nationalism in Latin America: A psychopolitical perspective

Montero, Maritza Caracas, Venezuela
The address will discuss, from a social and political psychology perspective: 1) New social identities and psychological factors emerging in Latin America during the last three decades. 2) Populism and authoritarianism and, characteristics associated with a historically developed dictatorial tradition 3) New forms of nationalism and supra-nationalism (forms of social identities transcending national identification). Political discourses; media information; official documents and historical research are sources providing data for the analysis. Main psychological categories considered include: A) Construction of political myths; B) Search for father-figures in mother-centred societies. C) Modes of understanding and interpreting leadership. D) Definition and attribution of power and legitimacy.

IA-092: Credibility and ethnicity: Theoretical and empirical perspectives

Rainer K. Silbereisen (Chair)

Sabourin, Michel Dept. of Psychology, University of Montreal, Montréal, Canada
The issue of credibility is relatively unexplored by previous research on the impact of ethnic factors on the criminal justice system. After addressing the shortcomings of prior research, we have tried to extend previous findings concerning ethnicity by using a more ecologically valid scheme. Results show that cues to deceit are not universally shared. Behaviors vary both according to ethnicity and credibility, and the stage of the interrogation process may also play an important role. Findings are discussed in line with past results, and a clear picture, both theoretically and empirically, of the relation between credibility and ethnicity is presented.

IA-093: Social responses and steroids: Cognitive mediators

Salvador, Alicia Valencia, Spain
Testosterone and Cortisol are steroid hormones that are closely associated with social behaviour. Studying the impact of competitive encounters on levels of these steroids contributes to a better understanding of the effects of social stressors. Several studies from our laboratory suggest that

when people are in a competitive situation, they assess it in such a way that it activates a psychobiological coping response. Their extent (or intensity) depends on several cognitive factors such as expectations and perceived possibilities of control of the outcome. The coping pattern displayed by the subject determines the steroid response while facing competition and its outcome.

IS-130: Personality and culture

Jüri Allik (chair)
Culture, cross-role consistency and adjustment
Church, A. Timothy Educ. and Couns. Psychology, Washington State University, Pullman, USA Anderson-Harumi, Cheryl Educ. and Couns. Psychology, Washington State University, Pullman, WA, USA del Prado, Alicia Educ. and Couns. Psychology, Washington State University, Pullman, WA, USA Curtis, Guy School of Psychology, University of Western Sydney, Sydney, Australia Tanaka-Matsumi, Junko Department of Psychology, Kwansei Gukuin University, Nishinomiya-City, Japan Valdez-Medina, Jose Dept. of Behavioral Sciences, National Autonomous University, Toluca, Mexico Mastor, Khairul Pusat Pengajian Umum, Univ. Kebangsaan Malaysia, Bangi, Kuala Lumpur, Malaysia White, Fiona School of Psychology, University of Sydney, Sydney, Australia Miramontes, Lilia Educ. and Couns. Psychology, Washington State University, Pullman, WA, USA Katigbak, Marcia Educ. and Couns. Psychology, Washington State University, Pullman, WA, USA
Trait and cultural psychology perspectives on cross-role consistency was examined in two individualistic cultures, the United States and Australia, and four collectivistic cultures, Mexico, Philippines, Malaysia, and Japan. Cross-role trait consistency was evident in all cultures, supporting trait perspectives. Cultural comparisons of consistency supported cultural psychology perspectives as applied to East Asian cultures (i.e., Japan), but not collectivistic cultures generally. Cross-role consistency predicted adjustment best in the American sample and least in the Japanese sample. Alternative constructs proposed by cultural psychologists—personality coherence, social appraisal, and relationship harmony—predicted adjustment equally well in both individualistic and collectivistic cultures.

Personality, personality disorders and culture
Rossier, Jérôme Inst. of Psychology, University of Lausanne, Lausanne, Switzerland
The Five-Factor Model (FFM) is a culturally stable dimensional model describing normal personality and personality disorders (PDs) are defined as "an enduring pattern [...] that deviates markedly from the expectations of the individual's culture". The aim of this research was to assess, the stability of the structures underlying the FFM and PDs and the relationship between them in a large sample from nine African countries and Switzerland. Results showed that the structures underlying the FFM and PDs and that the relationship between them was stable across cultures. However, the expressions of these PDs might vary according to the cultural context.

5 x 20: Comparing the big five dimensions of personality across 20 countries
Rammstedt, Beatrice gesis-zuma, Mannheim, Germany
Over the last decades the Big Five dimensions of personality have become the most well-accepted model of personality wordwide. The International Social Survey Programme (ISSP) now assessed for the first time the Big Five in 20 different countries based on population representative samples. The countries/regions investigated were West-Germany, East-Germany, United States, Ireland, Czech Republic, Russia, New Zealand, Philippines, Israel, Japan, Latvia, France, Denmark, Switzerland,

Flanders, Mexico, Taiwan, South Korea, Dominican Republic. Means of the five dimensions will be compared across countries and stability of gender differences in personality across countries will be examined. Results will be discussed against the background of societal and socio-economic differences among the countries.

Comparison of gender stereotypes with gender differences across generations
Kourilova, Sylvie Dept. of Psychology, Academy of Sciences, Brno, Czech Republic Hrebickova, Martina Institute of Psychology, Academy of Sciences of the CZ, Brno, Czech Republic
The research question was whether gender stereotypes correspond to real-people-ratings. The Five-Factor Model was used for assessing gender stereotypes and personality traits. Gender stereotypical characteristics were assessed using the National Character Survey (NCS). Two different age groups were asked to rate a typical young, middle-age, and old man or woman. Aggregate self-report and observer-rating scores from the Czech NEO-PI-R normative sample were used to test the correspondence with the rated gender stereotypes. The results showed that the assessed gender differences are largely consistent with gender stereotypes across different age periods as well as across judges of different age.

Russian character and personality survey
Allik, Jüri Dept. of Psychology, University of Tartu, Tartu, Estonia
Data were collected by the members of the Russian Character and Personality Survey from 40 samples in 34 administrative areas of the Russian Federation. Respondents (N = 10,862) either rated an ethnically Russian adult or college-aged man or woman whom they knew well using the Russian observer rating version of the NEO-PI-R or rated a typical Russian using the 30-item NCS. Analysis of other-ratings showed that Russian data replicated main features of an international sample combining data from 50 different cultures. Although in general personality traits in Russians closely followed the universal pattern, some reliable culture-specific effects were also found.

IS-131: Self-regulation and personal goals in different domains

Katariina Salmela-Aro (chair)
People direct their life by selecting and setting personal goals: they are active producers of their own life (Lerner, 1982). The aim of the symposium, including papers from five different countries, US, UK, the Netherlands, Switzerland and Finland, is to focus on the role of personal goals on different key domains of adult's life: career, children, interpersonal, health, financial and ecological issues, representing the key developmental tasks of adults' life. By using individual within-person approach, experimental data as well as longitudinal data sets, the results show how personal goals contribute to common good, career, health and well-being.

Self-regulation and goal appraisals: Predicting and explaining intra-individual variability in appraisal patterns
Cervone, Daniel Dept. of Psychology, University of Illinois, Chicago, USA Caldwell, Tracy L. Dept. of Psychology, North Central College, Naperville, Illinois, USA Orom, Heather Dept. of Gerontology, Karmanos Cancer Institute, Detroit, MI, USA Shadel, William G. Behavioral Sciences, RAND Corporation, Pittsburgh, PA, USA
People's appraisals of their capacity to achieve personal goals contribute substantially to self-

regulatory success. These appraisals also may vary substantially, within-person, across domains and social contexts. Predicting and explaining intra-individual variability, then, is a major challenge. We address it by employing idiographically tailored personality assessments that are guided by model of personality architecture, the KAPA (Knowledge-and-Appraisal Personality Architecture) model. Recent findings are presented from two areas of investigation: the regulation of addictive behavior, and the deployment of coping strategies in inter-personal behavior. In both, findings indicate that highly accessible self-knowledge contributes to idiosyncratic-yet-predictable patterns of goal ap-praisal and self-regulated action.

Money or ecology: Age-related differences in self-related vs. generative goals in a complex problem solving task
Freund, Alexandra M. Inst. für Psychologie, Universität Zürich, Zürich, Switzerland
Are there age-related differences in goal-orientation when pitting the personal and common good against each other? Younger, middle-aged, and older adults (N = 102) took part in a complex problem solving task that allowed either maximiz-ing personal financial gains or maintaining the ecological state of a hypothetical orchard. Younger adults made significantly more financial gains than middle-aged and older adults, while older adults outperformed younger and middle-aged adults concerning the ecological state. While younger adults maximize personal gains at the cost of a common good, older adults are willing to sacrifice personal gains to maintain a common good.

Reliability and validity of the Self-Regulation Skills Battery (SRSB)
Maes, Stan Dept. of Psychology, Leiden University, Leiden, Netherlands De Gucht, Veronique Dept. of Psychology, Leiden University, Leiden, Netherlands
The SRSB measures goal-ownership, self-determi-nation, goal-efficacy, planning, self-monitoring, help-seeking, social comparison, self-criticism, self-reward, attention and emotion control, coping with problems and self-efficacy enhancement. Various populations completed the SRSB, including a general population, adolescent, worksite and var-ious patient samples. All subscales have good internal consistency. There is a relationship between self-regulation skills and healthy life-style in various samples. The SRSB can be used as a diagnostic tool for health promotion initiatives and life-style interventions.

Letting go of your dreams: Adjustment of child-related goal appraisals and depressive symptoms during infertility treatment
Salmela-Aro, Katariina Dept. of Psychology, University of Jyväskylä, Jyväskylä, Finland Suikkari, Anne-Mari Infertility clinic, Family Federation, Helsinki, Finland
To examine child-related goal adjustment during infertility treatment 178 (86 men, 92 women; age for females M = 33.92, SD = 0.34, for males M = 35.68, SD = 0.45) adults at Infertility Clinic in Helsinki filled in personal goal and depressive symptoms questionnaires six times during the infertility treat-ment. Appraisals concerning child-related goal importance, attainability, and partner support increased among those with a successful treatment outcome, while they decreased among those with an unsuccessful treatment. Child-related goal affects changed in tandem with the treatment result. Goal adjustment contributes to depressive symptoms particularly after unsuccessful treatment.

Career aspirations and occupational attainment: The adaptiveness of ambitious aims
Schoon, Ingrid Inst. of Education, University of London, London, United Kingdom
Objective: To examine association between teenage career aspirations and career attainment among men from socially disadvantaged family back-ground. Method: In a follow-up study of over 7,000 men born in 1958 and 1970 respectively, the formation and realization of teenage career aspira-tions is investigated with particular focus on the wider socio-historical context in which aspirations are developed. Result: Evidence is provided for an increasing role of educational credentials and school motivation in shaping occupational careers. Conclusion: Findings are discussed in terms of adaptiveness of ambitious career aspirations for succeeding in an increasingly competitive world.

IS-132: Best practice assessment challenges in applied contexts

Cheryl D. Foxcroft (chair)
The purpose of the symposium is to reflect on/evaluate the practices in various applied contexts, identify good practices and suggest ways of addres-sing specific challenges in applied contexts.

Admissions assessment in higher education
Watson, Andrea Center for Access Assess., Nelson Mandela Metro Univ., Port Elizabeth, South Africa Foxcroft, Cheryl HEADS Management, Nelson Mandela Metro Univ, Port Elizabeth, South Africa
The purpose of this paper is to provide an overview of higher education (HE) admissions assessment practices with a view to highlighting good practices. While a global overview will be given, the main focus of the paper will be on current practices in South Africa, as illustrated by a case study of a recently merged comprehensive university. The Nelson Mandela Metropolitan University has had to re-engineer its admissions assessment practices, given the changes in HE legislature and the merger process that it has undergone. Suggestions will be made regarding how future practices in this new institution could be enhanced.

Challenges for neuropsychological assessment in South Africa
Watts, Ann Medical Center, Entabeni Hospital, Durban, South Africa Pillay, Basil Dept. of Medical Applied Psych, University of KwaZulu Natal, Durban, South Africa
The multilingual, transcultural, and unequal educa-tion and health status of the people in South Africa poses serious challenges for the best practice of neuropsychological assessment, particularly as most available tests are of Euro-American origin. Using data from common neuropsychological assessments and selected case studies, an evaluation of current assessment practices in this applied field will be illustrated and discussed. Given that ethnicity, language, educational background and other bar-riers significantly influence the outcome on neu-ropsychological assessments, suggestions will be made as to how practices can be enhanced and undesirable practices addressed.

Developmental assessment: Practices and challenges
Stroud, Louise Psychology Clinic, Nelson Mandela Metrop. Uni., Port Elizabeth, South Africa
The purpose of this paper is to provide an overview of developmental assessment in general and the Griffiths Mental Development Scales – Extended Revised (GMDS-ER) in particular, with a view to highlighting good practices. While international trends will be provided, the main focus will be on current practices in South Africa, especially with respect to the appropriateness of the measures used. The implications of revising a measure used widely

internationally, such as the GMDS-ER, based largely on the country of origin, will be explored. Suggestions will be made regarding how future practices in developmental assessment using the GMDS-ER could be enhanced.

Career assessment challenges in changing applied contexts
Watson, Mark Dept. of Psychology, Nelson Mandela Metro Univers., Port Elizabeth, South Africa McMahon, Mary School of Education, The University of Queensland, Brisbane, Australia
The dominant story in career assessment for over a century has focused on quantitative, psychometric, standardised tools. In the recent context of an increasingly diverse society, a complex and fluid world of work, and an evolving career theory base, career assessment has been challenged to keep pace and provide meaningful assessment experiences. The lesser told story is that of qualitative career assessment, the focus of this paper. Using the example of My System of Career Influences, guidelines for the development and conduct of qualitative career assessment will be discussed and application to diverse age groups and cultural contexts considered.

IS-133: Emotions and behaviors associated to children and adolescents' violence at school

Nelda Cajigas de Segredo (chair)
This Symposium presents Latin America research on interpersonal school violence: emotions and cognitions associated with aggression plus protec-tive and at-risk factors for prevention. Chair and Discussant integrate, comment and, with the audience, question panellists: Cajigas, Kahan, Luzardo and Ugo examine Uruguayan adolescent clusters resulting from anger, depression and bullying; Lisboa and Koller investigate Brazilian at-risk children, their bullying managing skills and resilience promotion; Berger and Rodkin analyse the effect of groups on Chilean adolescents' aggression; Pérez Algorta studies aggressive inter-actions between Uruguayan teachers and pupils; and Fernández, de Paula e Silva and Ferreira Salles highlight imaginary dimensions of violence phe-nomena.

Study of clusters generated from student anger, depression and bullying in a Uruguayan middle school
Cajigas de Segredo, Nelda School of Psychology, University of Uruguay, Montevideo, Uruguay Kahan, Evelina School of Psychology, University of Uruguay, Montevideo, Uruguay Luzardo, Mario School of Psychology, University of Uruguay, Montevideo, Uruguay Ugo, María del Carmen School of Psychology, University of Uruguay, Uruguay
Anger, depression and bullying were studied in 604 adolescents from a low-income school in Montevi-deo to better understand interpersonal violence and assist its reduction. The Students were self-adminis-tered the following scales: the STAXI-C(Spielber-ger) and the CDI (Kovacs) translated and validated (Del Barrio et al., 1999) and the Bullying and Fighting Questionnaire (Espelage, 2000) translated and validated by this team. After scale factorization and validation of this population, at risk students have been gathered according to their response patterns. Ward hierarchical cluster analysis has been applied and the different types of risk present in the students will be described.

Coping with peer bullying and resilience promotion: Data from Brazilian at-risk children

Lisboa, Carolina *Post-Grad Clinical Psychology, Vale do Rio dos Sinos Univer., São Leopoldo, Brazil* *Koller, Silvia Helena* *Dept. de Psicologia, Univers. Fed. do Rio Grande, Porto Alegre, Brazil*

The aim of the study was to investigate coping with peer bullying. There is evidence that victimization decreases if social skills are improved, which can be related to resilience. Forty-eight at-risk children (m age= 11.8, SD= 1.4) answered the SCAN – Bullying. A qualitative analysis shows that children referred nonchalance strategies to deal with bullying. Few differences between gender and role were observed: non-victims referred to use more non-chalance strategies. These few differences show that coping may be related to the problem's nature and the reference to nonchalance strategies emphasizes the influence of cognitions and emotional regulation in dealing with bullying.

The mediating role of group influence on individual aggression among Chilean early adolescents

Berger, Christian *Dept. of Psychology, Alberto Hurtado University, Santiago, Chile* *Rodkin, Philip* *College of Education, University of Illinois Urbana, Champaign, IL, USA*

The present study assessed the influence of the peer group on individual aggression over a one-year period. Criticizing an individual approach to aggression, this study departs from understanding aggression as part of group dynamics serving social functions, particularly those related to social status. Hierarchical Linear Model analyses were performed on a sample of 647 5th and 6th graders followed up after one year. Results showed that peer group norms on aggression predicted individual levels of aggression after controlling for baseline aggression levels. This effect was also mediated by individual scores on perceived popularity. Methodological and conceptual considerations are further discussed.

Violent relationships between teachers and pupils in Uruguay

Pérez Algorta, Guillermo *Dept. of Psychology, Catholic University of Uruguay, Montevideo, Uruguay*

The purpose of this study is to evaluate teachers' perception about teacher-pupil violent relationships, topic scarcely studied. A sample of 400 teachers from primary and secondary school is completing the Bullying Teachers and Teacher Bullying Questionnaire (adapted from by Twemlow S., Fonagy P., Sacco F. & Brethour J., 2004) starting September 2007 and continuing over a period of six months. Main study results will be presented, among others, the prevalence of this type of violence in schools; its significant dimensions; the extent of teachers admitting being victims of bullying when students; and the style differences between Bullying and No-Bullying Teachers.

Violence in schools: Interpersonal and imaginary dimensions

Fernández Villanueva, Concepción *School Political Cs and Socio., Complutense Univ. of Madrid, Madrid, Spain* *Adam de Paula e Silva, Joyce* *EDUCAÇAO, UNESP, RIO CLARO, Brazil* *Ferreira Salles, Leila* *EDUCAÇAO., UNESP, RIO CLARO, Brazil*

In previous research about violence in young people (Fernández Villanueva, Domínguez Revilla y Gimeno 1998) four dimensions explaining youth violence were identified: groupality, identity, ideology and "imaginary." This analytical schema was usefully applied in school violence research. This paper presents results about imaginary aspects of violence in secondary schools in Brazil as well as interpretation of secondary data about school violence perpetrated in other contexts. Using the concept of "imaginary" based in Lacan, Castoriadis, Durand, Giust des Prairies and ourselves, we identified imaginary representations of actors, victims, social contexts and even imaginarization of concrete acts of violence.

IS-134: Justice sensitivity

Manfred Schmitt, Anna Baumert (chair)

Recent research is presented on cognitive, emotional and behavioural consequences of Justice Sensitivity. Two sets of studies show that victim sensitive persons rather behave selfishly while persons sensitive to become beneficiaries of injustice behave fairly toward others. A third contribution explains why victim-sensitive persons tend to antisocial behaviour. Data show that the expectation that others will behave unfairly legitimises own unfair behaviour. In a fourth study, Justice Sensitivity moderates the impact of organisational injustice on job satisfaction. A fifth contribution reveals coping mechanisms involved in Justice Sensitivity. A sixth paper explains how Justice Sensitivity shapes the processing of justice-related information.

In search for the good guys and the bad guys: Justice sensitivity and pro-social vs. anti-social behavior

Schlösser, Thomas *Institut für Ökonomie, Universiät Köln, Köln, Germany*

In our talk we will give an overview of six studies (with a total of about 800 participants) that show a robust influence of the personality-scale justice sensitivity on participants' decision to act in an either fair or selfish manner. These studies include different game theoretical paradigms (dictator games, ultimatum games, altruistic punishment games), donations to a charitable organization and studies on moral hypocrisy. In all studies a high level of justice sensitivity from the perspective of an observer or a beneficiary predicted prosocial behavior, whereas a high level of justice sensitivity from the victim's perspective predicted rather antisocial behavior.

Do empathy, perspective taking, or justice sensitivity modulate fairness in the context of experimental games?

Edele, Aileen *Inst. für Psychologie, Humboldt Universität zu Berlin, Berlin, Germany*

The current study aimed to elucidate to what extent socio-affective, socio-cognitive and normative functioning explain fairness in the dictator game. We expected affective empathy and justice sensitivity to relate positively to fairness while persective taking would be unrelated. Different aspects of empathy, perspective taking, and justice sensitivity (four perspectives) were assessed in 35 young adults who played the dictator game. Empathy and two other-oriented perspectives of justice sensitivity explained fairness, but perspective taking did not. The results support the assumption that affective and selective normative dispositions explain differences in fair and prosocial behavior, whereas social cognition does not.

When justice sensitivity leads to antisocial behavior: The relation between victim sensitivity and assumptions about mean intentions

Rothmund, Tobias *Inst. für Psychologie, Universität Koblenz-Landau, Landau, Germany* *Gollwitzer, Mario* *Inst. für Psychologie, Universität Koblenz-Landau, Landau, Germany*

The present research addresses the question why Justice Sensitivity from the victim's perspective (JS-Victim) is related to antisocial behavior. We argue that JS-Victim encompasses both a motive to trust in the goodness of others and the expectation that others might be not trustworthy. When elicited by particular situational cues, both cognitions evoke a "suspicious mindset", which consists of an attributional bias regarding the immoral intentions of others and a legitimization for behaving immorally oneself. Findings from two laboratory experiments support these assumptions and help answering the question in which situations a trait effect of JS-Victim is most likely to occur.

How do I deal with injustice? Differences in coping patterns for justice sensitivity from a victim and perpetrator perspective

Nazlic, Tanja *Inst. für Sozial-Psychologie, Universität München, München, Germany* *Traut-Mattausch, Eva* *Inst. für Sozial-Psychologie, Universität München, München, Germany* *Frey, Dieter* *Inst. für Sozial-Psychologie, Universität München, München, Germany*

Research on relationships between Justice Sensitivity (JS) and other constructs (Schmitt et al., 2005) has not explicitly considered cognitive and behavioural coping. We expect more dysfunctional coping amongst JS from a victim-perspective whereas the perpetrator-perspective should be associated with more functional coping. A correlational study revealed evidence for our hypotheses: victim-sensitivity was e.g. associated with emotional coping and other-blame, the perpetrator-sensitivity with active coping and task-orientation. Two additional studies replicated this result through induction of victim- and perpetrator-perspective. Coping strategies can further clarify effects of JS on perception, thinking and behaviour. Successful induction of justice-perspectives will be discussed regarding intervention-strategies.

The moderating effect of justice sensitivity on organizational justice: Job satisfaction relationship in a health care setting

Ozer, Pinar *Business Administration, Dokuz Eylul University, Izmir, Turkey* *Gunay, Gonca* *Business Administration, Izmir University of Economics, Izmir, Turkey* *Basbakkal, Zumrut* *School of Nursing, Ege University, Izmir, Turkey*

Numerous studies have shown that perceptions of organizational justice have a positive relationship with job satisfaction. However, this relationship varies according to different individual factors. In this research, main emphasis was on justice sensitivity as an individual factor. Hence, this research attempted to identify the nature of the relationship between organizational justice and job satisfaction in a health care setting incorporating the moderating effect of justice sensitivity. Research was conducted applying a survey methodology and data was collected from nurses. The results indicate that justice sensitivity moderates the relationship between procedural justice and job satisfaction.

How justice sensitivity (JS) shapes attention and memory

Baumert, Anna *Inst. für Psychologie, Universität Koblenz-Landau, Landau, Germany* *Schmitt, Manfred* *Inst. für Psychologie, Universität Koblenz-Landau, Landau, Germany*

Attention and encoding processes shaped by JS are investigated: In an emotional Stroop task, interference for unjust words increased with increasing JS if injustice was primed (Study 1). In Study 2, high JS led to interpretations of ambiguous situations as less just, if injustice was primed. In Study 3, individuals high in JS were more focused in their information seeking when investigating potential injustice. Study 4 demonstrated that memory performance for justice-related information increased with increasing JS if the learning situation was framed as justice-related. Taken together, our research suggests that justice-related memory and attention function in congruency to JS.

Motivation, recall and information processing
Sanitioso, Bo Dept. of Psychology, Université Paris Descartes, Paris, France
The symposium concerns the influence of motivation on recall and information processing. The first three presentations focus on research showing the influence of (self-related) motivation on the semantic content and subjective experience of autobiographical memory recall (Sanitioso), the use of ease of remembering past behaviors as a basis for self-perception (Echterhoff), and processing of general information not directly related to the self (Augustinova). Next, research on the role of internal states in "if-then" plan implemented in goal striving is presented (Achtziger). Finally, Dunning presents data suggesting motivated reasoning can occur below awareness, related to inhibition and to visual stimuli preferences.

IS-135: Daily structure of cognitive performance

Rolf Ulrich (chair)
The multi-disciplinary research network Clock-WORK (initiated by the Daimler-Benz-Stiftung) investigates the daily structure of work with special emphasis on circadian timing of higher cognitive performance, such as task-switching, speech perception and fine motor control. This symposium aims to give an overview of the problems arising from the conflict between circadian and social timing and presents the latest results on daily cognitive performance produced by the team of Clock-WORK researchers in a series of constant routines.

The human circadian clock in real life
Rönneberg, Till Inst. für Med. Psychologie, Medizin. Universität München, München, Germany
Human life is controlled by the social, the sun, and the biological clock. We are most aware of the social clock, but the biological clock (synchronised by the sun clock) tells our body to do what when at all levels. When biological clocks run free in constant (time-less) conditions, they continue with a period close to 24 h (circadian) – in real life, they are synchronised to the 24-hour cycle of sun clock. Circadian clocks show large individual differences in their synchronisation – earlier or later – forming a normal distribution with the 'larks' and 'owls' forming the extremes.

Circadian variation in cognitive control
Bratzke, Daniel Inst. für Psychologie, Universität Tübingen, Tübingen, Germany Rolke, Bettina Inst. für Psychologie, Universität Tübingen, Tübingen, Germany Steinborn, Michael Inst. für Psychologie, Universität Tübingen, Tübingen, Germany Ulrich, Rolf Inst. für Psychologie, Universität Tübingen, Tübingen, Germany
In two studies, we investigated whether cognitive control mechanisms are subject to circadian variation. As measures of cognitive control, dual-task interference and task-switch costs were assessed. In order to reveal circadian variations in these two tasks, we used constant routine protocols. Dual-task interference and task-switch costs showed a time-of-day modulation resembling the circadian variation in overall reaction time performance. These findings suggest that tasks requiring cognitive control are particularly sensitive to the influence of the circadian system.

The triangle of sleep, clock and light in the context of shift-work
Juda, Myriam Inst. für Med. Psychologie, Medizin.Universität München, München, Germany Roenneberg, Till Inst. für Med. Psychologie, Medizin.Universität München, München, Germany
Although night shift-workers sleep during the day, they are still being exposed to daylight and therefore remain synchronised to the normal cycle of day and night. Night shift-workers want to sleep when the circadian clock tunes their physiology and alertness to normal day-time levels and they have to work when the body clock is set to night. Shift workers can also experience a social desynchronisation as their participation in the community is often being heavily compromised. By means of the Munich Chronotype Questionnaire for Shift Workers (MCTQshift) and by taking into account a multitude of relevant physiological, cognitive, and psycho-social factors, we find strong support for chronotype-specific differences in tolerance to shift work.

Circadian influences on sensorimotor control
Jasper, Isabelle Klinische Neuropsychologie, München-Bogenhausen Hospital, München, Germany Häußler, Andreas Hermsdörfer, Joachim
While a circadian rhythm is proved in gross motor performance, studies on circadian influences on different aspects of dexterous fine motor performances are scarce. Various sensorimotor tasks were performed every 3 hours by right-handed males in two 40 hour Constant Routine protocols. Fine motor skills of handwriting are subjected to a circadian rhythm with slower and smaller handwriting during the night. Circadian variations have also been found for maximum grip force and other fine motor skills. The similar circadian rhythmicity of fine and gross motor performance could devise strategies to optimize the structure of daily work concerning motor demands.

Circadian rhythm in speech perception
Pusch, Kathrin Inst. für Linguistik, Humboldt-Universität zu Berlin, Berlin, Germany Dietrich, Rainer Psycholinguistics, Humboldt University of Berlin, Berlin, Germany Sommer, Werner Biological Psychology, Humboldt University of Berlin, Berlin, Germany
This study deals with the question of circadian oscillations in phonetic speech perception. 12 subjects performed a behavioural discrimination task in a forced choice paradigm and a passive oddball paradigm every 3h during 40h of sustained wakefulness under controlled conditions. Acoustic and phonetic stimuli were presented to both ears via headphones in both auditory tasks. A significant circadian modulation of reaction time indicates circadian oscillations in phonetic speech perception which cannot be accounted for solely by effects of alertness. Analysis of pre-attentive mismatch negativity elicited by pitch deviants and vocal-consonant-deviants should give more information about construct validity of this result.

Circadian and homeostatic influences on interval timing
Späti, Jakub Zentrum für Chronobiologie, Psychiatr. Universitätsklinik, Basel, Switzerland Hofstetter, Marcel Zentrum für Chronobiologie, Psychiatr. Universitätsklinik, Basel, Switzerland Cajochen, Christian Zentrum für Chronobiologie, Psychiatr. Universitätsklinik, Basel, Switzerland
Duration judgments are essential in everyday life. During 40-h of sustained wakefulness, production and reproduction of 3.75-s, 5-s, 7.5-s, 10-s and 15-s were probed every 3-h in 12 young males. The tasks yielded antidromic response curves across the 40-h episode. Reproduction displayed wake-dependent changes for shorter (3.75-s, 5-s) and circadian modulation for longer intervals (10-s, 15-s); 7.5-s intervals were reproduced accurately during the entire protocol. The findings reveal a complex interaction between task type, interval length, circadian phase and state of the sleep-wake homeostat which are yet to be incorporated into models of interval timing.

IS-136: Analysis of causal effects in experiments and observational studies

Rolf Steyer (chair)
Treatment effects are traditionally analyzed with ANOVA, ANCOVA or regression models. There, treatment effects are identified with one or several parameters in these models. However, these parameters do not equal the treatment effects if there is systematic selection of subjects to treatments. Since the 70ties, Rubin revived Neyman's 1923-theory of individual and average causal effects developing procedures for estimating and testing average treatment effects such as matching on propensities. Leading experts will present and illustrate this and other new procedures and show how ANOVA and regression techniques can be integrated into a unified theory of individual and average causal effects.

Sufficient conditions for unbiased average and conditional causal treatment
Steyer, Rolf Inst. für Psychologie, Universität Jena, Jena, Germany
Self-selection of units into treatment conditions and systematic attrition may lead to severely biased treatment effect estimates. It is well-known that we can adjust for this bias under the assumption of strong ignorability, e.g., via propensity score analyses. I will present alternative sufficient conditions for unbiasedness and for successful adjustment. In contrast to strong ignorability, some of these other sufficient conditions are empirically testable, at least in the sense of falsifiability. This is also of practical importance, because these sufficient conditions for unbiasedness – again unlike strong ignorability – can also be utilized in choosing covariates on which adjustments are based. Alternatives to propensity score adjustments are presented as well.

Title to be announced
Rubin, Donald B. Dept. of Statistics, Harvard University, Cambridge, USA
For objective causal inferences from nonrandomized comparative studies, often called observational studies, they must be esigned to parallel, as closely as possible, randomized experiments. There are several aspects of this, the most obvious of which is the lack of any outcome data during this process, but there are several other activities that are critical. This presentation will describe these, which generally require a great deal of thought before any computing can begin.

Conditions under which adjustments for nonrandom assignment might be successful
Shadish, William R. Dept. of Psychology, University of California, Merced, CA, USA
When units self-select into conditions, effect estimates may be biased. In theory, bias can be reduced if the assumption of strong ignorability is met, but this is difficult to assess in practice. The present study examines several measures of strong ignorability. Results suggest that a necessary but not sufficient condition for successful adjustment is obtaining balance between conditions after propensity score adjustment, and that bias reduction is highly correlated with the indirect measures of strong ignorability—the more likely it is that strong ignorability is met, the greater the bias reduction.

Two conditions under which experiments and quasi-experiments have repeatedly given comparable causal estimates
Cook, Thomas D. Dept. of Policy Research, Northwestern University, Evanston, IL, USA
This paper describes the results from a set of studies where the results from a randomized experiment are

compared to those from a quasi-experiment sharing the same intervention group. Similar causal results are achieved when the experiment is compared to regression-discontinuity and to designs employing intact group matching. However, correspondence is rarer when attempts are made to equate two demonstrably non-equivalent groups through statistical adjustments or individual case matching. In this last case, covariates capturing the selection process are crucial. Yet there is rarely any way to know that one has indeed validly assessed the selection process.

Title to be announced

West, Stephen G. *Dept. of Psychology, Arizona State University, Tempe, USA*
In studies with non-random assignment the Campbell tradition has emphasized inclusion of design elements that address specific threats to interval validity. We illustrate this using an evaluation of a sales campaign in which (a) nonequivalent dependent variables and (b) multiple pre- and post-tests are employed. The Rubin tradition has emphasized careful specification of the causal estimand and propensity score procedures that provide close matches of treatment and control participants. We illustrate this using an evaluation of the effect of retention in grade on schoolchildren. Other modern statistical methods for equating groups are mentioned. The Campbell and Rubin approaches are compared.

Testing general hypotheses on individual causal effects using aggregate data

Erdfelder, Edgar *Lehrstuhl Psychologie III, Universität Mannheim, Mannheim, Germany* **Auer, Tina-Sarah** *Lehrstuhl Psychologie III, Universität Mannheim, Mannheim, Germany*
Experimental psychologists usually test hypotheses referring to the means of dependent variables calculated across individuals. However, a careful analysis of the underlying research questions reveals that the substantive hypotheses stimulating experimental research almost always conform to general hypotheses on individual causal effects (ICEs) rather than to statistical hypotheses on average causal effects (ACEs). We aim at bridging the gap between statistical and substantive hypotheses by analyzing under which conditions strong conclusions on ICE distributions can be inferred from aggregate data. A procedure of testing general hypotheses on ICEs is proposed and illustrated using examples from cognitive aging research.

IS-137: Test security applications of innovation in data forensics analysis

David Foster (chair)
This security symposium highlights the current threats to test security and new methods and technology to combat them. Participants will present research on the effectiveness of any of several new technologies in the area of test security. These include, but are not limited to security-friendly test and item designs, data forensics analyses, web monitoring systems, copyright infringement detection tools, item exposure controls and algorithms, and biometrics and other authentication technologies and methods.

Catching cheaters with better testing procedures and statistics

Hambleton, Ronald *School of Education, University of Massachusetts, Amherst, USA*
More and more often instances are being reported of cheating on tests. The goal of this paper will be to briefly describe some of the ways in which cheating is being done, and then to describe practices that might improve the validity of test scores to reduce

the level of cheating and catch at least some of the cheaters. These practices extend from better informing everyone about what is acceptable and unacceptable behavior concerning tests, to improving test security and administration procedures, to identifying cheaters based upon statistical analyses of their item response data.

Monitoring of suspicious response-time patterns on computerized tests

van der Linden, Wim *Faculty of Behavioral Sciences, University of Twente, Enschede, Netherlands* **Quo, Fanmin**
To identify aberrant response-time patterns on educational and psychological tests, it is important to separate the speed at which the test taker operates from the time the items require. A lognormal model for response times with this feature was used to derive a Bayesian procedure for detecting aberrant response times. A combination of the response-time model with a regular response model in an hierarchical framework was used in an alternative procedure for the detection of aberrant response times. The procedures are illustrated using a data set for the Graduate Management Admission Test® (GMAT®).

Applying data forensics to defend the validity of online employment tests

Burke, Eugene *Dept. of Psychometrics, SHL Group Limited, Thames Ditton, United Kingdom* **Maynes, Dennis**
SHL uses on-demand tests through the Internet which are unsupervised. Using Caveon's data forensics technology SHL has developed a security strategy to support the deployment and use of these tests. Regular data forensic audits of candidate data are undertaken to review a number of key indices such as high scores, collusion, highly speeded patterns of responding as well as score aberrance. The paper describes the data forensics indices for these analyses and results for over 60,000 live candidates who have been audited using these indices. How these audits are used to inform and improve test security is also described.

Using large-scale simulations to evaluate the effects of cheating

Wright, Dave *USA*
This paper shares results from large scale simulations used to evaluate the effect of cheating on the benefit from testing, and the benefits from verification of test scores in managing the impacts of cheating. Two examples are provided from over 1,000 simulations, one typifying an honest testing condition and one typifying high levels and impacts of cheating (1 in 5 candidates engage in cheating through proxy with a 2 SD gain in scores). These examples serve to show the loss of benefit from cheating and the recovery of that benefit offered by verification procedures.

IS-138: Language processing in Chinese

Hsuan-Chih Chen (chair)
To build a genuinely comprehensive theory of language processing, it is important and useful to conduct cross-language research. The Chinese language, due to its salient differences in structure from European languages, provides challenging opportunities to explore both universal and language-specific processes. Hence, selected recent studies on processing Chinese and their implications will be presented and discussed.

Morphemic ambiguity resolution in processing Chinese

Tsang, Yiu-Kei *Dept. of Psychology, Chinese Univ. of Hong Kong, Hong Kong, China, People's Republic of : Hong Kong SAR* **Chen, Hsuan-Chih** *Hong Kong, China, People's Republic of : Hong Kong SAR*
Chinese monosyllables typically represent morphemes and can be written down with individual logographic characters. A morphemically ambiguous situation occurs when a syllable is part of a compound word, but its dominant meaning bears no relationship to the word. We present results of two experiments designed to investigate meaning dominance and semantic context in morphemic ambiguity resolution using a visual world paradigm. Both meaning dominance and context showed reliable effects on the eye movement data. The results are discussed in terms of the time course of morphemic ambiguity resolution in processing spoken Chinese.

The role of semantic radicals in Chinese character recognition: Behavioural and electrophysiological findings

Weekes, Brendan S. *Dept. of Psychology, University of Sussex, Brighton, United Kingdom* **Su, I-Fan** *Dept. of Psychology, University of Sussex, Brighton, United Kingdom*
The semantic radicals of Chinese characters can convey meaning information to the reader. Previous research has demonstrated that radicals affect character identification and categorization. Our objective is to illustrate how radical consistency, transparency and combinability are involved in semantic access using lexical decision, semantic categorization and picture-word interference tasks as well as event related potentials. The results show areas of activity related to differential features of semantic radicals emerge at different spatial and temporal loci during pre-lexical and post-lexical processing. Our findings inform cognitive models of word recognition in Chinese and highlight challenges for the development of these models.

Involvement of cognitive control in Chinese sentence comprehension: Evidence from fMRI

Zhou, Xiaolin *Dept. of Psychology, Peking University, Beijing, People's Republic of China* **Ye, Zheng** *Dept. of Psychology, Peking University, Beijing, People's Republic of China*
We manipulated plausibility and syntax to examine the involvement of cognitive control to resolve conflicts between incompatible sentential representations in Chinese sentence comprehension. The results showed increased activations for implausible relative to plausible sentences over medial prefrontal cortex (mPFC), left middle frontal gyrus (LMFG), and left inferior frontal gyrus (LIFG). The LIFG activity was affected by both factors, while the activities of mPFC and LMFG were only influenced by Plausibility. Thus, processing implausible sentences needs brain regions responsible for the implementation of linguistic representation (LIFG) and those associated with the resolution of representational conflict regardless of information type.

Age-of-acquisition effects on naming characters in two Chinese dyslexic individuals

Law, Sam-Po *Speech and Hearing Sciences, University of Hong Kong, Hong Kong, China, People's Republic of : Hong Kong SAR* **Yeung, Olivia** *Speech and Hearing Sciences, University of Hong Kong, Hong Kong, China, People's Republic of : Macao SAR* **Wong, Winsy** *Speech and Hearing Sciences, University of Hong Kong, Hong Kong, China, People's Republic of : Macao SAR*
We examined dyslexic individuals' performance on reading aloud single characters varying in age-of-acquisition (AoA), consistencies related to the semantic and phonetic radicals, and other variables.

The results of initial assessment suggest that FWL showed a reliance on the non-semantic reading route with greatly reduced semantic input, while TWT's reading aloud was mainly mediated by the semantic reading route. Regression analyses were used to analyze their reading performance. It was found that AoA and phonological consistency significantly predicted FWL's performance, and AoA and semantic transparency significantly accounted for TWT's. The findings are consistent with the arbitrary mapping hypothesis.

Reading unspaced scripts: Eye movement in reading Chinese and Japanese

Feng, Gary Psychology and Neuroscience, Duke University, Durham, USA Mazuka, Reiko Psychology and Neuroscience, Duke University, Durham, USA Jincho, Nobuyuki /, REIKEN Brain Science Institute, /, Japan

Current theories of reading eye movements assume that explicitly marked word boundaries enable strategic eye-movement programming and parafoveal processing. The Chinese and Japanese scripts present a challenge because they do not mark word boundaries. Using a gaze-contingent paradigm, we show that Chinese and Japanese readers optimize their eye-movement planning by exploiting visual correlates of linguistic units. Adding spaces to the scripts result in shorter fixation duration but more fixations, thus does not substantially improve reading speed. Simulation studies also show that existing visual cues in the unspaced scripts afford useful eye-movement strategies that additional spaces get diminished returns.

Chinese and English speakers' perception of the time of an event

Chen, Jenn-Yeu Inst. of Cognitive Science, National Cheng Kung University, Tainan, Taiwan Su, Juiju Inst. of Cognitive Science, National Cheng Kung University, Tainan, Taiwan

We examined whether tense might affect English and Chinese speakers' time perception of an event. Chinese and English speakers described each presented pictures in their native languages. The pictures depicted action events that were happening, have happened, or were about to happen. Chinese speakers displayed a strong tendency of describing a past/future event as a present one and were less accurate in capturing the time of an event than English speakers. It appears that the particular linguistic forms adopted in a language can bias its speakers towards focusing on certain aspects of the world in exclusion of others.

IS-139: Individual stress resistance: Conceptual foundations and applied research

Anna Leonova (chair)
The symposium gives an overview of contemporary research in individual stress resistance. The goal of the presenters is an integrative representation of approaches to evaluation and upholding of stress resistance through a set of predictors of efficient behavior, well-being and mental health of the subject under influence of unfavorable environmental and psychosocial factors. The discussion comprises the role of genetic predispositions, resource investing coping, organizational support as well as emotional regulation in the framework of state-trait approach. New diagnostic and prevention tools are exemplified by results of empirical studies carried out in context of different subdisciplines of psychological science.

Individual differences in response to psychosocial stress – from genes to social interaction

Kirschbaum, Clemens Inst. für Psychologie, Technische Universität Dresden, Dresden, Germany Rohleder, Nicolas Inst. für Psychologie, Technische Universität Dresden, Dresden, Germany Mueller-Fries, Eva Inst. für Psychologie, Technische Universität Dresden, Dresden, Germany

The burdens of chronic or traumatic psychological stress are significant, both for the individual and society. Among the pathways responsible for the impact of adverse psychological stimulation, the hypothalamus-pituitary-adrenal (HPA) axis appears to be key. A combination of social-evaluative threat with a loss of controllability is the strongest predictors of HPA activation under laboratory and real-life conditions. Imaging studies suggest that prefrontal brain structures (including BA 9 and 10) control the stress-induced endocrine response. In addition, recent evidence from behavioral genetics suggests a role for neurotransmitter polymorphisms in the HPA response. Finally, intracellular signaling cascades are being unraveled describing how stress gets under the skin.

Preventing burnout and building engagement

Maslach, Christina Dept. of Psychology, University of California, San Francisco, USA

Burnout has been an issue of major concern in the workplace, given its high costs for both employees and organizations. Its presence as a social problem in many occupations has been the impetus for the research that is now taking place in many countries. Empirical findings show that burnout is largely a function of the social environment in which people work. The key causes lie in six critical areas of mismatch between the person and the job. Solutions to prevent burnout and to achieve its opposite, engagement with work, exist at both the individual and organizational level.

Psychological evaluation of individual stress resistance by the means of state-trait paradigm

Leonova, Anna Faculty of Psychology, Moscow State University, Moscow, Russia Velichkovsky, Boris Faculty of Psychology, Moscow State University, Moscow, Russia

An individual level of stress and its outcomes strongly depend on enduring personal attitudes and transitory appraisals of the situation. Accordingly, a psychodiagnostic model of stress resistance in the framework of state-trait paradigm was developed. It is based on integrative assessment of indicators of anxiety, aggression, depression, and exhaustion considered as dispositional traits and actual states crucial in the stress evoking process. The model was validated by an examination of contrast groups: psychosomatic patients and personnel with high/low job efficiency (745 persons). Furthermore, marked differences in the stress resistance profiles help to compile preventive programs appropriate for each individual case.

The role of resource investment coping in a development of individual stress resistance

Vodopyanova, Natalia Faculty of Psychology, St.Petersburg State University, St. Petersburg, Russia Starchenkova, Elena Faculty of Psychology, St.Petersburg State University, St.Petersburg, Russia

The concept of resource investment coping is considered through the modes of cognitive, emotional, and behavioral efforts' utilization for a conservation and/or enhancing individual capacities to cope with stressful situations. In the study of railroad dispatchers the interrelations between indicators of a stable job performance, current emotional states and coping styles were analyzed with including the measures of the Greenglass Proactive Coping Inventory and the Hobfoll Gain/Loss Checklist. The data suggest that dispatchers with a higher stress resistance use a wider

range of proactive coping strategies. It provides the use of better recovery strategies and anticipation of emerging stress events.

A complex non-drug technology for improving the level of individual stress-resistance

Glazachev, Oleg Inst. of Normal Physiology, Academy of Medical Sciences, Moscow, Russia Dudnik, Elena Inst. of Normal Physiology, Academy of Medical Sciences, Moscow, Russia Yartseva, Ludmila VNIIMI, Academy of Medical Sciences, Moscow, Russia Platonenko, Vyacheslav VNIIMI, Academy of Medical Sciences, Moscow, Russia

An individual level of stress resistance is considered as a human ability to retain efficient behavior and well-being by an adequate tension of regulatory mechanisms and homeostatic functions under the press of psychosocial stress-factors. This approach is exemplified by the results of empirical studies on psychosomatic patients and overtraining sportsmen. Different patterns of uncontrolled stress reactions are considered as the qualitative predictors of lowering stress resistance. Efficient prevention of such negative effects without drug assumption can be achieved by implementation of the complex rehabilitation system elaborated on the basis of physiotherapeutic multi-modal technology "Alfa Spa System" (Sybaritic INK, USA).

IS-140: New trends in clinical psychology

Winfried Rief, Stefan Hofmann (chair)
Clinical psychology is a fast developing field. This symposium will highlight a few of these new trends. An example of integrating new trends of genetics, brain imaging, and cognitive-emotional aspects will be reported by Joormann. Another new trend is to amplify the effect of psychological interventions using pharmacotherapy. A further emerging field is the use of the internet and virtual reality for enhancing the effect of psychological interventions (Botella). Finally, this symposium will be concluded by a presentation how psychological interventions can support the treatment not only of mental disorders, but also of medical conditions.

Amplifying the effect of psychological interventions through pharmacotherapy

Hofmann, Stefan Dept. of Psychology, Boston University, Boston, USA

Recent advances in the neuroscience of fear-reduction have led to novel approaches for combining psychological therapy and pharmacological treatments. Exposure-based therapy is partly based on extinction to reduce the fear response in anxiety disorders. Animal studies have shown that D-cycloserine (DCS), partial agonist at the glycine recognition site of the glutametergic N-methyl-D-aspartate receptor facilitates extinction learning. Similarly, a number of recent studies in humans have shown that DCS enhances fear reduction during exposure therapy of some anxiety disorders. This presentation will discuss the biological and clinical aspects of this emerging field of translational research.

Genetics, brain imaging and cognitive-emotional aspects and their relevance for psychopathology

Joormann, Jutta Dept. of Psychology, University of Miami, Coral Gables, FL, USA Gotlib, Ian Dept. of Psychology, Stanford University, Stanford, CA, USA

Important developments that promise to change clinical psychology in the coming years include advances in molecular genetics and brain imaging. In a sample of girls at high risk for depression, we investigated how a polymorphism in the serotonin transporter gene is related to neural correlates of emotion regulation and neuroendocrine responses to stressful situations thereby moderating the link between stressful life events and emotional disorders. This polymorphism was related to cognitive biases that have been implicated in depression. Our findings suggest an important role for the integration of genetic factors and brain imaging research into current models of emotional disorders.

The internet and virtual reality as tools to increase the efficiency of psychological interventions

Botella, Cristina Dept. of Psychology, Universitat Jaume I, Castellón, Spain *Gallego, M. Jose* Dept. of Psychology, University of Jaume I, Castellon, Spain *Garcia Palacios, Azucena* Dept. of Psychology, University of Jaume I, Castellon, Spain *Baños, Rosa* Dept. of Personality, University of Valencia, Valencia, Spain

In order to evaluate the efficacy of two Internet-based interventions seventy-seven participants with social phobia were randomized to: a) "Talk to me" a telepsychology treatment for fear of public speaking, b) a therapist-delivered treatment, or c) a waiting-list control group. Also, thirty-five participants with specific phobia were randomized to either: a) "Without fear", a telepsychology treatment for specific phobia animal type, or b) a therapist-administered treatment. These studies showed that both Internet-based treatments were equally effective than the therapist-administered treatment. Our work demonstrated that online cognitive-behavioral programs could be a good alternative in the treatment of specific phobias.

Psychological interventions for medical conditions

Rief, Winfried Inst. für Psychologie, Universität Marburg, Marburg, Germany

Even in medical conditions with clear organic pathology, psychological factors play a major role for illness-related disability and management strategies. This is confirmed in a study investigating 50 patients receiving heart surgery (e.g., valve replacement or bypass). Disability 3 months after the surgery was mainly predicted from illness perceptions and attitudes as assessed before the medical interventions, but not from medical status before or after surgery. Two randomized clinical trials, one including 120 chronic back-pain patients, the other including 110 tinnitus sufferers, further confirm the relevance of psychological approaches in medical conditions.

The psychological treatment of hallucination and dellusion

Kuipers, Elizabeth Dept. of Psychology, Institute of Psychiatry, London, United Kingdom

Delusions and hallucinations used to be thought of as 'unamenable' to rational discussion (Jasper 1913). However, since the 1990s cognitive behavioural approaches to anxiety, trauma and depression have been extended to the difficulties found in psychosis, in addition to antipsychotic medication. There have now been a number of randomised controlled trials and several meta analyses. The most recent of these confirm that medication resistant delusions and to some extent hallucinations are most responsive to these approaches usually via improvements in affect (depression). Treatment effects are moderate, at best. The mechanisms that may be involved, and the future development of such treatments will be discussed.

IS-141: Touching for learning: Contributions of haptic modality in learning to read, to write and to identify geometrical shapes in kindergarten children

Edouard Gentaz (chair)

The objective of this symposium is to show that incorporating the haptic modality in traditional training used in kindergarten children to prepare

reading, writing and mathematics improves their effectiveness. Firstly, we will describe the three principal functional characteristics of the haptic modality which are likely to support training: a good haptic identification of the objects, an analytical haptic perception and a haptic perception not dominated by the vision. Then, we will examine studies which reveal the positive effects of multisensory training (vision, audition and haptics) on the understanding of the alphabetic principle, the handwriting production of letters and the identification of geometrical shapes in the 5year old children. Finally, we will examine whether similar effects are also observed in adults.

Effect of visuo-haptic exploration of letters in the reading acquisition

Hillairet de Boisferon, Anne Grenoble, France

The visuo-haptic exploration of letters in reading interventions facilitates 5-year-old children's understanding of the alphabetic principle. The role of the sequentiality of the exploration was investigated in two interventions which proposed to develop phonemic awareness and letter knowledge and differed on the way the letters were explored: visually and haptically in multisensory intervention, only visually but in a biological sequential way in "biological" intervention. The number of decoded pseudo-words was higher after multisensory intervention than after biological intervention. The haptic exploration of letters per se, rather the visual perception of writing biological motion, explains the haptic effects.

A visuo-haptic device (Telemaque) increases the kindergarten children's handwriting acquisition

Palluel-Germain, Richard Grenoble, France

This study examines whether incorporating a visuo-haptic device 'Telemaque' may increase the fluency of handwriting production of cursive letters in kindergarten children. Forty two 5 year-old children were assigned an intervention involving either Telemaque or not. The results showed that the fluency of handwriting production for six letters (a b,f,i,l,s) was higher after the "Telemaque" intervention than after the control intervention: The movements were faster, exhibited less velocity peaks and children put up the pen less often during the letter production. These results showed that the Telemaque device may help children to increase the proactive strategy to control handwriting movements.

Evaluation of multisensory interventions intended for the acquisition of geometrical shapes in kindergarten children: A study on the contribution of the haptic modality

Pinet, Leatitia Grenoble, France

This study examines the effect of the incorporation of the haptic exploration in intervention intended to favor the acquisition of three geometrical shapes (squares, rectangles and triangles) in kindergarten children. The efficiency of two interventions was compared: In multisensory intervention, the visual and haptic modalities are used to explore the relief shapes while only the visual modality is mobilized in the classic intervention. Performances increased after both interventions but their magnitudes were higher after the multisensory intervention than after the classic intervention. These results were discussed in relation to the functional specificities of the manual haptic modality.

Learning of arbitrary association between visual and auditory unknown entities in adults: The "Bond effect" of the haptic exploration

Gentaz, Edouard Paris, France

The study examines whether the haptic exploration allows adults to better learn the arbitrary association between visual and auditory unknown entities. Adults must learn 15 associations in two interven-

tions: with their visual modality in the "classic" intervention and with their visual and haptic modalities in the "multisensory" intervention. Performances in the visual and audio intramodal recognition tests similarly increased after both interventions. In the visuo-auditory recognition test, the performances increased after both interventions but their magnitudes were higher after the multisensory intervention. The hypothesis of a haptic bond effect between visual and auditory entities is discussed.

Haptic guidance increases the visuo-manual tracking of untrained ellipses drawing

Bluteau, Jeremy St. Ismier, France *Coquillart, Sabine* i3D, INRIA, Saint Ismier, France *Payan, Yohan* GMCAO, TIMC-IMAG, la tronche, France *Gentaz, Edouard* LPNC, CNRS, Grenoble, France

This study examines whether two well-know types of haptic guidance –control in force or in position– increased the visuo-manual tracking of untrained ellipses drawing in terms of shapes and dynamics criterions. Three interventions were proposed in which completely defined ellipses were generated from the « two-third law » and learned. These interventions differed according to the haptic guidance (force, position or no guidance). Both position and force controller while generalized learning improve the fluidity of movements whereas no significant improvements was observed in term of trace shape.

IS-142: Perception, action and graphic representation

Annie Vinter, Christiane Lange-Küttner (chair)

The symposium offers a rich overview of the diversity of approaches in the study of drawing behaviour in children and adults. As indicated by the title of the symposium, relationships between drawing and perceptual functioning, between drawing and motor aspects of performance, between drawing and conceptual knowledge and memory will be explored and discussed. Data collected from individuals with typical development or with pathologies (blindness, autism) will be presented.

Drawings by blind people who had sight for an extended period

D'Angiulli, Amedeo Dept. of Psychology, Carleton University, Ottawa, Canada *Kennedy, John M.* Dpt. of Psychology, University of Toronto, Toronto, ON, Canada

Drawings by a blind child shortly after loss of sight at circa age 11 show a short-lived decline in developmental level with recovery of developmental level within one year. Drawings by a blind adult who gained sight for circa a decade in her 20s show use of stick figures and a novice developmental level. These observations support the hypothesis that drawing development may be the same in the sighted and the blind, and may depend on making drawings more than on the presence or absence of sight. We compare these two case-histories to observations of blind people making drawings that are literal copies of shapes of objects, and drawings that use metaphoric devices.

Beyond the global and analytical processing dichotomy: An approach through drawing in children

Vinter, Annie CNRS 5022, University of Bourgogne, Dijon, France

A large body of research in developmental psychology has been concerned with the extent to which processing visual objects or scenes begins with identifying the local elements or the complex whole. Most experiments have used perceptual judgments of similarity to investigate this question. However, a few of them have shown that the study of drawing behaviour constitutes a fruitful way of assessing how children parse objects into elements and integrate them into wholes. We will present results from two drawing experiments that suggest the necessity to define intermediary levels between local and global processing of object's structure.

Developmental differences in drawing performance of the dominant and non-dominant hand
van Mier, Hanneke Psychology, Cogn. Neuroscience, Maastricht University, Maastricht, Netherlands
The development of drawing performance of the dominant and non-dominant hand was assessed in the current study. Children between the ages of 4 to 12 years were presented with drawing tasks that differed in complexity with respect to motor planning and programming. For each task drawing time, percentage of stop time, drawing distance, velocity and errors were measured. With increasing age and use of the dominant hand, children performed the tasks faster, more accurate and with shorter stops. A significant interaction of age group and hand in several tasks suggests differential maturational changes for the dominant and non-dominant hand.

The impact of knowledge on copying and drawing accuracy in individuals with autism
Ropar, Danielle Dept. of Psychology, University of Nottingham, Beeston, United Kingdom Sheppard, Elizabeth, Dept. of Psychology, University of Nottingham, Beeston, United Kingdom Mitchell, Peter Dept. of Psychology, University of Nottingham, Beeston, United Kingdom
There is a general consensus among researchers that our conceptual knowledge proves to be a significant obstacle when attempting to illustrate an object accurately in typically developing children and adults. Since individuals with autism show difficulties with conceptual integration, we might expect them to be less likely to make knowledge associated errors when drawing or copying stimuli. Research providing evidence for a special advantage in accurately copying 2-dimensional stimuli (but not with drawing 3-dimensional stimuli) in autism will be presented. Implications of these findings will be discussed in relation to islets of ability in autism and previous drawing research.

Different repetition/training effects in spatial memory and drawing
Lange-Küttner, Christiane Dept. of Psychology, London Metropolitan University, London, United Kingdom
Can you actually train drawing skills like you can train memory by repetition ? 80 Children between ages 5 and 11 were asked to repeat the Draw-A-Person test three times plus three times they were drawing a police person. Repeated drawing caused deterioration in performance, however, in older children specificity interacted with sequence insofar as the Draw-A-Person Test had become robust to training, while the more challenging Draw-A-Police-Person was better in the beginning than in the end of the exercise. Spatial drawing deterioration vs. spatial memory improvement (see other conference contribution) is discussed in a DD model of diligence development.

IS-143: The brain basis of language comprehension

Angela D. Friederici (chair)
Our knowledge concerning the brain basis of language processing has increased considerably over the past decade due to the application of brain imaging techniques. The symposium will present five prominent views on the language-brain relationship. Dissociable neural networks supporting different aspects of language such as syntactic, semantic and thematic processes located in the left

hemisphere, are proposed by all views. The views differ, however, conceptually in their assumptions about the interactive character of these separable processing streams and of how domain-specific these processing systems are. Neuroanatomically, they differ with respect to the potential involvement of right hemispheric and subcortical structures.

From action to syntax: Evidence from ERPs and fMRI for common neural systems
Kuperberg, Gina R. Department of Psychology, Tufts University, Medford, USA
ERP and fMRI findings converge to suggest that semantic violations between verbs (actions) and their subject NP arguments (Agents) evoke a neural response that is distinct from that evoked by violations arising only at the level of real-world semantic knowledge, but similar to that evoked by morphosyntactic violations. These data are discussed in terms of a model in which comprehension proceeds along dissociable, parallel but highly interactive neural processing streams: one that is based on the frequency of co-occurrence of words or events, and another that builds up structure through the operation of both morphosyntactic and action-relevant (thematic) semantic constraints.

Language comprehension: Relevant brain systems and their temporal relation
Friederici, Angela D. CBS, Max-Planck-Institut, Leipzig, Germany
Based on neurophysiological data (ERP and fMRI) I propose a model comprising three neural networks in the left hemisphere: one semantic network and two syntactic networks, one for building local structure and one for computing grammatical relations. ERP data reveal that structure building takes place during a first phase, computation of semantic and grammatical relations during a second, and integration of these different information types during a third phase. The right hemisphere computes prosodic information which interacts with syntactic information on-line. Data from patients indicate that the corpus callosum, the brain structure connecting the two hemispheres, makes this interaction possible.

Contributions of memory brain systems to first and second language
Ullman, Michael T. Dept. of Psychology, Georgetown College, Washington, USA
Neurocognitive evidence – from behavioral, neurological, developmental, electrophysiological and neuroimaging studies, of both natural and artificial languages – is presented suggesting that in first language (L1), the lexicon of stored word-specific knowledge depends on the temporal-lobe based declarative memory system, whereas aspects of the mental grammar, which underlies the rule-governed composition of complex linguistic forms, depends on the frontal/basal-ganglia-based procedural memory system. In contrast, in later-learned second language (L2), both word-specific knowledge and complex forms depend largely on declarative memory, although with experience the grammar is gradually proceduralized, becoming increasingly L1-like. Neurocognitive evidence from explicit vs. implicit training paradigms is also presented.

The role of the basal ganglia in language processing
Kotz, Sonja A. Brain Sciences, MPI for Human Cognitive and, Leipzig, Germany
The functional role of the basal ganglia (BG) in language perception is controversial. Our recent event-related potential (ERP) work with BG patients shows that (i) syntactic reanalysis is affected, while (ii) selective attention is not, and (iii) syntactic reanalysis can be compensated by external and language inherent rhythmic stimulation. Latter data reveal that (iv) metric and

syntactic processes interact, but (v) that BGs can not detect metrical deviations, and (vi) the functional brain network supporting both syntactic and metric processing overlaps. Results will be discussed in relation to the functional nature of the BG in language processing and beyond.

The monitoring of language perception
Kolk, Herman Dept. of Cognitive Psychology, Radboud University Nijmegen, Nijmegen, Netherlands
Errors of human performance are common and it is generally assumed that the cognitive system is able to monitor for such errors and to repair them. The many current studies of monitoring have been exclusively devoted to production. However, we also make perceptual errors and are able to detect them. We have proposed that a strong conflict between what you perceive and what you expect signals the possibility of a perceptual error. This conflict brings the brain to reprocess the input and gives rise to a P600. This positivity thus has a general function, not just a syntactic one.

IS-144: Cutting it fine: Understanding and managing self-injurious behaviour

Penelope Hasking (chair)
This symposium aims to further our understanding of self-injurious behaviour. We examine the nature and extent of self-injury in adolescent and young adult samples, and explore the correlates of this behaviour. Qualitative analyses are utilised to gain a deeper understanding of one man's experience with self-harm. Finally we examine a solution-focussed treatment to assist nurses to treat those who self-injure.

Self-injurious behaviour in adolescents
Anderson, Holly Knox School of Psychology, Monash University, Victoria, Australia
Objectives: To establish the incidence of self-injurious behaviour in community and clinical samples of adolescents and differences between adolescents who self-injure and those who do not on psychopathology, coping strategies, alcohol use and emotion regulation. Methods: 446 adolescents recruited from secondary schools and 50 adolescents recruited from psychiatric units completed a self-report questionnaire. Results: A high incidence of self-injury was noted in both samples. Samples differed on all measures of psychopathology and in their attitudes towards self-injury. Conclusion: A high proportion of young people engaged in relatively mild self-injury, but still suffered significant psychological distress.

Assessing the intention to help those who self-injure: A test of the theory of planned behaviour
Thomas, Jodie School of Psychology, Monash University, Victoria, Australia
Objectives: To test the utility of the theory of planned behaviour to predict an intention to help those who self-injure using a general community sample. Methods: 220 participants completed self-report questionnaires assessing knowledge of self-injury, attitudes towards self-injury and intention to help someone who self-injures. Results: Positive associations were observed between subjective norms, perceived control, empathy and a less negative attitude and intention to help someone who self-injures. Subjective norms also interacted with attitudes to predict helping intention. Conclusion: The theory of planned behaviour may be a useful conceptual framework for assessing the intention to help someone who self-injures.

Knowing me, knowing you: How one gay man made meaning about and sense of his self-harm

Estefan, Andrew School of Nursing and Midwifer, Griffith University, Nathan, Australia

Objectives: To explore the experiences of gay men who self-injure. Methods: A qualitative narrative methodology was used to enable in-depth engagement with men's accounts of their self-injury. Results: One man used a quest narrative to organise his experience of his self-harm. The use of the quest narrative created possibilities for understanding this man's self-harm beyond conventional clinical discourses. Conclusion: Listening to stories of life provides insights that embed self-injury in rich contexts and therefore resist reductionist explanations. When heard, these stories generate insights for clinicians that might facilitate empathetic working.

From crisis management to turning point: An education intervention on self-harm and the emergency nurse's role

McAllister, Margaret School of Health and Sport Sci, University of Sunshine Coast, Maroochydore, Australia

Objectives: An education intervention using Solution Focused Nursing was designed to interrupt emergency nurses' tendencies to be concerned only about the client's problem. Methods: This mixed-method, pretest / posttest design involved test and comparison groups being administered surveys to explore professional self concept and perceptions of nursing. Qualitative methods included interviews and think aloud activities to explore clinical reasoning. Results: There were significant improvements in attitudes and clinical skills, particularly in relation to the client's future behaviours. Conclusion: By teaching nurses brief strategies the intervention helped nurses to see their role as transforming the present crisis into a turning point.

Coping, emotion regulation and alcohol use as moderators in the relationship between psychological distress and self-injury

Hasking, Penelope School of Psychology, Monash University, Victoria, Australia

Objectives: To examine whether coping skills, emotion regulation and alcohol use moderate the relationship between psychological distress and self-injury, in a non-clinical sample of young adults. Methods: 289 young adults completed self-report questionnaires assessing the variables of interest. Results: Adaptive coping strategies served to protect those who were psychologically distressed from severe self-injury. However for those who reported greater distress, this protective effect was negated by heavy alcohol use. Conclusion: Coping skills training may serve to protect young people from self-injury, however those who are severely distressed should also be screened for heavy alcohol use, as this may increase the risk of severe self-injury.

IS-145: Prenatal and early biological risk, genes and human development

Dieter Wolke (chair)

The last decade has seen an increasing interest in understanding the role of early biological risk, genetic factors, brain changes and plasticity for human cognitive and behavioural development. Three presentations will focus on prematurity and biological risk variation as a natural experiment to study the impact on brain and cognitive, behavioural and emotional development. The other two papers will explore the use of genetic sensitive designs to determine the impact of genes and environment (e.g. bullying) for psychopathology in childhood. The interaction between biological

risk, genetics, environment and functional outcome will be discussed.

Development of the fetal brain

Hueppi, Petra Dept. of Pediatrics, University Children's Hospital, Geneva, Switzerland

Adverse events during early life can result in changes in trajectories that may lead to the "programming" of adult-onset diseases or cognitive/behavioural deficits. Adverse events during gestation and early life can stem from unbalanced nutrition, exposure to stress and stress hormones. Prematurity often combines all these risk factors that can lead to developmental disruption and plasticity in the brain. Advanced magnetic resonance imaging (MRI) techniques have provided us with new modalities to study human cerebral development in vivo. Imaging data are presented illustrating developmental disruption and plasticity in the developing brain and its consequences to functional integrity of the brain.

Premature birth as a natural experiment for the study of human functional neuro-plasticity

Wolke, Dieter Dept. of Psychology, University of Warwick, Coventry, United Kingdom

The timing of premature birth is related to different stages of fetal brain development. Studying the outcome of prematurity (cognitive functioning, psychopathology, educational outcomes) provides a natural experiment for the study of functional neuroplasticity. Findings from several cohorts of premature children that vary from extreme (<25 weeks gestation) to mild prematurity (>32 weeks gestation) indicate that social environmental intervention can compensate for mild prematurity while extreme prematurity appears to lead to global aberrant brain development reducing the ability to take advantage of environmental stimulation. There appears to be a turning point for positive functional neuroplasticity at around 30-33 weeks gestation.

Early biological and psychosocial risk for hyperkinetic disorder

Esser, Günther Inst. für Psychology, Universität Potsdam, Potsdam, Germany

What are the differences between infants that develop hyperkinetic disorder compared to those with emotional or antisocial disorders or without mental disorder? Twenty-six children with hyperkinetic disorders, 25 with emotional disorders, 30 with antisocial disorders and 241 undisturbed children were followed from birth till the age of 8 years. The most important predictors for the onset of hyperkinetic disorders were low birth weight, the mother's origin from a broken home, early social impairments of the child and the mother's neglect of the infant.

Testing for environmentally-mediated effects: An example using bullying victimisation and children's internalizing problems

Arseneault, Louise SGDP Centre, Institute of Psychiatry, London, United Kingdom

Research has consistently indicated that being involved in bullying is associated with negative outcomes. However, the mechanisms by which bullying operates have not been fully investigated. Using data from a genetically-informative longitudinal cohort of 1,116 twin pairs, we tested whether the experience of being bullied has an environmentally-mediated effect on internalizing symptoms in young children. Results indicated that monozygotic twins who had been bullied had more internalizing symptoms compared to their co-twin who had not been bullied, indicating that bullying victimization has an environmentally-mediated effect on children's internalizing problems. This effect remained significant after controlling for pre-existing internalizing problems.

An extensive multi-centre study on genetics and gene x environment interaction of ADHD

Meyer, Jobst Neurobehavioral Genetics, Universität Trier, Trier, Germany

Attention Deficit/Hyperactivity Disorder (ADHD) is a complexly inherited childhood disorder affecting around 10% of school-aged children. Heritability estimates in the range of 0.6 - 0.8. Adult ADHD patients frequently develop symptoms of Major Depression, thus pointing to a contribution of stress-related endocrine systems and -genes to the disorder. We have recruited several multiplex as well as 200 nuclear families with ADHD. Extensive genetic studies using DNA-Chip technology were conducted, and combined with elucidation of the familial and school environment. Our results point to gene x environment interaction with respect to severity of symptoms, and monogenic inheritance in some cases.

IS-146: Psychological lay beliefs across cultures

Eun-Kook Mark Suh (chair)

Lay beliefs shared by cultural members, even if they are inaccurate, exaggerated, or simply wrong, are important vehicles for understanding the stability and change of various cultural syndromes. Despite the rich theoretical potentials, this topic has not been actively investigated with culture as a backdrop. This symposium will showcase the latest findings on how beliefs about self and others, fate, life goals, and happiness vary across cultures.

Culture and beliefs about a person's essence: Relative weight between visible versus invisible cues

Suh, Eun-Kook Mark Dept. of Psychology, Yonsei University, Seoul, Republic of Korea

Among the various aspects of the person, which ones are most reflective of his/her "essential" quality? In line with classic social psychology findings, Americans in this study thought that the relatively invisible aspects of the person (e.g., ambition) contained more of her essence than the visible cues (e.g., appearance). Koreans, on the other hand, emphasized the visible aspect more than the invisible aspect. Such contrasting cultural pattern emerged when participants engaged in an impression formation task, and also when they made evaluative judgments of a person whose behavior and intention mismatched.

Negotiable fate: Exercising agency under immutable constraints

Chiu, Chi Yue Psychology, University of Illinois, Champaign, USA *Chiu, Chi-Yue* Dept. of Psychology, University of Illinois, Champaign, USA *Au, Evelyn* Dept. of Psychology, University of Illinois, Champaign, USA

Negotiable fate, the belief that fate and personal agency jointly determine one's personal outcomes, challenges the assumption of incompatibility between fate and personal agency. In a series of four studies, we examine the impact of two societal-level factors that foster the development of negotiable fate: action-outcome contingency (the extent to which personal outcomes are contingent on one's actions), and constraint malleability (the degree to which societal constraints are perceived to be malleable). We propose that negotiable fate is most likely to develop when people are rewarded for their efforts, but face immutable societal constraints that affect their ability to attain these goals. The results from all four studies provide converging evidence in support of this hypothesis.

Life goals in the family: A three-generation cross-cultural study

Grob, Alexander Inst. für Psychologie, Universität Basel, Basel, Switzerland *Weisheit, Wibke Wibke, Weisheit* Inst. für Psychologie, Universität Basel, Basel, Switzerland

Assumptions about family resemblances are widely held among people all over the world. Old sayings like "it runs in the blood" or "like father, like son" reflect people's beliefs. Psychologists from various backgrounds propose mechanisms explaining why characteristics like life goals might run in the family. Yet there are convincing arguments for few overlap in life goals: Family members share different parts of their biographies with each other, belong to different societal cohorts, and have been socialized in different historical contexts. We will present data on life goals from three-generation families in four different cultural settings and answer the question about family resemblance in life goals empirically.

Fate attributions across cultures and religious groups

Norenzayan, Ara Dept. of Psychology, University of British Columbia, Vancouver, Canada

Studies examined attributions of life events to fate, the potential cultural influences on such attributions, and the underlying processes behind such influences. In several comparative studies, attributions to fate were consistently greater for Chinese Canadians than for European Canadians; these attributions were also greater for Christians than the non-religious, regardless of ethnicity. Mediational analyses identified two independent influences on fate attributions: the ethnic differences in fate attributions were partially mediated by holistic thinking, whereas religious differences were partially mediated by belief and devotion to God.

IS-147: Visual search and attention

Hermann Müller, Joseph Krummenacher (chair)
Current research into selective processing is presented. Wolfe shows that search efficiency depends on pre-knowledge about object features and (non-classic) information not related to visual features. Kumada reports that patients with right frontal lobe damage exhibit impaired performance in search for pre-cued target features; result interpretation is based on dimension weighting, the dynamics of which are addressed in Krummenacher's overview of experimental and imaging studies. Chun reports fMRI evidence for "filling-out" of scene representations by parahippocampal and retrosplenial cortices. Humphreys shows how single information items in working memory automatically guide selection by affecting eye movements, perceptual processes, and evoked potentials.

Classical and non-classical guidance of attention in visual search

Wolfe, Jeremy M. Harvard Medical School, Harvard University, Cambridge, USA

If observers are asked to search for a red letter among letters of various colors, they will guide their attention to red items, increasing the efficiency of search. This "classic" guidance has been extensively studied for several decades. Less is known about guidance in scenes. If observers are asked to search for a bottle in a natural scene, they seem to guide attention to surfaces that could hold bottles. In this talk, we will show that scene guidance can be very effective but that operates under different rules from classic feature guidance.

Feature-based control of attention for visual search in normal and damaged brains

Kumada, Takatsune Dept. of Human Informatics, AIST, Ibaraki, Japan

Feature-based top-down control of visual search was examined in patients with frontal lobe damage, in comparison with normal control participants. Feature singletons were presented in search displays, and participants responded to the presence or absence of feature singletons specified by a cue. The patients showed normal search performance when they detected any singletons in search displays. However, when they asked to detect only target singletons with features specified by a cue, they showed difficulty in searching for the targets. This result suggested that frontal lobe coded target template, and/or applied target template for bottom-up information.

Dynamics of dimension-based weighting mechanisms in visual search

Krummenacher, Joseph Inst. für Psychologie, Universität Fribourg, Fribourg, Switzerland *Müller, H.-J.*

Selective vision may be guided by non-spatial object features. A red object within green ones attracts attention seemingly automatically. Here, deployment of focal attention is determined by saliency activity based on multiple feature contrast signals. Summarizing recent own results, we discuss the role and computational dynamics of dimension-specific feature contrasts in visual search. The generation of dimension-specific saliency is mainly stimulus-driven and contrasts are weighted before integration. Dimension-specific activations may be top-down modulated. fMRI and EEG studies suggest that modulations of dimension-specific signals are achieved by a fronto-occipital cortical network, and that dimensional weighting affects early stages of perceptual analysis.

Scene representation and search

Chun, Marvin M. Dept. of Psychology, Yale University, New Haven, USA

Whether one can dissociate attention from eye movements is under debate. A spatiotopic (world-coordinate) system is required to maintain a sustained locus of spatial attention across saccades, and we've confirmed such updating across eye movements. However, we have novel evidence that the native coordinate system is retinotopic. During the first 100–200 ms after saccades, visual processing is facilitated at the retinotopic location, even when this location is task-irrelevant. When the retinotopic location is task-relevant, robust facilitation persists long after the saccade. The native system of endogenous spatial attention may be retinotopic, updated to spatiotopic coordinates when required by task.

Working memory and search

Humphreys, Glyn W. School of Psychology, University of Birmingham, Birmingham, United Kingdom *Soto, D. Rothstein, P.*

Current theories propose that information held in working memory (WM) can guide visual selection of a target. We have examined whether such guidance processes take place automatically, even when the information held in WM is irrelevant for search. We report that the WM stimulus affects the first eye movement even to pop-out targets, it affects perceptual processing of targets under brief exposure conditions and it affects early components of evoked response to search displays. fMRI results indicate that guidance from WM can be separated at a neural level from bottom-up priming, with selection mediated by a fronto-thalamic circuit.

IS-148: The appearance of colored objects

Karl Gegenfurtner (chair)
Human observers have the remarkable ability to assign constant color labels to objects, even though the wavelength composition of the light entering the eye can vary substantially. In this symposium the multitude of different mechanisms that contribute to color constancy will be considered, ranging from low level retinal cues to high level memory effects.

Are observers "opportunistic" Bayesians when using color for object identification?

Zaidi, Qasim Dept. of Optometry, State University of New York, New York, NY, USA

Color is primary in the identification of objects, particularly when objects do not differ in shape or texture, but changes in illumination with time, season, and weather, can lead to changes in the spectra of lights reflected from objects. We measured accuracy of object identification across two different illuminations on the basis of color cues. Patterns of correct and incorrect identifications ruled out color-constancy, contrast-constancy and inverse-optics. Instead of using information that could have led to accurate identifications, observers based identification on similarities in object colors as projected onto the illuminant color difference. This performance reflects an "Opportunistic" Bayesian strategy.

Perception of surface color in binocularly-viewed, three-dimensional virtual scenes

Maloney, Laurence Psychology and Neural Science, New York University, New York, USA

In everyday scenes, the intensity and chromaticity of light absorbed by a matte surface depends on the location and orientation of the surface. I describe recent experiments intended to investigate surface color perception in 3D rendered scenes. We found that the visual system partially compensates for changes in illumination due to changes in location and orientation of test surfaces. In carrying out these experimental tasks, observers effectively represents the spatial distribution, chromaticities and relative intensities of light sources in the scene. I'll describe additional experiments where we assess how the visual system estimates and discounts illumination.

On the functional role of the mechanism sensitive for the correlation between chromaticity and luminance

Golz, Jürgen Inst. für Psychologie, Universität zu Kiel, Kiel, Germany

In previous works Don MacLeod and I have argued that the correlation between chromaticity and luminance within the retinal image can play a functional role for achieving colour constancy and is used accordingly by the human visual system. Here I will present experiments showing that the effect of the chromaticity-luminance-correlation is substantially more global than reported by Granzier, Brenner, Cornelissen & Smeets [Journal of Vision,2005,5,20-27], who questioned that this scene statistic is used for the purpose of colour constancy. I will also discuss potential factors that may have lead in the experiments of Granzier et al. to an underestimation of the spatial extent to which the chromaticity-luminance-correlation is taken into account.

Colour constancy of natural objects

Hurlbert, Anya Dept. of Neuroscience, University of Newcastle, Newcastle, United Kingdom *Ling, Yazhu* Institute of Neuroscience, Newcastle University, Newcastle upon Tyne, United Kingdom *Vurro, Milena* Institute of Neuroscience, Newcastle University, Newcastle, United Kingdom

Colour constancy – the tendency of object colour to remain constant under changing illumination – is most likely mediated by multiple mechanisms. At the cognitive level, the memory colour of familiar objects may contribute to constancy, as Hering (1905) argued. We measured colour constancy of familiar and unfamiliar objects in an experimental setup which allows us to adjust the apparent colour of real objects while preserving natural cues to 3D shape. Observers reported whether particular colours 'matched' particular objects under varying illumination conditions. We find that the extent of colour constancy depends on object familiarity and the accuracy of colour memory.

Memory effects on color appearence

Gegenfurtner, Karl Inst. für Psychologie, Universität Gießen, Gießen, Germany

We asked human observers to adjust the colour of natural fruit objects until they appeared achromatic. The objects were generally perceived to be grey when their colour was shifted away from the observers' grey point in a direction opposite to the typical colour of the fruit. These results show that colour sensations are not determined by the incoming sensory data alone, but are significantly modulated by high level visual memory.

IS-149: Competition across psychological disciplines and cultures

Marta Fülöp (chair)

Competition is an interpersonal, an intergroup, an economical and a political phenomenon that has many different aspects and can be approached from different psychological disciplines. The present symposium brings together 5 papers that study competition from economic, social, developmental and personality psychological perspective. These studies have been carried out in societies that have been undergoing profound societal and economic changes in the last two decades: China, Hungary, Slovenia and Russia. In all these countries competition has been a key phenomenon of the changes. The symposium highlights how competition manifests itself across different cultures and psychological realms.

The competitive strategies of Hungarian business people

Fülöp, Marta Inst. for Psychology, Hungarian Academy of Sciences, Budapest, Hungary

Market economy has been established in the post-socialist countries almost for two decades. During this process those who has taken part in the business life has had to change their views and understanding of competition, as well as to alter their attitudes and values in connection with it. In our study 202 in-depth interviews were carried out with Hungarian business people on their attitudes towards competition, on their perception of the nature of competition in the Hungarian business life and the competitive strategies they employ in their private and professional life. The results of the qualitative analysis are presented in the paper.

Constructive versus destructive competitive tendencies as a function of perceptions of fairness

Berkics, Mihály Dept. of Social Psychology, Eötvös Loránd University, Budapest, Hungary

Previous studies have shown that morality or fairness can be an important factor in the perception of competition. This study investigated constructive versus destructive behavioral competitive strategies resulting from different perceptions of fairness. Participants were presented with hypothetical workplace scenarios, in which the level of perceived fairness was varied by manipulating the perceived correlation between work performance and outcomes (salaries). Participants were asked to judge each scenario in terms of fairness and satisfaction, as well as to make attributions for the outcomes and predict likely courses of action (among them, constructive vs destructive competition) for the hypothetical characters.

The representation of competition and its participants: Russian economics / business students' views

Garber, Ilya Dept. of Socio Economics, Saratov State University, Saratov, Russia

The goal of the study was to describe the image of competition and its participants from the Russian Economics/Business student's point of view as a part of a cross-cultural investigation. 231 students participated in the research (30% males and 70% females). In order to reveal the structure of the representation of competition a free associative technique was used and the results were analyzed according to Vergés's (1992) method. A questionnaire of closed-ended questions was applied to identify students' attitudes towards competition in the business world and their perception of the factors that lead to success in business.

Self-concept and competition in cross-cultural perspective

Kobal Grum, Darja Dept. of Psychology, University of Ljubljana, Ljubljana, Slovenia

The main focus of the study was to reveal the nature of the connection between competition as a personality dimension and self-concept in three countries: Slovenia, Serbia and Spain. University students filled in the Self-Description-Questionnaire to measure their general and specific domains of self-concept (Marsh & O'Neill, 1984) and Ryckman et al's (1990, 1996) two measures of competitiveness: hyper-competitiveness and personal development competitiveness. Personal development competitiveness in all three countries was more related to the social parts and to particular individual parts of the self-concept. Contrary, hyper-competitiveness was more related to individually oriented motivation. Culture also had a significant impact on self-concept and competition.

IS-150: The developmental significance of close relationships

Rita Zukauskiene (chair)

People live together with other people and they are forced to have relationships with others. Close relationships are important aspects of life and social development. Parents provide the first experiences in close relationships for children, but by adolescence, peers become more important than family as confidants and providers of emotional support. Later on romantic relationships play very important role in peoples' life. Considering that various relationships are very important for development, in this symposium we will cover several domains of interpersonal development: (a) parent-child relationships; (b) friendships and peer relationships; and (c) romantic and spousal relationships.

The influence of romantic relationships on youths' delinquency: Social-influence and/or social-amplification?

Eklund, Jenny Centre for Health Equity, Stockholm University, Stockholm, Sweden

Objectives: To investigate whether the influence of romantic relationships on youths' delinquency interacts with youths' delinquency propensity. Methods: The sample comprised Swedish 7th-8th grade girls and boys (n=686) who participated in three annual data collections. Variable-oriented statistical methods including regressions with post hoc probing of interaction effects were used. Results: Romantic relationships predicted subsequent delinquency for youths who were prone to delinquency, and indicated that romantic relationships amplified an already existing delinquency propensity. Conclusions: The findings further support the influence of romantic relationships on adolescents' delinquency, but emphasise the importance of investigating individual characteristics as potential moderators of this association.

Understanding leaving home and related developmental tasks: What is the right kind of parental support?

Seiffge-Krenke, Inge Inst. Entwicklungspsychologie, Universität Mainz, Mainz, Germany *von Irmer, Joerg* Inst. Entwicklungspsychologie, Universität Mainz, Mainz, Germany

Objectives: This longitudinal study examines the relationships between the pattern of leaving home and earlier developmental progression and parental support. Methods: data from a sample of 93 participants and their parents were used. Results: Paternal and maternal support during adolescence were found to be important predictors of the timing of leaving home. In-time leavers received lower levels of parental support and were more active in romantic relations during adolescence. No differences between the three groups emerged with respect to occupation or professional career. Conclusion: Developmental progression did not differ between in-time leavers and those who continued to reside in the family home.

Early temperamental unmanageability, harsh parenting profiles and romantic relationships in adolescence

Pakalniskiene, Vilmante Dept. of Psychology, Mykolas Romeris University, Vilnius, Lithuania

Objectives: It was examined the possible roles that different combinations of harsh parenting might play in the link between early unmanageable temperament and later romantic relationships. Methods: Prospective data from 3 months to 18 years in a sample of 212 children were used. Results: Latent class analysis revealed different patterns of harsh parenting. In mixture models, unmanageable temperament increased children's risk of having worse relationships. Children who experienced harsh treatment or only discordant relationships had bad relationships in adulthood. Conclusions: It seems that physical punishment has a different meaning in the context of good parent-child relationships than in the context of discordant relationships

Youths' psychopathic traits predict parenting: Examining the difference between boys and girls

Muñoz, Luna C. Dept. of Psychology, Univers. of Central Lancashire, Preston, United Kingdom

Objectives: Could the affective and interpersonal qualities (callous-unemotional and grandiose/manipulative traits) affect parenting beyond the effect of the behavioral and more observable qualities (impulsive/irresponsible traits) of psychopathic traits? Methods: Boys (n=250) and girls (n=277), from 13 to 15 years old, and their parents were surveyed over two years Results: Hierarchical regressions showed that impulsive/irresponsible traits accounted for much of the variance in predicting negative parenting, parental control, and parents' feelings about their child. The prediction was stronger for girls. For boys, callous-unemotional traits incrementally predicted to negative parenting Conclusions: The findings suggest that risky girls and remorseless boys are distressing to parents

Personality type and gender mediates the relation between parental rearing practices and youth behavioral problems
Zukauskiene, Rita Dept. of Psychology, Mykolas Romeris University, Vilnius, Lithuania
Objectives: It was examined whether personality in combination with gender plays a role in the association between parental rearing practices and youth behavioral problems. Methods: Prospective data from 14 to 17 years in a sample of 449 children were used. Results: Perceived parental rejection and overprotection was positively associated with aggression for girls, but not for boys. For boys, rejection by father and mother was associated with depression only. Personality type and gender moderated these associations. Conclusion: Several clear moderating effects of the personality type x gender groups were found on associations between perceived parental rejection, overprotection, depression and aggression.

Peer group selection and influence in adolescents' internal and external problem behavior
Kiuru, Noona Dept. of Psychology, University of Jyväskylä, Jyväskylä, Finland Nurmi, Jari-Erik Dept. of Psychology, University of Jyväskylä, Jyväskylä, Finland Salmela-Aro, Katariina Dept. of Psychology, University of Jyväskylä, Jyväskylä, Finland
The present study examined whether adolescents' peer groups are homogeneous in internal and external problem behavior and whether peer group selection and influence contribute to this group homogeneity. The Finnish adolescents (n = 611, median age = 15) answered questionnaires measuring their internal and external problem behavior and peer relations once before a transition to post-comprehensive schooling and twice after the transition. The results of multilevel modeling showed that peer group members resembled each other in both internal and external problem behaviour. Moreover, peer group selection operated in both behaviors. The analyses concerning peer group influence are in progress.

IS-151: Gender and health

Adriana Baban (chair)
The aim of this symposium is to argue that gender analysis is fundamental to the understanding of all dimensions of health, including health promotion, disease prevention, health-care and health policies. The papers focus on women's health in relation to their everyday lives, exploring how their embodied experiences are shaped by cultural beliefs, economic context, social institutions and health policies. Specific health issues, such as cervical cancer prevention, menopause, infertility, diabetes, heart disease will be discussed by the participants. Overall, this symposium demonstrates the implications of gender-sensitive strategies to improve women's physical, emotional and social health and well-being.

The effects of menopause on quality of life in a sample of Romanian women
Baban, Adriana Dept. of Psychology, Babes-Bolyai University, Cluj-Napoca, Romania Kallay, Eva Psychology, Babes-Bolyai University, Cluj-Napoca, Romania Colcear, Doina Cardiology, Medical University, Cluj-Napoca, Romania Zdrenghea, Dumitru Cardiology, Medical University, Cluj-Napoca, Romania
Aim: To investigate the effects of menopause on the Quality of Life in a sample of Romanian women. Method: Our study involved 145 Romanian women (age: 48 - 53), 65 at menopause and 80 not having any symptoms of menopause. All participants were assessed regarding their level of depression (13 - item BDI) and Quality of Life (SF-36). Results: Women at menopause have higher level of emotional distress, and lower level of social functioning and vitality. Conclusions: Counseling women at menopause may enhance their well-being.

Empowering infertility patients in the medical encounter: Effects on satisfaction with the encounter
Benyamini, Yael Dept. of Social Work, Tel Aviv University, Tel Aviv, Israel Csadai, Sharon Social Work, Tel Aviv University, Tel Aviv, Israel Gozlan, Miri Women's Health Center, Maccabi Health Services, Rishon LeZion, Israel Kokia, Ehud General Management, Maccabi Health Services, Tel Aviv, Israel
Objectives – to examine the effect of an intervention aimed at increasing female infertility patients' involvement in the medical encounter on their satisfaction with the encounter. Methods - 149 patients undergoing fertility treatments were randomly assigned to experimental and control groups. The experimental group received a brochure encouraging active participation in the encounter and structured instructions for preparation for the encounter. Satisfaction was assessed in both groups following the visit. Results – satisfaction with the medical encounter was higher in the experimental compared with the control group. Conclusions – preparing young women in a stressful situation for the medical encounter can increase their satisfaction.

Promoting women's heart health: Six-month follow-up results of a preventive trial
Julkunen, Juhani Dept. of Psychology, University of Helsinki, Helsinki, Finland Rantanen, Piia Research and development, Rehabilitation Foundation, Helsinki, Finland Vanhanen, Hannu medical, the Finnish Heart Association, Helsinki, Finland
Aim. To evaluate the effectiveness of two interventions in promoting women's heart health. Methods. High-risk women (n=126) were randomized into two groups: group-intervention and self-care group based on risk communication (simple cross-over design). Follow-up assessments were at 6 and 12 months. Results. At six months, significant positive changes in cardiovascular risk factors were observed in both experimental groups. Conclusions. Intervention based on individual risk communication and counselling by a nurse is as effective as a 10-session group intervention in producing positive changes in risk factors.

The role of gender in the prevention and attention of diabetes in the Mexico-US border
Givaudan, Martha IMIFAP, Mexico City, Mexico Vitela, Ana Laura Psychology, IMIFAP, Mexico City, Mexico
The aim: to present a program directed at acquiring knowledge and skills directed at the prevention of diabetes. Method: the target population is men and women in the US-Mexico Border States who are over 20 years of age and have never tested for their health status. We developed and implemented a training program of 266 nurses and physicians. They are replicating it in their clinics and communities. The results show that while men attend the health services much less than women they get significantly better attention in the home. Conclusion: health recommendations are made regarding differential gender role expectations.

IS-152: Culture and self: Independence, interdependence, and beyond

Shinobu Kitayama (chair)
Over the last two decades, an independence-interdependence theory of cultural self has been highly influential as a guiding hypothesis in investigating cultural variation in self, cognition, emotion, and motivation. The aim of this symposium is to take stock of empirical findings from the past, showcase some of the cutting-edge research on the topic, and then to explore new frontiers of research for the next decade. Five speakers will cover a wide range of topics including self, choice, parenting, and cognition. Moreover, this panel represents both a variety of methods and a wide range of populations.

Does interdependence equal weakness in the land of the free?
Markus, Hazel Rose Dept. of Psychology, Stanford University, Stanford, USA Hamedani, Maryam Dept. of Psychology, Stanford University, Stanford, USA
Whether the focus is politics, economics, the environment or the media, we live in an interdependent world. Yet given their history, founding ideology, institutions and everyday practices, Americans are likely to have relatively more elaborated schemas for independence than for interdependence. In two studies, products, people, cities, ideas and actions were framed as either independent or interdependent. Participants, both European American and Asian American, liked those targets characterized as interdependent, but also evaluated them as weak, passive, unsuccessful and not normal. In two subsequent studies, the focus was on the self. When primed with interdependence, European Americans but not Asian Americans, solved fewer anagrams and squeezed a handgrip with for a shorter period of time than when primed with independence.

Understanding cultural differences in the self: A neuroimaging approach
Han, Shihui Dept. of Psychology, Peking University, Beijing, People's Republic of China
Social psychological research shows that people from different cultures are characterized with distinct construals of the self. Our recent brain imaging work investigated the neural basis of cultural influence on self-styles and self-related processing. We found that Western/East Asian cultures that cultivate independent or interdependent self modulate neural representation of the self by excluding/including intimate others from/in the neural structure of the self in the ventral medial prefrontal cortex (MPFC). Religious cultures (Christianity) result in weakened neural coding of stimulus self-relatedness in the ventral MPFC but enhanced neural activity underlying evaluative process applied to self-referential stimuli in the dorsal MPFC.

Cognition and parenting
Keller, Heidi Inst. für Psychologie, Universität Osnabrück, Osnabrück, Germany
This study addresses cultural differences in parenting behavior, parenting cognitions and parental perception. Parents representing the cultural models of independence and interdependence, German middle class mothers and Cameroonian Nso farmers participated in this study. Parenting strategies were assessed in mother child free play situations, when the children were three months of age. Socialization goals and maternal perceptional style as expressed with the Framed Line Test were assessed. The data confirmed the expected relationships between maternal perceptional style, socialization goals and parenting behaviors. Cameroonian farmers embody the model of interdependence whereas German middle class mothers embody the model of independence.

Eco-cultural basis of cognition: Farmers and fishermen are more holistic than herders in rural Turkey

Uskul, Ayse K. Dept. of Psychology, University of Essex, Colchester, United Kingdom Kitayama, Shinobu Psychology, University of Michigan, Ann Arbor, USA Nisbett, Richard Psychology, University of Michigan, Ann Arbor, USA

It has been hypothesized that interdependent (versus independent) social orientations breed more holistic (versus analytic) cognitions. If so, farming and small-scale fishing, which require more co-operation (and represent a more interdependent mode of being) than does herding, may encourage a more holistic mode of cognition. To test this hypothesis we compared responses to tasks measuring categorization, reasoning, and attention by members of herding, fishing, and farming communities in North-Eastern Turkey. As expected, results indicate a greater degree of holistic mode of cognition preferred by fishermen and farmers than by herders. Implications for eco-cultural origins of cognitive differences are discussed.

Unconscious influences of social eyes: Choice and motivation in the U.S. and Korea

Kitayama, Shinobu Ann Arbor, USA Na, Jinkyung Psychology, University of Michigan, Ann Arbor, USA

Choice can be self-motivating, but this effect will depend on the nature of culturally sanctioned self. In independent cultures private choice will be most motivating, but in interdependent cultures public choice will be most motivating. In 2 studies, we tested this idea by inducing an awareness of public scrutiny in highly serendipitous fashion so that participants were not aware of their own awareness of the public scrutiny. Americans performed a task best when they chose the task in the absence of public scrutiny, but Korean performed a task best when they chose the task in the presence of such scrutiny.

IS-153: Adaptive testing in theory and application

Lutz F. Hornke (chair)

Adaptive tests are one of the most intriguing developments in psychological assessment of the last thirty years. Until recently, adaptive tests are routinely used in large-scale assessment programs but are not broadly implemented in day-to-day psychological assessment. The symposium addresses recent developments and future perspectives in adaptive testing. Special topics address the design of items banks, the role of item-response theory, the use of computers, and possible barriers to the application of adaptive testing in different domains of psychological and educational assessment.

Adaptive testing in the 21st Century

Bejar, Isaac I. Research Dept., Educational Testing Service, Princeton, USA

It seems inevitable that ultimately essentially all testing will be administered by computer. Advances psychometric models and models of adaptive testing will play a critical role in that future. I will argue that the content, the items have not received sufficient attention and that such attention is needed to insure sustainable and valid assessments. Specifically, the approach to assessment design that served us well last century needs to be updated to reflect advances in our understanding of the psychology behind test behavior, psychometric advances and technological developments. I will illustrate through examples of recent research and ongoing projects.

Impact of violations of the unidimensionality assumption in computer-adaptive testing

Walter, Otto B. Psychologisches Institut IV, Westf. Universität Münster, Münster, Germany

For the construction of item banks for computer adaptive tests an assumption of unidimensionality (i.e. all items of a test measure the same construct) is usually required. Violations of this assumption may affect the accuracy of item and person parameter estimates. Using both simulated and real data, we investigated the effect of a multidimensional latent trait (2, 3, and more dimensions) on item calibration and score estimation. Indices obtained from exploratory and confirmatory factor analysis were used to quantify the degree of multidimensionality and derive criteria for assessing the extent to which violations of unidimensionality still yield robust score estimates.

Item pool design

Reckase, Mark CEPSE, Michigan State University, East Lansing, USA

The positive features of computerized adaptive tests are only exhibited if they procedures operate on a test item pool wth sufficient items with an appropriate distribution of characteristics. The best procedures will not function well with a poor item pool. This presentation describes a methodology for designing the characteristics of an item pool that will support the proper function of the CAT. The design yields a target for the develoment of operational item pools. The target is based on the use of the test and the distribution of examinees.

Item writing rationales

Kubinger, Klaus D. Psychologische Diagnostik, Universität Wien, Wien, Austria

Adaptive testing only works if there is a big item pool. However, developing items just by professional eager leads in most cases to the deletion of many items when they were calibrated – by the Rasch model at best. For this item writing rationales will be needed. Besides of a lot of formal rationales, the content rationales are preferable be represented by some item generating rules. If there actually are such rules, Fischer's LLTM would master to calibrate them, as a consequence of which they enable the test author to construct an item with a difficulty on his/her particular demand.

Recent and future applications of computer-adaptive testing

Hornke, Lutz F. Inst. für Psychologie, RWTH Universität Aachen, Aachen, Germany Lang, Jonas W.B. Inst. für Psychologie, RWTH Universität Aachen, Aachen, Germany

The authors review applications of adaptive testing in different areas of assessment. While there has been a rapid emergence of adaptive tests in large-scale assessment programs, the breakthrough of adaptive testing methods in ordinary psychological assessment has been somewhat mixed. The authors found that only a very small proportion of psychological tests available to psychologists are adaptive tests in one sense or the other. Barriers to the use of adaptive testing outside of large-scale assessment programs are discussed as well as the many potential ways to foster the use of adaptive testing.

IS-154: Eating disorders

Brunna Tuschen-Caffier (chair)

The symposium will be focused on new developments and new data concerning psychotherapy with eating disordered patients. One speaker (Munsch) will present new data to evaluate short-term CBT. Another speaker (Schlup) will pay attention to predictors and moderators of treatment outcome. Two speaker will present new data of meta-analyses concerning psychotherapy for patients with bulimia

nervosa (deZwaan) and with binge eating disorder (Vocks). Finally, one talk will be about obesity of children (Braet).

Ecological Momentary Assessment (EMA) to evaluate efficacy of a cognitive behavioral treatment for binge eating disorder

Munsch, Simone Inst. für Psychologie, Universität Basel, Basel, Switzerland Milenkovic, Natasa Inst. für Psychologie, Universität Basel, Basel, Switzerland Meyer, Andrea H. Inst. für Psychologie, Universität Basel, Basel, Switzerland Schlup, Barbara Inst. für Psychologie, Universität Basel, Basel, Switzerland Margraf, Jürgen Inst. für Psychologie, Universität Basel, Basel, Switzerland Wilhelm, Frank Inst. für Psychologie, Universität Basel, Basel, Switzerland

Objective: To explore feasibility of EMA and to evaluate short-term CBT. Methods: Twenty-eight individuals were randomized to treatment or to wait-list condition. EMA was accomplished (7 days) before wait-list, before and after treatment. Results: Acceptance and compliance ratings were high. EMA exhibited less binges than retrospective instruments. Binge eating was significantly reduced. Craving, feelings of hunger and control remained stable. Conclusion: EMA is feasible and less susceptible to retrospective memory distortion. Short-term CBT is efficacious. Binge eating may be the tip of the iceberg, but craving and reduced feelings of control might represent more stable aberrations of impulse control.

Predictors and moderators of treatment outcome in a cognitive-behavioral (CBT) short- and long-term treatment for Binge Eating Disorder (BED)

Schlup, Barbara Inst. für Psychologie, Universität Basel, Basel, Switzerland

Objective: To examine whether rapid response, baseline negative affect or binge frequency predicted or moderated treatment outcome in two CBT treatments for BED. Method: 76 participants with BED participated in a 16- or 8-session CBT. Treatment response referred to remission from binge eating and reduction of binge episodes. Results: Rapid response and high negative affect did not predict nor moderate treatment outcome at posttreatment or at 1- and 2-year follow-up. Patients with higher initial binge eating showed higher remission rates in the shorter intervention. Conclusion: CBT, short or long-term, was effective for the majority of patients, regardless of predictors of treatment outcome.

The needs of carers: a comparison between eating disorders and schizophrenia

de Zwaan, Martina Abt. für Psychosomatik, Universitätsklinikum Erlangen, Erlangen, Germany

Objective: This pilot study compares the level of distress and the need for support between carers of patients with anorexia (AN) and bulimia nervosa (BN) and carers of patients with schizophrenia. Methods: Thirty-two carers of patients suffering from AN and BN and 30 carers of patients with schizophrenia filled out the General Health Questionnaire (GHQ-12) and the Burden Inventory (BI). In addition, they were interviewed with a semi-structured research interview, the Carers' Needs Assessment (CNA), to assess relevant problem areas as well as the need for helpful interventions. Patients with an eating disorder were interviewed with the Eating Disorder Examination (EDE) and patients with schizophrenia with the Positive and Negative Syndrome Scale (PANSS) to assess the severity of the disorder. Results: The mean duration of illness was 5.3 years in the patients with eating disorders and 7.3 years in the patients with schizophrenia. Most of the carers were mothers or partners. In the CNA we found high numbers of problems as well as high numbers of unmet needs for interventions. The most frequently mentioned problem areas in all groups of carers were "disappointment caused by the chronic course of the illness, concerns about the patient's future" and "problems in communication with the patient". The most frequently reported need for support in all groups was "counseling and support by a professional". Carers of patients with BN reported a significantly lower number of problems and of needs for interventions compared to the carers of patients with AN and schizophrenia. Also in the BI and the GHQ-12 we found significantly lower total scores in carers of patients with BN. Carers of patients with AN and schizophrenia did not differ significantly in any of the assessments. The severity or duration of illness of the patients did not correlate with the carers' burden or needs. Conclusions: Carers of patients with an eating disorder and carers of patients with schizophrenia are burdened with similar problems and have high levels of unmet needs which are usually not addressed in clinical practice. Carers of anorectic patients have higher levels of difficulties in various areas compared to carers of bulimic patients and did not differ from carers of patients with schizophrenia.

Meta-analysis on the effectiveness of various treatments for Binge Eating Disorder

Vocks, Silja Inst. für Klin. Psychologie, Universität Bochum, Bochum, Germany Tuschen-Caffier, Brunna Bielefeld, Germany Pietrowsky, Reinhard Kersting, Anette Herpertz, Stephan

Objective: The aim of the present meta-analysis is to integrate the findings of treatment studies concerning psychotherapy for Binge Eating Disorder. Method: Criteria for the inclusion of a study were that (a) the participants were diagnosed according to the DSM-IV, (b) at least one therapeutic intervention was applied and (c) symptom-specific outcome parameters were assessed. Results: Thirty-eight studies fulfilled these inclusion criteria and were assigned to the intervention categories psychotherapy, self-help, weight loss, pharmacotherapy and combination of various treatments. Conclusion: Based on these results, S3 treatment guidelines concerning the treatment of Binge Eating Disorder are developed.

Towards defining subtypes in overweight children

Braet, Caroline Dept of Develop. Psychology, Universtiät Gent, Gent, Belgium

Children with overweight are a heterogeneous group and differ on dimensions measuring dietary restraint and psychopathology. Whether these pre-treatment characteristics are related with differential treatment outcome is not explored yet. Two independent samples were subtyped along dietary restraint and negative affect dimensions using cluster analysis and then compared on disordered characteristics. Three robust subtypes emerged: a dietary restraint/ negative affect subtype (DR/NA), a pure negative affect group as well as a non-dietary/ non symptomatic group. Individual characteristics like degree of dietary restraint and negative affect can be helpful in typifying youngsters with overweight seeking treatment, stipulating specific treatment guidelines and making differential prognoses.

IS-155: Recovery from work stress

Sabine Sonnentag (chair)

Job stressors impair health. Recovery is assumed to be a process by which the negative effects of job stressors can be alleviated. This symposium brings together researchers from six countries that present and discuss research findings on recovery. The presentations will report empirical findings on recovery during vacations and during daily life. Findings from studies that examined physiological processes and indicators associated with (low) recovery will be presented. Overall, the studies

presented in this symposium suggest that research on recovery is necessary to fully understand the implications of job stress.

Do we recover from vacation?

de Bloom, Jessica Dept. of Work and Organization, Radboud University Nijmegen, Nijmegen, Netherlands Kompier, Michiel Dept. of Work and Organization, Radboud University Nijmegen, Nijmegen, Netherlands Geurts, Sabine Dept. of Work and Organization, Radboud University Nijmegen, Nijmegen, Netherlands de Weerth, Carolina Dept. of Work and Organization, Radboud University Nijmegen, Nijmegen, Netherlands Sonnentag, Sabine Dept of Psychology, University of Konstanz, Konstanz, Germany

The aim of this study is to investigate to what extent vacation has positive effects on health and well-being, how long such effects last after work resumption, and how vacation activities and experiences play a role in these relationships. Based on a systematic literature search (Psycinfo, Medline) and methodological inclusion criteria, we selected 8 studies to answer our research questions. The results indicated that vacation improves psychological health, but these effects seem to fade out rather quickly. Our research further demonstrated that vacation activities and experiences have hardly been studied. Based on our review, we come up with some methodological and theoretical recommendations for future research in this area.

Vacation fade-out in teachers

Kühnel, Jana A&O-Psychologie, Universität Konstanz, Konstanz, Germany Sonnentag, Sabine Universität Konstanz, Konstanz, Germany

Vacation, as a time off from work, offers the opportunity to recover from work demands. However, positive effects of vacations seem to fade-out quickly. One-hundred-thirty-five teachers filled in surveys before vacation, immediately, two weeks, and four weeks after vacation. Results showed the hypothesized increase of work engagement immediately after vacation which declined within two weeks. Emotional exhaustion decreased after vacation and reached its pre-vacation-level within four weeks. Experienced job stress after vacation fostered and experienced relaxation attenuated the fade-out in work engagement and emotional exhaustion. Our study suggests that accumulation of strains after vacation consumes resources gained during vacation.

Recovery experiences among Finnish employees

Kinnunen, Ulla Dept. of Psychology, University of Tampere, Tampere, Finland Siltaloppi, Marjo Dept. of Psychology, University of Tampere, Tampere, Finland Feldt, Taru Dept. of Psychology, University of Jyväskylä, Jyväskylä, Finland

The aim was to examine recovery experiences among Finnish employees in relation to potential predictors (job demands and resources) and consequences (burnout and work engagement). Specifically, four experiences, namely psychological detachment from work, relaxation, mastery and control, were assessed by 527 employees from a variety of different jobs. The recovery experiences showed moderate negative relations with job demands (e.g. work load) and positive relations with job resources (e.g. social support). The relations with burnout were stronger and in the opposite direction (i.e. negative) than those with work engagement. It seems that psychological detachment, due to its strongest relations, is the most relevant recovery experience.

Physical exercise as a daily recovery activity: A closer look on how it works

Feuerhahn, Nicolas Konstanz, Germany Sonnentag, Sabine Universität Konstanz, Konstanz, Germany

We examined the recovery potential of physical exercise during leisure on psychological well-being.

Based on earlier research we assumed that spending leisure time with physical activity will improve well-being before going to bed. Furthermore, we suggested that psychological detachment, positive experience, sense of belonging and physical self-concept mediate this relationship. One hundred and twenty-six participants from different occupations completed a diary twice a day over five consecutive workdays. Multilevel analyses showed that physical activity enhanced well-being before going to bed. Psychological detachment, positive experience, sense of belonging and physical self-concept were mediators in the relationship between physical activities and well-being.

Biological underpinnings of recovery from work in employed women and men

Lindfors, Petra Dept. of Psychology, Stockholm University, Stockholm, Sweden

This presentation summarizes findings from our studies on the biological underpinnings of recovery, asking respondents to complete a measure of self-rated recovery from work and to provide biological data. Examining the relationships between self-rated recovery and salivary cortisol in 25 white-collar workers revealed that high morning cortisol is associated with poor recovery. Analyses of linkages between self-rated recovery and biological dysregulation in 241 women employed within the health care sector showed that poor recovery increases the risk for biological dysregulation. These linkages between self-rated recovery and biological markers imply that poor recovery from work increases the risk for health problems.

Tell me why I don't like Mondays..

Walkowiak, Alicia Work and Social Psychology, University of Maastricht, Maastricht, Netherlands Zijlstra, Fred Dept. of Psychology, Maastricht University, Maastricht, Netherlands

In this study 70 participants kept a diary for 2 weeks, and reported sleeping times, working times, and so on, which revealed the weekly cycle of work and rest. Also on three days (before, during, and after the weekend) saliva samples were collected in order to determine levels of cortisol. The hypothesis tested in this study is that people start anticipating the demands of the week on Sunday evening. Our study findings appear to support our main hypothesis, and in particular ruminating about work seems to contribute to poor quality of sleep. Theoretical and practical implications will be discussed.

Stress and recovery of working parents in Berlin

Klumb, Petra Dept. of Psychology, University of Fribourg, Fribourg, Switzerland

This study investigated the antecedents of recovery processes in individuals facing high demands in more than one domains of life. With an intensive time sampling design, we observed 52 working couples with at least one preschool child. We collected data on productive activities on the labor market and in the household, mood and level of free cortisol over 6 consecutive days and modelled their relationships with multilevel analyses. Recovery processes as indicated by the decline of cortisol across the day and its level in the evening depended on characteristics of the productive activities, the person, and the couple.

IS-156: Dynamics of mind and body

Guy van Orden (chair)

Mind and body are traditionally explored as though they are separate entities. Recent findings of common dynamical principles begin to undermine this distinction as a working hypothesis, while an alternative hypothesis of interdependent systems gains credibility. The symposium presents representative examples of such findings.

Embodied cognitive dynamics in language comprehension

Spivey, Michael J. Cognitive Science Program, University of California, Merced, CA, USA

Saccadic eye movements and continuous reaching movements while carrying out spoken instructions have recently been providing rich insight into the online interaction between syntax, semantics, pragmatics, and even situational affordances. This presentation will describe several experiments that break down the barriers between these different information sources, and point to an account of language processing where perception, cognition, language, and action co-exist as a trajectory in a high-dimensional attractor landscape rather than being treated as a linear series of independent modules.

Cognition as the breaking and reforming of constraints

Stephen, Damian G. Dept. of Psychology, University of Connecticut, Storrs, USA

Our work deals with emergent cognitive structure in problem-solving research. In this paradigm, participants use a force-tracing strategy to determine the turning directions of the gears in an interlocking sequence of gears. With continued practice they discover an alternative strategy. We have modeled this discovery as a phase transition. The discovery of the alternative strategy can be predicted by changes in entropy and criticality of force-tracing motions (in hand and eye), using recurrence quantification analysis and power-law exponents, respectively. We propose a thermodynamic account of cognition as the breaking and reforming of constraints in a complex open system.

1/f scaling in speech

Kello, Christopher T. Dept. of Psychology, George Mason University, Arlington, VA, USA

Biological, behavioral and social systems are intricate beyond comprehension. Yet this complexity yields patterns of behavior that recur across scales and domains, suggesting fundamental principles at work. One such pattern is the scaling relation 1/f noise. This pattern is observed widely in the fluctuations of human brain activity as well as overt cognitive and motor behavior. Some explanations appeal to domain-specific mechanisms like the gating of ion channels or flux in vigilance or attention. I will present individual and dyadic speech data that contradict domain-specific explanations and favor instead common domain-general principles of coordination in biological, behavioral and social systems.

Coupling between cognition and locomotion

Riley, Michael Dept. of Psychology, University of Cincinnati, Cincinnati, CT, USA

Time intervals between treadmill strides are variable but not random. Stride variability carries a dynamical signature of healthy functioning called 1/f noise. Time intervals between cognitive responses share the same signature. Motor and cognitive tasks can be performed concurrently, resulting in well-known dual-task effects. However do concurrent task performances affect the respective dynamical signatures? Participants walked on a treadmill alone, while performing a cognitive task, or performed the cognitive task alone. Concurrent motor performance dramatically "whitened" the dynamical signature of cognitive performance, but not vice versa. Apparent spontaneous coupling between cognition and locomotion altered the dynamical signature of cognitive dynamics.

IS-157: The psychology of terrorism

Robert J. Sternberg, Karin Weis Sternberg (chair)
Hate is one of several precursors to terrorism. I describe in this talk a triangular theory of hate as well as data generated to test that theory. The theory, proposed originally by R. Sternberg, posits three components of hate: negation of intimacy, passion, and commitment. Each proves to be a distinct factor. Convergent-discriminant validation provides further support for the theory

From the terrorists' point of view: What they experience and why they come to destroy

Moghaddam, Fathali Dept. of Psychology, Georgetown University, Washington, DC, USA

Contemporary Islamic terrorism will only be defeated by first understanding the collaboratively constructed and collectively upheld worldview of terrorists. The metaphor of a staircase to and from terrorism, with particular psychological processes characteristic of each level on the staircase, is used to explain the terrorists' point of view. Nine different specializations are identified within terrorist networks. The conclusion focuses on radicalization underway on the ground floor, and some practical paths toward de-radicalization.

Hate as a precursor to terrorism

Weis Sternberg, Karin NPLI, Harvard University, Cambridge, MA, USA

Terrorism has many causes, such as religious fanaticism, economic deprivation or desire for more resources, and misplaced idealism. I will discuss one origin of terrorism, hatred. I draw upon R. Sternberg's duplex theory of hate, according to which hate has two basic aspects: a triangular structure and stories that generate this structure. Hate is viewed as comprising three components: negation of intimacy, passion, and commitment. Stories are diverse, but among them is viewing the object of hate either as a terrorist, an enemy of God, and a morally bankrupt individual. Terrorism is one device to extract vengeance against such targets.

IS-158: Intelligence and cognitive control

Edward Necka (chair)
The cognitive approach to intelligence is usually understood as an attempt to reveal mental processes that account for individual differences in IQ. We assume that the human ability to exert cognitive control over one's mental processes is essential for the general mental ability. Cognitive control may affect not only working memory capacity, but also efficiency of attention in tasks that require inhibition or distraction suppression. The symposium will be an occasion to present and discuss the state of the art in the studies that underscore the importance of various aspects of cognitive control to human intellectual performance.

Working memory as trait and state

Engle, Randall School of Psychology, Georgia Inst. of Technology, Atlanta, USA

Early conceptions of cognitive limitations were based on a limited number of chunks such as 4 ± 1. However, recent thinking also focuses on differences in cognitive control. It is further clear that working memory capacity (WMC) should be thought of as a construct that mediates between many other variables and other tasks in which control is useful. We can think of WMC as both a trait and state variable. Abiding individual differences are an important determinant of WMC but other variables from sleep deprivation to stereotype threat will lead to temporary reduction in capability for cognitive control in real-world cognition.

Intelligence, cognitive control, and working memory capacity: Three distinct relatives of selective attention

Cowan, Nelson Psychological Sciences, University of Missouri-Columbi, Columbia, USA

Many researchers have suggested that the control of cognition is a function of selective attention and that it is an important aspect of intelligence. My colleagues and I have suggested that the ability to save information in working memory also depends on selective attention. We review evidence on individual and developmental differences suggesting that the control and storage functions of selective attention overlap only partially, and that both of them are strongly related to intelligence.

Intelligence and working memory: A time accuracy function (TAF) approach

Brzezicka, Aneta Socia Psychology, Warsaw School of, Warsaw, Poland

The relationships between intellectual functioning and working memory have been investigated using different research paradigms. In the reported study, the time accuracy functions paradigm was used, which converts the presentation intervals into accuracy according to defined functions. Time accuracy functions were obtained on the basis of the PASAT test results. We compared performance of students with high and low Raven's scores. The findings of two experiments showed that students with lower intelligence scores were impaired in one aspect of performance only, namely the rate of processing. These results suggest that intelligence may be related to an ability to control the content of WM in spite of rapidly changing time intervals between consecutive trials.

Working memory capacity, attention control and conscious experience

Kane, Michael Dept. of Psychology, UNC Greensboro, Greensboro, USA

We present research on the relations among fluid ability (working memory capacity (WMC)), executive control, and attentional lapses. Prior research indicates that WMC variation predicts executive-control performance because lower WMC individuals fail to keep novel goals accessible in the face of competition from habit. Here we explored whether such "goal neglect" results from failures to keep conscious thoughts on task goals, which subjects experience as mind wandering. In both laboratory and daily-life studies, we probed subjects' thoughts at random intervals and found that WMC predicts mind wandering and that this association is partially responsible for the WMC-executive control relationship.

Executive control or focus of attention capacity? Working memory contribution to general fluid intelligence

Chuderski, Adam Inst. of Psychology, Jagiellonian University, Cracow, Poland

From two main theories of WM mechanism underlying general intelligence, one promotes the role of executive control, while the other – of the capacity to actively maintain and bind chunks. Our presentation reviews recent literature that shows these two views may not be mutually exclusive. We discuss our own results of n-back and dual-task experiments and structural equation models, which show that efficiency of control contributes to Gf. We will outline a theoretical model of intelligence as determined by the efficiency of control over mental processes.

IS-160: Contribution from psychology to active ageing

Rocio Fernández Ballesteros (chair)
From an evidence based point of view, it has been during the last decades, when from the fields of biomedicine and social sciences emerged the so

called "new paradigm" on the field of ageing: a positive view. The core of this new paradigm is a new construct: healthy, successful, optimal, active or positive ageing. After a systematic review on the field, four main psychological and behavioural domains emerged as the core of active aging: behavioural health and fitness, cognitive functioning, emotional and motivational functioning (affect, control, and coping), and social participation. The main objective of this Symposium is to examine some contribution from psychology on the field of positive ageing.

Lay concept of aging well: Cross-cultural comparisons

Fernández Ballesteros, Rocio Faculdad de Psicologia, Universidad Autónoma de Madrid, Madrid, Spain Luis, Garcia Faculdad de Psicologia, Universidad Autónoma de Madrid, Madrid, Spain Digma, Abarca NEN, National Elderly Network, Loja, Ecuador Lida, Blanc Faculdad de Psicologia, Catholic University of Uruguay, Uruguay, Spain Julia, Lerma Faculdad de Psicologia, Del Valle University, Cali, Colombia Victor, Mendoza Nuñez Estudios, Universidad Autónoma de Mexico, Mexico DF, Mexico Nidia, Mendoza Rubalcaba Faculdad de Psicologia, Autonomous Univ Guadalajara, Guadalajara, Mexico Teresa, Orosa Faculdad de Psicologia, National University Cuba, La Habana, Cyprus Constança, Paul Faculdad de Psicologia, Porto University, Porto, Portugal
Aging well is a relatively new domain of research in the study of aging.Trying to make cross-cultural comparisons in the elders' views,the same 20 items Questionnaire (plus a rank order for selecting the 5 more important aspects) used by Phelan et al. and by Matsubayashi, et al. was administered to elder adults in 7 Latin American (Brazil, Chile, Colombia, Cuba, Ecuador, Mexico, and Uruguay) and 3 European countries (Greece, Portugal and Spain).. Finally, results support that the scientific concept of successful aging seems to be disseminated around the world and perhaps this fact is expressing a positive globalization of this concept.

Psychological distress in women: Implications for active aging

Contança, Oscar Faculdad de Psicologia, University of Porto, Aveiro, Portugal Ribeiro, Paul
Psychological distress (mainly depression) is frequent in old women, although figures varied a lot between studies. Reducing the amount of suffering and dependence due to poor mental health in old age is a priority requiring a good understanding of the determinants of psychological distress as it emerges in association with poor self-perception of health and well-being, high levels of disability and low levels of social participation.We study the psychosocial correlates of psychological distress and discuss the implication of these data for psychological intervention to prevent negative results during the aging process, and to promote active aging. Findings are discussed within a gender lens.

The promotion of the active aging: Evaluation of the multumedia program vital ageing

Caprara, Maria Giovanna Faculty of Psychology, La Sapienza University, Rome, Italy
The interest for the promotion of the active aging and the research on its more important determinants constitutes one of the most relevant issues in the field of the Gerontopsychology. The principal aim of the present contribution is to present the results of three different applications of the program "Vital ageing", a multimedia course designed to promote the active aging. Results support the efficacy of the program "Vital Ageing"; it produces significant and positive changes in different aspects of the daily life of the elderly people. In sum, the carried out study allows to test that the Program "Vital Ageing" is an effective

instrument to produce changes in different domains.

Aging stereotypes, self-stereotypes and active ageing

Bustillos, Antonio Faculdad de Psicologia, Universidad Nacional a Distanc, Madrid, Spain Huici, Carmen Fernández Ballesteros, Rocio Faculdad de Psicologia, Universidad Autónoma de Madrid, Madrid, Spain
Stereotypes are simplified conceptions with specific meaning held by one group of people about another. Aging stereotypes are images about ageing, age and the aged held by social groups, including the aged group. It is assumed that social stereotypes about aging are influencing self-stereotypes and, also, that self-stereotypes about aging are predictor of longevity, good health and, therefore, active aging. It is assumed also that negative performance in old age could be accounted by stereotypes. After a review of the literature, three experiments about the link between social stereotypes, group identity, self-stereotypes and stereotype threat are going to be presented.

IS-161: On the suitability of direct brain-computer interfaces (BCI) for communication, control of robotic devices, and improvement of cognitive functioning

Christa Neuper (chair)
Brain-computer interfaces (BCI) transform signals originating from the human brain on-line into commands that can control devices or applications. This is achieved without any involvement of peripheral nerves and muscles. After almost 20 years of development and testing in the laboratory, BCIs have been applied and adapted in the field. Within several training sessions users can learn to control their brain response to achieve a specific behavior such as communication, grasping with the aids of a neuroprosthesis, or improvement of cognitive and motor functioning. BCI control depends upon progressive practice with feedback and reward and hence engages learning mechanisms in the brain. This symposium provides an overview of current BCI approaches and upcoming applications.

Short introductory presentation: Towards brain-computer interfacing: Applications and perspectives

Neuper, Christa Inst. für Psychologie, Universität Graz, Graz, Austria
Brain-computer interfaces (BCI) transform signals originating from the human brain on-line into commands that can control devices or applications. This is achieved without any involvement of peripheral nerves and muscles. After almost 20 years of development and testing in the laboratory, BCIs have been applied and adapted in the field. Within several training sessions users can learn to control their brain response to achieve a specific behaviour such as communication, grasping with the aids of a neuroprosthesis, or improvement of cognitive and motor functioning. BCI control depends upon progressive practice with feedback and reward and hence engages learning mechanisms in the brain. This symposium provides an overview of current BCI approaches and upcoming applications.

Brain-computer interfaces and quality of life in locked-in patients

Kuebler, Andrea Clinical and Health Psychology, Roehampton University, London, United Kingdom
Brain-computer interfaces (BCI) provide a new communication channel for patients who lost motor control due to injury or disease. Patients learn by

means of neurofeedback to control a BCI through regulation of brain activity such as slow cortical potentials or sensorimotor rhythms. Another approach is to present patients with stimulation paradigms known to elicit specific event-related potentials in the brain such as the P300 or visually evoked potentials. Both approaches proved to be suitable for locked-in patients such that they were able to spell words, select items or surf the internet with a BCI. Quality of life in locked-in patients can be maintained despite disease progression and extremely limited active behaviour and neither quality of life nor depression are related to physical disability or the need of life-sustaining treatment.

Motor imagery and brain-computer interfaces for restoration of movement

Neuper, Christa Inst. für Psychologie, Universität Graz, Graz, Austria
The development of motor brain-computer interface (BCI) systems grounded on the idea to bypass interrupted motor pathways and therewith, allow restoration of movement in paralyzed patients. This is achieved through combining a BCI with intelligent peripheral devices and electrical muscle stimulation. Motor imagery and associated oscillatory signals from the sensorimotor cortex form the basis of the Graz-BCI, which has been successfully used for the control of neuroprosthetic applications in high spinal cord lesions. Moreover, BCI neurofeedback training utilizing motor imagery is a topic of current research in chronic stroke. This novel BCI-based approach is devoted to enhance neural plasticity and the recovery of the stroke-affected brain area.

Inducing neural plasticity in neurological rehabilitation: Brain-computer interface use for the treatment of autism spectrum disorders

Pineda, Jaime Dept. of Cognitive Science, University of California, La Jolla, USA
Training-induced neural plasticity is seen as an important outcome of brain-computer interfaces (BCI) as neurological rehabilitation tools. The mirror neuron system has been theorized to be foundational for how humans understand the actions of others, the development of theory of mind, empathy and language. Autism spectrum disorders (ASD) are characterized by wide variations in symptoms and devastating impacts on these types of social skills. One EEG index of MNS activity is thought to be the suppression of the 8-13 Hz oscillations, or mu rhythms, recorded over sensorimotor cortex. While typically-developing individuals exhibit mu suppression during both self-movement and the observation of another's actions, ASD individuals exhibit mu suppression only in response to self-movement. Recent results suggest that training of mu rhythms using a BCI effects changes in behavior and electrophysiology of ASD children.

Machine learning methods for fast interfacing between brain and computer

Tangermann, Michael Inst. Machine Learning, Technische Universität Berlin, Berlin, Germany
Brain patterns of one and the same mental task (recorded e.g. by EEG) vary substantially from trial to trial and also between repeated sessions of the same user. As the analysis of single trials is necessary for the online use of BCI systems, this data characteristic poses a serious problem for most statistical methods. Intelligent data analysis methods from the field of machine learning enable the Berlin BCI system (BBCI) to deal with this variance. The BBCI learns typical brain patterns of e.g. a motor imagery task based on a short calibration recording. It adapts individually to the signals of a new user and eliminates the need of the time-consuming user training. Moreover, these machine learning methods also provide the possi-

bility to monitor the mental state of a user during task performance.

IS-162: Gender, identity, and collective action

Vindhya Undurti (chair)
This symposium will focus on the shaping and nature of gendered identities forged in varied contexts of collective action ranging from the post-tsunami reconstruction process in Indonesia, to peace promotion inititatives in post-apartheid South Africa, and to socio-political movements in India. Panellists will first, foreground women's activism as it is generally submerged in the master narratives of social movements and second, will identify the role collective action in turn, plays in the social construction of gender.

Social identity, gender and collective action
Sonpar, Shobna Private Practice, Delhi, India
This paper examines the intersection of gender with threatened social identity and forms of collective action in the politically violent context of the Indian state of Jammu-Kashmir. Using qualitative analysis of data, the study shows how conditions of collective and personal trauma have led to Muslim Kashmiri identity polarization that cuts across gender. The traumatic affects of humiliated rage and loss tend to find expression along gendered lines. Yet, polarities like masculine-feminine and violent-nonviolent are both reinforced and challenged in the ways that men and women act to preserve social identity.

Women's activism in post-conflict South Africa: The intersection of identity, culture and social agency
Suffla, Shahnaaz CVI Lead Programme, Medical Research Council, Kenwyn, South Africa
Following the transition from apartheid to democracy more than a decade ago, the role of South African women as agents of peace has expanded and reconfigured to address the essential mission of building a peaceful society in which the structural arrangements and cultural narratives are directed at promoting human security, and reducing inequality and oppression. Against this backdrop, the paper will explore the interface between personal and collective identities, the influence of culture, and the pursuit of social justice as constructed by a group of local women engaged in peace promotion initiatives within a historically marginalised context in South Africa.

The Durueng resilience
Nurdadi, Surastati Dept. of Psychology, University of Indonesia, Jakarta, Indonesia Purba, R.D. Marieta, J.R. Purba, Reno Dept. of Psychology, University of Indonesia, Jakarta, Indonesia Marieta, Josephine Dept. of Psychology, University of Indonesia, Jakarta, Indonesia
This paper focuses on the collective efforts of women participating in the post-tsunami reconstruction process in Durueng in Indonesia. Since more than a decade, these women have also been living under the shadow of violent ethnic conflict in the region. The research questions raised are what has been the progress in the reconstruction process? What are the issues that the women encounter? How can they develop their own resilience during the turbulence?

Bare bodies and bare life: Identity in "body politics"
Akoijam, Bimol Dept. of Psychology, CSDS, Delhi, India
Identity is not merely a psychological fact; it is in a critical sense a politico-cultural reality. After all, our existence is deeply embedded in, and critically mediated by, the politico-cultural milieu within which we exist. "Body", both literally and metaphorically, is a crucial site that registers the politico-cultural character of identity. Nothing seems to reflect this aspect of identity more expressively than in the case of women. Taking the case of women activists who protested against the Security Forces by baring their bodies on July 15 2004 in Imphal, Manipur (India), the present paper explores various layers of identity.

Guns and roses: Subjective well-being of women in the radical left movement in Andhra Pradesh, India
Undurti, Vindhya CESS, Hyderabad, India
Part of a larger project on social identity, self-efficacy, subjective well-being and gender in the context of a left movement in Andhra Pradesh, India, this paper explores the links between subjective well-being and participation in a movement that aims broadly to challenge existing relations of domination. Using qualitiative research techniques, the study attempts to capture the process of engaging in collective action that fosters empowering and postive feelings of well-being and helps to explain the sustainability of women's involvement in further struggle. The implications are discussed with reference to the gender inegalitarian culture in India.

S-044: Global promise: Quality assurance and accountability in professional psychology

Judy Hall (chair)
Changes in systems of education and training, ethical provisions, and licensing and credentialing of psychologists have been proposed, implemented or are undergoing change in many countries and regions. Presenters will consider how quality assurance and accountability are operating in one large region and one large country, followed by an overview of how ethical codes and standards contribute to accountability. Finally, how these developments currently affect mobility for psychologists will be presented. These developments will be framed in the context of the globalization of professional psychologists, today and tomorrow.

Quality assurance in the European Union
Lunt, Ingrid Dept. of Education, University of Oxford, Oxford, United Kingdom
The 27 countries of the European Union have developed very different education systems and arrangements for Quality Assurance. A number of recent developments have been implemented to achieve greater convergence and comparability across Europe. These include the formation of the European Network of Quality Assurance which brings together national QA agencies, the European process named the "Bologna" process which aims to create a European Higher Education Area by 2010, and a more psychology-specific initiative called the EuroPsy which has developed a European qualification or standard across Europe. The paper will present these developments and discuss the moves to greater accountability and quality assurance in psychology across Europe.

Quality assurance in Australia
Waring, Trevor Dept. of Psychology, University of Newcastle, New Lambton Heights, Australia
Australia's relatively small population of 21 million people is spread across a large continent governed by six sovereign states, two territory administrations and an overarching Federal Government. Professional psychologists train in one of 40+ universities and are registered with one of the state or territory Registration Boards each with its own standards of training and code of conduct. In such a context the risk of compromising standards was high. This potential was addressed by way of cooperation between registering authorities, training bodies and the professional association and has now been ratified by the introduction of a common national registration requirement.

Ethical codes as vehicles of accountability
Ritchie, Pierre L.-J. Dept. of Psychology, University of Ottawa, Ottawa, ON, Canada
The historic context for the emergence of ethics as a central component of psychology's public accountability as well as psychologists' accountability to the profession is reviewed. Codes and standards in various incarnations are examined, particularly the development of recognized documents at the national and multi-national levels, including recent work on meta-codes and a universal declaration of ethical principles. The advent of cultural competence is the object of focal attention because of its increasing pertinence in a world characterized by greater mobility. Concluding comments are offered within the perspective that ethical codes are the ultimate expression of a profession's shared values.

Global promise? International mobility
Hall, Judy National Register of HSPP, Washington, USA
Mobility for psychologists is an international issue. The co-author of a chapter on international mobility will address the many factors (education, training, licensure, & credentialing) that assist with mobility as well as identify what various organizations are doing to promote mobility for psychologists.

S-241: Analyzing interaction patterns in teams

Simone Kauffeld, Renee Meyers (chair)
This panel of European and American researchers will discuss five different research projects that all focus on interaction patterns in work team contexts. Results to be presented include investigations of the role of interruptions in group discussions, the impact of facilitator communication on group discourse, the role of moaning and complaining in decision-making work teams, the link between communication and outcomes in anesthesia teams, and the role of communication in promoting or inhibiting proposals in group discussion. Each presentation will describe and analyze the interaction patterns particular to their team context, and highlight the impact of communication on group outcomes.

Complaining and solution circles in group discussions
Kauffeld, Simone Inst. für Psychologie, Tech. Universität Braunschweig, Braunschweig, Germany Henschel, Angela Inst. für Psychologie, TU Braunschweig, Braunschweig, Germany Hilpert, Alexandra Inst. für Psychologie, TU Braunschweig, Braunschweig, Germany Lehmann-Willenbrock, Nale Inst. für Psychologie, Tech. Universität Braunschweig, Braunschweig, Germany
How does the mood of our colleagues affect our own mood in communication? We analyzed discussions of 50 real industrial groups from 2 companies with interaction coding (Cassel Competence Grid) and subsequent lag sequential analysis. We found evidence for complaining circles (continuous expressions of an inactive mood) as well as solution circles (continuous expressions of an active mood). Moreover, job characteristics (job rotation and autonomy) were positive predictors of solution circles and negative predictors of complaining circles. Theoretical and practical implications of these findings are discussed.

The influence of facilitator communication on the group discussion process

Lehmann-Willenbrock, Nale Inst. für Psychologie, Tech. Universität Braunschweig, Braunschweig, Germany Kauffeld, Simone Inst. für Psychologie, TU Braunschweig, Braunschweig, Germany

Facilitators are widely acknowledged to improve meetings by enhancing communication and providing procedures to make meetings more efficient. There is much written on the necessary skills for successful group facilitation. However, it is not clear how actual facilitation behaviors within a meeting affect the group process. We analyzed 59 real group discussions from 19 companies using interaction coding (Cassel Competence Grid, Kauffeld, 2006) and lag sequential analysis. The results show that structuring remarks such as goal orientation or procedural suggestions help to facilitate subsequent discussion. Implications for theory and practice in facilitation are discussed.

The role of interruptions in team decision making interactions

Meyers, Renee Dept. of Communication, Univ. of Wisconsin-Milwaukee, Milwaukee, USA Kauffeld, Simone Psychology, TU Braunschweig, Braunschweig, Germany Lazarides, Katina Dept. of Communication, Univ. of Wisconsin-Milwaukee, Milwaukee, WI, USA

The purpose of this study was to investigate interruptions in group decision-making interactions. Past research has typically conceptualized interruption behavior as dominant and inhibitive. In this study, we used the Cassel Competence Grid (Kauffeld, 2006) and lag-sequential analysis to analyze interruptions in 59 team discussions from 19 companies. Contrary to some past research, results showed that interruptions have the ability to enhance problem-solving and move groups in a positive direction. Conclusions touch on the dual nature of interruptions–both their inhibitive and facilitative characteristics. Implications for team decision-making practice and facilitation are discussed.

Communication in anesthesia teams

Kolbe, Michaela Organisation, Arbeit u.Techno., ETH Zürich, Zürich, Switzerland Künzle, Barbara Organisation, Arbeit u.Technol, ETH Zürich, Zürich, Switzerland Zala-Mezö, Enikö Grote, Gudela Organisation, Arbeit u.Technol, ETH Zürich, Zürich, Switzerland Wacker, Johannes Institute of Anesthesiology, University Hospital Zurich, Zürich, Switzerland

Anaesthesia teams have to handle high risks with failures potentially endangering human lives. Their ability to deal with work, which is characterized by routine as well as by rapidly shifting priorities, depends strongly on team communication. We analysed communication and performance in routine and non-routine events based on a taxonomy of communication and coordination behavior and a reaction-time based performance measure. Data were obtained from 15 inductions of general anaesthesia in a simulated setting where after minor changes in blood pressure an asystole occurred. We will present results of lag sequential and pattern analysis showing different communication patterns in well-performing groups and discuss implications for medical training.

The destiny of proposals in the course of group discussions

Boos, Margarete Inst. für Psychologie, Universität Göttingen, Göttingen, Germany Strack, Michaela

Based on the structurational theory of Poole et al. (1986, 1996), group decision-making is conceptualised as a process where individual cognitive contributions are intertwined with local and global interaction dynamics generating structure. In group decision making, proposals and their related argu-

ments form the critical contributions. Data from 21 5-person-groups show that the acceptance of the 956 proposals is predicted by the input variable proponent's positional power. Positional power is mediated by the process variable mode of argumentation. Thus, the destiny of a proposal becomes open again.

S-242: Recent advances in video game violence effects on brain function, aggression and violence

Craig Anderson (chair)

Researche teams will present results from five countries on the effects of playing violent video games on brain function and on aggressive and violent behavior. One presentation focuses on identifying neural areas that are activated and suppressed by violent and nonviolent action in video games. Three presentations include cross-cultural comparisons and context effects on aggression-related thoughts, feelings, and behaviors. Three presentations include longitudinal studies. One presentation focuses on factors that might reduce some harmful effects of violent games. Overall, the studies show remarkable consistency across cultures and ages, though there appear to be interesting context effects as well.

Media violence exposure and aggression among German adolescents: Individual and group differences

Möller, Ingrid Inst. für Psychologie, Universität Potsdam, Potsdam, Germany

The results of the first wave of a 4-year-longitudinal study will be presented. To examine the link between exposure to violent contents across different types of media and aggression and prosocial behavior, 2,000 7th and 8th graders were asked about their media violence consumption, normative beliefs about aggression, empathy and aggressive as well as helping behavior. Additionally, teacher nominations of aggression and prosocial behavior were obtained. The extent and type of media usage will be compared for German and migrant participants and similarities and differences of the relationships between the outcome variables will be examined.

The role of warning labels, wishful identification and empathy in reducing undesired effects from violent video games

Nije Bijvank, Marije Communication Science, VU University Amsterdam, Amsterdam, Netherlands

The relationship between violent video games and aggression has been established in numerous studies. Various factors may contribute to this relationship, leading to the question of how to protect minors who play those games. Our results show that the PEGI warning label system results in the opposite effect from what was intended, turning violent games into "forbidden fruits". We also find that players' "wishful identification" with an aggressive hero adds to aggressive behavior among adolescents. Finally, we show that a minor in-game manipulation can increase empathy with the victim. Implications for intervention techniques and media literacy programs will be discussed.

The long-term effects of presence and contexts of video game violence in Japan

Shibuya, Akiko Humanities and Social Science, Keio University, Tokyo, Japan Sakamoto, Akira Psychology, Ochanomizu University, Tokyo, Japan Ihori, Nobuko Psychology, Ochanomizu University, Tokyo, Japan Yukawa, Shintaro Psychology, University of Tsukuba, Tokyo, Japan

Japan is famous for a country of violent media but also with a low crime rate, and some researchers may wonder if there is no effect of violence media in

Japan. This presentation summarizes the video game violence studies in Japan, and indicates that Japanese children and adolescents are also influenced by video game violence. Authors also provide some empirical evidences that children in Japan are affected by the contexts of video game violence, possibly more than those in Western countries, and by their interpretation of violent scenes.

A cross-cultural comparison of violent video game effects on aggressive cognition

Gentile, Douglas Dept. of Psychology, Iowa State University, Ames, USA Khoo, Angeline Psychological Studies, National Institute of Educatio, Singapore, Singapore Liau, Albert Psychological Studies, National Institute of Educatio, Singapore, USA Brad, Bushman Dept. of Psychology, University of Michigan, Ann Arbor, USA Anderson, Craig Dept. of Psychology, Iowa State University, Ames, USA Huesmann, L. Rowell Dept. of Psychology, University of Michigan, Ann Arbor, USA

This session will report on two large-scale correlational studies of elementary and secondary children in Singapore (N = 3034) and the United States (N = 900). of violent video game exposure and multiple measures of aggressive cognition, including normative beliefs about the acceptability of violence, aggressive fantasies, empathy and perceived social and emotional competence. In both samples, violent video game exposure predicted aggressive cognitions, after controlling for several relevant potential confounding variables (e.g., sex, age, total amount of video game play). Similarities and differences between Singapore and the US are discussed.

Neural mechanisms of video game violence

Mathiak, Klaus Inst. für Psychiatrie, RWTH Aachen, Aachen, Germany Weber, Rene Dept. of Communication, University of California, Santa Barbara, CA, USA

Little is known about the neural correlates of playing video games. We provide an overview on past and ongoing research on neural substrates of playing violent video games. In two fMRI studies we analyzed the correlation between theory-based content analytical codings, cognitions after and during game play, and BOLD signal responses. The occurrence of violent episodes corresponded with a dominant activation pattern of the dorsal and deactivation of the rostral anterior cingulate cortex and amygdala. The interpretation of these findings, issues regarding the internal validity of our results, and the implications for current media violence theories will be discussed.

Violent video game effects: An overview

Anderson, Craig Dept. of Psychology, Iowa State University, Ames, USA

A new meta-analysis on the effects of violent video games will be presented. This meta-analysis is based on studies that meet stricter methodological criteria than past analyses. Included are studies using cross-sectional, experimental, and longitudinal designs from the U.S., Japan, Australia, and Western Europe. Results reveal strong support for the hypothesis that playing violent video games is a causal risk factor for aggression and violence, as well as for aggressive cognition, in both short and long term contexts. There also is evidence of significant effects on physiological arousal, aggressive affect, desensitization and lack of empathy, and prosocial behavior.

S-243: Neuro-cognitive mechanisms of conscious and unconscious visual perception

Markus Kiefer, Rolf Verleger (chair)

Elucidating human consciousness remains one of the greatest scientific challenges in the 21st century. Determining fundamental cognitive and neural mechanisms underlying conscious and unconscious visual perception can contribute to this endeavor. We present evidence that identifies processes relevant for forming a conscious percept from the visual input. Important information can be obtained from conditions which prevent the formation of a conscious percept. It will also be discussed which factors determine whether unconsciously perceived stimuli are processed and are able to influence behavior. Convergent evidence may help to identify general computational principles underlying conscious and unconscious visual perception.

Decoding conscious and unconscious visual processing from brain activity in humans

Haynes, John-Dylan Bernstein Zentrum, Universitätsmedizin Berlin, Berlin, Germany

Recent advances in human neuroimaging have shown that it is possible to accurately decode a person's conscious visual experience based only on non-invasive multivariate measurements of their brain activity. Here several studies will be presented that directly address the relationship between neural encoding of information (as measured with fMRI) and its availability for awareness. These studies include comparisons of neural and perceptual information, unconscious information processing, and decoding of the "stream of consciousness". Taken together these studies help reveal how the contents of visual awareness are encoded in the human brain.

How to become unconscious: Restrictions in the processing of word forms in rapid serial visual presentation

Niedeggen, Michael Experimentelle Psychologie, Freie Universität Berlin, Berlin, Germany

Illusory words are induced by rapid serial visual presentation: Two subsequently presented real words share a string of letters (RIVER – BEAVER). The free floating word fragment induced (BEA) is likely to be linked with a subsequently presented fragment (CH) if they combine to a word (illusory word: BEACH). Our behavioral and EEG experiments demonstrate an asymmetry in the level of processing of the word not reported: An illusory word is transiently activated although it does not elicit semantic priming. A real word is not decoded in the system and leaves no trace in the lexical system.

Non-conscious perception and uncontrolled action in a split brain: A case-study of a patient with anarchic-hand syndrome

Verleger, Rolf Neurologische Klinik, Universität Lübeck, Lübeck, Germany Friedrich, Monique Psychological Institute, TU Chemnitz, Chemnitz, Germany Binkofski, Ferdinand Neurologische Klinik, Universität Lübeck, Lübeck, Germany Sedlmeier, Peter Psychological Institute, TU Chemnitz, Chemnitz, Germany Kömpf, Detlef Neurologische Klinik, Universität Lübeck, Lübeck, Germany

Following an infarct lesion to the corpus callosum, G.H complains that the left hand does what it wants. In addition to extensive neuropsychological and neuroradiological examination, behavior and EEG-potentials were measured in a "Simon-paradigm" which task requires information exchange between the hemispheres. In the WAIS block-design test, G.H. evidenced split-brain behavior (video). EEG potentials recorded in the Simon task indicated that the right visual cortex was faster activated than the left, right centro-parietal areas were overactivated, and there was evidence of information transfer via the intact occipital hemispheric connection. Implications of this evidence for understanding the syndrome will be discussed.

Attentional capture by invisible colors and shapes

Ansorge, Ulrich Inst. Verhaltenswissenschaften, Universität Osnabrück, Osnabrück, Germany Horstmann, Gernot Inst. für Psychologie, Universität Bielefeld, Bielefeld, Germany

We tested whether invisible (backward masked) stimuli capture visuo-spatial attention in a top-down contingent fashion. In line with that hypothesis, we find that masked color stimuli capture attention once they match the set of searched-for colors, regardless of the color of the current or preceding target (Exp. 1). We observe a very similar pattern of results with masked shape stimuli (Exp. 2 and 3). The findings are discussed with regard to explanations of attentional capture.

How smart is unconscious perception? Complex mental operations on visual stimuli do not require awareness

Vorberg, Dirk Inst. für Psychologie, Tech. Universität Braunschweig, Braunschweig, Germany

The experiments to be presented explore the complexity limits of actions to be facilitated or inhibited by stimuli outside awareness, addressing the issue of whether the unconscious is "smart or dumb" (Loftus & Klinger, 1992). By studying priming of performance in categorization of visual stimuli based on logical rules, we tested the Feedforward-Sweep hypothesis (Lamme, 2001), which specifies the necessary conditions for stimuli to remain subliminal. As predicted, strong effects from masked congruent or incongruent primes were found for AND, OR, XOR, and relational rules. If well practiced, even complex mental operations can be performed automatically.

Constraining unconscious cognition: Top-down modulation of unconscious priming

Kiefer, Markus Inst. für Psychiatrie, Universität Ulm, Ulm, Germany

In classical theories, unconscious, automatic processes are usually thought to occur autonomously and independently of any cognitive resources. However, refined theories propose out that the cognitive system has to be configured in a certain way for automatic processes to occur. In this talk, electrophysiological evidence with the masked semantic priming paradigm will be presented which shows that masked priming effects crucially depend (i) on temporal attention to the masked prime and (ii) on the task set immediately before masked prime presentation. These results suggest a top-down gating mechanism which orchestrates the unconscious information processing stream.

S-244: Social and cognitive barriers of knowledge exchange

Ulrike Cress (chair)

Various research on knowledge exchange revealed that people do not share information in optimal way. The contributions aim to elaborate conditions that support effective knowledge exchange in different contexts: in decision making, complex problem solving, information-exchange dilemmas, and Wikipedia. For instance, the importance of interdependence structure, (a)synchronicity, visual representation of participating individuals, social motivation, relevance and distribution of information, and instrumentality perception is stressed. Experimental and field research is presented. The symposium will bring together international researcher dealing with related research projects and, thus, will enable fruitful discussion.

The effects of interdependence structure and anonymity on decision making and information processing

Mümken, Anke Ints. für Sozialpsychologie, Universität Münster, Münster, Germany Freytag, Clemens Ints. für Sozialpsychologie, Universität Münster, Münster, Germany Keil, Wolfgang Ints. für Pädagog. Psychologie, Universität Münster, Münster, Germany Piontkowski, Ursula Ints. für Sozialpsychologie, Universität Münster, Münster, Germany

Most research on hidden profile assumes that all group members are cooperative. Less attention is paid to competitive and mixed motive situations. We conducted a 3 x 2 factorial design to investigate the effects of interdependence structure (positive vs. mixed-motive vs. competitive) and anonymity (anonymous vs. non-anonymous) on decision making and information processing. Sixty-six 3-person-groups participated in the study. Data were analysed using mixed models. Results show an interaction effect of the interdependence structure and anonymity on the decision quality. Furthermore, both a competitive interdependence structure and anonymity reduce the willingness to share information and influence the interaction process.

Impact of temporal extension, synchronicity and group size on computer-supported information exchange

Kimmerle, Joachim Angew. Kognitive Psychologie, Universität Tübingen, Tübingen, Germany Cress, Ulrike Design and Implementation, Knowledge Media Research Cente, Tübingen, Germany

People's willingness to contribute information they have in a situation of computer-supported information exchange is influenced by the configuration of various circumstantial aspects. People's perception and their behavior depend on how long the period of cooperation persists, on whether the information exchange takes place synchronously or asynchronously, and on how large the cooperating group is. In an experimental laboratory study we investigated a prototypical situation of computer-supported information exchange examining those three factors: temporal extension, (a)synchronicity, and group size. With respect to each of these variables we describe their theoretical foundations and report their impact on behavior. Moreover we point out to the mediating influence of several psychological factors.

Application of SIDE: Different visual representation of group members and their effects on information exchange

Wodzicki, Katrin Knowledge Media Institut, Tübingen, Germany Cress, Ulrike KMRC, Tübingen, Germany

Two experimental studies elaborated what kind of visual representation of communicating group members is most effective in promoting exchange in information sharing dilemmas. For this purpose, we applied and expanded predictions of the Social Identity model of Deindividuation Effects (SIDE). In Study 1, no visualization was compared to visualization with personal pictures of all group members. In Study 2, no visualization was compared to visualizations with same-character and different-character pictures for all group members. The effects of the different visual representations depended on whether personal or social identity was salient. Only same-character visualizations enhanced knowledge sharing independently of salient identity.

Strategic information sharing: The effects of information sharedness, information relevance and social motivation

Utz, Sonja Dept. of Communication Science, VU University of Amsterdam, Amsterdam, Netherlands Steinel, Wolfgang Social & Organizational Ps, Leiden University, Amsterdam, Netherlands

Contributing information to a common pool is different from contributing money. Information can vary in quality (relevance; true vs. untrue). Thus, people can share several pieces of information to make a cooperative impression, but withhold the really important information. Social motivation is expected to moderate this behavior; proselfs should withhold more relevant and unshared information than prosocials. In two experiments, social motivation, sharedness and relevance of information were varied. Experiment 2 also included the option to lie. The results showed that people tend to contribute shared and irrelevant information, and that this tendency is even stronger for proselfs.

Information exchange and performance in dyadic complex problem solving
Meyer, Bertolt Inst. für Psychologie, Universität Zürich, Zürich, Switzerland
The study tested how the distribution of task-relevant information in a dyad influences its information exchange and performance in a complex problem-solving scenario. The members of 75 dyads received overlapping information on successful scenario control. Information overlap was altered over three conditions, information per group member was held constant. Dyads exchanged their information before working on the complex scenario. No information overlap led to more falsely communicated information than shared information. Analysis of variance reveals that dyads with partially shared information exhibited significantly better performance scores than dyads from other conditions. Implications for theories of informational diversity are discussed.

Voluntary engagement in an open web-based encyclopedia: From reading to contributing
Schroer, Joachim Inst. für Arbeitspsychologie, Universität Würzburg, Würzburg, Germany Hertel, Guido Inst. für Arbeitspsychologie, Universität Würzburg, Würzburg, Germany
Extending earlier research on active Wikipedia contributors (Schroer & Hertel, 2007), a longitudinal study was conducted to explore why Wikipedia readers would start to actively engage for Wikipedia. Online-survey data (N=256) were analyzed using PLS path modeling. Results revealed perceptions of costs-benefits, expected task enjoyment, and perceived instrumentality of personal contributions as main predictors of the intention to contribute. Active contributions 6 months later depended predominantly on costs-benefits and instrumentality perceptions, typically triggered by incomplete or incorrect Wikipedia articles in one's own field of expertise. Implications are instructive for organizational knowledge management and Web 2.0 websites.

S-245: The science of heuristics: Methodology and scope

Shabnam Mousavi (chair)
Heuristics are commonly perceived as second-best solutions, which result in inferior outcomes compared to exact methods such as optimization. We provide an overview of an alternative view: the fast and frugal heuristics program. We present philosophical and analytical arguments as well as experimental and simulation results demonstrating that even though heuristics do not conform to statistical or logical norms, they are not necessarily second-best solutions but are successfully and dominantly used by people. This session contributes to our understanding of how judgment and decision making relies on simple rules of thumb that exploit the informational structure of the environment.

Simple heuristics and the problem of strategy identification
Woike, Jan K. Ökonomie und Business Admin., Universität Lausanne, Lausanne, Switzerland Hoffrage, Ulrich Ökonomie und Business Admin., Universität Lausanne, Lausanne, Switzerland Hertwig, Ralph Department of Psychology, University of Basil, Basel, Switzerland
Decision strategies generate outcomes, but do outcomes allow for inferences regarding which strategy generated them? In a simulation study, various strategies (fast and frugal, linear, and Bayesian) solved paired-comparison tasks. We varied the percentage of missing cue values, of cue retrieval errors, and of strategy execution errors. Using a range of models, we subsequently modelled the decisions in an attempt to reconstruct the process that generated them. Because strategies often made identical decisions, they were barely separable. Thus, a good fit of a linear model does not necessarily exclude the possibility that a fast and frugal heuristic generated the decisions.

When cognitive processes exploit the environment rather than reflect it
Brighton, Henry Max-Planck-Institut, Berlin, Germany
Mirrors, lenses, and scissors are metaphors for how the mind is shaped by the environment. For Roger Shepard, much of cognition is done with mirrors: Key aspects of the environment are internalized in the brain. Egon Brunswik proposed his lens model to capture how accurately judgment captures the outside world. Herbert Simon proposed that human behavior is shaped by a pair of scissors whose two blades are cognition and the environment. I show how simple heuristics operate like scissors, how they exploit the statistical properties of environments, and how this process of exploitation enables them to outperform other cognitive models.

Even "No" information can become an information
Zurbriggen, Seraphina Inst. für Psychologie, Universität Zürich, Zürich, Switzerland Hausmann, Daniel Inst. für Psychologie, Universität Zürich, Zürich, Switzerland Läge, Damian Inst. für Psychologie, Universität Zürich, Zürich, Switzerland
Theoretical frameworks of decision making processes have not yet attributed any benefits to nondiscriminating cue information. In active and sequential information search, however, nondiscriminating information can substantially change the search order: Results from city inference task experiments show strong evidence that adaptive behaviour depends on the quality of nondiscriminating information (positive/positive vs. negative/negative cue values). We assume that nondiscriminating information points people towards city size classes such that they adapt their further information search accordingly, and explore whether this behaviour is influenced by the way they learn about cue information within a specific domain.

Heuristic processes in normatively superior judgment
Cokely, Edward T. Max-Planck-Institut, Berlin, Germany Kelley, Colleen M. Psychology, Florida State University, Tallahassee, USA
Some individuals consistently make "better" judgments and decisions. Yet little is known about the exact cognitive processes that give rise to this variation in judgment. To identify precise mechanisms, individual differences were assessed and process tracing was applied (i.e., protocol analysis) in the context of judgments under uncertainty. Results indicated that variation in expected-value type choices principally arose from variations in heuristic search processes. Heuristic depth of search also fully mediated the relationship between cognitive abilities and judgment. Implications for current models of cognitive control (e.g., dual-process

models) and decision-making (e.g., priority heuristic) are discussed.

The unnecessity of a simplicity-accuracy trade-off for heuristics
Martignon, Laura Mathematik und Informatik, Pädag. Hochschule Ludwigsburg, Ludwigsburg, Germany Mousavi, Shabnam Adaptive Behavior & Cognit, Max Planck Institute for Human, Berlin, Germany Katsikopoulos, Konstantinos Department of Mechanical Eng., MA Institute of Technology, Cambridge, USA
In the tradition of cognitive illusions, heuristics usually violate rational norms and produce errors by trading accuracy for simplicity. The fast and frugal heuristics (FFH) program takes an altogether different approach by showing that heuristics represent reliable strategies when used in matching environments. This match represents the ecological rationality of FFH, which are not necessarily subject to the same trade-off. We elaborate this characteristic of fast and frugal heuristics by reviewing the Take The Best (TTB) strategy. Specifically, we demonstrate that TTB coincides with DEBA for a specific choice of weights but is not a special case of DEBA.

S-246: Vicarious emotions: Antecedents, processes and consequences

Andreas Olsson, Jamil Zaki (chair)
Responding adequately to others' emotions is key to a normal development and an adaptive social life. Recent research in the social cognitive and affective neuroscience has provided new and exciting insights into the underlying processes involved when we watch and imagine others' emotional states. Beyond a better understanding of empathy and mental state inference, this research has begun to specify how these processes are affected by specific antecedents, such as the observer's previous experiences and contextual manipulations. In addition, this new research has suggested links between these processes and specific behavioral consequences, such as empathic accuracy and learning outcome.

Using self-knowledge to infer others' preferences
Mitchell, Jason Harvard University, Cambridge, USA
One useful strategy for inferring others' mental states may be to use knowledge of one's own thoughts, feelings, and desires as a proxy for those of others. These self-referential accounts of social cognition are supported by recent research suggesting that a single brain region – ventromedial prefrontal cortex (vMPFC) – is engaged both by tasks that require self-reference and those that require inferences about the minds of others. Additional studies suggest that one can increase vMPFC-mediated mentalizing by engaging in explicit perspective-taking of others. Together, these results suggest the vMPFC subserves both introspecting about one's own mind and considering the mind of others.

The role of the mirror neuron system in understanding emotional actions
Montgomery, Kim Columbia University, Princeton, USA Seeherman, Kimberly Dept of Psychology, Princeton University, Princeton, USA Haxby, James Dept of Psychology, Princeton University, Princeton, USA
Mirror neurons respond during the observation and execution of actions and may be related to the capacity for empathy since empathy is the ability to understand another by simulating their experience and emotions (Gallese et al, 1996; Gallese, 2003). Here we show that in individuals with high empathy, but not in those with low empathy, the

human mirror neuron system (hMNS) is more strongly activated by the perception of emotional facial expressions than by the perception of socially-irrelevant facial movements. These results indicate that the hMNS is an important component of the neural basis of empathic ability.

I've got me under your skin: direct and vicarious experience of social touch

Morrison, India Göteborg University, Sweden

Recent research suggests that selective nerve-brain pathways encode the type of gentle touch that occurs during affective social interactions, likely underpinning the affective perceptual correlates of directly-experienced "social touch". These pathways may also provide the basis for vicarious representations of observed touch between other individuals. We investigated this by comparing subjects' brain responses to "social touch" with responses to videos of others being similarly stroked. Touch and vision selectively activated a region of insula targeted by the relevant nerves. Altogether, the results suggest that cortical and psychophysical responses to observed touch are constrained by processing in pathways encoding social touch.

Beyond association: The role of empathy in vicarious fear learning

Olsson, Andreas Dept. of Psychology, Columbia University, New York, USA

Observing another individual's fear expression provides an efficient indirect means of emotional learning. Across species, observational fear learning (OFL) may involve the same basic learning mechanisms as classical fear conditioning. However, to provide adaptive learning in complex human social situations, OFL needs to be sensitive to both bottom-up driven empathic responses and mental attributions. This talk will present research suggesting that OFL comprises a flexible learning system drawing on both the brain's fear learning circuitry centered on the amygdala and prefrontal areas associated with empathy and mental state attributions.

I have been there: The evolution and neural mechanisms of shared emotional experience

Preston, Stephanie University of Michigan, Ann Arbor, USA

Supporting evolutionary and neurophysiological theories of empathy, brain-imaging studies have consistently found overlapping activation for experiencing and observing emotion. However, because these studies utilize simple, common states (like pain), they discount the most defining feature of empathy – the need for the observer to have previously experienced the relevant state/situation. Across studies, employing real, everyday experiences of emotion, we have consistently found that a similar past experience in the observer increases overlapping neural and psychophysiological activation, empathy, and even help offered. The data particularly point to the role of the ventral temporal cortex for mediating such representations of past experience.

The role of shared affect in empathic accuracy

Zaki, Jamil Dept. of Psychology, Columbia University, New York, USA *Bolger, Niall* Psychology, Columbia University, New York, USA *Ochsner, Kevin* Psychology, Columbia University, New York, USA

Previous work has demonstrated that perceivers sharing physiological arousal with social targets are more accurate about targets' affect. However, accuracy should depend on the coherence between targets' arousal and reported affect. We recorded autonomic arousal from targets discussing emotional events, who later rated the affect they felt while discussing. Perceivers then watched videotapes of targets and rated their affect. Coherent

targets were more emotionally readable by perceivers, an effect mediated by sharing of arousal between perceivers and targets. These results suggest that sharing arousal with someone may help us read their emotions, especially when their emotional state matches their arousal.

S-247: New developments in computer based assessment: Implications for competence assessment

Thomas Martens, Gilbert Busana (chair)

For the last ten years, empirical psychological and educational research has been concerned with the assessment of competencies. Particularly, the international comparative studies assessing students' achievement such as TIMSS, PISA and PIRLS have highlighted this subject. In order to assess and evaluate competencies, it is necessary to develop differentiated and proper diagnostic instruments. Computer-based test methods provide good conditions for this development, concerning objectivity, reliability, validity and economy. Furthermore, new item and test formats allow to assess complex and dynamic competencies often in more realistic situations. This symposium reports empirical results as well as future potentials of computer based assessment.

TAO: Paving the way to new assessment instruments using an open and versatile computer-based platform

Latour, Thibaud Technologies de l'information, CRP Henri Tudor, Luxembourg-Kirchberg, Luxembourg *Martin, Romain* EMACS research unit, Université du Luxembourg, Walferdange, Luxembourg *Plichart, Patrick* Technologies de l'information, CRP Henri Tudor, Luxembourg-Kirchberg, Luxembourg *Jadoul, Raynald* Technologies de l'information, CRP Henri Tudor, Luxembourg-Kirchberg, Luxembourg *Busana, Gilbert* EMACS research unit, Université du Luxembourg, Walferdange, Luxembourg *Swietlik-Simon, Judith* Technologies de l'information, CRP Henri Tudor, Luxembourg-Kirchberg, Luxembourg

The TAO framework provides a general and open architecture for computer-assisted test development and delivery, with the potential to respond to the whole range of evaluation needs. The TAO platform provides to all actors of the entire computer-based assessment process a comprehensive set of functionalities enabling the creation, the management, and the delivery of electronic assessments. In this contribution, we shall introduce the space of assessment needs from which are derived the required platform functionalities and architecture. Starting from the architecture, in a non-technical way, we shall then illustrate the numerous opportunities offered by the platform in terms of potentially new assessment instruments. http://www.tao.lu

A web-based system for the evaluation of information processing strategies in the domain of scientific literacy

Martin, Romain Faculté LSHASE, Université du Luxembourg, Walferdange, Luxembourg *Keller, Ulrich* Faculté LSHASE, Université du Luxembourg, Walferdange, Luxembourg *Reichert, Monique* Faculté LSHASE, Université du Luxembourg, Walferdange, Luxembourg *Schandeler, Ingo* Faculté LSHASE, Université du Luxembourg, Walferdange, Luxembourg *Busana, Gilbert* Faculté LSHASE, Université du Luxembourg, Walferdange, Luxembourg *Latour, Thibaud* CITI department, CRP Henri Tudor, Luxembourg-Kirchberg, Luxembourg

We will present a web-based system for exploring information processing strategies for the use of web-based content. Measurement takes place in two phases. In phase one, initial knowledge for a certain domain of scientific literacy is evaluated using a

standard multiple choice test. In phase two, testees have access to various web-based contents (videos, graphs, texts) which they can explore for a fixed amount of time in order to correct their answers given in phase one. Behavioral data of this second phase are used to infer different types of information processing. The possible added-value of behavioral data will be discussed.

Developing items for electronic reading assessment: The hypertext builder

Goldhammer, Frank Internat. Bildungsforschung, Deutsches Institut für, Frankfurt, Germany *Martens, Thomas* pädagogische Forschung, Deutsches Institut für intern., Frankfurt, Germany *Naumann, Johannes* pädagogische Forschung, Deutsches Institut für intern., Frankfurt, Germany *Rölke, Heiko* Pädagogische Forschung, Deutsches Institut für intern., Frankfurt, Germany *Scharaf, Alexander* Pädagogische Forschung, Deutsches Institut für intern., Frankfurt, Germany

The competence in reading electronic texts has become an important aspect of reading literacy. To account for this, an electronic reading assessment (ERA) will be carried out in PISA 2009. We present a new graphical front-end tool for TAO, the "ERA Hypertext-Builder", which was developed for item authoring in the PISA 2009 study. The tool enables the rapid development of complex electronic reading stimuli, such as websites, e-mail clients, or forums. In addition to presenting the ERA Hypertext-Builder itself and demonstrating its features, we report first evidence on the validity of ERA stimuli and items.

A web-based system for mathematical problem understanding and solving

Busana, Gilbert EMACS Research Unit, University of Luxembourg, Walferdange, Luxembourg *Martin, Romain* EMACS Research Unit, University of Luxembourg, Walferdange, Luxembourg *Langers, Christian* EMACS Research Unit, University of Luxembourg, Walferdange, Luxembourg

This work presents a Computer Assisted Mathematical Problem Understanding and Solving (CAMPUS) framework integrated to TAO. CAMPUS offers an environment that allows the student to develop mathematical problem-solving strategies in complex situations. The tool imposes no restrictions to the resolution process of the learner, but avoids him/her taking obviously wrong solution steps. We will present the tool as well as its characteristics and the first results from the field trial.

Online adaptive versus paper-pencil testing

Molnár, Gyöngyvér Inst. of Education, University of Szeged, Szeged, Hungary *Csapó, Ben* Inst. of Education, University of Szeged, Szeged, Hungary

This paper compares the advantages and disadvantages of traditional paper-pencil testing and online adaptive testing through the importance and power of assessment and feedback in learning and instruction. It shows the main steps from the fixed form of paper-pencil assessment to the flexibility of computer-based adaptive testing. It highlights the benefits and possibilities of using technology and IRT in testing and presents the perspectives and problems in computer based online adaptive testing.

S-248: Toward establishing common ground for an international evidence based psychology

Ann Marie O'Roark (chair)

The juggernaut of attention to evidence-based psychological practice (Levant, 2005) is driven by an interest in achieving accountability in applied sciences, in medicine, education, public policy, and architecture. In his call to have psychologists consider how a broader range of research evidence can be effectively included in evidence based practice in psychology (EBPP), Levant stated that "The zeitgeist is to require professionals to base their practice to whatever extent possible on evidence" (Levant, 2005, p. 1). The policy subsequently adopted by the American Psychological Association fails to address the practice of applied psychologists and fails to provide the foundation for global and international scientific agreements. The International Council of Psychologists (ICP) presents a panel of psychologists to discuss the development of agreements regarding a broader range of research designs, intervention decision-making, integration of multiple streams of evidence relevant to applications in cross-culture, cross-border, and diverse ortgeists. The panel consists of representatives of several professional associations, each experienced in international networks and committed to advancing human well-being and scientific knowledge. ICP, founded in 1941, was the first association to establish liaison relationships with international and national professional associations and continues to advocate collaborative research and alliances among colleagues.

S-249: Judgments of frequency and duration

Isabell Winkler *(chair)*
Frequency and duration are key units of the empirical world. They are of fundamental importance in behavioral adaptation. The workshop presents new empirical results and theoretical approaches on judgments of frequency and duration. The contribution by Pachur examines the roles of two cognitive mechanisms of frequency estimation. Betsch, Winkler, and Renkewitz show how judgments of frequency and duration influence each other under certain circumstances. Finally, Sedlmeier's model provides a basis for explaining both judgments about frequency and time. In sum, the objective of the workshop is to analyze memory and judgment mechanisms underlying estimations of quantity.

Cue and instance sampling in judgments of event frequencies
Pachur, Thorsten *Cognitive and Decision Science, Universität Basel, Basel, Switzerland* **Rieskamp, Jörg** *Adaptive Behavior & Cognit, MPI for Human Development, Berlin, Germany* **Hertwig, Ralph** *Cognitive and Decision Science, Universität Basel, Basel, Switzerland*
We contrast two kinds of cognitive mechanisms for making inferences about latent event frequencies (e.g., the prevalence of a disease in a population). Cue-based inference uses knowledge of semantic features of the events that are correlated with population frequency. Instance-based inference uses knowledge of instances of the events in a person's social network. We find that although cue-based strategies allowed to judge latent frequencies more accurately, people's frequency judgments were better predicted by instance-based strategies. Specifically, people often seemed to be using a fast and frugal instance-based strategy that exploits the social network structure to guide and to stop search.

The asymmetry in estimating frequency and duration
Betsch, Tilmann *Sozial- und Organisationswiss., Universität Erfurt, Erfurt, Germany*
There is a debate about how duration and frequency are stored in memory. In five experiments, duration/frequency of visual stimuli were varied within subjects. Participants estimated how long and how often each stimulus was presented. A

symmetric judgment pattern (bivariate sensitivity in judgment; bidirectional biases) was obtained if task or stimulus features encouraged participants to attend to the stimuli proportionate to their actual exposure durations. If this was not the case, an asymmetric judgment pattern was obtained (memory-based sensitivity for frequency but not for duration; frequency biases on duration judgment). Implications of results are discussed with reference to memory models.

Judgements of frequency and duration in waiting situations
Winkler, Isabell *Inst. für Psychologie, Universität Chemnitz, Chemnitz, Germany* **Sedlmeier, Peter** *Inst. für Psychologie, Universität Chemnitz, Chemnitz, Germany*
Typically, judgments of duration are influenced by the frequency of stimuli but the reverse does seldom hold. This might, however, be due to the relatively artificial stimuli commonly used, which could prevent a thorough encoding of their duration. Two studies examined the relationship between stimulus frequency and duration in realistic situations. In Study 1, participants watched a traffic video including waiting situations. In Study 2, participants working on a task were interrupted by pop-ups of varying frequency and duration. Contrary to former findings, frequency judgements are influenced by stimulus duration, presumably because of the participants' higher attention to this variable.

The impact of encoding strategies on the interdependence of time and frequency processing
Renkewitz, Frank *Erziehungswiss. Fakultät, Universität Erfurt, Erfurt, Germany* **Glauer, Madlen** *Erziehungswiss. Fakultät, Universität Erfurt, Erfurt, Germany*
In several former studies frequency estimates on serially encoded events were observed to be robust against variations of stimulus duration. A potential explanation for this finding is that the participants did not use the complete available time to encode the stimuli effectively. We tested this explanation by manipulating the encoding strategy used by the participants (imagery instructions versus no encoding instructions). In the imagery condition stimulus duration had an impact on the discrimination of frequencies and the magnitude of frequency estimates. In contrast, frequency estimates of participants who received no encoding instructions were generally not affected by stimulus duration.

PASS-T: An associative learning model that simulates judgments of frequency and duration
Sedlmeier, Peter *Inst. für Psychologie, Techn. Universität Chemnitz, Chemnitz, Germany*
PASS-T(ime) is an extension of PASS (Sedlmeier, 1999), a neural network model that simulates judgments of relative frequency and probability. PASS-T operates in discrete time steps elicited by an internal pacemaker. It encodes events and objects by their features and learns by continually updating the association-strengths between those features. The model assumes that the amount and time course of attention directed towards stimuli influences the strengths of associations. Moreover, PASS-T includes a mechanism that compares current memory contents with knowledge in long-term memory, which allows it to produce judgments of absolute frequency and duration that correspond well with empirical results.

S-250: Factors mediating the link between students' migration background and school success

Bettina Hannover, Petra Stanat *(chair)*
School achievement studies converge with respect to the finding that students from immigrant families

perform less well than students from native families in most countries. The symposium addresses the question which factors contribute to this performance gap. While some presentations focus on the influence of structural features, such as school vacation or social networks, other emphasize the impact of students' individual features, such as attitudes towards female teachers, or language proficiency. The discussant will integrate the findings in terms of how they further our understanding of immigrant students' school success.

The role of school vacations for the development of achievement differences between immigrant and native students
Becker, Michael *Inst. für Bildungsforschung, Max-Planck-Institut, Berlin, Germany* **Baumert, Jürgen** *Inst. für Bildungsforschung, Max-Planck-Institut, Berlin, Germany*
Based on the literature on causes of educational inequities, we examine the extent to which the out-of-school environment contributes to differential learning losses during the summer vacation in Germany, drawing on a sample of N = 1592 students from the city of Berlin and focusing on students from immigrant families. Controlling for prior achievement, we find disparities associated with ethnic background. These are partly, but not completely due to disparities in socio-economic background. Contrary to our hypotheses, specific differences in learning opportunities that may be associated with an immigrant background and children's activities were of minor importance.

The influence of social networks in multicultural schools on school performance
Fortuin, Janna *Education and Child Studies, Leiden University, Leiden, Netherlands* **Vedder, Paul** *Dept. of Education, University of Leiden, Leiden, Netherlands*
There is a long standing debate about the ways in which the social networks of youngsters influence their school performance. This debate is especially important in multicultural schools where migrant children face more obstacles on the road to school success than native children. We studied eight graders (14-year olds) in multicultural schools, to determine the effects that the social networks have on their performance. Preliminary analyses show that there is evidence for socialisation influences in the area of Dutch language competency. This effect is the same for both native and migrant students. Implications will be discussed during the presentation.

How students' sexist beliefs affect educational success
Rau, Melanie *School and Teaching Research, Freie Universität Berlin, Berlin, Germany* **Hannover, Bettina** *School and Teaching Research, Freie Universität Berlin, Berlin, Germany*
In German schools, native students outperform immigrant students and female students do better than male ones. School teachers are predominantly female, with the educational success of boys being strongly positively linked to the percentage of male teachers. We propose that (immigrant) boys cannot benefit as much from female teachers as from male teachers 1) due to the absence of a same-sex role model and 2) as a result of male students' sexist beliefs about female teachers, which should be particularly strong in immigrant students from paternalistic home countries. These assumptions were tested in a questionnaire study amongst 9th graders.

Evaluation of language assessment in pre-primary education
Roeder, Ute-Regina Inst. für Psychologie, Universität Dortmund, Dortmund, Germany Puca, Rosa Maria Institute of Education, University of Bochum, Bochum, Germany
Language support for children of immigrant families is an important topic in pre-primary education. One standardized observation survey (SISMIK) that is used in German speaking countries assesses linguistic proficiency and children's motivation to engage in language related learning activities. Data about the reliability and the validity of this instrument is, however, still sparse. In our study, 270 children from different kindergartens in North-Rhine-Westphalia (Germany) were repeatedly tested during a period of two years. Results from factor analyses and scale analyses are reported as well as correlations between the scores of the different SISMIK scales and scales of other language assessment tests.

Motivation and school perceptions among first and second generation immigrant youth: A cross-national comparison
Segeritz, Michael Inst. für Bildungsforschung, Freie Universität Berlin, Berlin, Germany Stanat, Petra Inst. für Bildungsforschung, Freie Universität Berlin, Berlin, Germany Christensen, Gayle Education Policy Center, The Urban Institute, Washington, USA
Despite the low performance levels of immigrant students in many countries, there is little research analyzing their school-related motivation from an international perspective. We explored aspects of motivation which are assumed to play an important role in educational success. Integrating different theoretical perspectives (immigrant optimism, assimilation, segmented assimilation), we tested three hypotheses using data from the PISA-study for 14 countries: 1) motivation is especially high among first-generation immigrants, 2) motivation is slightly lower among second-generation immigrants, 3) less successful immigrant groups show lower levels of motivation in the second-generation compared to native students. The findings largely corroborate our hypotheses.

S-251: Promoting environmental sustainability by effective social decision making

Susumu Ohnuma, Cees J.H. Midden (chair)
Sustainable development is in its essence a social issue requiring many social decisions and enduring commitment of everyone involved. This raises important questions for environmental sustainability like "what are good social decisions?" and "how should social decision processes be designed?" This symposium attempts to line out routes for addressing these complex questions. Issues of fairness and trust will be examined as well as dialogue factors that may facilitate or hamper the effectiveness of participation processes and information exchanges.

Effects of similarity and voice on procedural fairness and trust: Experiments in Japan and the Netherlands
Hiroshi, Nonami School of Sociology, Kwansei Gakuin University, Nishinomiya, Japan
Experiments were conducted in Japan and the Netherlands to clarify the effects of delegates' voice and opinion similarity on procedural fairness in public acceptance. In high voice condition where the delegates' voice reflected on the decision, fairness was higher in high similarity than in low similarity of opinion. On the other hand, fairness was low regardless of the similarity in low voice condition. In addition, the voice and similarity affected the trust in authority and delegates. Though these results were consistent both of the countries, the interactions were different. The

function of interaction between voice and similarity will be discussed.

When does procedural fairness influence acceptance of environmental plan? Moderating effect of trust in authority
Yukio, Hirose Graduate School of Environmen., Nagoya University, Nagoya, Japan
Our surveys clarified that main determinants of public acceptance of environmental planning through citizen participation were procedural and distributive fairness. But trust in authority had no impact on its acceptance. Instead, the trust had moderating effect between procedural fairness and public acceptance, that is, procedural fairness had more impact on the acceptance for the citizens having lower trust. These results that when the citizens have less trust, they are more likely to pay attention to the decision procedure, yielding more strong effect of procedural fairness on their acceptance. We will discuss the function of trust in environmental sustainability.

Bias in the exchange of arguments: The case of scientists' evaluation of lay viewpoints on GM food
Cuppen, Eefje Inst. for Environmental Psych., Vrije Universiteit Amsterdam, Amsterdam, Netherlands
In public participation dialogues, participants articulate and evaluate different views and knowledge claims. In this study we tested how three specific characteristics of a claim may bias this evaluation. In a survey-experiment among 73 biotechnology-scientists the effects were tested of 1) the claim's favourability towards GM-food, 2) the phrasing and 3) the source of the claim. The results indicated that claims congruent with the attitude of the respondent and cognitively phrased claims were evaluated more positively than incongruent claims affectively phrased claims. Contrary to our expectation, scientists evaluated claims of the public more positively than claims of experts.

Effects of participation in the social decision process on social acceptance
Ohnuma, Susumu Dept. of Behavioral Science, Hokkaido University, Sapporo, Japan
We have demonstrated that procedural fairness through citizen participation increases social acceptance and trust in authority, even for those who do not directly participate. This presentation focuses on comparing determinants of procedural fairness between participants and non-participants. We predicted that antecedent factors proposed in procedural fairness studies (e.g. opportunity of voice) would be more relevant for participants, while heuristics (e.g. perceived value similarity) would be more relevant for non-participants, who are not involved in participatory processes. Results from a Bavarian survey of citizen participation provided support for these hypotheses. Functions of procedural fairness for participants and non-participants will be discussed.

Not fair (for me)!: The influence of personal relevance on automatic versus controlled social justice inferences
Ham, Jaap Human-Technology Interaction, University of Technology, Eindhoven, Netherlands
This contribution argues that for designing social decision processes, the social psychology of making justice judgments is highly relevant. Specifically, social decision processes should assess people's automatic judgments next to people's controlled judgments. We present evidence that these two types of judgments are differently dependent on an important social-psychological variable—personal relevance. Two studies suggest that justice-relevant situations described from a first person perspective lead to different automatic cognitive responses than when described from a third person perspective,

even though controlled responses show an independence of personal relevance. The importance of these findings for designing social decision processes is discussed.

S-252: Early, automatic processing involved in the causation of emotion and affective responses

Agnes Moors (chair)
Appraisal theorists hold that events and emotions are mediated by an appraisal process consisting of several appraisal variables like goal relevance, intrinsic valence, goal conduciveness, and coping potential. In this session, the contributors present behavioral and neurophysiological data to address the questions of the automaticity of appraisal variables (Agnes Moors), the timing of some of these appraisal variables using EEG (Didier Grandjean), and the role of goal relevance in early attentional deployment (Tobias Brosch). A related question is whether affective vs nonaffective features take priority at encoding (Justin Storbeck, Adriaan Spruyt). The discussant is Dr. Nico Frijda.

Investigating the automaticity of appraisal variables
Moors, Agnes Dept. of Psychology, Ghent University, Ghent, Belgium
To accommodate the observation that emotions can arise spontaneously, appraisal theorists have argued that emotion-antecedent appraisal can be automatic (Frijda, 1993; Scherer, 1993). Previous studies support the automaticity of individual appraisal variables such as novelty, goal relevance, intrinsic valence, and goal conduciveness. To study the automaticity of coping potential, we developed a variant of the sequential priming task in which primes are events in a pacman game (signaling low or high coping potential) and targets are words. I describe the first results obtained with this task. I also discuss the difficulty to disentangle coping potential and valence.

Investigations of temporal unfolding of emotion-constituent appraisal using EEG
Grandjean, Didier Dept. of Psychology, University of Geneva, Geneva, Switzerland Scherer, Klaus R. Swiss Center for, University of Geneva, Geneva, Switzerland
Despite a growing consensus among appraisal theorists on which dimensions constituting the appraisal process are necessary to predict human emotional reactions, the question of the temporal dynamic remains unsolved. The sequence of the various appraisals is, according to authors, fixed or flexible. Scherer suggested that the appraisal process consists of a very rapidly occurring sequence of hierarchically organized stimulus processing steps. We designed two electroencephalographic studies in which we manipulated novelty, intrinsic pleasantness, goal relevance and goal conduciveness. The results, based on event-related potentials and frequency analyses are in favor of a sequential process despite massive parallel processes exist.

Appraisal mechanisms and rapid attention deployment
Brosch, Tobias Inst. für Psychologie, Universität Genf, Geneva, Switzerland
An alternative to the view that during evolution the human brain became specialized to preferentially attend to threat-related stimuli is to assume that all stimuli with high relevance are rapidly prioritized by the attention system during a multilevel appraisal process. We examined whether the baby schema, a prototypical biologically relevant stimulus configuration, captures attention in a dot probe task. Both behavioural data and event-related potentials revealed highly similar rapid attentional modula-

tion toward threat-related and baby stimuli. The findings support the notion that a common evaluative process is responsible for the emotional modulation of attention to relevant stimuli.

Semantic processing precedes affect retrieval: The neurological case for cognitive primacy in visual processing

Storbeck, Justin Dept. of Psychology, University of Virginia, Charlottesville, USA

According to the affective primacy hypothesis, visual stimuli can be evaluated prior to and independent of object identification and semantic analysis. I will argue that the affective primacy hypothesis is not likely correct. Although people can react to objects that they cannot consciously identify, such affective reactions are dependent upon prior semantic analysis within the visual cortex. I offer a preliminary neurological analysis of the mere exposure and affective priming effects that is consistent with the claim that semantic analysis is needed to elicit these effects. Thus, the brain must know what something is in order to evaluate it.

On the viability of the automatic stimulus evaluation hypothesis: Goal-dependency effects in affective and nonaffective stimulus processing

Spruyt, Adriaan Dept. of Psychology, Ghent University, Ghent, Belgium

Affective stimulus information can be processed rapidly, with minimal effort, and outside the reach of consciousness. Accordingly, it has been concluded affective stimulus processing is a fairly automatic and unconditional phenomenon. I will present new experimental evidence which suggests that affective stimulus processing may not be the unconditional phenomenon that several researchers have claimed it to be. Additionally, I will demonstrate that goal-irrelevant non-affective stimulus processing can proceed in an equally 'automatic' fashion as goal-irrelevant affective stimulus processing, provided that feature-specific attention allocation is taken into account. Implications for the affect primacy hypothesis will be discussed.

S-253: Emotional intelligence and cognitive processes

Richard D. Roberts, Gerry Matthews (chair)

The role of emotional intelligence (EI) in understanding and managing the challenges of everyday life requires further investigation. This symposium examines how EI infuses critical high-level cognitions supporting decision-making, coping, and adaptation. Scherer reviews a general framework for understanding emotional competence. Roberts et al. present new approaches to assessment. Turss reports on the role of EI in forecasting emotion. O'Sullivan discusses how expert lie detectors and controls may differ in emotion regulation. Zeidner addresses the role of EI in coping with threat. Finally, Schulze et al. present a meta-analysis of the relationship between EI and general cognitive ability and personality.

A functional approach to the definition and measurement of emotional competence

Scherer, Klaus R. CISA, Universität Genf, Genf, Switzerland

Work on "emotional intelligence" has suffered from the straightjackets imposed by the IQ and personality adjustment traditions respectively. It is suggested that emotional competence (EC) should be defined on the basis of the adaptive functions of the emotion mechanism. Based on the component process theory, three domains of EC are proposed: 1) Responding with appropriate emotions to pertinent events, 2) adaptation- and context-sensitive emotion regulation, and 3) efficient emotion recognition and communication. Relevant criteria

to measure competence and skills are discussed. In support of this new theoretical framework, data from experimental research and human resource assessments are presented.

Developing and validating situational judgment tests of emotional intelligence

Roberts, Richard D. Research and Development, ETS, Princeton, USA Ralf, Schulze Research and Development, ETS, Princeton, NJ, USA MacCann, Carolyn Research and Development, ETS, Princeton, NJ, USA

Previous research examining emotional intelligence (EI) has largely been restricted to numerous self-report instruments and the Mayer-Salovey-Caruso Emotional Intelligence Test. Neither measurement approach has proven entirely satisfactory; alternative assessments are needed. Four studies providing validity evidence for situational judgment tests of EI are reported. These EI assessments appear reasonably reliable, and with construct validity evidence demonstrated by relationships between EI and intelligence, personality (especially, Agreeableness), other emotions measures, and outcomes (e.g., grades). Although promising, the approach might be made more ecologically valid if use is made of multimedia technologies. We conclude with a demonstration of a video-based EI assessment.

Emotional understanding for self and others: The target makes a difference

Turß, Michaela Inst. für of Psychologie, Humboldt-Universität zu Berlin, Berlin, Germany Matthews, Gerald Department of Psychology, University of Cincinnati, Cincinnati, USA Scholl, Wolfgang Department of Psychology, Humboldt-University, Berlin, Germany

Emotional understanding is a branch of the ability model of emotional intelligence. To overcome scoring problems and to establish incremental validity, emotional knowledge is measured in real life situations. In two subsequent studies, participants predict emotions for upcoming exams and a mutual project. Results show that it is stereotype accuracy with later reported actual emotions that is associated with emotional intelligence (N= 143). When targets are further distinguished in a round robin design (N=171, 42 teams), accuracy for others relates to intelligence, emotional intelligence, and relationship success. Accordingly, emotional intelligence research can profit from the consideration of different targets.

Emotion regulation in the detection of deception

O'Sullivan, Maureen Human Interaction Laboratory, University of California, San Francisco, USA

Extensive cue utilization is one aspect of superior lie detection; another is the ability to regulate one's reaction to the knowledge of duplicity. Most people react negatively to being lied to: sadness or anger at betrayal, self-aggravation at being duped. One method of regulating these emotions is to pretend deception does not exist. This is consistent with the ubiquitous truth bias, Expert lie detectors, however, do not show a truth bias; they regulate the negative emotions involved in perceiving deception. The emotion regulation techniques used by expert lie detectors are contrasted with those of their matched controls.

Emotional intelligence and coping with threat

Zeidner, Moshe Dept. of Psychology, University of Haifa, Haifa, Israel Olenik-Shemesh, Dorit Dept. of Psychology, University of Haifa, Haifa, Israel Matthews, Gerry Dept. of Psychology, University of Cincinnati, Cincinnati, USA

This study examines the relationship between Emotional Intelligence (EI) and adaptive coping with stressful encounters in Israeli adolescents. EI was hypothesized to help adolescents cope more

adaptively with stressful situations, as mediated by social support, which, in turn, was hypothesized to improve well-being. The data (N=200) support the hypotheses. EI and its components were related to adaptive outcomes of coping with stress (even after controlling for ability and personality). Furthermore, social support was shown to mediate the effects of EI on adaptive outcomes. This research suggests that EI may predict adaptive outcomes, independent of other individual differences constructs.

Convergent and discriminant validity evidence for emotional intelligence tests and related measures: A meta-analysis

Schulze, Ralf Research and Development, ETS, Princeton, USA Roberts, Richard D. Research and Development, ETS, Princeton, NJ, USA MacCann, Carolyn Research and Development, ETS, Princeton, NJ, USA Orchard, Benjamin Research and Development, ETS, Princeton, NJ, USA

The availability of validity evidence for emotional intelligence (EI) tests is an important prerequisite to interpret and evaluate findings in this area of research. The results of a meta-analysis synthesizing the available validity evidence will be reported. This is done both for maximum performance EI tests and related self-report measures. The strength of relation between these two types of measures on the one hand and personality factors as well as traditional intelligence measures on the other will be reported. Valid EI measures are expected to evince strong relationships with other intelligence measures and weak relationships with personality factors.

S-254: Developmental aspects of text-picture-integration

Holger Horz, Nele McElvany (chair)

Most learning materials such as books, computer-based learning environments, worksheets etc. consists of texts and pictures. While the development of writing and reading skills has been examined extensively, the development of visualization ability and of combined processing of texts and pictures is a largely unknown field yet. This symposium aims at a deeper understanding of how cognitive processes involved in the combined processing and comprehension of text and pictures develops within individuals. Development of these processes will be focused from age of early childhood up to young adulthood.

The development of visualization ability

Horz, Holger Inst. für Pädag. Psychologie, Universität Koblenz-Landau, Landau, Germany Schnotz, Wolfgang Inst. für Pädag. Psychologie, Universität Koblenz-Landau, Landau, Germany

How abilities of visualizing complex content develop within individuals is an unknown field yet. In a field experiment 3x10 participants (7th and 11th graders, university students) worked in dyads of same age and visualized facts of a text (1800 words). Visualization processes were videotaped and visualizations were qualitatively classified. Younger dyads communicated less, produced the same kinds of visualizations, but made more mistakes regarding content and formal representation. Overall younger dyads seem to have too little capacities to cooperate and to produce at the same time because their ability to visualization is not fully developed at the age of 13.

Development of reading literacy using PISA-like test

Vidal-Abarca, Eduardo Dept. of Psychology, University of Valencia, Valencia, Spain Mañá, Amelia Dept. of Psychology, University of Valencia, Valencia, Spain Gilabert, Ramiro Dept. of Psychology, University of Valencia, Valencia, Spain Martínez,

Tomás Dept. of Psychology, University of Valencia, Valencia, Spain García, Victoria Dept. of Psychology, University of Valencia, Valencia, Spain

We developed a test of reading literacy following PISA test structure. The test contains three continuous and two non-continuous texts (i.e., including diagrams and graphics), and it measures retrieving, interpreting and reflection-evaluation skills. 798 students from 7th to 9th grade answered the test. Differences among students from different grades were significant. Reliability score for the test was .792. An electronic version of the test has been prepared based on the software called Read&-Answer, which records reading time measures and reading-answering question sequences. It aims at capturing developmental and individual differences on the question-answering processes.

Integrative processing of text and graphics by 5- and 6-graders at different levels of schooling

Schnotz, Wolfgang Inst. für Psychologie, Universität Koblenz-Landau, Landau, Germany Horz, Holger Inst. für Psychologie, Universität Koblenz-Landau, Landau, Germany Ullrich, Mark Inst. für Psychologie, Universität Koblenz-Landau, Landau, Germany

The competence of integrating text and graphics plays an increasingly important role in the acquisition of knowledge especially after primary school. However, reading and integrating verbal and pictorial information from multiple documents is not explicitly taught in many schools, and little is known about how this competence develops at different levels of schooling. In a field study with 48 classes of 5 and 6-graders from different school levels in Germany, we analyzed the effect of age and schooling on the development of competence of integrating text and graphics with science education materials. Results suggest alternative ways of instruction for schooling.

Text-picture integration in the school learning context: Teacher competence

McElvany, Nele Human Development, Max-Planck-Institut, Berlin, Germany Hachfeld, Axinja Human Development, Max-Planck-Institut, Berlin, Germany Baumert, Jürgen Human Development, Max-Planck-Institut, Berlin, Germany

While most learning materials in schools contain texts with integrated pictures, the combined processing of texts and pictures is not a common topic within teacher education. The study presented aims at A) the development of a theoretical framework and operationalization for teacher competence in this area, B) the investigation of teacher competence focusing on knowledge and diagnostic skills, C) the identification of determinants of inter-individual differences, and D) the analysis of the correlation between teacher competence and instructional quality. Data is collected in January 2008 from 144 biology, geography and German teachers (grades 5 to 8) within different school tracks in Germany.

A social psychological reading of multimodal scientific texts in online media

Roth, Wolff-Michael Applied Cognitive Science, University of Victoria, Victoria, BC, Canada

Reading multimodal (popularized) scientific texts predominantly is studied in terms of technical decoding skills said to be required (Street, 2008). In this paper I suggest that there are other interesting approaches to studying reading of multimodal (popularized) scientific texts grounded in social psychological concerns. These concerns include questions of what people read, how much they read, and the purposes and effects of reading" (Edwards, 2008). Here, I focus on reading practices and the kind of semiotic (meaning-making) resources (popularized) scientific texts in online media make available for the practices of reading, including the way in which membership categories are used to link different aspects of the text.

S-255: Evaluation of competence development in counselling and psychotherapy

Arthur Drexler *(chair)*

In today's knowledge economy lifelong learning has increasingly become an important factor on the path towards individual and organisational success. As a result, further education and trainings are a booming market and the quality of such professional development in the fields of psychotherapy, coaching and counselling depends on the quality of the underlying training. The presentations in this symposium focus on specific characteristics and soft skills of psychotherapists and counsellors and an evaluative approach to measure their development during the respective training. All contributions intend to collect "hard facts" instead of subjective self-assessments of the participants. The applied instruments cover a wide range of methods and present a framework for evaluating further education and trainings in general.

Effectiveness of psychotherapy training: On the evaluation of psychotherapeutic concept competence

Andreatta, Pia Inst. für Kommunikation, Universität Innsbruck, Innsbruck, Austria Kraler, Christian ILS, Universität Innsbruck, Innsbruck, Austria

We present a computer supported method evaluating the effectiveness of psychotherapy training by analysing written responses from of two groups of psychodrama trainees (beginners and finalists) with a special program. We assume that in order to cause psychotherapeutic change, psychotherapeutic trainees should be able to develop a clinical concept including the aetiology of the patients disorder(s), derivate a treatment concept and holistically deal with higher order complexities of clinical cases (cf. Beutler et al. 1994, Kahl-Popp 2004). According to our results, finalists show more coherency in case interpretations, a higher degree of cross-linking different psychotherapy concept elements, finalists' case items are more interlinked and show more complex circularity.

Emotion and relationship within psychotherapy-trainees

Benecke, Cord Inst. für Psychologie, Universität Innsbruck, Innsbruck, Austria Pauza, Elisabeth Inst. for Communication, Universität Innsbruck, Innsbruck, Austria

Most therapeutic schools consider personality variables of therapists as important for thera-peutic competence; therefore, the development of personality is part of therapists' training processes. Therapists are supposed to be empathic, capable of regulating their emotions, able to realise widespread relationship behaviour, etc. So far, there is no empirical evidence that these dimensions are developed through the training process. Aims: Investigation of the development of important dimensions like emotional experience, emotion regulation, emotion recognition, relationship patterns, introject-behaviour. Approxi-mately 90 trainees from different schools are investigated at the beginning and the end of their training. We present first results of the pre-training-data-ascertainment.

Communication and interaction in the counselling of psychotherapy trainees

Stippler, Maria Inst. für Kommunikation, Universität Innsbruck, Innsbruck, Austria

Referring to Rønnestad & Orlinskys findings that supervision is considered as essential for professional development of psychotherapists this study aimed to identify the special commu-nication styles and interaction patterns that are regarded by psychotherapy trainees across different orientations as helpful for their development. Quantitative and qualitative methods were combined. Anonymous questionnaires were filled out by supervisors and supervisees in the middle of the supervision process and after the ending of the supervisory relationship. In addition supervisors were asked to record every fourth supervision session. The qualitative analysis combines different analysis methods (e.g. content analysis, interaction analysis). First results are presented.

Research into course evaluation: Professional coach training

Drexler, Arthur Inst. für Kommunikation, Universität Innsbruck, Innsbruck, Austria

In this study we present a model for the evaluation of coach trainings, which we observe as prototypical for further education programmes and which leads to "hard facts" of the effects and the quality of such trainings. Up to now evaluations of trainings and seminars are mostly based on participants' self reports following events. In this study we use a multifaceted form of examination and thus we refer to different theoretical concepts, e.g. knowledge and problem solving, personality and emotion theories. Our generic yet multifaceted model for the evaluation of coach trainings should produce valid findings of the development of the trainees during the course and the quality of such trainings and should help to improve educational practice.

How to become a counsellor: Pre-post-testing of trainees and their counselling competence

Möller, Heidi Fachbereich 4, Universität Kassel, Kassel, Germany

Counselling as a professional field of applied psychology is dealing with questions on what training has to be provided and how it has to be organized to meet the requirements. This presentation shows a reasonably integrated qualitative-quantitative research design and preliminary results. Our research project poses questions concerning basic issues similar to psychotherapy outcome research: How does the theoretical knowledge and traits of trainees change in the course? Do different personality types tend to choose different types of counselling schools and what are the consequences? In this long-term study, we measure differences between beginners and advanced trainees and the development of individuals during training.

S-256: Dynamic Testing (DT) and the assessment of cognitive modifiability: Recent applications and methodological developments in educational and clinical settings

Karl Heinz Wiedl *(chair)*

"Dynamic Testing" is a diagnostic approach that integrates interventions into testing to come to a more precise estimation of cognitive ability and modifiability, particularly in subjects with problems of cognition and learning. Typical theoretical concepts are learning potential, plasticity of rehabilitation potential. The presentations deal with methods of assessing learning in ethnic minority, immigrant and special education children, plasticity of memory functions in elderly subjects and modifiability of executive performance in schizophrenic patients as a predictor of rehabilitation outcome. Also based on clinical data, measurement of change using a typological approach and analysis of modifiability with neuroimaging technology are addressed.

Using dynamic criteria for the validation of a learning potential test of analogical reasoning

Hessels, Marco Inst. für Psychologie, Unversität Genf, Genf, Switzerland

In this research, the validity of a standardized learning potential test (Hessels Analogical Reasoning Test) was examined with dynamic criteria. Two dynamic criterion tests were developed to evaluate how much pupils learned in a short training in Geography or Chemistry. The dynamic tests of school learning were used in two studies (N=570 and N=258, respectively) that included both Swiss and immigrant children, in mainstream primary education and special education classes. The results indicate an improvement of the validity, especially for minority children, as well as for low achieving children and children in special education.

Dynamic testing in children: Individual differences and learning patterns in indigenous and ethnic minority children

Resing, Wilma Dept. of Psychology, Universiteit Leiden, Leiden, Netherlands Tunteler, Erika Dept. of Psychology, Universiteit Leiden, Leiden, Netherlands de Jong, Froukje Dept. of Psychology, Universiteit Leiden, Leiden, Germany in't Velt, Arianne

Aim of the study was to examine both learning patterns and strategy use in groups of children after dynamic testing. Participants were 1st grade indigenously Dutch (N=50) and ethnic minority (N=50) primary school children. A pretest-posttest control group design was used. The dynamic test was an adapted version of Tzuriel's SeriaThink Instrument. Additionally, Raven's PM and a math test were administered. Children verbalized steps of their solving processes. Repeated measurement analyses significantly showed both positive group and cultural differences as a consequence of dynamic testing, including variability in learning patterns. As expected, most progression was found in ethnic minorities.

Estimation of cognitive plasticity in elderly subjects using dynamic evaluation techniques

Navarro, Elena Dept. of Psychology, University of Granada, Granada, Spain Calero, M. Dolores Faculty of Psychology, Granada University, Granada, Spain

Objectives: The present communication describes the techniques we have developed and results obtained from various practical studies designed to test them. Method: The experiments were carried out with Spanish elderly subjects from 60 to 95 years of age, who participated in diverse programmes of cognitive evaluation and intervention initiated by the University of Granada. Results and conclusions: These demonstrate that the techniques are useful for evaluating cognitive plasticity in old age, valid for diagnostic purposes, predictive of the efficiency of cognitive intervention measures for arresting cognitive decline, and prognostic with regard to the course of cognitive deterioration in elderly subjects.

Learning potential and rehabilitation outcome in schizophrenia: A longitudinal study

Watzke, Stefan Klinikum der Med. Fakultät, Universität Halle-Wittenberg, Halle, Germany Brieger, Peter

The relation between learning potential (LP) and the success of a vocational rehabilitation program in German community psychiatry was prospectively examined in n=41 schizophrenia patients. A dynamic test version of the WCST was completed at rehabilitation intake. Within a longitudinal study design, work capability, level of functioning, and vocational integration were assessed at rehabilitation intake, program course and termination and at 3-month follow-up. Hierarchical linear models showed that higher LP indicated better outcome in all measures during rehabilitation and at follow-up. LP added information beyond static cognitive

performance and, therefore, should be considered in the further development of rehabilitation programs.

Learning potential on the WCST: First results from fMRI, 1H-MRS- and genetic association studies in schizophrenia

Pedersen, Anya Abt. Psychiatrie, Universitätsklinik Münster, Münster, Germany Wilmsmeier, Andreas Psychiatrie, Universitätsklinik Münster, Münster, Germany Bauer, Jochen Psychiatrie, Universitätsklinik Münster, Münster, Germany Koelkebeck, Katja Psychiatrie, Universitätsklinik Münster, Münster, Germany Siegmund, Ansgar Psychiatrie, Universitätsklinik Münster, Münster, Germany Suslow, Thomas Psychiatrie, Universitätsklinik Münster, Münster, Germany Wiedl, Karl-Heinz Psychiatrie, Universitätsklinik Osnabrück, Osnabrück, Germany Arolt, Volker Psychiatrie, Universitätsklinik Münster, Münster, Germany Ohrmann, Patricia Psychiatrie, Universitätsklinik Münster, Münster, Germany

Objectives: Detailed instruction might remediate deficits on the Wisconsin Card Sorting Test (WCST) in some schizophrenic patients. Methods: 101 inpatients with schizophrenia (59 first-episode, 42 chronic) and 55 healthy controls completed a test-train-test version of the WCST as a measure of their learning potential. Results: "Nonretainers", who did not profit from detailed instruction, were identified in both schizophrenic groups, but not in the healthy control group. We present first results from a sub-sample in which we implemented imaging techniques (fMRT, 1H-MRS) and established associations with different genotypes. Discussion: Implications of the concept of 'learning-potential on the WCST' are discussed, considering the results of the brain imaging techniques.

Repeated administrations of the Wisconsin Card Sorting Test: A typological algorithm considering stability and practice effects

Waldorf, Manuel FB Humanwissenschaften, Universität Osnabrück, Osnabrück, Germany Schöttke, Henning Inst. für Psychologie, Universität Osnabrück, Osnabrück, Germany Wiedl, Karl Heinz FB Humanwissenschaften, Universität Osnabrück, Osnabrück, Germany

The Wisconsin Card Sorting Test (WCST) is a widely used measure in schizophrenia research. Although the specific deficits can be alleviated by means of a short training, the ascertainment of true change requires data concerning stability and practice effects in a pretest-training-posttest design. We carried out the WCST-64 three times without intervention. The sample consists of 100 non-psychiatric healthy participants with non-collegiate educational background. In contrast to earlier reports, the retest reliability of the WCST is satisfactory (i. e. rtt > .70). A statistically sound assessment of change thus seems feasible. An appropriate algorithmic, typological approach is presented.

S-257: Advances in complex data analysis and modeling

Andreas Klein (chair)

Topics discussed here address areas of causal relationships and measurement. Mutz investigates a structural equation modeling framework for assessing self-reported competencies of graduates based on causal effects theory. Klein proposes a new probability weighting technique providing an estimation formula for direct and indirect causal effects in mediator models. Brand et al. investigate the performance of LMS in analyzing moderated mediator models. Steinmetz and Schmidt investigate the consequences of partial measurement invariance for analyses of sumscore differences. Lloret-Segura et al. apply IRT modeling to pairs of

opposite affect items in order to locate the responses along the latent scale.

Modelling self-reported competencies of graduates: Psychology as an example

Mutz, Rüdiger Geistes-, Sozial- und, Swiss Fed. Inst. of Techn., Zürich, Switzerland

This contribution aims at suggesting a structural equation modeling framework for assessing self-reported competencies of graduates, based on the theory of causal effects of Steyer (2007). Competency will be defined as ability to do (person) what is needed (environment). This definition implies four model components: a) a measurement theory component (CTT), b) a person-environment fit component, c) a causality component (different instructions) and d) a latent state-trait component (competency as trait). A panel-study of 1490 psychology students in Germany provides for data to illustrate the proposal.

The problem of causal inference in mediator analysis

Klein, Andreas Dept. of Psychology, University of Western Ontario, London, Canada

In this paper, we discuss the difficulties related to the causal interpretation of mediator models. The problem of causal inference arises from the fact that the mediating variable plays the double role of an independent and a dependent variable and as such cannot be randomized. We adopt Holland's (1988) critique on the causal interpretation of conventional mediator models. As the main result, a new probability weighting technique is proposed that provides a novel solution to the problem and includes an estimation formula for the direct and indirect causal effects. The approach is illustrated by an example using depression data.

Analyzing latent nonlinear mediation models with LMS

Brandt, Holger Inst. für Psychologie, Universität Frankfurt, Frankfurt, Germany Schermelleh-Engel, Karin Inst. für Psychologie, Universität Frankfurt, Frankfurt, Germany Dimitruk, Polina Inst. für Psychologie, Universität Frankfurt, Frankfurt, Germany Kelava, Augustin Inst. für Psychologie, Universität Frankfurt, Frankfurt, Germany Moosbrugger, Helfried Inst. für Psychologie, Universität Frankfurt, Frankfurt, Germany

This presentation focuses on the difficulty to differentiate between different types of nonlinear effects in mediation models. Until now nonlinear mediation models have not been investigated on the level of latent variables. Therefore a simulation study was conducted in order to investigate the performance of LMS in analyzing such complex models. We systematically varied the number of variables, the number of nonlinear effects and the multicollinearity. The results show that LMS is able to differentiate between all different effects in the models when the models are not too complex. Limitations of the study are being discussed.

Effects of partial measurement (non)invariance on manifest sumscore differences across groups

Steinmetz, Holger Arbeits- und Org.-Psychologie, Universität Gießen, Gießen, Germany Schmidt, Peter Inst. für Politikwissenschaft, Universität Gießen, Gießen, Germany

Although the use of structural equation modeling has increased in the last decades, researchers still rely on traditional methods (e.g., ANOVA) when mean differences between constructs across groups are being investigated. A main problem is that traditional methods are only appropriate if the measurement model is invariant across groups. Whereas partial measurement invariance is regarded as sufficient for analyses of latent mean differences, its consequences for analyses of sumscore differences is still unknown. A Monte-Carlo simulation of multigroup analyses with varying noninvariant loadings, intercepts and latent mean differences reveals under which conditions partial invariance can bias sumscore differences.

S-258: Sleep, dreams, and emotion: Affective neuroscience approaches to the functions of sleep

Ullrich Wagner, Sophie Schwartz (chair)
Cognitive functions of sleep have been described since the beginning of experimental psychology. Only recently researchers have also begun to address this topic from the perspective of "affective neuroscience", investigating how sleep and dreaming specifically relate to emotional processes. This symposium will give an overview of findings from the internationally leading laboratories in this new field. Speakers will present data showing how sleep and different sleep stages affect emotional memory formation (Wagner, Payne), how emotional processes guide dream contents (Schredl, Valli), and how the brain processes emotional information in normally-sleeping healthy humans (Sterpenich) and in sleep-disturbed patients (Schwartz).

REM sleep and emotional memories
Wagner, Ullrich Inst. für Fundam. Neurowiss., Universität Genf, Geneva, Switzerland
Objectives: Sleep has been shown to support memory consolidation in many tasks. However, only recently researchers have begun to investigate also the role of emotions in this context. Methods: Recent studies will be presented which compared effects of sleep and different sleep stages (slow-wave sleep vs. REM sleep) on consolidation of emotional vs. neutral text contents. Results: Emotional as compared to neutral memories are particularly enhanced by post-learning sleep, especially by sleep periods rich in REM sleep. Conclusions: Emotional memories, critically depending on the amygdala, may particularly benefit from amygdala activations during sleep, which are selectively observed during REM sleep.

Sleep preferentially enhances memory for emotional components of scenes
Payne, Jessica Dept. of Psychology, Harvard University, Cambridge, USA Stickgold, Robert Dept. of Psychiatry, Harvard Medical School, BIDMC, Boston, MA, USA Swanberg, Kelley Dept. of Psychology, Harvard University, Cambridge, MA, USA Kensinger, Elizabeth Dept. of Psychology, Boston College, Chestnut Hill, MA, USA
Central aspects of emotional experiences are often well remembered at the expense of background details, but little is known about how emotional memories evolve over time. We examined the development of emotional scene memories between 30min and 12hrs including either wake or sleep. Wakefulness led to forgetting of entire emotional scenes, while sleep preserved memory for emotional objects, but not their backgrounds, suggesting that the two components undergo differential processing during sleep. Emotional memories develop differentially across time delays containing sleep and wake, with sleep selectively consolidating those aspects of a memory that are of greatest value to the organism.

Dream emotions: Prevalence and their continuity to waking life
Schredl, Michael Schlaflabor, ZI für Seelische Gesundheit, Mannheim, Germany
Objectives: Emotions play a major role in the dream experience. The continuity hypothesis of dreaming predicts that waking-life emotions are reflected in dreams. Methods: 444 participants kept a dream diary over a two-week period and completed several questionnaires eliciting current stress level. Results: The findings showed that stress exerts a strong effect ondream emotions but dream content (themes, images) are hardly affected and, thus, support the continuity hypothesis regarding emotions. Conclusions: Dreaming is a state in which emotions of the waking life are processed. Whether this has a functional significance has to be demonstrated.

Review of the threat simulation theory: Dreams portray the most salient emotional memory traces
Valli, Katja Centre for Cogn. Neuroscience, University of Turku, Turku, Finland
Objectives: According to the Threat Simulation Theory (TST) (Revonsuo, 2000), dreams have a strong tendency to simulate threatening events based on the most salient emotionally charged memory traces, in a way that suggests biological functionality. Methods: The TST has been tested in several empirical investigations (Revonsuo & Valli, 2000; Valli et al., 2005, 2006, 2007, in press). Results: The results of these studies mostly offer support for the predictions of the TST. Conclusions: In this presentation, the main results of the conducted dream content studies will be summarized and the TST discussed in the light of recent new evidence.

Sleep deprivation on the post-encoding night modifies the neural correlates of emotional memory retrieval after short and long retention period
Sterpenich, Virginie Cycloton Research Centre, University of Liàge, Liàge, Belgium
We used fMRI to characterize the influence of sleep on the consolidation of emotional memories. After learning emotional or neutral pictures, subjects slept (RS, n=17) or were totally sleep-deprived (TSD, n=15) on the post-training night.Retrieval sessions took place 3 days and 6 months later. Responses were larger in RS than TSD group and more so for emotional items in the hippocampus and the medial prefrontal cortex (MPFC) after 3 days, and in the amygdala and the MPFC cortex after 6 months. Post-training sleep supports the reorganization of brain representations subtending emotional memory, with an increased recruitment of MPFC.

Reward processing during game-playing in narcoleptic patients: A functional MRI study
Schwartz, Sophie Inst. für Fundam. Neurowiss., Universität Genf, Geneva, Switzerland
Narcolepsy with cataplexy (NC) is a sleep-wake disorder, associated with reduced hypocretin/orexin (a hypothalamic neuropeptide). NC is characterized by episodes of transient loss of muscle tone, called cataplexy, typically triggered by strong, mostly positive emotions. Cataplexy therefore represents a striking example of how emotions affect behaviour and motor control. We used functional magnetic resonance imaging to understand why emotions might elicit cataplexy. NC-patients showed exaggerated amygdala response to emotional stimuli such as humorous pictures or positive reward. Our data suggest that the hypocretin/orexin system, which is deficient in NC, modulates amygdala response to positively-loaded emotional signals.

S-259: Working memory and arithmetic problem solving

Dietmar Grube (chair)
There is ample evidence showing that working memory has an impact on arithmetic performance. However, available evidence is only partly able to answer the question of which characteristics of working memory affect certain kinds of arithmetic problem solving. This symposium includes further contributions to clarifying the relationship between working memory and arithmetic problem solving. The present studies included subjects from preschool age up to adulthood and followed experimental (dual-task) and longitudinal designs.

Development of arithmetical strategies in preschool age with and without promotion of numerical concept
Peucker, Sabine Inst. of Psychologie, Pädag. Hochschule Freiburg, Freiburg, Germany Weißhaupt, Steffi Inst. of Psychologie, Pädag. Hochschule Freiburg, Freiburg, Germany
This contribution investigates the development of arithmetical strategies in preschool age. In a longitudinal study 200 children were tested six months and two months before entering primary school with an instrument for assessing the development of numerical concepts (DEZ). For further analysis of childrens strategies the assessments were recorded on video. Half of the children took part on a programme for the development of numerical concepts (FEZ). For the trained children quantitative analysis revealed a better improvement of mathematical knowledge (such as counting strategies, numerical representation, part-whole-concept). Qualitative analysis showed that trained children used more elaborated strategies that also may reduce demands on working memory.

The impact of working memory, intelligence and domain-specific precursors on mathematics and spelling
Krajewski, Kristin Inst. für Psychologie, Universität Würzburg, Würzburg, Germany Schneider, Wolfgang Inst. für Psychologie, Universität Würzburg, Würzburg, Germany Nieding, Gerhild Inst. für Psychologie, Universität Würzburg, Würzburg, Germany
Results of a longitudinal study will be presented that tried to analyze the impact of working memory and intelligence on mathematics and spelling when domain-specific precursors were controlled. During their last year in kindergarten 108 children were tested three times regarding nonverbal intelligence, working memory, phonological awareness and early numerical competencies. Later on in school, at the end of Grade 1, children's spelling and mathematical competencies were investigated. Results show, that there is an impact of working memory on domain-specific precursors, but beyond this, no direct effect on school performances was found. Furthermore, phonological awareness and numerical competencies interacted with each other.

Working memory and individual differences math achievement: A longitudinal study from first to second grade
de Smedt, Bert Dept. of Educational Sciences, Katholieke Universiteit Leuven, Leuven, Belgium Janssen, Rianne Dept. of Educational Sciences, Katholieke Universiteit Leuven, Leuven, Belgium Verschaffel, Lieven Dept. of Educational Sciences, Katholieke Universiteit Leuven, Leuven, Belgium Ghesquiàre, Pol Dept. of Educational Sciences, Katholieke Universiteit Leuven, Leuven, Belgium
This longitudinal study examined the relationship between working memory (WM) at the start of first grade and later individual differences in math achievement in elementary school (N=106). WM-measures were administered at the start of first grade. Math achievement was assessed at the middle of first grade and the start of second grade. Results revealed that WM was significantly related to math achievement in both grades. Hierarchical regression analyses, controlling for IQ, showed that the visuospatial sketchpad and central executive were unique predictors of first-grade math achievement, whereas the phonological loop was the only

WM-component that uniquely predicted second-grade math achievement.

Development of solving simple addition problems in elementary school age: Changes in working memory demands

Grube, Dietmar Inst. für Psychologie, Universität Göttingen, Göttingen, Germany

Increasing knowledge of basic arithmetic facts is supposed to release working memory capacity involved in arithmetic problem solving. To test this hypothesis we had 54 first-graders and 50 fourth-graders solve simple addition problems (sums < 20) within a dual-task experiment. Performance was much more affected by simultaneous rapid tapping (secondary task) in first-graders than in fourth-graders. Error ratios were significantly increased by the dual-task condition only in first-graders. Results suggest that working memory load in solving simple addition problem decreases during elementary school years and that solving complex problems presupposes a certain quality of basic fact knowledge.

Children who perform poorly in arithmetic: Overload of working memory?

van Lieshout, Ernest C.D.M. Dept. of Special Education, University of Amsterdam, Amsterdam, Netherlands Berends, Inez Dept. of Special Education, University of Amsterdam, Amsterdam, Netherlands

It was expected that disturbance during a calculation task would affect high (HP) and poor (LP) performing children differently. Arithmetic problems were presented to 72 9.4 years old primary school children (half of the children HP, half LP) during an articulatory suppression condition, a central-executive interference condition or a no-interference condition. ANCOVAs showed that the HP-group was the least accurate during articulatory suppression and the slowest during both disturbing conditions. This study strengthens the claim of studies relating arithmetic performance to (offline) working memory tests, that lack of working memory resources is an important factor in poor arithmetic performance.

Instruction effects in mental arithmetic: The role of working memory and the influence of gender

Vandierendonck, André Experimental Psychology, Ghent University, Gent, Belgium Imbo, Ineke Dept. Experimental Psychology, Ghent University, Ghent, Belgium

This study aimed at testing instruction effects on adults' arithmetic performance: What happens when people are asked to respond as quickly and/or as accurately as possible? The role of working memory and the influence of gender were tested as well. Males and females solved simple additions (Exp.1) or simple multiplications (Exp.2) under load and no-load conditions and provided trial-by-trial strategy reports. The instructions affected participants' accuracies, response times, and strategy choices. No main effect of gender was observed, but several interactions were detected (gender x instruction and gender x load). The relevance of gender differences in mathematics will be discussed.

S-260: Ethical issues associated with test development and use in rapidly developing countries

Mark Leach (chair)

Although test use is universal, the availability and use of tests differs considerably among countries. Test development and use is likely to be associated with various ethical issues, particularly in developing countries and when national professional associations have not developed and enforced ethical standards for testing practices. This presentation discusses test-related ethical issues in four differing geographic locations, outlines strategies psychologists have used to address ethical dilemmas, and summarizes the results of recent studies of ethics related to test development and use.

Ethics and test use globally: Recent research

Leach, Mark Dept. of Psychology, Univ. of Southern Mississippi, Hattiesburg, USA

Although test use is universal, no research examined test development and use within international ethics codes. Testing standards in 31 ethics codes representing 35 countries were compared with those of the American Psychological Association's (APA) code. Ethics codes from approximately one third of the countries do not address test use, though there is overlap among some other countries ethics standards. Explaining results, using tests properly, and limiting their use by unqualified persons were most frequently found, while standards discussing test construction and restricting the use of obsolete tests were rare. Ethical issues impacting test development and use are discussed.

Conditions for testing equity in six sub-Saharan African countries

Mpofu, Elias Counselor Education and Reha., The Penn State University, University Park, USA Chireshe, Regis Educational Foundations, Great Zimbabwe University, Masvingo, Zimbabwe Folotiya-Jere, Jacquilene Psychology, University of Zambia, Lusaka, Zambia Mivanyi, Yuwanna Education, Kaduna Technical College, Kaduna, Nigeria Shumba, Almon Education, University of Fort Hare, Alice, South Africa Tchombe, Therese Education, University of Buea, Buea, Cameroon Maluwa-Banda, Dixie Educational Psychology, University of Malawi, Zomba, Malawi

Objective. We investigated local constructions of equity in educational testing in Cameroon, Nigeria, Malawi, South Africa, Zimbabwe, and Zambia. Method. Fifty-nine educationists responded to a regional survey of equity in assessment measure (Male = 37; Females = 21; Mean age = 43.5; SD = 8.01 years). The domains of equity in assessment surveyed included: fairness of assessment, sources of equity, and conditions of equity. Results. Participants perceived equity with alternative ways in which students can demonstrate learning, use assessments where students can work together, and teaching students test taking skills. Conclusion. Learner oriented assessment is important for perceived equity of testing.

Testing and ethics in the United Arab Emirates and the Arab world

Alghorani, Mohammad Adnan Dept. of Psychology, United Arab Emirates Univ., Al Ain, United Arab Emirates

Based on the results of the study on the status of the ethical codes for test development and use in Arab countries (Mhaisin, 2007), there is a dire need to develop relevant ethical codes to the Arab culture which is heavily loaded with Islamic values. Accordingly, a content analysis of the available Arabic and Islamic literatures related to psychological tests and scales was conducted in this study to come up with codes that are relevant to Arab and Islamic cultures. The new codes were integrated with the western codes that are suitable to the Arab culture.

Testing and ethics in the United Arab Emirates and the Arab world

Nassar, Khalaf Dept. of Psychology, United Arab Emirates Univ., Al Ain, United Arab Emirates

The objective of this study is to investigate what ethical codes the Arab universities and psychological associations use while developing and using psychological tests and scales. A questionnaire was distributed to a number of Arab universities, psychological associations, and individuals involved with developing and using tests and scales. The analysis of the data collected indicated that there are no locality-relevant ethical codes. However, they mostly refer to the western ethical codes when they have to address that issue.

Romanian psychologists' views on ethical test usage

Iliescu, Dragos Dept. of Test Publishing, D&D Research / Testcentral, Bucharest, Romania

Two major developments have marked the general environment of the psychological profession in Romania in the last 3-4 years. We now have a strong sdtream of test publishing and we now have a Psychological Commission, an institution based on statutory regulations, with the function of regsitering praticing psychologists and upholding ethical standards related to this profession. However, the attitude of psychologists towards test usage has not changed much. This paper is based on a survey of N~500 psychologists (from the ~3000 formally registered with the Commission), discussing their attitude towards test usage.

Test use and guidance in China

Yan, Greg Dept. of Psychology, Beijing Normal University, Beijing, People's Republic of China

China's three decade-old policy of economic reform and opening up to the outside world have lead to its great economic success. As a results, psychologists are being asked to play an increasingly important roles in the reconstruction of Chinese society. Psychological testing, a bridge that links theoretical advancements and application to real-life practice, is highly recognized by the society. This presentation reviews the stages of test development and use, summarizes the main challenges to be solved, and outlines new regulations and ethics codes for test-related professions.

S-261: Life times, timed life: The Berlin aging study

Ulman Lindenberger, Jacqui Smith (chair)

Longitudinal studies are pivotal in revealing individual differences and commonalities in lifespan development, and in delineating the causal structure, sequencing, and mechanisms of long-term ontogenetic change. Using data from the Berlin Aging Study (BASE), on on-going longitudinal study of 500+ individuals aged 70-103 years with up to 15 years of longitudinal observations, the various presentations in this symposium highlight conceptual and methodological advances in structuring the passage of time in longitudinal studies to arrive at multivariate descriptions and dynamic explanations of individual development in old and very old age. The discussion of Avron Spiro focuses on the promises and challenges of longitudinal studies to further our understanding of lifespan development.

Change in the third and fourth age: Overview of the Berlin Aging Study (BASE)

Smith, Jacqui Inst. for Social Research, University of Michigan, Ann Arbor, USA

Findings from the Berlin Aging Study (Baltes & Mayer, 1999) provide a multidisciplinary portrait of the differential aging and longevity of cohorts of young-old and oldest-old men and women (born between 1886 and 1920). Initial data were collected in 1990-1993 from a locally representative, heterogeneous, age-by-sex stratified sample of Berlin residents (M = 85 years). Six longitudinal follow-ups of the survivors have since been completed (1993-1994, 1995-1996, 1997-1998, 2000, 2004, and 2005). This presentation describes the study design, procedure, and sample evolution, and summarizes key psychosocial findings that reflect the combined influences of biogenetic factors and life history experiences.

Linking days to decades: Late life intraindividual variability across domains
Ram, Nilam Human Dev. and Family Studies, Pennsylvania State University, University Park, USA Gerstorf, Denis Human Dev. and Family Studies, Pennsylvania State University, University Park, PA, USA Lindenberger, Ulman Center for Lifespan Psychology, Max Planck Institute, Berlin, Germany Smith, Jacqui Institute for Social Research, University of Michigan, Ann Arbor, MI, USA
Each person is a complex of characteristics, some of which are changing from moment-to-moment, some from year-to-year. Development is characterized by changes in structure and behavior over time – along multiple time scales. Using data from the BASE we illustrate how "bursts" of measurement, wherein participants complete a battery of measures on multiple occasions within a wave, can be used to understand short-term processes (e.g., reactivity), and how such processes may relate to long-term changes. Specifically, we examine how short term changes in cognition (learning) relate to long-term aging-related decline, and present methods for quantifying intraindividual variability, the "hum" of every day life, across multiple domains of function.

On the dynamic interplay between cognition and emotion in old age: Evidence for dynamic linkages?
Staudinger, Ursula M. Zentr. für Lebenslanges Lernen, Jacobs Universität, Bremen, Germany Freund, Alexandra M. Institute of Psychology, University of Zurich, Zurich, Switzerland Gerstorf, Denis Human Dev. and Family Studies, Pennsylvania State University, University Park, PA, USA
Lifespan research has long been interested in studying associations between cognitive functioning and emotion regulation. In this study, we apply structural equation modelling to 13-year longitudinal data from the BASE in order to link level and change on indicators of positive and negative affect to both level of performance and trial-to-trial variability in perceptual speed. Our results provide evidence for dynamic cross-domain associations and also illustrate the role of health and personality variables for such relations. Our discussion focuses on conceptual implications and considers potentially underlying mechanisms.

Processes of decline in late life: Distance-from-birth vs distance-to-death
Gerstorf, Denis Human Development, Pennsylvania State University, University Park, USA Ram, Nilam Human Development, Pennsylvania State University, University Park, USA Ghisletta, Paolo Faculty of Psychology and Educ, University of Geneva, Genàve, Switzerland McArdle, John J. Department of Psychology, University of Southern Califor, Los Angeles, USA Smith, Jacqui Institute for Social Research, University of Michigan, Ann Arbor, MI, USA Lindenberger, Ulman Zentrum für Lebenserwartung, Max-Planck-Institut, Berlin, Germany
Using longitudinal data from the deceased participants of BASE we examine if, how, and in which domains old and very old individuals exhibit terminal decline in at the end of life. Relative to chronological age, distance to death often accounts for more variance in interindividual differences in change than does age, suggesting that late life decline in some domains is driven by mortality-related rather than age-related processes. Further, methodological advances combining growth and survival models highlight how these processes may be intertwined. We review findings from multiple domains, highlighting both theoretical and methodological implications for the study of developmental and selection processes.

Does social participation attenuate cognitive decline in old age? On testing dynamic developmental hypotheses with longitudinal panel data
Lindenberger, Ulman Zentrum für Lebenserwartung, Max-Planck-Institut, Berlin, Germany
Cross-sectional and longitudinal studies have revealed associations between age differences and age changes among different aspects of behavior. Due to basic limitations of cross-sectional designs and a reluctance to disentangle antecedent–consequent relations in longitudinal data, the functional significance and dynamics of these associations have remained unclear. To overcome this impasse, BASE is using advanced structural equation models representing multivariate longitudinal change as a function of time-based directed relations. I summarize the results of bivariate and quadrivariate analyses addressing antecedent–consequent relations within and across sensory, cognitive, social, and self-related functional domains, and discuss the prospects and constraints of this data-analytic strategy.

S-262: On misery with company: Dyadic perspectives on stress, coping, and intervention

Nina Knoll (chair)
Living in close relationships entails benefits and costs. Both may arise when stress interferes with partners' adaptive capacities. Five studies highlight different stages of partners' stress and coping in contexts including depression of a spouse, academic exams, assisted reproduction, and bereavement. Two studies focus on dyadic support interactions under stress: partners' support mobilization and outcomes (mood, performance) of daily supportive interaction. Studies 3 and 4 examine partners' stress appraisals and perceived coping abilities as predictors of emotional adaptation to potential and severe loss events. A fifth study compares effects of three couple interventions on spousal depression in couples receiving psychotherapy.

Mobilization of social support in dyads: Determinants, consistency and relations to supportive action
Klauer, Thomas Inst. für Psychosomatiks, Universität Rostock, Rostock, Germany
OBJECTIVES. Strategies of mobilizing social support were investigated with regard to their relations to gender, depression, relationship type and subsequent support as well as the consistency of self- vs. other-reports in dyads. METHODS. Subjects who had encountered a stressful event within the year before interview and their most important support sources were assessed using an item-parallel measure. The sample consisted of 133 dyads, 31 of them involving a depressive member. RESULTS. Depression and gender had independent effects on strategy use. Some mobilization strategies seemed to deter support. CONCLUSIONS. Implications for the design of coping interventions (i.e., mobilization trainings) are discussed.

Costs of daily support transactions: How long do they last?
Shrout, Patrick Dept. of Psychology, New York University, New York, USA Barry, Heather Dept. of Psychology, New York University, New York, USA Lane, Sean Dept. of Psychology, Columbia University, New York, USA Stadler, Gertraud Dept. of Psychology, Columbia University, New York, USA Paprocki, Christine Dept. of Psychology, Columbia University, New York, USA
During acute stress, daily emotional support receipt is associated with increased negative mood. Do these effects translate into worse performance on a professional examination and higher post-examination negative mood? Participants were 216 couples

where one partner was preparing to take an important examination. Both members of the dyad completed daily diary reports on support provision and receipt and mood for five weeks prior to the examination and one week following. Passing the examination was ascertained from public records. Receipt of emotional support during exam preparation was positively related to post-exam positive mood and relationship closeness but not to passing.

Situational appraisals and the transmission of depressive symptoms: A study with couples undergoing assisted reproduction treatment
Knoll, Nina Dept. of Medical Psychology, Charité Berlin, Berlin, Germany Schwarzer, Ralf Dept. of Psychology, Freie Universität Berlin, Berlin, Germany Kienle, Rolf Dept. of Medical Psychology, Charité Berlin, Berlin, Germany
Objectives: Partners' situational appraisals were investigated as indirect effects in the transmission of depressive symptoms in couples under stress. Methods: Situational appraisals and depressive symptoms of 82 couples undergoing assisted reproduction treatment were assessed at two times before and once after pregnancy test. Manifest pathanalyses were conducted. Results: Transmission of depressive symptoms from men to women was mediated by women's situational appraisals. Men were affected by their partners' depressive symptoms only indirectly via their partners' appraisals. Conclusion: Using a transactional dyadic stress framework for the study of emotional transmission should help to gain a better understanding of its underlying mechanisms.

A longitudinal approach to modeling individual differences in adjustment to bereavement
Burke, Christopher Dept. of Psychology, New York University, New York, USA Shrout, Patrick Dept. of Psychology, New York University, New York, USA
Bereavement research often focuses on adaptive versus maladaptive responses to loss. However, because few studies are longitudinal, many cannot distinguish transient reactions from long-term changes or chronic differences. Using data from a prospective survey of bereavement, we examined variability in trajectories of depressive symptoms from pre-loss to four years post-loss using nonlinear statistical methods. We found that higher pre-loss perceived coping ability predicted less distress overall and that greater pre-loss relationship satisfaction predicted less depression long after the loss but was unrelated to the severity of the immediate reaction. These results elucidate how the process of grieving unfolds over time.

Effects of coping-oriented couple therapy on depression
Widmer, Kathrin Inst. of Family Research, University of Fribourg, Fribourg, Switzerland Bodenmann, Guy Inst. of Family Research, University of Fribourg, Fribourg, Switzerland Plancherel, Bernard Dept. of Psychology, University of Fribourg, Fribourg, Switzerland Gabriel, Barbara Inst. of Family Research, University of Fribourg, Fribourg, Switzerland Charvoz, Linda Dept. of Psychology, University of Lausanne, Lausanne, Switzerland Meuwly, Nathalie Inst. of Family Research, University of Fribourg, Fribourg, Switzerland Hautzinger, Martin Dept. of Psychology, University of Tübingen, Tübingen, Germany Schramm, Elisabeth Dept. of Psychiatry, University of Freiburg, Freiburg, Germany
Interpersonal conditions play a crucial role for onset and relapse-probability of depression. Coping-oriented couple therapy (COCT) treats depression by improving dyadic competences - which at the same time help both partners to enhance relationship quality in the long term. Effects of COCT, Cognitive therapy (CT) and Interpersonal Psychotherapy (IPT) were compared. 60 patients

and their partners were randomized to one of the three treatments. Selfreport data over a study period of 1.5 years show that COCT was as effective in improving depressive symptoms as CT and IPT. Differential effects are presented and discussed with regard to clinical implications.

S-263: Time, space and culture: Chronogenesis in human life course

Tatsuya Sato, Jaan Valsiner (chair)
Time and space are central in all psychological existence. For long time there has been a tradition in psychology to view these categories as separate from everyday experiencing of the world by ordinary human beings, leading to infertile disputes about "Western" and "Eastern" understanding of the two concepts. We bring together international focus on time and space in real human life courses—and introduce the framework of chronogenesis for future psychological investigations. Basic human life activities include chronogenesis—in gender identity, desires for children, childbirth, and child-rearing, By creating new ways of acting human beings create actuality out of potentialities.

A dynamic system theory looks at gender identity
Ma, Chuan Dept. of Psychology, East China Normal University, Shanghai, People's Republic of China
The dynamic systems approach which provides a general framework for studying processes can be applied to the issue of gender identity. Presently, the interpersonal prospect is focused in research of it, though the prospects are multiform before, for instance, concept cognitive,scheme cognitive,social cognitive and etc. Gender identity is interactive with others and the circumstance, so the transition and the crisis emerge. The attractors hidden in them give the chance to explore the development of gender identity and the process is nonlinear. The methods of short-term processes, state space grid and mathematical models can assess it.

East Asian children and their pocket money: Development as negotiation of the cultural norm boundaries
Takahashi, Noboru Dept. of School Education, Osaka Kyoiku University, Kashiwara, Japan
Children who live in consumer society begin to know money at an early age. Money is not only a thing with exchange value, but also a cultural tool which mediates between children and other people. Young children use money under the strong parental control, but gradually they use money based on their own judgment, although they continue to behave in culturally adequate way. In this symposium, I will discuss how east asian children from the four countries become to use money in culturally appropriate way, though deviated from parental control, on the basis of our questionnaire research.

Transition and liminality: Changing identities of Sudanese refugees in Cairo
Mahmoud, Hala W. Social and Develop. Psychology, University of Cambridge, Cambridge, United Kingdom
Sudanese refugees in Cairo experience changes in their lives and identities as a result of their forced migration and the process of "waiting" for resettlement. Like other refugees, they are 'liminal' or transitional beings in the sense that they are no longer citizens of their home country but not yet citizens of another country. Their sense of suspension in time and place, and its associated disturbance in personal trajectories, both result in identities characterized by ambiguity and ambivalence. Those identity changes will be examined in

the light of time dynamics (past-present-future), and will draw on findings from my PhD fieldwork.

Time in life: Uncertainties in the infertility treatment in women
Yasuda, Yuko Graduate School of Education, Kyoto University, Hirakata, Kazakhstan
The aim of this study was to grasp women's experiences of infertility treatments up to stopping. From the viewpoint of highly developed medical science, only the success rate of treatments has become popular, but there are some women who still can't have children even after treatments. I investigated their infertility experiences by interview and narrative analysis. At first they placed all their hopes on treatments, but they gradually came to realize the difficulty in having children even with such treatment. Throughout the processes of treatments, they came to consider the meaning of having children and the view of their lives.

On chronogenesis
Valsiner, Jaan Dept. of Psychology, Clark University, Worcester, USA
Time can be viewed as proceeding irreversibly from the infinite past to the infinite future. In the course of evolution of physical, biological, and social systems this trajectory has become conditionalized through creation of quasi-stable periods in the development of these systems that turn irreversible time into periods that become characterized as homogeneous time units. The mapping of such time units onto actual (irreversible) time is possible through abstractive generalization (Karl Bühler) based on analogical reasoning. Time becomes curvilinear due to its links with the development of open systems in nature and society.

S-264: Top athletes' transition to new career horizons

Kiyoshi Takahashi, Toshihiro Kanai (chair)
The dual objectives of this research are to explore the intellectual developmental stages experienced by Japanese top athletes transitioning from sports careers to post-retirement career options, and to define the skills required for a successful transition. Interviews were conducted with ex-professional soccer players and Olympians. The intellectual stages for career transition correlate to those defined by Kübler-Ross(1969). Readiness for retirement and three kinds of skills by Kats (1955) are important to smooth transition. Conceptual skills and the human skills of top athletes are key components in coping with difficulties in retirement. Top athletes don't develop the necessary skills for career transition, and they need to develop them in the early period of post-retirement.

A narrative discourse of the developmental tasks for Japanese olympians
Toyoda, Norishige Biwako Seikei Sport College, Otsu, Japan
The objective of this study is to investigate the developmental tasks that confronted by the past Japanese Olympians. The study employed a qualitative research method, i.e., the simplified Grounded Theory Approach (GTA), administering a semi-structured interviews to five Japanese ex-Olympians who retired from the competition more than twenty years ago. The study found that the Olympians were encountered three developmental tasks in their processes of career transition; 1) changing of the self, 2) expanding of one's behavior, and 3) cultivating of relationships. Their distinctive, unique experiences were expressed in the narratives of 1) the changes of life patterns, 2) the formation of anchors, 3) the recognition of one's limit, and 4) the psychological sufferings.

Readiness and skills necessary for Japanese professional football players towards the retirement career
Takahashi, Kiyoshi Business Administration, Kobe University, Edinburgh, United Kingdom
Most of the top-athletes have a rough transition between athletic and occupational careers. Since they had been committed overwhelmingly to the sports, the loss of their loved objects hinders a smooth, successful transition. The purpose of this study is to investigate the transition processes among professional football players. Interviews were conducted to ex-football players in the Japanese league. Applying Kubler-Ross's (1969) theory of death and dying, the study found that professional football players experienced the resembling psychological process as dying with the optimistic view of the second life. It also suggested that the readiness for retirement as well as three skills i.e., conceptual, human, and technical skills (Kats, 1955) were important facilitators for smooth transition.

Overcoming incompatibilities with managers and professional players
Hattori, Yasuhiro Business Administration, Kobe University, Kobe, Japan
The objective of this study is to understand functions of compatibility between managers and professional players. Semi-structured interviews were conducted to ex-J League player. I asked them critical incidents with "the least-preferred manager" and "the most-preferred manager". The result showed that compatibility consisted of two dimensions: Cognitive compatibility refers to the awareness of (in)congruence in individual values and intentions between managers and players; Emotional/affective compatibility refers to individual affectivity and attachment to the other. Cognitive compatibility and emotional/affective compatibility influenced each other. To overcome incompatibility, one must attempt to communicate his values and intentions (that is cognitive compatibility) to the other person.

Internal support systems for Japanese top athletes in transition
Ogawa, Chisato Business Administration, Kinki University, Osaka, Japan
The purpose of this research is to explore the internal support systems required for a successful career transition by Japanese top athletes. Interviews were conducted with a randomly selected cohort of thirteen ex-professional soccer players from the Japanese professional football league. The data showed that they rarely explored alternative social networks during their sports careers, because they tended to be short-sighted about career choices outside of soccer. The key factor for the internal support systems is the courageousness in networking (Krumboltz and Levin, 2004). They also need to develop social skills.

External support systems for building a social network between athletes
Hara, Rie Business Administration, Kobe University, Kobe, Japan Ogawa, Chisato Business Administration, Kinki University, Osaka, Japan Sato, Yoshiaki Football Club, Osaka Sangyo University, Daito-shi, Japan
This research aims to investigate the key components of the external support systems supporting the transition from sports careers to post-retirement careers. Qualitative semi-structured interviews were conducted to thirteen retired soccer players in a Japanese league. The data showed that there was a gap between the players' conceptual and social needs to overcome hardship during the transition and the ability of formal career support functions to meet their needs. The most important factor was the approachability to the social networks of

persons who could accept them confidentially and discretely.

S-265: Psychological perspectives on cultural usability and human computer interaction

Torkil Clemmensen (chair)
This symposium analyzes the psychology of cultural usability. In industry, a wealth of usability evaluation methods is used to evaluate computer software user interfaces and other interactive products: Inspection methods, Workplace observation, Think-Aloud Usability Test, etc. Both in the industry and in research there is an interest in understanding cultural issues because there are many cultural factors that influence usability evaluation results. From an academic viewpoint, the psychology of 'cultural usability' should be analyzed within an expanded cultural and social diversity of users and contexts. The symposium will present current research into cultural usability.

Do Asian people take longer for warm-up during usability test?

Li, Huiyang *Inst. of Psychology, Chinese Academy of Sciences, Beijing, People's Republic of China* **Sun, Xianghong** *Inst. of Psychology, Chinese Academy of Sciences, Beijing, People's Republic of China* **Zhang, Kan** *Inst. of Psychology, Chinese Academy of Sciences, Beijing, People's Republic of China* **Clemmensen, Torkil** *Dept. of Informatics, Copenhagen Business School, Fredriksberg, Denmark* **Shi, Qingxin** *Department of Informatics, Copenhagen Business School, Copenhagen, Denmark*
Generally speaking, Asian people take longer time for warm-up during everyday communication. They need to ask each other some details about how everything is going before they discuss the topic they concern. Case is the same when they use instant message services on-line. Is this also true during usability test? In this paper, we analyze video record of usability tests in China and Denmark and encode the communication between evaluator and user. The whole process of usability test was divided into three stages: warm-up, formal test, and follow-up interview. It is found that Chinese people took longer in the warm-up stage, and also took longer in conversation management.

Effects of cultural influence while using likert scales in the context of product evaluation in China

Roese, Kerstin *Zentrum für Mensch-Maschine, Tech. Univers. Kaiserslautern, Kaiserslautern, Germany*
Likert scales are among the most abundant instruments applied in product development. However various effects, e.g. the reference-group effect, are known to affect the validity of cross-cultural application of likert scales. We compared the application of two- to six-staged likert scales in China. After normalizing the data in order to allow direct comparison, effects of the width of the applied scale on answering patterns were observed of which some in turn can be traced back to cultural effects.

User analysis for South East Asia. Does that work? A cross-check of two methods and two cultures: China and Korea

Braun, Björn-M. *Zentr. für Mensch-Maschine, Techn. Univer. Kaiserslautern, Kaiserslautern, Germany*
Analysis methods applied in the earliest stage of the product development process are expected to differ in their applicability across cultures. Certain method-traits serve as cultural dependent facilitators of method application while others hinder the efficient application. Reliability, validity and value of user analysis strongly depend on maximizing the prior kind of traits while minimizing the latter for

respective target-cultures and methods. Objective here is to elicit facilitators and obstacles of puzzle interviews and inspiration card workshops for China and Korea.

Communication pattern and usability problem finding in cross-cultural usability testing

Shi, Qingxin *Dept. of Informatics, Copenhagen Business School, Frederiksberg, Denmark*
Communication plays an important role for the evaluator to find accurate usability problems in formative thinking about usability testing in the industrial area. This study tries to investigate the communication pattern of evaluators in the cross-cultural usability testing, and the influence on usability problem finding by doing experiments with Danish users and Chinese users. It will be based on Nisbett's culture theory and Hong's dynamic constructivist approach to culture. The purpose of this research is to propose an effective communication pattern for evaluators to do usability tests with western users or eastern users.

Is cultural factors affect both evaluator's and test user's thinking in a usability test?

Sun, Xianghong *Institute of Psychology, Beijing, People's Republic of China* **Li, Huiyang** *Inst. of Psychology, Chinese Academy of Science, Beijing, People's Republic of China* **Clemmensen, Torkil** *Dept. of Informatics, Copenhagen Business School, Fredriksberg, Denmark* **Shi, Qingxin** *Department of Informatics, Copenhagen Business School, Copenhagen, Denmark*
Nisbett found Asians and European people understand the world in different ways. In our simulated usability test, the pictures that Nisbett mentioned in his study were used as experimental material. Test users were asked to describe the content and evaluate them, then pick one of them to make a greeting card for his/her friend. All their description, evaluation the evaluator's analysis was recorded. It was found that, both Danish and Chinese people paid attention to the background and salient objects. It was different from Nisbett's study in which western people only noticed salient objects and not sensitive to background and relationship among objects. It was concluded that ways of thinking was task-dependent.

Usability issues on the Chinese fire information display

Zhang, Liang *Inst. für Psychologie, Universität Hamburg, Hamburg, Germany* **Sun, Xianghong** *Institute of Psychology, Chinese Academy of Sciences, Beijing, People's Republic of China* **Qu, Weina** *Institute of Psychology, Chinese Academy of Sciences, Beijing, People's Republic of China*
The Fire Information Display (FID) is an essential part of high buildings, which helps firefighters' detection more efficiently. Recently, it is getting more widely used with the city's construction developing in China. The experiment was conducted to explore the Chinese FID prototype's usability and practicability, with ten Chinese firefighters participants. The prototype contained four levels of map: vicinity, neighborhood, street, floorplan, which are four typical levels in American FID, but didn't show the same significance for Chinese firefighters. The results also showed that the Chinese firefighters had the different understandings to the icons meaning and preference to the display frame.

S-266: User psychology and interaction design

Pertti Saariluoma (chair)
User psychology applies psychological knowledge in human-technology interaction design. It is not necessary to use psychological knowledge only in testing existent technologies or new prototypes. It is

also essential to apply it in designing new types of actions in ICT-environments. This is why psychologically grounded human requirements engineering shall be on of the important challenges for user psychological research. In this presentation a number of relevant problems shall be discussed.

From applied cognitive research to neuroergonomics: The quest for ecological validity

Velichkovsky, Boris M. *Dept. od Psychology, University of Technology, Dresden, Germany*
Recent progress in video-based eyetracking and in building virtual reality environments can be considered as a silent technological revolution in brain and behavioural sciences, approaching that of brain imaging methods. Both methodologies are of particular importance in the quest for more ecological validity. We demonstrate how eyetracking, virtual reality techniques and brain imaging can enrich each other by means of two lines of applied investigations. The first aimed at improving driving safety. The goal of our second study was to improve the productivity of computer-supported cooperative work. Both studies were done in collaboration with globally active automotive companies. Taken together, these studies demonstrate how productive the convergence of several technologies may be in usability research.

Modelling user psychlogy for efficient usability evaluation

Moeller, Sebastian *Deutsche Telekom Labs, Berlin, Germany*
In addition to its usefulness during system design and user testing, knowledge on user psychology might enable disruptively new evaluation techniques. For example, models which simulate user behaviour may be used for semi-automatic evaluation of interactive ICT services. In order to be successful, such models have to reflect the user psychology and take into account the perception processes, the user's aims and motivations, the previous experience, the user's mental model of the service, and other psychological factors. In this presentation, the need for such innovative approaches to evaluation is underlined, and the necessary steps for its implementation are outlined.

Emotion-based mobile services and content in public spaces

Saari, Timo *Information Technology, Cognitive Science, Jyväskylä, Finland*
Ubiquitous media is emerging based on mobile content and services as well as wireless sensor networks. However, what is lacking is a psychologically informed view on how ubiquitous, location-based mobile services evoke emotions and moods as part of the user experience and how this may explain the consumption and use of such services. In media studies, there is a vast literature on mood management, i.e. the motivation to use media to cancel or amplify certain emotional and mood states. A similar approach could be taken to conceptualizing and explaining uses of various mobile, location-based services and content. The presentation will address the relevant problems of emotion and mood-oriented ubiquitous media in public spaces.

S-267: Informal learning on the web: Individual differences and evaluation processes

Yvonne Kammerer, Peter Gerjets (chair)
Using the Web for information and learning purposes imposes high demands on the users. They have to determine their information need, navigate in Web sites and process conflicting contents. Particularly challenging is the evaluation of the

relevance and quality of available information. These processes are fundamentally influenced by individual differences of the users, e.g. prior knowledge, abilities, attitudes, epistemological or self-efficacy beliefs. Moreover, structure and design of the Web environment affect search and information evaluation. This symposium brings together empirical findings and theoretical perspectives that focus on the abovementioned aspects of informal learning on the Web.

What evaluation processes are performed during web search?: An eye-tracking study

Kammerer, Yvonne *Knowledge Acquis. Hypermedia, Knowledge Media Res. Center, Tübingen, Germany* **Werner, Benita** *Hypermedia, KMRC, Tübingen, Germany* **Gerjets, Peter** *Hypermedia, KMRC, Tuebingen, Germany*

Evaluating information with regard to relevance and quality is a fundamental part of Web search. In a first study, we recorded web search behavior of 5 students (without prompting evaluation processes). Gaze recording allowed for identification of each evaluated hyperlink (i.e. selected and rejected). However, by means of verbal protocols it could be shown that only 5 % of these hyperlinks seemed to be consciously evaluated. This discrepancy between the amount of evaluated hyperlinks visible in verbal and eye-tracking data is currently investigated in a study with 60 subjects testing experimentally how evaluation prompts influence search and evaluation processes.

Teaching students how to evaluate information on the WWW

Walraven, Amber *OTEC, Open University Netherlands, Heerlen, Netherlands* **Brand-Gruwel, Saskia** *OTEC, Open University of the Netherl, AT Heerlen, Netherlands* **Boshuizen, Henny P.A.** *OTEC, Open University of the Netherl, AT Heerlen, Netherlands*

Two educational programs based on two transfer theories have been designed and tested. The first theory advocates that transfer of complex cognitive skills is fostered through the development of a rich knowledge structure. The second theory advocates that transfer is fostered through the development of metacognitive skills. The complex cognitive skill central in the educational programs was evaluating results, information and sources while solving information problems using the WWW. Focus of the programs was on knowledge and use of evaluation criteria. Effects of the two programs on increase in knowledge and use of criteria and degree of transfer were determined.

Information search on the web and individual's epistemological beliefs

Kienhues, Dorothe *Psychologisches Institut III, Universität Münster, Münster, Germany* **Bromme, Rainer** *Psychological Institute III, University of Muenster, Muenster, Germany* **Stadtler, Marc** *Psychological Institute III, University of Muenster, Muenster, Germany*

When people search the web for medical information, they commonly come across conflicting evidence. This exploratory study focuses on the interplay between epistemological beliefs, medication attitudes, and ability beliefs and dealing with medical information from the web. Participants were 28 German students who had to gain information on cholesterol. 15 pre-selected websites modeling conflicting evidence concerning cholesterol were provided. Results from log-file data, different questionnaires and a retrospective interview indicate that discipline-specific epistemological beliefs are affected by dealing with conflicting evidence on the web. Furthermore, Internet search differs depending on attitudes, ability beliefs, and personal epistemology.

Internet-specific epistemic beliefs and internet-based learning activities among Norwegian physics undergraduates

Strømsø, Helge I. *Inst. of Educational Research, University of Oslo, Oslo, Norway* **Bråten, Ivar** *Institute of Educational Resea, University of Oslo, Oslo, Norway*

A sample of 84 Norwegian physics undergraduates answered questionnaires concerning epistemic beliefs about Internet-based knowledge and knowing, Internet self-efficacy beliefs, and Internet-search and -communication activities. Using two dimensions of epistemic beliefs, one concerning the certainty and simplicity of Internet-based knowledge, and one concerning the evaluation of knowledge claims encountered on the Internet, preliminary analysis indicated that students' epistemic beliefs predicted their self-reports of Internet-search and -communication activities in better and more consistent ways than did Internet self-efficacy beliefs.

Memory for information spaces: Effects of visuospatial abilities and representational aids

Rouet, Jean-François *LMDC, CNRS - University of Poitiers, Poitiers, France* **Vörös, Zsofia** *LMDC, CNRS - University of Poitiers, Poitiers, France* **Nivet, Clément** *LMDC, CNRS - University of Poitiers, Poitiers, France* **Fourmaux, Jérémy** *LMDC, CNRS - University of Poitiers, Poitiers, France* **Le Bigot, Ludovic** *LMDC, CNRS - University of Poitiers, Poitiers, France* **Pleh, Csaba** *Cognitive Science BME, Budapest University of Technol, Budapest, Hungary*

Prior research suggests that visuo-spatial abilities may be involved in hypertext learning. We investigated whether site maps help low-ability users learn the structure of hierarchical hypertext. 32 university undergraduates explored simple hypertexts organized in a hierarchical but arbitrary fashion. In half of the trials, the hypertexts included an interactive content map. After navigating, the participants were asked to reconstruct the hypertext layout and probed for their memory of page contents. We expected an interaction between the inclusion of a map and the participants' level of visuo-spatial ability. Data were being collected at the time of proposal.

Web information search in sign language

Fajardo, Inmaculada *Manchester Business School, University of Manchester, Manchester, United Kingdom* **Parra, Elena** *Department of Experimental Psy, University of Granada, Granada, Spain* **Cañas, José J.** *Department of Experimental Psy, University of Granada, Granada, Spain* **Abascal, Julio** *ATC, University of the Basque Count, San Sebastián, Spain* **López, Juan Miguel** *ATC, University of the Basque Count, San Sebastián, Spain*

Web information search is a challenge for minority language users such as Sign Language (SL). In one study we compared two navigation mechanisms based on textual hyperlinks linked to embedded SL videos: Multi-Videoframe vs. Unique-Videoframe. Whereas a group of Deaf SL users were comparably efficient in Web search using both mechanisms, only the second one correlated with their verbal categorization abilities and reading comprehension level. These results were interpreted as a higher efficiency of the first mechanism to facilitate SL use. We discuss the necessity of considering users individual differences in knowledge and language proficiency to improve information scent.

S-268: An (environmental) psychological perspective on technology transfer to developing countries

Melanie Jäger, Friederike Arnold (chair)

The transfer of technological innovations to developing countries is often seen as a motor of social development and a key to increase life quality in poor rural areas. But the requirements to realize this relationship are manifold and challenging. A goal of this symposium is to discuss these challenges to project partners, process design and the development and adaptation of technologies from the point of view of environmental and organizational psychology. Psychological theories and concepts to investigate the process of transfer will be considered as well as methods to monitor the transfer and evaluate the impact of technologies.

Everything flows: The importance of fluidity in rural electrification projects

Jäger, Melanie *Inst. für Psychologie, Universität Magdeburg, Magdeburg, Germany*

The nature scientific concept of fluidity, describing a substance or situation that can easily adapt itself or be integrated into something else is taken to evaluate a technological innovation in a rural electrification process in Madagascar. The adaptability of Renewable energy technologies to different environmental conditions, socio-cultural processes and human demands is researched in a field study using ethnographic methods and interviews with users and stakeholders. First results show the usefulness of the concept of fluidity to understand the different identities a technology can have on a micro, meso and macro level and also to describe social systems and individuals.

Supporting the transfer of water treatment technologies with the help of technology mediation

Arnold, Friederike *Geographisches Institut, Humboldt-Universität zu Berlin, Berlin, Germany*

When transferring water treatment technologies to so-called emerging countries, many problems may occur. Amongst the reasons for these problems is the fact that different phases of the innovation and transfer process take place at different places and involve different actors who have different perceptions, aims and habits. Intermediaries are persons or organisations who can bridge these differences. Within the Technology Mediation Approach (Arnold, Mieg & Hoffmann, 2007), the role of intermediaries is explored. Qualitative data on the functions and characteristics of intermediaries in the technology transfer process are presented.

Using the social network: Promotion of SODIS in a high density area in Simbabwe

Krämer, Silvie *SIAM, EAWAG, Dübendorf, Switzerland*

Solar water disinfection (SODIS), like other innovations to be introduced in developing countries, encounters problems in the uptake and usage process. For SODIS, untreated water in transparent PET-bottles is exposed to the sun for 6 hours. UV-radiation and heat cause microbiological disinfection of the water. To avoid slow uptake as experienced in past projects, social network and communication attributes have been analyzed and used to shape dissemination strategies. Results will be discussed. A pass-on-task will be compared with a request for talking about SODIS or to do SODIS and the impact of bottle centers to overcome bottle inavailability.

Successful long-term adoption of SODIS: Evaluating different commitment interventions in rural Bolivia

Tamas, Andrea *SIAM, EAWAG, Aquatic Research, Dübendorf, Switzerland*

SODIS (Solar Water Disinfection) is a simple drinking water treatment method designed for the use at household level. We conducted a study on the effective promotion of SODIS testing different commitment interventions to support especially habit formation. Interventions applied were prompts, public commitment, intention development, feedback and combinations. Investigation did not only focus on the influence on behaviour change, but also included behaviour determining factors such as beliefs, attitudes, and social norms. Results show an interesting pattern of associations between those factors, habits and behaviour intensity depending on the intervention. Further discussion includes recommendations for future field applications.

Socio-technical system analysis in the field of rural electrification with solar energy: A contribution to quality assurance of development cooperation projects

Vogt, Gisela Freiburg, Germany *Schüpbach, Heinz* Arbeits- & Organisationsps, Universität Freiburg, Freiburg, Germany

Around the world, rural electrification projects applying solar energy face major problems in being implemented and run sustainably. This study links the paradigm of socio-technical system analysis with the total quality management concept of the European Foundation for Quality Management (EFQM Model). Results indicate that there is empirical evidence to regard these projects as socio-technical systems, which has implications for the planning and realisation of these projects. The EFQM Model proves to be a useful framework to study and structure quality criteria in a systematic way and to judge the overall sustainability of the projects. Further research on psychological quality criteria is needed to adapt these better to the given context to support technology transfer.

Social aspects in the introduction of renewable energy in rural Indonesia

Djuwita Chaidir, Ratna FKMUI, Universitas Indonesia, West Java, Indonesia

Objectives of the study were to explore social & economical factors that determine if a PV-Hybrid System is socially accepted and will function technically well. Questionnaire and group discussions were used as data collection methods. Data was collected among adult villagers in 2 remote villages (Kalimantan and Sulawesi) and one less remote village in Java. Descriptive and qualitative methods were used to analyse the data. The results show that energy consumption is higher in less remote villages and that not only technical but also social-cultural management and finance skill should be trained more to influence consumption.

S-269: Decolonizing transgender psychology: Transgender identities and issues within cultural contexts

Vic Munoz (chair)

Culture is central to understanding transgender people in ways that move beyond the dominant white Western views of what it means to be lesbian, gay, bisexual, and transgender. Through research which focuses on the interactions between gender, sexuality, and culture within decolonizing movements (Maori, Native Hawaiian) and research that critiques the hegemony of Western views on gender we will address transgender identities and issues in ways that offer new understandings of LGBT people of color (psychoanalytical, culturally appropriate, as critique of the dominant). Research shows culturally grounded approaches are needed to support the self-determination of LGBT peoples across cultures.

Exploring Takatapui identity within the Maori community and implications for transgender identity

Aspin, Clive Dept. of Education, University of Auckland, Auckland, New Zealand

Increasing numbers of Maori, the indigenous people of New Zealand, are reclaiming the term

takatapui to describe their sexual identity. The term derives from the pre-colonial past and encapsulates the cultural and sexual components of one's identity. For many, it is a preferred descriptor over terms which derive from Western paradigms. Research suggests that takatapui identity provides beneficial outcomes for Maori, including transgender people, who are often marginalized because of their sexuality. This presentation will describe strategies that can be used to facilitate access to culturally appropriate support systems for indigenous transgender people and others from sexual minorities.

The accident of gender in the shadow of culture

Gozlan, Oren Gozlan Psychology, Toronto, Canada

This paper considers the desire to be "normal" as inhibition that prevents experimentation with the accidents of gender. Inhibition is viewed here as a guard against the clash between desire and culture. Analyzing the gender "experiments" of the character "Calliope" in J. Eugenides' Middle Sex, this paper offers a conceptualization of gender as an existential dilemma, lack, desire and defense against trauma; that is played out in and affected by the social. The author turns to Lacan and Verhaghea's emphasis on desire as a bridge between interiority and object relations arguing for a theory of gender that tolerates the inchoate.

A woman, ashamed: On shame, loss and mourning in transsexual transition within western culture context

Maurer, Offer Dept. of Psychology, Isr. Branch of Derby Univ., Tel Aviv, Israel

Many male-to-female transsexuals during a certain phase of the transsexual journey experience excruciating feelings of shame upon the realization of being a woman. Drawing upon clinical material I will demonstrate that this burden of shame stems from internalized western culture's views denigrating femininity. This intra-psychic conflict constitutes a normal phase of the transsexual transition; a phase resembling a gender-melancholic phase in the so-called 'regular' female development. In therapy, narcissistic losses of power and competence, subjectively felt to be 'naturally' masculine, need to be mourned, rediscovered and integrated as qualities existing also in the feminine.

Toward ethnic transgender psychologies: How can gender identities be decolonized?

Munoz, Vic Dept. of Psychology, Wells College, Aurora, USA

The master narrative of Gender Identity Disorder was written to make gender variance intelligible within a classed and racialized Western worldview. Globalization has further entrenched Western concepts of gender rigidity and the acceptance of GID. Using longitudinal data from the Gender Identity and Sexual Orientation Study and cultural psychological research this paper theorizes what it would mean to decolonize gender identities. Rather than affirm Western concepts of pathology and the abnormal, which have historically led to the marginalization of transgender people across cultures, this paper explores psychological self-determination and anti-colonial approaches to psychological health.

S-270: Depression in mainland China: Predictors, correlates and consequences

John Abela (chair)

Epidemiological studies suggest that the prevalence of depression in China has risen in recent decades - particularly among adolescents. With respect to adolescents, China has the second highest suicide rate in the world. Despite such alarming statistics,

little research has examined models of the etiology of depression in China. The speakers in the current symposium will present results from research examining the predictors, correlates, and consequences of depression in mainland China. Particular emphasis will be placed on highlighting both the cross-cultural similarities and differences between the findings presented and findings from research conducted in Western cultures.

Lifetime history of major depressive disorder in urban and rural adolescents in Hunan, China: Prevalence, course, symptom manifestation and correlates

Yao, Shuqiao Medical Psychological Research, The Second Xiangya Hospital, Changsha, People's Republic of China *Zhu, Xiongzhao* Medical Psychological Research, Second Xiangya Hospital, Changsha, People's Republic of China *Abela, John* Dept. of Psychology, McGill University, Montreal, Canada *Sun, Jiahong Starrs, Claire van Hammel, Anton Page, Gabrielle*

Epidemiological studies conducted within mainland China over the past decade suggest that depression is more common than was previously believed. Further, although no formal epidemiological studies have been conducted using child or adolescent samples, preliminary findings suggests that the prevalence rates of depression in these age groups exceed those seen in adults. The current study examined lifetime prevalence rates of major and minor depressive disorder in two samples of adolescents in mainland China: (1) 300 adolescents in urban Changsha and (2) 300 adolescents in rural Liuyang. In addition, we examined demographic correlates of depression in and across samples.

Chinese somatization and western psychologization: Is cognitive symptom emphasis a western culture-bound syndrome?

Ryder, Andrew Dept. of Psychology, Concordia University, Montreal, Canada *Abela, John* Dept. of Psychology, McGill University, Montreal, Canada *Zhu, Xiongzhao* Medical Psychological Research, Second Xiangya Hospital, Changsha, People's Republic of China *Yao, Shuqiao* Medical Psychological Research, The Second Xiangya Hospital, Changsha, People's Republic of China *Dere, Jessica*

The expectation that Chinese people present distress somatically is a central prediction of cultural psychopathology, but empirical research has been mixed. This study examined symptom presentation in Chinese (n=175) and Euro-Canadian (n=107) outpatients. Chinese outpatients reported more somatic symptoms on interview compared with Euro-Canadians, who themselves reported more psychological symptoms on both interview- and questionnaire-based assessment. The relation between culture and somatization was mediated by externally oriented thinking. Chinese somatization effects were weaker than Western psychologization effects, which were driven by cognitive rather than somatic symptoms. Other studies have shown somatization worldwide; cognitive emphasis may be unique to Western cultures.

Interpersonal vulnerability to depression: A multi-wave longitudinal study of adolescents in urban and rural China

Abela, John Dept. of Psychology, McGill University, Montreal, Canada *Sharp, Aaron Auerbach, Randy* Dept. of Psychology, McGill University, Montreal, Canada *Yao, Shuqiao* Medical Psychological Research, The Second Xiangya Hospital, Changsha, People's Republic of China *Zhu, Xiongzhao* Medical Psychological Research, Second Xiangya Hospital, Changsha, People's Republic of China

Interpersonal theories of depression posit that interpersonal factors serve as buffers against depression following negative events. Such interpersonal factors are hypothesized to buffer against the deleterious effects of stress by enhancing one's coping abilities. The current study examined theories of interpersonal vulnerability to depression in samples of adolescents in both urban (n=558) and rural (n=592) China using a multi-wave long-itudinal design. Results indicated that high quality interpersonal relations with both parents and peeres buffered against the deleterious effects of negative events on depressive symptoms.

Cognitive vulnerability to depression in adolescents from mainland China

Auerbach, Randy Dept. of Psychology, McGill University, Montreal, Canada Abela, John Dept. of Psychology, McGill University, Montreal, Canada Zhu, Xiongzhao Medical Psychological Research, Second Xiangya Hospital, Changsha, People's Republic of China Yao, Shuqiao Medical Psychological Research, The Second Xiangya Hospital, Changsha, People's Republic of China

In the present study, we examined whether cogni-tive vulnerability factors moderated the relationship between stress and depressive symptoms. At Time 1, 411 adolescents completed self-report measures assessing cognitive styles, stress, and depressive symptoms. Follow-up assessments occurred every four weeks (Time 2-6), and participants completed measures assessing stress and depressive symptoms. Results of multilevel modeling analyses indicated that individuals who reported higher levels of cognitive vulnerability, as compared to lower levels, reported greater increases in depressive symptoms following the occurrence of stress. These findings suggest that models of cognitive vulnerability developed with Western samples may be applicable to mainland China.

Negative attachment cognitions as a vulnerability factor to depressive and anxious symptoms in university students in Hunan, China

Zhu, Xiongzhao Medical Psychological Research, Second Xiangya Hospital, Changsha, People's Republic of China Yao, Shuqiao Medical Psychological Research, The Second Xiangya Hospital, Changsha, People's Republic of China Abela, John Dept. of Psychology, McGill University, Montreal, Canada Tong, Xi Auerbach, Randy Dept. of Psychology, McGill University, Montreal, Canada

This study examined whether negative attachment cognitions confer vulnerability to the development of depressive symptoms. Participants included 662 first-year university students from Hunan, China. During an initial assessment, participants com-pleted measures assessing attachment cognitions and depressive symptoms. Participants subse-quently completed measures assessing negative events and depressive symptoms once a month for six months. When examined as a continuous variable, results indicated that higher levels of negative attachment cognitions were associated with greater increases in depressive symptoms following negative events. When examined as a categorical variable, results did not provide indicate an association between specific attachment styles and vulnerability to depression.

Rumination as a vulnerability factor to depressive and anxious symptoms in urban and rural adolescents in mainland China

Parkinson, Carolyn Dept. of Psychology, McGill University, Montreal, Canada Abela, John Dept. of Psychology, McGill University, Montreal, Canada Auerbach, Randy Dept. of Psychology, McGill University, Montreal, Canada Yao, Shuqiao Medical Psychological Research, The Second Xiangya Hospital, Changsha, People's Republic of China Zhu, Xiongzhao Medical Psychological Research, Second Xiangya Hospital, Changsha, People's Republic of China

The current prospective study examined the applic-ability of the response styles theory of depression to

samples of adolescents in both urban (n=558) and rural (n=588) China. In line with hypotheses, in both samples, a greater tendency to engage in rumination in response to depressed mood was associated with increases in both depressive and anxious symptoms over time. Contrary to the response styles theory, and to results obtained in research examining the theory in samples of adolescents in Western countries, in both samples, girls did not report a greater tendency to engage in ruminative responses than did boys.

S-271: The wording effect: Structural models and consequences for validity

Wolfgang Rauch, Karl Schweizer (chair)
The symposium concentrates on methodological aspects of the effects resulting from including positively and negatively worded items into a scale. The prevention of acquiescence by means of such items has usually disadvantageous consequences: the structure of such a scale shows a deviation from the aspired unidimensionality. The presentations address the problem resulting from the combination of positively and negatively worded items from different perspectives: (1) in the search for the best representation of structure the appropriateness of various structural models is investigated; (2) the correlates of structural components are identified; (3) the dependency of the problem on the contents of the scales is considered.

The factor structure of self-report instruments comprised of positive and negative polarity items

Bors, Douglas A. Dept. of Psychology, University of Toronto, Toronto, Canada Vigneau, Francois Dept. of Psychology, Université de Moncton, Moncton, Canada

Using the multi-trait/multi-method technique we have analyzed several self-report instruments com-prised of positive and negative polarity Likert items: Need for Cognition, Tolerance of Ambiguity, and the State-Trait anxiety measure. Using con-firmatory factor analyses, these instruments were examined using various measurement models. In the trait/method model, the trait was defined as including all items for the particular scale, whereas the two method factors were defined by the polarity of the items. Using a range of indices, the trait/method model was consistently the best fit. These findings were consistent within a scale across languages (French and English) and across scales.

Personality correlates of method effects to negatively worded items on the RSES

Di Stefano, Christine Dept. of Psychology, University of South Carolina, Columbia, USA Motl, Robert Department of Kinesology, University of Illinois, UC, Urbana, IL, USA

This paper used a path analysis strategy to investigate the presence and correlates of method effects associated with negatively worded items on the Rosenberg Self-Esteem Scale (RSES; Rosen-berg, 1989). Seven personality measures were included and a MIMIC model was run using sex as a grouping variable. Path models included scales related to social desirability, evaluations by others, and self regulation of behavior. Identification of predictors related to the presence of method effects may help researchers identify personality traits of male and female subjects who are more prone to exhibit this response set due to negative item wording.

The investigation of the dimensionality of social optimism by means of the fixed-links model

Schweizer, Karl Inst. für Psychologie, Universität Frankfurt, Frankfurt, Germany

The paper reports on the investigation of social optimism data by means of a combination of the standard structural equation model and the fixed-links model. The standard structural equation model serves the estimation of loadings and the fixed-links model the estimation of the variances of latent variables. The investigation starts with a comprehensive model that includes latent variables representing bipolar and unipolar social optimism and pessimism. Since the maximum likelihood estimation method provides standard errors for the variances, the statistical significance of the latent variables can be investigated. The results suggest the elimination of the unipolar social pessimism latent variable.

Investigating the effect of item wording using the method effect model

Pohl, Steffi Inst. für Psychologie, Universität Jena, Jena, Germany

When positively and negatively worded items are used for the measurement of a construct, method effects often occur. The method effect (ME) model is introduced which allows modelling method effects in multitrait-multimethod designs. The definition of the method effects is here in line with a causal theory, allowing under certain conditions a causal interpretation of the method effects and, thus, a straightforward interpretation. Different forms of the ME model are presented in which trait and method factors are modelled in different ways with different interpretations. Recommenda-tions for choosing an appropriate model for a research question are given and illustrated on an example investigating the effect of item wording.

Ideal point response processes as an alternative explanation for the wording effect

Rauch, Wolfgang Inst. für Psychologie, Universität Frankfurt, Frankfurt, Germany Luu, Johanna Inst. für Psychologie, Universität Frankfurt, Frankfurt, Germany

Ideal point response models are explored as an alternative explanation for item-keying related factors. In ideal point models it is assumed that the probability of endorsing an item is highest when trait score and the item's position on the latent continuum coincide; in contrast, factor analyses assume that endorsement probability increases with increasing trait scores on the latent continuum and thus can be high even when trait score and item location are far apart. Data from an extended optimism questionnaire serve to illustrate the difference of the approaches and the consequences of assuming the wrong response model.

Temporal stability of wording effects: Empirical evidence from short-term test-retest designs

Vautier, Stéphane Dept. of Psychology, Université de Toulouse, Toulouse, France

Wording effects can be defined as true-score differences due to semantic nuances conveyed by the items used in rating scales. The effect of semantic nuances on the measurement process can be analyzed at the item level or at the level of composite scales. Wording effects can be viewed as individual difficulty parameters. We show that in short-term test and retest designs, temporal stability of method effects can be assumed, as shown by appropriate structural equation models. These models permit to assess how method effects do bias the measurement of inter-individual variability on target constructs.

S-272: Bologna process: New challenges on higher education

Edith Braun (chair)
45 European countries agreed upon the Bologna process: the adoption of comparable higher education degrees. During this process, university teaching is supposed to become more focussed on fostering key competences and employability. Furthermore, the quality of higher education is required to be proved empirically. We will bring together five national views: Looking at the relation of teaching aspects and enhancement of competences (Schaeper/ Germany), the relation between higher education and employment (Arthur & Little/ UK), the possibilities of competence assessment (Baartman/ the Netherlands, Bieri & Schuler/ Switzerland, Maier & Paechter/ Austria), and emotional resistance while the changing process (Braun/ Germany).

What is value of higher education?
Arthur, Lore Faculty of Education, The Open University, Milton Keynes, United Kingdom **Little, Brenda** CHERI, Open University, London, United Kingdom
In the main, UK undergraduates spend less time on higher education and feel less prepared for work after graduation than those in most other European countries. UK employers, therefore, carry a considerable burden for staff development, again more so than is the case in most other EU countries. We will look at the value and purpose of higher education in light of Bologna and the relationship between higher education and graduate employment. The paper is based on recent findings of a major study "The Flexible Professional in the Knowledge Society" (REFLEX) within 13 EU countries and Japan (N=30.000).

Assessment of learning outcomes using competence assessment programmes
Baartman, Liesbeth Dept. Educational Sciences, Utrecht University, Utrecht, Netherlands
Higher education in the Netherlands increasingly focuses on competence development. Adequate methods to assess competence acquisition are therefore needed. This research focuses on Competence Assessment Programmes (CAPs), including traditional knowledge tests and methods such as performance assessments. Eight schools evaluated their CAP on twelve variables, including stimulation of self-regulated learning and effects on learning processes. Results show differences between "traditional" and "innovative" approaches towards competence assessment. Based on the results, a theory was developed to study the relationship between different learning environments, students' learning conceptions, and their learning outcomes in terms of learning activities (process) and test results (products).

Assessing future teachers' competence in an assessment centre
Bieri, Christine Entwicklung, Berufsidentität, Pädagogische Hochschule Zürich, Zürich, Switzerland **Schuler, Patricia** Zürich, Switzerland
There is increasing interest in teachers' cross-curricular competencies as a result of reforms in teacher training and the "Bologna Process". Teachers need a variety of social skills in order to succeed in their professional career. At the University of Teacher Education in Zurich future students who do not have the appropriate formal qualification, are required to pass several examinations and participate in an Assessment Centre as well. The underlying model of competencies is currently being evaluated in a longitudinal study. The initial findings regarding assessment validity

and self-other agreement are presented. The implications for practice are discussed as well.

Emotion within change management of higher education
Braun, Edith Schul- & Unterrichtsforschung, Freie Universität Berlin, Berlin, Germany
It is argued that teaching that deals with learning as an active process of constructing knowledge ("student-focused approach") is more effective than teaching seen as the transfer of knowledge ("teacher-focused approach"). Hypothesising that teachers' behaviour is influenced by their conceptions of learning, we investigate the correlation between these conceptions and their use of teaching techniques. We go on to prove that students report higher gains in competences when their lecturers have adopted a more distinct student-focused approach. However, as found previously, teacher-focused and student-focused approaches are two independent scales in our sample.

Evaluation of university courses by students' assessment of gains in competences
Maier, Brigitte Inst. Pädagogische Psychologie, Universität Graz, Graz, Austria **Pächter, Manuela** Inst. für Päd. Psychologie, Universität Graz, Graz, Austria
A model for the evaluation of university courses is introduced which assumes that university education should impart the general competence to act and to solve problems. This competence comprises several spheres such as expertise in the knowledge domain, professional, social and personal competence, plus (in media-based courses) media competence. Questionnaires were developed in which students are to assess their gains in various competence domains in a course. The test quality of the questionnaires proved to be very satisfactory. Besides, bias variables such as prior knowledge or interest in the course topic have little or even no influence on students' assessments.

The role of key competencies in the Bologna process: Rhetoric and reality
Schaeper, Hilde Absolventenstudien, HIS, Hannover, Germany
The Bologna process places special emphasis on the outcomes of higher education in terms of employability and key competencies. Taking Germany as an example, the paper examines the question whether the higher education reform actually has led to an enhanced acquisition of key competencies. Based on constructivist learning theories we, in addition, test the hypothesis that an activating learning environment enhances both, the acquisition of disciplinary and key competencies. We use data of a survey among higher education graduates of the academic year 2005. The results of the linear regression analyses allow conclusions about the ingredients of a competence-oriented teaching.

S-273: Perception and performance in real, complex environments

Friedrich Müller (chair)
Experimental studies are introduced which deal with perceptual processes and performance in complex everyday life situations. The presentations focus on method and experimental designs which take the specific environments into account.

Assessment of occupational exertion and strain in laboratory- and real occupational environments
Müller, Friedrich Inst. für Exp. Wirtschaftsps., Leuphana Universität Lüneburg, Lüneburg, Germany
In order to obtain veridical level information of work related load, measures of physical exertion

and mental strain are proposed which are based on the Category Partitioning (CP) procedure. The requirements for the application of the CP-technique are introduced together with experimental foundations of the procedure and various examples of industrial applications which verify the reliability and validity of the proposed measures and demonstrate the successful use in real occupational environments.

Perception-action dynamics of locomotion with extension of the body
Higuchi, Takahiro Dept. of Health Promotion Sc., Tokyo Metropolitan University, Tokyo, Japan
I report several experimental studies regarding how individuals safely pass through narrow openings when the space required for passage is transiently extended with external objects (e.g., carrying a shopping bag) when walking, using a wheelchair, or wearing shoulder pads as American football players do). On the basis of on the results obtained from my kinematic and psychophysical studies, I will demonstrate that individuals are able to perceive altered action capabilities for aperture crossing under a variety of form of locomotion with extensions, although this is likely to occur only for well-learned actions performed in realistic settings.

Learning musical expressions using visual feedback
Sadakata, Makiko Inst. for Cognition, Radboud University Nijmegen, Nijmegen, Netherlands **Timmers, Renee** Nijmegen Inst. for Cognition, Radboud University Nijmegen, Netherlands **Brandmeyer, Alex** Nijmegen Inst. for Cognition, Radboud University Nijmegen, Nijmegen, Netherlands **Desain, Peter** Nijmegen Inst. for Cognition, Radboud University Nijmegen, Nijmegen, Netherlands
Expressive performance of music is a complex behavior and it is learned usually by imitation of master musicians. This learning process usually does not contain explicit instruction about the physical parameters of the sound, such as change in timing and loudness. We aim at developing a feedback system that monitors students' performance and provides real time visual feedback of these physical parameters. We examined the effect of providing different types of visual feedback on the success of imitation. In general, the method seems to be helpful, although size and direction of the effect depend on the types of visual feedback.

Reaction times in automobile driving under various arousal states
Mori, Shuji Fac. of Informat. Science, Kyushu University, Fukuoka, Japan
Driving automobiles is quite complex human performance, and erroneous performance is likely to result in serious consequences. Driver's arousal state is a crucial factor in automobile driving, and it affects driver's reaction times to external signals. This paper reports our ongoing study investigating quantitative relation between drivers' reaction times and their arousal states. We measured reaction times in simulated driving situation under various arousal states while monitoring temporal changes in width between lower and upper eyelid, or eye-opening rate, as a measure of arousal states. The results confirm close relation between driver's arousal state and reaction time.

Movement planning under risk, decision making under risk
Maloney, Laurence Psychology and Neural Science, New York University, New York, USA
I'll present a statistical decision theoretic model of ideal movement planning that takes into account a subject's spatial and temporal motor uncertainty. I'll summarize experiments in which subjects carried

out speeded motor tasks Subjects consistently chose movements that were close to optimal. This outcome is surprising: these motor tasks are equivalent to decision making under risk and subjects making decisions under risk typically do not maximize expected gain. I'll describe recent work in which we translate classical decision making experiments (concerning the independence axiom) into motor form and compare decision making under risk to movement planning under risk.

Implicit processes in moral decision making: Why milliseconds matter

Marquardt, Nicki Inst. Exp. Wirtschaftspsychol., Leuphana Universität Lüneburg, Lüneburg, Germany Höger, Rainer Inst. für Exp. Wpsy, Leuphana Universität Lüneburg, Lüneburg, Germany Roidl, Ernst Inst. für Exp. Wpsy, Leuphana Universität Lüneburg, Lüneburg, Germany

The present study examines the relationship between implicit mental processes and moral decisions in business. Based on the dual-process view in implicit social cognition, it is argued that moral judgments can rely on two different modes of information processing (implicit vs. explicit processes). In order to test this assumption, several experiments were conducted. The participants were supposed to work on a complex ethical decision-making task. Implicit processes were assessed with latency-based measures (e.g. Implicit Association Test, Eye-Tracking). Different questionnaires were used to diagnose explicit judgmental processes. The results show that latency-based measures are a good predictor for moral decision making.

S-274: Large survey research on well-being and health: Similarities and differences in findings from Europe and the USA

Jacqui Smith, Felicia A. Huppert (chair)
Health is highly salient to a sense of well-being in the second half of life, but specific individual and societal contexts may influence the strength of the relationship. Speakers in this symposium present findings from three comparable representative surveys of over-50 populations: the Health and Retirement Study (HRS) in the USA, the English Longitudinal Study of Ageing (ELSA), and the Survey of Health, Ageing and Retirement in Europe (SHARE). Beyond the similar role of socioeconomic disparities in health in each country, variations in reported well-being are associated with nation-specific contexts and subgroup and individual differences in social roles and health dynamics.

Health and well-being: International comparisons in Europe

Boersch-Supran, Axel Economics of Aging, Mannheim Research, Mannheim, Germany
The social gradient of health disparities is well-documented. Does this extend to well-being? We examined this question using comparable data on health and well-being from 11 European countries from the 2004 Survey of Health, Ageing and Retirement in Europe (N = 11,273). Older persons in the north of Europe are better off financially and are in better health, but this does not translate into corresponding mortality differences. The strong relation between health and socioeconomic status also holds for mental health and well-being. Europe exhibits large variations in health, well-being and socio-economic status, potentially caused by different welfare policies.

Health has different effects on well-being in England and the United States

Clarke, Philippa Inst. for Social Research, University of Michigan, Ann Arbor, USA Weir, David Institute for Social Research, University of Michigan, Ann Arbor, MI, USA Smith, Jacqui Institute for Social Research, University of Michigan, Ann Arbor, MI, USA
We compare psychological well-being among adults over age 50 in the United States (HRS) and England (ELSA), and examine cross-national differences in the effect of disability on well-being. In all age groups, American adults report lower life satisfaction than adults in England (controlling for gender, marital status, and race/ethnicity). However, in the young old (age 65 to 80) and in the midlife period, American adults report a higher sense of control. In both countries, disability is associated with lower life satisfaction and decreased control. Disability is more problematic for control among American adults than for their English counterparts. These results highlight the divergent consequences of disability for well-being across nations.

Emotional adaptation after the onset of a serious physical disability

Smith, Dylan M. Dept. of Internal Medicine, University of Michigan, Ann Arbor, MI, USA Brown, Stephanie Dept. of Internal Medicine, University of Michigan, Ann Arbor, MI, USA Kabeto, Mohammed Dept. of Internal Medicine, University of Michigan, Ann Arbor, MI, USA Langa, Kenneth Dept. of Internal Medicine, University of Michigan, Ann Arbor, MI, USA
Although emotional adaptation - recovery of well being in the face of difficult circumstances- is a widespread phenomenon, recent studies cast some doubt about whether people can recover a substantial part of well being after highly adverse life events, such as new disabilities. We examined this issue using HRS data, and found a pattern consistent with hedonic adaptation; loss of well being just before and especially after the onset of a new disability, followed by an increase in well being over time. Respondents had regained about half of their lost well being by 6 years after the onset of disability.

Caregiving behavior is associated with decreased mortality risk

Brown, Stephanie L. Dept. of Internal Medicine, University of Michigan, Ann Arbor, USA Smith, Dylan Dept. of Internal Medicine, University of Michigan, Ann Arbor, MI, USA Schulz, Richard Ctr for Social& Urban Rese, University of Pittsburgh, Pittsburgh, PA, USA Kabeto, Mohammed Dept. of Internal Medicine, University of Michigan, Ann Arbor, MI, USA Ubel, Peter Dept. of Internal Medicine, University of Michigan, Ann Arbor, MI, USA Poulin, Michael Dept. of Internal Medicine, University of Michigan, Ann Arbor, MI, USA Kim, Catherine Dept. of Internal Medicine, University of Michigan, Ann Arbor, MI, USA Yi, Jaehee Dept. of Internal Medicine, University of Michigan, Ann Arbor, MI, USA Langa, Kenneth Dept. of Internal Medicine, University of Michigan, Ann Arbor, MI, USA
Caregivers have been shown to be at-risk for health problems, including increased mortality. However these findings are based largely on studies that do not measure caregiving behavior separately from the circumstance of having an ailing spouse (spousal need). We examined the separate influences of caregiving behavior and spousal need on 7-year mortality risk using the HRS data. Results of models adjusted for health and other demographics demonstrated that high levels of caregiving behavior were predictive of decreased mortality risk. These results are consistent with the growing research on the health benefits of helping others.

Psychological well-being is associated with higher levels of cognitive function

Llewellyn, David J. Dept. of Clinical Medicine, University of Cambridge, Cambridge, United Kingdom Lang, Iain Epidemiology & Pub. Health, Peninsula Medical School, Exeter, United Kingdom Lang, Kenneth Dept. of Internal Medicine, University of Michigan, Ann Arbor, MI, USA Huppert, Felicia Department of Psychiatry, University of Cambridge, Cambridge, United Kingdom
While depression is related to poor cognitive function, little is known about the relationship between psychological well-being and cognitive function. We investigated this in 11,234 non-institutionalized adults aged 50+ in the English Longitudinal Study of Ageing (ELSA). Psychological well-being, measured by the CASP-19, was positively associated with cognitive function after adjusting for depressive symptoms, physical health, health-related behaviors, and sociodemographic factors. Similar associations were observed for men and women, and across several different domains of cognitive function. These findings are consistent with evidence that positive mental states can improve cognitive processes, and may have implications for rates of cognitive decline.

S-275: Coping with cancer

Shulamith Kreitler, Marek Blatny (chair)
The symposium deals with coping with cancer, focusing on major themes concerning intervention methods in psychooncology: quality of life of children with cancer (Blatny et al.), a psycho-educational intervention for improving the quality of life of children with cancer (Last et al.), the application of hypnotherapy as an intervention method in the first phase for adults with cancer (Banyai), psychoanalytic approaches to helping cancer patients in the course of their disease (Ayzenberg), assessing the results of intervention methods with cancer patients (Kryspin-Exner et al.), and identifying patients who may benefit most from social support (Kreitler).

The Brno Quality of Life Longitudinal Study of Pediatric Oncology Patients (QOLOP): Results from the pilot study

Blatny, Marek Dept. of Psychology, Academy of Sciences, Brno, Czech Republic Kepak, Tomas Dpt. of Paediatric Oncology, Children's Medical Center, Brno, Czech Republic Vlckova, Irena Dept. of Pediatric Oncology, Children's Medical Center, Brno, Czech Republic Pilat, Milan Dept. of Psychology, Children's Medical Center, Brno, Czech Republic Jelinek, Martin Inst. of Psychology, Academy of Sciences, Brno, Czech Republic Navratilova, Petra Inst. of Psychology, Masaryk Univ., Faculty of Arts, Brno, Czech Republic Slezackova, Alena Inst. of Psychology, Masaryk Univ., Faculty of Arts, Brno, Czech Republic
Along with a growing number of child cancer survivors the late effects of anticancer therapy and the quality of life have become the focus of attention. In the first part of the presentation we give information about the Brno Quality of Life Longitudinal Study of Pediatric Oncology Patients (qolop) that seeks to identify the main ways in which the quality of life of child cancer-survivors is affected, both in terms of objective indicators (mobility, sensory functioning) and subjective perceptions of wellbeing. In the second part we give overview of results from the first year of study.

Positive effects of a psycho-educational group intervention for children and teenagers with cancer: A pilot study

Last, Bob Psychosocial Pediatric, Academic Medical Center, Amsterdam, Netherlands Maurice-Stam, Heleen Psychosocial Pediatric, Academic Medical Center, Amsterdam, Netherlands Grootenhuis,

Martha Psychosocial Pediatric, Academic Medical Center, Amsterdam, Netherlands

OBJECTIVE: In two pilot studies the usefulness of a psycho-educational group intervention based on principles from cognitive behavior therapy was evaluated in children with cancer. METHODS: Evaluation of the group intervention was done by standardized measures. RESULTS: In study 1 a total of 20 patients (ages 12-18 years) participated. In study 2 a total of 11 patients (ages 8-12 years) took part. In both studies improvements were found in behavioral-emotional outcomes, social competence, information seeking, relaxation and positive thinking. CONCLUSIONS: The program appears to have a significant and positive impact on children and teenagers with cancer.

The "new look" in helping cancer patients: Conceptualizing cancer as a chance

Banyai, Eva Dept. of Psychology, Eötvös Loránd University, Budapest, Hungary

Since the shock of the seemingly life threatening diagnosis of cancer induces an altered state of consciousness, patients become extremely susceptible to suggestions. In this situation hypnotherapy and suggestive techniques may be especially helpful in making patients realize their chance for survival. Therapeutic cases from my practice illustrate how hypnotherapy can help patients make up their mistakes, straighten their relationships, set a new life-goal, promote experiencing the spiritual dimension of life, and facing death as the ultimate question of existence. Hypnotherapy is also very effective in communicating social support, thus it may help patients mobilize their inner resources.

Needs analysis and evaluation of psychosocial interventions for cancer patients

Kryspin-Exner, Ilse Inst. für Psychologie, Universität Wien, Wien, Austria *Winkler, Verena* Inst. für Psychologie, Universität Wien, Wien, Austria

Discrepancies exist between needs, offers and the requirement of psychological interventions for cancer patients. While a high percentage would need psychological support, only a few use appropriate offers. Reasons might be patients' fears of being labelled as mentally disordered and the incongruence between medical staff perceptions' and the actual patients' needs. The implementation of day hospitals and outpatient treatment necessitates psychooncological offers in this area. Therefore, outpatient psychological counselling services should be evaluated for enhancing their acceptance. To emphasize that, results of a pilot study evaluating psychosocial support offers for families with hereditary brestcancer will be presented.

When Kohut meets Sisyphus in oncology institute

Ayzenberg, Aviva Dept. of Oncology, Kaplan Medical Center, Rehovot, Israel *Efrat Ben Baruch, Noa* Dept. of Oncology, Kaplan Medical Center, Rehovot, Israel

Significant lengthening of life expectancy in metastatic patients and improvement in life quality, create exciting challenges for psychotherapy. In these stages of illness a patient can be metaphorically described as image of Sisyphus: carrying a heavy rock up the hill, never succeeding in climbing the top. Could he be happy, facing his human existence and fate? Psychotherapy should represent encounter of two traditions: Existential stance which deals with issues of "being" and "meaning" and Self psychology which tries to work through narcissistic pain enacted by illness. A case study integrating elements of those two psychotherapeutic attitudes will be presented.

The benefits of social support

Kreitler, Shulamith Dept. of Psychology, Tel-Aviv University, Tel-Aviv, Israel

The goal was to identify in cancer patients psychological correlates of readiness to use social support. The participants were 167 patients of both genders, with different cancer diagnoses and in different disease stages. They were administered questionnaires assessing the use of different kinds of social support and a cognitive orientation questionnaire assessing motivational tendencies for using social support. Discriminant and multiple regression analyses showed that the cognitive orientation variables provided good predictions of the use of social support. The results enable identifying patients who can benefit from social support and those who need help for using this coping resource.

S-276: Assessing serotonergic neurotransmission with Intensity Dependence of Auditory-Evoked Potentials (IDAEP): Neurochemical findings and clinical utility

Tilman Hensch, Ulrich Hegerl (chair)

This symposium will discuss recent progress in neurobiological underpinnings, methodological aspects and clinical applications of Intensity Dependence of Auditory-Evoked Potentials (IDAEP). After an overview of IDAEP research covering all data levels from genes to psychopathology (Hensch), animal (Juckel& Uhl) and human (O'Neill & Croft) studies validating the serotonin-hypothesis of IDAEP will be reported. Biological influences that should be considered in study-design (Gallinat) will be discussed. Technical aspects must be accounted for in assessments of intensity dependence with simultaneous EEG/fMRI registration (Mulert). Finally, the clinical value of IDAEP will be discussed: predicting treatment response to antidepressants (Hegerl) and assessing neurotoxity of Ecstasy (Daumann).

Correlates of intensity dependence of auditory-evoked potentials (IDAEP): From genes to behavior

Hensch, Tilman Inst. für Psychology II, Technische Universität Dresden, Dresden, Germany *Brocke, Burkhard* Psychology II, TU Dresden, Dresden, Germany

This talk gives an overview of correlates of IDAEP from genetic data, via biochemical, up to personality and psychopathology. The speakers' own recent results for each data level will also be given. The usefulness of IDAEP will be outlined. The discussion will consider that the revival of IDAEP only recently began when the theory of IDAEP as an indicator of serotonergic neurotransmission was introduced, thereby explaining the various associations with serotonergic modulated traits and solving apparent discrepancies. Furthermore, new applications could be derived from that theory. Open questions will be summarized, and a standardizing of the paradigm will be recommended.

Preclinical studies on the relationship between IDAEP and the central serotonergic neurotransmission

Juckel, Georg Inst. für Psychiatrie, Ruhr-Universität Bochum, Bochum, Germany *Uhl, Idun* Inst. für Psychiatrie, Ruhr-Universität Bochum, Bochum, Germany

Two animal studies validating IDAEP as an indicator of serotonergic neurotransmission are presented. In cats, the firing rate of dorsal raphe nucleus neurons was reduced or increased by microinjection of a 5-HT1A agonist and antagonist, respectively. AEPs were recorded from the auditory cortices. We found a stronger IDAEP at the

primary auditory cortex after inhibiting the firing rate of serotonergic neurons, and vice versa. In rats, we found negative correlations between extracellular serotonin in the auditory cortex (measured by in-vivo microdialysis) and the IDAEP recorded from the same area. These results support that IDAEP is inversely related to serotonergic activity.

IDAEP and the serotonin, dopamine and glutamate systems: Results from acute challenges in humans

O'Neill, Barry Brain Sciences Institute, Swinburne University of Techno, Hawthorn, Australia *Croft, Rodney James* Brain Sciences Institute, Swinburne Univ. of Technology, Hawthorn, Australia *Segrave, Rebecca* Brain Sciences Institute, Swinburne University of Techno, Hawthorn, Australia *Guille, Valerie* Brain Sciences Institute, Swinburne University of Techno, Hawthorn, Australia *Nathan, Pradeep J.* Dept. of Psychiatry, Cambridge University, Cambridge, United Kingdom

This presentation reports on five, double-blind, placebo-controlled repeated-measures studies, testing for effects of acute pharmacological manipulations on IDAEP. Results indicated only partial support for the sensitivity of IDAEP to acute 5-HT change, as 5-HT augmentation reduced IDAEP in one but not a second study, and 5-HT reduction did not affect IDAEP. Support for the selectivity of IDAEP to 5-HT was indicated in that neither dopamine augmentation nor reduction affected IDAEP, however, glycine reduced IDAEP, suggesting that systems other than 5-HT can modulate IDAEP. Results are interpreted in light of methodological issues (gender, and the acute/chronic and scalp EEG/DSA distinctions).

Genetics, biological aspects and environmental modulators of IDAEP

Gallinat, Jürgen Klinik für Psychiatrie, Charité Medizin Berlin, Berlin, Germany

Genetic variations of the serotonin transporter linked polymorphic region (S allele as well as LA and LG alleles) have been implicated in the pathogenesis of psychiatric disorders, which are themselves linked to dysfunctional serotonergic neurotransmission. IDAEP as a proposed in vivo indicator of central serotonergic neurotransmission has been shown to be abnormal in psychiatric diseases and is associated with genetic variations of the serotonin system. This presentation will focus on the retest reliability, heritability and methodology of the IDAEP as necessary preconditions for use in intermediate phenotype research. Additionally, smoking, alcohol consumption, and other modulating factors of IDAEP are discussed.

Multimodal data on intensity dependence: EEG and fMRI

Mulert, Christoph Inst. für Psychiatrie, Universität München, München, Germany *Pogarell, Oliver* Dept. of Psychiatry, University of Munich, Munich, Germany

Sound level dependence has been investigated for years with event related potentials (ERP). Recent fMRI studies described a pronounced intensity dependence only in the primary auditory cortex but not in auditory association areas. In the present simultaneous EEG and fMRI study we found a high correlation between the intensity dependent change of the extent of fMRI activation (number of activated voxels) and the corresponding changes of the mean current source density within the same region of interest covering the primary auditory cortex ($r=0.84$, $p<0.001$). Our findings suggest a close relationship between the fMRI signal and event-related potential activity.

Differential prediction of clinical response to antidepressants by IDAEP?

Hegerl, Ulrich *Inst. für Psychiatrie, Universität Leipzig, Leipzig, Germany* **Pogarell, Oliver** *Dept. of. Psychiatry, University of Munich, Munich, Germany*

A considerable proportion of patients with major depression do not respond to the first antidepressant administered. Non-response constitutes an enormous burden to the patient, as therapeutic outcome cannot be assessed for at least two to three weeks and antidepressants often involve side effects. In previous studies IDAEP could predict treatment response to antidepressants. This talk will discuss the status and usability of treatment response prediction with IDAEP and will also present the speaker's own recent data, including differential response prediction to serotonergic versus noradrenergic antidepressants.

IDAEP in ecstasy (MDMA) users: Evidence for serotonergic dysfunction

Daumann, Jörg *Inst. für Psychiatrie, Universität Köln, Köln, Germany* **Gouzoulis-Mayfrank, E.** *Dept. of. Psychiatry, University of Cologne, Cologne, Germany*

Animal studies demonstrated neurotoxic damage to central serotonergic systems after exposure to 3,4-methylenedioxymethamphetamine (MDMA, ecstasy). A high intensity dependence of auditory evoked potentials (IDAEP) is associated with a low functioning of serotonergic activity. Therefore, we used IDAEP for a possible neurotoxic damage in 18 polydrug ecstasy users at baseline and after 18 months. Ecstasy use was associated with the IDAEP at both measuring times. However, we failed to demonstrate any significant relationship between interim drug use and AEP changes. These data suggest, yet do not unambiguously confirm the hypothesis that abstinent ecstasy users present with diminished central serotonergic activity.

S-277: Cultural influences on identity development

Ulrich Schmidt-Denter, Claudia Quaiser-Pohl *(chair)*

The symposium deals with cultural influences on personal and social development across the lifespan. Papers presented focus on comparisons between different European countries. The studies analyze patterns of national identity and their relation to personal functioning, intergenerational transmission of attitudes towards minorities, sex differences in adolescence, cultural determinants of the transition to parenthood and acculturation orientations of naturalized immigrants. Results will be discussed in terms of the challenges of globalization and of multicultural societies.

Patterns of national identity in cross-cultural comparison

Schmidt-Denter, Ulrich *Inst. für Psychologie, Universität zu Köln, Köln, Germany*

The study examines the development of personal and social identity in ten European countries (N = 4312 adolescents and their parents). From intercultural perspective measures of national identity showed the most significant differences. Theories of national identity from the literature are critically discussed, because mostly an intercultural generalization has not been proved. According to our own approach data show that basic patterns of national identity are equal in all countries, but that there are also some specific differences. Across cultures similar relations were found between the types of national identity and variables of personal identity (e.g. self-esteem).

The role of intergenerational transmission for out-group rejection with female adolescents

Schick, Hella *Inst. für Bildung, Universität zu Köln, Köln, Germany*

The contribution investigates the effects of personal and familial variables on negative attitudes of adolescent girls towards foreigners and Jews. Personal variables (information seeking, self-evaluation, fear of future, tolerance) were considered in comparison to the agreement with the attitudes of their parents, education style and closeness of family relations. Relationships and mediator effects were examined by structural equation modelling (N=200). The proposed model explains 45% of the variance of out-group rejection. The transferability to several European countries is discussed. The results indicate that information seeking and the adoption of tolerant positions play a more prominent role than the parental influence.

Development of personal identity of adolescents in Austria in comparison to other European countries

Werneck, Harald *Fakultät für Psychologie, Universität Wien, Wien, Austria* **Rabl, Martina** *Faculty of Psychology, University of Vienna, Vienna, Austria* **Berger, Ute** *General and Social Psychology, University of Cologne, Cologne, Germany* **Maehler, Deborah** *General and Social Psychology, University of Cologne, Cologne, Germany* **Schick, Hella** *General and Social Psychology, University of Cologne, Cologne, Germany* **Schmidt-Denter, Ulrich** *General and Social Psychology, University of Cologne, Cologne, Germany*

The study presented in this paper is part of the research project "Personal and Social Identity in the Context of Globalization and National Differentiation". It focuses on the analysis of the development of personal identity, in particular on sex differences. Therefore a battery of questionnaires, taken from the framework project, concerning different aspects of personal identity was administered to 656 Austrian adolescents. The results show that girls score higher in self awareness than boys, corresponding e.g. with less self esteem and more being depressed. Besides female adolescents achieve earlier than male adolescents the status of identity achievement according to Marcia.

Parenthood from a cross-culutral perspective: Socio-cultural changes, values, and well-being of Spanish and German parents

Grohmann, Anna-Catharina *Institute of Psychology, Georg-August Uni. of Göttingen, Göttingen, Germany* **Quaiser-Pohl, Claudia** *Institute of Psychology, University of Siegen, Siegen, Germany* **Hasselhorn, Marcus** *Center Education & Develop, dipf, Frankfurt / Main, Germany*

In a questionnaire study the values and the well-being of 92 Spanish and 79 German parents during the first years after the birth of their child were compared. Contrary to expectation, Spanish mothers and fathers were more individualistic and less family-oriented, showed higher approval for traditional attitudes, and did not report higher parental well-being than German parents. These results can be interpreted with regard to changes in cultural and individual values accompanying the rapid development of the Spanish society during the last 30 years and against the background of the wide political discussion on day care in Germany nowadays.

Acculturation orientations of naturalized immigrants in Germany

Maehler, Debora *Inst. für Psychologie, Universität zu Köln, Köln, Germany*

The scope of the longitudinal study is the process of acculturation and identification of naturalized immigrants (N=300). This presentation deals with the acculturation orientations of "new Germans"

(first wave). Acculturation is based on the concept of Berry (1997), and is assessed by a two-statement method and analysed by a cluster-analytic and discriminant procedure. The analysis classifies three clusters: an integrated, an assimilated and an indifferent oriented group. The results do not exactly agree with Berry's assumption, rather a new profile is suggested. Moreover the different groups are distinguished by their socio-demographic background, motives for naturalization and identification.

S-278: Reactions to alarms and warnings

J. Elin Bahner, Monica De Filippis *(chair)*

Alarms and warnings indicate a state or situation that might result in danger. To prevent harm, an alarm has to be detected, understood, and complied with. Research focuses on different problems: First, warnings have to be noticed and understood. Open issues concern warning modalities and conveyed urgency levels. Second, no alarm system works totally reliable, therefore operators have to deal with false and missing alarms. This results in different levels of reliance and compliance. The symposium focuses on both, how an ideal warning should look like, and how erroneous warnings might affect human performance and trust.

Driving by the seat of your pants! A multisensory approach to capturing driver attention

Spence, Charles *Dept. of Psychology, University of Oxford, Oxford, United Kingdom*

The increasing availability of complex in-vehicle technologies means that 'driver inattention' still represent one of the leading causes of car accidents. The question therefore arises as to how best to alert 'distracted' drivers to potential road dangers. I will review the latest laboratory- and simulator-based studies from the Crossmodal Research Laboratory in Oxford detailing a novel brain-based approach to the design of auditory, tactile, and multisensory warnings signals. I will highlight the research that demonstrates the potential for improving driver behavior in potentially dangerous situations and so reducing the incidence of road traffic accidents that such multisensory warning signals offer.

Validity of uni-, cross-, and multimodal alarms: Effects on reactions

De Filippis, Monica *Inst. für Kognitive Ergonomiks, Technische Universität Berlin, Berlin, Germany*

Alarms are signals of a system to a user on any status that might result in danger. Therefore, the ideal alarm is detectable, understandable and acceptable, resulting in an appropriate and accelerated reaction. We investigated benefits of multimodal alarms - i.e. alarms presented in two modalities simultaneously - for perception, understanding, and reactions in a dual task paradigm. Subjects performed a driving-like tracking task while detecting auditory and visual signals. Visual and auditory alarms were presented in uni-, cross, as well as multimodal conditions. Results prove, that multimodal warnings have to be applied carefully and weighed up against unimodal warnings.

Responses to warnings reconsidered: Reliance and compliance in discrete and continuous tasks

Meyer, Joachim *Dep. of Indust. Engineering, Ben Gurion University, Beer Sheva, Israel*

Predicting users' responses to warning information is a challenge, because warnings can affect behavior both when they are given (compliance) and when they are absent (reliance). The paper discusses the measurement of the two types of responses to warnings in discrete tasks, where probabilities of responses can be computed, and in continuous tasks, such as driving, in which the effects of warnings are expressed as changes in driving speed. Experimental results supporting the distinction between these two responses in the different tasks are presented, and their implications for understanding the function of warnings in regulating behavior are discussed.

The effects of automation misses on reliance, complacency and automation bias

Bahner, J. Elin Arbeits- und Org.-Psychologie, Technische Universität Berlin, Berlin, Germany Elepfandt, Monika Work, Engin. & Organis. Ps, Berlin Univ. of Technology, Berlin, Germany Manzey, Dietrich Work, Engin. & Organis. Ps, Berlin Univ. of Technology, Berlin, Germany
Objective: The effects of misses of an automated alarm and fault diagnosis system (AFDS) on different manifestations of automation misuse were examined. Method: 24 participants interacted with an AFDS in a process control task. During training, they either experienced that the AFDS failed to detect a critical state or were only informed that such failures might occur. Results: Experience of misses reduced reliance on AFDS but did not affect complacency and commission errors in case of a correct alarm but false diagnosis. Conclusion: Results demonstrate the effects of failures on automation misuse and elucidate the interrelation of its manifestations in more detail.

The effects of automation bias and saliency on operator trust

Rice, Stephen Dept. of Psychology, New Mexico State University, Las Cruces, USA McCarley, Jason Dept. of Psychology, University of Illinois, Champaign, USA
Objective: To examine the effects of automation errors on operator responses to alerts (compliance) and non-alerts (reliance). Methods: Participants performed a mock luggage screening task aided by imperfectly reliable diagnostic automation. Framing of the automation's recommendations was manipulated such that errors were either explicit or implicit. Results: When errors were explicit, compliance and reliance were both reduced by automation false-alarms and misses. When errors were implicit, compliance was compromised only by FAs, and reliance only by misses. Conclusions: Crossover effects of automation FAs and misses are mediated the framing of the automation's recommendations.

Pilots' response time to complete alarm procedures as a function of alarm relevance

Newlin, Elizabeth Dept. of Psychology, Old Dominion University, Norfolk, USA Bustamante, Ernesto Psychology & Communication, University of Idaho, Moscow, ID, USA Bliss, James Dept. of Psychology, Old Dominion University, Norfolk, VA, USA Turner, Timothy Dept. of Psychology, Old Dominion University, Norfolk, VA, USA
Pilots often must prioritize task reactions. Past research has shown that low reliability degrades alarm reaction time. The purpose of this study was to investigate the role of alarm relevance on reaction time. Because cabin pressurization alarms occurring above 25,000 feet MSL are more relevant, we expected pilots to react to such alarms faster. Twelve commercial pilots completed a simulated flight using Microsoft Flight Simulator ™. They responded to 20 pressurization alarms presented at different altitudes. Repeated measures ANOVAs indicated that pilots reacted to relevant alarms significantly faster. These results suggest that alarm relevance may supersede reliability in piloting situations.

S-279: Human-machine interaction (Part II): Reliability and validity of usability-tests

Kai-Christoph Hamborg, Jürgen Sauer (chair)
Usability testing is considered the gold standard of formative design evaluation. But up to now basic concepts in usability testing are ill-defined. Moreover, standards defining procedures and methods of usability testing are still missing. Hence, usability tests suffer from a lack of validity and reliability. This symposium addresses factors that impair the validity and reliability of usability tests as well as conceptual and methodological remedies. These include a psychologically motivated definition of the term "usability problem" as well as findings about the impact of contextual fidelity and strengths and weaknesses of special testing methods on the quality of usability tests.

Quality assurance in usability-testing: Problems and approaches to solutions

Hamborg, Kai-Christoph Inst. für Psychologie, Universität Osnabrück, Osnabrück, Germany
Recent research has given reason to doubt the validity and reliability of usability tests. Beside lack of standardization of methods and procedures, one of the most serious reasons for this shortcoming is in our view, that the term "usability problem" is ill-defined. As a result theoretically derived criteria supporting a reasonable choice of testing methods and approaches for data analysis are missing. Therefore a psychologically motivated definition of the concept "usability problem" in terms of action theory will be presented, its application exemplified by empirical data and consequences concerning data gathering and analysis discussed from a methodological point of view

The concept of contextual fidelity in usability tests: Empirical evidence from a research programme

Sauer, Jürgen Dept. of Psychology, University of Fribourg, Fribourg, Switzerland Sonderegger, Andreas Dept. of Psychology, University of Fribourg, Fribourg, Switzerland
Guided by the framework of contextual fidelity, this paper presents findings from three empirical studies that examined various factors that may threaten the validity of usability tests. Different interactive consumer products (e.g., mobile phone) were examined in typical set-ups of usability tests. The work identified aesthetics of design as a product feature that influences the outcomes of usability tests with regard to perceived usability and user behaviour. Prototype fidelity (e.g., computer vs. paper prototypes) emerged as a further factor that influenced user performance but did not show effects on attractiveness and perceived usability. The implications of the work for usability practitioners are discussed.

Constructive interaction method in usability testing

Sonderegger, Andreas Inst. für Psychologie, Universität Fribourg, Fribourg, Switzerland Sauer, Jürgen Dept. of Psychology, University of Fribourg, Fribourg, Switzerland
In this paper, usability testing in pairs is compared with evaluation of individuals using the retrospective think-aloud method. In a 2x2 mixed design, testing method was used as between-subjects variable with 20 participants in the single evaluation condition and 20 dyads in the group condition. Task difficulty was varied at two levels: low and high (within-subjects variable). The results revealed an interaction effect of evaluation method and task difficulty with individuals performing better in simple tasks and groups in difficult tasks. The

implications on choice of evaluation method and tasks in usability tests are discussed.

Eye-tracking as a method in usbility-testing

Burmester, Michael Fakultät Information und Komm., Hochschule der Medien, Stuttgart, Germany Weinhold, Thomas Informationswissenschaft, University of Applied Sciences, Chur, Switzerland
The objective was to clarify whether eye tracking offers added value for usability testing. A classical formative usability test was conducted using thinking aloud and behaviour observation. During the tests all eye movements were registered and in a retrospective thinking-aloud session the test participants had to comment their eye movements and behaviour. Qualitative analysis was applied to verbal and observation protocols and statistical analysis to eye movement data. All usability problems were already identified in the formative usability test. Eye-tracking and retrospective thinking-aloud provided additional information in order to understand some of the usability problems in a more comprehensive way.

Reliability of eye trackingdata in usability testing

Lesemann, Elisabeth User Experience, SirValUse Consulting GmbH, Hamburg, Germany Wilms, Ulla PR- und Werbeagentur, Media Consulta, Berlin, Germany
Gaze paths and attention distributions of different users on websites show a high degree of variation, rendering the reliability and validity of eye tracking results in usability testing doubtful. In a large study involving 393 users we explored the issue of sample size in eye tracking of homepages by comparing the results of increasingly smaller sub samples to the results of the whole sample using the equivalence test (as suggested by Schlittgen, 1996). Our results indicate that the required sample size is far higher than the typical sample size of 10-15 users (according to Heinsen & Scheier, 2003).

S-280: Learning with dynamic visualizations: Cognitive and design issues

Mireille Betrancourt, Tim Kuehl (chair)
Animations are often used in educational software. However, the research failed to show a clear superiority of dynamic over static visualizations for learning. This symposium will present studies that tackle the cognitive processes underlying the comprehension of dynamic visualizations. Boucheix & Lowe investigated how information is extracted from dynamic visualizations. Kühl, Gerjets & Scheiter surveyed think aloud protocols from subjects learning with dynamic or other types of visualizations. The other three studies are dealing with related instructional factors - like realism (Imhof et al.), interactivity and learning setting (Bétrancourt & Borer) and speed and cueing (Fischer & Schwan). From an educational perspective, the results of the studies can provide guidelines on how to design more effective multimedia instructions.

Eye tracking as a basis for improving animation design

Boucheix, Jean-Michel LEAD, University of Burgundy, Dijon, France Lowe, Ric Department of Education, Curtin UNiversity, Perth, Australia
We explore the utility of eye tacking indicators such as fixations, transitions between areas of interest and "scan paths" as tools for understanding how individuals extract information from a technical complex animation. We report a series of experiments involving verbal description, the effect of cues on comprehension, and the development of comprehension during the course of the animation. The techniques used in these investigations and

their results will be discussed in terms of the opportunities that eye tracking approaches offer for studying the on-line processes involved in an individual's development of a high quality mental model from an animation.

Effects of dynamic and static visualizations in understanding natural science phenomena

Kuehl, Tim Institut für Wissensmedien, KMRC, Tübingen, Germany Scheiter, Katharina Applied Cognitive Psychology, University of Tuebingen, Tübingen, Germany Gerjets, Peter Knowledge Acquisition with Hyp, KMRC, Tübingen, Germany

The effects of dynamic and static visualizations in understanding physical principles of fish locomotion were investigated. Seventy-five students were randomly assigned to one of three conditions: text-only, text with static visualizations or text with dynamic visualizations. All subjects had to think aloud. Learning outcomes were measured by means of factual knowledge and transfer tasks. Learning performances did not differ between the static and the dynamic condition. However, learners of the two visualization conditions outperformed the text-only condition significantly for transfer tasks, but not for factual knowledge tasks. These results reveal the importance of visualizations for students understanding of natural sciences.

Realism in understanding fish locomotion from dynamic or static visualizations

Imhof, Birgit Institut für Wissensmedien, IWM - KMRC, Tübingen, Germany Scheiter, Katharina Applied Cognitive Psychology, University of Tuebingen, Tübingen, Germany Gerjets, Peter Knowledge Acquisition with Hyp, IWM - KMRC, Tübingen, Germany

The role of dynamism and realism in visualizations for knowledge acquisition in a dynamic domain (fish locomotion) was investigated. Eighty-nine university students were randomly assigned to four conditions (dynamic-realistic, dynamic-schematic, static-realistic, static-schematic). Learning outcomes were measured by factual-knowledge-tests, recognition-tests, and prediction-tests of future movement states. Data analyses revealed no differences in learning outcomes for factual knowledge. Learners recognized more fishes correctly in the dynamic than in the static conditions. And learners predicted more future states accurately in the schematic than in the realistic conditions. These results suggest a differentiated view of visualizations with regard to learning conditions and task demands.

Does interactivity benefit learning from dynamic visualizations in individual or collaborative setting?

Betrancourt, Mireille TECFA Psychology and Education, University of Geneva, Carouge, Switzerland Borer, Ruedi TECFA Psychology and Education, University of Geneva, Carouge / GE, Switzerland

This contribution reports a classroom study investigating the effect of the level of interactivity of dynamic visualizations explaining biological phenomena (osmosis and diffusion) on the memorization of explicit or incidental information. Two factors were involved in the design: the level of interactivity of the visualizations (interactive simulation or self-paced animation) and the learning setting (individual or in pair). The results show that in collaborative setting, interactivity did not affect learning performance for explicit information, while in individual setting, more interactivity decreased learning performance. These results are discussed in terms of cognitive processes involved in learning from dynamic visualizations.

Temporal manipulations for animation design: Presentation speed outperforms cueing

Fischer, Sebastian Inst. für Wissensmedien, IWM - KMRC, Tübingen, Germany Schwan, Stephan Knowledge Acquisition with Cyp, KMRC, Tübingen, Germany

Previous studies have shown that manipulating presentation speed of a clockwork animation affects distribution of attention and comprehension. To further investigate influence of attention guidance, normal vs. fast speed presentation was combined with cueing either relevant parts weight or pendulum, or an irrelevant gear, in a 2x3 between group design with 144 subjects. Results show whilst cueing had effects on subjective measures, comprehension measured by written descriptions of how the clock functions was solely influenced by presentation speed. We conclude that comprehension improvement through fast speed presentation is a result not merely of attention guidance, but of emphasising dynamic properties.

S-281: How political transitions affect the ethical practice of psychology

Michael Stevens, Jean Pettifor (chair)

Political events and forces impact the structure and dynamics of society. Psychology is susceptible to political transitions. Education, research, and practice in psychology mirror a society's political stability, health, and accessibility versus turbulence, dysfunction, and exclusiveness. Codes of ethics in psychology are not immune from political transitions. Ethics codes, designed to protect the public and guide psychologists, are often weakened by political transitions in ways that compromise psychological science and practice and, ultimately, may pose a threat to society. In this symposium, psychologists from five countries discuss the impact of political transitions on their country's psychological code of ethics.

Do ethics codes in psychology mirror political change?

Stevens, Michael Dept. fo Psychology, Illinois State University, Normal, USA

I examine how political events and forces shape codes of ethics in psychology, particularly when these macro-level events and forces transform the structure and dynamics of the society in which psychology is situated. I illustrate how ethics codes are socially constructed by sampling from the general principles and specific standards of ethics codes in countries that have transitioned from communism, military dictatorship, or racist oppression or from peacetime to wartime status. I offer a conceptual framework with which to identify ethics codes at-risk; that is, countries where political events and forces jeopardize the ethical practice of psychology.

Political change and professional ethics of psychology in East Germany

Rösler, Hans-Dieter Inst. für Medizin. Psychologie, Universität Rostock, Rostock, Germany

To disclose consequences of the German reunification for the professional orientation of psychologists in East Germany programmatic statements of psychological committees were analysed. Psychology in East Germany was supposed to contribute to forming a socialist system and its cadres. In West Germany, psychology primarily serves the individual and emphasizes on vigilance towards influences leading to malpractice of psychology. These principles entailed ideological relieve to psychologists of the former GDR, but transition problems occurred regarding changed professionalism in a free-market economy. Now, precise ethical guidelines ensure political freedom for them and

contribute to competition with colleagues and related professions.

A South American experience of the transition from dictatorship to democracy

Ferrero, Andrea Dept. of Human Sciences, National University, San Luis, Argentina

When psychology was striving to get its legal recognition, a military coup that took place in 1976 stopped this process. From 1976 to 1983, Argentina lived under a dictatorship: the House of Representatives and the Senate were closed, and many people were jailed or made disappeared. As psychology became an almost persecuted profession, the few initial psychologists' associations were closed, and psychologists worked without any legal support as no ethics codes had yet been developed. In 1983 democracy allowed the previous process to continue, and psychologists' associations were finally legally recognized and developed their own ethics codes.

Ethical code for psychologists: Relevance to post-apartheid South Africa

Wassenaar, Douglas School of Psychology, University of KwaZulu-Natal, Pietermaritzburg, South Africa

South Africa has undergone dramatic political and social changes since 1994. A new democratic dispensation and progressive national constitution enshrining human rights have been adopted. Ethical guidelines for psychologists have not changed dramatically during this period, however. This paper examines whether revisions to the South African ethical guidelines are necessary in the light of these social and political changes, and, if so, explores the nature of any changes that might be indicated. Guidelines are expected to accommodate the expectations of a culturally, socially, economically and politically diverse society, and guide psychologists in a wide range of activities and settings.

Ethical code for psychologists: Relevance to post-apartheid South Africa

Mkhize, Nhlanhla School of Psychology, University of KwaZulu-Natal, Pietermaritzburg, South Africa

South Africa has undergone dramatic political and social changes since 1994. A new democratic dispensation and progressive national constitution enshrining human rights have been adopted. Ethical guidelines for psychologists have not changed dramatically during this period, however. This paper examines whether revisions to the South African ethical guidelines are necessary in the light of these social and political changes, and, if so, explores the nature of any changes that might be indicated. Guidelines are expected to accommodate the expectations of a culturally, socially, economically and politically diverse society, and guide psychologists in a wide range of activities and settings.

S-283: Research in aviation psychology

Claudia Marggraf-Micheel (chair)

In the field of aviation psychology new research has been done regarding safety and comfort. The first of the two key topics, which will be presented, focuses on the development and optimization of personnel selection in operational working fields (situational awareness, multiple task performance, interpersonal competence). The second key topic emphasizes the analyses of occupational stress factors and passenger comfort within aircraft cabins. An analysis of stress in service work, which points out relevant resources and stressors, and research concerning thermal comfort and passengers well-being will be presented.

Group assessment of performance and behavior

Zinn, Frank *Aviation and Space Psychology, German Aerospace Center, Hamburg, Germany* **Oubaid, Viktor** *Aviation and Space Psychology, German Aerospace Center, Hamburg, Germany* **Klein, Jennyfer** *Aviation and Space Psychology, German Aerospace Center, Hamburg, Germany* **Johannes, Bernd** *Aviation and Space Psychology, German Aerospace Center, Hamburg, Germany*

Safe and effective performance in operational working groups (e.g. pilots) demands, apart from excellent technical knowledge, pronounced interpersonal competence; such as the selection and distribution of information, cooperative goal orientation and decision making as well as skills in leadership and conflict management. The development of a computer-based group test system will be presented, in which objective behavior measuring, behavior observation and physiological strain measuring are integrated into an overall evaluation. Basis of the multi-level observations are taxonomic derived complex scenarios, in which up to six participants gradually receive assignments through individual Touchscreens and interact face-to-face within the given situations.

Development and evaluation of computerized test battery for multiple task performance in pilot selection

Albers, Frank *Aviation and Space Psychology, German Aerospace Center, Hamburg, Germany*

The diagnostic of multiple task abilities in pilot selection is compulsory although there is no proof of a universal multiple task ability. A way of coping with this difficulty by developing a new modular battery of computerized cognitive and psychomotor tests will be presented. The tests were evaluated in test repetition studies with large samples (N>100 each) of pilot trainee program applicants. The evaluation provides reliable and valid results. Practice effects could be examined and have to be taken into account in the course of test evaluation as well as in the later personnel selection process.

Dyadic cooperation test: Predictive validity for captains upgrading

Stelling, Dirk *Aviation and Space Psychology, German Aerospace Center, Hamburg, Germany*

Computer-assisted teamwork scenarios provide an opportunity to simulate specific job requirements and to analyse the abilities of the applicant in dealing with complex systems. Since 1995 the German Aerospace Center uses the Dyadic Cooperation Test (DCT) to diagnose performance, as well as working and communicative behaviour in pilot - selection. In an analysis of 92 of captain-upgrading assessment records, the performance in aircraft system handling, flying and ground handling performance was rated. Previous DCT observer ratings regarding cooperation, decision-making and stress management showed even after years, predictive validity.

Changing demands in military pilot selection

Noser, Philip *Swiss Air Force, Insitute of Aviation Medicine, Dübendorf, Switzerland*

Demands for military pilots in Swiss Armed Forces have changed significantly within the last ten years. Changes in the selection system were urgently requested. Pilot candidates start in Switzerland at the age of 17 and are undergoing a long sequential way of selection. A new system with computer based testing and a subsequent basic flying training have been introduced with good success. The outcome of the screening has been measured against the success in the basic training and shows good results. Feedbacks of flight instructors were excellent. Swiss Air Force can satisfy their needs in personnel employment even though the amount of candidates is sinking.

Stress in service work of flight attendants

Bamberg, Eva *Inst. für Psychologie, Universität Hamburg, Hamburg, Germany* **Ronzheimer, Sandra** *A-B-U-Psychologie, Universität Hamburg, Hamburg, Germany* **Sparre, Angela** *A-B-U-Psychologie, Universität Hamburg, Hamburg, Germany*

Within two airline companies, one of them a traditional airline, one of them a low cost carrier, a study with 166 flight attendants was conducted. Results show that resources are especially important in predicting job satisfaction; stressors are important predictors of burnout. In this context task related stressors as well as customer- and emotion related stressors are relevant. In general, in the low-cost carrier organization, resources are higher and stressors are lower than in the traditional airline company.

Passengers subjective well-being in the aircraft cabin

Marggraf-Micheel, Claudia *Aviation and Space Psychology, German Aerospace Center, Hamburg, Germany* **Jaeger, Sabine** *Aviation and Space Psychology, German Aerospace Center, Hamburg, Germany*

The impact of air-stream and temperature to subjective well-being in an aircraft cabin was investigated in a mock-up (A380 Upper-Deck) with 70 subjects. The used instrument was validated inter alia, comparing subjective well-being with physical measurement in three climate-scenarios. Results of analyses of variance point out significant differences in experienced thermal comfort. It is shown that the degree of mental and physical well-being is lower for people with less emotional stability. In addition, airstream is more uncomfortable for less emotional stable persons and with regard to gender, women feel more uncomfortable with the affective climate than men.

S-284: Development of competencies during the transition from kindergarten to primary school

Bettina Hannover, Wolfgang Schneider *(chair)*

This symposium aims to bring together researchers studying the development of school-relevant competencies in children during the transition to primary school. So far, studies within Germany mostly dealt with children at the point of entry into primary school and mainly focussed on precursors of literacy acquisition, such as phonological awareness. To extend this research perspective, in our symposium we will particularly look at younger children (in kindergarten or preschool), at groups of children with disadvantaged learning preconditions (e.g., immigrants), on a wider range of competencies (e.g., mathematical achievement), and a wider range of factors potentially affecting the development of competencies (e.g., child-caregiver relationship quality, social skills).

Children's attachment to caregivers in kindergarten and the development of social behaviours supportive of learning

Glüer, Michael *Erziehungswi. und Psychologie, Freie Universität Berlin, Berlin, Germany* **Hannover, Bettina** *School and Teaching Research, Freie Universität Berlin, Berlin, Germany*

How does child-caregiver attachment quality in preschool affect the development of behaviours that prepare the child for successful learning in school? We expected securely attached children to most likely cooperate with the caregiver and to develop positive attitudes towards learning. In 75 child-caregiver dyads, attachment quality was observed. Children's social behaviour supportive of learning was measured by a) observation of child-caregiver interaction during a teaching task, b) observation of the child while working on different performance tests, c) caregivers' ratings of the child's behaviour. The discussion focuses on how to most effectively prepare children for school entry.

Prevention of math problems in school: Findings for the Würzburg kindergarten training program "Mengen, Zählen, Zahlen"

Schneider, Wolfgang *Inst. für Pädag. Psychologie, Universität Würzburg, Würzburg, Germany* **Krajewski, Kristin** *Psychology IV, University Wuerzburg, Würzburg, Germany* **Nieding, Gerhild** *Psychology IV, University Wuerzburg, Würzburg, Germany*

We present first findings of an evaluation study dealing with the mathematics kindergarten training program "Mengen, Zählen, Zahlen" ((MZZ: quantities, counting, numbers). During their last year in kindergarten, a total of 260 children participated in the training. Unspecific and specific predictor measures were assessed immediately before training and subsequently twice. The trained children showed considerable progress in the specific precursor variables of math competence (quantity assessment and counting). In contrast, non-specific precursor variables such as phonological awareness or working memory did not influence training success.

Prediction capability of early speech skills and working memory capacity on reading and spelling competencies at the age of eight years

von Goldammer, Ariane *Inst. für Pädag. Psychologie, Universität Göttingen, Göttingen, Germany* **Bockmann, Ann-Katrin** *Educational Psychology, University of Goettingen, Göttingen, Germany* **Mähler, Claudia** *Educational Psychology, University of Goettingen, Göttingen, Germany* **Hasselhorn, Marcus** *Education and Development, Internat. Educational Research, Frankfurt, Germany*

Phonological awareness has been demonstrated as a powerful predictor of childrens reading and spelling success during elementary school years. Less is known about the prediction capability of phonological working memory and early speech skills. Thus, 53 children took part in a longitudinal study, where related potential predictors were assessed at the age of four, five, and eight years. In addition, reading and spelling tests were administered at the age of eight by. The results underline the predictive power of early sentence memory and phonological working memory to explain later reading and spelling performance.

Development of school relevant competencies in preschool age: Effects of social status and migration

von Maurice, Jutta *BiKS, Universität Bamberg, Bamberg, Germany* **Weinert, Sabine** *Psychology I, University of Bamberg, Bamberg, Germany* **Dubowy, Minja** *Psychology I, University of Bamberg, Bamberg, Germany* **Ebert, Susanne** *Psychology I, BiKS, University of Bamberg, Bamberg, Germany*

School relevant competencies are based on developmental processes, which reach back to preschool years. The paper presents data from the longitudinal study BiKS-3-8 following 547 children from entry to preschool up to grade 2 in primary school. Amongst others we used standardized tests for different aspects of language and cognitive competencies every six months as well as detailed sociodemographic information. The results of the first three measurement points show effects of social status and migration on competence development in 3 to 5 year olds that are of theoretical and practical significance and that differ depending on the competence area analyzed.

Children's attachment to caregivers in kindergarten and acquisition of competencies

Wolter, Ilka School and Teaching Research, Freie Universität Berlin, Berlin, Germany Harwardt, Elena Human Science, University of Cologne, Cologne, Germany Glüer, Michael School and Teaching Research, Freie Universität Berlin, Berlin, Germany Ahnert, Lieselotte Human Science, University of Cologne, Cologne, Germany Hannover, Bettina School and Teaching Research, Freie Universität Berlin, Berlin, Germany

This research addresses the question how relationship quality between child and caregiver in kindergarten affects the development of precursors of literacy and mathematics competencies. We expected securely attached children to profit the most from kindergarten's educational offers, such that they should start off particularly well when entering primary school. In 75 randomly selected Berlin kindergartens, attachment quality in one child-caregiver dyad was observed. Precursors of competencies were measured using standardized tests. Results provide evidence for our expectations. Also, we found that girls were more frequently securely attached than boys and outperformed boys in reading and writing performance.

S-285: Conflicts, errors and emotions

Werner Sommer, Annekathrin Schacht (chair)
In everyday life conflicts and errors can elicit strong emotions; these emotions may influence the way we deal with conflict or error prone situations. This symposium investigates the presence, functional role and neurophysiological substrates of emotional and motivational aspects of conflicts and errors. The experimental situations studied range from sensorimotor experimental go-nogo and word recognition tasks to and gambling and social situations. Emotions are considered from many anglaes: as intrinsic or extrinsic results of conflicts and errors, as contributing to conflicts, or as factors in adaptation processes.

Emotions in Go/No Go conflicts?

Schacht, Annekathrin Inst. für Psychologie, Humboldt-Universität zu Berlin, Berlin, Germany Nigbur, Roland Department of Psychology, Humboldt-University at Berlin, Berlin, Germany Sommer, Werner Department of Psychology, Humboldt-University at Berlin, Berlin, Germany

In four experiments we investigated emotional reactions in a Go/NoGo paradigm which is held to evoke elementary but strong response conflicts. Emotional responses were examined with skin conductance responses (SCRs), M. corrugator supercilii activity, and startle blink elicitation. Our results indicate that NoGo trials modulate activity of the autonomic nervous system: SCRs and startle blinks were reduced while corrugator activity was prolonged in NoGo as compared to Go trials. Therefore, we suggest that NoGo trials temporarily suspend the approach system set into action by Go commands but seem to be neither arousing nor aversive.

Post-error adjustments

Ullsperger, Markus Inst. für Kognitive Neurologie, Max-Planck-Institut, Köln, Germany
Performance monitoring research suggests that the rostral cingulate zone (RCZ) signals the need for adjustments, whenever action outcomes deviate from the goals (e.g., on errors) or when goal achievement is at risk. These adjustments occur at motor, cognitive, motivational and autonomic levels and vary in time course from immediate compensatory actions to long-term strategy changes and learning. The presentation focuses on EEG and fMRI studies addressing the implementation of post-error adjustments. The relationship of RCZ

activity, reflected in the error-related negativity (ERN) and hemodynamic signal changes, with post-error slowing, post-error reduction of interference, and learning from errors will be demonstrated.

The influence of punishment on action monitoring

Masaki, Hiroaki School of Sport Sciences, Waseda-University, Tokorozawa, Japan Ogawa, Keiko Sommer, Werner Inst. für Psychologie, Humboldt-Universität zu Berlin, Berlin, Germany
We investigated the effect of punishment on action monitoring using the error-related negativity (ERN). In a series of experiments, we used a spatial Stroop task in which punishment sounds were presented for error responses. The first experiment suggested that the unpleasant and high-arousal sound might reduce the ERN. In the second experiment which compared 3 different sounds, the ERN was not influenced by punishment, although error rate became higher by delivery of noxious (vomiting) sounds. However, the ERN was larger with delivery of the neutral sound instead of punishment. These seemly contradictory results will be discussed.

Adaptation to gain? Effects of winning probability on feedback negativity in a gambling task

Nittono, Hiroshi Faculty of Integrated Arts, Hiroshima University, Hiroshima, Japan Otsuka, Yuka Cognitive Psychophysiology Lab, Hiroshima University, Higashi-Hiroshima, Japan Ullsperger, Peter BAuA, BAuA, Berlin, Germany
To examine whether the processing of gain and loss depends on the context, we asked 16 adults to perform a slot-machine-like gambling task. Each time a button was pressed, one of six outcomes (+10, +5, +1, −1, −5, and −10) occurred. The outcomes were first assigned equal probabilities, and subsequently, either +10 or −10 was presented more frequently. As compared to positive outcomes, negative outcomes elicited a larger negativity peaking around 300 ms in the even and losing conditions, but not in the winning condition. The results suggest that people change the level of expectation according to the context.

Making errors together

de Bruijn, Ellen R.A. Nijmegen Institute for Cognit., Radboud University Nijmegen, Nijmegen, Netherlands
Humans are social animals and participate in joint activities like dancing or sports. From a neurocognitive perspective, these seemingly simple actions are highly complex. Individuals not only have to plan and monitor their own actions, but they also have to keep track of and anticipate the actions of the person they are interacting with. So far, however, research has predominantly focused on action-monitoring processes in individual action. Little is therefore known about these processes in joint action. I will present data from recent ERP and fMRI studies in which we investigate monitoring processes that enable adaptive behaviour in social interactions.

S-286: Adolescents' multiple goals and academic learning

Manfred Hofer, Thea Peetsma (chair)
During adolescence, students have to pursue many goals. Therefore, learning might compete with leisure activities. One question is whether motivational and achievement outcomes depend on the quantity or quality of extracurricular activities. From a differential perspective, groups of adolescents differing in their future time perspectives may develop differentially regarding academic variables. From an instructional perspective, the congruence

between teacher's and student's goals should be an important factor. Finally, the question arises which interventions can be developed to effectively help students avoiding school-leisure conflicts, reaching a better integration of their goals, and consequently living a balanced life.

Students' well-being and academic achievement as a function of multiple role engagement: Not quantity but quality matters

Derous, Eva Inst. of Psychology, Erasmus University Rotterdam, Rotterdam, Netherlands Lens, Willy Institute of Psychology, University of Leuven, Leuven, Belgium
To understand students' wellbeing and academic achievement it is important to consider the number, strength and quality of competing action alternatives, such as students' work and leisure activities. This study investigates effects of students' multiple role engagement on their wellbeing and academic achievement. An electronic survey was held in two samples (n=868 Flemish and n=539 Dutch undergraduates). Hierarchical regressions showed that the quality of engagement in (extra)curricular activities (i.e., type of motivation to engage in activities) is a stronger predictor than the quantity of engagement (i.e., number of activities; time spent in (extra)curricular activities). Theoretical and practical implications are discussed.

Types of students motivated for leisure versus school

van der Veen, Ineke SCO-Kohnstamm Institute, University of Amsterdam, Amsterdam, Netherlands Peetsma, Thea SCO-Kohnstamm Institute, University of Amsterdam, Amsterdam, Netherlands
Increasing future time perspectives on leisure have been found to undermine students' academic motivation and achievement. Recognizing types of students strongly in favour for leisure time, makes it possible to respond to this early in their school career. Participants were about 1200 12-13 year old students attending pre-vocational education. Questionnaires on leisure perspectives and school motivation were administered four times during a year and report marks were collected. We could distinguish two groups of students: one with moderate and stable, another with high and increasing leisure perspectives. The developments in achievement and academic motivation of both groups will be discussed.

Goal (in)congruence between teachers and students in informal learning environments

Minnaert, Alexander Dept. of Educational Sciences, University of Groningen, Groningen, Netherlands
Secondary vocational education has undergone a major shift towards cognitive apprenticeship aiming at the acquisition and use of self-regulatory processes. Opposed to formal learning environments, informal learning pretents to be more realistic, learner-oriented, and in line with students' goals. The question remains open whether students' perception of informal learning settings are in line with teachers' goals. 192 students and 18 teachers participated in this study. Students perceived the learning context significantly less realistic and flexible than their teachers. The role of (dis)congruities between teacher goals and students' goal perceptions in promoting (self-regulated) learning is discussed.

The effects of a training program for minimizing school-leisure conflicts

Reiser, Goran Inst. für Kulturwissenschaften, Universität Bayreuth, Bayreuth, Germany
Pupils from the 6th, 7th and 8th grade (N=52) were trained with a self-regulation program in order to observe possible effects on motivational variables and homework according to the theory of motivational action conflicts (Hofer et al.,2004). In a

standardized dairy pupils had to note down the daily time spend for homework, learning and leisure activities as well as their attitudes toward homework and leisure. Both instruments were used before and after the self-regulation program. The results show positive effects on doing homework and the attitude towards it. Nevertheless the attitude towards leisure did not change. Keywords: Self-regulation, school-leisure conflict, homework

Resolving goal conflicts: An intervention study
Spaniol, Christina Educational Psychology, University of Karlsruhe, Karlsruhe, Germany Fries, Stefan Educational Psycholo, University of Karlsruhe, Karlsruhe, Germany

Conflicts between achievement goals and social goals of students can have negative consequences for goal attainment and subjective well-being. Based on an existing intervention, designed to foster students' goal achievement by increasing goal commitment and perceived attainability, a more comprehensive intervention was developed. The new intervention was tailored to help resolve goal conflicts by setting priorities. In a randomized control design 30 students received the new intervention, 29 received the original, and 26 served as a control group. Goal conflicts were only reduced in the group that received the new intervention. However, goal attainment and subjective well-being were not increased.

S-287: Assessing quality in higher education

Manuela Pächter, Edith Braun (chair)
Developments in Europe such as the declaration of Bologna and the European Qualification Framework have lead to a new view on quality in higher education. Quality is regarded from a holistic point of view as a process in which input, process and outcome variables are con-nected with each other. In the symposium approaches to will be presented which focus on the assessment of input variables (e.g., personnel, infrastructure) as well as process vari-ables (e.g., teaching and learning processes) and outcomes (e.g., competences). Further-more, the contributions regard the acquisition of competences for life-long learning as a core aspect of educational quality.

Internships in Bachelor programmes: Perspectives of different stakeholders
Hapkemeyer, Julia AB Evaluation, QS, QM, Freie Universität Berlin, Berlin, Germany Scheibner, Nicole FB 12, AB Evaluation, Free University Berlin, FB 12, Berlin, Germany Soellner, Renate FB 12, AB Evaluation, Free University Berlin, FB 12, Berlin, Germany

Objective: To identify supporting and inhibitory factors of successful students' internships against the background of the implementation of Bachelor programmes in Europe. Methods: An analysis of needs of different stakeholders involved in internships was conducted. Students, organizers at universities and supervisors in institutions were interviewed on expectations of internships and necessary competencies for successful performances. Results: Especially professional and personal competencies are required in internships. Students expect to gain professional and social competencies during internship. Recommendations about the organization of students' internships are derived, thus providing an important contribution to quality assurance in higher education.

Lecturer's expectations of academic course evaluation
Ulrich, Immanuel Inst. für Psychologie, Freie Universität Berlin, Berlin, Germany Spexard, Anna Psychology, Free University Berlin, Berlin, Germany

Braun, Edith Psychology, Free University Berlin, Berlin, Germany
According to the Bologna Process, universities should document the acquisition of competence as the outcome of the educational process. In 2007, 184 lecturers at the Freie Universität Berlin were surveyed to determine whether they judged key competences to have been sufficiently evaluated. In addition we investigated which evaluation items the lecturers preferred when being evaluated. Qualitative answers have been categorized and quantified. As expected, the areas of competence were rated as sufficient, but at the same time there was a preference for traditional process variables. We conclude that professional consultants are needed to train lecturers to meet the new demands.

German version of the Approaches to Teaching Inventory (ATI-R) for quality assurance processes in university teaching
Lübeck, Dietrun FB 12 - Psychologie, Freie Universität Berlin, Berlin, Germany Soellner, Renate Psychology, Free University Berlin, Berlin, Germany

Within the context of a study on academic teaching the revised version of the "Approaches To Teaching Inventory" (Trigwell, Prosser & Ginns, 2005) has been implemented as a web-based questionnaire that was completed by 620 lecturers of four universities in Germany and Switzerland in summer 2006. The study was aimed at conceptions (Kember, 1997) and associated teaching strategies of university lecturers in different teaching environments. Implications for quality assurance processes that focus on human resource development particularly for university lecturers will be discussed.

Course evaluations: New quality aspects in a questionnaire and three approaches for developing teaching skills
Lossnitzer, Tim Psychology, University of Jena, Jena, Germany Schmidt, Boris Psychology, University of Jena, Jena, Germany

Inspired by the Bologna Process, the functions and scopes of course evaluations in universities have changed. Formerly less recognized quality dimensions like learning outcomes are now being focused. We will present a recently developed questionnaire that integrates "traditional" and "modern" quality aspects. In three studies the goodness of this questionnaire will be analyzed, focusing on construct and criterion validity. Though commonplace, it is rarely implemented that course evaluations need to be integrated into specific approaches aiming at the development of teaching skills. Three such approaches are investigated in the finally presented interview study, involving superordinates, peers, and counselors.

Assessment of quality in higher education and vocational education and training in Austria
Pächter, Manuela Inst. für Päd. Psychologie, Universität Graz, Graz, Austria Lunger, Sigrun Psychology, University of Graz, Graz, Austria Maier, Brigitte Psychology, University of Graz, Graz, Austria

2005 a new system for quality assurance was introduced for the Higher Education and Vocational Education and Training institutions in Austria. The quality assurance system defines quality objectives which refer to key aspects of vocational education. To support the evaluation process questionnaires for online surveys were developed. In an empirical investigation carried out 2006 more than 60.000 students and more than 4.000 teachers took part. Based on these data the test quality of the instruments was analyzed (e.g. reliability and validity analyses). Besides, recommendations for the interpretation of evaluation data and for the assurance of quality could be derived.

S-288: Repetitive negative thinking across emotional disorders

Thomas Ehring, Karina Wahl (chair)
Because of its widespread presence across emotional disorders, repetitive negative thinking (RNT, e.g. worry, rumination) has been suggested to be an important transdiagnostic process. In addition, there is evidence from prospective and experimental studies supporting its role as a maintaining factor. The symposium comprises current research into the phenomenology, causes and effects of RNT. The contributions thereby cover a wide range of disorders (depression, GAD, OCD, PTSD) and methodological approaches (phenomenological, correlational, experimental and intervention studies). As a whole, the evidence presented further supports the role of RNT as a transdiagnostic maintaining factor and provides innovative perspectives for future research.

Differences and similarities between obsessive thoughts and ruminative thoughts in obsessive compulsive and depressed patients
Wahl, Karina Inst. für Psychiatrie, Medizin. Universität Lübeck, Lübeck, Germany Schönfeld, Sabine Dept. of Psychology, University of Dresden, Dresden, Germany Hissbach, Johanna Dept. of Psychology, University of Hamburg, Hamburg, Germany Küsel, Sebastian Department of Psychology, University of Hamburg, Hamburg, Germany Zurowski, Bartosz Dept. of Psychiatry, Medical University of Lübeck, Lübeck, Germany Kordon, Andreas Dept. of Psychiatry, Medical University of Lübeck, Lübeck, Germany

Introduction. The objective of the study was to compare obsessive and ruminative thoughts in depressed and obsessive-compulsive patients. Methods. Thirty patients diagnosed with OCD and 30 patients diagnosed with Major Depression were asked to identify both a personally relevant obsessive and ruminative thought and to subsequently evaluate these thoughts on a modified version of the Cognitive Intrusions Questionnaire (CIQ, Freeston et al., 1992). Results. In OCD patients, ruminative thoughts were more common and more distressing than predicted. In depressed patients, obsessive thoughts occur infrequently. Conclusions. Rumination appears to be inherently linked to obsessive thoughts and mental neutralising in obsessive-compulsive patients.

Worry and rumination in real life: Do dysphorics prefer to ruminate instead of worry?
Bohne, Antje Psychologisches Institut I, Universität Münster, Münster, Germany Thiemann, Pia Psychologisches Institut I, Universität Münster, Münster, Germany de Jong-Meyer, Renate Psychologisches Institut I, Universität Münster, Münster, Germany

Objective: Assessment of rumination, worry and response styles to daily hassles in dysphorics. Method: Dysphoric (n=68) and non-dysphoric (n=92) students (73% female, age: M=21.4 years) completed PSWQ-D, RSQ and the Daily Hassles Scale. Cognitive response styles to daily hassles experienced within the last month were assessed via retrospective self-ratings. Results: Preliminary analyses indicate that both, rumination and worry, are common in daily life of dysphorics. Discussion: The data can contribute to the identification of differential versus unique aspects of rumination and worry.

A test of a metacognitive model of rumination and depression in undergraduates and clinically depressed individuals

Roelofs, Jeffrey *Dept. of Clinical Psychology, Maastricht University, Maastricht, Netherlands*

This study sought to test out a clinical metacognitive model of rumination and depression in undergraduates and clinically depressed individuals. A total of 254 undergraduates of Maastricht University and 198 clinically depressed patients referred to the community mental health centre of Maastricht were included. Structural equation modelling was used to test the fit of the model in both samples. Following some modifications to the model, the model provided a good fit to the data in undergraduates and clinically depressed individuals. The findings have clinical implications including the implementation of metacognitive-focused cognitive therapy of depression.

The role of rumination and interpersonal behavior in depression

O'Mahen, Heather *Mood Disorders Centre, University of Exeter, Exeter, United Kingdom*

We examined pregnant women's willingness to disclose interpersonal needs on their perceptions of support, rumination, and depressive symptomatology. Ninety-seven women recruited in community obstetrics clinics who screened at risk for depression completed a clinical interview. Path analysis indicated that women with less social support, and higher levels of rumination and silencing the self, had more depressive symptoms. Women who reported less perceived social support endorsed stronger "silencing the self" views. "Silencing the self" views predicted level of rumination. The relationship between perceived social support and rumination was not significant. This study highlights specific interpersonal mechanisms involved in rumination and depression.

The role of reduced concreteness in trauma-related rumination

Ehring, Thomas *Dept. of Clinical Psychology, University of Amsterdam, Amsterdam, Netherlands* **Schaffrick, Christina** *Dept. of Psychology, University of Bielefeld, Bielefeld, Germany* **Szeimies, Anna-Kristina** *Dept. of Psychology, University of Braunschweig, Braunschweig, Germany*

Objectives: It was aimed to test the hypothesis that the negative effects of trauma-related rumination are partly due to its abstract nature. Method: In study 1, abstractness of rumination was rated from answers given by trauma survivors in a rumination interview. Study 2 experimentally manipulated abstractness of thinking in a subclinical group and investigated its short-term effects on mood and PTSD symptoms. Results: Results showed that abstractness of thinking was related to higher levels of PTSD symptoms in the correlational as well as the experimental design. Conclusions: The results support the view that reduced concreteness is a critical variable for the negative effects of repetitive thinking on emotional processing.

A targeted attention regulation training reduces intrusiveness of worrisome thoughts in subclinical GAD

Schönfeld, Sabine *Inst. für Klin. Psychologie, Technische Universität Dresden, Dresden, Germany* **Lange, Annika** *Department of Psychology, University of Bielefeld, Bielefeld, Germany*

Generalised Anxiety Disorder (GAD) is characterised by intrusive worrisome thoughts. This symptom might be partly caused by a deficit in the ability to inhibit negative task irrelevant and intrusive stimuli. The present study investigated whether a training of attention regulation reduces the intrusiveness of worries. 47 high worriers were randomly assigned to either an attention regulation training (ART) or a placebo training (PT), which

took one week and included daily exercises. Both trainings significantly reduced symptoms. However, the ART was over and above successful in reducing intrusiveness of worries. These results suggest that such targeted interventions could address transdiagnostically occurring symptoms.

S-289: Glucose and glucocorticoid effects on human memory

Jonathan Foster *(chair)*

Increases in blood glucose have been associated with memory facilitation in humans. Manipulation of arousal level has also been demonstrated to regulate memory functioning, an effect likely to be mediated by adrenaline (epinephrine) and cortisol. Given that adrenaline and cortisol are known to promote an increase in blood glucose concentration, it is possible that the impact of glucose and arousal on memory are associated. This symposium will present recent findings in the glucose, arousal and memory literature, with the aim of exploring whether a formal relationship exists between glucose, glucocorticoids and human memory.

Brain imaging investigations of glucose and cognition

Riby, Leigh *Division of Psychology, Northumbria University, Newcastle, United Kingdom*

Using the temporal precision of ERP methodology, the current work aimed to investigate further glucose-mediated cognitive processes. In the first study participants completed a visual three-stimulus oddball task. Consistent with behavioural evidence of memory-specific effects, glucose moderated the magnitude and latency of the P3b ERP component (memory updating effect). However, glucose also interacted with the P3a and P2 components (attention effects). Further ongoing work presented here shows the feasibility of combining ERP methods with standardised neuropsychological measures of attention and memory (e.g. Stroop, Verbal Learning Task) to reveal in more detail the neuro-cognitive mechanisms that can benefit from glucose ingestion.

Acute stress, cortisol and memory

Smeets, Tom *Dept. of Psychology, Universiteit Maastricht, Maastricht, Netherlands*

Exposure to stressful events is known to trigger a variety of physiological reactions, of which many are related to the activation of the stress-responsive hypothalamic-pituitary-adrenal (HPA) axis. A plethora of research has revealed that the secretion of cortisol due to HPA axis stimulation may modulate memory functioning. However, the precise direction of stress-induced cortisol effects on memory performance is far from clear. In this talk, I will highlight some of the latest research from our lab and discuss some promising avenues for future research.

Processing of emotionally arousing memory materials: effect on cognitive and physiological processes

Scholey, Andrew *Psychology & Sports Scienc, Northumbria University, Newcastle Upon Tyne, United Kingdom*

Increasing mental effort can reduce blood glucose levels and impair performance while processing emotional material raises blood glucose and can improve memory. In one study 72 young adults were randomised to a memory task condition according to a 2 (emotional, neutral words) x 2 (+/- secondary task) design. Blood glucose levels changed according to previous literature but independently of memory effects. In another study glucose preferentially enhanced a tracking task but not concomitant encoding of verbal material. These data suggest that the relationship between blood glucose changes and cognitive performance requires

consideration of multiple physiological, neurohormonal and cognitive processes.

Effect of glucose ingestion on recognition memory for emotionally arousing stimuli

Sunram-Lea, Sandra *Psychology, Lancaster University, Lancaster, United Kingdom* **Brandt, Karen** *Psychology, University of Keele, Keele, United Kingdom*

Previous data suggest that glucose administration facilitates recognition memory that is accompanied by recollection of contextual details and episodic richness. Research on emotion and memory has shown the presence of an emotional enhancement effect such that emotional stimuli are more memorable than their more neutral counterparts. This paper discusses whether the recognition memory facilitation effect associated with glucose would emerge for emotional material that already benefits from a memory advantage. The results suggest that the additive effect of glucose ingestion and a rise in glucose levels due to the emotional nature of the stimuli shifts the previously observed dose-response curve.

Stress, glucose and memory in adolescents

Smith, Michael *Paediatrics and Child Health, UWA, Crawley, Australia* **Foster, Jonathan** *Paediatrics and Child Health, UWA, Crawley, Australia* **Hii, Hilary** *Neurobiology, ICHR, Subiaco, Australia* **van Eekelen, Anke** *Neurobiology, ICHR, Subiaco, Australia*

Glucose administration has been observed to facilitate memory in humans and rodents. A number of factors are thought to modulate this facilitation effect, including glucoregulatory efficiency and cognitive demand. In a series of recent studies, we have investigated the impact of stress on this effect. Specifically, the effects of glucose on memory were investigated in adolescents who differed in self-reported and physiological (i.e. basal salivary cortisol) baseline stress levels, a) under conditions of acute stress, or b) under standard testing conditions. The potential role of stress in modulating susceptibility for glucose enhancement of memory will be outlined in this talk.

S-290: Meaning and personal growth in the context of cancer

Crystal Park *(chair)*

Personal growth following highly stressful experiences such as cancer is an area of great interest, but much remains to be learned about the experiences of growth, including the determinants of growth, the meaning of growth in the lives of those who experience it, and the clinical implications of growth for cancer survivors. In this symposium, five scientists will present their cutting edge research regarding growth in the context of cancer and then our discussant, Dr. Carolyn Aldwin, will integrate these findings, highlighting the underlying themes regarding the personal and coping factors that determine personal growth in those with cancer and others, and the meaning of this growth in terms of psychological adjustment.

Correlates of anticipated posttraumatic growth among cancer patients

Tallman, Benjamin *Dept. of Psychology, University of Iowa, Iowa City, USA* **Altmaier, Elizabeth** *Dept. of Psychology, University of Iowa, Iowa City, USA*

The current study examines relationships between anticipated posttraumatic growth (PTG) and demographics (e.g., age, gender), psychological functioning, physical functioning, personality characteristics (e.g., optimism), coping, and social support. Study participants (N = 100) have been diagnosed with gastrointestinal cancer, acute myelogenous leukemia (AML), or a condition that requires an autologous or allogeneic bone marrow transplant, and received treatment. Study participants complete three interviews: baseline (pre-treatment), 60 days, and 8 months after treatment. This is a correlational study: regression analyses will identify predictors of anticipated PTG. Data are currently being gathered; approximately 33% of patients have been enrolled to date.

Explanatory style and self-perceived posttraumatic growth among women with breast cancer in Hong Kong

Ho, Samuel Mun-Yin Dept. of Psychology, University of Hong Kong, Hong Kong, China, People's Republic of : Hong Kong SAR

Objectives: To investigate the relationship between explanatory styles and posttraumatic growth among women with breast cancer. Methods. This is a cross sectional study. 95 eligible patients completed a set of psychological inventories at the outpatient clinic. Results. Patients' tendency to attribute the causes of positive events to internal, global, and stable factors tended to have more self-reported posttraumatic growth. One's explanatory style for negative events was associated with posttraumatic stress symptoms but not with self-perceived posttraumatic growth. Conclusion. The explanatory style for positive events might affect later cognitive processing, such as meaning making, which will affect self-perceived posttraumatic growth.

Posttraumatic growth and posttraumatic stress in patients and their partners adapting to cancer

Znoj, Hansjörg Inst. für Psychologie, Universität Bern, Bern, Switzerland *Kuenzler, A.* Inst. für Psychologie, Universität Bern, Bern, Switzerland *Zindel, A.* Inst. für Psychologie, Universität Bern, Bern, Switzerland

Cancer patients' families are highly involved in the disease and its treatment. Few studies have examined the role of partners in adaptation or posttraumatic personal growth (PG), which involves increased personal strength, appreciation for life, compassion, and faith, and improved problem-solving abilities and relationships. With a longitudinal prospective design, we investigated the time-course of PG in 200 patients and partners assessed at diagnosis and six and 12 months post-diagnosis. Individual and dyadic factors predicting PG, including psychological stress, dyadic coping, and emotional, behavioral and cognitive reappraisal as well as cancer stage, treatment factors, and psychiatric medication will be presented.

Determinants and meaning of growth in cancer survivorship

Park, Crystal Dept. of Psychology, University of Connecticut, Storrs, USA *Blank, Thomas* Dept. of Family Studies, University of Connecticut, Storrs, USA *Edmondson, Donald* Dept. of Psychology, University of Connecticut, Storrs, USA

In a sample of 250 younger adult cancer survivors, we prospectively investigated, over a one year period, predictors of stress-related growth as well as the influence of growth on longer-term adjustment to cancer. Results suggested different models for men and women. For example, although religious coping was a strong predictor of increased growth over time for both men and women, emotional expression predicted growth only for women while a sense of control over the cancer predicted growth only for men. Additionally, controlling for time since diagnosis, growth was related to some measures of psychological well-being only for women.

The meaning of personal growth in the context of cancer: Research and clinical perspectives

Lee, Virginia Health Center, McGill University, Quebec, Canada

Learning to live a meaningful life within the limitations imposed by cancer or its treatment becomes the essence of many of the transitional

needs of cancer survivors from the moment of diagnosis and for the balance of his or her life. A number of meaning-oriented clinical interventions have emerged with varying outcomes. This presentation will critically review and discuss the theoretical and empirical questions arising from a research program examining the effects of a Meaning-Making intervention (MMi), using clinical examples from patients diagnosed with different types of cancer at various points along the cancer trajectory.

S-291: Career counseling in Europe: A future agenda for research and practices

Annelies van Vianen (chair)

Extant career theory, models and methods do not fit current and future job markets. Traditional career concepts and counseling practices refer to the notions of stability and predictability of people and environments. These notions will no longer hold. Europe in particular is facing demographic and job market changes that call for integrative approaches to careers. Yet, career theories and counseling practices within Europe seem diverge. This symposium includes contributions from five European countries that assessed their current career concepts and practices and seek to develop new career models and methods as a common basis for the training of career counselors.

Thinking global and acting local: Perspectives on career counseling with adults

Duarte, Maria Eduarda Fac. of Psychol. and Education, University of Lisbon, Lisbon, Portugal *do Rosário, Maria* Faculty of Psychology and Educ, University of Lisbon, Lisbon, Portugal

Objectives: Career counseling is examined along several approaches: the differential (do they impose constraints although allow freedom to counselee and counselor?), the developmental (do they stimulate exemption and therefore freedom?), the constructionism meta-model (do they respond to new challenges?), and the impact on guidance practices (do they restrain freedom?). Methods: A Portuguese adaptation of a Dutch Survey was administered to career counselors working in organizational settings. Results: The current aim of practitioners is to assess processes and outcomes as they occur in work environments. Conclusions: Evidence supports the role of theorists, but suggests the need to construct contextualized models.

Career counseling and career counselors in Italy

Soresi, Salvatore Dept. of Developm. Psychology, University of Padova, Padova, Italy *Nota, Laura* Department of Developmental Ps, University of Padova, Padova, Italy *Ferrari, Lea* Department of Developmental Ps, University of Padova, Padova, Italy

Objectives: One of the biggest vocational guidance challenges in Italy is increasing the professionalism of practitioners who do not have the requisites required by the SIO (Italian Society of Vocational Guidance, established in 2004) and the IAEVG (International Association for Educational and Vocational Guidance). Methods: A group of 100 Italian practitioners were administered the Italian adaptation of a Dutch Survey. Results: Data will be presented on the type of action carried out in different professional contexts by comparing them to client typology and amount of specific training received. Conclusions: Implications for training of practitioners will be discussed.

Current developments in the field of counseling: Evolution of practices and professions in France

Cohen-Scali, Valérie INETOP, Paris, France *Bigeon, Christine* INETOP, INETOP, Paris, France

Objectives: Providing an overview of the current developments regarding guidance practices and professions in France. Methods: This overview is based on an analysis of existing literature and responses to surveys among diverse groups of counselors. Results address: (1) the increasing number of counselors in many professional fields who get involved in supporting others; (2) the professionnalisation of counselors in the field of vocational guidance; (3) the growth of the company-executives' implication in the career development counseling. Conclusions: These results question the training of counselors (and particularly of the new actors) that obviously constitutes major economic, social and human issues.

Helping at-risk youth cope with multiple transitions: From career counselors to case managers

Massoudi, Koorosh Inst. für Psychologie, Universität Lausanne, Lausanne, Switzerland *Dauwalder, Jean-Pierre* Institute of Psychology, University of Lausanne, Lausanne, Switzerland

Objectives: Swiss statistics show a relatively new and risky phenomenon: a high rate of youth unemployment (Weber, 2004). Helping at-risk youth cope with complex and multiple transitions is a major challenge for career counseling. This presentation offers a review of current practices and a reflection about future needs. Methods: Impacts and specificities of different intervention programs (counseling, training, coaching) were studied. Results: Data analyze individual and environmental risk factors and counseling methods. Conclusions: The implementation of a case management system, aiming at the coordination of different interventions and a longitudinal follow up of at-risk youth during their life-span, is needed.

Current practices and future visions of career counseling in Europe

van Vianen, Annelies Work and Organizat. Psychology, University of Amsterdam, Amsterdam, Netherlands *de Pater, Irene* Work and organizational psycho, University of Amsterdam, Amsterdam, Netherlands

Objectives: The study summarizes current career counseling practices in Europe and the need for new approaches towards careers that fit recent labor market developments in Europe. Methods: Career counselors in Europe responded to a survey. Quantitative and qualitative analyses were performed among the participating countries. Results: Practitioners use traditional methods and instruments or develop new instruments that lack theoretical and empirical validation. Conclusions: European countries share many of their career guidance practices and they face similar changes in people's work lives, but are not yet prepared for these changes. Implications for career theory, concepts and methods are provided.

S-292: Partnership and parenthood in Germany

Sabine Walper, Johannes Huinink (chair)

This symposium informs about research questions, design, and findings of the priority program "Panel Analysis of Intimate Relationships and Family Dynamics" (pairfam). Pairfam addresses key issues in partnership development from mating to dissolution, fertility decision making, parenting, and intergenerational relationships. The piloting "Mini-Panel" employs a multi-actor and multi-informant design with three age cohorts of target participants (age 15-17, 25-27, and 35-37 years; n = 656) as well as their partners, parents, and children. The papers presented in this symposium illustrate the range of research questions as well as key methodological options to invite additional users of this data base.

The intergenerational transmission of relatedness and autonomy in adolescents' and adults' romantic relationships

Walper, Sabine Inst. für Bildung, Universität München, München, Germany Thönnissen, Carolin Inst. für Bildung, Universität München, Munich, Germany Wendt, Eva-Verena Inst. für Bildung, Universität München, Munich, Germany

This study focuses on relatedness and autonomy in adolescents' and adults' romantic relationships. In addition to age and gender differences as well as effects of partnership type (non coresiding, coresiding, married), special attention is paid to the intergeneration transmission of partnership quality. Data come from a three-cohort longitudinal study (subjects aged 15-17, 25-27, 35-37 years) conducted in Germany. Dyadic data analyses include both partners' perspectives on relationship quality (relatedness, emotional security, autonomy) as well as parental partnership quality. Results point to distinct transmission effects for each feature of partnership relations, and a high salience of father-offspring relationships for romantic relationships.

Attachment representation, sexual motives and emotional intimacy in young romantic relationships

Wendt, Eva-Verena Inst. für Bildung, Universität München, München, Germany Walper, Sabine Inst. für Bildung, Universität München, München, Germany

This paper addresses influences of general attachment-representations on sexual motives in young couples, focusing on long-term effects on the relationship development. Data come from N=57 romantic couples (mean-age 22.7), interviewed 2005, 2006 and 2007. Both partners' general attachment-representations, sexual motives and the emotional relationship-quality were assessed. Results show that sexual motives are primarily influenced by one's own attachment security as well as by the interaction of both partners' security. In general a high level of security is related to more positive, approach oriented sexual motives. Couples with secure attachment representations develop more sexual satisfaction and more emotional intimacy over time.

Individual resources, couple match and relationship stability

Arránz Becker, Oliver Inst. für Soziologie, RWTH Aachen, Aachen, Germany Hill, Paul B. Inst. für Soziologie, RWTH Aachen, Aachen, Germany

The present study investigates a variety of individual attributes as predictors of partnership stability, focusing on the role of partners' similarity (couple match). Effects of couple match are compared to those in terms of complementarity and independent additive effects of each partners' individual resources. Data come from 158 adult couples who participated in the PAIRFAM minipanel. Dyadic analyses suggest a positive effect of similarity for some characteristics (e.g., educational attainment), while for other domains the presence (or absence) of individual resources determines subjective relationship stability. A theoretical synthesis of the results is proposed considering processes at the individual and dyadic level.

Tenaciousness and flexibility in a model of childbearing intentions

Schröder, Torsten Inst. für Soziologie, EMPAS, Universität Bremen, Bremen, Germany Maul, Katharina Inst. für Soziologie, EMPAS, Universität Bremen, Bremen, Germany Huinink, Johannes Inst. für Soziologie, EMPAS, Universität Bremen, Bremen, Germany

Childbearing is a matter of resource intensive decision making. It frequently competes with other life projects (like work career). Sociological and economic models mostly focus on economic and normative factors, while the costs of failure to achieve personal goals remain largely unconsidered. The present paper closes this gap by using concepts of goal-management as suggested by psychological action theory. Based on a sample of n = 226 young adults (age 25 and older) our findings show that the effect of financial concerns on childbearing is moderated by tenaciousness and the salience of competing life goals.

Reasons to support old parents: Findings from the German study 'Panel analysis of intimate relationships and family dynamics'

Klaus, Daniela Inst. für Soziologie, Techn. Universität Chemnitz, Chemnitz, Germany Nauck, Bernhard Inst. für Soziologie, Techn. Universität Chemnitz, Chemnitz, Germany

Whereas many studies proved children as being the main caregivers for their aged parents the motivations behind their helping behavior are somewhat vague. The research question of this contribution is: To what extent grown-up daughters and sons are not only able but willing to care for their parents? Using data from a pre-study of the 'Panel Analysis of Intimate Relationships and Family Dynamics' four motivations are tested with respect to their relative power in explaining the degree of material and instrumental support given to parents. The findings suggest reciprocity as most decisive for parental support but also adult child's feeling of intimacy and altruism are uncovered as significant.

Parenting, coparenting and children's development

Geier, Boris Social Monitoring, German Youth Institute, München, Germany Alt, Christian Social Monitoring, German Youth Institute, München, Germany

Despite considerable international research on parenting and its relevance to child development, Germany still lacks representative data which allow to examine contextual influences on parenting styles as well as links between parenting and child outcomes. The present study seeks to provide appropriate instruments for assessing warmth and control in large-scale surveys. Based on nationwide surveys (n = 5,322 and 10,416), with parents of children aged 0 to 17, newly adapted short scales have been tested. The results indicate satisfactory psychometric quality. Not only parents' individual parenting style but also couples' co-parenting strategies seem to affect child development.

S-294: Emotion-cognition interactions in aging and dementia

Katja Werheid, Hakan Fischer (chair)

Over the past decade, Social Cognitive Neuroscience has provided a wealth of evidence supporting the intimate relationship of emotion and cognition. A rapidly growing research area investigates the impact of healthy and pathological aging on the interaction of emotion and memory. This symposium gathers investigators from different countries to provide an overview of current research on the influence of emotion on cognition from a lifespan perspective, to obtain an integrative perspective on current research on emotion-cognition coupling in 'normal' aging and dementia, and to discuss the methodological and clinical implications that arise from our current status of knowledge.

Age differences in emotional memory

Mather, Mara Dept. of Psychology, University of California, Santa Cruz, USA

Recent findings reveal that with age an increasing proportion of what people remember is positive instead of negative. One question is whether this positivity effect is the result of an increased focus on regulating emotions among older adults or the result of age-related decline in processes that detect and monitor negative, potentially threatening stimuli. In the current studies, we found that older adults' positivity effect in initial attention requires full attention and is eliminated when we distract participants. These findings suggest that older adults use top-down control mechanisms to enhance processing of positive stimuli and diminish processing of negative stimuli.

How emotion affects older adults' memories for event details

Kensinger, Elizabeth Dept. of Psychology, Boston College, Chestnut Hill, USA

Emotional experiences often are remembered with tremendous vividness and perceptual detail. In this talk, Dr. Kensinger will present behavioral and fMRI research examining the processes recruited as young and older adults process positive and negative information, and how those processes correspond with the way in which the information is later remembered. The results demonstrate that the amygdala and orbitofrontal cortices, through their interactions with other medial temporal-lobe and visual processing regions, mediate the effects of negative emotion on memory vividness. The engagement of this emotional memory network remains relatively preserved across the adult life-span.

Age differences in processing emotional and motivational information

Ebner, Natalie Center for Lifespan Psychology, Max Planck Institute for Human, Berlin, Germany Lindenberger, Ulman Center for Lifespan Psychology, MPI for Human Development, Berlin, Germany

Adults of all ages share the lifespan schema that young adults preferentially pursue growth goals, and older adults pursue loss-prevention goals. We used recognition memory to test: (a) whether young and older adults differentially rely on this schema when associating faces of different ages (young, old) with goals of different orientations (growth, loss-prevention); and (b) whether emotional expression (happy, sad) influences processing of face–goal associations. Individuals of either age group, but especially older adults, associated young faces with growth and happy expressions, and old faces with loss-prevention and sad expressions. Emotional and motivational aspects of lifespan schemata are discussed.

Remembering and forgetting of emotional information in the aging brain

Fischer, Hakan Aging Research Center, Karolinska Institute, Stockholm, Sweden

Forgetting begins immediately following the initial encoding of information and proceeds across time. The current objective was to investigate the neurobiological basis of the forgetting process by means of event-related fMRI. Of chief interest was the extent to which aging and the emotional valence of images affected patterns of brain activation. Memory performance and corresponding BOLD activations were measured on three occasions, with initial results indicating that both aging and emotionality influence the neural correlates of forgetting. The present results imply that the neurobiological basis of forgetting varies as a function of both age and the emotional content of images.

Emotional memory and memory distortions in Alzheimer's disease: Evidence form laboratory studies and the attacks of September 11th, 2001
Budson, Andrew Edith Nourse Rogers Memorial V, Boston University Alzheimer's, Bedford, USA
In two studies, emotional memory and memory distortions were investigated in patients with Alzheimer's disease. In the laboratory, patients and controls performed a false memory test in which they were tested on non-presented "lure" items that were semantically related to either emotional or non-emotional study items. Outside the laboratory, emotional responses to, and memory for, the 9/11/01 attacks were investigated in patients and controls in the initial weeks following the attacks, after 3 to 4 months, and finally after 1 year. Emotional intensity was similar between patients and controls, whereas memory distortions were more common in the patients.

Emotion-memory coupling in mild cognitive impairment
Werheid, Katja Inst. für Psychologie, Humboldt-Universität zu Berlin, Berlin, Germany
Recognition memory is sometimes distorted by emotion in terms of an 'emotion-induced recognition bias'. To examine whether this bias is robust to aging and memory decline we investigated recognition of positive, negative, and neutral faces in elder adults with amnestic Mild Cognitive Impairment (MCI), young and elder controls. Recognition performance was reduced in the elderly and even more so in MCI. The bias was preserved and pronounced for positive faces in both groups. Viewed together with findings on semantic relatedness of positive facial emotion and familiarity, biased recognition of emotional, especially positive, faces may serve as a compensatory memory strategy.

S-295: Positive and negative promotion of children's emotions

Victoria del Barrio (chair)
The aim of this symposium is to join different considerations about negative emotions in Spanish children found by the researchers in this field. They explore how the aggression in children is related to different types of mothers, how stressful life events and social skills deficits predict hopelessness, the link between empathy and prosocial behaviour versus emotional instability and aggressiveness and also how to improve emotional state in children affected by serious impairment like Asperger syndrome. The data from these studies will permit us to considerer the positive and negative elements related with children's emotional adaptation in order to build a useful plan for teachers and parents of a balanced emotional education

Empathy and personal disposition versus emotional instability and aggressiveness in childhood
Mestre, Vicenta Psicologia Basica, Universidad de Valencia, Valencia, Spain Samper, Paula Psicologia Basica, Universidad de Valencia, Valencia, Spain Tur, Ana Psicologia Basica, Universidad de Valencia, Valencia, Spain Bádenes, Mireia Psicologia Basica, Universidad de Valencia, Valencia, Spain
We present an empirical study conducted on the Spanish population with a view to determining the link between empathy and prosocial behaviour versus emotional instability and aggressiveness from an intercultural perspective. Sample are 593 boys and 638 girls, aged 10 to 12. Instruments were the Inventory of Empathy for Children and Adolescents (Bryant, 1982), the Prosocial Behaviour Scale, the Emotional Instability Scale and the Physical and Verbal Aggression Scale (Caprara and Pastorelli, 1993; Del Barrio, Moreno and López, 2001). Results show significant differences in

empathy and aggressiveness depending on the type of school (some schools had a greater presence of students from other countries).

The relationship between rearing types of mother and aggression in children and adolescents
Ángel Carrasco, Miguel Personality Dept., UNED, Madrid, Spain
The present study explore how the aggression in children is related to different subtypes of mothers. The sample consisted of 524 children (45,2% girls and 54,8 boys) ranging from 7 to 14 years old (means 11.11; Standar Desviation 1.56). Children completed the Childs Report Behavior Parenting Inventory (Shaefer, 1965) and The Physical and Verbal aggression Questionnaire (Caprara et al., 1993). Cluster analysis identified three distinct groups of mothers: hostile mothers, balaced mothers and affective mothers. Mothers profiles differed significantly on physical and verbal aggression in children. Membership in hostile mother cluster (high control and high hostility and low affect) was related with higher scores in physical and verbal aggression. From a bidirectional perspective aggression.

Stressfullife events and deficits in social skills as predictors of adolescents hopelessness expectancies
Rodriguez Naranjo, Carmen Personality Dept., University of Malaga, Malaga, Spain Cano Gonzalez, Antonio Basic Psychology., Malaga University, Malaga, Spain Sanchez, Alicia Personality Dept., Malaga University, Malaga, Spain
We explore an integration of the hopelessness theory and the social skills approach and test whether stressful life events and social skills deficits predict hopelessness expectancies. A sample of 642 students (12 to 18 years) completed the Life Experiences Survey, the Social Skills Inventory and the Hopelessness Scale. As expected, the regression analyses revealed that stressful life events, deficits in social expressivity, the tendency to be social sensitive, and deficits in social control skills, predicted hopelessness expectancies. Finally, stressful life events interacted with deficits in social control skills to predict hopelessness expectancies. These findings convey important implications regarding the focus of intervention for hopelessness depression in adolescents.

Assessment of emotional disorders by screening behavior in 5-to 12-year-old children
Maganto, Carmen Dept. of Clinical Psychology, University Basque Country, San Sebastián, Spain Garaigordobil, Maite Dept. of Clinical Psychology, University Basque Country, San Sebastián, Spain Pérez, Jose Ignacio Dept. of Clinical Psychology, University Basque Country, San Sebastián, Spain
Clinical assessment in children is not devoid of difficulties due to the need of hetero-reports for accurate evaluation (Cova & Maganto, 2005; Harrington, 2002; Stice). The purpose of this work is to present the Children's Behavior Problem Screening Test (SPCI, Maganto & Garaigordobil, 2005), an instrument that provides information about 11 diagnostic categories. The sample is made up of 1272 males and females -5 to 12- with and without emotional disorders. Relevant statistical analyses of the diagnostic categories confirmed the capacity of the screening test to discriminate between children with and without emotional problems, as well as revealing statistically significant gender differences in these problems.

Coping with aggression among schomates
Forns, Maria PETRA, University of Barcelona, Barcelona, Spain
Peer aggression is a significant problem among adolescents. This study aims to analyze peer

aggression, adolescents coping strategies and how they influence adaptive functioning. Participants were 400 adolescents aged 11-16 years from Barcelona Secondary Schools. Data were obtained from three self-report measures: a peer aggression and bullying questionnaire (instrument created ad-hoc for this investigation), Adolescent-Coping Orientation for Problem Experiences (Patterson,J. M., McCubbin, H), and Behavior Assessment System for Children Self-Report (Reynolds, C. R. & Kamphaus, R. W.). The results suggest that successful adaptation is related to the type of coping strategies used.

S-296: Advances in objective personality test development and research

Tuulia Ortner, Manfred Schmitt (chair)
Research on Objective Personality Tests (OPT) as proposed by Cattell almost disappeared during the last three decades due to insufficient convergence of T-data with Q-data and L-data. The rapid development of computer aided assessment procedures and recent advances in implicit measurement have fuelled a revival of OPT research. The symposium brings together recent work done to explore the validity and utility of newly developed OPTs. Presentations cover various domains of individual differences such as stress resistance, vocational interests, achievement motivation, and risk propensity. Emphasis is on moderators of the convergence between OPTs and explicit as well as implicit personality measures.

Using questionnaires and objective personality tests in a single setting for the assessment of vocational interests
Häusler, Joachim Psychological Assessment, SCHUHFRIED GmbH, Mödling, Austria Proyer, René T. Personality and Assessment, University of Zurich, Zurich, Switzerland
A test-battery for the assessment of vocational interests that consists of a questionnaire, a non-verbal test, and several objective personality tests is presented. It is suggested that each test-type has several advantages and disadvantages that make its usage preferable in a given situation. By incorporating measures of the vocational identity of the client and the degree of differentiation of his/her interest profile a sequential model of the usage of questionnaires, nonverbal tests, and objective personality tests is set up. The usefulness of the model is discussed with respect to the current literature.

New results on the validity of an objective test battery measuring the ability to work under pressure
Ortner, Tuulia Inst. für Psychologie, Humboldt-Universität zu Berlin, Berlin, Germany Kubinger, Klaus D. Psychology, University of Vienna, Vienna, Austria Vormittag, Isabella Psychology, Free University of Berlin, Berlin, Germany
Stress resistance is an important construct within occupational qualification. Due to problems of self report data as faking or introspective limitations, a behaviour based computerized battery was realized referring to the concept of objective personality tests. Following typical occupational demands, measured aspects are for instance: unfavorable working conditions; time pressure and stress resistance under avertion of working according to a plan. Results of different validation studies are presented, as predictive validity of aptitude assessment for university entrance, test data due to teacher's state of burnout and test characteristics of extreme groups. Hypotheses were only partly confirmed.

Would risk propensity be assessed using behaviorally-based tasks? A proposal for an objective personality testing of risk taking behavior

Rubio, Victor Dept. de Psicología, Universidad Autónoma de Madrid, Madrid, Spain *Hernández, José Manuel* Departamento de Psicología, Universidad Autónoma de Madrid, Madrid, Spain *Narváez, María* Departamento de Psicología, Universidad Autónoma de Madrid, Madrid, Spain *Márquez, Oliva* Departamento de Psicología, Universidad Autónoma de Madrid, Madrid, Spain *Santacreu, José* Departamento de Psicología, Universidad Autónoma de Madrid, Madrid, Spain

Risk propensity has been usually assessed using self-reports. Recently, several behaviorally-based alternatives have been presented. In this line, a set of objective personality tests (OPT) for assessing risk-taking behavior has been developed. The current paper presents five tests: the Betting Dice Test (BDT), the Roulette Test (RT), the Crossing the Street Test (CtST), the Risk Propensity Dilemmas Test (RPDT) and the Skillfulness Risk-Taking Behavior Test (SRTBT). It is presented some of the results regarding reliability and convergent as well as criterion validity (guessing tendency in a multiple choice test, risk-taking behavior in a investment simulation task) of these five tests.

The validity of the Objective Achievement Motivation Test (OLMT)

Schmidt-Atzert, Lothar Psychology, University of Marburg, Marburg, Germany *Krumm, Stefan* Psychology, University of Marburg, Marburg, Germany

The OLMT is a computer based objective personality test for the assessment of effort under different motivational conditions. Incentives are the task itself, personal goals, and competition. Different studies were conducted to explore the validity of the test. Participants (university students, trainees) worked on other achievement motivation measures (personality questionnaires, a semi-projective test) as well as on different performance tests (intelligence, sustained attention). In addition, the OLMT was used to predict study and training performance. Results concerning the construct validity were inconsistent, while the criterion validity of the test was confirmed in different studies.

Moderated convergence among implicit, explicit and objective risk propensitiy indicators

Schmitt, Manfred Inst. für Psychologie, Universität Koblenz-Landau, Landau, Germany *Dislich, Friederike* Inst. für Psychologie, Universität Koblenz-Landau, Landau, Germany *Zinkernagel, Axel* Inst. für Psychologie, Universität Koblenz-Landau, Landau, Germany

Based on theoretical models and previous studies on the consistency and predictive validity of implicit and explicit personality measures, the assumption was tested that the convergence among implicit, explicit, and objective risk propensity measures will depend on the relative strength of controlled versus automatic processes. The convergence of explicit and objective risk propensity measures was assumed to increase with the availability of control resources and the motivation to employ them. The opposite effect was expected regarding the convergence of implicit and objective measures. Hypotheses were tested and partly confirmed using several functionally equivalent indicators of control resources and control motivation.

The assessment of self-attributed need achievement using experiment-based behavioural tasks

Wagner-Menghin, Michaela Psychology, University of Vienna, Vienna, Austria

Assessing variables of the self-attributed need achievement (McClelland, Köstner and Weinber-

ger, 1989), like aspiration level, endurance, frustration tolerance and accuracy, is relevant in educational psychology as well as personnel psychology. Very often these constructs are assessed using self report measures out of questionnaires, which are afflicted with the problem of intentional answer distortion (Kubinger, 2002; Viswesvaran & Ones, 1999). The tasks under discussion here are constructed following the principles of experiment-based behavioural assessment (Kubinger, 2006), and allow standardized observation of the relevant behaviour. The paper focuses on the development of measures out of these tasks and their reliability and validity.

S-297: Conceptualizing predictors of risky behavior engagement amongst adolescents and young adults

Randy Auerbach (chair)
Adolescents and young adults engage in the highest frequency of risky behaviors, and such engagement often results in both short- and/or long-term negative consequences. In an effort to develop more effective prevention, intervention, and treatment programs, recent research has begun to examine factors that may underlie engagement in risky behaviors. The speakers in the current symposium will present results from research examining the predictors, correlates, and consequences of risky behavior engagement in Canada, China, and the USA. Particular emphasis will be placed on highlighting proximal and distal risk factors that shape the frequency and type of risky behaviors individuals utilize.

A double bind for emerging adults: Predicting risky behavior engagement

O'Donnell, Katherine Dept. of Psychology, McGill University, Montreal, Canada *Auerbach, Randy* Dept. of Psychology, McGill University, Montreal, Canada *Abela, John* Dept. of Psychology, McGill University, Montreal, Canada

The study examined factors that moderated the relationship between hassles and engagement in risky behaviors. At Time 1, 141 emerging adults completed self-report measures of neuroticism, emotional regulation, hassles, and risky behaviors. Follow-up assessments occurred every week for five weeks, and participants completed measures assessing hassles and risky behaviors. Multilevel modeling analyses indicated that higher levels of both neuroticism and emotion regulation deficits were significantly associated with greater engagement in risky behaviors following the occurrence of hassles. Consequently, a double bind was created whereby individuals who possessed both vulnerabilities were more likely to engage in risky behaviors.

Predicting risky behavior during early adulthood: Pinpointing the critical distal, developmental periods and experiences

Jager, Justin Dept. of Psychology, University of Michigan, Ann Arbor, USA *Schulenberg, John* Dept. of Psychology, University of Michigan, Ann Arbor, USA

This study examined how experiences during high-school and the college-years uniquely predict to early-adulthood risky behaviors. The sample included 6,000 U.S. respondents assessed in two-year intervals between the ages of 14 and 24. Using piece-wise growth modeling, growth of heavy drinking, 12-month marijuana use, and depressive affect during high-school and college was assessed, and the relation of each to age 24 risky behaviors was examined. While intercept levels and both growth pieces all uniquely predicted age 24 risky behaviors, growth during high-school was the most meaningful. Findings suggest the predominance of high-school experiences on early adult functioning.

An examination of gender differences: What role does coping play in predicting risky behavior engagement?

Auerbach, Randy Dept. of Psychology, McGill University, Montreal, Canada *Abela, John* Dept. of Psychology, McGill University, Montreal, Canada

Past research has found that adolescent males engage in a greater number of antisocial behaviors as compared to females. In the present study, we examined whether coping deficits were associated with increased engagement in risky behaviors following the occurrence of academic- and peer-related stress. Further, we explored whether gender moderated such an association. Using a multi-wave longitudinal design, adolescents (n=143) from the greater Montreal area were followed over the course of six months. Results of hierarchical linear modeling indicated that males, but not females, with coping deficits reported increased engagement in risky behaviors following both academic- and peer-related stress.

Positive and negative reinforcement mechanisms underlying riskiness in early adolescents

MacPherson, Laura Dept. of Psychology, University of Maryland, College Park, USA *Reynolds, Elizabeth* Dept. of Psychology, University of Maryland, College Park, USA *Duplinsky, Michelle* Dept. of Psychology, University of Maryland, College Park, USA *Wang, Frances* Dept. of Psychology, University of Maryland, College Park, USA *Lejuez, Carl* Dept. of Psychology, University of Maryland, College Park, USA

Early adolescence is a vulnerable period for onset of risk behaviors. Although research emphasizes the role of novelty seeking (positive reinforcement), less is known about risk behavior maintained by negative reinforcement (riskiness to avoid/escape aversive internal or external stimuli). This study focused on the use of laboratory risk taking tasks tapping positive and negative reinforcement processes, combined with self reported personality as well as affective and cognitive functioning, in relation to real world risk behaviors (n=286; 51% minority, ages 10-12). Findings indicated the differential importance of both reinforcement processes across demographic subgroups in the occurrence of risk behavior in youth.

Childhood sexual abuse and experiential avoidance: Escaping painful self-awareness?

Sarin, Sabina Dept. of Psychology, Centre Addic. and Ment. Health, Toronto, Canada *Nolen-Hoeksema, Susan* Dept. of Psychology, Yale University, New Haven, USA

Child sexual abuse (CSA) may produce emotion regulation deficits – specifically, a ruminative response style - which heightens distress and fosters aversive self-awareness, thus increasing risk for engaging in harmful escapist behaviours. To test this theory, community participants completed measures at three time points, one year apart. CSA survivors reported more substance use and dramatizing behaviours. Distress and rumination partially mediated the relationship between CSA and these escapist behaviours, with the model including both distress and rumination accounting for the most variance in escape behaviour scores. Results suggest that CSA survivors engage in escapist behaviors to avoid distress and aversive self-awareness.

Understanding risky behavior engagement amongst adolescents from mainland China

Zhu, Xiongzhao Medical Psychological Research, Second Xiangya Hospital, Changsha, People's Republic of China *Yao, Shuqiao* Medical Psychological Research, The Second Xiangya Hospital, Changsha, People's Republic of China

Epidemiological studies conducted within mainland China suggest that the prevalence of adolescent depression is rising. While individual differences exist in how adolescents respond to depressive symptoms, recent research has shown a strong association between such symptoms and broad-based engagement in risky behaviors (e.g., alcohol-use, unsafe sex, and violence). The present study examined risky behavior engagement amongst Chinese adolescents from Yue Yang, Hunan (n=411) using a multi-wave longitudinal design. Assessments occurred each month for six months (Time 2 – 7), and results of hierarchical linear modeling indicated that intrapersonal factors moderated the relationship between depressive symptoms and engaging in risky behaviors.

S-298: Ethics for European psychologists

Geoff Lindsay, Jean Pettifor (chair)
The European Federation of Psychologists Associations' Standing Committee on Ethics has worked from the early 1990s to develop psychological ethics across Europe. First came the Meta-code of Ethics, the template for the ethical codes of all EFPA member associations. This symposium is based on the latest venture, a book Ethics for European Psychologists which uses the Meta-code to provide guidance to individual psychologists in different European countries and cultures. Each presenter will develop a theme within the book taking into account similarities and differences among our practice contexts, with a discussion providing a Canadian perspective.

Generalisability of ethical principles across Europe
Lindsay, Geoff University of Warwick, Coventry, United Kingdom
How generalisable are ethical codes: principles and standards? And their implementation? Developing a pan-Europe ethical code and guidelines for psychologists forces us to consider similarities and differences, real and imagined, in both principles and standards. Freedom of movement within the EU should be an ethical as well as an economic process. I shall explore the commonalities and challenges for psychologists including those posed by new socio-political contexts such as large scale migration and perceived threats to national security. I shall also explore whether there is a particular 'European' dimension – or are the issues universal?

Procedures of ethical decision making
Lang, Fredi Referat Fachpolitik, BDP e.V., Berlin, Germany
Due to the nature of their work, psychologists frequently face ethical problems and decide on them in explicit as well as implicit ways. Guidance for decision making is given to them by ethical training, their National Code of Ethics and further available generic decision making models. The EFPA Meta Code on Ethics provides a high level of abstraction together with the coverage of all relevant ethical issues, both meaningful for decision making. This presentation will discuss models of guidance on decision making of the Canadian Psychological Society, Karl E. Tödt, an approach related to the EFPA Meta-Code, and others.

Decision making in a triad
Úvreeide, Haldor Ifru, Oslo, Norway
The ethical codes for psychologists addresses first of all the respect and caring for the individual person with whom the psychologist interacts. However, humans find their personal identity in attachments and dependencies in relationships; in their families and culture. Professionals are also embedded in relationships that form their practice and responsibility. The free-willed and self-determined individual client, and the corresponding professional, can thus be seen as a myth. I will argue that the triad is a necessary format for assessing ethical challenges

and obligations. The concept of the Third face, in the Other, will be presented as an entity for ethical assessment, parallel to the encountered and experiencing individual I.

FP-360: Clinical aspects of cognition II

Specificity of information-processing biases in patients with current and remitted depression and in patients with asthma
Fritzsche, Anja Inst. für Psychologie, Universität Hamburg, Hamburg, Germany Dahme, Bernhard Psychology, Hamburg University, Hamburg, Germany Gotlib, Ian Psychology, Stnford University, Stanford, USA Joormann, Jutta Psychology, Miami University, Coral Gables, USA Nutzinger, Detlev O. Psychology, Medical and Psychosomatic Clin, Bad Bramstedt, Germany Watz, Henrik Center of pneumology and thora, Pulmonary Research Institute, Großhansdorf, Germany von Leupoldt, Andreas Psychology, Hamburg University, Hamburg, Germany
We examined whether information-processing biases for sad stimuli that were found in currently depressed individuals, also exist in formerly depressed patients. Because asthma is highly comorbid with depression, we also examined biases in asthmatics. Three information-processing tasks assessing biases in memory and attention for emotional stimuli were administered to 20 currently and 20 formerly depressed participants, 20 asthmatics and 20 healthy controls. Compared to healthy participants, both currently and formerly depressed patients, but not asthmatic patients, demonstrated specific biases for sad stimuli. Our results suggest that information-processing biases exist even after recovery from depression, thus supporting cognitive theories of depression.

Information processing and selective attention in female adolescence students with eating disorders symptoms
Moradi, Alireza Dept. of Psycohlogy, Tarbiyat Moallem University, Tehran, Islamic Republic of Iran Yousefi Asl, Soureh Psychology, Tarbiyat Moallem University, Tehran, Islamic Republic of Iran
The purpose of this study is to investigate the selective attention in students with eating disorders symptoms. 53 female students with eating disorders symptoms (15anorexia and 38bulimia) and 46 normal students aged 14 to 18 years old who were matched by age and education participated in this study. All subjects responded to the computerized version of the dot probe task. The target words include food and body shape words. The results indicated that students with eating disorders symptoms showed attentional bias with avoidance from body shape stimuli, while no bias was found towards food stimuli.

The characteristics of emotion cognitive processing and regulation in alexithymia
Yi, Jinyao Central South University, Second Xiangya Hospital, Changsha, People's Republic of China Yao, Shuqiao Central South University, Second Xiangya Hospital, Changsha,Hunan, People's Republic of China Zhong, Mingtian Central South University, Second Xiangya Hospital, Changsha,Hunan, People's Republic of China Ling, Yu Central South University, Second Xiangya Hospital, Changsha,Hunan, People's Republic of China
712 university students finished the 2o-item Toronto Alexithymia Scale, the Cognitive Emotion Regulation Questionnaire and the Short Affect Intensity Scale. 51 alexithymic and 54 nonalexithymic gave scores to three dimensions (valence, arousal and dominant) of 120 affective pictures. Compared to the nonalexithymic, alexithymic got higher scores on negative coping dimension, while got lower scores on positive coping dimension, which suggested that alexithymia has deficit in

emotion regulation. Alexithymic had lower scores on positive intensity and negative intensity than nonalexithymic?which suggested that alexithymic have less intense affect. Alexithymic rated positive pictures less pleasurable and negative pictures less unpleasant, which supported that alexithymic have deficit in emotion cognitive processing.

Executive function and memory in posttraumatic stress disorder: A study of Bosnian war veterans
Koso, Maida Dept. of Psychology, Filozofski Fakultet, Sarajevo, Bosnia and Herzegovina Hansen, Stefan Psychology, Institute for Psychology, Gothenberg, Sweden
The present study assessed neuropsychological functions related to attention, executive function and everyday memory in a group of men with a diagnosis of combat-related posttraumatic stress disorder. Twenty Bosnian male combat veterans with a diagnosis of PTSD were tested using the Sustained Attention to Response Task, the Hayling Sentence Completion Test, the Trail Making Test, Rivermead Behavioural Memory Test and Wechsler Adult Intelligence Scale. The study disclosed pervasive cognitive impairments pertaining to attention, working memory, executive function, and memory. We speculate that, in the present group, PTSD was associated with dysfunction of a higher-level attentional resource which in turn affected the activity in other systems concerned with memory and thought.

Overgeneralization of autobiographical memories and emotional processes in opioid-dependent individuals and in methadone-maintained individuals
Gandolphe, Marie-Charlotte Dept. of Psychology, University of Lille3, Villeneuve d'Ascq, France Nandrino, Jean-Louis psychology, university of lille3, Villeneuve d'Ascq cedex, France
Objectives: To investigate the link between the strategies of overgeneralization of autobiographical memories and emotional processes in opioid-dependent individuals and in methadone-maintained individuals. Methods: The level of anxiety, depression, emotional awareness and the autobiographical memory of 30 opioid-dependent patients, 30 methadone-maintained patients and 30 control participants were measured. Results: Dependent individuals and methadone-maintained individuals retrieve more general emotional memories than control participants. Moreover, methadone-maintained patients recall more diversified memories than dependent patients. Conclusion: There is a link between overgeneralization processes and emotional disturbances in opioid-dependent individuals. The effect of substitution treatment on emotion regulation strategy is discussed.

A brief self-report scale on positive and negative affect in depressed and nondepressed subjects
Fiquer, Juliana Psicologia Experimental, Instituto de Psicologia-USP, São Paulo, Brazil Otta, Emma Psicologia Experimental, Instituto de Psicologia-USP, São Paulo, Brazil Yuan Pang, Wang Psiquiatria, Faculdade de Medicina-FMUSP, São Paulo, Brazil Hutz, Claudio Psicologia do Desenvolvimento, Instituto de Psicologia-UFRS, Porto Alegre, Brazil Geerts, Erwin Psychosocial Services, Un. Medical Center Groningen, Groningen, Netherlands Moreno, Ricardo Psiquiatria, Faculdade de Medicina-USP, São Paulo, Brazil Gorenstein, Clarice Farmacologia, LIM-23 IPq-HC-FMUSP, São Paulo, Brazil
A 10-item Affect Scale (AS) is presented. The development of AS was based on a sample of 487 Brazilian participants. Factor analysis revealed two factors: Positive Affect and Negative Affect that explain 57% of the total variance. The scores of AS were significantly correlated with the scores of the Subjective Well-Being Scale of Albuquerque and Trócolli and with the scores of Hamilton Depres-

sion Scale and Beck Depression Inventory. The external validity of AS was evaluated comparing scores of nondepressed and depressed individuals. The results show that AS is a reliable and valid brief self-report scale.

FP-361: Community, parenting style, and family relations

Family environment in divorced and non divorced families
Cortes Arboleda, Maria Rosario Developmental Psychology, Faculty of Psychology, Granada, Spain Cantón Cortés, David Developmental Psychology, Faculty of Psychology, Granada, Spain
The objective of the study was to analyse the differences in the family relationships depending on the home structure. The participants, 148 College student children of divorced families and a comparison group, completed the FES (Moos, Moos and Trickett; 1989). In order to analyse the data several mean comparisons and logistic regressions analyses were carried out. Results showed that divorced families had lower scores on Cohesion, Morality, Organization and Control and higher scores on Conflicts than the intact families. By the other hand, children of divorced families had higher scores on Autonomy and Recreational Orientation. To summarise, our data indicated that, overall, the family environment in divorced families was more negative.

Family education as part of an empowerment process: Helping parents raising healthy children
Berthoud, Cristiana Psychology, University of Taubate, Tremembe - SP, Brazil
The authors will present a preventive intervention conducted with low income families as part of a program for empowering communities. Parenting discussion groups last 8 to 10 sessions and are conduct in schools, social clinics or community associations by psychology students. The program is launched in every community at the Family Day – an event organized to promote family members interaction and to invite families to participate. Evaluation have shown that parents feel supported by the group and learn better alternatives to discipline and orient their children. After 5 years of implementation the program model can be considered a success.

The role of parenting style as perceived by children in the intrinsic motivation
Mesurado, Belén CIIPME, CONICET, Buenos Aires, Argentina
The purpose of this study is to analyze the effect of parenting style perception of children on intrinsic motivation and whether it changes with sex and/or age. The sample includes 270 participants, aged 9 to 10, of middle socioeconomic level, from Argentina. Parenting style was measured using Inventario de Percepción de Relaciones Parentales (Richaud de Minzi, 2007) and intrinsic motivation was computed according to Cuestionario de Experiencia Óptima (Mesurado, 2007). The regression analysis suggests that there is a strong influence of parenting style on the intrinsic motivation only for girls. Nonetheless, this effect decreases with age.

Predictors of family functioning amongst Malay single mother families in Malaysia
Baharudin, Rozumah Faculty of Human Ecology, Universiti Putra Malaysia, Selangor, Malaysia Doshi, Anjli Faculty of Human Ecology, Universiti Putra Malaysia, Selangor, Malaysia
The study determines what risk (RF) and protective (PF) factors influence the family functionings (FF) of Malay, single mother families in an urban area in Malaysia. The moderating role of PF on the relationships between RF and FF was also examined. Overall, the RF and PF accounted for 17-35%

of the variance in the FF. PF accounted for substantial variance in FF (28%); and greater than the risk measures (3%). The presence of PF tends to reduce the impact of RF. Parenting behavior provided the best protective barrier, and higher levels of PF seems to promote better FF.

Family therapy techniques and principles
Harutyunyan, Narine Dept. of Psychology, Yerevan State University, Yerevan, Armenia Gabrielyan, Levon Psychology, Urartu University, Yerevan, Armenia
In the process of working with families, family therapy techniques and principles should be taken into consideration. The idea that family therapy is one of the types of group therapy should be excluded. It must be noticed that in this case techniques play an important role. Moreover, the factors of ethno-psychology and the service period of the family (first five years and more) are to be taken into consideration as well. Family conflicts differ depending on family service period and family members, as well as generations existing in those families. As a result of research it turned out that in the process of resolution of conflicts in families the proper selection of techniques is of great importance.

The impact of factors effected of divorce incidence in Falavarjan township (one of Isfahan township)
Zargar, Fatemeh Clinical Psychology, Tehran Psychiatric Institute, Tehran, Islamic Republic of Iran Doost, Taher Neshat
The purpose of this study was investigate the factors effected in divorce from one of the Center of Prevention and Decrease of Divorce (CPDD) in welfare institute of Isfahan. The date were collected from all referred spouses in 1382- 1384 (march 2003- march 2005). The results of chi- square showed that the most cases were referred by Court. The most numbers of divorce appeal in females were in 28 to 31 years and in males were in 24 to 27 years. Divorce after 35 year was decrease in both of sex.The most important factors of divorce appeal were communication problems, addiction, interference of family and mental disorder of one or two couples.

FP-362: Psychotherapy - Research and treatment methods XI

The effectiveness of rational–emotional therapy to reduce depression in diabetes
Hodjatzadeh, Farahnaz Binesh Kara, Tehran, Islamic Republic of Iran Ghalkhani, Zahra clinical psychology, Binesh, Tehran, Islamic Republic of Iran
OBJECTIVE— the purpose of this study was to compare the effective of to reduce depression in diabetes& the associations between gender; age. RESEARCH DESIGN AND METHODS- prepost test of BDI was used to assess depressive symptoms in 96patients, at age 18-22 & 28-32, same gender. The treatment applies to Sample group. The theses were assessed by t-test, Mann- Whitney & two way analyses statistically& HSD. (α=95%) CONCLUSIONS— the therapy and age were significantly associated to reduce depression in diabetes after controlling for disease variables. No significant associations were found for gender in relation to depression in diameters. Farahnaz Hojatzadeh zahra Ghalkhani

Quantitative and qualitative comparative analysis of cognitive-behavioural and existential-humanistic therapist's speech
Kondratyuk, Nataliya Psychology, KNLU, Kiev, Ukraine
The current study was aimed at reconstructing and comparing structure and semiotics of therapist's speech in cognitive-behavioural and existential-humanistic therapies. The research material was

published sample dialogues, transcripts and videos of therapeutic sessions of C. Rogers, J.Bugental, A.Beck, A.Ellis, D.Meichenbaum, A.Lazarus. The therapists' replicas addressed to a client were analyzed by means of quantitative (computer content-analysis, syntax analysis) and qualitative (conversation analysis) research methods. Major differences revealed in cognitive-behavioural and existential-humanistic therapists' speech are: structure of therapeutic interaction, level of directiveness and therapist's position, time dimension, frequency and usage of different pragmatic types of utterances (interpretation, restatement, question etc.).

The method of imagery communication psychotherapy
Yuan, Yuan Psychology, Beijing, People's Republic of China
Imagery communication is a unique psychotherapy method created by a Chinese psychologist named Zhu Jianjun in 1990s. This study tested that we could use imagery to communicate with a client in unconscious world to change his mental status and treat his psychosomatic diseases, and even improve his personality state. The clinical research methods showed that imagery is a living and a close relationship between imagery and psyche. We will cite house imagery and a relevant case in illustration of the method.

The effect of art psychotherapy based on cognitive-behaviour approach to raise self-esteem and self-efficacy orphan children
Zadeh Mohammadi, Ali Shahid Beheshti University, Fanily Research Institute, Tehran, Islamic Republic of Iran Abedi, Ali Reza Shahid Beheshti University, Fanily Research Institute, Tehran, Islamic Republic of Iran
This exploratory, quasi-experimental study compared the impact of art psychotherapy cognitive-behavior approach on the self-esteem and self efficacy of 20 orphans' 13 to 16 years old. A control group pre-test/post-test design was implemented for this study. 10 children were provided cognitive behavior art psychotherapy services. Self Esteem was measured with questionnaire Rosenberg And self efficacy was measured with questionnaire Sherer. There were Significant differences on the questionnaire post intervention, With both groups. Result explained significant effects self efficacy and self esteem in P< .05 level in experiment group.

FP-363: Ethical issues

Academic-ethics in research methodology
Tayraukham, Sombat Dept. Educational Research, Mahasarakham University, Mahasarakham, Thailand
This research investigated academic-ethics in research methodology of 66 doctoral and 434 masters students of Mahasarakham University; compared academic-ethics among students; and constructed equations of factors related to academic-ethics behavior. The instruments consisted of tests on academic-ethics knowledge, behavior, and attitude. The data were analyzed by descriptive statistics and MRA. The results showed: that students' scores on all dependent variables were at high level; that the scores of masters students and those of doctoral students were not different; and that academic-ethics knowledge and attitude could predict academic-ethics behavior. The RY.123 was 0.908, and equations was ZBeh'=0.860Zknow+0.081ZAtt

Ethical dilemmas of the Portuguese psychologists
Coutinho, Vanessa Massamá, Portugal Cláudio, Victor Psicologia, ISPA, Lisboa, Portugal
The objective of this study was to identify the ethical dilemmas of the Portuguese Psychologists taking under consideration the lack of an updated

Ethical Code that would stand as an efficient guideline for professionals facing dilemmas. The results showed firstly that the most significant dilemmas rise from confidentiality issues. On second hand, they also showed that the Portuguese psychologists have not developed their knowledge's on ethical issues nor do they search for advice on the obsolete ethical codes that were available at the time of the research study, supporting the need for the elaboration of the Portuguese Psychologists Ethical Code.

Ethical issues in psychological research with indigenous peoples: Lessons from aboriginal street youth in Western Canada

Brunanski, Dana Counselling Psychology, University of British Columbia, Vancouver, Canada

This presentation will explore ethical issues in research with indigenous peoples, drawing on the author's experience conducting research with Aboriginal street youth in a large Canadian city. Street-involved indigenous youth are an especially vulnerable population, therefore researchers must take special ethical considerations. Examples from a photo-engagement project, a population-based survey using a participatory research design, and an interview-based qualitative study will be used to illustrate crucial ethical issues in research, including power imbalances; risks of coercion and exploitation; cross-cultural competence; cultural sensitivity in determining appropriate professional boundaries and negotiating multiple relationships; and authentic community consultation.

FP-364: Dual-task processing

Synthetic assessment model of cognitive load in a dual task environment

Jinbo, Li Psychology of Science, Zhejiang University, Hangzhou, People's Republic of China *Baihua, Xu* Psychology, Zhejiang University, Hangzhou, People's Republic of China *Wuheng, Zuo* Psychology, Zhejiang University, Hangzhou, People's Republic of China

On the basis of subjective evaluation, primary-task measures, secondary-task measures and eye movement measures, four techniques, principal components analysis, regression analysis, BP artificial neural network and self-organizing feature map, were respectively used to set up the synthetic assessment model of cognitive load during a dual task of web-searching and mental arithmetic. The result showed that BP artificial neural network modeling possesses the optimal evaluation efficiency among the four modeling techniques. This provided evidence for the use of generalized classification models in multitask cognitive load assessment.

A cognitive model of multi-tasking while driving

Deml, Barbara Human Factors Institut, Universität der Bundeswehr, Neubiberg, Germany *Halbrügge, Marc* Human Factors Institute, University of the Bundeswehr, Neubiberg, Germany *Neumann, Hendrik* Human Factors Institute, University of the Bundeswehr, Neubiberg, Germany

Understanding of how humans execute multiple, concurrent tasks is an important field of research. However, current literature on multi-tasking suffers mainly two problems: most often rather unrealistic settings are examined and most studies lack a proper theoretical foundation as they are limited to the analysis of experimental data. To overcome some of these constraints a common real-world task was studied here, namely driving on a highway while processing direction signs. By matching the experimental data (e.g. gaze behavior, lane keeping) acquired within a driving simulation with the results of a cognitive ACT-R model, it was possible to gain a better understanding of how everyday task-switching is controlled.

A cognitive model of visual search on direction signs alongside the Autobahn

Halbrügge, Marc Human Factors Institut, Universität Bundeswehr, Neubiberg, Germany *Deml, Barbara* Human Factors Institute, University of the Bundeswehr, Neubiberg, Germany *Neumann, Hendrik* Human Factors Institute, University of the Bundeswehr, Neubiberg, Germany

Guidelines for the design of direction signs are currently based on heuristics only. In order to examine whether signs on the autobahn can be processed during the time they are viewable to the driver, we conducted an experiment in a driving simulator. 19 subjects answered questions about randomly generated direction signs while they were driving on a three lane highway. The analysis of reaction times and gaze behaviour yielded both conformance and interesting differences with the already well researched visual search in simple lists. Based on the results, we created a cognitive model with ACT-R that can be used for further research and prospective design in the car driving domain.

FP-365: Cognitive development II

Supporting giftedness in preschool children

Veraksa, Nikolai social psychology, MCPPU, Moscow, Russia

Investigation was devoted to the problem of the general mental giftedness of children aged 5 to 7. According to L.S.Vygotsky's theory, development of giftedness is connected with development of mental ability. Our hypothesis was that special organization of children's activity that could support their initiative - adequate presentation of projects by children and their utility for the child environment - will develop creativity of preschoolers. The children were diagnostically selected using special methods (E.Torrance) so that three groups (37 children) included children with high and moderate level of cognitive and creative abilities. After two years all children had high level of creativity, what means that they are considered to be gifted.

Does the maximizer-satisficer distinction explain why older adults do not want new artefacts?: A questionnaire study of older-and younger-adults comparison

Harada, Etsuko Faculty of Social Sciences, Hosei University, Tokyo, Japan *Mori, Kenji* Gr Sch Social Well-being study, HOSEI University, Machida, TOKYO, Japan *Healey, Karl* Dept of Psychology, University of Toronto, Toronto, Ontario, Canada *Suto, Satoru* Life Science & Technology, AIST, Tsukuba, Ibaragi, Japan *Goldstein, David* Dept of Psychology, University of Toronto, Toronto, Ontario, Canada

Compared with younger adults, older adults are hesitant to adopt new technologies. Previous research has suggested that older adults avoid new products, especially IT-based equipment, because reduced cognitive resources leads to difficulty using and understanding the new equipment. However, there may be another cognitive explanation: If older-adults tend to satisfice rather than maximize, and they are satisfied with their current products, they may not be motivated to adopt new ones. We tested this hypothesis, by administering the maximizing/satisficing scale along with questionnaires about technology product use and satisfaction to a large sample of younger and older adults .

Building self-efficacy among adolescents: Assessing the role of parents and teachers

Mukhopadhyay, Lipi Centre for HRD and Beh Studies, Indian Inst. of Public Adm., Delhi, India

Self-efficacy provides the foundation for self-confidence, well being and personal accomplishment in all areas of life (Pajares, 2005). This belief was measured on Indian Adolescents from Metropolitan cities of Delhi and Kolkatta. High School Students (100 Male and 150 Females) with high academic performance and low performance were compared on self- esteem, social cognitive perspective, self–regulating motivation and emotional stability. Impact of school environment, peers, teachers and parents was also measured through a check list and interview. Results show positive correlation between school environment, parents' self-efficacy and self-esteem among students. Academic achievements and self-efficacy were not linked.

The process of taxonomic hierarchy formation: Cultural-historical view of concept development in the school age

Dziurla, Rafal Psychology, SWPS, Warsaw, Poland

The presentation concerns the problem of concept development of the child in the school age interpreted within cultural-historical psychology of L.S. Vygotsky. In that approach the conceptual system, understood as generalizations, is based on operations and relations between signs. The main problem of generalizations development in that age is the transition form meronimic hierarchy to taxonomic hierarchy. The research was based on method used in quantitative, cognitive semantics concerning building experimental hiperonimic strings, conceptual and lexical nests. It showed that generalizations used by students in the school age functioned as hybrids of meronimic (compelxive generalizations) and taxonomic (preconceptual generalizations) hierarchies.

FP-366: Cognitive aspects of aging

Words learning, spatial pair associated learning and movement time, three cognitive tasks for early Mild Cognitive Impairment (MCI) identification

Juncos Rabadán, Onésimo Dept. Developmental Psychology, Univ. Santiago de Compostela, Santiago de Compostela, Spain *Rodríguez, Nely* Developmental Psychology, University of Santiago de Comp, Santiago de Compostela, Spain *Facal, David* Developmental Psychology, University of Santiago de Comp, Santiago de Compostela, Spain

Our purpose was to study the relevance of several cognitive measures for early diagnosis of MCI. 41 individuals older than 55 years who presented at primary-care-centres complaining of memory failure without prior diagnosis of psychiatric disorder or dementia participated in this study. A neuropsychometric examination, composed by CAM-DEX-R and CANTAB-eclipse batteries and the California Verbal Learning Test, was given. The criteria for MCI were those proposed by Petersen et al. (1999) but adding decline in any area of cognitive functioning. ANOVAs and correlations analyses shown free words recall, PAL errors and movement time as appropriate measures for early MCI identification.

Negative priming in younger and older adults: Selection or response effect?

Behrendt, Jörg Georg-Elias-Müller-Institut, Universität Göttingen, Göttingen, Germany *Ihrke, Matthias* Georg-Elias-Müller-Institute, University of Göttingen, Göttingen, Germany *Schrobsdorff, Hecke* Institute for Nonlinear Dynami, BCCN Göttingen, Göttingen, Germany *Herrmann, J. Michael* Institute for Nonlinear Dynami, BCCN Göttingen, Göttingen, Germany *Gibbons, Henning* Georg-Elias-Müller-Institute, University of Göttingen, Göttingen, Germany *Hasselhorn, Marcus* Georg-Elias-Müller-Institute, University of Göttingen, Göttingen, Germany

The response retrieval theory assumes, that negative priming (NP) effects are due to conflicts between prime and probe responses. But at measures of reaction times target selection and response generation processes are confounded. In our study with 64 younger and older adults we realized a choice reaction NP-task. Varying the distance between stimulus and comparison word we used eye movement to record both, the time until selection is finished and the time until response is given. This process dissociation leads to identification of different reaction patterns for younger and older adults, showing age related changes in the processing of NP-trials.

FP-367: Aesthetic perception

Neural aesthetics of beauty: An event-related fMRI study

Osaka, Naoyuki Dept. of Psychology, Kyoto University, Kyoto, Japan *Ikeda, Takashi* Kyoto University, Department of Psychology, Kyoto, Japan *Rentschler, Ingo* University of Munich, Institute of MedicalPsychology, Munich, Germany *Osaka, Mariko* Osaka University, Department of Psychology, Osaka, Japan

Observers (n=14) viewed and rated number of Japanese paintings (landscape, still life and portrait) that they appreciate to be beautiful prior to fMRI session. Selected stimuli in 3 categories were viewed in the scanner for 2-s with an ITI of 3-4-s. Observers judged each painting ugly, neutral or beautiful by pressing buttons in the scanner. Major differentially activated brain regions were right orbitofrontal and amygdala for ugly while left parahippocampal area for beautiful with sharing common activation regions in anterior cingulate cortex, frontal pole, and medial prefrontal cortex. Thus neural aesthetics of sensing beauty and ugly could be dissociable.

Aesthetic perception of web sites

Thielsch, Meinald T. Psychologisches Institut 1, Münster, Germany

Aesthetic perception of web sites has been explored in two studies: A qualitative study (N=11) identified key aspects (colors, fonts, images). These were tested in a subsequent experiment which fully crossed the three factors in a 2x2x2 design. Based on a representative sample (N=364) the results showed that only the color manipulation has an effect on aesthetic judgements. Usability judgements are not affected, what conflicts with existing assumptions about the connection between both constructs; halo effects or effects of stereotypes caused by attractiveness can be rejected. Both constructs seem to be independent from personal variables like expertise or big five.

Aesthetic beauty and social justice in novels, histories and movies

Hector, Mark New Market, TN, USA

In her book "On Beauty and Being Just," Harvard aesthetics professor Elaine Scarry contends that the experience and contemplation of beauty leads to justice. She believes that "beauty assists us in our attention to justice." She illustrates how beauty and truth are closely allied; and when we encounter beauty we have a more capacious regard for the world. Scarry's contentions are examined in relation to Smith's novel "On Beauty," Suri and Bal's mathematical novel "A Certain Ambiguity," Gonzalez's historical biography "Sor Juana: Beauty and Justice in the Americas," and the German movie "The Lives of Others."

FP-368: Biases and reasoning

Perspective-taking in scientific and deductive reasoning

Thompson, Valerie Dept. of Psychology, University of Saskatchewan, Saskatoon, Canada *Beatty, Erin* Psychology, University of Saskatchewan, Saskatoon, Canada *Aspenlieder, Laura* Psychology, University of Saskatchewan, Saskatoon, Canada

Simply asking reasoners to think about evidence or inferences from another's perspective increases the proportion of valid inferences (Thompson, Evans, & Handley, 2005) and reduces belief-bias (Beatty & Thompson, under review). We hypothesise that reasoning from another's perspective promotes decontextualised, analytic thinking. To test this hypothesis, participants reasoned from two perspectives and either drew conclusions from scientific evidence or inferences from conditional premises. We expected the perspective manipulation to reduce cultural differences in analytic reasoning preferences (Nisbett, 2003) and to reduce differences between high- and low-capacity reasoners (Stanovich, 1999).

Systematic irrationality: A link between confidence bias and additivity

Kleitman, Sabina Psychology, The University of Sydney, Sydney, Australia *Stankov, Lazar* Psychology, The University of Sydney, A18, Sydney, Australia

This paper explores the nature of miscalibration as assessed by the over/underconfidence bias score and links it to another instance of non-normative (irrational) responding - the lack of awareness of the additivity principle of probability theory. Four studies employed a multiple-choice test of Verbal Reasoning to assess these two tendencies. The results indicate that over 60% of participants tend to violate the "additivity" postulate of probability theory. The manner in which participants violate the additivity principle – neglect of non-focal alternatives - is related to measures of confidence and miscalibration bias. The overlap between miscalibration and non-additivity is systematic and suggests that there exist tendencies towards irrationality that are independent of overall ability level.

Belief bias in transitive inference depends on premise integration difficulty

Andrews, Glenda School of Psychology, Griffith Unversity, Gold Coast, Australia

Belief bias involves accepting conclusions that are consistent with beliefs, irrespective of validity. We examined whether premise integration difficulty affects belief bias in transitive inference (A > B and B > C, therefore A > C). Undergraduates read premises of the form, A-B, B-C, C-D, D-E then evaluated B-D conclusions. Belief bias was estimated from acceptance rates for four item types differing in conclusion validity and believability. Belief bias was significantly larger when premise encoding time was briefer, unaffected by conclusion evaluation time, eliminated when premise displays facilitated integration. Reasoners succumb to belief bias when premise integration is difficult.

A comparative study on two types of high: Probability conclusion effects in conditional inference

Hu, Zhujing Dept. of Psychology, Jiangxi Normal University, Nanchang, People's Republic of China *Zhu, Liping* Psychological, Jiangxi Normal University, Nanchang, People's Republic of China

This research examines and compares two different types of high–probability conclusion effects in conditional inference proposed by Oaksford et al and Qiu Jiang et al respectively. 139 subjects were first asked to give their acceptance ratings for each of eight conditional rules and then perform a probability rating task for each antecedent and consequent of the eight conditional rules. The results support Oaksford et al's argument as well as Qiu Jiang et al's argument, that is, both the conditional probability and the probabilities of antecedent and consequent are main factors that have influence on people's conditional reasoning.

FP-369: Clinical / counseling psychology VII

Psychoeducational program for parents of paediatric cancer patients in Malaysia: A pilot study

Othman, Azizah School of Psychology (CE), University of South Australia, Adelaide, Australia *Shah, Ashiq Ali* Psychology, Kwantlen University College, Surrey, Canada

Objective: To evaluate a psychoeducational program for parents of Malaysian paediatric cancer patients. Methods: Parents received either 4 x 50 minutes sessions of information on childhood cancer and coping strategies, (n = 41) or standard care (n = 38). Assessments were conducted before and four weeks after the program. Results: Analyses revealed increased knowledge about cancer (p = .01) and reduced anxiety (p =.07) in the intervention parents compared to standard care. Intervention parents improved scores on interactions with children and children's behavioural problems but these were not significant. Conclusion: This psychoeducational program, the first of its kind in Malaysia, has the potential to decrease anxiety for parents of seriously ill children.

The effects of a combined training program on children with Attention Deficit Hyperactivity Disorder in the classroom activity

Kaymak Özmen, Suna Psychologie und Pychotherapie, Universität zu Köln, Köln, Germany *Lauth, Gerhard W.* Psychologie und Pychotherapie, Universität zu Köln, Köln, Germany

Abstract Attentional problems may lead to poor attainment in classroom because these children are recognized as troubled and impatient in school. In this research, effects of a combine training program (parent training, teacher training and child training) for classroom activity has been researched on tree children (aged 7-9) with ADHD. The aims of this research are to evaluate the effectiveness of combine training program on the children' behaviour problems in the classroom and effects on the teachers stress level. In this research single-case research design has been used. Collected data will be analysed by effect size method. The process of collecting data are being continued.

A contextually based intervention for victimized (bullied) children within elementary school settings

Kourkoutas, Elias Dept. Educational Psychology, University of Crete, Rethyno, Greece

The purpose of this paper is to present a contextually based intervention that has been applied in Greek primary school settings targeting victimized children. Fifteen children who have been systematically bullied by their peers have been included in this intervention program. The program lasted almost 2 years and more than 100 individual / group counseling sessions have taken place within school settings. Evaluation of children's emotional and behavioral states was carried with the use of CDI, RCMAS and ASEBA. Results of the intervention program, evaluated on the basis of a multisourced long term follow-up, suggest that a contextual resilient approach may be very useful in empowering victimized children.

FP-370: Communication and regulation behavior in intergenerational relationships I

The relationship between parental rearing behavior and mental health of undergraduate

Liu, Yingjie University, Inner Mongolia Normal, Huhhot, People's Republic of China *He, Jiaofei* Class 15, Grade 1, Hainan Middle School (senior), Haikou City, Hainan Province, People's Republic of China

Objective: To research the relationship between parental rearing behavior and mental health of undergraduate. Methods: 400 undergraduates were investigated with self-made questionnaire, SCL-90 and EMBU. Results: More than 20% undergraduates have the prevalence problems of mental. Correlation analysis showed that the total score and factors cores of SCL-90 had positive correlation with fathers' punishment, over interference, over protection, rejection, preference and mothers' over interference, rejection, punishment, preference. Parental warmth had negative correlation with the total score and factors cores of SCL-90. Conclusions: Parental rearing behavior is closely related to mental health in the medicinal undergraduate.

Relationship regulation between adult children and elderly parents across time

*Wagner, Jenny Inst. für Psychogerontologie, Universität Erlangen, Erlangen, Germany **Neyer, Franz J.** Department of Psychology, University of Potsdam, Potsdam, Germany **Lang, Frieder R.** Inst. für Psychogerontologie, Universität Erlangen-Nürnberg, Erlangen, Germany*

The project explored determinants of relationship regulation in intergenerational ties across a one-year interval. A total of 117 adult children and their elderly parents took part in the first assessment and the adult children in the follow-up. Traditional and non-traditional types of family situations of adult children were compared with respect to relationship-specific ratings of closeness and reciprocity in both generations. First analyses suggest a decrease in the perception of closeness to older parents but no change with regard to intergenerational reciprocity. Findings point to regulatory functions of closeness and reciprocity within a life-span framework of personality development.

Perceived sociocultural values of the elderly by the adolescents and young adults in Nigeria

Oluwatula, Olukunle Olusina Daniel Dept. of Behavioural Studies, Redeemer's University, Redemption City, Nigeria

The study examines the perceptions of Nigerian adolescents and young adults about the sociocultural values of the Nigerian elderly. Relationships between psychosocial variables such as sex, age, religious affiliation, self-esteem, personality and the perceived sociocultural values were also examined. 250 Nigerians were purposively sampled with the aid of some psychological measures. Analyses show some strong relationships between the variables and the sociocultural values (repository of historical knowledge, grandparenting, and custodian of religious beliefs) of the elderly Nigerians. The study concludes that Nigerian elderly are valuable and the implications of the findings are discussed.

FP-371: Clinical research methods I

Paralinguistic aspects of vocal communication: Implications for psychotherapeutic relationships

Cawthorpe, David R. L. Dept. of Psychiatry, University of Calgary, Calgary, Canada

Objective: Current theory of paralinguistic sensory information processing contends that utterances are processed for survival value in advance of cognitive awareness of linguistic meaning, and, as such, mental contents are offered up to consciousness with affective and emotional valences assigned a priori. Method: A quantitative method of analysis was used to examine specified paralinguistic aspects of utterances derived from a psychotherapeutic assessment paradigm: Adult Attachment Projective. Results: The measured paralinguistic features of human communication were related to the adult attachment classification. Conclusions: Paralinguistic features of vocal communication may influence mental state regarding attachment and other human relationships, including psychotherapeutic relationships.

Apparent motion evaluation in early diagnostics of mental diseases

Nedospasova, Veronika Dept. of Clinical Psychology, IEAP, Moscow, Russia

The structure of autokinetic movement is a predictor of early decease for some categories of patients. Original psychophysical method of apparent motion evaluation detects characteristics of visual perception changes at normal and pathologic development. This method showed high correlations with classical methods of neurophychology. Designed method reveals age dynamics of psychophysical characteristics of visual perception. Disorder of spatial characteristic of visual perception is one of specific mental disease symptoms. Shift of abstract visual perception characteristics e.g. coloration spaces was detected in certain cases of mental disease. Apparent motion evaluation has revealed certain evolution patterns of apparent motion characteristics.

Ego defense mechanisms and the issue of new research methods

Ochirjav, Myagmar Department of Psychology, State University of Education, Ulaanbaatar, Mongolia

The author has developed a new method on figuring out ego defenses based on the experiences of her 10 year research works. The purpose of the present scientific essay lays on the explanation of the aforementioned method. A questionnaire clearly showing each defense mechanism such as exclusion, projection, replacement, rationalization, counteraction, regression, denial, sublimation etc and attaching case studies was developed in the framework of the research. Subjects under the research were divided into three categories: high, medium and low defensive ones. Number of adults involved in the research has totaled 150. The result of the research clearly shows that the method was well suited for psychological counseling practices. Keywords: defense mechanisms, case questionnaire, level of defense

FP-372: Family issues: Parenting I

A multidimensional model of parental involvement in schooling

*Lorenz, Fiona Psychology, University of Bielefeld, Bielefeld, Germany **Wild, Elke** Psychology, University of Bielefeld, Bielefeld, Germany*

Both, the concept of authoritative parenting and self-determination theory specify characteristics of powerful learning environments. The present study integrates these approaches in a multidimensional model of parental involvement in schooling. In order to test the adequacy of this model, corresponding scales were administered to 133 German 3rd graders and their parents participating in a longitudinal study with annual measurements. Correlational analyses and confirmatory factor analyses support the construct and predictive validity of the four-dimensional model and substantiate requests for differentiated concepts of parental involvement in schooling.

The implicit beliefs about human nature and parenting behavior: The mediation process model

Lin, Wen-Ying Dept. of Psychology, Chung Yuan Christian Univers., Chungli, Taiwan

This study explores the unsolved contention that parenting beliefs do not have sufficient predictive power for parenting behavior. The mediation process model proposed that beliefs about human nature have a more important impact on parenting behavior than parenting beliefs via their influence on the attribution process. 525 participants completed scales measuring parenting beliefs and general beliefs about intelligence and responded to 4 vignettes that measured contingent beliefs about intelligence. Findings supported the main predictions of the mediation process model. The real determinants of parenting behavior are contingent beliefs about intelligence, which lead to varied attributions and parenting behaviors.

Investigation into the parental nursing style of female drug addicts

Liu, Yumei Dept. of Social Sciences, Hainan Medical College, Haikou, People's Republic of China

Objective: To investigate the mental health and parental nursing style of female drug addicts. Methods: The female drug addicts in the Drug Rehabilitation Center of Hainan Province in China were investigated using SCL-90 and face-to-face interviews. Results: The frustration and experience of early life, an unhealthy family background, and society were the most influential factors. Their health was worse than normal women's in terms of somatization, obsessive compulsive and depressive disorders. The parental nursing style of female drug addicts increased the feeling of rejection and incidences of denial. Conclusion: the parental nursing style cannot be ignored.

FP-373: Collective identities and collective action I

Psychological factors of Poles' accession to European Union

Zaleski, Zbigniew Dept. of Psychology, Catholic University Lublin, Lublin, Poland

A sample of 1309 Poles responded to questionnaire either in favour of or against joining the European Union which took place before and after the Accession Referendum in 2003. The results showed that those who were in favour of accession displayed higher level of patriotism, future goal-orientation, conformity, political leaders' influence and similarity to Western Europeans. Negative attitude was linked to national pride and future anxiety. The post-referendum data from 507 Ss revealed the decrease of emotions and expectations bound to country's accession. The author discusses the results in a psychopolitical context of decision-making for future generations.

Social responsibility: Analyses of mass political actions participants' discourse

*Naydonov, Mykhaylo ISPP, Kyiv, Ukraine **Grygorovska, Lyubov** Psychol. - Monitorig Research, Inst. of Social and Political, Kyiv, Ukraine*

Mass political actions participants are the silent group since politicians adopt the right to speak on behalf of them. The aim is to study the diversity of the discourse formed within the participants' environment during a mass action that is not presented by politicians. The discourse analyses of the social responsibility (SR) issue has been conducted in interviews of the mass political actions participants in Ukraine in 2004-2005 (n=380). Four types of the SR represented in the discourse (political, media, grassroots, personal) have been defined. Intersubject SR form means responsibility for trust, promise, mobilizing, intrasubject - for choice, words, deeds.

Friends attitudes to mass political action: During and after

Naydonova, Lyubov A. Psychol. of Mass Communication, ISPP, Kyiv, Ukraine

The subject of this investigation is the influence participants' friendship relations on their emotional attitudes to mass political action. The sampling covered 965 participants of the Ukrainian mass moves. Method of modality and emotional strength evaluation and the implicit association test were applied. Those participants who took part in the mass political movement together with their friends

(N=319) have the differences in emotional states which decrease the risk of development of uncontrolled crowd spanned with negative emotions (panic, aggressive). The context of friendly relationships has the influence on participants' more extensive inclusion into the emotional spin of positive states.

FP-374: Conditioning II

Two behavioral measures to prevent (conditioned) nausea: Synergistic or antagonistic?

Enck, Paul Psychosomatische Medizin, Universitätsklinik Tübingen, Tübingen, Germany *Klosterhalfen, Sibylle* Psychosomatic Medicine, University Hospital Tübingen, Tübingen, Germany *Hall, Geoffrey* Dept. of Psychology, University of York, York, United Kingdom

Latent inhibition (LI) and overshadowing (OS) are two conditioning procedures to reduce nausea. We tested whether they are synergistic or antagonistic. Methods: Rotation-nausea was induced in 32 subjects (16 women) randomly assigned to one of 4 groups: LI+OS+; LI+OS-, LI-OS+, LI-OS-. LI was induced by re-exposure to the rotation environment, OS was performed by providing salient drinks preceding rotation. Symptom ratings (SR), cortisol and TNF-α were compared between groups. Results: LI increased SR and cortisol, while OS reduced both. TNF-α decreased with LI, while it increased with OS. Conclusion: The combination of OS and LI has antagonistic effects on rotation-induced nausea.

I didn't feel like drinking beer but I don't know why: Evaluative conditioning changes drinking behavior and explicit attitudes

Schoenmakers, Tim Clinical Psychological Science, Maastricht University, Maastricht, Netherlands *Houben, Katrijn* Clinical Psychological Science, Maastricht University, Maastricht, Netherlands *Wiers, Reinout* Clinical Psychological Science, Maastricht University, Maastricht, Netherlands

We used a conditioning paradigm to change beer attitudes and drinking behavior in students. Participants had to spot an irrelevant target picture in a series of trials in which many different stimuli were presented. In a number of these trials beer-related pictures (CS's) were paired with negative words and pictures (US's). After conditioning, an ANOVA demonstrated less positive explicit beer attitudes and less beer consumption in a bogus taste test in the experimental compared to control (no exposure to US-CS pairs) condition. However, there was no effect on implicit attitudes. Results are discussed in terms of causality and clinical usefulness.

Training procedures that eliminate conditioned fear in rodents and prevent fear relapse

Thomas, Brian Psychology, Baldwin-Wallace College, Berea, USA

Rats were trained to fear a stimulus using a standard conditioned suppression procedure and were then given one of several different extinction procedures to see if fear could be eliminated and relapse prevented. Data from several effective procedures (explicitly unpaired, differential conditioning, conditioned inhibition, counterconditioning) will be presented and a theory of extinction learning will be described.

FP-375: Elementary information processing I

Differential connectivity of valenced person representations with and without subliminal priming of attachment-related stressors

Lemche, Erwin BCN Neuroimaging Center, Rijksuniversiteit Groningen, Groningen, Netherlands *Giampietro, Vincent P.* Brain Image Analysis Unit, Institute of Psychiatry, London, United Kingdom *Surguladze, Simon A.* Section Neuroscience & Emo, Institute of Psychiatry, London, United Kingdom *Phillips, Mary L.* Section Neuroscience & Emo, Institute of Psychiatry, London, United Kingdom

Objective The higher order cognitive networks of valenced mental representations of persons have not yet been elucidated. Methods We used an attachment priming experiment in fMRI with concurrent recording of skin conductance with single trials for positive and negative valence representations after a neutral prime or a stress prime in 12 healthy volunteer subjects and modeled effective connectivity. Results Increase in arousal was observed from positive to negative and from neutral to stress conditions. Model fits indicated shifts to subcortical regions in the stress condition. Conclusions Our results show that effective connectivity is altered for valence representations by induction of separation distress.

How to process a prime?: Semantic priming depends on task set

Bermeitinger, Christina Inst. Verhaltenspsychologie, Universität des Saarlandes, Saarbrücken, Germany *Frings, Christian* Cognitive Psychology Unit, Saarland University, Saarbruecken, Germany *Wentura, Dirk* Cognitive Psychology Unit, Saarland University, Saarbruecken, Germany

In a semantic priming task, we found an interaction of category-type (natural vs. artifactual) by sex: males showed positive priming for both category-types, whereas females showed positive priming for natural but not for artifactual categories. We hypothesized that this difference is due to different prime processing: females might dominantly focus on perceptual features in contrast to functional features. When we made functional features more relevant with an additional task, females showed priming for artifactual categories as well. Thus, the inclusion of a second task moderates category priming by making certain features more salient. In conclusion, semantic priming depends on task set.

Familiarity in the spotlight: Exploring the role of target familiarity in affective priming

Prada, Marília Social-Organizational Psych., ISPA, Lisbon, Portugal *Garcia-Marques, Teresa* UIPCDE, ISPA, Lisbon, Portugal *Silva, Rita*

Research in affective priming domain has mainly focused on how certain primes' characteristics may influence targets' processing, overlooking the role of the later. Given that some objects are able to automatically activate their associated evaluations, and that familiar objects' attitudes are taken to resist more to contextual influences, target's familiarity may moderate these effects. In a first study only the least familiar targets appeared to be evaluated in the direction of the activated valence. These results were then followed-up via an interference-paradigm, using valenced words as stimuli. Implications for affective priming research domain will be discussed.

FP-376: Cognition and work I

Cognitive load and human-machine interaction

Canas, Jose Dept. of Cognitive Ergonomy, University of Granada, Granada, Spain *Di Stasi, Leandro* Dept. of Experimental Psycho, University of Granada, Granada, Spain *Antoli, Adoración* Dept. of Exper.

Psychology, University of Granada, Granada, Spain *Alvarez, Vanessa* Dept. of Expe. Psychology, University of Granada, Granada, Spain *Madrid, Rafael I.* Dept. of Expe. Psychology, University of Granada, Granada, Spain

Cognitive load is a fundamental concept in explaining how people use technology to perform their tasks. It is related to the type and amount of resources required by the task, technology available and user goals. User efficiency and effort depend on the level of cognitive load. Therefore, new technologies must be designed to define new modes of interaction that reduce cognitive load. Methodological problems have limit research on measuring user's cognitive resources while performing a task. However, recent technical developments on psychophysiological measurement of cognitive load could now allow researchers and designers to evaluate on-line cognitive load during interaction with technology. Some of these techniques based on eye-movements parameters will be presented.

Assessing work-related knowledge using a free association technique and structure mapping: Validation studies

Rothe, Heinz-Jürgen Inst. für Psychologie, Universität Potsdam, Potsdam, Germany *Ceglarek, Petra* Institut für Psychologie, Universität Potsdam, Potsdam, Germany

Organisations rely heavily on techniques that allow the assessment individual's domain specific knowledge, for example, to evaluate the effectiveness of training interventions. We present a number of studies that support the validity of two such techniques; free association and structure mapping. They are based on the assumption that knowledge is structured in semantic networks, that those networks can be accessed through a stimulus-association technique and structure formation techniques. Validation studies indicate a relationship between supervisor performance ratings and results of both techniques. For example, the number of associations and the diameter of the semantic structure developed by participants correlated with the performance rating.

Action regulation theory: Are the characteristics of well designed tasks valid for interactive jobs as well?

Melzer, Marlen Institute f. General Psycholog, Technical Univ. of Dresden, Dresden, Germany *Hacker, Winfried* Institute f. General Psycholog, Technical Univ. of Dresden, Dresden, Germany

International standards (DIN EN 9241-2; DIN EN 614-2) demand compliance with "characteristics of well-designed tasks" in job design. However, for jobs including client or customer interaction - almost 70 percent of all jobs - the positive effects of job design in such manner have not been proven yet. Exemplarily 499 jobs in retail sales were examined using observation-based and subjective measures. Statistical analysis consisted in the comparison of differently well-designed retail jobs. The results recommend compliance with the standards for these jobs as well whereat adjustments for customer interaction especially with regard to the core characteristic "task completeness" are necessary.

FP-377: Determinants of environmental attitude and behavior

Responsibility for natural resources and the environment as a function of scientific competencies

Schütte, Kerstin IPN, Universität zu Kiel, Kiel, Germany *Schöps, Katrin* Educational Science, IPN, Kiel, Germany

Thorough comprehension of scientific concepts and processes is assumed to enhance persons' responsibility for natural resources and the environment and to foster its maintenance. PISA 2006 collected data from 15-year-old students from 57 countries. We used regression analyses to investigate the predictive power of the students' scientific competencies for their responsibility for natural resources and the environment and for their cognitions on environmental issues. Implications for interventions will be discussed. However, the results are confidential until the release of the international PISA report.

The impact of social economic status-human agency link on pro-environmental behaviors
Valencia, Marshall *Dept. of Psychology, De La Salle University, Manila, Philippines*
A structural model was hypothesized reflecting pro-environmental behaviors as a function of the social economic status (SES) and human agency (environmental efficacy and outcome expectations) link. Using mixed method design, questionnaire data from 348 college students were analyzed using structural equations modeling. Interview data provided further qualitative depth. Findings indicated that SES was negatively related with pro-environmental behaviors and indirectly related with efficacy. Outcome expectation positively relate to efficacy and pro-environmental behaviors. Qualitative data implied that environmental behaviors are unconsciously enacted. It was concluded that environmental behaviors are mostly cognitive scripts embedded by positioning in a social structure.

New ways to explain environmental attitudes and behaviors: An exploratory study
Caillaud, Sabine *Les Sables d'Olonnes, France*
The aim of the study was to explore different ways people use to think the link between environmental protection and economical constraints and to understand how these different representations explain environmental behaviors. Focus groups were conducted in France with students and were completely transcript. The analysis was conducted with Alceste, a software for lexical analysis, and with a dialogical content analysis. Results show the important role of new variables such as equity and rejection of consumer society. Finally, this exploratory study proposes to take account of these new variables to explain the gap between environmental attitudes and behavior.

Effects of the nature of information about global climate change and uncertainty on perception and sustainable behavior
Stone, Asako *Desert Researach Institute, Las Vegas, USA*
The objective of this study is to examine the effects of the nature of information and of uncertainty on human perceptions and sustainable behavior in the context of global climate change. The design of this study is 2 (information: logical vs. intuitive) x 2 (uncertainty: high vs. low) factorial experiment. The study hypothesized that logical information would be more effective than intuitive information to reduce uncertainty, change perception, and behavior relevant to global climate change. The results of the study will contribute valuable information to the current education and outreach efforts about global climate change.

Perspective-taking and the environment
Pahl, Sabine *Dept. of Psychology, University of Plymouth, Plymouth, United Kingdom* *Bauer, Judith* *School of Psychology - Social, University of Erlangen, Erlangen, Germany* *Zhou, Mi* *School o Psychology, University of Plymouth, Plymouth, United Kingdom*
Three experimental studies followed up the recent idea of using perspective taking (PT) to increase pro-environmental concern or behaviour. Study 1 had three conditions: PT with a person in the

future, objective and control. PT increased self-reported behaviour and information search. Study 2 tested the role of individual differences in PT. Only when participants were low in chronic PT did PT instructions affect reported behaviour. Study 3 compared PT with flood victims between Chinese and British participants and found an effect of PT on pro-environmental attitudes (NEP) that was stronger in the Chinese sample. Implications for interventions will be discussed.

Psychosocial factors related to Thais' mobile phone usage and battery disposal
Choochom, Oraphin *Behavioral Science Research, Srinakharinwirot University, Bangkok, Thailand*
The purpose of this study was to investigate and predict Thais' mobile phone usage and battery disposal. The sample consisted of 2,176 Thai mobile phone users in Bangkok. The data showed that most mobile phone users kept used batteries in their houses. The second method of mobile phone battery disposal was discarded with other waste garbages. The result also indicated that mobile phone users who disposed used mobile batteries mixed with other waste garbages had less appropriate intention of mobile phone battery disposal, less appropriate attitude towards mobile phone battery disposal, less mobile phone-battery knowledge, and more extrinsic motivation on mobile phone battery disposal.

FP-378: Family issues: Marriage

The study of relationship between couple privacy and marriage successes
Mehdizadegan, Iran *Dept. of Education, Islamic Azad University Khoras, Esfahan, Islamic Republic of Iran* *Atashpour, Hamid* *Psychology, Islamic Azad University Khoras, Esfahan, Islamic Republic of Iran*
The main purpose of this research is the study of couple privacy and marriage successes relationship. This research is a survey study. In this study 300 subjects selected via random sampling. The results of this research show that there is a significant negative relationship between tow variables (p=0.000). it also has been indicated that there is a significant and inverse relationship between the age and the subject group point of view (including process of marriage status group, hold married status and in process of divorce) for privacy. Other findings of the study show that there is significant relationship between the subjects level of job, gender, age and their point of view for privacy.

Brazilian men and women in the family: Can we speak of role reorganization?
Rocha Coutinho, Maria Lúcia *Dept. of Psychology, UFRJ / UNIVERSO, Rio de Janeiro, Brazil*
This work presents the results of an exploratory study conducted with two Brazilian middle-class couples in which the husband and wife have a paid job, in order to see how they share household duties and child care. Our data suggest that, although men's participation in the house increased, it continues to be seen as a "help" and is mostly related to recreational activities and food shopping. Women are still seen and see themselves as the main responsible for the household duties and family care, which includes providing children an adequate nutrition and physical care and supervising their activities.

The old story of marriage: An attempt to understand jealousy in Turkey?
Cetinkaya, Evrim *Dept. of Educational Sciences, Middle East Technical Univers., Ankara, Turkey* *Kemer, Gulsah* *Educational Sciences, Middle East Technical Universi, Ankara, Turkey* *Bulgan, Gokce* *Educational Sciences, Middle East Technical Universi, Ankara, Turkey* *Tezer, Esin* *Educational Sciences, Middle East Technical Universi, Ankara, Turkey*

This study examined the relationships of gender, infidelity type (emotional-sexual infidelity), and three dimensions of jealousy (emotional, behavioral, and cognitive) among 499 (264 female, 235male) married individuals. Factorial MANOVA results indicated that gender and infidelity types have significant main effect on the linear combination of three dimensions of marital jealousy. However, no significant interaction effect was found. Posthoc analysis showed that males were more emotionally jealous than females, and individuals who find sexual infidelity more upsetting were emotionally more jealous than the ones who find emotional infidelity more upsetting. The results were discussed in the light of the existing literature.

The influence of marital adjustment on sexual health
Gharaei, Vajiheh *Payamenoor University, University of Mashhad, Mashhad, Islamic Republic of Iran* *Alavi, Tahere* *Ferdowsi University, University, Mashhad, Islamic Republic of Iran*
This study aimed to investigate the effect of marital maladjustment on sexual problems in street women and to compare it with marital adjustment in normal women in Mashhad. A comparative-causative design was use. The data collection was carried out using a DAS questionnaire. Sample group was composed of 80 women, who were randomly allocated into two groups. The data analysis was taken place using SPSS version and independent t-test was used. The results revealed that there was a significant difference (α=0/01) between two groups in marital adjustment scores. The average marital adjustment scores in street women was lower than normal women.

The effect of communication skills training on communication patterns and positive feelings toward spouse on couples in Ahvaz, Iran
Khojasteh Mehr, Reza *Counseling Dept., Shahid Chamran University, Ahvaz, Islamic Republic of Iran* *Attari, Yoosef Ali* *Counseling, Shahid Chamran University, Ahvaz,kooye ostadane daneshgha, Islamic Republic of Iran* *Shirali, khadije* *Counseling, Shahid Chamran University, Ahvaz,kooye ostadane daneshgha, Islamic Republic of Iran*
This study has examined the effect of communication skills training on communication patterns and positive feelings toward spouse on couples in Ahvaz,Iran.24 couples were randomly assigned to experimental and control groups.Communication Pattern Questionnair and Positive Feelings Questionnair were administered in this study. The experimental group was exposed to communication skills training. The collected data were analyzed by using multivariate analysis of variance.The findings show that communication skills training had increased positive feelings and constuctive pattern and decreased demand withdrawl pattern and mutual avoidence pattern toward spouse.This study has implications for family therapists.

FP-379: Clinical neuropsychology II

Physiological and psychological stress responses in adult patients with Attention-Deficit/ Hyperactivity Disorder (ADHD)
Lackschewitz, Halina *Inst. für Klin. Psychologie, Universität Göttingen, Göttingen, Germany* *Hüther, Gerald* *Psychiatry and Psychotherapy, Georg-August University, Goettingen, Germany* *Kröner-Herwig, Birgit* *Clinical Psychology, Georg-August University, Goettingen, Germany*
The study examined psychological and physiological (salivary cortisol, heart rate, heart rate variability) stress responses in 18 adult ADHD subjects in comparison to 18 healthy controls under laboratory conditions (Trier Social Stress Test). Baseline levels in both groups were similar. While the ADHD group experienced significantly greater

subjective stress during the anticipation and stress phase, ANOVA results for the physiological variables were mixed. ADHD subjects revealed an attenuated HR during the stress phase. Trends were observed for the some HRV parameters and for cortisol, potentially indicating further alterations of specific aspects of the stress response in adult ADHD patients.

Electric brain patterns during pleasant and unpleasant emotions, induced by dangerous and neutral images in paranoid type of schizophrenia as intensification of instinct of self-preservation

Mironicheva, Alexandra psychology, Moscow State University, Moscow, Russia Arhipov, Andrey psychiatry, Medical center "Preobrazen, Moscow, Russia

The hypothesis is the intensification of instinct of self-preservation caused by cortical-subcortical reciprocal interaction. A visual seria of dangerous and neutral images, induced pleasant and unpleasant emotions, were showed to 7 patients with paranoid type of schizophrenia, 10 patients in remission and 10 healthy. Event related potentials and EEG coherent activity were studied with Mann-Witney test. In group of schizophrenia and control group amplitude and latence of both components of evoked potential change between healthy and schizophrenic patients. Evoked potentials correlation and coherent activity of patients with paranoid type of schizophrenia differ from healthy when neutral images were showed and didn't differ when it was images, connected with danger.

Neurocognitive impairment of bipolar patients and their healthy siblings

Tam, Wai-Cheong Carl Dept. of Psychology, ChungYuan Christian University, Chung Li, Taiwan Chiang, Shih-Kuang Clinical Psychology, Yu Li Veterans Hospital, Yuli Town, Taiwan Shiah, Yung-Jong General Education Center, Chienkuo Technology University, Changhua, Taiwan

Patients with bipolar disorder have been found to have neurocognitive impairment. If this impairment is genetically transmitted, the healthy siblings of these patients will also have some degree of the neurocognitive impairment. In this study, 58 bipolar patients, 59 healthy siblings, and 36 normal controls were recruited. A computerized battery of neurocognitive tasks were administered to each participant. Results indicated that both the patients and their healthy siblings had impairment on Wisconsin card sort, backward masking, and Asarnow continuous performance task. It appears that some neurocognitive tasks might be the biobehavioral markers of bipolar disorder.

FP-380: Personality and individual differences

Assessing resilience in HIV-infected mothers and their children

Eloff, Irma University of Pretoria, Pretoria, South Africa Ebersöhn, Liesel Educational Psychology, University of Pretoria, Pretoria, South Africa Boeving, Alex School of Medicine, Yale University, New Haven, USA Sikkema, Kathy School of Public Health, Duke University, Durham, USA Finestone, Michelle Educational Psychology, University of Pretoria, Pretoria, South Africa Forsyth, Brian Pediatrics, Yale University, New Haven, USA

In this paper we discuss the construct of resilience and describe the process of developing and culturally tailoring measures of resilience in a longitudinal study of HIV-infected mothers [n=440] and their children in South Africa. We describe the 18-month pilot study in the Kgolo Mmogo project, where the initial instrument battery for assessing resilience was adjusted to a final instrument battery which included instruments that assessed for emo-

tional intelligence, stress and coping, spiritual coping, self-concept, depression and developmental and behavioral factors. We adopted an iterative process for adjusting the instrument battery. This included trial assessments, feedback-groups, individual interviews, reflections, translations, back-translations, instrument-notations and exploring alternative instruments.

Investigating hackers' personality characteristics

Atashpour, Hamid Psychology, Azad University, Isfahan, Islamic Republic of Iran Salahshouri, Nasrin Psychology, Azad University, Isfahan, Islamic Republic of Iran Samsam Shariat, Mohamad Reza Psychology, Azad University, Isfahan, Islamic Republic of Iran Samavatyan, Hossein Psychology, Isfahan University, Isfahan, Islamic Republic of Iran

The purpose of this study was to compare the personality characteristics of internet hackers with normal users. Demographic and hacking desires as well as personality questionnaires were used. The collected data from 42 hackers and 33 normal users were analyzed and showed significant differences between the two groups (p<0.001). Also, the relationships between hacking desire and gender, the level of responsibility, tolerance, and independency were significant (p<0.001). The findings of the study would have some implications such as identifying the potential hackers on the basis of their personality.

Personality determinants of interpersonal professional behaviours in medical students

Munro, Don School of Psychology, University of Newcastle, Callaghan, Australia Bore, Miles School of Psychology, University of Newcastle, Callaghan, NSW, Australia Powis, David School of Psychology, University of Newcastle, Callaghan, NSW, Australia

We have been exploring aspects of personality that may be used to predict the interpersonal skills of medical students and doctors, including those relating to the treatment of patients/clients and those concerned with relationships between medical professionals (e.g., Munro, Bore & Powis, Australian Journal of Psychology, 2005). We describe an extension of the work with ten further facets of personality that have also emerged as relevant, centering on mental health and self control factors. The results suggest a revised model using three composite dimensions. This model will be discussed in relation to existing theories linking personality and interpersonal behaviours.

FP-381: Person perception & impression formation II

Social evaluation theory

Gifford, Robert Dept. of Psychology, University of Victoria, Victoria, Canada

Existing theories do not clearly postulate which types of persons might fulfill one's interpersonal needs and goals. To rectify this, social evaluation theory (SET) is introduced. SET posits that people routinely appraise the potential of others to fulfil their needs, and proposes the concept of need-satisfaction assessments (NSAs) to represent a taxonomy of eight archetypal person types. In 14 studies, scales for measuring NSAs were developed and located around a circumplex. Subsequent studies demonstrate that people do experience the need for these person types, and that NSAs play an important role in person perception and social interaction.

Dynamics of understanding others through a training session in social perception

Akhmadeeva, Diana Social Dept., Moscow State University, Moscow, Russia

The purpose of our research was to detect the main directions and the character of changes involved in understanding other people and in which areas of

understanding these changes occurs. The main method of research was interviewing participants before and after the training session of social perception, using the G.Kelly's Repertory Grids. The obtained Personal Constructs were processed by using content-analysis and quantitative analysis. The results show certain dynamics in cognitive area (categorial semantic structure of understanding) and affective area (changes in attitudes to others).

Better when together? Effects of distributed cognition in impression formation and person memory

Garrido, Margarida Social & Org. Psychology, ISCTE: Lisbon Univ Institute, Lisbon, Portugal Garcia-Marques, Leonel Psychology & Education, University of Lisbon, Lisbon, Portugal Hamilton, David Psychology, Univ. California, Sta Barbara, Santa Barbara, USA Ferreira, Mário Psychology & Education, University of Lisbon, Lisbon, Portugal

In two experiments we examined impression-formation and person-memory as socially-distributed cognitive processes. Participants' (N=156) individual and collaborative impression-formation and recall were compared. Non-collaborative performed better than collaborative-recall groups. This effect disappeared when impressions were formed collaboratively. Additionally, participants encoding collaboratively outputted a set of comments that moderated recall performance (comments reflecting elaborated processing led to higher recall when compared to simple trait-encoding or less elaborated processing). More elaborated processing led to better recall even when performed by others. These results extend the socially situated cognition approach to person memory suggesting that impression-formation and recall are often socially distributed cognitive processes.

Mental representations of poverty among poor women in Southern Philippines

Generalao, Flora Social Sciences Division, UP Cebu College, Cebu, Philippines

How is poverty construed by poor women in Southern Philippines? Interviews among 373 women from rural (n=145) and urban (n=288) Southern Philippines revealed representations that included a shortfall of daily food resources, internal causation, and positive affect. Respondents who were able to meet their quotidian food requirements tended to externalize poverty and as such, defined themselves as non-poor. Positive appraisals of their condition were significantly correlated with long-term poverty, with uncontrollable and permanent conceptions of poverty's cause, with better-off judgments of their condition compared to their neighbors, and with perceived entitlement of the rich.

FP-382: Work system school

Levers of institutional transformation: System-level working hypotheses in international group relations conferences

De Loach, Stan México City, Mexico

Aim: To document developing transformations of educational and learning models used in Tavistock group relations conferences, through recent verbatim working hypotheses focusing on system behaviors and psychodynamics. Method: Qualitative analysis to document the degree and types of institutional transformation resulting from verbal communication of staff-formulated interpretations of primitive latent and overt stresses in interactions among multinational social systems. Results: Participants reported gaining increased understanding of dynamic organizational behaviors and acquiring experiential learning skills applicable in institutional management. Conclusion: Interpreting, understanding, and reflectively participating in institutional system events (ISE) may improve collaboration in today's multinational world of intermingled commerce, ethnicity, religion.

The role of teachers' work values to the perception of principal's efficiency and behavior

Milasiunaite, Vilma Kaunas, Lithuania *Ma, Vita –, P.Vileisis secondary school, Kaunas, Lithuania*
Objective: To evaluate the links between the work related values and perception of principal's work. Methods: Case study limits the number of participants till fifty seven. The questionnaire measures principal's perceived efficiency, interpersonal behavior and personal work related values. Scales were composed using factor analysis. The connections were estimated using correlation analysis. Results: The values of control and respect are not connected with principal's perception. Workplace comfort and autonomy correlates with perception of principal's efficiency. Achievement and collaboration correlates both with efficiency and behavior. Conclusions: Values affect the perception of principal. He/ she is perceived as a leader when he/she is displaying behavior congruent with teacher's values.

Study of a reform process: Problems in building an analysis system

Crescentini, Alberto Scienze dell'Educazione, Alta Scuola Pedagogica, Locarno, Switzerland *Berger, Emanuele* Ufficio studi e ricerche, Ufficio studi e ricerche, Bellinzona, Switzerland *Pedrazzini-Pesce, Francesca* Ufficio Studi e Ricerche, Ufficio Studi e Ricerche, Bellinzona, Switzerland *Tamagni Bernasconi, Kathya* Ufficio studi e ricerche, Ufficio studi e ricerche, Bellinzona, Switzerland *Tozzini, Luana* Ufficio studi e ricerche, Ufficio studi e ricerche, Bellinzona, Switzerland
Inside Italian-speaking Switzerland is currently underway a reform process Our purpose is to produce an analysis grid to study this process in four case studies and in whole school system. All the public documents on the reform and some interviews with privileged witnesses have been analyzed; to check reliability we use a double blind coding system. Analysis helps in refinement of theoretical frame and in producing a detection and analysis grid to study our educational institutions and school system. Import investigating models from different contexts may be problematical for the evaluation of real weight of each dimension in the phenomenon.

Organizational effectiveness of school managers in Ukraine through the competing values model approach

Alla, Basina Organizational Psychology, Institute of Psychology, Kiev, Ukraine
Objective: To find out dominant models of school managers. Methods: The research was conducted on 230 school heads and deputy heads using R.Quinn Competing Values Instruments. Results: 1. School managers used Human Relations, Open Systems, Rational-Goal, and Internal Process Models; 2. Leadership roles influenced managerial effectiveness and organizational culture, with age and term in position being the main determinants. 4. 65% of the respondents had high performance and effectiveness in the Rational-Goal Model and Internal Process Model, 27% in Human Relations Model, and 7% in Open Systems Model. Conclusion: An effective management course has been successfully tested in the Central Institute of Post Graduate Pedagogical Training.

FP-383: Victims' reaction to violence and human rights violations

Post-conflict Aceh, Indonesia: Collectivism, worldview, and authoritarianism

Zain, Fajran Public Policy Analysis, Aceh Institute, Banda Aceh, Indonesia *Holtz, Rolf* Psychological Science, Ball State University, Muncie, IN, USA
Objectives: Civil war makes the world seem a dangerous place, which should mediate the relationship between vertical collectivism and authoritarianism. Methods: 215 Acehnese recalled brutal experiences from 1976-2005 military operations. Horizontal/vertical collectivism/individualism, Acehnese group identification, belief in a dangerous world (BDW), and right-wing authoritarianism (RWA) were also assessed. Results: AMOS modeling showed that wartime experiences predicted Acehnese identity [$\beta = .03$, $p < .002$]; and Acehnese identity predicted BDW [$\beta = .26$, $p < .001$]. BDW mediated the relationship between vertical collectivism and RWA. [RMSEA (.039), GFI (.97), and AGFI (.94)] Conclusions: Civil war predominantly influenced aggressiveness among vertical collectivists.

Identity salience: The contribution of trauma variables, collective identity commitment, and mental health to militancy and suicidality: The Palestinians case

Kira, Ibrahim Center for Cumulative Trauma, Hamtramck, MI, USA *Nasser, Abdul-Wahab* Field Studies, Center for Cumulative Trauma, Hamtramck, MI, USA *Abou-Median, Sharifa* Research, Center for Cumulative Trauma, Hamtramck, MI, USA *Mohanesh, Jamal* field research, Center for Cumulative Trauma, Hamtramck, MI, USA *Elamia, Hala* Research, Center for Cumulative Trauma, Hamtramck, MI, USA *Lewandowski, Linda* College of Nursing, Wayne State University, Detroit, MI, USA *Templin,, Thomas* Health Research, Wayne State University, Detroit, MI, USA *Ozkan, Bulent* Research, Wayne State University, Detroit, MI, USA
Why people, fearing death, kill themselves? ITMT suggests that the salience of identity, personal, and collective can explain. Using samples from Palestine' West Bank and Gaza, we developed a measure for collective identity salience. Exploratory and confirmatory factor analysis found two factors: Identity commitment and Militancy. Using measures of fear of death, annihilation anxiety, general anxiety, PTSD, CTD, depression and trauma types; multiple regression and path analysis revealed that personal identity trauma was associated with decrease in fear of death, mental health problems and increased clinical suicide and/ or militancy. Collective identity trauma, while it did not affect significantly fear of death, was associated with more of increase in identity commitment and militancy.

Reconciliation and mental health in traumatized victims of human right violations

Stammel, Nadine Research, Behandlungszentrum Folteropfer, Berlin, Germany *Knaevelsrud, Christine* Research, Behandlungszentrum Folteropfer, Berlin, Germany *Böttche, Maria* Research, Behandlungszentrum Folteropfer, Berlin, Germany *Neuner, Frank* Institut für Psychologie, Universität Konstanz, Konstanz, Germany
It is assumed that reconciliation has a positive effect on mental health in victims of human right violations. To asses the readiness to reconcile with the perpetrators a questionnaire was constructed. The interviewed sample (N=45) consisted of Kurdish refugees from Turkey. Factor Analysis revealed 3 questionnaire subscales. Reliability was high (Cronbach's α =.88). Validity was proved with Monotrait-Multimethod. First analysis showed a low correlation between the readiness to reconcile and PTSD (r=-.076; p=.65), Depression (r=-,284;

p=.115), Anxiety (r=-.275; p=.127) and Quality of Life (r=,174; p=,311). Results indicate that there is only a low connection between the readiness to reconcile and mental health in Kurdish victims of human right violations.

Longitudinal study on mental health and living conditions of refugees who are returning to their country of origin

von Lersner, Ulrike Inst. für Klin. Psychologie, Universität Konstanz, Reichenau, Germany *Rieder, Heide* Clinical Psychology, University of Konstanz, Reichenau, Germany *Wiens, Ulrike* Clinical Psychology, University of Konstanz, Reichenau, Germany *Elbert, Thomas* Clinical Psychology, University of Konstanz, Reichenau, Germany
In a study among refugees from the former Yugoslavia we study the impact of voluntary assisted return programs (VARP) on mental health. We investigate the psychiatric status (M.I.N.I., PDS), quality of life (EUROHIS) and living conditions before and after return in N= 90 refugees (40 returnees, 50 'stayers'). The prevalence of psychiatric disorders among returnees is high before return (48 %). Nine months after return the rate increases to 71 %. In 60 % the decision to return is forced by immigration officials. The results call for a redefinition of VARP taking into consideration the vulnerability of the participants.

FP-384: Visual processes

The sampling strategies for 3-D figures

Cao, Liren Dept. of Psychology, Zhejiang University, Hangzhou, People's Republic of China *Tian, Jia* Psychology Department, Zhejiang University, Hangzhou, People's Republic of China
The study was focused on the difference of sampling strategy between 3-D geometrical figures and their real objects. A eyelink system was used to record the eyes movements of subjects. The results were as follows: ① The first-sampling-point were mainly located at the critical features, such as corner, outline parts, both for 3-D figures and real objects. ② The scan-paths and the sampling order for figures were not different from their real objects. Most fixations located at the critical features and meaningful features. ③ The sampling orders were relative stable both for figures and their real objects.

Hue discrimination in the physiological meaningful DKL color space

Hansen, Thorsten General Psychology, University of Giessen, Gießen, Germany
Hue discrimination has been traditionally investigated by measuring detectable differences between wavelengths. Here we investigate hue discrimination in a physiologically meaningful color space. Discrimination thresholds are measured for 32 subjects along the cardinal axes and along intermediate axes in the isoluminant plane of the DKL color space. No gender differences were found. Hue discrimination was best along the cardinal directions, suggesting an important contribution of precortical processing stages in hue discrimination. Discrimination was worse along the main diagonal, in particular for magenta. Interestingly, discrimination was also good along the second diagonal for yellow/orange, the color of various flowers and fruits.

Differential seasonal processing in parvo- and koniocellular visual pathways in depression

Wesner, Michael Psychology, CBTC-Lakehead University, Thunder Bay, Canada *Pavlou, Dina* Psychology, CBTC-Lakehead University, Thunder Bay, Canada
Disruptive functioning of distinct parallel streams in the visual pathway can have important implications for understanding the pathophysiology of depression. Using noninvasive psychophysics, we

compared the spatiotemporal contrast sensitivity (CS) functions of non-depressed, seasonally depressed, and non-seasonally depressed individuals across seasons. Both depressed groups had an inferred parvocellular-mediated CS enhancement, with the NON-seasonally depressed showing neurovisual CS shifts between summer and winter. Also, shifts in inferred koniocellular operations were noted. This, coupled with our narrow-band short-wavelength adaptation studies, suggest that S-cones, as part of a photopic gain system, are also involved with nontraditional koniocellular retinogeniculate projections. Possible depressive neural mechanisms are discussed.

Binocular unmasking is important for the detection, categorization and identification of noise-masked real-life objects
de la Rosa, Stephan Dept. of Psychology, University of Toronto, Mississauga, Canada Schneider, Bruce Psychology, University of Toronto, Mississauga, Canada Moraglia, Giampaolo Psychology, University of Toronto, Mississauga, Canada
Binocular unmasking refers to the improved detection performance of noise-masked simple visual patterns (e.g. grating) in the presence compared to the absence of 3-D cues (stereoscopic depth cues). Here we investigated whether binocular unmasking is also important when perceiving noise-masked real-life objects. Specifically, we measured the detection, categorization, and identification thresholds of real-life objects in the presence and absence of stereoscopic depth cues. We found that the detection, categorization, and identification of objects was significantly better in the presence than in the absence of stereoscopic depth cues using hypothesis tests. Hence binocular unmasking seems important for object perception.

FP-385: Training and manipulation of values and moral skills

Sports-based prevention of violence/bullying and promotion of social and moral skills in adolescents: "fairplayer.sport"
Hess, Markus Freie Universität Berlin, Berlin, Germany Pawlizki, Christiane Erz.wissenschaft u. Psycholog, Freie Universität Berlin, Berlin, Germany Scheithauer, Herbert Erz.wissenschaften und Psych., Freie Universität Berlin, Berlin, Germany
Most of the programs developed to prevent violence/bullying and to promote socio-moral skills have been conceptualized for the school setting, leaving other domains of adolescent activities, like sports, unconsidered. We present a framework for a preventive intervention program aimed at promoting socio-moral skills within a team sports context. Adolescents (11 to 14 years of age) will take part in sequentially structured training sessions including physical and reflective elements. The preventive intervention will be evaluated using a randomized intervention-waiting-control group design. We will present data from the pre-evaluation study expecting improvements in a number of morally relevant skills like perspective-taking, empathy and emotion regulation.

Values and models of identification of adolescents and their parents
Frichand, Ana Institute of Psychology, Faculty of Philosophy, Skopje, The former Yugoslav Republic of Macedonia Surbanovska, Orhideja Institute of Psychology, Faculty of Philosophy, Skopje, The former Yugoslav Republic of Macedonia
The purpose of this study is to test the differences in value preferences and models of identification between adolescents and their parents. Three groups of hypothesis were tested. Subjects are 120 adolescents (14-20 years) and 240 parents (40-60 years). Significant differences (p<0.05; p<0.01) are found in value preferences and in the field from

which models of identification are selected, but not for characteristics of models. The results show that adolescents are less pro-socially oriented. With age more models are selected from culture, history and politics and less from sport and show-business. Subjects mostly choose characteristics from the group of humanity. Keywords: values, models of identification, adolescents, parents.

The unhappy moralist: Moral resilience and its emotional stress
Oser, Fritz Dept. of Education, University of Fribourg, Fribourg, Switzerland Hattersley, Lisa Education, University, Fribourg, Switzerland
We would like to present research results on the phenomenon of the so-called "Unhappy Moralist" effect. In different research projects we found - in contrast to the "Happy Victimizer" (Nunner-Winkler, 2001) - that in situations, in which moral courage contradicts economical success, subjects are discontent with the result of their action (negotiation, deal, discourse). The disadvantage of being moral and thus having less success leads to negative emotions and to a felt unsatisfactory result. We present outcomes of studies with children/adolescents aged 7-15 years. They are based on moral vignettes, in which the moral dimension conflicts with the success dimension.

Religious and laics values: Different relationships with religion and modern spirituality?
Muñoz-García, Antonio Educ. and Developm. Psychology, University of Granada, Granada, Spain
Values, as they are conceptualized by Schwartz's 10-value model, have showed a relatively pattern of relationships with religion (Saroglou et al, 2004): religious people tend to give high preference to values reflecting conservation (tradition, conformity) and limited self-transcendence (benevolence but not universalism), and low importance to values indicating openness to change and self-enhancement (self-direction, hedonism, stimulation, and in a less extended and systematic way, power and achievement). On the other hand, laics values (eg. tolerance, alterity, capacity of rebellion) are more and more relevant in secular societies and could be associated differently with religiousness and modern spirituality. We study those differences in preferences of values for religious and spiritual people.

FP-386: Development in adolescence and young adulthood II

Patterns of fulfilment in the domains of work, intimate relationship and leisure
Pinquart, Martin Inst. für Psychologie, Universität Marburg, Marburg, Germany Silbereisen, Rainer K. Inst. Entwicklungspsychologie, Universität Jena, Jena, Germany
We investigated patterns of fulfilment in the domains of work, partnership, and leisure among 1,977 German respondents. Eight groups were formed based on the combination of perceived career progress (yes/no), having a satisfying partnership (yes/no), and perceiving flow during leisure activities (yes/no). Individuals with high levels of flow during leisure reported the highest levels of positive affect. Lowest levels of depression were found in respondents who fulfilled at least two criteria of success. We conclude that for minimizing depressive symptoms and maximizing positive affect, individuals should have leisure activities combined with a positive intimate relationship or career progress.

Emerging adulthood and level of voice in different relational contexts
Kreyszig, Sheila Dept. of Psychology, University of Saskatchewan, Saskatoon, Canada
The researcher examined level of voice in relational contexts among 341 emerging adults at a Canadian university. Relationships between voice and relational context were found. In addition, differences in grade point average and level of voice in different contexts were uncovered. However, gender differences were not found on level of voice. Individuals (n=9) also participated in interviews providing rich information concerning their lives and experiences concerning level of voice. Results of this study indicate that emerging adulthood is truly a period where relationships and self-focus are of extreme importance and different contexts have been seen to affect level of voice.

Developmental trajectories from adolescence to young adulthood: The course of aggressive and rule-breaking behaviour
Winkler Metzke, Christa Kinder- und Jugendpsychiatrie, Universität Zürich, Zürich, Switzerland Zimprich, Daniel Psychologisches Institut, University of Zurich, Zürich, Switzerland Eschmann, Susanne Child & Adolescent Psychia, University of Zurich, Zürich, Switzerland Steinhausen, Hans-Christoph Child & Adolescent Psychia, University of Zurich, Zürich, Switzerland
Objectives: To examine trajectories of aggressive and rule-breaking behaviour and their concurrent and predictive validity. Methods: A longitudinal sample of 586 adolescents, four times of measurement. Longitudinal cluster analyses and semi-parametric mix-ture modelling. Results: Three similar trajectories were identified for both types of problem behaviour: persistent low levels, increasing and decreasing levels. A fourth most problematic trajectory began with a high level and continued with an increasing course of aggressive behaviour or had a late-onset-course of rule-breaking behaviour. Concurrent and predictive validity of these trajectories were established. Conclusions: Both general and specific processes in the development of aggressive and rule-breaking behaviour were observed.

FP-387: Communication and regulation behavior in intergenerational relationships II

Communication patterns perceived by adolescents about their mothers and adaptation variables
Armas Vargas, Enrique Person., Evaluat. & Psychology, Psychology Faculty, Tenerife, Spain
This study investigated the relationship between Communication Patterns & Problem-Solving Skills Questionnaire (Armas-Vargas, E.) with a group of teenagers, how do they communicate themselves with their mothers and the relationship with 4 areas of Adaptation. 182 students (12-14 years old). Factor analysis and reliability was conducted on the CPC-RC, 45% variance: 1) Help to Argue; 2) Ask/Give opinion; 3) Ask/Give an explanation; 4) Active listening and Wait turn; 5) Difficulty to reach Agreements. When boys perceived that their mothers give them an Explanation (3, the same with factors 1, 2 & 4) is positively related to all areas of adaptation. Difficulty to Reach Agreement affects negatively to familiar environment and the Self-esteem.

Parent /child ethnic prejudice relationship: Emerging moderators
Correia, Rita DEPSO/ ISCTE, CIS/ ISCTE, Lisbon, Portugal Monteiro, Maria Benedicta DEPSO/ ISCTE, DEPSO / ISCTE, Lisbon, Portugal
Although the contention that children's relation with their parents has an influence in the inter-

generational transmission of prejudice has been supported for various studies (Carlson & Iovini, 1985; Sinclair, Dunn & Lowery, 2004), some investigation shows no relation between parent and child prejudice (Aboud & Doyle, 1996; Branch & Newcombe, 1986). Those inconsistent results illustrate the need for deeper investigation. The current study examines the interactive effect of parents' prejudice and parent/children congruity of expectations on children's explicit and implicit pro-White/anti-Black prejudice. Results provide evidence that parents' racial attitudes influence their children's implicit racial prejudice but not their explicit prejudice.

Exploring the co-parenting family types of school-age children

Zou, Ping Normal College, Dalian University, Dalian, People's Republic of China Yang, Lizhu School of Education, Liaoning Normal University, Dalian, People's Republic of China Liu, Wen School of Education, Liaoning Normal University, Dalian, People's Republic of China

This presentation focused on exploring the co-parenting family types. Questionnaire method adopted with a sample of 775 couples of school-age children in Dalian of China, exploring the co-parenting family types of which were acquired distinguishingly. At the same time, through situational observations, coding analyses and evaluating for 28 nuclear families' parents, co-parenting behavior's actuality, characteristics were shown. Cluster analysis of fathers' and mothers' scores on the three co-parenting factors suggested five "types" co-parenting families: Mother high participant, Father high participant, opposite, cooperative and low participant co-parenting family.

FP-388: Clinical research methods II

Measuring emotional (dys-)regulation

Jasielska, Aleksandra Inst. of Psychology, Adam Mickiewicz University, Poznan, Poland Górska, Dominika INSTITUTE OF PSYCHOLOGY, Adam Mickiewicz University, POZNAN, Poland

The topic of our presentation will be the study revealing the difference between self-report measures and performance measures of emotional regulation and dysregulation in various populations. The first group of these methods implies existing the emotional self-knowledge and the second engages emotional processing in situations of emotion activations. There were questionnaire for emotional regulation and experimental performance test used. The investigation concerned two groups- disorder (ex. borderline personality disorder) and non-disorder. We selected them resting theoretical assumptions and empirical results, which indicate that emotional regulation process, proceed in distinct way. The results of ANOVA statistic would be discussed.

Turkish children's Bender Gestalt Test performance: The effects of social variables on visual spatial performance

Özer, Serap Dept. of Psychology, Dogus Universtity, Istanbul, Turkey

The Bender Gestalt test is an important educational assesment tool in Turkey. The present study was undertaken to test the hypothesis that SES is an important factor in this task. 515 children who came from either private or public schools, ranging in age from 5 years to 11 years were tested using the Bender Gestalt test. Results indicated that children's visual spatial performance as measured by the Bender Gestalt test differed not only based on age but also as a result of socioeconomic variables as indicated by school placement. The importance of cultural and social variables in visual motor tasks is discussed.

The application of partial list squares in clinical research

Tarroja, Maria Caridad Dept. of Psychology, De La Salle University, Manila, Philippines

This study looked into the application of Partial Least Squares (PLS) in clinical research, particularly adoptive family research as Brodzinsky (1990, 1998) calls for a more theory-driven research, systemic and sound theoretical models. PLS allows the examination of multiple interrelationships in small samples and an examination of both direct and indirect links among independent variables, defined by multiple measures. In this study, PLS proves to be useful in looking into the significant factors that influence the behaviors of Filipino adopted children. Among the preadoption risk and postadoption factors, family functioning is found to be the most significant direct predictor of adjustment of the Filipino adoptees.

FP-389: Family issues: Parenting II

Emotional reactivity and emotional disturbance following in vitro fertilization failure

Moura-Ramos, Mariana Faculdade de Psicologia e C. E, Universidade de Coimbra, Coimbra, Portugal Gameiro, Sofia Faculdade de Psicologia e C. E, Universidade de Coimbra, Coimbra, Portugal Canavarro, Maria Cristina Faculdade de Psicologia e C. E, Universidade de Coimbra, Coimbra, Portugal

The failure of an IVF treatment has proved to have a negative impact in infertile couples, generating stress, depression and negative emotional reactivity. The aim of the present work is to study emotional reactivity and psychopathology after an unsuccessful IVF cycle. 20 couples were recruited in a public medical centre. Psychopathology (BSI, Derogatis, 1993) and Emotional reactivity: (EAS – Carlsson et al., 1989) were assessed after an unsuccessful IVF cycle. Results obtained demonstrate that the failure in ART treatments has a deleterious effect in couples, indicating the presence of difficulties in adapting to IVF failure. Unsuccessful IVF treatments can have a negative impact in couples promoting adjustment difficulties.

Comparative study on the attachment style of the mothers who had abortion (induced and spontaneous) and mothers who had not abortion

Sadeghi, Mansoureh Alsadat Psychology, Family Institute, Tehran, Islamic Republic of Iran Mazaheri, Mohammad Ali psychology, family institute, tehran, Islamic Republic of Iran

This research has compared the attachment style of the mothers who had abortion (induced and spontaneous) and mothers who had not abortion. 86 mothers who had abortion (42 mothers with induced abortion and 44 mothers with spontaneous abortion) and 45 mothers who had not abortion were selected and filled out the adult attachment style Questionnaire (Hazan & Shaver, 1987). Statistical methods such as descriptive analysis, chi-squared, ANOVA analyze and two way analyze were employed. Analysis revealed secure attachment in mothers who had not abortion had more frequent and insecure attachment in mothers who had induced abortion had more frequent (P< 0.003).Attachment styles have impact on mothers attitude toward parenting and kind of mothers relationship to child.

The impact of parents' migration from rural to urban areas on the mental health of their children left behind in China

Wang, Ting Inst. of Psychology, Chinese Academy of Science, Beijing, People's Republic of China Gao, Wenbin Key Laboratory of Mental Healt, Institute of Psychology,CAS, Beijing, People's Republic of China Liu, Zhengkui Developmental Psychology, Institute of Psychology,CAS, Beijing, People's Republic of China

Objective: Exploring the impact of parents' migration form rural to urban areas on the mental health of their children left in hometown in China. Methods: Investigating anxiety and depression levels and some influencing factors in 876 children from three grades in rural schools in Chongqing and Guizhou. Results: Children left in rural areas have higher anxiety and depression levels than children whose parents don't leave. The quality and quantity of parent-child contact, as well as the family socio-economic status, influence child's mental health obviously. Conclusions: Children left in rural areas face more challenges during development, appropriate psychological interventions are needed.

FP-390: Collective identities and collective action II

Social identity and conflict intentions: The models of determination

Korostelina, Karina Dept. of Psychology, National Taurida University, Fairfax, USA

Numerous studies show that salient social identity leads to conflict. What are the factors that determine or moderate this impact? The paper analyze this question based on the results of survey (6,522 respondents) conducted in the autonomous republics of Russia and Ukraine. The analysis shows that different types of conflict intentions – discrimination, political mobilization, and quest for autonomy – have different models of determination: varying impact of social identities, including ethnic, religious, regional, and national identities as well as moderating effects of threats, intergroup trust, economic deprivation, confidence in public institutions, perception of fifth columns, and ethnic stereotypes.

The meanings of the antiglobalization movement as an expression of the new cultural discomforts

Urreiztieta Valles, María Teresa Ciencias y Tecnología del Comp, Simón Bolívar University, Caracas, Venezuela

This paper aims to analyze the collective action frameworks of the "antiglobalization movement" and its meanings, from a contextual perspective. From a socio-hermeneutical standpoint, the research presents a qualitative case study based on discourses produced and registered during selected collective action of this global movement. The results allowed the understanding of the most relevant psychosocial processes related with the configuration of collective subjectivity projects of the movement. The conclusions turn around its contribution to the new emerging forms of agency and social power in current democracies as an answer and expression of the new cultural discomforts.

Is third way possible? The national identity and its dilemma in Taiwan polarizing society

Huang, Li-Li Center for General Education, National Tsing-Hua University, Hsinchu, Taiwan

National identity in Taiwan is facing a dilemma of double identity, as both Taiwanese identity and Chinese identity are viable. This predicament has deep historical roots, but controversies of identity have been increasing. There are also diversity of Nationhood Imagination in Taiwan. Politically, most people favor independence. Militarily, China uses force against Taiwan for Taiwanese's searching for independent nation. In this study, questionnaires were conducted and 300 data were collected. The results will demonstrate the various opposite of Chinese identity and Taiwanese identity. Then, what is best favored future imagination for cross strait relation will be discussed.

FP-391: Work safety

Organizational culture and safety climate in U.S. Veterans administration hospitals
Hartmann, Christine CHQOER, Bedford VAMC, Bedford, USA Rosen, Amy CHQOER, Bedford VAMC, Bedford, USA Zhao, Shibei CHQOER, Bedford VAMC, Bedford, USA Meterko, Mark COLMR (152M), Jamaica Plain VAMC, Boston, USA Shokeen, Priti CHQOER, Bedford VAMC, Bedford, USA Gaba, David PSCI, VA Palo Alto HCS, Palo Alto, USA
Objectives: To identify organizational culture characteristics associated with higher levels of safety climate in 30 Veterans Administration hospitals. Methods: We administered the Zammuto and Krakower survey to employees to measure organizational culture (total n=1,428). We performed multiple OLS regressions. Results: Stronger group and entrepreneurial cultures were significantly associated with higher levels of safety climate, while stronger hierarchical culture was associated with lower levels of safety climate. Conclusions: Organizational culture characteristics are potentially mutable and have an impact on safety climate. Hospitals should devote greater attention to activities that promote stronger group and entrepreneurial cultures and reduce hierarchy within their institutions.

Perceptions of personal vulnerability to occupational health and safety (OHS) hazards in the Australian construction industry
Caponecchia, Carlo School of Safety Science, University of New South Wales, Sydney, Australia Sheils, Ian School of Safety Science, University of New South Wales, Sydney, Australia
Optimism bias is the belief that negative events are less likely to happen to oneself compared to others. Little research has been conducted on the presence of optimism bias, and its potential effect on safety practices in industry. 178 construction workers were surveyed regarding their perceived likelihood of workplace hazards occurring to themselves, and to the average worker of their age, doing their job. Significant optimism bias was observed for 7 of 10 events, including electrocution, falling from heights and being trapped in a confined space. Results are discussed in terms of their implications for workplace safety management.

The relationship between safety climate, safety performance and safety-related outcomes: A multilevel study in Chinese management context.
Jiang, Li Institute of Psychology, CAS, Beijing, People's Republic of China Yu, Guangtao and Economics, Central University of Finance, Beijing, People's Republic of China Li, Feng Institute of psychology, Chinese Academy of Sciences, Beijing, People's Republic of China Li, Yongjuan Institute of psychology, Chinese Academy of Sciences, Beijing, People's Republic of China
The aim of this study was to explore the effect of safety climate (SC) on safety performance, as well as the negative outcome. Individual and unit level SC, safety compliance and safety participation, and the injuries history data were collected in a chemical company. 384 employees responded the survey. Results showed that cross-level effects of Unit-level SC and Individual-level SC on safety compliance and safety participation were significant. The effect of Individual-level SC on injuries was fully mediated by safety participation. Implications of the study for management and safety climate research were discussed.

FP-392: Elementary information processing II

The mechanism of two-digit comparison: Evidence from priming effect
Hu, Qingfen Inst. of Developm. Psychology, Beijing Normal University, Beijing, People's Republic of China Lin, Chongde Inst of Development Psychology, Beijing Normal University, Beijing, People's Republic of China
Are multi-digit numbers decomposed or represented and compared holistically in number comparison? This is the focus of the controversy about the mechanism of multi-digit comparison recently. In the present experiment, we used priming design to investigate this process. In the primer, the decades of the two numbers (e.g., 54-69) are same as those of the two numbers in target pairs (e.g., 53-62) respectively. The results provide evidence for the process in which numbers are not compared holistically. Comparing a same-decades number pair successfully primed the comparison of target pair. The correct rate and response time were both improved significantly. Key Word: priming effect, number comparison, two-digit numbers

Stimulus-response compatibility based on affective arousal
Kleinsorge, Thomas Institut f. Arbeitsphysiologie, Dortmund, Germany
This study investigated effects of congruency between emotional arousal and response force. Participants responded with weak or strong forces to pictures varying with respect to arousal, the lightness of a frame surrounding the picture, and horizontal position. For different groups of participants, either of these stimulus dimensions was task relevant, with stimulus-response mapping varying between blocks of trials. The stimulus-response mapping of the two respectively task irrelevant dimensions varied unpredictably. Only when affective arousal was relevant, there was an advantage of the mapping arousing-strong, not arousing-weak over the reverse mapping. A similar pattern was observed for the nonaffective stimulus dimensions.

A new approach to research on mental rotation
Balaj, Bibianna Dept. Experimental Psychology, Catholic University of Lublin, Lublin, Poland
The presentation deals with the issue of mental rotation, which is tested not as an outcome but as a process. There is still lack of methods which allow us to analyse the process of this operation on-line. The indicator of mental rotation proposed by the author, apart from reaction time and the correctness of task performance, is an eye movement trajectory. The basic assumption is that there is a similarity between eye movement trajectory during the visual perception of a stable object and its visualisation (Laeng, Teodorescu 2002). This similarity, relating to the object rotation, will be tested.

FP-393: Cognition and work II

Intuition: Situated cognition and implicit control in managing complexity
von der Weth, Rüdiger Inst. für Allg. Psychologie, Universität Bamberg, Bamberg, Germany Starker, Ulrike Faculty of Social Work, University of Bamberg, Bamberg, Germany
The contribution summarizes the conclusions of our empirical studies about complex work activities of engineers, managers and spatial planners. The studies have shown that experienced professionals are often successful following their intuition without detailed planning and analysis. An information processing model was developed to explain how experts intuition works and on which information it relies. The main idea is that consciously planned behaviour is continuously embedded and modified

by a process of appraisal, which is based on implicit knowledge about critical signals for opportunities and threats. Conclusions for knowledge management, work design and change management have been drawn.

The relationship between shared mental models, team environment, and team creative performance: A field study
Bai, Xinwen Institute of Psychology, CAS, Beijing, People's Republic of China Ren, Xiaopeng CSEB, Institute of Psychology, CAS, Beijing, People's Republic of China Lin, Lin CSEB, Institute of Psychology, CAS, Beijing, People's Republic of China
This study examined the relationship between shared mental models (SMMs), team environment, and team creative performance (TCP) among 129 R&D and service teams of hi-tech companies. Results indicated that team environment moderated the relationship between SMMs and TCP. Specifically, the impact of SMMs on team TCP was more salient for teams that must react rapidly to the changing environment. In addiction, SMMs and environmental requirements also influenced TCP in a subtle way. High level of both SMMs and environmental requirements jointly reduced task conflict, which in turn reduced relational conflict within teams, and finally enhanced TCP.

Critical aspects of cognitive performance under military working schedules
Heiss, Andrea Central Institute, Federal Armed Forces, Koblenz, Germany Gorges, Willi Central Institute, Federal Armed Forces, Koblenz, Germany Sievert, Alexander Dept. of Physiology & Anat, German Sport University, Cologne, Germany Leyk, Dieter Central Institute, Federal Armed Forces, Koblenz, Germany
The introduction of computer-based technology added increased cognitive demands to a broad range of military tasks. Aim of our study was to assess the impact of military working schedules on critical aspects of cognitive performance. 40 soldiers were subjected to a test battery in a virtual environment before and after their working day. Tests assessed performance in vigilance, short term memory, mental arithmetic and simple reaction time. Eye movements were also recorded. Preliminary results indicate that performance was negatively affected in mental arithmetic and reaction time only. Results are discussed in terms of contemporary models of information processing.

FP-394: Child and adolescent psychopathology V

Trauma, psychopathology and resilience in former Ugandan child soldiers
Klasen, Fionna KJP, Universitätsklinikum Hamburg, Hamburg, Germany Oettingen, Gabriele Fachbereich Psychologie, University of Hamburg, Hamburg, Germany Adam, Hubertus Children for Tomorrow, Universitätsklinikum Hamburg, Hamburg, Germany
Objective: To investigate the association of trauma, psychopathology and resilience in child soldiers. Design: Cross-sectional field study of 394 former Ugandan child soldiers (age 11-18) in a school setting, conducted in 2006. Results: Despite a high level of exposure to traumatic events (e.g., 88.8% saw someone being killed, 51% had to kill someone themselves) 39.6% of the population were free of clinical relevant symptoms (measured by YSR; Achenbach, 2001). Conclusion: The study highlights factors of posttraumatic resilience (e.g. religious coping, absence of guilt). Strengthening these factors is crucial to successful psychological treatment of psychopathology in child soldiers.

Psychometric properties of the strengths and difficulties questionnaire in a sample of Turkish children

Eremsoy, Ekin Psychology, Dogus University, Istanbul, Turkey Karanc, Nuray Psychology, Middle East Technical Universi, Ankara, Turkey Kazak Berument, Sibel Psychology, Middle East Technical Universi, Ankara, Turkey

Strengths and Difficulties Questionnaire (SDQ) is a frequently used, brief questionnaire designed to evaluate the emotional and behavioral problems of children. The aim of this study was to evaluate the psychometric properties of the parent and teacher forms of the SDQ in a Turkish sample. According to the factor analysis, the Turkish version of the SDQ contained four factors, instead of five as in the original questionnaire. In general, the Turkish version of the SDQ showed reliable and valid results to evaluate the emotional and behavioral problems of children. Results will be discussed from a cultural perspective.

Cognitive behavioral intervention for childhood social phobia in a scholar setting

Gil Bernal, Flor Dept. of Psychology, UNAM, Mexico City, Mexico Hernández Guzmán, Laura Psychology, UNAM, Mexico, Mexico

In recent years the interest about the inclusion of social phobic children's parents in therapy has increased. Objective: To evaluate a 8 week CBGT program in a scholar setting and the additional value of a 4 session cognitive behavioral parent training program. Method: Twenty one children were assigned to a CBT condition. Ten parents were randomly assigned to a CB parent training program. Diagnostic interviews were conducted with parents and children separately before and after treatment and a 3 months follow-up Results: Children who received treatment as well as their parents showed more gains compared with the rest of the children. The gains were maintained at post-treatment and 3 months follow-up.

FP-395: Child and adolescent psychopathology VI

Bullying victimization in childhood and psychosis-like symptoms in a non-clinical population at 12 years of age: Results from the ALSPAC birth cohort

Schreier, Andrea Health Sciences Research Inst., University of Warwick, Coventry, United Kingdom

Objectives: The aim of the present study is to examine whether bullying victimization in childhood predicts the presence of psychosis-like symptoms (PLIKS) in early adolescence. Methods: Analyses are based on 6437 participants of the longitudinal ALSPAC birth cohort in Bristol, UK. PLIKS were assessed at age 12 and bullying at 8 and 10. Results: Bully victims had an elevated risk for PLIKS independent of various confounding factors. Associations were strongest for chronic and severe bullying. Conclusions: These results suggest that bullying predicts the presence of later PLIKS and could be an important target for early intervention and prevention of psychotic symptoms.

Video and computer game addiction

Wölfling, Klaus Medizinische Psychologie, Johannes Gutenberg-Universität, Mainz, Germany Grüsser, Sabine Miriam Medizinische Psychologie, Johannes Gutenberg Universität, Mainz, Germany Thalemann, Ralf Medizinische Psychologie, Johannes Gutenberg-Universität, Mainz, Germany

Computer games have become an ever-increasing part of many adolescents' day-to-day lives. To date, no reliable data for computer game addiction in Germany exist. The excessive usage of computer and video games can be seen as a rewarding behavior which can, due to learning mechanisms, become a prominent and inadequate strategy for adolescents to cope with negative emotions like frustration, uneasiness and fears. Data of several psychophysiological studies show that excessive computer game playing seems to parallel the mechanisms of development and maintenance of addiction. Results indicate the necessity of the implementation of effective strategies in prevention and treatment.

Emotional intelligence in parents of children with pervasive developmental disorders

Pouretemad, Hamid Psychology, Shahid Beheshti University, Tehran, Islamic Republic of Iran Jalali-Moghadam, Nilofar Psychology, Shahid Beheshti University, Tehran, Islamic Republic of Iran Saleh-Sedghpour, Bahram Psychology, Shahid Beheshti University, Tehran, Islamic Republic of Iran Khoshabi, Katayoun Psychiatry, University of Social Welfare a, Tehran, Islamic Republic of Iran

Objectives: The aim of this study was to investigate emotional intelligence in parents of children with Pervasive Developmental Disorders (PDD). Methods: Forty-three pairs of parents with PDD child recruited from the Center for the Treatment of Autistic Disorders - Tehran. They were asked to fill in the Bar-On Emotional Quotient Inventory (1997), individually. A similar procedure was implemented on a sex, age and education matched control group. Results: PDD parents scored less than controls on general EQ and three components: interpersonal, adjustability and global mood. Conclusion: The results provide some evidence in favor of sub-threshold autistic like behaviors in parents of children with PDD.

Parent-personality, parental attitudes, child-temperament and parent-child interactions as aetiological factors in the development of child-psychopathology

Rink, Klaus Inst. für Psychologie, Universität Zürich, Zürich, Switzerland Bachmann, Petra Psychological Institute, University of Zurich, Zurich, Switzerland Bernhard, Evelyn Psychological Institute, University of Zurich, Zurich, Switzerland Bolli, Catrina Psychological Institute, University of Zurich, Zuerich, Switzerland Fischer, Selina Psychological Institute, University of Zurich, Zurich, Switzerland Heule, Patricia Psychological Institute, University of Zurich, Zuerich, Switzerland Herrera, Isabel Psychological Institute, University of Zurich, Zurich, Switzerland Hochuli, Kathrin Psychological Institute, University of Zurich, Zuerich, Switzerland Müller, Rahel Psychological Institute, University of Zurich, Zuerich, Switzerland Müller, Sandra Psychological Institute, University of Zurich, Zuerich, Switzerland

Research-question: How strong is the development of child-psychopathology determined by parent-personality, child-temperament, parental attitudes and specific types of parent-child interactions? Method: 241 parents with a child of 1.5-6 years completed questionnaires on parent-personality (SCL-90-R, MMPI-2, EPI), parental attitudes (DysPAS), child-temperament (ECBQ/CBQ) and child-pathology (CBCL). 86 parents additionally sent protocols of parent-child interactions for 21 consecutive days (categorized into specific interaction-types). Correlations and structural equation models show that mostly mothers personality (18 subscales), Child-Temperament (14 subscales), parental attitudes, conflict management and interaction time with the child are significantly correlated with child-psychopathology.

FP-396: Cross-cultural comparisons III

A cross-cultural study of scientific creativity in adolescents

Shen, Jiliang Inst. Developmental Psychology, Beijing Normal University, Beijing, People's Republic of China

This study explored performances on 5 types of scientific creativity task in 1141 senior and junior high school students aged from 13 to 20 from China, Japan and England. Chinese students got the highest scores on problem posing, problem solving and scientific imagination, the lowest on product design and product improvement. Compared to figural task, Chinese students did better in reacting to verbal task, England and Japanese students performed reversely. In Chinese sample, the scores on fluency and flexibility are higher than that of originality, but in Japanese sample, the highest score was got on the dimension of originality.

Culture, illusory negative concerns, and social support seeking

Li, Chongliang Xili, Nanshan, People's Republic of China Wang, Lei Psychology, Peking University, Beijing, People's Republic of China

Our research aims to demonstrate that negative concerns in social support seeking are just illusions and exam its cultural difference. Study 1 found that the negative concerns in support seeking were indeed illusory that only shared by support seekers but not by the support providers. Moreover, Chinese were more illusive than Americans. In study 2, we reduced these illusions by role-image method and found that participants who imaged being asked for help showed more intentions for support seeking. Again, Chinese changed more for support seeking than Americans. Discussion centers on the theoretical and practical implications of the results.

The autonomous-related self among migrant and non-migrant students in Germany and Turkey

Otyakmaz, Berrin Özlem Inst. Bildungswissenschaften, Universität Duisburg-Essen, Essen, Germany Kagitcibasi, Cigdem Psychology, Koc University, Istanbul, Turkey

Individualism is assumed to entail both separateness and autonomy, while collectivism often implies relatedness and lack of autonomy. These construals are problematic because they confound two underlying dimensions of 'interpersonal distance' and 'agency.' There is empirical evidence for the distinctness of these dimensions and the coexistence of relatedness and autonomy. The autonomy-relatedness scale developed by Kağıtçıbaşı, allows measuring the co-existence of autonomy and relatedness. It was applied to German and Turkish-German students in Germany and to Turkish students in Turkey in order to assess the 'autonomous-related self' in these groups.

FP-397: Instruction, construction, and learning: Specific trainings, teaching practices, text-books II

The importance of self-regulation procedures in writing strategies trainings

Glaser, Cornelia Educational Psychology, Justus-Liebig-University, Giessen, Germany Brunstein, Joachim C. Educational Psychology, Justus-Liebig-University, Giessen, Germany

In two curriculum-integrated training studies, 4th grade students who were taught genre-specific strategies for planning and revising narratives in conjunction with self-regulation procedures (N = 101) were contrasted with students who were taught the same writing strategies but received no instruction in self-regulation (N = 94). At posttest and maintenance measures, strategy plus self-regulation students surpassed the writing performance of strategy-only students and were better able to transfer the learned strategies to untrained tasks. Findings will be discussed in terms of a need for decomposing self-regulatory trainings to identify their effective elements and integrate these elements into the classroom teaching of writing skills.

How words influence the learning behaviour: The impact of terminology on communication and learning performance in cooperative writing
Paus, Elisabeth Psychologisches Institut III, Universität Münster, Münster, Germany Jucks, Regina Psychologisches Institut III, Westf. Wilhelms-Universität MS, Münster, Germany
This study analyses how the exchange of text specific information in virtual cooperative writing can be improved. Based on the psycholinguistic concept of lexical alignment, we tested with 64 students, if there was a positive impact of the use of different terminology on the transfer of knowledge, the working result and the learning outcome. As assumed, dyads who had cooperated with material containing different terminology asked more questions, gave more explanations and performed better in a following learning test than dyads whose learning materials contained the same terminology. Also, their documents were formulated more independently. Implications for selecting and creating learning materials are discussed.

Linguistic imperialism in academia
Themistocleous, Eugenia Dept. of Liberal Arts, Intercollege, Limassol, Cyprus
A study (n=775)was conducted at Intercollege, Limassol Campus to examine cultural bias in college textbooks. Questionnaires were submitted to students for each course taught in English at Intercollege. The findings indicate that, although students perceive a slight cultural bias in their textbooks, they indicated that it does not affect their ability to understand the material. This does not mean that cultural bias does not exist in textbooks, but rather that students are multi-culturally literate What emerged very strongly from the study was the effect of language on student understandingl, indicating a type of linguistic, rather than cultural, bias.

Classroom management: An analysis of pedagogical jokes, management definitions, and punishment techniques
Ochirjav, Myagmar Department of Psychology, State University of Education, Ulaanbaatar, Mongolia
The article focuses on classroom management, and explores concerns, beliefs, and practices in that area. The research compare the responses of lecturers, student-teachers and practicum teachers, and use that comparison to draw conclusions for the teaching practicum.The study has been con-dacted in Ulaanbaatar and Bayan-Ulgii Mongo-lia.and draws from140 interviews and questionnaires.It uses different kinds of qualitative data analisis techniques.The author has conclude that a lot of emphasis is placed on preparing student-teachers on subject matter knowledge and content, bat not sufficient attention is given to strengthening student-teachers self- confidence and developin their pedagogigal skills of dealing with the individual student in the classroom.

FP-398: Interindividual differences in the experience of emotion II

When remembering the good times doesn't cheer you up: Neuroticism and mood regulation
Siemer, Matthias Dept. of Psychology, Miami University, Coral Gables, USA
In two studies the author demonstrated that participants with high levels of neuroticism have difficulties to repair induced sad mood states with happy memories. There were no differences be-tween participants with high and low levels of neuroticism in the initial reactivity to the sad mood induction or in the happiness of the memories recalled. Moreover, difficulties in participants with high levels of neuroticism to repair sad moods with happy memories were found for memories that differed in terms of self-relevance. The current results add to the notion that affective traits are not only related to affective reactivity but also to the ability to regulate affect.

The effect of mood and emotion on risky driving
Jie, Li Psychology Department, Peking University, Beijing, People's Republic of China Xiaofei, Xie Psychology Department, Peking University, Beijing, People's Republic of China Tianyi, Hu Psychology Department, Peking University, Beijing, People's Republic of China
Two studies were conducted to explore the relation-ship between affect and risky driving. Study one used POMS to measured 500 drivers' mood states in recent two weeks, and found that, dejection is negatively related to risky driving attitude. Dejec-tion and Anger are mediating factors between personality and risky driving behavior. Moods also moderate the relationship between risky driving attitude and risky driving behavior. Study two found drivers in the negative emotion, which was induced by video, showed more worry about involving in traffic accident. The impact of risk perception on risky driving attitude was moderated by emotion. The research displays the important role of affect in risky driving.

Behavioural activation and inhibition (BIS/BAS) are related to hippocampal volume
Cherbuin, Nicolas CMHR, Australian National University, Canberra, Australia Windsor, Tim D. CMHR, Australian National University, Canberra, Australia Anstey, Kaarin J. CMHR, Australian National University, Canberra, Australia Maller, Jerome J. APRC, The Alfred, Melbourne, Australia Meslin, Chantal CMHR, Australian National University, Canberra, Australia Sachdev, Perminder S. School of Psychiatry, University of New South Wales, Canberra, Australia
Objectives: Determine whether personality con-structs representing the behavioural inhibition and activation systems (BIS/BAS) are associated with volumetric measures of the hippocampus and amygdala in humans. Methods: Amygdalar and hippocampal volumes were measured in 430 com-munity-based volunteers. Associations between brain volumes and the BIS/BAS measures were assessed using multiple regression, controlling for age, sex, and education. Results: Hippocampal volumes were positively associated with BIS (Beta=0.167, p=.002) and BAS sensitivity (Beta=0.116, p=0.032). No association was found between amygdalar volume and BIS or BAS. Conclusions: These findings support a role of the hippocampus in the regulation of defensive/ap-proach behaviours and trait anxiety.

Analyzing mood variability in daily life by mobile phones
Courvoisier, Delphine Center for Affective, University of Geneva, Geneva, Switzerland Eid, Michael Faculty of Psychology, Freie Univ. Berlin, Berlin, Germany Lichetzske, Tanja Faculty of Psychology, Freie Univ. Berlin, Berlin, Germany
Using computerized mobile phone assessment (CMPA), we collected data on momentary mood 6 times per day for 7 consecutive days in the German-speaking and French-speaking part of Switzerland (N= 308). CMPA allows for collecting momentary reports of experiences or behavior, and thus minimize recall biases (e.g., "peak" and "recency" effects, use of semantic memory instead of true recall). Using latent state-trait models, we compared mood reliability and variability within work days, within week-end days and, more generally, within a week. We also analyzed whether intraindividual variability in mood differs between linguistic regions and between gender. Finally, we scrutinized the effect of weather on mood states.

FP-399: Interpersonal processes and relationship II

@ the tipping point: When "Enough is Enough" in email conversations
Svensson, Martin School of Management, Blekinge Tekniska Högskola, Ronneby, Sweden Westelius, Alf IEI, Linköping University, Linköping, Sweden
The reliance on IT-mediated communication in-volves interpersonal exchanges without face-to-face contact. However, this does not preclude emotional exchange. Have we not all at some point engaged in e-mail exchange where facts, fantasies and con-tagion caused us to get caught in spiraling exchanges of increasingly emotional and decreas-ingly rational e-mail? The purpose here is to explore e-mail conversations perceived as going awry, in terms of negative emotional escalation. Backtrack-ing e-mail conversations using discourse analysis and interviews, factors leading to an "emotional tipping point" and beyond were identified. Con-cludingly, psychological and managerial aspects on how then to avoid emotional escalation are derived.

The relationship between relationship styles, coping strategies, identity development status and mental health among Chinese young adult learners
Leung, Cynthia Educational Psychology, Counse, The Hong Kong Institute of Edu, Tai Po, China, People's Republic of : Hong Kong SAR Lung, Ching Educational Psychology, Counse, The Hong Kong Institute of Edu, Tai Po, China, People's Republic of : Macao SAR Moore, Susan Faculty of Life and Social Sci, Swinburne University, Melbourne, Australia Karnilowicz, Wally School of Psychology, Victoria University, Melbourne, Australia
Objective: To test a model integrating theories of attachment, coping and identity development to predict mental health of Chinese adolescents in the context of romantic relationships. Method: 181 Chinese tertiary students aged 18 to 25 completed a questionnaire assessing attachment, romantic rela-tionship style, coping, identity development, mental health. Results: Multiple regression indicated men-tal health was negatively predicted by avoidance and self-punishment coping strategies and positively predicted by accommodation coping and secure relationship style. Immature identity and insecure relationship styles were associated. Conclusions: Identity, coping and romantic relationship styles are important issues to consider in supporting adolescents facing issues of intimacy.

Reproduction of the Asch line-judgment experiment without using confederates

Mori, Kazuo Inst. of Symbiotec Science, Tokyo University, Tokyo, Japan

The Asch (1956) experiment was reproduced without using confederates. Twenty-six same-sex groups of four participated in the line judgment task. In each group, one participant saw different stimuli from what the other three saw without their noticing the duality by means of a presentation trick. The female minority participants showed a similar conforming tendency as Asch (1956); 28.6% of the responses were conformity errors. However, the male minority participants made far fewer conforming responses, 5.0%. It is notable that, contrary to previous findings, the conforming frequency was not affected by the breakage of unanimity among the majority group.

Cooperation and competition in the field of gene technology

Seuffert, Verena Inst. für Psychologie, Humboldt-Universität zu Berlin, Berlin, Germany Schulze, Anna Dorothea Institute for Psychology, Humboldt University, Berlin, Germany

Our study examined the relationship between cooperation and competition and researchers' innovative success. 146 scientists in Gene Technology were asked about their competitive/cooperative orientation, success within the last five years and newness of projects. Results: High performers were externally more cooperative than normal performers. Success was correlated with internal competitive and external cooperative orientation, newness with internal cooperativeness not excluding competition. Results indicate that scientists competing cooperatively are most successful in a field characterized by both competition and necessity to cooperate. Besides, scientists were externally more cooperative in universities than in R&D companies and Start-Ups.

FP-400: Management styles and organizational culture II

The order conception of organizational culture

Aksenovskaya, Liudmila Faculty of Psychology, The State University, Saratov, Russia

The order conception views organizational culture as a complex socio-psychological order of managing interactions, which are constituted and regulated by the systems of ethical notions of interaction participants. Basing on this approach a socio-psychological model of organizational culture has been built. With metaphors the model fixes three types of managerial interaction. Following this model the technology of change in organizational culture has been developed. The technology allows for diagnostics and development of the main characteristics of the organizational culture. The technology has been successfully applied to the projects on the change of the organizational culture of some Russian organizations

Discourse of organizational culture

Kiseleva, Anna Applied psychology institute, Kharkov, Ukraine

Discourse of organizational culture Objectives: research content and structure of organizational culture, to clarify the metaphor, which underpin culture Methods: sample 52 managers from 6 organizations, discourse-analyses of interview texts according with such criteria as identification, modality, transitivity; Results : we observe such organizational metaphors of organization as "functional mechanism", "administrative-bureaucratic mechanism", "fields for competition", "family", "association of autonomic single entrepreneurs", "compromises". Personal passivity of manager position accompany by non reflexive and non critical behavior and active requirements to "stabi-

lity of organizational mechanism". Personal activity of manager position accompany by passivity on forming of organization as a system.

Retirement preparedness and cultural differences

Franca, Lucia Graduate Studies in Psychology, UNIVERSO, Rio de Janeiro, Brazil

Brazil and New Zealand are contextually very different, especially in demography, cultural values, political, and socio-economical development. However both countries need to define policies to address the increasing numbers of retired people. This presentation is focused on how Brazilian and New Zealand executives from large organizations are planning for retirement. Factor analyses emerged four dimensions for Retirement Planning: (i) Personal and social activities; (ii) Work and network;(iii) Family relationships; and (iv) survival - finance and health. Family was evaluated as the most important dimension by both nationalities. Brazilians more than New Zealanders are concerned to personal/social activities and work/network dimensions.

FP-401: Neural bases of behavior II

Conscious and unconscious error processing

Stahl, Jutta University of Göttingen, Goettingen, Germany Gibbons, Henning Institute for Psychology, University of Göttingen, Goettingen, Germany

Error processing requires conscious and unconscious processing. We investigated error negativity (Ne/ERN) and error positivity (Pe) as two event-related potentials indicating error- processing activity. In two experiments (n=30; n=10) applying a visual backward masking task, we varied the onset between response stimulus (<<<, >>>) and mask (◇◇◇) onset (SOA: 0, 17, 51, 84, 119 ms). We could demonstrate a variation in Pe amplitude depending on SOA suggesting conscious error-processing activity. Ne/ERN, however, was not sensitive to SOA variation in the mixed-SOA design (Exp.1) but in the blocked-SOA design (Exp.2). A model of conscious and unconscious error processing is proposed. [supported by DFG, STA 1035/1-1]

Oscillatory brain activity during encoding predicts beneficial and detrimental effects of an internal context change

Pastötter, Bernhard Inst. für Experim. Psychologie, Universität Regensburg, Regensburg, Germany Hanslmayr, Simon Experimentelle Psychologie, Universität Regensburg, Regensburg, Germany Bäuml, Karl-Heinz Experimental Psychology, Regensburg University, Regensburg, Germany

If after study of a first list and before study of a second list subjects change their internal context, List-1 recall declines on a later test, whereas List-2 recall inclines. Measuring EEGs during encoding of the two lists, oscillatory brain activity was found to be related to both detrimental List-1 and beneficial List-2 performance. Whereas increases in theta and gamma phase coupling were predictive of List-1 forgetting, a decrease in relative alpha power was predictive of List-2 enhancement. Median-split analysis revealed that the oscillatory effects were selectively related to the two behavioral effects. The results point to separate neural origins of the two behavioral effects of an internal context change.

Neural encoding of object categories with and without awareness: A challenge for signal detection models of human decision making

Bode, Stefan Attention and Awareness, MPI CBS Leipzig, Leipzig, Germany Haynes, John-Dylan BCCN Berlin, Charité – Universitätsmedizin, Berlin, Germany

Object identity is encoded in distributed patterns of activity in human lateral occipital complex (LOC). However it has remained unclear whether object recognition also operates when stimuli are rendered

invisible due to masking. Here 16 subjects categorized masked target objects at either high or low visibility. Using a pattern classifier we were able to decode the categories of visible but not invisible objects from distributed fMRI signals in LOC. Interestingly the signals underlying the subjects' choices shifted to a different cortical location between high and low visibility conditions. This is incompatible with current signal detection models of perceptual decision making.

A neural network model of task-dependent movement preparation

Herbort, Oliver Inst. für Psychologie III, Universität Würzburg, Würzburg, Germany Butz, Martin V. Department of Psychology III, University of Würzburg, Würzburg, Germany Hoffmann, Joachim Department of Psychology III, University of Würzburg, Würzburg, Germany

Humans adapt their movements to changing tasks with astonishing ease, partially due to the ability to integrate information about goals, task constraints, and the motor system when preparing a movement. However, neural network models of motor control often neglect the role of movement preparation processes. We presented a novel neural network model, which emphasizes the importance of movement preparation for behavioral flexibility (Butz, Herbort, & Hoffmann, 2007, Psychological Review, 114(4),1015-1046). Now, we show that the model also accounts for recent experimental findings of a relationship between the duration of movement preparation and target distance.

FP-402: Assessment and prediction of the attainment of domain-specific and cross-curricular competencies II

Assessment of basic reading skill using IRT models for response times

Naumann, Johannes Pädagogische Forschung, Deutsches Inst. für Internat., Frankfurt, Germany Richter, Tobias Department of Psychology, University of Cologne, Cologne, Germany

This paper compares different approaches of adding response speed parameters to IRT-models, both theoretically and on the basis of their application to a new computer-based reading skills test that assesses the efficiency of basic reading processes through an integration of response correctness and speed. Two subtests, addressing sentence-level and local coherence processes respectively, were administered to 587 university students and 214 high-school students (age 12-16). Results indicate that for the assessment of individual differences in basic reading skills, incorporating response times into the measurement model is of crucial importance, with results for different modeling approaches being comparable.

Predicting statistics achievement in undergraduate psychology students

Hood, Michelle School of Psychology, Griffith University, Southport, Australia

Australian 2nd-year psychology students were surveyed 4 times regarding their attitudes to statistics, achievement goal orientations, statistics self-efficacy, outcome expectancies, past performance, and statistics test anxiety. Data were collected in the 2nd and 12th weeks of 1st and 2nd semester (semester = 13). There were 161 participants at Time 1 (89.4% response rate), of whom 131 remained at Time 3 (the start of 2nd semester). Models predicting statistics performance from these belief and goal variables were derived from achievement goal and social cognitive theories. Results confirmed the importance of self-efficacy, attitudes, goals, and anxiety to statistics achievement in psychology undergraduates.

Predictive validity of high school performance with respect to academic achievement at the university level
Saad, Intisar Abunagma Psychology, University of Khartoum, Khartoum, Sudan
Predictive Validity of High School Performance with Respect to Academic Achievement at the University Level This study aims at comparing students from different systems (Sudan and Gulf Arab States),thus investigating the relative potency of each system in qualifying its students for university education. Co relational and causal comparative models were employed. sample 1794. Findings:- 1- High school percentage was a reliable predictor of the academic achievement at the university level. 2- There were significant differences in the academic achievement between students with Sudanese high school certificate and those with certificates from Arabian countries. 3- No interaction was found between student sex and student choice of programme of study regarding their relation to the academic achievement.

Construct validation of the multidimensional school engagement scale (MSES)
Awang-Hashim, Rosna Dept. of Cognitive Sciences, University Utara Malaysia, Sintok, Malaysia Murad Sani, Azlina Fac of Cog Sc & Education, University Utara Malaysia, Sintok, Malaysia
The study examined the psychometric properties of the newly integrated Multidimensional School Engagement Scale (MSES). Data were gathered from 2,381 secondary school students (aged 14-16) from 40 day schools in Northern Malaysia. We posited an a priori hypothesis that the MSES could be explained by three first-order factors and also one second-order factor. Findings supported our hypothesis that the school engagement construct could be explained by one hierarchical factor comprising cognitive engagement, behavioural engagement, and psychological engagement sub-scales. Findings also showed acceptable internal consistency reliability for the overall scale and the three specific sub-scales of adolescent school engagement.

FP-403: Assessment and job performance II

Assessors' judgment policy in assessment centers: Further understanding of exercise effects
Li, Dezhong Business Administration, Zhejiang School of Admin., Hangzhou, People's Republic of China
The present study aimed to seek further understanding of exercise effects in assessment centers using data collected from 99 candidates who participated in a selection test for a high level management position conducted by a software company. The hierarchical linear modeling confirmed that assessors may identify one or more dimensions viewed as relevant to the task requirement. Noncompensatory strategies were the dominant mode used by assessors. A residual intraclass correlation of 21% suggesting that individual differed on the importance they placed on these dimensions. There were clearer differences in the information integration strategies among assessors in risky-choice task than in time-pressure task.

Development of an animated psychometric battery: Innovation to reduce traditional barriers to disadvantaged job seekers
Clifford, Ian Research Dept., Ballymun Job Centre, Dublin, Ireland Whelan, Nuala Research, Ballymun Job Centre, Dublin, Ireland
A Battery of Psychometric tools for a disadvantaged population was developed. These tools assist in matching individuals with appropriate vocational environments. This battery measures Career Interests, Personality and aptitudes. Tools were developed with a bottom-up approach using qualitative and quantitative techniques. Theories used include Holland's interests, the FFM model and Fleishman's Taxonomy. All items are online in written, audio and animated (flash) format. Psychometrics were tested using a sample of 400 participants in three languages English, Spanish and German. Results will be presented. The significance of these tools in the provision of appropriate career guidance to individuals will be discussed.

Big Five personality traits and educational choice of Serbian high school students
Hedrih, Vladimir Psychology, Faculty of Philosophy, Nis, Serbia Nesic, Vladimir Psychology, Faculty of Philosophy, Nis, Nesic, Milkica Medicine, Faculty of Medicine, Nis, Todorovic, Jelisaveta Psychology, Faculty of Philosophy, Nis,
The goal of this study was to explore relations between Big Five personality traits and educational choices of high school students. 383 last year high school students were examined by using a Serbian army inventory for measuring Big Five personality traits and were asked about the type of university level studies they were planning to enrol at. Each of these studies was then assigned a Holland's category based on properties of jobs typically held by people with that type of education. The results showed that people choosing studies assigned to different categories differ on O and A Big Five dimensions.

The academic and career readiness questionnaire: An early warning strategy
Brand, Handré Centre for Student Counselling, University of Stellenbosch, Stellenbosch, South Africa Du Plessis, Alten Traking System, University of Stellenbosch, Stellenbosch, South Africa
An online demonstration will be given of the Academic and Career Readiness Questionnaire (ACRQ). The questionnaire measures the degree of academic and career readiness of first year university students, and provide scores on four subscales viz., career exploration, knowledge of the academic environment, study and thinking skills and career directedness. The ACRQ consists of 67 items, and can be used as a diagnostic instrument during the process of academic counselling. A set of predetermined advisory responses is available for students as they complete the questionnaire. Statistical analyses of data include correlation analysis, item analysis, and reliability analysis.

FP-404: Theoretical and philosophical psychology II

Applying Hilbert's conception of meta-science to psychology
Garber, Ilya Dept. of Socio Economics, Saratov State University, Saratov, Russia
The objective of the study is to describe an approach by which German mathematician Hilbert's conception of meta-science may be applied to psychology. It is based upon theories and methods that were introduced recently: meta-system transition (V.F. Turchin), cliometric meta-theory (P. Meehl), categorial analysis (M.G. Yaroshevsky, L.M. Vekker), meta-analysis. The three-level structure of meta-psychology is represented with specific methods on each level used. Such approach may help to resolve methodological paradoxes of psychology and lead to the core methodology of psychology (M.S. Burgin, V.I. Kuznetzov).

H.M.Tutunjian's scientific contribution to the development of history of psychology
Katunyan, Araksya Psychology, Urartu University, Yerevan, Armenia
1.The problem of psychological historiography in different countries is generalization and reappraisal of scientific and experimental data produced by different psychological schools. Psychohistoriographic studies are not the end in itself. It is impossible to create common scientific psychological system without casting retrospective look on the history of psychology. 2. In that sense it is important to reveal the scientific contribution of H.M.Tutunjian (1918-1994), prominent historian and theorist of modern Armenian Psychology, to the development of history of psychology. Armenian psychological thought, being reserved for years on end, was not familiar with the history of psychology. By his investigations H.M.Tutunjian made a bridge between modern foreign psychological thought and Armenian psychological thought.

Levels of principle analysis in the study of B.F.Skinner's theory
Makhmutova, Anfisa Psychological Dept., Moscow State University, Moscow, Russia
One of the greatest theories of the XX century was the behavioral theory of B.F.Skinner. We decided to study it in the methodological way which was offered by Russian historical psychologist M.G.Yaroshevskij. Based on qualitative analysis of Skinner's works, we analyzed the origins of principles of his theory on different levels (personal, scientific, cultural). The results showed the coherence of information on these levels of principle analysis. Such approach helped to reveal the connections between Skinner's theory and theories of Russian psychologists.

Towards a psychological theory of situation
Mikhailova, Natalia Social Psychology, Psychologisches Institut, Moscow, Russia Grishunina, Elena Social Psychology, Psychologisches Institut, Moscow, Russia
The critical life situations were an object of our investigation. About a thousand probands were studied in the situations of unemployment, emigration and divorce. Our methods: Questionnaires, interviews, subjective scripts concerning the situation of life, expert assessments. The results: Cognitive representations and behavioural strategies are often not in accordance with each other. After a radical change in the life situation the chaotic-impulsive or a passive behavioural strategies predominate. Goal-orientated resultative behaviour of most probands is demonstrated in the second year of life in the new situation. CONCLUSION: the results influence the development of the psychological theory of situation.

FP-405: Teaching of psychology II

New guidelines for psychology courses in Brazil
Feitosa, Maria Angela Inst. of Psychology, University of Brasília, Brasília, Brazil
New curricular guidelines were established in Brazil in 2004. They have the standing of federal law and provide reference for values and attitudes, general skills, professional competences, and curricular contents. Curriculum design includes the establishment of reference duration of five years, with a minimum of 4.000 hours of activities, including a minimum of 600 hours of supervised practice. Courses are periodically evaluation by the Ministry of Education. The diploma entitles the psychology graduate to professional practice, provided a license in obtained from the Regional Psychology Council, which oversees standards of professional practice. Comparisons are made with EuroPsy standard.

Filling the gap in development of competences for different contexts of psychologists' activity: Undergraduate apprenticeship in communities of practice and situated learning of professional skills

Erausquin, Cristina Educational Psychology, Faculty of Psychology, Buenos Aires, Argentina Basualdo, María Esther Educational Psychology, Faculty of Psychology UBA, CAPITAL FEDERAL, Argentina

The work is focused on mental models tutors and students build in communities of practice for analyzing and solving problems in different contexts of psychologists activities: Clinic, Social, Justice, Labor and Research. Unit of analysis is examined through a four dimensions matrix, to study cognitive change in professional education. Questionnaires were administered to 45 tutors and 248 students of Psychology at the beginning and the end of Apprenticeship during 2004 and 2005. Results show diversity of competences built in different activity systems. The challenge is to widen social stages for the construction of heterogeneous and multidimensional profiles of professional skills

Clinical significance and reliable change in posttraumatic stress disorder: Supervisor instruction of meaningful change indicators optimizes outcome.

Rosqvist, Johan Professional Psychology, Pacific University, Portland, Oregon, USA

Traditional methods for evaluating treatment efficacy are problematic. Posttraumatic stress disorder is a phenomenon needing careful clinical decision-making to guide interventions. Correctly classifying patients as "changed" or "unchanged" help students optimize direct in treatment processes. Objectives: Using this robust approach for understanding patient progress aide student navigation to desirable end-states. Results: Patients met "recovered" status. Conclusions: Using meaningful change indicators facilitate student-delivered psychotherapy in producing "recovered" status, and increases student confidence in various treatment components for posttraumatic stress disorder. This mode of learning difficult cognitive-behavior therapy, while being a diligent empiricist, overcomes common obstacles to utilizing empirically supported treatments.

Dialogue in a critically oriented introductory psychology course

Sheese, Ron Dept. of Psychology, York University, Toronto, Canada

Typical North American Introductory Psychology courses rarely address historical and philosophical issues other than in a few brief pages of reading independently of all other course material. This presentation describes a York University course that introduces the subject matter of Psychology with an awareness of historical and cultural context, that problematizes the concepts of science, reductionism and universality, and does not limit itself to individualist, atomistic and apolitical methodologies. Emphasis will be placed on the means by which dialogue among students and instructors is facilitated in a manner that promotes integration of personal (cultural) experience and professional conceptions of psychological phenomena.

FP-406: Memory processes VI

The effect of enactment on frequency judgments

Olofsson, Ulrich Dept. of Behavioral Sciences, Linköping University, Linköping, Sweden

Enactment of action phrases improves recall and recognition of the phrases. The common view is that the effect is due to enhanced item-specific, rather than relational, processing. In the present study, the effect of enactment on judgments of frequency was studied. Action phrases were presented one, two or three times for verbal study or

enactment, and enactment resulted in significantly better frequency judgments. The results suggests that frequency judgments utilize item-specific information, and it is argued that this is more compatible with a recursive-reminding than a trace-strength explanation of frequency judgments.

Effects of emotional valence on memory for verbal and pictural stimuli in Alzheimer's disease

Blanc, Maïté Laboratoire de Psychologie, Université d'Angers, Angers, France Delaplace, Christelle Laboratoire de Psychologie, Université d'Angers, Angers, France Chainay, Hanna Laboratoire EMC, Université Lyon 2, Lyon, France

The contradictory effects of the emotional valence of the stimuli on their retention are reported with Alzheimer's patients. In order to better examine these effects, 16 moderate Alzheimer's patients and 16 controls performed two tasks: emotional judgment (assign negative, positive, neutral valence) and recognition. In the recognition task subjects discriminated new items from items (emotionally negative, positive or neutral) being presented in the judgment task. An effect of emotional valence of the stimuli (images and words) was observed for positive but not for the negative stimuli. The subjects were significantly faster for the positive than neutral items.

Cognitive processes in associative recognition: A multinomial modeling approach

Auer, Tina-Sarah Lehrstuhl Psychologie III, Universität Mannheim, Mannheim, Germany Erdfelder, Edgar Lehrstuhl Psychologie III, Universität Mannheim, Mannheim, Germany

We introduce a multinomial model that disentangles the cognitive processes underlying associative recognition. The model provides parameters separately measuring encoding and retrieval of associations in addition to word recognition and guessing parameters. The model parameters have been validated in two experiments. As predicted, the results showed that (1) a 'levels of processing'-manipulation influences encoding of associations selectively, (2) a retention interval manipulation reduces associative retrieval, and (3) a manipulation of the proportion target test items affects guessing parameters only. Future applications of the model can be seen in cognitive aging research to shed further light on the cognitive processes underlying the associative aging deficit.

Factorial structure of a computer memory battery: A preliminary approach

Ferreira, Aristides IEP, Minho University, Carvoeira-Mafra, Portugal Silva Almeida, Leandro IEP, Universidade do Minho, Braga, Portugal Prieto Adánez, Gerardo Facultad de Psicologia, Universidad de Salamanca, Salamanca, Spain

This study tests the construct validity of a computer memory battery formed by 6 subscales prepared to be used in adult population. These subscales intend to measure working memory (WM) and short-term memory (STM) constructs. Factor analysis has been conducted to assess their internal structure considering the results of 89 undergraduate students, and two orthogonal factors - STM and WM – have been found. This structure reproduces initial subscales organization. The Cronbach alpha coefficients showed acceptable to high internal item consistency levels for the 6 subscales. The potential utility of these memory tasks for psychological research and practice will be discussed.

FP-407: Categorization and conditional reasoning II

Categories are explained by causal reasoning rather than by associative learning

James, Nathalie Dept. of Psychology, UCLA, Venice, USA Cheng, Patricia Psychology, UCLA, Venice, CA, USA

To demonstrate that categories form around causal properties and that this cannot be explained by associative learning, participants examined objects whose features predicted either provenances or causal outcomes. Participants formed clearer categories around outcomes, a result that associative learning theories cannot explain. This suggests that causation plays a special role in category formation. Additionally, participants formed different categories to meet different goals set by the experimenter, indicating that categories are purpose-driven rather than merely descriptive. Finally, features that predicted goal-relevant outcomes (not provenances) weighed heavily on similarity judgments, indicating that similarity is a product of causal category formation.

On the nature of superordinate knowledge: Insights from superordinate and basic level feature norms

Marques, J. Frederico Centro de Invest.em Psicologia, Fundacao Uni. de Lisboa, Lisboa, Portugal

The classical perspective on the nature of superordinate knowledge (e.g. Rosch et al., 1976; Tversky & Hemenway, 1984) was reevaluated from the analysis of superordinate and basic level feature norms. Contrary to the classical perspective, results show that, in comparison to basic level concepts, superordinate concepts are not generally less informative; have similar feature distinctiveness and proportion of individual sensory features; but their features are less shared by their members. Implications for the explanation of cases of superordinate advantage/disadvantage in the degradation of semantic memory are also discussed.

Conditional reasoning with a moral content

Wiedenmann, Patrick Allg. Psychologie II, Universität Gießen, Gießen, Germany Knauff, Markus Allgemeine Psychologie II, Universität Giessen, Giessen, Germany

We used conditional reasoning problems with a moral or neutral content to investigate social decision making. Subjects had to decide whether presented conclusions were logically valid or not. This decision took significantly longer and was more prone to errors if the logically correct conclusion was immoral or when a morally correct decision was logically invalid. Overall, a conflict between logic and moral resulted in decreased reasoning performance. In a second experiment, we trained the participants in logical thinking. With these participants no such conflict-effects were found.

When a learning theory predicts the wrong response: Error of the model or of the learner?

Meeter, Maarten Dept. of Psychology, University of Amsterdam, Amsterdam, Netherlands

In probabilistic categorization tasks various cues are probabilistically (but not perfectly) predictive of class membership. There are two alternative conceptualizations of learning in such tasks: as rule-based learning, or as incremental learning. Analysis methods based on these conceptualizations can be used to predict responses of categorizers from their responses on preceding trials. They predict responses about equally well, but both suggest that on many trials the response of the categorizer is a toss-up. Here, we investigate whether categorizers on such trials really produce essentially random responses, or whether there are regularities that are not yet captured by learning theories.

FP-408: 'Social Media': Social processes and social interaction in mass media II

Accuracy of impressions based on social networking (Facebook) profiles

Gosling, Samuel *Dept. of Psychology, University of Texas, Austin, USA* **Evans, David** *YouJustGetMe, Psychster LLC., Kenmore, USA* **Vazire, Simine** *Department of Psychology, Washington University, St. Louis, USA* **Gaddis, Sam** *Department of Psychology, University of Texas, Austin, USA*

Social networking websites have become a major domain of social interaction. In two studies we examine the accuracy of impressions based on Facebook profiles. Study 1 draws on data gathered using a Facebook application, "youjustgetme" to examine impressions of over 4000 profile owners, comparing them with the profile owners' self-reports. Study 2 uses more extensive validity data to compare impressions based on 139 Facebook profiles with how the targets see themselves, how they are seen by close acquaintances and strangers. Results show generally strong patterns of convergence, although the accuracy correlations vary considerably across traits.

Does internet use reflect your personality?: Relationship between Eysenck's personality dimensions and internet use

Tosun, Leman Pinar *Dept. of Psychology, Middle East Technical Univ., Ankara, Turkey* **Lajunen, Timo** *Psychology, Middle East Technical Univ., Ankara, Turkey*

This study aims to investigate the relationship between three Eysenckian personality dimensions and the Internet use. A sample of 421 Turkish university students completed the Eysenck's Personality Questionnaire (EPQ) and an Internet Survey which contained questions about relational aims of Internet use, existence of "Internet only" friends, passion for Internet use, and the tendency to express one's self in the Internet communication. Psychoticism was found to be the only personality dimension related to establishing new relationships and having "Internet only" friends. Also, psychoticism and neuroticism were associated with revealing one's self in the Internet communication. Psychoticism was related to obsessive passion, neuroticism was related to harmonious passion, and extraversion was related to both types of passion for Internet use.

Proficiency and attitudes toward data analysis and information technologies use in psychology undergraduates

Cazares, Ana *Technology and Education. Mod., National Pedagogic University, Mexico City, Mexico*

This study had two aims: first, to evaluate the proficient use of data analysis and information technologies in psychology undergraduates. Second, to investigate the relationship between their proficiency level and attitude toward the technology's use for academic, social and personal activities. Two hundred students were asked about these issues by means of two short Likert scales which shown a high internal consistency (Proficiency α=0.93; Attitudes α=0.88) and a coherent factorial structure. A regression analysis showed that the proficient use of simple technologies as well as an efficient information searching strategy, can predict together (R2=.537) usage of complex technologies and abilities.

Relationships through ICT: A focus on Malaysian university students

Hashim, Intan H.M. *School of Social Sciences, Universiti Sains Malaysia, Pulau Pinang, Malaysia*

This paper describes a preliminary analysis of a study on how a group of university students maintain interpersonal relationships via information and communication technology (ICT). Participants were 339 Malaysian university students. Questionnaires were used to assess background information; usage of mobile phones, electronic mails and internets for contacting people and respondent's level of loneliness. Findings show there are specializations in the way technology was used to make interpersonal contacts and there is a significant relationship between the time spent on mobile phones and loneliness. Findings are discussed within general relationship theories and those that are more relevant to Malaysian culture.

FP-409: Agreement and information sharing in groups II

Constructing a network of shared agreement: A shared reality network model of negotiation process

Jochemczyk, Lukasz *Warsaw, Poland* **Nowak, Andrzej** *Faculty of Psychology, University of Warsaw, Warsaw, Poland*

Negotiation can be examined from two perspectives: either static – the entire situation of the negotiation, or dynamic – the process of getting to an agreement. The static perspective is widely described in the negotiation literature and it is known how various factors of the negotiation situation influence the outcome of a negotiation. On the other hand we still lack much information about the dynamics of the negotiation process. We will present a SRN (Shared Reality Network) model of negotiation that fills this gap.

The effect of shared task knowledge on team processes and team performance

Domeinski, Juliane *Institute of Psychology, TU Berlin, Berlin, Germany* **Frommann, Peggy** *Institute of Psychology and Er, TU Berlin, Berlin, Germany* **Manzey, Dietrich** *Institute of Psychology and Er, TU Berlin, Berlin, Germany*

Team cognition is a key component for successful teamwork. In this study the effect of one aspect of team cognition, i.e. the extent of team members shared task knowledge, on team performance and coordination has been investigated. Twenty-four 2-person teams performed a task under different levels of shared task knowledge. Team performances as well as team process variables were assessed by means of standardized observation protocols. As expected, teams with higher extent of shared task knowledge showed significantly (p<.01) higher performance (e.g. fewer errors) and more effective team processes (better coordination). Implications for team cognitions research will be discussed.

Effects of group incentives and status differences on knowledge sharing in computer-mediated groups

Rack, Oliver *Hochschule für Angew. Psychol., Fachhochschule Nordwestschweiz, Olten, Switzerland* **Hollingshead, Andrea B.** *Annenberg School, University of Sth. California, Los Angeles, USA* **Boos, Margarete** *Institute of Psychology, University of Goettingen, Goettingen, Germany*

In a laboratory experiment, we investigated the effects of monetary group incentives and its distribution strategies (factor I: equality strategy, equity strategy, no rewards) and status differences among group members (factor II: based on individual performance or age) on knowledge sharing in computer-mediated groups. Participants were divided randomly in 45 groups of three persons and performed a knowledge pooling task via chat. Multilevel analyses and qualitative analyses revealed that equally distributed rewards have positive effects on pay satisfaction and knowledge sharing behaviour. Additionally, the perceived fairness of status differences within the group moderates the effects of group incentives on knowledge sharing.

Preference consistent information distortion during group discussions

Vogelgesang, Frank *Inst. für Psychologie, Universität Göttingen, Göttingen, Germany* **Simon, Sabia** *Institut für Psychologie, Universität Göttingen, Göttingen, Germany* **Mojzisch, Andreas** *Institut für Psychologie, Universität Göttingen, Göttingen, Germany* **Schulz-Hardt, Stefan** *Institut für Psychologie, Universität Göttingen, Göttingen, Germany*

Wittenbaum et al. (2004) argue that group members strategically spin information about their preferred alternative upward (making it seem more positive) and information about the nonpreferred alternatives downward (making it seem more negative). Similarly, Cruz et al. (2000) propose that group members defend their preferences by bolstering preference-consistent information and discounting preference-inconsistent information. We tested these hypotheses by reanalyzing the data of a recent hidden profile study (Schulz-Hardt et al., 2006). Our results suggest that preference-consistent spinning, bolstering and discounting are the result of the ideosyncratic interpretation of information prior to discussion rather than the consequence of strategic information exchange.

FP-410: Aging and health II

Patterns of change in Big-Five personality in "young-old" age

Schilling, Oliver *Department of Psychological A, University of Heidelberg, Heidelberg, Germany* **Schmitt, Marina** *Dep. of Psych. Ageing Research, University of Heidelberg, Heidelberg, Germany*

Considering intraindividual change in Big-5 traits as interindividual differences variable, we asked whether persons in their "young-old" ages could be classified into different types in terms of Big-5 stability. We analyzed NEO-FFI measures from the Interdisciplinary Longitudinal Study of Adult Development. Significant interindividual slope-variation was found for extraversion and conscientiousness. A growth mixture approach in order to detect "clusters of change" in these traits revealed a three-group solution which further analyses suggested to be linked with physical health. The findings may be regarded as worth further research to confirm these patterns of personality change and its relation to physical health.

Examining satisfaction with retirement from a dynamic perspective

Potocnik, Kristina *Dept. of Social Psychology, University of Valencia, Valencia, Spain* **Tordera, Nuria** *Social Psychology, University of Valencia, Valencia, Spain* **Peiro, Jose Maria** *Social Psychology, University of Valencia, Valencia, Spain*

Grounding on the theoretical model of dynamic work satisfaction (Büssing, 1992), the main objective of the present study was to explore different forms of retirement satisfaction on a sample of 270 Spanish retirees. Applying a two-phase cluster analysis, we found different forms of retirement satisfaction, each showing a specific pattern. Furthermore, differences between clusters in potential antecedents of retirement satisfaction were explored. Results showed that members from each cluster differed in terms of their personal, work-life and retirement experiences, such as their intentions to retire, group norms, control over retirement, gender, or the level of retirement income. Our findings suggest that the nature of retirement transition and pre-retirement experiences are related to different patterns of retirement satisfaction.

Educational level in the diagnostic of dementias: A research with eldery patients

Barbosa, Cristina Monteiro Dept. de Psicometria, UFRJ, Rio de Janeiro, Brazil Bastos, Claudio Lyra HUAP, UFF, Niterói, Brazil Coelho, Cristina Lucia Maia Dep. Fund. Pedagógicos, UFF, Niterói, Brazil
Objectives: To analyze the relationship between gender and the level of education in verbal and performance dimension results. Methods: The WAIS-III and the Zülliger tests were employed in 10 males and 10 females. Results: Data indicated that male subjects with higher education presented lower scores in the performance subtest when compared to verbal subtest. Conclusions: The female sample, with lower level of scholarship, no differences was detected. A covariance analyses indicated that education level was the responsible variable for this difference. Depressive traits in the male sample are based on the devaluation that the disease causes in the social role.

General health and loneliness in elders living with their own families in compare to elders who were living in nursing homes in Tehran city

Hemati Alamdarlo, Ghorban Tehran, Islamic Republic of Iran Dehshiri, Gholam Reza psychology, psychology, tehran, Islamic Republic of Iran shojai, setare psychology, exceptional children, tehran, Islamic Republic of Iran Hakimirad, Elham psychology, exceptional children, tehran, Islamic Republic of Iran
Aim of the study was to compare general health and loneliness between two groups of elders, living with their families or in nursing homes in Tehran city. Two hundred eighteen elderly consisted our sample. GHQ and loneliness questionnaires were administered on them. Results of two way analysis of variance indicated that General health of elders living in nursing homes were significantly lower and their loneliness were significantly more than elders who were living with their families. Based on psycho-cultural situation of elders in Iran, home based environment is the best place of nurturing psychological needs of elderlies in Iran.

FP-411: Aggression and violence at school II

Violence prevention at primary schools

Frey, Anne München, Germany Speck-Hamdan, Angelika
The present study analysis the results of a violence prevention program (called "aufgschaut") in German primary schools. 155 teachers were asked before, directly after, three month and one year after the training. In addition 207 pupils (class 1 to 4) were asked at the beginning and at the end of the school year. The trainers evaluate the program very postive. After one year the estimated potential of violence in class was significantly lower and the team spirit in class higher. Also the pupils perceive significantly less violent behaviour and the numer of victims was reduced. Implications for prevention research will be discussed.

School climate as risk factor for microviolence

Pavalache-Ilie, Mariela Psychology, University Transilvania, Brasov, Romania Cocorada, Elena Psychology, University Transilvania, Brasov, Romania Luca, Marcela Rodica Psychology, University Transilvania, Brasov, Romania Clinciu, Aurel Ion Psychology, University Transilvania, Brasov, Romania
This correlational research is a contextualized approach focused on the school climate in evaluation settings and its interactions with personality variables involved in micro-violence. The participants are 629 students in 9 schools. An original 3-scale School Climate Inventory (Cocorada & al)

and usual personality inventories were used. The results indicate that the poor quality of school climate on the three dimensions – relational, equity and security climate is significantly associated with high scores for anger and dominance and low scores for control, responsibility and preference for exigency. The study gives a frame for preventing and treating micro-violence in evaluation settings.

Civil courage in schools: Perspectives on prediction and training

Pfetsch, Jan INSIDE, University of Luxembourg, Walferdange, Luxembourg Steffgen, Georges INSIDE, University of Luxembourg, Walferdange, Luxembourg Gollwitzer, Mario Inst. für Psychologie, Universität Koblenz-Landau, Landau, Germany
Civil courage is defined as a bystander's intervention reaction associated with potential risks in a situation where fundamental norms are being violated. The present talk reviews current research on civil courage and addresses two questions: (1) Which context- and person-variables predict civil courage? (2) How effective are civil courage trainings? Study 1 (N = 230) with vignettes shows that social responsibility and perceived costs for victims and bystanders are the most powerful predictors of civil courage. Study 2 (N < 1000) elucidates the individual- and class-level effects of a civil courage training that was implemented in different schools in Luxembourg.

Aggression and violence among school peers in basic education in Brazil: An exploratory research

Matos Coelho, Maria Inês Mestrado em Educação, UEMG, Belo Horizonte, Brazil Araujo, Frederico António Mestrado em Educação, UEMG, Belo Horizonte, Brazil
This paper presents a research about different manifestations of violence among school peers in the first part of basic education, in the brazilian context. In line with the conceptual definition of bullying discussed in the psychological literature, we have designed a questionnaire using a set of four cartoons each portraying different scenes of peer bullying which are combined to objective questions. The violence at school has been examined both as a consequence of a set of inadequate school practices, and as one of the aspects that characterizes the contemporary society, particularly, a socialization marked by aggressions and petty crime.

FP-412: Aggression and sexual abuse II

Posttraumatic stress disorder and depression in a sample of sexual abused patients

Pillay, Basil Dept. Behavioural Medicine, University of KwaZulu-Natal, Durban, South Africa Ngcobo, Maggie Behavioural Medicine, University of KwaZulu-Natal, Durban, South Africa
Objective As a result of the high incidence of sexual violence and abuse and the dearth of research on psychological outcomes of such trauma, this study investigated Posttraumatic Stress Disorder (PTSD) and depression in a cohort presenting at a general hospital. Method Adults and children who were sexually abused participated. A semi-structured interview, Depression Inventories and PTSD Scales were used. Results Adult participants obtained high scores on the measures. This was not so among children. Conclusion This paper highlights pertinent aspects of abuse among women, the difficulties researching sexually abuse in children and issues to consider in transcultural contexts.

The justification of the sexual violence against women and the attitudes toward rape

Coklar, Isil Family Court, Turkish Ministerey of Justice, Izmir, Turkey Mese, Gulgun Psychology Department, Ege University, Izmir, Turkey

The purpose of this study is to determine how ambivalent sexism toward women and general and gender related system justification tendencies are associated with rape myth acceptance. 323 paticipants completed Illinois Rape Myth Acceptance Scale (Payne, Lonsway & Fitzgerald), Ambivalent Sexism Inventory (Glick & Fiske, 1996), General System Justification Scale (Kay & Jost, 2003) and Gender Related System Justification Scale (Kay & Jost, 2005). Results demonstrated that gender related system justification, hostile sexism and benevolent sexism predicted rape myth acceptance. Hostile sexism and benevolent sexism mediated the relationship between gender related system justification and rape myth acceptance for male participants. For female participants only hostile sexism mediated this relationship.

In the aftermath: Interpersonal trauma and sexual health

Richmond, Kate Dept. of Psychology, Muhlenberg College, Allentown, USA Needle, Rachel Dept. of Psychology, Nova Southeastern University, Fort Lauderdale, USA
Domestic violence is a global problem (Amnesty International, 2005). Survivors are at a higher risk for developing multiple mental health and interpersonal concerns (Walker, 1994). In particular, sexual and domestic abuse can alter cognition and attitudes related to multiple aspects of sexuality. This study aims to examine the sexual functioning among survivors of violence. Using the Female Sexual Functioning Index (FSFI) and the Trauma Symptom Inventory (TSI), exploratory data, collected from an international sample of female survivors of violence, will be highlighted. Results will be discussed within the context of assessment and treatment of female survivors.

FP-413: The impact of students' family background on learning II

Media use and school achievement: A longitudinal intervention study

Kleimann, Matthias Forschungsinstitut Niedersach., KFN - Kriminologisches, Hannover, Germany Mößle, Thomas Forschungsinstitut Niedersach., KFN - Kriminologisches, Hannover, Germany
OBJECTIVES: The study examines how electronic media use affects children's social behaviour and school performance. A school based media education concept is developed and systematically evaluated. METHODES: Four year longitudinal control group study with 1.059 elementary school children. RESULTS: Multivariate Analyses show significant relations between poor school performance, problematic social behaviour and a high degree of daily media exposure. Analyses also show significant effects of an intervention program. CONCLUSIONS: Our findings show the potential benefits of reducing the time spend on electronic media. School based media education programes are strongly recommended.

Family influences on the creative experiences of children from grade five to six in China

Han, Cheng-Min Suzhou Vocational University, Suzhou, People's Republic of China
A sample of 823 children from different elementary schools was surveyed. It was found that, if parents preserved their children's works and valued children's creative ideas, their children would like to create, cherish their own works, be clear about the pros and cons of their works, and feel happy about their progress. Family's supportive climate exerted similar effects. If parents liked to design and decorate creatively their home, their children would also like to create novel things. Those findings have important implications for families as well as for schools with an emphasis on helping parents

nurture children's creativity. Keywords: childhood; creativity; family

School children's academic achievement: The effect of working mothers' role as home tutor/teacher

Singh, Priti Psychology, JB Shah Girls (PG) College, Jhunjhunu, India

This study examined the relation between the amount of home work put at home after school hours,teachers feedback and the growth of children's academic standing in class, knowledge enhancement over the year. Three main findings emerged. First, there were marked individual differences in children's conventional knowledge by 4 years of age that were associated with socio-economic status. Second, there were dramatic differences in the amount and quality of home work provided by working mother. Third, and most important, the amount of parental monitoring throughout the school year did matter but was unrelated to their cognitive skills and ability at the start of the academic session.

Academic performance and the use of slangs among city university students

Mivanyi, Yuwanna Jenny Education Technical, City University Kaduna, Kaduna, Nigeria Ojo, Felicia A. Languages, City University Kaduna, Kaduna, Nigeria Egwuda, Cecilia Education Technical, City University Kaduna, Kaduna, Nigeria

Language is an expression of the mind. The 'clearer the language, the more the understanding of the information communicated. Slangs is frequently used quoloqueally, for communication among tertiary students in Nigeria. The Objective of this research is to find out whether the use of slangs and its frequency affects the language skill of students' spoken and written english, and correlate the semesters results. using structured questionnaires, 200 students of the City University, would be interviewed on the use of slangs and its frequency cum science and arts and social sciences and male/female backgrounds.

FP-414: Psychological disorders VIII

An investigation of the aetiology of dental fear within the Cognitive Vulnerability Model

Buchanan, Heather Inst of Work, Health & Org, Nottingham University, Nottingham, United Kingdom

Dental anxiety (DA) has been established as a common fear, of which there are adverse effects for both patient and practitioner. Recently, Armfield (2007) has proposed a cognitive vulnerability model (CVM) in order to explain fear acquisition and has applied this model to DA. The objective of the present study is to explore the self-reported origins of fear, within the context of the CVM, of 85 individuals who accessed a DA Internet support group and completed our online study. Findings showed that the CVM was a satisfactory model for explaining origins of DA, though some extensions to the model are proposed.

'Action-versus-state-orientation' and successful treatment of anxiety

Geissner, Edgar Abt. Psychology, Roseneck Hospital, Prien am Chiemsee, Germany Kraft, Madlen Psychology, Roseneck Hospital, Prien am Chiemsee, Germany

The study examines if 'Action-Orientation' (AO) vs. 'State-Orientation' contributes to treating anxiety. AO comprises of 'AO after failure', 'AO in planning', 'AO during activities'. 200 panic disorder / agoraphobia pts filled out several anxiety measures and HAKEMP for AO. Examinations were 3 mths before, at admission, discharge, 6 mths FU. Intervention was cognitive-behavioral therapy (CBT) with exposures. Results show strong effects

in all but one measures. Above there were conditional effects confirming the hypotheses: The more pts exert AO, the less their anxiety. Anxiety reduction is best predicted by increase in AO 'after failure' and 'in planning'.

Social phobia and the use of online communication services

Lehenbauer, Mario Inst. für Klin. Psychologie, Universität Wien, Wien, Austria Stetina, Birgit U. Forschung und Ausbildung, Universität Wien, Wien, Austria Kryspin-Exner, Ilse Inst. für Psychologie, Universität Wien, Wien, Austria

Objectives: Social phobia includes the fear of social situations in real life. Internet communication-services allow low-threshold, anonymous conversation. This study investigated the online habits of users suffering from social phobia. Methods: 918 unpaid volunteers filled out our online questionnaire, consisting of questions about online habits and the SIAS (Social Interaction Anxiety Scale). Results: 20.3% of the sample suffered from social phobia and they use online communication-services more than healthy individuals do. Conclusions: There is a considerable danger that these individuals may use the internet as their sole method of acquiring social contacts and thus loose relevant social skills in real life.

How does exposure therapy work? A virtual reality study in aviophobia

Mühlberger, Andreas Department of Psychology, University of Würzburg, Würzburg, Germany Brütting, Johanna Department of Psychology, University of Würzburg, Würzburg, Germany Pauli, Paul Department of Psychology, University of Würzburg, Würzburg, Germany

While there is great evidence for the efficacy of in-vivo and virtual reality (VR) exposure for the treatment of specific phobias, studies on treatment mechanisms are rare. To investigate whether distraction during in vivo exposure has impairing effects on fear processing 37 aviophobic participants were randomly assigned to VR-flights with instruction to focus on their fear or to solve working memory tasks. While the distracted participants had less fear during turbulent flight periods, no difference between groups during a VR-flight in a second session were found. Focusing on fear during exposure might not be necessary for fear processing in aviophobia.

FP-415: Psychotherapy - Research and treatment methods XII

A comparison of the four therapeutic methods of cognitive behavioral, drug, mixed (cognitive - behavioral + drug) and placebo in the treatment of the generalized anxiety disorder

Abolghasemi, Shahnam Dept. of Psychology, Azad University, Tonekabon, Islamic Republic of Iran

In order to compare four therapeutic methods, 40 anxious subjects afflicted by generalized anxiety were assigned in the four therapeutic groups of 10 randomly. The methodology was a semi-experimental deign, and the instruments to collect the data were two questionries (Zung and Tylor anxiety scales). Two ways of analysis include the simplified form of ANOVA and Tuki tests. The results suggested that each of 4 ways was effective to treat the generalized anxiety, but the move effectiveness of the mixed way compared to teach of other 3 ways was not confirmed.

Empirical studies on trauma and dialogue-ability

Butollo, Willi Psychologie, Ludwig-Maximilians-Universität, München, Germany

Among the many ways in which people react to traumatic experiences the decay of interpersonal skills and especially the unability to interact in a dialogical way are most striking. Dialog-ability

implies sound self processes and the ability to establish personal exchange and contact. In a dialogical approach to trauma therapy ("dialogical exposure") different steps to re-establish dialogability are required. A multiphasic integrative therapeutic approach will be described which illustrates that healing traumatic impact implies step by step rebuilding and strengthening the abilities for dialogical encounters and contact-abilities. Now empirical results from applying this approach to trauma will be presented and discussed, with special focus on symptom reduction and changes in the contact process.

Comprehensiveness in clinical psychology: Why would we use it?

Carija, Martina Preventive Program, Association, Zagreb, Croatia Kulas, Kristina Preventive program, Association "Play", Zagreb, Croatia

A semi-structured interview will be applied to psychologists that work with individuals (counselling, psychotherapy, diagnostics,prevention,...). The goal is to find out an expert's opinion on the following questions: 1. What is comprehensiveness in the context of clinical psychology? 2. Is it important in working with individuals and in what way? 3. Can this kind of work be implemented in the clinical approach and how? 4. Some practical examples of a comprehensive way from our experience. A qualitative analysis of the collected data will be conducted and the results will be presented. Martina Carija, Kristina Kulas Association "Play"

Experience-based learning in psychotherapy

Wolf, Markus Mehl, Kilian Klinik Wollmarshöhe, Bodnegg, Germany

In a prospective controlled evaluation study on the effects of psychophysical exposure in 247 patients, the effects, effect sizes and processes of change through experience-based exposure to a ropes course were studied, the method being embedded in a multi-method inpatient psychophysical treatment concept. Instruments of evaluation were the routine quality control assessments conducted in our institution (Forschungsstelle Psychotherapie, Universität Heidelberg) as well as special instruments of higher sensitivity for measuring specific changes (locus of control, fear, depression, self-efficacy). Compared with controls, patients with exposure procedure showed significantly larger effect sizes with regard to impairment, depression, state and trait anxieties, locus of control and self-efficacy.

FP-416: Psychosocial problems and abuses in childhood and adolescence

Transgression and aggression. Object relations in street children

Alcalde, Aurea Lima, Peru Alcalde Alcalde, Maria Julia Education, Colegio Huerta Santa Ana, Seville, Spain

The present investigation is based on the probability that Street Children coming from dysfunctional families with unsatisfied basic needs, traumatic early experiences and who live in permanent risk conditions which can all affect their integrity and survival, should show aggressive behaviours and signs of borderline or narcissistic personalities as a consequence of their early frustrations. Three instruments were used with the purpose of exploring the presence, nature, quality and levels of extra-punitive answers and different adaptive and psychopathological levels of object relations internalized by a group of 36 male Street Children aged 12, 13 and 14 years old.

Child sexual abuse perpetrator strategies and survivor adjustment

Canton Cortes, David Developmental Psychology, University of Granada, Granada, Spain Cortes Arboleda, Maria Rosario Developmental Psychology, University of Granada, Granada, Spain

The objective of the study was to analyse the associations between the strategies employed by the CSA perpetrator in order to ensure secrecy of the child and the Posttraumatic stress disorder symptomatology of the victim. The study was carried out with a sample of 76 College students from the University of Granada, who had a history of CSA. Regression analyses showed that the re-experimentation and avoidance of the victims were higher when were threatened with getting into problems, while arousal and total score on PTSD were higher when were also threatened with physical damage. We can conclude that PTSD symptomatology of CSA survivors is related to the strategies employed by the perpetrator in order to ensure secrecy.

Psychological abuse over adolescents and its impact on cognitions about the self

Iovu, Mihai-Bogdan Valcea, Romania

Objective: This study investigates the presence of psychological abuse in educational and familal environments and its relation with the cognitions about the self. Method: 245 highschool children completed two questionnaires regarding the potential abusive experiences and the attached cognitions. Results: We found a correlation coefficient of .500, p<0.01 between the psychological abuse and the level of rationality. The abuse within their families had a deeper impact over the cognitions than those experienced within the schools (rfam= .453, rsch=.425, p<0.01). Conclusions: From these results psychological abuse needs increased attention from the research community.

Features of psychological problems among adolescents of different social situations

Samykina, Nataly Psychology, Samara State University, Samara, Russia Lisecky, Constantine Psychology, Samara State University, Samara, Russia

In 2005-2007 the study of features of adolescents of different social situations has been conducted. 450 adolescents have been studied: children from at-risk, single-parent, two-parent families, as well as children in families with high financial income. Research Methods: questionnaries, analysis autobiographies, psychosemantic methods. Typical psychological problems for each group were identified and the ways of their solving were proposed. It was noted that the typical problems of adolescence are relevant to any social situations. Features concerns differences of their solving. Adolescents in single-parent families or children in two-parent families appeared to be more able to solve them constructively.

FP-417: Interpersonal and peer relations in childhood and adolescence

Building strengths by positive peer culture: Results of an evaluation

Steinebach, Christoph Inst. für Angew. Psychologie, Universität Zürich, Zürich, Switzerland Steinebach, Ursula Inst. of Appl. Research, Cath. Univ. of Appl. Sciences, Freiburg, Germany

Concepts of resilience and self efficacy highlight possible positive effects of mutual help by adolescents. Accordingly the concept of Positive Peer Culture developed by Vorrath and Brendtro in the 1970s relies on the experience to be able to help. To line out the effects of Positive Peer Culture 163 male adolescents, parents and 47 staff members in a foster home were interviewed in a longitudinal study. In six different surveys quantitative as well as qualitative methods, questionnaires as well as

interviews have been applied. The results show an increasing self-worth and decreasing behavioral problems. Consequences for youth welfare services are being discussed.

Popularity and aggression: Direction of influences

Xie, Hongling Dept. of Psychology, Temple University, Philadelphia, USA Fleurant, Ngalula Department of Psychology, Temple University, Philadelphia, USA

This study recruited 329 6th-grade students (mean age = 12 47% African-American; 33% European-American) from 3 urban middle schools in North-eastern USA. Individual interviews yielded narrative accounts of what factors promote popularity and what behaviors are displayed by popular peers. Attractive appearance and affiliation with popular peers were most mentioned factors promoting popularity, while aggression and antisocial behaviors were rarely mentioned. In contrast, children viewed popular peers as being mean, snobby (dominant), and displaying poor studentship. Popular boys were perceived as being aggressive. These findings suggest a stronger direction of influence from popularity to aggression than from aggression to popularity.

Peer relationship and purchase deception in adolescence: The moderating role of vanity

Lin, Mei-Kuei Business Administration, National Taipei University, Sansia Township, Taiwan Hsu, Ya-Hui Business Administration, National Taipei University, Sansia Township, Taipei County, Taiwan Chen, Fang-Ping Business Administration, National Central University, Jhongli City, Taoyuan County, Taiwan

Previous studies rarely examine the relationship between peer relationships and purchase deceptions in adolescence, and frequently neglect the moderating effect of vanity. This study fills the research gap by exploring the influence of peer relationships and vanity upon purchase deceptions in adolescence. The analytical sample comprises a total of 287 high school students. Using hierarchical regression analysis reveals that (1) peer relationships have a significantly positive effect on purchase deceptions; (2) vanity significantly moderates the relationship between peer relationship and purchase deception.

FP-418: Gender differences and management

Differences between Czech male and female managers

Pauknerova, Daniela Manager. Psychology and Soc., University of Economics, Prague, Czech Republic

Objectives: The aim of this research was to analyze differences in leadership traits and skills among men and women in middle level managers from the financial sector. Methods: Personality questionnaires and observation by trained psychologists and human resources staff of leaders' performances in model situations were used as methods. Results: Male and female managers were found to differ significantly on assertiveness, motivation, and risk taking (p<.05 based on t-tests). They were no significant gender differences on other personality traits. Significant differences between men and women were not found regarding their leadership and communication skills.

Brazilian women in leadership positions in organizations: Career development and management style

Rocha Coutinho, Maria Lúcia Dept. of Psychology, UFRJ / UNIVERSO, Rio de Janeiro, Brazil Rocha Coutinho, Rodrigo Business, Strategy Consultat, São Paulo, Brazil

This work presents the results of a study in which we interviewed 20 Brazilian women in leadership

positions in organizations, aged 25 to 45. The resulting texts were submitted to a discourse analysis. Our data indicated that it is harder for women to prove their competence and efficiency so as to reach the highest positions and that, in general, women are more worried about the functioning of the team, have more sensibility to deal with subordinates, better communication skills and have a greater ability to manage different tasks simultaneously than men.

An analytical study of employment of educated women in Iranian labor force

Jazani, Nasrin Business Administration, Shahid Behshti University, Tehran, Islamic Republic of Iran

Purpose : Analysing structure and partipation of educated female labor force in Iran. Methodology:Applied-description type, meaning that its results may find application in removing barriers, once they are located and appropriately described. Questions: 1.Why the rate of women's participation in labor force is low regarding a high rate of Iranian educated women ? 2.Is job segregation the main reason for lower rate? 3.What are the main barriers facing them ? 4. What mechanisms should be used to diminish gap between male and female unemployment and participation in labor force? 5. Is legality a barrier? Key words: unemployment, job segregation, division of labor

What about differences of gender in the perception of occupational health?

Barros Duarte, Carla Faculty of Social and Human, University Fernando Pessoa, Porto, Portugal

This study falls within the theoretical and methodological framework of Work Psychology and Ergonomics of Activity, and consists of a research that seeks to understand the relations between Work, Health and Gender. The main goal was the analysis of the effects of the working conditions on occupational health through gender. An epidemiological study (Survey/Inquiry 329 workers) reveal the need to conduct a more specify analysis of the regulation processes for the preservation and construction of their health (case study). The results revealed gender differences and the need to understand the gender differences through the specificities of work division and task distribution. Keywords: Work, Health & Gender

FP-419: Group dynamics

A group conflict in dance therapy: Attempt of a group dynamic integration

Burbiel, Ilse Psychoanalyse, Deutsche Akademie für, München, Germany

Dance therapy is a successful nonverbal facet of the therapeutic network of Dynamic Psychiatry in addition to the predominantly verbal individual and group psychotherapy. The author's concern is to show, how a so called committer-victim conflict, which had been developed in a dance session, can be worked through and finally solved by means of group dynamic processes within verbal and dance therapy. So the "committer-victim" conflict changed into a group conflict. The fear to be excluded from the group, experienced by committer and victim likewise, as well as the experienced sense of shame and guilt can be diminished in this way.

Dissent in group decision making: Contrary effects of interpersonal liking

Klocke, Ulrich Department of Psychology, Humboldt University of Berlin, Berlin, Germany

Dissent can be promotional for group decision making. Liking between group members has contrary effects on dissent and its consequences. Study 1 manipulated dissent in interacting decision groups (90 students) and measured liking before discussion. In study 2, 77 students anticipated a decision with a partner. The partner's likability and expression of dissent was manipulated. On the one hand, liking reduced the perception of dissent (study 2) and enhanced opinion-consistent argumentation towards dissenting partners (study 1 and 2) presumably in order to reduce inconsistent dissent. On the other hand, liking enhanced a differentiated perception of the others' opinion (study 1).

Ultimate causes of egalitarianism: Factors influencing social order in Macaques and other primates

Lehmann, Hagen Computer Science, University of Bath, Bath Spa, United Kingdom Bryson, Joanna Computer Science, University of Bath, Bath Spa, United Kingdom
Primate social behavior is characterized along a continuum reaching from egalitarian to despotic. Despotic societies have strict hierarchies, few but intense aggressive interactions and less cohesive grouping. Egalitarian societies have less well-defined hierarchies, frequent but less violent aggressions, are more cohesive and group members execute a large repertoire of reconciliation behaviours. We present an agent-based computer model that describes this variation in terms of selective environmental pressures. Our model accounts for this variation entirely by adaptive environmental pressures that determine the optimal average distance between troop members. We validate our results by comparison to the social behavior of genus macaca.

FP-420: Industrial / organizational psychology

Factorial validity and consistency of Maslach burnout inventory: General survey across occupational groups in China

Li, Chaoping School of Public Admin., Renmin University, Beijing, People's Republic of China
First data from 294 employees was collected to validate the Chinese version MBI-GS. EFA analysis replicated the same three-factor structure as the original after item 13 was dropped. Then 1036 samples were got from four different occupation groups: nurses, teachers, policemen and IT employees. Both Separate CFA analyses of different occupations and combined analyses showed that the original three-factor model had a clearly better fit than the alternative one-factor and two-factor models. Alpha coefficients for all three subscales were above 0.80. The results support that MBI-GS provides a suitable measurement to assess burnout across a diversity of professions in China.

Psychological stress in the workplace: Measurement problems and integration of data into a physical and psychological stressor database

Windemuth, Dirk Research and Education, BGAG Institute Work and Health, Dresden, Germany Stamm, Roger BGIA, DGUV, Sankt Augustin, Germany
Psychological stress and strain in the workplace have received more attention. But how does one measure psychological stress reliably and scientifically but at the same time pragmatically? It appears that the current general consensus is for a graded approach with a minimum of scientific-based measurement. In the first part of the presentation these areas of contention will be outlined. In this relation there is a further question: How should the measurement results be interpreted and in which context? In the second part of the presentation a consolidated database will be presented as a possibility to handle these results.

Wording effects in the measurement of perceived organizational support

Xu, Xiaofeng CICP, Baoding, People's Republic of China Zhang, Enyou PSYCHOLOGICAL DEPARTMENT, Central institute justice pol, BAODING, People's Republic of China
Two researches explored the construct of Perceived Organizational Support(POS). Using a sample of 391 and 4402 employees respectively drawn from two of the largest SOEs in China, Study 1 and 2 examined the construct validity of 8 items SPOS developed by Eisenberger etc (1986). Factor analyses suggest separate factors associated with positively and negatively word items. Confirmatory factor analysis (CFA) and Multitrait-Multimethod (MTMM) matrix were used to evaluate the effect of item wording. The results indicated that method effects associated with negatively worded items was significant and wording factors explained a significant amount of item variance.

FP-421: Individualism / collectivism III

Self-criticism, dependency, and sense of coherence among Arab-Bedouin and Jewish students

Abu-Kaf, Sarah Psychology, Ben-Gurion University, Beer-Sheva, Israel Priel, Beatriz psychology, Ben-Gurion University, Beer-Sheva, Israel
Objective: To examine cultural differences in self-criticism, dependency, and sense of coherence among Arab-Bedouin and Jewish students. Methods: 100 Arab-Bedouin and 105 Jewish university students completed the Depressive Experiences Questionnaire (DEQ), the Center for Epidemiological Studies Depression (CES-D), Sense of Coherence Scale (SOC), and a questionnaire on demographic variables. Results: Arab-Bedouin students were found to present lower levels of SOC and higher levels of self-criticism and depression. SOC mediated part of the relationship between self-criticism and depression. Conclusion: Self-criticism appears as a severe vulnerability to depression. Self-criticism affects SOC which in turn causes depression in both collectivistic and individualistic cultures

Coping among Chinese: Self-dependent problem-focused as most adaptive strategy

Wong, Celia Ching-Yee Dept. of Psychology, CUHK, Hong Kong, China, People's Republic of : Hong Kong SAR Hui, Natalie Heung-Hung Psychology, CUHK, Hong Kong, China, People's Republic of : Macao SAR Lam, Fiona Wing-Chi Psychology, CUHK, Hong Kong, China, People's Republic of : Macao SAR Bond, Michael Harris Psychology, CUHK, Hong Kong, China, People's Republic of : Macao SAR
Many studies showed that social support is a protective factor against adversity (Aspinwall, Taylor, 1997; Seeman, 1996; Thoits, 1995). However, previous studies claim collectivistic people are less likely to adopt social support. The present study aimed at investigating and explaining psychological outcomes of various coping strategies in Chinese collectivistic culture. Specifically, we compared psychological outcomes of self-dependent and other-dependent coping and further classifying as problem-focused and emotion-focused. Negatively influences of other-dependent emotion-focused coping on self-perceived interpersonal satisfaction was revealed to support the speculation that social support may disrupt harmony in collectivist culture (Mortenson, Liu, Burleson, & Liu, 2006; Triandis, 1989)

FP-422: Cross-cultural comparisons IV

A study on the effects of socio-cultural factors on gender role stereotypes of two ethnic groups of Iranian students

Khamseh, Akram Women Research Center, Alzahra University, Tehran, Islamic Republic of Iran
The aim of the present study is understanding that how ethnicity and gender can influence the gender role characteristics and stereotypes of female and male students of two ethnic groups of Iran.Bem sex role inventory- Persian form- and a general demographic questionnaire were administered.The data were gathered from 156 Kurdish and Persian female and male students. Results show that there are no differences between two groups of female students in gender role stereotypes. But there are significant differences between two ethnic groups of male students according to femininity (t=2.5) Data also show that both ethnic groups evaluate masculine traits more positive than feminine traits.Results have been discussed on different theoretical bases .

Cultural differences in friendship

Sacharin, Vera Dept. of Psychology, University of Michigan, Ann Arbor, USA Gonzalez, Richard Psychology, University of Michigan, Ann Arbor, MI, USA
We examined the concept of friendship in American and German samples using Lewin's (1948) conceptual analysis of friendship differences between those cultures. In a paper and pencil study, 74 Americans and 47 Germans checked applicable statements about their friendships (73 items). Germans reported closer relationships with their acquaintances than Americans. No cultural differences were observed for closeness to good or best friends. The result was replicated in an online study where 49 Americans and 37 Germans assigned relationship terms to circle figures with varying "self-other" overlap. Our result can explain why Germans name fewer friends than Americans (Sleeth-Keppler, 2005).

A study about the relationship between Shutaiseil (self-direction) and feeling of adaptation in children: From comparison between Japanese and Canadian

Asami, Kenichiro Dept. of Human-Environment, Kyushu University, Fukuoka, Japan
In Japan, various research results indicate that many of the Japanese children's problems are related to children's lack of independence. Independence is "SHUTAISEI" in Japanese; it has a close meaning to "self-direction". I have created a scale to measure "self-direction" for children. I found out that there was a strong relationship between "self-direction" and "feeling of adaptation". This part of research is to collect the data in Canada, to find out the difference between Japanese and Canadians in terms of "self-direction" and "feeling of adaptation". For this statistical analysis, I distribute a questionnaire on the student's "self-direction" and "adaptation".

Self-disclosure as a relationship-strengthening strategy in Japan and the United States

Schug, Joanna Dept. of Behavioral Science, Hokkaido University, Sapporo, Japan Yuki, Masaki Behavioral Science, Hokkaido University, Sapporo, Hokkaido, Japan Maddux, William W. Organisational Behaviour, INSEAD, Fontainebleau Cedex, France
Various studies have shown that North Americans tend to self-disclosure more than East Asians. We hypothesized that this difference could be explained by the adaptive role self-disclosure plays in mobile social contexts. In societies high in relational mobility—or the number of opportunities to select new relationship partners—individuals must invest

energy in the formation and maintenance of interpersonal relationships, and self-disclosure is a useful tool for this means. We addressed this hypothesis by investigating the relationship between relational mobility and self-disclosure in Japan, as well as through a cross-cultural comparison, and found strong support for this hypothesis.

Poster Session Friday Morning 09:00

Professional identity as a characteristic of professionals' subjective reality.
Abdoullaeva, Mehirban Psychology, Moscow State University, Moscow, Russia
The aim of the empirical study is to contribute to the investigation of professional influences on the self, including perceived and construed aspects in its mental representations (self-concept and self-construals). 81 subjects of different occupations: lawyers, therapists, accountants, couturiers were involved. Methods: the multilevel technology of job analysis, semantic differential, statistical analysis of the data obtained. The results show the different semantic components of construction "by myself" (presentation of my real professional qualities in estimations of "real I", "ideal I" and so on), that made it possible to discuss positive and negative characteristics of professionals' subjective reality.

Influence of perceived support on vocational motive and application related behavior among Japanese university students
Adachi, Tomoko Behavioral Science, Osaka Kyoiku University, Osaka, Japan
The purpose of this study was to examine influence of perceived contextual support on vocational motive and application related behavior. Questioners were administrated to Japanese university students. Results of causal analysis using structural equation modeling indicated that perceived support influenced vocational motive which itself, influenced application related behavior, however, no direct linkage between perceived supports and application related behavior were obtained. Implications for career intervention for university students are discussed, including intervention using perceived support to maximize career decisions.

Altered representation of T-cell subsets in severely traumatized refugees with posttraumatic stress disorder (PTSD)
Aichinger, Hannah Klinische & Neuropsychologie, Universität Konstanz, Konstanz, Germany Sommershof, Annette Immunologie, Universität Konstanz, Konstanz, Germany Adenauer, Hannah Klinische & Neuropsycholog, Universität Konstanz, Konstanz, Germany Catani, Claudia Klinische & Neuropsycholog, Universität Konstanz, Konstanz, Germany Neuner, Frank Klinische & Neuropsycholog, Universität Konstanz, Konstanz, Germany Engler, Harald Elbert, Thomas Klinische & Neuropsycholog, Universität Konstanz, Konstanz, Germany Groettrup, Marcus Immunologie, Universität Konstanz, Konstanz, Germany Kolassa, Iris-Tatjana Klinische & Neuropsycholog, Universität Konstanz, Konstanz, Germany
This study investigated changes in T-cell differentiation through chronic stress in 15 patients with PTSD, due to war and torture experiences, and 15 matched controls. Results showed that the proportions of naïve T-cells (naïve cytotoxic T-cells, naïve T-helper cells) and regulatory T-cells were significantly reduced while memory T-cells (memory cytotoxic T-cells, central memory T-helper cells) were significantly enhanced in PTSD patients compared to controls. Thus chronic stress seems to compromise the maturation of new T-cells in the thymus. The downregulation of regulatory T-cells in PTSD patients might constitute a risk factor for the development of autoimmune disorders.

Correlated change in personality traits over twelve years: A comparison of middle aged and older adults
Allemand, Mathias Department of Psychology, University of Zurich, Zürich, Switzerland Zimprich, Daniel Department of Psychology, University of Zurich, Zürich, Switzerland Martin, Mike Department of Psychology, University of Zurich, Zürich, Switzerland
This research examines correlated change in personality traits in middle-aged and older adults over twelve years. Data from the Interdisciplinary Study on Adult Development (ILSE) were used. The sample consists of 300 older adults (60 to 64 years). The longitudinal follow-up for the middle-aged adults (42 to 46 years) is still in progress. Personality traits were measured with the NEO-FFI. Correlated change in personality traits was examined utilizing latent change models. First results indicated a number of statistically significant medium effect-sized latent change correlations among personality traits, except for neuroticism. The findings indicate substantive commonality in personality trait change over twelve years.

Mental health and work in a national survey of farm managers in the United States
Alterman, Toni NIOSH-DSHEFS-SB, CDC, Cincinnati, USA Li, Jia Contractor for NIOSH, SRA, Cincinnati, USA Steege, Andrea CDC/NIOSH/DSHEFS, National Institute for Occupat, Cincinnati, USA Petersen, Martin CDC/NIOSH/DSHEFS, National Institute for Occupat, Cincinnati, USA Muntaner, Carles CAMH, University of Toronto, Toronto, Canada
This study examines associations between mental health and working from a nationally representative survey of farm managers in the United States. The General Health Questionnaire (GHQ-20), a screening instrument used in many languages and settings to indicate severity of depression and anxiety, was administered. Logistic regression models showed that physical health, cutting down on work activity due to emotional or physical problems, considering oneself disabled, emergency room visits, and hospital stays were associated with GHQ scores. These associations did not differ with race, ethnicity, or gender. Mental health should be considered an important component of occupational health.

The study of excellence in science, sport and art in Portugal: Preliminary results and findings from a research program
Araújo, Liliana Inst. Educação e Psicologia, Universidade do Minho, Braga, Portugal Matos, Daniela Inst. Educação e Psicologia, Universidade do Minho, Braga, Portugal Almeida, Leandro Inst. Educação e Psicologia, Universidade do Minho, Braga, Portugal Cruz, José F. Inst. Educação e Psicologia, Universidade do Minho, Braga, Portugal
Trying to understand the development of excellence and exceptional performance, a Portuguese research team began a comprehensive study, searching for pathways for excellence in different achievement domains. The major goal was to integrate different theoretical approaches on excellence and superior performance, with data from participants' actual and past achievements, including their talent developmental process. Using a qualitative methodology, outstanding national scientists, athletes and artists were interviewed. Results suggest some core and common psychological characteristics ("what they are made of" and their "trademarks"), but also the important contribution of external factors to the development of excellence. Future research challenges are outlined.

Influence of consuming neurotoxic substances on prospective memory in a sample of teenagers and young adults
Arana, José M. Dept. of Psychology, University of Salamanca, Salamanca, Spain Blanco, Cristina Psychology, University of Salamanca, Salamanca, Spain Meilán, Juan J.G. Psychology, University of Salamanca, Salamanca, Spain Pérez, Enrique Psychology, University of Salamanca, Salamanca, Spain
Prospective memory is required for many aspects of everyday cognition and is essential for the autonomy of a person in their daily life. Aims. Considering the importance of drug consumption on young people, we decided to study how neurotoxic substances influence prospective memory in this population with a propotypic polyconsumption profile. Method. We applied three neuropsicological tests, the PMQ, some cognitive items and an objective PM task performed on a computer in our sample (n=164). Conclusions. Stepwise analysis showed that an important percentage of the worst performance in policonsumers is explained by the quantity of tobacco smoked and the years consuming tranquillizers.

Everyday life heroes (in white): The end of a dream job?- Burnout of general practitioners (GP)
Argyropoulos, Sophia Institut für Psychologie, Universität Innsbruck, Innsbruck, Austria Iwanowa, Anna Institut für Psychologie, Innsbruck, Austria
This quantitative study focuses on the investigation of burnout and mental health by GP. Specific resources, requirements in the job and socio-demographic variables were explored by interviews and questionnaires. A total of 2,500 completed questionnaires out of 10.000, were returned and evaluated. Job burnout was measured by MBI-D (Büssing & Glaser 1992) and general health by the GHQ (Goldberg & Williams). A new questionnaire of specific job requirements was developed to test the linkage between job characteristics, exhaustion, cynicism, perception of low personal accomplishment and general health. The mediating role of burnout was tested with Structural equation modelling analysis (AMOS).

A neural network model of category specific semantic memory impairments: Self-organizing mapping formation mediated by both temporal lobe and hippocampus area
Asakawa, Shinichi Centre for Information Science, Tokyo Woman's Christian Univ., Tokyo, Japan
Semantic memory representation in temporal lobe have been shown to depend on both cortico-cortico and cortico-hippocampus circuits. After damage of temporal lobe, we could observe category specific impairments, which might be modeled by self-organizing principles. The different roles of these two circuits might result in temporal encoding manners of information. Here we review self-organizing mapping principles in temporal lobe in which external information could be learnt via slow (cortical) and fast (hippocampal) learnings. We then describe a simple neural network model that captures some key features of category specific memory impairments of brain damaged patients.

Dynamic of change of understanding of civil liberties in early adolescence
Atanassova-Trifonova, Maria Institute of Psychology, Sofia, Bulgaria
The purpose of the experimental study was to investigate the dynamic of change in the adolescents' understanding of civil rights at the abstract level and at the level of their application in concrete situational contexts. The sample of 284 subjects of three age groups- 12-, 13- and 15-olds, evaluated concepts of eight civil liberties with the semantic differential technique. The same subjects were presented with an inventory with a wide range of

situations comprising applications of these civil rights. The significant age and gender differences were revealed with a multivariate analysis of variance either at the abstract level of understanding of civil rights and for their concrete application.

Emotional intelligence and underemployment in the youth labour market

Bayona, Jaime Andrés Social Psychology, University of Barcelona, Barcelona, Spain

The main objective of this study is to identify the emotional intelligence subscales that differ between underemployed, employed and not-working individuals in the youth labour market. The research is based on a work continuity framework (employment-underemployment-unemployment). 103 Spanish students ranged between 18 to 24 years old were tested using the Trait Emotional Intelligence Questionnaire (TEIQue). One-way ANOVA showed significant differences among all groups on: emotional expression, assertiveness, stress management and social skills (p < 0.05). Implications of these results for the work continuity framework will be discussed as well as some relevant suggestions for future research.

Development of speech synthesizer for the blind capabilities in Slavic language

Benediktov, Sergey Department of psychology, Belarus State University, Minsk, Belarus Naavgustova, Tatiana Department of psychology, Belarus State University, Minsk, Belarus Shulga, Oksana Department of psychology, Grodno State University, Grodno, Belarus

We currently train Blind people to use speech synthesizer in Belarus. It is difficult for Blind to perceive the speech from PC. This aspect has relating to engineering psychology. Unlike well-known JAWS-system for Blind we designed an intellectual program "Search Echo" which has internal speech comments in on human acts and computer answers. It reflects the computer's dynamics, but not the monitor's static. We have developed training programs on a keyboard, on reading, writing. Results: We have found 3 psychological phenomena: concerning space images, speech synthesizers is more human-like, a perfect command of the oral form

University students' critical thinking dispositions and emotional intelligence as a predictor variable

Berkant, Hasan Güner Educational Sciences, Cukurova University, Adana, Turkey Tümkaya, Songül Educational Sciences, Cukurova University, Adana, Turkey Çelik, Metehan Educational Sciences, Cukurova University, Adana, Turkey Aybek, Birsel Educational Sciences, Cukurova University, Adana, Turkey

The main purpose is to investigate the university students' critical thinking dispositions and to evaluate emotional intelligence as a predictor variable. The sample of the research consists of 205 students. Bar-On EQ Inventory, California Critical Thinking Disposition Inventory and Personal Information Form were used. T-test, one-way ANOVA, LSD test and multiple regression analyses were used. There is no meaningful difference between students' critical thinking dispositions according to their genders. There is meaningful difference between the students' critical thinking dispositions in favor of students attending to health science programme; between the students' critical thinking dispositions in favor of fourth grade students.

On the endogenous nature of personality traits: The continuity of adult personality and child temperament within the framework of Cloninger's model of personality

Blatny, Marek Dept. of Psychology, Academy of Sciences, Brno, Czech Republic Jelinek, Martin Inst. of Psychology, Academy of Sciences, Brno, Czech Republic Osecka-Pilatova, Terezie Inst. of Psychology, Academy of Sciences, Brno, Czech Republic Preiss, Marek Dept. of Psychology, Prague Psychiatric Center, Brno, Czech Republic

The study deals with the prediction of adult personality from behaviors observed in the nursling and toddler stages. The sample consisted of 83 participants (35 men and 48 women aged from 38 to 44 years) who had taken part in the longitudinal research of children (1961-1980) and agreed to participate in the follow-up study of adults (2000-onwards). Only child inhibition showed to be significant predictor of adult personality characteristics: inhibition is connected mainly to facets of Harm Avoidance trait – Worry/Pessimism and Fear of Uncertainty.

Sociopsychological indicators of successful and less successful entrepreneurs

Blumberga, Solveiga Pedagogy and Psychology, University of Latvia, Riga, Latvia

The purpose of this research is to determine, which sociopsychological indicators allow to differentiate successful entrepreneurs from less successful ones. The following sociopsychological indicators of successful entrepreneurs have been studied: personality (achievement motivation, risk taking, locus of control), cognitive skills (including intuition), social and other skills, social support, coping strategies, pshychological wellbeing (life satisfaction, happiness, job satisfaction). It was concluded that achievement motivation, risk taking, intuition, social skills, coping strategies and psychological wellbeing are indicators that significantly differentiate successful entrepreneurs from less successful ones.

Gender-dependent features of Heroin addiction in adolescents

Bokhan, Nikolay Addictive States Department, Mental Health Research Institu, Tomsk, Russia

There are no complex investigations carrying out comparative assessment of psychological and psychopathological peculiarities of gender-dependent addictive behavior. Taking into account the high social significance of the problem great significance is acquired by differentiated assessment of actual status and dynamic of dependence in this contingent, identification of typology and phenomenology of sex disadaptation, necessity of formation of differentiated graphic medication and psycho-correcting treatment programs. Among questions, which are supposed to be considered in detail, importance place will be allocated to features of phenomenology and regularities of clinical dynamic of gender-dependent heroin addiction in adolescents.

Psychological determinants of teacher's burnout

Borisova, Maria Dept. of Psychology, State Pedagogical University, Yaroslavl, Russia

The purpose of the research is to discover the determinants of a teacher's burnout. Methods: observation, expert assessment, documentation analysis; questionnaires: "Maslach Burnout Inventory", "Self-regulation", "Eysenck personality inventory", "Value Measuring", "Pedagogical activity management"; correlation and factor analysis, analysis of difference. 142 School teachers have taken part in the research. Results: teachers' burnout is mainly determined by neuroticism, inconsistence of values, lack of self-regulation, unsatisfactory psychological atmosphere, poor management of teachers' activity: poor autonomy,

irregular working load, poor work stimulation, insufficient professional growth and staying out of school running. These determinants prevent teachers' burnout from being corrected.

Activities of Daily Living (ADL's), depression, and social support in Turkish elderly citizens

Bozo, Ozlem Department of Psychology, Middle East Technical Uni, Ankara, Turkey Toksabay, N. Ece Ankara, Turkey Kurum, Oya Department of Psychology, Middle East Technical Uni, Ankara, Turkey

The aim is to examine the effects of activities of daily living and perceived social support on the level of depression in Turkish older adults. 102adults over the age of 60 participated. The hypotheses were (1) lower ADL's predict a higher level of depression; (2) an increased perceived social support would predict a lower depression; and (3) perceived social support would moderate the relationship between ADL's and depression. Both ADL's and perceived social support were significantly predicting the depression in Turkish older adults. Higher ADL's functioning and higher perceived social support predicted lower depression in older adults. The effect of ADL's-perceived social support interaction on the level of depression was insignificant.

Peer-parental influence, novelty seeking, reward dependence, risk taking, gender and alcohol consumption

Bozo, Özlem Psychology, Middle East Technical Uni., Ankara, Turkey Nan, Burcu Psychology, Middle East Technical Uni., Ankara, Turkey Güney, Mine Psychology, Middle East Technical Uni., Ankara, Turkey

The purpose of this study was to explore the relationships among peer-parental influence, risk taking, novelty seeking, reward dependence, gender, and alcohol consumption in young adults. One-hundred and twelve undergraduate students participated in the study. It was hypothesized that male participants high in risk-taking behavior, novelty seeking, and reward dependence, having parents and peers using alcohol would consume more alcohol than participants who did not have these characteristics. After multiple regression analysis it was found that peer influence, novelty seeking, and gender were significantly predicting alcohol consumption of young adults, while risk taking, reward dependence, and parental influence were not.

Experience of drug of choice: A phenomenological investigation

Carr, Erika Knoxville, USA Hector, Mark Psychology, University of Tennessee, Knoxville, USA

Drug of choice is an experience that recovering addicts speak of frequently when in recovery. The purpose of this study was to investigate the experience of drug of choice by using a qualitative method of phenomenological interviewing with eleven recovering drug/alcohol addicts as research participants. Verbatim transcripts were prepared and analyzed using a hermeneutic/existential/phenomenological method. A ground and main themes that emerged from the data were: void, name of the drug/drugs, death, spiritual illness, obsession, and relationships. Uses of this research for practitioners will be discussed and the literature review will include quantitative as well as qualitative research.

The different patterns of relation to work: Younger and older generations in the labour market

Carvalho, Sandra CIS, ISCTE, Lisbon, Portugal Soares, Célia CIS, ISCTE, Lisbon, Portugal Passos, Ana CIS, ISCTE, Lisbon, Portugal Castro, Paula CIS, ISCTE, Lisbon, Portugal

The study discusses the psychological implications and potential problems of the European labour context at the generations' level. Based on the articulation between qualitative (interviews to young and older workers from different sectors) and quantitative data (past relevant surveys) the different patterns of relation to work will be discussed. First, the results of the interviews showing those different patterns will be presented. And second, the main results of relevant surveys will be brought into the discussion in order to better understand the intricacies of the European labour context and the difficulties that younger and older generations face.

Theta-coupling during working memory maintenance of configural information in Magnetoencephalography (MEG)

Cashdollar, Nathan ICN, London, United Kingdom *Malecki, Ulrike* Department of Neurology II, O.v.G. University of Magdeburg, Magdeburg, Germany *Lavie, Nilli* Department of Psychology, University College of London, London, United Kingdom *Duzel, Emrah* ICN, University College of London, London, United Kingdom

We investigated interareal cortical synchronization (theta phase-coupling) during maintenance of configural information in working memory. In a delayed-match-to-sample MEG paradigm, configural maintenance engaged stronger theta-coupling between left lateral and posterior sensor groups during the delay period than non-configural maintenance. Increasing the number of items to be maintained during the delay, on the other hand, enhanced bi-lateral frontal synchrony. Additional behavioral testing after MEG revealed increased long-term recognition memory performance for configural stimuli compared to non-configural ($P< 0.01$). These results suggest that configural delay maintenance recruits a network of synchronous brain regions that is qualitatively different from non-configural and high-load maintenance.

The influence of language on spatial reasoning: The case of reading habits

Castelain, Thomas L2C2 CNRS UMR 5230, Bron, France *Van der Henst, Jean-Baptiste* Psychology, L2C2 CNRS UMR 5230, Bron, France

In the present study, we explore how reading habits (i.e. reading from left-to-right in French or reading from right-to-left in Arabic) influence the scanning and the construction of mental models in spatial reasoning. In two experiments, we analyse the wording of the conclusion (Experiment 1) and the time required to integrate the premises (Experiment 2) with French and Arabic readers. Our results show a strong influence of reading habits for French readers and a smaller influence for Arabic readers. This cultural factor seems to interact with a universal bias that prompts people to explore and construct mental models from left to right.

Predictors of OCB among blue and white collar employees in Turkey

Cem Ersoy, Nevra Psychology, Erasmus University, Rotterdam, Netherlands *Born, Marise* Psychology, Erasmus University, Rotterdam, Netherlands *Derous, Eva* Psychology, Erasmus University, Rotterdam, Netherlands

In a survey study using blue (N=379) and white collar employees (N=120) we examined the predictors of OCB namely, employees' general beliefs about world, their identification with their supervisor and colleagues, commitment to their career, colleagues and supervisors. Comparing blue and white collar employees' OCB was under-addressed therefore we aimed to examine the predictors of OCB among blue and white collar employees. Results showed that white collar employees were more committed to their career and they had higher scores on job dedication dimension of OCB than blue collars. Identification with the supervisor was an important predictor for blue collar employees.

Psychological response to collective and communicable responsibility among Chinese adolescents

Cen, Guozhen Applied Psychology, Shanhai Normal University, Shanghai, People's Republic of China

Aim: to explore the psychological response of adolescents to collective and communicable responsibility. Method: using projective method with situational stories for a sample of 386 Chinese adolescent students. Results: the psychological response to collective and communicable responsibility will depend on different ages, backgrounds ("not knowing the offender" and "not exposing the offender"), projections (general and role-taking) and events (three scenarios of school, society and history). Conclusion: adolescents in China showed their cognitive ane effective responses, and a tendency to take responsibility for behavior to the collective and communicable responsibility.

Addiction's and Dependence's Test to the Mobile Telephone (TADTeMo)

Chóliz, Mariano Psicologia Basica, Universidad de Valencia, Valencia, Spain *Villanueva, Verónica* Psicología Básica, University of Valencia, Valencia, Spain *Tejero, Pilar* Psicología Básica, University of Valencia, Valencia, Spain

The principal objective of this work is to develop a test to evaluate the abuse or dependence of the mobile telephone, following the DSM-IV diagnostics criteria. The population corresponds to all scholarly teens in educational centers, in ages understood among 12 and 18 years. We have accomplished a pilot study with 450 participants to depurate a first instrument of 101 items, that has remained reduced to 40. At the present time we are composing the definite test with principal diagnostic criteria of the disorder for dependence and abuse applied to the mobile telephone.

Chinese preschool children's literacy development: From creative to conventional writing

Chan, Lily Dept. Educational Psychology, Chinese Univer. of Hong Kong, Hong Kong, China, People's Republic of : Hong Kong SAR

Written Chinese has always been regarded as a logographic writing system. In recent years, theories of emergent literacy are beginning to have some impact in the teaching of Chinese writing. The present study introduces a unique learning experience of a 4 year old girl in Hong Kong who made a smooth transition from scribbles to conventional writing with full confidence and interest within a year. There is evidence that indicates that creative writing facilitated her understanding of the underlying principles of written Chinese, and in a later stage, she could understand both the forms and functions of strokes and stroke-patterns.

Determinants of alcohol use among university students: The role of stress, coping and expectancies

Chau, Cecilia Psychology, PUCP, Lima, Peru

The study explore the alcohol use among university students in Peru and the effect of psychosocial variables: perceived stress, alcohol consumption by peers/ parents, alcohol expectancies and coping styles. Questionnaires were administered to 1081 students. For the statistical analyses we used Chi-square, ANOVA, discriminant and Path analysis. The model for drinkers reported: best male best friends' alcohol use, gender, and the mother's and father's alcohol use all have a direct effect on the students alcohol use, while the best female friends' alcohol use has an indirect effect on alcohol use via positive personal and social alcohol expectancies. The effect of gender and of the best male friends' use is also modified by positive personal and social expectancies regarding alcohol.

The mediation effect of balanced need satisfaction on global life satisfaction

Chen, Chao Yu Taipei, Taiwan *Lin, Yi-Cheng* Psychology, National Taiwan University, Taipei, Taiwan

The previous study showed that a balanced life had a positive effect on global life satisfaction, even after the mean score across various life domains was controlled for. In this study, the authors further investigated the mechanism of a balanced life. The result demonstrated that the positive effect of balanced life domains on global life satisfaction was mediated by balanced need satisfaction. That is, those who are happy were due to be satisfied with multiple life domains which contribute to satisfaction with different needs. Implications on balanced need satisfaction were discussed further.

Stability and change of inhibition from two to ten years: A longitudinal observation

Chen, Huichang School of Psychology, Beijing Normal University, Beijing, People's Republic of China *Su, Ling* Office of International Comm., Child Center of China, Beijing, People's Republic of China

The present research aims to longitudinally explore the regularity of stability and change of temperamental inhibition from infancy to middle childhood. 31 children who assessed as extreme behaviorally inhibited and uninhibited children participated in this study. The children were observed in lab at 2 year, 4 year, 7 year and 10 year by using structured observation procedure, and questionnaire, mental tests, parent and teacher interview were used. Results show that the children's temperament is moderate stable from two to ten year, but there is an orientation that the inhibited or un-inhibited level regressed from extreme level to moderate level.

A survey on the relationship between job scope and sense of empowerment of career guidance counselors in Japanese special education schools

China, Aoko Sendai, Japan *Hosokawa, Toru* Education, Tohoku University, Sendai, Japan *Kumai, Masayuki* Educational Informatics, Tohoku University, Sendai, Japan

The purpose of this study was to investigate the relationship between job efficacy and sense of empowerment of career guidance counselors in Japan's special education schools for the intellectually disabled. A total of 303 guidance counselors (a 58.5% response rate) completed a questionnaire. A statistical analysis of 5 areas of the career guidance counselor's job scope: "assessment", "information dissemination", "job search/matching", "liaison", and "spearheading programs" was conducted. Results revealed a significant positive correlation between job efficacy and sense of empowerment. It was suggested that a framework providing a clear mandate for guidance counselors should be set up.

The effect of intervention messages on video lottery gambling perceptions and behaviour

Chua, Zhiren Singapore, Singapore *Tang, Catherine So-Kum* Psychology, National University Singapore, Singapore, Singapore

This study investigates the effectiveness of intervention messages in reducing erroneous beliefs and gambling behaviour in undergraduate slot machines players. The hypothesis is: A new type of intervention message (containing elements besides warning information) has a greater impact and a longer effect on reducing erroneous beliefs and gambling behaviour than an intervention message with only warning information or a neutral message. Participants are required to complete questionnaires and play a slot machine computer game in a laboratory setting. A three month follow-up study is included. Data obtained is examined using factor analysis.

Preliminary results will be presented at the conference.

Impact of the mental disorders on the employability of the homeless people

Combaluzier, Serge Dépt. de Psychologie, Université de Rouen, Mont-Saint-Aignan, France

If the mental disorders have been studied for many years in the homeless populations, their impact on the employment of this population has been estimated in very few works. In the Centre for Men were this studied has been done, only 10% have found a job six month after their entrance. 180 homeless men have been met in clinical interview at their entrance in a Centre for Men. Their admission in this Centre A multi-axial diagnosis have been done according to the APA. The estimations of measures of impact lead to the conclusion that the associations between clinical and personality disorders multiplies by 13 the risk of unemployment

Language functions in parent-child verbal exchanges: A comparative study

Comeeau, Judith Psychology, Universite de Montreal, Montreal, Canada Matte, Isabel Linguistics, Universite de Montreal, Montreal, Canada Leroux, Julien Psychology, Universite de Montreal, Montreal, Canada

The present study attempted to explore relationships between sex of parent, and functions of repetitions and reformulations when addressing their five-to-six-year old child. The sample included 20 parent-child dyads: 10 mother-daughter dyads and 10 father-son dyads. Each dyad was given the task of completing a model design using MacPaint and each interaction was videotaped. A classification of 12 functions was adapted from the pragmatic functions of repetitions by Greenfield and Savage-Raumbaugh (1995). Results indicated few differences between mothers and fathers. Both parents play the leadership role both in the verbal exchange and in the task to accomplish.

A two level growth model examinig risk factors for cigarette smoking in Canadian adolescents: Individual, family and school influences

Corbett, Bradley Dept. of Sociology, University of Western Ontario, London, Canada

This study uses data from Canada's National Longitudinal Survey of Children and youth to develop a growth model of adolescent smoking. Data was collected repeatedly from age 10 to 21 from a nationally representative sample of 4,500. The findings indicate smoking uptake for females is faster during adolescence but their rate of increase slows faster later in adolescence. Increased risk for smoking includes: being female, being francophone, having a mother and/or father who smokes, having lower family socio-economic status, knowing peer smokers at age 10, having lower self-esteem, and living with a single mother or with a stepparent.

Efficacy of a brief intervention for general hospital patients with prescription drug dependence: Does gender matter?

Crackau, Brit Psychiatrie und Psychotherapie, Uni-Klinik Schleswig-Holstein, Lübeck, Germany Löhrmann, Ira Psychiatry and Psychotherapy, University of Luebeck, Luebeck, Germany Otto, Christiane Psychiatry and Psychotherapy, University of Luebeck, Luebeck, Germany Zahradnik, Anne Psychiatry and Psychotherapy, University of Luebeck, Luebeck, Germany Bischof, Gallus Psychiatry and Psychotherapy, University of Luebeck, Luebeck, Germany Rumpf, Hans-Jürgen Psychiatry and Psychotherapy, University of Luebeck, Luebeck, Germany

Objectives: The prevalence of prescription drug dependence (PDD) is significantly higher in general hospital than in general population. Women are affected twice as often as men. Methods: In a randomised, controlled trial the efficacy of Motivational Interviewing in a proactive recruited sample of general hospital patients with PDD is tested. Gender differences in outcome and TTM-constructs are analyzed. Results: Forty-six men and 80 women gave their informed consent to participate. First results of the 3-Month-Follow-Up will be reported. Conclusions: If gender-differences are revealed, these results might provide a basis for gender-specific intervention for patients with PDD.

" Mobbying at work": A new concept in Portugal

Cruz, Marla Faculdade de Ciências Humanas, Universidade Fernando Pessoa, Angeja, Portugal Soares Martins, José Faculdade de Ciências Humanas, Universidade Fernando Pessoa, maia, Portugal

Mobbying at work is a new concept in Portugal. In other European countries, mobbying is commonly used to describe situations were someone persistently over a period of time is treated in a oppressive way.We investigated the prevalence of mobbying in work context and the relationships between symptoms of burnout among 8 people, which 4 were workers in a multi-industrial unit and 4 were worker-students. We concluded that out of our 8 people we've studied, 4 had experienced mobbying (80%) when compared to the other 4 which hadn't suffered from any type of mobbying at work. Mobbed workers had significantly higher levels of emotional exhaustion when compared with non-mobbed worker

Motivations in entrepreneurial choices: Successful and unsuccessful entrepreneurs

Cubico, Serena Psicologia e Antropologia, Università di Verona, Verona, Italy Bortolani, Elisa Psicologia e Antropologia, Università di Verona, Verona, Italy Favretto, Giuseppe Psicologia e Antropologia, Università di Verona, Verona, Italy

Entrepreneurship represents an interesting path of professional development: people are driven to be entrepreneurs by different motivations. This research aims at detecting whether successful entrepreneurs have different motivations in entrepreneurial choices when compared to unsuccessful entrepreneurs. 100 users (representative of population) of the Chamber of Commerce's New-Entrepreneurial-Service in Verona were contacted via telephone interview. Results reveal that successful entrepreneurs are significantly: less willing to conciliate work and family, more intent upon realizing new ideas, and more oriented to working without a boss. Effects of age and educational qualifications are provided.

Event-related potential and behavioral evidence for life-span changes in resolving response conflict during a cued task-switching paradigm

Czernochowski, Daniela Math. u. Verhaltenspsychologie, Universität Düsseldorf, Düsseldorf, Germany Nessler, Doreen CEPL, NY State Psychiatric Institute, New York, USA Cycowicz, Yael M. CEPL, NY State Psychiatric Institute, New York City, USA de Chastelaine, Marianne CEPL, NY State Psychiatric Institute, New York, USA Horton, Cort CEPL, NY State Psychiatric Institute, New York, USA Friedman, David CEPL, NY State Psychiatric Institute, New York, USA

The roles of conflict detection and resolution for age-differences in interference control were examined in children (9-10 years), young (20-25 years) and older adults (61-83 years). Participants responded to the questions "which" or "how many" numbers were presented in congruent (1; 333) or incongruent (3; 111) targets. In children and older adults, reaction time slowing for incongruent trials was pronounced, indicating heightened conflict detection. Children appeared unsuccessful in conflict resolution (i.e. elevated error rates). For older adults, a pre-response event-related negativity and slow, but accurate responses suggest successful upregulation of control. Thus, age-differences in interference control depend on conflict resolution.

A formative program evaluation of a hospital-based Eating Disorders Readiness Program

Czincz, Jennifer Dept. of Psychology, University of Ottawa, Ottawa, Canada Illing, Vanessa Psychology, University of Ottawa, Ottawa, Canada

Research has demonstrated that program evaluation is becoming an essential component of effective service delivery. A formative program evaluation was conducted for a hospital-based outpatient program that strives to prepare clients for an intensive eating disorders treatment program. A logic model was constructed to assess the program's inputs, activities, outputs, and immediate versus long-term outcomes. An evaluation matrix was then designed, outlining evaluation questions related to the rationale, design, delivery, impacts, and alternative strategies for the program. Methods included literature reviews, program database reviews, focus groups, and qualitative assessments of program sessions. Results and implications will be presented and discussed.

Moral development, moral audiences, and the enabling of terrorist behaviour

Day, James Meredith Psychology, Universite de Louvain, Louvain-la-Neuve, Belgium

Empirical research has shown that moral behaviour is at once influenced by moral reasoning, and the discursive worlds in which moral terms are given meaning, and moral language linked to moral conduct. This presentation is drawn from empirical research with Belgian and English adolescents whose moral decision-making processes were studied using standard questionnaires, narratives of moral problems and decisions, and structure, qualitative interviews. Clear relationships exist amongst reasoning, discursive, religious attitudes, and parenting styles amongst those who excuse, justify, and, at least in some sense, justify terrorist behaviour.

The teaching of psychoanalysis in the university

de Barros, Rita Maria Manso Psicologia Clinica, UERJ / PGPSA, Rio de Janeiro, Brazil

Objectives: To investigate the consequences of the teaching of psychoanalysis in the university. Its intends to be woman in the thought of girls between 13 and 17 years old in the school and its meaning in the magazines direct to those girls. Method: Interview and questionnaires with students. We analyzed the students' discourses about their thoughts to psychoanalysis theories. Results: The most of them like and learn a lot of things about human soul and thinking that this knowledge helps them to understand theirs students too. Conclusions: The teaching of psychoanalysis theory is important for the future teachers of children.

A functional measurement approach to the estimation of the differential impact of reward satisfaction dimensions on turnover intention

De Gieter, Sara I/O Psychology, Vrije Universiteit Brussel, Brussel, Belgium Mairesse, Olivier I&O Psychology, Vrije Universiteit Brussel, Brussel, Belgium De Cooman, Rein I&O Psychology, Vrije Universiteit Brussel, Brussel, Belgium Pepermans, Roland I&O Psychology, Vrije Universiteit Brussel, Brussel, Belgium

Previous studies indicated a significant relationship between reward satisfaction dimensions (e.g. pay level satisfaction, raises satisfaction, psychological reward satisfaction) and turnover intention using hierarchical regression analysis or structural equation modeling. The aim of this study is to calculate the differential weights of each reward satisfaction dimension in predicting employee's turnover intention, by using functional measurement (FM) methodology. In an experiment, participants estimate their turnover intention within a number of work-settings with changing satisfaction levels for each of the examined reward satisfaction dimensions. By means of FM the algebraic relation between different reward satisfaction dimensions can be investigated.

Gender differences in pay satisfaction: Testing the measurement invariance of the Pay Satisfaction Questionnaire

De Gieter, Sara I/O Psychology, Vrije Universiteit Brussel, Brussel, Belgium Hofmans, Joeri I&O Psychology, Vrije Universiteit Brussel, Brussel, Belgium De Cooman, Rein I&O Psychology, Vrije Universiteit Brussel, Brussel, Belgium Pepermans, Roland I&O Psychology, Vrije Universiteit Brussel, Brussel, Belgium

Regardless of their lower salary, women are at least as satisfied with their salary as their male colleagues. Studies examining this 'paradox of the contented female worker' often used the Pay Satisfaction Questionnaire (PSQ). Whether this instrument is measurement invariant across gender, however, has not been previously tested. To avoid rash conclusions, the present study submitted PSQ data of 699 female and 448 male employees to a series of measurement invariance tests. The results supported the gender invariance of the measurement of pay satisfaction by the PSQ, assuring now that it is an appropriate instrument to examine the illustrated paradox.

Teaching behavioral assessment to teachers of nursery school in Kobe City's project

Dojo, Yuki Dept. of Psychology, Kwansei Gakuin University, Kobe, Japan

Nursery school teachers in Japan are increasingly faced with the need to implement effective behavior management of their children. We conducted a three-day workshop for 15 supervising teachers of nursery schools and trained them in basic knowledge of applied behavior analysis, and then conducted practicum using videotapes in behavioral observation of appropriate and inappropriate child behaviors. We will report on the results of the workshop and follow-up.

Stress at work: A meta-analysis of longitudinal studies

Dormann, Christian Inst. of Psychologie, Universität Mainz, Mainz, Germany

The number of studies on organizational stress has been increasing since decades. Several meta-analyses were already published. However, since most studies were still cross-sectional, authors of reviews and meta-analyses frequently called for more longitudinal studies. A few reviews of longitudinal studies have already been published, but a quantitative approach to existing longitudinal results is lacking. Therefore we present a meta-analysis of longitudinal studies on organizational stress taking into account potential curvilinear relations between time lag and effect size. We also test for reversed causation. The results provide evidence for both stressors reducing subsequent well-being and poor well-being increasing subsequent stressors.

Temporal acuity and working memory

Dreszer, Joanna UMK in Torun, Torun, Poland Bedyska, Sylwia Department of Psychology, SWPS, Warsaw, Poland

Objectives A number of papers have suggested link between temporal acuity and working memory. Methods To better understand this relation, the rhythmical synchronization-continuation tapping task and working memory O-Span task were assessed. In tapping task different inter stimulus intervals (ISI) were used: 450-2400ms. We analyzed the correlation between synchronization /continuation error (SE/CE) and O-Span. Results Results

showed correlation depending on the ISI duration between SE/CE and O-Span. Conclusion These findings offer support for the notion that the timing in the synchronization-continuation tapping is controlled by automatic and cognitive mechanisms. Moreover results indicate relation between both working memory and timing acuity.

A psychodynamically oriented comparative study of impulsivity and life event stress among injecting drug users

Dutta, Tinni Psychology, Asutosh College, Kolkata, Kolkata, India Mallick, Debapriya Psychology, Asutosh College, Kolkata., Kolkata, India

Medication, Education and Training helps to overcome the conditions that facilitate the spread of HIV among (IDUs). Beyond this psychiatric medicine along with counseling can create the conditions of understanding that contribute to enhanced risk perception and being able to inculcate the risk reduction practices among them. In this context the Rorschach Ink Blot test(RIBT) and Life –Event Stress by Paykel were used for psychodynamic assessment on 100 IDUs and 100 normals. Psychodynamic assessment reflects that problem of IDUs are characterized by predominance of impulsive need, and loss of control in specific situations. Thus psychotherapeutic treatment is called for ameliorating maladaptive thoughts and actions among them.

Faces: A database of emotional facial expressions in young, middle-aged and older women and men

Ebner, Natalie Center for Lifespan Psychology, Max Planck Institute for Human, Berlin, Germany Riediger, Michaela Lifespan Psychology, Max Planck Institute for Human, Berlin, Germany Lindenberger, Ulman Lifespan Psychology, Max Planck Institute for Human, Berlin, Germany

Faces are widely used experimental stimuli, and interest in the development of their perception and processing is growing. Due to a lack of age-differential facial stimuli, most studies to date have exclusively used younger faces. We created a database comprising faces of young, middle-aged, and older women and men displaying six expressions (neutrality, sadness, disgust, fear, anger, happiness) and collected norm ratings from adults of different ages. This new database offers access to an age range of faces that is wider than that of other face databases and therefore more appropriate for the investigation of developmental research questions.

Asymmetry in the binding of verbal and spatial information in working memory

Elsley, Jane Dept. of Psychology, University of Plymouth, Plymouth, United Kingdom Parmentier, Fabrice Psychology, University of Plymouth, Plymouth, United Kingdom

We investigated the characteristics of bound verbal-spatial representations using a recognition task (Prabhakaran et al., 2000). Four consonants were presented simultaneously in locations followed by a single probe. In one task the identity of the single probe was judged, and in another the spatial location of the single probe was judged. Accuracy measures indicated binding when letters only were attended (p<.01), but not when locations only were attended (p=.31). The results suggest an asymmetry in association between verbal and spatial information whereby verbal information could not be processed independently of spatial information, while spatial information could be processed in isolation.

Mental models and activity systems for developing psychologists competences to teach psychology: Experiences and cognitions of tutors and students at university apprenticeship

Erausquin, Cristina Educational Psychology, Faculty of Psychology, Buenos Aires, Argentina Basualdo, Maria Esther Educational Psychology, Faculty of Psychology UBA, CAPITAL FEDERAL, Argentina Garcia Labandal, Livia Educational Psychology, Faculty of Psychology UBA, CAPITAL FEDERAL, Argentina Gonzalez, Daniela Educational Psychology, Faculty of Psychology UBA, CAPITAL FEDERAL, Argentina Ortega, Gabriela Educational Psychology, Faculty of Psychology UBA, CAPITAL FEDERAL, Argentina Meschman, Clara Educational Psychology, Faculty of Psychology, CAPITAL FEDERAL, Argentina

The work examines mental models to solve problems situated in school settings, built in communities of practice for teaching to teach Psychology. Descriptive ethnography includes quantitative and qualitative analysis. At the beginning and the end of Undergraduate Apprenticeship, one questionnaire about educational problems and another about conceptions on learning were administered to 22 tutors and 85 students. Results show differences between tutors and students in explicit knowledge, scientific hypothesis and professional involvement in activity systems. To raise awareness about diversity of interventions from psychologists and from psychology teachers is challenging for students. Developing competences to teach is challenging for University.

Relationship of critical thinking and thinking styles on college students of lima and Callao on Peru

Escurra-Mayaute, Luis Miguel Psychology, UNMSM, Lima, Peru Delgado-Vasquez, Ana Esther Psychology, UNMSM, Lima, Peru Torres, William Psychology, URP, Lima, Peru

Presents the relationships between attitude toward critical thinking and the thinking styles on college students. The participants were 830 college students of Lima and Callao, Peru. It was used Stenberg's Thinking Style Scale and a Scale was elaborated about Critical Thinking. The statistical analysis was done on three stages. The studens mean age were 20.6 year old, and 62.5% were female and 36.5% male. The findings show validity and reliability related to Attitude Toward Critical Thinking Scale and the Thinking Styles Scale respectively. There are significative correlations concerning areas of the critical thinking and the thinking styles. There are statistical differences considering college, sex, and field of study

Building emotional strength in business A redirection-moving towards the pain

Faye, Sharon Clear Perceptions Pty Ltd., Perth, Australia Hooper, Joel Research, the humex project, Berlin, Germany

Building Emotional Strength (ES) is built on the premise that whatever a business owner is experiencing in his business is a direct reflection of his experience of his internal world. The owner's perception is externally focused, blaming his employees or a set of circumstances for his stress. We have observed that facilitating the owner to reengage his emotions leads to a redirection of his attention from external circumstances to internal states, resulting in the identification of fundamental self-limiting beliefs that are mirrored at every level of his organisation which impacts organisational performance.

Personality types as predictors of premarital sex among tertiary education students in Nigeria

Fayombo, Grace Adebisi School of Education, University of West Indies, Bridgetown, Barbados Ogunsanya, Elizabeth Edu. Foundations &

Counselling, Olabisi Onabanjo University, Ogun,
Nigeria

Objective This study investigated thinkers and
feelers as predictors of premarital sex among
tertiary education adolescents Methods Sample
consisted of 407 adolescents randomly selected
from two universities in Nigeria. Adolescent Personality Assessment Questionnaire and Attitudes
towards Premarital Sex were used to collect the
data which were analysed using Multiple Regression analysis and t-test. Results Both thinkers and
feelers are prone to premarital sex, thinker is a
major personality variable in adolescents' premarital sex, feeler has impact on adolescents' premarital
sex,though not as serious as thinker, males predict
premarital sex more than females. Conclusion
Thinkers and feelers are both prone to premarital
sex.

The undergraduate psychology course offered at University of Brasília

*Feitosa, Maria Angela Inst. of Psychology, University
of Brasília, Brasília, Brazil Nunes da Cunha, Rachel
Psychology Institute, University of Brasília, Brasília,
DF, Brazil*

The Psychology Institute at University of Brasília
has a 45 year tradition at offering education in
Psychology. It currently offers an undergraduate
course with three degree options, a bachelor, a
teaching and a psychologist degree, and four
graduate courses comprising the master and doctoral levels. The undergraduate course is well
evaluated both by ex-students and the federal
government, and is distinguished as providing a
highly flexible and diversified curriculum, giving the
students ample contact with research activities of
the graduate programs. The presentation stresses
how the Institute interprets and applies recently
approved federal guidelines for psychology curricula.

Neural correlates of kinesthetic working memory

*Fiehler, Katja Inst. für Psychologie, Universität
Marburg, Marburg, Germany Burke, Michael
Psychology, Philipps-University Marburg, Marburg,
Germany Bien, Siegfried Neuroradiology, Philipps-
University Marburg, Marburg, Germany Rösler, Frank
Psychology, Philipps-University Marburg, Marburg,
Germany*

Separate neural pathways are proposed for somatosensory processing. A pathway for the guidance
of action that terminates in the posterior parietal
cortex can be dissociated from a pathway for
perception and memory that projects to the posterior insula and to the posterior parietal cortex. In an
fMRI study we aimed to test how the insular and
the posterior parietal pathways contribute to
kinesthetic movement memory by applying a
kinesthetic version of a delayed recognition task.
The results showed delay-related activity in the left
intraparietal sulcus, part of the posterior parietal
pathway, suggesting its important role in kinesthetic working memory.

Psychosemantic aspect of object relations in fishing vessel crews

*Frantsev, Alexander Tavryiski National Universtiy,
Kiev, Ukraine*

Objective. To find out effects of semantic 'nuclei' on
object relations in two fishing crews. Method.
J.Kelly Grid (1969) and hierarchical cluster analysis. Results. Crew 1 and crew 2 statistically
significantly differed in their psychosemantic areas:
1) the 'nucleus' of crew 2 consisted of three elements
having 5, 2, and 2 hardly conscious meanings
respectively which resulted in its heavy emotional
charge compared to crew 1 which consisted of 4
elements of 2 hardly conscious meanings each; 2)
work performance of crew 2 was much better than
that of crew 1. Conclusion. More fused nucleus of
hardly conscious meanings corresponds to object

relations of higher level and better work performance.

Motivational intervention for general hospital inpatients with unhealthy alcohol use

*Freyer-Adam, Jennis IES, Universität Greifswald,
Greifswald, Germany Coder, Beate IES, University of
Greifswald, Greifswald, Germany Bischof, Gallus
Psychiatry and Psychotherapy, University of Luebeck,
Luebeck, Germany Rumpf, Hans-Jürgen Psychiatry
and Psychotherapy, University of Luebeck, Luebeck,
Germany John, Ulrich IES, University of Greifswald,
Greifswald, Germany Hapke, Ulfert IES, University of
Greifswald, Greifswald, Germany*

Objective: To test the effectiveness of a brief
intervention among non-dependent general hospital
inpatients with unhealthy alcohol use, delivered by
either a specialized liaison service or hospital
physicians. Method: In a randomized controlled
trial, 595 inpatients with unhealthy alcohol use were
allocated to three groups receiving: counseling by a
liaison service, counseling by physicians or no
counseling. Results: Twelve months later the intervention resulted in increased motivation to reduce
drinking and to seek formal help. All groups
decreased their alcohol use significantly. Discussion: As the intervention was effective in increasing
motivation to change, brief intervention in general
hospitals is recommended.

The "Inner Patriarch": The exploration of an introjected part of our personality with the aid of drawings and qualitative interviews

*Friedrich, Sibylle Inst. für Psychologie, Universität
Hamburg, Hamburg, Germany*

By using the technique of a Focusing Process, a
form of superficial hypnosis, in a workshop
situation males and females were exposed to their
"Inner Patriarch", the part of our personality that
defends the traditional patriarchic rules and values
of our society. Afterwards the participants were
asked to visualize whatever they had experienced in
trance. Fifty drawings were analyzed. Additionally
20 qualitative one-to-one interviews were conducted
with participants shortly after the workshops.
Preliminary results indicate that the perceived
relationships between parents are reproduced as
inner matriachic and patriarchic archetypes. Complete findings will be presented at the conference.

The effect of covering trauma: A study with Russian journalists

*Friske, Oliver Psychology, Humboldt-Universität zu
Berlin, Berlin, Germany Weidmann, Anke
Psychotherapie u. Somatopsych., Humboldt-
Universität zu Berlin, Berlin, Germany*

Journalists are frequently sent out to cover possibly
traumatic events such as war or disaster. Previous
studies show that they are subsequently at risk of
posttraumatic symptoms; however, these studies
exclusively focused on journalists working in
Western media systems. We present the results of
a nearly completed study with about 30 Russian
journalists in order to replicate and extend earlier
findings. After exploring the level of traumatic
exposure and posttraumatic symptoms, data analyses focus on associations with the level of social
support, the way of coping, and several work-
related variables (e.g. differences between independent and government-related media).

Action fluency through childhood and early adolescence

*Galtier, Ivan Psicobiología y Metodología,
Universidad de La Laguna., La Laguna, Spain Suarez,
Marta Psicobiología y Metodología, Universidad de
La Laguna., La Laguna, Spain Nieto, Antonieta
Psicobiología y Metodología, Universidad de La
Laguna., La Laguna, Spain Barroso, Jose
Psicobiología y Metodología, Universidad de La
Laguna., La Laguna, Spain*

Fluency measures are commonly used in clinical
paediatric neuropsychology to assess executive
function. Little is know about age effects on Action
Fluency (AF) performance, a newly developed
fluency task that is particularly sensitive to frontal
systems damage. This study analyzes the effect of
age and gender on AF in 89 children between ages 5
and 15, divided into five groups according to grade.
Results revealed a significant age effect but no sex
effect or age x sex interaction. Performance showed
a clearly age-related improvement. The obtained
developmental trend is similar to that reported for
classical fluency measures.

Reactions to the professional injustices according to the statute and the gender of an Argentinean population

*Gangloff, Bernard Ciencias Sociais Aplicadas, Univ.
Federal da Paraiba, Joao Pessoa, Brazil*

The feelings of injustice can conduce to various
reactions, some resulting in passivity, others in
protest. We wanted to study here if the statute
(salaried employees versus unemployed persons)
and the gender (masculine versus feminine) had an
influence on these reactions. Thus we presented, in
a questionnaire, different cases of professional
injustices to Argentinean workers, differentiated
according to their statute and their gender, and we
asked them to indicate the reactions that they
would adopt. Our results, and their discussion, will
be about the different types of reactions induced by
our two independent variables.

Psychological symptoms and burnout in healthcare workers suffering aggressions

*Gascón, Santiago Medicina Legal, Universidad de
Zaragoza, Zaragoza, Spain Martínez Jarreta, Begoña
Medicina Legal, Universidad de Zaragoza, Zaragoza,
Spain Santed, Miguel Ángel Medicina Legal,
Universidad de Zaragoza, Zaragoza, Spain Sobradiel,
Natalia Medicina Legal, Universidad de Zaragoza,
Zaragoza, Spain*

Aggression against healthcare workers is a problem
of important consequences. However, its possible
effects on psychological health have not been
studied sufficiently. Material and methods: 1,845
healthcare workers. Instruments: • Record of
demographic and work data. • Questionnaire on
aggressions. • Record of psychological symptoms.
Results Eleven percent reported having suffered at
least one episode of physical aggression. Non-
physical aggression affected 64%. These rates were
much higher in large hospitals and in Services
(Emergency and Psychiatry). The association between non-physical violence and anxiety, burnout
and symptoms of Post-traumatic Stress Syndrome
was seen to be statistically significant.

Measure of the imbalance in assistance relationships: Validation of the TEEM questionnaire (Fears and stress factors in the medical profession)

*Gascón, Santiago Medicina Legal, Universidad de
Zaragoza, Zaragoza, Spain Martínez Jarreta, Begoña
Medicina Legal, Universidad de Zaragoza, Zaragoza,
Spain Andrés, Eva Medicina Legal, Universidad de
Zaragoza, Zaragoza, Spain Casalod, Yolanda
Medicina Legal, Universidad de Zaragoza, Zaragoza,
Spain*

To measure the degree of imbalance in assistance
relationships, the TEEM questionnaire was designed. METHOD 1,845 health professionals
TOOLS - TEEM Questionnaire... - MBI - List of
psychological symptoms RESULTS. Alpha coeffi-
cient ($\alpha = 0.91$). Statistically significant correlations
between the TEEM and the burnout dimensions.
By means of COR showed high rates of diagnostic
specificity/sensitivity. By means of a logistical
regression analysis, predicted emotional exhaustion,
depersonalization and the lack of professional
satisfaction. A factorial analysis showed that the

questionnaire had two dimensions: Fear of being harmed (30.81% variance), and Fear of being accused of malpractice (29.36% variance).

Cognitive-Behavioral Group-Therapy for smoking cessation

Genschow, Jan Berlin, Germany Mühlig, Stephan Klinische Psychologie, TU Chemnitz, Chemnitz, Germany

Aim of the study was to evaluate the efficacy and acceptance of a group-based behavioural-therapy for smoking cessation. A sample of 95 female and male smokers with different degrees of tobacco-addiction measured with DSM-IV and the "Fager-ström-Test for Nicotine-Dependence", was repeatedly assessed for post-treatment smoking status and relapse during a period of 6 months. Using a One-Group-Design the participants smoking status was obtained by self reports. An intent-to-treat approach showed an abstinence rate of 72,6% at the end of the intervention decreasing to 35,7% after 6 month, indicating that this programme performs well compared to already existing ones.

The effects of psychosocial programs of harm reduction model on general health level in injection drug users

Ghanimi, Farzaneh Psychology, Iran Welfare Organization, Karaj, Islamic Republic of Iran

Treatment for substance abuse problem is usually based on Harm Reduction Model as the third stage of prevention, in which a greater range of services are offered. It is viewed as a starting point for specially injection drug users (IDUs), who are not ready to change their high risk behaviors completely. So, 300 IDUs men within the age group of 20-50 were selected randomly and they completed the form of 28 items of General Health Questionnaire, voluntarily. The 100 of them that took psychosocial services. The GHQs were completed after a period of 6 months again. The analyses shows a significant difference between their general health level before and after taking these psychosocial services (p < 0.0001).

Efficacy of stress inoculation training in smellioration of depression and anxiety in multiple sclerosis

Ghorban Shirodi, Shoresh Dept. of Psychology, IAU of Tonekabon Branch, Tonekabon, Islamic Republic of Iran Khalatbari, Javad Dept. of Psychology, IAU of Tonekabon Branch, Tonekabon, Islamic Republic of Iran

Frist 65definitly diagnosed MS PAtients were selected from neurology clinic of different neurologist in city of Tehran.In second step they were tested by given three qerstionarries of ;depression pf Bec,anxiety of Zung and psychiatric distress of Markham.Than from them thirty patients who fulfilled the criteriaes of depression,anxiety and distress were selescted for our study..It was found the SIT group was significantly less depressed, anxious and distressed than control subjects(a<0.05).The study results suggest that SIT can be effectivly applied as a therapeutic tool in stressed,anxious and depressed MSpatients.

Not only performance: The link of emotional intelligence with organizational climate, workplace bullying, organizational context and socialization processes

Giorgi, Gabriele Psychology, University of Firenze, Firenze, Italy Majer, Vincenzo Psychology, University of Firenze, Firenze, Italy

The following research aimed to analyze the emergent relations between emotional intelligence and diverse constructs. Particularly, one aim was to verify if higher emotional intelligence people should have perceived a better organizational climate than lower emotional intelligence people. Data was collected on a sample of 566 employees. The findings confirmed the hypothesis. In order to verify this second aim data was collected on a sample of 412 employees. The bullying victims with lower emotional intelligence perceived more intensive and frequent negative acts. Also the relations of emotional intelligence with type of organization and socialization processes respectively were investigated.

The role of the motor coordination in the development of education ability at children of 3-6/7 years old: Pilot study of the PROMESED project

Giurgiu, Laura Faculty of Sciences, Sibiu, Romania Raluca, Sassu of Psychology, Faculty of Sciences, Sibiu, Romania Pierre, De Hillerin Human Performance, Sport Science Institute, Bucuresti, Romania Ioana, Bugner Faculty of Sciences, "Lucian Blaga" Univers, Sibiu, Romania Dragu, Anca

Objectives: - Evaluation of the subjects' motor coordination capacity by exercises on simulators of conditions, devices for neuromuscular control; - Elaboration of motor coordinative profiles on age groups; - Determination of a relation between motor coordinative profiles, levels of development and the education ability; - Methodology of: tests of motor coordination, events to evaluate the motor coordinative behavior, observation protocols; The subjects: a representative sample of the pre-school population from the city of Sibiu; Debates: the study aims to identify the necessary conditions to initialize a program of early psycho- motor instruction, targeting the efficient adjustment to the educational environment.

Culture of substance consumption in university campuses: A field of meanings and the context of their manifestation

Gonzalez-Gonzalez, Alejandro Dept. of Psychology, UNAM, Mexico-City, Mexico Reidl Martínez, Lucy Maria Psychology, UNAM, Mexico, City, Mexico Medina-Mora, Maria Elena Psychology, UNAM, Mexico, City, Mexico

Objetives: Analyze the alcohol and drug consumption culture in university students, using an etnographic approach and oriented interviews. The survey was performed in fifteen stages of sale and/ or consumption using observation and guided interviews. We try to identify and analyze actors, substances, practices, objects, rituals, rules, meanings, perceptions, physical conditions, control mechanisms, and accessibility to these substances inside university. From the results, a set of lines to be proposed were elaborated in order to contribute to the prevention of alcohol and drug consumption and the modification of the university environment, and reduce the presence of addictive behavior in students.

Neuropsychological assessment of Spanish-speaking adults with attention deficit/hyperactivity disorder

Gonzalez-Rodriguez, Rafael A. Clinical Psychology - Ph.D., Universidad Carlos Albizu, San Juan, Puerto Rico Velez-Pastrana, Maria C. Clinical Psychology - Ph.D., Universidad Carlos Albizu, San Juan, Puerto Rico Perez-Mojica, Deborah Neuropsychology, Colectivo de Servicios Psicolo, San Juan, Puerto Rico

This study examined the sensitivity, specificity and discriminatory capacity of a combination of neuropsychological measures and self report scale to assess Attention Deficit/Hyperactivity Disorder (ADHD) in Spanish-speaking adults. We compared the performance of 50 adults (with/without ADHD) on a neuropsychological battery and Wender-Utah Rating Scale (WURS). Student's t tests, discriminant function analyses and logistic regression were used to develop a prediction model. Neuropsychological and WURS test scores were graphed on a Relative Operating Characteristic (ROC) Curve. The combination of neuropsychological measures and self report evidenced an excellent discriminatory capacity (sensitivity 1.00; specificity .913). Clinical implications are discussed.

Ageism – a cause of personality, dominance or authoritarianism?

Grau, Andreas Inst. für Sozialpsychologie, Technische Universität Dresden, Dresden, Germany Zick, Andreas Social Psychology, University of Jena, Jena, Germany

Research on personality and prejudice has shown that social dominance orientation (SDO), rightwing authoritarianism (RWA) and the big five significantly correlate with prejudices. However, only a few studies focused ageism. That is surprising since ageism is one of three big isms in many societies. We tested the link by a German version of the Fraboni Scale of Ageism (N = 121). Results indicate significant correlations and effects of SDO, conscientiousness, and openness to experience on ageism. RWA, extraversion, agreeableness, and neuroticism do not explain ageism. An explanatory model on the link between ageism and dispositions is presented.

Burnout assessment and perceived negative consequences of working conditions

Grau, Armand Figueres Hospital, Figueres Hospital, Girona (Catalonia), Spain Font-Mayolas, Silvia Departament of Psychology, University of Girona, Girona, Spain Flichtentrei, Daniel Intramed Argentina, Intramed Argentina, Buenos Aires, Argentina Suñer, Rosa Departament of Nursery, University of Girona, Girona (Catalonia), Spain Gras, Maria Eugenia Departament of Psychology, University of Girona, Girona (Catalonia), Spain

Objective: Assess perceived negative consequences of working conditions, by two means of burnout assessment. Method: This research surveyed 631 health staff (52,8% male, mean average 38,97 years, SD =10,1). The participants were asked about personal and familiar impairment, medical errors and thoughts of giving up work. Burnout was assessed by a single item measure and with the Maslach Burnout Inventory (MBI). Results: Participants with higher scores in MBI and lower in single item measure presented more personal impairment, medical errors and thoughts about giving up work than those with lower scores in MBI and higher in single item measure. Conclusion: MBI scores seemed to be better related to negative perceived consequences of working conditions.

The Nestor-Effect: Extending evolutionary developmental psychology to a lifespan perspective

Greve, Werner Inst. für Psychologie, Universität Hildesheim, Hildesheim, Germany Bjorklund, David Department of Psychology, Florida Atlantic University, Florida, USA

Development has played a minor role in evolutionary theory until very recently. However, evolutionary developmental psychology has proven to be empirically fruitful. Yet the focus here still lies on maturing processes. Since human lifespan development is a result of evolution, human longevity begs for an evolutionary explanation. We argue for an interactive view of old age, focusing both on the adaptivity of grandparents and the cultural dynamics fueled by them, resulting in a better chance of survival for the grandoffspring and a culture that protects later periods of life and, thus, longevity.

Body's psychological meaning in risky groups

Guadarrama, Rodalinda CU UAEM Temascaltepec, UAEM, Tejupilco, Mexico Mendoza, Sheila Psycology, UAEM, Tejupilco, Mexico Valdez, José Luis CIENCIAS DE LA CONDUCTA, UAEM, Toluca, Mexico

The objective was to obtain the body's psychological meaning in different risky groups. It was carried out with a propositive type,no probabilistic sample. It was formed by 120 people. They were divided in 4 groups: 30 physical fitness people, 30 artists, 30 sportmen and 30 people that don't do any pevious activities. It was developed with a natural semantics nets technique, the application was realized in an individual way. The results determined that sportmen see their body as something that let them mobility, wereas, the artists group determined it as a projection aspect, and so on.

Pragmatic modulation in deontic conditional reasoning: An exploratory approach with prisoners

Guerreiro, Joao Psicologia Cognitiva, ISPA, Lisboa, Portugal *Quelhas, Ana Cristina* Psicologia Cognitiva, ISPA, Lisboa, Portugal

The present study focus on a mental model approach of deontic conditional reasoning, and envisages its recent developments in terms of pragmatic modulation (cf. Johnson-Laird & Byrne, 2002). A series of sentences with deontic content were presented to a group of prisoners, in order to study, from their experience, with what extent they would represent differently what is forbidden and what is allowed, in terms of mental models. The consequences of these different representations were also studied through an inferential task. The results were discussed, in terms of the role of the pragmatical variables in conditional reasoning.

Experiment on optic cognitive ability development of 3-6 years old infants by cognitive drawing course

Guo, Li-Yan School of Teacher Education, Shenyang Normal University, Shenyang, People's Republic of China *Wang, Bing* School of Teacher Education, Shenyang Normal University, Shenyang, People's Republic of China

The study examined infants' drawing education from the perspective of cognitive psychology and explored the effectiveness of drawing courses based on infants' cognitive development. A quasi-experimental design was conducted, and cognitive ability was measured from three aspects: optic memory ability, color perception ability, and figure perception ability. The results indicated an effective improvement of infant optic cognitive ability after accepting the relevant training for drawing skills. The study provided a kind of valuable way to the course development of kindergarten education.

Analysis of structural information in non-linear neural network models

Häusler, Joachim Psychological Assessment, SCHUHFRIED GmbH, Mödling, Austria

Based on simulation studies, methods of structural modelling for Neural Networks are presented and compared with respect to their ability to represent the structural relations in the simulated data and with respect to the risk of over-adaptation. Considering the results of the simulations, it can be concluded that the risk of over-adaptation to the data is not larger than it is for multivariate methods as long as the network architecture is determined on the base of parsimony indices. As well, structural analysis, beyond the point of selection of predictors and model complexity, appears possible based on a-priori pruning methods.

The defensive maintenance of egalitarian values: An idealistic fallacy

Hahn, Adam Psychology, University of Colorado Boulder, Boulder, USA *Cohen, Geoffrey* Psychology, University of Colorado Boulder, Boulder, USA

The present set of studies investigated how people protect their belief in equality within their societies. In Studies 1 and 2 an American sample evaluated a minority group (Arab-Americans) significantly more negatively after being reminded of their egalitarian values, but only when that group was presented as receiving unequal treatment. Study 3 investigated the process underlying the phenomen-

on and found activation of the concept of "threat" in the *egalitarian-threatening conditions. Study 3 also showed that the phenomenon emerges from identity-maintenance process, in that participants who received an esteem-boosting affirmation did not show the effect.

Education in psychology for Czech military health service staff

Halajàuk, Tomás Dept. of Military Hygiene, Faculty of Military Health, Hradec Králové, Czech Republic *Alena, Voseckova* Department of Military Hygiene, Faculty of Military Health Sci, Hradec Králové, Czech Republic *Zdenek, Hrstka* Department of Military Hygiene, Faculty of Military Health Sci, Hradec Králové, Czech Republic *Jan, Bydzovsky* Department of Military Hygiene, Faculty of Military Health Sci, Hradec Králové, Czech Republic

The Czech Army is already in the transformation process. All their components are significantly changing in last few years. Not only this area is necessary to keep in view when planning the system of education in the Czech Army. The most viewable area for publicity is the abroad missions. Because of a membership in NATO, the Czech Army participates on the NATO operations, nowadays in Afghanistan, Iraq or Kosovo. The most exploiting part of Czech Army in these missions are the health care service units, especially field hospitals. Conditions, especially the psychological are very difficult and it is necessary to prepare soldiers properly before the deployment.

The relationship between the quality of prosocial behavior and intelligence

Han, Ru Development and Education, The Institute of Psychology, Beijing, People's Republic of China *SHI, JianNong* Development and Education, The Institute of Psychology, BeiJing, People's Republic of China

This study attempts to distinguish the difference of several prosocial behaviors, and explores one of the relative stable determinations (cognitive ability). Participants were 200 university students. Their dispositional traits of prosocial behavior, the situational prosocial behaviors, the CCFT and Information processing ability test are examined. In the presence of the simpler prosocial tasks there is no significant difference of students' prosocial behavior between higher and lower cognitive abilities, while in the presence of the more complicated prosocial tasks children with higher ability have the higher probability to present prosocial behavior than children with lower ability.

Grounded theory examination of college student narratives

Hart, Alex Psychology, Clark University, Worcester, MA, USA *McGovern, Arthur* Psychology, Nichols College, Dudley, MA, USA

The goal of this research was to find what and how students write about when given the opportunity to express their feelings about the transition to college. Student narratives were examined using Grounded Theory. Students wrote on topics in three main areas- academics, socialization (about shyness and finding friends through commonalities and circumstance), and romantic relationships. Additionally, nearly all participants made concluding remarks at the end of the study- in an attempt to wrap up their thoughts and feelings. We discuss the implications of the students' experiences for college settings.

Teaching 'Counter Research'

Hart, Alex Psychology, Clark University, Worcester, MA, USA

The number of assumptions in psychology are numerous and growing. Students are taught rigorous methods of finding validity and reliability as a gold standard in many undergraduate courses. Students in one course were challenged to rethink the notions behind the empiricism of psychology as

a scientific discipline. Students were asked to engage in counter-research projects, those which do not fit the mold of standard research- to think critically about the most basic aspects of academic psychology. Students engaged in these projects with great joy and expressed higher levels of critical thinking about basic concepts. However, many students found this course difficult in confronting the apriori assumptions of traditional scientific, quantitative psychological methodology.

Progress and correlates of adolescent vocational development

Hartung, Paul J. Dept. of Behavioral Science, NEOUCOM, Rootstown, USA *Rogers jr., James R.* COUNSELING, THE UNIVERSITY OF AKRON, AKRON, OHIO, USA *Porfeli, Erik J.* BEHAVIORAL SCIENCES, NEOUCOM, ROOTSTOWN, OHIO, USA

Vocational development reflects patterns of change in vocational behavior observed over time and considered in terms of degree and rate. A prospective longitudinal design was used to investigate degree, rate, and correlates of vocational development in an age cohort of high school students (21 girls, 21 boys). Repeated measures MANOVA and Reliable Change Index results indicated significant increases in vocational development with age. These gains directly correlated to academic achievement, work-family role salience, and Investigative and Enterprising vocational personality types. Consistent with theory, career choice readiness increases during high school and remains a key concept for comprehending adolescent vocational development.

Validation of the evaluation of Teaching Competencies Scale (ETCS): Its relationship to measures of leadership and school commitment attitudes

Harvey, Steve Williams School of Business, Bishop's University, Sherbrooke, Canada *Catano, Victor* Department of Psychology, St-Mary's University, Halifax, Canada

We present a construct validation study of the newly developed Evaluation of Teaching Competencies Scale (ETCS) with students (N=660) at three universities. Students also completed measures of Leader Member Exchange (LMX), Transformational Leadership, as well as school commitment and intentions for involvement as alumnus. The ETCS substantially related to hypothesized perceptions of LMX (r=.50) and faculty's leadership styles of intellectual stimulation (r=.51), idealized influence (r=.54) and trustworthiness (r=.49). The ETCS also predicted school commitment (r=.32) and intentions for involvement as alumni (r=.26). These relationships are tested and reported within MR models as evidence of validity for the ETCS.

Work stress and causal attribution among hospital nurses

Haybatollahi, Sayyed M Social Psychology, University of Helsinki, Helsinki, Finland

To test a hypothetical model of path relationships between occupational attributional style and chronic work stressors, a sample of 934 Finnish hospital nurses was selected. In this study, negative pattern of occupational attributional style was assumed to be partly caused by chronic work stressors. The hypotheses of the study was mainly dealt with the mediation and moderation nature of cognitive coping, and in-group and out-group support, as the psychosocial variables along with work engagement, organizational identification, and turn over intention as organizational related affects. The results, in general, supported the existence of such processes of mediation for psychosocial and organizational related affects variables, and thus inline with the relevant theories and the expectations of the model.

An ERP study of naltrexone treatment for cue induced craving in opioid addicts

He, Shengxi The Institute of Psychology, Beijing, People's Republic of China Yu, Longchuan School of Life Sciences, Peking University, Beijing, People's Republic of China Jia, Shaowei Nuclear medicine department, Shenzhen Hospital, Shenzhen, People's Republic of China

We used ERP to explore the naltrexone treatment effective for opioid craving. Four groups subjects were recorded ERP when they saw two blocks pictures (drug relevant and neutral stimuli). The results showed that the latency and amplify of P200 for drug-cue reactivity in patients treated with naltrexone over 6 months did not differ significantly from healthy control; but addicted control and passive withdrawal group who abstained from drug over 6 months showed a significantly worse condition. The results suggested that patients treated with NTX showed normalization in P200.

Sense of coherence and quality of life measures among members of the narcotics anonymous fellowship

Hedzelek, Mateusz Dept. of Social Psychology, Faculty of Psychology, Warsaw, Poland Wnukiewicz, P. Silakowski, K. Wnuk, M.

The research concerns a comparison of a conglomerate of sense of coherence and subjective quality of life factors between people not addicted to drugs, and those addicted to drugs recovering in the Narcotics Anonymous Fellowship. Eighty participants were evaluated. Comparison has been done between fourty pairs standarized in socio-demographic data (control group – research group). The research indicated that there were no significant differences in sense of coherence and quality of life measures between non-addicts and recovering addicts in the Narcotics Anonymous Fellowship. Certain significant statistical differences among particular sense of coherence and quality of life factors were observed.

Extraversion and its positive emotional core: Further evidence from neuroscience

Hermes, Michael Inst. für Psychologie, Universität Trier, Trier, Germany Hagemann, Dirk Department of Psychology, University of Heidelberg, Heidelberg, Germany Naumann, Ewald Department of Psychology, University of Trier, Trier, Germany Walter, Christof Radiology and Neuroradiology, Hospital of the Barmh. Brüder, Trier, Germany

There is converging evidence from self-report data that extraversion and positive affect are systematically related. In the present study, we investigated whether positive affect forms the core of extraversion (as suggested by Watson & Clark, 1997) or vice versa. Baseline cerebral blood flow was measured in 38 participants and regressed to the personality and trait affect questionnaire scores. After partialing out the common variance of extraversion and positive affect voxel-based analyses suggested that positive affect forms the core of extraversion and not vice versa. The study thus demonstrates the usefulness of physiological data in evaluating psychological hypotheses.

Autobiographical memories and the role of involuntary memory in a case with hippocampal amnesia

Hirano, Mikio Medical Science and Welfare, Tohoku Bunka Gakuen University, Sendai, Japan Noguchi, Kazuhito SSER Center, Miyagi University of Education, Sendai, Japan Hosokawa, Toru Graduate School of Education, Tohoku University, Sendai, Japan

We report a case (Y.K.) with hippocampal amnesia since 1990. We conducted many neuropsychological tests and observed him carefully in his everyday life. The test results showed that his intellectual ability was within the normal range. He had severe anterograde amnesia and could not recall specific autobiographical episodes from his remote memories. Through our observations, he could not remember virtually any episodes after his onset, but sometimes could retrieve his personal semantics 'involuntary' in his everyday life. We think that involuntary memory was very important for him because he actually referred to it to manage his everyday life.

The self-reported psychological profile of six jobs in Romania

Holman, Andrei Iasi, Romania Havarneanu, Cornel Psychology, "Al. I. Cuza" Universi, iasi, Romania Dumitru, Marian Psychology, "Al. I. Cuza" Universi, iasi, Romania Dumitru, Alexandru Psychology, "Al. I. Cuza" Universi, iasi, Romania

We researched the psychological profile of six jobs in Romania, as it is reported by the professionals themselves: landscape architect, bank clerk, technologist engineer, officer of the court, PR officer and journalist. As such, we constructed a questionnaire in which subjects from all the four fields of work were required to relate to a typical representative of the respective profession, on three dimensions: cognitive abilities, social personality factors (on three levels: sociability, social presence and responsibility), and supplementary professional exigencies. The sample included both professionals and people in these respective academic domains, from different institutions/work places in several major cities.

Vertical collectivism and bias against disabled persons: The mediation of disgust sensitivity

Holtz, Rolf Psychological Science, Ball State University, Muncie, USA Gordon, Ellen R. Psychology, Ohio University, Athens, Ohio, USA

Objectives: The normative morality of vertical collectivists suggests that disgust mediates their bias against the severely disabled. Methods: 250 participants completed Triandis' (1996) horizontal/vertical individualism/collectivism measure, the Disgust Sensitivity Scale, and the Social Distance Scale (SDS) assessing bias against the severely disabled. Results: Regression analyses showed that only vertical collectivism (VC) predicted the SDS bias scores ($\beta = .08$, p < .04) and the disgust sensitivity scores ($\beta = .06$, p < .001). A Sobel test confirmed the complete mediation of VC-SDS by disgust ($z = 3.11$, p < .002). Conclusions: Disgust may elicit discriminatory practices within VC societies.

Creating monstrosity: How neo-nazi propaganda uses essentialist categorizations for the denigration of Blacks and Jews

Holtz, Peter Wirtsch.- u. Sozialpsychologie, Universität Linz, Linz, Austria

Psychological essentialism has become an important topic within the field of social psychology over the last two decades. We argue that because of the possible mutual exclusivity of essences, their inherence, and their immutability, essentialist categorizations are used in propaganda in order to create the impression of a social group being beyond any accepted category of things. This group is likely to be perceived as 'monstrous'. Evidence for the 'monstrification' of Jews and Africans in contemporary German Neo-Nazi propaganda is presented. The data derives from a qualitative analysis of app. 5000 postings in a German neo-Nazi online discussion board.

Analyzing the cost of prospective memory with the diffusion model

Horn, Sebastian Institut für Exp. Psychologie, Universität Düsseldorf, Düsseldorf, Germany Smith, Rebekah Department of Psychology, UTSA, San Antonio, USA Bayen, Ute Institut für exp. Psychologie, Heinrich-Heine Universität, Düsseldorf,

Germany Voss, Andreas Institut für Psychologie, Albert-Ludwigs Universität, Freiburg, Germany

Event-based prospective memory (PM) involves remembering to perform an action when an event occurs in the future. A current approach to detecting the potential cost of PM rests on the analysis of ongoing task performance. We used Ratcliff's (1978) diffusion model to analyze this cost to both speed and accuracy in an ongoing lexical-decision task. Model-based data revealed that PM intentions lowered information uptake and led to a more conservative response criterion in the ongoing task. This indicates that PM intentions can interfere with data-driven accumulation at an early stage and influence controlled processes in terms of strategic criteria.

The influence of self-efficacy and social support on occupational achievement and job satisfaction: Longitudinal analysis of middle school teachers enrolled in teacher training programs

Huhr, Hoe-Sook Dept. of Education, Inha University, Incheon, Republic of Korea Kim, Uichol Business administration, Inha University, Inchon, Republic of Korea Park, Young-Shin Dept. of Education, Inha University, Incheon, Republic of Korea

The purpose of this study is to examine the longitudinally the influence of self-efficacy and social support on occupational achievement and job satisfaction of middle school teachers enrolled in teacher training programs. A total of 431 teachers (119 males, 312 females) completed a questionnaire. Participants completed a questionnaire at three different phases: (1) prior to the onset of the training program, (2) after completing the training program, and (3) three months after completion of the training program. The results indicate that social support received from school administrators and fellow teachers raised their self-efficacy and job satisfaction. Self-efficacy has positive influence occupational achievement. Implications of the results for teacher training programs will be discussed.

Japanese life-patterns in the 2000s III: Full-time and part-time workers.

Ide, Wataru Humanities and Social Sciences, Osaka Prefecture University, Sakai, Japan Hashizume, Hiroko Research Institute, International Economy and Work, Osaka, Japan Maeda, Hiromitsu Graduate School of Sociology, Kansai University, Suita, Japan

The effects of full-time versus part-time employment status on attitudes toward performance appraisal were examined. The survey was conducted in cooperation with a Japanese supermarket labor union, and 2,600 full-time workers and 4,000 part-time workers answered the questionnaires. Using hierarchical linear modeling, this study demonstrated that full-time workers reported lower satisfaction with performance appraisal, and both individual and organizational level conditions were significantly associated with satisfaction: perceived justice and subordinate's evaluation of supervisor explained within-organization variance, and perceived justice aggregated to the organization level explained between-organization variance. Employment status moderated the relationship between perceived justice and individual satisfaction.

The effect of emotional valences of schedules on prospective memory

Ikegami, Kimiko Dept. of Education, Kanazawa University, Kanazawa, Japan

This study was conducted to investigate whether the emotional valences of schedules affect prospective memory in the same way as retrospective memory. Thirty-one undergraduate students were randomly assigned to the future condition to memorize pleasant, unpleasant and neutral schedules as future plans, or to the past condition to memorize them as past events. The result showed that the emotional valences did not affect prospective remembering, whereas pleasant events and neutral events were significantly more recalled than unpleasant events in the past condition. This result suggests that the underlying mechanisms of prospective memory differ from those of retrospective memory.

Strategies for random key pressing under cat-and-mouse conditions

Itagaki, Fumihiko Dept. International Relations, Asia University, Tokyo, Japan *Turk, David* School of Psychology, University of Aberdeen, Aberdeen, United Kingdom *Itoh, Kenji* Speech and Cognitive Science, University of Tokyo, Bunkyo-ku, Tokyo, Japan *Miura, Sachie* Neuropsychiatry, Fukushima Medical University, Fukusima, Japan *Niwa, Shin-Ichi* Neuropsychiatry, Fukushima Medical University, Fukushima, Japan *Kohno, Sou-Ichi* Neuropsychiatry, Fukushima Medical University, Fukushima, Japan *Gotoh, Daisuke* Neuropsychiatry, Fukushima Medical University, Fukushima, Japan *Kawasaki, Singo* Optical Topography Group, Hitachi Medical Corporation, Kashiwa-shi, Chiba-ken, Japan

Twenty-eight subjects performed random key pressing tasks under cat-and-mouse conditions. In the CAT condition participants attempted to predict the next number chosen by the computer. In the MOUSE condition participants attempted to outwit the computer that was attempting to predict their key press. Each condition required participants to make 163 key-press responses. Irrespective of the number key chosen, 18 responses were predetermined as hits (Cat wins and Mouse loses) and were accompanied by auditory feedback. Shifts in strategy between the CAT and MOUSE conditions are examined with relation to the activation of the frontal lobes measured by Near-infrared spectroscopy.

The relationship between job demands, job control, and subjective well-being (vitality, positive affect and negative affect, optimism) in job design among employees of a company

Jahanbakhsh Ganjeh, Madine Isfahan University, Isfahan, Islamic Republic of Iran *Orayzi, Hamid Reza* Psychology, Isfahan University, Isfahan, Islamic Republic of Iran *Molavi, Hosain* Psychology, Isfahan University, Isfahan, Islamic Republic of Iran *Nouri, Abolghasem* Psychology, Isfahan University, Isfahan, Islamic Republic of Iran

The purpose of this study was to investigate the relationship between job demands, job control, and Subject well-being (Vitality, Positive affect and Negative affect, Optimism) in job design among employees of a company. The participants were 100 employees who selected through a random sampling.The measurements were Desi and Rayan vitality questionnaire, Watson and Clark PANAS (Positive affect and Negative affect) questionnaire, and Wall at el job design questionnaire. Data were analyzed through multiple regressin.Findings indicated both job demands and job control were significantly related to vitality, positive affect and negative affect, and optimism. Keywords: Job demands, Optimism, Vitality

The relationship between job demands, job control, and stress in job design among employees of a company

Jahanbakhsh Ganjeh, Madine Isfahan University, Isfahan, Islamic Republic of Iran *Orayzi, Hamid Reza* Psychology, Isfahan University, Isfahan, Islamic Republic of Iran *Molavi, Hosain* Psychology, Isfahan University, Isfahan, Islamic Republic of Iran *Nouri, Abolghasem* Psychology, Isfahan University, Isfahan, Islamic Republic of Iran

The purpose of this study was to investigate the relationship between job demands, job control, and stress in job design among employees of a company.The participants were 110 employees who selected through a random sampling.The measurements were Eliot Stress Questionnaire and Wall Job Design Questionnaire.Data were analyzed by multiple regression. Findings indicated both job demands and job control were significantly related to stress.managers can reduce stress in employees by using Results of this study. Keywords: Job demands, Job control, stress, Job design

Exploring heterosexuals' experiences of being prejudiced toward gay men: An interpretative phenomenological analysis of homonegativity

Jewell, Lisa Dept. of Psychology, University of Saskatchewan, Saskatoon, Canada

This study documented the prevalence of anti-gay attitudes and behaviours on a Canadian university campus and described the lived experiences of heterosexuals who are perpetrators of homonegativity. A mixed-methods approach was used wherein a questionnaire was administered to 286 Canadian university students and interviews were conducted with eight individuals who are prejudiced toward gay men. Interviews were analyzed using Interpretative Phenomenological Analysis. The participants' lived experiences of homonegativity were characterized by their negative affective reactions toward homosexuality and their perceptions that gay men are feminine. Participants' homonegativity could best be understood in terms of their religious and gender role ideologies.

The study on Chinese children's sense of shame

Jie, Jing Dept. of Psychology, Liaoning Normal University, Dalian, People's Republic of China *Yang, Lizhu* Psychology, Liaoning Normal University, Dalian, People's Republic of China

To examine Chinese children's understanding of shame, 4- and 5-year-olds children were chosen and the method of semi-structured interviewing was adopted in this study. The results indicated that in no hint situation, a significant age-related difference in shame expression was found, while disappeared in hint situation. The shame expression in task failure scene was much more than that in transgression scene. There are significant age-related differences in understanding of sense of shame. The categories of definitions, antecedents and action tendencies of shame were consistent in both age groups, but only different in quantity.

Moderating effects of coping in the context of unemployment and job insecurity

Körner, Astrid Inst. für Entw.-Psychologie, Universität Jena, Jena, Germany *Reitzle, Matthias* Developmental Psychology, Friedrich Schiller University, Jena, Germany *Silbereisen, Rainer K.* Developmental Psychology, Friedrich Schiller University, Jena, Germany

Following stress and coping theories, the present study on 1,764 employed and unemployed German adults investigated the moderating role of coping on the connection between unemployment and psychological well-being. It was expected that active coping styles would buffer adverse effects of short-term unemployment, whereas it would not do the same for long-term unemployment. Instead, disengagement strategies were supposed to weaken this link. Multiple regression models including interaction terms of duration of unemployment and coping style partly confirmed these hypotheses. Furthermore, it was tested whether coping styles would yield similar effects among employed people with different degrees of perceived job-related insecurities.

Retrieval-induced forgetting: Eliminated by psychosocial stress, not by oral hydrocortisone

Kössler, Susanne Inst. für Psychologie, Universität Konstanz, Konstanz, Germany *Kissler, Johanna* Department of Psychology, University of Konstanz, Konstanz, Germany

Retrieval-induced forgetting refers to the phenomenon that the repeated retrieval of a subset of previously learned material can cause forgetting of the nonretrieved remaining material. However, the degree of retrieval-induced forgetting varies markedly between different subjects and conditions. We investigated the influence of psychosocial stress on retrieval-induced forgetting and found that the effect disappeared when subjects were exposed to stress before the retrieval practice phase. Though, replacing psychosocial stress by oral hydrocortisone did not reduce the effect. These results suggest that not solely cortisol, but the interplay of sympathetic activation and cortisol may lead to the disappearance of retrieval-induced forgetting.

Effects of an extended contact intervention on preventing prejudice in elementary school children

Küchel, Julia DFG-Forschungsgruppe, Universität Jena, Jena, Germany *Beelmann, Andreas* Institute of Psychology, University of Jena, Jena, Germany

The present study evaluates an extended-contact-intervention which aims to prevent prejudice and support positive intergroup relations. 38 elementary school children (mean age = 9) received the program, while comparable children served as control group (n=43). Several prejudice measures against black children and Russian German children were assessed prior, immediately after and six months after the intervention. In contrast to previous research, data revealed no significant differences between program and control group. These results are referred to the choice of the outgroup used in the extended contact condition and are discussed against the background of current research on prejudice development.

Truthful and untruthful behavior as a result of mental development in a pre-school age

Kankova, Alesia Department of Psychology, Belarusian State Pedagogical U, Minsk, Belarus

The present abstract describes the phenomenon of truthful and untruthful behavior between 3 and 7 year of age. Methods of research: technique "Carlson's button", methods D1/D2, D2/D2, D3/D3, D4/D4. It was calculated the Phi-square, coefficient of Spearman' rank-order correlation. The results show that there are correlations between different forms of truthful and untruthful behavior and certain mental functions (r=0,73, p=0,001). So, the disciplined truthful behavior correlates with function «realization» (ϕ=1,0, r=0,001). Undisciplined truthful behavior correlates with function «relation» (ϕ=0,5, r=0,001). Lying behavior correlates with function «understanding» (ϕ=0,4, r=0,001). Deceitful behavior correlates with function «reflection»(ϕ=0,4, r=0,001).

Effects of video game playing on empathy

Karatsu, Akari Osaka, Japan *Katsurada, Emiko* Psychology, Kwansei Gakuin University, Nishinomiya, Japan

This study investigated effects of video-game playing on emotional empathy. Twelve 4th graders and 30 undergraduates were shown various pictures to elicit emotional empathy before and after playing a video game. The results indicated that girls' level of empathy on piteous scenes tended to increase after playing video games. Children who had heard alarms while playing the game tended to have lowered their empathy on worrying scenes. For undergraduates, it was found that their level of empathy decreased on angry scenes but increased on painful scenes significantly. It was concluded that video-game playing has different effects on children and adults.

Values-ideals development at the transition from preschool to elementary-school age

Kashirsky, Dmitry Chair of Psychology&Pedagogics, Altai Academy of Economics&Law, Barnaul, Russia
The study investigates the peculiarities of value-system development at the first stage of its origin- at the period of transition from preschool to elementary school age. The hypothesis was that qualitative changes in values-ideals take place at age 6-7 and are closely connected with changes in social situation of child's development. Subjects were 114 children aged 5-8.Values were measured with "Ideal Man" and "Happy Animal" projective techniques and with the help of interview. Statistical analyses of the data was performed. The study revealed that the basic values-ideals of 6-7year-old children are security, recognition and communication. Implications of the findings for understanding the nature of 7-year developmental crises are discussed.

The meaning of working from employees' perspective

Kayaalp Ersoy, Esma Gorkem Business Administration, Beykent University, Istanbul, Turkey
Working has a cetral role to understand human behaviour. According to the many theorists and researchers, working is something more than achieving personal achievement. For this reason the aim of this paper is to investigate the attitudes of employees toward working. The relationship between working and psychology has a complex structure. In order to clarify this complex structure we create a questionary form about working life and its perception from the view of employees. Sample of this research is 200 acedemicians whom also work in cubicle office system so that the research points the effects of cubicle office system on employees psychology, organizational climate and effectiveness. To analize the data SPSS for Windows 11.00 is used.

The relation between personalities and loneliness in adolescents: The mediating effect of interpersonal competence

Kejia, Qu Psychological Department, Beijing Normal University, Beijing, People's Republic of China Hong, Zou Psychological Department, Beijing Normal University, Beijing, People's Republic of China
This study investigated the relations among inter-personal competence,personalities and loneliness.784 adolescents in China were used as subjects to complete the questionnaires of interpersonal competence, FFP and loneliness. Results?(1) There was significant gender difference on scores of loneliness,and boys scored higher than girls;(2)Most of the correlations among interpersonal competence, personalities and loneliness are significant;(3)Positive predictive effects were found in neuroticism and openness for the loneliness,while the predictive effects of extraversion, agreeableness and interpersonal competence were negative;(4)Interpersonal competence had partial mediating effect in the relations between extraversion, neuroticism,openness and loneliness, while in the relation between agreeableness and loneliness, interpersonal competence had full mediating effect.

The transtheoretical model of behavior change (TTM): Validation of the stages of change

Keller, Roger Sozial- u. Gesundheitspsychol., Universität Zürich, Zürich, Switzerland Hornung, Rainer Social and Health Ps, University of Zurich, Zurich, Switzerland
Objective To examine the validity of the Stages of Change (SOC) regarding the motivation for smoking cessation. Method A sample of 303 20- to 65-year-old smokers completed a questionnaire with smoking-specific TTM-scales. Data were analyzed by means of variance-, cluster- and discriminant analysis. Results At the precontemplation stage

three qualitatively different groups regarding their motivation to quit smoking could be identified. Differences emerged for twelve variables (e.g. readiness to reduce smoking, self-efficacy and processes of change). Conclusions The results show that the motivation of precontemplators for smoking cessation is underestimated when using the TTM. This misclassification impedes appropriate interventions.

Impact of family awareness and participation in educational program on successful cessation of illicit drugs.

Khasteganan, Noushin Forsat Clinic, Rasht, Islamic Republic of Iran
Aim: The present study examined whether family awareness were associated with successful cessation. Methods and Materials: A sample of 388 drug addicts was investigated at a quit addict clinic in north of Iran.Data were obtained from on site confidential interviews and individual drug use history was recorded. Results: The mean age of respondents was 31.6. 99.8% were male, 67.3% married.84.5% were treated by agonists. Successful cessation was not associated with family awareness or participation of them in educational program. Conclusion: It seems that families did not play their important role in supporting their family members to quit of drugs.

Are children's and adolescents' intuitive judgments about distributive justice linked to different school systems?: A comparative study between Germany and Italy

Kienbaum, Jutta Faculty of Education, Free University of Bozen-Bolza, Brixen, Italy
This study examined which principles (equity, equality, need) pupils choose when allocating a reward. Participants were 188 students from Germany (a country which tracks students into schools for high or low achievers) and 72 students from Italy (where tracking does not occur). The students, aged 9, 12 and 15 years, divided a reward between two protagonists who differed on the dimensions of need and effort. The German high achieving pupils rewarded effort much more than did their low achieving counterparts. The same age pupils from Italy resembled the high achievers in Germany. School tracking seems to make low achievers devalue effort.

The advantage of small memory capacity: Amplified correlation or simple strategy

Kikuchi, Ken Dept. of Psychology, Sophia University, Tokyo, Japan Michimata, Chikashi Psychology, Sophia University, Tokyo, Japan
People with small short-term memory capacity show better performance than people with large capacity in correlation detection tasks. Previous researches suggested two theories to explain this phenomenon; amplified correlation theory and simple strategy theory. We conducted the correlation detection task in which ϕ is .50, dividing participants into two groups based on the their immediate memory spans (8). The result supported the simple strategy theory. Males tended to avoid misses whereas females tended to avoid false alarms in the correlation detection task. This might be resulted from the sex difference of the cost for propagation.

The impact of specific attention retraining after traumatic brain injury

King, Andrea Ruprecht-Karls-University, Mannheim, Germany Kryspin-Exner, Ilse Inst. f. Klinische, Biolog. un, Universitaet Wien, Wien, Austria
The impact of a computerized cognitive training addressing four attention aspects was studied in patients with TBI. While 30 patients were specifically trained in attention domains, 20 patients received a non-specific training. Results indicate

that specific training led to a better performance in three attention domains, with alertness-training additionally enhancing quantitative performance in more complex aspects. Differences in the change of daily functioning and emotional state were absent. Improvements were also observed in single case analyses and mostly remained stable for 12 weeks. Results corroborate a hierarchic organization of attention functions and the necessity of each component being trained specifically.

The relationship between mental health, trauma dose, types, profiles and IQ discrepancy indexes in adolescents: The case of African-American and Iraqi refugees

Kira, Ibrahim Center for Cumulative Trauma, Hamtramck, MI, USA Lewandowski, Linda Nursing, Wayne State University, Detroit, MI, USA Somers, Cheryl Educational Psychology, Wayne State University, Detroit, MI, USA Yoon, Jina Educational Psychology, Wayne State University, Detroit, MI, USA Chiodo, Lisa Medicine, Wayne State University, Detroit, MI, USA Peterson, Barbara Nursing, Wayne State University, Detroit, MI, USA
Extreme stress and traumas can cause brain atrophy and ultimately impair hemispheric synchronization and cause significant discrepancy between major IQ indexes. To explore the effects of different traumas, on IQ discrepancies, we conducted a study on 401 adolescents African Americans and Iraqi refugees' adolescents. We used WISC IV, cumulative trauma, PTSD, APS and other measures. We used t-tests to check the significance of differences between groups. We conducted multiple regression analyses controlling for age, gender, full IQ, cultural background and other relevant variables. We conducted path analyses to check the mediation model of PTSD in these relationships. The results suggest linear and non-linear relationships between some trauma variables, e.g., sexual abuse, mental health variables and IQ discrepancies.

Types of burnout and intention to quit and continue working in nurses

Kishi, Taichi Toho University, Tokyo, Japan Yamada, Yukiko Faculty of medicine, Toho University, Tokyo, Japan Takeuchi, Shigeki
Burnout is one of the risk factor of turnover. We investigated the relationship between types of burnout and the intention to quit and continue working in nurses who work in a university hospital. 593 nurses answered the questionnaire involving MBI-GS Japanese version and the questions of intention to quit and continue working. The result of cluster analysis showed participants could be categorized into 4 types based on their burnout score, the result of ANOVA showed that high cynicism caused the intention to quit. Therefore, the cynicism seems the most important of all subscales of burnout for the intention to quit.

BIG5, motives and human capital variables have changing explanation power over the first five years of entrepreneurial success!

Klandt, Heinz Leadership, Strategy, EUROPEAN BUSINESS SCHOOL, Oestrich-Winkel, Germany Gese-Klier, Silke SOL, EUROPEAN BUSINESS SCHOOL, Oestrich-Winkel, Germany
Based on a still ongoing internet survey using as independent variables the BIG5, some motives, and aspects of human capital (experiences in industry etc.) with now more than 10,000 people, for the study to be presented we selected those who were/are self-employed (n > 800) and asked for entrepreneurial performance (dependent variables) like number of employees, sales per annum for a time span of five years from start. Beside other results it seems to be, that over a time period of 5 years different sets of variables contribute to the yearly entrepreneurial success in different ways.

Interpersonal action synchronization across the lifespan: A dyadic drumming study

Kleinspehn, Anna *Lifespan Psychology, Max Planck Institute, Berlin, Germany* **Riediger, Michaela** *Lifespan Psychology, Max Planck Institute/Human Dev, Berlin, Germany* **Schmiedek, Florian** *Department of Psychology, Humboldt University Berlin, Berlin, Germany* **von Oertzen, Timo** *Lifespan Psychology, Max Planck Institute/Human Dev, Berlin, Germany* **Li, Shu-Chen** *Lifespan Psychology, Max Planck Institute/ Human Dev, Berlin, Germany* **Lindenberger, Ulman** *Lifespan Psychology, Max Planck Institute/Human Dev, Berlin, Germany*

Although the ability to synchronize one's goal-directed behavior with others' is a fundamental characteristic of successful social interactions, little is known about its lifespan development. We propose that this ability develops based on changes in sensorimotor and social skills. Using a dyadic drumming paradigm, we examined age differences in interpersonal action synchronization. Participants from four age groups (5, 12, 20-30, 70-80 years) synchronized their constant-rate drumming at self-chosen frequencies in dyads with one participant from each age group. Results indicate developmental differences in interpersonal action synchronization across the lifespan as well as a relationship between synchronization accuracy and sensorimotor skills.

The influence of priming and expertise in the time course of real-world observation tasks

Koerber, Bernd *Inst. für Psychologie, Universität Regensburg, Regensburg, Germany* **Niepmann, Marcus** *Psychology, University of Regensburg, Regensburg, Germany* **Hammerl, Marianne** *Psychology, University of Regensburg, Regensburg, Germany*

We tested the hypothesis that the temporal dynamics of scanpath patterns depend heavily on previous knowledge and expertise. Eye movements were collected from four groups of partipiciants who viewed photographs of real-world scenes during an active search task. Experts (police officers) and laymen (students) who received preparatory scene priming were faster and needed fewer fixations than controls without any priming in order to detect dangerous objects in case- and security-relevant scenarios. Moreover, postidentificatory processes were significantly shorter only for experts who received preparatory priming compared to those without priming and to both control groups. We conclude that dissociable cognitive factors in the course of information processing account for typical temporal patterns of eye movement parameters during active search.

Young people and gambling

Koic, Elvira *Psychiatry, General Hospital, Virovitica, Croatia* **Per-Koznjak, Jasna** *Psychiatry, General Hospital, Virovitica, Croatia*

The aims of study: to examine the young people's attitudes about gambling. Material and Methods: The authors examined 213 subjects from nine different groups of high school students. The questionnaire used was designed for the purpose of this investigation. Results qualitative analyses how that young people experience gambling behavior as harmful. The authors conclude that, due to the size of the problem and its consequences, the prevention of pathological gambling is very important. The prevention can be carried out primarily through screening at the school level and primary health care services, whereas secondary screening may be conducted through the system of psychiatric care.

Computer modeling of concept-nets

Kolar, Gerald *Innsbruck, Austria* **Sachse, Pierre** *Psychology, University of Innsbruck, Innsbruck, Austria*

This study treats computer simulations from concept-nets to the knowledge representation in the semantic memory. An investigation with a system of 2500 connected real concepts is presented. The analysis ("activation spreading") took place with our program "Datamatrix". To that an experiment (N=50) is presented to the influence by term structuring on memory stability. Two questions were examined: 1. Are the conditions of scale-freeness fulfilled. 2. Has the term structuring an influence on memory stability. Methodical analyses showed that characteristics of scale-freeness are fulfilled. Real concept-nets make a higher robustness possible by the scale-freeness in relation to disturbances.

Drug addicted patients' social problem-solving abilities and goal during rehabilitation

Kolesnikova, Jelena *Dept. of Psychology, University of Latvia, Riga, Latvia*

The aim of the present research was to investigate differences changes in the social-problem solving abilities and goals of drug-addicted patients in different phases of rehabilitation. An experimental group of drug-addicted patients (N=35, 18-27 years of age) was compared with a control group of drug abusers (N=34, ages 18-27 years). The results indicated that the Social-Problem Solving Abilities and the Goals Scales in subscales changed significantly over the six month-period in the groups with improvement in the group undergoing therapy and no improvement or deterioration in the drug abuser group, except Rational problem solving subscale.

An investigation of the cognitive processing in multiply handicapped persons using event-related brain potentials (ERPs)

Konishi, Kenzo *Clinical Psychology, Kibi International University, Takahashi, Japan*

The purpose of this study was to investigate the cognitive processes of multiply handicapped persons especially on face perception. Stimuli consist of photographs of 5 kinds of objects including human faces were presented on monitor screen. Event-related brain potentials (ERPs) were recorded from 54 multiply handicapped persons during looking at the monitor screen. Face specific P170 ERP component was analyzed in its amplitude and latency. As the results, their appearance were not so relate with the degrees of severity by traditional classification scales but rather with the responsibility in daily life.

Gender-role conflict, job characteristics and psychosocial health: The case of male employees in female-dominated occupations

Korek, Sabine *Arbeits- und Org.-Pschologie, Universität Leipzig, Leipzig, Germany* **Wolfram, Hans-Joachim** *Work and Organizational Psycho, University Leipzig, Leipzig, Germany* **Mohr, Gisela** *Work and Organizational Psycho, University Leipzig, Leipzig, Germany*

Minority status may highlight the gender category. We hypothesized gender role self-concept and gender-role conflict to be important for psychosocial health. Hierarchical regression analyses based on survey data from 180 men working in female-dominated professions showed: Gender-role conflict predicted - as expected - depression, irritation, and low job satisfaction. Masculine, but not feminine gender role self-concepts were related to better health and higher job satisfaction. Furthermore, tenure and masculine gender role self-concepts were related to lower gender-role conflict, even though participants worked in female-dominated occupations. The impact of job characteristics as additional predictors will be explained.

A motivation to confirm is not necessarily problematic

Koslowski, Barbara *Human Development, Cornell University, Ithaca, USA* **Marasia, Joseph** *Human Development, Cornell University, Ithaca, New York, USA* **Liang, Victoria** *Human Development, Cornell University, Ithaca, New York, USA*

Trying to disconfirm a belief is said to be better scientific practice than trying to confirm it. To test this, we presented college students with several pieces of information that were causally consistent with an explanation, causally inconsistent with it, or neutral. Each participant was asked to choose information either to confirm or to disconfirm the explanation. Percentages of correct choices were analyzed with generalized estimating equations. When told to confirm, participants were more likely than when told to disconfirm to choose information that was either inappropriate or neutral. The motivation to confirm did not necessarily lead to better reasoning.

How children use language to express desires? Preliminary data on a Croatian sample

Kotrla Topic, Marina *Psychology, Institute Ivo Pilar, Zagreb, Croatia* **Sakic, Marija** *Psychology, Institute Ivo Pilar, Zagreb, Croatia*

Objectives of this study were to explore the linguistic means children use to express desires in Croatian, and to investigate developmental changes in their use frequency. The study was based on data from Croatian sample of children's speech utterances collected in the CHILDES database (McWhinney, 2000; Kovacevic, 2003). A number of linguistic means used to express desires was identified, and results revealed that their use frequency systematically varied from 10 to 38 months of age. Even very young children use a variety of linguistic means for expressing desires, and the number and frequency of used linguistic means changes during development.

Attention deficit hyperactivity disorder and substance use disorder: Is attention deficit hyperactivity disorder a risk factor?

Kousha, Maryam *Psychiatry, Gilan University, Rasht, Islamic Republic of Iran* **Shahrivar, Zahra** *Child Psychiatry, Tehran University, Tehran, Islamic Republic of Iran* **Alaghband-Rad, Javad** *Child Psychiatry, Tehran University, Tehran, Islamic Republic of Iran* **Kiani, Seyed Amir** *family Planning research cente, Gilan University, Rasht, Islamic Republic of Iran*

To assess the pattern SUD in adolescents with and without history of ADHD. in this case- control study, The participants were interviewed by a child psychiatrist and the measures included: k-SADS,Opium Treatment Index and GAF. adolescents divided to two groups: with history of ADHD (n=33) and without it (n=33). ADHD Adolescents had an earlier age of starting cigarette smoking, substance use, an earlier onset of substance dependence or abuse, more severe substance use and functional impairment. Early diagnosis and treatment of ADHD could be associated with better prognosis of SUD in adolescents and economically will diminish the costs of SUD .

Emotional and neuropsychological functioning in cardiac patients before and after surgery procedures with neuromonitoring during heart operation

Kowalska, Monika *Personality Psychology, UKSW/ Institute of Cardiology, Warsaw, Poland* **Wolski, Piotr** *Cardiosurgery, Institute of Cardiology, Warsaw, Poland*

NIRS is a non-invasive, similar to pulsoxymetry technique based on near infrared spectroscopy;monitoring reflects the balance between oxygen supply and demand of the forehead cortex. This study was prospectively performed on 110 operated on CPB patients. The purposes of this study are to introduce therapy targeted on maintaining rSO2 at the preoperative level during operation and to examine the correlation between the risk factors, mood and neuropsychological complications. Before and after operation patients were tested with psychological assessments: HADS, MMSE, ASEM and BLOCKS from WAIS-R. The results emphasize the importance of psychological support and neuropsychological rehabilitation for these patients.

Job demands and burnout: Is recovery a mediator or moderator?

Kubicek, Bettina Inst. Wirtschaftspsychologie, Universität Wien, Wien, Austria *Korunka, Christian* Economic Psychology, University of Vienna, Vienna, Austria *Bjelopoljak, Lejla* Economic Psychology, University of Vienna, Vienna, Austria

The study specifies the energetic process of the Job Demands-Resources model, according to which job demands lead to burnout, by building upon the Effort-recovery model. More specifically, we examined whether recovery accounts for (i.e., mediates) or influences (i.e., moderates) the effect of job demands on burnout among 210 nurses. Data were collected using self-administered questionnaires. Results show that recovery partially mediates the relationship between job demands and burnout. That is, high demands are directly and indirectly (via the intervening effect of recovery) related to burnout. Therefore leisure activities which allow for recovery seem to be important in the burnout process.

Increase of the adequate use of separate counseling communication skills after basic and advanced microskills training

Kuntze, Jeroen Psychology, Erasmus University Rotterdam, Rotterdam, Netherlands *Van der Molen, Henk* Psychology, Erasmus University Rotterdam, Rotterdam, Netherlands *Born, Marise* Psychology, Erasmus University Rotterdam, Rotterdam, Netherlands

Research into effectiveness of counseling communication skills trainings often reports overall effect sizes only. The aim of this study was to investigate the increase of the adequate use of separate basic and advanced counseling communication skills after respectively a basic and an advanced training. Participants were 583 bachelor students in psychology who took a video test. There were four groups: (1) freshmen, without receiving training in communication skills; (2) first year students, receiving basic skills training; (3) second year students, receiving advanced skills training and (4) a control group. All seven basic skills and four advanced skills showed large effect sizes.

Line motion illusion triggered by gradient bars: An end point hypothesis

Kuo, Chun-Yu Psychology Department, Chung Yuan Christian Unversity, TaoYuan, Taiwan *Chau, Hsuan-Fu* Psychology Department, Chung Yuan Christian Unversity, TaoYuan, Taiwan *Wang, Hsioa-Ling* Psychology Department, Chung Yuan Christian Unversity, TaoYuan, Taiwan

The goal of this study was to investigate the effect of perceived end point in line motion illusion, in which illusory motion was triggered by gradient bars. The contrast between the bar and the background was manipulated. Participants were asked to report if illusory motion was perceived as well as the motion direction. Results showed that gradient bars could induce line motion illusion. The perceived direction was from the low contrast end to the high contrast end, and luminance had no impact on perceived direction. These results suggest that the perceived end point could affect observers' perception of motion direction.

Anxiety and brain functional development

Kustubayeva, Almira Dept. of Psychology, Kazakh National University, Almaty, Kazakhstan

Objective: To investigate the anxiety level, emotional stability, motor asymmetry and brain functional development in orphans. Subjects and Methods: 120 healthy children (age-specific groups: 6-8; 11-12; 14-15 years old) were participants. Russian versions of Spielberger Trait-State Anxiety, Luscher Color test, Shtambok Test were used. EEG was registered monopolarly from the left and right frontal, central, parietal and occipital lobes with closed and open eyes. Spectral-coherence analysis was made by Vildavski's EEGlab. Results and conclusion: The significantly higher anxiety level and the left-handedness score in orphans compare to control group were found (p<0,05). The baseline brain activity testifies to differences of the brain functional development between orphans and control groups.

See no evil, there is no evil?: Controversial ethical dilemmas and the nature of morality

Kuttner, Simon Dept. of Psychology, University of Otago, Dunedin, New Zealand *Murachver, Tamar* Psychology, University of Otago, Dunedin, New Zealand

Are good acts motivated by evil thoughts virtuous? This is the type of question not investigated in traditional moral development research. This study examined how parental conditional regard (PCR) and spiritual connectedness relate to traditional and more controversial moral dilemmas. Participants (n=100, 18-23 years) made judgments on traditional and controversial moral dilemmas. PCR was significantly correlated with higher approval of the controversial acts. Spiritual connectedness was significantly correlated with intrinsic motivation to act morally. This study shows that internal thoughts and personal choices relate to morality and emphasize the importance of investigating individuals' conflicting beliefs regarding the nature of morality.

Knowledge of dementia and the image of elderly people

Kuze, Junko Handa Campus, Nihon Fukushi University, Handa, Japan *Okumura, Yumiko* Health and Welfare, Kawasaki Uni of Medical Welfar, Kurashiki, Japan

Purpose: Knowledge about elderly people affects their image. Relationship between knowledge of dementia and the image of elderly people was examined. Method: A test consisting of 10 items about dementia was administered to university students. According to the score, participants were divided into three groups: "Low", "Average", and "High". Result: The image of healthy elderly people and that of elderly people with dementia were compared among the three groups. Both images showed differences among groups. Conclusion: Knowledge of dementia has an effect not only on the image of elderly people with dementia but also on that of healthy elderly people.

Their stories: Group counseling with ten woman of substance use

Lang, Ya-Chin Counseling Center, Da-Yeh University, Changhwa, Taiwan

The 10 women in this study were prisoners in a jail and all of them were charged for substance use, and other charges were added for some of them. The main purpose of this 10-session group counseling is to help them review their relationship with men because some of them were battered or mistreated by their partners or husbands before. The researcher expected to let the participants realize their rights and regain their confidence and self-esteem. Narrative techniques and psychodrama will be used in this study. Self report and evaluation will be the

research method. The entire program will be finished by the end of December 2007.

Educational technology: Graduation and research

Lange, Elaine Dept. of Psychology, Universidade São Francisco, Ribeirão Pires- SP, Brazil *Pazzinato, Patrícia* Dept. of Psychology, Universidade São Francisco, São Paulo, Brazil

This study focalized educational practices on the pychological graduation, considering the social community around the university. The methods used were: needs raising of the differents ages inhabitants, culture and behaviour diversity, and social relationship. The projetc's paper offers organization data of the period of probation and academic activities, social and educational interference of the University within the community, development of interventive research, production of multidiscipline knowledge and group behaviour, variable of health raise. It was based on the humanitarian values: dignity, social compromise, respect for economic and cultural differences, ethics. It also contributed for human colective development, new parameters of research and elaboration of health politics.

Physical and psychological stressors differently affect the level of interleukin-2 in the brain

Lee, Yen-Ti Institute of Behavioral Medici, Cheng Kung University, Tai-Chung City, Taiwan *Wang, An-Li* Department of Life Sciences, National Chung Hsing Universit, Tai-Chung City, Taiwan *Wu, Yu-Han* School of Medical Laboratory, Chung Shan Medical University, Tai-Chung City, Taiwan *Fan, Chuen-Hui* School of Medical Laboratory, Chung Shan Medical University, Tai-Chung City, Taiwan *Pawlak, Cornelius R* Psychopharmacology, Central Institute of Mental He, Mannheim, Germany *Ho, Ying-Jui* School of Psychology, Chung Shan Medical University, Tai-Chung City, Taiwan

This study detected the effects of physical and psychological stressors on the levels of interleukin-2 (IL-2) in the rat brain. A two-day session of inescapable and escapable conditioning was administered for inducing psychological and physical stressors, respectively. IL-2 level in the prefrontal cortex and hippocampus was decreased when the rats encountered physical and psychological stressors simultaneously. All the physical, psychological, and the combination of theses two stressors were able to reduce the IL-2 level in the amygdala and cerebral cortex. Acute physical stress caused the reduction of IL-2 in the pituitary gland. These results showed that physical and psychological stressors differently affect the IL-2 levels in the brain.

Classroom climate, future perspective, and academic outcomes of secondary students

Legault, Frederic Special Education, UQAM, Montreal, Canada *Bourque, Isabelle* Special Education, UQAM, Montreal, Canada *Houle, Dominique* Special Education, UQAM, Montreal, Canada

Past research has provided support for the influence of perceived classroom climate on academic outcomes. More recently, some authors have studied the role of future perspective on these outcomes. The main objective of the present research was to evaluate the mediating role of future perspective on the relation between classrooom climate, motivational beliefs and academic engagement. Perceptions of 352 7th and 8th grade students were collected in their classrooms. Regression analyses showed that authoritative climate beared the highest correlations with academic outcomes, followed by authoritarian, and conflictual/disorganized climates. The mediating effect of future perspective was observed with authoritarian classrooms only.

Prospective memory and job instability: Their relationship in an Argentinean employees sample

Leibovich de Figueroa, Nora Instituto de Investigaciones, CONICET - F. Psicología, UBA, Buenos Aires, Argentina Injoque-Ricle, Irene Instituto de Investigaciones, CONICET - F. Psicología, UBA, Ciudad de Buenos Aires, Argentina Wilson, Maximiliano Instituto de Investigaciones, CONICET - F. Psicología, UBA, Ciudad de Buenos Aires, Argentina

Objectives. To study the relationship between job instability (JI) and prospective memory (PM) and to describe subject's characteristics by occupational adjustment. Methods. A PM task, an IL questionnaire (IMPIL) and the OSI were administered to 46 employees from Buenos Aires, Argentina. Pearson correlations among Age, IMPIL, PM and OSI were conducted. Regression analyses were performed with PM as dependent variable and the rest as independent ones. Results. JI and Age significantly accounted for 29% of PM variation. Conclusions. Results seem to support the hypothesis that workers affected by JI have less available cognitive resources for PM tasks.

The relationship among locus of control, job search self-efficacy, job search behaviors and outcomes in China

Li, Wenxi school of psychology, Beijing Normal University, Beijing, People's Republic of China Hou, Zhijin school of psychology, Beijing Normal University, Beijing, People's Republic of China

The purpose of this study was to examine the relationship among locus of control, job search self-efficacy, job search behaviors (informal and formal sources, job search intensity, and job search effort) and outcomes (job interviews, job offers, and employment status) in China. Questionnaires were used among a sample of 287 senior students. It was found that the relationships among locus of control, job search behaviors, and job search outcomes were vague. In addition, job search self-efficacy and job interviews can predict job offers. The implications of these results are discussed on the basis of Chinese labor market.

Conditions of disjuction effect

Li, Yanmei Institute of Psychology, Chinese Academy of Sciences, Beijing, People's Republic of China Li, Shu Institute of Psychology, Chinese Academy of Sciences, Beijing, People's Republic of China Liang, Zhe Institute of Psychology, Chinese Academy of Sciences, Beijing, People's Republic of China Yu, Yao Institute of Psychology, Chinese Academy of Sciences, Beijing, People's Republic of China

One experiment investigated whether disjunction effect (violation of Savage's sure-thing principle) appears in one-shot Prisoner's Dilemma (PD) games in the domain of losses, because results of the previous studies about disjunction effect were obtained mainly in the domain of gains. In our experiment, participants took part in a one-shot PD game, in which domain (loss or gain) and certainty (opponent's choice: cooperation, competition or unknown) were manipulated. Results showed that disjunction effect is more likely to appear in the domain of gains rather than in the domain of losses. Implications are discussed.

Effects of presentation modalities on imagined object location judgment

Li, Jing Inst. of Psychology, Chinese Academy of Sciences, Beijing, People's Republic of China Zhang, Kan Institute of Psychology, Chinese Academy of Sciences, Beijing, People's Republic of China

Imagined spatial working memory formed separately by literal and pictorial presenting modalities was compared, using Franklin and Tversky's experimental pattern. The response time in pictorial maps condition was the shortest in all the experimental conditions, while the accuracy and RT were equal between the narratives and literal maps. The results indicated that besides the shape information, pure spatial information was stored as a reference frame in the visuospatial component while only the names of the objects were stored in the verbal component of the working memory. The results are somewhat different from "What" and "Where" theory of Landau and Jackendoff.

Risky choice behavior and stimulant drug

Liao, Ruey-Ming Dept. of Psychology, National Cheng-Chi University, Taipei, Taiwan Lin, Wea-Lun Department of Psychology, National Cheng-Chi University, Taipei, Taiwan Yang, Jen-Hau Department of Psychology, National Cheng-Chi University, Taipei, Taiwan Yen, Nai-Shing Department of Psychology, National Cheng-Chi University, Taipei, Taiwan

Present study using animal investigated the effect of amphetamine on risky choice. In a T-maze, a goal arm was designated as certain low reward (CLR) arm providing 1 pellet of chocolate for every entry, whereas the other was designated as probabilistic high reward (PHR) arm providing 2 (or 8) pellets of chocolate to obtain based on a probability of 50% (or 12.5%). After training, the rats significantly chose more for CLR than for PHR as risk increased. Amphetamine (1mg/kg) treatment significantly produced more PHR arm entries. These data indicate that stimulant drug can facilitate the risky choice behavior.

Tug of war between intimacy and autonomy in romantic relationship

Lin, Wei-Fang Dept. of Psychology, National Taiwan University, Taipei, Taiwan Lin, Yi-Cheng Psychology, National Taiwan University, Taipei, Taiwan Huang, Chin-Lan General Education, NTUST, Taipei, Taiwan Chuang, Yu-Ying Psychology, National Taiwan University, Taipei, Taiwan

Previous research has shown that individuals with stronger intimacy goal showed more concern for their partner when conflicts emerged and also experienced greater relationship satisfaction. However, it still remains unclear how relationships change when one's desires are incompatible with partner's expectation. This study explored the relationship between the conflict resolution strategy and adjustment in romantic relationships. Moreover, East Asian Cultures value relationship harmony, this issue especially call for an indigenous approach, which may affect how individual deal with the clash. Implications in cultural interpretation of autonomy and its effect on interpersonal relationships were also discussed.

Effects of pro-inflammatory cytokines induced by lipoposaccharide on depressive-like behavior in rats

Lin, Wenjuan Institute of Psychology, Beijing, People's Republic of China Pan, Yuqin Brain Behavior Research Center, Institute of Psychology, Beijing, People's Republic of China

To examine the role of cytokines in depression, the effect of pro-inflammatory cytokines induced by lipoposaccharide (LPS) on depressive-like behavior and the sensitization effect of pro-inflammatory cytokines on depressive-like behavior induced by chronic cold swimming stress were investigated. The behavioral observations were carried out using saccharin preference test, open field test and elevated-plus maze. Data showed that LPS i.p administration could induce significant transient depressive-like behavior; no long-term effect in behavior was found. However, the stress-induced depressive-like behaviors in rats with LPS administration could be elicited earlier and kept longer than that in rats without LPS administration.

Event-related potentials' study of uncertainty monitoring

Lin, Chongde Inst. of Developm. Psychology, Beijing Normal University, Beijing, People's Republic of China Luo, Liang Institute of Development Psych, Beijing Normal University, Beijing, People's Republic of China Hu, Qingfen Institute of Development Psych, Beijing Normal University, Beijing, People's Republic of China Chen, Guang Institute of Development Psych, Beijing Normal University, Beijing, People's Republic of China Huang, Silin Institute of Development Psych, Beijing Normal University, Beijing, People's Republic of China

New experimental task paradigm was used to explore cognitive and brain mechanisms of uncertainty monitoring. Perception group and monitoring group performed severally comparison task of black-white diamonds. The results were as follows: the reaction time of monitoring group was longer than that of perception group, and amplitude of N2 (160ms-220ms) in anterior brain area and P2 (170ms-230ms) in posterior brain area of monitoring group were larger than those of perception group, and components of ERP of monitoring group were more negative than that of perception group in anterior brain area (340ms-440ms and 440ms-540ms).

The coherence of moral thinking from developmental perspective

Lin, Hui-Tzu Psychology, Fo Guang University, Yilan, Taiwan

The purpose of present research is to investigate whether the global coherence of moral thinking is increased by age. The author utilized four moral situations to evaluate the subjects' responses to two contradictive arguments concerning behavior. The correlation of the two responses indicated the degree of coherence. Since the material should be developed differently for younger children and older subject, the author designed two studies to study two age groups; Study 1 for elementary school children, Study 2 for older subjects. Taking study 1 and study 2 into account, coherence of moral thinking is increased by age which support the implication by Piaget and Kohlberg's theoretical hypothesis.

Am I your friend depends on how I interpret secret sharing priority

Lin, Wei-Fang Dept. of Psychology, National Taiwan University, Taipei, Taiwan Lee, Yi-Chen Psychology, National Taiwan University, Taipei, Taiwan

Previous researches have shown that secret sharing helps individuals feel more intimate with friends. However, the previous result could be affected by the priority of secret sharing. This study explored the association between the friendship quality and the way individuals interpreted the priority of secret sharing. 41 participants completed a questionnaire which aimed at assessing their feelings, thoughts and friendship when they found they were not told the secret first. Results showed that individuals who viewed the priority as an index of the intimacy or importance of friends reported stronger negative impacts on friendships. Implications of interpersonal interactions were discussed.

Can anti-stigma campaigns be improved? A test of the impact of biogenetic versus psycho-social causal explanations on attitudes to schizophrenia

Lincoln, Tania Klinische Psychologie, Philipps Universität, Marburg, Germany Arens, Elisabeth Klinische Psychologie, Philipps-Universität Marburg, Marburg, Germany Berger, Cornelia Klinische Psychologie, Philipps-Universität Marburg, Marburg, Germany Rief, Winfried Klinische Psychologie, Philipps-Universität Marburg, Marburg, Germany

Existing anti-stigma campaigns emphasize the medical view of schizophrenia. This study compares the impact of biogenetic and psychosocial educational interventions on stigma in medical and psychology students (n=121). Information was presented via information brochures and video case presentation. Explicit and implicit attitudes were assessed before and after interventions. Both interventions produced a significant decrease in stereotypes, compared to a neutral condition. The biogenetic intervention decreased the attribution of blame, unpredictability and social distance but increased negative outlook on prognosis. The psychosocial intervention reduced the stereotype of dangerousness and social distance. The proposal for anti-stigma-campaigns is to take a multidimensional approach.

System and personality: Ontopsychological aspects in the education of leaders

Linde, Nina Educational Planning, Ministry of Education - Latvia, Rome, Italy *Zoppolato, Alessandro* Leadership and communication, Berlin FOIL, Rome, Germany

The leader, inended as a person who carries the responsibility for the organisation of a social sector, needs not only technical, fiscal, administrative, marketing and management skills, but also instruments to verify if her/his choices are free from forms of individual stereotypes. The authors will explain the methodological aspects of the training of the leader to increase the knowledge of the real dynamics of relationship here and now, as well as the overcoming of the non functional interpretative styles of reality. Results in entrepreneurial, political and socio-educational field will be discussed.

A longitudinal study on the relationship between children's activity and parenting

Liu, Wen Dept. of Psychology, Liaoning Normal University, Dalian, People's Republic of China *Guo, Zhifeng* Department of Psychology, Liaoning Normal University, Dalian, People's Republic of China

The purpose of this research is to explore the relationship between children's activity and parenting style by the longitudinal study. 101 children were studied by questionnair,observation,and laboratory experiment. The results showed that: 1. there existed a certain stability on children's activities; 2.there was stable gender differences in Children's activity. 3.It was transformative between parenting and devlopment of children's activity. Doting and activity which was still significantly positive correlation; and the permissive parents of children with different activity had stabilized.

Memory-based preattentional processing in visual mismatch negativity

Liu, Tongran Institute of Psychology, Chinese Academy of Sciences, Beijing, People's Republic of China *Shi, Jiannong* Institute of Psychology, Chinese Academy of Sciences, Beijing, People's Republic of China

Objectives: To investigate whether visual mismatch negativity could be evoked by different light wavelengths. Methods: We designed an oddball task, and electroencephalograms were recorded, and visual MMN and attention specific N2-P3 complex waveforms were evoked and distinguished. Results: It is indicated that visual MMN was an occipital generation component with 270-310 ms peak latency, and N2b and P3a were in 310-400 ms and 400-600 ms range, respectively. All the VMMN, N2b and P3a components were affected by the amount of deviation between the infrequent stimuli and frequent stimuli. Conclusions: The study further proofed that VMMN existed under preattentional condition.

Interactions between working memory and selective attention

Liu, Zhaomin Psychology Department, Beijing, People's Republic of China *Guo, Chunyan* Psychology Department, Capital Normal University, Beijing, People's Republic of China

Event-related potential (ERP) was used to examine the interactions between working memory and selective attention. The ERP results revealed that both congruent and incongruent stimuli in the selective attention task evoked an N400 component. The N400 evoked by incongruent stimuli was more negative than that of congruent, which indicated the difference of semantic N400. Furthermore, working memory load had a significant influence on the N400 evoked by selective attention task in parietal region. And working memory load showed difference in the ERPs of working memory retrieval in central and parietal regions.

Emotional intelligence and academic performance: An overview

Lopez Zafra, Esther Dept. of Social Psychology, Universidad de Jaén, Jaén, Spain *Jiménez, María Isabel* Social Psychology, Universidad de Jaén, Jaén, Spain *Rodríguez Espartal, Noelia* Social Psychology, Universidad de Jaén, Jaén, Spain

Our society has spread the values of productivity to educational context, and therefore, there is now a great interest in the field of Emotional Intelligence (EI). Recent studies have been conducted to explore the relationship between EI and academic performance. Results are inconsistent due to the lack of consensus on the definition, construct and methodology. This work deepens this relationship as well as the need to further investigate the mechanisms through which the skills and emotional skills affect performance. Behavioural problems reflect the growing need to implement psychosocial programs to develop skills needed to cope with the emotional demands. Finally, we propose objectives and benefits that provide such programs and action to come

The use of Freudian concept of ritual in research of drug addiction in present-day Czech society

Lorencova, Radmila FF KSV, University of Pardubice, Pardubice, Czech Republic

Abuse of psychoactive drugs is often motivated by an internal/external conflict, feelings of failure and frustration and seeking for well-being restoration. Suppressed and tabooed desires and ambitions inducing inner psychological conflict can be calmed down by therapeutic effect of ritual (Freud, 1997; Turner, 1957). From this view we can approach abuse of marijuana and alcohol, which provide quick leaving of everyday social problems and frustrations. The present study aims to show how this ritual concept approach can help us to understand motivation for drug abuse and frustration coping among young Czech addicts.

Virtual reality, computer helmet: A new coil by Vigotsky in development of human image thinking

Losik, George Lab. Identification System, Institute Information Problem, Minsk, Belarus

According to Vigotsky theorie filogenesis, ontogenesis thinking by images was supplemented with thinking by signs. Genesis of human scull volume limited further growth of cerebral cortex. Biological development was becoming impossible. While using the virtual reality helmet person get a possibility to think in computer 3D images. Thinking in images reaches a new third coil. Conclusions: in anticipation of a child's acquisition become the way to think relying on virtual reality. Prediction of image and verbal pathology phenomena is also possible. Human practical activity is going to lose its significance. Share of scholastic processes is going to become larger.

Traffic sign perception: Holistic and analytic strategies

Luna, Rafaela Psicología y Metodología, Facultad Psicología, Málaga, Spain

The aim of the present experiment is to generalize the hypothesis of global precedence to daily perceptive situations: vertical signalling perception -two traffics signs-. Participated 50 subject (24 men and 26 women), with aged between 19 and 25 years. All the statistics tests were used alpha 0.05, ANOVA for reaction time and regression logistics for accuracy. The results indicated interaction between the factors "Figure of the vertical sign" x "Element of the vertical sign" x "Colour of the vertical sign", in both dependent variables, which suggests the holistic and analytic strategies utilization in the traffic signs recognition.

Work in the Chinese restaurants: A qualitative research

Lung, Tzyy-Jiun Dept. International Business, Hsuan Chuang University, Hsinchu, Taiwan

Before the globalization of McDonald, Chinese restaurants are already well-known in the world. In our research, we interviewed the workers of 3 Chinese restaurants. We found firstly, through the blood and family, they made the relationship between their personal needs and the objectives of organization; secondly, instead of specialization or formalization of works, they always spent their time to share their experience and knowledge to each other; and thirdly, in the restaurants, they tried to substitute customized and varied products for speed, because they hoped their customers could eat delicious and health food.

Interactions between spatial working memory and delayed interval interference task

Luo, Liang Inst. of Develop. Psychology, Beijing Normal University, Beijing, People's Republic of China *Lin, Chongde* Institute of Development Psych, Beijing Normal University, Beijing, People's Republic of China *Hu, Qingfen* Institute of Development Psych, Beijing Normal University, Beijing, People's Republic of China *Chen, Guang* Institute of Development Psych, Beijing Normal University, Beijing, People's Republic of China *Huang, Silin* Institute of Development Psych, Beijing Normal University, Beijing, People's Republic of China

By event-related potential, we investigated interaction between spatial working memory and delayed interval interference task. Results were as follows: (1) P1 and N1 amplitudes in interference task in occipital lobe were larger in the congruent condition than in the incongruent condition. Compared to occipital lobe, the P1 and N1 amplitudes of both conditions in parietal lobe showed different trend. (2) P1 and N1 amplitudes in occipital lobe were larger in positive memory probe trials than in negative memory probe trials. Compared to occipital lobe, the P1 and N1 amplitudes of both memory probe conditions in parietal lobe showed different trend.

The effect of emotional contents on belief bias in category syllogism reasoning

Luo, Rufan Dept. of Psychology, Peking University, Beijing, People's Republic of China *Su, Yanjie* Department of Psychology, Peking University, Beijing, People's Republic of China

This study investigated the belief-bias effect in syllogistic reasoning contained emotional and neutral materials, and explored the cause of belief-bias effect in reasoning about emotional syllogisms. The syllogistic evaluation task and the children's gambling task were used with 163 children to test reasoning ability and executive function. The results indicated that children showed weaker belief bias in emotional condition than in neutral condition. Children with better executive function had stronger ability to overcome the belief bias in emotional condition. The results suggested that belief-bias effect was existed in emotion reasoning, and might be caused by deficiency of inhibitory ability.

The compiling of faking detection scale in occupational selection situations

Luo, Fang School of Psychology, Beijing Normal University, Beijing, People's Republic of China
The use of personality test becomes more and more popular in Chinese Occupational Selection Situations. However, its validity is challenged due to fake answers. The most commonly used method dealing with faking is to employ social desirability scale measure faking for controlling exaggerated scores or detecting faking candidates. However, SD Scale is unfit for measuring faking. Based on the special character of faking, this research developed "Faking Detection Scale". The scale is effective to identify faking candidates. However, there is a dilemma as to the setting of the cut-off score. Setting up higher cut-off score is suggested.

Executive cognitive functioning and reward sensitivity in relation to alcohol consumption by university undergraduates

Lyvers, Michael Psychology, Bond University, Gold Coast, Australia Czerczyk, Cameron Psychology, Bond University, Gold Coast, Australia Follent, Anna Psychology, Bond University, Gold Coast, Australia Lodge, Phoebe Psychology, Bond University, Gold Coast, Australia
Undergraduates were administered the Alcohol Use Disorders Identification Test (AUDIT), Frontal Systems Behavior Scale (FrSBe), Sensitivity to Punishment and Reward Questionnaire (SPSRQ) and Wisconsin Card Sorting Test (WCST). AUDIT scores were correlated with total FrSBe scores and Disinhibition subscale. SPSRQ Reward Sensitivity scores were negatively correlated with age at onset of regular drinking. High risk drinkers had higher FrSBe, Disinhibition, Executive Dysfunction, and Reward scores than low risk drinkers, and made more WCST failures to maintain set. Findings show associations between indices of prefrontal cortex dysfunction and alcohol consumption, suggestive of traits that predispose to heavy drinking.

Cognitive-behavioral group-therapy for smoking cessation

Mühlig, Stephan Inst. Klinische Psychologie, Tech. Universität Chemnitz, Chemnitz, Germany
Aim of the study was to evaluate the efficacy and acceptance of a group-based behavioural-therapy for smoking cessation. A sample of 95 female and male smokers with different degrees of tobacco-addiction measured with DSM-IV and the "Fagerström-Test for Nicotine-Dependence", was repeatedly assessed for post-treatment smoking status and relapse during a period of 6 months. Using a One-Group-Design the participants smoking status was obtained by self reports. An intent-to-treat approach showed an abstinence rate of 72,6% at the end of the intervention decreasing to 35,7% after 6 month, indicating that this programme performs well compared to already existing ones.

AktivA: A social-cognitive group program to improve health for long-term unemployed

Mühlpfordt, Susann Arbeits- und Org.-Psychologie, Technische Universität Dresden, Dresden, Germany Rothländer, Katrin Arbeits- und Organisationspsy, Technische Universität Dresden, Dresden, Germany
In a follow-up to a study from 2007 we tested whether a socio-cognitive training program, aiming to assist long-term unemployed persons, leads to a reduction in health complaints and an improvement in social-support, self-efficacy, and personal initiative. The program, 24 hours long, provides training in planning balanced activities, cognitive restructuring, social competence, and problem solving. A sample of 200 long-term unemployed persons

responded to a questionnaire at three different points of measurement: before, immediately after, and three month following the training. A pilot-study showed significant positive effects for the treatment-group –but not for the control- group.

Recognition memory in Parkinsons disease without dementia: Research implications

Maranon, Daniel Dept. of Psychology, University of Deusto, Bilbao, Spain Amayra, Imanol Psychology, University of Deusto, Bilbao, Spain Martinez, Silvia Psychology, University of Deusto, Bilbao, Spain Uterga, Juna Maria Neurology, Basurto Hospital, Bilbao, Spain
Recent findings suggest that Parkinsons disease (PD) patients exhibit deficits in recognition memory. Thirty nondemented patients and thirty controls were evaluated with the California Verbal Learning Test (Spanish version). The groups did not differ in recognition memory scores and they did not show any relationship between recognition and disease severity. However, PD group performed significantly worse than controls on false positive errors and discriminability. Both measures were predicted by processing speed and verbal fluency. These results revealed that we will find recognition memory impairment depending on the performance of the clinical sample in processing speed and executive function measures.

Do what you want or do what fits best?: Job and academic outcomes related to congruence with overt vocational preferences versus covert RIASEC interests

Marcus, Bernd Inst. für Psychologie (I/O), Fern Universität Hagen, Hagen, Germany Wagner, Uwe Psychology, Chemnitz U of Technology, Chemnitz, Germany Kitunen, Michelle Rae Psychology, University of Western Ontario, London, ON, Canada
Two studies related Holland's (1997) RIASEC vocational interests and conscious vocational preferences with job and academic outcomes (e.g., job performance, counterproductive behavior, job satisfaction, grades). In study 1 (272 German job apprentices), congruence with overt preference accounted for incremental variance beyond RIASEC congruence in five out of six criteria, whereas subjective and objective RIASEC congruence each were incrementally valid for only one criterion. Study 2, using a predictive design, largely replicated these findings in an academic setting in Canada (N = 81). These results point to the previously overlooked relevance of conscious vocational preferences for career counseling and applicant selection.

Evaluation of a self-instructional manual to teach instructors to conduct discrete-trials teaching to children with autism

Martin, Garry St. Paul's College, University of Manitoba, Winnipeg, Canada Arnal, Lindsay St. Paul's College, University of Manitoba, Winnipeg, Canada Thiessen, Carly St. Paul's College, University of Manitoba, Winnipeg, Canada Fazzio, Daniela St. Paul's College, University of Manitoba, Winnipeg, Canada Yu, Dickie St. Paul's College, University of Manitoba, Winnipeg, Canada
Early intensive behavioral intervention based on Applied Behavior Analysis (ABA) is the most effective treatment for children with autism. An essential component of ABA programs is Discrete-Trials Teaching (DTT). In Experiment 1 we developed and field tested a self-instructional manual for DTT with university students teaching confederates role-playing children with autism. Based on Experiment 1, we revised the manual, and replicated the study, and assessed generalization of DTT to a child with autism. Results indicate that the changes in the manual resulted in marked improvement in participants' post-manual DTT performance from Experiment 1 to Experi-

ment 2, with good inter-observer agreement, treatment integrity, and social validity results.

Investigation of behavioral inhibition in association with maternal psychopathology and self regulation in toddlers

Martini, Julia Technische Universität Dresden, Dresden, Germany Junge-Hoffmeister, Juliane TU Dresden, Inst. of Clinical Psychology, Dresden, Germany
Objectives: The aim is an assessment of the temperamental factor Behavioral Inhibition (BI) and the investigation of associations to early regulation disorders. Additionally, maternal factors, which may have an impact on the children's temperament, are examined. Methods: Based on the behavior observation paradigm of Kagan & Snidman (1991), the temperament is assessed in 30 toddlers. An interview with the mothers is used to clarify potential associations with maternal factors (e.g., maternal psychopathology during pregnancy, maternal BI) and early regulation disorders (e.g., excessive crying, sleep disorders, feeding disorders). Results: Results and implications for diagnostics and early preventative interventions will be presented.

Confirmation bias revisited: Prior belief influences the evaluation of research findings and explanations (whether explanations are present or not)

Masnick, Amy Psychology, Hofstra University, Hempstead, USA Zimmerman, Corinne Psychology, Illinois State University, Normal, USA
We examined two factors that could influence evaluation of research findings: having one's belief confirmed or disconfirmed by evidence, and presence/absence of an explanation for the findings. Participants (n=273) expressed a belief about a study's outcome before reading a research report. When belief was confirmed, the study's methodology was subsequently evaluated more positively, and findings were rated as more obvious, credible, interesting and important (p's < .05). Interestingly, when belief was confirmed, evaluations of the explanation's adequacy were higher, regardless of whether an explanation was actually present. Prior belief strongly influences the process of evaluating research findings (and explanations).

Attitudes of Italians toward African immigrants: Ingroup favoritism and acculturation process

Matera, Camilla Psychology, University of Florence, Firenze, Italy Stefanile, Cristina Psychology, University of Florence, Firenze, Italy
Intergroup bias, defined as the systematic tendency to evaluate the in-group more favorably than the out-group, was studied in reference to the acculturation process in Italy. Host community members (N=180) completed a questionnaire in which their attitude toward African immigrants was assessed, together with other variables. Hierarchical multiple regression showed the success of national identity, feeling of security as an Italian and acculturation attitude predicting in-group favoritism. This was confirmed for each of the acculturation attitudes considered (integration, integration with transformation, assimilation, exclusion, segregation and individualism). The study provides useful indications for intergroup bias reduction in inter-ethnic contexts.

Researching peer bullying in Brazilian basic schools

Matos Coelho, Maria Inês Mestrado em Educação, UEMG, Belo Horizonte, Brazil Araujo, Frederico Antônio Mestrado em Educação, UEMG, Belo Horizonte, Brazil
The present poster describe a methodology of researching manifestations of violence among school peers in the first part of basic education, in

the brazilian context. The peer bulling is defined as a kind of violence at school that has been analysed both as a consequence of a set of inadequate school practices, and as one of the aspects that characterizes the contemporary society, particularly, a socialization marked by aggressions and petty crimes. We analysed how the ethnography approach is basis to design a questionnaire using a set images of different peer bullying scenes and objective questions directed to children.

Disabled students' experiences of higher education in Japan
Matsubara, Takashi Dept. of Human Sciences, Osaka University, Osaka, Japan Atsumi, Tomohide CSCD, Osaka University, Suita city, Osaka, Japan

This study examined how disabled students experience higher education in Japan. Recent statistics showed they had a greater presence in higher education. But it is still unclear how they experienced these provisions, especially from their own perspectives. Hence, we conducted interviews to five disabled students in Osaka University. Interview data were analyzed by KJ method (Kawakita, 1967), in consultation with interviewees. Then, we extracted three categories from interview data; identity, education and equal opportunity. Consequently, we indicated that disabled students were forced to narrate the barriers by individualized and medical terms within the context of education that sights on individual students, though those barriers were structural in nature.

Development of a job-hunting anxiety scale for college students
Matsuda, Yuko Comprehensive Human Sciences, Tsukuba University, Tsukuba, Japan

The purpose of the study was to construct a scale to assess the job-hunting anxiety and to examine the relation between job-hunting anxiety and indicators of concurrent validity such as "a lack of information and confidence," and state anxiety. Questionnaires were completed by 288 Japanese college students who have started job-hunting. Explorative factor analysis extracted five factors such as "appeal anxiety," "a lack of readiness anxiety," "test anxiety," "activity persistence anxiety," and "support anxiety". Correlational analysis confirmed sufficient concurrent validity. These results suggested that job-hunting anxiety may be controlled by providing information about job and self.

Conceptual versus perceptual influences in picture detection
Matsukawa, Junko Dep. of Psychology, Kanazawa University, Kanazawa, Japan

Participants detected a target from picture stimuli containing natural or artificial common objects. The target and the other stimuli were from the same category, either natural or artificial, in the congruent condition, and were from the different category in the incongruent condition. The shape of the target was similar to or different from those of other stimuli on both conditions. The results showed that targets were detected more quickly in the incongruent than the congruent condition and were detected more quickly in the different-shape than the similar-shape condition, indicating the interference effects of semantic and perceptual contexts in picture detection.

The international communication of Japanese and Chinese in a 3D online virtual space: The effects of conversation topics and avatar costumes
Matsuo, Yumi Kasiwa, Japan Sakamoto, Akira Letters and Education, Ochanomizu University, Tokyo, Japan

In this study, Japanese students communicated with Chinese confederates at "Second Life". And they talked about personal topics or cultural topics while their avatar (i.e., a vicarious agent) wore native

dress or daily cloths. Their feelings toward the partner such as trust and their attitudes toward Chinese people were measured. Results revealed that participants who talked about personal topics more greatly trusted their partner when they wore native dress than daily cloths. No such effect was indicated when they talked about cultural topics. In addition, the results also indicated that Japanese attitudes toward Chinese were improved after experiencing that communication.

Communication as an important factor for the establishment of fairness in small groups
May, Mareike Osnabrück, Germany

Which conditions are necessary for the establishment of fairness in a small group? To answer this question 120 participants took part in a social exchange experiment. Each group consisted of three players communicating by means of a computer network. The communication groups exchanged both money and messages. In the control groups only money could be transfered. After the experiment all participants received the amount of money earned by their group members during the session. The results show no significant differences in the outcomes of the communication groups because of the establishment of fairness strategies.

Pathological buying: An internet survey in a German sample
Meiners, Sinje Münster, Germany de Jong-Meyer, Renate Klinische Psychologie, Universität Münster, Münster, Germany Bohne, Antje Klinische Psychologie, Universität Münster, Münster, Germany

Objective: Assessment of pathological buying and related syndromes including the validation of pathological buying questionnaires. Method: Internet survey with German versions of compulsive buying questionnaires (e.g., Compulsive Buying Scale, Compulsive Acquisition Scale), depression, anxiety, impulsivity, and obsessive-compulsive symptom measures as well as DSM-IV-based screenings for differential diagnoses. Results: Data of more than 500 participants (80% female, age: M = 26.6) have been collected. Data collection is still in progress. Conclusion: The results will contribute to the understanding of pathological buying and its relation to co-occurring syndromes.

Lightness estimation in real 3D scene
Menshikova, Galina Dept. of Psychology, Moscow State University, Moscow, Russia

We investigated the role of perceived illumination (PI) in lightness (L) estimation in real 3D scene. According to albedo hypothesis PI and L are coupled and their correlation depends on a perceived slant of a surface. Twelve observers viewed pictures attached to a surface perceived as convex or concave depending on conditions of viewing: through the pseudoscope or without it. Lightness illusions (LI) were used as pictures. Observers matched patches from pictures and Muncell neutral scale in lightness. The expression of LI (ELI) was measured for both conditions. Changes in ELI could be explained in accordance with albedo hypothesis.

Object substitution masking affects the visibility of equiluminant coloured stimuli
Mereu, Stefania Dipartimento di Psicologia, Universita di Roma, Roma, Italy Casagrande, Maria Dipartimento di Psicologia, "Sapienza" Università, Roma, Italy Caldarola, Sabrina Dipartimento di Psicologia, "Sapienza" Università, Roma, Italy Martella, Diana Dipartimento di Psicologia, "Sapienza" Università, Roma, Italy Marotta, Andrea Dipartimento di Psicologia, "Sapienza" Università, Roma, Italy Martelli, Marialuisa Dipartimento di Psicologia, "Sapienza" Università, Roma, Italy

In object substitution masking (OSM) a target becomes inaccessible to consciousness when a

lateral mask stays on the screen after it disappears. Similarity between target and distractors along certain properties, seems to affect this effect. Particularly, the role of inhomogeneous colours between target and distractors in modulating OSM is debated. This study was aimed to evaluate the magnitude of OSM on isoluminant stimuli in both colour and letter identification. Results show high individual variability on target detectability and the same amount of OSM on both color and letter identification tasks, suggesting that it affects feature binding as much as feature detection.

A dynamic 4-dot mask: The size of masking on coloured stimuli
Mereu, Stefania Dipartimento di Psicologia, Universita di Roma, Roma, Italy Casagrande, Maria Dipartimento di Psicologia, "Sapienza" Università, Roma, Italy

The visibility of a target is reduced when a lateral mask remains on the display after the target disappears. This effect seems to be independent of the image-level characteristics of the stimulus. This study would verify the efficacy of a 4-dot masking, in which an apparent motion illusion is added on coloured stimuli otherwise difficult to mask. Both localization and colour identification tasks are assessed, in both masked and unmasked conditions. Results show the efficacy of this dynamic masking on coloured stimuli, and seem to confirm the independence of 4-dot masking from the visual characteristics of stimuli.

Understanding motivational predictors in severely obese people
Mestre, Sonia Det. of Health Psychology, Psychology University, S. João da Talha, Portugal Pais Ribeiro, Jose Health Psychology, FPCE-UP, Porto, Portugal

In accordance with Self-Determination Theory and Regulatory Focus Theory, this study provides a comprehensive relationship between motivational regulations (autonomous and controlled), perceived competence and motivational focus (promotion and prevention). Participants were 30 severely obese individuals who enrolled in a weight loss program at a community hospital. SPSS analyses revealed that controlled motivation was associated with promotion focus, while prevention focus was correlated with greater feelings about behaving in healthy way. Furthermore, body mass index revealed negative association with autonomous motivation. Results indicate that two different theories can provide researchers new tools to better understand motivated behavior in obese people.

Psychological education in Russia: Student's ideas (knowledge, responsibilities) about future profession correspond with reality
Mileshkina, Yulia Dept. of Psychology, St. Petersburg State Univer., St. Petersburg, Russia Manichev, Sergey S.

The purpose: understand differences between system of psychological education and needs of practice in Russia. Psychological education does not meet needs of practice. A method: the questionnaire Job analysis of psychologists. Sample: professional psychologists (241), students (91). The statistical analysis data was compared by criterion Mann-Whitney U. Significant differences on frequency of occurrence of responsibilities are revealed on 19 responsibilities. As a whole in representations of students the most rare responsibilities (supervision colleagues etc) meet more often, than at experts. The insignificant quantities of differences on content areas are revealed in all areas, except for area - Ethical problems.

A study of validating creative climate questionnaire

Min, Ji-Yeon Seoul National University, Seoul, Republic of Korea Seo, Eun-Jin

A study is to develop CCQ(Creative Climate Questionnaire) which is valid and reliable as a norm of evaluating the elementary school classroom environment and to examine the relationship among creative thinking, personality and motivation. It included 266 elementary 6th grade students by conducting CCQ through exploratory factor analysis and reliability analysis. It shows that the CCQ was a valid and reliable Questionnaire. The names of CCQ's sub-factors are Support, Trust, Tension, Playfulness, Conflict, Challenge and Communication. And there were significant correlations among creative thinking, personality and motivation. Especially, creative motivation was influenced more by the environment.

Oscillatory-field computer modeling of perception and consciousness

Miroshnikov, Sergey Psychology Faculty, St.Petersburg State University, Saint-Petersburg, Russia

The proposed model of perception and consciousness is programmed as the system of auto-oscillatory elements cooperating through the uniform field. They are able to play different information-processing functions (sensory, memory, motor) and to self-organize dynamical relations through the field, creating classical cycles of informational synthesis of the sensory and memory content. Analogical experiments on model and man reveal analogies in reflecting stimuli: specific role of subliminal perception; stochastic misrecognizing; stochastic normal distribution of the response time; interferential, stroboscopic effects, priming effect and other features of perception. The conclusion is that the model reflects specific laws and mechanisms of human perception.

Stress and coping among Malaysian university students

Mohd Zaharim, Norzarina School of Social Sciences, Universiti Sains Malaysia, Malaysia

The study explored common stressors facing multicultural Malaysian university students (N = 380, mean age = 21.63) and their coping strategies. The most common coping strategies were direct problem solving, avoidance, cognitive shift, social problem solving, and social support. Coping strategy affected coping outcome and was predicted by stressor, race, general self-efficacy, and religiosity but not by sex and optimism. Religious coping was frequently used; it was predicted by religiosity and general self-efficacy but not by stressor, sex, race and optimism. Based on these findings, a stress-and-coping model was built. Cultural contexts for Malaysian students facing stress were examined.

Impact of age of onset of cigarette smoking on heavy drug use.

Mohtasham Amiri, Zahra Community Medicine, Guilan University, Rasht, Islamic Republic of Iran Khasteganan, Nooshin Community Medicine, Forsat quit addiction clinic, Rasht, Islamic Republic of Iran

Objective: the study presents data about age of onset of cigarette smoking and its association with later heavy drug use. Methods: A diverse sample of 388 drug addicts was investigated at a quit addict clinic in north of Iran.Data were obtained from on site confidential interviews. AResults: Opium and cannabis were used more than other drugs, respectively 51.3 and 31.7 percent. 67.5% patients were on methadone maintenance. Heavy use of substances is associated with use of cigarettes before 18 (OR = 1.6, CI: 1.3 – 1.9). Conclusion: Early onset of cigarette smoking users shows increasing probabilities of heavy drug use patterns.

Emotional intelligence and social-emotional learning program in schools

Mokhtaripour, Marzieh Education, University of Isfahan, Isfahan, Islamic Republic of Iran Seyed Ali Education, University of Isfahan, Isfahan, Islamic Republic of Iran

Nowadays emotional intelligence has basic role in human interactions is effective in activities related to home,school, employment and other situations. Therefore it is not surprising if we claim that schools can take into account as centres for fostering of emotional intelligence schools are first social places thet can reform shortages of childs in emotions and social interactions. Therefore schools are face challenges to educate and reform emotional skills of childs. This challenges can disappear replacement and eliminating existing ambiguities concerning emotions through administering education standardized programs that cause to foster and evolution emotional skills and their correct application.In this article will be stated emotional intellignece and social-emotional learning program educational applications.

The paradigm of preattention: A new method to study the effects of preattentional processing of grouped patterns on selective attention

Montoro, Pedro R. Dept. of Basic Psychology 1, UNED, Madrid, Spain Luna, Dolores Dept. of Basic Psychology 1, UNED, Madrid, Spain

Our aim was to study the effect of preattentional grouping on selective attention by means of a new task called Paradigm of Preattention. This task is composed of two sequential stages: (1) preexposure of grouped patterns concurrent with a demanding rapid visual series presentation, and, (2) an identification or visual search tasks involving grouped patterns. The results showed that preattentional grouping can enhance or interfere subsequent attentional task depending on the preexposure duration of grouped patterns. Grouped patterns can be processed without attention and influence selective attention as a function of the temporal course of preattentional processes.

A differential approach to prejudice and the religious beliefs and practices of Islam and Christianity

Moral Toranzo, Felix Facultad de Psicologia, Universidad de Malaga, Málaga, Spain Nunez-Alarcon, Maximo Social Psychology, Malaga University, Malaga, Spain Moreno-Jiménez, Pilar Social Psychology, Malaga University, Malaga, Spain

The objectives of this research were: validate prejudice scales in the Spanish context, analyze the correlations between different measures of prejudice, and know the relationships between the religious beliefs and practices and the prejudice toward people of a different religion. We have analyzed two samples both Muslim (N=210) and Christian (N=244) samples. The variables analyzed: beliefs, anti-immigrants and pro-immigrants judgments, emotions, discrimination, favorability, linking, internal and external motivation to respond without prejudice. Our results show that there isn't a high level of prejudice in these groups. The study suggests that there is a correlation between Islam and some to measures of prejudice.

Values system and ethical position as determinants of prosocial behaviour

Moreno, José Eduardo CIIPME, CONICET, Buenos Aires, Argentina Regner, Evangelina Raquel CIIPME, CONICET, Buenos Aires, Argentina

The main objective of this paper was to evaluate the influence of the Values System and Ethical Positions (absolutism and relativism) on Prosocial Behaviour. The participants were 700 young adults ranging in age from 18 to 30 years old, from both sexes. It was administered the following tests: Values Survey (Rokeach), Ethical Positions Questionnaire (Forsyth) and Prosocial Behaviour Scale (Caprara et al.). It was determined by regression analyses the values and ethical positions that influence positively and negatively, or not, on prosocialness, helpfulness, sharing, consoling, supportiveness, and cooperativeness. Besides, the values profile of relativistic and absolutists young adults were compared.

No category-specificity in Alzheimer's disease: An exaggerated normal aging effect

Moreno-Martínez, F. Javier Psicología Básica I, U.N.E.D., Madrid, Spain Laws, Keith R. School of Psychology, University of Hertfordshire, Hatfield, United Kingdom Goñi-Imízcoz, Miguel Servicio de Neurología, Hospital Divino Vallés, Burgos, Spain Moriano-León, Silvia Pediatría, Hospital Universitario La Paz, Madrid, Spain

Objective: Does Alzheimer's disease (AD) differentially affect semantic domains? The great variability across studies has been attributed to a failure to control for intrinsic variables and the issue of ceiling effects in control data. Methods: We examined category effects on tasks of picture naming, naming to definition and word-picture matching in 38 AD patients and 30 healthy controls. Results: AD patients showed a profound semantic impairment on all three semantic tasks, but we did not observe any evidence of a category-specific effect. Conclusions: Our results suggest that the category effect is not influenced by intrinsic variables, but is largely an exaggeration of the normal healthy elderly semantic processing.

Longitudinal patterns of semantic fluency impairment in dementia: A role for "nuisance variables"

Moreno-Martínez, F. Javier Psicología Básica I, U.N.E.D., Madrid, Spain R Laws, Keith School of Psychology, University of Hertfordshire, Hatfield, United Kingdom R Montoro, Pedro Psicología Básica I, U.N.E.D., Madrid, Spain

Objective: A strongly debated subject in Cognitive Neuropsychology arena is the possible occurrence of domain-specific semantic impairments in Alzheimer disease (AD) patients. Methods: We present longitudinal fluency data in 9 AD patients and 9 healthy controls evaluated in 14 semantic categories. Results: As expected, AD patients showed a profound semantic fluency impairment that gradually increased. We found no evidence of a domain effect (living-nonliving), but intrinsic variables (i.e. name agreement, familiarity) did affect fluency. Conclusions: Our results suggest an important role for intrinsic variables in contrast with the role of the semantic domain (living-nonliving).

Change of fixation point during Gestalt collapse of Chinese character

Mori, Terunori Engineering Dept., Tamagawa University, Machida, Japan

The eye movement during Gestalt collapse was measured in order to investigate the relation between the fixation point and the object recognition. The time when the Gestalt collapse happened, the first saccade time after stimulus presentation and the fixation point are measured. Result shows that the fixation point moved from the center of Chinese character to the center of a part consisting the character at 8.4±2.8sec before subject becomes aware the Gestalt collapse. The result seems to support the hypothesis that subject recognizes the object putting the fixation point on the center of selected object area.

Conformity among cowitnesses sharing same or different information about an event in experimental collaborative eyewitness testimony

Mori, Hideko Dept. of Nursery, Bunka Womens University, Nagano, Japan *Mori, Kazuo* Inst. of Symbiotec Science, Tokyo University, Tokyo, Japan

Using the MORI technique (Mori, 2003), in which two different movies presented on the same screen are viewed separately by two groups without them noticing the duality, two experiments were carried out with a total of 138 undergraduates in groups of varying sizes to examine the effects of co-witnesses with the same or different information on witnesses' memory distortion. Experiment 1 investigated the co-witness effects in a one-versus-two situation, while Experiment 2 investigated the effects in a two-versus-two situation. Results showed that isolated eyewitnesses who had no supporting co-witnesses changed their minds more frequently in accordance with the majority, and when they had a co-witness who shared the same information, they tended to stick to their original reports even after being confronted with conflicting information in a discussion.

The relationship between stress and intervening variables for Japanese workers

Morishita, Takaharu Psychology, Tezukayama University, Nara, Japan

This study was undertaken to explore the problems of stress on Japanese Workers. We have strain as a dependent variable and Stressor as a independent variable, and have intervening variable that enter into relation between both variables. What relationship are found in their coping behavior, social support from leader or co-worker an intervening variables? Coping behavior is 3 types, active, passive, emotional coping type. Social support is 2 types, emotional and instrumental type. S's are office holders and company's workers.

Examination of relationship among negative rumination, interpersonal stress-coping, and depression in undergraduates, using a month longitudinal data

Moriwaki, Aiko Teikyo University, Tokyo, Japan

The purpose of the study was to examine relationship among negative rumination, interpersonal stress-coping, and depression, using a month longitudinal data. 162 undergraduates completed negative rumination scale and Interpersonal Stress-Coping Inventory(ISI). ISI includes positive relationship-oriented strategies(PRS), negative relationship-oriented strategies(NRS), and postponed-solution coping(PSC). A month later, Self-Rating Depression Scale(SDS) was assessed. Path analyses indicated that negative rumination increases PRS and NRS, while negative rumination decreases PSC. They also indicated that PRS and NRS increases depression, while PSC decreases SDS. The findings suggest that interpersonal stress-coping have effects on depression and that interpersonal stress-coping mediates the relationship between negative rumination and depression.

Is spirituality always transcendent as is defined in psychology?

Muñoz-García, Antonio Educ. and Developm. Psychology, University of Granada, Granada, Spain

Articles, edited and authored-book, and conferences about Spirituality have increased in last years as a element with specifics characteristics separated from religion although previously was included in literature about religion and Psychology. Recent literature show that spirituality has also different and more extended meanings than religion (eg. McDonald, 2004; Paloutzian y Park, 2005). On the other hand, some of those meanings particularly, could not have the sense of transcendence or could have a limited transcendence in a traditional sense. We analyze how transcendence is present in traditional spirituality (religious) and definitions and dimensions of modern spirituality, and how this transcendence could not be the same in traditional and modern perspectives of spirituality.

Minority influence: The role of ambivalence toward the source

Mucchi-Faina, Angelica Istituzioni e Società, Università di Perugia, Perugia, Italy *Pagliaro, Stefano* Scienze Bio-Mediche, Università di Chieti-Pescara, Chieti, Italy

This study aimed at providing empirical support for the theoretical assumption, advanced by the Conversion Theory (Moscovici,1980), that minorities may indirectly influence group members by fostering ambivalent reactions toward themselves. Participants were exposed to a counter-attitudinal message advocated by a fictitious minority group. We focussed on two possible antecedents of ambivalence, consistency of the minority and personal relevance of the topic for participants. We found that ambivalence mediates the effects of the two factors on indirect influence. This study provides evidence of the importance of ambivalence in minority influence, an early assumption that still lacked in empirical support.

What is the most real for you? Predominant ontological orientations at different life stages

Mudyñ, Krzysztof Inst. Applied Psychology, Jagiellonian University, Krakow, Poland

According to the concept of ontological orientations, different people treat different things as the most real, and therefore most important. Presumably, things absorbing mostly our daily attention become a central elements of our subjective realities. Six orientations were distinguished: theoretical, economical, esthetical, social, political, and religious. To explore how they evolve along a lifespan, 1590 subjects (both gender), age 16-85, were administered RN-2002 method. They chose the most real "objects" in 58 different concept's sets. Results: in the youngest group (16-23) prevails social orientation, in the "intermediate age" (24-59) - economic, in the advanced age (60-85) - religious...

The effect of online conducted team building procedures on initial cohesion and performance of virtual teams

Muellner, Herbert confidere.at, Matzen, Austria

The aim of the study was to investigate the effect of team building procedures of exclusively online conducted kick off meetings on cohesion and group performance of virtual teams. Sixty-six ad-hoc three member groups of unacquainted and spatial separated students were randomly assigned to one of 4 experimental online conducted team building conditions. After attending the initial meeting, the groups had to accomplish a disjunctive group task via chat during a session of 25 minutes. The hierarchical analysis of variance revealed that the degree of cohesion depends on the extent the members became acquainted by virtual communication but teams with a medium degree of cohesion achieved the best group performance.

Converting of occupational stress to eustress: Role of official hierarchy

Mukherjee, Debjani Bhilai - Chattisgarh, India *Singh, Promila* Psychology, Pt.R.S.University, Bhilai - Chattisgarh, India

Occupational-stress(O.S) is perceived as threatening to the person's well-being and predictably reduces quality of work. There is also a positive side of stress, called eustress that refers to the healthy, positive, constructive outcome of stressful events and the stress response. Official hierarchy is found to play an integral role in perceptual overhauling of stress into favorable outcomes. On a sample of 400 executives from steel plants, 3x3 ANOVA was found between the variables. Findings show that O.S does affect work-involvement in an inverse manner, but top-management significantly showcased positive outcomes of stress, (F-3.59,p<.01) confirming cognitive conversion of O.S to eustress.

Secondary exposure to trauma and self reported distress among young people orphaned by AIDS

Mumah, Solomon Psychology, Kenyatta University, Nairobi, Kenya *Muga, Richard* Community Medicine, Great Lakes University, Nairobi, Kenya

The research questions were: to what extent do AIDS orphans exhibit symptoms consistent with secondary traumatic stress; and to what extent are those symptoms explained by exposure to parents' trauma, personal history of trauma, and/or gender? Respondents were orphans aged 10-18, all of whom had been involved as caregivers. Using survey research design, 86% male and 81% females were found to be experiencing emotional distress consistent with STS. Caregiver role exposure and work-related personal traumas were strongly associated with presence of STS. Evidence suggests that levels of exposure on a short-term basis may contribute more to the development of STS.

Secondary traumatic stress: The effects of orphanhood on mind, body, and soul

Mumah, Solomon Psychology, Kenyatta University, Nairobi, Kenya *Muga, Richard* Community Medicine, Great Lakes University of Kisu, Nairobi, Kenya

The study objective was to assess the prevalence and severity of secondary traumatic stress symptoms among a sample of young people orphaned by AIDS. Up to 86% male and 81% female respondents were found to be experiencing levels of emotional distress consistent with STS. Only 18% of the respondents enjoyed good quality of life, while levels of caregiver role related traumas were strongly associated with presence of those symptoms. To promote our understanding and potential to help orphans, we need further information about the process of how some orphans develop these symptoms, while others appear not to be in distress.

Children with disruptive behavior problems: Differences between subgroups on continuous performance test measures

Munkvold, Linda Faculty of Psychology, University of Bergen, Bergen, Norway *Manger, Terje*

Measures of executive function deficits, particularly response disinhibition, have been the main focus of the laboratory-based assessment inquiry into of AD/HD and oppositonal defiant disorder/conduct disorder (ODD/CD). The continuous performance test (CPT) is a widely used instrument for this purpose, but its utility for distinguishing between sub-groups of children with disruptive behaviour problems is still unclear. The objective of this study is to compare ODD/CD-children with and without comorbid AD/HD on specific CPT-measures in a sample of 328 children (9-12 yrs old) derived from the population-based, longitudinal "Bergen Child Study" in Norway.

Luck resource belief in Asia

Murakami, Koshi Kobe Yanate University, Kobe, Japan

Our research indicates that Luck Resource Belief (Murakami, 2004), which is the tendency to perceive luck as like resources, is believed popular in Japan. In order to survey Luck Resource Belief is unique to Japan, investigation was conducted in several Asian countries by interview method. As a result, the factor of society which people are whether or not able to grasp success with effort such as more social class have influence on aspects of "luck" than religion factor.

Nationalism, patriotism and national stereotypes in Japan

Murata, Koji Dept. of Social Psychology, Hitotsubashi University, Tokyo, Japan Takabayashi, Kumiko Social Psychology, Hitotsubashi University, Tokyo, Japan Sakuma, Isao Information and Communication, Bunkyo University, Chigasaki, Japan

This study examined how patriotism and nationalism shaped national stereotypes. Patriotism represents feelings of attachment to one's country but nationalism includes feelings of superiority over others. A model of stereotype content demonstrated that we perceived stereotyped groups on warmth and competence dimensions, based on structural relations between the groups. Japanese undergraduates rated 15 national peoples on bipolar scales and responded to a measure of patriotism and nationalism. Multiple regression analyses showed that in general patriotism related to the warmth positively, but nationalism predicted the competence negatively. We discussed these effects in terms of ingroup and outgroup relationships.

Electrophysiological correlates of object and spatial memory: Dissociations and interactions

Murphy, Jonathan Dept. of Psychology, NUI Maynooth, Maynooth, Ireland Roche, Richard Psychology, NUI Maynooth, Maynooth, Ireland Commins, Sean Psychology, NUI Maynooth, Maynooth, Ireland

128-channel electroencephalography was used to record event-related potentials while participants performed an object and/or location recognition test. Using the 'Spatial Grid Task', objects were presented repeatedly in various locations during the study phase and participants were required to learn and remember each object in its specific location. In the test phase participants were instructed to respond to the object presented, its location or a combination of the two. Early results show the operation of disparate brain regions for each task as well as differences in waveform topography but areas of convergence also emerge as schemas interact.

Social selection or causation: A longitudinal assessment of social support and psychiatric symptomatology

Murray, Linda M. T. Social Work - Psychology, University of Manitoba, Winnipeg, Canada Frankel, Sid I. Social Work/Psychology, University of Manitoba, Winnipeg, Manitoba, Canada

Social support and psychiatric illness are inversely related. Social Causation and the Social Selection theoretical models explaining the relationship between social support and psychiatric symptoms are evaluated. Literature supports both opposing positions. A Reciprocal Causation Model is proposed to explain divergent findings. Social functioning variables (socioeconomic status [SES], education, income, employment, and financial adequacy perceptions) were evaluated for impact upon social support and psychiatric symptoms Response rate at Time-1 was 36%, N = 232 and was N = 146 at Time-2). Evaluation of data via path analysis using cross-lagged panel regression models demonstrated support for both Social Causation and Selection Theories, resulting in support for a type of Reciprocal Action Model.

Wanting more is not always better: Associations of goal-orientation with age, outcome vs. process focus, and subjective indicators of well-being

Mustafic, Maida Applied Psychology, University of Zurich, Zurich, Switzerland Freund, Alexandra M. Applied Psychology, University of Zurich, Zurich, Switzerland

A study of N = 136 young, middle-aged, and older adults investigated the relationship between age, goal orientation towards growth, maintenance, or prevention of loss and process versus outcome goal focus. With increasing age, adults reported a higher goal orientation towards maintenance and prevention of loss. Moreover, maintenance orientation was negatively associated with focusing on the outcome of a goal and positively associated with subjective well-being and satisfaction during goal pursuit. In contrast, goal orientation towards growth was related to higher goal concreteness and higher difficulty of goal pursuit.

The effects of social support and social control on cardiovascular reactivity during problem disclosure

Nagurney, Alexander Psychology, Texas State University, San Marcos, TX, USA Bagwell, Brandi Psychology, Texas State University, San Marcos, TX, USA

This study compared the physiological effects of social support with those of social control. In a lab setting, participants (n = 150) disclosed a relationship problem to a same-sex or opposite-sex confederate who provided either supportive or controlling feedback. Results indicated that males were more reactive in the short run to social control but demonstrated better long-term recovery from control relative to females. Those participants who were controlled by a male rather than a female confederate demonstrated a similar pattern of results. In general, males and females did not differ in terms of their reactions to receiving social support.

Attentional bias for threat in infancy

Nakagawa, Atsuko School of Humanities, Nagoya City University, Nagoya, Japan Sukigara, Masune Sch.of Humanities & Social, Nagoya City Univ., Nagoya, Japan Mizuno, Rie Dept. of Psychology, Chukyo Univ., Nagoya, Japan

The purpose of this study is to investigate the temperamental basis for a bias toward affect in attention to threat in infants of about 12 months. The experiment required to infant to disengage from a central stimulus that was either a fearful, happy, or neutral facial expression. A peripheral attractive target was presented to the right or left of the fixation stimuli. The latency to make a saccade towards a peripheral target was measured. Three conditions were examined: overlap, no-overlap, and 300-ms gap. The results will be discussed in terms of possible interactions of attention and emotion in infant development.

Is rational person fair? The ultimatum game and logical reasoning

Nakamura, Kuninori Tokyo, Japan

Previous studies reveal that people weigh fairness principle even when it prevents them from the subjective expected utility maximization. Then, one question arises: How does rational person who can solve logical tasks behave when his/her maximization of the expected utility is not compatible with social rationality? We examined this question by using ultimatum game (Guth et al, 1982) and Wason's selection task (Wason, 1966). In this study, participants answered various kinds of the selection tasks and then performed the ultimatum game. The results indicated that, regardless of the performance of the selection task, participants opted for fair allocation.

An empirical study of the developmental process of infant intersubjectivity

Nakano, Shigeru Clinical Psychology, Hokkaido Health Sciences Univ., Sapporo, Japan

It has been hypothesized that infant intersubjectivity develops from the primary intersubjectivity at 2-3 months, via engaging objects at 4-5 months, to the secondary intersubjectivity at 9-10 months. However, none of empirical studies has been done. In this longitudinal study 50 mother-infant dyads were observed from 2 weeks to 10 months of infant's age. Results showed that inter-relationships between the primary and the secondary intersubjectivity were not found, but they showed individual differences. The some infants showed preference to engaging objects from earlier months. Those results were considered as suggesting that the developmental process of intersubjectivity contains individual differences.

Relations among teacher's classroom management, classroom structure and children's multiple goals

Nakaya, Motoyuki Grad. Sch. of Human Sciences, Osaka University, Suita, Japan

In classroom settings, teacher behavior influences children's motivation and academic achievements, mediated by children's cognition of the classroom. This study examined the relations among teacher's classroom management behavior (e.g. explanation, affiliation), classroom structure (e. g. norms, commitments), and children's multiple goals (e.g. social, academic). Classroom observation and questionnaires were administered to 100 six graders and teachers in three classes. Results indicated that the relations between teacher behavior, cognition of classroom structure and children's types of goals differed for each class. The importance of social influence in children's learning processes was discussed.

Complexity matters: When natural frequencies are not enough

Navarrete, Gorka Psicologia Cognitiva, Universidad de La Laguna, La Laguna, Spain Santamaría, Carlos Psicologia Cognitiva, Universidad de La Laguna, La Laguna, Spain Orenes, Isabel Psicologia Cognitiva, Universidad de La Laguna, La Laguna, Spain

We compared performance in probabilities and natural-frequencies versions of the classical HIV diagnose problem with a modified version using even base rates (50/50). In terms of computational complexity, this modification should make comparable the difficulty of both representation formats. Indeed, although according to the Frequentists predictions the advantage of natural frequencies should withstand this slight modification of the classical paradigm, all differences between probabilities and natural frequencies disappeared. Accordingly, computational complexity should be more carefully considered as a possible explanation for the classical superiority of frequencies over probabilities.

Social support and mental health among young Eastern European migrants in Germany

Naydenova, Vihra Public Health Medicine, Universität Bielefeld, Bielefeld, Germany

Objectives and Background: Little is known about the social support and mental health of young Eastern European migrants in Germany. We examined the depressive symptoms and social support among the educational migrants in Germany. Methods: 102 Eastern European migrants and 159 Germans as control sample were surveyed using a standardized self-administered questionnaire. Results and conclusions: The prevalence of depressive symptoms in the sample was relatively high among the migrants. A significantly bigger part of the migrants showed higher clinical depression as compared to the Germans (p=.029), (29.3% in migrants and 16.5% in Germans with M-BDI score above 35). Higher depression scores were associated with little social support (p=.045).

Personality development in children that play theatre

Neagu, Diana-Elena Galati, Romania

This study focuses on the pozitive influence that theatre play as an extracurricular activity has on the development of children and adolescents. To this end we have measured by self-report scales features described in pozitive psychology as psychological well-being, self-esteem, perceived social support and self-efficacy, as well as the ability to understand oneself and the others and to express oneself. It was a longitudinal study implying over 100 subjects (ages 9-16) and it analyses the correlations between being or not a participant in theatre clubs and the development of these features. The resulted interactions have practical implications in children's education.

Empirical dissociations between hindsight components

Nestler, Steffen Psychology, University of Leipzig, Leipzig, Germany
Two studies investigated a tripartite model of the hindsight bias, involving (1) increased foreseeability impressions, (2) increased necessity impressions and (3) memory distortions. In both studies, I manipulated a third variable that should lead to an increase in necessity impressions while memory distortions should remain constant (Experiment 1), and that should influence foreseeability impressions (i.e., the event outcome is perceived as unforeseeable) but not necessity impressions (Experiment 2), respectively. The results showed the expected diverging effects on the components, and they support the idea of separate hindsight components and contradict a unitary phenomenon view of the hindsight bias.

Psychosomatics in angiocardiology

Neu, Eva Dept. Physiology, Inst. Umweltmedizin/ICSD e.V., Muenchen, Germany Martin, Daniele Dept. Physiology, Inst. Umweltmedizin/ICSD e.V., Muenchen, Germany Welscher, Ursula Dept. Physiology, Inst. Umweltmedizin/ICSD e.V., Muenchen, Germany Michailov, Michael Ch. Dept. Physiology, Inst. Umweltmedizin/ICSD e.V., Muenchen, Germany
Objectives: Cardiovascular patho-physiology implies high complex interaction of psychic, neuro-hormonal, drug-factors, leading to arrhythmia, hypertension. Method: Psychophysiological effects after psychosomatic-training [9.&8.Eur.-Congr.-Psychol., Granada/CD:3493.html/2005, ISBN:923717-6-5; Psychol.-in-Österreich 2-3/221/2003; Urol.-70/3A/232-3/2007]. Cardiovascular animal-experiments [Acta-Physiol.-Scand.-191/S.658:49/2007]. Results: High positive influence on psychic items (patients: "polar-attitude-list"/n=31). Possible correlation with effects of psychotropic hormones/drugs, participated in cardiovascular-regulation/n=50). Conclusions: Recommendation for systematic investigations on psychophysiological effects of psychotropic hormones/drugs concerning angiocardial pathogenesis/therapy.

Prioritizing visual selective attention is not diminished by high concurrent working memory loads

Neumann, Ewald Dept. of Psychology, University of Canterbury, Christchurch, New Zealand
De Fockert et al. (2001, Science) postulated that working memory is crucial for reducing distraction by maintaining the prioritization of relevant over irrelevant information in visual selective attention tasks. This hypothesis was examined by assessing the influence of working memory load on visual attention in a dual selective attention and memory task. University students ignored famous faces while categorizing conflicting superimposed celebrity names, under low or high memory loads. Within-subjects ANOVAs showed that interference and negative priming effects were invariant, regardless of the memory load, suggesting that prioritization capacities were undiminished. A methodological resolution to the incompatible findings is provided.

How does expressive writing take effect?: Studying differential mechanisms of writing about stressful life events

Niedtfeld, Inga Psychosomatik - Psychotherapie, ZI für Seelische Gesundheit, Mannheim, Germany Schmidt, Alexander F. Sozial- & Rechtspsychologi, Institut für Psychologie, Bonn, Germany
Writing about stressful events can lead to improvements in well-being, while the mechanisms behind these benefits from experimental disclosure are still not clarified. The present study investigated whether writing about stressful events would influence long-term measures of mental health. Furthermore, two possible mechanisms to which benefits might be attributable, namely improvements in self-efficacy or healthy emotion regulation strategies, were examined. The results indicate that writing diminishes hyperarousal and the occurrence of negative affect. Self efficacy and the use of different emotion regulation strategies cannot account for the observed improvements, albeit perceived intensity is proved to be a mediator.

Changes in job autonomy: The role of maladaptive routines

Niessen, Cornelia Inst. für Psychologie, Universität Konstanz, Konstanz, Germany
When work environments change, routines have to be adapted to the new requirements. In an experiment with a simulated office task (n = 56), it was examined how persons with routines respond to an increase in job autonomy (i.e., selection, use of working methods) rendering a new working strategy optimal. Multi-level analyses showed that compared to participants with no change in job autonomy, participants with low autonomy tended to retain their suboptimal routine when job autonomy was increased. Thinking aloud protocols revealed that routines narrowed reflection about a new working strategy (planning and evaluating of strategy options).

Relation between worry domains and health related quality of life in medical sciences students, 2006

Nikbakht Nasrabadi, Alireza Tehran School of Nursing, Tehran, Islamic Republic of Iran Mazloom, Reza Tehran School of Nursing and M, Room 31, Tehran School of Nurs, Tehran, Islamic Republic of Iran Nesari, Maryam Tehran School of Nursing and M, Room 31, Tehran School of Nurs, Tehran, Islamic Republic of Iran Goodarzi, Fatemeh Tehran School of Nursing and M, Room 31, Tehran School of Nurs, Tehran, Islamic Republic of Iran
The objective of this study is to assess relationship of worry domain with quality of life in Medical Sciences students. In this descriptive correlation study, 400 medical university students from 7 different schools completed corresponding versions of QOL and worry domain questionnaires. The results of the present study indicated that worry was in a severe level in 4.8 % and in medium level in 34.3% of students while the mean scores of QOL was 76.3 (from 100) and 5% of students had also low level of QOL. The results also indicated that worry and quality of life were negatively direct related.

Reducing effects of stress reaction with brainstorming card game

Nishiura, Kazuki Devel. and Clinical Psychology, Miyagigakuin Women's Univ., Sendai, Japan Tayama, Jun Cardiovascular Division, Tohoku Rosai Hospital, Sendai-city, Japan Watanabe, Satoshi ?, Miyagi Prefecture, Sendai-city, Japan Ito, Toshinori Industrial Technology Institut, Miyagi Prefectural Government, Sendai-city, Japan Ishii, Rikie Graduate School of Engineering, Tohoku University, Sendai-city, Japan
[Objective] The purpose of this study was to develop a card game for Brainstorming, and to show by

means of evidence that psychological stress reaction would be alleviated with the card game. [Method] The card game had 50 TOI cards and 4 kinds of 10 cards for role-play; Defer Judgment, Strive for Quantity, Seek Wild and Unusual Ideas, Build on Other Ideas. 35 Subjects played it, and we measured the effects of stress reaction; depression and anxiety. [Result and Discussion] The results found that their depression reaction reduces with time going.

Shrinkage of functional field of view induced by emotion

Nobata, Tomoe Human-Enviroment Studies, Kyushu University, Fukuoka, Japan Hakoda, Yuji Human-Enviroment Studies, Kyushu University, Fukuoka, Japan Ninose, Yuri Engineering, Fukuoka University, Fukuoka, Japan
This study examined whether positive or negative emotion influenced the functional field of view. Participants' task was to identify a digit in any of four corners of an emotional picture on the display presented, while discriminating an alphabet on the center of the display. There were two conditions in stimulus onset asynchrony (SOA) between an emotional picture and a digit (500ms and 3000ms). In the result, only negative emotion disturbed the identification of digit in both SOA conditions. This result indicated that negative emotion shrunk the functional field of view, while positive emotion didn't.

The role of affective states in interpreting thoughtless behaviors taken by acquaintances

Noda, Masayo Department of Psychology, Kibi University, Takahashi, Japan
The role of affective states in interpretation of acquaintances' behaviors was examined. A total of 204 participants were induced to positive, neutral or negative mood and were presented with vignettes describing behaviors that lacks in interpersonal considerations, taken by acquaintances. The participants were asked to rate to what extent they felt the behaviors lacked in interpersonal considerations. The behaviors were evaluated more negatively among the participants in the positive and negative affective states compared to neutral affective state. The authors concluded that people are more likely to rely on their subjective affect states when interpreting behaviors taken by their acquaintances.

Someone to watch over me: The effect of the egalitarian norms on gender stereotype-activation

Nodera, Aya Nagoya University, Nagoya, Japan Karasawa, Kaori Social Psychology, the University of Tokyo, Tokyo, Japan
We hypothesized that the egalitarian norms can have automatic influences on stereotype-activation. The salience of the egalitarian norms was manipulated by presenting a picture of other person's faces which were looking at participants or not. Participants performed a gender role IAT in which either a face with direct gaze or that with averted gaze was presented. We found that the IAT effect was smaller in the direct gaze condition than in the averted gaze condition, only among the female participants who didn't express the attitudes as an egalitarian. The relationship between the salient norm and stereotype-activation is discussed.

The relationship between role stress and burnout syndrome in Japanese care staffs

Noriko, Okuta Health and Welfare, YMCA collage of Human Services, Atsugi-shi, Japan Matsuda, Yoriko Graduate school of internation, J.F.OBERLIN University, machida-shi, Japan Shibata, Keiko nurse's office, J.F.OBERLIN University, machida-shi, Japan Ishikawa, Rie human science, J.F.OBERLIN UNIVERSITY, machida-shi, Japan Kamba, Naoko

Graduate school of internation, J.F.OBERLIN
University, Machida-shi, Japan **Seino, Junko**
Graduate school of internation, J.F.OBERLIN
University, Machida-shi, Japan
The purpose of this study was to investigate the relationship between Role stress and burnout syndrome in Japanese care staffs, and to examine licenses differences. 223 care staffs were asked to complete the questionnaire containing the measures of Role Questionnaire (RQ), Maslach Burnout Inventory (MBI), and licenses. 97 respondents got the national license. Analyses of Role stress scores indicated that care staffs got the national license in technical collage showed significantly higher score on "Role ambiguity" than others. All showed significant correlation between "Role ambiguity"and "Depersonalization". This study indicated that Role stress have effects on burnout syndrome.

Non-verbal memory in experienced actors and controls

Notthoff, Nanna Dept. of Psychology, Stanford
University, Stanford, USA **Jonides, John** Department
of Psychology, University of Michigan, Ann Arbor,
USA
Objectives: Do actors perform better than controls in non-verbal memory tasks? Hypothesis: Actors use visual and spatial cues to remember scripts, resulting in experimentally-verifiable superior non-verbal memory. Methods: We tested experienced actors' short-term spatial (Corsi Blocks) and visual (VPT), long-term visual (RVDLT), and working memory (Reading & Operation Span). Results: Actors performed better on Corsi (meanA=17.90;-meanC=16.00;p=0.0156), VPT (meanA=11.24;-meanC=10.38;p=0.0351), Reading Span (meanA=56.05;meanC=47.79;p=0.0383), had greater improvement in RVDLT (meanA=8.00;-meanC=6.13;p=0.0026), organized material more consistently. No difference in Operation Span. Conclusions: Experience in theatrical acting confers advantage in non-verbal memory.

Projecto integrado de intervenção precoce: Evaluation of fourteen years of early intervention in Portugal

Nunes, Helga Loulé, Portugal **Almeida, Susana**
Psychology, University of the Algarve, Faro, Portugal
Pacheco, Andreia Psychology, University of the
Algarve, Faro, Portugal
This investigation aims to collect and evaluate the information given by all the families, supported between 1989 and 2004, by the Direct Intervention Team of Coimbra, of the Projecto Integrado de Intervenção Precoce. Fifty-two families answered three questionnaires, and the data were analyzed using the software SPSS. Through the results, it is possible to reflect about the quality of the practice in Early Intervention, so that the services that are available to Portuguese children and their families resemble more the theoretical and practical guidelines.

Program of inductive methodologies of behavior appropriate in class

Nunes Caldeira, Suzana Ciências da Educação,
Universidade dos Açores, Ponta Delgada - Azores,
Portugal
This study is part of a wider research project greatly inspired by Rutter's work. It involves a program of educational intervention centered on the practice of inductive methodologies of behavior appropriate in class, based on the introduction of variability and reciprocal modulation. The researcher (psychologist) assumed the role of facilitator before the group of teachers. Initially, the target group was a group of students exhibiting lack of discipline, but the focus quickly fell on the class as a social unit. Analysis of the percentage differences indicates improvement in student behavior. The teachers

manifested satisfaction in having participated in the project.

Experiments on binocular stereopsis with inverting view glasses

Ohta, Masao Kanazawa, Japan
The assumption was "when both eyes are rotated 180 degrees at the center of the distance between both eyes entailing the optic chiasma, retinal images which have been turned over by each lens are reversed, and upright retinal images with normal stereoscopic vision can be obtained". Tasks were "writing", "walking", and so forth wearing inverting view glasses which can turn retinal images by crossing cords to connect video cameras with liquid crystal screens similar to the optic chiasma. Trials repeated 20 times. Errors and the required time were measured. Results showed that normal binocular stereopsis of reversed image was obtained and coordinated behaviors were established. The assumption was supported.

Sleeping time relates to perceived health and psychoneuroimmunological responses

Okamura, Hisayoshi Dept. of Medicine, Kurume
University, Kurume, Japan **Tsuda, Akira** Department
of Psychology, Kurume University, Kurume, Japan
Yajima, Jumpei Dept. of Human Studies, Beppu
University, Beppu, Japan **Horiuchi, Satoshi** Graduate
School of Psychology, Kurume University, Kurume,
Japan **Matuishi, Toyojiro** Dept. of Medicine, Kurume
University, Kurume, Japan
The present study was to assess the relationship between sleeping time and the health of mind-body. Subjects were 205 healthy university students. These subjects were divided by habitual sleeping time. Therefore we had 3 groups (35 adequate sleepers, 33 short sleepers and 28 long sleepers). Subjects completed the questionnaire of GHQ-28 while the saliva samples were collected. The results of this study indicated that sleeping time relates to perceived health and change in PNI function. Moreover, the results of change in PNI responses and GHQ-28 suggest that sleeping time is very important factor for prevention of stress disease and health promotion for university students.

Investigations on the evaluation estimation Item groups in a young person group, a middle-aged group and an elderly group

Okuda, Hiroki Kinjo University, Hakusan-City, Japan
This study examined the difference of recognition concerning development by the age of the subjects. A young person group (18-22), a middle-aged group (40-59) and an elderly group (65+) were asked to evaluate five development estimation item groups to see to what degree 1, 3, 5, 10, 20, 40, 60 and 80 year-old people could perform independently and adequately. Concerning 60 year-old, average scores of the five item groups of the middle-aged and elderly groups were higher than average scores of the young person group. This suggests that younger people evaluate the various abilities of 60 year-olds as relatively low.

Factors related to the students' image of elderly people

Okumura, Yumiko Health and Welfare, Kawasaki Univ
Medical Welfare, Kurashiki, Japan **Kuze, Junko** Social
& Information Scien, Nihon Fukushi University,
Handa, Japan
Purpose: Improvement of nursing care for elderly people might be achieved by caregivers' expert knowledge and positive image of elderly people. The formation of the image of elderly people during developing years was examined. Method: The image of elderly people was measured in university students and the factors related to image formation were investigated. Result: Interactive experiences with elderly people including grand parents, and parents' attitude toward elderly people could affect

the image of elderly people. Conclusion: Having interactive experiences with elderly people in the developing stage of life, and growing up observing the positive attitudes of parents regarding elderly people are important.

The relationship of job characteristics with job involvement of personnel

Omidi Arjenaki, Najmeh Psychology, Isfahan
University, Isfahan, Islamic Republic of Iran **Oreyzi,
Hamid Reza** Psychology, Isfahan university, Isfahan,
Islamic Republic of Iran **Nouri, Abolghasem**
Psychology, Isfahan university, Isfahan, Islamic
Republic of Iran
The purpose of this study was to examine the relationship between job characteristics and job involvement of personnel. The relevant sample consisted of 115 personnel of a company who selected through a random sampling. To measure variables has been used the Job Characteristics Inventory(JCI) of Sims et al, and Kanungo job involvement questionnaire.The results of multiple regression analysis showed that job characteristics have significant relationship with job involvement. The findings could be used for job design. Keywords: Job characteristics, Job involvement, Job design

The relationship of job characteristics with organizational commitment of personnel

Omidi Arjenaki, Najmeh Psychology, Isfahan
University, Isfahan, Islamic Republic of Iran **Oreizy,
Hamid Reza** Psychology, isfahan university, Isfahan,
Islamic Republic of Iran **Nouri, Abolghasem**
Psychology, isfahan university, Isfahan, Islamic
Republic of Iran
The purpose of this study was to investigate the relationship between job characteristics and organizational commitment among employees of a company. The relevant sample consisted of 100 personnel of a company who selected through a random sampling. To measure variables has been used the Job Characteristics Inventory(JCI) of Sims et al, and Allen and Meyer organizational commitment questionnaire. The results of canonical correlation showed that job characteristics have significant relationship with organizational commitment components(affective, normative and continuance commitment). The findings could be used for job design.Keywords: Job characteristics, organizational commitment, Job design

Emotional intelligence, occupational stress, and social support among Japanese workers

Omori, Mika Psychology, Ochanomizu University,
Bunkyo, Tokyo, Japan
Recent interests in emotion and emotional intelligence (EI) draw attention to the role of emotion in the stress process. The present study was designed to examine the role of EI on relationships between occupational stress and psychological response among Japanese company employees. A web survey was conducted and data was collected from 254 participants (113 men and 141 women). The mean age of the participants was 38.59 (SD = 11.00; age range 20-59). Structural equation modeling analyses revealed that higher EI was related to higher perceived social support, which in turn resulted in lower stress responses.

The effect of motion in depth on time perception

Ono, Fuminori Dept. of Neurophysiology, Juntendo
University, Tokyo, Japan **Kitazawa, Shigeru**
Department of Neurophysiology, Juntendo
University, Tokyo, Japan
The present study examined the effect of approaching and receding motion on time perception. We required participants to estimate the length of a short empty interval that started from the offset of the first marker and ended at the onset of the second marker. We changed the size of the markers

so that a visual object was perceived as approaching or receding. The empty interval was perceived as shorter when the object was approaching straight to the face than when it was receding. We conclude that anticipated collision decreased the perceived duration of the moving object.

Relation between the bullying term and social skill of bullies

Ono, Akiko Psychology, Japan Women's University, Kawasaki, Japan Honma, Mitiko psychology, Japan Women's University, kawasaki, Japan

This study was conducted to test the hypothesis that bullies have some kind of characteristics to prolong their bullying behavior. We used questionnaires and asked 122 university students about their bullying experiences, suffering experiences, social skills and the bullying term during their junior high school period. The results indicated that the bullying tended to be prolonged when the score of the social skill was high in both Ringleader bullies and follower bullies (who join in the bullying). Thus, it appears that the length of bullying is related to the social skill on the side of the bullies.

Psychological distress in radiotherapy patients and needs for psychological support

Oppenauer, Claudia Inst. für Klin. Psychologie, Universiätsklinik Wien, Wien, Austria Jagsch, Reinhold Inst. für Psychologie, Universität Wien, Wien, Austria Six, Nicola Radiotherapy, Universitätsklinik Wien, Wien, Austria Wölfl, Hedwig Radiotherapy, Universiätsklinik Wien, Wien, Austria Pötter, Richard Radiotherapy, Universiätsklinik Wien, Wien, Austria Kryspin-Exner, Ilse Inst. für Psychologie, Universität Wien, Wien, Austria

This study aims to measure attitudes towards the psychooncological outpatient clinic (POC) and to measure the distress and quality of life of radiotherapy patients. 108 radiotherapy patients including 24 clients of the POC were interviewed in this study. Data were assessed by the means of the Stress Index Radiooncology (SIRO), the Hornheider Questionnaire, the EORTC QLQ C-30 and an evaluation form of the POC. In general clients of the POC were more distressed than other radiotherapy patients. Only a few differences in distress and quality of life data were found between radiotherapy patients with and without psychological support.

Distinct mechanisms in "where", "what", and "how" visual feature processing

Osaki, Hirotaka Human Environment Studies, Kyushu University, Fukuoka, Japan Kawabata, Hideaki Faculty of Education, Kagoshima University, Kagoshima-city, Japan Hakoda, Yuji Human Environment Studies, Kyushu University, Fukuoka-city, Japan

Using a one-shot paradigm with visual search display, we examined differential accuracy in change blindness responding to localizing where target changed, discriminating what visual feature changed, and identifying how the feature changed. In the display with face or letter-string elements, the changed feature of a target was its orientation or swapping to same distracter element. The result showed an advantage in the order of identification, discrimination, and localization, regardless of changed feature and of stimulus type. The results indicated distinct mechanisms processing where, what, and how the target changed, irrespective of visual mechanisms pertaining to visual characteristics to be presented.

Researching on relationship between self identity and social identity of undergraduates

Ouyang, Wen School of Art & Law, Changsha Uni.of Science&Techn., Changsha, China, People's Republic of : Macao SAR Deng, Zhiwen political school,

changsha university of science, Changsha, China, People's Republic of : Macao SAR

Objective: Probing on relationship between self identity and social identity. Methods: 438 undergraduates are surveyed by "Chinese undergraduate self-identity status scale (a=0.871)" and "social identity scale(a=0.908)".Regression-linear analysis is used. Results: (1) Self-identity is slightly related to social identity, and self-identity effects on social identity about 12.4%.(2) The second layer of self-identity(especilly,IDDIF,IDFOR,INDIF,INMOR) makes the most great and directive influences on social identity.(3) Social identity influences self-identity very slightly. Conclusion: The second layer of self-identity influence on social identity

A relational study of attachment styles, emotional intelligence and quality of relationship

Ozabacý, Nilüfer Dept. of Educational Sciences, Eskiehir Osmangazi University, Eskiehir, Turkey

The aim of this study was to determine the relationship between attachment styles emotional Intelligence and relationship quality of university students. The sample of the study consists of 314 university students that selected randomly from Eskişehir Osmangazi University..Datas were collected by "The Inventory of Close Realtionship" that developed by Brennan and et.all (1998) and adapted by Güngör (2000) for attachment styles, "EQ-NED" that was developed by Ergin, Işmen and Özabacı (1999) for Emotional Intelligence and "Inventory of Relationship Quality" that adapted by Özabacı (2007) for relationship quality and Pearson Moment Corelation were used for analyze the data.

Event related potentials associated to distraction processes caused by events related to pending intentions

Pérez, Enrique Psychology, University of Salamanca, Salamanca, Spain Meilán, Juan J. G. Psychology, University of Salamanca, Salamanca, Spain Arana, José M. Psychology, University of Salamanca, Salamanca, Spain

This work aims to study the importance of attentional processes on the realization of delayed intentions (prospective memory). We analyze, through event related potentials recording, the attentional capture processes which occurs when recovering, spontaneously, a delayed intention when faced with an event related with the intention. Moreover, we have checked the type of attentional processes (automatics vs. strategics) used to remember the tasks to do. How deep is the processing of stimuli related with an intention? Is it only the switch of the attentional focus (orientation attention)? Or, on the contrary, is it a semantic processing of delayed task?

Work of preference and wellbeing in different types of permanent employees

Pérez, Lorena Social Psychology, University of Valencia, Valencia, Spain Caballer, Amparo SOCIAL PSYCHOLOGY, UNIVERSITY OF VALENCIA, VALENCIA, Spain Sora, Beatriz STRATEGICAL PROJECTS, CIEMAT, BARCELONA, Spain

Previous research suggests that not having a work of preference has specially negative outcomes in permanent employees when compared to temporaries because it may be associated with feelings of being locked into one's job. This study investigates the influence of having or not a job of choice on the well-being of different types of permanent employees. Hierarchical moderated regression analysis indicated that lifelong civil servants were more negatively influenced by not having a job of preference than employees with an open ended contract. Results are discussed in relation to the "locked-in" phenomenon. Proposals to guide future research are discussed.

Attentional bias to smoking cues and reactivity to rewarding stimuli in nicotine dependence

Paelecke-Habermann, Yvonne Department of Psychology, Martin-Luther-University Halle, Halle/ Saale, Germany Rummel, Kristin Department of Psychology, Martin-Luther-University Halle, Halle/ Saale, Germany Paelecke, Marko Department of Psychology, Martin-Luther-University Halle, Halle/ Saale, Germany Leising, Daniel Department of Psychology, Martin-Luther-University Halle, Halle/ Saale, Germany Leplow, Bernd Department of Psychology, Martin-Luther-University Halle, Halle/ Saale, Germany

Nicotine consumption causes neuronal changes within the brain-reward-system that lead to the experience of craving, which includes an increased sensitivity for smoking cues and a decreased sensitivity for natural reinforcers. The aim of our study was to test the assumption of a substance-related attentional bias to nicotine-related stimuli and a reduced reactivity to primary and other secondary reinforcers in dependent smokers. We compared dependent and occasional smokers (according to DSM-IV criteria) to a matched control group of non-smokers in tests of attentional bias (emotional Stroop paradigm), decision making (go-no go-task with reward and punishment) and reward learning (probabilistic classification learning).

Work design and psychological work reactions: The mediating effect of psychological strain and the moderating effect of social support

Panatik, Siti Aisyah Hamilton East, New Zealand

The aims of the present study were twofold: First, I examined the moderating influence of social support on the relationship between job design (job demands and job control) and psychological strain, job satisfaction and turnover intentions. Second, in providing a more comprehensive link between job design and work reactions, I examined psychological strain as a mediator of that relationship. Participants were 443 technical workers at Telecom Malaysia. Social support was found to moderate the job design-psychological work reactions. Moreover, psychological strain significantly mediated the job design-job satisfaction and turnover intentions. Implications of this study are discussed from theoretical and applied perspectives

Perceived intensity of physiological measures as a function of the degree of neuroticism under different levels of shock induced stress

Papachristou, Efstathios Athens, Greece

Differences between perceived and actual intensity of blood pressure, Galvanic Skin Response and heart rate were examined on 72 undergraduate students as a function of their stress level induced by electric shocks (0, 45, 90 Volt) and their degree of neuroticism, as measured by the Florida OCD Inventory. Physiological measurements followed by subjective estimations of intensity showed consistent overestimation of activation of the SNS and the heart rate but not blood pressure. Specifically, increasing levels of stress and number of obsessive-compulsive symptoms lead to greater discrepancy between perceived and actual physiological measures. Findings suggest that neurotic individuals exaggerate at the intensity of physical symptoms under stressful circumstances.

False memory due to working memory span and cognitive load

Park, Mi-Cha BK21 Group of Multi-Cultural, Sung Kyun Kwan University, Seoul, Republic of Korea Lee, Soon-Mook Psychology, SungKyunKwan University, Seoul, Republic of Korea

This study examined the role of working memory span and cognitive load on veridical memory and false memory. Sixty undergraduate students performed a working memory span task and other memory tasks utilizing DRM procedure. Cognitive load at encoding was experimentally manipulated within subjects. Without cognitive load, working memory span was positively correlated with correct recall and correct recognition. When there was cognitive load, however, subjects with shorter working memory span produced significantly more false memories. These results imply that working memory plays a role in generating false memory via executive function.

Do we all dream about balanced work-life?
Parts, Velli *Psychology, Tallinn University, Tallinn, Estonia*
Work-life balance is often held up as an ideal for all employees. The hypothesis guiding this study is that different non-balanced work-life orientations exist in addition to balanced one. K-mean cluster analysis was used to develop a typology of work-life preferences using data from three surveys of work-aged population in Estonia (total n = 2400). In all samples ca 40% of employees preferred balanced work-life (work, family, leisure equally important) whereas 10% were predominantly leisure-oriented, 25% family-centered, and 20% work-oriented. Socio-demographic characteristics are important when predicting work–life orientations. Work attitudes also vary according to work-life preferences.

Semantic long-term knowledge leads to distortions in working memory
Patterson, Michael *Dept. of Psychology, Nanyang Technol. University, Singapore, Singapore* **Chin, Zhen Hui** *Psychology, Nanyang Technological Universi, Singapore, Singapore* **Tan, Kelda** *Psychology, Nanyang Technological Universi, Singapore, Singapore*
In several studies we examined the effect of long-term semantic knowledge on working memory for briefly (1.5sec/pair) presented word-pairs. Immediately after the presentation of pairs, participants were asked to select the word that had been paired with a single word probe. Participants remembered pairs that were grouped according to expectations significantly more accurately than unexpected groupings. Participants tended to falsely group unexpected pairs to match semantic expectations. As unexpected pairs per trial increased, accuracy significantly decreased. Thus, contrary to working memory for single items, working memory for pair bindings relies strongly upon long-term semantic knowledge.

Coping and personality disorders in substance-addicts: Integration of Hobfoll's and Millon's models
Pedrero Pérez, Eduardo J. *CAD-4-San Blas, Instituto de Adicciones Madrid, Madrid, Spain* **Santed Germán, Miguel Ángel** *Psicología de la Personalidad, UNED, Madrid, Spain* **Pérez García, Ana María** *Psicología de la Personalidad, UNED, Madrid, Spain*
Hobfoll's Strategic Approach to Coping Scale – Dispositional Form (SACS-D), and Millon Clinical Multiaxial Inventory–II (MCMI-II) were administered to a clinical sample of 712 individuals diagnosed with substance abuse or dependence (heroine, cocaine, alcohol or cannabis). Participants started a rehabilitation programme in a public outpatient treatment centre for addictive disorders. The strategic profiles of coping in each personality disorder were explored. Results showed that each pathological personality faces the difficulties in an specific way, predominating the avoidance, indirect, instinctive, and antisocial coping strategies. Present results were discussed in terms of clinical implications for treatment in addictive disorders.

Clinical trial: Brief intervention programs for adolescents who initiate the alcohol consumption
Pedroza Cabrera, Francisco Javier *Dept. of Psychology, Universidad de Aguascalientes, Aguascalientes, Mexico* **Martínez Martínez, Kalina Isela** *Psychology, Universidad de Aguascalientes, Aguascalientes, Mexico* **Salazar Garza, Martha Leticia** *Psychology, Universidad de Aguascalientes, Aguascalientes, Mexico* **Herrera Rodroguez, Jacobo** *Psychology, Universidad de Aguascalientes, Aguascalientes, Mexico*
The Brief Intervention and Brief Advise programs have been demonstrated to be effective in reducing the alcohol consumption pattern of teenagers who have not developed a dependency. However, each program has been evaluated separately. The goal of this investigation was to compare the effectiveness of Brief Intervention and Brief Advice on patterns of alcohol consumption among teenagers, through a random clinical trial. We worked with 72 participants divided into four clinical groups and two control groups on the waiting list. The results indicated that the Brief Intervention and Brief Advise programs were effective in reducing the drinking pattern to safe levels compared with the control groups.

A study of the relationships among employees' fairness, job satisfaction and turnover intention in the state-owned enterprises
Peng, Jianfeng *LHR, Renmin University of China, Beijing, People's Republic of China*
This study focused on the relationships among employees' fairness, job satisfaction and turnover intention in the Chinese state-owned enterprises. The samples for this study were drawn from 417 employees of 7 state-owned enterprises in Chinese mainland, and the statistic techniques such as stepwise regression and path analysis were used for analyzing data. The conclusions are: 1. Distributive fairness, participation at company level and participation at job level had significantly positive impacts on job satisfaction; however appeal mechanism had not significant impact on job satisfaction. 2. Job satisfaction had a significantly negative impact on turnover intention.

Interest, group adherence and knowledge and their impacts in ufological beliefs
Pereira, Marcos *Dept. of Psychology, Universidade Federal da Bahia, Salvador, Brazil* **Silva, Joice** *Psychology, Universidade Federal da Bahia, Salvador, Brazil* **Silva, Paula B. e** *Psychology, Universidade Federal da Bahia, Salvador, Brazil*
This research aims to identify the beliefs shared by people who are taking part or not in ufological research groups. The variables studied for their influence on the belief in UFOs and aliens were degree of knowledge, interest taken in research and adherence to ufological groups, as well as religion, age, gender and education. The questionnaire was made available on-line and 617 people completed it. Results point to a differential adherence pattern, with participants with a deeper knowledge, interest, and linked to research groups tend to embrace the beliefs of other participants more faithfully than participants with dissimilar behavior.

Influence of attributions, motivation and self-concept on academic achievement
Perez Sanchez, Antonio Miguel *Evolutive Psychology, University of Alicante, Alicante, Spain* **Quiros-Bravo, Soledad** *EVOLUTIVE PSYCHOLOGY AND DIDAC, UNIVERSITY OF ALICANTE, ALICANTE, Spain* **Garcia-Fernandez, Jose Manuel** *EVOLUTIVE PSYCHOLOGY AND DIDAC, UNIVERSITY OF ALICANTE, ALICANTE, Spain* **Valero-Rodriguez, Jose** *EVOLUTIVE PSYCHOLOGY AND DIDAC, UNIVERSITY OF ALICANTE, ALICANTE, Spain*

Objective: To find out the extent of variance of the dependent variable, DV (academic achievement) that can be attributed to independent variables, IV (attributions, motivation, self-concept). Method: The participants were 201 girls in first year of Compulsory Secondary Education (average age, 12). The data was obtained from the qualifications attained by the students and through questionnaires such as "Self-Description Questionnaire I" (Marsh, 1988). Hierarchical Regression Analysis was used as statistical technique. Results: IVs were found to explain 62.8% of the variance of the DV. Conclusions: The IVs dealt with in our study must be included in the school curriculum.

Differential effects of self-efficacy and perceived behavioural control on skin cancer risk behaviours
Pertl, Maria *Dept. of Radiation Therapy, Trinity College Dublin, Dublin, Ireland* **Hevey, David** *Psychology, Trinity College Dublin, Dublin, Ireland* **Thomas, Kevin** *Psychology, Trinity College Dublin, Dublin, Ireland* **Maher, Laura** *Radiation Therapy, Trinity College Dublin, Dublin, Ireland* **Ni Chuinneagain, Siobhán** *Radiation Therapy, Trinity College Dublin, Dublin, Ireland* **Craig, Agnella** *Radiation Therapy, Trinity College Dublin, Dublin, Ireland*
Objectives: to test the Theory of Planned Behaviour's (TPB) efficacy for understanding intentions to use sunscreen and sunbeds. Methods: Questionnaire data from 590 young adults were analysed using multiple regression. Results: The TPB accounted for 43% and 46% (p < .001) of the variation in intentions to use sunscreen and sunbeds respectively. Perceived behavioural control (PBC) was only a significant predictor for sunbed use, while self-efficacy (SE) only predicted sunscreen use. Conclusion: SE and PBC had different effects on intentions to perform skin cancer risk behaviours. Results support the conceptual distinction between the two components of perceived control.

Effect of sex stereotypes on school adolescents' sexual behaviour in south-western Nigeria
Popoola, Bayode *Educational Found & Counseling, Obafemi Awolowo University, Ile Ife, Nigeria*
The study investigated the prevalence of sex stereotyping and its effects on sexual behaviour of Nigerian adolescents. Participants were 658 adolescents selected randomly from secondary schools in South Western Nigeria. An instrument measuring the extent of the internalization of sex-stereotypes and another instrument measuring dimensions of sexual behaviour were administered. Findings revealed that male participants demonstrated a higher degree of sex-stereotypical behaviour than their female counterparts and that sex stereotyping had significant negative effects on sexual behaviour of male and female adolescents. The study highlights the need for virile and radical programmes of sexual re-conditioning for Nigerian adolescents

Peer sexual harassment and coping mechanisms of female students in a Nigerian university
Popoola, Bayode *Educational Found & Counseling, Obafemi Awolowo University, Ile Ife, Nigeria*
The study investigated the prevalence, nature and coping mechanisms of peer sexual harassment among 387 female students of the Obafemi Awolowo University, Nigeria. Participants selected by convenience sampling from three Faculties responded to a questionnaire on peer sexual harassment. Results indicated that verbal harassment was the most frequent type of peer sexual harassment and that victims did not report their harassment to authorities but adopted strategies that did not involve direct confrontation with their harassers. The study stressed the need for a virile counselling programme in Nigerian universities to stem down the incidence of peer sexual harassment.

Indexes of fatigue for the workers of a railway transport police

Popova, Galyna of Railway Transport Ukraine, State Scientific-Research Cent, Kiev, Ukraine
Purpose: determination of basic factors of fatigue nature, analysis of dynamics of attention indexes and emotional states for the workers of railway transport police. Methods: questioning, tepping-test, Shulte's tables, M. Lyusher's modified test, correlation analysis. Results. The factors of fatigue: innormativ working day, stress loadings, absence of abilities, skills of states self-regulation. Research of parameters of attention (stability, switching) and dynamics of the emotional states for transport police before and after their duty testify to worsening. Relationship between the central nervous system force and fatigue indexes are set. Conclusions. Maintenance of perception is probed the workers from point of their emotional tension. Way of policemen functional states optimization: self-regulation receptions teaching.

The transmission of work affectivity and experiences from adults to children

Porfeli, Erik Dept. of Behavioral Sciences, NEOUCOM, Rootstown, USA Wang, Chuang Educational Leadership, UNC-Charlotte, Charlotte, USA Hartung, Paul Behavioral Sciences, NEOUCOM, Rootstown, USA
Children may develop vicarious orientations toward work that are appreciably influenced by family members' work experiences and emotions. Cross-sectional data from 100 grade-school children and confirmatory factor analysis are employed to assess new measures of work affectivity and experiences. Structural equation modeling is employed to test hypotheses suggesting that family work experiences and emotions influence children's orientation toward work. The results suggest that children's anticipated work emotions and experiences mediate the relationship between perceived family members' work emotions and experiences and children's school and work motivation. The family serves as an influential context for career development during the childhood period.

Changing counseling perspectives regarding older immigrants: Addressing diversity and provision of services in graduate education

Poulakis, Michael PSYCHOLOGY, University of Indianapolis, Indianapolis, USA Beggs, Katy PSYCHOLOGY, UNIVERSITY OF INDIANAPOLIS, INDIANAPOLIS, USA
Older adult immigrants are perceived to be a growing population within the United States. The number of adults over 65 is expected to double in the next 40 years (2043), as well as increased ethnic diversity. By 2030, the older adults will consist of 25% of the population. The project is an educational component, designed to add an educational module in the Life Span Development course in graduate psychology. The project will increase awareness of future mental health clinicians regarding the effects of immigration, acculturation, and how to improve their counseling needs.

Infants do not imitate novel actions modeled by an unreliable person

Poulin-Dubois, Diane Dept. of Psychology, Concordia University, Montreal, Canada Brooker, Ivy Dept. of Psychology, Concordia University, Montreal, Canada Polonia, Alexandra Dept. of Psychology, Concordia University, Montreal, Canada
This study examined whether the credibility of an individual's gaze influences infants' decision to imitate novel actions modeled by that individual. Infants aged 16-18-months first observed an experimenter show excitement while looking inside an empty box. Infants then observed the same experimenter turn on a light-box with her forehead rather than with her hands. In contrast to previous research with an unfamiliar experimenter, the majority of infants (76%) were more likely to imitate the action with their hands than with their forehead. This suggests that infants who mistrust a person's gaze infer that this person is not a rational agent.

Non-work activities and well-being

Prizmic, Zvjezdana Dept. of Psychology, Washington University, St. Louis, USA Kaliterna Lipovcan, Ljiljana Psychology, Institute of Social Science, Zagreb, Croatia
Worker satisfaction with non-work activities was examined as predictors of well-being. Subjects, 180 health care workers, completed the Survey of Health Care Professionals (including 15 non-work activities and job satisfaction), the Life satisfaction, and the Fordyce Happiness Measure. Regression analyses examined the effects of non-work activities on well-being, controlling for age and gender. Different predictors for each well-being measure were found: satisfaction with exercise was the best predictor of life satisfaction, raising children best predicted happiness and balancing work/family responsibilities best predicted job satisfaction. Results are discussed in light of previous findings in the work and well-being literature.

Inverted event-related potentials response to illusory contour in boys with autism

Prokofyev, Andrey Dev. psychophysiol., MSUPE, Moscow, Russia Orekhova, Elena Clinical Neurophysiology, Sahlgrens University Hospital, Moscow, Sweden Posikera, Irina Developmental psychogenetics, PIRAO, Moscow, Russia Morozov, Alexey Laboratory 144, IREERAS, Moscow, Russia Morozov, Vladimir Laboratory 144, IREERAS, Moscow, Russia Obukhov, Yuriy Laboratory 144, IREERAS, Moscow, Russia Stroganova, Tatiana Developmental psychogenetics, PIRAE, Moscow, Russia
Objective: to study lower-level processing of perceptual grouping in boys with autism (BWA) aged 3-6 years. Methods: non-parametric analysis of event-related response to visual elements that either formed illusory contour or were arranged in a noncoherent way. Subjects: healthy boys (19 children) and BWA (19 children) aged 3-6 years. Results: healthy boys demonstrated the enhanced negativity of N1 peak whereas BWA demonstrated more positive N1 amplitude to illusory contour. Conclusions: we hypothesized that BWA were sensitive to difference between illusory contour and control figures basing on collinearity processing mechanisms implemented in neural circuitry of primary visual cortex.

Analyzing the student's point of view in school violence

Pulido, Rosa Dept. Educational Psychology, Alcala University, Madrid, Spain Martin Seoane, Gema Educational Psychology, Alcala University, Madrid, Spain
The general objective of the present research is to determine the relevance of different protective and risk factors in adolescences violence behaviour. Participants were 1.635 students (aged 14-18 years), from a representative sample of Spanish high schools. A combination of qualitative and quantitative approach was used. Students filled out questionnaires that included measures of several situations of violence (exclusion, verbal violence, physical violence and vandalism), different contexts (school and spare time) and the related roles (victim, aggressor and observant). Deep analysis, through individual interviews, point out several relevant variables like guilty feelings, attitudes, etcetera. The results are generally in line with previous studies, and the implications will be discussed.

Critical periods for visual and multisensory functions in humans

Putzar, Lisa Inst. für Psychologie, Universität Hamburg, Freiburg, Germany Goerendt, Ines Department of Psychology, University of Hamburg, Hamburg, Germany Büchel, Christian Dpt. of Systems Neuroscience, University of Hamburg, Hamburg, Germany Schicke, Tobias Department of Psychology, University of Hamburg, Hamburg, Germany Röder, Brigitte Department of Psychology, University of Hamburg, Hamburg, Germany
The aim of the present brainimaging study in people suffering from early visual deprivaton was to identify critical periods for the development of both visual and multisensory functions. Compared to normally sighted controls, patients treated for dense, bilateral, congenital cataracts showed significantly reduced lipreading-specific activations (fMRI) in superior and middle temporal cortex, accompanied by lower lipreading scores. The same patients did not show any enhancement of speech comprehension when stimuli were presented audio-visually as compared to auditorily. Therefore, adequate sensory input during the first months of life is necessary for a normal development of brain systems mediating higher visual and crossmodal functions.

Confirmed/disconfirmed expectation in success/ failure attribution among Indian college adults

Qazi, Tabassum Humanities and Social Sciences, Indian Institute ofTechnology, Kanpur, India Krishnan, Lilavati Humanities and Social Sciences, Indian Institute of Technology, Kanpur, India
Some unresolved effects of Confirmed/ Disconfirmed expectation of success and Attribution Dimensions on Success/ Failure attribution and subsequent behaviour were examined in two studies involving Indian subjects. Responses based on a scenario, as well as actual task performance, revealed a significantly higher Success attribution rating compared to Failure attribution rating. Contrary to predictions, the pattern of attribution in terms of various internal /external dimensions was similar between Success and Failure, with the exception of attribution to Task Difficulty. The implications of these findings for both cognitive and motivational interpretations of achievement attribution in the context of confirmed/disconfirmed expectations have been discussed.

Fluoxetine reverses disrupted activities of the extracellular signal-regulated kinase (ERK)-cyclic AMP responsive element binding protein (CREB) signal system and depressive-like behaviors in rats exposed to chronic forced swim stress

Qi, Xiaoli Brain-Behavior Center, Institute of Psychology, Beijing, People's Republic of China Lin, Wenjuan Brain-Behavior Center, Institute of Psychology, Beijing, People's Republic of China Li, Junfa Department of Neurobiology, Capital University of Medical, Beijing, People's Republic of China Pan, Yuqin Brain-Behavior Center, Institute of Psychology, Beijing, People's Republic of China Wang, Weiwen Brain-Behavior Center, Institute of Psychology, Beijing, People's Republic of China
The extracellular signal-regulated kinase (ERK)-cyclic AMP responsive element binding protein (CREB) signal system was proposed to be involved in molecular mechanisms of antidepressant actions. To investigate the hypothesis, the present experiment treated animals with daily saline injection, forced swim stress (FSS), fluoxetine injection, or FSS followed by fluoxetine injection for 21 days. The results demonstrated stress induced disrupted activities of the ERK-CREB signal system and depressive-like behaviors, and such effects were reversed by fluoxetine treatment, suggesting the normalization of the disrupted activities of ERK-CREB signal system may represent a molecular mechanism fluoxetine reverses stress-induced depressive-like behaviors.

Experiment study on three factors affecting schema induction and analogical transfer

Qiu, Qin Dept. of Psychology, Jiangxi Normal University, Nanchang, People's Republic of China Hu, Zhujing Psychology, Jiangxi Normal University, Nanchang, People's Republic of China Yu, Daxiang Psychology, Jiangxi Normal University, Nanchang, People's Republic of China

In this article, we adopt three-factor randomized experiment to investigate the influence of cognitive style, the clearness of problem structure, and content similarity on schema induction and analogical transfer. The main results are as follows:(1) field-independent subjects had better schema induction than field-dependent subjects. Further, this difference only appeared in ill-organized problem structure conditon;(2)the subjects on the condition of well-organized structure had better performance of schema induction and transfer than those on the condition of ill-organized structure. The conclusion suggests that well-organized problem structure can improve field-dependent subject's schema representation and eliminate the negative influence of cognitive style. Well-induced schema isn't necessary condition for successful analogical transfer.

The influence of the effects of text signals on analogical transfer

Qiu, Qin Dept. of Psychology, Jiangxi Normal University, Nanchang, People's Republic of China Hu, Zhujing Psychology, Jiangxi Normal University, Nanchang, People's Republic of China Yu, Daxiang Psychology, Jiangxi Normal University, Nanchang, People's Republic of China

Since the artificial problems are presented in the form of text reading, we hypothesis the effects of text signals in text reading understanding is likely to affect analogical transfer. The experiment adopted three-factor randomized design. Three independent variables are macro-signals, micro-signals and no signal. The results showed that there were better analogical transfer performance in the macro-signals and micro-signals conditions than in the no-signal condition and the performance difference between macro-signals condition and micro-signals condition was significant. After farther analyzing, we discover text signals don't directly influence analogical transfer but the quality of problem representation. Text signals would benefit to form high quality problem representation and facilitate the subsequent analogical transfer.

Optimism, pessimism and continuity: Individual differences in subjective temporal assessments of life satisfaction across adulthood

Röcke, Christina Inst. für Psychologie, Universität Zürich, Zürich, Switzerland Lachman, Margie E. Psychology, Brandeis University, Waltham, USA

We examined subjective trajectories of life satisfaction and biopsychosocial and demographic correlates of profile differences. 3631 adults (24-75 years) from the Midlife in the U.S. survey rated their life satisfaction at present, 10 years ago, and 10 years into the future on two measurement occasions 10 years apart. Cluster analyses of the temporal life satisfaction ratings identified three groups at both occasions, representing patterns of expected increase, decrease, and stability. Subgroups differed in age, mean levels, and 10-year change in biopsychosocial variables. Perceptions of continuously high satisfaction were more adaptive than optimism about future increases or low and pessimistic expectations.

The contribution of achievement motivation to Stroop interference: An event-related fMRI study

Radke, Sina Osnabrück, Germany Nüsser, Corinna Medical Psychology, University of Bonn, Bonn, Germany Erk, Susanne Medical Psychology, University of Bonn, Bonn, Germany Kuhl, Julius Personality Research, University of Osnabrück, Osnabrück, Germany Walter, Henrik Medical Psychology, University of Bonn, Bonn, Germany

Objectives: Stroop interference can be reduced after exposure to positive achievement-related word primes (Kazén & Kuhl, JPSP, 2005). The underlying neural mechanisms were investigated during fMRI. Methods: 25 men (age 20-28) participated. Induction of need-specific positive affect preceded each Stroop task. Data were acquired on a 1.5T Scanner and analyzed using SPM2. Furthermore, personality measures were assessed. Results: Focusing on a subgroup showing decreased Stroop interference after achievement-related primes, the superior prefrontal cortex displays an interaction of motivation and Stroop interference (uncorrected p<.001). Interference was significantly correlated with high implicit achievement motive (p<.05). Conclusions: Mastering the Stroop conflict can be dissociated from Stroop conflict per se.

The relationship between positive and negative symptoms and cognitive disorders in schizophrenia

Rahimi Taghanaki, Changiz Clinical Psychology, Shiraz University, Shiraz, Islamic Republic of Iran

This study examined the relationship between positive symptoms, negative symptoms and cognitive disorders related to frontal lobe dysfunctions in schizophrenic patients (36 with negative and 32 with positive symptoms), using a series of tests related to frontal lobe dysfunctions. In opposite of the theories, t test revealed that schizophrenic patients with positive symptoms showed significantly more cognitive disorders (P<0.01) than those with negative symptoms. It is concluded that frontal lobes' cognitive disorders in schizophrenia are not related to kinds of symptoms, but they could be explained using other factors like the severity of symptoms.

The study of parietal lobe disorders in schizophrenic patients

Rahimi Taghanaki, Changiz Clinical Psychology, Shiraz University, Shiraz, Islamic Republic of Iran

Many studies have revealed that schizophrenic patients show cognitive disorders related to frontal and temporal lobes but not parietal lobe dysfunctions. This study examined the functional disorders related to parietal lobe in schizophrenic patients. Schizophrenic patients and the patients with unipolar psychotic depression, the last one as a control group, completed the Line Bisection Test a test sensitive to parietal lobe dysfunctions. T test showed that, schizophrenic patients had significantly(P<0.01) more problem than depressive patients in this test. It is concluded that schizophrenic patients have parietal lobe functional disorders, specially in the right hemisphere of the brain.

The role of positive emotions in stress among student teachers and school teachers

Rajala, Raimo Dept. of Education, University of Lapland, Rovaniemi, Finland

The role of positive emotions (PE's) in stress and coping is a neglected field of research. The purpose of this study is to investigate effects of initial PE's on later problems, cognitions, coping efforts, coping resources and negative emotions. The subjects of the study were student teachers (n= 180) and schoolteachers (n=316). The data were gathered via a stress and coping questionnaire on two occasions during student teaching and school-teaching. Multiple regressions were used to find out whether PE's had predicted effects. The results indicated that PE's increase favorable cognitions and constructive coping efforts and decrease negative emotions. In conclusion, PE's shape mediating factors between problems and stress.

Impact of stress and daily hassles on mental health of children in public care in Croatia

Rajhvajn Bulat, Linda Department of social work, Faculty of Law, Zagreb, Croatia Branica, Vanja DEPARTMENT OF SOCIAL WORK, FACULTY OF LAW, ZAGREB, Croatia

Study investigates in what way mental health of children in public care is affected with stress, daily hassles and ways of coping with it. A longitudinal study completed in 2007 (5 years between follow-up) was conducted with 139 children placed in public care. At the first study children were 12.65 years old in average and 17.71 years at the follow-up. In order to establish the level of stress, self-concept and children's mental health we used 6 questioners. Regression analysis showed that earlier seeking and getting social support and present more positive self-concept and less daily hassles prevents developing children's' external and internal problems.

Stereotypes as threat in relationships: A comparative analysis between Brazilian and Polish society

Ramos De Oliveira, Diana Dept. of Social Psychology, University of Basque Country, San Sebastián, Spain Pankalla, Andrzej Psychology of Institute, University of Adam Mickiewicz, Poznań, Poland

Stereotypes have for a long time been associated with the negative attitudes of an outgroup. Stephan & Stephan(1996) postulated that because NE represent negative expectations about outgroup, appear together with negative emotions towards the outgroup that intensifies negative attitude of outgroup. The present study investigates how stereotypes reflect the cognitive component of prejudicial attitudes in Brazil and Poland. To assess we applied the Negative Stereotype Index. Participants were asked to indicate the percentage of citizens of another country who possessed each of 12 traits. Results showed that negative stereotype traits in Poland and Brazil, when attributed to outgroup, resulted in more unfavourable evaluations.

Emotional intelligence and stress resiliency: A relationship study

Rastogi, Renu Humanities and Social Sciences, Indian Institute of Technology, Roorkee, India Garg, Pooja Humanities and Social Sciences, Indian Institute of Technology, Roorkee, India

This paper delves into the relationship study between emotional intelligence and stress resiliency among students of technical institute. Pearson correlation and multiple stepwise regression analysis unfold positive relationship between emotional intelligence and stress resiliency and conclude with certain important guidelines for inculcating emotional intelligence and stress resiliency among students.

First evidence of positive effects of cognitive skill training on cognitive and psychosocial aspects in unemployed subjects

Rehberger, Maria-Christina Inst. für Psychologie, Universität Innsbruck, Innsbruck, Austria Bliem, Harald Rudolf Department of Psychology, University of Innsbruck, Innsbruck, Austria

Although there is some evidence that job loss may be associated with cognitive difficulties, it is still unclear if and/or how these difficulties can be managed. The present work investigates the effects of cognitive skill training on cognitive performance and on identified psychosocial difficulties. Results reveal clearly positive effects on most cognitive parameters, i.e. logical analysis, word fluency, verbal memory and psychosocial parameters. Integrating the neuropsychology-based cognitive training research into the existing research of unemployment represents a new scientific approach. Future perspectives of this new approach beyond unemployment research are discussed.

Madness, discontent and touristic's growth of cities: Challenges to contemporary social psychology

Reinecke Alverga, Alex Dept. of Psychology, UFRN-Brazil, Natal, Brazil Dimenstein, Magda Psychology, UFRN - Brazil, Natal - RN, Brazil Ferreira Leite, Jáder Psychology, UFRN- Brazil, Natal - RN, Brazil Sales Macedo, João Paulo Psychology, UFRN- Brazil, Natal - RN, Brazil

Objective: To discuss the invention of urban's territory and styles of living in everyday life. Method: Theoretical discussion about relations between city/madness, city/discontent in psychologists work and city/contemporary and hegemonic process of privatization and turistification. Results: Contemporaneity has been characterized by creation of global and flexible identities that change according to market movements. Conclusion: There is a continuity between development of sociability and subjectivity, urban and subjective changes. There exist a very close relation between our style of live and subsist in cities and the possibility of resisting or not against effects of power, domination and formation of life.

Warri players and working memory

Retschitzki, Jean Dept. of Psychology, University of Fribourg, Fribourg, Switzerland Minore, Raphaela Psychology, University of Fribourg, Fribourg, Switzerland

This research investigates the role of working memory in warri players, mainly in Antigua. In experiment 1, players memorised a situation while performing (or not) a secondary task aimed at suppressing selectively one of the components of working memory. In experiment 2 players chose the best move in a given situation while performing the same secondary tasks. Results indicate that good players do not use specifically visual aspects in representing the situations both when they have to memorize a situation or to choose the best move. Tentative explanations of the contrasts with Robbins & al.'s results will be proposed.

The encoding and integration of premises in easy conditional and syllogistic deductive tasks

Reverberi, Carlo Charité - Universitätsmedizin, Bernstein Center, Berlin, Germany Cherubini, Paolo Psychology department, Università Milano - Bicocca, Milan, Italy Frackowiak, Richard Functional Imaging Laboratory, University College London, London, United Kingdom Paulesu, Eraldo Psychology department, Università Milano - Bicocca, Milan, Italy Macaluso, Emiliano Neuroimaging Laboratory, Santa Lucia Foundation, Rome, Germany

Deductive reasoning can be applied to several problem types. We tested whether the same cognitive operations underlie solutions for them all. We used fMRI to compare reasoning-related activity associated with conditionals and syllogisms. Activity was assessed separately during the encoding and the integration of premises. The left-inferior frontal gyrus (BA44) was the only brain area active during integration, both for conditionals and syllogisms. No reasoning-specific activity was observed for encoding. The hypothesis that different kinds of deduction engage the same cognitive operations at the integration stage is corroborated. These operations involve BA44, an area linked to syntax and abstract rule application.

Parents underestimate the severity of stressful events and health symptoms reported by their children

Reyes, Ana Marina Dept. of Psychology, National University of Mexico, Mexico City, Mexico Acuna, Laura Psychology, National University of Mexico, Mexico City, Mexico

Elementary-school children (N=156) answered the Social Readjustment Rating Scale (SRRS) and the Scale of Physical and Psychological Symptoms (SPPS). In addition, parents also answered both questionnaires for each of their children. Children reported having experienced more stressful events and more symptoms than those reported by their parents. The reports from girls, older children, and children from families with a low income were more consistent with their parents' reports than the reports from their counterparts. These results confirm previous reports that parents tend to underestimate the stress and the symptoms actually experienced by their children.

Age-related gains in empathy: Subjective and behavioral evidence

Richter, David Inst. Entwicklungspsychologie, Universität Leipzig, Leipzig, Germany Kunzmann, Ute Entwicklungspsychologie, Universität Leipzig, Leipzig, Germany

Recent life-span theories have suggested that a deficit-model of social-emotional aging is inappropriate. This laboratory study investigated age differences in empathic concern on subjective and behavioral levels in a sample of 80 young and 73 older adults. Eight film clips, each depicting a person talking about a significant life event, were presented as stimuli. The age-relevance of the life-event was varied (young vs. old). First results suggest that older people report and express greater empathic concern toward others than young adults when being confronted with a life-event relevant in old age. This evidence gives a positive outlook on getting older.

Subsidized employment as predictor of personal initiative among long-term unemployed

Rigotti, Thomas Inst. für Psychologie II, Universität Leipzig, Leipzig, Germany Steinhorst, Katrin Institute of Psychology II, University of Leipzig, Leipzig, Germany Mohr, Gisela Institute of Psychology II, University of Leipzig, Leipzig, Germany

In Leipzig a program, called "Aktiv-Office" has been set up to promote the reintegration of long-term unemployed persons into the labour market. The aim of our study was to investigate the impact of this program on personal resources and well-being of participants. In a sample of 210 persons from this program, working for the public transport system, we could find that the time spent within "Aktiv-Office" was positively related to self-initiative and was negatively related to psychosomatic complaints. As a consequence it may have a positive impact on re-employment or at least the psychosocial situation of the participants.

Health and conflict in couples

Rivera Aragon, Sofia Psychology Faculty, UNAM, Mexico City, Mexico Díaz Loving, Rolando Psychology Faculty, UNAM (Mexico), Mexico, Mexico Velasco Matus, Pedro Wolfgang Psychology Faculty, UNAM (Mexico), Mexico, Mexico Montero Santamaria, Nancy Psychology Faculthy, UNAM (Mexico), Mexico, Mexico

Various theories attempt to explain the development of close relationships. However, the way individuals react when their relationships deteriorate has not been systematically studied or reported. Hence, this study is aimed at studying the relationship between conflict, anxiety and depression in men and women. Three scales were therefore applied to 321 volunteers, 164 males and 157 females: the scale evaluating the content of conflict, Spilbergers Anxiety and Beck's Depression Inventory were applied. Results show that conflict is related to anxiety and depression, observing that the greater the number of conflicts, the more the former increase. Results can therefore be explained based on mishandling of anxiety produced by different couple situations, which are an important source of conflict.

Switching off from work: The role of psychological detachment and rumination in workplace bullying

Rodriguez Muñoz, Alfredo Biological and Health Psychol., Universidad Autonoma de Madrid, Madrid, Spain Garrosa, Eva Biological and Health Psycho, Universidad Autonoma de Madrid, Madrid, Spain Morante, Maria Eugenia Biological and Health Psycho, Universidad Autonoma de Madrid, Madrid, Spain Moreno-Jimenez, Bernardo Biological and Health Psycho, Universidad Autonoma de Madrid, Madrid, Spain

A recent number of studies have focused on the relations between psychosocial factors and sleep disturbances. Several models have highlighted the importance of cognitive factors in the development and maintenance of insomnia. The aim of this study is to examine the moderating role of psychological detachment and rumination on the relationship between workplace bullying and insomnia. We used a design in which we collected data at two points in time separated by 1 month. A total of 511 individuals responded to both phases. The results of the regression analysis provide evidence for the moderating role of psychological detachment and rumination in bullying process.

Visual and spatial memory in fibromyalgia patients.

Roldan-Tapia, Lola Neurociencias y CC Salud, University of Almeria, Almeria, Spain Canovas, Rosa Neurociencias y CC Salud, University of Almeria, Almería, Spain León, Irene Neurociencias y CC Salud, University of Almeria, Almería, Spain Cimadevilla, Jose Manuel Neurociencias y CC Salud, University of Almeria, Almería, Spain Valverde, Matias Neurociencias y CC Salud, University of Almeria, Almería, Spain

Fibromyalgia (FM) is a chronic, painful musculoskeletal disorder of uncertain etiology, that it seems related with cognitive alterations, as memory and attention. This study evaluates FM patients for the presence of visual and spatial memory deficit using traditional neuropsychological test and a virtual reality test. Neuropsychological assessment was conducted on twenty women with FM. Assessment include measures of working memory, attention, spatial memory and intellect, relating performances with age and demographical variables and clinical signs. Cognitive data were also correlated with performance on a new virtual task to evaluate human place learning, showing a decline in the speed of processing and in some cases, low execution group, a deficit in the spatial learning. Keywords: Fibromyalgia, memory, attention, virtual reality

Temporal preparation facilitates perceptual identification of letters

Rolke, Bettina Kognitive Psychologie, Universität Tübingen, Tübingen, Germany

Recent evidence suggests that perceptual processing of single stimulus features improves when participants are temporally prepared for the occurrence of visual stimuli. In this study, a visual backward masking paradigm was employed to investigate whether the benefit of temporal preparation generalizes to perceptual identification of more complex stimuli such as letters. Visual discrimination performance improved when participants were temporally prepared. Therefore, the present results support the notion that perception benefits from temporal preparation not only at the feature level but also at subsequent levels that integrate feature information.

Executive processes and overgenerality in non-clinical population

Ros Segura, Laura Psychology, Castilla La Mancha University, Albacete, Spain Latorre Postigo, Jose Miguel Psychology, Castilla La Mancha University, Albacete, Spain Serrano Selva, Juan Pedro PSICOLOGÍA, Facultad de Medicina, Albacete, Spain Aguilar Córcoles, José Psychology, Castilla La Mancha University, Albacete, Spain Navarro Bravo, Beatriz Psychology, Castilla La Mancha University, Albacete, Spain

The present study investigates the role of executive processes plays in overgenerality (OGM) in non-clinical population. 50 young adults and 46 older adults took part in the study. We obtained measures of working memory, short-term memory, sustained attention and specificity of autobiographical memories. Data were analyzed with the statistical softwares SPSS 14.0. and AMOS 6.0 Older adults showed more OGM than young adults $(F(1,93) = 5.80, p = .018)$. There was a positive correlation between specificity and working memory $(r = .31, p < .01)$. The findings showed that OGM increases with normal ageing and it is negative correlated with working memory.

Posttraumatic stress disorder: Supervising student-delivered exposure therapy for optimal clinical outcome.

Rosqvist, Johan Professional Psychology, Pacific University, Portland, Oregon, USA

Posttraumatic stress disorder is often disabling, and a complex phenomenon commonly recalcitrant to treatment. Fortunately, empirical evidence supports using exposure therapy, but many practitioners shy from using this robust approach. In fact, dissemination has largely failed. Objectives: Novel dissemination method better prepares students to use this gold-standard procedure. Methods: "Live" training was delivery model for exposure therapy, and end-state functioning was used to gauge clinically meaningful change. Results: Patients met "recovered" status. Conclusions: This form of teaching exposure therapy overcomes common utilization obstacles, and does not interfere with outcome. "Live" training may represent true dissemination, and may actually enhance outcome.

Psychosocial stress: Negative life events in TEDDY (The Environmental Determinants of Diabetes in the Young)

Roth, Roswith Inst. für Psychologie, Universität Graz, Graz, Austria Johnson, Suzanne B. Dept of Med Human Soc Science, Florid State Univ Coll of Med, Talahassee, USA Lernmark, Babro Department of Clinical Science, Lund University, Malmö, Sweden Baxter, Judith Dept. of Preventive Medicine, Univers of Colorado at Denver, Aurora, CO, USA Simell, Tuula Department of Pediatrics, University of Turku, Turku, Finland Mcleod, Wendy Data Coordination center, University of South Florida, Tampa, USA

TEDDY is an international study to identify environmental triggers of type 1 diabetes in genetically at-risk children, identified at birth. Children were enrolled in TEDDY prior to the age of 4.5 months. The aim was to evaluate frequencies of occurrence and categories of negative events affecting mothers (N=3755) and children during pregnancy and the first three months after birth. Negative life events were more common during pregnancy than during the three postnatal months but the proportion of different negative life events was similar during both time periods. Half of negative events were health-related. Events differed between the participating four countries.

The effect of a hardiness program on call center agents' restorative well-being

Roxas, Maryfe Guidance and Counseling Center, TIP, Manila, Philippines

Several studies correlated shift work with stress. Stressful events are assumed to decrease life satisfactions. Such events may increase a shift worker's vulnerability to burnout. Burnout may lead to physical and mental health problems and emotional exhaustion. This study sought to determine the effect of a hardiness program on call center agents' well-being recovery. Findings of this study showed that there is a significant increase in all levels of the Multi Dimensional Wellness Indices of the experimental group after the intervention program. This study confirmed that the hardiness program facilitated the use of coping appraisal and adaptation. This in turn has positive effect in the recovery process of their well-being.

Eye-tracking the classic Sally-Ann task: A real-time investigation of adult theory of mind

Rubio Fernandez, Paula Psychology Department, Princeton University, Princeton, USA

Two experiments investigated Boaz Keysar's claim that egocentricity is an automatic bias in adults and Theory of Mind only a correction mechanism. I tested adults (allegedly as a control group) on a computer version of the Sally-Ann task for children, incorporating eye-tracking. The story included a control True Belief condition and two critical False Belief conditions, each with a mind-reading question. No errors were expected. Response times, gaze direction and fixation latencies were recorded. Eye-movements showed that, despite being sometimes the dominant initial response, the egocentric perspective is not an automatic bias across conditions. Moreover, Theory of Mind does not operate as an effortful correction mechanism, even though curse-of-knowledge effects were observed.

Increasing levels of students' self-realization

Rustanovich, Zoya Organizational Psychology, Institut of Psychology, Kiev, Ukraine

Objective. Finding effects of student psychological support training on students' self-realization. Method. The investigation was done on a sample of 30 university students in Mykolaiv in 2006 using the Self-Actualization Test (SAT) and SPSS. Results. The investigation found statistically significant differences between the respondents' pre- and post-training scores on the following SAT scales: time competence (p=0.042), support (p=0.0001), value orientations (p=0.003), behavioral flexibility (p=0.001), sensitivity (p=0.041), self-respect (p=0.0001), self-perception (p=0.0001), synergy (p=0.0001), aggression admittance (p=0.025), sociability (p=0.0001), cognitive needs (p=0.0001), creativity (r=0.049), and self-control (p=0.0001). Conclusion. The student psychological support program proved to be effective in enhancing students' self-realization.

Description of sexual harassment that occurs to young adulthood women in Jakarta

Rutyanto, Iriani Roesmaladewi Psychology, Tarumanagara University, Jakarta, Indonesia

Aim of this study is to get an information on the sexual harassment toward young adulthood woman.Sexual harassment is an unwanted sexual behavior that harms the victim, that consist of verbal, non-verbal, and physical. There are 336 women (20–40 years old)from all level of society.The result 200 are a victim. 20% as a victim of heavy sexual harassments.Commonly type of physical sexual harassment is a gaze/glimpse with sexual desire.The side effect that arises are emotional imbalance,insomnia. Most of the victims tend to ignore and doesn't take action to againt

their sexual harassment Keyword: sexual harassment, young adulthood woman

Comparing the long-term predictive power of a singe-item of perceived work stress on need for recovery for managers and manual workers

Rydstedt, Leif Behavioural Studies, University West, Trollhättan, Sweden Devereux, Jason Robens Centre f Health Ergonom, University of Surrey, Guildford, United Kingdom

This study analysed the predictive power of one work stress item ("In general, how do you find your job; 1=not at all stressful—5=extremely stressful) to long-term need for recovery for "managers" (n=216) and "elementary trades" (n=100). There were no group differences in need for recovery managers reported significantly higher baseline work stress. Controlling for baseline need for recovery and demographic factors, the work-stress item significantly predicted outcome need for recovery (R2=.051; df=1,93; p<.01) for manual workers but not for managers. Possibly managers may perceive their job demands as positively challenging which may explain the different reactions to work stress.

Types of social desirability effect on the multifactor tolerance inventory scores

Sabadosh, Pavel Psychology of Abilities, Institute of Psychology RAS, Moscow, Russia Babaeva, Julia Psychology, Moscow State University, Moscow, Russia

Aim of present study: to investigate how questionnaire-measured tolerance level is affected by social desirability. Validated on more than 1000 subjects, authors' Multifactor Tolerance Inventory was used, comprising scales of 2 types: "objects of tolerance" and "subject variables". 242 Moscow students of both sexes aged 14-16 years completed the questionnaire twice, with the second instruction suggesting socially desired answers. While the social desirability significantly augmented the tolerance summary index, there were scales "religion" and "strangers" that decreased. Moreover, the summary index decreased in 32% of the sample. Conclusion: depending on subject, social desirability induces opposite changes in the manifested tolerance.

Development of emotional traits in early childhood: Relationship between primary emotions and the self-regulative functions

Saiki, Hisayo Takarazuka, Japan

Relationship between primary emotions and self-regulative functions, as well as the developmental process in early childhood was investigated. The participants were 253 children (aged: 43-78 months). Their homeroom teachers were asked to rate them on 12 items measuring emotional traits and seven items measuring self-regulation. Children with high self-regulation showed high "fear," "acceptance," and low "surprise," "disgust," and "anger." Those with high self-assertiveness showed high "acceptance," "joy," "disgust" and "surprise," and low "fear," and "sadness." Moreover, 5- 6 year-old children were ambivalent in emotional regulation.

Intention to change organization and to change occupation: From a view point of mental health

Sakai, Keiko Graduate School, Chuo University, Hachioji, Japan

This study aimed to examine differences between intention to change organization and to change occupation from a viewpoint of mental health. A questionnaire was administered to 231 Japanese young adult workers (age25-39) who engage in work more than 40 hours a week. Partial correlation analyses showed that "intention to change organization" has significant negative correlation with subjective happiness, and that "intention to change occupation" has significant negative correlation with self-esteem and significant positive correlation with general health questionnaire and anxiety for the future. Results implied that "intention to change occupation" is more maladaptive than "intention to change organization".

Does face stimulus capture both young and older Japanese adults' attention?

Sakata, Yoko Dept. of Psychology, Aichi Shukutoku, Aich, Japan Kamei, So Psychology, NILS, Aich-gun, Japan Kumada, Takatsune Psychology, AIST, Aich-gun, Japan

This study examined age-related differences in attentional capture for the face stimulus. Participants were instructed to move their eyes as quickly as possible to a color singleton target and identify whether a small face or sign was located inside it. The two age groups were analyzed individually. However the tendencies were alike. Namely, for both groups, eye saccadic latencies to the face stimulus by the eye mark recorder were equal to the sign. On the other hand, response times to the face stimulus were shorter than to the sign. These contradictory results are discussed in terms of peripheral vision.

Gender and occupational class differences in the effect of work stress on depressive symptoms

Salavecz, Gyöngyvér Institute of Behavioral Scienc, Semmelweis University, Budapest, Hungary László, Krisztina Institute of Behavioral Scienc, Semmelweis University, Budapest, Hungary Kopp, Mária Institute of Behavioral Scienc, Semmelweis University, Budapest, Hungary

The aim of this study was to analyse occupational class differences in the effect of work stress on depression in a sample taken from the Hungarian Epidemiological Panel. Binary logistic regression was used to determine the effect of work stress. The results showed higher effort-reward imbalance and overcommitment significantly predicted higher depressive symptoms in both genders. A significant interaction between overcommitment and occupational classes was found among men. Men who were manual workers with high overcommitment had the highest risks of depressive symptoms (OR=3,4 p<0,001). Higher occupational class may buffer against the health damaging effects of overcommitment among men.

The 'non-self' belief across the life span

Sano, Ayako Waseda University, Tokyo, Japan Ishii, Yasutomo Letters,Arts and Sciences, Waseda University, Tokyo, Japan Takaki, Hiroko Letters,Arts and Sciences, Waseda University, Tokyo, Japan

Today a fifth of Japanese people is over 65 year old. This study examined a cross-sectional age-difference of the 'non-self' belief which was 'the state of seeing things just they are and having respect for not only oneself but also others as well'.This belief is assumed to be helpful for successful aging. Japanese people(18-82 year olds?N=455) answered questionnaires about the 'non-self' and other psychological states. ANOVAs revealed that older people have stronger belief of 'non-self' than younger one.And the 'non-self' belief had correlations with subjective happiness(r=.47,p<.01) and depressive state(r=-.41,p<.01).

Perceived organizational support and well-being at work

Santos, Joana Dept. of Psychology, University of Algarve, Faro, Portugal Gonçalves, Gabriela Department of Psychology, University of Algarve, Faro, Portugal Gomes, Alexandra Department of Psychology, University of Algarve, Faro, Portugal

The main goal of the present research is to study the influence of perceived organizational support on well-being at work; those are fundamentals issues when we are interested in organizational performance. 150 questionnaires were applied to Portu-

guese teachers. The regression analysis showed a systematic and positive association between organizational support and well-being at work. The organizational support explains significantly more the well-being than the contributions brought by demographic variables. These results showed the importance of organizational support in the study of well-being. However, further research is needed in order to explore this problem more deeply, from theoretical and empirical perspectives.

Drug addiction: Salomé case study

Santos Gomes, Patricia Faculdade de Ciências Humanas, Universidade Fernando Pessoa, Porto, Portugal Soares Martins, José Faculdade de Ciências Humanas, Universidade Fernando Pessoa, maia, Portugal

The aim of this study was to know a woman history, once there is a lack of knowlege about drug addicts women. In this case study, it had been conclued, there are therapeutic outcomes in the treatment process which is still happen and her recuperation is really being made, also result of her personal contribution. This is the reason our choice of a clinical case to suport one monography: description of a sucessful case, despite the whole negative life events and interferents in this life course. Key words: drug addiction; drug addicts women; qualitative research; female drug addict case study; treatment; therapeutic community; therapeutic outcomes.

Recovery strategies: Mitigating the negative effects of work-family conflict on employee's well-being

Sanz Vergel, Ana Isabel Biological and Health Psychol., Universidad Autónoma de Madrid, Madrid, Spain Garrosa, Eva Biological and Health Psycho, Universidad Autónoma de Madrid, Madrid, Spain Gálvez, Macarena Biological and Health Psycho, Universidad Autónoma de Madrid, Madrid, Spain Sebastián, Julia Biological and Health Psycho, Universidad Autónoma de Madrid, Madrid, Spain

The present study links the work-family interface (i.e. work-family conflict (WFC) and family-work conflict (FWC) with the concept of recovery. The authors hypothesized that two recovery strategies - psychological detachment from work and verbal expression of emotions- moderated the relationship of the two types of conflict with well-being. The sample was composed of 128 emergency professionals from Spain. Results of regression analyses revealed that psychological detachment from work moderated the relationship between WFC and psychological strain and between FWC and life satisfaction. Verbal expression of emotions moderated the relationship between both types of conflict and psychological strain. Findings are discussed in terms of their theoretical and practical implications.

History of social psychology in Japan

Sato, Tatsuya Dept. of Psychology, Ritsumeikan University, Kyoto, Japan

Both McDougall (a psychologist) and Ross (a sociologist) coincidentally wrote the first textbook(s) on social psychology in 1908. But in Japan, the first book on "social psychology (SHAKAI SHINRIGAKU)" appeared in 1906 by the sociologist Tokuya. And in 1908, Higuchi published the "Study on social psychology". These authors might have been influenced by psychological sociology. After the Taisho Political Crisis (TAISHO SEI-HEN), Higuchi (1913) defined the social situation of Japan as the "era of the crowded" after Gustav Le Bon. The implication of psychological sociology to the history of Japanese social psychology is discussed.

The evaluation of a multimodal intervention program to prevent prejudice and promote intergroup relations in elementary school children

Saur, Michael DFG Forschungsgruppe, Universität Jena, Jena, Germany Ziegler, Petra DFG Research Group, University of Jena, Jena, Germany Beelmann, Andreas Institute of Psychology, University of Jena, Jena, Germany

The present study evaluates the PARTS-program, a multimodal prevention program that combines intercultural learning methods, extended contact stories, and social-cognitive skills exercises to prevent prejudice and promote intergroup relations among elementary school children. Effectiveness was studied within a treatment-control-group design with a total of n = 500 third-graders. Assessments on prejudice, discrimination and interpersonal tolerance were made prior, immediately after and three-month after the termination of the program. The results showed positive outcomes for the program group compared to the control group on proximal measures (e.g., prejudice), while effects on distal outcomes (e.g., interpersonal tolerance) were only weak.

The influence of perceptual grouping on visual contextual modulation

Sayim, Bilge BMI-LPSY, EPFL, Lausanne, Switzerland Herzog, Michael H. BMI-LPSY, EPFL, Lausanne, Switzerland Westheimer, Gerald Dept.of Molecular & Cell B, UC Berkeley, Berkeley, USA

Embedding a target within contextual elements can influence performance on this target. For example, when a vernier is flanked by two lines, discrimination deteriorates strongly compared to an unflanked presentation. This contextual modulation is usually explained by local spatial interactions. Here we show that this explanation is inadequate. Instead, we propose that flanks interfere most strongly with the vernier when they are grouped with the vernier. We show that "ungrouping" the flanks from the vernier by embedding them in figurative configurations improves performance. Our results show that global figural aspects are crucial in visual contextual modulation.

Addiction and co-morbidity

Scheibenbogen, Oliver Frauenabteilung, Anton Proksch Institut, Wien, Austria Feselmayer, Senta Frauenabteilung, Anton Proksch Institut, Wien, Austria

At in-patient treatment facilities psychopathologic disturbances are more noticeable in female alcohol-addicts than in male alcohol-addicts. The following studies try to identify the relationships between co-morbidity and the potential course of dependencies and to derive gender and disorder-specific treatment approaches. 170 female and male in-patients at the Anton Proksch Institute participated in the study. Standardized questionnaires, short diagnostic interviews and rating scales were used. First results show a mental co-morbidity in 75% of the women and in 53% of the men (t=2,255; df=97). Women suffer significantly more frequently from depressive episodes and agoraphobia and social phobia. Resulting therapeutic consequences are shown and discussed.

Does prior strategy use affect on subsequent strategy choice?: Insights from a numerosity judgement task

Schillemans, Viki Educational Sciences, Katholieke Universiteit Leuven, Leuven, Belgium Luwel, Koen Educational Sciences, Katholieke Universiteit Leuven, Leuven, Belgium Onghena, Patrick Educational Sciences, Katholieke Universiteit Leuven, Leuven, Belgium Verschaffel, Lieven Educational Sciences, Katholieke Universiteit Leuven, Leuven, Belgium

Three experiments tested the hypothesis that repeated prior strategy use affects subsequent strategy choice. Adults were presented sequences of items that either strongly elicited an addition-based or a subtraction-based strategy for judging numerosities in a rectangular grid. Each sequence was followed by a "neutral" item that equally elicited both strategies. Experiment 1 and 2 revealed that strategy choices on a neutral item were affected by the repeated use of the strategy on the previous items, but only for a small range of neutral items. Experiment 3 showed that this effect was – unexpectedly – not strengthened by the length of the sequence.

Are infant regulatory disorders predictive of intelligence in preschool children: Results of a prospective longitudinal study

Schmid, Gabriele Department of Psychology, University of Basel, Basel, Switzerland Schreier, Andrea Department of Psychology, University of Warwick, Coventry, United Kingdom Meyer, Renate Department of Psychology, University of Warwick, Coventry, United Kingdom Wolke, Dieter Department of Psychology, University of Warwick, Coventry, United Kingdom

Objective: To evaluate whether infant regulatory problems are predictive of cognitive development in children. Method: The sample consisted of n=4427 infants. Regulatory problems, i.e. excessive crying and feeding problems were assessed at 5 months of age, and IQ (CMM), language and vocabulary (AWST) at 56 months. Results: 19.7% of infants suffered from regulatory problems. Feeding and number of regulatory problems were predictive of lower vocabulary, whereas socioeconomic status, breastfeeding, neurological problems, and family adversity were predictive of all three IQ scales. Conclusion: Infant feeding problems and number of regulatory problems are predictive of lower verbal IQ when controlled for other social factors.

Capitalize the potential of interdisciplinary teams: Evaluation of the knowledge integration training for teams

Schmidtborn, Adrienne Stuttgart, Germany Wittmann, Werner W. Dept. of Psychology, Chair II, Universität Mannheim, Mannheim, Germany Kremer, David CC Personalmanagement, Fraunhofer IAO, Stuttgart, Germany

Today's growing business complexity frequently asks for work in interdisciplinary teams. However, these teams are challenged by problems that emerge from different functional backgrounds of team members. The Knowledge Integration Training for Teams was developed to improve efficiency of interdisciplinary teams. Based on a sample of 36 students, the present study evaluated six training-modules. The evaluation followed the five-data-box conception (Wittmann, 1985; 1990) and the four-level model proposed by Kirkpatrick (1975). All six modules seem to promote the work in interdisciplinary teams; furthermore three of them promote the ability of knowledge integration. These results encourage further use of this training.

Representation of the elderly in textbooks: Diagnosis and recommendation

Schoenenberger, Sandrine Dept. de Psychologie, Université Paul Verlaine, Metz, France Wagner, Anne-Lorraine Psychology, université Paul Verlaine, Metz, France Tisserant, Pascal Psychology, université Paul Verlaine, Metz, France Sinigaglia, Sabrina Sociology, université Paul Verlaine, Metz, France

Negative stereotypes about the elderly are present in children before they start school, especially because of television and the limited number of good relationships between generations. Textbooks are common tools for children and they must not contain stereotypes about the elderly. Our study is based on a quantitative analysis of textbooks, a survey among teachers and book publishers, and interviews of an association for the elderly. The

elderly are hardly ever presented in textbooks and they are usually in retirement situations. They are absent from work situations. We will give recommendations to improve the representation of the elderly in textbooks.

Are ERN/Ne and CRN amplitudes affected by people's uncertainty?

Schreiber, Melanie Department of Psychology, Humoldt-University at Berlin, Berlin, Germany Endrass, Tanja Department of Psychology, Humoldt-University at Berlin, Berlin, Germany Kathmann, Norbert Department of Psychology, Humoldt-University at Berlin, Berlin, Germany

This study aims to investigate whether age effects on ERN/Ne and CRN are related to uncertainty. We expect a replication of the smaller ERN/Ne in elderly compared to young adults and the ERN/Ne and CRN to vary with task difficulty. 20 younger/older participants performed a perceptual decision task with four difficulty levels. The EEG and EOG were recorded from 65 channels. Elderly had smaller ERN/Ne and CRN amplitudes compared to younger adults. Both groups showed attenuated ERN/Ne and enhanced CRN amplitudes with higher difficulty. Task difficulty and thereby uncertainty does not differentially affect performance monitoring in younger and older adults.

Mistaking the instance for the rule: A critical analysis of the truth-table paradigm and implications for theories of conditional reasoning.

Schroyens, Walter Psychology, University of Gent, Gent, Belgium

Many studies investigate <if A then C>'s interpretation by having people evaluate truth-table cases as making the rule true or false, or being irrelevant. We argue that a single case can never prove a general rule to be true. The impossible 'true' option would therefore bias results. Experiment 1 accordingly showed an increase in not-false vs. true evaluations. Experiment 2's experimental group (N=67) could also indicate cases make the rule more plausible, but neither true nor false. This significantly reduced irrelevant evaluation-rates as compared to the standard true/false/irrelevant task (N=61). Results challenge 30 years of research with tasks using the impossible "true" option.

A critical review of thinking about what is true, possible and irrelevant in reasoning from or reasoning about conditional propositions: Corrective meta-analyses and reconsiderations of theoretical argumentation based on the truth-table task literature

Schroyens, Walter Psychology, University of Gent, Gent, Belgium

Truth-table tasks investigate <if A then C>'s interpretation by having people evaluate truth-table cases (e.g., <A_C>, <A_not-C>, <not-A_C>, <not-A_not-C>) as making a rule true or false, or being irrelevant. Recent studies looking at truth-table task performance have used their conclusions about the 'facts' presented in the literature to evaluate the explanatory adequacy of theories of human reasoning. Mental-models theory has recently been the focus of many critiques. Focusing on those critiques based on truth-table task results, our meta-analyses suggest they are in need of a critical analysis: critics have presented mistaken generalizations as fact, thus constructing arguments that are at best unsound.

A crucial test for the suppositional-conditional theory of conditional reasoning

Schroyens, Walter Psychology, University of Gent, Gent, Belgium

Suppositional-conditional theory explains the relevance of false-antecedent cases – as evidenced by truth-table studies, in which <not-A_not-C> is

often judged consistent with <if A then C> rules – by means of pragmatic implicatures: <if A then C> invites its converse <if C then A> and/or its inverse <if not-A then not-C>. Neither the converse, nor inverse implicature yields a pattern of truth-table task evaluations that is consistent with the material-implication interpretation, in which only <A_not-C> makes the rule false, while other cases are neither irrelevant nor false. Evidence shows that a significant minority of people do exhibit material-implication patterns/interpretations; thus showing suppositional-conditional theory is false/incomplete.

Adolescents' knowledge, attitude and performance regarding Ecstasy

Seyedfatemi, Naiemeh Psychiatry, Faculty of Nursing, Tehran, Islamic Republic of Iran Khoshnavayefoomeni, Fatemeh psychiatry, Faculty of Nursing, Tehran, Islamic Republic of Iran Behbahani, Nasrin psychiatry, Faculty of Nursing, Tehran, Islamic Republic of Iran Hoseini, Fatemeh psychiatry, Faculty of Nursing, Tehran, Islamic Republic of Iran

Introduction: Illicit drug use appears to be increasing among youth. Ecstasy is a psychoactive illegal drug which has numerous side effects. Methods: This cross-sectional study was carried out to determine adolescents' knowledge, attitude and performance regarding Ecstasy. Eight hundred adolescents resided in west of Tehran participated in this study. Results: Adolescent's Knowledge about Ecstasy in 53.8% was moderate, 78.9 % had a negative attitude toward using Ecstasy and 7.6% of them used Ecstasy once at least. Conclusion: Based on the study findings, Prevention programs which address the drug abuse side effects and reinforce adolescents' life skills is recommended.

Assessment of the effects of the first phase of the cardiac rehabilitation program on the level of anxiety in patients hospitalized for coronary arteries bypass surgery

Shaban, Marzieh Faculty of Nursing, Tehran University, Tehran, Islamic Republic of Iran

Surgical operations are among the most stressful events which might take place in everyone's life. This is a quasi-experimental research of the type clinical trial in which 60 patients who were hospitalized for coronary arteries bypass heart surgery. Findings of the research indicated that on the average, the level of anxiety and vital sign were no significant difference in both experience and control groups. the first phase of the cardiac rehabilitation program including physical exercises and conversation with the patient. During this process, patients are encouraged to do their ordinary daily activities in order to reduce their anxiety .

The difference of paternity of adolescences: Discussion from the Jung's perspective

Shimoda, Hiroko Dept. of Medicine, Kyoto University, Kyoto, Japan Keskinen, Soili Dept of teacher education, Turku university, Kyoto, Japan Keskinen, Esko Department of psychology, Turku university, Kyoto, Japan Hadano, Kazuo Department of medicine, Kyoto university, Kyoto, Japan Hayashi, Takuji Department of medicine, Kyoto university, Kyoto, Japan

Maternal affection is necessary for children. People have masculinity and femininity from Jungian theory. Young adolescence is cooperative for child rearing. However, how do men enthusing business manage both maternal affection and business? We executed survey for Japanese and Finnish university students using questionnaire. We found not only for women but for men have maternal affection, from the standpoint of intention of future lifestyle. However, Finnish adolescences do not want to be both motherly men and also paternity men. Finding is that the cross-point of identities and social expectation is important. We discuss how to unite maternal affection and masculinity.

Psychological change in children who attended Japanese traditional pilgrimage Ohenro

Shinto, Takaaki University Extension, University of Tokushima, Tokushima, Japan Fujihara, Nobuhiko Center for Collaboration in Co, Naruto University of Education, Naruto, Japan Yamasaki, Yoko Literature, Mukogawa Women's University, Nishinomiya, Japan Kohno, Michiyuki Elementary School, Kataji School, Kami, Japan

It was investigated that the effect of Japanese traditional pilgrimage "Ohenro" on children (8-14 y.o.). They walked for a part of Ohenro, that is, approx. 40 km and visited 4 Buddhist temples in 3 days. Questionnaires were administered to the children (pre- and post-test, n = 20) and their parents (post-test). The results showed (1) the children had reduced feeling of sadness (p < .01, by paired t-test), (2) they had reduced the use of resignation coping for stressor (p < .05, by paired t-test), and (3) they had increased confidence and feeling of growth (by post-test).

Work engagement and communication processes at work place in Japan

Shitara, Saeko University of Tsukuba, Tsukuba, Japan Arai, Kunijiro Psychology, University of Tsukuba, Tsukuba, Japan

The present study examines how work engaged employees recognize and form their relationships at their work place. 11 Japanese employees who were high on work engagement (Schaufeli et al., 2002) were given individual semi-structured interviews. Based on the 45 concepts, 14 categories and 6 category groups created by analyzing the data using M-GTA (Modified Grounded Theory Approach; Kinoshita, 2006), a model describing communication processes, more particularly, mentally and objectively focused ones, was developed. The findings indicate that work engaged employees are characterized by curiousness, persistence, flexibility and positiveness concerning relationships. They purposely join colleagues and try to develop interactions.

Maternal behavior toward directing an infant's attention to foods during mealtime

Shizawa, Miho Nursing, Nagoya University, Nagoya, Japan Shizawa, Yasuhiro Psychology, Osaka University, Suita, Japan Hinobayashi, Toshihiko Psychology, Osaka University, Suita, Japan Minami, Tetsuhiro Psychology, Osaka University, Nagoya, Japan

We examined the manner in which mothers direct their infants' attention to foods during mealtime. The directing behaviors of mothers toward infants were divided into "following" and "redirecting." Fourteen pairs of mothers and infants aged from nine to fourteen months were observed. The results showed that mothers, under monitored infants' behaviors, used "following" or "redirecting" for directing infants' attention to foods. While previous studies suggested that "redirecting" is less effective than "following" in play situation, our results indicate that "redirecting" is effective in some situations.

Employment dispute resolutions in New Zealand: What affect employers' satisfaction?

Shulruf, Boaz Faculty of Education, University of Auckland, Auckland, New Zealand

This study attempts to identify the reasons for employers' dissatisfaction with the employment relationship problems resolution (ERPR) provisions in New Zealand. Data was received from a national survey asking employers about their ERPR experiences. Results showed that the total cost of employment relationship problems was about 0.4-0.6% of private sector annual wages and salaries. Regression models suggest that the level of satisfaction was negatively associated with the change in productivity, recruitment costs and the length of the resolution process. It was concluded that employers' concerns about the high cost of ERPR were likely to be based on perception rather than on concrete evidence .

The relationship between social support and emotional well-being in daily life

Siewert, Kerstin Inst. für Psychologie, Universität Greifswald, Greifswald, Germany Antoniw, Katja Institute of Psychology, University of Greifswald, Greifswald, Germany Kubiak, Thomas Institute of Psychology, University of Greifswald, Greifswald, Germany Weber, Hannelore Institute of Psychology, University of Greifswald, Greifswald, Germany

We examined the impact of discrepancies in desired and received social support on emotional well-being in daily life. A total of 30 undergraduates took part in a hand-held computer based experiences sampling study. In a series of multilevel analyses, we found that, in comparison to an optimal matching, insufficient received support in terms of desired support was significantly negatively associated with well-being. In contrast a surplus of received compared to the desired support was only for emotional support significantly positively associated with well-being. The results highlight the importance of optimal matching between desired and received support for emotional well-being.

Controlling the impact of mood in persuasion: Contrasting correction and suppression

Silva, Pedro UIPCDE, ISPA, Lisboa, Portugal Garcia-Marques, Teresa UIPCDE, ISPA, Lisboa, Portugal

The control of undesired influences in our judgments, by thought suppression, has been associated with ironic effects given the paradoxical hiperaccessibilty of those thoughts. In this study, we contrast suppression and correction strategies, presenting a direct comparison of their processes and consequences. We first manipulated participants' mood (positive vs. negative) and subsequently gave them suppression or correction instructions, in order to control its influence on the evaluation of a following persuasive message. Results reveal a differential impact of these strategies in the persuasive message processing, as well as in a subsequent mood measure, associating rebound effects only with suppression.

Sex differences in basic and social emotion recognition

Simão, Cláudia Olhão, Portugal Justo, Mariline Psychology, Universidade do Algarve, Olhão, Portugal Martins, Ana Teresa Psychology, Universidade do Algarve, Faro, Portugal

Gender has been suggested as an important factor in emotion processing. The main objective of this study was to understand the sex differences in emotion recognition. We applied a cognitive test battery to characterize sixty participants (30 males and 30 females), and a visual emotion paradigm. The visual paradigm was composed by 54 stimulus of six basic emotions (happiness, sadness, anger, fear, disgust and surprise) and 27 stimulus of three social emotions (arrogance, guilt and jealousy). The results suggest that males recognize anger with inferior reactions times and display that females had a superior accuracy for social emotions in study.

Kohlberg and a "fair community": Promoting the citizenship in school

Simão, Márcia Mestrado in Psychology, Universo Niteroi, Niteroi, Brazil Barreto, Marcia Simão Linhares MESTRADO IN PSYCHOLOGY, UNIVERSO, Niteroi-RJ, Brazil

This work had as main objective to describe a technique for moral education entitled "Fair Community" as proposed by Kohlberg and his collaborators at the University of Harvard and which has its fundamentals in the theory of moral judgement by the same author. Starting from the discussion technique of hypothetical dilemmas in group, it is resumed in a program in the type of "fair community" implemented in the city of Niterói, Rio de Janeiro, Brazil and presents a statistical analysis by which it was verified an increase of scores in the moral maturity of students within the program. It was also discussed the broad implementation of such program in a Brazilian context.

Explanatory style and coping

Singh, Maneesha Department of Psychology, University of Allahabad, Allahabad, India Kohli, Neena Department of Psychology, University of Allahabad, Allahabad, India

An exploratory study was carried out to understand the possibility of any relationship between explanatory style and coping on 30 women (age range 35-55). Data was elicited through in-depth interview. The interview focused on questions relating to background information, explanatory style and ways of coping. Thematic analysis showed that women who were optimists relied on planning, self control, positive reframing as a way of coping. Women, who were pessimists preferred denial, behavioural disengagement, distancing as a way of coping. This study has implication for designing interventions to promote positive approach towards life and to counsel individuals to be more optimists.

Social-pedagogical reflective self-images of students of psychological and pedagogical specialities

Sitnikov, Valery St. Petersburg, Russia Karagachova, Maria psychology, Railway University, St Petersburg, Russia Kedich, Svetlana psychology, LGU, St Petersburg, Russia

Social - pedagogical reflective self-images of students of psychological and pedagogical specialities The present study explores the possible link between self- and reflective images of students. The purpose of the study was to analyze the content and the structure of actual and reflective images (Myself in the opinion of my favorite and unfavorite teachers). To develop this we used a method of free characteristics (Sitnikov, 2001). Data analysis indicated a significant positive correlation between reflective self-images and images of favorite and unfavorite teachers. Findings showed little correlation between actual and reflective self-images of students. The results underline the importance of self-perception in the opinion of emotional-significant teachers on formation of self-image.

Stereotype threat impacts in uniformly minority contexts may require both majority presence and majority-involved evaluation.

Sloan, Lloyd Psychology, Howard University, Washington, DC, USA Wilburn, Grady Psychology, Howard University, Washington, DC, USA Van Camp, Deborah Psychology, Howard University, Washington, DC, USA Barden, James Psychology, Howard University, Washington, DC, USA Glover, Crystal Psychology, Howard University, Washington, DC, USA Martin, Daniel Management, Calif. State U. East Bay, East Bay, USA

Does Stereotype Threat require outgroup evaluative presence and stereotype related testing of minorities? 307 African American students at a historically Black College completed SAT verbal tests under conditions represented as diagnostic or as nondiagnostic of their personal ability. White experimenter's or White co-actor/test-taker's presence produced stereotype threat performance decrements. Black experimenters didn't produce performance decrements even when a White researcher appeared briefly before testing, or when a merely present, White male sat uninvolved near the front of the test room. These findings suggest that continuous outgroup presence and potential outgroup comparison-evaluation may be required to produce substantial Stereotype Threat impacts.

The effects of message framing on minority influence impact

Smith, Christine *Dept. of Psychology, Grand Valley State University, Allendale, USA* **McDonald, Melissa** *Psychology, Grand Valley State University, Allendale, USA* **Lord, Jennifer** *Psychology, Grand Valley State University, Allendale, USA* **Galen, Luke** *Psychology, Grand Valley State University, Allendale, USA*
Opinion minorities can increase their impact by linking arguments to a common normative principle shared by both the majority and the minority. Message framing as an influence strategy has been demonstrated in a variety of contexts and the present study expands and contextualizes this effect. Participants observed a videotape of five individuals discussing the legal marriage between homosexuals. We manipulated whether or not the minority framed its arguments and assessed its perceived impact upon the group, attitude change, and information processing of the message via thought-listing. Results support the notion that framing is a powerful influence strategy for minority sources.

Unemployement and psychosocial impact of the outplacement

Soares Martins, Jose Manuel *Faculdade de Ciências Humanas, Universidade Fernando Pessoa, Maia, Portugal* **carvalho, joana** *Faculdade de Ciências Humanas, Universidade Fernando Pessoa, Famalicão, Portugal*
This study evolves around the employee separation process, the unemployment phenomenon and its psychosocial impact. The aim is to analyse whether there are differences in terms of self-esteem and the discouragement learned between two groups, one consisting of individuals with access to the Outplacement program and another without Outplacement or any other kind of employee separation program. This is a prospective study in which it's predicted that the self-esteem of the subject with access to Outplacement programs is higher compared with the subjects not included in that kind of employee separation programs; the disappointment learned, in contrary, is expected higher in the group without Outplacement. Keywords: Unemployment, Untying labour, Employee Separation, Outplacement.

Weight bias in early childhood

Solbes, Irene *Developmental Psychology, Universidad Complutense Madrid, Pozuelo de Alarcón, Spain* **Enesco, Ileana** *Developmental Psychology, Universidad Complutense Madrid, Pozuelo de Alarcón (Madrid), Spain* **Lago, Oliva** *Developmental Psychology, Universidad Complutense Madrid, Pozuelo de Alarcón (Madrid), Spain* **Rodríguez, Purificación** *Developmental Psychology, Universidad Complutense Madrid, Pozuelo de Alarcón (Madrid), Spain*
The general purpose of this study was to examine weight bias in young children. A great number of empirical studies show weight-based stigmatization toward overweight children in boys and girls as young as age three. Participants of this study were 280 pres-school and Primary School children (3 to 8 years of age). They were individually assessed following a semi-structured interview. Participants had to successively select among 4 drawings depicting children differing in body shape (from "very slim" to "very fat") one of the figures for several tasks (preferences and rejections task, identification tasks, playmate preferences and adjective attributtion task). Overall, most children

showed positive bias toward thinner figures and negative bias toward fatter ones.

But next time, I will win: On the relation between irrationality and probability estimates in a game of chance

Spörrle, Matthias *Dept. for Psychology, Ludwig-Maximilians University, München, Germany* **Paulini, Anke** *Psychology, LMU München, München, Germany*
Based on Rational Emotive Behavior Therapy (REBT) we tested the hitherto unexplored assumption that irrationality as conceptualized by REBT (demandingness, self evaluation, low frustration tolerance), is associated with erroneous statistical reasoning. We assessed trait irrationality of 216 respondents and individual estimates of future winning probabilities in the context of the Wortman (1975) perceived control design. Results indicate that an increased (i.e. unrealistically optimistic) as well as a decreased (i.e. unrealistically pessimistic) estimation of future winnings is associated with irrationality. Findings substantiate an association between erroneous probability estimates and therapeutically relevant cognitions which do not imply any mathematical or statistical contents.

Toys and children's games in a gender's study

Spinelli, Nilton *LIRES, Universidade Gama Filho, Rio de Janeiro, Brazil* **Teves, Nilda** *LIRES, UNIVERSIDADE GAMA FILHO, Rio de Janeiro, Brazil*
To investigate cultural stereotypes signaled by children of 8 and 9 years old, boys and girls pupils of elementary school in Rio de Janeiro, they having as base the symbolic dimension of the toys and tricks. Methodology - Quali/ Quantitative study. The Subjects were 300 children. Hypothesis: the children choose toys and tricks that had adequate culturally to its sex. Result - 33 % of the girls breach with stereotypes of previous generations. They point to culture change in the woman image. 78% of boys reproduce stereotypes of the Brazilian culture where the exchange of social papers still resists the rupture.

Possibilities for and effects of health-promoting work organization in nursing

Stab, Nicole *Inst. für Psychologie, Techn. Universität Dresden, Dresden, Germany* **Hacker, Winfried** *Arbeitsgruppe, TU-Dresden, FR Psychologie, Dresden, Germany*
The characteristics of work organization have an essential impact on the quality of working life. Unfortunately there are only a few studies in the impact of hospital and ward organization on strain and well-being of nurses. Therefore the main question is, wether there are different kinds of work organization in hospital nursing? The main sample consists of 44 wards and 220 graduated nurses. The results show that it is possible to develop kinds of work organization on the ward level and the individual level of the nurses. Emotional exhaustion and perceived task-specific strain differ in favour of the most favourably organized wards and individual strategies. The organizational characteristics are discussed mainly with respect to primary prevention.

Theoretical grounds of educational psychology

Stepanova, Marina *Faculty of Psychology, Moscow State University, Moscow, Russia*
Educational psychology is actively developing in Russia but many practical problems of education remain unsolved. One of the reasons is diversity of approaches to the goals of psychological service in education,. We consider educational psychology not as independent brunch of educational process but as an aspect equal with medical, social and methodical ones. It's goals are derived from the general goals of education. The goal of modern education is not the translation of ready-made

knowledge but the training of pupils in dealing with different tasks in changing environment. So the task of school psychological service is the formation of vide social outlook in accordance with P.J.Galperin's concept of psyche as orienting process.

Studying explicit and implicit ethnic attitudes and ethnic categorization effects in the Russian Federation

Stepanova, Elena *Dept. of Psychology, Washington University, Saint Louis, USA* **Strube, Michael** *Psychology, Washington University, Saint Louis, MO, USA* **Yablonsky, Gregory** *Chemical Engineering, Washington University, Saint Louis, MO, USA* **Pehrson, Kali** *Psychology, Washington University, Saint Louis, MO, USA* **Shuman, Saskia** *Psychology, Washington University, Saint Louis, MO, USA*
We studied ethnic attitudes and ethnic categorization judgments in Russia. Participants judged 100 faces varying on facial physiognomy (Eurocentric to Afrocentric) and skin color (light to dark) and completed implicit and explicit ethnic attitude measures. Explicit and implicit attitudes were pro-Russian; negative explicit attitudes were expressed towards some ethnic groups. Implicit and explicit attitudes towards non-Russian groups were independent. Participants used skin color when categorizing faces as "Russian" or "non-Russian," and relied on facial physiognomy to make finer distinctions among lighter faces. Participants high on implicit ethnic prejudice judged racial typicality more variably than individuals low on implicit ethnic prejudice.

Fostering language development of migrant children: Results of an evaluation study

Strehmel, Petra B *Social Work, University of Applied Sciences, Hamburg, Germany*
Fostering migrant children to learn the national language before visiting school is a crucial topic of early education in child care institutions. A programm was evaluated in a 1-year controlled pre-post-design and followed up 2 years after start with 100 children, initially 2, 3 and 4 years old. Language status was measured by a standarsized observation scale run in the institutions. Context data from families and institutions were collected by questionaires, Young children with early entrance into the program catched up or even outdid elder children.The program showed: compensatory effects reducing differences between children from lower and higher education families.

How do teachers react to stress? Work related coping styles and psychophysiological correlates

Stueck, Marcus *Institute of Psychology, University of Leipzig, Leipzig, Germany* **Rigotti, Thomas** *Institute of Psychology, University of Leipzig, Leipzig, Germany* **Balzer, Hans Ullrich** *Technology, Akademy of Arts, Viena, Germany*
The aim of this study is the investigation of differences in galvanic skin response regarding behavioural coping styles, measured with the Workrelated Risk Factors Questionnaire (WRFQ). The sample consists of 20 female teachers. In a 24-hour-monitoring a skin response diagnostic was performed. According to the under-arousal-theory, risktype A (high work involvement and low dissociation from work) and risktype B (high resignation and low life-satisfaction) showed lower physiological arousal and at the same time more changes between arousal and relaxation. The latter can be interpreted as a decreased ability to relax. Thus, in person-oriented interventions activating techniques should be used.

Behavioral change of drug users visiting rehabilitation centers in Jakarta

Suci, Eunike Dept. of Psychology, Atma Jaya Catholic University, Jakarta, Indonesia
Objectives: find a new knowledge of relapse and drop outs among those who visited rehabilitation centers in Jakarta Methods: longitudinal qualitative study in Jakarta greater area. Participants were drug users who have been in rehabilitation centers and selected by backgrounds (i.e., sex, age, educational level, social economic status, and type of drugs). After baseline interview, participants were followed up every four months for two years. Results: 12 participants have been in rehabilitation centers at least once. During the study they were not in rehabilitation centers but stayed using drugs. Conclusion: rehabilitation program for drug users needs to be evaluated

The influence of occupation-related gender stereotypes on self-reported service satisfaction

Suen, Mein-Woei Taichung, Taiwan Wang, Jui Sing China Medical University Hospi, China Medical University Hospi, TAICHUNG city, Taiwan
Stereotype Threat Theory indicates that individuals' performance can be influenced and conform to their stereotypes (Steele & Aronson, 1995). Our aim is to tests whether the activation of occupation-related gender stereotypes (doctor is suitable for males & nurse is for females) causes participants' inappropriate evaluation of service satisfaction about particular targets (male nurses or female doctors). Participants were asked to read a manipulation article, look at target photographic, and then rate their satisfaction if they are serviced by this target. Our results reveal participants in experiment condition rate lower satisfaction than in control condition. More details and findings are discussed.

Attention enhances the perception of backscroll illusion

Sugimoto, Fumie Dept. of Psychology, Kwansei Gakuin University, Nishinomiya, Japan Fujimoto, Kiyoshi Psychology, Kwansei Gakuin University, Nishinomiya-shi, Hyogo, Japan Yagi, Akihiro Psychology, Kwansei Gakuin University, Nishinomiya-shi, Hyogo, Japan
When a movie presents a walker against an ambiguously moving background of vertical counterphase grating, the background appears to move in the opposite direction of her/his locomotion. We examined an effect of spatial cueing on this backscroll illusion. When a dot stimulus preceded the movie clip at the same location, participants perceived the backscroll illusion at higher probabilities than under no-cueing conditions. In addition, this effect occurred in peripheral vision but not in central vision. These results suggest that the spatial attention enhances the motion perception which relies on high-level object-centered signals.

Improvement of university students' communication skills through sports education classes

Sugiyama, Yoshio Inst. of Health Science, Kyushu University, Fukuoka, Japan Nagao, Yuichi Grad Sch Hum-Environ Stud, Kyushu University, Kasuga, Fukuoka, Japan Yamazaki, Masayuki Grad Sch Hum-Environ Stud, Kyushu University, Kasuga, Fukuoka, Japan Kawadu, Keita Grad Sch Hum-Environ Stud, Kyushu University, Kasuga, Fukuoka, Japan
The purpose of this study was to investigate the change of communication skills through sports education classes in a university. One hundred and eighty-seven students participated in two badminton or three table tennis classes. The participants were twice administered communication skills questionnaires including the Encoding-Decoding Skills Test Ver.2 (Horike, 1994) and the Affective Communication Test (Friedman et al., 1980). The results indicated that the communication skills of the participants improved significantly through the sports education classes with more improvement in the badminton classes than the table tennis classes.

Perceptual bias and attentional bias on chimeric faces processing

Sui, Guangyuan Zhejiang Normal University, Jinhua, People's Republic of China
An experiment was conducted using the chimeric face paradigm to investigate the perceptual bias and attentional bias on chimeric face processing. The results indicated that: (1) the left perceptual bias was significant when faces were upside, significant perceptual bias was not found when faces were upside down; (2) participants produced more first saccades on the right and longer fixation time on the right side of faces significantly. These results suggested that perceptual bias and attentional bias on chimeric faces were separated, eye movements were not required in perceptual bias producing on chimeric face judgements.

Students' judgments and teachers' self-judgments of empathy: The empathy judgment consistency based on the Interpersonal Reactivity Index (IRI)

Sun, Binghai Dept. of Psychology, Zhejiang Normal University, Jinhua, People's Republic of China Li, Weijian Dept. of Psychology, Zhejiang Normal University, Jinhua, People's Republic of China
To examine the consistence between students' and their teachers' judgments of empathy, a sample of 525 adolescents and their teachers completed the Interpersonal Reactivity Index(IRI) with four subscales: empathy concern(EC), perspective taking(PT), fantasy(FS), and personal distress(PD). The average-achieving students(AAS) scored significantly lower than others on all subscales; The inferior students(IS) scored lower on EC but higher on PD than excellent students(ES) ; The teachers scored significantly higher than others on PD and FS. The hypothesis of close effect was supported, the ES gained more caring while the IS gained more sympathy. PD and FS might be implicit elements of empathy.

Effects of received training quantity in the elaboration of derived research inquiries

Suro, Ana CEIC, University of Guadalajara, Guadalajara, Mexico Padilla, Antonia CEIC, University of Guadalajara, Guadalajara, Mexico Tamayo, Jairo CEIC, University of Guadalajara, Guadalajara, Mexico
An essential activity in the scientific work is making research inquiries derived from a certain knowledge area. An experimental task was designed to study the relation of different mastery in a theory and the capability to formulate inquiries derived from that theory. Twenty-five participants were evaluated in the formulation of research inquiries, being exposed to different training quantities: Definitions, examples and experiments; Definitions and experiments; Definitions; and Experiments. Data shows that complexity and pertinence in the questions elaborated by the participants, increases with an increased quantity of received training. The implications that these results have for teaching sciences are discussed.

Gender stereotypes on the rebound in Japan

Tadooka, Yoshika Dept. of Social Science, Hitotsubashi University, Tokyo, Japan Takabayashi, Kumiko social science, Hitotsubashi University, Naka, Kunitachi, Tokyo, Japan Murata, Koji social science, Hitotsubashi University, Naka, Kunitachi, Tokyo, Japan
This study investigated the rebound effect in the context of stereotypes of traditional women in Japan. First, participants were told to write a description of a traditional woman on a holiday. Half of them were instructed to avoid using stereotypes in their description, others were not. After a filler task, they rated another woman on twenty items which were consisted of four kinds of trait; gender type (masculine vs. feminine) x valence (positive vs. negative). Results indicated that the rebound effect occurred only in female participants on the negative-feminine traits. We discuss gender differences in this stereotype rebound effect.

Assessment parents' idea with epileptic children about stressor and their coping.

Taghavi Larijani, Taraneh Psychology, Nursing&Midwifery of Tehran U., Tehran, Islamic Republic of Iran Salmani Barough, Nasrin Psychology, Nursing&Midwifery of Tehra, Tehran, Islamic Republic of Iran
Objective:determination of parents' idea with epileptic children about stressor and their coping.-Methods:The sample was 400 parents with children 5to14 years old.The instrument was questionnaire with 3 parts about demography informations,stressor and coping.The t-test and analyze variance were applied.Results:there was significant difference between mothers' and fathers' stress(p=0.001)and there wasn't significant coping(p=0.866).There was significant and converse relationship between stress and coping in parents.Conclusion:There was significant and converse relationship with stress and coping in parents with epileptic children and increasing stress lead to decrease coping.

General health in runaway and non-runaway girls

Tahbaz, Sahar Dept. of Psychology, University of Tehran, Tehran, Islamic Republic of Iran
This study examined differences between runaway and non-runaway girls' general health through a case-control design. The sample group of runaway girls involved 25, 17-25 years of age runaway girls being kept at the shelters in Tehran. Non-runaway girls were 25 college students matched with runaway girls in all demographic features. General Health Questionnaire (GHQ) was administered on subjects for measurement of general health. The results showed a significant difference between two groups in all subscales of somatization, anxiety and insomnia, social dysfunction, depression and total score of GHQ. Running away from home, needs more consideration and the author suggests strengthening social preventive and protective systems to deal with this pathology.

Japanese students' images of the elderly: An analysis by the Semantic Differential (SD) method

Takahashi, Ikko Faculty of Buddhism, Minobusan University, Tokorozawa, Japan Tanaka, Mayumi Child Psychology Department, Tokyo Future University, Tokyo, Japan
Our purpose is to compare the Japanese students' images of the general elderly with those of their own old age. The Semantic Differential (SD) test with 23 items was used. The subjects were 362 Social Science (SS) major students and 279 Social Welfare (SW) majors. Japanese students' images of the general elderly were not coincident with their own elderly images. Their images of the general elderly were similar in all students. However, SS students evaluated their own elderliness more positively than SW students. The factor analysis showed 5 factors in the general elderly and 4 in their own elderliness.

Figure - ground organization on Watercolor effect and Sumi painting effect

Takashima, Midori Dept. of Psychology, Nihon University, Tokyo, Japan Fujii, Teruo Economics, Keiai University, Inage-ku, Chiba-city, Japan
Watercolor effect is new color spreading effect. On the other hand, when background color was middle gray and the border colors were lighter gray and darker gray, we observe a spreading effect into both sides. This phenomenon is Sumi painting effect.

This study examined figure - ground organization on Watercolor effect and Sumi painting effect. This result indicated that Sumi painting effect dose not influence the organization of both depth and form. However, Watercolor effect strongly affected organizations of depth, and the organizations of form were more affected by a factor of equal width than Watercolor effect.

A school-based long-term intervention for reduction of students' trauma-related distress in a Japanese school

Takino, Yozo National Mental Support Center, Osaka Kyoiku University, Ikeda, Japan Iwakiri, Masahiro National Mental Support Center, Osaka Kyoiku University, Ikeda, Japan Motomura, Naoyasu National Mental Support Center, Osaka Kyoiku University, Ikeda, Japan

A school-based long-term intervention for reducing students' post-traumatic stress-related symptoms, somatic complaints, functional impairment, and anxiety due to exposed to a school crisis is reported and examined. The tragic incident occurred on June 8, 2001. Eight students were killed and thirteen students and two teachers were seriously injured by a intruder with a knife. Many students witnessed and suffered from psychological trauma. After early intervention, authors have kept on supporting to the students, parents and teachers on psycho education, counseling, consultation on class contents and school events and so on. This intervention results in students adjustment at school. The implementation and effectiveness of the school-based long-term intervention in a Japanese school is discussed.

Teacher's classroom management and children's behavior at the beginning of the semester

Tanaka, Yasuhiro Dept. of Human Science, Osaka University, Sasayama, Japan

This study investigated the relations between teacher's classroom management and children's behavior at the beginning of the semester. Teacher's discourse and behaviors and children's behavior were observed in one of the six grade classroom in Japan (20 boys and 19 girls) from April to July. Also, interviews about classroom management were administered to the teacher. The main results were as follows: First, teacher's instructional belief was reflected on teacher's behavior to children. Second, the teacher coped with problem children considering overall classroom management. And the teacher's behavior to children changed as to the forming grade of his class.

Can the type of goal and critical thinking ability affect the evaluation of enthymeme?

Tanaka, Yuuko Graduate School of Education, Kyoto University, Kyoto, Japan Kusumi, Takashi Graduate School of Education, Kyoto University, Kyoto, Japan

This study examined the effect of two types of goal ("to make correct judgments" and "to enjoy things") and critical thinking ability, assessed using part of the Watson-Glaser Critical Thinking Appraisal, on the evaluation of enthymemes. An enthymeme is defined as a syllogism without a major premise that is logically invalid. Thirty-five Japanese nursing students were asked to evaluate the acceptability of 30 enthymemes. The results showed that the enthymemes tended to be more accepted when the students were "enjoying things" and students who had lower critical thinking ability scores tended to more accept the enthymemes.

Relationship between humor and friendships

Tani, Tadakuni Dept. of Social Psychology, Osaka University, Osaka, Japan Daibo, Ikuo Social Psychology, Osaka university, Suita, Osaka, Japan

This study was investigated how assistive sense of humor affected the satisfaction and influence derived from their friends. A questionnaire was administered to 357 Japanese undergraduates. Results indicated that participants with high in assistive sense of humor rated higher scores on the satisfaction and influence derived from their friends with sense of humor, while they rated lower satisfaction and influence to their friends without having the sense. Furthermore, the higher the score on the sense people had, the more notably the discrepancy of those two rates expanded.

Mental grouping in multiple-object tracking

Tanner, Thomas Computational Psychophysics, Max-Planck-Institut, Tübingen, Germany

We report that during multiple-object tracking (MOT, Pylyshyn & Storm 1988) a strategy of grouping several targets into "mental objects" and overtly following their centers is more consistent with eye movement data then a theory of moving multiple foci of attention (FINST). 18 subjects showed significantly (p < 0.01) higher performance when they had to track objects by freely moving their eyes than by fixating in the screen center. The eye movements are well predicted by a model following centers of groups of 3-4 targets and occasionally inspecting collisions of targets.

Main types of high school students' career orientations and effects of gender on their development

Taras, Karamushka Psychology, Kiev national university, Kiev, Ukraine

Objectives. To find out main types of high school students' career orientations and effects of gender on their development. Methods. The investigation was done on 120 high school students (33.3% boys and 66.7% girls) from Kiev in 2007 using E.Schein Career anchors and SPSS. Results. 1. Three types of the students' career orientations were found: autonomous-professional, managerial-entrepreneurship, and traditional. 2. The most developed was the managerial-entrepreneurship type (37.0% of the respondents). 3. The managerial-entrepreneurship type was mainly oriented toward by men (r<0.01) while the traditional type by women (r<0.01). Conclusion. The research findings can be helpful in professional counseling of high school students.

The value system of students of Iran

Tarkhorani, Hamid Tehran, Islamic Republic of Iran

Introduction: The value types proposed by Schwartz were: power, achievement, hedonism, stimulation, self-direction, universalism, benevolence, conformity, tradition and security. This study designed to determine values preferences in students of Tehran city. Methods: The sample size consists of 1000 students that educating in Tehran high schools. We used clustering method for sampling. Each student was given Schwartz value survey Results: the value ranking in sample was Conformity, security, Self-direction, universalism, benevolence, achievement, hedonism, power, stimulation, tradition. Discussion: The Conformity, the first value in the ranking introduces the life-adjustment as the most important challenge among adolescent population.

Explaining the role of coping styles in mental health and marital satisfaction

Tashk, Anahita Psychology and Education, Tehran University, Tehran, Islamic Republic of Iran

An extensive analysis was performed to assess the kind of association among coping styles (problem-focused, positive emotional-focused, negative emotional- focused), marital satisfaction and mental health. 276 students were included in this study. The result revealed that positive emotional-focused strategies were positively associated with marital satisfaction and psychology well-being, and negatively associated with psychology distress. It was found that negative emotional-focused coping style as an ineffective strategy was negatively associated with marital satisfaction and psychological well-being, and positively associated with psychological distress. The results suggested that couples marital satisfaction and mental health could be explained by different coping styles

The relationship between goal orientation and feedback seeking motives

Tayfur, Özge Ankara, Turkey Sümer, Hayriye Canan Department of Psychology, Middle East Technical Universi, Ankara, Turkey

This study examined the relationship between goal-orientation and feedback seeking motives. Two-hundred-two people working in transportation, banking, and pharmaceutical sectors in Turkey filled out a questionnaire package including goal-orientation and feedback seeking motives scales. Regression analyses showed that learning-goal orientation predicted desire-for-useful information motive (DUIM) positively and defensive motive (DM) negatively. While performance-prove orientation (PPO) predicted both DUIM and DM positively, performance-avoid orientation (PAO) predicted DM only. It seems that for learning-oriented employees the primary motive for seeking feedback is to obtain diagnostic information about their performance whereas for PAO employees the primary motive is to protect their ego and self-image.

Professionals' work locus of control and quality of life

Teichmann, Mare Psychology, Tallinn Univ. of Technology, Tallinn, Estonia

The present study examined the relationship between work locus of control and quality of life among three occupations (N=654), namely managers, engineers, and bookkeepers in Estonia. Research has held by Work Locus of Control Scale (WLCS) and WHO Quality of Life Instrument (WHOQOL-100). Results showed that professionals' internal work locus of control associated with their higher quality of life (r= .43). Moreover, all six domains of quality of life, e.g. physical health, psychological well-being, level of independence, social relationships, environment, spirituality/religion/personal beliefs were significantly (p ≤ .001), related to internal work locus of control, correlations ranged from .39 to .24.

Bookstart: Evaluation of a head start program that supports early language development of children in Hamburg

Thoma, Ester Kinder- und Psychosomatik, UKE Hamburg-Eppendorf, Hamburg, Germany Schulte-Markwort, Michael Kinder- und Psychosomatik, UKE Hamburg-Eppendorf, Hamburg, Germany Barkmann, Claus Kinder- und Psychosomatik, UKE Hamburg-Eppendorf, Hamburg, Germany

This research project evaluates the Hamburg bookstart program. Core of bookstart is the distribution of free book packages at the U6 preventive medical checkup to all parents residing in Hamburg. Additionally, special playgroups are offered to support the families. The evaluation combines specific designs, subjects, methods of data collection and statistical analyses in a multimethod approach to answer diverse research questions. First results indicate a high acceptance of the program among parents and a positive rating by pediatricians. Besides structure and process quality, the effectiveness of bookstart concerning parental skills of language teaching and infantile language development will be observed.

The effects of stress and failure on mood and performance of functional, dysfunctional and non-perfectionists

Thurner, Florian Arbeitsgruppe DDPM, Universität Koblenz-Landau, Landau, Germany *Altstötter-Gleich, Christine* Arbeitsgruppe DDPM, University of Koblenz-Landau, Landau, Germany *Dislich, Friederike* Arbeitsgruppe DDPM, University of Koblenz-Landau, Landau, Germany

Longitudinal studies have shown that perfectionism acts as a vulnerability factor for distress in response to failure and stressful live events. It is hypothesized that this holds especially for achievement related stress. Usually the amount of experienced stress is measured by self-assessment, and consequences of failure and other forms of stress are not differentiated. In the presented study (N=70), achievement related stress and failure were manipulated experimentally by using two forms of a concentration test and positive versus negative feedback. Effects on mood and performance varied across different types of perfectionists. Implications for perfectionism theory and measurement will be discussed.

Adaptive disengagement from unattainable demands in adulthood: The concept of developmental barriers

Tomasik, Martin J. Sonderforschungsbereich 580, Friedrich-Schiller-Universität, Jena, Germany *Silbereisen, Rainer K.* Developmental Psychology, Friedrich Schiller University, Jena, Germany *Heckhausen, Jutta* Psychology and Social Behavior, University of California, Irvine, USA

When individuals are confronted with serious barriers for development, then opportunities for primary control are limited. We hypothesized that the most adaptive way of coping with developmental barriers rather is to employ secondary control strategies. This hypothesis was tested and confirmed utilizing a sample of N = 806 adults who lived in different contexts and who reported many challenging demands in their work and family life. Results showed positive associations between secondary control and subjective well-being if developmental barriers were high. This implies that under certain circumstances giving up may be more adaptive than persistence.

Intolerance of ambiguity, interpersonal life events, and mental health

Tomono, Takanari Department of Psychology, Doshisha University, Kyoto, Japan

This study examined whether the interactions between intolerance of ambiguity and interpersonal-related life events have effects on mental health. Two hundred thirty six Japanese university students participated in the study. They were asked to complete 4 scales including Intolerance of Ambiguity Scale, Stress Response Scale, Happiness Scale, and Interpersonal Life Event Scale. Hierarchical regression analysis showed that in males, the interaction among intolerance of ambiguity, negative life events and positive life events predicted the increase of stress response significantly. However among females, no significant interaction effects were obtained.

Prospective memory failure and the metacognitive experience of "blank in the mind"

Touroutoglou, Alexandra School of Psychology, Thessaloniki, Greece *Efklides, Anastasia* School of Psychology, Aristotle University of Thessa, Thessaloniki, Greece

This study tested the hypothesis that prospective memory (PM) failure is related to the metacognitive experience of "blank in the mind" (BIM). A computerized, event-based PM task was administered to 68 university students of both genders. After the completion of the PM task participants responded to a series of questions tapping metacognitive awareness of PM failures and BIM experience. Results showed that participants were aware of PM failures and of BIM experience. The frequency of self-reported BIM was a function of task demands on working memory and correlated with the accuracy of response and response time on the PM task.

The role of direct experiences in evaluation shifts

Tsuchiya, Koji Graduate School of Education, Nagoya University, Nagoya, Japan *Yoshida, Toshikazu* Graduate School of Education a, Nagoya University, Nagoya, Japan

The present study aimed to clarify the role of direct experiences in evaluating attitude objects. Although past researches showed evaluation shifts in some context (e.g., attitudes) after having direct experiences, it is still not clear how people give meanings to the events according to the way they experience. The authors manipulated the manner of experience (direct/indirect) in an experiment setting. A total of 52 participants were asked to solve the five sets of puzzles under different conditions. Findings of the present study provided evidences supporting the importance of direct experiences in decision making.

Positive affect and cortisol awaking response on work day and weekend in women

Tsuda, Akira Dept. of Psychology, Kurume University, Fukuoka, Japan *Okamura, Hisayoshi* School of Medicine, Kurume University, Kurume, Fukuoka, Japan *Horiuchi, Satoshi* Psychology, Kurume University, Kurume, Fukuoka, Japan *Yajima, Jumpei* Psychology, Beppu University, Beppu, Japan *Tsuda, Shigeko* Nursing, Ibaraki Christian University, Oomika, Ibaraki, Japan *Chida, Yoichi* Epidemiology and Public Health, University College London, London, United Kingdom *Grant, Nina* Epidemiology and Public Health, University College London, London, United Kingdom *Steptoe, Andrew* Epidemiology and Public Health, University College London, London, United Kingdom

Positive affective states such as psychological well-being are associated with reduced cortisol awaking response (CAR) which is the change in cortisol levels that occurs during the first hour after waking from sleep, ie., allostatic response. here we show that higher positive affect level in Japanese women, 20-50 years old (N=58), is associated with reduced CAR on work day when compared to the subjects with lower positive affect level. However, there were no significant differences in CAR on weekend between subjects with higher positive affect level and with lower one. These findings suggest that positive affective states directly buffer the impact of working day.

The study of peer-assisted learning strategy system for elementary students

Tsuei, Mengping Dept. of Computer Science, TMUE, Taipei, Taiwan

The aim of this study was to develop the peer-assisted learning strategy system (PALSS) for elementary students. A hierarchical cluster analysis was carried out based on students' online involvement profiles. The results indicated that the patterns of online peer interaction varied as a function of types of language arts activities. The findings suggested a critical connection among learners' achievement level, self-concept, and online interaction. There was a positive correlation between students' self-concept and their online tutor's/tutee's behaviors. The results indicated that PALSS was an effective tool for enhancing students' Chinese reading ability as well as self-concept of those passive participants.

Relationships between elementary children's reading, writing, and mathematical abilities: Does working memory play a role?

Tzoneva, Irina Faculty of Education, Simon Fraser University, Burnaby, BC, Canada *Hoskyn, Maureen* Faculty of Education, Simon Fraser University, Burnaby, BC, Canada

One potential source of individual and age-related differences in elementary school children's ability to perform on reading, writing, and mathematical tasks and the focus of the current study is working memory (WM). In this study, we test two competing models of WM. The first model posits that individual and age related differences in reading, writing, and mathematical ability are related to a processing efficiency model of WM where the fluency of lower order component processes mediates these relations. In contrast, the second model assumes that storage capacity within a WM executive system allocates resources to lower order operations.

Promotion of the self-efficacy of junior high school students by contrived success using a presentation trick

Uchida, Akitoshi High School, Shinonoinishi Junior, Nagano, Japan *Mori, Kazuo* Institute of Symbiotic Science, Tokyo Univ of Agricult & T, Tokyo, Japan

The purpose of the study was to promote the self-efficacy of junior high school students and to examine whether academic achievement can be positively affected by artificially promoted self-efficacy. Twenty-four junior high school students with academic achievement in the 26-50 percentile solved easier anagram tasks surreptitiously presented using the fMORI technique (Mori, 2007), while other 183 students solved more difficult tasks, without being aware of the duality. The target students preformed the anagram task significantly better than their class mates. Success on the tasks significantly promoted students' self-efficacy and showed a sign of subsequent academic achievement. (97 words)

"(Don't) worry, live?!" – An empirical review of the theory of learned carefreeness

Ullrich, Bastian Muenchen, Germany

The Theory of learned carefreeness deals with the question of why people often repeatedly violate precautions and ignore warning-signals in combination with a comfortable state of well-being (positive illusions, hedonism). The Validation study presents a confirmatory factor analysis and behavioural measures of a new scale to detect carefreeness (= .88, N=581) as well as correlations with related concepts. As a reliable instrument the carefreeness-scale provides numerous starting points for prevention strategies in all areas where human behaviour can be seen as a risk factor for sanitary, social or material damages (environmental pollution, health care, traffic- or financial behaviour, etc.).

Neural correlates of action and size information during working memory retention and retrieval from long-term memory

Umla-Runge, Katja Department of Psychology, Saarland University, Saarbrücken, Germany *Zimmer, Hubert D.* Department of Psychology, Saarland University, Saarbrücken, Germany *Krick, Christoph M* Department of Neuroradiology, Saarland University Hospital, Homburg/Saar, Germany *Reith, Wolfgang* Department of Neuroradiology, Saarland University Hospital, Homburg/Saar, Germany

We hypothesized that working and long-term memory are represented by the same content-specific neural structures (e.g. visual sensory, auditory sensory, motor). In an fMRI study with sixteen healthy participants, working memory retention and long-term memory retrieval of size and action information were investigated. Whole brain analyses revealed a jointly activated posterior region (BA 17) for size information whereas action tasks yielded a common frontal region (BA 47) considered representing semantic information. Motor structures for action information were confined to Regions of Interest (ROI) analyses. It can be concluded that information-specific configurations exist pertaining to both working and long-term memory.

Individual differences in the attentional blink: The important role of irrelevant information

Valchev, Nikola Groningen, Netherlands

A well-established phenomenon in the study of attention is the attentional blink (AB): A deficit in reporting the second of two targets when it occurs 200-500 ms after the first. We present evidence for large individual differences in the level of distractor processing and subsequent interference with target identification processes. In two experiments we present streams with or without additional distracters besides the target's masks. The results thus seem to support the hypothesis that non-blinkers (participants who systematically show no blink) are more efficient in ignoring irrelevant information than blinkers are.

Identification of work styles in children between 4 and 5 years old

Valero Rodriguez, Jose Evolutive Psychology and Didac, University of Alicante, Alicante, Spain Gomis Selva, Nieves Evolutive psychology and didac, University of Alicante, Alicante, Spain Pérez Sánchez, Antonio Miguel Evolutive psychology and didac, University of Alicante, Alicante, Spain Castejón Costa, Juan Luis Evolutive psychology and didac, University of Alicante, Spain

The main aim of our research is to determine whether children between 4 and 5 years old work at school with different working styles in the different areas of the curriculum. 104 children have participated. The observation has been carried out by six teachers using the assessment protocol of Gardner, Feldman and Krechevsky (1998). The results suggest that children use different work styles depending on the knowledge area. The most significant conclusion is that teachers can identify the predominant style with which children take part in each of the curriculum subjects.

Styles of work in children on first stage of primary education (6 and 7 years old)

Valero Rodriguez, Jose Evolutive Psychology and Didac, University of Alicante, Alicante, Spain Castejón Costa, Juan Luís Evolutive psychology and didac, University of Alicante, Alicante, Spain Gomis Selva, Nieves Evolutive psychology and didac, University of Alicante, Alicante, Spain Pérez Sánchez, Antonio Miguel Evolutive psychology and didac, University of Alicante, Alicante, Spain García Fernández, Jose Manuel Evolutive psychology and didac, University of Alicante, Alicante, Spain

The investigation's aim is to verify the existence of different work styles in children between 6 and 7 years old. They have 93 children participated and evaluation has been carried out by six teachers who have used the observation protocol adapted by Ballester (2004). The results show that children at this age have various work styles. The findings indicate that children use in each activity a different work style depending on the area they are studying.

To be a volunteer: Motivational and ideological underpinnings

Valor-Segura, Inmaculada Social Psychology, University of Granada, Granada, Spain Willis, Guillermo Byrd SOCIAL PSYCHOLOGY, UNIVERSITY OF GRANADA, GRANADA, Spain Rodriguez-Bailon, Rosa SOCIAL PSYCHOLOGY, UNIVERSITY OF GRANADA, GRANADA, Spain

Volunteering is an important social phenomenon nowadays. Many volunteers are young people, most of them are university students. Then, it seems relevant to study the reasons that lead university students to enrol in volunteer activities. The current research tried to explore whether motivational factors, ideological variables and previous experiences can influence the willing to do volunteer work. In order to investigate these factors, two different studies were conducted. A sample of volunteers participated in both studies. Results show that altruistic motivation and legitimizing ideologies play important roles in volunteers' enrolment and commitment. Discussion will be focus on the importance of these results for promoting volunteers active participation and long term commitment.

Does sense of coherence mediate the relationship of hardships and psychological distress during unemployment?

Vastamäki, Jaana Chair of Psychology, University of ErlangenNürnberg, Nürnberg, Germany Moser, Klaus Chair of Psychology, University of ErlangenNürnberg, Nürnberg, Germany Paul, Karsten Chair of Psychology, University of ErlangenNürnberg, Nürnberg, Germany

Individuals exposed to hardships during unemployment experience greater distress than their non-exposed counterparts. We investigated whether the reactions to hardships could be explained through greater vulnerability caused by weakened resistant resources, i.e. sense of coherence (SOC). Our method was a longitudinal study with unemployed respondents participating in an intervention program. Results: Individuals subjected to impaired work ability, problem drinking and financial strain have weaker SOC than other individuals. Moreover, we found that SOC acts as a mediator of relationships between experienced hardships and psychological distress. Conclusion: Low SOC can be an important psychological background factor underlying the negative effects of hardships during unemployment on mental health.

The Estonian students' and teachers' coping patterns in the academic domain

Veisson, Marika Inst. of Education, Tallinn University, Tallinn, Estonia

In this empirical research the method of gathering data about students' and teachers coping strategies was based on the system of coping categories created by Skinner and Wellborn (1997). Main hypothesis was that a school can potentially either support or inhibit students' capacity to overcome problems with academic copying. We distributed questionnaires to the 7th, 9th and 12th grade students (N = 3838) with 2 years interval and their teachers (N = 620). Results: teachers' and students' coping patterns, sex, national differences will be analysed.

Couple's attachment and adjustment to the transition to parenthood

Velotti, Patrizia Dynamic and Clin. Psychology, University of Rome, Rome, Italy Castellano, Rosetta Dynamic and Clinical Psycholog, University of Rome, Rome, Italy

As shown by wide research, childbirth determines remarkable changes in couple's relationship; it is a period in which attachment is extremely important for the successful transition. The aim of this study is to investigate the role of adult/couple's attachment on marital adjustment in this period. 104 subjects were recruited; Adult Attachment Interview, Current Relationship Interview, and Dyadic Adjustment Scale were administered. Repeated measures General Linear Models were applied for the analyses. Results showed the role of couple's attachment on adjustment after childbirth (p = .033), underlining the importance to analyze the

recent conceptualizations of adult attachment states of mind.

Physiotherapist work in the habilitation team in elementary school

Ventaskrasta, Luize Education and Sport Medicine, Latvian Academy of Sport, Riga, Latvia Grinberga, Sabine Dep. of Rehabilitation, Riga Stradins University, Riga, Latvia

The possibilities in the work of a physiotherapist dealing with the habilitation of the grade 1-4 schoolchildren in the Center of Children Development and Education are investigated in the research. The theoretical conclusions about the junior grade schoolchildren physical and mental development and studies are drawn. The ideas about the peculiarities of the children musculoskeletal system are presented. Especially poor posture in childhood and the possibility to correct it are discussed. Particular attention is paid to the therapeutic exercises and swimming. The survey of different professional work experience has been carried out in Secondary School in the Center of Children Development and Education.

Gender perception and stereotypical beliefs: Application for diversity management

Venturini, Beatrice verona, Italy Cubico, Serena Psicologia e Antropologia, Università di Verona, Verona, Italy Martini, Massimo Psyhc.&Cult.Anthropology, University of Verona, verona, Italy Bellotto, Massimo Psych.&Cult.Anthropology, University of Verona, verona, Italy

Given the growing presence minorities in organizations, diversity researchers have focused on the process underlying the diversity perception, and they mostly studied the effects of social category differences in race, ethnic background and gender. Focusing on induction-deduction paradigm, on a sample of (N= 249) students the stereotyping processes underlying relations were assessed. Relying on gender as a salience social category, 2(Gender)x2(Target)x2(Individual)x2(Traits stereotypical-non streotypical) ANOVA analysis was conducted and it revealed a main effect of stereotype relevance (M=.31), F(1,232)=14.95 p<.001.Taking into account these processes, suggestions may arise for further research in the field of diversity management.

Interpretation patterns of counterfactuals, absurd conditionals, prospective and retrospective conditionals

Verbrugge, Sara Lab. Experimental Psychology, University of Leuven, Leuven, Belgium

In three experiments we investigated the preferred interpretation of counterfactuals, absurd, prospective and retrospective conditionals. Subjects could pick out of a list of four paraphrases, matching the inference types of propositional logic. For prospective conditionals, participants primarily chose Modus Ponens (p, therefore q); for retrospective conditionals Modus Ponens and Affirmation of the Consequent (q, therefore p); for counterfactuals Denial of the Antecedent (not p, therefore not q); for absurd conditionals Modus Tollens (not q, therefore not p). Contrary to the regular inference task, this new method displays a very clear distribution among the inference types.

Extraversion and agreeableness as personality characteristics associated with sense of community

Vignale, Paula Dept. de Psicologia, CONICET - CIIPME, Buenos Aires, Argentina Regner, Evangelina Raquel Psicologia, CONICET - CIIPME, Capital Federal - Buenos Aires, Argentina

The objective of this investigation was to study the influence of the personality factors, specifically the quality and intensity of interpersonal relationships in the sense of community. The sample was composed by 400 adults from Argentina. The Revised Inventory of Personality NEO (NEO PI-R) by Costa and McCrae (1992) and the Sense of Community Scale (Vignale, in press) were administered. Regression analyses were done between Extraversion and Agreeableness factors and the sense of community. According to the studied sample, we can conclude that the personality factors contributed significantly to the prediction of the sense of community.

The relationship between working expectancies and burnout syndrome among Mexican health professionals

Villa George, Fabiola Itzel Universidad Autonoma de Madrid, Madrid, Spain Moreno Jiménez, Bernardo Facultad de Psicología, Universidad Autonoma de Madrid, Madrid, Spain Villalpando Uribe, Jessica Psicología, Servicios de Salud de Puebla, Puebla, Mexico Villamil Delgado, Sagrario

Objective: Analyze the relationship between working expectancies (Professional development, Users relationship, Compensation, Work characteristics) and the burnout syndrome components (emotional exhaustion, despersonalisation, and personal accomplishment) Method: Participants were 236 mexican health professionals. The working expectancies were evaluated through the "Working Expectancies Questionnaire" (CEL), and Burnout through the "Short Burnout Questionnaire" (CBB) Results: The results of the multivariate analysis of variance showed a positive relation between whole working expectancies index and whole burnout index. The relations between the different types of expectations and the components of Burnout Syndrome are discussed. Conclusions: The analysis of the job expectations contributes to the development of a burnout cognitive model.

Prediction of moral decisions and actions

Villegas de Posada, Cristina Dept. of Psychology, University of Los Andes, Bogotá, Colombia

Three studies were designed to test a model for the prediction of moral decisions and actions. The model comprises moral development and expectancies x values of costs, benefits and feelings. The studies tested the model in hypothetical moral decisions and in game situations: in the prisoners dilemma (PD) the first two studies and in the dictator game (DG) the third study. Participants were university students and employees. Regressions showed a high percentage of variance predicted by the model in the hypothetical decisions, and a lower but significant variance of the behavior predicted in the games.

Better late than never: How onsets and offsets influence prior entry and exit

Vingilis-Jaremko, Larissa Psychology, Neuroscience, McMaster University, Hamilton, ON, Canada Ferber, Susanne Department of Psychology, University of Toronto, Toronto, ON, Canada Pratt, Jay Department of Psychology, University of Toronto, Toronto, ON, Canada

Three experiments examine visual prior entry (determining which of two stimuli appeared first) and prior exit (determining which of two stimuli disappeared first) effects with a temporal order judgment (TOJ) task. In addition to using onset and offset targets, the preceding cues were either onset or offset stimuli. Typical, and equivalent, prior entry effects were found when either onset or offset cues preceded the onset targets. Unexpectedly large prior exit effects were found with the offset targets, with offset cues producing greater capture effects than onset cues. These findings suggest that more attention is allocated to searching the visual field when targets are difficult to find.

Role of virtual reality helmets in the development of human image thinking

Volodina, Kate Dept. of Psychology, Belarus State Pedagogical Uni., Minsk, Belarus Borisevich, Nataly Psychology, Belarus State Pedagogical Univ, Minsk, Belarus Pilipenec, Nataly Psychology, Belarus State Pedagogical Univ, Minsk, Belarus Tishuk, Anna Psychology, Belarus State Pedagogical Univ, Minsk, Belarus Yatcenko, Anna Psychology, Belarus State Pedagogical Univ, Minsk, Belarus Multan, Tatiana Psychology, Belarus State Pedagogical Univ, Minsk, Belarus

According to the phased and cultural-historical (Vigotsky) theories of mental development exteriorization results in interiorization. On a certain stage of filogenesis human thinking by images was supplemented with thinking words. It makes thinking more effective. thanks to virtual reality helmets and gloves people get a possibility to think in computer images, virtually forming skills and habits, experiencing emotions. Results of our experiment shows: Children's early assimilation of methods allowing interacting with virtual reality suppresses the defense and the newness reflexes. Verbal thinking and verbal communication play a less significant part. Nevertheless orientation, cognitive reflexes develops at earlier periods.

Interests and competence beliefs of elementary school students: Effects on secondary school track choice

von Maurice, Jutta BiKS, Universität Bamberg, Bamberg, Germany Bäumer, Thomas Lehrstuhl EFP, Universität Bamberg, Bamberg, Germany

In a sample of about 900 elementary school students we analyze relations between motivational variables and the choice of secondary school track. Data are taken from BiKS-8-12, a longitudinal study on competence development and educational decisions in 8 to 12 year olds. Substantial differences in interests and especially competence beliefs between academic and non-academic track can already be shown in primary school age. Interests and competence beliefs are based on school subjects as well as broader domains of activity. The sample will be traced until grade 7, allowing further analyses of mutual influences between individual differences and school contexts.

Beyond logics and deontic logics: The rational role of action options and goals in the Wason selection task

von Sydow, Momme Inst. für Psychologie, Universität Göttingen, Göttingen, Germany Rietz, Chantal Department of Psychology, University of Göttingen, Göttingen, Germany Beller, Sieghard Department of Psychology, University of Göttingen, Göttingen, Germany

Normatively, testing a conditional (p→q) traditionally involves logics and checking p and non-q cases. We tested our hypothesis that participants, checking conditional obligations or prohibitions, deviate from logic not in an irrational, but systematic way, using deontic logic, different social goals (cheater and cooperator detection, cf. v. Sydow & Hagmayer, 2006), and action options. In the first experiment we varied rules and goals, in the second goals and action options. Both studies confirmed our prediction of rational knowledge-based answers that systematically transcend the norms of standard logics.

Perception of affordances for standing on an inclined surface depends on center of mass and experience

Wagman, Jeffrey Dept. of Psychology, Illinois State University, Normal, USA Regia-Corte, Tony Psychology, Illinois State University, Normal, Illinois, USA

Objectives. We investigated whether changes in the height of center of mass influence perceptual boundaries for standing on inclined surface. Methods. Participants adjusted a surface until it was the steepest angle that would support standing on that surface. Participants wore a weighted backpack that raised their center of mass. Results. Perceptual boundaries occurred at smaller slopes while wearing the weighted backpack but decreased over the course of six trial blocks regardless of whether the backpack was worn. Conclusions. Perceptual boundaries for standing on an inclined surface depend on both the height of the center of mass and experience.

La place des stéréotypes et discriminations dans les manuels scolaires

Wagner, Anne-Lorraine Psychology, Université Paul Verlaine-Metz, Metz, France Schonenberger, Sandrine Psychology, Université Paul Verlaine-Metz, Metz, France Tisserant, Pascal Psychology, Université Paul Verlaine-Metz, Metz, France

Textbooks must remain neutral and must not convey stereotypes which participate in the advent of discrimination. However, in reality, stereotypes can remain. We analyse, with a quantitative methodology, different textbooks of civic-education, history, geography, French literature, English, mathematics and biology in order to identify potential discrimination. Some textbooks present different situations between men and women. Foreigners and seniors are rarely present. Finally, disabled people and homosexuals are absent in textbooks. The results enable us to suggest some recommendations to book publishers so that they can reduce the amount of stereotypes present in textbooks.

Recognition memory impairment after intentional suppression as an all-or-none phenomenon: Electrophysiological evidence

Waldhauser, Gerd Psychology, Lund University, Lund, Sweden Bovim, Tone Psychology, Lund University, Lund, Sweden Johansson, Mikael Psychology, Lund University, Lund, Sweden

This study employed event-related potentials (ERPs) to investigate the effects of intentional suppression on recognition memory in a think/no-think experiment. Participants were cued to either suppress or think of previously learned words, 18 or 0 times. Subsequent old/new discrimination was attenuated for repeatedly suppressed in contrast with zero-repetition items. Early frontal and late parietal ERP old/new effects, reflecting familiarity and recollection, were present for all correctly recognized items and did not differ between conditions. These results indicate that intentional suppression diminishes item recognition, but that it does not alter the relative contributions of familiarity and recollection to correct recognition memory.

A comparative study on validities of two indicators for dependent variable in the running memory paradigm

Wang, Shuzhen School of PublicAdministration, Northwest University, China, Xi'an, People's Republic of China Gao, Xiaocai School of PublicAdministration, Northwest University, China, Xi'an, People's Republic of China Zheng, Zijian School of PublicAdministration, Northwest University, China, Xi'an, People's Republic of China Zhang, Fuchang School of PublicAdministration, Northwest University, China, Xi'an, People's Republic of China

To explore validities of dependent variables in the running memory paradigm, two indicators of two Jonides and Smith's running memory experiments (n=78; 1.75s task, 1.25s task) were employed. Indicator 1 is that a number string symbols one score; indicator 2 is that different lengths of number strings represent different scores, which depend on lengths and capacities of active memory for number strings. As results, factor loadings of indicator 1 in two tasks are 0.21 and 0.26 respectively; those of indicator 2 are 0.80 and 0.97 respectively. In conclusion, indicator 2 is more valid than indicator 1 for running memory paradigm.

A multilevel analysis on high school teachers' job burnout

Wang, Peng School of Psychology, Shandong Normal University, Jinan, People's Republic of China Gao, Fengqiang School of Psychology, Shandong Normal University, Jinan, People's Republic of China

Objectives This paper explored the indicating effect on teachers' job burnout, which was caused by individual and collective variables. Method HLM was used to analyze how the collective variable (teacher collective efficacy) influenced the individual variables (teacher efficacy, coping self-efficacy, teacher work stress, and teacher job burnout) within 763 teachers Results TCE could predict positively the relation between WS and depersonalization, and CSE and personal accomplishment. TCE could explain higher percent on variance of CSE, compared to TE. Conclusions People ought to pay more attention to school culture, such as TCE, and reduce the sense of TJB effectively.

Academic self-presentation of primary school student: Styles and mechanics

Wang, Xiaoli Shanghai, People's Republic of China Li, Xiaowen psychology, East China Normal University, Shanghai, People's Republic of China

The present research aimed to explore the academic self-presentation styles in pupils and the reciprocity of self-presentation and self-evaluation. Assertive, ambivalent and protective styles were identified by projection test. Different relationships between self evaluation and conceived other's evaluation were also found. 3 experiments were conducted to explore the interaction of self evaluation and other's evaluation. it was found that a passive feedback within a limit and an positive feedback would invoke self-promotion. Pupils with passive self-evaluation would like to present themselves better than before, and try to change themselves in the new environment.

Working memory span, central executive functions and reasoning ability: A relationship study on uncultured mountainous youth in China

Wanhua, Ge Xi'an, People's Republic of China Fuchang, Zhang collage of life science, Ins. of Population & Healt, Xi'an, People's Republic of China Shuzhen, Wang Management, Ins. of Population & Healt, Xi'an, People's Republic of China Qiwei, Yang Management, Ins. of Population & Healt, Xi'an, People's Republic of China Xiaocai, Gao Collage of life science, Ins. of population & Healt, Xi'an, People's Republic of China Zijian, Zhen Management, Ins. of population & Healt, Xi'an, People's Republic of China

Objectives: To explore the relationships among working memory capacity(WMC), reasoning ability and the central executive functions(CEF) including three subcomponents. Method: The WMC, reasoning achievements and CEF of 84 volunteers were assessed using cognitive mesaures, which based on DMDX software package and Raven's Standard Progressive Matrices in Qinba areas in China. Results: The correlations were significantly among reasoning ability, WMC and some of CEF subcomponents exluding the shifting function. However no significant correlation were found between WMC, reasoning ability vs. the shifting function. Conclusion: The results suggested significant correlation between WMC, CEF vs. reasoning ability.

E-Leadership and personality of team leaders: Are personality factors relevant in virtual teams ?

Waschina, Tanja Wien, Austria

The aim of the study was to investigate the influence of personality factors on emergent leadership in virtual teams. Sixty-six ad-hoc three member

groups of unacquainted students of technical colleges had to nominate a leader after accomplishing a disjunctive group task via chat in a session of 25 minutes. Results obtained by discriminant analysis revealed that emergent leadership was associated most strongly with extraversion followed by openness to experience (big five) respectively extraversion followed by acting (self monitoring scale). Further analyses showed that the influence of these personality traits is of relevance if the group is heterogenic in their composition regarding personality.

Developmental study of relations among shame, orientation toward others and self-esteem

Watanabe, Hirozumi Dept. Educational Psychology, Ehime University, Matsuyama, Japan

The purpose of the study was to clarify the developmental changes in the relations between five types of shame–that is inferiority, social nonconformity, being gazed at, self-criticism, and reflected–and orientation toward others and self-esteem. A questionnaire was administered to junior high school, high school, and university students. Results showed that higher orientation toward others was associated with higher degrees of shames were, especially self-critical shame, in early adolescence. Also, self-esteem was negatively related to various types of shame, in particular, in late adolescence. Findings were discussed in terms of the individualism-collectivism dichotomy applied on a personal level.

Relationship between four requirements of assertiveness and internal adjustment

Watanabe-Matsumi, Asami Comprehensive Human Sciences, University of Tsukuba, Tsukuba, Japan

This study examined relationship between assertiveness and internal adjustment. Assertiveness was dealt with in terms of four requirements in this study. Theoretical concept of assertiveness included "open expression", "control of emotion", "consideration for others" and "self-direction". 359 students completed a questionnaire which contained UCLA isolation scale, general health questionnaire(GHQ) and original items to measure four requirements assertiveness. Correlation analysis revealed that "control of emotion" and "self-direction" had positive correlation with internal adjustment. However, "consideration for others" had negative correlation with internal adjustment. The results suggested consideration for others had appropriate revel to keep internal adjustment.

Remembering and knowing personality traits: Figure/ground asymmetries in person-related retrieval experience

Wehr, Thomas Psychology, University of Trier, Trier, Germany

The retrieval experience in social information processing was investigated. Subjects rated typicality or concreteness of personality traits that differed in stereotype reference. Remember/know responses indicated an impact of category salience. Only after typicality ratings (high salience), stereotype-consistent traits were more often "remembered" than inconsistent traits. After a change of the attention focus (i.e., after untypicality ratings), the remember/know rate was reversed. The results suggest that metacognitive trait representations depend on principles of figure/ground asymmetries rather than on functional principles of social information processing. This conclusion was confirmed by a perceptual identification task (i.e., traits were hidden within a word puzzle).

Teachers burnout : Strategies to cope with it

Weintraub, Elena Adolescence, Hospital J.M.Ramos Mejia, Buenos Aires, Argentina

Nowadys the educational system in Argentina is going through a profound crisis. Rapid changes and

permanent pressures to which teachers are exposed, impose them continuous adaptations that turn them more and more prone to distress. When stressors are intense or extended in time, exceeding personal abilities to cope with them, the individual gets exhausted and collapses. This may lead to burnout syndrome, affecting teachers health as well as the educational structure as a whole. We will describe a Prevention and Management Program for Teachers Stress which aim is to prevent and/or to reduce its effects, by offering physiological, cognitive and behavioural techniques as well as group dynamics strategies to cope with stress situations at work.

Nonlinear and interactive effects of stressors and resources in occupational stress: A structural equation modeling approach using multimethod data

Werner, Christina Inst. für Psychologie, Universität Frankfurt, Frankfurt, Germany Zapf, Dieter Inst. für Psychologie, Universität Frankfurt, Frankfurt, Germany Schermelleh-Engel, Karin Inst. für Psychologie, Universität Frankfurt, Frankfurt, Germany

A previously collected sample of 404 steel workers provided multimethod data of job analysis measurements (self and oberserver ratings, coworker data from the same workplace). Hypothesized interactive effects of work stressors and resources on health outcomes were re-analyzed using the data from multiple methods simultaneously by nonlinear structural equation modeling. Nonlinear and interactive effects of stressors (problems of work organization) and resources (task control, communication possibilities) were found. However, adequately taking the multimethod structure and nonlinear effects into account at the same time proved to be challenging. Limitations of different methods of analysis and potential remedies will be discussed.

Relationships among the Big Five, emotional intelligence and coping in a naturally occurring stressful encounter

Weyl, Anja Inst. Recht und Psychologie, Humboldt-Universität zu Berlin, Berlin, Germany Turss, Michaela Psychology, Humboldt University, Berlin, Germany

Emotional management is a part of emotional intelligence (ability EI) and its relation to stress and coping is not fully clarified. This study amongst 141 civil service trainees investigated the links between emotional intelligence, coping, and personality traits in a potentially highly stressful examination that contributes to a grade which is important for further employment. Results suggest a mediational model in which neuroticism leads to worse coping strategies which in turn leads to higher states of anxiety. Notably, emotional intelligence does not contribute to this relationship.

Parents' satisfaction from inclusive education of their children

Wiacek, Grzegorz Rehabilitative Psychology, Catholic University Lublin, Lublin, Poland

The purpose of the study was to describe satisfaction of parents from inclusive educational settings of their children, and it's basic differentiation and correlations. The study was conducted in 13 inclusive classrooms (primary schools, 1-3 grade); 277 parents participated (ca. 135 couples). Self-constructed method was used to measure parents' satisfaction; several other variables were measured and used in analysis. Parents' satisfaction correlates with their attitudes towards people with disability, and differs regarding parents' gender and school grade. Both correlation and differences interact with the presence of child's disability. The received outcomes are important for future organisation of inclusive classrooms.

Reward processing and decision-making in cannabis-addiction and schizophrenia

Wiesner, Christian Dirk *Inst. für Psychologie, Universität zu Kiel, Kiel, Germany* **Manecke, Marite** *Psychology, University of Kiel, Kiel, Germany* **Raack, Ninja** *Psychology, University of Kiel, Kiel, Germany* **Hermanns, Jean** *Therapieleitung, PKH Rickling, Rickling, Germany* **Ferstl, Roman** *Psychology, University of Kiel, Kiel, Germany*

As recent studies showed cannabis addiction not only increases the risk for psychosis but also changes functions on the neuronal and neuropsychological levels, what can be used to improve the differential diagnosis of schizophrenia. Models of decision-making and reward-processing emphasize the role of the fronto-striatal loops, especially dopaminergic projections to the ventral striatum and PFC implicated in both diseases. We tested groups of 20 Patients suffering from cannabis-addiction and/or schizophrenia and matched controls with a comprehensive neuropsychological test-battery. Primarily the Iowa-Gambling-Task and a probabilistic-selection task revealed specific profiles of deficits and strengths in the domains of decision-making and reward-processing respectively.

Work-life-conflict as a mediator between job stressors and strain: The moderating role of family status

Wilde, Barbara *Inst. für Psychologie, Universität Freiburg, Freiburg, Germany* **Bahamondes Pavez, Carolina** *Institute of Psychology, University of Freiburg, Freiburg, Germany* **Hinrichs, Stephan** *Institute of Psychology, University of Freiburg, Freiburg, Germany* **Schüpbach, Heinz** *Institute of Psychology, University of Freiburg, Freiburg, Germany*

This study examined whether the mediative effect of work-life-conflict (WLC) between job stressors and strain depends on family status. Data were obtained from German employees (N=149). Time pressure as job stressor, irritation and somatic complaints as strain parameters and WLC were measured by questionnaire. As expected, total mediations were found in the group of employees living together with a partner (sobel-test, p<.05) but not in the group of employees living alone. The results show that living conditions should be recognized in researching WLC. Regarding the data, companies should use differentiated strategies to reduce their employees' strain.

Emotional influences upon perceptions of group deviants (or how I learned to stop worrying and love deviance)

Williams-Eliyesil, Sion *Experimental Psychology, University of Oxford, Oxford, United Kingdom*

The present study assessed the role of emotions in the process of creating a normative framework the make deviance more acceptable. Perceived legitimacy was found to have a significant effect upon the acceptability of group deviance, and illegitimate conditions were accompanied by significantly more negative emotional states that legitimate conditions. These findings lend support to the argument that emotional states interact with social perceptions to affect group norms and influence group behaviour.

Irrationality as a determinant of gender stereotyping towards women

Wimmer, Birgit *Inst. für Psychologie, Universität München, München, Germany* **Haupt, Tobias C.** *Psychologie, Ludwig-Maximilians-Universität, München, Germany* **Spörrle, Matthias** *Dept. for Psychology, Ludwig-Maximilians University, München, Germany*

Irrational thinking can be considered to be the key concept of Rational Emotive Behavior Therapy (REBT) and has been conceptualized as rigid und inflexible adherence to absolutistic thinking and person evaluations. Based on this definition we predicted a positive relation between irrationality and gender stereotyping towards women. Established reliable scales were used to asses the constructs in a non-student sample (N = 240). In line with assumptions we were able to detect a significant positive relation between irrationality and gender stereotyping while controlling for the Big Five, life satisfaction, sex and age. Implications for interventions concerning stereotypes are outlined.

Creative behavior predicted by stages of the creative process

Winzen, Julia *Inst. f. Sozialwissenschaften, Universität Hohenheim, Stuttgart, Germany* **Gelléri, Petra** *Inst. f. Sozialwissenschaften, Universität Hohenheim, Stuttgart, Germany* **Görlich, Yvonne** *Inst. f. Sozialwissenschaften, Universität Hohenheim, Stuttgart, Germany* **Schuler, Heinz** *Inst. f. Sozialwissenschaften, Universität Hohenheim, Stuttgart, Germany*

When predicting creative behavior, in addition to divergent thinking, further abilities considered in creativity process models should be analysed regarding their importance for creative performance. Based on a process-oriented creativity test, we examined the predictive power of eight process stages for different criteria of creative performance in a sample of 742 employees and students. Regression analyses indicated significant (p < .05) beta weights for several stages depending on the criterion taken into account. To gain incremental validity, a self-description inventory was included, which lead to an increase in R^2. Thus, considering multiple criteria in process-oriented assessment helps explaining creative performance.

Does synaesthesia enhances memory: Short review

Wrzalka, Bartlomiej *Faculty of Psychology, University of Warsaw, Warsaw, Poland*

In psychological literature concerning memory one can find suggestions that synaesthesia enhances memory. Is it really a fact? Does current psychological knowledge entitles us to such claims? The main purpose of the presentation is to review scientific research conducted in this field, with special consideration of methods of gathering data used in those experiments. Author's own research (case study) concerning memory of two synaesthetes will also be shown. A short theoretical introduction containing basic information about synaesthesia is included. Data from literature concerning synaesthesia along with data concerning superb memory will be presented and analyzed.

Researching on the relationship among social categorization, depersonalization, and group behaviour

Wu, Licun *and Technology, Changsha University of Science, Changsha, People's Republic of China* **Deng, Zhiwen** *schoolofpolitical&administ, universityofscience&techno, changsha city in hunan provinc, People's Republic of China*

Based on Tajfel's SIT, especially Turner's SCT, we argue that social categorization influences social processes and structures within groups through self-categorization and prototype-based depersonalization. Because social categorization place people in categories. Meanwhile, depersonalization can make people in groups appear attitudinally, affectively, and behaviorally, furthermore relatively homogenous. Social categorization links to the ingroups behaviors through prototype-based depersonalization. The bound that social categorization and depersonalization effects on processes within groups is wide, it covers conformity, normative behavior, crowd behavior, group polarization, the behavioral expressions of attitudes cohesion, deviance, leadership and power, roles, status, diversity, subgroups, and organizational mergers.

The mixed effect of psychological empowerment towards emotional exhaustion

Wu, Jieqian *School of Management, Fudan University, Shanghai, People's Republic of China* **Wang, Zhen** *Institute of Psychology, Chinese Academy of Sciences, Beijing, People's Republic of China*

Emotional labor workers experience high level of emotional exhaustion. Most previous research demonstrated that psychological empowerment reduced emotional exhaustion. The purpose of this study was to explore whether all psychological empowerment dimensions would definitely lower emotional exhaustion. Hypotheses were tested by doing a field investigation of 369 employees in a customer service center in a big telecom company. Hierarchical regression analysis revealed that meaning was negatively related to emotional exhaustion, whereas impact was positively related to it. Female workers perceived more emotional exhaustion. The result indicates it is important to consider the mixed effect of psychological empowerment towards emotional exhaustion.

Probe the relationship between collective identity and personal identity

Wu, Chengsheng *School of Political&Administer, Changsha University of S&T, Changsha, People's Republic of China* **Deng, Zhiwen** *School of Political&Admini, Changsha University of S&T, Changsha, People's Republic of China*

Based on the three level of self representation, namely collective, relational, and personal, and the two distinct component, namely collective versus private self, from the Tajfel's SIT and Turner's SCT, we have probed the relationship between collective identity and personal identity. Three factors play very important role in turning personal identity into collective identity: a. Depersonalization and social categorization; b. Mutable self-category. Individual develop a taxonomy of situations to reflect the different concerns and motives that play as a result of threats to personal and group identity and degree of commitment to the group. c. self-esteem and uncertainty reduction.

An exploratory study on job seeking self-efficacy of university students in China

Wu, Xin *School of Economics & Managemt, Beihang University, Beijing, People's Republic of China* **Li, Dan** *School of economics & mana, Beihang University, beijing, People's Republic of China*

This study explored the dimensionality, antecedents and consequences of job seeking self-efficacy (JSSE) of Chinese university students. Survey data were collected from 220 university student job seekers and newly employed graduates. Factor analysis revealed two dimensions of JSSE, information and decision efficacy (IDE), and personnel selection efficacy (PSE). Results indicated that vicarious experience and emotional arousal were positively related to IDE, and vicarious experience was positively related to PSE. Positive effects of JSSE on job seeking consequences were found. The study has significance for university students counseling and training during the expansion of enrollment in higher education in China.

Top-down processes based on color cues in preview search

Xu, Baihua *Psychology, Zhejiang University, Hangzhou, People's Republic of China* **Cui, Xiangyu** *Psychology, Zhejiang University, Hangzhou, People's Republic of China*

Two experiments were conducted to determine the role of color cues in preview search. In experiment one, the color of probe dot was either that of the preview items or an irrelevant color. The results showed that subjects detected the irrelevant-color probe dot faster than the preview-item-color probe dot. In experiment two, the color of search items and the irrelevant color were alternatives. It was found that the reaction time to the search-item-color probe dot was shorter than the one to the irrelevant-color probe-dot. The authors reduce that there might be two types of top-down processes based on color cues: inhibition set and anticipatory set.

The role of emotion in the individual investor's decision making behavior

Xu, Helen Shanghai, People's Republic of China
Under the background of financial behavior, this study is to explore the role of emotion in the individual investor's Decision Making behavior. Through systematic manipulation of a stock price in a simulated situation, experimenter record (a)subjects' reaction time of every price; (b)subjects' behavior of buying, selling and maintaining; (c)subjects' heart rate during the experiment; (d)the anticipatory emotion elicited by the price and(e)the final score the subjects get by buying, selling or maintaining the price-manipulated stock as subjects' response. The findings show that different anticipatory emotion will produce different influence on participants' Decision Making behavior. Keywords: Emotion; Decision Making behavior; Heart rate

The color-based anticipatory set in preview search: Evidence from a colored dot probing task

Xu, Baihua Psychology, Zhejiang University, Hangzhou, People's Republic of China *Cui, Xiangyu* Psychology, Zhejiang University, Hangzhou, People's Republic of China
A colored dot probing task was created to certify the role of color-based anticipatory set in preview search. In experiment one, preview items were initially displayed, followed by a colored dot or search items. The color of probe dot was either as same as the search items or irrelevant to both of search and preview items. The results showed that subjects responded faster to the search-item-color probe dot than the irrelevant-color one. In experiment two, an attentional blink paradigm was combined with the task of experiment one. The results showed that the effect once observed in the first experiment became weaker, supporting the hypothesis that attentional resources are required for anticipatory set.

Nicotine use, problem solving styles and depression levels of university students

Yüksel, Muazzez Merve Dept. of Psychology, Middle East Techn. University, Ankara, Turkey *Torun, Cagla* PSYCHOLOGY, BILKENT UNIVERSITY, ANKARA, Turkey
Backround: The aim of the study is to determine the relationship between perceived problem solving styles, depression levels and nicotine/alcohol use among university students. Method: University students in Ankara [n:110] had completed Problem Solving Inventory and Beck Depression Inventory. The sociodemographic data as well as addictive behaviours were recorded. Results: The results of the current study showed that the prevalence of nicotine/alcohol use is highly correlated with the depression level and problem solving styles of the students. Conclusion: Preventative efforts such as education about problem solving and coping styles could be beneficial on increasing the nicotine/alcohol use and depression levels.

Relationship between the PNEI response and the subjective well-being

Yajima, Jumpei Dept. of Human Studies, Beppu University, Beppu, Japan *Tsuda, Akira* Dept. of Psychology, Kurume University, Kurume, Japan *Okamura, Hisayoshi* Institute of Brain Diesease, Kurume University, Kurume, Japan *Horiuchi, Satoshi* Graduate school of Psychology, Kurume University, Kurume, Japan

This study investigated relationship between the PNEI response (saliva free-MHPG, s-IgA, and cortisol) and the subjective well-being was evaluated using WHO-SUBI. We carried out the WHO-SUBI to 100 volunteers and extracted the healthy group and the poor group. Subjects were exposed to the speech task after a rest for 10 minutes. The speech task increased the saliva level of free-MHPG, s-IgA, and cortisol. The level of s-IgA in the healthy group was higher than the poor group during the session. These results show that the acute stress coping skill in the healthy group was better than in the poor group.

Combining representations of visible and invisible motion in estimating time-to contact

Yamada, Yuki Dept. of Behavioral and Health, Kyushu University, Fukuoka, Japan *Kawabe, Takahiro* Human-Environment Studies, Kyushu University, Fukuoka-city, Japan *Miura, Kayo* Human-Environment Studies, Kyushu University, Fukuoka-city, Japan
This study investigated the effect of speed change of task-irrelevant moving objects (distractors), which accompanied a moving target, on time-to-contact estimation. In a prediction motion task, the target passed behind a rectangle and observers estimated the exit timing of the target. The variation of speed, spatial offset, luminance, occlusion, and motion direction of the distractors were controlled as experimental factors. As a result, the speed change altered the estimation only if the distractor motion paralleled the estimated target motion. The results imply that reliable visible motion information affected invisible motion in estimating time-to contact.

The effects of olfactory stimulus on cognitive function of stroop task measured by near infrared spectroscopy

Yamada, Hiroshi Department of Dairy Science, Rakuno Gakuen University, Ebetsu, Japan
Oxyhemoglobin (oxy-Hb) was measured by near infrared spectoroscopy (NIRS) at eight positions of head while performing Stroop task to test the effects of olfactory stimulus on the cognitive function. NIRS and blood pressure were monitored and saliva was collected for six male students performing Stroop task for 10 min. Within the task, one of the lavender, lemon or odorless air was presented. Blood pressure and cortisol level were not affected by odor presentation. NIRS revealed that, in odorless air condition, oxy-Hb was increased at forehead and near Broca's area while performing task, and lavender odor supressed its increase on forehead.

Measurement of the Ponzo illusion in the picture drawings

Yamagami, Akira Psychology Department, Konan Women's University, Kobe, Japan
The Ponzo illusion in the picture drawing of room-walls (Rock, I., 1984, Perception) and its variants were measured to test the validity of the perspective theory. Eight variant figures were made by gradual degradation of the original figure. The results of 13 human observers in the experiment on the PC display by the method of adjustment of vertical lines showed a rapid change of the illusion magnitude between geometrical perspective line drawings (about 20%) and more picture-like drawings of the room-walls (about 40%). A new explanation of the illusion was proposed based upon these results.

Effects of training on visual attentional function in olders

Yamamura, Yutaka Psycholosy, Rissho University, Saitama-ken Hukaya-shi, Japan *Hohri, Jyuri* Psychology, RISSHO University, Tokyo-to Shinagawa-ku, Japan *Yamashita, Fumiyo* Psycholosy, RISSHO

University, Saitama-ken Hukaya-shi, Japan *Yamada, Kenata* Psycholosy, RISSHO University, Tokyo-to Mlnato-ku, Japan *Kosuge, Hanae* Psycholosy, Dennoo Co.,Ltd., Tokyo-to Mlnatao\KU, Japan
In this study, we investigated the effects of training on the visual attentional function of the olds. Two kind of the visual-search tasks were used. One was the feature search (FS), and the other was the conjunction search (CS). In each task, the targets were divided by the level of familiarity. The results showed that the reaction time in the olders faster than in the younger, especially in the FS when the targets were more familiar. The similar results were found also when the targets were presented in the center region. These results suggest that the simple and familiar stimuli were more efficient as the training tool for the olds.

An inquiry into depression consultancy system

Yan, Danniang Faculty Lodging House 6-3-302#, South-Central Nationality Uni., Wuhan, People's Republic of China
An increasing number of Chinese undergraduates are committing suicide because of depression. This article describes the establishment of a computer program for depression consultancy. The consultancy system can help undergraduates to measure themselves whether or not they are suffering from depression, to adjust their behavior and to decide whether or not it is necessary to seek therapy. The author has 18 years of working experience as a psychological counselor in universities. She has collected large numbers of first-hand data, and used systems analysis method to construct a reasonable database. Based on this, she established the depression consultancy system.

The effect of verbal self-guidance training for overcoming employment barriers: A study of Islamic women

Yanar, Basak OB & HRM, University of Toronto, Toronto, Canada *Latham, Gary P.* OB & HRM, University of Toronto, Toronto, Canada *Budworth, Marie-Hélàne* Management, York University, Toronto, Canada
Women, over the age of 40, in an Islamic society were trained in verbal self guidance. Subsequently, they (n=27) had significantly higher self-efficacy with regard to re-employment than their counterparts who had been randomly assigned to a control group (n=28). In addition, they persisted in job search behaviors significantly more so than those in the control group. Job search self-efficacy completely mediated the effect of the training program on job search behaviors. Consequently, they were more likely to find a job in their area of interest within six months and one year of training than were women in the control group.

The microgenetic study of visual self-recognition in infancy

Yang, Lizhu Dept. of Psychology, Liaoning Normal Universtiy, Dalian, People's Republic of China *Liu, Ling* Dept. of Psychology, Liaoning Normal Universtiy, Dalian, People's Republic of China
The microgenetic approach was adopted to assess 15 toddlers weekly from 15 to 23 months by video. It was designed to evaluate the occurring time and the individual differences of visual self-recognition, and its sequence of the indices as well. The results showed: (1) visual self-recognition occurred at the 2nd week of the 17th month and it developed gradually rather than abruptly while this process had individual differences; (2) the indices of visual self-recognition occurred in order: the mirror self-recognition came the first, then was followed by object-locating from its mirror image, and the photo identification emerged at last.

The brain mechanism of implicit self-esteem and N400

Yang, Juan school of psychology, southwest university, Chongqing, People's Republic of China Qiu, Jiang school of psychology, southwest university, Chongqing, People's Republic of China Zhang, Qinglin school of psychology, southwest university, Chongqing, People's Republic of China
Event-related brain potentials (ERPs) were measured when the participants finished the implicit association test (IAT) for implicit self-esteem. Behavioral data indicated that the participants responded relatively rapidly in the congruent condition when associating self with positive items. Scalp event-related brain potentials analysis revealed that self items in the incongruent condition elicited a more negative ERP deflection than those in the congruent condition between 350 and 450 ms after the onset of the self items. N400 has been shown to be sensitive to semantic processing, which is consistent with the nerve net model of the IAT.

The neural basis of risky decision making in a blackjack task

Yang, Juan school of psychology, southwest university, Chongqing, People's Republic of China Qiu, Jiang school of psychology, southwest university, Chongqing, People's Republic of China Zhang, Qinglin school of psychology, southwest university, Chongqing, People's Republic of China
Event-related potentials were recorded when participants engaged in a modified blackjack game. We focused on the high-conflict condition (probability of losing ~50%) and low-conflict condition (probability of losing ~20%). We were also interested in the difference between risky and conservative responses in high-conflict conditions. In the 220–320 ms and 500–600 ms time windows, high-conflict conditions elicited more negative event-related potential deflections than low-conflict conditions. In the latter time window, risky conditions elicited more negative event-related potential deflections than conservative conditions. The N2 and N500 provide evidence for the dissociation of neural circuits between perceptual conflicts and response conflicts.

Understanding of the scientific texts by the freshmen

Yaroslavtseva, Diana Psychology and Education, Moscow State University, Moscow, Russia
Our research deals with the problem of understanding of the scientific texts. The purpose of the research is to distill the main properties and typical errors in understanding of the complex scientific texts by the freshmen. The main method of the research is the interview which is conducted after reading of the experimental text. The preliminary results of the research allow to formulate several common characteristics of the text understanding. The results of the research show the actuality of the topic and necessity of the further research.

The effect of career information exploratory behavior on the outcomes of job hunting in Japan.

Yazaki, Yumiko Education and Human Developmen, Nagoya University, Nagoya, Japan Saito, Kazushi Communication, Aichi Shukutoku University, Nagoya, Japan
The purpose of this study was to examine the effect of career information exploratory behavior on the outcomes of job hunting. 200 fourth-year Japanese undergraduates (72 males, 128 females) reported a Big Five, career information exploratory behavior and one's own outcomes of job hunting. Path analysis showed the following results; 1) Conscientiousness was significantly related with the first-hand information, and neuroticism or extroversion were also significantly related with the company characteristics. 2) Exploring the first-hand informa-

tion from alumni and the company characteristics predicts the outcomes of job hunting such as satisfaction for one's own job hunting or career decision.

Hypothyroidism affects behavioral inhibition in rats

Yonezaki, Kumiko Hokkaido University, Sapporo, Japan Wada, Hiromi Hokkai-do, Hokkaido University, Sapporo, Japan
We investigated the relationships between impulsiveness and thyroid hormone inhibition in rats. Pregnant rats were treated with Methimazole by adding it to the drinking water at the dose of 0, 0.002 or 0.02% from the gestational day 15 to the postnatal day 21. Their offspring performed the DRL 20s schedule. In the schedule, the animals were required to press a lever greater than or equal to 20 s after the previous response to get a food reward. The hypothyroid rats tended to induce greater burst responses than the control rats. The results indicate the possibility that hypothyroidism causes impulsiveness.

Affective effects generated by motions: Different impression made by the direction of movement

Yoshida, Hiroyuki Dep. of Psychology, Nihon University, Setagaya-ku, Japan
In this study, effects of direction on impressions for a moving dot were investigated by two experiments using the SD method. Stimuli are made by controlling some variables (direction, motion pattern, changes of acceleration, and color). In experiment 1, factor analysis indicated three factors: Activity, Evaluation, and Smoothness. In experiment 2, factor analysis indicated five factors: Activity, Potency, Evaluation, Lightness, and Smoothness. In both experiments, observers felt that movement from right to left was more active than the opposite direction, even if these movements had the same motion pattern. The results confirmed the descriptions of creators based on subjective experiences.

The bullying in junior high schools in Japan (1): Factors of restraining bullying in the view point of group dynamics

Yoshitake, Kumiko Dept. of Humanities, Nagasaki Junshin University, Nagasaki, Japan Fujiwara, Tamae Dept. of Humanities, Nagasaki Junshin University, Nagasaki, Japan
This study investigated the bullying in the view point of group dynamics which consisted of bully (minority), targets and observers (majority). Subjects?120 University students. Methods? retrospect about bullying in their junior high school days: questionnaire. The results are 1) higher friendship in classes, 2) closer relationship with teachers and 3) higher degree of enjoyment in school, these three influenced high normative consciousness of observers significantly. Those with high normative consciousness tended to react against bully. But because of observers' no reactions bully often regarded themselves as being attached in class. Reasons of no reactions were discussed.

Factors which impact the vocational choice of Chinese college students

Yu, Yonghong CUFE, Beijing, People's Republic of China
With the development of economy and innovation in policy of China, college students' behavior and conception of employment have changed. According the investigation in Chinese college students studying at different university, we found that it is a common conception that after graduation one should find a job to make a living independently. The vocational choice of them is not only affected by their demography, such as grade, gender, major, but by family economic situation, parents' education and location where the university is. Further

more these factors impact their wills to obtain a job. The result is consistent with social cognitive theory.

Relations between working memory and reasoning about spatial and nonspatial relations in nonverbal learning disabilities NLD

Yu, Guoliang Inst. of Psychology, Renmin University, Beijing, People's Republic of China Jiang, Zhao-ping Philosophical School, Wuhan University, Wuhan, People's Republic of China
This study examined the relations between working memory and reasoning about spatial and nonspatial relations in three groups of children aged 11-14: children with NLD, children with verbal learning disabilities (VLD), and children without learning disabilities. Experiment 1 explored four working memory spans: phonological loop, central executive, static and dynamic visual working memory. Experiment 2 tested the secondary task effects on reasoning about spatial and nonspatial relations. Experiment 1 found the NLD group had lower performance than other groups in dynamic visual tasks. Children with VLD experienced deficits in central-executive tasks. Experiment 2 found spatial and nonspatial reasoning loaded different working memory components. The implications of the data for the working memory requirements of reasoning were discussed.

Researching on social identity in CCP of university students

Yue, Living political school, Changsha university of science, Changsha, People's Republic of China Deng, Zhiwen political school, changsha university of science, changsha city in Hunan provinc, People's Republic of China
According to Tajfel'theory of social identity, after measuring 546 CPA and positive member of university students and interviewing with 23 CPA of university students, structural equation modeling and correspondence analysis was used to explore the data, four findings are discovered by us: a. a questionnaire of social identity in CPA of university students; b. setting up a model of influence on behavior that university students participate in CPA. c. status of social identity in CPA of university students; d. the four factors of influencing social identity in CPA of graduate students, namely cognition, motivation, appraisal and relationship among personal, in-group and out-group.

Individual differences between formal and informal leaders within the groups of high school students

Zaharescu, Loredana Brasov, Romania Negovan, Valeria Faculty of Psychology, University of Bucharest, Bucharest, Romania
The research aims to investigate the differences of personality between the formal, informal – professional and informal – affective leaders within the groups of high school students. The informal leaders were selected in each class (we worked with 30 classes) as a result of applying a sociogram, whereas the formal leaders were the ones named by the main teacher to be responsible for their classes. After the leaders answered the 16 PF questionnaire, we used inferential statistics to verify the hypothesis. The preliminary results show statistically significant differences between certain personality factors, which have implications for the educational psychology.

The impact of psychiatric comorbidity on brief intervention outcome in dependence on prescription drugs

Zahradnik, Anne Psychiatrie und Psychotherapie, Uni-Klinik Schleswig-Holstein, Lübeck, Germany Crackau, Brit Psychiatry and Psychotherapy, University of Luebeck, Luebeck, Germany Löhrmann, Ira Psychiatry and Psychotherapy, University of Luebeck, Luebeck, Germany Otto, Christiane Psychiatry and

Psychotherapy, University of Luebeck, Luebeck, Germany **Bischof, Gallus** Psychiatry and Psychotherapy, University of Luebeck, Luebeck, Germany **Rumpf, Hans-Juergen** Psychiatry and Psychotherapy, University of Luebeck, Luebeck, Germany

Objectives: The impact of psychiatric comorbidity on the efficacy of Motivational Interviewing in persons with a dependence on prescription drugs (DPD) will be examined in a randomised, controlled trial. Methods: Of 128 proactive recruited persons with a DPD in a general hospital 60 (49.9%) participants were diagnosed with a current psychiatric diagnosis on Axis I. Results: At baseline no significant differences in behavior change constructs assumed by the Transtheoretical Model between groups were found. Currently collected 3-month-follow-up-data will be presented at conference. Conclusions: The study results might reveal a basis for implementing interventions for dually diagnosed persons with DPD.

Social representations about the image of politician: Theoretical aspects

Zakrizevska, Maija ALBERTA College, Riga, Latvia

The political perception in the level of mass consciousness, that has its own values, stereotypes and attitudes, structure and functions of political leader, basic indicators of political leader that shows a potential of personality and main factors that influence forming the image of the politician are analyzed in the framework of article. Social representations are value, ideas, and collectively practiced forms of cognitions shared within society, which facilitate the understanding and communication of the knowledge of the world. The paper is aimed reviewing the relevant theoretical knowledge to form a basis for empirical studies of social representations about image of politician.

Does N450 reflect both semantic and response conflict in stroop task?: Evidence from the interaction between inhibition of return and stroop effect

Zhang, Yang Dept. of Psychology, Northeast Normal University, Changchun, People's Republic of China **Ming, Zhang** psycology, NortheastNormal university, Changchun, Germany

Objective: The goal of current study is to determine whether the N450 reflect both semantic and response conflict in Stroop task or only reflect response conflict with the combination of a spatial cueing task and Stroop paradigm? Methods: Seventy undergraduate students from Northeast Normal University were recruited as participants. Results and Conclusions: Although the Stroop effect was eliminated in cued location in behavioral performance, there was no suppression of N450 component at cued location(F<1). These results suggested that the N450 only reflect response conflict rather than both semantic and response conflict in the classical Stroop task.

Stress, coping strategies, and their relationship with adjustment in middle childhood

Zhang, Yinna Psychology, Beijing Normal University, Beijing, People's Republic of China **Wu, Chunxia** Psychology, Univ of California,Riverside, Riverside, CA, USA **Chen, Huichang** Psychology, Beijing Normal University, Beijing, People's Republic of China

91 children were randomly selected in Chinese cities. According to a semi-structured interview and teacher's rating, the data of children's stress, coping strategies and adjustment were collected. The results showed that: (1) the main stresses in children's daily life were peers' collision, tests' losing, parent-child collision, social evaluation stress, and loneliness. Most children's stress of tests' losing were from parents, then peers, and the teachers. (2) active coping, avoidance, seeking help, and distraction were coping strategies children

mainly and consistently used when facing stress. (3) active coping is a mediator of tests' losing and anxiety.

Researches of characteristic of college students' informal reasoning and its measurement criteria

Zhang, Li psychology, Liaoning Normal University, dalian, People's Republic of China **Zhang, Qi** psychology, Liaoning Normal University, dalian, People's Republic of China

Everydaylife problems and socialscientific issues tests were administered to debaters and college students with non-debating experience by experiment method and clinical interview method. Results showed that: debaters offered significantly more effective reasons, counterarguments to the arguments and reasons, non-debaters offered significantly more ineffective reasons; Non-debaters made significantly more concept representational mistakes and reasoning discontinuity; Debaters achieved significantly more scores on factors of thinking quality; No significant differences were found in my-side bias index between debaters and non-debaters; The debaters offered significantly more alternative-based objections, argument-based objections and assertion-based objections. Conclusion: based on this research, a systematical measurement criteria were constructed.

The neural basis of insight problem solving: An event-related potential study

Zhang, Qinglin School of Psychology, Southwest University, Chongqing, People's Republic of China **Qiu, Jiang** School of Psychology, Southwest University, Chongqing, People's Republic of China

The electrophysiological correlates of successful insight problem solving (Chinese logographs) were studied in 18 healthy subjects using high-density Event-Related Potentials (ERPs). Results mainly (see figure 1) showed that Successful logographs elicited a more negative ERP deflection than did Unsuccessful logographs in the time window within 1500-2000 ms (N1500-2000) and 2000-2500 ms (N2000-2500). Dipole analysis localized the generator of the N1500-2000 in the anterior cingulate cortex (ACC) and of the N2000-2500 in the posterior cingulate cortex (PCC). This result mainly indicates that the ACC might play an important role in the breaking of mental set successfully and the forming of novel associations in insight.

An empirical research of the relationship between entrepreneurial strategies and venture growth in high-tech enterprises

Zhang, Wei School of Management, Hangzhou Dian Zi University, Hangzhou, People's Republic of China

The research tried to probe into the way of which human resource strategies and technology strategies influenced venture growth performance. It had investigated 65 small and medium Hi-tech enterprises via multilevel behavioral questionnaires. The result of study showed that commitment human resource strategy had a prominent positive effect on potential performance. Control human resource strategy had a prominent positive effect on competitive performance and potential performance, and support human resource strategy had a medium level positive effect on competitive performance and potential performance. Meanwhile, the study revealed that the technology strategies had remarkably positive effect on competitive performance and potential performance.

Concealable stigma in the schools: Cognitive and behavioral control of students with learning disabilities under the condition of learning-related information being concealed

Zhao, Jun-yan Institute of Psychology, Chinese Academy of Sciences, Beijing, People's Republic of China **Zhang, Bao-shan** Institute of Psychology, Chinese Academy of Sciences, BeiJing, People's

Republic of China **Yu, Guoliang** Institute of Psychology, Renmin University of China, BeiJing, People's Republic of China

The present study examined the LD children's cognitive and behavioral control related to concealable stigma under the condition that learning-related information was concealed. A group of middle school students with learning disabilities (LD) and those without learning disabilities (NLD) were assigned separately into the concealed or disclosed conditions. Results showed that the LD group in the concealed condition exhibited more mental and behavioral control with a higher level of suppressing learning-relevant thoughts and higher accessibility of these thoughts than the NLD group. Furthermore, the LD group exhibited a strong tendency than the NLD group in attending to the learning environment and monitoring their own behavior.

Angelica injection reduces cognitive impairment during chronic cerebral hypoperfusion through brain-derived neurotrophic factor and nerve growth factor

Zheng, Ping Psychology, Huazhong Normal University, Wuhan, People's Republic of China **Zhang, Junjian** Neurology, Wuhan University, Wuhan, People's Republic of China **Liu, Hanxing** Neurology, Wuhan University, Wuhan, People's Republic of China **Xu, Xiaojuan** Psychology, Grand Valley State University, Allendale, USA

The study investigated whether chronic cerebral hypoperfusion (CCH) produced by 2-vessel occlusion (2-VO) induced cognitive impairment and whether angelica injections alleviated the impairment. Spatial learning in Morris water maze and the expression patterns of brain-derived neurotrophic factor (BDNF) and nerve growth factor (NGF) in the hippocampus of all rats were examined. The results showed that 2-VO significantly impaired spatial learning and memory, and angelica injections significantly reversed the learning and memory impairment. Furthermore, 2-VO resulted in significantly decreased BDNF protein, NGF protein, and NGF mRNA expression in the hippocampus. Thus, angelica injections might alleviate cognitive impairment during CCH through BDNF and NGF.

Understanding flaming through the lens of victimization in the work place.

Zheng, Xinyi Applied Psychology, Fuzhou University, Fuzhou, People's Republic of China **He, Shaoying** Applied Psychology, Fuzhou University, 350008, People's Republic of China

Flaming refers to aggressive or hostile communication occurring via computer –mediated channels. This study was to examine how, when and why flaming happens through the lens of victimization. The objective of the study is to increase work productivity by controlling the cost of work conflict generated by flaming actors. A qualitative approach was used. One of citical results was found. With the increase of frequency of flaming, victimization was seen to provoke the episodic flaming shifting to institutional flaming especially when both victim and perpetrator have incompatibility personality. The implications of management for the negative working behavior were recommended.

Procrastination types revisited: Passive non-procrastinator versus active procrastinator

Zhu, Chaowei Organizational Behavior Dep., School of Business, Beijing, People's Republic of China **Li, Junlan** School of Foreign Languages, Yichun University, Yichun, Jiangxi Province, People's Republic of China **Song, Lynda J.** School of Business, Renmin University of China, Beijing, People's Republic of China

This article argued against the traditional dichotomy of non-procrastination and procrastination through the development of a matrix of four procrastination types, namely active/passive non-procrastinator and active/ passive procrastinator. Especially, contrary to the prevailing assumption on non-procrastinators, we attempted to identify a passive type of non-procrastinator and compare it with positive procrastinators. An empirical test on 150 Chinese university students indicated that while passive non-procrastinators tend to finish tasks on time, they are more similar to passive procrastinators than to positive procrastinators in terms of Need for Achievement, Perceived Self-Efficacy, Stress Felt and Performance. Theoretical contributions and implications were discussed.

Emotional memory in Iranian older and younger adults

Ziaei, Maryam Psychology, Shahid Beheshti University, Tehran, Islamic Republic of Iran *amiri, sholeh* psychology, university of Isfahan, Isfahan, Islamic Republic of Iran *Jokar, Sanaz* psychology, university of Isfahan, Isfahan, Islamic Republic of Iran

The purpose of this study was to investigate the differences in emotional memory among older and younger adults in Iran. 161 subjects from 17-27 and 50-76- years old were selected. emotional memory tasks were presented which followed by immediate recall. Two-way ANOVA analysis was used. The results showed that younger groups recalled more positive (P< 0.03) and negative (P< 0.01) words; positive (P< 0.00) and negative (P< 0.003) faces than older adults. In addition, results showed that females recall more positive (P< 0.000) words; positive (P< 0.009) and negative (P< 0.000) faces than males. It seems significant differences in emotional memory could reflect cultural effects.

How many routes to persuasion are there? The research on the dual-process models of persuasion and the unimodel

Ziaja, Joanna Inst. of Psycholology, Jagiellonian University, Krakow, Poland *Plaskocinski, Adam* Inst. of Psychology, Jagiellonian University, Krakow, Poland

Current research on persuasion is dominated by two dual-process theories: the elaboration likelihood model and the heuristic-systematic model. According to them, persuasion can be accomplished via two distinct routes. Lately, there has appeared an alternative approach - the unimodel, which views persuasion in terms of a single process. The aim of the experiment was an attempt to verify both models. The experimental design included all the variables recognized as important from the perspective of both approaches (involvement, source expertise, source information length, argument quality, argument length, evidence appearance order). The experiment concerned attitudes toward introducing final exams to the universities.

Psychological distress and marijuana use in adolescence: A three year follow-up

Ziba-Tanguay, Kali Psychology, University of Montreal, Montreal, Canada *Claes, Michel* Psychology, University of Montreal, Montreal, Canada *Lacourse, Eric* Sociology, University of Montreal, Montreal, Canada

The present study aims at identifying the role of psychological distress in the development of marijuana use in adolescence. A sample of 780 adolescents from Montreal (Canada) was assessed on three occasions 1999 (T1), 2000 (T2), 2001 (T3). Participants completed a self-report questionnaire on marijuana use and symptoms of psychological distress. Logistic regression analysis indicated that the level of psychological distress at T1 was associated with the presence of psychological distress at T3 only for adolescents' girls. Further analysis will include SES, family structure and ethnicity. This study underscores the importance of internalized problems in the prevention of marijuana use.

A model's competence influences the imitative behaviour of 14-month-olds

Zmyj, Norbert Inst. für Psychologie, Max-Planck-Institut, Leipzig, Germany *Buttelmann, David* Dev. and Comp. Psychology, Max Planck Institute EVA, Leipzig, Germany *Carpenter, Malinda* Dev. and Comp. Psychology, Max Planck Institute EVA, Leipzig, Germany *Daum, Moritz M.* Psychology, Max Planck Institute CBS, Leipzig, Germany

Previous studies show that children learn novel words from competent rather than incompetent models. In our study, 14-month-olds were presented with video sequences showing a model acting either competently or incompetently. Then they saw the model 1) choosing one of two novel objects and 2) operating apparatuses using unusual actions (counterbalanced order) before being given the objects and apparatuses themselves. The model's competence did not influence participants' preference for novel objects. However, infants imitated the unusual actions significantly more often when the model was competent than incompetent (t(45)=2.24; p=.03) This is the earliest demonstration of 'the competence effect' in infancy.

Concepts and evaluation of psychological models of empathy

Zoll, Carsten Inst. für Allg. Psychologie, Universität Bamberg, Bamberg, Germany *Enz, Sibylle* Human Sciences, General Psychology, Bamberg, Germany *Schaub, Harald* Human Sciences, General Psychology, Bamberg, Germany

Most psychological researchers agree on the differentiation between two empathic processes (affective and cognitive empathy). Several models of empathy for the use in virtual agents that users can interact with have been created and evaluated. These models have been optimized regarding different criteria like simplicity, psychological plausibility, and computability. The models have been evaluated by psychological experts and users. The former evaluated the theoretical models while the latter evaluated the running models, i.e. after interacting with the virtual agents featured with one of the models in a virtual environment.

Attachment and stress reactivity in adolescents

Zulauf-Logoz, Marina Kinderpsychiatrie, Universität Zürich, Zürich, Switzerland

The purpose of this study was to examine the stability of attachment quality, stress reactivity (saliva cortisol) and the influence of adverse life events on attachment quality and continuity. Methods: 51 children participated in the 'Ainsworth Strange Situation' at age one year. At age 9 and age 15 subject's attachment was examined again. Life events were assessed with the 'Zürcher Lebensereignisliste' (Steinhausen & Winkler Metzke, 2001) at the age of 15. Results: While there was a significant continuity between the first and the second measurement, attachment was not stable between between age 9 and age 15.

Author Index

INTERNATIONAL PLATFORM FOR PSYCHOLOGISTS

Congresses and scientific meetings

July 1 - 3, 2008
4th Biennial Psychology Learning and Teaching 2008 (PLAT2008) Conference
Bath, UK
URL: http://www.psychology.heacademy.ac.uk/plat2008

July 3 - 6, 2008
2nd International Congress on Interpersonal Acceptance and Rejection
Rethymno, Crete, GREECE
URL: www.isipar08.org

July 8 - 12, 2008
III European Congress of Methodology
Oviedo, SPAIN
URL: http://methodology.cop.es/

July 12 - 16, 2008
3rd International Conference on the Teaching of Psychology (ICTP-2008)
St. Petersburg, RUSSIA
URL: http://www.ictp-2008.spb.ru

July 13 - 17, 2008
20th Biennial ISSBD-Meeting
Würzburg, GERMANY
URL: www.issbd2008.com

July 13 - 17, 2008
XXVI CINP (Collegium Internationale Neuro-Psychopharmacologicum): 50th Anniversary of the CINP
Munich, GERMANY
URL: www.cinp2008.com

July 14 - 15, 2008
3rd International Conference on Child and Adolescent Psychopathology
London, UK
URL: http://www.roehampton.ac.uk/childandadolescentpsychopathology/index.html

July, 14 - 16, 2008
6th International Conference, International Test Commission: The Public Face of Testing
Liverpool, UK
URL: www.intestcom.org

July 14 - 17, 2008
2nd International Conference on Psychology
Athens, GREECE
URL: http://www.atiner.gr/docs/Psychology.htm

July 15 - 18, 2008
8th International Conference on Grief and Bereavement
Melbourne, AUSTRALIA
URL: http://www.icgb08.com/

July 15 - 18, 2008
The 26th CICA Meeting & the 2nd STR Conference on aggression and terrorism
Zakopane (near Cracow), POLAND
URL: http://psps.psychologia.pl/conference/index.php

July 15 - 19, 2008
66th Annual Meeting, International Council of Psychologists (ICP)
St. Petersburg, RUSSIA
URL: http://www.icpweb.org/conference.html

July, 16 - 20, 2008
14th European Conference on Personality
Tartu, ESTONIA
URL: www.ecp14.ee

July 17 - 19, 2008
Sixth International Conference on Emotions and Organizational Life 'EMONET VI'
Fontainbleau, FRANCE
URL: http://www.uq.edu.au/emonet/
Deadline for receipt of papers March 31, 2008
(submission http://www.aomonline.org)

---

* Please send details of forthcoming events as far in advance as is possible to Dr Merry Bullock, Deputy Secretary-General, International Union of Psychological Science and Associate Editor of the International Journal of Psychology, Science Directorate, APA, 750 First Street NE, Washington DC 20002, USA; E-mail: mbullock@apa.org; URL: http://www.iupsys.org

July 20 - 25, 2008
XXIX International Congress of Psychology
Berlin, GERMANY
URL: http://www.icp2008.de

July 27 - 31, 2008
4th Latin American Regional Congress of Cross-Cultural Psychology
Mexico City, MEXICO
Contact: loving@servidor.unam.mx

July 27 - 31, 2008
XIX International Congress of the International Association for Cross Cultural Psychology
Bremen, GERMANY
URL: http://www.jacobs-university.de/iaccp2008/

July 28 - August 1, 2008
20th Conference of IAPS (International Association for People-Environment Studies)
Rome, ITALY
URL http://www.iaps2008.com

August 14 - 17, 2008
116th Annual Convention of the American Psychological Association
Boston, Massachusetts, USA
URL: www.apa.org/convention

August 18 - 22, 2009
XIVth European Conference on Developmental Psychology
Vilnius, LITHUANIA
URL: http://www.ecdp2009.com.

August 19 - 22, 2008
20th Annual Congress of the International Association of Empirical Aesthetics
Chicago, Illinois, USA
URL: http://users/ipfw.edu/bordens/IAEA08/IAEAcall.pdf

August 19 - 23, 2008
Understanding Conflicts - Cross-Cultural Perspectives
Aarhus, DENMARK
URL: http://www.understandingconflicts.net/

August 26 - 29, 2008
6th International Conference on Methods and Techniques in Behavioral Research
Maastricht, THE NETHERLANDS
URL: http://www.noldus.com/mb2008/

August 31 - September 4, 2008
4th International Conference on Traffic & Transport Psychology
Washington DC, USA
URL: http://www.icttp.com/index.htm

September 9 - 12, 2008
The Annual Conference of the European Health Psychology Society (EHPS) and the Division of Health Psychology (DHP) of the British Psychological Association (BPS)
Bath, UK
URL: www.bath2008.org.uk

September 9 - 13, 2008
Second International Congress of the International Society for Cultural and Activity Research (ISCAR)
La Jolla, California, USA
URL: www.iscar.org

September 19 - 22, 2008
Social Capital Foundation International Conference
MALTA
URL: http://www.socialcapital-foundation.org/

September 24 - 27, 2008
4th International Conference on Research and Developmental Education
San Juan, PUERTO RICO
URL: www.ncde.appstate.edu/cfp

October 9 - 11, 2008
14th Biennial Meeting, International Society for Comparative Psychology
Buenos Aires, ARGENTINA
URL: http://www.comparativepsychology.org/

October 13 - 17, 2008
V Conferencia Internacional de Psicología de la Salud
Havana, CUBA
URL: http://psicosalud2008.sld.cu /
www.cpalco.com

November 20 - 24, 2008
49th Psychonomic Society Annual Meeting
Chicago, Illinois, USA
URL: http://www.psychonomic.org/meet.htm
2009

January 24 - 28, 2009
European Congress of Psychiatry - AEP 2009
Lisbon, PORTUGAL
URL: http://www.kenes.com/aep/

February 11 - 14, 2009
International Neuropsychological Society (INS) Annual Conference
Atlanta, Georgia, USA
URL: http://www.the-ins.org/meetings

April 1 - 5, 2009
Society for Research in Child Development Biennial Meeting
Denver, Colorado, USA
URL: http://www.srcd.org/biennial.html

May 21 - 24, 2009
21st Annual Convention, Association for
Psychological Science
San Francisco, California, USA
URL: http://www.psychologicalscience.org/
convention/

May 27 - 30, 2009
Association for Psychological Science 21st Annual
Convention
Boston, Massachusetts, USA
URL: www.psychologicalscience.org/convention/
future_conventions.cfm

June, 2009
First World Congress on Positive Psychology
Details to be announced

June 11 - 13, 2009
Canadian Psychological Association (CPA) Annual
Convention
Montreal, Quebec, CANADA
URL: www.cpa.ca

June 28 - July 2, 2009
XXXII Interamerican Congress of Psychology
Guatemala, GUATEMALA
URL: www.sip2009.org

July 7 - 10, 2009
11th European Congress of Psychology
Oslo, NORWAY
URL: www.ecp2009.no

August 6 - 9, 2009
117th Annual Convention of the American
Psychological Association
Toronto, Ontario, CANADA
URL: www.apa.org/convention

2010

TBD
3rd Congress ASEAN Regional Union of
Psychological Societies
MALAYSIA

May 27 - 30, 2010
21st Annual Convention, Association for
Psychological Science
Boston, Massachusetts, USA
URL: http://www.psychologicalscience.org/
convention/

June 3 - 5, 2010
Canadian Psychological Association (CPA) Annual
Convention
Winnipeg, Manitoba, CANADA
URL: www.cpa.ca

July 11 - 16, 2010
International Congress of Applied Psychology
Melbourne, AUSTRALIA
URL: www.icap2010.com

July 11 - 16, 2010
8th International Conference on Teaching Statistics
Ljubljana, SLOVENIA
URL: http://www.stat.auckland.ac.nz/~iase/index.php

August 12 - 15, 2010
118th Annual Convention of the American
Psychological Association
San Diego, California, USA
URL: www.apa.org/convention

2011

March 31 - April 2, 2011
Biennial Meetings of the Society for Research in Child
Development
Montreal, CANADA
URL: www.srcd.org

August 4 - 7, 2011
119th Annual Convention of the American
Psychological Association
Washington, DC, USA
URL: www.apa.org/convention

Summer, 2011
XIIth European Congress of Psychology (ECP)
Istanbul, TURKEY
URL: www.psikolog.org.tr

2012

July 22 - 27, 2012
International Congress of Psychology
Cape Town, SOUTH AFRICA

TBD
4th Congress ASEAN Regional Union of
Psychological Societies
PHILIPPINES

August 2 - 5, 2012
120th Annual Convention of the American
Psychological Association
Chicago, Illinois, USA
URL: www.apa.org/convention

2013

July 31 - August 4, 2013
121st Annual Convention of the American
Psychological Association
Honolulu, Hawaii, USA
URL: www.apa.org/convention